W9-CHK-841

Congressional Quarterly's

Guide to the Presidency

Everett C. Johnson, Folio Inc.

North Portico entrance to the White House, facing Pennsylvania Avenue

Congressional Quarterly's

Guide to the Presidency

Michael Nelson
Editor

Washington, D.C.

Congressional Quarterly Inc.

Congressional Quarterly Inc., an editorial research service and publishing company, serves clients in the fields of news, education, business, and government. It combines Congressional Quarterly's specific coverage of Congress, government, and politics with the more general subject range of an affiliated service, Editorial Research Reports.

Congressional Quarterly publishes the *Congressional Quarterly Weekly Report* and a variety of books, including college political science textbooks under the CQ Press imprint and public affairs paperbacks on developing issues and events. CQ also publishes information directories and reference books on the federal government, national elections, and politics, including the *Guide to Congress,* the *Guide to the U.S. Supreme Court,* the *Guide to U.S. Elections, Politics in America,* and *Congress A to Z: CQ's Ready Reference Encyclopedia.* The *CQ Almanac,* a compendium of legislation for one session of Congress, is published each year. *Congress and the Nation,* a record of government for a presidential term, is published every four years.

CQ publishes *The Congressional Monitor,* a daily report on current and future activities of congressional committees, and several newsletters including *Congressional Insight,* a weekly analysis of congressional action, and *Campaign Practices Reports,* a semimonthly update on campaign laws.

An electronic online information system, Washington Alert, provides immediate access to CQ's databases of legislative action, votes, schedules, profiles, and analyses.

Acknowledgments: Box, The Great Communicator, p. 758, is reprinted by permission of Pantheon Books, a Division of Random House, Inc. The following photographs are reproduced by permission of the Smithsonian Institution, Division of Political History: p. 135, photo no. 73845; p. 215, photo no. 736473; p. 246, photo no. 52271; p. 247, photo no. 45995; p. 298, photo no. 742802; p. 362, photo no. 67656.

1414 22nd Street N.W., Washington, D.C. 20037

Printed in the United States of America

Library of Congress Cataloging-in-Publication Data
Congressional Quarterly's guide to the presidency/Michael Nelson, editor.
p. cm.
Bibliography: p.
ISBN 0-87187-500-4: $137.50
1. Presidents--United States. I. Nelson, Michael, 1949-
II. Congressional Quarterly, inc. III. Title: Guide to the presidency.
JK516.C57 1989 89-7184
353.03' 13--dc20 CIP

Project Director: Margaret Seawell Benjaminson
Editor: Michael Nelson
Associate Editors: Sabra Bissette Ledent, John L. Moore
Production and Picture Editor: Jane Gilligan
Developmental Editor: Nola Healy Lynch
Writers: Harold F. Bass, Jr.; Margaret Seawell Benjaminson; W. Craig Bledsoe; Dom Bonafede; Christopher J. Bosso; Mark E. Byrnes; Daniel C. Diller; Harrison Donnelly; Charles C. Euchner; Richard A. Karno; John Anthony Maltese; Sidney M. Milkis; Michael Nelson; Dean J. Peterson; Stephen L. Robertson; Robert J. Spitzer; Margaret C. Thompson; James Brian Watts; Margaret Jane Wyszomirski
Contributing Editors: Carolyn Goldinger, Robert E. Healy, Kerry V. Kern
Production Assistant/Researcher: Jamie R. Holland
Proofreaders: Catherine W. Ballay, Joe Fortier, Carla Gately, Kerry V. Kern, Jodean Marks, Steve F. Moyer, Mark Skuta, Susanna Spencer, Tracy W. Villano
Indexer: Patricia R. Ruggiero
Graphic Artists: Carlos Cornelio, Roy Gallop, Hördur Karlsson, Dmitri Lipczenko, Douglas L. Parkhurst, Ron Silberberg
Cover Designer: Robert O. Redding and Douglas L. Parkhurst

Summary Table of Contents

Table of Contents

Part I
Origins and Development of the Presidency

Part II

Selection and Removal of the President

Part III
Powers of the Presidency

Part VII

The Presidents and the Vice Presidents

Appendix

Foreword

The presidency eloquently expresses a vision of the Framers of the Constitution. Yet no other institution has been more transformed by the forces of history. To understand the meaning of the Constitution today, we must remind ourselves of the shape the Founders conceived for that office. But we can understand American politics today only if we see how the forces of history and technology have reshaped the office in the late twentieth century. Congressional Quarterly's *Guide to the Presidency* brings together past and present into a portrait of the presidency illuminated by the accidents, trends, and forces that have made its present character.

When the Framers created the office of president, they described an institution unprecedented, at least in modern history. Therefore, working out the details of the office was one of the more troublesome tasks of the Constitutional Convention. There was disagreement about the precise mode of election, the length of the president's term and whether the president could serve more than one term, the powers of the office, and the procedure for impeachment.

On August 6, 1787, the Committee of Detail proposed: "The Executive Power of the United States shall be vested in a single person. His stile shall be, 'His Excellency.' He shall be elected by ballot of the Legislature. He shall hold his office during the term of seven years; but he shall not be elected a second time." Some of these details were changed after further debate. But the essentials, a president elected by the people for a fixed term, remained. These, too, were what made the office a new departure in modern political institutions.

The fixed term, though modified in detail, remains one of the most significant if least celebrated features of the office. It expressed the Framers' confidence—which history has justified—in the civility of American politics. Seeing the advantage of a predictable term of four years for the chief executive, they believed that here the opposition would never be so violent or rebellious that the opposing party would not allow presidents to serve out their terms. We have seen many advantages to this arrangement, which prevents a flurry of unfavorable public opinion from causing the ouster of a popular and effective president. The salient and most remarkable feature of American political life (interrupted only by the traumas of the Civil War and the Vietnam War) has been the refusal of the American people to allow ideology or special interests to disrupt the orderly constitutional conduct of national politics. The rise of political parties has become a way of adjusting the ebb and flow of political sentiments to the enduring frame of the Constitution.

To avoid the direct popular election of the president, the Framers provided complicated electoral college machinery, which remains a fossil among our evolving institutions. But their concern over the procedure for electing presidents and vice presidents was not misplaced. The expansion of the nation, the increasing ethnicity of the national politics of an immigrant people, the primary system of selecting party candidates, and the powers of costly campaign technology have created new problems for which there are not apt to be "solutions."

Although the essentials of the office of president in our tripartite constitutional structure survive, two great forces have reshaped the problems of candidacy, the office and the tasks of the president, and the president's capacity to perform those tasks.

The first is the vast expansion of the powers of the whole federal government, of the executive branch over which the president presides, and, incidentally, of the size and complexity of the White House staff. George Washington's federal government consisted of five departments—State, Treasury, War, Justice, and Post Office—with an annual budget of about $4 million. In 1801, when a president was first inaugurated in Washington, Thomas Jefferson's annual budget was still only about $9.4 million. American history is a story of the growth of the federal government, which has been preponderantly in the executive branch.

The climax of this proliferation has come in the twentieth century. The Budget and Accounting Act of 1921 marked the modern tendency toward increasing federal expenditures. The expanded military establishment in two world wars and against the Soviet challenge, the rise of welfare services and entitlements sparked by the Great Depression and the New Deal, the expansion of foreign aid, and the support of wobbly foreign governments, all have multiplied the employees and the costs of the federal government. The White House staff has grown to thousands—exceeding the whole number of government employees at the founding of the Republic. Is it any longer possible for the president to manage the executive branch? Nearly every president since Franklin Roosevelt has recognized the urgency of this question by appointing a commission to improve presidents' control over the offices for which they are responsible. The commissions generally have suggested additions to one or another executive office, but few critics believe that they have come to grips with the problem.

Meanwhile, over all the categories of government familiar to the Framers of the Constitution broods a vast and amorphous new power that complicates, and sometimes nullifies, the best efforts at traditional reform. This is, of course, the power of technology. Not only has technology provided extensive new areas of federal responsibility—from the control of air and water pollution, and the regulation of motor vehicles and air travel, to the allotting of television channels, and the provision of nuclear power and control of nuclear waste. No less traumatic has been the way technology has reshaped the processes and increased the price of electing a president. The rise of the news and opinion media to gargantuan proportions in this century has created a vast advertising industry and its offspring, a science of opinion polling, and the arts of public relations. These in turn have recast presidential elections into matters of technology and money and redesigned the tasks of a sitting president. No one has suggested that there is—or should be—any way of getting the private forces of public information "under control" in a free society. The momentum of opinion technology advances and accelerates, and the office of the president must accommodate that momentum.

It is desirable, then, in our free society, that the debate over the proper shape, or possible reshaping, of the presidency should go on. Is the presidency today too strong? Does an "imperial presidency" menace the control of Congress over the war powers and over the dangerous associated powers of ensuring internal security? Or is the presidency too weak? Does the Congress now have a menacing power to veto the president's "national voice" and to dilute what Woodrow Wilson called the national "zest for action" that the urgencies of our world demand? This question must be asked again in every generation. The ingredients of the problem are always changing, with new ingredients constantly being added in our immigrant-enriched and technologically advancing nation.

Congressional Quarterly's *Guide to the Presidency* provides a needed resource for our continuing efforts to understand this momentous question. Here is an unexcelled treasury of facts about the presidency past and present and helpful access to all other sources. The presidency, as we study it in this volume, is a laboratory where we can see how uniquely American institutions have been shaped by the forces of history and technology. What we see here can help us reflect on how these institutions can be preserved and improved and can keep us alert to the caution of President Washington in his first inaugural address—more relevant today than when he uttered it: "The preservation of the sacred fire of liberty, and the destiny of the Republican model of government, are justly considered as *deeply,* perhaps as *finally* staked, on the experiment entrusted to the hands of the American people."

Daniel J. Boorstin
Librarian of Congress Emeritus
Author of *The Discoverers, The Image,* and the trilogy *The Americans*

Preface

At any given moment, the powers and duties of the office of president of the United States are entrusted fully to the person who occupies the office. To some degree, then, the presidency has been shaped and defined by the forty individuals who, as of today, have held the office. Historical periods often are described in terms of the presidents who dominated them: the "Age of Jackson," the "Lincoln years," the "New Deal period" of Franklin D. Roosevelt, the "Reagan era." But the presidency is more than the persons who have served as president. It is also an institution, an enduring and evolving office.

Plan of the Book

By design and execution, *Guide to the Presidency* reflects the individualism of the presidency. Throughout the book, an effort is made to describe every president's accomplishments and failures, virtues and foibles. Even a quick glance at the index will attest to the detailed information the book provides on each president. Part VII includes illustrated biographies of every president from George Washington to George Bush, and of their vice presidents; Part V recounts the lives of the individual first ladies. Part V also gives close attention to the daily life of the president and to the developing role of former presidents.

The institutional character of the presidency is manifested in several ways, all of which are described in this book.

~ *The presidency is a constitutional office,* shaped by its design at the Constitutional Convention in 1787 and by subsequent constitutional amendments, Supreme Court decisions, and customs and precedents. Part I includes an extensive description of the constitutional beginnings of the presidency, and Part III gives thorough consideration to the various powers of the office, most of them constitutional in origin. Constitutional aspects of the presidency also are noted throughout the book; Part II, for example, examines the processes of presidential succession and removal.

~ *The presidency is a historical office.* During its more than two centuries of existence, the presidency has evolved in response to changing social, economic, political, and international conditions. Part I, which provides an extensive chronological history of the development of the presidency, is one of but several places in the book where the office's history is described. Part II includes an election-by-election history of presidential contests.

~ *The presidency is the nation's supreme elective office.* Part II offers full treatment of presidential selection—not just the history, rules, strategies, and processes of presidential nominations and elections but also the methods provided by the Constitution for presidential selection under special circumstances, such as the death, resignation, or disability of the president.

~ *The presidency is a highly public and political office.* Indeed, it is as public and political after the election as it is during the campaign. Presidential leadership depends heavily upon the support or acquiescence of those groups outside government whose relations with the presidency are described in Part IV—the political parties, the mass media, interest groups, and the general public.

~ *The presidency is the chief office of the executive branch,* including the White House staff, the cabinet, and the numerous departments and agencies of the federal bureaucracy. The executive branch—its major players and major components—is closely described in Part V. The president's relationship with the bureaucracy is treated in Part VI.

~ *The presidency is part of a multibranch system of government.* Throughout the entire book attention is paid to the separation of powers and the checks and balances that characterize the U.S. constitutional system, but the interactions of the presidency with Congress, the bureaucracy, and the Supreme Court are specifically the subject of Part VI.

The vice presidency also is covered in *Guide to the Presidency*—its origins and history (in Part I), the processes of vice-presidential selection and removal (in Part II), and the office of the vice president (in Part V).

Thus *Guide to the Presidency* explains in one volume the origins, evolution, and contemporary workings of the most important office of the U.S. political system. The book has been written and edited to make this material readily accessible. The thirty-seven chapters of the *Guide,* grouped into seven parts, each focus on a particular subject. But these topics are not discrete, for few aspects of the presidency are unrelated to others. The subject of one chapter therefore may be mentioned in several different contexts throughout the book. The president's relationship with the public, for example, is the focus of Part IV, but this relationship is discussed also in Part I (in the chapter on the history of the office) and in Part II (in the chapter on the electoral process). Cross-references within each chapter guide the reader to other relevant discussions. This overlap provides complete treatment of a topic in one place but allows as well for the discovery and pursuit of related subjects.

Continuing the tradition of Congressional Quarterly's other major reference works—*Guide to Congress, Guide to the U.S. Supreme Court,* and *Guide to U.S. Elections*—the material in *Guide to the Presidency* is descriptive, factual, unbiased, and easy to understand. In a highly readable style, the authors have distilled for the average nonexpert reader the widely accepted expertise on the presidency. For readers who want to delve further into the scholarly literature, the footnotes and selected bibliographies at the end of each chapter show the way.

The Appendix to the *Guide* supplements the text with tables, charts, and documents. Included are excerpts from forty documents significant to the presidency, with explanatory headnotes. Unique to this volume is the complete listing of cabinet members from the administration of George Washington through that of George Bush. Notable also are the charts showing Gallup poll ratings of Presidents Harry S Truman through Ronald Reagan.

A word on the photographs. The *Guide* is by far the most thoroughly illustrated of CQ's reference books, containing more than four hundred pictures chosen to instruct as well as to illustrate. Some were selected to familiarize students with the classic pictures from the presidency—such as the shot of an exuberant Truman displaying a "Dewey Defeats Truman" headline, or the picture of a solemn Lyndon B. Johnson taking the oath of office aboard *Air Force One*. Others highlight little-known facts of presidential history—such as the cartoon from the 1840 election showing the origin of the expression *OK*. The inclusion of early political cartoons points out that political commentary in the United States is nearly as old as the presidency itself.

Acknowledgments

The efforts of many people have brought this project to completion, but the work of a few deserve individual mention. David R. Tarr, director of Congressional Quarterly's Book Department, kept alive the idea of the *Guide* in its conceptual stages, then provided thoughtful direction and support until the project reached completion. Nola Healy Lynch, former developmental editor at Congressional Quarterly, wrote the first working outline of the volume. Presidential scholar Thomas E. Cronin of The Colorado College reviewed the initial plan of the book.

The authors of the *Guide* displayed unusual dedication in meeting the demands of a rigorous review and editing process. We commend them for their stamina as well as their scholarship. The contributors and their affiliations are: Harold F. Bass, Jr., Ouachita Baptist University; W. Craig Bledsoe, David Lipscomb University; Dom Bonafede, *National Journal;* Christopher J. Bosso, Northeastern University; Mark E. Byrnes, Vanderbilt University; Daniel C. Diller, Congressional Quarterly; Harrison Donnelly, freelance writer, Washington, D.C.; Charles C. Euchner, The Johns Hopkins University; Richard A. Karno, freelance writer, Washington, D.C.; John Anthony Maltese, University of Georgia; Sidney M. Milkis, Brandeis University; Dean J. Peterson, University of Illinois; Stephen L. Robertson, Vanderbilt University; Robert J. Spitzer, State University of New York at Cortland; Margaret C. Thompson, freelance writer, Washington, D.C.; James Brian Watts, Emory University; and Margaret Jane Wyszomirski, Georgetown University.

The following persons and organizations were especially helpful in researching and providing photographs: the American Political Science Association; the Bettmann Archive; the Smithsonian Institution, Division of Political History; the Library of Congress, Prints and Photographs Division; Wallace F. Dailey of the Theodore Roosevelt Collection, Harvard College Library; Mark Renovitch at the Franklin D. Roosevelt Library; the Harry S. Truman Library; the Dwight D. Eisenhower Library; James Hill at the John F. Kennedy Library; E. Philip Scott at the Lyndon B. Johnson Library; the Nixon Project, National Archives; Richard Holzhausen at the Gerald R. Ford Library; and David Stanhope at the Jimmy Carter Library.

Rex Scouten, curator of the White House, and Betty Monkman, associate curator, generously shared their time and their knowledge of White House history.

We owe special thanks to five other persons who have worked on the project. John L. Moore, assistant director of CQ's Book Department, edited several chapters and compiled parts of the Appendix. His years of experience with CQ references and broad knowledge of U.S. politics guided the project throughout. Nancy A. Lammers, managing editor of the Book Department, time and again found creative ways to meet our goals within the finite resources of time, budget, and staff. Freelance editor Sabra Bissette Ledent has that rare mix of professional skill, commitment, and realism essential to a fine editor. Her work with the authors and their manuscripts helped ensure the integrity of this volume. Production and picture editor Jane Gilligan supervised the transformation of more than five thousand edited manuscript pages and a list of five hundred picture ideas into the typeset, illustrated material that follows. Her organizational skills, keen eye for detail, and boundless patience made the nigh-impossible possible. In fact checking and picture research, Jamie R. Holland provided the resourceful and diligent support essential to producing a reference book.

Finally, we and the other writers and staff owe a great deal to our friends and especially our families who stood by while we worked on the *Guide*. Their support and good cheer count for much.

Margaret Seawell Benjaminson
Project Director
Congressional Quarterly

Michael Nelson
Editor
Vanderbilt University
April 1989

Library of Congress

The Constitution was written at Independence Hall in Philadelphia, pictured here.

Part I

Origins and Development of the Presidency

Constitutional Beginnings

The American presidency was an invention of the Constitutional Convention, unlike any other national executive position in history. Its inventors—the fifty-five convention delegates—drew on their experience, philosophy, study of history, understanding of political reality, and individual and collective wits in designing the office.

The convention's most important decisions involved number and selection (the series of choices that made the presidency a single-person office whose incumbent is selected by an independent national constituency), term and removal (the former fixed in length, the latter difficult to achieve), and powers and institutional separation (which made the presidency one of three separated institutions sharing powers).

Although the presidency has been modified several times by constitutional amendments, the basic design of the Framers remains as it was two centuries ago.

Antecedents

As with any invention, the presidency had antecedents, all of which influenced the form it took in the Constitution. The delegates to the convention had long acquaintance with British executives—the king in London and his appointed governors in the American colonies. Delegates also were influenced by their careful study of political philosophy. Finally, after independence was declared in 1776, delegates had the benefit of a decade's worth of experience with governments of their own design, both the various state constitutions and the Articles of Confederation, which defined and created a national government. The decade was a troubled one for the new nation. Experience, more than anything else, set the stage for the calling of the Constitutional Convention and the creation of the presidency.

British and Colonial Executives

The colonists were well-acquainted with the British form of government, which may be described as a constitutional monarchy. Great Britain was headed by a king (or, less frequently, a queen) who assumed the throne through inheritance and reigned for life. The monarch's power was limited by the power of Parliament, the British legislature. The king could order the nation into war, for example, but his order would prevail only if Parliament was willing to appropriate the funds to finance it. (Conversely, Parliament could pass laws, but the king could veto them.) Parliament was a bicameral, or two-house, legislature—it consisted of the House of Commons, which was elected by the people, and the House of Lords, which was made up of hereditary peers with lifetime tenure.

The British form of government was more than just the most familiar one to the American colonists—they also regarded it as the best that human beings ever had devised. Basic liberties seemed better safeguarded by Britain's constitutional monarchy than by any other government in history; British wealth and power exceeded that of any other nation. Indeed, Great Britain seemed to have answered what once was regarded as an insoluble problem of classical political philosophy—the inherent limitations of each of the three basic forms of government, namely, monarchy (rule by one person), aristocracy (rule by an elite group), and democracy (rule by the people). Because, as the problem usually was formulated, those who were entrusted to reign on behalf of the whole society ended up using power for their selfish ends, monarchy inevitably degenerated into despotism, aristocracy into oligarchy, and democracy into anarchy. The British remedy, developed over several centuries, was to meliorate these tendencies both by blending elements of all three forms of government into one—monarchy in the king, aristocracy in the House of Lords, and democracy in the House of Commons—and by allowing each element to check and balance the others.

The governments of most of Britain's American colonies were similar in structure to the British national government: a governor, appointed by the king; an upper house of the legislature, which in most colonies was appointed by the governor; and a lower house of the legislature, elected by the people. Governors were armed with substantial powers, including the right to cast an absolute, or final, veto over colonial legislation, the right to create courts and appoint judges, and even the right to prorogue, or dissolve, the legislature. But politically astute governors exercised these powers cautiously, because only the legislature was empowered to appropriate the funds to finance a colony's government and pay its governor's salary.

For all their virtues, the British and colonial govern-

By Michael Nelson

The Framers' Philosophy

In his book *1787: The Grand Convention,* Clinton Rossiter, a preeminent scholar of the founding period, summarized the basic political philosophy of the Framers by enumerating the clusters of interconnected ideas about human nature and public institutions that underlay their approach to the writing of the Constitution.[1]

The first of these clusters involved natural law and the basic human nature that derives from it:

"The political and social world is governed by laws as certain and universal as those which govern the physical world. Whether direct commands of God, necessities of nature, or simply hard lessons of history, these laws have established a moral order that men ignore at their peril. . . .

"The nature of man, which is an expression of the law of nature, is a durable mix of ennobling excellencies and degrading imperfections. Man's 'good' qualities, which need all the support they can get from education, religion, and government, are sociability, reasonableness, generosity, and the love of liberty; his 'bad' qualities, which flourish quite unaided, are selfishness, passion, greed, and corruptibility.

"Many things can corrupt a man, but none more drastically than the taste and touch of political power. . . ."

In the Framers' philosophy, Rossiter continues, the law of nature guarantees people certain fundamental rights—notably life, liberty, property, the pursuit of happiness, and conscience—to which every individual is equally entitled.

From these rights flow an understanding of the proper role of government:

"The purpose of government is to protect men in the enjoyment of their natural rights, secure their persons and property against violence, remove obstructions to their pursuit of happiness, help them to live virtuous and useful lives, adjust the complexity of their social relations, and in general fill those limited but essential collective needs that they cannot fill as individuals or in families."

The proper design of government is a different matter, more difficult to determine than government's proper role:

"The nature of government, like the nature of man, is a mixture of good and bad — 'good' because it has been ordained by the law of nature to serve some of the most basic needs of men, 'bad' because it can always get out of hand and turn arbitrary, corrupt, wicked, and oppressive. . . .

"The best form that has ever been devised or even imagined is republican government, which is to say, popular, representative, responsible, and non-hereditary. . . .

"The one agency essential to republican government is a representative legislature. Its basic function is to act as an instrument of consent through which the people tax and restrict themselves.

"The fact of legislative primacy does not mean, however, that all authority should be lodged in the representative assembly. In those governments that are stable as well as republican the total sum of permissible power is divided among three branches: a legislature, preferably bicameral; an executive, preferably single; and a judiciary, necessarily independent." Divided government "is most likely to strike the right balance between the urges of liberty and the needs of authority."

1. All of the quotations that follow are from Clinton Rossiter, *1787: The Grand Convention* (London: MacGibbon and Kee, 1968), 60-64.

ments were prone to abuse by executives who were hungry for power. King George III, who reigned during the American Revolution, used government contracts, jobs, and other forms of patronage as virtual bribes to ensure the support of members of Parliament. Some colonial governors employed similar practices with their legislatures. In 1776, the colonists' anger over these abuses of power was expressed fervently in the Declaration of Independence, which consisted mainly of a long and detailed indictment of executive "injuries and usurpations, all having in direct object the establishment of an absolute tyranny over these states."

The lesson many Americans learned from their experience with the British and colonial governments was that liberty was threatened by executive power and safeguarded by legislative power. As James Wilson, who fought in the revolutionary war and later served as a Pennsylvania delegate to the Constitutional Convention, observed:

> Before [the Revolution], the executive and judicial powers of the government were placed neither in the people, nor in those who professed to receive them under the authority of the people. They were derived from a different and a foreign source: they were regulated by foreign maxims; they were directed to a foreign purpose. Need we be surprised, then, that they were objects of aversion and distrust? . . . On the other hand, our assemblies were chosen by ourselves: they were guardians of our rights, the objects of our confidence, and the anchor of our political hopes. Every power which could be placed in them, was thought to be safely placed: every extension of that power was considered as an extension of our own security.[1]

Political Philosophy

Various scholars have argued that the Framers were guided in their thinking about government in general and the executive in particular by one or another book or school of political philosophy. *The Second Treatise on Government* (1690), by John Locke, the British philosopher; *L'Esprit des Lois (The Spirit of Laws)* (1748), by the French philosopher Baron de Montesquieu; and numerous writings of David Hume and other philosophers of the Scottish Enlightenment—all have their champions as the main inspiration of the Constitution.

In truth, the Framers were guided by all of these works, as well as by their own studies of modern and ancient government. James Madison, for example, compiled a document called "Vices of the Political System of the United States," which catalogued his objections to the state and national governments of the 1770s and 1780s on the basis of general precepts of governance that he had derived from his own research. John Adams, although not present at the Constitutional Convention (he was in London serving as the U.S. Ambassador to the Court of St. James) wrote and circulated a book in 1787 called *Defense of the Constitutions of Government of the United States of America.* Although rather aristocratic in tone, it argued for a government of separation of powers and for a bicameral legislature.

Drawn from these varied sources, the basic political philosophy of the Framers was grounded in several widely shared ideas: a belief in the fundamental and universal human rights of life, liberty, and property; an understanding of the threat that human nature's darker side posed to the preservation of these rights; and a commitment to the importance of having a republican form of government, characterized by separation of powers, as a means of averting this threat. *(See box, The Framers' Philosophy, p. 4.)*

State Constitutions

During the course of the revolutionary war, seventeen constitutions were written by the thirteen newly independent former colonies. (Some states began with one constitution, then replaced it with another.) Revulsion against their experience with the British executive—the king in London and the royal governors in the state capitols—led almost all of the authors of state constitutions to provide for weak governors and strong legislatures. As James Wilson wryly observed, under independence, "the executive and the judicial as well as the legislative authority was now the child of the people; but to the two former, the people behaved like stepmothers. The legislature was still discriminated by excessive partiality; and into its lap, every good and precious gift was profusely thrown." [2]

Typically, state governors in the decade after independence was declared were elected by the legislature for a brief term (one year, in most cases) and were ineligible for reelection. They were forced to share their powers with a council of some sort, which made them, in the assessment of the historian Gordon Wood, "little more than chairmen of their executive boards." [3] (Indeed, at the Constitutional Convention, Gov. Edmund Randolph of Virginia would oppose the proposal to make the presidency a unitary office by saying that, as governor, he was merely "a member of the executive.") Such powers as the governors had were meager. Most state constitutions made vague grants of authority to their chief executives and, by specifically denying them the right to veto legislation and to make appointments, rendered them incapable of defending even those from legislative encroachment. In his *Notes on Virginia,* Thomas Jefferson described the result in his home state:

> All the powers of government, legislative, executive and judiciary, result to the legislative body.... The [state constitutional] convention, which passed the ordinance of government, laid its foundation on this basis, that the legislative, executive and judiciary departments should be separate and distinct, so that no person should exercise the powers of more than one of them at the same time. But no barrier was provided between these several powers. The judiciary and executive members were left dependent on the legislative for their subsistence in office and some of them for their continuance in it. If therefore the legislature assumes executive and judiciary powers, no opposition is likely to be made; nor, if made, can it be effectual; because in that case they may put their proceedings in the form of an act of assembly, which will render them obligatory on the other branches.[4]

The constitution of the state of New York offered a striking exception to the general practice of weak governors and strong legislatures. New York's governor was elected by the people, not the legislature, for a term of three years, not one, and, rather than being confined to one term, could be reelected as often as the people chose. (George Clinton, the first governor to be elected under the New York constitution, was elected six times, for a total of eighteen years.) The executive power of New York was unitary, exercised by the governor alone and not shared with a council. The powers of the governor were defined by the constitution in detail, much as the powers of the president would be in the U.S. Constitution:

> Article XVIII.... The governor ... shall by virtue of his office, be general and commander in chief of all the militia, and admiral of the navy of this state;... he shall have power to convene the assembly and senate on extraordinary occasions; to prorogue them from time to time, provided such prorogations shall not exceed sixty days in the space of any one year; and, at his discretion, to grant reprieves and pardons to persons convicted of crimes, other than treason and murder, in which he may suspend the execution of the sentence, until it shall be reported to the legislature at their subsequent meeting; and they shall either pardon or direct the execution of the criminal, or grant a further reprieve.
>
> Article XIX.... It shall be the duty of the governor to inform the legislature of the condition of the state so far as may concern his department; to recommend such matters to their consideration as shall appear to him to concern its good government, welfare and prosperity; to correspond with the Continental Congress and other States; to transact all necessary business with the officers of government, civil and military; to take care that the laws are executed to the best of his ability; and to expedite all such measures as may be resolved upon by legislature.

Finally, the governor of New York was empowered to veto legislation, subject to a vote to override by the legislature, and to make appointments, subject to legislative confirmation.

The Articles of Confederation

The decision by the Continental Congress to declare independence from Great Britain in summer 1776 was accompanied by another decision that, as stated in the motion by Virginian Richard Henry Lee, "a plan of confederation [shall] be prepared and transmitted to the respective Colonies for their consideration and approbation." Such a step was militarily necessary. Although the Declaration of Independence made each of the states, in effect, an independent nation, they could not fight a common war against the British without a common government.

But the states, jealous of their independence and reluctant to substitute a new central government (even one that was homegrown) for the British government they had

They Shaped the Presidency

Of the fifty-five delegates who attended the Constitutional Convention, fewer than half played roles of any consequence in the creation of the presidency. Of those who did, eight stand out. James Wilson and Gouverneur Morris urged the convention to make the presidency the leading institution of the new national government. Wilson and Morris did not achieve all they had hoped for, but they were effective in persuading their fellow delegates to create a stronger executive than they originally had been disposed to do. Alexander Hamilton was less effective, George Washington less vocal, and James Madison less certain in their support of a strong executive, but, in various ways, the influence of each was crucial. Roger Sherman and Edmund Randolph were staunch opponents of the presidency as it developed during the convention, but their contributions in debate helped to shape the delegates' deliberations. Charles Pinckney's suggestions about the presidency and other offices were influential beyond his historical reputation. *(See box, The Puzzle of the Pinckney Plan, p. 16.)*

just rejected, surrendered power grudgingly. They stipulated to their members in Congress that the confederation was to be no stronger than was absolutely necessary to conduct the Revolution. Reacting against their experience with British rule, the states also made clear that the confederation's executive component must be minimal. Nothing remotely resembling a national king would be tolerated.

On June 11, 1776, a Committee of Thirteen (one from each state) was formed in the Continental Congress to draft a plan of confederation. The committee, acting expeditiously, submitted its recommendation on July 12. More than a year later, on November 15, 1777, Congress adopted a revised version of the plan, calling it the Articles of Confederation and Perpetual Union. Ratification by the states came slowly, the last state voting approval on March 1, 1781. But the Articles were so much like the ad hoc arrangement that the states already were using under the Continental Congress that the delayed ratification posed no serious problems.

The articles more than embodied the states' dread of central government and executive power. Indeed, they hardly created a government at all—more like an alliance or league of nations. Its president was no more than a presiding officer. Eventually, Congress created departments headed by appointed officials—the task of making all financial, diplomatic, and military decisions and executing all legislative enactments was more than Congress as a body could handle—but their activities underwent close legislative monitoring. In truth, few laws of consequence were passed by Congress. To pass a law required the support of nine of the thirteen states: amendments to the articles had to be approved unanimously.

In addition to a weak institutional structure, the articles undermined the power of the national government in other ways. Technically, Congress was empowered to declare war, make treaties and enter alliances, raise an army and navy, regulate coinage and borrow money, supervise Indian affairs, establish a post office, and adjudicate disputes that arose between states. Funds and troops were to be supplied by the states according to their wealth and population. But Congress had no power to tax the states or to enforce its decisions. When, as often happened, one or two states balked at meeting an obligation, other states followed suit. "Each state sent what was convenient or appropriate," the historians Christopher Collier and James Lincoln Collier have observed, "which usually depended on how close to home the fighting was going on." [5] After the revolutionary war was won and the common threat from the British removed, states felt even less incentive to honor the requests of the national government.

National Problems

For all its weakness, the Articles of Confederation did not prevent the United States from winning independence from Great Britain. The revolutionary war effectively ended on October 17, 1781, when Gen. George Washington's American army and a French fleet, anchored off Yorktown, Virginia, forced the surrender of the British forces led by Lord Cornwallis.

The problems of a weak, purely legislative national government became more apparent in the half-decade that followed victory. No longer joined by a common foe, the states turned their backs almost completely on Congress and on each other.

Discord among the states was one result of national weakness. Overlapping claims to western lands brought some states into conflict—Connecticut settlers and Pennsylvania troops even clashed violently in a disputed area. The western territories were the nation's most valuable resource, but until the rival claims were settled, it was difficult to develop and profit from them. On the East Coast, some states with port cities—New York, Massachusetts, South Carolina, and Pennsylvania—placed taxes on goods imported from overseas by merchants in neighboring states.

The nation also was burdened by a crippling debt. Money was owed to soldiers who had fought and merchants who had provided supplies during the revolutionary war. Threatened in many cases with bankruptcy or foreclosure, they were angry and sometimes violent. By 1789, foreign creditors held more than $10 million in notes and were owed $1.8 million in unpaid interest. Unless paid, they were unwilling to engage in further trade with the United States. Yet Congress was unable to persuade the states to contribute to the Treasury. The total income of the national government in 1786, for example, was less than one-third of the interest due that year on the national debt.

The United States faced numerous problems on and outside its borders as well as at home. The nation's northern, southern, and western boundaries were under siege, with only an ill-equipped, poorly financed, seven hundred-member army to defend them. British soldiers continued to occupy two Great Lakes forts that they had promised to vacate under the Treaty of Paris, which had been concluded in 1783 to settle the revolutionary war. Similarly, Spain closed the Mississippi River to U.S. ships and claimed land east of the river that, according to the treaty,

James Wilson

No delegate contributed more to the creation of the presidency than James Wilson of Pennsylvania. Wilson, forty-six years old at the time of the convention, was born in Scotland. The son of a small dirt farmer, he studied law and emigrated to America when he was twenty-four. He became a highly successful lawyer and, in the opinion of many, the preeminent legal scholar of his time. In addition, observed William Pierce, a Georgia delegate who wrote perceptive short profiles of his colleagues at the convention, Wilson

> is well acquainted with Man, and understands all the passions that influence him. Government seems to have been his peculiar Study, all the political institutions of the World he knows in detail, and can trace the causes and effects of every revolution from the earliest stages of the Grecian commonwealth down to the present time. No man is more clear, copious, and comprehensive than Mr. Wilson, yet he is no great Orator. He draws the attention not by the charm of his eloquence, but by the force of his reasoning.

Being foreign born, Wilson was much more devoted to the United States as a nation than to any particular state. He signed the Declaration of Independence and helped to write the Articles of Confederation. One of the few lowborn delegates, he had a high regard for the common sense and good instincts of the people. Indeed, he believed that the president should be popularly elected, but, realizing the hopelessness of persuading the convention to adopt that idea, he became the first delegate to propose a scheme of presidential election by electors chosen by the people. Wilson also worked hard and effectively to have the executive power entrusted to a single person, who would be unshackled by a council and eligible for reelection. Along with Roger Sherman, Wilson spoke as often at the convention as any delegate except Madison, whose support he rallied for a strong presidency.

Wilson's achievements at the Constitutional Convention are all the more remarkable because of the personal travails he was suffering at the time. His beloved wife, Rachel, had died one year earlier, leaving him to care for their six young children; and his personal fortune, built mainly on land speculation, was beginning to unravel. Wilson's financial decline continued and probably caused his early death in 1797—he actually was jailed for debt in New Jersey while serving as a justice of the U.S. Supreme Court.

---

rightfully belonged to the United States. Both nations encouraged Indian raids on American frontier settlements. (Spain, in particular, roused Indians in Florida to harass settlements in Georgia.) Abroad, U.S. ships were preyed on by pirates in the Mediterranean Sea and denied entry by the British to Britain's colonies in Canada and the West Indies, two lucrative markets for U.S. trade.

To a large degree, British hostility to the United States was caused, or at least rationalized, by the U.S. failure to comply with two provisions of the Treaty of Paris. One provision compelled the United States to reimburse British loyalists for property that had been seized from them during the war; the other required that prewar debts to British merchants be paid. States actively resisted both these requirements, and the national government was powerless to enforce them.

In the midst of foreign and domestic difficulties, another problem developed that mixed elements of both. A currency crisis occurred in the United States, partly because Americans had gone on a buying spree after the revolutionary war was over, frantically importing "luxuries" like clocks, glassware, and furniture from Great Britain. As money—that is, gold and silver—flowed out of the country to pay for these products, it became scarce at home. Many debtors, including farmers who had left the land to fight for independence and still had not been paid by the financially destitute national government, faced bankruptcy or foreclosure. They put pressure on the legislatures of their states simply to print vast sums of paper money that they could use to pay off their debts. Creditors, horrified at the prospect of being reimbursed in depreciated currency, fought back, with limited success. State legislatures, being both powerful and democratic, often were more responsive to the greater number of debtors than to the smaller number of creditors.

The problems that beset the United States under the strong legislative governments of the states and the weak legislative government of the Articles of Confederation taught certain lessons, particularly to conservatives and people of property. As the political scientist Charles Thach has written, "experience with the state governments during the period following the cessation of hostilities served . . . to confirm the tendencies toward increasing confidence in the executive and increasing distrust of the legislature." Along with the ineffectiveness of the national government, it also taught certain lessons about the proper design of an effective executive:

> It taught that executive energy and responsibility are inversely proportional to executive size; that, consequently, the one-man executive is best. It taught the value of integration; the necessity of executive appointments, civil and military; the futility of legislative military control. It demonstrated the necessity of the veto as a protective measure . . . [for] preventing unwise legislation. . . . It demonstrated the value of a fixed executive salary which the legislature could not reduce. It discred-

> ited choice by the legislature, though without teaching clearly the lesson of popular choice. . . . And, above all, it assured the acceptance of, if it did not create, a new concept of national government—the fundamental principles of which were the ruling constitution, the limited legislature, and the three equal and coordinate departments.[6]

A Convention Is Called

Of all the problems that plagued the new nation after independence, none seemed more amenable to solution than those involving commerce among the states. Few benefited, and many suffered, from the protectionist walls that states had built around their economies. At the urging of James Madison and others, the Virginia state assembly called for a trade conference to be held at Annapolis, Maryland, in September 1786 and urged all the other states to send delegations.

In some ways, the Annapolis Convention was a failure. Only three states (Virginia, New Jersey, and Delaware) sent full delegations; and seven states, suspicious of Virginia's intentions, boycotted the meeting altogether. The convention made no proposals to remedy the nation's trade difficulties.

But the delegates who did come to Annapolis, notably Madison and Alexander Hamilton of New York, rescued the enterprise by issuing a bold call to Congress to convene an even more wide-ranging meeting. They urged that the states be enjoined to choose delegates to "meet at Philadelphia on the second Monday in May next [1787], to take into consideration the situation of the United States, to devise such further provisions as shall appear to them necessary to render the constitution of the Federal Government adequate to the exigencies of the Union."

Congress initially was cool to the summons of the Annapolis Convention, but an event occurred within weeks that lent urgency to the nationalist cause. Mobs of farmers in western Massachusetts, saddled with debts and unable to persuade the state legislature to ease credit, closed down courts and stopped sheriffs' auctions in order to prevent foreclosure orders from being issued and executed against their land. Although similar outbreaks had occurred in other states, they had been easily suppressed; this one, dubbed Shays's Rebellion after one of its leaders, the revolutionary war hero Daniel Shays, threatened for a time to rage out of control. The reaction around the country among people of property and, more generally, among believers in law and order was one of shock and horror, both at the class warfare that seemed to be breaking out and the inability of the national government to deal with it. On February 21, 1787, Congress decided to act on the request of the Annapolis Convention:

> RESOLVED, That in the opinion of Congress it is expedient that on the second Monday in May next a Convention of delegates who shall have been appointed by the several states be held in Philadelphia for the sole and express purpose of revising the Articles of Confederation and reporting to Congress and the state legislatures such alternations and provisions therein as shall when agreed to in Congress and confirmed by the states render the federal constitution adequate to the exigencies of government & the preservation of the Union.

The states were, of course, no more compelled to follow this summons of Congress than any other—Rhode Island never did send delegates to the convention But when a sufficient number of states—whether frightened by the prospect of further Shays-style rebellions, concerned about

Gouverneur Morris

Gouverneur Morris was one of the more flamboyant delegates at the Constitutional Convention, yet his brilliance earned him respect as a strong and effective advocate of executive power.

As William Pierce observed:

> Mr. Gouverneur Morris is one of those Genius's in whom every species of talent combine to render him conspicuous and flourishing in public debate:—He winds through all the mazes of rhetoric, and throws around him such a glare that he charms, captivates, and leads away the senses of all who hear him. With an infinite stretch of fancy he brings to view things when he is engaged in deep argumentation, that render all the labor of reasoning easy and pleasing. But with all these powers he is fickle and inconstant,—never pursuing one train of thinking,—nor ever regular. . . . This Gentleman . . . has been unfortunate in losing one of his Legs, and getting all the flesh taken off his right arm by a scald, when a youth.

Morris blended the character of the successful businessman with that of the stylish rake. (Indeed, he fostered the rumor that his leg had been lost after he injured it leaping from a married woman's second-story window to escape her husband—the truth was that he had hurt it in a carriage accident.) At the convention, Morris fought hard and successfully against having the executive be chosen by the legislature, a process that he felt would degenerate into "the work of intrigue, of cabal, and of faction: it will be like the election of a pope by a conclave of cardinals." Morris also urged that the president be permitted to stand for reelection, in order to take advantage of "the great motive to good behavior, the hope of being rewarded by a reappointment." Aware of his fellow delegates' reluctance to entrust as much power as he would have liked to a single executive, Morris shrewdly argued that an impeachment provision be included in the Constitution.

Alexander Hamilton

Alexander Hamilton's role in the framing of the Constitution was of enormous significance, but his contributions at the Constitutional Convention were less significant. Before the convention, it was Hamilton and James Madison, more than anyone else, who transformed the failed Annapolis Convention of 1786 into a vehicle to persuade Congress to summon delegates to a more far-reaching convention.

After the Constitutional Convention was over, Hamilton recruited Madison and John Jay to help him write an eighty-five part newspaper series to urge the ratification of the Constitution. (Hamilton wrote fifty-one numbers.) The collection of articles, which were written under the pen name "Publius" and later compiled into a book called *The Federalist Papers,* generally is regarded as the greatest work of political philosophy ever written in the United States. *(See box,* The Federalist Papers *on Powers of the Presidency, p. 38.)*

At the convention itself, however, Hamilton was a minor figure. This was partly because the three-member New York delegation to which he belonged also included Robert Yates and John Lansing, two opponents of a stronger central government who consistently outvoted Hamilton. Frustrated, Hamilton left Philadelphia early in the convention, returning only after Yates and Lansing themselves decided to leave.

Another reason for Hamilton's small influence at the convention was his arrogant, impatient manner, which was ill-suited to the deliberative, sometimes tedious work of the convention. The thirty-two-year-old Hamilton had always been a man in a hurry. A child of illegitimate birth in the British West Indies, he had made his way to New York as a teenager, fought in the revolutionary war, and even won a command (at age twenty-one) under Gen. George Washington. According to William Pierce's description,

> [T]here is something too feeble in his voice to be equal to the strains of oratory;—it is my opinion that he is rather a convincing Speaker, [than] a blazing Orator. Colo. Hamilton requires time to think,—he enquires into every part of his subject with the searchings of philosophy, and when he comes forward he comes highly charged with interesting matter, there is no skimming over the surface of a subject with him, he must sink to the bottom to see what foundation it rests on.... He is ... of small stature, and lean. His manners are tinctured with stiffness, and sometimes with a degree of vanity that is highly disagreeable.

A final reason for Hamilton's minor role at the convention is that his ideas were far more radical than either the country or his fellow delegates were willing to accept. As much as possible, Hamilton wanted to transplant the British form of government onto American soil. The Senate, like the British House of Lords, would have life tenure. So, like the British monarch, would the "supreme Executive Authority," which he proposed to call "Governor." Only the House of Representatives would be elected for brief terms, as was the House of Commons.

For all his disappointment with the convention and his role in it, Hamilton defended the Constitution in *The Federalist Papers* as enthusiastically as if he had written every jot and tittle in it. Indeed, in No. 69, he took great pains to persuade his readers not only that the American president was *not* like the British king but that it was to be preferred for that very reason.

the nation's growing domestic and international weakness, or inspired by the example of George Washington, who decided to attend as a delegate from Virginia—selected delegations, other states fell into line for fear of having their interests ignored.

The Constitutional Convention

The Constitutional Convention has been variously described over the years: an "assembly of demigods" (Jefferson), a "miracle at Philadelphia" (author Catherine Drinker Bowen), and a "nationalist reform caucus" (political scientist John Roche), to cite but three descriptions. The convention may have been all of these things and more. But, more mundanely, it also was a gathering of fifty-five individuals (the delegates) in a particular place (Philadelphia) at a specific moment in history (Summer 1787).

From May to September, the delegates used debate and drafts, compromises and committees to work through the many issues that faced them. The design of the presidency not only took a great deal of their time and effort in its own right; it also was interwoven with the design of the other institutions and processes of the new government.

The Delegates

Some sixty to seventy-five delegates were selected by the various states to represent them at the convention in Philadelphia, of whom fifty-five actually attended. Self-selection had much to do with determining who was selected and who went. Political leaders who were committed to the idea that the system had to be dramatically improved leaped at the opportunity to attend the convention. Most of those who were basically satisfied with the status quo and disapproved of the convention—including such

Library of Congress

Library of Congress

Library of Congress

Library of Congress

Satisfied with the status quo, these four prominent Americans refused to attend the Constitutional Convention because they disapproved of creating a new system of goverment. From left, Patrick Henry and Richard Henry Lee of Virginia, George Clinton of New York, and Samuel Adams of Massachusetts.

prominent Americans as Patrick Henry and Richard Henry Lee of Virginia, Samuel Adams of Massachusetts, and George Clinton of New York—stayed away. ("I smelt a Rat," said Henry.) Had they attended and fought stubbornly for their position, the political scientist Clinton Rossiter has observed, the convention "would have been much more perfectly representative of the active citizenry of 1787. It would also, one is bound to point out, have been crippled as a nation-building instrument."[7]

The fifty-five delegates were generally united, then, in their belief that a stronger national government was vital to the health of the new American nation. In part, this was because many of them had shared similar experiences. Forty-two were current or former members of Congress; twenty-one had risked life and livelihood by fighting in the revolutionary war; eight had signed the Declaration of Independence. They were, wrote Rossiter:

> men who had been out together in all sorts of weather and were still not afraid of storms. [George] Washington could look around the room and see a half-dozen men who had voted him into command far back in 1775, a dozen who had been with him at Trenton, Monmouth, or Yorktown, . . . and another dozen who had won his friendship by supporting him in Congress or fishing with him in the Potomac.[8]

Other shared characteristics of the delegates contributed to their common outlook on many fundamental issues. Almost all were prosperous—around half were lawyers and another quarter owned plantations or large farms. (Only two delegates were small farmers, who made up 85 percent of the nation's white population.) All had held public office—more than forty currently occupied positions in their state governments, including ten judges, thirty legislators, and three governors. Several had helped to write their state constitutions. All were well known in their states; around one-fourth had national reputations.

All of the delegates to the convention were white males. All but two Roman Catholics were Protestant in affiliation, but most were rationalist in outlook. Twenty-six had earned college degrees, at a time when a college education was rigorous and rare. The College of New Jersey (now Princeton University), the College of William and Mary, and Yale University were the most frequently represented alma maters. Collectively, the delegates were surprisingly young. Madison, age thirty-six, was older than eleven other delegates, including several who were to play significant roles at the convention, such as Gouverneur Morris (thirty-four), Edmund Randolph (thirty-three), and Charles Pinckney (twenty-nine). Jonathan Dayton of New Jersey was the youngest delegate (twenty-six); Benjamin Franklin, age eighty-one, was the oldest. The average age of the delegates was forty-three.

Still, there were differences among those who attended the convention. Some represented small states, some large. Some were southerners, some from the middle Atlantic region, some from New England. (Regardless of region, however, most lived in the coastal parts of their states; the backcountry was hardly represented.) Temperamentally, wrote the Colliers, they were "as diverse as any group of people is likely to be. Some were bold, some cautious; some shy, some outspoken; some politically adept, some bristly and rancorous."[9]

The wealth of most of the delegates derived from personal property (money, government securities, and investments in manufacturing, shipping, and land speculation); other delegates grounded their prosperity in real property, notably agricultural land and slaves. (The historian Charles A. Beard believed that the enactment of the Constitution, more than anything else, was a triumph of the "personalty"—that is, financial and commercial—interests over the "realty, or landed" interests.)[10] In the realm of political philosophy, delegates who agreed on basic goals often differed on the proper means to achieve them.

Delegates also varied in the extent of their participation at the convention. Of the fifty-five who came to Philadelphia, only twenty-nine were there at the beginning and stayed through until the end. (This number, however, included Madison, Randolph, Washington, and George Mason of Virginia, Wilson and Franklin of Pennsylvania, Elbridge Gerry of Massachusetts, Roger Sherman of Connecticut, Charles Pinckney of South Carolina, and most of the other leading members of the convention.) The twenty-six others were part-timers to varying degrees, although some of them also played important roles, such as Pennsylvania's Gouverneur Morris, Oliver Ellsworth of Connecticut, and William Paterson of New Jersey. These delegates either arrived late at the convention (in some cases because their states had been tardy in choosing them) or left early because of illness, dissatisfaction with the proceedings, the need to attend to state or personal business, or, in the case of James McClurg of Virginia, an overwhelming sense of personal inadequacy to the task at hand. Thus, most sessions of the convention were attended by thirty to forty delegates, of whom the majority were regulars and the rest a shifting cast.

The Setting

Philadelphia was the site of the Constitutional Convention. The capital of Pennsylvania at the time (Harrisburg replaced it in 1812), Philadelphia was in many ways the nation's capital as well, even though Congress met in New York. Philadelphia was by far the largest U.S. city, with a population of around 45,000. It also was the commercial, cultural, and intellectual center of the United States. Not least among its virtues was its central location. Travel was arduous and time consuming in the late eighteenth century—few southerners wanted to travel to New York or Boston and few New Englanders to Charleston, South Carolina, which were the other leading cities of the day.

One of Philadelphia's least appealing qualities was its notoriously hot, humid, and insect-ridden summers. The summer of 1787, especially after a heat wave struck on June 11, was no exception. The city sweltered for almost the entire duration of the Constitutional Convention. The delegates found that although closed windows made the heat even more stifling, open windows were invitations to Philadelphia's infamous black flies during the day and mosquitoes at night.

As in most other cities, much of the social and business life of Philadelphia during this period took place in taverns, which were more like inns than bars or saloons. The leading tavern in Philadelphia was the Indian Queen, described by one New England traveler as "a large pile of buildings, with many spacious halls and numerous small apartments," each equipped with a bed, bureau, table, mirror, and one or two chairs. Many of the delegates stayed at the Indian Queen, and even those who did not (Madison and most of the Virginia delegation, for example, stayed at the boardinghouse of Mrs. Mary House, and Washington was the house guest of Robert Morris, a Pennsylvania delegate to the convention) helped make the tavern the convention's after-hours social and, in many cases, business center.

During the convention, the delegates' days settled into a routine. After breakfast and a morning walk or ride, most of them would stroll over to Independence Hall—then called the State House and used as the capitol building for the government of Pennsylvania—where they met from nine-thirty or ten o'clock in the morning until three or four

Roger Sherman

"Mr. Sherman exhibits the oddest shaped character I ever remember to have met with," William Pierce observed. "He is awkward, un-meaning, and unaccountably strange in his manner. . . . [T]he oddity of his address, the vulgarness that accompany his public speaking, and that strange New England cant which runs through his public as well as his private speaking make everything that is connected with him grotesque and laughable."

For all his strangeness of speech and manner, Sherman was one of the most influential political leaders of his time. He had signed and helped to write both the Articles of Confederation and, along with Thomas Jefferson, John Adams, and Benjamin Franklin, the Declaration of Independence. After the Constitution took effect, Sherman was elected a representative from Connecticut in the first Congress and a senator in the second. At the Constitutional Convention, Sherman spoke more frequently than anyone other than James Madison and, perhaps, James Wilson and was the author of the Connecticut Compromise on representation in Congress, the issue that had stymied the convention more than any other. Even Pierce agreed that Sherman "deserves infinite praise,—no Man has a better Heart or a clearer Head. If he cannot embellish he can furnish thoughts that are wise and useful. He is an able politician, and extremely artful in accomplishing any particular object;—it is remarked that he seldom fails."

Sherman was fifty-six years old in 1787. He was unusual among the delegates in two obvious ways. First (like Wilson), he was lowborn, the son of a small family farmer. (The house Sherman grew up in contained nine people and three beds.) Second, he was a career politician who, during most of his life, earned his living from holding office.

Sherman was one of the most effective opponents of a strong presidency at the convention. He regarded the ideal executive "as nothing more than an instrument for carrying the will of the legislature into effect." For that reason, he believed, the legislature should be free to create and revise the executive as it saw fit. Specifically, Sherman wanted the legislature, not the Constitution, to define the executive's powers as it found convenient; "he wished the number might not be fixed, but that the legislature should be at liberty to appoint one or more as experience might dictate"; and he urged that "the national Legislature should have power to remove the Executive at pleasure." To Sherman, in fact, an "independence of the executive on the supreme legislative was in his opinion the very essence of tyranny."

George Washington

George Washington spoke hardly a word during the debates at the Constitutional Convention—he thanked his fellow delegates on the first day of the convention for choosing him to preside and urged them on the last day to pass a minor motion involving representation in Congress. But, perhaps as much as any other delegate, Washington's presence was felt at the convention, especially on the subject of the presidency.

Washington's decision to attend the Constitutional Convention lent the proceedings an otherwise unattainable legitimacy. William Pierce wrote:

> Having conducted these states to independence and peace, he now appears to assist in framing a Government to make the People happy. Like Gustavus Vasa, he may be said to be the deliverer of his Country; —like Peter the Great he appears as the politician and the States-man; and like Cincinnatus he returned to his farm perfectly contented with being only a plain Citizen, after enjoying the highest honors of the Confederacy, —and now only seeks for the approbation of his Country-men by being virtuous and useful.

Despite the silence in debate he maintained as president of the convention, Washington clearly favored a stronger central government and a strong executive within that government. This is attested to not just by his correspondence and one of his few recorded votes at the convention (in favor of a unitary executive rather than a council), but also by the record of his life.

Washington, who was fifty-five at the time of the convention, already had been, as commander in chief of the revolutionary army, the closest thing to a national executive in the young nation's experience. His fears were less of government power than of the disorder that the absence of power invited. These views were made known to his fellow delegates, not in formal debate, but in private and informal discussions.

Washington influenced the creation of the presidency in various ways. His fellow delegates' certain knowledge that he would be the nation's first president increased their willingness to resolve doubts about executive power in favor of the presidency. The constitutional powers of the president "are full great," wrote South Carolina delegate Pierce Butler to a British kinsman after the convention, "and greater than I was disposed to make them. Nor, entre nous, do I believe they would have been so great had not many of the delegates cast their eye on General Washington as President; and shaped their Ideas of the Powers to be given to a President, by their opinions of his Virtue."

in the afternoon. The two-story building, although plain, was attractive because of its large windows and graceful horizontal spread. From the street, delegates would enter into the State House's great hallway through the main door. To the right were the chambers of the state supreme court; straight ahead and up the stairs were the offices of Pennsylvania's Supreme Executive Council (Franklin was its president); and to the left was the forty-by-forty room in which the state legislature usually met.

The legislature's room was used by the delegates during the convention, just as it had been used by the Continental Congress from 1775 to 1783. (Among other things, the Declaration of Independence was signed there.) The room was high-ceilinged and simple—only the speaker's mahogany chair and inkstand lent any ornamentation. The speaker, or presiding officer, sat behind a table with only a small bell (no gavel) to call meetings to order. Thirteen other tables were spread about the room, covered, like the speaker's, with green baize (a thick wool cloth). Each was equipped with inkstands, goose quill pens, sand, and writing paper. (Delegates added their own materials, including papers, books, and snuff and tobacco boxes.) Each table was reserved for a state delegation—the southern tables on one side, the New England tables on the other, and the middle states' tables in the middle. Washington, after being elected president of the convention, sat in the speaker's chair. Madison, although a Virginia delegate, found a chair near the front and middle so that he could keep thorough notes on the debates.

Rules and Procedures

Congress had called upon the convention to assemble on Monday, May 14, but not until Friday, May 25, were the seven state delegations that were needed for a quorum present in Philadelphia. Most of the other delegations arrived within a few days, but some came later. Rhode Island, whose legislature was fiercely opposed to any effort to strengthen the national government, boycotted the convention entirely.

The first order of business on May 25 was to elect a president, a word that, in the usage of the day, suggested a "presiding officer" more than a "leader" or "chief executive." [11] Not surprisingly, George Washington was the delegates' unanimous choice. Washington spoke out on only one minor issue during the convention—he rose on the last day in support of a proposal to amend the Constitution so that members of the House of Representatives would represent at least thirty thousand people rather than forty thousand. (Not surprisingly, the delegates agreed unanimously.) But clearly he played more than a ceremonial role. According to the Colliers, "during that long, hot summer, this gregarious man was constantly having dinner, tea, supper with people, and one must assume of course that he was actively promoting his position," namely, a strong national government and a strong executive within that government.[12]

After Washington's election, a secretary was chosen—Maj. William Jackson of Pennsylvania. Jackson kept the convention's official journal, which was little more than a record of motions and votes. Fortunately, Madison decided to keep a more extensive record of the delegates' debates and deliberations. Madison had been frustrated in his studies of other governments by the near-impossibility of determining what their founders had in mind. Although he was acting on his own initiative, the other delegates knew what he was doing. In fairness to them, he decided to keep his notes secret until the last delegate died. This turned out to be himself. (Madison died in 1836, at the age of eighty-six.) Along with the rest of Madison's papers, his notes on the Constitutional Convention were purchased by Congress and published in 1840.

The only other business of the convention's first day was to accept the credentials of the various state delegations. In doing so, the delegates implicitly agreed that the then-customary procedure of having each state cast an equal vote in any national body would be followed. Wilson of Pennsylvania was displeased by this arrangement (he felt that the large states should have a greater voice) but was persuaded by Madison and others that to alienate the small states at such an early stage would abort the entire proceedings.

On Monday, May 28, the delegates adopted additional rules and procedures. None was more important to the success of the convention than the rule of secrecy. The rule was simple: no delegate was to say anything to anyone, including their families, about the convention's discussions and deliberations.

Thomas Jefferson, then the U.S. ambassador to France, wrote John Adams, the ambassador to Great Britain, that he was appalled by "so abominable a precedent [as secrecy] .... Nothing can justify this [decision] but the innocence of their intentions and ignorance of the value of public discussions." But in a letter to Jefferson, Madison explained the delegates' action. "It was thought expedient in order to secure unbiased discussion within doors, and to prevent misconceptions & misconstructions without, to establish some rules of caution which will for no short time restrain even a confidential communication of our proceed-

James Madison

Even as admiring a scholar as the political scientist Charles Thach, who wrote in his book *The Creation of the Presidency* that "Madison has with much justice been called the father of the Constitution," conceded that "the claims for his paternity do not extend to the fundamentals of Article II."

Madison himself claimed no paternity of the presidency—as he wrote George Washington on April 16, 1787, less than a month before the scheduled opening of the convention, "I have scarcely ventured as yet to form my own opinion either of the manner in which [the executive] ought to be constituted or of the authorities with which it ought to be cloathed." Madison's Virginia Plan left the number and term of the executive unspecified and offered only a vague definition of what the executive's powers would be. The plan was more specific in providing that the legislature would select the executive, but James Wilson and Gouverneur Morris persuaded him otherwise—Madison actually argued against the legislative selection on July 19 and spoke favorably of election by the people.

Indeed, far from being preoccupied with the design of the executive, Madison's primary concern was for the creation of a government by the people, not the states. This purpose would be achieved, he believed, mainly through the legislature, which he felt should be checked and balanced internally but apportioned according to population and empowered both to pass laws that acted directly on individuals and to veto state laws.

Madison was thirty-six years old, a member of the Virginia aristocracy who had been educated at the College of New Jersey in Princeton. Always fearful of power, Madison's main battles as a member of the Virginia state government had been against British tyranny and the established church. In Congress, his target became what he saw as the runaway state governments and the threat they posed to property. Madison's solution was a central government strong enough to curb the power of the states but thoroughly saddled with internal checks and balances so that its own power did not become excessive.

At the Constitutional Convention (which he and Alexander Hamilton had worked so hard to arrange), Madison made a deep and positive impression on his fellow delegates. William Pierce observed:

> [E]very Person seems to acknowledge his greatness. He blends together the profound politician, with the Scholar. In the management of every great question he evidently took the lead in the Convention, and tho' he cannot be called an Orator, he is a most agreeable, eloquent, and convincing Speaker. From a spirit of industry and application which he possesses in a most eminent degree, he always comes forward the best informed Man of any point in debate. The affairs of the United States, he perhaps, has the most correct knowledge of, of any Man in the Union.... [Yet] Mr. Madison is ... a Gentleman of great modesty,—with a remarkable sweet temper. He is easy and unreserved among his acquaintances, and has a most agreeable style of conversation.

Edmund Randolph

Edmund Randolph was thirty-four years old at the time of the convention, a member of one of Virginia's most aristocratic families. A tall, somewhat portly man with a commanding presence (William Pierce described him as "a young Gentleman in whom unite all the accomplishments of the Scholar, and the Statesman.... He has a most harmonious voice, a fine person and striking manners"), Randolph was a political protégé of the state's elite. He had been the youngest delegate at the Virginia constitutional convention in 1776, George Washington's legal counsel, and the state's first attorney general. As president, Washington later named Randolph to be the nation's first attorney general.

At the time of the convention, Randolph was governor of Virginia, a position to which he was elected by the legislature. Because he made the speech that introduced the Virginia Plan, Randolph sometimes is linked with James Madison and Washington as a proponent of strong central government. In truth, he was mainly concerned about political opinion in Virginia, which he feared would begrudge ceding the state's power to a new government. During the course of the convention, Randolph expressed particularly heated opposition to proposals for a strong executive. He told the delegates that, as Virginia's governor, he was "a member of the executive" and that he regarded a unitary executive as the "foetus of monarchy." Randolph proposed instead a committee-style executive that would consist of representatives from each region of the country. Disappointed with the convention's final decisions, Randolph was one of three delegates who refused to sign the Constitution.

ings." In other words, secrecy permitted delegates to think through issues and to change their minds when necessary without appearing weak or vacillating. It also kept opponents of the convention from sensationalizing particular ideas or decisions as a means of discrediting the whole undertaking. Years later, Madison told historian Jared Sparks that "no Constitution would ever have been adopted by the Convention if the debates had been made public." [13]

Another important rule adopted by the convention was to permit its decisions to be reconsidered at even a single delegate's request. Because issues could always be raised and decided again, those who were on the losing side of a crucial vote were encouraged to stay and try to persuade the others, rather than walk out and go home in protest and frustration.

Convention Overview

The Constitutional Convention was not a scripted or even an especially orderly proceeding. The delegates' decision to allow issues to be redecided, reinforced by their twin desires to build consensus among themselves and to create a government whose parts would mesh with one another, meant that their proceedings "could not, and did not, proceed in a straight line, neatly disposing of one issue after the next until all were dealt with. [The convention] moved instead in swirls and loops, again and again backtracking to pick up issues previously debated." [14]

Still, the Constitutional Convention was not a completely chaotic undertaking. Various plans (submitted by delegates) and committees (appointed by the convention) helped to order its deliberations. These plans and committees structured the convention's deliberations into seven main stages:

~ the introduction of the Virginia Plan and the Pinckney Plan (May 29)
~ the convention's decision to recast itself as a committee of the whole, originally for the purpose of considering the Virginia Plan in detail but later to evaluate the Hamilton and New Jersey plans as well (May 30-June 19)
~ clause-by-clause debate by the convention of the decisions of the Committee of the Whole (June 20-July 24)
~ the five-member Committee of Detail, appointed by the convention to produce a draft of the new Constitution that reflected its manifold decisions on particular issues (July 24-August 6)
~ convention debate on the report of the Committee of Detail (August 7-31)
~ the eleven-member Committee on Postponed Matters (or Committee of Eleven), created to propose acceptable solutions to problems that continued to divide the delegates (August 31-September 8)
~ final adjustments, including the work of the Committee of Style, which was charged to write a polished and final draft of the Constitution, and last-minute tinkering by the convention, culminating in the signing of the proposed plan of government (September 9-17).

Virginia Plan and Pinckney Plan (May 29)

The Virginia Plan, introduced on May 29 by Gov. Edmund Randolph but written mainly by Madison, proposed a radical departure from the weak, one-branch government of the Articles of Confederation. The plan proposed to create a three-branch national government and to elevate it to clear supremacy over the states, partly through its power to veto state laws that were in conflict with the Constitution or national laws.

The heart of the national government was to be a bicameral (two-house) legislature, with the lower house elected by the people, the upper house elected by the lower house, and both apportioned according to population. The legislature's powers would include broad authority not just to pass laws, but also to appoint judges and most government officials and to conduct foreign policy.

A national judiciary, organized into a "supreme tribunal" and various "inferior tribunals" and appointed (with life tenure) by the legislature, would form a second branch. Its broad-ranging powers included "impeachments of any National officer."

The government also would have an executive branch, although it was vaguely defined in the Virginia Plan. The "national executive" (the plan left unresolved the question of whether this was to be a person or a group) was "to be chosen by the National Legislature for a term of ______ years." Its powers were obscure: "besides a general authority to execute the National laws, it ought to enjoy the Executive rights vested in Congress by the [Articles of] Confederation."

Finally, a "council of revision," consisting of "the executive and a convenient number of the National Judiciary," was empowered to veto laws passed by the national legislature, subject to override if a vetoed law was repassed.

The Virginia Plan was one of two offered to the convention on May 29. Madison recorded in his notes for that day that Charles Pinckney of South Carolina also introduced a plan. *(See box, The Puzzle of the Pinckney Plan, p. 16.)* But because Madison (who had long loathed Pinckney from their days together in Congress) neither described the Pinckney Plan nor included its text, scholars have had to try to reconstruct it as best they could from other documents (in particular, some notes found in the papers of James Wilson).

The Pinckney Plan probably resembled the Virginia Plan in many ways. It, too, provided for a strong, three-branch national government. It seems to have been more specific regarding the executive, however. The executive was to consist of a single person (called "president") serving a seven-year term and empowered, among other things, to recommend laws to the legislature, oversee the executive branch, and act as commander in chief of the military. Pinckney borrowed most of the elements of his plan from the Articles of Confederation, the Massachusetts constitution, and, especially, the New York constitution.

The delegates' response to the Virginia and Pinckney plans was remarkably placid, especially considering the radical departure in the direction of a strong national government that each proposed. "So sharp a break was Virginia asking the other states to make with the American past that one wonders why at least one stunned delegate . . . did not rise up and cry havoc at the top of his lungs," Rossiter has written. "Instead, the delegates ended this [May 29] session by resolving to go into a 'committee of the whole house' " on the next day to "consider the state of the American union." [15]

Committee of the Whole (May 30-June 19)

In becoming a Committee of the Whole, the convention was, in a sense, simply giving itself a different name—the same group of delegates made up the committee as made up the convention. But as a Committee of the Whole

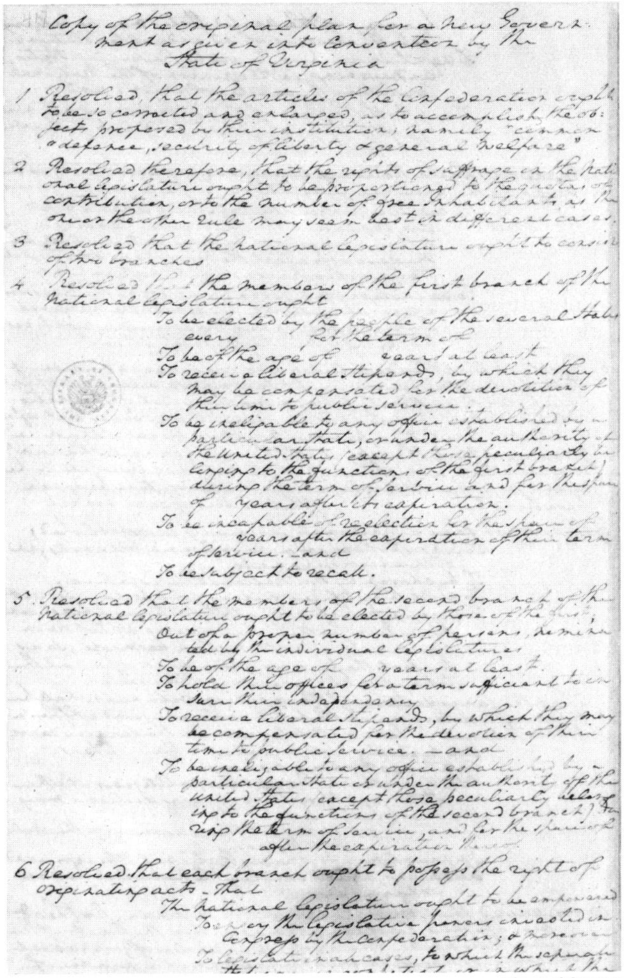
Copy of the original plan for a new Government as given into Convention by the State of Virginia

1 Resolved, that the articles of the Confederation ought to be so corrected and enlarged, as to accomplish the objects proposed by their institution; namely "common defence, security of liberty & general welfare"

2 Resolved therefore, that the rights of suffrage in the National Legislature ought to be proportioned to the quotas of contribution, or to the number of free Inhabitants, as the one or the other rule may seem best in different cases.

3 Resolved that the National Legislature ought to consist of two branches

4 Resolved that the members of the first branch of the National Legislature ought
To be elected by the people of the several States every for the term of
To be of the age of years at least
To receive liberal stipends, by which they may be compensated for the devotion of their time to public service.
To be ineligable to any office established by a particular State, or under the authority of the United States (except those peculiarly belonging to the functions of the first branch) during the term of service and for the space of years after its expiration.
To be incapable of reelection for the space of years after the expiration of their term of service. —and
To be subject to recall.

5. Resolved that the members of the second branch of the National Legislature ought to be elected by those of the first,
Out of a proper number of persons, nominated by the individual Legislatures
To be of the age of years at least.
To hold their offices for a term sufficient to ensure their independency
To receive liberal stipends, by which they may be compensated for the devotion of their time to public service. —and
To be ineligable to any office established by a particular State or under the authority of the United States (except those peculiarly belonging to the functions of the second branch) during the term of service, and for the space of after the expiration thereof

6 Resolved that each branch ought to possess the right of originating acts. That
The National Legislature ought to be empowered
To enjoy the Legislative powers vested in Congress by the Confederation; & moreover
To legislate in all cases, to which the separate

Library of Congress

"Copy of the original plan for a New Government as given into Convention by the State of Virginia" – the Virginia Plan – in George Washington's hand.

they could operate more informally. (To symbolize this, Washington temporarily stepped down as president, and Nathaniel Gorham of New Hampshire was chosen to preside.) In addition, any decision made by the delegates while meeting as Committee of the Whole would be in the form of a recommendation to the convention that would have to be voted on again.

From May 30 to June 13, the Committee of the Whole spent most of its time going over the Virginia Plan, clause by clause. Much of the plan was accepted. But some of it was altered, and some ambiguous provisions were clarified. For example, the executive was defined as a unitary (one person) office. The executive would be elected for a single, seven-year term by the legislature and was subject to impeachment and removal on grounds of "malpractice or neglect of duty." The executive, not a council of revision, was empowered to veto laws passed by the legislature, subject to override by a two-thirds vote of both houses.

In deference to the states, members of the upper house of the national legislature, who had to be at least thirty years old, would be chosen by the various state legislatures. They would serve seven-year terms and be eligible for

The Puzzle of the Pinckney Plan

Did James Madison cheat Charles Pinckney of South Carolina of proper credit for his role in crafting the Constitution?

Madison, the author of the highly significant Virginia Plan and sometimes called the "Father of the Constitution," kept the only set of thorough notes on the debates and resolutions of the Constitutional Convention. Yet when Pinckney presented "the draught of a federal government which he had prepared" to the convention on May 29 (just after Gov. Edmund Randolph of Virginia introduced the Virginia Plan), Madison failed to describe it in his notes. He also omitted any description of Pinckney's later speech about the plan on June 25. Yet convention records show that the Pinckney Plan was referred for consideration to the Committee of the Whole and the Committee of Detail.

In 1818, noting these discrepancies while reviewing the convention's records, Secretary of State John Quincy Adams wrote Pinckney to ask for a copy of his plan. Pinckney replied that he had several rough drafts in his papers, but sent Adams "the one I believe it was."

The document Pinckney sent to Adams resembled Madison's Virginia Plan in some ways—for example, it called for a strong, three-branch national government—but went beyond it in other ways that seemed to foreshadow the convention's ultimate decisions. Pinckney's president was unitary and vigorous; his Senate was apportioned partly by state and partly by population; his House had the duty of impeachment; his enumerations of the powers of the three branches was detailed; and so on.

Pinckney freely admitted that he had borrowed widely in creating his plan, notably from the Articles of Confederation, the Massachusetts constitution, and, especially, the New York constitution. Still, depending on how one does the counting, somewhere between twenty-one and forty-three specific contributions to the Constitution seem to have been made by Pinckney.[1]

Ever since Adams published the records of the convention, including the Pinckney Plan, Madison and his admirers have attempted to discredit Pinckney. Madison biographer Irving Brant has branded Pinckney "a sponger and a plagiarist," accusing him of stealing ideas from the Virginia Plan that Madison had shared with him in preconvention conversations. Clinton Rossiter's account of the convention says that the Pinckney Plan was "at best merely a source of familiar phrases for the members of the Committee of Detail." Madison himself, through historian Jared Sparks, suggested that Pinckney had sent Adams a bogus draft that made his own role in creating the Constitution seem far more important than it really was. In truth, studies of the ink and paper on which the draft Pinckney sent Adams appeared dated it at 1818, not 1787, but this may mean only that Pinckney kept the original and had a copy made for mailing.[2]

What seems indisputable is that Madison disliked Pinckney intensely. Beyond this, he had a personal stake in making his own role at the convention seem central. Pinckney was in truth, an unlovely character—ambitious, vain, egocentric, aggressive, and not always truthful. (Twenty-nine years old, he told the other delegates that he was twenty-four so that he, not the twenty-six-year-old Jonathan Dayton of New Jersey, would seem the youngest delegate.) But Pinckney had been a staunch advocate of a stronger central government for years. And the historical record—not just his own writings but documents found in the papers of delegate James Wilson of Pennsylvania and others—accords Pinckney a greater share of the credit for writing the Constitution than Madison and his partisans have allowed.

Charles Pinckney

1. S. Sidney Ulmer, "James Madison and the Pinckney Plan," *South Carolina Law Quarterly* 9 (Spring 1957); Ulmer, "Charles Pinckney: Father of the Constitution?" *South Carolina Law Quarterly* 10 (Winter 1958); Christopher Collier and James Lincoln Collier, *Decision in Philadelphia: The Constitutional Convention of 1787* (New York: Ballantine, 1986), 97.
2. Irving Brant, *James Madison,* vols. 1-6 (Indianapolis: Bobbs-Merrill, 1941-1961), 3:28; Clinton Rossiter, *1787: The Grand Convention* (London: MacGibbon and Kee, 1968), 171; Collier and Collier, *Decision in Philadephia,* chap. 7.

reelection. (Members of the lower house, also eligible for reelection, would serve three-year terms.) All members of the national legislature would be barred from holding any other government office, mainly to prevent conflicts of interest from arising. Judges would be appointed by the upper house of the legislature.

New Jersey Plan

One plank of the Virginia Plan was especially controversial—the provision that both houses of the national legislature be apportioned according to their population. Delegates from large states (specifically, those from Virginia, Massachusetts, Pennsylvania, and the three states whose populations were growing most rapidly, Georgia, North Carolina, and South Carolina) favored the idea. They split sharply with delegates from small states, who feared that their states would be hopelessly outnumbered in the legislature and who favored instead the existing arrangement, namely, equal representation in Congress for each state. A compromise plan, proposed by Roger Sherman of Connecticut on June 11, would have apportioned the lower house of the legislature according to population and the upper house on a one state, one vote basis; but few delegates were ready for compromise. Instead, small staters responded to the Virginia Plan with a sweeping counter plan of their own. It was introduced on June 15 by William Paterson of New Jersey.

The New Jersey Plan came in the form of amendments to the Articles of Confederation, rather than as a new constitution. It proposed to create two new branches in the national government—a plural (committee-style) executive, to be elected by Congress, and a supreme court, to be appointed by the executive—and to empower Congress to regulate commerce and to impose taxes. But the main point of the New Jersey Plan was an unstated one, namely, that the structure of Congress would remain the same as under the articles—a single house in which each state, regardless of size, would cast one vote.

Hamilton's Plan

On June 18, Alexander Hamilton of New York delivered a four-to-six-hour speech to the delegates in which he urged them to consider his plan for an avowedly British-style government. "He had no scruple in declaring," according to notes kept by Madison, "supported as he was by the opinions of so many of the wise & good, that the British Government was the best in the world: and he doubted much whether any thing short of it would do in America."

Specifically, Hamilton proposed that, as in Great Britain, the national government be all powerful—state governors would be appointed by the national legislature and granted the right to veto any laws passed by their own state legislatures. Members of the upper house of the national legislature, like members of the British House of Lords, would serve for life. As to the executive, "the English model is the only good one on this subject," Hamilton asserted. Although he did not suggest that the United States create a hereditary monarchy, he did propose that an executive be chosen by electors and granted vast powers and lifetime tenure.

Hamilton's speech was admired for its brilliance by many of the delegates, but his plan was dismissed as being far beyond the bounds of what the people or the states would accept. As for the New Jersey Plan, it was defeated on June 19 by a vote of seven states to three. Later that day, the Virginia Plan, as modified by the Committee of the Whole, was approved and referred to the convention for further consideration. The conflict between the delegates from the large and from the small states over apportionment in the national legislature, however, was far from resolved.

Convention Debate (June 20-July 24)

On June 20, with Washington again in the chair as president of the convention, the delegates began their clause-by-clause consideration of the plan of government laid out by the Committee of the Whole.

Among the changes they voted in the plan were these:

~ Members of the lower house would be elected for a term of two years, not three; they also would be required to be at least twenty-five years old.

~ The term for members of the upper house would be six years rather than seven. Their terms would be staggered so that one-third were elected every two years.

~ The national legislature would not have the power to veto state laws, much to Madison's dismay.

~ A property requirement for members of the executive, legislative, and judicial branches would be established. (This idea later was abandoned.)

~ Sufficient displeasure was expressed with the provision for legislative election of the president to a single, seven-year term as to guarantee that it would not remain in the final document, but no generally satisfactory alternative was proposed.

More than any other issue, legislative apportionment consumed the convention's time, attention, and endurance during these five weeks of debate. Delegates from the small states pressed relentlessly for equal representation of the states in Congress: large state delegates were equally adamant in their insistence on representation according to population.

A special committee with members from all the states was appointed on July 2 to propose a compromise. On July 5, after a break to celebrate Independence Day, the committee recommended a plan of equal representation for each state in the upper house, apportionment according to population in the lower house (with each slave counted as three-fifths of a person), and, as a sop to delegates from large states who might fear that the upper house would push for spending programs that would impoverish their states, exclusive power in the lower house to originate all legislation dealing with money.

After more than a week of sometimes bitter and complex debate (new questions were raised, for example, about whether states yet to be admitted to the Union should receive as much representation as the original thirteen and whether apportionment in the lower house should reflect wealth as well as population), the convention narrowly voted on July 15 to approve the main points of the special committee's compromise proposal, sometimes called the Connecticut Compromise in honor of its original author, Roger Sherman. On July 23, the delegates decided that each state should have two members in the upper house, with each free to vote independently.

Committee of Detail (July 24-August 6)

On July 24, the convention voted to appoint a Committee of Detail to review all of its actions to date and to draft a plan of government that incorporated them. The five-member committee was representative of the three main regions of the country—Nathaniel Gorham of New Hampshire and Oliver Ellsworth of Connecticut (a protégé of Sherman) from New England, James Wilson of Pennsylvania from the middle states, and Edmund Randolph of Virginia and John Rutledge of South Carolina from the South. The committee worked while the rest of the convention adjourned until August 6.

One index of the committee's influence is that it took

convention-passed resolutions amounting to twelve hundred words and transformed them into a draft of thirty-seven hundred words. It drew also from a wide range of other sources in compiling its report—the Pinckney Plan, the New Jersey Plan, the Articles of Confederation, the rules of Congress, and some state constitutions, notably those of New York and Massachusetts.

Most of the memorable phrases in the Constitution were written by the Committee of Detail, including "state of the Union" and "We the People." Institutions were named: the executive became the "president"; the national tribunal, the "Supreme Court"; and the legislature, "Congress," with its upper house called the "Senate," and the lower house the "House of Representatives."

For the most part, the committee, in keeping with its name, simply fleshed out the details of earlier convention decisions. It set procedures for the president's veto, defined the jurisdiction of the courts, and adjusted certain relations between the states. In some instances, however, the committee substituted its own judgments for the convention's. The power to impeach, for example, was vested in the House; the power to convict, in the Supreme Court. No property requirement for officeholders was included.

Perhaps the most important decision of the Committee of Detail was to transform general grants of power into specific ones. What had been Congress's broadly stated authority "to legislate in all cases for the general interests of the Union" became a list of eighteen enumerated, or defined, powers, including the power to "lay and collect taxes," regulate interstate commerce, establish post offices, make war, elect a national treasurer, and set up inferior courts—all culminating in a sweeping grant "to make all laws" that appeared "necessary and proper" to carry "into execution" these and "all other powers vested" in the government. The states were forbidden certain powers, notably to make treaties with other nations, to print money, and to tax imports.

The committee granted the president the power to recommend legislation to Congress, make executive appointments, receive ambassadors from other nations, issue pardons, "take care" that the laws be executed, and command the armed forces. (An oath to "faithfully execute the office" of president also was included, as was a provision that the president of the Senate would exercise the powers and duties of the presidency if the president died, resigned, or became disabled.) The judiciary—a Supreme Court and other "inferior courts" to be created by law—was given jurisdiction over impeachments, controversies between states or the citizens of different states, and cases arising under the laws of the national government.

Finally, responding to a threat from Gen. Charles Cotesworth Pinckney of South Carolina, the committee forbade Congress to tax or ban the importation of slaves and the exportation of goods. In another concession to the South, which feared that Congress might legislate navigation acts requiring that U.S. exports be shipped on U.S. ships (a boon to northern shipbuilders, but a burden to southern agricultural exporters), the committee required that such acts would have to pass by a two-thirds vote.

Convention Debate (August 7-31)

As they had with the Virginia Plan and the report of the Committee of the Whole, the delegates reviewed the draft constitution that was proposed by the Committee of Detail clause by clause. Much of the draft was approved. However, some parts were modified, and others became matters of serious controversy.

Modifications

The delegates tinkered with several provisions of the committee draft.

~ Citizenship requirements for legislators (seven years for members of the House, nine years for senators) were enacted, along with a requirement that they be inhabitants of the states they represented in Congress.

~ The requirement that a two-thirds vote of both houses of Congress was needed to override a president's veto was raised to three-fourths. (Near the end of the convention, the two-thirds figure was restored.)

~ Congress's power to "make war," judged too sweeping to protect the national security when Congress was out of session, was revised to read: "declare war."

~ Congress was forbidden from passing both ex post facto laws—that is, retroactive criminal laws—and bills of attainder (laws that declare a person guilty of a crime without a trial).

~ The government was barred from granting "any title of nobility," and government officials were forbidden to receive "any present, emolument, office, or title of any kind whatever from any king, prince, or foreign state."

~ Congress was empowered to call forth the militia of any state "to execute the laws of the Union, suppress insurrections, and repel invasions."

~ The two-thirds requirement for the passage of navigation acts was dropped.

~ A procedure was created to amend the Constitution: "on the application of the legislatures of two-thirds of the states in the Union for an amendment of this Constitution, the legislature of the United States [Congress] shall call a convention for that purpose."

~ Religious tests were prohibited as a requirement for holding office.

~ The Committee of Detail had proposed that the new constitution take effect when ratified by a certain number of state conventions (not state legislatures), but had left the number unspecified. The convention now voted to set it at nine.

~ The president's oath was expanded to include these words: "and will to the best of my judgment and power preserve, protect, and defend the Constitution of the United States." (Still later, "to the best of my judgment and power" became "to the best of my ability.")

Controversies

The draft constitution's slavery provisions came under fierce assault by northern delegates, both the three-fifths rule for counting slaves as part of the population and the prohibition of laws banning imports. (Much of the North's concern derived from fear of slave rebellions, which might attract foreign invaders and, in any event, would require northern arms and money in order to be subdued.) Southern delegates not only defended the provisions protecting slavery but insisted that their states would not ratify any constitution that placed slavery in jeopardy.

As with the large state-small state controversy, a special committee was appointed on August 22 to find a compromise solution. Two days later, it proposed that Congress

Benjamin Franklin

Benjamin Franklin was eighty-one years old in 1787—old enough to be the father of even the oldest of the other delegates, the grandfather of most of them, and the great-grandfather of some. (He was twenty-six years older than George Washington, forty-five years older than James Madison, and fifty-five years older than the youngest delegate to the Constitutional Convention, Jonathan Dayton.) Franklin's health was very bad. When he was able to attend sessions of the convention, he had to be carried from his home in a sedan chair by prison trusties. Often his speeches were delivered by someone else, usually his fellow Pennsylvanian, James Wilson.

Franklin had few clear ideas of what the new government the convention was creating should be like, and most of these were voted down. He favored a unicameral legislature and a plural executive. He opposed salaries for government officials. He urged that a clergyman be brought into the convention to open each of its sessions with a prayer. These suggestions typically were received with respectful tolerance by most of his fellow delegates. Franklin's motion against salaries, for example, "was treated with great respect," wrote James Madison, "but rather for the author of it than from any conviction of its expediency or practicability."

William Pierce of Georgia described Franklin as "the greatest philosopher of the present age.... But what claim he has to the politician, posterity must determine. It is certain that he does not shine much in public council; he is no speaker, nor does he seem to let politics engage his attention."

For all his feebleness, Franklin was one of the most important delegates at the Constitutional Convention. His presence lent lustre to the enterprise—no American, other than Washington, enjoyed Franklin's national and international prestige as scientist, inventor, author and publisher, diplomat, and statesman. Equally important, Franklin deliberately played the role of conciliator at the convention. Although he lacked clear ideas about government himself, he did his best to calm his colleagues' tempers and assuage their differences so that the convention would stay together to produce something tangible.

On September 17, the day the Constitution was signed, Franklin offered the convention's most memorable benedictions, both publicly and privately. To the delegates, he presented a long speech (read by Wilson), which said in essence:

> Mr. President, I confess that there are several parts of this constitution which I do not approve, but I am not sure that I shall never approve them. For having lived long, I have experienced many instances of being obliged by better information, or fuller consideration, to change opinions even on important subjects, which I once thought right, but found to be otherwise.... I doubt too whether any other convention we can obtain may be able to make a better constitution.... It therefore astonishes me, Sir, to find this system approaching so near to perfection as it does; and I think it will astonish our enemies.... Thus I consent, Sir, to this constitution because I expect no better, and because I am not sure it is not the best.

Later that day, leaving the hall, someone asked Franklin, "Well, Doctor, what have we got? A republic or a monarchy?" "A republic, if you can keep it," Franklin replied.

be authorized, if it so decided, to end the importation of slaves after 1800; in the meantime, Congress could tax imported slaves at a rate no higher than ten dollars each. (A euphemism—not "slaves," but "such persons"—was used in the Constitution.) General Pinckney persuaded the convention to change 1800 to 1808. The committee recommendation, as amended, was passed.

Two other controversies caused the convention to bog down: the powers of the Senate (which delegates from large states wanted to minimize and delegates from small states wanted to maximize) and a cluster of issues regarding presidential selection. Nearing the end of its labors, the convention on August 31 appointed a Committee on Postponed Matters, with a member from each state delegation, to resolve these vexing issues.

Committee on Postponed Matters

On September 4, the Committee on Postponed Matters, chaired by David Brearley of New Jersey, made several recommendations concerning the presidency. It proposed a term of four years rather than seven, with no restriction on the president's eligibility for reelection.

The president was to be chosen by an electoral college, not by Congress. Under the electoral college, each state would be assigned the right to select, by whatever means it chose, electors equal in number to its representatives and senators in Congress. Each elector would vote (at a meeting with other electors from the same state) for two different presidential candidates from two different states. The various states' votes would then be forwarded to Congress for counting. The candidate who received the greatest number of electoral votes, assuming the support of a majority of electors, would become president. The candidate who finished second would become vice president. If no candidate received a majority, the Senate would select a president and vice president from among the five candidates who had received the highest number of electoral votes.

As a corollary to its proposal for an electoral college, the committee recommended that certain responsibilities be assigned to the vice president, namely, to serve as president of the Senate, with the right to cast tie-breaking votes, and to act as president if the office became vacant before the expiration of the president's term. Finally, the committee recommended that qualifications for president be stated in the Constitution: at least thirty-five years old, a natural-born citizen of the United States (or a citizen at the time of the Constitution's enactment), and at least fourteen years a resident of the United States.

For several days, the delegates gave critical scrutiny to the committee's complex and surprising proposal. On September 7, they passed it after making only one substantive change: the House of Representatives, rather than the Senate, would choose the president in the event of an electoral college deadlock, with each state delegation casting one vote. The Senate still would choose the vice president if the electoral college failed to produce a winner.

Having approved the electoral college, the convention quickly took other actions to reduce the powers of the Senate in response to the demands of the delegates from the large states. The president was granted authority to make treaties and to appoint ambassadors and other public ministers and consuls, Supreme Court justices and other federal judges, and all other officers whose appointments were not otherwise provided for. Senate confirmation remained a requirement for all these appointments and a two-thirds vote by the Senate was stipulated to ratify treaties.

On September 8, the convention approved two final proposals of the Committee on Postponed Matters. The president was to be impeached by the House and, upon conviction by the Senate, removed from office on grounds of "treason or bribery or other high crimes and misdemeanors against the United States." (The delegates added the vice president and other civil officers to the roster of those subject to impeachment but raised the majority needed for Senate conviction from a simple to a two-thirds majority.) In addition, the House was empowered to originate "all bills for raising revenue."

Having thus completed (they believed) their work on the Constitution, the delegates ended their business on September 8 by voting to create a five-member Committee of Style to write a polished, final draft for signing. Among the committee's members were Madison, Hamilton, and Gouverneur Morris, who seems to have done most of its work.

Final Adjustments (September 9-17)

Even as the Committee of Style labored, the convention continued to modify its earlier decisions. On September 10, Madison urged that special conventions not be a part of the process of amending the Constitution but rather that amendments be initiated by a two-thirds vote of Congress or by two-thirds of the state legislatures, with subsequent approval by three-fourths of the states needed for ratification. The Committee of Style incorporated his idea into their draft.

On September 11, Hugh Williamson of North Carolina successfully moved that the requirement for overriding a president's veto be reduced from a three-fourths vote of each house of Congress to a two-thirds vote.

Meanwhile, more fundamental reservations were expressed by some delegates. Randolph worried that the delegates had gone far beyond their original charter and urged that the approval of not just state ratifying conventions but also of Congress and the state legislatures be sought for the proposed constitution. George Mason objected to the absence of a bill of rights.

The Committee of Style reported to the convention on September 13. Its draft not only reduced the number of articles from twenty-three to seven, but included some significant innovations. The most memorable of these was the preamble:

> We the People of the United States, in Order to form a more perfect Union, establish Justice, insure domestic Tranquility, provide for the common defence, promote the general Welfare, and secure the Blessings of Liberty to ourselves and our Posterity, do ordain and establish this Constitution for the United States of America.

The preamble it replaced was blander and more state-centered: "We the people of the states of New Hampshire, Massachusetts," etc.

The Committee of Style also added a provision that barred states from passing laws to impair the obligations of contracts. Finally, a pair of vesting clauses for Congress and the president were written that, intentionally or not, suggested that the president might have executive powers beyond those enumerated in the Constitution. *(See " 'The Executive Power,' " p. 29, in this chapter.)*

The committee's draft met with widespread approval from the delegates, but their tinkering continued. Congress was stripped of its power to choose the national treasurer. A provision was added that the Constitution could not be altered to deprive a state of equal representation in the Senate without the state's consent. And a compromise procedure for amending the Constitution was created, at the initiative of Gouverneur Morris and Elbridge Gerry, that incorporated both the Committee of Detail and the Madison proposals. As finally agreed upon, a constitutional amendment could be proposed either by a two-thirds vote of both houses of Congress or by a convention that Congress was to call if two-thirds of the state legislatures requested one. In either case, three-fourths of the states would have to ratify an amendment for it to become part of the Constitution.

Randolph and Mason remained unhappy. Now joined by Gerry, they again expressed their doubts about the magnitude of the changes the convention was about to recommend. But their motion for a subsequent constitutional convention to consider the objections and recommendations that might be raised at the state ratifying conventions was defeated by a vote of eleven states to none.

The convention's labors complete, the delegates assembled on September 17 to sign an engrossed, or final, copy of the Constitution. (This is the copy on public display at the National Archives in Washington, D.C.) Forty-one of the original fifty-five delegates still were present at the convention; all but Randolph, Mason, and Gerry signed the document. Even then they could not resist some fine tuning, unanimously approving a Washington-supported motion to alter slightly the apportionment formula for the House of Representatives.

As the last few delegates waited to affix their signatures to the Constitution, an informal benediction was offered by Benjamin Franklin. Franklin gestured to Washington's chair and said to those standing nearby:

> Painters have found it difficult to distinguish in their art a rising from a setting sun. I have often in the course of this session and the vicissitudes of my hopes and fears as to its issue, looked at that sun behind the President without being able to tell whether it was rising or setting. But now, at length, I have the happiness to know that it is a rising and not a setting sun.[16]

The Creation of the Presidency

During the course of the Constitutional Convention, two main developments occurred with regard to the presidency. First, the rather loosely designed executive of the Virginia Plan took on greater clarity and specificity. Second, the weak executive, subordinate to the legislature, that most of the delegates initially seemed to favor was made stronger. These two main developments manifested themselves in a variety of specific issues of executive design, including number, selection, term, removal, institutional separation, and enumerated powers.

Overview of the Creation of the Presidency

The design of the executive was one of the most vexing problems of the Constitutional Convention. Other issues were more controversial, but these typically lent themselves to compromise solutions: small states split the difference with large states and provided for a bicameral legislature; the North and the South worked out the three-fifths rule for counting slaves; and so on. When it came to the nature and powers of the executive, the delegates labored in a realm of such intellectual and political uncertainty that the politics of compromise was largely irrelevant.

One problem the delegates encountered was that their experience offered several models of what they did not want in an executive but few that they found attractive. The British monarch and the royal colonial governors had been, in their eyes, tramplers of liberty. The state constitutions that were written after independence provided for nonoppressive governors but also rendered them weak to the point of impotence. The national government of the Articles of Confederation, such as it was, had no chief executive at all. The plethora of proposals for an executive that various delegates offered during the convention (listed by the writer Fred Barbash) is more a mark of their uncertainty than of any strongly held desires:

> Three executives, each from a different part of the country.
>
> An executive joined with a council.
>
> A single executive, with a life term.
>
> A President, without a life term, chosen by the people.
>
> A single executive, chosen by the Congress and eligible for reelection.
>
> A single executive, chosen by the Congress and ineligible for reelection.
>
> An executive chosen by the governors of the states.
>
> A President chosen by members of the Congress, to be drawn by lot, or chosen by the Congress the first time and by electors the second time, or chosen by electors all the time. Electors chosen by state legislatures. Electors chosen by the people.[17]

A second problem that stymied the delegates derived from their general ambivalence about executive authority. They wanted an executive branch that was strong enough to provide the government with "energy" to check a runaway legislature, but not so strong as to become despotic. This ambivalence was shared by the American people, whose hatred of monarchy existed side-by-side with their longing to make George Washington king. As the political scientist Seymour Martin Lipset has shown, Washington was a classic example of what Max Weber, the great German sociologist, called a charismatic leader, one "treated as endowed with supernatural, superhuman, or at least specifically exceptional powers or qualities." The historian Marcus Cunliffe recorded:

> Babies were being christened after him as early as 1775, and while he was still President, his countrymen paid to see him in waxwork effigy. To his admirers he was "god-like Washington," and his detractors complained to one another that he was looked upon as a "demigod" whom it was treasonous to criticize. "Oh Washington!" declared Ezra Stiles of Yale (in a sermon of 1783). "How I do love thy name! How have I often adored and blessed thy God, for creating and forming thee into the great ornament of humankind!"[18]

But the public's longing for Washington—shared by the delegates, although in a more restrained manner—was just that: a longing for Washington, not for a monarchy.

Despite these difficulties, the presidency slowly took shape as the convention wore on. For all their intellectual uncertainty, the delegates moved steadily in the direction of a rather clearly designed executive. For all their ambivalence, they made the executive stronger as well.

Clarity

Madison offered the convention a shadowy and vaguely defined executive in the Virginia Plan. Even the basic structure of the plan's executive—was it to be a single person or a committee?—was undefined. In addition, the length of the term was unspecified, and the powers of the executive were not enumerated.

Madison's fellow delegates seem to have shared his uncertainty. The only issues they resolved to their satisfaction during the convention's first two months were the unitary nature of the executive and its power to veto laws passed by the legislature (subject to override). Other issues left them floundering, as evidenced by the Colliers' account of their efforts during the week of July 17:

> The delegates appeared to be struggling to create an executive that was strong without being strong. Over the week the Convention reversed itself again and again. On July 17 it constructed a weak executive dominated by Congress. On the nineteenth and twentieth it created a strong executive independent of Congress. On July 24 it went back to the executive chosen by Congress. At various times it was suggested that his term might be eight, fifteen, and, even though the proposal was facetious, thirty years.[19]

The Committee of Detail, which begin its work on July 24, helped matters some: it gave the executive the name of president, provided for succession, and enumerated its powers. But the main issues that fragmented the delegates—selection, term, and reeligibility—were not resolved until September, when the Committee on Postponed Matters proposed selection by an electoral college, a term of four years with no limit on reeligibility, and the creation of the vice presidency.

Strength

For all its vagueness of conception, the national executive of the Virginia Plan generally accorded with what most delegates at the start of the Constitutional Convention seem to have been looking for, namely, an agent of restraint in a basically legislative government. The executive in

Number of the Executive

The executive Power shall be vested in a President of the United States of America.

—from Article II, section 2

Madison's proposed goverment was weak (it was bound by a council and devoid of enumerated powers), but it certainly was stronger than in the government of the Articles of Confederation. The executive was subordinate to the legislature, which was empowered to elect it, but not subservient, as demonstrated by its fixed seven-year term, the veto power, and the bar on legislative reductions of the executive's salary.

Dissatisfied with the convention's early consensus on a subordinate executive, a coterie of committed and talented delegates worked diligently and effectively to strengthen its constitutional power. They were led by James Wilson, who envisioned the executive as a "man of the people," and by Gouverneur Morris, who regarded the executive as "the general guardian of the national interests." During the course of the convention, the pro-executive group won victory after victory:

~ The executive was defined as a unitary, not a committee-style office, and unshackled of a council.

~ The executive, instead of being chosen by the legislature for a single term, was given its own popular electoral base and the right to run for reelection. (Indispensable to this victory was Wilson's conversion of Madison, who declared on July 19 that "it is essential . . . that the appointment of the Executive should either be drawn from some source, or held by some tenure, that will give him a free agency with regard to the Legislature. This could not be if he was appointed from time to time by the Legislature.")

~ The Committee of Detail spelled out a detailed list of executive powers, including those of military command, involvement in the legislative process, pardon, and the execution of the laws.

~ After the Connecticut Compromise transformed the Senate into the small states' bastion in Congress, large-state delegates allied with pro-executive delegates to transfer some of the Senate's powers to the executive, notably those of appointment and treaty making.

For all their victories, Wilson, Morris, and the other delegates who favored a strong executive did not get everything they wanted, such as life tenure, an unqualified veto, and easier procedures for Senate ratification of treaties. But they moved the convention much further in the direction of a strong executive than it initially had been inclined to go.

Number of the Executive

The number of the executive was the first issue to rouse the delegates. The debate on number took two forms. First, should the executive be unitary or plural, that is, a single-person or a committee-style office? Second, should the executive be forced to consult with a council before exercising some or all of its powers?

Unitary or Plural?

The Virginia Plan said nothing about the number of the executive, perhaps because its author, James Madison, had no clear opinion on the issue or perhaps because, like Roger Sherman, Madison felt that the legislature should be free to define the executive as it saw fit.

On June 1, the convention, meeting as the Committee of the Whole, heard a motion from James Wilson that the executive be a single person. The delegates evidently lapsed into silence for a time. Historians differ as to why: Catherine Drinker Bowen attributes their silence to awe at the prospect of creating a potentially king like office; Charles Mee suggests that the delegates were uneasy about discussing the issue in the presence of George Washington, who presumably would be the leader of whatever executive they created.[20] After Benjamin Franklin admonished his colleagues of their obligation to speak freely, however, the debate was joined, and the issue became an early test for the pro-executive and anti-executive forces at the convention.

Edmund Randolph led the fight against Wilson's motion. Randolph argued both that the people would reject a constitution that bore any "semblance of monarchy" and that this rejection would be justified: a single executive, by its nature, would be the "foetus of monarchy." Randolph proposed instead a three-person committee, with one member of the executive from each region of the country.

Wilson was shrewd in defending his motion. To be sure, he argued that a single executive would be a source of "energy" and "dispatch"—that is, of leadership and action—in the new government. But Wilson also urged that a single executive was indispensable for controlling executive power—how could responsibility for incompetence or for abuses of power be assigned to a committee? This argument was persuasive to most delegates. They feared monarchy but realized how much the national government had suffered under the Articles of Confederation from the diffusion of executive responsibility. As property owners, they also feared threats to order such as Shays's Rebellion and saw a single executive as more likely to respond quickly and effectively to riot and discord than would a committee.

On June 4, the convention voted overwhelmingly in favor of a unitary executive. One of Washington's few recorded votes was in favor of this motion.

A Council?

The Virginia Plan provided that a "council of revision" consisting of the executive and "a convenient number of the National Judiciary" would be empowered to veto laws passed by the legislature. All thirteen state constitutions provided for a council of some sort; Sherman, who voted for the single executive, said he had done so only because he assumed it would be forced to share power with a council. Wilson, however, opposed a council because he believed that it would dilute the virtues of the unitary executive—energy, dispatch, and responsibility.

The proposal for a council was tabled on June 4 after two Massachusetts delegates, Elbridge Gerry and Rufus King, injected a new argument into the debate—they questioned the wisdom of having judges participate in making laws that they later would be asked to rule upon.

Election of the President

Each State shall appoint, in such Manner as the Legislature thereof may direct, a Number of Electors, Equal to the whole Number of Senators and Representatives to which the State may be entitled in the Congress: but no Senator or Representative or Person holding an Office of Trust or Profit under the United States, shall be appointed an elector.

[The Electors shall meet in their respective States, and vote by Ballot for two Persons, of whom at least one shall not be an Inhabitant of the same State with themselves. And they shall make a List of all the Persons voted for, and the Number of Votes for each; which List they shall sign and certify, and transmit sealed to the Seat of the Government of the United States, directed to the President of the Senate. The President of the Senate shall, in the Presence of the Senate and the House of Representatives, open all the Certificates, and the votes shall then be counted. The Person having the greatest Number of Votes shall be President, if such Number be a Majority of the whole Number of Electors appointed; and if there be more than one who have such Majority, and have an equal Number of Votes, then the House of Representatives shall immediately chuse by Ballot one of them for President; and if no Person have a majority, then from the five highest on the List the said House shall in the like manner chuse the President. But in chusing the President, the Votes shall be taken by States, the Representatives from each State having one Vote. A quorum for this purpose shall consist of a Member or Members from two thirds of the States, and a Majority of all the States shall be necessary to a Choice. In every Case, after the Choice of the President, the Person having the greatest Number of Votes of the Electors shall be the Vice President. But if there should remain two or more who have equal Votes, the Senate shall chuse from them by Ballot the Vice President.]*

The Congress may determine the Time of chusing the Electors and the Day on which they shall give their Votes; which Day shall be the same throughout the United States.

—from Article II, section 1

* Superseded by the Twelfth Amendment

Confusion also existed among the delegates about what the real effect on executive power of a council would be—some saw it as a check on the executive but others thought that a council would buttress the executive with the support of the judiciary, thus strengthening it in its relations with the legislature.

The council idea recurred in various guises and at various times throughout the convention. As late as September 4, George Mason suggested that the House of Representatives or the Senate be charged to appoint an executive council. ("The Grand Signor himself had his Divan," he argued.) But no consensus ever formed about the wisdom of the idea or the form that it should take.

Selection and Succession

James Wilson was as much opposed to the part of the Virginia Plan that provided for the executive "to be chosen by the National Legislature" as he was in favor of a unitary executive. Legislative selection would make the executive a creature of (and thus subservient to) the legislature, Wilson believed. On June 1, he proposed instead that the executive be elected by the people. He realized, Wilson said, that his idea "might appear chimerical," but he could think of no better way to keep the executive and legislative branches "as independent as possible of each other, as well as of the states"—that is, to achieve the goals of separation of powers and government by the people.

The delegates virtually ignored Wilson's proposal for popular election. In principle, the idea was too democratic for their taste (they thought of democracy as mob rule) and, by requiring voters to pass judgment on candidates from distant states of whom they knew little or nothing, it was impractical as well. (Later in the convention, Mason vividly stated both of these objections cogently: "It would be as unnatural to refer the choice of a proper character for chief Magistrate to the people, as it would, to refer a trial of colours to a blind man.")

Undiscouraged, Wilson returned to the convention on June 2 with a proposal to elect the executive with an electoral college. Each state would be divided for purposes of election into a few large districts; these would each choose electors who would gather to select an executive. A plan like Wilson's later was adopted, but at this stage of the convention it was still too novel. The delegates voted instead to affirm the legislative selection provision of the Virginia Plan.

But the decision for legislative selection, although it was confirmed in several votes taken in July and August, was not a happy one. The reason was that, in the delegates' minds, a legislatively selected executive could not be allowed to stand for reelection, lest the powers and patronage of the office be used for the purpose of, in effect, bribing legislators for their votes. But the delegates believed that eligibility for reelection was a valuable incentive to good performance in office and regretted that legislative selection of the executive ruled it out. *(See "Term of Office," p. 24, in this chapter.)* The result was an ongoing search for a selection process that was desirable in its own right and also allowed for reelection. This was no easy task. Among the ideas the delegates considered and rejected, wrote the political scientist Clinton Rossiter, were some rather far-fetched ones:

> election by the state governors or by electors chosen by them, neither a scheme that could muster any support; nomination by the people of each state of "its best citizen," and election from this pool of thirteen by the national legislature or electors chosen by it, an unhelpful proposal of John Dickinson; election by the national legis-

> lature, with electors chosen by the state legislatures taking over whenever an executive sought reelection, a proposal of [Oliver] Ellsworth that found favor with four states; and, most astounding of all, election by a small group of national legislators chosen "by lot".... [21]

The search for an alternative to legislative selection became more urgent after August 24. Until that day, no consideration had been given to the matter of how the legislature was to choose the president. Now, by a vote of seven states to four, the convention approved a motion that Congress would select the president by a "joint ballot" of all the members of the House of Representatives and Senate. This decision, by giving the large states a clear majority in presidential selection (there were many more representatives than senators), threatened to reignite the large state-small state controversy that already had split the convention once. To avert this catastrophe, Roger Sherman, who had written the Connecticut Compromise between the large and small states on legislative apportionment, moved on August 31 to refer the whole issue of presidential selection to the Committee on Postponed Matters.

On September 4, the committee proposed the electoral college as a method for electing the president, with no restrictions on the president's right to be reelected. The president would be selected by a majority vote of the electors, who were to be chosen by the states by whatever methods they individually adopted. Each state would receive a number of electoral votes equal to its representation in Congress. If no presidential candidate received votes from a majority of electors, the Senate would elect the president from among the five highest electoral vote recipients. In addition, to prevent a "cabal" from forming in the electoral college, electors would never meet—instead, they would vote in their state capitals, then send the results to the Senate for counting. Finally, to ensure that the electors would not simply vote for a home-state favorite, each was required to vote for two candidates for president from two different states, with the runner-up in the presidential election filling the newly created office of vice president.

The electoral college proposal was generally well received by the delegates. As Fred Barbash has argued, it was the ideal political compromise, "baited" with something for virtually every group at the convention:

> For those in the convention anxious for the President to be allowed reelection, the committee made him eligible without limit.
>
> For those worried about excessive dependence of the President on the national legislature, the committee determined that electors chosen as each state saw fit would cast ballots for the presidency.
>
> For the large states and the South, the committee decided that the number of electors would be proportioned according to each state's combined representation in the House and Senate....
>
> For the small states, the committee determined that when no candidate won a majority of electoral votes, the Senate would choose the president from among the leading contenders.[22]

Only one aspect of the proposed electoral college was controversial among the delegates, that of Senate selection in the absence of an electoral college majority. Large-state delegates objected to Senate election because the Senate underrepresented them in favor of the small states. What is more, not foreseeing the development of a two-party system, most delegates believed that after Washington (the obvious choice for the first president) left office, electoral college majorities would seldom form and the Senate would choose most presidents. Mason estimated that the electoral college would fail to reach a majority in nineteen elections out of every twenty.

Once again, Sherman proposed an acceptable compromise: let the House of Representatives elect the president when the electoral college failed, but assign each state delegation a single vote. Quickly, on September 6, the convention agreed.

One issue that the creation of the vice presidency resolved, at least partially, for the delegates was: What happens if the president dies, resigns, becomes disabled, or is impeached and convicted? The Committee of Detail was the first to deal with the matter. It recommended that the president of the Senate be designated "to discharge the powers and duties of [the Presidency] ... until another President of the United States be chosen, or until the disability of the President be ended." Madison and other delegates objected to this proposal because it seemed to give the Senate an incentive to remove a president, and the matter was referred to the Committee on Postponed Matters.

The committee proposed that the vice president, not a senator, be president of the Senate; it also designated the vice president to step in when a vacancy occurred in the presidency. The convention agreed, but only after passing an additional motion that seemed to call for a special presidential election before the expiration of the departed president's term. Somehow this intention was lost when the Committee of Style wrote its final draft of the Constitution. No one caught the error. As a result, the Constitution was vague on two important matters: Was the vice president to become president in the event of the president's death, resignation, disability, or removal or merely to assume the powers and duties of the presidency, and was the vice president to serve out the unexpired balance of the president's term or only fill in until a special election could be held to pick a new president? *(See "The Vice Presidency," p. 34, in this chapter and Selection by Succession chapter in Part II.)*

Term of Office

He shall hold his Office during the term of four Years, and, together with the Vice President, chosen for the same term, be elected . . .*

—from Article II, section 1

* Supplemented by the Twenty-second Amendment

Term of Office

Questions of length of term, eligibility for reelection, and selection were interwoven in the minds of the delegates, and they could not resolve one independently of the others. Indeed, one political scientist has compared their efforts to sort out these questions to a game of "three-dimensional chess." [23]

The Virginia Plan left the question of the executive's term of office blank—literally. ("Resolved, That a national executive be . . . chosen by the National Legislature for a term of years.") The plan also stipulated that the executive was "to be ineligible a second time." When these provisions came before the Committee of the Whole on June 1, a variety of alternatives were proposed, including a three-year term, with no limit on reeligibility; a three-year term with two reelections allowed; and a seven-year term, with no reeligibility. Although the delegates approved the single seven-year term, the vote was narrow, five states to four.

Underlying the delegates' uncertainty was a basic choice between two alternatives concerning the executive that they regarded as incompatible, namely, eligibility for reelection or legislative selection. The reason that, in their view, one could not have both was well stated by Mason: if the legislature could reelect the executive, there would be a constant "temptation on the side of the Executive to intrigue with the Legislature for reappointment," using political patronage and illegitimate favors in effect to buy votes.

On July 17, the convention voted for both legislative selection and reeligibility, but when James McClurg of Virginia pointed out the contradiction between these two decisions, ineligibility for reelection was reinstated. (McClurg, supported by Gouverneur Morris and Jacob Broom of Delaware, offered a different way out of the dilemma: election of the executive by the legislature for a life term. But this smacked too much of a king to suit the other delegates.)

On July 26, the delegates voted again to have the legislature elect the executive for a single term. But the advantages the delegates saw in reeligibility were so powerful that the issue remained alive. Reeligibility not only would give the nation a way of keeping a good executive in office, it also would give the executive what Morris called "the great motive to good behavior, the hope of being rewarded with a re-appointment." Even an executive whose behavior was governed by such personal motives as "avarice," "ambition," or "the love of fame," Alexander Hamilton later argued in *Federalist* No. 72, would do a good job in order to hold on to the office that could fulfill those desires.

To complicate their task further, the delegates' decision between legislative selection and reeligibility implied a related decision between a shorter term for the executive and a longer term. If the executive were to be chosen by the legislature for a single term only, the delegates believed, the term should be long. If the executive were eligible for reelection, a shorter term was to be preferred.

In late August, the convention changed course for the last time. The delegates decided against legislative selection of the president, then created the Committee on Postponed Matters to propose an alternative. The committee's recommendation, adopted by the delegates, was that an electoral college choose the president for a four-year term, with no limit on reeligibility. *(See "Selection and Succession," p. 23, in this chapter.)*

Impeachment

The President, Vice President, and all civil Officers of the United States shall be removed from Office on Impeachment for, and Conviction of, Treason, Bribery, or other High Crimes and Misdemeanors.

—from Article II, section 4

The House of Representatives . . . shall have the sole Power of Impeachment.

—from Article I, section 1

The Senate shall have the sole Power to try all Impeachments. When sitting for that Purpose, they shall be on Oath or Affirmation. When the President of the United States is tried, the Chief Justice shall preside: And no Person shall be convicted without the concurrence of two thirds of the Members present.

Judgment in Cases of Impeachment shall not extend further than to removal from Office, and disqualification to hold and enjoy any Office of honor, Trust or Profit under the United States: but the Party convicted shall nevertheless be liable and subject to Indictment, Trial, Judgment and Punishment, according to law.

—from Article I, section 3

Removal

During the course of the convention, the delegates decided to provide for situations in which the executive needed to be removed from office before the expiration of the term. Serious abuse of power by the president was one such situation—the remedy was impeachment. Disability was the other, but, even at the end of the convention, the delegates were less than clear about what ought to be done when the executive was disabled.

Impeachment

Although the Virginia Plan made no specific provision for impeaching the executive, most of the delegates agreed from the outset that some mechanism should be included in the Constitution. Even proponents of a strong executive quickly came to realize that their goal would be achieved only if the other delegates felt confident that an out-of-control executive could be removed from office.

The convention's consensus on impeachment was revealed on June 2, when the Committee of the Whole quickly passed Hugh Williamson's motion that the executive be "removable on impeachment and conviction of malpractice or neglect of duty." (Impeachment is comparable to indictment by a grand jury; it must be followed by a trial and conviction in order for the impeached official to be removed from office.)

This consensus was confirmed and strengthened on July 19, when Morris suggested to the convention that if the executive were assigned a short term, there would be no need for impeachment—the passage of time would lead to the executive's removal soon enough. Morris was answered

Succession and Disability

In Case of the Removal of the President from Office, or of his Death, Resignation, or Inability to discharge the Powers and Duties of the said Office, the Same shall devolve on the Vice President, and the Congress may by Law provide for the Case of Removal, Death, Resignation, or Inability, both of the President and Vice President, declaring what Officer shall act accordingly, until the Disability be removed, or a President shall be elected.*

—from Article II, section 1

* Modified by the Twentieth and Twenty-fifth Amendments

by Gerry, Randolph, Franklin, and Mason, each of whom made clear that he regarded impeachment not only as a vital safeguard against and punishment for abuses of power, but also (at least in Franklin's case) a way of removing tyrants without resorting to assassination. Morris quickly retreated, declaring that he was persuaded by his colleagues' arguments.

The Committee of Detail tried to clarify Williamson's definition of the grounds for presidential impeachment (from "malpractice or neglect of duty" to "treason, bribery, or corruption") and also created a mechanism for removal ("impeachment by the House of Representatives and conviction in the Supreme Court"). The convention did not take up the impeachment provision of the committee's report until August 27, when Morris asked that it be tabled. His reason was that if, as still seemed possible, the convention decided to create a council of revision for the president that included the chief justice of the Supreme Court, the court should not be involved in the impeachment process. The delegates agreed to Morris's motion without objection. Later that week, on August 31, the Committee on Postponed Matters was formed and took charge of the impeachment issue, among others.

The committee made its three-part recommendation on September 4: first, impeachment by the House; second, conviction by a two-thirds vote of the Senate, not the Supreme Court, but with the chief justice presiding over the trial; and third, impeachment on grounds of treason or bribery, but not the vague offense of "corruption." On September 8, Mason complained that simply to bar treason and bribery "will not reach many great and dangerous offenses," including certain "attempts to subvert the Constitution." He proposed that "maladministration" be added to the list of impeachable offenses. After Madison objected that "so vague a term will be equivalent to a tenure during pleasure of the Senate," Mason replaced it with "other high crimes and misdemeanors," which passed despite Madison's continuing objection.

Disability

As thoroughly as the delegates considered the grounds for and process of presidential impeachment, that is how cavalierly they treated the situation of a president who is disabled. The matter first was put before the convention on August 6, as part of a provision of the Committee of Detail's report that dealt mainly with succession. It read: "In the case of his . . . disability to discharge the powers and duties of his office, the President of the Senate shall exercise those powers and duties, until another President of the United States be chosen, or until the disability of the President be removed."

On August 27, when this provision of the committee's report came before the convention, John Dickinson of Pennsylvania complained that "it was too vague. What is the extent of the term 'disability' & who is to be the judge of it?" The delegates decided to postpone their discussion of disability until another time, presumably to supply answers to these questions. That time never came, nor were answers ever supplied, leaving *disability* an undefined term in the Constitution and creating no process either to determine whether a president was disabled or to transfer the powers and duties of the presidency to a temporary successor. Instead, the Committee on Postponed Matters merely named the vice president, rather than the president of the Senate, as successor and substituted "inability" for "disability" (without explaining what difference, if any, this substitution made).

Institutional Separation from Congress

Many of the delegates were very much influenced by the idea that in order to preserve liberty, government should be designed to incorporate the principle of separation of powers. Various contemporary or recent political philosophers, including John Locke, had articulated this idea, but none was more familiar to the delegates than Baron de Montesquieu. Montesquieu, the author of *L'Esprit des Lois,* was "the oracle who is always consulted and cited" on the subject of separation of powers, according to *Federalist* No. 47. In a passage the delegates knew well, Montesquieu had written:

> The political liberty of the subject is a tranquility of mind, arising from the opinion each person has of his safety. In order to have this liberty, it is requisite the government be so constituted as one man need not be afraid of another.
>
> When the legislative and executive powers are united in the same person, or in the same body of magistracy, there can be no liberty; because apprehensions may arise lest the same monarch or senate should enact tyrannical laws, to execute them in a tyrannical manner.

The separation of powers principle did not require a strict division of labor, in which each branch of government was assigned exclusive power to perform certain functions. Indeed, the Constitution assigns few powers to the federal government that are not shared by two or more branches. *(See "Enumerated Powers," p. 27, in this chapter.)* Separation of powers actually meant something more like "separated institutions" to the delegates, a separation in which the membership of one branch does not overlap or persecute the membership of the other.[24]

From the beginning, the convention imposed two prohibitions to preserve institutional separation within the government. The first prohibition was against alterations in the incumbent executive's salary; the other was against simultaneous membership in the legislative and executive branches. Both prohibitions were stated in the Virginia

Plan, and they remained substantially unaltered in the final Constitution.

Salary

Immediately after the clause stating that the executive shall be chosen by the legislature, the Virginia Plan provided that the executive shall "receive punctually at stated times, a fixed compensation for the services rendered, in which no increase or diminution shall be made so as to affect the Magistracy existing at the time of increase or diminution." In view of the Virginia Plan's brevity and generality, the detail in this provision is remarkable, as is the priority assigned to it. Clearly, Madison feared that a legislature either might infringe on an executive's independence by lowering or delaying the salary or might reward or entice the executive with an increase in salary.

During the course of the convention, the provision for executive salary was modified only slightly. (The delegates eventually added a provision that "he shall not receive within [his term of office] any other Emolument from the United States, or any of them.") On June 2, Franklin wrote (and, because of his frailty, asked Wilson to read) a long, almost wistful speech urging that the executive not be compensated at all because to attach a salary to the position "united in view of the same object" two "passions which have a powerful influence on the affairs of men. These are ambition and avarice, the love of power, and the love of money.... Place before the eyes of men a post of *honor* that shall be at the same time a place of *profit*, and they will move heaven and earth to obtain it." The delegates gave Franklin's speech a courteous listening and no more: their concern was to protect the executive from the legislature, not to create an office that only the rich could afford to occupy.

Membership

As with the ban on alterations of an incumbent president's salary, the delegates' commitment to separate membership for Congress and the president did not waver. The Virginia Plan said that legislators were "ineligible to any office established by a particular State, or under the authority of the United States, except those peculiarly belonging to the functions of the first branch [the legislature], during the term of service, and for the space of   after the expiration of their term of service." The final document, although lifting the bar on legislators holding executive office for a period after they left Congress, included essentially the same provision: "no Person holding any Office under the United States, shall be a Member of either House during his continuance in Office." The Constitution also prohibited members of Congress from serving as electors in presidential elections.

The reason for keeping the membership of the legislative and executive branches separate was to prevent the executive from increasing power by, in effect, bribing members of Congress with jobs and salaries. On June 22, Pierce Butler, supported by Mason, "appealed to the example of G[reat] B[ritain] where men got into Parlt. [Parliament] that they might get offices for themselves or their friends. This was the source of corruption that ruined their Govt." On June 23, Butler added: "To some of the opposer she [George III] gave pensions—others offices, and some, to put them out of the house of commons, he made lords. The great Montesquieu says, it is unwise to entrust persons with power, which by being abused operates to the advantage of those entrusted with it." The office-holding issue was raised again on August 14, when John Mercer of Maryland took the opposite side of the debate. He argued that since "governments can only be maintained by *force* or *influence*" and the president lacks force, then to "deprive him of influence by rendering members of the Legislature ineligible to Executive offices" was to reduce the president to "a mere phantom of authority." Still, the delegates did not alter their earlier decision.

Nothing was said during the convention about judges holding executive offices. The New Jersey Plan would have prohibited them from doing so, but the subject never was discussed or debated on the convention floor. Indeed, most proposals that delegates made for a council of revision included one or more federal judges as members. *(See "Number of the Executive," p. 22, in this chapter.)* The political scientist Robert Scigliano has argued that this was not an oversight on the delegates' part. Instead, they regarded the executive and judicial powers as joined in some ways. (Both involved carrying out the law.) They also believed that Congress would be the most powerful branch in the new government unless the executive and the judiciary could unite when necessary to restrain it.[25]

Institutional Separation from Congress

No Senator or Representative shall, during the Time for which he was elected, be appointed to any civil Office under the Authority of the United States, which shall have been created, or the Emoluments whereof shall have been increased during such time; and no Person holding any Office under the United States, shall be a Member of either House during his Continuance in Office.

—from Article I, section 6

The President shall, at stated Times, receive for his Services a compensation, which shall neither be encreased nor diminished during the Period for which he shall have been elected, and he shall not receive within that Period any other Emolument from the United States, or any of them.

—from Article II, section 1

Enumerated Powers

The delegates were slow to enumerate the powers either of the presidency or of the other branches of the government they were creating. Indeed, their initial inclination was to give each branch a general grant of powers rather than a specific list. The Virginia Plan, for example, empowered the legislature simply "to legislate in all cases to which the separate states are incompetent, or in which

Enumerated Powers

Every Bill which shall have Passed the House of Representatives and the Senate, shall, before it become a Law, be presented to the President of the United States; If he approve he shall sign it, but if not he shall return it, with his Objections to that House in which it shall have originated, who shall enter the Objections at large on their Journal, and proceed to reconsider it. If after such Reconsideration two thirds of that House shall agree to pass the Bill, it shall be sent, together with the Objections, to the other House, by which it shall likewise be reconsidered, and if approved by two thirds of that House, it shall become a Law. But in all such Cases the Votes of both the Houses shall be determined by Yeas and Nays, and the Names of the Persons voting for and against the Bill shall be entered on the Journal of each House respectively. If any Bill shall not be returned by the President within the ten Days (Sundays excepted) after it shall have been presented to him, the Same shall be a Law, in like Manner as if he had signed it, unless the Congress by their Adjournment prevent its Return, in which Case it shall not be a Law.

Every Order, Resolution, or Vote to which the Concurrence of the Senate and House of Representatives may be necessary (except on a question of Adjournment) shall be presented to the President of the United States; and before the Same shall take Effect, shall be approved by him, or being disapproved by him, shall be repassed by two thirds of the Senate and House of Representatives, according to the Rules and Limitations prescribed in the Case of a Bill.

—from Article I, section 7

The executive Power shall be vested in a President of the United States of America. . . .

—from Article II, section 1

The President shall be Commander in Chief of the Army and Navy of the United States, and of the Militia of the several States, when called into the actual Service of the United States; he may require the Opinion, in writing, of the principal Officer in each of the executive Departments, upon any Subject relating to the Duties of their respective Offices, and he shall have power to grant Reprieves and Pardons for Offenses against the United States, except in Cases of Impeachment.

He shall have Power, by and with the Advice and Consent of the Senate, to make Treaties, provided two thirds of the Senators present concur: and he shall nominate, and by and with the Advice and Consent of the Senate, shall appoint Ambassadors, other public Ministers and Consuls, Judges of the Supreme Court, and all other Officers of the United States, whose Appointments are not herein otherwise provided for, and which shall be established by Law; but the Congress may by Law vest the Appointment of such inferior Officers, as they think proper, in the President alone, in the Courts of Law, or in the Heads of Departments.

The President shall have Power to fill up all Vacancies that may happen during the Recess of the Senate, by granting commissions which shall expire at the End of their next Session.

—from Article II, section 2

He shall from time to time give to the Congress Information of the State of the Union, and recommend to their Consideration such Measures as he shall judge necessary and expedient; he may, on extraordinary Occasions, convene both Houses, or either of them, and in Case of Disagreement between them, with Respect to the Time of Adjournment, he may adjourn them to such Time as he shall think proper; he shall take Care that the Laws be faithfully executed, and shall Commission all the Officers of the United States.

—from Article II, section 3

the harmony of the United States may be interrupted by the exercise of individual legislation." The executive, in addition to having a veto, was to execute the national laws.

The advantage the delegates saw in a general grant of powers (which they approved both while meeting as the Committee of the Whole and afterward) was that the alternative, a specific enumeration, risked limiting the government to a list of powers that the passage of time could render obsolete. But they were uneasy—"incompetent" was a vague word, easily subject to abuse, but so was any other phrase they might invent for a general grant.

Reading the delegates' mood, the Committee of Detail included an enumeration of each branch's powers in the draft constitution it presented to the convention. The committee anticipated the convention's reaction correctly—although the delegates debated each proposed power separately, they never questioned the decision to enumerate.

The powers of the presidency are detailed in Article II of the Constitution (except for the veto power, which is in Article I, section 7). They are discussed here in the order of their appearance in the Constitution. Three other provisions examined in this section—the president's title, oath of office, and qualifications—also are spelled out in Article I.

Veto

The right to veto acts passed by the legislature was the only specific grant of power to the executive in the Virginia Plan. The states' recent experience with weak governors and powerful legislatures was proof enough to the delegates that the veto was indispensable to executive self-defense against legislative encroachments. Even so, they were initially reluctant to cede too much responsibility to the executive—the Virginia Plan provided that the executive could exercise its veto power only with the cooperation of a council of judges. Vetoes could be overridden (and the vetoed act become law) by vote of an unspecified majority of both houses of the legislature.

On June 4, Wilson and Hamilton urged the delegates, then meeting as a Committee of the Whole, to grant the executive an absolute veto—that is, a veto not subject to legislative override. Franklin, Sherman, and Mason rose to speak in opposition to this suggestion, invoking their own and the public's memories of the British king and the royal governors, who had cast absolute vetoes against the acts of American legislatures in colonial times. "We are not constituting a British monarchy, but a more dangerous monarchy, an elective one," argued Mason, who wanted to empower the executive merely to postpone the enactment of offensive laws in the hope that the legislature would revise them. James Madison found a middle ground that was acceptable to the delegates: an executive veto, subject to override by a two-thirds vote of each house of the legislature. The recommendation that the executive share the veto power with a council was tabled.

In its report of July 26, the Committee of Detail, while faithfully reflecting the decisions of the Committee of the Whole regarding the veto, also sought to clarify two unresolved issues. First, the right to cast vetoes was assigned to the president alone. Second, it was stipulated that after a bill was passed and presented, the president would have seven days in which to respond. If the bill was neither signed nor vetoed by the president in that period, it would become law. An important exception was made, however, in order that Congress not try to get its way by adjourning before the president had a chance to cast a veto. If Congress adjourned within the seven-day period, the president had merely to ignore the bill for it to be vetoed. (Such vetoes later came to be called "pocket vetoes.") *(See "Pocket Veto," p. 454, in Legislative Leader chapter of Part III.)*

On August 15, the convention voted to modify the Committee of Detail report in ways that strengthened the president's veto power. The two-thirds requirement for congressional override of a veto was raised to three-fourths. In addition, to prevent Congress from evading a veto by passing legislation and calling it something other than a "bill," the veto power was extended to "every order, resolution, and vote" of Congress. Finally, the period in which a president could cast a veto was extended from seven days to ten days, not including Sundays.

Only one further modification was made in the veto power. On September 12, in a gesture to delegates suspicious of presidential power that was designed to win their signatures on the Constitution, the convention voted to restore the two-thirds requirement for legislative override.

"The Executive Power"

The Virginia Plan introduced the executive article by stating "that a national executive be instituted." The Committee of the Whole had modified this provision of the plan only by adding "to consist of a single person." The Committee of Detail, however, proposed "vesting" clauses for all three branches of government:

> The legislative power shall be vested in a Congress. . . .
>
> The Executive Power of the United States shall be vested in a single person. His title shall be "The President of the United States."
>
> The Judicial Power of the United States shall be vested in one Supreme Court, and in such inferior courts as shall, when necessary, from time to time, be constituted by the Legislature of the United States.

The vesting clause that the committee proposed for the president was particularly important because it made clear that the powers of the presidency derived directly from the Constitution, not from discretionary grants by Congress.

The clause was less instructive on another important aspect of presidential power. As the political scientist Richard Pious noted, " 'Executive Power' was a general term, sufficiently ambiguous so that no one could say precisely what it meant. It was possible that the words referred to more than the enumerated powers that followed, and might confer a set of unspecified executive powers."[26] Chief among these would be prerogative powers, which had been discussed at length in a book that was widely familiar among the delegates, John Locke's *Second Treatise on Government*. Locke had argued that in times of crisis, inadequate laws and constitutions temporarily might have to "give way to the executive power, viz., that as much as may be, all the members of society are to be preserved." Prerogative was "the people's permitting their rulers to do several things of their own free choice, where the law was silent, or sometimes, too, against the direct letter of the law, for the public good, and their acquiescing in it when so done."[27]

The theory that the powers of the presidency extend beyond those listed in the Constitution is supported by the language of the document itself, thanks to a "joker," as Charles Thach has called it, that Gouverneur Morris, the chief draftsman for the Committee of Style, tossed into the final draft. The committee's charge was merely to put the Constitution into polished language. "Positively with respect to the executive article," noted Thach, Morris "could do nothing." His pro-executive biases were so well known that any substantive changes would have been quickly detected. Morris left the vesting clause for the presidency unaltered ("The Executive Power shall be vested in a President of the United States of America") but quietly changed the vesting clause for Congress to read: "All legislative powers herein granted shall be vested in a Congress of the United States."

Thach suspects that Morris did his tinkering "with full realization of the possibilities," namely, that presidents later could claim that the different phrasing of the branches' vesting clauses implies that there is an executive power beyond those "herein granted," else why would the Constitution not apply those restricting words to the president? "At any rate," Thach concluded, "whether intentional or not, it admitted an interpretation of executive power which would give the president a field of activity wider than that outlined by the enumerated powers."[28]

Commander in Chief

Because nothing was said in the Virginia Plan about control of the armed forces, the delegates took it for granted during the early stages of the convention that Congress would have this power, as it had under the Articles of Confederation. The issue did not come up for debate in the Committee of the Whole. The Committee of Detail, however, included a military role for the president in its detailed enumeration of the suggested powers of each branch.

The committee proposed that the president "shall be commander in chief of the Army and navy of the United States, and of the Militia of the several states." But it also suggested that Congress be empowered "to make war; to raise armies; to build and equip fleets; [and] to call forth the aid of the militia, in order to execute the laws of the Union; enforce treaties; suppress insurrections, and repel invasions." The meaning of these provisions confused the delegates when they took them up for consideration on August 17. Clearly, Congress's power to "make" war included the actual conduct of the fighting, but so did the president's power as "commander in chief of the Army and the navy." Which branch, then, would actually order soldiers into action? Which would tell them where to go and what to do when they got there?

Debate on the convention floor was brief and went only part way toward resolving the ambiguities created by the Committee of Detail. Pierce Butler, doubting that Congress (or even the Senate alone) would be able to act quickly enough on military matters should the need arise, urged the convention to vest the power to make war in the president alone, "who will have all the requisite qualities, and will not make war but when the Nation will support it." Madison and Gerry, agreeing that Congress might be unable to respond to foreign invasions promptly (perhaps because it was not in session) but not willing to entrust the president with such vast military powers, "moved to insert *'declare'* [war], striking out *'make'* war; leaving to the Executive the power to repel sudden attacks." Sherman agreed: "The Executive shd. be able to repel and not to commence war." Madison's motion passed.

As for control of the various state militias, on August 27, the convention approved without discussion a motion by Sherman that the president be commander in chief of the militia only "when called into the actual service of the United States." Thus, the clause as finally written in the Constitution reads: "The President shall be Commander in Chief of the Army and Navy of the United States, and of the Militia of the several States, when called into the actual Service of the United States." *(See "Appointment and Commissioning Power," p. 31, in this chapter.)*

"Require the Opinion"

The Constitution includes a provision that empowers the president to "require the Opinion, in writing, of the principal Officer in each of the executive Departments, upon any Subject relating to the Duties of their respective Offices." This curious clause (Hamilton described it in *Federalist* No. 74 "as a mere redundancy in the plan, as the right for which it provides would result of itself from the office") was proposed by the Committee on Postponed Matters and adopted by a unanimous vote of the state delegations on September 7. But its origin lies in the Virginia Plan's proposal for an executive council, an idea that recurred frequently during the convention.

Although most delegates seem to have favored some sort of council, they never created one because they held such varied opinions about who should be on such a council and whether its relationship to the president should be merely advisory or involve the shared exercise of executive powers. *(See "Number of the Executive," p. 22, in this chapter.)* One version of the council idea was included in a sweeping plan for the organization of the executive branch that Gouverneur Morris and Charles Pinckney introduced on August 20. The Morris-Pinckney plan provided for five departments to be created, which were to be headed by, respectively, a secretary of domestic affairs, of commerce and finance, of foreign affairs, of war, and of marine. All five of these "principal officers" were to be appointed by the president and serve at the president's pleasure. Together with the chief justice of the Supreme Court, they were to constitute a Council of State whose purpose would be to

> assist the President in conducting the Public affairs.... The President may from time to time submit any matter to the discussion of the Council of State, and he may require the written opinion of any one or more of the members: But he shall in all cases exercise his own judgment, and either Conform to such opinions or not as he may think proper; and every officer abovementioned shall be responsible for his opinion on the affairs relating to his particular Department.

The Morris-Pinckney plan was not debated by the delegates, but the proposal to empower the president to require written opinions from individual department heads on matters related to their responsibilities seems to have underlain the Committee on Postponed Matters' September 7 recommendation. Although Mason, Franklin, Wilson, Dickinson, and Madison again urged that a council be created, their colleagues, frustrated by their inability to agree on a specific proposal and eager to conclude the convention's business, approved the committee's recommendation as written.

Pardon

Hamilton was the first to suggest to the convention that it grant the president the power to pardon criminals. In his long and generally unpersuasive speech to the delegates on June 18 he urged that the executive "have the power of pardoning all offences except Treason; which he shall not pardon without the approbation of the Senate." *(See "Hamilton's Plan," p. 17, in this chapter.)* Perhaps inspired by Hamilton's proposal, the Committee of Detail included a provision that the president "shall have power to grant reprieves and pardons; but his pardon shall not be pleadable in bar of an impeachment" (that is, to prevent an impeachment).

Remarkably (the pardon power is a power of kings and the only unchecked power granted to the president), the delegates resisted efforts to modify the committee's recommendation in any substantive way. Sherman's August 25 motion to require the president to gain Senate consent for a pardon was defeated by a vote of eight states to one. Two days later, Luther Martin moved to allow pardons only "after conviction"; he withdrew the motion after Wilson objected that "pardon before conviction might be necessary in order to obtain the testimony of accomplices." On September 12, the Committee of Style clarified one aspect of the pardon power by limiting it to "offences against the United States," that is, to violations of national rather than state law. A September 15 motion by Edmund Randolph to disallow pardons for treason ("The President may himself be guilty. The Traytors may be his own instruments.") was defeated by a vote of eight states to two after Wilson argued that if the president "be himself a party to the guilt he can be impeached and prosecuted."

No thoroughgoing case for granting the pardon power to the president ever was offered at the convention, but Hamilton's defense of it in *Federalist* No. 74 may have reflected the delegates' thinking. Hamilton began by pleading the need for leeway in the criminal justice system to "make exceptions in favor of unfortunate guilt." As to pardons for treason, he argued (perhaps with Shays's Rebellion in mind), "The principal argument for reposing the power of pardoning in this case in the Chief Magistrate is this: in seasons of insurrection or rebellion there are often critical moments when a well-timed offer of pardon to the insurgents or rebels may restore the tranquility of the commonwealth; and which, if suffered to pass unimproved, it may never be possible afterwards to recall."

"Make Treaties"

At the start of the convention, most delegates seemed to assume that the treaty power would be vested in Congress. That had been the practice under the Articles of Confederation, and although the Virginia Plan said nothing explicitly about treaties, it did provide that "the National Legislature ought to be impowered to enjoy the Legislative Rights vested in Congress by the Confederation."

The first suggestion that the treaty power should be shared between the legislative and executive branches seems to have been made at the convention by Alexander Hamilton. Among the specific provisions of the lengthy plan of government he proposed on June 18 was that the executive should "have with the approbation and advice of the Senate the power of making all treaties." There was no discussion of Hamilton's suggestion, and it appeared to be dead when the August 6 report of the Committee of Detail proposed that "the Senate shall have the power to make treaties." But the committee's proposal sparked heated debate on the convention floor.

George Mason said the proposal would enable the Senate to "sell the whole country by means of treaties." James Madison thought the president, representing the whole people, should have the treaty-making power. Regional concerns also were expressed: Southern delegates worried that their right to free navigation of the Mississippi River might be surrendered in a future treaty; New Englanders expressed similar fears about their right to fish in the waters near Newfoundland. The delegates, having reached an impasse, referred the treaty issue to the Committee on Postponed Matters.

On September 4, the Committee on Postponed Matters recommended that "the president, with the advice and consent of the Senate" be granted the treaty-making power and that no treaty could be approved "without the consent of two-thirds of the members [of the Senate] present." The provision for a two-thirds vote, designed to assuage the concerns of the southerners and New Englanders that they would be outnumbered on issues of regional importance, was highly controversial and brought on numerous motions to revise. One would have deleted the two-thirds requirement in favor of a simple majority vote. Another would have strengthened the requirement by requiring a two-thirds vote of the entire membership of the Senate. Another would have included the House of Representatives in the treaty power. Yet another—which initially passed and then was rejected—would have applied the simple majority rule to peace treaties. In the end, though, the committee's recommendation of a two-thirds vote of the senators present was accepted.

The proposal to involve the president with the Senate in treaty making was relatively uncontroversial, reflecting an alliance between pro-executive delegates and small-state delegates that had come about after the convention decided that states would be represented equally in the Senate. Only one motion was made to modify the president's role: Madison moved to allow two
Senate, acting alone if it chose, to conclud
Madison argued that the president wo
rive so much power and importance
that he might be tempted to "impe
His motion failed when Nathaniel
that Congress could end a war by simp
priate funds to continue the fighting.

Appointment and Commissioning P

Article II, section 2, of the Constitution, as fin
written, provides three methods of appointment for federa
judges and other unelected government officials: presidential appointment with Senate confirmation (the ordinary method); presidential appointment without Senate confirmation (when the Senate is in recess); and, when Congress so determines by statute, appointment of certain "inferior Officers" (officers subordinate to the heads of the departments or the courts of law) by the heads of the departments or the courts of law. Clearly the delegates moved a long way from both the Articles of Confederation, which vested the appointment power entirely in Congress, and the Virginia Plan, which proposed to continue that practice.

The appointment power was one of the first, last, and (in between) the most contentious issues at the convention regarding the powers of the national government. On June 1, meeting as the Committee of the Whole, the delegates did accept Madison's motion to modify the Virginia Plan slightly by adding to the then-limited powers of the executive the ambiguous phrase: "to appoint to offices in cases not otherwise provided for." This decision opened the door to stronger advocates of executive power, such as Wilson and Hamilton, who wished to make the appointment of judges, ambassadors, and other government officials a purely executive responsibility, with no involvement by the legislature at all.

Hot debate periodically ensued during the months of June and July over which branch of government would be most prone to favoritism in appointments, which would know the most about the qualifications of prospective appointees, and other such issues. Many delegates, mindful of how George III and his royal governors in the colonies had used government appointments as patronage plums to curry support among legislators, dreaded giving this power to any executive.

On July 21, meeting as the Committee of the Whole, the delegates voted to confer sole responsibility for the appointment of judges on the Senate. The Committee of Detail added the appointment of ambassadors to the Senate's list of powers, then stipulated that Congress as a whole should elect the treasurer (that is, the secretary of the Treasury) and confirmed the convention's earlier decision that the president "shall appoint officers in all cases not otherwise provided for by this Constitution." The committee also empowered the president to "commission all the officers of the United States." It remained unclear, however, where responsibility would lie for appointing the heads of the departments or other department officials and employees.

During August, as the delegates were generally turning more in the direction of increased presidential power, they passed a motion that, although not altogether clear, seemed to expand the president's power to make appointments, while leaving complete responsibility for choosing judges and ambassadors in the Senate's jurisdiction. The motion stated: the president "shall appoint to all offices established by this Constitution, except in cases herein otherwise provided for, and to all offices which may hereafter be created by law." The delegates rejected George Read's motion to allow the president to appoint the treasurer, however. They still wanted anything to do with money firmly in Congress's hands.

As with the treaty power, the Committee on Postponed Matters proposed in early September to increase further the president's role in the appointment process. Judges, ambassadors, ministers, and other officers that the delegates already had provided for—all would be appointed by the president with the advice and consent of the Senate. (A simple majority vote of the senators present would suffice to confirm a presidential appointment.) Wilson tried again to persuade the delegates to make appointments a unilateral power of the president (to involve the Senate, he argued, had "a dangerous tendency to aristocracy"), but his motion was unsuccessful.

The convention accepted the committee's recommendation with three additions: the power to appoint the Treasury secretary was transferred from Congress to the president, the president was given the power to fill vacancies that occurred while the Senate was in recess, and control over certain forms of patronage was distributed between the two branches by giving Congress the power to "vest the appointment of such inferior officers as they think proper" in the president, the courts, or the heads of the departments.

Advisory Legislative Powers

In enumerating the proposed powers of the presidency, the Committee of Detail enjoined that: "He shall, from time to time, give information to the Legislature, of the state of the Union: he may recommend to their consideration such measures as he shall deem necessary, and expedient." The latter of these provisions, both of which were uncontroversial, was modified slightly in response to an August 24 motion by Gouverneur Morris. Morris argued that it should be "the *duty* of the President to recommend [measures to Congress], and thence prevent umbrage or cavil at his doing it." The convention approved his specific suggestion that the words "he may" be replaced by "and." Thus, the Constitution as finally written reads: "He shall from time to time give to the Congress Information of the State of the Union, and recommend to their Consideration such Measures as he shall judge necessary and expedient."

Powers to Convene and Adjourn Congress

The Committee of Detail also recommended that the president be empowered to "convene them [the legislature] on extraordinary occasions," that is, to call Congress into special session. Further, "In case of disagreement between the two Houses, with regard to the time of their adjournment, he may adjourn them to such time as he thinks proper."

Elbridge Gerry, wishing to grant the president the option to call only the Senate back into session (presumably to consider a treaty or presidential appointment), persuaded the delegates to amend the special session clause to that effect on September 8. In the end, the Constitution read: "he may, on extraordinary Occasions, convene both Houses, or either of them."

"Receive Ambassadors"

The president's power to "receive Ambassadors" was proposed by the Committee of Detail. The committee joined this power to another—permission to "correspond with the supreme Executives of the several States," that is, state governors—that the convention rejected on August 25 as "unnecessary and implying that he could not correspond with others" (according to Morris). As for receiving ambassadors, the absence of debate or discussion by the delegates makes it unclear whether they meant this power to be merely ceremonial or substantive. In practice, it has made the president the sole recipient of communications from foreign governments and the sole maker of decisions about which governments the United States will recognize diplomatically.

"Take Care"

According to the Virginia Plan, the executive was to have "general authority to execute the National Laws." On June 1, Madison sought to revise this to read: "power to carry into effect the national laws . . . and to execute such other powers not Legislative or Judiciary in their nature as from time to time be delegated by the national Legislature." The stipulation about legislative and judicial powers reflected Madison's acceptance of a suggestion by Charles Cotesworth Pinckney who felt it useful to prevent "improper" powers from being delegated to the executive. The other South Carolina Pinckney (Charles) persuaded the delegates to strike the amendment as "unnecessary." No further controversy over the "take care" clause ensued. The Committee of Detail's formulation—"he shall take care that the laws of the United States be duly and faithfully executed"—was adopted without discussion by the convention and survived virtually intact in the final Constitution: "he shall take Care that the Laws be faithfully executed."

Title

During the first two months of their deliberations, the delegates usually referred to the head of the executive branch as the "national executive," "supreme executive," or "governor." On August 6, the Committee of Detail, borrowing from the plan proposed to the convention on May 29 by Charles Pinckney, included the term "president" in its report to the convention. *(See box, The Puzzle of the Pinckney Plan, p. 16.)* The title had been used for the presiding officer of Congress and many other legislative bodies, including the convention itself. It was familiar and unthreatening to those who feared that the delegates might be creating a monarchical or tyrannical office. Once proposed by the committee, "president" was accepted without debate by the convention.

Oath of Office

"Before he enter on the Execution of his Office," the Constitution requires of the president, "he shall take the following Oath or Affirmation:—'I do solemnly swear (or affirm) that I will faithfully execute the Office of President of the United States, and will to the best of my Ability, preserve, protect and defend the Constitution of the United States.' " Although another provision of the Con stitution states that all legislators, judges, and other officials of both the national government and the various state governments "shall be bound by Oath or Affirmation, to support this Constitution," the actual language of only the president's oath is included in the document. Some scholars regard the wording of the presidential oath (it pledges the president to execute "the office" rather than the laws) as further support for the claim that there are implied prerogative powers in the Constitution. *(See " 'The Executive Power,' " p. 29, in this chapter.)*

Virtually no debate or discussion accompanied the writing of the president's oath by the Constitutional Convention. The first half of the oath was proposed by the Committee of Detail on August 6: "I ______ solemnly swear (or affirm) that I will faithfully execute the office of President of the United States of America." On August 27, Mason and Madison moved that the phrase "and will to the best of my judgment and power preserve protect and defend the Constitution of the U.S." be added to the oath. Wilson objected that a special presidential oath was unnecessary, but Mason's and Madison's motion passed handily. Finally, on September 15, the delegates substituted "abilities" for "judgment and power," but, again, no discussion is recorded to explain this alteration.

In contrast to the prevailing practice in most of the states at the time, the Constitution bars the imposition of religious oaths on the president and other officials of the national government. Some state constitutions required an adherence to Christianity as a condition for serving as governor, others to Protestant Christianity. (North Carolina, for example, insisted that its governor affirm the existence of God and the truth of Protestantism and hold no religious beliefs that were inimical to the peace and safety of the state.) On August 30, Pinckney moved that "no religious test shall ever be required as a qualification to any office or public trust under the authority of the U. States." Sherman said he "thought it unnecessary, the prevailing liberality being a sufficient security agst. such tests." Nonetheless, Pinckney's motion was approved.

Qualifications

No statement of qualifications for president was included in the Constitution until September 7, when the convention, unanimously and without debate, approved the recommendation of the Committee on Postponed Matters that the president be thirty-five years or older, a natural-born citizen (or a citizen at the time of the Constitution's adoption), and a resident of the United States for at least fourteen years.

The lateness of the convention's actions on presidential qualifications was the result of deliberation, not tardiness. Throughout their proceedings, the delegates seem to have operated on the principle that qualifications for an office needed to be stated only if qualifications were not stated for those who choose the person who will fill the office.[29] Thus, as early as the Virginia Plan, qualifications, which were not stated for voters, were included for members of the national legislature. (Ultimately, the qualifications for a member of the House of Representatives were established as at least twenty-five years old, seven years a citizen, and an inhabitant of the state; senators had to be at least thirty years old, nine years a citizen, and an inhabitant of the state.) Conversely, qualifications for judges and other appointed offices never were included in the Constitution because they were selected by the president and by members of the Senate, government officials for whom qualifications were stated.

Through most of the convention's deliberations, the majority of delegates remained wedded to the idea that Congress, a body for whose members qualifications were stated, would elect the president. *(See "Selection and Succession," p. 23, in this chapter.)* Thus, no need was seen to include qualifications for president in the Constitution. By mid-August, however, it was obvious that most delegates had changed their minds about legislative selection of the executive. Although they had not yet decided upon an alternative, whatever procedure they eventually devised for choosing the president clearly would involve selection by an "unqualified" body, since members of Congress were the only officials for whom constitutional qualifications were stated. This new election procedure, in turn, would necessitate the writing of qualifications for president. What is more, these qualifications would have to be high, since the delegates also seem to have agreed that the greater the powers of an office, the higher the qualifications for it should be.

On August 20, Elbridge Gerry moved that the Committee of Detail propose a list of qualifications for president. Two days later, it did: at least thirty-five years old, a U.S. citizen, and an inhabitant of the United States for at least twenty-one years. On September 4, the Committee on Postponed Matters submitted a revised statement of qualifications: at least thirty-five, a natural-born citizen (or a citizen at the time of the Constitution's adoption), and at least fourteen years a resident. The delegates approved the revised recommendation on September 7.

Each element of the presidential qualifications clause was grounded in its own rationale. The age requirement had two justifications. First, the delegates presumed, age would foster maturity—as Mason said in the debate on establishing a minimum age for members of the House of Representatives, "every man carried with him in his own experience a scale for measuring the deficiencies of young politicians, since he would if interrogated be obliged to declare that his political opinions at the age of 21 were too crude & erroneous to merit an influence on public measures." Second, age left a record for voters to assess. According to John Jay, the author of *Federalist* No. 64,

> By excluding men under 35 from the first office [president], and those under 30 from the second [senator], it confines the electors to men of whom the people have had time to form a judgment, and with respect to whom they will not be liable to be deceived by those brilliant appearances of genius and patriotism which, like transient meteors, sometimes mislead as well as dazzle.

Oath of Office

Before he enter on the Execution of his Office, he shall take the following Oath or Affirmation: —"I do solemnly swear (or affirm) that I will faithfully execute the Office of President of the United States, and will to the best of my Ability, preserve, protect and defend the Constitution of the United States."

—from Article II, section 1

Qualifications

No person except a natural born Citizen, or a Citizen of the United States, at the time of the Adoption of this Constitution, shall be eligible to the Office of President; neither shall any Person be eligible to the Office who shall not have attained to the Age of thirty five Years, and been fourteen Years a Resident within the United States.

—from Article II, section 1

The residency and citizenship requirements for president were grounded less in principle than in the politics of the moment. The stipulation that the president must be at least fourteen years a resident of the United States was designed to eliminate from consideration both British sympathizers who had fled to England during the American Revolution and popular foreign military leaders, notably Baron von Steuben of Prussia, who had emigrated to the United States to fight in the Revolution. As to the length of the residency requirement, the Committee of Detail's recommendation of twenty-one years seems to have been reduced to fourteen because the longer requirement—but not the shorter—would have barred three of the convention's delegates from the presidency.

The reason for requiring that the president be a natural born citizen was similarly tied to contemporary politics. Rumors had spread while the convention was meeting that the delegates were plotting to invite a European monarch—Prince Henry of Prussia and Frederick, Duke of York, who was King George III's second son, were the most frequently mentioned names—to rule the United States. (The practice of importing foreign rulers was not uncommon among the European monarchies of the day and would not have seemed outlandish to people who heard the rumor.) The delegates, aware that the mere fact of an independent executive in the Constitution was going to provoke attacks by those who suspected the presidency of being a latent monarchy, seem to have believed that they could at least squelch the foreign king rumor by requiring that the president be a natural born citizen of the United States.[30]

A property qualification for president was not included in the Constitution, even though most state constitutions required that their governors be property owners and the delegates had approved a similar requirement for the president more than a month before they enacted the presidential qualifications clause. On July 26, the convention adopted a motion by Mason and Pinckney that a property qualification be stated for judges, legislators, and the executive. The Committee of Detail neglected the motion in its proposed draft of the Constitution, which provoked both a complaint and another motion by Pinckney. John Rutledge, the chairman of the committee, apologized and seconded Pinckney's motion. He said the committee had made no recommendations about property "because they could not agree on any among themselves, being embarrassed by the danger on one side of displeasing the people by making them too high, and on the other of rendering them nugatory by making them low."

Franklin then rose to attack the very idea of property qualifications—"Some of the greatest rogues he was ever acquainted with were the richest rogues," he told the delegates—and Pinckney's motion, noted Madison, "was rejected by so general a no, that the States were not called." In truth, the practical difficulty of establishing an acceptable property requirement, more than any belief that such a requirement should not be included on principle, seems to explain why the Constitution was silent regarding property ownership by the president.

The Vice Presidency

The idea of an office like the vice presidency was not unknown to the delegates to the Constitutional Convention. During the period of British rule, several colonies had lieutenant governors (known in some states as deputy governors or by another title) whose ongoing duties were minor but who stood by to serve as acting governor if the governor died, was replaced, or was ill or absent from the colony.

After independence, five states (New York, Connecticut, Rhode Island, Massachusetts, and South Carolina) included lieutenant governors in their constitutions. Each was elected in the same manner as the governor and was charged to act as governor when needed. (New York's lieutenant governor also was ex officio president of the state senate, empowered to vote to break ties.) Other states handled the matter of gubernatorial death, absence, or inability differently. In Virginia and Georgia, for example, the head of the privy council, a cabinet-style body, was the designated gubernatorial successor; in Delaware and North Carolina it was the speaker of the upper house of the legislature; in New Hampshire, the senior member of the state senate.[31]

It is difficult to say whether the experience of the states had much influence on the decision of the Constitutional Convention to create the vice presidency. No reference was made to the state lieutenant governors in the convention debates. Nor was any proposal made to include a vice president in the Constitution until very late in the proceedings. Indeed, the invention of the vice presidency seems to have been an afterthought of the convention, a residue of its solution to the problem of presidential selection.

The convention initially had decided that the legislature should choose the executive, who, to remove the temptation to use the powers and duties of the office to trade favors for votes with legislators in a quest for reelection, was to be allowed only one term. But as the convention wore on, delegates became so enamored of the incentive to excellent service in office, which eligibility for reelection brings, that they removed the bar to a single term and, with it, the legislative method of presidential selection. They eventually replaced legislative selection with the electoral college, an invention of the Committee on Postponed Matters in which each state's delegates were to choose electors, who in turn would choose the president, by majority vote. A possibly fatal defect of this procedure was that state electors simply would vote for a variety of favorite sons, preventing the choice of a nationally elected president. But the committee remedied this potential problem by assigning the electors two votes each for president, requiring that they cast at least one of their votes for a candidate who "shall not be an Inhabitant of the same State with themselves," and attaching a consequence to both votes: the

An Ambiguous Office

The constitutional status of the vice presidency is a matter of some confusion. A variety of practices and opinions have emerged through the years. Vice President Thomas Jefferson, dwelling on the vice president's role as president of the Senate, said, "I consider my office as constitutionally confined to legislative duties." John Nance Garner, a twentieth-century vice president, placed the vice presidency in "a no man's land somewhere between the executive and legislative branch." Walter F. Mondale said that as vice president he was "a member of both ... branches."

As part of both the executive and legislative branches (or as part of neither), the vice presidency has never been fully at home in either one. In this century, the Senate has become steadily less receptive to vice presidents who hoped to play a formal role there. Nothing illustrates this better than the rebuff that Senate Democrats handed Lyndon B. Johnson, arguably the most effective Senate leader is history, when he asked to be allowed to continue presiding over meetings of the Senate Democratic Caucus at the start of his term as vice president in 1961. As Sen. Clinton Anderson, who had been one of Johnson's closest political allies, protested, the office of vice president is not a legislative office.

Neither is the vice presidency fully executive. To be sure, a number of developments, notably the establishment by President Franklin D. Roosevelt of the presidential nominee's right to designate a running mate, have moved the vice presidency more clearly into the executive orbit—in practice, if not in constitutional theory.

The difference between theory and practice was decorously observed in the working relationship between President Dwight D. Eisenhower and Vice President Richard Nixon. Eisenhower firmly believed that the vice president "is not legally a member of the executive branch and is not subject to direction by the president." Thus the president would never tell his vice president to do anything. Instead, recalls Nixon, Eisenhower would "wonder aloud if I might like to take over this or that project." Nixon, of course, never refused these requests; indeed, he estimated after seven years as vice president that about 90 percent of his time had been spent on executive branch activities, and only 10 percent on legislative matters. But, following constitutional form, Eisenhower said he regarded Nixon's efforts on the administration's behalf as "working voluntarily."

In one very important sense, however, theory really does guide practice. The vice presidency, being an elective office with a fixed four-year term, is constitutionally independent. However closely the vice president may be associated with the administration, presidents are reluctant to assign certain important tasks to vice presidents, knowing that, unlike department heads and other executive officials, they cannot be commanded, removed, or otherwise held formally accountable for their words and actions. Historically, the two major efforts to assign a vice president supervisory responsibility for an agency or staff unit ended in failure and disappointment—when President Franklin Roosevelt named Vice President Henry A. Wallace to chair the three-thousand-member Economic Defense Board and when President Gerald R. Ford allowed Vice President Nelson A. Rockefeller to head the White House Domestic Council. *(See History of the Vice Presidency chapter in Part I.)*

runner-up in the election for president would be awarded the newly created office of vice president.

Thus, as North Carolina delegate Hugh Williamson, a member of the Committee on Postponed Matters, testified, "Such an office as vice-President was not wanted. It was introduced only for the sake of a valuable mode of election which required two to be chosen at the same time." But, having invented the vice presidency, the committee proposed that the office also be used to solve two other problems that had vexed the convention.

The first was the role of president of the Senate. Some delegates had fretted that if a senator were chosen for this position, one of two problems inevitably would arise. If the senator were barred from voting on legislative matters except in the event of a tie (which was customary for presiding officers, because it guaranteed that tie votes would be broken), the senator's state would be effectively denied half its representation on most issues. If the senator were allowed to vote on all matters, the state would be effectively overrepresented in the Senate. The Committee on Postponed Matters recommended that, as a way around this dilemma, the vice president serve as president of the Senate, voting only to break ties. An exception was made for impeachment trials of the president, when the chief justice of the Supreme Court would preside over the Senate.

The second loose end that the committee used the vice presidency to tie off was presidential succession. This, too, was a matter to which the convention had turned rather late. The Virginia Plan, New Jersey Plan, and (probably) the Pinckney Plan had been silent about succession. On June 18, as part of his sweeping proposal for a national executive chosen by electors to serve for life, Alexander Hamilton had suggested that in the event of the executive's death, resignation, impeachment, removal, or absence from the country, the president of the Senate (a senator) should "exercise all the powers by this Constitution vested in the President, until another shall be appointed, or until he shall return within the United States, if his absence was with the Consent of the Senate and Assembly [House of Representatives]." But Hamilton's plan, as we have seen, received little consideration from the delegates and was never formally discussed. *(See "Hamilton's Plan," p. 17, in this chapter.)*

Serious attention first was given to the succession question by the Committee of Detail. Deliberately or not, the committee followed Hamilton's lead in its August 6 report to the convention, providing that: "In the case of his [the president's] removal as aforesaid, death, resignation,

Vice President

The Vice President of the United States shall be President of the Senate, but shall have no Vote, unless they be equally divided.

The Senate shall chuse . . . a President pro tempore, in the Absence of the Vice President, or when he shall exercise the Office of the President of the United States.

—from Article I, section 3

(See boxes on term, election, succession and disability, impeachment, and constitutional amendments in this chapter.)

or disability to discharge the powers and duties of his office, the President of the Senate shall exercise those powers and duties, until another President of the United States be chosen, or until the disability of the President be removed." When the delegates discussed this provision of the committee report on August 27, considerable dissatisfaction was voiced. James Madison feared that the Senate would have a stake in presidential vacancies if its own president were the designated successor and suggested that a "Council to the President" fill that role instead. (Gouverneur Morris suggested the chief justice as successor.) Finally, Williamson asked that the question be postponed, placing it in the hands of the Committee on Postponed Matters. The convention agreed.

The committee, which reported to the convention on September 4, proposed that: "in the case of his [the president's] removal as aforesaid, death, absence, resignation, or inability to discharge the powers or duties of his office the Vice President shall exercise those powers and duties until another President be chosen, or until the inability of the President be removed." Three days later, Edmund Randolph, in an effort to supplement the committee's proposal with one that would provide a method of presidential succession if there were no vice president, moved that: "The Legislature may declare by law what officer of the United States shall act as President in the case of the death, resignation, or disability of the President and Vice President; and such Officer shall act accordingly until the time of electing a President shall arrive." Madison moved to replace the last nine words of Randolph's motion with "until such disability be removed, or a President shall be elected." The motion passed, as amended.

Madison's reason for amending Randolph's motion is clear: he wanted to allow for a special presidential election to replace a departed president, or, in his words, to permit "a supply of vacancy by an intermediate election of the President." Other evidence from the records of the convention suggests that most of the delegates intended that the president's successor would serve only as acting president until a special election could be called.[32] But sometime during the period September 8-12, when the Committee of Style was working to fulfill its charge to produce a smooth, final draft of the Constitution, that intention was, probably unwittingly, lost. The committee took the September 4 motion of the Committee on Postponed Matters and Randolph's September 7 motion and merged them into one passage, which, with minor modification, became paragraph 6 of Article II, section 2, of the Constitution:

> In case of the Removal of the President from Office, or of his death, Resignation, or Inability to discharge the Powers and Duties of the said Office, the Same shall devolve on the Vice President, and the Congress may by law provide for the Case of Removal, Death, Resignation, or Inability, both of the President and Vice President, declaring what Officer shall then act as President, and such officer shall act accordingly, until the Disability be removed, or a President shall be elected.[33]

Clearly, the delegates' intentions regarding succession were obscured by the Committee of Style. Grammatically, it is impossible to tell—and in its rush to adjournment, the convention did not notice the ambiguity—whether "the Same" in this provision refers to "the said office" (the presidency) or, as the delegates intended, only its "powers and duties." Nor can one ascertain if "until . . . a President shall be elected" means until the end of the original four-year term or, again as intended, until a special election is held.[34]

The vice presidency was not a very controversial issue at the Constitutional Convention. On September 4, when the delegates were considering the Committee on Postponed Matters's proposal for the electoral college, Nathaniel Gorham worried that "a very obscure man with very few votes" might be elected because it was required only that the vice president be runner-up in the presidential election, not the recipient of a majority of votes. Roger Sherman replied that any of the top vote-getters would likely be qualified.

The role of the vice president as president of the Senate became a subject of minor controversy on September 7. Elbridge Gerry, seconded by Edmund Randolph, complained about the mixing of legislative and executive elements: "We might as well put the President himself at the head of the Legislature. The close intimacy that must subsist between the President & vice-president makes it absolutely improper." Gerry was "agst. having any vice President." Gouverneur Morris doubted that the presumed intimacy that fretted Gerry would arise, observing wryly that "the vice president then will be the first heir apparent that ever loved his father." Sherman added that "if the vice-President were not to be President of the Senate, he would be without employment." He also reminded the convention that for the Senate to elect a president from among its own members probably would deprive that member of a vote. George Mason ended the brief debate by branding "the office of vice-President an encroachment on the rights of the Senate; . . . it mixed too much the Legislative and Executive, which as well as the Judiciary departments, ought to be kept as separate as possible." After Mason's speech, the convention voted overwhelmingly to approve the vice presidency. Interestingly, no serious attention was given to the vice president's responsibilities as successor to the president.

Ratifying the Constitution

The original call by Congress for a convention in Philadelphia had charged the delegates only to propose amendments to the Articles of Confederation, not to design an entirely new system of government. By itself, the delegates' decision to ignore this charge ensured that controversy would ensue when, having met so long in secret, they published the Constitution in September. In addition, several provisions of the draft constitution, including the enhanced powers of the national government and the design of the legislative branch, were certain to be controversial. But nothing astonished the nation more than the convention's decision to recommend that a national executive be established—unitary, independently elected, and empowered with its own grant of powers.

In the debates that the various state ratifying conventions held on the Constitution, Anti-Federalists (those who opposed the Constitution) concentrated much of their fire on the presidency. Federalists (those who wanted the Constitution ratified) rose to its defense, their intellectual arsenal well stocked with arguments from a series of newspaper articles that Alexander Hamilton, James Madison, and John Jay were publishing under the name "Publius." In the end, the Federalists prevailed, although the outcome of the battle for ratification was not certain until the very end.

The Anti-Federalist Critique of the Presidency

Anti-Federalists attacked the presidency as a disguised monarchy that, in collaboration with a supposedly aristocratic Senate, eventually would rule the United States much as the British king, assisted by the House of Lords, was said to rule England.

The most strenuous opposition to the presidency was registered by Patrick Henry of Virginia. On June 7, 1788, speaking with unvarnished fervor, Henry voiced the Anti-Federalists' fears of a presidential monarchy to his state's ratifying convention:

> This Constitution is said to have beautiful features, but when I come to examine these features, Sir, they appear to me to be horridly frightful: Among other deformities, it has an awful squinting; it squints towards monarchy: And does this not raise indignation in the breast of every American?
>
> Your President may easily become a King; . . . if your American chief, be a man of ambition, how easy it is for him to render himself absolute: The army is in his hands, and if he be a man of address, it will be attached to him; . . . I would rather infinitely, and I am sure most of these Convention are of the same opinion, have a king, Lords, and Commons, than a Government so replete with such insupportable evils. If we make a King, we may prescribe the rules by which he shall rule his people, and interpose such checks as shall prevent him from infringing them: But the President, in the field, at the head of his army, can prescribe the terms on which he shall reign master, so far that it will puzzle any American ever to get his neck from under the galling yoke. . . . And what have you to oppose this force? What will then become of you and your rights? Will not absolute despotism ensue? [35]

Other Anti-Federalists directed their fire at the close relationship they saw the Constitution fostering between the "monarchical" president and the "aristocratic" Senate, the two bodies that, without the involvement of the "democratic" House of Representatives, shared the powers of appointment and treaty making. A group of delegates at the Pennsylvania ratifying convention published a report on December 18, 1787, asserting that the Constitution's provisions regarding treaties virtually invited foreign meddling. The Senate would consist of twenty-six members, they noted, two from each of the thirteen states. Fourteen senators would constitute a quorum for that body, of whom only ten were needed to provide the two-thirds vote to ratify a treaty proposed by the president. "What an inducement would this [small number] offer to the ministers of foreign powers to compass by bribery *such concessions* as could not otherwise be obtained," the Pennsylvania dissenters concluded.[36]

Although monarchy was the Anti-Federalists' main fear, scarcely a feature of the presidency was immune from their criticism. The Virginia and North Carolina ratifying conventions urged passage of a constitutional amendment that would limit a president to eight years in office in any sixteen-year period. George Clinton, writing as "Cato" in the *New York Journal* in November 1787, argued that the president's term was too long and cited Montesquieu's prescription of one-year terms. The absence of a council meant that the president will "be unsupported by proper information and advice, and will generally be directed by minions and favorites." Instead of direct election by the people (which Clinton, as Cato, favored), the president "arrives to this office at the fourth or fifth hand." [37]

Interestingly, the presidency drew criticism from two future presidents—Thomas Jefferson, who observed archly that a president who could be reelected indefinitely and commanded the armed forces "seems a bad edition of a Polish king," and James Monroe, who fretted about the possibility of a president being reelected into life tenure. The office also was attacked by two future vice presidents—Elbridge Gerry, one of three delegates to the Constitutional Convention who refused to sign the document, and Clinton, who, as governor of New York, was jealous of the presidency's resemblance to his own office. "This government is no more like a true picture of your own than an Angel of Darkness resembles an Angel of Light," he warned his fellow New Yorkers.[38]

The Federalist Defense of the Presidency

Article II posed a political problem to Federalists who were trying to persuade the states to ratify the Constitution. Not only was the presidency the most obvious innovation in the new plan of government, but its unitary nature roused fears of the most horrifying specter Americans could imagine—an all-powerful monarchy like the one they had overthrown in the revolutionary war. Anti-Federalists, as we have seen, inflamed these fears.

Proponents of the Constitution at the state ratifying conventions stressed both the virtues of the presidency and the restraints that the Constitution placed upon it. In doing so, they relied to some degree on the explanations and defenses of the Constitution that Hamilton, Madison, and Jay were putting forth in the series of eighty-five newspaper articles that Hamilton had commissioned. These articles, later gathered together in a book called *The Federalist Papers,* appeared pseudonymously under the name "Publius" in several New York newspapers. (We now know that Hamilton wrote fifty-one of them, Madison twenty-six, Jay five, and Hamilton and Madison jointly three.) They were reprinted and disseminated widely through the states. *(See box,* The Federalist Papers *on Powers of the Presidency, p. 38.)*

Hamilton wrote *Federalist* Nos. 69-77, the articles that

The Federalist Papers on Powers of the Presidency

With regard to the presidency, *The Federalist Papers* is most famous for Nos. 69-72, in which the nature of the office is explained, defended, and contrasted to the British monarchy. In *Federalist* Nos. 73-77, the enumerated powers of the presidency are treated individually, in the order they are stated in Article II of the Constitution. In all cases, the author, Alexander Hamilton, labored to demonstrate to readers that the powers of the presidency, far from being threatening, were modest and essential to the operations of good government. Excerpts from his arguments follow.

Veto. "The propensity of the legislative department to intrude upon the rights, and to absorb the powers, of the other departments has been already more than once suggested.... Without [the veto,] ... he might gradually be stripped of his authorities by successive resolutions or annihilated by a single vote.... But the power in question has a further use. It not only serves as a shield to the executive, but it furnishes an additional security against the enaction of improper laws.... Nor is this all. The superior weight and influence of the legislative body in a free government and the hazard to the executive in a trial of strength with that body afford a satisfactory security that the negative would generally be employed with great caution; and that there would oftener be room for a charge of timidity than of rashness in the exercise of it."

Commander-in-Chief. "Even those [constitutions] which have in other respects coupled the Chief Magistrate with a council have for the most part concentrated the military authority in him alone. Of all the cares or concerns of government, the direction of war most peculiarly demands those qualities which distinguish the exercise of power by a single hand."

Require the Opinion of Department Heads. "This I consider as a mere redundancy in the plan, as the right for which it provides would result of itself from the office."

Pardon. "As the sense of responsibility is always strongest in proportion as it is undivided, it may be inferred that a single man would be most ready to attend to the force of those motives which might plead for a mitigation of the rigor of the law, and least apt to yield to considerations which were calculated to shelter a fit object of its vengeance.... But the principal argument for reposing the power of pardoning in this case in the Chief Magistrate is this: in seasons of insurrection or rebellion, there are often critical moments when a well-timed offer of pardon to the insurgents or rebels may restore the tranquility of the commonwealth; and which, if suffered to pass unimproved, it may never be possible afterwards to recall. The dilatory process of convening the legislature, or one of its branches, for the purpose of obtaining its sanction to the measure, would frequently be the occasion of letting slip the golden opportunity."

Treaties. "With regard to the intermixture of powers [between the president and the Senate,] ... the essence of the legislative authority is to enact laws, or, in other words, to prescribe rules for the regulation of the society; while the execution of the laws and the employment of the common strength, either for this purpose or for the common defense, seem to comprise all the functions of the executive magistrate. The power of making treaties is, plainly, neither the one nor the other.... It must indeed be clear to a demonstration that the joint possession of the power in question, by the President and Senate, would afford a greater prospect of security than the separate possession of it by either of them."

Appointment. "I proceed to lay it down as a rule that one man of discernment is better fitted to analyze and estimate the peculiar qualities adapted to particular offices than a body of men of equal or perhaps even of superior discernment. The sole and undivided responsibility of one man will naturally beget a livelier sense of duty and a more exact regard to reputation. He will, on this account, feel himself under stronger obligations, and more interested to investigate with care the qualities requisite to the stations to be filled, and to prefer with impartiality the persons who may have the fairest pretensions to them.... It is also not very probable that his nomination would often be overruled. The Senate could not be tempted by the preference they might feel to another to reject the one proposed; because they could not assure themselves that the person they might wish would be brought forward by a second or by any subsequent nomination.... To what purpose then require the co-operation of the Senate? I answer, that the necessity of their concurrence would have a powerful, though, in general, a silent operation. It would be an excellent check upon a spirit of favoritism in the President, and would tend greatly to prevent the appointment of unfit characters.... The possibility of rejection would be a strong motive to care in proposing."

Other Powers. "The only remaining powers of the executive are comprehended in giving information to Congress on the state of the Union; in recommending to their consideration such measures as he shall judge expedient; in convening them, or either branch, upon extraordinary occasions; in adjourning them when they cannot themselves agree upon the time of adjournment; in receiving ambassadors and other public ministers; in faithfully executing the laws; and in commissioning all the officers of the United States. Except some cavils about the power of convening *either* house of the legislature, and that of receiving ambassadors, no objection has been made to this class of authorities; nor could they possibly admit of any."

dealt with the presidency. The first of these squarely addressed the Anti-Federalist charge that the presidency was a latent monarchy. Hamilton argued that in contrast to the British king, who secures his office by inheritance and serves for life, the president is elected for a limited term. The president may be impeached; the king may not. The king has an absolute veto on laws passed by Parliament; the president's vetoes can be overridden by Congress. The king can both declare war and raise an army and navy; the president can do neither. The king can prorogue Parliament for any reason at any time; the president can adjourn Congress only when the House of Representatives and the Senate cannot agree on an adjournment date. The king can create offices and appoint people to fill them; the president cannot create offices and can fill them only with the approval of the Senate.

Hamilton dissembled to some degree in drawing these contrasts—the powers he ascribed to the British monarch were more characteristic of the seventeenth century than of the eighteenth, during which the influence of Parliament and the prime minister had grown—but his article was effective in deflating the Anti-Federalists' caricature of the presidency. Indeed, in many cases, Hamilton deftly argued, the power of the presidency was less than that wielded by the governor of New York, the staunchly Anti-Federalist George Clinton.

Federalist No. 70, less defensive in tone than the first article, describes the virtues of the presidency. Its theme is "energy," a quality that, according to Hamilton, is requisite to good government:

> It is essential to the protection of the community against foreign attacks; it is not less essential to the steady administration of the laws; to the protection of property against those irregular and high-handed combinations which sometimes interrupt the ordinary course of justice; to the security of liberty against the enterprises and assaults of ambition, of faction, and of anarchy.

Energy, in the government created by the Constitution, was provided by the presidency, mostly because of its unitary character. Unity provides the presidency with a whole host of virtues—"decision, activity, secrecy, and dispatch . . . vigor and expedition." In contrast, a plural, or committee-style executive, would be riven by disagreements that would render it slow to act and prone to create factions. The nation also would find it hard to hold a plural executive responsible for failure, since each member of the executive could blame the others.

In *Federalist* Nos. 71-77, Hamilton defends the presidency as having other qualities that are indispensable to energy. "Duration," the theme of No. 71, is one—the four-year term provides the president with enough time to act with firmness and resolve but is not so long as "to justify any alarm for the public liberty."

Hamilton claims that eligibility for reelection, which he discusses in No. 72, soundly acknowledges that "the desire of reward is one of the strongest incentives of human conduct"; without it, a president would be tempted either to slack off on the job or, at the opposite extreme, to usurp power violently. (Presidential reeligibility also allows the nation to keep a president in office if it so desires.)

"Adequate provision for its support" is a third energy-inducing quality of the presidency. Interestingly, Hamilton attaches great importance to the prohibition that the Constitution places on Congress not to raise or lower an incumbent president's salary. In the first part of No. 73, he argues that without such a bar, Congress could "reduce him by famine, or tempt him by largesse" and thus "render him as obsequious to their will as they might think proper to make him."

Later in No. 73, then in Nos. 74-77, Hamilton defends the enumerated powers of the presidency, which, along with unity, duration, and adequate support are the indispensable ingredients of presidential energy.

The Vice Presidency in the Ratification Debates

"Post-convention discussion of the vice presidency was not extensive," notes attorney John D. Feerick, the author of two books on the vice presidency.[39] The only mention of the office in *The Federalist Papers* is in No. 68, written by Hamilton. Like the delegates' debate, it, too, is concerned mainly with the vice president's role as president of the Senate:

> The appointment of an extraordinary person, as Vice-President, has been objected to as superfluous, if not mischievous. It has been alleged, that it would have been preferable to have authorized the Senate to elect out of their own body an officer answering to that description. But two considerations seem to justify the ideas of the Convention in this respect. One is, that to secure at all times the possibility of a definitive resolution of the body, it is necessary that the President should have only a casting [tie-breaking] vote. And to take the Senator of any State from his seat as Senator, to place him in that of President of the Senate, would be to exchange, in regard to the State from which he came, a constant for a contingent vote. The other consideration is, that, as the Vice-President may occasionally become a substitute for the President, in the supreme Executive magistracy, all the reasons which recommend the mode of election prescribed for the one, apply with great if not with equal force to the manner of appointing the other.[40]

Hamilton may have been responding in part to concerns raised by leading Anti-Federalist George Clinton. Clinton was later to serve as vice president in the administrations of Thomas Jefferson and James Madison, but in November 1787, writing as Cato, he argued that the vice presidency was both "unnecessary" and "dangerous": "This officer, for want of other employment is made president of the Senate, thereby blending the executive and legislative powers, besides always giving to some one state, from which he is to come, an unjust preeminence."

Luther Martin, who opposed ratification, expressed concern that a large state like New York, of which Clinton was governor, typically would benefit from the vice president's Senate role:

> After it is decided who is chosen President, that person who has the next greatest number of votes of the electors, is declared to be legally elected to the Vice-Presidency; so that by this system it is very possible, and not improbable, that he may be appointed by the electors of a *single large state;* and a very undue influence in the Senate is given to that State of which the Vice-President is a citizen, since, in every question where the Senate is divided, that State will have two votes, the President having on that occasion a casting voice.

Mason, another delegate to the convention who opposed ratification in his state, also complained about the vice president's right to vote in the Senate and the office's mix of legislative and executive roles. His fellow Virginia

Anti-Federalist, Richard Henry Lee, wondered about the absence of stated qualifications for the vice president.[41]

Defenders of the vice presidency made a virtue of the office's role as Senate president. In their view, the vice president's election by the nation as a whole was a powerful advantage. "There is much more propriety to giving this office to a person chosen by the people at large," urged Madison, "than to one of the Senate, who is only the choice of the legislature of one state." William R. Davie of North Carolina felt that a nationally elected vice president would cast tie-breaking votes "as impartially as possible." Answering another argument of the Constitution's critics, Oliver Ellsworth and Roger Sherman wrote separately that the vice president did not wield a mix of legislative and executive powers, but rather that the vice presidency was a part of the legislative branch except in the event of a succession, at which time it became part of the executive branch.[42]

In all, Feerick has concluded the vice presidency "received scant attention in the state ratifying conventions. . . . The discussion of the vice-presidency that did occur centered mostly around the fact that the office blended legislative and executive functions." [43] As in the convention, almost nothing was said about the vice president's successorship duties.

The Politics of Ratification

Most historians agree that a majority of Americans were initially opposed to the Constitution. Certainly there was intense and vocal opposition in many states. But the Federalists had two compelling advantages in the battle for ratification. First, their cause was defended in most of the state ratifying conventions by leaders who had been at the Constitutional Convention and could knowledgeably explain the Constitution's provisions, defend its virtues, and answer any criticisms. Second, whatever doubts people may have entertained about ratification, there was no better alternative. "It was clear enough that the old government was finished," noted the Colliers. "If the Constitution was not ratified, the union would dissolve, and with what result nobody could calculate." [44]

Delaware, a small state that regarded the new government as protection against its large-state neighbors, became the first state to ratify, on December 7, 1787. Pennsylvania, by a vote of 46-23, followed five days later, but only after considerable doubts were expressed about the absence of a bill of rights. (Similar complaints were voiced in many states, prompting Federalists to promise that the first Congress would propose such a bill in the form of amendments to the Constitution.) Three more small states—New Jersey, Georgia, and Connecticut—were next to ratify, the first two states unanimously, the last by an overwhelming vote of 128-40. Massachusetts, in which opposition was intense, ratified by a paper-thin vote of 187-168 after the Constitution was endorsed by John Hancock, the state's popular governor. (Hancock seems to have been convinced that if Virginia did not ratify, he, not George Washington, would be elected as the first president.) In April, over the intense opposition of Luther Martin, Maryland ratified by a 63-11 vote; South Carolina followed in May by 149-73. New Hampshire, by a close vote of 57-47, became the ninth state to ratify on June 21.

New Hampshire's endorsement meant that the Constitution was enacted. Although ratification by the two remaining large states, Virginia and New York, probably was essential if the new government were to be successful, Virginians and New Yorkers in turn realized that their states would be weakened if they voted to remain isolated. In both states, the Federalists prevailed even though they were initially outnumbered by the Anti-Federalists. On June 25, Virginia voted 89-79 to ratify. (Governor Randolph may have turned the tide when, after defending his refusal to sign the Constitution at the convention, he declared that in light of the decisions of the other states, he would vote to ratify rather than see the union dissolved.) New York's July 26 decision to ratify (by a vote of 30-27) was similarly grudging. North Carolina (November 19, 1789) and Rhode Island (May 29, 1790) followed, but not until after the first president and Congress had been elected and the new government gotten under way.

Constitutional Amendments

Article V of the Constitution defines several processes—all of them difficult—by which the Constitution may be amended. An amendment may be *suggested* by one or more members of Congress, by the president in a message to Congress, or by resolutions passed and sent to Congress by two-thirds of the state legislatures. If the suggested amendment originates with the president or from within Congress, it may then be considered by Congress, which can *propose* (that is, approve) it only by a two-thirds vote of both the House of Representatives and the Senate. If the suggested amendment originates in the state legislatures, Congress is enjoined to call a national convention to consider and possibly propose it. In either case, Congress then sends the proposed amendment to the states for *ratification.* If three-fourths of the states ratify a proposed amendment, it becomes part of the Constitution. Congress decides whether ratification should be by the state legislatures or by specially called conventions within each state.

Some provision for amending the Constitution was made at every stage of the Constitutional Convention. The Virginia Plan, reflecting the delegates' apprehensions about the accountability of the stronger national government they were designing, said only that a procedure ought to be created to enact constitutional amendments that did not require the consent of the national legislature. The Committee of Detail proposed such a procedure: a convention called by Congress to enact any amendment that was requested by two-thirds of the state legislatures. Although the delegates initially accepted the committee's proposal, disquiet about the nature of such a convention—its composition, rules, powers, and likely biases (some delegates predicted that conventions would be pro-state government power, some that they would be anti-state government power)—surfaced on September 10. Madison then suggested the current arrangement of either state or congressional initiative, followed by state ratification. The delegates accepted his proposal, and the Committee of Style drafted the final language.[45]

In practice, every amendment that has been added to the Constitution since 1789 has been considered and proposed by Congress and every amendment but one (the Twenty-first Amendment, which ended Prohibition) has been ratified by the state legislatures.[46] Since 1918, Congress sometimes has required that a proposed amendment be ratified within a seven-year period.[47]

The Constitution does not specify how a constitutional convention would be called if two-thirds of the states asked for one, how its members would be chosen, or what its rules, procedures, and agenda would be. Nor has Congress, jealous of its role in the amendment process and fearing a "runaway convention" that would exceed its original charge (like the original constitutional convention in Philadelphia), been willing to create such procedures. In the 1960s, thirty-three states (just one fewer than the required two-thirds) requested a convention to reconsider the "one person, one vote" rule regarding the apportionment of seats in the state legislatures that the Supreme Court had instituted in *Baker v. Carr* (1962).[48] During the 1970s, thirty-two state legislatures requested a convention to consider a "balanced-budget" amendment to the Constitution.

Amending the Constitution, although an easier task to accomplish under the Constitution than under the Articles of Confederation (which required ratification by all of the state legislatures for any proposed amendment), is an arduous undertaking nonetheless. One-third-plus-one of the members of either the House or the Senate can prevent Congress from proposing an amendment. If an amendment is proposed, barely thirteen of the ninety-nine houses of the fifty state legislatures (all but the Nebraska legislature are bicameral, or two-house, legislatures) can deny it ratification, since the approval of the full legislatures of thirty-eight (three-fourths) of the states is required.[49] The consequence, according to constitutional scholar James Sundquist, is that:

> Within the political elite, for an amendment to clear the barriers to passage, its acceptance must come close to unanimity.... [A] proposed amendment either must have no adverse effect on anybody—as, say, the amendment that rescheduled inauguration day and congressional sessions—or must distribute its adverse effects so nearly neutrally that no substantial interest is offended.[50]

Since the Bill of Rights (the first ten amendments) was added to the Constitution in 1791, the Constitution has been amended only sixteen times.[51] (Seven other amendments have been proposed by Congress but failed to be ratified.) Four of these sixteen amendments dealt explicitly with the presidency and vice presidency:

- Twelfth Amendment (1804): instituted separate balloting by electors for president and vice president in presidential elections; House of Representatives to choose the president from among the three highest vote-getters if no candidate has an electoral vote majority; constitutional qualifications for president applied to vice president.
- Twentieth Amendment (1933): set January 20 as inauguration day for the president, January 3 as beginning of term for members of Congress; provided vice president-elect would become president if president-elect died or was disqualified.
- Twenty-second Amendment (1951): imposed a two-term limit on the president.
- Twenty-fifth Amendment (1967): defined the full successorship rights of the vice president should a presidential vacancy occur; created procedures for responding to presidential disabilities; provided for the filling of vice-presidential vacancies.

Three of the four presidency amendments did little more than clarify or correct minor flaws in the original Constitution. The Twelfth Amendment adapted the electoral college to the rise of national political parties. The Twentieth Amendment answered some unresolved procedural questions. The Twenty-fifth Amendment established a process that would satisfy the original Constitution's provision that the vice president should step in during a presidential disability; it also guaranteed that a vice president would always be available to fulfill this responsibility. Only the Twenty-second Amendment altered a fundamental component of the presidency's original design. The Framers had strongly rejected efforts to limit the president's eligibility to reelection.

In addition, five other constitutional amendments have expanded the right to vote, which has affected participation in presidential elections. Three of these amendments—the Fifteenth (1870), Nineteenth (1920), and Twenty-sixth (1971)—extended the suffrage to blacks, women, and eighteen-year-olds, respectively. The Twenty-third Amendment (1961) granted three electoral votes in presidential elections to the District of Columbia. The Twenty-fourth Amendment (1964) banned the poll tax, which some states had required citizens to pay as a prerequisite to voting. Interestingly, the five voting amendments took less time to ratify—an average of fewer than twelve months each—than any other category of constitutional amendments.[52]

Numerous other amendments to alter the presidency have been suggested in recent years. Some have been endorsed by the public in opinion surveys, by one or more presidents, and by several members of Congress. None, however, has been proposed by Congress for ratification by the states. The suggested amendments would:

- Abolish the electoral college and choose presidents by direct vote of the people. This highly popular alteration of the Constitution would bring the presidency into line with virtually all of the nation's other elective offices and remove the possibility of either an electoral college stalemate or the election of a president who had less than a plurality of popular votes. Critics say direct election would subvert the principle of federalism that the current, state-centered system upholds.
- Limit the president to a single term, but extend the term to six years. Advocates, including presidents Andrew

Amending the Constitution

The Congress, whenever two thirds of both Houses shall deem it necessary, shall propose Amendments to this Constitution, or, on the Application of the Legislatures of two thirds of the several States, shall call a Convention for proposing Amendments, which, in either Case, shall be valid to all Intents and Purposes, as part of this Constitution, when ratified by the Legislatures of three fourths of the several States, or by Conventions in three fourths thereof, as the one or the other Mode of Ratification may be proposed by the Congress; Provided that . . . no State, without its Consent, shall be deprived of its equal Suffrage in the Senate.

—from Article V

Jackson, Dwight D. Eisenhower, Lyndon B. Johnson, Jimmy Carter, and others, claim that a single, six-year term would free the president from the political pressures of reelection and grant the administration more time to accomplish its long-term goals. Opponents point out that under a single six-year term, an unpopular president would serve two more years as president than under the current system, and a popular president two fewer years.

~ Repeal the Twenty-second Amendment's two-term limit. President Ronald Reagan, a strong advocate of repeal, argues that the voters should not be denied the opportunity to extend a president's tenure for as long as they like. Critics warn of an overly personalized presidency.

~ Abolish the vice presidency and fill presidential vacancies by special election. Proponents, such as the historian Arthur M. Schlesinger, Jr., differ with critics on the issue of how valuable an institution the vice presidency is and how politically disruptive succession by special election would be.

~ Make the vice presidency an appointive office, with confirmation by both houses of Congress. By extending the Twenty-fifth Amendment's procedure for filling vacancies in the vice presidency to all vice-presidential selections, the main effect of this proposal might be either to enhance the quality of vice presidents or to deny the vice presidency the legitimacy of election.

~ Empower the president with an item veto, which could be used to remove specific items from spending legislation. President Reagan asserted that this power would have enabled him to control federal spending; critics argue that the president already has ample means to influence the budget without upsetting the constitutional balance of power between the president and Congress.

~ Repeal the part of Article I, section 6, that bars members of Congress from holding positions in the executive branch, thus allowing presidents to draw cabinet members from Congress. Such joint membership is a feature of parliamentary systems, a point that both defenders and opponents of the idea invoke in making their arguments.

~ Allow a "no-confidence" vote of three-fifths (or two-thirds) of both houses of Congress to trigger a special election of the president and all members of Congress. This would be a means of resolving interbranch deadlock short of impeachment, argue proponents such as former representative Henry Reuss (D-Wis.). Critics say a special election would violate the constitutional principle of fixed terms and create national disruption.

As these examples illustrate, most proposals to amend the Constitution stem from ongoing political controversies—the threat of electoral college stalemate by a popular third party candidate, the four-term presidency of Franklin D. Roosevelt, a mutual pointing of fingers by president and Congress on the issue of budget deficits, and the like. Because they are mired in partisan politics, it is virtually impossible to pass them through the arduous process of approval by Congress and ratification by the states.

Twelfth Amendment (1804)

Paragraphs 2 through 4 of Article II, section 1, which created the electoral college method of choosing the president, were among the least controversial provisions of the Constitution during the state ratification debates. "The mode of appointment of the Chief Magistrate of the United States," wrote Alexander Hamilton in *Federalist* No. 68, "is almost the only part of the system of any consequence, which has escaped without severe censure, or which has received the slightest mark of approbation from its opponents." It is all the more ironic, then, that the electoral college was the first institution of the new government to undergo a major constitutional overhaul.

The main effect of the Twelfth Amendment was to change a system in which electors cast two votes for president, with the candidate receiving the largest majority elected president and the second place finisher elected vice president, to a system in which electors were charged to vote separately for president and vice president, with a majority of electoral votes required to win each office.

The Twelfth Amendment also reduced the number of candidates from which—in the event that no candidate received a majority of electoral votes for president—the House could elect the president from the five highest electoral vote recipients to the three highest. Selection of the vice president in the event of an electoral college failure was lodged exclusively in the Senate, not partially, as in the original Constitution. (The amendment empowered the Senate to choose from the two highest electoral vote recipients for vice president, with a majority of the whole membership of the Senate required for election.) The Constitution's age, residency, and citizenship requirements for president were extended to the vice president. Finally, the amendment stated that if a vice president, but no president, had been chosen by the March 4 following the election, "the Vice President shall act as President as in the case of the death or other constitutional disability of the President."

The Old System Breaks Down

The original electoral college was designed by the Constitutional Convention on the assumption that political parties would not arise and dominate the presidential election process. States and ad hoc groups, it was believed, would nominate candidates for president, of whom the most popular (and, presumably, best qualified) would be elected as president and the second most popular as vice president.

Despite the Framers' intentions, two political parties—the Federalists and the Democratic Republicans—formed during George Washington's first term as president and, within a very few years, began nominating complete national tickets: Federalist and Democratic-Republican candidates for president and Federalist and Democratic-Republican candidates for vice president. In 1800, the inevitable happened. All seventy-three Democratic-Republican electors (a majority of the electoral college) cast one of their votes for president for Thomas Jefferson and the other for Aaron Burr. Despite their intention that Jefferson be elected as president and Burr as vice president, the vote was constitutionally recorded as a tie between Jefferson and Burr for the office of president. Under Article II, section 1, paragraph 3, the House of Representatives was then forced to choose between them.

Dominated by a lame duck Federalist majority, the House, through thirty-five ballots, denied Jefferson the majority of state delegations that was required for election. On the thirty-sixth ballot, prodded by Hamilton to cease its mischief making and do the right thing, the House elected Jefferson as president and Burr as vice president. But some disgruntled Federalists began plotting for the 1804 election: if the Democratic-Republican candidates won, they decided, Federalist electors would cast one of their votes for the opposition party's vice-presidential nominee, thus electing him, not the presidential nominee, as president and the presidential nominee as vice president.

Proposal and Ratification

Aware both of the unsuitability of the original Constitution's presidential election process to the new reality of party politics and of the Federalists' willingness to continue exploiting the process's weaknesses, the Democratic-Republican-controlled Congress voted to propose the Twelfth Amendment in December 1803. All but the most ardent Federalist states quickly ratified (Massachusetts finally ratified in 1961), and the amendment became part of the Constitution in June 1804, in time for the 1804 presidential election.

Separate Balloting for President and Vice President

The Twelfth Amendment's requirement that electors vote separately for president and vice president completely solved the problem that had occasioned the amendment's enactment. Not since 1800 has there been any confusion over who was running for president and who for vice president.

Less benign, however, were the amendment's effects on the vice presidency. The position, always constitutionally powerless and now stripped of its status as the office awarded to the second most successful presidential candidate, became a political backwater. Even before the Twelfth Amendment was enacted, parties had begun using the vice-presidential nomination mainly to "balance the ticket" with someone from either a different region or a different faction of the party than the presidential nominee. But with the office now bereft of status as well as power, ambitious and talented political leaders shunned such nominations. The vice presidency sank into a century-long torpor and was occupied frequently by aged or incompetent politicians.

At least some members of Congress anticipated the Twelfth Amendment's likely effect on the vice presidency and, during congressional debate, moved to abolish the office. They failed to persuade a sufficient number of their colleagues, however. *(See History of the Vice Presidency chapter in Part I.)*

One aspect of electoral voting that emerged as an issue only much later was that of the "faithless elector." Whatever the Framers' intentions may have been, in practice electors have never been chosen to exercise their own judgment in deciding whom to support, but rather to vote for the candidate supported by their state.[53] There is no constitutional requirement that they do so, however. Twenty states and the District of Columbia currently have laws that require electors to support the candidates whom they are pledged to represent, but these laws may well violate the Twelfth Amendment. In any event, only nine of the more than seventeen thousand electors who have been chosen since 1789 have been "faithless," and none have been punished for violating their pledges.[54]

Twelfth Amendment (1804)

The Electors shall meet in their respective states and vote by ballot for President and Vice President, one of whom, at least, shall not be an inhabitant of the same state with themselves; they shall name in their ballots the person voted for as President, and in distinct ballots the person voted for as Vice President, and they shall make distinct lists of all persons voted for as President, and of all persons voted for as Vice President, and of the number of votes for each, which lists they shall sign and certify, and transmit sealed to the seat of the government of the United States, directed to the President of the Senate;—The President of the Senate shall, in the presence of the Senate and House of Representatives, open all the certificates and the votes shall then be counted;—The person having the greatest number of votes for President, shall be elected the President, if such number be a majority of the whole number of Electors appointed; and if no person have such majority, then from the persons having the highest numbers not exceeding three on the list of those voted for as President, the House of Representatives shall choose immediately, by ballot, the President. But in choosing the President, the votes shall be taken by states, the representation from each state having one vote; a quorum for this purpose shall consist of a member or members from two-thirds of the states, and a majority of all the states shall be necessary to a choice. [And if the House of Representatives shall not choose a President whenever the right of the choice shall devolve upon them, before the fourth day of March next following, then the Vice President shall act as President, as in the case of the death or other constitutional disability of the President.]* The person having the greatest number of votes as Vice President, shall be the Vice President, if such number be a majority of the whole number of Electors appointed, and if no person have a majority, then from the two highest numbers on the list, the Senate shall choose the Vice President; a quorum for the purpose shall consist of two thirds of the whole number of Senators, and a majority of the whole number shall be necessary to a choice. But no person constitutionally ineligible to the office of President shall be eligible to that of Vice President of the United States.

* Possibly superseded by the Twentieth Amendment

House Election of the President

The Twelfth Amendment reduced the number of candidates from which the House of Representatives, in the event of an electoral college deadlock, must choose the president from the five highest electoral vote recipients to the three highest. The reduction was an acknowledgement both that a two-party system had developed, in which even three candidates were unlikely to receive electoral votes in most elections, and that the parties had taken over the presidential nominating function. In 1824, when four presidential candidates received electoral votes, the House's freedom to choose from only three may have eased its difficulties in reaching a decision in time for the inauguration.

The House had to clarify several procedural ambiguities in the Twelfth Amendment before voting for president in 1825. One of the most important rules it adopted required that, in order for the vote of a state delegation to be cast for a candidate, a majority of the state's entire delegation (not just of the members present) was needed. Another stated that "the House shall continue to ballot for a President, without interruption by other business, until a President be chosen." Finally, House members were allowed to vote by secret ballot, in individual ballot boxes for each state. These rules were not enacted as law, however, and a future House could use or replace them at its discretion.

The Twelfth Amendment is unclear on yet another potentially important matter, partly because of complications introduced by the recent enactment of the Twentieth and Twenty-fifth amendments. *(See "Twentieth Amendment," p. 45, and "Twenty-fifth Amendment," p. 48, in this chapter.)* The Twelfth Amendment states that "if the House of Representatives shall not choose a President whenever the right of choice shall devolve upon them, before the fourth day of March next following, then the Vice President shall act as President, as in the case of the death or other constitutional disability of the President." Harvard University law professors Laurence H. Tribe and Thomas M. Rollins argue that this provision was superseded by the Twentieth Amendment and that the House is obliged to keep balloting until either it elects a president or the president's four-year term expires. Conceivably, then, a Senate-elected vice president could serve as acting president for a full presidential term. Allan P. Sindler, a political scientist, maintains that not only does the Twelfth Amendment still apply, but it means that if the House has not elected a president by March 4, balloting ceases and the vice president becomes president. Under the Twenty-fifth Amendment, the vice-president-turned-president would then nominate a new vice president.[55]

Senate Election of the Vice President

Only once since the Twelfth Amendment was enacted has the electoral college failed to choose a vice president: in 1836, the Democratic party's presidential candidate, Martin Van Buren, received a majority of electoral votes, but his running mate, Richard M. Johnson, fell one vote short of being elected vice president when Virginia's twenty-three electors, disapproving Johnson's dalliances with a succession of slave mistresses, denied him their support. The Senate, charged to choose a vice president from among the top two electoral vote recipients by a majority vote of all its members, quickly elected Johnson over the Whig party vice-presidential nominee, Francis Granger, by a vote of 33-16. The straight party nature of the vote, however, leaves one to wonder what would have happened if the Whigs had controlled the Senate. Another open question—given the amendment's requirement that a quorum of two-thirds must exist in order for the Senate to elect a vice president—is what would happen if a party's senators boycotted the Senate chamber.

These circumstances notwithstanding, the Twelfth Amendment makes it easier for the Senate to elect a vice president than for the House to elect a president. The Senate chooses between two, not three, candidates, and a simple majority of its members, not a majority of state delegations, is all that is required.

Legislative Elaboration of the Twelfth Amendment

Under federal laws passed in 1792, 1934, and most important, 1887, and state laws passed at various times, procedures have been established for the selection, certification, and tabulation of electoral votes beyond the very general provisions offered in the Constitution. Electors are chosen on the first Tuesday after the first Monday in November. Since 1860, every state's laws have provided that electors shall be chosen by popular vote, although each state is free under the Constitution to choose its electors by some other method.[56] All but Maine have decided to employ a "winner take all" system in which the candidate who receives a plurality of popular votes in the state wins all the state's electoral votes.[57] If there is any dispute about the result of the presidential election in a state, federal law authorizes the state to resolve the dispute in accordance with its own existing procedures.[58]

The electors meet to vote in their states on the first Monday after the second Wednesday in December. (The electoral college never meets as a single body.) Electors send the results of their votes to Washington, where they are counted in front of a joint session of Congress by the vice president, acting in the capacity of president of the Senate, on January 6. Two recent vice presidents—Richard Nixon in 1961 and Hubert H. Humphrey in 1969—have announced their own defeats for president. In 1989, George Bush announced his own election.

Proposed Reforms

More suggested constitutional amendments (well over five hundred) have been offered in Congress to alter or abolish the electoral college than any other feature of the Constitution. In recent years, four major amendments have been widely discussed.[59]

The Automatic Plan. Some reformers, including presidents John F. Kennedy and Lyndon Johnson, have proposed that each state's electoral votes be automatically cast for the candidate who receives the most popular votes in the state. As the political scientist Stephen J. Wayne has observed, the plan "keeps the electoral college intact but eliminates the electors."[60] It also eliminates both the "faithless elector" problem and the possibility that if third party candidates prevent a majority from forming in the electoral college, they could use their electors as bargaining chips to negotiate a deal with either of the major party candidates.

Politically, the main problem with the automatic plan is that it has roused little public or congressional interest. The flaws it seeks to remedy are relatively minor. Some oppose the plan because they like the electoral college the way it is, others because they want to overhaul the electoral college in more fundamental ways.

The Proportional and District Plans. Popular in the 1950s, when it was sponsored in Congress by Sen.

Henry Cabot Lodge, Jr. (R-Mass.), and Rep. Ed Lee Gossett (D-Texas), the proportional plan would eliminate not just electors, but the winner-take-all principle of awarding state electoral votes. Instead, electoral votes in each state would be divided among the presidential candidates in proportion to their share of the state's popular vote. The purported advantage of the Lodge-Gossett proposal is that it would encourage candidates to campaign in every state, even those in which they expect to get fewer popular votes than their opponent. The proportional plan also would heighten the incentive for third party candidates to run, however, and would substantially increase the chances that presidential elections would end up in the House and vice-presidential elections in the Senate.[61] Politically, large states regard the proportional plan as a threat to their primacy in presidential politics.

The district plan, under which candidates would receive two electoral votes for each state they carried and one for each congressional district, would extend Maine's arrangement to the entire nation. It has all of the advantages and disadvantages of the proportional plan and also seems to favor Republican presidential candidates.[62]

The National Bonus Plan. Proposed by a Twentieth Century Fund task force, the national bonus plan would retain the electoral college but weigh it more heavily to the popular vote winner. The candidate who received a plurality of popular votes nationally would receive a "bonus" of 102 electoral votes.[63] This would virtually eliminate the possibility of a presidential election being decided in Congress. A problem with the bonus plan, however, is that in an especially close election, like 1960, it might take a long time to decide who had received the most popular votes and, thus, who should receive the 102-vote bonus and be elected president.[64]

Direct Election. The most popular proposal to reform presidential elections has been to abolish the electoral college and elect the president by direct vote of the people. In most versions of the direct election plan, a minimum plurality of 40 percent would be needed for election; if no candidate received 40 percent, there would be a runoff election between the two highest vote getters. Several recent presidents, notably Nixon, Ford, and Carter, have endorsed direct election. The House of Representatives approved a direct election amendment in 1969 by a vote of 338-70. The Senate voted 51-48 in favor of direct election in 1979, which was fifteen votes less than the necessary two-thirds majority. The public regularly expresses its approval of direct election in Gallup polls by margins of anywhere from three-to-one to seven-to-one.[65]

The main arguments for direct election are that it would bring presidential elections into line with virtually all other U.S. elections, making the process more comprehensible and legitimate to the public; that it would eliminate the possibility of an electoral college deadlock and a House election; and that it would prevent a candidate who lost the popular vote from winning the election, as happened in 1824, 1876, and 1888.

Opponents assert that direct election would violate the constitutional principle of federalism on which the electoral college is based; encourage the formation of third parties, whose hope would be to deny any candidate 40 percent, then bargain for support in the runoff election; and, as with the national bonus plan, increase the possibility for confusion and delay in a close national election.

Twentieth Amendment (1933)

Section 1. The terms of the President and Vice President shall end at noon on the 20th day of January, . . . and the terms of their successors shall then begin. . . .

Section 3. If, at the time fixed for the beginning of the term of the President, the President elect shall have died, the Vice President elect shall become President. If a President shall not have been chosen before the time fixed for the beginning of his term, or if the President elect shall have failed to qualify, then the Vice President elect shall act as President until a President shall have qualified; and the Congress may by law provide for the case wherein neither a President nor a Vice President elect shall have qualified, declaring who shall then act as President, or the manner in which one who is to act shall be selected, and such person shall act accordingly until a President or Vice President shall have qualified.

Section 4. The Congress may by law provide for the case of death of any of the persons from whom the House of Representatives may choose a President whenever the right of choice shall have devolved upon them, and for the case of the death of any of the persons from whom the Senate may choose a Vice President whenever the right of choice shall have devolved upon them.

Politically, direct election amendments have been defeated in Congress by a coalition of small states, which are especially well represented in the Senate and which fear losing what little advantage they have in the electoral college, and liberal interest groups, which argue that minority, union, and urban voters, who are concentrated in the large states, would lose their strategic advantage if these states were no longer as central to the fortunes of presidential candidates as they are in the electoral college.

Twentieth Amendment (1933)

The Twentieth Amendment, also known as the "lame duck" amendment, was written mainly to shorten the time that separated the election of the president and members of Congress from their inauguration. The hiatus for newly elected representatives and senators (unless the president called them into special session) had been thirteen months—from the first Tuesday after the second Monday in November (election day) until the first Monday in December of the following year (the date established by Article I, section 4, paragraph 2, of the original Constitution as the initial meeting day for Congress). The delay for presidents had been approximately four months, from election day until the following March 4. The source of this date for presidential inauguration was a decision by the "old Congress" of the Articles of Confederation. After the Constitution was ratified, Congress had declared March 4, 1789, the date "for commencing proceedings under the said Constitution." A law passed by the House and Senate in 1792 confirmed March 4 as the starting date for future presidential terms.

Sen. George W. Norris (R-Neb.), the main author of the Twentieth Amendment, sought to remedy three main flaws he saw in the traditional arrangement, which he regarded as better suited to an age when travel was difficult and time-consuming and the business of the federal government relatively minor. The first flaw was the biennial "lame duck" session of Congress, which lasted from the December after the election until the following March and which included many members of the defeated party. Second, by not having Congress begin its term before the president, existing procedures empowered the lame duck Congress, not the most recently elected one, to choose the president and vice president in the event of an electoral college deadlock. Finally, four months was regarded as too long a time for the nation to have, in effect, two "presidents"—an outgoing incumbent and an incoming president-elect.

Section 1

To remedy the lame duck and two-presidents problems, Section 1 of the Twentieth Amendment set noon on January 20 as the beginning of the president's and vice president's four-year terms and noon on January 3 as the start of the term for representatives and senators. The wisdom of moving up the president's inauguration seemed vindicated when, in the last transition to take place under the old system, a nation gripped by the Great Depression had to endure four months of awkward stalemate between President-elect Franklin D. Roosevelt and the incumbent president he had defeated in the 1932 election, Herbert C. Hoover. Yet nearly a half century later, the political scientist Richard E. Neustadt bemoaned one quality of the January inauguration—the "eleven week scramble" between the election and the start of the term that a president-elect now must undergo in order to get people and policies in place for the beginning of the administration.[66]

Section 3

Norris also used the Twentieth Amendment as a vehicle to address two other potential problems in the presidential and vice-presidential selection process. Section 3 provides that if a president-elect were to die before the start of the term, the vice president-elect would be inaugurated as president.[67] (Under Section 2 of the Twenty-fifth Amendment, which was to become part of the Constitution in 1967, the vice president-elect who thus succeeded to the presidency then would appoint a new vice president, pending congressional approval.)

In addition to death, Section 3 also stipulated that if, by inauguration day, no presidential candidate had received the electoral vote majority or, failing that, the majority of state delegations in the House of Representatives that is required for election, the vice president-elect would become acting president until a president were chosen. (The same would be true if a president-elect were found to be unqualified under Article II, section 1, paragraph 5, by virtue of age, citizenship, or residency.) The amendment also authorized Congress to legislate for the possibility that a vice president-elect might not be chosen either, whether through failure to secure an electoral vote majority or inability to win a Senate election. Congress passed such a law in 1947, the Presidential Succession Act. It stipulated that the Speaker of the House would serve as acting president until a president or vice president were elected.[68]

Section 4

The possibility that either a winning presidential or vice-presidential candidate might die before officially receiving "elect" status when Congress counts the electoral votes on January 6 underlay the writing of Section 4.[69] It simply calls upon Congress to legislate for these contingencies. Congress never has done so, however, which means that if such a death were to occur, it would have to improvise. One of Congress's options, in counting the votes, would be to declare the dead candidate elected, thus triggering either Section 1 of the amendment (if it were the presidential candidate who had died), under which the vice president-elect would become president, or Section 2 of the Twenty-fifth Amendment (if it were the winning vice-presidential candidate who had died), under which the vice president-elect-turned-president would nominate a new vice president after being sworn in. Congress's other choice—less absurd than electing a dead person but politically more problematic—would be to allow the House of Representatives to elect one of the election's losing presidential candidates as president.[70]

Proposal and Ratification

The Twentieth Amendment passed easily through Congress on March 2, 1932, and was ratified without controversy on February 6, 1933. The wisdom of the amendment seemed confirmed when—on February 15, 1933—an assassin shot at President-elect Franklin D. Roosevelt on a speaker's platform in Miami, Florida. All the state legislatures eventually voted to ratify the amendment.

Twenty-second Amendment (1951)

The Twenty-second Amendment prohibits any person from being elected president more than two times. It also prevents successor presidents from being elected more than once if they have served more than two years of a departed president's four-year term. (If they serve two years or less of an unexpired term, they may be elected two times on their own, for a maximum tenure of ten years.) The amendment was written in such a way as to exempt Harry S Truman, who was president at the time, from its coverage.

The Two-Term "Tradition"

Thomas Jefferson was the first president to argue that no president should serve more than two terms. Responding on December 10, 1807, to a letter from the Vermont state legislature requesting him to run for a third term (seven other states had sent similar letters), Jefferson replied:

> If some termination to the services of the Chief Magistrate be not fixed by the Constitution, or supplied by practice, his office, nominally four years, will in fact become for life, and history shows how easily that degenerates into an inheritance. Believing that a representative Government responsible at short periods of election is that which produces the greatest sum of happiness to mankind, I feel it a duty to do no act which shall essentially impair that principle, and I should unwillingly be

> the person who, disregarding the sound precedent set by an illustrious predecessor [George Washington], should furnish the first example of prolongation beyond the second term of office.[71]

Jefferson's invocation of Washington for his argument was not altogether appropriate—Washington had stepped down from the presidency voluntarily after two terms, but said in his Farewell Address that he had done so not as a matter of principle, but because he longed for "the shade of retirement." [72] Still, Jefferson's defense of a two-term limit took root quickly in presidential politics.[73] Indeed, the Whig party and many Democrats soon argued for a one-term limit. Andrew Jackson was the last president until Abraham Lincoln to be elected to two terms, and even Jackson said he would prefer a constitutional amendment barring more than one presidential term (albeit a six-year term). Of the first thirty presidents (Washington to Herbert Hoover), twenty served one term or less.

In the late nineteenth and early twentieth centuries, the issue of a third term arose only occasionally. Ulysses S. Grant (in 1876) and Woodrow Wilson (in 1920) probably would have liked to serve another four years but were too unpopular at the end of their second terms even to be renominated by their parties. Theodore Roosevelt's situation was more complicated. He was elected president only once, in 1904, but, as vice president, had served all but six months of the term of his assassinated predecessor, William L. McKinley. In 1908 Roosevelt declined a certain renomination and, considering his great popularity, a probable reelection, calling the two-term limit a "wise custom." Four years later, however, he ran for president again, first as a Republican, then as a third party candidate. That he had declined a "third cup of coffee" in 1908, Roosevelt said, did not mean that he never intended to drink coffee again. "I meant, of course, a third consecutive term." [74]

FDR

The two-term tradition was broken in 1940, by President Franklin D. Roosevelt. In 1937 Roosevelt, while not flatly ruling out a third term, had declared that his "great ambition on January 20, 1941" (the day his second term would expire) was to "turn over this desk and chair in the White House" to a successor. A number of Democrats, including Postmaster General James A. Farley, Vice President John Nance Garner, and former Indiana governor Paul V. McNutt, began preparing their own presidential candidacies. But as Roosevelt's second term wore on, he became increasingly frustrated by congressional resistance to his policies and programs. In 1939, World War II broke out in Europe in response to German, Italian, and Soviet aggression, with little hope that the United States would be able to remain above the fray. Waiting until the Democratic convention in July 1940, Roosevelt finally signaled his willingness to be renominated. The delegates overwhelmingly approved.[75]

Polls had shown that the public was deeply divided over the propriety of Roosevelt's candidacy, and Republicans took up the cry "No third term" on behalf of their nominee, business leader Wendell Willkie. Roosevelt won the election, but by a much narrower popular vote margin than in 1936—five million votes, compared with eleven million. In 1944, with the United States and its allies nearing victory in World War II, Roosevelt won another term, by three million votes. Ill at the time of his fourth election, he died less than three months after the inauguration.

Twenty-second Amendment (1951)

No person shall be elected to the office of the President more than twice, and no person who has held the office of President, or acted as President for more than two years of a term to which some other person was elected President shall be elected to the office of the President more than once. But this Article shall not apply to any person holding the office of President when this Article was proposed by the Congress, and shall not prevent any person who may be holding the office of President, or acting as President, during the term within which this Article becomes operative from holding the office of President, or acting as President, during the remainder of the term.

Proposing the Amendment

Congress never had been fully satisfied with the original Constitution's provision for unrestricted presidential reeligibility: from 1789 to 1947, 270 resolutions to limit the president's tenure had been introduced in the House and Senate, sixty of them—an average of three per year—since 1928.[76] But the Roosevelt years added a partisan dimension to this longstanding concern. In 1932, Republicans, who formed the nation's majority party from 1860 to 1928, were driven from power. Conservative Democrats, mostly southern, lost control of their party at the national level.

In the midterm elections of 1946, Republicans regained a majority of both houses of Congress. On February 6, 1947, less than five weeks after the opening of the Eightieth Congress, the House passed a strict two-term amendment to the Constitution by a vote of 285-121. The House bill provided that any president who had served one full term and even one day of another would be barred from seeking reelection. Republicans supported the amendment unanimously (238-0); Democrats opposed it by 121-47, with most of the yea votes coming from southerners.

Five weeks later, on March 12, the Senate passed a slightly different version of the amendment by a vote of 59-23—it allowed a president who had served one full term and less than half of another to seek an additional term. Republican senators, like their House colleagues, were unanimous in their support (46-0); Democrats opposed the amendment by a vote of 23-13. The differences between the two houses were ironed out quickly in favor of the Senate version; final congressional action took place on March 24, 1947.

Debate on the Twenty-second Amendment was framed in philosophical, not partisan terms. Republicans contended that a two-term limit would protect Americans against the threat of an overly personalized presidency; besides, argued Rep. Leo Allen (R-Ill.), "the people should be given the opportunity to set limits on the time an individual can serve as Chief Executive." Democrats such as Rep. Estes Kefauver of Tennessee rejoined that the people, "by a mere majority vote, have the opportunity of deciding every four years whether they want to terminate the services of the President if he stands for reelection."[77] Little, if any, consideration was given to the Framers' original decision to place no restrictions on presidential reeligibility. Nor did Congress foresee the beneficial political effect of the amendment on the vice presidency. With second-term presidents barred from reelection, vice presidents could openly campaign for their party's presidential nomination without jeopardizing their standing within the administration, as Richard Nixon did in 1960 and George Bush did in 1988.

Ratification

The proposed Twenty-second Amendment received a mixed response from the states—no amendment to the Constitution has taken longer to ratify (three years, eleven months) than the two-term limit. Eighteen state legislatures—exactly half the needed number—ratified the amendment in 1947, all of them in primarily Republican states. Afterward, ratification proceeded slowly, with most victories coming in the South, until the needed three-fourths was reached in early 1951. The adoption of the Twenty-second Amendment was certified and declared part of the Constitution by Jess Larson, administrator of the General Services Administration, on February 27, 1951. (Previously, amendments had been certified by the secretary of state.) Five more states later ratified, bringing the total to forty-one.

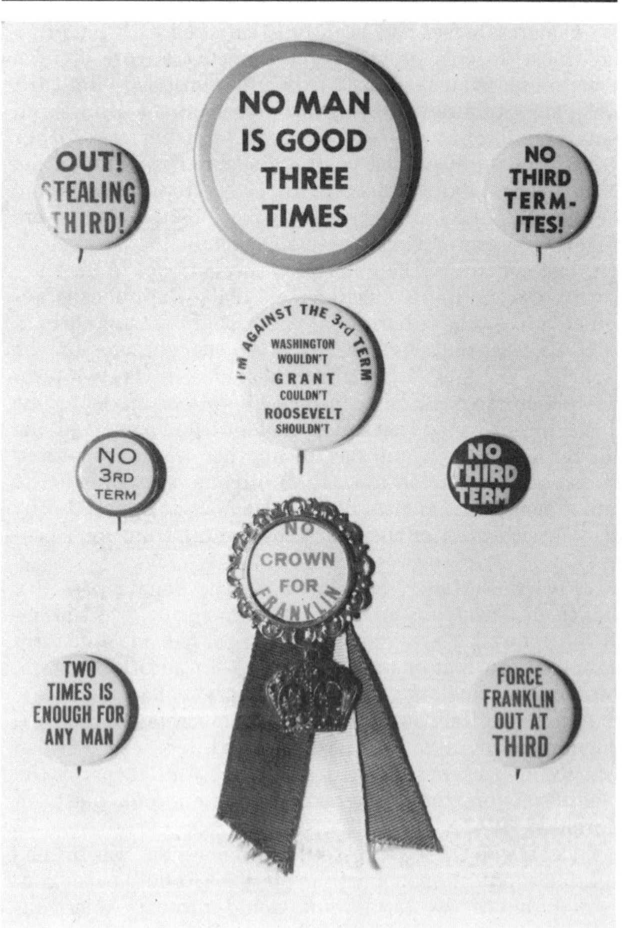

The Franklin D. Roosevelt Library

Franklin Roosevelt's candidacy for a third term prompted deep divisions among the electorate. Republicans nominated business leader Wendell Willkie and took up the cry "No third term."

Conclusion

So few presidents have served even two full terms since the Twenty-second Amendment was enacted that its effects on the modern presidency are hard to measure. John Kennedy was assassinated late in the third year of his first term. Because Lyndon Johnson, who succeeded to the presidency on November 22, 1963, served less than half of Kennedy's term, the amendment allowed him to run for two full terms of his own. But Johnson's political unpopularity in 1968 led him to withdraw from the race. Nixon was elected to a second term in 1972, but resigned less than two years later. Gerald R. Ford served more than half of Nixon's second term, which limited him to only one elected term as president. But Ford failed to win even that. The candidate who defeated him in 1976, Jimmy Carter, was defeated in turn by Ronald Reagan in 1980.

The constraints of the two-term limit, then, have been felt by only two presidents, both of them Republicans. Dwight Eisenhower, the first president to whom the Twenty-second Amendment applied, would have run for a third term in 1960, according to John Eisenhower, his son and deputy chief of staff. While president, Eisenhower expressed "deep reservations" about the two-term limit. Reagan was the second president to be denied the opportunity to run for reelection by the Twenty-second Amendment.[78] During his second term, he campaigned for a constitutional amendment that would repeal the two-term limit (although not in such a way as to apply to him), a campaign he pledged to continue after he left office.

The American people, despite the popularity of presidents Eisenhower and Reagan, the restriction the two-term limit places on their right to choose, and their general support for a strong presidency, show little sign of wanting to abandon the Twenty-second Amendment. In 1966, the political scientist Roberta Sigel summarized the presidential job description implicit in American public opinion in terms that more recent studies generally confirm: "Wanted is a man who is strong, who has ideas of his own on how to solve problems, and who will make his ideas prevail even if Congress or the public should oppose him. . . . Finally, this powerful man should exit from his office after eight years lest he become too powerful."[79]

Twenty-fifth Amendment (1967)

The Twenty-fifth Amendment was proposed by Congress and ratified by the states mainly to provide for two separate but related situations: vacancies in the vice presidency and presidential disabilities.[80] According to Section 2 of the amendment, vice-presidential vacancies were to be filled by presidential nomination, pending confirmation by a majority of both houses of Congress. A set of procedures for handling presidential disabilities was created by Sections 3 and 4. Either the president alone or the vice president and a majority of the cabinet may declare a president disabled and temporarily transfer the powers and duties of the office to the vice president. Congress is charged to resolve disagreements about presidential disability between the president and the rest of the executive branch.

Presidential Disabilities

The original Constitution stated in Article II, section 1, paragraph 6, that, as with presidential deaths, resignations, or impeachments, "in case of the ... inability [of the President] to discharge the powers and duties of the said Office, the same shall devolve on the Vice President." The Constitution gave no guidance as to what a disability (inability) was, how the vice president was to step in should the need arise, or even whether the vice president was actually to become president in response to a presidential disability or merely to assume temporarily the powers and duties of the office. (Did "the same" refer to "the powers and duties" or to "the said Office"?)

The problems created by the Constitution's vagueness became dramatically apparent during the long disabilities of presidents James A. Garfield and Woodrow Wilson. Garfield lay dying for eighty days after he was shot in 1881. His cabinet met to discuss the situation but concluded that if Vice President Chester A. Arthur were to invoke paragraph 6, he would legally become president and thus prevent Garfield from resuming the office should he recover.

Wilson's cabinet and many members of Congress were more disposed to transfer power temporarily to Vice President Thomas R. Marshall during Wilson's long illness in 1919 and 1920, but the Constitution's lack of guidance and a protective White House staff stayed their hands. When Secretary of State Robert Lansing raised the possibility with Joseph Tumulty, Wilson's secretary, Tumulty replied, "You may rest assured that while Woodrow Wilson is lying in the White House on the broad of his back I will not be a party to ousting him." Marshall confided to his secretary, "I am not going to seize the place and then have Wilson—recovered—come around and say, 'Get off, you usurper.' "[81] Although Garfield's and Wilson's disabilities were unusual in their length, one third of the nation's presidents have been disabled for at least brief periods of their terms.[82]

Vice-Presidential Vacancies

The vice presidency becomes vacant when the vice president dies, resigns, or is impeached or when the vice president succeeds to the presidency after a president dies, resigns, or is impeached. Such circumstances left the nation without a vice president sixteen times between 1789 and 1963: seven times because the vice president died (all of natural causes), eight times because the president died, and once because the vice president resigned.[83] *(See Removal of the Vice President chapter in Part II.)*

Changing succession laws provided for the possibility of a double vacancy in the presidency and vice presidency by placing the president pro tempore of the Senate and the Speaker of the House, respectively, next in line to the presidency from 1792 to 1886 (pending a special presidential election); the secretary of state and the other department heads next in line (pending an optional special election) from 1886 to 1947; and the Speaker of the House and the Senate president pro tempore, respectively, next in line, with no special election, after 1947. By merest chance, a double vacancy never occurred.

Library of Congress — Michael Evans, The White House

Two presidents have felt constrained by the Twenty-second Amendment's two-term limit: Republicans Dwight Eisenhower and Ronald Reagan.

Addressing the Problem

Public and congressional concern about the problems of presidential disability and vice-presidential vacancy was minor and episodic through most of U.S. history, usually rising for brief periods while a president was disabled, then waning when the crisis passed. From 1945 to 1963, however, a combination of events took place that placed these problems high on the nation's constitutional agenda.

The invention and spread of nuclear weapons and intercontinental ballistic missiles after 1945 heightened concern that an able president be available to wield the powers of the office at all times. Then, in rapid succession, President Dwight D. Eisenhower suffered a series of disabling illnesses—a heart attack in 1955, an ileitis attack and operation in 1956, and a stroke in 1957. Finally, the assassination of President John F. Kennedy in 1963 left the nation with a president, Lyndon B. Johnson, who had a history of heart trouble and whose legally designated successors, in the absence of a vice president, were an old and ailing House Speaker, John W. McCormack (D-Mass.), and, as Senate president pro tempore, an even older and more ill Carl Hayden (D-Ariz.).

The first tangible result of this series of developments was a letter, released to the public on March 3, 1958, that President Eisenhower sent to Vice President Richard Nixon. The letter stated that if Eisenhower ever were disabled again, he would instruct the vice president to serve as acting president until the disability passed, at which time the president could reclaim his powers. If Eisenhower were disabled but unable to communicate with Nixon for some reason, Nixon could make the decision himself. Again, Eisenhower would determine when it was time to resume the powers of his office.

The Eisenhower letter was later adopted by President Kennedy and Vice President Johnson, President Johnson and Speaker McCormack, and (after the 1964 election) President Johnson and Vice President Humphrey. But it hardly solved the problem of presidential disability. For one thing, a letter lacks the force of law. For another, Eisenhower's letter made no provision to relieve a president who was disabled, perhaps mentally, but who refused to admit it. Finally, the letter did not—nor could it—address the related problem of the vacant vice presidency.

Twenty-fifth Amendment (1967)

Section 1. In case of the removal of the President from office or of his death or resignation, the Vice President shall become president.

Section 2. Whenever there is a vacancy in the office of the Vice President, the President shall nominate a Vice President who shall take office upon confirmation by a majority vote of both Houses of Congress.

Section 3. Whenever the President transmits to the President pro tempore of the Senate and the Speaker of the House of Representatives his written declaration that he is unable to discharge the powers and duties of his office, and until he transmits to them a written declaration to the contrary, such powers and duties shall be discharged by the Vice President as Acting President.

Section 4. Whenever the President and a majority of either the principal officers of the executive departments or such other body as Congress may by law provide, transmit to the President pro tempore of the Senate and the Speaker of the House of Representatives their written declaration that the President is unable to discharge the powers and duties of his office, the Vice President shall immediately assume the powers and duties of the office as Acting President.

Thereafter, when the President transmits to the President pro tempore of the Senate and the Speaker of the House of Representatives his written declaration that no inability exists, he shall resume the powers and duties of his office unless the Vice President and a majority of either the principal officers of the executive departments or of such other body as Congress may by law provide, transmit within four days to the President pro tempore of the Senate and the Speaker of the House of Representatives their written declaration that the President is unable to discharge the powers and duties of his office. Thereupon Congress shall decide the issue, assembling within forty-eight hours for that purpose if not in session. If the Congress, within twenty-one days after receipt of the latter written declaration, or, if Congress is not in session, within twenty-one days after Congress is required to assemble, determines by two-thirds vote of both Houses that the President is unable to discharge the powers and duties of his office, the Vice President shall continue to discharge the same as Acting President; otherwise, the President shall resume the powers and duties of his office.

Proposing the Amendment: Disability

In December 1963, less than a month after the Kennedy assassination, Sen. Birch Bayh (D-Ind.), chairman of the Senate Judiciary Committee's Subcommittee on Constitutional Amendments, announced that he would hold hearings in early 1964 to consider constitutional remedies to the disability and vacancy problems. Coordinating his efforts with a special committee of the American Bar Association, Bayh drafted an amendment that formed the basis for the subcommittee's hearings and that, with minor modifications, later entered the Constitution as the Twenty-fifth Amendment.

The Senate approved the amendment on September 29, 1964, by a vote of 65-0. The House did not act in 1964, possibly because to propose an amendment to fill vice-presidential vacancies would be perceived as a slap at Speaker McCormack, who under current arrangements was first in line to succeed President Johnson. In 1965, however, after the election of Vice President Hubert Humphrey in November 1964, the House joined the Senate (which had reaffirmed its support of the amendment by a vote of 72-0 on February 19) and, on April 13, voted its approval by a margin of 368-29.

From the beginning, most of Congress's concerns about the Twenty-fifth Amendment were directed at its disability provisions. As drafted by Bayh (and eventually enacted by Congress), three very different situations were covered by Sections 3 and 4 of the amendment. In the first, the president is "unable to discharge the powers and duties of his office" and recognizes the condition, say, before or after surgery. A simple letter from the president to the Speaker of the House and the president pro tempore of the Senate is sufficient to make the vice president acting president; a subsequent letter declaring that the disability is ended would restore the president's powers.

In the second situation, the president is disabled but, having perhaps lost consciousness, is unable to say so. Should this happen, either the vice president or the head of an executive department may call a meeting of the vice president and cabinet to discuss the situation. If both the vice president and a majority of the heads of the departments declare the president disabled, the vice president becomes acting president. The rationale for this procedure was explained by attorney John Feerick, who assisted Bayh in writing the amendment:

> The vice president, it was said, should have a voice in the process because it would be his duty to act as president once the determination had been made. Consequently, he should not be forced to take over under circumstances which he felt to be improper. On the other hand, it was urged that he not have the sole power of determination since he would be an interested party and therefore possibly reluctant to make a determination.[84]

Some critics of the Bayh proposal argued that it vested too much power in the executive branch in making disability determinations. Suggestions were made to create a disability commission that included members of all three branches, perhaps joined by a number of physicians. Bayh defended his proposal by saying that any move to strip power from the president by officials outside the administration risked violating the constitutional principle of separation of powers. In the end, both to satisfy the critics and to preclude the possibility that a president might fire the cabinet to forestall a disability declaration, the amendment empowered Congress, at its discretion, to substitute another body for the cabinet.

The third situation covered by the disability portions of the amendment is the most troubling, involving situations (such as questionable mental health or sudden physical disability) in which the president's ability to fulfill the office is in doubt—the president claims to be able, but the vice president and cabinet judge differently. The amendment provides that should this happen, the vice president would become acting president pending a congressional resolution of the matter. Congress would have a maximum of three weeks to decide whether or not the president is disabled, with a two-thirds vote of both the House and the Senate needed to overturn the president's judgment. (The reason for the requirement of an extraordinary majority was the presumption that the president should receive the benefit of any doubt.) But because the Twenty-fifth Amendment only transfers power to the vice president for as long as the president is disabled, a subsequent claim of restored health by the president would set the whole process in motion again.

Interestingly, the Twenty-fifth Amendment, while creating an elaborate set of procedures for disability determinations, includes no definition of *disability* itself. It is clear from the congressional debate that disability is not to be equated with incompetence, laziness, unpopularity, or impeachable conduct. As to what disability is, Congress thought that any definition it might write into law in 1965 would likely be rendered obsolete by changes in medical technology.[85]

Proposing the Amendment: Vice-Presidential Vacancies

Widespread agreement existed in Congress about the need to replace the vice president when the office becomes vacant, both to increase the likelihood of a smooth succession to the presidency, if needed, by a member of the president's party and to ensure that the presidential disability provisions of the amendment would always have a vice president on hand to execute them. Bayh's proposal—that the president nominate a new vice president when the office becomes vacant and that a majority of both houses of Congress, voting separately, confirm the nomination—prevailed and became Section 2 of the amendment, but not before consideration was given to a variety of other suggestions to have Congress or the electoral college from the previous election choose the vice president. Proposals to impose a time limit on Congress either to vote on a president's nominee for vice president or to forfeit its right to reject the nomination also were considered and rejected.

Ratification

No serious opposition to the Twenty-fifth Amendment arose during the ratification process. The needed approval of thirty-eight state legislatures was attained on February 10, 1967, barely a year and a half after Congress proposed the amendment. In the end, all but three states voted to ratify.[86]

Conclusion

Section 2 of the Twenty-fifth Amendment—the vice-presidential vacancy provision—was put to use rather quickly, albeit in surprising circumstances. Vice President Spiro T. Agnew, facing prosecution in federal court on a variety of bribery-related charges, resigned from office as part of a plea bargain on October 10, 1973. President Nixon nominated House Republican leader Gerald R. Ford to replace Agnew on October 12. After a thorough, nearly two-month investigation, the Senate approved Ford's nomination on November 27 by a vote of 92-3, and the House gave its approval on December 6, voting 387-35. Barely eight months later, after President Nixon resigned on August 9, 1974, to avoid being impeached for his involvement in the Watergate coverup, Ford became president. On August 20, he nominated Gov. Nelson A. Rockefeller of New York to be vice president. Congress investigated and debated the nomination for four months before approving Rockefeller by a vote of 90-7 in the Senate (December 10) and 287-128 in the House (December 19).

Wide World Photos

The White House

Under the provisions of the Twenty-fifth Amendment, President Nixon appointed Gerald Ford, left, vice president after the scandal leading to Spiro Agnew's resignation in 1973. When Nixon resigned, Ford himself appointed a vice president, Nelson Rockefeller, right.

Use of the Twenty-fifth Amendment's presidential disability provisions (Sections 3 and 4) has been infrequent and grudging. No occasions of disability arose until March 30, 1981, when President Ronald Reagan was wounded by an assassin's bullet. Although conscious and lucid before surgery, he did not sign his powers over to Vice President George Bush. Meanwhile, presidential aides stifled discussion at the White House about the possibility of a cabinet-voted transfer. In July 1985, before undergoing cancer surgery, Reagan did sign his powers over to Bush, but only after arguing that the Twenty-fifth Amendment was not meant to apply to such brief episodes of disability.

Election Amendments

Three constitutional amendments—the Fifteenth, Nineteenth, and Twenty-sixth—have broadened the suffrage. Two other amendments—the Twenty-third and Twenty-fourth—have changed some of the rules of voting in presidential elections. In all five cases, presidential politics has affected and been affected by the amendments.

Fifteenth Amendment (1870)

Before the Union's victory in the Civil War, only nine states allowed blacks to vote. (They were the nine northernmost states of New England and the upper Midwest and had the fewest blacks.) After the war was ended, the eleven states of the Confederacy were forced by the Reconstruction Act of 1867, which was passed by the Republican-controlled Congress, to extend the suffrage to blacks as a condition for readmission to the Union. The votes of south-

Twenty-third Amendment (1961)

The District constituting the seat of government of the United States shall appoint in such manner as the Congress may direct: A number of electors of President and Vice President equal to the whole number of Senators and Representatives in Congress to which the District would be entitled if it were a State, but in no event more than the least populous State; they shall be in addition to those appointed by the States, but they shall be considered for the purposes of the election of President and Vice President, to be electors appointed by a State; and they shall meet in the District and perform such duties as provided by the twelfth article of amendment.

ern blacks were indispensable to at least the popular vote victory of Ulysses S. Grant, the Republican candidate for president, in 1868.

Fearing that southern blacks might lose their franchise to white politicians in their states and eager for the support of blacks who lived in the northern and border states that did not practice universal manhood suffrage, Republicans pushed the Fifteenth Amendment through a lame duck session of Congress in February 1869. The amendment provided simply that neither the United States nor any individual state could deprive a citizen of the right to vote "on account of race, color, or previous condition of servitude." (As one Republican member of Congress said, "party expediency and exact justice coincide for once.") The Fifteenth Amendment was ratified on February 3, 1870, by a combination of New England, upper midwestern, and black-controlled southern state legislatures.

The amendment secured the Republicans' major short-term political goal by effectively safeguarding the right to vote for northern blacks. But southern states, which once again came under the control of conservative whites after Union troops left in 1876, found extra-constitutional ways to disfranchise blacks. These included not just violence and intimidation, but also legal subterfuges such as literacy tests (illiterate whites were exempted from taking the test if their ancestors had been eligible to vote before 1867—the so-called grandfather clause) and white primaries (political parties, as "private" organizations, were authorized to exclude blacks from membership and participation).

Although the Supreme Court eventually declared both these practices to be unconstitutional under the Fifteenth Amendment—the grandfather clause in *Guinn and Beall v. United States* (1915) and the white primary in *Smith v. Allwright* (1944)—voter registration among southern blacks remained below 30 percent as late as 1960.[87] Not until the Voting Rights Act was passed in 1965 was the Fifteenth Amendment effectively implemented in the South. The act suspended literacy tests (banned permanently in 1970) and authorized the federal government to take over the registration process in any county in which less than 50 percent of the voting age population was registered or had voted in the most recent presidential election. Since 1960, the registration rate for southern blacks has doubled.

Until the 1930s, most enfranchised blacks, grateful to the party of Abraham Lincoln for freeing the slaves and granting them the vote, supported the Republicans. During the Great Depression of the 1930s, Franklin D. Roosevelt and the Democratic party won roughly two-thirds of their support with New Deal social and economic relief programs. The Democratic party-sponsored civil rights laws and Great Society social programs of the 1960s made black voters into a virtually monolithic Democratic constituency. For example, according to the Gallup poll for the 1984 election, 87 percent of black voters supported Walter F. Mondale even as he was losing the election to Ronald Reagan by a margin of 59 percent to 41 percent.[88]

Nineteenth Amendment (1920)

Securing the vote was a stated goal of the women's movement from the moment of its birth at the first women's rights convention in Seneca Falls, New York, in 1848. In 1890, women were granted full suffrage by Wyoming; by 1919, women had the vote in fifteen states and the right to vote in presidential elections in fourteen others. As time went by, the only significant political opposition to granting women the vote came from the liquor industry, which feared that women would support Prohibition. Even without national women's suffrage, however, Prohibition entered the Constitution when the Eighteenth Amendment was enacted in 1919.

The Nineteenth Amendment passed easily through the House of Representatives on May 21, 1919, and the Senate on June 4, 1919, and was ratified by the required number of state legislatures on August 26, 1920, in time for the 1920 elections. It followed the form of the Fifteenth Amendment: neither the United States nor any state can deny or abridge the right to vote "on account of sex."

For more than a half-century after the enactment of the Nineteenth Amendment, women and men usually voted very much alike. The only "gender gap" was in voter turnout: fewer women voted. By the 1980s, however, the disparity in turnout rates had closed, and significant differences between men's and women's views on some issues and candidates had emerged. Women tend to be more concerned than men (and have more liberal views) about issues such as social welfare, public policies concerning families and children, and war and peace. Although women supported Reagan in 1980 and 1984, for example, their margin of support was narrower than for men (55 percent to 40 percent, according to the Gallup poll).[89]

Twenty-sixth Amendment (1971)

The Fourteenth Amendment (1868) set twenty-one as the highest minimum age that a state could require for voters. By 1970, only four states had exercised their right to establish a voting age lower than twenty-one.

Political pressure to reduce the voting age by constitutional amendment rose during the late 1960s, spurred by the combination of an unusually large number of young people in the population (the post-World War II "baby boom" generation) and the Vietnam War, a controversial undertaking that conscripted hundreds of thousands of eighteen-year-olds into the army. Bowing before the slogan, "Old enough to fight, old enough to vote," Congress passed a law in 1970 to lower the voting age in all elections to eighteen. The Supreme Court, in *Oregon v. Mitchell* (1970), ruled that the law was constitutional in its application to federal elections but not to state elections.[90] The decision, which would have required states to establish two sets of voting procedures for state and federal elections, threatened to throw the 1972 elections into chaos.

Responding to *Oregon v. Mitchell,* Congress passed the Twenty-sixth Amendment expeditiously, on March 23, 1971. As with the Nineteenth Amendment, it followed the form of the Fifteenth Amendment: the right to vote for citizens who are eighteen years or older shall not be denied or abridged by the United States or any state "on account of age." Ratification by the states, which was completed on July 1, 1971, took only 107 days, less than half the time required to ratify any other constitutional amendment.

As with newly enfranchised women, young voters departed from their elders mainly by registering and voting at a much lower rate—barely one-third of eighteen- to twenty-year-olds have voted in recent elections, compared with roughly two-thirds of people forty-five and older.[91] This upset the pre-amendment forecasts of many political experts, who believed that masses of young people would turn out in the 1972 elections and move the political system dramatically to the left.[92]

Twenty-third Amendment (1961)

Until the Constitution was written, the location of the capital of the United States was precarious and ever changing—at various times, it moved or was forced to move to Philadelphia, Trenton, New York, and elsewhere. To prevent this migration from happening again, the Constitutional Convention stipulated in Article I, section 8, paragraph 17, that the new capital would be a federal city, governed by Congress and carved out of territory "not exceeding ten miles square" that was ceded to the federal government by the states.[93]

One result of being neither a state nor a part of a state was that the District of Columbia (Washington) was not represented in the federal government. It lacked senators and representatives in Congress and electoral votes in the presidential election. Over the years, this became the source of much resentment among the tax-paying citizens of Washington.

The Twenty-third Amendment, proposed by Congress on June 16, 1960, granted the District a "number of electors of President and Vice President . . . in no event more than the least populous state," that is, three. The amendment was ratified quickly, on March 29, 1961, although Tennessee was the only southern state to vote its approval. Overwhelmingly black and Democratic, the District of Columbia has never given less than 75 percent of its vote to the Democratic candidate for president.

In 1978, Congress proposed a constitutional amendment to repeal the Twenty-third Amendment and expand the voting rights of District residents. The proposed amendment would have granted the District some of the electoral rights of states—power to ratify proposed constitutional amendments, two senators, and a number of representatives and presidential electors commensurate with its population.[94] Partly for partisan and racial reasons, the necessary thirty-four states failed to ratify by the time the seven-year deadline for state action expired.

Twenty-fourth Amendment (1964)

The right of citizens of the United States to vote in any primary or other election for President or Vice President, for electors for President or Vice President, or for Senator or Representative to Congress, shall not be denied or abridged by the United States or any State by reason of failure to pay any poll tax or other tax.

Twenty-fourth Amendment (1964)

Proposed by Congress on August 27, 1962, and ratified by the states on February 4, 1964, the Twenty-fourth Amendment barred the United States or any state from requiring citizens to pay a "poll tax" in order to vote in primary or general elections for president and other federal officials. Although once used by many southern states as a tool to disfranchise blacks and poor whites, the poll tax already had been abandoned by all but five states at the time the Twenty-fourth Amendment was passed. Congress's main purpose in proposing the amendment seems to have been to make a positive gesture to the growing civil rights movement.

The Twenty-fourth Amendment said nothing about poll taxes for state and local elections. But in 1966, in the case of *Harper v. Virginia Board of Electors,* the Supreme Court ruled that they too were unconstitutional because they violated the Fourteenth Amendment's guarantee of "equal protection of the laws."[95] In a sense, this ruling rendered the Twenty-fourth Amendment superfluous.

Notes

1. Quoted in Charles C. Thach, Jr., *The Creation of the Presidency, 1775-1789* (Baltimore, Md.: Johns Hopkins University Press, 1969), 27.
2. Ibid.
3. Gordon S. Wood, *The Creation of the American Republic, 1776-1787* (Chapel Hill: University of North Carolina Press, 1969), 138.
4. Thomas Jefferson, *Notes on the State of Virginia,* ed. William Peden (Chapel Hill: University of North Carolina Press, 1955).
5. Christopher Collier and James Lincoln Collier, *Decision in Philadelphia: The Constitutional Convention of 1787* (New York: Ballantine, 1986), 5.
6. Thach, *Creation of the Presidency,* 49, 52-53.
7. Clinton Rossiter, *1787: The Grand Convention* (London: MacGibbon and Kee, 1968), 141.
8. Ibid., 152.
9. Collier and Collier, *Decision in Philadelphia,* 104-105.
10. Charles A. Beard, *An Economic Interpretation of the Constitution* (New York: Macmillan, 1913).
11. Unless otherwise noted, the source for these discussions of the Constitutional Convention is Max Farrand, ed., *The Records of the Federal Convention of 1787,* vols. 1-4 (New Haven, Conn.: Yale University Press, 1913), or James H. Hutson, ed., *Supplement to Max Farrand's The Records*

of the Federal Convention of 1787 (New Haven, Conn.: Yale University Press, 1987). An excellent chronological account of the convention may be found in William Peters, *A More Perfect Union: The Making of the United States Constitution* (New York: Crown, 1987).

12. Collier and Collier, *Decision in Philadelphia,* 108.
13. John Roche has argued that the preservation of secrecy by the delegates is great testimony to their sense of shared enterprise: even when they disagreed strongly over particular issues, they were sufficiently committed to the effort to keep their objections within the convention's walls. John P. Roche, "The Founding Fathers: A Reform Caucus in Action," *American Political Science Review* 55 (December 1961): 799-816.
14. Collier and Collier, *Decision in Philadelphia,* 120.
15. Rossiter, *1787,* 171.
16. Quoted in Collier and Collier, *Decision in Philadelphia,* 341.
17. Fred Barbash, *The Founding: A Dramatic Account of the Writing of the Constitution* (New York: Linden Press/ Simon and Schuster, 1987), 175.
18. Seymour Martin Lipset, *The First New Nation* (New York: Basic Books, 1963), chap. 1; Max Weber, *The Theory of Social and Economic Organizations* (New York: Oxford University Press, 1947), 358; Marcus Cunliffe, *George Washington: Man and Monument* (New York: New American Library, 1958), 15.
19. Collier and Collier, *Decision in Philadelphia,* 300.
20. Catherine Drinker Bowen, *Miracle at Philadelphia* (Boston: Little, Brown, 1966), 55; Charles L. Mee, Jr., *The Genius of the People* (New York: Harper and Row, 1987), 118.
21. Rossiter, *1787,* 199.
22. Barbash, *The Founding,* 182.
23. Roche, "The Founding Fathers," 810.
24. Richard E. Neustadt, *Presidential Power* (New York: Wiley, 1960), 35.
25. Robert Scigliano, "The Presidency and the Judiciary," in *The Presidency and the Political System,* ed. Michael Nelson (Washington, D.C.: CQ Press, 1984), 392-418.
26. Richard M. Pious, *The American Presidency* (New York: Basic Books, 1978), 29.
27. John Locke, *The Second Treatise on Government* (Indianapolis: Bobbs-Merrill, 1952), 91-96.
28. Thach, *Creation of the Presidency,* 138-139.
29. Michael Nelson, "Constitutional Qualifications for the President," *Presidential Studies Quarterly* 17:2 (Spring 1987): 383-399.
30. Another reason the convention decided to include a requirement of natural born citizenship for the president may be found in a letter that John Jay sent to George Washington on July 25. "Permit me to hint," Jay wrote, "whether it would not be wise and reasonable to provide a strong check on the admission of foreigners into the administration of our National Government, and to declare expressly that the command in chief of the American Army shall not be given to, nor devolve upon, any but a natural *born* citizen." On September 2, two days before the Committee on Postponed Matters proposed the natural born citizen requirement to the convention, Washington replied to Jay, "I thank you for the hints contained in your letter."
31. John D. Feerick, *From Failing Hands: The Story of Presidential Succession* (New York: Fordham University Press, 1965), chap. 2.
32. See Farrand, *Records of the Federal Convention,* vol. 2, 137, 146, 163, 172.
33. On September 15, 1787, delegates discovered a clerical error in the committee's draft and changed "the period for chusing another president arrive" to "a President shall be elected."
34. For a thorough comparison of the convention's decisions on succession and the Committee of Style's rendering of them, see Feerick, *From Failing Hands,* 48-51. Feerick speculates that the committee may have omitted presidential "absence" from the list of situations requiring a temporary successor because it was covered by the term *inability.*
35. Quoted in Ralph Ketcham, ed., *The Anti-Federalist Papers and the Constitutional Convention Debates* (New York: New American Library, 1986), 213-214.
36. Ibid., 251.
37. Quoted in Cecelia M. Kenyon, ed., *The Antifederalists* (Indianapolis: Bobbs-Merrill, 1966), 302-309.
38. Quoted in Pious, *American Presidency,* 39.
39. Feerick, *From Failing Hands,* 51.
40. Quoted in Kenyon, ed., *The Antifederalists,* 305.
41. Feerick, *From Failing Hands,* 52, 53-54.
42. Quotes are drawn from ibid., 52-55.
43. Ibid., 53.
44. Collier and Collier, *Decision in Philadelphia,* 347.
45. Madison, perhaps aware of how far afield the Philadelphia convention had strayed from its original charter, dreaded the prospect of additional amending conventions. In January 1789, he expressed a strong preference that Congress propose a bill of rights rather than convene another convention to do so. In a letter to George Eve, Madison wrote: "The Congress who will be appointed to execute as well as to amend the Government, will probably be careful not to destroy or endanger it. A convention, on the other hand, meeting in the present ferment of parties, and containing perhaps insidious characters from different parts of America, would at least spread a general alarm, and be but too likely to turn everything into confusion and uncertainty" (quoted in Walter E. Dellinger, "The Recurring Question," *Yale Law Journal* [October 1979]: 1979).
46. Congress feared that Prohibition repeal would not be ratified by a sufficient number of states if the decision were left to rural-dominated legislatures.
47. The Eighteenth (Prohibition), Twentieth (inauguration day), Twenty-first (Prohibiton repeal), and Twenty-second (two-term limit for presidents) amendments included a seven-year ratification deadline. So did the Equal Rights Amendment (ERA), proposed by Congress in 1972, and the amendment that would have granted the District of Columbia full representation in Congress and a potentially larger share of electoral votes in presidential elections, proposed in 1978. Neither of the latter two amendments was ratified by a sufficient number of states, even after Congress, in a move of questionable constitutionality, later extended the ERA ratification deadline by three years.
48. *Baker v. Carr,* 369 U.S. 186 (1962).
49. Seven state constitutions require the approval of an extraordinary majority of either two-thirds or three-fifths of the members of both houses of their legislatures in order to ratify.
50. James L. Sundquist, *Constitutional Reform and Effective Government* (Washington, D.C.: Brookings, 1986), 13.
51. Nothing threatened the ratification of the proposed Constitution more than the absence of a bill of rights. Delegates to the Philadelphia convention believed that individual rights were safeguarded in the Constitution because it created a government of delegated powers that was not granted the power to infringe upon basic rights. This argument carried little weight politically. Pro-ratification delegates at several state conventions promised that the new Congress would approve a bill of rights to the Constitution in the form of constitutional amendments. Congress did so expeditiously.
52. The Bill of Rights took fourteen and one-half months to ratify. The eleven other nonvoting amendments have required an average of twenty-two months.

    Two other constitutional amendments have affected the presidency strongly but indirectly: the Sixteenth Amendment (1913), which declared a federal income tax constitutionally permissible, and the Seventeenth Amendment (1913), which required that U.S. senators be elected by the people rather than the state legislatures.

53. In forty states and the District of Columbia, the electors' names do not even appear on the ballot, just the names of the presidential and vice-presidential candidates to whom they are pledged.
54. Of the twenty states that legally bind electors, only five—New Mexico, North Carolina, Oklahoma, South Carolina, and Washington—stipulate penalties for violators. The nine "faithless" votes were cast in 1796, 1820, 1948, 1956, 1960, 1968, 1972, 1976, and 1988. The first electoral vote for a woman was cast in 1972 by Roger MacBride, a Virginia elector pledged to the Republican ticket of Richard Nixon and Spiro T. Agnew. He voted for the Libertarian party ticket of John Hospers for president and Theodora Nathan for vice president.
55. Laurence H. Tribe and Thomas M. Rollins, "Deadlock: What Happens If Nobody Wins," *The Atlantic*, October 1980, 49; Allen P. Sindler, "Presidential Selection and Succession in Special Situations," in *Presidential Selection*, ed. Alexander Heard and Michael Nelson (Durham, N.C.: Duke University Press, 1987), 393.
56. South Carolina was the last state to allow its legislature to choose electors. All the other states had abandoned the practice by 1828.
57. Maine uses a district plan—two electors are awarded to the candidate who carries the state, with one each for every congressional district that a candidate carries.
58. In 1876 no such law existed. The electoral votes of three southern states were in dispute that year. Congress improvised a solution by creating a special commission. The commission awarded all the votes in question to the Republican candidate, Rutherford B. Hayes. Hayes, who had lost the national popular vote to Democrat Samuel K. Tilden, was thus elected by a margin of one electoral vote (185-184). Charges of corruption and foul play were rampant. In 1887, Congress decided to charge states to resolve similar disputes regarding their own electoral votes in the future.
59. This discussion draws heavily on Stephen J. Wayne, *The Road to the White House: The Politics of Presidential Elections*, 3d ed. (New York: St. Martin's Press, 1988), 287-293.
60. Ibid., 288.
61. The proportional plan would have denied any candidate a majority in three of the last eight elections (1960, 1968, and 1976).
62. Interestingly, Nixon would have defeated Kennedy in 1960 under the district plan, by a vote of 278-245. The district plan would have produced a tie vote (269-269) between Ford and Carter in 1976.
63. The principle underlying the 102 figure is two votes times the fifty states and the District of Columbia.
64. In 1960, one consideration that kept Nixon and the Republicans from challenging possible vote fraud in Chicago, Illinois, was that even if it had turned out that Nixon had carried Illinois, he still would have lacked an electoral vote majority. With 102 bonus votes in addition to those of Illinois, however, he may have been less reluctant to do so, thus prolonging the election indefinitely.
65. Wayne, *Road to the White House*, 296.
66. Richard E. Neustadt, *Presidential Power*, 3d ed. (New York: Wiley, 1980), 219.
67. Section 2 said nothing about the presidency. It merely stated that Congress must assemble at least once a year, convening on January 3 or, if it chose, some other day.
68. To do so, the Speaker not only would have to meet the qualifications for president, but also would have to resign from Congress. Next after the Speaker in the line of temporary succession is the president pro tempore of the Senate, followed by the secretary of state and the other department heads in the order their departments were created. Since cabinet officials serve until they resign or are replaced by the president, they would of necessity be members of the outgoing president's administration.
69. Section 4 also pertains to the death of a presidential candidate after an election in which no candidate receives an electoral vote majority.
70. Technically, Congress would declare the dead candidate ineligible to be president, then count the electoral votes of the losing candidates, and let the House of Representatives choose among the three highest electoral vote recipients who had lost the election. In almost all presidential elections, however, there is only one main rival to the winning candidate.
71. Quoted in Edward S. Corwin, *The President: Office and Powers*, 4th ed. (New York: New York University Press, 1957), 332. In 1788, while the Constitution was still awaiting ratification, Jefferson had written to George Washington: The "perpetual reeligibility" of the president "will, I fear, make an office for life. I was much the enemy of monarchy before I came to Europe. I am ten thousand times more so since I have seen what they are.... I shall hope that before there is danger of this change taking place in the office of President the good sense and free spirit of our countrymen will make the change necessary to prevent it" (ibid., 332-333).
72. Indeed, Washington wrote in a 1788 letter that "I differ widely myself from Mr. Jefferson ... as to the necessity or expediency of rotation in that department [the presidency].... I can see no propriety in precluding ourselves from the services of any man who in some great emergency shall be deemed universally most capable of serving the public." Even Jefferson later told the Vermont legislature that "one circumstance could engage my acquiescence in another election; to wit, such a division about a successor, as might bring in an monarchist" (ibid., 333, 332).
73. For example, John Quincy Adams described the two-term tradition as "tacit subsidiary Constitutional law" (quoted in Arthur B. Tourtellot, *The Presidents on the Presidency* [Garden City, N.Y.: Doubleday, 1964], 34-35).
74. Quoted in Corwin, *The President*, 36.
75. In his acceptance speech, delivered over the radio from the Oval Office to the convention in Chicago by a president "too busy" to leave his "post of duty," Roosevelt said: "I find myself ... in a conflict between deep personal desire for retirement ... and that quiet invisible thing called conscience.... Lying awake, as I have on many nights, I have asked myself whether I have the right, as Commander-in-Chief of the Army and Navy, to call on men and women to serve their country or to train themselves to serve, and at the same time decline to serve my country in my personal capacity, if I am called upon to do so by the people of my country."
76. Paul G. Willis and George L. Willis, "The Politics of the Twenty-second Amendment," *Western Political Quarterly* 5 (September 1952): 469.
77. Quoted in Willis and Willis, "Politics of the Twenty-second Amendment," 470.
78. Michael R. Beschloss, *Mayday: Eisenhower, Khrushchev, and the U-2 Affair* (New York: Harper and Row, 1986), 3.
79. Roberta S. Sigel, "Image of the American Presidency: Part II of an Exploration into Popular Views of the Presidential Power," *Midwest Journal of Political Science* 10 (February 1966): 125-126. Sigel also reported a public opinion poll that showed six-to-one support for the two-term limit.
80. A third matter—the right of the vice president to succeed to the office, not just the powers, of the presidency—is also treated in the Twenty-fifth Amendment. The original Constitution was vague as to whether the vice president was to become president or merely acting president when the president died, resigned, or was removed. John Tyler had asserted the vice president's right of full successorship when he succeeded President William Henry Harrison in 1841, which set the precedent for future successions. Section 1 of the Twenty-fifth Amendment simply wrote this practice into the Constitution: "In case of the removal of the President from office or of his

death or resignation, the Vice President shall become President."

81. John D. Feerick, *The Twenty-fifth Amendment* (New York: Fordham University Press, 1976), 9; Irving G. Williams, *The Rise of the Vice Presidency* (Washington, D.C.: Public Affairs Press, 1956), 112, 114.
82. In addition to Garfield and Wilson, there were James Madison, William Henry Harrison, Chester A. Arthur, Grover Cleveland, William McKinley, Warren G. Harding, Franklin D. Roosevelt, Dwight D. Eisenhower, John F. Kennedy, and Ronald Reagan. Feerick, *Twenty-fifth Amendment,* chap. 1.
83. The seven vice presidents who died in office were: George Clinton (1812), Elbridge Gerry (1814), William R. King (1853), Henry Wilson (1875), Thomas A. Hendricks (1885), Garret A. Hobart (1889), and James S. Sherman (1912). The eight presidents who died in office were: William Henry Harrison, who was succeeded by Vice President John Tyler (1841), Zachary Taylor, succeeded by Millard Fillmore (1850), Abraham Lincoln, succeeded by Andrew Johnson (1865), James A. Garfield, succeeded by Chester A. Arthur (1881), William McKinley, succeeded by Theodore Roosevelt (1901), Warren G. Harding, succeeded by Calvin Coolidge (1923), Franklin D. Roosevelt, succeeded by Harry S Truman (1945), and John F. Kennedy, succeeded by Lyndon B. Johnson (1963). The vice president who resigned was John C. Calhoun (1832).
84. Feerick, *Twenty-fifth Amendment,* 61.
85. Ibid., 200-202.
86. Georgia, North Dakota, and South Carolina voted against ratification.
87. *Guinn and Beall v. United States,* 238 U.S. 347 (1915); *Smith v. Allwright,* 321 U.S. 649 (1944).
88. Wayne, *Road to the White House,* 74-75.
89. Ibid., 75.
90. *Oregon v. Mitchell,* 400 U.S. 112 (1972).
91. Wayne, *Road to the White House,* 60.
92. See, for example, Frederick G. Dutton, *Changing Sources of Power: American Politics in the 1970s* (New York: McGraw-Hill, 1971).
93. Maryland and Virginia contributed the land to build a capital city.
94. Currently, the District's population is about the same as Delaware's, so it would continue to have three electoral votes.
95. *Harper v. Virginia Board of Electors,* 383 U.S. 663 (1966).

Selected Bibliography

Barbash, Fred. *The Founding: A Dramatic Account of the Writing of the Constitution.* New York: Linden Press/Simon and Schuster, 1987.

Beard, Charles A. *An Economic Interpretation of the Constitution.* New York: Macmillan, 1913.

Bowen, Catherine Drinker. *Miracle at Philadelphia.* Boston: Little, Brown, 1966.

Collier, Christopher, and James Lincoln Collier. *Decision in Philadelphia: The Constitutional Convention of 1787.* New York: Ballantine, 1986.

Corwin, Edward S. *The President: Office and Powers.* 4th ed. New York: New York University Press.

Farrand, Max, ed. *The Records of the Federal Convention of 1787.* New Haven, Conn.: Yale University Press, 1913.

Hutson, James H., ed. *Supplement to Max Farrand's The Records of the Federal Convention of 1787.* New Haven, Conn.: Yale University Press, 1987.

Ketcham, Ralph, ed. *The Anti-Federalist Papers and the Constitutional Convention Debates.* New York: New American Library, 1986.

Kenyon, Cecelia M., ed. *The Antifederalists.* Indianapolis: Bobbs-Merrill, 1966.

Locke, John. *Second Treatise on Government.* Indianapolis: Bobbs-Merrill, 1952.

Mee, Charles L., Jr. *The Genius of the People.* New York: Harper and Row, 1987.

Nelson, Michael. "Constitutional Qualifications for the President." *Presidential Studies Quarterly* 17:2 (Spring 1987): 383-399.

Peters, William. *A More Perfect Union: The Making of the United States Constitution.* New York: Crown, 1987.

Roche, John. "The Founding Fathers: A Reform Caucus in Action." *American Political Science Review* 55 (December 1961): 799-816.

Rossiter, Clinton. *1787: The Grand Convention.* London: MacGibbon and Kee, 1968.

Sundquist, James L. *Constitutional Reform and Effective Government.* Washington, D.C.: Brookings, 1986.

Thach, Charles C., Jr. *The Creation of the Presidency, 1775-1789.* Baltimore, Md.: Johns Hopkins University Press, 1969.

Wood, Gordon S. *The Creation of the American Republic, 1776-1787.* Chapel Hill: University of North Carolina Press, 1969.

History of the Presidency

The Constitution of 1787 provides only the barest outline of the duties and responsibilities of the president. Article 2 was the most loosely drawn constitutional chapter and thus left considerable leeway for future presidents and events to shape the executive office. By stating that "the Executive Power shall be vested in a President of the United States" and that "he shall take care that the laws be faithfully executed," without in most cases stipulating what those executive and administrative responsibilities would be, the Constitution has given rise to two centuries of conflict over the appropriate extent of presidential authority.

This chapter tells the story of the major developments that have shaped the idea of presidential power in U.S. history, as well as the institutional changes that have followed from the debates and furious struggles over the proper definition of executive authority.

The Presidency of George Washington

The election of George Washington in 1789 as the first president of the United States was never in doubt. Yet, as one historian has written, "Never was the election of a president so much a foregone conclusion and yet so tortuous in consummation." [1]

The electoral college met on February 4, 1789, but its unanimous vote for Washington could not be official until the president of the Senate, temporarily elected for the purpose, opened the ballots in the presence of both houses. According to the Constitution, Congress was due to convene in New York, the first capital, on March 4 (in 1933, the Twentieth Amendment changed the date to January 3). Legislators "dribbled" into the city, however, and on March 30, there were still too few members to form a quorum. Any man other than George Washington might have been in the capital in time for the opening of Congress, which finally occurred when the House obtained a bare quorum on April 1, the Senate on April 6. But Washington was concerned with the requirements of correct behavior. Since he would not be elected officially until a joint session of Congress tallied the votes of the electors, he waited in frustration at Mount Vernon and worried over the "stupor or listlessness" being displayed by the members of the newly forming legislative body on whom the success of the Constitution largely would depend.[2]

Yet, the start of the government was further delayed by Washington himself. Upon finally receiving word of his election at his home on April 14 from the secretary of the Congress, Charles Thomson, Washington took his time getting to New York, "lest unseemly haste suggest that he was improperly eager for the office." [3] Since he believed that the future of the government depended largely on its acceptance by the people, he was concerned with the way his progress through the states to the presidency would be received. The popular adulation that greeted him during the trip made obvious his country's devotion to him. The nation's first president finally arrived in New York in time to be inaugurated on April 30.

The long and complicated business involved both in the election of Washington and his assuming the responsibilities of the chief executive foretold of the major task of his administration—"to make the government which had been adopted, often by the thinnest of majorities, and in only eleven out of thirteen states, happily acceptable to the overwhelming majority of the entire population." [4]

That the "more perfect union" framed by the Constitution included a strong executive authority was particularly controversial, even "radical" in the American context, for executive power had been the object of distrust in America for a long time. In most of the state constitutions and in the Articles of Confederation, executive power was very weak. Indeed, the author of the Declaration of Independence, Thomas Jefferson, wrote James Madison in December 1787 to register his opposition to the Constitution's creation of a strong president: "I own that I am not a friend to a very energetic government. It is always oppressive." [5]

Given such a tradition, the establishment of the presidency was a great achievement, one that might have been impossible without the great popularity and propriety of General Washington. George Washington was, as Madison wrote in 1789, the only aspect of the government that had really caught the public imagination.[6]

Making the Presidency Safe for Democracy

Washington's awe-inspiring personality and popularity made him an indispensable source of unity and legitimacy

By Sidney M. Milkis

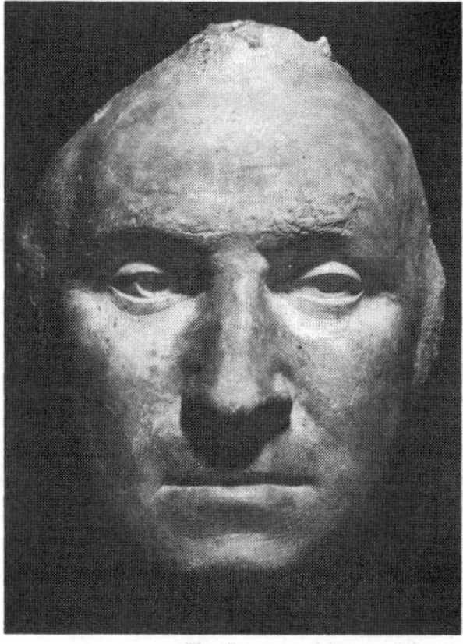
The Pierpont Morgan Library

The Pierpont Morgan Library

George Washington was the subject of many sculptors and painters in his day. French sculptor Jean Houdon made these life masks in 1785, when the future president was fifty-three.

to the newly formed government, but it also made him seem, to people who were suspicious of strong executive power, extremely dangerous. Thus, many of the conflicts of Washington's administration and that of his successor, John Adams, revolved around efforts to make strong executive power compatible with representative democracy. Washington's conduct of the office revealed his great sensitivity to the difficult tasks of attaining popular support for the institution of the presidency and his understanding that the activities of the executive office's first occupant were of great symbolic importance:

> Washington established two occasions a week when any respectably dressed person could, without introduction, invitation, or any prearrangement, be ushered into his presence. One was the President's "levee," for men only, every Tuesday from three to four. The other was Martha's tea party, for men and women, held on Friday evenings. Washington would also stage dinners on Thursdays at four o'clock in the afternoon. To avoid any charges of favoritism or any contests for invitations, only officials and their families would be asked to the dinners, and these in an orderly system of rotation.[7]

A more controversial issue of etiquette was the form of address for the president. A committee of the House of Representatives suggested simply "the president of the United States," as in the Constitution. But the Senate in May 1789, at the behest of Vice President John Adams rejected the House report. Adams, believing that "titles and politically inspired elegance were essential aspects of strong government," supported the title "His Highness the President of the United States and protector of their Liberties." Washington himself felt that the whole business of titles was a bit silly and made known his annoyance at Adams's efforts "to bedizen him with a superb but spurious title." On May 27, it was agreed that the chief executive should have no fancier title than "the President of the United States."

Forming the Executive Department

During Washington's first term, Congress passed bills setting up three major departments of government: the Departments of State, Treasury, and War. The heads of these departments were duly nominated by the president and ratified by the Senate.

For secretary of state, Washington chose Jefferson, who as minister to France had shown himself to be an excellent diplomat. Alexander Hamilton, a recognized expert on finance and commerce, became head of Treasury. Gen. Henry Knox, a diligent administrator, who as chief of artillery had served Washington reliably during the revolutionary war, was selected to be secretary of war. Edmund Randolph of Virginia became the first attorney general. At this time the office of attorney general occupied a unique position in the executive branch. It did not yet possess the status and dignity of a department, but after 1792 its incumbent regularly attended cabinet meetings and served as legal adviser of the president and of the department heads.

In forming the cabinet and the executive branch, the Washington administration employed highly informal procedures. In general, administration was ad hoc and personal. Indeed, the notion of a "president's cabinet" did not even take form during the early years of Washington's tenure: Washington did not use the word *cabinet* until April 1793, and he did not call formal meetings of the department heads until close to the end of his first term.

This informality did not mean, however, that there was no purpose to the administrative appointments and procedures of Washington's presidency. Recognizing the need to invest the national government with talent and moral character that would advance the acceptability of the new government, Washington sought the most brilliant people possible in carrying out its functions. The president's three principal aides—Hamilton, Jefferson, and Madison, a member of the House of Representatives from Virginia—formed a remarkable constellation of advisers who became the most important American statesmen in the generation after Washington. Washington deserves great credit not only for recognizing such talent but also for being able to get three such independent-minded men in a "single harness."[8] His ability to do so and the general success he achieved as an administrator helped "plant in the minds of the American people the model of a government which commanded respect by reason of its integrity, energy, and competence."[9]

Washington's appointments to minor jobs in the government also were made with attention to the need to establish the legitimacy of the fledgling national government. As the various enactments creating the major departments became law during his first term, the president found himself with nearly a thousand offices to fill. Considering these appointments important, Washington devoted an enormous amount of time to them: "no collector of customs, captain of a cutter, keeper of a lighthouse, or surveyor of revenue was appointed except after specific consideration by the President."[10]

Although besieged by applicants, directly or through intermediaries, Washington "scrupulously declined to exploit the opportunity to create a patronage system." His appointments were only partisan in the sense that he appointed only persons "of known attachment" to the new government.[11] Washington also was less concerned with expertise as such than he was in a strong commitment to the Constitution and the applicants' reputation for "good character," that is, both personal integrity and standing in one's local community. Washington's personnel policies were part of his close attention to the exigencies of nation building.

Presidential "Supremacy" and Conduct of the Executive Department

In assuming the tasks of nation building, the Washington administration established a critical precedent in favor of the view that executive authority was solely the president's. This view, held by Washington, prevailed against competing general philosophies of public administration that foresaw either the Senate or individual cabinet officers sharing fully in the operations of the executive department.

One controversial bill, for example, turned on where the power to dismiss an executive official should lie. Opponents of a strong presidency argued that the constitutional provision that presidents could appoint officials only with Senate approval implied that they could dismiss officials only with Senate approval. Favoring a strong presidency, President Washington and James Madison, his chief congressional ally in this matter, argued that presidents would be rendered impotent if they were denied the power of removal. Madison effectively led the fight in the House against senatorial interference with presidential removals; but the Senate was evenly divided, and the final vote was tied. Vice President Adams, as presiding officer, broke the tie by supporting presidential supremacy over the executive department. From then on, Congress followed Madison's leadership in passing laws establishing the major departments of government that were carefully designed to minimize the legislature's influence on the executive branch.

The eventual acquiescence of the Congress to presidential supremacy over the executive departments was probably a tribute to Washington's demonstrated devotion to the separation of powers. Washington did make recommendations to Congress, albeit sparingly, but he made no special effort to get his program through, "nor did he attempt during his first term to achieve by executive orders any matter which the strictest interpretation of the Constitution could regard as within the legislative domain." [12] Washington adhered to the view that the presidential veto power properly extended only to constitutional questions and not to policy questions.

Washington's propriety in executive-legislative relations extended even to foreign policy. Washington did not hesitate to assert his primacy in diplomatic affairs, but he worked hard to develop lines of communication between the chief executive and the Senate, which he believed the Constitution required in its stipulation that the president seek the Senate's "advice and consent" on treaties. Washington initially considered this constitutional requirement to mean prior consultation with the Senate, before the actual treaty negotiations began. But his efforts to involve the Senate fully in the making of treaties resulted in an awkward and embarrassing incident that established a precedent contrary to his desire to consult the upper chamber.

Having drafted instructions for a commission he had appointed, with Senate approval, to negotiate a treaty with the Creek Indians, Washington accompanied acting Secretary of War Knox to the Senate chamber in August 1789, seeking "advice and consent." After the treaty was read to the Senate by Vice President Adams, however, the president's appeal for consultation was met by a "dead pause," an awkward silence broken reluctantly by the senators, who proceeded to engage in a rather confused and feeble discussion of the treaty. Finally, Sen. William Maclay of Pennsylvania, sensing that there was "no chance of a fair investigation of subjects while the President of the United States sat there," recommended that the papers of the president be submitted to a committee for study. As the senator sat down after making this recommendation, Washington started up in what Maclay described as a "violent fret," and cried out: "This defeats every purpose of my coming here." [13]

Although in the end Washington achieved his purpose—the treaty was ratified with only minor changes—neither he nor any subsequent president ever again consulted the Senate in person. Most significant, Washington's

Library of Congress

After Congress established the major executive departments, President George Washington chose well-known figures for his first cabinet. On Washington's left are Henry Knox, secretary of war; Alexander Hamilton, secretary of the Treasury; Thomas Jefferson, secretary of state; and Edmund Randolph, attorney general.

failure to obtain the active cooperation of the Senate in the preliminary work of making treaties firmly established presidential supremacy in matters of diplomacy. The president did not come into possession of an unhampered power to make treaties, to be sure. Yet the Washington administration resulted in a precedent whereby the Senate was relegated to approving or rejecting a treaty that was negotiated by the chief executive without prior consultation.

Presidential Nonpartisanship and the Beginning of Party Conflict

Washington's actions as president reflected his perception of the presidency as a nonpartisan office. Like most of the Framers of the Constitution, he disapproved of "factions" and did not see himself as the leader of any political party. Although Washington insisted on being master of the executive department, it was contrary to his principles to try to influence elections or the legislative process. It was his primary duty, he believed, to enforce the laws.

Hamilton and Jefferson

Washington's conception of the presidency did not endure, however. Party conflict grew out of the sharp differences between Hamilton and Jefferson, differences that began during Washington's first term and became irreconcilable during the second term. These differences first surfaced in response to Hamilton's financial measures for the "adequate support of public credit," which he proposed in a series of reports presented to Congress between 1790 and 1791. These measures called for the assumption by the national government of the war debts of the states, the creation of a national bank, and a tariff system designed to protect infant industries in the United States.

Jefferson did not oppose all of Hamilton's measures—for example, he approved payment of the domestic and foreign debt. But Jefferson, and eventually Madison, opposed Hamilton's program for a national bank, which was contained in the Treasury secretary's report presented to Congress in December 1790. According to Jefferson and Madison, Hamilton's plan would establish national institutions and policies that transcended the powers of Congress. Furthermore, the proposed domestic and international initiatives presupposed a principal role for the president in formulating and carrying out public policy. This necessarily subordinated, Jefferson and Madison believed, the more decentralizing and democratic institutions—Congress and the states—to the executive, thus undermining popular sovereignty and pushing the United States toward a British-style monarchy.

The Neutrality Proclamation of 1793

The rift between Hamilton and Jefferson was aggravated by a foreign policy controversy during Washington's second term, centering on the war between Britain and France that broke out in 1793. As with domestic policy, the conflict over foreign affairs was inextricably linked to contradictory perceptions of the appropriate extent of presidential power. On the Anglo-French question, a bitter exchange of views over executive power in foreign affairs came about because of President Washington's issuance of the Neutrality Proclamation of 1793.

The 1793 proclamation declared that the duties and interests of the United States required "that they should with sincerity and good faith adopt and pursue a conduct friendly and impartial to the belligerent powers." To Americans, it prohibited "committing, aiding, or abetting hostilities against any of the said powers, or by carrying to them any of those articles which are deemed contraband by the modern usage of nations." [14]

The great controversy stirred by this policy prompted Hamilton to defend the issuance of the executive proclamation in a series of newspaper articles under the pseudonym "Pacificus." Madison, at the urging of Jefferson, replied to these articles in the "Helvidius" letters. The issues broached in this dialogue illuminated the fundamental nature of what would become an ongoing conflict, not only in foreign affairs but in domestic matters pertaining to the legitimate authority of the president.

Supporting the neutrality proclamation, Hamilton put forth a sweeping defense of discretionary presidential power. In doing so, he distinguished between the grants of legislative and executive power. Article I of the Constitution states: "All legislative powers herein granted shall be vested in a Congress of the United States." Article II provides a much more general grant: "The executive power shall be vested in the President of the United States." Hamilton argued that the broad language of Article II, not having the words *herein granted,* clearly indicates that the national executive power was completely lodged in the president, "subject only to the exceptions and qualifications which are expressed in the Constitution."

In foreign affairs these qualifications and exceptions went no further than the right of the Senate to approve treaties and of the Congress to declare war. These rights of the legislature, insisted Hamilton, should be strictly construed and should not hinder the executive in all other matters of foreign policy, which "naturally" was the domain of the president.[15] Thus, Hamilton not only set forth a theory of presidential power that delegated to the chief executive nearly absolute discretion in foreign affairs but also proposed a broad conception of "emergency powers which later Presidents, particularly those in the twentieth century, would generously draw upon." [16]

Although these arguments in support of a broad conception of presidential power influenced development of the executive, especially in the twentieth century, they did not go unanswered. The alternative view of presidential authority in foreign affairs offered by Madison in the Helvidius letters became one of the most important causes of the opposition that he and Jefferson led.

This view denied that foreign policy was "naturally" an executive power. The tasks of foreign policy—the powers to declare war, to conclude peace, and to form alliances—were among "the highest acts of sovereignty; of which the legislative power must at least be an integral and preeminent part." In foreign policy, as in domestic matters, Madison argued, representative government required that the president's power be confined to the execution of laws. To suggest, as Hamilton did, that foreign policy was within the proper definition of executive power, implying in effect that the executive department naturally included a legislative power, was "in theory an absurdity—in practice a tyranny." [17]

The precedent established during the Washington administration for the executive to enunciate a policy of neutrality was less important than the larger principle in the debate that took place between his leading advisers. The issue was whether the president was to be limited by the letter of constitutionally prescribed functions or be considered a proper sovereign head of state with discretion to act independently of legal restraints except in those instances where the Constitution specifically "enumerated" exceptions and limitations. Thus, the debate between Pacificus and Helvidius turned on "the classical debate between the broad and narrow construction, the loose and strict interpretations of the Constitution." [18]

Ultimately, this debate caused strains that made open party conflict inevitable. The full implications of this conflict between the Federalists, who shared Hamilton's point of view, and the Democratic-Republicans, who shared Jefferson's, became clear during the presidency of John Adams, who took office in 1797. Still, this party conflict never became as raw and disruptive as the Framers feared factional strife might be. The enduring limits of "factionalism" in the United States were probably attributable largely to Washington's forceful example of nonpartisanship. To some extent Washington sought to deal with the divisive conflict between the Hamiltonians and Jeffersonians by avoiding it, by choosing to continue to "preside" rather than to lead and direct.[19] He thereby exerted a moderating influence at a time when maintaining unity was critical to the survival of the new government. In domestic and foreign policy Washington did take stands, usually tilting to the Hamiltonian point of view. Yet his extraordinary personal charisma and popularity, combined with a commitment to the existence of a strong and independent legislature, restrained partisan strife as long as he presided over the nation. Moreover, Washington renounced the role of party leader, clearly articulated in his Farewell Address, an enduring legacy of presidential "impartiality" that was not completely eclipsed by the advent of party politics. *(See "Washington's Farewell Address," p. 1365, in the Appendix.)* Even with the emergence of a formal party system, the full potential of the executive office demanded that the chief executive be leader of the nation, not simply the head of a party governing the nation.

The Rise of Party Politics and the Triumph of Jeffersonianism

The end of Washington's administration marked an important change in the executive office. This change is best characterized as the transformation of the presidency from a nonpartisan to a partisan institution. This change did not entail a complete metamorphosis; those who were leaders in the first great party conflicts in the United States—John Adams, Alexander Hamilton, Thomas Jefferson, and James Madison—viewed partisanship with great disfavor. Yet the furious struggles that followed Washington's return to Mount Vernon made open party conflict a central part of the American presidency. Thereafter, presidents might attempt to rise above party, but partisanship had become an unavoidable condition of effective presidential leadership.

Washington's Retirement and the 1796 Election

As the end of the year 1795 approached, the paramount question for most public figures in the United States was whether Washington would accept another term as president. The Constitution originally imposed no limit on presidential reeligibility, and Washington, although slightly tarnished by the partisan animosities that afflicted the unity of his cabinet, surely could have stayed in office had he chosen to do so.

Washington was anxious to return to Mount Vernon, however, and in September 1796 he announced his retirement, an event marked by the release of his Farewell Address, published without ceremony. Washington's voluntary retirement set a precedent for limiting presidents to two terms, a practice that endured for nearly a century and a half. This development allayed the Jeffersonian concerns about the dangerous use of executive power and converted Jefferson from his original idea of a single seven-year presidential term of office.[20]

Washington's retirement also resulted in a more partisan form of presidential politics. As long as the first president was on the scene, he was able by dint of his prestige to restrain open party conflict. But Adams, although a distinguished and respected statesman, lacked Washington's stature as well as his reputation for impartiality. In the division between Federalists and Democratic-Republicans, Adams was clearly identified with the Federalists. His role in the titles controversy and his well-known admiration for the British form of government marked him in the eyes of Jeffersonians as a "monarchist." Thus, when Washington's retirement became known and Adams, as the incumbent vice president, assumed the position of heir apparent, the presidential campaign of 1796 began in earnest.

In this campaign, generally considered one of the most bitter and scurrilous in U.S. history, the appearances of nonpartisanship gave way to competition between national political parties. For the first time in a presidential election, a contest was organized around two party tickets. The Federalists supported John Adams and Thomas Pinckney for president and vice president, respectively. The Democratic-Republicans chose Jefferson for president and Aaron Burr for vice president.

The issues that divided the Federalists and Democratic-Republicans in the election of 1796 were crystallized by the controversial Jay Treaty, signed in London in November 1794. Through this treaty, the United States secured a promise from Britain to evacuate by 1796 the northwest posts, which had sustained a British presence on U.S. soil since the Revolution, and a limited right of U.S. vessels to trade with the British West Indies. As such, this treaty secured the territorial integrity of the United States and ameliorated dangerous conflicts at sea, resulting from Britain's war with France, that had brought the United States and Britain to the brink of war. Yet, when the terms of this treaty were released November 2, 1795, a firestorm of controversy ensued that made the Washington administration and John Jay (the chief justice of the Supreme Court who, as a presidential envoy, negotiated the agreement with Great Britain) the target of vicious party attacks.

Democratic-Republican opposition to the treaty was animated by a strong dislike of the British, a contempt reinforced by Britain's use of western posts as vantage points for the arming of Indian and rebel slaves to attack settlers in the Northwest Territory. To Democratic-Republicans, the Jay Treaty reflected the Washington administration's preference for the British monarchy over the French Republic. Jay's Treaty thus became the first national partisan issue in U.S. political history, and, as such, set the tone for the campaign of 1796.[21]

In spite of the stark difference between the Federalists and the Democratic-Republicans, contestants in the partisan strife of the 1790s were reluctant warriors. It was still not considered respectable in U.S. politics to have one's political activities associated with partisanship; nor was it expected that candidates for the presidency would actively seek the office. Paradoxically, both Adams and Jefferson made efforts to stay above party conflicts, even as they (Jefferson especially) worked behind the scenes to achieve the triumph of the parties they represented. Neither Adams nor Jefferson made the slightest public effort to influence the outcome of the election, as both considered it unethical to campaign on their own or their parties' behalf.

The result of the 1796 election was a narrow Federalist victory. Adams obtained the presidency with seventy-one electoral votes. Jefferson's sixty-eight votes made him vice president, as the nonpartisan constitutional mechanism for selecting the president and vice president had not yet been changed to accommodate the outbreak of partisan competition. The Constitution originally directed that every elector vote for two persons, without designating the office to which either was to be chosen. This mechanism did not easily accommodate the selection of a party ticket, a fact that was not changed until the Twelfth Amendment was ratified in 1804. Hence, the election of 1796 yielded a presidential administration shared by the leaders of deeply divided political organizations.

The Embattled Presidency of John Adams

Few presidents in U.S. history have faced a more difficult set of national circumstances than John Adams. No other chief executive would have the unenviable task of succeeding a leader of Washington's stature. Moreover, Adams faced much more trying circumstances than had Washington. Contemplating the transition of power in 1797, vice president-elect Jefferson stated, "The President [Washington] is fortunate to get off just as the bubble is bursting, leaving others to hold the bag." [22]

Most significant, the foreign situation Adams faced in 1797 was more difficult than Washington's. The Jay Treaty had greatly worsened U.S. relations with an aggressive French government, which, after Napoleon Bonaparte had beaten Austria in October 1797, was at the height of its power. The French interference with U.S. commerce at sea made Britain's interference in 1793 seem mild in comparison. Moreover, what amounted to a virtual naval war with France was severely aggravated when Adams's diplomatic attempts to maintain Washington's policy of neutrality resulted in insulting and humiliating treatment by the French foreign ministry.

The French foreign minister, Talleyrand, sent three representatives of the French government (referred to in dispatches as "X, Y, and Z") to confront the U.S. emissaries in Paris and to find out how much the United States was willing to pay in bribes to French officials and loans to the French government to secure a treaty. When the "XYZ affair" became public early in 1798, a furor broke loose in the United States that seemed to make war with France inevitable.

Adams's efforts to come to terms with this international crisis were hindered by members of his own party as much as they were by the opposition. Although it was expected that the Democratic-Republicans, led by the vice president, would oppose Adams's actions, "the Federalists were often as recalcitrant or bitter toward the president." [23] His most influential intraparty critic was Hamilton, who believed the president to be too moderate politically and thereby incapable of dealing with the problems the nation faced.

Adams was a party man, but he intended to follow Washington's example of standing as much as possible above party. This conviction was evident in his approach to the problems with France. Unlike the so-called Arch-Federalists, led by Hamilton, the president was willing to accept war if declared by France, but he hoped to avoid it. His primary objective was to protect U.S. commerce, through diplomacy and naval expansion, and to force the French Republic to respect the American flag. Hamilton and his allies in the party, however, did not want to contain the conflict with France but to exploit it. They wanted to undertake strong measures immediately that would prepare the nation for war, as well as to suppress the Democratic-Republican opposition. Ultimately, these different objectives generated an irreconcilable split within the Federalist party, prompting Jefferson to write in May 1797 that the "Hamiltons" were "only a little less hostile [to Adams] than to me." [24]

The conflict between Hamilton and the president culminated in a disruption of the administration that contributed to the triumph of the Democratic-Republicans in the election of 1800. Before that contest, however, several developments severely tested the authority of the president as chief executive. The crisis of presidential authority stemmed from Hamilton's determination to guide the policy of the government, although he was not one of its members. He retired from the Treasury at the end of January 1795, but during the latter days of Washington's second term and throughout Adams's tenure he remained the dynamic center of the Federalist party. Hamilton's influence was enhanced after 1797 as a result of Adams's decision to retain Washington's cabinet, a judgment he made both out of deference to the stature of his predecessor and his belief that good government depended upon the labor of skilled and experienced administrators.[25]

Three members of Washington's cabinet, Secretary of State Timothy Pickering, Secretary of War James McHenry, and Oliver Wolcott, who succeeded Hamilton as head of the Treasury, largely owed their government positions to Hamilton, and in all important questions they looked to him, and not Adams, as the suitable guide of their actions. Only Charles Lee, the attorney general and the least powerful cabinet member, and Benjamin Stoddert, who joined the cabinet as head of the newly established Navy Department in 1798, were loyal to Adams. Consequently, unity of executive policy was achieved only when the president agreed with Hamilton, a coincidence most obviously absent in addressing the threat of war with France. Thus, in Adams's administration there emerged "an extraordinary situation in which the control of public policy became the prize of a struggle between a New York lawyer and a president who apparently was not fully aware of the activity of his rival." [26]

The conflict between Adams and the Arch-Federalists culminated in 1799 as Adams prepared to send a second mission to France in an effort to avoid war. On February 1799, without previous consultation with the secretary of state or the cabinet, he nominated William Vans Murray, then minister to the Netherlands, as minister plenipotentiary to the French Republic. Murray was chosen because of his good relations with France; it was through Murray, in fact, that Adams learned of France's willingness to receive a new U.S. mission and desire to avoid war with the United States. The Senate, which was sympathetic to Hamilton's views, would have rejected the nomination, but Adams's quick and unilateral action caught its members by surprise. So the Senate compromised by asking for a commission of three, to which the president consented.

After further attempts orchestrated by Secretary of State Pickering to postpone the sailing of the second mission, Adams, while sending signals that he was not opposed to a delay, took unilateral action to place the mission on board a U.S. frigate. Thus, the mission arrived in time to take advantage of France's uncertain situation, one created by a series of military defeats at the hands of the British. Adams's bold action cost him the support of influential men in his cabinet and in the ranks of the Federalist party but achieved a commercial agreement with France that ended the threat of war, thus preserving the principle of neutrality in the wars of Europe that he inherited from the Washington administration.

More significant, Adams rescued the authority of the presidency from a severe assault. Adams's position was shaken by this incident; in all likelihood it cost him his chance for reelection. But, as Leonard White, a scholar on the early development of the U.S. presidency, has written:

> the outcome was a resounding affirmation of the authority of the President as chief executive and of the subordination of the department heads to his leadership and direction. Adams confirmed the character of the presidency as the Constitutional Convention had outlined it and as Washington had already formed it—but only after events which stirred grave doubts concerning its future.[27]

Seeking to end the events that led up to this crisis of executive authority, Adams attempted to rid the cabinet of the two men most disloyal to him. In May 1800, he asked for McHenry's resignation and summarily removed Pickering, when the latter refused to resign. Thus, Timothy Pickering, the secretary of state who actively sought to scuttle the second peace mission to France, became the first cabinet officer to be removed by a president.

Although historians frequently have praised John Adams for upholding the authority of the presidency in the face of a badly divided cabinet and party, he has been condemned for his role in the passage and enforcement of the Alien and Sedition Acts in 1798. The Alien Act gave the president authority to expel any foreigner considered dangerous to the public peace; the Sedition Act, which caused most of the anger and dispute in the nation, made it a crime, punishable by fine or imprisonment, to bring "false, scandalous and malicious" accusations against the president, the Congress, or the government.

The Alien Act generally was viewed as a defensible measure in support of the national government's right of self-protection, although it was severely challenged by the Democratic-Republican opposition for vesting extraordinary powers in the hands of the president and thus violating the separation of powers. The sedition law, however, was widely denounced as violating sacred constitutional principles. To be sure, it was not as oppressive as similar European statutes, as it posed on the prosecution the necessity of proving an "intent to defame" and required a jury trial. But it was enforced in such a way that it led to a confounding of sedition (that is, an effort to conspire against the federal government) and legitimate political opposition. As such, it violated the First Amendment of the Constitution, forbidding Congress to pass any law abridging the freedom of speech or the press.

Adams was not in sympathy with the more extreme purposes underlying Federalist support of the Alien and Sedition Acts. For example, he resisted the intention of Secretary of State Pickering to use the alien laws to deport large numbers of people who were not citizens. He also opposed the Arch-Federalists' proposal to establish a large standing army. But Adams's unwillingness to go along with the more extreme members of his party came with a price.

The "Revolution" of 1800

Although Adams's effort to rise above party conflict may have avoided civil war, it could not prevent his defeat at the hands of Thomas Jefferson in the 1800 election. Ironically, Adams's dislike of party politics contributed to the evolution of a formal two-party system, for the avoidance of war with France and the triumph of the more moderate Federalist party allowed for the first peaceful transition of power in a presidential election. But the ascent of the Democratic-Republican party to power, a development Jefferson referred to as "the Revolution of 1800," was preceded by an odd set of events that precipitated a constitutional crisis and nearly abrogated the results of the presidential election.

These events were the result of fully developed party competition operating for the first time under constitutional provisions that did not make allowances for a formal party system. *(See "Emergence of Parties," p. 157, in The Electoral Process chapter of Part II.)* As noted, the Constitution, originally written without party tickets in mind, arranged for no separate designation of presidential and vice-presidential candidates. Consequently, when in the close election of 1800, seventy-three Democratic-Republican electors were chosen to sixty-five for the Federalists, each cast both presidential ballots for Thomas Jefferson and his running mate, Aaron Burr.

Apparently, one vote was to have been withheld from the vice-presidential candidate, but because of a lapse in party planning, Jefferson and Burr turned up with the same number of electoral votes. According to procedures established by the Constitution, the presidential election of 1800 therefore became the first of only two elections in U.S. history that had to be decided in the House of Representatives since no candidate had a majority in the electoral college.

Federalist leadership in Congress saw an opportunity to make a president of Aaron Burr, a less principled, and, therefore, perhaps more pliable politician than Jefferson. But under the Constitution a majority of the representatives of each of nine states was needed to elect in the House, and the Federalists could not produce the votes. This stalemate lasted through thirty-five ballots, and it was not until February 17, 1801, that Jefferson was finally elected.

The electoral contest of 1800-1801 led to the adoption of the Twelfth Amendment, a decisive step "toward constitutional recognition of the role played by parties in the federal government." [28] The electoral college was changed, allowing for separate ballots for president and vice president. Thus, an important constitutional obstacle was removed from the formal institutionalization of the two-party system. Neither the Democratic-Republicans nor

Federalists were comfortable in taking such a step; but the harrowing experience of 1801 and the desire to avoid such incidents in the future took precedence over the strong dislike of party that characterized partisans during the early history of the presidency.

Jefferson's triumph in the 1800 election marked a critical realignment of political forces in U.S. politics, resulting in the political dominance of the Democratic-Republican party from 1801 to 1824. During the last decade of his life, in a letter to the eminent lawyer and legal scholar Spencer Roane, Jefferson spoke of the "revolution of 1800," saying that although effected peacefully in the course of a popular election, it was "as real a revolution in the principles of our government as that of 1776 was in its form." [29]

Jefferson's understanding of revolution did not mean what it does in the twentieth century—massive social and economic upheaval. Rather, he meant that the election of 1800 had brought about a change, supported by a majority of the people, that marked a return to the principles of the American Revolution. In Jefferson's view those principles had been perverted by the Federalists in their commitment to extending the power of the executive and expanding the responsibilities of the national government. In effect, the domestic and international initiatives of the Federalists constituted an attempt to establish a monarchy. The task of the Democratic-Republican revolution, according to historian Forrest McDonald, was to restore limited democratic government to the American polity, an effort that entailed casting off the Federalist institutions and instilling "the people with the historical knowledge and true principles that would prevent them from losing their liberties ever again." [30]

Jefferson's concern with ensuring the integrity of majority decisions motivated the war he carried on with the federal judiciary. In a desperate attempt to maintain a foothold on the national government, the Federalists tried to "pack" the courts before leaving office. The Judiciary Act of 1801 increased the number of federal judgeships, and these positions were hurriedly filled by the "midnight" appointments of the Adams administration before leaving office. To the Jeffersonians the judiciary constituted "the final barrier to be assaulted in the advance of popular government and political liberty." To the Federalists the courts represented "the last bastion of moderation and sanity arresting the progress of mob rule and anarchy." [31]

More was at stake than power relationships, however. The Democratic-Republicans opposed the courts being vested with a broad grant of authority that would enable them to override the actions of the elected representatives. The Federalists, to the contrary, supported the judiciary possessing a power of judicial review that would make it the ultimate arbiter of constitutional issues. Although Jefferson and his followers did not challenge the right of the courts to decide matters of constitutionality, they insisted that each branch of government, and the state governments as well, shared that right equally.

These issues of power and principle came to a head in the case of *Marbury vs. Madison* (1803). Chief Justice John Marshall decided in favor of Jefferson, but on grounds that claimed powers for the judiciary that Jefferson denied it had. In effect, Marshall gave Jefferson a free hand to dismiss Federalist appointees (while he scolded Jefferson for wishing to do so), but only on condition that the president accept the Court's power to pass upon the constitutionality of acts of Congress.[32] *(See "Judicial Review," p. 1150, in The President and the Supreme Court chapter of Part VI.)*

Jefferson was unwilling to accept such a condition, but, because of Marshall's adroit ruling, he was unable to deal with the chief justice and the judiciary as he had hoped. Soon after the Marbury case, when he failed to remove Supreme Court Justice Samuel Chase by impeachment, Jefferson ended his war with the judiciary. Indeed, developments during his first term seemed to make this war unnecessary, because by that time much of the Democratic-Republican program was completed. Nevertheless, although the judiciary weathered the storm of Jefferson's first term, and the power of judicial review became rooted in the U.S. political system, the question that gave rise to the conflict between Jefferson and the courts was never fully resolved. That question—whether ultimate authority rests with elected representatives in the Congress and the White House or in a standard of "fixed" law as interpreted by the judiciary—has arisen again and again in U.S. history.

Library of Congress

Thomas Jefferson won the election of 1800, but the contest had to be decided by the House of Representatives after Jefferson and his running mate, Aaron Burr, tied in the electoral college vote.

The Democratic-Republican Program and Adjustment to Power

In important respects, a great deal of the Democratic-Republican program was negative. It aimed at repealing Federalist policies that Jeffersonians believed had undermined the Constitution.

In short order Congress, which the Democratic-Republicans also captured in the 1800 election, repealed the Alien and Sedition Acts that had not already expired. In addition, Jefferson pardoned all ten persons (mostly Democratic-Republican newspaper publishers) who had been convicted under the Sedition Act, and Congress voted to restore with interest all fines that had been levied under the act. During Jefferson's first term, Congress also abolished most of the internal taxes, including the very unpopular excise tax (levied on the production and sale of certain commodities) and direct property tax, that Federalists had enacted in 1798 to help pay for war preparations undertaken in the wake of the conflict with France. As part of the same package, Congress reduced the military establishment, severely cutting army and naval appropriations.

Although Jefferson's views stressed the need to restrain the role of the national government, he was not narrowly doctrinaire in his conception of the proper limits of government. The emphasis on strictly construing the role of the national government and states' rights did not

New York Public Library

Thomas Jefferson, depicted here as being robbed by King George and Napoleon, found himself in 1805 in the middle of the war between England and France. The cartoon symbolizes the war's effect on U.S. trade.

reflect an animus against government in itself, but a concern to make government more responsive to the will of the people.

"His faith in the people," as one scholar has remarked, "gave to his views on power a flexibility that permitted the use of power in positive ways to emphasize the freedom *from* government." [33] In those areas where the national government's responsibility was properly exercised, that is, in matters pertaining to external affairs and the regulation of relations between the states, Jefferson believed that the powers of the central government should be exercised with energy and efficiency.

Given certain compelling conditions, he was willing to tolerate government action that even seemed to contradict his stated principles. Thus, in 1803 Jefferson consented to the purchase of Louisiana, which doubled the territory of the United States, although, as he granted in a letter to Sen. John Breckinridge, he did not feel the Constitution provided "for our holding foreign territory, still less for incorporating foreign nations into our union." [34] Seeking to maintain the longstanding U.S. commitment to neutrality in struggles between Britain and France, Jefferson also was willing to pronounce and enforce an embargo on all foreign commerce in 1804, which involved coercion rivaling that of the notorious Alien and Sedition Acts.

Thus, Jefferson's actions as president reflected a "duality that was to underlie the whole of the [Democratic-Republican] era and to account for many of its frustrations." [35] Such tensions in the Democratic-Republican philosophy of government were clearly evident in the Jeffersonians' view of and effect on executive power. Opposing conceptions of executive power had been at the center of the bitter conflict between the Federalists and Democratic-Republicans. Given these discrepant views, one might have expected important changes in the executive when Jefferson and his friends took over the government. But the Democratic-Republicans maintained the essence of the Federalist concept of executive power.

Jefferson, in particular, with the able support of his secretary of the Treasury, Albert Gallatin, exercised an executive influence and control over domestic policy that equaled that of Hamilton during the Washington administration. Indeed, Jefferson secured from a Democratic-Republican Congress a grant of authority to enforce the embargo policy that exceeded any grant of executive power undertaken by the Federalists. Moreover, he used those powers with all the energy that the Democratic-Republican partisans in opposition had denounced as a mark of tyranny.

In important respects, then, the "revolution" of 1800 did not bring about any sweeping changes in the existing constitutional arrangements. Hamilton, in fact, was among those who recognized that Jefferson was not opposed to the firm exercise of executive power and assured his colleagues in 1801 that "it is not true, as alleged, that he [Jefferson] is for confounding all the powers in the House of Representatives." [36] Hamilton's observations predicted accurately how Jefferson was to act as president.

Nevertheless, while it is true that the Democratic-Republicans in general maintained the Federalist concept and institutions of the executive, Jefferson's presidency marked an important change in the executive's relationship to the people.[37] Put simply, Jefferson's predecessors, Washington and Adams, believed that presidential power derived from its constitutional authority; but Jefferson, while not rejecting this view out of hand, maintained that the strength of the presidency ultimately depended upon the "affections of the people." Jefferson clearly implied in his first inaugural address that the program of the Democratic-Republican party should be enacted because of its endorsement by a majority of the people in the 1800 election.

Washington and Adams viewed their task as one of maintaining some distance from the people and serving as a moderating force in the clash of parties and interests in Congress. But Jefferson believed that the most effective and responsible way to lead the government was through the institutions that were rooted in a popular base. Rather than stand apart from developments occurring in the legislature, he sought to direct them. Whereas Hamilton's conception of a strong presidency emphasized the necessity of independent initiatives on the part of the executive, Jefferson assumed the role of party leader as a device to combine the separated branches of U.S. government. Jefferson, as noted, was uncomfortable with party politics, yet he created the role of party leader as a means of making effective his political philosophy and program, a means he considered more consonant with the principles at the heart of the American Republic than the Federalists' view of the executive.

Informed by such a conception of the presidency, Jefferson brought about important institutional changes that resulted in a closer relationship between the president and the people than had existed before. One such change was the decline in the ceremonial trappings of the executive office. Jefferson did not emulate Washington by employing a coach and an assemblage of liveried outriders. Instead, he rode his own horse, with only one servant in attandance. He also stressed republican simplicity in his dress, a practice that offended some who felt his personal appearance unsuitable for a head of state.

He simplified as well his relations with Congress. His decision to submit his first annual message to Congress in writing rather than deliver it in person was "a calculated political act, designed to reduce the "relics" left by the Federalists and to underline the return to sound republican simplicity." [38] Jefferson thereby began a century-long practice of presidents' sending their State of the Union messages to be read to Congress by the clerk of the House rather than delivering them in person.

It is appropriate that the adoption of simpler etiquette in the conduct of the executive office corresponded with the move of the capitol from Philadelphia to Washington, D.C. This transition left members of Congress, executive branch officials, and diplomats, who had been accustomed to the well-developed culture and the comforts of Philadelphia, "stranded" on the banks of the Potomac. One historian described Washington in the early 1800s was "a village pretending to be a capital, a place with a few bad houses, extensive swamps, hanging on the skirts of a too thinly peopled, weak and barren country." [39] Yet Jefferson, who was never comfortable in cities, appreciated the change in the location of the capital. In the relatively simple surroundings of Washington, Jefferson established an informality of social activity that was compatible with his image of the executive office.

The Limits of "Popular" Leadership

It is important, however, to take note of the limits on the popular leadership of the presidency that continued during the Jeffersonian era. Neither Jefferson nor his Democratic-Republican successors—James Madison (1809-1817), James Monroe (1817-1825), and John Quincy Adams (1825-1829)—sought to enhance their power as party or popular leaders by bartering patronage (or other sorts of favors that the executive might bestow) for legislation. Members of Congress, increasingly eager for appointments, made some inroads on the executive domain, but the practice of using federal positions to get votes in either House was rare and would have been thought corrupt. The institution of presidents using the "spoils" of federal appointment to facilitate party unity or obtain desired legislation did not begin until 1829.

Nor was it considered respectable during the Jeffersonian era for presidents to seek influence by appealing to the public. Not only were the facilities lacking for presidents to make such rhetorical appeals, but it was considered irresponsible demagogy to do so.[40] Until the twentieth century, popular leadership in the executive office was exercised through influence over the party mechanisms in the Congress and in the state governments, not by making appeals to the country "over the heads" of other elected representatives.

The self-imposed limit on the power of presidential persuasion is revealed by Jefferson's refusal to take the controversial embargo issue to the people. Jefferson was able to get this policy adopted by using his enormous popularity to influence party leaders in Congress, both chambers of which were dominated by the Democratic-Republican party. Yet over the course of its fourteen-month existence the embargo policy began to unravel and eventually was repealed by a rebellious legislature.

Jefferson was deeply disturbed by congressional and public opposition to this and other of his policies. Still, he remained silent and acquiesced to it rather than seek to influence the court of political opinion. While Democratic-Republican leaders received behind-the-scenes directives from the president, Jefferson presented "an imperturbable, almost sphinx like silence to the nation." [41] To do otherwise would have been to violate the well-established custom prohibiting presidents from seeking directly to affect public views.

The defeat of Jefferson's embargo policy marked the first striking example of the limits of presidential power. It also marked the beginning of a long decline in the influence of the presidency that affected the administrations of Jefferson's three Democratic-Republican successors. A combination of personal factors and institutional developments caused the presidency after Jefferson to shrink to its limited constitutional role as prescribed by the orthodox Democratic-Republican doctrine.

The Presidency of James Madison

The decrease in presidential power was especially evident during James Madison's two terms in office. During his tenure, major institutional developments occasioned the transfer of power from the executive to the legislative branch. One such development was the advent of the congressional nominating caucus as an independent source of power.

The nomination of Jefferson in 1800 and 1804 was a foregone conclusion, but the Democratic-Republican caucus of 1808 was the first to make a vital decision. Madison was generally viewed as the heir apparent to Jefferson, but the leader of the anti-Jefferson faction in the Democratic-Republican party, John Randolph, sought to secure the nomination for James Monroe. Although Madison was duly nominated and elected, the fact that he had to win over his party members in the Congress for this to occur suggested that the nomination of presidential candidates could now become an occasion "to make explicit executive subordination to congressional president-makers." Indeed, in 1812 there is reason to believe President Madison's renomination by the Democratic-Republican caucus was delayed until he gave assurances of his support of congressional war policy.[42]

The emergence of the House Speaker as a major force in the Congress and the extraordinary use of that office by Henry Clay was another major development during the Madison presidency that reduced the power of the executive relative to that of Congress. Before Clay's election as Speaker in 1811, party leadership in the lower chamber usually fell to a designated floor leader; until that time, the Speaker had been only a moderator. This practice changed dramatically with the first of Henry Clay's six almost unanimous selections to this office:

> Clay was chosen Speaker on an issue that President Madison was unable to grip, and with the intention of forcing national action despite the President's incapacity to act—war with Great Britain. Clay succeeded in this purpose, and until the last day of Madison's administration the initiative in public affairs remained with Clay and his associates in the House of Representatives.[43]

Under Clay's direction, the capacity of the House of Representatives to meet its broader obligations was strengthened by the expanding number and influence of standing committees, providing legislators for the first time with the opportunity to specialize and obtain competence in an area of interest. Because this institutional development was coordinated by the party leadership, the House became an effective instrument of action. Consequently, from 1811 to 1825, Henry Clay was arguably the most powerful man in the nation.

The decline of the presidency was most dramatically illustrated by developments during the War of 1812. Madison's message of war to Congress on June 1, 1812, was the first by a president. Yet while subsequent developments in U.S. history were to establish formidable wartime powers for the president, Madison's command of the nation's military effort was singularly undistinguished. He was handicapped not only by his inability to exert influence over the Congress but also by personal qualities that were poorly suited for the tasks at hand. Madison's service to the country before his presidency was prodigious; of all the members of the Founding generation, no one played a more important role in framing the U.S. Constitution and influencing its early operations. Yet, as even a sympathetic biographer wrote of Madison's war leadership:

> The hour had come but the man was wanting. Not a scholar in governments ancient and modern, not an unimpassioned writer of careful messages, but a robust leader to rally the people and unite them to fight was what the time needed, and what it did not find in Madison.[44]

Not surprisingly, given the weakness of the executive office at this critical time, the War of 1812, from a military point of view, was the most unsuccessful in U.S. history. The low point in the war occurred in August 1814, when President Madison had to evacuate the capital for three days as a British force of fewer then five thousand men moved unchecked up the Chesapeake Bay and marched with little resistance into the heart of Washington, burning the Capital, the White House, the Navy Yard, and most other public buildings in Washington.

The nation's morale was boosted by Gen. Andrew Jackson's victory at New Orleans on January 8, 1815, which, although gratifying to national pride, had no effect on the outcome of the war, for peace had been concluded two weeks before the engagement. In the wake of Jackson's triumph, the end of the war was greeted with joy by the American people, enabling James Madison to retire with honor in 1816 and rendering the Federalists, many of whom opposed the war from the start, a fatally wounded opposition. But the War of 1812 was at best a stalemate, which revealed the shortcomings of Madison as president.

In important respects, Madison's failures transcended his personal limitations and were attributable to the difficult circumstances he inherited from the Jefferson administration and a Democratic-Republican tradition of which he had been one of the major architects. He and Jefferson

Library of Congress

The White House was among the many public buildings burned by British forces in 1814 during the War of 1812.

had preached economy and had taken measures to undo the military preparations undertaken during the Adams administration, opposing the creation of even a minimal standing army. They were thus completely dependent on solving the country's foreign policy problems with France and Britain through diplomatic channels. Failing this, the Democratic-Republicans were forced to resort to an impractical policy of "peaceful" coercion, which proved disastrous for the U.S. economy, without influencing either Britain or France to stop interfering with U.S. ships. The collapse of the embargo left Madison no alternative but to resort to war when provocations, especially at the hands of the British, continued, although he knew the country was neither prepared for war nor united behind it.

Years later, Madison recounted how he hoped to overcome the nation's obvious unpreparedness by "throw[ing] forward the flag of the country, sure that the people would press onward and defend it." [45] Yet the decline in the status of the executive office left Madison in a poor position to rally the Congress and nation. Contrary to his expectations, Democratic-Republican doctrine of hostility to centralized power was not abandoned during war time. Congress was willing to declare war but not to provide the revenue required to carry it out. Moreover, the Madison administration's war strategy of using the state militias was scuttled by the state governments' lack of cooperation. The governors of Massachusetts and Connecticut, for example, refused to release their militias for the purpose of fighting the war, while the president, a strong advocate of states' rights as a member of the opposition, "offered no suggestion for stopping so grave a defiance of federal authority." [58]

The Presidencies of James Monroe and John Quincy Adams

James Madison's Democratic-Republican successors, James Monroe (1817-1825) and John Quincy Adams (1825-1829), were unable to restore the strength of the presidency that had dissipated after Jefferson's retirement. Monroe, although a forceful statesman and a stronger personality than his predecessor, was stiff and formal in his personal dealings, which made it difficult for him to lead the party effectively. Like Washington and Adams, he was more suited to the task of presiding than directing.

Library of Congress

Library of Congress

Henry Clay and John C. Calhoun dominated the National Republicans—the new wing of the Democratic-Republican party—after the War of 1812.

Monroe also was hindered by a growing split within his party between "old" Democratic-Republicans, who inclined toward a strict construction of the Constitution, and "new" Democratic-Republicans, or National Republicans, who were more nationalist in outlook. Monroe was identified with the former group; the latter, represented by prominent figures such as Henry Clay, John C. Calhoun, and Monroe's successor, John Quincy Adams, dominated the party after the War of 1812.

One of the major domestic issues of the day, "internal improvements," turned on whether it was constitutional for the national government to construct roads and canals. Monroe informed Congress of his belief that an amendment to the Constitution would be required for the national government to undertake such a responsibility. Nevertheless, Congress, under the strong direction of Clay, defied Monroe and passed a bill for the repair of the Cumberland Road. The president's veto of this bill signaled a breakdown within the ranks of the Democratic-Republicans that was to plague Monroe throughout his two terms.

This split in the Democratic-Republican ranks reinforced the transfer of power from the executive to the legislative branch. In his battle with Clay and the Congress, Monroe, adhering to the prevailing custom, rarely used the veto power; his action in the Cumberland Road controversy was the exception rather than the rule. Following the practice begun under Washington, Monroe vetoed only legislation he deemed unconstitutional.

Monroe's deference to the legislature went beyond custom; he was motivated by an unprecedented Democratic-Republican commitment to legislative supremacy. Hence, he abstained almost completely from involvement in the greatest issue of the day: the admission of Missouri to the Union. For the first time admission of a state led to a debate in Congress over the status of slavery in the Louisiana Territory. Jefferson observed this bitter debate with great concern. Writing to Rep. John Holmes of Maine, he said: "This momentous question, like a fire-bell in the night, awakened and filled me with terror. I considered it at once the knell of the Union." [47] The Missouri Compromise of 1820 settled the slavery controversy for a time, but President Monroe had virtually no hand in resolving this crisis, save for signing the final bill hammered out in Congress.

The character of Monroe's administration prompted Supreme Court Justice Joseph Story to remark in 1818 that "the Executive has no longer a commanding influence. The House of Representatives has absorbed all the popular feeling and all the effective power of the country." [48]

The development lamented by Justice Story was not as salient in foreign affairs, however, as it was in domestic matters. In fact, Monroe reinforced the right of presidents to take the initiative in foreign affairs, by issuing the Monroe Doctrine, which became one of the pillars of U.S. foreign policy in the nineteenth and twentieth centuries. The Monroe Doctrine resulted from the president's attempt to respond to the revolt of Spanish colonies in Latin America that nearly liquidated the Spanish empire. The Monroe administration was alarmed at reports that European powers, France in particular, had designs on several Latin American nations. Simultaneously, there were reports that Czar Alexander I of Russia was interested in staking out claims to the territory on the northwest coast of Oregon country. By authority of the maintenance of a trading

Culver Pictures

After the Russians established Fort Ross, a trading station in northern California, Czar Alexander I issued a decree claiming territory on the coast of Oregon. The Monroe Doctrine precluded such claims in the Western hemisphere.

station at Fort Ross in Bodega Bay, near San Francisco, the czar issued a decree claiming exclusive trading rights to the area north of the fifty-first parallel. In response, the president included in his State of the Union address to Congress on December 2, 1823, a sweeping statement that denounced colonization in the western hemisphere and proclaimed the independence of the American nations from interference by the European powers.[49]

The Monroe Doctrine provided an important example, at a time of general executive weakness, that the president was paramount in the formulation of foreign policy. Indeed, it placed a greater burden on the presidency, for such a defiant expression of independence committed the United States to additional diplomatic and military responsibilities, most of which would inevitably fall upon the chief executive. For a time, this commitment had no important effect, but its potential to become a guiding influence on foreign policy was realized by the end of the nineteenth century.

The end of the Monroe presidency marked the end of a dynasty of sorts. James Monroe was the last member of the famous Virginia "triumvirate"—Jefferson, Madison, and Monroe—to serve as president. Each of these men played important roles in the formation and early history of the Republic; moreover, they were at the center of the founding of the Democratic-Republican opposition and its rise as a governing party. With the end of the Virginia dynasty, the Democratic-Republican party no longer had a leader of nationwide stature to hold the party together. Monroe was the last of the revolutionary presidents, the generation that had successfully prosecuted the War of Independence. With the passing of this generation, subsequent presidential candidates found it difficult to achieve consensus.

The problem of consensus was made more acute, ironically, by the extraordinary electoral success of the Democratic-Republican party. Creation of the role of party leader for the president during the Jeffersonian era made presidents largely dependent on the energy that could be derived from "a clear division between parties that could stir popular enthusiasm or provide vindication for a platform presented during the contest." The mobilization of popular support for a governing party presupposed a credible opponent. Yet during Monroe's first administration, the Federalist party disappeared as a national organization; in fact, Monroe was unopposed in his reelection of 1816. An "Era of Good Feelings" followed the second war with England, a term applied to the period between 1812 to 1820, when it became clear that Democratic-Republican dominance over the nation was unassailable.

With the Federalists vanquished, the 1824 presidential election became a contest of individuals rather than issues. Rival and sectional leaders, each supported by his own personal organization and following, contested for the presidency in one of the most bitter and fragmented elections ever staged. The results of this contest caused a storm of controversy and led to a revolt against the party procedures that had prevailed for a quarter of a century. Moreover, John Quincy Adams, the eventual winner of the 1824 election, inherited an impossible governing situation, one that ended the Democratic-Republican era amidst bitter conflicts that endured for a generation.

In 1824, for the second time in U.S. history, an election was determined not by the voters, but by the House of Representatives. Sen. Andrew Jackson of Tennessee, the hero of the battle of New Orleans, received the most electoral votes, 99, which was far short of the 131 necessary for a majority and election. Adams, who felt that as secretary of state he occupied the logical stepping stone to the presidency, came in second with 84 electoral votes. Monroe's secretary of the Treasury, William Crawford, was the choice of the Democratic-Republican caucus; but the party machinery had run down badly by 1824, and its support was no longer tantamount to nomination. Crawford finished third with 41 votes. The powerful Speaker of the House, Henry Clay of Kentucky, finished fourth with 37 votes.

According to the Twelfth Amendment, the House was to choose from the top three candidates, which removed Clay from consideration for the presidency. Still, he exercised considerable influence in the House. His use of that influence on Adams's behalf secured Adams's election, and the new president rewarded Clay with the position of secretary of state.

Not surprisingly, Jackson's supporters were furious, asserting that Clay's support was attained by Adams in a corrupt bargain that violated the will of the people. Although the charge of conspiracy against Adams and Clay was in all likelihood unfounded, the controversial election of 1824 ensured the demise of what had come to be called "King Caucus" and precipitated reform of party and election procedures that formed the basis of Jacksonian democracy.

The last, unhappy administration of the Jeffersonian era, that of Adams, was severely constrained by the general view that the incumbent was a "minority president." Nevertheless, this administration did not readily accept the difficult circumstances it faced. Adams was a statesman of considerable talent and accomplishment, and, not content to remain in the shadow of Congress, he undertook to renew the strength of the presidential office. In fact, he was the first president in U.S. history who attempted to lead Congress in an active program of governmental achievement.

In his first annual message, Adams recommended a broad program of internal improvements, a national university, an observatory, scientific exploration, and voyages of discovery. His three Democratic-Republican predecessors had strong reservations about the constitutional power of Congress to mandate such enterprises and to appropriate funds for them. Madison and Monroe followed Jefferson in believing that a constitutional amendment was necessary for such a program. But Adams boldly rejected this narrow interpretation of the Constitution as well as the deference of his predecessors to legislative primacy in most domestic affairs. In spite of the reservations of his cabinet members, who believed Adams's ambitious plans expressed in the State of the Union were impractical, Adams was determined to go ahead. Recounting the resistance of his cabinet to his program, Adams wrote in his diary, "Thus situated, the perilous experiment must be made. Let me make it with full deliberation, and be prepared for the consequences." [50]

Adams was the first president "to demonstrate the real scope of creative possibilities of the constitutional provision to 'recommend to their [Congress's] consideration measures as he shall judge necessary and expedient.' " [51] But Adams had no decisive mandate either from the country or from the electoral college. And, although a strong personality, his formal and stern manner was ill-suited to the tasks of building a political coalition. Finally, the legacy of the Jeffersonian presidency had not prepared the country for the sort of assertive executive leadership that Adams attempted. Thus, his proposals were largely ignored or ridiculed.

Adams influence, never very great, was effectively ended with the congressional elections of 1826. His political opponents, representing Jackson's opposition to the administration, won control of both the House and the Senate—the first time that the executive and legislative branches of government were controlled by different parties. The Democratic-Republican era of the presidency ended with Congress, not the president, at the center of government power.

The Jacksonian Presidency

The presidency of John Quincy Adams was characterized by one long and acrimonious campaign for reelection. As Adams struggled in Washington with a recalcitrant Congress, a well-organized opposition formed around Andrew Jackson, who was intent upon rectifying the "corrupt bargain" between Adams and Clay that had denied Jackson the presidency in 1824.

By the election of 1828, the confused situation of the previous presidential campaign, in which four candidates ran for office, had been replaced by a new party alignment. The Democratic-Republicans now were divided into two major factions. Adams and Clay, who stood for the more national aspirations of the "new" Republicans (or National Republicans, as they were sometimes called), led one group; and Andrew Jackson and John C. Calhoun, the vice president during Adams's administration, led the opposition, which dedicated itself to the "old" Democratic-Republican causes of states' rights and a strict interpretation of the national government's powers. By 1832, these factions developed into the Whig and Democratic parties, which dominated the U.S. political landscape until the eve of the Civil War.

The Jacksonian Democrats had the better of this competition. From 1828 until 1856, the electoral success of the Democrats was interrupted in only two presidential campaigns: the election of Whigs William Henry Harrison 1840 and Zachary Taylor in 1848. Jackson's victory in 1828 marked the culmination of a trend that began during the Jeffersonian era, whereby the emerging agrarian and frontier interests of the South and West triumphed over the commercial and financial interests of the East, which previously had controlled national politics. The purchases of Louisiana in 1803 and Florida in 1819 had added millions of acres to the territory of the United States and afforded greater influence to those who formerly had stood outside of the regular channels of political power.

Jackson, in fact, was the nation's first "outsider" to become president of the United States. Jackson's predecessors in office had undergone extensive apprenticeships in national politics and diplomacy. Jackson had less formal education than any of them; he had only limited experience in Congress and none in public administration. He was a self-made man, one who had risen from a small cabin in the pine woods of South Carolina to the majestic White House in Washington. A powerful symbol of his times, Jackson's principles and presence were to hold sway over the country for nearly three decades. This period in U.S. history deservedly is called the "Age of Jackson." [52]

Jacksonian Democracy

The most important aspect of this age was the desire for equality of opportunity, that is, a society in which no one had special privileges that worked to the disadvantage of others. Jackson followed Jefferson in believing that the elimination of special privilege in society presupposed a limited role for the national government. The rapid expansion of the country was accompanied by a dynamic society and economy that seemed to foster unlimited opportunity. Within the expansive environment of U.S. society, Jacksonians believed that the best approach to government was to keep power as much as possible in the less obtrusive state governments.

The philosophy of the Jacksonians resulted in a much more strident assault on national institutions and programs than the generally more flexible Jeffersonians undertook. Jackson forcefully withdrew the federal government from the field of internal improvements. Military power, especially the army, was kept at a minimum. Fiscal policy centered on a commitment to hold down expenditures. And the Bank of the United States, which Jeffersonians had learned to live with, was dismissed as an instrument of privilege. The Jackson administration dismantled the bank and placed its deposits in selected state banks.

Jackson's View of the Presidency

Yet the age of Jackson had its contradictory and compensating aspects when it came to the authority of the national government. The Jacksonians had a concept of the presidency as the "tribune" of the people, a view that invested the executive, in an age dominated by democratic aspiration, with tremendous influence. During the Jeffersonian era, the presidency began to develop a closer relationship to the people. But this development took place on the authority of political principles and attendant institutional arrangements that supported the supremacy of the legislature. Jackson's presidency marked an effort to establish a direct relationship between the executive and the people, thus challenging the status of Congress as the principal representative institution. The strengthened presidency, especially during Jackson's two terms, "gave voice in a new age to the rising spirit of democratic nationalism," one that sustained and strengthened the Union in the face of serious sectional conflict over the tariff and slavery.[53]

Jackson was a states' rights man, but during his presidency he personified and fought for the sovereignty of the nation, a conviction demonstrated in the nullification crisis. Seeking to compel the federal government to accede to its demands for a lower tariff, South Carolina's legislature summoned a convention on November 24, 1832, that declared the existing 1832 tariff law "null and void." Propounding the nullification doctrine proposed by John Calhoun, South Carolina claimed that any state had a right to declare a federal law null and void within its boundaries whenever it deemed such a law (like the tariff) unconstitutional.

In the face of this threat to the Union, Jackson issued a proclamation that vigorously rejected South Carolina's right to disobey a federal statute. The power to annul a law of the United States, assumed by one state, he argued, was "incompatible with the existence of the Union, contradicted expressly by the letter of the Constitution, unauthorized by its spirit, inconsistent with every principle on which it was founded, and destructive of the great object for which it was formed."[54] In 1861, Abraham Lincoln based his actions on the same reasoning.

In expressing this doctrine, Jackson rested the defense of the Union squarely upon the shoulders of the president. It was the people, acting through the state legislatures, who formed the Union, and the voice of the people, and not the states, was represented in the Executive branch. In defending the Union, then, Jackson asserted that he embodied the will of the people, thereby appealing to the concept that the president—and not the Congress or the states—was the direct representative of the American electorate. Jackson's concept of the presidency then "transcended the older categories of nationalism versus states' rights" and portrayed a new understanding of national sovereignty.[55]

The evolution of the view that the president was the direct representative of the people was grounded in the political developments associated with Jacksonian democracy. Jackson's election as president coincided with changes in election laws in the various states that ended the dominance of state legislatures over the choice of electors, making popular election the principal means of their selection. In the first three presidential elections, the electors were chosen chiefly by the state legislatures. By 1824 electors were chosen by popular vote in all but six states; and by 1832, in all states except South Carolina, which retained legislative selection until the Civil War. Consequently, Jackson was arguably the first popularly elected president of the United States, thus strengthening his conviction and that of his supporters that he held a mandate directly from the hands of the "sovereign" people.[56]

The perception of the president as the direct representative of the people was advanced also by the expansion of the electorate. Jacksonian democracy advocated the widest possible extension of suffrage, a commitment that accelerated the push to eliminate property qualifications for voting and established virtually universal white manhood suffrage by 1832.

This development brought into the electorate farmers, mechanics, laborers—those Jackson referred to as "the humble members of society"—who saw the executive office under "Old Hickory's" supervision as a rallying point. The reform of election laws rescued the presidency from the dominance of Congress that characterized presidential administrations from James Madison to John Quincy Adams. Indeed, with the collapse of the party caucus, which was, in effect, the congressional caucus, Jackson was the first president since Washington not to be chosen in an election involving the national legislature. He found himself in the position, therefore, to revitalize the independence of the president and to remake the office he held so that its powers were invested with a new scope and vitality.[57]

Party Conventions

The advent of the Jacksonian presidency was associated with important developments in the party system. The decline of King Caucus as a nominating device in presidential campaigns left a vacuum that was filled by the national convention. *(See "Development of Party Conventions," p. 164, in The Electoral Process chapter of Part II.)* The party convention did not exist when Jackson became president but was employed by the Democrats in 1832 and accepted by the Whigs in the campaign of 1836.

Delegates to the national convention were selected by party conventions in the states, which in turn were built on local urban and rural organizations of party members. These delegates did not simply speak for the people; but the development of an elaborate national party organization that reached far beyond the halls of Congress, and eventually penetrated every corner of the Union, enabled presidents to build an independent basis of political support. Backed by a far-reaching party organization, Jackson became the first president in U.S. history to appeal to the people over the heads of their representatives.[58]

Jackson's Struggle with Congress

The transformation of the presidency from a congressional to a popular institution did not take place without a tremendous struggle. The Whig party, although able to carry only two presidential elections between 1828 and 1856, was a powerful opposition.

Reflecting the ideas of Henry Clay and John Quincy Adams, the Whig party took a national approach to the nation's problems; that is, it advocated policies, known as the "American plan," that envisioned an active role for the federal government, including rechartering the Second Bank of the United States, the passage of a protective tariff, and the development of an internal improvements program. These policies contradicted the states' rights policies of the Democrats and conformed to a liberal construction of the Constitution, like Hamilton's interpretation. Yet the Whigs, formed as a party of opposition to Jackson, resisted the expansion of executive power and defended the legislature as the principal instrument of representative democracy. President Jackson and the Democratic party firmly controlled the House; but the Senate, led by such forceful Whig statesmen as Clay and Daniel Webster, was in a position to challenge Jackson's policies and pretensions to executive prerogative.

The Whigs did not control a majority of Senate seats but forged a coalition with southern Democrats, led by Calhoun, who resented Jackson's defense of the Union in the nullification crisis of 1832. Between 1832 and 1836, especially, this bipartisan Senate coalition consistently resisted Jackson's aggressive use of executive power.

New York Historical Society

Although President Jackson, left, and the Democratic party controlled the House, forceful Whig senators such as Henry Clay, right, and Daniel Webster, center, challenged Jackson's policies and use of executive prerogatives.

Veto of the Bank Bill

The conflict between the president and the Whigs came to a head in July 1832, when Jackson vetoed the bill to recharter the National Bank four years before the expiration of its charter. Jackson's veto of the bank bill and the defense of this action in his message to Congress of July 10, 1832, was, according to historian Robert Remini, "the most important veto ever issued by a president." [59]

Indeed, this action established a critical precedent that significantly strengthened the presidency. Federalist and Democratic-Republican presidents had agreed that the veto power should be used sparingly; it should be exercised, Jackson's predecessors argued, only when the legislation in question was unconstitutional.

In forty years under the Constitution only nine acts of Congress had been struck down by the chief executive, and only three of those dealt with what could be considered important issues. Yet Jackson believed, and so stated in his veto message, that a president could kill a bill for any reason if he felt it injured the nation or the people. He rested his veto of the bank bill on constitutional grounds, but he also legitimized his action, and other veto actions, on grounds of "expediency." For Jackson, that is, a veto was justified if the president had a policy disagreement with Congress. In demanding the right to be involved in the development of legislation, Jackson "essentially altered the relationship between the executive and legislative branches of government." [60]

Two other aspects of Jackson's famous veto message are worth recalling. First, it contained Jackson's view—one that Jefferson first articulated—that the president, as well as the Congress, possessed coordinate power with the courts to determine questions of constitutionality. President Jackson articulated such a view in maintaining that the national bank was an illegitimate exercise of congressional authority, a claim that his Whig opponents considered outrageous, given Chief Justice John Marshall's decision in *McCulloch v. Maryland* (1819) that it was not unconstitutional for Congress to charter a bank.[61]

Jackson insisted, however, that the executive was no more bound in such matters by judicial rulings than it was by acts of Congress. The Congress, the executive, and the court, he asserted, "must each for itself be guided by its opinion of the Constitution." [62] Thus, Jackson's veto message dramatically reopened the question, seemingly settled by *Marbury v. Madison,* of the appropriate authority to be allowed the federal courts.[63] His claim in support of the president and Congress, the popularly elected branches of government, to make constitutional determinations marked still another example of his interest in forging a stronger link between the people and their government.

Indeed, an additional notable feature of Jackson's war with Congress over the bank was the manner by which he laid the controversy before the American people. The last paragraph of the veto message, anticipating the president's impending campaign for reelection, indicated that the final decision rested with the American people. "If sustained by his fellow citizens," said Jackson (speaking of himself), he would be "grateful and happy."

Concerned about the political effects of the bank war, the Congress failed to override Jackson's veto. His overwhelming victory in the 1832 campaign, which largely was fought over the bank measure, convinced even his political opponents, as the weekly *Niles Register* reluctantly reported after the election, that the president "had cast himself upon the support of the people against the acts of both houses of Congress" and had been sustained. Never before in U.S. history had a chief executive gone to the people over the heads of their representatives, and Jackson's victory in this endeavor ratified his conviction that the president, and not Congress, was the immediate and direct representative of the American public.[64]

Aftermath of the Veto

The aftermath of the bank fight further extended the Jacksonian revolution. Regarding his reelection in 1832 as a vindication of his veto, Jackson decided to kill off the bank once and for all. He decided that the best method of ministering such a blow was to withdraw public funds from the bank three years before the expiration of the charter, placing them in selected state banks. But this action required the cooperation of the secretary of the Treasury.

Congress had refused Jackson's request to pass a measure authorizing the president to remove the bank's funds; the authority to do so remained with the head of the Treasury Department, who was so authorized in precise language that was included in the 1816 chartering of the second bank. When Jackson's then secretary of the Treasury, Louis McLane, opposed removal of deposits, he was transferred to the State Department and replaced by William J. Duane. Duane also resisted the president's efforts to kill the bank and was dismissed within four months of taking the oath of office. His replacement, Roger B. Taney, formerly the attorney general, finally gave Jackson the cooperation he was looking for but not without the Senate passing a resolution of censure that accused the president of assuming "authority and power not conferred by the Constitution and laws." [65]

The dismissal of Duane, the removal of public deposits from the national bank, and the Senate's censure of Jackson's action involved a stuggle over a fundamental constitutional question: Can the President of the United States, through his constitutionally implied powers of dismissal, dictate to an executive officer how he should exercise discretionary power vested exclusively in a department headed by Congress? This struggle, capping a longstanding battle between the president and the Congress over the control of executive administration, was decisively won by Jackson. Jackson's "Protest" to the Senate's resolution of censure became the commanding issue in succeeding elections to the Senate, enabling Jackson's Democratic allies to command majority support in the upper chamber of the legislature by 1837. Thus, before Jackson left office, he had the satisfaction of seeing the Resolution of Censure formally expunged on January 16, 1837. This vote signified a political triumph for Jackson that symbolically confirmed his broad interpretation of executive power over the activities of the executive department.

The Limits of the Jacksonian Presidency

According to the Whig opposition, the legacy of Jackson's presidency was the dangerous expansion of presidential prerogatives. The bank controversy demonstrated, they argued, that the chief executive now possessed powers that dwarfed the influence of the Congress as well as the judiciary, thus undermining the separation of powers.

It was during the bank controversy that anti-Jackson forces assumed the party name of "Whig." Historically, the term carried the connotation of opposition to executive prerogative, a meaning derived from the party in England that was opposed to the power of the king and attached to parliamentary—or legislative—superiority. The Whigs in the United States meant by their name to imply that the Jackson wing of the Democratic-Republican party—the Democrats—had abandoned Jeffersonian principles, supporting the coronation of an elected monarch, "King Andrew the First." [66]

The legacy of Jackson's two terms in office, however, were much more ambiguous than his political opponents implied. The extension of executive powers during his presidency did not simply expand the opportunities for unilateral executive action. This extension depended upon the emergence of the president as popular leader that was mediated in critical ways by party organization. For example, Jackson's "appeal to the people" in his war on the national bank was not truly direct; instead, the bank battles were fought within the framework of party.

The Party Press

These battles were carried on by the party press that emerged during the 1830s. In this respect, the close relationship Jackson had with party journalists such as Amos Kendall and Francis Blair added an important dimension to his presidency: these men provided the president with a newly acceptable tool of political influence by translating "White House decisions into forceful language and announce[ing] them with persuasive eloquence to the American people." [67] Blair's *Globe,* in fact, became the official organ of both the Jackson and the succeeding Van Buren administrations. As such, the paper enjoyed special access to official circles as well as financial support from perquisites and profits controlled by the government. Yet this "administration press" was also a party press, dedicated to a party program and organization.[68] Hence, a more assertive presidency was linked inextricably to the formation of a more aggressive and popular version of party politics.

Every president from Andrew Jackson to James Buchanan secured one important newspaper that was solidly devoted to his personal support as well as the program of his party. These newspapers were supported by the profits derived from government printing contracts routinely awarded to a favored party press.

Advent of Patronage

Jackson's presidency also initiated a system of rotation in government personnel practices, whereby the enhanced power of removal that was evident in the bank controversy was used to remove subordinate officers and employees for partisan reasons. Before the Jackson presidency, an ethos of forming a stable and neutral career service dominated personnel practices. Beginning in 1829, however, Jackson and every one of his successors until 1861 rejected this principle and deliberately removed or sanctioned the removal of hundreds, even thousands, of subordinates for partisan reasons. The commitment to forming a public sector insulated from the vagaries of public opinion and elections was thus displaced by a system whose credo was, as New York senator William L. Marcy put it, "to the victor belongs the spoils." [69]

In theory, the system of rotation expanded the powers of the president enormously. The chief executive was now

Library of Congress

In this 1832 cartoon, "King Andrew the First" is depicted as a tyrant trampling the Constitution, a ledger of the Court decisions, and the watchwords *Virtue, Liberty,* and *Independence.*

in a position, as Jackson's dismissal of Duane illustrated, to enforce conformity within the executive departments. In practice, however, the system of rotation was controlled by the party in a manner that circumscribed presidential influence on the conduct of government.

In particular, patronage greatly increased the power of *local* party organizations, which dominated the more decentralized partisan system that emerged with Jacksonian democracy. Local party leaders demanded influence over offices as recompense for returning majorities in congressional and presidential elections, a demand even powerful executives such as Jackson and James K. Polk were not inclined to reject. Moreover, after 1829, many federal officeholders, especially those who served in the widely scattered custom houses and postal offices, were progressively brought under the influence of the local party machine and subjected to various requirements as a condition of continuing their employment. These requirements included obligations to return part of their salaries to the party organization that sponsored the office held, to do party work at election time, and to "vote right." [70]

Thus, especially during the tenure of less dominant chief executives between 1829 and 1860, presidential influence over patronage was subordinate to the advantage of party, particularly in the conduct of the postal system, which became the focal point of partisan favors. Beginning with the Jackson administration, and continuing well into the twentieth century, it became common practice to appoint as postmaster general an individual who served as the principle agent of patronage, representing the interests of the party to the president.

Presidents who were insensitive to partisanship paid a severe price in loss of political support. James Buchanan, for example, was attacked by many influential Democratic party leaders when he removed many officeholders appointed by his predecessor Franklin Pierce, even though many of these individuals were loyal Democratic partisans.[71]

The powers of the presidency ushered in by the Jacksonian era were not only limited by the party system but by the doctrine of the Democratic party that was organized to advance Jacksonian principles. This doctrine, as evidenced by Jackson's veto of the bank bill, was dedicated to limiting the role of the national government. Jackson defended the principle of Union against the extreme states' rights claim of South Carolina in the nullification controversy; generally, however, he was a strong advocate of the rights of the state governments and opposed expanding the responsibilities of the national government and executive. Thus, as Alexis de Tocqueville wrote about the executive in the 1830s, "General Jackson's power is constantly increasing, but that of the president grows less. The federal government is strong in his hands; it will pass to his successor enfeebled." [72]

Martin Van Buren and the Panic of 1837

Jackson's successor, in fact, the able and shrewd Martin Van Buren, did assume office under the most difficult of circumstances. As a result, Van Buren became the first president to face a domestic crisis that shaped his entire presidency.

No sooner had he assumed office than the economy began a downward spiral, a decline that was at least in part the legacy of Jackson's assault on the national bank. The Panic of 1837, as the crisis was called, was caused in large measure by speculation. A boom in western land, manufacturing, transportation, banking, and several other business enterprises began in 1825 and brought about an overextension of credit.

By removing the deposits from the conservative Bank of the United States and placing them in selected—"pet"—state banks, the Jackson administration contributed to the liberal expansion of credit. Then, conscious of the problems posed by an overextended economy, Jackson issued a Treasury order, the so-called Specie Circular, in July 1836, requiring that hard currency be used in payment for all federal lands. This order aroused concern that Jackson and his successor would do all they could to contract the currency, causing banks to call in loans and consequently helping to bring on the panic.

By early 1837, American mercantile houses began to fall, and there were riots in New York over the high cost of flour. In short order, almost every bank in the country had suspended specie payments, and the state banking system that Jackson set up to replace the national bank collapsed, costing the Treasury some $9 million.

Van Buren was a more pragmatic statesman than his predecessor, but he was sufficiently wedded to Jacksonian principles to resist government-sponsored solutions to the economic crisis. He rejected any notion of reviving a national institution such as the Bank of the United States to regulate currency. Similarly, he rejected the view that the Treasury ought to provide a paper medium to facilitate domestic exchange. The Treasury was to attend to its own affairs and let business do the same.

Rejecting the "constant desire" of the Whigs "to enlarge the power of government," Van Buren's response to the panic was remarkably measured, given its severity. This response centered on a proposal to establish an independent treasury, which would hold government funds in federal vaults instead of depositing them in state banks. The proposed subtreasury, however, was to have limited power, leaving state banks free from federal regulations. Even this modest measure was not put into effect until

An 1840 woodcut sold by Huestis & Co.; Library of Congress

This 1840 campaign cartoon shows Jackson leading Van Buren to the White House for a second term. Van Buren, known as "Old Kinderhook" after his New York home, lost to the "hard cider and log cabin" candidate, William Henry Harrison. But his partisan rallying cry, "OK," entered the language as an expression of agreement or approval.

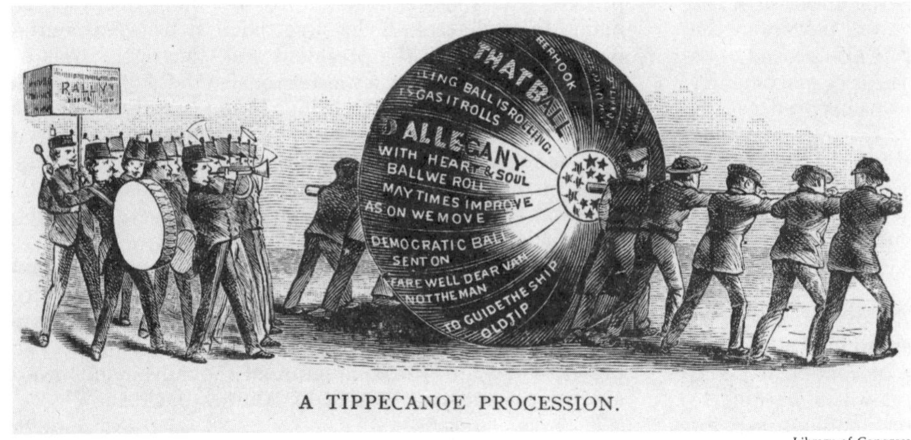

A TIPPECANOE PROCESSION.

Library of Congress

Supporting candidates William Henry Harrison, known for his victory over the Indians at the Battle of Tippecanoe, and John Tyler, Whig partisans rolled a huge paper ball from city to city, singing, "It is the ball a-rolling on for Tippecanoe and Tyler too." Thus the expression "Keep the ball rolling" came into the language.

1840, as it was resisted for most of Van Buren's tenure by a coalition of conservative Democrats and Whigs, most of whom favored a stronger role for the national government in the economy. Thus, the presidential election of 1840 was held in the midst of a depression, for which the Democratic party was held responsible.

The Jacksonian Presidency Sustained

The triumph of the Whig candidate William Henry Harrison in the election of 1840 posed a challenge not only to the domestic program of the Democrats but to the institutional achievements of the Jacksonians as well. The triumphant Whig party was united above all else by its opposition to the expansion of executive prerogatives that took place during Jackson's administration. Accordingly, its leaders, such as Henry Clay and Daniel Webster, saw the Panic of 1837 as an opportunity to assert the rights of Congress.

Clay was the most obvious candidate to head the Whig ticket in 1840. He was the architect of the program to oppose Jackson and had been the real founder of the Whig coalition. But instead the Whigs nominated General Harrison, the aged (he was sixty-seven years old at the time of his election) hero of the Battle of Tippecanoe, believing him to be more electable than Clay. It might have been some consolation to Clay and his allies that the old general had put himself on record in favor of the leading Whig principles. Harrison had in 1838 proclaimed support for the Whig assault on the executive, thus dedicating himself to a program that would: (1) confine the executive's service to one term; (2) establish the Treasury free from the president's control; and (3) strictly limit the veto power, confining its exercise principally to legislation deemed unconstitutional.[73] Although the 1840 campaign was not distinguished by its attention to serious discussion of issues, Harrison continued his attack on the power of the presidency, pledging to step down after one term.

Thus there was reason to believe that the Whig victory in 1840 would undo Jackson's reconstruction of the presidency. Indeed, Harrison's inaugural address proclaimed it "preposterous" to suppose that the president could "better understand the wants and wishes of the people than their representatives." This speech, which Webster and Clay helped write, raised suspicion among Jacksonians that designing Whig leaders may have practically persuaded the aged Harrison to accept the status of figurehead, delegating the accrued powers of the executive to the Congress.[74]

Yet, the major characteristics of the Jacksonian presidency were destined to prevail in the face of the Whig challenge. The importance of the presidency was so firmly established in the popular mind by 1840 that the executive was unlikely to be restored to the weak position to which it was reduced during the latter stages of the Jeffersonian period.

The Whigs, in fact, unwittingly contributed to the permanent transformation of the presidency in the way they conducted the 1840 campaign. Jackson's political enemies had looked with disfavor upon the popular campaign tactics employed by the Democratic party during the three previous presidential campaigns. But having been the victims of the effective Democratic efforts on behalf of Jackson and Van Buren, the Whigs did everything in their power to "go to the people" in 1840. They bought up newspapers for party propaganda, held great mass rallies, used popular party spokesmen for speech-making tours, and concentrated on mobilizing the largest possible number of voters.

As a result, the 1840 campaign reinforced the Jacksonian concept of the president as popular leader. This contest stimulated tremendous interest and enthusiasm in the country, resulting in a substantial increase in turnout. The 2.4 million voters who cast their ballots constituted 80.2 percent of the eligible voters in the country, a percentage that has been surpassed only twice (in 1860 and 1876) in presidential elections since that time. Hence, by accepting and expanding on the successful campaign techniques of the Democrats, the Whigs ratified the Jacksonian concept of popular leadership. The Whig antiexecutive doctrine notwithstanding, thereafter it was not possible for the presidency to be restored to its pre-1828 status, however inept the incumbent of the office might be.[75]

John Tyler and the Problem of Presidential Succession

This "ratification" of the Jacksonian presidency became more pronounced when Harrison died after only a month in office. John Tyler thus became the first vice president in U.S. history to become president by succession. Not only did Tyler help to resolve the question of the right of a vice president to assume the full powers of the executive office in such a situation, but he also proved to be a less enthusiastic proponent of Whig theories, particularly as they applied to the presidency, than was his predecessor. Whig leaders were soon disappointed to discover that they had in Tyler no willing ally in dismantling the Jacksonian presidency.

Leaving absolutely no doubt about his intention to be president in his own right, Tyler went before "the people," assembled in the capital on April 9, 1841, to give an inaugural address after the manner of an elected president. Tyler's taking this opportunity to provide an "exposition of the principles" that would govern *his* administration, was a signal to the country that he would not be content to stand in the shadow of Harrison. Similarly, it was a warning to Whigs that Tyler did not intend to be a compliant servant to party leaders such as Clay and Webster.

In fact, Tyler represented a faction of the Whig party that dissented from many of the views preached by its nationalist leaders. As became a frequent practice in U.S. party politics, his nomination was made in an effort to balance the Whig ticket; Tyler's selection had been a gesture of compromise from the National Republican Whigs to the southern states' rights members of the party. Yet this gesture was made with the view that Tyler was safely embalmed in the virtually powerless office of the vice presidency where his antinationalist ideas, decidedly a minority in Whig circles, would not cause trouble. This plan backfired, however, when Tyler decisively seized the reins of the presidency after Harrison's death and proceeded to exercise the powers of the Jacksonian presidency to thwart Whig plans to put in place Clay's "American plan." [76]

As a result of Tyler's opposition to much of the Whig domestic program, he used the veto power more than any of his predecessors except Jackson. He shared with other Whigs opposition to Jackson's use of the removal power, especially in regard to Jackson's efforts to control the activities of the Treasury Department. Yet, unlike the Whig party leaders, he believed the creation of a national bank was unconstitutional, and he vetoed two successive bills Congress sent him that resembled the old bank legislation that Jackson had killed. Immediately after the second veto a cabinet crisis ensued in which all cabinet members except Secretary of State Daniel Webster resigned. Had Webster not resisted pressure from Senator Clay to join this "conspiracy," which included plans to prevent Tyler from reconstructing his cabinet, Tyler very likely would have been forced to resign.

The battles over restoring the national bank were only the beginning of the struggle between Tyler and his party. His veto of a tariff measure a year later provoked the first attempt in U.S. history to impeach a president of the United States. The fact that there was a movement to impeach Tyler simply for exercising the veto power demonstrated the Whigs' passionate commitment to curtailing the powers of the executive and their frustration at failing to implement their plans even after having won a presidential election. The assertive exercise of the veto power was irreconcilable with the Whig theory of executive subordination to Congress; this along with political considerations led Clay to propose a constitutional amendment whereby Congress could overcome a veto by a mere majority.

In his veto of the tariff bill, Tyler defended his action on *policy,* rather than *constitutional* grounds, thus claiming a right for the president to participate in the legislative process that was very similar to the claim Jackson had made. Like Jackson, Tyler asserted that where a conflict developed between the president and Congress, it was for the nation to decide who was responsive to the popular will. With the overthrow of the Whigs in the congressional election of 1842, Tyler believed that his defense of the executive had been thoroughly vindicated. Moreover, nothing came of the movement to impeach the president, and the proposal for a constitutional amendment to curb the veto power elicited only public indifference.

Thus, although he lost the support of his party and therefore any chance to be reelected in 1844, Tyler prevented a potentially damaging setback in the evolution of the presidential office. As one scholar wrote, Tyler "prepared the way for the completion of the movement toward executive leadership started by Andrew Jackson." [77]

The Presidency of James K. Polk

Few would have guessed as John Tyler's term came to an end that his Democratic successor, James K. Polk, would lead a successful administration. Yet if Tyler saved the presidency from a debilitating setback, Polk moved it forward, successfully assuming responsibilities for the office that either were resisted by or denied to his predecessors.

The achievements of the Polk administration did not come easily. He faced militant Whig minorities in both houses of Congress, and he was elected as the head of a Democratic party that had begun to reveal the first serious signs of breaking apart as a result of the slavery issue. The conflict over slavery, in fact, especially its role in the expanding United States territory, was the issue that led to Polk's surprising election to the presidency.

Winning the Nomination

It was widely expected that Martin Van Buren would receive the 1844 Democratic nomination, but then the issue of Texas, and its annexation to the United States, intervened. Just before the nominating conventions of the Whigs and the Democrats, Calhoun, Tyler's secretary of state, concluded a treaty with the Republic of Texas for its annexation. As a result, the two principal contestants for president, Van Buren and Clay, the leading Whig contender, were forced to announce their views on annexation, an issue that aroused serious disagreements over the desirability of expanding the cotton-growing and slave-holding territory of the United States.

Clay's opposition to annexation caused little controversy, but when Van Buren took the same position, a firestorm erupted in the Democratic party. The Democrats, and their hero, Andrew Jackson, had long supported territorial expansion, an issue sacred to the emerging frontier interests in the South and the West. Moreover, the Democrats, in order to defeat the Whigs, depended upon strong support in the South, where states' rights advocates looked to areas such as Texas as a base for expanding slavery. This dependence upon southern support encouraged most Democratic leaders to support expansionist policies, regardless of slavery. Yet the pragmatic politician Van Buren chose this moment to follow what he called "the path of duty" and resist the extension of slavery, an act that cost him his chance to return to the White House. With Van Buren's candidacy seriously compromised, Polk emerged at the deadlocked Democratic convention as a compromise choice between North and South, thus becoming the first "dark-horse" candidate in the history of U.S. presidential elections.[78]

Reasserting Presidential Power

By a combination of shrewd political maneuvering and forceful statesmanship, Polk was able to overcome successfully the centrifugal forces that were beginning to dominate U.S. politics during the late 1840s. After winning the Democratic nomination, he stole one of the Whigs' main issues by disclaiming any intention of seeking a second term. Yet during his four years in office, Polk asserted vigorously and effectively executive functions that reinforced, even expanded, the Jacksonian concept of presidential power.

Presidents before Polk, including Andrew Jackson, had failed to achieve a day-to-day, regularized supervision over the executive departments. Important precedents were set before 1844 that established the president's superiority over his domain; and in dramatic fashion Jackson, with his dismissal of Secretary of the Treasury William Duane, asserted his control over the conduct of administrative activities. It fell to Polk, however, to establish a tradition for the president to assume a routine and consistent influence over the major departments of the executive branch.

This form of executive influence was particularly absent in the president's relations with the Treasury Department. Before Polk's administration it had been firmly established that the president had no responsibility over the departmental budgetary estimates that were submitted to Congress. In the Treasury Act of 1789 Congress had made it the duty of the secretary of the Treasury, not the president, to prepare and report estimates of expenditures to the legislature.

George Washington's Treasury secretary, Alexander Hamilton, set the precedent of not even consulting the president, an arrangement that generally prevailed up through the administration of John Tyler. The initiative for budgetary policy occasionally was with the secretary of the Treasury, as was true of Hamilton and Albert Gallatin, who served the Jefferson and Madison administrations. Usually, however, the only function of the Treasury was to gather the various estimates together and submit them to Congress under one cover. In 1839, for example, Van Buren's secretary of the Treasury, Levi Woodbury, denied any responsibility for a composite budget or for a review of budget items submitted to him by other departments.[79]

One of Polk's major achievements was to begin to coordinate the formulation of budgetary policy; for the first time in the history of the presidency there was an executive budget. Not only did Polk review the budget requests, he insisted that the department heads revise their estimates downward. Polk faced the need for tight fiscal control after the Mexican War began in 1846, especially since he was operating under the reduced tariff rates of the Walker Tariff, which he considered one of the major accomplishments of his administration.

Like his fellow Tennessean Andrew Jackson, Polk displayed a strong commitment to limiting government expenditures and a hatred of public debt. Intent upon establishing a record of sound fiscal economy for his administration and determined to assert aggressively the prerogatives of the chief executive, Polk functioned as, in twentieth-century terms, the director of the budget. *(See "The Budgeting Power," p. 415, in the Chief Executive chapter and Chief Economic Manager chapter, both in Part III.)* That Polk was successful in his efforts to control the budget was demonstrated by the tight rein he imposed on fiscal matters after the end of the Mexican War, directing his reluctant secretary of war, William Marcy, to force his bureau chiefs to accept a return to the prewar level of expenditures.

The precedents Polk established in fiscal policy were not followed by any of his successors until 1861. But his actions deliberately established the Jacksonian concept of the presidency more firmly in the U.S. constitutional system. By effectively reinforcing this concept of the presidency, Polk gave an example of the functioning of the new type of chief executive that had emerged after 1828, thereby institutionalizing many of its characteristics. He succeeded, wrote historian George Bancroft, who served as Polk's secretary of the navy, "because he insisted on being its [his administration's] center and in overruling and guiding all his secretaries to act as to produce unity and harmony." [80]

Perhaps the most important contribution of the Polk presidency in this respect was the forceful manner by which he assumed the role of commander in chief during the Mexican War, which broke out in 1846 and was not settled until 1848. According to the administrative historian Leonard White, "Polk gave the country its first demonstration of the *administrative* capacities of the presidency as a war agency." [81] That is, he proved for the first time that a president could run a war.

Polk was only the second U.S. president to wield power as commander in chief in wartime, and James Madison, who during the War of 1812 became the first to assume this role, had done little to reveal the potential of this grant of constitutional authority. Polk did not push the power of commander in chief to its outer limits; this task was accomplished by Abraham Lincoln during the Civil War. He did establish the precedent, however, that a president without previous military experience could control and dominate the military commanders. During the war, in fact, Polk insisted on being the controlling and decisive authority in all military matters.

Polk's significant contribution to the presidential role as commander in chief was not without partisan motivation and serious blunders. Polk was a loyal Democrat and thus was disconcerted that the war was making a hero of Gen. Zachary Taylor, who was a Whig and potentially a formidable opponent for the Democrats in 1848. He thus, in a mean and petty partisan action, refused to sign an order requiring the troops to fire a salute in honor of Taylor's victory in Buena Vista.

The president's relations with the army's top commander, Gen. Winfield Scott, also a Whig, were similarly governed by a partisan outlook. Polk attempted, for example, to create a post of lieutenant general for Democratic senator Thomas Hart Benton, so that the senator could supersede General Scott as the commanding officer in the field. Since Benton's limited military experience was greatly inferior to his political importance, this scheme did Polk little credit, and the Senate failed to support the president in this action, albeit by only one vote.[82]

Polk's problems with his two top military commanders reflected the close relationship between the advent of the Jacksonian presidency and the institutionalization of the party system. The conduct of the Mexican War confirmed that partisan practices, which had become a more central part of presidential politics during the 1830s and 1840s, were not to be driven from the field by union to win a war with a foreign power.

The intrusion of partisan practices on the Mexican War notwithstanding, President Polk's command of the war was, on the whole, very able. The general strategy he personally devised and commanded realized a decisive victory by 1848, resulting in the acquisition of New Mexico and California. Thus Polk obtained the major objective of the war and became, except for Jefferson, the president who brought the most territory under the domain of the United States. By asserting and, in the final analysis, demonstrating that the president as commander in chief could direct the overall strategy of a large-scale military operation, Polk effectively asserted the principle of presidential responsibility over the military operations of the United States.[83]

Slavery and the Twilight of the Jacksonian Presidency

The presidency of James Polk was the last of the Jacksonian era that was not consumed by the slavery question. The annexation of Texas and the Mexican War greatly expanded the southwest territory of the United States, making the question of the status of slavery in this area an explosive one. The slavery issue began to split apart the Democratic party in 1844, a development that was avoided by the compromise choice of Polk. But the spoils of the Mexican War made a similar rapprochement impossible in 1848; and Martin Van Buren, the organizational genius who did so much to bring the Democratic coalition together, now split from his party to run as the third party Free Soil candidate.

Although Van Buren managed to win only 10 percent of the vote, his candidacy drew support away from the Democratic candidate Lewis Cass, thereby benefiting the Whig candidate Zachary Taylor. In all likelihood, the Van Buren candidacy did not determine the outcome of the 1848 election—Taylor, the hero of the Mexican War, probably would have been the winner in any case. But the Free Soil party drew enough votes to affect the outcome in many states, and it gained the support of many prominent statesmen. Accordingly, Van Buren's campaign in 1848 made it difficult for the Democrats and the Whigs to ignore the slavery issue any longer, foreshadowing the collapse of the party system that dominated the Jacksonian era and the emergence of a new governing coalition.

The Presidency of Zachary Taylor

Because of its strong base in the South, the Democratic party would survive the slavery controversy and Civil War, although in a greatly weakened state. But the election of Taylor in 1848 was to be the last major political success of the Whig party, which collapsed soon thereafter. The Whigs stood for national unity, a concept that was rendered irrelevant by the emerging slavery controversy. Moreover, the Whig opposition to executive power was shown decisively to be unworkable by the last Whig to be elected to the executive office. Taylor's inaugural address contained the sort of self-denying declaration regarding executive power that suggested support for Whig principles. But Taylor's brief administration (he died in 1850) was hardly true to his promise of self-denial.

The chief significance of Taylor's presidency was his consistent and unyielding opposition to the Compromise of 1850, legislation that achieved a temporary peace on the slavery issue. Taylor's opposition to the compromise, which put no restrictions on slavery in territories acquired from Mexico and strengthened the national fugitive slave law, angered southerners and threatened a major crisis. Yet the president stood firm in the face of the threat of disunion; he told southern congressional leaders that he would take the field in person and hang those taken in rebellion "with as little mercy as he had hanged deserters and spies in Mexico." Since no president after Jackson had played a "hands off" role with respect to Congress, Taylor found that he could not return to the self-effacing precedents of Madison and Monroe. The slavery controversy and Jackson's legacy had made this impossible by 1849.

The Presidency of Millard Fillmore

Taylor died before the crisis created by the 1850 debate over slavery matured. His successor, Vice President Millard Fillmore of New York, repeated Whig assurances in favor of restraint over executive power yet proved no more willing to leave critical domestic matters to Congress than was Taylor. But Fillmore was as determined to see the Compromise of 1850 passed as his predecessor was committed to preventing its enactment. Fillmore's accession to the presidency then affected an about-face in the attitude of the executive toward this critical legislation, and his support played an important part in getting the slavery compromise through the Congress. For example, one member of the House reported that there were between twenty and thirty representatives who before Taylor's death adamantly opposed the provisions of the compromise legislation that would allow for an expansion of slavery into the territories acquired in the Mexican War but who did a dramatic turnabout in the face of Fillmore's support of the slavery compromise.[84]

Having seen this controversial legislation through, the new president detèrmined to enforce the new and stringent Fugitive Slave Act vigorously. The passage of this act resulted in a new form of nullification, this time centering on the North, as Massachusetts refused to cooperate in the prosecution of its citizens who violated the Act. Fillmore committed his administration to executing this law, admitting "no right of nullification North or South," although his determination to defend the Union never really yielded a reliable means of securing compliance in those areas of the country where there were efforts to obstruct the seizure and removal of fugitive slaves.[85]

The Presidency of Franklin Pierce

The presidency of Millard Fillmore demonstrated that the Jacksonian era had irrevocably transformed the presidency, yet this strengthened executive was no match for the crisis engendered by the slavery question. The last two presidents of this era, Franklin Pierce and James Buchanan, were irresolute northern Democratic leaders who sought vainly to hold the northern and southern factions of their party together. They attempted to do so by seeking to diffuse, rather than come to terms with, the slavery question, and it was too late for such a strategy to work. The polarization of the nation over slavery was only aggravated by the efforts of Pierce and Buchanan to dismiss the issue.

The passage of the Kansas-Nebraska Act in 1854 was

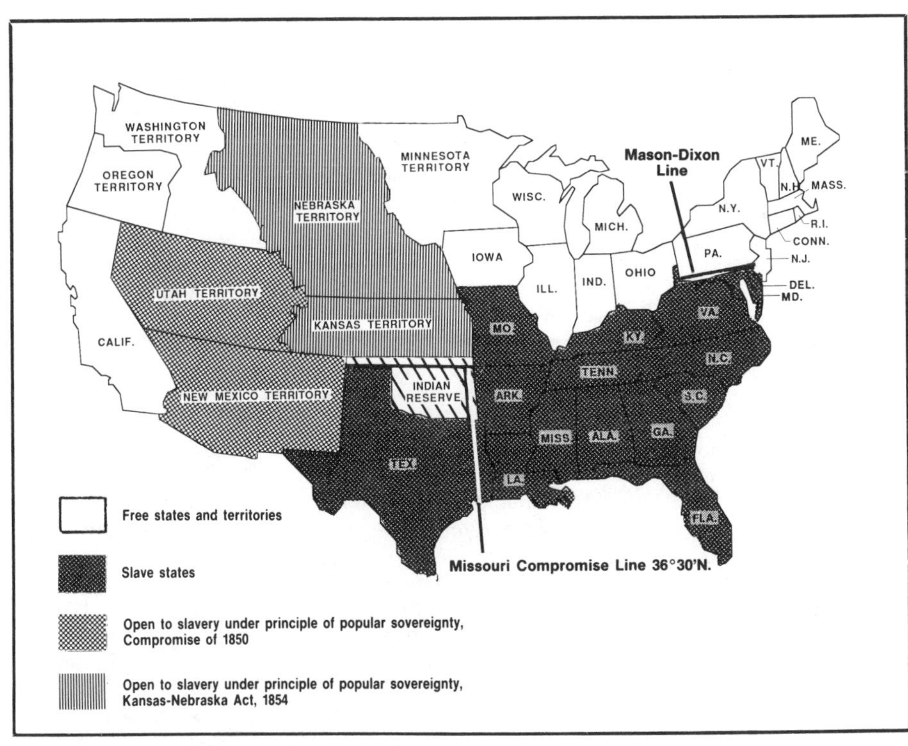

The Kansas-Nebraska Act, 1854

the most telling failure of Pierce's attempt to allay sectional conflict. This legislation, the brainchild of influential Illinois senator Stephen Douglas, was an effort to bury the slavery question by resting the determination of slavery's status in a new territory on the principle of "popular sovereignty." According to this principle, the people of the new territory would decide whether or not they would have slavery as soon as they obtained a territorial legislature. The Kansas-Nebraska Act would apply "popular sovereignty" in organizing the Great Plains territory, encompassing Kansas and Nebraska, thereby repealing a central ingredient of the 1820 Missouri Compromise that prohibited slavery north of Missouri's southern boundary, latitude 36° 30′. The debate over this bill dragged on for three months, and Pierce made every effort to employ the power of his office, including patronage, to ensure its passage. Party discipline prevailed.

On May 25, 1854, the Kansas-Nebraska bill passed the Senate by a comfortable margin and was signed into law by President Pierce. Within six months, however, it became apparent that the repeal of the Missouri Compromise had not quelled the slavery controversy but had greatly aggravated it. Hence, Pierce's forceful leadership of the Democratic party signaled its demise as a governing institution. His effective support of the Kansas-Nebraska legislation and the furious provocation elicited by its enactment prompted presidential scholar Wilfred E. Binkley to declare that "even the ineptitude of the President revealed the enormous significance of the presidency." [86]

A new political alignment emerged in the election of 1856. The collapse of the Whigs after 1852 and the northern crusade against slavery in Kansas (that Nebraska would become a free territory was never in doubt) led to the emergence of a new party dedicated to saving the West from slavery. Offering a platform that stood squarely against any further expansion of slavery, the newly formed Republican party nominated John C. Fremont for president in 1856. The Republicans made a good showing, but they received no support in the South and were not yet sufficiently organized in the North to overcome this handicap. Winning his home state of Pennsylvania, as well as Indiana, New Jersey, California, Illinois, and all 112 of the southern electoral votes, the Democratic candidate, James Buchanan, was elected president. Thus, the Jacksonian party and the Union were given another chance.

The Presidency of James Buchanan

Buchanan was just as anxious as Pierce to avoid the slavery controversy, but he was determined to avoid the damaging consequences that Pierce suffered from supporting and leading the fight for ameliorative legislation. In his inaugural address, Buchanan identified himself with an as yet unannounced Supreme Court decision, arguing that the resolution of the slavery question in the territories rightfully belonged to the federal judiciary. Referring to the pending suit by a sixty-two-year-old slave, Dred Scott, who claimed that residence in free territories had made him a free man, Buchanan pledged that he would "in common with all good citizens . . . cheerfully submit" to the decision of the Supreme Court.[87]

Such a pledge, Binkley notes, "was a strange abdication of executive claims by a member of the party of Jackson who . . . had emphatically denied the right of the judiciary thus to determine public policies through the medium of court opinions." [88] But, in fact, Buchanan's announced deference to the Supreme Court was disingenuous, for he had corresponded with Justice James Grier, a critical swing vote on the Court, pressuring him to resolve the issue by joining a majority of the Court in denying either the Congress or a territorial legislature the right to prohibit slavery.[89] Buchanan's pretended innocence as to the nature of the forthcoming Supreme Court verdict and his improper communication with Justice Grier reflected a last, desperate attempt by a Jacksonian president to preserve the Union while seeking to avoid addressing the slavery question.

Buchanan's attempt to settle the agitation over slavery by forming a surreptitious alliance with the Court failed miserably. The Court's decision, *Dred Scott v. Sanford*, opened the entire West to slavery, regardless of what the opinion of the popular majority in the territories might be.[90] This aggressive foray of the Supreme Court into the realm of policy, albeit one that was welcomed by President Buchanan, not only badly damaged the prestige of the Court but also resulted in a provocation of sectional strife that catapulted an obscure Illinois Republican, Abraham Lincoln, to the candidacy for the Senate in 1858 and to the presidency in the election of 1860.

The secession of South Carolina followed the election of Lincoln, who was the first president not satisfactory to the supporters of slavery. In effect, the reaction of the southern states to Lincoln's election was dramatic confirmation of the transformation of the presidency during the Jacksonian era. While a few southern statesmen counseled against secession, arguing that Lincoln's power would be limited, such advice meant nothing to people who had witnessed an important expansion of executive power since 1829. To be sure, the executive's authority was exaggerated in the popular mind. Yet the myth that the executive was an all-important organ of the national government was symptomatic of important precedents established during the previous four decades that had, in effect, made the office of the chief executive one of power and influence. The formal constitutional authority of the president was not changed by the Jacksonian Democrats, but they were responsible for giving vigor and power to an office destined for national leadership.

The Presidency of Abraham Lincoln

Abraham Lincoln made the last important contribution to the theory and institutions of the presidency during the nineteenth century. In the role of commander in chief, especially, the administration of Lincoln established important precedents that demonstrated the great potential of the executive to assume extraordinary powers during a national emergency. This record as president has led many historians to assess Lincoln not only as a forceful leader who demonstrated the vast powers inherent in the presidency, but as a dictator, although in many accounts a benevolent dictator.[91]

Lincoln, certainly, did not see his presidency this way. He offered a defense of his actions on the basis of a conception of the Constitution and executive power that, while respectful of procedural regularity and formal legality, was concerned above all with the need to uphold the principles that were the foundation of the American constitutional order. Thus, Lincoln's presidency not only marked a critical moment in U.S. political history but also raised anew, under conditions of unprecedented urgency, questions about the appropriate place of executive power.

It is remarkable that Lincoln so forcefully extended the boundaries of executive power. As a Whig member of Congress, he had criticized Polk's assertive leadership during the Mexican War, upholding the view that the Constitution gave the "war-making power to Congress," a view grounded in Lincoln's embrace of the Whig tenet that "the will of the people should produce its own result without executive influence." [92] Lincoln emerged as an impressive spokesman for Republican principles during the 1850s in a way that suggested a determination to deal forcefully with the slavery question and the threat of disunion. Yet he gave no indication during the 1860 campaign that he would boldly and deliberately assert the prerogatives of the executive.

The 1860 Election

Lincoln's audacious assertion of executive power was all the more remarkable in that this was the work of a "minority" president. The election of 1860 was a fragmented contest among four candidates, the result of the old Whig and Democratic coalitions being supplanted by a fierce brand of sectional politics. The northern vote was split between Lincoln and Stephen Douglas, who had the support of northern Democrats. The southern electorate divided between John C. Breckinridge of Kentucky, the standard-bearer of southern Democrats, and John Bell of Tennessee, who was nominated by the Constitutional Union party, formed from the remaining supporters of the Whig party who resided south of the Mason-Dixon line.

This fragmented contest yielded a decisive electoral college victory for Lincoln, who won every northern state but New Jersey. Yet Lincoln received only about 40 percent of the popular vote, and he commanded a plurality of these votes only because of the disarray that afflicted the opposition. He received 1.9 million votes to 1.4 million for Douglas, the runner-up; but if Douglas had received the votes cast for southern Democrats, he would have had a considerable majority over Lincoln. Lincoln managed to become president because the Republican party was more united than the Democrats, but he assumed office without winning decisive popular support, and his victory was greeted throughout the South with ominous threats of secession. "Well boys," he told newsmen the day after his election, "your troubles are over now, mine have just begun." [93]

Lincoln, Slavery, and Secession

In the face of such dire political circumstances, Lincoln's inaugural address of March 4, 1861, sought to reassure southerners that his policy toward them was one of forbearance, not coercion. Southerners seemed afraid that he threatened their property, their peace, and their personal security; yet, Lincoln said, there had never been any "reasonable cause for such apprehension." [94] Although Lincoln had spoken eloquently about the evils of slavery, he believed Congress had no enumerated powers to eliminate the institution of slavery in the states. Thus, Lincoln renounced any "purpose, directly or indirectly, to interfere with the institution of slavery in the states where it exists." [95]

The "only substantial dispute" that faced the country, therefore, centered on the extension of slavery, Lincoln asserted. "One section of the country believes slavery is *right* and ought to be extended," he pointed out, "while the other believes it is *wrong* and ought not to be extended." [96] This moral dispute was not, Lincoln maintainted, a matter that could be settled by "legal right," as the Supreme Court had claimed in the *Dred Scott* decision, which ruled that Congress could not prohibit slavery from existing in the territories.

Lincoln's irresolute predecessor, James Buchanan, had shifted the burden of resolving the slavery controversy to the judiciary, hoping in this way to diffuse the issue. But Lincoln denied that the policy of the government upon vital questions could be "irrevocably fixed by decision of the Supreme Court." He differed from the view of Jefferson and Jackson that each branch of government could follow its own interpretation of the Constitution; yet he claimed that the Court's intrusion into matters of policy that were not explicitly attended to by the written law could not be accepted as settled doctrine, for then "the people will have ceased to be their own rulers, having to that extent practically resigned their government into the hands of an eminent tribunal." [97] Thus, Lincoln argued, the question of slavery in the territories had to be determined by the elected representatives, for "a majority held in restraint by constitutional checks and limitations, and always changing easily with deliberate changes of popular opinions and sentiments, is the only true sovereign of a free people." [98]

As one scholar has aptly put it, Lincoln's first inaugural address "held up the iron fist, despite a velvet glove of measured reassurances." [99] He insisted that rebellion—the secession of the slave-holding states—was not an acceptable means of thwarting the principles and programs of the Republican party.

On December 20, 1860, South Carolina had become the first state to take itself out of the Union. Echoing its Ordinance of Nullification, which was issued in 1832 during the tariff controversy, South Carolina asserted that secession was constitutional, declaring itself restored to a "separate and independent place among nations." By the time of Lincoln's inauguration, six other states from the Deep South had also seceded. Lincoln, following Jackson's example, used the occasion of his inaugural address to pronounce the secessionist movement as treasonous: "I hold that in contemplation of universal law and of the Constitution the Union of these states is perpetual. . . , that no state upon its own mere notion can lawfully get out of the Union." [100] Thereupon, the newly installed president vowed to enforce federal laws in all the states, just as the Constitution enjoined him to do, and to defend and maintain the Union.

Lincoln's appeal for a peaceful resolution of the slavery controversy was quickly rejected by southern leaders. On March 5, the day after Lincoln's inauguration, rebel batteries in South Carolina surrounded Fort Sumter, outside Charleston, thus making inevitable the outbreak of hostilities. Once the southern states abandoned the Union, Lincoln believed his oath to the Constitution allowed for extraordinary measures—including emancipation of the slaves—if such measures were required to save the nation. As he wrote to a Kentuckian, A. G. Hodges, in April 1864, it was senseless to observe legal niceties while the end of the law itself—the preservation of the Union—was threatened:

> Was it possible to lose the nation and yet preserve the Constitution? By general law, life and limb must be protected, yet often a limb must be amputated to save a life; but a life is never wisely given to save a limb. I felt that measures otherwise unconstitutional might become lawful by becoming indispensable to the preservation of the nation.[101]

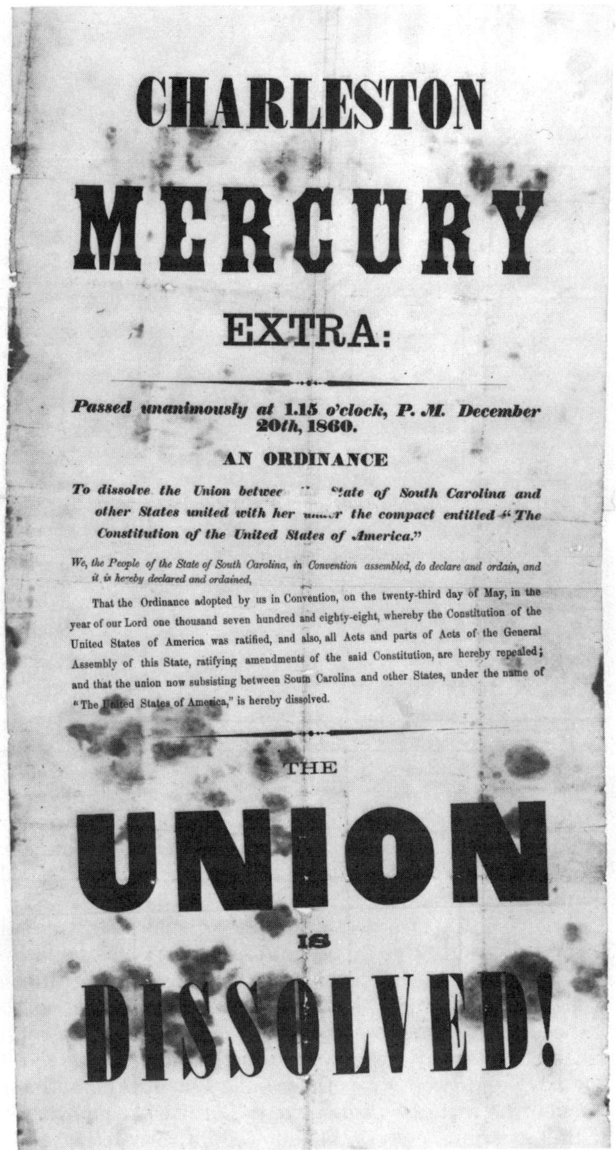

CHARLESTON

MERCURY

EXTRA:

Passed unanimously at 1.15 o'clock, P. M. December 20th, 1860.

AN ORDINANCE

To dissolve the Union betwee [illegible] State of South Carolina and other States united with her [illegible] the compact entitled "The Constitution of the United States of America."

We, the People of the State of South Carolina, in Convention assembled, do declare and ordain, and it is hereby declared and ordained,

That the Ordinance adopted by us in Convention, on the twenty-third day of May, in the year of our Lord one thousand seven hundred and eighty-eight, whereby the Constitution of the United States of America was ratified, and also, all Acts and parts of Acts of the General Assembly of this State, ratifying amendments of the said Constitution, are hereby repealed; and that the union now subsisting between South Carolina and other States, under the name of "The United States of America," is hereby dissolved.

THE

UNION

IS

DISSOLVED!

Library of Congress

On December 20, 1860, South Carolina became the first state to take itself out of the Union. By Lincoln's inauguration March 4, 1861, six more Southern states had seceded and formed the Confederate States of America.

Lincoln's Wartime Powers

Lincoln did not hesitate to undertake such extraordinary measures once the Confederates bombarded Fort Sumter on April 12, 1861. From that day until Congress convened on July 4, all the measures taken to protect the Union and prosecute the war against the Confederacy were taken by or upon the authority of the president. Hence, the

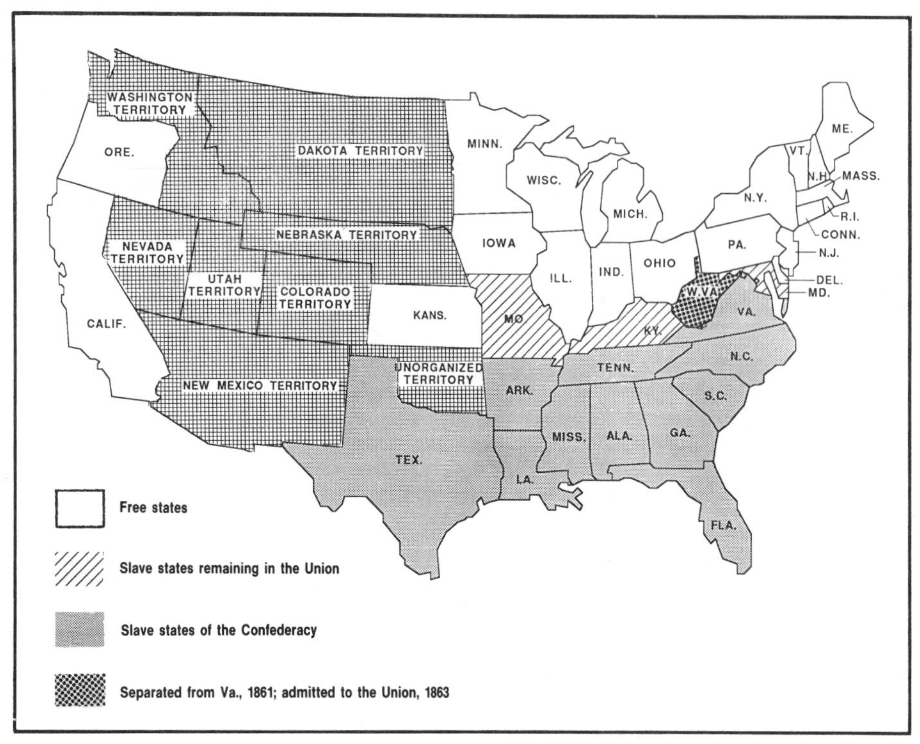

Alignment of states, 1861

early stages of civil conflict marked the first dramatic example of a chief executive taking the law into his own hands; to that extent Lincoln's actions constituted a "presidential war." [102]

Some of the measures Lincoln took, such as the mobilization of seventy-five thousand militia, were clearly within the proper sphere of presidential authority. Yet Lincoln went well beyond this. Hoping to bring the insurrection to a speedy end, he imposed a blockade of the southern coast, enlarged the army and navy (adding eighteen thousand to the navy and twenty-two thousand to the army), and suspended the writ of *habeas corpus.* This suspension carried with it sweeping powers that allowed officials acting under the authority of the president to make arrests without warrant for offenses undefined in the laws, without having to answer for such acts before the regular courts.

Many of these actions raised grave doubts about the constitutionality of the prosecution of the war. The enlargement of the military in the absence of legislative authorization seemed blatantly to disregard the clearly expressed constitutional delegation of power to Congress "to raise and support armies." Indeed, in referring to his proclamation of May 3, 1861, calling for enlistments in the regular army far beyond the existing legal limits, Lincoln himself frankly admitted that he had overstepped his legal authority.

Suspension of the Writ of *Habeas Corpus*

Moreover, the power to suspend the writ of *habeas corpus* during a national emergency was mentioned in Article I of the Constitution, which stipulated the authority of the legislature. Thus, Lincoln's critics argued, the suspension of this privilege rightfully belonged to Congress. This was an especially controversial matter, for Lincoln's suspension of *habeas corpus* struck at what presidential scholar Edward Corwin has called "the greatest of all muniments of Anglo-American liberty." [103]

Given the severity of Lincoln's war measures, it was not surprising that they prompted charges of "military dictatorship," even from some members of Lincoln's own party. These charges were apparently supported by the president's deliberate postponement of the special session of Congress until Independence Day, even though the call for such a session was issued on April 15.

The alleged unconstitutionality of this conduct of Lincoln became an issue before the Supreme Court in the *Prize Cases* (1863).[104] As was to be expected, given the circumstances prevailing in 1863, the Court upheld the legality of the war from the time of Lincoln's proclamation establishing a blockade, sustaining completely the executive acts taken while Congress was in recess. In rendering such a decision, the Court, paradoxically, recognized the importance of congressional legislation of July 1861 that ratified these executive orders, while refusing to admit that such legislative confirmation of Lincoln's war measures was necessary. "If it were necessary to the technical existence of the war that it should have a legislative sanction," said the Court, "we find it in almost every act passed at the extraordinary session of . . . 1861." [105] The Supreme Court's decision thereby supported Lincoln's claim that his measures were justified not only because of the threat to public safety but also because his actions were taken in the *expectation* that Congress would eventually approve of them.

The extraordinary powers accorded Lincoln must be understood in relation to the conditions that he confronted. It was of considerable significance that, from the standpoint of the government in Washington, the Civil War began as an "insurrection." [106] The president may not declare war, but he may proclaim the existence of rebellion or insurrection; and it was Lincoln's view, a view to which Congress and the courts generally subscribed, that treasonous activity called for quick and unilateral action by the president that might not have been appropriate in a formally declared war against a recognized, independent power. An internal rebellion, Lincoln proclaimed, imposed a special burden on regular legal protections, for the execution of the laws was "obstructed ... by combinations too powerful to be suppressed by the ordinary course of judicial proceedings. . . ." [107]

Lincoln's conception of the executive's responsibilities to suppress treasonous activity justified not only the suspension of the *habeas corpus* privilege, but the establishment of martial law in many areas of the country as well. Thus, not only was the executive accorded sweeping powers to arrest and detain those it suspected of rebellious activity, but citizens residing in peaceful regions of the country were subjected to trials before military tribunals. Moreover, as the Civil War progressed and the scope of conflict expanded, Lincoln took more sweeping and independent measures to deal with the insurrection.

The executive acts undertaken during the outset of the war were relatively circumscribed and put before Congress for ratification, but by the latter part of 1862, Lincoln was proclaiming more comprehensive powers for military authorities without apparent thought of Congress.[108] On September 24, 1862, for instance, an executive order of nationwide application proclaimed that all rebels and insurgents and all persons discouraging enlistment, resisting the draft, or guilty of any disloyal practice were subject to martial law and liable to trial by courts martial or military commissions. Regarding such persons, wherever found, the *habeas corpus* privilege was suspended.[109]

Imposition of Martial Law

Lincoln's more far-reaching measures establishing martial law were eventually challenged by the Supreme Court, although not until the Civil War was over. In the case of *Ex Parte Milligan,* decided in 1866, the Supreme Court declared illegal the use of military tribunals for the trials of citizens in districts unaffected by actual invasion and remote from the presence of armies.[110] *(See "War Power and Civil Rights," p. 1189, in The President and the Supreme Court chapter of Part VI.)* The Court declared that the constitutional guarantees of a fair trial were violated by the unrestricted exercise of martial law and that these freedoms could not be set aside because of the existence of a state of insurrection alone. Rather, the conditions of the insurrection had to be so grave as to close the civil courts and depose the civil administration. Martial law, the Court's opinion read, "could never exist where the Courts are open" but had to be "confined to the locality of actual war." [111]

The *Milligan* case lessened somewhat the effect of the precedents established during Lincoln's presidency. But the powers the executive assumed during the Civil War, and the prerogatives Lincoln claimed, demonstrated conclusively "that in meeting the domestic problems that a great war inevitably throws up an indefinite power must be attributed to the president to take emergency measures." [112]

Although the Lincoln administration took extreme measures, neither Congress nor the Courts exercised effective restraints upon the president. Congress did challenge the suspension of *habeas corpus* in an 1863 statute, which directed the release of prisoners unless indicted in the civil courts; but it did not put an end to extralegal imprisonments, nor did it succeed in shifting the control of punishments from the military to the civilian tribunals. Similarly, the Court, in the *Milligan* case, declared martial law unconstitutional in regions remote from actual hostilities; but the Courts had refused to interfere with the operation of a military commission in a similar case while the war was in progress.[113] Legally, then, the Civil War stands out as an exceptional period in U.S. history, "a time when constitutional restraints did not fully operate and the rule of law largely broke down." [114]

Although Lincoln's grasping of power caused him to be denounced as a dictator, there was another side to his leadership, one that showed him to be a constitutionalist faithful to the purpose for which the Union and Constitution were ordained.

The extent of the measures taken by Lincoln were far-reaching, offering the opportunity for the abuse of power, but the application of these powers was remarkably measured, given the extent of the danger posed by a full-scale civil war. For example, although the suspension of standard legal protections led to the arbitrary arrest of a very large number of individuals, in most cases a short military detention was followed by release or parole. As for the military trial of civilians, such commissions were commonly used to try citizens in military areas for military crimes. Circumstances such as those leading to the *Milligan* case, involving military trials of citizens for nonmilitary crimes in peaceful areas, were rare.

Thus, the Constitution, while stretched severely, was not subverted during the Civil War. It is a "striking fact," as one scholar noted, "that no life was forfeited and no sentence of fine and imprisonment [was] carried out in any judicial prosecution for treason arising out of the 'rebellion.' " [115] Lincoln was driven by circumstances to use more arbitrary power than perhaps any other president, yet he was criticized for leniency as often as for severity in his exercise of these powers.

The Emancipation Proclamation

Lincoln's regard for maintaining the integrity of the Constitution was clearly revealed by his cautious handling of the issues of emancipation. Lincoln had argued consistently that the emancipation of the slaves in the existing states was beyond the constitutionally enumerated powers of Congress. Yet the duties of commander in chief allowed the president to assume powers in war that he believed were forbidden in peace.[116] Nevertheless, the celebrated Proclamation of Emancipation, issued on January 1, 1863, was actually a cautious measure, one more limited than members of Lincoln's cabinet or the so-called Radical Republicans in Congress had hoped for. It did not proclaim a comprehensive and sweeping policy of emancipation; in fact, Lincoln had declared unauthorized and void declarations by two of his generals that went so far. Rather, Lincoln based his proclamation solely upon the "war power" and viewed it as "a fit and necessary war measure for suppressing rebellion." [117] *(See "Emancipation Proclamation," p. 1370, in the Appendix.)*

As an act based upon "military necessity," the Emancipation Proclamation had an important, albeit limited, practical effect. Well over 100,000 soldiers were taken from slave labor and added to the Union soldiery, thus vindicating Lincoln's defense of emancipation as a critical war measure. Yet the 1863 proclamation included neither a defense of a principle adverse to slavery nor any guarantee that the institution of slavery would be abolished once the war was over. Lincoln believed that such a comprehensive strike at this vile institution could not occur as a result of either regular legislation or executive order, even during the war. Accordingly, his veto of the Wade-Davis bill of 1864, which included the sort of sweeping emancipation and reconstruction measures that Lincoln believed the federal government had no right to impose upon the states, expressed the hope that the abolition of slavery could be achieved by constitutional amendment.

Lincoln pressed the Thirteenth Amendment through a reluctant Congress, believing as he did that such a sweeping social reform was eminently just, yet incompatible with the existing framework of U.S. constitutional government. The ratification of this amendment in 1865 eliminated slavery "within the United States, or any place subject to their jurisdiction." Thus, paradoxically, the disregard for legal restrictions evident in the wide extent of the war power assumed by Lincoln went hand in hand with a deep and abiding commitment to the principles and institutions of the U.S. Constitution.

The Election of 1864

The most important evidence weighing against the view that Lincoln conducted the war in a dictatorial fashion was the continuation of party competition in the election of 1864.[118] The stakes in this contest were great, for the opposition Democrats declared in their platform that "after four years of failure to restore the Union by the experiment of war . . . justice . . . and the public welfare demand that immediate efforts be made for a cessation of hostilities." [119] The victory of their candidate, Gen. George B. McClellan, therefore, might very well have meant a compromise with the Confederacy and the continuation of slavery.[120] In facing such a forceful challenge in 1864, one that Lincoln and many Republicans believed might end in a Democratic victory, Lincoln, one scholar pointed out, "accepted a risk and permitted his power to be threatened in a way that no dictator, constitutional or not, would have tolerated." [121]

Lincoln's commitment to popular sovereignty was quite evident in the lenient attitude of his administration throughout the war in dealing with the rights of press and conscience. Although there were some notable and unfortunate exceptions, as a rule, anti-Lincoln and anti-Union organs were left undisturbed.[122]

The election campaign of 1864 was characterized by a remarkably open and strident debate in the midst of hostilities, "adding not a little," as Lincoln granted after the election, "to the strain" caused by civil insurrection. But the election was a necessity, the president told a crowd of supporters who gathered at the White House on November 10, 1864, to celebrate his victory, because as he put it, "we cannot have free government without elections; and if rebellion could force us to forgo or postpone a national election, it might fairly claim to have already conquered and ruined us." The election of 1864, Lincoln concluded, "demonstrated that a people's government can sustain a national election in the midst of a great civil war. Until now, it has not been known to the world that this was a possibility." [123]

These were revealing words, for the principal task of Lincoln's presidency was to demonstrate that a democratic republic could survive a national struggle that threatened its survival. As he remarked on one occasion, "It has long been a grave question whether any government, not too strong for the liberties of its people, can be strong enough to maintain its existence in great emergencies." [124] The conduct of the Civil War apparently answered this question in the affirmative. As the constitutional historian J. G. Randall wrote:

> In a legal study of the war the two most significant facts are perhaps these: the wide extent of the war powers; and, in contrast to that, the manner in which the men in authority were nevertheless controlled by the American people's sense of constitutional government.[125]

> Neither slavery nor involuntary servitude, except as a punishment for crime whereof the party shall have been duly convicted, shall exist within the United States, or any place subject to their jurisdiction.
> —Thirteenth Amendment, section 1

Andrew Johnson and the Assault on Executive Authority

Andrew Johnson faced extraordinarily difficult circumstances upon assuming office in April 1865. The Civil War had settled the question of Southern independence and emancipated the slaves in the Confederate states, but the end of hostilities left the enormous problem of reconstruction. How were the Confederate states to rejoin the Union, and what would the future status of emancipated slaves be in America? These were issues that had begun to divide the Republican party toward the end of Lincoln's first term. Lincoln's principal concern was to restore the Union as quickly as possible, without exacting undue recrimination or posing extensive conditions on the rebellious states. The "Radicals" of his party, however, led by Massachusetts senator Charles Sumner believed that high-ranking Confederates should be punished severely for their treason, that the Southern states should not be granted full membership rights in the Union until they were thoroughly reconstructed and their loyalty ensured, and that blacks should be guaranteed the rights of full citizenship.

This conflict within the Republican party remained unresolved as the war ended. In 1863, Lincoln had promulgated for three Confederate states that had been conquered by the Union army—Louisiana, Arkansas, and Tennessee—a lenient program of reunification, requiring only that 10 percent of the voters on taking an oath of allegiance to the United States could form state governments and elect members of Congress. The Republican-dominated Congress rejected Lincoln's program as too lenient and refused to seat the elected members from the three conquered states, declaring that reconstruction was a legislative, not an executive, function.

Congress's answer to Lincoln's policy was the passage of the Wade-Davis bill that disenfranchised all high-ranking Confederates, stipulated that 50 percent of the voters in a rebel state must take a loyalty oath before elections could be held, and made the abolition of slavery a condition for readmission to the Union. Lincoln's pocket veto of this legislation, accompanied by a message propounding that reunification should be an executive function, elicited the Wade-Davis Manifesto from Republican leaders in Congress, a bold attack on Lincoln's Reconstruction program and a defense of the "paramount" authority of Congress reminiscent of the Whig's assault on Andrew Jackson. The Republican members' concept of the proper relation of the executive to the legislature as well as their Reconstruction program apparently were rejected in the election of 1864, which was a plebiscite of sorts on the issues raised. But the strength of the Radical Republicans was restored after the assassination of Lincoln. As historian Wilfred E. Binkley has written:

> To those who had applauded the furious blast of the Wade-Davis Manifesto against Lincoln only to see its effect nullified by the triumphant re-election of the President it must have now seemed as if fate, through the assassin's bullet, had at last delivered the government into their hands. Their glee was but ill concealed.[126]

The Radicals' confidence in Johnson was not unreasonable. Before Lincoln appointed him military governor of Tennessee in early 1862 (a post he held until his nomination as Lincoln's running mate in 1864), Johnson had been one of them, serving as a member of the Radical-dominated Congressional Joint Committee on the Conduct of the War. This committee had been the censor of Lincoln's wartime initiatives, charging the president with usurping the prerogatives of Congress. Only a few hours after Lincoln died this committee paid a visit to Johnson, and its chairman, Senator Wade, cosponsor of the Wade-Davis Bill, declared, "Johnson, we have faith in you. By the gods, there will be no trouble now in running the government!"[127]

This faith did not last long. Johnson kept Lincoln's cabinet, spurning the Radicals' advice "to get rid of the last vestige of Lincolnism." Then, without consulting Congress, he proceeded to put Lincoln's Reconstruction policies into effect by executive proclamations during the spring and summer of 1865. Congressional Republicans were furious yet unable to respond. Johnson refused to call a special session of Congress, and the legislature would not convene until December. Thus, the Radicals suffered the humiliation of standing by helplessly for several months while Reconstruction policies they deemed unacceptable were aggressively pursued by the Johnson administration.

Johnson's bold unilateral actions were no doubt influenced by the success Lincoln had in repeatedly executing major policy decisions while Congress was in recess, leaving the legislature with little choice but to ratify the *faits accomplis* when it returned. But Johnson lacked Lincoln's political stature and skill; this and the end of hostilities gave congressional Republicans the opportunity to establish their dominance over policy. They seized their opportunity as soon as the regular session of Congress convened in December 1865, threatening to destroy in the process the balance of government branches that had been achieved from the time of Washington's presidency.

Johnson's struggle with Congress was aggravated by the sharp difference of principle that distinguished him from most members of the Republican party. He was a strong defender of the Union; in fact, during the secession crisis of 1860-1861, Johnson was the only Southern senator to take such a stand. Yet in background and belief, he was a Jacksonian Democrat, and, although he gave up that affiliation to join Lincoln's "Union" ticket in the 1864 presidential campaign, Johnson was never very comfortable in the Republican party. His commitment to states' rights inclined him to oppose not only the Radicals of his party, but the moderate Republicans as well. Thus, Johnson vetoed a bill to continue the Freedman's Bureau in February 1866, asserting in his message to Congress that it was unconstitutional in time of peace to sustain this agency, which was created during the war to promote the welfare of Southern blacks. In vetoing this legislation, sponsored by moderate Republican senator Lyman Trumbull of Illinois, Johnson did not merely challenge the Radicals; he went against a Republican party measure that had the unanimous support of its congressional members.

The link between Johnson and his party was irrevocably broken about a month later when he vetoed the Civil Rights Act, which, like the Freedman's Bureau legislation, enjoyed the unanimous support of congressional Republicans. This bill, which was eventually made part of the fundamental law as the Fourteenth Amendment, declared blacks to be citizens of the United States and bestowed on all persons born in the United States (except Indians) an equal right to make and enforce contracts, to sue and be witnesses in the courts, to own land and other property, and to enjoy equal protection under the law.

Had Johnson supported this legislation, he would have satisfied the North's desire to protect blacks in the South and kept the moderate Republicans, who did not insist on immediate black suffrage, divided from the Radicals, who did. But his veto of the civil rights bill united his party and public opinion against him. On April 6, the Senate by a vote of 33-15 passed the bill by overriding the president's veto; three days later the House did the same, 122-41. Congress's passage of the civil rights legislation over Johnson's head was a landmark in constitutional development, as it was the first time in history that Congress had overturned a presidential veto on an important issue. It was also important as a political event, signifying that Congress, not the president, was the master of the Reconstruction program.[128]

Congress Assumes Control of Reconstruction

The congressional election of 1866 was widely viewed as a referendum on the question of congressional versus executive Reconstruction. The verdict of the voters was overwhelmingly in favor of the Radical Republicans. Influenced by the unanimous rejection of the Fourteenth Amendment by the states that had been reconstructed by presidential proclamation, the voters routed Johnson's followers, giving the Radicals firm control over both houses of Congress. Particularly damaging to Johnson was that the Southern states had followed his advice in deciding not to grant constitutional status to the rights of citizenship established by the Civil Rights Act.

Spurred by the public mandate of the 1866 elections, Congress passed a series of measures that not only deprived Johnson of his control over Reconstruction but systematically stripped the president of his authority to conduct the affairs of the executive department. The Military Reconstruction Act, passed in 1867, abolished the state governments established by Johnson and divided the South into military districts subject to military commanders who were granted almost total independence from presidential directives. Congress ensured this autonomy by tacking riders to the 1867 Army Appropriations Bill requiring the president and secretary of war to transmit all orders to military commanders through the general of the army (Ulysses S. Grant) and forbidding the president to relieve, suspend, or transfer from Washington the general of the army without the Senate's consent. This direct challenge to the president's authority as commander in chief was instigated and designed by Johnson's secretary of war, Edwin Stanton, who, along with Grant, conspired with Republican leaders to strip Johnson of his influence over the administration of Congress's Reconstruction program.

Johnson vetoed the Military Reconstruction Act, stating that the act would create an absolute despotism in the South; and he protested the riders attached to the military appropriations bill, maintaining that these clauses were an assault on his authority as commander in chief. Yet Congress quickly overrode the president's veto and ignored his protest against the riders attached to the appropriations bill. Moreover, to prevent Johnson from reasserting control over Reconstruction, Congress made provisions to stay in session permanently. This both nullified the constitutional privilege of the president to pocket veto legislation passed with less than ten days remaining in a congressional session and usurped the president's authority to call special sessions of Congress. As a result, without any call by the president as the Constitution requires, there were three extra sessions of Congress in 1867, that body staying in continual session to prevent the president from interfering with the congressional Reconstruction policy.[129]

Having stripped Johnson of his influence on legislation and the conduct of military rule in the South, Congress proceeded next to divest Johnson of his control over the personnel of the executive branch. In March 1867 it passed over Johnson's veto the Tenure of Office Act, prohibiting the president from removing any official appointed with the Senate's consent without that body's prior approval. The enactment of this legislation was a reversal of the first Congress's momentous decision in 1789 to uphold the president's authority to remove executive officials. After seven decades of unbroken theory and practice, the right of presidential removal had become settled constitutional principle. But the struggle between President Johnson and the Congress had reached a point where neither settled precedents nor explicit prescriptions of the Constitution would deter Radical Republicans from their attack on the prerogatives of the executive.

By the spring of 1867, Andrew Johnson had little political power left. He was helpless to block any legislation that Congress saw fit to pass. Johnson fought stubbornly against the emasculation of the presidency, but his only recourse was to make a direct appeal to public opinion. More than any of his predecessors, Johnson attempted to establish a direct link with the people with speeches, messages, and press interviews. *(See "The Age of Reform," p. 290, in The Electoral Process chapter of Part II.)* Jefferson and especially Jackson had sought to establish closer ties between the presidency and the public, but in doing so had worked through the party organization. But Johnson was without the support of any party once he refused to sign the civil rights legislation that was passed in 1866 with virtually unanimous Republican support. Thus, beginning with the 1866 congressional campaigns, Johnson attempted to influence popular opinion over the heads of party and congressional leaders, hoping that rhetoric could restore his severely weakened presidency.

This was a vain hope. Johnson fancied himself a good orator, but, especially when goaded by hecklers, his forceful attack on the Congress was prone to excess. For example, on the evening of February 22, 1866, Washington's Birthday, he told a crowd of supporters who had marched on the White House to demonstrate their support for his veto of the civil rights bill that new rebels had appeared in the country, this time in the North. These men, the Radical leaders in the Congress, "had assumed nearly all the powers of government" and prevented the restoration of the Union. Johnson charged Thaddeus Stevens, the Pennsylvania representative who led the Radicals in the House, and Charles Sumner of Massachusetts, Johnson's major opponent in the Senate, with being just as treasonable as the leaders of the Southern Confederacy.[130]

This sort of rhetoric backfired. The vast majority of northerners felt outraged and ashamed as they read, or read about, Johnson's speeches, most of which were closely patterned after the Washington's Birthday harangue. They resented his attack on Stevens and Sumner, who, whatever else they might be, were no traitors to the Union. Moreover, the purpose of his speeches, to rouse public opinion in support of his policy initiatives in Congress, was considered illegitimate, a form of demagogy that was beneath the dignity of the presidential office. The use of rhetoric to sway public opinion became acceptable, even commonplace, in the twentieth century; but during the nineteenth century, such popular rhetoric was considered a violation of constitutional norms.

The Impeachment of Andrew Johnson

Johnson's "improper" rhetoric not only strengthened his opposition but served as the basis for one of the eleven articles of impeachment brought against the president by the House of Representatives on February 24, 1868. It charged that the president ignored the duties of his office in seeking to impugn Congress and by making and delivering "with a loud voice certain intemperate, inflammatory, and scandalous harangues ... amid cries, jeers, and laughter of the multitude then assembled...." [131] The charge of "bad and improper" rhetoric was not the major reason for the impeachment proceeding against Johnson; the president's violation of the Tenure of Office Act was the major issue. Furthermore, many members of Congress doubted that inflammatory speech was an impeachable offense. Yet the charge directed at Johnson's perceived demagogy was not frivolous; instead, it suggested the severe limitations on direct popular leadership that applied to the executive office until the twentieth century.

Johnson's dismissal of Secretary of War Stanton was the principal issue in the impeachment proceedings carried out by Congress. In taking this action against Stanton, who in spite of his position in the cabinet was regularly conspiring with the president's enemies in Congress, Johnson disregarded the requirements established by the Tenure of Office Act, thus intending to get this legislation into the courts for a test. Yet the Radicals made the most of the president's breaking a law to test its constitutionality, proceeding quickly with the preparation of the articles of impeachment. As a result, the constitutionality of Johnson's dismissal of Stanton was decided by the Senate, not the courts, in the course of its judgment on the impeachment charges that the House approved by a vote of 126-47. Thus, for the first—and so far only—time in U.S. history, a president had been impeached.

Johnson's impeachment trial, which lasted one and a

James E. Taylor; Library of Congress

In 1868 the House of Representatives impeached President Andrew Johnson. This sketch by James E. Taylor depicts Johnson's trial in the Senate, where by one vote he was acquitted and allowed to remain in office.

half months, threatened not only Johnson's presidency, but the independence of the executive office. The Senate proceedings did not resemble a trial to determine whether Johnson had committed "high crimes and misdemeanors." Rather, the proceedings constituted virtually a convention of the Republican party to put Andrew Johnson out of office. The Republican leadership did all it could to bring the pressure of public opinion upon the senators' deliberations. Moderate Republicans, in particular, who had broken with Johnson but feared that his removal from office would destroy the constitutional system of checks and balances, were threatened in the party press and from home as part of a nationwide campaign to coerce the wavering "judges" into submission to the party's decree.[132]

Had Johnson been convicted under such conditions, the presidency might have suffered irreparable damage to its power and prestige. Yet seven Republicans stood up to the pressure of party discipline and public opinion, leaving the Radicals one vote shy of the two-thirds plurality they needed to depose Johnson.

Ulysses S. Grant and the Abdication of Executive Power

The failure of the Senate to impeach Andrew Johnson did not restore either the president or the executive office to a position of strength. The remainder of Johnson's term was characterized by a relatively quiet deadlock between the executive and the legislature. Nor did the election of Ulysses S. Grant to the presidency in 1868 revive the power of the executive. If the American people, made uneasy by the subordination of the president to the Congress, thought they were electing a forceful leader in Grant, they were sorely mistaken. Whereas Grant's military career justified a belief that he had unusual executive ability, he was unable to transfer this success into the office of the presidency. Andrew Jackson had done as much, but by temperament and philosophy Grant was ill-suited for such a task. Unlike Jackson, who had served in the House and Senate, Grant had no experience in civil administration. Grant had neither the detailed knowledge of the political process required to perform the tasks of chief executive nor the political experience needed to bend other men to his purposes.

Grant's shortcomings as a civilian leader were demonstrated almost immediately. The president let it be known upon his election that he favored the repeal of the Tenure of Office Act and that he would not make any appointments beyond his cabinet until such action was taken. The House soon complied with Grant's wishes, but the Senate, under the control of the Radical Republicans, approved a "compromise" amendment that essentially continued its control over the removal of executive officials. Had Grant asserted himself at this point in favor of repeal, he would in all likelihood have prevailed, given the popularity and stature he had at the time of his election to the presidency. Yet, not realizing the implications of his actions, Grant capitulated to Senate leaders, whereupon congressional Republicans in both legislative chambers joined ranks to support the compromise. An advocate of repealing the Tenure of Office Act, Gideon Welles, reflecting the disappointment of those who hoped Grant would lead them into an era of reform, remarked: "The lawyers duped and cowed him. The poor devil has neither the sagacity and obstinacy for which he has credit, if he assents to this compromise, where the Executive surrenders everything and gets nothing." [133]

Grant had the people and a majority of the press on his side, yet he failed to press his political advantage. This error, which dramatically revealed Grant's inability to apply his military talents to the presidency, set the tone for his entire two terms in office. Grant never recovered the prestige and power he lost in his first showdown with Republican leaders in the Senate.[134]

Grant's acquiescence to the Senate on the question of whether to repeal the Tenure of Office Act was no doubt influenced by his concept of the presidency. He considered himself purely an "administrative officer," and "except on rare occasions he was, as President, disposed to accept without question the work of Congress as the authoritative expression of the will of the American people."[135] This view of executive leadership fit well with the conceptions of the powerful Republican leaders in the Senate who embraced the Whig principles of legislative supremacy. Whereas this ideal was thwarted by Lincoln and obstinately resisted by Johnson, congressional Republicans had in Grant a man who was manageable. As a result, the Senate achieved the peak of its power under Grant. George F. Hoar, a Republican member of the House at this time, described the attitude of the Senate with respect to the president:

> The most eminent Senators—Sumner, Conkling, Sherman, Edmunds, Carpenter, Frelinghuysen, Simon Cameron, Anthony, Logan—would have received as a personal affront a private message from the White House expressing a desire that they should adopt any course in the discharge of their legislative duties that they did not approve. If they visited the White House, it was to give, not to receive advice.... Each of these stars kept his own orbit and shown in his sphere within which he tolerated no intrusion from the President or from anybody else.[136]

Grant's virtual abdication of presidential responsibility made his administration among the most pathetic in American history. His passive concept of the office he held resulted not only in weakness but in scandal. Patronage practices were tolerated that left the staffing and conduct of federal offices to a small number of weak and unreliable party loyalists holding seats in Congress and in high executive office. During Grant's second term especially, his administration was rocked with one scandal after another.

The most dramatic and probably the most damaging scandal involved the evasion of internal revenue taxes on distilleries—the so-called Whiskey Ring. The Whiskey Ring included Gen. John A. McDonald, collector of internal revenue in St. Louis, who, with the collusion of Treasury officials and the president's private secretary, Gen. Orville E. Babcock, defrauded the government of millions of dollars in taxes. Perhaps the most disconcerting aspect of this scandal was Grant's efforts to protect Babcock, who was acquitted on the strength of a deposition in his favor that was prepared by the president. The honest but hopelessly naive Grant "rewarded" Secretary of the Treasury Benjamin H. Bristow's efforts to break the Whiskey Ring and to bring its perpetrators, including Babcock, to justice by making it clear that he was no longer welcome in the cabinet. It was a mark of the moral degeneration of Grant's administration that, when the Whiskey Ring was broken, Babcock received the president's appointment as inspector of lighthouses, while Bristow, having successfuly fought corruption in the revenue service, was forced into private life.[137]

Grant's unfortunate actions in the Whiskey Ring incident notwithstanding, he was neither unaware of nor unconcerned about the problems with the existing system of public administration. In 1870 he asked for reform of the Civil Service, declaring, "the present system [of party pa-

Mathew Brady; National Portrait Gallery

Gen. Ulysses S. Grant, shown here in 1864 during the Civil War, had no experience in civil administration when he became president. His successful military career suggested unusual executive ability, but he was unable to transfer that success to the presidency.

tronage] does not secure the best men and often not even fit men, for public place."[138] Receiving the necessary authority from Congress in March of that year, Grant proceeded to set up a board, which soon became known as the Civil Service Commission, with the responsibility to devise rules and regulations to effect reform. George William Curtis, the leader of the civil service reform movement in the United States, was appointed as chairman of the commission, and a competitive examination system was established in each department to conduct agency examinations under the supervision of the commission. Thus, perhaps the most corrupt presidential administration in U.S. history also made the first earnest attempt to reform the civil service system.

Despite a promising beginning, however, the trend of events during Grant's second term worked against reform and reformers. The patronage system had been seized by and used to the benefit of members of Congress, most of whom fought against reform. Sen. Roscoe Conkling of New York, the leader of the "Stalwart" wing of the Republican party, led an assault on the commission; he was supported not only by the controlling wing of his party, but by Democrats seeking patronage as well. The "Liberal" Republicans, who supported reform, were, after having nominated Horace Greeley to run against Grant in 1872, anathema to the president and unable, thereby, to work cooperatively with him in fending off the congressional attack on the commission's authority. In the face of resistance from Congress, which refused to allocate funds for the Civil Service Commission in 1874, Grant, characteristically, abandoned the system. In strict accord with his belief that Congress was the body to determine policy, the president announced in his annual message of December 7, 1874, that if Congress adjourned without passing positive legislation for civil service reform, he would discontinue the system. Congress adjourned having taken no action, and on March 9, 1875, Grant ordered the abolition of the examining boards throughout the country.[139]

Harper's Weekly; Library of Congress

The Fifteenth Amendment, ratified in 1870, allowed black men to vote. Women were not granted that right until 1920.

The Fight to Restore Presidential Power

When Grant retired from the presidency a year later, the office he had occupied for eight years had reached its lowest ebb. The Senate, its leaders believed, was "secure in its mastery over the executive."[140] Yet Grant's successor, Rutherford B. Hayes, was intent upon emancipating the executive from congressional dominance. During his administration, the prerogatives of presidential power would be defended persistently and effectively for the first time since the Civil War.

Rutherford B. Hayes

During the presidency of Republican Rutherford B. Hayes (1877-1881), a full decade of executive decline abruptly came to an end. Yet this administration had its start under the most inauspicious of circumstances.

Republican defeat seemed certain in the election of 1876, given the moral bankruptcy of the Grant presidency. In fact, the Democratic candidate, New York governor Samuel J. Tilden, who had exposed corrupt political rings in his state, seemed to have won the election. But the electoral votes of three southern states, still subjected to military rule, and of Oregon were doubtful. Without them, Tilden had only 184 electoral votes; if Hayes carried those four states, he would have 185 votes and would win the election.

From all four disputed states came two sets of electoral votes. Congress dealt with the problem by setting up an electoral commission of fifteen members, eight Republicans and seven Democrats. At this point a deal apparently was worked out between Republicans and southern Democratic leaders, by virtue of which Republicans, in return for the Democrats' acquiescence to Hayes's election, promised to end military rule in the South. Both sides kept their side of the bargain. On March 2, 1877, the electoral commission by a strict party vote rejected the Democratic returns from the doubtful states and declared Hayes the winner by one electoral vote. Hayes, in turn, removed troops from the South, ending virtually any attempt to enforce the conditions of the Fourteenth Amendment to the Constitution, which guaranteed civil rights to the freedman. Nor, thereafter, was any effort made to uphold the conditions of the Fifteenth Amendment, added to the Constitution in 1870, which affirmed the right of citizens of the United States to vote, regardless of "race, color, or previous condition of servitude." *(See "The Compromise of 1876," p. 286, in The Electoral Process chapter of Part II.)*

It is ironic that such an unsavory bargain brought to power a president who uncompromisingly dedicated his administration to breaking the grip of the Senate over the operations of the executive office and to reforming the civil service, a reform, Hayes announced in his inaugural address, that should be "thorough, radical, and complete." [141] The battle between Hayes and Congress centered on control of appointments to the executive branch over which, by the end of Grant's second term, senators and, to a lesser extent, representatives had substantial influence.

Hayes first offended Republican leaders in the Senate by making his choices for the cabinet without consulting them. Not only did this action disrupt the plans of Senate Stalwarts to dictate the appointment of Hayes's cabinet, but, with the nomination of former Confederate David M. Key as postmaster general, it also aroused their patriotic wrath. Yet the major "insult" Hayes perpetrated upon the senators who were accustomed to controlling the details of personnel policy was his appointment of the civil service reformer Carl Shurz to the Department of the Interior, where members of Congress feared the new secretary would wage war on the patronage system.

Even though Hayes's appointments were a distinguished and qualified group of men, the senatorial "oligarchy" did not hesitate to accept the president's challenge. When the cabinet appointments were submitted to the Senate for approval, as required by the Constitution, the entire list was referred to committees for examination and report. Hoping to force the president's hand in this way, the Senate did not make an exception even for their fellow senator John Sherman, nominated as secretary of the Treasury, although it was customary for fellow members, especially those as well qualified as Sherman, to be confirmed without investigation.

This move by the Senate to delay confirmation of an entire list of cabinet nominations was unprecedented, and a storm of indignation swept the country. The Senate's audacious attempt to block the president's appointment of such well-qualified individuals aroused public sympathy for Hayes, whose office was flooded with telegrams and letters urging him to stand firm. Within a few days the Senate capitulated to public opinion and confirmed the whole list of cabinet nominations almost unanimously. Thus, "for the first time since the Civil War," Wilfred E. Binkley has written, "the Senate had been vanquished on a clear cut issue between it and the President. The Senate had passed its zenith." [142]

Yet, the great battle between Hayes and Congress was still to come. Having installed a cabinet of his choice, the president now set his sights on the patronage system: "Now for Civil Service Reform," Hayes wrote in his diary on April 22, 1877.[143] One of his first moves was to appoint a number of independent commissions to investigate the federal customhouses in New York, San Francisco, New Orleans, and elsewhere. These federal outposts were controlled by local party machines and had fallen into some outrageous practices in the course of collecting federal revenues. While changes were quickly carried out in many areas of the country, the customhouse in New York, which collected more than two-thirds of all the customs revenues of the federal government, continued to serve the state and local party machines. The independent commission that inquired into the practices of the New York customhouse cited practices of hiring employees on the basis of political pressure (to which customs officials admitted), revealed the existence of a system whereby employees were expected to contribute a certain percentage of their salaries to the party coffers, and called attention to widespread incompetence and corruption among customhouse personnel.

Upon receiving the report on the New York customhouse, Hayes sought to replace its three top officials, Collector Chester A. Arthur, Surveyor General George H. Sharpe, and naval officer Alonzo B. Cornell, all of whom were prominent members of the New York state Republican organization. Yet the president's intention to take decisive action was impeded both by custom and by law. One obstacle was the practice of "senatorial courtesy" that had emerged since the Civil War. Under this practice (still observed today), senators of the president's party who object to a nominee from their state, or an aspirant to a federal office in their state, can rely on the support of their fellow senators in refusing confirmation should the president not withdraw the nomination. The Stalwart New York senator Roscoe Conkling, for whom the New York customhouse was a critical source of political power, called on his colleagues to thwart the president and to deny confirmation to those Hayes selected to replace the Republican spoilsmen.

When the nominations were submitted to the Senate, they were referred to the Committee on Commerce, chaired by Senator Conkling, who invoked the power of the Senate over removals under the Tenure of Office Act, and the session of Congress ended without confirmation of the nominations. Under the amended terms of this legislation, the Senate was not authorized to confirm a presidential removal, yet its approval of the president's choice to succeed the suspended official was necessary to consummate the firing in question. Thus, when Hayes's nominations, which were greeted in the Senate with derisive laughter, were rejected, Conkling and the New York Republican machine retained its grip on the federal customhouse; and Arthur, Sharpe, and Cornell retained their federal posts.

Still, the stubborn Hayes was determined to continue the fight. On December 12, 1877, he recorded in his diary, "In the language of the press, Senator Conkling has won a great victory over the administration. . . . But the end is not yet. I am right and I shall not give up the contest." [144] After Congress had adjourned in 1878, Hayes once again dismissed the three officials in question, made recess appointments, and in December again sent his nominations for these vacant posts. Conkling was able to hold up action for two months but finally defeated himself by resorting to a bitter speech against the president in which he alienated many senators by stooping to the reading of private correspondence of cabinet members.[145] The Senate finally voted to confirm Hayes's nominations on February 3, 1879.

In his letter of congratulations to Arthur's replacement, Gen. E. A. Merritt, the president laid down the principles for a complete overhauling of the personnel system of the New York customhouse. Besides insisting that Merritt's office be conducted "on strictly business principles," Hayes prescribed that the new collector restrict the area of patronage to the narrowest possible limits. "Let no man be put out merely because he is a friend of the late collector," he wrote, "and no man be put in merely because he is our friend." [146]

President Hayes's battle with Senator Conkling was successful, but the cost was extremely high. It took almost eighteen months to remove Arthur, Cornell, and Sharpe, and during this period the president was virtually helpless as the administrative head of government. Thus, even though Hayes's triumph restored some of the executive powers that had been lost since the assassination of Lincoln, his administration would be noted largely for "holding its ground, rather than for developing new frontiers." [147] But Hayes expressed satisfaction with the blows he had struck against the power of the senatorial group that for so long had been directing the government. A year after his success in the battle for control over the New York customhouse, he wrote in his diary:

> The end I have chiefly aimed at has been to break down congressional patronage. The contest has been a bitter one. It has exposed me to attack, opposition, misconstruction, and the actual hatred of powerful men. But I have had great success. No member of either house now attempts even to dictate appointments. My sole right to make appointments is now tacitly conceded.[148]

James A. Garfield

The battle between the president and Congress over the conduct of the executive office was not settled by Hayes's victories over Conkling. In fact, the first weeks of James A. Garfield's administration led to a renewal of the battles that had dominated Hayes's term in office. The ferocity of these battles was unexpected. Garfield was nominated by the Republican party on the thirty-sixth ballot as a compromise choice between the Stalwarts, led by Conkling, and the moderate faction of his party (the so-called Half-breeds, led by Sen. James G. Blaine[149] of Maine). The convention completed the job of bandaging party wounds by selecting Conkling's lieutenant and former head of the New York customhouse, Chester A. Arthur, as the vice-presidential candidate. Unlike Hayes, Garfield was by nature prone to conciliation and compromise, and he would have preferred to work cooperatively with both factions of the Republican party. Against his will, however, Garfield was forced to continue the assault against senatorial courtesy that his successor had begun.

Garfield's attack on the Senate was a response to the attempt by the Conklingites to dictate his choice for secretary of the Treasury. They demanded that the president appoint Levi P. Morton, a New York banker, to this post. When Garfield resisted the idea, arguing that the banker's Wall Street connections and his extremely conservative views on the economy made him unacceptable to western Republicans, his conciliatory offer to name Morton as secretary of the navy and to consider alternative recommendations for the Treasury post was boldly refused by the Stalwarts; their answer was simple: Morton must be secretary of the Treasury.

Garfield was not so conciliatory that he was willing to yield to this stubborn challenge to executive authority. He generously recognized the Conkling wing of the New York Republicans by placing many in federal positions, but he insisted upon his own choices for the cabinet. He now realized, as clearly as had Hayes, that the constitutional independence of the executive "could be preserved only by a bold challenge of the pretentions of the Senate and a duel to the finish with the most militant champion of senatorial courtesy." [150]

Garfield left no doubt about his intention to make such a challenge when he nominated William H. Robertson as collector of the port of New York. Robertson was Conkling's political enemy in New York and a friend of Conkling's chief rival, Blaine. This appointment, then, was an even more distinct challenge to Conkling and the practice of senatorial courtesy than Hayes had ever given. Garfield wrote to his longtime friend, B. A. Hinsdale, the president of Hiram College:

> This [nomination] brings on the contest at once and will settle the question whether the President is registering clerk of the Senate or the Executive of the United States.... Summed up in a single sentence this is the question: shall the principal port of entry in which more than ninety percent of all our customs duties are collected be under the control of administration or under the local control of a factional senator?[151]

The enormous weight of Senator Conkling's political machine, which included Vice President Arthur, was used in a vain attempt to compel Garfield to withdraw Robertson's nomination. But the president refused to budge. Indeed, when the senators under Conkling attempted to outwit the president by preparing to confirm all the nominations except the one in question, Garfield withdrew all his nominations except that of Robertson. There would be no further nominations, Garfield insisted, until the issue of control over the conduct of the executive office was settled. This bold move left the Stalwarts practically helpless. On May 16, 1881, seeing that Robertson's confirmation was now inevitable, Conkling and fellow New York senator Thomas C. Platt resigned, hoping that the New York legislature would enable them to save face by reelecting them. The legislature refused to do so, and after a long struggle, two other men were chosen to fill the Senate vacancies.

Garfield's victory was complete; Robertson's nomination was unanimously confirmed, and Conkling never resumed public office. This event, which ended a long struggle that began with Hayes's attempt to reform the New York customhouse, marked, the historian James A. Garraty has written, a "milestone in the revival of the power and prestige of the White House." Thereafter, the Senate's influence in suggesting persons for presidential consideration still remained substantial, but its claim to govern executive discretion was denied.[152]

Chester A. Arthur and the Enactment of Civil Service Reform

Fate did not grant Garfield the time to pursue a more comprehensive program of civil service reform. On July 2, 1881, Charles J. Guiteau, a deranged lawyer, shot President Garfield in the back in a Washington railroad station. The president died of his wound September 19, thus elevating Arthur, the former spoilsman at the center of the New York customhouse crisis, to the presidency. Civil service reformers had little reason to expect anything positive from this New York Stalwart. Indeed, former president Hayes predicted that Arthur's former patron, Conkling, would be "the power behind the throne." [153]

The new president, however, soon laid to rest the worst fears of those who expected him to turn control of the White House over to the Stalwarts. In fact, Arthur quickly realized that he had little choice but to lend his support to civil service reform, lest he jeopardize the dominant position the Republican party had enjoyed since the Civil War. Garfield's assailant was apparently a disappointed office seeker, who, upon being arrested, blurted out that he was a Stalwart and that Arthur would now be president. As a result, Garfield's death aroused public opinion against the spoils system.

Intent upon strengthening his position in the country, Arthur, to the pleasant surprise of his critics, expressed support for limited civil service reform in his first annual message to Congress. This support was strengthened as a result of the 1882 congressional elections, which saw the

Democrats achieve dramatic gains. Arthur and congressional Republicans believed that by acting quickly they could pose as reformers to their constituents, while protecting the tenure of their officeholders in the event that the Democrats won the 1884 presidential election.

Thus, in his second annual message to Congress, Arthur called for the passage of the Pendleton Act, legislation introduced in 1881 by the Democratic senator from Ohio, George Hunt Pendleton. This bill contained measures such as competitive examinations and the banning of assessments that Arthur originally had opposed. But after the sobering results of the 1882 congressional elections, the president endorsed the provisions of the Pendleton Act. When this legislation easily passed the House and Senate in early 1883, Arthur signed it. With this action, Chester A. Arthur, once removed as collector of the port of New York for flagrant partisan abuses, launched the civil service in the United States.

The Pendleton Act had a limited application, as it was restricted to officials in Washington and to employees in major customhouses and post offices. The vast majority of federal employees, including many postal workers, as well as all municipal and state ones, still were not protected. In fact, when the bill was passed, it covered only 11 percent of the government employees—some 14,000 of a total of 131,000. Indeed, the struggle over the rich supply of remaining patronage was to be the primary source of conflict between Arthur's successor to the presidency, Grover Cleveland, and Congress.

Nevertheless, the achievement of civil service reform in 1883, the administrative historian Leonard White has written, "was a fundamental turning point in the history of the federal administrative system." The Pendleton Act contained provisions that limited the assessment of federal workers' salaries for party coffers and restricted the solicitation of campaign funds by officials from employees and in public buildings. Moreover, the Pendleton Act established a bipartisan Civil Service Commission of three members appointed by the president with the advice and consent of the Senate. The Civil Service Commission was vested with two crucial powers—control of examinations and authority to investigate enforcement of its rules. Finally, of great significance was the authority conferred upon the president to extend the classified service by executive order from time to time. Therefore, limited as was its initial application, the Pendleton Act was a solid foundation upon which the public service could be built in succeeding decades. The extension of the civil service in the twentieth century was to be a vital ingredient in establishing new energy and responsibility for a transformed executive office.

The First Term of Grover Cleveland

Neither the support of civil service reform nor the nomination of the leader of the half-breed, more moderate, faction of the party, James G. Blaine, for president could save the Republicans from defeat in the 1884 election. In comparison with the Democratic sweep in the 1882 congressional elections, the Republicans made a remarkable recovery in 1884, managing to retain control of the Senate and to gain twenty-two seats in the House of Representatives. But the Democratic standard-bearer, Gov. Grover Cleveland of New York, won a close election, thus becoming the first Democratic president in a quarter of a century.

Moderate men in every section of the country viewed the election of Cleveland as heralding the true end of the bitter conflicts generated by the Civil War. Cleveland was anxious to prove them correct, and, as the head of the party that received its greatest support from the South, he appointed many southerners to high office, including two to posts in his cabinet. To be sure, Republicans were not yet prepared to stop waving the "bloody shirt" and continued to paint the Democrats as unworthy to control the councils of power. Yet Cleveland's victory signaled a shift in the nation's attention from the Civil War conflicts to economic controversies relating to tariffs and the currency, which dominated U.S. politics after 1884.

Cleveland's election, however, did not result in a moratorium on the struggles between the president and Congress for control of appointments to the federal government. Hayes and Garfield had won major victories against the Senate, restoring some of the prestige of the executive that had been so badly diminished during the Johnson and Grant years. It fell to Cleveland, however, to fight one last battle over appointments that finally brought about the repeal of the Tenure of Office Act.

This battle resulted from Cleveland's attempt to reward with appointments loyal Democrats, who, after being out of office for so long, were hungry to partake of the patronage system. The president certainly was no spoilsman; indeed, he had established a reputation for reform both as mayor of Buffalo and governor of New York. He enforced the Pendleton Act and devoted an enormous amount of his time to scrutinizing the qualifications of candidates for federal positions that were not covered by the newly established civil service procedures. This approach yielded a number of outstanding appointments and won Cleveland the praise of civil service reformers.

Still, fashioning himself a Jacksonian Democrat, the president was not an enemy of the patronage system, and in time he was amenable to placing deserving Democrats in posts formerly held by Republicans. Operating under the constraints of the amended Tenure of Office Act, however, he was able to suspend but not remove individuals from their jobs. In effect, Cleveland could replace officials only when the Senate was in session and could approve those individuals selected as replacements. Yet the Republican-dominated Senate had determined to retain a degree of control over the administration by slowing down Cleveland's appointments, especially those tapped to replace Republicans. As a result, of the 643 suspensions (and corresponding appointments) that Cleveland made during the early days of his presidency, the Senate, after being in session for three months, had considered only seventeen, and only fifteen had been confirmed.

Before long, the issue between the president and the Senate was clarified by focusing on one particular office, the position of United States attorney in Alabama. When Cleveland suspended the incumbent, George M. Duskin, and nominated John D. Burnett as his replacement, the chairman of the Senate Judiciary Committee, George F. Edmunds of Vermont, prepared to place this nomination under intense and protracted scrutiny. He asked Cleveland's attorney general to send to his committee the papers covering not only Burnett's appointment, but all the information relating to Duskin's dismissal as well. Cleveland directed his attorney general to comply with the request for information covering Burnett's appointment; but, determined to settle once and for all the president's prerogative to remove federal officials without suffering congressional interference, he refused to put before the Senate any material relating to the suspension of Duskin.

Cleveland's refusal to comply stung Senate Republicans, and they responded with a resolution condemning the administration for its unwillingness to cooperate. The president, in turn, sent a message up to the "Hill" defending his actions and accusing the Congress of infringing on his constitutional responsibilities as chief executive. Of the requests and demands from the Senate for information covering his suspension of federal officials, Cleveland said:

> They [requests for information] assume the right of the Senate to sit in judgment upon the exercise of my exclusive discretion and executive function, for which I am solely responsible to the people from whom I have so lately received the sacred trust of office. My oath to support and defend the Constitution ... compels me to refuse compliance with these demands.[154]

Cleveland's message dramatized the issue with the Senate, and it quickly caught the attention of the nation. As in previous battles of this sort, public opinion supported the president. Recognizing that it was beaten, the Senate fell upon a means of retreat. It was discovered that during the controversy, Duskin's term had expired, thus making unnecessary his suspension by the president. Duskin's successor was quickly confirmed, ending still another struggle over the removal power, which resulted in total victory for the president. Although this incident concluded so anticlimactically, Cleveland's position was vindicated when a few months later, with overwhelming support from Democrats and Republicans, Congress passed a bill to repeal the Tenure of Office Act. "Thus," wrote Cleveland long after the event, "was an unhappy controversy happily followed by an expurgation of the last pretense of statutory sanction to an encroachment upon constitutional Executive prerogatives, and thus was a time-honored interpretation of the Constitution restored to us." [155]

Prelude to a More Active Presidency

In the twenty years from the end of the Grant administration to the end of Cleveland's second administration (1877-1897), the decline of executive prestige had been halted. The Senate's grip upon the details of executive branch administration, especially the removal power, had been loosened somewhat as a result of the defeats administered to the legislature by Hayes, Garfield, and Cleveland. The struggle to rejuvenate the independent status of the presidency was advanced further by the enactment of civil service reform, which began the process of insulating federal appointments from the local concerns of party spoilsmen.

The achievements of Grant's immediate successors notwithstanding, the office of the presidency remained small in scale and limited in power during the latter half of the nineteenth century. In effect, the struggles that emancipated the executive from congressional dominance restored presidential control over the president's own domain, but that province remained a constricted one. Late-nineteenth-century presidents had little control over either government expenditures or the policies of federal bureaus and departments. *(See "Early Presidential Economic Management," p. 639, in Chief Economist chapter of Part III.)*

In budgetary policy, the end of the Civil War marked the transition from emergency executive discretion in fiscal matters to renewed efforts on the part of Congress to reassert its authority over the level and purposes of executive expenditures. Hayes and Cleveland used the veto power effectively and aggressively to ward off the most egregious efforts of Congress to impose its will on government expenditures. Hayes, for example, successfully vetoed an Army Appropriations Bill of 1879 that included riders attached by the Democratic-controlled House of Representatives intended to short-circuit Reconstruction legislation.

Yet the use of the veto in such cases was strictly a defensive measure that did not exert executive authority over fiscal policy; indeed, until the passage of the Budget and Accounting Act in 1921, executive authority in this area was "almost, if not entirely, lacking." [156] Presidents were not consulted on the preparation of department and agency estimates; they were rarely consulted on the disposition of those estimates by the congressional committees handling appropriations. The secretary of the Treasury was merely a compiler, not a minister of finance. The absence of executive leadership in fiscal matters resulted in an irresponsible and disorderly budgetary policy, made worse by the congressional practice of dispersing fiscal authority among a number of appropriations committees.

The president's capacity to provide guidance in public policy and to enlist Congress's support to advance a program of the president's choosing also was very limited during the latter half of the nineteenth century. Indeed, no president at this time advanced a concept of executive power in support of the president playing such a role.

Cleveland, for example, fiercely defended the independence of the executive, but he made little effort to exert policy influence over his party or Congress. He did not believe that his responsibilities in this regard went beyond the recommendation of programs for Congress's consideration, and he expressly declined to use any other means of pressing his programs upon the legislature. Even on the tariff, an issue central to the conflict between Democrats and Republicans in the 1880s, Cleveland did little to bend Congress to his will. After the Democrats fared poorly in the 1886 congressional elections, Cleveland delivered a forceful message, demanding that Congress, in conformity with Democratic principles, cut tariff rates sharply. But having done so, the president did little to control events or even to maintain the sense of urgency and public purpose that had led him to focus attention on tariff reform. As one historian has written, "Like a great lethargic bear, Cleveland had bestirred himself ... and shaken the political hive, but then he slumped back into querulous inactivity." [157]

Benjamin Harrison

The limits of presidential power during the second half of the nineteenth century prompted Woodrow Wilson to declare in 1885, the second year of Cleveland's first term, that "unquestionably, the predominant and controlling force, the center and source of all motive and of all regulative power, is Congress." [158] But if Cleveland failed to challenge legislative supremacy, his successor, Benjamin Harrison, who thwarted Cleveland's bid for reelection in 1888, enthusiastically endorsed it.

Harrison, a Republican senator from Indiana, won a very close election; in fact, Cleveland, by piling up big margins in the South, won a plurality of the popular vote, but he lost the big northern states and thus the electoral college. This unusual development (there has not been such a discrepancy between the popular and electoral college votes since the 1888 election) brought to the presidency a man who understood perfectly congressional efforts to retain control over the conduct of government. Harrison came from the dominant group of Senate leaders who had clashed with Cleveland over the president's power of dismissal. He, therefore, did not require much urging to accept the advice that Republican senator John Sherman offered him a few weeks after the election about how the office of the presidency should be conducted. "The President," Sherman wrote Harrison, "should have no policy distinct from his party and that is better represented in Congress than in the Executive." Suggesting that "Cleveland made a cardinal mistake in [seeking to dictate] a tariff policy to Congress," Sherman urged the new president to cultivate friendly relations with legislators and to follow the dictates of, rather than seek to lead, the Republicans in the House and Senate.[159]

Thus, in spite of his unquestioned industry and dignified supervision of the nation's affairs, Harrison's term in the White House marked a retreat in the struggle to revive the status of the executive office. Garraty wrote of his conduct as president: "Cleveland had surrendered to the patronage system after a battle; Harrison embraced it from the start. Cleveland squabbled with Congress, and fumbled [in the tariff controversy] toward presidential leadership at least once; Harrison cheerfully submitted to being practically a figurehead." [160]

The absence of presidential leadership during Harrison's term, and the triumph of the doctrine of congressional sovereignty, gave rise to efforts to put the business of the legislature in order and to prepare the House and Senate to perform their functions more efficiently. Before the 1880s, Congress was primarily a deliberative and legislative body; by the end of the nineteenth century, it was less a forum for debate than a complex and well-disciplined body organized to reign over the affairs of the nation.

In the House, especially, law making increasingly came under the control of the congressional leadership, that is, the heads of leading committees and the Speaker. The Republican Speaker during Harrison's tenure, Thomas B. Reed, imposed rules in the House that greatly streamlined its chaotic conditions. Confronted with the dilatory tactics of the minority Democrats in the form of a "disappearing quorum"—where members sat mute during attendance calls, thus blocking the quorum necessary to conduct the business of the House—Reed counted the recalcitrants whether they signified their presence or not and faced down the protests of the opposition. The Supreme Court in 1891 upheld this and other "Reed rules," such as a no-filibustering rule, thus sanctioning the transformation of the House into a more disciplined body.[161]

A similar change occurred in the Senate, prompting the distinguished and critical English observer of the American political system, James Bryce, to write in 1890 that the Senate was "modern, severe, and political." [162] A forceful leadership represented by men such as Finance Committee chairman Nelson W. Aldrich of Rhode Island and the Appropriations Committee head, William B. Allison of Iowa, imposed controls on the Senate paralleling those that "Czar" Reed had established in the House, thus enabling Republicans to bring a previously unknown degree of party and procedural discipline to the Senate.

The Harrison administration, then, was one during which Congress and party organization reigned supreme. An outburst of important legislation during the first half of Harrison's term, including the protectionist McKinley Tariff of 1890, marked the rise of party discipline and institutional efficiency. As such, Harrison's presidency afforded a striking example of party government according to the model once celebrated by the Whigs but now put into practice for the first time by the Republicans.[163]

Yet no sooner had the Whig-Republican model of party government triumphed than developments rendered it obsolete. Massive social and economic changes were increasing the scale and complexity of American life, resulting in jarring economic dislocations and political conflict. In the face of these changes, pressures mounted for a new form of governance, one requiring a more expansive role for the national government and a more regularized administration of public affairs. Thus, the limited, nineteenth-century polity that was compatible with the dominance of decentralized party organizations and patronage practices, and the "sovereignty" of Congress, began to give way to a new order, one that provided a fertile environment for more consistent and forceful presidential leadership. The rise of a more intensely ideological politics in the 1890s,

Puck; Library of Congress

Cartoonist Joseph Keppler shows President Benjamin Harrison as being too small to wear the hat of his grandfather, President William Henry Harrison. Secretary of State James Blaine, who disagreed with Harrison over an important tariff bill, is depicted here as "The Raven."

culminating in the Bryan-McKinley presidential contest of 1896, and the growing role of the United States in world affairs, marked by the Spanish-American War (1898), set the stage for a significant transformation of presidential leadership.

The Second Term of Grover Cleveland

Most of these changes had roots in the late 1880s and early 1890s, and the effect of the new political order on the presidency first became evident during the second term of Grover Cleveland, who defeated Harrison in the 1892 election. Cleveland had a second chance at the White House because the probusiness Republican program had failed to assuage concerns in the nation about the economic dislocations of industrialization.

Although the Republican-controlled Fifty-first Congress (1889-1891) passed the Sherman Antitrust Act in 1890 to ameliorate the concentration of economic power in the country and responded to inflationist pressures by expanding the coinage of silver, it proved to be one of the most unpopular on record. In 1890, the Democrats regained control of the House by a huge margin, a preface, as it turned out, to Cleveland's victory two years later. Yet the Democrats were caught in power by the severe depression of 1893, a development that both enabled the Republicans to regain control of Congress in 1894 and created conditions that led Cleveland to employ presidential power more vigorously, albeit not more successfully, than any president since Lincoln. Thus, the "panic of 1893" and its enormous political repercussions were a prelude to the emergence of a new form of presidential leadership in the early twentieth century under Theodore Roosevelt and Woodrow Wilson.[164]

Cleveland's vigorous response to the economic crisis tested the limits of executive power but cost him the support of his party. His calling of a special session of Congress and securing the repeal of the Sherman Silver Purchase Act represented effective leadership in defense of the gold standard. Yet this marked departure from the hands-off approach to the legislative process that dominated his first term insulted not only inflationist Democrats such as William Jennings Bryan, but also key legislative leaders who resented the president's aggressive intervention in domestic policy.

The Democratic party's repudiation of Cleveland was ensured by the president's action in the Pullman strike of 1894. In the face of this railway strike, Cleveland, without consulting the governor of Illinois, dispatched troops to Chicago to protect U.S. property and "to remove obstructions to the United States mails." This action infuriated the Democratic governor, John P. Altgeld, who denounced the president's actions as both gratuitous and insulting to the constitutional protection of local self-government. "To absolutely ignore a local government in matters of this kind," Altgeld asserted in a telegram to Cleveland, "when the local government is ready to furnish assistance needed, and is amply able to enforce the law, not only insults the people of this State by imputing to them an inability to govern themselves or an unwillingness to enforce the law, but is in violation of a basic principle of our institutions."[165] Unimpressed, Cleveland replied that "in this hour of danger and public distress, discussion may well give way to active efforts on the part of all in authority to restore obedience to law and to protect life and property."[166]

Library of Congress

This banner celebrates the return of Grover Cleveland and his wife, Frances, to the White House in March 1893.

Cleveland's actions in the Pullman strike marked an important expansion of the president's domestic authority. His use of federal troops was unprecedented both in relying on constitutional, rather than more explicit statutory, authority and in circumventing state officials and assistance from beginning to end. Nevertheless, this action was ringingly endorsed by the Supreme Court in the *Debs* case, which upheld the arrest of Eugene Debs and other labor leaders of the Pullman strike for conspiring to obstruct the mails.[167] This decision ruled, in effect, that regardless of any statutory power, the president was justified under his general powers, as stated in Article II of the Constitution, in taking any measures for protecting the peace of the United States.[168]

Cleveland's action was successful, but it was expensive politically. Although the conservative wing of the Democratic party praised the president, his intervention in this labor dispute so aroused laborers and friends of labor that they turned not only against him but temporarily against the Democratic party.[169] The rift between the Democrats and workers was completed when the party nominated the rural-oriented William Jennings Bryan for president in 1896 and fought the campaign mainly on the issue of free silver.

Since the industrial-urban element was the fastest-growing segment of the population, the heavy losses the

Democrats suffered among workers and other city voters in 1896 precipitated a major political realignment from which the Republicans emerged as the party of the future.[170] The dramatic triumph of Republicans in this critical election brought an astute and skilled politician, William McKinley, to the White House, whose incumbency initiated a new era in the operation of the national government. This new era eventually placed the president at the center of U.S. politics in a way that dramatically altered the character of the executive office.

William McKinley

McKinley's presidency often is regarded as a mediocre prelude to the vigor and energy of Theodore Roosevelt's administration. But no less than the forceful leadership of Cleveland's second term, McKinley's administration marked an important change in the presidency.

In one important respect, however, McKinley's tenure was a "throwback." He, like Harrison, was a regular Republican who came to the presidency after a long apprenticeship in the Congress. Consequently, McKinley believed that good government could come only through party organization, and he carried into the White House a deep and abiding respect for legislative prerogatives. Still, he did not permit the executive branch to decline, as Harrison had. Instead, McKinley displayed remarkable skill as party leader, thus exerting tremendous influence over the legislature. Indeed, McKinley was the first Republican president to exercise any considerable initiative without arousing the resentment of his party in Congress.[171]

In displaying such effective party leadership, McKinley's presidency did not necessarily mark a fundamental advance of executive power. His influence over Congress, in fact, was similar to Jefferson's use of the congressional caucus to enact the Democratic-Republican program nearly a century earlier. Jefferson's successors were unable to match his influence over Congress, thus demonstrating the limits of party government as an instrument of sustained executive leadership.

McKinley's presidency, however, was dominated by a foreign policy that established a new position for the United States in world affairs, a development that enormously increased McKinley's power and that began dramatically to reshape the presidency. Especially important was the Spanish-American War in 1898. McKinley favored a peaceful resolution of the conflict with Spain but ultimately yielded to public sentiment, which, aroused by propaganda, expressed a distinct consensus for war. McKinley carried out a "day by day, and sometimes . . . an hour by hour" supervision of the war effort that laid the foundation for a greater level of presidential involvement and control over foreign policy.[172] The hostilities were so brief, the victory so complete, and, most important, the expansion of territory so considerable that no reaction set in against executive power as it had after the Civil War.

The acquisition of the Philippines and the greater influence over Cuba that resulted from the defeat of Spain broadened the international obligations of the country and blurred party lines. This development allowed the president for the first time in the nineteenth century to attain a status above party politics. U.S. participation in China during the Boxer uprising of 1899 and the successful U.S. push for an "open door" policy reinforced the public's view that the United States had a new position in world affairs.[173] McKinley himself expressed awareness of this change and its effect on the executive when he said, "I can no longer be called the President of a party; I am now the President of the whole people." [174]

McKinley's tenure, then, marked an important transformation of the executive office. To be sure, his presidency gave only a hint of what was to come. Committed to a limited role for the national government in the economy, McKinley did not seek to articulate a positive program to deal with major domestic issues such as race relations, trusts and their regulation, labor relations, and the civil service. Nor did he attempt to influence public opinion outside of the regular channels of party politics. Following the tradition of the nineteenth-century executive, McKinley did not attempt to employ popular rhetoric to influence policy. Indeed, his speeches did not even allude to the Spanish-American War, the sinking of the *Maine,* the problem of racially discriminatory "Jim Crow" laws, or U.S. policy toward the Philippines—all major issues faced by his administration.[175] Nevertheless, McKinley's influence with Congress and his role as "world leader" was an important preface to the transformation of the executive in the twentieth century.

Theodore Roosevelt to Woodrow Wilson

During the last three decades of the nineteenth century, major changes in American life placed increased burdens upon the national government, and particularly upon the office of the president. The population of the United States doubled during these years but did not keep pace with industrial development, urbanization, and immigration, all of which increased at extraordinary rates. These changes were incident to the Industrial Revolution, the shift from small-scale manufacturing and commerce to large-scale factory production, which began to transform American life dramatically after the Civil War.

The concentration of economic wealth at the turn of the century yielded giant "trusts" that had become, according to reformers, uncontrolled and irresponsible units of power within American society. These industrial combinations aroused fears in the United States that opportunity would no longer be equal, that the growing corporation might threaten the freedom of individuals to earn a living. Moreover, it was feared that great business interests had captured and corrupted the men and methods of government for their own profit.

The first wave of protest against the financial exploitation and political corruption unleased by industrial growth was the Populist revolt that culminated in William Jennings Bryan's ill-fated crusade for the presidency in 1896. The Progressive Era emerged after the collapse of populism; it was a period of urban and middle-class protest against many of the same forces of expanding industrialization and unrestrained finance capitalism that caused the agrarian revolts of the late nineteenth century. Unlike the Populist movement, however, it focused on problems that were of greater concern to the urban and industrial element that was the fastest growing segment of the population. As a result, Progressivism had a major impact on the nation. As the historian Richard Hofstadter noted, it "enlarged and redirected" agrarian discontent, resulting in industrial reform and changes in government institutions that "affected in a striking way . . . the whole tone of American political life." [176]

Progressive reform was closely related to significant changes in the office of president. Although the executive office had undergone significant development at the hands of strong leaders such as Washington, Jefferson, Jackson, and Lincoln, the role and power of the president remained severely restricted until the twentieth century. The emergence of Theodore Roosevelt changed this pattern.

Roosevelt and the Expansion of Executive Power

On September 6, 1901, President McKinley was shot by an anarchist while attending the Pan-American Exposition in Buffalo, New York. *(See "William McKinley," p. 362, in Removal chapter of Part II.)* The president died a week later, elevating the vice president, Theodore Roosevelt, to the presidency on September 15, 1901. Disregarding the advice of friends who warned that he would seem but a "pale copy of McKinley," Roosevelt announced his intention to continue unchanged McKinley's policies and cabinet. "If a man is fit to be President," T R wrote, "he will speedily so impress himself in the office that the policies pursued will be his anyhow, and he will not have to bother as to whether he is changing them or not. . . ." [177]

The prospect of Theodore Roosevelt "impressing himself" upon the executive office, his assurances of continuity notwithstanding, greatly troubled those who dominated U.S. politics at the turn of the century. The conservative members of the Republican party, especially, were concerned that the young president (at only forty-three years of age he was the youngest man ever to assume the office) was not to be trusted. Throughout his political career, including his tenure as governor of New York, he had established a reputation as a progressive and impetuous statesman, one who lived uneasily with the patronage practices and probusiness policies that dominated the Republican party. Indeed, as governor he was so troublesome to New York party regulars that they took pains to secure his nomination as McKinley's running mate in 1900.

"Anything can happen now that that damn cowboy is in the White House," remarked Mark Hanna, chairman of the Republican National Committee, when his friend McKinley died. Conservative public figures in New York and Washington openly hoped for the best, yet privately they agreed with Hanna.

Roosevelt's plain-speaking and unconventional style of leadership aside, he was not the "madman" Hanna feared. He was no enemy of business interests or party. Like most progressive reformers, he accepted the new industrial order that had grown up since the Civil War, but he wished to curb its worst abuses and bring it under government regulation. Similarly, his view of the presidency did not lead to a jarring departure from past practices; instead, especially during the early days of his administration, he was a *conservative* reformer who hoped to preserve constitutional government by placing a strengthened executive office in the service of a moderate program of change.

Roosevelt's Concept of Presidential Power

In both foreign and domestic matters, presidential scholars Samuel and Dorothy Rosenmen have written, "Roosevelt extended executive authority to the furthest limit permitted in peacetime by the Constitution—if not further." [178] Theodore Roosevelt himself viewed the expansion of executive authority as the principal ingredient in his remarkably successful tenure as president. "The most important factor in getting the right spirit in my administration," he wrote in his *Autobiography,* "was my insistence upon the theory that the executive power was limited only by specific restrictions and prohibitions appearing in the Constitution or imposed by Congress in its constitutional powers." [179] Believing that the delimitation of presidential power during the nineteenth century had rendered the American political system impotent and subject to capture by special interests, Roosevelt expressed the view that the president, and every executive officer in high position, was "a steward of the people bound actively and affirmatively to do all he could for the people, and not to content himself with the negative merit of keeping his talents undamaged in a napkin." [180]

In his belief that the president possessed a special mandate from the people, Theodore Roosevelt was a conscious disciple of Andrew Jackson. Unlike Jackson, however, he did not adhere to Jeffersonian (that is, states' rights) principles, but he tried to link popular leadership to a greater sense of national purpose. Roosevelt dedicated himself to a "new nationalism," as he and his progressive allies called it, which presupposed an unprecedented expansion of the national government's responsibility to secure the social and economic welfare of the people.

In important respects, Theodore Roosevelt's exposition of executive power drew upon the defense of a broad discretionary authority for the president articulated by Alexander Hamilton in 1793 under the pen name of "Pacificus." *(See "The Presidency of George Washington," p. 57, in this chapter.)* In his defense of the issuance of the 1793 Neutrality Proclamation, Hamilton espoused a view of the presidency that was largely unacceptable until Theodore Roosevelt entered the White House. "The general doctrine of our Constitution," Hamilton argued, "is that the executive power of the nation is vested in the president; subject only to the exceptions and qualifications which are expressed in the instrument." [181] Washington, Jackson, and Lincoln acted on a broad view of the president's authority, especially when they were faced by a national crisis. Theodore Roosevelt, however, was the first chief executive to embrace the Hamiltonian position as a recipe for the day-to-day administration of the nation's affairs.

Yet this embrace of Hamilton's principles was certainly not complete. Hamilton supported an energetic executive in which a dominant president would curb, rather than abet, popular influence. In contrast, Theodore Roosevelt expressed and embodied the progressive aspiration to establish the president as an agent of social and economic reform. "Men who understand and practice the deep underlying philosophy of the Lincoln school of American political thought," wrote T R, "are necessarily Hamiltonian in their belief in a strong and efficient National Government and Jeffersonian in their belief in the people as the ultimate authority, and in the welfare of the people as the end of government." [182]

Beginning of the Rhetorical Presidency

T R's determination to use the executive office to serve the interests of the people, as he understood them, brought about a number of significant changes in the conduct of the executive office. Arguably, the most important of these changes was the advancement of the president's role as the leader of public opinion. Roosevelt's administration marked the advent of the "rhetorical presidency," that is, the use of popular or mass rhetoric as a principal tool of presidential governance.[183]

The rise of the rhetorical presidency signified a dramatic transformation in the founding theory and early history of the executive. The Framers of the Constitution explicitly proscribed popular leadership; and during the nineteenth century, presidential efforts to rouse public opinion in support of policy initiatives in Congress were considered illegitimate, a form of demagogy that was beneath the dignity of executive office. Roosevelt's "stewardship" theory of the executive, however, demanded the forging of stronger, more direct links with the public.

The great skill Roosevelt displayed in his rhetorical campaigns and the popularity of the programs he championed made popular rhetoric a more acceptable, if not yet commonplace, form of leadership. Much of this program centered on regulatory policies designed to, as T R put it, "subordinate the big corporation to the public welfare." [184] But the Republican party was controlled by conservative congressional leaders who continued to adhere to a "laissez-faire" creed in the face of the massive social and economic changes at the turn of the century, a view that eschewed the regulation of business, transportation, or finance. (Leaders in the Senate were Nelson Aldrich of Rhode Island and Eugene Hale of Maine; the House bridled under the grip of the Speaker, Joseph Cannon of Illinois.) "Gradually," however, T R wrote of his relationship with the Republican Old Guard, "I was forced to abandon the effort to persuade them to come my way, and then I achieved results only by appealing over the heads of the Senate and House leaders to the people, who were the masters of both of us." [185]

Perhaps the most important result achieved by going to the people in this way was the passage of the Hepburn Act in 1906, which delegated power to the Interstate Commerce Commission (ICC) to regulate railroad shipping rates and to maintain and enforce compliance with these regulations. The president's proposal had been received favorably in 1904 by the House of Representatives, which quickly passed railroad rate legislation in early 1905; but it ran into trouble in the Senate, where the Committee on Interstate Commerce conducted long public hearings, mostly given over to the opposing testimony of railroad executives.

As the Senate hearings proceeded, the president left the capital for a long vacation in the West, giving rise to speculation that he had given up on rate regulation.[186] In fact, Roosevelt's trip during April and May of 1905 through the Middle West and Southwest turned out to be a campaign for the Hepburn bill. The first blast of his rhetorical campaign came from Chicago, where, speaking before the Iroquois-Republican Club, he demanded that ICC have "ironclad powers" to set rates.[187] This speech and similar addresses given in Dallas, San Antonio, and Denver received extensive and favorable coverage in the press.

The campaign for rate regulation continued in the early fall of 1905 on a swing through the Southwest and culminated in Roosevelt's annual message to Congress in December. Although addressed to Congress, Roosevelt's message had a larger audience in mind, the American people, and the pressure of public opinion eventually overcame resistance to the Hepburn Act. Soon after the president's annual message, Secretary of War William Howard Taft reported to his brother on a confidential talk he had with the president of the Rock Island Railroad. The railroad executive had admitted that the senators he had counted on for "allegiance," while still opposed to the Hepburn bill, were yielding, since the president had so "roused the people that it was impossible for them to stand against the popular demand." [188] On May 18, 1906, Roosevelt's bill was passed into law by an exceptionally large majority, with only three senators voting against it.

The Hepburn Act, the historian George Mowry has written, "was a landmark in the evolution of federal control of private industry." [189] Among other things, it gave the ICC the power to set aside a railroad rate schedule on complaint of a shipper and prescribe a reasonable rate subject to review. This substantial expansion of federal administrative power marked the first important step away from laissez faire and toward regulation and control of the nation's business practices.

Roosevelt's remarkable success was helped considerably by the press. He was the first president to recognize the value of the press as a means of communication with the nation and to understand that access to this potential had to be pursued actively and continuously. It was his good fortune that the years of his presidency coincided with the development of mass circulation of newspapers and popular magazines.

Roosevelt's grasp of the potential of the media is revealed by the use he made of the mass circulation magazines. Partly by inspiring articles by intimates, and partly through the force of his personality and ideas, he "kept the pages of the popular magazines glowing with support" of his crusades.[190] As the journalist Mark Sullivan has noted, "Roosevelt, in marshalling public opinion for the railroad rate bill, had, as always, help from the magazine writers," [191] including Henry Beech Needham, Ray Stannard Baker, and Walter Hines, all intimates of the president.[192]

Roosevelt's triumph in the matter of rate regulation signaled a change whereby the president's key relationship was with the public rather than with his party or with Congress. But Theodore Roosevelt's administration marked only the beginning of a new form of leadership. His rhetorical flourishes notwithstanding, Roosevelt believed that a balance had to be maintained between presidential initiative and congressional deliberation in order to maintain the U.S. system of government. Accordingly, although he insisted that the president had to assume a more prominent place in the political system than was possible in the nineteenth century, T R made assiduous efforts to court support in the Congress and to work compatibly with his party's leadership in the Senate and the House.

Roosevelt and Policy Leadership

The rise of the rhetorical presidency during the Progressive era went hand-in-hand with an expansion of the executive's responsibility to provide guidance in the formation of public policy. The capacity of the president to exert leadership in policy matters and to bend an often factious and defiant Congress to his will was very limited during the latter half of the nineteenth century. T R's respect for the legislative process notwithstanding, his presidency resulted in a fundamental shifting of federal power from Congress to the White House, a change that slowly, but ineluctably, moved the executive to the center of government activity.

Roosevelt's all-out campaign for the Hepburn Act and the principle behind it came to symbolize his whole domestic policy. Roosevelt called his policy the "Square Deal," naming a principle he felt described the proper function of government: to maintain a "just balance" between management and labor, between producer and consumer, and between the extremists at both ends.

The important fact about T R's enunciation of the Square Deal in the development of the presidency is that it summoned consideration of a principle of fairness as he, rather than his party or Congress, understood it.[193] Nearly all subsequent presidents would define their administrations in similar terms: the New Freedom, the New Deal, the Fair Deal, the Great Society, the Opportunity Society. The routine effort after Roosevelt to advertise a catchy phrase in order to symbolize a president's idea of appropriate government action was symptomatic of a new style of presidential leadership, one where, for better or worse, the executive, not Congress, assumed the major burden of managing public policy.

The President As World Leader

Theodore Roosevelt's innovative executive activism in domestic politics was quite modest in comparison with his actions in foreign affairs. Although during the nineteenth century the president's authority to initiate foreign policy and negotiate treaties became settled practice, Roosevelt took action to assert the primacy of the president's role in foreign affairs over the legislature in *executing* such policy as well, even when clear direction from the legislature was lacking.

T R's executive theory had a policy purpose. Looking toward the future, Roosevelt saw the distinct need for a more energetic and ambitious U.S. foreign policy. "Whether we desire it or not," he told Congress in his first annual message, "we must henceforth recognize that we have international duties no less than international rights." [194] This view was rooted in philosophical and practical considerations. Just as many progressives believed the doctrine of laissez faire must give way to a greater sense of national purpose in domestic affairs, they urged a departure from the nineteenth-century commitment to isolation from world affairs. Progressives couched the belief in U.S. manifest destiny in ethical terms, arguing that an expansion of U.S. territory and influence was not imperialism but the opposite of it. Roosevelt was in hearty accord with Herbert Croly's assertion that "peace will prevail in international relations, just as order prevails within a nation, because of the righteous use of superior force—because the power which makes for pacific organization is stronger than the power which makes for war like organization." [195]

More practical considerations also prompted a more active foreign policy. The Spanish-American War of 1898 resulted in an expansion of U.S. territory in the Caribbean and the Pacific. This newly acquired empire created responsibilities that required dominance in Central and South America, a new emphasis on the Pacific basin, and an isthmus canal so that naval power could be efficiently transformed from one ocean to another.

The Panama Canal. Roosevelt considered the building of a canal especially important. His first annual message to Congress, dated December 3, 1901, declared, "No single great material work which remains to be undertaken on this continent is of such consequence to the American people as the building of a canal across the isthmus connecting North and South America." [196] The site eventually chosen for this project, Panama, belonged to Colombia, which to Roosevelt's surprise and embarrassment, was not willing to grant the United States the right to build the canal according to the terms offered by the president. There ensued a complicated round of diplomacy and intrigue that revealed some of the most important characteristics of the Theodore Roosevelt era in U.S. foreign policy.

On January 22, 1903, Roosevelt's secretary of state, John Hay, negotiated and signed a treaty with the Colombian minister in Washington, Thomas Herran, known as the Hay-Herran Treaty. Under the treaty, the New Panama Canal Company was to construct the project, and complete sovereignty of the three-mile zone was to be given to the United States in perpetuity. These conditions were rejected by the Colombian dictator, José Manuel Marroquin.

Instead of negotiating further, however, Roosevelt formulated a policy to attain by force what he had failed to achieve by diplomacy. First, he gave tacit support to efforts, instigated by those with interests in the New Panama Canal Company, to foment a revolution in Panama to secede from Colombia. If the Panamanian revolution had not succeeded, Roosevelt gave clear indication that he would have acted to take possession of the isthmus anyway. On the tenuous legal foundation of an 1846 treaty with Colombia, in which both countries had guaranteed the right of transit across the isthmus, T R was prepared to recommend to Congress that the United States should at once occupy the canal zone without any further negotiation with Colombia; he had actually drafted a paragraph in early October to be included in his 1903 annual message to Congress recommending this course of action.[197] When the more cautious Mark Hanna, who was now a leading figure in the Senate, was informed of this plan, he counseled that patience was necessary and expressed confidence that Colombia would come around. But the president answered Hanna's entreaty in a way that typified his preference for decisive action in such matters of diplomacy: "I think it is well worth considering whether we had not better warn those cat-rabbits that great though our patience has been, it can be exhausted. . . . I feel that we are certainly justified in morals and . . . justified in law under the treaty of 1846, in interfering summarily and saying that the canal is to be built and that they shall not stop it." [198]

A successful revolution in Panama made it unnecessary for Roosevelt to take direct action against Colombia. But the president's rapid and unilateral action did aid and protect the revolution when it broke out on November 3, 1903; a U.S. warship, the U.S.S. *Nashville,* conveniently docked in Colón on the eve of the uprising and on the following days prevented Colombian troops from reinforcing their outnumbered forces in Panama. On November 6, Panama became a free and independent nation, and within an hour and a half it was recognized by the United States. Shortly after the new republic had been proclaimed, the Panamanian government signed a treaty granting the United States canal rights in return for $10 million, the amount originally offered to Colombia.

Roosevelt's action in taking control of the canal zone was emblematic of his "stewardship" theory of the presidency as it applied to foreign policy. He was not reluctant to act quickly and independently, even when the support of Congress and the legal foundation for his maneuvers seemed uncertain. Roosevelt treated the criticism of his policy in regard to the canal as unconstitutional with disdain. "At different stages of the affair," he wrote, "believers in a do-nothing policy denounced me has having 'usurped authority'—which meant, that when nobody else could or would exercise efficient authority, I exercised it." [199]

Roosevelt succeeded in building the canal and proclaimed some years later that this accomplishment was "by far the most important action that I took in foreign affairs during the time I was President." [200] This policy, however, was to cause problems in the future. Colombia felt cheated and continued to press its claims for justice. Later, in the Wilson and Harding administrations, over former President Roosevelt's protest, an apology was extended to Colombia, along with an indemnity award of $25 million. Yet, as one historian has written, "the wounds in this incident were never really eradicated. . . . An unfortunate pattern of overbearing American domination in Latin American affairs was established, and even when they were at least partially abandoned in later years, the memory remains to plague future American Presidents." [201]

The taking of the canal zone signified a new policy toward Latin America following the Spanish-American War and the acquisition of new territory, a policy that entailed an expanded U.S. role in foreign affairs and enlarged presidential powers in support of this new policy.

In 1903, an incident in Santo Domingo prompted Roosevelt to modify significantly the Monroe Doctrine. *(See "The Presidencies of James Monroe and John Quincy Adams," p. 68, in this chapter.)* A corrupt dictatorship had left Santo Domingo bankrupt and unable to meet its obligations, and a revolution had left the island in chaos. In the early winter of 1903, France, Germany, and Italy were threatening intervention, and by the end of the year there were rumors that a German naval squadron was heading across the Atlantic to protect the German interests in the Caribbean. Roosevelt, facing an election year, acted cautiously; but he began to articulate a policy that proclaimed the duty of the United States to intervene in the affairs of Latin American countries that acted wrongfully or were rendered impotent by a mismanagement of their industrial and political affairs. The president officially proclaimed this policy to Congress in his December 1904 annual message. The Roosevelt Corollary to the Monroe Doctrine, as it became known, was a bold statement of future policy toward the debt-ridden, unstable governments of Latin America:

> If a nation shows that it knows how to act with reasonable efficiency and decency in social and political matters, if it keeps order and pays its obligations, it need fear no interference by the United States. Chronic wrongdoing, or an impotence which results in a general loosening of the ties of civilized society may in America, as elsewhere, ultimately require intervention by some civilized nation, and in the western hemisphere the adherence of the United States to the Monroe Doctrine may force the United States, however reluctantly, in flagrant cases of such wrongdoing or impotence, to the exercise of an international police power.[202]

The Roosevelt Corollary altered Monroe's doctrine from one denying the right of European intervention in the Americas to one sanctioning the process when conducted by the United States. At the end of the month in which Roosevelt announced this doctrine, the worsening of conditions in Santo Domingo forced him to translate his words into action. Confronted with a nation facing bankruptcy, on the one hand, and European powers demanding satisfaction for their accounts, on the other hand, Roosevelt forced an "agreement" on Santo Domingo in early 1905 establishing a U.S. financial protectorate over the island. When the Senate, resentful of the president's acting unilaterally to develop a novel foreign policy, failed to ratify the treaty, Roosevelt went ahead and implemented the protectorate anyway, considering it an executive agreement. The Dominican agreement was in operation for two years before the Senate finally acquiesced and approved it with minor modification in 1907.

Roosevelt's dominance over the development of policy, as well as its execution, even in the face of congressional opposition, signaled a major shift of power in the area of foreign relations from Congress to the president. Before Roosevelt's administration, it was not uncommon for Congress, especially the Senate, to intervene in foreign policy. Theodore Roosevelt defended and asserted a role for the president in foreign affairs that was not bounded by the specific authorizations of power granted by the Constitution, the statutes passed by the legislature, or even the power of the Senate to ratify treaties. "The Constitution did not explicitly give me power to bring about the necessary agreement with Santo Domingo," Roosevelt wrote in 1913. "But," he added, "the Constitution did not forbid my doing what I did."[203]

The Russian-Japanese War. Roosevelt's policy in Latin America was an important departure from the nineteenth-century doctrine of isolation. This departure was even more clearly revealed by T R's bold initiatives in Asia. Most significant was his unprecedented intervention in a conflict between the Russians and Japanese in 1905. This conflict centered on the imperialistic designs of these two powers in China.

When Russia took action in 1903 that threatened the Open Door Policy in China, Japan staged a devastating surprise attack on the Russian fleet anchored at Port Arthur. Because Roosevelt considered Russia a greater imperialistic threat in Asia, his sympathies lay with Japan. Indeed, the Japanese were fortified in their attack upon the Russians by the secret verbal assurances of President Roosevelt that the United States would support Japan if any of the European powers came to the aid of the Russians. This extraordinary commitment included an agreement of Japan's recognition of U.S. jurisdiction in the Philippines and the denunciation of all aggressive interest in that direction in return for the U.S. recognition of Japan's claim to Korea. Thus, for the first time, a president of the United States had committed this country to possible future military action, and to the recognition of one power's claim upon another nation's territory and sovereignty, without any consultation with the Senate.

This audacious action ended in diplomatic triumph for Roosevelt. Although the president favored the Japanese as a countervailing force to Russian designs on China, he feared that an overwhelming Japanese victory might establish that nation as a danger in the Pacific. Therefore, when the war tilted dramatically in Japan's favor, Roosevelt intervened, without the knowledge of the cabinet or Congress, or even most of the State Department, and eventually won consent from both Russia and Japan to meet in a peace conference at Portsmouth, New Hampshire. The U.S. president then managed through what Mowry has called "patient, tactful and brilliant diplomacy" to bring about the Peace of Portsmouth in September 1905. This settlement achieved a balance of power in Asia, satisfying not only the interests of the warring nations, but, because its Open Door policy in China was maintained, those of the United States as well.[204]

Roosevelt's actions in the Russian-Japanese War marked the end of a tradition, supported by all previous presidents, that kept the United States out of the affairs of the European nations and their imperialistic designs in Asia and Africa. Yet his bold actions in the Pacific basin were taken without consulting Congress or the cabinet. This policy was further advanced in 1907, when the president, once again without consulting Congress or the cabinet, sent the U.S. battle fleet on a tour around the world, a daring and brilliant maneuver that won public support for an expanded navy and demonstrated to the Japanese the intention and ability of the United States to protect its interests in Asia.

Nevertheless, Roosevelt's foreign policy, although singularly successful, did not establish the U.S. as a world power. The expansion of the U.S. role in the world and the expansion of executive responsibility in foreign affairs took place largely without any meaningful examination of their implications by the American people or their representatives in Congress. Roosevelt's great popularity notwithstanding, he initiated a new era of U.S. foreign policy without nurturing the sort of democratic consensus that could consistently sustain such a departure from past practices. This was a disconcerting aspect of what was generally a very favorable presidential legacy. As Goldsmith has written, "Theodore Roosevelt set the stage for the American President to play a world historical role that in many instances successive Presidents were neither capable of nor inclined to follow, nor were the American people prepared to support it."[205] T R's presidency paved the way for strong and dynamic presidential leadership in foreign affairs, but this was to create problems, as well as opportunities, for future presidents.

Theodore Roosevelt Collection, Harvard College Library

Theodore Roosevelt stands with his hand-picked successor, William Howard Taft.

The Troubled Presidency of William Howard Taft

Roosevelt left the office of the presidency more important and more the focus of national attention than it had ever been. Had T R wanted to stand for a third term, he certainly could have been renominated and most likely would have been reelected.[206] But he had promised in November 1904 that he would not run again. The three and a half years he had already served, Roosevelt stated at the time, constituted his first term; and because he considered the custom that limited presidents to two terms a wise one, on election night he issued a statement declaring that he would not be "a candidate for or accept another nomination."[207]

Although Roosevelt was clearly tempted to go back on this promise in 1908, the fact that he did not do so revealed his commitment to the traditions and institutions of constitutional government. Roosevelt believed strongly that the powers of the president needed to be expanded for the good, indeed the survival, of the nation. But he was also acutely aware that representative government would be poorly served by the concentration of too much power in its first citizen.

Roosevelt's self-denial, however, did not go so far as to prevent him from selecting his successor, William Howard Taft, his secretary of war and closest adviser during the second term. Nor did it stop him from "throwing his hat in the ring" in 1912 and challenging Taft's renomination, once he feared that his successor had betrayed progressive principles. Indeed, it is fair to say that William Taft spent the entire four years of his presidency dwelling uncomfortably in the shadow of Theodore Roosevelt. Taft sincerely intended to carry on the policies of his predecessor, and he had some success in doing so. But he was ill-suited, by philosophy and personality, to match T R's "stewardship" of the executive office.

In the wake of Roosevelt's presidency, Taft seemed like an anachronism in the office. Although he never said so publicly, Taft never approved of T R's theory that it is the president's duty "to do anything that the needs of the nation demand, unless such action is forbidden by the Constitution or the law." Taft's view of executive power was much closer to the understanding that prevailed during the latter half of the nineteenth century, one that eschewed a broad interpretation of the executive's discretionary powers. As he wrote some years after leaving office:

> The true view of the executive function ... is that the President can exercise no power which cannot be reasonably or fairly traced to some specific grant of power or justly implied or included within such express grant as necessary and proper to exercise. Such specific grant must be either in the Constitution or in an act of Congress passed in pursuance thereof. There is no undefined residuum of power which he can exercise because it seems to be in the public interest.[208]

Because he narrowly construed the president's power, Taft denied that it involved the exercise of either popular or policy leadership. He rejected the notion that he bore any special mandate from the people and refused to make any special effort to court public opinion or the press. Taft also did not take advantage, as T R did, of "swings around the circle," or speaking tours around the country, to advance his program or bring the pressure of public opinion upon Congress to support his policies. Taft did go on speaking tours; but unlike Roosevelt, who enjoyed such trips, Taft made tours at the urging of his aides and with considerable reluctance. "The Taft administration," political scientist Elmer Cornwell has noted, "represented a hiatus in the presidential leadership of opinion, if not actually a retrograde step." [209]

Taft's passive view of presidential power also was reflected in his relations with Congress. On the one hand, Taft dedicated himself to an ambitious legislative program, seeing his task as enacting into legislation, or institutionalizing, the reform that Roosevelt's vigorous and independent executive action had begun. On the other hand, he had serious misgivings about interfering in the legislative process, telling the Senate majority leader, Nelson Aldrich, "I have no disposition to exert any other influence than that which it is my function under the Constitution to exercise. . . ." [210] For example, Taft stood by passively in 1910 as his most important legislative proposal, to alter the protectionist tariff policies of the Republican party, was badly compromised in the Senate, which added over eight hundred amendments to the much stronger bill passed by the House. Taft signed the bill that came out of conference, although the final product was closer to the Senate bill, with high rates, than to that of the House.[211]

Taft's public deference to the prerogatives of Congress was not necessarily an obstacle to achieving an impressive legislative record. Jefferson and McKinley before him had worked quietly within the party councils to forge strong links between the executive and the legislature, thus exercising considerable influence over Congress. But Taft lacked the deft political touch to provide this kind of party leadership. In fact, his experience before reaching the presidency had been confined to judicial and administrative posts, so that he came, like Herbert Hoover later, to the White House relatively inexperienced in the political functions that worked to combine the separate branches of government.[212]

Taft also suffered from changing political conditions. By the time Roosevelt left office, the Republicans were badly divided between an increasingly stubborn conservative, probusiness majority and a growing progressive minority whose reform claims were inspired by Roosevelt's successful challenge of the regular party leadership. Taft was far more conservative than Roosevelt; and although his friendship for Roosevelt and his recognition of the public's support for reform inclined him to push for what was genuinely a progressive program, he seemed all too willing, in the eyes of progressive Republicans, to accept compromise and to allow the conservative leadership—Aldrich in the Senate and Cannon in the House—a free hand in the management of his legislative program. Indeed, Taft's feeble efforts to mediate the differences between conservatives and reformers only aggravated the situation, resulting eventually in an irreparable split.

The outbreak of virtual civil war in the Republican party began with a progressive revolt in the House of Representatives that ended in significant institutional change. Unwilling to tolerate any longer the policies and arbitrariness of Speaker Cannon, the House insurgents, under the leadership of George Norris of Nebraska, united with the House Democrats at the opening of the new Congress in March 1910 to strip the speakership of most of its power. Although Cannon was not removed from his chair, the institutional power of the Speaker over legislation was limited substantially. Before the insurgent movement, the Speaker served as presiding officer and, simultaneously, controlled committee assignments and the all-important Rules Committee, which was in charge of the legislative agenda. After insurgency, the office of Speaker was stripped of all major duties except the constitutional role of presiding officer; that role itself was narrowed, however, by the passage of rules limiting the Speaker's discretionary parliamentary prerogatives.[213]

The weakening of party leadership in the House, a bulwark of congressional government, reinforced and institutionalized the fundamental shift of power from Congress to the White House that first became noticeable during Theodore Roosevelt's presidency. The same progressive revolt that toppled the speakership in the House also began to weaken the foundation of party government in the Senate during Taft's presidency, depriving party leaders of their control over Senate deliberations. Power in Congress devolved to committee members, especially chairs, who became masters of legislation. The decline of party in the House and Senate badly fragmented power in Congress, making the country more dependent upon the sort of dynamic and independent presidential leadership that Theodore Roosevelt had provided.

Taft, his narrow construction of executive power notwithstanding, was not insensitive to the new demands for leadership both in congressional and party matters. In fact, toward the end of his presidency, he began to offer proposals and take actions that suggested a partial acceptance of the expansion of executive authority. Very late in his term he suggested that the presidential and legislative branches be brought closer together by giving cabinet members nonvoting seats in Congress. Furthermore, he endorsed the report of a presidential commission that called for the president to exert greater influence over the administrative affairs of the executive branch by holding the various departments and agencies to a comprehensive budgetary program. Taft submitted an executive budget in 1913 just before he went out of office.

These proposals to strengthen the executive were ignored by Congress. But it is misleading to view Taft's term in office merely as a throwback to the nineteenth century. Rather, his halting acceptance of the Roosevelt legacy served to ratify, rather than challenge in any serious way, the emergence of a new form of presidential leadership.

Woodrow Wilson and the Defense of Popular Leadership

After the midterm election of 1910, it became unlikely that Taft would be reelected president. This election marked, Mowry has written, "one of those significant decades in American history which signalize a reversal in trends before a complete transfer of power occurs." [214] For the first time in sixteen years the Democratic party controlled the House of Representatives, and although the Republicans kept their majority in the Senate, it was a purely nominal one. The insurgent Republicans, who strengthened their position in the primary and general elections of that year, held the balance of power between the almost evenly divided regular Republican and Democratic forces. The 1910 election also went far to rehabilitate the Democratic party because it furnished it with a number of progressives, most of whom were unattached to William Jennings Bryan, whose fiery message of rural populism had taken the party to disastrous defeat in three of the past four presidential campaigns.

Among these new Democrats was Woodrow Wilson, formerly a professor and president of Princeton University, who in 1910 was elected governor of New Jersey. Two years later, the Democrats, after a long deadlock in the convention, nominated the erstwhile professor for president on the forty-sixth ballot. The Democrats, unable for the past two decades to offer a program that addressed the challenges of the Progressive Era, suddenly found themselves led by an articulate and forward-looking statesman whose candidacy appeared to offer the party its best opportunity since the Civil War to govern the nation. Wilson's victory in 1912 was only the third by a Democrat since the Civil War, and his victory helped to sweep enough Democrats into office so that his party controlled both houses of Congress.

Yet the Democratic opportunity to govern might not have been realized had the Republicans not self-destructed in 1912. Persuaded that his candidacy was indispensable to the progressive cause and bored by inactivity, T R reconsidered his 1904 pledge not to run again for the presidency. His announcement of candidacy on February 21 was followed by a bitterly contested fight for the nomination that ended with Taft's renomination and Roosevelt's bolt from the GOP convention to run on the ticket of the newly formed Progressive party.

Roosevelt lost, but his second-place finish signaled a decisive rejection of the Republican Old Guard. The incumbent, Taft, was able to carry only two states, Vermont and Utah. Moreover, if one totals the combined votes of Wilson, Roosevelt, and Eugene Debs, the Socialist party candidate, all three advocates of progressive policies, over 75 percent of the American people who voted endorsed progressivism of one variety or another.[215] Thus, Wilson, although receiving less than a majority of votes cast, was in a position to reap the benefits of a reform movement that crested as he entered the White House. He took advantage of the opportunity afforded him not only to advance social and economic reforms but to extend further the restructuring of presidential leadership that began with Theodore Roosevelt's presidency.

Wilson's Theory of Executive Leadership

Woodrow Wilson had long expressed the need to reform the principles and institutions that governed the U.S. political system to ameliorate what he believed to be a disconcerting lack of energy and inconsistency of action. As a student at age twenty-three he published an article in 1879 that called for major institutional reforms that would establish closer ties between the executive and the legislature. At this point in his career, Wilson believed this link would best be formed by centering power in Congress, which dominated the political system during the second half of the nineteenth century, rather than in the presidency. Thus, he called for the adoption of the British cabinet system, which concentrated leadership in an executive agency responsible to the legislature (or Parliament, as it was called in Britain). He proposed that the Constitution be amended "to give the heads of the Executive departments—the members of the Cabinet—seats in Congress, with the privilege of the initiative in legislation and some part in the unbounded privileges now commanded by the Standing Committees."[216] With power so concentrated in the legislature, the president, who, in Wilson's view, had been rendered virtually useless by developments since the Civil War in any case, would become a mere figurehead, assuming a position similar to that of the monarch in England.

Although Wilson never abandoned his view that the system of checks and balances should be replaced by an American version of the parliamentary system, his views did change dramatically during the early 1900s about the possibilities of presidential leadership. He now stressed that the greatest promise for the establishment of more concentrated leadership in the United States lay in the strong assertion of presidential leadership.[217] No doubt Wilson's changed view on the possibility of strong leaderhip in the presidency was influenced by Theodore Roosevelt, who demonstrated the potential powers of the executive office by his vigorous and independent stewardship of the nation. Wilson had some strong disagreements with T R about institutional and policy matters, but he gave Roosevelt credit for charting the path toward a new era of presidential leadership. "Whatever else we may think or say of Theodore Roosevelt," he said in 1908, "we must admit he was an aggressive leader. He lead Congress—he was not driven by Congress. We may not approve of his methods but we must concede that he made Congress follow him."[218]

Wilson's theory of presidential power called for a more comprehensive rethinking of the U.S. constitutional order than that of Theodore Roosevelt. Roosevelt's "stewardship" model of the executive accepted the essential characteristics of the system of checks and balances, seeking only, by reviving and modifying Hamiltonian nationalism, to strengthen the prevailing constitutional order and prepare it to address the problems of an industrial society. T R was not hesitant to go to the people and bring the pressure of public opinion upon Congress, yet he did so in a way to preserve the independence of both the president and Congress.

Wilson agreed with T R that the president must focus more attention on national problems, but he believed that such leadership would be ineffective or dangerous unless accompanied by a fundamental change in constitutional arrangements. This change would be marked by *combining* the usually *separated* branches of government. Thus presidential leadership and practices had to be recast so as to destroy the wall between the executive and legislative branches in the formulation and adoption of public policy. Most significant, it was necessary to strengthen the role of the president as party leader so that the executive as the leader of national opinion could fuse the executive and legislative branches in his own person. Instead of limiting executive power, as had been the case for much of the nineteenth century, the party system had to be modified so that it would serve the president.

Wilson's Presidency and the Art of Popular Leadership

As president, Wilson acted both to perfect the methods of popular leadership already developed by Theodore Roosevelt and to apply them in a way in which he might establish leadership of Congress and achieve mastery over the Democratic party. The president was not completely successful in this endeavor, to be sure. Still, Wilson's two terms in office brought about major changes in the executive office, prompting his biographer Arthur Link to assert that "historians a century hence will probably rate the expansion and perfection of the powers of the presidency as his most lasting contribution."[219]

Wilson employed a number of methods during his two terms in office to strengthen the hand of the president vis-à-vis Congress and the party. The first of these techniques was to assert the position of the president as the spokesman of the people and to use public opinion as a spur on Congress.

Whereas Roosevelt had viewed popular rhetoric and "swings around the circle" as methods to be used infrequently and in defense of specific pieces of legislation, Wilson believed that inspirational leadership of public opinion was the primary responsibility of executive leadership. Wilson's effective use of oratory and public messages established a new standard of popular rhetoric, requiring the president to articulate a vision of the future and to impel the populace toward it. As he announced in his first inaugural address:

> We know our task to be no mere task of politics but a task which shall search us through and through, whether we be able to understand our time and the need of our people, whether we be indeed their spokesmen and interpreters, whether we have the pure heart to comprehend and the rectified will to choose our high course of action.[220]

At his best, Wilson was a spellbinder who not only grasped the aspirations of his day but also was able to translate them into words that had a major influence, first on the American people and then, during the war and afterward, on people throughout the world. In the course of doing so he consciously defended and established by example the legitimacy of popular rhetoric as a principal tool of governance.

Wilson's interest in forming an intimate relationship with the people led him to establish important precedents in the executive's relationship with the press and Congress. For example, Wilson was the first president to have formal press conferences, which were held frequently during his first two years in office. Less gregarious than Roosevelt and more concerned above all with the pristine conveyance of his ideas on national affairs, he found the informal and personal relations that T R carried on with journalists to be painful and unsatisfactory. Yet, unlike Taft, Wilson did not feel that he could afford to be reticent—he considered regular contact with the press necessary in order to take the people fully into his confidence. Regular press conferences enabled the president to assume more formal and restricted relations with journalists yet gave him access to a valuable channel of communication to Congress and the public. Furthermore, this restricted yet liberalized relationship with journalists set an important precedent that institutionalized the president's link with the press.[221]

Wilson also revived the practice of appearing in person before Congress to deliver the State of the Union address and other important public messages. Thomas Jefferson had abandoned the custom (established by George Washington and carried on by John Adams) of appearing before Congress on the ground that this sort of exercise attached too much ceremony to the executive duties, detracting thereby from the republican character of the presidency; it resembled too much the king's speech from the throne.

Going before Congress, however, was Wilson's way of establishing once and for all the president's role as the true representative of public opinion. Progressive democracy required a departure from Jeffersonian methods and traditions and a stronger sense of national purpose to satisfy the Jeffersonian commitment to equality of opportunity. And this departure could not take place unless the president as the only representative of national opinion could find devices to make direct appeals to the people.

Wilson's Relations with Congress

Going before Congress also served Wilson's purpose of breaking down the wall that had so long divided the executive from the legislative branch. Wilson delivered his first speech to Congress, an address on tariff reform, on April 8, 1913. He began his tariff address to the somewhat tense members of Congress by highlighting this concern as a major purpose of his appearance:

> I am very glad indeed to have this opportunity to address the two houses directly and to verify for myself the impression that the President of the United States is a person, not a mere department of government hailing Congress from some isolated island of jealous power, sending messages, not speaking naturally with his own voice—that he is a human being trying to cooperate with other human beings in a common service. After this pleasant experience I shall feel quite normal in all our dealings with one another.[222]

Wilson's precedent-shattering gesture was well received by Congress, and it launched the first successful campaign for tariff reform since before the Civil War. Moreover, Wilson's dramatic overture confirmed his supremacy as the leader of Congress. With the blurring of party alignments and with the traditional mechanisms for asserting discipline over the legislative process under attack, new methods were required to bring the executive and the legislature into harness. In devising such methods and having the capacity to use them effectively, Wilson advanced the development of the presidency beyond the path-breaking efforts of Theodore Roosevelt. The president's wife, Ellen Axson Wilson, remarked to her husband as they were driving back to the White House after the tariff reform speech that this was the kind of thing T R liked to do. Wilson is reported to have said with a laugh, "Yes, I think I put one over on Teddy."[223]

Wilson's speeches before Congress on behalf of tariff reform and subsequent measures advanced by his administration were an important part of advancing his legislative leadership. But also significant were other innovations, such as his practice of visiting Capitol Hill to meet with members of Congress personally as legislative deliberations proceeded. For example, he followed up the advantage gained from his dramatic tariff address by appearing the very next day in the president's room of the Senate for a conference with the members of the Finance Committee, who would be responsible for the new tariff legislation. No president since Lincoln—and that was in wartime—had ventured to make such a call.

Perhaps the most significant factor in Wilson's leadership of Congress was his assertion of control over the Democratic party. The Democrats were at least as divided as the Republicans between conservative and progressive elements. Nevertheless, Wilson decided to work through and with his party in Congress rather than to govern by a coalition of progressive Democrats and Republicans, as he might have done. Wilson considered party debate and organization to be a vital ingredient of responsible executive leadership, without which the rhetorical presidency would degenerate into idle chatter or, even worse, vicious demagogy. But he felt that the center of party responsibility had to shift from the party organizations in Congress, where it had resided since Jefferson's administration, to the president; such a change was necessary if parties were to be freed from their antiquated fix on local politics and spoils.

Thus, Wilson conceived of himself as the responsible leader of his party, as the only leader who could speak for it and the nation. He worked assiduously to formulate a comprehensive policy program and engaged in tireless efforts to establish this plan as a *party* program. He was even successful in getting the Democrats in the House to adopt a rule binding members to support the administration's policies. Similar party discipline was obtained in the traditionally more recalcitrant Senate, where the Democratic caucus declared important legislation, such as the tariff bill, to be party measures and urged all Democrats to support them.

Owing to his effective leadership of Congress and the Democratic party, Wilson was able to drive the major policies of his 1913 electoral platform—entitled the New Freedom—through Congress. The New Freedom concept expressed Wilson's own understanding of progressivism, one that he believed was rooted in the traditional Democratic hostility to the centralization of government power. Theodore Roosevelt's New Nationalism campaign in 1912 accepted the evolution of great corporations as inevitable and considered them to be the most efficient units of industrial organization; all that was necessary was to bring them under strict public control through regulation of their activities by a powerful trade commission. Wilson, in contrast to this position, called for reform that would free business from the plague of monopoly and special privilege, thus making unnecessary a dangerous centralization of administrative power. "As to monopolies, which Mr. Roosevelt proposes to legalize and welcome," remarked Wilson during the 1912 campaign, "I know that they are so many cars of juggernaut, and I do not look forward with pleasure to the time when the juggernauts are licensed and driven by commissioners of the United States." [224] As the leader of the Democratic party, Wilson promised remedial policies, such as tariff reform, an overhaul of the banking and currency system, and a vigorous antitrust program that would "disentangle" the "colossal community of interest" in the United States and restore fair competition in the U.S. economy.[225]

To the astonishment of Wilson's friends and enemies, most of the elements of the New Freedom concept were achieved by 1914. The tariff reform legislation, entitled the Underwood Tariff Act, was enacted in October 1913. It was followed by the passage of the Federal Reserve Act in late December of that year, which reconstructed the national banking and currency system. Finally, two statutes passed in 1914, the Clayton Anti-Trust Act and the Federal Trade Commission Act, strengthened the government's authority to prevent unfair competition.

The scope of Wilson's legislative achievements was remarkable. In a few short months Wilson had turned his fractious party into a disciplined body, and, in the course of doing so, enacted many programs that progressives had been demanding for two decades. Yet the progressive program promised by the New Freedom legislation was to be severely compromised by weak administration and a conservative judiciary, which still adhered to a restrictive view of the federal government's powers. And the New Freedom program was, to begin with, rather narrowly conceived. Given the strength of laissez-faire doctrine in the United States, it was a notable achievement: but the mission of the New Freedom was to restore competition in the business world, not to provide government support for the impoverished or to enact laws for the benefit of the laborer.

Nevertheless, Woodrow Wilson substantially transformed the U.S. presidency. His leadership consolidated and extended Roosevelt's achievements. The Constitution had not been formally amended, but its powers as they pertained to the presidency had been given new meaning.

The Presidency under Conditions of Total War

Theodore Roosevelt expanded the role of the president and reduced the effectiveness of Congress in foreign affairs. The expansion of executive authority during his presidency was partly a result of the expanding U.S. role in the world; but Roosevelt did much to encourage the growth of U.S. influence in international relations and to redefine the president's role in initiating and executing American responsibilities abroad.

Wilson's actions in foreign affairs were just as ambitious as, if somewhat more idealistic than, those of Theodore Roosevelt. Roosevelt's diplomatic initiatives were rooted in a mixture of progressive philosophy and *realpolitik* that did not shrink from the vigorous pursuit of U.S. strategic and economic interests. Wilson and his secretary of state, William Jennings Bryan, took a more idealistic course; they assumed somewhat naively, one historian has written, "that moral force controlled the relations of peace, that reason would prevail over ignorance and passion in the formation of public opinion, and that men and nations everywhere were automatically progressing toward an orderly and righteous international society." [226] Thus, Wilson was determined to pursue an energetic foreign policy, yet he hoped to inaugurate a new era in U.S. foreign relations, one based more upon altruism and less upon sheer considerations of national and material interests.

Wilson's most severe test in foreign affairs came during World War I, when executive power was exercised for the first time under conditions of world war. U.S. participation in this war began when the president signed a proclamation declaring a state of war with Germany on April 6, 1917. This declaration of war was passed by the Congress after the president's moving and eloquent appeal to the legislature on April 2, in which he reluctantly called on the United States to end its traditional position of neutrality when faced with war in Europe: "It is a fearful thing to lead this great peaceful people into war, into the most terrible and disastrous of all wars," said Wilson on this solemn occasion. "But," he added, "the right is more precious than the peace, and we shall fight for . . . a universal domination of right by such a concert of free peoples as shall bring peace and safety to all nations, and make the world at last free." [227]

This fight to make the "world safe for democracy," as Wilson called it, placed new demands upon the war powers of the president. To fight this kind of "total war" successfully required the mass production of complex weapons and the mobilization as well as deployment of troops on a massive scale at a great distance from the United States. The president, therefore, was responsible for leading a national effort that demanded the organization and control of an industrial economy and the coordination of the transportation and communications industries so that they would be geared to meet the requirements of a large scale military commitment. Under such conditions, the president's duties of commander in chief went far beyond the arduous task of directing the country's military efforts to the responsibility of overseeing the extensive controls established over the economy and society that were necessary for war production.

The need to impose such controls strained the settled procedures of U.S. constitutional government in a way that had not been seen since the Civil War. Wilson did not rely upon statutory power for everything he did as commander in chief. When Congress failed to pass a bill that authorized the president to arm merchant vessels, for example, he went ahead and armed them anyway, realizing full well that he had the constitutional power to do so. But Wilson believed that the full flowering of presidential authority required linking executive action to legislative leadership, even in the area of foreign policy, where expansive presidential authority was better established by constitutional precedents and historical developments.

Of the many congressional delegations of power to the president that followed Wilson's declaration of war, the most striking was passage of the Lever Food and Fuel Control Act in the summer of 1917. This legislation granted the power "to regulate by license the importation, manufacture, storage, mining or distribution of necessaries"—meaning, in effect, that the president had the authority to control the activities of industry, the distribution of food, and the utilization of means of transportation in the U.S. economy. Such a grant of power was without precedent in American history, and it was assailed by many legislators who feared dictatorship. Yet Wilson was able to beat back an effort to write into the Lever Act a provision to set up a bipartisan committee in both houses to oversee activities of the war, a watchdog provision which would have saddled Wilson with the same arrangement "Radical" Republicans imposed on Lincoln during the Civil War. *(See "The Presidency of Abraham Lincoln," p. 81, and "Andrew Johnson and the Assault on Executive Authority," p. 85, in this chapter.)*

Thus, the emergency powers Wilson assumed during the war were extraordinary, and, as Corwin has noted, the contrast between Wilson's and Lincoln's "dictatorship" was not one of "tenderness for customary constitutional restraints"; rather, it was one of "method." [228] Once obtaining such extraordinary authority, Wilson divested himself of everything but ultimate responsibility, appointing competent administrators—such as Bernard Baruch, who chaired the powerful War Industries Board; Herbert Hoover, who served as Food Administrator, and Secretary of the Treasury William Gibbs McAdoo, who managed the railroads—to manage day-to-day problems and administration. Similarly, Wilson left the management of military affairs to his European commander, Gen. John J. Pershing; he intervened only when large political and diplomatic considerations were involved.[229]

The pattern of war leadership Wilson established, then, was one of delegating detailed tasks to trusted members of his administration while he assumed responsibility for overall control and direction of the nation's war effort. This not only suited Wilson's approach to government, which emphasized moral leadership as the president's principal duty, but was an understandable adaptation to the exigencies of modern warfare. By the twentieth century, warfare was far too massive and complex for the president to contribute directly to the development of strategy and tactics as Polk, Lincoln, and McKinley had done. But the mobilization of popular support and the overall direction of economic activity that undergirded the modern war effort was established by Wilson's outstanding moral and legislative leadership.

The Defeat of the League of Nations

Ironically, Wilson's greatest failure during the war resulted from his effort to provide leadership where he believed his influence and talents could best be employed—the securing of peace. Indeed, Wilson was reluctant to assert his prerogatives as commander in chief so as not to jeopardize the opportunity to play a leading role at the peace table. As the historian Ernest R. May has argued, "From the first day of the war to the last, all that Wilson sought was a peace that could be secured by the League of Nations, a peace that would make the world safe for democracy." [230]

Wilson's plan for a League of Nations was the most controversial of his Fourteen Points, a program he formulated, in early 1918. *(See "Wilson's 'Fourteen Points' Speech," p. 1375, in the Appendix.)* He hoped to persuade the Allies and the Senate to accept these policies, which, in addition to the proposal for the formation of an international peace-keeping association, advocated lenient terms for the defeated Axis powers.

The president had to compromise on some points with U.S. allies, particularly on those pertaining to the conditions that were to be imposed on the Germans. But many of his objectives were incorporated into the Treaty of Versailles, signed by the major powers in June 1919, including his most cherished objective, the formation of a League of Nations "for the purpose of affording mutual guarantees of political independence and territorial integrity to great and small states alike."

Wilson had little doubt that he would be able to win approval of the armistice in the Senate; nor did he have any cause to doubt his ability to do so. He had displayed throughout his presidency an almost unsurpassed ability to enlist the public in the causes he championed. Yet the same methods that had succeeded magnificently in the New Freedom program failed disastrously in his fight for the League.

The limits of Wilson's influence first became evident in the 1918 elections, before the Treaty of Versailles was signed. No sooner had the Fourteen Points been pronounced and peace negotiations started than Congress, tiring of Wilson's independent course in seeking a settlement, began to challenge the president's conduct of foreign affairs. Ex-president Theodore Roosevelt, who had returned to the Republican party, abetted this opposition by urging the Senate to repudiate Wilson's Fourteen Points. On October 25, 1918, T R sent a telegram to Republican leaders: "Let us dictate peace by hammering guns and not chat about peace to the accompaniment of clicking typewriters." [231]

Flustered by the effort of Republican leaders to discredit him with the public before the November congressional elections, Wilson sought to rally the nation in support of his war policy. The day after Roosevelt's telegram, he appealed to the voters to return a Democratic majority to Congress in the upcoming elections. "If you have approved of my leadership and wish me to be your unembarrassed spokesman in affairs at home and abroad," his announcement to the press read, "I earnestly beg that you will express yourself unmistakably to that effect by returning a Democratic majority to both the Senate and the House of Representatives." [232]

President Wilson's 1918 campaign efforts proved to be a serious error. He was loudly criticized for suggesting the Democrats had a monopoly on loyalty; in doing so he seemed to have overlooked that many Republicans had supported his leadership during the war, while many Democrats had uniformly opposed him. Moreover, the 1918 campaign, occurring as it did in the midst of an international crisis, seemed an inappropriate occasion for an appeal to party loyalty. So intent was Wilson upon leading through his party in Congress that he was seemingly incapable of nonpartisan statesmanship, even when the occasion so clearly required it. The negative response to Wilson's message contributed to the Republicans making substantial gains in the November elections and, for the first time since 1911, the Republican party took control of both legislative chambers.

The results of the 1918 election lessened the president's prestige abroad and in Congress, adding immeasurably to the difficulties he was to encounter at the Peace Conference and, especially, with Congress. Although Wilson managed to salvage much of his program at Versailles, he was not able to get his peace plan through the Senate, where opposition to the bill was led by the implacable Wilson foe, Massachusetts senator Henry Cabot Lodge. Lodge, as a result of the 1918 elections, was now chairman of the Senate Foreign Relations Committee and the most vocal force in Congress in international affairs. Unwilling to compromise with Lodge, Wilson left Washington on September 3, 1919, on a month-long speaking tour of the western states, where he hoped to create a groundswell of public opinion in favor of the League that would force his Senate opponents to support it.

Wilson's swing around the country, however, only further diminished his influence. His presidency, and that of Theodore Roosevelt, had enhanced vastly the image of the executive office; but the presidency was not yet large enough to overcome the opposition in the press and in Congress elicited by Wilson's defiant campaign for the League of Nations.

Wilson's abortive campaign for the League was dramatic evidence that the presidency, which had gained considerable influence since the turn of the century, was still limited by a powerful, if no longer dominant, Congress as well as by the vagaries of public opinion. Because of Wilsons efforts, Americans no longer considered it inappropriate for presidents to attempt to move the public by programmatic speeches over the heads of Congress, but there was certainly no guarantee that such campaigns would succeed.

The final chapter of Wilson's presidency revealed a serious dilemma that future occupants of the White House would have to face: the changing character of the nation at the turn of the century seemed to demand strong presidential leadership, but a president determined to alter fundamentally the connection between the executive and the legislature risked losing the support of Congress and the public. The results of the 1920 election, in which conservative Republican senator Warren G. Harding, an opponent of Wilson's peace plan, won by an overwhelming popular vote, and the final defeat of the Treaty of Versailles in the Senate that soon followed, constituted a setback not only for progressivism but for Wilson's theory of presidential power.

Warren Harding to Herbert Hoover

The election of Warren Harding by a huge majority in 1920 signified the end of the Progressive Era. In May 1920, Harding told the Home Market Club in Boston, "America's present need is not heroics, but healing; not nostrums but normalcy; not revolution but restoration ... not surgery but serenity." [233]

The term *normalcy* captured the temper of the times not only in regard to policy matters but with respect to the presidency as well. Senator Lodge's address after the 1920 Republican national convention, officially notifying the candidate of his nomination, contained some subtle warnings for Harding. Alluding to the shift of power from Congress to the White House during Wilson's administration, Lodge reminded his audience that the Constitution provided for three coordinate branches of government, no one of which was to usurp the powers of the others. Lodge added that Harding would run the executive branch "in that spirit" and maintain that condition.[234]

Neither Harding nor his two Republican successors, Calvin Coolidge (1923-1929) and Herbert C. Hoover (1929-1933), took exception to the sentiment expressed by Lodge. As before in U.S. history, a period of strong executive leadership had again been followed by passivity or drift.

The Harding Era

True to the theme of his campaign, Harding made little effort to exert leadership over Congress. His model

Library of Congress

President Woodrow Wilson rides with President-elect Warren G. Harding to Harding's inauguration March 4, 1921. Harding promised a "return to normalcy" after the Progressive Era and tumultuous war years.

was William McKinley, whose legislative influence was achieved through quiet consultation and compromise with his party's congressional leadership.[235]

McKinley's legislative leadership techniques were no longer possible, however. The congressional revolt of 1910, which had dethroned the Speaker, had weakened party ties in the House. Gone were the days when the president and the Speaker could bring together the executive and legislative branches of government by quiet consultation. The Senate, too, had been affected by the insurgent revolt against party leadership. Moreover, the enactment of the Seventeenth Amendment in 1913, providing for the direct election of senators, replacing the method of selection by state legislatures, accentuated the lack of party discipline in the upper chamber. The senator, one observer wrote in 1922, "came to think more in terms of himself and his own reelection, nearly always an impelling motive, and less in terms of party." [236] Harding's forbearance in the legislative process guaranteed congressional deadlock and confusion.

Even had Harding been a gifted and determined statesman, it is unlikely that he could have shaped Congress to his will. The defeat of the Versailles treaty signaled congressional and popular reaction against the sort of leadership Wilson had provided; and Republican members of Congress were determined that the 1920 Republican victory would restore the power of Congress, not of the president. Congress displayed its determination by actively directing foreign affairs throughout Harding's term. Most significant, the Senate took the initiative in curbing the naval race that had engaged the major powers since the beginning of World War I. Progressive Republican senator William E. Borah amended the 1921 naval appropriations bill by calling on the president to invite Great Britain and Japan to a naval disarmament conference to reduce naval expenditures. This rider passed Congress in spite of Harding's efforts to replace it with a weaker resolution. Harding was not opposed to having a conference, but he felt it prudent to build up U.S. forces first.

Still, Harding was not one to engage Congress in a bitter and protracted struggle. Bowing to congressional and popular pressure, he called an international disarmament conference, which took place in Washington from the end of 1921 to early 1922. Ironically, the accord reached at the Washington Naval Disarmament Conference proved to be Harding's most significant foreign policy achievement.

Teapot Dome and Other Scandals

Harding's presidency began slowly and ended disastrously. By 1923, it became clear that there was a heavy price to be paid for his passive leadership and deference to the regular party apparatus. The president's pledge to restore normalcy included a renewed enthusiasm for patronage practices. Thus the extension of the merit system that followed the passage of the Pendleton Act in 1883, which covered a majority of the federal service by the end of Theodore Roosevelt's incumbency, went no further during Harding's administration. "By the middle of the summer of 1921 the spoils efforts of the Republicans began to assume the proportions of a sizable if not full scale raid," the administrative historian Paul Van Riper has written.[237]

Nor was the Harding administration reluctant to manipulate the unclassified service, now constituting 20 to 30 percent of the total civil employment. Some of Harding's appointments were excellent, notably his selection of Herbert C. Hoover as secretary of commerce and Charles Evans Hughes as secretary of state. Many others, however, were more characteristic of the Grant era than the twentieth century and resulted in the worst fraud and corruption since the advent of civil service reform.

The first disturbing situation to come to light involved Charles Forbes, director of the Veterans' Bureau. In early 1923 Harding learned that Forbes had been selling government supplies from the medical supply base in Perryville, Maryland, to private contractors at ridiculously low prices and was engaging in undercover deals relating to hospital building contracts and site selections. Forbes had to resign, and on March 14, 1923, his principal legal adviser, Charles F. Cramer, committed suicide.

When revelations about the attorney general's office soon followed, Harding had final proof that his administration was deeply tainted with corruption. Fearing for his reputation and the fortunes of his party, he is reported to have remarked to the journalist William Allen White, "My God, this is a hell of a job! I have no trouble with my enemies.... But my damned friends, my God-damned friends, White, they're the ones that keep me walking the floor nights." [238]

Despondent and in poor health, Harding decided to escape by venturing on a trip that would take him across the country and up to Alaska. It was on this journey that his presidency came to end, just as another scandal was about to come to light. In the course of his return from Alaska, Harding fell ill of ptomaine poisoning, then pneumonia, and died of an embolism in San Francisco on August 2, 1923.

His death preceded by a few months the uncovering of a complicated and subtle plot to defraud the government, known as the Teapot Dome scandal. Albert B. Fall, secretary of the interior, entered into a corrupt bargain with the oil companies of Edward L. Doheny and Harry F. Sinclair to turn over to them valuable petroleum deposits, which President Wilson had reserved for the navy. The Elk Hill oil reserve in California was leased to Doheny, and the Teapot Dome oil reserve in Wyoming to Sinclair. Fall personally received at least $100,000 from Doheny and $300,000 from Sinclair.

Armed with these facts, and other damaging revelations unearthed by a Senate investigation, a special commission appointed by Harding's successor, Calvin Coolidge, initiated prosecutions in early June 1924. The resultant trials and legal maneuvering went on for almost six years, after which Fall was sentenced to a year in jail and a $100,000 fine and Sinclair was sentenced to six months in jail. But Doheny was acquitted, a ridiculous verdict in view of the fact that Fall recently had been convicted of bribe taking. This verdict caused George Norris, progressive Republican senator from Nebraska, to remark in reference to Doheny's expensive legal fees that it is "very difficult, if not impossible to convict one hundred million dollars." [239]

The Budget and Accounting Act of 1921

Harding's reputation suffered tremendously because of the scandals that rocked the nation after his death, but his administration was not without its achievements. During Harding's presidency, for example, a national budget system was created, significantly enhancing the president's authority to oversee the expenditures of the executive departments and agencies. This authority was achieved by the enactment of the Budget and Accounting Act of 1921.

The budget act called for a comprehensive executive

budget, which assigned to the president the fundamental responsibility for coordinating an overall estimate of the needs of the administration and the responsibility of preparing an estimate of the probable revenues the government could collect during the coming fiscal year. Moreover, it established a Bureau of the Budget to support presidential use of this new budget authority. Although formally assigned to the Treasury Department, the Budget Office was intended to serve as the president's staff agency to aid in the preparation of the budget and to strengthen the president's authority over the activities of the executive branch. Finally, the budget act created the General Accounting Office, headed by the comptroller general (serving a fixed tenure of fifteen years in office), which was to be an auditing arm of Congress, reserving, thereby, a place for the legislature in the government's fiscal operations.

With the passage of the budget act, presidents finally attained the legal authority to influence the allocation of expenditures of the government over which they presided. Thus, the practitioner-scholar Herbert Emmerich judged the budget act to be "the greatest landmark of our administrative history except for the Constitution itself." [240]

Public Relations during the Harding Era

Neither Harding nor his successor, the taciturn New Englander Coolidge, saw themselves as law givers, governmental expansionists, or tribunes of the people in the sense that Roosevelt and, especially, Wilson had. But just as they were to find that they could not effect their laissez-faire prescriptions without assuming a strong hand in administering the executive departments and agencies, they could not succeed without public support.

Although Harding's presidency ended disastrously, he made significant contibutions to the development of presidential techniques for the leadership of public opinion. Having been the editor-publisher of the *Marion Star* in Ohio before entering politics, Harding understood the workings of the press. He developed an intimacy with journalists that greatly benefited his presidential campaign and, until the scandals of 1923, his image as president. Harding was the first participant in presidential politics to recognize that public opinion could be courted in leisurely as well as more formal and ceremonial ways. During the 1920 campaign, for example, a three-room cottage was built near the Harding home in Marion to accommodate the press, and there Harding would meet them daily and discuss developments frankly.

Once he became president, he revived the regular press conference, open to all accredited correspondents, which Wilson had started but allowed to taper off after 1915. Harding also established the device of the "White House spokesman" whereby information could be conveyed from the administration to the public that was not directly attributable to the president. Harding was also the first president to benefit from "photo opportunities." He willingly posed for photographers several times a week.

Willing to court public opinion on those few matters with which he was concerned, Harding delivered messages to Congress in person and immensely enjoyed speech-making tours. In fact, the mounting burden of the rhetorical presidency was recognized by Harding's appointment of the first presidential speechwriter, newspaperman Judson Welliver.

President Harding died before the American people realized his shortcomings. Although he enjoyed the glitter and attention that had become part of the executive office, he found its burdens unbearable. Poring over an immense stack of correspondence, he is reported to have remarked to an aide, "I am not fit for this office and should never have been here." [241]

Nevertheless, the death of this president, who had served barely two years and whom history would count as one of the least successful and least admirable of all White House occupants, caused an extraordinary outpouring of national emotion. Such a reaction was a tribute to the growing importance of the U.S. president. The stature of the office did not shrink but, to a surprising degree, continued to grow during the Harding era. "More than ever before," one scholar has remarked about the reaction to Harding's death, "thanks to the media and use made of them on the President's behalf, the presidency was destined to blow up the man to heroic proportions and project this image constantly on the national screen." [242]

The "Silent" Politics of Calvin Coolidge

Calvin Coolidge was an unlikely figure to assume an office that had grown to such proportions. Very plain in appearance, so sparing in speech that he was dubbed, "Silent Cal," Coolidge's persona was one of ordinariness when the executive office appeared to require individuals of heroic stature. Still, Coolidge emerged from the White House as one of the most popular presidents of all time.

It might be said that Coolidge's popularity was attributable in part to his ability to exalt inactivity to a fine art. When it came to leading Congress and exerting his will in matters of public policy, he felt even less responsible for leadership than his immediate predecessor. Less a party man than Harding, he made little effort to confer with the Republican leadership in Congress to advance a legislative program. And by philosophy and personality, he was more doctrinaire than Harding in his opposition to the bold measures employed by Wilson to combine the separated branches of government. "I have never felt it was my duty," Coolidge wrote in his autobiography, "to attempt to coerce Senators or Representatives, or to take reprisals." [243]

Such forbearance in legislative matters was compatible with Coolidge's general disdain for programmatic initiatives. "The key to an understanding of the presidential career of Calvin Coolidge is to be found in the fact that he had a distaste for legislation," the historian Wilfred E. Binkley has written.[244] Like Taft and Harding before him, Coolidge believed that there were too many programs in place already and that his energies should be devoted to an economical and efficient administration of the nation's affairs. One of the few legislative measures he pushed vigorously was the Mellon tax reduction plan of 1923, named for the conservative secretary of the Treasury during the Harding and Coolidge administrations, Andrew Mellon.

Aside from measures such as this one, which reduced the national government's role in the economy, Coolidge maintained a public silence on legislative issues typical of a nineteenth-century executive. Even in the matter of ratification of the protocol of the World Court, which the president had recommended, Coolidge gave neither encouragement nor direction to Republican senators. Instead, he uttered barely a word as his supporters in the Senate fought a valiant but losing battle to win support for this measure, which would have committed the United States to participate in a court of international justice, in the face of the isolationist sentiment that gripped the nation after World War I.

President Coolidge's lack of success with Congress notwithstanding, he managed to form a strong bond with the American people. To some degree, one suspects, Coolidge's limitations were an asset; his stern Yankee demeanor and businesslike administrative style were a welcome respite from the scandals that had rocked the country in 1923. The restrained Coolidge was also the perfect man to preside over the prosperity of the postwar economy. The Harding-Coolidge economic program, emphasizing free markets at home and protection from competition abroad, put "business in the saddle," as *Harper's* magazine described it in 1925.[245] For a time, business was up to the job; throughout the spring of 1924, the scandal disclosures of the Harding administration had to compete on the front pages of the newspapers with dramatic evidence of increasing dividends, profits, and spiraling sales.[246] These good times seemed to call for someone who was content to "sit tight."

Coolidge's link with the people was reinforced by political shrewdness and publicity sense. Paradoxically, this doleful and reticent man was a master of public relations who perfected some of the emerging White House communications practices. Extraordinarily faithful in discharging what he felt to be his obligations to reporters and the American public, he held during his five years in office 520 press conferences, more in an average month than the gregarious Franklin Delano Roosevelt. Not surprisingly, this sense of obligation to the press corps won Coolidge a considerable measure of favorable coverage.

On occasion, Coolidge's exceedingly cordial relations with the press were employed to exert legislative leadership. In no fewer than ten press conferences held between December 1923 and June 1924, Coolidge urged Congress to enact the Mellon tax reduction package. But, given the president's minimal aspirations in the area of legislation, much of his public relations focused on selling himself rather than public policy. At the very moment that Republican senators, without an encouraging word from their leader in the White House, were fighting a losing battle on the administration's World Court measure, Coolidge was at the executive mansion lunching with outstanding editors and authors who would return home and disseminate pleasant impressions about the president.[247]

Such incidents reflected Coolidge's keen recognition of the nation's interest in the human side of the presidency. Harding was the first to exploit human interest stories in the press, but Coolidge displayed an even greater readiness to benefit from the nation's growing fascination with the personal lives of those who resided in the White House. Accepting the fact that news about his personal doings could pave the way for ready acceptance of his public pronouncements, the shy Coolidge showed an unprecedented willingness to throw open his private life as well as his official activity to public scrutiny. One contemporary reporter noted that "Mr. Coolidge would don any attire or assume any pose that would produce an interesting picture. He was never too busy. . . ."[248]

Important as the newspapers were to Coolidge, his most important contribution to the development of White House communications was the use of the radio. Coolidge was the first president to come into office after radio had been developed into a practical medium, and he and his advisers exploited this medium deliberately. "I am fortunate I came in with the radio," he told Sen. James Watson of Indiana. "I can't make an engaging, rousing, or oratorical speech to a crowd as you can, . . . but I have a good radio voice, and now I can get my messages across to them without acquainting them with my lack of oratorical ability."[249]

Coolidge did not make use of the radio for the specific shaping of public opinion for policy objectives—that purpose had to await Franklin Roosevelt. But Coolidge did use the radio effectively to enhance his personal popularity; moreover, had he not formed a strong bond with the public in this way, he might not have been nominated by his party in 1924 and elected president in his own right. Before the Republican convention in June, Coolidge made sure that he entered the homes of the American people at least once a month with carefully staged broadcasts that conveyed an impression of his own personality and ideas.

Coolidge was nominated overwhelmingly on the first ballot, which signified an important step, as Coolidge himself recognized, in the emergence of the president as "the sole repository of party responsibility."[250] The conservative Republican senators who controlled their party after 1912 had little regard for Coolidge. Unlike Harding, this taciturn New Englander, the former governor of Massachusetts, was not one of them. As William Allen White wrote in 1925, "the reason why the senatorial group ceased hoping to defeat Coolidge for the Republican nomination was the obvious fact that Coolidge was getting stronger and stronger with the American people."[251] Noting that the radio in no small measure had made this possible, Cornwell has written: "Here was the first President in history whom more than a tiny fraction of the populace could come to know at first hand. Small wonder that the man developed a tangible meaning for millions—more so perhaps than any of his predecessors."[252]

Herbert Hoover and the Great Depression

When Herbert Hoover, capitalizing on Coolidge's refurbishing of the presidency and the Republican party, defeated Al Smith in 1928, there was much reason to expect that he would be an able—even brilliant—leader. "The Great Engineer," as Hoover was called, brought to the White House a tremendous reputation earned in his service as Food Administrator during the Wilson administration and as secretary of commerce under Harding and Coolidge. Dedicated to the probusiness program of Harding and Coolidge, yet confident that knowledgeable and efficient administration of the nation's affairs could build a stronger foundation for prosperity, Hoover seemed the perfect man to consolidate the gains of the postwar economic recovery.

Nevertheless, this president who entered office with such high qualifications left as the focus of scorn. The startling reversal was attributable in part to the Great Depression, perhaps the worst economic crisis in the nation's history, which struck only nine months after Hoover assumed office. But Hoover's presidency was in trouble even before the stock market crash of October 29, 1929. The nation's image of him cannot be attributed only to the intractable conditions he faced.

Much of Hoover's difficulty as president derived from his desire to effect important changes in the economy and society without assuming the leadership that might have made these changes possible. Like Harding and Coolidge,

Hoover feared big government, but Hoover's fear coexisted with a progressive faith in the government's ability to improve the condition of society.[253]

Shortly after the inauguration, Hoover called a special session of Congress and asked it to consider a program of significant reform. The new president called for major reform in agriculture, taxes, conservation, and government organization. Hoover believed his administration should play a leading role in mobilizing industrial and civic organizations to facilitate better economic coordination and enhanced opportunity. He was concerned that the nation's prosperity was marred by several problems: an imbalance between production and consumption; a weak agricultural sector; the lack of orderly, rational, and bureaucratic procedures in industrial organization; feverish speculation that was fueled by unsound currency and lending policies; and the weak condition of labor, which allowed for a disproportionate share of profits to go to capital. The solution to these problems, Hoover believed, did not lie in directly expanding the role of the national government but in using the powers of the presidency and executive branch agencies to encourage the development of more rational and just economic arrangements.

By philosophy and personality, however, Hoover proved incapable of providing such leadership, especially under the hammer blows of the depression. Sharing Coolidge's respect for the autonomy of Congress, Hoover failed to provide legislative leadership during the special session of Congress that he called in 1929. The following passage describes his views throughout much of his presidency:

> The encroachments upon our liberties may not be overt—by repeal of any of the Constitutional guarantees—but they may be insidious and no less potent through encroachment upon the checks and balances which make its security. More particularly does the weakening of the legislative arm lead to encroachment by the executive upon the legislative and judicial functions, and inevitably that encroachment is upon individual liberty.[254]

Hoover wrote these words in 1934 as a warning against the aggressive leadership of Franklin D. Roosevelt, but this doctrine of legislative independence was not a mere afterthought—to a remarkable degree it fit the president's actual relations with Congress. For example, he called for the special session of Congress to pass legislation that would help the ailing agricultural sector, aid that he believed should come in the form of loans and increased tariff rates on farm imports. But, considering tariff rates and farm relief to be among the prerogatives of Congress, Hoover refused to offer a detailed program of action. Nor did he provide any leadership as farm relief and tariff measures bogged down in Congress.

Although Congress passed a farm relief bill that Hoover found acceptable, it did not approve the tariff legislation. The president favored a limited revision of tariff schedules to aid stricken farmers. Without his active engagement in the legislative process, however, Congress, particularly the Senate, increased tariffs on nonfarm as well as farm commodities, resulting in a bill that raised schedules to the highest levels in history. When this protectionist measure reached Hoover's desk, he signed it despite innumerable pleas from all parts of the country that he veto it and despite his private characterization of the bill to his friends as "vicious, extortionate, and obnoxious."[255]

Hoover's passivity seemed incongruous given his ambitions for the nation. As one scholar has concluded, "no

Library of Congres

This Charles Dunn caricature of Herbert Hoover is said to be the former president's favorite. Hoover kept twenty thousand cartoons of himself in a White House room he called his "Chamber of Horrors."

activist president in this century has kept his distance from the Congress as did Hoover."[256] By the fall of 1929, the congressional leadership of the president's party was severely criticizing Hoover's apolitical approach, and the press seemed mystified. One commentator remarked, "It is hardly too much to say that a strange paralysis seemed to rest upon Mr. Hoover during the first year after Congress met."[257]

This "strange paralysis" caused concern and confusion during the early days of the administration, but it resulted in biting jest and scorn with the onslaught of the depression. Hoover's dignified silence in the face of congressional indifference to his program was one thing, but his reluctance to act seemed appalling and heartless as economic conditions worsened and 25 percent of the work force lost their jobs. Yet he resisted growing demands that he step into the role of legislative leader and help produce a body of law authorizing federal departments and agencies to take over more of the tasks of economic coordination and social service provision.

This stance became especially crippling after the Democrats took control of the Congress in the 1930 elections. When the Democrats refused to cooperate with the president, he was left with two choices: to battle publicly with the Democratic-controlled legislature or to maintain public silence with the hope of getting somewhere by conferring quietly with the hostile opposition. Hoover chose silence, then bewailed the intransigence of Congress rather than attempt to go to the people over the heads of Congress. As he later wrote in his memoirs:

> I had felt deeply that no President should undermine the independence of the legislative and judicial branches by seeking to discredit them. The constitutional division of powers is the bastion of our liberties and was not designed as a battleground to display the prowess of Presidents. They just have to work with the material that God—and the voters—have given them.[258]

Hoover had risen to prominence as a builder of businesslike economic and civic organizations rather than as a politician forging workable coalitions or a popular following. He was comfortable in dealing with facts, which he would attempt to marshal in support of a given course of action. But, as the journalist Walter Lippmann wrote, Hoover was characteristically "diffident in the presence of the normal irrationality of democracy." [259] He fought losing battles to keep both his negotiations over public policy and his private life screened from view. His administration "served to make painfully plain," one scholar has observed, "that no future President could hope to emerge from his White House ordeal unless he was prepared in talent and temperament to cope with and master the demands of an age of mass communications." [260]

Hoover was hardly a do-nothing president as Franklin D. Roosevelt and the Democrats charged in the 1932 election. He supported programs such as the Reconstruction Finance Corporation, which would provide federal loans to banks, railroads, and certain agricultural organizations, to treat the nation's economic maladies. But he would not, and probably could not, provide the sort of bold political leadership required to gain popular support for such programs or to ensure their energetic operation.

In a sense, Hoover was both the last of the old and the first of the "modern" presidents. For nearly a century and a half the executive office had operated in a political environment founded on principles dedicated to a balance of power and limited government. Americans continued to embrace these principles, even after the path-breaking developments of the Progressive Era. The "return to normalcy" during the 1920s, although it did not restore the old order, meant that government leaders and the public still wanted to limit the sphere of White House and government activity. Hoover defended those limits, although his conception of the president's duties and the responsibilities of government was positive. He repeatedly called for and actively encouraged efforts by various segments of the economy and the general public to pursue more rational and just business practices. But Hoover was willing to go only so far.

He rigidly refused to support direct government relief of human suffering. Thus, in seeking to come to terms with the great drought of 1930 and 1931, he seemed to be haggling to persuade the Red Cross to feed the people, rather than have the federal government do it. When the Red Cross balked and Congress demanded a relief package, Hoover still demurred, for he believed that direct federal relief was unconstitutional and beyond the competence of the national government. It was a sorry spectacle: the president standing on a perceived constitutional prohibition and Congress pleading for human relief.[261]

Seeking to come to terms with the new conditions of the U.S. political system and a national emergency, Hoover actively put traditional political practices and principles to their greatest test. But his unalterable commitment to preserving these traditions in the face of the pressing needs that arose from the Great Depression served only to diminish further, if not to discredit, their place in U.S. politics. In this way, Hoover prepared the nation for a fundamental break with the past.

Franklin D. Roosevelt to Ronald Reagan

The 1932 election marked a new political era. Franklin D. Roosevelt became the first Democratic candidate to be elected president with a popular majority since Franklin Pierce in 1852. FDR's victory indicated, in the opinion of the progressive Republican journalist William Allen White, "a firm desire on the part of the American people to use government as an agency for human welfare." [262]

Roosevelt did not disappoint his supporters. He not only accepted the progressive reformers' commitment to regulate business, so as to curb its worst abuses, but also believed it was the responsibility of the federal government to guarantee the economic security of the American people.

Franklin Roosevelt's extraordinary leadership in expanding the role of the state to meet the demands of a national crisis, the Great Depression, and later an international one, the Second World War, had a profound effect on the presidency. The "modern" presidency, the executive office as we know it today, begins with his thirteen-year tenure in the White House.

The presidency that emerged from this dramatic transformation was different from the traditional executive office in the following respects:

1. From a state of affairs where there was still some question about the right of the president to intervene in legislative affairs, it has come to be taken for granted that he should regularly initiate and seek to win support for legislative action as part of his continuing responsibilities.
2. From a presidency that exercised few unilateral powers, especially in domestic matters, there has been a shift to one with many more occasions to take actions not formally ratified by Congress.
3. From a presidency with extremely modest staff support, there has evolved one in which the President has at his disposal in the Executive Office of the President, first formed during FDR's administration, an extensive presidential bureaucracy to implement his initiatives.
4. Finally, the "modern" president has become by far the most visible actor in the political system, overshadowing even the most influential legislators.[263]

FDR and the Breakthrough to the Modern Presidency

So great an impression did FDR leave on the executive office that in the most recent survey of historians he was ranked as the second greatest in U.S. history, surpassed only by Abraham Lincoln.[264] Above all, this high ranking is explained by the role he played in leading the American people through the Great Depression.

Roosevelt came to office in the fourth year of a world economic crisis that raised grave doubts about the U.S. political system—indeed, about the future of the Western world. As Roosevelt prepared to take the oath of office, 15 million Americans were unemployed. Every bank in thirty-two states had been closed by state government edict. On

Wide World Photos

In the 1932 presidential election, Franklin D. Roosevelt's image of strength and optimism provided a devastating contrast to his 1932 Republican opponent, President Hoover.

the very morning of FDR's inauguration, March 4, 1933, the New York Stock Exchange had shut down, causing the editor of *Nation's Business* to describe the national mood as one of "fear, bordering on panic, loss of faith in everything, our fellowman, our institutions, private and government." [265]

This sense of national despair notwithstanding, Roosevelt's arrival in Washington was greeted by a mood of distinct hopefulness. Everyone who watched and waited, wrote *New York Times* columnist Arthur Krock, was "ready to be enthusiastic over any display of leadership," eager to be convinced that the new president would exhibit the kind of bold statesmanship that the American people had demanded, but failed to receive, from Herbert Hoover.[266]

Unlike Hoover, Roosevelt was admirably suited in personality and background to provide such leadership. "The essence of Roosevelt's presidency," Clinton Rossiter has written, "was his airy eagerness to meet the age head on." [267] This confidence stemmed not only from a privileged, albeit challenging, upbringing in Hyde Park, New York, but also from an admirable political education: state senator, assistant secretary of the navy in the Wilson administration, his party's vice-presidential nominee in 1920, and two-term governor of New York (then the largest state in the Union). Roosevelt's composure was matched by a willingness to experiment and a spirit of innovation.

The Critical Early Days

Roosevelt began his presidency with a compelling inaugural address. *(See "Franklin D. Roosevelt's First Inaugural Address," p. 1376, in the Appendix.)* Laying the blame for the economic crisis on the laissez-faire doctrine and halting leadership of his immediate predecessors, the president called the nation to a higher purpose: "The money changers have fled from their high seats in the temple of our civilization. We may now restore that temple to ancient truths. The measure of that restoration lies in the extent to which we apply social values more noble than mere monetary profit." [268]

FDR's determination to lead the nation to a more noble calling was stated just as boldly:

> It is to be hoped that the normal balance of executive and legislative authority may be wholly adequate to meet the unprecedented task before us.... But in the event that ... the national emergency is still critical.... I shall ask the Congress for one remaining instrument to meet the crisis—broad executive power to wage a war against the emergency, as great as the power that would be given to me if we were in fact invaded by a foreign foe.[269]

After taking the oath of office, Roosevelt lost no time in translating his intentions into action. The next day he issued the "Bank Holiday Proclamation," directed to suspending "the heavy and unwarranted withdrawals of gold and currency from our banking institutions." This action, an unprecedented exercise of executive prerogative during peacetime, declared that from March 6, 1933, to March 9, 1933, banking institutions in the United States would be required to suspend all transactions.[270] Four days later he introduced the Emergency Banking Bill, providing for a number of immediate steps to place the full resources of the Federal Reserve Board behind the faltering banks and to restore the confidence of the people in the banking system. This bill, enacted by both legislative houses in fewer than eight hours, was the first to be passed during the extraordinary "One Hundred Days." From noon on March 9, to 1 a.m. on June 15, 1933, a relentless succession of bills was passed by a special session of Congress. *(See box, The First Hundred Days of Franklin D. Roosevelt, p. 462.)*

Having taken official action to ameliorate the banking crisis, FDR announced that he would go directly to the people three days later, on Sunday evening, March 12, to give a radio address explaining what he had done and why he had done it. This was to be the first of Roosevelt's "fireside chats," which marked a revolutionary advance in the presidential use of mass communications. Coolidge and Hoover had used radio but only to broadcast fixed, formal policy pronouncements like the State of the Union message. The twenty-seven fireside chats FDR delivered during his presidency were informal messages intended to shape public opinion.

Of all the fireside chats Roosevelt was to give, none was more successful than the banking crisis address. Both Roosevelt's unmatched radio style and the phrasing of the talk were ideally suited to his purpose of reassuring the populace and restoring hope and confidence in the U.S. financial system:

> It was the government's job to straighten out the situation and do it as quickly as possible. And the job is being performed.... Confidence and courage are the essentials of success in carrying out our plan. You people must have faith; you must not be stampeded by rumors or guesses. Let us unite in banishing fear. We have provided the machinery to restore our financial system; it is up to you to support it and make it work.[271]

Grave problems remained unsolved, but Roosevelt's fireside chat of Sunday, March 13, ended the banking crisis, for there were no runs on the banks the next day. On the contrary, deposits far exceeded withdrawals as hoarded currency poured back into bank vaults all over the country. A few days later, the New York Stock Exchange, closed since March 3, opened and within five hours recorded the greatest single-day rise in the history of the exchange. Thus, there was some justification for the dramatic declaration made by Roosevelt's aide Raymond Moley that "capitalism was saved . . . in eight days." [272]

Indeed, the first two weeks of Roosevelt's presidency marked a remarkable and enduring change in the spirit of the country. The despair and political paralysis of the Hoover years were gone. In their place were an ebullient national mood and a refashioned presidency, which formed the basis of a vital link between the government and the American people. Almost overnight, the chief executive was transformed from the passive entity it had been since the Wilson presidency to a vivid focal point of national attention. Whereas one man had been able to handle all of Hoover's mail, a staff of fifty had to be hired to take care of Franklin Roosevelt's incoming correspondence, which averaged five thousand letters a day.

The New Deal

The advent of the welfare state, marking a massive shift of responsibility from the states and private groups to the national government, meant new responsibility for the president. Roosevelt played a critical role in instigating this shift, masterfully preparing the nation for the revolutionary departures in public policy that took place during the 1930s.

The centerpiece of this program was the Social Security Act, passed in 1935, which initiated a comprehensive federal system of unemployment and old-age insurance. Although the depression had focused attention on the plight of potential beneficiaries of social security to an unprecedented extent, there was no general willingness to accept such a scheme, nor even understanding of the basic problems.

Roosevelt's campaign for social security did not entail rousing public oratory to focus the pressure of public opinion on Congress. Rather, he saw his task as one of civic education, requiring that he demonstrate to the American people that the reform being advocated was not alien to American values but a rediscovery and refurbishing of elements already present.

The development of industrial society, Roosevelt believed, no longer made it possible for security to be achieved within the simple bonds of the small community and the family. Rather, the complexities of great communities and of organized industry required the more active interest of the nation as a whole through government to secure the welfare of the individuals who composed it. To bring this lesson home to the American people, Roosevelt's fireside chat of June 28, 1934, included a highly effective yet homey illustration that masterfully alluded to the need to refurbish both the national government and the executive office—the then-current remodeling of the White House. Referring both to the refurbished White House and to social insurance, he said, "Our new structure is part of and a fulfillment of the old. . . . All that we do seeks to fulfill the historic traditions of the American people." [273]

Thus, Roosevelt's moral leadership involved, as one presidential scholar has written, "a careful process of grafting social security onto the stalk of traditional American values." [274] At the end of this process Roosevelt had moved the nation beyond the notion that "rights" embodied only guarantees against denial of freedom of expression to the conception that government also had an obligation to ensure economic security. It was just such a new understanding of rights that Roosevelt had in mind when, at the 1932 Democratic convention, he pledged himself to "a new deal for the American people." [275]

The New Deal program was a series of legislative acts, executive orders, and proclamations that sought not only to secure the economic welfare of the individual but also to remedy the economic problems rooted in the Great Depression. Programs were established to provide aid to the handicapped and to dependent children and to provide work relief projects, financed by the greatest single peacetime appropriation in history. Moreover, for the first time the national government fostered unionization. When Roosevelt took office, almost no factory worker belonged to a union. By the time his tenure was over industrial unionism was firmly established, in part because of the enactment of the Wagner Act in 1935. Under this act the government broke precedent by entering factories to conduct elections in which workers could choose whether to join a union and which union to join.

Not all of these major departures in public policy were the result of Roosevelt's leadership. Some of the New Deal programs, such as the Tennessee Valley Authority, had long been on the public agenda but needed the impetus of a national crisis to achieve approval.[276] And certain other parts of the new "economic constitutional order," as FDR called it, such as the Wagner Act, redounded to the president's credit, even though he backed such measures haltingly, and the principal credit for their enactment belonged to others. That FDR was given credit for the initiatives of others illustrates a tendency during his administration for people to think increasingly of the president as the symbol of government.

The Institutionalization of the Modern Presidency

The 1936 election ensured that the important political changes that had taken place in the country since 1932 would endure. FDR won 60 percent of the popular vote—the largest plurality that had ever been won by a presidential candidate—and all but two states in the electoral college. This election, which also strengthened the hold of the president's party on both houses of Congress, marked the emergence of the Democrats as the new majority party, a position they were to enjoy for nearly half a century.

The increasing demands for active leadership signified by the rise of the modern presidency meant that the nation had come to look to the White House as the preeminent source of moral leadership, legislative guidance, and public policy. Because of the mushrooming responsibilities of the executive office, the staff support of the president had to be increased. Previously an office with very modest staff support, the presidency developed after the 1930s into an *institution,* a veritable government unto itself. Roosevelt made a significant contribution to this development when he named three of the country's foremost scholars of public administration—Louis Brownlow (chairman), Charles E. Merriam, and Luther Gulick—to a President's Committee on Administrative Management. Making the claim that "the President needs help," the Brownlow Commission, as it came to be called, proposed that an Executive Office of the President be established, including a White House Office staffed by loyal and energetic aides who were to have "a passion for anonymity." In addition to the White House Office, the first Executive Office of the President included the National Resources Planning Board (a long-term planning agency) and a strengthened Bureau of the Budget, which was moved from the Treasury Department. After a protracted battle in Congress, the Executive Reorganization Act of 1939 was passed and implemented by Roosevelt's Executive Order 8248, thus carrying out many of the Brownlow Commission's recommendations.

The Modern Presidency and Constitutional Crisis

The expansion of the national state and the advent of the modern presidency resulted in a serious constitutional crisis by the end of Roosevelt's first term. Roosevelt argued that the modern presidency, like the welfare state, was not a departure from sound constitutional principles. "The only thing that has been happening," he told the nation in his fireside chat of May 7, 1933, "has been to designate the President as the agency to carry out certain of the purposes of Congress. This was constitutional and keeping with past American traditions." [277]

In 1935 and 1936 the Court struck down more important national legislation than in any other comparable period of U.S. history. Roosevelt responded in February 1937 with the most controversial action of his presidency, the so-called court-packing plan: for every justice who failed to quit within six months after reaching the age of seventy, the president could appoint a new justice. Six of the nine justices were already over seventy, so Roosevelt conceivably could have made six new appointments, enlarging the Court to fifteen members, and, thus, overcoming the judicial resistance to the New Deal. *(See "Franklin D. Roosevelt and the 'Court Packing' Episode," p. 1168, in The President and the Supreme Court chapter of Part VI.)*

Although Roosevelt did not get his plan through Congress, he was able to claim that he had lost the battle but won the war, for the Court never struck down another New Deal law. In fact, as a consequence of the "Constitutional Revolution of 1937," the Supreme Court never again has invalidated a statute on the grounds that it was an unconstitutional delegation of authority to the executive.[278]

This achievement did not come without considerable political cost. The issue of Court reform served as a lightning rod, sparking a resurgence of congressional independence and the formation of a bipartisan legislative coalition, composed of conservative Democrats and Republicans, which would block presidential reform initiatives for many years to come.

The Modern Presidency and Foreign Policy

The stronger presidency that emerged from the volatile political developments of the 1930s was to prevail. In addition to the domestic crisis that dominated Roosevelt's first two terms in office came the Fascist menace to Europe and the Second World War. Total U.S. involvement in that conflict intensified the focus on the national government and its administrative apparatus and on the president himself. Significantly, it was this foreign policy crisis that led Roosevelt to believe that he should stand for reelection in 1940; thus, FDR became the only president to break the barrier against election to a third term. During the latter stages of the war, he won a fourth term as well. Only death cut short his protracted tenure.

In 1937 the Roosevelt presidency began to confront the isolationism that had dominated the polity since the League of Nations' dispute.[279] In doing so, FDR acted from a very strong constitutional position, which, ironically, had been fortified by the very Court that had been such a problem for him in the sphere of domestic action.

The major development in this regard had come in late 1936, when the Supreme Court in *U.S. v. Curtiss-Wright Export Corp.* upheld a 1934 measure authorizing the president to embargo the sale of arms to countries engaged in armed conflict. President Roosevelt had placed an arms embargo on two such countries, Bolivia and Paraguay, in the so-called Chaco War. This measure had been challenged as an unlawful delegation of authority; but in a somewhat surprising opinion, written by conservative justice George Sutherland, the Court laid down a sweeping doctrine of presidential authority in foreign affairs.

With only one dissenter, the Court held that the president's powers in domestic and foreign matters were fundamentally different. In foreign affairs, the Court argued, the federal government's actions, and more specifically the actions of the executive as the "sole organ" of the federal government in the field of international relations, depended neither on an affirmative grant by the Constitution nor on an act of Congress. Rather, the executive's authority in foreign matters was a "plenary and exclusive power." [280]

The *Curtiss-Wright* case established a constitutional doctrine that supported Alexander Hamilton's sweeping defense of the executive's prerogatives in foreign affairs. In 1936 the Court in *U.S. v. Belmont* justified executive agreements (presidential treaties made without the participation of the Senate). These two cases made virtually impossible any constitutional challenge to Roosevelt's increasingly internationalist posture as World War II approached.[281]

On the basis of such a broad understanding of the executive's foreign policy authority Roosevelt concluded the controversial Lend-Lease agreement with Great Britain in 1941. This deal, which paved the way for the United States to send fifty naval destroyers to help England in its desperate battle with Nazi Germany, marked a departure from the official U.S. position of neutrality.

World War II continued this development, allowing Roosevelt to assert an executive prerogative more boldly than he could have before the attack on Pearl Harbor. Under the conditions of total war, he assumed, the presidency could call upon sweeping executive prerogatives not only to direct military operations abroad but to manage affairs at home as well. In a bold—his critics claimed brazen—expression of such power, the president demanded an effective price-and-wage-control statute. "I ask the Congress," FDR said in his Labor Day message of September 7, 1941, "to take . . . action by the first of October." In the event that Congress did not act, Roosevelt warned, "I shall accept the responsibility, and I will act." [282]

Congress did enact the economic controls the president demanded, and Roosevelt never had to follow through on his threat. But the legislature's reluctant acquiescence in this matter indicates that "as depression gave way to war, another expansion of presidential authority was under way, linked chiefly now to the creation of a national security and warfare state rather than a welfare one." [283]

Harry S Truman and Dwight D. Eisenhower

FDR dominated American political life for over a decade. His legacy was a more powerful and more prominent presidency, but Roosevelt also had established unrealistic and contradictory standards by which citizens would judge his successors.

Truman and the Roosevelt Inheritance

When the Senate session of April 12, 1945, ended at about five o'clock, Vice President Harry Truman made his way over to the office of Speaker Sam Rayburn to join his friends for their afternoon round of bourbon and tap water. No sooner had his drink been poured than the vice president received a call from White House Press Secretary Steve Early, who told him to come to the executive mansion as soon as possible. Upon his arrival, Mrs. Roosevelt came up to him, put her arm around his shoulders, and said softly, "Harry, the president is dead." After a moment of shock, Truman asked Mrs. Roosevelt, "Is there anything I can do for you?" She replied, "Is there anything we can do for you? For you are the one in trouble now." [284]

Eleanor Roosevelt was not the only one who felt Truman was in deep trouble. The country was still at war, and it seemed incomprehensible that anyone, let alone this "little man" from Missouri, as his contemporaries often disdainfully referred to Truman, could replace Roosevelt as president of the United States.

That Truman eventually was able to emerge from FDR's shadow had little to do with his ability to move the public. A poor speaker and awkward in the presence of the press, Truman was very uncomfortable in the limelight of the modern presidency, especially in comparison with the self-command and bonhomie displayed by Roosevelt. Truman's personal and rhetorical shortcomings contributed to his low popularity: his public approval was lower than 50 percent for much of his time in office, including the entire final three years of his second term.[285] *(See Presidential Approval Ratings, p. 1465, in the Appendix.)*

In many respects, however, Truman was an ideal successor to Roosevelt. Truman understood and deeply believed in the changes that Roosevelt's tenure had made in the United States. He recognized that FDR's dynamic leadership and the expansion of government responsibilities demanded active leadership. He liked to remark that "being a president is like riding a tiger. You have to keep on riding or be swallowed." [286] Truman's determination to carry on the developments that FDR's momentous stay in the White House had set in motion enabled him to be—his personal deficiencies notwithstanding—one of the most important and successful of twentieth-century presidents.

Truman's Fair Deal. Truman made it quite clear that he was no back-to-normalcy Harding when he set forth in a message to Congress on November 6, 1945, a program that followed Roosevelt's New Deal commitment. Truman's twenty-one-point program called for extension of social security, increases in minimum wages, national health insurance, urban development, and a full employment bill.

Truman achieved little of his domestic program, however, and the 1946 congressional election appeared to be a dramatic rejection of the Fair Deal. That campaign was organized around the theme that the country had "had enough" of Roosevelt-Truman liberalism. For the first time in sixteen years the Republicans won control of Congress.[287]

Truman fought aggressively against any attempts on the part of the Eightieth Congress (1947-1949) to dismantle the New Deal. Truman used the veto more than two hundred times during his presidency, most vigorously in the areas of tax and labor policy. Truman's most significant veto was of the 1947 Taft-Hartley bill, legislation widely viewed as an attack on labor unions. The veto, although overridden, caused labor and middle-class liberals to line up solidly behind Truman.

Truman turned the 1948 presidential campaign into a referendum on the Roosevelt era. When Truman caught nearly everyone by surprise by winning a stunning come-from-behind victory over his Republican opponent, New York governor Thomas Dewey, he appeared to be finally out of FDR's shadow. Not only had he waged a successful fight to save the New Deal and rebuild the Roosevelt coalition, but the assertiveness he displayed in his battles with Congress confirmed the preeminence of the modern presidency in legislative affairs.

Truman's legislative leadership could not break the stalemate in domestic policy making that prevailed throughout his presidency; but he could claim some success with his Social Security, minimum wage, and public housing proposals during the Eighty-first Congress (1949-1951), which, after the 1948 election, was controlled by the Democrats. And his administration was remarkably successful in assembling a large bipartisan foreign policy coalition to authorize the Truman Doctrine, the Marshall Plan, and other postwar reconstruction and cold war initiatives that maintained the international commitments of the United States after the Second World War.

Truman's Use of Executive Power. Truman's battles with Congress encouraged him to stake out a substantial sphere for independent presidential action. In doing so he was acting on his long-held belief in a presidency with substantial autonomous powers. By executive order on December 5, 1946, Truman established the President's Committee on Civil Rights (PCCR), which was authorized "to determine whether and in what respect current law enforcement measures and the authority and means possessed by Federal, State, and local governments may be strengthened and improved to safeguard the civil rights of the people." [288] He recommended legislative action based on the PCCR's report; and when Congress proved unresponsive, the president acted on his own in the areas in which he had authority as chief executive. Most significant was his 1948 executive order establishing a policy of equal opportunity in the armed services.

Truman's most daring and politically costly unilateral actions came in the realm of international relations: the 1945 decision to use atomic weapons against Japan to end World War II and the decision to commit troops to Korea. In the latter action, following North Korea's invasion of South Korea in June 1950, U.S. troops were deployed in a full-scale war for the first time without a congressional declaration of war.

In part, Truman's action in Korea followed logically from the emergence of the United States after World War II as a superpower, actively engaged in international affairs. In 1945 the Senate overwhelmingly ratified the United Nations (UN) charter, and Congress passed the United States Participation Act, which would subject the United States to certain decisions taken by the UN. Truman cited this treaty as his primary justification for the deployment of troops in Korea; after the UN Security Council had called for action, the president argued, he had a duty to respond under Articles 29 and 42 of the UN charter.

Truman's actions in Korea also were defended on the basis of a sweeping presidential claim of authority to use

U.S. armed forces without consulting Congress. Truman clearly believed that the cold war against Communism and the president's position as leader of the free world had greatly diminished the role of Congress in foreign policy. As he said in March 1951, "the congressional power to declare war has fallen into abeyance because wars are no longer declared in advance."[289] There were still limits, however, on the powers of the modern presidency, even in the area of foreign policy. Truman would pay a price in congressional sniping at his foreign and military policies as the war in Korea dragged on. Moreover, his assertion that the war in Korea justified the president's assuming emergency economic powers was rebuffed by the Supreme Court in its 1952 decision in *Youngstown Sheet and Tube Co. v. Sawyer*. *(See "Sustaining the War Effort," p. 1188, in The President and the Supreme Court chapter of Part VI.)*

Truman and the Institution of the Modern Presidency. In the final analysis, Truman's almost seven years in office reaffirmed the modern presidency. He demonstrated that a president without the extraordinary political gifts and popularity of Roosevelt could make use of the refurbished executive office to achieve important objectives, define the terms of political debate, and control the main lines of domestic and foreign policy.

Truman both formalized and expanded the *institution* of the presidency. Although Franklin Roosevelt had created the Executive Office of the President, FDR's staff support was unstructured during his tenure, reflecting his penchant for improvisation and ad hoc arrangements. But Truman was a more diligent administrator. During his presidency responsibilities within the White House Office became more clearly defined. Truman also made more extensive use of the Bureau of the Budget than Roosevelt had. During his tenure, it became a regular BOB duty to clear and coordinate all legislative requests originating within federal departments, to draft legislation emanating from the White House, and to clear and draft executive orders.[290] As a result, Truman developed an advisory process in which political issues came to him for *decision*, instead, as was the case with FDR, for *development*.

Truman had help from Congress in this further institutionalization of the presidency. Congressional statutes, for example, established the Council of Economic Advisers (CEA) in 1946 and the National Security Council (NSC) in 1947 to aid the president in the formulation of fiscal and foreign policy, respectively; and Congress appropriated funds for larger staffs to assist him. Although the NSC and CEA initially were conceived by many in Congress as a check on the president's autonomy in fiscal and security matters, Truman acted effectively to make these agencies part of the president's team.

Dwight D. Eisenhower: The Reluctant Modern President

Eisenhower's administration marked the reluctant acceptance of the changes in the executive office since the 1930s. Eisenhower had no intention of dismantling the "Roosevelt revolution," but he came to the White House with aspirations and a perception of the presidency very different from Roosevelt's. "Ike," as he was known to the nation, was a soldier, not a political reformer, who served as supreme Allied commander in Europe (a position to which FDR appointed him) and who emerged from that experience as the most celebrated of World War II military officers. In many respects Eisenhower, like Coolidge, intended to preside over a national healing process after the controversies of the Roosevelt-Truman years rather than actively lead the country.

Eisenhower was no partisan Republican; in fact, as a career soldier he considered it his duty to remain above politics; he did not even cast his first vote until he was fifty-eight years old. But he did accept the Republican party's position that the balance between Congress and the White House had been upset by his immediate Democratic predecessors. In support of this view, the Republican-controlled Eightieth Congress (1947-1949) had passed the Twenty-second Amendment imposing a two-term limit on the presidency, which was ratified by the requisite number of states and made part of the Constitution in 1951. As the first Republican president since 1933, Eisenhower did not even send forward a legislative program during his first year in office.

Yet Roosevelt's presidency had accustomed the country to focus intensely on the early days of a presidency, thus taking the measure of the incumbent and his plans for the country. Like every chief executive in the post-Roosevelt era, Eisenhower found that the press insisted on grading him at the end of his "First Hundred Days," and he did not fare well when measured by FDR's standard.

The Hidden Hand. Eisenhower was not, however, simply a passive figure in the White House; in fact, he exercised power with much more relish and shrewdness than his contemporaries surmised. His was a "hidden-hand" presidency, as political scientist Fred Greenstein has put it, where power was exercised behind the scenes, while he presented the public image of a man detached from the political machinations taking place in the nation's capital.[291]

Although Eisenhower, compared with Roosevelt and Truman, was a domestic political conservative without a desire to innovate except in modest, incremental ways, he believed that the New Deal had become a permanent part of the U.S. government. When his conservative brother Edgar criticized him for carrying on liberal politics, the president replied angrily, "Should any political party attempt to abolish social security and eliminate labor laws and farm programs, you should not hear of that party again in our political history."[292] Moreover, unlike many members of his party, Eisenhower shared the internationalist aspirations of FDR and Truman.

Given the New Deal legacy and the emergence of the United States as leader of the free world, it was not possible for the president simply to preside. Instead, the task, as Eisenhower understood it, was to lead actively without seeming to do so, to obscure his steady involvement in political controversy while publicizing his status as a national hero and his congenial outward manner.

The most instructive example of Eisenhower's hidden-hand approach to government was his handling of the national crisis caused by Republican senator Joseph McCarthy, who chaired the Senate Committee on Operations and its Permanent Subcommittee on Investigations. The nation was traumatized by McCarthy's charges of Communist infiltration of the government, but Eisenhower refused to attack McCarthy publicly, although he recognized his irresponsible "red-baiting" as demagogy of the worst type. Eisenhower's critics maintained that by not taking McCarthy on publicly, he abetted the Wisconsin senator in unjustly ruining many lives and careers. "Unopposed by the one public leader who could have discredited him," wrote the historian Alonzo Hamby, "McCarthy ran amok." [293]

Eisenhower's public silence did not, however, indicate timidity or quiet approval. Rather, he feared that taking McCarthy on publicly would diminish the dignity of the presidency and undermine the unity of the Republican party, thus jeopardizing the chances for satisfying the internationalist aspirations reflected in his administration's foreign policy. "I will not," Eisenhower told his brother Milton, "get into a pissing contest with that skunk." [294]

Instead, the president worked closely with his press secretary, James Hagerty, and used the media and congressional allies to end McCarthy's political effectiveness.[295] Through Hagerty, Eisenhower helped manage the congressional hearings that culminated in McCarthy's censure in December 1954. Moreover, Eisenhower added to the mounting attacks on McCarthy by indirectly criticizing his actions; the overall strategy was for Eisenhower and Vice President Richard Nixon systematically to avoid direct mention of McCarthy but condemn the types of actions in which McCarthy engaged.

Eisenhower, then, did not reject the modern presidency; rather, he attempted to manage its responsibilities in a way that suited his own strengths and political goals. Many of his contemporaries in the press indicted Eisenhower's style of presidential leadership, asserting that it reflected weakness and forfeiture of moral leadership. Yet Eisenhower was extraordinarily popular with the American people. Surely, one suspects, his capacity to maintain a dignified distance from the contentiousness of modern presidential politics helps explain his popularity.

Eisenhower's Legacy. Eisenhower has been criticized frequently for what he left undone. To most liberals Eisenhower, who was as popular as FDR, failed to lead the country politically to redress problems of civil rights, education, and social justice. In Eisenhower's defense, however, it might be said that he recognized that there were limits to what a president could do. Arguably, by confronting those limits and displaying a political style to circumvent them, Eisenhower made an important contribution to the development of the modern presidency.

Eisenhower also played a significant part in institutionalizing the modern presidency. Drawing on his long military exposure to staff work, Eisenhower enlarged and more formally organized the White House Office. He established a line of command originating with a chief of staff, whose title was "the assistant to the president"; the chief of staff reported directly to him. Sherman Adams was the first person to hold this influential position, zealously protecting the president from the everyday demands of the White House.[296] *(See "Eisenhower and the Formalized Staff," p. 922, in White House Office chapter of Part V.)*

Eisenhower also instituted the first White House legislative liaison office to promote the president's program on Capitol Hill. There was no such office during Eisenhower's first year, but pressures from several quarters eventually forced the administration to become more actively involved in legislative affairs. Thus a legislative program accompanied Eisenhower's January 1954 State of the Union message, and Eisenhower and his legislative liaison office made systematic efforts to have it enacted. The president became increasingly involved in legislative matters during his tenure in office and managed to hold his own with a Congress that, after 1954, was under Democratic control.

Eisenhower's "special triumph" in legislative matters, as one historian has noted, was to hold down defense spending.[297] This former military man wished to avoid an arms race with the Soviet Union, fearing that it would lead to uncontrollable inflation and eventually bankrupt the United States, without providing any additional security. The Democrats, led by Sen. John F. Kennedy, criticized Ike for putting a balanced budget ahead of national defense. But as long as Eisenhower was president, there was no arms race; inheriting a $50-million defense budget from Truman, he reduced it to $40 billion and held it there for the eight years of his presidency.

Thus, Eisenhower upheld the prerogatives of the modern presidency. Perhaps the best evidence of this was his active involvement in the campaign that successfully defeated the Bricker Amendment, which called for Congress to alter a president's constitutional authority in the conduct of foreign policy. By its terms, executive agreements with other nations would become the law of the land only if they were approved by Congress and did not conflict with state laws. Its author, Republican senator John Bricker of Ohio, and its adherents held isolationist sentiments that, according to Eisenhower, threatened the international role of the United States and the future of the Republican party.

In the Senate, largely because of the president's personal influence, the amendment fell one vote short of the necessary two-thirds for ratification. This close vote reflected widespread public support for the proposed amendment, which indicated that many Americans still questioned a chief executive's exercise of initiative in foreign affairs. It was the reluctant modern president— "Dwight D. Eisenhower—nobody else," an embittered Senator Bricker maintained—who preserved the executive's prerogative to make unilateral international agreements, without the need to attain Senate approval.[298]

JFK and the Personalization of the Modern Presidency

John F. Kennedy was elevated to the presidency in 1960 to get the country moving again, to pull it out of the complacency that had settled over it in the twilight of the Eisenhower years. A sluggish economy, a simmering civil rights problem, and the Soviet threat abroad had created doubts about the country's future, producing a Democratic victory, although by a very narrow margin.

Tragically, on November 22, 1963, less than three years after Kennedy took the oath of office, he was assassinated by Lee Harvey Oswald in Dallas, Texas. At age forty-three, Kennedy had been the country's youngest elected president. Yet despite his truncated term, or perhaps because of it, Kennedy has found a lasting place in U.S. history. Or, as one historian has observed, Kennedy has become "part not of history but of myth," a myth that much of the American public has embraced.[299]

The persistence of Kennedy's popularity is due not only to his tragic death but to his inspirational qualities as president. His inaugural address set the tone for his administration. Hoping to broaden his support, Kennedy delivered a universalistic and stirring speech, many parts of which immediately entered the political lexicon.[300] Among his most memorable words were: "Ask not what your country can do for you; ask what you can do for your country." *(See "Kennedy's Inaugural Address," p. 1382, in the Appendix.)*

The First Television President

Kennedy's administration marked a revolutionary advance in the use of television in politics. Eisenhower had been the first president to appear on television regularly, but as JFK's biographer Carl Brauer has written, "It was under and because of Kennedy that television became an essential determinant—probably the essential determinant—of a president's ability to lead the nation." [301]

Kennedy's principal forum for reaching the public was the press conference, which was given a new prominence during his time in office. Eisenhower's press conferences were the first to be televised; but they were filmed, and the White House had retained the power to edit them and revise the transcript. Kennedy had benefited greatly from his television debates with Richard Nixon during the 1960 campaign and had come to see the medium of television as an ally.

The live, televised press conference relegated reporters to playing the part of stage props, thus allowing the president to establish direct communication with the public. Under Kennedy's auspices the press conference became the functional equivalent of the fireside chat; that is, it provided a relatively informal and personal way for the president to reach the public over the heads of Congress and the proprietors of the print media. President Kennedy held sixty-four press conferences, and his pleasing personality, quick wit, and impressive knowledge of government set a standard that his successors have struggled to meet.[302] Just as Franklin Roosevelt had been, in a sense, the first radio president, John Kennedy was the first television president.

The Personal Presidency

With Kennedy and the advent of television politics, the splendid isolation of the president, or what has been called the *personal* presidency, came into its own.[303] Kennedy's effective use of the media was only one important part of this development. His campaign for the presidency—run by members of his family, especially his brother Robert—undercut the traditional campaign roles of the party chair and the party organization. Henceforth, presidential campaigns would be directed by the candidate's own principal advisers and strategists, and coordination and liaison with party campaign efforts would become problematical.[304]

The Kennedy organization also made its mark on government. Most of the personnel from the campaign staff were relocated in parallel or comparable positions in the White House Office. This development was reinforced by greater concentration of policy responsibility in the executive office than there had been in past administrations. For example, Kennedy's White House assistant for national security, McGeorge Bundy, carried out many duties traditionally reserved for the secretary of state.

The Kennedy Legacy

Kennedy was a very popular president during his brief stay in the White House, and he passed from life to an enshrinement as the "best of the modern presidents." But Kennedy certainly had faults, made mistakes, and did not always live up to his public image.

His administration was responsible for a disastrous invasion of Cuba on April 17, 1961, by a brigade of some fourteen thousand anti-Castro exiles. They were crushed three days after arriving in Zapata Swamp at Cuba's Bay of Pigs. The Bay of Pigs affair was a humiliating defeat for Kennedy, who had been in office less than one hundred days when the invasion took place. Kennedy also can be faulted for initiating the ill-fated U.S. involvement in Vietnam. "Though [Kennedy] privately thought the United States 'overcommitted' in Southeast Asia," a historian generally sympathetic to JFK has written, "he permitted the commitment to grow. It was the fatal error of his presidency." [305]

Still, Kennedy's presidency was certainly not without its acomplishments. For seven days in October 1962, after the discovery of Soviet intermediate missile bases in Cuba, the world seemingly stood on the brink of nuclear war as Kennedy and Soviet Premier Nikita Khrushchev engaged in what Secretary of State Dean Rusk characterized as an eyeball-to-eyeball confrontation. This crisis was resolved when, in response to a U.S.-imposed quarantine of Cuba, the Soviets agreed to dismantle the missiles. Throughout this incident, Kennedy acted not only with firmness but with restraint, thus making it possible for Khrushchev to comply with U.S. demands without being humiliated.

Kennedy's triumph in the missile crisis demonstrated that he had matured considerably since the Bay of Pigs fiasco. This growth was also evident as he pursued initiatives to reduce U.S.-Soviet tensions. The United States and the Soviet Union concluded their first arms control agreement—a nuclear test ban treaty—on August 5, 1963. This agreement on atmospheric nuclear tests was a small step forward (it did not ban underground tests, for example), but it raised hopes for much more substantial progress in the future.

In domestic matters, one of the most frequent criticisms of Kennedy was that he promised much more than he delivered. In particular, JFK was faulted for his failures as a legislative leader. His New Frontier program included proposals for medical aid, support of education, and civil rights. But his relations with Congress were extraordinarily difficult. Several measures Kennedy sought, particularly Medicare and federal aid to education, were stalled during his administration; and two others, civil rights and tax reduction, had not been passed when he died.

Kennedy's problems with Congress and the difficulties he faced in foreign affairs pointed to a troubling paradox of the modern presidency. By the end of Kennedy's tenure, the evolution of the executive office had given rise to a more powerful and prominent chief of state, an elaborate and far-reaching institution with considerable autonomous power. At the same time, however, the president was increasingly cut off from the Congress and the party, thus making it difficult to satisfy public demands and achieve lasting reform.

Lyndon B. Johnson and Presidential Government

Kennedy's assassination left the nation in the hands of Lyndon B. Johnson, a Texan who had been selected as Kennedy's running mate to balance the ticket. Before his election as vice president, Johnson had earned a reputation as the consummate political operator in the Senate, where as majority leader he exercised enormous influence during the Eisenhower years. It remained to be seen whether this quintessential power broker could successfully adapt the experience and skills of a legislative insider to the presidency. But Johnson quickly grasped the reins of power. He

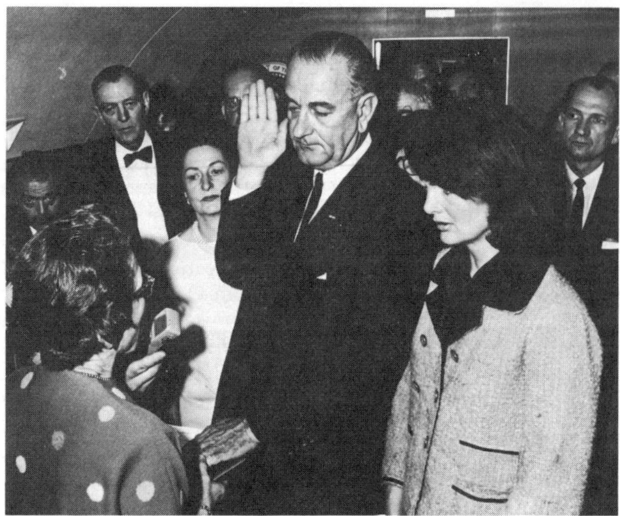

Cecil Stoughton, National Park Service

Lyndon Johnson takes the presidential oath aboard Air Force One just minutes after John F. Kennedy's assassination.

did more than reassure the nation and build confidence in his leadership: he continued—even accelerated—developments of the Kennedy era that accentuated the power and independence of the executive. Arguably, his administration marked the height of "presidential government." Yet LBJ's failings also brought into serious question for the first time since the 1930s the assumption that it was desirable for a president to dominate the affairs of state.

LBJ's Great Society

Johnson defined his first task as the completion of key elements of Kennedy's New Frontier—civil rights, the 1964 tax cut, Medicare, and voting rights. Each of these controversial measures was enacted under his leadership. Especially notable was the passage of civil rights legislation. When Kennedy died, the civil rights bill was bogged down in the Senate; but by drawing on the memory of a fallen leader and using his extraordinary skill and experience in legislative affairs, Johnson prevailed. On July 1, Congress passed the Civil Rights Act of 1964, which Johnson signed on July 2. The act extended the nondiscrimination principle to private as well as public establishments, forbidding discrimination in hotels, restaurants, and stores.

Johnson's successful battle for civil rights dazzled the liberal members of his party, many of whom resented his elevation to the presidency. But the Civil Rights Act was only the beginning. Johnson unveiled his plans for reform on May 22, 1964, in a speech at the University of Michigan. In those remarks he boldly set the tone for the Great Society, viewing past reform aspirations as only a point of departure:

> The Great Society rests on abundance and liberty for all. It demands an end of poverty and racial justice, to which we are totally committed in our time. But this is just the beginning.
>
> The Great Society is a place where every child can find knowledge to enrich his mind and to enlarge his talents. It is where leisure is a welcome chance to build and reflect, not a feared cause of boredom and restlessness. It is a place where the city of man serves not only the needs of the body and the demands of commerce but the desire for beauty and the hunger of the community.[306]

This vision of reform gave rise to a program of extraordinary scope, which was put before the Eighty-ninth Congress when it convened in 1965, two months after Johnson's landslide victory in the 1964 election. *(See "Lyndon B. Johnson's 'Great Society' Speech," p. 1384, in the Appendix.)* Johnson meant to demonstrate in sponsoring such a program that he was deeply concerned with the "quality" as well as the "quantity of life in America." Johnson and the Eighty-ninth Congress left an unparalleled record. In 1965 alone Congress passed eighty of the Johnson administration's proposals, denying him only three. These measures included important policy departures such as Medicare, Medicaid, the Civil Rights Act of 1965 (pertaining to voting rights), the Elementary and Secondary Education Act, the War on Poverty, and the Air Pollution and Control Act.

LBJ and the Institution of the Presidency

Johnson's dominance of the political process had enduring effects on the institution of the presidency, some of them extensions of developments begun under Kennedy. The programs of the Great Society gave new meaning to the idea of a *president's* program. More and more policies began to be invented by the politically appointed policy advocates in the West Wing of the White House, who were dedicated to moving quickly on the president's agenda. Concomitantly, career staff in the regular line agencies and the longtime policy analysts in the budget bureau became less influential in legislative program development.

This personalization of the executive office was not only extended during the Johnson years, but institutionalized. White House aide Joseph Califano supervised the creation of several task forces, comprising government officials and leading academics, which were given the responsibility of formulating new and challenging proposals for the president's domestic policy program. This new policy process, which was under the supervision of the presidency and free of traditional institutional restraints, was able to break through what Johnson and his advisers considered the timidity and conservatism of the old system. Califano's group was the precursor of the Domestic Policy Council, established by Johnson's successor, Richard Nixon, and of the domestic policy staffs of later administrations.[307]

Soon, however, Johnson overextended himself. It was, ironically, the "personalization" of the Johnson leadership that led to its undoing. LBJ was a gifted government politician, but he could not be the kind of leader that was required by the very office he had helped create. As Johnson aide Harry MacPherson put it, LBJ was incapable of "rising above the dirt of 'political governing,' so that he could inspire the nation." [308] His best words and teachings were laws and policies, but he was unable to cultivate a stable basis of popular support for his domestic program. Johnson himself felt that his most serious disadvantage as president was "a general inability to stimulate, inspire, and unite all the public in the country." [309]

LBJ's Downfall

It was the war in Vietnam, however, which most clearly revealed Johnson's shortcomings and the troubling aspects of presidential government. In 1965 the president had reached the conclusion that a Communist takeover in

South Vietnam could be prevented only by the commitment of a large contingent of U.S. forces to actual fighting. Johnson's extraordinary political skill at building political consensus in 1965 helped legitimize the Americanization of the war in Vietnam. With little resistance from Congress or, at the start, the public, U.S. forces rose from 23,000 at the end of 1964 to 181,000 a year later, 389,000 a year after that, and 500,000 by the end of 1967.

The war in Southeast Asia became, in an unprecedented way, the president's war. As political scientist Richard Pious has written, "No treaty obligations or other commitments required the United States to intervene." [310] Nor was there a declaration of war by Congress, only the Tonkin Gulf resolution, rushed through Congress in August 1964 after an alleged attack on U.S. destroyers off the coast of North Vietnam. This resolution held that Congress "approves and supports the determination of the President, as Commander-in-Chief, to take all necessary measures to repel any armed attack against the forces of the United States and to prevent further aggression."

By 1967, Johnson's political consensus had crumbled. The war was militarily unsuccessful and politically unpopular. LBJ was trapped politically at home, strategically in Vietnam. He told his advisers on November 2, 1967, "I am like the steering wheel of a car without any control." [311] When he announced in March 1968 that he would not be a candidate for reelection, the president, who only two years before commanded the political process, no longer held the allegiance of the American people.

Drawing by David Levine. Reprinted with permission from *New York Review of Books*.

This famous caricature shows LBJ displaying his gall bladder scar, drawn by the artist in the shape of South Vietnam.

Richard Nixon and the Twilight of the Modern Presidency

In 1968, the disarray within the Democratic party that followed Johnson's presidency enabled Richard Nixon to capture the office he had long coveted. But Nixon did not win a decisive mandate to govern. The Democrats retained control of both houses of Congress, thus making Nixon the first president since 1849 to be elected without his party's having gained a majority in either house of Congress.

Congress was not the only quarter from which the new president could expect opposition. Because the country had elected only one other Republican since Franklin Roosevelt's path-breaking presidency had begun thirty-six years earlier, Nixon faced a bureaucracy with a large number of Democratic holdovers. Many of these holdovers were protected by civil service procedures, which had been extended "upward, outward and downward" since the New Deal, encompassing most of the federal service. In his memoirs Nixon explained that "one of our most important tasks would be to place our stamp on the federal bureaucracy as quickly and firmly as we possibly could." [312]

Nixon's New Federalism

Nixon aggressively sought to expand presidential prerogatives. His administration was the first to look to the possibility that the modern presidency could be characterized as a double-edged sword, which could cut in a conservative as well as a liberal direction. This is not to say that Nixon was rigidly ideological in his opposition to the welfare state. His program of New Federalism called for sorting out government responsibilities so that national problems would be handled by the federal government, while those more suited to community control would be assumed by state and local authorities. Nixon believed that welfare, for example, required uniform standards and should be brought under the jurisdiction of the national government, whereas job training required a more flexible approach and should be managed by the states.

Nixon's New Federalism was conservative only in that it was the first challenge to the presumption underlying the New Deal—that societal problems are most effectively addressed at the national level. This challenge was enough to arouse opposition to Nixon's domestic policies in Congress and in the bureaucracy. Tensions between the White House and the bureaucracy were especially severe. To enhance the role of the states and localities and to give the poor greater opportunity to make their own decisions, Nixon's policies entailed removing power from the specialized bureaucracies of the federal government.[313] Faced with opposition from Congress, civil servants, and, often, even his own appointees to cabinet posts, Nixon increasingly ran the government out of the White House. Leonard Garment, of the Nixon White House legal staff, observed that the "central paradox of the Nixon administration was that to reduce *federal* power, it was first necesary to increase *presidential* power." Or, in Nixon's own words, "Bringing power to the White House was necessary to dish it out." [314]

Nixon and Vietnam

The aggrandizement of presidential power during the Nixon years was reinforced by foreign policy considerations. It was in Nixon's political self-interest to obtain "peace with honor" in Vietnam as soon as possible. But there was neither peace nor honor by the time the war was finally concluded on January 27, 1973. In the interim, Nixon had actually escalated U.S. involvement by covertly bombing North Vietnamese sanctuaries in Cambodia, a neutral country. Nixon next informed the nation on April 30, 1970, that he was sending troops to Cambodia, a venture that led to massive demonstrations in the United States and to unprecedented debate and hostility in Congress.

Nixon's policies in Vietnam not only reinforced but made more rigid and controversial his aggressive use of presidential power. He was to find, as had Truman and Johnson, that toleration for sweeping presidential power was not automatically accorded a president engaged in an undeclared war, particularly in the face of increasing opposition from Congress and the public.

The Administrative Presidency

The administrative presidency was born of Nixon's inability to achieve policy change by the enactment of legislation. During his first two years in office, most of his proposals, notably welfare reform and environmental initiatives, bogged down in Congress. Thus, Nixon shifted to a managerial strategy that would give him control of the executive departments and allow for the achievement of policy objectives through administrative action.

The first phase of the Nixon administrative strategy entailed an expansion and reorganization of the Executive Office of the President (EOP). The White House Office doubled in size, swelling from a staff of 292 under Johnson to 583 by the end of Nixon's first term. Nixon loyalists assumed responsibility not only for formulating policy, as Johnson's staff had done, but for carrying out that policy, thus dramatically undercutting the authority of the departments and agencies of the bureaucracy.

In foreign policy, Nixon's assistant for national security affairs, Henry Kissinger, created for the first time a system for the management of international affairs that was completely dominated by the White House. So marginal was the Department of State in Nixon's foreign policy making that Secretary of State William P. Rogers was not even informed in advance of the administration's most innovative foreign affairs departure—the opening to China.[315]

Similarly, White House assistant John Ehrlichman headed the newly formed Domestic Council, which dominated the domestic policy process. And the Bureau of the Budget (BOB) was reorganized and expanded to strengthen the president's influence over domestic affairs. On July 1, 1970, by executive order BOB was transformed into the Office of Management and Budget (OMB), signifying an added cadre of presidentially appointed assistant directors for policy who would stand between the OMB director and the bureau's senior civil servants. The budget office therefore attained additional policy responsibility and was "further domesticated" so as to be more responsive to the president.

Although Nixon expanded the EOP, he still did not achieve as much control over public policy as he had hoped. Early in his second term, therefore, Nixon undertook a reorganization intended to rebuild the bureaucracy in his own image. The White House sought to place its proven loyalists in the regular program departments and agencies and to consolidate leadership of the bureaucracy in a "super-cabinet" of four reliable secretaries who would implement Nixon's policies. But Nixon was forced to abandon this plan when the Watergate scandal began to unfold.

The Watergate affair was the principal cause of Nixon's becoming the first president in U.S. history to resign his office. Nixon's impeachment was ensured by the Supreme Court action in *United States v. Nixon,* which rejected Nixon's sweeping claim of executive privilege and forced the release of tapes that showed the president had known all along of the cover-up.[316] *(See "The Case of Richard Nixon," p. 373, in Removal of the President chapter of Part II and box, The President versus the Supreme Court:* United States v. Nixon, *pp. 1160-1161.)* But, as political scientist Fred I. Greenstein has noted, "the willingness of Congress to take the extraordinary step of removing a president was in part a response to Nixon's continuing failure to use persuasion to win Congressional support and to his repeated efforts to circumvent Congress."[317]

An Imperiled Presidency: Gerald Ford and James Carter

The shock of Nixon's resignation in August 1974 reinforced concerns created by the Vietnam War, resulting in a dramatic and widespread recognition that the president's power was subject to abuse. When asked in 1959 whether the president or Congress should have "the most say in government," a representative sample of Americans overwhelmingly favored presidential dominance by 65 percent to 17 percent. A similar survey in 1977, however, indicated a striking reversal: 58 percent of the public believed Congress should have the most say in government; only 26 percent supported presidential dominance.[318]

Rallying to this change in public opinion, Congress passed a flurry of legislation during the 1970s designed to curb the unilateral exercise of presidential power. One important example of this legislation was the Congressional Budget and Impoundment Control Act of 1974, which put restrictions on the president's power to impound funds (requiring that such "rescissions" be approved by Congress). *(See "Presidents and the Budget," p. 652, in Chief Economist chapter of Part III.)* Congress also created budget committees in the House and Senate to coordinate and strengthen legislative action in fiscal matters. The budget reform legislation established the Congressional Budget Office (CBO), a legislative staff agency that would make available to Congress the same sort of expertise on fiscal matters that OMB provided the executive branch.

Congress also enacted statutes to reassert its influence on foreign affairs. The War Powers Resolution, passed over Nixon's veto in 1973, required the president to consult Congress "in every possible instance" before committing troops to combat and to submit a report of presidential action to Congress within forty-eight hours. After sixty days, the act further stipulated, troops were to be removed unless Congress had passed a declaration of war or some more specific authorization to continue troop deployment. *(See "War Powers Act," p. 543, in Commander in Chief chapter of Part III.)*

These laws would have only a marginal effect on presidential power, but their enactment reflected Congress's determination to reestablish itself as an equal partner, if not the dominant force, in the governance of the nation.

Gerald Ford and the Post-Watergate Era

Gerald Ford assumed office under some of the most difficult circumstances any president has ever faced. Ford had never run for national or statewide office; his electoral constituency was confined to the fifth district of Michigan. He was representing this district in the House, where he served as minority leader, when the incumbent vice president, Spiro Agnew, was forced to resign over revelations about his improprieties while serving as governor of Maryland. Ford was then nominated by Nixon to replace Agnew and was confirmed by both houses of Congress under conditions of the Twenty-fifth Amendment, ratified in 1967. When the Watergate scandal forced President Nixon to resign, Ford became the first president in U.S. history to hold the offices of vice president and president without having been elected to either.

That Nixon resigned in disgrace made the start of Ford's presidency especially difficult. Ford entered the Oval Office when the country was still deeply polarized and scarred by the Vietnam War, when respect for the institution of the presidency was greatly diminished, and when the nation's economy and foreign relations were in disarray. Ford made an earnest effort to restore the integrity of the presidency and purge the nation of the effects of the Watergate experience by symbolic actions and shifts in policy.[319] Many of the trappings of the so-called imperial presidency were removed. Ford reduced the White House staff by 10 percent, from 540 to 485. The principal section of the White House—the living quarters and state rooms—were referred to as "the residence" rather than "the mansion." After three days in office Ford accepted the recommendation of a Senate resolution calling for a White House summit conference on the economy.

The change in style and policy in the early days of the Ford administration brought the president much goodwill. His self-effacing manner did not seem to diminish the presidency but to give it an endearing folksiness. In his first week in office Ford received a 71 percent approval rating; only 3 percent disapproved, and 26 percent were undecided.[320] Almost overnight, however, Ford's standing with the public crumbled. The cause was his decision on September 8, 1974, to grant Nixon a full and unconditional pardon. By the end of September, Ford's popularity in the public opinion polls had dropped from a favorable rating of 71 percent to 50 percent. *(See Presidential Approval Ratings, p. 1485, in the Appendix.)*

No one ever challenged Ford's integrity, and—the public outcry over the Nixon pardon notwithstanding—he restored confidence in the presidency. Ford did much, as his successor Jimmy Carter observed in his inaugural address, "to heal our land." But Ford was unable to restore the power of the modern presidency. The limits of executive influence were most clearly revealed by Ford's inability to exert his will on an aggressive and hostile Democratic Congress. The results of the 1974 midterm election made the task of legislative leadership more difficult, swelling the Democratic majority by forty-four seats in the House and three in the Senate.

Ford did not shrink in the face of this opposition, and he had some success with Congress in tax cutting and deregulation. But for the most part his influence was negative; he cast sixty-six vetoes during his short time in office, mostly against spending bills, and was upheld forty-nine times. Such a role was more characteristic of the nineteenth-century executive than it was of the modern presidency.

Ford's difficulties with Congress did not stop at the water's edge. The legislature refused to respond to a number of Ford's most urgent foreign policy proposals: request for emergency aid to the disintegrating forces of South Vietnam, a plea to lift an embargo on aid to Turkey, and a request for aid to the enemies of the Marxist forces in Angola. It was the lack of congressional support in foreign affairs, especially, that caused President Ford to express concern in March 1976 that "there had been a swing of the 'historic pendulum' toward Congress, raising the possibility of a disruptive erosion of the president's ability to govern." [321]

As he turned the White House over to former Georgia governor Jimmy Carter, who defeated him in the 1976 election, Ford had every reason to believe that the presidency was slipping into receivership. Carter's four years in the White House would not prove him wrong.

A President Named Jimmy

James Earl Carter, Jr.—he preferred "Jimmy"—represented the extremes of promise and disappointment to which the contemporary executive office is prone. His elevation to the White House and initial popularity as president was a remarkable personal triumph. Yet, as one presidential scholar has noted, "at the time he left office his reputation had nowhere to go but up." [322]

A one-term governor of Georgia and a virtual unknown outside of his state before his run for the presidency, Carter won the Democratic nomination, although he was not supported by the leaders of his party. To emphasize his personal relationship with the people, Carter went further than Ford in eliminating the imperialistic trappings of the presidency. In his inaugural parade, he and his wife, Rosalynn, broke precedent by stepping from their limousine onto the street and walking the mile from the Capitol to the White House; he banned the playing of "Hail to the Chief" at presidential appearances; and he carried his own luggage. Such behavior had worked well before the election as he campaigned to win the votes of ordinary citizens, but it worked to his detriment once he occupied the Oval Office and sought to wield power. Carter failed to recognize at the beginning of his administration that presidential authority depended upon a dignified image and that the very symbols he eliminated contributed to that dignity.

Carter's problems went beyond symbolism, however. Before the end of his first year as president, it was clear that he was having serious conflicts with Congress. In budgetary matters especially, since passage of the Congressional Budget and Impoundment Control Act of 1974, disagreements between the president and Congress had become institutionalized. Although less conservative than his Republican predecessors, Carter tried to hold budget costs down, especially as inflationary pressures mounted during the later part of his term. He was no more successful than Nixon or Ford, however, in getting the liberal Democratic Congress to respond to his call for fiscal restraint.

Carter was able to learn from his mistakes, and after his first year in office he established better relations with Congress. The president's record with the Ninety-sixth Congress (1979-1981), in fact, was quite respectable. Congress ratified the Panama Canal treaties and enacted airline deregulation, civil service reform, and the natural gas pricing bill, which completed a comprehensive energy package; Congress also eliminated some of the most egregious pork-barrel works projects.

This success was attributable in part to creation of an effective White House Office of Public Liaison, a significant addition to the institution of the presidency. The purpose of this office, headed by Anne Wexler, was to make it possible for a president who lacked great rhetorical ability to form a link with the public. As political scientist Erwin Hargrove has written: "The Wexler office compensated for Carter's limitations as a presidential persuader by institutionalizing the persuasion function, not with Congress, but by bringing groups of citizens to the White House for briefings by the president and others on current legislative issues." [323]

In addition to his legislative achievements, Carter scored a personal diplomatic triumph with the signing of the Camp David agreement by Egyptian president Anwar Sadat and Israeli prime minister Menachem Begin on September 17, 1978, a significant turning point in Middle East history. Frustrated with the difficulty of getting the two parties together, Carter devised the novel solution of inviting Begin and Sadat to Camp David. It was Sadat who first made a dialogue between Israel and Egypt possible; and it was his willingness to acquiesce to an agreement favoring Israel that allowed for a concrete accord to be reached. But Carter's determination and keen mind for detail, displayed throughout the thirteen days of diplomacy among the three leaders, was essential to achieving the first rapprochement between an Arab nation and Israel.

Despite the successes of Carter's last two years in office, his presidency never recovered from the damage caused by the confusion and ineptness of his early days in the White House. A full resurrection of his standing was not possible because of an inability to establish a bond with the public. Carter's personal presidency depended upon popular leadership, which appealed over the heads of interest groups and legislators. Yet this was not really Carter's style.[324] He was an effective campaigner in making general appeals to the public and selling himself as a trustworthy statesman. But he lacked a *public* vision that could focus the nation's attention and enable him to lead it in a particular direction. Having offered a bewildering array of legislative proposals on energy, welfare, education, and urban decay, among other issues, Carter failed to provide integrating themes by which the American public or the Democratic party could make sense of these measures. Carter had not given the nation an idea to follow; instead he offered a host of incremental responses. "I came to think," wrote his speechwriter James Fallows, "that Carter believes fifty things, but not one thing." [325]

Frank Johnston, *Washington Post*

President Carter, center, grasps hands with Egyptian president Anwar Sadat and Israeli prime minister Menachem Begin at the signing of the Camp David peace accords on March 26, 1979.

Thus, even when some of Carter's proposals were enacted, the public never got the impression that he was in control of events. In fact, the last two years of Carter's presidency were overcome by events for which he was not to blame and were beyond the president's control, notably the inflationary pressures of the oil price increases of the Organization of Petroleum Exporting Countries and the Iranian hostage crisis. Any leader, no matter how gifted, would have had trouble dealing with these matters. But Carter's style of leadership brought the full brunt of these problems down upon him. His tendency to personalize the problems of state was especially damaging in the hostage situation.

The consuming events of his last two years in the White House did not prevent Carter from fending off a serious challenge from Massachusetts senator Edward M. Kennedy for the 1980 Democratic nomination. But Carter entered the 1980 campaign bearing the public image of a weak and indecisive leader. His defeat at the hands of Ronald Reagan in the general election marked the first time an elected president had been defeated since Herbert Hoover lost to Franklin Roosevelt in 1932. So decisive was the American people's rejection of Carter in 1980 that it created the opportunity for his successor to move the country away from the policies that had governed the nation for nearly a half a century.

Ronald Reagan: Restoration of the Modern Presidency

"Among the consequences of Reagan's election to the presidency," political scientist Jeffrey Tulis wrote in 1987, "was the rewriting of textbooks on American government." It was no longer possible to claim, he noted, that the fragmented and demoralized conditions in U.S. politics "would frustrate the efforts of any president to accomplish substantial policy objectives, to maintain popularity, and to avoid blame for activities beyond his control." [326] In contrast to Carter, Reagan was able to advance a legislative program successfully. Unlike Carter and Ford, he was renominated without opposition and reelected handily. He retired from the White House as the most popular president since Franklin Roosevelt.

The Reagan Revolution

The results of the 1980 election were somewhat ambiguous. In a three-man race between Reagan, Carter, and independent candidate John Anderson, Reagan won 489 electoral votes. Yet he won only 51 percent of the popular vote. Nor were the results of the congressional races decisive. For the first time since 1953-1955, the Republicans held the majority of the Senate seats, and several liberal senators were defeated. Nevertheless, although the GOP did manage to pick up thirty-three seats in the House, the Democrats retained control of the lower chamber. Thus, Reagan faced political conditions considerably more favorable than those Nixon and Ford were forced to deal with, but there was no unambiguous turning of the tide.

It was to Reagan's credit that he was able to present

this ambiguous victory as a national mandate and bring about important policy departures during the first year of his presidency. Reagan's ability to transform his electoral victory into concrete achievements testified to his considerable rhetorical gifts. Critics dismissed his ability to communicate effectively as the talent of a former actor who still could learn and deliver his lines. But Reagan's supporters maintained that there was logic and substance to his message, that he was not the "Great Communicator" but the "Great Rhetorician," who, like Wilson, the two Roosevelts, and Kennedy before him, articulated a vision that inspired the nation.[327] His inaugural address *(see "Reagan's First Inaugural Address," p. 1354, in the Appendix)* was the first by a president in almost fifty years to make an appeal for limited government, defining clearly his intention to preside over a redirection of public policy for the country:

> In this present crisis, government is not the solution to our problem; government is the problem. From time to time we've been tempted to believe that society has become too complex to be managed by self-rule, that government by an elite group is superior to government for, by, and of the people. Well, if no one among us is capable of governing himself, then who among us has the capacity to govern someone else? [328]

Reagan's effective rhetoric was matched by his skill as a legislative leader. In contrast to Carter's numerous and diverse legislative proposals, the Reagan administration focused on one major issue—shrinking the influence of government in domestic policy.[329] Reagan concentrated on an economic program based on two legislative proposals: a three-year tax cut and a major reduction in domestic spending. The results brought a dramatic departure in fiscal policy: $50 billion in program cuts, $700 billion in tax cuts, and a three-year, 27 percent increase in defense spending.

Reagan's hastily conceived economic package suffered from some of the same defects of Johnson's Great Society legislation. The premise of the administration's "supply-side" economics was that reducing federal spending and cutting taxes would stimulate the economy. In theory, tax savings would be invested by upper-income people, who benefited most from the tax act. This investment, in turn, would trigger productivity, increase employment, decrease welfare, and lead to an increased income base for taxation and, ultimately, a balanced budget with reduced interest and inflation rates. Yet, as budget director David Stockman admitted, "None of us really understands what's going on with all these numbers." [330] The Reagan administration later became saddled, contrary to supply-side projections, with the largest national debt in U.S. history.

This debt was an ironic legacy for a fiscal conservative. Yet the unanticipated consequences of Reagan's fiscal program did not harm the president's standing with the public. Despite the deficit, the economy performed well after the severe recession of 1982. And when he did face adversity, Reagan managed to give the impression that he was still on the march.

Reagan as Party Leader

Reagan's confidence, one suspects, reflected his comfort with the office of the presidency and his faith in the principles he so effectively conveyed to the American people. It was Reagan's hope that these principles would animate a fundamental realignment in U.S. history in which the philosophy of FDR and the New Deal would no longer hold sway because conservative thought had become the American mainstream. The 1984 presidential election—in which the Republican ticket won the electoral votes of all but one state (Minnesota) and the District of Columbia, as well as 59 percent of the popular vote—convinced the president that such a realignment was indeed taking place.

Reagan worked very hard at strengthening the organization and popular support of the GOP, surprising even his own White House political director with his "total readiness" to shoulder such partisan responsibilities as making numerous fund-raising appearances for the GOP and its candidates. In his effort to bring about a new political era, Reagan helped to galvanize the renewal of party politics. The erosion of old-style partisan politics allowed for a more national and issue-oriented party system, which, in turn, made possible closer ties between presidents and their parties. Reagan's presidency accelerated such a development, and during his administration the Republican party became solidly right of center.

It may be, then, that the 1980s will mark the watershed of a new political era and of a strengthened link between presidents and the party system. As political scientist James Sundquist has noted, the Democrats have become a more national and programmatic party as well, with an ideology decidedly left of center; thus, "the Democrats, if and when they elect a president, will demonstrate a cohesion that will astound those who recall the schismatic party of thirty or even twenty years ago." [331]

Reagan and the Administrative Presidency

It is premature, however, to celebrate the dawn of a new form of party government, one that reflects Woodrow Wilson's concept of responsible party politics and one that will serve rather than restrain presidential ambitions. In fact, Reagan's personal popularity was never converted into Republican control of government. His landslide in 1984 did not prevent the Democrats from maintaining control of the House of Representatives. And despite his plea to the voters in the 1986 House and Senate campaigns to elect Republican majorities, the Democrats recaptured control of the Senate, thus restoring the divided government that had existed during the Nixon and Ford years.

Reagan, to be sure, did enjoy considerably more support in the country and in Congress than had his two Republican predecessors, especially during his first six years in office. Still, the president suffered a number of reversals, and by the end of his term Congress had demonstrated its ability to challenge him for control over the councils of power. After 1982, Congress refused to cut domestic spending any further and required the administration to slow the pace of its rearmament program. Congress also restricted the president's ability to aid the contra rebels battling the Marxist regime in Nicaragua by enacting a series of amendments—the Boland Amendments—to foreign military assistance bills.

In the face of the mounting opposition from Congress, the Reagan presidency was relegated to employing the same sort of tactics that characterized the institutional combat of the Nixon years. To effect its policies on Nicaragua, the administration undertook to build an alternative intelligence apparatus attached to the National Security Council. This apparatus enabled the White House to conduct covert operations (such as aiding the contras) that the Congress had refused to approve and activities (such as the sale of weapons to Iran) that Congress almost certainly would not have countenanced. Thus, the damaging Iran-contra scandal was not simply the result of a president's being asleep at his watch. Rather, it was the unfortunate consequence of the Reagan administration's attempt to assume a forceful anti-Communist posture in Central America in the face of a recalcitrant bureaucracy and Congress.

Nor was this assertion of the "administrative presidency" in the case of Nicaragua an aberration. Especially in the area of social regulation, "regulatory relief"—the Reagan administration's attempt to weaken environmental, consumer, and civil rights regulation—became the product not of legislative change but of administrative action, delay, and repeal. Executive Orders 12291 and 12498, which mandated a comprehensive review of existing and proposed agency regulations, respectively, and centralized review in the Office of Management and Budget, demonstrated quite clearly the extent to which emphasis was placed on *administrative* regulatory relief.

Thus, the Reagan presidency was not merely a rhetorical one. It marked the resumption of the trend in modern presidential leadership to concentrate power in the White House, a trend that had been suspended in the wake of Vietnam and Watergate. Moreover, Reagan's administrative presidency dramatically confirmed the acceptance by conservatives of the need to centralize power in order to carry out their objectives. As one presidential scholar has written, "Nixon and Reagan had the courage to act on what was once the convictions of liberals, taking it for granted that the president should use whatever power he can muster, including power to administer programs, to shape policy."[332]

The success of the Reagan administration perhaps can be viewed as a remarkable triumph of the administrative presidency. Unlike Nixon, Reagan did not resign in disgrace; instead, he retired to his ranch in California as the most popular president in over a half century.

Notes

1. James Thomas Flexner, *George Washington and the New Nation: 1783-1793* (Boston: Little, Brown, 1970), 171.
2. Ibid.
3. Forrest McDonald, *The Presidency of George Washington* (Lawrence: University Press of Kansas, 1974), 24.
4. Flexner, *George Washington*, 398.
5. Thomas Jefferson to James Madison, December 20, 1787, in *The Portable Thomas Jefferson*, ed. Merrill D. Peterson (New York: Viking Press, 1975), 431.
6. Flexner, *George Washington*, 193.
7. Ibid., 196.
8. Ibid., 106.
9. Leonard White, *The Federalists: A Study in Administrative History, 1789-1801* (New York: Macmillan, 1948), 101.
10. Ibid., 106.
11. McDonald, *Presidency of George Washington*, 38.
12. Flexner, *George Washington*, 221.
13. "Account by William Maclay of President George Washington's First Attempt to Obtain the Advice and Consent of the Senate to a Treaty," August 22, 24, 1789, in *The Growth of Presidential Power: A Documented History*, ed. William M. Goldsmith (New York and London: Chelsea House, 1974), 1:392-396.
14. Printed in *Letters of Pacificus and Helvidius on the Proclamation of Neutrality of 1793* (Washington, D.C.: Gideon, 1845), 3.
15. Ibid., 5-15.
16. Goldsmith, *The Growth of Presidential Power*, 1:398.
17. *Letters of Pacificus and Helvidius*, 53-64.
18. Goldsmith, *Growth of Presidential Power*, 1:411.
19. McDonald, *Presidency of George Washington*, 114.
20. Leonard White, *The Jeffersonians: A Study in Administrative History, 1801-1829* (New York: Macmillan, 1951), 30.
21. McDonald, *Presidency of George Washington*, 160.
22. Quoted in Ralph Adams Brown, *The Presidency of John Adams* (Lawrence: University Press of Kansas, 1975), 22.
23. Ibid., 25.
24. Letter to Elbridge Gerry, May 13, 1797, in Peterson, *The Portable Thomas Jefferson*, 471-474.
25. Brown, *The Presidency of John Adams*, 26-27.
26. White, *The Federalists*, 241.
27. Ibid., 237.
28. Richard Hofstadter, *The Idea of a Party System* (Berkeley: University of California Press, 1969), 139.
29. Thomas Jefferson to Spencer Roane, September 6, 1819, in *The Writings of Thomas Jefferson*, ed. Albert Ellery Bergh (Washington, D.C.: Thomas Jefferson Memorial Association, 1903), 15:212-216.
30. Forrest McDonald, *The Presidency of Thomas Jefferson* (Lawrence: University Press of Kansas, 1976), 34.
31. Robert M. Johnstone, Jr., *Jefferson and the Presidency* (Ithaca, N.Y.: Cornell University Press, 1978), 162.
32. McDonald, *Presidency of Thomas Jefferson*, 50-51.
33. Johnstone, *Jefferson and the Presidency*, 46.
34. Letter, Thomas Jefferson to John Breckinridge, August 12, 1803, in *The Portable Thomas Jefferson*, 494-497.
35. White, *The Jeffersonians*, 3.
36. Quoted in Johnstone, *Jefferson and the Presidency*, 53.
37. The discussion of the change in the presidency during the Jeffersonian era is derived from James Ceaser, *Presidential Selection: Theory and Development* (Princeton, N.J.: Princeton University Press, 1979), 88-122; and Johnstone, *Jefferson and the Presidency*, 52-75.
38. Johnstone, *Jefferson and the Presidency*, 58-59.
39. Merrill D. Peterson, *Thomas Jefferson and the New Nation: A Biography* (New York: Oxford University Press, 1970), 653.
40. Jeffrey Tulis, *The Rhetorical Presidency* (Princeton, N.J.: Princeton University Press, 1987).
41. Leonard W. Levy, *Jefferson and Civil Liberties: The Darker Side* (Cambridge: Harvard University Press, 1963), 95.
42. White, *The Jeffersonians*, 53-54. See also Gaillard Hunt, *The Life of James Madison* (New York: Russell and Russell, 1902), 316-319.
43. White, *The Jeffersonians*, 55.
44. Hunt, *Life of James Madison*, 325.
45. Ibid., 318-319.
46. Ibid., 329-330.
47. Thomas Jefferson to John Holmes, April 22, 1820, in *The Portable Thomas Jefferson*, 567-569.
48. White, *The Jeffersonians*, 39.
49. James Monroe, "State of the Union Address," December 2, 1823, in *Messages and Papers of the Presidents*, ed. James D. Richardson (New York: Bureau of National Literature, 1897), 1:778.
50. John Quincy Adams, "Diary Account of Cabinet Discussions of His First State of the Union Message," November 25-26, 1825, in Goldsmith, *Growth of Presidential Power*, 1:325.
51. Ibid.
52. Robert V. Remini, *Andrew Jackson and the Course of American Democracy, 1833-1845* (New York: Harper and Row, 1984), 7.
53. Major L. Wilson, *The Presidency of Martin Van Buren* (Lawrence: University Press of Kansas, 1984), 13.
54. Richardson, *Messages and Papers of the Presidents*, 3:1206.
55. Wilson, *Presidency of Martin Van Buren*, 13.
56. Wilfred E. Binkley, *The Powers of the President: Problems of American Democracy* (Garden City, N.Y.: Doubleday, Daron, 1937), 68.
57. Edward S. Corwin, *The President: Office and Powers, 1787-1957*, 4th ed. (New York: New York University Press, 1957), 20-21.

58. Ibid.; see also Leonard D. White, *The Jacksonians: A Study in Administrative History, 1829-1861* (New York: Macmillan, 1954), 24-25.
59. Robert V. Remini, *Andrew Jackson and the Course of American Freedon, 1822-1832* (New York: Harper and Row, 1981), 369.
60. Richardson, *Messages and Papers of the Presidents,* 3:1152; Remini, *Andrew Jackson and the Course of American Freedom,* 370. Jackson vetoed twelve bills in all and used the "pocket veto" for the first time.
61. *McCulloch v. Maryland,* 4 L.Ed. 579 (1819).
62. Richardson, *Messages and Papers of the Presidents,* 3:1144-1145.
63. *Marbury v. Madison,* 1 Cranch 138 (1803).
64. *Niles Register,* November 17, 1832, quoted in White, *The Jacksonians,* 23; Remini, *Andrew Jackson and the Course American Freedom,* 373.
65. Quoted in Binkley, *Powers of the President,* 81.
66. Ibid., 83.
67. Remini, *Andrew Jackson and the Course of American Freedom,* 325.
68. On the development of the "administration press," see White, *The Jacksonians,* chap. 15.
69. Quoted in ibid., 320.
70. Ibid., 332-343.
71. Ibid., 313. The deleterious effects of the system of rotation on public administration often have been exaggerated (ibid., 308, 343).
72. Alexis de Tocqueville, *Democracy in America,* ed. J. P. Mayer (Garden City, N.Y.: Doubleday, 1969), 394.
73. Gen. William Henry Harrison, letter to Rep. Harmer Denny, December 2, 1838, in Goldsmith, *The Growth of Presidential Power,* 2:637-641.
74. Binkley, *Powers of the President,* 92-93.
75. Ibid., 112.
76. Robert J. Morgan, *A Whig Embattled: The Presidency under John Tyler* (Lincoln: University of Nebraska Press, 1954), chap. 2; Binkley, *Powers of the President,* 96-104.
77. Binkley, *Powers of the President,* 103.
78. On the nomination of Polk as the first "dark horse," see Charles A. McCoy, *Polk and the Presidency* (Austin: University of Texas Press, 1960), chap. 2; on Van Buren's actions in 1844, see Donald B. Cole, *Martin Van Buren and the American Political System* (Princeton, N.J.: Princeton University Press, 1984), chap. 13.
79. McCoy, *Polk and the Presidency,* 74-75; White, *The Jacksonians,* 77-79.
80. Quoted in Binkley, *Powers of the President,* 105.
81. White, *The Jacksonians,* 50.
82. Ibid., 51.
83. McCoy, *Polk and the Presidency,* 119-120; White, *The Jacksonians,* 66.
84. Binkley, *Powers of the President,* 110.
85. White, *The Jacksonians,* 522, 529.
86. Binkley, *Powers of the President,* 112.
87. Richardson, *Messages and Papers of the Presidents,* 7:2962.
88. Binkley, *Powers of the President,* 112.
89. Elbert B. Smith, *The Presidency of James Buchanan* (Lawrence: University Press of Kansas, 1975), 23-29.
90. *Dred Scott v. Sandford,* 19 Howard 1393 (1857).
91. For a critical examination of the view that Lincoln's presidency was one of "constitutional dictatorship," see Herman Belz, *Lincoln and the Constitution: The Dictatorship Question Reconsidered* (Fort Wayne, Indiana: Louis A. Warren Lincoln Library and Museum, 1984).
92. Corwin, *The President,* 451; Binkley, *Powers of the President,* 107.
93. Quoted in Stephen B. Oates, *With Malice toward None: The Life of Abraham Lincoln* (New York: Harper and Row, 1977), 195.
94. Richardson, *Messages and Papers of the Presidents,* 7:3206.
95. Ibid.
96. Ibid., 3211 (Lincoln's emphasis).
97. Ibid., 3210.
98. Ibid.
99. Robert K. Faulkner, "Lincoln and the Constitution" (Paper prepared for the annual meeting of the Northeast Political Science Association, Boston, Mass., April 1986), 34.
100. Richardson, *Messages and Papers of the Presidents,* 7:3208.
101. *Complete Works of Abraham Lincoln,* ed. John G. Nicolay and John Hay (Harrogate, Tenn.: Lincoln Memorial University, 1894), 10:66.
102. J. G. Randall, *Constitutional Problems under Lincoln,* rev. ed. (Urbana: University of Illinois Press, 1951), 51.
103. Corwin, *President: Office and Powers,* 144.
104. *Prize Cases,* 67 U.S. 635. For a discussion of this case, see Randall, *Constitutional Problems under Lincoln,* 52-59.
105. 67 U.S. 670.
106. For a discussion of the importance of the legal distinction between an insurrection and a war against an independent nation, see Randall, *Constitutional Problems under Lincoln,* 59-73.
107. "Proclamation of April 15, 1861," in Richardson, *Messages and Papers of the Presidents,* 7:3299.
108. Corwin, *The President,* 145-147.
109. Richardson, *Messages and Papers of the Presidents,* 7:3299.
110. *Ex Parte Milligan,* 71 U.S. 2. For a discussion of this case, see Randall, *Constitutional Problems under Lincoln,* 180-186.
111. 71 U.S. 127.
112. Corwin, *The President,* 234.
113. See the *Vallandigham* case (1 Wall 243), decided in 1864, which found acceptable the arrest and sentencing of a prominent antiwar agitator who was detained for a speech given in Mount Vernon, Ohio.
114. Randall, *Constitutional Problems under Lincoln,* 521.
115. Ibid., 91.
116. For a discussion of Lincoln's policy of emancipation, see Faulkner, "Lincoln and the Constitution," 23-29.
117. Richardson, *Messages and Papers of the Presidents,* 7:3359.
118. Belz, *Lincoln and the Constitution,* 15.
119. Quoted in Lord Charnwood, *Abraham Lincoln* (Garden City, N.Y.: Garden City Publishing, 1917), 413.
120. Ibid., 414-415.
121. Belz, *Lincoln and the Constitution,* 16.
122. Randall, *Constitutional Problems under Lincoln,* chap. 9.
123. *Works of Abraham Lincoln,* 10:263-264.
124. Ibid., 263.
125. Randall, *Constitutional Problems under Lincoln,* 522.
126. Binkley, *Powers of the President,* 135. For a discussion of the Reconstruction controversy inherited by Johnson, see Albert Castel, *The Presidency of Andrew Johnson* (Lawrence: University Press of Kansas, 1979), 17-20.
127. Quoted in Castel, *Presidency of Andrew Johnson,* 20.
128. On the struggle between Johnson and Congress over civil rights legislation, see ibid., 68-76; and Binkley, *Powers of the President,* 141-145.
129. Binkley, *Powers of the President,* 147.
130. Castel, *Presidency of Andrew Johnson,* 68-70.
131. "The House of Representatives, Articles of Impeachment against President Andrew Johnson," March 2-3, 1868, printed in Goldsmith, *Growth of Presidential Power,* 2:1068-1069.
132. David Miller Dewitt, *The Impeachment and Trial of Andrew Johnson* (Madison: State Historical Society of Wisconsin, 1967), 517-518.
133. Quoted in Goldsmith, *Growth of Presidential Power,* 2:1102.
134. Ibid.
135. Binkley, *Powers of the President,* 159.
136. George F. Hoar, *Autobiography of Seventy Years* (New York: Scribner's, 1903), 2:46.
137. Leonard D. White, *The Republican Era: 1869-1901: A Study in Administrative History* (New York: Macmillan, 1958), 372-376.
138. President Ulysses S. Grant, "First Statement to Congress on Civil Service Reform," December 5, 1870, printed in Goldsmith, *Growth of Presidential Power,* 2:986.

139. White, *The Republican Era,* 281-287.
140. Binkley, *Powers of the President,* 163.
141. Rutherford B. Hayes, "Inaugural Address," March 5, 1877, in *Messages and Papers of the Presidents,* ed. Richardson, 6:4396.
142. Binkley, *Powers of the President,* 167.
143. Charles Richard Williams, ed., *Diary and Letters of Rutherford B. Haye,* 5 vols. (Columbus: Ohio State Archeological and Historical Society, 1924), April 22, 1877, 3:430.
144. Ibid., December 12, 1877, 3:454.
145. Binkley, *Powers of the President,* 170.
146. President Rutherford B. Hayes, "Letter to General E. A. Merritt Defining Criteria for Appointments to the New York Custom House," February 4, 1879, printed in Goldsmith, *Growth of Presidential Power,* 2:1112.
147. Ibid., 2:1113.
148. Williams, *Diary and Letters of Rutherford B. Hayes,* July 4, 1880, 3:612-613.
149. The Stalwarts had dubbed Blaine's followers "Half-breeds," implying that they were deficient in GOP loyalty. In reality, however, the partisanship of the Blaine Wing, although it paid lip service to civil service reform, was just as strong.
150. Binkley, *Powers of the President,* 172.
151. Quoted in Theodore Clark Smith, *James Abram Garfield: Life and Letters* (New Haven: Yale University Press, 1925), 2:1109.
152. John A. Garraty, *The New Commonwealth: 1877-1890* (New York: Harper and Row, 1968), 273; White, *The Republican Era,* 34-35; Binkley, *Powers of the President,* 173-174.
153. Quoted in Justus D. Doenecke, *The Presidencies of James A. Garfield and Chester A. Arthur* (Lawrence: University Press of Kansas, 1981), 54.
154. President Grover Cleveland, "Message to the Senate on the President's Power of Removal and Suspension, March 1, 1886," printed in Goldsmith, *Growth of Presidential Power,* 2:1121.
155. Grover Cleveland, *Presidential Problems* (New York: Century, 1904), 76.
156. White, *The Republican Era,* 66.
157. Garraty, *The New Commonwealth,* 295.
158. Woodrow Wilson, *Congressional Government* (Boston: Houghton Mifflin, 1885; New York: Meridian Books, 1956), 31.
159. Quoted in Binkley, *Powers of the President,* 199.
160. Garraty, *The New Commonwealth,* 305.
161. Morton Keller, *The Affairs of State: Public Life in Late Nineteenth Century America* (Cambridge: Harvard University Press, 1977), 302-303.
162. James Bryce, *The American Commonwealth* (London: Macmillan, 1891), 1:115.
163. Binkley, *Powers of the President,* 199-200.
164. Garraty, *The New Commonwealth,* 306-308.
165. Gov. John P. Altgeld, "Telegram to President Grover Cleveland on the Use of Federal Troops in Illinois," July 5, 1894, printed in Goldsmith, *Growth of Presidential Power,* 2:1155.
166. President Grover Cleveland, "Telegram to Governor John P. Altgeld on the Use of Federal Troops in Illinois," July 6, 1894, ibid., 2:1157.
167. *In re Debs,* 158 U.S. 564 (1895).
168. Corwin, *The President: Office and Powers,* 134.
169. J. Rogers Hollingsworth, *The Whirligig of Politics: The Democracy of Cleveland and Bryan* (Chicago: University of Chicago Press, 1963), 24-25.
170. Garraty, *The New Commonwealth,* 306.
171. Binkley, *Powers of the President,* 207.
172. Lewis L. Gould, *The Presidency of William McKinley* (Lawrence: University Press of Kansas, 1980), 93.
173. Binkley, *Powers of the President,* 209.
174. Quoted in ibid.
175. Tulis, *The Rhetorical Presidency,* 87.
176. Richard Hofstadter, *The Age of Reform: From Bryan to F.D.R.* (New York: Knopf, 1956), 5.
177. Theodore Roosevelt, *The Works of Theodore Roosevelt* (New York: Scribner's, 1926), 20:340.
178. Samuel and Dorothy Rosenman, *Presidential Style: Some Giants and a Pygmy in the White House* (New York: Harper and Row, 1976), 123.
179. Roosevelt, *Works,* 20:347.
180. Ibid., 347.
181. Hamilton and Madison, *Letters of Pacificus and Helvidius,* 10.
182. Roosevelt, *Works,* 20:414. Lincoln's defense of the Union and audacious use of executive power occurred under the stress of a domestic rebellion. His understanding of the national government's powers in less dire circumstances was far more restricted than Theodore Roosevelt's.
183. Tulis, *The Rhetorical Presidency,* 97-116.
184. Roosevelt, *Works,* 20:416.
185. Ibid., 20:342.
186. George Mowry, *The Era of Theodore Roosevelt: 1900-1912* (New York: Harper and Brothers, 1958), 201.
187. Ibid., 201.
188. Ibid., 203.
189. Ibid., 205.
190. Mark Sullivan, *Our Times: Pre-War America* (New York: Scribner's, 1930), 3:80.
191. Ibid., 3:240.
192. Mowry, *Era of Theodore Roosevelt,* 203.
193. Tulis, *The Rhetorical Presidency,* 96.
194. Roosevelt, *Works,* 15:117.
195. Herbert Croly, *The Promise of American Life* (New York: Dutton, 1963; New York: Macmillan, 1909), 313. The concept of Manifest Destiny became prominent at the end of the nineteenth century and was employed by President McKinley in defending the acquisition of territory during his administration. It proclaimed for the United States an inevitable and natural right to grow and expand as necessary for freedom and democracy to prosper and survive.
196. Roosevelt, *Works,* 15:114.
197. Ibid., 20:549-550.
198. T.R. to Marcus Alonzo Hanna, October 5, 1903, in *The Letters of Theodore Roosevelt,* ed. Elting E. Morrison (Cambridge: Harvard University Press, 1951), 3:625.
199. Roosevelt, *Works,* 20:501.
200. Ibid., 501.
201. Goldsmith, *Growth of Presidential Power,* 2:1233.
202. Roosevelt, *Works,* 15:256-257.
203. Ibid., 20:490.
204. Mowry, *Era of Theodore Roosevelt,* 185.
205. Goldsmith, *Growth of Presidential Power,* 2:1269.
206. Mowry, *Era of Theodore Roosevelt,* 226.
207. Ibid., 180; Roosevelt, *Works,* 20:378.
208. Quoted in Binkley, *Powers of the President,* 219.
209. Elmer E. Cornwell, Jr., *Presidential Leadership of Public Opinion,* (Bloomington: Indiana University Press, 1965), 27.
210. Quoted in Mowry, *Era of Theodore Roosevelt,* 245.
211. Ibid., 246.
212. Binkley, *Powers of the President,* 220. The only office that Taft ever ran for, except the presidency, was that of justice of the State Superior Court in Ohio.
213. For a discussion of the revolt in Congress against the regular party leadership, see Lawrence C. Dodd and Richard L. Schott, *Congress and the Administrative State* (New York: Wiley, 1979), 58-100.
214. Mowry, *Era of Theodore Roosevelt,* 272.
215. Goldsmith, *Growth of Presidential Power,* 3:1343.
216. Woodrow Wilson, "Cabinet Government in the United States," *International Review* 7 (August 1879): 150-151.
217. Wilson's mature thought on presidential leadership and constitutional change is expressed in his *Constitutional Government in the United States* (New York: Columbia University Press, 1908).
218. David Lawrence, *The True Story of Woodrow Wilson* (New York: Doran, 1924), 39.
219. Arthur S. Link, *Wilson and the New Freedom* (Princeton, N.J.: Princeton University Press, 1956), 145.

220. Woodrow Wilson, *The Papers of Woodrow Wilson,* ed. Arthur S. Link (Princeton, N.J.: Princeton University Press, 1966-1985), 27:151. On Wilson's contribution to the expansion of popular leadership in the United States, see Tulis, *The Rhetorical Presidency,* 117-144.
221. Cornwell, *Presidential Leadership of Public Opinion,* 32-44.
222. Wilson, *Papers,* 27:269-270.
223. Ray Stannard Baker, *Woodrow Wilson: Life and Letters* (London: Heinemann, 1932), 4:109.
224. Quoted in Arthur S. Link, *Woodrow Wilson and the Progressive Era: 1910-1917* (New York: Harper and Row, 1954), 21.
225. Woodrow Wilson, "Monopoly or Opportunity," in Goldsmith, *The Growth of Presidential Power,* 3:1334-1342, 1341.
226. Link, *The New Freedom,* 277.
227. Wilson, *Papers,* 41:526.
228. Corwin, *The President: Office and Powers,* 237.
229. Goldsmith, *Growth of Presidential Power,* 3:1705, 1711.
230. Ernest R. May, "Wilson (1917-1918)," in *The Ultimate Decision: The President as Commander in Chief,* ed. Ernest R. May (New York: Braziller, 1960), 131.
231. Quoted in Rosenman and Rosenman, *Presidential Style,* 241.
232. Wilson, *Papers,* 51:381.
233. Quoted in Robert K. Murray, *The Harding Era: Warren G. Harding and His Administration* (Minneapolis: University of Minnesota Press, 1969), 70.
234. Ibid., 44.
235. Binkley, *Powers of the President,* 237.
236. George Rothwell Brown, *The Leadership of Congress* (New York: Arno Press, 1974; Indianapolis., Ind.: Bobbs-Merrill, 1922), 258.
237. Paul P. Van Riper, *History of the United States Civil Service* (Evanston, Ill.: Row, Peterson, 1958), 287.
238. William Allen White, *The Autobiography of William Allen White* (New York: Macmillan, 1946), 619.
239. Quoted in Murray Myers, *The Harding Era, 418.*
240. Herbert Emmerich, *Federal Organization and Administrative Management* (Tuscaloosa: University of Alabama Press, 1971), 40-41. For a discussion of the enactment and early history of the Budget and Accounting Act, see Goldsmith, *Growth of Presidential Power,* 3:1478-1495.
241. Emmerich, *Federal Organization,* 418.
242. Cornwell, *Presidential Leadership of Public Opinion,* 73.
243. Calvin Coolidge, *The Autobiography of Calvin Coolidge* (New York: Cosmopolitan, 1929), 232.
244. Binkley, *Powers of the President,* 244.
245. Quoted in Murray, *The Harding Era,* 514.
246. Ibid., 505.
247. Binkley, *Powers of the President,* 246.
248. Quoted in Cornwell, *Presidential Leadership of Public Opinion,* 79.
249. Quoted in ibid., 90.
250. Coolidge, *Autobiography,* 231.
251. William Allen White, *Calvin Coolidge: The Man Who Is President* (New York: Macmillan, 1925), 137.
252. Cornwell, *Presidential Leadership of Public Opinion,* 92.
253. Ellis Hawley (Dept. of History, University of Iowa), "The Constitution and the Presidency in the Depression Era: 1930-1939," in *The Constitution and the American Presidency,* ed. Martin L. Fausold and Alan Shank, (forthcoming).
254. Herbert Hoover, *The Challenge to Liberty* (New York: Scribner's, 1934), 125-126.
255. Quoted in Binkley, *Powers of the President,* 254.
256. Martin L. Fausold, *The Presidency of Herbert C. Hoover* (Lawrence: University Press of Kansas, 1985), 49.
257. Quoted in Binkley, *Powers of the President,* 251.
258. Herbert Hoover, *The Memoirs of Herbert Hoover: The Great Depression, 1929-1941* (New York: Macmillan, 1952), 3:104.
259. Walter Lippmann, "The Peculiar Weakness of Mr. Hoover," *Harper's Magazine,* 161 (June 1930), 5.
260. Cornwell, *Presidential Leadership of Public Opinion,* 113.
261. Fausold, *The Presidency of Herbert C. Hoover,* 111.
262. Quoted in Stefan Lorant, *The Presidency: A Pictorial History of Presidential Elections from Washington to Truman* (New York: Macmillan, 1951), 594.
263. Fred I. Greenstein, "Introduction: Toward a Modern Presidency," in *Leadership in the Modern Presidency,* ed. Fred I. Greenstein (Cambridge: Harvard University Press, 1988), 4; and Greenstein, "Change and Continuity in the Modern Presidency," in *The New American Political System,* ed. Anthony King (Washington, D.C.: American Enterprise Institute, 1978), 45-46.
264. Robert K. Murray and Tim H. Blessing, "The Presidential Performance Study: A Progress Report," *Journal of American History* 70:3 (December 1983): 542.
265. Quoted in Robert M. Collins, *The Business Response to Keynes* (New York: Columbia University Press, 1981), 28.
266. Quoted in Kenneth S. Davis, *FDR: The New Deal Years, 1933-1937* (New York: Random House, 1986), 23.
267. Clinton Rossiter, *The American Presidency* (New York: Harcourt Brace, 1956), 114.
268. Franklin D. Roosevelt, *Public Papers and Addresses,* 13 vols. (New York: Random House, 1938-1950), 1:12.
269. Ibid., 1:15.
270. Ibid., 2:24-26.
271. Ibid., 2:65.
272. Quoted in Davis, *FDR,* 61.
273. Roosevelt, *Public Papers and Addresses,* 3:317-318.
274. Cornwell, *Presidential Leadership of Public Opinion,* 131.
275. Roosevelt, *Public Papers and Addresses,* 1:659.
276. Fred I. Greenstein, "Nine Presidents in Search of a Modern Presidency," in *Leadership in the Modern Presidency,* ed. Greenstein, 299.
277. Roosevelt, *Public Papers and Addresses,* 2:161.
278. William E. Leuchtenburg, "Franklin D. Roosevelt's Supreme Court 'Packing' Plan," in *Essays on the New Deal,* ed., Harold M. Hollingsworth and William F. Holmes (Austin: University of Texas Press, 1969).
279. Hawley, "Constitution and the Presidency."
280. *United States v. Curtiss-Wright Export Corporation,* 299 U.S. 304 (1936).
281. *United States v. Belmont,* 301 U.S. 324 (1936).
282. Quoted in William E. Leuchtenburg, "Franklin D. Roosevelt: The First Modern President," in *Leadership in the Modern Presidency,* ed. Greenstein, 36.
283. Hawley, "Constitution and the Presidency."
284. William E. Leuchtenburg, *In the Shadow of FDR: From Harry Truman to Ronald Reagan,* rev. ed. (Ithaca and London: Cornell University Press, 1985), 1.
285. Alonzo L. Hamby, "Harry S. Truman: Insecurity and Responsibility," *Leadership in the Modern Presidency,* ed. Greenstein, 42-43.
286. Quoted in Larry Berman, *The New American Presidency* (Boston: Little, Brown, 1987), 212.
287. Leuchtenburg, *Shadow of FDR,* 23.
288. President Harry S Truman, "Executive Order 9308 Establishing the President's Committee on Civil Rights," December 5, 1946, printed in Goldsmith, *Growth of Presidential Power,* 3:1568-1569.
289. *Public Papers of the Presidents of the United States: Harry S. Truman* (Washington, D.C.: Government Printing Office, 1961-1966), March 1, 1951, 176.
290. Greenstein, "Nine Presidents," 334.
291. Fred I. Greenstein, *The Hidden-Hand Presidency: Eisenhower As Leader* (New York: Basic Books, 1982).
292. Quoted in Leuchtenburg, *Shadow of FDR,* 49.
293. Alonzo L. Hamby, *Liberalism and Its Challengers: FDR to Reagan* (New York: Oxford University Press, 1985), 126.
294. Quoted in Stephen E. Ambrose, "The Eisenhower Revival," in *Rethinking the Presidency,* ed. Thomas E. Cronin (Boston: Little, Brown, 1982), 107.
295. Greenstein, *The Hidden-Hand Presidency,* chap. 5.
296. Greenstein, "Nine Presidents," 307-311.
297. Ambrose, "The Eisenhower Revival," 108.
298. Quoted in Elmo Richardson, *The Presidency of Dwight D. Eisenhower* (Lawrence: University Press of Kansas, 1979), 53.
299. Leuchtenburg, *Shadow of FDR,* 119.

300. Carl M. Brauer, "John F. Kennedy: The Endurance of Inspirational Leadership," *in Leadership in the Modern Presidency,* ed. Greenstein, 119.
301. Ibid., 119.
302. Ibid., 118.
303. Theodore Lowi, *The Personal President: Power Invested, Promise Unfulfilled* (Ithaca and London: Cornell University Press, 1985).
304. Ibid., 75-76; Harold F. Bass, "The President and the National Party Organization," in *Presidents and Their Parties: Leadership or Neglect?* ed. Robert Harmel (New York: Praeger, 1984), 62.
305. Arthur M. Schlesinger, Jr., *The Cycles of American History* (Boston: Houghton Mifflin, 1986), 414.
306. *Public Papers of the Presidents of the United States: Lyndon Baines Johnson, 1963-1964* (Washington, D.C.: Government Printing Office, 1965), 1:704.
307. Greenstein, "Nine Presidents," 329.
308. Author's interview with Harry McPherson, July 30, 1985.
309. *CBS Cronkite Interview with Lyndon Johnson,* no. 1, December 27, 1969: "Why I Chose Not To Run," 5 (Austin, Texas: Lyndon Baines Johnson Library).
310. Richard M. Pious, *The American Presidency* (New York: Basic Books, 1979), 399.
311. Quoted in Larry Berman, "Lyndon B. Johnson: Path Chosen and Opportunities Lost," in *Leadership in the Modern Presidency,* ed. Greenstein, 153.
312. Richard Nixon, *RN: The Memoirs of Richard Nixon* (New York: Warner, 1978), 1:440-441.
313. Richard Nathan, *The Administrative Presidency* (New York: Wiley, 1983), 27.
314. Quoted in Joan Hoff-Wilson, "Richard M. Nixon: The Corporate Presidency," in *Leadership in the Modern Presidency,* ed. Greenstein, 177.
315. Greenstein, "Nine Presidents," 332. For a balanced account of Nixon's "administrative presidency," see Nathan, *The Administrative Presidency,* 43-56.
316. *United States v. Nixon,* 418 U.S. 683 (1974).
317. Greenstein, "Nine Presidents," 334.
318. These surveys are discussed in James MacGregor Burns, J. W. Peltason, and Thomas Cronin, *Government by the People,* 11th ed. (Englewood Cliffs, N.J.: Prentice-Hall, 1981), 359.
319. These changes are discussed in Roger Porter, "Gerald Ford: A Healing Presidency," in *Leadership in the Modern Presidency,* ed. Greenstein, 206-213.
320. Berman, *New American Presidency,* 293-294.
321. Quoted in ibid., 297.
322. Greenstein, "Nine Presidents," 340.
323. Erwin C. Hargrove, "Jimmy Carter: The Politics of Public Goods," in *Leadership in the Modern Presidency,* ed. Greenstein, 251.
324. Hargrove, "Jimmy Carter," 233.
325. James Fallows, "The Passionless Presidency," in *Behind the Scenes in American Government,* 4th ed., ed. Peter Woll (Boston: Little, Brown, 1983), 171.
326. Tulis, *The Rhetorical Presidency,* 189.
327. On Reagan's use of rhetoric, see William K. Muir, Jr., "Ronald Reagan: The Primacy of Rhetoric," in *Leadership in the Modern Presidency,* ed. Greenstein, 260-295.
328. "Inaugural Address of President Ronald Reagan," January 20, 1981, printed in Nathan, *The Administrative Presidency,* 159.
329. Marc Landy and Martin A. Levin, "The Hedgehog and the Fox," *Brandeis Review* 7:1 (Fall 1987): 17-19.
330. William Greider, *The Education of David Stockman and Other Americans* (New York: Dutton, 1982), 33. See also David A. Stockman, *The Triumph of Politics: Why the Reagan Revolution Failed* (New York: Harper and Row, 1986), 79-99.
331. James L. Sundquist, "The New Era of Coalition Government in the United States," *Political Science Quarterly* 103:4 (Winter, 1988-1989): 626, n. 39.
332. Greenstein, "Nine Presidents," 345.

Selected Bibliography

Arnold, Peri E. *Making the Managerial Presidency.* Princeton, N.J.: Princeton University Press, 1986.

Binkley, Wilfred E. *The Powers of the President.* Garden City, N.Y.: Doubleday, Daron, 1937.

Ceaser, James. *Presidential Selection: Theory and Development.* Princeton, N.J.: Princeton University Press, 1979.

Cornwell, Elmer E., Jr. *Presidential Leadership and Public Opinion.* Bloomington: Indiana University Press, 1965.

Corwin, Edward. *The President: Office and Powers, 1787-1984.* 5th rev. ed. New York University Press, 1984.

Goldsmith, William, ed. *The Growth of Presidential Power.* New York and London: Chelsea House, 1974.

Greenstein, Fred I., ed. *Leadership in the Modern Presidency.* Cambridge: Harvard University Press, 1988.

Letters of Pacificus and Helvidius on the Proclamation of Neutrality of 1793. Washington, D.C.: Gideon, 1845.

Randall, J. G. *Constitutional Problems under Lincoln.* Rev. ed. Urbana: University of Illinois Press, 1951.

Tulis, Jeffrey. *The Rhetorical Presidency.* Princeton, N.J.: Princeton University Press, 1987.

White, Leonard. *The Federalists: A Study in Administrative History.* New York: Macmillan, 1948.

———. *The Jacksonians: A Study in Administrative History, 1829-1861.* New York: Macmillan, 1954

———. *The Jeffersonians: A Study in Administrative History, 1801-1829.* New York: Macmillan, 1951.

———. *The Republican Era: A Study in Administrative History, 1869-1901.* New York: Macmillan. 1958

Wilson, Woodrow. *Constitutional Government in the United States.* New York: Columbia University Press, 1908.

History of the Vice Presidency

Almost since its creation, the vice presidency has been an easy and frequent target of political humor. Benjamin Franklin quipped that the vice president should be addressed as "Your Superfluous Excellency." Mr. Dooley, the invented character of writer Finley Peter Dunne, described the office as "not a crime exactly. Ye can't be sint to jail f'r it, but it's kind iv a disgrace. It's like writin' anonymous letters." The popular 1930s musical, *Of Thee I Sing,* featured a fictitious vice president whose name (which no one in the play could remember) was Alexander Throttlebottom. Vice President Throttlebottom spent most of his time feeding pigeons in the park and trying to find two people willing to serve as references so that he could get a library card.

Even some vice presidents have poked fun at the office. Thomas R. Marshall, who occupied the vice presidency during Woodrow Wilson's two terms as president, said that the vice president is like "a man in a cataleptic fit; he cannot speak; he cannot move; he suffers no pain; he is perfectly conscious of all that goes on, but has no part in it." (Marshall also told the story of the two brothers: "One ran away to sea; the other was elected vice president. And nothing was heard of either of them again.") John Nance Garner was a fairly active vice president during the first two terms of Franklin D. Roosevelt's administration, but his pithy assessment of the office is probably the most frequently quoted of all: "The vice presidency isn't worth a pitcher of warm spit." [1]

Many a truth—about the vice presidency as well as other things—has been spoken in jest, of course. Constitutionally, the vice presidency was born weak and has not grown much stronger. But lost in all the laughter is an appreciation of the importance—ongoing in U.S. history but growing in recent years—of the position the vice presidency occupies in the American political system. *(See Office of the Vice President chapter in Part V.)*

The vice presidency is most significant when, cocoonlike, it empties itself to provide a successor to the presidency. ("I am vice president," said John Adams, the first person to hold the office. "In this I am nothing, but I may be everything." [2]) Nine vice presidents, more than one-fifth of those who have served in the office, have become president when the incumbent chief executive died or resigned. Collectively, they led the nation for forty-two years. Each of the five twentieth-century vice presidents who succeeded to the presidency—Theodore Roosevelt, Calvin Coolidge, Harry S Truman, Lyndon B. Johnson, and Gerald R. Ford—subsequently was nominated by his party for a full term as president, and all but Ford were elected. In 1965, Congress determined that the advisability of having a vice president to stand by at all times was so strong that it passed the Twenty-fifth Amendment, which established a procedure for filling vice-presidential vacancies. In addition, the amendment, which was ratified by the states in 1967, stated unequivocally the right of the vice president, in the event of a presidential death, resignation, or impeachment, to serve as president for the unexpired balance of the term and created a mechanism by which the vice president could assume the powers and duties of the presidency for as long as a president was disabled.

Besides its longstanding role as presidential successor, the vice presidency also has become an important electoral springboard to the presidency. The modern vice president is not only a presumptive candidate for president, but the presumptive front-runner as well. Fifteen of nineteen twentieth-century vice presidents (not counting Dan Quayle) have gone on to seek the presidency. (Death or ill health accounts for three of the exceptions—James S. Sherman, Charles Curtis, and Nelson A. Rockefeller—and criminal conviction the fourth, Spiro T. Agnew.)

In the history of the Gallup poll, which extends back to 1936, Garner and every vice president since Richard Nixon have led in a majority of surveys that measure the voters' preferences for their party's presidential nomination.[3] In all three of the elections since 1956 in which the president did not or could not run for reelection, the incumbent party has nominated the vice president as its presidential candidate. Six of the eight most recent vice presidents later were nominated for president in their own right: Nixon, Johnson, Hubert H. Humphrey, Ford, Walter F. Mondale, and George Bush. Even a vice-presidential nomination now is a springboard of sorts: five of the seven losing vice-presidential candidates since 1956—Henry Cabot Lodge, Edmund Muskie, Sargent Shriver, Robert A. Dole, and Mondale—later showed support in presidential nominating contests.

Finally, recent changes in the vice presidency have made the office itself increasingly substantial. The vice presidency has become "institutionalized" to some degree. This is true both in the narrow sense that it is organizationally larger and more complex than in the past (the vice president's staff, for example, has grown from twenty in

By Michael Nelson

1960 to around seventy today) and in the broader sense that certain kinds of vice-presidential activities now are taken for granted. These include: regular private meetings with the president and attendance at many other important presidential meetings, membership on the National Security Council, full national security briefings, frequent diplomatic missions, public advocacy of the president's leadership and programs, and party leadership. Modern vice presidents have a lot more to do than, in Vice President Marshall's gibe, "to ring the White House bell every morning and ask what is the state of health of the president." [4]

The vice presidency, then, as successor and springboard to the presidency and as an institution in its own right, has become an important office. But its history is a problematic one, and not all of those problems have been solved.

The Founding Period

The vice presidency was invented late in the Constitutional Convention, not because the delegates saw any need for such an office, but rather as a means of perfecting the arrangements they had made for presidential election and succession and, to some degree, for Senate leadership. The original Constitution provided that the vice presidency was to be awarded to the person who received the second highest number of electoral votes for president. (If two or more candidates finished in a second-place tie in the presidential election, the Senate would choose among them.) The office's only ongoing responsibility was to preside over the Senate, casting tie-breaking votes. The most important duty of the vice president was to stand by as successor to the presidency in the event of the president's death, impeachment, resignation, or "inability to discharge the Powers and Duties" of the office. But the Constitution was vague both about whether the vice president was to assume the office of president or only its powers and duties and about whether the succession was to last until the end of the departed president's four-year term or until a special election could be held to choose a new president. The Constitution also left the term *inability* undefined and provided no procedure for the vice president to take power in the event the president became disabled. Finally, by giving the vice presidency both legislative and executive responsibilities, it deprived the office of solid moorings in either Congress or the presidency. *(See "The Constitutional Convention," p. 9, in Constitutional Beginnings chapter of Part I.)*

Thus, although the vice presidency solved several problems related to the presidency and the Senate, it was plagued from birth by inherent problems of its own. The office's hybrid status was bound to make it suspect in legislative councils because it was partly executive and in executive councils because it was partly legislative. The single ongoing responsibility of the vice president, to preside over the Senate, was not very important. The poorly defined successor role was to be an inevitable source of confusion and, perhaps, of tension between president and vice president: the fabled "heartbeat away" that separates the vice president from the presidency is, after all, the president's. Finally, more than any other institution of the new government, the vice presidency required the realization of the Framers' hope that political parties would not develop. The office would seem less a brilliant than a rash improvisation of the convention if it were occupied as a matter of course by the president's leading partisan foe.

John Adams was the first person to be elected vice president. *(See "Election of 1796," p. 267, in The Electoral Process chapter of Part II.)* Midway through his tenure, Adams lamented to his wife Abigail Adams that "my country has in its wisdom contrived for me the most insignificant office that ever the invention of man contrived or his imagination conceived." [5] Little did Adams realize that the vice presidency was at a peak of influence during the period he served. Because the Senate was small and still relatively unorganized, he was able not only to cast twenty-nine tie-breaking votes (still the record), but also to guide the upper house's agenda and to intervene in debate. Adams also was respected and sometimes consulted on diplomatic and other matters by President George Washington, who invited him to meet with the cabinet in his absence. Moreover, having won the vice presidency by receiving the second largest number of electoral votes for president in 1789 and 1792, it is not surprising that Adams was elected president after Washington left office.

Adams's election as president was different from Washington's, however. The Framers' hopes notwithstanding, two political parties, the Federalists and the Democratic-Republicans, emerged during the Washington administration. The result in 1796 was the election as vice president of the Democratic-Republicans' presidential nominee, Thomas Jefferson. Adams tried to lure Jefferson into the administration's fold by urging him to undertake a diplomatic mission to France, but Jefferson, eager to build up his own party and win the presidency away from Adams, would have no part of it. He justified his refusal by claiming that, constitutionally, the vice presidency was a legislative office. By Jefferson's own testimony, that was the end of his dealings with President Adams, except on formal occasions. He did make a mark as Senate president, writing a book—*Manual of Parliamentary Practice*—that, although never formally adopted by the Senate, became its working procedural guide. But most of his congressional activities involved behind-the-scenes opposition to President Adams and the Federalists.

Unsatisfied with the divided partisan result of the 1796 election, each party nominated a complete ticket in 1800, instructing its electors to cast their two votes for its presidential and vice-presidential candidates. The intention was that both would be elected; the result was that neither was. The electors having voted as instructed, Jefferson and his vice-presidential running mate, Aaron Burr, ended up with an equal number of votes for president. This outcome was doubly vexing: not only was Jefferson the party's clear choice for president, but there was little love lost between him and Burr, who had been placed on the ticket to balance the Virginia and New York wings of the party. Under the Constitution, the House of Representatives was called upon to choose between them. It eventually did, picking Jefferson, but not before Federalist mischief-makers kept the result uncertain through thirty-six ballots. Burr was elected vice president.

One result of the election of 1800 was the Burr vice presidency, which was marked by bad relations between him and Jefferson and by various misdeeds, including a duel in which Burr shot and killed Alexander Hamilton. Another was the widespread realization that something had to be done about the electoral college so that it could accommodate the existence of party competition. Vice-presidential selection was the problem; one obvious solution was to require electors to vote separately for president and vice president. In opposing this suggestion, some members of Congress argued that it would create a worse problem than it solved. Because "the vice president will not stand on such high ground in the method proposed as he does in the present mode of a double ballot" for president, predicted Samuel Taggert, the nation could expect that "great care will not be taken in the selection of a character to fill that office." Sen. William Plumer of New Hampshire warned that such care as was taken would be "to procure votes for the president."[6] In truth, as the nomination of Burr indicated, the parties already had begun to degrade the vice presidency into a device for balancing the ticket.

In 1804, motions were made in Congress to abolish the vice presidency rather than continue it in a form degraded from its original constitutional status as the position awarded to the second-most-qualified person to be president. These motions failed by votes of 12-19 in the Senate and 27-85 in the House. Instead, the Twelfth Amendment was passed and entered the Constitution in 1804. The amendment provided that electors "shall name in their ballots the person voted for as President, and in distinct ballots the person voted for as Vice President." It also stipulated that if no one received a majority of electoral votes for vice president, then "from the two highest numbers on the list, the Senate shall choose the Vice President; a quorum for the purpose shall consist of two-thirds of the whole number of Senators, and a majority of the whole number shall be necessary to a choice." The amendment's final provision regarding the vice presidency extended the Constitution's original age, citizenship, and residency qualifications for president to the vice president. *(See "Constitutional Amendments," p. 40, in Constitutional Beginnings chapter of Part I.)*

The Vice Presidency in the Nineteenth Century

The development of political parties and the enactment of the Twelfth Amendment sent an already constitutionally weak vice presidency into a tailspin that lasted until the end of the nineteenth century. Party leaders, not presidential candidates (who often were not even present at national nominating conventions and who, if present, were expected to be seen and not heard), chose the nominees for vice president, which certainly did not foster trust or respect between the president and vice president in office. Aggravating the tension were the main criteria that party leaders applied to vice-presidential selection. One criterion was that the nominee placate the region or faction of the party that had been most dissatisfied with the presidential nomination, which led to numerous New York-Virginia, North-South, Stalwart-Progressive, hard money-soft money, and other such pairings. Another was that the nominee be able to carry a swing state in the general election where the presidential candidate was not popular.

In addition to fostering tension within the government, ticket balancing as the main basis for vice-presidential selection also placed such a stigma on the office that many politicians were unwilling to accept a nomination. (Daniel Webster, declining the vice-presidential place on the Whig party ticket in 1848, said, "I do not propose to be buried until I am dead.")[7] Those who did and were elected found that fresh political problems four years after their nomination invariably led party leaders to balance the ticket differently: no first-term vice president in the nineteenth century ever was renominated for a second term by a party convention. Nor, after Vice President Martin Van Buren in 1836, was any nineteenth-century vice president elected or even nominated for president. Finally, the vice president's role as Senate president (which most vice presidents, following Jefferson's lead and for want of anything else to do, spent considerable time performing), became more ceremonial as the Senate institutionalized and took greater charge of its own affairs. John C. Calhoun, for example, who served from 1825 to 1833, was the last vice president whom the Senate allowed to appoint its committees.

Library of Congress

In 1828, Daniel Webster declined the Whig nomination for vice president, saying, "I do not propose to be buried until I am dead."

Not surprisingly, then, the nineteenth-century vice presidents make up a virtual rogues' gallery of personal and political failures. Because the office was so unappealing, an unusual number of the politicians who could be enticed to run for vice president were old and in bad health. Six died in office, all of natural causes: George Clinton, Elbridge Gerry, William R. King (who took his oath of office in Cuba and died the next month), Henry Wilson (who was born with the name Jeremiah J. Colbath), Thomas A. Hendricks, and Garret A. Hobart. Some vice presidents became embroiled in financial scandals: Daniel D. Tompkins was charged with keeping inadequate financial records while serving as governor of New York during the War of 1812, and Schuyler Colfax and Henry Wilson were implicated in the notorious Crédit Mobilier stock scandal of the 1870s.

Other vice presidents fell prey to personal scandals. Tompkins and Andrew Johnson were heavy drinkers. (Johnson's first address to the Senate was a drunken harangue.) Richard M. Johnson kept a series of slave mistresses, educating the children of one but selling another when she lost interest in him. Clinton, Calhoun, and Chester A. Arthur each publicly expressed his dislike for the president. Clinton refused to attend President James Madison's inauguration and openly attacked the administration's foreign and domestic policies. Calhoun alienated two presidents, John Quincy Adams and Andrew Jackson, by using his role as Senate president to subvert their policies and appointments, then resigned in 1831 to accept South Carolina's election as senator. Arthur attacked President James A. Garfield over a patronage quarrel. "Garfield has not been square, nor honorable, nor truthful. . . ," he told the *New York Herald.* "It's a hard thing to say of a presi-

Library of Congress

John Tyler was the first vice president to succeed to the presidency. When William Henry Harrison died in 1841, Tyler set a precedent by assuming the office of president, not just its powers and duties, and by serving out his predecessor's full term, rather than calling a special election.

dent of the United States, but it's only the truth." [8] Finally, some vice presidents did not even live in Washington—Richard Johnson left to run a tavern for a year.[9]

The history of the nineteenth-century vice presidency is not entirely bleak. A certain measure of comity existed between a few presidents and vice presidents—notably Andrew Jackson and Van Buren, James K. Polk and George M. Dallas, Abraham Lincoln and Hannibal Hamlin, Rutherford B. Hayes and William A. Wheeler, and William McKinley and Hobart—but even in their administrations, the vice president was not invited to cabinet meetings or entrusted with important tasks. What strengthened most of these relationships was the president's respect for the vice president's advice, which was sought informally, and the vice president's willingness and effectiveness as an advocate of the administration's policies in the Senate.

More important, in one area of vice-presidential responsibility—presidential succession—the nineteenth century witnessed a giant step forward. *(See Selection by Succession chapter in Part II.)* The succession question did not even arise until 1841, when William Henry Harrison became the first president to die in office. The language of the Constitution provided little guidance about whether the vice president, John Tyler, was to become president for the remainder of Harrison's term or merely acting president until a special election could be held; the records of the Constitutional Convention, which could have clarified the Framers' intentions, had long been kept secret by James Madison and still were not widely available. In this uncertain situation, Tyler's claim to both the office and the balance of Harrison's term was accepted with little debate, setting a precedent that the next successor president, Vice President Millard Fillmore, was able to follow without any controversy at all. (Fillmore succeeded to the presidency in 1850, after President Zachary Taylor died.)

But even this bright spot in the early history of the vice presidency was tarnished. Tyler's presidency was marred by debilitating disagreements with the party, especially in Congress, and with the late president's cabinet. Fillmore and the other two nineteenth-century successor presidents, Andrew Johnson and Arthur, encountered similar problems. (Johnson was impeached by the House and came within one vote of being removed by a two-thirds majority of the Senate.) None of the four is regarded as having been a successful president. In the most recent round of historians' rankings, Johnson was rated a failure, Tyler and Fillmore as below average, and Arthur as average.[10] *(See Rating the Presidents chapter in Part I.)* Nor were any of the nineteenth-century successor presidents nominated for a full term as president in their own right, much less elected.

Unresolved issues of succession and disability also vexed the vice presidency during the nineteenth century. Taken together, six vice-presidential deaths, one vice-presidential resignation, and four presidential deaths left the nation without a vice president during eleven of the century's twenty-five presidential terms. (President Taylor's death in July 1850 and Vice President King's in April 1853 meant that, with the trivial exception of the month King spent in Cuba after taking the oath of office in March 1853, the vice presidency was vacant for seven consecutive years, until March 1857.) Fortunately, no president died while the vice presidency was vacant. (In the twentieth century, the vice presidency has been vacant for parts of six presidential terms.)

The issue of vice-presidential responsibility in periods of presidential disability also remained unresolved. Five nineteenth-century presidents seem to have been disabled for measurable lengths of time.[11] In 1881, for example, during the seventy-nine days that President Garfield lay comatose before dying from an assassin's bullet, Vice President Arthur could only stand by helplessly, lest he be branded a usurper.

Theodore Roosevelt to Truman

The rise of national news media (specifically mass-circulation magazines and newspaper wire services), a new style of active presidential campaigning, and alterations in the vice-presidential nominating process enhanced the status of the vice presidency during the first half of the twentieth century. In 1900, the Republican nominee, Theodore Roosevelt, became the first vice-presidential candidate (and, other than William Jennings Bryan, the Democratic nominee for president in 1896, the first member of a national party ticket) to campaign vigorously nationwide. While President William McKinley waged a sedate "front-porch" reelection campaign, Roosevelt gave 673 speeches to three million listeners in twenty-four states.

The national reputation that Roosevelt gained through travel and the media stood him in good stead when he succeeded to the presidency after McKinley was assassinated in 1901. Roosevelt was able to reverse the earlier pattern of successor presidents and establish a new one: unlike Tyler, Fillmore, Johnson, and Arthur, Roosevelt was nominated by his party to run for a full term as president in 1904, thus setting the precedent for Calvin Coolidge in 1924, Truman in 1948, Johnson in 1964, and Ford in 1976. Roosevelt's success also may help to explain another new pattern that contrasts sharply with nineteenth-century practice. Starting with Sherman in 1912, every first-term vice president in the twentieth century who has sought a second term has been nominated for reelection. Finally, Roosevelt helped to lay the intellectual groundwork for an enhanced role for the vice president in office. In an 1896 article, he argued that the president and vice president should share the same "views and principles" and that the vice president "should always be ... consulted by the president on every great party question. It would be very well if he were given a seat in the Cabinet ... a vote [in the Senate], on ordinary occasions, and perchance on occasion a voice in the debates." [12]

Roosevelt was unable to practice what he preached about the vice presidency, either as vice president or president. Just as party leaders imposed the vice-presidential nomination of Charles W. Fairbanks on him to balance the ticket in 1904 (Roosevelt was from the progressive wing of the party, Fairbanks from the Old Guard), so had Roosevelt's nomination as vice president been forced on McKinley in 1900, and for the same reason. Neither McKinley nor Roosevelt liked or trusted his vice president, much less consigned him responsibilities. (President Roosevelt often repeated the humorist Dunne's response when the president said that he was thinking of going down in a submarine: "Well, you really shouldn't do it—unless you take Fairbanks with you.")[13]

Still, the enhanced political status of the vice presidency soon began to make it a more attractive office to at least some able and experienced political leaders, including Charles Dawes, who had served in three administrations and won a Nobel Prize; Curtis, the Senate majority leader; and Garner, the Speaker of the House. And, with somewhat more talent to offer, some vice presidents were given more responsibilities by the presidents they served. John Adams had been the last vice president to meet with the cabinet, for example, but when President Woodrow Wilson went to Europe in 1918 to negotiate the treaty that ended World War I (the first time a president had ever left U.S. soil), he asked Vice President Marshall to preside in his absence. Wilson's successor as president, Warren G. Harding, invited Vice President Coolidge to meet with the cabinet as a matter of course, as has every president since Franklin Roosevelt.[14]

Franklin Roosevelt, like his cousin Theodore, had both run for vice president before becoming president (he lost in 1920) and written an article urging that the responsibilities of the vice presidency be expanded. In the article, Roosevelt had identified four roles that the vice president could perform helpfully: cabinet member, presidential adviser, liaison to Congress, and policy maker in areas "that do not belong in the province" of any particular department or agency.[15]

As president, Roosevelt initially had so much respect for his vice president, House Speaker Garner, that even though the conservative Texan's nomination had been imposed on him at the 1932 Democratic convention, the president relied on him during the first term as "a combination presiding officer, cabinet officer, personal counselor, legislative tactician, Cassandra, and sounding board." [16] Most significant, the vice president served as an important liaison from Roosevelt to Congress—it was Garner's suggestion that led to the practice, which subsequent presidents have followed, of meeting weekly with congressional leaders. Garner also undertook a goodwill mission to Mexico at Roosevelt's behest, another innovation that virtually all later administrations have continued.

During the second term, Roosevelt and Garner had a falling out over the president's Court-packing plan, support for organized labor, and other liberal policies—Garner even challenged Roosevelt for the party's 1940 presidential nomination. This rupture between the president and the vice president set the stage for an important modification of the vice-presidential selection process whose purpose was to foster greater harmony between presidents and vice presidents. In 1936, at Roosevelt's insistence, the Democrats already had abolished their two-thirds rule for presidential nominations, which meant that candidates for president no longer had to tolerate as much trading of vice-presidential nominations and other administration posts to win at the convention. (They also abolished the two-thirds rule for vice-presidential nominations, reducing the degree of consensus needed for that choice as well.) In 1940, Roosevelt completed his coup by seizing the party leaders' traditional prerogative to determine nominations for vice president and making it his own. His tactic was simple: he threatened that unless the convention nominated Secretary of Agriculture Henry A. Wallace for vice president (which it was loath to do), he would not accept its nomination for president.

Unlike Garner and many of his other predecessors, Wallace never had been a member of Congress and, while in office, spent little time on Capitol Hill. But he did

Smithsonian Institution

Theodore Roosevelt was the first vice-presidential candidate to participate actively in a presidential campaign. Here he addresses an outdoor rally in Hillburn, New York, in 1901.

Vice Presidents Often Attain Top Spot

As of January 1989 when George Bush became president, fourteen of the forty-one individuals who have served as president of the United States were first vice presidents, but only four of them got to the Oval Office by being elected to it. The others made it because of the death or resignation of their predecessors.

Of the five vice presidents elevated by election, two—John Adams and Thomas Jefferson—were elected when there was no direct mass participation in the presidential nomination or election process. Martin Van Buren was elected directly to the presidency in 1836, as was Bush in 1988. Richard Nixon narrowly lost his bid to move up from the vice presidency in 1960 but was elected eight years later.

Few other vice presidents have come close to attaining the Oval Office. Hubert H. Humphrey was the only other sitting vice president to win a major party presidential nomination; he lost narrowly to Nixon in 1968. Walter F. Mondale won the Democratic presidential nomination in 1984, nearly four years after his term as vice president ended, but lost to Ronald Reagan.

Two other vice presidents who never won the White House ran as third party presidential candidates: John C. Breckinridge, Democrat James Buchanan's vice president (1857-1861), was the nominee of the Southern Democrats in 1860; and Henry A. Wallace, Franklin D. Roosevelt's second vice president (1941-1945), was the candidate of the Progressive party in 1948.

In the following chart are the names of the vice presidents who became president as well as those who won a major party presidential nomination. The party affiliation of the vice presidents and the names of the presidents under whom they served are noted.

Assumed Presidency on Death or Resignation	Year Assumed Presidency
John Tyler, Whig (W. H. Harrison)	1841
Millard Fillmore, Whig (Taylor)	1850
Andrew Johnson, D (Lincoln)	1865
Chester A. Arthur, R (Garfield)	1881
Theodore Roosevelt, R (McKinley)	1901
Calvin Coolidge, R (Harding)	1923
Harry S Truman, D (F. D. Roosevelt)	1945
Lyndon B. Johnson, D (Kennedy)	1963
Gerald R. Ford, R (Nixon)	1974

Elected President Directly from Vice Presidency	Year Elected President
John Adams, Federalist (Washington)	1796
Thomas Jefferson, D-R (Adams)	1800
Martin Van Buren, D (Jackson)	1836
George Bush, R (Reagan)	1988

Elected President Later	
Richard Nixon, R (Eisenhower)	1968

Nominated for President but Lost	Year Sought Presidency
Richard Nixon, R (Eisenhower)	1960
Hubert H. Humphrey, D (Johnson)	1968
Walter F. Mondale, D (Carter)	1984

1. Although nominated to run with Republican Abraham Lincoln, Andrew Johnson was identified as a Democrat.

become the first vice president to be appointed as head of a government agency. In July 1941, Roosevelt named Wallace to chair the new Economic Defense Board, a three-thousand member wartime preparation agency that, after World War II was declared in December, was renamed the Board of Economic Warfare and assigned major procurement responsibilities. Unfortunately, the powers and duties of Wallace's agency overlapped with those of several cabinet departments, notably State and Commerce. These overlaps generated interagency conflicts over jurisdiction and policy that weakened both the war effort and Wallace's authority. But because the vice president is a constitutionally independent official whom the president cannot command or remove, at least not in the usual sense, Roosevelt felt compelled to abolish the warfare board, which left Wallace embarrassed and devoid of function. What initially had seemed to be the birth of new vice-presidential power turned out to be a false labor. No subsequent president has ever asked the vice president to head an executive agency.

Nonetheless, the steadily growing involvement of the vice presidency in executive branch activities continued under Wallace. The vice president continued to sit with the cabinet, advise the president, and travel abroad as an administration emissary. Even Wallace's lack of involvement with Congress exemplified, although to an unusual degree, a developing characteristic of the twentieth-century vice presidency, namely, the atrophy of the office's role as president of the Senate. To some degree, the first development explains the second—to the extent that vice presidents became more involved with the presidency, they had less time to spend on the floor of the Senate and less ability to win its trust. But changes in the Senate also help to account for the decline of the vice president's constitutional responsibilities in that institution. For one thing, the admission of new states caused the Senate to grow larger, making tie votes statistically less probable. The Senate also became ever more institutionalized, developing its own body of rules and procedural precedents, which the president of the Senate was expected merely to announce, on the advice of the parliamentarian.

Advances in the visibility, stature, and extraconstitutional responsibilities of the vice presidency may help to explain the office's improved performance of its main constitutional duty: to provide an able successor to a departed president. Historians rate two of the five twentieth-century successor presidents (Theodore Roosevelt and Truman) as near-great, one as above average (Johnson), and only Coolidge as below average.[17] But for all its gains, the vice presidency on the eve of mid-century remained a fundamentally weak office. Its constitutional status was substantially unaltered, although the Twentieth Amendment (1933) did establish the full successorship of the vice president-elect in the event of the president-elect's death. Ticket balancing to increase the party's appeal on election day continued to dominate vice-presidential selection. All the ambiguities of the vice president's rights and duties in times of presidential disability still were unresolved, as dramatized by the passive role Marshall felt compelled to play during the prolonged illness of Woodrow Wilson. *(See "Presidential Disability," p. 378, in Removal chapter of Part II.)* Tension continued to mark some presidential-vice presidential pairings, although less frequently after Franklin Roosevelt won for presidential candidates the right to choose their running mates.

Even the glimmerings of enhanced vice-presidential influence sometimes seemed to be no more than that. Roosevelt replaced the unpopular Wallace with Senator Truman when he ran for a fourth term in 1944. On inauguration day 1945, the president was ill, and World War II was racing to a close. Yet Truman later was to say that in his eighty-two days as vice president, "I don't think I saw Roosevelt but twice ... except at cabinet meetings." [18] He was at most dimly aware of the existence of the atomic bomb, the contents of the Allies' plans for the postwar world, and the serious deterioration of the president's health. In this woeful state of ignorance and unpreparedness, Truman, upon Roosevelt's death on April 12, 1945, immediately succeeded to the office of president and to its full range of powers and duties. He told a friend later that day, "I feel like I have been struck by a bolt of lightning." [19]

The Modern Vice Presidency

Truman's lack of preparation in 1945, along with the subsequent development of an ongoing cold war between the United States and the Soviet Union and the proliferation of intercontinental ballistic missiles armed with nuclear warheads, heightened public concern that the vice presidency should be occupied by leaders who were not just willing but ready and able to step into the presidency at a moment's notice if the need for a succession should arise. This concern has had important consequences for vice-presidential selection, activities, succession and disability, and political status.

Selection

To meet the new public expectations about vice-presidential quality, most modern presidential candidates have paid considerable attention to experience, ability, and political compatibility in selecting their running mates. Winning votes on election day is as much the goal as in the days of old-style ticket balancing, but presidential nominees realize that voters now care more about competence and loyalty—a vice-presidential candidate's ability to succeed to the presidency ably and to carry on the departed president's policies faithfully—than they do about having all regions of the country or factions of the party represented on the ticket. This realization has helped to create a climate for a more influential vice presidency. As attorney Joel Goldstein has shown, the president is most likely to assign responsibilities to the vice president when the two are personally and politically compatible and when the president believes that the vice president has talents the administration needs.[20] These conditions now are likely to be met (and have been, in every administration since 1974) as a consequence of the new selection criteria.

Little is left to chance in modern vice-presidential selection, at least when the presidential nominating contest is settled, as has been typical since 1952, well in advance of the convention. Jimmy Carter set a precedent in 1976 when he conducted a careful, organized preconvention search for a running mate. A list of four hundred Democratic officeholders was compiled and scrutinized by aides, then winnowed down to seven finalists who were investigated and, ultimately, interviewed by Carter. (He tapped Walter F. Mondale at the convention.) Mondale and Michael S. Dukakis followed similar procedures as the Democratic presidential nominees in 1984 and 1988, respectively. Ronald Reagan did nothing so elaborate in 1980 because he hoped to lure former president Ford onto the ticket, but he and his aides did give considerable thought to the kind of running mate they wanted. George Bush searched hard before choosing Dan Quayle in 1988.

The fruit of both the new emphasis on loyalty and competence and the new care that is invested in the selection process can be seen in the roster of postwar vice-presidential nominees. The modern era has been marked by an almost complete absence of ideologically opposed running mates, and those vice-presidential candidates who have differed even slightly on the issues with the heads of their tickets have hastened to gloss over past disagreements and to deny that any exist in the present. The record is even more compelling with regard to competence: from 1948 to 1984, the vice-presidential candidate as often as not has been the more experienced member of the ticket in high government office, including John Sparkman in 1952, Estes Kefauver in 1956, Johnson and Lodge in 1960, Mondale in 1976, Bush in 1980, and Lloyd Bentsen in 1988.[21]

There is, to be sure, no guarantee that reasoned, responsible vice-presidential nominations will be made on every occasion. Politicians do not always see their interests clearly. Nixon, the Republican presidential nominee in 1968, was too clever by half when, acting on the theory that a relatively unknown running mate would have few enemies and cost the ticket few votes, he chose Agnew as his candidate for vice president. In 1984 many observers thought Mondale seemed too eager to placate women's groups within the party when he selected Geraldine Ferraro, a three-term member of the House of Representatives with no notable foreign affairs experience, just as George McGovern may have been overly concerned about satisfying organized labor in picking Thomas Eagleton in 1972. (It was revealed soon after Eagleton's nomination for vice president that he had undergone electroshock treatment for a nervous breakdown, which led to his being dropped from the ticket.) What seems certain, however, is that the presidential candidate who pays insufficient attention to competence and loyalty in choosing the vice-presidential nominee will suffer for it in the election: the news media will present critical stories, the other party will run harsh commercials, and the now-traditional vice-presidential debate, which is nationally televised, may reveal the nominee as an unworthy presidential successor.

A concern for competence and loyalty in the vice presidency characterized the solution Congress invented to a recurring problem of the executive that the challenges of the postwar era had made urgent: vice-presidential vacancies. The Twenty-fifth Amendment, which was passed in 1965 and ratified in 1967, established a procedure for selecting vice presidents in unusual circumstances. Before then, the vice presidency had been vacant for parts of sixteen administrations, leaving the presidency without a designated successor.[22] The new amendment stated that "whenever there is a vacancy in the office of the Vice President, the President shall nominate a Vice President who shall take office upon confirmation by a majority vote of both Houses of Congress," voting separately. This procedure came in handy, albeit in circumstances its authors scarcely had imagined, in 1973, when Vice President Agnew resigned as part of a plea bargain and was replaced by Ford, and in 1974, when Ford became president after President Nixon resigned to avert impeachment proceedings and appointed Nelson A. Rockefeller to fill the vacated vice presidency. *(See "Filling Vice-Presidential Vacancies," p. 341, in Selection by Succession chapter of Part II.)*

Activity

One thing modern presidents do to reassure the nation that the vice president is prepared to succeed to the presidency is to keep them informed about matters of state. As President Dwight D. Eisenhower's remark at a news conference indicates, to do otherwise would invite public criticism: "Even if Mr. Nixon and I were not good friends, I would still have him in every important conference of government, so that if the grim reaper would find it time to remove me from the scene, he is ready to step in without any interruption."[23] In 1949, at President Truman's behest, the vice president was made a statutory member of the National Security Council. (The only other task assigned to the vice president by law is membership on the Board of Regents of the Smithsonian Institution.) Vice presidents also receive full national security briefings as a matter of course.

As a further means of reassurance, most presidents now encourage the vice president to stay active and in the public eye. Since Garner began the practice, vice presidents have traveled abroad in the president's behalf both with growing frequency—Nixon made seven foreign trips, Humphrey twelve, Mondale fourteen, and Bush (during the first term) twenty[24]—and in pursuit of a variety of diplomatic missions, ranging from simple expressions of American good will to actual negotiations. Vice presidents since Garner also have met regularly with the cabinet and served, to some degree, as legislative liaison from the president to Congress—counting votes on Capitol Hill, lobbying discreetly, and listening to complaints and suggestions.

Library of Congress

As Franklin Roosevelt's vice president, John Nance Garner began the practice of traveling abroad on the president's behalf.

Alben W. Barkley, who served as vice president in the Truman administration, elevated the ceremonial duties of the vice presidency to center stage. Some of these, like crowning beauty queens (a Barkley favorite), are inconsequential; but others, such as commencement addresses and appearances at events that symbolize administration goals, need not be. Nixon, whose president did not enjoy partisan politics, carved out new vice-presidential roles that were as insignificant as chair of a study commission and as important as public advocate of the administration's policies, leadership, and party. The advocacy role exposed the vice president to a wide range of audiences, including interest groups, party activists, journalists, and the general public.

During the 1960s and 1970s, vice presidents began to accumulate greater institutional resources to help them fulfill their more extensive duties. Johnson, the vice president to President Kennedy, gained for the vice presidency an impressive suite of offices in the Executive Office Building, adjacent to the White House; Agnew won a line item in the executive budget—between them they freed vice presidents from their earlier dependence on Congress for office space and operating funds.

Even more significant institutional gains were registered by Ford and Rockefeller, the two vice presidents who were appointed under the Twenty-fifth Amendment and whose agreements to serve were urgently required by their presidents, for political reasons. Ford, who feared becoming too dependent on a president who might well be removed from office, persuaded Nixon to increase dramatically his budget for hiring staff. The new personnel included support staff for press relations, speech writing, scheduling, and administration (which meant vice presidents no longer had to depend on the often unreliable White House staff for those functions), policy staff (enabling vice presidents to develop useful advice on matters of presidential concern), and political staff (to help vice presidents protect their interests and further their ambitions). Rockefeller secured a weekly place on the president's calendar for a private meeting.[25] He also enhanced the perquisites of the vice presidency—everything from a better airplane to serve as *Air Force Two* to an official residence (the Admiral's House at the Naval Observatory) and a redesigned seal for the office. (The old seal showed an eagle at rest; the new one, a wingspread eagle with a claw full of arrows and a starburst at its head.)

The vice presidency came into full flower during Mondale's tenure in the administration of President Carter. As a candidate in 1976, Mondale participated in the first nationally televised debate between the vice-presidential candidates. His most tangible contributions to the institution during his term as vice president, building on earlier gains, were the authorization he won to attend all presidential meetings, full access to the flow of papers to and from the president, and an office in the West Wing of the White House. More important, perhaps, Mondale demonstrated that the vice president could serve the president (who, as stated earlier, had selected him with unprecedented care and attention) as a valued adviser on virtually all matters of politics and public policy. Some vice presidents in each of the earlier eras of the office's history, and most vice presidents in the modern era, had been consulted by their

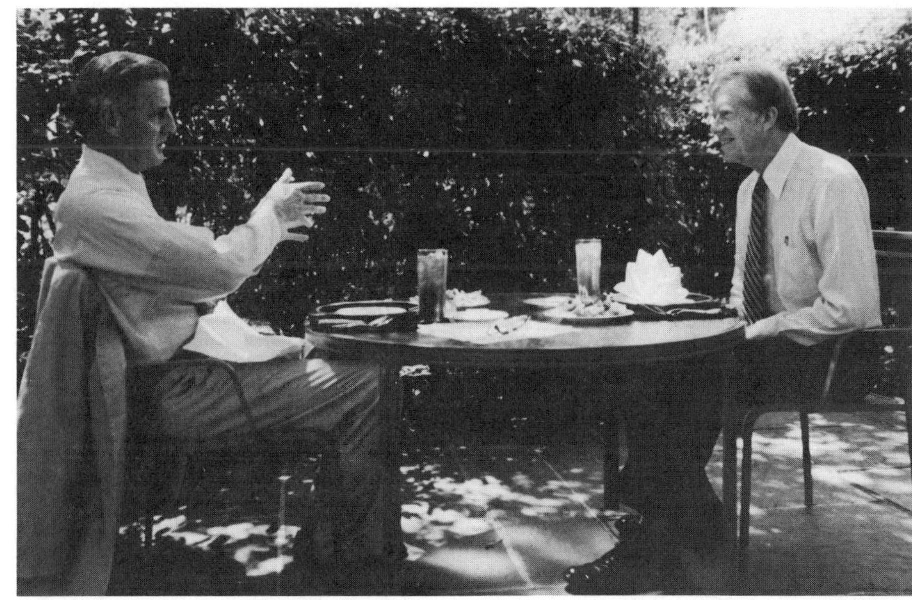

Jimmy Carter Library

As President Jimmy Carter's vice president, Walter Mondale was one of the most influential vice presidents. Unlike his predecessors, he had his own office in the West Wing of the White House.

presidents on at least some important matters—Johnson on space issues, Humphrey on civil rights, Rockefeller on domestic policy. But no vice president ever had attained Mondale's status as a general adviser to the president.

Bush, as vice president to President Reagan, was heir to all the institutional gains in both roles and resources that his recent predecessors had won. Although he did not enter office enjoying the same sort of personal relationship with Reagan that Mondale had with Carter, Bush worked hard and, for the most part, successfully to win the president's confidence. As Bush (and, later, his own vice president, Quayle) realized, the degree to which the new activities of the vice presidency translate into real influence within the White House still depends in large part on the president's perception of the vice president's ability, energy, and perhaps most important, loyalty. But, because of the new vice-presidential selection criteria, this perception is more likely to be favorable than at any previous time in history. And, because of the institutionalization of numerous roles and resources in the vice presidency, the vice president has a greater opportunity than ever to be of real service to a president.

Succession and Disability

In addition to creating a procedure to fill vice-presidential vacancies, the Twenty-fifth Amendment accomplished two other purposes. One was to state explicitly the right of the vice president to assume the office of president and to serve for the remainder of the departed president's term, an uncontroversial measure that conferred constitutional sanction on a long-established tradition. The other was to establish a set of procedures to handle situations of presidential disability. Disability had been a recurring problem of the presidency, but President Eisenhower's heart attack and other ailments during the 1950s brought matters to a head. In an age of nuclear confrontation, he and many others felt, the nation could not run the risk of being leaderless even briefly. Eisenhower's short-term solution was to write Vice President Nixon a letter in 1958 stating that if the president ever were disabled again, he would instruct the vice president to serve as acting president until the president announced that he was once again able. If Eisenhower were unable to communicate for some reason, Nixon could make the decision himself.

Presidents Kennedy and Johnson endorsed this arrangement when they took office, but it hardly solved the disability problem. The Eisenhower letter lacked the force of law and made no provision to relieve a president who was disabled but, like President Wilson, refused to admit it. The Twenty-fifth Amendment provided constitutional methods both for the president, by means of a letter to the leaders of Congress, to name the vice president as acting president during a time of disability and for the vice president and a majority of the heads of the departments to make that decision if the president were unable to do so. The amendment even created a procedure to be followed if the vice president and cabinet believed the president to be disabled and the president disagreed: the vice president would become acting president, but the president would be restored to power within twenty-one days unless two-thirds of both the House of Representatives and the Senate voted against the president.

Only two clear situations of presidential disability have arisen since the Twenty-fifth Amendment was passed, both during the Reagan administration. The first occurred when Reagan was shot on March 30, 1981. Some thought was given, then and in the days afterward, to naming Vice President Bush as acting president, but White House aides discouraged any such action on the grounds that it might make Reagan appear weak or might confuse the nation.[26]

Criticism of the administration's failure to act shaped its preparation for the second instance of presidential disability, Reagan's cancer surgery on July 13, 1985. This time Reagan did relinquish his powers and duties to Bush before undergoing anesthesia. Curiously, however, he did not explicitly invoke the Twenty-fifth Amendment in doing so, instead saying that he was not convinced that the amendment was meant to apply to "such brief and temporary

The White House

Library of Congress

In 1988, George Bush became the first incumbent vice president to be elected to the presidency since Martin Van Buren in 1836.

periods of incapacity" as his surgery. As for Bush, he spent his eight hours as acting president quietly at home, chatting and playing tennis with friends.

Political Status

The vice president enjoys a curious political status. Until Bush's 1988 victory, no incumbent vice president had been elected president since 1836, when Van Buren accomplished the feat. Yet, in a marked departure from previous political history, the modern vice presidency has been an effective steppingstone to a major party presidential nomination. Of the other recent vice presidents, Nixon, Humphrey, and Mondale were nominated directly for president; and Truman, Johnson, and Ford were nominated for full terms after succeeding to the presidency. (Barkley, Agnew, and Rockefeller did not actively seek a presidential nomination.)

What accounts for the recent ascendancy of the vice presidency in the politics of presidential nominations? First, the two-term limit that was imposed on presidents by the Twenty-second Amendment (1951) made it possible for the vice president to step forward as a presidential candidate, as Nixon did in 1960 and Bush in 1988, during the president's second term without alienating the president. (This effect of the amendment was wholly unanticipated.) Second, the roles that Vice President Nixon developed, with Eisenhower's encouragement, as party builder (campaigning during election years, raising funds between elections) and as public advocate of the administration and its policies uniquely situate the vice president to win friends among the political activists who influence presidential nominations. Finally, the recent growth in vice-presidential activities has made it a more prestigious office, and thus a more plausible steppingstone to the presidency. Foreign travel and the trappings of the office—the airplane, mansion, seal, West Wing office, and so on—are physical symbols of prestige.[27]

Perhaps more important, in their efforts to assure the nation that they are fulfilling their responsibility to prepare for a possible emergency succession, presidents may make inflated claims about the role of the vice president in the administration. Thus, the typical modern vice president can plausibly argue, as Mondale frequently did, that the vice presidency "may be the best training of all" for the presidency:

> I'm privy to all the same secret information as the president. I have unlimited access to the president. I'm usually with him when all the central decisions are being made. I've been through several of those crises that a president inevitably confronts, and I see how they work. I've been through the budget process. I've been through the diplomatic ventures. I've been through a host of congressional fights as seen from the presidential perspective.[28]

Yet vice presidents who are nominated by their party for president carry certain disadvantages into the fall campaign that are as surely grounded in the office as are the advantages they bring to the nominating contest. Indeed, some of the very activities of the modern vice presidency that are most appealing to the party activists who influence nominations may repel members of the broader electorate that decides the election. Days and nights spent fertilizing the party grass roots with fervent, sometimes slashing rhetoric can alienate voters who look to the presidency for unifying, not partisan, leadership. In addition, although only the president can plausibly take credit for an administration's successes, the vice president is fair game for attack by the other party's presidential candidate for its shortcomings. (Because of the Vietnam War, that was the fate of Vice President Humphrey in 1968.) Such attacks allow no good response. A vice president who tried to stand apart from the administration would alienate the president and cause voters to wonder why the criticisms were not voiced earlier, when they might have made a difference. The vice president may say instead that loyalty to the president forecloses public disagreement (an argument Bush frequently made), but that course is no less perilous. Strength, independence, vision, and integrity are the qualities voters most seek in a president, not loyalty.

To be sure, vice presidents are not destined to lose in general elections any more than they are destined to win presidential nominations. Before Bush's election in 1988, Nixon in 1960 and Humphrey in 1968 came within a few percentage points of victory. But the electoral tensions vice presidents face, which inhere in the office, were well stated by President Eisenhower: "To promise and pledge *new* effort, *new* programs, and *new* ideas without appearing to criticize the current party and administration—that is indeed an exercise in tightrope walking." [29]

Conclusion

In selection, activity, succession and disability, and political status, the vice presidency has come a long way during the twentieth century, especially since 1945. But the curious political status of the vice presidency is a reminder that, for all its progress as an institution, some weaknesses of the office endure. Although new selection criteria make the nomination of vice-presidential candidates who are qualified to be president more likely, the recent examples of William E. Miller in 1964, Agnew in 1968, Eagleton in 1972, Ferraro in 1984, and Quayle in 1988 indicate that older forms of ticket balancing are not yet extinct. New selection criteria may foster greater harmony in office between president and vice president, but they do not guarantee it. (Perhaps it is not surprising that the two modern presidents who inflicted the greatest pain on their vice presidents, Johnson and Nixon, once were vice presidents themselves.[30]) Finally, although vice presidents enjoy more resources, responsibilities, and influence than ever before, they do so mainly at the sufferance of the president. The price of power for a vice president can be high—unflagging loyalty, sublimation of one's own views and ambitions, and willing receptiveness to the president's beck and call. But, in view of the inherent constitutional weakness of the office, no other path to influence exists.

Notes

1. These familiar quotations about the vice presidency may be found in Michael Dorman, *The Second Man: The Changing Role of the Vice Presidency* (New York: Delacorte Press, 1968), 6-7.
2. Quoted in Paul C. Light, *Vice-Presidential Power: Advice and Influence in the White House* (Baltimore, Md.: Johns Hopkins University Press, 1984), 13.
3. Joel K. Goldstein, *The Modern American Vice Presidency* (Princeton, N.J.: Princeton University Press, 1982); various editions of *The Gallup Poll* (Wilmington, Del.: Scholarly Resources, 1982-1987).
4. Thomas R. Marshall, *Recollections* (Indianapolis: Bobbs-Merrill, 1925), 368.
5. Quoted in Light, *Vice-Presidential Power,* 13.
6. Quoted in Goldstein, *Modern Vice Presidency,* 6.
7. Quoted in Thomas E. Cronin, "Rethinking the Vice Presidency," in *Rethinking the Vice Presidency,* ed. Thomas E. Cronin (Boston: Little, Brown, 1982), 326. Rather than being buried, of course, Webster would have succeeded to the presidency when Zachary Taylor died in 1850.
8. Quoted in Irving G. Williams, *The Rise of the Vice Presidency* (Washington, D.C.: Public Affairs Press, 1956), 66.
9. Johnson was the protagonist in two other unique events in the history of the vice presidency. In the election of 1836, Virginia's Democratic electors refused to vote for Johnson because they objected to his interracial sexual extravagances. This left Johnson one vote short of the required electoral vote majority, so the Senate elected him by 33-16. Four years later, Johnson refused to withdraw as a candidate for the Democratic nomination for vice president, dividing the party convention to such an extent that it selected no vice-presidential candidate at all. (The Democrats lost the election.)
10. Robert K. Murray and Tim H. Blessing, "The Presidential Performance Study: A Progress Report," *Journal of American History* 70:4 (December 1983): 535-555.
11. The five nineteenth-century presidents who were disabled for a measurable period of time were Madison, William Henry Harrison, Arthur, Garfield, and Grover Cleveland. John D. Feerick, *The Twenty-fifth Amendment* (New York: Fordham University Press, 1976), chap. 1.
12. Theodore Roosevelt, "The Three Vice-Presidential Candidates and What They Represent," *Review of Reviews,* September 1896, 289.
13. Quoted in Williams, *Rise of the Vice Presidency,* 89.
14. Marshall's decision to accept Wilson's invitation to meet with the cabinet was made with some misgivings. Although he once had described the president as "my commander-in-chief" whose "orders would be obeyed," Marshall believed that, constitutionally, the vice president, as president of the Senate, was a "member of the legislative branch," ill-suited to executive responsibilities. Thus, he told the cabinet, he wanted it clearly understood that he was present only "informally and personally" and would "preside in an unofficial and informal way." Before his inauguration in 1925, Vice President Dawes said publicly that he would not accept an invitation from President Coolidge to meet with the cabinet, if, as seemed likely, one were forthcoming. "The cabinet and those who sit with it should always do so at the discretion and inclination of the president. . . ," Dawes told reporters, neglecting the possibility that Coolidge might wish to exercise his discretion to have the vice president present. "No precedent should be established which creates a different and arbitrary method of selection" (Williams, *Rise of the Vice Presidency,* 108-110, 134).
15. Franklin D. Roosevelt, "Can the Vice President Be Useful?" *Saturday Evening Post,* October 6, 1920, 8.
16. Williams, *Rise of the Vice Presidency,* 158-159.
17. Murray and Blessing, "Presidential Performance Study."
18. Quoted in Williams, *Rise of the Vice Presidency,* 219.
19. Quoted in Robert J. Donovan, *Conflict and Crisis: The Presidency of Harry S Truman, 1945-1948* (New York: Norton, 1977), 15.
20. Goldstein, *Modern Vice Presidency,* 147-148.
21. Ibid., 85.
22. Vice-presidential vacancies occurred seven time because the vice president died, once because the vice president resigned, and eight times because the president died.
23. *Public Papers of the Presidents* (Washington, D.C.: Government Printing Office, 1957), 132.
24. Joseph A. Pika, "A New Vice Presidency?" in *The Presidency and the Political System,* 2d ed., ed. Michael Nelson (Washington, D.C.: CQ Press, 1987).
25. Rockefeller also headed the White House Domestic Council, an assignment that, like Henry Wallace's, ended in failure.
26. Lawrence I. Barrett, *Gambling with History: Ronald Reagan in the White House* (Garden City, N.Y.: Doubleday, 1983), chap. 7.
27. As Vice President Ford remarked in 1974, "I am now surrounded by a clutch of Secret Service agents, reporters and cameramen, and assorted well-wishers. When I travel I am greeted by bands playing 'Hail Columbia' and introduced to audiences with great solemnity instead of just as 'my good friend, Jerry Ford'" (quoted in Light, *Vice-Presidential Power,* 10).
28. Quoted in Cronin, "Rethinking the Vice Presidency," 338.
29. Dwight D. Eisenhower, *Waging Peace* (Garden City, N.Y.: Doubleday, 1965), 596.
30. Paul Light calls this the "abused child syndrome" (*Vice-Presidential Power,* 108).

Selected Bibliography

Cronin, Thomas E., ed. *Rethinking the Vice Presidency.* Boston: Little, Brown, 1982.

Dorman, Michael. *The Second Man: The Changing Role of the Vice Presidency.* New York: Delacorte Press, 1968.

Goldstein, Joel K. *The Modern American Vice Presidency.* Princeton, N.J.: Princeton University Press, 1982.

Light, Paul C. *Vice-Presidential Power: Advice and Influence in the White House.* Baltimore, Md.: Johns Hopkins University Press, 1984.

Nelson, Michael. *A Hearbeat Away.* New York: Unwin Hyman, 1988.

Pica, Joseph A. "A New Vice Presidency?" In *The Presidency and the Political System.* 2d ed. Washington, D.C.: CQ Press, 1987.

Williams, Irving G. *The Rise of the Vice Presidency.* Washington, D.C.: Public Affairs Press, 1956.

Rating the Presidents

One approach that historians have taken to the history of the presidency is to rate the presidents' performances in office, then rank them in relation to one another. In doing so, historians participate in the great American pastime of listing and ranking almost everything, from the ten best movies to the top forty songs. But historians also hope to learn certain things from their rankings. What makes a president great, average, or a failure? Have different eras in U.S. history been marked by notable differences in presidential quality? Were the "good old days" really that much better than the recent past?

Presidential ratings also try to shed some light on a larger historical issue, namely, has the American presidency been a generally successful institution, or has it been on the whole a failure? James Bryce, the distinguished nineteenth-century British observer of U.S. politics, took one position on this question in a chapter titled "Why Great Men Are Not Chosen Presidents," from his book *The American Commonwealth.* The answer, according to Bryce, was that the political party bosses who controlled the selection of candidates for president preferred "safe," or mediocre, men to "brilliant" men. Harold J. Laski, another British student of the American presidency, rejoined that the United States had a remarkable record of finding great presidents when they were needed to lead the nation in times of crisis, such as the Civil War and the Great Depression.[1]

The Schlesinger Polls

Arthur M. Schlesinger, the Harvard University historian, conducted the first of the presidential ratings surveys in 1948. He wrote to fifty-five distinguished historians and asked them to evaluate each president as either great, near great, average, below average, or a failure. (William Henry Harrison and James Garfield were left off the list because they died so soon after taking office; Harry S Truman was not included because he was the incumbent president.) The only yardstick Schlesinger offered his colleagues was that their evaluations were to be based solely on "performance in office, omitting anything done before or after." Schlesinger reported the results of his survey in the November 1, 1948, issue of *Life* magazine.[2]

"Those who believe that in a democracy people generally get the kind of government they deserve will be heartened by the results of [my survey]," Schlesinger wrote. "Only two of our past Presidents were labeled 'failure'; four were judged 'near great'; and six received the accolade 'great.' "[3] He noted a high degree of consensus among the participants in the poll about which presidents belonged in each of these categories. The six presidents judged as great were Abraham Lincoln, George Washington, Franklin D. Roosevelt, Woodrow Wilson, Thomas Jefferson, and Andrew Jackson, in that order. The four near-great presidents, ranked seven through ten among the twenty-nine presidents evaluated in the poll, were Theodore Roosevelt, Grover Cleveland, John Adams, and James K. Polk, respectively. Only Ulysses S. Grant and Warren G. Harding were judged to have been failures. All the other presidents scored as average or below average, with less consensus among the experts about exactly how they should be ranked.

Schlesinger repeated his poll in 1962, this time drawing on the judgments of seventy-five participants, including several political scientists and journalists and Justice Felix Frankfurter of the U.S. Supreme Court. The results, which appeared in the July 29, 1962, issue of the *New York Times Magazine,* were quite similar to those of the first survey.[4] Lincoln, Washington, Franklin Roosevelt, Wilson, and Jefferson again were judged great presidents, in the same order as in 1948. Jackson remained sixth, but slipped to near-great status, along with Theodore Roosevelt, Polk, Truman (a new addition), John Adams, and Cleveland. Grant and Harding still were the sole occupants of the failure category. Dwight D. Eisenhower, whose presidency occurred between the dates of the two polls, ranked twenty-first, near the bottom of the average presidents. John F. Kennedy, the incumbent president in 1962, was not evaluated, but as the Pulitzer Prize-winning author of the historical book *Profiles in Courage,* was invited by Schlesinger to fill out a ballot. He declined. "A year ago I would have responded with confidence. . . ," Kennedy wrote, "but now I am not so sure."[5]

Assessing the results of his two polls, Schlesinger drew some conclusions about the perceived qualities that cause a president to be ranked high, low, or somewhere in between by historians. The great presidents were, among other things, "lucky in their times: they are all identified with some crucial turning point in our history."[6] Washington

By Michael Nelson

Table 1 The Schlesinger Ratings, 1962 and 1948

Presidential Rating	
1962 (*N* = 75)	1948 (*N* = 55)
Great	Great
Lincoln	Lincoln
Washington	Washington
F. Roosevelt	F. Roosevelt
Wilson	Wilson
Jefferson	Jefferson
	Jackson
Near great	Near great
Jackson	T. Roosevelt
T. Roosevelt	Cleveland
Polk	J. Adams
Truman	Polk
J. Adams	
Cleveland	
Average	Average
Madison	J. Q. Adams
J. Q. Adams	Monroe
Hayes	Hayes
McKinley	Madison
Taft	Van Buren
Van Buren	Taft
Monroe	Arthur
Hoover	McKinley
B. Harrison	A. Johnson
Arthur	Hoover
Eisenhower	B. Harrison
A. Johnson	
Below average	Below average
Taylor	Tyler
Tyler	Coolidge
Fillmore	Fillmore
Coolidge	Taylor
Pierce	Buchanan
Buchanan	Pierce
Failure	Failure
Grant	Grant
Harding	Harding

Note: *N* = number of respondents to each survey.

and the birth of the Republic, Jefferson and the opportunity for national expansion, Jackson and the rise of agrarian democracy, Lincoln and the Civil War, Wilson and the Progressive movement and World War I, Franklin D. Roosevelt and the depression and World War II—each served at a time in which the opportunity for presidential leadership was unusually great.

The great presidents shared some personal and political qualities as well, according to Schlesinger. Notable among these were strength and the desire for power. "Washington apart," Schlesinger wrote, "none of [the great presidents] waited for the office to seek the man; they pursued it with all their might and main." Once in office, their greatness was established by the fact that "every one of [them] left the Executive branch stronger and more influential than he found it." When dealing with Congress, they knew "when to reason and to browbeat, to bargain and stand firm, . . . and when all else failed, they appealed over the heads of the lawmakers to the people." Nor did the great presidents shy away from confrontations with the Supreme Court. They were, to be sure, inattentive to their duty to administer the departments and agencies, but this freed them, according to Schlesinger, for the more important task of "moral leadership." All the great presidents were castigated by the press and by powerful political opponents. Finally, each "took the side of liberalism and the general welfare against the status quo." [7]

The near-great presidents shared the great presidents' desire to dominate the nation's political course but were less fortunate in their times, less skillful as leaders, or both. The average and below-average presidents were marked as a group by a belief in "negative government, in self-subordination to the legislative power," Schlesinger observed. The failure category was reserved for presidents "who, by their moral obtuseness, promoted a low tone in official life, conducting administrations scarred with shame and corruption." [8]

Schlesinger was heartened by the results of his polls. He regarded the generally positive ratings of the presidents as "favorable not only to them, but also the political system which made it possible for them to rise to power." Even the average presidents "rendered useful services according to their gifts," he suggested; besides, "there are moments indeed when the general welfare may call for rest and recuperation." Ultimately, however, "what endows a country with greatness is the ability to produce greatness when greatness is needed. Measured by such a standard, America has been served well by her Presidents." [9]

Later Surveys

The Schlesinger surveys spawned a number of successors. Gary Maranell, a sociologist at the University of Kansas, tried to improve on the earlier polls by including a broader array of historians in his sample and asking them to rate the presidents not only according to their overall prestige,

Table 2 The Maranell Rating, 1968

Presidential Rating (*N* = 571)	
Lincoln	Hoover
Washington	Eisenhower
F. Roosevelt	A. Johnson
Jefferson	Van Buren
T. Roosevelt	McKinley
Wilson	Arthur
Truman	Hayes
Jackson	Tyler
Kennedy	B. Harrison
J. Adams	Taylor
Polk	Coolidge
Cleveland	Fillmore
Madison	Buchanan
Monroe	Pierce
J. Q. Adams	Grant
L. Johnson	Harding
Taft	

Note: *N* = number of respondents to the survey.

Changes in Rank

The rankings of most presidents have not changed very much since Arthur M. Schlesinger conducted his first survey of historians in 1948. The top seven presidents then—Abraham Lincoln, George Washington, Franklin D. Roosevelt, Woodrow Wilson, Thomas Jefferson, Andrew Jackson, and Theodore Roosevelt—remained the top seven presidents in the poll conducted by Robert K. Murray and Tim H. Blessing in 1981, although not in precisely that order. (So did the bottom two presidents, Ulysses S. Grant and Warren G. Harding.) But for some presidents, substantial rises and falls in ranking have occurred. Equally dramatic changes may await other presidents in the near future.

Two Who Have Risen, Two Who May Rise

Dwight D. Eisenhower. The most striking rise in stature has involved Eisenhower, who ranked twenty-first in 1962 and eleventh in 1981. Part of the explanation for Eisenhower's increased standing is that previously secret papers and documents from his administration have recently been released for public inspection. After studying the Eisenhower papers during the 1970s, political scientist Fred Greenstein wrote, he felt compelled to abandon the then-common scholarly view of Eisenhower as "an aging hero who reigned more than he ruled and who lacked the energy, motivation, and political skill to have a significant impact on events." Greenstein's book, *The Hidden-Hand Presidency,* instead portrayed Eisenhower as a president "politically astute and informed, actively engaged in putting his personal stamp on public policy, [who] applied a carefully thought-out conception of leadership to the conduct of his presidency." [1] Events of the 1960s and 1970s also made Eisenhower's presidency seem more successful in hindsight. The restraint he showed in withholding U.S. troops from the war in Indochina and his personal integrity stood in sharp contrast to the later record of Vietnam and the Watergate scandal.

Franklin D. Roosevelt. The Murray-Blessing poll placed Roosevelt second among the presidents, instead of his previous position of third behind Washington. Roosevelt's original high rating in 1948 was controversial. One New Yorker wrote to *Life* magazine, "I will agree that FDR was great if by that is meant great liar, great faker, great traitor, great betrayer." [2] But, as Schlesinger noted, the passage of time could only enhance Roosevelt's stature—"all the great Presidents have been held in lower esteem by their contemporaries than by later generations." [3] The Murray-Blessing poll proved Schlesinger correct.

Richard Nixon. Corruption in office is the mark of the failed president, according to historians. This explains why Nixon ranked just one notch above Grant and Harding in the Murray-Blessing poll. "Yet there is the nagging fact," observed Geoffrey Ward, editor of *American Heritage* magazine, in 1982, "that his administration saw solid accomplishments, of which the opening to China is the most obvious. I suspect that ten years from now—or twenty—Nixon's name will have crept up the list." [4]

Jimmy Carter. Ranked twenty-fifth in the Murray-Blessing poll, Carter has maintained that "history" will treat him more kindly than his contemporary critics have. Some scholars agree. "He'll be remembered as an average president," predicted Thomas Cronin, a political scientist. Biographer David McCullough said, "He will begin to gain in statute much as Eisenhower has done because of the Panama treaties, because of the Camp David accords, and because he maintained peace." [5]

Two Who Have Fallen, Two Who May Fall

Andrew Johnson. An average president in the opinion of historians in 1948 (he ranked nineteenth), Johnson descended to the failure category (thirty-second) in 1981. Johnson had long been treated kindly because historians believed that he had been impeached unjustly. But recent studies argue that Johnson was a reckless and incompetent president who may have deserved to be stripped of his office.[6]

Grover Cleveland. Historians in 1948 evaluated Cleveland in the afterglow of Allan Nevins's admiring biography, *Grover Cleveland: A Study in Courage.*[7] Accordingly, they ranked Cleveland eighth among the presidents, in the near-great category. As the influence of Nevins's book has waned, and as Cleveland's brand of conservative Democrat has faded from the scene, he has dropped in each successive survey, scoring seventeenth in the Murray-Blessing poll.

Woodrow Wilson and Harry S Truman. Wilson already has been demoted from the ranks of the great presidents to the near-great category. Truman seems likely to decline in reputation as well. One reason, Murray and Blessing report, is that both presidents are much more highly regarded by older generations of historians than by the younger ones replacing them.

1. Fred I. Greenstein, *The Hidden-Hand Presidency: Eisenhower as Leader* (New York: Basic Books, 1982).
2. Thomas A. Bailey, *Presidential Greatness* (New York: Appleton-Century, 1966), 32.
3. Arthur M. Schlesinger, *Paths to the Present* (New York: Macmillan, 1949), 96.
4. Quoted in Steve Neal, "Our Best and Worst President," *Chicago Tribune Magazine,* January 10, 1982, 12.
5. Ibid., 13.
6. James David Barber, "Adult Identity and Presidential Style: The Rhetorical Emphasis," *Daedalus* 97 (Summer 1968): 938-968; Michael L. Benedict, *The Impeachment and Trial of Andrew Johnson* (New York: Norton, 1973).
7. Allan Nevins, *Grover Cleveland: A Study in Courage* (New York: Dodd, Mead, 1932).

but also according to their strength, activeness, idealism, flexibility, and accomplishments. Of 1,095 members of the Organization of American Historians whom Maranell asked to participate in March 1968, 571 returned questionnaires.

The results of the Maranell poll were generally similar to those Schlesinger obtained. But some interesting differences also could be seen. Jefferson now was ranked higher than Wilson, and Truman higher than Jackson and Polk. Eisenhower, Herbert C. Hoover, James Monroe, and Andrew Johnson each had been moved up the list; William McKinley, among others, had been graded down. Of the presidents who were rated for the first time, Kennedy ranked ninth and Lyndon B. Johnson sixteenth.[10]

Maranell also discovered, through statistical analysis of his results, which criteria were important to historians in assessing the presidents' prestige. His findings confirmed Schlesinger's insights. The significance of a president's accomplishments, the strength of the role he played in directing the government and shaping the events of his day, and the activeness of his approach toward his administration—all were closely tied to the historians' overall assessment of his presidency. In contrast, the idealism that underlay a president's actions and the flexibility of his approach to implementing his programs and policies mattered little.

In 1981, journalist and biographer Steve Neal conducted a presidential rating survey for the *Chicago Tribune Magazine,* drawing on the views of forty-nine historians and political scholars (including four who had participated in the 1962 Schlesinger survey). His object was to obtain the experts' list of the ten best and ten worst presidents. Interestingly, two of the five most recent presidents at the time of the survey (excluding the incumbent, Ronald Reagan) scored among the ten worst: Richard Nixon (second worst for the corruption in his administration) and Jimmy Carter (tenth worst for the weakness of his presidency). None of the three other recent presidents ranked in the top group, but Kennedy and Johnson came close. (Gerald R. Ford scored somewhere in the middle.) The biggest changes in rank from previous surveys were Eisenhower, who ranked ninth, McKinley (just below the top group), and Theodore Roosevelt, now fourth on the historians' list.[11]

Like Schlesinger and Maranell, Neal discovered a close identity between presidential strength and presidential prestige in the minds of the experts. "The best presidents have been strong political leaders with a vision, if not a complete program, of where they think the country should go," said one historian. Eisenhower's rise in stature was linked to some degree to new scholarship that transformed his image from a weak and passive president to "hidden-hand leader," orchestrating events behind the scenes while maintaining a calm and pleasant facade.[12]

The largest effort to measure how historians rate the presidents, in terms of both the number of scholars canvassed and the number of questions asked of them, was conducted in 1981 by Robert K. Murray and Tim H. Blessing, two historians at Pennsylvania State University. They sent questionnaires to every Ph.D.-holding American historian with the rank of assistant professor or above, a total of 1,997. (Nine hundred fifty-three filled out their questionnaires in full.) Each questionnaire contained detailed queries about the presidential office in general and various presidential actions in particular, as well as about the respondent.[13]

The overall rankings obtained by Murray and Blessing differ to some degree from those of previous polls. Lincoln, Washington, and Franklin Roosevelt remained the three most highly rated presidents, but Roosevelt passed Washington for second place. Eisenhower's recent ascendancy was confirmed (he ranked eleventh), but not McKinley's. Cleveland's steady slide continued, from near-great status in the first Schlesinger poll to seventeenth in the Murray-Blessing survey. So did that of Rutherford B. Hayes (from thirteenth to twenty-third) and Andrew Johnson (from nineteenth to thirty-second). Interestingly, Murray and Blessing found that the historians in their poll differed widely in their assessments of Nixon, Lyndon Johnson, Hoover, and Jackson but were virtually unanimous in their praise for Lincoln, Franklin Roosevelt, and Washington. Finally, certain kinds of historians—those who were older,

Table 3 The *Chicago Tribune* Rating, 1981

Presidential Rating (N = 49)	
Ten best	Ten worst
Lincoln	Carter
Washington	Tyler
F. Roosevelt	Coolidge
T. Roosevelt	A. Johnson
Jefferson	Fillmore
Wilson	Grant
Jackson	Pierce
Truman	Buchanan
Eisenhower	Nixon
Polk	Harding

Note: N = number of respondents to the survey.

Table 4 The Murray-Blessing Rating, 1981

Presidential Rating (N = 953)	
Great	**Average**
Lincoln	McKinley
F. Roosevelt	Taft
Washington	Van Buren
Jefferson	Hoover
Near great	Hayes
T. Roosevelt	Arthur
Wilson	Ford
Jackson	Carter
Truman	B. Harrison
Above average	**Below average**
J. Adams	Taylor
L. Johnson	Tyler
Eisenhower	Fillmore
Polk	Coolidge
Kennedy	Pierce
Madison	**Failure**
Monroe	A. Johnson
J. Q. Adams	Buchanan
Cleveland	Nixon
	Grant
	Harding

Note: N = number of respondents to the survey.

The Public Rates the Presidents

Since the early 1970s, the Gallup and Harris polling organizations have assayed the public's views of the presidents. The pollsters have discovered that average citizens have a somewhat different set of presidential heroes than do scholars.

Gallup

In 1975 and 1985, Gallup asked Americans, "Which three U.S. presidents do you regard as the greatest?" The results in both polls were dominated by recent presidents. In 1985, for example, John F. Kennedy ranked first, Harry S Truman fourth, Ronald Reagan sixth, Dwight D. Eisenhower seventh, Richard M. Nixon eighth, Jimmy Carter ninth, and Lyndon B. Johnson twelfth. Almost all of the other presidents mentioned by citizens came from the roster of those rated great by scholars: Abraham Lincoln (second), Franklin D. Roosevelt (third), George Washington (fifth), Thomas Jefferson (tenth), Theodore Roosevelt (eleventh), and Woodrow Wilson (thirteenth).

In contrast to the historians' judgment, Eisenhower's stature among the general public dropped from 1975 to 1985 (24 percent to 16 percent) and Nixon's rose (5 percent to 11 percent).

Harris

Unlike Gallup, Harris asked citizens to rate only the presidents since Franklin Roosevelt. From 1972 to 1977, the pollster showed respondents a list of the recent presidents, then asked: "If you had to choose, which *one* president would you say did the best job in the White House?" Kennedy and Roosevelt usually were chosen by about one-fourth each, with the other presidents trailing behind. (As in the Gallup poll, Eisenhower's support dropped during the period.) Starting in 1985, Harris changed the question to who "likely will be viewed as the best president by history?" In 1985, Roosevelt led with 35 percent, followed by Kennedy (25 percent), Reagan (12 percent), Truman (9 percent), Eisenhower (6 percent), Carter and Nixon (2 percent), and Gerald R. Ford and Johnson (1 percent). In 1987, Kennedy passed Roosevelt (29 percent to 28 percent), with the order of the remaining presidents substantially unchanged.

Detailed questions elicited extreme reactions in the cases of Carter and Nixon. Carter was ranked second among the modern presidents in the 1987 survey for setting moral standards but was judged worst in foreign affairs and in getting things done. Nixon, who ranked high in foreign affairs, was chosen as having set the lowest moral standards.

The Gallup Polls, 1975 and 1985
(percent)

Question: "Which three U.S. presidents do you regard as the greatest?"

President	Year 1975	1985
John F. Kennedy	52	56
Abraham Lincoln	49	48
Franklin D. Roosevelt	45	41
Harry S Truman	37	26
George Washington	25	25
Ronald Reagan	—	21
Dwight D. Eisenhower	24	16
Richard M. Nixon	5	11
Jimmy Carter	—	9
Thomas Jefferson	8	7
Theodore Roosevelt	9	7
Lyndon B. Johnson	9	5
Woodrow Wilson	5	1
Herbert Hoover	0	1
All others	9	3
Don't know	3	2

Source: Compiled by the author from Gallup poll data.

The Harris Polls, Selected Years, 1972-1987
(percent)

Question: "Here is a list of the last seven Presidents of the United States. (Hand respondent card.) If you had to choose, which one president would you say did the best job in the White House?" (1972, 1976, 1977); "I'd like to ask you about the last nine presidents of the United States. Please keep in mind Roosevelt, Truman, Eisenhower, Kennedy, Johnson, Nixon, Ford, Carter, and Reagan. If you had to choose one, which president do you think likely will be remembered as the best president by history?" (1985, 1987)

President	Year 1972	1976	1977	1985	1987
John F. Kennedy	25	23	23	25	28
Franklin D. Roosevelt	23	29	23	35	28
Ronald Reagan	—	—	—	12	13
Harry S Truman	8	19	17	9	9
Dwight D. Eisenhower	10	12	8	6	6
Richard M. Nixon	20	2	2	2	3
Jimmy Carter	—	—	—	2	2
Lyndon B. Johnson	3	2	2	1	1
Gerald R. Ford	—	2	8	1	1
Not sure	10	11	17	7	8

Source: Compiled by the author from Harris poll data.

male, and specialized in the era of the president they rated—tended to be less severe in their judgments of the presidents than their colleagues.

Critics of the Ratings

Historians' efforts to rate and rank the presidents have drawn fire from a number of critics, including at least two presidents. Asked by a reporter about the second Schlesinger survey, in which he ranked ninth (near great), Truman said, "The historians didn't know any more than the pollsters did when they said I wouldn't win [the election] in 1948. Nobody will be able to assess my administration until about thirty years after I'm dead." Kennedy, after declining to participate in Schlesinger's 1962 poll, told Arthur M. Schlesinger, Jr., a White House aide and a historian himself, "How the hell can you tell? Only the President himself can know what his real pressures and his real alternatives are. If you don't know that, how can you judge performance?"[14]

Some scholars also have taken the polls to task. The historian Thomas A. Bailey, in his book *Presidential Greatness*, argued that two forms of bias cloud historians' judgments when they rate the presidents. First, like all Americans, the historian "is in some degree brainwashed before he reaches maturity." Surrounded by parks, memorials, cities, and other places named after presidents such as Lincoln, Washington, Jefferson, and Jackson, culturally imprinted with the monumental granite image of Lincoln, Washington, Jefferson, and Theodore Roosevelt on Mt. Rushmore, and used to seeing certain presidents' faces on coins and currency (Lincoln on the penny and five-dollar bill, Jefferson on the nickel, Frankin Roosevelt on the dime, Washington on the quarter and the one-dollar bill, Kennedy on the half-dollar, and Jackson on the twenty-dollar bill), how can one grow up in the United States without taking for granted that these presidents are great? Second, Bailey suggested, it was no coincidence that historians, who tend to be Democrats, selected a group of great presidents that is mostly Democratic and a group of failures that is entirely Republican. "One wonders if a man can quickly switch a partisan's derby for a scholar's mortarboard without getting the two mixed," he wrote.[15]

In addition to bias, Bailey found a more fundamental flaw in the ratings. "Judging presidents is not like judging those who play duplicate bridge," he argued; "no two incumbents were ever dealt the same hand." Nineteenth-century presidents served in an era when strong presidential leadership generally was not desired, which may explain why so many of them rate as average or below average. The great presidents, in contrast, each were " 'lucky' enough to serve in a time of great crisis" when extraordinary presidential power was encouraged.[16]

Nelson Polsby, a political scientist, has criticized the presidential rating game from a different perspective, namely, its effect on current and future presidents. Presidents know they will someday be rated and hope to be ranked highly. But, Polsby has argued, "the aspiration to presidential greatness ... leads to a variety of difficulties. For fear of being found out and downgraded, there is the temptation to deny failure, to refuse to readjust course when a program or a proposal doesn't work out. There is the temptation to hoard credit rather than share it.... There is the temptation to offer false hopes and to proclaim spurious accomplishments to the public at large."[17]

Eras of Presidential Success and Failure

As critics of the historians' polls suggest, surveys that rate the presidents may reveal as much about the scholars who do the rating as about the presidents themselves. At the very least, such surveys indicate the criteria by which historians evaluate presidents, notably political strength (if untainted by corruption) and the desire to be strong.

To the extent that the presidential ratings surveys are valid, however, one of the most interesting insights they offer is that different eras in U.S. history have been marked by widely different levels of presidential quality. The nation's first half-century (1789-1837) produced, according to the Murray-Blessing poll, seven presidents who were above average or better (two were great, one near great) and none who rated average or below. The next century stood in sharp contrast. Only five of the twenty-one rated presidents who served from 1837 to 1933 were graded great (one), near great (two), or above average (two). Of the sixteen others, seven were judged average, five below average, and four as failures. Perhaps, then it is encouraging to see that the present era more closely resembles the distant past than the recent past. Since 1933, the nation has been served by five presidents who rate above average or better in the Murray-Blessing poll (including one great and one near great), and only three who rate average (two) or below (one failure).

Notes

1. James Bryce, *The American Commonwealth*, vol. 1 (New York: Macmillan, 1924), 77. (Originally published in 1888.) Harold J. Laski, *The American Presidency: An Interpretation* (New York: Harper and Row, 1940), 49-53.
2. Arthur M. Schlesinger, "The U.S. Presidents," *Life*, November 1, 1948; Schlesinger, *Paths to the Present* (New York: Macmillan, 1949), chap. 5.
3. Schlesinger, "The U.S. Presidents."
4. Arthur M. Schlesinger, "Our Presidents: A Rating by 75 Historians," *New York Times Magazine*, July 29, 1962, 12ff.
5. Quoted in Thomas A. Bailey, *Presidential Greatness* (New York: Appleton-Century, 1966), 43.
6. Schlesinger, "The U.S. Presidents," 68.
7. Schlesinger, "Our Presidents."
8. Ibid.
9. Schlesinger, *Paths to the Present*, 110-111.
10. Gary Maranell, "The Evaluation of Presidents: An Extension of the Schlesinger Polls," *Journal of American History* (June 1970): 104-113.
11. Steve Neal, "Our Best and Worst Presidents," *Chicago Tribune Magazine*, January 10, 1982, 9-18.
12. See, for example, Fred I. Greenstein, *The Hidden-Hand Presidency: Eisenhower as Leader* (New York: Basic Books, 1982); Murray Kempton, "The Underestimation of Dwight D. Eisenhower," *Esquire*, vol. 68 (September 1967), 108-109, 156; and Garry Wills, *Nixon Agonistes: The Crisis of the Self-Made Man* (Boston: Houghton-Mifflin, 1970).
13. Robert K. Murray and Tim H. Blessing, "The Presidential Performance Study: A Progress Report," *Journal of American History* (December 1983): 535-555. The results of all the polls discussed in this chapter are listed in this article.
14. Bailey, *Presidential Greatness*, 40-41, 43.
15. Ibid., chaps. 4-5.
16. Ibid.
17. Nelson Polsby, "Against Presidential Greatness," *Commentary*, January 1977, 61-64.

General Dynamics

Campaign buttons are symbolic of the U.S. electoral process.

Part II

Selection and Removal of the President

The Electoral Process

By contemporary standards, the early days of presidential politics seem quaint. The Founders premised their insulated system on the ability of an "electoral college" of the nation's most virtuous and learned men to rise above petty factions and select leaders with national vision. The early system aspired to be a *republic,* in which sovereign power resides in the electorate and is exercised by elected representatives of the people. *Democracy,* in the sense of *direct* rule by the people, was considered a pejorative term.

Since George Washington was first elected in 1789, voter participation in U.S. presidential elections has grown steadily. In the nation's early elections, only the upper economic classes could participate. Over the years, however, as different political factions sought national leadership, the electoral process has been opened up. By 1971 virtually every adult citizen at least eighteen years of age was eligible to vote. The presidential campaigns of Andrew Jackson, Abraham Lincoln, William Jennings Bryan, Theodore Roosevelt, Woodrow Wilson, Franklin D. Roosevelt, and Lyndon B. Johnson all appealed, in different ways, to expanding electoral participation.

The process for electing the president not only has shifted political power from the few to the many; it also has become longer and more complex, more subject to the unintended consequences of reform and the changing technologies of business and everyday life.

Elections never have been as simple as candidates making appeals to greater and greater numbers of citizens. Today, every campaign organization mediates the relations between the candidate and the voter. It may seem at times as if the candidate is speaking directly to a voter, but every move has been influenced by campaign workers, the media, consultants, and public attitudes. A vast array of interlocking elements now require consideration in the campaign to elect one person president. People involved in a campaign include the candidate and his or her family, a running mate, political allies, campaign strategists, lawyers and accountants, television producers and consultants, schedulers and advance people, advertising experts, issues experts, fund-raisers, pollsters, computer analysts, and sometimes the incumbent president. Organizations affecting the campaign include corporations, labor unions, interest groups, public action committees, the national party, state parties, and third parties. Constitutional requirements for candidates and complex national and state campaign laws establish rules for the campaign. The campaign must direct itself toward state primaries and caucuses, conventions, televised debates, and the vote of the electoral college (and possibly the Congress). And not least among these diverse elements are the substantive and symbolic issues of the day.

By Charles C. Euchner and John Anthony Maltese

History of Presidential Elections

Presidential elections have been perhaps the most influential events in national politics, giving shape to dominant issues, the makeup of national parties and interest groups, regional economic and political alignments, and the way citizens understand and talk about society.

Campaigns for the White House have shaped U.S. politics in several stages and cycles. As the franchise has expanded and electronic media have exercised greater influence, presidential politics have become more broadbased and concerned about the way government can address the needs and demands of innumerable groups.

Presidential elections throughout U.S. history have been at the center of political controversies involving disputes between the branches of government, federalism, banking, tariffs and other taxes, economic change, corporate power, unions, international affairs, social welfare programs, and consumer issues.

Meanwhile, presidential politics also have moved in cycles of conservatism and liberalism, activism and consolidation, elitism and populism, isolationism and internationalism. Presidential elections have articulated the changing moods of the nation since the very first election.

Original Constitutional Provisions

The method of choosing the president proved to be but one of many vexing problems for the fifty-five men who assembled in Philadelphia in May 1787 to draft the Constitution. The Articles of Confederation, which the Constitution would replace, was riddled with weaknesses. *(See "Articles of Confederation," p. 1354 in the Appendix.)* Adopted in 1781, the Articles established an impotent federal government consisting of a weak congress and no single executive (although there was a "Committee of States" with no power worth speaking of that sat when the congress was not in session). By the time the Constitutional Convention convened, the Confederacy was but a "cobweb." [1]

From the start of the convention, it was clear that the federal government would be strengthened and that there would be some sort of executive branch. The convention was split, however, between those who wanted a strong executive (the "presidentialists") and those who were wary of executive authority and wanted to increase the power of the national legislature instead (the "congressionalists").[2]

There was also the question of whether the "national executive" should consist of several individuals or just one. Congressionalists wanted a plural executive with minimal power. Presidentialists wanted a strong executive with power vested in the hands of one individual. Debate over this point was extremely heated. *(See "Number of the Executive," p. 22, in Constitutional Beginnings chapter of Part I.)*

As it became clear that the executive power would be singular, the tension between the two camps shifted to the question of presidential selection. Congressionalists, anxious that the executive remain subservient to the legislature, wanted the president to be elected by Congress. Presidentialists, however, did not want Congress to exercise that power.

This issue remained unresolved for most of the summer. By the end of August there was still not a consensus on how to select the president. Therefore, that issue—along with other "questions not settled"—was sent to the Committee on Postponed Matters for resolution. Since the committee was dominated by presidentialists, it pushed for a proposal that would avoid legislative appointment. The result was a compromise that was reported to the convention on September 4, 1787, and that served, with little alteration, as the basis for the actual constitutional provision.

The compromise, as finally approved, provided for indirect election of the president by the so-called electoral college.[3] This system allowed each state to appoint (in the manner directed by its own legislature) the same number of electors as it had senators and representatives in Congress. (Virginia, for example, had two senators and ten representatives in Congress and so could choose twelve electors.) Those electors would then meet in their respective states and vote by ballot for two persons (at least one of whom must be from a state other than that inhabited by the elector). When the ballots of all the electors from all the states were tallied, the candidate with the greatest number of votes would become president (assuming it was a majority), and the second-place candidate would become vice president. In case of a tie, or if no candidate received a majority, the decision would be made by the House of Representatives.[4]

The compromise won the support of the convention because it so successfully placated all parties concerned. First of all, it provided for the president to be selected by electors. This satisfied the presidentialists who were opposed to appointment by Congress. It also satisfied those who were wary of direct election by the masses. Electors, it was thought, would infuse an element of reason into the selection process, thereby stabilizing the whims of mass opinion.

Second, individual state legislatures were allowed to determine how electors would be chosen in their respective states. The language of the clause left open a wide range of options for that process. As a result, the convention did not have to agree upon one method of appointing electors for all the states.

Third, if no candidate received a majority, the election would be decided by the House of Representatives. Since it was widely assumed that no candidate after George Washington would receive a majority of votes from the electors, many thought that selection by the House would become the norm. Thus, congressionalists could argue that they had lost the battle but won the war. From their perspective, electors usually would nominate candidates, and the House would select the winner.

Finally, since each elector voted for two persons—one of whom could not be the from the elector's state—"favorite son" candidates would tend to cancel one another out. This helped to dispel the fear that large states would consistently elect their own favorite sons. Nevertheless, since the number of electors from each state would equal the state's total number of senators and representatives in Congress, the relative weight of more populous states would not be discounted.

The Framers' View of Parties

Whatever the particular motivations of the Framers, it is clear that they were proponents of moderation. It is also clear that they held a quite different understanding of the presidential selection process than that which is generally accepted today. Most notably, the Framers envisaged a nonpartisan process. Political parties (or "factions") were viewed as a political evil. The goal of the selection process was to promote men of civic virtue who would be able to exercise unfettered judgment.

The Framers' view of political parties was a natural outgrowth of the Anglo-American tradition. Opposition parties are now considered an essential part of representative democracy, but the Framers believed they would cause tumult and discord. Political scientist Richard Hofstadter has argued that, in eighteenth-century British political thought, there were three archetypal views of party that could have influenced the Framers.[5]

The first, which he called "the Hamiltonian view" (since it is a position associated with Alexander Hamilton) was based on the antiparty doctrine of Bolingbroke, an English statesman, who wrote two important pamphlets on politics in the 1730s. For Bolingbroke, the best sort of state would be led by a "patriot king"—a benign monarch who would subdue factions by good statecraft. To him, parties were by definition antithetical to the common good. Nevertheless, he conceived of instances when a uniting "country party" speaking for the nation as a whole rather than particular interests could be used to restore stability in a state.

The second view, which Hofstadter termed "Madisonian" after James Madison was based on the writings of the eighteenth-century Scottish philosopher David Hume. Like Bolingbroke, Hume thought that parties were evil, but unlike Bolingbroke he thought that their existence was inevitable in a free state. Champions of liberty could check and limit the excesses of parties, but they could not abolish them. Madison expressed this view in *Federalist* No. 10, concluding that the only satisfactory method of "curing the mischiefs of faction" was to control their effects. To remove their cause would be to destroy liberty.

Finally, Hofstadter pointed to the views of British statesman Edmund Burke, who felt that parties were not only inevitable, but—for the most part—good. But Burke's writing, published in 1770, came too late to influence the Framers at the Constitutional Convention. Instead, both the Federalists and Anti-Federalists condemned parties. Each side hoped to eliminate the other, thus forming a united nonpartisan state. From their perspective, the common good would triumph over the petty rivalries and selfish interests that political parties would produce.

Thus, the Framers adhered to one or the other of Hofstadter's first two archetypes. It was the resulting doctrine of nonpartisanship that allowed for the original vice-presidential selection process. Since the Framers did not contemplate partisan contests among candidates, they did not foresee a problem with having the second-place candidate become vice president.

Voting Requirements

Aside from the Framers' views of political parties, the electorate in the eighteenth century was quite different from the electorate today. The Constitution left it up to the states to determine voting requirements. In all states, only men could vote. Furthermore, in many states property ownership was a prerequisite for the right to vote. Indeed, property qualifications had existed in all the colonies and endured in many of the states, although the exact qualifications differed among states. Colonial restrictions tended to be harsher than those adopted by the states and were often based on a measure of real estate. Some colonies, such as Massachusetts, even had religious qualifications for voting.[6]

Virginia—the home of some of the most important members of the Constitutional Convention and four of the first five presidents—is a good example. Property possession had been a prerequisite for the vote there since 1677. From 1705 until 1736, the laws were quite liberal: any male tenant who held land for life (his own or that of another person such as his wife or child) was considered a "freeholder" and could vote. In other words, as a qualification to vote, leasing property for the duration of one's own lifetime or for that of a family member was the equivalent of owning property. From 1736 onward, the definition of *freeholder* was more restrictive. A man living in the country had to hold twenty-five acres of cultivated land with a house, or one hundred acres (changed to fifty in 1762) of uncleared land with no settlement, in order to vote. A man living in town had to hold a house with a lot.[7] By the standards of the time, those requirements were not excessive.[8]

The American Revolution brought no suffrage reform to Virginia, although it did to other states. The Virginia constitution of 1776 stated that voting requirements "shall remain as exercised at present."[9] Thus, even those who paid taxes or fought in the militia could not vote unless they held the requisite amount of land. By 1800, Virginia was one of five states that retained real estate property qualifications. (At the other extreme, four states had established universal manhood suffrage by 1800.) While various other states allowed personal property or the payment of taxes to substitute for holding real estate, Virginia held on to its old property qualifications until 1830. By that time it was the only state to retain freehold suffrage throughout. Even the reform of 1830 brought little change. Householders were added to the franchise—a very modest step toward universal manhood suffrage.[10]

Property requirements of one sort or another were not abandoned by all the states until 1856. It is not entirely clear how much of the electorate was excluded by property requirements; historians differ on this point, sometimes quite markedly.[11] However, one should keep in mind that the effect of property qualifications—while certainly restrictive—can be overstated. Because the United States was predominantly a middle class society with fairly widespread ownership of property, such qualifications were not as significant a limit as they may first appear.

Different conceptions of political parties and suffrage than we are accustomed to today were part of the milieu in which the original constitutional provision for presidential selection was created. Elements of that provision soon proved to be flawed and were superseded by the Twelfth Amendment, which provided for presidential and vice-presidential votes to be tallied on separate ballots. Nevertheless, the provision met the needs of the moment: it was an acceptable compromise of the diverse positions both within the Constitutional Convention and among the states that would ratify it.

Early Experience, 1789-1828

The years 1789 to 1828 saw a tremendous change in many of the concepts and institutions that the Framers had envisaged. Nonpartisan elections did not last even a decade. Deadlock in the election of 1800 forced the young nation to change the method of choosing the vice president. Restrictions on the right to vote were eased. A system of nominating presidential candidates by congressional caucus was developed, then overturned. And the original understanding of the function of electors was significantly altered.

Selection of Electors and the Role of the Electoral College

The Constitution provided that each state appoint electors "in such manner as the legislature thereof may direct." As a result, diverse methods for choosing electors were used throughout the country. In some states the legislature appointed the electors, either by joint ballot (both houses voting together) or a concurrent vote (both houses voting separately). Others used popular election on a statewide general ticket; still others, popular election by districts. There were also mixed systems in which electors were chosen partly by the people in districts and partly by the state legislature, or by the legislature from nominees voted by the people, or by the legislature from among the top candidates if there was no majority in the popular vote.[12] It was even suggested during the Constitutional Convention that electors be chosen by lot, although no state adopted that method.[13]

The first group of presidential electors was chosen on the first Wednesday of January 1789. Only three states (Maryland, Pennsylvania, and Virginia) used direct popular election. New Hampshire also called for popular election, but required that an elector receive a majority vote to win. When a majority was not forthcoming, the election was thrown to the legislature. Five states (Connecticut, Delaware, Georgia, New Jersey, and South Carolina) used legislative appointment to choose electors. Massachusetts preferred a mixed system, and New York—deadlocked between its Federalist senate and its Anti-Federalist house—could not agree and chose no electors. North Carolina and

Library of Congress

A war hero from Virginia and presiding officer of the Constitutional Convention, George Washington, more than six feet tall, was the very symbol of legitimacy for the new republic.

Rhode Island had not yet ratified the Constitution and therefore did not participate.

It seems that members of Congress assumed that state legislatures would appoint the electors, at least for the first election. They had allowed less than four months (from September 13, 1788, to the first Wednesday in January 1789) for the electoral system to be implemented—not much time given the slowness of communication and the amount of work to be done. Distant states would not learn of Congress's directive for two weeks or more. The states then had to call their legislatures into session (itself time-consuming), pass laws providing for the selection of electors (which often entailed lengthy and acrimonious debate), canvass and choose the electors, and arrange for the electors to meet and vote. Often there was not time to make the necessary provisions for popular election, even if that were the preferred method of selection.[14]

Nevertheless, appointment of electors by state legislatures continued to be the norm in the election of 1792; nine states—Connecticut, Delaware, Georgia, Kentucky, New Jersey, New York, Rhode Island, South Carolina, and Vermont—used that method. Electors were chosen by popular election on a general ticket in Maryland and Pennsylvania, and by popular election with districts in Virginia. Massachusetts also called for popular election within districts but required a majority to win. In five districts, majorities were achieved; in the nine others, the General Court (the Massachusetts legislative body) chose the electors. New Hampshire had a mixed system in which both the people and the legislature chose the electors.[15]

By 1792, Congress had changed the dates for elections. Electors were required to cast their votes on the first Wednesday in December, with electors to be chosen in each state within the thirty-four days preceding that.[16] This change caused a problem for North Carolina, which had undergone reapportionment after the 1790 census. The reapportionment became law on April 13, 1792, but North Carolina's legislature was out of session and did not meet again until November 15. Since electors had to be chosen by December 5, there was not time to provide for popular election. As a result, the state was divided into four districts. Members of the state legislature residing in each district met on November 25 and chose three electors. That unusual arrangement was never used again in any state. Before adjourning, the legislature made a provision for electors to be chosen by popular election in districts in future years.[17]

After the first three presidential elections (1788, 1792, and 1796), popular vote increasingly became the preferred method of choosing electors. By 1824, only six of twenty-four states still used legislative appointment (Delaware, Georgia, Louisiana, New York, South Carolina, and Vermont).[18] From 1832 until 1860, all states except South Carolina chose electors by popular vote. Since 1860, only Colorado in 1876 has used legislative appointment.[19]

After 1832, *popular vote* came to mean popular vote by general ticket. The notion of election by a general ticket encompassed three things. First, it meant that the electors were chosen by the people of the state at large (as opposed to in districts). Second, it involved the so-called unit rule. The unit rule meant that electors for each party were grouped together on a general ticket for each party and were elected as a bloc. In other words, a vote for one elector on a general ticket was equivalent to a vote for all the electors of that ticket. Often electors' names did not even appear on the ballot; instead people voted for the ticket of a particular party. Third, general tickets involved the concept of "winner take all." The general ticket with a plurality of votes won. Thus, the winning ticket consisted of all the electors representing that state. Electors were not divided in proportion to the popular vote.[20]

General tickets were closely associated with the rise of partisan contests, since under the general ticket system, voters selected a party rather than individual electors. In the process, the nature of the electoral college was changed. The Framers of the Constitution had expected electors to act as free agents, exercising individual (that is, nonpartisan) judgment in their selection of the president. Instead, the electoral college was transformed into a contingent of party proxies. As Supreme Court Justice Robert Jackson wrote in *Ray v. Blair:* "Electors, although often personally eminent, independent, and respectable, officially became voluntary party lackeys and intellectual nonentities.... As an institution the electoral college suffered atrophy almost indistinguishable from *rigor mortis.*"[21] In addition to increasing the power of political parties, the general ticket system allowed states to maximize their influence in the election. Rather than scattering their electors among many candidates, the system consolidated each state's electors behind the candidate who received the most votes.

In 1801, Alexander Hamilton drafted a constitutional amendment that would have prohibited the selection of electors by general ticket or by state legislatures, but it was rejected.[22] Rather, the selection of electors by general ticket became so much the norm that when Michigan passed a law in 1891 providing for the election of presidential electors by congressional districts instead of by general ticket, the law was contested and ultimately made its way to the Supreme Court. In that case (*McPherson v. Blacker*), the Court stated that the Constitution had clearly provided state legislatures with plenary, or full, power to prescribe the method of choosing electors; the fact that states had come to adopt a uniform method of selection did not in any way reduce that power.[23] Since then, only Maine (from 1972 on) has used the district system; all other states (including Michigan, which quickly returned to its former system) have chosen their electors by general ticket.

Emergence of Parties

Although the electoral system was undemocratic by modern standards, George Washington's unanimous election as president in 1788 and 1792 has been described as "a triumph of popular will."[24] More than six feet tall, he was—at the age of fifty-five—the very symbol of legitimacy: a hero who held the confidence of virtually all the people. As the presiding officer of the Constitutional Convention he had lent credence, if not discourse, to their enterprise. (During the entire span of the convention, he spoke only once, and on a minor issue.)[25] Now he would lend credence to the new government.

There is no record of any elector expressing opposition to the election of Washington. Each elector had to vote for two persons, however, with the candidate having the second highest number of votes becoming vice president. In the days before the electors met, it was the "talk about town" that the vice president should be a person who complemented Washington: he should be from a northern state and be a civilian. It was also suggested that he should not have to vacate an office in which his services were needed. John Adams—a short, stocky, bald New Englander—fit all of those qualifications, and he soon came to be regarded as the candidate for vice president.

Adams, however, was a proud man who felt he was on an equal footing with Washington: technically they were, after all, both candidates for the presidency. There was no separate ballot for the office of vice president; whoever came in second would fill that post. As a result, some of the electors began to worry: if Adams came to be regarded as the candidate for vice president, he could conceivably get the same number of votes as Washington. At best, such a situation would be an embarrassment; at worst, it could degenerate into a divisive power struggle. To avoid this situation, Hamilton maneuvered to siphon votes away from Adams. In so doing, he earned Adams's scorn, thus creating a split that would prove to be important in the coming years. In the end, all of the electors cast one of their votes for Washington, giving him a total electoral count of sixty-nine. Adams received thirty-four electoral votes, and the thirty-five other votes were divided among ten other candidates.[26]

Washington expressed no particular liking for politics, and after two terms in office he decided not to run for reelection (although there was nothing in the Constitution, nor was there any law, that would have prevented him from doing so). Although much has been made of Washington's precedent of serving only two terms, his decision to retire seems mainly personal. Indications are that he would have preferred to retire after one term had he felt able to do so without adversely affecting the young nation.[27] He informed his closest associates of his decision early in 1796, and by autumn it was public knowledge. The first two presidential elections had been nonpartisan; in each, the will of the people had been clear. Neither would be the case again.

Library of Congress

A civilian and former minister to France and Great Britain, John Adams, a short, stocky, bald New Englander, was considered an excellent complement to Washington. He soon come to be regarded as the candidate for the vice presidency.

There is marked difference of opinion over just when political parties really emerged in this country and what specific events triggered their development.[28] George Washington was avowedly nonpartisan. Still, he did not appoint staunch Anti-Federalists (or Democratic-Republicans, as they were also known) to positions in his administration. To do so, he thought, would put the Constitution at risk. *(See box, When and Why Did Parties Begin? p. 59.)*

Nonetheless, splits developed within the new government. Secretary of the Treasury Alexander Hamilton lobbied Congress for passage of administration programs such as an excise tax and the establishment of a national bank, but opposition arose from James Madison (then a member of the House of Representatives) and others. In the cabinet, Hamilton and Secretary of State Thomas Jefferson often disagreed. Federalists, such as Hamilton, believed in a strong central government led by a vigorous executive; Democratic-Republicans, such as Jefferson and Madison, were more concerned with states' rights and the will of the people as expressed through the legislature.

Newspapers both reflected and widened those splits. In 1789, Hamilton established a newspaper—the *Gazette of the United States*—to serve as the official mouthpiece of the administration and, not coincidentally, of the Federalist position.[29] In return, the newspaper was awarded government patronage in the form of printing orders from the Treasury Department and, for a time, through the printing of the laws.[30]

In 1791, Jefferson was instrumental in establishing a rival newspaper—the *National Gazette*—to serve as the voice of the Democratic-Republican position. When Jefferson left Washington's cabinet in 1793, his *Gazette* was replaced by the rabidly pro-Democratic-Republican paper, the *Aurora*. The polarized positions of the rival papers and their exchanges of editorial attacks attracted attention thoughout the country. Such exchanges went to extremes in both personal and policy-oriented attacks. The *Aurora*, for instance, deemed most of President Washington's acts unconstitutional, accused the president of overdrawing his salary, and labeled him "a frail mortal, whose passions and weaknesses are like those of other men, a spoiled child, a despot, an anemic imitation of the English kings." [31] On another occasion, the *Aurora* proclaimed: "If ever a nation was debauched by a man, the American nation has been debauched by Washington. If ever a nation has suffered from the improper influence of a man, the American nation has suffered from the influence of Washington. If ever a nation was deceived by a man, the American nation has been deceived by Washington." [32]

Events abroad exacerbated splits in the government. The French Revolution was under way, and in 1793 France declared war on England. Although the United States remained officially neutral, passions ran high. Federalists denounced the Democratic-Republicans as being populist radicals who wanted to undermine the authority of the executive through a powerful legislature. Democratic-Republicans condemned the Federalists as being a pseudo-British party of aristocratic monarchists.[33]

The 1796 Election. Although there was no formal party machinery, the election of 1796 was a de facto contest between the Federalists and the Democratic-Republicans. The Democratic-Republicans had recently formed a congressional caucus, but it was not convened for the purpose of choosing candidates. That Jefferson would be chosen as the presidential nominee was obvious, and although there was no clear agreement on a vice-presidential candidate, that problem was not considered of sufficient importance to call the caucus into session.[34] An informal meeting on the choice of a running mate ended with the issue unresolved.

Federalist members of Congress appear to have discussed their choice of candidates in the summer of 1796. Hamilton was considered but rejected since he had made many enemies during the Washington administration. John Jay also was rejected, primarily because he had negotiated a controversial treaty with England. The Federalists finally placed their support behind Vice President Adams. Thomas Pinckney of South Carolina was the Federalists' choice for vice president since it was thought that he would take votes away from Jefferson (a Virginian) in the South.

In September 1796, Washington delivered his famous Farewell Address. *(See "Washington's Farewell Address," p. 1365, in the Appendix.)* The speech, written with Hamilton's help, warned against the dangers of parties. While the speech was largely a response to the divisiveness of recent events, it is likely that his denunciation of parties was a veiled attack on the Democratic-Republicans.[35] He cited "the common and continual mischiefs of the spirit of Party" and said that this was "sufficient to make it the interest and the duty of wise people to discourage and restrain it." Elaborating on the spirit of parties and its baneful effects, Washington said:

> It serves always to distract the public councils and enfeeble the public administration. It agitates the community with ill founded jealousies and false alarms, kindles the animosity of one part against another, foments occasionally riot and insurrection. It opens the door to foreign influence and corruption, which find a facilitated access to the government itself through the channels of party passions. . . . A fire not to be quenched; it demands a uniform vigilance to prevent its bursting into flame, lest instead of warming it should consume.[36]

Despite Washington's warning, the election of 1796 quicky became an intensely partisan contest. Newspapers fanned the flames as the Federalist press attacked Jefferson and the pro-Democratic-Republican *Aurora* attacked Adams.[37]

By the time the campaign was in full swing, it was understood that the Democratic-Republicans' vice-presidential candidate was Aaron Burr from New York. When the electors met to choose the winners, however, the weakness of the selection process became apparent. As designed, the system did not take into account partisan contests. No provision was made for candidates from the same party to be elected as a team. Although Pennsylvania, for example, chose electors by party tickets, party organization was largely ephemeral. The electors of South Carolina, for example, did not follow party lines in their choice. There the electors voted for an all-southern ticket with the Democratic-Republican Jefferson and the Federalist Pinckney splitting the votes equally. In the North, electors did not give equal support to Adams and Pinckney since they were fearful that Pinckney's vote might exceed that of Adams. It appears that Hamilton, who urged northern electors to give equal support to the two Federalist candidates, actually hoped that Pinckney would upset Adams.

There was still no separate ballot for vice president, so the candidate with the second highest number of electoral votes was assigned that office. As a result, John Adams was elected president with seventy-one electoral votes, and his rival from the Democratic-Republican party, Thomas Jefferson, was named his vice president with sixty-eight electoral votes. Pinckney came in third with fifty-nine electoral votes, and Burr trailed a distant fourth with thirty.

The 1800 Election. The election of 1796 had served as a portent to the problems of the existing presidential selection process. The election of 1800 proved them. Adams and Gen. Charles Cotesworth Pinckney of South Carolina were nominated as the Federalist candidates by a caucus of Federalist senators and representatives in the spring of 1800. Around the same time, a caucus of forty-three Democratic-Republican senators and representatives convened. Once again there was no question that Jefferson would be the candidate for president. Rather, the caucus met to designate a candidate for vice president and unanimously nominated Aaron Burr.[38]

When the electors voted in December 1800, it turned out that the two Democratic-Republican candidates, Jefferson and Burr, tied for first place. In accord with the constitutional provision, the election was thrown to the

When and Why Did Parties Begin?

Although there is no precise date for the beginning of parties, both Alexander Hamilton (a Federalist) and Thomas Jefferson (a Democratic-Republican) referred to the existence of a Jeffersonian republican "faction" in Congress as early as 1792.

The two competing parties developed as a result of public sentiment for and against adoption of the Constitution. The Federalist party—a loose coalition of merchants, shippers, financiers and other business interests—favored the strong central government provided by the Constitution. Their opponents were intent upon preservation of state sovereignty. Underlying the controversy was the Federalists' desire to create a government with power to guarantee the value of the currency (and thus protect the position of creditors) and the desire of the Democratic-Republican agrarians and frontier settlers to maintain easy credit conditions. The Democratic-Republicans also wanted to protect state legislatures against encroachments by a remote federal government.

Although party organization became more formalized in the 1790s and early 1800s, the Federalists never considered themselves a political party but rather a gentlemanly coalition of interests representing respectable society. What party management there was, they kept clandestine, a reflection of their own fundamental suspicion of parties. The Jeffersonians achieved a high degree of organization but never acquired a nationally accepted name. They most commonly referred to themselves as "Republicans." (In his conciliatory inaugural address of 1801, Jefferson said, "We are all republicans; we are all federalists.") Their opponents labeled them "Anti-Federalists," "disorganizers," "Jacobins," and "Democrats"—the latter an unflattering term in the early years of the Republic. To many Americans in the late eighteenth century, a democrat was considered a supporter of mob rule and revolution and often ideologically identified with the bloody French Revolution.

The designation "Democrat-Republican" was used by the Jeffersonians in several states but was never widely accepted as a party label. Historians often refer to the Jeffersonians as the "Democratic-Republicans," however, to avoid confusion with the later and unrelated Republican party founded in 1854.

Although the early American political leaders acknowledged the development of parties, they did not foresee the emergence of a two-party system. Rather, they often justified the existence of their own party as a reaction to an unacceptable opposition. Jefferson defended his party involvement as a struggle between good and evil: "[When] the principle of difference is as substantial and as strongly pronounced as between the republicans and the Monocrats of our country, I hold it as honorable to take a firm and decided part, and as immoral to pursue a middle line, as between the parties of Honest men, and Rogues, into which every country is divided."

House of Representatives (which was dominated by Federalists). Although it was common knowledge that Jefferson was the presidential candidate and Burr was the vice-presidential candidate, some Federalists considered Burr the lesser evil and plotted to elect him president. Hamilton, cognizant of the new nation's delicate balance, roundly discouraged the idea. In a letter to Gouverneur Morris he wrote: "I trust the Federalists will not finally be so mad as to vote for Burr.... His elevation can only promote the purposes of the desperate and profligate. If there be a man in the world I ought to hate, it is Jefferson. With Burr I have always been personally well. But the public good must be paramount to every private consideration." [39] Nevertheless, most Federalists continued to support Burr.

The Constitution required that when the election was thrown to the House, a majority of all the states was required to elect. On Wednesday, February 11, 1801, the House met to vote. On the first ballot, Jefferson received the votes of eight states, and Burr the votes of six. Two states were divided. There was no majority. The House balloted eighteen more times that day with no change in the outcome. Balloting continued through Saturday, February 14, and resumed on Monday. In all, there were thirty-six ballots. The tide finally turned on Tuesday, February 17. Jefferson received a majority, with the votes of ten states. On March 4, there was a peaceful transfer of power. In his inaugural address, Jefferson offered a conciliatory note: "We are all republicans; we are all federalists."

The Twelfth Amendment

It was evident from the problems of 1796 and 1800 that the constitutional provision for presidential selection was flawed. Even before the election of 1800, Vermont had adopted a resolution calling for a constitutional amendment. Similar resolutions were introduced in Congress in 1802, but they were defeated. When the Eighth Congress convened in October 1803, the matter of a constitutional amendment was considered at great length. After much debate, the resolution for an amendment was passed December 8, 1803. The amendment was ratified by the states with unusual speed. It was officially adopted as the Twelfth Amendment to the Constitution September 25, 1804. Thirteen states ratified it; three (Connecticut, Delaware, and Massachusetts) dissented.[40] *(See box, Twelfth Amendment, p. 43.)*

The Twelfth Amendment called for electors to vote for president and vice president on separate ballots. If none of the candidates for president had a majority, the House of Representatives would choose the winner from no more than the top three candidates. As before, a majority of the states in the House was needed to elect. If none of the candidates for vice president had a majority, the winner would be chosen from the top two vice-presidential candidates by a majority of the whole number of senators. As a result, the vice presidency was no longer awarded to the runner-up (in theory, the second-most-qualified person to be president). *(See also "Twelfth Amendment," p. 42, in Constitutional Amendments chapter of Part I.)*

Congressional Caucus Nominating System

By 1804, it was customary for presidential candidates to be nominated by a caucus comprising members of Congress from their party. To some degree, this approximated what the congressionalists had wanted at the Constitutional Convention: selection of the executive by the legislature. The Democratic-Republican caucus nominated Jefferson in 1800 and 1804, although the real purpose of the caucus in those two years was the selection of a candidate for vice president. In 1808, the Democratic-Republican caucus nominated James Madison for president and George Clinton of New York (already vice president under Jefferson) as his running mate. Madison was renominated by a near unanimous vote of the caucus in 1812. Initially, John Langdon of New Hampshire was chosen as his running mate, but he declined the nomination because of his age. (He turned seventy-one in 1812.) At a second caucus, Massachusetts governor Elbridge Gerry was nominated for vice president. In 1816, James Monroe was nominated by a vote of sixty-five to fifty-four over William H. Crawford of Georgia, with New York governor Daniel D. Tompkins as his running mate.

By 1820, the Federalist party was virtually dead. The Federalists had performed dismally in presidential elections ever since their narrow loss in 1800. There is no record of how they selected their candidates in 1804. In 1808 and 1812, their candidates were chosen by secret meetings of Federalist leaders in New York. By 1816 they had given up nominating candidates for president. According to historian Edward Stanwood, "Nothing whatever was done to nominate candidates in opposition to Monroe and [Daniel C.] Tompkins. On December 3, the day before the electors were to vote, the 'Boston Daily Advertiser,' published in one of the three states which had chosen Federal electors, remarked: 'We do not know, nor is it very material, for whom the Federal electors will vote.' "[41] (They voted for Rufus King.) In 1820, Monroe ran unopposed. With virtual one-party rule, nomination by the Democratic-Republican's "King Caucus" was tantamount to election.

In 1824, however, King Caucus was dethroned. There had been objections to the caucus system from the start. In 1808, when Sen. Stephen Bradley of Vermont conveyed notice to the Democratic-Republican members of the House and Senate that the caucus would meet, a representative from Virginia published a response that said, in part: "I cannot ... countenance, by my presence, the midnight intrigues of any set of men who may arrogate to themselves the right, which belongs only to the people, of selecting proper persons to fill the important offices of president and vice president."[42] After Madison's nomination by the caucus in 1808, seventeen Democratic-Republican members of Congress signed a protest against the system. Even Vice President Clinton, who was nominated by the caucus, expressed disapproval of it. They did so because they felt the caucus system was undemocratic. Citizens had no direct say in the nomination, and those states and districts not represented by the party in Congress were effectively disenfranchised.

At the Democratic-Republican caucus in 1824, only 66 of 261 members of Congress were present (three-quarters of whom were from only four states). By the time the caucus met, five serious candidates had emerged—all with roughly equal strength: John Quincy Adams, John C. Calhoun, Henry Clay, William H. Crawford, and Andrew Jackson. Crawford won the caucus nomination, and Albert Gallatin of Pennsylvania was chosen as his running mate. The other candidates, however, refused to follow the decision of the caucus. In his home state of Tennessee, Jackson was nominated by the state legislature, which also passed a resolution condemning the caucus system. Kentucky did the same for Clay. Among the candidates, Calhoun was the only one to withdraw.

When the electoral college met to determine the winner of the general election, Crawford came in third with forty-one votes. His running mate had withdrawn from the race in October. Jackson received the most popular and the most electoral votes, but not a majority of either (ninety-nine electoral votes to Adams's eighty-four). Clay came in fourth with thirty-seven. Since there was no majority in the electoral college, the election was thrown to the House of Representatives. In the House, John Quincy Adams was elected president.

Ironically, the Democratic-Republican caucus died when its party was at its zenith, largely because other candidates within the party would not acquiesce to the choice of the caucus. But the demise of the caucus also reflected the growing democratization of the political system. By 1824, only six states still chose electors by legislative appointment; all the other states did so by popular election. Mass participation in presidential elections was increasing dramatically. Furthermore, there was a trend toward expansion of suffrage (the right to vote). As early as 1791, Vermont had instituted universal manhood suffrage. Kentucky and New Hampshire followed suit in 1792, as did Indiana in 1816. By 1824, most states had dropped property restrictions on voting, although several still retained tax-paying restrictions. Mississippi, which entered the Union in 1817, was the last state to institute tax-paying restrictions, and these were dropped in 1832.[43] The caucus system was a holdover from an age that distrusted mass democratic sentiments. That age was dying.

Finally, the caucus's selection of the staid William Crawford over the frontier hero Andrew Jackson and the subsequent House selection in 1824 of second-place Adams over the popular favorite Jackson was the kiss of death—not only to the Democratic-Republican caucus but to the Democratic-Republican party as well.

Major Developments, 1828-1988

After the election of 1828, party alignments crystallized, and the United States began to develop what would become the most stable two-party system in the world. Party conventions were held regularly beginning in 1831, and presidential primaries took their place in party politics shortly after the turn of the century. Throughout the nineteenth and twentieth centuries, the electorate continued to expand as blacks, women, and other groups in U.S. society won the right to vote.

The Two-Party System

In 1828, Jackson swept into the presidency as the head of the newly formed Democratic party. The Democratic-Republicans had split earlier in the decade over an issue that would divide U.S. politics to the present day—the

Drawing by Howard Pyle for Harper's Weekly, 1881; Library of Congress

Andrew Jackson was greeted by enthusiastic crowds as he traveled from Tennessee to Washington for his inauguration in 1829. Capturing the spirit of America's expanding frontier, "Old Hickory" inaugurated the age of popular politics.

protective tariff. *(See box, Tariffs in U.S. Politics, p. 195.)* Under the "American system" of Henry Clay, the United States would use high tariffs both to protect nascent domestic industries and to fund internal improvements. After his election as president in 1824, Adams adopted much of Clay's program. Agrarian interests resisted the high tariffs because of the higher costs for finished products and the investment bias given to the North and West. Jackson emerged as the agrarian hero.

The geographic and economic expansion of the nation and the development of a more broad-based national party organization reached a peak under Jackson, who inaugurated an age of popular politics.

The Democrats and the Whigs. Jackson was an activist president from the start. His programs for internal improvements, decentralization of the U.S. Bank's assets, and control of the federal bureaucracy were landmarks in U.S. history. *(See "The Jacksonian Presidency," p. 70, in History of the Presidency chapter of Part I.)*

In reaction to Jackson's populism, a collection of aggrieved interests pulled together under the Whig party. The Whigs aimed to restore moderate policies and end what they considered to be an era of "mob rule" that gave the president excessive authority. Two military heroes, William Henry Harrison and Zachary Taylor, won presidential elections under the Whig banner. But the Whigs suffered two ills: the lack of a sophisticated national organization and contradictions within the party that could not be overcome—such as the diverse geographic, economic, and cultural backgrounds of its members. The rise of industrialism and a religious-based abolition movement in the North made Whig party unity impossible at midcentury.

In the 1836 election the Whigs fielded a set of regional candidates against Jackson's vice president, Democrat Martin Van Buren. By running several regional candidates rather than one national candidate, the Whigs hoped to send the election to the House. Van Buren easily won, however. The fact that their presidential victories came with the nomination of military heroes points to the organizational weakness of the Whigs. Only charismatic leadership could temporarily overcome growing Whig schisms and the lack of organization.

Slavery split the Whigs badly. As the abolitionist movement grew in northern states, the Whigs had difficulty appealing to southerners. By 1856, the Whigs were replaced by the Republican party.

Library of Congress

The Whigs nominated two military heroes for president: William Henry Harrison in 1840, left, and Zachary Taylor in 1848, right. The party picked such charismatic figures for leadership to compensate for deep schisms and poor organization.

The Republicans ran their first national campaign in 1856, when John Charles Fremont ran against Democrat James Buchanan. The Republicans lost in 1856 but won the White House in 1860 when a former Whig, Abraham Lincoln, defeated the divided Democratic party. The Republicans dominated U.S. politics for the next seven decades. The Republican founding stemmed from anger over the Kansas-Nebraska Act of 1854, which allowed new territories to decide whether to enter the union as either slave or free states. Republicans were a collection of groups antagonized by the major parties. Many Whigs were abolitionists, but even more Whigs simply opposed the extension of slavery into new territories. Republicans favored a homestead law (which would give settlers land in exchange for their commitment to settle and develop it), an extensive system of internal improvements, the protective tariff, and principles of more centralized control of the federal government. The Republicans were able to overcome the divisions that the slavery issue created in the 1840s and 1850s. But the Democrats were increasingly vulnerable. By supporting extension of slavery into the new territories and opposing high tariffs, the Democrats lost any hope of building an alliance with northern industrialists who were becoming a greater force in U.S. politics.

Republican Dominance. After the Union won the Civil War, the Republicans dominated U.S. politics with little opposition. Between 1860 and 1932, the Democrats won the presidency only in 1884 and 1892 (with Grover Cleveland on the ticket) and 1912 and 1916 (with Woodrow Wilson).

The electoral bargain that settled the election of 1876—in which Republican Rutherford B. Hayes won the presidency even though Democrat Samuel Tilden won the popular vote—created an electoral crisis that eventually led to creation of a new party alignment. After long negotiations, Hayes was declared the winner. As part of the election deal, the Republicans agreed to pull federal troops out of the South and increase federal funding for internal improvements. As soon as the troops left the old Confederacy, the Democrats took over and disenfranchised blacks through an elaborate set of racially discriminatory, or "Jim Crow," laws. The Republicans maintained national hegemony through vigorous pursuit of a national economic policy. The federal government aided economic expansion with a high-tariff system, funding of exploration and transportation, limitations on labor unions, and tight-money policies. When the Democrats won the presidency under Cleveland, the nation still followed conservative policies. Particularly on labor relations and monetary policy—the most important issues of the time—Cleveland pursued basically Republican policies.

The Democrats became vulnerable toward the end of the century as discontent among the nation's farmers reached an almost revolutionary pitch. Farmers were hurt by the high-tariff and tight-money policies that Republicans promoted, which depressed farm prices and inflated the costs of the manufactured and imported goods that farmers needed to buy. One solution to the problem was unlimited coinage of silver to expand the money supply.

Not only did the Democratic party develop splits because of the Populist uprising in western states, but it also faced a Republican party that established better financing and organization to meet the challenge. The 1896 election, in which the Republican William McKinley defeated Democrat William Jennings Bryan for the presidency, solidified Republican dominance of U.S. politics.

Woodrow Wilson, a former political scientist at Princeton University who became a reform governor of New Jersey, was the only Democrat to win the White House in the quarter-century after the McKinley-Bryan showdown in 1896. Elected to the first of two terms in 1912, Wilson helped the Democrats take control of Congress and produced a unique period of party-government activism. Wilson's reforms covered antitrust laws, labor relations, banking regulations, women's suffrage, and international law.

But the Democrats' ascendance in national politics was short-lived, largely because of the bitterness that accompanied the end of World War I. President Wilson's failed attempt to get Senate approval of the Versailles treaty, which would have brought the United States into the League of Nations, shattered the career of the Democratic party's leader and split the party badly. Republicans in 1920 were able to exploit the national mood of cynicism about liberal activism abroad and at home. Republicans won the presidency in the elections of 1920, 1924, and 1928.

The Age of the New Deal. Republican dominance ended with the stock market crash of October 29, 1929, when Herbert C. Hoover was in the White House. Hoover reluctantly took a number of measures to provide relief for victims of the nation's greatest economic catastrophe, but his lack of empathy for those victims and his failure to understand the fundamental nature of the crisis made him into a political scapegoat. To many Americans, Hoover was an object of enmity for most of his four-year term. Any Democrat promoting change in 1932 was practically guaranteed victory.

Democrat Franklin D. Roosevelt, the former assistant secretary of the navy and governor of New York, not only won the presidency in 1932 but changed the face of U.S. politics. Under the coalition that Roosevelt built, the Democrats were the dominant national party for the next three decades. The New Deal coalition included international business leaders, bankers, southerners, blacks, organized labor, urbanites, Catholics, and Jews. The Democrats won seven of the next nine presidential elections. The only Republican winner between 1932 and 1964 was Dwight D. Eisenhower (in 1952 and 1956), who was originally wooed by the Democrats.

The issue of race and a variety of economic developments started to pull the Democrats apart in the years after World War II. When the party adopted a strong civil rights platform in 1948, a group of southerners led by Gov. J. Strom Thurmond of South Carolina bolted the convention and formed their own party. *(See "Third Parties," p. 248, in this chapter.)* With the defection the same year of the liberal former vice president Henry Wallace, the Democrats and President Harry S Truman retained the middle-of-the-road vote and the White House. But the party's once-strong hold on the South was gone. Thurmond won more than 22 percent of the popular vote in the South in 1948 as well as the electoral college support of electors from Alabama, Mississippi, South Carolina, and Louisiana (and one "faithless elector" from Tennessee).

Republicans suffered splits of their own during this period. The party's isolationist, high-tariff wing was still strong under the leadership of Sen. Robert Taft of Ohio. But other party leaders, such as Eisenhower, Thomas Dewey, Nelson A. Rockefeller, and Richard Nixon, propounded an American role as bulwark against the Soviet Union in world politics and economic expansion at home and abroad. The more traditional GOP wing remained strong until the late 1960s, however.

The Postwar Party System. Two major economic changes and the race issue shifted the balance of power in U.S. politics in the years following World War II. First, the locus of economic activity in the United States shifted from the urban Northeast to the suburbs and the South and the West. The loosening of economic ties led to the loosening of social and political ties. Second, the United States faced growing competition in world markets from the countries rebuilding after the devastation of World War II. By the late 1960s, the U.S. share in world markets had been cut in half, the position of the dollar in international finance was in decline, and inflation posed a threat to domestic prosperity. An explosion in social spending created resentment among some middle- and upper-class groups. The American economic "pie" was not growing fast enough to satisfy all the elements of the Democratic coalition, which started to compete with one another.

The Democratic coalition split not only over race and economic issues but also over the proper U.S. role in international affairs. The Vietnam War divided the party into "hawk" and "dove" factions. Other developments fragmenting the party in the 1960s and 1970s included the emergence of a post-colonial Africa and Latin America, revelations about certain notorious activities of the Central Intelligence Agency, a thaw in relations with the Soviet Union and the People's Republic of China, and the emergence of the Organization of Petroleum Exporting Countries.

The Republicans won slim control of Congress during parts of the Truman and Eisenhower years and of the Senate for six years of the Reagan administration, but the Democrats remained the leading party. The Democrats led in party identification by voters and dominated Congress and most state governments. Democratic skill in responding to constituency demands also helped the party in local politics. Democrats have dominated governorships and legislatures in most states since the Roosevelt revolution.[44]

But the Republicans showed impressive gains. The GOP won four of the six presidential elections from 1968 to 1988, three by landslides. The only Democrat to win the once-solid Democratic South during this period was the Georgian Jimmy Carter in 1976. The Republicans had a strong hold on the West and made strong inroads into the blue-collar and northeastern suburban votes. The Republican party became competitive in the South below the presidential level for the first time since Reconstruction, even though Democrats held control of most state governments. By the time of the 1990 census, the eleven states of the South from Texas to Virginia were expected to have one-third of all House seats and more than half of the electoral votes needed to win the presidency. This area, which boomed with suburbanization and the development of the defense and space industries, could hold the balance of power in U.S. politics for the next generation.

Although southern resistance to the increasingly liberal policies of the Democrats created an opening for the GOP, the Democrats still had strong natural bases. Since 1964, no Democratic presidential candidate has won less than 84 percent of the black vote. In the 1986 Democratic takeover of the U.S. Senate, the black vote was crucial in five southern states that went Democratic. Populist appeals on economic issues also have brought results in state elections in the South.

The key to party alignments in the 1990s could be the way different social and economic groups cluster geographically. Urban-suburban segmentation and redrawing of legislative district lines after the 1990 census could affect the way coalitions are created or maintained. If social groups are separated by geographic boundaries, it could be difficult to build a broad political coalition in which diverse groups see common interests.

The way political parties develop could be crucial for the same reasons. Political scientists studying the party system in the 1970s and 1980s were reluctant to proclaim a "realignment" of political forces. They were more confident with the term "dealignment," which suggests a breakup of traditional alliances without an obvious set of new alliances. The Democrats were too strong in the states and in Congress to suggest that they were a minority party. But the Democrats clearly lost much of the financial backing on which they had relied for four decades, and many groups in the New Deal coalition were lukewarm in their support. Especially because of unprecedented numbers of independent voters, a new party alignment could take a long time to develop.

The Development of Party Conventions

Since the adoption of nomination reforms by both parties, national conventions have been more media events than deliberative bodies. But conventions still serve an important role by ratifying the party's choice for president and vice president and by adopting a platform, or statement of party principles. Perhaps because the Constitution's Framers resisted the idea of partisan contests for the presidency, they did not outline any procedures for party selection of candidates. The party convention for selecting nominees developed as a reaction to the nation's first system—"King Caucus." Under this early system, congressional caucuses, or meetings of top party leaders, were responsible for the selection of candidates until 1824. A popular reaction against the closed nature of the caucus system led to the development of conventions of party leaders from all the states.

The Anti-Masonic party held the first party convention in September 1831. Delegates from thirteen states nominated William Wirt for president. The National Republican, or Whig, party held a convention that December and nominated Henry Clay for president. The following May, Democrats convened to nominate Andrew Jackson. Although they were a repudiation of the Framers' dislike for partisanship, conventions still were in tune with the nation's federalist ideals: states could decide on their own how they wished to select delegates, but once they met with other states' representatives, they were forced to bargain and consider more than parochial concerns. The convention system strengthened state party organizations because each state selected its own delegates.

Library of Congress

In September 1831, the Anti-Masonic party held the first national nominating convention in U.S. history. Delegates from thirteen states nominated William Wirt for president. Wirt lost the 1832 election to Democrat Andrew Jackson.

The convention system was open and deliberative. Party leaders often met without any idea which candidates would head the national ticket or how the party would stand on major issues. Those matters were subject to debate and bargaining.

Conventions were sufficiently open to deliberation to allow the emergence of several "dark-horse" candidates. James K. Polk, who won the Democratic nomination in 1844, is considered the first true "outsider" candidate to lead a party. A number of conventions were so badly divided that party leaders were forced to stay in session longer or even convene a second time. The Democrats, split by the slavery issue, needed a second convention in 1860 to nominate Stephen A. Douglas, and then a rival faction ran its own ticket in the fall election. The 1924 Democratic convention went through seventeen days, 103 ballots, and sixteen candidates in New York's sweltering Madison Square Garden before nominating John W. Davis. Republican donnybrooks include the 1880 rejection of Ulysses S. Grant's bid for a third term and the 1940 emergence of Wendell Willkie despite his having no political experience.

"Drafts" of candidates are usually arranged before the convention. Horatio Seymour's 1868 Democratic draft was genuine, but others have been scripted by political operatives. Franklin Roosevelt was disappointed that his 1940 draft for a third term did not work out as he had planned because other Democratic candidates sought the nomination.

The way the party frames controversial issues during a convention can have a dramatic effect on debate during the fall campaign. Democratic platforms set the debate in 1888 (tariffs), 1896 (currency), 1948 (civil rights), and 1984 (taxes). GOP platforms set the debate in 1860 (preservation of the Union), 1952 (the Korean War and economic controls), 1964 (Goldwater conservatism), and 1980 (taxes and foreign policy).

Because of the development of state presidential primary elections at the beginning of the twentieth century, conventions became more representative of the electorate. Party leaders increasingly referred to the importance of public opinion rather than their duty to use their independent political judgment. To use the terminology of political scientist Richard Fenno, conventioneers became less like "trustees" and more like "delegates."[45]

By the end of World War II, conventions were losing control over the nomination process. In 1952 the convention battle between Dwight D. Eisenhower and Sen. Robert A. Taft of Ohio was important, but the outcome was shaped by results from Republican primaries. The last open bargaining for the national ticket was the jockeying for the Democratic vice-presidential nomination in 1956. Since then, nomination front-runners have had to hold on to the coalition they built before the convention rather than continue building at the convention. The nomination victories of Democrats John F. Kennedy (1960) and Jimmy Carter (1980) and Republican Gerald R. Ford (1976) were secured when the front-runners avoided an erosion of support in key early convention votes.

Conventions today are considered by many to be meetings to ratify the choice of voters in the states. Almost all states now offer party members the opportunity to select the candidates in primaries and caucuses. The candidate

Library of Congress

When conventions were still deliberative events, the Democrats, in the summer of 1924, went through seventeen days, 103 ballots, and sixteen candidates before choosing John W. Davis as the presidential nominee. Davis lost to Republican Calvin Coolidge.

with enough delegates to win the nomination usually is determined before the convention. The votes of the states' voters are held to be more legitimate than convention bargaining. Gov. Mario Cuomo of New York, once considered a possible draft candidate in 1988, said it would be "immoral" to win the nomination without entering primaries.

One of the factors working against open conventions is the adoption of the majority-vote rule. Before the change, candidates in the Democratic party needed to get the support of two-thirds of all convention delegates to win the nomination. The two-thirds rule made winning the nomination difficult without bargaining with opponents within the party. President Franklin Roosevelt insisted on the abolition of the two-thirds rule in 1936. Rivals to Roosevelt in 1940 tried to restore the two-thirds rule as a way to block a third Roosevelt term. Other reasons behind the predetermined convention result include the rise of media politics and the use of proportional representation for delegate allocation in primaries and caucuses. Media politics undermine the legitimacy of political "deals" made among elites at conventions. Proportional representation prevents longshot candidates from winning big chunks of delegate support with narrow primary and caucus wins.

Attempts to open the convention to deliberation have failed. Former California governor Ronald Reagan failed in his 1976 attempt to establish a requirement that candidates name a running mate before the convention; if he had succeeded, delegates would have been free to reassess their allegiance based on the vice-presidential candidate. Sen. Edward M. Kennedy led the unsuccessful movement for an "open convention" in 1980.

Battles over the credentials of convention delegates have been among the livelier aspects of modern conventions. In 1912, Theodore Roosevelt unsuccessfully contested the seating of delegates for William Howard Taft. Taft's son, Ohio senator Robert Taft, lost an important credentials dispute and the nomination to Eisenhower in 1952. The Democrats endured divisive credentials disputes in 1968 and 1972.

History of the Primary System

One of the progressive movement's greatest effects on presidential politics was the introduction of the primary election in the nomination process at the turn of the century. The most persistent complaints of progressives concerned the undemocratic way urban and state political machines selected leaders. The progressives' solution was to put selection of high officials in the hands of the electorate. A purer democracy was the rationale behind reforms such as the Seventeenth Amendment (which provides for direct election of U.S. senators, previously selected by state legislatures), provisions for referendums and recall votes in state constitutions, and voter initiatives (which are similar to referendums but are instigated by citizen petitions rather than legislative action).

The logical extension of pure democracy to presidential politics was the direct primary. The idea was to bypass completely the vested interests that controlled nominations and thereby limited the people's choices in the general election. Some proponents of the primary wanted complete abolition of the deal making that had been characteristic of the nomination process throughout U.S. history. Primaries would provide for the direct election of delegates, or an election in which voters express their preferences for the presidential candidates themselves, or some combination of the two.

Early Days. Florida passed the first presidential primary law in 1901, but the primary got its biggest impetus when the 1904 Republican convention refused seating to the backers of progressive leader Robert M. La Follette. As a result, La Follette in 1905 successfully promoted legislation in Wisconsin that provided for primary election of delegates to national party conventions. In 1906 Pennsylvania established a primary.

Oregon in 1910 established the first "beauty contest," a primary election in which voters express an unbinding preference for the candidates themselves. Oregon voters, appropriately enough, approved the plan in a referendum. Delegates were legally bound to vote for candidates according to the results of the beauty contest.

By 1916, twenty-five states had passed laws for presidential primaries. The greatest surge of support for primaries, and the system's greatest disappointment, came with the 1912 Republican nomination struggle. Former president Theodore Roosevelt used the primaries to battle his handpicked successor, William Howard Taft, for the nomination. Despite his nine primary victories, compared with La Follette's two and Taft's one, Roosevelt lost the nomination to Taft. Roosevelt maintained that Taft had "stolen" the nomination. Running on his own "Bull Moose" ticket, Roosevelt called for national primaries to decide nominations.[46]

Resistance to primaries persisted for years. Even as the states enthusiastically moved toward direct voter selection of presidential nominees in the years before World War I, conservatives in state legislatures, courts, and local election boards worked against the new system.

Time, however, did what opponents of primaries could not manage. The coming of the First World War, the political apathy of the 1920s, and the struggle for economic survival during the Great Depression brought about the collapse of the system. The high costs of primaries, the low voter turnout, and the avoidance of the contests by presidential candidates made them irrelevent vestiges of the progressive movement.

Eight of the twenty-five states that had adopted primaries during the progressive surge abolished them by 1935. Only a three-way Republican race in 1920 created any local interest or candidate activity in primaries—and even then, the biggest vote getter, Hiram Johnson, was denied the nomination. The disaster that befell Republican

Table 1 Votes Cast and Delegates Selected in Presidential Primaries, 1912-1988

	Democratic Party			Republican Party			Total	
Year	Number of primaries	Votes cast	Delegates selected through primaries (%)	Number of primaries	Votes cast	Delegates selected through primaries (%)	Votes cast	Delegates selected through primaries (%)
1912	12	974,775	32.9	13	2,261,240	41.7	3,236,015	37.3
1916	20	1,187,691	53.5	20	1,923,374	58.9	3,111,065	56.2
1920	16	571,671	44.6	20	3,186,248	57.8	3,757,919	51.2
1924	14	763,858	35.5	17	3,525,185	45.3	4,289,043	40.4
1928	16	1,264,220	42.2	15	4,110,288	44.9	5,374,508	43.5
1932	16	2,952,933	40.0	14	2,346,996	37.7	5,299,929	38.8
1936	14	5,181,808	36.5	12	3,319,810	37.5	8,501,618	37.0
1940	13	4,468,631	35.8	13	3,227,875	38.8	7,696,506	37.3
1944	14	1,867,609	36.7	13	2,271,605	38.7	4,139,214	37.7
1948	14	2,151,865	36.3	12	2,653,255	36.0	4,805,120	36.1
1952	16	4,928,006	38.7	13	7,801,413	39.0	12,729,419	38.8
1956	19	5,832,592	42.7	19	5,828,272	44.8	11,660,864	43.7
1960	16	5,686,664	38.3	15	5,537,967	38.6	11,224,631	38.5
1964	16	6,247,435	45.7	16	5,935,339	45.6	12,182,774	45.6
1968	15	7,535,069	40.2	15	4,473,551	38.1	12,008,620	39.1
1972	21	15,993,965	65.3	20	6,188,281	56.8	22,182,246	61.0
1976	27	16,052,652	76.0	26	10,374,125	71.0	26,426,777	73.5
1980	35	18,747,825	71.8	35	12,690,451	76.0	31,438,276	73.7
1984	30	18,009,217	52.4	25	6,575,651	71.0	24,584,868	59.6
1988	37	23,312,931	66.6	37	12,169,003	76.9	35,481,934	70.2

Sources: Guide to U.S. Elections, 2d ed. (Washington, D.C.: Congressional Quarterly Inc., 1985). The percentages of delegates selected by party for the years 1912-1976 were computed by F. Christopher Arterton and are contained in F. Christopher Arterton, "Campaign Organizations Confront the Media-Political Environment," in *Race for the Presidency,* ed. James David Barber (Englewood Cliffs, N.J.: Prentice-Hall, 1978), 7. For 1980, *Congressional Quarterly Weekly Report,* June 5, 1980, 1870-1873; for 1984, calculations by CQ staff from data supplied by the Democratic National Committee, and *Congressional Quarterly Weekly Report,* August 25, 1984, 2128; for 1988, *Congressional Quarterly Weekly Report,* February 27, 1988, 532; July 9, 1988, 1894; August 13, 1988, 2254; and updates by CQ staff.

Wendell Willkie in 1944 when he tried to use the Wisconsin primary as a springboard to a second nomination—he won only 4.6 percent of the vote—seemed to indicate that primaries offered great risk and little potential for gain.

But a comeback for primaries was not far away. Former Minnesota governor Harold E. Stassen almost captured the Republican nomination in 1948 when he won the Wisconsin, Nebraska, and Pennsylvania primaries. Stassen lost his chance for the nomination when he took on Sen. Robert A. Taft in the latter's home state of Ohio and lost. New York governor Thomas E. Dewey, the eventual nominee, then beat Stassen in the critical Oregon primary after campaigning there for three weeks.

After the dramatic events of 1948, interest in primary selection surged. A number of states, such as Indiana, Minnesota, and Montana, reinstated primaries in time for the 1952 election. Voter participation in primaries jumped from 4.8 million in 1948 to 12.7 million in 1952. Enthusiasm was not as strong as it was during the Progressive Era, and some states even repealed primary laws during the 1950s. But primaries had found an important niche. *(See Table 1.)*

The Mixed System. Presidential nomination politics evolved into a "mixed system" in the 1950s and 1960s. Under a mixed system, candidates could restrict their public campaign to a few primaries that would supplement other strengths, such as fund-raising ability, endorsements, control of state and local machines, regional and ideological distinctiveness, and skill in negotiations with other political forces. In many cases, the nomination was settled only during negotiations at the summer convention.

The major function of primaries under the mixed system was to allow the candidate to demonstrate an ability to campaign and to appeal to voters; primaries served to supplement—but not replace—other strengths such as ties to the party leadership, to organized labor, or to the business community. Primaries were a rough test of "electability." John F. Kennedy used West Virginia's Democratic primary in 1960 to demonstrate to skeptical party leaders that he could overcome resistance to a Catholic candidacy. Kennedy's victory in Wisconsin's primary demonstrated an ability to appeal to the more liberal elements of the party. In 1968, Richard Nixon used a string of primary victories to demonstrate that he was not a "loser" with the voters, despite losses in the 1960 presidential and 1962 California gubernatorial campaigns.

Except for candidates whose vote-getting ability was viewed skeptically, the primary under the mixed system was considered a risk. Performing below expectations could be fatal to a campaign, as Harry S Truman in 1952 and Lyndon B. Johnson in 1968 learned. Good primary showings, moreover, did not ensure a nomination, as Estes Kefauver learned in 1952.

Primaries always have been springboards for dark-horse candidates. Eugene J. McCarthy's second-place finish to President Johnson in the 1968 New Hampshire primary established him as a serious candidate. Other dark-horse candidates who became instant contenders after important primary showings include Estes Kefauver (1952), George S. McGovern (1972), Jimmy Carter (1976), George Bush (1980), and Gary Hart (1984).

Under the mixed system, a candidate who dominated the primary season could lose the nomination if enough state party organizations rallied behind other candidates—a highly unlikely event today. Kefauver lost the 1952 Democratic nomination to Adlai E. Stevenson despite attracting 64.5 percent of the total primary vote to Stevenson's 1.6 percent. In 1968, McCarthy had 38.7 percent of the total primary vote, and the other major antiwar candidate, Robert F. Kennedy, had 30.6 percent; yet Vice President Hubert H. Humphrey, closely associated with the Vietnam War, won the nomination although he did not enter any primaries.

The candidacies of Lyndon Johnson in 1960 and Barry Goldwater in 1964 illustrate the possibilities for conducting a candidacy under the mixed system without depending on the primaries. Although Johnson did not announce his candidacy formally until just before the Democratic convention—stating that his duties as Senate majority leader had been too pressing—he still managed to build a strong base of support in the preceding months. By delivering a series of weekend speeches before state conventions, attending fund-raisers, and appearing before other party groups, Johnson won high visibility for his "noncandidacy" and gained the support of some four hundred southern and Rocky Mountain delegates. But LBJ was painted by rivals as a regional candidate, and his strength going into the convention was limited to a possible vice-presidential nomination to "balance" the national ticket.

Goldwater lined up enough delegates to win the 1964 Republican nomination before the primary season began. Goldwater's support from state party organizations, however, needed some primary wins to convince party leaders of his popular appeal. Primary victories such as California were helpful to his effort. The surprise, come-from-behind victory dissipated the chances for a late entry by Pennsylvania governor William Scranton.

Selective participation in primaries no longer appears to be a viable option for a presidential campaign. Hubert Humphrey hoped that the Democratic party would turn to him in a deadlocked convention in both 1972 and 1976, but McGovern and Carter controlled the process before the convention. Gov. Edmund G. (Jerry) Brown, Jr., of California was considered a "stalking horse" in 1976 by many Humphrey backers, but he always insisted that he was running for himself. Brown's run was the last serious mixed strategy for a candidate on the sidelines. The last nominee who took part in only a limited number of primaries was Nixon in 1968. Humphrey in 1968 won the Democratic nomination without running in any primaries.

Recent Years. Since 1968, primaries have been at

Theodore Roosevelt Collection, Harvard College Library

In 1912, former president Theodore Roosevelt won nine out of twelve GOP primaries but was outmaneuvered by William Howard Taft at the Republican convention.

In reaction, Roosevelt ran on his own "Bull Moose" ticket, calling for national primaries to decide the presidential nomination.

How Primaries Work

There are two basic types of presidential primaries. One is the presidential preference primary in which voters vote directly for the person they wish to be nominated for president. The second is the type in which voters elect delegates to the national conventions.

States may use various combinations of these methods:

~ A state may have a preference vote but choose delegates at party conventions. The preference vote may or may not be binding on the delegates.

~ A state may combine the preference and delegate-selection primaries by electing delegates pledged or favorable to a candidate named on the ballot. Under this system, however, state party organizations may run unpledged slates of delegates.

~ A state may have an advisory preference vote and a separate delegate-selection vote in which delegates may be listed as pledged to a candidate, favorable, or unpledged.

~ A state may have a mandatory preference vote with a separate delegate-selection vote. In these cases, the delegates are required to reflect the preference primary vote.

For those primaries in which the preference vote is binding upon the delegates, state laws may vary as to the number of ballots through which delegates at the convention must remain committed.

Most primary states hold presidential preference votes, in which voters choose among the candidates who have qualified for the ballot in their states. Although preference votes may be binding or nonbinding, in most states the vote is binding on the delegates, who either are elected in the primary itself or chosen outside of it by a caucus process, by a state committee, or by the candidates who have qualified to win delegates.

Delegates may be bound for as short a time as one ballot or as long as a candidate remains in the race. National Democratic rules in effect in 1980 required delegates to be bound for one ballot unless released by the candidate they were elected to support. The rule was repealed for 1984.

Until 1980 the Republicans had a rule requiring delegates bound to a specific candidate by state law in primary states to vote for that candidate at the convention regardless of their personal presidential preferences. That rule was repealed at the July 1980 convention.

Delegates from primary states are allocated to candidates in various ways. Most of the methods are based on the preference vote—proportional representation, statewide winner-take-all (in which the candidate winning the most votes statewide wins all the delegates), congressional district and statewide winner-take-all (in which the high vote-getter in a district wins that district's delegates and the high vote-getter statewide wins all the at-large delegates), or some combination of the three. Still another method is the selection of individual delegates in a "loophole," or direct election, primary. Then the preference vote is either nonbinding or there is no preference vote at all.

In the proportional representation system, the qualifying threshold for candidates to win delegates can vary. After a decade of intensive debate, Democratic leaders voted to require proportional representation in all primary and caucus states in 1980. But by 1984, after more rules changes, states were given the right to retain proportional representation only if they wished, awarding delegates to any candidate who drew roughly 20 percent of the vote. This threshold was changed for the 1988 election to 15 percent of the vote.

The Republicans allow the primary states to set their own thresholds, which in many states were lower than the Democrats'. In Massachusetts, for example, a GOP candidate in 1980 had to receive only 2.4 percent of the vote to win a delegate.

In nearly half the primary states, major candidates are placed on the ballot by the secretary of state or a special nominating committee. The consent of the candidate is required in only three states—Kentucky, Michigan, and North Carolina. Elsewhere, candidates must take the initiative to get on the ballot. The filing requirements range from sending a letter of candidacy to elections officials (the case in Puerto Rico) to filing petitions signed by a specified number of registered voters and paying a filing fee (the case in Alabama).

On many primary ballots, voters have the opportunity to mark a line labeled "uncommitted" if they do not prefer any of the candidates.

the center of the nomination process. *(See box, How Primaries Work, this page.)* The number of primaries has increased from thirteen in 1968 to thirty-eight in 1988. Early contests such as the Iowa caucus and New Hampshire primary are vital to any campaign since the media and campaign professionals use those tests to determine a "front-runner." Candidates now routinely campaign for two years before the first electoral test. Early contests eliminate all but a few candidates, and the survivors battle until one wins enough delegates for a first-ballot nomination at the convention.

Caucuses. Since the passage of Democratic reforms after the 1968 election, the nomination process has been dominated by open primaries and caucuses. Caucuses represent a middle ground between primary elections, dominated by the voters, and state conventions, dominated by the party professionals. Before the 1970s, state conventions had been the center of nomination battles. *(See box, How Caucuses Work, p. 169.)*

Caucuses are neighborhood or precinct meetings at which party members debate the merits of the candidates before voting for them; backers of candidates try to persuade other caucus-goers to change sides. At the end of as much as three hours of debate and deal making, each precinct meeting votes on which delegates it will send to

How Caucuses Work

Caucuses, long the quiet backwater of the Democratic nominating process, became controversial in 1984 as they gained in popularity at the expense of presidential primaries. A strong showing in the caucuses by Walter F. Mondale led many Democrats—and not only supporters of his chief rivals—to conclude that caucuses are inherently unfair.

Mondale's caucus victories might be termed the revenge of the insiders. More so than the primaries, the often complex, low-visibility world of caucuses is open to takeover. The mainstream Democratic coalition of party activists, labor union members, and teachers was primed to dominate the caucuses in Mondale's behalf.

The influence of caucuses had decreased in the 1970s as the number of primaries grew dramatically. During the 1960s a candidate sought to run well in primary states mainly to have a bargaining chip with powerful leaders in the caucus states. Republicans Barry M. Goldwater in 1964 and Richard Nixon in 1968 and Democrat Hubert H. Humphrey in 1968 all built up solid majorities among caucus state delegates that carried them to their parties' nominations. Humphrey did not even enter a primary in 1968.

After 1968, candidates placed their principal emphasis on primaries. In 1972, Democrat George McGovern and in 1976 Republican president Gerald R. Ford and Democratic challenger Jimmy Carter won nomination by securing large majorities of the primary state delegates. Neither McGovern nor Ford won a majority of the caucus state delegates. Carter was able to win a majority only after his opponents' campaigns collapsed.

Complex Method

Compared with a primary, the caucus system is complicated. Instead of focusing on a single primary election ballot, the caucus presents a multi-tiered system that involves meetings scheduled over several weeks, sometimes even months. There is mass participation at the first level only, with meetings often lasting several hours and attracting only the most enthusiastic and dedicated party members.

The operation of the caucus varies from state to state, and each party has its own set of rules. Most begin with precinct caucuses or some other type of local mass meeting open to all party voters. Participants, often publicly declaring their votes, elect delegates to the next stage in the process.

In smaller states such as Delaware and Hawaii, delegates are elected directly to a state convention, where the national convention delegates are chosen. In larger states such as Iowa, there is at least one more step. Most frequently, delegates are elected at the precinct caucuses to county conventions, where the national convention delegates are chosen.

Participation, even at the first level of the caucus process, is much lower than in the primaries. Caucus participants usually are local party leaders and activists. Many rank-and-file voters find a caucus complex, confusing, or intimidating.

In a caucus state the focus is on one-on-one campaigning. Time, not money, is the most valuable resource. Because organization and personal campaigning are so important, an early start is far more crucial in a caucus state than in most primaries. Because only a small segment of the electorate is targeted in most caucus states, candidates usually use media advertising sparingly.

Although the basic steps in the caucus process are the same for both parties, the rules that govern them are vastly different. Democratic rules have been revamped substantially since 1968, establishing national standards for grass-roots participation. Republican rules have remained largely unchanged, with the states given wide latitude in the selection of delegates. Democratic caucuses are open to Democrats only. Republicans allow crossovers where state law permits, creating a wide range of variations. The first step of the Democratic caucus process must be open, well-publicized mass meetings. In most states Republicans do the same. Generally, voters participate only in the election of local party officials, who meet to begin the caucus process.

1988 Contest

Caucuses in Iowa and a few other states drew attention in the opening weeks of the 1988 presidential campaign. But after March 8, "Super Tuesday," the spotlight turned to states holding presidential primaries. In every Democratic and Republican nominating campaign since 1972, more delegates were chosen in primaries than in caucuses. In 1988 the primary-caucus ratio was particularly one-sided.

Thirty-five Republican primaries (in thirty-three states plus the District of Columbia and Puerto Rico) selected more than three-fourths of the 2,277 delegates to the GOP convention. Nineteen Republican caucuses (seventeen states plus Guam and the Virgin Islands) selected only 23 percent.

Delegates elected in thirty-four Democratic primaries cast nearly two-thirds of the 4,162 votes at the Democratic national convention. The rest of the delegates were almost equally divided between those elected in twenty-three caucuses (nineteen states plus American Samoa, Guam, the Virgin Islands, and Democrats Abroad) and "super-delegates"—those guaranteed delegate slots by virtue of their party or elected position.

---

county, congressional district, and state conventions. The sparsely attended caucus meetings covered by the national media, then, are just the first step in allocating delegates to the national party convention. Bargaining continues as a select few party members move from the precinct to the county, congressional district, and state conventions. The whole process often takes months, so a candidate who wins in the early rounds does not always succeed at higher levels. The media usually cover the outcomes of early caucus maneuverings as if they were straightforward primary balloting. The Iowa caucus and the New Hampshire primary receive more media attention than other nomination contests.

One reason the preelection year activities of today's candidates are more public than those of Kennedy and Goldwater is that today's early efforts are unambiguous tests of strength. More sophisticated, open tallying and reporting techniques enable the media to report hundreds of precinct caucuses and conventions quickly. This gives early organizing maneuvers the appearance of being conclusive tests of voter appeal.

The Franchise and the Electorate

The history of U.S. elections has been the story of efforts to break down legal barriers to voting and widen the size of the electorate. *(See Table 2.)* The counterpoint to that history, however, has been a wide range of practices to exclude certain groups from exercising the ever-widening franchise.

Since passage of the Bill of Rights, only sixteen new amendments have become part of the Constitution. Nine of those amendments address the way citizens participate in elections.[47] *Smith v. Allwright* (1944) held that where parties are the chief organizing institution of democracy, all-white primaries are unconstitutional. *Harman v. Forssenius* (1965) struck down the poll tax for federal elections, and *Harper v. Virginia State Board of Elections* (1966) found the poll tax unconstitutional for state and local elections as well.[48] Some of the nation's most storied legislative battles have been fought over regulation of elections. Voting rights have been a continuous source of contention in U.S. politics for the nation as a whole as well as for the individual states.

Almost every U.S. citizen at least eighteen years old is now entitled to vote. Restrictions based on wealth and property, sex, and race no longer exist. Today, only convicted felons and the insane are denied the vote. Limits on electoral participation are based on registration requirements and the drawing of jurisdictional lines.

The Framers of the Constitution left regulation of voting rights in the hands of the states. These rights have been expanded at two levels. First, many states have moved to liberalize voting requirements. Second, the federal government has intervened to forbid the states from excluding certain classes of voters. "Nationalization" of economic and political life has been accompanied by nationalization of election laws. In the first few decades after the United States won independence from Great Britain, the thirteen states allowed only male property-holders or taxpayers to vote. Seven of those states required ownership of land; the others required a certain value of possessions or evidence of having paid taxes. About half of all white males were qualified to vote in the Republic's early days. Religious restrictions on voting, prevalent in the colonial period, no longer existed. Still, in 1790, women, blacks, Indians, and indentured servants could not vote. Tax-paying requirements gradually replaced property requirements, and by 1850 most states had eliminated this restriction as well.[49]

Blacks and the Right to Vote. The group facing the most persistent discrimination has been blacks. The Constitution sanctioned slavery, and in the infamous 1857 *Dred Scott* case the Supreme Court held that slaves are property. The constitutional provision that declares a black to be three-fifths of a person, for census considerations, is perhaps the most convoluted expression of early American disrespect for blacks.

Table 2 Growing Franchise in the United States, 1932-1988

Presidential election year	Estimated population of voting age	Vote cast for presidential electors: Number	Percent
1932	75,768,000	37,732,000	52.4
1936	80,174,000	45,643,000	56.9
1940	84,728,000	49,900,000	58.9
1944	85,654,000	47,977,000	56.0
1948	95,573,000	48,794,000	51.1
1952	99,929,000	61,551,000	61.6
1956	104,515,000	62,027,000	59.3
1960	109,672,000	68,838,000	63.1
1964	114,090,000	70,645,000	61.8
1968	120,285,000	73,212,000	60.7
1972	140,068,000	77,625,000	55.4
1976	150,127,000	81,603,000	54.4
1980	162,761,000	86,515,221	53.2
1984	173,936,000	92,652,793	53.3
1988	182,628,000	91,609,673	50.2

Sources: U.S. Bureau of the Census; *Congress and the Nation: 1977-1980* (Washington, D.C.: Congressional Quarterly Inc., 1982); *Congressional Quarterly Weekly Report,* October 30, 1981, 2749; February 19, 1983, 387; April 13, 1985, 687; Committee for the Study of the American Electorate.

Because blacks were at first considered indentured servants who could eventually gain citizenship, blacks in all but three southern states enjoyed some voting rights in the early 1800s. But the extension of slave status to the black's entire lifetime steadily reduced the number of potential black voters. By the outbreak of the Civil War, all but six of the thirty-three states barred blacks from voting at any time, solely because of their race.

The Civil War was not fought over the morality of slavery, as romantic versions of U.S. history assert, but over the issue of states' rights and the regional balance of power in U.S. national politics.

The war, however, led to the extension of the vote to blacks. President Abraham Lincoln issued the Emancipation Proclamation on New Year's Day 1863. The proclamation—which had questionable legal status and had derived at least partly from a desire to enlist blacks as soldiers for the Union—granted freedom to slaves in states fighting the Union. Lincoln expressed a desire in writings and public and private talks to move slowly to include blacks in the democratic process. He wished to give priority to "very intelligent" blacks and to blacks who fought for the Union.

In response to the passage of "black codes" in many southern states, which barred blacks from voting and holding office, Radical Republicans who controlled Congress after the Civil War passed a number of measures to bring blacks into U.S. political life. The most important was the Reconstruction Act of 1867, which set up military governments in the Confederate states and tied readmission to the Union to passage of the Fourteenth Amendment, which that year failed to win ratification.

The Fourteenth Amendment is probably the most important constitutional addition besides the Bill of Rights. The amendment—particularly after more expansive readings by the Supreme Court in the twentieth century—bans states from limiting the "privileges and immunities" of U.S. citizens. It orders states to respect all citizens' rights to "due process" and the more general "equal protection of the laws." The amendment also reduces the representation of states that deny the franchise to any male over twenty-one years of age. It passed in 1868. The Fifteenth Amendment, which grants the franchise to all adult males regardless of race or "previous condition of servitude," passed in 1869.

The addition of blacks to the electorate was crucial in Ulysses S. Grant's slim 300,000-vote margin of victory over Horatio Seymour in the 1868 presidential election. Also in that year, blacks for the first time won election to state and federal offices. Between 1870 and 1900, twenty-two southern blacks won election to Congress. Two blacks, Mississippi Republicans Hiram R. Revels and Blanche K. Bruce, served in the U.S. Senate. Federal troops with ties to the Republican party enforced voting rights.

Federal resolve to guarantee civil rights to blacks died during the maneuvering over the 1876 presidential election results. As part of a deal that gave the disputed election to Republican Rutherford B. Hayes, the Republicans agreed to pull federal troops out of the South and allowed southern states to pass laws restricting blacks' ability to participate in politics and economic and social life.

The old Confederacy kept blacks from the polls with a variety of racially discriminatory measures, known as "Jim Crow" laws: poll taxes, literacy tests, "grandfather clauses" (which exempted poor whites from the measures by guaranteeing the franchise to citizens whose ancestors voted or served in the state militia), property requirements, tests of "morality," and the "white primary" (which banned blacks from the Democratic party with the legal reasoning that the party is a private organization not subject to the Fourteenth Amendment). When these legal means did not block black political activity, violence did. By the turn of the century, southern politics was solely a white man's vocation.

Around the turn of the century, the states passed a wide range of voter registration requirements that restricted ballot access to blacks and other vulnerable groups, such as illiterates and voters who could be intimidated, by creating voter qualification hurdles. The total vote in southern states fell by as much as 60 percent between 1884 and 1904.[50] Ballot restriction during this period was aimed at white agrarian radicals who backed the 1896 presidential campaign of William Jennings Bryan, but it had the effect of tightening exclusion of blacks.

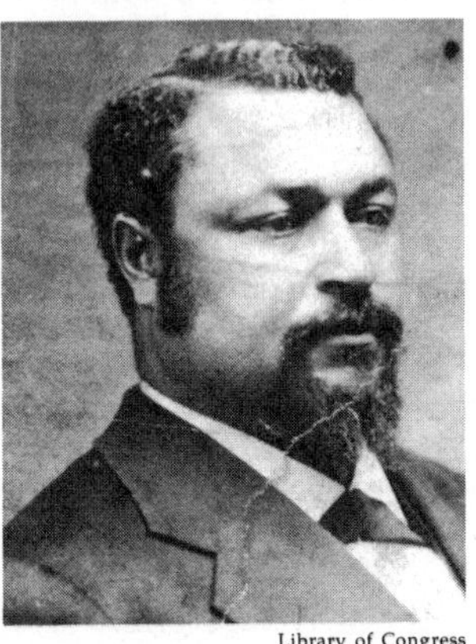

Library of Congress Library of Congress

The first black to serve in Congress was Republican Hiram R. Revels of Mississippi, left, who served in the Senate from 1870 to 1871. In 1874, Mississippi Republican Blanche K. Bruce, right, was elected to the Senate. He was the first black member to serve a full term in that chamber.

Congress and the federal courts gradually chipped away at voting discrimination against blacks. In 1915, the Supreme Court struck down the use of grandfather clauses. The Court banned all-white primaries in 1944, and it banned poll taxes in 1966.[51]

The Civil Rights Act of 1957 established the Civil Rights Commission, which was empowered to study voter discrimination, and expanded the attorney general's authority to bring federal lawsuits against anyone restricting blacks' right to vote. A 1960 law extended the attorney general's court standing and authorized the appointment of federal officials to monitor elections. The Civil Rights Act of 1964 required states to adopt uniform election procedures for all citizens, required states to show sufficient cause for rejecting voters who had completed the sixth grade or demonstrated an equivalent level of intellectual competence, and eased procedures for federal consideration of voting rights cases.

Constitutional revisions further advanced voting rights. The Twenty-fourth Amendment banned the use of poll taxes in federal elections. Congressional action was crucial to enforcing the constitutional provisions.

The Voting Rights Act of 1965 suspended literacy tests in seven southern states and parts of another. It also required federal supervision of voter registration in states and counties that on November 1, 1964, still had literacy tests or other qualifying tests and where less than 50 percent of all voting-age citizens had voted in the 1964 presidential election. Jurisdictions under federal supervision needed to receive federal approval for any changes in election procedures. This act led to the addition of one million blacks to the voting rolls.

A 1970 amendment to the Voting Rights Act suspended for five years all literacy tests, whether they were discriminatory or not. In 1970 the Supreme Court upheld that law's constitutionality, and the tests were banned by law permanently in 1975. The "trigger" for federal involvement was applied to additional states and jurisdictions by amendments passed in 1970, 1975, and 1982.

The 1982 law extended for twenty-five years the provisions requiring nine states and parts of thirteen others to get Justice Department approval for election law changes. The law also included: "bail-out" procedures for states that had demonstrated a clean ten-year record on voting rights; tests for discrimination based on results rather than intent; and bilingual ballot provisions. On cases involving voting requirements, district lines, and nomination processes, the federal courts consistently have backed up the federal laws extending suffrage to blacks who had been "locked out" of the system.

Women and the Vote. Women won the right to vote with passage of the Nineteenth Amendment in 1920. The battle for suffrage lasted more than a century, with victories accumulating in the new states before a movement developed nationwide. As in other nations, such as Great Britain, the women's suffrage question involved bitter pro-

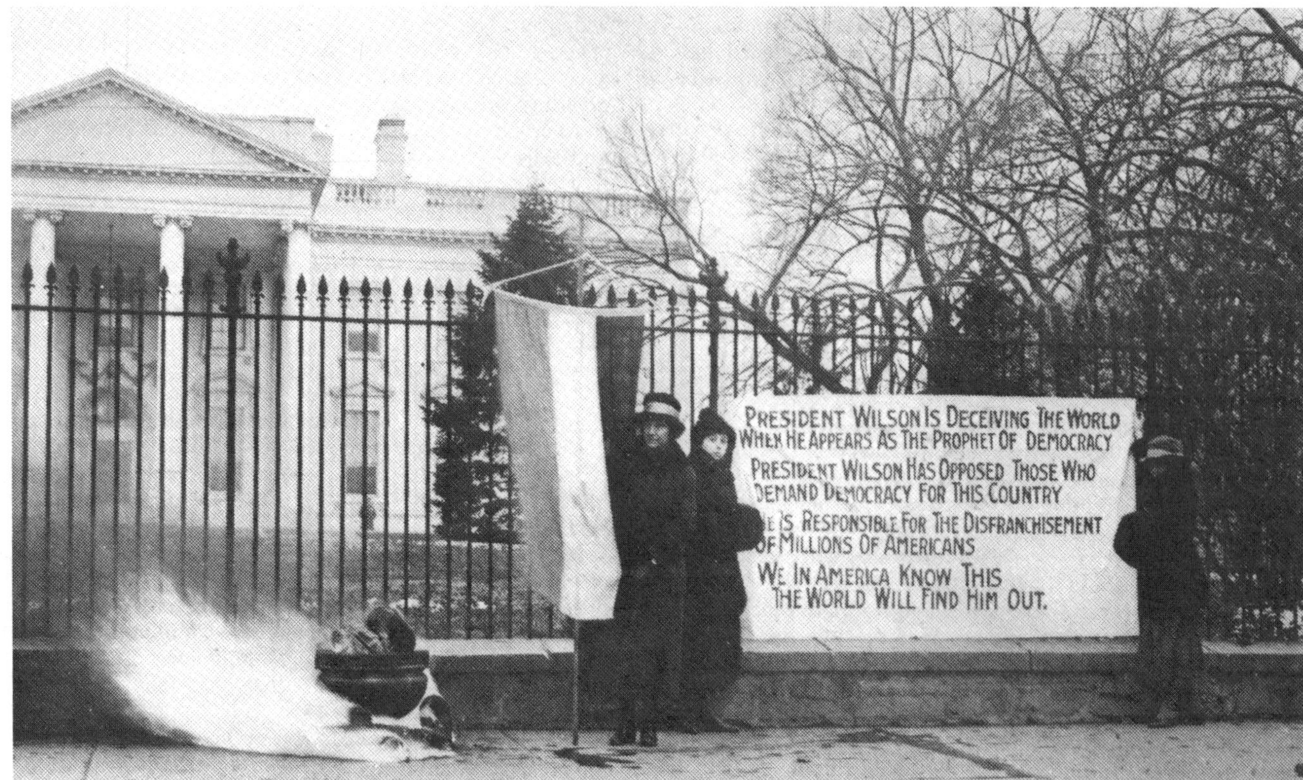

Supporters of the Nineteenth Amendment picket the White House in 1916.

tests such as calls for single-issue voting and hunger strikes.

Several states granted women the vote in school board elections in the nineteenth century. The Women's Rights Convention in Seneca Falls, New York, in 1848 marked the unofficial beginning of the feminist movement in the United States. In the late nineteenth century, Susan B. Anthony led a suffragist movement that claimed the right to vote under the Fourteenth Amendment and sought a constitutional suffrage amendment. In 1887 Congress defeated legislation for a constitutional amendment.

Western states led the way in complete women's suffrage. Full voting rights were granted women in Wyoming in 1890; Colorado in 1893; Utah and Idaho in 1896; Washington in 1910; California in 1911; Arizona, Kansas, and Oregon in 1912; Montana and Nevada in 1914; and New York in 1917. These states formed the foundation of the movement and helped secure quick passage of the Nineteenth Amendment once Congress sent the amendment to the states in 1919.

Debate over women's suffrage was not always enlightened. Assertions that women's suffrage would usher in a utopian era of open political action and respect among all citizens were countered with the argument that the amendment would wipe away distinctions between the sexes.[52] The movement did not link up with the civil rights movement; in fact, some suffragists argued that the women's vote would be a bulwark against black demands because women presumably would be more regular and conservative voters. The movement for women's suffrage peaked in 1914 when a more militant group led a campaign against congressional candidates who opposed the amendment regardless of their positions on other issues. President Woodrow Wilson initially opposed a constitutional amendment, arguing that state action was more appropriate. But protests escalated to hunger strikes, and in 1918 Wilson announced his support for the amendment. In 1919 Congress passed the amendment on its third try in three years, and the states approved it in 1920.

Other Impediments to Voting. Residency laws have long posed difficulties for millions of mobile citizens. Many states have required residency in the state of two years, and lesser periods for residency in the county and election district. The 1970 voting rights legislation guaranteed the vote in presidential elections if the citizen had lived in the voting district at least thirty days before the election. This measure made an additional five million people eligible to vote in the 1972 election.

Congress passed legislation in 1976 guaranteeing the vote to Americans living overseas. Absentee ballots now go to overseas citizens according to their last U.S. address.

In 1973, the Supreme Court ruled in *Marston v. Lewis* that states may not deny the franchise to people who had not lived in a state for a year and in a county for three months.[53] By 1980, seventeen states had no residency requirement, and all but one had requirements of thirty days or less.

The most recent constitutional change affecting the right to vote was the lowering of the voting age to eighteen. Before World War II, no state allowed citizens to vote before age twenty-one. Led by Georgia's change in the voting age to eighteen in 1943, after a campaign marked by the slogan "Fight at 18, Vote at 18," several states passed the more liberal requirement. President Dwight D. Eisenhower proposed a constitutional amendment in 1954, but it failed in the Senate. The Voting Rights Act of 1970 set a minimum voting age of eighteen for all federal, state, and local elections, but the act was declared unconstitutional for state and local elections. In 1971, however, the voting age was approved under the Twenty-sixth Amendment.

Low voter participation in the United States has been a constant source of concern among democratic theorists and leaders of movements for poor people. No state or federal laws ban any significant class from voting, but only slightly more than half of all eligible citizens vote in presidential elections, and only a third vote in congressional elections. Explanations for the disappointing turnout range from a lack of meaningful choice to a contentedness with the current policies of the government. The highest percentage of voter participation in recent years was in 1960, when 60.1 percent of all eligible citizens voted in the presidential race. By 1976, the participation rate had fallen to 50.3 percent; in 1984, it was 53 percent.

The one difference between the United States and Western nations with high turnout—such as Great Britain, West Germany, Canada, and Australia—is the method of registering citizens to vote. The United States is the only nation that places the burden of qualifying for electoral participation on the citizen. In other nations government agencies sign up voters. Registration is inconvenient in many U.S. jurisdictions.

In 1977 and 1978 President Jimmy Carter backed congressional measures to allow voters to register on election day, but the legislation failed. By the late 1980s, the majority of U.S. citizens lived in states that allowed postcard registration. Public interest groups worked throughout the 1980s to extend postcard registration to more states and eventually to achieve passage of congressional legislation. Oregon and Wisconsin allow registration on the day of the election, and the participation rate in those states is about 10 percentage points higher than the national rate.

The ways state legislatures have drawn lines for legislative districts has been a constant source of voting rights controversy. District lines are important for presidential politics because many primaries and caucuses use congressional districts as a geographic unit. Candidates who win a congressional district get delegate bonuses. The Supreme Court has approved city annexation programs, even if annexation diluted black representation, and redistricting that created "safe" racial districts. The Court has stated that consideration of race is sometimes appropriate in drawing district lines.

Campaign Practices and Technology

In the early days of partisan politics, newspapers were the dominant means of conveying campaign messages. Newspapers were unabashedly biased. In the tradition of the Federalist and Anti-Federalist newspaper arguments, leading politicians and interest groups started newspapers specifically for campaigns. Alexander Hamilton started the *Gazette of the United States,* and his rival Thomas Jefferson founded the *National Gazette.* *(See "Historical Background," p. 705, in Media chapter of Part IV.)* As popular participation in presidential selection grew in the early nineteenth century, parties organized partisan appeals and get-out-the-vote drives. Democrats and Whigs developed hierarchical party organizations. One Whig supporter described a prevalent model:

> The fundamental idea is borrowed from the religious organizations of the day. The model of my primary local association is the Christian Church. The officers, the exercises, the exhortations, the singing, the weekly meetings (on Wednesday night), the enrolment of members, the contributions, and all are to be on the primitive apostolic model.... These little unit associations are to be mutually fraternized and affiliated to County, District—and state central associations, with regular and definite means of communication....[54]

Tammany Hall, the most famous organization in U.S. politics, began as a fraternal society in New York City in the late 1700s. Tammany came to typify the party organizations of the nation's states and cities. Those "machines" were marked by pyramidal organization with top-down control, door-to-door recruitment, demands of loyalty, extensive use of patronage, exacting vote-counting, aggressive poll tactics, close relations with businesses and utilities seeking government protection, recreational activities, and parochial concerns. As sociologist Robert Merton has argued, party organizations gained hegemony not only because of their discipline but also because they fulfilled many social needs that governments did not address.[55]

State and local party organizations were central to U.S. politics for more than a century. Since the advent of the New Deal in the 1930s, government at all levels has assumed a vast number of functions. Specific interest groups increasingly bore the burden of making demands on the political establishment. The government bureaucracy and interest groups, in effect, took over much of the function of making demands; rather than going to a party leader for action, citizens today approach government agencies and interest groups, as well as legislative representatives. In addition, organizations loyal to specific candidates rather than the parties gradually took over the presidential selection process.

The importance of money and patronage grew along with the size of the electorate. One of the earliest public relations blitzes was the U.S. Bank's expenditure of $42,000 from 1830 to 1832 on pamphlets against the efforts of President Andrew Jackson to abolish the Bank. By 1896, political strategist Mark Hanna had raised as much as $16 million for the presidential campaign of William McKinley. Richard Nixon's reelection campaign in 1972 cost more than $60 million. The total cost of elections at all levels in 1988 was more than $2 billion.

It was not until the late 1800s and early 1900s that candidates were impelled to tour the country making speeches on their own behalf. Not all candidates took to the campaign trail, however; in some campaigns, the candidates assumed at least the appearance of a nonpartisan stance. Candidates often were content to stay at home and occasionally issue statements or answer questions while the party organizations mobilized voters. In 1920, for example, Republican Warren Harding spent most of the fall campaigning from his front porch in Marion, Ohio. As late as 1932, when Franklin D. Roosevelt sought the White House, candidates struck a disinterested, nonpartisan pose during the nomination process. Many candidates did not attend party conventions, at least until the nomination was finished.

As the public philosophy of "democracy" replaced the more elitist "republicanism" in the 1800s, and as political messages came to be delivered through mass media, candidates dropped their reluctance to "barnstorm" the country to give a series of speeches. The harbinger of future campaign practices was the 1896 underdog campaign of William Jennings Bryan. Bryan traveled eighteen thousand miles and delivered some six hundred speeches to approximately five million people. The development of the state primary election in the first decade of the twentieth century, and of advanced transportation communications systems later on, contributed to the evolving tendency of the candidate to set out on the hustings.

Primaries demanded that candidates make public appeals for support. Theodore Roosevelt's participation in the 1912 Republican primaries against his handpicked successor as president from four years earlier, William Howard Taft, set the standard for political barnstorming that stands to this day. The primary and Roosevelt institutionalized the kind of public campaign that Bryan inaugurated.

Before the 1960s, primaries were just part of the presidential nomination process. Since a series of Democratic party reforms were put in place before the 1972 election, primaries have dominated the nomination process. *(See "History of the Primary System," p. 165, in this chapter.)* Nowadays, a candidate cannot win the nomination without undertaking a long public campaign.

The rise of mass media contributed to the need to make public appeals. Some cities at the turn of the century had as many as a dozen newspapers and many more radio stations. In addition, dozens of mass circulation magazines helped to shape political debate. *(See "Historical Background, " p. 705, in Media chapter of Part IV.)* Citizens came to demand to know more about the candidates' personal background and demeanor as well as policy positions. Franklin Roosevelt excelled in making mass media appeals. His campaign talks and "fireside chats" on radio set a new standard for political communication.

The acquisition of television by middle-class American families in the years after World War II ushered in a new age of political discourse. The first presidential candidate to use television advertising was Dwight D. Eisenhower in 1952. By the 1960s television advertising was an integral element in political campaigning. Every aspect of today's presidential campaign is shaped by considerations of television coverage. The simplicity and visual impact of television messages shape the way candidates are able to present themselves and the way experts judge the strength of a campaign.

Sophisticated polling methods developed after World War II with the use of computer analysis and telephone sampling techniques. A Princeton University professor's assessment of consumer demands and shortages during World War II was among the first polls to move beyond simple "snapshots" of candidate strength.[56] Today, media, campaign staffs, and contributors use polls to determine the "viability" of campaign strategies. Privately held polls have become central to the internal strategy of the candidates—helping them to understand the importance of issues and voters' psychological makeups. Eisenhower in 1952 used polling data to develop themes for television advertising and to target specific socioeconomic voter blocs for appeals. John F. Kennedy used polling extensively in his 1960 campaign. Kennedy's strategy for dealing with public resistance to his Catholicism was developed partly with such data.

Candidates today demand information about the way a wide variety of voting groups approach different issues. Candidates receive information about attitudes of groups with specific economic, ethnic, religious, geographic, educational, occupational, and residential characteristics. Polling data were crucial to the political victories of George S. McGovern in 1972, Jimmy Carter in 1976, and Ronald Reagan in 1980.

Campaigns in 1984 began using instant polling procedures to determine the effect of specific candidate performances. Selected voters watch candidates in debates and other appearances and register their feelings at intervals of several seconds by adjusting knobs on a handheld computer device. The knobs indicate whether they were feeling "positive" or "negative" toward the candidate's specific statements or actions.

Many theorists of democracy have expressed concern about the effect of technology—such as sophisticated polling and use of media—on democracy; others maintain that technology offers new possibilities for involving citizens in key electoral and governmental decisions. *(See Public Support and Opinion chapter in Part IV.)*

Rules Changes in the Democratic Party

Since 1968 there have been numerous efforts to reform the presidential nominating process. *(See Table 3.)* The most notable of these took place within the Democratic party, although once the Democrats had made changes, the Republicans followed suit. The roots of such reform can be traced in part to the tumultuous political climate of 1968, a year of disillusionment.[57] In 1968 protests against the Vietnam War reached their height, and Martin Luther King, Jr., and Robert F. Kennedy were assassinated. There were race riots in major cities, student uprisings throughout the country, and bitter confrontations between demonstrators and police. In Washington, President Lyndon B. Johnson was forced to call out federal troops to protect the White House.

The Tet offensive, launched against South Vietnam in January 1968, brought massive U.S. casualties and provoked renewed opposition to the Vietnam War. In the New Hampshire Democratic primary race, which occurred shortly thereafter, Sen. Eugene McCarthy of Minnesota campaigned against the Vietnam policies of President Johnson. In response, Democratic party regulars waged a last-minute write-in campaign for the president. They managed to beat McCarthy by 49.6 to 41.9 percent, but the media—impressed by McCarthy's showing against the president in a conservative state—portrayed Johnson as the big loser.

McCarthy's "victory" underscored the lack of popular support for Johnson's policies and prompted Sen. Robert F. Kennedy of New York to enter the race against the president on March 16. Two weeks later, on March 31, with a McCarthy victory predicted in the Wisconsin primary, Johnson withdrew his candidacy. Nevertheless, divisiveness within the Democratic party continued. Vice President Hubert Humphrey entered the race as Johnson's heir apparent on April 27, having purposely delayed his formal entry into the campaign to avoid participating in the Democratic primaries. With the support of party regulars (who commanded delegate votes), Humphrey banked on a victory at the Democratic national convention. That victory was ensured when Robert Kennedy was assassinated on June 5. But it was a hollow victory, won at a bitterly divided convention that was shaken by violent protests and ugly confrontations between the police and demonstrators. Humphrey, who had campaigned on the theme "the politics of joy," was nominated amidst the politics of anger.

Beyond the rancor of the antiwar demonstrators, the

hurling of rocks and feces in the streets, and the clubbings and gassing by the police, there was anger on the convention floor. State delegations who opposed the nomination of Humphrey felt excluded from the process, and they let their bitterness be known. Supporters of McCarthy were particularly angry. During the campaign, they had formed the ad hoc Commission on the Democratic Selection of Presidential Nominees, chaired by Iowa governor Harold Hughes. Just before the start of the convention the commission issued its report, which told of unfair representation of McCarthy during the delegate selection process and of manipulation by party leaders.

As it stood, the nomination process allowed for relatively little influence by rank-and-file Democrats. Nearly one-third of the delegates to the Democratic national convention had already been chosen by the time McCarthy announced his candidacy.[58] As political scientist William Crotty has written: "Presidential selection [in the Democratic party] was controlled from the top down. The rules governing the process, to the extent that they existed, were made and enforced by those in power, the party regulars in charge of party operations. Such things as primary victories and popular support among grassroots party elements had little effect on the choice of a presidential nominee." [59] In short, the Hughes Commission report concluded that the Democratic party's delegate selection process displayed "considerably less fidelity to basic democratic principles than a nation which claims to govern itself can safely tolerate." [60]

The McGovern-Fraser Commission. Examples of perceived abuses received widespread attention at the Democratic convention and served to increase animosity toward Humphrey and the party regulars. In the wake of Humphrey's nomination, many elements of the Democratic party were determined to change the rules of the game. The report of the convention's Credentials Committee echoed that sentiment. The report alleged unfair and exclusionary practices in the delegate selection process and proposed the establishment of a committee to examine the problem and offer recommendations. As a result, in Feburary 1969 the party established the Commission on Party Structure and Delegate Selection, chaired by Sen. George McGovern and, later, by Rep. Donald Fraser. (The commission came to be known as the McGovern-Fraser Commission.) Its report, issued a little more than a year later, included eighteen detailed "guidelines" for the state delegate selection processes.

The commission's guidelines were designed to counteract rules and practices that either inhibited access to the process or diluted the influence of those who had access. They condemned discrimination due to race, color, creed, sex, or age and required that affirmative steps be taken to give delegate representation to minorities, women, and young people in proportion to their population in each state. The guidelines further required that restrictive fees (defined as those over $10) and petition requirements for delegate candidates be eliminated and "urged" that undue restrictions on voter registration (such as literacy tests, lengthy residency requirements, and untimely registration periods) be alleviated. To help prevent dilution of influence, the guidelines banned the "unit rule" (whereby a majority of delegates bound the rest to their will) and "proxy voting" (which allowed votes to be cast for someone who was absent from a meeting) at every level of the delegate selection process; set minimum quorum provisions for party committees; and disallowed ex officio delegates (who were automatically appointed because of their public or party position). In addition, the guidelines limited the influence of party committees in the selection of delegates, required written rules for governing the process, demanded adequate public notice of all meetings pertaining to delegate selection, and called for standardized apportionment.

The McGovern-Fraser Commission finished its work early and stressed that its guidelines were mandatory. By the time the 1972 Democratic national convention met, the commission could claim that virtually all the states were in at least substantial compliance with the guidelines, that only 1.1 percent of the convention delegates were still elected by state party committees, and that the percentages of black, women, and young delegates had increased three to four times over their percentages in 1968.[61]

The effects of this compliance were considerable. On the one hand, it substantially democratized the system by opening avenues for citizen participation. On the other hand, it greatly reduced the power of party leaders, prompting some observers to say that the reforms had "dismantled" the party.[62] In the process, delegate selection systems were fundamentally altered. For instance, "party caucuses" and "delegate primaries" were abolished in favor of "participatory conventions" and "candidate primaries." In the "party caucus" system, national convention delegates were chosen by delegates who were chosen by low-level party officers. In the "participatory convention," selection of the intermediary delegates was not limited to party officers but was open to any party member. In the "delegate primary" system, the names of delegates to the national convention (rather than the names of presidential candidates) appeared on the ballot. The "candidate primary" required that the names of presidential candidates, instead of just the names of their potential delegates, be listed on the ballot.[63]

In addition, the McGovern-Fraser guidelines urged a move toward "proportional representation"—or what they called "fair representation"—which is common in European electoral systems but unusual in the United States. Under proportional representation, delegates are assigned in proportion to the relative percentage of the total that each candidate receives. (The alternative is a "winner-take-all" system, in which the candidate who wins a plurality of the popular vote receives all of the delegate votes in his or her electoral district.) Furthermore, the guidelines were interpreted as requiring mandatory "quotas" for the representation of minority groups.

Although states were in substantial compliance with the guidelines by 1972, there was considerable resistance to the reforms. Compliance was achieved because a state's delegation at the convention could not be seated unless the state had followed the guidelines. More than 40 percent of the convention's membership and more than half of the states challenged some aspect of the guidelines.[64]

Criticism of the reforms increased after the Democratic party's debacle in the 1972 election. Some observers argued that the new rules contributed to George McGovern's overwhelming loss to Richard Nixon. They argued that a demographically balanced slate of delegates was not necessarily representative of the constituency of the Democratic party. They pointed out that the rules had produced a slate of delegates that was significantly more liberal than the rank-and-file of the party. Political scientist Jeane J. Kirkpatrick, for instance, argued that the policy preferences of the average Democrat were better represented by

Table 3 Democratic Party's Reform Commissions on Presidential Selection

Known as	Formal name	Years in operation	Chair	Size	Mandating body
McGovern-Fraser Commission	Commission on Party Structure and Delegate Selection	1969-1972	Sen. George McGovern (S.D.), 1969-1970; Rep. Donald M. Fraser (Minn.), 1971-1972[a]	28	1968 national convention
Mikulski Commission	Commission on Delegate Selection and Party Structure	1972-1973	Barbara A. Mikulski, Baltimore city councilwoman	81	1972 national convention
Winograd Commission	Commission on Presidential Nomination and Party Structure	1975-1976 1976-1980[b]	Morley Winograd, former chairman of Michigan Democratic party	58	1976 national convention
Hunt Commission	Commission on Presidential Nomination	1980-1982	Gov. James B. Hunt, Jr., of North Carolina	70	1980 national convention
Fairness Commission	Fairness Commission	1984-1986	Donald Fowler, chairman of South Carolina Democratic party	53	1984 national convention

Source: Reprinted by permission from William J. Crotty, *Party Reform* (New York: Longman, 1983), 40-43. Updated by the authors.
a. Fraser assumed chair January 7, 1971.

Republican delegates than by those of their own party in 1972.[65] While it is not clear whether the reforms themselves were as responsible for the situation in 1972 as some critics have contended,[66] there was no denying the magnitude of the Democrats' loss.

The Mikulski Commission. The 1972 Democratic convention called for the establishment of another delegate selection commission. The call was largely in response to the controversy over some of the McGovern-Fraser reforms. By the time it was actually appointed, the new Commission on Delegate Selection and Party Structure (chaired by Baltimore city councilwoman Barbara Mikulski) was facing a Democratic party even more badly split between those who wanted a return to traditional procedures and those advocating further reforms. The commission responded by trying, at least rhetorically, to appease both sides.[67]

Since the strongest reaction against the McGovern-Fraser Commission had been over quotas, the Mikulski Commission sought to placate critics by making it clear that quotas were not required, although they were permitted. (Indeed, the McGovern-Fraser Commission had not originally intended for them to be mandatory.)[68] The Mikulski Commission dictated, however, that "affirmative action programs" be adopted to expand the participation of women and minority groups in party affairs. As further concessions to the critics of McGovern-Fraser, the Mikulski Commission allowed party regulars to appoint up to 25 (instead of 10) percent of a state's delegation; loosened proxy voting and quorum requirements; extended convention privileges (not including voting rights) to public officials and party regulars (although it retained the ban on ex officio members); and loosened the formula for apportioning delegates within states.

Nevertheless, advocates of reform won a major victory in the decision of the Mikulski Commission to require proportional representation of all candidates receiving a minimum of 10 percent of the vote (later changed to "from 10 to 15 percent," to be decided by individual state parties)—something that McGovern-Fraser had "urged" but not required. In short, the Mikulski Commission advanced, to the extent that it could, the goals of the McGovern-Fraser Commission. To the degree that it loosened earlier requirements, it did so not to emasculate them but to make the reforms more palatable to those within the Democratic

Major recommendations	Distinctive features	Principal report
"Quotas"; rules for opening delegate selection to 1972 national convention	First, most ambitious, and most important of reform groups. Completely rewrote rules for presidential selection; made them mandatory for state parties and state practices; changed power distribution within Democratic party; set model other reform commissions attempted to follow.	*Mandate for Change* (1970)
Modified McGovern-Fraser rules; revised quotas; provided for proportional representation of presidential candidates' strength; increased role of party regulars in delegate selection	Commission had a stormy, if brief, life. Its principal recommendations were intended to placate regulars and modify most controversial aspects of McGovern-Fraser rules. Its major achievement, however, was in *not* seriously revising the McGovern-Fraser provisions. With the work of this commission, the assumption underlying the reforms became generally accepted within the party.	*Democrats All* (1973)
10% "add-on" delegates for party officials; steps to close system at top	Vehicle of party regulars and Carter administration to tighten system, increase role of party regulars, and adopt rules expected to help Carter's renomination. Developed complicated procedures that are heavily dependent on national party interpretation.	*Openness, Participation and Party Building: Reforms for a Stronger Democratic Party* (1978)
25% quota for party officials	Expanded role of party and elected officials in national conventions.	*Report of the Commission on Presidential Nomination* (1982)
Loosened restrictions on "open primaries"; lowered the threshold for "fair representation" to 15%; increased number of "super-delegates."	Tried to satisfy both wings of the party by simultaneously increasing the power of party leaders (by increasing the number of super-delegates) and by lowering the threshold for fair representation.	No formal report.

b. The original Winograd Commission was not authorized by the national convention. It was created by the national chairman, Robert Strauss. The post-1976 committee membership was expanded.

party who had opposed the reforms established by the McGovern-Fraser Commission.[69]

In the wake of the Democratic party's reforms, the number of presidential primaries mushroomed. Between 1968 and 1976 they nearly doubled (increasing from sixteen to thirty). Most state party leaders felt that the adoption of a presidential primary was the easiest way to conform to the rules and thereby prevent a challenge to their delegates at the next national convention. Party regulars also feared that reformed caucuses would bring activists into wide-ranging party decision making—a consequence that they felt was worse than turning to a primary system.

Members of the McGovern-Fraser Commission had not intended for there to be such an increase in primaries. As Austin Ranney, a distinguished political scientist and member of the commission, has written:

> I well remember that the first thing we members of the [commission] agreed on—and about the only thing on which we approached unanimity—was that we did *not* want a national presidential primary or any great increase in the number of state primaries. Indeed, we hoped to prevent any such development by reforming the delegate-selection rules so that the party's nonprimary processes would be open and fair, participation in them would greatly increase, and consequently the demand for more primaries would fade away. . . .
>
> But we got a rude shock. After our guidelines were promulgated in 1969 no fewer than eight states newly adopted presidential primaries, and by 1972 well over two-thirds of all the delegates were chosen or bound by them. . . . So here was a case in which we had a clear objective in mind; we designed our new rules to achieve it; we got them fully accepted and enforced; and we achieved the opposite of what we intended.[70]

The Winograd Commission. Whether or not it was directly caused by the McGovern-Fraser reforms,[71] the proliferation of presidential primaries was disturbing to party regulars since primary elections tend to weaken the role of state political parties in selecting candidates. The result was the formation of yet another Democratic party commission in 1975: the Commission on the Role and Future of Presidential Primaries (later changed to the Commission on Presidential Nomination and Party Structure), headed by Michigan Democratic chairman Morley Winograd. Despite its original purpose, the Winograd Commission ultimately skirted the question of primaries. With the election of Jimmy Carter in 1976, the commission was

Table 4 Republican Party's Reform Committees on Presidential Selection

Known as	Formal name	Years in operation	Chair	Size	Mandating body
"DO" Committee	Committee on Delegates and Organization	1969-1971	Rosemary Ginn, member, Republican National Committee, from Missouri	16	1968 national convention
Rule 29 Committee	Rule 29 Committee	1973-1975	Rep. William A. Steigler (Wis.)	57	1972 national convention

Source: Compiled by the authors.

recast to reflect at least partially the interests of President Carter (which included protecting the incumbent). When it issued its final report, the commission stated that it could not reach a consensus on the issue of primaries. As a result it offered no recommendations in that area.

Unlike its earlier counterparts, the Winograd Commission worked without the fanfare of publicity. For the most part, the media had lost interest in the reform process. Political scientist William Crotty suggested that this lack of publicity played into the hands of the White House.[72] A number of the commission's recommendations seem to bear this out. First, the nomination season was shortened to three months, from the second Tuesday in March to the second Tuesday in June (although exemptions to go earlier were later given to several states including Iowa and New Hampshire). This change tended to favor the incumbent president because in a tightened time frame, the effect of early primaries and caucuses (where long shots can be thrust onto center stage) is diminished, and there is less time for unknown candidates to gain name recognition and money.

Second, the Winograd Commission proposed that filing deadlines for a candidate to enter a primary or a caucus be at least fifty-five days before the selection of delegates. This, too, would favor an incumbent by discouraging last-minute challengers. The Democratic National Committee (DNC) later amended the proposal and allowed deadlines to fall within a more flexible thirty- to ninety-day range.

Third, the commission proposed that the threshold for a candidate to be eligible for a proportional share of delegates be based on an increasing scale of 15 to 25 percent as the nomination season progressed. Although it was argued that this system would give a fair chance to long shots in the early phase of the campaign, the proposal made it extremely difficult for a candidate to wage a successful challenge to a front-runner (incumbent) over the entire course of the season. Again, the DNC overruled the proposal and set a threshold range of from 15 to 20 percent.

Finally, the commission proposed the "bound delegate" rule, which required that a delegate who was elected on behalf of a particular candidate be bound to vote for that candidate at the national convention. This became a major point of contention at the 1980 Democratic convention when Sen. Edward Kennedy of Massachusetts—hoping to upset the renomination of Carter—forced a floor fight over the rule. Kennedy's argument was that the bound delegate rule prevented delegates from taking into account events since their selection (such as the entry of a new candidate into the field). Nevertheless, this rule is problematic since it also weakens the role of the national convention (and thus, arguably, party regulars) by allowing delegates no discretion on early ballots, while ostensibly promoting the grass-roots participatory ethos of earlier reforms.

As we have seen, the Democratic National Committee ultimately altered a number of these proposals, making them less favorable to the White House. Indeed, the influence of the White House on the commission can be overstated. Some of the proposals were adopted because of considerations other than simply protecting an incumbent. Many reformers saw the shortening of the primary season, for instance, as a way of "reducing the fragmentation" of the nominating process—of cutting costs and streamlining a process they felt was unnecessarily long.[73]

Other proposals of the Winograd Commission included a ban on open primaries (meaning that a registered Republican could no longer vote in a Democratic primary); a suggestion that state party committees be able to appoint an additional 10 percent of the delegates to the national convention; continued support of affirmative action programs to represent women and minorities; and a rejection of the idea that state delegations should be equally divided between men and women, since such a recommendation too closely resembled quotas. The Democratic National Committee later overturned this last point in its call to the 1980 convention.

Finally, the commission eliminated so-called loophole primaries, which had served to undermine proportional representation. In such primaries, citizens voted directly for individual delegates (rather than the delegates being distributed in proportion to the relative vote tallies of the presidential candidates). The individual delegates receiving pluralities won. Since such primaries generally produced winner-take-all results, they were a "loophole" to the proportional representation requirement of the party rules.[74]

The Hunt Commission. By 1980, the establishment of commissions on party rules at the Democratic national convention was becoming a tradition. That year the party created the Commission on Presidential Nomination, chaired by North Carolina governor James B. Hunt, Jr. The express purpose of the Hunt Commission was to strengthen the party.

One of its most important recommendations was to increase the number of delegate slots reserved for party

Major recommendations	Distinctive features	Principal reports
Proposals for increasing participation in delegate selection process.	The committee's recommendations were not binding; designed "to implement the Republican party's Open Door policy."	No formal report.
Implement "positive action" to open delegate selection process; institute RNC review of such actions.	Most ambitious reform effort by the Republican party. However, the committee's major recommendations were rejected by the RNC and by the 1976 national convention.	No formal report.

leaders and elected officials (who have come to be known as super-delegates). The Hunt Commission went beyond the 10 percent "add-on" of the Winograd Commission to one of approximately 25 percent. Negotiations for the add-on had been complicated. The final proposal called for two delegate slots from each state for the chair and vice-chair of its Democratic party; 100 additional slots to be distributed among the states in proportion to the size of their base delegation; and a guarantee that every state have enough slots to accommodate its "core" Democratic officials (governor, members of Congress, and mayors of cities with a population of more than 250,000). Although the 10 percent add-on provided by the Winograd Commission had consisted of delegates entirely pledged to candidates, the scheme adopted by the Hunt commission allowed for a relatively large increment (almost twice the number of the original 10 percent) that would not be pledged.[75]

Another important move by the Hunt Commission was its decision to cut back on the trend toward proportional representation. Most notably, it rescinded the Winograd Commission's ban on loophole primaries. Furthermore, the threshold for receiving proportional representation was raised to 20 percent in caucus states and to 25 percent in primary states, and states were allowed to give "bonus delegates" to the winner of the primary to better reflect that candidate's strength (the "winner-take-more" option).

In addition, the Hunt Commission repealed the bound delegate rule that had caused controversy at the 1980 convention. This action returned delegates to the pre-Winograd Commission "good conscience" standard. Finally, the Hunt Commission retained the affirmative action rule; maintained the policy that delegations be equally divided between men and women (the "equal division" rule); continued to allow candidates to approve their delegates; and reaffirmed the Winograd Commission's shortening of the nomination season to three months. (The commission gave specific exemptions—notably to Iowa and New Hampshire—but with strict limits as to how much earlier than the other states they could be.)

The Fairness Commission. The most recent of the longstanding series of reform efforts within the Democratic party has been the so-called Fairness Commission, headed by Don Fowler, chairman of the state Democratic party in South Carolina. In its report, adopted by the DNC on March 8, 1986, the commission reiterated many of the recommendations of earlier commissions. Most notably it provided an opportunity for some states (such as Wisconsin and Montana) to hold open primaries. The rule, however, was tightly worded so that states that traditionally restricted participation to Democrats could not move to open systems.

The Fairness Commission also eased the mechanism for loophole primaries. At the same time, however, it lowered the threshold for "fair" (proportional) representation to 15 percent. In addition, it further increased the number of delegate slots that were reserved for unpledged superdelegates. In 1988 Jesse Jackson won primaries in ten states plus the District of Columbia, Puerto Rico, and the Virgin Islands. At the Democratic national convention, however, Jackson won only two states (South Carolina and Mississippi), the District of Columbia, and the Virgin Islands because of the votes of super-delegates.[76] As a concession to Jackson, the Rules Committee recommended at the convention that the number of super-delegates be reduced in 1992.

Effects of Democratic Reforms. The combined effects of the Democratic party's quadrennial reform efforts has been significant. First of all, the codification of rules that were binding upon state parties led to a centralization of power within the national Democratic party and a loss of autonomy of state party leaders. At the same time, the reforms greatly increased the participation of rank-and-file members, leading to the rise of a more "plebiscitary" system (that is, a system based on the vote of the people). The proliferation of primaries that accompanied the reforms also bolstered the rise of direct democracy. Finally, the reforms transformed the national party convention. Although many had thought that the rise of proportional representation would increase the role of the convention by creating a situation where there were many candidates and no front-runners, this has not happened. Instead, the convention has become a rubber stamp—formally adopting a decision already made by the popular vote of rank-and-file. Indeed, no major party presidential nomination has required more than a single vote since the Democrats nominated Adlai Stevenson on the third ballot in 1952.

Rules Changes in the Republican Party

Although the proliferation of primaries that accompanied the reforms of the Democratic party also affected the Republicans, they did not experience the same sort of internal pressures to reform as the Democrats did.[77] While liberal insurgents within the Democratic party found that party's rules to be a barrier to their participation, prompting them to push for reform in 1968, the Republicans faced no such problem. To a large degree, this was because the Republicans were a smaller, more ideologically cohesive party than the Democrats. The Republicans also had far fewer minority members, which meant that there was less demand for equal representation from within its ranks.

To the extent that ideological factions did exist within the Republican party, they did not find the rules problematic. Indeed, conservative insurgents had been quite successful in 1964. In short, a grass-roots movement promoting specific policy goals (an "amateur" movement, to use the terminology of James Q. Wilson) was apparently more feasible among the Republicans than among the Democrats. It was the failure of a similar "amateur" movement against party "professionals" within the Democratic ranks that helped to spawn that party's reform.[78]

There were also differences in the structure of the two parties. Republican rules were strictly codified and could be changed only with the approval of the national convention. The Democrats' rules were quite different. Existing in a very loose fashion, they were not codified, and changes did not have to be approved by the national convention. The ad hoc (or "common law") tradition of the Democratic rules at the national level made changes easy and invited reform.

Finally, the Republicans already had achieved several reforms sought by Democrats. Use of the unit rule at the Republican national conventions had been banned since the mid-nineteenth century. A similar ban of proxy voting at the national convention had long been in force. Leaders of the Republican party were quick to state that the reforms the Democrats were getting around to in 1968 had been accomplished in their party years before.

Clearly, the Democrats' reform went beyond the existing rules of the Republican party. Nevertheless, rank-and-file Republicans were not overly anxious to keep up the pace. The Democrats were more amenable to the centralization of national party control, and a number of the Democrats' more far-reaching efforts—such as quotas or strictly enforced affirmative action programs—were discouraged by the conservative ideology of the Republican party. Indeed, after the initial reforms of the Democrats, the Republicans warned against the effects that "McGovernizing" their party could bring about.

Nonetheless, the Republicans did institute some reforms in the post-1968 era, often along somewhat the same lines as the Democrats. *(See Table 4.)* Why? David Price, a political scientist and U.S. representative from North Carolina who served as staff director of the Hunt Commission, has written that the Republicans' efforts were partly "imitative," oftentimes "reactive," and to a degree "defensive."[79]

They were imitative in the sense that the Republicans were anxious to garner some of the publicity that the Democrats had engendered from their early reforms. The Republicans were also anxious to reduce discrimination and to broaden their demographic base—especially to young voters who had recently been enfranchised.

Republican reforms were reactive in that Republicans did not want to adopt what they perceived were debilitating aspects of the Democrats' reforms. This is what they feared when they warned against "McGovernizing." The Republican national convention amended its rules in 1976 so that a subcommittee of the Republican National Committee (RNC) would undertake all future rules review—an effort to prevent "run-away" commissions.

Finally, the Republican reforms were defensive in the sense that reforms by the Democratic party often prompted changes in state laws that also affected the Republicans. As a result, Republicans had to accommodate those changes—whatever their own rules may have been. More recently they have tried to anticipate Democratic rules changes that would affect them.

In 1968 the Republican national convention passed a resolution that called for the establishment of a committee to consider party rules changes. This resulted in the creation of the Committee on Delegates and Organization, chaired by Rosemary Ginn of Missouri. All sixteen members of the so-called DO Committee came from the Republican National Committee. Unlike the McGovern-Fraser Commission, its recommendations were not binding. Indeed, the report contained no enforcement or compliance mechanism at all, which reflected the states' rights orientation of the Republican party.

Among its recommendations were proposals to ban ex officio delegates, to eliminate proxy voting in meetings on delegate selection, and to "attempt" to have an equal number of men and women in each state's delegation to the national convention. The 1972 national convention later approved these recommendations but rejected a DO Committee proposal that delegations attempt to include youths under the age of twenty-five in numerical proportion to their population in each state. Nevertheless, the convention strengthened the rule to end discrimination and increase participation. It also established a new reform committee under Rule 29 of its bylaws.

The Rule 29 Committee was chaired by Rep. William A. Steigler of Wisconsin. Its fifty-eight members included not only members of the RNC but also state party leaders, governors, members of Congress, young people, and other representatives of the Republican party. Among its recommendations was a proposal that state parties be required to take "positive action" to broaden participation and, most important, that state action be reviewed by the RNC. Although there were no sanctions attached to the review procedure, and quotas were not a part of the recommendation, the RNC objected to the proposal on the grounds that it interfered with the states' rights outlook of the party. The 1976 national convention rejected the establishment of any compliance procedures.

Since 1976, subcommittees of the RNC have undertaken all rules review. To date, such subcommittees have not brought about any significant changes affecting the delegate selection process.

Constitutional Change

After Franklin D. Roosevelt won four terms to the White House, Republicans in Congress succeeded in initiating a constitutional amendment that would limit future presidents to two terms. By 1951, the Twenty-second Amendment, barring third terms, was part of the Constitution. The incumbent president, Harry S Truman, was exempted from the limit, which took effect with the election of Dwight D. Eisenhower in 1952. The Twenty-second Amendment has changed the dynamics of national elections. To the extent that a president derives bargaining strength by appealing to possible future electoral tests, a second-term president is less powerful. *(See "Twenty-second Amendment," p. 46, in Constitutional Beginnings chapter of Part I.)*

The two-term limit had been followed as a matter of

tradition before FDR. The precedent George Washington set when he refused to seek a third term held until 1940. An effort to pass a two-term amendment in 1876, to prevent Ulysses S. Grant from seeking a third term, failed. (He was denied renomination by his party.) Other presidents, such as Woodrow Wilson, indicated that they would like a third term, but they did not receive the nomination again. Even if a third term was in practice not probable, the mere possibility that a president always could seek reelection affected the power maneuverings between the president and Congress. Franklin Roosevelt was the only president to run for a third term. Members of the administration who had become candidates on their own—such as Vice President John Nance Garner and Postmaster General James Farley—found themselves undercut by the maneuvers of their boss. After months of speculation about whom the president might tap as his successor, Roosevelt accepted a "draft" for the Democratic nomination in 1940.

Since its passage, prominent figures including Eisenhower and Ronald Reagan have questioned the wisdom of the Twenty-second Amendment. In 1984, with President Reagan's popularity at an all-time high and no other Republicans developing a similarly loyal following, a brief movement to repeal the Twenty-second Amendment developed. The movement probably never had a chance because Reagan was by far the oldest president in history. The movement died when Reagan became embroiled in a controversy over the arms-for-hostages deal with Iran and the secret use of profits from the arms sales to support Nicaraguan rebels.

Significant Elections

Several elections since 1828 have fundamentally altered the population's voting habits and the discourse of U.S. politics. Scholars differ over the proper definition of terms such as *critical election* and *realignment,* but a number of elections stand out as turning points. *(See "Chronology of Presidential Elections," p. 266, in this chapter.)*

The Rise of Andrew Jackson: 1828. The hold of the so-called Virginia dynasty on U.S. politics was routed by the ascendance of Andrew Jackson, a hero of the War of 1812. The rough-hewn Tennessean lost the 1824 election to John Quincy Adams after the electoral college deadlocked and sent the contest to the House of Representatives. *(See "The Age of Jackson," p. 272, in this chapter.)* Jackson asserted that Adams stole the election by making a deal with Henry Clay, and Jackson plotted revenge. In 1828, Jackson won easily with his broad appeal among farmers and common laborers, especially in the West. As the nation expanded economically and geographically, Jackson's appeal for democratic processes to replace elite maneuverings was bound to get a sympathetic hearing.

Under the tutelage of Vice President Martin Van Buren of New York, Jackson developed a strong national Democratic party based on patronage. Strict party organization soon became a prerequisite for competition in national politics. The Whigs' 1836 presidential campaign was the last in which a party eschewed a unified national ticket. Van Buren easily defeated the Whigs that year.

Preservation of the Union: 1860 and 1864. After passage of the Kansas-Nebraska Act in 1854, which reopened the slavery question by allowing several new territories to decide the issue by popular sovereignty, the nation became irreparably divided over whether slavery should be extended into new territories. The legislation undermined the delicate balance of power between slave and nonslave states and aroused dissension over a wide variety of sectional issues such as internal improvements, protective tariffs, economic regulation, and the currency. Abraham Lincoln defeated two candidates from the Democratic party and one from the Constitutional Unionist party on a platform of containment of slavery. After Lincoln's election in November 1860, Southern states seceded and in February 1861 formed the Confederate States of America. For the next four years, the Union and the Confederacy fought a civil war. Lincoln won reelection in 1864 under the banner of the National Union party. The war was the most technologically sophisticated and one of the bloodiest in U.S. history at the time; but in the end, the Confederacy was restored to the Union.

Radical Reconstruction: 1868. Northern Republicans were bent on revenge in 1868, particularly since the stubborn Southern Democrat Andrew Johnson became president after Lincoln's assassination. The Republicans nominated Gen. Ulysses S. Grant, who narrowly defeated Democrat Horatio Seymour. With Republicans in control of Congress, the South came under a set of retributive policies. The Republicans controlled the South through military governors and proceeded with industrial expansion in the North and West aided by high tariffs. Grant's administration is considered one of the most corrupt in history. Republican Reconstruction policies—motivated partly by humanitarian concern for the recently freed slaves and partly by a desire for revenge—embittered the South perhaps as much as the war. Once Reconstruction was over, the Democrats dominated the old Confederacy for years to come.

Electoral Legitimacy and the Rise of Jim Crow: 1876. Disputed election results in the contest between Republican Rutherford B. Hayes and Democrat Samuel Tilden created a constitutional crisis and brought fears that another civil war was imminent. The crisis was solved with backroom bargaining that gave the Republicans the presidency in exchange for a pledge to pull federal troops out of the Confederacy and commit federal money to internal improvements in the South. The deal essentially left southern politics in the hands of many of the same figures who led the Confederacy. In the years that followed, Democrats took control of the political apparatus and passed a series of racially discriminatory measures—known as "Jim Crow" laws—that disfranchised blacks.

Defeat of Populism: 1896. After decades of falling agricultural prices, debt, and bankruptcy, farmers took over the Democratic party and in 1896 nominated one of their own, William Jennings Bryan of Nebraska, for president. Bryan called for unlimited coinage of silver to expand the money supply and to lighten the financial burden of farmers. Republican William McKinley spent ten times as much as Bryan, and voter turnout was at an all-time high. Bryan failed to bring labor into his "common man" coalition, probably because his criticism of high tariffs threatened the jobs of protected U.S. industries. The competitive two-party system that existed in most parts of the United States shifted to stronger Republican domination in the North and Democratic domination in the South. Less-competitive, one-party politics developed in all regions of the country as sectional rhetoric undermined populist appeals for a more class-oriented politics.

The Republicans Self-destruct: 1912. Between 1860 and 1932, only two Democrats won the presidency—Grover Cleveland in 1884 and 1892 and Woodrow Wilson in 1912.

In Wilson, a former university professor and governor of New Jersey, the Democrats elected a real liberal. But Wilson probably would not have won without a bitter battle in the Republican party that pitted the incumbent, William Howard Taft, against the popular former president Theodore Roosevelt. Wilson left a lasting legacy not only in domestic and foreign affairs, but also in the style of presidential leadership.

The Taft-Roosevelt feud stemmed largely from Roosevelt's feeling that Taft had betrayed the trust-busting, environmental, and foreign policies that Roosevelt had pursued between 1901 and 1908. (Some historians actually give Taft credit for being more vigorous than Roosevelt in these areas, but Roosevelt grew increasingly critical of Taft because of the deliberative way Taft approached those policies.) Roosevelt was a proud advocate of the presidential "bully pulpit," and Taft was ill-suited to much of the rough-and-tumble of public controversies.

While Roosevelt challenged Taft in the GOP primaries—the first exhibition of a popular campaign for the nomination—Wilson plotted and plodded to the Democratic nomination. Wilson won the nomination on the forty-sixth ballot at the convention in Baltimore, after maneuvering by William Jennings Bryan, House Speaker Champ Clark, antiprotectionist Oscar Underwood, and a cast of governors, favorite sons, and party leaders.

Wilson took to the hustings in the fall campaign, urging Americans to seek a moral awakening and to approve a program of liberal reforms involving labor relations, regulation of corporations and financial institutions, agriculture, and relations with other nations.

Wilson won when Roosevelt bolted the Republican party to run his own Progressive ("Bull Moose") party campaign. The politically inexperienced Wilson won the presidency with 41.8 percent of the vote, while the upstart Roosevelt finished second with 27.4 percent and the incumbent, Taft, pulled up the rear with 23.2 percent (less than half of his winning percentage of 51.6 percent in 1908). It was the most unusual of U.S. presidential election results, with a newly created third party outpolling the incumbent and both losing to a candidate with little political experience.

Dawn of the New Deal: 1932. After three years of Republican Herbert C. Hoover's uncertain leadership following the stock market crash of 1929, Democrat Franklin D. Roosevelt won the presidency and oversaw the greatest shift in political alignments in U.S. history. The Democratic coalition included a variety of groups: urbanites, blacks, Jews, Catholics, laborers, farmers, and southerners. The New Deal changed the scope and discourse of American government forever. For the first time, the federal government was involved in almost every aspect of economic and social life. By Roosevelt's third term, Republicans did not oppose the basic structure of the New Deal, only the Democrats' implementation of its programs. The United States also permanently adopted an activist role in international affairs.

Mandate for the Great Society: 1964. After John F. Kennedy's assassination in 1963, Lyndon B. Johnson became president and moved to enact Kennedy's unfinished agenda. Johnson needed a landslide not only to enact that agenda but also to move out from under Kennedy's shadow. Johnson got his landslide and oversaw one of the most prolific sessions of Congress in history. Congress passed ambitious programs affecting civil rights, medical care, education, welfare, urban development, and housing. Many of those programs created a "backlash" against social planning, especially after riots in Los Angeles in 1965 and other cities in 1968. Meanwhile, Johnson increased U.S. involvement in the Vietnam War, which eventually gave rise to a widespread protest movement. Many of the traditional groups of the Democratic coalition broke away from the party and in 1968 elected Richard Nixon president.

The Reagan Revolution: 1980 and 1984. Ronald Reagan, a former movie star and television personality, won the hearts of America's right wing with a televised speech for Barry Goldwater in 1964. For a quarter-century, Reagan delivered a standard speech that attacked government involvement in the U.S. economy and called for an aggressive foreign policy toward the Soviet Union and other Communist countries. After serving two terms as California governor, Reagan almost defeated a sitting Republican president, Gerald R. Ford, for the party nomination in 1976.

In 1980 and 1984, Reagan won landslide elections over President Jimmy Carter and Walter F. Mondale. Reagan shepherded dramatic cuts in taxes and the domestic budget through Congress in 1981 and promoted the largest military buildup ever in peacetime. Reagan put a conservative stamp on a wide range of issues: the environment, federalism, welfare, education, intervention in civil wars from Afghanistan to Nicaragua, civil rights, and energy. He also filled more than half of the federal judiciary, mostly with young conservatives. Reagan also helped to rekindle American awe of the presidency; scholars had wondered whether anyone could handle the pressures of the modern office. At the end of Reagan's second term, however, it was still doubtful whether the Reagan era constituted a political realignment, since Americans expressed steady support in the polls for the very programs Reagan attacked.

The Campaign Finance System

The role of money in politics always has been a matter of great dispute. From the first national elections, dominated by the "Virginia dynasty," until the most recent ones, dominated by federal funding and interest group donations, citizens have debated whether money strengthens or undermines democracy.

Money presents a more difficult problem than do other resources, such as polls, media, computer-generated direct mail operations, and even "machine" party organizations. The reason is simple: money, as the "universal equivalent" commodity, is the only resource that can be converted quickly into other resources.[1] A campaign with a good money supply has the potential to develop a wide range of strategies. Further, the sources and uses of money may be concealed from the public.

Money has been called both the ultimate corrupter and a major source of vigorous competition. "The kind of person who might enter national politics is changing," wrote journalist Elizabeth Drew. "Politicians who ... do not have great wealth of their own to spend, are signed up on a systematic basis by interests who wish to enjoy influence over their official conduct. Until the problem of money is dealt with, it is unrealistic to expect the political process to improve in any other respect." [2]

Taking a different point of view, another journalist, Robert J. Samuelson, wrote of proposals for finance reform: "Groups need to feel they can express themselves and participate without colliding with obtuse rules intended to shut them out. Our politics is open and freewheeling. Its occasional excesses are preferable to arbitrary restraints." [3]

Much of the debate about money in politics can be traced to the explosion in campaign spending after World War II. Presidential campaign costs increased from $37 million in 1968 to $92.2 million in 1988. Congress has attempted to control the influence of private donors on the political process. In the early 1970s Congress passed major reform legislation—the Federal Election Campaign Finance Act and subsequent amendments to that act. Reform has been limited, however, by the institutional interests of Congress. On the major issue of political action committees (PACs), for example, Congress has moved slowly, arguably because PAC contributions go to incumbents over challengers by a margin of almost four to one.[4]

The campaign finance debate turns on the extent to which private money affects a candidate's behavior both before and after the election and on whether electoral competition is stifled by private money.

Extensive statistical research by political scientist Gary C. Jacobson has found that obtaining a threshold amount of campaign contributions is critical to the fortunes of challengers for congressional seats: "In contests between incumbents and challengers, the critical variable is the amount spent by the challenger." [5] Incumbents benefit from name recognition, franking privileges, and their staffs' constituency-service and pork-barrel efforts on behalf of voters.[6] In presidential races, money was arguably the difference in the 1968 election of Richard Nixon and a factor in the 1980 election of Ronald Reagan.

Understanding the link between contributions and the positions candidates take on issues can be difficult because of the circularity and subtlety of candidate-donor relations. Contributors usually eschew a "hard sell" and insist only that their views on relevant issues be heard. But if their concerns are rejected frequently, the contributor may abandon a politician—a prospect likely to enter the calculations of election-conscious officials.

Sen. Dale Bumpers of Arkansas, frequently mentioned as a possible Democratic presidential contender in 1984 and 1988, has argued that fund raising affects the entire governmental process: "You can't have a sensible debate about how much is enough for defense when those PACs [representing defense contractors] are contributing so much. The decisions aren't based on what the likely mission of the Pentagon is going to be." [7]

Supporters of unlimited campaign spending maintain that even if "elites"—the wealthiest and most influential groups and individuals—contribute the most money, so many factions exist that they tend to check the influence of one another. To use the language of economist John Kenneth Galbraith, the goals of one interest will serve as a

'Your honor, my client believes that campaign spending limitations are a curb on free speech because everybody knows money talks!'

"countervailing force" against the goals of another interest. [8]

Many studies of campaign finance explain U.S. politics in economic terms: the U.S. political system is an "economy" of public views with a "demand" side and a "supply" side. By forming interest groups to express their concerns and by casting a ballot on election day, voters send "signals" to politicians. These signals are the demand side of the political economy. They force the suppliers of political goods—the politicians—to be responsive to the wishes of the electorate. These studies emphasize the voters' ability to shape the political environment by making independent choices: that is, demand is presumed to shape the supply of political goods. The political science literature dealing with party systems analyzes the ways that groups attach themselves to the two major parties and the ways that various coalitions shape the political debate. Coalitions display great consistency in what they demand from the political system. [9]

Political scientists Thomas Ferguson and Joel Rogers take a different view, however. They have argued that the American citizenry is disorganized and fragmented and that it therefore does not exert anywhere near the amount of control over the system that the traditional studies of campaign finance in U.S. politics suggest. Instead, the authors have contended, the system is dominated by elites who "invest" in the system: "The real market for political parties is defined by major 'investors'—groups of business firms, industrial sectors, or, in some (rare) cases, groups of voters organized collectively." [10]

The upshot of the Ferguson-Rogers analysis is that campaign contributions are a way of participating in the political process that is more important than voting, since campaign donors are better able to coordinate action and their actions help shape the choices offered to voters. The concerted action of independent oil producers in the 1980 election, for example, did much to shape debate about taxes and business regulation. Low voter participation—slightly over half of the electorate votes for president and about a third of the electorate votes in midterm elections for members of Congress—is just one of many pieces of evidence that most Americans are not sufficiently organized as voters to press their political demands. The upper-class bias of interest groups underscores the difficulties that many groups have in organizing to make their view known.[11]

Economist Mancur Olson analyzed the difficulty of forming groups to press broad social demands. Large groups of individuals, he argued, often do not pull together to promote common concerns because the possible benefits of the group seem too distant or indirect to potential group members. Only direct incentives and compulsion enable large groups to form and stay together.[12]

The U.S. labor movement, for example, reached a peak electorally during the years of the Great Depression. The economic crisis offered an opportunity for unity and, later, mandatory union membership and dues-paying gave specific unions a cohesion they had not previously experienced.

History of Campaign Finance

The extensive role of money in politics can be traced to the requirements of the American party system. When John Adams was elected president in 1796, Thomas Jefferson formed newspapers to promote Republican opposition views. But only with expansion of the electorate between 1824 and 1828, when all but two states voted directly for presidential candidates, did money become a central element in campaigns. Reaching an expanded pool of voters required mass propaganda, which, in turn, required money.

Campaign Finance in the Nineteenth Century

In 1828 Andrew Jackson challenged John Quincy Adams in the fiercest battle for the presidency in the forty-year history of that office. Jackson decried the "corrupt bargain" of the previous election, in which the House of Representatives decided the deadlocked election. Adams's supporters, meanwhile, spread gossip about Jackson's character. Adams's allies urged him to use patronage to support newspapers critical of Jackson's character. Adams recalled the dilemma:

> To pay money [in an election] directly or indirectly, was in my opinion incorrect in principle. This was my first and decisive reason for declining such a contribution. A second reason was that I could not command such a sum as $5,000 without involving myself in debt for it; and the third was, that if I once departed from my principle and gave money, there was no rule, either of expediency or of morality, which would enable to limit the amount of expenditure which I ought to incur.[13]

When Jackson defeated Adams in 1828, the age of mass popular politics began. Money thenceforth would be crucial in reaching an expanding electorate.

Henry Clay, who took up the opposition to Jackson, did not share Adams's reservations about money's corrupting influence. President Jackson's opposition to the U.S. Bank stirred urban financiers to action; between 1830 and 1832, the bank spent $42,000 on pamphleteering. Clay wrote: "It seems to me that our friends who have ability should contribute a fund for aiding the cause; and if that be deemed advisable, the appeal should be made in the large cities where alone the Capital is to be found."[14]

The parties attracted large donors long before the Civil War. Whig sponsors included the Weed and du Pont families, and Democratic sponsors included the Rothschild family, August Belmont, and Samuel Tilden. The parties attempted to build systems to extract regular contributions from members at all levels.

By the time of Abraham Lincoln's election in 1860, a presidential campaign required $100,000. Money could make or break a campaign. Stephen Douglas's losing 1860 campaign suffered from poor fund raising; Salmon P. Chase's abortive 1864 race for the GOP nomination was made possible by the largesse of financier Jay Cooke and others. Cooke also contributed $1,000 to Lincoln in the 1864 race—one of the first recorded instances of private interests contributing to both contestants to ensure access to the eventual winner.

Industrialism fed the campaign cost spiral. Wealthy entrepreneurs who donated money to Ulysses S. Grant in the 1868 election included Cooke, Cornelius Vanderbilt, A. T. Stewart, Henry Hilton, and John Astor. One historian wrote: "Never before was a candidate placed under such great obligation to men of wealth as was Grant."[15] Expenses grew to $16 million—mostly because of advertising and travel costs—for William McKinley's winning effort in 1896.[16]

The first major effort toward electoral finance reform stemmed from concern about the power of trusts and the role of campaign professionals such as Mark Hanna. Hanna, an Ohio mining magnate and a key strategist for McKinley, raised money for the Republican party through a systematic assessment of banks and corporations. He used the money to make McKinley financially solvent, to influence possible delegates, and to pay for the kind of mass propaganda campaign that would change the face of national politics forever.[17]

McKinley's successor, Theodore Roosevelt, accepted large gifts in his 1904 campaign. Roosevelt was ambiguous about the role of money in politics. He refused to return major contributions, arguing that "the wrong lies not in receiving the contribution" but in exercising improper pressure or making promises to get it.[18]

Campaign Finance in the Twentieth Century

After revelations by "muckraking" journalists about campaign finances and agitation by the progressive leader Sen. Robert La Follette (R-Wis.), Congress in 1907 passed the Tillman Act banning bank and corporate gifts to candidates seeking federal office. The legislation was ineffective because it contained no formal mechanism for monitoring the far-flung activities of various campaigns.

The Federal Corrupt Practices Act of 1910 set disclosure requirements for candidates for the House of Representatives. The law required committees and individuals "which shall in two or more states . . . attempt to influence the result" of House races to provide a complete record of

Library of Congress

Mining magnate and financier Mark Hanna (standing between President and Mrs. McKinley) raised millions of dollars for McKinley's 1896 and 1900 campaigns. His fund-raising practices sparked the first major effort toward campaign finance reform.

campaign transactions. That record was to include the names and addresses of donors giving $100 or more and all candidates receiving $10 or more. The law did not enable voters to use the information before the election. Disclosure did not take place until after the election.

The following year, Congress extended the requirements to Senate campaign contributors. The 1911 law also required House and Senate candidates to submit campaign expense reports. The legislation contained a provision that would be controversial throughout the rest of the century: a limitation on spending by candidates. Senate candidates could spend no more than $10,000, and House candidates were limited to $5,000. Congressional candidates might be more restricted if state laws dictated.

The Federal Corrupt Practices Act of 1925 was the most important finance legislation until 1971. It continued contribution bans and required campaigns to report receipts and expenditures. But neither the 1910 nor the 1925 legislation contained enforcement mechanisms to monitor the activities and connections of political campaigns. Spending limits were avoided by breaking up party and campaign committees into smaller parts and by selling advertising in party publications and selling copies of the publications at inflated prices.

The Hatch Act, passed in 1939, all but eliminated the last vestiges of the federal patronage system that was once prominent in U.S. elections. The law stemmed from a series of newspaper reports that Franklin D. Roosevelt's administration was improperly using the Works Progress Administration to bolster the reelection campaign of a Senate ally. Democratic senator Carl Hatch of New Mexico led a coalition of Republican and anti-New Deal Democrats.

The act banned federal employees from taking part in organized national political activity. It also banned solicitation from anyone receiving any federal relief funds. President Roosevelt considered a veto but instead signed the bill and led an effort the next year to extend the restrictions to employees in state agencies receiving federal funds.

Admendments to the Hatch Act, passed in 1940, banned federal contractors from contributing to political campaigns, asserted the authority of Congress to regulate the nominating process, limited contributions to a federal candidate or committee to $5,000 a year (contributions to a "state or local committee" were exempt), and limited the spending of committees operating in two or more states to $3 million. The last provision underscored the toothlessness of the law. Single political forces could evade the spending limits by simply breaking up into many legally distinct but coordinated committees.

The Hatch Act continued a long process of removing the executive establishment from campaign politics. Since the passage of the Pendleton Act in 1883, the federal government has been filled with greater numbers of civil servants. *(See "The Federal Civil Service," p. 844, in Pay and Perquisites chapter of Part V.)* Political appointees in the civil service declined from 90 percent in 1882 to 50 percent in 1896 to 20 percent in 1932.[19] Political appointees now make up less than 1 percent of the civil service.

In 1942 Congress passed the War Labor Disputes Act, which included labor unions along with national banks and corporations in the 1907 ban on contributions to political campaigns. That provision was made permanent in the Taft-Hartley Labor-Management Relations Act of 1947.

By the campaign of 1952, both parties were well financed. In the race for the Republican nomination, opponents of California governor Earl Warren spent between $500,000 and $1 million in the California primary while Warren backers spent between $50,000 and $100,000. Supporters of Sen. Robert A. Taft spent $58,000 in Ohio; Dwight D. Eisenhower spent $65,000 to Taft's $50,000 in New Hampshire; and Eisenhower outspent Taft in South Dakota $44,000 to $40,000. Eisenhower, the 1952 Republican nominee, was the first presidential candidate to make television commercials a central part of his campaign. He spent $500,000 on television compared with his Democratic rival Adlai Stevenson's $77,000.[20]

UPI/Bettmann Newsphotos

Vice-presidential candidate Richard Nixon, seen here as he appeared to millions on television Sept. 23, 1952, denied allegations of personal "slush funds" in his famous "Checkers" speech.

Allegations of personal "slush funds" were made during the campaign in 1952 and were capped by the tearful denial of Republican vice-presidential candidate Richard Nixon—in the now-famous "Checkers" speech—that he had improperly received contributions.[21]

From 1952 to 1968, campaign spending steadily climbed with the rise of television advertising, professional campaign consultants, polling, and more public barnstorming by candidates. Concern about campaign spending rose alongside developments such as John F. Kennedy's extensive use of family money to win the 1960 Democratic nomination, Goldwater's need to use many small donors in 1964, and Nixon's two-to-one spending advantage over rival Hubert Humphrey in 1968.

Congress considered several election finance reform initiatives in the 1950s and 1960s, but they were all unsuccessful. In 1962 President Kennedy's Commission on Campaign Costs issued its report and made a number of recommendations, including: tax credits for campaign donors, the removal of limits on interstate political committees, reporting requirements for presidential campaigns, government funding of transitions, and establishment of a federal agency to enforce campaign regulations. In May 1962, Kennedy proposed five bills pertaining to election finance reform, but none passed.

The 1971 Legislation

Congress in 1971 passed two major reform laws: the Federal Election Campaign Act of 1971 (FECA) and the Revenue Act of 1971. President Nixon signed the 1971 legislation only after congressional leaders agreed to delay its provisions until after Nixon's reelection campaign in 1972.

The Federal Election Campaign Act of 1971. The FECA was the most important piece of campaign finance legislation since the 1925 Federal Corrupt Practices Act. The law attacked the growing influence of the media and private contributors with blunt instruments: a limit on the amount of money that could be spent on media campaigns (repealed in 1974), per-voter spending limits on the nominating process, and a requirement for periodic disclosure of campaign spending and of funds provided by private sources.

The legislation passed by a bipartisan majority, with both parties concerned about protecting their sources of financial support and limiting private influence. Republicans were determined to protect their business support, and Democrats were determined to keep an effective electoral alliance with labor unions.

The idea behind the legislation was to reduce what was seen as the insidious influences of private money by bringing it into the light of day. Like many "sunshine" ordinances of the era, the FECA logic was that illicit influence thrives in secret and healthy contests for influence thrive in public view.

Media spending limits would be based on a formula of 10 cents per voter and pegged to the inflation rate. *Media* was defined as newspaper, magazine, television, and radio advertising. Of total media spending, only 60 percent could be earmarked for television and radio. The overall media limit for 1976, the first year of operation, was $14.3 million, of which no more than $8.5 million could be used for television and radio. In the 1968 election, Nixon had spent $12.6 million of his general election treasury of $24.9 million on media broadcasting; Humphrey had spent $6.1 million of his $10.3 million for broadcasting.[22] The legislation also included a requirement that broadcasters charge the lowest unit cost for the same advertising time that would be charged to other advertisers.

The FECA disclosure provisions called for federal candidates to file quarterly reports on spending and receipts. Candidates who contributed had to list the names, businesses, and addresses of donors who contributed $100 or more. Candidates were required to file additional reports fifteen and five days before election day. Donations of $5,000 and more had to be disclosed publicly within forty-eight hours of receipt.

Congress required that the disclosure be made during primary, caucus, convention, and runoff periods as well as during the general election. Any political committee with assets greater than $1,000 had to make public disclosures—partly closing a loophole in which campaigns hid actual expenses by creating separate campaign organizations that were technically independent of the main campaign committee.

The law still had enforcement difficulties. One notable loophole, for example, made it possible for wealthy persons to coordinate the donations of family members and friends of amounts less than $100 in order to keep the source of gifts secret.

Even more limiting was the prospect for making use of the information provided by candidates. True disclosure requires thorough examination and dissemination of the information. Listings of contributions are often so bulky and complex that no group can adequately determine the sources of influence. A flood of contributions late in a campaign cannot be examined before the election. Newspapers generally report on the top donors to the campaigns and list other donors. But finance stories usually last only a day or two; disclosure and the effect of the donations is rarely explored.

Campaign finance experts David W. Adamany and George E. Agree wrote:

> The effectiveness of disclosure depends entirely on the transmission of campaign finance information to the voters. The media may simply find this too burdensome, or they may cover it in ways consistent with editorial preferences. Nor can candidates be relied on to transmit campaign finance information. When candidates are well funded both are likely to count big givers and interest groups among their contributors; neither has an interest in raising the political finance issue.[23]

The Income Tax Checkoff. Congress passed the Revenue Act of 1971 after a long and bitter partisan struggle between congressional Democrats and the Nixon administration.

The legislation, now a centerpiece of the government financing of presidential elections, created the Presidential Election Campaign Fund for federal financing of general election campaigns. The amount of money that candidates would receive was determined by a per-voter spending formula. A candidate qualifies for matching funds by raising at least $100,000 in twenty or more states, with at least $5,000 from each state in individual contributions of $250 or less. Candidates accepting federal funds would not be allowed to accept private contributions. The act's sponsors hoped federal campaign funding would "level the playing field" for the two candidates. In the 1968 election, Nixon had outspent Humphrey two-to-one.

The federal campaign money would be raised through a "checkoff" option for taxpayers. When filling out tax forms, taxpayers could designate that $1 of their tax payment be put into a campaign fund earmarked for the major presidential candidates. Couples filing joint returns could designate $2 to go into the fund.

The Democrats, long the debt-ridden party, contended that the legislation was needed to control the amount of influence that the wealthy could exert in a presidential campaign. Republicans, looking forward to a bountiful presidential election in 1972 with one of their own seeking reelection, opposed the measure. The legislation passed but with the 1972 election exempted.

The tax checkoff has come to be accepted by both parties, partly because of loopholes that allow independent groups to spend unlimited amounts of money on behalf of favorite candidates. The legislation has not ended private influence; instead, it has redirected private funds and served as a guaranteed minimum campaign war chest. The expansion of public financing into the nomination process has allowed numerous candidates to compete, at least in the early stages of the campaign.

The Watergate Election

The last completely privately financed election was the 1972 race. Although broadcast expenses fell, overall campaign costs soared. President Nixon's campaign organization spent $61.4 million, while the Democratic campaign of George McGovern spent $21.2 million.

The Committee to Re-elect the President (or "CREEP," as it became known) relied mostly on large contributions. Nixon's chief fund-raiser, Maurice Stans, got the campaign off to a fast start by raising $20 million before April 7, the date after which contributions were required to be made public under the FECA. Some $5 million came into the Nixon coffers on April 5 and 6 alone. Leading contributors included insurance magnate W. Clement Stone, who gave $2 million, and Richard Scaife, an heir to the Mellon oil and banking fortune, who gave $1 million.[24] The Nixon campaign troubled outsiders because of some large donors' apparent expectation that they would receive government favors in return for their generosity. Stans was reported to have informed wealthy individuals and corporations that they had to contribute 1 percent of their net worth or gross annual sales to the campaign if they wished to have a good working relationship with the White House.[25]

Perhaps the most blatant single example of influence buying was the offer from International Telephone and Telegraph (ITT) to provide $400,000 in services at the Republican national convention in San Diego. The Nixon campaign eventually turned down the offer from ITT, which had an important antitrust case settled by the Justice Department, and moved the convention to Miami Beach to avoid the further appearance of impropriety.[26] Other large contributors with an interest in influencing government policy included Robert Vesco, under investigation by the Securities and Exchange Commission; Dwayne Andreas, seeking a federal bank charter; the dairy industry, seeking higher milk price supports; and the Seafarers International Union, seeking a Justice Department dismissal of an indictment.[27]

Besides access to key administration officials, the rewards for hefty donations apparently included positions in the administration. Nine of Nixon's appointees as ambassadors or heads of foreign missions contributed more than $20,000 to the 1972 campaign. Fifteen of Nixon's thirty-four noncareer appointees as heads of foreign missions contributed a total of $252,000 to the 1968 campaign.[28]

The Nixon campaign did not rely solely on large donors. It also continued the party's 1964 efforts to raise money from small donors. The Committee to Re-elect the President spent $4 million on direct mail appeals. Subse-

Form **1040A** Department of the Treasury—Internal Revenue Service
U.S. Individual Income Tax Return 1987
OMB No. 1545-0085

Step 1 Label
Use IRS label. Otherwise, please print or type.

Your first name and initial (if joint return, also give spouse's name and initial) Last name
Present home address (number and street). (If you have a P.O. Box, see page 9 of the instructions.)
PLACE LABEL HERE
City, town or post office, state, and ZIP code

Your social security no.
Spouse's social security no.
For Privacy Act and Paperwork Reduction Act Notice, see page 31.

Presidential Election Campaign Fund
Do you want $1 to go to this fund? ☐ Yes ☐ No
If joint return, does your spouse want $1 to go to this fund? ☐ Yes ☐ No
Note: *Checking "Yes" will not change your tax or reduce your refund.*

By marking "yes" on their federal income tax forms, taxpayers may designate one dollar of their tax payments for the Presidential Election Campaign Fund. This fund has subsidized presidential campaigns since 1976.

quent legislation, which provided candidates with matching funds for small amounts collected in at least twenty states, institutionalized the system of massive small-donor appeals.

Post-Watergate Finance Laws

Congress passed the most sweeping campaign finance legislation ever amidst the climate of electoral reform following the Watergate scandal. *(See "The Case of Richard Nixon," p. 373, in The Removal of the President chapter of Part II.)* Gerald R. Ford, who rose to the presidency with the resignation of Richard Nixon, reluctantly signed into law the Federal Election Campaign Act Amendments in October 1974. *(See box, Current Laws for Campaign Finance, p.189.)*

Congress was not the only body to get involved in campaign finance reform. By the time Nixon was driven from the White House because of his campaign's electoral scandals, some seventeen states had imposed limitations on the amount of money that individuals could donate to campaigns. New Jersey's limit of $600, which was eligible for state matching funds, was the lowest in the nation.[29]

The federal law was most important for presidential politics. Technically just an amendment to the 1971 law, the post-Watergate statute superseded some of the previous law's provisions and expanded others. The Federal Election Campaign Act Amendments contained provisions for the following:

~ Establishment of a federal election commission. The makeup of the commission was later found unconstitutional.

~ A limit of $1,000 per election for an individual's annual donation to a candidate for a federal office. The presidential nominating contest was considered a separate election. Gifts made in nonelection years would be counted toward the gifts for the election year.

~ A limit of $25,000 on total individual contributions for all national offices.

~ Spending limits of $10 million for the nominating process and $20 million for the general election. Spending in the nominating process would also be limited in each state according to the state's voting-age population. In future elections, these sums would rise along with the inflation rate.

~ A system of matching funds for candidates in nomination campaigns. Candidates who raise $100,000 on their own initiative—$5,000 in each of twenty states in denominations of $250 or less—could collect up to $5 million in federal matching funds.

~ A limit of $5,000 per election on the contributions of independent political committees to campaigns. To qualify as an independent committee, a group must register six months before making the donation, receive contributions from at least fifty persons, and make gifts to five to more candidates. Any group not qualifying would be bound by the $1,000 individual contribution limit. Under this provision, an organization with legally independent federal, state, and local branches could give three gifts of $5,000 to a single candidate.

~ Inclusion of indirect donations in tallies of donations. Gifts made to ancillary committees that end up in the campaign's treasury would be considered a direct contribution to the campaign.

~ A requirement that gifts greater than $100 be made by check. Any combination of cash gifts exceeding $100 would be illegal. This provision was intended help track donations and make "laundering" of money difficult.

~ A limit of $50,000 on candidates' contributions to their own presidential campaign and a limit of $1,000 per person on contributions from family members of the candidates' family.

~ Donation of $2 million to each major party for staging the national summer conventions. That amount would be increased in later elections according to the inflation rate.

~ A ban on contributions by foreign nationals. This provision was designed to prevent laundering of money.

~ A requirement that candidates establish a single organization through which all campaign spending would flow and which would submit regular reports.

Court Cases and Constitutional Issues

The 1974 law faced an important federal court challenge, *Buckley v. Valeo*, soon after it took effect. The Supreme Court's final 1975 ruling reduced congressional authority over campaign activity.

A broad ideological coalition challenged the 1974 law on a wide range of constitutional grounds. The main argument was that restrictions on campaign contributions amounted to restrictions on political expression and association. Another argument was that the financial disclosure requirement violated the right to privacy. The coalition also argued that the law posed unreasonable barriers to minor political parties and violated the separation of powers. In all, the plaintiffs said, the law violated the First, Fourth, Fifth, Sixth, and Ninth amendments to the Constitution. The coalition opposing the law included James Buckley, Conservative Republican senator from New York; former Democratic senator Eugene McCarthy of Minnesota, a prospective third party presidential candidate; the New York Civil Liberties Union; the American Conservative Union; and *Human Events*, a conservative periodical.

Many analysts were concerned that the law would quell third party candidacies and "maverick" movements within the two major parties. Such dissident movements have been a crucial element in forcing major parties to respond to the changing demands of the electorate. The "threshold" provision, which required a party to receive at least 5 percent of the vote in the previous election in order to receive federal funding, effectively ended the life of George Wallace's 1968 American Independent party. Limitations on legal donations could have crippled McGovern's 1972 run, since it depended in its early stages on large donations from figures such as General Motors heir Stewart Mott.

The U.S. Court of Appeals for the District of Columbia upheld the law on August 14, 1975; the coalition appealed the decision to the Supreme Court. On January 30, 1976, the high court issued a 137-page unsigned opinion in *Buckley v. Valeo* that upheld some of the law's provisions and struck down others. In five separate decisions, the justices concurred and dissented with various parts of the main ruling. Congress responded to the Court's ruling the same year with amendments that answered many of the decision's objections, but Congress was unable to restore all of the law's tough provisions.

The Court approved limitations on how much individuals and organizations could contribute to national candidates as well as the disclosure provisions. The Court also approved the federal financing of presidential nominating campaigns and general election campaigns.

One of the most controversial elements of the reform—

Current Laws for Campaign Finance

Since Congress started legislating the financing of national elections, a number of provisions have come and gone. The provisions no longer on the books have either been superseded by congressional action or been declared unconstitutional by the Supreme Court.

The following provisions regulating presidential campaigns, listed in order of the progress of the nomination and general election campaigns, are still on the books. The provisions are followed by a reference to the appropriate legislation or ruling. When one year's amendments superseded previous law, both citations are listed.

~ Federal regulation. The Federal Election Commission (FEC) is the federal agency responsible for enforcement of campaign laws (Federal Election Campaign Act of 1971 [FECA], amendments of 1976).

~ Disclosure. Presidential candidates must file regular reports listing campaign contributions and expenditures (1971). Donors of $200 must be listed on the reports (1971, 1979 amendments). Any organization spending more than $5,000 on campaigns must establish formal political committees (FECA 1971, 1979). Those reports go to the FEC (1974, 1976 amendments). Candidates must establish a single organization for their campaigns (1974). The name of the candidate must be listed on campaign materials (1979).

Certain expenses of local party organizations—such as get-out-the-vote drives and voter education activities—do not have to be reported (1979). Up to $1,000 in voluntary services, such as lending a home for meetings and lodging, do not have to be reported as contributions (1979).

Independent spending of $250 or more must be reported to the FEC (1971, 1979). Organizations without formal ties to campaign organizations do not have to adhere to spending limitations (1974).

~ "Lowest-unit" rule. Broadcasters can charge campaigns only as much as they charge other advertising clients for spot commercials (1971).

~ Political action committees (PACs). Corporations and labor unions may establish separate units to promote political ends and not be in violation of federal prohibitions on direct contributions (1971).

~ Equal time. Broadcasters selling or giving time to a federal candidate must provide equal time to the candidate's campaign opponents (section 315 of the Federal Communications Act). Typically, this law gives spokespersons for both parties a chance to respond to the remarks of the other. After a State of the Union address, for example, a representative of the other party delivers a statement. Hollywood movies featuring Ronald Reagan were not permitted to be aired on television during his 1976, 1980, and 1984 campaigns because of this provision.

~ Taxpayer checkoff. Citizens may indicate on their tax forms that they would like $1 ($2 for joint filings) of their tax money to be put into the Presidential Election Campaign Fund. This fund has been used to help finance nomination and general election campaigns (1971).

~ Matching funds during primaries. Candidates may receive federal "matching funds" if they raise at least $100,000 in twenty or more states. Each of those states must contribute a total of $5,000 to the candidate in individual donations of $250 or less (1974).

~ Limits on contributions. Citizens may contribute only $1,000 to each primary or general election campaign, a total of $25,000 to federal candidates overall, and $20,000 to committees of national parties (1976). Candidates may spend only $50,000 of their own or their family's money on their campaigns if they accept federal funding (1971, 1976).

Multicandidate committees—most commonly PACs—may contribute only $5,000 per candidate and $15,000 to committees of the national parties (1976).

~ Federal funding of national conventions. The parties receive $3 million each for their summer conventions (1974, 1979).

~ Spending limits. Candidates receiving federal matching funds may spend limited amounts during the nomination season and other limited amounts in each of the states (state limits are determined by population). The limit in 1976, the first year, was $10 million; the limit has been adjusted to account for inflation.

~ Federal funding of general election campaigns. The federal government offers the nominee of the major parties equal sums of money for the general election campaign. Candidates who accept the money may not raise or use additional campaign funds. The figure was $17 million in 1976; the amount has been adjusted each election year according to the inflation rate (1974).

---

limits on spending by individuals—was overturned. The Court agreed with the plaintiffs' First Amendment argument that restrictions on spending amounted to abridgment of free speech. The Court ruled, however, that campaign organizations could be required to honor spending limits if they accepted federal money.

The Court stated: "A restriction on the amount of money a person or group can spend on political communication during a campaign necessarily reduces the quantity of expression by restricting the number of issues discussed, the depth of their exploration, and the size of the audience reached. This is because every means of communicating ideas in today's mass society requires the expenditure of money." Only Justice Byron White rejected the reasoning. White noted the "many expensive campaign activities that are not themselves communicative or remotely related to speech." [30]

An important Supreme Court ruling, overlooked at the time, was that the $25,000 limitation on personal donations to federal candidates could not be extended to political action committees. This opened the way for PACs to spend as much as they could gather on behalf of a candidate as long as they did not have a formal connection with the candidate. Later legislation allowing donations of $5,000 to PACs, compared with $1,000 to candidate committees, also promoted PAC growth.

The Court struck down the FECA limit of $50,000 on presidential candidates' spending of their own money for their campaigns if they received federal funds. The Court, however, also accepted limits on outside contributions. The rationale for the apparent double standard was that allowing candidates to spend unlimited amounts on their own behalf would free them from the same outside influences that limits on outside contributions were intended to curb.

The majority opinion reads: "The use of personal funds reduces the candidate's dependence on outside contributions and thereby counteracts the coercive pressures and attendant risks of abuse to which the act's contribution limits are directed." Justice Thurgood Marshall, in a dissenting opinion, wrote: "It would appear to follow that the candidate with a substantial personal fortune at his disposal is off to a significant 'head start.'" Marshall added that the Court's reasoning on this issue could have the effect of encouraging wealthy candidates more than others to enter the political process.[31]

The Supreme Court also struck down the provision for creation of a federal election commission because the makeup of the panel would violate the separation of powers and appointment provisions of the Constitution. In its *Buckley v. Valeo* decision, the Court maintained that members of the commission appointed by Congress should not be permitted to exercise executive authority. The decision stated that a commission with congressional appointees could only investigate and gather information. A commission with administrative and enforcement powers would require executive appointments.

More FECA Amendments

Congress was unable to reconstitute the section of the legislation pertaining to a federal election commission within the Court's thirty-day stay of the decision. Rather than simply rework the legislation to fit the Court's dictates about the separation of powers, Congress in 1976 passed a completely new set of amendments to the FECA. President Ford had wanted only some minor tinkering with the commission to satisfy the high court.[32]

The Federal Election Commission (FEC) of the 1976 law was a six-member panel appointed by the president and confirmed by the Senate. Commission members were not permitted to take part in any outside business matters. The commission was given the authority to prosecute civil violations of campaign finance law and jurisdiction over violations formerly covered only in the criminal code.

Also in response to the Court ruling, Congress passed an amendment limiting independent spending. The Court had declared unconstitutional the 1974 law's limitations on independent political expenditures. In 1976 Congress required individuals and committees making independent expenditures over $100 to swear that the expenditures were not made in collusion with the candidate.

The 1976 amendments set new spending limits. An individual could give no more than $5,000 to an independent committee and $15,000 to the national committees of a political party. The new amendments also set a total limit of $50,000 on donations from families to candidates receiving federal funds.

In 1979 Congress passed new FECA amendments designed to strengthen state and local parties and reduce red tape. The legislation did not involve any major partisan controversies. President Jimmy Carter signed the legislation in 1980.

The legislation's most important provisions addressed complaints that federal regulation strangled state and local party organizations. The bill allowed unlimited spending by state and local organizations on voter registration and get-out-the-vote drives. Those organizations also were permitted to buy unlimited campaign materials for volunteer activities. The items included buttons, bumper stickers, yard signs, posters, and hand bills. Mentioning a presidential candidate in local campaign literature no longer counted as a contribution under the 1979 amendments. Determining the value of such mention had been the source of bookkeeping nightmares.

Volunteer activities were encouraged by doubling to $1,000 the amount of money a person could spend on providing home, food, or personal travel on behalf of a candidate without reporting the amounts to the FEC. A person could spend $2,000 on such expenses on behalf of a party.

The amendments reduced the number of reports required of federal candidates from twenty-four to nine in the two-year election cycles, reduced the amount of detail required in financial disclosure reports, and eliminated disclosure requirements for candidates spending less than $5,000.

Money in Presidential Primaries

The pursuit of a presidential nomination always has been expensive. In 1920, Gen. Leonard Wood spent $1.8 million in thirteen primaries in his unsuccessful campaign against Warren Harding for the Republican nomination. Other big spenders in the nominating process have included Herbert Hoover, Franklin Roosevelt, Robert A. Taft, and John F. Kennedy.

From 1928 to 1948, the average cost of taking part in a single contested primary rose from $50,000 to $100,000. The costs increased much faster in the postwar years. By 1960, the average cost of a single contested primary had risen to $200,000; in 1964 the figure was $400,000. Costs of primaries in later presidential elections have varied so widely that an "average" is not meaningful. But it is clear that costs have soared. In 1972, for example, Democrat George S. McGovern spent $316,000 in Massachusetts; $182,000 in Pennsylvania; $231,000 in Ohio; $159,000 in Oregon; and $4.2 million in California, more than a third of what he spent on his entire nomination drive. By contrast, Hubert Humphrey, McGovern's top rival, was able to spend only $500,000 in California.[33]

Yet money does not ensure success. The record for futile big spending belongs to former Texas governor John B. Connally, who spent $13 million in the 1980 Republican primaries and won just one delegate. Sen. Henry M. Jackson of Washington spent $2.4 million in his losing two-month 1976 effort. President Carter outspent Sen. Edward Kennedy $722,000 to $215,000 in the 1980 Pennsylvania primary but lost badly.

Congress did not pass fund-raising legislation until the 1970s, in response to the inflation of campaign costs and the fear that only wealthy candidates or those indebted to large donors could run for office. Congress first encouraged small political donations with the Revenue Act of 1971, which allowed a tax credit or a deduction for political contributions in primaries and general elections. (The tax break was eliminated in 1986.)

In 1974, the Federal Election Campaign Act offered

offered matching funds to contenders for party nominations who raised a minimum of $100,000 on their own. The FECA also provided for federal financing of nominating conventions. Partial federal funding encourages campaigns to seek small donations. To be eligible for federal money, a candidate must raise $100,000, with at least $5,000 coming from each of twenty states in donations of $250 or less. In previous years, a small number of "sugar daddies" underwrote major nomination expenses. General Motors heir Stewart Mott, for example, gave liberals Eugene J. McCarthy $300,000 in 1968 and George McGovern $400,000 in 1972. Mott also made a practice of giving large loans to candidates—such as $200,000 to McGovern in 1972.

In addition to the $250-rule for matching funds, no contributor is permitted to give more than $1,000 to a candidate's nomination drive. Large donors have evaded the spirit of the law by persuading friends and family members to donate money. Donors may give $5,000 to PACs.

Matching funds have accounted for about 40 percent of the total nomination campaign expenditures. Some $31.3 million in federal money was disbursed to candidates meeting matching-fund requirements in 1980, $30.9 million in 1984, and $66.7 million in 1988. [34]

The FECA limited the money that candidates could spend in primaries. In 1976, the first year of the law's operation, no candidate could spend more than 16 cents per voting-age person in a state. That figure is adjusted for inflation each election year. [35]

Presidential hopefuls traditionally have followed an unwritten rule against public campaigns early in the election cycle. In recent years, however, the need to raise money in small sums has spurred candidates to conduct formal fund-raising drives early. By February 1975, a year before the first primary test, five Democrats had announced their candidacies. Republican George Bush met matching-fund requirements in January 1979, a full year before the 1980 race began. Candidates began their efforts just as early in previous elections, but the efforts were not as public.

Early fund raising can be crucial to a campaign because of the high costs of organization and the need to demonstrate viability. Two key rules of fund raising are to "find some fat cats, quick" and "go where the money is." Because of individual donor limits, a presidential campaign must have access to fund raisers with "lots of rich friends." The best states for fund raising have been California, New York, Florida, and Texas, which supply about one-half of all campaign donations. One observer says: "A modern presidential campaign is designed to suck money out of New York and California and spend it in Iowa and New Hampshire." [36]

Matching funds are limited to candidates who receive at least 10 percent of the vote in at least one of the last two succeeding primaries they enter. Candidates seeking delegates face a dilemma: risk missing out on the delegate hunt or risk losing matching-fund eligibility.

The matching funds "threshold" is a crucial factor in the campaign's high dropout rate after the first three or four primaries. Poor primary performances—and the fund-raising drought and loss of federal matching funds that result—have forced candidates Alan Cranston, Ernest F. Hollings, and Reubin Askew in 1984 to quit the campaign before they could reach friendly political turf. In previous years, candidates stayed in the race much longer. In contrast, the first dropout in the 1972 presidential race was John V. Lindsay in April; in 1984, candidates began dropping out in February.

Table 5 1988 Prenomination Campaign Receipts and Expenditures, by Candidate (millions of dollars)

Candidate	Total receipts	Individual contributions	Matching funds
Bruce Babbitt	3.40	2.28	0.99
Joseph Biden	3.74	3.72	—
George Bush	31.72	22.31	8.36
Robert Dole	26.41	16.88	7.55
Michael Dukakis	28.57	19.31	8.73
Pierre du Pont	8.06	5.42	2.55
Richard A. Gephardt	9.68	6.10	2.77
Albert Gore, Jr.	12.13	7.77	3.32
Alexander Haig	1.98	1.37	0.53
Gary Hart	4.44	2.29	1.08
Jesse Jackson	18.69	11.99	5.76
Jack Kemp	16.26	10.06	5.62
Marion G. Robertson	29.24	19.75	8.95
Paul Simon	9.33	5.89	3.13

Source: Federal Election Commission.

Notes: Figures through July 31, 1988. Individual contributions plus matching funds do not equal total receipts because the federal government gives matching funds only for particular kinds and amounts of contributions.

Candidates survived somewhat longer in 1988 than they did in the previous three nomination campaigns. George Bush defeated virtually all of his rivals in 1988 on March 8 "Super Tuesday," winning seventeen of the eighteen primaries and caucuses. Sen. Robert Dole decided to quit the race after he lost the March 15 Illinois primary, but he delayed his announcement so that his campaign could qualify for additional federal matching funds.

Among the Democrats, Michael Dukakis, Albert Gore, Jr., Jesse Jackson, Richard Gephardt, and Paul Simon survived Super Tuesday. But the Gephardt, Gore, and Simon campaigns weakened or collapsed shortly thereafter, and Dukakis was considered the winner of the nomination after he defeated Jackson in the New York primary April 19.

Candidates with strong voter appeal have found their prospects damaged because they failed to meet the threshold in two consecutive primaries. Gore ended his 1988 campaign after failing to meet the threshold in the New York primary, which cut off his federal matching funds. Arizona representative Morris K. Udall did not receive federal matching funds for nine weeks in 1976, partly because the implementation of federal regulations was uncertain in its maiden year of operation.

Spending limits do not apply to candidates who decline federal assistance. John Connally bypassed federal money in 1980 and spent $13 million raised mostly from the business community. Ronald Reagan briefly considered declining the federal money in his 1980 campaign, as did Marion G. (Pat) Robertson in 1988.

The spending restrictions and expansion of the primary schedule have created a problem: candidates must compete in as many primaries as possible with as little money as possible. The conventional wisdom after Maine senator Edmund Muskie's ill-fated Democratic 1972 drive was that he had squandered money by competing in too many primaries. But in 1975, Jimmy Carter won the nomination by winning seventeen primaries. Carter was more

Critiques of the Campaign Finance System

The system of financing presidential and congressional campaigns in the United States is not the result of any coherent design but rather the haphazard development of vague laws passed during crisis periods in U.S. electoral history.

The result, critics say, is a system in which some campaigns are overfinanced and others are underfinanced. Rather than creating elections in which the candidates have an equal opportunity to present themselves to voters, a few leading candidates for party nominations dominate fund raising.

Almost anyone exposed to presidential campaigns agrees that the time required for fund raising is a distraction that binds prospective candidates to special interests.

Limits on campaign contributions also damage the strength of the two-party system, other critics say. The $1,000 individual limit on donations to the national parties pales in comparison to the $5,000 limit on donations to political action committees. Those different limits encourage big donors to give to PACs, which usually concentrate on single issues rather than on the coalition building of parties.

Many critics, eyeing the threefold increase in real campaign expenditures since 1960, maintain that too much money is in circulation. Heavily financed campaigns, according to this view, are dangerous because of the superficial media images they produce. Of greater importance, perhaps, is the amount of influence expensive campaigns give to special interests that make contributions. Journalist Elizabeth Drew's *Politics and Money* is the most prominent such critique.[1]

David Adamany and George Agree, long-time experts on campaign finance, argue that any limits on campaign spending or donations might work against education of voters. They point out that spending on campaigns is slight compared with spending by the rest of the advertising industry. Since most Americans are ill-informed about the presidential candidates, what is needed is more, not less, spending.[2] Some have proposed allocating free television time for the candidates to talk about issues.

The requirements for disclosure of campaign receipts and spending are often criticized for being "too little, too late." Critics argue that the information is so voluminous and newspaper reports so skimpy that voters do not get much useful information when they are making their decisions.

1. Elizabeth Drew, *Politics and Money: The New Road to Corruption* (New York: Macmillan, 1983).
2. David Adamany and George Agree, *Political Money: A Strategy for Campaign Financing in America* (Baltimore, Md.: Johns Hopkins University Press, 1975).

adept at trimming costs and taking advantage of free media exposure.

An important element of campaign "momentum" is fund-raising ability. Carter's early fund-raising and electoral tests in 1976 enabled him to increase total monthly receipts from $125,000 in January to $400,000 in February, $612,000 in March, and $732,000 in April. Just as previous candidates relied on a few wealthy candidates, Carter depended on a strong base of regional pride: almost half of his $900,000 primary treasury came from his home state of Georgia.[37] Massachusetts governor Michael S. Dukakis benefited from the contributions of fellow Greek-Americans and businesses associated with his state's government.

Insurgent campaigns always have depended on small contributions from loyal followers. Goldwater in 1964, McCarthy in 1968, and McGovern in 1972 all relied on small donors. It now appears that even establishment candidates need a broad base of small contributors.

Spending is much heavier in the early stages of the campaign. Reports on recent presidential races found that campaigns spent about 85 percent of their state limits in the early states, then dropped to 30 to 40 percent in March, and 25 to 30 percent in April.[38] (Each state contest has its own limit according to population.)

But early spending is not always wise spending. Gary Hart's 1984 campaign spent most of its reserves in the campaign's early stages, neglecting costly organizing in later states that could have earned him more than a hundred additional delegates. The major 1976 candidates displayed the same inability to save their money for the important battles. For the 1976 race, eleven Democratic and Republican candidates spent in 1975 $13 million of the $13.3 million they had raised that year. Carter understood the importance of frugality and paid his 1976 campaign staffers one-third the salaries of staffers working for Washington senator Henry Jackson. The Carter campaign never faced a cash-flow crisis.[39]

In 1980, Sen. Edward Kennedy "spen[t] himself virtually out of existence" on high staff salaries, first-class travel, and extravagant headquarters—$2.4 million in two months compared with the Carter campaign's expenses of $2.8 million in ten months.[40]

An election's unpredictability can create enormous difficulties in making financial decisions, for candidates make spending decisions based on their primary strategy for winning nomination. Walter Mondale's "early knockout" strategy in 1984 led the Mondale campaign to use most of its funds in early states. When Hart surprised Mondale with strong showings in Iowa, New Hampshire, and the South, Mondale had to scramble to win New York, Illinois, Pennsylvania, and Ohio—with less money than Hart.

Campaigns have been ingenious in getting around the state limits, especially in the early contests. Campaign workers in New Hampshire, for example, rent cars and set up lodging in neighboring Massachusetts. They also list headquarters expenses as the cost of complying with federal regulations, which are exempt from the spending limits.

The 1984 Mondale campaign deliberately violated state limits. Mondale spent $2.85 million in the New Hampshire primary (and lost), despite a legal limit of $404,000; he later accepted a $400,000 fine. "It wasn't a lot, and that's the whole point," said Mondale aide Robert Beckel. "The FEC is not one of the great enforcement agencies of modern politics." [41]

One harmful effect of the spending limits is that campaigns are forced to shut down their headquarters in a state right after the caucus or primary takes place. Efforts to continue to organize staffs and educate voters are dropped until the general election. If the headquarters could remain in operation, the state organizations could build strong links between state and national party officials and keep the campaign atmosphere alive all year. *(See box, Critiques of the Campaign Finance System, p. 192.)*

Even though campaigns pump millions of dollars into television and radio outlets, the stations often are wary of doing business with them. Campaign spending is minor compared with the overall advertising budgets of the stations, and campaigns provide only a short burst of business that may endanger the standing of regular clients. Furthermore, the ad hoc nature of many campaigns makes doing business with them difficult. Broadcast outlets therefore set stringent standards for campaign advertising. Candidates often must contract for broadcast spots weeks in advance, and they must pay in advance to comply with FEC standards.

The mood and content of a campaign can change dramatically in a matter of days, which makes the broadcast spending decisions even more difficult. It is not always possible to pull advertising spots off the air, as the Hart campaign discovered when it failed to halt a television commercial during the 1984 Illinois primary that was critical of the Chicago Democratic machine.

Money in the General Campaign

Under the Federal Election Campaign Act, the campaigns of the major party nominees for president are financed entirely by the federal government. Participants say federal provision of campaign funds has improved the process. Between the conventions and election day, no presidential nominee must spend precious campaign time seeking money. But private money and nominally independent organizations have continued to play an important role in the general election.

The first campaign underwritten by public money was the 1976 race. In that year, both candidates were given $22 million. Because of inflation, funding rose to $29 million in 1980, $41 million in 1984, and $46 million in 1988.

The federal funding goes directly to the presidential candidates' campaign organizations. Direct support reduces the role of the two parties in the daily operations of the fall campaign.[42]

Federal financing of presidential elections has not served so much to eliminate private interests from the election as to redirect their money into independent committee efforts. In 1980, committees independent of the campaign organizations spent $13.7 million on the presidential election and another $2.3 million on congressional elections. Some $12.2 million of the independent presidential campaign spending supported Republican Ronald Reagan. Four years later, independent expenditures rose to $18.5 million, with $15.5 million spent for Reagan and only $160,000 against Reagan. (The remainder was spent for Mondale and other efforts such as interest group appeals and general civic messages that cannot be called either pro-Reagan or pro-Mondale.) Groups supporting Reagan tended to be large operations. Five conservative organizations, for example, spent more than $14.5 million. Mondale's largest donor was the Senior Political Action Committee, which spent $218,000.

Table 6 Funds Raised by Democratic and Republican National Committees, 1977-1988 (millions of dollars)

Election cycle	Democratic party	Republican party
1977-1978	26.4	84.5
1979-1980	37.2	169.5
1981-1982	39.3	215.0
1985-1986	64.8	255.2
1987-1988[a]	59.84	166.19

Sources: 1977-1986, FEC press release, May 5, 1988; 1987-1988, FEC press release, August 29, 1988.

a. Through June 1988.

Many of the independent expenditures went for direct mail operations, which often require spending a dollar to raise a dollar. Direct mail efforts are the most expensive form of fund raising. The value of direct mail is not limited to the money it attracts. Appeals for contributions advertise and make an argument as well. The appeals also provide a campaign with important feedback (information passed along informally or published in direct mail newsletters) that some of the most sophisticated survey techniques cannot match.

Federal funds are supplemented by the treasuries of the national committee of each of the major parties. The Republicans have had a strong advantage. They raised $211.1 million to the Democrats' $43.5 million in the 1985-1986 election cycle. *(See Table 6.)*

Those funds are important in setting the terrain of national political contests. In 1981, for example, the Republicans spent $6 million to support selected party candidates. Some $2.8 million went for communications systems, $2.3 million to promote President Reagan's tax-cutting policies, and $800,000 to national and state polling operations. These expenditures do much to complement the party's efforts in presidential campaigns.[43]

Similar ends are served with donations to party organizations in states that do not have restrictions on fund raising. The money is used for "party-building" activities such as voter registration efforts, polling, and advertising. *(See Table 7.)*

The Democratic ticket in 1988 countered the Republican advantage in outside spending with heavy spending in the Texas Senate race. Lloyd Bentsen, the vice-presidential candidate, spent $8 million on his reelection campaign against a weak opponent, Rep. Beau Boulter.

Bentsen ran both for vice president and for reelection to his Senate seat under a 1959 state law designed for Lyndon Johnson. In 1959, Johnson, the Senate majority leader, was planning a presidential race, but he did not want to forfeit his Senate seat if he did not make it to the White House. When Johnson won the vice presidency in 1960 on a ticket with John F. Kennedy, he resigned his Senate seat.

In his well-financed Texas campaign, Bentsen almost never mentioned his race for the Senate. Republicans charged that the Dukakis-Bentsen campaign was violating the spirit if not the letter of federal campaign finance legislation, which gives both presidential tickets equal

Table 7 Mondale-Ferraro Committee Expenditures, General Election, 1984

Expenditure class	Amount
Payroll and benefits	$ 3,487,332
Consulting contracts	2,987,659
Casual services	135,694
Computer services	333,955
Rent	368,878
Postage and delivery	468,951
Telephone	1,284,247
Printing and reproduction	898,629
Stationery and supplies	284,079
Furniture and equipment	1,102,234
Travel	10,998,581
Petty cash	263,748
Media space/time	18,550,994
Media production	1,425,608
Direct mail	500
Teleconferencing	77,896
Meetings	389,496
Campaign materials	556,222
Refundable deposits	133,250
Polling	1,115,256
Voter contact	123,930
Interest expense	49,482
Total	$45,036,621

Source: Herbert E. Alexander and Brian A. Haggerty, *Financing the 1984 Election* (Lexington, Mass.: Lexington Books, 1987), 369.

amounts for the fall campaign. The GOP asked the Federal Election Commission to count some of Bentsen's Senate money toward the Dukakis campaign limit of $46 million. The FEC and federal courts rejected the requests.

Expenses for the primary and general election campaigns can be broken down into four main categories:

~ Advertising. About half of a campaign's funds are spent on the media—the researchers and producers who design the advertising spots and the television and radio stations that air the spots. The campaigns must be careful to save enough funds until the end of the campaign for an advertising blitz when the voters are most attentive.

~ Staff salaries. In 1984, the Reagan campaign employed three hundred full-time staff members; Mondale employed half as many. Salaries range from $60,000 annually for the top staff members to $125 a week for menial jobs such as clerical work. Strategists, pollsters, fund-raisers, and speechwriters occupy the most visible positions in the campaign and usually have a one-on-one relationship with the candidate. But the campaign depends on a variety of other staffers that the candidate might not get to know, such as "advance" experts, issues researchers and analysts, bookkeepers, experts on state delegate selection and allocation rules, office managers, secretaries, and receptionists.

~ Polling and other professional services. The cost of polling has increased as pollsters have adopted more sophisticated techniques—such as "longitudinal" (long-term) analyses of selected groups of voters, "multivariate" studies of smaller population segments, which examine many variables in different combinations, and focus group studies, which involve intense interviews with small groups of voters. The complexity and expense of surveys today are mind-boggling compared with the sorting of postcards relied upon just a half-century ago. The Mondale campaign spent $1.1 million on polling in the fall 1984 campaign. Consulting contracts cost almost $3 million.

~ Travel and headquarters expenses. National campaigns today do not have any choice but to travel all over the country by chartered airplane. Candidates often must appear in three or four states in a single day, bringing with them key staffers. In addition to the cost of planes, the campaign also must pay for room and board for staff on the road. The Mondale campaign spent $10.9 million on travel expenses in the fall 1984 campaign.

Rent for campaign headquarters—usually located in the high-priced real estate market of Washington, D.C.—is several thousand dollars a month. And costs of business furniture, office supplies, and telephone service are astronomical.

Major Donors in U.S. Politics

Enthusiasm for the candidates has varied, but the major financial supporters of the Democratic and Republican parties have remained basically the same for much of the twentieth century. Republicans are backed by a relatively unified and wealthy business coalition but also have been much more successful than the Democrats at raising money from small contributors. The Democrats are backed by an uneasy alliance of business and liberal groups. The different makeups of the parties produce different public images: the Republicans have a single coherent message, while the Democrats more often are best by conflicting internal demands.

Democratic Donors

The Democratic coalition since the New Deal has been built around the notion of a growth economy that allows the party to attract the less economically fortunate members of society with a variety of social programs. Big financial backers have included multinational corporations, real estate developers, and elements of the communications and entertainment industries. The manufacturing concerns that ally with the Democrats have tended to be capital-intensive firms, seeking new markets abroad as a way of spurring growth. (Capital-intensive firms are those that rely more on machinery in mass production than on cheap labor.) The Democratic commitment to "international liberalism" came in the form of low tariffs, an international monetary system dominated by the dollar and U.S. banks, and international development programs. *(See box, Tariffs in U.S. Politics, p. 195.)*

The U.S. economy was so strong in the post-World War II era that the demands of the less well-off groups—farmers, organized labor, blacks, the elderly, and the poor—did not antagonize the party's more conservative members of the business establishment. There was room in the party for both the masses of people seeking government protection and the financial supporters. Rogers and Ferguson noted: "Because they were capital-intensive, firms in the bloc were less threatened by labor turbulence and organization. They could thus 'afford' a coalition with labor. Because [these firms] were world, as well as U.S., pacesetters, they stood to gain from global free trade."[44]

The New Deal coalition included large, growing corporations such as General Electric, International Business

Tariffs in U.S. Politics

Tariffs—taxes levied on goods imported to the United States to protect domestic producers and raise revenues—have been a constant issue in U.S. presidential politics. Positions on tariffs reveal much about the kinds of social and political alignments each party supports.

Determining just who is for "high tariffs" can be tricky because of the large number of imported products. The tendency of politicians to deal with interest groups one by one leads them to approve high duties for some industries but not for others. Which industries to protect depends as much on political expediency—whom one represents—as on economic philosophy or the nation's resources.

Early Tariffs

Early tariffs were passed to promote national self-sufficiency. The Tariff of 1816 passed in part because of resentment toward Great Britain during the War of 1812 and in part out of fear that Britain's economy would dominate the United States when its military could not. Whigs advocated tariffs along with "internal improvements" as part of a general plan of balanced development.

Opinion on tariffs has divided consistently along regional lines. Southern and western agricultural interests in the nineteenth century opposed tariffs because these taxes increased the cost of goods they did not produce and had to buy. Northern manufacturers favored the duties because they increased profits and protected development.

As the United States became a world economic power, regional alignments shifted. U.S. manufacturers became advocates of open markets. Regions with little industrial development—which depended on labor-intensive production processes—sought protection.

The Republican party historically has supported high tariffs. The party's alliances with business concerns led to duties that protected manufacturers in the nineteenth century as they rose to world prominence. As late as 1964, Republicans favored high tariffs to protect labor-intensive industries.

The Democrats under Franklin D. Roosevelt developed broad national dominance with their open-trade policies. Low duties in the United States corresponded with growing U.S. penetration of foreign markets. With the low-tariff policies of the New Deal years and after, the United States expanded its role in foreign affairs and was able to pursue economic growth policies that allowed expansion of social welfare programs at home. Between 1938 and 1967, for example, world trade grew at an average annual rate of 4.8 percent—twelve times the rate between 1913 and 1937.[1]

With the resurgence of European and Asian economies in the years after World War II, the U.S. share of foreign markets declined. The U.S. share of the world's gross national product fell from 40 to 22 percent between 1950 and 1980.[2] Tougher world trade competition—part of the reason for the loss of U.S. manufacturing jobs—led to various movements for protectionist legislation.

Tariffs Today

Today, party alignment on the tariff issue is fuzzy. Leading proponents of limits on imports and higher duties on incoming products have been mostly Democrats, but prominent Republicans also have sought limits and higher taxes on imports.

The issue has become important in the 1980s because of the unprecedented trade deficits under Ronald Reagan's administration. Economists attribute the deficits to the high value of the dollar, which makes American products expensive overseas. But politicians blame other nations' import duties and government subsidization of private industry. They have called for higher U.S. tariffs to balance world trade competition.

Unions have been important forces behind calls for higher tariffs. Two Democratic presidential candidates with strong union support—former vice president Walter F. Mondale in 1980 and Missouri representative Richard Gephardt in 1988—backed higher duties. Democrats also have pushed congressional efforts for trade legislation. But a wing of the Democratic party has resisted calls for higher duties. Senators Gary Hart of Colorado and Bill Bradley of New Jersey have argued for more aggressive U.S. competition in world markets rather than protection of domestic markets.

In 1980, Texas Republican John B. Connally ran for president on a strongly protectionist platform remarking: "Unless the Japanese ease trade barriers for U.S. products they should be made to sit on the docks of Yokohama in their own Toyotas watching their own Sony television sets."[3] Despite the best-financed primary campaign, Connally was badly beaten in the GOP primaries.

Republicans have moved toward strong support of the free-market philosophy but have compromised on specific proposals. President Reagan and 1988 presidential candidate Rep. Jack F. Kemp of New York spoke forcefully against protectionism, but under the Reagan administration, many tariffs increased. The portion of goods imported by the United States that were subject to trade restrictions rose from one-eighth to one-fourth between 1980 and 1987, according to the Institute for International Economics in Washington, D.C.

1. Thomas Ferguson and Joel Rogers, *Right Turn: The Decline of the Democrats and the Future of American Politics* (New York: Hill and Wang, 1986), 50.
2. Ibid., 81.
3. Richard Harwood, ed., *The Pursuit of the Presidency 1980* (New York: Berkley Books, 1980), 146.

Machines, and R. J. Reynolds, as well as big oil concerns and commercial and investment banks. Until the post-Watergate era of campaign reform and the Carter administration's windfall profits tax and emphasis on conservation, the oil industry favored many Democrats.

The importance of growth to the Democratic coalition is underscored by prominent party fund-raisers. Two of Mondale's top fund-raisers in 1984 were real estate developers Nathan Landow of Maryland and Thomas Rosenberg of Chicago. Rosenberg has based his career on subsidized housing projects and says bluntly, "My business would be a lot better if the Democrats were in power." [45]

The alliance of the "haves" and the "have nots" was strained in the 1970s and 1980s because of slower economic growth. After World War II, U.S. firms controlled 60 percent of all manufacturing production in the West and 40 percent of the total goods and services. The U.S. share of manufactured goods dropped from 26 to 18 percent between 1960 and 1980. The U.S. share of world gross national product dropped from 40 percent in 1950 to 22 percent in 1980. In 1956, forty-two of the world's largest corporations were American; by 1980, only twenty-three were.[46]

Since U.S. business entered a precarious age in the 1970s, it has been less willing to accommodate liberal causes. Business concerns increasingly rely on the Republican party to represent their interests. But business issues and support remain an important element in the Democrats' strategy, since about half of all Democratic campaign contributions come from business sources.

Since the administration of Franklin Roosevelt, the labor movement has been an integral element of the Democratic party. Critics of contribution limits argue that the Democrats' labor support neutralizes any advantage that Republicans may enjoy from corporate support. Because union workers often are organized as campaign volunteers, Democrats benefit from nonfinancial benefits that are as influential as the straight cash contributions to the GOP. Furthermore, unions may spend unlimited funds on internal communications that aid their mobilization efforts.

It is difficult to determine just how much the union workers' volunteer hours would translate into dollars. According to figures from the Federal Election Commission (FEC), unions spent $4.4 million in the 1984 election to educate their members and encourage them to become active in the campaigns. But since the 1950s union strength has experienced a steady decline. In 1950, membership stood at 23 percent of the U.S. work force; in 1984, 16 percent.[47] A study by David R. Cameron of Yale University found the U.S. labor movement to be among the weakest in the Western industrialized world.[48]

Relations between labor and the Democratic party have been strained since the late 1960s. Democratic support for labor initiatives—such as a proposed abolition of a provision in the 1947 Taft-Hartley Act that impedes organizing efforts, import protection for vulnerable labor-intensive industries such as textiles, and minimum-wage and training bills—has not been unanimous as had Democratic support for previous prolabor measures. Many Democratic presidential candidates criticized labor's demands. Much of the labor movement, meanwhile, has criticized the party's liberal foreign policy stances.

Republican Donors

The Republican party traditionally has been the bastion of domestic businesses. Labor-intensive businesses demand protectionist and antilabor policies to survive, and the GOP has responded. The party began the century as the champion of protective tariffs to spur industrialization. The Republicans continued to support policies that would protect industry from floods of cheap imports from countries with lower labor costs. Supporters of Republican presidential candidate Barry Goldwater in 1964 included George Humphrey of National Steel, Roger Milliken of the textile firm Deering Millikin, and independent oil producers John Pew and Henry Salvatori.[49] Goldwater's platform included a strong plank in favor of protectionist legislation.

The financial bases of the two parties evolved with the emergence of new issues in the 1960s and 1970s: the ascendance of Japanese and Western European economies, expanded relations with the Soviet Union and the People's Republic of China, oil shortages, political unrest in Africa and Latin America, the "internationalization" of the economic system, environmentalism, soaring budget deficits, imbalances in trade relations with other countries, and the combination of high inflation and high unemployment rates, or "stagflation."

As the economy stagnated in the 1970s, business became more involved in the political process. Groups that had been hostile to one another coalesced. Large and small oil producers, for example, moved fully into the Republican camp in the period of price increases after the oil crises of 1973 and 1979. Worldwide oil inflation spurred the growth of independent producers; when President Carter in 1979 pushed a windfall profits tax, those interests moved to the GOP. In the 1981-1982 election cycle, some 26 percent of the individual contributions to the Republican National Committee came from Texas, Louisiana, and Oklahoma—the nation's leading oil states.[50] In 1980, independent oil producers contributed $25.7 million to the Republican party, the Reagan campaign, and non-oil state Republican candidates.[51]

By building on Goldwater's 1964 fund-raising efforts, the Republicans have established an impressive list of small contributors. The party receives an average donation of $25 from people responding to direct mail initiatives, according to 1982 figures.[52] The names come from lists provided by the Carte Blanche credit card, the *Wall Street Journal*, McGraw-Hill business publications, and stock and investment firms. As *Washington Post* reporter Thomas Byrne Edsall has noted, "Those willing to give $25 a year to a political party come overwhelmingly from an economic elite." [53] Goldwater raised some $5.8 million from 651,000 such donors—that is, an "elite" comprising not simply wealthy individuals but middle-class and upper-middle-class persons with more disposable income than the average American.

President Richard Nixon's 1972 campaign drew on the Goldwater initiative, seeking more contributions from small donors and building up mass-mailing lists. Republicans expanded their mailing lists and relied almost entirely on smaller contributors in 1976. Republican committees received 58 percent of their funds from donors of less than $100. By 1980, 73 percent of GOP funds came from small contributions.[54]

The Democrats have been forced to play "catch-up" in the direct mail fund-raising game. George S. McGovern developed a mailing list with 600,000 names from various liberal causes in his 1972 campaign, but Democratic chairman Robert Strauss dumped the lists four years later and stressed fund raising from large donors, telethons, and

Table 8 Growth of PACs, 1974-1988

Category	1974	1976	1978	1980	1982	1984	1986	1988[a]
Corporate	89	433	785	1,206	1,469	1,682	1,744	1,806
Labor	201	224	217	297	380	394	384	355
Trade, membership, and health	318[b]	489[b]	453	576	649	698	745	766
Nonconnected			162	378	723	1,053	1,077	1,066
Cooperative			12	42	47	52	56	60
Corporations without stock			24	56	103	130	151	143
Totals	608	1,146	1,653	2,551	3,371	4,009	4,157	4,196

Source: FEC press release, July 18, 1988.

Note: Membership PACs are mostly the PACs of professional associations such as trial lawyers, real estate, and medical and academic organizations. Nonconnected PACs do not have any connection with a specific business firm, union, party, or candidate. Examples include the Auto Dealers and Drivers for Free Trade and Democrats for the '80s. Cooperative PACs are mostly industry coalitions. Figures for each year listed indicate the number of PACs registered with the FEC at year's end.

a. As of July 1988.

b. Numbers represent all noncorporate and nonlabor PACs; no further categorization was made.

special events.[55] Only 20 percent of the Democratic National Committee's receipts came from small contributors in the 1979-1980 election cycle.

Political Action Committees

Political action committees have been the source of great controversy in recent years because of their explosive growth, negative campaign tactics, special interest messages, and limited accountability. A PAC is a committee designed to raise and distribute money for political purposes. Many PACs are affiliated with corporations, trade and professional associations, or labor unions. Many others are independent.

Between 1974 and 1988 the number of PACs grew from 608 to 4,196. *(See Table 8.)* Independent PAC spending on campaigns has grown even faster—from about $14.2 million in 1972 to $266.8 million in 1984. Independent PAC spending was an important element in Ronald Reagan's 1984 victory. In the general election campaign, political action committees favorable to Reagan spent $7.2 million, while those favorable to Democratic challenger Walter Mondale spent $657,000.[56] This spending took place in the system of federal financing where spending levels are supposed to be equal.

Legal limits on campaign and PAC contributions are, for all practical purposes, unenforceable. Wealthy political activists can work around limits on individual donations by persuading their family and friends to give money to a number of PACs and campaigns. Once donors run up against limits to national campaign contributions, they can start giving "soft money," that is, donations to unregulated state party organizations. One indication of the importance of soft money is Reagan's 1980 campaign in Texas, one of the most important states in the nation.[57] The Reagan campaign spent virtually no money in that state because the Texas Republican organizations spent so much in his behalf.

PAC growth can be traced to the provision in federal law allowing larger donations to independent committees than to the candidate's own campaign organizations. Individuals may donate $5,000 annually to PACs but only $1,000 (one-time) to presidential candidates. The five-to-one donation advantage encourages prospective donors to give to the multicandidate PACs more than to parties or candidates.

Another cause of PAC growth is organized labor's 1972 request for "clarification" of a federal law on independent spending. Concerned that the Nixon administration would attempt to bar independent spending by unions, the American Federation of Labor-Congress of Industrial Organizations (AFL-CIO) solicited the clearance for unlimited PAC spending. The resulting 1972 amendment stated that a ban on direct campaign contributions by unions and corporations did not also imply a ban on creation of independent organizations by unions and corporations to advertise and conduct political campaigns for whatever cause they wished. The amendment also held that union and corporate money could be used for get-out-the-vote drives and intramural communications such as meetings, newsletters, and surveys. When Congress passed the 1972 amendment to the previous year's Federal Election Campaign Act sanctioning political action committees, few organizations had PACs.[58] In the decade after the amendment's passage, business PACs grew twenty-three times as fast as labor PACs.[59]

Years before the election, presidential candidates often create their own PACs to finance travel and expenses. The PACs ostensibly are designed to promote a wide range of congressional and state campaigns across the country. In reality, the bulk of the PAC money goes to support the PAC founder's presidential aspirations.[60]

Candidates initially form PACs rather than formal campaign organizations for several reasons. First, donors may contribute $5,000 annually to a multicandidate PAC compared with only $1,000 to a presidential campaign. Second, PACs are not subject to the campaign spending ceilings and other regulations that formal campaign organizations must heed.

Missouri representative Richard Gephardt's PAC, the Effective Government Committee, spent more than $1 million in 1985 and 1986, but only $65,597 on campaigns for fellow Democrats. The rest of the money paid for Gephardt's travel to early caucus and primary states and for the salaries and expenses of many campaign workers. More than a third of the money for other campaigns went to candidates from Iowa and New Hampshire. Most people involved with Gephardt's PAC made no serious attempt to hide its status as an arm of Gephardt's presidential bid.[61]

Gephardt was not the only presidential aspirant to establish a nominally independent PAC. In 1985 and 1986, PACs associated with Republican presidential candidates George Bush, Robert Dole, and Jack Kemp raised $10.4 million and distributed only $1.2 million to Republican congressional candidates. Democrats Gary Hart, Joseph Biden, and Bruce Babbitt collected $577,000 during the same period.[62]

Candidates can evade spending limits—illegally—by creating several PACs or "independent committees." The 1984 Democratic campaigns of Walter Mondale and his chief challenger, Gary Hart, did not accept any PAC money during the primaries. But Mondale allowed the creation of a number of nominally independent state committees that accepted PAC money and spent it to promote his candidacy. More than one hundred "delegate committees" solicited PAC money and enabled Mondale to avoid limits on total primary spending. After weeks of Hart's hectoring—"Give the money back!"—Mondale agreed to return the contributions from business and labor committees. Rather than giving the money back, however, Mondale made a financial settlement with the Federal Election Commission.[63]

The delegate committee expenditures were crucial. Because Mondale's "early knockout" strategy failed, his campaign nearly ran out of money during the middle stages of the primary season. Delegate committee spending enabled Mondale to stay alive during a period when Hart appeared to have enough "momentum" to win the nomination.

PACs have a middle- and upper-class bias. Business, banking, real estate, and communications are among the largest PAC interests. Middle-class interests also are central to fund raising around the issue of Social Security, the most lucrative liberal, direct mail appeal. Environmentalism, peace, and abortion are other liberal causes dominated by middle-class constituencies. Even unions, the most class-conscious of donors, have a middle-class bias. Labor appeals stress the needs of workers already enjoying wage and workplace protection. Because of interest in economic growth, labor often adopts probusiness stances.

Kansas senator Robert Dole, a presidential candidate in 1980 and 1988 and national GOP chairman from 1971 to 1973, rejects the argument that PAC dollars balance each other and allow all major positions to be heard on issues: "There aren't any Poor PACs or Food Stamp PACs or Nutrition PACs or Medicare PACs."[64] PACs must be independent of campaigns for their expenditures to be exempt from the legal limits on campaign spending. The independence is often a facade. PACs with common interests find ways to plot strategy together and receive signals from campaign organizations. Leaking the results of polls—an expensive and strategic part of any campaign—is common. The leaks help coordinate the efforts of the various groups working for a candidate. "Social" visits—such as receptions or fund-raisers where people with common political goals gather—are enough for PACs to know how to direct their efforts. Coordination can be completely unstated. Said Georgetown University professor Roy Schotland: "Any dummy can figure out where it will help the candidate to spend money. And the candidate is going to observe that money is being spent. No communication is necessary."[65]

Public appeals by PACs and campaign organizations often complement one another. PAC ads on issues such as Nicaragua, Social Security, tax policy, and defense policy dovetail presidential and congressional ads. PAC commercials even attack specific candidates. In 1980 the National Conservative Political Action Committee sponsored a campaign of broadcast commercials attacking Democratic senators George McGovern, Frank Church, Birch Bayh, and John Culver. This "negative campaigning" was considered instrumental in the senators' defeat and in Ronald Reagan's overall campaign against the Washington establishment.

PACs depend on direct mail solicitation. Republicans have a strong advantage in such operations. Goldwater's 1964 campaign pioneered the technique when wealthy contributors balked from supporting him. The Republicans had a basic direct mail list of about 1.7 million people in 1984, compared with the Democrats' list of about 200,000.[66]

Trends in Campaign Spending

Perpetual fund raising is the electoral equivalent of an arms race. Candidates are so concerned with survival that they spend more and more time and use more and more sophisticated technology to gain an advantage over rivals. Candidates raise money not according to objective standards of need but out of a fear of falling behind their rivals. The arms race mentality, said Drew, affects every aspect of politics. "It is not relevent whether every candidate who spends more than his opponent wins. What matters is what the chasing of money does to the candidates, and to the victors' subsequent behavior. The point is what raising money, not simply spending it, does to the political process."[67] Hubert Humphrey, who sought the presidency in 1960, 1968, and 1972, described the ways that fund raising affects the tenor of the campaign:

> Campaign financing is a curse. It's the most disgusting, demeaning, disenchanting, debilitating experience of a politician's life. It's stinky, it's lousy. I just can't tell you how much I hate it. I've had to break off in the middle of trying to make a decent, honorable campaign and go up to somebody's parlor or to a room and say, 'Gentlemen, and ladies, I'm desperate. You've got to help me.' ... And you see the people there—a lot of them you don't want to see. And they look at you, and you sit there and you talk to them and tell them what you're for and you need help and, out of the twenty-five who have gathered, four will contribute. And most likely one of them is in trouble and is someone you shouldn't have had a contribution from.[68]

Concern about money in politics has increased as spending at all levels of electoral politics has increased. Total costs for presidential campaigns jumped from $30 million in 1960 to $160 million in 1976 and approximately $500 million in 1988.[69] *(See Table 9.)* Because general elections are federally funded, their costs have not risen as dramatically as the costs of the nominating process, which have exploded in recent years. The New Hampshire primary alone costs millions of dollars. Even with federal funding of general elections and matching funds for primaries, private donors have continued to influence the process through their contributions to the national parties and to political action committees.[70]

The inflation of campaign costs stems from several factors: increased radio and television advertising, the rise of interest groups operating on a national scale, the decline of state and local party organizations, the shift of many campaign operations to paid political consultants, more public tests of candidate strength such as primaries and caucuses, and greater geographic dispersal of voters.

Compared with other democracies, however, the

United States spends little per voter on elections, especially considering the fragmentation inherent in its federal system. The 1983 West German parliamentary elections cost about $3.20 per voter, and the 1981 Irish parliamentary elections cost about $3.93 per voter. In addition, in both of these countries the government pays for broadcast expenses. In the United States the 1980 congressional elections cost about $1.51 per voter.[71]

Critics of interest group influence contend that the major problem of U.S. elections is that candidates do not have enough money to deliver their message. Any limitation on private donors, they say, must be accompanied by a significantly larger contribution to elections by the government. Only massive public financing will both reduce the influence of special interests and provide enough money for competitive campaigns.[72]

Many experts have suggested that Congress arrange with television and radio stations, which are under the jurisdiction of the Federal Communications Commission, to provide free air time to major candidates so that candidates can deliver their messages without undue private influence. Broadcast expenses have been the major element in the inflation of campaign costs. One proposal, modeled after the French system, would require television networks to give presidential candidates free air time during which they would speak in front of a simple backdrop; that is, the candidates would not be permitted to use the time to present slick commercials. Free air time would be limited to "talking heads" spots ranging from five minutes to an hour. The emphasis would be upon presentation of issues rather than on marketing.[73]

Comparative Party Strength

The parties' financial strength always has been unequal, but the disparity has grown in recent years. In every presidential election since World War II, the Republican party has outspent the Democratic party. With the exception of President Lyndon B. Johnson's 1964 landslide, the Republicans have received more money in large donations than the Democrats.[74] Presidential nominees since 1976 have accepted equal amounts of campaign funds from the federal government, but the funding disparity has remained. The efforts of the national party organizations, state and congressional candidates, and independent committees have combined to give the Republican candidate a strong financial advantage, which might have been decisive in some elections.[75]

In 1968 Richard Nixon spent more than twice as much money as Hubert Humphrey—$24.9 million to $10.3 million—in winning one of the closest elections in history. Humphrey was unable to afford television advertising during several weeks of the fall campaign. In 1980, Ronald Reagan benefited from a lopsided spending advantage by the national party organization and by PACs. In the 1979-1980 election cycle, the major committees of the Republican party raised $169.5 million to $37.2 million raised by the Democratic party.[76] *(See Table 6.)* The PAC targeting of Senate Democrats in the 1980 election put the party's national campaign in particular danger in several states.

Regulations and Experts

More expensive electioneering, complex federal regulation, and the rise of public primary campaigns have combined to give finance experts a central role in campaigns.

Table 9 Presidential Spending: 1960-1988 (millions of dollars)

Year	Actual spending	Adjusted spending
1960	30.0	30.0
1964	60.0	57.3
1968	100.0	85.1
1972	138.0	97.7
1976	160.0	83.2
1980	275.0	98.9
1984	325.0	96.3
1988[a]	500.0	126.5

Sources: Herbert E. Alexander and Brian A. Haggerty, *Financing the 1984 Election* (Lexington, Mass.: Lexington Books, 1987), 84; Citizen's Research Foundation.

Note: All spending figures include prenomination, convention, and general election costs.

a. Actual spending is an estimate from Herbert E. Alexander as of October 1988; adjusted spending accounts for inflation.

Because candidates need to reach voters in a more public way, and because federal regulations are tight, the most effective professionals are those who can meet legal requirements and find loopholes in federal and state election laws.

The Federal Election Campaign Act requires candidates to submit reports quarterly until the late stages of the campaign, when the reports must be submitted more frequently. Campaigns must employ several full-time staffers just to fill out forms. Accountants, lawyers, and other staff members responsible for compliance with election laws play an important role not only in complying with the law but also in planning the campaign.[77]

Five percent of a presidential campaign's expenses can be tied to compliance with a plethora of often conflicting legal structures and disclosure requirements, according to political scientist and campaign finance expert Herbert Alexander of the University of Southern California. The 1980 campaigns of Jimmy Carter and Ronald Reagan, for example, spent some $3.5 million on legal counsel for financial issues. Former FEC attorney Benjamin Vandergrift says no candidate for national office can be isolated from legal problems: "Very few decisions at any level can be made by politicians without consulting their attorneys because money is always involved, and you've got to be so careful."[78]

The FEC's incremental decision-making process makes compliance difficult. The FEC outlines its standards through case decisions; the law's status, therefore, is often in flux. The complexity is further aggravated because FEC members are political appointees with ties to politicians with national ambitions; these appointees often gear their decisions to the specific plans of their benefactor.

Even more complexity arises from changing campaign technology and interest group activity. Some technological innovations, such as video cassettes distributed to individuals and groups, raise questions about whether they should be regulated as media or other tools of the campaign. The short lifespan of political campaigns also makes it hard to comply with the rules. Institutional memory is impossible for a campaign staff to achieve, despite the elite group of campaign professionals who work in several election years.

Often the best that campaign officials can do is make decisions about spending practices after examining the cases the FEC has addressed. Because of time pressures, however, many campaigns proceed with questionable actions without carefully resolving their legality. The effect is to delay the consequences of the questionable practices until the campaign is over. Walter Mondale's 1984 campaign, for example, delayed the consequences of its one hundred illegal "delegate committees" until the primary season was over. Mondale had to pay a penalty to the FEC, but only long after the campaign had benefited from his excessive spending during the close race against Colorado senator Gary Hart. The Mondale campaign considered the $400,000 fine just one of the costs of important nationwide organization.

The time and expense of bookkeeping have become such a burden that the FEC allows campaigns to exempt the costs of compliance with federal regulations. The exemption has become a loophole. Campaigns list many expenses—including rent, telephone charges, and staff salaries—as compliance costs in order to exempt them from spending limits.

Campaign finance regulation has contributed to the nationalization of the two parties. Whether the regulations have strengthened or weakened the party system as a whole is a subject of debate. The parties have become more centralized organizations, mainly because of the complexity of complying with regulations. Before finance reform, party committees at all levels operated independently and therefore had more leverage in dealing with the national party. The need for presidential campaigns to account for the activities of state and local organizations has brought about central control. Federal funding also has produced centralization. Election efforts in previous years relied on coordination of state and local fund-raising machines, but they are now barred from donating funds directly to presidential campaigns.

How Other Campaigns Affect the Presidential Race

Debate about the financing of congressional and state elections has been more intense than debate about financing presidential elections. Those contests rely entirely on private money and are more difficult to monitor and control because hundreds take place every two years.

Even though presidential and congressional elections are separate—in contrast to the parliamentary systems of Great Britain and France—the finance system of nonpresidential elections has a profound effect on presidential politics. The system in the United States depends on campaigns at all levels for its political education and energy. Spending at lower levels is an important supplement to the presidential campaign.

Nonpresidential campaigns can reinforce presidential campaign themes and activities. Candidates for lower offices often adopt the campaign themes of the standard-bearer, so any spending in these contests augments spending for the presidential race. The condition of the economy and foreign affairs regularly become important campaigning issues for congressional candidates as well as presidential candidates. Perhaps more significant, many activities important to national politics, such as voter registration, can be undertaken by local party organizations.

Local contests have become "nationalized" as interest groups with national organization such as anti-abortion and senior citizen activists have become involved in the local contests. Congressional races, then, are shaped by many of the same interest groups that are active in presidential politics. Local races still have a parochial quality, but the way those parochial interests find expression increasingly is influenced by nationally based interest groups.[79]

Two-thirds of the contributions made by political action committees goes to incumbents, according to the public interest group Common Cause. The bias in campaign contributions fosters a high reelection rate for incumbents in Congress. Low congressional turnover, in turn, helps determine the shape of presidential politics.[80]

Presidential candidates have to piece together states to win election. They therefore must make parochial appeals, especially in swing states. In 1988, for example, Michael Dukakis made a concerted effort to appeal to southerners with campaign swings stressing crime, national defense, and the oil industry. The terms of debate in the states—influenced by contributions to Senate and House candidates—are therefore important for presidential appeals.

Even when parochial interests are not shaped by national interest groups, they can influence the national debate. Especially when they cluster together at the regional level, parochial concerns create boundaries for political debate. Candidates seeking votes in states dominated by agriculture, military spending, manufacturing, or the elderly must work within the confines of those dominant interests. The electoral college system—which encourages national candidates to assemble a coalition of states rather than attract a simple national majority—gives weight to clusters of regional and local concerns.[81]

The Nominating Process

Observers of the American political system since James Madison have pointed out that control over the selection of candidates results in control over the direction of the country. As political scientist E. E. Schattschneider has noted, in a large society a small group of active political participants controls the selection and sets the "agenda." The rest of the system—the citizens themselves—can respond in only a limited way: "The people are a sovereign whose vocabulary is limited to 'yes' and 'no.' This sovereign, moreover, can speak only when spoken to." [1]

In U.S. presidential politics, the vast majority of voters have a chance to say "yes" or "no" at two points—the nominating process and the general election. But less than a third of the eligible electorate participates in the nominating process, and in some states as little as 4 or 5 percent. The nomination contest is "biased" not only by this low participation but also by the structure of the process. The result of the nomination is a narrow yes-or-no choice in the general election.

The ability of the most active political participants to include or exclude other participants, issues, and even elements of political language goes a long way toward determining a system's bias. Schattschneider illustrated his point with the example of the schoolyard fight, the outcome of which depends on the combatants' pulling spectators into the fight.[2] By determining the national candidates and a party platform, the Democratic and Republican parties include some concerns and exclude others.

Presidential Nominating Process

Before 1968

Party-Dominated

The nomination decision is largely in the hands of party leaders. Candidates win by enlisting support of state and local party machines.

Few Primaries

Most delegates are selected by state party establishments, with little or no public participation. Some primaries are held, but their results do not necessarily determine nominee. Primaries are used to indicate candidate's "electability."

Short Campaigns

Candidates usually begin their public campaign early in the election year.

Easy Money

Candidates frequently raise large amounts of money quickly by tapping a handful of wealthy contributors. No federal limits on spending by candidates.

Limited Media Coverage

Campaigns are followed by print journalists and, in later years, by television. But press coverage of campaigns is not intensive and generally does not play a major role in influencing the process.

Late Decisions

Events early in the campaign year, such as the New Hampshire primary, are not decisive. States that pick delegates late in the year, such as California, frequently are important in selecting nominee. Many states enter convention without making final decisions about candidates.

Open Conventions

National party conventions sometimes begin with nomination still undecided. Outcome determined by maneuvering and negotiations among party factions, often stretching over multiple ballots.

Since 1968

Candidate-Dominated

Campaigns are independent of party establishments. Endorsements by party leaders have little effect on nomination choice.

Many Primaries

Most delegates are selected by popular primaries and caucuses. Nominations are determined largely by voters' decisions at these contests.

Long Campaigns

Candidates begin laying groundwork for campaigns three or four years before the election. Candidates who are not well organized at least 18 months before the election may have little chance of winning.

Difficult Fund Raising

Campaign contributions are limited to $1,000 per person, so candidates must work endlessly to raise money from thousands of small contributors. PAC contributions are important in primaries. Campaign spending is limited by law, both nationally and for individual states.

Media-Focused

Campaigns are covered intensively by the media, particularly television. Media treatment of candidates plays crucial role in determining the nominee.

"Front-loaded"

Early events, such as the Iowa caucuses and New Hampshire primary, are important. The nomination may be decided even before many major states vote. Early victories attract great media attention, which gives winners free publicity and greater fund-raising ability.

Closed Conventions

Nominee is determined before convention, which does little more than ratify decision made in primaries and caucuses. Convention activities focus on creating favorable media image of candidate for general election campaign.

With its two-party system, the American process has usually proved to be a consensual, moderating, incremental method for generating electoral options. The system's candidate-centered nature, length, expense, complexity, media saturation, and tedium create choices—that is, candidates—that are uniquely American.

Eligibility

The résumé of prospective presidential candidates must meet certain constitutional requirements, but just as important are a number of unwritten, informal requirements. American political culture demands that its chief executive meet standards of political and managerial expertise as well as moral and social standing.

Constitutional Requirements

Article II of the Constitution stipulates that all presidents be "natural born citizen[s]" who have "been 14 years a Resident within the United States" and are at least thirty-five years old. Under the Twelfth Amendment, those requirements also apply to the vice president. The requirements were intended to ensure that candidates have absolute fidelity to the nation and (in the case of the age requirement) maturity. The Founders were wary of the new nation coming under foreign influence.[3]

The presidency's most important requirement stems from the Framers' concern for separation of powers in the federal government—the Article I ban on serving simultaneously as president and as a member of Congress. That ban precludes the possibility of the United States becoming a parliamentary system like Great Britain; it also can break down party solidarity and prevent swift action on the president's agenda. The Twenty-second Amendment, which forbids a president from serving more than two full terms, also affects the president's relations with Congress, since much of the president's leverage is based on public appeals for support.[4] *(See "Institutional Separation from Congress," p. 27, and "Twenty-second Amendment," p. 46 in the Constitutional Beginnings chapter of Part I.)*

The Constitution does not have property or class qualifications. The Framers were wary of duplicating the aristocratic bent of British government, which made high social class a prerequisite for membership in the House of Lords and property a requirement for voting and hence inclusion in the House of Commons. State property qualifications for voting privileges and political candidacy were eliminated by 1856.

Unwritten Requirements

More important for screening potential presidential candidates are cultural norms. Political scientist Clinton Rossiter's classic study of the American presidency describes a limited pool of candidates: middle-aged, white, Protestant males who embody small-town family values, have legal and state government experience, and come from large northern states.[5] Since Rossiter's study, however, two southerners (Lyndon B. Johnson in 1964 and Jimmy Carter in 1976), one man more than sixty-five years old (Ronald Reagan in 1980 and 1984), and another less than forty-five (John F. Kennedy in 1960), one Catholic (Kennedy), and four candidates who were not lawyers (Johnson, Carter, Reagan, and Bush) have been elected president.

Geraldine Ferraro's Democratic vice-presidential nomination in 1984 broke the exclusion of women from serious consideration for high offices. Ferraro's nomination followed a long period of public lobbying by organizations such as the National Organization for Women.[6] Democratic representative Patricia Schroeder of Colorado and Republican Jeane J. Kirkpatrick, Reagan's first United Nations ambassador, each considered a 1988 campaign. The percentage of the electorate professing a willingness to vote for a woman jumped from 52 percent in 1958 to 80 percent in 1983. The number of women holding elective office has grown dramatically in recent years, increasing the pool of women who might pursue more ambitious political goals.[7]

Jesse Jackson's pursuit of the Democratic nomination in 1984 and 1988 might have weakened the race barrier. Jackson, leader of the civil rights group Operation PUSH, attracted 18 percent of the vote in the 1984 primaries. In 1988 Jackson won the near-unanimous support of black leaders—many of whom had been wary of him four years earlier—and made inroads into white farm and industrial votes.[8] In 1988, Jackson finished second out of the eight Democratic candidates who began the primary and caucus season. At the end of the nomination contest, Jackson was the only surviving candidate besides the eventual nominee, Gov. Michael Dukakis of Massachusetts.

Rossiter's portrait is obsolete, but it still captures the desire of Americans for a leader who combines the often contradictory qualities of political involvement and nonpartisanship, majesty and simplicity, experience and freshness, morality and toughness, friendliness and detachment. The electorate seeks candidates who can fill the symbolic functions of the head of state as well as the policy-oriented functions of the executive.[9]

Thanks in part to Geraldine Ferraro's Democratic vice-presidential nomination in 1984, women have won consideration as serious candidates for high offices.

Moral Values. The disastrous beginning of Sen. Edward M. Kennedy's 1980 campaign and the implosion of Gary Hart's 1988 candidacy are powerful evidence of the importance many Americans place on certain "moral" qualities. Kennedy was dogged by questions about his behavior following a 1969 automobile accident at Chappaquiddick, Massachusetts, in which a woman passenger was killed. In 1987 Hart's front-runner status collapsed within a week after the appearance of newspaper reports alleging adultery.

Other character traits such as "toughness" are also expected by the electorate and the media. Gov. George Romney of Michigan, a strong contender for the 1968 Republican nomination, dropped out early when he said that he had been "brainwashed" about the U.S. role in the Vietnam War. Sen. Edmund Muskie's 1972 Democratic campaign faltered when he appeared to cry as he issued a strong attack on the tactics of the *Manchester Union Leader*.[10]

Wealth often is viewed as a positive trait simply because the candidate is presumed free of a selfish interest in government, just as Plato's ideal *polis* separates the "guardians" from pecuniary motives. The "Virginia dynasty" that ruled the nation in its early years embodied this principle. Since the administration of Andrew Jackson, a down-to-earth image has been important to a candidate's success. Lyndon Johnson, Richard Nixon, Carter, Reagan and Bush were millionaires when they won the presidency, but each presented himself as an ordinary citizen.

Political Experience. The political experience of presidential nominees has undergone three distinct phases in the twentieth century. Until 1960, governors were predominant among the nominees, and state organizations led by governors dominated party conventions. William McKinley, Theodore Roosevelt, Woodrow Wilson, James Cox, Calvin Coolidge, Alfred Smith, Franklin D. Roosevelt, Alfred Landon, Thomas E. Dewey, and Adlai Stevenson all were former governors. Other candidates included members of Congress, judges, cabinet members, a business leader, and a military hero.

From 1960 to 1972, the nominees were former senators: John Kennedy, Nixon, Johnson, Barry Goldwater, Hubert H. Humphrey, and George S. McGovern. In this period the electorate was preoccupied with unique national concerns, such as the civil rights movement, the Vietnam War, the welfare state, environmentalism, and the "space race."

From 1976 to 1988, governors again dominated the nominating process. Long, media-controlled campaigns and an anti-Washington mood brought nomination victories to governors such as Jimmy Carter, Ronald Reagan, and Michael Dukakis. Nominees who were not governors were a president, Gerald R. Ford, and two former vice presidents, Walter F. Mondale and George Bush.

When experience in elective politics has not been enough to convince voters of their qualifications, candidates have boasted other experience. Wendell Willkie and Dwight D. Eisenhower, the Republican nominees in 1940 and 1952, respectively, claimed executive experience as a business leader and a general. Democrat Jimmy Carter in 1976 augmented his short political résumé—two years as a state legislator and four years as governor of Georgia—with entries of nuclear engineer, farmer, and businessman. Reagan often mentioned his term as the head of the Screen Actors Guild to augment his political experience as California governor. In his campaigns Democrat Jesse Jackson stressed his civil rights activities and leadership of Operation PUSH. Republican Marion G. (Pat) Robertson, an evangelist, introduced himself as a businessman and lawyer in 1988.

Lawyers dominate the ranks of politicians at all levels, but a number of serious candidates—including Eisenhower, Johnson, McGovern, Carter, Reagan, and Bush—were not lawyers.

Foreign Policy Experience. Voters regularly list foreign policy experience as an important electoral consideration. Members of Congress who seek the White House regularly invoke their experience in issues such as arms control, the North Atlantic Treaty Organization, international trade, military engagements, and intelligence activities as reasons they should be elected.

In the nuclear age, a perceived inability to manage foreign affairs could cripple a campaign. Goldwater, Johnson, Carter, Reagan, and Dukakis all faced criticism of their foreign policy experience. In 1988, Rep. Patricia Schroeder attempted to overcome doubts about a woman's candidacy by stressing her experience on the House Armed Services Committee: "Every year I have been on the committee, I have submitted an alternative defense budget." Referring to the Reagan administration's inability to find the proper type of ships for military maneuvers in the Persian Gulf, Schroeder said, "[My defense budgets] have always included mine sweepers." [11]

In recent years, candidates with negligible foreign policy experience have been elected president. The only experience that Carter and Reagan had was their efforts to attract foreign trade as governors and, for Carter, membership in organizations such as the Trilateral Commission. Inexperience has been countered by emotional vows to shift the foreign policy goals of the nation. In 1976 and 1980 Reagan punctuated his campaigns with bitter denunciations of the Soviet Union, arms control initiatives, treaty negotiations with Panama, and U.S. "abandonment" of allies in Taiwan.

Library of Congress

Library of Congress

Former governors William McKinley and Theodore Roosevelt were the first two twentieth-century presidents. Five other twentieth-century presidents also held governorships before becoming president.

Age. A candidate's age has on occasion been an issue, but it has not deterred the candidacies of some old and some young men. John Kennedy—who asked headline writers to call him "JFK" rather than the youthful-sounding "Jack"—was the youngest elected president in 1960 at age forty-three. His opponent, Richard Nixon, was forty-seven. Edmund G. (Jerry) Brown, Jr., and Albert Gore, Jr., ran for the presidency when they were still in their thirties. Reagan was elected in 1980 at the age of sixty-nine. His vigorous campaigning in the primaries eliminated questions about his ability to meet the job's physical demands. In 1984, when asked about his age in a debate, Reagan deflected the question with a quip; he did not, he said, intend to exploit his opponent's "youth and inexperience."

Party Identification. Close party identification has declined in recent years. In fact, some candidates since the early 1960s have found it useful to switch parties. Reagan was a Democrat for much of his adult life and, as a television personality, headed a "Democrats for Nixon" effort in 1960. But he switched parties before the Republican convention of 1964. Republicans John B. Connally and Pat Robertson, candidates in 1980 and 1988, were former Democrats. Many candidates also have downplayed the party label after winning the nomination. Campaign paraphernalia has stressed the candidate rather than the party.

Still, involvement with the party can help candidates earn "IOUs" for the campaign. Ford, who served in Congress for twenty-four years, was able to use party ties to withstand a nomination challenge from Reagan in 1976. Two major candidates in recent years, Vice President George Bush and Senate leader Robert Dole, had chaired the Republican National Committee. Those positions enabled Bush and Dole to develop a national identity, work

Library of Congress

Michael Evans, The White House

At forty-three, Kennedy was the youngest elected president; Reagan, at sixty-nine, was the oldest. Theodore Roosevelt, at forty-two, succeeded to the presidency when President McKinley was assassinated and therefore holds the record as the youngest person to become president.

with a wide variety of office seekers, and pick up important financial contacts.

The Decision to Compete

The decision to seek the presidency is among the most mysterious and difficult in American politics. In one respect, it is highly logical, even scientific. The decision involves complicated calculations about financial and time requirements; the tangle of party and state rules and the states' electoral makeups; and the need to master a complex set of policy issues, to attract endorsements, to recruit a competent and enthusiastic staff, and to develop an "image" suitable for media presentation. The prospective candidate must also consider the effect a national campaign will have on his or her family, the psychological demands of the office, and possible revelations about personal "skeletons" that might hinder a campaign.

In other ways, the decision is as idiosyncratic as the psychological makeups of the potential candidates. Some candidates, such as the sons of former ambassador to Great Britain Joseph P. Kennedy, are instilled with high political ambition from their youth. Others are groomed from childhood for great deeds; John Quincy Adams, Benjamin Harrison, and both Roosevelts were such presidents. Others come to the ambition late in life. Ronald Reagan did not run for political office until he was fifty-five. Wendell Willkie, a businessman, never ran for any office besides the presidency in 1940.

Some presidents come to the White House driven by ambition that many consider unhealthy and maybe even psychologically dangerous. Woodrow Wilson, Richard Nixon, and Lyndon B. Johnson are examples.[12]

Still others seem to be uninterested in the presidency until it comes to them. Calvin Coolidge was a little-known governor from Vermont when he was selected for vice president; he moved to the White House when President Warren G. Harding died. Rep. Gerald R. Ford of Michigan never aspired to any office above House majority leader until President Nixon appointed him vice president after major administration scandals.

Prospective candidates gradually develop confidence that they can handle the office's demands. Jimmy Carter decided to run for president soon after being elected governor of Georgia. Carter says he first considered the idea after meeting several past presidential candidates who, he said, did not impress him as possessing any more raw intelligence or energy than he had.[13] Occasionally, candidates in the presidential race will shift their hopes to the vice-presidential nomination. Presidential candidates who received the vice-presidential nomination instead include Estes Kefauver, Lyndon Johnson, Walter Mondale, and George Bush.

Many presidential campaigns have been undertaken as symbolic crusades, designed not to win the White House but to publicize certain issues. For these candidates, campaign calculations are reduced to a question of visibility. Ellen McCormack's 1976 campaign in the Democratic primaries, for example, was based on a single issue: banning abortion. McCormack did not attract more than 4 percent of the vote in any primary, but her campaign forced other candidates to address the divisive issue. Her campaign may have played a role in the "New Right" mobilization on the issue in 1980.

The Reverend Jesse Jackson's 1984 Democratic campaign followed months of deliberation among black leaders about how to counter a perceived rightward drift of U.S. politics. Many black leaders opposed his candidacy and backed former vice president Mondale instead. The Jackson candidacy—with its religious fervor and cries of "Our time has come"—was seen as strictly symbolic from the start. Partly because he did not expect to win, Jackson was not forced to moderate his positions. If Mondale had not won enough delegates to secure the nomination before the convention, Jackson could have played a pivotal role in a brokered convention.

Sen. George McGovern's brief 1968 campaign was a symbolic effort designed to help the Democratic party heal the wounds it developed during the tumultuous nomination struggle. McGovern stood in for the assassinated senator Robert F. Kennedy.

Many observers considered Barry Goldwater's 1964 campaign to be at least partly symbolic since Goldwater did not appear to have any chance of defeating President Johnson. In his primary battles with New York governor Nelson A. Rockefeller, Goldwater stressed the party's need to change its ideology rather than to field a candidate capable of defeating Johnson. Goldwater's campaign is credited with transforming the party and thus enabling Reagan to be elected president in 1980.

The Exploratory Stage

Candidates have always maneuvered for position long before the election year. In the past, however, the maneuvering took place behind the scenes and was designed to impress party leaders across the nation rather than gain a high public profile. John Kennedy's 1956 convention bid for the vice-presidential nomination and his 1958 polling of many primary states, for example, helped him establish credibility for a run for the presidency in 1960. Sen. Barry Goldwater's organization of conservative activists at the local level in October 1961 was a crucial element in his "insurgency" strategy for the 1964 Republican nomination struggle.

Contenders traditionally have delayed announcing their candidacy until late in the year before the election to avoid the disadvantages of candidacy, such as legal spend ing limits and strong public scrutiny. In recent years, however, politicians have not considered an early announcement the sign of a weak candidacy. Jimmy Carter's surprise election in 1976, after a two-year public campaign, caused Republican candidates to get started right after the 1978 congressional elections.[14]

Political Action Committees

It has been customary in recent years for politicians to create political action committees (PACs) to broaden their visibility from state and local politics to national politics and to test their appeal and fund-raising ability. Many politicians form PACs with little chance that they will run for president. PACs enable a prospective candidate to raise money, to assess strength with interest groups and geographic regions, to undertake polling and other marketing operations, to recruit political professionals, and to travel around the country.

PACs also allow the candidate to pick up important political IOUs. Since Richard Nixon's successful barnstorming on behalf of Republican state and congressional candidates in the 1966 election, when the GOP made major gains in congressional races, presidential hopefuls have built their base of support by making campaign appearances for other politicians. Walter Mondale's 1984 Democratic nomination can be attributed partly to the endorsements that he garnered after extensive travel on behalf of other candidates. Mondale held a particularly strong edge in support from "super-delegates," that is, Democratic elected officials who made up almost 15 percent of the party convention.

Ronald Reagan was one of the first major political figures to organize his national candidacy around a PAC. After losing his 1976 bid for the Republican presidential nomination, Reagan used $1 million in leftover funds to keep Citizens for the Republic operating in preparation for his eventual 1980 run. Reagan planned to keep a PAC after his presidency ended in 1989. By 1986, several candidates' PACs paid for early travel and office expenses of the 1988 campaign. Democrats Richard Gephardt, Gary Hart, Joseph Biden, and Jesse Jackson, and Republicans George Bush, Jack Kemp, and Robert Dole all got off to an early start with their PACs.[15]

Fund Raising

Because of the lack of competition in the pre-election-year maneuvering, fund raising is one of the few tangible ways to assess a candidate's early strength. For some, fund-raising success is the most important element in campaign decisions. In 1987, Colorado representative Patricia Schroeder announced that she needed to raise $2 million in five months to make a run; she raised less than $1 million and decided not to run.

Public Opinion Polls

Candidates make extensive use of public opinion polling to help them determine their chances. Modern polling techniques indicate the candidate's potential on a number of issues and with a number of groups. Besides polling broad demographic groups, campaigns also intensively interview smaller groups of people from selected demographic groups.

Campaign buttons courtesy of Rhodes Cook; Photo by Garrison Studio

Since the early 1960s, candidates have downplayed their party label. Campaign buttons usually stress the candidate rather than the party.

Exploratory Committee

When prospective candidates form an "exploratory committee," they are in effect announcing their presidential ambitions. While PACs are crucial in giving a candidate a base of a national campaign, the exploratory committee undertakes a sober analysis of the candidate's prospects for a presidential run. The members of the committee consider possible campaign themes and strategies, write speeches and position papers, line up major endorsements, recruit professionals and volunteers, assemble campaign organizations in key primary and caucus states (such as Iowa and New Hampshire), hire pollsters and campaign consultants, and develop media appeals.

The model for detailed organization in the exploratory stage is the 1984 Mondale campaign. More than any other candidate, Mondale understood the changes in party rules and was prepared to take advantage of them. He was able to parlay his long Senate career into a bevy of congressional endorsements, especially helpful under the super-delegate system of elite party representation. Mondale beat out other Democrats for a number of union endorsements, raised more money than any other candidate, and hired an experienced campaign staff.

Straw Polls

Candidates' primary and caucus successes often are presaged by skirmishes at the exploratory stages of the campaign. In October 1975, Jimmy Carter gained national press attention by winning 23 percent of the vote in a straw poll conducted at the annual Jefferson-Jackson Day dinner in Iowa. Supporters of both President Carter and Senator

Kennedy spent $1 million on a Florida straw poll in November 1979 (which Carter won handily). Sen. Howard H. Baker, Jr., of Tennessee damaged his Republican presidential prospects in November 1979 with a poor performance at a similar contest in Maine.[16] In 1987, Pat Robertson made headlines with his displays of organizational strength in the Michigan and Iowa skirmishes.

The object of efforts such as straw polls is mostly public relations. The idea behind the straw polls—in which supporters of the various campaigns pay fees to take part in a mock election—is simply to demonstrate organizational strength in a very public way to the media, to election professionals, and to the public.

The Primary and Caucus Schedule

The sequence of electoral tests is an important strategic element. Concern about the length and divisiveness of campaigns caused the Democratic party to shorten the campaign schedule and push many contests to the early part of the calendar in 1980. Party reformers hoped to limit the campaign to three months to sustain voter interest, to attract candidates with nationwide support, and to reduce party infighting.

Before the 1980 campaign the Democratic National Committee adopted a rule restricting delegate selection to the period from the second Tuesday in March until the second Tuesday in June. The "window" exempted Iowa and New Hampshire, which by the law and tradition of that state has always been the first to hold a primary. Attempts by other states to schedule their primaries at earlier dates have met with discipline by Democratic officials.

Iowa has attracted national attention with its first-in-the-nation caucus. Michigan officials have used a complex, many-tiered delegate selection process to gain national attention even before election year. The results of the Michigan tests are tentative and uncertain, however; it is difficult to ascribe more importance to that process than various straw polls and debates held during the same period.

Even though New Hampshire and Iowa have a secure hold on the first nomination contests, other states have moved their contests to the beginning of the year to attract greater attention. "Front-loading"—concentration of nomination contests at the beginning of the calendar—has resulted from the jockeying of states for national media attention, the manipulations of candidates seeking to establish name recognition, and a more general concern for controlling the length of the campaign.

Before the party reforms expanded the number of primaries in 1972, the spacing of primaries was fairly even. Few states held contests in March, and the bulk of the contests took place in April and May. By 1984, seventeen states scheduled primaries or caucuses in the first twenty-two days of the season. In 1988, more than half of the delegates were selected at the conclusion of the twenty primaries and caucuses that states scheduled on Super Tuesday, March 8.

The Early Contests

The early stages of the campaign for the presidency have become important because the nominating process has shifted its emphasis to primaries and caucuses. Especially when the campaign does not have an obvious front-runner, early contests determine a possible leader. Since the country has not had a national electoral contest for more than three years, Iowa and New Hampshire provide the first tangible results.

After several early tests, the field of candidates shrinks. The "winnowing" process was most evident in the Democratic contest in 1984, when five candidates withdrew less than three weeks after the New Hampshire primary. Within a few more days, all but two candidates quit the 1980 Republican race. In 1988, most Republican candidates

UPI/Bettmann Newsphotos

Vice President George Bush, GOP presidential candidate, appears before supporters after winning the New Hampshire presidential primary in 1988.

lost their public profile after New Hampshire and were soon out of the race. All the original Democratic candidates except Jimmy Carter and Morris K. Udall withdrew within nine weeks in 1976.[17] Within a month and a half after the New Hampshire primary in 1972, four major candidates had left the Democratic field.[18]

Media pay far more attention to Iowa and New Hampshire than other states with larger, more representative populations. An analysis of 1984 media coverage found that the New Hampshire primary received 19.2 percent of the total nomination coverage, and the Iowa caucus received 12.8 percent, although together they make up only 2.9 percent of the U.S. population.[19] One reason for the attention to New Hampshire, however, may be that no one has ever been elected president without winning the New Hampshire primary. Larger states such as New York and California receive extensive coverage later in the year, but by then the winnowing of candidates has taken place. "To put matters in perspective," wrote William Adams, professor of public administration at George Washington University, "if one-third of all European media coverage were about Luxembourg and Portugal, it would be small consolation that the balance of the coverage were apportioned more sensibly." [20]

The early primaries and caucuses are important also because they give contributors an idea which candidates have a chance for the nomination. Since making a contribution is in many ways an investment in the next government, it makes greater sense to give money to someone with a good chance of heading that government than to someone unlikely to win. Money flows to some candidates but not to others once the contributors have an idea of who the "viable" candidates will be.

Many experts have criticized the role of New Hampshire and Iowa in the nominating process. Both states are predominantly rural with a largely white, Anglo-Saxon, Protestant populations. Iowa's economy is dominated by agriculture, and New Hampshire boasts a burgeoning electronics industry; candidates therefore pay almost no attention to major problems such as the decline of U.S. industry. Activists in both states pull the political debate to the outside margins of the parties' mainstream. The antiwar movement dominated the 1968 and 1972 New Hampshire campaigns, for example, and the controversial Seabrook nuclear power plant dominated later contests.

Critics complain that the priority given those states leads to the selection of bad candidates. Professor William Mayer said: "Why in the world would we want to give an unknown, inexperienced person a good chance to be president in the first place? Given that the presidency is one of the most difficult and important jobs in the world it seems absurd to me to argue that we want to confer it on a person who has temporarily caught the fancy of a few New Hampshire voters." [21]

Not everyone, however, is critical of the disproportionate influence of the Iowa and New Hampshire contests. Several observers have lauded the old-fashioned American values of industry, family, and community that seem to exist in those two rural states. Sen. Albert Gore, Jr., a 1988 Democratic aspirant, told an Iowa gathering: "All of us who have come to your state have noticed the approach you take. You are almost worried you might make a mistake and choose the wrong candidate, because you have such an impact." *Washington Post* columnist David Broder wrote of the event: "If there was a winner, democracy was its name." [22]

For several weeks after the Iowa caucus and the New Hampshire primary, the goal of the remaining candidates is to attract media attention by winning, or performing "better than expected," in the following contests. Especially with proportional representation rules, the number of delegates at stake in the early contests is significant compared with the media attention those states receive.

In 1984, for example, Democrats Gary Hart and Walter Mondale concentrated their attention on winning as many states as possible in the March Super Tuesday electoral marathon. The candidates were less concerned with the delegates at stake than with the broad vote-getting ability they could demonstrate. Hart won more states, but Mondale was able to convince the media and political professionals that his wins constituted a "comeback." Regardless of the delegate count, Carter in Pennsylvania in 1976, Reagan in North Carolina and Texas in 1976, and Kennedy in New York and Pennsylvania in 1980 got big boosts with primary wins.

Carter's 1976 campaign turned on scheduling changes that Carter initiated. Winning a southern state over Alabama governor George Wallace was central to Carter's strategy, and Florida was probably Carter's best bet. With the help of governor Reubin Askew, Carter had the Florida primary scheduled ahead of the primaries in other southern states. Carter beat Wallace and swept the South.

Carter continued his "sequence as strategy" approach in 1980 when he arranged to move a number of southern primaries forward in the calendar and to mix states favorable to his rival, Senator Kennedy, with states that were favorable to him. Walter Mondale's 1984 campaign arranged to push forward favorable states such as Rhode Island, Massachusetts, and Michigan.

The Late Contests

After most of the primaries have been held, attention begins to turn to the question of which candidate leads in the delegate race and how many delegates are needed for a first-ballot convention victory. Candidates try not so much to win primaries as to accumulate the delegates allocated by various systems of proportional representation.

A candidate who enjoys a delegate lead late in the race will attempt to accumulate as many delegates as possible in the later primaries and caucuses. The goal of the late stages of the nomination process, especially for the front-runner, is less to win specific primaries and caucuses than to accumulate delegates. The candidates also will woo the delegates who were once allied to candidates who have dropped out, the delegates who are linked to "favorite son" candidates, and the bloc of super-delegates (elected officials) that constitute 15 percent of the convention.

Carter in 1976 managed to accumulate enough delegates for a first-ballot Democratic nomination by finishing in second or third place in many late primaries, but Carter had a commanding delegate lead that enabled proportional delegate allocations to clinch the nomination.[23] Mondale, the eventual 1984 Democratic nominee, followed a similar strategy, but he also dominated the super-delegate competition.[24]

Strategy Considerations

Early in the campaign, the candidates devise a strategy for emerging from the field or maintaining an early lead.

Delegate Selection Calendar for 1988

This calendar includes 1988 presidential primary and first-round caucus dates. The Republican contests selected 2,277 delegates to the GOP convention (1,751 in primaries and 526 in caucuses). Democratic contests selected 3,517 out of the 4,162 delegates to their national party convention (2,771 in primaries and 746 in caucuses). The Democrats' remaining 645 delegates were guaranteed slots by virtue of the party or elected position that they held ("super-delegates"). States that selected Republican and Democratic delegates on different dates are designated by a "D" or an "R." States listed in normal type held caucuses; states listed in **bold** type held primaries.

Date	State
Jan. 27	Hawaii (R)
Feb. 8	Iowa
Feb. 16	**New Hampshire**
Feb. 23	Minnesota
	South Dakota
Feb. 28	Maine (D)
March 1	**Vermont (non-binding)**
March 5	**South Carolina (R)**
	Wyoming
March 8	**Alabama**
	Arkansas
	Florida
	Georgia
	Hawaii (D)
	Idaho (D)
	Kentucky
	Louisiana
	Maryland
	Massachusetts
	Mississippi
	Missouri
	Nevada (D)
	North Carolina
	Rhode Island
	Tennessee
	Texas
	Texas (D)
	Virginia
	Washington
	American Samoa (D)
March 10	Alaska (D)
March 12	South Carolina (D)
March 13	North Dakota (D)
March 15	**Illinois**
March 19	Kansas (D)
March 20	**Puerto Rico**
March 22	**Democrats Abroad** [1]
March 26	Michigan (D)
March 29	**Connecticut**
April 2	Virgin Islands (D)
April 4	Colorado
April 5	**Wisconsin**
April 16	Arizona (D)
April 18	Delaware (D)
April 19	**New York**
	Vermont (D)
April 24	Guam
April 25	Utah
April 26	Vermont (R)
	Pennsylvania
May 3	**District of Columbia**
	Indiana
	Ohio
May 10	**Nebraska**
	West Virginia
May 17	**Oregon**
May 24	**Idaho**
June 7	**California**
	Montana
	New Jersey
	New Mexico
June 14	**North Dakota**
July 18-21	Democratic national convention
August 15-18	Republican national convention

1. Any U.S. citizen of voting age who lives abroad may participate in the March 22 mail-in primary collectively designated "Democrats Abroad."

The strategy depends on a wide variety of considerations, such as the nature of the competition, the primary schedule, the candidate's fund-raising ability and endorsements, media requirements, and the tenor of the electorate.

Size and Makeup of the Competition

Different strategies work for different candidates. A candidate successful in a one-on-one contest could be inadequate at playing a number of other candidates off each other. A liberal candidate might deal well with a conservative opponent but struggle against another liberal or moderate.

Going into the 1976 Democratic primaries, most experts rated Indiana senator Birch Bayh and Arizona representative Morris K. Udall top prospects for the nomination because they had strong liberal backing. The candidates' combined 37.9 percent (Udall, 22.7 percent; Bayh, 15.2 percent) share of the New Hampshire primary vote was an impressive start, but former Georgia governor Jimmy Carter's 28.4 percent was enough to win the primary. Udall, Bayh, Fred Harris, R. Sargent Shriver, Frank Church, and Jerry Brown split the liberal vote throughout the primaries. Carter received only 39 percent of the total primary vote, but he won the nomination because his opposition was fragmented.

If Carter had faced a single politician with national experience, he might have lost. A poll of Democrats before the Pennsylvania primary showed Minnesota senator Hubert H. Humphrey, perhaps the most prominent liberal in the party, with a commanding lead over all rivals including Carter. But with Humphrey not in the race, Carter was a strong winner.[25]

In 1980 California governor Brown planned to run against Carter on a platform stressing economic and environmental limits—a campaign that would address directly the national discontent that came with the energy crisis of 1979. When Kennedy joined the race, however, Brown's voice was drowned out.

Scheduling of Primaries and Caucuses

Candidates must compete in the early stages of the campaign in order to gain the national visibility they need to survive the whole campaign. Colorado senator Gary Hart's 1984 bid for the Democratic nomination is an example of a campaign sustained in later stages by the burst of success at the beginning. But to win the nomination, a candidate must stay in the race long enough to participate in the primaries and caucuses of "friendly" states. Candidates who suffer early defeats may not be able to show their real strength. Whatever strategy a candidate takes, early primary contests have had a disproportionate influence. Success in Iowa and New Hampshire can transform a candidate from dark horse to front-runner in a matter of weeks in poll standings, delegate counts, endorsements, financial backing, and media play. If a leading candidate fails in these contests, that candidate's campaign faces a crisis. Most candidates drop out early in the campaign, often before testing their strength on friendly political turf.

In recent years, all but two or three candidates have dropped out after a few early contests because they could not finance a sustained drive. Gov. George Romney in 1968, Sen. Henry Jackson in 1976, and Sen. Ernest Hollings in 1980 did not have the opportunity to bring the campaign to favorable turf because of early losses. Speculation about a possible late bid by New York governor Mario Cuomo in 1988 turned on whether he could remain viable until the New York and California primaries.

Candidates must focus attention on the string of state contests that show them in a favorable light. After the Iowa caucus and the New Hampshire primary, the attention the media give to state contests varies greatly, and candidates differ widely on which of the later contests they would like to see highlighted in the press.

Once the nomination struggle eliminates most candidates, the delegate count becomes the major focus of attention. States such as Pennsylvania, New York, Ohio, New Jersey, and California—which hold primaries late in the campaign—arguably deserve more media attention as indicators of the political leanings of the U.S. electorate. But by the time they hold their primaries, the focus of the campaign is likely to be the number of delegates the candidates have. The large states, then, are viewed according to how they affect the candidates' tedious quest for a majority of delegates.

If a delegate race is deadlocked in the late stages of a campaign, victories in the large states can help "tip the balance." A victory by Gary Hart in New Jersey as well as California on June 5, 1984, might have enabled him to wrest the Democratic nomination from Walter Mondale. A big victory can also breathe new life into a moribund campaign, as Kennedy's 1980 Pennsylvania and New York victories over President Carter and Reagan's 1976 North Carolina victory over President Gerald Ford attest. It is the delegate race that ultimately is important, however. Especially in an age of proportional representation, late surges of support are unlikely to change the mathematics of delegate counts.

Fund-raising Ability

One of the few measures of candidate strength in the preprimary stage is fund raising. Financial disclosure reports to the Federal Elections Commission are reported in the media as indications of campaign strength.

Candidates face important decisions about how to allocate money—whether to spend most funds early with the hope of making an electoral "breakthrough," which could bring a windfall of contributions, or to spend frugally and extend the time for making their case to the primary voters.

Because of spending limitations in various stages, important decisions are forced on the candidates. Long-shot candidates usually must spend most of their money on early contests to spur greater contributions. If long shots bide their time, they risk missing fund-raising opportunities completely. The Iowa and New Hampshire contests likely will produce two or three early favorites who dominate donations until the convention.

Fund-raising success stories, like endorsements, have their risks, however. One is a false sense of security. Senator Kennedy's 1980 campaign was marked by profligate staff spending and poor planning that undercut the early momentum built around the fame of the Kennedy family. Spending mistakes early in the race reduced the amount of money the campaign was legally permitted to use in the later stages.

Another risk is getting tagged as the candidate of special interests. In 1988, Massachusetts governor Michael Dukakis led other candidates in contributions by as much as eight to one; his opponents quickly dubbed him the candidate of "moneyed interests." In 1980, the lavish spending of former Treasury secretary John Connally in the Republican primaries aggravated uneasiness among voters about his honesty.[26]

Economic and Political Makeup of the States

Candidates are famous for donning the popular garb and eating the foods typical of the region in which they campaign. But more important is the way the candidates fashion their rhetoric to the conditions of the states.

Candidates are guaranteed to discuss farm problems, energy costs, and trade issues in distinctive ways in Iowa and New Hampshire. The prevalence of farm and "small town" concerns in those two states might alienate the rest of the electorate. Some observers have attributed nationwide voter apathy in the early stages of the contest to the emphasis on the smaller states.[27]

Attention later turns to industrial concerns in north-

Wide World Photos

On the campaign trail in 1948, Republican presidential candidate Thomas Dewey lets himself be "kidnapped" by members of the Oregon Cavemen Club.

ern "rustbelt" states and to defense and social issues in the southern states. Senator Kennedy's populist rhetoric on unemployment in New York and Pennsylvania produced important primary victories during his troubled 1980 bid for the Democratic nomination.[28]

Jimmy Carter achieved a bond with voters of Iowa and New Hampshire in 1976 partly because of the background they shared as farmers and rural dwellers. In contrast, Tennessee senator Albert Gore developed problems in the 1988 New York primary when he became embroiled in the bitter racial politics of New York City. Gore was endorsed by Mayor Edward I. Koch, who offended many voters with his attacks on Rev. Jesse Jackson.

Media Requirements

When Democratic senator Paul Simon of Illinois began his 1988 presidential campaign, analysts argued that his chances were minimal not only because he was an old-fashioned "New Deal liberal" but also because of his "frumpy" appearance. The small man with the horn-rimmed glasses and bow tie, it was said, was not what the "new generation" of media-saturated voters in the Democratic party were seeking.[29]

The conventional wisdom of contemporary presidential politics stresses cosmetic requirements in the media age. With references to John Kennedy, some argue that good looks are required for a candidate to have widespread appeal. Others state that a candidate must simply appear to be "presidential"—calm, sincere, knowledgeable, fatherly, tough, gentle, and commanding.

Some analysts assert that Kennedy prevailed over Vice President Richard Nixon in 1960 solely because of his appearance in the first televised debate. After President Reagan's landslide victory in the 1984 election, Democratic candidate Walter Mondale complained that television requires candidates to be masters of "the 20-second snip, the angle, the shtick, whatever it is." [30]

The primary process requires making appeals to what political scientist Nelson Polsby has called "mass publics"—and, to make those appeals, the candidate needs access to the media. Jimmy Carter's foresight in being available in New York City for morning television programs after his 1976 Iowa caucus victory is a good example of the importance of media in modern politics. Spending on television commercials is the main reason for the tremendous increase in campaign costs in recent years.[31]

Strength of State Parties and Other Institutions

Until 1968, state party organizations held hegemony over the presidential nominating system. In recent years, the state parties have been overshadowed by candidate organizations and state and national interest groups.

The leaders of state parties tend to be political executives—usually the governor or a mayor. Executives have control over patronage and contracts that are the glue of parties. Parties tend to be organized hierarchically, with state leaders playing important roles in the national organization.

Because of the media saturation of campaigns, the rise of interest groups, and changes in the rules for selecting presidential candidates, state party organizations have lost much of their influence on national politics in recent years. Parties at all levels have lost influence also because of a growing cynicism about politics among the populace. The share of the electorate declaring themselves members of national parties declined from 80 to a low of 67 percent between 1940 and 1976, and the share of independents increased from 20 to 33 percent.[32] *(See Table 10.)*

At the same time, ticket splitting and issue voting increased.[33] Most analysts trace the disillusionment to the tumultuous events of the 1960s and 1970s: assassinations; the Vietnam War; urban riots and increases in crime; and scandals involving the Nixon administration, Congress, the Federal Bureau of Investigation, and the Central Intelligence Agency.

State parties still play major roles in recruiting people for political activity, in organizing elections and governmental institutions, in providing "cues" for voters, and in mediating some important policy issues. Because its main goal is to win election for its slate of candidates, the party is more likely to compromise on specific issues and to occupy the center of the ideological spectrum. State parties are concerned about the "coattail" effects of national campaigns. A strong national candidate could add as much as 5 percent to the vote of statewide candidates.[34]

Presidential candidates must know the relative strengths of state party organizations. States with strong, hierarchical organizations have provided reliable, if sometimes limited, bases for support. These organizations tend to be more pragmatic and compromising in their approach to issues, especially divisive issues that might alienate important elements of the party coalition. States with weak top-down control allow candidates to make more direct appeals to voters.

In 1964, Goldwater was able to recruit loyalists to join local and state party organizations to "take over" the organizations. Nelson Polsby and Aaron Wildavsky wrote: "The absence of central leadership on a state-by-state basis meant that delegates were freer to follow their personal preferences and also free to weigh ideological considerations more heavily than if they had been responsible to a leader who would suffer badly if Republicans were defeated for state offices. Similar considerations have affected Democrats in recent years. . . ."[35]

Interest groups by their very definition—organizations designed to further a specific cause by donating money to campaigns—are less likely than parties to be concerned about a wide range of issues. Most interest groups are geared to specialized areas of national policy and lobbying before legislatures and agencies.[36]

Endorsements

Voters often judge candidates by the company they keep. Endorsements by prominent politicians, business and labor leaders, and citizens organizations can give credibility to a presidential candidate, but endorsements also can cause trouble if they make the candidate appear beholden to special interests.

Perhaps the most prominent example of an endorsement-based candidacy was Mondale's 1984 effort. Before the primaries even began, Mondale had won endorsements from a wide variety of labor organizations, women's groups, and civil rights organizations.[37] The endorsements—and the volunteers and fund-raising capabilities that they offered—helped to give Mondale the status of front-runner and even an air of invincibility in the months before the primaries. But the endorsements also had a negative side for Mondale. Although all the Democratic candidates had sought endorsements, Mondale was tagged throughout the primaries as the candidate who had compromised his leadership ability because of "favors" he owed backers. The criticism from fellow Democrats later was used skillfully by President Reagan's reelection campaign.

Table 10 Party Identification, 1940-1988 (percent)

	Republican	Democratic	Other
1940	38	42	20
1950	33	45	22
1960	30	47	23
1964	25	53	22
1968	27	46	27
1972	28	43	29
1976	22	45	33
1980	26	43	31
1984	31	40	29
1988	29	43	28

Source: Gallup polling organization, press office, telephone interview, October 1988.

Note: Data for 1988 are second-quarter composites. Data for other years are yearly composites.

Grass-roots Organizations

In 1975 Jimmy Carter gained an advantage on the competition for the Democratic nomination by visiting Iowa almost a year before the caucuses. His win there was central to his string of primary victories. But in the 1988 race, a dozen presidential candidates concentrated early on the Iowa caucuses, spending more than eight hundred days in the state. Democratic representative Richard Gephardt of Missouri typified the candidates' concern with Iowa: he actually rented an apartment in the state and kept his family there to campaign when he was not able to be on hand.

The organizational demands of both Iowa and New Hampshire are based on the likelihood that voter turnout will be light and candidates need to ensure that their supporters get to the voting booths and to caucus meetings. Pat Robertson did not hesitate to bus his supporters to key "straw votes."[38]

The early tests entail more than get-out-the-vote drives, however. The candidates need state political operatives, who know the political makeup of the localities, and local fund-raising experts in addition to the usual office staffers, speechwriters, and issues experts. When Gary Hart and Joseph Biden dropped out of the Democratic race in 1987, other candidates scrambled for the backing of their local organizations.

For the later states, which are dominated by media appeals, other aspects of grass-roots organizing become important. It is still essential to get voters to the polls, but the candidates also must recruit slates of delegates and develop ties to newspaper and broadcast journalists. The move from intimate, grass-roots politicking to states large in area and population requires a campaign organization to prepare the stage for the state-hopping candidate and to target appeals and polling information to large blocs of voters, such as residents of nursing homes, religious organizations, and veterans groups.

The Tenor of the Electorate

A number of scholars have asserted that U.S. history

follows distinct "cycles" and that candidates must fashion messages that parallel the dominant psychological mood of the electorate. James David Barber has argued that politics is shaped by quadrennial shifts in the national mood from "conflict" to "conscience" to "conciliation." The cycle recurs again and again in U.S. history, Barber has argued, because the excesses of each stage create a backlash; the backlash forms the basis of the next stage.[39]

Campaigns of conflict, according to Barber, include those of Harry S Truman in 1948, John Kennedy in 1960, and George McGovern in 1972. Campaigns of conscience include those of Woodrow Wilson in 1916, Wendell Willkie in 1940, Barry Goldwater in 1964, and Jimmy Carter in 1976. The politics of conciliation motivated the campaigns of Warren G. Harding in 1920, Franklin Roosevelt in 1932, Dwight Eisenhower in 1956, and Richard Nixon in 1968. Yet Barber's fitting of elections into the twelve-year cycle can be criticized as arbitrary. The 1968 election, for example, which Barber described as the "politics of conciliation," was marked by a great deal of conflict—including President Lyndon Johnson's bitter defeats and withdrawal from the primaries, political assassinations, urban riots, and Nixon's "southern strategy." Still, Barber's argument about national moods shaping elections is provocative.

Another cyclical theorist is historian Arthur M. Schlesinger, Jr., who has argued that politics swing from periods of activism to periods of preoccupation with private interests. Intervals of minimalist government include the late nineteenth century, the 1920s, the 1950s, and the years beginning with Nixon's election in 1968. Periods of activism include the Progressive Era of the early twentieth century, the New Deal Era, and the Kennedy and Johnson years.[40]

Erwin Hargrove and Michael Nelson have argued that political cycles move according to the stage of policy development and implementation.[41] Government activism waxes and wanes depending on the cycles of policy preparation, achievement, and consolidation. According to this view, activism depends less on the "mood" of the people than on whether the ground is laid for action.

The presidents of achievement include Woodrow Wilson, Franklin Roosevelt, Lyndon Johnson, and Ronald Reagan. Their administrations oversaw major changes in domestic legislation, regulation, tax policy, and defense and foreign policies.

The Wilson, Roosevelt, Johnson, and Reagan presidencies also stood in the middle of major shifts in electoral politics. The only lasting realignment was Roosevelt's New Deal era. Wilson temporarily moved the national government to the Democrats, and Johnson helped to strengthen Democratic dominance. Scholars question whether Reagan produced a "realignment" of the parties, but they agree that he was central to a growing conservatism that dominated U.S. politics in the late 1970s and 1980s. Under Reagan, the Republicans held the U.S. Senate for six years (for the first time since the 1950s) and developed national strength.

The presidents of achievement exploit the groundwork of the presidents of preparation. During these administrations, policy proposals percolate in the bureaucracy and in academic and media circles. The nation is not yet ready for broad-based initiatives but is preparing for an era of activism. Preparation presidents include Theodore Roosevelt, John Kennedy, and Jimmy Carter.

Presidents of consolidation make innovations part of the norm of government. Even presidents who may oppose programs for philosophical reasons will work to implement the programs well. The Republican presidents of the 1920s, Dwight Eisenhower, and Richard Nixon may be considered in this category.

In addition to the cycles of history, some scholars have argued that modern candidates must deal with a "sullen" political mood that is a byproduct of the age of media politics. They contend that the decline of parties and fixed ideologies in recent years has created a political climate in which candidate personalities have taken on greater importance than ever before.

James MacGregor Burns has argued that "lacking the moorings of party or the anchors of ideology . . . a profound, perverse, almost revolutionary change" in national politics has occurred since the rise of the welfare state and of active government regulation of the economy (especially since the 1960s when growth was fastest).[42] The rise of interest groups with cross-cutting purposes—in which alliances last only as long as a particular issue is under public consideration—has undermined the "cues" that voters traditionally have used to orient themselves to national campaigns. The result, Burns and others say, is a politics dominated by media attention to many personal and trivial aspects of a candidate's life. Before even the first caucus or primary of the 1988 race, for example, the media concentrated on the perceived personality disorders of candidates Gary Hart, Joseph Biden, Michael Dukakis, Jesse Jackson, Pat Robertson, and George Bush.

Past Electoral Performances

More than ever, candidates must demonstrate widespread voter appeal whether they are considered front-runners or underdogs. Candidates with little national exposure need to perform better than others just to receive serious consideration by politicians, campaign professionals, and financial donors.

In 1968 Nixon needed a series of primary victories to shed the "loser" image he developed in his unsuccessful 1960 presidential and 1962 California gubernatorial campaigns. Because he had been out of elective office for almost eight years, there were doubts about his "electability." Nixon eliminated those concerns with victories in the New Hampshire, Wisconsin, Pennsylvania, Oregon, and New Jersey primaries. Other strong contenders with questionable past performances include Walter Mondale (who dropped out of the 1976 campaign early) in 1984 and George Bush and Robert Dole in 1988.

Hubert Humphrey's strong 1968 presidential campaign gave his 1972 bid more credibility. Reagan's string of primary victories in 1976 established him as a proven vote-getter in 1980.

Electability

Numerous voting studies have indicated that some voters are so concerned about "wasting" a vote that "electability" is a major aspect of their decision making. Assertions about which candidate has the best chance of winning in November reverberate throughout the nominating process. The electability issue is most prominent toward the end of the primary season. The candidates try to show the public, the media, and political professionals that they would do best against the likely nominee of the other party.

President Gerald Ford used the electability issue effectively against Reagan in 1976, and President Jimmy Carter used it well against Kennedy in 1980. Those candidates stressed polls that showed them leading the other party's possible nominees. They also argued that the party would suffer if it denied the nomination to a sitting president.

The Complexity of Primary and Caucus Rules

The states have a wide variety of rules for ballot qualifications and allocation of delegates. When Colorado representative Patricia Schroeder announced that she would not seek the Democratic nomination in 1988, she cited the complexity of state rules as a major consideration. A late-starting campaign is practically impossible, even for long-time national figures, because of the complexity of state laws. Candidates not only must follow legal requirements to qualify for state contests, but they also have to adapt campaign strategy to the state's imperatives.

The state rules differ on many aspects of the contest, including: eligibility of nonparty members to participate, filing requirements and entry deadlines, allocation of delegates, stages in the selection of delegates, timing of the contests, and the choice of super-delegates.

Eligibility of Nonparty Members

Most states limit participation in primary and caucus voting to registered party members, but many welcome independents and members of the other party. When nonparty members participate, they usually sign a form stating that they would like to join the party.

"Open" primaries can have an important effect on the campaign. John Kennedy won the 1960 Democratic primary in Wisconsin largely on the basis of crossover Catholic Republican voters, dealing his opponent, Sen. Hubert Humphrey of Minnesota, a severe defeat in his home region. In 1984, Colorado senator Gary Hart augmented his strength among technocratic "Atari Democrats" with crossover votes of Republicans in many states. Open primary victories often are termed "illegitimate" by the losers because of the involvement of nonparty members. Humphrey complained that Kennedy's 1960 Wisconsin victory was unimportant for that reason.

Filing Requirements and Deadlines

The first step in the competition for delegates is to get on the ballot. Most states require petitions (at either the state or local level), filing fees, or both to get on the primary ballot. Other states leave the makeup of the ballot to state or party officials and committees.

South Dakota requires only that the candidate file a letter of intent to run. Louisiana requires proof that the candidate has appeared on the ballot in two other states or a petition or a filing fee. North Carolina automatically lists candidates who have qualified for federal matching funds. Most states require a minimal test of strength statewide, but some also require proof of backing in each of the state's congressional districts.

The range of laws that candidates must meet to put delegates on the ballot at the congressional district and state levels requires extensive planning. In 1984 Hart neglected to recruit delegate candidates in all states; consequently, he received few delegates in later Democratic primaries in which he polled well. Hart's failure to field full slates of delegates was partly intentional. His strategy depended on allocating resources to early stages of the campaign, since it would have been foolish for him to spend time and energy on the later primaries if he was not assured of surviving until then.

Allocation of Delegates

The diverse ways that states allocate delegates for the national convention constitute a major organizational concern for candidates. Systems for determining the number of delegates that a candidate wins in a primary or caucus are complicated and, if neglected, could deal major setbacks to a strong candidate. Understanding the different systems is crucial to allocating scarce campaign time and resources. If a candidate spends a lot of time in a state with a delegate-allocation system more favorable to a competitor, the results can be disastrous.

Party members in "binding presidential preference" states vote directly for candidates, and delegates are allocated to the candidates in a number of ways. "Beauty contest" states use the vote simply as a rough measure of popular preference for the candidates; binding selection of delegates takes place later. Voters in "delegate selection" states choose delegates without indicating which candidate the delegates will support.

Delegates are allocated at different levels. Some states require candidates to recruit delegates to run in each congressional district; other states allow delegates to be recruited from anywhere in the state.

In some states, delegates are allocated proportionally ("proportional representation"). In 1976, 80 percent of Idaho's delegates were allocated proportionally to the candidates receiving at least 5 percent of the vote. In Kentucky, only the top four finishers with at least 15 percent of the vote receive proportional allocation of delegates.[43]

Because of the "thresholds" required by proportional primaries, an allocation bias favors the top candidates. Jimmy Carter received 5.1 percent more delegates than his vote totals would have suggested in the fourteen proportional Democratic primaries of 1976. President Gerald Ford was overrepresented by 2.1 percent in proportional Republican states.[44]

Candidates in Illinois, Pennsylvania, West Virginia, and New Jersey operate under a "winner-take-all" system at the local level. In these "loophole" states, a candidate may win a bare plurality in every congressional district and end up winning all of the delegates in the state. It is conceivable for candidates finishing in second or third place statewide to win an overwhelming majority of delegates.

A number of other states use "bonus proportional representation" systems in which candidates receive delegate bonuses for winning congressional districts, in addition to an allocation based on their overall share of the vote.

The results of beauty contests might not have any effect on delegate selection. A candidate with good contacts among party activists in the state but little widespread popular support could win the majority of delegates after losing the primary.

In some states—such as New Jersey, Pennsylvania, Vermont, West Virginia, and Illinois—voters are required to make two decisions. First, voters cast a presidential preference ballot for the candidate of their choice; they then vote for the slate of delegates, which may or may not be listed as supporters of particular candidates.

Winner-take-all primaries are largely obsolete. Reformist Democrats were the first to do away with this system. Republicans eventually were compelled to drop winner-take-all contests because they fell under the jurisdiction of Democrat-dominated state legislatures. Winner-take-all contests had been big boosts. Reagan's 1976 campaign against Ford was boosted by winner-take-all victories in his native California and in Georgia, Montana, and Texas.[45] McGovern was boosted by a winner-take-all primary victory in California in 1972.

Stages of the Delegate-Selection Process

Many states select their delegates in several stages. Although the media sometimes convey the impression that party members automatically select delegates when they vote, the public balloting often is just the start of the process.

Caucuses are the starkest example of multistage delegate selection. In some caucus systems, party members meet several times before making final decisions on the presidential candidates. This explains why candidates who appear to do well on the major caucus day sometimes end up with a smaller number of delegates than was first projected.

The multistage system is more sensitive to fluctuations in candidate strength throughout the process. In the 1988 Iowa precinct caucuses, for example, Rep. Richard Gephardt of Missouri and Sen. Paul Simon of Illinois led a Democratic field of seven candidates. But as the delegate-selection process moved up to the county, congressional district, and state levels, Gephardt and Simon dropped out of the race. Massachusetts governor Michael Dukakis, who had finished third, took most of the Iowa delegates.

Timing of State Electoral Contests

States follow varying practices for scheduling state and presidential electoral contests. Some states schedule primaries for gubernatorial, senatorial, and mayoral contests to coincide with the presidential contest. Depending on the strength of state and local politics, such a move could tilt presidential contests toward parochial concerns. The candidate's grasp of state politics becomes more important when the presidential and state contests coincide.

Holding presidential and state primaries on the same day can cause trouble for some state politicians. According to the conventional wisdom, a state's influence on presidential selection depends on holding its primary or caucus in the spring. Many state officials, however, favor a September primary for state offices in order to open up the process for challenges. Other states assiduously separate their statewide and local contests from the presidential primaries. The effect of the separation usually is to keep voter turnout to a minimum in both selection processes.

About two-thirds of the states do not have important statewide elections in a presidential election year, although a third of the states have senatorial races every two years. Governors are selected in off-years in New York, Massachusetts, Tennessee, and Maryland, for example.

Super-delegates

The Democratic party in 1984 adopted a rule requiring it to apportion a bloc of super-delegates—delegate positions reserved for elected officials and party officials. The purpose of the rule was to create a stronger link between the concerns of the government and the selection process. Super-delegates were intended to give the selection process more stability.

Party members had complained that the selection process was biased in favor of primary voters who were susceptible to "image" politics and caucus participants promoting ideological or single-issue politics. Low voter turnout and the domination of the process by ideological extremists also was said to be a reason for the rule. Discontent over former president Carter's inability to establish good relations with Congress also was a factor.

The super-delegates were integral to former vice president Walter Mondale's strategy in 1984. Mondale won 450 of the 568 super-delegates—about 80 percent—compared with Hart's total of 62.[46] Mondale and his delegate-tracking team spent hours on the telephone courting the super-delegates. Without any super-delegates, Mondale would have fallen short of a majority. The "inevitability" of his nomination might not have existed.

Who Participates?

The American system continuously has increased the size of the electorate in response to the demands of different factions for a greater role in politics. The widening "scope of conflict" has given more groups access to the system.[47] Yet this apparently open system suffers from low turnout in both the nominating process and the general election. Only a third of all party members typically votes in primaries; a mere tenth, or less, participates in caucuses. In the general election, just over half of the electorate actually votes.

Austin Ranney found in a study of competitive presidential primaries between 1948 and 1968 that the mean voting turnout was 39 percent. Ranney defined "competitive" primaries as those with two or more candidates in which no candidate got more than 80 percent of the vote. The mean turnout in such states was 28 percent in 1976—an eleven-point drop. The decline in primary participation was larger than the drop in the general election turnout from its high point of 62.8 percent in 1960 to 54.4 percent in the 1976 general election.[48]

Only in Oregon and Wisconsin has the participation rate come close to half of all eligible party members. The crucial New Hampshire primary usually attracts about a third of the voters. Delegates awarded in the California primary—the most of any state—are allocated by less than 40 percent of eligible party members.[49]

Low turnout rates for nominating contests give the process a bias toward well-organized and well-staffed campaigns. Especially in caucuses—which are more demanding on party members than the simple voting requirements of the primary—the ability to get supporters to the polls takes on great importance. With a low overall turnout, control over certain blocs of voters could be tantamount to control over a large part of the overall voting population.

Low turnouts give primaries and caucuses a "wild card" aspect that can undo the best-laid plans. Bad weather in Iowa and New Hampshire, for example, can undermine the efforts of candidates to get elderly supporters to the polls. An especially salient issue such as social security or farm policy can spur certain groups to show up at polling places more than others. The controversy over the Vietnam War—exacerbated by the Tet offensive in early 1968—spurred students to become more active than ever in the nomination.

The primary system is unrepresentative because of a class bias in turnout. Studies of voting behavior have found that the citizens most likely to vote are "plugged into" party organizations and feel they can effect change. The level of education is crucial to the citizen's level of activity. A set of sometimes onerous registration requirements also works against a high degree of participation by people of lower socioeconomic status.[50]

Groups in the Republican coalition tend to have higher voter turnout than Democratic groups. In the general election, for example, the poor made up 28 percent of the Democratic coalition in 1952 but only 5 percent in 1980. Young people, southerners, blacks, people with little education, and the unemployed are the main groups with low participation.[51]

Political scientist James Q. Wilson's study of the amateur-club movement of the 1950s suggests the kinds of party members that presidential contenders must attract. The "amateur" is a party activist devoted to the public pursuit of issue-oriented, "clean" politics. Modern-day examples of amateurs include environmental groups, antiwar and civil rights activists of the 1960s, and supporters of the Proposition 13 tax-reduction movement in California in the 1970s. "Professionals" are party members less concerned with ideological and policy matters than with maintaining the party as a long-term organization.[52]

The tug-of-war between amateurs and professionals could be a key indicator of a presidential candidate's most favorable strategy. The strong performances of Barry Goldwater (1964), Eugene McCarthy (1968), George McGovern (1972), Jimmy Carter (1976), and Ronald Reagan (1976 and 1980) can be attributed to their appeal to the amateurs. The strong performances of Hubert Humphrey (1968), Gerald Ford (1976), Carter (1980), and Walter Mondale (1984) might be attributed to their appeal to professionals.

Political scientists have argued that preconvention participants tend to be "activists" with more of an ideological bent than the rest of the party and electorate. To win the nomination, candidates must package their messages so they are acceptable to the more rigid, issue-oriented parts of the electorate. In recent years, for example, Democrats have needed liberal positions on arms control, world human rights, civil rights, abortion, and the environment in order to be successful. Republicans have needed conservative positions on taxes, military spending, domestic spending, and U.S.-Soviet relations. Candidates who deviated from these basic requirements, such as Republican John Anderson in 1980 and Democrat Reubin Askew in 1984, failed.

Besides appealing to the activists, candidates often stake out fringe positions to distinguish themselves from the competition. Democratic Alabama governor George Wallace, who complained that there was not "a dime's worth of difference" between Democrats and Republicans, articulated populist right-wing positions in 1968 and 1972. Tennessee senator Albert Gore, Jr., attempted to assume a more activist military stance than his Democratic rivals in 1988.

Centrists, however, often have enjoyed better success in primary contests. In 1976, Carter won the nomination when liberal candidates split the vote among themselves. Also that year, President Ford withstood a strong challenge from former California governor Ronald Reagan to win the nomination. Reagan's campaign was based on highly charged, conservative complaints about détente with the Soviet Union and the negotiation of a treaty to cede control of the Panama Canal to Panama. George Bush emerged as the main competition to Reagan in the 1980 Republican primaries on the basis of his being a "moderate" alternative to Reagan. Hart established himself as an alternative to Mondale's traditional liberalism.

Marie Bagnowski, Smithsonian Institution

Alabama governor George Wallace, who complained that there was not "a dime's worth of difference" between Democrats and Republicans, articulated right-wing positions in his 1968 and 1972 campaigns. Here he addresses a Baltimore rally in May 1972.

Types of Strategy

All presidential aspirants must have a detailed strategy for attracting voter support and delegates before announcing their candidacy. The plan incorporates analyses of the candidate and the nominating environment, and it attempts to forecast likely high and low points of the campaign. The strategy is often so detailed that the candidate will know at prescribed points whether the campaign continues to be viable. The approaches a candidate may pursue are: the insider strategy, the outsider strategy, the early knockout, trench warfare, the slow buildup, and the wait-and-see strategy.

~ Insider strategy. Heavily dependent on the endorsements and resources of major party and government figures, this approach was dominant in the period before the party reforms of 1968. Franklin Roosevelt (1932, 1936, 1940, 1944), Harry Truman (1948), Robert A. Taft (1952), John Kennedy (1960), Richard Nixon (1960), and Hubert Humphrey and Nixon (1968) all used this approach. Walter Mondale's 1984 Democratic campaign included elements of an insider strategy in an age of outsider politics.

~ Outsider strategy. The candidate presents a "fresh face" to voters weary of the current state of politics, then stages an insurgent "takeover" of the system. Barry Goldwater in 1964, Eugene McCarthy and Robert Kennedy in 1968, Jimmy Carter in 1976, and Ronald Reagan in 1976 and 1980 based their campaigns on moralistic rhetoric critical of the Washington establishment.

~ Early knockout. Front-runners hope to parlay their early strength in polls, fund raising, and endorsements into decisive primary victories at the beginning of the primary season. The hope is that the candidate will build such an impressive early lead that the competition quickly drops out. Nixon in 1968 and Reagan in 1980 both won their nominations early. Mondale in 1984 planned an early knockout but was forced to adopt a more gradual approach with the emergence of Gary Hart.

~ Trench warfare. No candidate's favorite strategy, this approach requires candidates to struggle through the primaries with the hope of barely outpacing opponents. The danger lies in sapping the party's resources to the extent that the eventual nominee is handicapped in the general election. The races between McCarthy, Kennedy, and Humphrey in 1968; McGovern, Humphrey, and Wallace in 1972; Ford and Reagan in 1976; Carter and Kennedy in 1980; and Mondale and Hart in 1984 are examples of trench warfare. In 1988, Michael Dukakis won the Democratic nomination with a deliberate, plodding strategy designed to outlast seven rivals. Dukakis never made a spectacular breakthrough but managed to accumulate enough delegates to win the nomination.

~ Slow buildup. The idea here is to build support for the campaign slowly so that the candidate can avoid early traps and criticism and gain the aura of party savior when other candidates look weak. New York senator Robert F. Kennedy entered the 1968 campaign late and appeared to be in good position for the nomination when he won the winner-take-all California primary to cap the season. In 1976 Sen. Henry Jackson of Washington hoped to win the nomination with victories in the states holding primaries late in the schedule. This strategy might be obsolete today since early losses are considered almost fatal.

~ Wait and see. Even though all but one nomination since 1960 has been decided largely by results of primaries and caucuses, a number of politicians have tried to sit on the sidelines and eventually emerge as the consensus candidate after an indecisive primary season. Humphrey won the 1968 Democratic nomination after a divisive primary season without entering a single contest, and he hoped to win the same way in 1976. In 1980, New York governor Hugh Carey joined a movement to free delegates from obligations to vote for a particular candidate with the hope that another candidate might emerge in a deadlocked convention. In 1988, New York governor Mario Cuomo refused to enter the primaries but said he would accept a convention draft.

Carter's 1976 victory was the product of a classic outsider strategy. In an astute 1972 memo, Carter aide Hamilton Jordan had urged the candidate to travel extensively to build up foreign policy "experience," to get involved in national party politics, and to stress innovative programs of his governorship in order to supplement his "good guy brand of populism." Jordan wrote: "It will take more than the hand-shaking and the projection of the 'I understand the problems of the average man' image to put Carter over. This is still his greatest asset and it must still be projected but he will also have to convince the press, public, and politicians that he knows how to run a government." [53] Carter conducted an anti-Washington campaign based on his reputation as a leader of the "New South" and his appeals for the nation to heal the wounds of the Watergate scandal and the Vietnam War. By the time the media began exploring his record in Georgia, Carter had become a strong front-runner. The party's new proportional representation system meant that Carter needed to win just ten of the last twenty-one primaries to secure enough delegates for the nomination.

In contrast, Carter's 1980 nomination campaign followed a classic insider strategy. Carter consciously used the advantages of incumbency to line up the support of party and business elites. He also successfully manipulated the primary and caucus calendar to his advantage. Carter staffers arranged for three southern states where Carter was strong—Alabama, Florida, and Georgia—to hold their primaries together on March 11, which ensured a big sweep for Carter. They also arranged to switch the date of Connecticut's primary from March 4 to March 25 to avoid a possible Kennedy sweep on March 4, the day Massachusetts—Kennedy's home state—was holding its primary.

Issues and Other Elements of Discourse

The "spatial model" of politics perhaps best explains the way presidential candidates approach issues. Economist Anthony Downs and others have argued that the nomination process pulls candidates away from the national ideological center and toward the ideological extremes; the general election battle between the two parties then pulls the candidates back to the center.

According to this model, candidates search for the party's ideological midpoint during the nomination contest. The party's midpoint is off-center of the entire electorate, however. In the general election, then, candidates have to move away from party orthodoxy and toward the national center to attract wide support. The candidate presumably will retain the support of the more extreme party members when moving to the center since the party members have no better place to go.[54]

In 1976, Jimmy Carter originally positioned himself as a moderate to set himself apart from liberal candidates such as Morris Udall and Birch Bayh. To stave off late challenges by Frank Church and Edmund G. Brown, Jr., and a possible draft of Hubert Humphrey, Carter moved to the left. Carter's proposals for cuts in the defense budget, a national health system, and full employment allayed suspicions of the party's left. Once the fall campaign began, Carter shifted to conservative themes, such as family issues, government reorganization, and federal deficits. Democrats stood behind Carter because he was more compatible than the conservative incumbent president Gerald Ford.

Ronald Reagan moderated many of his emphases in the 1980 campaign after winning the Republican nomination. Reagan rebutted President Carter's charges that he would dismantle important social welfare programs such as Social Security and Medicare. Reagan also shifted the focus of his call for a military buildup, saying that it would make arms negotiations more productive rather than enable the United States simply to be more aggressive in world affairs.

The spatial model, however, obscures a number of elements of the campaign dynamic. Often it is more important to appeal to activists in the party than to abandon them for the center. In 1960, for example, the efforts of Massachusetts senator John Kennedy on behalf of jailed civil rights leader Martin Luther King, Jr., not only solidified black and liberal support but also provided an example of the vigorous leadership that Kennedy promised the electorate. In 1980, Republican Ronald Reagan found he was able to broaden his overall support with strongly conservative statements and backers. "New Right" groups such as the Moral Majority—which called for a constitutional ban on abortion, reinstatement of prayer in public schools, and policies to restore "traditional" family structure—actively worked for his election. The groups sponsored advertising and brought to the polls people who had never voted. The effort did not alienate centrists who were more concerned about the economy and foreign policy.[55]

The system of state-by-state delegate accumulation causes important variations in a candidate's issue appeals. Candidates will make separate pitches to appeal to the mainstream of the separate states in which they are campaigning. A candidate's overall message must have some consistency, but the emphasis of political arguments can vary greatly from state to state. The disadvantage of this practice is its potential effect on the president's ability to govern. President Carter experienced difficulties building coalitions for energy and welfare reform proposals, and President Reagan was limited by his separate promises to Social Security recipients, military weapons producers, and business leaders. Reagan's political appointments often were threatened by some of his own allies on the right.

U.S. politicians always have pulled together disparate factions to build electoral and governing coalitions. What is different, according to many analysts, is that parties no longer serve as a cohesive political force. With the decline of party discipline and the increase in organized factions, party and public officials have less "bargaining" authority and must respond to the discrete and contradictory signals of the factions. Furthermore, voters' signals become indecisive when they cannot be directed at a comprehensive party program.[56]

Whenever possible, a candidate will try to appeal both to party activists and to the general public with "fuzzy" statements. Jimmy Carter's 1976 stance on abortion—he personally opposed abortion but was ambivalent about the proper role of government—was designed to appeal to all sides of the divisive issue. Carter's promise to offer pardons rather than amnesty to Vietnam War draft resisters was a gesture both to liberals who wanted to end punishment and to conservatives who wanted a statement that draft resistance is wrong. Patrick Caddell, Carter's pollster, wrote in a memorandum to the candidate: "We have passed the point when we can simply avoid at least the semblance of substance. This does not mean the need to outline minute, exact details. We all agree that such a course could be disastrous. However, the appearance of substance does not require this. It requires a few broad, specific examples that support a point."[57]

The Use of Polls

Polling data are used extensively during the nominating campaign, even though it is not always helpful. Media, campaign staffs, and contributors use polls to determine the "viability" of various campaigns. Privately held polls have become central to the internal strategy of the candidates—helping them to understand which issues are impor-

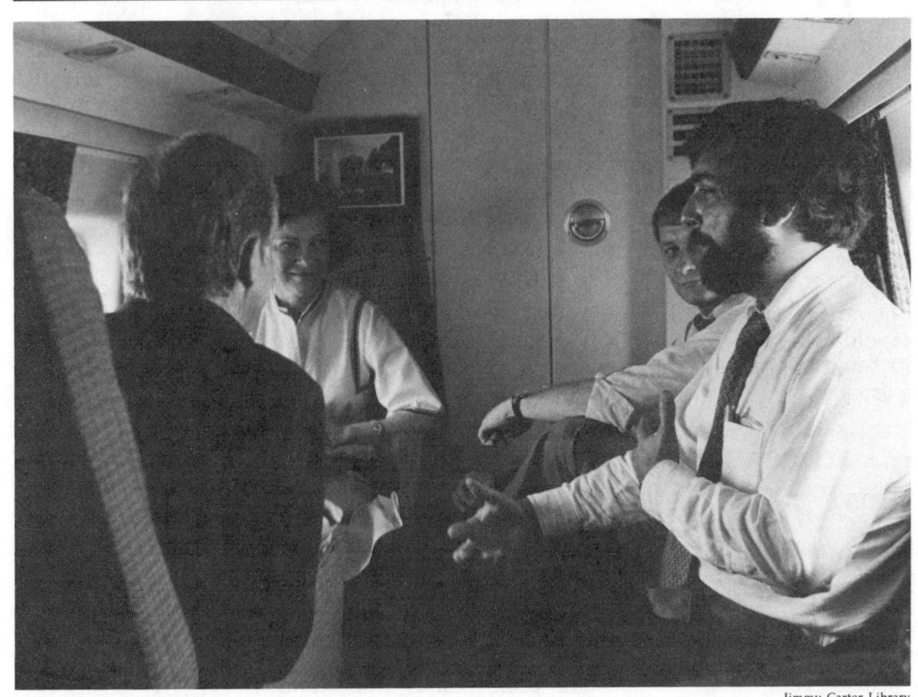

Jimmy Carter Library

Pollster Patrick Caddell, front-right, worked closely with Carter in both campaigns and in the White House.

tant to voters and the electorate's complex psychological makeup.

Scientific polls have been a regular part of campaigns since the 1936 election, when the accuracy of George Gallup's forecasts provided a stark contrast to a *Literary Digest* reader survey that predicted a victory of Alfred Landon over President Franklin Roosevelt.

Until 1952, however, campaign polling remained restricted to simple "snapshots" of the strength of the candidates. Republican presidential candidate Dwight Eisenhower used polling data to develop themes for television advertising and to target specific socioeconomic voter blocs for appeals. When he ran for reelection to the Senate in 1958, John Kennedy of Massachusetts hired Louis Harris to conduct polls of several important 1960 presidential primary states to prepare for a possible national candidacy. Kennedy's concern that his Catholicism could be a political liability and his selection of West Virginia as an important primary test state both stemmed from the Harris polls.

President Lyndon Johnson and several other candidates in 1964 used extensive "image" polling and determined that Sen. Barry Goldwater's chief liability was a widespread perception that he was an ideologue with a dangerous tendency to act "without thinking." Both New York governor Nelson Rockefeller and Johnson hammered away at the issue in their primary and general election battles against Goldwater.

In more recent years, polling has moved beyond broadbrush portraits of the electorate to sophisticated geographic, ethnic, and issue breakdowns. Polling is one of the most expensive elements of a modern campaign because campaigns now receive information on countless groups and issues. Candidates receive information about groups with specific economic, ethnic, religious, geographic, educational, occupational, and residential characteristics and how those characteristics affect attitudes about a wide range of policy issues.

In his surprising second-place finish in the 1972 New Hampshire primary, George McGovern had followed pollster Patrick Caddell's advice and concentrated his campaign on university towns, blue-collar workers, and the young professionals living on the southern border of the state. Similarly, Jimmy Carter in 1976 concentrated on the southern and middle parts of Florida in his important primary win over George Wallace.

In the 1984 election, campaigns began using a process pioneered by the advertising industry: instant polling procedures to determine the effect on voters of specific candidate performances. Selected groups of voters watched candidate debates; throughout the debate, they registered their feelings by adjusting knobs on a handheld computer device. The knobs indicated whether their response was "positive" or "negative" toward the candidate's specific statements or actions. Campaign analysts could then tabulate and analyze the reactions of whole groups.

Political Professionals, Parties, and Interest Groups

The modern campaign is dominated by professional, technically oriented staffs with loyalty to the candidate rather than to the party as a whole.

With an emphasis on appealing to activist voters in primaries and caucuses, the presidential candidate no longer relies on state party leaders. The primary campaign, especially, turns on how successfully candidates fashion and transmit their campaigns to blocs of likely voters and how well the candidates' staffs get those voters to the polls and caucus meetings. Party machinery frequently is ignored in these tasks.

Perhaps the most important stage of any campaign is recruitment of campaign professionals, such as fund-raisers, strategists, pollsters, speechwriters, media advisers, issues experts, delegate rules experts, and volunteers. Newspaper reporters and other students of presidential selection closely watch the shaping of the candidate's staff as the first indication of the campaign's viability.

The extent to which campaigns turn on their professional help is underscored by the 1988 Democratic campaign. Gary Hart recruited many of the top campaign professionals but dropped out of the race in spring 1987. Although Hart later reentered the race, he was unable to attract his former professional supporters. Sen. Joseph Biden picked up many of Hart's aides and was considered a top contender, but then he quit the campaign in fall 1987. At that point, Sen. Paul Simon hired many of Biden's top Iowa operatives—and zoomed to the top of state polls. Simon ran a strong campaign in Iowa caucuses, but his third place finish in New Hampshire was considered inadequate to expand his base significantly.

Almost every aspect of a campaign is now scripted by professionals. Aides determine the "theme of the day" for the nonstop campaign and brief the candidate between stops about the day's events and issues. Not since Adlai Stevenson in 1956 have major candidates written their own speeches.[58]

Campaign professionals make up a well-defined, if transient, lot. Most rise to the top by working in previous elections, then, after a period of "candidate shopping," hitching up with a presidential effort. William Henkel, the head of President Reagan's advance team in 1984, did similar work for Richard Nixon and Gerald Ford. Howard Druckman, the head of Mondale's 1984 advance team, began campaign work with Edmund Muskie's 1972 effort.

Many campaign experts have become legendary figures because of their ability to shape a campaign. John Sears (Nixon, 1968); Gary Hart (McGovern, 1972); Hamilton Jordan (Carter, 1972); Patrick Caddell (McGovern, 1972; Carter, 1976); Oliver Henkel (Hart, 1984); and Edward Rollins (Reagan, 1984) are among the more prominent campaign strategists of recent years. Less well known figures have fame within the world of campaign staffers. Experts on campaign finance, delegate selection rules, media, and advertising are widely sought by budding presidential candidates.

Because modern candidates run in all regions, they must delegate much of the campaign authority to other people. The way candidates manage their organizations can be a double-edged sword. On the one hand, management of the campaign can present a good indication of the candidate's executive ability. On the other hand, trivial events within an organization of strangers often can have a profound effect on the shape of the campaign.

Candidates frequently receive criticism for the actions of their subordinates and events. The 1988 campaign of Gov. Michael Dukakis stumbled after revelations that two top aides had secretly prepared a videotape critical of Biden. Sen. Gary Hart suffered when he was unable to pull from Chicago television stations controversial commercials during the 1984 Illinois primary.

The professionals' importance is underscored by the

United Press International Photo

The 1984 Democratic presidential candidates pose for a picture before their debate at Dartmouth College in Hanover, N.H.

From left to right: John Glenn, Alan Cranston, Ernest Hollings, George McGovern, Gary Hart, Walter Mondale, Jesse Jackson, and Reubin Askew.

campaigns that failed to organize delegate pursuits adequately. After victories in Florida and Michigan, Wallace was ineligible to compete in the 1972 winner-take-all California primary because he missed the state filing deadline. Four years later, Rep. Morris Udall was left off the Indiana Democratic ballot because he fell fifteen signatures short of the petition requirement in one congressional district. In 1984 Hart did not receive all the delegates that his electoral performance would allow in several states because he had failed to recruit slates of delegates.

The development of formal training programs is an indication of the professionalization of campaigns—and of their separation from state party structures. In 1987 Rutgers University announced the creation of a graduate program in campaign management. The program provides technical training for the major phases of campaign work—polling, strategy, canvassing, fund raising, speech writing, office management, and advance work. Designed for people from all parts of the political spectrum, the program has been criticized for not stressing the moral dilemmas of the democratic process.

Although state party organizations have assumed a secondary role in presidential politics, they still can be decisive. State parties are crucial in writing the rules of primaries and caucuses, and they have extensive lists of political activists and technical knowhow on matters from polling to media. Political scientist Kay Lawson has argued that state parties have withered because they have not been able to control their own affairs. The imposition of primaries by state legislatures, she says, is "a form of legalized theft." Primaries take control of the parties away from those who work to build the organization and give it to those who take only occasional interest in politics. The states also have limited party strength with campaign finance regulations, which encourage contributions to political action committees and interest groups rather than parties, and by banning straight-ticket voting, which reduces party identification. The decline of parties is perhaps most stark in Florida and California, which are not allowed by state law to endorse candidates before the primary.[59]

State legislatures are not the only factor behind state party decline. The rise of organized interest groups also has reduced the roles of state parties in political education and mobilization. Citizen allegiance to causes usually does not take the form of party membership—where different interests would have to accommodate one another—but of specialized interest groups.

Candidate Debates

Debates among candidates have become a prominent and perhaps even institutionalized part of the nominating process.

When the chairs of the Democratic and Republican parties in 1987 committed their nominees to a series of debates in the general election campaign, the effect might have been to increase the importance of debates during the nominating process since the nominee must have excellent debating skills and an ability to project a good television image. Even without the fall commitment, however, debates during the nominating process have become commonplace.

The central importance of open primaries in which masses of voters select candidates, and the increasing tendency for the parties to have large fields of contenders, means that voters and political pundits rely on debates to sort out and get to know the candidates. Especially in the early stages of a campaign, debates are important because they offer the only large event at which candidates can be judged.

Debates among party contenders were prominent parts of the 1980, 1984, and 1988 campaigns. Debates in Iowa and New Hampshire in 1980 were considered crucial turning points in the Republican nomination season. Ronald Reagan became vulnerable in Iowa when he refused to debate his opponents: he fell from 50 percent to 26 percent in the preference polls between December and the day after the January 5 debate. Trivial as it may seem, Reagan's posturing in the Nashua, New Hampshire, debate gave his campaign an important lift. Reagan invited other GOP candidates to join a one-on-one debate he had scheduled with only Bush. When Bush resisted the inclusion of the others and debate moderator Jon Breen ordered Reagan's microphone cut off, Reagan, misstating Breen's name, declared angrily: "I paid for this microphone, Mr. Green." The righteous declaration won applause for Reagan and made Bush appear stiff and uncompromising.

The 1984 Democratic debates first chipped away at Walter Mondale's status as front-runner, then dealt a devastating blow to Gary Hart's candidacy. Mondale's mocking of Hart's "new ideas" campaign with an allusion to a popular television commercial—"Where's the beef?"—left Hart on the defensive in a major Atlanta debate. Hart also stumbled when asked if U.S. military pilots could distinguish between military and civilian aircraft intruding on U.S. air space; he said they could tell the difference by looking into the plane to see if its occupants were wearing uniforms. Throughout the 1984 and 1988 campaigns, Jesse Jackson used the debates to portray himself as a mediator of party disputes.

The intramural debates started earlier than ever in the 1988 campaign. In summer 1987, a group of Democrats gathered for a debate under the auspices of the television program "Firing Line." The Republicans debated on the same program in the fall. The 1988 campaign also included one-on-one matchups, such as the trade debate between Democrats Richard Gephardt and Michael Dukakis and a debate between Republican Pierre du Pont and Democrat Bruce Babbitt.

Incumbency and the Primary Process

Despite the real advantages of incumbency for a presidential campaign, recent years have shown that renomination is not inevitable. Harry Truman, Lyndon Johnson, Gerald Ford, and Jimmy Carter all faced strong challenges when they sought a new four-term lease on the White House. Vice-presidential candidates have been even more vulnerable, whether they have sought to retain the second spot or succeed their bosses as president.

If the incumbent appears at all vulnerable, another candidate likely will emerge to oppose the president for the nomination. The decline of party solidarity and the rise of candidate-centered campaigns and organized interest groups means that an incumbent could be vulnerable when economic or foreign policy crises develop. Since World War II, presidents have not had a political anchor that strongly ties their fortunes to those of the rest of the party.

Although challenges are more likely today, the president still has a powerful command of media attention, budgetary and regulatory operations, and foreign policy initiatives—an advantage that helps defeat rivals. In addition, the prestige of the office is so great that most party members are reluctant to reject an incumbent. Fears that a prolonged intraparty battle could cripple the eventual nominee in the fall campaign are a major consideration. No president has lost a renomination effort at a party convention since 1884. Even then, whether President Chester A. Arthur actually wanted the nomination is a matter of dispute among historians.[60]

When President Carter confronted the challenges of Massachusetts senator Edward Kennedy and California governor Jerry Brown for the 1980 nomination, the unemployment and inflation rates were both high, and the country had experienced foreign policy crises with Iran and the Soviet Union. The administration's relations with the Democratic Congress also were bad. Brown had long planned to oppose Carter, and Kennedy entered the race when polls showed him leading Carter by a margin of more than two-to-one.

But President Carter defeated Brown and Kennedy by using the powers of incumbency. His chief advantage was his Rose Garden strategy. Instead of campaigning and directly countering the criticism of his administration, Carter displayed a preoccupation with governmental affairs by staying at the White House. When Kennedy and others criticized his performance in the Iranian hostage crisis, Carter intimated that they were being unpatriotic.

After public and private posturing failed to dissuade Kennedy from making a run, Carter's campaign manager, Hamilton Jordan, developed a strategy that unabashedly used the powers of the White House. (Jordan argued that Ford had lost the presidency in 1976 because he failed to take full advantage of his incumbency.) On the morning of the Wisconsin primary, for example, Carter announced an imminent breakthrough in the hostage crisis; the breakthrough fizzled, but he won the primary. Carter operatives also were able to manipulate the primary schedule, pushing southern primaries to the early part of the schedule and mingling likely Carter states with likely Kennedy states.

Drawing further on the power of the office, Carter enticed voters with promises of federal funds. But he was by no means the first to use this advantage of incumbency. In 1976, for example, while campaigning against challenger Ronald Reagan in the Florida primary, President Gerald Ford promised a Veterans Administration hospital in St. Petersburg, an interstate highway in Fort Myers, and an aerospace plant contract and mass transit funds in Miami. Referring to the president's campaign promises, Reagan quipped to a crowd of supporters in North Carolina, "If he comes here with the same bag of goodies to hand out that he's been giving away elsewhere, the band won't know whether to play 'Hail to the Chief' or 'Santa Claus is Coming to Town.' "[61]

One built-in advantage of incumbency is a reluctance of voters to jettison a known commodity for a newcomer. The campaign slogans of incumbents usually stress the stability that reelection of the president will bring; the Carter-Mondale slogan in 1980 was "A Tested and Trustworthy Team." Party members also are reluctant to turn out an incumbent because it would appear to be an admission that they had erred in selecting their standard-bearer.

National Party Conventions

The establishment of national conventions for the purpose of nominating presidential candidates in 1831 marked the formalization of political parties in this country. As we have seen, the Framers neither anticipated nor wanted partisan elections. Certainly, they made no provision for the nomination of candidates by political parties. Instead, that process emerged incrementally.

The elections of George Washington followed the selection process set out in the Constitution—they were nonpartisan, and the choice of candidates was made by the electoral college with no prior nomination. The practice of nominating candidates by congressional caucus emerged with the rise of partisanship that followed Washington's administration. It reflected the desire of competing factions to have candidates that would represent their political positions.

Associated with this rise of partisanship was a fundamental change in the nature of the electoral college. Rather than exercising their own individual judgment in electing presidents, electors became instructed agents of political parties. Thus, the choice of particular electors was tantamount to a choice for a particular candidate.

When two-party competition between the Federalists and the Democratic-Republicans gave way to single-party Democratic-Republican rule during the "Era of Good Feeling" (a term used to describe the presidency of James Monroe, 1817-1825), nomination by "King Caucus," as it was called by its detractors, virtually guaranteed one's election. With no opposition party to challenge its candidate, the congressional caucus was sovereign. The caucus system came under attack and was finally dismantled by the election of 1824.

In the transitional phase between King Caucus and the national convention system, a variety of methods were used to nominate candidates. These included nomination by state legislative caucuses, by state party conventions, by "mixed" state conventions (consisting both of party members of the state legislature and elected delegates from those sections of the state not represented by that party in the legislature), and by mass meetings of rank-and-file voters. All of these were decentralized systems, however, which did not generate the degree of mass support that the national convention system later would.

The first national party nominating convention was held by the Anti-Masons (a short-lived splinter party) in Baltimore, Maryland, in September 1831. *(See "Third Parties," p. 248, in this chapter.)* With 116 delegates from thirteen states, the convention nominated William Wirt for president and Amos Ellmaker for vice president. Within the next eight months, two other parties followed suit. In December, the National Republicans held a convention where they nominated Henry Clay and John Sergeant, and in May 1832 the Democrats convened to nominate Andrew Jackson and Martin Van Buren. The convention system was born and has remained intact ever since.

Sites

Baltimore proved to be a popular spot for the first conventions. From 1831 to 1852, ten conventions (including the Democratic party's first six) were held there. To a large degree, the choice of Baltimore was a matter of convenience. Transportation was slow, and a central location was desirable. Most other sites (such as Harrisburg, Pennsylvania; Philadelphia; and Pittsburgh) conformed to that rule, although Buffalo, New York, hosted the Liberty party in 1843 and the Free Soilers in 1848.

The choice of convention sites after 1856 reflected the country's westward expansion. Since then, Chicago has been the most popular choice (having hosted twenty-four major party conventions). Cincinnati and St. Louis were two other popular sites in the latter part of the 1800s. The

Wood engraving in *Harper's Weekly*, May 19, 1860; Library of Congress

Chicago has been the most popular site for political conventions, having hosted twenty-four since 1856. At the Republican convention of May 1860, Abraham Lincoln won the nomination and went on to become the first Republican president.

South, however, seldom has been the site of a convention. The Democrats held a tumultuous one in Charleston, South Carolina, in 1860 that ultimately deadlocked—forcing a second convention to be held in Baltimore. The Democrats did not hold another southern convention until 1928, when Houston, Texas, was chosen (largely in an effort to appease southerners, who party leaders knew would be unhappy with the nomination of Al Smith, a Catholic from New York). The Republicans did not hold a southern convention until 1968 (if, indeed, Miami Beach, Florida, qualifies as "southern"). In 1988, however, both parties chose to hold their conventions in the South—the Democrats in Atlanta, the Republicans in New Orleans.

In more recent years, the issue of a central location gave way to a more pressing one: money. For a time, the major consideration in choosing a convention site was the amount of money that the city in question would donate to the national party committee in cash and services. Local businesses, after all, stood to gain a considerable profit from the influx of thousands into their city. In 1976 it was estimated that a convention would generate about $10 million of business a day.[62] Aside from that, a convention offers a city tremendous exposure in the form of media attention. By 1968, contributions from cities were approaching $1 million.

The practice of city donations to national committees ended in 1972 when it was discovered that an antitrust suit against International Telephone and Telegraph (ITT) was settled in ITT's favor by the Justice Department of Richard Nixon's administration shortly after the Sheraton Corporation (an ITT subsidiary) offered to supply $400,000 worth of services to the Republicans if they would locate their 1972 convention in San Diego. The offer was part of a package put together by that city. Campaign finance legislation passed in the wake of Watergate prohibited corporate contributions and free services and provided for each national party to receive $2.2 million from the government to finance their conventions. Although that amount has since increased to reflect inflation, it is still far less than that needed to fund conventions. As a result, the Federal Election Commission loosened its restrictions to allow private businesses to offer services (such as free hotel accommodations) as long as the other party receives comparable benefits. It also allowed state and local governments to offer a number of services free of charge (such as security and the use of a convention hall). Thus, the 1976 Democratic national convention received some $3.63 million in direct subsidies from New York City.[63] In 1988, the Republican national convention received $5.5 million in subsidies from New Orleans.

The choice of a convention site now rests primarily on the facilities that are available. For instance, there must be adequate accommodations—20,000 rooms or more—to house all the people associated with the convention, including delegates, party officials, members of the press, television crews, and the candidates' advisers and staff. Lack of hotel space prevented Philadelphia from hosting the Democrats in 1968. In addition, the city must have a convention hall large enough to seat all the delegates and to facilitate the media—including space for overhead booths for the television networks.

In 1988, the Omni Coliseum in Atlanta proved to be a tight fit for the Democrats. The stage alone—a huge structure that soared eighty-five feet into the air and included two large screens, space for an orchestra, and a podium that could be adjusted by hydraulic lifts to make everyone appear to be the same height—took up space for 7,200 seats. As a result, the Omni provided fewer than 10,000 seats and a maximum capacity of 12,500 people. That capacity was far less than was needed to accommodate everyone who wanted to get in, including 5,373 delegates and alternates, more than 12,000 members of the press, and thousands of other guests.[64] On several occasions, the fire marshal determined that the building was overcrowded and would not allow delegates and others with credentials to enter. During Jesse Jackson's speech to the convention, hundreds were stranded outside, including Martin Luther King III.

In contrast, the New Orleans Superdome proved to be too *big* for the 1988 Republican convention. The building, which can seat more than 97,000 people, was divided by a curtain that rose nine stories high and weighed three tons. Behind the curtain were twenty-seven trailers that served as offices. The rest of the building was used to accommodate the convention itself. A side effect of the cavernous interior was that many of those in the hall could not hear the proceedings. It seemed that the vast open space of the Superdome (some twenty-four stories high) simply swallowed the sound.

Security considerations also can play a major role in the choice of a convention site. Miami Beach proved to be a popular site in 1968 and 1972 partly because it is an island; its being set off from the mainland discouraged protests and other security threats, such as those that had plagued the 1968 Democratic convention in Chicago.

The choice of a site may also serve as a gesture to a particular part of the country or reflect the personal preferences of an incumbent president running for another term. Ronald Reagan, for instance, was anxious that Dallas be selected as the site of the 1984 Republican convention because of the support he had received from Texas conservatives in 1976 and 1980. Nevertheless, according to an unwritten rule, states with contenders for a party's nomination do not host that party's convention. Finally, choice of a site may be symbolic of a theme that the party wishes to convey. Hence, the Republicans chose Detroit in 1980 because it was "a back-from-trouble renaissance city, much as the GOP sees itself as a party restored to health."[65]

A site is usually chosen about a year in advance of the convention by a committee of a dozen or so members appointed by the party's national chair. The national party committee then officially announces the convention's date and site, allocates convention delegates to each state, and appoints its officers and committees. An occasional suggestion that a permanent national convention center be built for use by both parties never has generated much enthusiasm.

Delegates

Setting the number of votes that each state delegation shall have at the national convention is one of the most important parts of the formal call to the convention. This distribution of votes (known as *apportionment*) originally coincided with the number of votes each state had in the electoral college (which, in turn, was determined by the size of the state's congressional delegation). From the beginning, however, states often sent more representatives than the number of their electoral votes. In 1848, the Democrats tried (without success) to limit the actual voting power of a state delegation to its electoral college vote, regardless of the actual number of delegates from the state. In an effort to deal with the problem of extra delegates, the Democrats passed a rule in 1852 giving every state twice as many delegates as it had electoral votes (with each delegate receiving a half vote). To do away with fractional votes, the number of votes was doubled in 1872, giving each delegate a whole vote.[66]

At its start in 1856, the Republican party also followed a system of apportionment that was roughly analogous to the electoral college. In 1856, it gave each state six delegates at large, plus three delegates for each congressional district. This was changed in 1860 to four at-large delegates, plus two delegates for each congressional district.

Both parties, then, followed a system that allocated convention delegates mainly according to population rather than their voting strength in a given state. That system of apportionment came under attack after the Civil War with the rise of "one-party" states. In such states, a minority party (such as the Republicans in the post-Reconstruction South) would be overrepresented at their convention. The term *rotten borough* is often used to describe districts that were so represented.

Since overrepresentation was more of a problem for the Republicans than the Democrats, Republican apportionment has been more complicated. Although the problem has been addressed by the party since 1880, the Republicans did not change their method of apportionment until after their disastrous loss in the presidential election of 1912.

Beginning in 1916, the Republicans adopted a system of "bonus delegates," which were apportioned according to Republican voting strength in that state. Initially, the system called for each state to receive four at-large delegates, one delegate for each congressional district, and one bonus delegate for each congressional district that had cast at least 7,500 Republican votes in the presidential race in 1908 or in the congressional race in 1914. In 1924 the number of votes necessary for bonus delegates was raised to 10,000. In addition, the Republicans instituted a new system for awarding bonus delegates that gave three at-large delegates (instead of individual delegates to particular congressional districts) to each state that the party carried in the last presidential election.

Over the years, the Republicans have increased the number of bonus delegates that they award and have made it easier to receive those delegates.[67] Since 1972 the Republicans have followed a complicated formula that gives each state six at-large delegates, three delegates for each congressional district, four-and-a-half bonus delegates (plus 60 percent of its electoral vote total, rounded up) if it carried the Republican ticket in the last presidential election, one bonus delegate for each Republican senator, one bonus delegate for a House delegation that is at least one-half Republican, and one bonus delegate for states with a Republican governor. In addition, fourteen at-large delegates are awarded to the District of Columbia, eight to Puerto Rico, and four each to Guam and the Virgin Islands. The rule also ensures states that they will receive at least the number of votes that they had in the previous election.[68]

The Democrats did not institute a "bonus" system until 1944. At that point they simply awarded two bonus delegates to each state that the Democrats carried in the last presidential election. The number of bonus delegates was increased to four in 1948. Since then, various delegate allocation formulas have been used. Beginning in 1972, the Democrats used an apportionment formula that based nearly half of a state's voting strength on its Democratic vote in the last three presidential elections. The remaining strength was based on the state's electoral college votes.[69]

The number of delegates attending national conventions has increased dramatically through the years. The first convention, held by the Anti-Masons in 1831, boasted 116 delegates. The Democratic convention the next year had 283. In 1856 the first Republican convention was attended by 567 delegates. By the early 1900s, both parties had approximately 1,000 delegates. That number remained fairly stable until the 1950s, when the Democratic party began its efforts to increase participation in the national convention.

In 1956 the Democrats allowed states to send delegates on a "half-vote" basis. Under that system, states could send twice as many delegates while still having the same voting power. Between 1952 and 1956, the number of Democratic delegates increased from 1,642 to 2,477. At the same time, the number of delegate votes was increasing as well. This increase initially reflected the use of bonus delegates and was later spurred by the greater democratization of its conventions (brought about by the party's post-1968 reforms). Thus, the number of delegate votes at Democratic conventions increased from 1,230 in 1952 to 3,331 in 1980. In 1988, 3,531 regular delegates and 672 super-delegates (elected officials and party leaders who have automatic seats at the convention) were able to cast total and partial votes adding up to 4,162—even though their total ranks equalled 4,203.[70]

The size of Republican conventions has not increased quite so dramatically. Nevertheless, party reform in the early 1970s provided for a 60 percent increase in delegate strength. As a result, the number of delegates at the Republican convention increased from 1,333 in 1972 to 2,259 in 1976.[71] In 1988, there were 2,277 Republican delegates.

The number of delegates, however, is only part of the number of people in attendance at modern-day national conventions. For instance, there were 26,594 "official" credentials distributed each day during the 1976 Democratic convention, although the actual number of credentials topped 30,000 each day. These included not only the 3,353 delegates and their 2,086 alternates, but 5,200 for the media; 869 for officeholders and members of the Democratic National Committee; 1,500 for security officials; and more than 10,000 for "guests," or observers. For that convention, credentials tags were printed on specially laminated layers of paper with blue on the interior. This allowed security personnel to detect counterfeits by tearing a corner of the tag.[72]

The reforms that helped to increase the size of conventions also formalized the method of choosing delegates. In the nineteenth century, delegates usually were chosen by "closed" caucus meetings of state or local party regulars, or they were appointed by the governor or another state party leader. In the early part of the twentieth century, primaries evolved in which delegates were chosen by direct popular vote (usually restricted to party members). By 1968, the two dominant forms of delegate selection were the caucus and primary systems.

Since 1968, reforms instituted by the Democrats (and to a lesser extent, the Republicans) have set specific criteria for delegate selection. These criteria were instituted to counteract rules and practices that either inhibited access to the delegate selection process or diluted the influence of those who had access. *(See "Rules Changes in the Democratic Party," p. 174, in this chapter.)* The result was the democratization of the selection process—the demise of "closed" caucuses and the rise of grass-roots participation through primaries and "participatory" caucuses that are open to every voter in the party. The reforms also altered the characteristics of the delegates themselves by decreasing the number of party professionals and public officeholders and increasing the number of rank-and-file members (especially women, minorities, and young people).

Preconvention Committees

Three major committees carry out the work of the national convention: credentials, platform, and rules. These committees have traditionally met before the start of the national convention—usually in the week before it begins. More recently, the Democrats have begun holding committee sessions several weeks before the convention.

The Credentials Committee reviews all disputes arising over delegates to the convention. Before the start of the convention, the committee receives a list of the delegates from each state. It then holds hearings on any challenges to those delegates (usually based on the procedures by which they were chosen) and makes its recommendation to the convention, which makes the final decision on the matter. When there is a close presidential nominating contest, the Credentials Committee can significantly influence who is nominated. A notable instance was the 1912 Republican convention when President William Howard Taft was locked in a bitter nomination battle with former president Theodore Roosevelt. In those four states holding primaries, Roosevelt was the overwhelming winner. Taft, however, controlled the party machinery, so in caucus states he had the advantage. In particular, that control all but guaranteed that the Republicans' rotten boroughs in the South would go for Taft. Ironically, Roosevelt had hand-picked Taft as his successor in 1908, using that very machinery to guarantee Taft's success.[73]

The preconvention fight between Taft and Roosevelt is one of the most bitter on record. Roosevelt forces contested 254 pro-Taft delegates, but the Credentials Committee recommended that all but 19 of them be seated. The convention upheld that recommendation, virtually guaranteeing Taft's renomination. The problems caused by rotten boroughs in 1912 were decisive in bringing about reform of the delegate apportionment process.

A similar battle brewed in 1952 in the fight between Gen. Dwight D. Eisenhower and Ohio senator Robert A. Taft (son of William Howard Taft) for the Republican nomination. Like his father in 1912, Taft controlled the party machinery. Sixty-eight pro-Taft delegates from Georgia, Louisiana, and Texas were contested. The Credentials Committee recommended that they be seated, but after a series of emotional speeches in support of Eisenhower stressing the theme "Thou shalt not steal," the convention overturned the recommendation. Eisenhower went on to win the election.

The Democrats experienced a major credentials dispute in 1968 during the struggle between Vice President Hubert H. Humphrey and Minnesota senator Eugene McCarthy. The Credentials Committee dealt with seventeen different challenges from fifteen states—an unprecedented number for the Democrats. Humphrey forces (who controlled the party machinery) won all of the contested seats.

Many of the credentials disputes at the 1972 Democratic convention centered on whether or not states had complied with the guidelines of the McGovern-Fraser Commission, but there were also bitter skirmishes between George McGovern and the opposing "ABM" ("Anybody But McGovern") forces. Over eighty challenges involving more than 1,300 delegates were brought before the committee.[74] Since 1972, both parties have reformed their rules to help ensure fair decisions by their credentials committees.

The Rules Committee is responsible for determining the operating rules of the convention. Until 1972, the Democrats did not have a formal set of rules that were retained from convention to convention. Instead, the rules evolved in an ad hoc fashion, although many rules from the previous convention were readopted. In comparison, Republican rules were strictly codified.

Among the most controversial rules used by the Democrats were the "two-thirds" rule and the "unit" rule. The two-thirds rule required that any nominee for president or vice president receive not just a simple majority, but a full two-thirds of the convention vote. Since the two-thirds rule made it more difficult to receive the nomination, protracted balloting was commonplace. While the Republican party (which nominates by simple majority, that is, more than 50 percent) has had just one convention in its entire history that required more than 10 ballots (36 in 1880), the Democratic party has had seven (requiring 49 ballots in 1852, 17 in 1856, 59—spread over two conventions—in 1860, 22 in 1868, 46 in 1912, 43 in 1920, and an unending 103 in 1924).

Proposals were introduced to abolish the two-thirds rule in the wake of the 1924 marathon convention and again in 1932 by supporters of Franklin Roosevelt who feared that he might not be able to gather the votes necessary to win the nomination. Despite considerable opposition, the Democrats finally eliminated the two-thirds rule at the 1936 convention. The South, in particular, objected to its elimination since the two-thirds rule had allowed that region a virtual veto power over any nominee. To make up for that loss, the South received more votes at later conventions.

The unit rule allowed the majority of a delegation (if so authorized by its state party) to cast all of the votes of that delegation as a "unit" for the candidate or position supported by a majority of the state's delegation. Again, this rule was never used by the Republicans. Proponents of the unit rule argued that it muted conflict within the party (since dissident minorities would be overridden) and therefore strengthened state party organizations. Detractors of the rule argued that the rule was undemocratic. Conceivably, a candidate with a minority of the delegates could win the nomination under the rule by simply controlling the votes of a dozen or so of the largest state delegations. Furthermore, it was argued that the unit rule undermined the notion of participatory democracy by ignoring the popular sentiments of minority factions. As used in the Democratic party, the unit rule largely served to consolidate the voting strength of the South.[75] In 1968, the Democratic Rules Committee recommended that the unit rule be repealed. That action was later ratified by the 1968 convention and has been supported by subsequent reforms.

Actions by the Rules Committee also can influence the outcome of a convention. In 1976, Ronald Reagan—who had announced his intention to nominate Pennsylvania senator Richard Schweiker as his running mate if he won the Republican presidential nomination—proposed a rules change to force his opponent, Gerald R. Ford, to name his own choice. Reagan, with a 110-delegate vote deficit, hoped that he might be able to win over enough delegates alienated by Ford's choice to secure the nomination. But Ford forces voted down the rules change, and Ford went on to become the Republican nominee.

The so-called "bound delegate" rule (which required delegates to vote according to their pledge at the time of their selection) was the subject of a major rules fight at the 1980 Democratic convention. President Jimmy Carter was in favor of the rule, since it bound his delegates to vote for him. Carter's rival, Massachusetts senator Edward M. Kennedy, fought to overturn the rule in the hopes that those delegates would turn their support to him. The Carter forces won the rules fight and went on to win the nomination.

The Platform Committee is responsible for preparing a statement of party principles (called a *platform*) that is presented to the convention for its approval. Since party leaders are anxious to mute conflict within the party and appeal to as wide a base as possible, platforms seldom have much punch. Wendell Willkie (the Republican nominee in 1940) called them "fusions of ambiguity." Nevertheless, their adoption sometimes causes bitter fights. The passage of a strong civil rights plank in the 1948 Democratic platform provoked opposition from southern states and prompted the walkout of the entire Mississippi delegation and thirteen members of the Alabama delegation. Some of the disgruntled southerners then formed their own party—the States' Rights Democratic party, or the Dixiecrats—who held their own convention in Birmingham, Alabama, and nominated South Carolina governor J. Strom Thurmond for president and Mississippi governor Fielding L. Wright for vice president.

Since 1852, most conventions have adopted their platform before nominating their candidates. As a result, platform fights can serve as yet another indicator of the relative strength of rival candidates, especially when those candidates hold different ideological positions. Platform fights also can signal splits within the party that may prove fatal in the general election. Such was the case for the Republicans in 1964 and the Democrats in 1968. In contrast, consideration of the platform at the 1988 Democratic convention was more a debate than a fight. The approved platform was the party's shortest in fifty years and was filled with generalizations rather than specific promises. Its aim was to promote unity. Republicans assailed the Democrats for vagueness. Their platform was six times longer than the Democrats' (more than thirty thousand words) and reflected a strong conservative stance.

For many years, the Committee on Permanent Organization confirmed the national chair's choice of permanent officers for the convention and then recommended that slate to the convention itself. Since the post-1968 reforms, the Democrats have had no such committee. Rather, their choice of permanent officers has been made by the Rules Committee.[76] The Republicans have retained their Committee on Permanent Organization.

Convention Officers

National party conventions are called to order by the national committee chair, who presides until a temporary convention chair is appointed. The temporary chair then presides until the convention acts on the recommended slate of candidates for permanent officers. For the first half of this century, the temporary chair usually served as the "keynote" speaker at the convention. There was also a tradition that the temporary chair be a U.S. senator. Since 1952, when Gen. Douglas MacArthur delivered the keynote

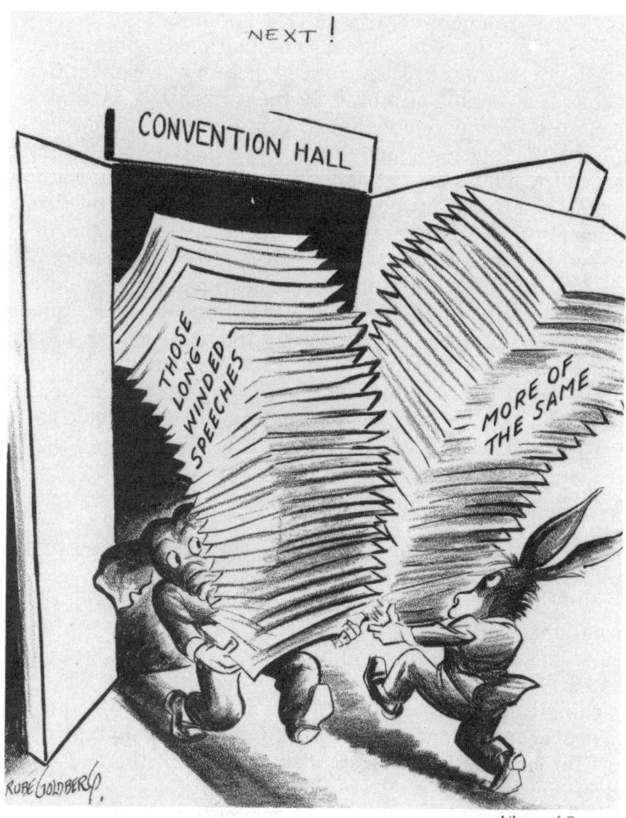

Library of Congress

address at the Republican convention, the keynote speaker usually has been someone other than the temporary chair. And in recent years, the tradition of appointing a senator to be temporary chair has been less frequently observed.

The temporary chair usually does not hold great power at a convention, and the appointment is usually routine. Nevertheless, there have been exceptions. The 1912 Republican convention again serves as a case in point. In the feverish fight between Taft and Roosevelt, maneuvering in the early part of the convention was essential to victory. The permanent chair was not chosen until credentials contests had been decided (as is standard practice).[77] Since contested delegates are seated until the convention acts on the recommendations of the Credentials Committee, and since the temporary chair rules on motions brought from the floor and generally controls the proceedings, the temporary chair was in a position to exert considerable influence in 1912. The Roosevelt forces supported Wisconsin governor Francis E. McGovern, but Sen. Elihu Root of New York—the favorite of the Taft supporters—won the post of temporary chair.

The choice of Root played an important role in Taft's eventual nomination. With the engineering of Root, the Taft forces won the credentials fight. Many accused Root of "steam roller" tactics, and in the galleries, pro-Roosevelt forces rubbed sandpaper and blew horns to imitate the sound of a steam roller. Dissension on the floor was rampant. Police squads stood ready to uphold the rulings of the temporary chairman should he meet with violent resistance. Indeed, party officials were taking no chances. Even the decorations around the rostrum were used to conceal barbed wire should violence erupt.

The permanent chair usually is appointed on the second day of the convention. The national committee's choice for the post is announced before the convention begins. It is usually approved by the convention itself with no contest. The permanent chair presides during the adoption of the platform and during the actual nomination procedure. Thus, the permanent chair also is in a position to exercise strategic rulings that can help or hinder particular candidates. Indeed, the permanent chair is often described as the most important officer of the convention.[78]

In the 1880s, prominent leaders in state and local politics usually filled the post of permanent chair. Since the 1930s, it has been the custom for the party leader in the House of Representatives to serve as permanent chair of the national convention. Since 1972, the Democrats have required that the position alternate every four years between the sexes.

Oratory and Films

H. L. Mencken once wrote that convention orators are "plainly on furlough from some home for extinct volcanoes." [79] Indeed, oratory—and lots of it—plays a major role at national party conventions. During much of the behind-the-scenes maneuvering and unfinished committee work in the early phase of the convention, speeches are a way of marking time. They are also a means of staking out positions over important rules or platform fights, rallying support for candidates, or reestablishing unity at the end of a bitter convention.

The first major speech of the convention is the keynote address, usually heard on the first day of the convention. Keynote speakers usually are chosen for their oratorical skills, since they are there to whip up enthusiasm among the delegates. Before the age of television, keynote addresses often lasted well over an hour. Until the 1950s, it was the custom for the temporary chair of the convention to deliver the address. In more recent years, someone other than the temporary chair has served as keynoter. That address is surrounded by millions of other words: the call to order; the invocation; addresses by party notables, former presidents, and presidential candidates; the reading of committee reports; entertainment; nomination speeches; and roll calls.

In recent times, the acceptance speeches of the candidates for vice president and president have been the climax of the convention. Acceptance speeches were not a part of conventions, however, until 1932, when Franklin D. Roosevelt broke precedent. Anxious to show that his physical disability would not hinder his activities, Roosevelt made a dramatic flight from Albany to Chicago to address the Democratic national convention that had nominated him for president. To mark a turning point for the nation in the grip of the Great Depression, Roosevelt triumphantly entered the convention hall as a band played "Happy Days Are Here Again." Noting that he was the first candidate ever to deliver an acceptance speech to a national convention, he said: ". . . I am here to thank you for the honor [of nominating me]. Let it be symbolic that in so doing, I broke traditions. Let it be from now on the task of our party to break foolish traditions." [80] In 1944, New York governor Thomas E. Dewey became the first presidential nominee to deliver an acceptance speech at a Republican convention.

The drafting of acceptance speeches is now a major endeavor, often involving the work of many writers. Strategic lines are inserted to satisfy specific voting blocs and interest groups, and the overall structure and delivery of the speech is designed to capture the interest of the millions of viewers who watch it on television. Even light touches are added by comedy writers. Two such writers, Jack Kaplan and John Barrett, sent Jimmy Carter a memorandum suggesting an opening for his acceptance speech to the 1976 Democratic convention. Although not included in advance texts of the speech, Carter took their advice. Their memo, including parenthetical directions, suggested the following: "(AFTER THANK YOUs, JIMMY TURNS TO THE AUDIENCE AND SAYS:) HELLO, I'M JIMMY CARTER. (LAUGH) AND I'M RUNNING FOR PRESIDENT OF THE UNITED STATES. (APPLAUSE)." That use of Carter's campaign line from the days when he was an unknown candidate became one of the most famous passages in his acceptance speech.[81]

Much convention oratory is neither riveting nor profound. More often than not, scant attention is paid to the speakers, and their words are quickly forgotten. But in the millions of words that have poured forth from national conventions, a few have struck a chord and galvanized a convention. Often the phrases live on: Franklin Roosevelt's promise of a "new deal" in his 1932 acceptance speech; the coinage of the term "G.I. Joe" by Clare Booth Luce in her keynote address to the Republicans in 1944; and the invocation of the phrase "Our time has come!" by the Reverend Jesse Jackson in his speech to the 1984 Democratic convention.

Perhaps the greatest convention speech of all occurred in 1896 when William Jennings Bryan—a young leader of the Nebraska delegation—stunned the Democratic national convention with what has become known as his legendary "Cross of Gold" speech. By the end of the convention he was that party's nominee for president. The speech evolved out of the platform fight over the currency issue (whether the U.S. should maintain the gold standard or allow unlimited coinage of silver). The Democratic National Committee favored the gold standard, but prosilver forces had much support at the convention. Bryan's speech was instrumental in leading the convention to a prosilver stance. Throughout the speech Bryan held some twenty thousand spectators spellbound. He later recalled that the vast crowd would "rise and sit down as one man" as it responded to his oratory.[82]

Couching his appeal for free silver as a fight for "the struggling masses," Bryan intoned: "We have petitioned, and our petitions have been scorned. We have entreated, and our entreaties have been disregarded. We have begged, and they mocked when our calamity came. We beg no longer, we entreat no more, we petition no more. We defy them." And from the wellspring of the convention hall, the thousands echoed: "We defy them." In the hush that fell back over the hall as Bryan spoke, he concluded, ". . . we will answer their demand for a gold standard by saying to them: You shall not press down upon the brow of labor this crown of thorns, you shall not crucify mankind upon a cross of gold." [83]

In recent times, New York governor Mario Cuomo was catapulted into the public eye by his memorable keynote address at the 1984 Democratic convention. Had he delivered such a speech in an earlier age, he might have found himself nominated for president practically on the spot. Playing off President Reagan's use of the phrase "a shining city on a hill" to describe the United States, Cuomo responded: "The president is right. In many ways we are 'a shining city on a hill.'... But there's another part of that city, the part where some people can't pay their mortgages and most young people can't afford one, where students can't afford the education they need and middle-class parents watch the dreams they hold for their children evaporate.... There is despair, Mr. President, in faces you never see, in the places you never visit in your shining city." Invoking the image of family and community, he called for the new president of the United States to be "a Democrat born not to the blood of kings but to the blood of pioneers and immigrants." [84]

Since the advent of television, both parties have complemented convention oratory with the showing of films. Often they are used to introduce the candidates—extolling their achievements in carefully produced packages of propaganda. A film on President Nixon at the 1972 Republican convention chronicled his accomplishments in Peking, Moscow, and Washington. It brought hushed attention even to the three thousand reporters in the press gallery—people who were usually inattentive at such presentations.[85] In 1976, the Democrats showed a fourteen-minute film about Carter: a "Lincolnesque story of a determined barefoot boy from the peanut fields of Plains, Georgia, working his way to a presidential nomination." [86] A biographical film about Reagan shown at the 1980 Republican convention tried to broaden his appeal, stressing such things as his early ties with labor unions when he was president of the Screen Actor's Guild.[87]

Films also are used to celebrate party greats from the past. In 1980, the Republicans showed a filmed tribute to their one-time presidential nominee Alfred M. Landon. In 1968, the Democrats screened a filmed memorial to Robert F. Kennedy, followed by a mass singing of "The Battle Hymn of the Republic."

The great appeal of films is that they are virtual campaign commercials beamed free of charge across network television. Such films can reach over fifty million Americans. Convention organizers were careful to plan the films for the prime-time viewing hours, often scheduling them just before the nominee's acceptance speech. In the days when there was gavel-to-gavel coverage of the conventions, networks were especially bound to carry the films. Because house lights were shut off during their showing, television was unable to cover other events from the floor. Since 1980, the networks have been more restrictive in their coverage. They balked, for instance, at airing a film on Ronald Reagan prepared for the Republican convention in 1984. Ultimately, only CBS refused to carry it—a practice the network continued for both conventions in 1988. That year, the Republican film introducing George Bush again caused problems. NBC, for instance, had aired the short, six- to seven-minute films introducing Michael Dukakis and Jesse Jackson at the Democratic convention but said that the Republican film—lasting twenty minutes—was too long. NBC agreed to show it only after Bush aides desperately trimmed it down to seven minutes and seven seconds.[88] Although the parties still have free air time for their major speeches, the days of unquestioned airing of political films appears to have gone.

Presidential Nomination

Recent reforms have helped transform national conventions into ratifying assemblies. Since 1952, all candidates of the two major parties have been nominated on the first ballot. A number of factors help to account for this. The abolition of the unit rule and the two-thirds rule by the Democrats helped reduce the protracted balloting that was common in that party. But even more important was the changing nature of the political landscape: the rise of primaries (which bind delegates to candidates before the convention), the increased cost of campaigning (which has added to the "winnowing" process of candidates since losers in early primaries quickly find themselves without contributors), and the televising of conventions (in which the appearance of party unity is of utmost concern). Indeed, the democratization of the selection process makes an old-style "brokered" convention (in which the candidate is chosen by party bosses behind closed doors) all but impossible. For such an event to happen today, all of the "normal" channels of selecting a president would have to end in stalemate—a highly unlikely occurrence.

In order to corral votes at the convention, campaign managers and strategists always have kept in close contact with the state delegations. Candidates have floor leaders and "whips" to direct voting on the floor and to deal with any problems that may arise among state delegations. In addition, there are "floaters" who wander the floor in search of any signs of trouble. Today, all such people have access to virtually instant communication with their candidate's command post via walkie-talkies, direct phone lines, television monitors, and the like. Floor leaders, whips, and floaters often wear specially colored clothing or caps so they can be spotted easily on the floor.[89] Candidates go to these lengths at the convention because they are eager to please the delegates and to ensure their support. In 1976, Carter met and shook hands with each of the more than 1,800 delegates pledged to him.[90]

Nominating speeches mark the beginning of the formal selection process. The convention of the National Republican party (which met in Baltimore in December 1831, three months after the Anti-Masons held the first national party convention) is said to have had the first nominating speech.[91] In the early years, such speeches were short. In 1860 Abraham Lincoln's name was placed into nomination with only twenty-seven words; the name of his chief rival for the nomination, William H. Seward of New York, was put forward with only twenty-six.[92] Over the years the length of nomination speeches has increased. It has also become the tradition for the nomination speech to be followed by a series of shorter seconding speeches. These are interspersed with floor demonstrations to show candidate support.

Television, however, has reshaped nomination and seconding speeches—just as it has reshaped so much of the activity at national conventions. Anxious that coverage of the event be streamlined and entertaining to television viewers, convention managers have encouraged a return to shorter nomination speeches and have seen to it that there are fewer seconding speeches (in 1936 Franklin Roosevelt was seconded fifty-six times), but things can still go awry. At the 1988 Democratic convention, Arkansas governor Bill Clinton was allotted fifteen minutes to nominate Michael Dukakis, and seconding speeches were eliminated altogether. To the dismay of Dukakis organizers, Clinton soon lost the attention of the delegates and then spoke for more than half an hour through all manner of signals to desist. Dukakis later joked that Clinton was available "to do the same fine job at the Republican convention as he did for me at the Democratic convention." [93]

Sometimes the persons who nominate candidates or second them are strategically chosen to display party unity.

Thus, New York governor Nelson Rockefeller—a longtime foe of Richard Nixon—was chosen to nominate Nixon in 1972. Similarly, after an unsuccessful effort by Harold Stassen to "dump" Vice President Nixon and replace him with Massachusetts governor Christian Herter in 1956, Nixon was renominated for vice president by Herter and seconded by Stassen. In 1968, Maryland governor Spiro Agnew was nominated for vice president by another frequently mentioned contender for the nomination, New York mayor John Lindsay. Those who nominate the candidates can also be chosen for other strategic reasons. In 1988, George Bush was nominated by his daughter-in-law as part of an effort by the Republicans to stress the importance of family.

Once the nominating and seconding speeches are over, the roll call begins. When the name of each state is called, the chair of the state's delegation rises and gives the vote of that delegation.[94] At early conventions, the order of the roll call was determined partly by geographical location and partly by the order in which states had entered the Union. Since the latter part of the 1800s, however, both parties have called the roll in alphabetical order, except in 1972. In that year, the Democrats determined the order of the roll call by lottery, thereby giving states that came later in the alphabet the chance to be called earlier and to have the honor of pushing the nominee "over the top." The roll call that year started with California and ended with Oklahoma but was a disaster since delegation chairs were not familiar with the new order and were seldom ready to announce their delegations' votes when called upon. In 1988, computer terminals were installed for each delegation at the Democratic convention. That allowed virtually simultaneous electronic voting. Only the roll calls for the nomination of the presidential and vice-presidential candidates were done the "old fashioned way"—by voice vote in alphabetical order.[95] Still, Dukakis organizers tinkered with the process to ensure that California, the state where Dukakis clinched the nomination in its June 7 primary, would also officially clinch the nomination for him at the convention. To do this, California and several other strategically chosen state delegations passed when called upon to vote. According to plan, the alphabetical rotation began a second time. California then voted and pushed Dukakis to victory.[96]

Often a candidate is chosen on the first ballot. On numerous occasions, however, more than one ballot has been required. Among the most famous deadlocked conventions were those of the Democrats in 1860 and 1924. The 1860 Democratic convention that met in Charleston, South Carolina, was turbulent from the start because of major splits between Northern and Southern delegates. When the convention adopted a platform plank that took a Northern "moderate" stance on slavery, forty-five delegates from nine states (including the majority of six Southern delegations) walked out of the convention. Chairman Caleb Cushing of Massachusetts then ruled that the two-thirds rule necessary to nominate a candidate would be based on the total number of delegates originally allocated, rather than on the number that remained present and voting. As a result, it was almost impossible for any candidate to receive the nomination. After fifty-seven ballots, the convention disbanded and reconvened in Baltimore the next month. There, Stephen A. Douglas of Illinois was nominated on the second (or fifty-ninth) ballot.

The 1924 Democratic convention at New York's Madison Square Garden spawned 103 roll calls and crawled on for an unprecedented seventeen days. At that convention, the split was between urban and rural delegates. The leading contenders were New York governor Alfred E. Smith and William Gibbs McAdoo of California, but fourteen others also were nominated at the convention. With so many candidates, the two-thirds rule prevented anyone from being nominated. Balloting went on and on. During the 38th ballot, William Jennings Bryan (who was serving as a delegate from Florida) stood and spoke in opposition to Smith. Unlike his triumphant "Cross of Gold" speech twenty-eight years before, Bryan's last convention speech was drowned out in a chorus of boos from urban delegates.

As balloting continued, McAdoo consistently came out ahead. After the 82d ballot, a resolution was passed that released all delegates from their commitments to candidates. On the 86th ballot, Smith topped McAdoo, but without the requisite two-thirds majority necessary for the nomination. It eventually became obvious that neither of the two major candidates could garner the support necessary for nomination. On the ninth day of balloting and the 103d ballot, the Democrats nominated John W. Davis of New York for president. That was the first Democratic convention to be broadcast live on radio, and listeners got an earful.

The most notable deadlock in the Republican party came in 1880, when former president Ulysses S. Grant sought the nomination for a third term. After thirty-six ballots, James A. Garfield was nominated for president.

More recently, Thomas E. Dewey entered the 1940 Republican convention the clear front-runner. Ohio senator Robert Taft was close behind. But there was growing support at the convention for Wendell Willkie, a Wall Street lawyer and former Democrat. On the first ballot, Dewey received 360 votes against 189 for Taft, 105 for Willkie, and 76 for Sen. Arthur Vandenberg of Michigan. As the balloting proceeded, Willkie worked his way up. In the galleries there were chants of "We want Willkie," and an outpouring of public sentiment for Willkie came in the form of thousands of letters and telegrams urging his nomination. On the sixth ballot, Willkie won and the convention went wild. As *Newsweek* magazine reported: "Nothing exactly like it has ever happened before in American politics. Willkie had never held public office or even sought it. Virtually a neophyte in politics, he had entered no primaries, made no deals, organized no campaign." [97] The "amateur" movement had succeeded in nominating a candidate—although there was help from big-business backers who had very effectively publicized his campaign.

A genuine draft of a reluctant candidate at a conven-

Library of Congress

In 1868, New York governor Horatio Seymour did not want the Democratic presidential nomination, declaring "Your candidate I cannot be!" He was drafted anyway.

tion is very rare. The first was New York governor Horatio Seymour who was nominated by the Democrats in 1868. Again, it was a convention with protracted balloting. The chief contenders for the nomination were President Andrew Johnson, George H. Pendleton of Ohio, and Gen. Winfield Scott Hancock of Pennsylvania. On the fourth ballot, North Carolina voted for Seymour, who promptly let it be known that he did not want the nomination: "I must not be nominated by this convention. I could not accept the nomination if tendered, which I do not expect."

The Johnson and Pendleton candidacies eventually collapsed, leaving General Hancock the front-runner. Opponents of Hancock introduced a new opponent, Sen. Thomas A. Hendricks of Indiana. Determined that an eastern candidate be nominated, the Ohio delegation voted for Seymour on the twenty-second ballot, and suddenly the tide turned toward him. Seymour rushed to the rostrum shouting, ". . . your candidate I cannot be!" Friends pulled him from the platform and hustled him to the Manhattan Club. There he learned of his nomination. His response, with tears streaming down his face, was "Pity me! Pity me!"[98] Since then there have been two other drafts of reluctant candidates: the selection of Supreme Court Justice Charles Evans Hughes by the Republicans in 1916 and the selection of Illinois governor Adlai Stevenson by the Democrats in 1952.

In the age of brokered conventions, nominations were often decided by powerful party bosses in "smoke-filled rooms." Mark Hanna—who was instrumental in achieving the nomination of William McKinley by the Republicans in 1896—is one of the most famous of those bosses. The reforms instituted by the parties since 1968 were largely an effort to reduce the influence of such people and increase rank-and-file participation in a democratization of the selection process.

For many years, a good deal of convention time was taken up by the nomination of "favorite son" candidates (that is, candidates nominated by their own state's delegation). Such nominations were seldom taken seriously by the convention as a whole. Since 1972, the Democrats have required that every name placed into nomination have the written support of at least fifty delegates from three or more delegations and that no more than twenty signatures come from one delegation. That action streamlined the proceedings and effectively ended favorite-son nominations.[99]

Vice-Presidential Nominee and Party Chair

After the nomination of the presidential candidate, the convention chooses a vice-presidential candidate. Until relatively recently, presidential candidates had little success in choosing their running mate. The 1920 Republican convention ignored Warren G. Harding's choice of Sen. Irwin L. Lenroot, and chose Massachusetts governor Calvin Coolidge instead. Sometimes presidential candidates (such as William McKinley and William Jennings Bryan in 1900) did not even bother to indicate a preference for their running mate. Such a choice had become the prerogative of the party leaders.

This practice changed in 1940 when Franklin Roosevelt threatened not to run unless the convention accepted his vice-presidential choice—Secretary of Agriculture Henry A. Wallace. The convention acquiesced, but Wallace was persuaded not to deliver an acceptance speech.[100]

Although it has come to be done routinely, the method of nominating the vice-presidential candidate mirrors the procedure for presidential nominations: there are nominating and seconding speeches, demonstrations, and balloting. In recent years, likely nominees have selected their running mates before the convention begins. Democrats Walter Mondale in 1984 and Michael Dukakis in 1988 chose their running mates early to clear the convention agenda for shows of unity. In 1976, Ronald Reagan, who finished second to Gerald Ford in the primaries, chose Pennsylvania senator Richard S. Schweiker in a futile effort to expand his appeal.

The actual choice of the vice-presidential candidate often is motivated by geographical considerations in an effort to "balance the ticket." For years, a balanced ticket was one that boasted an easterner and a midwesterner. More recently, the balance has shifted so that the split is more often between a northerner and a southerner. Ideological considerations also play a part in the balance. Thus, a liberal presidential candidate may be paired with a more conservative running mate to attract a broader base of votes. Finally, the choice of the vice-presidential candidate may be used to appease factions of the party who are unhappy with the presidential candidate. With the increasing number of vice presidents who go on to be president, more attention is given to the abilities of the person who is chosen (and more prominent figures are willing to accept the nomination).[101] In 1972, the Democrats' vice-presidential nominee, Missouri senator Thomas F. Eagleton, was forced to withdraw from the ticket when it was revealed that he had been hospitalized for "nervous exhaustion and fatigue" three times during the 1960s. The Democratic National Committee subsequently chose R. Sargent Shriver of Maryland to replace him.

In 1980, Reagan gave brief but apparently serious consideration to nominating former president Ford as his vice president with expanded powers. This plan for what media observers termed a "co-president" fell apart, and Reagan went on to nominate his former rival, George Bush. In 1984, Democrat Geraldine Ferraro of New York became the first woman to be nominated for vice president. Candidates seldom campaign openly for the vice-presidential nomination, but Jesse Jackson made it clear in the days before the 1988 Democratic convention that he wanted the number-two spot. Massachusetts governor Michael Dukakis ultimately chose conservative Texas senator Lloyd M. Bentsen, Jr., as his running mate in an effort to offer a Democratic ticket with a balance of ideology, experience, and regional background and to evoke images of the Massachusetts-Texas team of John F. Kennedy and Lyndon B. Johnson in 1960.

At the 1988 Republican convention, sixty-four-year-old vice president George Bush chose forty-one-year-old conservative Indiana senator Dan Quayle to bring the ticket an image of youth. Quayle was the first such candidate to be born after World War II. Almost immediately, there were allegations that Quayle's wealthy family had helped secure him a spot in the National Guard in 1969 to prevent him from serving combat duty in Vietnam. The allegations embarrassed the Republicans, who took pride in asserting their patriotism and military service.

Once the candidates have been chosen, it is the prerogative of the presidential nominee to select the national party chair. The nominee does so by informing the national committee of the choice. The committee then convenes to elect the individual formally. This power to appoint carries over into the nominee's term in office if the candidate

Bettmann Newsphotos

The 1952 conventions were the first to be broadcast to a coast-to-coast television audience. Republican nominees Eisenhower and Nixon were seen by approximately seventy million television viewers.

succeeds in winning the White House. Since the average tenure of party chairs is two years, presidents have an opportunity to influence significantly the workings of their party.[102] *(See "Selection of the Party Chair," p. 602, in the Chief of Party chapter of Part III.)*

Television and Other Press Coverage

National party conventions are media events par excellence. The most powerful leaders of a political party and hundreds of other notables are all to be found in one spot—a flamboyant setting with cheering crowds and mob demonstrations, candidates involved in a "horse race" for delegate votes, passionate speakers and poignant appearances by party elders, and limitless opportunities for on-the-spot interviews and human-interest stories. Of course, there are times when conventions are hard upon both "the cerebral centers and the *gluteus maximus,*" [103] as Mencken said. But on the whole, conventions are the breeding ground of drama, and drama is the grist for news.

The convention system originated in an age before the telegraph or telephone, when newspapers were highly partisan mouthpieces of political parties. Communication and transportation were slow, so conventions took place with relative anonymity. Today, all of that has changed. Thousands of reporters attend conventions, and millions of Americans are privy to the action via television and radio.

The 1924 conventions were the first to be broadcast on the radio. The 1940 Republican convention was televised on an experimental basis, but it was seen by only a tiny audience. Likewise, the 1948 Democratic convention was televised, but it reached an audience of only about 400,000 along the eastern seaboard. The Democrats also used television that year so that an overflow crowd of some 6,000 could watch the proceedings in an auditorium adjacent to the convention hall.[104] The 1952 conventions were the first to be broadcast to a coast-to-coast television audience.

The advent of this new age has had a tremendous effect upon national party conventions. Television brought the 1952 conventions into the living rooms of sixty-five to seventy million Americans. All three networks held gavel-to-gavel coverage of the convention itself, as well as considerable coverage of Credentials Committee hearings that took place before the conventions convened and while they were in recess.[105] It soon became clear that under the close scrutiny of the television eye, the use of "unfair" tactics against the opposition could have disastrous consequences.

Credentials fights between the Taft and Eisenhower forces at the Republican convention were played out for all the world to see. Eisenhower forces introduced a famous "Fair Play" amendment and won their fight after emotional "Thou shalt not steal" speeches by Eisenhower's floor leaders. As ABC commentator Elmer Davis said, it was "no longer possible to commit grand larceny in broad daylight." [106] Steamroller tactics such as blatantly unfair rulings by the convention chair, or forced recesses during roll calls to deflate enthusiasm for a candidate or mobilize opposition support, are largely things of the past.

Since the key to electronic media is "image," conventions are now choreographed for television. Convention planners are careful to prevent boring lulls in the action, to keep potentially divisive rules or platform fights out of prime-time viewing hours, and to orchestrate "spontaneous" demonstrations and telegenic events such as the release of hundreds of colorful balloons on the convention floor. Television consultants coach speakers and give hints on makeup, wardrobe, and how to read the TelePrompTer. The party leader warns state delegations about how to act. Even the chair is coached on how many times to bang the gavel. Eric Lieber, a television consultant for the Democrats in 1976, said that gavel banging was a sign of disorder. Subsequently, use of the gavel was restricted to three times a session—regardless of what was happening on the floor.[107] Individual speakers are often astute as well. When Mary Anne Krupsak, the lieutenant governor of New York, mounted the podium to give a short five-minute speech to the Democrats in 1976—an opportunity often taken to cut away for commercials or commentary—the networks stayed with her because she used a sign-language interpreter.[108]

Still, attempts at image control are not always successful. The 1968 Chicago convention was a disaster for the Democrats. Bloody confrontations between antiwar demonstrators and helmeted police outside the hall and anger and divisiveness among participants inside the hall set the tone for television coverage. In 1972, George McGovern, the Democratic nominee for president, had the ignominious distinction of delivering his acceptance speech at 2:48 a.m. because of a long string of symbolic vice-presidential nominations brought about by the "open politics" of the new Democratic party rules. On the first day of their 1976 convention in New York's Madison Square Garden, Democrats were aghast to see television pointing to some three thousand empty seats. Harried convention aides were instructed to hand out credentials passes along Seventh Avenue to anyone who walked by.

The media age has changed conventions substantively as well. Lengthy Credentials and Rules committee sessions are now scheduled to meet before the start of the convention so as to cut down on the delays while the convention awaits their reports. The Democrats have passed rules that effectively eliminate lengthy favorite son nominations. Limits have been set on the number and length of seconding speeches. Roll calls have been streamlined, and the old practice of state chairs delivering a short speech on behalf of their state and candidate is gone.[109]

Those covering the convention also are concerned with image. Officials of the television networks are anxious about winning higher ratings than their competitors, and they assign their most important reporters to cover the event. Many Americans are more familiar with the reporters than with the politicians. Anchors and analysts cover the convention from overhead booths, while scores of reporters rove the floor in search of fast-breaking stories. The networks hire "spotters" to scan the floor for people who might make for interesting interviews.

Television often produces images just as misleading as those the media consultants conjure up for the political parties. In particular, television cultivates an illusion of action to maintain viewer interest. Activities taking place at various locations are all covered at once. Cameras switch back and forth between events to maintain a sense of constant action. As a result, television sometimes exaggerates or creates a false sense of confusion and disorder at conventions.[110] As Theodore H. White has written, television "displays events, action, motion, arrival, departure; it cannot show thought, silence, mood or decision. And so [television catches] the carnival outer husk of the convention in all its pageantry. . . ." [111]

So that the anchor can talk intelligently about everything that is going on at the convention at any given time, "gophers" scramble through reference books or call researchers for background about persons the camera might focus on, and researchers stand by to explain what is happening on the platform or on the floor.[112] Likewise, directors shout instructions into the earpieces that anchors and floor reporters wear. To be sure they never have to miss any of the action, some floor reporters wear waste bags developed for astronauts by the National Aeronautics and Space Administration. One correspondent told a colleague: "I won't have to come off the floor to go to the bathroom for 28 days." [113]

The amount of money spent for network coverage of national party conventions is enormous. In 1980, one network executive indicated that such coverage cost approximately $10 million.[114] Since 1980, television networks have pulled away from gavel-to-gavel coverage of conventions. In 1988, the three major networks scheduled live coverage of only two prime-time hours a day. After the Democratic convention, where everything—including the vice-presidential choice—was wrapped up before the convention even convened, some commentators questioned the utility of even that much live coverage.[115]

Both parties treated their conventions as four-day television commercials. Recognizing this, networks frequently cut away from the proceedings themselves and offered their own commentary or interviews with party officials. In particular, Republican efforts to shape the television image of the convention were thwarted by network coverage that was dominated by the vice-presidential selection process. Coverage of the first two days centered on speculation over who would be selected. Coverage of the last two days centered on controversy surrounding the choice of the young Indiana senator Dan Quayle as George Bush's running mate. [116]

Functions of National Party Conventions

National party conventions perform many functions.[117] They serve as a forum for officially selecting candidates and determining party policy and rules. In so doing, they make the actions of the party legitimate. Furthermore, since all factions of the party are brought together at conventions, they serve as a place for bargaining and compromise.

The ultimate aim is to foster party unity by closing ranks behind the nominee—even though divisiveness before the nomination may have been bitter. This process of consensus-building is aided by the fact that most factions are ultimately loyal to the party. Bitterness is diffused since any given group has multiple opportunities to score success. If they are unsuccessful in nominating a presidential candidate, they may have success in winning a key platform plank or gaining a favorable vice-presidential nominee. Furthermore, there is always the possibility of future victories if their party wins the general election campaign, such as political appointments and the passage of legislation that their group espouses.

Especially since the advent of television coverage, conventions also serve a publicity function. Through television, millions of Americans learn about the personalities of candidates and the policies espoused by the party. Televised conventions set the image of the party for millions of outsiders. In addition, conventions are a way to rally support among party activists so that they will work hard for the party during the general election campaign.

In short, conventions are rituals that legitimize the selection process. They aim toward conciliation and unity while allowing for the expression of disparate viewpoints. Especially because today's conventions tend merely to ratify the choice voters expressed in the primaries, they serve as a means of wedding the candidate and the party and provide a basis for mass support of the ticket during the general election campaign.

Death or Resignation of Convention Nominee

If a nominee dies or resigns from the ticket before election day, Democratic and Republican rules call for the national party committee to meet and choose a replacement. Thus, the Democratic National Committee chose R. Sargent Shriver as their vice-presidential nominee when Thomas Eagleton resigned from the Democratic ticket in 1972.

If the death or resignation takes place after election day but before the date in December when the electors cast their ballots, the national committee would probably still choose a replacement in an effort to guide the vote of the electors. That was what happened when Republican vice president James S. Sherman died on October 30, 1912.

If the death or resignation takes place after the electoral votes are counted and announced by Congress, but before the inauguration, the selection process is governed by the Twentieth Amendment to the Constitution. That amendment specifies that if the president-elect dies or resigns, the vice president-elect will become president. If both were to die or resign during that period, the Presidential Succession Act would take effect.

The procedure is less clear if the death or resignation takes place between the time that the electors cast their votes and the time that they are counted by Congress. Since the electoral votes are technically not valid until counted by Congress, there would be no real president-elect or vice president-elect during that period. Thus, the Presidential Succession Act could not be used. If the candidate who died or resigned during that period did not have a majority of the electoral votes, the majority candidate simply would win. If, however, the candidate who died or resigned did have a majority of the electoral votes, the choice of a president would be thrown to the House of Representatives, and the choice of a vice-president to the Senate.[118]

Proposals to Reform the Nominating Process

Does the existing nominating process lead to the selection of the "best" candidates—those who are most qualified or who are most likely to win in the general election? Does it weaken the power of political parties? Does it give too much influence to particular states or regions of the country? Is it "deliberative" enough? Is it responsive to voter preferences? Is it too long? Too fragmented? Too oriented to the media?

These are some of the questions raised by observers of the nominating process. Different observers have different opinions as to what the process should achieve.[119] As a result, they have different answers to the above questions. Nevertheless, many analysts and political figures are unhappy (for a variety of reasons) with the current system. As a result, there have been numerous proposals to reform the nominating process.

The post-1968 reforms served to open the system, making it more responsive to the rank-and-file and less responsive to party elites. For many, this was good. Indeed, a more participatory system was the aim of most of the reformers. Others, however, argue that the reforms went too far. This group wants to increase the influence and involvement of party elites in the selection process. Such critics argue that the post-1968 reforms explicitly weakened the parties. Nonetheless, as political scientist Michael Nelson has pointed out, the parties were already in a state of decline in the 1950s and 1960s. Indeed, he has argued that the decline has been halted, and in many cases reversed, in the last decade—partly by the reforms themselves since they helped the parties adapt "to the changed social and political environment that underlay their decline."[120]

Those who want to strengthen the power of party elites are often said to adhere to an "organizational" (or "party regular") model of presidential selection. Those favoring a more open system are said to adhere to a "participatory" (or "reform") model of selection.[121] There are, of course, a range of positions between the extreme versions of these two models. Indeed, most proposals to increase the power of party elites have been far from radical. Usually such proposals have called for increased participation by party officials at the national convention through the reservation of delegate slots for them and for increased power of state parties to design their delegate selection systems.[122] Both of these proposals were incorporated in the recommendations of the Hunt Commission. *(See "The Hunt Commission," p. 178, in this chapter.)* More radical proposals, such as the suggestion that Congress require that nominating conventions consist only of party leaders and elected officials (with the total elimination of primaries) are seldom taken seriously. As political scientist Thomas E. Mann has written, most proposals "move in the direction of increasing or channeling, not eliminating, participation by rank-and-file party identifiers."[123]

The National Primary

Another set of reform proposals aims at further democratizing the system. One of the most frequently mentioned of these is the suggestion that the United States adopt a national primary. Such a system was proposed in Congress as early as 1911 (and endorsed by Woodrow Wilson shortly thereafter).[124] Since then, numerous versions of such a system have been presented. One of the best known of these would allow each party a single national primary on a designated day. To appear on the ballot, candidates would have to file a petition containing signatures equivalent to 1 percent of the votes cast in the last presidential election, or almost one million names. This primary (with a runoff election, if necessary), would determine the presidential nominee, although a convention could still be held to choose a vice-presidential nominee, adopt a platform, and conduct other party business. Another variation of the plan would have the national primary select two-thirds of the delegates to a national convention. The other third would consist of party elites. When a national primary was not decisive, this system would allow for a deliberative convention rather than a runoff election.[125]

Those who support a national primary argue that it would simplify the process by having one uniform system of candidate selection. They further argue that it would make the system more democratic: votes would count equally, the candidate would be representative of the rank-and-file, and voter participation might even increase. In the process, the campaign season would be shortened, particular states would no longer be accorded special weight, issues of national concern would be addressed, and the effect of the media's interpretation of early primaries and caucuses would be eliminated.[126]

Opponents of a national primary argue that it would

severely weaken—if not destroy—the party system and would all but eliminate grass-roots campaigning. They further argue that it would increase candidates' use of the media and allow for no "winnowing" of candidates through the campaign season.[127] Finally, they contend that the system would be biased against unknown candidates (who, in the present system, can make a name for themselves in the early primaries) and could lead to the selection of a candidate with ephemeral or even demogogic appeal. This would be so, they argue, since candidates would not have to survive a string of contests and continually prove themselves over a long primary season.[128]

A change to a national primary would itself be quite complicated. It would require, at the least, national legislation, and possibly even a constitutional amendment. There is no doubt that it would be bitterly contested by many factions including party regulars and those who favor a states' rights approach to the election process.[129]

The Regional Primary

Another frequently mentioned proposal to reform the nominating process is the idea of regional primaries. Those who have introduced proposals for such a system include Sen. Bob Packwood (R-Ore.) and Walter Mondale, then a Democratic Senator from Minnesota. Under these proposals, the country would be divided into regions (five in Packwood's proposal; six in Mondale's). Each state within that region would be required to hold its primary or caucuses on the date assigned that region. These dates would fall at intervals of two weeks (Mondale) or one month (Packwood). The order of the regional primaries would be chosen by lot, and therefore the order would change from one election year to the next.[130] Under both plans, state primaries would be optional. Others have suggested that the primaries be mandatory.[131] Such primaries would be used to select delegates to a national nominating convention.

The regional primary plan is an attempt to correct a system that critics say is too fragmented. By requiring that all states within a particular region hold their primary on a set day, the undue influence of individual states that hold early primaries (such as New Hampshire) would be eliminated. That advantage would be transferred to a region as a whole, but the shifting order of the primaries would prevent any one region from enjoying an advantage for long. As political scientists William Crotty and John S. Jackson III have written, such plans attempt "to resolve some of the difficulties of the current system of scattered primaries, while retaining the strengths both of the party system and of reform era democratization."[132]

Critics of regional primaries say such plans would severely weaken the role of the states in the presidential selection process. Not only would the process be nationalized under a uniform system, but candidates would focus less attention on the needs of individual states. In short, they see such plans as merely a modified version of national primary plans. Like the national primary, they say, regional primaries would undermine the need for grass-roots campaigning, be biased against unknown candidates, and increase the candidates' use of media. In 1988, Super Tuesday served as a de facto regional primary for the South. A variant of the regional primary plan, introduced by Rep. Morris K. Udall (D-Ariz.), would require states that hold primaries to do so on one of four dates. Under this plan, the grouping of states would be voluntarily chosen rather than set by region.[133]

As reformers continually discover, proposals for change often bring unanticipated consequences. Thus, it is difficult to say with full assurance what would happen if any of the reform proposals were instituted. Michael Nelson, for one, has suggested that we stick with our current system. Even though strong cases can be made for certain reforms, he has argued that continued tampering with the process lends instability to the system since continued rules rewriting is not only distracting, but subversive of the system's legitimacy.[134]

General Election Campaign

Once they have won their party's nomination, presidential candidates focus their attention on winning the general election. They must choose a strategy that they think will propel them to victory and interact with a complex political environment that includes a scrutinizing news media, the opposition party, and interest groups. Not least among their problems is organizing their own staff—including pollsters, media consultants, and other senior advisers—and coordinating activities with state and national organizations of their own party.

Types of Strategy

The choice of a particular strategy is based on several factors, including: the standing of the candidates in the polls, the relative strengths and weaknesses of the candidates, the source of the candidates' core support (for example, regional or national, partisan or personal, ideological or consensual), the strength of the parties, the mood of the electorate, the expected voter turnout, and the chances of winning the election in November.[1]

Most strategies entail geographical considerations. Democratic candidates usually are strongest in large industrial states; Republicans, in the Midwest and western states. Until recently, the South was a Democratic stronghold, but conservatives there increasingly have been attracted to Republicans in presidential elections. *(See map, Party Strength in Presidential Elections.)*

To appeal to a large geographic constituency, most tickets include presidential and vice-presidential candidates from different parts of the country—one element of "ticket balancing" (which also includes such considerations as ideology). *(See "The Vice President's Campaign," p. 244, in this chapter.)* When Walter Mondale chose Geraldine Ferraro as his running mate in 1984, Ronald Reagan's strategist, Lee Atwater, was elated. He predicted that the Democrats' choice of a "North-North" ticket had given the South to the Republicans and guaranteed victory for Reagan.[2]

Regional strength does not tell all, however. Since states do not count equally in the electoral college, candidates often concentrate their efforts on certain key states with large electoral vote counts. Indeed, the electoral votes of twelve key states are enough to secure victory in the general election. For instance, a candidate in 1984 needed only to carry California, New York, Texas, Pennsylvania, Illinois, Ohio, Florida, Michigan, New Jersey, North Carolina, Massachusetts, and either Georgia, Virginia, or Indiana in order to win the election. Given victories there, votes

Party Strength in Presidential Elections, by State, 1952-1988, and Electoral Votes, 1988

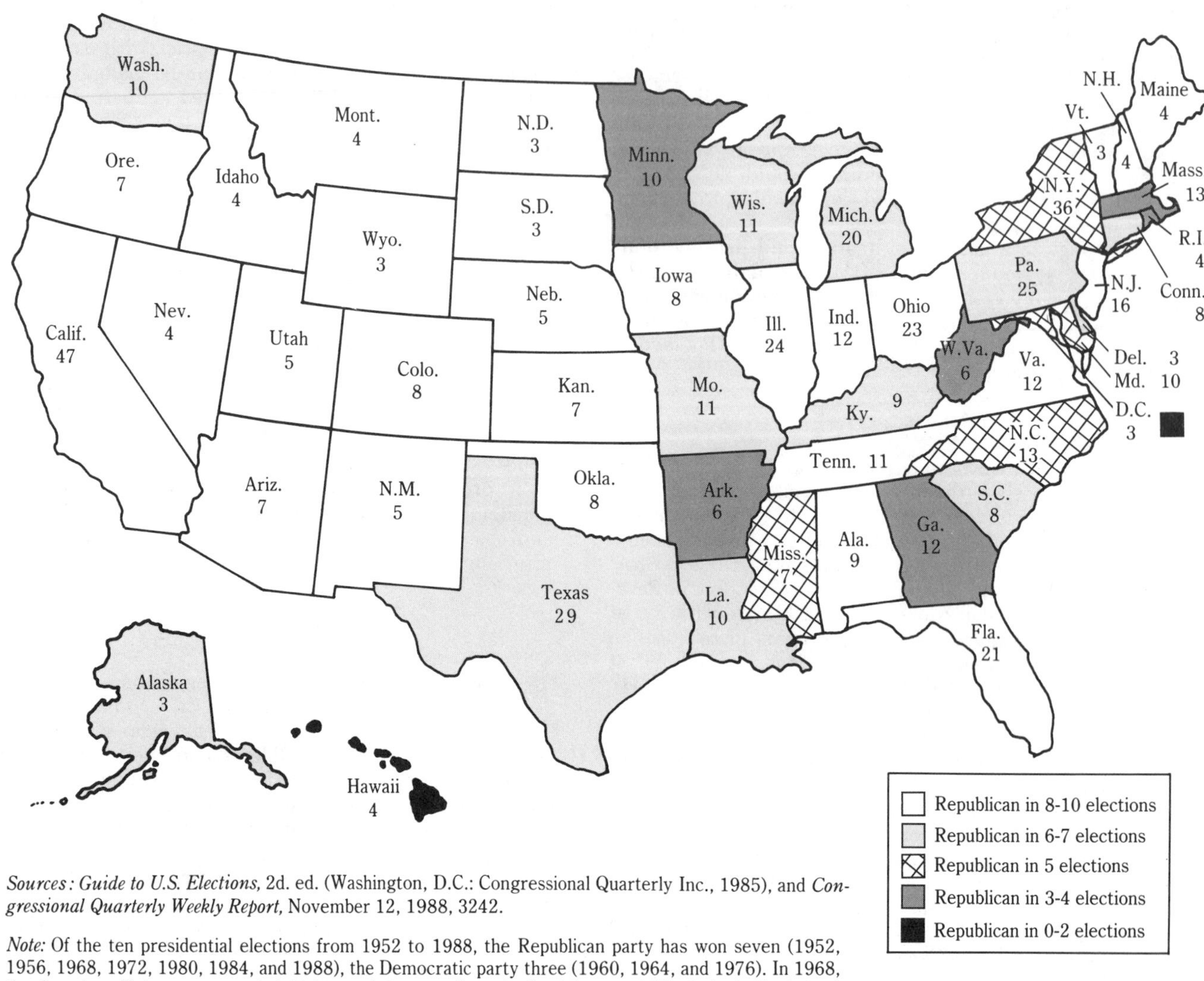

Sources: Guide to U.S. Elections, 2d. ed. (Washington, D.C.: Congressional Quarterly Inc., 1985), and *Congressional Quarterly Weekly Report,* November 12, 1988, 3242.

Note: Of the ten presidential elections from 1952 to 1988, the Republican party has won seven (1952, 1956, 1968, 1972, 1980, 1984, and 1988), the Democratic party three (1960, 1964, and 1976). In 1968, the American Union party carried Alabama, Arkansas, Georgia, Louisiana, and Mississippi. Alaska and Hawaii first voted for president in 1960; the District of Columbia in 1964.

in the thirty-eight other states would not matter.

To concentrate time and attention on all the states can be a waste of resources. Richard Nixon promised to visit each of the fifty states when he ran for president in 1960. He came to regret that decision when he was forced to waste valuable time visiting states with almost no influence, while his rival, John Kennedy, was targeting key states. This point was driven home on the last weekend before the election when Nixon had to fly to Alaska to fulfill his promise, while Kennedy visited important northeastern states including New York, New Jersey, and Massachusetts. When Nixon ran again in 1968 he was careful to target particular states. For instance, he did not visit Kansas that year. As Robert Ellsworth, a campaign aide from that state, said: "If you have to worry about Kansas, you don't have a campaign anyway." [3]

Aside from deciding what sort of geographic strategy to pursue, candidates are faced with other strategic choices. Should they stress their party affiliation or their individual merit? Should they run a strictly ideological campaign or emphasize conciliation and consensus? Should they concentrate on style or on substance?

Since the New Deal, the Democrats consistently have had more registered voters than the Republicans. As a result, it is more advantageous for the Democrats to follow a strictly partisan campaign than it is for the Republicans. Since they have a larger pool of registered voters than do the Republicans, it also behooves the Democrats to encourage a large voter turnout. This can be done either through "neutral" efforts stressing the civic obligation to vote, or through more specific efforts, such as providing baby-sitters and transportation to the polls.[4] Such efforts appear to have secured victory for John F. Kennedy in 1960.[5]

Republicans can be hurt by a large voter turnout or by running an intensely partisan campaign. While maintaining their base of support, they must also reach out to independents and Democrats with weak party ties.[6] To do this, Republican candidates sometimes deemphasize their party. In 1976, Gerald Ford's official campaign poster contained his picture, but no indication of his party affili-

Figure 1 Victorious Party in Presidential Elections, by State, 1952-1988

State	1952	1956	1960	1964	1968	1972	1976	1980	1984	1988
Ala.	D	D	D	R	I	R	D	R	R	R
Alaska	—	—	R	D	R	R	R	R	R	R
Ariz.	R	R	R	R	R	R	R	R	R	R
Ark.	D	D	D	D	I	R	D	R	R	R
Calif.	R	R	R	D	R	R	R	R	R	R
Colo.	R	R	R	D	R	R	D	R	R	R
Conn.	R	R	D	D	D	R	R	R	R	R
Del.	R	R	D	D	R	R	D	R	R	R
D.C.	—	—	—	D	D	D	D	R	D	R
Fla.	R	R	R	D	R	R	D	R	D	R
Ga.	D	D	D	R	I	R	D	D	R	R
Hawaii	—	—	D	D	D	R	D	D	R	D
Idaho	R	R	R	D	R	R	D	R	R	R
Ill.	R	R	D	D	R	R	R	R	R	R
Ind.	R	R	R	D	R	R	R	R	R	R
Iowa	R	R	R	D	R	R	R	R	R	D
Kan.	R	R	R	D	R	D	D	R	D	R
Ky.	D	R	R	D	R	R	R	R	R	R
La.	D	R	D	R	I	R	D	R	R	R
Maine	R	R	R	D	D	R	R	R	R	R
Md.	R	R	D	D	D	R	D	D	R	R
Mass.	R	R	D	D	D	D	D	R	R	D
Mich.	R	R	D	D	D	R	R	R	R	R
Minn.	R	R	D	D	D	R	D	D	D	D
Miss.	D	D	D	R	I	R	D	R	R	R
Mo.	R	D	D	D	R	R	D	R	R	R
Mont.	R	R	R	D	R	R	R	R	R	R
Neb.	R	R	R	D	R	R	R	R	R	R
Nev.	R	R	D	D	R	R	R	R	R	R
N.C.	D	D	D	D	R	R	D	R	R	R
N.D.	R	R	R	D	R	R	R	R	R	R
N.H.	R	R	R	D	R	R	R	R	R	R
N.J.	R	R	D	D	R	R	R	R	R	R
N.M.	R	R	D	D	R	R	R	R	R	R
N.Y.	R	R	D	D	D	R	D	R	R	D
Ohio	R	R	R	D	R	R	D	R	R	R
Okla.	R	R	R	D	R	R	R	R	R	R
Ore.	R	R	R	D	R	R	R	R	R	D
Pa.	R	R	D	D	D	R	D	R	R	R
R.I.	R	R	D	D	D	R	D	D	R	D
S.C.	D	D	D	R	R	R	D	R	R	R
S.D.	R	R	R	D	R	R	R	R	R	R
Tenn.	R	R	R	D	R	R	D	R	R	R
Texas	R	R	D	D	D	R	D	R	R	R
Utah	R	R	R	D	R	R	R	R	R	R
Vt.	R	R	R	D	R	R	R	R	R	R
Va.	R	R	R	D	R	R	R	R	R	R
Wash.	R	R	R	D	D	R	R	R	R	D
W.Va.	D	R	D	D	D	R	D	D	R	D
Wis.	R	R	R	D	R	R	D	R	R	D
Wyo.	R	R	R	D	R	R	R	R	R	R

Key: R = Republican; D = Democrat; I = Independent; — = Did not vote

Sources: Guide to U.S. Elections (Washington, D.C.: Congressional Quarterly Inc., 1985); *Congressional Quarterly Weekly Report*, November 12, 1988, 3242.

ation—something that might also have reminded voters of the Watergate debacle that drove Richard Nixon from office in 1974.[7] Likewise, Nixon's campaign organization in 1972—the Committee to Re-elect the President—was a blatant attempt to bypass the Republican party. Earlier, the nomination of the World War II hero, Gen. Dwight D. Eisenhower, successfully deemphasized partisanship.

Despite a decline in importance, party labels are still important cues to voters. Nelson W. Polsby and Aaron Wildavsky have argued that even independents have party preferences: "About two-thirds of all independents have leanings; scratch an independent and underneath you are likely to find an almost-Republican or a near-Democrat, and those who are left are least likely to turn out." [8]

Unlike partisan campaigns, which stress party loyalty, ideological campaigns stress a strict adherence to a particular political ideology. In so doing, ideological campaigns can alienate those who are opposed to the ideological stance of the candidate (including members of the candidate's own party). This alienation solidifies the opposition, prompts defection, and decreases the likelihood of broad-based support.[9] Yet another strategy is a "consensus" campaign, which makes broad appeals beyond the confines of either partisanship or ideology. The campaigns of Republican Barry Goldwater in 1964 and Democrat George McGovern in 1972 are two examples of ideological campaigns that failed. Their opponents, Lyndon Johnson and Richard Nixon, respectively, both waged successful consensus campaigns.

Candidates must also decide how specific they will be on the issues. Fearful of antagonizing portions of the electorate, many candidates couch their positions in generalities. Stock phrases are repeated in speech after speech, and candidates are careful to tell their audiences what they want to hear. A few candidates, such as Adlai Stevenson, took pride in crafting new speeches for every occasion, but this is not the norm. In fact, that tactic ultimately hurt Stevenson. Since he was not repeating a well-worn text, his delivery suffered. Furthermore, he often was accused of speaking "over people's heads" and of not being sure that his speeches were tailored to his audience.[10]

In 1984, Walter Mondale tried to appear honest and straightforward by taking specific stands on controversial issues. He promised, for instance, to raise taxes. He also lost. But most candidates—Democrat and Republican alike—are cautious and repetitive. What they strive for are short "extractables" or "sound-bites" that can be lifted from their speeches and included in fifteen- or thirty-second spots on the evening news. Thus, Ronald Reagan saying "There you go again!" to Jimmy Carter in 1980, or Walter Mondale asking "Where's the beef?" in 1984 are more memorable than the substance that surrounded those lines.

Incumbents are faced with a broader set of strategic options than their opponents. Often the simple fact that they are in office gives them certain advantages. The office of president lends them credibility and respect. They are, in a sense, "tried and true." They have on-the-job experience and, with some luck, accomplishments that they can tout. They also are guaranteed to be known. But beyond that, they are in a position to influence events and benefit key constituencies. *(See "Incumbents Seeking Reelection," p. 237, in this chapter.)*

These advantages have led to the so-called Rose Garden strategy in which presidents avoid active campaigning, make official appearances in carefully controlled settings (such as greeting heads of state and signing legislation), and act "presidential" by wrapping themselves in the symbols and backdrop of the office. This strategy isolates presidents from the press (while not diminishing their visibil-

Princeton University Library

Unlike most candidates, Adlai Stevenson crafted new speeches for every occasion – a tactic that ultimately hurt him. By not repeating a well-worn text, his delivery suffered, and he was accused of speaking over people's heads.

Gerald R. Ford Library

Behind in the polls, President Ford chose a campaign strategy that included televised debates with Gov. Jimmy Carter.

ity), reduces the likelihood of their committing a costly blunder, saves money, and appears to put the president above petty politics. Such a strategy was used most effectively by Nixon in 1972 and by Reagan in 1984.[11]

Both the Rose Garden strategy and incumbency itself can have their drawbacks, however. Presidents are blamed for failures as well as remembered for successes. Even events over which presidents have little control may be blamed on them. Oil shortages, military upheavals, and adverse economic conditions may arise through no particular fault of the incumbent president. Indeed, adopting a Rose Garden strategy in times of trouble can lead to the accusation that the president is hiding in the White House rather than attending to official duties. Jimmy Carter was accused of this in 1980, when there was widespread public displeasure over his handling of the Iranian hostage crisis and he was facing a serious challenge for his own party's presidential nomination from Sen. Edward Kennedy of Massachusetts.

In 1976, Ford's Rose Garden strategy included challenging his opponent, Carter, to a series of televised debates. The plan was suggested in a memorandum to Richard Cheney, Ford's White House chief of staff, in June of that year.[12] As Cheney has written, the debate option was "part of a 'no campaign' campaign strategy," with the debates serving as "a means of deemphasizing traditional campaigning, maximizing the advantages of incumbency, and forcing Governor Carter to deal substantively with the issues."[13] As journalist Martin Schram noted, they were also "a chance for the President to dispel the notions that he was not intelligent and not capable of running the country.... The debates would be a chance for the President to demonstrate competence and poise."[14]

Ford chose that strategy largely because he was very far behind in the polls. He generally was perceived to be poor on the stump but well prepared for debates. Ford and his advisers calculated that he had little to lose and much to gain in a debate. There had been no debates of that sort since 1960, and they were bound to be a decisive element in the campaign.

As a rule, however, incumbents stand more to lose than their opponents in face-to-face debates. Such debates allow opponents to prove their mettle. They are put on an equal footing with the president and given the opportunity to demonstrate that they, too, can deal with substantive issues. Because the incumbents are tied to their record and their policies, they easily are placed on the defensive.

Deciding whether to participate in televised debates is but one of many tactical decisions facing candidates. Candidates must decide whether potential voters should be targeted primarily through the mass media, personal campaigning, party organization, or independent political action committees (PACs). Techniques used through these various avenues include spot commercials on television, door-to-door canvassing, direct mail, and endorsements by organizations such as labor unions that can turn out a large number of votes.[15]

Incumbents Seeking Reelection

Once the general election campaign is under way, the two major-party nominees are in many ways equals. Since 1976, they have received identical grants from the federal government to finance their campaigns. The media dispatch teams to cover the two candidates on a roughly equal footing. Even when third-party candidates such as John Anderson in 1980 run for the presidency, the spotlight usually stays trained on the Democratic and Republican nominees.

When a sitting president is running for reelection, however, the balance of power can tilt. The incumbent not only already has the stature of the presidency but is able to influence media coverage with official presidential actions and to use pork-barrel politics to appeal to specific constituencies. The president also benefits from the public's reluctance to reject a tested national leader for an unknown quantity.

The emotional bond of the people with the president is an important, if unquantifiable, factor in a president's reelection advantages. Perhaps the greatest examples in recent years are Lyndon B. Johnson's 1964 reelection, which benefited from the nation's deep psychological desire for continuity in the wake of the assassination of President John F. Kennedy, and President Ronald Reagan's evocation of patriotic themes in his 1984 campaign for reelection.

In times of economic or foreign policy crisis, the president's prominence can have a negative effect on the campaign. President Jimmy Carter's bid for reelection in 1980 was doomed by "stagflation"—the combination of high unemployment and high inflation rates—and the continued holding of U.S. citizens as hostages in Iran. Carter's credibility on foreign policy also was damaged by his apparent surprise at the Soviet Union's invasion of Afghanistan in November 1979 and the resentment of many groups about his actions against the Soviets (an embargo of grain sales to the Soviets and a U.S. boycott of the 1980 Moscow Olympics).

Most first-term presidents appear intent on managing the economy so that the inevitable cyclical slump occurs early in the administration. The hope is that by the time the reelection campaign begins, the economy will rebound and voters will have confidence in the administration's economic management. President Reagan presided over the highest unemployment rate since the Great Depression early in his first term, but by the time he sought reelection in 1984 both the unemployment and inflation rates had declined significantly.

Well-timed announcements of government statistics on the economy or of plans for domestic initiatives can also help the incumbent.

Managing foreign relations probably provides the greatest opportunity for an incumbent to enhance the chances for reelection. In 1972, President Richard Nixon orchestrated a number of major foreign policy initiatives that guaranteed him continued media coverage. Nixon coopted many Democratic calls for greater efforts to negotiate solutions to difficult world problems. He visited both the Soviet Union and the People's Republic of China and oversaw the negotiation of a ceasefire treaty in the long and bitter Vietnam War. The China trip was especially dramatic: it was the first time a U.S. president had visited that nation since the 1949 revolution.

As the campaign neared its end, the Nixon administration expressed greater confidence about the prospects of a settlement of the Vietnam War. In late October, Secretary of State Henry A. Kissinger announced that "peace is at hand." The public pronouncements on Vietnam undercut the antiwar campaign of Nixon's Democratic rival, Sen. George McGovern of South Dakota.

Even foreign policy difficulties can be an advantage for an incumbent. Vice President Hubert H. Humphrey's 1968 campaign got a late boost when President Lyndon Johnson announced a halt in bombing of Vietnam. Initially at least, Carter got a temporary boost from the crises in Afghanistan and Iran. After the tragic truck-bombing of U.S. Marine barracks in Lebanon in 1983—a policy disaster since Reagan had been explicitly warned about the dangers of such an attack—Reagan benefited politically from the nation's willingness to "rally 'round the flag." Two days after the Lebanon attack, Reagan stirred up more feelings of patriotism with the invasion of the tiny Caribbean island of Grenada.

As the defeats of Presidents Ford and Carter demonstrate, the incumbent's advantages in the general election do not guarantee victory. The existence of negative symbolic issues—such as Ford's pardon of the disgraced president Nixon and Carter's handling of economic and foreign policy crises—can doom an incumbent. Factors such as heavy campaign expenditures by political opponents—one of Carter's problems in 1980—can badly damage the sitting president. Both Ford and Carter suffered from bitter struggles for their party nominations.

Role of the Campaign Staff and Advisers

In modern elections, important tactical decisions are made by professional campaign consultants. Such consultants form the core of a candidate's personal campaign organization—a complex superstructure of pollsters, media producers, accountants, advertising executives, and other advisers. Usually, these consultants are engaged in highly specialized tasks such as public opinion sampling, data processing, policy formulation, fund raising, and the production of television commercials.

Presidential elections in the media age are elaborate, multimillion-dollar operations. The rise of professional campaign consultants is, in part, an attempt to use the expertise that is necessary (or perceived to be necessary) in this complex environment. Such consultants also helped fill the void left by the weakening of party organizations that used to coordinate campaigns.[16]

Pollsters

Candidates have always had advisers of some sort to guide them through their campaign, but the technological advances that spawned the new breed of consultants—most notably, advances in communications and data processing—are relatively recent. Polling, for instance, has been around since 1824 when the *Harrisburg Pennsylvanian* published a survey of the presidential preferences of the voters of Wilmington, Delaware.[17] That was the year King Caucus fell, and the crowded field of candidates (including Andrew Jackson, John Quincy Adams, William H. Crawford, and Henry Clay) sent the election to the House of Representatives. But surveys such as the one published that year were unsophisticated and were published primarily as a form of "entertainment." Candidates themselves did not use the advice of pollsters until the 1930s, when advances in communications and sampling techniques made polls more reliable.

Polls tell the candidates where their base of support lies, what the electorate thinks of them personally, and what issues are important to the electorate.[18] Thus, polls can be used by candidates to decide whether or not to run,

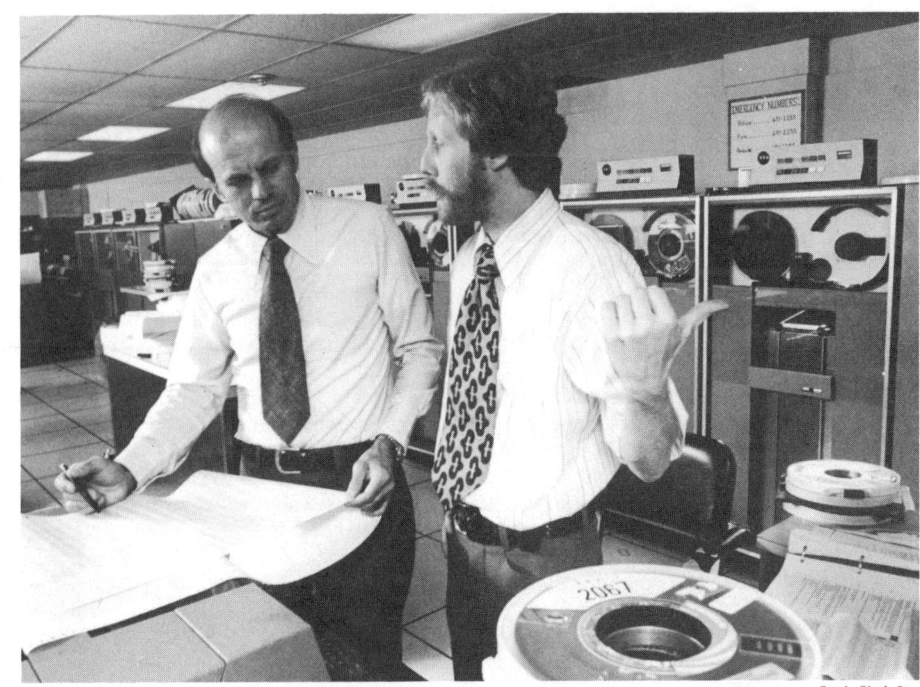

Brack, Black Star

Candidates use computerized direct-mail operations, like this one run by consultant Richard Viguerie, to reach a wide base of small contributors. Viguerie's organization maintains "an in-house list of eleven million proven contributors."

to improve name recognition and image, to target opposition weakness, to formulate mass media advertising, to allocate resources, and to build coalitions.[19] Pollster Louis Harris maintains that the use of polls can change the outcome of an election by as much as 4 percent if candidates use the data to target their resources most efficiently.[20] Since 1960, when John F. Kennedy hired Harris, every presidential candidate has made extensive use of polls. Succeeding presidents also have kept close tabs on survey data once they are in office. For instance, Jimmy Carter's close association with pollster Patrick Caddell strongly influenced his decisions both on the campaign trail and at the White House.[21]

Quite simply, no modern-day presidential candidate would dream of entering the electoral fray without the benefit of research data. In the 1980 campaign, Carter spent $2 million on polling; Reagan spent $1.3 million.[22] But the fact that candidates focus so much attention on them does not suggest that polls are infallible. Particularly in the primary season (when the field is full of candidates and there are many uncommitted voters), polls can be volatile. In 1988, polls did not predict George Bush's third-place showing in Iowa's Republican caucus or his victory in the New Hampshire primary. Even in the general campaign, there is room for errors both in polls themselves and in their interpretation.[23] The most famous example is from 1948, when virtually all pollsters predicted that Thomas E. Dewey would beat Harry S Truman. For a variety of reasons—including poor sampling techniques, the fact that polling stopped too early in the campaign, and mistaken assumptions about how the uncommitted would vote—the pollsters were wrong. Many pollsters also substantially underestimated the size of Ronald Reagan's victory in 1980.[24]

Nonetheless, polls that forecast the actual outcome of elections are only one of many types of polls used by candidates. Sociologists James R. Beniger and Robert J. Giuffra, Jr., have identified several types of polls that play a major role in campaigns. Preliminary "benchmark" or "baseline" surveys of the entire nation provide basic information about candidate strength and the political mood of the nation. These can be useful in deciding whether or not to run.

"Follow-up" surveys are used to gather more in-depth data about particular concerns raised in initial benchmark surveys. These are often conducted state by state and are used in planning campaign strategy.

"Panel" surveys are used to refine strategy further by reinterviewing previous respondents to determine opinion shifts on specific issues within various demographic categories. These are supplemented by continuous "tracking polls" that measure fluctuations in general voter support for the candidate across time.

Continuing developments in computer technology have also allowed for new techniques such as the "geodemographic targeting system" in which census data and specially programmed voter registration lists pinpoint swing voters.[25] Used together, such surveys are a source of information that candidates feel they cannot do without. Polls can be particularly helpful in forming a candidate's image and in deciding how to use the media to cultivate that image and target specific voting blocs.

Media Consultants

Image building has become especially important since the development of television. Urging symbolic actions that would play well on television (such as holding folksy town meetings and carrying one's own luggage), Caddell warned Carter in a 1976 political strategy memorandum that "too many good people have been beaten because they tried to substitute substance for style."[26] Increasingly, a candidate's style has been cultivated by a media consultant. With the help of polls and survey data, such consultants "market" their candidate.

Dwight D. Eisenhower was the first to make extensive use of television commercials and an advertising agency when he ran as the Republican nominee in 1952. Nixon shunned the use of an advertising agency and most modern media techniques in the 1960 campaign. Even his participation in televised debates with John Kennedy was marred by his poor makeup, haggard appearance, and lack of attention to his wardrobe. Nixon lost the election. His subsequent campaign for president in 1968 was a paradigm for campaigning via marketing techniques.[27] Since then, media consultants have become an integral part of presidential campaigns, coordinating everything from the personal appearance of the candidates to the color of their bumper stickers.

Media consultants also have fine-tuned the production and use of television advertisements. For instance, Nixon's foreign policy experience was stressed in 1968 after polls showed that viewers thought this was important. After Vietnam and Watergate, Carter's commercials stressed that he was an honest, folksy candidate—"a leader, for a change." Even the color of his campaign literature (green) stressed his difference from mainstream politicians.[28]

Technological advances have led also to the use of direct mail. Through the help of computers, "personalized" mailings are sent to "targeted" individuals whose names are culled from lists of contributors to the candidate's party or to related causes, from the mailing lists of magazines that indicate an ideological preference, and from membership lists of various organizations, among other sources. Names and addresses of individuals can also be bought from list brokers in any major city.

Direct mail is used primarily as a fund-raising device. It was first employed in 1952 by Dwight Eisenhower, who compiled a donor list with the aid of *Reader's Digest* publisher DeWitt Wallace. But it was not until the 1970s that vigorous use of direct mail was spurred by campaign finance legislation that limited individual contributions to $1,000 per candidate. In such a climate, direct mail served as a grass-roots approach to reaching a wide base of small contributors. Through a well-coordinated program that contacts both potential contributors ("prospective mailings") and those who have given money in the past ("in-house" or "contributor mailings"), a relatively small investment can reap a tremendous profit.[29]

The goal of such mailings is to establish a degree of intimacy that will encourage the recipient to make a donation. In 1980, for instance, mailings for George Bush included reprints of newspaper articles with "personal notes" laser-printed in the margin: "To [recipient's name] — I thought you might be interested in these recent clippings—G.B." [30] The facade of intimacy, coupled with careful packaging and emotional pleas, is designed to draw the recipient into the campaign by giving money.

Perhaps the most famous direct mail consultant is conservative activist Richard Viguerie. Viguerie came to prominence in 1976 when he managed a highly successful direct mail operation for George Wallace, who was seeking the Democratic nomination for president. Four years later, Viguerie helped the Republican party broaden its financial base and usher in the presidency of Ronald Reagan and the first Republican Senate since 1955. By 1982, the Viguerie Company employed more than three hundred people and directed several subsidiaries, including American Mailing Lists Corporation, American Telecommunications Corporation, Diversified Mailing Services, and the Viguerie Communication Corporation (which published *Conservative Digest* and *The Right Report*).[31] Viguerie himself maintained that his operation had amassed an "in-house list of eleven million proven contributors." [32]

In addition to direct mail, candidates use telephone banks to recruit volunteers and to target potential voters. Contacting households by phone is quick and easy—a way to reach many more voters with less effort than door-to-door canvassing.[33] Likewise, telephones are used in conjunction with fund-raising drives. Hoping to generate contributions by impulse, some media ads encourage voters to call a toll-free number and pledge money on credit cards.[34]

The effect of media consultants on the outcome of political campaigns is debatable. Their effect on the process itself, however, is clear. They have driven up costs, further weakened the link between candidates and parties, and made the emphasis on style and image (which has always been a part of campaigns) more glaring.[35] The danger, as political scientist Larry Sabato has concluded, lies not so much in the techniques that are used (indeed, Sabato points out that they could be used to strengthen the party system), but with the type of candidates those techniques may create—candidates who confuse the style of campaigning for the substance of policy making.[36] Such candidates may be well-suited to win elections but ill-equipped to handle the rigors of governing, thus weakening our governmental structure.

Role of Parties and Interest Groups In the General Election

In the past, the general election often was won by the candidate best able to mobilize support. Traditionally, state party organizations have organized party appeals, but interest groups have played a greater role in the post-World War II years.

State Party Organizations

State parties once were the center of the presidential selection process, but they have declined with the rise of candidate-centered organizations, special interest groups, and the media. The proportion of citizens claiming party membership has declined from about three-fourths to two-thirds since the 1950s. Despite their diminished role in national politics, state and local party organizations can be an important supplement to the efforts of the national campaign.

Coordination of a party's national, state, and local campaign efforts is informal. The national campaign's receipt of federal funds requires it to limit spending, so the efforts of other groups must be formally separate. By setting campaign priorities, the national campaign organization gives important cues to its allies.

State and local organizations offer a wide variety of important campaign services. Foremost among those services is the grass-roots effort to register likely supporters and get them to the polls on election day. Party organizations own extensive lists of supporters and "leaners." As election day approaches, the organization sends these voters letters and cards urging them to vote, and volunteers call them on the telephone to urge them to vote.

Under 1979 amendments to the Federal Election Cam-

League of Women Voters

Because voter turn-out often is low, state and local organizations work to register voters and get them to the polls on election day.

paign Act, state and local organizations may spend unlimited amounts of money on get-out-the-vote drives and political paraphernalia such as bumper stickers, buttons, and lawn signs. Those organizations can also produce and distribute media appeals that promote the whole party—appeals that usually follow the national campaign theme set by the presidential candidate.

State parties are loose coalitions of the state's many distinctive social groups. Many of these organizations still have influence over patronage, construction and service contracts, and routine political operations. Many also control the mechanics of the electoral process. Ohio law, for example, requires that registration officials be approved by county party leaders. In addition, twenty-one states allow single-ticket voting (where voters cast their ballot for all candidates of a party by pulling a single lever or using one ballot), which increases the importance of intraparty cooperation by creating strong party competition in all races simultaneously. Many political struggles are fought within the party structure.

State and local party positions on a variety of political issues often provide the starting point of political debate. It is true that single-issue interest groups have increased in importance, but party cohesion is still possible. The unity of congressional delegations in states like California and New York, dominated by one party, frames a wide variety of policy concerns. New York City's Democratic delegation, for example, was unified enough to press successfully both presidential candidates in 1976 for aid to the fiscally distressed city.

Political scientist Kay Lawson argues that national party rules and state legislation have undermined the organizational integrity of state parties. Even if parties do not enjoy the autonomy they once did, they still play a permanent and independent role in state and national politics.[37]

National Party Organizations

In addition to state party organizations' working to get out the vote and spread the national ticket's word, the national party organization provides an important organizing function. In particular, committees of the national party raise large sums of money and develop long-range strategies. The efforts of party chairs, such as Republican William Brock and Democrats Charles T. Manatt and Paul Kirk, have been instrumental to presidential politics. These three developed wide-ranging strategies for coordinating presidential campaigns and reaching out to important political groups. Brock was central in developing the GOP as a broad-based party after the disaster of Watergate. Manatt developed ties to influential persons in business whom the Democrats had neglected; Kirk worked to diminish the Democrats "special interest" tendencies.

The fund-raising abilities of the Republican party committees have outstripped their Democratic counterparts in recent years. In the 1985-1986 election cycle GOP committees raised $211.1 million compared with the Democrats' $43.5 million.[38] *(See Table 6.)* The money enables the Republicans to undertake important party-building activities, including: funding congressional and state candidates; advertising campaigns; get-out-the-vote drives; polling; lobbying state legislatures on matters such as redistricting; direct-mail appeals; and hiring consultants.

The GOP has systematically identified "marginal," or close, elections and pumped money into the Republican campaigns. In 1982, for example, Democratic candidates came within ten percentage points of their Republican rivals in twenty-nine races for Congress; the GOP candidates, who outspent the Democrats by two-to-one margins, won most of those races.[39] Democratic resources have always been more scarce than GOP resources, and they have been allocated disproportionately to incumbents' "safe" seats. Political scientist Larry J. Sabato argues that the Republican wealth has led to wasteful spending, and the Democrats are now aware of targeting their money to close races.[40]

Interest Groups

Whatever metaphor is most appropriate—"melting pot" or "mosaic"—the United States is a collection of social and ethnic groups with distinctive identities. Successful candidates must make separate appeals to social groups while tying those discrete interests together with broad appeals. Groups with distinctive political interests and voting habits include Catholics, Jews, blacks, Hispanics, Asians, Irish, Greeks, women, bankers and insurance company executives, real estate developers, laborers, professionals, farmers, environmentalists, young people, senior citizens, urbanites, southerners, members of "New Right" groups, and the poor.

Candidates are sensitive to the participation rates of the different groups, that is, how many of the group members vote. Robert Axelrod has estimated that the proportion of the poor in Democratic vote totals fell from 28 percent to 5 percent between 1952 and 1980.[41] It is probably no accident, therefore, that Democratic appeals to the poor have declined in recent years. Candidates must consider the cost of appealing to different groups. While two-thirds of all unregistered voters are at the bottom of the economic ladder, Democrats have been unwilling to risk the costs of a massive registration program or of antagonizing current supporters.

In recent years political action committees—organizations designed to promote the concerns of ideological or social groups, business, and labor mainly by funding election campaigns—have played an important role in supplementing the direct mail and mass media appeals of the two major candidates, who may spend only the money they receive from the federal government. The number of PACs has grown tremendously in the 1970s and 1980s and PAC spending has increased along with that growth. *(See Table 8.)* PAC expenditures increased from $19.2 million in 1972 to $266.8 million in 1984.[42] Their spending patterns give an enormous advantage to the Republican party. In 1980, for example, independent expenditures for Republican Ronald Reagan totaled $12.5 million; independent expenditures for Democratic president Jimmy Carter totaled $1.2 million. *(See "The Campaign Finance System," p. 182, in this chapter.)* PACs enjoy an advantage over campaign organizations because individuals are permitted to donate $5,000 to a PAC and only $1,000 to a campaign under federal law. The effect of these diverse political action committees is an increase the number of narrow or single-issue appeals at the expense of the broader concerns of candidates and parties.

Role of the Media

In recent years, the media—television, newspapers, magazines, and radio—have played an increasingly important role in presidential elections. For a variety of reasons, they have come to perform many of the functions that party leaders once did in the presidential selection process.[43] Indeed, the media are the primary source of information about candidates and elections for most Americans (as opposed to information from family, friends, associates, and direct contacts with political parties and candidate organizations).[44] As a result, the media have helped to change the type of candidate who is likely to succeed. Increasingly, the emphasis has been on style and image, and an ability to communicate well on television.

News values themselves influence the campaign. News is drama, and drama thrives on conflict.[45] As a result, the media often emphasize the game-like characteristics of presidential campaigns. Strategy, momentum, competition, and error are often treated at the expense of candidates' records and policy pronouncements. Journalists covering presidential debates, for instance, are more concerned with who "won" than with the issues articulated. In the process, news coverage is personalized; that is, issues are subordinated to personalities, and electoral outcomes focus on the individual's personal victory or defeat rather than on the process (the implications of that outcome for the system as a whole).[46] Thus, the media can impinge upon the ability of candidates to set the agenda and articulate their positions.

Nevertheless, the modern media also provide candidates with an unprecedented ability to take their message directly to the people. Television, in particular, is often said to have transformed electoral politics. Cutting across all socioeconomic divisions, television reaches nearly 98 percent of all households in the continental United States.[47] One study shows that as recently as 1982, more Americans had televisions than refrigerators or indoor plumbing.[48]

In analyzing the media content of candidate appeals, political scientists David Paletz and Robert Entman have identified three types of content: unmediated messages, partially mediated messages, and mostly mediated messages.[49] *Unmediated messages* are those in which the candidate's message is passed to the people unfettered by commentary or criticism—those over which the candidates exercise total control, such as paid political advertisements.

Since they were first used by Dwight Eisenhower in 1952, television advertisements have played an ever more sophisticated role in presidential elections. Between them, Ronald Reagan and Walter Mondale spent $50 million on television advertising in 1984.[50] This use of television, in turn, has led to the increased importance of professional media consultants who oversee the production and targeting of such appeals.

The precise effect of such commercials is difficult to determine.[51] In trying to assess the effect of the media on public attitudes in this and other areas, many have echoed the wry sentiments of sociologist Bernard Berelson who concluded some years ago that "some kinds of communications on some kinds of issues, brought to the attention of some kinds of people under some kinds of conditions, have some kinds of effects." [52] The relatively few studies undertaken to determine the effect of televised commercials seem to indicate that they have little influence on the outcome of presidential general election campaigns (a finding that does not appear to be true for lower political offices, where commercials can be instrumental in building name recognition and securing victory).[53]

Paletz and Entman have argued that unmediated messages such as televised ad campaigns are the most difficult for candidates to use to sway voters since many people realize that they are self-serving. In addition, such messages are "vulnerable to the Gorgons of selective exposure, selective perception, and selective retention." [54] As

UPI/Bettmann Newsphotos

In 1960, Vice President Richard Nixon speaks during the first televised presidential debate while his opponent, Sen. John F. Kennedy, left, takes notes. Since 1976, televised debates have become a regular part of each presidential campaign.

political scientist Doris Graber concluded: "Commercials are perceiver-determined. People see in them pretty much what they want to see—attractive images for their favorite candidate and unattractive ones for the opponent." [55]

In contrast to unmediated messages, *partially mediated messages* are those passed along through vehicles such as televised press conferences, debates, talk shows, and interviews. Here candidates have an opportunity to air their views and repeat well-worn phrases, but these messages are constrained by the questioning of media representatives (and, in debates, the responses of opposing candidates).

First used in 1960, televised debates have become a part of presidential campaigns in each election since 1976. Although they are a vehicle for the transmission of policy positions, viewers often seem to be more impressed by the style of the debaters than by their stands on specific issues. Richard Nixon is widely considered to have lost his first debate with John Kennedy in 1960 because of his personal appearance, not because of the substance of his arguments. Likewise, Ronald Reagan succeeded against Jimmy Carter in the 1980 debates largely because of his style: the warm image that he conveyed through his folksy anecdotes, his rejoinders to the president ("There you go again. . ."), and the fact that he structured his answers in simple rhetorical terms.

The effect of debates is also hard to measure, especially because they are quickly followed by a barrage of media commentary and speculation over who won. According to political scientist Stephen Wayne, surveys taken immediately after the second debate between Gerald Ford and Jimmy Carter in 1976, for example, indicated that viewers, by almost two to one, felt that Ford had won. However, media attention on Ford's "gaffe" (his statement that Eastern Europe was not dominated by the Soviet Union), dramatically reversed that opinion within three days.[56] Nevertheless, it appears that as a rule, debates do not significantly alter voter perceptions of the candidates.[57]

Finally, *mostly mediated messages* are those over which the candidates have the least control, such as news stories that are constructed by the media about the candidate. Paletz and Entman contended that mostly mediated messages have the greatest effect on public opinion precisely because the candidates do not appear to control their content. Candidates' campaign staffs therefore use a wide variety of techniques to try to influence such coverage, including timing and staging events, restricting access to the candidate, and controlling the flow of information from the campaign organization.[58] Incumbents are particularly able to attract coverage through such activities. Only an incumbent, for instance, can schedule an event in the Rose Garden or the East Room of the White House, or participate in foreign "summit meetings" as did Richard Nixon in 1972. Ronald Reagan was also able to combine the backdrop of the presidency with precisely coordinated campaign appearances before ecstatic crowds to remarkable effect.

Recent criticism has focused on the role of the media in their early projections of winners and losers on election day coverage. Such projections (which are based on exit polls) could unfairly influence voting behavior, especially in western states. For instance, in 1980 NBC projected the victory of Ronald Reagan at 8:15 p.m. Eastern Standard Time, potentially reducing late voter turnout on the West Coast where polls would still be open for several hours. Four years later, CBS projected a Reagan victory at 8:01 p.m., followed by ABC and NBC by 8:30. The precise effect of such projections has not been determined.[59] Nonetheless, since 1985 ABC, CBS, NBC, and CNN have refrained voluntarily from election-eve forecasting until after 9:00 p.m. Eastern Standard Time.

Modern elections are inextricably intertwined with the media. As such, the media have done much to transform the campaign process. Although it is easy to overestimate the effect of the media, that effect, nonetheless, is significant. The media appear to be most influential, however, in the preconvention phase of the presidential selection process when "horse-race" coverage of the primaries often accelerates the winnowing process of candidates.[60] At that time the media also help to form impressions of a large field of candidates that the public may not yet be very familiar with. By the time of the general election, however, voters are more likely to have set feelings about the candidates—making it more difficult for media coverage to influence them.

The Vice President's Campaign

Vice presidents played important policy roles in the administrations of Jimmy Carter and Ronald Reagan, but the vice presidency traditionally has served mostly to help the president get elected in the first place. The second spot is often used to "balance" the national ticket.

The vice presidency's importance has been likened to "a pitcher of warm spit" by John Nance Garner and "a cow's fifth teat" by Harry S Truman. Although the vice presidency is a possible step on the way to the presidency, Martin Van Buren in 1836 was the last vice president to win the White House until George Bush did so in 1988.[61] Nonetheless, the vice presidency is just "a heartbeat away" from the presidency. The assassination and resignation of two recent presidents—John F. Kennedy and Richard Nixon—have increased the public's awareness that the vice president could someday become president. Nine presidents have become president after the president died in office or resigned the position: John Tyler (1841), Millard Fillmore (1850), Andrew Johnson (1865), Chester A. Arthur (1881), Theodore Roosevelt (1901), Calvin Coolidge (1923), Truman (1945), Lyndon B. Johnson (1963), and Gerald R. Ford (1974).

Presidential nominees insist that their running mates are "perfectly compatible" with their approach to government. But especially in tight elections, the vice-presidential candidate is selected to balance the national ticket in terms of geography, religion, ideology, government experience, and political style. In the Republic's early years, the vice presidency went to the person who finished second in the voting of the electoral college. Early vice presidents such as Thomas Jefferson actually were defeated presidential candidates. With ratification of the Twelfth Amendment in 1804, presidential and vice-presidential candidates were expected to run on the same national ticket. Republican Abraham Lincoln of Illinois was an adept ticket-balancer. In 1860, he picked Hannibal Hamlin of Kentucky, a southern or border state. In 1864, he selected Andrew Johnson of Tennessee, a Democrat, for the ticket renamed the National Union party.

One of the most famous modern ticket-balancing maneuvers was Massachusetts senator John Kennedy's selection of Senate Majority Leader Lyndon Johnson as a running mate. Kennedy's Catholic background, support for civil rights, and northern urban appeal required some sort of gesture to conservative southern Democrats. Kennedy and his top aide, brother Robert F. Kennedy, were reportedly alarmed that Johnson would accept the second spot, which was offered as a conciliatory gesture. But as the candidate's father, former ambassador Joseph P. Kennedy, remarked, it was the shrewdest move of the campaign.

In 1968 Richard Nixon based his "southern strategy" on the selection of Maryland governor Spiro T. Agnew. Agnew was once considered an urban liberal, but he attracted conservative support nationwide by publicly blaming black leaders for not doing enough to end the urban riots that rocked the nation in 1968.

Carter picked Sen. Walter F. Mondale of Minnesota as his running mate in 1976 to counteract his inexperience in national politics and to appeal to some of the traditional Democratic constituencies such as urbanites, blacks, and organized labor. The same year, the conservative Ronald Reagan selected moderate senator Richard S. Schweiker of Pennsylvania to broaden his appeal before the party's national convention; the ploy failed to win Reagan the nomination, however. President Ford in 1976 was forced to abandon his vice president, Nelson A. Rockefeller, when he came under criticism from party conservatives suspicious of the New York moderate. From the time of his battle with Barry Goldwater for the 1964 Republican nomination until his death in 1979, Rockefeller was the target of much dislike in his own party.

At other times, running mates are selected to bind party wounds opened during nomination struggles. Kennedy's selection of Johnson and Reagan's 1980 selection of Bush fits that description.

Still, some nominees have refused to accept the ticket-balancing wisdom. In 1964 Goldwater picked an obscure New York member of the House of Representatives, William Miller, whose conservative credentials were as consistent as his own. In 1984, Walter Mondale's selection of Rep. Geraldine Ferraro of New York as his Democratic running mate created a ticket of two northern liberals. In 1976, President Gerald Ford selected a fellow midwesterner, Sen. Robert J. Dole of Kansas, as his running mate.

The vice-presidential nomination provides a point of entry to groups traditionally excluded from the political process. Ferraro's selection as Mondale's Democratic running mate in 1984—the first woman to run on a major-party national ticket—is perhaps the most notable example of the breakthrough phenomenon.

How vice-presidential candidates fashion their pitch depends on the party ticket's overall strategy. In general, presidential candidates appeal to the broad electorate while their running mates appeal to specific groups. In 1968, for example, Republican presidential candidate Richard Nixon took the "high road" by campaigning for a negotiated end to the Vietnam War while his running mate, Spiro Agnew, appealed to southern resistance to the civil rights and antiwar movements. In 1976, GOP standard-bearer Gerald Ford ran a campaign stressing his role as a national conciliator after the Watergate scandal and Vietnam while Dole, his vice-presidential candidate, took "the lead in implementing the Attack [Democratic Jimmy] Carter plan." [62]

Vice-presidential candidates must take part in the

televised debates that have become a mainstay of campaigns. Experts closely watch the debates not only because the vice president could be president if anything happened to the standard-bearer, but also because he or she could be a party leader in the future regardless of the election outcome. Many experts consider Dole's debate performance to have damaged the 1976 GOP ticket—perhaps enough to lose the close election. Reports on Ferraro's debate with Vice President George Bush in 1984 were mixed.

In general, the vice-presidential candidate serves to reinforce or break down the electorate's attitudes toward the presidential candidate. If a presidential candidate has little foreign policy or Washington experience as was true of Reagan and Carter, a running mate with that experience can reassure voters. A vice-presidential candidate whose character or issue stances bother voters can turn away undecided voters.

Like the family of the presidential candidate, the family of the vice-presidential candidate plays an active role in campaigning. Often unknown before the party nominating convention, family members become instant celebrities. Their personal appearance at campaign events can lend excitement to the campaign.

The families of the vice-presidential candidates also can be liabilities. Ferraro's husband caused the Democratic ticket embarrassment when the media reported his questionable real estate, trusteeship, and tax activities.

Personal Campaigning by Presidential Candidates

Today we take it for granted that presidential candidates will actively campaign on their own behalf, but for many years this was not the case. As Stephen Wayne has written: "Personal solicitation was [once] viewed as demeaning and unbecoming of the dignity and status of the Presidency." [63] Thus, while their supporters engaged in propaganda, public relations, mass rallies, and other sorts of hoopla, the candidates themselves sat quietly in the sidelines.

The first major party candidate to break that tradition was Stephen A. Douglas in his 1860 race against Abraham Lincoln. The two had held public debates in 1858 when they both ran for the same Senate seat from Illinois, but in the presidential race Lincoln made a vow not to "write or speak anything upon doctrinal points." [64] Instead, he remained in Springfield, Illinois, receiving visitors and shunning rallies and political meetings.

Douglas, in contrast, set out on a personal campaign to try to mend the splits in the Democratic party caused by the slavery issue. Southern Democrats had nominated their own candidate, John C. Breckinridge, on a proslavery platform. Douglas soon realized that he would not win the election, but he ardently fought to save the Union. The speaking tour took him from New England to the South, and then to the Midwest where he heard some initial electoral vote returns. Aware that Lincoln would be the next president, Douglas returned to the South in a last-ditch effort "to lift the voice of reason in behalf of Union." [65]

The circumstances of 1860, however, were unique. Thus, it was thirty-six years before another candidate actively campaigned on his own behalf. In the election of 1896, William Jennings Bryan—whose stunning "Cross of Gold" speech at the Democratic convention had secured his nomination—traveled over eighteen thousand miles and delivered more than six hundred speeches.[66] His opponent, William A. McKinley, followed a more traditional approach. Although he was an excellent public speaker who had engaged in a speaking tour on his own behalf when seeking the Republican nomination, McKinley felt that pleading his own cause once he was his party's nominee was unbecoming to his position. Nevertheless, he did not want to stay completely out of the picture and therefore made a compromise: he stayed home and waged a "front porch" campaign. Instead of going to the people, the people came to him; and they came by the droves. Historian Eugene H. Roseboom has referred to those excursions as "mass pilgrimages." [67] From his front porch, McKinley greeted his visitors and—when appropriate—delivered a formal speech. McKinley won the election.

In 1900, McKinley and Bryan were again pitted against each other. As in 1896, Bryan engaged in a lengthy speaking tour. Although McKinley stayed in the White House, he sent his running mate, Theodore Roosevelt, to campaign on his behalf. Outspoken in his views, flamboyant on the podium, and vigorous in his rhetoric, Roosevelt was an immediate success with his audiences. "Buffalo Bill" Cody referred to him as the "American cyclone." [68] Roosevelt appeared in many of the same places as Bryan, and the campaign quickly emerged as a contest between the two orators. Indeed, it often seemed that it was Roosevelt rather than McKinley who was running for president.[69]

With the election of 1904, the candidates reverted to a more traditional approach. Roosevelt (who had been elevated to the presidency with the assassination of McKinley) did not engage in a speaking tour, although his running mate, Charles Fairbanks, campaigned for the Republican ticket. Their Democratic opponent, Alton B. Parker—cautious, colorless, largely unknown, and politically conservative—stayed out of the fray. So did his running mate, the eighty-one-year-old West Virginia millionaire Henry G. Davis. Democrats had hoped that Davis would use his millions to help fund the campaign. He did not. The Republicans won.[70]

Although Republican candidates remained less likely to campaign actively than their counterparts in the Democratic party, it was clear that traditions were changing. Bryan, nominated yet again in 1908, hit the campaign trail, as did his Republican opponent, Taft. Both Woodrow Wilson and Theodore Roosevelt (on the Bull Moose ticket) campaigned strenuously in 1912. (Taft, recognizing that his cause was hopeless, did little.) *(See "Chronology of Elections," p. 266, in this chapter.)* By 1932, personal campaigning had become the norm. In that year, Herbert Hoover became the first incumbent to campaign actively for his own reelection.[71]

Today direct appeals to the people are an integral part of a campaign-centered selection process—a process that may begin years before the election takes place. With the development of jet travel, candidates are now able to crisscross the country extensively. At the height of the campaign, it is not uncommon for candidates to visit several states in one day. But personal campaigning has also been revolutionized by developments in communications. Such developments have made new forms of direct mass appeals available. Televised debates, campaign commercials, and direct mail operations are all relatively new ways of taking candidates' messages directly to the people. Even personal campaign appearances are now designed more for the me-

Smithsonian Institution

In the 1896 election, William Jennings Bryan, left, traveled over eighteen thousand miles and delivered more than six hundred speeches.

dia than for those actually in attendance at the event. Enthusiastic crowds, colorful backdrops, and telegenic symbols are carefully coordinated at every campaign stop. In the process, personal campaigning has become an elaborate enterprise, dependent upon the advice of pollsters, media consultants, advertising experts, and speechwriters. Thus, present-day campaigns are a far cry from those of our forebears.

Highlights of General Election Campaigns

The traditional "opening day" for the presidential election campaign is Labor Day, when most Americans have returned to work and school from summer vacations and the election is just two months away. The period before Labor Day is reserved at least partly for the candidates to develop strategy with close aides.

The issues that the nominees consider as they head into the fall campaign include: whether to concentrate their appeals on certain sections of the country, how many issues to stress throughout the campaign, how many and what kind of broadcast commercials to buy, what kind of collaboration to undertake with groups interested in helping the campaign, and how to organize state and local campaign efforts. The candidates also try to anticipate the opposition's style of attack.

The party nominees often must undertake "fence-mending" efforts with rivals of their own party. In 1984, Democratic nominee Walter Mondale made overtures to his nomination rivals, Gary Hart and Jesse Jackson, who had distinctly different blocs whose support he would need to run a competitive race in the fall.

In recent years, candidates have been unwilling to bypass campaigning before the Labor Day opener. In 1980, for example, Republican Ronald Reagan gave a number of speeches to groups such as the Veterans of Foreign Wars to develop campaign themes. Reagan used the month before Labor Day as a learning period. He was able to test campaign themes and make the major mistakes of his campaign—such as suggesting that the United States adopt a "two-China" policy, that is, recognizing the governments of both Taiwan and the People's Republic of China—during the period when the media and public were least attentive.

The campaign organization for the general election in the fall is usually an extension of the nomination organization, and it is separate from the national and state party organizations. Nominees have the prerogative of naming their own party national committee chair to help coordinate the campaign.

The national campaign committee, usually based in Washington, receives its funding from the Federal Election Commission (FEC). The campaign must agree to limit spending to the amount received from the FEC in exchange for federal funding. Since 1975, when federal funding of elections began, all candidates have chosen to accept the government funds rather than raise their own money. In 1988, both major party candidates received $46 million from the FEC.

Although the presidential campaign is limited in its expenditures, a number of allied organizations supplement the campaign with more or less independent efforts. State and local party organizations, political action committees,- independent committees established to help specific candi-

In 1896 Bryan's opponent, William A. McKinley, took a more traditional approach by staying at home and waging a "front porch" campaign. People traveled to McKinley's home to hear him speak.

Smithsonian Institution

dates, and labor unions contribute time, money, and volunteers to assist the candidate of their choice.

The campaign begins with Labor Day parades and speech making at symbolic sites. In their first day of campaigning, the candidates signal the issues they will highlight and the strategy they will use to win the presidency. Democrat Jimmy Carter opened his 1976 campaign in Warm Springs, Georgia, the former retreat of Franklin D. Roosevelt, symbolizing not only Carter's southern roots but also the party's dream of reassembling Roosevelt's New Deal coalition.

Once the campaign begins, the media scrutiny of candidates becomes intense. The candidates must attempt to steer the campaign coverage to the issues that they would like to address. Reagan in 1980 and Mondale in 1984 designated whole weeks for concentrating on major themes such as military preparedness and budget deficits.

Even though the candidates and their advisers map out a campaign strategy before Labor Day, the campaign inevitably shifts its tactics according to polls, political events, and each candidate's instincts about which approaches will be successful. The Nixon-McGovern race in 1972 shifted with developments in the Vietnam War, and the Reagan-Carter race in 1980 shifted with developments in the Iran-hostage crisis. It is often difficult for a challenger to highlight events, however. George McGovern failed to make the Nixon campaign's burglary of the Democratic National Committee's headquarters a major issue in 1972.

One element of campaign strategy that usually remains intact is the decision about where to campaign. The winner-take-all electoral college system, in which the leading vote-getter in a state wins all of that state's electoral votes, encourages candidates to win as many large states as possible rather than build up strength in states in which they are weak. Candidates generally spend most of their time in closely contested states, and just enough time in "likely win" states to ensure victory. Appearances in unfavorable states are usually symbolic efforts to show that the candidate is not conceding anything.

Candidates usually try to determine the states in which they are strongest and then build on that base. A Democrat, for example, might solidify a northeastern industrial base by making appeals in bordering states such as Minnesota, Wisconsin, Kentucky, and Maryland. A Republican with southern appeal will try to build strength in border states such as Tennessee and Kentucky as well as in more western states such as Texas and Oklahoma.

Competing in all regions of the country can be difficult. Richard Nixon in 1960 gave some 212 speeches in fifty states but lost the election to John F. Kennedy. If he had spent less time in states that heavily favored Kennedy and more time in close states such as Illinois and Missouri, he might have won the election. In 1984, Democrat Walter E. Mondale and his running mate, Geraldine Ferraro; missed the opportunity to solidify their support in northeastern states when they campaigned in the solid Republican South and West.

The ideological tone of the presidential campaign usually moderates once the parties have determined their nominees. To win the nomination, Democrats must appeal to the more liberal sections of their party, and Republicans must appeal to the more conservative sections. But once they win the nomination, they must try to attract independents and voters from the other parties. The candidates usually can depend on the support of the most ideological members of their own party, so they are able to shift their sights in the fall.

The exception to this rule comes when a candidate has suffered a bruising nomination battle and must persuade the backers of the defeated candidates to go to the polls. In 1980, after President Carter defeated Sen. Edward M. Kennedy for the Democratic nomination, Carter continued to make liberal appeals to satisfy the disappointed Kennedy supporters.

Whether to highlight specific issue stances or provide a "fuzzy" ideological stance is a major question facing every campaign. Campaign consultants often advise against being too specific. Mondale's pledge to raise taxes shows both the opportunity and the risk of being specific. For a while, the proposal put President Reagan, who presided over historic budget deficits, on the defensive; but the proposal backfired when Reagan regained the offensive and charged Democrats with fiscal and taxing irresponsibility.

Daily campaign activities are geared to getting impressive visual "bites" on the national and local television news programs. The ill fortunes of the 1984 Mondale campaign were underscored on Labor Day, when the television networks stressed the poor turnout at a rainy parade Mondale attended in New York City while President Reagan's campaign opener was a sunny, balloon-filled rally in southern California. Strategists try to adapt the day's "news" events to reinforce the campaign's overall themes and broadcast commercial appeals.

Depending on their standing in the polls, and on whether they are running for or against the party in power, the candidates switch back and forth between appeals to bolster their own image and appeals to undermine their opponent's credibility. Challengers such as Mondale in 1984 have a dual task: Mondale first had to break down the positive image of the popular President Reagan, then he had to portray himself as a worthy replacement. It was too great a task. If a candidate already has an unfavorable image, as President Carter did in 1980, the opponent only needs to convince voters that he or she is a trustworthy alternative. Reagan succeeded at that task.

The candidates use television and radio throughout the fall to advertise their campaigns, but the pace quickens at the end of October when many voters are just beginning to pay close attention to the race.

Whether the broadcast spots address specific issues or confine themselves to images of the candidate depends on the target audience, the salience of the issues, the stage of the campaign, and the closeness of the race. In 1984, the Reagan campaign used "feel-good" commercials with vague images of Americana because it needed to reinforce a positive mood in the nation rather than sway many voters. Mondale used issue-oriented spots that year in an attempt to loosen Reagan's coalition of support.

Televised debates of both presidential and vice-presidential candidates have become a fixture of campaigns. Before 1976, candidates leading in the polls resisted debates because they had little reason to give an opponent a boost in stature by appearing on the same stage. Front-runners also feared "gaffes" that might undermine their advantages in the polls or give opponents ammunition for the campaign trail.

In recent years, front-runners have been obliged to take part in debates to avoid the charge that they were "hiding" from the opponent. President Reagan agreed to debate Mondale in 1984 despite Reagan's huge leads in the polls. The chairs of the Democratic and Republican national committees got commitments from their candidates to participate in debates the year before the 1988 campaign.

Presidential candidates have displayed different attitudes toward the campaigns of fellow party members in state and congressional elections. Republican Richard Nixon and Democrat Jimmy Carter were not willing to use their campaigns to help other candidates. Republican Ronald Reagan, determined to spur a "realignment" of party loyalties in the United States, devoted much time and attention to campaigning for other candidates.[72]

One of the biggest jobs of state and local party organizations is getting out the vote. Voter turnout has hovered just over the 50 percent mark in recent elections, despite the voter registration efforts of liberal civil rights organizations and conservative religious groups. With participation so low, it is vital for both parties to get their certain voters to the polls. The major efforts consist of telephone canvassing and election-day transportation for people who have difficulty getting to the polls.

Third Parties

Although the United States has a two-party system, third parties often have entered the electoral fray. Third parties usually are transient bodies that garner little support and quickly die. Since 1832, third parties have received more than 10 percent of the total popular vote only seven times, and more than 20 percent only twice. *(See Table 11.)* Most third parties have grown up in times of intense conflict.[73] Often their base of support is regional rather than national. Whenever and wherever they evolve, they are a sign of dissatisfaction with the two major parties.

Political scientist James Q. Wilson has identified four types of third parties: ideological parties, one-issue parties, economic protest parties, and factional parties.

Ideological Parties

Ideological parties possess a "comprehensive view of American society and government that is radically different from that of the established parties." [74] These include parties at both ends of the political spectrum, such as the Socialist and Libertarian parties. Although ideological parties appeal to a narrow base of support, they have proven to be the most enduring type of third party (largely because of the ideological commitment of their members).

The longest established type of ideological parties are those that have embraced Marxism. The Socialist Labor party, for instance, was established in 1888 and ran its first presidential candidate in 1892. Although the party still exists (and has continued to run presidential candidates), its doctrinal rigidity and increasingly militant stance caused moderate members to bolt and form the Socialist party with Eugene V. Debs as its leader in 1902. In 1912, running with vice-presidential candidate Emil Seidel, Debs received 6.0 percent of the popular vote for president. During World War I, Debs was convicted of sedition for making a speech espousing the Socialist party's antiwar stance. In 1920, he ran for president from the federal penitentiary in Atlanta, Georgia, and won 3.4 percent of the popular vote. (Seymour Stedman was his running mate that year.) The party has run national candidates in most presidential elections since then.

The most recent variant of the socialist movement is the Socialist Workers party, formed in 1938 by followers of the Soviet Communist Leon Trotsky who were expelled from the U.S. Communist party. The Socialist Workers have run candidates for president in every election since 1838. The Communist party, from which the Socialist Workers split, formed in the early 1920s and ran presidential candidates from 1924 through 1940. Throughout the 1950s, the party was outlawed by restrictive legislation passed by the U.S. Congress. In the later 1960s, however, the party was reconstituted. Since 1972 Gus Hall has run as its presidential candidate.

At the opposite end of the political spectrum is the Libertarian party, formed in 1972. Libertarians are dedicated to the concept of individual freedom, and they oppose government intervention in both the personal and economic spheres. They have run candidates in every presidential election since 1972 when Roger MacBride, as a "faithless" Republican elector, cast the only electoral vote the Libertarians have ever received. In 1976, the Libertarians chose MacBride as their presidential candidate and David Bergland as his running mate. They appeared on the ballot in thirty-two states, more than independent Eugene J. McCarthy or any other third party candidate. They won 173,000 popular votes—only 0.2 percent of the national vote and far fewer votes than McCarthy, but more than any other minor party candidate that year. In 1980 the Libertarian party was on the ballot in all fifty states and the District of Columbia. Presidential nominee Edward E. Clark of California and vice-presidential nominee David Koch of New York garnered 921,000 votes, or 1.1 percent of the vote nationwide. In 1984, the Libertarians appeared on the ballots of thirty-eight states and the District of Columbia—more than any other minor party presidential candidate. Bergland and vice-presidential nominee Jim Lewis won 228,000 votes, or 0.3 percent of the popular vote.

UPI/Bettmann Newsphotos

Gus Hall, U.S. presidential candidate on the Communist party ticket, takes questions at a 1976 press conference at the party's national headquarters in New York.

One-Issue Parties

Dissatisfaction with the major parties often centers on their stance toward a particular issue. Thus, many third parties have arisen around a single policy concern. These have included such diverse issues as slavery, states' rights, currency, opposition to immigration ("nativism"), abortion, and even hostility to lawyers.[75] Once such an issue ceases to be of importance, the basis for the party's existence disappears. Since most issues provoke intense feelings for a relatively short time—or, if they persist, eventually are addressed adequately by the majority parties—one-issue parties tend to be short-lived.

One exception to that rule is the Prohibition party. Dedicated to banning the sale of liquor, the Prohibition party has existed since 1869 and has run a presidential candidate in each election since then (although the name was temporarily changed to the National Statesman party in 1980). As such, it is the longest-running third party in U.S. history. Although primarily dedicated to the temperance issue, the Prohibition party was closely linked to the early feminist movement. Indeed, it was the first party to endorse women's suffrage.

Many of the earliest third parties evolved out of the slavery issue. The best-known of these was the Free Soil party (which was formed in 1848 as a coalition of three anti-slavery movements—the Liberty party, the Barnburners, and the Conscience Whigs). The Free Soil party held a convention in Buffalo, New York, in 1848 and nominated former Democratic president Martin Van Buren as its presidential candidate and Charles F. Adams (son of former president John Quincy Adams) as his running mate. Although it lost the election, the Free Soil party succeeded in winning thirteen congressional seats.[76]

The American party—better known as the "Know-Nothings" because its members told outsiders they knew nothing of its secret rituals and greetings—is another notable single-issue party of the 1800s. The Know-Nothings emerged in the 1850s in opposition to European immigration (which was at a pre-Civil War peak because of severe economic conditions abroad). The party was particularly hostile to Catholics. In 1854 and 1855, the Know-Nothings were extremely successful. They elected five senators, forty-three members of the House of Representatives, and seven governors and won control of the state legislatures in six states (and came close to doing so in many others). In 1856, the Know-Nothings held a national convention in Philadelphia, nominating former Whig president Millard Fillmore for president and Andrew Jackson Donelson for vice president. The party was split, however, over slavery. Most Northern Know-Nothings turned to the Republican party; Southern and border factions later joined with former Whigs to form the Constitutional Union party.

Economic Protest Parties

Economic protest parties evolve in opposition to depressed economic conditions. The Greenback party, for instance, was an outgrowth of the Panic of 1873 (a post-

Civil War economic depression). Farmers who called for the issuance of "greenbacks" (paper money) to stem the shortage of capital organized the Greenback party. Since paper money was inflationary, farmers also hoped that the use of greenbacks would lead to an increase in the price of their goods.

The Greenback party held its first national convention in 1876. With Peter Cooper—an eighty-five-year-old New York philanthropist—as their presidential candidate and Samuel F. Corey as the vice-presidential nominee, the Greenbacks won less than 1 percent of the popular vote. But as hard times continued, they mobilized more support. Most important, they joined forces with labor groups. In 1877 and 1878, they won fourteen House seats and showed strength in state and local elections. By 1880, however, economic conditions were improving. Although they held conventions and nominated candidates for the presidential elections of 1880 and 1884, support for the Greenbacks dwindled. By 1888 the party was effectively dead. Supporters of the movement later turned to the People's party (better known as the "Populists").

Prompted by the return of bad economic conditions, the Populists held a national convention in Cincinnati, Ohio, in 1891. Currency was again a prime concern, although the issue now hinged on the free coinage of silver. The Populists, with James B. Weaver as their presidential candidate and James G. Field as his running mate, won 8.5 percent of the popular vote in the 1892 presidential election. Four years later, however, the Democrats embraced the Populists' issue and nominated William Jennings Bryan on a free-silver platform. The Populists ran candidates in presidential elections through 1908 but with no appreciable accumulation of support.

UPI/Bettmann Newsphotos

In 1948 southerners split off from the Democratic party over Truman's civil rights program. They formed the "Dixiecrat" party and nominated South Carolina governor J. Strom Thurmond, left, for president and Mississippi governor Fielding H. Wright, right, for vice president.

Factional Parties

Factional parties evolve from splits in one of the major parties. They usually form to protest "the identity and philosophy of the major party's presidential candidate." [77] In the twentieth century, they have been the most successful at winning votes. Examples include three twentieth-century candidacies that have used the Progressive party label (although the party itself was not a continuous organization).

The Progressive party was first formed to support the candidacy of former president Theodore Roosevelt after the raucous Republican convention of 1912 in which Roosevelt and president William Howard Taft went head to head. Dubbed the "Bull Moose" party, it held a convention in Chicago where it nominated Roosevelt for president and Hiram Johnson for vice president and drew up a party platform. Although defeated by Woodrow Wilson, Roosevelt on the Bull Moose ticket proved more successful than Taft on the Republican ticket, winning 27.4 percent of the popular vote to Taft's 23.2 percent and eighty-eight electoral votes to Taft's eight. *(See "Wilson and the Divided Republicans," p. 293, in this chapter.)* In 1912 the Bull Moose, or Progressive, party also ran candidates in state and local races and even won thirteen House seats. But the Progressives' appeal was generated by Roosevelt, and when he later defected, the party disintegrated. Wilson's Democratic administration incorporated many of the Progressives' reform proposals and therefore drew away much of the Progressives' support.

Like Teddy Roosevelt, Sen. Robert M. La Follette of Wisconsin represented the liberal wing of the Republican party. In 1924 he split off from the Republicans and revived the Progressive party label. The Progressives held a convention in Cleveland where they nominated La Follette for president and Burton K. Wheeler for vice president. La Follette went on to receive an impressive 16.6 percent of the popular vote but only thirteen electoral votes. Again, the party relied primarily on La Follette's personal appeal. When he died in 1925, the party collapsed.

In 1948 the Progressive party label revived yet again. This time, however, it split off from the liberal wing of the Democratic party. Henry A. Wallace (former vice president under Franklin D. Roosevelt) was nominated as the Progressives' presidential candidate and Glen H. Taylor as the vice-presidential candidate at a convention in Philadelphia. That same year, southerners also split off from the Democratic party over a dispute concerning President Harry S Truman's civil rights program. They walked out of the Democratic convention, formed the States' Rights ("Dixiecrat") party, and convened in Birmingham, Alabama, where they nominated South Carolina governor J. Strom Thurmond for president and Mississippi governor Fielding L. Wright for vice president.

Although both the Progressives and the Dixiecrats received close to the same popular vote nationwide (Wallace received 1.157 million votes to Thurmond's 1.169 million), the Dixiecrats received more than 22 percent of the vote in the South. As a result of their southern support, the Dixiecrats captured four states and thirty-nine electoral votes, while the Progressives won none. The Dixiecrats' success

Table 11 Top Vote-Winning Third Parties, 1832-1988

Party	Election year	Candidate	Popular vote (percent)	No. electoral votes
Anti-Masonic	1832	William Wirt	7.8	7
Free-Soil	1848	Martin Van Buren	10.1	0
American ("Know-Nothing")	1856	Millard Fillmore	21.5	8
Southern Democrats	1860	John C. Breckinridge	18.1	72
Constitutional Union	1860	John Bell	12.6	39
Populist	1892	James B. Weaver	8.5	22
Socialist	1912	Eugene V. Debs	6.0	0
Progressive (Bull Moose)	1912	Theodore Roosevelt	27.4	88
Progressive	1924	Robert M. LaFollette	16.6	13
American Independent	1968	George C. Wallace	13.5	46
Independent	1980	John B. Anderson	6.6	0

Source: Guide to U.S. Elections, 2d ed. (Washington, D.C.: Congressional Quarterly Inc., 1985).

Note: These parties received more than 5.6 percent of the popular vote, the average third party vote historically cast for president (Daniel A. Mazmanian, *Third Parties in Presidential Elections* [Washington, D.C.: Brookings, 1974], 4-5). No significant third parties in 1984 or 1988.

illustrates the system's bias toward third parties with a regional base. Despite the fracturing of his party, Harry Truman managed to win the election over his Republican challenger, Thomas E. Dewey.

There were more defections from the Democratic party twenty years later when Alabama governor George C. Wallace bolted and formed the American Independent party in 1968. He did not hold a convention and chose as his running mate the retired Air Force general Curtis LeMay. Wallace had come to national attention in 1963 when he stood in the doorway of the University of Alabama to block the entrance to two black students. The next year he ran in the Democratic presidential primaries in opposition to the 1964 Civil Rights Act.

Wallace's third party candidacy in 1968 gained support from whites and blue-collar workers who were fed up with civil rights activism, antiwar demonstrations, urban riots, and the perceived liberal ideology of incumbent president Lyndon B. Johnson and Hubert H. Humphrey. In the general election Wallace received 13.5 percent of the popular vote and forty-six electoral votes. There was fear at the time that he would stalemate the election and throw it to the House of Representatives, but the Republican candidate, Richard Nixon, managed to outpoll Wallace in many southern states.

Wallace returned to the Democratic party after 1968, but candidates have continued to run under the American Independent party's label. By 1976, two splinter groups had formed—the American party and the American Independent party—each of which ran candidates in the 1976 election. Since the defection of Wallace, however, support for these parties has been virtually unnoticeable.

Illinois representative John B. Anderson formed the National Unity Campaign as the vehicle for an independent candidacy in 1980 when he failed to win the Republican nomination. He chose Wisconsin governor Patrick J. Lucey, a Democrat, as his running mate. In a year when many citizens were dissatisfied with the candidates of the two major parties, Anderson received widespread publicity for his acumen and his oratory, as well as for his willingness to take often-controversial stands on issues. Despite considerable support in early polls, he ultimately captured only 6.6 percent of the popular vote and no electoral votes.

The Decline of Third Party Organization

In the nineteenth century, third parties (even when they were primarily issue oriented) tended to mirror the organization of majority parties: they often ran a slate of candidates for offices other than president, held nominating conventions, drew up a platform, and existed for at least two elections. The American (Know-Nothing) party, for instance, elected seven governors, five senators, and forty-three members of the House of Representatives and controlled several state legislatures,

In contrast, third parties of this century have usually been associated with the candidacy of one person. As we have seen, the Bull Moose party of 1912 was more a platform for the candidacy of Theodore Roosevelt than an enduring minority party. Once Roosevelt ceased to be a candidate, the party died. The candidacies of George Wallace, Minnesota senator Eugene J. McCarthy (who ran against Gerald Ford and Jimmy Carter in 1976), and John Anderson have existed with little or no party organization.

Each of these men sought the presidency more as independent candidates than as a part of a broader-based third party effort. To a large extent, these candidates were the result of technological innovations in transportation and communication, which have decreased the need for an established party organization to rally voter support.[78]

When McCarthy waged his independent candidacy in 1976, he chose no running mate and purposely refrained from establishing any party machinery.[79] Running simply as an independent candidate, he successfully challenged many states' ballot access laws. That, rather than his 0.93 percent of the popular vote, is the most significant aspect of his candidacy.[80]

What Makes Third Parties "Significant"?

Since 1832, over forty third parties have waged more than 150 races for the presidency.[81] Some commentators have suggested that "significant" third parties are those that have received more than 5.6 percent of the total popu-

When Minnesota senator Eugene J. McCarthy waged his independent campaign in 1976, he chose no running mate and purposely refrained from establishing any party machinery.

lar vote—the average third party vote historically cast for president.[82] By that criterion, eleven parties qualify as significant.[83] *(See Table 11.)*

Popular support does not tell all, however. The States' Rights (Dixiecrat) party, for instance, received 7.3 percent of the electoral college vote in 1948, even though its candidate, J. Strom Thurmond, received only 2.4 percent of the popular vote. Conversely, Anderson—whose 1980 campaign is deemed significant by his popular vote—did not receive a single electoral vote.[84]

Even candidacies with only a small share of the popular or electoral vote can influence an election significantly. For instance, the Liberty party—a movement dedicated to the abolition of slavery—received only 2.3 percent of the popular vote and no electoral college votes in 1844, yet it is widely assumed that Liberty candidate James G. Birney drained enough votes from the Whig party to guarantee the election of the Democratic candidate, James K. Polk. The thirty-six electoral votes that Polk narrowly won in New York were particularly important. As political scientist James L. Sundquist has written: "The New York *Tribune* estimated that 90 percent of the Liberty party vote in New York came from Whigs. Secretary of War John C. Spencer put his estimate at 75 percent." [85] Thus, the outcome of the election might well have been different had the Liberty party not run. In that sense the party was certainly significant.

Third parties that ultimately do not garner much support in the general election also may have significant influence by publicizing important issues or options that the major parties had ignored.[86] Since major parties do not want third parties to siphon away their votes, the major parties may even adopt positions they otherwise would not have adopted in an effort to lessen the effect of (or "co-opt") their third party rivals.

Finally, some third parties are notable for the long periods of time that they have endured, even though they may never have captured a "significant" portion of the popular or electoral vote. The Prohibition party is an excellent example.

Obstacles to Success

Third parties face considerable legal, political, cultural, and psychological barriers. Often, voters do not cast their ballots for third parties because of their loyalties to one of the two major parties. The greater their loyalty to a party, the less likely they are to vote for a third party movement. Instead, loyal members will tend to work within their party to promote change. Only as a last resort will such members exit their party.[87] This was particularly the case in the nineteenth century, when voters established third parties with the expectation that they would endure. Now a vote for a one-time, independent candidacy (such as Anderson's) may be considered more a "boycott" of the major parties than a real "exit."

Often when there is disillusionment with the major parties, people simply do not vote. Indeed, when third parties prosper, voter participation nationwide declines.[88] People with weak party allegiances (such as new voters) are most likely to vote for third parties.

The fact that third parties have little chance of winning further diminishes their support. People often feel that a vote for a third party is a "wasted" vote. Many people also have the sense that third parties are somehow illegitimate, that they disrupt the "normal" two-party system.[89] Of particular concern is the fear that third parties will lead to a deadlock in the electoral college, thus throwing the election to the House of Representatives. Major parties benefit from (and therefore encourage) the feeling that third parties are illegitimate.

Even more potent than these psychological barriers are the legal ones. Most notable are statutory obstacles. Since the 1890s, states have used the so-called Australian ballot, which means that states prepare official ballots listing party slates. These are provided to voters, who then mark them in secret. Before that time, parties prepared the ballots themselves. Voters then chose the ballot of the party that they wished to vote for and simply dropped it in the ballot box.[90]

Most states that adopted the Australian ballot also adopted some sort of ballot access laws to keep their official ballots from being too long. The two major parties automatically appeared on the ballot, but minor parties had to pass a series of hurdles that were different in each of the fifty states and the District of Columbia, including petition requirements, filing deadlines, fees, and even loyalty oaths. Meeting these requirements was time consuming, costly, and complicated. At times it was purposely exclusionary. Since the late 1960s, a series of court cases has eased ballot access laws to prevent rules that are blatantly unfair to third parties. Nevertheless, such laws (which continue to differ from state to state) still serve as a considerable hurdle for third parties.

In addition to ballot access laws, the 1974 Federal Election Campaign Act (FECA) has served as a barrier to third parties. The act allows major party candidates to receive some $45 million each in public funds during the campaign, but third parties are allowed public funds only after the election is over *and* only if they appear on the ballot in at least ten states and receive at least five percent of the popular vote nationwide.[91] (Five percent of the popular vote guarantees them funding in the next election, too.) Receiving public funds after the fact (rather than during the campaign when they are needed) puts third parties at a significant comparative disadvantage to the major parties. Not only is the money not in hand, but valuable time must be spent on fund raising rather than on other campaign activities. Fund raising itself is more difficult because third parties do not have the organizational structure or expertise of the major parties.

Initially, FECA discriminated against "independent" candidates as opposed to "real" third parties. Eugene McCarthy would not have been eligible to receive public funding in 1976 even if he had received more than 5 percent of the popular vote because he was technically an independent candidate, not a "minor party" nominee. The rule was changed for Anderson's benefit in 1980. In making the change, the Federal Election Commission said that Anderson was the functional equivalent of a third party.[92]

The electoral college itself is sometimes seen as a barrier to third parties, largely because of the "general ticket" system. *(See "Early Experience, 1789-1828," p. 155, in this chapter.)* Under that system, the candidate with the most votes in any given state—whether it be a plurality or majority—wins all of that state's electors. It is argued that this "winner-take-all" approach hurts third parties because it overrepresents the power of the majority parties. However, the electoral college can magnify the support of minority parties as well. Thurmond, for example, won a disproportionate share of electoral votes in 1948 by carrying four southern states. In such cases, the existing system can help third parties with a geographical base.

An alternative to the existing system would be a direct popular election (or a proportional system of election). It is often said that such a system would benefit third parties, since every candidate would receive his or her percentage of the popular vote. Indeed, many fear that such a system would lead to a proliferation of small parties seeking a share of the vote.

Under a direct, or proportional, system, third parties would be most influential if runoff elections were held. This would allow them to form coalitions in the period between the general election and the runoff. That influence would be most significant, however, if runoffs were required when no candidate received a majority (that is, more than 50 percent) of the votes. If the winner could be elected by a plurality (that is, simply by receiving more than anyone else), third parties would gain little. The greater the proportion of votes needed to win, the greater the influence of third parties. This is because the greater the proportion of votes needed to win, the less likely it will be that any one party will receive that proportion—thus forcing a runoff election (and thereby increasing the influence of third parties).[93] Third parties can still play an important role under the electoral college system by winning a large enough share of the vote to send the election to the House of Representatives. Especially if the third party were represented in the House, its influence could be significant.

The rise of direct party primaries also has been said to help maintain the two-party system. Through primaries, dissident groups within parties have an opportunity to air their views, vent their frustrations, and resolve their differences within the party itself. Without such an opportunity, such groups might be more inclined to leave the party.[94]

In addition to psychological and legal barriers, third parties also face political barriers. Because third parties tend to be short-lived, they lack the base of voter support that major parties enjoy. Furthermore, their party organization tends to be weaker and less experienced. Often their candidates are less experienced and less known than those of the major parties, and they have less money to publicize their cause. Without much money, publicity—such as expensive television air time for commercials—is difficult to come by.

Likewise, third parties receive less free media coverage. They often are excluded from televised debates between the two major party candidates; their nominating conventions (if they hold any) are not beamed into American homes by television; and—with rare exceptions—they are ignored or given slight attention in news coverage and commentary. Even in 1980, when Anderson received considerable media attention, the two major party candidates received ten times more coverage than he and all ten of the other candidates combined.[95]

Finally, the U.S. political culture may help to reinforce the two-party system. Ours is a politics of moderation. Both of the major parties are—relatively speaking—centrist and ideologically similar. As a whole, our political spectrum does not run the gamut of some European countries. This leads to fewer irreconcilable differences. As a result, political factions in this country "coalesce around pragmatic issues within the two major parties" rather than fragmenting over fundamentals.[96] This spirit of moderation, consensus, and compromise is not conducive to vigorous and persistent third party movements.

Whether this is good or bad is open to debate. Some see third parties as a threat to the stability of the democratic system in the United States. Others see them as a vital element in expressing minority sentiments and as a breeding ground of issue-awareness and innovation.[97] Whatever their merits, and despite obstacles to their success, third parties persist. In so doing they often perform important functions: they focus attention on issues or ideas that might otherwise be ignored, they provide a testing ground for the presentation of new ideas or policies, and they serve as a vehicle for the free expression of opposition sentiments. As a result, they may force major parties to respond in important and beneficial ways. Thus, the threat of exit as well as the exercise of voice helps to make parties responsive to the people.

The Election

The presidential election in the fall does not present as complex a process as the nomination process in the first half of the year. Not only has the field been limited to two or three "serious" nominees, but the rules of balloting are virtually identical throughout the nation (with some exceptions for third party candidates). The fall election, however, has the potential to be complicated. Despite the campaign's national scope, campaigns direct their efforts to states and regions. Once the people vote, the selection of the president can move from the electoral college to the House of Representatives and the Senate.

The Popular Vote

When almost 100 million people go to the polls across the United States on a presidential election day, the great American political and media machines go into gear for the last time of the quadrennial election cycle. It is a day of parties for the frazzled campaign staffs and of aggressive competition for the media. In recent years, the media have been criticized for approaching their election-day competition too aggressively. Some observers have suggested that broadcasters have undermined the democratic process with their zeal to report the winners.

Ballots are tallied electronically in most parts of the United States. The controversy that once swirled around the tampering of paper ballots has declined in recent years.

Figure 2 Percentage of Voting-Age Population That Voted for President, 1920-1988

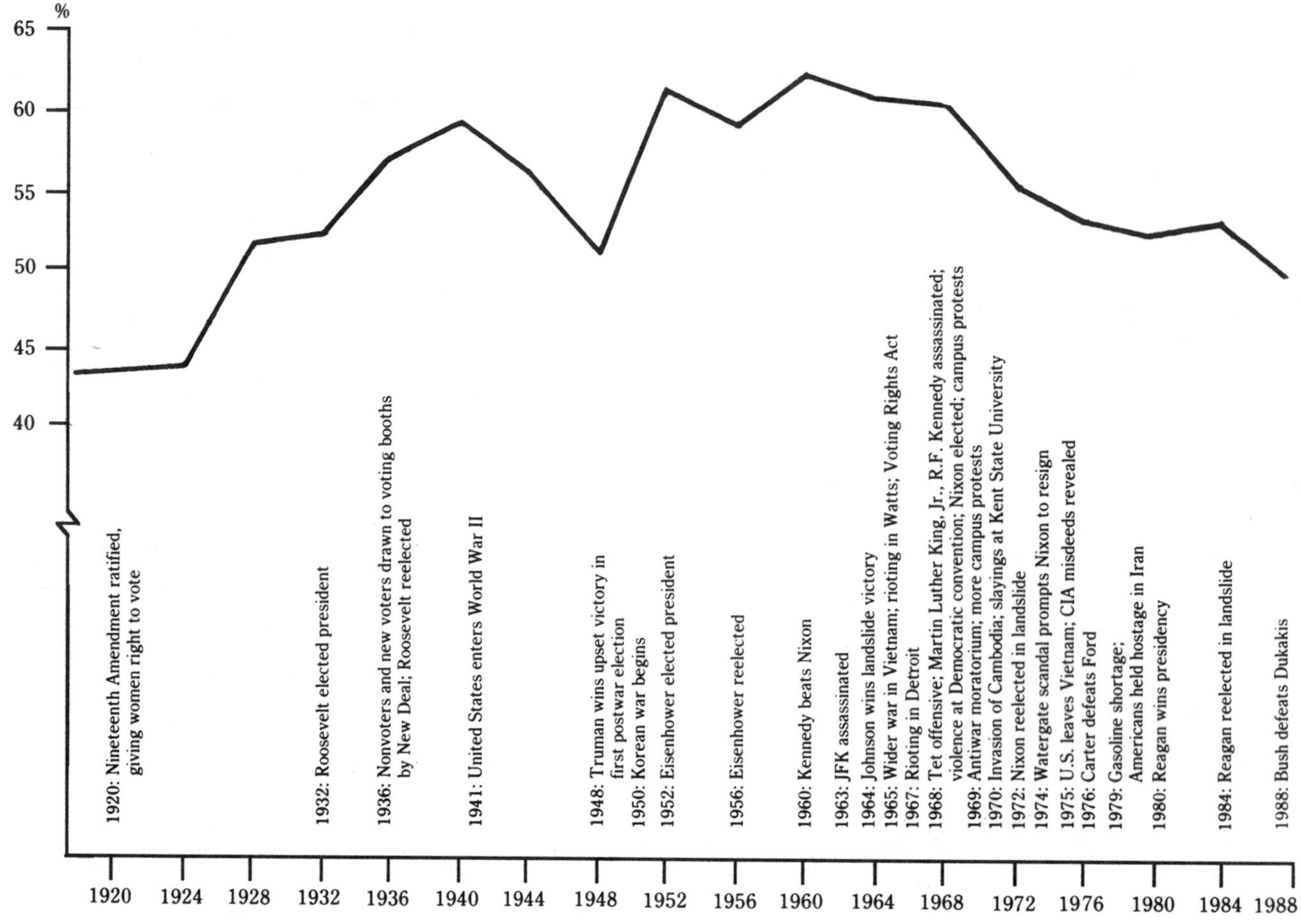

Source: Elections '88 (Washington, D.C.: Congressional Quarterly Inc., 1988), 141.

Ballot counting now consists of collecting and reporting the electronically recorded results from voting booths.

For most Americans, the tabulation of the actual votes is a minor part of the election-night ritual. The major television networks have developed a variety of ways of making their own counts of the elections in all states—and of reporting the results as soon as they come in. The networks project winners in the states on the basis of their analyses of as few as 5 percent of the state's precincts; the precincts chosen for analysis are considered to be representative of the state's overall voting patterns. Through "exit polls"—surveys of voters as they leave the polls—the networks are able to make projections even before the polls close.

The networks' practice of declaring winners on the basis of incomplete information caused a major controversy in 1980. All three networks declared Republican Ronald Reagan the winner over President Jimmy Carter before the polls closed in the western states, and Carter conceded the election at 8:45 p.m. Eastern Standard Time. Media critics argued that the early projection discouraged western voters from going to the polls since the national election was apparently a foregone conclusion; the scholarly evidence is mixed.[1] A higher turnout could have changed the outcome of close state and congressional races in the West.

Congress considered action to restrict network pronouncements on election day, and the networks pledged to withhold results until polls closed in the states, but the basic problem of news outracing events is likely to remain. Only a longer balloting period—a full twenty-four hours or a full weekend, as was the case in some states in the nineteenth century—would be likely to control the media's imperative to report news instantly.

Whether the presidential election is close or not, the networks stay on the air with special election coverage into the wee hours of the next day. The candidates watch the returns on television in hotel suites before going to their election headquarters either to celebrate or to commiserate with supporters.

Few elections have aroused counting controversies in recent years. The 1960, 1968, and 1976 elections were close enough that a change in five thousand votes in four or five states would have changed the result. In 1960, Richard Nixon considered declaring a recount of his losing contest with John F. Kennedy after ballot tampering was reported in Texas, Illinois, and other closely contested states. Almost two weeks after the election Nixon decided against the call for a recount. He later wrote in his memoir *Six Crises* that he made that decision because of the constitutional crisis in presidential succession that a recount might have provoked.

Scholars disagree about the effect of *coattails* during

presidential election years. The *coattails effect* is the positive or negative influence that a presidential candidate has on the fortunes of other party members running for office. Strong presidential candidates such as Franklin D. Roosevelt and Ronald Reagan have helped other candidates get elected. In 1980, the Republican party gained control of the U.S. Senate for the first time since 1955 as Reagan not only ran a strong national race but also campaigned personally for other Republicans.

Because the kinds of issues that voters consider important are usually different for presidential and congressional campaigns, the coattails effect is usually considered to be of minor importance. Congressional candidates stress local concerns and their role as liaison between citizens and the federal government; presidential candidates, in contrast, stress broad themes. Political scientist James MacGregor Burns has argued that American politics is best understood not as a single system but as an uneasy marriage of separate presidential and congressional systems. While presidents set broad themes for the national political system, Congress tends to the parochial concerns of constituents; voters therefore have different standards for presidential and congressional selection.

The Electoral College

The Founders intended the selection of the president to be the work of the nation's most learned and public-spirited citizens who would form a group called "the electoral college." The electors were to be selected by the states as they saw fit; the electors then would meet in their separate states sometime after their selection to pick the next president.

The Constitutional Convention included advocates of direct presidential elections, but most delegates were as concerned about the dangers of "mob rule" as they were concerned about excessive government power. As George Mason of Virginia stated: "It would be as unnatural to refer the choice of a proper magistrate to the people as it would to refer the choice of colors to a blind man." [2]

As it operates today, electors meet in state capitals on the first Monday after the second Wednesday of December and prepare a statement of their vote to send to Washington, where Congress counts the votes January 6.

The Framers expected a plethora of state "native son" candidates to produce regular electoral college deadlocks, sending the elections to the House. Such a situation would create a variant of a parliamentary system.

Since 1836, all the states except Maine have allocated delegates to candidates on a "winner-take-all" basis. (Maine allocates delegates by special presidential-elector districts.) States receive one elector for each representative and senator in Congress. If no candidate wins an electoral majority, the House of Representatives decides the election, with each state casting one vote. Each state's delegation votes on which candidate to support. If a precedent set in 1825 were followed, a state could cast a House vote only if a majority of its whole delegation supported a candidate (as opposed to a majority of House members present for the vote). This requirement could disenfranchise a state with strong two-party competition if some of its House members were to be absent from the vote. The Senate selects the vice president. *(See "When the Electoral College Is Deadlocked," p. 256, in this chapter.)* This system was part of the web of compromises between large and small states during the constitutional convention.

The electoral college system favors the very small and very large states. The smallest states are favored because they have, regardless of their population, at least two electors representing the state's two Senate seats plus at least one elector for the delegation to the House of Representatives. Large states are favored because their large bloc of electoral votes ensures that the candidates will pay close attention to their demands.

The winner-take-all system is a moderating influence on U.S. politics. Political strategies depend on attracting as many diverse groups as possible under the same political banner in order to win the whole state rather than only a part of the state. Systems of proportional representation (in which parties or candidates receive representation according to their percentage of the popular vote) tend to complicate bargaining and to fragment coalitions by giving representation to minority parties.

The state-by-state system of allocation of electors encourages candidates to identify a base of strength and attempt to build slowly on that base. Candidates typically make appeals to groups in states just outside their strong base of support to lure these voters into their camp. Modern Democrats, for example, usually have industrial regions in the Northeast and Midwest as a strong base of support; their job is to appeal to groups with common concerns in other states with geographic and ideological proximity. Modern Republicans appear to have a strong hold on the West and many states of the South.

Democrat Jimmy Carter's winning 1976 campaign won over not only the solid South but also border states from Maryland to Ohio and Illinois. The "across the board" strategy of Walter Mondale's losing 1984 campaign prevented him from building on his natural strength in traditionally liberal areas.

Critics of the electoral college system point out several possible sources of an electoral crisis. The fact that a candidate with a popular-vote lead can lose the electoral vote is said to present the nation with a possible problem of legitimacy. John Quincy Adams in 1824, Rutherford B. Hayes in 1876, and Benjamin Harrison in 1888 won the presidency with a smaller popular vote than their opponents. The elections of Adams and Hayes were decided in the House. The legitimacy of both elections came under serious ques-

Library of Congress

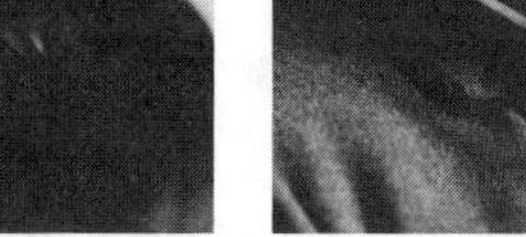

Library of Congress

Despite losing the popular vote by 100,000 ballots, Benjamin Harrison, left, won the 1888 presidential election with 233 electoral votes to 116 for Grover Cleveland, right.

tion. Corrupt deals allegedly thwarted the will of the people in both cases. Harrison attracted about 100,000 fewer votes (of almost 12 million cast) than President Grover Cleveland, but he won the electoral college vote by 233 to 168.

More concern has been expressed about a possible deadlock in the electoral college if the election involves more than two candidates. If no candidate wins a majority of all electoral votes, the election is to be decided by the House. If a third-party candidate wins one or two states in a close race, he or she could play an important "broker" role either in the electoral college or in the House. The legitimacy of a race decided by backroom deals would be in serious question.

In 1968 George Wallace's candidacy on the American Independent party ticket presented such a threat. Republican Richard Nixon and Democrat Hubert Humphrey ran one of the closest races in history. Despite earlier hopes of winning the whole South, Wallace won only five states and forty-six electoral votes. If Nixon had lost just California or two or three smaller states that were close, he would have been denied an electoral majority. Wallace's electoral votes would have made the difference. In exchange for that support, Nixon might have needed to promise important appointments or policy concessions. *(See "Threats," p. 259, in this chapter.)*

A related controversy surrounds the instructions that electors have when they meet to vote. About a third of the states require electors to cast their ballot for the candidate who won the popular vote in the state. The Constitution does not require electors to adhere to the party line. In theory, they may vote however they like, but electors who do so—known as "faithless electors"—are rare. Still, in 1960 Sen. Harry Byrd of Virginia, who was not listed on any ballot, won fifteen electoral votes from unpledged electors and one faithless elector. An organized movement could produce even more electoral vote defections—and a constitutional crisis. The outcome of an election could depend on the willingness of a candidate with only minority or regional support to cooperate with a major candidate.

Numerous reforms have been proposed to alter both the fundamental concept of the electoral college and some of its obsolete and odd aspects. One reform would eliminate faithless electors by automatically casting a state's electoral votes for the candidate receiving the most popular votes. A second reform would allocate electoral votes by congressional district rather than by state and would give the state's two electors who represent its senators to the top presidential candidate as a bonus. A third proposal would provide for proportional allocation of a state's electoral votes—which could lead to more deadlocks and congressional selection of presidents because there would be more opportunity for third and fourth parties to garner electors. A fourth proposal would do away with the electoral college altogether through direct election of the president, with a runoff if no candidate achieved a majority. Another reform would give the popular-vote victor "bonus" electors for each state. A final proposal would alter the way Congress voted in the event of an electoral college deadlock by allowing House members to vote individually rather than having one vote for each state.

Congress has never passed a constitutional reform of presidential elections for submission to the states, although the Senate passed a direct election proposal in the 1970s. Any of these changes would require a constitutional amendment, and amending the Constitution is a long and arduous process. Under the most prominent method, Congress submits the proposed amendment to the states for ratification, and two-thirds of all state legislatures must approve the amendment for it to become law. In the absence of a major crisis, an overhaul of the electoral college is unlikely. The way that the electoral college highlights state identity has many supporters. The most serious efforts to reform the electoral college failed in 1950, 1969, and 1977.

When the Electoral College Is Deadlocked

When no presidential candidate receives a majority of the electoral vote, the Constitution directs that the election be decided by the House of Representatives. Originally, the House also selected the vice president in such a situation (as it did in 1800) since there was then no separate ballot for presidential and vice-presidential candidates. Under that system, the second-place candidate became vice president. That changed in 1804 with the ratification of the Twelfth Amendment, which directed that electors vote for president and vice president on separate ballots. Since then, the House has been directed to select the president and the Senate the vice president when there is a deadlocked election.

The Framers of the Constitution originally thought that most presidential elections would be deadlocked. George Mason, for one, predicted that nineteen out of twenty elections would be decided by the House.[3] In fact, only two presidential elections—those of 1800 and 1824—have been so decided.

Procedure

If an election is thrown to the House, the newly elected representatives select the president from among the three candidates with the most electoral votes. The fact that the new House, rather than the "lame-duck" House, selects the president is provided for by statute. The Twentieth Amendment to the Constitution (ratified in 1933) specifies that the new Congress convene on January 3 and the inauguration take place January 20. Before that amendment, both the new Congress and the new presidential term began on March 4; thus, the old lame-duck Congress was forced to select the president.

The changes brought about by the Twentieth Amendment mean that Congress now would have considerably less time to choose a president if the electoral college were deadlocked. Originally, the Twelfth Amendment gave the House until March 4 to select the president. If the House did not make a decision by that date, the amendment called for the vice president-elect (chosen, if necessary, by the Senate) to "act as president as in the case of the death or other constitutional disability of the president."[4] Under the current system, the House has only about two weeks to make a choice before the inaugural date of January 20. If the House is deadlocked and cannot make a choice by that date, the Twentieth Amendment directs that the vice president-elect "shall act as president *until a president shall have qualified.*"[5]

The language surrounding that provision can be read in different ways. For instance, legal scholars Laurence H. Tribe and Thomas M. Rollins of Harvard have argued that the House, if deadlocked, "could go on voting, with interruptions for other business and indeed with an infusion of members in midterm, for four full years." They pointed out that this would transform our government into a "quasi-parliamentary system," since the acting president would be "subject to termination at any time until the House deadlock is finally broken."[6] Political scientist Allan P. Sindler has argued, however, that the deadline of March 4 that was imposed by the Twelfth Amendment was not superseded by the Twentieth Amendment. As such, he argues that the House can replace the acting president only *until* that time. If the House acts before March 4, the acting president becomes vice president.[7]

When selecting the president, each state delegation in the House has one vote, and no vote is cast if the delegation is evenly divided. Members of the delegation vote by secret ballot, and an absolute majority of the delegations (twenty-six of the fifty states) is necessary for election.[8]

If no vice-presidential candidate receives a majority of votes in the electoral college, the selection is made by the Senate between the two candidates with the most electoral votes. Unlike the House procedure, each senator has one vote. Again, an absolute majority—fifty-one votes—is needed for the election. Since the Senate chooses among only the top two candidates and is not beset with the potential problems of split delegations, the vice-presidential selection process is somewhat less complicated than the presidential selection process. By statute, the new Senate (as convened on January 3) makes the decision.

The selection process is further complicated if neither a president nor a vice president can be decided upon by the date set for inauguration. In such an event, the Twentieth Amendment empowers Congress to decide by law "who shall then act as President, or the manner in which one who is to act shall be selected, and such person shall act accordingly until a President or Vice President shall have qualified."[9]

The Presidential Succession Act of 1947 now covers such a circumstance. The act calls for the Speaker of the House and the president pro tempore of the Senate, in that order, to serve as acting president until a candidate qualifies. To so serve, they must resign their seat in the legislature.[10] If they refuse, the line of succession reverts to members of the cabinet of the incumbent (previous) administration in the order the cabinet offices were established (starting with secretary of state). Although there were two earlier presidential succession acts (in 1792 and 1886), the 1947 act—in conformity with the Twentieth Amendment—was the first to deal with vacancies caused by the failure of candidates to qualify.[11]

Neither the constitutional provisions nor the succession act specify what criteria legislators should use in choosing among the designated candidates. As many commentators have pointed out, this raises several problems. Should legislators vote for the candidate with the most electoral votes or the most popular votes? If they base their decision on the popular vote, should they look at the popular vote in their district, or their state, or in the nation as a whole? Or should they simply vote for the candidate of their party or of their conscience? Could they bargain away their votes to the "highest bidder," so to speak?[12] Although there is little to guide legislators in making such decisions, there no doubt would be considerable pressure to act in a fashion that would foster an orderly and legitimate transfer of power.

Library of Congress

Library of Congress

Only two presidential elections – those of 1800 and 1824 – have been decided by the House of Representatives. In 1800, Thomas Jefferson, left, and the intended vice-presidential candidate, Aaron Burr, right, tied in the electoral college vote.

Precedents: 1800 and 1824

Presidential elections have been thrown to the House of Representatives only twice in our history: in 1800 and 1824. In the first case, the deadlock was brought on by the old method of electors voting for the president and vice president on the same ballot. Each elector had two votes, and when all the votes were tallied the second-place candidate became vice president. The Federalist ticket consisted of John Adams for president and Charles Cotesworth Pinckney for vice president; the Republican ticket consisted of Thomas Jefferson and Aaron Burr. When the electors voted in December 1800, the two Republican candidates tied for first place.

This example illustrates some of the pitfalls of the legislative selection process. Under the provisions then in effect, the old lame-duck House (which had a Federalist majority) selected the president. Many Federalists considered Aaron Burr less repugnant than Thomas Jefferson and therefore plotted to elect him president (even though it was clear that Jefferson was the presidential candidate and Burr was the vice-presidential candidate).

Although Alexander Hamilton strongly discouraged the idea, the majority of Federalists in the House backed Burr. If the Constitution had allowed the decision to be made by the vote of individual members (rather than by the bloc votes of state delegations), Burr would have won. As it stood, the situation remained deadlocked. Balloting began on February 11, 1801, but no candidate received a majority. It soon became apparent that the House deadlock would not be broken soon. As one observer recalled: "Many [congressmen] sent home for night caps and pillows, and wrapped in shawls and great-coats, lay about the floor of the committee rooms or sat sleeping in their seats. At one, two, and half-past two, the tellers roused the members from their slumbers, and took the same ballot as before."[13]

Seven days and thirty-six ballots later, the tide turned. The day before, Federalist representative James Bayard of Delaware told a party caucus that balloting had gone on long enough. To delay the process any longer would run risk to the Constitution. After receiving word from Maryland Republican boss Samuel Smith that Jefferson would preserve the Hamiltonian financial system, respect the integrity of the navy, and refrain from dismissing Federalists

"Minority" Presidents

Under the U.S. electoral system, fifteen presidents have been elected, either by the electoral college itself or by the House of Representatives, who did not receive a majority of the popular votes cast in the election. Three of them—John Quincy Adams, Rutherford B. Hayes, and Benjamin Harrison—actually trailed their opponents in the popular vote.

The following table shows the percentage of the popular vote received by candidates in the fifteen elections in which a "minority" president (designated by boldface type) was elected:

1824	Jackson 41.34	**Adams** 30.92	Clay 12.99	Crawford 11.17
1844	**Polk** 49.54	Clay 48.08	Birney 2.30	
1848	**Taylor** 47.28	Cass 42.49	Van Buren 10.12	
1856	**Buchanan** 45.28	Fremont 33.11	Fillmore 21.53	
1860	**Lincoln** 39.82	Douglas 29.46	Breckinridge 18.09	Bell 12.61
1876	Tilden 50.97	**Hayes** 47.95	Cooper 0.97	
1880	**Garfield** 48.27	Hancock 48.25	Weaver 3.32	Others 0.15
1884	**Cleveland** 48.50	Blaine 48.25	Butler 2.74	St. John 1.47
1888	Cleveland 48.62	**Harrison** 47.82	Fisk 2.19	Streeter 1.29
1892	**Cleveland** 46.05	Harrison 42.96	Weaver 8.50	Others 2.25
1912	**Wilson** 41.84	T. Roosevelt 27.39	Taft 23.18	Debs 5.99
1916	**Wilson** 49.24	Hughes 46.11	Benson 3.18	Others 1.46
1948	**Truman** 49.52	Dewey 45.12	Thurmond 2.40	Wallace 2.38
1960	**Kennedy** 49.72	Nixon 49.55	Others 0.72	
1968	**Nixon** 43.42	Humphrey 42.72	Wallace 13.53	Others 0.33

in subordinate government jobs simply on the grounds of politics, Bayard was convinced that the Federalists must relent. Thus, on the thirty-sixth ballot, Bayard and the Burr supporters from Maryland, South Carolina, and Vermont cast blank ballots, giving the presidency to Jefferson and the vice-presidency to Burr.[14]

The election of 1824 is the only one thrown to the House since the adoption of the Twelfth Amendment. The fact that no candidate received a majority of the electoral vote count that year was largely a result of the crowded field of candidates. By 1824, the Federalist party was dead. It appeared that whoever was nominated by the Republicans' "King Caucus" would surely be elected president. The congressional caucus, however, was subject to increasing criticism. The caucus system was a holdover from an age that distrusted mass democratic sentiments, and that age was coming to an end.

As it turned out, attendance at the caucus was meager. The caucus nominated William H. Crawford (who had served as secretary of the Treasury under President James Monroe), but others balked at the choice, for two reasons. First, Crawford had suffered a paralytic stroke the year before that left him greatly impaired. Second, populist sentiment was rising, and Crawford's selection by a small group of legislators smacked of political manipulation. State legislatures promptly nominated John Quincy Adams, John C. Calhoun, Henry Clay, and Andrew Jackson for president.

Attempts were made to limit the field of candidates, but they were to little avail. Crawford's men dropped his running mate, Albert Gallatin, in the hopes that they could persuade Clay to take his place. Their plan was that Clay supporters, recognizing that Crawford might not live out his term, would push Crawford to victory. Clay, preferring to gamble on the possibility of winning on his own merits, refused.[15] Among the candidates, only Calhoun withdrew from the presidential race.

When the votes of the electoral college were in, no candidate had a majority. Jackson stood in front with ninety-nine electoral votes, followed by Adams with eighty-four, Crawford with forty-one, and Clay with thirty-seven. In accord with the Twelfth Amendment, the names of Jackson, Adams, and Crawford were placed before the House. It was immediately evident that the support of Clay would tip the balance between the two front-runners.

Clay was not fond of either candidate, but he clearly felt that Adams was the lesser of two evils. In early January, Clay and Adams conferred, and Clay let it be known that he would support Adams in the House election. Soon thereafter, a letter in a Philadelphia newspaper alleged that Adams had offered Clay the post of secretary of state in return for his support. Jackson was furious, and his rage was all the worse when Adams won the House election with a bare minimum of thirteen out of twenty-four state delegations and proceeded to name Clay secretary of state. Thus, Jackson, who had more popular and electoral votes than any of the other candidates in the general election, did not become president.

The Senate has chosen a vice president only once, in 1837. Martin Van Buren was elected president that year with 170 of 294 electoral votes. However, his running mate—Richard M. Johnson of Kentucky—received only 147 electoral votes (one less than a majority). A group of twenty-three Virginia electors who supported Van Buren boycotted Johnson because of his long-term romantic entanglement with a black woman.[16] The remainder of the electoral votes were split among three other candidates. Francis Granger of New York received seventy-seven electoral votes, John Tyler of Virginia received forty-seven, and William Smith of Alabama received twenty-three.

The names of the top two candidates were sent to the Senate. In making the selection, the Senate adopted a resolution that called for the senators to vote by voice vote in alphabetical order.[17] The Senate confirmed Johnson's election by a vote of thirty-three to sixteen.

Library of Congress

Library of Congress

In the election of 1824, none of the candidates won an electoral majority. Although Andrew Jackson, left, outpolled his competitors, John Quincy Adams, right, was chosen by the House of Representatives.

Threats

Although no presidential election has been thrown to the House since 1824, several have come close. The elections of Abraham Lincoln in 1860 and John F. Kennedy in 1960, for instance, would have gone to the House given a shift of only 30,000 popular votes.[18] A relatively small shift of vòtes could also have sent the elections of 1836, 1856, 1892, 1948, 1968, and 1976 to the House. *(See "Chronology of Elections," p. 266, in this chapter.)*

Often threats are precipitated by the presence of a third party candidate in the race. In 1948, a group of disgruntled southern Democrats formed the States' Rights (or "Dixiecrat") party in opposition to a strong civil rights plank adopted at the Democratic national convention. The Dixiecrats' candidate, Gov. J. Strom Thurmond of South Carolina, captured thirty-nine electoral votes.

In 1968 Alabama governor George C. Wallace ran as a strong third party candidate, receiving forty-six electoral votes. There was widespread fear that year that Wallace would deadlock the election and throw it to the House. Well aware of his strategic position, Wallace elicited written affidavits from his electors promising that they would vote as he instructed them to. Wallace took a hard stance on the terms that he required for delivering those votes to another candidate. Among other things he called for the repeal of all civil rights legislation, the repeal of the federal antipoverty program, and the criminal indictment of anyone advocating Viet Cong victory in the Vietnam War.[19]

Although the independent candidacy of John Anderson failed to win any electoral votes in 1980, and Ronald Reagan won the race by a wide margin, there was fear early on in the campaign that Anderson's presence would deadlock that election. At the 1980 Republican convention, former president Gerald R. Ford predicted precisely such an outcome.[20] Similar fears were expressed about the third party candidacies of Theodore Roosevelt in 1912 and Robert La Follette in 1924. *(See "Chronology of Elections," p. 226, in this chapter.)*

To an extent, such fears are fanned by party regulars in an attempt to discount the influence of a third party candidate. A vote for such a candidate is worse than just a wasted vote, they argue; it is one that could lead to a "constitutional crisis." However, it is not just the presence of third party candidates that threatens to deadlock presidential elections. Neck-in-neck races between Kennedy and Nixon in 1960 and between Carter and Ford in 1976 came close to such a deadlock.

Ironically, the Constitution's Framers took great pride in the same system of House election that we now view with great fear. Whether that fear is justified or not is a matter of debate. Nonetheless, it is a fear that periodically haunts our political landscape.

Taking Office

Some of the president's most fateful decisions take place before the administration takes the reins of power. In making appointments, developing budget priorities, and taking command of foreign policy leadership, the president-elect does much to determine the possibilities and limits of the new administration.

The Transition Period

In the period between the election and the inauguration of a president, the media are filled with reports about likely cabinet selections and the managerial style of the new president. The incumbent invites the president-elect to the White House to ensure a smooth transition, and the new chief executive and incoming staff get a battery of briefings on matters ranging from budget deficits to nuclear strategy.

Media and academic accounts stress the cooperative nature of the transition period. Only in the United States, the analysts say, can the government be turned over to political opponents with good cheer and cooperation. Transitions rarely involve active recrimination, and, almost never is there struggle over the legitimacy of the electoral outcome. The transition is a rare celebration of a stable democracy based on parties that differ on specific policies but achieve consensus on the most important matters of state.

In recent years Congress has appropriated $2 million for the incoming president to organize the new administration. Ronald Reagan's 1980 transition used $3 million, $1 million from private sources. The money is used for talent

Library of Congress

After finishing last in the election of 1824, Henry Clay threw his support to John Quincy Adams, making him president. Adams subsequently appointed Clay secretary of state.

Table 12 Growth of Transition Teams and Expenditures, 1952-1989

President	Size of transition team	Expenditure dollars (in millions) Public funds	Private funds	Total funds
Eisenhower (1952-1953)	100	0	0.4	0.4
Kennedy (1960-1961)	50[a]	0	1.3	1.3
Nixon (1968-1969)	125-150	0.5	1.0	1.5
Carter (1976-1977)	300	1.7	0.2	1.9
Reagan (1980-1981)	1,550	2.0	1.0	3.0
Bush (1988-1989)	150[b]	3.5	0	3.5

Sources: Laurin L. Henry, *Presidential Transitions* (Washington, D.C.: Brookings, 1960); Frederick C. Mosher, W. David Clinton, and Daniel G. Lang, *Presidential Transitions and Foreign Affairs* (Baton Rouge: Louisiana State University Press, 1987); Herbert E. Alexander, *Financing the 1968 Election* (Lexington, Mass.: Lexington Books, 1971), *Financing the 1976 Election* (Washington, D.C.: CQ Press, 1979), *Financing the 1980 Election* (Lexington, Mass.: Lexington Books, 1983); General Services Administration; Bush transition staff.

a. Estimate based on statement by Richard Neustadt that Carter's transition staff was six times the size of Kennedy's (Richard Neustadt, *Presidential Power* [New York: Macmillan, 1980], 218).

b. Plus 100-150 volunteers.

searches, policy deliberation, and public relation activities. Separate funds are used for inaugural ceremonies.

Presidential transitions are the opening acts of administrations, when the successful candidate's strengths and weaknesses are part of the governmental process for the first time. New presidents often are so confident in the wake of their electoral success that they pay little attention to the perils awaiting them at the White House. Presidents-elect have their own agendas and sometimes are unwilling to listen to the counsel of political adversaries.

Historian Carl M. Brauer, in one of the few academic studies of presidential transitions, wrote:

> Transitions are filled with peril and opportunity.... Newly elected presidents have ended wars or prolonged them. They have demonstrated acumen or ineptitude on national security and foreign policy issues. They have maximized their mandates and led Congress, or squandered their mandates and failed to lead Congress. They have inspired or failed to inspire the public through their statements and actions. They have established economic and social policies with widely varying results. They have wisely or imprudently adopted or discarded inherited policies. They have appointed people who helped them achieve their goals and who graced public service and others whom they came to regard as liabilities and mistakes.[1]

The question of electoral "mandate" is central to a transition period. John F. Kennedy's slim victory in 1960 did not stop him from an aggressive approach. Kennedy stated after the election: "The margin is narrow, but the responsibility is clear. There may be difficulties with Congress, but a margin of only one vote would still be a mandate."[2] But Kennedy had numerous problems with Congress. Reagan's 1980 landslide election led to more policy victories than a slimmer electoral triumph would have allowed.

The transition can be crucial in determining what kind of "honeymoon" the new president is likely to have with Congress and the public. The length of the honeymoon, in turn, has a great effect on whether the new president can be a decisive and strong leader in the first term.

Appointments

Perhaps the most important matter the president-elect addresses is staffing. The men and women chosen to fill the upper levels of the bureaucracy and the White House staff, and the "management style" of the new administration, will determine the administration's success or failure. As of 1988, the president appoints some 5,200 people to a federal bureaucracy of 3.1 million. The major sources of staff for the new president are:

~ Close associates. Most presidents fill the White House staff with close political associates, many of whom have little experience in government. The new president's trust for former campaign strategists is the key factor in filling positions such as chief of staff, press secretary, congressional liaison, and various presidential assistants.

~ Business men and women. The private sector has been a rich recruiting ground for all presidents, but Republicans have been most enthusiastic about applying business techniques to government. Dwight D. Eisenhower preferred business and finance leaders for his cabinet, especially for the Treasury and Defense departments. Kennedy's most fateful appointment probably was Robert S. McNamara, the head of Ford Motor Company, as secretary of defense. McNamara became a key figure in Johnson's unsuccessful Vietnam War policy.

~ Academic figures. Government officials often are recruited from universities and think tanks. Academics usually make contact with the future president during the campaign, when they provide briefings, position papers, and "instant advice" as different issues develop. These people often move in and out of academe according to which party holds the White House. The most notable academic in recent years to hold a position of influence was Henry Kissinger, a Harvard University professor who became Richard Nixon's top foreign policy adviser. Other academics to join administrations include Arthur M. Schlesinger, Jr., and John Kenneth Galbraith under Kennedy; Daniel P. Moynihan under Nixon and Ford; Zbigniew Brzezinski and Ray Marshall under Jimmy Carter; and Jeane J. Kirkpatrick, Terrel H. Bell, and Martin Feldstein under Reagan.

~ Constituency representatives. The new president faces a tension between a desire to control the executive bureaucracy and a desire to reach out to constituencies served by the various departments. Many departments—such as Agriculture, Commerce, Labor, Education, Veterans' Affairs, and Housing and Urban Development—were created to represent constituent groups. Those groups expect one of their "own" to head the department. A president who wants to control that group's influence, however, might appoint someone from outside the interest group's community, such as James Watt, the first secretary of interior in the Reagan administration. Watt, a lawyer for the development-oriented Mountain States Legal Foundation, worked against many environmental groups who had dominated the department in recent administrations.

~ Party leaders and elected officials. Many presidential appointments serve to reward the efforts of party leaders and workers. George Bush, a one-time GOP national chairman, received a number of appointments in the Nixon and Ford administrations. Many party officials receive lesser appointments in the White House and in government agencies, but the possibility of rewarding party faithful on a large scale has diminished with the professionalization of the civil service. Less than 1 percent of federal workers are appointed by the president.

The postal service was the traditional government agency for rewarding party faithful because of its geographic scale, relatively straightforward tasks, and large number of employees. The postal service was a good place for a president to build a party machine. Franklin D. Roosevelt's postmaster general, James Farley, was the consummate party builder with a federal post. Other positions also have gone to party faithful, but with less of a patronage-minded strategy.

Appointing party leaders and elected officials now is done more to bring different kinds of managerial and policy expertise into the administration. President Carter's appointment of Robert Strauss as a special negotiator for the Middle East, for example, was intended to take advantage of the mediation skills Strauss developed as party leader. Carter appointed former Florida governor Reubin Askew as his special trade representative on the strength of Askew's foreign investment efforts in state government. Carter's later appointment of New Orleans mayor Moon Landrieu to head the Department of Housing and Urban Development was oriented to Landrieu's experience with the problems of big cities. Each of these appointments was a payment of a political debt, but more important in each case was the recipient's governmental expertise.

~ Opposition figures. Especially after a close election, a president-elect might feel the need to "reach out" to the opposition party to build consensus for policies. In 1968 Nixon asked Democratic senator Henry M. Jackson to be secretary of defense; Jackson declined. Reagan appointed then-Democrat Jeane Kirkpatrick ambassador to the United Nations.

Staff turf battles can have an important effect on appointments and the whole style of the new presidency. A struggle between Jack Watson and Hamilton Jordan, in which Jordan won control over key personnel decisions, was an important development in the Carter administration. Watson and Jordan had markedly different approaches to management, as well as different sets of political contracts. John Ehrlichman's role as referee of a struggle between Daniel Moynihan and Arthur Burns over domestic policy was pivotal in shaping the Nixon White House.

Management Style

The president's management style is an important focus of transition-watchers. Presidents-elect usually promise to involve cabinet members in the decision-making process, but a strong White House staff can reduce the influence of the cabinet. Eisenhower was the last president to have anything like a true "cabinet government." Recent presidents, determined to control the bureaucracy, have relied more on a White House staff with a strong chief of staff. Nixon said the hundreds of cabinet meetings under Eisenhower were "unnecessary and boring." [3] Much like Franklin Roosevelt and Eisenhower before him, Kennedy insisted on playing advisers off one another. "I can't afford to confine myself to one set of advisers," he said. "If I did that I would be on their leading strings." [4]

Largely because of the important roles that White House staff members played in the Watergate scandal, Carter was reluctant to appoint a chief of staff. Carter instead served as his own chief of staff, providing direct access to a number of competing advisers. Carter maintained that the position encouraged overzealous aides to insulate the president. Reagan, who always espoused delegation of authority on a wide range of issues, appointed a chief of staff at the beginning of his administration.

Perhaps more important than the loyalty of the cabinet officers is the loyalty of their subordinates. Presidents allow their cabinet secretaries to choose their own assistant secretaries at the risk of losing control over initiatives in the bureaucracy. Nixon in his first term and Carter did not exert control over mid-level appointments, as many other presidents have done, and found that the departments were "captured" by career bureaucrats and the interest groups connected with the agencies.

The administration's congressional liaison—though not a household name outside Washington—could be the most important member of the administration. Carter's liaison, Frank Moore, lacked experience on Capitol Hill and was ineffective as the president's lobbyist. Reagan's liaisons, Max Friedersdorf and Kenneth Duberstein, won high marks, especially for their efforts on behalf of the administration's tax- and budget-cutting initiatives.

Early Advice

Incoming presidents have outside allies who offer advice on appointments and policy options. In 1980, the Heritage Foundation provided Reagan's transition team with a three-thousand-page report urging a quick selection of top aides and several policy initiatives. Kennedy benefited from a Brookings Institution study of the 1952 transition difficulties.

The outgoing administration's briefings of the president-elect and the incoming team could be important, but the different styles of the two sides often block meaningful exchanges. The most important briefing deals with the nuclear capacities of the superpowers—a briefing that never fails to shake the new president from the intoxication of the recent electoral success.

The meeting between the incoming and outgoing president is usually cordial, but the new executive is reluctant to take much advice. When Truman offered Eisenhower advice on staff operations, Truman remarked, "I think all this went into one ear and out the other." [5] Carter reports that Reagan was inattentive during their Oval Office meeting. The Reagan transition team's cooperation with other agencies such as the Office of Management and Budget was more sustained.

Early Considerations

A president's early signals to the bureaucracy could be decisive in setting the terms of relations in the executive branch. Nixon encouraged bureaucratic resistance with his repeated statements about the Democratic and liberal bias of civil service workers.[6] Reagan appointed lower-level administrators only after a thorough screening by his transition team to ensure ideological purity and loyalty to the administration.

The size of the legislative agenda is an important consideration for the new administration. Carter's initiatives—economic stimulus, arms limitation, reorganization of the bureaucracy, the Panama Canal treaties, water projects, management of the energy crisis—were so wide-ranging that the president was not able to project broad themes. Asked about his top priorities, Carter said: "I have no preference; my preference is to move on everything at once." [7] Even when his efforts succeeded, Carter did not receive much credit because of the failures along the way. Eisenhower had the same difficulty. Reagan, by contrast, emphasized issues directly pertaining to the budget—taxes, cuts in domestic spending, and increases in military spending. The work of budget director David Stockman was crucial to Reagan's desire to "hit the ground running."

From John Quincy Adams's "midnight" judge appointments to Carter's unsuccessful efforts to free American hostages from Iran, the outgoing president's last days have been fateful moments. The outgoing administration prepares a budget for the next fiscal year and issues administrative regulations. In addition, the outgoing president often delivers a "farewell address" to draw attention to the major problems of the nation. George Washington's call for limited foreign engagements remains the most famous farewell address. Prominent recent addresses include Eisenhower's warning about the "military-industrial complex" and Carter's plea for recognition of environmental and economic limits. *(See "Washington's Farewell Address," p. 1365, and "Eisenhower's Farewell Address," p. 1381, in the Appendix.)*

The Inauguration

Ritual acts permeate politics. They reassure us. They bind us together. They legitimize existing power relationships. Each presidential election is capped by a ceremony of grand proportions—the inauguration of the new president. Such ceremonies are overt political rituals that instill patriotism, unite the nation behind its leader, and provide for an orderly transfer of power. They do so through a combination of symbolism, pageantry, and rhetoric.[8] Yet almost none of that ceremony is formally required. Most of it has evolved by way of tradition.

Oath of Office

The only part of the inaugural ceremony that is required by the Constitution is the taking of the oath of office. Article II, section 1, clause 8, sets out the words that every president has repeated: "I do solemnly swear (or affirm) that I will faithfully execute the office of President of the United States, and will to the best of my ability preserve, protect, and defend the Constitution of the United States." Only Franklin Pierce in 1853 affirmed (rather than swore) to faithfully execute the office that he was about to enter. The practice of adding the words "so help me God" at the conclusion of the oath was begun by George Washington at the first inaugural ceremony.

Washington was also the first president to take the oath of office with his left hand placed on the Bible and his right hand raised toward heaven. Although not required by the Constitution, the practice of taking oaths upon Bibles was deeply ingrained in English and American colonial history. For centuries, the kings and queens of Britain had taken their coronation oaths on Bibles, and the use of a Bible was an established practice in the administration of oaths in civil and ecclesiastical courts.[9]

Nevertheless, no one thought to secure a Bible for Washington's inauguration until shortly before the general's arrival at Federal Hall in New York City for his swearing in. Chief justice of the New York state judiciary, Chancellor Robert R. Livingston, who was to administer the oath, feared that the oath would lack legitimacy without a Bible, but none could be found in the building. One was finally borrowed from St. John's Masonic Lodge No. 1, a few blocks away on Wall Street, and used during the oath.[10]

There is no definite record of a Bible being used again at a swearing-in ceremony until James K. Polk's inauguration in 1845 (although it is believed that Andrew Jackson used one in 1829 and again in 1833). Since James Buchanan in 1857, every president has taken the oath on a Bible except for Theodore Roosevelt in 1901, when he was hastily sworn in after the assassination of William McKinley. The oldest inaugural Bible was the one used by Franklin D. Roosevelt in all four of his inaugurations. It was printed in Amsterdam, Holland, around 1686 (in Dutch) and contained the Roosevelt family records—the earliest of which was the birth of Jacob Roosevelt in "1691/92." [11]

The page that the Bible is opened to during the administration of the oath is sometimes a random choice and sometimes carefully chosen. During Washington's first inauguration, it was randomly opened to Genesis 49-50. Rutherford B. Hayes placed his hand on Psalm 118:11-13, which reads, in part, "Thou has thrust sore at me that I might fall: but the Lord helped me." These words were significant, given the circumstances of his fiercely contested election. Franklin Roosevelt's Bible was opened to I Corinthians 13 for all four of his inaugurals ("Though I speak with the tongues of men and of angels, and have not charity, I am become as sounding brass. . . ."). Richard Nixon, entering office in the midst of the Vietnam War in 1969, placed his hand on Isaiah 2:4— ". . . and they shall beat their swords into plowshares, and their spears into pruning hooks: nation shall not lift up sword against nation, neither shall they learn war any more." [12]

After Washington's first inauguration, the oath of office was administered indoors until 1817. Washington's second inauguration, as well as that of John Adams, was held in Philadelphia. There the oath was administered in the Senate chamber of Independence Hall. Thomas Jefferson was the first president to be inaugurated in the District of Columbia, where in 1801 he took his oath in the original Senate chamber. In later years the ceremony was moved to the old House chamber. It was not until James Monroe's inauguration in 1817 that the ceremony was moved outdoors—to a platform erected in front of the east portico of the Capitol.

With rare exceptions, the oath of office has been administered by the chief justice of the United States, although the Constitution makes no provision for that. At Washington's first inauguration, the Supreme Court had not yet been appointed, and at his second inauguration Associate Justice William Cushing filled in for Chief Justice John Jay, who was out of the country on official business. Thus, John Adams was the first president to take the oath of office from the chief justice (who was then Oliver Ellsworth). Other judges have administered the oath in times of unexpected presidential succession.

Such times raise questions. For instance, can a person assume the presidency without having taken the oath of office? The first president to die in office was William Henry Harrison in 1841. His vice president, John Tyler, initially thought that he need not take the presidential oath. In his mind, the vice-presidential oath sufficed. Nevertheless, Tyler eventually took the presidential oath on April 6, 1841 (two days after Harrison's death) for "greater caution"—a practice that has been followed in similar circumstances since then.[13]

Still, the period between the death of a president and the swearing in of his successor remains a gray area. As recently as the assassination of John F. Kennedy in 1963, there was some question whether Lyndon B. Johnson should take the oath immediately in Dallas or wait until his return to Washington. Attorney General Robert F. Kennedy advised that the oath should be administered immediately, and it was, by federal district judge Sarah Hughes aboard *Air Force One*.[14]

Ceremony and Celebration

From the beginning, inaugurations have involved far more than just the swearing in. When George Washington set out from his home at Mt. Vernon on his journey to New York City (then the seat of government) for his swearing in, he desired a quiet trip. He had only recently recovered from a severe bout of rheumatism, and he was depressed about leaving the home that he loved. On April 16, 1789, he wrote in his diary: "About ten o'clock I bade adieu to Mt. Vernon, to private life, to domestic felicity, and with a mind oppressed with more anxious and painful sensations than I have words to express, set out for New York. . . . "[15]

But along the way, Washington was met by crowds, celebrations, speeches, ringing bells, cavalry troops, and cannon fire. In Philadelphia, thousands turned out to watch him ride down Market and Second streets. By the time he finally reached New York, the crowds had worked themselves into a frenzy. They were so loud when Washington stepped off the barge at Murray's Wharf that even the ringing church bells were drowned out.

On April 30, 1789—the morning of his inauguration—Washington traveled from his quarters at Franklin House to Federal Hall in an ornate horse-drawn coach. Upon his arrival at Federal Hall, he was escorted to the balcony where he took the oath of office in front of a huge crowd. After yet more pandemonium, he moved inside the Senate chamber to deliver a brief speech—thus establishing the precedent for inaugural addresses. That night the celebration was capped by a fireworks display.

Since then, inaugurations have usually been a time for much pomp and circumstance. When the office changes hands, it has been customary for the president-elect to come to the White House and make the trip to the Capitol with the incumbent president. On occasion, this has been an awkward ride. Herbert Hoover and Franklin Roosevelt barely exchanged glances during the trip in 1933. In 1869, president-elect Ulysses S. Grant refused to ride in the same carriage with Andrew Johnson. As a result, President Johnson boycotted the inauguration, as had John Adams in 1801, John Quincy Adams in 1829, and Martin Van Buren in 1841 (although Van Buren had made a point of meeting president-elect William Henry Harrison during the interregnum). Most presidents, however, have made the trip. Even Woodrow Wilson, partially paralyzed and on the verge of death, drove with Warren G. Harding to the Capitol in 1921, although the bitter cold prevented him from witnessing the ceremonies.[16]

In the early days, inaugural parades were made *to* the Capitol before the swearing in. Initially, these were relatively simple events with small escorts and spontaneous crowds. James Madison in 1809 was the first to wrap the parade in military formality when he was escorted by cavalry. With the exception of Andrew Jackson—who vetoed the idea of any kind of parade and simply walked to the Capitol on the sidewalk—successive presidents saw larger and larger parades.

Printed by A. Doolittle, 1790; Library of Congress

On April 30, 1789, at Federal Hall in New York City, George Washington took the oath of office. The practice of adding the words "so help me God" at the end of the oath was begun by Washington at this first inaugural ceremony.

With William Henry Harrison in 1841 came a parade filled with bands, loyal supporters, and militia units, and James Buchanan's parade in 1857 added a huge float representing the goddess of liberty. It was not until Benjamin Harrison's inauguration in 1889 that parades came *from* the Capitol after the swearing in. Harrison was also the first president to watch the parade from a reviewing stand rather than participate in it.[17]

Today, inaugural parades are elaborate events that are broadcast live on television with presidents watching the proceedings from behind bullet-proof glass. Ronald Reagan's 1985 inaugural parade—cancelled because of extremely cold weather—was scheduled to include 12,000 people, 730 horses, 66 floats, and 57 marching bands. Just the cost of building the reviewing stand and bleachers and housing the horses reached nearly $1 million. All told, the estimated cost of the 1985 inauguration was $12 million, with some $800,000 to have been raised from the selling of twenty-five thousand parade tickets (ranging in price from $12.50 to $100 apiece).[18]

Actions taken during an inaugural ceremony are often highly symbolic. To the horror of Secret Service agents, Jimmy Carter—in an act reminiscent of Jackson—walked

The Jimmy Carter Library

In a democratic gesture reminiscent of Andrew Jackson, Jimmy Carter walks with his wife and family down Pennsylvania Avenue from the U.S. Capitol to the White House in his inaugural parade, January 20, 1977.

back to the White House from his swearing-in at the Capitol in 1977 with his wife and children at his side. Yet the ease with which presidents can mingle with the public has changed markedly over the years. In 1789 George Washington thought nothing of walking home through crowds of people in New York after watching the evening fireworks display with friends. In 1829, Jackson's swearing-in was followed by an open reception at the White House for anyone who cared to attend. It has been said that refreshments were prepared for twenty-thousand people. Nevertheless, the organizers did not anticipate the full force of a hungry throng of people anxious to greet "Old Hickory." The crowd soon became an unruly mob—surging towards Jackson and the food, destroying furniture, tracking in mud, breaking windows, and ultimately forcing the president to flee.[19]

Despite the mayhem that year, later presidents continued to greet virtually anyone who stood in line to meet them at the White House after the inauguration. After Abraham Lincoln's second inauguration in 1865, however, the crowd broke out of line and descended upon the reception that was reserved for official guests. Romping through the White House, they stole food, silver, and even tore off parts of draperies to take home as souvenirs.[20]

In the evening, festivities have traditionally ended with an inaugural ball. The first such ball was held by James and Dolley Madison in 1809. With a few exceptions the tradition has continued since then. There was no ball after Jackson's first inauguration because of the recent death of his wife, and Wilson—appalled at the idea of being paraded around in front of hundreds of gawking people—scuttled plans for balls in 1913 and 1917. Harding wanted a ball in 1921, but after complaints that his plans were too extravagant, he reluctantly cancelled all postinaugural festivities. Calvin Coolidge simply went to bed in 1925 (even though there was an unofficial ball held at the Mayflower Hotel), and Franklin Roosevelt suspended the practice of balls after his first inauguration because of the crises of the Great Depression and the Second World War.[21]

Since then, however, balls have been a prominent part of the inaugural day landscape. In recent years, to accommodate the throngs that have wanted to attend, several balls have taken place throughout the city with the president and his wife making appearances at all the official ones. In 1977, Jimmy Carter had inaugural "parties" rather than "balls" to symbolize a new era of simplicity in government. In 1985, Ronald and Nancy Reagan visited nine balls attended by some fifty thousand people who had paid $125 each.[22]

Inaugural Addresses

When George Washington entered Federal Hall after taking the oath of office in New York City on April 30, 1789, he proceeded to the Senate chamber and gave a brief speech. That was the first inaugural address, and every inaugural ceremony since then has included one—even though a speech is not a constitutional requirement.

Initially, such speeches were made to a joint session of Congress and were held in either the House or Senate chamber. Beginning with James Monroe in 1817, inaugural addresses were delivered outdoors for the general public. Inclement weather has sometimes made this tradition uncomfortable. The most tragic example was the inauguration of 1841. Although the day was damp and extremely cold, General Harrison insisted on delivering his inaugural address—the longest in history, taking over an hour and forty minutes to read—without an overcoat. To make matters worse, he had traveled to the Capitol on horseback (again with no coat or hat) in a very slow procession, even though he was sixty-eight years old and exhausted from the campaign and a long journey to Washington. The exposure brought on pneumonia, and Harrison died exactly one month after his inauguration. When the wind chill factor sent temperatures plummeting well below zero in 1985, seventy-three-year-old Ronald Reagan (the oldest president to be sworn in) moved the ceremony indoors to the Capitol Rotunda and canceled the parade. Four years earlier, Reagan had enjoyed one of the warmest January inaugurations, when temperatures soared close to sixty degrees. The average high temperature for a January 20 in Washington is forty-four degrees.

Every inaugural address since Harry Truman's in 1949 has been carried live on television. Today we take such instant communication for granted, but early in our history the distribution of the president's remarks to all parts of the country took a long time. In 1841, a record was set when the text of President Harrison's address was dashed by train from Washington to New York in only ten hours.[23] Four years later, Samuel Morse stood on the platform and transmitted an account of the proceedings to Baltimore via his telegraph machine as Polk was sworn in.[24] Calvin Coolidge's 1925 inaugural address was the first to be broadcast by radio. The earliest known photograph of an inauguration is from James Buchanan's swearing-in on March 4, 1857. In 1981 Ronald Reagan moved the site of the ceremony from the East to the West Front of the Capitol. *(See Documents and Texts section of the Appendix for ad-*

dresses of Jefferson, Lincoln, Roosevelt, Kennedy, Ford, Reagan, and Bush.)

After the divisiveness of a presidential election, inaugural addresses usually stress unity and nonpartisanship. Jimmy Carter—having beaten incumbent president Gerald R. Ford in the 1976 election—opened his inaugural address with conciliatory words: "For myself and for our nation, I want to thank my predecessor for all he has done to heal our land." Jefferson reminded the joint session of Congress that listened to his inaugural address that "every difference of opinion is not a difference of principle. We have called by different names brethren of the same principle. We are all Republicans, we are all Federalists." And when Wilson entered the White House in 1913, he said: "This is not a day of triumph; it is a day of dedication. Here muster, not the forces of party, but the forces of humanity."

In troubled times, an inaugural address is an opportunity for reassurance and supplication. Franklin Roosevelt, entering office in the midst of economic crisis, recognized that "only a foolish optimist can deny the dark realities of the moment." But he preached the gospel of restoration and entreated his audience with memorable words: "... the only thing we have to fear is fear itself—nameless, unreasoning, unjustified terror which paralyzes needed efforts to convert retreat into advance."

Lincoln—entering office for a second term in 1865 as Civil War ravaged the nation—told a hushed crowd: "Fondly do we hope, fervently do we pray, that this mighty scourge of war may speedily pass away.... With malice toward none, with charity for all, with firmness in the right as God gives us to see the light, let us strive on to ... bind up the nation's wounds...."

One hundred years later, our nation was once again faced with civil unrest. On that occasion, Lyndon Johnson reminded his audience: "We are one nation and people." Those, he said, "who seek to reopen old wounds and to rekindle old hatreds ... stand in the way of a seeking nation.... For the hour and the day and the time are here to achieve progress without strife, to achieve change without hatred—not without difference of opinion, but without the deep and abiding divisions which scar the union for generations."

When Ford became the first unelected president after Nixon resigned in 1974, he addressed a crowd in the East Room of the White House, saying: "... I assume the presidency under extraordinary circumstances never before experienced by Americans. This is an hour of history that troubles our minds and hurts our hearts.... We must go forward now together.... [O]ur long national nightmare is over. Our Constitution works. Our great Republic is a government of laws and not of men. Here, the people rule...."

Such optimism is probably the most common theme of inaugural addresses. That theme was perhaps best represented by Kennedy's inauguration in 1961. As the nation's youngest elected president, he set the tone for change: "Let the word go forth from this time and place to friend and foe alike, that the torch has been passed to a new generation of Americans—born in this century, tempered by war, disciplined by a hard and bitter peace, proud of their ancient heritage—and unwilling to witness or permit the slow undoing of those human rights to which this Nation has always been committed.... [L]et us begin...."

As George Bush put it in 1989: "The new breeze blows, a page turns, the story unfolds—and so today a chapter begins: a small and stately story of unity, diversity and generosity—shared and written together."

Architect of the Capitol

This is the earliest known photograph of an inauguration, taken at James Buchanan's swearing-in on March 4, 1857.

Chronology of Presidential Elections

The presidential selection process has changed significantly since George Washington was elected to his first term in 1789. In part, this is because the constitutional provisions for presidential selection are so vague.

There are no provisions for organizing political parties, for nominating candidates, or for campaigning for office. Indeed, the Framers assumed (incorrectly) that the selection process would be a reasoned one that would transcend petty partisanship. Furthermore, the original provision for balloting by the electoral college was flawed and had to be superseded by the Twelfth Amendment in 1804. *(See "The Twelfth Amendment," p. 159, in this chapter.)*

As a result of the Constitution's ambiguities, the method of choosing presidential and vice-presidential candidates has gone through several distinct phases. Political scientist Richard P. McCormick has identified four such phases.[1]

The first phase was a period marked by uncertain and hazardous rules that lasted until the Twelfth Amendment was ratified in 1804. The second phase, continuing through 1820, was dominated by the Democratic-Republicans and is associated with the nomination of candidates by congressional caucus. The third phase was precipitated by the demise of "King Caucus" in 1824 and was characterized by factional politics and a period of time when the rules for selecting candidiates were in flux. The fourth phase—ongoing today—evolved between 1832 and 1844 and is characterized by a two-party system that nominates candidates by national conventions.

Election of 1789

The Constitution was ratified in July 1788—nearly nine months after the close of the Constitutional Convention in Philadelphia. The Continental Congress then decided that the seat of government would be New York City. There, on September 13, 1788, Congress passed a resolution that the states should appoint electors on the first Wednesday in January, that those electors would assemble and vote in their respective states on the first Wednesday in February, and that the new government would convene on the first Wednesday in March.

The method of choosing electors was left up to the individual state legislatures. *(See "Selection of Electors and the Role of the Electoral College," p. 155, in this chapter.)* The fact that all electors had to be chosen on the same day proved to be troublesome for the states, however. Some did not have time to call elections. In New York, for example, where electors were to have been chosen by the legislature, dissension between the two houses led to stalemate and prevented the state from participating in the election.

In 1789 there was no formal nomination of candidates. It had been obvious since the close of the Constitutional Convention that George Washington of Virginia would be president, even though he was not anxious to serve. The only real question was who would be his vice president. Federalist leaders ultimately decided to support John Adams of Massachusetts.

Under the existing constitutional provision, each elector cast two votes. The two votes had to be for different persons—one of whom could not be from the same state as the elector. The individual receiving the votes of a majority of the electors was named president, and the person receiv-

Woodcut from John Frost, *History of the United States*, 1836; New York Public Library

After riding his horse for a full week, Charles Thomson, secretary of the Continental Congress, arrived at Mt. Vernon on April 14, 1789, with the official news of George Washington's election as the first president of the United States.

ing the second highest total was named vice president. Since no distinction was made between balloting for president and vice president, it was possible for both candidates to receive an equal number of votes, thus throwing the election to the House of Representatives. It also was possible that the candidate for vice president—through fluke or machination—actually could end up with the most votes and therefore become president.

Federalist leader Alexander Hamilton recognized the danger all too clearly. Hamilton's concern was further fueled by his personal animosity toward Adams. He therefore plotted to siphon away votes from Adams. In a letter to James Wilson of Pennsylvania, Hamilton wrote: "Everybody is aware of that defect in the constitution which renders it possible that the man intended for vice president may in fact turn up president." To prevent that, Hamilton recommended that several votes that would otherwise have gone to Adams be thrown away on other candidates: "I have proposed to friends in Connecticut to throw away 2 [votes], to others in New Jersey to throw away an equal number and I submit to you whether it would not be well to lose three or four in Pennsylvania. . . ."[2]

Hamilton's efforts were successful. Washington was unanimously elected president with sixty-nine electoral votes. Adams, however, won the vice presidency with only thirty-four electoral votes. Only two states—New Hampshire and his own Massachusetts—voted solidly for Adams. In other states, Federalist leaders withheld support from Adams and sometimes worked against him. Adams did not receive *any* votes from Delaware, Georgia, Maryland, or South Carolina, and he received only one vote from New Jersey. The remaining votes were spread among ten other candidates, including John Jay, John Hancock, Robert Harrison, John Rutledge, and George Clinton.

Although the new government was supposed to begin on March 4, 1789, not enough members of Congress had arrived in New York City by that date to have a quorum. The Senate finally convened on April 6 to count the electoral votes. A messenger was dispatched by horse to deliver news of the election's outcome to president-elect Washington who was in Mount Vernon. He received the news on April 14. Washington then set out for New York where he was sworn in on April 30. *(See "The Inauguration," p. 262, in this chapter.)*

The election of 1789 demonstrated the potential for partisanship and intrigue in presidential contests. It also pointed out the weaknesses of the existing election calendar (which had made it difficult for New York to participate in the election) and reminded participants of the danger of the constitutional "defect" in the selection process that made it possible for the person intended to be vice president to become president.

Washington's Reelection: 1792

The election of 1792 was different from its predecessor in at least two ways. First, the election calendar was changed and made more flexible by an act of Congress. That law remained in effect until 1845. It allowed states to choose electors within a thirty-four day span before the first Wednesday in December when the electors met to vote. The second difference was that an overtly partisan contest broke out between the Federalists and the Democratic-Republicans over the vice presidency when the Democratic-Republicans decided to contest the reelection of Adams. No attempt was made to displace President Washington.

Thomas Pinckney, the Federalist vice-presidential candidate, lost in the 1796 election, although his running mate, presidential candidate John Adams, won. Democratic-Republican Thomas Jefferson won the vice presidency. The Twelfth Amendment (1804) precluded future split-ticket administrations.

Library of Congress

Thomas Jefferson, the leader of the Democratic-Republicans, chose not to run for vice president, in part because he came from the same state as President Washington. (Since electors could vote for only one candidate from their own state, Jefferson was tacitly precluded from receiving the large electoral vote of Virginia. Besides, a "balanced ticket" required a regional diversity.) Instead, Democratic-Republican leaders from New York, Pennsylvania, Virginia, and South Carolina chose New York governor George Clinton as their candidate at a meeting in Philadelphia in October 1792. The endorsement of Clinton was a milestone in the evolution of the presidential nominating process and a step away from the Framers' original understanding of the selection process.

Both Washington and Adams were reelected, although Clinton scored well in the electoral college. Adams received 77 electoral votes to Clinton's 50 (with 4 votes going to Jefferson and 1 to Aaron Burr), and Washington was reelected president by a unanimous electoral vote of 132.

The First Contest: 1796

George Washington chose not to run for president again in 1796, although there was no prohibition against his doing so. With Washington out of the race, the United States witnessed its first partisan contest for president.

On the Democratic-Republican side, there was no opposition to Jefferson as the presidential candidate, and he was considered the party's standard-bearer by a consensus of party leaders. A caucus of Democratic-Republican senators was unable, however, to agree on a running mate, producing a tie vote for Sen. Aaron Burr of New York and Sen. Pierce Butler of South Carolina that ended with a walk-out by Butler's supporters. As a result, there was no formal Democratic-Republican candidate to run with Jefferson.

The Federalists, by contrast, held what historian Roy F. Nichols described as a "quasi caucus" of the party's members of Congress in Philadelphia in May 1796.[3] The gathering chose Vice President Adams and Minister to Great Britain Thomas Pinckney of South Carolina as the

New York Historical Society

This 1807 anti-Jefferson cartoon compares Washington and Jefferson in contrasting images of good and evil.

Federalist candidates. The choice of Adams was all but obligatory given that he was Washington's vice president. Nonetheless, Adams was unpopular in the South, and he continued to be disliked by Hamilton. As a result, Hamilton tried to use the "defect" in the Constitution to make Pinckney rather than Adams president. He urged northern electors to give equal support to Adams and Pinckney in the hopes that the South would not vote for Adams and that Pinckney would therefore win the most votes.

Had northern electors followed Hamilton's advice, Pinckney might have won the presidency. Instead, eighteen votes were thrown to other Federalists. As a result, Adams won the presidency with seventy-one electoral votes, but Pinckney—with fifty-nine votes—was not even able to win the vice presidency. Instead, Jefferson (from the opposing Democratic-Republican ticket) came in second with sixty-eight votes and thus was named Adams's vice president. Although the results again played up the defects in the constitutional procedure for electing presidents, Federalists and Democratic-Republicans did not seem unduly concerned that the president and vice president were of opposing parties. Both sides felt that they had prevented the opposition from gaining total victory.

Jefferson's 1800 Victory

The election of 1800 was the first in which both parties used congressional caucuses to nominate candidates for their tickets. Such caucuses were an important innovation in the development of the presidential selection process. They were illustrative of partisan alignments in Congress and demonstrated the emergence of organized political parties.

Federalist members of Congress met in the Senate chamber in Philadelphia on May 3, 1800, to choose their candidates. As in previous presidential election years, Federalists were divided in their support of Adams. Nonetheless, Federalists felt that they had to nominate Adams since he was the incumbent president. Because of their ambivalence toward Adams, they nominated both Adams and Maj. Gen. Charles Cotesworth Pinckney of South Carolina without giving preference to one or the other for president. Pinckney was the elder brother of the Federalist vice-presidential candidate in 1796.

The choice of Pinckney was made at Hamilton's insistence. Once again Hamilton was plotting to use the constitutional defect against Adams. In 1796, South Carolina had voted for an all-southern ticket—Jefferson and Thomas Pinckney—even though the two were of opposing parties. Hamilton hoped that South Carolina would vote the same way in 1800, and that all other Federalist electors could be persuaded to vote for Adams and Charles Pinckney. That would give Pinckney more votes than Adams, thus making him president.

Although the deliberations of the Federalist caucus were secret, the existence of the meeting was not. It was described by the local Democratic-Republican paper, the Philadelphia *Aurora*, as a "Jacobinical conclave." Further denunciations by the paper's editor, Benjamin F. Bache, earned him a personal rebuke from the U.S. Senate.

The Democratic-Republicans once again chose Jefferson as the presidential candidate by consensus. On May 11, a caucus of Democratic-Republican members of Congress met at Marache's boarding house in Philadelphia to choose a running mate. Their unanimous choice was Aaron Burr. Although there was no such thing as a formal party platform in 1800, Jefferson wrote fairly detailed statements of principle in letters to various correspondents. Partisan newspapers also helped to spread the Democratic-Republican position. Among other things, the Democratic-Republicans believed in states' rights, a small national government, and a relatively weak executive. They opposed standing armies in peacetime, a large naval force, and alliances with other countries. And they denounced the Alien and Sedition Acts, which had been passed by the Federalists in 1798 for the ostensible purpose of protecting the nation from subversives given the threat of war with France. *(See "The Embattled Presidency of John Adams," p. 62, in History of the Presidency chapter of Part I.)*

When the electors voted in December, the constitutional defect did not work as Hamilton had hoped. Instead of resulting in a Pinckney victory, the defect produced an unexpected tie vote between the two Democratic-Republican candidates, Jefferson and Burr—each of whom had seventy-three electoral votes. Adams came in third with sixty-five, and Pinckney followed with sixty-four. In accord with the constitutional provision, the election was thrown to the Federalist-controlled House of Representatives. *(See "Jefferson's 1800 Victory," p. 268, in this chapter.)*

Some Federalists felt that Burr was the lesser of the two evils and plotted to elect him president instead of Jefferson—even though Jefferson was clearly the presidential candidate. Hamilton helped to squelch the idea. After thirty-six ballots, Jefferson received a majority in the House of Representatives. The crisis—which could have fatally wounded the nation by calling into question the legitimacy of the new president—was over. Jefferson was elected president and Burr vice president.

The near disaster brought about by the constitutional defect led to the passage of the Twelfth Amendment to the Constitution in September 1804. It called for electors to vote for president and vice president on separate ballots, thereby clarifying who was the presidential candidate and eliminating the possibility of a tie between the principal candidate and the running mate.

The election of 1800 is also important because it was the first to witness active campaigning designed to rally voter support for particular political parties. Despite attempts by the Federalists to muzzle the opposition press with the passage of the Sedition Act of 1798, partisan newspapers on both sides actively defamed the opposition. In fact, the Sedition Act ultimately worked against the Federalists since it helped to turn the Democratic-Republicans into champions of a free press.

Finally, increased partisan activity spurred voter participation. Since electors still were chosen indirectly in twelve of the sixteen states, voters often expressed themselves through state legislative elections as a means of influencing future presidential elections.[4] The seeds were being sowed for a new phase in the development of the presidential election process.

Jefferson's Reelection: 1804

The 1804 election was the first one held after the Twelfth Amendment to the Constitution went into effect, requiring electors to cast separate votes for president and vice president. With ratification of the amendment, parties in 1804 and thereafter specifically designated their presidential and vice-presidential candidates.

The Democratic-Republicans retained the caucus system of nomination in 1804, as they did for the next two decades, and for the first time they publicly reported their deliberations. The party caucus met on February 25, 1804, and attracted 108 of the party's senators and representatives. President Jefferson was renominated by acclamation, but Vice President Burr, who had fallen out with his party, was not considered for a second term. On the first nominating roll call publicly reported in U.S. political history, New York governor George Clinton was chosen by the caucus to run for vice president. He received sixty-seven votes and easily defeated Sen. John Breckinridge of Kentucky, who collected twenty votes. To "avoid unpleasant discussions" no names were placed in nomination, and the vote was taken by written ballot.

Before adjourning, the caucus appointed a thirteen-member committee to conduct the campaign and promote the success of Democratic-Republican candidates. A forerunner of party national committees, the new campaign group included members of both the House and Senate, but with no two persons from the same state. Since the Twelfth Amendment had not yet been passed when the caucus met, the committee was designed to "manage" the vote of Democratic-Republican electors to make sure that the events of 1800 were not repeated. In fact, that precaution was not necessary since the Twelfth Amendment was ratified in September—well before the electors voted.

By 1804, the Federalist party had deteriorated badly. The new era of dominance by the Virginia-led Democratic-Republicans had begun. The Federalists did not even hold a congressional caucus to select their nominees. Instead, Federalist leaders in 1804 informally chose Charles Cotesworth Pinckney for president and Rufus King of New York for vice president. The exact details of how Federalists formulated this ticket are not clear. There is no record in 1804 of any formal meeting to nominate Federalist candidates.

The Federalists mounted a disorganized and dispirited national campaign. Despite concerted efforts to win at least the votes of New England, the Federalists failed miserably. Pinckney received only 14 electoral votes—those of Connecticut and Delaware, plus 2 from Maryland. Jefferson, the Democratic-Republican candidate, was the overwhelming victor with 162 electoral votes.

Madison's 1808 Victory

President Jefferson refused to seek a third term of office, and the authority of the Democratic-Republican congressional caucus to choose a candidate to succeed Jefferson was put to a test. The caucus met on January 23, 1808. For the first time a formal call was issued. Sen. Stephen R. Bradley of Vermont, chairman of the 1804 caucus, issued the call to all 146 Democratic-Republicans in Congress and several Federalists sympathetic to the Democratic-Republican cause. Several party leaders questioned Bradley's authority to call the caucus, but various reports indicate that eighty-nine to ninety-four members of Congress attended.

As in 1804 the balloting was done without the formal placing of names in nomination. For president, Jefferson's handpicked successor, Secretary of State James Madison, was the easy winner with eighty-three votes. Despite earlier support for James Monroe among Democratic-Republicans in Virginia, and Vice President Clinton's own desire to be president, each received only three votes at the caucus. For vice president, the caucus overwhelmingly renominated

Clinton. He received seventy-nine votes, while runner-up John Langdon of New Hampshire collected five.

The Democratic-Republican caucus also repeated its practice of appointing a committee to conduct the campaign. Membership was expanded to fifteen House and Senate members, and it was formally called the "committee of correspondence and arrangement." The committee was authorized to fill any vacancies on the national ticket, should any occur. Before the caucus adjourned, it passed a resolution defending the caucus system as "the most practicable mode of consulting and respecting the interest and wishes of all." Later caucuses adopted similar resolutions throughout the history of the system.

Still, there were divisions among Democratic-Republicans. Forty percent of the Democratic-Republican members of Congress refused to attend the nominating caucus. Monroe refused to withdraw from the presidential race even after being defeated at the caucus. Even Clinton, although he was nominated for vice president, was angry at not being nominated for president. Clinton publicly denounced the caucus, as did Monroe's supporters. Pro-Clinton newspapers in New York launched harsh attacks on Madison and even suggested a Clinton-Monroe ticket. Some Clinton supporters went so far as to hope that Federalists would nominate Clinton for president later in the year. Such a thought was unpalatable to the Federalists, who ultimately nominated Charles Cotesworth Pinckney.

The Federalists chose their ticket at a secret meeting of party leaders in New York City in August 1808. The meeting was initially called by the Federalist members of the Massachusetts legislature. Twenty-five to thirty party leaders from seven states, all north of the Potomac River except South Carolina, attended the national meeting. Despite the suggestion from Massachusetts representatives that Clinton be nominated, the gathering decided to run the same ticket they had chosen in 1804—Pinckney and King.

Federalists did not actively publicize their ticket. The party itself was divided and devoid of leadership. Many Virginia Federalists formally endorsed Monroe, even though he was a Democratic-Republican. Others preferred to align themselves with Clinton. In the end, Madison achieved a wide margin of victory with 122 electoral votes. For the sake of future party unity, Democratic-Republicans retained Clinton as their vice-presidential nominee even though he had tried to subvert Madison's candidacy. Clinton received 113 electoral votes for vice president, thus winning that office; he received six electoral votes from New York for president. Pinckney came in second for president with 47 electoral votes. Monroe received no electoral votes.

Madison's Reelection: 1812

The Democratic-Republican party held its quadrennial nominating caucus on May 18, 1812. Only 83 of the 178 Democratic-Republicans in Congress participated. New England and New York delegations in particular were poorly represented. Many of the New Yorkers supported the candidacy of their state's lieutenant governor, De Witt Clinton (George Clinton's nephew), who also was maneuvering for the Federalist nomination. New England was noticeably upset with Madison's foreign policy, which was leading to war with England. Others did not attend the caucus because they opposed the system in principle.

Madison was renominated by a near-unanimous vote of the caucus, receiving eighty-two votes. John Langdon of New Hampshire was chosen for vice president by a wide margin, collecting sixty-four votes to sixteen for Gov. Elbridge Gerry of Massachusetts. But Langdon declined the nomination, citing his age (seventy) as the reason. As a result, the Democratic-Republicans held a second caucus on June 8 to select another vice-presidential candidate. Gerry was the clear winner with seventy-four votes. He responded with a formal letter of acceptance. Ten members of Congress who had not been present at the first caucus also took the opportunity to endorse the presidential candidacy of Madison.

Democratic-Republicans from New York were unwilling to accept the choice of Madison. They therefore held their own caucus, consisting of nearly all of the ninety-five Democratic-Republicans in the New York state legislature. They unanimously nominated Clinton, who issued an written "Address" that was a precursor to party platforms. Later, Clinton also was nominated by the Federalists. As they had four years earlier, Federalists convened a three-day secret meeting in New York City. The September meeting was more than twice the size of the 1808 gathering, with seventy representatives from eleven states attending. Delegates were sent to the conference by Federalist general committees, with all but nine of the delegates coming from the New England and Middle Atlantic states.

Debate centered on whether to run a separate Federalist ticket or to endorse the candidacy of Clinton. After much debate, they decided to endorse Clinton. They nominated Jared Ingersoll of Pennsylvania as vice president. Originally, the caucus's decision was meant to be kept a secret, but leaks eventually were reported by Democratic-Republican newspapers.

The United States had declared war on England in June, making the presidential election of 1812 the first wartime election. Federalists aligned themselves with the cause of peace and unimpeded commerce. In some northern states, the Federalists even adopted the Peace party label. Still, Clinton lost with 89 electoral votes to Madison's 128. That vote reflected the growing split between southern agricultural states, which supported Madison, and northern commercial states, which supported Clinton. Indeed, the common bond that held the Clinton coalition together was a hatred of Virginia—the kingmaker of the Democratic-Republican party.

Monroe's 1816 Victory

The Federalist party was nearly extinct by 1816. Rufus King had tried to win the governorship of New York and thus revive the party, but he was defeated in April 1816. Afterwards, he said it was a "fruitless struggle" to maintain the party. Despite efforts by Federalists in Philadelphia to convene another secret meeting to nominate candidates for president and vice president, the party did not hold any type of meeting for such purposes. With the Federalists not running candidates, nomination by the Democratic-Republican caucus was tantamount to election.

Despite his opposition to Madison in 1808, Monroe had been accepted back into the Democratic-Republican fold in the years that followed. In 1811, Madison named him secretary of state. By 1816, he was Madison's heir apparent, but many states were increasingly jealous of the Virginia dynasty that had held a grip on the presidency since 1804. Democratic-Republicans in such states opposed Monroe (himself a Virginian) and favored Secretary of War William H. Crawford of Georgia.

A Democratic-Republican caucus met in the House chamber on March 12, 1816, but only 58 members of Congress—mostly Crawford supporters—attended. With the expectation of better attendance, a second caucus was held on March 16. It drew 119 of the 141 Democratic-Republicans in Congress. There, Monroe narrowly defeated Crawford by a vote of 65-54. Forty of Crawford's votes came from five states: Georgia, Kentucky, New Jersey, New York, and North Carolina. The vice-presidential nomination went to New York governor Daniel D. Tompkins, who easily outdistanced Pennsylvania governor Simon Snyder, 85-30.

The nominations of Monroe and Tompkins revived a Virginia-New York alliance that extended back to the late eighteenth century. With the lone exception of 1812, every Democratic-Republican ticket from 1800 to 1824 was composed of a presidential candidate from Virginia and a vice-presidential candidate from New York.

With the Federalist party in disarray, the Democratic-Republican ticket won easily. Monroe received 183 electoral votes. Three states—Connecticut, Delaware, and Massachusetts—chose Federalist electors, who cast their 34 electoral votes for Rufus King.

Although the collapse of the Federalists ensured Democratic-Republican rule, it also increased intraparty friction and spurred further attacks on the caucus system. Twenty-two Democratic-Republican members of Congress were absent from the second party caucus, and at least fifteen were known to be opposed to the system. Historian Edward Stanwood wrote that there were mass meetings around the country to protest the caucus system.[5] Opponents asserted that the writers of the Constitution did not envision the caucus, that presidential nominating should not be a function of Congress, and that the caucus system encouraged candidates to curry the favor of Congress.

Monroe's Reelection: 1820

The 1820 election came during the "Era of Good Feelings," a phrase coined by a Boston publication, the *Columbian Centinel*, to describe a brief period of virtual one-party rule in the United States. Yet, that phrase glosses over serious sectional divisions that were growing during Monroe's presidency. Indeed, sectional strife was on the brink of explosion during Monroe's first term over the admission of Missouri as a new state. Tensions had grown in recent years between northern and southern states. In the Senate a tenuous balance existed between the two regions, with eleven free states and eleven slave states. The admission of Missouri threatened that balance. The two sides finally agreed to a compromise in which both Missouri and Maine would apply for statehood at the same time. Maine would apply as a free state and Missouri as a slave state. Monroe remained neutral in the debate leading up to the compromise. Despite a financial panic in 1819, he retained overwhelming popular support, bolstered by peace and a wave of nationalistic feeling that overshadowed any partisan divisions.

Although several rival Democratic-Republican candidates aspired to win the presidency when Monroe retired in 1824, none wanted to challenge his reelection in 1820. A nominating caucus was called for early March, but fewer than forty members of Congress showed up. The caucus voted unanimously to make no nominations and passed a resolution explaining that it was inexpedient to do so. Although Monroe and Tompkins were not formally renominated, electoral slates were filed on their behalf.

Because the Federalist party was dead, Monroe ran virtually unopposed. Even John Adams, the last Federalist president, voted for Monroe as an elector from Massachusetts. Only one elector, a Democratic-Republican from New Hampshire, cast a vote against Monroe, supporting instead the young John Quincy Adams, son of the former president.

Last of the Old Order: 1824

With virtual one-party rule in 1820, nomination by the Democratic-Republicans' King Caucus had all but ensured election. There was still only one party in 1824, but within that party an abundance of candidates were vying for the presidency: Secretary of State John Quincy Adams of Massachusetts, Sen. Andrew Jackson of Tennessee, Secretary of War John C. Calhoun of South Carolina, House Speaker Henry Clay of Kentucky, and Secretary of the Treasury William H. Crawford. The number of candidates, coupled with the growing democratization of the U.S. political system, led to the demise of King Caucus in 1824. As McCormick has written, the events of 1824 led to the rise of an interim period of factionalism that characterized the next phase in the evolution of the presidential selection process.

Early on, Crawford was the leading candidate. He had strong southern support and appeared likely to win the support of New York Democratic-Republicans. Since it was assumed that he would win a caucus if one were held, Crawford's opponents joined the growing list of caucus opponents. But Crawford's apparent invincibility suddenly ended in September 1823 when he suffered a paralytic stroke. Nearly blind and unable even to sign his name, he was incapacitated and kept in seclusion for months.

In early February 1824, 11 Democratic-Republican members of Congress issued a call for a caucus to be held in the middle of the month. Their call was countered by 24 other members of Congress from fifteen states who deemed it "inexpedient under existing circumstances" to hold a caucus. They claimed that 181 members of Congress were resolved not to attend if a caucus were held.

The caucus did convene in mid-February, but only 66 members of Congress were present. Three-quarters of those attending came from just four states—Georgia, New York, North Carolina, and Virginia. Despite his illness, Crawford won the caucus nomination with sixty-four votes. Albert Gallatin of Pennsylvania was selected for vice president with fifty-seven votes. The caucus adopted a resolution defending its actions as "the best means of collecting and concentrating the feelings and wishes of the people of the Union upon this important subject." The caucus also appointed a committee to write an address to the people. As written, the text of the address viewed with alarm the "dismemberment" of the Democratic-Republican party.

In fact, the action of the caucus actually led to the further dismemberment of the party. Since so few members of Congress—almost all of them Crawford supporters—attended the caucus, opponents could argue that the choice was not representative even of the Democratic-Republican voice in Congress, much less "the people of the Union." As a result, Crawford was roundly criticized as being an illegitimate candidate. His opponents derided King Caucus, and Crawford's physical condition made it even easier for them to reject his nomination. As it stood, other candidates simply refused to follow the caucus's decision. Never again were candidates chosen by the caucus system.

With the caucus devoid of power and the party lacking unity or leadership, there was no chance of rallying behind a single ticket. In addition, many political issues proved to be divisive. Western expansion and protective tariffs, for example, benefited some parts of the country but hurt others. Thus, the various candidates came to represent sectional interests.

The candidates themselves recognized that such a crowded field was dangerous. The election would be thrown to the House of Representatives if no candidate received a majority. The candidates therefore made efforts to join forces. Adams tried to lure Jackson as his running mate. Adams was a short, stocky, aloof, well-educated New Englander who came from a family of Federalists, while Jackson was a tall, thin, hot-tempered war hero with little education who came to epitomize a new brand of populist democracy. In trying to lure Jackson onto their team, Adams supporters envisaged a ticket of "the writer and the fighter," but Jackson would have nothing of it.

In the meantime, Crawford dropped Gallatin as his vice-presidential running mate. His supporters then tried to get Clay to drop his own quest for the presidency and join the Crawford team. They hinted that Crawford's physical condition was such that he would probably not finish out a term of office if elected (in fact, he lived ten more years). But Clay was not swayed. Instead, Calhoun dropped his race for the presidency and joined efforts with Crawford.

Still, four candidates remained in the field and each collected electoral votes. None, however, received a majority. Jackson received the most with ninety-nine, followed by Adams with eighty-four, Crawford with forty-one, and Clay with thirty-seven. Thus, the election was thrown to the House of Representatives.

In accordance with the Twelfth Amendment, the names of the top three candidates—Jackson, Adams, and Crawford—were placed before the House. Clay, who had come in fourth place and was Speaker of the House, would play a major role in tipping the balance in favor of one of the candidates. In contrast to Jackson, Adams actively lobbied for support, and Washington rocked with rumors of corruption. Clay informed Adams in January that he would support Adams in the House election—a major blow to Jackson. Shortly thereafter, a letter in a Philadelphia newspaper alleged that Adams had offered Clay the post of secretary of state in return for his support. Adams went on to win the House election narrowly. Each state delegation had one vote, and Adams won the vote of thirteen out of twenty-four states. Jackson came in second with seven, and Crawford third with the remaining four. *(See "When the Electoral College Is Deadlocked," p. 256, in this chapter.)* Thus, the candidate who won the most electoral votes and the most popular votes did not win the presidency.

Jackson was furious at what he considered unfair bargaining between Adams and Clay. He felt that the will of the people had been thwarted, and he seethed when President Adams proceeded to name Clay secretary of state as rumor had indicated he would. The events of 1824 kindled the flame of popular democracy. The stage was set for a rematch between Adams and Jackson in 1828.

The Age of Jackson

Andrew Jackson was in many ways the perfect man to usher in an age of popular politics, although his rhetoric was more populist than his true style of governing. The textbook version of U.S. history depicts Jackson as a coarse man of the frontier, a war hero, a battler of banks and moneyed interests, and a leader of the unschooled and exploited men who built a mass party on patronage and charismatic leadership. Jackson was the first politician to break the Virginia dynasty that had governed the country since the Revolution. After his bitter defeat in the 1824 election, Jackson fought back and grabbed the reins of government in a turbulent election in 1828. These two elections signaled the passing of elite politics and the rise of popular politics. In 1828 Jackson roused the people to turn Adams and his aristocratic clique out of office.

But the Jacksonian folklore has serious flaws. Jackson traveled in elite business circles, for example, and one of his greatest contributions as president was the creation of a more rationally organized bureaucracy.[6] Still, the textbook depiction suffices to show some trends in U.S. politics, including the development of a stable mass party system, sectionalism, urbanization, and shifts in the debate about U.S. expansionism.

As President Adams struggled with the factions and turf battles in Washington, an opposition force gathered strength. The opposition was able to deal the president a number of humiliating defeats. Adams's desire for a national program of roads and canals, education, and research in the arts and sciences antagonized even the most nationalistic groups in the country. U.S. participation in a conference of countries from the Western Hemisphere and the imposition of a tariff (a tax on imported goods designed either to raise revenues and to protect domestic industries from foreign competition) were also divisive issues. But even though Adams was under constant personal attack, the opposition was divided on the same issues. The opposition was united, however, behind Old Hickory.[7]

Jackson, the Battle of New Orleans hero in the War of 1812, had a strong appeal to the common man even though he traveled in the circles of southern gentlemen. People who met with Jackson talked of his unerring "intuition." Jackson's decision to push for reforms of the punishment of debtors was an important gesture to small businessmen and workers who were held to a kind of indentured servitude. Martin Van Buren said the people "were his blood relations—the only blood relations he had."[8]

Jackson's 1828 Victory

Jackson and his running mate, John C. Calhoun, easily beat Adams in their 1828 rematch; Jackson won 178 electoral votes, and Adams won 83. (Calhoun also had been vice president under John Quincy Adams.) Of the popular vote, Jackson received 643,000 votes (56.0 percent) to Adams's 501,000 (43.6 percent). Sectional splits showed in the vote distribution. Adams held all but 1 of New England's electoral votes, all of Delaware's and New Jersey's, 16 of New York's 36 votes, and 6 of Maryland's 11 votes. Jackson took all the rest—the South and the West. The election was decided by the thousands of votes from newly enfranchised voters in the burgeoning regions of the country. The U.S. electorate was expanding not only in the West but also in the original states. Voter participation grew from 3.8 percent to 16.7 percent of the total popula-

GENERAL JACKSON SLAYING THE MANY HEADED MONSTER.

Library of Congress

This 1836 cartoon depicts Jackson attacking the Bank of the United States with his veto stick. Vice President Van Buren, center, helps kill the monster, whose heads represent Nicholas Biddle, president of the bank, and directors of the state branches.

tion between 1824 and 1856.[9]

Jackson had only begun to exert his electoral influence with his revenge victory over Adams. The expanded pool of politically involved citizens that brought Jackson victory also brought him demands for patronage jobs with the federal government. Van Buren, a master machine politician from New York State, tutored the beleaguered new president on dealing with the office seekers. Jackson replaced fewer than one-fifth of the government's employees, which he defended as a perfectly reasonable "rotation in office" that would keep the ranks of the bureaucracy fresh. But the effect of his system was greater. Appointees of previous administrations were able to retain their jobs only when they expressed loyalty to Jackson and his party. Far more important than any government turnover, Jackson's spoils system inaugurated an age in which mass party loyalty was a paramount concern in politics.

The central element of the Jacksonian program was expansion. Much as twentieth-century politicians would talk about economic growth as the key to opportunity, Jackson maintained that movement West "enlarg[ed] the area of freedom."[10] The administration fought to decentralize the management of expansion. Jackson railed against the "corrupt bargain" between the government and banks, joint-stock companies, and monopolies, which, he said, were squeezing out the average person seeking opportunity. Jackson opposed the Bank of the United States and promoted state banks because of his desire to free finance capital from central control.

The increased importance of loyalty, to the president and to the party, became clear with Jackson's dispute with Vice President Calhoun and the subsequent purging of the cabinet. A growing feud between Jackson and Calhoun came to a head when a personal letter by Calhoun became public. The letter criticized Jackson's conduct of the Seminole Indian campaign and the 1818 invasion of Florida. In a letter to Calhoun during the crisis, Jackson wrote: "Et tu, Brute." A purge of Calhoun men in the cabinet followed the incident. Secretary of State Van Buren enabled the president to make the purge when he and Secretary of War John Eaton, both Jackson allies, resigned their posts; the president then called on the whole cabinet to quit.

Jackson's political strength was further underscored with the introduction of a quintessentially party-oriented institution: the national party convention. *(See "The Development of Party Conventions," p. 164, in this chapter.)* Jacksonians from New Hampshire proposed the Democratic convention of 1832, and the president and his advisers jumped at the opportunity. The only previous national convention had been held by the Anti-Masonic party in 1831. Conventions had been the principal means of selecting candidates for local offices since the early part of the century. Especially compared with the caucus system that preceded it, the convention system was a democratic leap forward.

The convention system enabled the parties to gather partisans from all geographic areas, and it welded them together as a cohesive unit that ultimately was accountable to the electorate, if only in a plebiscitary way. Voters had the opportunity to give approval or disapproval to a party program with one vote. Historian Eugene H. Roseboom has written: "It was representative in character; it divorced nominations from congressional control and added to the independence of the executive; it permitted an authoritative formulation of a party program; and it concentrated the party's strength behind a single ticket, the product of compromise of personal rivalries and group or sectional interests."[11]

Jackson's presidency was activist from the beginning. The president in his first term carried on a long-running battle with Nicholas Biddle, the head of the Bank of the United States, and with Congress over the status of the bank. Alexander Hamilton created the bank to manage the nation's monetary policy and investment but Jackson opposed it as a tool of the eastern financial establishment. Jackson failed to close the bank but neutered it when he placed its deposits in a number of regional institutions.

The Jackson administration also negotiated treaties with France, the Ottoman Empire, Russia, and Mexico. Jackson established a distinctive system of federalism when he vetoed a number of public improvements bills as unconstitutional infringements of local affairs. Jackson also called for a tariff that would yield revenues for dispersal to the states for their own public projects—an early form of "revenue sharing." Jackson signed the Indian Removal Act of 1830, which provided for settlement of the territory west of the Mississippi River. Late in his first term, Jackson's strong stand defeated the South Carolina legislature's claim to "nullify," or declare "null and void," federal tariff legislation that the state disliked.

Jackson's 1832 Victory

There was never any doubt that Jackson would be renominated in 1832; in fact, several state legislatures endorsed him before the convention. The purpose of the convention was to rally behind the president and select a new vice-presidential candidate. Van Buren got the nomination, despite lingering resistance from Calhoun supporters and various "favorite sons" (prominent state and local figures).

Jackson's opposition was fragmented as usual. The Whigs—the opposition party that developed from grassroots protests in the North and West against Jackson's tariff and development policies—met in convention in Baltimore in December 1831, and unanimously nominated Henry Clay of Kentucky. Eighteen states used a variety of selection procedures to determine who would be their convention delegates. The party's platform sharply criticized the administration's patronage practices, relations with Great Britain, criticism of Supreme Court decisions, and ill-tempered congressional relations.

The incumbent easily dispatched the opposition in 1832. "The news from the voting states blows over us like a great cold storm," wrote Rufus Choate, a prominent lawyer, to a friend.[12] Despite last-minute maneuvering to unite the opposition to Jackson and a well-financed campaign by the National Bank, the president won 219 electoral votes to Clay's 49, Independent John Floyd's 11, and Anti-Mason William Wirt's 7. Jackson won all but seven states. Clay won Kentucky, Massachusetts, Rhode Island, Connecticut, and Delaware, plus five electors from Maryland. Jackson won 702,000 popular votes to Clay's 484,000 and Wirt's 101,000.[13]

Before Jackson finally left the political stage in 1837, he had changed the face of U.S. politics. Even if his pretensions to being an everyman were overstated, he did open up the system to mass participation and force politicians to listen to popular demands. He developed the notion of a strong party organization. He fought, and eventually defeated, the National Bank by withdrawing its funds and placing them in state banks. He strongly opposed two forces that could have torn the nation apart—the nullification principle of state sovereignty and the Supreme Court's bid for broader discretion over political issues—by simply proclaiming the law to be "unauthorized by the Constitution" and "therefore null and void."

Van Buren's 1836 Win

Many historians consider the election of 1836 to be the most important event in the development of the party system. Van Buren, a Democratic follower of Jackson and a theorist on the role of political parties in a democratic system, easily won the election over an uncoordinated Whig party. The defeat eventually convinced Whig leaders of the need for a permanent organization for political competition. The emergence of two permanent parties extinguished the American suspicion of the morality of a party system based upon unabashed competition for the levers of power.

Van Buren, who had allied with Jackson during the cabinet controversies and promoted his philosophy of parties and patronage, received the Democratic nomination in 1836 at a convention packed with Jackson administration appointees. The vice-presidential nomination of Richard M. Johnson of Kentucky, whose past relationship with a mulatto woman caused controversy, damaged the ticket in the South, but the Democrats won anyway.

The Whigs' campaign strategy was to run several favorite sons to prevent any candidate from getting a majority of the electoral votes, thereby throwing the election into the House of Representatives. As one Whig put the matter: "The disease [Democratic rule] is to be treated as a local disorder—apply local remedies."[14] The Whig expectation was that Gen. William Henry Harrison of Ohio or Hugh Lawson White of Tennessee would be selected by the House after the electoral college vote proved inconclusive.

Van Buren, however, had Jackson's machine and his personal backing and was able to overcome the Whigs' local strategy. In the last race for the White House before presidential elections became dominated by two national parties, Van Buren took 170 electoral votes—22 more than he needed for election. Of the Whig candidates, Harrison received 73 electoral votes; White 26; and Daniel Webster of Massachusetts, 14. Willie Mangum, an Independent Democrat from North Carolina, received 11 electoral votes from the South Carolina legislature, which was hostile to White because of his role in nullification politics. Van Buren won 764,000 popular votes (50.8 percent); Harrison, 551,000 (36.6 percent); White, 146,000 (9.7 percent); and Webster, 41,000 (2.7 percent). For the only time in history, the Senate selected the vice president, Richard M. Johnson, who fell one vote shy of election by the electoral college and defeated Francis Granger by a 33-16 Senate vote.

Van Buren was besieged practically from the minute he took the oath of office in March 1837. The economy crashed after years of feverish business growth, overspeculation in land and business, huge private debt accumulation, and unregulated financial and trade practices. Van Buren's approach to the economic crisis was either stubborn refusal to fix a mess that he had not created or action that was guaranteed to antagonize key interest groups.

When Van Buren moved to create an independent treasury to give the federal government insulation from state financial institutions, he was opposed by conservative Democrats who were supporters of the state financial institutions that Jackson had promoted in his legendary National Bank battles. When Van Buren was not hit from the right, he was hit from the left. The nascent labor movement called for protection of jobs and wages and made protests against monopoly and privilege.

The Idea of a Party System

Whatever problems Van Buren had in governing, he can receive credit at least for helping to establish the principle of party government in the United States. That principle—much derided in the early days of the nation's history—has come to enjoy unquestioned allegiance in the United States.

Van Buren's arguments on behalf of a party system—contained in his 1867 book, *An Inquiry into the Origin and Course of Political Parties in the United States*—are similar to the economic principle of Adam Smith that the pursuit of selfish ends redounds to the good of the entire community. American leaders from George Washington through John Quincy Adams had stated that self-interested factions endangered the functioning and virtue of the Republic. These leaders also warned against the dangers of democracy, which they often called "mob rule." The worst of all possible scenarios pictured permanent parties with strong ideological stances appealing to the mass public for support. Most of the Framers feared that democratic institutions would undermine the ability of national leaders to guide public virtue.[15]

The basic tension that Van Buren had to resolve was the system's need for stability and responsible leadership and the party system's imperative to gain office. How could a party's selfish desire to run the government and award patronage and contracts to political allies benefit the whole system?

Van Buren argued that the absence of parties—collections of people from disparate backgrounds—resulted in a system of personal politics that fueled demagogy, perpetual campaigns, and a lack of accountability. Personal presidential politics was more polarizing than the politics of consensus or of coalition building. Presidents should be able to do their job without constant carping from outsiders who fancy themselves to be prospective presidents. Mass parties with certain partisan principles would enable presidents to get the backing they needed to do their work.

The existence of two parties would enable the nation to move beyond its many cleavages—toward the general interest and away from simple clashes of particular interests. Competition among parties, like competition among economic enterprises, would bring about a situation in which disparate demands are promoted by a party. The key is to achieve a balance of competing forces. Political scientist James W. Ceaser has written:

> Established parties . . . may stand 'over' the raw electoral cleavages, possessing some leeway or discretion about which potential issues and electoral divisions will be emphasized and which will be suppressed or kept at the fringes. This discretion is exercised according to the interests of the organizations and the judgement of their leaders. But it is important to keep in mind that the degree of this discretion is limited. . . . Their discretion is always threatened or held in check by the possibility that they might be displaced by a new party having as its goal the advancement of a certain policy. . . . When a sufficiently powerful and enduring issue exists, an impartial reading of American party history suggests that the party system in the end will have to respond to it, regardless of how the established parties initially react.[16]

The Age of Jackson brought a fundamental shift from republican to democratic values as the nation's territory and activities expanded. Republicanism was the product of a variety of strains of thought—from the Romans Cicero and Tacitus and the Greek Polybius to the Frenchman Montesquieu—that stressed the need for a balancing of interests to produce public virtue. Republicans worried about excess in any single form of governance. Of particular concern was "mob rule"—the excess of democracy. *Democracy* was a term of derision. The Constitution contained many buffers against this and other forms of excess.

Republicanism declined in many stages. A greater stress on the individual's role in society, embodied in the work of Adam Smith and David Hume, reduced the sphere open to public pursuits.

The pace of economic change undermined established patterns. As the nation demanded large-scale projects, and as rival factions looked to the mobilization of larger and larger parts of the electorate to augment their strength, democratic rhetoric gained respectability. Mass party participation became a vehicle for pursuing civic virtue and balance. The notion of a constant opposition party gained strength. If the democratic process had enough "checks," political thinkers now reasoned, the harmful "mob" aspects of democracy could be tempered. The development of the Jacksonian party as a way of arbitrating interests was the final stage in republican decline and democratic ascendance.

Political scientist Russell Hanson has noted that the new democratic ethos sprang from one of the same goals as the old republican ethos: development of a public spirit by rising above particular restraints. "Support for popular sovereignty became the lowest common denominator for a Democratic Party composed of interests seeking liberation from a variety of sectionally specific restraints on the 'will of the people.' "[17]

A two-party system persisted as the nation drifted toward civil war, but it was not a simple two-party system. The Democrats and Whigs competed for the presidency and other political offices until 1856, when the Republican party fielded its first national ticket and made the Whigs obsolete. But the parties were so unstable that their many elements were constantly forming and breaking up coalitions—and threatening to bolt from the system itself. A series of third parties entered the national electoral arena for short periods, applying or relieving pressures on the two major parties.[18]

Only by examining the parties and their various factions and struggles can one understand the presidential contests in the years before the Civil War, and the way that the Civil War revealed the basic fault lines of U.S. politics.

The Whigs' 1840 Victory

The Whigs developed to fill the role of their British namesake, which had been to mount a republican opposition to the royal ruling power. The rise of Andrew Jackson and his supposedly imperial presidency threatened the "balance" of the United States, and the Whigs rose to restore that balance. The Whigs saw Jackson's Democrats as a faction of the most dangerous variety—a majority faction that had the ability to trample liberties in its mad scramble for spoils.

The key to Whiggery was the notion of balanced development. The Whigs opposed the war with Mexico and other expansionist programs because they feared the perils of overextending the nation's abilities and getting entangled with foreign powers. The Whigs favored internal improvements, but only as a way of maintaining balance and staving off the corruption of the Jackson era. The protective tariff was central to the Whigs' program of internal development and protection from outsiders. Political scientist Russell Hanson has described the Whig philosophy:

> Even in America, which was uniquely blessed by an abundance of natural resources and a citizenry of hardy stock, there was need for informed guidance and direction of progress. For the Whigs, government was the primary agent of this progress. Government represented a strong and positive force to be used in calling forth a richer society from the unsettled possibilities of America. In the economic realm this meant that government was responsible for providing the essential conditions for a sound economy, namely, a reliable currency, ample credit, and the impetus for internal improvements. And in the social realm, the government was responsible for promoting virtue in its citizenry through education and exhortation.[19]

The Whig desire for balance and compromise was intended to give the party a national rather than a sectional identity. A series of Senate battles with President Jackson, especially the tariff battles of 1833, which resulted in an unsatisfying compromise, gave impetus to grass-roots organizations in the North and West and to southern Democratic opponents. The tendency of the Whigs to nominate widely popular military heroes helped create at least the illusion of a party of national dimensions. The Whigs developed first in the South where voters were dissatisfied with Jackson's selection of Van Buren as his running mate. Loose coalitions elected candidates in the 1834 and 1835 state and congressional elections in the South. Westerners also organized to oppose the Democratic party that was headed by a New Yorker.

The first serious Whig presidential contest was a loss, but an encouraging one. In 1836, the Whig ticket headed by Harrison showed surprising appeal in the loss to the Democrat Van Buren. The Whig strategy was to run a number of favorite sons and produce inconclusive results in the electoral college, sending the contest to the House of Representatives for resolution. The Whigs won Jackson's home state of Tennessee and the neighboring Georgia, as well as three border slave states, and were strong competitors elsewhere. Harrison carried the old Northwest (now the Midwest) and came close in northern states like Pennsylvania.

Because of the rise of the antislavery "conscience Whigs," the Whigs eventually moved to a completely different base of support—the North rather than the South and West—but their early organizing at least broke the Democratic stranglehold on the latter two regions. The Whigs nominated Harrison in 1840 after a nomination struggle with Clay. A Clay supporter, John Tyler of Virginia, was the vice-presidential nominee. This time, the popular if politically inexperienced hero of the War of 1812 won his ticket to the White House. Harrison defeated the incumbent Van Buren in an electoral vote landslide, receiving 234 of the 294 electoral votes—all the states except Alabama, Arkansas, Illinois, Missouri, New Hampshire, South Carolina, and Virginia. Harrison won 1.3 million popular votes (52.9 percent) to Van Buren's 1.1 million (46.8 percent).

According to Richard P. McCormick:

> The campaign of 1840 brought the American party system at last to fruition. In every region of the country, and indeed in every state, politics was conducted within the framework of a two party system, and in all but a handful of states the parties were so closely balanced as to be competitive. In broad terms, it was the contest for the presidency that shaped this party system and defined its essential purpose.[20]

Harrison's campaign was as vague as his government experience was unimpressive. The image of Harrison as a sort of frontier everyman—which received its popular expression when a Baltimore newspaper mocked him as a sedentary man who would sit in a log cabin and drink cider rather than perform great deeds of leadership—was the theme of numerous parades and mass meetings. On issues from banking and currency to slavery, Harrison spoke in generalities. He did not have an opportunity to do much as president besides discipline the aggressive Clay. Clay assumed that he and the rest of the congressional leadership would play the leading role in the government, and Harrison wrote a quick note rebuking him. But one month after his inauguration, the sixty-eight-year-old Harrison, physically weakened by the pressures of office, developed pneumonia and died. On April 6, 1841, the burdens of the presidency fell upon Vice President John Tyler.

The rift between the White House and Congress widened under Tyler. Clay acted as if he were prime minister during a special session of Congress, pushing through a legislative program that included a recharter of the long-controversial National Bank, higher import taxes, and distribution of proceeds from land sales to the states. Tyler, a lifetime states' rights advocate, vetoed two bills for a national bank, and the Whigs in Congress and his own cabinet entered a bitter feud with the president. In 1842 Clay left the Senate to promote his presidential aspirations, and everyone in the cabinet except Secretary of State Daniel Webster quit. Tyler was all alone, but he did manage to defeat the Whig program in his four years as president.

Polk's Dark-Horse Victory in 1844

The Democrats were transformed into a well-organized mass by Andrew Jackson and Martin Van Buren between 1828 and 1836. But, like the Whigs, the Democratic party became vulnerable because of the irreconcilable difference among many of its parts.

From the beginning, the Democratic party had contained contradictory elements. According to Sundquist: "The party had been formed originally as an alliance between Southern planters and New Yorkers and had always spanned both regions. Northern men of abolitionist sympathies were accustomed to sitting with slaveholders in presidential cabinets and collaborating with them in the halls of Congress." [21] Northerners went so far as to organize anti-abolitionist rallies in their cities and towns, and newspapers and churches also defended slavery.

The deepest Democratic divisions—which eventually would lead to the failure not only of the party but also of the nation—were the regional differences based on slavery. Although slavery and the regional split it engendered were a constant and growing theme in U.S. politics, other, more complex divisions also affected the operation of the Democratic party. When the party was able to reconcile or even delay action on the divisive issues, it won. When the divisions burst into the open, the party was in trouble.

James K. Polk of Tennessee, the first "dark-horse" candidate in history, defeated the Whig Henry Clay in 1844 by supporting an expansionist program and winning the support of the solid South. One of the key issues in the campaign was whether Texas should be admitted to the Union and, if so, whether it should be slave or free. President Van Buren in 1840 opposed annexation—opposition that might have cost him the presidency—and the Democrats and Whigs hedged on the issue for the next eight years. In 1844, Polk endorsed the annexation of Texas as a slave state; that was enough for him to lock up the South.

During the 1844 nominating convention, the Democrats finessed the sectional dangers of the Texas issue by combining it with a call for occupying Oregon and for eventually bringing that state into the Union. The Democrats also appealed to Pennsylvania and the rest of the Northeast by supporting a high tariff. Both parties spoke out against the growing foreign elements in the cities, but the Whigs were more effective because of the Democrats' swelling immigrant ranks.

Polk defeated Clay, winning 1.34 million votes (49.5 percent) to Clay's 1.30 million (48.1 percent) and 170 electoral votes to Clay's 105. Clay received his strongest support from five northeastern states and five border slave states. Of the expansionist Northwest, only Ohio fell in the Clay column.

The Liberty party's abolitionist campaign may have been the deciding factor in the 1844 race. Although it received only 2.3 percent of the popular vote and no electoral votes, the Liberty party was strong enough in New York to prevent the Whigs from winning that state's crucial thirty-six electoral votes. Those votes went to the Democrat Polk rather than to the Whig Clay.

The depth of the Democrats' divisions were agonizingly evident even when the party won elections and started to pass out spoils and make policy. Like Harrison, the Whig who had won the presidency four years before, President Polk faced the antagonisms of party factions when he began making appointments after his 1844 win. Westerners were angry when they were shut out of the cabinet and Polk vetoed a rivers and harbors bill. Supporters of both Van Buren and John Calhoun were angry that their faction did not win more prominent positions. Northeasterners were upset at tariff cuts. The New York split between the reformist "Barnburners" and the party-regular "Hunkers"—who disagreed on every issue, including banks, currency, internal improvements, and political reforms—also disrupted the administration.

Creating still more dissension was the war with Mexico (1846-1848), fought because of the dispute over the Texas border and the possible annexation of California. Patronage was intensely controversial, and Northerners resented the country's fighting Mexico over a slave state. Among the war's more prominent opponents was Henry David Thoreau.

Whig Success under Taylor in 1848

In 1848 the Whigs recaptured the White House behind another military hero, Gen. Zachary Taylor, who was vague on most political issues. Taylor defeated the irrepressible Clay and Gen. Winfield Scott for the nomination on the fourth convention ballot. Clay mounted an impressive public campaign that drew large crowds, but the Whigs had lost too many times with Clay. The Whig ticket was headed by the Louisiana slave-owning Taylor, and his running mate was New Yorker Millard Fillmore.

The Whigs were so determined to avoid sectional and other issue splits that they not only nominated the popular Taylor but also eschewed writing a platform. Despite such extreme measures to maintain unity, the convention was disturbed by squabbles between pro- and antislavery forces on the question of the Wilmot Proviso, which would ban slavery in any territory obtained from Mexico.

Sen. Lewis Cass of Michigan defeated Sen. James Buchanan of Pennsylvania and Supreme Court Justice Levi Woodbury for the Democratic nomination, and Gen. William Butler was picked as his running mate. But the convention experienced splits between the New York factions of the Barnburners, who were part of the antislavery movement, and the Hunkers, who had ties to Southerners. The Barnburners defected from the party to become part of the Free Soil party. *(See "Third Parties," p. 248, in this chapter.)*

The Democrats behind Cass praised the administration of the beleaguered Polk, defended the war with Mexico, congratulated the French Republic that emerged from the wave of revolution in Europe, and did everything it could to avoid the nasty slavery issue. The nomination of Cass—a "doughface," or Northerner with Southern principles—was expected to appeal to both sides of the simmering issue.

Taylor defeated Cass, winning 1.4 million popular votes (47.3 percent) to Cass's 1.2 million (42.5 percent). New York Democrat Martin Van Buren, the former president, running on the Free Soil ticket, won 291,500 votes (10 percent) but no electoral votes. Taylor received 163 electoral votes to Cass's 127, with a strong showing in the North. Taylor won Connecticut, Massachusetts, New Jersey, New York, Pennsylvania, Rhode Island, and Vermont in the North; Delaware, Kentucky, Maryland, North Carolina, and Tennessee in the border states; and Florida, Georgia, and Louisiana in the Deep South. This combination was enough to beat Cass's coalition of seven slave states, six northwestern states, and two New England states.

On July 10, 1850, Fillmore succeeded to the presidency when President Taylor suddenly died. After consuming too many refreshments at a Fourth of July celebration, Taylor developed cramps, then a fatal illness, probably typhoid fever. Fillmore, however, was unable to secure the party nomination in 1852 despite an early lead in convention polling. General Scott won the nomination, and the Whigs entered into permanent decline.

Slavery Divides the Whigs

Try as they might with the selection of military heroes as candidates and vague issue statements, the Whigs could not cover over the nation's disagreements forever. When divisive issues burst into the open, the party was in trouble. The tariff issue and their mildly probusiness stance gave the Whigs strength in the North. But the Whigs, like the Democrats, needed to attract support also in the South; so they tried to keep the slavery question out of their rhetoric. The Whigs could count on being competitive in the border slave states, but not in the rest of Dixie. In 1844, Clay had won only the northern rim of slave states (Delaware, Kentucky, Maryland, North Carolina, and Tennessee).

As political scientist James L. Sundquist has noted, both the Whig and Democratic parties in the pre-Civil War era attempted to ignore the slavery issue, but the Whigs had less room to maneuver. The Democrats' agrarian and populist position gave them the solid South as a foundation, and they could make a variety of antiabolitionist appeals to the rest of the electorate. Democrats could argue that their support for slavery in the South was compatible with many "moderate" positions. The appeal of Stephen Douglas and Buchanan rested on such a coalition-building strategy. The Whigs, however, included vociferous opponents of slavery that could not be reconciled easily with "moderate" positions. Abolitionism had upper-class and religious roots that were difficult to use as a foundation. The support the Whigs were able to retain in the South was based on their positions on local issues. In sum, the Whigs did not have the same potential to build a national party organization as the Democrats.

Both parties contained slavery sympathizers and opponents; neither was willing to make a principled stand against the institution, particularly where it already existed. The parties were more competitive over issues such as westward expansion, banking questions, public improvements, the tariff, and foreign relations. It was up to third parties such as the Liberty and Free Soil parties to press the slavery issue. Sectional cleavages were so strong that Congress in 1836 passed a "gag rule" that forbade the reading of antislavery statements in Congress. Such attempts to silence abolitionist fervor were in vain, however, as politics were entering an age of mass communication and organization. The slavery issue would become irrepressible.

The beginning of the abolitionist movement, which may be dated to the founding of William Lloyd Garrison's newspaper, *The Liberator*, in 1831, posed problems for the Whigs that eventually proved fatal. The antislavery belt developed in the Whigs' strongest territory—New England—and westward into what today would be called the Midwest. Abolitionism was largely an upper- or middle-class and religious cause. But it also was a partisan issue: the Whigs, the party out of power for years, needed an issue with which to confront the Democrats. Slavery was a useful issue, even if the Whigs' antislavery stance in the North contradicted their accommodating stance in the South.

The slavery issue split the Whigs badly with the controversy over the admission of Texas to the Union in 1845. A splinter group of young party members calling themselves the "Conscience Whigs" argued for a straightforward statement of principle against slavery. An opposition group called the "Cotton Whigs" wanted to defuse the slavery issue by ignoring moral arguments and simply calling for a halt to annexation. The party split became complete with Clay's Compromise of 1850, which admitted California as a free state, ended slave trade in the District of Columbia, and admitted Texas but reduced its size by splitting off the New Mexico territory. After agitation from Conscience Whigs and General Scott's nomination in 1852, the party was irreparably rent by the slavery issue.

The Whigs attempted to make concessions to the South, but many of their efforts only antagonized Northern supporters. The 1852 Whig convention platform contained several statements supporting states' rights and the principles behind Clay's compromise.[22] Northern Whigs made these concessions to win Southern support for their presidential favorite, General Scott. When no Whigs voted for the Kansas-Nebraska Act in 1854, which permitted state determination of the slavery question, the Whigs' remaining ties to Dixie were severed.

The Whigs' strength in the Northwest was almost nonexistent. Only Ohio, in 1844, went for the Whigs even once over the course of the 1844, 1848, and 1852 presidential elections. Previously strong ties between the "lake region" and the South deteriorated as immigrants and others moved from the Northeast to the Northwest and, after the completion of railroad links, the two regions developed strong economic ties.

The Whigs' last gasp came in 1852, when Scott was demolished by Democrat Franklin Pierce. Pierce won all the states except two in New England (Massachussetts and Vermont) and two border states (Kentucky and Tennessee). Pierce won twenty-seven states and 254 electoral votes to Scott's four states and 42 electoral votes.

Whig divisions were most evident in 1856 as the Whigs split their votes among the Democrat Buchanan, the former Whig Fillmore, and the Republican John C. Fremont. Not all Whigs were ready yet to join the nascent Republican party, because of the extremism of some of the party's abolitionists. The majority of Whigs folded into the Republicans in 1860 when Abraham Lincoln avoided a white "backlash" by insisting that he supported slavery where it existed and opposed its spread only because of how it would affect the economic fortunes of poor Northern whites.

Slavery Divides the Democrats

The Democrats suffered a North-South cleavage that Lincoln exploited in the 1860 election against Stephen Douglas. Southern Democrats were intent on protecting slavery, and they felt that control of Congress was necessary to their strategy. Extension of slavery to the new states joining the Union was necessary to maintain congressional strength.

Northern Democrats were willing to allow Dixie to maintain its peculiar institution but were scared about their own electoral prospects if slavery should expand. Northern Democrats at first rallied to Douglas's doctrine of "popular sovereignty" (under which the people of new states could decide whether to adopt slavery), but they got nervous when Lincoln hammered away at his argument that any unchecked slavery threatened the freedom of whites as well as blacks. Lincoln argued that Democrats such as Douglas wanted to make slavery a nationwide, rather than a selective state-by-state, institution.

Lincoln planted seeds of doubt about partial solutions to the slavery question by asserting that slavery could extend to whites if it were nationalized: "If free negroes should be made *things,* how long, think you, before they will begin to make *things* out of poor white men?"[23] Lincoln also maintained that the extension of slavery into new territories would close off the territories for whites seeking upward mobility: "The whole nation is interested that the best use be made of these Territories. We want them for homes of free white people. This they cannot be, to any considerable extent, if slavery shall be planted within them."[24]

The growing movement against the extension of slavery was based on a concern for the upward mobility of labor. Rather than stressing the common interests of blacks and poor, Northern, white laborers, the antiextension movement followed Lincoln's lead in playing up the competition between the two groups. Horace Greeley's vision of the frontier as "the great regulator of the relations of Labor and Capital, the safety valve of our industrial and social engine"[25] left little room for the extension of slavery into the new territories. The extension of slavery was the issue that most divided the Democratic party.

Democrat Pierce's Victory

Clay's congressional compromise on slavery in the territories, known as the Compromise of 1850, turned out to be the major reason for the Democrats' 1852 victory. President Taylor stalled action for months and even suggested that California and New Mexico might become independent nations. But his successor, Fillmore, threw his support behind the compromise. The Whigs were divided on the proposal. The compromise addressed the slavery question in all of the new U.S. territories by making concessions to both sides of the struggle. For the North, California would be admitted as a free state, and the slave trade (but not slavery itself) would be abolished in the District of Columbia. For the South, fugitive slave laws would be strengthened, and the New Mexico territory would be divided into two states where popular sovereignty would decide the slave issue.

The compromise was designed to settle the issue of slavery in new territories once and for all. But the slavery issue could not be contained by region; it had an increasingly important "spillover" effect. Because of concerns for the congressional balance of power and the difficulties of enforcing slavery provisions such as the fugitive-slave law in states that opposed slavery, it was impossible to isolate the slavery question into particular regions as Clay intended.

General Scott won the Whig nomination in 1852 after platform concessions to the party's Southern delegation. Scott's appeal was always limited to the North, while Fillmore appealed to the South and Daniel Webster appealed to New England. Scott won on the fifty-third ballot.

Franklin Pierce of New Hampshire, a dark horse who gained fame with his Mexican War record, won the Democratic nomination in 1852. The vice-presidential candidate was Sen. William Rufus de Vane King of Alabama. The party held together a coalition of groups with contradictory positions on the slavery issue and regional affairs. The convention, meeting in Baltimore, pledged to "abide by, and adhere to" Clay's compromise and to do what it could to smother the slavery issue.

Attempts to inject issues of economics and foreign affairs into the election failed, and the campaign degenerated into squabbles over personalities. Pierce easily won with 1.6 million popular votes (50.4 percent) to Scott's 1.4 million (43.9 percent). Pierce had twenty-seven states and 254 electoral votes to Scott's four states and 42 electoral votes.

The Democrats' Bruising 1856 Victory

By 1856, the North-South split had eliminated the Whigs as a national party and fatally damaged the Democrats' chances for winning a national election for decades.

Congress opened the slavery issue by passing the Kansas-Nebraska Act of 1854. *(See map, The Kansas-Nebraska Act, 1854, p. 79.)* The act declared "null and void" the Missouri Compromise, which prohibited slavery in new territories north of the 36°30′ parallel except in Missouri. The 1854 legislation created two territories (Kansas and Nebraska) from the original Nebraska territory and left the slavery issue to be determined by popular sovereignty there and in the Utah and New Mexico territories.

The Kansas-Nebraska Act was a vehicle to spur the development of the West. Such development was part of a longstanding American approach to creating opportunity and freedom via growth. Sen. Stephen A. Douglas of Illinois—the promoter of the law and the main advocate of popular sovereignty—held that the law was necessary if the country was to be bound together by rail and telegraph lines and was to drive Great Britain off the continent. The latter goal was intertwined with a widely held suspicion that Britain was exploiting the slavery issue to distract American politics and stunt American growth.

Whatever the economic motives for unification, the Kansas-Nebraska Act was bitterly divisive. Northern state legislatures passed resolutions denouncing the law. The development of sectional parties continued.

A flood of new settlers into Kansas, and the terror-filled balloting over whether Kansas was to be a free or a slave state, further inflamed passions. Neighboring Missourians took part in the controversy, arguing that their status as slave owners would be undermined if Kansas voted to be free. Especially with the Supreme Court's infamous 1857 *Dred Scott* decision, which defined slaves as property, and the Lincoln-Douglas debates in Illinois in 1858, the slavery question was becoming decisive in American politics.

The Democrats won the White House in 1856 when the party endorsed the Kansas-Nebraska Act and nominated the pro-Southern James Buchanan as its presidential candidate. John Breckinridge of Kentucky, who later served in the Confederate Army, was Buchanan's running mate. The Democrats, who were becoming almost exclusively a Southern party, benefited from close wins in Buchanan's home state of Pennsylvania and in New Jersey, and in western states such as Illinois, Indiana, and California. But the only strong region for the Democrats was the South. Buchanan won all the slave states except Maryland. Overall, Buchanan won 1.8 million popular votes (45.3 percent) to Fremont's 1.3 million (33.1 percent). The electoral college gave Buchanan a 174-114 victory.

The nativist American party—or the "Know-Nothings," as they were called—nominated former Whig president Millard Fillmore, but the party was never able to move beyond an urban strength based on parochial resistance to immigration and Catholicism. Fillmore won only the state of Maryland; overall, he got 873,000 popular votes (21.5 percent) and 8 electoral votes. *(See "Third Parties," p. 248, in this chapter.)*

After an 1854 meeting in Ripon, Wisconsin, where a new national party was first proposed, the Republican party developed quickly. The Republicans had a strong grass-roots organization in the Northwest after the Kansas-Nebraska Act and attracted Whigs, Know-Nothings, and Northern Democrats who were troubled by the possible extension of slavery. Uncertainty about how the extension of slavery would affect laborers who sought opportunity in the territories also helped unite the new coalition.

The first GOP presidential convention met in Philadelphia in 1856 with delegates from all of the free states, four border states, three territories, and the District of Columbia. The party's opposition to slavery was far from unanimous, but its willingness to address rather than suppress the issue enabled it to redefine the political dialogue. Besides strong antislavery statements, the party platform contained proposals for several internal improvements

Mathew Brady; Bettmann Archive

Stephen Douglas, at 5′4″, was the 1864 Democratic candidate for president.

advantageous to the North. The party did not offer anything to the solidly Democratic South. To win a national election, it would have to sweep the North. Col. John Charles Fremont was named the Republicans' first presidential candidate. Former Whig senator William Dayton of New Jersey received the vice-presidential nomination.

In 1860, the Democratic split was complete when the party's Southern elements supported Vice President Breckinridge and Northerners backed Stephen Douglas. The Buchanan administration earlier had waged war on Douglas by ousting Douglas allies from the federal bureaucracy for opposing the administration's pro-Southern stance on the Kansas issue.

When the time came for the 1860 presidential campaign, the Democrats were hopelessly split over slavery. The biggest sticking point was the *Dred Scott* decison, which held that Congress had no power to prohibit the slave trade in a territory. The decision was just what Southerners favoring popular sovereignty wanted, but it also created uncertainty about any legislature's authority over slavery. If the federal legislature could not regulate slavery, could state legislatures? The Republicans were able to use the decision as a rallying point for popular control of government; the Democrats were in the uncustomary position of defending the Supreme Court, which since Thomas Jefferson they had pictured as elitist. Douglas, the eventual Democratic nominee and architect of the platform, insisted on state resolution of the issue. Jefferson Davis of Mississippi, the eventual president of the Confederate States of America, fought in Congress for the right of Congress to promote and protect slavery in new territories.

Eventually, the Davis Democrats held their own convention and nominated Vice President Breckinridge for the presidency. Although these "Dixiecrats"—a term used to distinguish Southern from Northern Democrats—insisted that they were the backbone of the party and had been strong enough to elect Buchanan four years before, the party divided would not be able to win a national election.

Democratic party splits enabled Lincoln to win the 1860 election, resulting in the secession of seven Southern states from the Union even before his inauguration. (The remaining four states forming the Confederacy seceded after the fall of Fort Sumter, April 13, 1861.)

The Fateful Election of 1860

The regional splits that had been tearing the nation apart for decades reached their peak in 1860. None of the four major candidates who sought the presidency could compete seriously throughout the nation. The winner would probably be a candidate from the North, the region with the most electoral votes. The two Northern candidates were former U.S. representative Abraham Lincoln of Illinois and Stephen Douglas, a Democrat, who defeated Lincoln for the Illinois Senate seat in 1858. Moderate Constitutional Union nominee John Bell of Tennessee and Democrat John Breckinridge of Kentucky were the candidates competing in the South.

The Republican party developed out of disgruntled elements of the Whigs, the Know-Nothings, abolitionists, members of the Liberty and Free-Soil parties, anti-imperialists, high-tariff supporters, temperance activists, and states' rights advocates. The Republicans succeeded in 1860 because they were able to pull together a variety of potentially warring factions. Above all else, the Republicans stood against the extension of slavery into new territories. By accepting slavery where it already existed but warning against the nationalization of the system, the Republicans divided the Democrats and picked up support from a diverse array of otherwise contentious factions—abolitionists, moderate abolitionists, and whites who feared for their position in the economy.

The *Dred Scott* decision enabled the Republicans to rail publicly against the high court in the tradition of Jefferson and Jackson. While opposing the Democratic doctrine of popular sovereignty, the Republicans picked up some states' rights sympathizers.

Lincoln won the nomination at a frenzied convention in Chicago. After the convention blocked several radical candidates, Lincoln emerged as the consensus compromise choice. Lincoln was known widely throughout Illinois, which improved his chances at the Chicago convention.

Among the Democrats, Douglas was Lincoln's principal rival. Douglas managed several moderate platform victories at the Democratic convention in Charleston, S.C., defeating resolutions that called for acceptance of the *Dred Scott* decision and protection of slavery in the territories. But Douglas's success prompted delegates from ten Southern states to bolt the convention. After disputes over quorum rules and fifty-seven ballots, the Democrats were unable to muster the necessary two-thirds majority for Douglas. The convention adjourned, reassembled at Baltimore, and faced disputes about the seating of delegates that caused further defections from the South. With Southern radicals effectively eliminated from the convention, Douglas swept to a unanimous nomination victory.

The Democratic defectors named Vice President Breckinridge to run for president in the South. The Constitutional Union party, which developed as a futile attempt to repair the nation's geographic divisions, nominated Bell to oppose Breckinridge. *(See "Third Parties," p. 248, in this chapter.)* These two candidates were doomed from the start, however, since the South's electoral-vote total was significantly below that of just a few major Northern states.

The Republicans assembled the wide-ranging coalition that eluded the Whigs in their last years of existence. Lincoln could count on strength in the areas that Fremont had won in 1856—New England and the upper Northwest, as well as New York and Ohio. The GOP offered an internal-improvements program to attract settlers in the frontier. Lincoln's local ties would help him in Illinois and Indiana, and his Whig background was a plus in the Ohio valley. The coal and iron regions of Pennsylvania and Ohio were attracted to the party's high-tariff policy. Urban immigrants, particularly Germans, were attracted by the GOP support of homestead (that is, frontier settlement) legislation and the Lincoln campaign's "Vote Yourself a Farm" appeal.[26] The vice-presidential selection of Hannibal Hamlin of Maine, a former Democrat, broadened the coalition beyond partisan lines. Lincoln's oft-stated desire to protect slavery where it then existed was an appeal to border states.

Lincoln easily won with a total of 180 electoral votes to Breckinridge's 72, Bell's 39, and Douglas's 12. Lincoln's closest competitor in the popular vote was Douglas. Lincoln had 1.9 million popular votes (40.0 percent); Douglas had 1.4 million (29.5 percent) spread out geographically. The two other principal candidates received much less support, which was concentrated in the South: Breckinridge won 848,000 popular votes (18.1 percent); Bell, 591,000 (12.6

Library of Congress

Republican presidential candidate Abraham Lincoln stood tall at 6'4".

President of the Confederacy

In 1861, two weeks before Abraham Lincoln was inaugurated in Washington, D.C., as the sixteenth president of the United States, another president was inaugurated in Montgomery, Alabama. On February 18, 1861, Jefferson Davis became the first and only president of the Confederate States of America.

Davis was born in Christian (now Todd) County, Kentucky, on June 3, 1808. He was the youngest of the ten children of Samuel and Jane Davis, who moved their family to a small Mississippi plantation when Jefferson was a boy. He attended private schools and Transylvania University in Lexington, Kentucky, before his oldest brother, Joseph, secured his appointment to West Point in 1824.

After graduating from the academy, Davis was stationed in Wisconsin under Col. Zachary Taylor. There he saw action in the Black Hawk War during the early 1830s and fell in love with Taylor's daughter, Sarah Knox. In 1835 he left the army, married Sarah, and settled on a one-thousand-acre plantation in Mississippi, which was given to him by his brother Joseph. Tragically, Sarah died from malaria three months after the wedding, and for several years Davis devoted himself to developing his land and wealth.

In 1845 Davis married Varina Howell, a member of the Mississippi aristocracy, and was elected to the U.S. House of Representatives. He served in Washington less than a year before the Mexican War began, and he gave up his seat to accept a commission as a colonel. He became a national hero when his company made a stand at the Battle of Buena Vista that was said to have saved Gen. Zachary Taylor's army from defeat.

Jefferson Davis

In 1847 he left the army and was elected to the Senate. He served there until 1851, when he ran unsuccessfully for governor of Mississippi. He returned to Washington in 1853 after being appointed secretary of war by President Franklin Pierce. Davis was credited with strengthening the armed forces during his time in office. He also was influential in bringing about the Gadsden Purchase from Mexico in 1853, which added areas of present-day Arizona and New Mexico to the United States.

In 1857 Davis was reelected to the Senate. Although he became a leading spokesman for the South, he did not advocate secession until 1860 when it had become inevitable. Davis hoped to be appointed commanding general of the South's army, but instead he was chosen as president by a convention of the seceding states.

Davis believed his first priority as president was to preserve Southern independence. He tried to secure French and British assistance for the Confederacy, but he was largely unsuccessful. Like Lincoln he helped develop military strategy and on occasion interfered with the plans of his generals. In managing the war effort, Davis was hampered by his paradoxical position. The South could fight most effectively as a unified nation run by the central government in Richmond, but the Southern states had seceded in part to preserve their rights as independent states. Davis took actions, including the suspension of *habeas corpus* and the establishment of conscription, that were regarded as despotic by many Southerners.

When the Union's victory appeared imminent in early 1865, Davis fled south from Richmond and was captured by federal troops. He was indicted for treason and imprisoned for two years, but he never stood trial. He lived in Canada and Europe for several years before retiring to Mississippi. There he wrote his *Rise and Fall of the Confederate States*, which was published in 1881. He died in New Orleans on December 6, 1889.

percent).

Southerners had vowed to secede from the Union if Lincoln won the election. In the period before Lincoln's inauguration, congressional committees sought to put together a compromise that would save the nation from civil war, but they always failed because of Lincoln's refusal to abandon his policy of containment of slavery. Lincoln rejected proposals for popular sovereignty or a slave-free geographic division of Western states. Lincoln would not comment on proposals for constitutional amendments or popular referenda on the issue.

After Lincoln was elected, South Carolina, Louisiana, Mississippi, Alabama, Georgia, Texas, and Florida seceded from the Union and on February 7, 1861, adopted a constitution forming the Confederate States of America. After a protracted standoff between Union soldiers who held Fort Sumter and the Confederate soldiers who controlled South Carolina, the Confederates fired on the fort. Virginia, Arkansas, North Carolina, and Tennessee then joined the Confederacy, and the Civil War was under way.

The Civil War Election

The Union's military difficulties in 1861 and 1862 created resentment and impatience with President Lincoln, and splits that developed in the Republican party seemed to imperil his chances for renomination and reelection.

From the very beginning of his administration Lincoln suffered because of the difficulty he had finding a general who could successfully prosecute the war. Repeated military setbacks and stalemates—such as the battles of Fredericksburg and Chancellorsville, Confederate general Robert E. Lee's escape after the battle of Antietam (Sharpsburg), and heavy casualties in the drive to Richmond—hurt the Republicans. Publicized conflicts with generals such as George McClellan caused further damage. In addition to the military problems, the president's announcement of the emancipation of slaves in rebellious states in September 1862 (the Emancipation Proclamation) created legal and political controversy.

The Republicans experienced widespread losses in congressional and state elections in the 1862 midterm elections. Among the more bitter defeats for Lincoln was John Stuart's victory in the president's old congressional district in Illinois. By the time of the election, Stuart, a former law partner of the president, was an ardent political foe.

The military frustrations gave rise to deep divisions within Lincoln's own cabinet. Treasury Secretary Salmon P. Chase led a radical faction of the administration, and the Philadelphia banker Jay Gould briefly led a movement for Chase's nomination for president in 1864. Chase withdrew only after the Lincoln forces dealt him a severe blow at the party caucus in his home state of Ohio. Other radicals met in Cleveland in May 1864 and named John Fremont to run against Lincoln in the fall. Fremont withdrew only after a series of Union military victories strengthened Lincoln's political standing.

The president manipulated the GOP convention in Baltimore brilliantly, ensuring not only his own renomination but also the selection of pro-Union governor Andrew Johnson of Tennessee as the vice-presidential candidate. Lincoln professed indifference about a possible running mate. "Wish not to interfere about V.P. Cannot interfere about platform," he said in a letter. "Convention must judge for itself."[27] Nonetheless, he maneuvered to build support for Johnson. Johnson's selection was in accord with the desire of the party, which called itself the Union party as a way to attract Democrats and to develop nationwide unity. Yet Lincoln's reelection drive was so uncertain that he obliged his cabinet in August 1864 to sign a statement pledging an orderly transition of power if he lost. The statement read: "This morning, as for some days past, it seems exceedingly probable that this Administration will not be reelected. Then it will be my duty to so cooperate with the President-elect, as to save the Union between the election and the inauguration; as he will have secured his election on such ground that he cannot possibly save it afterwards."[28]

The man for whom Lincoln anticipated arranging a wartime transition was General McClellan, the Democratic nominee whom Lincoln had fired as general in January 1863. McClellan had won the Democratic nomination with the strong backing of "peace Democrats" such as Clement L. Vallandigham of Ohio, who was arrested by Union general Ambrose E. Burnside after making a series of antiwar speeches. (Vallandigham later took up exile in Canada.) McClellan's running mate was Rep. George Pendleton of Ohio, who would later sponsor landmark civil-service reform legislation.

McClellan was a vocal critic of the administration. The general did not win a single major battle despite constant infusions of extra troops, but he blamed Lincoln for the losses. McClellan was popular with the soldiers, and his campaign was built around a call for a cease-fire and a convention to restore the Union. McClellan and other peace Democrats also criticized the administration's violation of civil liberties and other unconstitutional actions.

Lincoln's fortunes improved in the two months before the election. When Gen. William Tecumseh Sherman took Atlanta after a scorched-earth march through the South, the Confederacy was left badly divided geographically. The military victory cut off Gulf states from the Confederate capital of Richmond. Gen. Philip Sheridan had important successes in the Shenandoah Valley, and Gen. Ulysses Grant did well in Virginia.

Not only did the Democrats face a GOP reconstituted for the war election as the Union party and united by recent military victories, but McClellan also had a difficult time developing consistent campaign themes. He was at various times conciliatory toward the Confederacy and solicitous of the soldiers who fought for the Union. The balancing problem was underscored by the inclusion of both war and peace songs in the *McClellan Campaign Songster*, a piece of campaign literature.[29] McClellan also had a difficult time selling his message to Northern industrialists who profited from munitions procurement.

Not until the arrival of election results from three state elections on October 11 were Lincoln and the Unionists confident that they would win the national election in November. Republican victories in Indiana, Ohio, and Pennsylvania were the first concrete indications that Lincoln's fortunes had turned around.

Lincoln overwhelmed McClellan by winning all of the loyal states except Delaware, Kentucky, and New Jersey for a 212-21 electoral-vote victory. Lincoln garnered 2.2 million popular votes (55.0 percent) to McClellan's 1.8 million (45.0 percent). The electoral votes of Louisiana and Tennessee, the first Confederate states to return to the Union, were not accepted by Congress.

Postwar Radicalism

The Civil War's end left the nation almost as divided as it had been in the antebellum years. Concerns about punishment of the rebel states, the status of the freedmen, and economic development replaced slavery as the principal sources of disagreement

The nation undoubtedly would have experienced bitter splits no matter who served as chief executive, but the assassination of President Lincoln on April 14, 1865, shortly after the Confederate surrender, created a crisis of leadership. Lincoln's vice president, Andrew Johnson, ascended to the presidency and immediately came into conflict with the radical Northern Republicans who controlled Congress. Johnson, a Democrat from Tennessee, was stubborn, which only aggravated the troubles that were inevitable anyway because of his party and regional background.

Johnson intended to continue Lincoln's plans for a reconstruction of North and South "with malice toward none," but the Congress was intent on establishing political institutions that would respect the rights of former slaves and promote economic growth.[30] A states' rights politician, Johnson attempted to put together a coalition of moderates from all parts of the country that would bring about a quick reconciliation. He chafed at the notion of the South as a conquered territory. Johnson and Congress fought over bills that would extend the life of the Freedmen's Bureau and guarantee the franchise and equal protection to blacks. Johnson vetoed both bills. Johnson also opposed the Fourteenth Amendment, which guaranteed equal protection, as well as the stipulation that Confederate states approve the amendment as a condition of their readmission to the Union.

When the Radicals took over Congress in the 1866 midterm elections, the war with Johnson began in earnest. In March 1867 Congress established limited military rule in recalcitrant Southern states and passed the Tenure of Office Act limiting the president's right to dismiss his appointees. Johnson contemptuously disregarded the tenure act and fired Edwin Stanton, his secretary of war. For this action Johnson was impeached by the House and tried by the Senate. When the Senate voted in May 1868, he avoided conviction by a single vote (35-19). *(See "Impeachment of Andrew Johnson," p. 369, in Removal of the President chapter of Part II.)*

The Grant Years, 1869-1877

Ulysses S. Grant was more than a concerned citizen during the dispute between Johnson and Congress. Despite its portrayal in many history books as a clear instance of congressional abuse of power, the affair was more complicated. All of the players in the drama negotiated their way with care, and almost none of them escaped without major scars. Grant was a central figure, and his style of maneuvering was dictated by his ambition to succeed Johnson as president.

Radical Republicans in Congress achieved a lasting victory when they secured passage of the Civil Rights Act of 1866 over President Johnson's veto, but they were increasingly disturbed by reports that the statute was not being enforced. A congressional investigation of violence against blacks in Memphis concluded that the Freedmen's Bureau could not enforce civil rights without help. Radicals began to look to Secretary of War Stanton to enforce the law that the president clearly disliked and repeatedly subverted.

Stanton indicated that he would carry out the law in the Confederacy as Congress intended, and Johnson began to think about replacing him. Congress passed the Tenure of Office Act over Johnson's veto in May 1867, reasoning that its constitutional "advise and consent" powers over appointments extended to removal as well. Johnson decided to test the law's constitutionality. Johnson's concern—and indeed the concern of all involved—was who could be given the post with minimal threat to his own position. Johnson first considered General Sherman but decided to appoint Grant on a temporary basis. Originally a Democrat and supporter of moderate Southern policies, Grant worried about appearing too close to the unpopular president. After vaguely assuring Johnson that he would accept a temporary appointment, Grant hedged. He increasingly expressed support for the notion that appointees should interpret and obey laws according to congressional intent. Eventually, Grant told the president in a letter that he could not accept the appointment.

After the drama of impeachment, Grant was in a good position to seek the White House. He had avoided allying himself with controversy both during Johnson's search for a replacement for Stanton and in the ensuing impeachment battle. Everyone but Grant and Chief Justice Salmon Chase was tainted by the affair. Grant even managed to maintain his public posture of disinterested duty. Thus during one of the nation's ugliest political episodes, Grant looked clean. He was ready for a presidential campaign.

As Johnson endured his Senate impeachment trial in March, Grant won his first electoral victory. A New Hampshire congressional campaign, which normally would favor the Democrat, became an early Grant referendum when Republican candidate Donald Sickles told voters that a vote for a Republican was a vote for Grant; Sickles won. Just before the GOP convention in May, a Soldiers and Sailors Convention "nominated" Grant. Grant avoided an excessively military image when he vowed to reduce the size of the standing army. Grant was on his way.

Grant won the nomination without opposition. The real battle at the 1968 Republican convention was for the vice-presidential nomination. Schuyler Colfax of Indiana, the Speaker of the House, won on the sixth ballot.

The Democrats had a difficult time finding a nominee. Johnson sought the Democratic nomination, but his appeal was to the South; and, because many Southern states were still outside the Union, Northern politicians were selecting the nominee. Chase, highly regarded for his fairness during Johnson's Senate trial, was a possibility, but his strong stand for black suffrage was a barrier. Thomas Hendricks of Indiana was strong in the East, and George Pendleton of Ohio was strong in the West. Gen. Winfield Hancock of Pennsylvania presented the opportunity of running one military hero against another.

After twenty-three bitter ballots in a sweltering New York City, Horatio Seymour, the party chair and popular war governor of New York, accepted the Democratic nomination against his will. Gen. Francis P. Blair, Jr., of Missouri was the vice-presidential nominee. The party platform called for a rapid reentry of Confederate states to the Union, state authority over suffrage questions, and the "Ohio Idea," which set an inflationary money supply and helped the indebted South.

Both sides were well-financed in the election, but the Republicans had the edge. The GOP's positions on the tariff, railroad grants, and the currency attracted millions of dollars. Newspapers and magazines tended to be pro-Republican.

Grant ran his campaign from his home in Galena, Illinois. He was vague about issues ranging from the currency to voting rights. Appearances in Colorado with fellow generals Sherman and Sheridan were taken to be endorsements. Everything seemed to go Grant's way. Even the traditional campaign gossip about the sexual activities of candidates did not hurt him. Charges that Grant was excessively pro-black—"I am Captain Grant of the Black Marines, The stupidest man that was ever seen" were the lyrics of one ditty[31] —helped him with the recently enfranchised citizens. Without the black vote, Grant probably would have lost the popular vote and maybe the electoral vote. Results from October state elections that favored the Republicans created a brief movement for Seymour and Blair to quit the contest so that the Democrats could name a new ticket. Seymour instead took the October results as an incentive to get to the campaign stump. Seymour was a good speaker, but nothing he could do could help the Democrats.

Grant defeated Seymour 3.0 million (52.7 percent) to 2.7 million votes (47.3 percent). The electoral vote tally was 214 for Grant and 80 for Seymour. Grant won all but eight of the thirty-four states taking part in the election. He benefited from Radical Republican reconstructionist sentiment in the North and newly enfranchised blacks in the South.

With Grant's ascension to the presidency in 1869, the Republican party entered a new era—what the German sociologist Max Weber would call a shift from "charismatic" to "rational" institutional authority. The party shifted its devotion from a great moral cause to its own survival as an organization. The party began as a coalition of activists fervently opposed to the expansion of slavery (many opposed to slavery itself) and to the rebellion of Southern states from the Union. The Republicans' 1868 victory under Grant was the first not dominated wholly by crisis conditions.

The Republicans had a strong base of support: Eastern bankers, manufacturers, railroads, and land speculators. With the old Confederacy under the control of military governments and with blacks given the franchise, the Republicans had strength in the South. The West was restive, however, because of depressed farm prices, high taxes, and debt. The industrial-agrarian split between North and South before the Civil War would be resumed as an East-West split in the years after the war.

Republican leadership was turning over to new hands. Age was claiming a number of the early Republican leaders, such as Thaddeus Stevens, William Seward, Benjamin Wade, Charles Sumner, James Grimes, Stanton, and Chase. New party leaders included Senators Roscoe Conkling of New York, Oliver Morton of Indiana, Simon Cameron of Pennsylvania, and Zachariah Chandler of Michigan, and Representatives Benjamin Butler of Massachusetts, John Logan of Illinois, James Garfield of Ohio, and James G. Blaine of Maine.

The Grant administration was undistinguished. The new president's inaugural address—spoken without the traditional company of the outgoing president, since Grant neglected to respond to Johnson's polite letters—was decent but uninspiring. Grant vowed that "all laws will be faithfully executed, whether they meet my approval or not," that debtors would not be tolerated, and that blacks should get the vote throughout the country, and Indians should be offered "civilization and ultimate citizenship." [32] With a few important exceptions, cabinet positions went to old Grant cronies.

The nation experienced a financial panic when financiers Jay Gould and Jim Fisk attempted to corner the world's gold market. Their scheme led to "Black Friday," September 24, 1869. Gould and Fisk met with President Grant and urged him not to sell government gold—therefore keeping the price of gold high. At the last minute, however, Grant decided to reject their advice and dumped $4 million worth of gold on the market. That dumping caused a severe drop in gold prices, breaking up the Gould-Fisk conspiracy but also causing tremendous losses for thousands of speculators. It was the worst disaster on Wall Street up to that time. Although it did not cause a depression, the South and West were hard hit by the financial retrenchment program that followed. Tariff rates remained high on most manufactured goods, despite tentative efforts to reform the system. The spoils system was in full swing during the Grant years. Grant himself was not involved in the scramble for booty, but his family and aides were often shameless in their greed. When Grant learned that liberal Republicans were planning an independent presidential campaign against him in 1872, he took the edge off the spoils issue by creating the Civil Service Reform Commission, but his neglect of the commission made it ineffective.

Currier & Ives; Library of Congress

The 1872 Republican campaign called voters' attention to the humble backgrounds of presidential candidate Ulysses S. Grant and his running mate, Henry Wilson.

Before the 1872 election, the *New York Sun* exposed the Crédit Mobilier scandal. The newspaper reported that the firm's board of directors had many of the same members as the Union Pacific Railroad Company, which hired it to build a transcontinental route, and that Crédit Mobilier had paid its board exorbitant profits. To avoid a public investigation, Crédit Mobilier offered stock to Vice President Colfax and Representative Garfield (later president). Colfax lost his place on the Republican ticket for his role in the scandal; Sen. Henry Wilson of New Hampshire took his position as the vice-presidential candidate in 1872.

Liberal Republicans, discontent with protective tariffs, spoils, and uneven administration of the Southern states, bolted the party in 1872. The group was interested in policies such as civil service and free trade that would promote individual virtue in a laissez-faire economic system. The reformers thought they had a chance to win. The German-born senator Carl Schurz of Missouri wrote to a friend that "the administration with its train of offices and officemongers [is] the great incubus pressing upon the party. . . . The superstition that Grant is the necessary man is rapidly giving way. The spell is broken, and we have only to push through the breach." [33]

Candidates for the nomination from this group of Republicans included former ambassador to Great Britain

Charles Francis Adams, son of President John Quincy Adams and grandson of President John Adams; Supreme Court Justice David Davis; Salmon Chase; Sen. Lyman Trumbull of Illinois; and Horace Greeley, editor of the *New York Tribune*. Greeley won the nomination on the sixth ballot. The Democrats were so weak that they did not field a candidate of their own. They endorsed the Greeley ticket.

Since his early days as a newspaper reporter, when he described President Van Buren as an effeminate failure, Greeley won fame as a pungent social critic. He was a crusading, abolitionist editor and a dedicated reformer, but his rumpled appearance and unpolished speaking style made him appear "unpresidential." Greeley was unable to parlay an amalgam of promises to various interest groups—blacks, soldiers, immigrants, and laborers—into a victory over Grant. Groups that Greeley actively courted found him wanting for a variety of reasons, and even though Greeley advocated the tariff favored by the North, he could not cut into Grant's northeastern strength. A Republican cartoon showed Greeley's difficult task: Sitting on the fence are a laborer, skeptical because of Greeley's stand against strikes, and a black, concerned because of Greeley's advocacy of amnesty for Confederates. Sitting on the sidelines is a German upset because of Greeley's prohibitionist stance. He says: "Oh! Yaw! You would take my Lager away, den you must get widout me along!" [34]

Even though he went on the stump and delivered a series of impressive speeches, Greeley never had a chance. Republican gubernatorial victories in North Carolina in August and in Pennsylvania, Ohio, and Indiana in October were clear harbingers that the GOP would do well in November. Grant took the entire North and the newly admitted South with 3.6 million popular votes (55.6 percent). Greeley won three border states, as well as Tennessee, Texas, and Georgia, with 2.8 million popular votes (43.9 percent). Less than a month after the election, Greeley died. Of the electoral votes, which were cast after Greeley's death, Grant received 286; the Democrats' 63 electoral votes were scattered among various candidates, and 17 Democratic electoral votes were not cast.

The Compromise of 1876

The pattern of Republican, Northern, and business domination of presidential politics was institutionalized in the 1876 election. Republican Rutherford B. Hayes, the three-time governor of Ohio, lost the popular vote and had a questionable hold on the electoral-college vote, but he managed to beat Democrat Samuel J. Tilden for the presidency when the election was settled by a special commission created by Congress. (Hayes won 4.0 million votes to Tilden's 4.3 million, or 48-51 percent of the vote.) Perhaps the most controversial election outcome in history, some feared it would set off a second civil war.

The problem arose when the vote tallies in Florida, South Carolina, and Louisiana were called into question. Violence attended the voting in all three states, but President Grant did not send in federal troops to ensure fair balloting. On those states hung the electoral outcome. There was good reason to be suspicious of any vote count in those and other Southern states. While the Republicans controlled the balloting places and mounted vigorous drives to get blacks to the polls, the Democrats used physical intimidation and bribery to keep blacks away. The bitterness between Northern interests and Southern whites was apparent in the violence that often took place at polls.

State election board recounts and investigations did not settle the question, and Congress took it up. An electoral commission made up of five senators (three majority party Republicans, two minority Democrats), five representatives (three majority party Democrats, two minority Republicans), and five Supreme Court justices (two from each party, one independent) assembled to hear complaints about the disputed states. At the last minute the independent justice could not serve; his place was taken by a Republican who was accepted by Democrats because they considered him to be the most independent of possibilities. Weeks of bargaining followed, during which the Republican vote totals of the disputed states were confirmed, and the Southern Democrats extracted promises of financial aid and political independence from the federal government.

When the validity of the Florida vote count for Hayes was challenged, the commission responded that it did not have the capacity to judge the actual conduct of the balloting, only the validity of the certificates presented to Congress. That decision gave the state to Hayes. Challenges to the vote counts of Louisiana, South Carolina, and Oregon were dismissed in a similar way, so Hayes was awarded the presidency.

The compromise not only settled the partisan dispute between Hayes and Tilden; it also established a rigid alignment of political interests that would dominate U.S. politics for the next half-century. Although Democrats won occasional victories, the Republican, eastern, conservative, business-oriented establishment held sway over the system until Franklin Roosevelt's election in 1932. The institutional form of the regional splits created by the compromise remained much longer.

Historian C. Vann Woodward has argued that secret wheeling and dealing among congressional and party leaders institutionally divided the political system by party, region, economic interest, and governmental branches. Northern Republican industrial interests were given control of the presidential election process, and Southern Democratic agricultural interests were given autonomy over their regional politics that led to domination of Congress.[35] This alignment was not completely dislodged until the passage of important civil rights legislation in the 1960s. In return for throwing the election to the Republican Hayes, Northern politicians agreed to pull federal troops out of the South and to allow Southern whites to take over the system. Within months, Southern states were erecting a powerful edifice of racial discrimination that would last until the 1960s. Former South Carolina governor Daniel H. Chamberlain later summed up the deal:

> What is the president's Southern policy? [I]t consists in the abandonment of Southern Republicans and especially the colored race, to the control and rule not only of the Democratic Party, but of that class of the South which regarded slavery as a Divine Institution, which waged four years of destructive war for its perpetuation, which steadily opposed citizenship and suffrage for the negro—in a word, a class whose traditions, principles, and history are opposed to every step and feature of what Republicans call our national progress since 1860.[36]

The Age of Republicanism

From 1860 until 1908, the Republicans won nine elections; the Democrats won only two. Only Grover Cleveland could put together a Democratic win, and he was as conservative on most issues as the Republicans of the period. Presidential election winners after the Great Compromise were Hayes (1876), James Garfield (1880), Cleveland (1884), Benjamin Harrison (1888), Cleveland (1892), William McKinley (1896 and 1900), Theodore Roosevelt (1904), and William Howard Taft (1908).

The political aspirants of the day were required to adhere to the religion of high tariffs, laissez-faire economics, and tight money. Tight money policies—the restricted issuance of currency, which favored bankers and other established interests but hurt debtors and those seeking more rapid expansion of some kinds of investment and spending—provided rare openings for resistance to Republican hegemony. Resistance also developed when the scramble for tariff protections created obvious inequities among businesses and hardships for the consumer. Populist uprisings such as Democrat William Jennings Bryan's 1896 campaign faltered, however, because of strong mobilization by the Republicans and divisions within the Democratic ranks. Bryan failed to bring a likely Democratic constituency—the worker—into the fold. Eastern businessmen were able to portray their interest in industrial growth as a common concern with labor and Bryan's western agrarian alliance as a danger to that growth.

While the GOP dominated presidential politics, the parties were well-balanced in Congress and in state governments until the class and sectional cleavages of the 1890s. The Senate was split in 1881, 37-37, and two years later the Republicans had a 38-36 edge. Democrats made gains in Northern congressional races, and Republicans were making smaller gains in the South. The House tended to provide a majority for the presidential party in power.

Garfield Carries the GOP Banner

Hayes honored his pledge to serve only one term, setting off a scramble for the parties' nominations in 1880. When the momentum for a third term for Grant faltered, the Republican contest became a battle between Grant, House Speaker James Blaine, and General John Sherman. Grant was able to muster a first-ballot plurality but could not attract new supporters as the balloting proceeded. A stalemate between Blaine and Sherman ensued.

Rep. James Garfield of Ohio, a former preacher who was impressive in his oratory and organization for Sherman, was the compromise choice for the nomination. He selected as his running mate Chester A. Arthur, the collector of the Port of New York, an important patronage job.

The Democrats named Gen. Winfield Hancock and former Rep. William English to head their ticket. The Democrats' platform advocated the gold standard, a tariff to raise revenue, civil service reform, restrictions on Chinese immigration, and a belated criticism of the 1876 deal that gave the presidency to Hayes. Except for the tariff and 1876 questions, the Democrats' platform was close to the Republicans' statement of principles.

The regional breakdown of support, with most of the North and West falling in Garfield's camp and the South lining up behind Hancock, gave the presidency to Garfield. The popular vote was close—4.45 million (48.27 percent) to 4.44 million (48.25 percent)—but Garfield won a 214-155 electoral-vote victory.

The festering issue of patronage and civil service came to a head shortly after Garfield's inauguration. On July 2, 1881, Charles Guiteau, a man history textbooks have described as a "disappointed office-seeker," shot Garfield in a railroad depot while Garfield was traveling to Williams College to deliver a commencement address. Garfield died in September, and Arthur became president. *(See "Government by the Common Man, 1829-1883," p. 846, in the Pay and Perquisites chapter of Part V.)* The outstanding feature of Arthur's presidency was the easy passage of the Pendleton Act. The legislation set up a commission to regulate the provision of federal jobs and the behavior of civil servants. The number of federal workers removed from the patronage system was at first small, but successive presidents widened the coverage of nonpartisan workers so that today less than 1 percent of all federal workers are appointed by the White House.[37]

The tariff question also emerged as crucial. The Tariff Act of 1883 "gave little or no relief to the consumer and took care of every important industrial interest." [38] The Democrats opposed the bill and later worked for gradual lowering of rates, but failed. The tariff would be a major issue in later elections.

The next three elections, 1884, 1888, and 1892, revolved around Democrat Grover Cleveland of New York, a city politician who worked his way up to the governorship. Cleveland defeated Blaine for the presidency in 1884, lost to Harrison in 1888, then came back to defeat Harrison in 1892. Even after his two staggered terms, Cleveland remained involved in Democratic presidential politics. He emerged as the chief foe of Bryan in 1896 and was even considered for the presidency in 1900.

Democrat Cleveland Wins

Arthur wanted the Republican nomination in 1884, and his record as stand-in for the assassinated Garfield arguably should have earned him the nomination. Not only was he an important player in the civil service reform and the tariff issue, but he began the modernization of the navy and vetoed the Chinese Exclusion Act of 1883. He was a model of fiscal probity with his veto of the $19 million river and harbor bill.

James G. Blaine of Maine—secretary of state in Arthur's own administration—stood in Arthur's way. After months of public appeals by old-line Republicans interested in stronger leadership and more generous patronage from their own party, Blaine quit his administration position and opposed Arthur for the nomination.

Blaine was the most charismatic figure of the period. A former teacher, editor, state legislator, and member of Congress, Blaine's fiery oratory captured the imagination of the political establishment. He had made a national name for himself when he opposed an 1876 congressional resolution expressing forgiveness to Civil War rebels including the Confederate president, Jefferson Davis. Col. Robert G. Ingersoll, a rising political figure in the Republican party, said of Blaine: "Like an armed warrior, like a plumed knight, James G. Blaine marched down the halls of the American Congress and threw his shining lance full and fair against the brazen forehead of every traitor to his country." [39]

The Republican convention in Chicago praised Arthur's administration and fudged the tariff issue. *(See box, Tariffs in U.S. Politics, p. 195.)* The tariff that passed in 1883 was the product of swarms of lobbyists for private interests. The GOP platform promised better protection

Library of Congress

The fiery oratory of 1884 Republican candidate James G. Blaine captured the imagination of the political establishment, but it was not enough to win him the election over Democrat Grover Cleveland.

for raw wool interests, angered by their treatment in 1883, and a generally protective stance for domestic industry. The platform also called for an international currency conference, railway regulation, a national agency for labor affairs, and further improvements in the navy.

At a frenzied convention, Blaine took the lead over Arthur on the first ballot. Old-line party leaders quickly united behind Blaine, while Arthur was unable to consolidate the support of reform Republicans still skeptical of his leadership abilities from his days as a patronage politician and collector of the Port of New York. Blaine won the nomination on the fourth ballot. Gen. John Logan of Illinois received the vice-presidential nomination.

The Democrats nominated Grover Cleveland after skirmishes with Sen. Thomas Bayard of Delaware and Sen. Thomas Hendricks of Indiana. Hendricks, whose liberal expansionist currency stance would balance the more conservative stance of Cleveland, was named the vice-presidential candidate. The Democratic platform vaguely promised reform of the tariff laws to make them more fair and, even more vaguely, promised a more honest and efficient administration.

Cleveland was a former teacher, lawyer, assistant district attorney, and reform mayor of Buffalo who had won the governorship of New York only two years before. Members of both parties consistently underestimated Cleveland's intellect and resolve. As governor, he made enemies through vetoes of low public-transit fares and aid to sectarian schools. He also defied Tammany Hall, the Democratic party organization that dominated New York politics, especially in New York City.

Cleveland's nomination signaled a triumph for the "educational politics" characteristic of urban progressivism. In a move away from the highly partisan and vitriolic campaigns of the post-Civil War era, Cleveland and other disciples of former New York governor Samuel Tilden promoted their program through a "literary bureau" that distributed pamphlets describing the party's policy positions. Campaign themes were developed at the national level and disseminated via the mails and meetings with the many professional and community organizations. The educational style was adopted by Republican Harrison in 1888.[40]

Blaine's campaign was one of the dirtiest in U.S. history. Blaine first attempted to spark sectional antagonisms with his "bloody shirt" warnings that the South was trying to reassert its rebel ways through Cleveland. Blaine also tried to rouse business fears with claims that Cleveland would institute free trade policies damaging to domestic industries. That appeal failed because the Democratic platform's plank on the tariff laws specifically supported protection of those interests. Finally, Blaine tried to make a scandal of Cleveland's fathering of a child out of wedlock years before. Among the charges against Cleveland was that he kidnapped and immured both the mother and child to cover up the story.

The campaign eventually turned on Cleveland's victory in New York, which resulted from a number of blunders by Blaine. One blunder had occurred years before, when Blaine mocked New York party boss Roscoe Conkling: "The contempt of that large-minded gentleman is so wilted, his haughty disdain, his grandiloquent swell, his majestic, supereminent, overpowering, turkey-gobbler strut, has been so crushing to myself that I know it was an act of the greatest temerity to venture upon a controversy with him."[41] Conkling was so peeved by the turkey image that he spent his whole career battling Blaine, including the presidential campaign of 1884. Blaine's own running mate, Logan, sympathized with Conkling in the dispute.

The other Blaine faux pas occurred a week before the election when a Protestant minister praised Blaine and proclaimed, "We are Republicans, and do not propose to leave our party and identify ourselves with the party whose antecedents have been rum, Romanism, and rebellion." Blaine did not separate himself from the remark, which angered New York Democrats and cost him votes. Later the same day, Blaine attended a formal dinner with a number of wealthy persons that became known as "the millionaires dinner"; the event belied Blaine's claims to speak for ordinary people.

Blaine, of Irish background, appealed to Irish immigrants in New York for their votes. But Cleveland countered Blaine's Irish tactic with the last-minute endorsement of the powerful Tammany leader Edward Kelly. Cleveland made two campaign speeches and attended a public rally in Buffalo. On the Saturday before the election, he attended a parade in New York City that attracted forty thousand people chanting: "Blaine, Blaine, James G. Blaine, the Monumental Liar from the State of Maine!" With the help of an economic downturn and the "Mugwumps"—independents and liberal Republicans offended by Blaine—Cleveland won the presidency.

The race however, was close. Cleveland received 4.9 million votes (48.5 percent) to Blaine's 4.8 million (48.3 percent). He won the solid South, Indiana, Connecticut, New Jersey, and, most important, New York (although by only 1,047 out of 1.13 million votes cast). Still, the election controversy did not end with the balloting. The *New York*

Tribune reported that Blaine won the race, fueling fears about an election deadlock similar to the Hayes-Tilden contest of 1876. But Cleveland received 219 electoral votes to Blaine's 182, making the Democrat the clear winner.

Cleveland's first two years in the White House were productive. His inaugural address and cabinet selections won wide praise. His style of leadership—examined closely in the newspapers—appeared refreshingly unassuming. The Cleveland agenda included issues like tariff reform (cutting rates on the "necessaries of life"), navy modernization, civil service, expansion, and land law reform. The president oversaw passage of the Presidential Succession Act and the Electoral Count Act, changes in currency policy, and labor controversies.

As during his terms as mayor of Buffalo and governor of New York, Cleveland icily refused to compromise his values. But when he became party leader, this steadfastness proved to be a problem. Thousands of Democratic party workers went to Washington seeking jobs in the new administration only to be disappointed. "Ah, I suppose you mean that I should appoint two horse thieves a day instead of one," Cleveland said in response to one party leader.[42] In vetoing pension bills, Cleveland called their sponsors "blood-suckers," "coffee-boilers," "pension leeches," and "bums."[43] The president appeared just as aloof to labor when a record number of strikes and disturbances swept the nation in 1886; the federal troops that Cleveland sent to the Haymarket riot in Chicago killed thirty people.

When Cleveland did bend to political realities, his timing was off. After standing firm against patronage when party enthusiasm was at its height, Cleveland disappointed reformers when he allowed lieutenants such as First Assistant Postmaster Adlai E. Stevenson to distribute favors.

The biggest controversy of the Cleveland administration involved tariffs. Concerned about federal budget surpluses that threatened to stall economic activity, Cleveland prodded the House of Representatives to pass tariff reductions. The Senate responded with a highly protective tariff measure. The unpopular tariff issue propelled the two parties into the 1888 election. The Democrats nominated Cleveland by acclamation and chose seventy-five-year-old judge Allen G. Thurman of Ohio for the vice presidency. The Democrats tried to soften their low-tariff image by promising that domestic industries would get larger markets. Lower tariffs were said to be necessary for avoiding disastrous federal budget surpluses, preventing the development of monopolies, and ensuring consumers reasonable prices for basic goods.

The 1888 Republican Recovery

A politics-weary James Blaine sent word from Florence and Paris that he would not be a candidate in 1888. The race was left open to some lesser lights, including Sen. John Sherman of Ohio, Gov. Russell Alger of Michigan, Sen. William Allison of Iowa, and Sen. Benjamin Harrison of Ohio. Sherman led the early balloting but quickly lost ground to Alger and Harrison. After extensive back-room maneuvering, including a last-minute plea to Blaine to accept the nomination, Harrison, who had the backing of state party bosses, won on the ninth ballot. Levi Morton, a banker, got the vice-presidential nomination.

Harrison, a senator from Indiana, was a former Civil War brigadier and the grandson of President William Henry Harrison with a scandal-free if colorless demeanor. Harrison was a good speaker, but often appeared aloof. One historian wrote: "Those who talked with him were met with a frigid look from two expressionless steel grey eyes; and their remarks were sometimes answered in a few chill monosyllables devoid of the slightest note of interest."[44] Harrison pledged a modernized navy, civil service reforms, and traditional Republican protective trust and trade policies.

The election turned, as in 1884, on New York and Indiana—both states with extensive evidence of voter intimidation and manipulation of counting. Harrison won the two states narrowly—New York by only 14,373 votes—and won the White House. Except for Connecticut and New Jersey, Harrison swept the North and West. Cleveland won the South. Overall, Harrison won 5.4 million popular votes (47.8 percent) and 233 electoral votes; Cleveland won 5.5 million popular votes (48.6 percent) and 168 electoral votes.

Cleveland left the White House with an unusual amount of good will among the public because of his honest tariff campaign. His popularity increased during the next four years as the economy hit slumps and as the former president, while practicing law, delivered speeches calling for a more egalitarian brand of politics. Cleveland would be back in 1892 for vindication.

With the first one-party majority in both the executive and legislative branches in a dozen years, the Republicans went about their business briskly after the election. Postmaster General John Wanamaker dispensed patronage with zeal. President Harrison signed into law the McKinley Tariff Act and the Sherman Silver Purchase Act. The former raised duties on manufactured goods to their highest level ever but also included provisions for negotiating with other countries to bring the rates down. The silver act

After Frank Beard in *Judge;* Library of Congress

Captioned "Another Voice for Cleveland," this 1884 cartoon played on Cleveland's admission that he had fathered an illegitimate son.

loosened the money supply, which stimulated economic activity (but angered creditors and bankers since money, when it is more readily available, is worth less).

Cleveland's Comeback, 1892

The 1890 midterm elections brought huge Democratic gains. Voters all over the country—but especially in the depressed farm belt—rebelled against the inflation that high tariffs brought. The Republicans held on to the Senate, but the new House of Representatives had 235 Democrats, 88 Republicans, and 9 Farmers' Alliance members. The brief experiment in party government ended with two years of stalemate.

President Harrison evoked widespread discontent in 1892 both for his demeanor and policies, but no Republican could mount an effective challenge. Through their strong party government, Republicans had cast their lot with Harrison and had few places to turn for an alternative. Political wizard Mark Hanna, a wealthy coal magnate who became a powerful behind-the-scenes political strategist, promoted William McKinley, and Secretary of State Blaine became an alternative when he abruptly quit the administration just before the GOP convention. But Harrison received a first-ballot nomination. Former minister to France Whitelaw Reid of New York got the vice-presidential nomination.

Cleveland enjoyed widespread backing among rank-and-file voters, but party leaders were suspicious. New York governor David B. Hall got a head start when he called a "snap" state convention and won the delegation. An "anti-snapper" convention from New York sent a rival delegation to the national party convention. Democrats across the country rebelled at Hall's move and rapidly switched their support to Cleveland.

Another problem for Cleveland was the rising sentiment in agrarian states for free and unlimited coinage of silver—a way of boosting sagging farm prices by inducing inflation in the overall economy. Cleveland always had opposed this solution. The former president's consistent, principled stance on the issue not only added to his reputation for integrity but kept business- and finance-dominated states in the Northeast in the Democratic camp. Cleveland defeated Hill for the nomination on the first ballot and selected Stevenson of Illinois as his running mate.

The fall campaign was uneventful. Historian Eugene Roseboom wrote: "Honest bearded Benjamin Harrison confronting honest mustached Grover Cleveland in a tariff debate was a repeat performance that did not inspire parades with torches or the chanting of campaign ditties.... Democrats, out of power, could assail Republican tariff policy without clarifying their own position." [45]

Cleveland won easily. He received 5.6 million popular votes (46.1 percent) to Harrison's 5.2 million (43.0 percent) and 277 electoral votes to Harrison's 145. Populist general James B. Weaver, advocating expansion of currency and limits of interest rates, won 1.0 million popular votes (8.5 percent) and 32 electoral votes.

The Age of Reform

Throughout the period dominated by Republican conservatism—from Grant's election in 1868 until William C. McKinley's 1896 win—movements for reform of political and economic institutions gathered strength at all levels of the American political system. The so-called Populists and progressives did not overturn the system, as their rhetoric sometimes suggested, but over time they made major changes in the operation and discourse of U.S. politics.

Depending on the time and place, people who called themselves "Populists" and "progressives" promoted such contradictory ideas as strict morals and free spirits, tight money and loose money, redistribution to the masses and control of the economy by elites, federal intervention and local control of politics, the opening and closing of electoral participation, technological progress and a return to a pastoral ideal long gone, individualism and community action, ethnic celebration and immigration barriers, scientific investigation and religion, and internationalism and isolationism.

Reformism was the response to the pressures of national expansion, urban development, and growth. Both major parties had adopted probusiness, laissez-faire policies in the latter part of the nineteenth century; the parties existed to make sure the terrain was suitable for economic expansion. But the lack of any program to deal with the undesired consequences of explosive growth led to an accumulation of problems that demanded attention. The most obvious problems evolved on the opposite ends of the rural-urban continuum: on the farms and in the cities.

The farm problem developed as the U.S. became a major economic power in the world. Agriculture expanded on a vast scale to feed the booming cities and, with international trade, to bring foreign capital to the United States. By 1880, the value of U.S. wheat and flour exports nearly equaled that of cotton exports.[46] As agriculture became part of the international market, farmers became dependent not only on the vagaries of the weather but also on the fluctuations of currency in the larger economy.

In the thirty years after the Civil War, prices for farm staples fell steadily. A debt that could have been paid by producing one thousand bushels of grain immediately after the war required three thousand bushels in 1895. The more farmers produced to meet their obligations, the more prices fell to exacerbate their problems. Confronting the problem required attention to a wide array of issues, including tight money, bankers who charged 20 percent interest for loans, monopolies among farm-equipment producers, high tariffs, railroad gouging, shipping inflation, warehouse monopolies, and land speculation. Throughout the farm belt, particularly in the West, tens of thousands of farmers developed an "intense class consciousness."[47]

All of these issues received attention from a variety of third parties and independent organizations, but the two major parties were usually inattentive. The Granger Movement of the 1870s, for example, took hold in several farm states and elected new legislatures and high state officials. The Greenback party attempted to merge a labor-farmer alliance with a doctrine of silver use for public debts. Later, the Farmers' Alliance politicized the same issues. In 1892, the Populist party won 8.5 percent of the vote on a platform calling for free coinage of silver. *(See "Third Parties," p. 248, in this chapter.)*

Another site of growing reformist strength was the city. The dominance of machines of both parties in the cities established an electoral system based on patronage but stubbornly opposed to any coherent program for addressing urban ills, such as poverty, poor housing, unsanitary conditions, transportation, education, and unfair workplace practices. Electoral fraud spurred mostly middle-class reformers to devise new electoral and city government machinery, while social problems spurred some insurgent class politics.[48] The labor movement developed strength during this period.[49]

Other parts of the progressive agenda developed with a greater understanding of the nationalization of the economic and political systems. The wider sphere of economic activities created calls for regulation of economic corporations, railroads, and banks, attention to health and environmental concerns, and product safety.

Until the ascendance of William Jennings Bryan, the Democratic presidential nominee in 1896, 1900, and 1908, the reformers were unable to capture a major party. Partly because political activism was based at the state and local level, neither national party adopted the reformers' widely variegated program as its own. The depression of 1888 caused the Populist forces to pull together more than they had during previous economic downturns, probably because of the accumulated effects of inaction. The panic of 1873 created a sectional rather than a party split, with the Democrats eventually adopting a more conservative stance on the debate over whether the currency should be expanded to spur economic activity and redistribute social burdens.[50]

The Republican presidential candidates steadfastly opposed the class-oriented proposals of the progressive movement, especially the loose-money demands.

The only Democrat to win the presidency since the Civil War was Cleveland, a stubborn advocate of hard money and other conservative economic policies, in 1884 and 1892. President Cleveland vetoed dozens of private pension bills, only grudgingly accepted railroad regulation, and did not address domestic problems in any comprehensive way. Cleveland's public statements on the currency question were especially strong. He called the use of silver "a dangerous and reckless experiment" that was "unpatriotic."[51] On the question of labor, Cleveland was just as conservative: he called out federal troops to put down the Pullman strike of 1894, and regularly preached about the evils of disorder that the labor movement seemed to foster.

Despite the complexity of the agriculture issue, the most concerted Populist action concentrated on the currency question alone. The drive to overturn the prevailing conventional economic thought by moving from a gold (tight) to a gold and silver (loose) money standard captured the imagination of the entire farm belt stretching from the Southeast to the prairie and silver-producing states of the West. The silver standard was a very simple answer to the problem of farm prices: "If money was scarce, the farmer reasoned, then the logical thing was to increase the money supply.[52]

Gold-runs on banks, manipulation of the gold crisis by J. P. Morgan and other leading financiers, procorporation Supreme Court decisions, and antilabor actions all stirred up resentment in the South and West. Silver sentiment escalated. The Democratic convention in 1896 called for the issuance of silver and rejected a resolution praising President Cleveland.[53] The movement for a silver currency found an eloquent advocate in Bryan, a member of the House of Representatives from Nebraska, who defeated Richard P. Bland of Missouri for the 1896 Democratic presidential nomination on the strength of his fiery "Cross of Gold" speech.

That speech was one of the most emotional and successful in U.S. history. Bryan attacked eastern financiers and businessmen who exploited farmers. In an important theme to which his fall campaign would return, Bryan sought to expand the traditional Democratic conception of the independent working man to include farmers and factory workers.[54] In his speech's fortissimo, Bryan declared: "You shall not press down upon the brow of labor this crown of thorns, you shall not crucify mankind upon a cross of gold."[55]

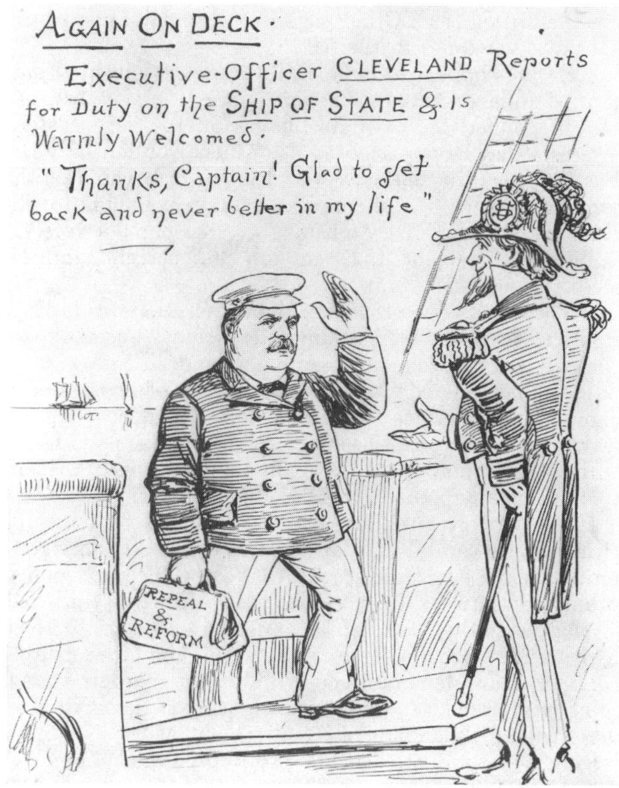

G. Y. Coffin, 1893; Library of Congress

Grover Cleveland is welcomed back on board the "Ship of State" in this 1893 cartoon. Having served as president from 1885 to 1889, he lost the 1888 election but regained the White House in the 1892 contest. Cleveland remains the only president to serve two nonconsecutive terms.

In 1896 the Republicans nominated Ohio governor William McKinley after brilliant maneuvering by his manager, Mark Hanna. Hanna's chief strengths were fund raising and his mastery over state party organizations.

McKinley had little difficulty defeating Bryan. McKinley outspent the prairie populist by as much as ten to one, and he attracted the disaffected progold wing of the Democratic party.[56] The GOP platform called for retention of the gold standard unless international negotiations could produce a bimetallic (that is, silver and gold) currency system. The platform also called for restored tariff protections and an aggressive foreign policy in the Western Hemisphere.

Bryan's campaign was a political hurricane. He spent just $650,000, most of it donated by silver interests, compared with the millions McKinley spent. But Bryan traveled eighteen thousand miles and gave some six hundred speeches, and his campaign staffers put out an impressive quantity of literature. Several million copies of *Coin's Financial School,* a prosilver pamphlet, were distributed during the fall of 1896. Other silverites also maintained busy speaking schedules in the fall.

Bryan's appeal to industrial workers to join his coalition of independent businessmen failed, largely because they depended for their livelihoods on the very eastern interests that Bryan attacked. McKinley won not only the East but also the small cities and towns in Bryan's southern and western belt of support. Bryan was unable to win rural areas of the East. McKinley won the popular vote 7.1 million (51.0 percent) to 6.5 million (46.7 percent) and the electoral vote 271-176.

The effect of the 1896 presidential election was lasting. Political scientist James Sundquist wrote: "For 20 years the two-party system had been based on dead issues of the past. It had offered the voters no means of expressing a choice on the crucial issues of domestic policy around which the country had been polarizing.... Then suddenly, with the nomination of Bryan in 1896, the party system took on meaning once again." [57]

The new Republican coalition included residents of cities, where capital and labor were both reasonably content with the economic growth that the GOP tariff policy promoted; farmers in the East and Midwest, who had strong ties to the "party of Lincoln" and who came to favor high tariffs; Catholic, German Lutheran, and other liturgical Christian denominations; and some border states. Sundquist noted: "It was the persistence of the Civil War attachments that made the realignment of the North so largely a one-way movement—pro-Republican." [58]

After 1896, the competitive party balance that had prevailed for years gave way to lopsided party strength according to region—Democrats in the South, Republicans in the North. Strong opposition parties disappeared in all regions of the country, vesting political power in the hands of those already part of the system.

As political scientist E. E. Schattschneider has observed:

> The 1896 party cleavage resulted from the tremendous reaction of conservatives in both major parties to the Populist movement.... [S]outhern conservatives reacted so strongly that they were willing to revive the tensions and animosities of the Civil War and the Reconstruction in order to set up a one-party sectional southern political monopoly in which nearly all Negroes and many poor whites were disenfranchised. One of the most important consequences of the creation of the Solid South was that it severed permanently the connection between the western and the southern wings of the Populist movement. [59]

Conservative Republicans won the White House in all but two (1912 and 1916) of the nine elections from 1896 to 1928.

The country experienced economic prosperity that blunted the possible activism of workers and the previous activism of farmers. With good harvests and rising commodity prices, the agrarian revolt fizzled. The development of new ore extraction methods and discovery of new gold deposits made calls for silver to expand the currency supply superfluous. The war with Spain, which McKinley reluctantly entered and the burgeoning mass media publicized, created a patriotic fervor.

McKinley's reelection in 1900 was even stronger than his 1896 election. He won 7.2 million popular votes (51.7 percent) to Bryan's 6.4 million (45.5 percent), and 292 electoral votes to Bryan's 155. McKinley swept to victory with all states except the silver states of the West (Colorado, Montana, Idaho, and Nevada).

The Rise of Theodore Roosevelt

To replace Vice President Garret A. Hobart, who died in office in 1899, the Republicans selected New York's Progressive governor Theodore Roosevelt to run with McKinley. Roosevelt, an independent-minded environmentalist and trust-buster, was promoted for vice president by New York GOP boss Thomas Platt to rid the state of progressive politics. Roosevelt was reluctant to take the job—"I am a comparatively young man yet and I like to work.... It would not entertain me to preside in the Senate" [60]—but accepted when a convention movement and McKinley prevailed upon him.

When McKinley was assassinated in 1901 and Roosevelt became president, U.S. presidential politics came under the influence of a variant of the progressive movement. As Gabriel Kolko and other historians have demonstrated, Roosevelt's administration was friendly to many of the traditional conservative allies. But Roosevelt's rhetoric and his legacy of regulation and conservation had strong progressive or reformist elements.[61]

Roosevelt's leadership of progressives is an example of generational politics. The new president grew up in an era in which economic expansion strained the nation's fabric, causing political figures to seek idealistic but pragmatic solutions to a wide variety of problems. The previous generation had grown up in a simpler age when "politics were devoid of substance, built around appeals to tradition and old loyalties and aimed at patronage." [62]

Roosevelt steered his party toward conservation of natural resources, enforcement of antitrust laws, promotion of the concerns of labor, and railroad regulation. The government's suit to dissolve the Northern Securities Company under the Sherman Anti-Trust Act and Roosevelt's intervention in the anthracite coal miners' strike, both in 1902, established the tenor for an activist presidency. TR (the first president identified by his initials) also used his office as a "bully pulpit" to promote his increasingly sophisticated progressive ideology.

Roosevelt had no trouble winning nomination for election as president in his own right in 1904. The Republican convention, arranged in advance at the White House, unanimously voted for Roosevelt and his platform of trust-busting, tariffs, labor relations, and activist foreign policy. Sen. Charles W. Fairbanks of Indiana was the GOP vice-presidential nominee.

To oppose the rambunctious Roosevelt, the Democrats selected a sober-visaged judge. Alton Parker, the chief justice of the New York State Court of Appeals, received the backing of the Democratic party's conservative establishment when former president Cleveland turned down entreaties to make a fourth presidential run. Parker was opposed by William Randolph Hearst, a member of Congress and newspaper magnate. Bryan forced the party to adopt a liberal platform, as a balance to the conservative judge.

The Roosevelt victory was a landslide. He won 7.6 million votes (56.4 percent) to Parker's 5.1 million (37.6 percent) and won all but the southern states. Roosevelt won 336 electoral votes to Parker's 140. Both houses of Congress were overwhelmingly Republican.

President Roosevelt pledged not to seek a second term of his own because he had served most of McKinley's second term. He occupied himself with his progressive agenda and groomed his secretary of war, William Howard Taft, as his successor.

Roosevelt Picks Taft

Roosevelt appeared to be genuinely dismayed by talk in 1907 of a possible third term, so he made public shows of support for Taft. Roosevelt was able to line up state delegations for Taft, and the nomination was never in doubt. Taft, through Roosevelt, was particularly strong among Republicans in the South. Attempts to restrict southern representation and pass a more liberal party platform were defeated.

Taft had impressive government experience. Before joining Roosevelt's cabinet, he had been a Cincinnati judge, U.S. solicitor general, federal circuit judge, head of the U.S. Commission on the Philippines, and the first civil governor of the Philippines.

Roosevelt's only problem in pushing Taft at the convention was avoiding a stampede in his own favor. Despite a highly disciplined convention, the galleries demonstrated wildly for Roosevelt. But Taft—a newcomer to electoral politics—easily won the nomination on the first ballot. He had 702 votes to the runner-up's 68. Rep. James S. Sherman of New York was selected as his running mate.

The Democrats nominated Bryan for the third time. The electoral disaster that befell Judge Parker in 1904 was said to be evidence that the party needed an aggressive challenger to the Republicans rather than another conservative candidate. The Democrats were bereft of new talent, especially in close states in the East and Midwest, and turned to Bryan despite his disastrous campaign record and the warnings of former president Cleveland.

The campaign was void of serious discussion. Taft campaigned on the Roosevelt record. Bryan called for government ownership of railroads and other liberal measures—such as a lower tariff, campaign finance reform, a graduated income tax, labor reforms, and greater enforcement of antitrust and other business regulations.

With Roosevelt and Taft promoting much of the progressive agenda, Bryan's message was no longer distinctive. Taft easily won. He gathered 7.7 million popular votes (51.6 percent) to Bryan's 6.4 million (43.1 percent), and 321 electoral votes to Bryan's 162. The North, most of the West, and the border states went into the Republican column.

Wilson and the Divided Republicans

Taft was not, by temperament, an ideal executive. His lifelong ambition had been to serve on the Supreme Court, and his disciplined legal mind and collegial nature eventually would enable Taft to become one of the high court's most able chief justices. But Taft foundered in the presidency. He carried out Roosevelt's program of business regulation and conservation, yet Roosevelt responded not with gratitude but with a series of nasty statements and plans for a campaign against Taft.

The tariff issue proved to be Taft's early trouble spot. Taft was committed to reducing tariffs—he was less political than Roosevelt, who fudged the divisive issue—and quickly became embroiled in a fight with Congress, which wanted to raise tariffs. The Senate remolded House legislation to push up various duties, and Taft publicly promoted the legislation after he managed to secure new corporate taxes and tariff reductions for raw materials. Taft proved ineffective and indecisive on the tariff issue and, as a consequence, began losing the party.

Library of Congress

Harvard College Library

The Democrats selected sober-visaged judge Alton B. Parker to run against the outgoing Theodore Roosevelt in the 1904 election. Roosevelt won by a wide margin.

The Glavis-Ballinger affair further muddied the image of the administration. The scandal broke when the chief forester of the Interior Department, Gifford Pinchot, charged that Secretary Richard A. Ballinger had betrayed the cause of conservation and had even engaged in corrupt practices regarding minerals and water power. Pinchot also charged that Ballinger had wrongly fired another Interior official, Louis Glavis, for trying to expose the scandal. Pinchot took his complaints directly to Taft, but Taft sided with Ballinger and urged Pinchot to drop the matter. After an indignant Pinchot went public with the issue, Taft fired him, fueling suspicion of a coverup at Interior. The incident was a major embarrassment to Taft because of the priority that conservation had received under Roosevelt and because of the inevitable complaints that Taft was betraying his mentor on the issue.[63]

Divisions within the Republican party eventually created the movement toward rival Taft and Roosevelt factions. Tariffs, Arizona's new state constitution (which included a provision that Taft opposed for recall of the governor), treaties, and antitrust issues split the former president and the sitting president. In many ways, the dispute was over personalities. Taft carried out Roosevelt's program, but lacked his evangelical fervor and decisiveness. In a still conservative age, progressives felt they needed more aggressive leadership than the judicially tempered Taft would ever give them.

Roosevelt spent more than a year of Taft's term hunting in Africa, but he was an active speaker and campaigner when he returned to the United States. He gave a detailed accounting of his philosophy of government at a 1912 speech in Columbus, Ohio, calling for voter referenda and initiatives, recall of elected officials, and curbs on judicial power. When a dump-Taft movement decided that Wisconsin's Sen. Robert La Follette had no chance to defeat the president for the GOP nomination, party discontents turned to the energetic and still young (fifty years) Roosevelt.

Roosevelt made an all-out effort for the Republican nomination, entering twelve primaries and winning all but three. Roosevelt won 278 delegates in states with primaries to Taft's 48 and La Follette's 36. In today's system, Roosevelt probably would have marched to a first-ballot nomination (because today more delegates are allocated by popular votes than by the party organizations, which then dominated the process). Three crucial Republican states—Pennsylvania, Illinois, and Ohio—went for Roosevelt. Roosevelt clearly had great popular appeal and vote-getting ability—perhaps more than ever.

But Taft won the nomination. The president controlled the party machinery, and most of the convention's delegates were sent by the state machines. Roosevelt challenged the credentials of Taft delegates at the Chicago convention, and the nomination's outcome turned on battles over almost one-fourth of the delegates. The fight went to the floor of the convention, but Taft's smooth operation defeated Roosevelt. Roosevelt appeared at the convention to buoy his forces and cry foul.

When Roosevelt, after the defeat, urged his supporters to continue their fight, some bolting progressive delegates organized a convention in August to mount a third party effort. The bolters formed the Progressive party for the effort. When Roosevelt remarked to a reporter during the GOP convention, "I'm feeling like a bull moose," his vigorous campaign had a symbol. With the Republicans divided, the Democrats saw their first opportunity to win the presidency since Cleveland.

As the 1912 Democratic convention in Baltimore neared, several national candidates and favorite sons were vying for the nomination. The front-runner was House Speaker James Beauchamp (Champ) Clark of Missouri, a party regular who had party organization support and years of experience to recommend him.

Library of Congress

Woodrow Wilson traveled widely in the 1912 election campaign. His dynamic presence and reformist rhetoric appealed to the crowds who came to hear him.

Gov. Woodrow Wilson of New Jersey—who held a doctorate in political science and moved into politics after a distinguished career as professor and president at Princeton University—was another strong candidate. Wilson's virtues were the opposite of Clark's. He did not have an extensive record for opponents to attack, and he was supported enthusiasticallly because of his dynamic presence and reformist rhetoric rather than a long political apprenticeship. The New Jersey machine had brought Wilson into politics, but he quickly asserted his independence and became something of a crusader. Wilson had guided an election bill, an anticorruption act, public utilities regulation, and worker's compensation legislation through the state legislature. Although he had dealt with the state's party bosses, he also put a distance between himself and the machine.

Other Democratic candidates were the conservative representative Oscar Underwood of Alabama, author of a historic tariff act; another conservative, Gov. Judson Harmon of Ohio; and four favorite-son governors.

Clark appeared to have won the nomination when a Tammany bloc of delegates moved to support him after he won a tenth-ballot majority. The requirement for a two-thirds majority, however, gave other candidates time to maneuver. Wilson almost dropped out of the race, but Bryan's late transfer of his support from Clark to Wilson created a bandwagon effect for Wilson. On the forty-sixth ballot, Wilson accumulated the necessary two-thirds of delegates for the nomination. Gov. Thomas Marshall of Indiana, one of the favorite-son candidates, was picked to be the vice-presidential candidate because Underwood, Wilson's choice, would not accept.

The Democratic platform was progressive. It called for tariff reduction, utility regulation, banking reforms, legislation to curb monopolies, a national income tax, direct election of senators, campaign finance reforms, and a national presidential primary.

Wilson easily won the election, receiving 435 electoral votes to Roosevelt's 88 and Taft's 8. The Republican splits obviously helped Wilson; if Roosevelt and Taft had combined their totals of 4.1 million votes (27.4 percent) and 3.5 million votes (23.2 percent), they would have topped Wilson's 6.3 million (41.8 percent). But even though Wilson was a minority president, there was a clear Democratic trend, since the Democrats had taken over the House and replaced several Republican governors in the 1910 midterm elections. It was the worst showing ever for an incumbent president—third place with only two states.

Whatever the strength of Wilson's "mandate," he acted as though he had won by a landslide. His first term was one of the most productive in U.S. history. With the Democrats in control of Congress, and with a shrewd political adviser in Col. Edward M. House, Wilson adopted a reform agenda that had been percolating at various levels of government for years. He broke precedent by delivering his first State of the Union message to Congress in person. At the center of the message was a call for reductions in tariff rates. After a bitter fight raged for a month, Wilson went public with a demand that members of Congress reveal their property holdings. The revelations showed close links between their holdings and the kinds of tariff protections on the books. Congress soon was shamed into passing tariff cuts of 15 percent. Some one hundred items were placed on a free-trade list for the first time.

Wilson also addressed other areas successfully: taxes (institution of a graduated income tax in 1913); banking regulation (the Glass-Owen Act of 1913, which created the Federal Reserve System); antitrust legislation (the Clayton Anti-Trust Act of 1914, creation of the Federal Trade Commission in 1914); labor relations (Section 6 of the Sherman Anti-Trust Act, which exempted unions from antitrust strictures); agriculture (the Smith-Lever Act of 1914, the Federal Farm Loan Act of 1916); environmentalism (creation of the National Park Service in 1916); and the judiciary (the appointment of Louis Brandeis to the Supreme Court).

Despite his strong leadership—highlighted by his stirring oratory—Wilson still faced the prospect of a tough reelection. He had won the presidency in 1912 with only 41.8 percent of the popular vote, and the growing war in Europe was beginning to disturb the American process of contented economic growth.

Public opinion on the war was volatile, largely because more than a third of the U.S. population was either foreign-born or offspring of foreign-born parents. Some eleven million Americans surveyed in the 1910 census were of direct German or Austrian descent, and another five million were from Ireland. Other immigrants were Russian, Italian, Hungarian, British, and French. Wilson sought to diffuse feelings for the immigrants' native lands when he denounced "hyphenism"—the tendency of many citizens to identify themselves with appellations that linked their ethnic origins and American status—but politicians at lower levels tailored their campaigns to specific nationality voting blocs.[64]

Wilson and Vice President Marshall won renomination without any opposition. The most significant event of the Democratic convention was the passage of the platform, which indicated the party's main campaign theme. By calling for national universal suffrage, Wilson helped himself in the eleven western states where women had already won the vote. The platform praised "the splendid diplomatic victories of our great president, who has preserved the vital interests of our government and its citizens, and kept us out of war." The latter phrase would be repeated endlessly during the fall.[65]

The Republicans nominated Supreme Court Justice Charles Evans Hughes. Hughes was silent in the months before the convention, but a number of party leaders lined up enough delegates for him to win a third-ballot nomination. Other potential candidates that year included former president Roosevelt, former senator Elihu Root of New York, former vice president Fairbanks, and senators John Weeks, Albert Cummins, and Lawrence Sherman. Fairbanks won the vice-presidential nomination.

Prosperity and reformism limited the campaign themes of the Republicans. The GOP railed against Wilson's foreign policy as "shifty expedients" and "phrasemaking" that put the United States in danger of entering the war. Hughes turned out to be a bad campaigner, but he bridged the gap between conservative and progressive Republicans that cost the party the 1912 election. Wilson was occupied with Congress throughout the summer of 1916, but he emerged to give a series of speeches in the fall. Democratic strategists, meanwhile, conceived and executed a masterful strategy to return Wilson to the White House. The Democrats concentrated all their resources on "swing states" and ignored states they thought Wilson was sure to lose. Illinois, for example, was ignored since it was a certain Republican state. Bryan, Wilson's secretary of state, toured the West.

Wilson won one of the closest elections in history. California, an uncertain state, ensured Wilson's victory when, because of the urban vote, it went the president's way late in the campaign. The margin of victory was 3,420 votes in that state. The president defeated Hughes by a margin of 9.1 million (49.2 percent) to 8.5 million popular votes (46.1 percent). The electoral college gave Wilson 277 votes and Hughes 254.

The "Return to Normalcy" and the Roaring Twenties

After the tumult of Woodrow Wilson's domestic reforms, the First World War, and the divisive battle over the Versailles treaty, the time was ripe for a period of conservatism and Republican government. Deep resentments developed toward Wilson and the Democratic party, and the Democrats were divided over many issues, including economic regulation, Prohibition, and race relations.

Blessed with good luck, strong financial backing, and a strong trend toward split-ticket voting, the Republicans were able to resume their dominance over national politics with three successful presidential campaigns. Warren G. Harding was elected in 1920, Calvin Coolidge in 1924, and Herbert C. Hoover in 1928.

The 1920s are usually pictured as a time of steady, unexciting politics. The conservatives dominated the federal government, and occupying the White House were men who spoke of "normalcy" and a noninterventionist brand of politics in both domestic and foreign affairs. One of the symbols of the age is President Coolidge's program of tax cuts, which reduced the rates on the wealthy. The wartime Revenue Act of 1918 had driven tax rates to the highest point in U.S. history. The total tax rate in the highest brackets was 77 percent. In 1921, 1923, and 1926, Secretary of the Treasury Andrew Mellon presented to Congress proposals to cut taxes, the most controversial being the reduction in the maximum surtax from 77 to 25 percent. Congress eventually cut the surtax to 40 percent in 1924 and 20 percent in 1926.[66]

But the three sober men who filled the presidency met challenges from progressives of both parties in Congress and in the state governments. On a wide range of issues—including relief of the poor, subsidies for the depressed farm sector, regulation of utilities, immigration, race relations, states' rights, tax cuts, and Prohibition—the conservative presidents encountered strong challenges. They frequently responded by vetoing legislation, but such an expedient would not prevent the pressures for a more activist government from developing.

Harding and "Normalcy"

Sen. Warren Harding, a product of the GOP machine of Ohio, emerged from a crowded and largely unknown pack to win the Republican nomination in 1920 at a convention dominated by economic interests such as oil, railroads, and steel.

The early candidates were Gen. Leonard Wood, an old Roosevelt ally; Gov. Frank Lowden of Illinois, who married into the Pullman family and therefore had ample financing for a campaign; and Sen. Hiram Johnson of California, whose progressive and isolationist stances put him in good stead with voters in many states. A dozen favorite sons hoped that a deadlocked convention might bring the nomination their way. All of the candidates were on hand in Chicago to maneuver for the nomination.

While Wood, Johnson, amd Lowden performed reasonably well in the primaries, Harding won only his home state of Ohio and did not arouse much popular enthusiasm. Under the direction of a shrewd campaign manager, Harry Daughtery, Harding gained the support of the party's bosses and won the nomination on the tenth ballot after a brief interview in the "smoke-filled room" that was synonymous with boss control. Gov. Calvin Coolidge of Massachusetts, a favorite-son contender for president, became Harding's vice-presidential candidate.

The Democrats selected Gov. James Cox, also from Ohio, after lengthy platform battles and balloting for the nomination. Early balloting put former Treasury secretary William McAdoo and Attorney General Mitchell Palmer in the lead, but Cox gained steadily and had the nomination by the forty-fourth roll call. Franklin D. Roosevelt of New York, the assistant secretary of the navy, was the quick selection for Cox's running mate.

The image of Woodrow Wilson hung over the convention and would hang over the fall campaign. The Democratic platform praised Wilson's conduct of the war and his domestic reform program. The results in the November election indicated deep unease over the Democratic administration, however. Harding's landslide victory was termed "election by disgust" by political analysts.

Harding amassed 16.1 million popular votes (60.3 percent) to Cox's 9.1 million (34.2 percent), and 404 electoral votes to Cox's 127. Harding carried the North and West including Oklahoma and all of the southern and border states except Tennessee and Kentucky.

The sacrifices demanded under Wilson were widely perceived as the cause of Harding's victory rather than a desire for the ideology or policy proposals that Harding offered. The *New York Post* editorialized: "We are in the

Franklin D. Roosevelt Library

Democratic presidential candidate James M. Cox of Ohio, left, and vice-presidential candidate Franklin D. Roosevelt (one year before he was stricken with polio), campaign in the 1920 election. They lost to Republican presidential candidate Warren G. Harding and his running mate, Gov. Calvin Coolidge of Massachusetts.

backwash from the mighty spiritual and physical effort to which America girded herself when she won the war for the Allies.... The war has not been repudiated, though the administration that fought it has been overwhelmed. We are now in the chill that comes with the doctor's bills." [67]

The electorate's ability to shift allegiances from the Republicans to the Democrats and back again—from one period to the next, and from one level of government to the next—suggested a dissolution of partisan alignments. The addition of women to the electorate after the Nineteenth Amendment in 1920 and increasing independence among all voters added uncertainty. Apathy resulted from the national exhaustion from the war and the lack of sharp ideological differences between the candidates. The electorate's instability was suggested by the divisions within both parties on high-profile issues such as Prohibition, the League of Nations, agricultural policies and other social and economic issues such as technical assistance and trust busting. The appearance of numerous "blocs" in both parties represented "little if anything more than a transitory alignment upon a particular vote or issue." [68]

The shifts in control of congressional and state offices also indicated electoral instability. The Democrats had comfortable control of Congress under Wilson, but in 1920 the Republicans gained a majority of 301 to 131 in the House and 59 to 37 in the Senate. Impressive liberal gains in congressional and state elections in 1922 appeared to be a slap at the Harding administration. The high turnover of votes also indicates unstable party affiliations: the 14.2 percentage point increase in the Republican vote between the 1916 and 1920 presidential elections was the largest since the Civil War, obviously a time of turmoil.[69]

President Harding died on August 2, 1923, of a heart attack, just as revelations of kickbacks and favoritism in the administration began to surface and several members of the administration quit and two committed suicide. The investigation into the so-called Teapot Dome scandal—so named after the site of naval oil reserves that were transferred to private hands in exchange for bribes—would last five years. The Democrats hoped to make the scandal a major issue in 1924, but Democratic complicity in the wrongdoing and the integrity of Harding's successor, Calvin Coolidge, defused the issue.

Coolidge Cleans Up

President Coolidge fired Attorney General Harry M. Daugherty and other members of Harding's clique and projected an image of puritan cleanliness. Coolidge—a taciturn man who had slowly climbed the political ladder in Massachusetts from city council member, city solicitor, mayor, state legislator, lieutenant governor, and governor before he became vice president—expounded a deeply individualistic Yankee philosophy that helped to separate him from the corrupt men in the Harding White House.

Except for appointing as attorney general Harlan Fiske Stone, former dean of the Columbia University School of Law, Coolidge allowed others to clean up the mess left behind by Harding. The new president was concerned about unnecessarily alienating himself from party leaders.

By the time Coolidge sought the presidency in his own right in 1924, the economy had rebounded. One of the most conservative presidents ever, Coolidge's platform called for additional tax cuts but said nothing substantive about increasingly salient agriculture and labor issues. Coolidge also pushed an isolationist foreign policy plank. He won the nomination on the first ballot.

While the Republicans were able to "Keep Cool with Coolidge," the Democrats spent sixteen days in a seemingly endless attempt to pick a nominee in New York's sweltering Madison Square Garden. The fight developed because the party was badly split between its northeastern urban bloc and its more conservative southern and western rural bloc. New York governor Alfred Smith and former Treasury secretary William McAdoo of California were the key combatants at the convention until the delegates were freed from boss instructions on the 100th ballot.

Suspicions between the two regions were intense. A platform plank denouncing the Ku Klux Klan created the most controversy. Northerners wanted an explicit repudiation of the society that preached hatred of Catholics, Jews, and blacks; in the end, southerners would settle only for a vaguely worded rebuke. The Klan infiltrated the party in many rural areas. Another divisive issue was Prohibition, with northerners attacking the initiative and southerners supporting it. These sectional splits would cripple the Democrats in the next two elections.

After the delegates were freed from instructions, a stampede developed for John W. Davis of West Virginia, a lawyer with Wall Street connections. The ticket was balanced with the vice-presidential selection of Charles Bryan of Nebraska, the younger brother of three-time presidential candidate William Jennings Bryan.

The Progressive candidacy of Robert La Follette complicated the calculations of voters, particularly those on the liberal end of the spectrum. Since the Democrats had a nearly impenetrable hold on the South, La Follette was not given a reasonable chance of winning. But the conservatism of both Coolidge and Davis meant that La Follette was the only genuine liberal in the race. Still, many liberals voted for Davis or even Coolidge because of the fear of an inconclusive election that would have to be resolved in the House of Representatives.

Coolidge won the election easily, with the Democrats polling their smallest percentage ever. Coolidge won 54.1 percent of the vote, Davis won 28.8 percent, and La Follette won 16.6 percent. Coolidge attracted 15.7 million popular votes and 382 electoral votes; Davis 8.4 million and 136; and La Follette 4.8 million and 13.

On August 2, 1927, when Coolidge announced his decision not to seek reelection by passing out a brief note to reporters and then refusing further comment, the Republicans began jockeying for the nomination for the 1928 election.

The Hoover Succession

Secretary of Commerce Herbert Hoover was the obvious choice to replace Coolidge at the head of the GOP ticket. A native of Iowa who learned mining engineering at Stanford University, Hoover was immensely popular to most of the party. Hoover's administration of Belgian relief and food distribution programs during World War I had earned him the status of statesman and humanitarian.

Hoover began working for the nomination soon after Coolidge dropped out, spending $400,000 in the nomination phase of the election. He won the nomination on the

Smithsonian Institution

"Keep Cool with Coolidge" was the Republican incumbent's 1924 campaign slogan, used on posters, banners, buttons, and decorative stamps such as this one from Wisconsin.

first ballot over Lowden and Gov. Charles Curtis of Kansas. Curtis was named Hoover's running mate.

Hoover was religious in his zeal for what he called "the American system" of free enterprise and individualism. He did not see any inconsistency in having the government vigorously support businesses with tax breaks, tariffs, public provision of infrastructures, and police protection, while at the same time denying relief to people in need. Hoover appeared to be less rigid than Coolidge, however. He proposed creation of a special farm board and said he would consider legislation to protect labor unions from abuses in the use of court injunctions.

Al Smith, the Tammany-schooled governor of New York, was the Democratic nominee. Smith had the support of all the party's northern states, and he won a first-ballot nomination. Sen. Joseph Robinson of Arkansas was the vice-presidential candidate.

Smith's candidacy polarized the electorate, particularly the South. He was the first Catholic to be nominated for president by a major party, and he endured religious slurs throughout the fall. He favored repeal of Prohibition, still a divisive issue. He was an urbanite, a problem for a nation that had nurtured a rural ideal since Thomas Jefferson. He was a machine politician, a problem for anyone outside (and many people inside) the nation's great cities. He was a strong opponent of the Klan, which put him in trouble in the South. Finally, he was an unabashed liberal who proposed public works, farm relief programs, stronger protection of workers, and regulation of banking and industry.

During the fall campaign, Hoover acted like the incumbent and Smith barnstormed the country, trying in vain to pick up support in the South and West. The 1928 campaign was the first with extensive radio coverage, and Hoover generally fared better than Smith on the airwaves. Hoover, the small-town boy who made good, represented fulfillment of the American Dream; Smith, the inner-city boy who made good, also embodied that ideal, but he had too many alien traits for much of the nation to realize it.

The November election produced another Republican landslide. Hoover carried forty states with 21.4 million popular votes (58.2 percent) and 444 electoral votes, while Smith carried only eight states with 15.0 million popular votes (40.8 percent) and 87 electoral votes. As disastrous as the election appeared to be for the Democrats, it put them in position to build a wide-ranging coalition in future years.

Smith carried only six southern states, but the defection of the others was temporary. More important to the Democrats' long-range fortunes was the movement of cities into the Democratic column, probably for the rest of the century. In all, Smith diverted 122 northern counties from the GOP to the Democratic party. Catholics, whose turnout previously was low, turned out in record numbers. Immigrants in cities also expanded their vision from local politics to the national stage for the first time. Smith also seemed to pick up some of the Progressive farm vote that La Follette had tapped before; in Wisconsin, for example, the Democratic vote jumped from 68,000 to 450,000 from 1924 to 1928. Smith's candidacy also put the Democrats solidly in the "wet" column, just as the national temper began to resent Prohibition.

President Hoover impressed political observers with his managerial skills and "coordinating mind." With passage of the Agricultural Marketing Act in June 1929, the administration appeared to address the most pressing economic problem for the business-minded president. He met some legislative setbacks, but overall the Great Engineer appeared to be in good political condition as the nation looked back over his record when Congress began its recess in the summer of 1929.

The national economic and social fiesta that began at the close of World War I came to an abrupt end on October 29, 1929. After climbing to dizzying new heights for months, the stock market crashed. First described by economists and politicians as a temporary interruption of the good times, the crash quickly led to a wave of business and bank failures, mortgage foreclosures, wage cuts, layoffs, and a crisis of political leadership. By the end of Hoover's term in 1932, more than twelve million workers had lost their jobs; the unemployment rate was approximately 25 percent. An October 1931 advertisement for 6,000 jobs in the Soviet Union brought 100,000 American applications.[70]

President Hoover, who had celebrated his inauguration with a prediction that poverty and hunger were near an end, did not know how to cope with the crisis. In a special session that Hoover called, Congress created the Federal Farm Board to coordinate marketing of agricultural products, but Hoover steadfastly opposed further moves, especially subsidies. Hoover also signed the Smoot-Hawley tariff bill to protect manufacturers, but, true to the predictions of economists and bankers, the tariff only aggravated economic conditions by hurting foreign trade.

Hoover later approved agricultural relief and public works programs and established the Reconstruction Finance Corporation. The president refused to approve direct relief to the unemployed and businesses, but he did approve some loans and aid to specific sectors of the economy.

Despite his earnest and tireless efforts, Hoover became a figure of widespread enmity. The low point of his distinguished career came when World War I veterans petitioned for early receipt of their service bonuses, which, by contract, were not to be paid until 1945. They set up camp in Washington, singing old war songs and carrying placards that bore their pleas. The "Bonus Army" numbered twenty thousand at its height. When Hoover feared a protracted protest, he ordered federal troops to take buildings over where some veterans were camping. In two skirmishes, two veterans were killed. The president then sent in Gen. Douglas MacArthur with tanks, infantry, and calvary soldiers. (MacArthur's junior officers included Dwight D. Eisenhower and George Patton.) After successfully removing the veterans, the military forces overran nearby veterans' camps in a rain of fire and tear gas. Thousands of veterans and their families fled the burning district.

The administration's tough stance against a defeated, ragtag band of former war heroes shocked and embittered the nation. The barricaded White House and administration statements about "insurrectionists" symbolized a dangerous gulf between the government and the people.

Partly because of the economic crisis he did not create, but also because of a dour and unimaginative demeanor, Hoover probably never had a chance to win reelection. The 1930 midterm elections indicated a loss of confidence in the administration. The House went Democratic, 219 to 214, and the Senate came within a seat of going Democratic as well.

Those election results did not convey the bitterness and despair that the depression would aggravate before the next presidential campaign. Hoover was mercilessly ridiculed in newspapers and in Democratic speeches. The Democratic party coordinated a comprehensive anti-Hoover campaign that made the president politically impotent.

Election of 1932

Franklin D. Roosevelt, fifth cousin to Theodore Roosevelt, was the perfect candidate to oppose Hoover. The New York governor had been an activist in state politics, first opposing the state's Tammany machine and then pioneering many relief and reconstruction programs that Hoover refused to expand to the national scale. Roosevelt had been the party's vice-presidential candidate twelve years before, and he had served in the federal government as assistant secretary of the navy.

Perhaps more important than any of his political accomplishments was FDR's image of strength and optimism and his deft handling of hot issues and disparate members of the potential Democratic coalition. Although he was a polio victim, Roosevelt often smiled—a devastating contrast to Hoover. (Gutzon Borglum, the sculptor, wrote: "If you put a rose in Hoover's hand, it would wilt." [71]) Roosevelt was able to campaign for the presidency without putting forth a comprehensive program: the simple promise of a change in leadership was enough.

Some observers found the man from Hyde Park wanting. Journalist Walter Lippmann, for example, complained that Roosevelt was "a pleasant man who, without any important qualifications for the office, would like very much to be president." [72] But those detractors and a large field of Democrats were not able to keep Roosevelt from his "rendezvous with destiny." [73]

The Democratic field included the 1928 Democratic standard-bearer, Al Smith; John Nance Garner, the Speaker of the House; Gov. Albert Ritchie of Maryland; Gov. George White of Ohio; Gov. Harry Byrd of Virginia; and Sen. James Reed of Mississippi. Most considered Smith more of a "stalking horse" for the anti-FDR forces than a serious candidate in his own right. Garner had impressive backing from the newspaper magnate William Randolph Hearst amd former Democratic candidate William G. McAdoo.

The many favorite sons in the race threatened to deadlock the convention and deny the nomination to the front-runner, as they had done so often in the past. Roosevelt had difficulty with his own region of the country because of his opposition to the Tammany machine in New York. The goal of the two-thirds vote of delegates for the nomination for Roosevelt or any other candidate was difficult, but FDR eventually won on the fourth ballot when he promised the vice-presidential slot to Garner.

Franklin Roosevelt was the first candidate to appear before the convention that nominated him. In an acceptance speech to the conventioneers who had staged wild rallies in his support, Roosevelt made passing reference to

The Bettmann Archive

In 1932, World War I veterans, seeking early receipt of their service bonuses, staged a protest by setting up camps near the Capitol. On July 28, President Herbert C. Hoover ordered federal troops, headed by Gen. Douglas MacArthur, to disperse the veterans with tear gas.

Franklin D. Roosevelt Library

Franklin D. Roosevelt campaigns in West Virginia, October 19, 1932.

a "new deal" that his administration would offer Americans. That phrase, picked up in a newspaper cartoon the following day, would symbolize the renewal that Americans yearned for as riots and radicalism seemed to threaten the nation's spirit and the legitimacy of its institutions.

Roosevelt conducted an active fall campaign, traveling twenty-three thousand miles in all but seven states to quell suspicions that his physical handicaps would deter him from performing his job. Besides barnstorming the nation, Roosevelt also took to the radio airwaves—he was the first sophisticated electronic media candidate—and conveyed a sense of warmth and confidence. He also showed an intellectual bent and an open mind when he called on academics and professionals—the famed "brains trust"—for their expert advice on the issues.

Roosevelt won 22.8 million votes (57.4 percent) to Hoover's 15.8 million (39.6 percent). Forty-two of the forty-eight states and 472 of the 531 electoral votes went for Roosevelt. The election was a landslide and a realignment of the major forces in U.S. politics.

The New Deal Coalition

The profound effect of Roosevelt's victory on U.S. politics can hardly be overstated. The New Deal coalition that Roosevelt assembled shaped the political discourse and electoral competition of the United States until the late 1960s. In many respects, that coalition is a central element of politics today.

The new Democratic coalition brought together a disparate group of interests: southerners, blacks, immigrants, farmers, capital-intensive producers, international businessmen, financiers, urbanites, trade unions, Catholics, and Jews. Rexford Tugwell called it "the most miscellaneous coalition in history."[74] These blocs were not always in perfect harmony—for example, the Democrats juggled the demands of blacks and white southerners with great difficulty—but they were solid building blocks for national political dominance.

The dominance was impressive. Between 1932 and 1964, the Democrats won seven of nine presidential elections. The only successful Republican, Eisenhower, could just as easily have run as a Democrat. Party leaders in fact asked him to run as a Democrat in 1948 and 1952, and his name was entered in some Democratic primaries in 1952.

The strength of the Roosevelt rule is attributable partly to the president's personality. He could be soothing. When he gave his first "fireside chat" about the banking crisis, the nation responded with cooperation; the raids and violence at banks ended in a matter of weeks. More important than his soothing nature was his ability to experiment and shift gears. Professor James David Barber described Roosevelt's many public postures:

> Founder of the New Deal, modern American democracy's closest approximation to a common political philosophy, Roosevelt came on the scene as the least philosophical of men—"a chameleon in plaid," Hoover called him. Firm fighter of yet another Great War, Roosevelt appeared to H.L. Mencken in 1932 as "far too feeble and wishy-washy a fellow to make a really effective fight." Architect of world organization, he introduced himself as totally concerned with America's domestic drama. His name is inseparable from his generation's great social revolution; in 1932, nearly all the heavy thinkers scoffed at him as just another placebo politician—a "pill to cure an earthquake," said Professor [Harold] Laski.[75]

More important than personality was what Roosevelt had to offer the many groups in his coalition. As historian Richard Hofstadter has noted, the New Deal was "a series of improvisations, many adopted very suddenly, many contradictory."[76] The Roosevelt credo was: "Save the people and the nation, and if we have to change our minds twice a day to accomplish that end, we should do it."[77]

Until the vast expenditures of World War II, there was not enough pump-priming to end the depression, but Roosevelt's initiatives touched almost everyone affected by the slump.[78] For the jobless, there were unemployment insurance and public works programs like the Works Progress Administration and the Civilian Conservation Corps. For the poor, there were categorical aid programs. For westerners, there were conservation measures. For the banks, there was the famous holiday that stopped runs on holdings, and there were currency and securities reforms. For farmers, there were incentives and price supports and cooperatives. For the aged, there was Social Security. For the southeasterners, there was the Tennessee Valley Authority. For southern whites, there was a hands-off policy on race matters. For blacks, there was sympathy. For those living in rural areas, there was electrification. For families, there were home loans. For the weary worker eager for a few rounds at the local pub, there was the repeal of Prohibition. For laborers, there was acknowledgment of the right to negotiate for their share of the national wealth. For business, there were the Federal Emergency Relief Act and the National Industrial Recovery Act, as well as negotiation to reduce trade barriers.

The remarkably divergent interests in the coalition were underscored by the politics of race. Blacks moved en masse to the Democratic party from their traditional position in the "Party of Lincoln," partly because of Hoover's failure but also because of the inclusive rhetoric of the New Deal. Yet, Roosevelt was too concerned about his bloc of southern support even to accept antilynching legislation.

Scholars have argued that the New Deal coalition did not indicate a wholesale shift in existing political loyalties, but rather that new forces had joined an already stable alliance to tip the competitive balance of U.S. parties. The political discourse in the United States changed not because all or even most groups changed their behavior, but because new groups and issues became involved.[79]

The core of Roosevelt's winning coalition is easy to describe: "Southern white Protestants, Catholics, and non-Southern white Protestants of the lowest socioeconomic stratum together accounted for roughly three-fourths of all Americans of voting age in 1940 who thought of themselves as Democrats. By way of contrast, these three groups provided only about 40 percent of the smaller cadre of Republican identifiers." [80] Within this coalition, there were both new and old elements.

Although the Democratic party encompassed new constituencies and addressed new issues, it retained many of its traditional supporters. The "Jim Crow" South had consistently been in the Democratic column; in 1896, for example, the South's percentage support for Democrat William Jennings Bryan exceeded that of the rest of the nation by 15.3 points. Even in 1928, when Al Smith's Catholicism brought the Democratic support for the Democrats below 50 percent for the only time, the Deep South supported the Democrats more than the border South.[81] To the South, the Democrats were reliably the party of white supremacy and agricultural interests, while Republicans favored the industrial interests of the North.

Outside the South, the Democrats were the party of immigrants and Catholics. Since Andrew Jackson's day, the overwhelming monolithic Democratic voting patterns of Catholics contrasted with the split vote of Protestants in the United States. The Catholic-Protestant divisions "represent not so much religious as more general ethnocultural traditions." [82] The Democratic hold on the Catholic vote was reinforced by the heavy immigration into northern cities in the last half of the nineteenth century. While the anti-Catholic Ku Klux Klan received Democratic backing in the South, it received Republican backing in the North, pushing Catholics decisively into the Democratic party.

A steady base in the Democratic party consisted of laborers and the poor. From the first party machines in the early nineteenth century to William Jennings Bryan's campaign on behalf of the depressed farm belt in 1896 to Woodrow Wilson's acceptance of labor bargaining in 1914, the Democrats had shown sympathy for the less privileged classes. Such sympathies were often constricted by prejudice, but the Democrats offered more hope of representation than the business-oriented Republicans. Roosevelt solidified the support of the poor and laboring classes.[83] Sundquist has written: "The party system undoubtedly reflected some degree of class before the realignment, but there can be little doubt that it was accentuated by the event. It was in the New Deal era that tight bonds were formed between organized labor and the Democratic Party, that ties equally close if less formal and overt were formed between business and the GOP, and that politics for the first time since 1896 sharply accented class issues."[84] Roosevelt consistently received the support of more than two-thirds of the voters of low socioeconomic status.[85]

New converts to the Democratic party included blacks and Jews. The inclusion of blacks into the New Deal coalition underscores a "multiplier effect" at work with thriving interest-group politics. The Republicans received the black vote in the seventeen elections from Reconstruction to 1932. Roosevelt received 35 percent of the black vote in 1932, and his black support was as low as 23 percent in Chicago and 29 percent in Cincinnati.[86] Even though Roosevelt did little to promote black interests in the South, where most blacks lived, the black vote for him increased to 70 percent in 1936 and 1940. Migration of blacks to the North and spillover effects of Roosevelt's many domestic programs brought blacks to the Democratic party.

Jews, who had voted Republican since their numbers swelled during immigration around the turn of the century, turned to the Democrats as they became the more liberal party. Roosevelt got 85 percent of the Jewish vote in 1936 and 84 percent in 1940. New Deal assistance programs and Roosevelt's efforts to fight Nazism appealed to Jews, but perhaps more important was "the historic pattern of discrimination which forced or disposed Jews to oppose conservative parties." [87] The class division that split other social groups was absent in the Jewish population.

In many ways, the whole of the New Deal was greater than the sum of its parts. Political scientist Samuel Beer has argued that two long-competing visions of U.S. politics—the national idea and the democratic idea—at last came together during Roosevelt's administration. With the New Deal, the Democratic party was able to combine its traditional concern for local, individualistic interests with a national vision. By bringing "locked-out" groups into the system, the Democrats enhanced both nation building and individual freedoms. The parts, put together, created a stronger whole. Beer quotes the French sociologist Emile Durkheim: "The image of the one who completes us becomes inseparable from ours. . . . It thus becomes an integral and permanent part of our conscience. . . ." [88]

The political genius of "interest-group liberalism" [89] was not just that it offered something to everyone, but that it created a new age of consumerism in which everyone's interest was in growth rather than structural change. The general good was defined as growth. The potentially divisive competition over restricted and unequally distributed resources was avoided with a general acceptance of growth as the common goal. When there was growth, everyone could get a little more. That public philosophy became a permanent part of American political discourse.

The Four-term President

Roosevelt's coalition and leadership were so strong that he became the only president to win more than two elections. He won four elections and served a little more than twelve years in the White House before dying in office.

Roosevelt's four electoral triumphs caused Republicans to fume about his "imperial" presidency; all they could do in response to FDR was promote a constitutional amendment to limit presidents to two terms. More important was the way Roosevelt shaped the American political agenda. For many people of the time, it was difficult to imagine the United States under any other leadership.

Roosevelt's three successful reelection drives evoked a changing response from Republicans. Roosevelt's first reelection opponent, in 1936, was Gov. Alfred M. Landon of Kansas, who strongly criticized every aspect of the New Deal. After 1936, Republican candidates did not criticize federal intervention in economic and social affairs but rather the speed and the skill of Democratic intervention. In the third election, the Republicans argued that Roosevelt was a "warmonger" because he tilted toward Great Britain in World War II. The GOP argued in the third and fourth elections that Roosevelt threatened to become a "dictator" by breaking the traditional two-term limit.

Landon was the early favorite for the Republican nomination in 1936. Sen. Charles McNary of Oregon, Sen. Arthur Vandenberg of Michigan, and *Chicago Daily News* publisher Frank Knox provided weak opposition. Landon was attached to neither the old-guard nor the younger liberal Republicans. A Republican bolter for Theodore Roosevelt's "Bull Moose" candidacy in 1912, Landon was consistently to the left of the GOP. Historian James MacGregor Burns observed: "Landon had just the qualities of common sense, homely competence, cautious liberalism and rocklike 'soundness' that the Republicans hoped would appeal to a people tiring, it was hoped, of the antics and heroics in the White House." [90]

In 1936 the Republicans could not have stated their opposition to the popular New Deal in any stronger terms. The platform read: "America is in peril. The welfare of American men and women and the future of our youth are at stake. We dedicate ourselves to the preservation of their political liberty, their individual opportunity, and their character as free citizens, which today for the first time are threatened by government itself." [91]

The Republicans called for ending a wide range of government regulations, returning relief to state and local governments, replacing Social Security, balancing the budget, and changing tariff and currency policies. Landon's only innovation was a call for a constitutional amendment allowing the states to regulate the labor of women and children; the Supreme Court had struck down a New York minimum-wage law. After Landon won the nomination on the first ballot, he selected Knox as his running mate.

The only time the two presidential candidates met was at a meeting Roosevelt called with state governors to discuss farm relief and a recent drought. The candidates sparred inconclusively.

Landon's campaign possessed a lavish war chest of $9 million, the defections of Democratic stalwarts such as Al Smith and John Davis, well-coordinated campaign work by business lobbies, and smear campaigns that portrayed Social Security as a simple "pay reduction" measure and Roosevelt as physically and mentally ill. Landon also argued that New Deal spending was just another form of spoils politics, a charge Roosevelt addressed by folding postmasters into the civil service system.

The only important departure at the Democratic convention was the repeal of the party's requirement that a candidate receive two-thirds of the delegates to win the nomination. After some arm twisting, southern delegates backed the change, but the governor of Texas wondered aloud if the change was designed for a third Roosevelt run in 1940. Roosevelt was renominated without opposition. He asked Garner to run with him a second time.

In response to Landon's GOP nomination and agitation by leaders of the left—including Huey Long of Louisiana, Father Charles Coughlin of Detroit, Dr. Francis Townsend of California (who espoused a federal pension plan for senior citizens), and the Socialist Norman Thomas of New York—President Roosevelt in his acceptance speech launched a rhetorical war against "economic royalists" who opposed his programs. He dropped the idea of a "unity" campaign in favor of a partisan ideological attack intended to gain a mandate for a variety of stalled programs rather than a personal vote of confidence. [92]

Roosevelt at first had planned a low-key campaign of "conciliation" but decided to wage the more aggressive campaign when Landon got the GOP nomination. Landon had run an impressive nomination campaign and was thought to appeal to American pinings for governmental stability. In the early stages of the fall campaign, Roosevelt pretended not to be a partisan politician. He moved around the country to make "official" inspections of drought states and public works programs and to deliver speeches on electrical power, conservation, social welfare programs, among other topics. Roosevelt assigned Postmaster General James Farley the task of addressing party rifts and Republican charges of spoils.

At the end of September, Roosevelt returned to his role as partisan leader. The president answered Republican charges point by point, then lashed out at the Republicans in biting, sarcastic terms. As the campaign progresssed and Roosevelt sensed a strong response from the large crowds to his attacks, the attacks became stronger. At the close of the campaign, he said:

> We have not come this far without a struggle and I assure you that we cannot go further without a struggle. For 12 years, our nation was afflicted with a hear-nothing, see-nothing, do-nothing government. The nation looked to the government but the government looked away. Nine mocking years with the golden calf and three long years of the scourge! Nine crazy years at the ticker and three long years at the breadlines! Nine mad years of mirage and three long years of despair! And, my friends, powerful influences strive today to restore that kind of government with its doctrine that that government is best which is most indifferent to mankind.... Never before in all of our history have these forces been so united against one candidate as they stand today. They are unanimous in their hate for me—and I welcome their hatred.[93]

Especially to sophisticated campaign technicians of the modern age, a poll that predicted a big Landon victory provides some amusement. The *Literary Digest*, which had

Library of Congress
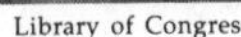

Library of Congress

New York Historical Society

President Franklin D. Roosevelt's Republican opponents during his three reelection campaigns were, from left: Gov. Alfred M. Landon of Kansas in 1936; former Democrat and business executive Wendell L. Willkie in 1940; and Gov. Thomas E. Dewey of New York in 1944.

predicted past elections with accuracy, conducted a post-card poll that pointed toward a Landon landslide. The heavy middle- and upper-class bias of the magazine's readership meant that the views of the voters on the lower rungs of the economic ladder were left out of the sample. To this day, the poll is cited as the prime example of bad survey-group selection.

The failure of the *Literary Digest*'s survey pointed to the most salient aspect of the election results: the heavy class divisions among the voters. Polls show that class divisions widened starting around the midpoint of Roosevelt's first term. The broad support FDR had enjoyed because of a common economic disaster hardened along class lines by 1936.

Roosevelt won 27.7 million popular votes (60.8 percent) to Landon's 16.7 million (36.5 percent). Roosevelt won all but two of the forty-eight states, and he took 523 of the 531 electoral votes. In addition, the Senate's Democratic majority increased to 75 of 96 seats, and the House majority increased to 333 of 435 seats. Roosevelt ran ahead of candidates such as gubernatorial candidate Herbert Lehman of New York, who had been recruited to boost his vote totals in various states. The Democratic victory was almost too overwhelming, Roosevelt suggested, because it would encourage Democrats to fight among themselves rather than with Republicans.

The Third Term

Soon after his landslide, Roosevelt tempted fate with a proposal that would have increased the size of the Supreme Court from nine to fifteen members in order to "pack" the court with justices closer to the president's political philosophy. The high court had constantly struck down important New Deal initiatives such as the Agriculture Adjustment Act, the National Recovery Administration, and the tax on food processing.

Roosevelt shrouded his proposal in statements of concern for the capacities of some of the court's older and more conservative justices. In a fireside speech, Roosevelt said the Court's failure to keep pace with the other "horses" in the "three-horse team" of the federal government constituted a "quiet crisis." [94] The elderly chief justice Charles Evans Hughes belied that charge with the energy he brought to the tribunal. Roosevelt refused to compromise on the bill, and it became an executive-legislative dispute. The proposal was widely seen as a brazen power play, and by the summer Congress had defeated it.

President Roosevelt eventually got the judicial approval he wanted for his initiatives—what wags called "the switch in time that saved nine." The Court appeared to shift its philosophy during the court-packing affair, and, before long, enough justices had retired so that Roosevelt could put his own appointees on the Court.

Other problems awaited Roosevelt in the second term. Splits in the labor movement gave rise to violence during organizing drives, and the president responded haltingly. After his rift with business over the full range of New Deal policies, Roosevelt appeared to be drifting. Conservatives in Congress were more assertive than ever in opposing the "socialist" measures of the Roosevelt years. The only major New Deal legislation in the second term was the Fair Labor Standards Act of 1938, which abolished child labor and set a minimum wage and an official rate of time-and-a-half for overtime.

As Roosevelt looked toward a third term in 1940, the widening war in Europe posed a difficult problem. Nazi Germany had invaded the Rhineland, Poland, France, Norway, Denmark, Holland, Belgium, and Luxembourg and had made alliances with Italy and the Soviet Union, while Japan invaded China. Adolf Hitler launched the Battle of Britain in the summer of 1940 and all-night air raids of London soon afterwards.

British prime minister Winston Churchill desperately petitioned President Roosevelt to provide fifty destroyers. Britain's need for the destroyers was so great that Roosevelt balked at asking Congress for help. He reasoned that congressional action probably would take three months, and isolationists might even block action—dealing a crippling blow to Britain. After lengthy administration debate, Roosevelt agreed to send Churchill the destroyers as part of a "lend-lease" agreement. The United States would receive bases in the Carribbean as part of the deal.

A favorite parlor game as the 1940 election approached was guessing whom Roosevelt might tap as his successor. Roosevelt publicly maintained that he did not want another term, but he refused to issue a definitive statement begging off the race. Despite the historic precedent against third terms, however, Roosevelt wanted to remain president. To avoid the appearance of overzealousness, Roosevelt wanted the Democrats to draft him in 1940.

While the nation waited for Roosevelt to act, Vice President Garner announced his candidacy. Postmaster General Farley and Secretary of State Cordell Hull also wanted to be president, and Roosevelt gave both vague assurances of support. Roosevelt, whose relations with Garner had been sour for years, simply watched the vice president struggle to gain a respectable public profile. The Farley and Hull prospects withered without the help of the old master.

From a distance, Roosevelt watched state Democratic delegations declare their support. Polls showed Roosevelt's fortunes rising with the deepening European crisis. Just before the GOP convention, Roosevelt appointed Republi cans Henry Stimson and Frank Knox to his cabinet. Roosevelt did not reveal his plans even to his closest aides. The president did not forbid aides such as Harry Hopkins to work on a draft, but he did not get involved because he wanted the Democrats to call on him and not the other way round.

At the Chicago convention, Sen. Alben Barkley told the convention: "The president has never had, and has not today, any desire or purpose to continue in the office of president.... He wishes in all earnestness and sincerity to make it clear that all the delegates of this convention are free to vote for any candidate."[95] The statement was followed by an hour-long demonstration and Roosevelt's first-ballot nomination.

The convention mood turned sour, however, when Roosevelt announced that he wanted the liberal secretary of agriculture, Henry Wallace, as his running mate. The announcement disgruntled delegates who had already lined up behind other candidates. Wallace eventually beat Alabama representative William Bankhead, his strongest opponent for the nomination.

The Republicans mounted their strongest challenge to Roosevelt in 1940, largely on their charge that Roosevelt was moving the United States toward involvement in the world war. Several moves toward military preparedness had failed at the hands of isolationists in Congress. When Roosevelt asked for increases in defense spending after Gen. Francisco Franco's victory in Spain and Hitler's invasion of Austria in 1938, critics asserted that the president was attempting to cover up domestic failures with foreign adventures. Roosevelt pressed on, however, and Congress passed the Selective Service Act and increases in military spending in 1940.

The Republican field in 1940 included several fresh faces—Sen. Robert A. Taft of Ohio, son of the former president; District Attorney Thomas E. Dewey of New York City; and Sen. Charles L. McNary of Oregon and Sen. Arthur H. Vandenberg of Michigan who had sought the Republican nomination in 1936. The freshest face of all was Wendell L. Willkie, a utility executive who had never run for political office. A large and affable man, former Democrat Willkie had barnstormed the country for seven years speaking in opposition to the New Deal.[96]

Hundreds of "Willkie clubs" sprang up in the summer of 1940, and a number of publications including Henry Luce's *Time* magazine chronicled Willkie's career and encouraged the Willkie groundswell. Despite concern about Willkie's lack of political experience that led to a "stop Willkie" movement, the Indianan won a sixth-ballot nomination by acclamation. Senator McNary, the Republicans' Senate floor leader, reluctantly accepted the vice-presidential nomination.

Traveling thirty thousand miles in thirty-four states, Willkie gave some 540 speeches. By the time his campaign ended, his already husky voice turned hoarse. The Republicans spent lavishly and organized grass-roots clubs for Willkie across the country. Charges against Roosevelt of managerial incompetence, "warmongering," and imperial ambitions punctuated the Willkie effort. A dramatic moment came when labor leader John L. Lewis called on workers to back Willkie.

After a period of strictly "presidential" behavior, Roosevelt took to the campaign trail with partisan vigor. He answered Willkie's warmongering charges with a promise never to involve the United States in "foreign wars" (which left Roosevelt free to respond to a direct attack).

The importance of alienated Democratic and independent voters was symbolized by Vice President Garner, who did not even vote. Roosevelt won, but by the slimmest margin of any race since 1912. Roosevelt received 27.3 million popular votes (54.7 percent) to Willkie's 22.3 million (44.8 percent). The electoral vote tally was 449-82.

The War and Its Legacy

Roosevelt's third term and fourth election were dominated by the Second World War. Japan attacked U.S. bases at Pearl Harbor, Hawaii, on December 7, 1941. The president, speaking before Congress, declared the surprise attack "a day that will live in infamy," and Congress shook off its isolationist inclinations to declare war.

The war did for the economy what the New Deal, by itself, could not: it brought economic prosperity. The number of unemployed workers fell from eight million to one million between 1940 and 1944. The boom brought seven million more people, half of them women, into the job market. Inflation, worker shortages, and occasional shortages in raw materials posed problems for wartime agencies. The number of U.S. families paying taxes quadrupled, and by 1945 tax revenues were twenty times their 1940 level. Budget deficits reached new heights.[97]

The war effort was grim for two years of the president's new term. Isolationist sentiment built up in Congress, with the Midwest proving the region most resistant to Roosevelt's foreign policy. Criticism of war administration was rampant. The administration won key congressional votes on the war but faced stubborn resistance on domestic measures. In the 1942 midterm elections, the Republicans gained ten seats in the Senate and forty-seven seats in the House—a major repudiation of Roosevelt.

After several setbacks, the Allied forces won impressive victories. Roosevelt and Churchill worked together closely. Allied forces led by Gen. Dwight D. Eisenhower routed the Axis powers in North Africa in 1942. The Soviet Union beat back a Nazi assault on Stalingrad in the winter of 1942-1943. The Allies took over Italy in 1943 and struggled with the Nazis in France. By September 1944, British and American troops entered Germany. In the Pacific war, American offensives secured Australia in 1942 and the Philippines in 1944.

Despite the bitterness that prevailed through much of his administration, Roosevelt had no trouble winning a fourth term in 1944. The Allies found greater success on the battlefield and on the sea, and the nation did not appear willing to risk untested leadership to prosecute the war. The Republicans turned to the smooth governor of New York, Thomas Dewey. Willkie wanted another shot at the White House, and his best-selling book *One World* put him in the public eye, but old-line conservatives blamed him for the 1944 election defeat. Governors John Bricker of Ohio and Harold Stassen of Minnesota and Gen. MacArthur were the other hopefuls.

Dewey's primary victories over Willkie in the Wisconsin, Nebraska, and Oregon primaries finished Willkie's public career. Dewey was too far in front to stop. At the convention, he won a nearly unanimous, first-ballot nomination after Bricker and Stassen dropped out. After Gov. Earl Warren of California refused the vice-presidential nomination, Bricker accepted it.

The party platform extolled the virtues of free enterprise but did not criticize the concept of the New Deal and even made bids for the votes of blacks and women. In his acceptance speech, Dewey criticized "stubborn men grown old and tired and quarrelsome in office." [98]

The 1944 election marked the early resistance of the South to the modern Democratic party. Roosevelt was a shoo-in for the nomination, but southerners wanted a replacement for Wallace as vice president, restoration of the two-thirds nominating rule, and a platform declaration of white supremacy. Unsatisfied Dixiecrats threatened to bolt the party in November, but when the party adopted only a vague civil rights plank in its platform, southern discontent dissipated. The rest of the platform called for an internationalist thrust in foreign policy and further New Deal-style reforms domestically.

Roosevelt expressed support for Wallace but said he would allow the convention to pick his running mate. Wallace gave a stirring convention speech but disturbed conservatives with his stand against the poll tax and for equal opportunity for all "regardless of race or sex." Sen. Harry S Truman of Missouri, who had won fame as a critic of defense spending, beat Wallace for the vice-presidential nomination on the second ballot.

The Democratic campaign was dominated by references to the need for wartime unity and reminders of the Republican rule under Hoover. One leaflet bore the words "Lest We Forget" and a photograph of an unemployed man selling apples in front of a "Hoover Club"; an inset photograph showed Dewey conferring with former president Hoover. The Republicans spent nearly as much money as they did in the record-setting 1936 election.

Roosevelt won with 25.6 million popular votes (53.4 percent) to Dewey's 22.0 million (45.9 percent). The electoral vote score was 432-99. President Roosevelt—who reshaped U.S. politics at all levels—did not have the opportunity to see the end of the war or to participate in the making of the postwar world. On April 12, 1945, less than two months after his fourth inauguration, Roosevelt collapsed while sitting for a portrait in Warm Springs, Georgia.

The Truman Presidency

The shock of President Roosevelt's death was perhaps greatest for the former haberdasher and machine politician who succeeded him. Truman had been a last-minute choice as FDR's running mate the previous year, and he never became a part of Roosevelt's inner circle. Truman did not have any knowledge of the most important military program of the age—the Manhattan Project, which, in a race with the Nazis, was developing a nuclear bomb in the secrecy of the brand-new town of Oak Ridge, Tennessee.

Truman also faced a problem of stature. Roosevelt had done nothing less than redefine the presidency in his twelve years in office. He not only effected the longest-lasting partisan realignment in U.S. history, but he changed the very scope of government activity. As would become clear during the Eisenhower presidency, even conservative Republicans came to accept, grudgingly, the notion that the government ought to play an active role in stimulating the economy and addressing the needs of specific constituency groups. Many people could not fathom a presidency without Roosevelt. One member of the White House staff said later: "It was all so sudden, I had completely forgotten about Mr. Truman. Stunned, I realized that I simply couldn't comprehend the presidency as something separate from Roosevelt. The presidency, the White House, the war, our lives—they were all Roosevelt." [99] Other aides could not bring themselves to call Truman "Mr. President," as if so doing would dishonor the late president.

Truman's personality could not have presented a greater contrast to Roosevelt. Plain-speaking, blunt, middle-class, midwestern, not college educated, wheeling-and-dealing, and surrounded by old pals from the Pendergast machine of Missouri (the Democratic organization that dominated politics in the state), Truman offended people who had been accustomed to the charisma of Roosevelt. Truman's wife, Bess, also paled in comparison to the dynamic, more public Eleanor Roosevelt as First Lady. Truman showed absolute loyalty to the New Deal, but that would never be enough for many old Roosevelt hands and a nation entering a difficult period of postwar readjustment.

By the time the 1948 elections neared, Truman was in grave political shape. He brought former president Hoover back from exile for special projects—one of the many ways he rankled the sensibilities of former Roosevelt aides and Mrs. Roosevelt. Truman professed a desire to "keep my feet on the ground" and avoid the "crackpots and lunatic fringe" that had surrounded FDR.[100] Toward that end, Truman got rid of Commerce Secretary Henry Wallace and others. The independent journalist I. F. Stone wrote of Truman's personnel moves: "The little nameplates outside the little doors . . . began to change. In Justice, Treasury, Commerce and elsewhere, the New Dealers began to be replaced by the kind of men one was accustomed to meeting in county court-houses." [101]

The politics of postwar adjustment were difficult. The Republican Congress elected in 1946 sought to dismantle many New Deal programs, and it frustrated anti-inflation efforts. Truman duelled with Congress, vetoing 250 bills (eleven of these vetoes were overridden). Tentative civil rights initiatives disgruntled the South. Labor unrest was on the rise. Postwar mapmaking and subsequent efforts to "contain" Soviet geopolitical ambitions not only created splits among Democrats but also brought attacks from Republican isolationists. Truman also was said to have performed inadequately at Potsdam, the summer 1945 conference of World War II victors that established many geographic borders in Europe.

The situation was so bad that Roosevelt's own son promoted General Eisenhower and Supreme Court Justice William O. Douglas for a 1948 run for the Democratic nomination against Truman. Truman, in other words, was doing a good job antagonizing both the left and the right. The Democratic convention in August 1948 appeared to show a dangerously polarized nation. The convention began with a feeling of desperation when Eisenhower and Douglas refused to run. Then a "states' rights" plank offered by southern delegates was defeated, and, after strong speeches by Minneapolis mayor Hubert H. Humphrey and others, a strong northern plank passed. The party's New Deal and northern machine elements decided that southern defection would be less damaging than northern defection.

Defect is just what the southerners did. The Dixiecrats, under the leadership of South Carolina's governor J. Strom Thurmond, left the convention to conduct their own fall campaign. Thurmond's candidacy ran under the Democratic party label in four states (Alabama, Louisiana, Mississippi, and South Carolina) and under the States' Rights party elsewhere in the south. Meanwhile, the party's left wing, behind Henry Wallace, protested Truman's Marshall Plan, military buildup, and confrontational stance toward the Soviet Union; it, too, ran its own fall campaign under the banner of the Progressive Citizens of America (the Progressive party).

The seeds of Dixie defection were planted long before the convention. In 1947 the President's Committee on Civil Rights issued a report calling for the protection of the rights of all minorities. It was just the kind of spark southern segregationists needed to begin a dump-Truman drive and to organize their own campaign in 1948. The Southern Governors Conference in March 1948 recommended that southern states send delegates to the Democratic convention and electors to the electoral college who would refuse to back a pro-civil rights candidate.

As political scientist V. O. Key, Jr., has shown, the degree of resistance to civil rights in southern states depended on two basic factors: the proportion of blacks and the strength of the two-party system. Key argued that the existence of a large black population led to stronger Democratic measures against black enfranchisement and led whites to support the party in greater numbers. "To them [the whites in such districts], a single Negro vote threatened the whole caste system."[102] Alabama, Louisiana, Mississippi, and South Carolina ended up voting for the Thurmond ticket. Other southern states found broader economic and political issues more compelling than race.[103]

Many of FDR's old political allies eventually got behind the new man, but Truman's election prospects looked bleak. Some support was grudging—Mrs. Roosevelt offered a straightforward endorsement only to rebut newspaper reports that she favored the Republicans. While the Democratic party was badly fractured, the Republican party united behind Dewey.

Dewey was part of a new breed of Republican leaders—pragmatic and accepting of the New Deal and the international role that the United States would play in the postwar era. He expressed support for the basic tenets of postwar liberalism, including Social Security, civil rights, and the United Nations. In the 1948 campaign, Dewey planned to put himself above the slashing attack style of President Truman. His constant calls for national unity—spoken in a baritone voice and perfect English—expressed acceptance of the vast changes in U.S. politics over the previous twenty years.

Dewey, the 1944 GOP candidate, survived a large field in 1948 to become the nominee once again. Senator Taft of Ohio was the main threat, but his isolationism and dull public demeanor were liabilities. The most spirited opposition came from Governor Stassen of Minnesota, who appealed to the more liberal and internationalist wing of the party. An anathema to party bosses, Stassen proved his strength in a series of primary victories. Other candidates or potential convention contenders included generals Eisenhower and MacArthur, Governor Warren, and Senator Vandenberg. Polls showed all of the Republicans but Taft beating Truman.[104]

Dewey gained the preconvention momentum he needed with an impressive primary victory over Stassen in Oregon. Dewey spent three weeks in the state, while Stassen frittered away his time and resources with a hopeless challenge to Taft in the Ohio primary. Dewey was especially tough in a primary debate about Communism. Dewey also had impressive organizational strength and mastery

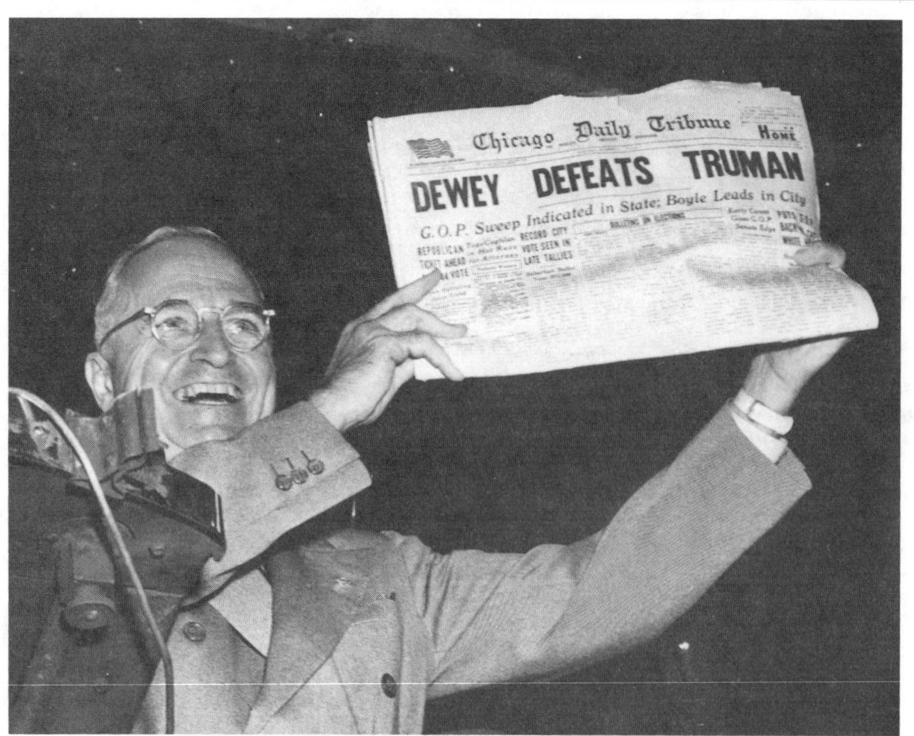

UPI/Bettmann Newsphotos

In 1944, pollsters and the media fed Republican candidate Thomas E. Dewey's overconfidence in his campaign to unseat President Harry S Truman. Truman had the last laugh on the press and his opponent.

over convention mechanics, and he won the nomination on the third ballot. Warren was selected the vice-presidential nominee.

From the beginning of the campaign, the media and professional politicians gave Truman little chance of retaining the White House. Early polls showed Dewey with such a strong lead that pollsters simply stopped surveying voters. But the polls failed because of a bias in the way the questions were asked and a presumption that the large undecided vote would cast their ballots in the same way as the rest of the population, when it in fact heavily favored Truman.[105]

Dewey was so certain of victory that he ran as if he were the incumbent. He made a series of bland, almost diplomatic statements rather than energetic campaign speeches. Dewey appeared confident that his advice to one audience—"Vote your own interests"—would attract an amalgam of disaffected groups. Never even mentioning the president's name, Dewey calmly canvassed the country and just smiled when people called him "President Dewey." Dewey was careful to avoid the overaggressive posture that he thought ruined his 1944 campaign against Roosevelt. He even made some initial cabinet and policy decisions.

From the beginning, Truman's strategy was simply to mobilize the New Deal coalition. The biggest danger was apathy, he and campaign aide Clark Clifford reasoned, so the best strategy was to give the voters a reason to go to the polling booths. Since the Democrats were the majority party, they had to concentrate mainly on getting their longtime supporters to the polls.

Truman ran a scrappy and blunt underdog campaign that could have been mistaken for an outsider's effort. Truman was the president, but he ran against the Washington establishment. Crisscrossing the nation on a "whistle-stop" train tour, Truman traveled some thirty-one thousand miles and spoke before six million people. He turned his record of vetoes into an asset, claiming that the "do nothing" Republican Eightieth Congress made him do it. He assailed the conservative Republican record on inflation, housing, labor, farm issues, and foreign affairs. The president drew large crowds—sometimes many times the size of Dewey's crowds—but he was the only political professional who thought he would win.

Truman himself predicted in October that he had 229 solid electoral votes to Dewey's 109 and Thurmond's 9; he said 189 votes could go either way. The best anyone would say about the Truman campaign was that its fighting spirit improved the Democrats' chances to win the Senate. Truman answered the Republicans' claims of liberalism and reformism by criticizing the GOP for obstruction of his policies. Truman's outsider taunt was constant: "that no-account, do-nothing, Republican 80th Congress!"[106]

Despite the *Chicago Tribune*'s now famous headline—"Dewey Defeats Truman"—President Truman prevailed. Early returns put Truman in front, but it was expected that the later-reporting western states would give Dewey the win. When California and Ohio went into the Truman column mid-morning Wednesday, Dewey conceded defeat. Especially considering the Democratic defections, Truman's appeal was widespread. Truman won twenty-eight states with 24.11 million votes (49.51 percent) and might have won more in the South and North with a united party. Thurmond won 22 percent of the vote in the South. Dewey won 21.97 million votes (45.12 percent), and Thurmond polled 1.17 million votes (2.40 percent). Henry Wallace won some 1.16 million votes (2.38 percent) but no electoral votes. Wallace's candidacy may have cost Truman New York, Michigan, and Maryland. On the other hand, Wallace may have done Truman a favor by freeing him from the taint of being the most liberal candidate in a time when the electorate was weary of liberalism. Particularly because the Republicans did not have a midwesterner on their ticket and talked about cutting back agricultural subsidies, farmers felt safer with Truman. In all, Truman won 303 electoral votes, Dewey 189, and Thurmond 39.

This campaign button from the 1952 election expresses support for a candidate coveted by the Democratic and Republican parties.

Dwight D. Eisenhower Library

The Democratic defections might have helped Truman by making him the candidate of the center. The Wallace campaign freed the president from suspicions on the right, and the Thurmond defection strengthened Truman's more liberal northern constituency. In addition, the defections might have inspired Democratic voters to turn out in larger numbers than they would have had victory seemed certain.

In the end, the election merely confirmed long-held partisan allegiances. In the words of political scientist Angus Campbell and his colleagues, it was a "maintaining" election: "The electorate responded to current elements in politics very much in terms of its existing partisan loyalties. Apparently very little of the political landscape attracted strong feeling in that year. But what feeling there was seemed to be governed largely by antecedent attachments to one of the two major parties."[107]

The Eisenhower Years

Truman's political fortunes worsened during his second term to the extent that he belatedly decided against making a bid for the Democratic nomination. In 1952, for the first time in twenty-four years, neither party had an incumbent president as its nominee.

Election of 1952

The Democrats suffered from a weariness that is bound to affect any party that has been in power for twenty years. Problems and opponents' frustrated ambitions were piling up, and in Dwight Eisenhower the Republicans were able to recruit a candidate with universal appeal who was coveted by both parties. The national mood in the years before the 1952 election was sour. The nation was tiring of the Korean War, which the administration had entered in 1950 but did not appear interested in winning or leaving; price controls; and recurring scandals among members of the White House staff. The Republicans asked for a chance to "clean up the mess" in Washington and punctuated their appeals with the question: "Had Enough?"

The Truman administration met with repeated frustration in dealing with the Congress that the president ran against in 1948. On civil rights, tariffs, taxes, labor reform, and the sensationalized question of Communist sympathizers in the government, Truman met a stubborn Democratic Congress—which, in turn, became more stubborn after Republican gains in the 1950 midterm elections. When Truman seized control of the steel mills because he said the steelworkers' strike threatened the nation's security, he was rebuffed by the Supreme Court.[108]

Truman's biggest problems, however, concerned cronyism and war. Republicans in congressional investigations and on the stump hammered away at conflict-of-interest scandals in Truman's administration—creating nationwide sentiment to "clean up" Washington with a new administration. Meanwhile, the United States was mired in a stalemate in Korea—a distant war that was being fought inconclusively under the aegis of the United Nations, with uncertain goals (was it to protect South Korea or replace North Korea as well?) and uncertain enemies (was the People's Republic of China an opponent as well as North Korea?). Truman evoked ire with his firing of General MacArthur, who wanted to take the war into China, and with the slow movement toward a settlement. Just as the nation tired of sacrifices in World War I under Woodrow Wilson, it tired of sacrifices under Truman.

General Eisenhower—who had just left the presidency of Columbia University to take charge of the forces of the North Atlantic Treaty Organization (NATO)—was recruited by Republicans to run when it appeared that other GOP candidates lacked the national appeal to win the White House. Senator Taft was again running, but his isolationism was considered a liability in the postwar age of internationalism. Stassen, MacArthur, and Warren were other likely Republican candidates.

Eisenhower's popular appeal was revealed when he attracted 50.4 percent of the vote in the New Hampshire primary to Taft's 38.7 percent and Stassen's 7.1 percent. Eisenhower performed well in the Northeast, and Taft generally performed well in the Midwest. A write-in campaign for Eisenhower almost upset Stassen in his home state of Minnesota.

When the GOP convention finally met in Chicago, Taft had the lead in convention delegates. In crucial delegate-seating contests, many of them played out on national television, Eisenhower defeated Taft and won the right to seat pro-Eisenhower insurgents from the South. Taft had relied on the old strategy of mobilizing state machines, but such tactics looked unsavory on television. Eisenhower had undisputed popular appeal, and he won on the first ballot after his early lead turned into a stampede.

In 1952, Dwight D. Eisenhower selected Sen. Richard Nixon of California as his running mate. The thirty-nine-year-old conservative had won national recognition with his activities on the controversial House Committee on Un-American Activities.

Eisenhower selected Sen. Richard Nixon of California as his running mate. The thirty-nine-year-old conservative had won national recognition with his activities on the controversial House Committee on Un-American Activities, which investigated the alleged Soviet ties of Alger Hiss, a former State Department official. Hiss served time for a perjury conviction.

The Democrats moved haltingly toward putting together a ticket. Truman did not announce his decision to stay out of the race until April, after two primary losses. Sen. Estes Kefauver of Tennessee, who gained fame with his televised hearings of organized crime, ran an aggressive primary campaign and entered the convention with the lead in delegates. Other candidates included Gov. Averell Harriman of New York, Vice President Alben Barkley, Sen. Robert Kerr of Oklahoma, and Sen. Richard Russell of Georgia.

The eventual nominee was Gov. Adlai Stevenson of Illinois, son of Grover Cleveland's second vice president. Stevenson had experience in the Navy and State departments before running for governor. President Truman privately recruited Stevenson for the race—at first unsuccessfully. Truman and Illinois backers set up a draft movement for Stevenson, which the governor disavowed until the last minute. Kefauver was the early leader in convention balloting, but Stevenson was always close, and he pulled into the lead on the third ballot.

Stevenson's campaign was an eloquent call to arms for liberals and reformers. Years later, Democrats would recall that the campaign had inspired the generation that would take the reins of power under John F. Kennedy. Democratic politics at all levels in subsequent years would revolve around battles of party regulars and reformers.

Stevenson did not have a chance, however, against the popular Eisenhower. Some southern states bolted the party in response to Stevenson's pro-civil rights stance. While the Republicans had them as a gift, they hammered away at the misdeeds of the Democratic administration under Truman. Issues like the Communist revolution in China of 1949 ("Who lost China?"), the protracted Korean War, administration corruption, and the alleged Communist infiltration of the government captured the nation's attention more than Stevenson's oratory.

More than anything, however, the desire for party change rather than policy change determined the election. The Republican evocation of the theme of "Corruption, Korea, and Communism" did not challenge the policies that the Democrats offered the nation as much as the way they executed those policies. Eisenhower was a proven administrator and was free of the taint of everyday U.S. politics. Stevenson was a reformer himself, but his campaign had the conspicuous backing of President Truman. Stevenson's divorce and public support of Hiss were constant if only vaguely stated issues.

The campaign's biggest controversy developed when newspaper reports alleged that Nixon used a "secret fund" provided by California millionaires to pay for travel and other expenses. To a Democratic party weary of charges of impropriety, the revelation offered an opportunity to charge that Nixon was beholden to special interests. Nixon admitted the existence of the fund but maintained that he used the money solely for travel and that his family did not accept personal gifts.

Nixon originally reacted to the story by asserting that it was a Communist smear. When Eisenhower would not publicly back his running mate, speculation developed that Ike would ask him to leave the ticket—and the Republican *New York Herald-Tribune* openly called for him to drop out. When Nixon decided to confront his accusers with a television speech, campaign aides told him he would be dropped if the public reaction was not favorable.

Nixon's speech was remarkable. He denied any impropriety and stated that the Stevenson campaign was hypocritical in its criticisms because it had similar funds. He denied that he accepted gifts such as a mink coat for his wife, Pat; he said that his wife wears a "Republican cloth coat." Nixon acknowledged receiving a pet dog named Checkers from a Texas admirer: "And you know, the kids love that dog, and I just want to say this right now, that regardless of what they say about it, we're going to keep it." [109] His folksy message and appeal for telegrams created a wave of sympathy, which Eisenhower rewarded with a pledge of support. The crisis was over.

In a personal victory—surveys showed that the nation still favored the programs of the New Deal and simply wanted to put the cronyism, sacrifices, and Korean War behind it—Eisenhower swept to the White House. Ike won the entire North and West, parts of the South, and some border states—a total of thirty-nine states to Stevenson's nine. His 442 electoral votes and 33.9 million popular votes (55.1 percent) overwhelmed Stevenson's 89 electoral votes and 27.3 million popular votes (44.4 percent). The election of 1956 would bring more of the same.

Election of 1956

Despite his age and a heart attack in 1955, Eisenhower was the strong favorite to be the GOP nominee for another term. Close cooperation with the congressional leadership and a "hidden-hand" leadership style seemed to comport with the electorate's wishes for normalcy. [110] The White House apparatus was ably run by the chief of staff, Sherman Adams, and foreign policy was supervised by Secretary of State John Foster Dulles. The genius of Eisenhower's management style was the use of aides as "lightning rods" for unpopular policies.

Even without lightning rods, Eisenhower probably would have fared well. The economy was booming, and Eisenhower quickly brought the Korean War to a close. His nuclear policy gave the nation a "bigger bang for the buck" in defense spending and kept the troop requirements low. Federal housing and highway programs gave impetus to suburbanization, now considered part of the middle-class American Dream. Issues that would in the future become divisive, such as civil rights, were muffled.

The only unsettled Republican issue was whether Nixon would again be the vice-presidential candidate. Eisenhower offered him a cabinet post, and Stassen mounted a campaign to replace Nixon with Massachusetts governor Christian Herter. After some hesitation, however, Eisenhower stood by his controversial running mate.

Kefauver challenged Stevenson for the right to face Eisenhower in the fall. After impressive primary victories in New Hampshire and Minnesota, the Stevenson campaign fought back with a string of primary wins in states as varied as California, Florida, and Oregon.

Former president Truman continued his stormy relationship with Stevenson when he endorsed New York governor Harriman at the opening of the Democratic convention. A variety of other favorite sons entered the race. With the help of Eleanor Roosevelt, Stevenson was able to win the nomination for a second time with careful campaigning among the convention's delegations. Stevenson won on the first ballot.

Stevenson left the vice-presidential slot open to the convention delegates. Kefauver, after battling senators John Kennedy, Albert Gore, and Hubert Humphrey and New York mayor Robert Wagner, eventually won. The open contest highlighted the future potential of Kennedy, who, according to later accounts, mainly intended not to win the second spot but to gain visibility for a 1960 presidential run.

The campaign was bereft of real issues. Eisenhower's campaigning was a tempered appeal to American values and bipartisan consensus. To Nixon was left the job of hacking away at the opposition; he called Stevenson "Adlai the Appeaser" and a "Ph.D. graduate of Dean Acheson's cowardly College of Communist Containment." [111] Overall, however, the campaign was an example of what James David Barber calls "the politics of conciliation," with little conflict or desire for change.

Whether or not the electorate was "asleep," as frustrated critics charged, Eisenhower won another strong victory. He won forty-two states, 457 electoral votes, and 35.6 million popular votes (57.4 percent), compared with Stevenson's six states, 73 electoral votes, and 26.0 million popular votes (42.0 percent). In an unprecedented development, however, both houses of Congress went to the opposition.

Kennedy and the Politics of Change

The periodic national desire for change came at the expense of the Republicans in 1960, when Sen. John F. Kennedy of Massachusetts became the youngest person elected president by defeating Vice President Richard Nixon in the tightest election in history.

The presidential election took shape in the 1958 midterm election, when the Democrats made impressive gains in Congress. An economic recession and generational politics created the first major shift toward liberalism since the administration of Franklin D. Roosevelt. The "Class of '58" decisively changed the discourse of U.S. politics. After the election the Democrats held 64 of 98 Senate seats and 283 of 435 House seats, and thirty-five states had Democratic governors. The time appeared ripe for reopening issues that had long been stifled.[112]

The 1960 Democratic field was dominated by senators—Kennedy, Lyndon B. Johnson of Texas, Hubert H. Humphrey of Minnesota, and Stuart Symington of Missouri. Each had important advantages and disadvantages. Kennedy was from a wealthy and politically minded family, but his Catholicism and undistinguished Senate record were liabilities. Johnson was a masterful majority leader, but no southerner had won the White House since James K. Polk in 1844. Humphrey was popular in the Midwest, but he lacked financial backing and was considered too loquacious and liberal. Symington had a strong Senate record and Harry S Truman's backing, but he was considered colorless, and Truman's backing carried liabilities.

Former Illinois governor Adlai E. Stevenson, the par-

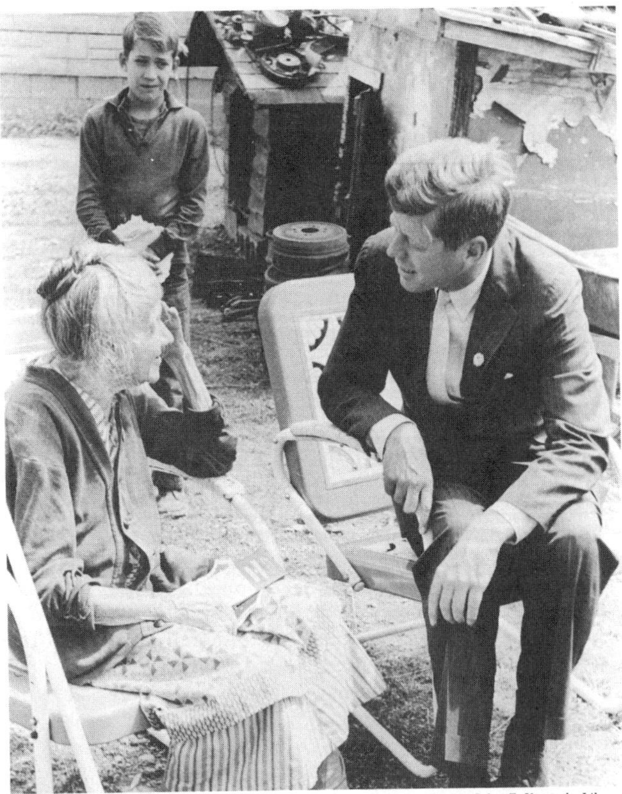

Charleston Gazette; John F. Kennedy Library

In the 1960 presidential campaign, John F. Kennedy worked hard to win the West Virginia primary. His victory in this overwhelmingly Protestant state blunted the issue of his Catholicism and set him on the way to a first-ballot nomination.

ty's nominee in 1952 and 1956, and Sen. Estes Kefauver of Tennessee stood on the sidelines, hoping that a convention deadlock or draft movement would finally bring them a ticket to the White House. Early speculation was that the convention would be deadlocked and a compromise candidate would have to emerge. It appeared likely that the nomination would go to Symington, Johnson, Humphrey, or one of the two senior candidates, Stevenson and Kefauver; the other candidates were good bets for the vice-presidential slot.

Kennedy presented the most intriguing candidacy. He was the son of Joseph P. Kennedy, the millionaire who had been Franklin Roosevelt's ambassador to Britain before their bitter break over U.S. involvement in World War II. John Kennedy was also an Ivy League graduate (of Harvard University), a war hero (described in the book *P.T. 109*), and a Pulitzer Prize-winner (for *Profiles in Courage*). With an experienced campaign staff, he had won an overwhelming reelection to the Senate in 1958. Moreover, he had been planning a run for the White House for years.

There were Kennedy skeptics, however. No Catholic since Alfred Smith had been a major-party nominee, and Smith's bitter loss and the anti-Catholic sentiments he aroused made political professionals wary of naming another Catholic. Others focused on the influence of Joseph Kennedy, who bankrolled his sons' political careers.[113] Some considered Kennedy, at age forty-three, to be too young. Truman's comment captured the crux of Kennedy's liabilities: "It's not the Pope I'm afraid of, it's the Pop." [114]

To address the doubts, Kennedy entered political primaries that would enable him to demonstrate vote-getting ability and to confront the religion problem. The two key primaries were Wisconsin and West Virginia. In Wisconsin, Kennedy would answer the charge that he was too conservative and uncommitted to expanding the New Deal. The Kennedy strategists were divided about whether to oppose Senator Humphrey of nearby Minnesota; Wisconsin's growing independence in party politics eventually convinced them it would present a low risk for the possibility of beating Humphrey in his native region. In West Virginia, Kennedy would attempt to blunt the religion issue by attracting the votes of an overwhelmingly Protestant electorate.

Kennedy defeated Humphrey in Wisconsin, a state close to Humphrey's home state of Minnesota not only geographically but also culturally and ideologically. Kennedy's impressive campaign treasury enabled him to staff offices in eight of the ten congressional districts in the state; Humphrey had only two offices. Humphrey maintained that the defeat stemmed from crossover Republican Catholic votes and was therefore illegitimate. (Most of the state's Catholics, 31 percent of the population, belonged to the GOP.) But to Kennedy and many political observers, it was still an important victory.

Humphrey wanted to even the score in West Virginia. If Humphrey had quit the campaign and left Kennedy with no opponents, as many advised him to do, a Kennedy victory would have attracted little attention.[115] But Kennedy was able to use the Appalachian state as a way to deflect the religion issue as well as the "can't win" problem. Kennedy had a thorough organization in the state, and he worked hard. He had commissioned polls in the state as far back as 1958 in anticipation of the presidential race.

Kennedy's handling of the religion question in the primaries was shrewd and would be repeated in the fall campaign. He framed the question as one of tolerance—which put Humphrey on the defensive since he had never tried to exploit the religion issue. Kennedy had his campaign workers plant questions about how his religious beliefs would affect his loyalty to the nation, to which the candidate replied with a stock answer: "When any man stands on the steps of the Capitol and takes the oath of office as president, he is swearing to uphold the separation of church and state; he puts one hand on the Bible and raises the other hand to God as he takes the oath. And if he breaks the oath, he is not only committing a crime against the Constitution, for which the Congress can impeach him—but he is committing a sin against God." [116]

Kennedy's direct confrontation of the religion issue worked to his benefit. Kennedy had the money to get his message across: his television expenditures alone in the state totaled $34,000, while Humphrey had only $25,000 for the whole primary campaign in West Virginia.[117] Early polls gave Humphrey wide leads, and interviews elicited strong reservations about Kennedy's Catholicism. As the commercials aired and the primary neared, the lead became smaller, and voters privately said they would vote for Kennedy.

JFK, as he asked headline writers to call him instead of the youthful-sounding "Jack," easily won the primary. He was on his way to a first-ballot nomination.

The Kennedy campaign staffers managed the convention with consummate skill. Had they failed to gain a majority by the first ballot, pressure might have developed for another candidate. But the Kennedy team efficiently lobbied delegations to augment support; the vice-presidential slot was vaguely offered to several politicians. In the end, Johnson was the surprise choice for running mate. Even Kennedy supporters had doubts about Johnson, but the selection of the southerner was a classic ticket-balancing move.[118]

Central to Kennedy's winning campaign was his younger brother Robert F. Kennedy. A former counsel to Republican senator Joseph McCarthy, Robert developed into the consummate political operative. He was JFK's confidant, chief strategist, delegate counter, fund-raiser, taskmaster, and persuader. Biographer Arthur M. Schlesinger, Jr., wrote that Robert Kennedy's strength "lay in his capacity to address a specific situation, to assemble an able staff, to inspire and flog them into exceptional deeds, and to prevail through sheer force of momentum." [119]

Vice President Richard Nixon was the overwhelming choice for the Republican nomination. Nelson A. Rockefeller, elected governor of New York in 1958, was a liberal alternative, but he announced in 1959 that he would not run. There was a brief surge for Rockefeller when he criticized the party and its "leading candidate," but meetings with Nixon settled the differences. Some conservatives were disgruntled with Nixon, but their efforts for Sen. Barry Goldwater of Arizona would have to wait until 1964.

Nixon selected United Nations Ambassador Henry Cabot Lodge as his running mate, and the party platform and rhetoric stressed the need for experience in a dangerous world. Nixon promised to continue President Dwight D. Eisenhower's policies. He attempted to portray Kennedy as an inexperienced upstart, even though he was Kennedy's senior by only four years and the two had entered Congress the same year. Nixon led in the polls at the traditional Labor Day start of the fall campaign.

Kennedy's campaign was based on a promise to "get the nation moving again" after eight years of calm Republican rule. Specifically, he assured voters he would lead the nation out of a recession. The real gross national product increased at a rate of only 2.25 percent annually between 1955 and 1959. Economists puzzled over the simultaneously high unemployment and high inflation rates.[120] Kennedy repeatedly called for two related changes in national policy: pumping up the economy and increasing defense spending dramatically.

The Democrat faced up to the religion issue again with an eloquent speech before the Greater Houston Ministerial Association, and he attracted attention from civil rights leaders when he offered moral and legal support to the Rev. Martin Luther King, Jr., after King was arrested for taking part in a sit-in at an Atlanta restaurant. While Kennedy appealed to the party's more liberal and moderate wing, Johnson toured throughout the South to appeal to regional pride and to assuage fears about an activist government.

The high point of the campaign came on September 26, 1960, when the candidates debated on national television before seventy million viewers. Kennedy was well-rested and tanned and spent the week before the debate with friends and associates. Nixon was tired from two solid weeks of campaigning, and he spent the preparation period by himself. Their appearances alone greatly influenced the outcome of the debates.

Kennedy's main objective had been simply to look relaxed and "up to" the presidency. He had little to lose. Nixon was always confident of his debating skills, and he performed well in the give-and-take of the debate. But the rules of debating—the way "points" are allocated—are different in formal debating from what they are in televised encounters. Kennedy's managers prepared their candidate better for the staging of the debate. Nixon's five-o'clock shadow reinforced the cartoon image of him as darkly sinister. Polls of radio listeners found that Nixon had "won" the debate, but polls of television viewers found that Kennedy had "won" the debate. Historian Theodore H. White wrote: "It was the picture image that had done it—and in 1960 it was television that had won the nation away from sound to images, and that was that." [121]

While Kennedy called for a more activist and imaginative approach to world problems, Nixon stressed the candidates' similarities so much that their differences paled into insignificance. Kennedy called for a crusade to eliminate want and to confront tyranny. Nixon responded: "I can subscribe completely to the spirit that Sen. Kennedy has expressed tonight." [122] With ideology an unimportant part of the debate, the images of personal character the candidates were able to project gained in importance.

The candidates held three more debates and addressed issues including Fidel Castro's Cuba, the Chinese offshore islands of Quemoy and Matsu, and relations with Nikita Khrushchev's Soviet Union. None of the debates had the effect of the first, which neutralized Nixon's incumbency advantage. Nor was Nixon greatly helped by President Eisenhower, who did not campaign for his protégé until late in the campaign.

The election results were so close that Nixon did not concede his defeat until the afternoon of the day following the election. Nixon later said he considered contesting some returns more than a week after the election. After a vacation in Florida and Nassau, Nixon returned to Washington on November 19 to consider a series of charges that voter fraud had cost him the election. A shift of between eleven thousand and thirteen thousand votes in a total of five or six states could have given Nixon the electoral vote triumph. Nixon said he decided against demanding a recount because it would take "at least a year and a half" and would throw the federal government into turmoil.[123]

When the electoral college voted, Kennedy won 303 electoral votes to Nixon's 219. Democratic senator Harry F. Byrd of Virginia attracted 15 electoral votes. Kennedy won twenty-three states to Nixon's twenty-six. (A slate of eight independent electors won Mississippi; these eight, plus six from Alabama and one from Oklahoma voted for Byrd.) The overall popular vote went 34.2 million for Kennedy and 34.1 million for Nixon. The margin was about one-tenth of 1 percent, or 115,000 votes. The margins in many states were very close. Kennedy won Illinois by 8,858 votes and Texas by 46,242 votes. Despite statements that the religion question would hurt Kennedy, it probably helped him by mobilizing Catholics on his behalf. Gallup polls showed that 78 percent of Catholics voted for JFK. Although Catholics were a traditional Democratic constituent group—by margins of three or four to one—they had voted for Eisenhower by large margins.[124] In addition, Kennedy put together a predictable coalition: he won the support of voters in the Northeast, in most of the South, and in cities, plus blacks and union workers. Upper New England, the Midwest, and the West went primarily to Nixon.

In an informal way, Kennedy and Goldwater discussed the way they would conduct their campaigns for the presidency in 1964. The two expected to win their party nominations easily, and they talked about crisscrossing the nation in head-to-head debates, which would set a new standard for national campaigns.[125]

U.S. News & World Report; Library of Congress

In accepting the 1964 Republican presidential nomination, Sen. Barry Goldwater called for a moral crusade, declaring, "Extremism in defense of liberty is no vice; moderation in pursuit of justice is no virtue."

The Kennedy-Goldwater campaign never came. On November 22, 1963, while riding in a motorcade in Dallas, Texas, President Kennedy was assassinated by a gunman named Lee Harvey Oswald.[126] Vice President Johnson assumed the presidency.[127]

In his brief administration, Kennedy had compiled a record disappointing even to many of his supporters. The Bay of Pigs fiasco in which a Central Intelligence Agency plan to overthrow the Cuban government failed miserably, the inability to obtain passage of landmark civil rights legislation, budget deficits and a drain of gold supplies from the United States, confrontations with the Soviet Union in Cuba, Hungary, and Berlin, and the nascent U.S. involvement in the Vietnam War created doubts about the young president's control of the government.

Still, Kennedy had made a start on many important issues. Arms control initiatives such as the test-ban treaty, economic growth through tax cuts, modernization of the military, the successful management of the Cuban missile crisis, civil rights and other domestic initiatives, the Peace Corps and Alliance for Progress, and growing world stature all offered hope for the second term. It would fall to Johnson, the legendary former Senate majority leader, to bring the Kennedy plans to fruition. First acting as the loyal servant of the slain president, then as his own man, Johnson was able to bring to legislative enactment many of the long-cherished initiatives of the U.S. liberal establishment—most notably the Civil Rights Act of 1964, which was considerably stronger than the Kennedy bill that had stalled in Congress.

"All the Way with LBJ"

From the time of his sad but graceful ascension to the White House, Johnson was never in doubt as the Democrats' 1964 nominee. He was expected to select an eastern or midwestern liberal as his running mate, and he did so when he tapped Senator Humphrey of Minnesota at the convention, which his campaign organization stage-managed to the last detail. The only dissent from the Democratic unity was provided by Gov. George C. Wallace of Alabama, whose segregationist campaign took advantage of a backlash against the civil rights movement. Wallace entered three primaries against Johnson-allied favorite sons. He polled 43 percent of the vote in Maryland. Wallace talked about mounting a third party bid in the fall, but he backed off.

The Republicans were divided into two bitter camps led by Senator Goldwater of Arizona, the eventual nominee, and Governor Rockefeller of New York. The nomination contest was a struggle for the soul of the party. Other active and inactive candidates included Ambassador to Vietnam Henry Cabot Lodge, former vice president Nixon, and Gov. William Scranton of Pennsylvania. After a New Hampshire primary victory by Lodge, achieved through a well-organized write-in drive while he was still ambassador to Vietnam, Goldwater and Rockefeller scrapped through a series of primaries. The moderate Lodge later helped Scranton in a late effort to recruit uncommitted delegates to stop Goldwater, but by then it was too late. Goldwater lined up strong delegate support to get the nomination before the primary season even began, but he needed to use the primaries to show that he had vote-getting ability. The state organizations that backed him needed evidence that his conservative message would find popular acceptance.

In the "mixed" system then in place, candidates were able to pick and choose the primaries that best suited their strategy. Front-runners avoided risks, and long shots entered high-visibility and often risky contests as a way to attract the attention of party professionals. As expected, Goldwater won widespread support in the southern state conventions and had strong primary showings in Illinois and Indiana. Rockefeller beat Lodge in Oregon, but the decisive test came when Goldwater narrowly upset Rockefeller in California.

More important than the confusing preconvention contests was the rhetoric. Both the conservative Goldwater and the liberal Rockefeller vowed to save the party from the other's ideology. Goldwater, who rode the bestseller success of his *Conscience of a Conservative* to hero worship among conservatives, made a vigorous case against New Deal politics and for American sway in world politics: "I don't give a tinker's damn what the rest of the world thinks about the United States, as long as we keep strong militarily." [128] Rockefeller implied that Goldwater risked nuclear war and would recklessly dismantle basic social programs.

The nomination contest was a regional as well as an ideological struggle. The westerner Goldwater—backed by labor-intensive manufacturers, small business and agricultural enterprises, and domestic oil producers—opposed internationalist banking and commercial interests.[129] Goldwater made eastern media the objects of scorn. Rockefeller and his family, of course, represented the apex of the eastern establishment. Because of his strategy, Goldwater made himself an outsider to the growth-oriented consumer politics of the period.

Bitter battles over the party platform and unseemly heckling of Rockefeller displayed the party's divisions at the convention. When the conservatives won the nomination and the platform, there was no reconciliation. Goldwater selected Rep. William Miller of New York, another conservative, as his running mate and vowed to purify the party of liberal and moderate elements.

In a defiant acceptance speech, Goldwater painted a picture of the United States as inept in international affairs and morally corrupt in domestic pursuits, and he vowed an all-out crusade to change the situation: "Tonight there is violence in our streets, corruption in our highest offices, aimlessness among our youth, anxiety among our elderly, and there's a virtual despair among the many who look beyond the material successes toward the inner meaning of their lives.... Extremism in defense of liberty is no vice; moderation in pursuit of justice is no virtue." [130]

To a nation experiencing prosperity and unaware of the true proportions of its involvement in Vietnam, the "choice, not an echo" that Goldwater offered was a moral crusade. But the American consensus was built on material, consumer foundations, and an "outsider" appeal would have to wait until the system's foundations became unstable.

The divided GOP made for easy pickings for Johnson. The fall campaign was dominated by Goldwater's gaffes, which started long before the campaign began. He said, for example, that troops committed to the North Atlantic Treaty Organization (NATO) in Europe "probably" could be cut by "at least one-third" if NATO "commanders" had the authority to use tactical nuclear weapons in an emergency.[131] Goldwater also proposed a number of changes in the Social Security system, called for selling off the Tennessee Valley Authority, criticized the civil rights movement, and denounced the Supreme Court, the National Labor Relations Board, and the federal bureaucracy. Except for use of nuclear weapons and changes in Social Security, most of Goldwater's proposals when taken alone were not shocking. But the sum of his proposals—and his sometimes halting explanations—scared many voters.

President Johnson campaigned very actively to win a mandate for an activist new term. He traveled throughout the country making speeches to build a consensus for his domestic programs as well as his reelection. Johnson resisted Goldwater's constant calls for televised debates. The nation's prosperity was probably enough to keep the president in the White House.[132]

Johnson desperately wanted a personal mandate to pursue a variety of domestic programs that fell under the rubric "the Great Society"—a term that Johnson used in a 1964 commencement address (borrowed from a book of the same title by British socialist Graham Wallas). The desired landslide—underscored by his campaign slogan, "All the Way with LBJ"—was essential to initiatives in civil rights, health care, community action, education, welfare, housing, and jobs creation. Central to the landslide was not only economic prosperity but also peace in the world's trouble spots. Johnson therefore ran as a "peace" candidate.

But while he was trying to build a coalition that would sustain his domestic initiatives, Johnson faced an increasingly difficult dilemma about U.S. involvement in Vietnam. The United States had been involved in opposing Ho Chi Minh's revolution against French colonial rule in the 1940s and 1950s, and under presidents Eisenhower and Kennedy the United States had made a commitment to the leaders of South Vietnam (created after the failure of the 1954 Geneva accord) as a bastion against Communist expansion in Asia. But talk of war would likely imperil the domestic initiatives of the Great Society.

So while Johnson was campaigning as the peace candidate in 1964, he also was preparing for a major increase in U.S. involvement in Vietnam. As early as February 1964 the administration began elaborate covert operations in Southeast Asia and prepared a resolution to give the president a "blank check" in Vietnam.[133] By June the resolution was ready, and the Pentagon had chosen ninety-four bombing targets in North Vietnam and made provisions for bombing support systems. But on June 15, Johnson decided to delay major offensives until after the election.[134] In August Johnson sent to Congress what would be known as the Tonkin Gulf Resolution, which passed quickly and nearly unanimously. The president instructed congressional leaders to get an overwhelming majority so his policy would be bipartisan.

Johnson also seized on Rockefeller's use of the peace issue during the Republican primaries against Goldwater. He alluded to some of Goldwater's scarier statements about war, and he pledged that "we are not about to send American boys nine or ten thousand miles away from home to do what Asian boys ought to be doing for themselves." [135] A week before the election, Johnson said: "The only real issue in this campaign, the only one you ought to get concerned about, is who can best keep the peace." [136]

Johnson's landslide was the largest in U.S. history. He won 61 percent of the popular vote to Goldwater's 38 percent (or 43.1 million to 27.2 million votes). In the electoral college Johnson received 486 votes to Goldwater's 52, and he carried forty-four states—all but Goldwater's home state of Arizona and five southern states. In addition, the Democratic party amassed huge majorities in both the Senate (67-33) and the House of Representatives (295-140).

On election day Johnson created a working group to study "immediately and intensively" the U.S. options in Southeast Asia.[137] The war was increasing far beyond what most supporters of the Tonkin Gulf Resolution or "peace" supporters of the president imagined. In 1965 alone the number of U.S. troops in Vietnam increased from 15,000 to nearly 200,000.[138]

The Breakup of Consensus

A long period of uncertainty in American politics began sometime after Johnson's landslide victory over Goldwater in 1964.

By 1968, some thirty thousand Americans had been killed in action, and television was bringing the war into the living rooms of American families. Despite repeated assertions that the United States was defeating the North Vietnamese enemy, U.S. bombing efforts and ground troops did not break the resolve of the Communists in the North or their sympathizers who had infiltrated the South. The corrupt South Vietnamese government and army appeared to lack the resolve to fight the war on their own.

The opposition to the war developed as the casualties mounted, and the administration experienced a "credibility gap" because of its statements about the war. Before the United States left Vietnam in 1975, fifty-five thousand Americans had died in combat. Perhaps more important than the number of casualties—about the same as in the Korean War—was the long-term commitment that the

United States appeared to make with little evidence of progress. The "quagmire," as *New York Times* reporter David Halberstam called the war, was perhaps typified by the program of intense U.S. bombing raids that were judged by many experts to be ineffectual against the North's guerrilla warfare strategy.[139]

As opposition to the war grew among an increasingly vocal and well-organized minority, strains developed in Johnson's economic and domestic programs. Starting with the Watts riots in Los Angeles in 1965, urban areas sizzled with resentment to the mainstream liberal establishment. Detroit, Newark, and many major U.S. cities erupted in riots that burned miles of city streets and caused millions of dollars in damage. The assassination of civil rights leader Martin Luther King, Jr., in Memphis April 4, 1968, led to riots throughout the nation. Even before the riots, however, a conservative reaction against the Great Society had developed.

The activities of the Great Society were many and varied: the Civil Rights Act of 1964, the Voting Rights Act of 1965, Head Start, Model Cities, mass transit legislation, food stamps, Medicaid, the Elementary and Secondary Education Act, college loans, housing programs that included subsidies for poor, to name just the most prominent programs.

The conservative backlash was apparent before many programs had time to do their work. Efforts such as the Model Cities program and the Community Action Program, which mandated that poverty programs promote "maximum feasible participation" by the poor themselves, were often badly organized. They also were the source of additional struggles over jurisdiction in cities that already were notorious for divisive politics. Liberal efforts that predated the Great Society, such as school desegregation, created other tensions in cities.

One of the greatest sources of backlash in the late 1960s was an alarming increase in street crime. Even though blacks and the poor were the chief victims of the increase, the issue was most salient for conservative whites. Many tied the breakdown in order to the growth of the welfare state inspired by the Great Society. The crime rate seemed to many to be nothing less than ingratitude on the part of the poor. James Sundquist writes: "While increasing millions were supported by welfare, rising state and local taxes made the citizen more and more aware of who paid the bill. And while he armed himself for protection against thieves or militants, the liberals were trying to pass legislation to take away his guns." [140]

The crime problem was an important element in both national and metropolitan politics. Polls showed that half the women and a fifth of the men in the country were afraid to walk alone in their own neighborhoods at night.[141] In Alabama, Gov. George Wallace was whipping up his supporters in a frenzy of prejudice and resentment. The fear of crime also would be an important element in Richard Nixon's 1968 campaign.

The Election of 1968

With the nation divided over the war and domestic policy, the Democrats entered the 1968 campaign in an increasingly perilous state. In December 1967, Sen. Eugene McCarthy of Minnesota challenged President Johnson for the Democratic nomination, a move based almost entirely on his antiwar stance. McCarthy did unexpectedly well against Johnson's write-in candidacy in the New Hampshire primary on March 12, 1968 (drawing 42.4 percent of the vote to Johnson's 49.5 percent). Anticipating a devastating defeat in the Wisconsin primary April 2, Johnson dramatically announced his withdrawal from the campaign in a televised address March 31.

After the New Hampshire primary, New York senator Robert F. Kennedy declared his antiwar candidacy, which put in place all the elements for a Democratic fight of historic proportions. Vice President Humphrey took Johnson's place as the administration's candidate; he eschewed the primaries but eventually won the nomination on the strength of endorsements from state party organizations.

McCarthy and Kennedy fought each other in the primaries, and Kennedy appeared to have the upper hand when he closed the primary season with a victory in California on June 5. But after making his acceptance speech, he was assassinated, and the party was in greater turmoil than ever.

At the party convention in Chicago, a site Johnson had chosen for what he thought would be his own nomination, Humphrey became the Democratic party's candidate. The vice president took the nomination on the first ballot after Mayor Richard Daley of Chicago committed the Illinois delegation to his effort. Humphrey won with support from the traditional elements of the Democratic coalition—labor, blacks, urban voters—plus the backers of President Johnson. Humphrey appealed to many of the party's "moderates" on the Vietnam War.

Preliminary battles over rules and delegate seating, the representativeness of the party, and Vietnam War policies caused ugly skirmishes on the convention floor. The party's platform eventually endorsed the administration's war policy, including bombing, but strong opposition to this plank left the party divided.[142]

Outside the convention halls, demonstrations for civil rights and an end to the war met brutal rejection from the police. After three days of sometimes harsh verbal and physical battles with antiwar demonstrators in parks, the police charged a group of protesters that planned a march on the convention. Theodore H. White described the scene that played on national television:

> Like a fist jolting, like a piston exploding from its chamber, comes a hurtling column of police from off Balbo into the intersection, and all things happen too fast: first the charge as the police wedge cleaves through the mob; then screams, whistles, confusion, people running off into Grant Park, across bridges, into hotel lobbies. And as the scene clears, there are little knots in the open clearing—police clubbing youngsters, police dragging youngsters, police rushing them by their elbows, their heels dragging, to patrol wagons, prodding recalcitrants who refuse to enter quietly.[143]

Humphrey and his running mate, Sen. Edmund Muskie of Maine, faced an uphill fight.

The Republicans united behind Richard Nixon, the 1960 nominee whose political career seemed at an end after a loss in the 1962 California gubernatorial election. The GOP did not have to deal with any of the divisiveness of the 1964 Goldwater-Rockefeller battle. Nixon outspent Humphrey two-to-one, and followed a carefully devised script that avoided the exhausting schedule of his 1960 campaign. Nixon capitalized on the national discontent created by the Vietnam War, urban riots, political assassinations, and general concern about the speed of change wrought by the Great Society. Nixon traveled the high road

Wide World Photos

Popular support for Richard Nixon won him the 1968 presidential election. Promising an "open administration," his main campaign promise was change.

in his own campaign by calling for the nation to unite and heal its wounds. Promising an "open administration," Nixon's main offer was change. "I must say the man who helped us get into trouble is not the man to get us out."[144] To avoid scrutiny by the national media, Nixon gave few major addresses, preferring instead a series of interviews with local newspapers and broadcasters.

As President Johnson resisted calls for a halt in the bombing of North Vietnam, Nixon said he had a "secret plan" to end the war. He appealed to weary Democrats with his pledge of an activist administration and alternative approaches to dealing with some of the problems the Great Society addressed. Nixon promised to give blacks, in his words, "a piece of the action with a program to encourage entrepreneurial activity in cities." The "new Nixon" appeared willing to deal with the Soviet Union, which he had scorned earlier in his career. Meanwhile, his vice-presidential nominee, Gov. Spiro T. Agnew of Maryland, offered a slashing critique of the Democrats to middle-class and blue-collar Americans who resented the civil rights laws, government bureaucracy, Vietnam War protesters, and the young protest generation.

Wallace ran one of the strongest third party campaigns in U.S. history. Governor Wallace of Alabama ran as an antiestablishment conservative, railing away at desegregation, crime, taxes, opponents of the war in Vietnam, social programs, and "pointy-head" bureaucrats and "intellectual morons." His American Independent party was the strongest effort since Theodore Roosevelt's Bull Moose campaign in 1912 and Robert La Follette's Progressive run in 1924. Like the earlier third party campaigns, the Wallace run caused concern about the soundness of the electoral college system. Because the race was so close, it was conceivable that no candidate would win an electoral college victory. In that event, Wallace could have held the balance of power.[145]

Despite the early disadvantage, Humphrey made steady inroads into Nixon's support by disassociating himself from Johnson's Vietnam policies. When Johnson on November 1 ordered a halt to all bombing of North Vietnam, Humphrey appeared to be free at last from the stigma of the administration. But this change in administration policy was not enough to win the election for Humphrey.

The 1968 election was one of the closest in U.S. history. Nixon's victory was not confirmed until the day after the election when California, Ohio, and Illinois—each with very close counts—finally went into the Nixon column. Nixon attracted 31.8 million votes (43.4 percent of all votes cast); Humphrey 31.3 million votes (42.7 percent); and Wallace 9.9 million votes (13.5 percent). Nixon won 32 states and 301 electoral votes, compared with Humphrey's 13 states and 191 electoral votes. Nixon won six southern states (Wallace won five others), all of the West except Texas, Washington, and Hawaii, and all the midwestern states except Michigan and Minnesota. Humphrey won all of the East except New Hampshire, Vermont, New Jersey, and Delaware, plus West Virginia, Maryland, and the District of Columbia.

One long-lasting effect of 1968 was a transformation of the nomination process. In response to the bitter complaints about the 1968 Democratic convention, the party adopted rules that would make the primaries the center of the nomination process. The Chicago convention, dominated by party professionals at the expense of many important constituencies—blacks, women, youths—nominated a candidate who did not compete in any primaries. The key reform was a limit on the number of delegates that state committees could choose—after 1968, no more than 10 percent of the delegation. *(See "Rules Changes in the Democratic Party," p. 174, in this chapter.)*

Nixon's Reelection

McGovern was the miracle candidate of 1972, but his miracle did not last long enough.

Edmund Muskie, a veteran of the U.S. Senate and the vice-presidential nominee in 1968, was the early favorite to win the Democratic nomination. But because of party reforms enacted in response to the disastrous 1968 convention, the nomination process was bound to create surprises and confusion.

No fewer than fifteen contenders announced their candidacy, twelve with serious hopes of winning or influencing the final selection. Some twenty-two primaries to choose 60 percent of the party's delegates—a third more than in 1968—were to take place over four months. The marathon would be decided by accidents, media strategy, and a confusing array of voter choices that changed with each new development.

Muskie was badly damaged before the primary when he appeared to cry while lashing back at the *Manchester Union Leader*'s vicious and unrelenting attacks on his campaign and on his outspoken wife, Jane. The *Union Leader* had printed a series of attacks on Jane, then falsely reported that Muskie had laughed at a derogatory joke about French Canadians. Muskie later said of the incident: "It changed people's minds about me, of what kind of a guy I was. They were looking for a strong, steady man, and here I was weak." [146]

Muskie won the first-in-the-nation New Hampshire primary, but his 46.4 percent of the vote was considered a "disappointing" showing. McGovern of South Dakota, the antiwar candidate who won 37.1 percent of the vote, was pronounced the real winner by media and pundits. His strong showing—engineered by imaginative young political operatives, such as Gary Hart and Patrick Caddell, and a corps of youthful volunteers—was a surprise.

After New Hampshire, the Democrats battled through the summer. Wallace parlayed his antibusing rhetoric into an impressive victory in the Florida primary. Better organized than the others, McGovern swept the Wisconsin delegation by winning 29.6 percent of the state vote. McGovern then won an easy Massachusetts victory with 52.7 percent of the vote to Muskie's 21.3 percent. Humphrey edged McGovern in Ohio by 41.2 to 39.6 percent, but McGovern claimed a moral victory.

In the popular primary vote before the late summer California primary, McGovern actually stood in third place behind Wallace and Humphrey. But the delegate allocation rules gave the edge to the candidate who could squeeze out narrow victories in congressional districts, and that was McGovern. McGovern had 560 delegates to Humphrey's 311. Wallace had 324 delegates, but he was paralyzed after being shot in a Maryland shopping center and therefore no longer appeared to have a chance at the nomination.

The big McGovern-Humphrey showdown was California, which offered 271 delegates to the winner. It was a spirited campaign that included a head-to-head debate and strong Humphrey assaults on McGovern's positions on welfare and defense spending. McGovern went on to beat Humphrey by five percentage points in the winner-take-all primary. McGovern also won a majority of the delegates in New Jersey, South Dakota, and New Mexico in the last day of the primary season.[147]

After platform battles over welfare, busing, and the Vietnam War, McGovern won the nomination handily. He then selected Sen. Thomas Eagleton of Missouri as his running mate after several others declined. McGovern did not get to deliver his acceptance speech—perhaps the best speech of his career—until 2:48 a.m., when most television viewers were already in bed.

President Nixon and Vice President Agnew were renominated with barely a peep out of other Republicans. Rep. Paul N. (Pete) McCloskey of California opposed Nixon in the primaries but won only one delegate (from New Mexico).

McGovern would have been an underdog in the best of circumstances, but his chances were badly damaged by what came to be known as the "Eagleton affair." As the McGovernites celebrated their hard-won nomination, rumors circulated that Eagleton had been hospitalized for exhaustion after the 1960 campaign. Eagleton finally told McGovern operatives that he had been hospitalized three times for nervous exhaustion and fatigue, and his treatment included electroshock therapy. Despite McGovern's public statement that he was "1,000 percent for Tom Eagleton, and I have no intention of dropping him," Eagleton left the ticket less than two weeks after his nomination.

McGovern eventually replaced Eagleton with his sixth choice, R. Sargent Shriver, the former Peace Corps and Office of Economic Opportunity executive. But the aura of confusion that surrounded the Eagleton affair and the search for a new vice-presidential candidate hurt the campaign badly. The columnist Tom Braden likened it to a school teacher who could not control the class: "Nice people, too. One looks back with sympathy and a sense of shame. But at the time—was it that they were too nice?—their classes were a shambles. The erasers flew when they turned their backs." [148]

Nixon was in command of the fall campaign. He paraded a litany of accomplishments—the Paris peace talks over the Vietnam War, the diplomatic opening to China, the arms limitation treaty with the Soviet Union, and a number of domestic initiatives. Most of all, he was a strong figure; and if he still aroused suspicion, he was at least a known commodity.

Nixon won all but Massachusetts and the District of Columbia in the fall election. His popular vote margin was 47.2 million to McGovern's 29.2 million; the electoral college cast 521 votes for Nixon and only 17 for McGovern. Nixon's 60.7 percent share of the popular vote stood second only to Johnson's 61.1 percent in 1964.

The Watergate Scandals

On the surface, it appeared in 1972 that American politics were entering an age of calm consensus. At the time of the election, the economy was temporarily strong: opposition to the Vietnam War had faded as the two sides negotiated in Paris for an end to the war; the United States had signed an important nuclear arms treaty with the Soviet Union and had made important diplomatic moves with that country and the People's Republic of China. Nixon's landslide victory appeared to be a mandate and a vote of confidence.

But trouble loomed behind the apparent stability and consensus. The war in Vietnam continued, as did the antiwar protests, and generational cleavages remained. The economy experienced the first of many "shocks" in 1973 when the Organization of Petroleum Exporting Countries agreed to increases in the world prices of oil. The economic turmoil was topped off with a wage and price freeze. In addition, a warlike atmosphere between the White House and the media (as well as other perceived enemies of the administration that appeared on Nixon's "enemies list") and the mushrooming Watergate scandal combined to create a dark side to U.S. politics in the 1970s.[149]

The Watergate affair was perhaps the greatest political scandal in U.S. history. For the first time, a president was forced to leave office before his term expired. President Nixon resigned on August 9, 1974, when it became apparent that the House of Representatives would impeach him for "high crimes and misdemeanors" and the Senate would convict him. *(See "The Case of Richard Nixon," p. 373, in Removal of the President chapter of Part II.)* In addition, a number of Nixon aides, including his first attorney general and campaign manager, John Mitchell, would spend time in jail because of the scandal.

At its simplest level, the Watergate affair was "a third-rate burglary" and a subsequent coverup by President Nixon and his aides. In the summer of 1972, several employees of the Committee to Re-elect the President were arrested after they were discovered breaking into and bugging the Democratic National Committee's offices at the posh Watergate complex in Washington. The break-in was not a major issue in the 1972 election, but the next year congressional committees began an investigation.

During the investigation, a presidential aide revealed that Nixon had secretly taped Oval Office conversations with aides. When the Watergate special prosecutor, Archibald Cox, ordered Nixon to surrender the tapes in October 1973, Nixon ordered Cox fired. Nixon's attorney general and assistant attorney general refused to fire Cox; eventually, the solicitor general, Robert Bork, fired Cox, and a constitutional crisis dubbed the "Saturday night massacre" ensued. Nixon soon handed over the tapes Cox sought. In the summer of 1974, the Supreme Court ruled that Nixon had to surrender even more tapes, which indicated that he had played an active role in covering up the Watergate scandal. Nixon resigned the presidency when his impeachment and conviction appeared certain. The impeachment articles charged him with obstruction of justice, abuse of presidential powers, and contempt of Congress.

Many students of the Watergate affair maintain that the illegal campaign activities were just part of a tapestry of illegal activities in the Nixon administration—including secretly bombing Cambodia, accepting millions of dollars of illegal campaign contributions, offering government favors in return for contributions, "laundering" money through third parties, wiretapping and burglarizing a wide variety of people thought to be unsupportive of the president, offering executive clemency to convicted campaign workers, engaging in "dirty tricks" to discredit other political figures, compromising criminal investigations by giving information to the people under scrutiny, and using government funds to renovate the president's private residence.

The decade saw other political scandals as well. In 1973, Nixon's vice president, Spiro T. Agnew, resigned after pleading "no contest" to charges of bribe-taking while he was governor of Maryland. Members of Congress became enmeshed in the "Koreagate" and "Abscam" influence-peddling scandals. Congressional investigations uncovered massive abuses by the Federal Bureau of Investigation and the CIA reaching back into the 1950s.

After Agnew's resignation on October 10, 1973, Nixon named House Minority Leader Gerald Ford, a longtime GOP stalwart, to become vice president under the Twenty-fifth Amendment for presidential succession.

Ford, who had never entered a national election, became president upon Nixon's resignation and quickly attracted the support of the American public with his modest, earnest disposition. Ford responded to the widespread feeling that Nixon's isolation in the Oval Office contributed to his downfall by promising to work closely with Congress and to meet with the press regularly.

Less than two months after becoming president, however, Ford ignited a firestorm of criticism with his full pardon of Nixon for crimes he may have committed while president. Ford testified before Congress that he believed Nixon had suffered enough and that the nation would have been badly torn if a former president were brought to court to face criminal charges. Critics asserted that Ford had made a "deal" in which Nixon resigned the presidency in exchange for the pardon.[150]

Ford selected former New York governor Nelson Rockefeller to be his vice president. Rockefeller received Senate and House confirmation on December 10 and 19, respectively, after long and difficult hearings that centered on his financial dealings.

Jimmy Who?

With the benefit of the Watergate scandal and Ford's pardon of Nixon, the Democrats won resounding victories in the 1974 midterm elections. The Democrats' gains of fifty-two House seats and four Senate seats not only created stronger majorities but also cut the number of members with allegiance to the old system of organizing congressional business.

The moralistic zeal of the "Watergate class" forced major changes on Congress that affected not only the legislative process but also the presidency and the nation's process of pluralistic political bargaining. The new crop of legislators was so large that it was able to undermine the seniority system that had ordered the way Congress had operated for years. The new system of committee assignments led to a proliferation of subcommittees on which most members had prominent roles. That, in turn, created a fragmented policy-making process—less susceptible to coercion by presidents and party leaders and more susceptible to interest group politics.[151]

The 1976 campaign was the first governed by campaign finance reform legislation enacted in 1971 and 1974. The Federal Election Campaign Act (FECA) of 1971 limited campaign expenditures and required disclosure of campaign receipts and expenditures. The Revenue Act of 1971 created a tax check-off in which taxpayers could designate $1.00 of their taxes to be allocated for public financing of elections. The FECA amendments of 1974 limited spending and donations for both primary and general election campaigns, established a system of partial public funding of elections, and created the Federal Election Commission to monitor campaign activities.

The Democrats and their eventual nominee, Jimmy Carter, were able to continue exploiting the nation's discontent through the 1976 election. Ronald Reagan, the former movie actor and California governor, added to the Republican party's vulnerability by waging a a stubborn primary campaign against President Ford.

The Democrats appeared headed for a long and bitter nomination struggle for the third time in a row. A few candidates—such as senators Henry Jackson of Washing-

Arthur Grace, Sygma Photos

Virtually unknown to the nation at the outset of the 1976 presidential campaign, former Georgia governor Jimmy Carter emerged from a field of candidates to win the Democratic nomination and the presidency. His casual and honest approach appealed to many voters.

ton and Birch Bayh of Indiana and Governor Wallace of Alabama—had greater stature than others, but their appeal was limited to specific factions of the Democratic coalition. Other candidates included Rep. Morris Udall of Arizona, Sen. Fred Harris of Oklahoma, Sen. Frank Church of Idaho, and Gov. Edmund G. Brown, Jr., of California. Church and Brown entered the race late, and senators Humphrey of Minnesota and Edward M. Kennedy of Massachusetts awaited a draft in the event of a deadlocked convention.

The moderate Carter, whose name recognition in polls stood in single figures as the campaign began, executed a brilliant campaign strategy to win the nomination on the first ballot. Constructing strong organizations for the Iowa caucus and the New Hampshire primary, Carter won both contests by slim margins. Although liberal candidates Udall and Bayh together polled better than Carter, it was Carter who received cover billings on national magazines and live interviews on morning television talk shows.[152] Within a matter of days, Carter changed from long shot to front-runner.

Udall performed well in the primaries but never won a single state. He and other liberals constantly split their vote; Udall's chance for a Wisconsin primary win fizzled when Harris refused to back out to create a one-on-one matchup of a liberal with Carter.[153] Carter ran into strong challenges from Church and Brown in later primaries, but he had the delegates and endorsements by the time of the Democratic convention in New York for a first-ballot nomination.

The Democratic convention was a "love-feast" with the Democrats united behind Carter and his running mate, Sen. Walter F. Mondale of Minnesota.

The GOP was divided between Ford and Reagan. Ford won the early contests, but Reagan scored big wins in the North Carolina and Texas primaries. Reagan was put on the defensive with his proposals for transferring welfare obligations to the states, but when he focused on foreign policy issues he had success. He attacked Ford for his policy of détente with the Soviet Union and his negotiation of a treaty that would forfeit U.S. control of the Panama Canal.

With Ford and Reagan locked in a close contest for delegates in the late summer, Reagan tried to gain advantage by breaking precedent and naming his vice-presidential candidate before the convention. Reagan's choice was Sen. Richard Schweicker of Pennsylvania, a moderate who widened Reagan's ideological appeal but angered many of his conservative supporters. Reagan tried to force Ford to name a vice-presidential candidate in advance, and the convention vote on the issue was a crucial test of the candidates' delegate strength. Ford won that test and the nomination. He selected the acerbic senator Robert Dole of Kansas as his running mate as a consolation prize for disappointed conservatives.

Carter emerged from the Democratic convention with a wide lead over Ford, but the race was too close to call by election day. A number of gaffes—such as Carter's interview with *Playboy* magazine, his ambiguous statements about abortion, and his confused observations on tax reform—hurt the Democratic contender.[154] Ford also gained in the polls when he began to use the patronage powers of the presidency and effectively contrasted his twenty-seven years of Washington experience to Carter's four years as governor of Georgia.

For the first time since 1960, the major candidates took part in televised debates. As the outsider, Carter helped himself by demonstrating a good grasp of national issues and by appealing to Democrats to vote the party line. Ford hurt himself with a claim that Eastern European nations did not consider themselves to be under the control of the Soviet Union.[155] The remark was intended to be testimony to the Europeans' sense of national identity, but it was interpreted as evidence of the president's naiveté.

Carter's main advantage was regional pride. The Democrats had long since lost their hold over the south, but Carter gained widespread support as the first candidate nominated from the region on his own in more than a century. The Democratic party's many factions—including big-city mayors such as Daley of Chicago and Abraham Beame of New York, civil rights activists, and organized labor—put on a rare display of unity.

Carter defeated Ford by a slim margin, winning 40.8 million votes (50.1 percent) to Ford's 39.1 million (48.0 percent). In the electoral college, 297 votes went to Carter, 240 to Ford. Carter won by pulling together the frazzled New Deal coalition of industrial and urban voters, blacks, Jews, and southerners. Ford won the West, and Carter won the South, except Virginia. Ford won all the states from the Mississippi River westward except Texas and Hawaii, plus states in his native Midwest like Iowa, Illinois, Michigan, and Indiana. Ford also won Connecticut and the three northernmost New England states—New Hampshire, Vermont, and Maine.

Carter's Uncertain Leadership

After his election, President Carter's ability to hold the coalition together was limited. The growing influence of nationalized media politics and interest group politics, poor relations with Congress, and difficult "crosscutting" issues—inflation and unemployment, oil shocks and the more general energy crisis, the Iran hostage crisis, relations with the Soviet Union, and budget austerity moves such as proposed cutbacks in water projects and social welfare—all damaged Carter's governing ability.

As the 1980 election approached, Carter appeared to have lost all but his institutional strength and the reluctance of voters to reject a president for the fourth time in a row. Carter controlled party processes, such as the primary schedule; he had access to key financial support and skilled political operatives; and he shaped much of the political agenda. But Kennedy hit him hard from the left, and Reagan and others hit him hard from the right. Carter was unable to forge a lasting consensus on important issues. Kennedy led Carter in polls by a two-to-one margin when he announced his challenge to Carter in November 1979. But Carter overcame that lead by the start of the nominating season when the seizure of American hostages in Iran rallied the nation around the president and Kennedy made a series of political mistakes. Kennedy was unable to develop campaign themes or answer questions about his personal conduct in the 1969 Chappaquiddick incident, in which a woman died after a car he was driving went off a bridge. Other "character" issues, such as Kennedy's alleged "womanizing," and more substantive issues, such as his liberal voting record, also hurt him in a year dominated by conservative themes. Kennedy's campaign also was in financial jeopardy early because of lavish spending on transportation, headquarters, and other expenses.

The campaign of Governor Brown of California was unable to find much support for his appeal for recognition of economic and environmental limits. He dropped out of the race on April 1, 1980.

The president was able to manipulate the primary and caucus schedule to bunch states favorable to him and to match pro-Kennedy states with pro-Carter states. The result was an early, strong Carter lead in delegates. Kennedy came back with some strong primary wins in New York and Pennsylvania, but his campaign by then was reduced to a vehicle for anti-Carter expressions. Many Kennedy voters hoped for a deadlocked convention at which a third candidate could win the nomination.

Carter won the nomination on the first ballot despite a variety of stop-Carter efforts and Kennedy's attempt to free delegates to vote for any candidate. When Carter won the crucial floor vote on the "open convention" question, Kennedy did not have a chance. The Carter-Mondale ticket entered the fall campaign as a wounded army with little enthusiasm from the troops.

The Republicans united early behind Reagan. By April 22, 1980, less than two months after the New Hampshire primary, six candidates had dropped out of the race, and George Bush, Reagan's only surviving competitor, was desperately behind in the delegate count. Reagan's campaign experienced an early scare when Bush beat Reagan in the Iowa caucus; but Reagan rebounded, changed campaign managers and tactics, and won a string of primaries and caucuses. By the time of the convention, Reagan was the consensus candidate, and he improved party unity by adding Bush to the fall ticket.

Reagan called for the electorate to replace politics that he said were marked by "pastels," or compromising and uncertain policies, with "bold colors." Reagan's proposed bold strokes included a 30 percent reduction in marginal tax rates based on a "supply-side" economic theory—which even some Republicans said was a dangerous kind of "voodoo economics"—and massive increases in military expenditures. Reagan criticized at the same time Carter's alleged vacillation and his commitment to liberal policies.

President Carter—vulnerable as the hostage crisis neared its first anniversary (which was November 4, election day) and high inflation and unemployment rates persisted—attempted to portray Reagan as a dangerous, heartless, and inexperienced amateur. Reagan managed to use Carter's attacks to his own advantage by assuming a posture of hurt feelings at the unfair criticism. When in a televised debate Carter attacked Reagan's previous opposition to social welfare programs, Reagan cut him off with a line, "There you go again," that suggested Carter was unfairly and relentlessly distorting Reagan's record.

Carter strategists also were concerned about the independent candidacy of Rep. John B. Anderson of Illinois, a moderate who dropped out of the Republican race when it became clear that conservatives would dominate that party. After some stronger support in the polls, Anderson stood at about 10 percent for the final two months of the campaign. Carter was concerned that Anderson would take more votes from him than from Reagan, even though analysis of Anderson support suggested otherwise.[156]

Private money almost doubled the amount that Reagan was legally entitled to spend under the federal financing system. Well-organized groups on the "new right" that opposed abortion, gun control, détente, and many social welfare programs spent lavishly on television commercials and efforts to register like-minded voters. These groups also made a "hit list" of leading liberals in Congress; these candidates were so weakened by the new right's attacks that they put a local and regional drag on an already dragging Democratic ticket.[157]

Polls before election day predicted a close race. Reagan, however, won all but six states and took the White House in an electoral landslide, 489 electoral votes to 49. Reagan won 51 percent of the vote, while Carter managed 41 percent and Anderson 7 percent. Carter ran tight races in ten additional states that could have gone his way with a shift of less than one and a half percentage points. In twenty-one states, Anderson's vote totals made up most or all of the difference between Reagan and Carter. Despite these factors and polls that regularly showed preference for Carter's policy positions, Reagan's victory was impressive. He beat Carter by better than a two-to-one margin in nine states.

Even more surprising than Reagan's electoral landslide was the Republican takeover of the Senate. The new right's targeting of several Senate liberals—such as McGovern, Bayh, Gaylord Nelson of Wisconsin, John Tunney of California, and John Culver of Iowa—created the biggest Senate turnover since 1958. The Republicans now held the Senate by a 53-to-46 margin.

President Reagan was able to parlay his claims of an electoral mandate into wide-ranging changes in tax, budget, and military policies. Reagan won passage of a three-year, 25 percent cut in tax rates that would reduce federal revenues by $196 billion annually by the time the three-stage program was in place. He also secured omnibus legislation that cut the domestic budget by $140 billion over four years and increases in defense spending of $181 billion over the same period. The media hailed Reagan as the most successful handler of Congress since Lyndon Johnson.

Reagan's 1984 Landslide

Reagan's popularity dipped to 44 percent in 1983—about the average for modern presidents—but Reagan rebounded when the economy later picked up.[158] As the 1984 election approached, Reagan faced no opposition from Republicans, but a large field of Democrats sought the right to oppose him in the fall.

The Democrats' early front-runner was former vice president Mondale, who accumulated a wide range of endorsements (AFL-CIO, National Education Association, United Mine Workers, and the National Organization for Women) and an impressive campaign treasury. The more conservative senator John Glenn of Ohio, the first American to orbit earth, was considered a strong challenger. Other candidates included senators Gary Hart of Colorado, Alan Cranston of California, and Ernest Hollings of South Carolina, civil rights leader Jesse Jackson, former presidential candidate George McGovern, and former governor Reubin Askew of Florida.

UPI/Bettmann Newsphotos

Democratic presidential candidate Walter F. Mondale and his running mate, Geraldine Ferraro, the first woman to receive a major party nomination for national office, campaign in the 1984 presidential race.

The early results eliminated all but Mondale, Hart, and Jackson just sixteen days after the New Hampshire primary. Hart became the serious challenger to Mondale when he finished second in Iowa and first in New Hampshire, creating an explosion of media coverage. Mondale recovered, and the two fought head-to-head until the convention. Jackson, the second black to run, stayed in the race to promote his liberal party agenda.[159]

After interviewing a wide range of candidates, Mondale selected Rep. Geraldine Ferraro as his running mate—the first woman ever to receive a major-party nomination for national office. Representative Ferraro's vice-presidential candidacy probably was a drag on the ticket, not so much because she is a woman but because of the controversy created by her husband's finances and her stand on the abortion question. The controversies hindered the Democratic campaign's effort to articulate its own vision for the nation.[160]

Ferraro appeared knowledgeable and strong in her debate with Vice President Bush, and she often drew large and enthusiastic crowds. But she was stuck in controversy when details of her husband's questionable real estate, trusteeship, and tax practices became public. Opponents of abortion held prominent and often loud protests at the sites of her speeches, and she got involved in a lengthy public dispute over abortion with Catholic archbishop John O'Connor. Ferraro also did not help the ticket in regions where the Democrats were weak, such as the South and West.

Mondale ran a generally conservative campaign, concentrating on a proposed tax increase to address the unprecedented budget deficit of over $200 billion and proposing no new social programs. Mondale criticized Reagan's record on the arms race, but did not outline basic disagreements on other foreign affairs issues. He charged that Reagan, the oldest president in history, was lazy and out of touch. Only late in the campaign, when his speeches became unabashedly liberal and combative, did Mondale create any excitement.

Just once—in the period after the first presidential debate—did Mondale appear to have a chance to defeat President Reagan. Political pundits had marked Mondale as a poor television performer, but the challenger outfoxed Reagan in the debate and afterwards appeared to be gaining ground for a few days. Before the debate, Mondale aides leaked erroneous information that suggested he would make a slashing attack. But Mondale surprised Reagan. At the advice of strategist Patrick Caddell, Mondale adopted a "gold-watch approach" suitable to a family business retiring an oldtimer—"sort of embracing a grandfather, and gently pushing him aside." [161] Mondale gave the president credit for helping to restore national patriotism and beginning a national debate on education reform, but he said it was time for new leadership. Reagan appeared confused and, in the rush to demonstrate statistical knowledge of policies, he failed to outline broad themes.

Although the first debate boosted the Mondale campaign's morale, it never brought Mondale within striking range of Reagan. He never came within ten percentage points of Reagan in the polls. Reagan's campaign was a series of rallies with masses of colorful balloons and confident talk about the United States "standing tall" in domestic and world affairs. Reagan was so sure of victory that he

National Archives

Although Reagan's popularity dipped to 44 percent in 1983, he rebounded when the economy later picked up. Here, Reagan campaigns with Vice President George Bush.

made a last-minute trip to Mondale's home state of Minnesota with the hope of completing a fifty-state sweep of the nation.

Reagan's triumph was resounding almost everywhere. He won 54.5 million votes (58.8 percent) to Mondale's 37.6 million (40.6 percent). In the electoral college, he received 525 votes to Mondale's 13 votes. Reagan won forty-nine states, with 2-to-1 margins in eight states. Idaho, Nebraska, and Utah each gave Reagan more than 70 percent of the vote. Mondale won only the District of Columbia and his home state of Minnesota, where he beat Reagan by only two-tenths of 1 percent.

Reagan's two landslides and the conservative discourse of his administration led many experts to wonder if they were witnessing a "realignment"—that is, a major shift in political alliances among a variety of social, economic, and ethnic groups.[162] The noteworthy aspect of U.S. politics in the last two decades appeared to be the Democratic hold on congressional and state elections and the Republican dominance of presidential elections. Some experts pointed to the electorate's ticket-splitting tendencies as evidence of "dealignment"—that is, breakdown of the old system without development of an entirely new system.[163]

Perhaps the most noteworthy development of recent years, which fits the dealignment thesis, has been the convergence of the appeal of the two parties. Michael Barone, in *The Almanac of American Politics,* wrote:

> Political preferences in the America of the 1940's correlated to a fair degree with income. Republican strength was greater than average in high income states . . . , while Roosevelt and Truman carried virtually every state with incomes below the national average. But today there is virtually no correlation between income level and political preference. Utah, with one of the lowest per capita incomes, was one of the nation's most Republican states in 1980. . . . In the Midwest, high income Illinois is more Democratic than low income Indiana.[164]

The New Conservative Discourse

Reagan's rise ushered in a new age of conservatism in the American political discourse. The vigorous conservative campaigns for the presidency and Congress were accompanied by a host of new "think tanks" and publications with a restyled set of philosophical and policy pronouncements.

The most celebrated event of the conservative revival was the publication of George Gilder's *Wealth and Poverty,* a far-reaching attack on welfare state policies that rested on supply-side economic theory. Gilder argued that free markets and low taxes promoted not only economic efficiency and growth but also other benefits such as family strength and artistic creativity. Gilder's book was a central element of Reagan's campaign for major tax cuts.[165] But the supply-side tracts of Gilder and others were only the most prominent signs of the conservative movement. Reagan's criticism of the Supreme Court decisions on abortion and school prayer helped to bring evangelical Christians into the political process. Businesses and conservative philanthropists, meanwhile, sponsored an unprecedented level of public policy research that shaped the debate of elections and government policy.[166]

Reagan's political appeal, according to scholar Garry Wills, turned on his ability to blend contradictory elements of American culture such as capitalism, conservatism, and individualism. While Reagan decried the decline of "traditional American values," for example, he extolled the dynamic economic system that demanded constant change. Wills writes: "There are so many contradictions in this larger construct that one cannot risk entertaining serious challenge to any of its details. In Reagan, luckily, all these clashes are resolved. He is the ideal past, the successful present, the hopeful future all in one."[167]

Using the "bully pulpit" of the presidency, Reagan was able to overwhelm his opponents with his vision. When Democrats criticized specific Reagan policies, Reagan deflated them with expressions of disdain for "little men with loud voices [that] cry doom." [168] Jeane Kirkpatrick's depiction of Democrats as the "blame America first crowd" neatly expressed the way the Reagan rhetoric foreclosed debate on major policy issues such as the budget and trade deficits, military spending, the U.S. role in the third world, and U.S.-Soviet relations.

By the time the 1984 campaign took place, much of the nation had adopted Reagan's terms of debate. Mondale's strongest performance, in fact, was in the first debate when he congratulated Reagan for restoring national pride and suggested not that Reagan should be ousted but rather given a graceful retirement. Mondale's campaign was basically conservative: he did not propose a single new social program and called the federal budget deficit the nation's top problem.

The Post-Reagan Era

The election of 1988 was the first since 1968 in which an incumbent president did not run. With no major figure and no major issues, the campaign was a tumultuous affair. As fourteen candidates struggled to develop an identity with the voters, the campaign lurched from one symbolic issue to the next and never developed the overarching themes of previous campaigns.

In the absence of any major new issues, and in a time of general peace and prosperity, Republican vice president George Bush won the presidency. Bush defeated Democratic Massachusetts governor Michael S. Dukakis by a margin of 54 percent to 46 percent—47.9 million votes to 41.0 million votes. Bush's electoral vote margin was more impressive, 426-112. A negative campaign and limited voter-registration efforts resulted in the lowest voter turnout in modern times. Just more than 50 percent of all eligible citizens voted for president.

Bush won with the Nixon-Reagan presidential coalition. He won all the states of the old Confederacy, the entire West except Oregon and Washington, and several northern industrial states. Dukakis originally hoped to crack the South by selecting a favorite son, Sen. Lloyd Bentsen of Texas, as his running mate; but that failed. Dukakis lost crucial states that he fought for to the end, such as California, Pennsylvania, Illinois, Ohio, and Missouri. He won New York, Massachusetts, Wisconsin, Minnesota, Oregon, Washington, West Virginia, Iowa, Rhode Island, Hawaii, and the District of Columbia.

President Ronald Reagan's retirement after two full terms created a void as the campaign began. By most accounts, Reagan was the most popular president since Dwight D. Eisenhower. His dominance of national politics left little room for other figures to establish presidential stature.

Reagan's fiscal and social policies reduced the possibility for candidates to offer ambitious new programs. The national government's huge budget deficits—which exceeded $200 billion, compared with the previous high of about $80 billion in the last year of the Carter administration—checked any grandiose new spending plans. The Reagan debt exceeded the debt of the previous thirty-nine presidents.

President Reagan also reshaped the dialogue on foreign affairs. He maintained strong opposition to the Soviet Union and other "Marxist" nations with his policies in Nicaragua, Afghanistan, and Angola. He also projected an image of strength with military action in Libya and Grenada. At the same time, however, he co-opted critics by meeting Soviet leader Mikhail Gorbachev several times and signing a nuclear arms control agreement. Reagan even asserted that the Gorbachev regime was fundamentally different from previous Soviet regimes, which he had called the "evil empire."

The early Republican front-runners were Bush and Sen. Robert J. Dole of Kansas; former senator Gary Hart of Colorado was considered the early Democratic leader. The campaign got scrambled before it began, however. Hart left the race in 1987 when the Miami *Herald* augmented rumors of Hart's infidelity with a report that he had spent the night with a young model. Hart, considered by many to be the brightest and most issue-oriented candidate, had long faced criticism about his "character."

Sen. Joseph R. Biden, Jr., of Delaware was the next casualty of the media's 1987 concern with "character" issues.[169] Media reports that he had committed plagiarism on a law school paper and in campaign speeches led to Biden's early exit from the campaign. Biden had been considered a leading candidate because of his experience and strong speaking style.

With Hart and Biden out of the race, the Democrats were in disarray. Dubbed "dwarfs," the remaining candidates—Rev. Jesse Jackson of Illinois, Gov. Dukakis, Rep. Richard A. Gephardt of Missouri, Sen. Albert A. Gore, Jr., of Tennessee, Sen. Paul M. Simon of Illinois, and former Arizona governor Bruce Babbitt—lacked the combination of extensive government experience and strong national bases many observers thought necessary to win the presidency.

The Republicans had problems of their own. Vice President Bush was the early favorite, and he benefited from his association with President Reagan. But Bush's public fealty to Reagan created a problem: he was considered a "wimp," unable to stand on his own. Every major position Bush had held in his political career was the result of appointment: ambassador to the United Nations, chairman of the Republican National Committee, envoy to China, director of the Central Intelligence Agency, and vice president. Bush had represented Texas for two terms in the House and lost two Senate races.

Dole, too, was considered strong at the outset of the race. As Republican leader in the Senate, he had a high profile in national politics and proven fund-raising abilities. His wife, Elizabeth, was prominent as secretary of transportation. Dole also had an acerbic wit, which gave spark to his campaigning style but also irritated some voters. Other GOP candidates were Rep. Jack Kemp of New York, former secretary of state Alexander M. Haig, Jr., of Pennsylvania, former Delaware governor Pierre S. (Pete) du Pont III, and television minister Marion G. (Pat) Robertson of Virginia.

The marathon campaign for the nomination began with the Iowa caucuses, a significant event only because of intense media attention. Gephardt barely edged Simon in the Democratic contests, and Dole won the Republican race. The big story was just how badly Bush performed: he finished third behind Dole and Robertson.

The Iowa loss caused the Bush campaign to emerge from its isolation. Bush had been the most restrained and cautious candidate as he tried to benefit from the prestige of the White House. But in the New Hampshire primary, Bush beat Dole. Bush won with a series of television advertisements charging that Dole would raise taxes. Bush also was more animated on the campaign trail than he had been before. Dole failed to respond quickly to the Bush offensive, and when he snapped on national television about Bush's "lying about my record," he reinforced his image as a mean-spirited candidate.

Among the Democrats, Governor Dukakis easily won the New Hampshire primary. Capitalizing on his regional popularity, Dukakis beat Gephardt and Simon. Most of the Democratic fire in that race took place between the two runners-up. Dukakis escaped without any major criticism, and his already strong fund-raising machine went into high gear.

The decisive stage of the GOP campaign was Super Tuesday—March 8—when twenty-two states held presidential primaries or caucuses. Benefiting from a well-organized campaign, Bush won seventeen of the eighteen GOP contests. Dole staked his campaign on the ensuing Illinois primary, but he lost badly, and Bush was virtually ensured the Republican nomination.

The one issue that threatened Bush throughout 1988 was the Iran-contra scandal. Revelations that the administration had traded arms to Iran in exchange for the release of hostages, then used the proceeds illegally to fund the war in Nicaragua, raised questions about Bush's role. Administration officials admitted lying to Congress, destroying evidence, and operating outside normal government channels; one top official even attempted suicide. But the question of Bush's involvement fizzled after months of inconclusive questioning of Bush.

The Democrats sorted things out slowly on Super Tuesday. Dukakis won Texas and Florida and five northern states and confirmed his shaky front-runner status. Civil rights leader Jesse Jackson was the big surprise, however, winning five southern states. Gore won seven states.

The Democratic marathon continued into Illinois, Michigan, and New York. Dukakis took and maintained the lead in delegates with steady wins over Jackson and Gore. Gore dropped out after finishing third in a divisive New York primary, and the rest of the campaign was a one-on-one race between Dukakis and Jackson. Only once—after his victory over Dukakis in the Michigan caucuses—did Jackson appear to have a chance to win the Democratic nomination.

Jackson was a mixed blessing for the party. An energetic campaigner, he attracted support from blacks and from farmers and blue-collar workers who were disgruntled by the uneven rewards of economic growth. But Jackson was considerably to the left of the rest of the party and never had held any government office. Race also was a factor: no political professional believed that a black could be elected president.

Dukakis practically clinched the nomination with his victory over Jackson in the New York primary. The issue of race was at the center of the campaign. New York City mayor Edward I. Koch, a Gore supporter, called Jackson a "radical" and said Jews would be "crazy" to vote for him. Such remarks aggravated tensions between blacks and Jews that had festered since the 1960s. Dukakis avoided the race issue and won the primary.

As the summer conventions approached, Bush and Dukakis each had the full support of his party. The parties' internal divisions were on display as the prospective nominees considered possible vice-presidential candidates. Blacks lobbied for Jackson's selection by Dukakis, while "New Right" GOP leaders lobbied against a "moderate" running mate.

Dukakis selected conservative senator Lloyd M. Bentsen, Jr., of Texas as his running mate before the Atlanta Democratic convention. Jackson complained publicly and privately, but he eventually embraced Bentsen for the sake of party unity. Dukakis hoped Bentsen would be able to help carry Texas: no Democrat has won the presidency without winning Texas since the state became part of the nation in 1845.

The July convention was a success for the Democrats. After a week of Bush-bashing and Democratic conciliation, Dukakis gave an effective acceptance speech peppered with statements in Spanish and Greek. Dukakis left the conven-

David Valdez; The White House

On August 18, 1988, George Bush and his vice-presidential running mate, Dan Quayle, celebrate their victory at the Republican national convention.

tion with a double-digit lead over Bush in the polls.

The Republican convention in August did not start out as well. Bush announced his selection of Sen. Dan Quayle of Indiana as he arrived in New Orleans. After revelations that Quayle had avoided military service in the Vietnam War by enlisting in the Indiana National Guard, many Republicans criticized Bush's choice. Some even said Quayle might have to be dropped from the ticket. By the end of the convention, however, the Republicans had weathered the storm. Bush delivered a crisp address, which provided the self-portrait that the vice president needed, and moved into the fall campaign for a close battle with Dukakis.

Bush took the offensive immediately after the August GOP convention and hit Dukakis as a "liberal" out of touch with American "values." Bush attacked Dukakis for his membership in the American Civil Liberties Union, his veto of a bill requiring Massachusetts teachers to lead children in the Pledge of Allegiance, and a Massachusetts program allowing prisoners time off for weekends. As he pounded away at these symbolic issues, Dukakis's "negative" ratings with voters soared. Not believing the attacks would affect his standing with undecided voters—and believing they might even hurt Bush—Dukakis did not respond forcefully to the attacks until October. By then, however, Bush had effectively defined Dukakis, a newcomer to national politics. Dukakis's counteroffensive in the last two weeks of the campaign came too late.

Other major national issues—the national debt, the trade deficit, housing, education, U.S.-Soviet relations, the environment, and ethics in government—were drowned out by the emphasis on symbolic issues.

As Dukakis fell behind Bush, his campaign pinned its hopes on two nationally televised debates. Dukakis performed well in the first debate, but Bush appeared to "win" the second debate. Dukakis failed to gain on Bush.

The only major problem for Bush was Quayle. Most political professionals considered Quayle a "lightweight." The forty-one-year-old Quayle was a poor student and marginal member of Congress.[170]

Dukakis said Bush's selection of Quayle amounted to failure in his "first presidential decision." Dukakis compared Quayle with the more experienced Bentsen, who performed much better in a vice-presidential debate. Public polls revealed that most voters thought that Quayle was a bad choice.

The Bush campaign minimized the damage by limiting Quayle's public exposure and carefully scripting his statements. Quayle rarely spoke in major media markets; many of his campaign stops were accessible only by bus. While Bush delivered speeches in several states each day, Quayle often made just one speech before schoolchildren or partisan audiences.

After months of inconsistent and confusing strategy, Dukakis finally developed a strong appeal in the last two weeks of the campaign. He told voters he was "on your side" and portrayed Bush as a toady to the wealthy. Dukakis said the middle class was "squeezed" by the policies of the Reagan administration and that the Democrats would provide good jobs, affordable housing and health care, and tough enforcement of environmental protection laws.

It was not enough. Bush, who had made a fortune in the oil business before entering politics and was the son of a former U.S. senator, convinced more voters that his experience and values were what they wanted in the very personal choice of a president.

Democrats gained one seat in the Senate and three seats in the House of Representatives—a warning to Bush, since winning presidential candidates usually help their party gain seats in Congress. A period of divided government appeared in the offing, as congressional Democrats developed their own agenda for the next four years.

Notes

History of Presidential Elections

1. Richard M. Pious, *The American Presidency* (New York: Basic Books, 1979), 22.
2. Ibid., 25-29.
3. The term *electoral college* does not appear in the text of the Constitution. Citing Andrew C. McLaughlin, Edward Corwin wrote that the term "was used by Abraham Baldwin in 1800 and by John Randolph in 1809, and 'officially' in 1845" (Edward S. Corwin, *The President: Office and Powers,* 4th ed. [New York: New York University Press, 1957], 339 n.21).
4. The original compromise called for the Senate to make the final decision in such circumstances.
5. Richard Hofstadter, *The Idea of a Party System* (Berkeley: University of California Press, 1969), 16-39.
6. John F. Hoadley, *Origins of American Political Parties* (Lexington: University Press of Kentucky, 1986), 34.
7. A. E. Dick Howard, *Commentaries on the Constitution of Virginia,* vol. I (Charlottesville: University Press of Virginia, 1974), 318-19; ibid.
8. Howard, *Commentaries,* 320.
9. Quoted in ibid., 323.
10. Ibid., 325-26.
11. See, for example, Hoadley, *Origins,* 34-35; Robert E. Brown, *Charles Beard and the Constitution* (Princeton: Princeton University Press, 1956), 61-72.
12. *McPherson v. Blacker,* 146 U.S. 1 (1892) at 29; Eugene H. Roseboom, *A History of Presidential Elections,* 2d ed. (New York: Macmillan, 1964), 15.
13. Corwin, *The President,* 39.
14. Edward Stanwood, *A History of the Presidency from 1788 to 1897,* revised by Charles Knowles Bolton (Boston: Houghton Mifflin, 1928), 21-22.
15. Ibid., 38-39.
16. Roseboom, *History of Presidential Elections,* 28.
17. Stanwood, *History of the Presidency,* 38-39.
18. Ibid., 136.
19. Corwin, *The President,* 39-40.
20. Nelson W. Polsby and Aaron Wildavsky, *Presidential Elections,* 6th ed. (New York: Scribner's, 1984), 298 n.94.
21. *Ray v. Blair,* 343 U.S. 214 (1962), quoted in Harold W. Chase and Craig R. Ducat, *Edwards S. Corwin's The Constitution and What it Means Today,* 13th ed. (Princeton: Princeton University Press, 1973), 380.
22. Stanwood, *History of the Presidency,* 78.
23. *McPherson v. Blacker,* 146 U.S. 1 (1892).
24. Roseboom, *History of Presidential Elections,* 17.
25. Margaret Horsnell, "Who Was Who in the Constitutional Convention," *This Constitution* 15 (Summer 1987): 38.
26. Stanwood, *History of the Presidency,* 27. According to Stanwood: "Although in all the newspaper references to the coming election . . . Mr. Adams was spoken of as a candidate for Vice-President, that gentleman did not so regard himself, but rather as a candidate for the presidency. If he received more votes than Washington, he would be President; if the votes were equal, the House of Representatives would choose one of the two. He showed plainly that he regarded his own merits as equal to those of Washington" (page 26).
27. Roseboom, *History of Presidential Elections,* 33.
28. James S. Chase, *Emergence of the Presidential Nominating*

Convention: 1789-1832 (Urbana: University of Illinois Press, 1973), 8.
29. Richard L. Rubin, *Press, Party, and Presidency* (New York: Norton, 1981), 11.
30. Culver H. Smith, *The Press, Politics, and Patronage* (Athens: University of Georgia Press, 1977), 13.
31. John Tebbel, *The Compact History of the American Newspaper* (New York: Hawthorn Books, 1963), 64, 65.
32. From the December 23, 1796, issue of the *Aurora,* quoted in Willard Grosvenor Bleyer, *Main Currents in the History of American Journalism* (Boston: Houghton Mifflin, 1927), 116.
33. James MacGregor Burns, *The Deadlock of Democracy* (Englewood Cliffs, N.J.: Prentice-Hall, 1963), 29.
34. Chase, *Presidential Nominating Convention,* 11. But see others who say that the caucus did meet: *CQ's Guide to U.S. Elections,* 2d ed. (Washington, D.C.: Congressional Quarterly Inc., 1985), 9; Noble E. Cunningham, Jr., *The Jeffersonian Republicans: The Formation of Party Organization, 1798-1801* (Chapel Hill: University of North Carolina Press, 1957), 91. Austin Ranney, in *Curing the Mischiefs of Faction* (Berkeley: University of California Press, 1975), notes that it is not clear when the first caucuses were, but that most historians agree that both parties held caucuses in 1800 (p. 64).
35. Noble E. Cunningham, Jr., ed., *The Making of the American Party System: 1789-1809* (Englewood Cliffs, N.J.: Prentice-Hall, 1965), 14.
36. From text of the speech in ibid., 16-17.
37. Stanwood, *History of the Presidency,* 45-46.
38. Chase, *Presidential Nominating Convention,* 12.
39. Quoted in Stanwood, *History of the Presidency,* 70.
40. The history of the amendment is covered in some detail in ibid., 77-82.
41. Ibid., 111.
42. Quoted in ibid., 90.
43. William J. Crotty, *Political Reform and the American Experiment* (New York: Crowell, 1977), 11.
44. By the mid-1970s Republicans were becoming competitive for the first time in the South, but the Democrats still held most legislatures. In 1954, only 86 of 1,559 state legislators, or 5.5 percent, were Republicans; by 1972, the figure had climbed to 280 out of 1,516 (18.5 percent). See Everett Carll Ladd, Jr., and Charles D. Hadley, *Transformation of the American Party System* (New York: Norton, 1975), 150.
45. Richard Fenno, *Home Style: House Members in Their Districts* (Boston: Little, Brown, 1978), 160-162.
46. Woodrow Wilson also called for national primaries in his first message to Congress as president in 1913, but the initiative died because of neglect. Polls since World War II have found steady majorities favoring national primaries, but there has never been any serious effort to bring about such a system.
47. The nine amendments that affect the way citizens participate in elections are: the Twelfth (1804), placing the presidential and vice-presidential candidates on a single ticket; the Fourteenth (1868), providing for equal protection under the law and for a decrease in the number of House members of any state that denied citizens the vote; the Fifteenth (1870) specifying that the right to vote cannot be denied because of race; the Seventeenth (1913) providing for direct election of senators; the Nineteenth (1920), giving women the right to vote; the Twenty-second (1951), limiting presidents to two terms; the Twenty-third (1961) giving the District of Columbia electoral votes; the Twenty-fourth (1964), eliminating the poll tax; and the Twenty-sixth (1971), giving eighteen-year-olds the right to vote.
48. *Smith v. Allwright,* 321 U.S. 649 (1944); *Harman v. Forssenius,* 380 U.S. 528 (1965); *Harper v. Virginia State Board of Elections,* 383 U.S. 663 (1966).
49. Some jurisdictions below the state level retained tax-paying requirements into the twentieth century.
50. E. E. Schattschneider, *The Semisovereign People* (Hinsdale, Ill.: Dryden Press, 1975), 82.
51. *Guinn v. United States,* 238 U.S. 347 (1915); *Smith v. Allwright,* 321 U.S. 649 (1944); *Harper v. Virginia State Board of Elections,* 383 U.S. 663 (1966).
52. Charlotte Perkins Gilman's *Moving the Mountain,* for example, pictures a utopian state that would exist if there were true equality of the sexes. Gilman's study, *Women and Economics,* analyzed the way gender discrimination and repression deformed the economy. See *Charlotte Perkins Gilman Reader* (New York: Pantheon, 1980). Gilman and other feminists of the late nineteenth century designed schemes for cooperative cooking and housekeeping that they hoped would release women for full participation in the world of work and politics. See Delores Hayden, *The Grand Domestic Revolution* (Cambridge, Mass.: MIT Press, 1981).
53. *Marston v. Lewis,* 410 U.S. 679 (1973).
54. Jasper B. Shannon, *Money and Politics* (New York: Random, 1959), 19-20.
55. Robert Merton, *Social Theory and Social Structure* (New York: Free Press, 1957), 71-82.
56. Professor Hadley Cantril's department of psychology at Princeton University conducted a wide variety of polls both about domestic production and consumption during the war and about the attitudes and needs of troops on the front. See James R. Beniger and Robert J. Giuffra, Jr., "Public Opinion Polling: Command and Control in Presidential Campaigns," in *Presidential Selection,* ed. Alexander Heard and Michael Nelson (Durham, N.C.: Duke University Press, 1987), 190.
57. This account draws on William Crotty, *Party Reform* (New York: Longman, 1983); Nelson W. Polsby, *Consequences of Party Reform* (New York: Oxford University Press, 1983); and David E. Price, *Bringing Back the Parties* (Washington, D.C.: CQ Press, 1984), chap. 6
58. From the McGovern-Fraser Commission Report, quoted in Crotty, *Party Reform,* 25.
59. Ibid., 26.
60. Quoted in Price, *Bringing Back the Parties,* 146.
61. Crotty, *Party Reform,* 62.
62. For an overview of the literature on this point, see Austin Ranney, "The Political Parties: Reform and Decline," in *The New American Political System,* ed. Anthony King (Washington, D.C.: American Enterprise Institute, 1978), 214-215.
63. Polsby, *Consequences of Party Reform,* 34-35, quoting Byron Shafer.
64. William J. Crotty, *Political Reform and the American Experiment* (New York: Crowell, 1977), 245.
65. Terry Sanford, *A Danger of Democracy: The Presidential Nominating Process* (Boulder, Colo.: Westview Press, 1981), 20-21.
66. For examples of those who take issue with these critics, see: Robert T. Nakamura, "The Reformed Nominating System: Its Critics and Uses," *PS* 16, no. 4 (Fall 1983): 667-672; and Kenneth A. Bode and Carol F. Casey, "Party Reform: Revisionism Revised," in *Political Parties in the Eighties,* ed. Robert A. Goldwin (Washington, D.C.: American Enterprise Institute, 1980), 3-19.
67. James W. Ceaser, *Presidential Selection: Theory and Development* (Princeton: Princeton University Press, 1979), 284.
68. Price, *Bringing Back the Parties,* 151.
69. Crotty, *Political Reform,* 246.
70. Austin Ranney, "Changing the Rules of the Nominating Game," in *Choosing the President,* ed. James David Barber (Englewood Cliffs, N.J.: Prentice-Hall, 1974), 73-74.
71. While it is generally accepted that the reforms led to the proliferation of presidential primaries, Kenneth Bode and Carol Casey (both members of the McGovern-Fraser Commission) have suggested that other factors played a role as well. See Bode and Casey, "Party Reforms," 16-17. For a refutation of their position, see: Polsby, *Consequences of Party Reform,* 57-58.
72. Crotty, *Party Reform,* 76-77.
73. Price, *Bringing Back the Parties,* 154.
74. Ibid., 151; and James W. Davis, *Presidential Primaries: Road to the White House* (Westport, Conn.: Greenwood Press, 1980), 66.
75. Price, *Bringing Back the Parties,* 170.

76. Michael Oreskes, "Jackson Still Irked by Delegate Vote Tally," *New York Times*, July 22, 1988, A11.
77. This account of the Republican party's reform efforts is based on Crotty, *Party Reform*, chap. 17 and 18; Robert J. Huckshorn and John F. Bibby, "National Party Rules and Delegate Selection in the Republican Party," *PS* 16, no. 4 (Fall 1983): 656-666; and Price, *Bringing Back the Parties*, 156-159.
78. For a discussion of this, see Ceaser, *Presidential Selection*, 265-271.
79. Price, *Bringing Back the Parties*, 156.

The Campaign Finance System

1. Robert L. Heilbroner, *The Nature and Logic of Capitalism* (New York: Norton, 1985), 55.
2. Elizabeth Drew, *Politics and Money: The New Road to Corruption* (New York: Macmillan, 1983), 2, 4.
3. Robert J. Samuelson, "The Campaign Reform Fraud," *Newsweek*, July 13, 1987, 43.
4. Jeffrey Berry, *The Interest Group Society* (Boston: Little, Brown, 1984), 168.
5. Ibid., 51.
6. Thomas Byrne Edsall, *The New Politics of Inequality* (New York: Norton, 1984), 82-84.
7. Drew, *Politics and Money*, 96.
8. John Kenneth Galbraith, *American Capitalism: The Concept of Countervailing Power* (Boston: Houghton Mifflin, 1952), esp. chap. 2.
9. A number of academic debates fall within the demand-side school of electoral behavior. The debate whether voters address issues "prospectively" (by estimating how the candidates' issue stances will affect their own fortunes in the future) or "retrospectively" (by judging the effects of candidates' past policy positions) emphasizes the voters' ability to shape the system (see Morris P. Fiorina, *Retrospective Voting in American National Elections* [New Haven, Conn.: Yale University Press, 1981]). Debates whether a winning candidate has a "mandate" for particular policies assume that the system operates according to the signals that voters send (see Walter Dean Burnham, "The 1980 Earthquake: Realignment, Reaction, Or What?" in *The Hidden Election: Politics and Economics in the 1980 Campaign*, ed. Thomas Ferguson and Joel Rogers [New York: Pantheon, 1981], 98-140). The debate about the winning candidate's differing roles as "delegate" or "trustee" also falls into this school of U.S. election studies (see Richard Fenno, *Home Style* [Boston: Little, Brown, 1978]).
10. Thomas Ferguson and Joel Rogers, *Right Turn: The Decline of the Democrats and the Future of American Politics* (New York: Hill and Wang, 1986), 45.
11. Ira Katznelson, "A Radical Departure: Social Welfare and the Election," in *Hidden Election*, ed. Ferguson and Rogers (New York: Pantheon, 1981), 332-334.
12. Mancur Olson, *The Logic of Collective Action* (Cambridge, Mass.: Harvard University Press, 1965).
13. Jasper P. Shannon, *Money and Politics* (New York: Random, 1959), 15.
14. Ibid., 17-18.
15. Ibid., 25.
16. Ibid., 31.
17. By the time of McKinley's reelection drive in 1900, Hanna had refined his fund-raising system to the point where it was "unofficial taxation." Corporations were expected to contribute "according to [their] stake in the general prosperity of the country." Hanna returned $50,000 of the Standard Oil Company's $250,000 donation because it was considered more than the company's fair "share" for the campaign. See Michael E. McGerr, *The Decline of Popular Politics: The American North, 1865-1928* (New York: Oxford University Press, 1986), 44-45, and Shannon, *Money and Politics*, 33.
18. Shannon, *Money and Politics*, 37.
19. Michael Nelson, "A Short, Ironic History of American Bureaucracy," *Journal of Politics* 44 (Winter 1982): 767.
20. Samuel Kernell, *Going Public: New Strategies of Presidential Leadership* (Washington, D.C.: CQ Press, 1986), 100, 109.
21. Shannon, *Money and Politics*, 60-61.
22. Herbert E. Alexander, *Money in Politics* (Washington, D.C.: Public Affairs Press, 1972), 10.
23. David W. Adamany and George E. Agree, *Political Money: A Strategy for Campaign Financing in America* (Baltimore: Johns Hopkins University Press, 1975), 113-114.
24. Ibid., 32. Of the money raised before the disclosure requirement took effect, eighty-seven contributors of $50,000 or more gave a total of $12.4 million. Some $4.4 million of the $43.3 million raised after that point came from thirty-seven contributors of $50,000 or more.
25. Adamany and Agree, *Political Money*, 39.
26. Nelson W. Polsby and Aaron Wildavsky, *Presidential Elections* (New York: Scribner's, 1984), 66. As might be expected, the sequence of events is as disputed as it is crucial. From 1969 to 1971, the Nixon administration negotiated with International Telephone and Telegraph (ITT) over the suit. President Nixon was involved personally. Tapes revealed that at the same time, administrative officials knew of ITT's offers for campaign and convention assistance. See Herbert E. Alexander, *Financing the 1972 Elections* (Lexington, Mass.: Lexington Books, 1976), 263-268.
27. Stephen Hess, *The Presidential Campaign* (Washington, D.C.: Brookings, 1974), 82. Long after the 1972 election, the public continued to associate John Connally, the administration's Treasury secretary, with influence peddling. During his losing presidential campaign in 1980, Connally faced persistent questions about the dairy scandal, for which he was indicted and acquitted. Connally tried to defuse the issue by saying, "I'm the only certified non-guilty political figure in the country," a posture that seemed to betray a certain cynicism about the nonlegal, moral standards of politics. See Richard Harwood, ed., *The Pursuit of the Presidency 1980* (New York: Berkley, 1980), 145.
28. Adamany and Agree, *Political Money*, 41.
29. Ibid., 48.
30. From *Buckley v. Valeo*. Cited in *Guide to Congress*, 3d. ed. (Washington, D.C.: Congressional Quarterly Inc., 1982), 680.
31. Ibid.
32. The delays in revamping the FEC had an immediate effect on the 1976 presidential nomination contests. Arizona representative Morris Udall and former California governor Ronald Reagan did not receive federal funds they had planned to use, and they had to trim their primary efforts in several states. It is conceivable that both candidates could have won their party nominations if they had had the money at the critical periods. See Jules Witcover, *Marathon: The Pursuit of the Presidency, 1972-1976* (New York: Viking Press, 1977), 219-221.
33. James W. Davis, *Presidential Primaries: Road to the White House* (Westport, Conn.: Greenwood Press, 1980), 217-218; Alexander, *Financing the 1972 Election*, 110-159.
34. Federal Election Commission, press release, March 8, 1989.
35. Michael J. Malbin, "You Get What You Pay For, But Is That What You Want?" in *Before Nomination: Our Primary Problems*, ed. George Grassmuck (Washington, D.C.: American Enterprise Institute, 1985), 86.
36. Davis, *Presidential Primaries*, 206. Committees to draft reluctant candidates are not automatically subject to campaign spending limits. The money spent by the 1979 draft committees for Massachusetts senator Edward M. Kennedy did not count against Kennedy's overall spending limits.
37. Ibid., 207.
38. Xandra Kayden, "Regulating Campaign Finance: Consequences for Interests and Institutions," in *Presidential Selection*, ed. Alexander Heard and Michael Nelson (Durham, N.C.: Duke University Press, 1987), 261.
39. Davis, *Presidential Primaries*, 206-207.

40. Harwood, *Pursuit of the Presidency,* 102-103.
41. "Manufacturing the Next President," *Harper's,* December 1987, 49.
42. Reducing the party's role can have enormous repercussions for the political system. It is wrong to assign complete responsibility for the separation of presidential politics and the party system to the finance system. A variety of other developments—such as the increasing dominance of media and campaign professionals in the process—are just as important. Furthermore, the split between the campaign organization and the rest of the system was evident before federal financing. Perhaps the best example of a campaign cut off from the rest of the system was Richard Nixon's 1972 reelection campaign, which operated completely on privately raised funds. The 1972 Nixon campaign illustrates the perils involved in an isolated presidential campaign—whether it is publicly or privately financed. The independence of the Committee to Reelect the President was probably a major reason behind the committee's illegal activities, from influence-peddling to dirty tricks to espionage activities. When the so-called Watergate affair reached its climax in the summer of 1974, Nixon could not count on the loyalties of Republican members of Congress he had declined to support vigorously in 1972.
43. Edsall, *New Politics of Inequality,* 91-92.
44. Ferguson and Rogers, *Right Turn,* 47.
45. Peter W. Bernstein, "Fritz's Fat Cats Shake the Money Tree," *Fortune,* August 20, 1984, 153.
46. Ferguson and Rogers, *Right Turn,* 73-83.
47. Allen R. Thompson, *Economics* (Reading, Mass.: Addison-Wesley, 1988), 372.
48. David R. Cameron used measures of labor's membership rates, unity, and centralized bargaining strength to rank eighteen countries (Edsall, *New Politics of Inequality,* 145-147).
49. Ferguson and Rogers, 53.
50. Edsall, *New Politics of Inequality,* 99.
51. Ibid., 100.
52. Ibid., 98.
53. Ibid., 98.
54. Herbert E. Alexander, "Political Parties and the Dollar," *Society,* January/February 1985, 55.
55. Ibid.
56. Herbert E. Alexander and Brian A. Haggerty, *Financing the 1984 Election* (Lexington, Mass.: Lexington Books, 1987), 109, 110, 359, 381.
57. See Edsall, *New Politics of Inequality,* 252.
58. The most notable PACs were run by the AFL-CIO, the American Medical Association, and the National Association of Manufacturers.
59. Berry, *Interest Group Society,* 159.
60. The following discussion relies on David Corn, "Inside Gephardt's PACscam," *The Nation,* May 2, 1987.
61. Telephone calls to the PAC were answered: "Gephardt for President." Queries about the PAC were referred to Gephardt's formal campaign staff. PAC donors—who also gave to the formal presidential campaign—acknowledged that the PAC, ostensibly formed to help other Democrats, really operated to promote Gephardt: "I gave under the assumption that I was giving to Gephardt" (Corn, "Inside Gephardt's PACscam," 575).
62. Ibid., 577. The Federal Election Commission has been lenient in interpreting the role of multicandidate PACs. In a 1986 case, the FEC ruled 4-2 that George Bush's Fund for America's Future was not acting as part of Bush's campaign when it recruited, assisted, and donated money to Republican party members in Michigan who were attempting to become delegates to the 1988 national convention. As long as the PAC helps a variety of candidates it can also promote Bush's presidential bid, the FEC held. Thomas Harris, an FEC member, issued a dissenting opinion in the decision. "Only persons just alighting from a U.F.O.," he wrote, "can doubt that activities of these sorts will promote the candidacy of the [PAC's] founding father. That, of course, is why so many would-be presidents, of both parties, have created and utilized PACs of this sort in recent years. The commission, however, is willing to turn a blind eye to the realities."
63. Rogers and Ferguson, *Right Turn,* 181-182.
64. Drew, *Politics and Money,* 96.
65. D. M. Alpern, "Reforming the Reforms," *Newsweek,* September 3, 1984, 25.
66. Drew, *Politics and Money,* 131-132.
67. Kayden, "Regulating Campaign Finance," 276.
68. Herbert Asher, *Presidential Elections and American Politics* (Homewood, Ill.: Dorsey Press, 1980), 279-280.
69. The estimates for campaign spending vary, depending on what elements are included. The Federal Election Commission uses only figures that fit within its official limits and campaign reports, such as money raised for primaries, the nominating process, matching funds, official convention budgets, and the federal government's equal allotments for the fall campaign organizations. Herbert Alexander and his associates at the Citizens' Research Foundation, however, include figures that fall outside the official reports, such as third party candidates; labor, corporate, and association spending; the costs of complying with federal laws; spending by "independent" organizations formed to back or oppose presidential candidates; spending by party organizations; and total spending on conventions.
70. "Behind All the Fuss over Election Money," *U.S. News & World Report,* October 8, 1984, 74.
71. American advertisers spend more than even the most lavish political campaigns. The industry spent $19 billion in 1985. Procter and Gamble alone spent some $652 million—more than double the total amount spent by all organizations in the 1984 presidential campaign (Kayden, "Regulating Campaign Finance," 276). Elections logically should cost more than promotion of other public and private activities because they are so intermittent and fragmented. Campaign organizations must start afresh every two or four years, preventing any continuity in the delivery of the message.
72. Adamany and Agree, *Political Money,* 113-114.
73. Joseph Nocera, "Why American Voters Should Watch French Television," *Washington Monthly,* September 1981, 40-42.
74. See charts in Edsall, *New Politics of Inequality,* 86, 91, 133.
75. Ibid., 91. Democratic money as a percentage of Republican money fell from 30.1 percent to 21.9 percent to 18.1 percent during those cycles.
76. Edsall, *New Politics of Inequality,* 91.
77. Kayden, "Regulating Campaign Finance," 262-263.
78. "Reforming the Reforms," *Newsweek,* September 3, 1984, 25-26.
79. William M. Lunch, *The Nationalization of American Politics* (Berkeley: University of California Press, 1987), 112-114.
80. "Behind All the Fuss over Election Money," 75.
81. The explosion in campaign spending in state and congressional races has mirrored that of presidential races. In the 1986 congressional elections, candidates spent $450 million, an average of more than $500,000 per campaign. The thirty-six gubernatorial elections that year cost $200 million, an average of $15.5 million. Campaigns for various state offices and legislative seats cost $300 billion.

    Higher election costs have been most apparent in the Senate races. In 1980, the most expensive Senate races were five close elections that cost between $2.1 million and $2.7 million. By 1986, the average cost of Senate races was $3 million, and some races were costing around $10 million. California senator Alan Cranston spent $2.7 million in 1980 but $11 million in 1986.

    The costs for congressional races vary widely. Differences in spending depend on the costs of commercial media blitzes, the density of population, the strength of state and local party organizations, the competitiveness of the two-party system, and the importance of primary contests.

    Congressional elections were under few enforceable regulations before the passage of the Federal Election Campaign Act in 1971. The law and its subsequent amendments and regulatory rulings have redirected spending patterns rather than limit them. The most important element of the FECA turned out to be disclosure requirements. The law required quarterly financial statements from all candidates or political committees taking part in a federal election. The effectiveness of the requirements is difficult to gauge. It is hard for local newspapers to examine the candidates' reports critically before the campaign.

In 1974, Congress passed a number of amendments to the FECA that affected congressional elections. The major provision was a $1,000 limit on donations to federal candidates in each of the major stages of the campaign—the primary, runoff, and general election. Donors could not spend more than $25,000 for all federal candidates. Political action committees, however, could spend up to $5,000 per candidate per election, with no overall national limitation. Congress has moved slowly on further reform. Despite the support of President Jimmy Carter, proposals for public financing of congressional elections failed in 1977, 1978, and 1979. A bill to limit PAC contributions in House races failed in 1980.

The Nominating Process

1. E. E. Schattschneider, *Party Movement* (New York: Holt, Rinehart, and Winston, 1942), 52.
2. E. E. Schattschneider, *The Semisovereign People* (Hinsdale, Ill.: Dryden Press, 1975), 1-3.
3. The continuous-residency requirement has not been followed to the letter. Herbert Hoover lived overseas for several years before his election in 1928, and Gen. Dwight D. Eisenhower was commander of the North Atlantic Treaty Organization (NATO) in Europe before his successful 1952 candidacy. Other prospective candidates—such as Ambassador Anne Armstrong in 1976 and NATO commander Alexander Haig in 1980—also lived overseas. A person born of American parents on foreign soil would presumably be permitted to seek the presidency. See Charles Gordon, "Who Can Be President of the United States," *Maryland Law Review* 28 (Winter 1968): 1-32.
4. For recent examinations of the president's need to make public appeals for support of policy initiatives, see Jeffrey K. Tulis, *The Rhetorical Presidency* (Princeton, N.J.: Princeton University Press, 1987), and Samuel Kernell, *Going Public: New Strategies of Presidential Leadership* (Washington, D.C.: CQ Press, 1986).
5. Rossiter's portrait of the president reads in part:

   > He must be, according to unwritten law: a man, a white, a Christian. He almost certainly must be: a Northerner or Westerner, less than 65 years old, of Northern European stock, experienced in politics and public service, healthy. He ought to be: from a state larger than Kentucky, more than forty-five years old, a family man, of British stock, a veteran, a Protestant, a lawyer, a state governor, a Mason, a Legionaire, or Rotarian—preferably all three, a small-town boy, self-made man, especially if a Republican, experienced in international affairs, a cultural middle-brow who likes baseball, detective stories, fishing, pop concerts, picnics, and seascapes. It really makes no difference whether he is: a college graduate, a small businessman, a member of Congress, a member of the Cabinet, a defeated candidate for the Presidency, providing that he emerged from his defeat the very image of the happy warrior.... He almost certainly cannot be: a Southerner..., of Polish, Italian, or Slavic stock, a union official, an ordained minister. He cannot be, according to unwritten law: a Negro, a Jew, an Oriental, a woman, an atheist, a freak....

   See Clinton Rossiter, *The American Presidency* (New York: Harcourt Brace, 1960), 193-194.
6. Polling data before the 1984 campaign showed that women differed greatly from men in both their level of support of the Reagan administration and opinions on several major issues. A number of state and congressional races also appeared to turn on women's support. See Eleanor Smeal, *Why and How Women Will Elect the Next President* (New York: Harper and Row, 1984), 1-16. On the basis of that evidence, several organizations including the National Organization for Women lobbied the Democratic party to nominate a woman for vice president.
7. In 1983, 13 percent of state legislators were women—still far below their share of the population at large but three times their share in 1969. See Erwin D. Hargrove and Michael Nelson, *Presidents, Politics, and Policy* (Baltimore: Johns Hopkins University Press, 1984), 142.
8. The ambivalence of white voters toward a black candidacy is suggested in Andrew Kopkind, "A Populist Message Hits Home," *The Nation,* July 18/25, 1987, 55. One Iowa voter, asked whether she might vote for a black such as Jackson, said farm issues were more important than race: "The presidency is so far away. Now if he was going to marry my daughter, that might be a different story."
9. Hargrove and Nelson, *Presidents, Politics, and Policy,* 20-24.
10. David S. Broder, "The Story That Still Nags at Me," *Washington Monthly,* February 1987, pp. 29-32.
11. David S. Broder and T. R. Reid, "Schroeder Garners Encouragement, Money," *Washington Post,* August 22, 1987, A5.
12. A variety of psychological studies of political leadership have argued that a candidate's insecurities can be an important part of his or her energy but also an unhealthy distraction from rational political behavior. See James David Barber, *The Presidential Character* (Englewood Cliffs, N.J.: Prentice-Hall, 1972) for portraits of Wilson, Johnson, and Nixon. Among the most prominent "psychobiographies" are Alexander George and Juliette George, *Woodrow Wilson and Colonel House* (New York: John Day, 1956), and Bruce Mazlish, *In Search of Nixon* (New York: Basic Books, 1972).
13. Jimmy Carter, *Why Not the Best?* (New York: Bantam Books, 1976), 158-159.
14. Nelson W. Polsby and Aaron Wildavsky, *Presidential Elections* (New York: Scribner's, 1984), 95.
15. See David Corn, "Inside Gephardt's PACscam," *The Nation,* May 2, 1987.
16. Elaine Ciulla Kamarck, "Structure as Strategy: Presidential Nominating Politics since Reform" (Ph.D. diss., University of California, Berkeley, 1986), 46-47.
17. Two others, Jerry Brown and Frank Church, entered the campaign late.
18. William G. Mayer, "The New Hampshire Primary: A Historical Overview," in *Media and Momentum: The New Hampshire Primary and Nomination Politics,* ed. Gary Orren and Nelson W. Polsby (Chatham, N.J.: Chatham House, 1987), 24.
19. William C. Adams, "As New Hampshire Goes...," in *Media and Momentum,* Orren and Polsby, 45.
20. Ibid., 49.
21. Quoted in Theodore J. Lowi, "Constitution, Government, and Politics," in *Before Nomination: Our Primary Problems,* ed. George Grassamuck (Washington, D.C.: American Enterprise Institute, 1985), 7.
22. David S. Broder, "Listening Carefully in Iowa," *Washington Post,* August 12, 1987, A23. Gore, struggling in Iowa polls, later attacked the prominence of Iowa in the nomination process and pulled all but a few campaign workers out of the state.
23. Jules Witcover, *Marathon: The Pursuit of the Presidency, 1972-1976* (New York: Viking Press, 1977), 327-354.
24. Jack Germond and Jules Witcover, *Wake Us When It's Over: Presidential Politics of 1984* (New York: Macmillan, 1985).
25. James W. Davis, *Presidential Primaries: Road to the White House* (Westport, Conn.: Greenwood Press, 1980), 185.
26. A television call-in show in Iowa included the following exchange between Connally and a Connally supporter who could not persuade his wife to vote for the former Texas governor:

   "What's the problem?" asked Connally.

   "She thinks you're a crook."

   "I'm the only certified non-guilty political figure in the country," Connally answered after an explanation of his acquittal in a federal bribery case.

"I told my wife all of that."

"What did she say?"

"She still thinks you're a crook."

See Richard Harwood, *The Pursuit of the Presidency 1980* (New York: Berkley, 1980), 145.

27. New York governor Mario Cuomo argued that the "stature problem" of the 1988 Democratic candidates would fade as soon as one or two candidates emerged from the field in the Iowa caucus and New Hampshire primary.
28. Norman H. Nie, Sidney Verba, and John R. Petrocik, *The Changing American Voter* (Cambridge, Mass.: Harvard University Press, 1979), 210-242.
29. The stress that political pundits place on appearance was underscored by the reaction of two observers of the first debate of Democratic candidates in 1987. One said of Sen. Paul Simon: "He may have the highest IQ, but he's never going to photograph well. . . . His earlobes are unbelievable." Another said Simon "does not project the vigor and youthfulness" of other candidates (David S. Broder, "Gephardt, Simon, Dukakis Score Well Among Viewers," *Washington Post,* July 3, 1987, A16).
30. Stephen Hess, "Why Great Men Are Not Chosen Presidents: Lord Bryce Revisited," in *Elections American Style,* ed. A. James Reichley (Washington, D.C.: Brookings, 1987), 81.
31. Davis, *Presidential Primaries,* 213-219, 224-239.
32. Polsby and Wildavsky, *Presidential Elections,* 149.
33. On the nexus of parties and issues in voting, see Nie, Verba, and Petrocik, *Changing American Voter,* 47-73, 156-73. For a discussion of the different vote orientations toward presidential politics and congressional politics, see James MacGregor Burns, *The Deadlock of Democracy: Four-Party Politics in America* (Englewood Cliffs, N.J.: Prentice-Hall, 1963), esp. 241-264.
34. The effect of presidential coattails should not be overstated. More important may be the "drag" effect that an unpopular president may have on the party's candidates. See Warren E. Miller, "A Study in Political Myth and Mythology," *Public Opinion Quarterly* 19 (Winter 1955-1956): 26-39.
35. Polsby and Wildavsky, *Presidential Elections,* 49.
36. See Jeffrey Berry, *The Interest Group Society* (Boston: Little, Brown, 1984).
37. The organizations backing Mondale included the American Federation of Labor-Congress of Industrial Organizations, the United Auto Workers, the National Education Association, the National Organization for Women, and a number of members of Congress and other politicians such as Atlanta mayor Andrew Young.
38. Maureen Dowd, "New Model Iowa for '88: Less Corn, More Silk," *New York Times,* November 25, 1987, B12.
39. See James David Barber, *The Pulse of Politics* (New York: Norton, 1980), 3-4:

> The stress on conflict is the clearest case: the campaign is a battle for power. Like a real war, the political war is a rousing call to arms. Candidates mobilize their forces for showdowns and shoot-outs, blasting each other with rhetorical volleys. It is a risky adventure; its driving force is surprise, as the fortunes of combat deliver setbacks and breakthroughs contrary to the going expectation, and the contenders struggle to recover and exploit the sudden changes. . . . Over the next four years, reaction sets in. Uplift is called for. Political conflict seems more and more like mere politics, in the low sense of stab and grab, a clash of merely selfish interests. . . . [In the next stage,] we worry about the drift from disagreement to disruption, from civil conflict to civil war, threatening the union so laboriously patched together over all those years of mutual adjustment and forbearance. The public yearn for solace, for domestic tranquility, for the politics of conciliation.

40. Arthur M. Schlesinger, Jr., *The Cycles of American History* (Boston: Houghton Mifflin, 1986).
41. Erwin C. Hargrove and Michael Nelson, "The Presidency: Reagan and the Cycle of Politics and Policy," in *The Elections of 1984,* ed. Michael Nelson (Washington, D.C.: CQ Press, 1985), 189-213.
42. James MacGregor Burns, *The Power To Lead* (New York: Simon and Schuster, 1984), 163.
43. Davis, *Presidential Primaries,* 65.
44. Ibid., 71.
45. Ibid., 67-68.
46. Paul R. Abramson, John H. Aldrich, and David W. Rohde, *Change and Continuity in the 1984 Elections,* rev. ed. (Washington, D.C.: CQ Press, 1986), 25.
47. For a classic account of the widening scope of conflict, see Samuel H. Beer, "Liberalism and the National Interest," *Public Interest,* no. 1 (Fall 1966): 70-82.
48. Davis, *Presidential Primaries,* 139.
49. Ibid., 139-142.
50. On the "plugged-in" hypothesis, see Sidney W. Verba and Norman H. Nie, *Participation in America* (New York: Harper and Row, 1972), 125-137; Angus Campbell, Gerald Gurin, Warren E. Miller, *The American Voter* (New York: Wiley, 1960), 475-481. On the effect of registration laws on voter turnout, see Raymond Wolfinger and Stephen Rosenstone, *Who Votes?* (New Haven, Conn.: Yale University Press, 1980), 61-88. See also Stanley Kelley, Jr., Richard E. Ayres, and William G. Bowen, "Registration and Voting: Putting First Things First," *American Political Science Review* 61 (June 1967). Useful overviews are contained in Walter Dean Burnham, "The Turnout Problem," and Eddie N. Williams and Milton D. Morris, "Is the Electoral Process Stacked against Minorities?" in *Elections American Style.*
51. Polsby and Wildavsky, *Presidential Elections,* 24-29.
52. James W. Wilson, *The Amateur Democrat* (Chicago: University of Chicago Press, 1962).
53. Martin Schram, *Running for President* (New York: Pocket Books, 1976), 64.
54. See Anthony Downs, *An Economic Theory of Democracy* (New York: Harper and Row, 1957).
55. Theodore H. White, *America in Search of Itself: The Making of the President, 1956-1980* (New York: Harper and Row, 1982), 318-319.
56. James W. Ceaser, *Presidential Selection: Theory and Development* (Princeton, N.J.: Princeton University Press, 1979), 325, 343, 345. Ceaser writes:

> Polarization is a necessary component of building constituencies anew. . . . [T]here are certain values, such as restraint on the pursuit and exercise of power, that are more important than adhering to the formulae of full democracy. If the existence of parties with intermediary power brokers—modern bosses if you like—can provide an informal check on the presidency and discourage candidates from going to the roots in quadrennial crusades, then the cost in terms of deviation from some abstract notion of 'democratic ethic' is well worth bearing. . . . The 'leverage' that parties possess enables them to withstand, at least temporarily, undesirable currents of opinion and extreme movements.

57. Polsby and Wildavsky, *Presidential Elections,* 45.
58. See Kathleen Hall Jamieson, *Eloquence in an Electronic Age* (New York: Oxford University Press, 1988).
59. Kay Lawson, "How State Laws Undermine Parties," in *Elections American Style,* 247.
60. Howard L. Reiter, *Selecting the President: The Nominating Process in Transition* (Philadelphia: University of Pennsylvania Press, 1985), 49, 165.
61. Davis, *Presidential Primaries,* 159.
62. James W. Davis, *National Conventions in an Age of Party Reform* (Westport, Conn.: Greenwood Press, 1983), 45.
63. Ibid., 77-78; see also, Nelson W. Polsby and Aaron Wildavsky, *Presidential Elections,* 6th ed. (New York: Scribner's, 1984), 66.
64. Maureen Dowd, "Democrats Confront 'The Thing That Ate the Hall,' " *New York Times,* July 14, 1988, A21.
65. Morton Krondracke, quoted in Davis, *National Conventions,*

47; see also Polsby and Wildavsky, *Presidential Elections,* 115-116.
66. Paul T. David, Ralph M. Goldman, and Richard C. Bain, *The Politics of National Party Conventions* (Washington, D.C.: Brookings, 1960), 165.
67. Ibid., 166-168.
68. Davis, *National Conventions,* 58-59.
69. Ibid., 54.
70. Andrew Rosenthal, "Poll Finds Atlanta Delegates More Liberal Than the Public," *New York Times,* July 17, 1988, A17.
71. Davis, *National Conventions,* 42-44.
72. Richard Reeves, *Convention* (New York: Harcourt Brace Jovanovich, 1977), 39-40.
73. Eugene H. Roseboom, *A History of Presidential Elections,* 2d. ed. (New York: Macmillan, 1964), 361.
74. Davis, *National Conventions,* 93.
75. David, Goldman, and Bain, *Politics of National Party Conventions,* 203-208.
76. Davis, *National Conventions,* 49-50.
77. Ibid., 87.
78. David, Goldman, and Bain, *Politics of National Party Conventions,* 66.
79. Quoted in Malcolm Moos and Stephen Hess, *Hats in the Ring* (New York: Random, 1960), 119.
80. Quoted in Stefan Lorant, *The Glorious Burden* (New York: Harper and Row, 1968), 592-594.
81. Martin Schram, *Running for President: A Journal of the Carter Campaign* (New York: Pocket Books, 1976), 254-255.
82. Quoted in Roseboom, *History of Presidential Elections,* 309.
83. Quoted in Lorant, *The Glorious Burden,* 440.
84. Text of keynote address by Gov. Mario Cuomo, *New York Times,* July 17, 1984, A16.
85. Theodore H. White, *The Making of the President 1972* (New York: Atheneum, 1973), 244.
86. Reeves, *Convention,* 207.
87. Davis, *National Conventions,* 201.
88. "Rift Over Campaign Films," *New York Times,* August 11, 1988, D19; Maureen Dowd, "A Man Is Chosen, but a Verb Is Born," *New York Times,* August 18, 1988, A23.
89. Jules Witcover, *Marathon: The Pursuit of the Presidency* (New York: Viking, 1977), 487.
90. Reeves, *Convention,* 19.
91. Terry Sanford, *A Danger of Democracy* (Boulder, Colo.: Westview Press, 1981), 31.
92. Moos and Hess, *Hats in the Ring,* 124.
93. "We Point with Pride," *New York Times,* August 10, 1988, A14.
94. Moos and Hess, *Hats in the Ring,* 130-131.
95. Warren Weaver, Jr., "A Choice Seat Is More Luck Than Politics," *New York Times,* July 20, 1988, A19.
96. Andrew Rosenthal, "For Delegate Trackers, Timing Is Everything," *New York Times,* July 22, 1988, A12.
97. Quoted in Lorant, *Glorious Burden,* 638.
98. Ibid., 302-304. See also Roseboom, *History of Presidential Elections,* 215.
99. Davis, *National Conventions,* 203.
100. Joel K. Goldstein, *The Modern American Vice Presidency* (Princeton, N.J.: Princeton University Press, 1982), 47.
101. Moos and Hess, *Hats in the Ring,* 144-158.
102. Harold F. Bass, "The President and the National Party Organization," in *Presidents and their Parties,* ed. Robert Harmel (New York: Praeger, 1984), 73-81.
103. H. L. Mencken, quoted in Moos and Hess, *Hats in the Ring,* 15.
104. Irwin Ross, *The Loneliest Campaign: The Truman Victory of 1948* (New York: New American Library, 1968), 93-94.
105. Kurt Lang and Gladys Engel Lang, *Politics and Television* (Chicago: Quadrangle, 1968), 78-79.
106. Quoted in ibid., 24.
107. Reeves, *Convention,* 35-36.
108. Ibid., 68.
109. Davis, *National Conventions,* 202-203; Moos and Hess, *Hats in the Ring,* 131.
110. David L. Paletz and Martha Elson, "Television Coverage of Presidential Conventions: Now You See It, Now You Don't," *Political Science Quarterly* 91 (Spring 1976), discussed in Davis, *National Conventions,* 206-207.
111. Theodore H. White, *The Making of the President 1960* (New York: Atheneum, 1961), 151-152.
112. Reeves, *Convention,* 108-109.
113. Ibid., 34.
114. Davis, *National Conventions,* 204.
115. Walter Goodman, "Desultory Coverage of Convention," *New York Times,* July 21, 1988, A20.
116. Michael Oreskes, "Convention Message Is Garbled by Quayle Static," *New York Times,* August 19, 1988, A16.
117. This section is based on Davis, *National Conventions,* 5-11 and 150-156.
118. Walter Berns, ed., *After the People Vote: Steps in Choosing the President* (Washington, D.C.: American Enterprise Institute, 1983), 18-20.
119. For an overview, see William Crotty and John S. Jackson, *Presidential Primaries and Nominations* (Washington, D.C.: CQ Press, 1985), 213-220.
120. Michael Nelson, "The Case for the Current Presidential Nominating Process," in *Before Nomination: Our Primary Problems,* ed. George Grassmuck (Washington, D.C.: American Enterprise Institute, 1985), 24.
121. Ibid., 217 (citing Robert T. Nakamura and Denis G. Sullivan, "Party Democracy and Democratic Control," in *American Politics and Public Policy,* ed. Walter Dean Burnham and Martha Wagner Weinberg [Cambridge, Mass.: MIT Press, 1978], 26-40).
122. Thomas E. Mann, "Should the Presidential Nominating System Be Changed (Again)?" in *Before Nomination: Our Primary Problems,* ed. George Grassmuck (Washington, D.C.: American Enterprise Institute, 1985), 39.
123. Ibid., 40-41.
124. Michael Nelson, "Two Cheers for the National Primary," in *Rethinking the Presidency,* ed. Thomas E. Cronin (Boston: Little, Brown, 1982), 55.
125. Mann, "Should the Presidential Nominating System Be Changed (Again)?" 44-45.
126. Nelson, "Two Cheers," 55-58.
127. Crotty and Jackson, *Presidential Primaries and Nominations,* 222.
128. Mann, "Should the Presidential Nominating System Be Changed (Again)?" 43. For a further discussion of the costs and benefits of such a system, see Austin Ranney, *The Federalization of Presidential Primaries* (Washington, D.C.: American Enterprise Institute, 1978), chap. 5.
129. Crotty and Jackson, *Presidential Primaries and Nominations,* 223.
130. Ibid., 225-227.
131. Mann, "Should the Presidential Nominating System Be Changed (Again)?" 42.
132. Crotty and Jackson, *Presidential Primaries and Nominations,* 227.
133. Ibid., 227-228; Mann, "Should the Presidential Nominating System Be Changed (Again)?" 42
134. Nelson, "Case for the Current Process," 33.

General Election Campaign

1. Paul R. Abramson, John H. Aldrich, and David W. Rohde, *Change and Continuity in the 1984 Elections,* rev. ed. (Washington, D.C.: CQ Press, 1986), 49.
2. Ibid., 51.
3. Lewis Chester, Godfrey Hodgson, and Bruce Page, *The American Melodrama: The Presidential Campaign of 1968* (New York: Viking, 1969), 620.
4. Nelson W. Polsby and Aaron Wildavsky, *Presidential Elections,* 6th ed. (New York: Scribner's, 1984), 148.
5. Richard M. Pious, *The American Presidency* (New York: Basic Books, 1979), 104.
6. Richard M. Pious and Robert C. Weaver, "Presidential Cam-

paigns: Strategies and Tactics," in *Selection/Election: A Forum on the American Presidency,* ed. Robert S. Hirschfield (New York: Aldine, 1982), 121.
7. Stephen J. Wayne, *The Road to the White House,* 2d ed. (New York: St. Martin's Press, 1984), 182.
8. Nelson W. Polsby and Aaron Wildavsky, *Presidential Elections* (New York: Scribner's, 1984), 149.
9. Pious and Weaver, "Presidential Campaigns," 118.
10. Polsby and Wildavsky, *Presidential Elections,* 170, 182.
11. Wayne, *Road to the White House,* 188-191; Polsby and Wildavsky, *Presidential Elections,* 82-85.
12. The complete text of the memorandum, prepared by Mike Duval and Foster Channock of the White House staff and dated June 11, 1976, is included in: Martin Schram, *Running for President: A Journal of the Carter Campaign,* expanded edition (New York: Pocket Books, 1978), 320-324.
13. Richard B. Cheney, "The 1976 Presidential Debates: A Republican Perspective," in *The Past and Future of Presidential Debates,* ed. Austin Ranney (Washington, D.C.: American Enterprise Institute, 1979), 110.
14. Schram, *Running for President,* 326.
15. Wayne, *Road to the White House,* 194-199.
16. Richard Joslyn, *Mass Media and Elections* (Reading, Mass.: Addison-Wesley, 1984), 32.
17. Larry J. Sabato, *The Rise of Political Consultants* (New York: Basic Books, 1981), 69.
18. Howard L. Reiter, *Parties and Elections in Corporate America* (New York: St. Martin's Press, 1987), 159-160 (based on a 1984 memorandum from Stuart Spencer to Ronald Reagan).
19. James R. Beniger and Robert J. Giuffra, Jr., "Public Opinion Polling: Command and Control in Presidential Campaigns," in *Presidential Selection,* ed. Alexander Heard and Michael Nelson (Durham, N.C.: Duke University Press, 1987), 189-215.
20. Bruce E. Altschuler, *Keeping a Finger on the Public Pulse: Private Polling and Presidential Elections* (Westport, Conn.: Greenwood Press, 1982), 7.
21. Sabato, *Political Consultants,* 70.
22. Joslyn, *Mass Media and Elections,* 21.
23. See Sabato, *Political Consultants,* 92-104.
24. Stephen J. Wayne, *The Road to the White House,* 3d ed. (New York: St. Martin's Press, 1988), 243-244.
25. Beniger and Giuffra, "Public Opinion Polling," 194-196.
26. Altschuler, *Public Pulse,* 3.
27. Sabato, *Political Consultants,* 113-115. For an account of Nixon's 1968 campaign, see Joe McGinniss, *The Selling of the President: 1968* (New York: Trident Press, 1969).
28. Beniger and Giuffra, "Public Opinion Polling," 192; Wayne, *Road to the White House,* 215-216.
29. Sabato, *Political Consultants,* 224-229.
30. Ibid., 238.
31. Dom Bonafede, "Part Science, Part Art, Part Hokum, Direct Mail Now a Key Campaign Tool, " *National Journal,* July 31, 1982, 1334-1335.
32. Reiter, *Parties and Elections,* 189 (note 13).
33. Sabato, *Political Consultants,* 201.
34. Ibid., 254.
35. Reiter, *Parties and Elections,* 162-168.
36. Sabato, *Political Consultants,* 337.
37. Kay Lawson, "How State Laws Undermine Parties," in *Elections American Style,* ed. A. James Reichley (Washington, D.C.: Brookings, 1987).
38. Thomas Byrne Edsall, *The New Politics of Inequality* (New York: Norton, 1984), 91.
39. Ibid., 81-82.
40. Larry J. Sabato, *The Party's Just Begun* (Glenview, Ill.: Scott, Foresman, 1988), 75-90.
41. Robert Axelrod, "Where the Votes Come From: An Analysis of Electoral Coalitions, 1952-1968," *American Political Science Review* 66 (March 1972).
42. Herbert E. Alexander and Brian A. Haggerty, *Financing the 1984 Election* (Lexington, Mass.: Lexington Books, 1987), 110.
43. See, for example: Nelson W. Polsby, "The News Media as an Alternative to Party in the Presidential Selection Process," in *Political Parties in the Eighties,* ed. Robert A. Goldwin (Washington, D.C.: American Enterprise Institute, 1980), 50ff; Donald R. Matthews, "Winnowing," in *Race for the Presidency,* ed. James David Barber (Englewood Cliffs, N.J.: Prentice-Hall, 1978), 55ff.
44. F. Christopher Arterton, *Media Politics: The News Strategies of Presidential Campaigns* (Lexington, Mass.: Lexington Books, 1984), 1.
45. David L. Paletz and Robert M. Entman, *Media Power Politics* (New York: Free Press, 1981), 16.
46. W. Lance Bennett, *News: The Politics of Illusion* (New York: Longman, 1983), 7-8; Paletz and Entman, *Media Power Politics,* 52.
47. Barry Cole, ed., *Television Today: A Close-Up View* (New York: Oxford University Press, 1981), 183.
48. National Institute of Mental Health, *Television and Behavior,* vol. 1 (Washington, D.C.: Government Printing Office, 1982), 1.
49. Paletz and Entman, *Media Power Politics,* 45-49.
50. Stephen J. Wayne, *The Road to the White House,* 3d ed. (New York: St. Martin's Press, 1988), 209.
51 See Richard Joslyn, *Mass Media and Elections* (Reading, Mass.: Addison-Wesley, 1984), chap. 7, for an overview of this question.
52. Bernard Berelson, quoted in Joseph T. Klapper, *The Effects of Mass Communication* (Glencoe, Illinois: Free Press, 1960), 4.
53. Graber, *Mass Media,* 179.
54. Paletz and Entman, *Media Power Politics,* 45.
55. Graber, *Mass Media,* 179.
56. Wayne, *Road to the White House,* 223.
57. Joslyn, *Mass Media and Elections,* 210 (see 203-214 generally for a discussion of the effects of presidential debates).
58. Wayne, *Road to the White House,* 227.
59. Graber, *Mass Media,* 213.
60. Wayne, *Road to the White House,* 231.
61. Joseph Ernest Kallenbach, *The American Chief Executive* (New York: Harper and Row, 1966), 232-233.
62. Jules Witcover, *Marathon: Pursuit of the Presidency, 1972-1976* (New York: Viking Press, 1977), 535.
63. Stephen J. Wayne, *The Road to the White House,* 3d ed. (New York: St. Martin's Press, 1988), 171.
64. Quoted in Stefan Lorant, *The Glorious Burden* (New York: Harper and Row, 1968), 246.
65. Ibid., 249.
66. Wayne, *Road to the White House,* 172.
67. Eugene H. Roseboom, *A History of Presidential Elections,* 2d ed. (New York: Macmillan, 1964), 313-314.
68. Lorant, *Glorious Burden,* 466.
69. Roseboom, *History of Presidential Elections,* 331.
70. Lorant, *Glorious Burden,* 486.
71. Wayne, *Road to the White House,* 173.
72. Sabato, *Party's Just Begun,* 59-61.
73. Daniel A. Mazmanian, *Third Parties in Presidential Elections* (Washington, D.C.: Brookings, 1974), 27-28.
74. James Q. Wilson, *American Government: Institutions and Policies* (Lexington, Mass.: D.C. Heath, 1980), 155.
75. Steven J. Rosenstone, Roy L. Behr, and Edward H. Lazarus, *Third Parties in America* (Princeton, N.J.: Princeton University Press, 1984), 5.
76. Sundquist, *Dynamics of the Party System,* 60-65.
77. Wilson, *American Government,* 155.
78. Rosenstone, Behr, and Lazarus, *Third Parties in America,* chaps. 3 and 4 (esp. pp. 78-79, 119-121).
79. Eugene McCarthy had no national running mate because he favored eliminating the office of vice president. But because laws in various states required a running mate, McCarthy chose different ones in different states—amounting to nearly two dozen—all political unknowns.
80. Rosenstone, Behr, and Lazarus, *Third Parties in America,* 115.

81. This number, based on Appendix A in Rosenstone, Behr, and Lazarus, *Third Parties in America,* includes only those parties and candidates that received popular votes in more than one state in any given election.
82. Mazmanian, *Third Parties in Presidential Elections,* 4-5 (drawing upon William Nisbet Chambers).
83. Some would discount the Anti-Masons in 1832 since two-party competition was not yet firmly established throughout the country. See Rosenstone, Behr, and Lazarus, *Third Parties in America,* 10-11.
84. Ibid., 17.
85. James L. Sundquist, *Dynamics of the Party System,* 58 (notes omitted). Sundquist notes that analysis of the election returns also supports this view (p.58 n.23).
86. Rosenstone, Behr, Lazarus, *Third Parties in America,* 8.
87. For a full discussion of the dynamics of the use of "exit" versus "voice" by members of organizations, see Albert O. Hirschman, *Exit, Voice, and Loyalty: Responses to Decline in Firms, Organizations, and States* (Cambridge, Mass.: Harvard University Press, 1970).
88. Mazmanian, *Third Parties in Presidential Elections,* 77.
89. Rosenstone, Behr, Lazarus, *Third Parties in America,* 40.
90. This discussion of legal constraints is based on ibid., 19-27.
91. The major candidates may forgo public funds if they prefer private financing. Candidates are not eager to take that option, however; although acceptance of the public funds precludes them from raising funds privately, it does not preclude independent organizations (such as political action committees—PACs) from spending an unlimited amount on their behalf, nor does it preclude state and local parties from raising money for voter registration and other volunteer activities. The amount of public funding, originally set at $20 million for each major party candidate, has increased annually in response to cost-of-living adjustments calculated by the Department of Labor (Polsby and Wildavsky, *Presidential Elections,* 6th ed., 64 and 302 n. 27).
92. Rosenstone, Behr, and Lazarus, *Third Parties in America,* 26.
93. Ibid., 17-18.
94. Mazmanian, *Third Parties in Presidential Elections,* 3.
95. Rosenstone, Behr, and Lazarus, *Third Parties in America,* 33.
96. Mazmanian, *Third Parties in Presidential Elections,* 1.
97. Ibid., 67.

The Election

1. John E. Jackson, "Election Night Reporting and Voter Turnout," *American Journal of Political Science* 27 (November 1983): 615-635.
2. Richard A. Watson and Norman C. Thomas, *The Politics of the Presidency* (Washington, D.C.: CQ Press, 1988), 68.
3. Laurence H. Tribe and Thomas M. Rollins, "Deadlock: What Happens if Nobody Wins," *Atlantic Monthly,* October 1980, 49.
4. U.S. Constitution, Amendment XII, Section 1.
5. U.S. Constitution, Amendment XX, Section 3.
6. Tribe and Rollins, "Deadlock," 60-61.
7. Allan P. Sindler, "Presidential Selection and Succession in Special Situations," in *Presidential Selection,* ed. Alexander Heard and Michael Nelson (Durham, N.C.: Duke University Press, 1987), 355.
8. Ibid.
9. U.S. Constitution, Amendment XX, Section 3.
10. Sindler, "Presidential Selection," 356.
11. Edward S. Corwin, *The President: Office and Powers,* 4th ed. (New York: New York University Press, 1957), 55-56.
12. Sindler, "Presidential Selection," 355; Tribe and Rollins, "Deadlock," 58-60.
13. Quoted in Tribe and Rollins, "Deadlock," 60.
14. Milton Lomask, *Aaron Burr: The Years from Princeton to Vice President (1756-1805)* (New York: Farrar, Straus, Giroux, 1979), 291-294.
15. Eugene H. Roseboom and Alfred E. Eckes, Jr., *A History of Presidential Elections,* 4th ed. (New York: Macmillan, 1979), 38.
16. Tribe and Rollins, "Deadlock," 60.
17. Edward Stanwood, *A History of the Presidency from 1788 to 1897,* rev. by Charles Knowles Bolton (Boston: Houghton Mifflin, 1926), 187.
18. Tribe and Rollins, "Deadlock," 50.
19. Ibid., 56. Wallace's terms were delivered in a press conference on February 19, 1968.
20. Ibid., 50.

Taking Office

1. Carl M. Brauer, *Presidential Transitions* (New York: Oxford University Press, 1986), xiv.
2. Ibid., 62.
3. Presidents usually start their term stating that they desire cabinet government, with the Oval Office likened to the center of a wheel and the different departments reaching from the spokes. As a symbol of the difficulty of such a system, President Ford's chief of staff, Richard Cheney, gave incoming Carter officials a badly mangled bicycle wheel.
4. Brauer, *Presidential Transitions,* 127.
5. Ibid., 65.
6. Ibid., 16.
7. Brauer, *Presidential Transitions,* 177.
8. For a more thorough discussion of rituals and symbols in politics, see Murray Edelman, *The Symbolic Uses of Politics* (Urbana: University of Illinois Press, 1964).
9. *Presidential Inaugural Bibles: Catalogue of an Exhibition (November 17, 1968-February 23, 1969)* (Washington, D.C.: Washington Cathedral, 1969), 6-7.
10. Ibid., 12.
11. Ibid., 43.
12. Ibid., 12, 29, 43; 1969 Inaugural Committee, *The Inaugural Story: 1789-1969* (New York: American Heritage, 1969), 67.
13. Edward S. Corwin, *The President: Office and Powers, 1787-1957,* 4th rev. ed. (New York: New York University Press, 1957), 54.
14. Harold W. Chase and Craig R. Ducat, *Edward S. Corwin's The Constitution and What It Means Today,* 13th ed. (Princeton, N.J.: Princeton University Press, 1973), 119.
15. Quoted in Edna M. Colman, *Seventy-five Years of White House Gossip: From Washington to Lincoln* (Garden City: Doubleday, Page, 1925), 4.
16. *The Inaugural Story,* 42-45.
17. Ibid., 86-87.
18. Phil Gailey, "The Cold Bottom Line: No Parade and No Profit," *New York Times,* January 22, 1985, A19. Ticket holders could receive a refund if they made their request before February 10, 1985.
19. Colman, *Seventy-five Years,* 155.
20. *The Inaugural Story,* 103.
21. Ibid., 97-107.
22. Irvin Molotsky, "Nine Grand Balls: The Reagans and Thousands of Well-Wishers Go Dancing," *New York Times,* January 22, 1985, A19.
23. Colman, *Seventy-five Years,* 186.
24. *The Inaugural Story,* 56.

Chronology

1. Richard P. McCormick, *The Presidential Game: The Origins of American Presidential Politics* (New York: Oxford University Press, 1982), chap. 1.
2. Ibid., 33-34.
3. Roy F. Nichols, *The Invention of the American Political Parties* (New York: Macmillan, 1967), 192.
4. Edward Stanwood, *A History of the Presidency* (Boston: Houghton Mifflin, 1898), 63.
5. Ibid., 110.
6. Matthew A. Crenson, *The Federal Machine* (Baltimore:

Johns Hopkins University Press, 1971), 11-30.

7. Jackson biographer Robert V. Remini explains the nickname "Old Hickory." In an ardous, five-hundred-mile march, Jackson gave his three horses to wounded soldiers and marched on foot with his troops to give them moral support. The soldiers serving under him agreed that their general was as tough as hickory. "Not much later," Remini writes, "they started calling him 'Hickory' as a sign of their respect and regard; then the affectionate 'Old' was added to give Jackson a nickname . . . that admirably served him thereafter throughout his military and political wars" (Robert V. Remini, *Andrew Jackson* [New York: Harper and Row, 1969], 54).
8. Arthur M. Schlesinger, Jr., *The Age of Jackson* (New York: New American Library, 1945), 34.
9. *Guide to Congress,* 2d ed. (Washington, D.C.: Congressional Quarterly Inc., 1982), 613.
10. Russell L. Hanson, *The Democratic Imagination in America: Conversations with Our Past* (Princeton, N.J.: Princeton University Press, 1985), 125.
11. Eugene H. Roseboom, *A History of Presidential Elections* (New York: Macmillan, 1970), 106.
12. Schlesinger, *Jackson,* 55.
13. Estimates of vote totals vary, especially in the years before standardized methods of balloting. Discrepancies developed because of disputes about stuffing ballot boxes, the eligibility of some voters, absentee ballots, and simple counting and reporting difficulties in the pre-media age.
14. Roseboom, *Presidential Elections,* 112.
15. Hanson, *Democratic Imagination,* 54-120.
16. Ibid., 140-141.
17. Ibid., 136.
18. See Albert O. Hirschman, *Exit, Voice, and Loyalty* (Cambridge: Harvard University Press, 1970).
19. Hanson, *Democratic Imagination,* 138.
20. Richard P. McCormick, "Political Development and the Second Party System," in *The American Party Systems: Stages of Development,* ed. William Nisbet Chambers and Walter Dean Burnham (New York: Oxford University Press, 1967), 102.
21. James L. Sundquist, *Dynamics of the Party System,* rev. ed. (Washington, D.C.: Brookings, 1983), 51.
22. Roseboom, *Presidential Elections,* 143.
23. Richard Hofstadter, *The American Political Tradition* (New York: Vintage, 1948), 113.
24. Ibid.
25. Hanson, *Democratic Imagination,* 176.
26. Roseboom, *Presidential Elections,* 177-181.
27. Paul N. Angle, ed., *The Lincoln Reader* (New York: Pocket Books, 1954), 523.
28. Ibid., 531.
29. Roseboom, *Presidential Elections,* 201.
30. Eric Foner, *Reconstruction: America's Unfinished Revolution, 1863-1877* (New York: Harper and Row, 1988).
31. William S. McFeely, *Grant* (New York: Norton, 1981), 283.
32. Ibid., 288-289.
33. Ibid., 381.
34. Bernhard Bailyn, et al., *The Great Republic: A History of the American People* (Boston: Little, Brown, 1977), 802.
35. C. Vann Woodward, *Reunion and Reaction* (New York: Doubleday Anchor Books, 1951).
36. Kenneth M. Stampp, *The Era of Reconstruction, 1865-1877* (New York: Vintage, 1965), 210-211.
37. Michael Nelson, "A Short, Ironic History of American National Bureaucracy," *Journal of Politics* 44 (Winter 1982): 747-777.
38. Roseboom, *Presidential Elections,* 264.
39. Harry Thurston Peck, *Twenty Years of the Republic, 1885-1905* (New York: Dodd, Mead, 1906), 20.
40. Michael E. McGerr, *The Decline of Popular Politics: The American North, 1865-1928* (New York: Oxford University Press), 82-106.
41. Peck, *Twenty Years of the Republic,* 41.
42. Ibid., 78.
43. Ibid., 144.
44. Ibid., 169.
45. Roseboom, *Presidential Elections,* 290.
46. Bailyn et al., *Great Republic,* 786.
47. Sundquist, *Party System,* 107.
48. For a concise account of the machine-reform struggle, see Dennis R. Judd, *The Politics of American Cities* (Boston: Little, Brown, 1984), 50-110.
49. See David Montgomery, *The Fall of the House of Labor* (New York: Cambridge University Press, 1987).
50. Sundquist, *Party System,* 116-118.
51. Ibid., 143, 152.
52. Hofstadter, *American Political Tradition,* 187.
53. Sundquist, *Party System,* 149-152.
54. Hofstadter, *American Political Tradition,* 192-193.
55. See "William Jennings Bryan, Cross of Gold Speech," in *Great Issues in American History: From Reconstruction to the Present Day, 1864-1969,* ed. Richard Hofstadter (New York: Vintage, 1969), 166-173.
56. Jasper B. Shannon, *Money and Politics* (New York: Random House, 1959), 30-32.
57. Sundquist, *Party System,* 158.
58. Ibid., 169; for a general discussion of the 1896 election's resulting realignment, see pp. 160-169.
59. E. E. Schattschneider, *The Semisovereign People* (Hinsdale, Ill.: Dryden Press, 1975), 76-77.
60. Edmund Morris, *The Rise of Theodore Roosevelt* (New York: Ballantine, 1979), 718.
61. See Gabriel Kolko, *The Triumph of Conservatism* (New York: Free Press, 1963).
62. Sundquist, *Party System,* 176.
63. See Alpheus I. Mason, *Bureaucracy Convicts Itself* (New York: Viking Press, 1941); and James Penick, Jr., *Progressive Politics and Conservation* (Chicago: University of Chicago Press, 1968).
64. J. Leonard Bates, *The United States, 1898-1928* (New York: McGraw-Hill, 1976), 187.
65. Roseboom, *Presidential Elections,* 384.
66. John L. Shover, ed., *Politics of the Nineteen Twenties* (Waltham, Mass.: Ginn-Blaisdell, 1970), 148.
67. Ibid., 4.
68. Ibid., 12.
69. Ibid., 10.
70. James David Barber, *The Pulse of Politics* (New York: Norton, 1980), 239.
71. William E. Leuchtenberg, *Franklin D. Roosevelt and the New Deal* (New York: Harper and Row, 1963), 13.
72. Frank Friedel, *Franklin D. Roosevelt: The Triumph* (Boston: Little, Brown, 1956), 248-249.
73. Barber, *Pulse of Politics,* 243.
74. Ibid., 244.
75. Ibid., 238.
76. Hofstadter, *American Political Tradition,* 332.
77. Barber, *Pulse of Politics,* 244.
78. See Robert Lekachman, *The Age of Keynes* (New York: Random, 1966).
79. Schattschneider argues in *The Semisovereign People* that the key element of any conflict is the extent to which the protagonists are able to control how many people get involved. Every "scope of conflict" has a bias. The size of the group involved in the conflict is almost always open to change. Schattschneider writes: "A look at political literature shows that there has indeed been a long-standing struggle between the conflicting tendencies toward the privatization and socialization of conflict" (p. 7). The New Deal was a stage of socialization of conflict.
80. Everett Carll Ladd, Jr., and Charles D. Hadley, *Transformations of the American Party System* (New York: Norton, 1978), 86.
81. Ibid., 43.
82. Ibid., 46.
83. Ibid., 64-74, 112; Sundquist, *Party System,* 214-224.
84. Sundquist, *Party System,* 217.

85. Ladd and Hadley, *American Party System,* 82.
86. Ibid., 58-59.
87. Ibid., 63.
88. Samuel H. Beer, "Liberalism and the National Interest," *The Public Interest,* no. 1 (Fall 1966): 81.
89. Theodore J. Lowi, *The End of Liberalism* (New York: Norton, 1969). See also Russell Hanson, *The Democratic Imagination in America* (Princeton, N.J.: Princeton University Press, 1985), 257-292.
90. James MacGregor Burns, *Roosevelt: The Lion and the Fox* (New York: Harcourt, Brace, and World, 1956), 282-283.
91. Roseboom, *Presidential Elections,* 447.
92. Burns, *Lion and the Fox,* 269-271.
93. Burns, *Roosevelt,* 282-283.
94. Ibid., 300.
95. Ibid., 427.
96. James David Barber, *The Pulse of Politics* (New York: W. W. Norton, 1980) tells the story behind the Willkie movement and the role played by Henry R. Luce, the founder of Time, Inc.
97. See Lekachman, *Age of Keynes,* esp. chaps. 5 and 6.
98. Roseboom, *Presidential Elections,* 483.
99. William E. Leuchtenberg, *In the Shadow of F.D.R.: From Harry Truman to Ronald Reagan* (Ithaca, N.Y.: Cornell University Press, 1983), 1-2.
100. Ibid., 15.
101. Ibid., 21.
102. V. O. Key, *Southern Politics in State and Nation* (Knoxville: University of Tennessee Press, 1984), 649.
103. Ibid., 330-344.
104. Barber, *Pulse of Politics,* 50.
105. Nelson W. Polsby and Aaron Wildavsky, *Presidential Elections* (New York: Scribner's, 1984), 205-206.
106. Barber, *Pulse of Politics,* 61.
107. Angus Campbell, Gerald Gurin, and Warren E. Miller, *The American Voter* (New York: Wiley, 1960), 532.
108. Richard Neustadt, *Presidential Power* (New York: Wiley, 1980), 10, 12-14, 16, 18, 19, 22-25, 43, 67-68, 178.
109. Garry Wills, *Nixon Agonistes* (New York: New American Library, 1969), 91.
110. Fred Greenstein, *The Hidden-Hand Presidency* (New York: Basic Books, 1982).
111. Barber, *Pulse of Politics,* 269.
112. Eric F. Goldman quipped, "The returns, as the gangsters said, made even Alf Landon look good" (*The Crucial Decade* [New York: Vintage, 1960], 326).
113. The elder Kennedy always planned for his sons to enter national politics. He originally pushed his eldest son, Joseph, Jr., but the son died in combat in World War II. John was next; he ran for Congress in 1946. Robert, the third Kennedy son, served as an aide to Sen. Joseph McCarthy before managing John's 1960 presidential campaign and serving as his attorney general. Edward, the youngest, worked on the 1960 campaign and won a Senate seat in 1962.
114. Merle Miller, *Plain Speaking* (New York: Berkley, 1974), 199.
115. Theodore H. White, *The Making of the President 1960* (New York: Atheneum, 1961), 114-116.
116. Ibid., 128.
117. Ibid., 130.
118. Ibid., 198-204.
119. Arthur M. Schlesinger, Jr., *Robert F. Kennedy and His Times* (Boston: Houghton Mifflin, 1978), 193.
120. Henry Fairlie, *The Kennedy Promise* (New York: Dell, 1972), 30-31.
121. White, *Making of the President 1960,* 329.
122. Ibid., 327.
123. Richard M. Nixon, *Six Crises* (Garden City, N.Y.: Doubleday, 1962), 412.
124. White, *Making of the President 1960,* 397-401.
125. Sen. Barry Goldwater, letter to the author, January 25, 1988.
126. The Warren Commission, appointed by Johnson, concluded that Oswald acted alone, but Oswald himself was killed before he had a chance to give full testimony. Many experts dispute the Warren Commission conclusion.
127. The Kennedy assassination fomented passage of the Twenty-fifth Amendment, which provides for a more orderly system of replacement. Previously, when a vice president ascended to the White House after the death or removal of a president, the vice presidency was left vacant. The amendment provides for presidential appointment of a vice president to fill the vacant spot. It also provides for at least temporary replacement of the president in the case of disability. The latter provision developed out of a concern that the country could have become leaderless had Kennedy been physically or mentally impaired but not killed.
128. Barber, *Pulse of Politics,* 167.
129. Thomas Ferguson and Joel Rogers, *Right Turn: The Decline of the Democrats and the Future of American Politics* (New York: Hill and Wang, 1986), 53.
130. Theodore H. White, *The Making of the President 1964* (New York: New American Library, 1965), 261.
131. Ibid., 353.
132. The central importance of economic conditions to electoral politics is widely documented. See, for example, Stanley Kelley, Jr., *Interpreting Elections* (Princeton, N.J.: Princeton University Press, 1983); Edward R. Tufte, *Political Control of the Economy* (Princeton, N.J.: Princeton University Press, 1978); and Angus Campbell, Gerald Gurin, and Warren E. Miller, *The American Voter* (New York: Wiley, 1960). On the link between economic conditions and the 1964 election, see Kelley, *Interpreting Elections,* 194.
133. Stanley Karnow, *Vietnam: A History* (New York: Viking, 1983), 358.
134. Ibid., 362.
135. Ibid., 395.
136. James David Barber, *The Presidential Character* (Englewood Cliffs, N.J.: Prentice-Hall, 1972), 34.
137. Karnow, *Vietnam,* 403.
138. Ibid., 479.
139. David Halberstam, *The Best and the Brightest* (New York: Random, 1969).
140. Sundquist, *Party System,* 384.
141. Ibid., 383.
142. The administration plank supported a bombing halt only when it would not endanger the lives of our troops in the field, did not call for a reduction in search-and-destroy missions or a withdrawal of troops until the end of the war, and advocated a new government in Saigon only after the war had ended. The minority plank, drafted by McCarthy and McGovern, called for an immediate halt to the bombing, reduction of offensive operations in the South Vietnamese countryside, a negotiated troop withdrawal, and encouragement of the South Vietnamese government to negotiate with Communist insurgents. After nearly three hours of debate, the minority plank was defeated, 1,567-3/4 to 1,041-1/4.
143. White, *Making of the President 1968,* 371.
144. Roseboom, *Presidential Elections,* 603.
145. See Russell Baker, *The Next President* (New York: Dell, 1968).
146. David Broder, "The Story That Still Nags at Me," *Washington Monthly*, February 1987, 29-32; see also White, *Making of the President 1972,* 82.
147. White, *Making of the President 1972,* 129.
148. Ibid., 207.
149. On the politics of the period, see Sundquist, *Party System,* 393-411; and Theodore H. White, *America in Search of Itself* (New York: Harper and Row, 1981). Good accounts of the Watergate scandal include Theodore H. White, *Breach of Faith* (New York: Atheneum, 1975); Jonathan Schell, *The Time of Illusion* (New York: Knopf, 1976); and Lewis Chester, et al., *Watergate* (New York: Ballantine, 1973).
150. Seymour Hersch, "The Pardon," *Atlantic,* August 1983, 55-78.
151. David J. Vogler, *The Politics of Congress* (Boston: Allyn and Bacon, 1977), 15-20, 25-26, 34, 147-155, 243-245.
152. For a good account of Jimmy Carter's 1976 Iowa victory, see

Hugh Winebrenner, *The Iowa Precinct Caucuses* (Ames: University of Iowa Press, 1987), 67-93.

153. Jules Witcover, *Marathon* (New York: Viking, 1977), 274-288.
154. Ibid., 545-560.
155. Responding to a question during a debate, Ford said: "There is no Soviet domination of Eastern Europe, and there never will be under a Ford administration.... I don't believe ... that the Yugoslavians consider themselves dominated by the Soviet Union. I don't believe that the Rumanians consider themselves dominated by the Soviet Union. I don't believe that the Poles consider themselves dominated by the Soviet Union" (Ibid., 597, 598).
156. Richard Harwood, ed., *The Pursuit of the Presidency 1980* (New York: Berkley, 1980), 305-307.
157. Thomas Byrne Edsall, *The New Politics of Inequality* (New York: Norton, 1984), 77-78.
158. Thomas Ferguson and Joel Rogers, *Right Turn* (New York: Hall and Wang, 1986), 26.
159. Rep. Shirley Chisholm of Brooklyn, New York, was the first black to seek a major-party nomination. Her participation in the 1972 Democratic primaries won 151 delegates.
160. Geraldine Ferraro, with Linda Bird Francke, *Ferraro: My Story* (New York: Bantam, 1985), 164.
161. Paul R. Abramson, John H. Aldrich, and David W. Rohde, *Change and Continuity in the 1984 Elections,* rev. ed. (Washington, D.C.: CQ Press, 1986), 58.
162. V. O. Key, Jr., "A Theory of Critical Elections," *Journal of Politics* 17 (February 1955): 3-18.
163. Abramson, Aldrich, and Rohde, *Change and Continuity*, 286-287.
164. Michael Barone and Grant Ujifusa, *The Almanac of American Politics: 1984* (Washington, D.C.: National Journal, 1983), xiv. See also Ladd and Hadley, *American Party System,* 237-249.
165. George Gilder, *Wealth and Poverty* (New York: Basic Books, 1980). Another prominent supply-side tract is Jude Wanniski, *The Way the World Works* (New York: Basic Books, 1978). A sympathetic summary of the whole movement can be found in Robert Craig Paul, *The Supply-Side Revolution* (Cambridge, Mass.: Harvard University Press, 1984).
166. Ferguson and Rogers, *Right Turn,* 86-88, n. 245.
167. Garry Wills, *Reagan's America: Innocents at Home* (Garden City, N.Y.: Doubleday, 1987), 387.
168. Ibid., 385.
169. Also that year, two Supreme Court nominees, Robert H. Bork and Douglas H. Ginsburg, failed to win Senate confirmation. Bork lost because of his views on a wide variety of social issues, but many criticisms focused on his personality. Ginsburg withdrew from consideration after revelations that he had smoked marijuana as a student and law school professor.
170. Quayle did not meet the requirements set for political science majors and failed the first general examination at DePauw University in Indiana. He also failed to gain admission to law school under the usual application procedure. A study of Quayle's congressional career concludes that Quayle had no policy achievements in the House of Representatives but mastered some policy issues in the Senate. See Anthony Lewis, "The Intimidated Press," *New York Times*, January 19, 1989, 27, and Richard F. Fenno, Jr., *The Making of a Senator: Dan Quayle* (Washington, D.C.: CQ Press, 1988).

Selected Bibliography

Abramson, Paul R., John H. Aldrich, and David W. Rohde. *Change and Continuity in the 1984 Elections.* Rev. ed. Washington, D.C.: CQ Press, 1987.

Alexander, Herbert E., and Brian A. Haggerty. *Financing the 1984 Election.* Lexington, Mass.: Lexington Books, 1987.

Altschuler, Bruce E. *Keeping a Finger on the Public Pulse: Private Polling and Presidential Elections.* Westport, Conn.: Greenwood Press, 1982.

Arterton, F. Christopher. *Media Politics: The News Strategies of Presidential Campaigns.* Lexington, Mass.: Lexington, 1984.

Barber, James David, ed. *Choosing the President.* Englewood Cliffs, N.J.: Prentice Hall, 1974.

——. *The Presidential Character.* Englewood Cliffs, N.J.: Prentice Hall, 1972.

——. *The Pulse of Politics: Electing Presidents in the Media Age.* New York: Norton, 1980.

Bennett, W. Lance. *News: The Politics of Illusion.* New York: Longman, 1983.

Berkman, Ronald, and Laura W. Kitch. *Politics in the Media Age.* New York: McGraw-Hill, 1986.

Burnham, Walter Dean. *Critical Elections and the Mainsprings of American Politics.* New York: Norton, 1970.

Burns, James MacGregor. *The Deadlock of Democracy.* Englewood Cliffs, N.J.: Prentice Hall, 1963.

Campbell, Angus, Philip E. Converse, Warren E. Miller, and Donald E. Stokes. *The American Voter.* Beverly Hills, Calif.: Sage Publications, 1976.

Ceaser, James W. *Presidential Selection: Theory and Development.* Princeton, N.J.: Princeton University Press, 1979.

——. *Reforming the Reforms.* Cambridge, Mass.: Ballinger, 1982.

Chambers, William Nisbet, and Walter Dean Burnham, eds. *The American Party Systems: Stages of Development.* New York: Oxford University Press, 1967.

Chase, James S. *Emergence of the Presidential Nominating Convention: 1789-1832.* Urbana: University of Illinois Press, 1973.

Cheney, Richard B. "The 1976 Presidential Debates: A Republican Perspective." In *The Past and Future of Presidential Debates,* ed. Austin Ranney. Washington, D.C.: American Enterprise Institute, 1979.

Cole, Barry, ed. *Television Today: A Close-Up View.* New York: Oxford University Press, 1981.

Crotty, William J. *Political Reform and the American Experiment.* New York: Thomas Y. Crowell Company, 1977.

Crotty, William J., and John S. Jackson III. *Presidential Primaries and Nominations.* Washington, D.C.: CQ Press, 1985.

Cunningham, Noble E., Jr., ed. *The Making of the American Party System: 1789-1809.* Englewood Cliffs, N.J.: Prentice Hall, 1965.

Davis, James W. *National Conventions in an Age of Party Reform.* Westport, Conn.: Greenwood Press, 1983.

——. *Presidential Primaries: Road to the White House.* Westport, Conn.: Greenwood Press, 1980.

Drew, Elizabeth. *Politics and Money: The New Road to Corruption.* New York: Macmillan, 1983.

Edsall, Thomas Byrne. *The New Politics of Inequality.* New York: Norton, 1984.

Ferguson, Thomas, and Joel Rogers, eds. *The Hidden Election: Politics and Economics in the 1980 Presidential Campaign.* New York: Random, 1981.

——. *Right Turn: The Decline of the Democrats and the Future of American Politics.* New York: Hill and Wang, 1986.

Fiorina, Morris P. *Retrospective Voting in American National Elections.* New Haven: Conn., Yale University Press, 1981.

Graber, Doris A. *Mass Media and American Politics.* 2d ed. Washington, D.C.: CQ Press, 1984.

Hanson, Russell L. *The Democratic Imagination in America: Conversations with our Past.* Princeton, N.J.: Princeton University Press, 1985.

Harmel, Robert, ed. *Presidents and Their Parties.* New York: Praeger, 1984.

Heard, Alexander. *Made in America.* New York: Basic Books, forthcoming.

Heard, Alexander, and Michael Nelson, ed. *Presidential Selection.* Durhan, N.C. Duke University Press, 1987.

Hirschman, Albert O. *Exit, Voice, and Loyalty: Responses to Decline in Firms, Organizations, and States.* Cambridge, Mass.: Harvard University Press, 1970.

Hofstadter, Richard. *The Idea of a Party System.* Berkeley: University of California Press, 1969.

Joslyn, Richard. *Mass Media and Elections.* Reading, Massachusetts: Addison-Wesley, 1984.
Klapper, Joseph T. *The Effects of Mass Communication.* Glencoe, Illinois: Free Press, 1960.
Ladd, Everett Carll., Jr., and Charles D. Hadley. *Transformations of the American Party System.* New York: Norton, 1978.
Lang, Kurt, and Gladys Engel Lang. *Politics and Television.* Chicago: Quadrangle Books, 1968.
Lowi, Theodore J. *The Personal President.* Ithica, N.Y.: Cornell University Press, 1985.
Lubell, Samuel. *The Future of American Politics.* New York: Harper Colophon Books, 1963.
McGinniss, Joe. *The Selling of the President: 1968.* New York: Trident Press, 1969.
Mann, Thomas E. "Should the Presidential Nominating System Be Changed (Again)?" In *Before Nomination: Our Primary Problems,* ed. George Grassmuck. Washington, D.C.: American Enterprise Institute, 1985.
Marshall, Thomas R. *Presidential Nominations in a Reform Age.* New York: Praeger, 1981.
Matthews, Donald R. "Winnowing." In *Race for the Presidency,* ed. James David Barber. Englewood Cliffs, New Jersey: Prentice-Hall, 1978.
Mazmanian, Daniel A. *Third Parties in Presidential Elections.* Washington, D.C.: Brookings, 1974.
Moos, Malcolm, and Stephen Hess. *Hats in the Ring.* New York: Random, 1960.
National Institute of Mental Health. *Television and Behavior.* Vol. 1. Washington, D.C.: Government Printing Office, 1982.
Nelson, Michael. "Two Cheers for the National Primary." In *Rethinking the Presidency,* ed. Thomas E. Cronin. Boston: Little, Brown, 1982.
Orren, Gary R., and Nelson W. Polsby. *Media and Momentum: The New Hampshire Primary and Nomination Politics.* Chatham, N.J.: Chatham House, 1987.
Paletz, David L., and Martha Elson. "Television Coverage of Presidential Conventions: Now You See It, Now You Don't." *Political Science Quarterly* 91 (Spring 1976).
Paletz, David L., and Robert M. Entman. *Media Power Politics.* New York: Free Press, 1981.
Patterson, Thomas E. *The Mass Media Election.* New York: Praeger, 1980.
Pious, Richard M. *The American Presidency.* New York: Basic Books, 1979.
Pious, Richard M., and Robert C. Weaver. "Presidential Campaigns: Strategies and Tactics." In *Selection/Election: A Forum on the American Presidency,* ed. Robert S. Hirschfield. New York: Aldine, 1982.
Piven, Frances Fox, and Richard A. Cloward. *Why Americans Don't Vote.* New York: Pantheon, 1988.
Polsby, Nelson W. "The News Media as an Alternative to Party in the Presidential Selection Process." In *Political Parties in the Eighties,* ed. Robert A. Goldwin. Washington, D.C.: American Enterprise Institute, 1980.
Polsby, Nelson W., and Aaron Wildavsky. *Presidential Elections: Strategies of American Electoral Politics.* New York: Scribner's, 1984.
Pomper, Gerald. *Nominating the President.* Northwestern University Press, 1963.
Ranney, Austin. *The Federalization of Presidential Primaries.* Washington, D.C.: American Enterprise Institute, 1978.
Reeves, Richard. *Convention.* New York: Harcourt Brace Jovanovich, 1977.
Reichley, A. James, ed. *Elections American Style.* (Washington, D.C.: Brookings, 1987.
Roseboom, Eugene H. *A History of Presidential Elections.* 2d ed. New York: Macmillan, 1964.
Rosenstone, Steven J., Roy L. Behr, and Edward H. Lazarus. *Third Parties in America.* Princeton, N.J.: Princeton University Press, 1984.
Ross, Irwin. *The Loneliest Campaign: The Truman Victory of 1948.* New York: New American Library, 1968.
Sabato, Larry J. *The Party's Just Begun.* Glenview, Ill.: Scott, Foresman, 1988.
——. *The Rise of Political Consultants.* New York: Basic Books, 1981.
Sanford, Terry. *A Danger of Democracy.* Boulder, Colo.: Westview, 1981.
Schlesinger, Arthur M., Jr., ed. *History of U.S. Political Parties.* Vol. I. New York: Chelsea House, 1973.
Schram, Martin. *Running for President: A Journal of the Carter Campaign.* Exp. ed. New York: Pocket Books, 1978.
Sundquist, James L. *Dynamics of the Party System.* Rev. ed. Washington, D.C.: Brookings, 1983.
Wayne, Stephen J. *The Road to the White House: The Politics of Presidential Elections.* 3d ed. New York: St. Martin's Press, 1988.
Witcover, Jules. *Marathon—The Pursuit of the Presidency: 1972-1976.* New York: Viking, 1977.
White, Theodore H. *The Making of the President 1960.* New York: Atheneum, 1961.
Wolfinger, Raymond, and Stephen Rosenstone. *Who Votes?* New Haven, Conn.: Yale University Press, 1980.

Selection by Succession

The original Constitution—supplemented by the Twentieth Amendment (1933), the Twenty-fifth Amendment (1967), the succession acts of 1792, 1886, and 1947, the rules of the Republican and Democratic parties, and a number of informal precedents and practices—provides that under certain circumstances, the president may be selected not by election, but by succession.

Historically, nine presidents have reached the White House through succession—four of them when the incumbent president died of natural causes, four when the president was assassinated, and one when the president resigned. Four succeeded to the presidency in the nineteenth century, five in the twentieth century. None of the nineteenth-century vice presidents were subsequently nominated by their parties, much less elected, for a term in their own right. All five twentieth-century successors were nominated, and four were elected.

Each of the nine successor presidents was vice president at the time he succeeded to the presidency.

~ Vice President John Tyler became president when President William Henry Harrison died of an illness just one month after his inauguration in 1841.

~ Vice President Millard Fillmore succeeded to the presidency in 1850 when President Zachary Taylor died of natural causes during the second year of his term.

~ President Abraham Lincoln, who was assassinated six weeks after the start of his second term in 1865, was succeeded by Vice President Andrew Johnson.

~ Vice President Chester A. Arthur became president in 1881 after the death of President James A. Garfield, who also was assassinated near the start of his term.

~ In 1901, an assassin killed President William McKinley. Vice President Theodore Roosevelt succeeded to the presidency, served out the remaining three and one-half years of McKinley's term, and was elected president in 1904.

~ President Warren G. Harding died of natural causes with nineteen months left in his term in 1923. He was succeeded by Vice President Calvin Coolidge, who ran for president and was elected in 1924.

~ President Franklin D. Roosevelt died of natural causes three months after the start of his fourth term in 1945 and was succeeded by Vice President Harry S Truman. Truman was elected president in 1948.

~ Vice President Lyndon B. Johnson succeeded to the presidency in 1963 after President John F. Kennedy was assassinated with fourteen months remaining in his term. Johnson was elected in his own right in 1964.

~ Under threat of imminent impeachment and removal, President Richard Nixon resigned in 1974, after serving less than two years of his second term. Vice President Gerald R. Ford became president. Ford was nominated for a full presidential term by his party in 1976 but was narrowly defeated in the general election.

Another vice president, George Bush, served briefly as acting president when President Ronald Reagan was disabled for cancer surgery in 1985.

Assassination attempts, impeachment proceedings, and illness made succession an active concern during twenty of the nation's first forty presidencies (George Washington through Ronald Reagan).[1] With the exception of Walter F. Mondale, every vice president in the period 1945-1989 aroused public concern because of some event or condition of health that raised the possibility that he would succeed to the presidency.

Vacancies also have occurred in the vice presidency on eighteen occasions. The vice presidency became vacant nine times because the vice president succeeded to the presidency. In addition, seven vice presidents died in office—George Clinton (1812), Elbridge Gerry (1814), William R. King (1853), Henry Wilson (1875), Thomas A. Hendricks (1885), Garret A. Hobart (1899), and James S. Sherman (1912). Two vice presidents—John C. Calhoun (1832) and Spiro T. Agnew (1973)—resigned.

The original Constitution provided, but not fully, for presidential selection through succession by the vice president. (It said nothing about filling vacancies in the vice presidency.) But the Constitution was neither clear nor complete. Presidential succession practices had to be clarified and supplemented over the years: by precedent (Tyler's succession to the office of the president, not just to its powers and duties, and for the full balance of the president's unexpired term, not just until a special election could be called), by law (succession acts passed by Congress in 1792, 1886, and 1947 to extend the line of succession beyond the vice president), and by constitutional amendment (the Twentieth Amendment, enacted in 1933, to provide for succession during the period between the election and the start of the president's term, and the Twenty-fifth Amendment, which entered the Constitution in 1967, to provide both for presidential disabilities and for vice-presidential vacancies).

By Michael Nelson

The Constitutional Convention

The Framers of the Constitution were aware that merely to elect a president to a four-year term was no guarantee that the president would be able, willing, or deserving to fulfill the term. At the Constitutional Convention in 1787, they provided for four circumstances that might require presidential selection not by election, but by succession: the president's resignation from office; the president's death, whether by assassination or natural causes; the temporary or permanent inability of the president to meet the responsibilities of the office; and the impeachment and removal of the president by Congress for "Treason, Bribery, or other High Crimes and Misdemeanors."

As prudent as the delegates were in anticipating that circumstances might arise that would require a president to be chosen by succession, they were less than thorough in addressing six related issues.

First, who would be the successor? In August the Committee of Detail suggested the president of the Senate, but this idea ultimately was rejected for fear that it would create an incentive for senators to convict a president who had been impeached by the House of Representatives in order to replace the president with one of their own. Individual delegates proposed the chief justice of the Supreme Court (Gouverneur Morris of Pennsylvania) or a council of state (James Madison of Virginia) as the designated presidential successor. When, late in the convention, the vice presidency was invented by the Committee on Postponed Matters as a way of making the electoral college work, the vice president—almost offhandedly—was made successor to the president. *(See "The Vice Presidency," p. 34 in Constitutional Beginnings chapter of Part I.)*

Second, in the event that the presidency were to become vacant, would the vice president serve out the unexpired balance of the president's four-year term, or would succession to the presidency be temporary, pending a special presidential election? Although history's answer has been full succession, the convention almost certainly intended that succession be temporary.

The delegates' intentions regarding succession and a special election were obscured because of what can only be called a clerical error. The Committee of Style, created at the end of the convention to put the delegates' myriad decisions into a final, polished draft of the Constitution, was given two succession resolutions to incorporate, one from a report by the Committee on Postponed Matters that was submitted to the convention on September 4, 1787, the other from a motion that was made on the floor by Edmund Randolph of Virginia on September 7.

The first resolution stated: "In case of [the president's] removal as aforesaid, death, absence, resignation, or inability to discharge the powers of duties of his office the Vice President shall exercise those powers and duties until another President be chosen, or until the inability of the President be removed."

The second resolution, which was intended to supplement the first by providing a method for presidential succession if there were no vice president, read: "The Legislature may declare by law what officer of the United States shall act as President and Vice President in the case of death, resignation, or disability of the President; and such Officer shall act accordingly, until such disability be removed, or a President shall be elected." The last eleven words of this resolution—"until such disability be removed, or a President shall be elected"—were Madison's amendment to Randolph's motion. They were inserted, Madison told the delegates, expressly to permit "a supply of vacancy by an intermediate election of the President."

What appeared in the final draft by the Committee of Style, which was mildly modified by the convention, was the product of the committee's effort to compress the two resolutions into one—now paragraph 6 of Article II, section 2 of the Constitution:

> In case of the Removal of the President from Office, or of his Death, Resignation, or Inability to discharge the Powers and Duties of the said Office, the Same shall devolve on the Vice President, and the Congress may by law provide for the case of Removal, Death, Resignation, or Inability, both of the President and Vice President, declaring what Officer shall then act as President, and such officer shall act accordingly, until the Disability be removed, or a President shall be elected.

Clearly, the delegates' intentions regarding succession were obscured, no doubt unwittingly, by the Committee of Style.[2] Grammatically, it is impossible to tell—and in their rush to adjournment the delegates did not notice the ambiguity—whether "the Same" in the provision refers to "the said Office" (the presidency) or, as the convention intended, to its "Powers and Duties." Nor can one ascertain if "until ... a President shall be elected" means until the end of the original four-year term or, again, as intended, until a special election is held.

Third, the delegates left Congress to legislate for the matter of presidential selection by succession when the vice presidency was vacant, either because the vice president had died, resigned, or been impeached and removed or because the vice president had succeeded to the presidency.

Fourth, the original Constitution was silent as to what would happen if a person whom the electoral college had chosen to be president or vice president died, withdrew, or was found to be constitutionally unqualified by virtue of age, residence, or citizenship before being inaugurated.

Fifth, the delegates made no provision for succession to the vice presidency or replacement of the vice president when the office became vacant.

A final issue regarding selection by succession that the delegates dealt with incompletely involved determinations of presidential inability. Death, resignation, impeachment and removal—these were well-defined events. Little doubt could exist as to when succession was needed. The presence of an inability, whether mental or physical, was a more subjective matter and would not always be so readily apparent. Nor did the delegates create any procedure for determining whether a presidential disability existed. "What is the extent of the term 'disability,' " John Dickinson of Pennsylvania asked the convention on August 20, "and who is to be the judge of it?" No one answered him.

The Vice President as Full Successor

Fifty-two years elapsed between the ratification of the Constitution in 1789 and the occurrence of the first vacancy in the presidency in 1841, when William Henry Harrison died shortly after his inauguration. (Since 1841, the nation has never gone more than twenty-six years without the presidency becoming prematurely vacant.) Because the language of the Constitution was vague, official and unofficial records of the Constitutional Convention had not yet been published, and no delegates to the convention were still alive, it was impossible to say authoritatively what was supposed to happen next.

Initially, Harrison's cabinet and some others seemed to think that the president's death made Vice President John Tyler only the acting president. Tyler believed differently. He quickly took the oath of office as president, delivered a sort of inaugural address, declared his intention to serve out the remainder of Harrison's term, and moved into the White House. Tyler's decisiveness prevailed in a constitutionally and politically uncertain situation. An effort in Congress to address Tyler officially in correspondence as "Vice President, on whom, by the death of the late President, the powers and duties of the office of President have devolved" overwhelmingly failed to pass.[3]

Tyler's action set a precedent that Millard Fillmore (nine years later) and future vice presidents were able to follow without controversy. Not until the Twenty-fifth Amendment was enacted in 1967, however, did the Constitution explicitly codify the vice president's right, when the presidency became prematurely vacant, to succeed to the office and serve for the balance of the unexpired term.[4] Section 1 of the amendment states: "In case of the removal of the President from office or of his death or resignation, the Vice President shall become President."

Other Officials in the Line of Succession

Article II, section 2, paragraph 6, of the original Constitution did not delineate a line of succession that extended past the vice president. Instead, it charged Congress to provide by law for situations in which the vice presidency was vacant when a successor to the president was needed.

The second Congress passed the Succession Act in 1792. It stipulated that a double vacancy in the presidency and vice presidency should be remedied by a special election to a full four-year term the following November unless the vacancy occurred during the last six months of the departed president's term. In the meantime, the president pro tempore of the Senate (or, if there were none, the Speaker of the House of Representatives) would "act as President." Madison, then a representative from Virginia, objected to this provision of the act, partly beause he thought that the presence of legislators in the line of succession violated the principle of separation of powers, and partly because the line bypassed the leader of his party, Secretary of State Thomas Jefferson.

Although the double vacancy provided for in the 1792 succession act never has occurred, the nation has frequently been at risk: sixteen of the first thirty-six presidents (Washington to Lyndon Johnson) served without a vice president for part of their terms. A particular problem arose in 1881. President Garfield was assassinated at a time when there was neither a Senate president pro tempore nor a House Speaker—if anything had happened to Vice President Arthur, his successor, the nation would have been without a president.[5] Congress did nothing to correct this problem, and it arose again in 1885, when President Grover Cleveland, a Democrat, was president. Republicans con-

Line of Succession

On March 30, 1981, President Ronald Reagan was shot by assassin John Hinckley outside a Washington hotel and rushed to an area hospital for surgery. Vice President George Bush was on a plane returning to Washington from Texas. Presidential aides and cabinet members gathered at the White House, where questions arose among them and the press corps about who was "in charge."[1] Secretary of State Alexander M. Haig, Jr., rushed to the press briefing room and, before an audience of reporters and live television cameras, said, "As of now, I am in control here in the White House, pending the return of the vice president.... Constitutionally, gentlemen, you have the president, the vice president, and the secretary of state."

Haig was, as many gleeful critics subsequently pointed out, wrong. The Constitution says nothing about who follows the vice president in the line of succession. The Succession Act of 1947 (later modified to reflect the creation of new departments) establishes congressional leaders and the heads of the departments, in the order the departments were created, as filling the line of succession that follows the vice president.

The line of succession is:

vice president
Speaker of the House of Representatives
president pro tempore of the Senate
secretary of state
secretary of the Treasury
secretary of defense
attorney general
secretary of the interior
secretary of agriculture
secretary of commerce
secretary of labor
secretary of health and human services
secretary of housing and urban development
secretary of transportation
secretary of energy
secretary of education
secretary of veterans affairs

A different "line"—not of succession to the presidency, but of National Command Authority in situations of wartime emergency—was created according to the National Security Act of 1947. The command rules are detailed in secret presidential orders that each new president signs at the outset of the term. Among other things, the orders authorize the secretary of defense to act as commander in chief in certain specific, limited situations in which neither the president nor the vice president is available. Presumably, such situations would follow a nuclear attack on Washington.

1. "Confusion over Who Was in Charge Arose Following Reagan Shooting," *Wall Street Journal*, April 1, 1981.

trolled the Senate that year, which drew attention to another problem with the 1792 act: a successor drawn from Congress might well be of a different political party than the president.

Responding at last to the double vacancy problem, Congress passed the Succession Act of 1886. The new law located the line of succession in the president's cabinet in the order the departments were created, beginning with the secretary of state. Some members of Congress (including a future president, Rep. William McKinley of Ohio) opposed the measure on the grounds that it violated democratic principles by allowing the president to appoint the successors. What is more, the statute was unclear as to whether succession would be temporary (pending a special election) or permanent in the event of a double vacancy.

The issue of selection by succession was reopened by President Truman, who succeeded to the presidency when President Roosevelt died near the beginning of his fourth term in 1945. Rejecting the idea that, in the absence of a vice president, the secretary of state should be next in line to the presidency, Truman said: "It now lies within my power to nominate the person who would be my immediate successor in the event of my own death or inability to act. I do not believe that in a democracy this power should rest with the Chief Executive." In 1945, Truman called for a reversion to the 1792 act, although with the Speaker of the House first and the president pro tempore of the Senate (now largely an honorific office awarded to the most senior senator of the majority party) second. Truman also wanted the old act's special election provision restored.[6]

After the 1946 midterm elections, in which Republicans regained control of both houses, Congress selectively accepted Truman's recommendation by passing the Succession Act of 1947. Although Congress rejected special elections for fear that they would produce an excessive discontinuity of leadership within a four-year term, it did rearrange the line of succession as speaker of the House, president pro tempore of the Senate, then the cabinet. *(See box, Line of Succession, p. 339.)* In the absence of a vice president, this placed Republican speaker Joseph Martin, not Secretary of State George C. Marshall, next in line to the presidency until after the 1948 election.

The Twenty-fifth Amendment did not repeal the 1947 succession act. But by providing for the filling of a vacant vice presidency, it reduced the possibility that a double vacancy ever would occur. *(See "Filling Vice-Presidential Vacancies," p. 341, in this chapter.)*

Preinauguration Selection by Succession

A combination of legislation, constitutional amendments, and political party rules cover, albeit incompletely, the variety of circumstances under which a president-elect or presidential candidate must be replaced before being inaugurated as president when the term begins at noon on January 20 following the election.

The possibility that a president-elect might die before taking office was dramatized less than three weeks before the inauguration of Franklin Roosevelt in 1933: an anarchist named Joseph Zangara shot at Roosevelt on a speaker's platform in Miami, Florida. (The bullet missed Roosevelt but killed Chicago mayor Anton Cermak, who was also there.) Later that year, the Twentieth Amendment became part of the Constitution. *(See "Twentieth Amendment," p. 45, in Constitutional Beginnings chapter of Part I.)* Section 3 of the amendment dealt in various ways with the problem of presidential succession before the inauguration.

One clause of section 3 states clearly that if the presi-

UPI/Bettmann

On April 12, 1945, Vice President Harry S Truman succeeded Roosevelt to the presidency when FDR died three months into his fourth term. Bess Truman, the vice president's wife, watches her husband take the oath of office.

dent-elect dies, the vice president-elect becomes president at the beginning of the term. Another provides that if neither the electoral college nor the House of Representatives is able to fulfill its responsibility under the Twelfth Amendment to elect a constitutionally qualified president by inauguration day, the vice president-elect shall serve as acting president until a president is elected. Finally, section 3 states that Congress may provide by law for the situation in which neither a qualified president nor a qualified vice president has been chosen by inauguration day. (Congress did so by designating the Speaker of the House, followed by the president pro tempore of the Senate and the other presidential successors listed in the 1947 succession act.)

As clear as section 3 is, it covers at most the period from January 6 (the day that, by law, Congress counts the electoral votes for president and vice president and, assuming one pair of candidates has received a majority, declares who is president-elect and vice president-elect) and January 20, the day fixed by section 1 of the Twentieth Amendment as the start of the president's term.[7] The Constitution is no guide as to what would happen if a presidential candidate died, withdrew, or was found to be constitutionally unqualified before Congress certified the victory of the president-elect on January 6.

The Republican and Democratic parties have completed part of the preinaugural succession puzzle, the piece that fits between the national nominating conventions in July or August and the first Monday after the second Wednesday in December, which is when the electors who are chosen by the people on election day in November meet in their state capitals to cast the electoral votes that constitutionally elect the president and vice president. National Republican party rules provide that if the Republican presidential (or vice-presidential) candidate should die in this period, the party's national committee would meet to choose a replacement. Democratic rules assign the national nominating convention's "super-delegates" the responsibility to make such a choice. *(See "Super-Delegates," p. 214, in The Electoral Process chapter of Part II.)* Presumably, both parties ordinarily would nominate the vice-presidential candidate for president should the need arise.[8]

What would happen if the presidential candidate who had won a majority of electoral votes died, withdrew, or was found to be constitutionally unqualified in the period between the first Monday after the second Wednesday in December (when the electoral votes are cast) and January 6 (when the electoral votes are counted by Congress)? Section 4 of the Twentieth Amendment calls upon Congress to legislate for this possibility. But Congress never has done so.

Thus, in counting the electoral votes on January 6, Congress would have to improvise. One course of action would be for Congress to declare that no qualified candidate for president had received a majority, in which case the House of Representatives would have to choose the president under the Twelfth Amendment. Since the House's choice is constitutionally confined to the three highest electoral vote recipients in the presidential election, its only alternatives would be to elect a defeated candidate or no one at all. In the latter case, the amendment's provision that the vice president would serve as acting president for the entire four-year term would apply.

The other course Congress could take would be to count all the electoral votes and declare the departed presidential candidate elected. That would produce a more pleasing result, for the vice president would be inaugurated as president (under section 3). But as a procedure, it would mock both common sense and the Constitution's requirement that to be eligible for president, a person must be at least thirty-five years old, a natural-born citizen, and fourteen years a resident of the United States—that is, alive.

Filling Vice-Presidential Vacancies

In contrast to the presidency, no provision was made in the original Constitution to fill vacancies in the vice presidency. As it happened, vacancies in the vice presidency occurred sixteen times between 1789 and 1963, an average of once every eleven years. Seven vacancies occurred because the vice president died, one because the vice president resigned, and eight because the president died and the vice president succeeded to the presidency. In 1965, Congress passed the Twenty-fifth Amendment, part of which established a mechanism to replace departed vice presidents, not by succession but by presidential appointment and congressional confirmation. The amendment was ratified and became part of the Constitution in 1967. Since then, it has been invoked on two occasions—when Vice President Spiro Agnew resigned in 1973 and was replaced by House minority leader Gerald Ford and when Vice President Ford succeeded to the presidency after President Richard Nixon resigned in 1974 and was replaced as vice president by New York governor Nelson A. Rockefeller.

Vice-Presidential Vacancies, 1789-1963

The vice presidency may become vacant when either the vice president dies, resigns, or is removed after conviction for impeachment or the president dies, resigns, or is removed after conviction for impeachment. (In the latter case, the vice presidency becomes vacant because the vice president succeeds to the presidency.) Taken together, the sixteen occasions on which these situations arose during the nation's first thirty-six vice presidencies—that is, before the passage of the Twenty-fifth Amendment—left the office vacant for thirty-seven years.

From 1789 to 1912, the most frequent cause of a vacancy in the vice presidency was a vice-presidential death. Six vice presidents died during this period, all of natural causes. Most were old; some were in ill health when elected. The nineteenth-century vice presidency was a weak, even despised office, and vigorous, ambitious young political leaders typically shunned vice-presidential nominations. *(See History of the Vice Presidency chapter of Part I.)*

The first vice president to die in office was George Clinton, who served under presidents Thomas Jefferson and James Madison. Clinton died in 1812, with ten months remaining in his term. Madison's second vice president, Elbridge Gerry, died two years later, with two years and three months left in his term. President Franklin Pierce's vice president, William R. King, died just six weeks after his inauguration, in 1853. (In the meantime, John C. Calhoun, the vice president to presidents John Quincy Adams and Andrew Jackson, had resigned in 1832, with three

Should Presidential Vacancies . . .

The constitutional process of selection by succession is not bereft of critics, most of whom regard it as inadequate to the task of ensuring the nation effective leadership and would prefer that vacancies in the presidency be filled by special election. Vice presidents are not likely to be of presidential caliber, proponents of a special election argue. (As former Democratic representative James G. O'Hara put it, presidential candidates will not choose running mates "to succeed them. They will choose them to succeed.") Nor is the experience of being vice president helpful preparation for the presidency. Historian Arthur M. Schlesinger, Jr., frequently has called service as vice president "a maiming, not a making, experience."

Arguments for Special Election

Critics of vice-presidential succession are as convinced of the virtues of special election as they are of the weaknesses of the vice presidency. One line of advocacy is avowedly idealistic: American practice should conform to the original constitutional intent that the president "be elected," an ideal later enshrined, at least in part, in the 1792 succession act, which provided for a special election in the event of a double vacancy in the presidency and vice presidency. The other main argument for a special election, practical in nature, draws attention to the experience of the French Fifth Republic. The constitution of France—which, like that of the United States, established a presidential system—provides that in the event of a vacancy in the presidency, the president of the Senate shall serve as the government's caretaker until a special election is held within five weeks to choose a new president for a full term of office. In 1974, when President Georges Pompidou died, the special election took place thirty-three days afterward, followed by a runoff two weeks later and the inauguration of a new president eight days after that.

In the most advanced version of the special election proposal, Schlesinger suggests some American variations on the French practice. Because any designated caretaker from Congress could well be a leader of a party different from the late president's, the acting president should be a member of the administration, preferably the secretary of state. Because U.S. political parties are large and diffuse, the special election should not take place until ninety days after the vacancy, with the parties' national committees choosing the candidates. Finally, to allow the usual presidential selection process to run its course, no special election should be held if a vacancy occurs during the final year of a president's tenure. Instead, the caretaker should serve out the term.[1]

What of the vice presidency in this new scheme? Logically, the office need not be abolished in the course of instituting special elections. The vice presidency still would have its constitutional duties as the Senate president and the vital figure in situations of presidential disability, as well as certain of its ongoing modern activities and, perhaps, a new responsibility as caretaker pending the special election. But, as Schlesinger realizes, the office would best be eliminated under the special election proposal. It would be difficult to attract competent people to the vice presidency if its successor role were stripped from it, in which case even the office's limited powers would be exercised poorly. Also, after the special election brought in a new president, the vice presidency might well be occupied by a member of the opposition party, a problem best headed off by abolition.

Arguments against Special Election

Appealing as the special election idea may be, it has attracted a variety of critics. Some identify problems in the proposal itself. Unlike France, the United States is a superpower; it cannot afford the uncertainty that would attend caretaker leadership, especially in view of the frequency with which presidential vacancies have occurred.

months left in his term, to accept South Carolina's election as U.S. senator.) Henry Wilson, the vice president during the second term of President Ulysses S. Grant, died in 1875, with fifteen months remaining in his term. Thomas A. Hendricks died in 1885, nine months after his inauguration as vice president in the administration of President Grover Cleveland. Finally, President William Howard Taft's vice president, James S. Sherman, died in 1912, with four months left in his term. Although Sherman died days before the 1912 election, his name remained on the ballot and three million citizens voted for electors pledged to him and Taft. (After the election, the Republican National Committee nominated Nicholas Murray Butler, the president of Columbia University, to replace Sherman as the party's nominee for vice president and to receive Sherman's eight electoral votes.)

During this period, presidential deaths left the vice presidency vacant on five occasions: William Henry Harrison (1841), Taylor (1850), Lincoln (1865), Garfield (1881), and McKinley (1901). From 1913 to 1963, the vice presidency became vacant three times, but only because the president died: Harding (1923), Franklin Roosevelt (1945), and Kennedy (1963).

Because the vice president's ongoing constitutional duties are meager—namely, to preside over the Senate and cast tie-breaking votes—the absence of a vice president seldom created serious problems before 1963. Still, each time the vice presidency became vacant, the nation lacked a constitutionally designated successor to the president. The original Constitution simply had called upon Congress to legislate a line of presidential succession that extended past the vice president. Congress did so in 1792, 1886, and 1947.

Remarkably, the nation never experienced a presidential term in which both the president and vice president died; as a result, the statutory line of succession never had

. . . Be Filled by Special Election?

Unlike France, presidential selection in the United States is an inherently lengthy undertaking: the nominating process is diffuse, the pool from which presidents are drawn is broad, and time is required for voters and political activists to sort through all the alternatives. Staffing a new president's administration and developing its policies also is time consuming. In practice, the proposed ninety-day interregnum, itself long, might effectively last thirty to sixty days longer, with the added time serving as a de facto transition period for the new president.

Other critics of the special election proposal concern its actual operation. For example, would the caretaker president be allowed to run in the special election? If not, the nation would be guaranteed a lack of continuity in leadership and, perhaps, deprived of an able president. If so, how would the caretaker's candidacy influence the conduct of the temporary "administration"? And how would the selection of people to fill the office that provides the caretaker be affected? The qualifications of a good acting president and those of, say, a good secretary of state may be quite different. Other questions come to mind. Could the parties' national committees do an adequate job of nominating the presidential candidates, an assignment for which they have little experience? Would presidential and congressional elections remain forever unsynchronized? Would the caretaker be granted the full range of presidential powers and duties?

In addition to attacking the special election idea, some have defended the virtues of vice-presidential succession. Above all, they argue, the traditional procedure of instant, certain, and full succession by the vice president is a source of stability in the political system. Presidential deaths are, in a literal sense, traumatic events for many citizens, triggering feelings not only of personal grief but of fear for the Republic.[2] In this uncertain and emotional setting, Americans historically have accepted the vice president's succession as legitimate; indeed, survey data for the last three successions show the public rallying to each new president's support to an extent unrivaled by even the most popular newly elected president.[3] Legitimacy and stability are qualities of the historic system of vice-presidential succession; they are not qualities that a polity can take for granted on occasions of leadership change.

Beyond the virtues of vice-presidential succession as a procedure in its own right, some argue that the system also works well in practice, by providing able presidents when needed. In the view of historians, the five twentieth-century successor presidents actually rate slightly higher, as a group, than the century's ten elected presidents.[4] Voters have agreed, electing four of the five successors to full terms while rejecting the reelection bids of three of the ten elected presidents.

Changing electoral incentives mean that vice presidents in the late twentieth century are chosen more with their successor role in mind, and are better prepared for it while in office, than at any time in history. In a real sense, critics say, proponents of a special election are prescribing a cure for an ailment that is healing of its own accord.

1. Schlesinger most recently has made the argument for abolishing the vice presidency and substituting a special presidential election for vice-presidential succession in *Cycles of American History* (Boston: Houghton Mifflin, 1986), chap. 12.
2. Paul B. Sheatsley and Jacob J. Feldman, "The Assassination of President Kennedy: Public Reactions," *Public Opinion Quarterly* 28, no. 2 (Summer 1964): 189-215.
3. See the data reported in Erwin C. Hargrove and Michael Nelson, *Presidents, Politics, and Policy* (Baltimore: Johns Hopkins University Press, 1984), 21-22.
4. Calculated from the results of the Murray-Blessing poll: Robert K. Murray and Tim H. Blessing, "The Presidential Performance Study: A Progress Report," *Journal of American History* 70 (December 1983): 535-555. Reagan was not included in the survey.

to be invoked. Still there were some periods of high risk. The deaths of President Taylor and Vice President King left the vice presidency vacant for all but six weeks from July 9, 1850, until March 4, 1857. From September 19, 1881, when President Garfield died, until March 4, 1889, when Vice President Levi P. Morton was inaugurated, the vice presidency was vacant for all but the few months that Vice President Hendricks served in 1885 before dying. The vice presidency also lay vacant during parts of both President Madison's two terms and for more than three-fourths of the terms of Presidents Tyler, Andrew Johnson, Arthur, Cleveland, Theodore Roosevelt, and Truman.

The Twenty-fifth Amendment

The possibility that a vice president would not be available to succeed to the presidency was not regarded as intolerable until after the assassination of President Kennedy on November 22, 1963. To be sure, the importance of having an able and informed successor standing ready to become president had become dramatically clear when Vice President Truman, ignorant of the nation's wartime plans and of the existence of the atomic bomb, succeeded to the presidency in 1945. But the absence of a vice president during the first fourteen months of Lyndon Johnson's presidency seemed especially distressing because the next two offices in the 1947 line of succession were occupied by aged and ill members of Congress, Speaker of the House John W. McCormack of Massachusetts and President Pro Tempore of the Senate Carl Hayden of Arizona. As the legal scholar John D. Feerick writes in *The Twenty-fifth Amendment*, "Neither had been chosen for his position with an eye toward possible succession to the presidency, and neither was viewed by the public as a person of presidential stature." [9]

Lyndon Baines Johnson Library

On February 23, 1967, Lyndon B. Johnson signed into law the Twenty-fifth Amendment, which addresses the issue of presidential disability and empowers the president to nominate a vice president when that office becomes vacant.

On December 12, 1963, less than three weeks after the Kennedy assassination, Democratic senator Birch Bayh of Indiana, who chaired the Subcommittee on Constitutional Amendments of the Senate Committee on the Judiciary, proposed a constitutional amendment that, in addition to addressing the issue of presidential disability, empowered the president to nominate a vice president when the office became vacant, pending confirmation by a majority of both houses of Congress. In presenting his amendment, Bayh argued:

> The accelerated pace of international affairs, plus the overwhelming problems of modern military security, make it almost imperative that we change our system to provide for not only a president but a vice president at all times. The modern concept of the vice presidency is that of a man "standing in the wings"—even if reluctantly—ready at all times to take the burden. He must know the job of president. He must be current on all national and international developments. He must, in fact, be something of an "assistant president"... [10]

The hearings that were held by the constitutional amendments subcommittee during January, February, and March of 1964 revealed near-unanimous support for finding a solution to the problem of the vacant vice presidency. Witnesses differed, however, about the best method to fill such vacancies. Senator Bayh's proposal for presidential nomination and congressional confirmation, which was supported by the American Bar Association and numerous scholars, was grounded in the idea that, as Harvard law professor Paul Freund stated at the hearings, "the vice presidency should have a popular base and at the same time be in harmony with the presidency. These objectives can best be achieved by associating the Congress and the president in the selection, with the opportunity for informal consultation to be expected in such a process." Even those who supported Bayh's proposal, however, wondered whether a time limit should be placed on congressional confirmation and whether confirmation should come from a joint meeting of both houses of Congress or from each house voting separately. Democratic senator Frank Church urged that the president be required to submit a list of several names to the Senate and that those ratified by the Senate be passed on to the House for a final selection.

Other proposals emerged during the hearings. Democratic senator Sam Ervin of North Carolina, arguing that "the potential president should be democratically elected," wanted to entrust the selection of a new vice president to Congress alone. New York Republican Jacob K. Javits worried that such a vice president might be unacceptable to the president and urged that the president be empowered to veto Congress's choice. Democrat Frank Moss of Utah rejoined that presidents should not be forced to rebuke Congress in order to get the vice presidents they wanted. Former vice president Richard Nixon proposed that the president submit the vice-presidential nomination to the electoral college from the previous election, which had formally elected the departed vice president and which was, almost by definition, controlled by the president's party. But, as Bayh argued, "the electoral college is not chosen, as is Congress, to exercise any considered judgment or reasoning"—indeed, since it meets simultaneously in all the state capitals, it is not a body at all.

After tinkering slightly with Bayh's original proposal, the Constitutional Amendments Subcommittee voted on May 27, 1964, to recommend a new amendment to the Constitution that said in part: "Whenever there is a vacancy in the office of the Vice President, the President shall nominate a Vice President who shall take office upon confirmation by a majority vote of both Houses of Congress." The full Judiciary Committee approved the amendment on August 4; the Senate passed it by voice vote on September 28 and, at the request of Democratic senator John Stennis of Mississippi, by a roll call vote of 65-0 on September 29.

The House of Representatives took no action in 1964, partly because the Senate did not act until late in the second year of the 88th Congress, but mainly because one effect of the proposed amendment would have been to remove Speaker McCormack from his statutory place in the line of succession. Once a new vice president was elected in 1964, however, the House moved swiftly. (The Senate, having already considered and passed the amendment in 1964, whisked it through by a 72-0 vote on February 19, 1965.) After commencing hearings on February 9, the House Judiciary Committee approved the amendment on March 24; one week later, on March 31, the Rules Committee cleared it for floor consideration by a 6-4 vote; and on April 13, the full House passed the amendment by a vote of 368-29. Minor differences in the versions of the amendment that were passed by the House and Senate required the calling of a conference committee, which eventually agreed on a common version and brought it back to both houses for final passage. Section 2 of the amendment, the part that dealt with vice-presidential vacancies, remained unchanged from the version that had been in the original Senate Judiciary Committee recommendation.

On June 30, the House voted final passage of the Twenty-fifth Amendment by voice vote. The Senate followed on July 6 with a 68-5 vote. Ratification by the states proceeded quickly and uncontroversially. The amendment was approved by the necessary three-fourths, or thirty-eight, state legislatures on February 19, 1967, and was formally proclaimed the Twenty-fifth Amendment to the Constitution at a White House ceremony on February 23, 1967. Although the process of amending the Constitution does not involve the presidency, President Johnson had supported the amendment in press conferences and speeches and took special pleasure in its enactment.

The smooth passage of the Twenty-fifth Amendment through the process of congressional affirmation and ratification by the states belied the numerous concerns raised along the way by critics, some of which later would seem prescient. One was the absence of a time limit on either the president to nominate a vice president or, especially, on Congress to confirm. Clearly, a long delay would thwart a main purpose of the amendment, which was to ensure that the nation always would have a vice president standing at the ready to succeed to the presidency if the need should arise. A second concern was that the amendment allowed for not just the vice presidency but the presidency to be transformed into an appointed office in the event that an appointed vice president were to succeed to the presidency. Indeed, if that happened, the next vice president to be appointed would be chosen by a president who originally had been appointed, and so on, ad infinitum. Finally, there was the matter of vice-presidential disability, which the amendment did not address. Specifically, if the vice president were disabled, the nation still would lack a qualified successor to the presidency.

In all cases, these concerns were considered by Congress but not addressed in the amendment for fear that it would grow too cumbersome and complex and that any attempted solutions would create problems of their own.

Two Vice-Presidential Vacancies

The authors of the Twenty-fifth Amendment assumed both that vacancies in the vice presidency would occur fairly frequently and that death, either the president's or the vice president's, would be the usual cause. These were reasonable assumptions: from 1789 to 1963 all but one of the sixteen vice-presidential vacancies had come about because the vice president died or the president died and was succeeded by the vice president.

The assumption about frequent vice-presidential vacancies was born out rather quickly: the vice presidency became vacant in both 1973 and 1974. But in each case it was resignation in the face of impeachment, not death, that left the nation without a vice president.

The Nomination of Gerald R. Ford

On October 10, 1973, Vice President Spiro Agnew resigned as part of a plea bargain with the Justice Department that allowed him to avoid prosecution on most of the bribery and income tax evasion charges that the government was preparing to bring. *(See Removal of the Vice President chapter of Part II.)* Later that day, Ronald Ziegler, the president's press secretary, told reporters that "President Nixon intends to move expeditiously in selecting a nominee and he trusts the Congress will then act promptly to consider the nomination."

Nixon's first choice for vice president seems to have been former Treasury secretary John B. Connally, a Democrat-turned Republican who had supported the president in the 1972 election and whom Nixon greatly admired. But Democrats in Congress, joined by some Republicans, resisted the idea of naming a potential candidate for president in the 1976 election as vice president. At the same time, a groundswell began to form among members of both congressional parties in favor of the House Republican leader, Gerald Ford, who was widely liked and respected but not regarded as ambitious to be president. Wishing to avoid a prolonged confirmation battle and possible defeat, Nixon announced Ford's nomination in a televised speech from the East Room of the White House on the evening of October 12, 1973. He told the nation that Ford met the three criteria he had set for a vice president—that he should be qualified to be president, able to work with Congress, and in harmony with the president's domestic and foreign policy views. It was widely reported that Nixon privately expressed the opinion (which turned out to be errant in the extreme) that Congress would be reluctant to impeach and remove him if to do so meant that Ford would become president.

Hearings on the Ford nomination began promptly in both houses of Congress. Although there was some disagreement about which committee should conduct the Senate's hearings, the nomination eventually was referred to the Committee on Rules and Administration because of its traditional jurisdiction over matters relating to presidential succession and presidential and vice-presidential elections. (The Judiciary and Government Operations committees also had claimed jurisdiction; others had suggested that a special committee be formed.) The House referred the nomination to its Judiciary Committee.

Ford's nomination prompted the most extensive investigation ever conducted into the background of a nominee for government office. At Congress's request, approximately 350 agents of the Federal Bureau of Investigation (FBI) conducted more than one thousand interviews of people who had known Ford. The Library of Congress, the Internal Revenue Service (IRS), and staff members detailed from the General Accounting Office (GAO) and various congressional committees pored over Ford's public career, tax returns, medical records, campaign finance reports, bank accounts, and payroll records. Nothing seriously detrimental was uncovered.

The ongoing investigation of President Nixon's involvement in the Watergate affair that took place while Congress was considering the Ford nomination lent an air of special urgency to the confirmation process. As Senate Rules Committee chairman Howard W. Cannon of Nevada said at the beginning of his committee's hearings, the "committee should view its obligations as no less important than the selection of a potential president of the United States." For his part, Ford assured the committee that "I have no intention to run [for president in 1976], and I can foresee no circumstances where I would change my mind."

One concern of both congressional committees was the proper criteria to use in evaluating a president's nominee for vice president. Democratic representative Robert F. Drinan of Massachusetts, a member of the Judiciary Committee, argued that "this is really an election by the House, that it doesn't really compare with the 'advice and consent' [standard for other presidential nominations].... [P]olitical ideology is relevant and to some extent partisan concepts may be employed, and compatibility [with the president] is not the sole consideration." Representative Drinan's view differed from that expressed by Senator Bayh, who noted that the intent of the Twenty-fifth Amendment "was to get a vice president who would be compatible and could work harmoniously with the president," assuming the nominee had "honesty, integrity, [and] no skeletons in the closet."

Because confusion and disagreement existed over the appropriate bounds of Congress's investigation of a vice-presidential nomination, the questions that were put to Ford in the House and Senate committee hearings ranged widely. According to attorney Joel Goldstein, Senate committee members asked 50 percent of their questions about "institutional" matters (the proper operations of the institutions of government, such as executive privilege, openness, and the government's right to lie), 33 percent about "personal" matters (tax returns, associations, past political conduct), and 17 percent about "issues" (welfare, civil rights, foreign policy). In the House, 50 percent of the questions asked of Ford were personal, 35 percent were institutional, and 15 percent concerned issues. In both houses, questions about issues were asked almost exclusively by Democrats.[11]

Ford answered all the questions that committee members asked patiently and committed no gaffes. In responding to Watergate-related questions, Ford was careful not to contradict positions that had been stated by Nixon. But he did emphasize his respect and concern for good relations with Congress. "I believe I can be a ready conciliator and calm communicator between the White House and Capitol Hill," Ford told one questioner, "between the reelection mandate of the Republican president and the equally emphatic mandate of the Democratic 93rd Congress."

When the hearings were over, most members of Congress seemed to have accepted Senator Bayh's argument that Congress's proper role in reviewing vice-presidential nominations was to defer to the president except when defects of character, competence, or integrity made a nominee unacceptable. On November 20, 1973, the Senate Rules Committee voted 9-0 to approve Ford's nomination. After brief floor debate on November 27, the Senate confirmed the nomination by 92-3. Two days later, the House Judiciary Committee recommended Ford's nomination by a vote of 29-8; on December 6, the full House followed suit, 387-35. Although all of the votes against Ford came from Democrats, the vast majority of Democrats voted to confirm. As Democratic representative James G. O'Hara of Michigan argued, "I submit that to allow ourselves to be caught up in measuring Mr. Ford's qualifications for office against the subjective yardstick of our own philosophies would be to disserve the American people who expect Congress, at this critical moment in history, to rise above partisanship."

On December 6, 1973, immediately following the House vote, Ford was administered the oath as vice president by Chief Justice Warren Burger before a joint session of Congress, with President Nixon in attendance. The entire confirmation process, from nomination to swearing in, had lasted seven weeks.

The Nomination of Nelson A. Rockefeller

Gerald Ford served only eight months as vice president. When President Nixon resigned on August 9, 1974, Ford became president, and the vice presidency was once again vacant. Ford's succession posed an early test for the legitimacy of the vice-presidential appointment process that had been created by the Twenty-fifth Amendment. Not only was Ford, in a sense, the "handpicked" choice of his discredited predecessor, but his own nomination of a new vice president would mean that for the first time the nation would be led by an unelected president and an unelected vice president.

Hours after he took the oath as president, Ford told congressional leaders that he considered the nomination of a new vice president to be his first important decision as president and that he planned to make a selection within ten days. On August 11, Ford decided that Gov. Nelson A. Rockefeller of New York was his choice for vice president. Rockefeller was a national leader of demonstrated competence in the fields of administration, urban problems, and foreign policy. Although he had declined offers to run for vice president in 1960 and 1968, Rockefeller now expressed a willingness to serve. At age sixty-six, his own ambitions for the presidency largely extinguished, he regarded the vice presidency as a crown to his career. For his part, President Ford was sufficiently self-confident so as not to fear that Rockefeller's long-established reputation in politics and government would overshadow his own.

On August 20, after soliciting the views of Republicans in Congress and around the country, President Ford announced his selection, to wide press and public acclaim. (Ford had worried that prominent party conservatives, like Sen. Barry Goldwater of Arizona and Sen. John G. Tower of Texas, might oppose a Rockefeller nomination and was pleased to find that they did not.) Shortly afterward, Rockefeller declared that he would not campaign in the fall congressional elections until his nomination as vice president had been confirmed. This may have been a tactical error—Congress, controlled by Democrats who had no desire to see Rockefeller out on the campaign trail, responded by dragging its feet in considering his nomination. The Senate Rules Committee did not begin its hearings until September 23; the House Judiciary Committee waited until November 21. Meanwhile, the FBI, at Congress's request, conducted an even more extensive investigation into Rockefeller's background than it had into Ford's—more than three hundred agents interviewed more than fourteen hundred sources.

For all the delay, there seemed little doubt at the outset of the congressional confirmation process that ap-

Gerald R. Ford Library

On December 6, 1973, Gerald R. Ford was sworn in as vice president by Chief Justice Warren Burger before a joint session of Congress, with President Nixon in attendance. Ford replaced Spiro T. Agnew who resigned.

proval of Rockefeller's nomination to be vice president would be forthcoming. But two political bombshells exploded during the course of the Senate hearings that clouded his prospects. First, Rockefeller disclosed that during the previous seventeen years he had given $1.97 million in gifts to twenty present and former staff members, including $625,000 to William Ronan, the chairman of the Port Authority of New York and New Jersey, and $50,000 to Henry A. Kissinger, a former Rockefeller aide who currently was President Ford's secretary of state. Second, the FBI suggested to the House Judiciary Committee that Rockefeller, through intermediaries, may have financed the writing of a critical biography of his Democratic opponent in the 1970 New York gubernatorial election. (The book, written by Victor J. Lasky, was called *Arthur J. Goldberg: The Old and the New.*) The fundamental question that both incidents seemed to raise was whether Rockefeller had used his wealth to buy political power.

Rockefeller defended the practice of giving financial gifts to aides on the grounds that it had enabled them to stay in public service despite relatively low salaries. He claimed that his long record of public service demonstrated his commitment to the public interest rather than to personal gain. He also offered a "sincere and unqualified apology" to Goldberg. Both congressional committees probed deeply into the issue of Rockefeller's wealth—in contrast to the Ford hearings, 77 percent of the questions asked by members of the Senate Rules Committee, and 63 percent of those asked by members of the House Judiciary Committee, concerned "personal" matters. (Seven percent of the Senate committee's questions and 13 percent of the House committee's questions dealt with institutional matters; 16 percent of the Senate committee's questions and 24 percent of the House committee's questions involved issues.)[12] Annoyed by the amount of time that Congress was taking to probe into Rockefeller's background, President Ford stated in a news conference November 14 that it was time for Congress to "fish or cut bait." He further urged that the Twenty-fifth Amendment be altered to impose a time limit on congressional confirmation of vice-presidential nominations. The nation "needs a vice president at all times," Ford argued.

Prodded by Ford and persuaded by Rockefeller's testimony, the Senate Rules Committee approved the nomination on November 22, by a 9-0 vote. On December 10, the full Senate voted 90-7 for confirmation. Approval by the House Judiciary Committee came on December 12, by a vote of 26-12; on December 19, the full House voted 287-128 in Rockefeller's favor, completing the process of confirmation four months after Ford had made his nomination. Immediately after the House voted, President Ford and Rockefeller went to the Senate chamber, where Rockefeller was sworn in as vice president by Chief Justice Warren Burger.

Some commentators marked the irony that on July 4, 1976, the bicentennial of the nation's birth, the government was presided over by an unelected president and an unelected vice president. That no question was raised about the legitimate right to rule of either President Ford or Vice President Rockefeller seemed powerful testimony to the confidence Americans have in the Constitution. Nonetheless, within a short time, both were expelled from office. In response to pressure from conservatives in the Republican party, Ford encouraged Rockefeller to withdraw as a possible candidate for renomination in the 1976 election. Rockefeller complied, making him only the second vice president in the twentieth century to be dropped from the ticket after only one term. For his own part, Ford ran for president in 1976, was barely renominated by his party, and narrowly lost in the general election. He thus became the century's only successor president not to be elected to a term in his own right.

Temporary Succession When the President Is Disabled

Presidential disability was a minor concern at the Constitutional Convention, a recurring inconvenience during much of U.S. history, and a potentially grave crisis in the nuclear age. *(See "Disability," p. 26, and "Twenty-fifth Amendment," p. 48, in Constitutional Beginnings chapter of Part I.)*

The original Constitution provided that, as in the case of a president's death, resignation, or impeachment and removal, "in case of ... Inability [of the president] to discharge the Powers and Duties of the said Office, the Same shall devolve on the Vice President ... until the Disability be removed, or a President shall be elected." No debate accompanied the enactment of this clause, so it is impossible to determine what the delegates meant by "inability" or "disability." Nor was any procedure created to determine whether a president was disabled.

By one estimate, eleven presidents who served in the period 1789-1967 were disabled during at least part of their administration, including Garfield, who hovered near death for eighty days after being shot in 1881, and Woodrow Wilson, who was felled by a stroke in 1917 that incapacitated him during most of his final seventeen months in office.[13] Discussions took place within both presidents' cabinets about transferring power to the vice president, but the absence of constitutional guidance made them reluctant to act.

Presidential disability became a pressing issue after World War II, with the invention of nuclear weapons launched by intercontinental ballistic missiles. Awareness spread that the nation no longer could afford to be leaderless even for brief periods—the president might be called on at a moment's notice to make a decision that could literally destroy the world. After a series of severe health problems in the mid-1950s, President Dwight D. Eisenhower improvised an arrangement with Vice President Richard Nixon under which Eisenhower, by letter, would temporarily transfer the powers and duties of the presidency to Nixon if he again were disabled. The arrangement also provided that Nixon could take those powers if the president were unable to transfer them voluntarily. Presidents John Kennedy and Lyndon Johnson made similar arrangements with their vice presidents.

In 1965, a constitutional answer was offered to the disability question when Congress proposed the Twenty-fifth Amendment (ratified by the states in 1967). Although the amendment did not define *disability,* it created a set of procedures for determining when a president is disabled and for transferring the powers and duties of the presidency to the vice president until the disability is ended.

The amendment authorizes a disabled president to make the vice president acting president simply by sending a letter to the Speaker of the House of Representatives and the president pro tempore of the Senate. (The president, when once again able, can regain the powers and duties of the office by writing another letter.) Should the president be unable or unwilling to declare that a disability exists, the vice president *and* a majority of the heads of the departments may declare the vice president to be acting president. Again, a letter from the president to the leaders of Congress would restore the president to power. But if the vice president and a majority of the cabinet were to disagree with the president's claim of restored capacity, Congress would have to decide who was right. (In the meantime, to prevent the president from simply firing the cabinet, Congress could substitute another body for it.) Unless two-thirds of both the House and Senate sided with the vice president and the cabinet, the president's claim would prevail.

George Bush, who served with President Ronald Reagan, is the only vice president to have become acting president under the Twenty-fifth Amendment. Criticism of Reagan and his aides for not transferring the powers and duties of the presidency to the vice president when Reagan was shot in 1981 prompted the president to send the constitutionally required letter to congressional leaders before undergoing cancer surgery in 1985. Bush spent his eight hours as acting president at home, playing tennis, and chatting with friends.

Notes

1. Joel K. Goldstein, *The Modern Vice Presidency* (Princeton, N.J.: Princeton University Press, 1982), 207-208.
2. See, for example, Ruth C. Silva, *Presidential Succession* (Ann Arbor: University of Michigan Press, 1951); Edward S. Corwin, *The President: Office and Powers,* 4th ed. (New York: New York University Press, 1957), chap. 2; and John D. Feerick, *From Falling Hands: The Story of Presidential Succession* (New York: Fordham University Press, 1965), chap. 1.
3. Leonard Dinnerstein, "The Accession of John Tyler to the Presidency," *The Virginia Magazine of History and Biography* 70, no. 4 (October 1962): 447-458; Stephen W. Stathis, "John Tyler's Presidential Succession: A Reappraisal," *Prologue* 8, no. 4 (Winter 1976): 223-236.
4. Amendments to the Constitution only clouded the issue. The Twelfth Amendment (1804) seemed to suggest, albeit offhandedly and not by clear congressional intent, that the vice president was to be acting president. In providing for the failure of both the electoral college and the House of Representatives to elect a president by the scheduled start of the term, the amendment said that "the Vice President shall act as President, as in the case of the death or other constitutional disability of the President." The provision was replaced in 1933 by the Twentieth Amendment, which said more blandly that, if a president had not been elected by inauguration day, "the Vice President shall act as President until a President shall have qualified." The Twenty-second Amendment (1951) left the matter explicitly unresolved, stating that "no person who has held the office of President, or acted as President for more than two years of a term to which some other person was elected President shall be elected to the office of the President more than once."
5. Nor had the 1792 act provided for the possibility that there might not be a qualified Senate president or House Speaker should the need arise. Yet congressional leaders, unlike presidents, need not be natural-born citizens or thirty-five years old. (Henry Clay was elected Speaker at age thirty-four in 1811.)
6. Quoted in Arthur M. Schlesinger, Jr., *The Cycles of American History* (Boston: Houghton Mifflin, 1986), 351.
7. Not until January 6 does Congress count the electoral votes and declare who is elected, after an opportunity is provided to consider objections to any of the votes. Walter Berns, ed., *After the People Vote: Steps in Choosing the President* (Washington, D.C.: American Enterprise Institute, 1983), 19-20.
8. No presidential nominee has ever failed to live until or qualify for election. In 1912, Vice President James S. Sherman, the

Republican nominee for reelection as vice president, died on October 30. The Republican National Committee replaced him with Nicholas Murray Butler, the president of Columbia University. In 1972, the Democratic vice-presidential nominee, Thomas Eagleton, withdrew from the ticket when information was uncovered shortly after the convention about treatments for mental illness that he had undergone. The Democratic National Committee, which was responsible for filling vacancies on the ticket until 1988, approved presidential nominee George McGovern's nomination of ex-Peace Corps director Sargent Shriver for vice president.

9. John D. Feerick, *The Twenty-fifth Amendment* (New York: Fordham University Press, 1975), 59.
10. Quotations from the debate over the proposed Twenty-fifth Amendment and from the Ford and Rockefeller confirmations are drawn from Feerick, *Twenty-Fifth Amendment.*
11. Goldstein, *Modern American Vice Presidency,* 242-243.
12. Ibid., 245.
13. The other temporarily disabled presidents, according to John D. Feerick, were: James Madison, William Henry Harrison, Chester A. Arthur, Grover Cleveland, William McKinley, Warren G. Harding, Franklin D. Roosevelt, Dwight D. Eisenhower, and John F. Kennedy (Feerick, *The Twenty-fifth Amendment,* chap. 1).

Selected Bibliography

Berns, Walter, ed. *After the People Vote: Steps in Choosing the President.* Washington, D.C.: American Enterprise Institute, 1983.

Corwin, Edward S. *The President: Office and Powers.* 5th ed. New York: New York University Press, 1984.

Feerick, John D. *From Falling Hands: The Story of Presidential Succession.* New York: Fordham University Press, 1965.

——. *The Twenty-fifth Amendment.* New York: Fordham University Press, 1975.

Goldstein, Joel K. *The Modern Vice Presidency.* Princeton, N.J.: Princeton University Press, 1982.

Silva, Ruth C. *Presidential Succession.* Ann Arbor: University of Michigan Press, 1951

Removal of the President

The four-year presidential term specified in the Constitution may be cut short by one of three events: death (from either natural causes or assassination), impeachment, or resignation. As of 1988, nine of the forty men who have served as president have failed to serve out the term of office to which they were elected for one of these reasons.

During the first fifty years of the Republic, the American political system did not encounter any of these eventualities. It was only upon the death of President William Henry Harrison in 1841 that the possibility of a nonelectorally triggered executive succession became a reality. Since that time three other presidents have died in office of natural causes: Zachary Taylor in 1850, Warren G. Harding in 1923, and Franklin D. Roosevelt in 1945. Abraham Lincoln was the first president to be felled by an assassin (1865), followed by James A. Garfield (1881), William McKinley (1901), and John F. Kennedy (1963). Two presidents—Andrew Johnson in 1868 and Richard Nixon in 1974—faced the serious possibility of being removed from office through impeachment. Johnson survived the impeachment attempt and completed his term of office; Nixon short-circuited the possibility of removal through impeachment by becoming the first president in American history to resign from office.

Issues in Presidential Succession

Article II, section 1, of the Constitution requires that both the president and the vice president "be elected" and provides for succession as follows:

> In Case of the Removal of the President from Office, or of his Death, Resignation, or Inability to discharge the Powers and Duties of the said Office, the Same shall devolve on the Vice President, and the Congress may by Law provide for the Case of Removal, Death, Resignation or Inability, both of the President and Vice President, declaring what Officer shall then act as President, and such Officer shall act accordingly, until the Disability be removed, or a President shall be elected.

This section eventually gave rise to three issues. The first concerned the status of a vice president who succeeded upon a disability or a vacancy in the presidency. Some historians have argued that the Founders intended "a Vice President or an officer designated by Congress merely to *act* as president" and not actually inherit the office.[1] This interpretation was disproved by the test of the first vice-presidential succession, in 1841. Although controversy ensued when John Tyler succeeded William Henry Harrison, Tyler became president rather than simply a vice president acting as president. When Zachary Taylor died in office less than a decade later, no one questioned the new interpretation or the vice president's right to full successorship.

The second issue was the congressional practice of providing for a line of succession when unexpected vacancies occurred in both the presidency and the vice presidency. Congress has passed succession acts three times. While the same set of officers was considered part of the legitimate line of succession in all three acts, the succession law of 1792 began the line, after the vice president, with the president pro tempore of the Senate followed by the Speaker of the House of Representatives. Either of these officials would have become acting president, and provision was made for a special election. In 1886 Congress passed a law that dropped the special election provision and shifted the succession to the cabinet, starting with the secretary of state and working through the cabinet in the order in which departments were established. Finally in 1947, at the request of successor president Harry S Truman, Congress again changed the order to begin with the Speaker of the House, followed by the president pro tempore of the Senate and the cabinet secretaries in rank seniority order.[2]

The third issue—hinted at but not dealt with explicitly—was presidential disability. Just as experience helped solve the "easier" succession problems, it also spurred efforts to formalize disability procedures. This did not occur until passage of the Twenty-fifth Amendment in 1967, which still leaves many questions unanswered. *(See "Twenty-fifth Amendment (1967)," p. 48, in Constitutional Beginnings chapter of Part I.)*

Over the history of the presidency three circumstantial conditions have emerged as being vital to workable and legitimate presidential succession arrangements. First, the succession must be certain; there should be no question about who will accede to the presidency. This assurance is particularly important for successor presidents, who will lack the customary legitimacy of electoral endorsement. Vice presidents are not elected in their own right; they are merely the running mate of the president.

By Margaret Jane Wyszomirski

Second, the succession must be speedy, if not immediate. While a short time lag might have been acceptable in earlier years when the pace and magnitude of national affairs were not so great, it is now imperative that there be a president. The need for a speedy transition always has been implicit, and all possible haste has been employed in notifying and administering the oath of office to the successor president.

Third, the provisions for presidential succession must be mindful of maintaining political continuity. While each past successor president has pledged to maintain the policies of his predecessor and to remain faithful to his programmatic legacy, this often has been a problem in practice. Vice presidents generally maintain partisan continuity, but since originally many were chosen for their differences from the presidential candidate to better balance an electoral ticket, they may be naturally predisposed to policy or philosophical positions that differ from those of their predecessors. The more profound these differences, the more difficulties these successors have faced in maintaining their political support and effectively exercising presidential power and leadership. Similar problems might afflict congressional leaders or cabinet members should succession proceed that far.

If succession passed to the congressional leadership, other problems might arise as well. For example, the Speaker of the House or the president pro tempore of the Senate might not belong to the same party as the president they are replacing. While such an eventuality has never occurred in this nation's history, it has become highly probable during the modern presidency, which frequently has seen different parties in control of the White House and of Congress.

Death from Natural Causes

Four presidents have died in office of natural causes: two in the nineteenth century (William Henry Harrison in 1841 and Zachary Taylor in 1850) and two in the twentieth century (Warren Harding in 1923 and Franklin Roosevelt in 1945). The natural death of a president is less traumatic than an assassination because it generally follows a period of illness in which both public sentiment and the political system have begun to prepare themselves for a transition of leadership. Nonetheless, the death of a president is an occasion of public loss.

This loss seems particularly acute in two circumstances. One is when a new president's term is mortally terminated soon after assumption of office—for example, the death of President Harrison only a few short months after entering office—leaving a sense of unfulfilled potential and unrealized expectations. The other circumstance is when a long-serving and popular president dies in office, thereby closing an era of familiar and effective leadership. The death of President Franklin Roosevelt after serving for more than twelve years in the presidency was a case in point. Indeed, when Roosevelt died he left behind an entire political generation that had never known any other model of the presidency.

While the natural death of a president allows the political system some opportunity to plan for the succession, presidential illnesses are always viewed with optimism for recovery or improvement, thus impeding the effort and weakening the desire to plan for the eventual transition. In fact, the onset of illness in the presidency is usually an unexpected occurrence; frequently, concern for the health of prospective presidents is raised during election campaigns. In only one case—that of Franklin Roosevelt in 1944—has a public aware (although not fully informed) of an incumbent's failing health chosen to reelect a president who had little chance of serving out his term in office.

William Henry Harrison

William Henry Harrison, a frontier general and war hero who became famous in the 1811 Battle of Tippecanoe and later fought in the War of 1812 as the commander in chief of the Army of the Northwest, was one of the first presidential candidates to be selected by a national party convention. The 1840 Whig convention that nominated Harrison of Ohio as its presidential standard-bearer also endorsed John Tyler, a Democrat from Virginia, to be his running mate. Despite Tyler's party stance and his opposition to important Whig programs—including protective tariffs, internal improvements, and a national bank—he was nonetheless acceptable to the Whigs because he was a staunch defender of states' rights and because he could help win the electoral votes of the southern states.[3] The 1840 Whig convention adopted no party platform, and the campaign generally avoided serious discussion of public issues. Thus, any policy differences between Harrison and his running mate remained muted.

The Whig ticket of the hero of "Tippecanoe and Tyler too" easily defeated its Democratic opponents, and, at age sixty-eight, Harrison became the oldest president to be inaugurated to that date. Although he came to office without a clearly defined program, he was, as his biographer James A. Green has noted, "a President around whom more high hopes were centered, from whom more was expected and who enjoyed a greater degree of the love and affection of the people than any of his fellows since the days of Washington."[4]

Harrison launched his administration with great promise and public impression. Upon being sworn in on the east portico of the Capitol by Supreme Court chief justice Roger B. Taney on March 4, 1841, Harrison proceeded to deliver the longest inaugural address in history. For two hours the new president stood in the cold March weather without hat or coat and delivered an address that was printed immediately by Horace Greeley's *Daily National Intelligencer* and distributed as far away as New York City within the unprecedented time of ten hours.[5] Thus, within hours of taking office Harrison's presidential presence and style had been conveyed, via the press, to a broader public than theretofore possible.

Harrison then assembled a distinguished cabinet, composed of men with national reputations. Among others, it included Daniel Webster as secretary of state, Thomas Ewing as head of the Treasury, and John J. Crittenden as attorney general. With the core of his administration in place, the president called Congress into special session—scheduled for May 31—to consider the nation's revenue and finance policies.[6] And, because the Whig administration had displaced the Democratic governments of Andrew Jackson and Martin Van Buren, Harrison found himself besieged with Whig office seekers and pressed by the attendant problems of staffing a new government and rewarding partisan supporters. Thus the president quickly found himself nearly overwhelmed by the daily cabinet meetings, the incessant visitors, and the numerous social events.

Fatigued by this initial schedule, President Harrison appears to have been caught in a rain shower during his morning walk on March 27, and he subsequently took to his bed with a cold. Initially, he was diagnosed as having pneumonia, but later consulting physicians found Harrison's condition to be complicated by congestion of the liver and neuralgia, and they changed their diagnosis to bilious pleurisy. Consequently, the president was subjected to a host of different, and at times contradictory, remedies, only to have his condition worsen.[7] On April 4, 1841, a week after taking ill and a mere month after taking office, William Henry Harrison became the first American president to die in office.

Upon Harrison's death Secretary of State Daniel Webster dispatched his son Fletcher, who was chief clerk in the State Department, to notify Vice President Tyler at his home in Williamsburg, Virginia. Tyler immediately set out for Washington, arriving on April 6. Upon meeting informally with members of the cabinet, the vice president asked them all to continue to serve in their present positions, and he indicated that he intended to remain faithful to Harrison's policies. Tyler then took the presidential oath of office. Some observers believed that Tyler did not need to take the presidential oath because his vice-presidential oath required him to discharge the succession duty if necessary. William Cranch, chief judge of the Circuit Court of the District of Columbia, who administered the presidential oath to Tyler, noted that although the vice president considered himself qualified to perform the duties and exercise the powers of the office of the president without more than his prior vice-presidential oath, he nonetheless took the presidential oath of office "for greater caution" and to allay any doubts that might arise.[8]

In taking the presidential oath of office, Tyler set what later became known as the "Tyler Precedent," whereby the vice president succeeds to the office of the president upon the death of an elected president, rather than merely assuming responsibility for its powers and duties. Indeed, there was some political opposition to this interpretation, including that of former president John Quincy Adams, who was then a Whig member of the House from Massachusetts. Adams maintained that Tyler did not become president; rather he was acting as president upon the death of President Harrison. Webster countered that the office and the powers of the presidency were inseparable; therefore, the vice president assumed the responsibilities and the office of the president when the president died in office. Similarly, the leading Whig newspaper of the day, the *Daily National Intelligencer,* argued: "By this original election as Vice President, he was provisionally elected President; that is elected to the office of President upon the happening of any one of the conditions provided in the Constitution."[9]

Although President Tyler succeeded in establishing the status of an accidental president, two other unresolved problems would trouble future successor presidents. One was the issue of the line of succession beyond the vice president. This issue arose in February 1844 when a naval gun on board the first propeller-driven warship, the U.S.S. *Princeton,* exploded during a demonstration while the ship was on an inspection cruise. The explosion killed the secretaries of state and navy as well as five other people on board and wounded eleven more. President Tyler, who was below deck at the time, escaped injury. Since his accession to the presidency, Tyler had served without a vice president. Thus, according to the succession law of 1792, if Tyler had been killed in this incident, the presidency would have passed on to a legislative officer, the president pro tempore of the Senate, Whig senator Willie P. Mangum of North Carolina.[10]

Library of Congress

Within a mere month of his inauguration, William Henry Harrison became the first president to die in office. In memorium, many Americans wore armbands like this one.

The second problem—and one of more immediate political significance—was the continuation of policy between the successor president and his elected predecessor. Although Tyler had intended to maintain Harrison's policies, his administration became notable for its opposition to various Whig programs as President Tyler's original Democratic sentiments reasserted themselves. Tyler's September 1841 veto of a bill proposing the establishment of a national bank resulted in the wholesale resignation of his entire cabinet, except Daniel Webster. Two days after this mass resignation, President Tyler was expelled officially from the Whig party by a caucus of congressional Whigs.

In part, the Tyler case may have raised the problem of political continuity with particular clarity because Tyler was the first vice president to accede to the presidency and because the elected president died so early in his term of office. Another important factor was that Tyler was a member of the opposition party who had been brought onto the Whig national ticket as a campaign tactic without thought given to the possibility that he actually might succeed to office if President Harrison died.

Despite these problems, Tyler's administration was responsible for a number of achievements, among them reorganization of the U.S. Navy, establishment of a weather bureau, negotiation of a trade treaty with China, termination of the Seminole War, and the successful annexation of Texas into the United States.[11] Perhaps his most lasting legacy was the Tyler Precedent, which established that a vice president succeeded to the presidency upon the death of the elected president.

Zachary Taylor

Less than a decade after William Henry Harrison died in office, the twelfth president, Zachary Taylor, died after having served only sixteen months of his term. Upon his death Vice President Millard Fillmore succeeded to the presidency. No one questioned his status or suggested that he merely was acting as president; thus the Tyler Precedent was confirmed.

Zachary Taylor was the first member of the regular army to become president. During his more than forty years in the army, he advanced rapidly, first winning merit as an Indian fighter and later becoming the hero of the Mexican War. "Old Rough and Ready" (as his troops called him) was a man of meager formal schooling. Taylor knew little of law and government, and he had no interest in politics before becoming president in 1849. It is said that before his nomination in 1848, Taylor had never cast a vote in his life. The Whig party nominated Taylor with little knowledge of where he stood on the issues of the day; rather, it sought his general appeal as a war hero and his diverse sectional appeal—to the South as a southern slaveholder and to the North where his military record was admired. Millard Fillmore of New York was the compromise choice to be his running mate.

During the campaign of 1848 Taylor adopted a low-profile strategy. He remained on active duty throughout the campaign as commander of the Western Division and relied on his reputation as Old Rough and Ready to attract the voters. Meanwhile, more adept Whig politicians, led by John Crittenden, actually waged the campaign and spoke for the presidential nominee.[12]

Upon his election Taylor delayed his arrival in Washington, D.C., to begin assembling his administration. His resignation from the army did not become effective until February 28, 1849—less than a week before the inauguration. Taylor, unlike virtually all of his predecessors, came to the presidency with no political experience or acumen; rather he possessed the "naive assumption that good intentions and a genuine dedication to the common good would triumph." He also took office with a less well-formed administration and less well-defined policies than any of his predecessors.[13]

Taylor's election did little to unite or strengthen the Whig party, which largely was held together by its opposition to the Jackson Democrats. Whig party leaders Daniel Webster and Henry Clay declined to join Taylor's cabinet, as did the architect of Taylor's successful campaign strategy, John Crittenden. Taylor thus was able to assemble only a relatively weak cabinet of secondary party leaders. These officials did not even perform effectively for the duration of Taylor's tenure. By the time the president died at age sixty-five, six of his seven cabinet members were under heavy partisan attack for abuse of patronage, corruption, and incompetence. Indeed, shortly before his death President Taylor had decided that he would replace his entire cabinet, and he was in the process of selecting a new official family. Thus, his successor, Millard Fillmore, did not inherit a strong cabinet on which he could rely during his early months in office.[14]

In 1850 the nation and Congress was in the middle of the debate over California's statehood and admission to the Union, with the attendant problem of retaining the senatorial balance between free and slave states. The more general, and thorny, questions concerned conditions for the admission of new states in the southwest territories, the retention of slavery in the South, and how to deal with fugitive slaves. In the midst of this intense controversy, in which the country seemed to totter on the brink of civil war, President Taylor was taken ill.

During a long Fourth of July celebration the president apparently became overheated and thus consumed large quantities of ice water, chilled milk, and fresh cherries—all items that Washingtonians had been warned away from for fear of an Asiatic cholera epidemic that was sweeping parts of the country. Over the next two days the president began to develop various symptoms, diagnosed by army surgeon Dr. Alexander Witherspoon as cholera morbus, a catchall nineteenth-century term for various intestinal maladies not related to the dread Asiatic cholera. Initially, President Taylor responded to treatment, but then he began to weaken, to develop intermittent fevers, and eventually to suffer intense dysentery and vomiting. By July 8 the president was predicting that "in two days I shall be a dead man." Late in the evening of July 9, 1850, President Taylor bid farewell to his wife, Margaret Smith Taylor, beseeching her not to grieve, and said: "I have always done my duty. I am ready to die. My only regret is for the friends I leave behind me." Soon thereafter he lost consciousness and died.

Vice President Fillmore was notified immediately, as was the cabinet, which formally announced the death of the president. The next day at noon in the House of Representatives, Millard Fillmore took the presidential oath of office and became the thirteenth president of the United States. The oath was administered by William Cranch, the same federal justice who had sworn in John Tyler as the first successor president in 1841. Congress appointed a joint committee to make funeral arrangements and delivered a round of eulogies. On Friday, July 12, a public viewing of the body was held in the East Room of the White House, and a funeral was scheduled for the following day. An estimated 100,000 people congregated along the funeral route.

It often was said that Vice President Fillmore looked more like a president than President Taylor.[15] Despite appearances, however, the vice president had played only a minor role in the Taylor administration. Although Fillmore was a national political figure by virtue of his leadership of the House Ways and Means Committee at the time of his nomination, he lacked a strong political base in his home state of New York because he was in opposition to the dominant Seward-Weed faction of the New York Whigs.[16] Prior to the 1849 inauguration, Fillmore had called upon the president-elect to discuss possible cabinet appointments, only to be informed that Taylor already had made those decisions after consulting John Crittenden for advice. As Whig senator William H. Seward from New York increasingly won Taylor's confidence and friendship over the course of the administration, it had the effect of freezing out another New Yorker—Millard Fillmore—from influence with the president.[17] Thus, Fillmore succeeded to the presidency following only a distant relationship with his predecessor. The discredited cabinet that he inherited tendered their pro forma resignations to the new president, and he accepted them all. Although Fillmore asked the cabinet to stay on for a month to afford a smooth transition, the disgruntled officials agreed to remain for only one week, thus plunging the new president into feverish activity to establish a new administration.[18]

Fillmore also inherited the smoldering tension between the North and South and their free and slave interests. President Taylor had indicated his intention to veto any omnibus compromise bill, thereby limiting the possibilities for successfully defusing the territorial issues crisis. In contrast, Fillmore the experienced legislator took a more flexible stance, seeking peace as his primary goal. With strategic presidential maneuvering and the herculean efforts of Whig senators Daniel Webster (Massachusetts) and Popular Sovereign Democrat senator Stephen A. Douglas (Illinois), a set of bills was enacted and signed by September that effected the Great Compromise of 1850.[19] Although this achievement helped postpone war for a decade, Fillmore's signing of the Fugitive Slave Act weakened his political position in both the North and the South.

Increasingly, Fillmore found himself in a lame duck position, losing support from his own party while confronting a divisive political situation. From the very beginning of his presidency Fillmore exhibited no strong desire for a second term and was ambivalent about the possibility of seeking or accepting renomination. In 1852 Daniel Webster was intent upon making a last, although ultimately weak, bid for the nomination. Fillmore's rival, William Seward, was championing the candidacy of Winfield Scott. When the Whig convention met in Baltimore, it became clear that neither anti-Scott candidate—Fillmore or Webster—had the votes necessary for victory. After forty-six ballots, the convention remained stalemated and suspended proceedings for Sunday, June 20. During this hiatus both Webster and Fillmore simultaneously but separately decided that they would withdraw and that each would throw his support to the other. When he realized the coincidence, Fillmore tried to retract his withdrawal, but in the ensuing confusion convention support shifted to Scott, who finally succeeded in winning the nomination on the fifty-third ballot.[20] Four years later Fillmore attempted another run at the presidency as the candidate of the American, or Know-Nothing, party, only to suffer a humiliating defeat, while carrying only the state of Maryland. Thus, like President Tyler, Fillmore inherited the office, powers, and responsibilities of his predecessor, but not his general popularity or political support. Consequently, both saw the erosion of their political position, culminating in their rejection for renomination in the next election.

Warren G. Harding

Warren G. Harding's editorials for the *Marion Star* in Marion County, Ohio, provided a platform for his entry into public office. He won election to the state senate, ran unsuccessfully for lieutenant governor, and eventually gained a seat in the U.S. Senate. His 1914 campaign for the Senate demonstrated that he was a strong vote-getter in a changing electoral system. Harding won the Republican nomination for the Senate seat in the first statewide direct primary in Ohio's history. Later, he won the general election with a majority of 100,000 votes in the first popular election of senators since passage of the Seventeenth Amendment.[21]

In Washington, Harding proved an affable colleague but an unimpressive legislator. Nevertheless, he rose in the ranks of the Republican party, which selected him to deliver the keynote address at its national convention in 1916 and thereafter elected him permanent chairman. As a member of the powerful Senate Foreign Relations Committee, Harding was immersed in the controversy over the League of Nations treaty. His decision to side with the anti-League reservationists provided a useful launching pad for his presidential campaign in 1920. Conducting a masterful and gentlemanly campaign, Harding seemed to personify the "normalcy" that he advocated restoring. As historian Robert K. Murray has noted, "Harding represented solid ground, stability, a return to national tranquility."[22] The public responded overwhelmingly, electing Harding in a landslide that constituted the largest popular majority recorded to that date in the nation's history (60.2 percent). He carried thirty-seven of the forty-eight states. In addition, his party seized control of the House of Representatives (303-131), while acquiring a majority of twenty-two seats in the Senate.[23]

At first, Harding enjoyed the public role of the presidency, but later he began to feel almost overwhelmed by the scope of his executive responsibilities. Labor strikes, recurring difficulties over patronage, the problems of dealing with a resurgent Congress following the League of Nations battle, and the difficulties of enforcing Prohibition all combined to make Harding feel inadequate and unhappy as president. By the fall of 1922 the president had begun to lapse into a general mental depression that was only compounded by the illness of his wife, Florence Kling De Wolfe Harding, whose kidney ailment put her almost at death's door for six weeks during September and October. Then in 1923, as the improprieties that would become known collectively as the Teapot Dome scandal began to emerge, Harding's own health suffered as his worry and anxiety mounted. An attack of influenza in January of that year triggered a rapid deterioration in his health; his blood pressure rose precariously, and he was generally listless and tired.

Despite these inauspicious circumstances, President Harding launched a much-publicized cross-country trip to Alaska in mid-June. Intended in part to resolve administrative in-fighting over the management of the territory and its resources and in part to be a grand politicking junket, the trip included a heavy speaking schedule. The president's itinerary called for travel by rail through St. Louis, Kansas City, Denver, Salt Lake City, Helena, Spokane, Portland, and Tacoma, from where he would sail to Alaska. He was to return three weeks later through Vancouver, Seattle, San Francisco, Los Angeles, and San Diego, before boarding a ship for the return trip to Washington via the Panama Canal and Puerto Rico. As Harding progressed on this two-month-long trip, he delivered speeches, often in searing heat, outlining his political and economic beliefs and elaborating on his December 1922 State of the Union message.[24]

The first part of the journey went well, but by late July the president was tiring noticeably and experiencing nausea and abdominal pains and a rapid pulse rate. By July 29 it was clear that Harding was suffering from both cardiac problems and bronchopneumonia. By August 1, however, the president had appeared to rally. It thus was announced that the crisis had passed and the presidential party would soon return to Washington. On the night of August 2, as Mrs. Harding was reading to the president while he was propped up on pillows in bed at a San Francisco hotel, Harding twisted convulsively. She immediately ran from the room calling for the doctors, who administered stimulants to the president's heart but to no avail. President Harding was dead. Officially, the death warrant reads "apoplexy," but the actual cause of death remains uncertain. It may have been a cerebral hemorrhage caused by a burst sclerotic blood vessel in the brain or a ruptured wall of the heart—either cause related to the president's high blood pressure.

A cross-country funeral procession followed, as throughout the nation people turned out to mourn the president's passing. The crowds were immense; an estimated million and a half people lined the rails in Chicago alone. Pennies were placed on the tracks to be flattened by the passing funeral train and retrieved as historic souvenirs. Arriving in Washington on the evening of August 7, the president's casket was placed in the East Room where Mrs. Harding maintained a solitary vigil. The next morning the coffin was carried on a caisson to the Capitol and placed in the rotunda; ten truckloads of flowers banked the walls. After a brief service and a viewing by over thirty-five thousand mourners, the casket was borne to Union Station for the final train trip back to Marion, Ohio, for burial.

Between August 4 and President Harding's burial on August 10 the nation was in an official period of mourning. The world press deplored the loss of "a man of peace," and many observers remarked that his devotion to his job had made him a martyr to the presidency.[25] Secretary of Commerce Herbert C. Hoover captured the public sentiment about Harding's passing: "When he came into responsibility as President he faced unprecedented problems of domestic rehabilitation. It was a time when war-stirred emotions had created bitter prejudices and conflict in thought. Kindly and genial, but inflexible in his devotion to duty, he was strong in his determination to restore confidence and secure progress." [26]

The mantle of office then fell to Vice President Calvin Coolidge as his father, a notary public, administered the oath of office to his son, who was vacationing at the family home in Plymouth, Vermont. Coolidge had been the Republican convention's choice as a running mate for Harding in 1920. As governor of Massachusetts, Coolidge had won national recognition during a Boston police strike when he declared, "There is no right to strike against the public safety by anybody, anywhere, any time." [27] Harding, however, did not seem to find Coolidge personally compatible, and he did not rely on Coolidge for advice or much campaign support. Indeed, Coolidge was not an exciting stump speaker and avoided such occasions whenever possible. Upon his election as vice president, Coolidge received a congratulatory message from the current vice president, Thomas R. Marshall: "Please accept my sincere sympathy." [28]

After the ticket had triumphed, Coolidge made few contributions to the Harding administration. He participated in neither political nor administrative decision, although he did sit with the cabinet at its Tuesday and Friday meetings as an ex officio member. Instead, Coolidge acquired many social responsibilities, becoming the "official diner-out of the administration." [29] He also spent considerable time at the Capitol where he found presiding over the Senate a fascinating experience. Being taciturn and somewhat somber and aloof, Coolidge was a marked contrast to the gregarious and affable Harding. Yet these characteristics stood him in good stead upon his succession, because they set him apart from the poker-playing, carousing, and scandalous image that eventually tarnished the Harding administration when the Teapot Dome scandal was uncovered after Harding's death. *(See "Teapot Dome and Other Scandals," p. 108, in History of the Presidency chapter of Part I.)*

Initially, the change from Harding to Coolidge was more a matter of style than of top-level personnel or programs. The Harding cabinet was retained until public and congressional pressure forced out two members, Secretary of the Navy Edwin Denby and Attorney General Harry M. Daugherty. Not until after the election of 1924 did Coolidge take the initiative and make significant changes in cabinet, ambassadorial, and regulatory personnel.

Upon announcing Harding's death Coolidge pledged to continue the policies of the Harding administration. In foreign affairs he thus supported the collection of all war debts, U.S. participation in the World Court, and improved relations with Latin and South America. In domestic and economic affairs Coolidge promised to follow the Harding lead to further restrict immigration, to seek economy in government, to maintain protective tariffs, and to aid the farmer. Like his predecessor, Coolidge was opposed to the recognition of the Soviet government in Russia and to the payment of a soldiers' bonus at home.[30] And unlike many earlier successor presidents who failed to honor initial pledges of continuity, Coolidge remained remarkably faithful to the legacy of his predecessor until after 1925.

When Coolidge entered office on August 3, 1923, Congress as not in session and would not return until December. Europe was in disarray and devastated from World War I, the Philippines were in political turmoil, and a domestic coal strike seemed imminent. Administratively, Coolidge soon had to face the legacy of oil scandals and other corruption charges that were only beginning to emerge as he took office.

Unlike many other successor presidents, Coolidge met the challenges of the presidency while retaining the support of his party and of the general public. He also was fortunate that his predecessor had bequeathed to him an economic and political philosophy that was suited to the times. Moreover, Harding's quest for "normalcy" had left few major unsettled policy questions.[31] From the moment in December 1923 when Coolidge formally announced that he would seek a second term, he had little serious opposition within the Republican party. With the disarray in the opposing Democratic party and the general state of business prosperity, circumstances were propitious for Coolidge's political prospects. He thus had no difficulty winning nomination and election to a second term in 1924. In 1927, having occupied the presidency both as a successor and in his own right, Coolidge announced that he would not seek reelection.

Franklin D. Roosevelt

Franklin Roosevelt served as president longer than any other person in American history. Although his death was sudden, rumors about his health had circulated for years. It was alleged that Roosevelt had suffered a series of small strokes as early as 1938, but the president's health was not a serious concern until midway through World War II and his third term of office. Not only were the long years of his tenure and the pace of the wartime presidency wearing on FDR, but the need to consult personally with British prime minister Winston Churchill and Soviet leader Joseph Stalin demanded that Roosevelt undertake frequent international travel to engage in extensive and exhausting conferences. Late in 1943, following one of these wartime conferences in Teheran, Roosevelt underwent a pronounced change in health and vigor as the strain of leadership began to show. During the next four months the president suffered an alarming loss of weight, appetite, and strength. His face became haggard and gaunt, the circles around his eyes deepened, he had a persistent cough, and his concentration began to wander. Indeed, his staff and family became so concerned that they finally prevailed upon him to undergo a thorough medical checkup at Bethesda Naval Hospital in March 1944. The results were not heartening.

Dr. Howard Bruenn, a heart specialist, reported that FDR was suffering from hypertension, a general degeneration of the cardiovascular system, and an enlarged heart. In short, the diagnosis was that Roosevelt was, at sixty-two years old, a seriously ill man, who might, at best, live for another year or two.[32] A program of rest, restricted diet and gradual weight reduction, codeine to control the cough, and digitalis for the heart condition were prescribed. Dr. Bruenn was brought into the White House to serve as the president's physician-in-residence. He was not permitted to discuss the president's condition with anyone (including the patient and his family) except navy surgeon general and White House physician Adm. Ross McIntire. Thus, the state of the president's health was kept a closely guarded secret, even from the president.

During the campaign of 1944 questions were asked frequently about Roosevelt's health, but they were countered largely by the president's increased and vigorous campaigning and by medical reports that claimed to certify his good health. Indeed, FDR's campaign stamina did much to allay fears about his health, particularly his October campaign appearance in New York City, where he rode in an open limousine through a cold rain for a four-hour parade. Exuberant and exhilarated by the experience, the president not only rallied but also seemed to recapture his old buoyancy and energy. It was a masterful performance that reassured the public and stilled talk about his poor health.

Roosevelt won his fourth election to the presidency by a wide electoral college margin (432-99)—and the smallest percentage (53.4 percent) of the popular vote of any of his victories. The weeks following the election were intensely busy, leaving the president little time to rest. Political activities at home, the war effort abroad, as well as plans for the forthcoming Yalta Conference to secure the Soviet entry into the war in the Far East and to begin drawing the map of postwar Europe, all preoccupied Roosevelt and left him exhausted. His 1945 inauguration was brief and somber, and the day was raw and overcast. The president looked pained and haggard as he delivered the shortest inaugural address on record.[33] Two days later Roosevelt left Washington for Yalta to meet with Churchill and Stalin.

When he returned at the end of February his spirit seemed refreshed, but his physical condition was strained. Symptomatic of his decline was the delivery of his report to a joint session of Congress on March 1, 1945. Unprecedentedly, Roosevelt was wheeled to a table below the rostrum, where he delivered his speech seated in the well of the House of Representatives. His speech was halting and imprecise; the effects of twelve years in the presidency were vividly evident and gave rise to renewed morbid speculations about his health. Pale, tired, sometimes listless and depressed, and with the circles around his eyes darkening and his hands trembling, Roosevelt complained of a poor appetite and sleeplessness. Finally, he was persuaded to leave Washington to go to Warm Springs, Georgia, for a long rest and to regain his strength before hosting the upcoming United Nations Conference on International Organization. Delegates from some fifty nations were meeting to draft a charter for an international organization for the promotion of peace (the United Nations).

After arriving at Warm Springs on March 30, 1945, Roosevelt began to improve, regaining color, appetite, and good spirits. On the morning of April 12 the president awoke well rested but complaining of a slight headache. Then, after a productive morning, he suddenly complained of a severe occipital headache and lapsed into unconsciousness. By 3:35 in the afternoon the president was dead from a massive cerebral hemorrhage.

In Washington the president's wife, Eleanor, was notified, and she calmly began the process of notifying her children of their father's death. She also asked that Vice President Harry S Truman be called to the White House. Word reached Truman at the Capitol, where he was sharing a relaxed drink and talk of inside politics with House Speaker Sam Rayburn (D-Texas). When the call came in, Truman was asked simply to leave quietly and come to the White House, where upon arriving he was escorted up to Mrs. Roosevelt's study. The new widow put her arm around Truman's shoulders, and said, "Harry, the president is dead." For a few moments Truman was stunned and speechless as he tried to comprehend what had happened and what it would mean for himself and the country. When he finally found words, he asked Mrs. Roosevelt, "Is there anything I can do for you?" She replied, "Is there anything we can do for you? For you are the one in trouble now." [34]

By dinnertime the news of the president's death was on the wire services and on the radio; the tragic news quickly spread far and wide. The public seemed to feel a sense of personal loss, bereavement, and bewilderment. Roosevelt had so long dominated the public life of the nation and had been such a vital force in defining the country's course and fortunes, that it was stunning to contemplate his passing. At the announcement of his death many wept; others prayed. Quietly that evening a cluster of three to four hundred people gathered at Lafayette Square, across from the White House, to keep a hushed vigil.

By seven o'clock that evening, the members of the cabinet, the vice president's wife and daughter, and the chief justice of the Supreme Court had been assembled in the cabinet room. At 7:05 Harry S Truman was sworn in as the thirty-third president of the United States. By 7:15 President Truman was convening his first cabinet meeting and issuing his first decision: the United Nations conference scheduled to open in San Francisco would indeed go on as planned.[35] Truman asked all the cabinet members to remain at their posts and told them that he intended to continue both the foreign and the domestic policies of the Roosevelt administration. As the meeting adjourned, Secretary of War Henry L. Stimson remained to speak to the new president on a matter of great urgency. He then told Truman about the Manhattan Project and the nearly completed development of the atomic bomb.[36] Thus, Truman assumed the presidency while the nation was still at war in the Pacific and on the brink of the nuclear age. Ahead of him stretched the prospect of having to complete an almost entire presidential term and to replace a president that seemed irreplaceable.

Historian Cabell Phillips has written that Truman's

"tenure was one of the most torturous of any President in history ... marked by intense and sometimes paralyzing political strife, by personal denigration such as no President since Andrew Johnson has had to endure." [37] Indeed, Truman enjoyed nothing approximating the political stature of Roosevelt, inherited an administration that was exhausted from twelve years of governance and the war effort, and faced a Congress and an opposition party that were eager to reassert themselves once Roosevelt and the war had passed. Moreover, Truman was new to the Roosevelt administration. He had spoken to the president fewer than ten times since his nomination as the vice-presidential candidate in the summer of 1944. Roosevelt had been away from Washington for most of the three months that Truman had been vice president.

Like many successor presidents, Truman faced significant political difficulties during the remainder of his term. His party suffered substantial congressional losses at the 1946 midterm elections, and the polls showed that he had lost popular support. As the opposition mounted, the leaders of his own party sought to deny him renomination in 1948, and when this failed they distanced themselves from him during the campaign. Indeed, his party splintered, as candidates from both the right (South Carolina governor Strom Thurmond of the Dixiecrats) and the left (former vice president Henry A. Wallace of the Progressives) sniped at him and drained his electoral support.

Despite these trials, Truman succeeded in winning a cliff-hanger election against New York governor Thomas E. Dewey, which, however narrow, vindicated his performance as Roosevelt's successor. Indeed, history has come to value Truman's courage, determination, and common sense approach and to rank him as a "near great" president. *(See Rating the Presidents chapter in Part I.)*

Presidential Assassinations

Half of the presidents who have died in office were felled by assassins. The first presidential victim was Abraham Lincoln in 1865, and the most recent was John F. Kennedy in 1963. All of these assassinated presidents, except for Kennedy, were killed very early in their terms of office. Presidents Lincoln, James A. Garfield, and William McKinley each died within approximately six months of their inauguration, leaving their successors to fill out nearly full terms of office. Lincoln was the only president known to have been killed as part of a larger conspiracy. Although William Henry Harrison was the first president to die in office (of natural causes), Andrew Jackson came close to being the first presidential fatality. On January 30, 1835, while Jackson was attending the funeral of South Carolina representative Warren Davis in the rotunda of the Capitol, house painter Richard Lawrence attempted to shoot him. Aiming from a distance of only seven feet, Lawrence fired both of his pistols at the president at point-blank range. Both guns misfired, however, and Lawrence was captured and later found to be insane.[38]

Abraham Lincoln

The death of a president is always a shock to the body politic as well as the nation's citizens. Compared with other presidential deaths, however, the death of Abraham Lincoln had even greater effect on both because it was the first instance of a presidential assassination and because it was the third in a tragic series of presidential deaths within a twenty-five-year period (following the natural deaths of President Harrison in 1841 and of President Taylor in 1850). The unprecedented assassination was, in itself, shocking to a people who had come to pride themselves on the peaceful and orderly transfer of executive power. Its occurrence at a time when the public was just beginning to see an end to the terrible bloodshed of the Civil War was a harsh harbinger of the passionate controversy that would continue to haunt the peoples of the restored Union for years to come.

Throughout his first term of office Abraham Lincoln had been a controversial president. The demands of leadership during the nation's only civil war had led Lincoln to assert expansive, indeed prerogative, presidential powers, which had in turn prompted congressional and partisan criticism even in the midst of war. Early in 1864 it appeared that Lincoln would have a hard time winning renomination, much less reelection, to a second term. Nonetheless, the Republicans, calling themselves the National Union party, renominated Lincoln and chose a Democrat but Union loyalist, Andrew Johnson, as his running mate. Lincoln went on to win a resounding victory with 212 of 233 electoral college votes against a Democratic opponent, Stephen A. Douglas, whose party's main source of strength, the South, had seceded.[39]

The second term began auspiciously—within a month of the inauguration, Richmond, Virginia, the capital of the Confederacy, fell. A few nights later and just before the surrender of Gen. Robert E. Lee to Gen. Ulysses S. Grant on April 9, 1865, the president was said to have had an ominous and prophetic dream. Lincoln dreamed that he had awakened to the sound of many people weeping in the White House. He made his way to the East Room, only to find himself lying in a coffin on a catafalque, while people wailed, "The President is dead." [40] In the rejoicing at the prospect of peace that followed the raising of the American flag once again over Fort Sumter, the dream was brushed aside. Instead, the president and his wife, Mary Todd Lincoln, planned to celebrate by attending a play at Ford's Theater in Washington on the night of April 14.

While watching a performance of *Our American Cousin,* President Lincoln was shot by John Wilkes Booth, an actor and Confederate sympathizer. Booth, who had been plotting for months either to kidnap or kill the president (a month earlier a kidnap plan intended to hold Lincoln as a hostage to bargain an end to the war on Confederate terms had failed), learned that the president would be at the theater that evening and so set his plan in motion. The defeat of the South had led Booth to feel that "our cause being almost lost, something decisive and great must be done." [41] His conspiracy plan entailed assassinating not only the president, but also Vice President Johnson and Secretary of State Seward. Booth's target was to be the president, while his coconspirator George Atzerodt was to kill Johnson at his home in the Kirkwood House, and Lewis Thornton Powell was to kill Secretary Seward as he lay in bed recovering from a recent carriage accident.

Booth, who was known at Ford's Theater as an actor, had no trouble gaining access to the building. And, as fate would have it, he also encountered no difficulty entering the president's box, since the president's guard had left his post to watch the play. Standing less than six inches from

Table 1 Assassinations of and Assaults on Presidents, Presidents-Elect, and Presidential Candidates

Date	Victim	Length of administration at time of attack; president-elect; candidate	Location	Type of weapon and result	Assailant, outcome, professed or alleged reason for assaults
Jan. 30, 1835	Andrew Jackson (D)	Six years	Washington, D.C.	Pistol, misfired	Richard Lawrence, declared insane. Said Jackson was preventing him from obtaining money.
April 14, 1865	Abraham Lincoln (R)	Four years, one month	Washington, D.C.	Pistol, fatal	John Wilkes Booth, killed by police pursuers. Loyalty to the Confederacy, revenge for defeat, slavery issue.
July 2, 1881	James A. Garfield (R)	Four months	Washington, D.C.	Pistol, fatal	Charles J. Guiteau, convicted. Disgruntled office seeker, supporter of opposite faction of Republican party.
Sept. 6, 1901	William McKinley (R)	Four years, six months	Buffalo, New York	Pistol, fatal	Leon F. Czolgosz, convicted. Anarchist.
Oct. 14, 1912	Theodore Roosevelt (Progressive-Bull Moose)	Candidate	Milwaukee, Wis.	Pistol, wounded	John Schrank, declared insane. Had vision that McKinley wanted Schrank to avenge his death.
Feb. 15, 1933	Franklin D. Roosevelt (D)	President-elect, three weeks before first inauguration	Miami, Fla.	Pistol, bullets missed FDR, killed Chicago mayor	Joseph Zangara, convicted of murdering Chicago mayor. Hated rulers and capitalists.
Nov. 1, 1950	Harry S Truman (D)	Five years	Washington, D.C.	Automatic weapons, prevented from shooting at president	Oscar Collazo, convicted of murdering guard; Griselio Torresola, killed. Puerto Rican independence.
Nov. 22, 1963	John F. Kennedy (D)	Three years	Dallas, Texas	Rifle, fatal	Lee Harvey Oswald, murdered by Jack Ruby. Motive unknown.
June 4, 1968	Robert F. Kennedy (D)	Candidate and U.S. senator	Los Angeles, Calif.	Pistol, fatal	Sirhan Sirhan, convicted. Opposed candidate's stand on Israeli-Arab conflict.
May 15, 1972	George C. Wallace (D)	Candidate	Laurel, Md.	Pistol, wounded	Arthur Bremer, convicted. Motive unknown.
Sept. 5, 1975	Gerald R. Ford (R)	One year	Sacramento, Calif.	Pistol, misfired	Lynette Alice Fromme, convicted. Member of extremist "Manson family."
Sept. 22, 1975	Gerald R. Ford (R)	One year	San Francisco, Calif.	Pistol, missed target	Sara Jane Moore, convicted. To bring about "the upheaval of needed change," revolutionary ideology.
March 30, 1981	Ronald Reagan (R)	Ten weeks	Washington, D.C.	Pistol, wounded	John W. Hinckley, Jr., arrested and indicted.

Source: Derived from Frederick M. Kaiser, *Presidential Protection: Assassinations, Assaults and Secret Service Procedures* (Washington, D.C.: Congressional Research Service, 1981). Data for the incidents through 1968 were drawn from James E. Kirkham, Sheldon G. Levy, and William J. Crotty, *Assassination and Political Violence: A Report to the National Commission on the Causes and Prevention of Violence* (Washington, D.C.: Government Printing Office, 1969), 8:22.

Charles DeForest Fredricks; National Portrait Gallery

John Wilkes Booth, a Confederate sympathizer, shot Abraham Lincoln on April 14, 1865, while the president was watching a play at Ford's Theater. Lincoln died the following day.

the president, Booth fired. The single bullet struck the president behind the left ear, drove through his skull and brain, and came to rest behind the right eye. A guest, Maj. John Rathbone, attempted to seize the assassin, who dropped his pistol, drew a dagger, and slashed at the major. Booth then vaulted the railing of the theater box, declaring "sic semper tyrannis" (ever thus to tyrants); landed on the stage, breaking a bone in his leg; and ran out a rear exit, where he mounted his waiting horse and escaped.

Concurrently, Powell had gone to the secretary of state's home. Forcing his way in, Powell beat Seward's son senseless in the process. Then he stabbed at the secretary's face and neck several times, slashing Seward's right cheek so severely that one could see his tongue through the bloody and gaping hole in his face.[42] Eventually, a second son, a nurse, and a hapless State Department messenger also were wounded in the struggle and escape of the would-be assassin. The vice president was spared by a change of mind after his intended assailant instead fled to Maryland.

Immediately after the shooting two doctors who happened to be in the theater dashed to the president's side to render what aid they could. They managed, through artificial respiration, to restore the president's breathing, and they directed that he be carried to the nearest bed. Unconscious, President Lincoln was carried across the street to a private home, where the helpless doctors tried to make the unknowing and unfeeling victim comfortable. Because the president's six-foot-four frame was too long for the bed, he was arranged diagonally with his head settled on two overhanging pillows propped against a door. Throughout the night these pillows soaked up the life blood as it drained from Lincoln, until they were so saturated that a crimson pool began to form on the carpet below. Nothing could be done for the president, except to keep vigil over his final hours. During the night members of the cabinet, government officials, the vice president, members of the president's family, the surgeon general, the president's pastor, and others visited, waiting for the inevitable. At 7:22 on the morning of April 15, Lincoln died at the age of fifty-six. As a brief requiem prayer was pronounced, Secretary of War Edwin M. Stanton sobbed, "Now he belongs to the ages."

Later that morning Vice President Johnson was notified officially of Lincoln's death, and the presidential oath of office was administered at ten o'clock by Supreme Court chief justice Salmon P. Chase. Johnson's succession would be troubled and turbulent. Although he would try to remain faithful to Lincoln's Reconstruction plans, he had neither the political skills nor the support to carry them past rabid congressional opposition. Indeed, he would be politically disgraced and very nearly removed from office. Thus, hopes for a reconciliation of North and South died with Lincoln; instead, a bitter and vindictive Reconstruction ensued that would scar the political and national psyche for decades.

The outpouring of national grief at Lincoln's death was unprecedented.[43] The funeral services, held in Washington, took the better part of a week. On Tuesday the president lay in the East Room atop a four-foot-high catafalque called the "Temple of Death." All day long the line of mourners filed past. Special trains ran into the city bringing sixty thousand spectators to watch the funeral parade planned for forty thousand on Wednesday.

Funeral services at the White House on Wednesday morning were followed by a journey to the Capitol rotunda where the president would lie in state. The funeral procession included officer contingents from the army, navy, and Marine Corps, a detachment of black soldiers, twenty-two pallbearers, marshals, clergy, attending doctors, officials, and family. Just behind the hearse was Lincoln's favorite and now riderless horse with his master's boots reversed in the stirrups. Many convalescent soldiers left their hospital beds to hobble in the funeral march in tribute to their fallen leader. Perhaps one of the most impressive sights was a group of four thousand black citizens, holding hands, marching in lines of forty across, and wearing high silk hats and white gloves.

On Friday the president's coffin began its long and sorrowful journey back home to Springfield, Illinois. For twenty days and over sixteen hundred miles the funeral train crept through Baltimore, Harrisburg, Philadelphia, New York City, Albany, Buffalo, Cleveland, Columbus, Indianapolis, Michigan City, and Chicago, on its way to Springfield. At each city the president's coffin was moved off the train to lie in state on prominent catafalques in public squares, allowing the people to bid Lincoln farewell. A million Americans actually passed his coffin; thirty million attended religious services or watched the train or the hearse pass by.

Thus, the legend of Lincoln as a national martyr was established, marked by the breadth of public mourning, the perception of Lincoln's death as the final sacrifice of the Civil War, and its poignant occurrence at the moment that the nation was expressing its relief at the war's end and hope for the restoration of peace.

James A. Garfield

A scholar, a soldier, and a politician, James Garfield was nominated for the presidency as a dark-horse compromise candidate on the thirty-sixth ballot of the Republican convention of 1880. The forty-eight-year-old senator from Ohio had been a member of the 1876 Electoral Commission that had resolved the disputed electoral college votes in the Rutherford B. Hayes-Samuel J. Tilden election. He had served as well as the Republican floor leader in the House of Representatives. Chester A. Arthur, a product of the New York Republican political machine, was selected as his running mate. Arthur played a crucial role in the campaign, acting as perhaps the first "advance man" in American political history, coordinating rallies and meetings as well as the campaign tours of General Grant and New York Republican boss Roscoe Conkling.[44] In the close election that followed, the Garfield-Arthur ticket won by less than one-tenth of 1 percent of the popular vote. Although the electoral college margin, 214-155, was more comfortable, it was the ability of Arthur to carry his home state of New York with its thirty-five electoral college votes that was pivotal to the Republican victory.[45]

Following his election Garfield confronted a host of political and administrative problems related to the spoils system. Assembling a cabinet from a badly divided and divisive Republican party was a delicate and complex task that consumed much of the president-elect's time and energy during the transition period. He did not succeed in completing his cabinet until the day after his inauguration.[46] This was, however, only the beginning of Garfield's troubles with government appointments; the line of job applicants awaiting him after the oath of office stretched down Pennsylvania Avenue. Concurrently, the expectations of civil service reformers were at odds with those of many of his political supporters and advisers who felt entitled to patronage appointments.

President Garfield also encountered patronage problems with Senate factions, each of which claimed broad senatorial prerogatives over executive appointments subject to Senate confirmation—each faction was using appointments as ammunition to punish its enemies and reward its allies. This controversy peaked in May 1881, when the two senators from New York, Republican Thomas C. Platt and Union Republican Roscoe Conkling, resigned from the Senate in protest against the president's intrusion into the Senate's influence over appointments. Meanwhile, the president had come to see the struggle as one in which he was protecting the independence of the executive. Although both senators intended to seek reelection and thus vindication for their cause, both found that their political base in the New York State legislature was insufficient to return them to Washington.[47]

Finally, personnel problems extended into the administration of departments. Soon after Garfield took office, a scandal erupted in the Post Office Department about the contracting of mail routes; it became known as the Star Route affair. After a full-scale investigation a general departmental overhaul was ordered in April, and grand jury indictments were prepared for charges of fraud.

Thus, Garfield inherited a host of problems associated with the spoils system and political patronage and found at various levels and in various institutions of government. Certainly the nation and its beleaguered chief executives were ripe for civil service reform. And while Garfield was not as committed a reformer as his predecessor, Rutherford B. Hayes, he nonetheless recognized the need for such reforms.

Four months after his inauguration President Garfield began a two-week tour of New England, including Massachusetts, where he planned to attend commencement exercises at Williams College, his alma mater. On the morning of July 2, 1881, as the president and Secretary of State James G. Blaine walked through the Washington depot of the Baltimore and Potomac Railroad, shots rang out and the president fell to the floor, bleeding. He had been hit by two shots, one grazing his arm and the other lodging in his spinal column. The would-be assassin was captured immediately and identified as Charles J. Guiteau, a disappointed office seeker.

Upon being taken into custody, Guiteau declared: "I did it and will go to jail for it. I am a Stalwart; now Arthur is president!" In his pocket were two letters. The first, addressed to the White House, maintained that "the President's tragic death was a sad necessity, but it will unite the Republican Party and save the Republic. . . . His death was a political necessity." The second, addressed to Vice President Arthur, informed him of the assassination and his succession to the presidency. It went on to recommend cabinet appointments. At first, these letters led investigators to suspect that Guiteau was part of a conspiracy, and they even cast suspicion on Vice President Arthur. The conspiracy notion was quickly discarded, however, but the likelihood that Guiteau shot Garfield in the name of Arthur and the Stalwarts diminished Arthur's popularity and placed him in a difficult political position in dealing with the president's disability.[48]

At first, little hope was held for Garfield's recovery. Then as the president rallied the doctors became optimistic. During the first three weeks of July, Garfield seemed to make steady progress. Thus, a day of national thanksgiving was declared for July 18, only to be followed by a presidential relapse and weakening the next week. August was a roller coaster of gains and setbacks, recovery and relapse. Finally after another rally, the president asked to be moved from the White House to a cottage on the New Jersey shore at Elberon. After making the trip on September 6, the president again seemed to improve before suffering the effects of blood poisoning. On the night of September 19 Garfield complained of a sudden pain in his chest, and then he died. An autopsy revealed that the immediate cause of death was a rupture of the peritoneum caused by a hemorrhage of the mesenteric artery in the chest. It also was discovered that several abscesses had formed along the path of the bullet that was lodged in Garfield's spine, causing the blood poisoning. In the late 1800s there was little that doctors could have done to save the president. Even if he had survived, he would have been crippled.

For the eighty days during which Garfield was disabled the nation lacked a leader, and almost no executive functions were carried out. Immediately after the president was shot, the doctors announced that his only chance for survival was to be "kept perfectly quiet." Fortunately, Congress was not in session at the time, thereby minimizing the press of legislative business. In fact, during his disability Garfield signed only one official document. For almost the entire month of July only the president's wife, Lucretia Rudolph Garfield, and attendants were allowed to enter the president's sickroom. When a member of his cabinet, the secretary of state, finally was permitted to visit on July 21, his visit was limited to ten minutes. Other members of the cabinet were not allowed to visit, even briefly, until after the president had been moved to Elberon in September. The vice president never saw or spoke with the president after the assassination attempt.

In late August, as the president's condition seemed to worsen, the cabinet considered asking the vice president to assume the executive duties. When consulted, Arthur indicated that he had no wish to come to Washington to take over these duties and that he was averse to any appearance that he was waiting for Garfield's death so that he might assume office.[49] When the president rallied for what was the last time, the cabinet decided against pursuing the matter. Thus, Arthur spent most of the period that Garfield was disabled in New York at his home. It was there that he received on September 20, 1881, the telegram informing him of the president's death. The same day he took the oath of office from Judge John R. Brady of the New York Supreme Court. Later that day, Arthur was joined by Secretary of State Blaine and Secretary of War Robert Todd Lincoln, who journeyed with him to Elberon to pay their respects to the dead president and to call on Mrs. Garfield.

Upon arriving in Washington on September 22, Arthur retook the oath of office to establish a federal record of it, delivered a brief inaugural address, and held a formal cabinet meeting. The following day he issued a proclamation calling the Senate into special session on October 10 to elect a president pro tempore.

When Arthur succeeded to the presidency the office of vice president became vacant. According to the then-valid Succession Act of 1792, the next in line for the presidency was the president pro tempore of the Senate, followed by the Speaker of the House. At Garfield's death, however, there was no president pro tempore. Before Arthur's accession, he had had to cast deciding votes in the Senate as it was divided evenly between Republicans and Democrats. Consequently, the Republicans had been unable to command the votes needed to elect a president pro tempore. When the special session was convened—following the resignations of New York senators Platt and Conkling—the Democrats had the majority of votes needed to control the election of the president pro tempore. The country thus faced the prospect that, after Arthur, a Democrat was next in line to complete the term of the elected Republican administration—a possibility fraught with political controversy and consequences.

Because the new House of Representatives was not scheduled to convene until December, there also was no Speaker of the House. (At that time the Speaker's term corresponded with the length of time that the House was actually in session.) Thus when Arthur succeeded to the presidency, there were vacancies in the next three positions in the line of succession: there was no vice president, no president pro tempore, and no Speaker. Aghast at this situation, President Arthur tried three times during his tenure to prod Congress into acting on proposals dealing with the issues of presidential disability and succession. But with the immediate crisis past, Congress refused to act.[50]

Arthur assumed the presidency encumbered with a number of disadvantages. A machine politician who had obtained the vice-presidential nomination through sharp dealing and who hailed from a faction of the Republican party different from that of Garfield, Arthur had little national experience and inspired little public confidence. Furthermore, he inherited a divided and factionalized party in which other leading figures were jockeying to position themselves for the 1884 nomination.

To his benefit, however, Arthur had conducted himself with dignity and diplomacy during President Garfield's disability, thereby winning the public's sympathy. Upon becoming president, he sought to cease acting like a "Gentleman Boss" and to begin acting in the best interests of the country as a whole. He took particular care to appoint talented, capable officials, while embracing Garfield's policy of supporting civil service reform. Indeed, in 1883 Arthur signed the Pendleton Civil Service Act, which created the merit-based civil service. In repudiating his machine politics orientation and support for the spoils system, Arthur lost considerable political support within his own party; he became "virtually a President without a party."[51] Thus, although Arthur proved to be an honest administrator and a conscientious president, he was unable to retain the political support needed to capture his party's presidential nomination in 1884. Upon leaving office in March 1885 President Arthur retired from public life and resumed the practice of law in New York City. He died in 1886.

William McKinley

During the 1880s, control of the federal government wavered between the Republican and Democratic parties, as in 1884 the Republican party lost control of the White House for the first time since Abraham Lincoln. Democrat Grover Cleveland, however, lost his bid for relection in 1888 to Republican Benjamin Harrison. Once reinstated in the White House, the Republicans pursued policies of tariff protectionism, which included passage of the McKinley Tariff and the Sherman Antitrust Act. But such activist trade policies made voters warry of the threat of higher prices. They demonstrated their displeasure by handing congressional Republicans a resounding defeat in 1890, followed by the victorious return of Grover Cleveland to the White House in 1892. Unfortunately for Cleveland and the Democrats, prior economic policies brought on the Panic of 1893 and its attendant economic distress and social protest. The subsequent public repudiation of the Democrats resulted in the realigning election of 1896, which firmly established the Republican party as the majority party for the next thirty years. William McKinley led the Republicans to that signal victory in 1896.

A former member of Congress and two-term governor of Ohio, McKinley was a champion of the protective tariff. He combined this stance with both a brand of nationalism and an appeal to American labor. During his first term in office McKinley worked to restore prosperity to an economically troubled nation, leading him to observe at his second inauguration in 1901, "Now every avenue of production is crowded with activity, labor is well employed, and American products find good markets at home and abroad."[52] His successful conduct of the Spanish-American War of 1898 was crowned by his acquisition of the Philippine islands, Puerto Rico, and Guam by right of conquest or as indemnity for wartime losses. That same year he also annexed the Hawaiian islands. This decision set the stage for the expansionist and imperialistic tendencies of his successor, Theodore Roosevelt. Roosevelt initially joined the McKinley administration as assistant secretary of the navy, a position he left to organize the Rough Riders. His notorious heroics in charging Cuba's San Juan Hill during the Spanish-American War then helped catapult him to the governorship of New York in 1898. From that position he was drafted at the 1900 Republican convention to become McKinley's running mate for a second term.[53]

Six months after his second inauguration President McKinley traveled to the Pan-American Exposition in Buffalo, New York. On President's Day at the exposition, McKinley delivered a speech that outlined the policy goals of his second term while also summing up the accomplishments of nineteenth-century Republicanism and looking forward to a new era of Republicanism.[54] The president participated as well in a public reception held at the Temple of Music on the afternoon of September 6. Even though the president was accompanied by a newly assigned contingent of Secret Service agents, as well as four special guards and a number of soldiers, he was shot as he greeted people in a receiving line. Leon Czolgosz, the assassin and an anarchist, fired two bullets at McKinley. One bounced off a button, and the other hit the fifty-eight-year-old president in the stomach. The assassin was subdued quickly and later tried, convicted, and executed in a mere fifty-three days. The wounded president thought his assailant "some poor misguided fellow" and worried considerably about how his frail wife, Ida Saxton McKinley, would respond to the news.[55]

An operation to remove the bullet was attempted immediately, but it could not be located. The wounds then were bathed, and the president seemed to be on the road to recovery. On September 10 the vice president, as well as the majority of the cabinet, who had joined him in Buffalo, were told that the president's condition was so improved that they might disperse. Vice President Roosevelt thus departed for a vacation with his family in the Adirondacks. During the next three days fever, gangrene, and infection set in, weakening the president. Once again the vice president and the cabinet were summoned to Buffalo. President McKinley died in the early morning hours on Friday, September 14, 1901. Theodore Roosevelt was sworn in as the new president the following afternoon. He then returned to Washington and held his first cabinet meeting, where he asked the members to stay on and help him carry out McKinley's program.

In the remaining three and a half years of the term Roosevelt proved to be an energetic and forceful leader. He embarked on a "Square Deal" program of social reform, supported the organization of trade unions and greater social and industrial justice for laborers, and launched his trust-busting campaign. He also won passage of the Reclamation Act of 1902 for western lands, oversaw the creation of the Department of Commerce and Labor in 1903, and signed a treaty for the construction of the Panama Canal. In foreign affairs he announced the "Roosevelt Corollary" of the Monroe Doctrine and did much to enhance American prestige abroad.

Indeed, Roosevelt was twice blessed as an accidental president: he inherited a legacy of successful policies, prosperity, and party support, and he built upon his own political record to become a forceful and popular president. So effective was his performance that Roosevelt was nominated at the 1904 Republican convention by acclamation and went on to win the election by a margin of over two and a half million votes. Thus, Roosevelt broke the jinx that had seemed to haunt successor presidents. He won election in his own right instead of following the pattern of Tyler, Fillmore, Johnson, and Arthur, who saw their support erode and culminate in their political repudiation.

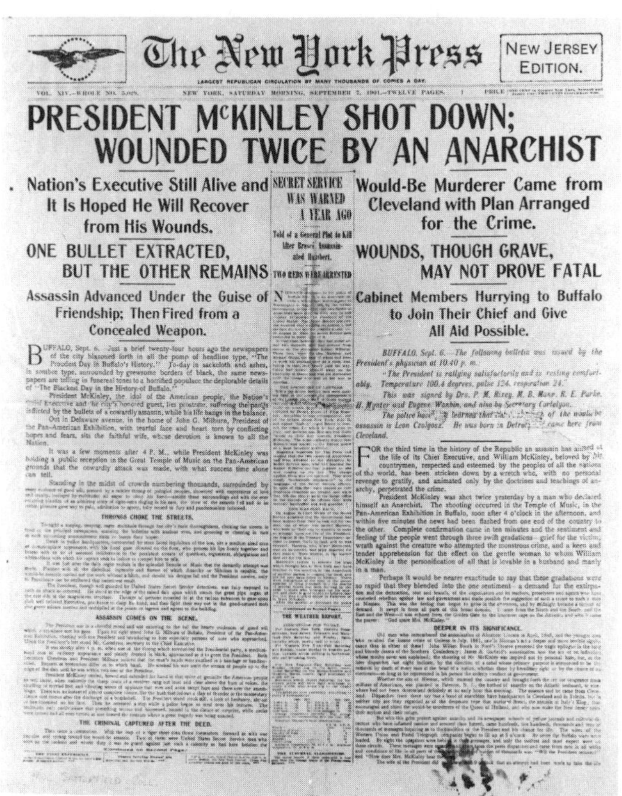

The New York Press

NEW JERSEY EDITION.

LARGEST REPUBLICAN CIRCULATION BY MANY THOUSANDS OF COPIES A DAY.

NEW YORK, SATURDAY MORNING, SEPTEMBER 7, 1901.—TWELVE PAGES.

PRESIDENT McKINLEY SHOT DOWN; WOUNDED TWICE BY AN ANARCHIST

Nation's Executive Still Alive and It Is Hoped He Will Recover from His Wounds.

ONE BULLET EXTRACTED, BUT THE OTHER REMAINS

Assassin Advanced Under the Guise of Friendship; Then Fired from a Concealed Weapon.

BUFFALO, Sept. 6.—Just a brief twenty-four hours ago the newspapers of the city blazoned forth in all the pomp of headline type, "The Proudest Day in Buffalo's History." To-day in sackcloth and ashes, in sombre type, surrounded by gruesome borders of black, the same newspapers are telling in funereal tones to a horrified populace the deplorable details of "The Blackest Day in the History of Buffalo."

President McKinley, the idol of the American people, the Nation's Chief Executive and the city's honored guest, lies prostrate, suffering the pangs inflicted by the bullets of a cowardly assassin, while his life hangs in the balance.

Out in Delaware avenue, in the home of John G. Milburn, President of the Pan-American Exhibition, with tearful face and heart torn by conflicting hopes and fears, sits the faithful wife, whose devotion is known to all the Nation.

SECRET SERVICE WAS WARNED A YEAR AGO

TWO REDS WERE ARRESTED

Would-Be Murderer Came from Cleveland with Plan Arranged for the Crime.

WOUNDS, THOUGH GRAVE, MAY NOT PROVE FATAL

Cabinet Members Hurrying to Buffalo to Join Their Chief and Give All Aid Possible.

BUFFALO, Sept. 6.—The following bulletin was issued by the President's physician at 10.40 p. m.:

"The President is rallying satisfactorily and is resting comfortably. Temperature 100.4 degrees, pulse 124, respiration 24."

This was signed by Drs. P. M. Rixey, M. B. Mann, R. E. Park, H. Mynter and Eugene Wasdin, and also by Secretary Cortelyou.

Ralph E. Becker Collection, Smithsonian Institution

Despite the protection of Secret Service agents, special guards, and soldiers, President William McKinley was shot as he greeted people at the Pan-American Exposition in Buffalo, New York. The next day's headlines of September 7, 1901, held out hope that the president would recover, but he died eight days later.

John F. Kennedy

When he entered office in January 1961, forty-three-year-old John F. Kennedy was the youngest man ever elected president. Succeeding, as he did, the oldest president to that date (Dwight D. Eisenhower), Kennedy and his administration seemed to inject new vitality and energy into government. Nonetheless, it was an energy that was, of necessity, politically restrained. Kennedy had won an extremely close election, and he faced considerable conservative opposition from his own party in Congress. Thus, he looked forward to a stronger showing and another victory in 1964 and to finally capitalize on the political and policy foundations he had laid during his first term. Indeed, the November 1963 presidential trip to Dallas, Texas, was made with the 1964 election campaign in mind. Kennedy was concerned about retaining and increasing his support in the South, including Texas. Toward that end, he hoped to reconcile quarreling factions of Texas Democrats with the help of his vice president, Lyndon B. Johnson, who was well versed in the politics of his home state.[56]

Texas, especially Dallas, did not promise, however, to be particularly hospitable to the president. Dallas was an odd city: it was newly oil rich, yet imbued with fundamentalist self-righteousness and Old West macho. These

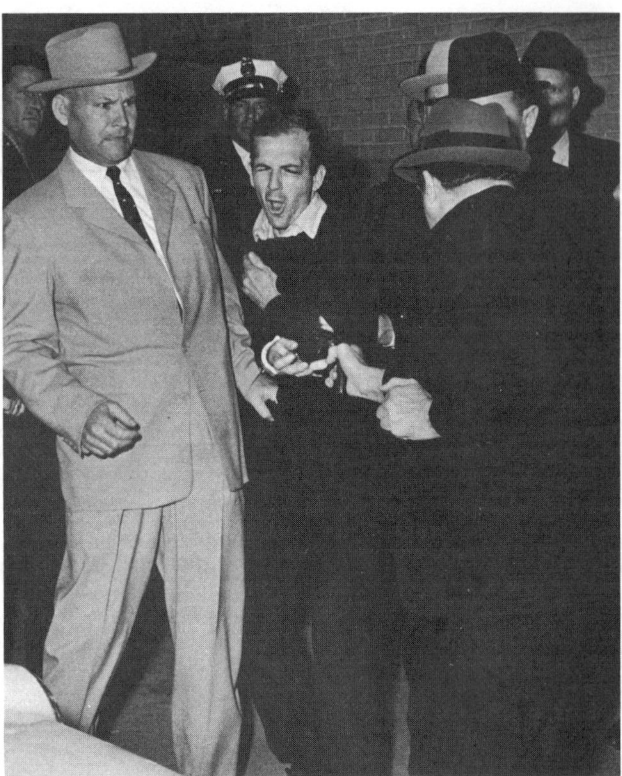

Shouting, "You killed the president, you rat!" Jack Ruby, a Dallas club owner, shot and killed Lee Harvey Oswald as the accused assassin of President Kennedy was being transferred to another jail. Millions witnessed the event on national television.

characteristics produced an atmosphere of aggressive intolerance that was evident in the state and city homicide levels. Texas had one of the highest homicide rates in the country (higher than New York, for example); in Dallas the murder rate was twice the national average.[57] Even Texas native son Lyndon Johnson had been hissed and spat at in Dallas when campaigning there for Kennedy in 1960. And just four weeks before President Kennedy's 1963 trip the administration's ambassador to the United Nations, Adlai Stevenson, had been heckled speaking at a United Nations Day event in Dallas. Moreover, on the way to his car a crowd of picketers had closed in on him; one woman hit him over the head with a sign and a man spat at him. Stevenson had been so shaken by the experience that he told the president that he had found the atmosphere "ugly and frightening"; he urged the president to reconsider his scheduled trip.[58] Nevertheless, John Kennedy went to Dallas.

On the morning of Friday, November 22, 1963, a motorcade was formed at Love airfield outside the city to bring the presidential party through downtown Dallas. The president and first lady, Jacqueline Bouvier Kennedy, as well as Texas governor John B. Connally and his wife, were in the lead car. Vice President and Mrs. Johnson and Sen. Ralph W. Yarborough (D-Texas) were in the following car. Just as the motorcade was turning onto its final stretch, Mrs. Connally was pleased to be able to comment, "You can't say Dallas doesn't love you, Mr. President," to which Kennedy replied, "No, you can't." [59] Although the crowds were neither unusually large nor effusive, they gave the president a warm welcome, which seemed to hold political promise.

As the cars turned off Main Street onto Elm and rolled past the Texas School Book Depository, a series of short, sharp noises startled everyone. Some thought they were firecrackers being set off; others thought an engine was backfiring. The Texas hunters in the party instinctively identified it as rifle fire. The first shot that hit the president entered the back of his neck, bruising his right lung, tearing his windpipe, and exiting from his throat to strike Governor Connally's back, chest, right wrist, and left thigh. In the seconds of stunned disbelief that followed, the assassin lined up the second, and fatal, shot, which tore into Kennedy's cerebellum. Suddenly the president's car was awash in blood. As Mrs. Kennedy cradled her husband's shattered head, the motorcade dissolved, and the lead car raced for the nearest hospital. Meanwhile, Secret Service agents covering the vice president's car pushed him and his guests down, and his car, too, raced for the hospital.

Instantaneously, word of the shooting went out over the wire services. Military forces in the Washington, D.C., area were put on special alert. A plane with half the cabinet aboard, including Secretary of State Dean Rusk, received word while in midflight to Japan, and it turned around to return to Washington.

Medical efforts made at the hospital in Dallas were futile; the wound was too damaging. As in the case of Lincoln nearly one hundred years earlier, the doctors could do little but confirm the inevitable. In another hospital room security personnel and staff were urging Vice President Johnson to leave Dallas as soon as possible. Fears of a larger conspiracy prompted them to return the new president to the kind of security that could be found only in Washington.[60]

At two o'clock in the afternoon the television networks interrupted their regular programming to bring word to a stunned nation that President Kennedy was dead. (The president was pronounced dead officially at 1:15, but the announcement of his death was delayed until the vice president was safely on board *Air Force One.*) In no other case of a president's death in office, not even Lincoln's, had the tragic finality occurred so suddenly. Before most Americans even knew that the president had been hurt, he was dead.

Vice President Johnson was whisked back to the airfield and boarded *Air Force One.* There the mournful party awaited the arrival of the now former first lady and the president's casket. Meanwhile, the Dallas police had identified and apprehended the suspected assassin, Lee Harvey Oswald, a maladjusted worker at the book repository who had Marxist leanings. Before the plane took off, a brief swearing-in ceremony was held; local federal district judge Sarah T. Hughes administered the oath of office to Lyndon Johnson.

Upon its return to Washington, President Kennedy's body lay in state in the East Room of the White House, where a steady stream of family, Washington officialdom, and diplomatic representatives paid their respects. On Sunday, November 24, shortly before the funeral procession in Washington was scheduled to begin, Lee Harvey Oswald was shot and killed as he was being transferred to a different jail. Jack Ruby, a Dallas club owner, had elbowed through the crowd of security and reporters, pointed a .38 revolver at Oswald, and pulled the trigger, shouting, "You killed the president, you rat!" An act of impulsiveness, the event was caught on film and would be broadcast repeatedly in the days and even years ahead. While retribution against presidential assassins generally had been speedy, never had an assassin's execution been so immediate or so public.

At one o'clock in the afternoon of November 24 the funeral procession began the journey from the White House to the Capitol; the presidential caisson was followed by the riderless horse. The casket was placed in the rotunda for public viewing. An estimated quarter of a million people then lined the streets and sought to file past the closed casket. Millions more, both in the United States and abroad, joined in the proceedings via television. Indeed, the television coverage was unprecedented. It was estimated that 95 percent of the adult U.S. population was following television or radio accounts of the funeral. Networks cancelled virtually everything else, including commercials, weather, news, and sportscasts. Domestic broadcasts were relayed by satellite to Europe and parts of Asia; the funeral was even telecast in the Soviet Union.[61] The entire country and much of the world was mesmerized by the ceremony of mourning for the young, assassinated president.

On Monday morning, November 25, the caisson reclaimed the president's casket and carried it to St. Matthew's Cathedral for a requiem mass and then on to Arlington National Cemetery where President Kennedy was interred. Afterward the country, and especially the new president, Lyndon Johnson, turned to the business of trying to carry on. Within days of the funeral the president was persuading Supreme Court chief justice Earl Warren to head an independent investigatory commission into the assassination. Ten months later the Warren Commission report declared that Oswald was the sole assassin and dismissed the possibility that Oswald was part of a wider conspiracy. That possibility, however, has maintained public credibility. Decades after Kennedy's death speculation about possible conspiracy plots continues.

Only a year away from a presidential election, President Johnson succeeded in maintaining the legacy of his predecessor while establishing his own record. He was nominated by his party to head the ticket in 1964 and to turn the "New Frontier" into the "Great Society." Unlike many other successor presidents, Lyndon Johnson was a resounding success at the polls. He won the election of 1964 by one of the greatest landslides in history, carrying additional liberal Democrats into Congress on his coattails. This outcome, combined with his own considerable legislative skills and the policy groundwork laid by Kennedy, helped President Johnson to enact many of Kennedy's proposed programs into law and to amass a legislative success record that has been compared to that produced by Franklin Roosevelt's first one hundred days in office.

Another important but indirect result of the Kennedy assassination was a renewed concern for the presidential line of succession and for the problem of presidential disability. The circumstances in Dallas made it painfully clear that a president and vice president might be killed simultaneously. While this was not a new thought—indeed, just such a situation had been part of the Lincoln assassination plot—Vice President Johnson's presence in President Kennedy's fatal motorcade, potentially within yards of being shot himself, seemed to make planning for such a possibility, especially in the nuclear age, a necessity. And if one looked past the vice president to the line of succession as it stood in 1963, other problems were evident as well. After the vice president, the next two officials in line to accede to the presidency were the Speaker of the House, John W. McCormack (D-Mass.), and the president pro tempore of the Senate, Carl T. Hayden (D-Ariz.). Both lawmakers were advanced in age; McCormack was in his seventies and Hayden in his eighties. Thus, while the stress of entering office under the exceptional circumstances of a dual assassination would have strained anyone, it was not unreasonable to speculate that such a situation might have proven

John F. Kennedy Library

On November 24, 1963, the presidential caisson, accompanied by the riderless horse, carried the body of John F. Kennedy from the White House to the Capitol. The slain president's widow, family, and the new president, Lyndon B. Johnson, are at right.

insupportable for these elderly leaders.

The character of President Kennedy's wounds also raised once again the problem of presidential disability. As Sen. Kenneth B. Keating (R-N.Y.) noted, "A matter of inches spelled the difference between the painless death of John F. Kennedy and the possibility of his permanent incapability to exercise the duties of the highest office of the land." [62] Consequently, a significant and constitutional legacy of the Kennedy assassination was the passage of the Twenty-fifth Amendment, which addresses presidential disability and the ability to nominate a replacement vice president. A joint resolution proposing the amendment was introduced in January 1965 and approved with virtually no opposition six months later. Ratification moved swiftly and was completed by February 1967. *(See "Passage of the Twenty-fifth Amendment," p. 381, in this chapter.)*

Other Assaults and Issues of Presidential Security

In addition to the four presidents who have died at the hands of assassins, five other presidents have withstood six assassination attempts. Threats of attempts to gain unauthorized entry to the Executive Mansion have occurred as well, dating back to John Quincy Adams (1825-1829), who was accosted and threatened by a court-martialed army sergeant demanding reinstatement. President John Tyler (1841-1845) was the target of rocks thrown by an intoxicated painter. And there is evidence of a plot against Richard Nixon (1969-1974) in which the potential assailant intended to hijack an airplane and crash it into the White House. During the Ford administration (1974-1977), a man wired with explosives threatened to crash his car through the White House gates, while another intruder scaled the White House security fence armed with what appeared to be a bomb. He was fatally shot by security officers.[63]

Most of the early, serious assassination attempts were successful, with the exception of Andrew Jackson's lucky escape from an attempted shooting in 1835. In the years following President Garfield's assassination in 1881 the need for greater protection of the president began to be recognized. For example, Secret Service agents accompanied President Cleveland to his summer vacation home in Buzzard's Bay, Massachusetts. Such protection was used more regularly during the McKinley administration (1897-1901), when the president requested that an agent accompany him on formal outings. Indeed, because of prior threats three agents were with President McKinley when he was mortally wounded in Buffalo, New York, in 1901.

Secret Service protection for presidents was formally authorized by Congress in 1906, with two agents normally assigned to presidential guard duty. Eight agents provided twenty-four-hour coverage when the president was on extended vacation. In 1908 such protection was extended to the president-elect and in 1945 to the vice president. After the 1950 attempted attack on President Truman by terrorists espousing the cause of Puerto Rican independence, the Secret Service instituted procedures to limit public access to their protectee by varying the time and location of the president's leisure activities (for example, Truman's morning walks) and by restricting access to the presidential residence and its vicinity. Until the mid-1960s the essential protective strategy of the Secret Service was to increase security personnel (that is, a "more-is-better" strategy) and to restrict access to the president in public settings. *(See "Protecting the President: The Secret Service," p. 905, in Daily Life of the President chapter of Part V.)*

In addition to the fatal McKinley and Kennedy assaults, attempts have been made on five other presidents during the twentieth century.[64] The first of these occurred in Bayfront Park in Miami, Florida, on February 15, 1933. Less than a month before his inauguration President-elect Franklin Roosevelt narrowly escaped shots fired by Joseph Zangara, an apparent anarchist who hated rulers and capitalists. Roosevelt's companion in the car, Chicago mayor Anton J. Cermak, was fatally wounded. And in 1950, although one of the two terrorists and a White House policeman were killed in the attack upon President Truman while he was residing temporarily at Blair House, the president himself was not harmed.

The assassination of President Kennedy in Dallas in 1963 prompted the most extensive changes in Secret Service protective procedures, made in response to the findings and recommendations of the Warren Commission. Indeed, an added protective strategy was devised that involved closer association and liaison between the Secret Service and other support agencies, particularly the Federal Bureau of Investigation (FBI). It was discovered that although the FBI was aware of Lee Harvey Oswald as a Communist supporter with revolutionary viewpoints, this information was not transmitted to the Secret Service before or during the fateful Dallas trip. As a reform measure, the Secret Service and FBI drew up joint guidelines for the regular dissemination of FBI reports to the Secret Service. Revised guidelines issued in 1976 curtailed this routine communication to the provision of investigative services only upon the specific written request of the director of the Secret Service.

In September 1975 two attempts were made on President Gerald R. Ford's life, both in California. In each instance protective actions by Secret Service agents and others succeeded in deflecting the attack and guarding the president from harm. On September 5, 1975, as President Ford was in Sacramento to appear before the California General Assembly, Lynette (Squeaky) Fromme emerged from the crowd and pointed a gun at the president from two feet away. A Secret Service agent walking behind the president saw the gun, grabbed it, and wrestled the would-be assassin to the ground. Approximately two weeks later, on September 22, 1975, a single gunshot rang out as the president was walking from his hotel to his car in San Francisco. Two Secret Service agents and presidential assistant Donald Rumsfeld pushed the president down beside his car, then onto the floor of the backseat, shielding him with their bodies until the motorcade could make a hasty departure for the airport. The individual who had fired the gun, Sara Jane Moore, was quickly identified and apprehended. In both cases the assailants attributed their assassination attempts to vaguely articulated nihilist or revolutionary ideologies.

On March 30, 1981, an attempt on the life of a president was perpetrated by John W. Hinckley, Jr., whose gunfire outside a Washington, D.C., hotel wounded President Ronald Reagan, seriously injured his press secretary, James Brady, and also wounded a Secret Service agent and a District of Columbia policeman. The twenty-five-year-old assailant was arrested at the scene of the shooting. Less than a month later a grand jury indicted him for attempting to assassinate the president and for twelve other counts related to the injuries inflicted on Brady, the Secret Service agent, and the policeman. Hinckley, who had been under psychiatric care, suggested that his infatuation with a teen-aged movie actress and his need to impress her was his motive for shooting the president.

Following the shooting President Reagan was rushed to the hospital with a chest wound and a bullet lodged in his left lung. The operation to remove the bullet lasted two hours, and the president remained hospitalized until April 11. He made his first major public appearance on April 28, when he delivered a televised speech on the economy to a joint session of Congress.[65] Thus, Ronald Reagan became the only president to have fully recovered from injuries sustained in an attempted assassination.

AP/Wide World

On March 30, 1981, psychiatric patient John W. Hinckley, Jr., shot Ronald Reagan as the president was leaving a Washington, D.C., hotel. Reagan quickly recovered, making his next public appearance less than one month later.

Impeachment

Within the American constitutional scheme, impeachment is an extraordinary legislative check on both executive and judicial power. As such, it is one of the most potent, yet least exercised, powers of Congress. Since 1789 impeachment proceedings have been initiated by the House of Representatives more than sixty times. Only fourteen of these proceedings led to the adoption of impeachment charges against eleven federal judges, one president, one senator, and one cabinet member. One of these individuals resigned from office before the House sent charges to the Senate, and two other cases were dismissed before a Senate trial because the offenders resigned. Ten cases underwent a Senate trial, resulting in six acquittals and four convictions; the convictions were of federal judges. The two most significant cases, both of which resulted in acquittals, involved Supreme Court justice Samuel P. Chase in 1805 and President Andrew Johnson in 1868. In both instances the proceedings were motivated largely by partisan and political conflicts between the branches of government.

In essence, impeachment is a political action framed in legal terminology and directed against a high-ranking federal official. The House of Representatives acts as the grand jury by considering and adopting impeachment charges, and then as the prosecutor by appointing a group of its members (called managers) to present the charges to the Senate. The Senate chamber becomes the courtroom, with the Senate acting as both judge and jury. Conviction on impeachment charges results in removal from office and may disqualify the individual impeached from ever holding public office again.

Origins and Purposes of Impeachment

In *Federalist* No. 65 Alexander Hamilton called impeachment "a method of national inquest into the conduct of public men."[66] The Constitution stipulates that impeachment proceedings may be brought against "the President, Vice President and all Civil Officers of the United States. . . ." The Constitution was not specific, however, about who was or was not a civil officer. In practice, most impeachment efforts have been directed at federal judges, who hold lifetime appointments "during good Behaviour" and who otherwise cannot be removed from office. One early impeachment case raised the possibility of its application to members of Congress, but this idea was dismissed by the Senate in favor of its informal equivalent, expulsion from the chamber. In other instances impeachment has been sought against executive officials such as cabinet members, diplomats, customs collectors, and a U.S. district attorney. Removal of such officials seldom requires full impeachment proceedings, however, since they can be dismissed from office.

English Origins: Constraining the Executive

The impeachment process dates from fourteenth-century England, where the fledgling Parliament used it as a device to make the king's advisers accountable. While the monarch himself was immune from such oversight, ministers and judges believed guilty of breaking the law or of implementing unpopular orders of the king were liable to impeachment by Parliament. Both criminal and noncriminal activities were possible grounds for impeachment. As described by historian Joseph Story, these offenses included not only "bribery and acting grossly contrary to the duties of their office," but also misleading the sovereign by unconstitutional opinions and . . . attempts to subvert the fundamental laws and introduce arbitrary power."[67]

By the mid-fifteenth century impeachment had fallen into disuse, largely because the strong Tudor monarchs of the period had succeeded in forcing Parliament to remove contentious officials by way of bills of attainder or pains and penalties. Later, during the early seventeenth-century reigns of the Stuart kings, Parliament revived the impeachment power as a means of curbing the monarch's absolutist tendencies by removing his favorite aides and advisers.

In 1642 the power struggle between executive and legislature—king and Commons—peaked with the impeachment of the earl of Strafford, a minister to Charles the First. The success of this effort—through impeachment by the Commons and a bill of attainder in the House of Lords—has been regarded as critical to preventing "the English monarchy from hardening into an absolutism of the type then becoming general in Europe." [68]

During the seventeenth and eighteenth centuries more than fifty impeachment trials were held in the House of Lords. Indeed, even as the American Constitution was being drafted, the long impeachment and trial of Warren Hastings, the first governor general of India, was under way in London. By the time Hastings was acquitted in 1795, parliamentary impeachments were considered unnecessary because ministerial responsibility to Parliament had been established. The last British impeachment trial occurred in 1806.

Constitutional Convention

American colonial governments adopted the English system under which impeachment charges were brought by the lower house of the legislative body while the upper house sat in judgment. Although early state constitutions incorporated such a pattern, the Constitutional Convention debated whether the Senate was the appropriate site for trials on impeachment charges. Founders James Madison and Charles Pinckney opposed that role for the Senate, arguing that it would make presidents too dependent on the legislative branch. Suggested alternatives included the Supreme Court, a "national judiciary," or a convocation of the chief justices of the state supreme courts. In the end, however, the Senate was selected as the trial arena.

The Convention also debated the definition of impeachable crimes. Initially, it was proposed that the president be subject to impeachment and removal for "mal or corrupt conduct" or for "malpractice or neglect of duty." Later, these crimes were changed to "treason, bribery, or corruption" and still later, to simply "treason and bribery." George Mason argued that these grounds were "too narrow" and proposed including "mal-administration" which Madison opposed as too broad. Eventually, impeachable crimes were defined as "Treason, Bribery, or other high Crimes and Misdemeanors."

The constitutional provisions pertaining to impeachment are scattered among the first three articles of the Constitution. The House is given the "sole Power of Impeachment," while the Senate is accorded "the sole Power to try all Impeachments." "The President, Vice President and all Civil Officers of the United States" are subject to impeachment for "Treason, Bribery, or other high Crimes and Misdemeanors." The consequences of a conviction on impeachment charges extend no further "than to removal from Office, and disqualification to hold and enjoy any Office of honor, Trust or Profit under the United States. . . ."

Impeachment Procedures

The impeachment process has been used so little that almost no uniform practice for its initiation has evolved. Impeachment proceedings have been initiated in several ways: by the introduction of a resolution by a member of the House, by a letter or message from the president, by a grand jury action forwarded to the House from a territorial legislature, by a memorandum setting forth charges, by a resolution authorizing a general investigation, and by a resolution reported by the House Judiciary Committee. In the five cases that have reached the Senate since 1900 the preferred method of initiating impeachment proceedings has been House action on impeachment charges following a resolution of the Judiciary Committee.

Once the impeachment issue has been joined, a House committee investigates the changes. If probable cause for impeachment is found, the committee reports out an impeachment resolution, which generally includes articles of impeachment. In the twentieth century the House Judiciary Committee has filled this role. In earlier times the House Speaker named a select committee to investigate the charges and, if warranted, to report an impeachment resolution. If the House, by majority vote, approved the resolution, articles of impeachment were drawn up. Both the impeachment resolution and the articles of impeachment are subject to amendment and adoption by majority approval in the House.[69]

After the adoption of an impeachment resolution and articles, the House selects managers who will serve as prosecutors at the Senate trial. Selection of the managers—usually an odd number ranging from five to eleven—has been accomplished either by a resolution fixing the number of managers and empowering the Speaker to appoint them, by a resolution establishing the number and naming the appointees, or by ballot with a majority vote required for election. Once selected, the House managers present the articles of impeachment to the Senate and inform it of the impending necessity to hold a trial. The entire House may attend the trial, but the House managers are its official representatives at the Senate proceedings.

The Senate trial is similar to a criminal proceedings. Both sides may present evidence and witnesses, and the defendant is allowed counsel and has the right to testify in his or her own behalf and to cross-examine witnesses. If the president or vice president is on trial, the Constitution stipulates that the chief justice of the U.S. Supreme Court must preside. There is no constitutional specification about the presiding officer for other defendants, however. In the past either the vice president or the president pro tempore of the Senate has presided over nonpresidential impeachment trials.

The presiding officer rules on all questions of evidence, and this ruling stands unless the officer decides to submit the question to a vote of the Senate or a senator calls for such a vote. Customarily, questions about the admissability of evidence and other procedural issues are submitted to the Senate for a decision by majority vote. The presiding officer also questions witnesses and asks questions submitted in writing by Senate members, who are not permitted to question witnesses directly.

At the conclusion of the hearing the Senate goes into closed session to debate the question of guilt or innocence. During this session each senator is limited to fifteen minutes of debate. According to the Constitution, conviction requires the approval of two-thirds of the senators present. A separate vote is taken on each article of impeachment. If no article is approved by two-thirds of the senators present, the impeached official is acquitted. A two-thirds approval for even one article of impeachment is sufficient for conviction. Upon conviction the Senate then votes on removal of the convicted official from office. Later, the Senate may also by majority vote disqualify the convicted official from holding federal office in the future. Disqualification is not mandatory and has followed only two of the four convictions in the past two hundred years.

Controversial Questions

The grounds for and the character of impeachment often have been the subjects of debate. Clearly, treason and bribery are grounds for impeachment, and their definitions have been well established. Treason and the requirements for its proof are defined in the Constitution, and bribery is specified in statutory law and is generally understood to mean the giving, offering, or acceptance of rewards in payment for favors. The remaining grounds—"other high Crimes and Misdemeanors"—are anything but clear and have been the object of much discussion.

Broad constructionists (and generally those seeking the impeachment of a particular officeholder) have tended to advocate an inclusive definition of the phrase that covers not only indictable offenses but also actions that constitute abuse of office and political crimes. As a 1974 staff report of the House Judiciary Committee proposed:

> Impeachment conduct . . . may include the serious failure to discharge the affirmative duties imposed on the president by the Constitution. Unlike a criminal case, the cause for removal . . . may be based on his entire course of conduct in office. . . . It may be a course of conduct more than individual acts that has a tendency to subvert constitutional government. . . . Impeachment was evolved to cope with both the inadequacy of criminal standards and the impotence of the courts to deal with the conduct of great public figures. . . .[70]

Perhaps the most vivid example of this broad interpretation can be found in a statement made by Gerald Ford (R-Mich.)—then serving as House minority leader—when attempting to impeach Supreme Court justice William O. Douglas in 1970: "An impeachable offense is whatever a majority of the House of Representatives considers it to be at a given moment in history; conviction results from whatever offense or offenses two-thirds of the other body considers to be sufficiently serious to require removal of the accused from office." [71]

Conversely, narrow constructionists (and generally the counsel for the accused) contend that "other high Crimes and Misdemeanors" refers only to indictable offenses. This, for example, was the interpretation put forth by President Richard Nixon's lawyers, who argued, "Impeachment of a president should be resorted to only for cases of the gravest kind—the commission of a crime named in the Constitution or a criminal offense against the laws of the United States. . . ." [72]

The constitutional debates seem to indicate that, when conceived, impeachable offenses were not limited to indictable crimes; they also included abuses of office and political crimes. Furthermore, the criminal code defines as crimes many actions of insufficient gravity to merit impeachment.[73] (But "misdemeanor" here does not mean a traffic violation, for example.) Thus, neither the broad nor the narrow interpretation of "other high Crimes and Misdemeanors" is fully acceptable. Not all indictable crimes constitute grounds for impeachment, yet indictable crimes are not the only valid grounds for impeachment.

The character of the impeachment process has engendered considerable debate as well—is it a political process or a judicial one?[74] The view that impeachment is a judicial proceeding on criminality is prompted by the terminology of the Constitution. Article II provides for removal from office upon "conviction," and Article III guarantees a jury trial for "all Crimes, except in cases of Impeachment." The interpretation of impeachment as a judicial proceeding has ramifications for the due process that should be accorded those accused as well as their right to judicial review and vulnerability to double jeopardy.

The opposing interpretation views impeachment as a political process. Accordingly, the purpose of impeachment is to protect the state against gross official misconduct by divesting the offender of his or her public office. It does not "punish" the accused by any deprivation of life, liberty, or property. As a political process, impeachment proceedings may adopt judicial trappings and procedures, but they are not bound to conform to all legal requirements, such as a jury trial or judicial appeal.

In the final analysis, both by the intent of the Framers and as demonstrated by experience, impeachment is essentially a political process.

Impeachment of Andrew Johnson

Andrew Johnson has the dubious distinction of being the only president against whom impeachment charges were brought and who underwent a trial in the Senate. The primary formal reason for his attempted removal in 1867-1868 was the charge that in violating a federal statute, the Tenure of Office Act (1867), he had failed to faithfully execute the law. This specific charge was leveled against a backdrop of broader issues: control of the Republican party, the character and control of Reconstruction policy, the treatment and protection of the freed slaves, as well as monetary and economic policy matters.

Beyond these issues the impeachment attempt also held significant implications for the separation of powers. These implications were twofold. First, it has been argued that Johnson was the victim of a resurgent Congress seeking to reassert its prerogatives at the expense of the presidency after the "constitutional dictatorship" of Abraham Lincoln.[75] Historian Arthur M. Schlesinger, Jr., carried this argument further in speculating that had Johnson been removed from office, "the constitutional separation of powers would have been radically altered . . . and . . . the presidential system might have become a quasi-parliamentary regime." [76] Another historian, Michael L. Benedict, argued that "Johnson had usurped the rightful legislative powers of Congress by inaugurating his own system of Reconstruction. . . ." [77] From this perspective Congress undertook impeachment proceedings to preserve the separation of powers and, indeed, the integrity of the presidency itself.

Johnson's Leadership Style

Benedict also has argued that the attempt to impeach Andrew Johnson was precipitated by the president's "inept" political leadership and "stubborn refusal to accommodate." [78] This interpretation raises the so-called presidential character factor. According to the presidential personality typology developed by James David Barber,[79] Johnson was an active-negative president, who turned a political controversy into a personal crusade and stubbornly refused to accommodate valid political differences. Thus, Andrew Johnson's cause was that of "the battling champion of the common man, valiantly resisting cynical radicals bent on the vindictive destruction of southern society and the subjugation of southern whites before ignorant and venal blacks led by corrupt white Carpetbaggers. . . ."[80]

In describing President Johnson's stubborn leadership style historian William Goldsmith observed:

> Once he finally made up his mind, he was unprepared to change it; his record of failure only stimulated him to fight for his policy all the harder. He resented criticism of any kind, . . . he refused to admit . . . mistakes and frequently compounded his error(s) by continuing rigidly along his chosen path.[81]

Historian David Donald has noted that Johnson was:

> temperamentally unable to understand the Northern mood in 1865, much less yield to it. . . . Few Northerners felt vindictive toward the South, but most felt that the rebellion that had been crushed must never rise again. Johnson ignored this postwar psychosis gripping the North and plunged ahead with his program of rapidly restoring the Southern States to the Union.[82]

Certainly, personality was not the cause of Andrew Johnson's impeachment, but it was an element in the dramatic events of 1867-1868. Indeed, "if the critical importance of Reconstruction for the security of the nation provided the kindling for the impeachment crisis, it was the torch of Andrew Johnson's personality that ignited that flame."[83]

Political Situation of a Successor President

In many ways Andrew Johnson rose from humble origins similar to those of Abraham Lincoln. Like Lincoln, Johnson was born in a log cabin—but in North Carolina. Both men lacked formal schooling and were essentially self-taught. Both had earned an early political reputation and succeeded through skillful public debate. Johnson was left fatherless at age four and was apprenticed to a tailor at age ten. With the help of a shop supervisor, he taught himself to read; later his young wife taught him to write.

Such similarities in their backgrounds had different impacts upon the characters of the two presidents, however. Lincoln had triumphed over his informal education; he enjoyed matching wits with anyone, had an open mind, and was the consummate politician. Johnson, in contrast, was embarrassed by the deficiencies of his education. He developed a rigid cast of mind which sought refuge from complex problems in adherence to principles, and a tenacity in maintaining his position despite the political or personal costs.[84]

Johnson rose quickly in politics. Upon moving to Greeneville, Tennessee, in 1827 to open his own tailor shop, Johnson joined the local debating society and hosted a developing political club in his shop. Elected a city alderman before he was twenty-one, Johnson was soon elected mayor of the town. During the next thirty years he climbed the Democratic political ladder, moving from state representative to state senator to representative to Congress to governor of Tennessee, before finally returning to Washington as U.S. senator from Tennessee in 1857. When the Civil War broke out, Johnson was the only senator from a seceding southern state to remain loyal and to support Lincoln's use of military force to preserve the Union. Later during the war Lincoln appointed Johnson to serve as military governor of Tennessee, where he served courageously and with considerable success despite the abrogation of his confederates.

On the basis of this record of loyalty to the Union and in an attempt to strengthen the Union party coalition through an appeal to War Democrats such as Andrew Johnson, Lincoln secured Johnson's nomination as his running mate for 1864 on the first ballot. Although for a time Lincoln's own reelection looked uncertain, his prospects were improved by news of impressive battlefield victories as the tide of war turned in the Union's favor. Lincoln was assassinated only a few weeks after his second inauguration, leaving a successor who was considered a political anomaly as well as politically suspect.

Johnson was a southerner at a time when the South had rebelled against the Union and former officeholders in the South were automatically suspected of disloyalty. He was a Jacksonian Democrat who believed in states' rights, hard money, and minimal federal government activity,[85] and who adhered rigidly to his own strict interpretation of the Constitution.[86] Yet Johnson was vice president to a president who had exercised unprecedentedly broad executive power and was pursuing expansive policies for both the money supply and the role of the federal government.

Because he was vice president for less than six weeks before the assassination catapulted him into the Oval Office, Johnson had little time to become reacquainted with the mood in Washington (and especially in Congress), to establish acquaintances with Republican party leaders in Congress, and to learn of Lincoln's plans. Thus, by background and circumstance Johnson was viewed by the Republican party as an outsider who was sympathetic with the South. Although Johnson had served in the Senate, he had not spent the war years in Washington and thus had little firsthand understanding of the attitudes and opinions that were dominating Congress. His initial Reconstruction plans were similar to those Lincoln had pursued during the final phase of the war, but Johnson did not appreciate that the president had sustained his moderating efforts only by expansive use of his war powers. Once the war ended, these prerogative powers lost much of their thrust, making it necessary to reach an accommodation with Congress.[87]

Controversy over Reconstruction Policy

The developers of a Reconstruction policy faced three central problems: the status of the insurrectionist states, the status of individuals participating in the insurrection, and the status of the newly freed slaves. On each point the president's policy preference differed from that of Congress. Thus, increasingly Johnson's ideas on Reconstruction clashed with the wishes of the majority in Congress, and especially with the views of the minority, but activist, radical Republicans.

Both Lincoln and Johnson favored reconstructing the southern states as quickly and as simply as possible. Before his death Lincoln had begun the Reconstruction process in Tennessee, Louisiana, and Arkansas. Using his war powers, the commander in chief had imposed military rule upon the recaptured territories during the war and set up provisional governments. The basic elements of Reconstruction then required that a substantial proportion of the former voters of each state swear allegiance to the Union and that each new state government ratify the Thirteenth Amendment, thereby nullifying its previous secession, repudiating the debts of its Confederate government, and abolishing slavery.[88]

Even Lincoln encountered considerable opposition to what some in Congress regarded as too lenient a Reconstruction policy. Indeed, an alternative and stiffer plan was embodied in the Wade-Davis Bill of 1864. Although Lincoln pocket-vetoed the bill, it was clear that different executive and congressional positions were being formulated. By the time Johnson acceded to office, it also had become evident that while positions on the status of insurrectionist states and individuals might be accommodated, the question of the status of the freed slaves had taken on an importance equal to, if not greater than, the restoration of a functioning political Union.

By the war's end, protecting the new freedoms of the ex-slaves had become a minimal condition of Reconstruction for most northerners and for the majority of congressional Republicans, both moderate and radical. Thus, congressional Reconstruction plans emphasized the far-reaching restructure of southern economic and social institutions and included more difficult and exclusive conditions for establishing the loyalty of the insurrectionist states and individuals in order to reclaim their political rights and privileges. These conditions were intended to guarantee that control of the new South would not fall into the hands of those who had led the old South into secession and rebellion, and to guarantee that slavery and its vestiges would be eliminated. In pursuing these goals, congressional Republicans wanted a Freedmen's Bureau to protect and provide services for ex-slaves and a civil rights bill to enforce the protection of their rights and privileges of citizenship.

In 1865 Congress passed a Freedmen's Bureau bill and a civil rights act; President Johnson vetoed both. The split between moderate and radical Republicans in Congress prevented it from overriding the Freedmen's Bureau veto. But the president's veto of the civil rights bill estranged him from moderate Republicans, who then joined with the radicals to form a majority coalition against the president. After the override of the civil rights veto, most legislators began to believe that the president intended to disregard congressional opinion and obstruct a significant congressional policy-making role in Reconstruction. Furthermore, many believed that President Johnson had betrayed a sympathy with southern attitudes toward blacks that was inconsistent with the thrust of northern opinion.

Throughout 1866 Congress and the president battled over Reconstruction both in Washington and across the nation during the midterm congressional elections. The November elections gave the radicals a landslide, thereby increasing their numbers as well as their resolve to confront and control the president. Indeed, as historian David Miller DeWitt has written:

> The Congressional majority came back to their seats . . . flushed with triumph and bent on vengeance. They meant to strip the President of the prerogatives and functions of his office, as far as they could do so by statute, and, if he struggled against the process of emasculation, as they had every reason to believe he would, to impeach and remove him out of the way.[89]

When the Thirty-ninth Congress of the winter of 1866-1867 returned to Washington after the midterm elections, it quickly enacted legislation designed to limit presidential power and to impose its own design upon Reconstruction. The Tenure of Office Act was reported out of committee in December and was enacted speedily, by mid-February 1867. The bill was aimed at stripping the president of his independent power to remove appointed government officials, thus allowing those officials who might respond to congressional, as opposed to executive, Reconstruction policies to remain in office.

Other measures to establish new Reconstruction policy and procedures, and in the process to further constrain executive administrative discretion, were enacted by Congress as well. The new Reconstruction act, passed in the spring of 1867, marked the end of attempts to reconcile North and South; rather, it imposed northern retribution upon the vanquished South. This act abolished the provisional governments established by Lincoln and Johnson and divided the South into five military districts under the command of high-ranking military officers. New conditions for the readmission of states also were announced, including ratification of the Fourteenth Amendment, which granted the full rights and privileges of citizenship to all native-born Americans regardless of race. Furthermore, any former federal or state government officials who had repudiated their allegiance to the United States during the insurrection were excluded from holding civil or military office under the reconstituted southern governments.[90]

A third bill, attached as a rider to an army appropriations bill, deprived President Johnson of his real authority as commander of the armed forces and thus blocked his ability to control military implementation of the congressionally mandated Reconstruction process. The spring 1867 Reconstruction act had transferred provisional governing authority during Reconstruction to the military commanders of the five districts. This rider required that all orders to subordinate military officers be channeled through the general of the army, Ulysses S. Grant. Under this arrangement General Grant, who could not be removed from office without Senate approval, was largely responsible to Congress for carrying out the legislatively determined Reconstruction program. Concomitantly, it foreclosed the president from either countermanding or bypassing the general with his own orders. Combined, these three acts emasculated executive power and established congressional hegemony over Reconstruction policy.

Johnson believed the Tenure of Office Act and the army appropriations rider to be unconstitutional. Although he vetoed both the Tenure of Office and the Reconstruction acts, his vetoes were easily overridden. Indeed, thereafter the president's veto power was largely ineffectual as he saw thirteen of his fifteen vetoes overridden during the final two years of his term.[91]

Meanwhile, in early 1867 relations between President Johnson and Secretary of War Edwin M. Stanton had deteriorated beyond repair. According to DeWitt, although the president never liked or trusted Stanton—initially he suspected Stanton of underhanded dealings with his adversaries, the Radical Republicans—he hesitated to dismiss any of the cabinet members appointed by Lincoln.[92] As the controversy over Reconstruction policy raged between the president and Congress, Stanton's support from the Radical Republicans increased even as the president's tolerance of him faded. Indeed, as it became clear that the president wanted to be rid of his secretary of war, Congress moved to protect the cabinet, and especially the secretary of war, from executive removal with passage of the Tenure of Office Act.[93]

At about the same time the first moves toward impeachment were made. Rep. James M. Ashley (R-Ohio), who called for the president's impeachment, charged him with usurpation of power and corrupt use of the appointment, pardon, and veto powers, which constituted "high Crimes and Misdemeanors." Although these general charges were recognized to be political grievances rather than illegal acts, Ashley's resolution was sufficient to prompt an inquiry by the House Judiciary Committee. Just before the end of the Thirty-ninth Congress the committee reported that it had reached no conclusions. On March 7, 1867, as the Fortieth Congress convened, Representative Ashley reintroduced his impeachment resolution, which again was referred to the House Judiciary Committee for investigation. The committee's investigation proceeded throughout the year, and on November 25 it reported out an impeachment resolution. On December 6, 1867, the House refused, by a resounding vote of 108-57, to impeach Johnson, at least in part because many lawmakers did not believe that he had specifically violated any law.[94]

The House Moves to Impeach

Apparently buoyed by the defeat of the impeachment movement, Johnson moved to eliminate War Secretary Stanton from his cabinet. Six days after the failed impeachment resolution the president suspended Stanton from office. Simultaneously, he sent word to the Senate of his reasons, seeking its concurrence in the removal. He also convinced General Grant to accept an ad interim appointment to replace Stanton. Grant promised as well that he would remain in office regardless of Senate action, which would force Stanton to take the matter to court. If this happened, the president was certain that the courts would find the Tenure of Office Act unconstitutional. On January 13, 1868, the Senate refused its concurrence. Thus, under the provisions of the Tenure of Office Act, Secretary Stanton was to be reinstated.

At this point Grant broke his promise to the president and vacated the office, which Stanton reoccupied. On February 21 Johnson, frustrated in his attempt to force the issue but loath to take Stanton back, directed the army adjutant general, Maj. Gen. Lorenzo Thomas, to assume the duties of the secretary of war until a formal appointment could be made. Thomas presented a letter stating this direction, as well as one removing Stanton from office, to the secretary at the War Department. Feigning compliance, Stanton asked Thomas for time to gather and remove his personal property. Thomas agreed and left to spend the evening celebrating his own new appointment. Meanwhile, Stanton alerted his supporters in Congress and had a warrant sworn out for Thomas's arrest for violation of the Tenure of Office Act. Before breakfast the next morning Thomas found himself under arrest. But, released on bond, Thomas returned to the War Department later in the day to confront Stanton and demand his surrender of the office. Stanton, surrounded by a delegation of representatives from Congress, refused and instead ordered Thomas from the office. After some discussion and a shared drink, Thomas departed and Stanton barricaded himself in his office. For each of the next two days Thomas returned to Stanton and renewed his claim to the office, but each time he was rebuffed and he withdrew.[95] Matters at the War Department were at a standoff.

In contrast, the congressional response was swift and decisive. When the House met on February 21 it immediately reopened the question of impeachment. Conservative Republicans and Democrats, who had supported the president and voted against impeachment in December because they found no specific illegal act justifying such action, now confronted what seemed to be an incontrovertible instance of such illegal conduct. With his dismissal of Secretary Stanton and his appointment of General Thomas as an interim replacement, the president had violated the Tenure of Office Act. This violation constituted not only an illegal action but also, under the terms of the act itself, a "high misdemeanor" and therefore an impeachable offense. A resolution on impeachment thus was introduced immediately in the House and referred to the Committee on Reconstruction, headed by the notorious Radical Republican Thaddeus Stevens of Pennsylvania. The resolution was reported out of committee with a recommendation in favor of impeachment. Two days later the House concurred by a vote of 126-47. A week later it approved eleven specific articles of impeachment and appointed seven managers to argue the case against the president at the Senate trial: George S. Boutwell (R-Mass.), Benjamin F. Butler (R-Mass.), James F. Wilson (R-Iowa), Thomas Williams (R-Pa.), John A. Bingham (R-Ohio), John A. Logal (R-Ill.), and Stevens.

The Senate Trial

The first eight articles of impeachment dealt with President Johnson's removal of Secretary of War Stanton, and they thus charged the president with intent to violate the Tenure of Office Act and the Constitution of the United States. Article I specifically referred to the allegedly illegal and unconstitutional attempt to remove Stanton, while the next seven articles concerned various aspects of that action, including conspiracy. Article IX contended that Johnson had violated the law contained in the rider to the army appropriations bill by attempting to bypass the general of the army when giving an order to Gen. William H. Emory. Finally, Articles X and XI accused the president of seditious libel against the Congress through speeches made during the 1866 midterm election campaign. These speeches allegedly sought to bring Congress into "disgrace, ridicule, hatred, contempt, and reproach" and questioned the authority and legitimacy of the Thirty-ninth Congress because its membership represented only some of the states of the Union.

The president's lawyers, led by Henry Stanbery who resigned as attorney general to lead the defense, argued his case in the Senate. The defense's case rested on three major points.[96] First, it sought to demonstrate that in removing the secretary of war from his cabinet position, the president had acted within constitutional parameters and in accord with well-established custom followed by every president since Washington. In raising this defense, counsel also questioned the constitutionality of the Tenure of Office Act. It asked if the president was to be impeached for upholding his oath of office to "preserve, protect and defend" the Constitution, arguing that the president sought action that would prompt a judicial decision on whether the executive was indeed correct in believing that the act was unconstitutional.

Second, the defense contended that the president had not in fact acted in violation of the Tenure of Office Act. The relevant portion of the act read as follows:

> That the Secretaries of State, of the Treasury, of War, of the Navy, and of the Interior, the Postmaster-General and the Attorney-General shall hold their offices, respectively, for and during the term of the President by whom they may have been appointed and one month thereafter, subject to removal by and with the advice and consent of the Senate.[97]

Under these provisions, Johnson's counsel argued, the president was not constrained from removing Secretary Stanton from office. Stanton had been appointed to office not by Johnson but rather by President Lincoln during his first term of office. At most then Stanton was entitled to serve for one month after Lincoln's death and Johnson's succession to office. Thereafter, he served essentially at the pleasure of the president and thus could be removed without Senate approval. In this case, even if the Tenure of Office Act proved to be constitutional and the president was therefore obligated to execute it faithfully, Johnson was not in violation of that act in removing Secretary Stanton from office.

Third, the defense argued that, aside from either the constitutionality issue or the applicability of the law to the situation of Secretary Stanton, the president had done nothing that violated the law, since he had not, in fact, removed Stanton from office. Stanton remained physically barricaded in his office at the War Department, and no formal removal had occurred. The remaining charges found in Articles X and XI were dismissed as more complaints "that the President made speeches against the Congress . . . not the entire constitutional body . . . [but] the dominant majority in Congress" and that surely the Constitution protected such freedom of speech.[98]

The Senate trial proceedings themselves were marred by serious violations of due process and obvious political passion rather than legal objectivity. One of the House managers of the case against the president exhorted the Senate that in this matter it was "bound by no law," rather it was a law unto itself.[99] The defense was denied adequate time to prepare its case, important evidence that it tried to present was ruled inadmissible, and the normal rights and courtesies generally accorded the defense were denied.[100]

After weeks of argument and testimony the Senate took a test vote on Article XI, because as the catchall charge it was the most likely to attract a convicting coalition. The votes of fifty-four senators were in question. Twelve senators—nine Democrats and three conservative Republicans—were certain to support the president. Equally certain were the guilty votes of thirty of the remaining senators. That left a dozen Republicans whose opinions and votes were uncertain. Many of those senators had serious reservations about the consequence of a Johnson impeachment: under the succession law then in effect, Senate president pro tempore Benjamin Wade of Ohio, the most radical of the Republicans and a Reconstruction hardliner, was next in line for the presidency.[101]

The partisan pressure put upon these members was unprecedented. According to DeWitt, once the hearing was concluded and the Senate went into closed session to deliberate its verdict, Republican leaders:

> went into caucus and organized a far-reaching combination to coerce the suspected judges into submission to their party's decree.... They were threatened in the party press; their constituents were stirred up to threaten them from home; letters were sent to them from all quarters filled with threats of political ostracism and even of assassination, in the event of their treason.[102]

Thirty-six votes were required for conviction and removal from office. On May 16, 1868, the vote on Article XI saw seven Republicans join the twelve Democratic and conservative Republican senators in supporting Johnson for a vote of nineteen not guilty to thirty-five guilty. Identical votes on Articles II and III, taken on May 26, demonstrated that the die was cast. The Senate abandoned the remaining articles and adjourned, thus abruptly ending the trial. President Johnson had been acquitted of impeachment charges by the narrow margin of a single vote.

Epilogue

Although the political passions that had prompted the attempt to impeach and remove President Johnson from office had failed to achieve this objective, politics continued to affect the remainder of Johnson's term in office. Within months the president had been repudiated by the Republican party, which chose General Grant as its presidential candidate for the 1868 election. Thus, Andrew Johnson finished out the last year of his term as perhaps the lamest of lame duck presidents. He returned to Tennessee, where eventually he succeeded in making a political comeback. In 1874 he was once again elected U.S. senator from his state, and upon his return to the Senate he was greeted by the applause of the gallery and the congratulations of his colleagues.[103]

The seven recusant Republican senators who had voted for Johnson's acquittal were vilified by the press and their constituents and ostracized by the colleagues. By 1870 all were out of favor with the Republican administration and the mainstream of the party. Two left politics because of illness, two retired at the end of their Senate terms, two others switched to the Democratic party, and one joined the Liberal party.

The circumstances that had prompted the attempted impeachment resulted in imposition of the harsh Reconstruction policy of the Radical Republicans and subsequently caused relations between North and South, blacks and whites, to fester for decades to come. Ironically, the Tenure of Office Act was soon amended, at President Grant's insistence, to be somewhat less constraining of the executive removal power. It was formally repealed in 1887 and declared unconstitutional in 1926 by Supreme Court justice William Howard Taft in *Myers v. United States*.[104]

Although President Johnson succeeded in defending himself and his office from complete domination by the legislative branch, constitutionally the incident had upset the delicate balance of power between the branches and paved the way for a period of congressional ascendancy. The impeachment and trial of Andrew Johnson demonstrated the problems and dangers of invoking this ultimate check upon the executive. The political implications of its invocation were serious and the political costs extremely high. Furthermore, the highly partisan nature of its application risked violating democratic principles, particularly the rights of the accused. As legal historian Raoul Berger has noted, "The chief lesson which emerges from the Johnson trial is that impeachment of the President should be a last resort." Indeed, Sen. William P. Fessenden (Whig-Maine), one of the seven recusant Republican senators who voted for Johnson's acquittal, observed that impeachment must "be exercised with extreme caution" and in "extreme cases" and be limited to causes that would win the agreement of "all right-thinking men," not merely a politicized or partisan majority opposition.[105]

The Case of Richard Nixon

The effort to impeach President Richard Nixon marked only the second time in American history that

Congress has seriously considered removing an incumbent president from office. The move toward impeachment stemmed from the revelations of official misconduct, corruption, and abuse of power that arose after the June 17, 1972, burglary of Democratic National Headquarters in the Watergate Office Building in Washington, D.C. The burglary was perpetrated by individuals associated with the Committee to Re-elect the President (CREEP) and was later covered up by members of Nixon's White House staff. It was the so-called "Saturday night massacre," when President Nixon fired Archibald Cox, the special prosecutor appointed to investigate the break-in and its cover-up, that actually prompted the House to take up the question of impeachment. The final catalyst was the Supreme Court's decision that the president must surrender certain subpoenaed tapes of White House conversations held after the break-in. When released, these tapes, including the one for June 23, 1972, showed clearly that the president had participated in the Watergate cover-up. These tapes thus provided the "smoking gun" of incontrovertible proof of presidential wrongdoing. The House then quickly indicated that it likely would approve three articles of impeachment and then schedule the full House to begin debate on the charges on August 19. On August 8, 1974, President Nixon resigned from office; the ends of impeachment—removal from office—were thus accomplished.

Political Situation

Richard Nixon staged an accomplished political comeback when he succeeded in winning his second bid for the presidency in 1968. Yet he came to office confronting a country divided over the Vietnam War and a Congress controlled by the opposition Democratic party. During much of his first term President Nixon moved carefully, seeking to achieve a record in office that would help him win a strong reelection and public endorsement. Indeed, while he only narrowly won election in 1968, his 1972 victory was the third largest landslide of the twentieth century. As would be revealed eventually, however, he and his supporters took extraordinary, and illegal, measures to ensure that the 1972 electoral victory was certain and strong. One of these measures was the break-in at Democratic National Headquarters by five agents of the Committee to Re-elect the President and subsequent attempts to cover up White House involvement in the incident. Thus, in seeking the political resources he felt he needed to govern boldly and effectively, President Nixon undermined the very legitimacy of his presidency.

Events of 1973 provided diplomatic drama, economic consternation, and growing revelations of political scandal. The year began with the president's announcement of a Vietnam "peace with honor" agreement. Having reopened diplomatic communications with the People's Republic of China in 1972, President Nixon then turned his attention to relations with the Soviet Union. In June the warming of détente with the Soviet Union was marked by the signing of several executive agreements on commercial, scientific, and cultural matters during a week-long visit by Soviet leader Leonid Brezhnev to the United States.

Economically, inflation continued to soar despite a wage and price freeze, and the dollar became progressively weaker on the international money market. In October the Arab oil embargo occurred in the wake of the Yom Kippur War, sending economic shocks through the United States, and indeed the world.

Although confronted with serious economic problems both domestically and internationally, President Nixon seemed to be working his way out of the Vietnam quagmire and achieving considerable diplomatic successes in dealing with the major Communist nations. Buoyed by his election results, he also turned to the task of strengthening his administrative control. His "super cabinet" consolidation plan would have established a two-tier cabinet with the top-level secretaries serving simultaneously as White House counselors to the president. Thus, Nixon hoped to effect an "administrative presidency," which would allow him stronger control over policy implementation by the bureaucracy as well as policy planning and initiation, despite the opposition-controlled Congress.[106]

Watergate Investigations

Amidst these challenges and accomplishments, political scandals began to emerge. By early 1973, investigative articles begun in 1972 by *Washington Post* reporters Bob Woodward and Carl Bernstein were focusing public and political attention on the Watergate burglary, its origins and its aftermath. Also early in the year, at the confirmation hearings for the new director of the Federal Bureau of Investigation, L. Patrick Gray, it was revealed that presidential counsel John W. Dean III had been inappropriately involved in an FBI investigation of the Watergate break-in. This information turned the corruption and cover-up trail toward the White House, and although White House press secretary Ronald L. Zeigler initially tried to dismiss the Watergate incident as a "third-rate burglary attempt," it was later revealed that the incident included a host of misdeeds committed by or in the name of the president.[107]

Following the hints of a White House cover-up that emerged during Gray's confirmation hearing, the Senate launched its own inquiry. On February 7, 1973, the Senate voted 77-0 to establish the Select Committee on Presidential Campaign Activities to investigate "the extent ... to which illegal, improper or unethical activities" occurred in the 1972 campaign and election.

During the first phase of the committee's hearings numerous employees from the Committee to Re-elect the President and former White House aides testified. The hearings revealed the existence of a special White House investigative unit known as the "Plumbers," which used such tactics as harassment to "plug leaks" in the administration; Daniel Ellsberg, who had released the Pentagon Papers to the press, was one of its victims. Former White House counsel John Dean documented a systematic effort both to identify "enemies" of the administration and to elicit suggestions for dealing with them. In April two of the president's closest White House aides, H. R. Haldeman and John D. Ehrlichman, were forced to resign because of their apparent implication in the widening pattern of political sabotage and cover-up that was emerging from the Watergate investigations. The surprise revelation of an elaborate White House taping system during the June testimony of another former White House assistant, Alexander P. Butterfield, marked a turning point in the investigations and touched off a nine-month political and legal battle for release of those tapes.

Throughout the summer the nationally telecast Watergate hearings brought the sordid details of administration misconduct to the American public, whose support for the president began to erode. The committee's live audience was strongly anti-Nixon and generally made its feelings known. Indeed, committee chairman Samuel J. Ervin, Jr., (D-N.C.) was given standing ovations when he entered the room, and reaction to the testimony of various witnesses was vocal and demonstrable. By midsummer 1973 "Watergate" had come to refer to a range of illegal activities and to what seemed right or wrong about the presidency, about politics, and about America.[108]

The Watergate hearings also damaged the power of the president and marked a new phase in the resurgence of congressional power. In the midst of the Watergate hearings Congress passed the War Powers Resolution, designed to limit the executive's ability to exercise war-making powers unilaterally and without the consultation or consent of Congress. Although President Nixon vetoed the bill, Congress succeeded in overriding the veto.

The hearings pitted the testimony of former presidential aide John Dean against the president's contention that he had never approved clemency offers to the Watergate defendants, that he was unaware of payoffs to them, and that he had played no part in any attempted cover-up. Thus when Butterfield told the Ervin committee about the secret White House taping setup, he also revealed a possible way to settle the discrepancy in testimony: subpoena the tapes of key meetings.[109] The president refused to hand over the tapes, citing executive privilege.

Late in July the U.S. district court decided unanimously that the president should turn over sixty-four tapes of White House conversations that Special Prosecutor Archibald Cox had sought to subpoena. The administration appealed the decision to the U.S. court of appeals.

Although untouched by the Watergate scandal, Vice President Spiro T. Agnew added another dimension to the picture of corruption within the administration. Under investigation for alleged conspiracy, extortion, and bribery, the vice president resigned on October 10, 1973, as part of a plea bargain that involved his pleading nolo contendere to a charge of income tax evasion and not being jailed. He maintained that he had resigned because "the American people deserve to have a vice president who commands their unimpaired confidence and trust" and because he did not want to "subject the country to a further agonizing period of months without an unclouded successor for the presidency." [110] Two days later President Nixon announced his nominee to fill the vacancy in the vice presidency under the provisions of the Twenty-fifth Amendment. Thus, the process of making House minority leader Gerald Ford the first nonelected vice president in history began. Ford's confirmation hearings moved quickly in both houses of Congress. Although he repeatedly maintained that he did not intend to seek the presidency in 1976, his confirmation created considerable interest because of speculation that he would become president if President Nixon either resigned or was impeached.

On the same day that Ford's nomination was announced the U.S. appeals court upheld the district court's earlier ruling directing President Nixon to surrender the Watergate-related tapes. The president then offered Special Prosecutor Cox a compromise—transcripts of certain verified tapes—if Cox agreed not to subpoena additional tapes or documents. Cox rejected the compromise offer. The president in turn felt that Cox had now exceeded his authority and had deliberately challenged presidential authority. Nixon thus decided to fire the special prosecutor and directed Cox's immediate superior, Attorney General Elliot L. Richardson, to carry out that order. Richardson, stating that he was pledged to uphold the independence of the special prosecutor, refused and tendered his resignation. Deputy Attorney General William Ruckelshaus also chose to resign rather than carry out the order. Finally, the third-ranking Justice Department official, Solicitor General Robert H. Bork, acting as attorney general, fired Cox. This sequence of events, which became known as the "Saturday night massacre," prompted swift adverse public reaction. In the firestorm of protest that followed, House Democratic leaders introduced impeachment resolutions, which later were referred to the Judiciary Committee.

The Move to Impeach

In February 1974 the House Judiciary Committee began to hold hearings on possible impeachment charges against the president. Conscious of the highly politicized Johnson impeachment proceedings held over a century earlier, the Judiciary Committee took particular care to dampen partisanship and to proceed in a bipartisan manner. Meanwhile, the new special prosecutor, Leon Jaworski, proceeded with the prosecution of a host of Nixon administration officials. In March several Nixon aides, including Haldeman and Ehrlichman as well as former attorney general John N. Mitchell, were indicted for conspiracy to cover up the Watergate burglary. The president was named an unindicted coconspirator. In April the Internal Revenue Service reported that Nixon owed nearly half a million dollars in back taxes and interest on improperly filed income tax returns for the period 1969-1972. The issue of possible illegal conduct was coming very close to the president himself.

During May the House Judiciary Committee began closed hearings to consider grounds for impeachment. In response to the subpoenas of the committee and the special prosecutor, Nixon released over thirteen hundred pages of edited transcripts of taped materials, but he retained the actual tapes and other materials under the cloak of executive privilege. Simultaneously, Special Prosecutor Jaworski, citing an urgent need for a final judicial ruling on the tapes and executive privilege issue, asked the Supreme Court to take up the controversy before it recessed for the summer. As the Supreme Court hearing proceeded, President Nixon repeatedly implied that he might not abide by the Court's ruling, particularly if it were not a unanimous decision.

On July 24, 1974, Warren Burger announced an 8-0 decision of the Court, acknowledging for the first time judicially that the constitutional underpinnings for a presidential claim of executive privilege existed, but finding that privilege was superseded in the present circumstances by the "demands of due process of law in the fair administration of criminal justice." [111] The president then announced through his attorney, James D. St. Clair, that he would turn over the tapes. On the same day the House Judiciary Committee began broadcasting its debates over the adoption of articles of impeachment against the president. Within hours it became clear, as each member of the committee expressed his views, that seven of the seventeen Republican members were inclined to vote for impeachment. On the second day of the debate all of the committee's more conservative Democratic members expressed their support as well for certain articles of impeachment.

Within the week the Judiciary Committee had approved three articles of impeachment. Article I charged the president with violating his oath of office to faithfully uphold the laws by taking actions that obstructed the administration of justice. These charges referred primarily to deeds undertaken in conjunction with the Watergate conspiracy and attempted cover-up and included: withholding of evidence, condoning perjury, approving the payment of "hush money," interfering with lawful investigations, and making false and misleading statements to investigators as well as the public. Article II contended that the president had misused and abused executive authority and the resources of various executive agencies. Finally, Article III charged the president with contempt of Congress. If convicted under this article, the president would have been guilty of a misdemeanor because he had refused to honor subpoenas issued by the House Judiciary Committee, and he had violated the separation of powers by interfering with the ability of the House to exercise the sole power of impeachment granted it by the Constitution.

Article I was approved by a bipartisan vote of 27-11, Article II by 28-10, and Article III by a weaker but still bipartisan vote of 21-17. Indeed, the impressively bipartisan character of the committee vote not only rebutted the White House's contention that the inquiry was a partisan "witch hunt" conducted by a "kangaroo court," but also served notice that the full House probably would adopt the impeachment charges and send them to the Senate for trial.

Each of the impeachment charges contained elements of indictable offenses as well as the political consequences of undermining the public trust "to the manifest injury of the people of the United States." The two additional articles that were debated (and later rejected) confirmed the compound nature of what were considered to be impeachable offenses. An article faulting the president for the secret expansion of the Vietnam conflict into Cambodia was rejected. Clearly, the question of war making was a political one as well as one with substantial partisan overtones. While some might consider the president's actions in this regard a political crime, it was not an indictable offense and therefore was rejected as a possible impeachable offense. Conversely, a second rejected article concerning the president's admission of income tax evasion also failed to satisfy the dual definition of an impeachable offense. While an indictable crime, it was not a recognized political offense.

During the first week of August President Nixon, in compliance with the Supreme Court ruling, turned over the tapes of White House conversations that had been subpoenaed by Special Prosecutor Jaworski. Included in these was the so-called smoking gun tape of June 23, 1972, which was produced just six days after the burglary and bugging of Democratic headquarters at the Watergate. During the conversation, White House Chief of Staff Haldeman told President Nixon that campaign manager John Mitchell had approved the illegal operation. Nixon then ordered that the FBI be told not to go any further into the case. Release of this taped conversation made it clear that, contrary to President Nixon's repeated public statements that he had not known about the cover-up until much later (March 1973), the president had indeed been involved in the cover-up virtually since it began. With the president's part in Watergate revealed by this incontrovertible evidence of presidential wrongdoing, the remaining congressional support evaporated. One measure of how much release of the tapes damaged the president's case was seen in the shift—from opposition to support of impeachment charges—of all ten of his Republican supporters on the House Judiciary Committee. His defenders had argued that the case against President Nixon lacked hard evidence; the released tapes provided just such evidence. Whereas before, impeachment had been a strong possibility, now it seemed a certainty.

A President Resigns

As support for President Nixon eroded during the first few days of August, he called congressional Republican leaders to meet with him at the White House on Monday, August 5, to assess the situation. House Minority Leader John J. Rhodes (R-Ariz.) and Senate Minority Leader Hugh Scott (R-Pa.) informed the president of conditions in both chambers. Scott characterized the situation as "very gloomy" with no more than ten votes in the House and fifteen in the Senate in his favor and against impeachment.

By Wednesday night President Nixon had made his decision. On Thursday, August 8, it was announced that he would meet with congressional leaders that evening and then address the nation. In his televised resignation speech Nixon made no reference to the impending impeachment proceedings. Rather, he attributed his decision to resign to the lack of a "strong enough political base in Congress to justify continuing" to stay in public office.

Although President Nixon's resignation would end the impetus for impeachment, the process was in motion and had to be brought formally to a conclusion. Furthermore, the work of the House Judiciary Committee had historical and precedential value that needed to be preserved for the record. Thus, despite the president's resignation, the committee persevered in the preparation of its report, explaining the bases for its decisions to recommend impeachment. The 528-page report was then filed and accepted by a 412-3 vote of the House of Representatives. By accepting rather than approving the report, the House took official notice of the committee's recommendations and authorized the printing of the report without adopting the articles of impeachment and thereby setting a Senate trial in motion. Thus, while the House did not formally approve impeachment charges against Richard Nixon, its acceptance of the committee's report established a record of evidence that, as Rep. Charles B. Rangel (D-N.Y.) noted, made "it abundantly clear ... that he [Nixon] committed impeachable crimes and that on the available evidence he would have been impeached by the House of Representatives." [112]

On the morning of August 9, 1974, Nixon bid an emotional farewell to his cabinet and staff and left the White House for his residence in San Clemente, California. Nixon's terse letter of resignation reached the appropriate official—Secretary of State Henry Kissinger—shortly after 11:30 the same morning.[113] The first and only president to resign from office and only the second president to face the prospect of impeachment, Richard Nixon had become a part of American political history.

At noon Vice President Gerald Ford was sworn in as the thirty-eighth president of the United States. He declared: "Our long national nightmare is over. Our Constitution works." Popular and congressional support rallied to the new—and first unelected—president. Because Ford had been well liked as a member of Congress, it was hoped that relations between the executive and the legislature would improve. Addressing a joint session of Congress, Ford called for an "era of good feelings" with Congress and expressed confidence that the legislature would be both his "working partner" and a "constructive critic."

UPI/Bettmann Newsphotos

With the impending possibility of House impeachment, President Richard Nixon announces his resignation in an emotional television address on August 8, 1974. His wife, Pat, and daughter, Tricia, are at right. He was the first and only president to resign from office.

President Ford quickly took steps to provide for the presidential line of succession by nominating Nelson A. Rockefeller as vice president. Earlier in his career Rockefeller had twice turned down the vice presidency. In 1960, 1964, and 1968, he had made a run for the presidency, and many observers thought he was going to try again in 1976. Indeed, Rockefeller may have been the de facto Republican front-runner following the demise of the Nixon presidency. Nonetheless, under these extraordinary circumstances Rockefeller put aside his presidential ambitions and accepted the nomination to the vice presidency.

Despite the initially favorable reaction to his nomination, Rockefeller's substantial personal wealth generated considerable controversy and concern. During four months of grueling confirmation hearings, Congress questioned Rockefeller's practice of making loans and gifts to former members of his New York State administrations. It also wondered about the wisdom of placing the power of such wealth "only a heartbeat away" from the power of the presidency. Eventually, confirmation was secured, and on December 19, 1974, Nelson Rockefeller was sworn in as vice president. For the first time in American history both the president and vice president had been selected under the provisions of the Twenty-fifth Amendment rather than by national election.

Perhaps the second most far-reaching act of the new Ford administration was the granting to former president Nixon of a "full, free and absolute pardon . . . for all offenses against the United States which he . . . has committed or may have committed" during his years in office. Ford offered the pardon in the hope of ending the bitter and divisive national debate that had raged for the past year and a half. This exercise of the presidential pardoning power drew strong congressional and public criticism, effectively ending the new president's "honeymoon." The critics argued that the pardon circumvented the judicial process, and the House Judiciary Subcommittee on Criminal Justice convened hearings to investigate why it was granted. In an unprecedented appearance President Ford became the first incumbent president to testify formally before a congressional committee. He vigorously denied that he had made any secret arrangement with Nixon to grant a pardon in exchange for his resignation.

Nevertheless, some House members were so incensed by the Ford pardon that they called for a revival of impeachment hearings against the former president as one of the few options available to Congress for countering certain consequences of the pardoning action. Even Senate Majority Leader Michael J. Mansfield (D-Mont.) expressed regret that "the constitutional process of impeachment . . . was 'cut off at the pass.' " Despite such initial agitation, the effort to revive impeachment proceedings soon faded. House Judiciary Committee chairman Peter W. Rodino, Jr., (D-N.J.), who was opposed to any reconvening, argued that the major purpose of impeachment was removal from office (which had been accomplished by resignation) and should not be used as a tool to achieve any other objectives.[114]

Although President Ford had wanted to reestablish the legitimacy and credibility of the presidency and to revive public trust in the executive, these two early decisions tainted him and his administration with suspicions of deception and potential corruption. The public reaction to the pardon and the Rockefeller nomination also distracted the new administration from quickly assuming control of the government and taking advantage of the latent goodwill that Nixon's successor might have enjoyed.

During the next two years President Ford found that differences between Congress and the executive persisted, and that he could make little programmatic progress. When he changed his mind about seeking the presidential nomination he confronted serious opposition within his own party. His liabilities in seeking the 1976 nomination included the perception of him as a caretaker president who had never before run a national campaign and his association with the disgraced Nixon presidency. Strongly challenged for the nomination by Ronald Reagan, Ford narrowly succeeded in winning the Republican nomination, but he entered the election burdened by the backlash against Republicans in general that followed the Nixon resignation and hamstrung by the meager record of his own presidency (albeit one that had operated under severe political constraints). Thus, Ford could not convince a sufficient number of the voting public that he represented the trustworthiness and competence they were seeking in a president. Like so many other successor presidents, Gerald Ford failed to win reelection in his own right.

Presidential Disability

The Constitution anticipates the possibility that a president may fall victim to serious illness or death and provides as well for the need to remove a president from office through impeachment procedures. But the death of a president and the need to provide for the swift transfer of power to a successor is a relatively clear-cut matter compared to the problem of executive disability. According to the calculations of one scholar, the periods of presidential disability have left the country cumulatively without a president for nearly a full year.[115]

For most of the nation's history the issue of disability has been guided solely by a provision of Article II of the Constitution:

> In Case of ... Inability to discharge the Powers and Duties of the said Office, the Same shall devolve on the Vice President, and the Congress may by Law provide for the case of ... Inability, both of the President and Vice President, declaring what Officer shall then act as President, and such Officer shall act accordingly, until the Disability be removed, or a President shall be elected.

As presidential scholar Louis Koenig has noted, this "quagmire of ambiguity" left many questions unanswered.[116] What is meant by *disability*—does it include both mental and physical disabilities? Might it be a temporary condition or only a permanent one? Who is authorized to declare that a presidential disability exists—Congress, the vice president, or some combination of the Congress, the vice president, and the cabinet? To what does a vice president succeed in the case of a presidential disability—the "Powers and Duties of the said Office" or to the office itself? For the first hundred years of the Republic these questions did not have to be answered. Beginning with the eighty-day disability of President James Garfield in 1881, however, the problem of how to deal with a presidential disability arose.

The First Presidential Disability

The attempted assassination of James Garfield left him incapacitated from a gunshot wound that pierced his spinal column and generally unable to fulfill the duties of his office for the eighty days between the shooting and his death. During that period the problem of presidential disability was discussed widely.

According to one opinion, the disability must be limited to mental incapacity, or, as former senator William W. Eaton (D-Conn.) maintained, "there could be no disability that the President can be conscious of." [117] Others took the more general position that a disability could be either mental or physical and temporary or permanent in duration. And still others used a more situational approach, such as that of former senator Lyman Trumbull (R-Ill.), who argued that a presidential disability combined an incapacity that was generally known with an urgent need for executive action.

Similarly, the consequences of a vice president's assumption of presidential authority in the case of a disability were debated. The predominant view was that a vice president should act as president only temporarily, until the disabled president had recovered. Others believed, however, that once the duties of the presidency "devolved" upon the vice president, that individual became president for the remainder of the term, thereby dispossessing the elected president.

Opinion about who might declare a president disabled was divided between those who thought it a legislative function and those who saw it as a vice-presidential responsibility. The Garfield cabinet unanimously decided that Vice President Arthur should assume the executive responsibilities. When they proposed this to the vice president, he adamantly opposed any such assumption while Garfield was alive, seeing such action as politically charged and constitutionally ambiguous.

When he later became president, Arthur repeatedly expressed his concern about the ambiguities of the succession provision, particularly the proper response to a presidential disability. His concern did not stem, however, only from his experience with the Garfield disability. In the summer of 1882 President Arthur learned that he was suffering from a fatal kidney disease. Thus, he faced the possibility that his own disability might occur at a time when there was no incumbent vice president. A year later the illness forced Arthur to reduce his schedule to a half day, and the work of government slowed down noticeably. Nonetheless, President Arthur did not disclose publicly the full nature of his illness for political reasons, nor did he succeed in directing congressional attention to the succession and disability issue.[118]

The Secret Disability

Shortly after Grover Cleveland took office in March 1893 a financial panic struck the country: major industries went bankrupt, banks closed their doors, businesses shut down, and millions of people were thrown out of work. President Cleveland believed that a primary cause of the depression was the Sherman Silver Purchase Act of 1890; therefore he sought its repeal. On June 30, 1893, he called a special session of Congress to consider the proposed repeal.

The night that he called the special session, Cleveland boarded the yacht *Oneida* in New York City and embarked on a five-day cruise of Long Island Sound. For the next month he alternated between visits to his summer home on Buzzards Bay in Massachusetts and cruising on the yacht. On August 5, he returned to Washington, where he addressed the special session of Congress on August 7.

Unknown to the public and virtually all members of the government, including the vice president, President Cleveland had undergone an operation during that initial cruise and spent the subsequent weeks recuperating.[119] A surgeon had removed a cancerous growth from the roof of his mouth as well as a major part of his upper jaw. The entire operation, which had taken place while the unconscious president was strapped in a chair propped against the yacht's mast, had taken less than an hour and had required no external incision, thus leaving no scar. Later at his summer home Cleveland was fitted with an artificial jaw so that he could speak intelligibly. In late July, during a second cruise, the president underwent a second operation for removal of suspicious tissue noticed during the first operation.

By early August the president was sufficiently recovered to address the special session of Congress. At the end of the summer the *Philadelphia Press* published an account of the operations that was denounced officially as a hoax. Others claimed that the president simply had had a toothache that required the extraction of some teeth. The president's doctors as well as government officials neither denied nor confirmed the story. As the president seemed to be in fine health with no noticeable changes in his facial structure or speech, the story faded.

Not until twenty-four years later, with the 1917 publication of a story in the *Saturday Evening Post* by one of Cleveland's doctors, were the facts revealed to the public. Cleveland had insisted on complete secrecy because he feared further unsettling a public that was in the throes of a financial panic. As the doctor-author commented, "What the consequences would have been had it become known at once we can only surmise and shudder!" [120]

The Wilson Disability

On September 25, 1919, as he was conducting a speaking tour of the country to gain support for the League of Nations, President Woodrow Wilson fell ill. The public was informed that the president had suffered a complete nervous breakdown brought on by overwork and the effects of an earlier attack of influenza. The rest of the speaking trip was cancelled, and the president returned to Washington where on October 2 he suffered a stroke that paralyzed the left side of his body.

Thereafter the White House was turned into a nursing ward under the direction of Dr. Cary Grayson, the president's close friend and physician, and Mrs. Wilson, with the assistance of the presidential secretary Joseph P. Tumulty. Vague and ambiguous health bulletins sparked wild rumors about the president's condition. Nevertheless, Edith Bolling Galt Wilson's first concern was trying to save her husband, and if that meant shielding him from the responsibilities and decisions of the presidency, then she was determined to do so.[121]

For more than six months after his stroke President Wilson was bedridden and saw very few people. Meanwhile, the country was in the midst of a difficult transition from war to peace, with the attendant issues of readjusting the economy to a peacetime footing, demobilizing the armed forces, and considering the Versailles peace treaty with its controversial League of Nations provisions.

Clearly, executive leadership was necessary in such circumstances. Mrs. Wilson and Tumulty did what they could to marshall and focus the president's meager energies for occasional demonstrations of competency and official tasks such as the approval of papers or speech drafts and the dictation of strategy instructions for the treaty fight. Secretary of State Robert Lansing was concerned about the potential drift in government affairs, and the day after Wilson's stroke he spoke to Tumulty about the possibility of calling upon Vice President Thomas R. Marshall to act as president. At that meeting Lansing read the succession provision of the Constitution to Tumulty, who replied that he was in no need of any tutoring on the subject. He then declared, "You may rest assured that while Woodrow Wilson is lying in the White House on the broad of his back I will not be a party to ousting him." [122] At a cabinet meeting on October 6 (called at Lansing's initiative), a discussion of presidential disability was ended abruptly by the arrival of Tumulty and Grayson. They informed the cabinet not only that the president was irritated that a cabinet meeting had been convened without his authority, but also that they, the president's secretary and physician, respectively, would repudiate any attempt to declare Wilson disabled.

As the weeks and months passed there were repeated calls for Vice President Marshall to act as president. But in the face of ambiguous constitutional guidelines, no useful historical precedents, and the decided reluctance of the vice president, affairs of state continued to drift. Indeed, Vice President Marshall was quite concerned that he not give the appearance of attempting to usurp executive power, and he certainly was loath to incur the wrath of Mrs. Wilson. Marshall reportedly said, "I am not going to get myself entangled with Mrs. Wilson. No politician ever exposes himself to the hatred of a woman, particularly if she's the wife of the President of the United States." [123] The possibility of Wilson's resignation also arose, but one doctor opposed it, telling Mrs. Wilson that such action might remove the president's main incentive for recovery.

During the next five months Secretary of State Lansing tried to coordinate government affairs somewhat by convening informal cabinet meetings. Between October 1919 and February 1920 he called more than twenty such meetings, but because the United States has never had a system of cabinet government, there were many matters that the cabinet could not handle. For example, it could not sign bills into law; nearly thirty bills became law by default for want of any executive action during this period. And because the cabinet could not make presidential appointments, many government vacancies went unfilled. Also unable to provide executive leadership in foreign relations, the cabinet could not manage the ratification controversy with the Senate or accept the credentials of foreign representatives.

Perhaps it was a sign of Wilson's partial recovery that in February 1920 he wrote Lansing to voice his objection to the secretary's convocation of the cabinet. In replying to the president's letter Lansing wrote that his actions betrayed no intention of assuming or exercising presidential powers. Wilson responded with the blunt suggestion that Lansing submit his resignation, which he did on February 12, 1920. Wilson reportedly told Tumulty, "It is never the wrong time to spike disloyalty. When Lansing sought to oust me, I was upon my back. I am on my feet now and I will not have disloyalty about me." [124]

Following Lansing's dismissal a number of disability proposals were considered by Congress. One plan sought to empower the Supreme Court to declare a president disabled if authorized by congressional resolution. Another sought to have a presidential disability certified by a majority declaration of the cabinet. Although hearings were held on these proposals, no action was taken. On April 13, 1920, President Wilson held his first cabinet meeting in six months. Although he never fully recovered, the president became more active in government affairs and finished out the remaining months of his second term of office.

The Wilson disability demonstrated at least two important lessons. First, a presidential disability could last for months, rather than simply a few days or even weeks, and might reoccur. Second, a formal mechanism was needed to declare a president disabled. Clearly, informal attempts to draft the vice president to act as president or to have the cabinet try to provide executive leadership were bound to prove inadequate and likely to appear disloyal. Yet nothing was done to demonstrate the benefit of these lessons.

The Eisenhower Disabilities

The presidency of Dwight Eisenhower brought the disability issue into vivid and repeated focus. Between 1955 and 1957 President Eisenhower suffered three illnesses that left him partially disabled for a total of almost twenty-three weeks. Paradoxically, this succession of illnesses led to the development of informal precedents and procedures for dealing with presidential disabilities.

While vacationing in Colorado in September 1955, the president suffered a moderate heart attack that required complete rest for about a month. Fortunately, the illness struck when there were no crises in either domestic or foreign affairs and when Congress was out of session. Thus, the press of public business was routine and helped to mitigate the impact of the disability.

Other factors also facilitated the administration's ability to deal with the presidential disability. For example, fortunately Vice President Nixon was an established participant in the National Security Council and cabinet meetings. Indeed, Nixon often had presided over these bodies in the president's absence. Furthermore, President Eisenhower had an extensive White House support staff as well as cabinet secretaries accustomed to broad delegations of authority. Thus, the administration was structured so that it could shoulder the added burden of a temporary presidential disability. Finally, both the president and the secretary of state, John Foster Dulles, were fully aware of the problems presented by the Wilson disability, and they were determined to avoid them whenever possible. Because President Eisenhower remembered how the vague reports about President Wilson's condition had led to wild rumors, he was determined to keep the public fully informed about his condition and progress.[125] Similarly, Secretary Dulles recalled how the apprehensions and misinterpretations stemming from the cabinet meetings called by his uncle Robert Lansing during the Wilson disability had led to Secretary Lansing's dismissal.[126] Thus, Dulles was determined to avoid even the slightest appearance of impropriety or disloyalty. When combined, these conditions allowed the relatively smooth handling of the president's first illness.

By the end of the president's first week in the hospital both the National Security Council and the cabinet had met at their scheduled times, with the vice president presiding. At the cabinet meeting a set of administrative operating principles were agreed upon, including the assignment of White House assistant Sherman Adams to act as the primary liaison with the president. Thus, the administration team of White House staff and cabinet officers under the direct of de facto chief of staff Adams quietly assumed responsibility for maintaining the regular operations of the executive branch. Simultaneously, Vice President Nixon carried on with certain ceremonial and established functions.[127]

The president's recuperation progressed well: he was receiving visitors after the second week and was discharged from the hospital in six weeks. He met with the cabinet in late November and returned to the White House, fully recovered, by mid-January 1956. Indeed, the president's fast recovery not only defused the disability issue; it also put to rest speculation over Eisenhower's intention and ability to run for a second term.

Not nine months after his heart attack, however, the president was struck by another illness, an attack of ileitis (inflammation of the ileum, a part of the small intestine). The president was hospitalized, and he underwent successful exploratory surgery on June 9, 1956. Within two days he was allowed to meet with staff and was walking about. Although President Eisenhower needed to rest, he was quite aware and capable of performing official acts. On July 21 the president embarked on a trip to Panama to attend a meeting with South American presidents. Although fully recovered, the president was nonetheless distressed by his illness. He especially was disturbed that the country had been without an able president while he was on the operating table.

The president's third illness, a mild stroke, occurred seventeen and a half months later, on November 25, 1957, at a time of considerable international tension. The United States was still reeling from the shock to its military and technological prestige prompted by the Soviet launching of *Sputnik I* in October. Simultaneously, there were troubling signs of the developing acute recession of 1958, and a meeting of heads of state organized by the North Atlantic Treaty Organization (NATO) was three weeks off. Fortunately, the president's mild stroke caused him only some brief difficulty in speaking, and by December 2 he was back to his normal routine.

In the aftermath of this third illness the president asked the Justice Department to recommend a procedure for dealing with the presidential disability problem. Eventually, it was decided to propose a constitutional amendment that recommended how to declare and terminate a presidential disability. The amendment's recommendations were met with little enthusiasm from the Republican congressional leaders and by strong opposition from the Democrats. Confronted with congressional reluctance to deal with the problem, Eisenhower and Nixon worked out their own informal arrangement through a letter of agreement made public on March 3, 1958. This agreement also was adopted by President John Kennedy and Vice President Lyndon Johnson in August 1961, by President Johnson and Speaker John McCormack in December 1963, and by President Johnson and Vice President Hubert H. Humphrey in January 1965.

Several other occurrences of presidential disability also incited discussion of presidential succession. One such occurence was in 1813, when James Madison suffered an illness that left him unable to perform his presidential duties for almost three weeks. Although as on previous occasions the vice president assumed command, in this case both the president and the vice president, Elbridge Gerry, were ill. These circumstances placed a new importance upon the more extended line of succession, which at that time passed first to the president pro tempore of the Senate and then to the Speaker of the House. This concern was reinforced again a year later when Vice President Gerry died, thus leaving a vacancy in the line of succession. Since then, the problem of providing for an extended line of succession in the absence of a vice president has arisen eighteen times, or for a total of forty years, when the United States has been without a vice president because the vice president either succeeded to the presidency, died, or resigned.[128]

Passage of the Twenty-fifth Amendment

Although the nation's experience with presidential illness had prompted discussion of how to deal with presidential disability and the vice-presidential vacancy created by succession upon the death of a president, in each case the passing of the immediate crisis removed the incentive for formal action. The assassination of President Kennedy, however, helped generate an irresistible momentum for dealing with these issues, since it was agreed that the nation should not find itself without executive leadership in the nuclear age.

Awareness of the disability and succession issue was multifaceted and came at the end of a sequence of troubling experiences. Indeed, since the decline and death of Franklin Roosevelt in 1944-1945, each presidency has confronted the problems of presidential disability and succession. Harry Truman served for nearly four years without a vice president. And Dwight Eisenhower was temporarily disabled by a succession of illnesses during the mid-1950s. After Eisenhower's 1955 heart attack the House Judiciary Committee set up a special subcommittee chaired by Rep. Emanuel Celler (D-N.Y.) to study the problem of presidential disability. The subcommittee could not reach agreement, however, and it reported to the parent committee on May 16, 1957, without making any recommendations. Thus, congressional action languished until after President Eisenhower's third illness when Sen. Estes Kefauver (D-Tenn.), chairman of the Subcommittee on Constitutional Amendments of the Senate Judiciary Committee, held hearings on the issue in January and February of 1958. Again these proceedings failed to produce procedures for determining the existence and termination of a disability. They did seem to demonstrate, however, that there was an emerging consensus about two matters: (1) following the death, resignation, or removal of the president the vice president becomes president (not merely acting president) for the remainder of the term, and (2) in cases of presidential disability the vice president merely acts for the president for the duration of the president's disability.[129]

In the early 1960s, both senators Kefauver and Kenneth B. Keating (R-N.Y.) joined forces to promote reconsideration of the matter. In reconvening hearings on the issue in June 1963, Senator Kefauver noted that the incumbency of a young and obviously healthy president would allow the exploration of the topic "without any implication that the present holder of that high office is not in good health" and would allow the nation "to prepare now for the possible crises of the future." [130] But a double tragedy delayed action once again: the sudden death of Senator Kefauver in August brought the congressional proceedings to a temporary halt, and the assassination of President Kennedy emphasized anew the need to prepare for the unexpected.

The Kennedy assassination also revived concern about the vacancy that occurred in the vice presidency. When Lyndon Johnson acceded to the presidency the nation faced a period of over a year in which there would be no vice president. This prompted particular concern at the time because of the advanced age of the next two officials in the line of succession: House Speaker John McCormack was seventy-one, and President Pro Tempore of the Senate Carl Hayden was eighty-six. It was uncertain how a congressional succession would work if found necessary. For example, if one day the Speaker acceded to the presidency and resigned from the House, would the newly elected Speaker then have precedence over the president pro tempore of the Senate, who ostensibly was next in the line of succession? Thus, congressional intent in fashioning the line of succession to go through both houses of Congress appeared frustrated. There were also unanswered questions about the workability of a Speaker temporarily serving as president in the case of a president's disability when there was no vice president. To do so, the Speaker would have to resign from the House with little possibility of regaining that legislative position once the executive disability had passed. A Speaker would thus be reluctant to fill a temporary vacancy, thereby impeding the intention of Congress in providing for an extended line of succession.[131]

Kefauver's young successor as chairman of the Subcommittee on Constitutional Amendments, Sen. Birch E. Bayh (D-Ind.), brought new energy to consideration of a constitutional amendment to deal with the subject of presidential disability and the subsequent vice-presidential vacancy, and the American Bar Association mobilized to assist Congress in the process. During hearings held the first three months of 1964, a consensus was forged on acceptable procedures for declaring and terminating a period of presidential disability and on confirmation procedures for filling a vacancy in the vice presidency. These arrangements were embodied in a joint resolution proposing the Twenty-fifth Amendment, which was introduced in January 1965. Six months later, the proposed amendment was approved by both houses of Congress with virtually no opposition. Ratification by the states required 219 days and the amendment took effect on February 10, 1967.

According to the new amendment, the vice president would become acting president under one of two circumstances: if the president informed Congress that he or she was unable to perform the presidential duties or if the vice president and a majority of the cabinet each found the president incapacitated. In each case the vice president would become acting president until the disability had ended. In the event of a dispute over the termination of a president's disability, Congress was given twenty-one days to resolve the dispute. A two-thirds vote of each house was required to deny the president office. And finally, when a vacancy occurred in the office of vice president, whether upon the death or resignation of a vice president or upon the vice president's succession to the presidency, the president was empowered to nominate a vice president, who was subject to confirmation by a majority vote of both houses of Congress.

Applications of the Twenty-fifth Amendment

Since ratification of the Twenty-fifth Amendment, three of its four sections have been invoked. Section 1, which confirmed the Tyler Precedent, accorded constitutional certainty to the practice that a vice president succeeding a president who died or resigned thus becomes president, not merely acting president.

Section 2, on filling a vacancy in the vice presidency, has been used twice. The first instance occurred when President Nixon nominated Gerald Ford on October 12,

1973, following the resignation of Vice President Spiro Agnew. Ten months later, in August 1974, President Ford nominated Nelson Rockefeller to fill the vacancy created when Ford himself succeeded to the presidency following President Nixon's resignation.

Section 3, on provisions for the declaration of a temporary presidential disability, has been invoked once, when President Reagan was hospitalized for colon cancer surgery in July 1985. Although President Reagan was mindful of this section of the Twenty-fifth Amendment, he did not think it applied to the situation in which he was unconscious for surgery. Observing that he did not wish to set a precedent that would be binding upon his successors, he nonetheless passed "to the vice president his powers and duties . . . commencing with the administration of anesthesia . . . in this instance." The president went on to note that he would notify the Speaker of the House when he determined that he was "able to resume the discharge of the constitutional powers and duties" of his office.[133]

Section 4 deals with the declaration that a president is unfit to fulfill his or her responsibilities. Prior to passage of the Twenty-fifth Amendment there was no mechanism, short of impeachment, for dealing with an unfit president who would not resign or who was mentally incapable of resigning from office. Impeachment was, however, an inadequate procedure; it was designed to deal with "high Crimes and Misdemeanors," not health problems. Although this provision has stood unused since ratification of the amendment in 1967, in retrospect one can hypothesize that it might have been applicable to the final period of Woodrow Wilson's presidency or the final months of the Roosevelt presidency.

Thus, lawmakers in passing the Twenty-fifth Amendment sought to embody the wisdom and lessons gained from previous experiences and to provide for unforeseen exigencies in the future. Although the amendment did not resolve all problems and ambiguities, it was, as Walter Lippmann observed, "a great deal better than an endless search . . . for the absolutely perfect solution . . . which will never be found, and . . . is not necessary." [134]

Notes

1. Ruth C. Silva, *Presidential Succession* (Ann Arbor, Mich.: University of Michigan Press, 1951), 8.
2. For a discussion of the lines of succession, see John D. Feerick, *From Failing Hands* (New York: Fordham University Press, 1965), 264-269.
3. Ibid., 87-88.
4. James A. Green, *William Henry Harrison, His Life and Times* (Richmond, Va.: Gerrett and Massie, 1941), 393.
5. Ibid.
6. James D. Richardson, *Messages and Papers of the Presidents, 1789-1897* (Washington, D.C.: Bureau of National Literature, 1897), 4:21.
7. For details of what Green considers Harrison's mistreatment by physicians, see *William Henry Harrison,* 398-399.
8. Richardson, *Messages and Papers,* 4:31-32.
9. *Daily National Intelligencer,* April 15, 1841, 3.
10. Robert Seager II, *And Tyler Too, A Biography of John and Julia Gardiner Tyler* (New York: McGraw-Hill, 1963), 149.
11. Feerick, *From Failing Hands,* 98.
12. For more on the campaign, see K. Jack Bauer, *Zachary Taylor: Soldier, Planter, Statesman of the Old Southwest* (Baton Rouge, La.: Louisiana State University Press, 1985), 239-247.
13. Ibid., 254-255.
14. For further discussion of the disunion of the Whig party and the disarray of the Taylor cabinet, see Benson Lee Grayson, *The Unknown President: The Administration of Millard Fillmore* (Washington, D.C.: University Press of America, 1981), 2-5.
15. John Durant and Alice Durant, *Pictorial History of American Presidents* (New York: Barnes, 1955), 94.
16. Bauer, *Zachary Taylor,* 237. William H. Seward was the senior U.S. senator from the state of New York and a major figure in the Whig party there. Thurlow Weed was Republican party boss in the state of New York.
17. Ibid., 308.
18. Robert J. Rayback, *Millard Fillmore, Biography of a President* (Buffalo, N.Y.: Henry Stewart, 1959), 242.
19. For more on the legislative and executive tactics used to achieve the Great Compromise, see ibid., 246-253.
20. Grayson, *The Unknown President,* 137-143.
21. Robert K. Murray, *The Harding Era* (Minneapolis: University of Minnesota Press, 1969), 13-14.
22. Ibid., 69.
23. Ibid., 66-67.
24. For the details of this final trip, see ibid., 439-445.
25. Ibid., 456-457.
26. As quoted in ibid., 457-458.
27. Durant and Durant, *Pictorial History,* 243.
28. Feerick, *From Failing Hands,* 182.
29. Murray, *The Harding Era,* 499.
30. Ibid., 500-501.
31. For an assessment of the Harding-Coolidge transition and legacy, see ibid., 498-514.
32. See Jim Bishop, *FDR's Last Year* (New York: Morrow, 1974), 3-12.
33. Cabell Phillips, *The 1940's, Decade of Triumph and Trouble* (New York: Macmillan, 1975), 242-243.
34. Bishop, *FDR's Last Year,* 596-598.
35. Ibid., 609-610.
36. Harry S Truman, *Memoirs* (Garden City, N.Y.: Doubleday, 1955), 1:9-10.
37. Phillips, *The 1940's,* 252.
38. Marquis James, *Andrew Jackson* (New York: Bobbs-Merrill, 1937), 390-391.
39. Durant and Durant, *Pictorial History,* 128.
40. Recounted in Dorothy Meserve Kunhardt and Philip B. Kunhardt, Jr., *Twenty Days* (North Hollywood, Calif.: Newcastle, 1985), 12.
41. Quoted in Feerick, *From Failing Hands,* 109.
42. For more on the attack on Seward, see Kunhardt and Kunhardt, *Twenty Days,* 50-53.
43. For more on the funeral arrangements in Washington, D.C., and on the trip back to Springfield, Illinois, for burial, see ibid., 119-302.
44. Justus D. Doenecke, *The Presidencies of James A. Garfield and Chester A. Arthur* (Lawrence: Regents Press of Kansas, 1981), 27.
45. Ibid., 29.
46. For more on the negotiations and maneuvering to form the Garfield cabinet, see ibid., 30-35.
47. Ibid., 41-45.
48. Feerick, *From Failing Hands,* 118-120.
49. Ibid., 127-128.
50. For more on the problems in the line of succession following Arthur, see Birch Bayh, *One Heartbeat Away: Presidential Disability and Succession* (Indianapolis, Ind.: Bobbs-Merrill, 1968), 17-18.
51. As quoted in Doenecke, *The Presidencies,* 181.
52. Inaugural address quoted in Lewis L. Gould, *The Presidency of William McKinley* (Lawrence: Regents Press of Kansas, 1981), 240.
53. McKinley's first vice president, Garret Augustus Hobart, died of a heart attack in November 1899. Hobart was widely reputed to have restored the vice presidency to a position of dignity and importance. Indeed, the press often called him

the "Assistant President." Despite this favorable precedent, Theodore Roosevelt resisted the call to the vice presidency. As support for his nomination grew, Roosevelt issued a statement, which said, "Under no circumstances could I, or would I, accept the nomination for the Vice Presidency." Nevertheless, it was the unanimous first ballot consensus of the Republican convention that it wanted Roosevelt, and Roosevelt found this to be an invitation that he could not refuse. For more on the Hobart vice presidency and the Roosevelt nomination, see Feerick, *From Failing Hands,* 152-155.

54. See Gould, *The Presidency of William McKinley,* 250-251.
55. Ibid., 251.
56. For more on the purpose of Kennedy's visit to Texas, see Arthur M. Schlesinger, Jr., *A Thousand Days* (New York: Fawcett, 1977), 1017-1019.
57. Ibid., 1022.
58. Ibid., 1021.
59. William Manchester, *The Death of a President* (New York: Harper and Row), 153.
60. Ibid., 233.
61. Ibid., 530.
62. Quoted in Feerick, *From Failing Hands,* 243-244.
63. For further information about the various assaults and assassinations of presidents as well as their impact on protective services and practices and politics, see Frederick M. Kaiser, "Presidential Assassinations and Assaults: Characteristics and Impact on Protective Procedures," *Presidential Studies Quarterly* 11: 4 (Fall 1981): 545-558, and William C. Spragens, "Political Impact of Presidential Assassinations and Attempted Assassinations," *Presidential Studies Quarterly* 10: 6 (Summer 1980): 336-347.
64. In 1912 an attempt was made to assassinate former president Theodore Roosevelt who was then a presidential candidate after being out of office for almost four years. Although the assailant, John Schrank, wounded Roosevelt, the wound was not fatal. Attempts also have been made on two other presidential candidates, Sen. Robert F. Kennedy (D-N.Y.) in 1968 and Alabama governor George C. Wallace in 1972. Kennedy died, and Wallace was severely injured.
65. For more details on the Reagan assassination attempt, see *Reagan's First Year* (Washington, D.C.: Congressional Quarterly Inc., 1982), 3-9.
66. *The Federalist Papers,* No. 65, with an introduction by Clinton Rossiter (New York: Mentor, 1961), 397.
67. Joseph Story, *Commentaries on the Constitution of the United States* (Boston: Hilliard Gray, 1833), vol. 2, sec. 798.
68. Raoul Berger, *Impeachment: The Constitutional Problems* (Cambridge.: Harvard University Press, 1973), 31, where he quotes G. M. Trevelyan's *Illustrated History of England* (London: Longmans Green, 1956), 391.
69. For more on House impeachment procedures, see U.S. Congress, House, Committee on the Judiciary, *Impeachment: Selected Materials on Procedure,* 93d Cong., 1st sess., 1973, and 93d Cong., 2d sess., 1973.
70. See U.S. Congress, House, Committee on the Judiciary, *Constitutional Grounds for Presidential Impeachment,* 93d Cong., 2d sess., January 1974.
71. As quoted from the *Congressional Record* in Louis Fisher, *Constitutional Conflicts between Congress and the President* (Princeton, N.J.: Princeton University Press, 1985), 200-201.
72. "An Analysis of the Constitutional Standards for Presidential Impeachment," February 1974, prepared by James D. St. Clair, John J. Chester, Michael A. Sterlacci, Jerome Murphy, and Loren A. Smith (attorneys for the president).
73. Fisher, *Constitutional Conflicts,* 202.
74. For a discussion of this debate, see Berger, *Impeachment,* 78-85.
75. The concept was proposed by Edward S. Corwin in *The President: Office and Powers, 1787-1948* (New York: New York University Press, 1948), 369. He wrote that initially Lincoln claimed an interim war power authority that was operative only until Congress could ratify his actions. Later the Supreme Court's decision in the *Prize Cases* (2 Black 635, 1863) led to a more expansive claim, which in turn "led him to break over constitutional bounds and become a dictator even exceeding the Roman model."

    Later, Clinton Rossiter used the term "constitutional dictator" to describe Lincoln's expansive use of presidential powers during a time of national emergency. See Clinton Rossiter, *The American Presidency,* rev. ed. (New York: New American Library, 1960), 142.
76. Arthur M. Schlesinger, Jr., *The Imperial Presidency* (Boston: Houghton Mifflin, 1973), 74.
77. Michael L. Benedict, *The Impeachment and Trial of Andrew Johnson* (New York: Norton, 1973), 21.
78. In a historiographical essay discussing changing interpretations of the Johnson presidency, his impeachment, and histories of the Reconstruction period, Benedict noted that the earliest historians of the period placed much of the blame for Johnson's political troubles on the president himself. See ibid., 202.
79. For a typology of presidential personalies, see James David Barber, *The Presidential Character,* 3d ed. (Englewood Cliffs, N.J.: Prentice-Hall, 1985).
80. According to the Benedict historiographical essay (*The Impeachment and Trial of Andrew Johnson,* 202), historians of the 1920s had come to develop a new appreciation for President Johnson and had begun to cast him as something of a heroic figure attempting to curb the excesses of the Reconstruction congresses.
81. William M. Goldsmith, *The Growth of Presidential Power* (New York: Chelsea House, 1974), 2:1036.
82. David Donald, "Why They Impeached Andrew Johnson," *American Heritage* (December 1956): 22.
83. Benedict, *The Impeachment and Trial of Andrew Johnson,* 3.
84. See commentary in ibid., 3.
85. *Guide to Congress,* 3d ed. (Washington, D.C.: Congressional Quarterly Inc., 1982), 250.
86. Benedict, *The Impeachment and Trial of Andrew Johnson,* 5.
87. Goldsmith, *The Growth of Presidential Power,* 2:1033-1035.
88. Abraham Lincoln, "Last Public Address on Reconstruction, April 11, 1985," in ibid., 2:1020-1023.
89. David Miller DeWitt, *Impeachment and Trial of Andrew Johnson* (New York: Macmillan, 1903), 135.
90. Goldsmith, *The Growth of Presidential Power,* 2:1054.
91. Compiled from *Presidential Vetoes, 1789-1976* (Washington, D.C.: Government Printing Office, 1978).
92. DeWitt, *Impeachment and Trial of Andrew Johnson,* 269.
93. DeWitt quotes a private letter from General Grant to the president about the possible removal of Secretary of War Stanton. In the letter of August 1, 1867, Grant comments that Stanton's "removal cannot be effected against his will without the consent of the Senate.... It certainly was the intention of the legislative branch of the Government to place cabinet ministers beyond the power of Executive removal and it is pretty well understood that ... [the Tenure of Office Act] was intended specifically to protect the Secretary of War" (ibid., 272).
94. Benedict, *The Impeachment and Trial of Andrew Johnson,* 102.
95. For more on the attempt to remove Stanton from office and on the interchanges between Stanton and Thomas, see DeWitt, *Impeachment and Trial of Andrew Johnson,* 339-356.
96. For more on the trial, see ibid., chap. 6; on Johnson's defense, see 422-514.
97. See the text of the Tenure of Office Act reprinted in Goldsmith, *The Growth of Presidential Power,* 2:1045-1047, particularly sec. 1.
98. DeWitt, *Impeachment and Trial of Andrew Johnson,* 436.
99. Berger, *Impeachment,* 264.
100. Ibid., 267-269.
101. In *The Impeachment and Trial of Andrew Johnson,* Bene-

dict wrote that a number of Republicans feared that a Wade administration would be disastrous for both the country and the party. Benedict quoted a May 1868 letter from Garfield to James Harrison Rhodes in which Garfield wrote that Wade is "a man of violent passions, extreme opinions, and narrow views; . . . a grossly profane coarse nature who is surrounded by the worst and most violent elements in the Republican Party . . ." (134-135).

102. DeWitt, *Impeachment and Trial of Andrew Johnson*, 517-518.
103. Ibid., 623-624.
104. The opinion written by former president and Chief Justice William Howard Taft in *Myers v. United States*, 272 U.S. 52 (1926), enunciated a broad interpretation of the president's removal power, declaring it unrestricted, even in the presence of statutory limits.
105. Berger, *Impeachment*, 300.
106. Richard Nathan, *The Administrative Presidency* (New York: Wiley, 1983).
107. For a full account of the Watergate investigations and their political impact, see *Watergate: Chronology of a Crisis*, 2 vols. (Washington, D.C.: Congressional Quarterly Inc., 1974) and Theodore H. White, *Breach of Faith: The Fall of Richard Nixon* (New York: Dell, 1975).
108. George A. Nikolaieff, *The President and the Constitution* (New York: H.W. Wilson, 1974), 38.
109. "Judge John Sirica: Standing Firm for the Primacy of Law," *Time*, January 7, 1974, as reprinted in ibid., 64-65.
110. Eleanora W. Schoenebaum, ed., *Profiles of an Era: The Nixon-Ford Years* (New York: Harcourt Brace Jovanovich, 1979), xvi.
111. Quoted by Nikolaieff from "A Very Definitive Decision," *Newsweek*, August 5, 1974, 23-26.
112. As reported from the committee report in *Presidency, 1974* (Washington, D.C.: Congressional Quarterly Inc., 1975), 32.
113. For the text of Nixon's televised address as well as his farewell remarks the following day, see Richard M. Nixon, *The Public Papers of the President, 1974* (Washington, D.C.: Government Printing Office, 1975), 626-633. According to 62 Stat. 678, dated June 25, 1948, the secretary of state is the designated recipient of any resignation letters by presidents and vice presidents.
114. *Presidency, 1974*, 38.
115. Richard Hansen, *The Year We Had No President* (Lincoln: University of Nebraska Press, 1962), as quoted in Louis W. Koenig, *The Chief Executive*, 4th ed. (New York: Harcourt Brace Jovanovich, 1981), 79.
116. Koenig, *The Chief Executive*, 114.
117. Quoted by Feerick in his discussion of the Garfield disability. See *From Failing Hands*, 133-139, especially 133.
118. John D. Feerick, *The Twenty-Fifth Amendment* (New York: Fordham University Press, 1976), 10-11.
119. On the Cleveland case, see Feerick, *From Failing Hands*, 147-151 and ibid., 11-12.
120. Quoted in Feerick, *From Failing Hands*, 151.
121. In her memoirs, Mrs. Wilson said that "Woodrow Wilson was first my beloved husband whose life I was trying to save, fighting with my back to the wall—after that he was the President of the United States." Quoted in a discussion of the Wilson disability in ibid., 173.
122. Joseph P. Tumulty, *Woodrow Wilson As I Know Him* (Garden City, N.Y.: Doubleday, 1921), as quoted in Feerick, *The Twenty-Fifth Amendment*, 13.
123. Quoted in Feerick, *The Twenty-Fifth Amendment*, 14.
124. For more on the exchange of letters between Wilson and Lansing, see Feerick, *From Failing Hands*, 176-177. Wilson's comments on Lansing's disloyalty are quoted on p. 179.
125. Ibid., 215-216.
126. For more on Dulles's awareness of the Lansing experiences, see Feerick, *The Twenty-Fifth Amendment*, 18.
127. Koenig, *The Chief Executive*, 83.
128. John C. Calhoun resigned as vice president on December 28, 1832, to become a U.S. senator, and Spiro T. Agnew resigned on October 10, 1973.
129. For more on the preliminary hearings and discussions on the disability issue during the 1950s and early 1960s, see Feerick, *From Failing Hands*, 237-257.
130. Quoted in ibid., 243.
131. Many of these arguments were summarized in a *Washington Post* article of December 2, 1963, which is reprinted in Bayh, *One Heartbeat Away*, 9-10.
132. For an assessment of how the Twenty-fifth Amendment has worked since its ratification twenty years ago, see *Report of the Miller Center Commission on Presidential Disability and the Twenty-Fifth Amendment* (Lanham, Md.: University Press of America, 1988).
133. From a letter from President Reagan to the Speaker of the House of Representatives, dated July 13, 1985, as summarized and quoted in White Burkett Miller Center of Public Affairs, *Miller Center Commission Report* (Lanham, Md.: University Press of America, 1988), 6.
134. Quoted in Koenig, *The Chief Executive*, 86.

Selected Bibliography

Bauer, K. Jack. *Zachary Taylor: Soldier, Planter, Statesman of the Old Southwest*. Baton Rouge, La.: Louisiana State University Press, 1985.

Bayh, Birch. *One Heartbeat Away: Presidential Disability and Succession*. Indianapolis, Ind.: Bobbs-Merrill, 1968.

Benedict, Michael L. *The Impeachment and Trial of Andrew Johnson*. New York: Norton, 1973.

Berger, Raoul. *Impeachment: The Constitutional Problems*. Cambridge: Harvard University Press, 1973.

Corwin, Edward S. *The President: Office and Powers 1787-1948*. New York: New York University Press, 1948.

DeWitt, David Miller. *Impeachment and Trial of Andrew Johnson*. New York: Macmillan, 1903.

Doenecke, Justus D. *The Presidencies of James A. Garfield and Chester A. Arthur*. Lawrence: Regents Press of Kansas, 1981.

Donald, David. "Why They Impeached Andrew Johnson." *American Heritage* 8 (December 1956): 20-25.

Feerick, John D. *From Failing Hands*. New York: Fordham University Press, 1965.

Feerick, John D. *The Twenty-Fifth Amendment*. New York: Fordham University Press, 1976.

Fisher, Louis. *Constitutional Conflicts between Congress and the President*. Princeton, N.J.: Princeton University Press, 1985.

Goldsmith, William M. *The Growth of Presidential Power*, vol. 2. New York: Chelsea House, 1974.

Grayson, Benson Lee. *The Unknown President: The Administration of Millard Fillmore*. Washington, D.C.: University Press of America, 1981.

Green, James A. *William Henry Harrison, His Life and Times*. Richmond, Va.: Gerrett and Massie, 1941.

Hansen, Richard. *The Year We Had No President*. Lincoln: University of Nebraska Press, 1962.

Kaiser, Frederick M. *Presidential Protection: Assassinations, Assaults, and Secret Service Protective Procedures*. Washington, D.C.: Congressional Research Service, 1981.

Manchester, William. *The Death of the President*. New York: Harper and Row, 1967.

McKitrick, Eric. *Andrew Johnson: President on Trial*. New York: Farrar, Straus and Giroux, 1960.

Moe, Ronald C. *Presidential Succession*. Washington, D.C.: Congressional Research Service, 1979.

Murray, Robert K. *The Harding Era*. Minneapolis: University of Minnesota Press, 1969.

Rayback, Robert J. *Millard Fillmore, Biography of a President*. Buffalo, N.Y.: Henry Stewart, 1959.

Report of the Miller Center Commission on Presidential Disability and the Twenty-Fifth Amendment. Lanham, Md.: Univer-

sity Press of America, 1988.
Rossiter, Clinton. *The American Presidency.* Rev. ed. New York: New American Library, 1960.
Seager, Robert, II. *And Tyler Too, A Biography of John and Julia Gardiner Tyler.* New York: McGraw-Hill, 1963.
Silva, Ruth C. *Presidential Succession.* Ann Arbor: University of Michigan Press, 1951.
Sindler, Allan P. *Unchosen Presidents.* Berkeley: University of California Press, 1976.
U.S. Congress. House. Committee on the Judiciary. *Impeachment: Selected Materials.* Washington, D.C.: Government Printing Office, October 1973.
U.S. Congress. House. Committee on the Judiciary. *Impeachment: Selected Materials on Procedure.* Washington, D.C.: Government Printing Office, January 1974.
U.S. Congress. House. Committee on the Judiciary. *Constitutional Grounds for Presidential Impeachment.* Washington, D.C.: Government Printing Office, February 1974.
Watergate: Chronology of a Crisis, vol. 2. Washington, D.C.: Congressional Quarterly Inc., 1974.
White, Theodore H. *Breach of Faith: The Fall of Richard Nixon.* New York: Dell, 1975.

Removal of the Vice President

Like the presidency, the vice presidency is subject to frailties of its incumbents that can cause the office to become vacant. Vice presidents may die, resign, become disabled, or be impeached and removed. They also may succeed to the presidency, vacating the vice presidency in the process. Historically, seven vice presidents have died, two have resigned, and nine have become president by succession. These eighteen vice-presidential vacancies have left the nation without a vice president for nearly one-fifth of its history.

Other than impeachment, the original Constitution made no mention of how vice presidents might be removed. It also created no procedure for replacing departed vice presidents. The Twenty-fifth Amendment, which became part of the Constitution in 1967, included a section that remedied these problems in part.

Constitutional Convention

The Constitutional Convention showed little concern for the vice presidency in general and for vice-presidential removal in particular. No provision was made for the death, resignation, or disability of the vice president, nor was any discussion devoted to these possibilities by the delegates. The reason may have been that the convention thought it had provided in other ways for the fulfilling of the only two constitutional responsibilities of the vice presidency—as Senate president and presidential successor—in the event that there was no vice president. Article I stipulates that the Senate shall elect a president pro tempore to preside "in the absence of the Vice President." Article II calls upon Congress to "by Law provide for the Case of Removal, Death, Resignation, or Inability, both of the President and Vice President, declaring what Officer shall then act as President."

The convention did vote on September 8, 1787, to include the vice president and "other civil officers of the United States" in the roster of officials who may be impeached for "Treason, Bribery, or other High Crimes and Misdemeanors" by a majority vote of the House of Representatives and removed by a two-thirds vote of the Senate. The decision, which came after no discussion, was unanimous.

By Michael Nelson

Death

Seven vice presidents have died in office, all of them of natural causes and all in the century-long period 1812-1912. The political weakness of the vice presidency seems to have made it an unappealing target for assassins, in contrast to the presidency. Nor is the concentration of vice-presidential deaths in one period entirely coincidental. Until the Twelfth Amendment was ratified in 1804, the vice presidency was awarded to the runner-up in the presidential election. The vice presidents elected before 1804—John Adams, Thomas Jefferson, and Aaron Burr—were, not surprisingly, relatively young and vigorous. The Twelfth Amendment, which enjoined electors to vote separately for president and vice president, diminished the vice presidency by stripping it of its status as the office held by the person who, presumably, was the second most qualified individual in the country to be president. As a result, a large share of the political leaders who could be persuaded to run for vice president were old, in ill health, or past their political prime. Later, in the twentieth century, the vice presidency regained some of its lustre as a steppingstone to the presidency, and younger political leaders, who were less likely to fall prey to fatal diseases, once more were attracted to the office. *(See "History of the Vice Presidency" in History of the Presidency chapter of Part I.)*

George Clinton, who served in the administrations of Presidents Jefferson and James Madison, was the first vice president to be elected under the Twelfth Amendment and the first to die in office, three years into his second term on April 20, 1812, at age seventy-three. Clinton had been renominated unanimously for vice president in 1808 despite his bad health. (Sen. Stephen Bradley described him to John Quincy Adams in January 1808 as "too old [to be president]; and we are all witnesses that his faculties are failing.") His successor as vice president under President Madison, Elbridge Gerry, was in bad health throughout his term and died of a hemorrhage on November 23, 1814, after twenty months in office. (Gerry was seventy.)

William R. King, who was elected as vice president with Franklin Pierce in 1852 at age sixty-seven, was in Cuba on inauguration day and took his oath of office there. He also died in Cuba, barely six weeks later, on April 18, 1853.

Henry Wilson was the fourth vice president to die in office. Elected with President Ulysses S. Grant in 1872, he served almost three years before dying, at age sixty-one, on

November 22, 1875. Ten years later, Vice President Thomas A. Hendricks died on November 25, 1885, at age sixty-six, after serving eight months under President Grover Cleveland. Garret A. Hobart, who was both vice president and close adviser to President William McKinley, died on November 21, 1899, at age fifty-five, almost three years into his term.

The last vice president to die in office was the fifty-seven year old James S. Sherman. Sherman had been renominated for a second term as vice president on the ticket headed by President William Howard Taft in 1912—the first vice president ever to be renominated by a party convention. He died on October 30, 1912, just before the election. The Taft-Sherman ticket lost, and the Republican National Committee chose Nicholas Murray Butler, the president of Columbia University, to receive Sherman's electoral votes.

Taken together, vice-presidential deaths have left the office unoccupied for thirteen years. Added to the twenty-six years that the vice presidency has been vacant because presidents died and vice presidents succeeded to the presidency, the nation has been without a vice president for thirty-nine years. This includes a seven-year stretch—interrupted only by Vice President King's six-week stint in the office—from July 9, 1850, when Vice President Millard Fillmore succeeded to the presidency after President Zachary Taylor died, until March 4, 1857, when John C. Breckinridge was inaugurated as vice president in the administration of President James Buchanan.

Until recently, a vacant vice presidency was not regarded as a serious problem. The president pro tempore of the Senate took the place of the vice president as Senate president. And, in accordance with the Constitution, Congress passed a succession act in 1792 that placed the president pro tempore next in line to succeed to the presidency. In 1886 Congress replaced the Senate president with the secretary of state in the line of succession; in 1947, it replaced the secretary with the Speaker of the House of Representatives.

In 1965, however, for reasons discussed in the following section, Congress passed the Twenty-fifth Amendment. One of its sections provided that when the vice presidency became vacant, the president would nominate a new vice president, subject to confirmation by both houses of Congress. (The amendment was ratified in 1967.)

Resignation

Only two vice presidents—John C. Calhoun and Spiro T. Agnew—have resigned from the vice presidency. In some ways, this low number is surprising, especially for the period before 1940. Until that year's Democratic convention, when President Franklin D. Roosevelt threatened not to run for reelection unless the party accepted his choice of Henry A. Wallace as his running mate, vice-presidential nominees were placed on the ticket by party leaders. Not only was the presidential nominee largely excluded from this decision, the vice president often was chosen to balance the ticket with someone from a different, often hostile wing of the party. Discord was almost built into the relationship between the president and vice president. Most vice presidents were frozen out of the policy process. Some responded by leaving Washington for long periods; others by actively undermining the president's policies and leadership; still others by suffering in silence.

Only one nineteenth- or early twentieth-century vice president resigned, however, perhaps because he had a better offer: in December 1832, near the end of his second term as vice president, South Carolina offered Vice President Calhoun a U.S. Senate seat, and he accepted. Calhoun had first been elected vice president in 1824, after convincing supporters of both of the leading presidential candidates, John Quincy Adams and Andrew Jackson, that he was in their camp. Calhoun, whose real ambition was to be president, accepted the second office in the hope that both the electoral college and the House of Representatives would deadlock in the presidential election, leaving him as acting president for four years. Although the electoral college did fail to elect a president, the House did not, choosing Adams. *(See "Congressional Caucus Nominating System," p. 160, in The Electoral Process chapter of Part II.)*

Vice President Calhoun used his position as president of the Senate to undermine President Adams by stacking committees with Adams's opponents, delaying presidential appointments, and tolerating vicious speeches against the president by certain senators. These activities endeared Calhoun to Jackson, who made the vice president his own running mate in 1828 and did nothing to discourage Calhoun's hope of being his successor. But Calhoun feuded bitterly after the election with the president's other protégé, Martin Van Buren, and broke with President Jackson over his strongly pro-Union policies. When Jackson learned that Calhoun, as secretary of war in the administration of President James Monroe, had criticized his activities in 1818, the break became irreparable. "I never expected to say to you . . . Et tu, Brute," Jackson wrote Calhoun.

Calhoun's method of resigning—no procedure was provided in the Constitution—set the precedent for future presidents and vice presidents. He sent a one-sentence letter to the secretary of state: "Having concluded to accept of a seat in the United States Senate, I herewith resign the office of Vice-President of the United States."

Vice President Agnew's resignation in 1973 was the product of an entirely different set of circumstances. The vice president's relationship with President Richard Nixon was reasonably harmonious, and his popularity with rank-and-file Republicans made him the early favorite for the party's 1976 presidential nomination. What undid Agnew was a federal criminal investigation into bribes he had received from contractors, architects, and engineers while serving as county executive of Baltimore County, Maryland, governor of Maryland, and vice president. Agnew revealed and denied the charges at a televised news conference on August 8, 1973, and vowed as late as September 29 that "I will not resign if indicted." On October 10, however, he pleaded nolo contendere (no contest) to one count of income tax evasion. In return for a Justice Department agreement not to prosecute him on other charges and to seek a lenient sentence for the tax evasion conviction, Agnew resigned as vice president that same day. His resignation letter to Secretary of State Henry Kissinger read: "I hereby resign the Office of Vice-President of the United States, effective immediately." U.S. District Court Judge Walter E. Hoffman sentenced Agnew to a fine of $10,000 and three years of unsupervised probation.

Impeachment

The one procedure for vice-presidential removal that was provided for in the original Constitution—impeachment—has never been implemented. Impeachment proceedings, which require investigation and debate by the House in order to bring an indictment, then a full-scale trial and a two-thirds vote to convict in the Senate, are inherently lengthy and controversial undertakings whose only effect is to remove the impeached and convicted official from office. This may explain why two vice presidents who committed arguably impeachable offenses—Aaron Burr and Schuyler Colfax—were allowed to complete their terms without undergoing impeachment and why Congress preferred that Vice President Agnew resign rather than be impeached.

Vice President Burr's offense was to shoot and kill Alexander Hamilton in a duel on July 11, 1804. Burr was indicted for murder in New York and New Jersey, although never arrested and prosecuted. Sen. William Plumer, a Federalist from New Hampshire, reacted by writing, "We are indeed fallen on evil times. . . . The high office of president is filled by an infidel, that of the vice president by a murderer." But because Burr's term was set to expire March 4, 1805, no impeachment proceedings were begun.

Similarly, the timing of certain revelations about Vice President Colfax was fortunate—evidence against him did not surface until he already had been dropped from the Republican ticket in 1872 and was in the last months of his term. Colfax was found to have received, while still in Congress, twenty shares of the notorious Crédit Mobilier, a dummy construction company that the Union Pacific railroad had created to receive the proceeds of government contracts. The *New York World* called for his impeachment, and a House committee investigated Colfax in December 1872. But the committee concluded that, constitutionally, impeachment is intended to remove a person from an office only for offenses committed while occupying it.

On September 25, 1973, after Vice President Agnew learned that the Justice Department was about to seek an indictment for bribery, corruption, and income tax evasion, he met with Speaker Carl Albert and other House leaders to ask them to begin an impeachment investigation against him. Agnew's strategy seems to have been to preempt the criminal investigation. The next day, Albert declined, on grounds that Agnew's request "relates to matters before the courts." Albert also was concerned that Congress not be tied up with a vice-presidential impeachment when impeachment proceedings against President Nixon seemed possible. The vice president resigned two weeks later.

Replacing the Vice President

When Vice President Lyndon B. Johnson succeeded to the presidency after the assassination of President John F. Kennedy on November 22, 1963, the vice presidency became vacant for the sixteenth time in thirty-six presidencies. This was particularly distressing because Johnson had a history of heart trouble and the two congressional leaders who were first in line to succeed to the presidency, Speaker of the House John W. McCormack and Senate President Pro Tempore Carl Hayden, were both old and in poor health.

There also had developed a more general concern about the appropriateness of congressional succession to the presidency in the absence of a vice president. One reason for this concern was that, in the not uncommon situation in which Congress is controlled by a party different from the president, succession would bring about a change in partisan control of the presidency. Another reason was that congressional leaders, having been selected for their legislative talents or seniority and representing only individual states or congressional districts, might not be qualified to assume the presidency. In contrast, the vice president is elected by the nation, is of the same party as the president, and, in modern times, is chosen with attention to the ability to succeed ably and faithfully to the presidency and is prepared for succession while in office.

Concern that the nation always should have a vice president standing next in line to the presidency contributed to the passage of the Twenty-fifth Amendment in 1965 and its ratification in 1967. Section 2 of the amendment provides that "whenever there is a vacancy in the office of the Vice-President, the President shall nominate a Vice President who shall take office upon confirmation in a majority vote of both Houses of Congress." The authors of the amendment anticipated that death, either of the president or the vice president, would be the occasion for most vice-presidential vacancies, as it had been in fifteen of the sixteen previous instances. (Calhoun's resignation was the only exception.)

In reality, although section 2 has been invoked twice since its passage, it has been in circumstances different from those that had been foreseen: Vice President Agnew's resignation in 1973 and President Nixon's resignation in 1974. On October 12, 1973, two days after Agnew resigned, Nixon nominated House Republican leader Gerald R. Ford to be vice president. Congress conducted an extensive investigation of Ford, including a background probe by the Federal Bureau of Investigation, and confirmed his nomination by a vote of 92-3 in the Senate on November 27 and 387-35 in the House on December 6.

The vice presidency soon became vacant again. Vice President Ford became president when President Nixon resigned on August 9, 1974. On August 20, Ford nominated New York governor Nelson A. Rockefeller as vice president. Congress conducted an even more wide-ranging investigation of Rockefeller than it had of Ford before approving the nomination by a vote of 90-7 in the Senate on December 10 and 287-128 in the House on December 19. One consequence of the new Twenty-fifth Amendment procedure was that, for the first time in history, the United States had an unelected president and vice president.

Disability

Although section 2 of the Twenty-fifth Amendment provides for the filling of vice-presidential vacancies that are caused by the death, resignation, or impeachment of the vice president, it is silent on the matter of vice-presidential disabilities. This is a curious omission. Other sections of the amendment create procedures for handling presidential disabilities; what is more, some of these procedures make the vice president the main figure in determining whether a disability exists, and all of them stipulate that the vice president will be acting president for as long as a president remains disabled. Clearly, the presidential disability provisions of the Twenty-fifth Amendment assume that a vice president will always be both available—indeed, that was one of the reasons for including section 2 in the amendment—and able. Yet neither the amendment nor any other provision of the law or the Constitution offers the nation any protection against a disabled vice president.

Susan Biddle, White House

George Bush became the forty-first president on January 20, 1989.

Part III

Powers of the Presidency

Chief Executive

The powers of the president can be divided into two categories, *formal powers* and *inherent powers*. The president's formal powers originate in the Constitution, in acts of Congress, and in judicial interpretations. The Constitution, for example, empowers presidents to appoint members of their administrations and some federal judges. Congressional acts instruct presidents to submit annual budget requests. Supreme Court decisions authorize them to desegregate public school systems.

Inherent powers reside in the office of president and come from the job itself rather than through constitutional or statutory law. Most inherent powers derive from the loosely worded statements in the Constitution that "the executive Power shall be vested in a President" (Article II, section 1) and that the president "shall take Care that the Laws be faithfully executed" (Article II, section 3). Emergency powers invoked by presidents during wartime are examples of inherent powers. When the Japanese bombed Pearl Harbor, Franklin D. Roosevelt used his inherent powers to relocate the Japanese living in the United States.

Even though all presidents have the same formal and inherent powers, different chief executives use these powers in different ways depending on their skills, their personalities, the people who serve them, and, often, circumstances that are beyond their control. Most presidential scholars classify presidential powers according to the categories devised by presidential scholar Clinton Rossiter in *The American Presidency*. Rossiter divided the presidency into several presidential jobs, entailing both formal and inherent powers. These are the administration of government, domestic policy development and leadership, foreign policy development and leadership, the promotion of national unity, and party leadership.[1]

Over the years, presidential scholars have changed greatly in their understanding of the use of presidential power. In 1884, long before he became president, Woodrow Wilson wrote *Congressional Government*, a study of U.S. politics. Wilson described the president's business as "usually not much above routine" and "mere administration." Placing most of the burden for directing the government squarely on the shoulders of Congress, Wilson saw the president as little more than a civil servant.[2]

Presidents have always had considerable power at their disposal, however. Wilson underestimated the significance of the powerful administration of Abraham Lincoln, who took the reins of the federal government firmly in hand during the Civil War. He also overlooked the ambiguities present in the constitutional grants of power to the presidency. The Constitution's designation of the president as commander in chief means much more in the twentieth century than simply directing U.S. military forces. It also means directing the nation's economy and foreign policy.

One hundred years after *Congressional Government* was published, political analysts' perceptions of presidential power have changed drastically to accommodate a more realistic approach. As president, Wilson himself quickly changed his view of the demands of the job. In fact, Rossiter was so impressed with the demands of the presidency that he introduced his study with a quotation from Shakespeare's *Macbeth:* "Methought I heard a voice cry 'Sleep no more!' " A few days before he was assassinated on November 22, 1963, President John F. Kennedy wrote Rossiter to comment on the use of the quote from *Macbeth.* Kennedy believed the quote to be apt but thought an even more appropriate one could be found in Shakespeare's *King Henry IV, Part I*: Glendower boasts, "I can call spirits from the vasty deep," and Hotspur replies, "Why so can I, or so can any man; but will they come when you do call for them?" Kennedy pointed to the difference between presidents' calling for action and actually accomplishing their desired goals. After almost three years in office, he understood the paradoxical nature of presidential power and its limitations.

Article II of the Constitution lists the president's powers. Although it grants far fewer explicit powers to the president than it does to Congress in Article I, the ambiguity and vagueness of the article have made it possible for presidents to expand their powers. Article II, section 1, clearly grants executive power to the president. Section 3 makes the president responsible for the execution of federal laws.

In theory, these directives make the president responsible for carrying out or executing the laws of the federal government. In practice, however, the ambiguity of this mandate often has increased the power of the presidency. For example, by broadly interpreting the authority to execute the law, Grover Cleveland used federal troops to break a labor strike in the 1890s and Dwight D. Eisenhower sent troops to help integrate a public school in Little Rock, Arkansas, in 1957.

From the beginning the Framers of the Constitution expressed a great deal of uncertainty over the exact nature

By W. Craig Bledsoe and James Brain Watts

> The executive Power shall be vested in the President of the United States of America.
>
> —from Article II, section 1

of the executive. They derived many of their political ideals from seventeenth- and eighteenth-century European writers such as John Locke, Jean Jacques Rousseau and Montesquieu, whose theories emphasized both popular sovereignty and individual liberty. If the political beliefs of these writers were adopted, the chief executive would not come from a ruling class or hereditary base but instead would represent the popular will. The presidency would not be set up as a monarchy, not even a limited one. The president would be an elected public official responsible only to the people.

Still, Framers feared the effects of an unrestrained democracy. They were afraid that the chief executive might be too inclined to appeal to popular demands in ways harmful to minority rights. Consequently, they attempted to insulate the office of president by having the public participate in presidential selection only indirectly through the electoral college.

This debate on the strength of the executive spilled over into the effort to define the exact nature of the president's administrative duties. Influenced by classical liberal writers, such as Montesquieu, the Framers dispersed power by structuring an executive branch separate and independent from the legislature. In doing so, they gave the presidency sweeping administrative responsibilities to "faithfully execute" the law. But to keep the presidency from becoming too powerful, they subjected it to certain constraints by giving Congress immense powers of its own. The president has the power to appoint officials of the executive branch, but the Senate must confirm many of the appointments. And the president is in charge of administering the federal laws and programs, but Congress creates them, and it may change them at any time. Specifically, Congress can create and destroy agencies, and it determines whether they are going to be located in the executive branch or outside it. In other words, if it chooses, Congress can make an agency completely independent of the president.

The legislature also has the power of appropriation, which gives it ultimate control over federal agencies. Congress can define exactly what an agency has the power to do and not do. Consequently, as political scientist Peter Woll has observed, "Congress has virtually complete authority to structure the administrative branch and determine where formal lines of accountability shall be placed. It may or may not decide to let the President exercise various types of control." [3]

In *The Federalist Papers,* Alexander Hamilton defined the presidents' administrative activities as "mere execution" of "executive details." His was a narrow interpretation, for he in no way understood what would develop later. Hamilton, however, saw the president as the person solely responsible for administrative action. In *Federalist* No. 72 he wrote,

> The persons, therefore to whose immediate management these different [administrative] matters are committed, ought to be considered as the assistants or deputies of the chief magistrate, and on this account they ought to derive their offices from his appointment, at least from his nomination, and ought to be subject to his superintendence. This view of the subject will at once suggest to us the intimate connection between the duration of the executive magistrate in office and the stability of the system of administration.[4]

Since the 1930s Congress has delegated to the president the broad authority to achieve several general goals. Congress will often pass laws, leaving to the president and the executive branch the discretion to define the regulations and programs to be put into effect. This practice has come into being through political events, not by design. Americans increasingly look to the president for leadership in times of crisis and in everyday affairs, making the chief executive responsible for a growing portion of the nation's successes and failures. Consequently, the administrative responsibilities of the presidency have grown tremendously. As the presidency evolved, presidents found themselves serving as chief administrators, chief personnel officers, chief financial officers, and chief law enforcers—all part of the job of "chief executive."

The President as Chief Administrator

Although the Founders placed a high priority on the presidency's executive duties, the Constitution provides very few instructions about the president's tasks as head of the executive branch. Specific presidential administrative powers have evolved as the presidency has matured.

The Constitution does not make direct provisions for the vast administrative structure that the president must oversee. It does, however, authorize the president to demand written reports from the "principal Officer in each of the executive Departments, upon any Subject, relating to the Duties of their respective Offices" (Article II, section 2). This clause implies a division of labor within the executive branch and clearly establishes an administrative hierarchy with the president as the chief administrative officer.

Similar to chief executives in private corporations, the chief executive in the White House tries to persuade subordinates in government to conform to presidential objectives. The chief executive tries to give direction to the administration. Presidents do not have time to follow through on every action taken by the bureaucratic departments and agencies directly under their control. They sit atop a federal executive structure that has 2.7 million civilian employees. They must develop techniques that give them control over this vast administrative organization. Because this organization has grown tremendously since the early days of the Republic, analysis of the president's power as chief executive entails discussion of the structure of the executive branch.

> [H]e shall take Care that the Laws be faithfully executed.
>
> —from Article II, section 3

Structure of the Executive Branch

Often the term *bureaucracy* is considered pejorative, for to many it suggests red tape, inflexibility, and confusion. Opposition to "big government" has become almost synonymous with opposition to bureaucracy. Political candidates from both major political parties usually decry the evils of the burgeoning U.S. bureaucracy, denouncing it for removing Americans from the decision-making process of their federal government.

Those who work in the federal bureaucratic structure—"bureaucrats"—are often criticized for being unproductive and obstinate. Political scientist Charles Goodsell has written that "the employee of bureaucracy, that 'lowly bureaucrat,' is seen as lazy or snarling, or both. The office occupied by this pariah is viewed as bungling or inhuman, or both. The overall edifice of bureaucracy is pictured as overstaffed, inflexible, unresponsive, and power-hungry, all at once." [5]

Bureaucracy, however, has a technical meaning. The German sociologist Max Weber saw the bureaucratic model of organization as one distinguished by its large size, its formulation of rules and procedures, the presence of a clear hierarchy, the systematic maintenance of records, and the employment of a full-time appointed staff who performed specific duties using technical knowledge.[6]

By this definition, a large corporation or university is a bureaucracy, and so is a government. The departments, agencies, bureaus, commissions, and offices of the executive branch make up most of the federal bureaucracy. Although not as large and usually not as visible as the executive branch, Congress and the courts have their own bureaucracies.

Despite the negative connotations of the term, a bureaucrat is simply an administrator who carries out the policies of the elected officials of government. The structure of the federal bureaucracy under the president's control can be broken down into the Executive Office of the President (EOP), the cabinet departments, the executive agencies, and the regulatory commissions.

Executive Office of the President

In 1939 Executive Order 8248 created the Executive Office of the President to advise the president and to help manage the growing bureaucracy. The EOP includes the White House Office, the Council of Economic Advisers, the National Security Council (NSC), and the Office of Management and Budget (OMB)—agencies conceived to help the president more effectively control the expanding executive branch.

Since then the EOP has grown tremendously, employing approximately eighteen hundred people in the late 1980s. Its most important components are the White House Office, the NSC, and the OMB.

The White House Office consists of the president's closest assistants. Their actual titles vary from one administration to another, but under each new president it is this group who oversees the political and policy interests of the administration. Serving as a direct extension of the president, they do not require Senate confirmation. The creation of the White House Office has allowed the president to centralize executive power within the White House at the expense of the cabinet secretaries. Henry A. Kissinger, for example, Richard Nixon's assistant for national security affairs, forged such a strong power base in foreign affairs that his authority eventually eclipsed that of the secretary of state. *(See White House Office chapter in Part V.)*

In 1947, early in the cold war, Congress passed the National Security Act, which created the NSC to help coordinate military and foreign policies. Responsible for organizing activities between the State Department and the Defense Department, the NSC has four statutory members: the president, the vice president (added in 1949), the secretary of state, and the secretary of defense. The act further names the chairman of the Joint Chiefs of Staff and the director of the Central Intelligence Agency (CIA) as advisers to the NSC. In addition to the NSC but distinct from its formal mmbers is the NSC staff. Made up of foreign policy advisers and headed by the national security adviser, the NSC staff has evolved into an apparatus used by many presidents to implement their own foreign policy goals. Since the role of the NSC and its staff is purely advisory, presidents have used it to varying degrees. President Kennedy, preferring his own close advisers, used the NSC infrequently. President Nixon, however, gave the NSC formal authority in formulating and executing foreign policy. *(See "National Security Council," p. 955, in Supporting Organizations chapter of Part V.)*

In 1970 President Nixon created the Office of Management and Budget to replace the Bureau of the Budget (BOB), established in 1927. As the largest of the EOP agencies, its six hundred staff members help presidents achieve their political objectives by formulating and administering the federal budget. Departments and agencies of the executive branch must submit annual budget requests to OMB. Besides preparing the budget, OMB serves as an important managerial tool of the president by reviewing the organizational structure and management procedures of the executive branch, assessing program objectives, and developing reform proposals. OMB has tremendous power within the federal government. President Ronald Reagan relied heavily on OMB Director David Stockman for the technical expertise necessary to implement his political objective of cutting the budget. *(See "Office of Management and Budget," p. 950, in Supporting Organizations chapter of Part V.)*

Cabinet Departments

The cabinet is made up of the heads—or "secretaries"—of the major departments of the government. Originally, there were only three cabinet departments—State, War, and the Treasury. By 1989, the number had grown to fourteen. Lacking any constitutional or statutory base, the cabinet is primarily an advisory group. Although presidents may work closely with individual cabinet officers, they rarely use the collective cabinet for advice. Once President Lincoln, opposed by his entire cabinet on an issue, remarked, "Seven nays, one aye; the ayes have it." President Eisenhower, holding regular cabinet meetings and listening to opinions of others, came closer than any modern president to making the cabinet a truly deliberative body.

Each cabinet secretary is appointed to head a specific department with a specific constituency. Although presidents makes their own appointments, with Senate confirmation, the power they have over a specific department is limited. One reason is that the president can appoint only a limited number of a department's employees. When President Reagan came into office in 1981, for example, he could appoint only about one hundred people to positions in the Department of Transportation, less than 1 percent of its employees. *(See Cabinet and Executive Departments chapters in Part V.)*

Executive Agencies

Executive agencies are agencies or commissions that are not considered a part of the cabinet and that by law often have quasi-independent status. Examples of these executive agencies include the National Aeronautics and Space Administration, the Peace Corps, and the CIA.

The difference between a "presidential" agency and an "independent" agency is often vague. Generally, heads of presidential agencies and commissioners serve at the discretion of, and may be removed by, the president. Independent agency heads and commissioners are appointed for fixed terms of office and have some independence from the president in their operations.

Government corporations, such as the Tennessee Valley Authority (TVA), also fall under the category of executive agencies. Similar to private corporations, these organizations perform business activities such as operating a transportation system (Amtrak) or selling electricity (TVA). Government corporations are primarily controlled by a board of directors, allowing them to be run more like a business. Since the president appoints these boards and their chairs, they have come increasingly under the control of the presidency. *(See Government Agencies and Corporations chapter in Part V.)*

Regulatory Commissions

Regulatory commissions are responsible for regulating certain segments of the economy. Many of them, such as the Food and Drug Administration (FDA) and the Occupational Safety and Health Administration (OSHA) are located within the regular departments. FDA is a part of the Department of Health and Human Services, and OSHA is in the Labor Department. Other regulatory agencies, such as the Interstate Commerce Commission, are independent in their relationship to the executive branch and so are insulated from regular presidential control and policy direction.

By statutory law each regulatory agency is governed by a bipartisan board of commissioners, who serve overlapping terms of five years or more. Although presidents have the power to appoint board members, they do not have the power to remove these appointees from office unless they can prove reasons of incompetence. This regulation ensures a certain amount of independence from executive control. Presidents cannot fire commission members simply because they do not like the policy direction of the agency, nor can they veto agency actions.

Still, presidents influence regulatory commission policies by choosing the commissioners and the chairs. Bipartisanship rarely means much in the composition of these boards, for presidents always have been able to name board members who share their views regardless of political party affiliation. Many conservative Democrats share the same policy beliefs as Republicans, and many liberal Republicans share the same policy beliefs as Democrats. Although commissioners serve long, overlapping terms, presidents still have the opportunity to place a majority of their appointees in any given agency. *(See Government Agencies and Corporations chapter in Part V.)*

Bureaucratic Growth and Reform

In 1789 President George Washington's administration consisted primarily of his three cabinet departments (State, Treasury, and War) and employed only a few hundred people. By 1816 the number of federal civilian employees had grown to only a little over 4,800. Only about 500 of these worked in Washington. Most of the rest were scattered throughout the country providing mail service as employees of the Post Office Department. By 1931, however, the number of federal civilian employees had reached slightly more than 600,000, and by 1953 the number had expanded to approximately 2.5 million.

Although the number of federal employees has remained relatively constant since the 1950s, federal expenditures have continued to increase. Between 1965 and 1984, federal expenditures jumped from $118 billion to $850 billion. This period also saw an increase in the number of people working for the federal government as either contractors or consultants or through grant-in-aid programs administered by state or local governments. Federal employment figures usually overlook the large and growing number of people who work indirectly for the federal government as employees of private firms and state and local governments that are largely, or entirely, funded by U.S. taxpayers. In 1978 Secretary of Health, Education and Welfare Joseph Califano observed that although his department employed almost 144,000 people, it indirectly paid the salaries of about 980,000 more in state and local governments through numerous grant-in-aid programs.[7]

Every president, eventually frustrated by the large and often unresponsive bureaucracy, talks of bureaucratic reform. When Carter came into office, he vowed to make a wholesale overhaul of the ninety-five-year-old Civil Service system, but the Civil Service Reform Act (1978) that finally passed Congress in Carter's second year in office had little effect. Campaigning for office, Carter promised to reduce the nineteen hundred existing federal agencies to two hundred. After he took office, however, the campaign promise was quickly forgotten and never appeared in the civil service reform law. In fact, in attempting to win their support for the reform measure, Carter promised Civil Service employees, "No one will be demoted, have their salaries decreased, or be fired as a result of reorganization. You need not fear that."[8]

Even the most reform-minded presidents move slowly. They must convince key members of the bureaucracy that proposed changes are worth making for the country as a whole and that they will not hurt individual bureaucrats. Thus, presidents cautiously try to persuade bureaucracies to favor their reforms. In addition, and far more important, presidents are subject to the same clientelism that afflicts an individual agency. By the time they reach office, presidents have become indebted to people who have contributed to their campaigns and helped them achieve their political stature. Rarely do they bite the hand that feeds them. Presidents are very reluctant to undermine an agency that might serve one of their clientele groups.

This is not to say that presidents have never attempted to reform the bureaucracy, however. In fact, the evolution of the federal bureaucracy has been largely a history of attempts at reform. Although these efforts were aimed at reducing the power of the bureaucracy, instead they gradually increased it. In examining these recurring efforts, presidency scholar Michael Nelson has pointed out the irony in bureaucratic reform: the disparity that existed between what the reform intended and the actual result led not to a reduction in the power and scope of bureaucracy but an increase.[9]

The Founders were ambivalent about the exact nature of the government's administrative structure and about who was to control it. The subject was not mentioned in convention debates; consequently, it was not mentioned in the Constitution. Nelson has argued that this ambivalence helped create the rapid growth that later characterized the American bureaucracy. By not specifically spelling out the exact nature of the government's administrative structure, the Founders created a situation that allowed the bureaucracy to come under the simultaneous control of both the president and Congress in the nineteenth century. As a result, the system of dual control allowed administrators to increase their own independence by playing one institution off the other. Nelson observed:

> The Constitutional Convention, in loosing the agencies from their old legislative moorings (politically necessary if the support of executive power adherents was to be won) without tying them securely to the presidency (equally politic if anti-federalist support was to be kept) forced agencies to find and exercise relatively independent power. Agencies began to learn to play one branch off another; if neither president nor Congress was supreme, then law was, and the agencies interpreted and implemented the law.[10]

Nelson concluded that the power of bureaucracy has grown in part because of the attempts to control it. For example, reformers, intent on controlling the bureaucracy by making it less susceptible to corruption, actually made it less efficient and responsible. To make it harder for public employees to defraud the government, agencies developed elaborate systems of internal checks and balances. These checks and balances took time. Efficiency, responsiveness, or some other value often was sacrificed for the sake of preventing official cheating. The cause of this irony is that administrative institutions were scarcely mentioned in the Constitution and have remained somewhat illegitimate in U.S. political culture ever since. This has forced bureaucratic agencies to rely on independent bases of political support, such as their constituent groups, for their organizational goals, coincidentally freeing them from political control.

This historical account of bureaucratic reform points out that bureaucratic power endures even throughout the most challenging of reforms. Although the historical record indicates that reformers have unintentionally increased the power and scope of bureaucracy, attempts at reform will undoubtedly continue. Future presidents, like their predecessors, will become frustrated with the sluggishness and unresponsiveness of their administrations. Efforts at deregulation, civil service reform, and cutbacks in government expenditures that aim at removing the financial support for various bureaucratic agencies therefore will continue. Political scientist Robert Sherrill has outlined the problem: "Because so many portions of the bureaucracy are no longer responsive to the needs of the general public, and because they do their narrowly selfish work without fear of reprisal from the public, it may seem useless to talk of reform. But it isn't useless to talk of reform; it is only naive to expect much."[11]

Control of the Bureaucracy

Presidents often complain that they lack sufficient control over the executive branch bureaucracy. They are quick to blame the bureaucracy for the many problems that hinder the implementation of presidential programs. Franklin Roosevelt provided one of the best-known illustrations of a president's lack of control over the bureaucracy. He is reported to have told one of his aides:

> "When I woke up this morning, the first thing I saw was a headline in the *New York Times* to the effect that our Navy was going to spend two billion dollars on a shipbuilding program. Here I am, the Commander in Chief of the Navy having to read about that for the first time in the press. Do you know what I said to that?"
>
> "No, Mr. President."
>
> "I said: 'Jesus Chr-rist!' "[12]

Other presidents faced similar frustrations later. Contemplating what it would be like for Eisenhower to be president rather than a general, Harry S Truman once said, "He will sit here and he will say, 'Do this! Do that!' And nothing will happen. Poor Ike—it won't be at all like the Army! He'll find it very frustrating."[13]

Chief executives expect to have their orders obeyed and their programs set in motion. Yet upon assuming office, they often find that their programs rarely are implemented as promptly or as efficiently as they would like. They must face, and learn how to manage, an obstinate and unruly bureaucracy. Frank Carlucci, President Nixon's chief assistant for bureaucratic reorganization, stated that it takes "from six to eight months for a presidential directive to be translated into agency guidelines and reach the action level." In some cases, Carlucci maintained, it could take the policy two to three years to be put into action.[14]

Controlling the bureaucracy has become a major priority for most presidents. All presidents after Franklin Roosevelt, whether liberal or conservative, have shared the desire to make the bureaucracy more responsive to their program objectives. Historian Arthur M. Schlesinger, Jr., commented, "As any sensible person should have known, the permanent government has turned out to be, at least against innovating presidents, a conservatizing rather than a liberalizing force."[15]

Presidents face a tremendous task when they try to manage the bureaucracy and make it work for them. To control a specific agency, the chief executive must know what the agency does and what it did in the past. The president must know the preferences and inclinations of its members and the pressures being put on the agency from clientele groups. In addition, the president must anticipate the political implications of the agency's actions. Ideally, the chief executive should be able to do this for the hundreds of departments, bureaus, boards, commissions, independent commissions, and pubic corporations under White House supervision. But even with the help of the Executive Office of the President, it is an almost impossible task. Presidential scholar Richard Pious wrote, "It takes a few weeks for a new administration to learn how to intervene in the affairs of a bureau; it may take a few years for the president to know enough to stay out of them."[16]

Instead of being intimately involved in every little detail of an agency's affairs, a president must learn to delegate; that is, the president must be a manager. Presidential scholar Thomas E. Cronin wrote:

> He must constantly delegate, he must be most precise about what he is delegating, and he must know whether and for what reasons the agencies to which he is delegating share his general outlook. He must be sensitive to bureaucratic politics, to the incentives that motivate bureaucrats, and to the intricacies of their standard operating procedures. He must have some assurance (and hence an adequate intelligence system) that what he is delegating will be carried out properly.[17]

Unfortunately, most presidents have not done well in this respect. They often have misunderstood the bureaucracy and have concentrated on the choice rather than the implementation of policy. Political scientist Richard Rose has argued that "once in office, a president is much more concerned with choosing what to do than he is with how these decisions are implemented (that is, how choices are turned into routine government activities) or the conduct of program activities on a continuing basis." [18]

In addition to the problems of understanding the exact nature of the bureaucracy, presidents must face problems inherent in the political process itself that make it difficult to control their administrations. Upon entering office, presidents find that most bureaucratic institutions are already fixed. If they want to reorganize, as did Nixon, they run the risk of a confrontation with Congress. Consequently, few presidents attempt to risk an outcry of disapproval from a Congress that tries to protect the interests of its constituencies, who are often the clients of the existing bureaucratic agencies. Instead, newly elected presidents attempt to do the best they can with the bureaucratic structures already at their disposal.

Constitutional inhibitions also make it difficult for the chief executive to fashion the bureaucracy into a more responsive institution. Presidential programs require legislative approval and appropriations, and they are subject to review, and possible nullification, by the courts. Even with statutory and constitutional authority, the president often faces untold difficulty in making the bureaucracy more responsive. Although the Constitution charges presidents with the execution of the laws, the formal authority to take that action is often statutorily vested in a cabinet secretary or the head of a specific agency. In theory, such presidential appointees will carry out the president's objectives. In practice, however, heads of departments and agencies often operate independently of the president and are more attuned to their clientele groups than to the administration's goals.

Instruments of Presidential Control

Although the obstacles to effective management of the bureaucracy are great, presidents do have two tools that afford them at least a small measure of influence: their authority to appoint top officials and their own centralized management staff—the Executive Office of the President.

Appointments. Presidents appoint fourteen cabinet heads and some 5,200 other executive officials, including all members of the independent and regulatory agencies. In other words, presidents may hire or fire almost all of their top officials at will, except the heads of independent regulatory commissions. This authority gives them great control over their immediate aides and department and agency heads, but not over the vast majority of the executive branch.

In addition to the power of removal, presidents may also attempt to make appointments that are ideologically compatible with their policies. President Reagan attempted to transform departments and agencies by appointing officials who shared his desire to curb the size and influence of the federal establishment. For example, Reagan appointed Thorne Auchter, an opponent of "unnecessary" federal rules, to head the Occupational Safety and Health Administration and Robert F. Burford, who helped lead a novement to return greater control of federal lands to the states, as director of the Interior Department's Bureau of Land Management. Largely successful in his efforts, Reagan proved that the federal bureaucracy can be controlled by appointing officials whose political ideology is similar to the president's. By placing loyal appointees in bureaucratic leadership positions, the chief executive can ensure that the policies bureaucracies carry out are those of the White House.

Centralized Executive Power. In 1933, Franklin Roosevelt found himself facing a bureaucracy staffed by holdovers from preceding conservative Republican administrations. He feared that his New Deal programs, if left to the discretion of these bureaucrats, would never be put into effect, at least not in the way they were intended. To ensure compliance with the intent of the New Deal legislation, he established numerous new agencies, such as the short-lived National Emergency Council, to coordinate directives through new and old agencies committed to his liberal programs. By adding on to the existing bureaucracy, Roosevelt created an organizational monster.

Roosevelt found it difficult to get the information he needed to implement his policies. Frustrated by the bureaucratic mess of his administration, he asked Congress to expand his supervisory staff. Congress agreed, and on September 8, 1939, Roosevelt issued Executive Order 8248, which established the Executive Office of the President. In so doing, Roosevelt created a miniature bureaucracy to help him control the vast executive apparatus and thus expanded the modern presidency. Rossiter described the creation of the EOP as a "nearly unnoticed but nonetheless epoch-making event in the history of American institutions." [19]

Roosevelt maintained that only a strong, well-staffed presidency could provide unity and direction to the federal government. Later presidents agreed and continued trying to centralize power within the White House to control the bureaucracy. More often than not, however, such attempts overloaded the White House staff and undermined the effectiveness of the presidency. By the early 1970s, the presidency was attempting to centralize all policy at the White House by using White House staff to oversee programs of high presidential priority.[20] In attempting to centralize power within the White House, Nixon structured his staff in a way that limited his associates to those over whom he had the most control. This attempt at centralization isolated him and put him out of touch with the rest of the government.

However interested presidents might have been in centralizing power, it did not work. The White House staff was simply not large enough to control the massive executive branch, which in the early 1970s comprised nearly 5 million military and civilian employees and spent over $300 billion annually. This points to the reality that no presidential mechanism has ever been large enough or powerful enough to control the bureaucracy.

Some scholars maintain that presidents should not be

in complete control of the bureaucracy.[21] They contend that the president's role in overseeing the success or failure of federal programs should be relinquished to the executive departments. Most federal laws, they argue, deliberately provide for discretion to be given to top departmental and agency officials. Presidential scholar Richard Rose has pointed out that the work of the executive branch is carried out by operating departments granted specific powers and responsibilities by acts of Congress, and not by presidential delegation.[22] Therefore, both appointed and career executives should have the liberty to apply standards, revise regulations, and interpret legislative intent to fit specific situations. The president and the EOP should not be involved in most situations. These scholars hold the view that Congress is as much in charge of administration as the president, for it is Congress that creates the laws, funds the programs, and confirms the appointments.

Most presidents oppose this view. They argue that only the presidency can provide the coordination necessary to master the complexity of the federal bureaucracy. Cronin summarized the presidential perspective: "Only the president should have discretion over budget choices and the administration of federal policies. He is the one charged with faithfully executing the laws.... a strong presidency makes a major difference in the way government works, and ... this difference will be in the direction of a more constructive (desirable) set of policy outcomes." [23]

This is the position that Hamilton advocated in *Federalist* No. 70: "A feeble Executive implies a feeble execution of the government. A feeble execution is but another phrase for a bad execution; and a government ill-executed, whatever it may be in theory, must be, in practice, bad government." [24] *(See* "Federalist *No. 70," p. 1364, in the Appendix.)*

At the heart of this argument is the idea that the government bureaucracy has become so large and diverse that the White House itself spends more time reacting to the whims of the bureaucracy than controlling it. Former presidential adviser McGeorge Bundy maintained that the executive branch often "more nearly resembles a collection of badly separated principalities than a single instrument of executive action." [25] The answer, according to this logic, is more hierarchy. An accountable president must be able to control the bureaucracy.

Information Management

Part of the problem of management is the control of information. The maxim "Knowledge is power" is never more true than in the executive branch.

Obtaining Information. Presidents must deal with a highly specialized and expert bureaucracy. How does a president gather information necessary to make informed decisions? One way is to rely on information supplied by bureaucratic agencies themselves. But if this is the chief executive's only source of information, then the presidency runs the risk of being dominated by, or dependent upon, the bureaucracy itself.

To a large extent this dependence on the bureaucracy is unavoidable. Compared with the rest of the executive branch, the president's management staff—the Executive Office of the President—is quite small, usually comprising fewer than one thousand employees.

Thus the president and the EOP must make decisions on the facts and opinions supplied by the agencies themselves, a dependence that puts the president at an obvious disadvantage. But even if the EOP were enlarged to give the presidency greater information-gathering capability, it could never become large enough to provide the president with relevant information for *all* policy decisions for every agency. As Woll has written, "The scope and technical complexity of administrative legislation and adjudication alone precludes this, even if there were no legal and political obstacles to presidential control. What is of greater importance is the fact that the president alone cannot personally comprehend these areas." [26]

Those who insist upon expansion of the EOP argue that presidents need larger staffs to channel information from the multitude of agencies for which they are responsible. Since the offices within the EOP, such as the Office of Management and Budget, are not dependent upon any clientele or constituency group but serve as the president's staff, they are viewed as being independent of the political pressures that other agencies endure. But the EOP suffers from political tensions just like any other executive bureaucracy. In examining the effects of information within the EOP, Woll described the need for presidents to be sensitive also to other major departments and agencies, such as the OMB, which have powerful support from Congress. He has observed, "Such political support has a way of showing up in the White House sooner or later, and if OMB were continually at odds with the agencies it supposedly supervises, its job would be made impossible both politically and practically." [27]

Not only do agencies outside the EOP constantly seek to channel their points of view to the White House, but EOP offices inevitably become advocates of particular viewpoints of their own. Such advocacy within the president's own management staff poses a serious problem for chief executives who attempt to remain detached from many of their top advisers in the EOP. On the one hand, such detachment allows key EOP staffers to make decisions based on their own particular interests and without presidential supervision. On the other hand, it becomes increasingly difficult for presidents to maintain the type of information surveillance necessary to remain knowledgeable and up-to-date. According to the *Report of the President's Special Review Board (Tower Commission Report),* the involvement of Oliver North and John Poindexter in the Iran-contra scandal was the result of detachment from their key advisers. Their strong advocacy of the pro-contra position coupled with the president's lack of direction in the activities of his aides resulted in a policy disaster for the Reagan administration.[28]

Transmitting Information. Not only gathering information but transmitting information can be a big obstacle for presidents. Transmitting information from one level of the administrative hierarchy to another provides the opportunity for a portion of the information to be screened out by those who receive it and in turn send it on. Screening out information may be deliberate by those who wish to frustrate the efforts of a president, or it may be unintentional. Economist Anthony Downs estimated that as much as 98 percent of information can be lost or distorted this way.[29] With as large a bureaucratic structure as the president must attempt to control, the task of disseminating information is particularly formidable. Presidents cannot simply assume that their instructions, statements of policy, or program directives are traveling down the bureaucratic hierarchy as they intended.

To ensure that presidential communications from the EOP have been received and accurately understood, presidents must do follow-ups, that is, check for agency compliance and require regular feedback. Since administrative agencies resist supplying feedback in the same way that they resist sending information through regular channels, presidents must conscientiously monitor bureaucratic activity to maintain control at the top of the bureaucracy. The extra personnel that this requires is one reason most presidents have called for a larger EOP.

Permanent versus Presidential Government

Beneath this desire to manage the transmission of information throughout the federal bureaucracy more deliberately is an equally important motivation for greater presidential control of the bureaucracy—an antipathy and a contempt for the bureaucracy's ability to frustrate presidential policy. Most presidents never completely trust civil servants and are not completely at ease with their own political appointees. They fear that bureaucrats and department appointees develop loyalties that would obstruct presidential policy objectives. With this view comes a widely accepted belief among presidential scholars that an administration's failures result from ineffective management of the bureaucracy. Or, more specifically, an administration's failures result from the attempts of careerists (career civil servants who have made their careers in a particular department or agency) to supplant the policies of the president with those of their own agencies.

Arthur M. Schlesinger, Jr., a former Kennedy staffer, said of the Kennedy administration:

> Our real trouble was that we had capitulated too much to the existing bureaucracy. Wherever we have gone wrong . . . has been because we have not had sufficient confidence in the New Frontier approach to impose it on the government. Every important mistake has been the consequence of excessive deference to the permanent government. . . . The problem of moving forward seemed in great part the problem of making the permanent government responsive to the policies of the presidential government.[30]

Consequently, many presidents have sought to reform the executive branch to make the bureaucracy more responsive to their policy initiatives. They want to provide the EOP with a larger staff and greater resources for coordination of the various departments and agencies and their programs. According to Cronin, these presidents see themselves as "the recipients of endless special-interest pleas and narrow-minded agitation, even from many of their own cabinet members. In its crudest form, their goal is to presidentialize the executive branch." [31] To gain control over what they perceive to be hostile environments, they push for strong bureaucratic reform measures.

Presidential scholar Louis Koenig has argued for reforms that would give presidents powerful administrative control over the bureaucracy:

> The strong presidency will depend on the chief executive's capacity to control and direct the vast bureaucracy of national administration. Ideally, the president should possess administrative powers comparable to those of business executives. What the president needs most can be simply formulated: a power over personnel policy, planning, accounting, and the administration of the executive branch that approaches his power over the executive budget.[32]

Nixon stands out among recent presidents for the depth of his animosity toward the bureaucracy and his suspicion that it sought to sabotage his administration. In line with his view of a hostile bureaucracy, he attempted to adopt strategies of governance designed to decrease the role of bureaucracy and increase the power of the White House staff. After abandoning a legislative strategy to put his stamp on domestic policy, Nixon turned to an administrative strategy that would take over the bureaucracy and concentrate on achieving policy objectives through administrative action.

Public administration scholar Richard P. Nathan referred to the Nixon administration as the "anti-bureaucracy administration." He noted that over the course of Nixon's tenure in office "there was no reduction in mistrust of the bureaucracy. On the contrary, these attitudes hardened to the point where unprecedented reorganizational steps were planned for the second term to take control of the machinery of domestic government." [33]

Hostility toward the bureaucracy could be found in several statements of Nixon's aides. One staff member referred to the "White House surrounded"—apparently by a bureaucracy more attuned to the policies of interest groups than those of the president. Another Nixon aide, former White House staff assistant Michael P. Balzano, described the federal bureaucracy in June 1972 in the following terms: "President Nixon doesn't run the bureaucracy; the civil service and the unions do. It took him three years to find out what was going on in the bureaucracy. And God forbid if any president is defeated after the first term, because then the bureaucracy has another three years to play games with the next president." [34] This view of a hostile bureaucracy probably contributed greatly to some of Nixon's later difficulties in the Watergate affair.

Nathan pointed out that Nixon's 1973 decision to develop an administrative strategy for his second term brings up an important question. What should be the role of the elected chief executive in influencing the career professionals of the executive branch agencies? Should Congress, the courts, interest groups, the press, and the public be as powerful in controlling the executive branch, or even more so? Nathan argued that the president "should have the most important role in this area of modern government. Purely as a practical matter, the chief executive is in a much better position than a large group of people in a legislative body or the courts to give cohesive policy direction and guidance to the work of large public bureaucracies." [35]

The President's Administrative Style

How the chief executive organizes the EOP affects the success of any administration. Eisenhower, pointing to the necessity of a president giving considerable thought to administrative organization, wrote, "Organization cannot make a genius out of an incompetent. On the other hand, disorganization can scarcely fail to result in inefficiency and can easily lead to disaster." [36]

Presidents have used different styles in running their administrations. Some are more comfortable with a system that is tidy and neat; others prefer a chaotic system that allows them to be innovative. In choosing their administrative style, they determine how much advice and information they want to receive from within government and how much they want to receive from outside. Their decisions on administrative style determine whether they will give competing assignments and have overlapping jurisdictions or rely on aides with specific and narrowly defined responsibilities.

The Circular System

Some presidents, such as Franklin Roosevelt and John Kennedy, did not adopt a system with rigid lines of responsibility. They gave staffers different jobs over time and nurtured a competitive spirit. In this way they hoped to find the best person for any given task. Political scientist Stephen Hess described this style of staff organization as "circular," with the president at the hub of the wheel.[37] With no chief of staff to filter out less important information or decide who can and cannot see the president, this system permits large numbers of people—staffers, cabinet secretaries, members of Congress—to have relatively easy access to the Oval Office. Top staffers report directly to the chief executive.

Roosevelt is the clearest example of a hub-of-the-wheel president. Choosing a wide-open, free-wheeling, conflict-loaded system, Roosevelt delighted in encouraging and cultivating chaos in his staff. Although it was seldom clear either to outsiders or insiders where the lines of authority ran, there was never the slightest doubt that Roosevelt was in charge.

It was not unusual for Roosevelt to assign two of his top assistants to work on the same problem without informing either of them that the other had the same task. For example, Roosevelt pitted Secretary of State Cordell Hull against Assistant Secretary of State Raymond Moley at the International Monetary and Economic Conference held in London in 1933. Assigned the responsibility of working out a policy on protective tariffs, the two men had widely differing views. Hull considered protective tariffs a terrible mistake, and Moley was convinced that they were indispensable to industrial recovery at home during the New Deal. Hull, who was chairing the U.S. delegation at the conference, was surprised when Roosevelt sent Moley as his personal liaison when the conference stalled. Who had the most authority? Which view was closer to Roosevelt's? No one knew until Roosevelt sided with Hull. Infuriated by the whole episode, Moley resigned.

At whatever cost, Roosevelt had no intention of being isolated in the White House. He was determined to get as much information from as many people as he could, even if doing so meant duplicating assignments or bruising egos. Political scientist Frank Kessler described the Roosevelt system:

> One hundred or so persons could get to him directly by telephone without being diverted by a secretary. He employed no chief of staff and permitted few of his staffers to become subject matter specialists. Except for Harry Hopkins, to whom he turned almost exclusively for foreign policy assignments, staffers were assigned problems in a variety of areas. He wanted to be sure that no staffer would become so steeped in an issue area that he would be forced to lean on that person for advice. Everyone but FDR had to be expendable.[38]

The Hierarchical System

Other presidents, such as Dwight Eisenhower and Richard Nixon, valued formal, hierarchical relationships. They felt more comfortable with an arrangement that placed greater coordinating and integrating responsibilities upon a chief of staff. According to Hess, these presidents designed a highly structured pyramidal system with themselves at the pinnacle.[39]

Leaning heavily on his experience in the army, Eisenhower set up a pyramid with himself at the top and delegated as much responsibility to his staff as possible. The key to the operation was Chief of Staff Sherman Adams, who served, in effect, as a deputy president. Adams, a former member of Congress and governor of New Hampshire, came to the Eisenhower administration with a great deal of government experience. Eisenhower placed much confidence in Adams and would not read memos or reports coming across his desk unless his chief of staff had seen them first. Adams wrote, "Eisenhower simply expected me

The White House

Chief of Staff H. R. Haldeman, left, was called the "Berlin Wall" because he jealously guarded the entrance to the Oval Office. He is shown here meeting with President Nixon and aide C. Stanley Blair.

to man a staff that would boil down, simplify and expedite the urgent business that had to be brought to his attention and keep ... work of secondary importance off of his desk." [40]

The Nixon administration epitomized the pyramid staffing pattern. Similar to the Eisenhower system, Nixon constructed a highly stratified organization with himself at the top and a chief of staff standing between him and the rest of the executive branch. Preferring to make decisions from option papers rather than through face-to-face communications, Nixon allowed papers to get through to him more easily than people. Nixon's chief of staff (before the Watergate scandal forced his resignation), H. R. Haldeman, became known as the "Berlin Wall" because he jealously guarded the entrance to the Oval Office. Few staff members could get around Haldeman to see the president. Kessler has told the following story: "Once Federal Reserve Board Chairman Arthur Burns met Nixon for his allotted ten minutes but, on his way out, he remembered something else he wanted to tell the president. Haldeman reportedly thrust his arm across the doorway telling Burns to make another appointment." [41]

While Nixon's operation was successful in freeing the president to think out broad policy initiatives, Haldeman often was criticized for keeping too tight a reign on who got in to see the president. Critics argued that Haldeman took too much responsibility upon himself. But two other chief Nixon aides, speechwriter William Safire and National Security Adviser Henry A. Kissinger, contend that Haldeman was performing the very role that the president assigned him. They maintain that Nixon wanted to be protected from the "unnecessary" intrusions of his lower staff.[42] Haldeman himself reportedly once insisted, "Every president needs an S.O.B., and I'm Nixon's."

Hybrid Systems of Carter and Reagan

Jimmy Carter and Ronald Reagan provide an interesting contrast in presidential leadership styles. Neither fits neatly into either the hub-of-the-wheel or the pyramid administrative system; rather, they adopted hybrids of each style. Carter is an example of a president devoted to details and involved in the minutiae of office. Reagan, more in line with the traditional pyramid style of management, is an example of a president who values delegation, one who prefers to be free from all the small details of the presidency.

When Carter entered office, he professed to be a proponent of cabinet government and promised a decentralized system of administration, one in which great amounts of authority would be delegated to the department secretaries. He proclaimed, "I believe in cabinet administration. There will never be an instance while I am president where members of the White House staff dominate or act in a superior position to the Cabinet." [43] Yet, just two and one-half years after his inauguration, power within his administration had concentrated in the office of presidential assistant Hamilton Jordan. As Carter's term progressed, the role of the White House staff increased at the expense of the various departments and agencies in the executive branch.

Part of the reason Carter's commitment to cabinet government did not last can be found in a personal work style that proved cumbersome in the White House. Because of his predilection for immersing himself in detail, Carter spent much time consuming large amounts of factual information. Early in his administration, senior career civil servants from OMB were astounded to learn that they were to brief Carter personally rather than his top aides on the defense budget. Once, in a meeting that lasted from 3:00 p.m. to 11:00 p.m., the president devoured every piece of information that OMB could feed him. This commitment to detail pushed the administration away from a hub-of-the-wheel approach to a more structured one. Political scientist Colin Campbell has suggested, "Every fiber of Carter's personal makeup had actually been conspiring all along to run a highly centralized administration. Here the president's tendency to engross himself in details served as the fifth column." [44]

Carter originally organized his staff along functional lines rather than strict lines of command. He devised three administrative levels: the president at the top, nine key aides on the next level, and the rest of the bureaucracy below. He planned no pecking order. All of his aides, especially those on the level right below him, would have equal access to the president. Yet, despite Carter's commitment to cabinet government, a natural hierarchy developed

Jimmy Carter Library

Even though President Jimmy Carter organized his White House staff with no formal pecking order, Hamilton Jordan, right, and Jody Powell became his closest advisers. By Carter's third year in office, Jordan had become his official chief of staff.

Treasury Department

Sue Klemens

Roger Sandler

In the early years of Ronald Reagan's White House, authority was divided among these advisers: from the left, James A. Baker III, chief of staff; Edwin Meese III, counselor to the president; and Michael K. Deaver, who scheduled appointments.

within the presidential staff. By the end of the second year of the Carter administration, two long-time campaign aides, Hamilton Jordan and Jody Powell, became Carter's closest advisers. By July 1979 Jordan had moved from the second level of equals in Carter's initial staff structure to his de facto chief of staff.

Thirty-one months into his administration, Carter finally appointed Jordan as his formal chief of staff. The addition of a chief of staff should have freed Carter from the minutiae of the presidency, but his passion for details continued throughout his tenure in office. Kessler wrote, "Often he overlooked the big picture because he was bogged down in particulars. Memos that crossed his desk in the Oval Office were often returned to the sender with Carter's comments penciled in the margin. He went so far as to correct his young staffer's grammar." [45]

Under Jordan's direction, the White House began to solidify its control over bureaucratic operations. In the first few months of the Carter administration, cabinet secretaries and the heads of many other agencies had enjoyed great latitude in appointing people to fill vacancies. Personnel officers in each of the departments eventually were told, however, that the White House wanted to be consulted on all appointments to high government positions—a major blow since the departments had been promised great flexibility and control over their own affairs.

In contrast to Carter, Reagan cared little for the details of the presidency. Throughout his administration, he conveyed almost a nonchalance about such specifics. Preferring one page mini-memos that boiled down even the most complex issues to the bare essentials, Reagan operated largely through massive delegation of duties. He maintained a "nine-to-five" schedule characteristic of pyramid presidents who prefer delegation to detail.

During the 1980 campaign, however, Reagan, like Carter, had stated his intention to establish a cabinet government. And, like Carter, he gradually discarded the idea. He chose instead a modified pyramid form of staffing in which authority was divided between Chief of Staff James A. Baker III and Edwin Meese III, who served as counsellor to the president. Baker was charged with handling political matters and selling the president's programs to the public, the press, Congress, and interests groups. Meese was charged with policy formulation. In addition, Michael K. Deaver became part of the inner circle of advisers who had easy access to Reagan. Deaver's responsibilities included scheduling, appointments, and travel.

Reagan's modified pyramid incorporated some important aspects of the hub-of-a-wheel approach to organizing the presidency. By dividing power among Baker, Meese, and Deaver, he gave these three aides almost unlimited access in his first term. This arrangement kept him from becoming completely isolated, as Nixon had become by having only a single chief of staff in Haldeman. Meese served as Reagan's political conscience, keeping him true to his conservative policy goals. And Baker and Deaver helped him undertake the practical aspects of policy implementation. It was a system that suited Reagan's personality and one with which he was quite comfortable.

Once in office Reagan exercised great control over the appointment process in the departments and agencies, thereby imposing exceptional discipline on his administration. By ensuring the ideological compatibility of his nominees, Reagan could delegate and not worry about subordinates sabotaging his programs. Reagan's most effective source of discipline early in his administration, however, was the OMB under the direction of David Stockman (1981-1985). By mastering the intricacies of the budget process and controlling the budgets of the various departments and agencies, Stockman was able to impose a stringent regimen on the departments and agencies and bring them under the policy directions of the Reagan administration.

How successful was Reagan's tight discipline and modified pyramid in formulating and implementing presidential initiatives? Many who served in the Reagan administration give the president credit for energetically involving himself in important issues such as tax reform and contra funding. One aide stated:

> One thing that Reagan does is, when push comes to shove, he'll stay up all night. I mean he will get involved at the important moment.... Reagan is usually above the fray except where he thinks the president's getting involved will make a difference.... But he has a ruthless sense of priorities. He really knows that he can accomplish a few things. He's going to pick some good people and let them handle the rest. [46]

The success of the kind of system Reagan used depends on the president's knowing when to become involved in details and which issues merit concentrated attention. Yet the president must have a certain amount of knowledge even to decide which issues not to concentrate on. In several instances Reagan lacked the depth of knowledge in a specific policy area to make this determination. In 1982 a member of the NSC staff made the following statement about Reagan's lack of background in national security policy:

Karen Ruckman

David Stockman, Reagan's first director of the Office of Management and Budget, imposed strict budgetary discipline on the administration's departments and agencies.

> We really operate a bottom-up system. The president has a good overall idea of where he wants to go. When specific decisions are brought to him, I think he makes them with enormous good sense and skill. But, there's not really much push coming from him in the form of initiatives or unifying policies at an early stage. It's more waiting for the issues to come up when they get critical.[47]

In 1987 the *Tower Commission Report* confirmed this assessment of Reagan's delegation of power. Charging that President Reagan delegated too much authority to the NSC without following up on its activities, the report noted that Reagan did not give enough attention to important details of security policy. His inattention resulted in the secret sale of military equipment to Iran and the diversion of funds to assist U.S.-backed forces in Nicaragua during 1985 and 1986. This undertaking, which came to be known as the Iran-contra affair, became the subject of much public attention and embarrassment to the Reagan administration. The *Tower Commission Report* concluded that Reagan's management style put too much responsibility for policy review and implementation on the shoulders of his advisers. It stated, "The president should have ensured that the NSC system did not fail him. He did not force his policy to undergo the most critical review of which the NSC participants and the process were capable.... Had the president chosen to drive the NSC system, the outcome could well have been different."[48]

Congressional Oversight

Article I, section 1, of the Constitution states that "all legislative powers herein granted shall be vested in a Congress of the United States, which shall consist of a Senate and a House of Representatives." Section 8 lists specific congressional powers and gives Congress all powers "necessary and proper" to implement them. Over the years these provisions have been used to establish administrative agencies such as the General Accounting Office to implement congressional policies. The constitutional grants of authority have given Congress the power of life and death over these administrative agencies.

Since Congress has the power to enact laws and create and abolish executive branch agencies without presidential consent, members of Congress have significant opportunities to tell the bureaucracy what to do and how to do it. Most programs enacted into law by Congress are technical and complex, however. As a result, Congress usually states general goals to be achieved by programs administered through bureaucratic agencies.

The Economic Opportunity Act of 1964, for example, states that the poor should have "maximum feasible participation" in the administration of the programs of the Office of Economic Opportunity (OEO). The interpretation of the act was left entirely to OEO and its local branches. Congress occasionally specifies very precise standards that eliminate bureaucratic discretionary power, as it did in the Securities Act of 1933, but not often.

The very size of the *Federal Register,* a journal published each weekday in which agencies announce and publicize all the new rules and regulations used in administering programs, indicates the amount of freedom agencies have in interpreting congressional intent. Delegating this authority to the bureaucracy allows Congress to keep its workload manageable. Otherwise, the volume and complexity of its work would allow Congress to accomplish little.

By giving agencies considerable leeway in realizing their objectives, however, Congress abrogates a certain amount of control over the bureaucracy. Thus, a great deal of public policy is made by the bureaucracy, without any direct input from Congress. Since administrative agencies have wide latitude in promulgating regulations and establishing policies, the burden of reconciling conflicts among competing interest groups often falls on the bureaucracy rather than on Congress. Woll has written, "Theoretically, Congress still retains the primary legislative power, and is merely appointing an agent to act for it; in fact, however, virtually complete legislative discretion is given to the designated agency or to the President."[49]

Although Congress delegates to executive branch agencies much of its authority to make and implement policy, it retains considerable influence through a variety of activities known collectively as *congressional oversight.*

Through laws and precedents, Congress has developed procedures that allow it to monitor the way the bureaucracy exercises its delegated authority.

The Legislative Reorganization Act of 1946 requires congressional committees continuously to oversee those agencies that they created or that fall under their jurisdiction. For many years after passage of this act, members of Congress were more interested in creating new laws than in monitoring ones they had already made; oversight, therefore, was not a major concern of the committees. With the growth of grant-in-aid programs in the 1960s and 1970s, which gave state and local governments federal funds to administer specific programs in areas such as highways, hospitals, and welfare services, interest groups and state and local officials encouraged legislative oversight of agencies providing goods and services to constituents.

The Legislative Reorganization Act of 1970 increased the capability of Congress to oversee federal programs by giving committees additional staffing and funds to retain outside experts. In addition, the 1970 legislation increased the resources of the General Accounting Office (GAO)—created by Congress in 1921 to oversee the expenditures of the executive branch—and gave it power to review and analyze government programs whenever a congressional committee ordered it to do so. As a consequence GAO hired economists, systems analysts, engineers, and management consultants to help monitor and analyze programs requested by Congress. Despite the Pentagon's objections, during the 1970s approximately twelve hundred of GAO's twenty-seven hundred professional staff spent their time auditing and evaluating Department of Defense programs.[50]

Since legislation can allow considerable latitude in an agency's interpretation of congressional intent, the tools provided by GAO go a long way in giving committees a better capacity to monitor agency actions. In addition to GAO monitoring, committees can hold either regular hearings or special investigations on specific aspects of a program. They also can monitor an agency's actions through informal means, such as phone calls and visits with bureaucrats, lobbyists, and constituents. Program evaluations, done by either the committee's staff or GAO, often provide ways in which the agency's actions can be changed to bring it into line with what Congress intended.

The Legislative Veto

Congressional committees increasingly require bureaucratic agencies to meet specifications for their programs set forth by the committees themselves. These requirements provide committees a formal veto over executive actions and give them authority to approve or disapprove specific actions of the agency. In recent years the Armed Services committees have controlled the openings and closing of military bases; the public works committees have controlled contracts for capital expenditures; the House Interior and Insular Affairs Committee has controlled locations of regional offices; and the House Post Office and Civil Service Committee has located postal buildings, all through the legislative veto system. Describing the effects of legislative control over the bureaucracy, political scientist Allen Schick had noted that by 1983 "Congress had adopted more than 250 veto provisions; of these, more than half were enacted during the 1970s."[51]

The legislative veto was first written into legislation used by President Herbert C. Hoover in his attempt to reorganize the executive branch. In 1932 Congress passed a joint resolution that allowed Hoover to reorganize executive agencies but specified that his changes would not take effect for ninety days. During this time either house of Congress by a simple resolution could veto his reorganizations, but they did not.

Perhaps the best example of the use of a legislative veto comes from the Joint Committee on Atomic Energy (JCAE) in the 1950s. In setting up the Atomic Energy Commission, Congress required that agency to keep the JCAE informed on the development of its nuclear reactor programs. As Pious concluded, "In effect that provision made the committee a 'board of directors' that supervised the peaceful development of atomic energy. The committee determined what technology would be advanced, the location of experimental facilities, and policies relating to the private development of commercial power plants."[52]

Congress argues that the legislative veto is the most effective tool possible to ensure that the president and the bureaucracy conform to the intent of legislation. Many presidents, however, view the legislative veto as a violation of the doctrine of the separation of powers and as an unconstitutional encroachment into the powers of the presidency. Although the legislative veto has been challenged by various presidents and their attorneys general, not until 1983 did the Supreme Court rule on this congressional power, finding it unconstitutional.

Critics of congressional oversight and the legislative veto also argue that rather than allowing committees to oversee agencies effectively, the legislative veto gives too much influence to interest groups. They contend that "alliances" between the agency, its constituent group, and its congressional committee supersede the ability of the committee to monitor agency activities objectively. According to this theory, because the congressional committee is "captured" by the interest groups it serves, its oversight of agencies and programs will be biased to benefit the constituent groups.

Problems of Presidential Control

Congressional oversight and the legislative veto make it much more difficult for the president to control the bureaucracy. Through a variety of oversight techniques, Congress has made significant gains in controlling both foreign and domestic bureaucratic agencies. Congressional oversight helped thwart the efforts of the executive branch in its bombing of Cambodia in 1973 and inhibited various other covert intelligence activities during the Nixon years. In fact, political scientists Thomas Franck and Edward Weisband argued that executive dominance in foreign policy has been replaced by a system of policy codetermination in which power is shared by the president and Congress.[53]

As a result, presidents have learned to live with congressional efforts at bureaucratic control, often signing bills that include oversight and veto provisions not completely to their liking. Franklin Roosevelt signed the lend lease bill under which he lent American destroyers to Great Britain before the United States officially entered World War II, and other wartime measures that gave him extensive war powers, despite the constraints that Congress put on him. Nixon signed the 1974 Impoundment Control Act granting him authority to defer the spending of funds already appropriated by Congress, although either house could veto his actions. Almost any provision that delegates congressional authority to the executive branch will contain provisions for legislative review.

Presidential control of the bureaucracy, however, has not been replaced by congressional control. Congress is much too large and much too overworked to provide effective control over the bureaucracy. According to Pious, "Although Congress' oversight role has increased in recent years, it should not be exaggerated. It is still intermittent, especially in the Senate, where members are spread too thin, serving on too many committees and subcommittees to develop expertise in agency operations."[54]

In June 1983, *Immigration and Naturalization Service v. Chadha*, the Supreme Court held the legislative veto to be unconstitutional. It found that the Constitution positively requires in Article I that "every order, resolution, or vote to which the concurrence of the Senate and House of Representatives may be necessary . . . shall be presented to the president of the United States" who must either approve it or veto it.[55] In other words, the president must concur in any action that Congress takes that has the force of law, including the legislative veto. Yet, since the *Chadha* decision, Congress has passed several laws containing legislative vetoes. And these laws have yet to be challenged in court.

Reorganization Power

Because the president and Congress often find themselves opposing each other for control of the bureaucracy, presidents frequently look to reorganization as a means of gaining the upper hand and increasing their ability to manage their administrations. Presidents have attempted countless reorganization plans, however, only to find that the affected agencies are strongly protected by their sponsoring congressional committees. Without the cooperation of Congress, it is extremely difficult for presidents to effect any reorganization plan for making the bureaucracy more efficient.

Every president wants to coordinate policy-making efforts as much as possible, but because the number of federal programs has increased rapidly, coordination of the the many agencies and departments is difficult. In the area of transportation policy alone, the president must work not only with the Department of Transportation but also with the Interstate Commerce Commission, the National Transportation Safety Board, and the Federal Maritime Administration, and other agencies involved in transportation policy. This overlap among the agencies means that the executive branch often wastes time and effort trying to manage the development and implementation of public policy.

Brownlow Commission

The first real effort at administrative reorganization recognized these problems of inefficiency in the executive branch. Franklin Roosevelt wanted to establish a line of command that ran directly from the White House through the department secretaries to their subordinates. In March 1936 he created the Committee on Administrative Management and gave it the task of planning the overhaul of the executive branch. With Louis D. Brownlow as its chairman and political scientists Charles E. Merriam and Luther Gulick as the other members, the Brownlow Commission concluded in 1937 that the executive branch under Roosevelt had become so complex that "the president needs help." [56]

The Brownlow Commission specifically recommended that the president receive increased administrative support. It proposed the creation of six new presidential assistants, "possessed of high competence, great physical vigor, and a passion for anonymity," who would be assigned at presidential discretion. In addition, it recommended that discretionary funds be put at the presidency's disposal to allow him to acquire more help as needed. Finally, the commission proposed a major organizational addition to the presidency, consisting of the Executive Office of the President with the Bureau of the Budget as its centerpiece.[57]

With the exception of placing the Civil Service Commission under the control of the White House, Roosevelt won approval from Congress in 1939 for most of the Brownlow Commission's recommendations. He was given reorganization authority for a two-year period. In addition, Roosevelt was permitted to hire the six assistants that the Brownlow Commissison recommended.

In Reorganization Plan No. 1, the president moved three EOP offices—the Bureau of the Budget, the Central Statistical Board, and the National Resources Planning Committee—into the State, War, and Navy Building next-door to the White House. Soon after Reorganization Plan No. 1, Roosevelt issued an executive order that delineated the organization and responsibilities of the newly expanded presidency. This order detailed the formal relationships in the EOP between the White House Office, the BOB, and the remaining agencies of the executive branch.

Although Roosevelt got much of what the Brownlow Commission had recommended, the reorganization bill that finally passed Congress in 1939 was less than what he had hoped. The original bill was introduced in 1937 and became embroiled in Roosevelt's attempt to modify the composition of the Supreme Court. The final bill was a compromise and lacked most of Roosevelt's initial proposals. Peri E. Arnold has written, "It [the Reorganization Act of 1939] was on its face a congressional product, drafted under the guidance of Representative Lindsay Warren (Dem., N.C.) as a way of short-circuiting the intense, negative connection between presidential strength and the reorganization program." [58]

Even so, the main thrust of the Brownlow Commission recommendations were preserved, not only in the commission's structural recommendations but also in its desire to strengthen the president's control over the administration. Although Congress has been reluctant to go along completely with presidential recommendations to extend top-level management, it has allowed presidents gradually to centralize control over the bureaucracy in the EOP.

First Hoover Commission

The next major effort at centralizing presidential control occurred during the Truman administration. After large gains in the congressional elections of 1946, Republicans anticipated the end of the Truman presidency in 1948. The Republican-controlled Congress approved legislation to help a new president grapple with the problems of executive branch organization by setting up the Commission on the Organization of the Executive Branch of the Government. In 1947 Truman appointed former president Herbert Hoover as chairman.

Hoover set about the task of evaluating the effectiveness of executive branch organization with much enthusiasm. Truman, who could have viewed the commission as a means of criticizing his administration, also was enthusiastic about the project and gave it his full cooperation. It is one of the ironies of the U.S. presidency that Truman would be the one to benefit from the Hoover Commission's efforts when the Republicans failed to capture the presidency in 1948.

The Hoover Commission report recommended 277 specific measures that would institute "a clear line of control from the president to these departments and agency heads and from them to their subordinates ... cutting through the barriers that have in many cases made bureaus and agencies practically independent of the chief executive." [59] The commission's report charged that the executive branch was unmanageable; its lines of communication and authority were confusing, and there were too few tools at the top for the development of effective policy.

The commission suggested three major areas of reform. First, department heads should assume the major authority within their departments rather than allowing it to reside in the bureau chiefs. This recommendation was aimed at overcoming the congressional practice of vesting statutory powers directly in agency chiefs. With department heads more easily held responsible to the president, the lines of authority and responsibility would be more distinct. Second, the commission wanted to achieve greater clarity of direction and greater control by grouping the executive branch agencies into departments "as nearly as possible by major purposes in order to give a coherent mission to each department." [60] Third, the commission recommended that the EOP be strengthened by giving the president a stronger staff, including a staff secretariat in the White House. The president should have absolute freedom in dealing with this staff, giving it shape and appointing its members.

Truman enthusiastically supported the commission's recommendations. In addition, both Congress and the public gave their support to most of the report's proposals. The most important recommendations were realized. Recommendations for increased presidential staff and discretion in the use and organization of the EOP were implemented. And, following the commission's proposals, the Post Office, and the Departments of Interior, Commerce, and Labor were reorganized. The NSC and a number of independent agencies, including the Civil Service Commission and the Federal Trade Commission, also were reorganized.

By and large, the success of the reforms reflected the depoliticized nature of the report. Hoover and his commission approached the presidency solely in managerial terms without engaging in political ideology. Arnold has observed, "At one and the same time, reorganization planning aimed at strengthening the presidency while presenting the issue of enhanced presidential capacity as merely managerial and irrelevant to politics. Herbert Hoover and his commission of 1947-1948 present perhaps the most successful application of that logic within reorganization planning's history." [61]

Second Hoover Commission

When Dwight Eisenhower came to office in 1952, he faced a bureaucracy that had grown tremendously since Hoover, the last Republican president. After twenty years of Democratic control of the presidency, few Republicans had experience in running the federal government. In fact, after years of opposing big government and big spending, Republicans now found themselves in charge of the same bloated government they had criticized. Further complicating things for Eisenhower was a bureaucracy composed mostly of Democrats appointed under Democratic presidents. Searching for a way to make the executive branch more responsive to his leadership, Eisenhower in 1953 called once more on Hoover—at that time seventy-nine years old—to head the second Commission on the Organization of the Executive Branch of Government (the Second Hoover Commission).

The First Hoover Commission had been interested primarily in improving the administrative management of the executive branch; the Second Hoover Commission centered on issues of policy and function. At the heart of its recommendations was the idea that the executive branch should reduce its scope, saving money, reducing taxes, and eliminating competition with the private sector. The Second Hoover Commission had a specific conservative ideological agenda that aimed at reducing the growth of the government since the time of the New Deal. It argued that many of the Roosevelt era programs and agencies had become counterproductive.[62] The commission was more concerned with prescribing what government should do rather than how it should be organized and managed.

Most of the commission's recommendations were of only indirect value to the Eisenhower administration as it wrestled with the problems of a massive executive bureaucracy. For the first time, however, a major reorganization report dealt with the relations between political appointees and career public servants. Among its specific recommendations was the creation of a "Senior Civil Service" comprising approximately three thousand upper-level career executives serving in administrative positions. The commission proposed that these senior civil servants be able to transfer from one agency to another, if their particular skills and competencies suited those agencies. These senior civil servants would constitute a personnel pool that would be rotated regularly to improve management quality. The idea finally became incorporated into general personnel practices in the executive branch with the establishment of the Senior Executive Service in 1978.

Ash Council

In April 1969, Richard Nixon sought to simplify the domestic side of policy making in the executive branch by creating the Advisory Council on Executive Organization. Intending to use private sector reform in reorganization planning for his administration, Nixon appointed industrialist Roy Ash, president of Litton Industries, as chairman and four other private citizens to the council. Known as the Ash Council, the reorganization group set out to address three problems. First, it examined the executive branch's response to increasing demands on the federal government. Second, it gave attention to the organization problems that occurred among the more than 150 departments, offices, and agencies in the executive branch. Third, the council evaluated the organizational complications resulting from intergovernmental relations.[63]

The Ash Council recommended that the executive branch's domestic programs should be directed by a small number of major purpose super-departments. The council believed that this reorganization not only would save the government money but also would increase the effectiveness of executive branch management. Specifically, the council proposed that departments be set up in which the secretary would be assisted by a small number of secretarial officers who held department-wide responsibilities. Secretarial officers would include a deputy secretary who would serve as an alter-ego and department manager for the secretary, two under secretaries, several assistant secretaries, and a general counsel. The recommendations pointed to a desire to "facilitate decentralized management while simultaneously providing for effective secretarial control and department cohesion." [64]

President Nixon sent four departmental reorganization proposals to Congress on March 25, 1971. These proposals would have abolished seven existing departments and replaced them with four new super-departments. The new Department of Natural Resources would have merged the Interior Department with parts of Agriculture, Defense, and Commerce. The Department of Health, Education, and Welfare would have become the Department of Human Resources. The Department of Community Development would have combined Housing and Urban Development with some of the remaining parts of the Agriculture. The Department of Economic Affairs would have combined Labor with parts of Commerce. None of the departmental bills ever got out of their congressional committees, and Nixon eventually lost interest in the super-departments.

Some of the Ash Council's recommendations did become important to executive branch reorganization, however. In its recommendations on the EOP, the council proposed the creation of a Domestic Council and the conversion of the Bureau of the Budget into the Office of Management and Budget. Nixon incorporated these proposals into his Reorganization Plan No. 2, which he submitted to Congress on March 12, 1970.

The Ash Council intended for the Domestic Council to serve as a domestic counterpart to the NSC. It would be a cabinet-level advisory group composed of the president, vice president, attorney general, and the secretaries of Treasury, Interior, Agriculture, Commerce, Labor, Transportation, Housing and Urban Development, and Health, Education, and Welfare. The important changes to the Bureau of the Budget included expanding its managerial, policy coordination, and program information functions in its reincarnation in OMB. Both President Nixon's reorganization efforts and the Ash Council's recommendations sought through reorganization to centralize executive branch policy formation in the EOP.

Under the authority granted by Congress through the periodic extension of the Reorganization Act of 1949, presidents could reorganize executive branch entities as they pleased. Congress retained oversight of such reorganizations through a legislative veto provision in the reorganization act.

President Carter used this method several times while in office. In 1978, for example, he ordered four thousand workers involved in border inspection to move their operations from the Justice Department to the Treasury Department. He also shifted thirty-five hundred people from the firearms and explosives division of the Treasury Department to the Justice Department. In 1977 Carter exerted his reorganization powers to their fullest when he established a whole new Energy Department, absorbing two independent agencies—the Federal Power Commission and the Atomic Energy Commission. In 1979, he divided the Department of Health, Education, and Welfare into two new departments, the Department of Education and the Department of Health and Human Services.

Congress, however, refused to renew the reorganization act after the Supreme Court declared legislative vetoes unconstitutional in 1983. As a result, executive branch reorganizations must now be achieved through normal legislative procedures.

The Appointment Power

As the size of the federal government has grown, presidents have been forced to delegate more and more of their administrative responsibilities to a growing number of political executives. No single chief executive can make all the important policy and administrative decisions necessary to carry out the functions of the U.S. government. Consequently, one of the most important administrative powers that presidents have at their disposal is their ability to recruit and appoint people to fill high-level positions in their administrations.[65]

Article II, section 2, of the Constitution gives the president the power to appoint top political executives. *(See box, this page.)*

The language of the Constitution separates the appointment process of major executive officers into a two-step procedure shared by the president and the Senate. The president recruits and nominates potential appointees, and the Senate either confirms or rejects the president's appointments. The Constitution also gives Congress the ability to place other appointments within the prerogative of the president (such as the White House staff), of the courts (such as special independent counsels), or of the department heads without Senate confirmation.

Although the Constitution gives the chief executive the responsibility for selecting the approximately 2.7 million civilian employees (as of 1987) of the executive branch, over the years the chief executive has given up much direct participation in the process to the federal civil service system. Until the 1880s most executive branch jobs were apportioned through *patronage,* the system of granting favors and filling jobs as political rewards. Nineteenth-century presidents placed their friends and allies in federal government positions. With the passage of the Pendleton Act in 1883, which created the Civil Service Commission, most agencies must now choose their employees according to their qualifications and ability to do the job. *(See "The Federal Civil Service," p. 844 in Pay and Perquisites chapter of Part V.)*

Because over 90 precent of executive branch positions are covered by the Civil Service, only the most senior executive positions are filled by presidential appointees. By choosing personnel for these positions, presidents send their political goals to the bureaucracy.

At the beginning of a new administration, Congress publishes *Policy and Supporting Positions*—known as the "plum book"—which lists the top executive branch positions available for direct presidential appointment, many of which require Senate confirmation. Each new presidential administration must appoint approximately 200 members of the White House staff, 14 department heads, 400-500 members of the subcabinet, and approximately 150 ambassadors. In addition, agency and department heads appoint 600-800 members of the Senior Executive Service and about 1,800 special aides in Schedule C positions, which are exempted from the testing and qualification requirements of the civil service merit system. Altogether, presidents and their subordinates must appoint about 5,200 people to the executive branch.[66] Political scientist Hugh Heclo estimates that presidents are most interested in approximately 300 top political executive posts—cabinet secretaries, undersecretaries, assistant secretaries, and bureau chiefs.[67]

Since executive appointees link the president to the vast organizational components of the executive branch, the right to recruit and appoint these people is extremely

> . . . he shall nominate, and by and with the Advice and Consent of the Senate shall appoint Ambassadors, other public Ministers and Consuls, Judges of the supreme Court, and all other Officers of the United States, whose Appointments are not herein otherwise provided for and which shall be established by Law; but the Congress may by Law vest the Appointment of such inferior Officers as they think proper in the President alone, in the Courts of Law, or in the Heads of Departments.
>
> —from Article II, section 2

important to the chief executive's ability to control the disparate components of the federal government. To ensure effective leadership, presidents look for quality and loyalty in their appointees.

The sixteenth-century political theorist Niccolo Machiavelli observed, "The first opinion that is formed of a ruler's intelligence is based on the quality of men he has around him." [68] This observation suggests that an administration is only as good as the people the president appoints to fill it. The immense size of the executive branch makes it impossible, however, for presidents to know most of the people they appoint, much less to make personal assessments of their quality. Upon winning the presidency after several months of campaigning, John F. Kennedy complained about trying to fill many of his top positions: "People, people, people! I don't know any people. All I know is voters! How am I going to fill these 1,200 jobs?" [69] Kennedy knew fewer than half of his final cabinet appointments.

Some new appointees come to their positions well qualified, but others do not. What occupational and educational characteristics do presidential appointees have? Between 1982 and 1985 a National Academy of Public Administration survey found that 40 percent of federal appointees are transferred or promoted from other positions in the government. Sixty percent, however, come from occupations outside the federal government: 24 percent from business, 16 percent from academic and research communities, 12 percent from the legal profession, 7 percent from state and local governments, and 1 percent from other organizations. The education level of presidential appointees is relatively high: 19 percent hold bachelor's degrees, 21 percent hold master's degrees, 17 percent hold Ph.D.s, and 34 percent hold law degrees.[70]

In addition to quality and loyalty, presidents consider other factors as well when they make their selections. Most presidents have accumulated quite a few political debts on their way to the White House. Numerous groups and individuals have contributed both money and votes to their victories, and presidents look for ways to reward their chief supporters with major political appointments. Although these selections usually do not constitute the majority of a president's appointments, they are an important consideration. President Harry S Truman, for example, appointed banker John Snyder and Democratic National Chairman Robert Hannegan, both old friends from Missouri, to the positions of Treasury secretary and postmaster general, respectively. Hannegan also served as chairman of the Democratic National Committee. Early in his administration, President Ronald Reagan appointed political advisers Lyn Nofziger, Michael K. Deaver, and Edwin Meese III, all friends and longtime supporters.

Presidents also make many appointments for purely political reasons. The very first presidential personnel selections are the most important politically. In fact, the appointments that presidents make as they establish their administrations generally set the tone and priorities of their presidencies. These selections are important for symbolic reasons and are subject to very close public scrutiny. In his study of presidential cabinets, political scientist Richard Fenno commented: "The presidential decisions leading to the composition of a new 'official family' are taken during the peak period of public interest which attends the national election campaign. As executive decisions go, they are pre-eminently concrete and visible. Among the earliest of presidential moves, they are treated as symbolic acts of considerable significance." [71]

Table 1 Number of Employees and Political Appointments in Cabinet Departments, 1989

Department	Total number of employees	Schedule C appts.	Total number of appts.[a]
Agriculture	124,706	226	308
Commerce	44,347	107	190
Defense	1,057,842[b]	119	248
Education	4,602	125	348
Energy	17,316	68	108
Health and Human Services	125,331	79	152
Housing and Urban Development	13,436	91	135
Interior	77,994	54	111
Justice	75,605	59	281
Labor	18,480	72	107
State	26,272	162	1,053
Transportation	63,386	73	136
Treasury	164,541	43	93
Veterans Affairs	246,529	9	190
Total	2,060,387	1,287	3,460

Sources: Office of Personnel Management; Center for Excellence in Government.

a. Includes noncareer employees in the Senior Executive Service and public law positions, such as State Department Foreign Service officers.

b. Total civilian employees.

In addition, presidents consider in what ways future political relationships will be affected by their early choices. An administration's success often depends on the ability of the president to forge political allies and broaden the presidency's base of support. Expanding political allies frequently can be accomplished through the appointment process. In addition to rewarding those who have supported them in the past, presidents often use appointments to get on the good side of members of their own political party, interest groups whose support they seek, and, often, members of Congress.

This strategy can backfire, however. William Howard Taft, quoting Thomas Jefferson, used to lament, "Every time I make an appointment I create nine enemies and one ingrate." As political scientist Calvin Mackenzie wrote: "The selection process, particularly in the early stages of a new administration is governed by scarce resources and multiple, competing demands. Opportunities exist for gaining some political advantage from these early personnel choices, but, if used unwisely, those opportunities are easily squandered." [72]

Another important consideration in presidential appointments is the presidency's managerial needs. As the bureaucracy has become more technologically complex, presidents have had to choose appointees that bring with them managerial and administrative capabilities. The larger the department or agency, the greater the need for management expertise. Departments such as Defense and Health and Human Services and agencies such as the U.S. Postal Service are examples of large government organizations requiring consideration of administrative competence as a standard for appointment.

Although many presidents desperately seek better

management, rarely are appointments made on the basis of such an objective consideration as management ability. Most jobs are filled immediately after the presidential election, when presidents have the largest number of appointments to make and the least amount of time to consider them. Ironically, at this point in their administrations, when they are best able to lure potential appointees, presidents are unable to take full advantage of one their greatest administrative powers. More often than not, the ability to manage becomes one of the last considerations given a potential appointee. Political considerations, as well as an administration's inability to judge its management needs, often outweigh managerial skill. Characteristics such as an appointee's geographic or ethnic background are often much more obvious and easy to consider than administrative ability.

Constraints on the Appointment Process

The postelection rush to fill vacancies in the new administration places a number of constraints on the appointment process. Between the election and the inauguration, the president works to establish the policy objectives of the administration. While still forming their policy objectives, presidents or their subordinates must make the vast majority of their most important appointments. Cronin has noted: "Too frequently appointees are not carefully related to policy. Many subcabinet appointments, for example, are made by subordinates, with the president hardly aware of whether the appointee is matched with the position. . . ." [73] Once in office many appointees adopt new attitudes as a result of new institutionalized responsibilities; or some, perhaps ill-suited for institutional management, may become rigidly wedded to the views of the interest groups with which they most frequently interact.

Presidents often find it difficult to persuade their potential nominees to give up high-paying positions in the private sector and move to Washington, D.C. In 1980 the Commission on Executive, Legislative, and Judicial Salaries concluded: "There is growing evidence that low salaries are a major reason for highly talented people declining appointment to key positions in the federal government." [74]

Other presidents have found it difficult to persuade potential nominees to disclose their financial background and income. Because the American public expects executive branch officials to perform their duties without undue regard for special interests, Congress passed strict financial disclosure laws in 1965. Certain top executive branch employees were required to report information about their personal finances to the head of the Civil Service Commission, who could report this information to the president if there seemed to be a conflict of interest. Title II of the Ethics in Government Act of 1978 broadened disclosure provisions by requiring all presidential appointees to complete the Executive Personal Financial Disclosure Report, which publicly discloses their personal financial information. These provisions have been a source of great concern for many potential appointees. E. Pendleton James, President Reagan's assistant for personnel, stated that "literally hundreds" of potential presidential nominees lost interest as a result of demanding disclosure provisions.[75]

Similarly, presidents must sometimes pass up potential nominees because of the person's involvement with a past administration, a scandal, or even the appearance of wrongdoing. For example, Peter Flanigan, a former Nixon aide, was nominated by President Gerald Ford as ambassador to Spain, but he had to withdraw under opposition from Congress over his relationship with the Watergate-plagued Nixon administration. In short, presidents face enormous difficulties in finding appropriate candidates in a shrinking pool of potential nominees who are willing to go to Washington and face public scrutiny and who have avoided any conflict of interest.

The Role of the Senate

The Senate is an integral part of the appointment process and serves as one of the most important limits to the presidential appointment privilege. Constitutionally, presidents share the appointment of many political executives with the Senate, and the Senate must confirm most of the president's major appointments. As a result, the Senate has come to view the appointment procedure as a process in which its members should have a considerable say. As Mackenzie has observed, "For Senators and Senate committees, the confirmation process is both a responsibility and an opportunity." [76] It is a constitutional responsibility and a political opportunity. Senators view the appointment process as a way to influence government policy. Cronin has noted that senators even try to influence presidential policy by getting the president to nominate their choices: "They ... often have candidates of their own. This is especially the case in recent years, for as the staffs of Congress have expanded ... there are more and more aides to Congress who seek top executive branch appointments." [77]

The number of presidential nominations sent to the Senate for confirmation is staggering. The Senate must process between 90,000 and 170,000 nominations each session (two-year period). Usually, the vast majority of these nominations are routine military commissions and promotions that require very little of the Senate's time. Although the number of civilian appointments is much lower, the Senate must still spend a great deal of time and energy processing them. For example. the Ninety-eighth Congress in 1983-1985 processed 7,581 civilian nominations. This figure includes routine nominations to such civilian organizations as the Foreign Service, the Public Health Service, and the National Oceanic and Atmospheric Administration. However, more highly scrutinized nominations to top-level policy-making positions in the executive branch—averaging only about 700 per session—require much attention from the Senate.

Like most other matters before Congress, the nomination process is handled mostly by standing committees. Although each committee has different sets of procedures for managing appointments referred to them, most committees have developed their own standard sets of structured proceedings. Usually, these procedures require additional background checks and financial disclosures, other than those already required by the president's personnel director and the Ethics in Government Act of 1978, and extensive hearings. The average length of time required by the Senate to confirm presidential nominees during the Reagan administration was 14.6 weeks. The result of this rigorous and lengthy investigative process has been an increase in demands on potential appointees. In his study of the Senate's role in the presidential appointment process, political scientist Christopher J. Deering pointed out that this demanding investigatory process has made the Senate's role in the nomination process not only more thorough but also more demanding: "Unfortunately, the process has ... become more tedious, time-consuming, and intrusive for the nominees. For some the price is too high...." [78]

The Founders intended the Senate's constitutional role in the presidential appointment process to serve as a check on executive power. To what extent has the Senate checked presidential power through its confirmation power? All presidents have been successful in getting the majority of their nominees confirmed. Over 92 percent of all civilian presidential nominations were confirmed by the 98th Congress. Most nominations are defeated in committees. Since 1960 only six nominees have been defeated on the floor of the Senate. Many, however, have had a few of their potential appointees rejected. The Senate regularly thwarted the efforts of James Madison and Ulysses S. Grant to nominate their choices for executive branch positions freely. John Tyler perhaps had the most difficulty with the Senate in attempting to fill vacancies. His appointees were frequently rejected by the Senate, including four cabinet and four Supreme Court appointees. In one day in 1843, the Senate rejected Tyler's nomination of Caleb Cushing as secretary of the Treasury three times. In 1984 President Reagan's nominee for associate attorney general, William Bradford Reynolds, was turned down by the Senate Judiciary Committee. His opponents argued that Reynolds had been negligent in enforcing antidiscrimination laws during his tenure as chief of the Justice Department's Civil Rights Division. Although the Senate does not often reject a presidential nominee, the occasions on which it has done so, and the thoroughness of its investigations of those who are confirmed, indicate that the Senate does exert some control over the president's prerogative to appoint key members to the administration.

In some cases, however, the Senate may use its confirmation power more as a political bargaining chip than anything else. It will often "hold" the nominee in limbo until the president agrees to support a political position. For example, President Reagan's nomination of Edwin Meese as attorney general was used by the majority leader as leverage to exact a promise to support farm aid legislation. During the 1980s Sen. Jesse Helms (R-N.C.) repeatedly held up nominations because he found them politically unacceptable or he wished to force political opponents to compromise on policy issues. Deering has written, "On numerous occasions in recent years, members of the Senate of both parties have placed holds on particular individuals. In some cases, the nominee is the target, in other cases merely a pawn, but in either case the use of nominees as, in effect, hostages has undermined the integrity of the system." [79]

The Presidential Personnel System

The presidential appointment process remained relatively unchanged throughout the first 150 years of U.S. history. Presidents had little, if any, staff to help them make their appointments; political parties usually controlled personnel selection for the president. *(See "Presidential Party Leadership within the Executive," p. 610, in Chief of Party chapter of Part III.)* Even when chief executives did become actively involved in the selection process, they often used the existing political party structure. Other nominees were usually suggested to the president by party leaders or members of Congress from the president's party. Too often this dependence on the party resulted in administrations filled with top-level appointees with little loyalty to presidential objectives.

Roosevelt and Truman Administrations

Since Franklin D. Roosevelt entered the White House, however, newly elected presidents have needed significant staff support and a centralized procedure for choosing personnel because of the vast number of appointments that must be made in a short period of time. Perhaps more important, a centralized appointment process under the president's control ensures faithfulness to White House policies and objectives.

Until the 1960s, the selection of presidential appointments was haphazard and unfocused. Presidential personnel operations relied heavily on chance to place the right people in the right positions. During the 1940s, however, President Roosevelt attempted to alleviate much of the problem by introducing a number of governmental reforms that removed presidential patronage from the national political parties. For example, he appointed an assistant to handle personnel matters in an effort to improve presidential control over the appointment process. In the following decades the presidency experienced an increase in its administrative powers, allowing it more discretion in personnel selection.

Journalist Dom Bonafede has attributed the growth of a more centralized selection procedure within the White House after 1940 to three factors. First, political reforms that increased the number of state primaries and emphasized grass-roots politics "hastened the decline of the national parties and minimized their brokerage role as conduit and clearinghouse for appointments." Presidents were no longer obligated to party leaders for their election and, therefore, had less need to reward them with government jobs. Second, the movement toward a strong administrative presidency, which centralized power in the White House, further strengthened the president's hand vis-à-vis Congress and the bureaucracy. Third, "the complexity of domestic and foreign issues, such as arms control, tax reform, federal deficits and trade imbalances, necessitated elaborate institutional support, placing a premium on substantive knowledge and managerial competence." [80]

Specific recommendations by the Committee on Administrative Management, headed by Louis D. Brownlow, and the two Hoover Commissions helped centralize more power into the presidency. *(See "Reorganization Power," p. 406, in this chapter.)* In 1939, acting on Brownlow Commission recommendations, Congress created the Executive Office of the President (EOP) and brought the Bureau of the Budget under the control of the president within the EOP. These measures began what has become known as the "institutional presidency." The first and second Hoover Commissions further increased the administrative power of the presidency by giving it more control over the vast federal bureaucracy and substantial authority over the appointment process.

President Truman appointed the first full-time staff member responsible only for personnel matters. Although this aide, Donald Dawson, addressed mostly routine concerns and spent a good deal of time in contact with the

Democratic National Committee, the new position signaled the growing importance of staffing issues.

Eisenhower Administration

Dwight D. Eisenhower came to office in 1953 with a strong desire to improve the management of the executive branch but with a dislike for personnel matters. He frequently wrote in his diary that patronage was one of the great banes of his administration and one of the things most likely to cause him to lose his temper. Consequently, he delegated personnel concerns to members of his staff, primarily to Sherman Adams, his chief of staff. Adams, however, soon found the job of personnel director too demanding when added to his other responsibilities. The president then approved the position of special assistant for executive appointments, which several people held during the eight years Eisenhower was in office. These special assistants did not choose the president's appointees. Rather, they managed the appointment process by narrowing the president's choices to candidates with the best qualifications and the fewest political liabilities. More than anything else, Eisenhower sought appointees who were loyal to his political philosophy and his programs.

Kennedy and Johnson Administrations

Shortly after his election, president-elect Kennedy put together a personnel selection staff called "Talent Hunt." Comprising some of the best people from the campaign, Talent Hunt was a loosely organized operation with two objectives. First, it tried to determine the president-elect's political obligations—supporters who helped him win the election—and find appropriate jobs to pay off those debts. Second, it attempted to identify the most important jobs the president would have to fill and to find the best people for those positions. After the inauguration, Talent Hunt broke up, and its members went to their own jobs in the administration.

In mid-1961 Kennedy appointed Dan Fenn of the Harvard Business School faculty to take over the day-to-day personnel responsibilities of the White House. Asked to recommend changes in the traditional method of filling executive positions, Fenn concluded that the procedure was too limited. The most important jobs in the federal government were being filled by a very unsophisticated "Whom do you know?" system—a process he called "BOGSAT," that is, a "bunch of guys sitting around a table."

John F. Kennedy Library

Dan Fenn, President John F. Kennedy's personnel aide, created a White House appointment process that gave the president recruiting ability independent of the political parties.

Fenn attempted to correct this problem by creating a systematic White House appointment operation consisting of three major stages. First, he and his staff developed reliable job descriptions that allowed them to match candidates with positions, something most administrations had not been able to do. Second, Fenn offered the president a wider selection of candidates from which to choose. He believed that the range of people with whom presidents normally come into contact was too narrow to provide the talent necessary for a successful administration. Third, since he could offer a wider range of choices only by reaching beyond traditional political sources for appointments, Fenn established a network of well-positioned people throughout the country whose opinions the president trusted and who could provide Kennedy with candid information about potential nominees. Although the system Fenn established never worked quite as well as it might have, it nonetheless marked the first time a president had significant independent recruiting ability, separate and apart from the influence of the political parties.

During Lyndon B. Johnson's administration, the centralization of presidential personnel selection took a giant leap forward. Although Kennedy had put together a significant staff for selecting nominees, he would often bypass the process by selecting appointees without using the system Fenn had established. Johnson, too, would sometimes circumvent his personnel staff, but he always maintained the appearance that the selection had been made through the White House personnel system. The authors of one study of the presidential selection process concluded:

> Those who wanted to influence [Johnson's] appointment decisions quickly got the message that their contact point for this was the personnel staff and that efforts to evade the established personnel selection procedures would be difficult to pull off. This focused more attention on the White House and significantly strengthened its role at the hub of the appointment process.[81]

The Kennedy and Johnson presidencies effected three important long-term changes in presidential personnel management. First, a full-time personnel staff became a regular component of the White House Office. Second, presidents have attempted to maintain their independence from traditional political party pressures by recruiting their own candidates. Third, each administration has developed and followed routine procedures for scrutinizing the background, competence, integrity, and political loyalty of each potential appointee.

Nixon Administration

When Richard Nixon took office in 1969, he at first failed to incorporate in his presidency many of the advances made in personnel selection in preceding administrations. He had little interest in personnel matters and delegated most of the responsibility for filling offices to his staff. His initial appointment process was slow and cumbersome, and too many times the White House appointed people who had little loyalty to the president's programs. As a result, in 1970 Nixon appointed Frederic V. Malek to study the personnel staff and recommend improvements. His recommendations called for a personnel system similar to those of Nixon's predecessors: centralization of the recruiting process in the White House, recruitment outreach beyond traditional political party sources of potential nominees, and a more rigorous clearance process.

In 1971 Nixon appointed Malek director of his personnel operation. Malek, acting on his own recommendations, set up the White House Personnel Office (WHPO). Following the examples of the organizations set up by Fenn and John W. Macy, personnel assistant to President Johnson, Malek made the WHPO a tightly organized operation that employed a highly professional staff. The WHPO employed professional headhunters whose sole responsibility was to find the right person for the right job in the administration. In addition, the WHPO developed a much more sophisticated evaluation system than had ever been used before in the White House. After two years of haphazard personnel selection, the Nixon White House emerged with a firm commitment to centralized personnel decision making for almost all noncareer positions in the federal government. Eventually, the WHPO lost much of its intensity, and some of its members went beyond the limits of propriety in attempting to control the appointment process. The WHPO outlined ways in which the civil service could be manipulated by the administration. One way was to write job descriptions to fit specific applicants loyal to Nixon. Those unsympathetic were to become transfers to undesirable locations or assignments requiring a great deal of travel. The press and Congress finally intervened, forcing the WHPO to retreat from its continued efforts at centralization.

Frederic V. Malek, President Richard Nixon's personnel director, established the White House Personnel Office in 1971.

Nixon Project, National Archives

Ford and Carter Administrations

Gerald R. Ford's personnel staff spent much of its time trying to clean up the image of the aggressive WHPO under Nixon. The first thing that Ford changed was the name. The WHPO became the Presidential Personnel Office. In addition, Ford reduced the size of the personnel operation and narrowed the focus of its activities to positions traditionally viewed as presidential appointments rather than most noncareer appointments.

Jimmy Carter was the first president who began planning for his presidency while still running for election. In the summer of 1976, he set up a small staff in Atlanta to begin working on the staffing of his administration. Carter chose Jack Watson to head up the operation, which became known as Talent Inventory Program (TIP). After Carter won the election, Watson moved his operation to Washington. Once there he became locked in a power struggle with Carter's campaign manager, Hamilton Jordan, over who would control the appointment process. As a result of this struggle, the Presidential Personnel Office floundered for almost two years. Although a personnel staff was established in the White House, its ability to manage the appointment process effectively was hampered by the rivalry between Watson and Jordan. Throughout the Carter administration, there was no central coordination of appointments in the White House, and much of the early work of TIP was ignored.

Carter contributed to the disorder in the appointment process by insisting that cabinet heads be given almost total discretion in choosing their subordinates. At various times in the campaign, he had proclaimed: "There will never be an instance while I am president where members of the White House staff dominate or act in a superior position to the members of our Cabinet." [82] This promise made good campaign rhetoric, but it diminished Carter's ability to control his administration by decentralizing the decision-making process. Some departments made appointments after a rigorous search procedure. Others resorted to "politics as usual" and used the insiders' network to select potential nominees whose main qualifications were friendship and loyalty to department secretaries. As Bonafede described the results, "In an unseemly brief period it became clear to the president's top lieutenants—and only later to Carter himself—that he had made a major mistake in giving secretaries carte blanche authority to hand-pick their assistants." [83]

Reagan Administration

Reagan viewed the appointment process as an integral part of his plans for changing the direction of the federal government. Determined to avoid the mistakes of the Carter administration, he centralized the appointment process squarely within the White House.

Reagan also made a determined effort to appoint only persons who shared his political philosophy. E. Pendleton James, Reagan's postelection talent search manager and eventual assistant to the president for personnel, declared, "You can't separate personnel from policy." [84] This outlook pervaded the administration's appointment efforts. From the "kitchen cabinet" made up of Reagan's elite, conservative California advisers who chose politically acceptable potential nominees before his election, to the personnel office, which managed appointments during the administration, the strategy was to choose nominees whose political philosophy matched the president's.

The Reagan appointment process benefited from some of Carter's mistakes. James gave the process a consistency it lacked under Carter. During the transition and throughout the first eighteen months of the Reagan administration, James presided over the day-to-day operation of the administration's personnel selection. As a result, there was very little confusion over the process itself or who was in charge. Also, Reagan visibly involved himself in the appointment process. He made the final decision on all of the important appointments during the transition and the first year. The authors of one study noted:

> This proved to be an effective deterrent to those in the departments and agencies and in Congress who might try and wrest control of appointment decisions away from the White House. It is one thing to attempt that when low-level White House staff members are making appointment decisions; it is quite another when those decisions are being made in the Oval Office.[85]

Since Franklin Roosevelt's administration, presidents have relied on increasingly sophisticated methods of cen-

Washington Star; courtesy Martin Luther King, Jr., Library

E. Pendleton James, Ronald Reagan's assistant to the president for personnel, saw to it that all appointees shared Reagan's political philosophy.

tralizing the appointment power in the White House in their attempts to strengthen control over their administrations. The personnel office is now a permanent part of the White House organizational structure. Succeeding presidents have significantly increased the number of staff assigned to find competent and loyal political executives. And presidential personnel operations have come to rely on professional recruiting techniques. Yet, as important as the office is to presidential control, it is not at the top of the executive branch hierarchy. Bonafede has concluded that, in most administrations, the presidential personnel office

> lacks institutional stability; the process varies from one presidency to another, and it even varies in the zeal and orderliness with which it is conducted within the same administration. Each incoming administration, distrustful of past personnel procedures, feels compelled to reinvent its own system. Few presidents have been willing to lend their prestige to the office.[86]

The Removal Power

The ability of presidents to control their administrations is often dependent on their authority to remove subordinates from office. This issues lies at the very heart of the chief executive's power over the bureaucracy. The power of presidents to remove officials from office who are not doing their jobs properly or who disagree with presidential goals and programs is, however, controversial and has been significantly limited by the Supreme Court. Because the Constitution does not explicitly grant presidents power to remove officials from office, the legitimacy of the power often has rested on court interpretations of specific presidential removal actions.

Preferring to avoid the issue as long as possible, the Supreme Court refused to make a definitive ruling on the issue of presidential removal of public officeholders until 1926—just a few years before the growth of modern presidential power. In *Myers v. United States* the Court ruled that an 1876 law that limited the president's removal power over postmasters was unconstitutional. In 1917 President Woodrow Wilson had appointed Myers to be a postmaster in Portland, Oregon, for a term of four years. Attempting to make his administration responsive to his policy goals, Wilson removed Myers from office in 1920 without consent of the Senate, although the 1876 statute provided that postmasters should be appointed and removed by the president by and with the advice and consent of the Senate. Myers sued for his salary in the U.S. Court of Claims. When he received an adverse judgment, he took his case to the Supreme Court.

In delivering the opinion of the Court, Chief Justice William Howard Taft, a former president, strongly argued that presidents cannot effectively administer the executive branch unless they can control their subordinates with the threat of removal for political and other reasons. He stated that the power of removal was implied in the constitutional provision in Article II, which gave the presidency the responsibility to see that the laws be faithfully executed. Furthermore, Congress could not constitutionally restrain or limit that power. Taft contended that presidents cannot carry out their constitutional responsibilities if Congress interferes with their ability to control the executive branch.[87]

The *Myers* case arguably had given presidents sweeping authority to remove not only immediate executive subordinates but also members of independent regulatory commissions, such as the Interstate Commerce Commission and the Federal Trade Commission. Independent regulatory commissioners are appointed under the provisions of statutes that confer upon them a certain amount of independence and freedom from the political control of the president. In these agencies, Congress had carefully outlined the provisions by which a commissioner could be removed in an attempt to free these executives from political control. If the *Myers* case applied to all political executives, then the political independence of the regulatory commissions would no longer exist. Sooner or later the question of unlimited presidential power of removal would be challenged.

The question of the president's ability to remove independent regulatory commissioners quickly came up during Franklin Roosevelt's administration and was settled in 1935 by the Supreme Court in *Humphrey's Executor v. United States.* President Herbert C. Hoover had nominated William E. Humphrey to the Federal Trade Commission (FTC) in 1931. Under the terms outlined by Congress in the Federal Trade Commission Act of 1914, FTC commissioners were supposed to serve a term of seven years. The act stated that commissioners could be removed by the president only for "inefficiency, neglect of duty, or malfeasance in office." After his election to office, Roosevelt wrote Humphrey and requested his resignation from the FTC so that "the aims and purposes of the administration with respect to the work of the Commission can be carried out most effectively with personnel of my own selection." After Humphrey's initial reluctance to resign, Roosevelt again wrote him, this time stating: "You will, I know, realize that I do not feel that your mind and my mind go along together on either the policies or the administering of the Federal Trade Commission, and frankly, I think it is best for the people of the country that I should have full confidence." [88] When Humphrey refused to resign, Roosevelt notified him that he had been removed. Humphrey died in 1934, never having agreed to his removal. The executor of Humphrey's estate decided to sue for salary he believed was due Humphrey but never paid him.

The court of claims asked the Supreme Court to answer two questions before it could render a judgment. First, did the Federal Trade Commission Act limit the president's power to remove commissioners except for reasons stated in the act? Second, if the act did indeed limit the president's power to remove commissioners, was it constitutional?

Roosevelt had made clear that the removal of Humphrey was for political reasons. Justice George Sutherland delivered the Court's opinion that the *Myers* case did not apply to Humphrey because the FTC was "an administrative body created by Congress to carry into effect legislative policies." Therefore, it could not "in any sense be characterized as an arm or an eye of the Executive." Sutherland continued:

> Whether the power of the president to remove an officer shall prevail over the authority of Congress to condition the power by fixing a definite term and precluding the removal except for cause will depend upon the character of the office; the *Myers* decision, affirming the power of the president alone to make the removal, is confined to purely executive officers.[89]

The *Humphrey* decision not only invalidated Roosevelt's removal of Humphrey but also generally limited presidential removal power to officials who could be classified as "purely executive officers." Except for appointees immediately responsible to the president and those exercising nondiscretionary or ministerial functions, such as White House aides, the president's power of removal could be limited by Congress.

The Supreme Court attempted to make a distinction between "executive" and "administrative" functions within the federal bureaucracy. Presidents have complete control over executive functions, or those that deal with the execution of the policy of the administration and are under the direction of the president, such as members of the EOP and cabinet members. The Court ruled that presidents do not, however, have complete control over administrative functions, or those that have quasi-judicial or quasi-legislative roles, such as those of the independent regulatory commissions. Only when Congress chooses specifically to give presidents control over these agencies can they remove officials for merely political reasons.

In 1958 the Supreme Court further clarified the removal power of presidents. In *Wiener v. United States,* the Court held that if officials are engaged in adjudicative functions presidents may not remove them for political reasons. In 1950 President Truman had appointed Wiener to serve on the War Claims Commission. When Eisenhower assumed office, he requested Wiener's resignation. When Wiener refused, Eisenhower removed him from office. Similar to Roosevelt's removal of Humphrey, Eisenhower's removal of Wiener rested on purely political reasons. Congress had created the War Claims Commission to adjudicate damage claims resulting from World War II. It made no provisions for removing commissioners. Wiener sued for his lost salary.

Noting the similarity between the *Wiener* and *Humphrey* cases, the Supreme Court ruled in favor of Wiener. The Court argued that in both cases presidents had removed persons from quasi-judicial agencies for political purposes. Calling the War Claims Commission a clearly adjudicative body, Justice Felix Frankfurter concluded for the Court:

> Judging the matter in all the nakedness in which it is presented, namely, the claim that the President could remove a member of an adjudicative body like the War Claims Commission merely because he wanted his own appointees on such a Commission, we are compelled to conclude that no such power is given to the President directly by the Constitution, and none is impliedly conferred upon him by statute simply because Congress said nothing about it. The philosophy of *Humphrey's Executor,* in its explicit language as well as it implications, precludes such a claim.[90]

These cases have defined more clearly the legal and constitutional authority of presidents over the federal executive branch by addressing their power to remove certain officers. The *Myers* case gave presidents considerable authority to fire executive branch officials appointed by the president and confirmed by the Senate. The *Humphrey* and *Wiener* cases limited presidential removal authority over agencies that exercise quasi-legislative or quasi-judicial functions, such as independent regulatory agencies.

Generally, presidents may remove all heads of cabinet departments and all political executives in the Executive Office of the President. In addition, they may remove at any time the directors of the following agencies: ACTION, the Arms Control and Disarmament Agency, the Commission on Civil Rights, the Environmental Protection Agency, the Federal Mediation and Conciliation Service, the General Services Administration, the National Aeronautics and Space Administration, the Postal Service, and the Small Business Administration.

The Budgeting Power

The power to control the budget process is one of the most important administrative prerogatives of the presidency. The chief executive is an important participant in the budget process, for often it is the president who decides where and how money is spent. As presidential scholar Richard Pious has noted, "To budget is to govern. In a system of separated institutions that share power, the question is which institution, and by what authority, determines spending levels for the departments?" [91] In the last part of the twentieth century, the presidency has assumed an increasingly important role in determining federal spending and thus more responsibility in governing. Although Congress technically controls the purse strings, the president controls the formulation and development of the budget.

The Constitution does not clearly establish a budgetary process or specifically spell out the presidency's role in such a process. Because of this ambiguity, presidents have been able to bring much of the process under their control. Article I of the Constitution gave Congress the powers to tax and spend. Article II, section 3, gave presidents the power to recommend to Congress such measures as they deemed appropriate. ("He shall from time to time give to the Congress Information of the State of the Union, and recommend to their Consideration such Measures as he shall judge necessary and expedient.") Implied in this power is the idea that presidents may present to Congress a financial program.

Historically, presidents have not taken part in budget planning. Even in modern times, presidential involvement in the process has varied from one administration to another. For many presidents, preparing a budget is a job not readily cherished because it has proven to be tedious and time consuming. President Lyndon B. Johnson once wrote, "The federal budget is a dry, unfathomable maze of figures and statistics—thicker than a Sears-Roebuck catalogue and duller than a telephone directory." [92] Some presidents have been able to maintain consistent interest in the budget's complexities throughout their terms in office; others have not. Political scientist Lance T. LeLoup examined the roles that past presidents played in the budget process and found that shortly after the first year in office, Dwight D. Eisenhower and Richard Nixon tired of the tedious budget process. Harry S Truman and Gerald R. Ford, however, were able to maintain their enthusiasm throughout their administrations.[93]

Budgeting gives the presidency a tremendous amount of administrative power, and most presidents have recognized the importance of the budget in controlling their administrations. They usually approach their first budget optimistically, excited about the potential power to eliminate or cut back programs that they may feel have outlived their usefulness. Describing his involvement in his first budget, Lyndon Johnson wrote, "I worked as hard on that budget as I have ever worked on anything.... Day after day I went over that budget with the Cabinet officers, my economic advisers, and the Budget Director. I studied almost every line, nearly every page, until I was dreaming about the budget at night." [94] Yet, LeLoup found that often this enthusiasm wanes after presidents are confronted with the recurring difficulty of the whole process.[95]

Although their enthusiasm may fade, presidents continue to seek to control the budget process. They see their participation in the process as a way of doing things that can benefit the national economy and their own political fortunes. In the words of President Ford, "The budget is the president's blueprint for the operation of government in the year ahead." [96] According to Dennis S. Ippolito in his study of the budget process, presidents become involved in the budget process to achieve a means of administrative management and control: "By affecting the resources available for agencies and programs, the president can seek to promote better planning of what is done, more effective supervision of how it is done, and more systematic evaluation of how well various objectives are accomplished." In addition, Ippolito has pointed out that budget decisions can affect political support. He has written, "By emphasizing particular programs or criticizing others, by challenging Congress' spending preferences, by trumpeting the need for fiscal responsibility, or by reiterating commitments to greater economy and efficiency, a president can attempt to dramatize his leadership role and to generate public support for his economic policies and program preferences." [97]

Attempts to control the budget process often force presidents to play a public relations game. Most presidents want to be considered fiscal conservatives. The overwhelming majority of Americans want a balanced budget and want the president to curtail the growth of federal expenditures. Yet presidents must continue to fund existing programs for various groups and for the American public in general. In addition, presidents are expected to present new initiatives, some of which benefit groups to whom presidents have political obligations. The dilemma is one of holding down public expenditures while trying to solve public problems. It is not an easy task, and it makes presidential participation in the budget process much more demanding and important.

The President's Role in the Budget Process

In the role of chief administrator, presidents had little influence in managing executive branch funds before passage of the Budget and Accounting Act of 1921. Previously, agency budget requests went to the House of Representatives without much interference from the White House. There was very little budget coordination by presidents or their staffs. Congress believed it could handle the budget without much help from the presidency. By the end of World War II, however, both the executive and legislative branches had developed an awaremess that the federal government needed better management.

Budget and Accounting Act of 1921

The Budget and Accounting Act of 1921 gave presidents important managerial controls over the budgeting process and made them the dominant force in budgetary politics. Ironically, this act was passed by Congress in an attempt to bring order into its own chaotic budget process. An earlier House committee pointed to the haphazard nature of a budget process that lacked a coherent review of the executive branch's budget request. But in attempting to alleviate the problem, the act placed the presidency squarely in the budgetary process by requiring presidents to submit to Congress annual estimates of how much money it will take to run the federal government during the next fiscal year. (A fiscal year is the twelve-month span in which financial accounting is made. This period for the federal government runs from October 1 to September 30.)

The annual budget messages delivered by the president contain recommendations on how much money should be appropriated by Congress for each department of the federal government. The White House first evaluates all agency budget requests and decides which to accept or reject before submitting the annual budget message. Consequently, presidents become very much involved in the process. They receive more information about the budget than most members of Congress, allowing them to initiate budget discussions on their own terms.

In addition, the Budget and Accounting Act created the Bureau of the Budget (BOB) and placed it under the control of the Treasury Department. Its role was to "assemble, correlate, revise, reduce, or increase the estimates of the several departments or establishments." [98] In 1939, as a result of a growing need for coordination of New Deal programs and recommendations from the Committee on

Administrative Management (the Brownlow Commission), President Roosevelt moved BOB into the Executive Office of the President (EOP).

BOB began instituting a form of "budget clearance" so that the departments could not bypass its budget review process either for authorizations or for appropriations. No longer were the departments on their own in requesting funds from Congress. Bureaus and agencies made requests for funds to their departments, and the departments went through BOB for consideration by the president. From 1939 to 1969, BOB evolved into a highly influential component of the EOP.

Office of Management and Budget

In 1970 President Richard Nixon changed the name and function of BOB. Emphasizing the management functions of the budget agency, Nixon renamed it the Office of Management and Budgeting (OMB). As the word *management* implies, new emphasis was placed on providing departments with advice on ways to improve their efficiency and to reduce the costs of their operations.

Nixon specifically had four major roles for OMB. First, it was to continue many of BOB's functions, especially writing the federal budget. Second, it was to serve as a clearinghouse for programs and new legislation. Third, Nixon wanted some part of the Executive Office of the President to have the capability to track legislation as it moved through Congress. OMB was vested with this capacity. Fourth, OMB was given the specific authority to provide management advice to the various departments and agencies. Since its inception, OMB has served as the centerpiece of presidential budgeting.

Although the president's budget is not submitted to Congress until the January before the first day of the new fiscal year (October 1), the presidential budget process begins at least nineteen months before the submission of the finished budget proposal. *(See Table 2.)* The budget cycle begins in early spring with OMB informing the departments of the fiscal outlook and the spending priorities of the president. During the summer, the OMB director (also called the "budget director") issues specific revenue projections and imposes specific guidelines for departmental spending. On September 1 agencies submit their initial budget requests to OMB. OMB then holds formal hearings on these requests at which departmental officials justify their proposed budgets before OMB examiners.

OMB's director examines the entire budget from November 1 to December 1. Often the director will invite the National Security Council (NSC), the Council of Economic Advisers, and several White House aides to participate in the review. The OMB director makes final decisions subject to the economic forecast and communicates these decisions to the departments. The departments may appeal the decisions directly to the president. Usually, however, each department will revise its formal budget to coincide with the budget director's wishes, for presidents rarely reverse their budget director's decisions.

Congress receives the first official hint of what the president wants in the State of the Union address at the end of January, and specifics are then spelled out in the president's budget message in February. Pending approval by Congress, the budget goes into effect with the new fiscal year, October 1.

Not all agency requests are treated equally. Until the Nixon administration, the Defense Department's budget requests were exempt from control by the president's budgeting organization. During the administrations of John F. Kennedy and Lyndon Johnson, the Pentagon submitted its budget directly to the president without review by the Bureau of the Budget. If BOB believed budget items to be too high, it could appeal to the president. This practice, a reversal of the traditional procedure, placed the burden of proof on the budget office rather than on the department. President Nixon changed the procedure for the Pentagon by leaving final decisions with the NSC and OMB and giving the Defense Department the right of appeal. Subsequent presidents have continued to use OMB as a counterbalance to the Pentagon's budget requests.

Current Services Budget

Under the provisions of the 1974 Congressional Budget and Impoundment Act (PL 93-344), presidents must submit two budget proposals. When they submit their budget for the upcoming fiscal year, they must also submit, through the supervision of OMB, a *current services budget.* The current services budget provides Congress with an indication of the cost of existing budget obligations and a guide for evaluating additional budget proposals. Specifically, the current services budget includes the "proposed budget authority and estimated outlays that would be included in the budget for the ensuing fiscal year . . . if all programs were carried on at the same level as the fiscal year in progress . . . without policy changes."[99]

Although this procedure was intended to provide Congress with a basis for determining the overall size and direction of existing budget commitments and for assessing and evaluating the president's budget proposals, it has never quite lived up to its potential. Political scientist Howard E. Shuman has noted that the current services budget has little significance or meaning: "Only budget buffs and perennial budget watchers pay much attention to it. It is, however, a useful document in assessing whether any or how much fundamental change has been made in the old budget to produce the new one."[100]

Uncontrollable Spending

In any given year, much of OMB's current service estimates can be classified as *uncontrollable spending,* expenditures mandated by current law or some previous obligation. *(See Table 3.)* To change the spending on these mandated programs would require congressional action. By 1980, 75 percent of the federal budget could be classified as uncontrollable spending. These expenditures can be broken down into three major categories.

The first category, fixed costs, consists of legal commitments made by the federal government in previous years. These require the government to spend whatever is necessary to meet these expenses. The largest and most important component of this category is interest on the national debt. Another fixed-cost expenditure is public housing loans. Fixed costs are virtually "uncontrollable" because they can be eliminated only by such extreme measures as default.

The second category is large-scale government projects that require long-term financing. These multiyear contracts and obligations include the building of dams, weapons systems, aircraft, and the space shuttle. Many of these projects are reviewed annually, and expenditure levels are occasionally modified. Most, however, are not.

Table 2 Budget Timetable in the Executive Branch and Congress

Executive branch	Timing	Congress
Agencies subject to executive branch review submit initial budget request materials.	September 1	
Fiscal year begins.	October 1	Fiscal year begins.
President's initial appropriation order takes effect (amounts are withheld from obligation pending issuance of final order).	October 1	
	October 10	Congressional Budget Office (CBO) issues revised report to Office of Management and Budget (OMB) and Congress.
OMB reports on changes in initial estimates and determinations resulting from legislation enacted and regulations promulgated after its initial report to Congress.	October 15	
President issues final sequester order, which is effective immediately, and transmits message to Congress within 15 days of final order.	October 15	
Agencies not subject to executive branch review submit budget request materials.	October 15	
	November 15	Comptroller general issues compliance report.
Legislative branch and the judiciary submit budget request materials.	November-December	
President transmits the budget to Congress.	1st Monday after January 3	Congress receives the president's budget.
OMB sends allowance letters to agencies.	January-February	
	February 15	CBO reports to the budget committees on the president's budget.
	February 25	Committees submit views and estimates to budget committess.
OMB and the president conduct reviews to establish presidential policy to guide agencies in developing the next budget.	April-June	
	April 1	Senate Budget Committee reports concurrent resolution on the budget.
	April 15	Congress completes action on concurrent resolution.
	May 15	House may consider appropriations bills in the absence of a concurrent resolution on the budget.
	June 10	House Appropriations Committee reports last appropriations bill.
	June 15	Congress completes action on reconciliation legislation.
	June 30	House completes action on annual appropriations bills.
President transmits the mid-session review, updating the budget estimates.	July 15	Congress receives mid-session review of the budget.
OMB provides agencies with policy guidance for the upcoming budget.	July-August	
Date of "snapshot" of projected deficits for the upcoming fiscal year for initial OMB and CBO reports.	August 15	
	August 20	CBO issues its initial report to OMB and Congress.
OMB issues its initial report providing estimates and determinations to the president and Congress.	August 25	
President issues initial sequester order and sends message to Congress within 15 days.	August 25	

Source: Office of Management and Budget, Circular No. A-11 (1988).

The third category of expenditures officially designated as uncontrollable is the largest. These programs, called "entitlements," commit the federal government to pay benefits to all eligible individuals. Any attempt at controlling these expenditures would require changing the laws that set them up. Entitlements include Social Security, Medicare, Medicaid, Supplemental Security Income, food stamps, public assistance, and federal retirement. In some cases the federal government will pay individuals directly; in other cases, the states determine eligibility and administer the programs. Most of these programs have no limit on the amount of spending they may entail. As more people become eligible for benefits, expenditures increase.

From time to time presidents will try to increase or decrease these so-called uncontrollable expenditures. Nixon and Ford, for example, attempted to decrease entitlement expenditures by restricting eligibility and establishing a limit on benefit increases on several programs. In his first full budget year, Reagan proposed an entitlement cut of $11.7 billion. His budget proposal reflected the frustration that many presidents have felt in attempting to deal with uncontrollable expenditures. It said in part, "The explosion of entitlement expenditures has forced a careful reexamination of the entitlement or automatic spending programs. . . . when one looks behind the good intentions of these programs, one finds tremendous problems of fraud, waste, and mismanagement. Worse than this, the truly needy have not been well served." [101]

Controllable Spending

The president does have some control over several categories of expenditures. Sixty percent of expenditures that can be classified as controllable are used for salaries and fringe benefits for both civilian and military personnel. Although these expenses technically fit the category of controllable expenditures, the practical problems surrounding spending on salaries and fringe benefits make it difficult for a president to control them completely. Seniority and civil service rules protect so many federal employees that it is futile to attempt real cutbacks in expenditures going to salaries.

A second category of controllable federal expenditures is the general operating expenses of the various agencies. Spending for operating expenses constitutes 22 percent of the budget. Although economical measures can be undertaken on such things as heating, cooling, electricity, transportation, and supplies, expenses will always continue if operations continue. And operating expenses usually increase as inflation increases.

The third category of controllable expenditures, research and development of new programs, makes up 18 percent of the controllable portion of the federal budget. Medical research, weapons research, and grants to state and local governments encompass a large proportion of this category. Again, budget cuts can be made in this category, but only within limits. As a result, even the controllable categories of the federal budget give the president little latitude in budget decisions.

Table 3 Uncontrollable Spending, 1970-1980 (billions of dollars)

Category	1970	1975	1980
Open-ended programs and fixed costs			
Payments to individuals			
Social Security and railroad retirement	31.3	68.4	120.4
Federal employees' retirement and insurance	5.6	13.3	25.7
Unemployment	3.7	14.0	13.2
Veterans' benefits	6.6	12.4	13.7
Medicare and Medicaid	9.9	21.6	46.2
Housing assistance	.5	2.1	5.1
Public assistance and related programs	4.7	17.1	26.2
Interest	14.4	23.2	46.2
Revenue sharing	—	6.1	6.9
Farm price supports	3.8	.6	2.8
Other	3.8	8.0	9.8
Outlays from prior-year contracts and obligations[a]			
Defense	24.1	22.3	37.1
Civilian	17.4	28.4	50.8
Total	125.8	237.5	404.1

Source: Office of Management and Budget, *The Budget of the United States Government, Fiscal Year 1980* (Washington, D.C.: Government Printing Office, 1980), 560.

a. Excluding prior year contracts and obligations for activities shown as "open-ended programs and fixed costs."

Budgeting Theories

One of the most important functions served by the budget is to increase presidential administrative control and management of federal agencies and programs. However, the budget process has always been the subject of criticism aimed at improving the efficiency of government management. Over the years, critics, both within the presidency and outside it, have complained about the lack of coordination and centralization in the executive branch's efforts to control the federal administration. Consequently, since the early 1960s various presidents have introduced reforms aimed at making budgeting more efficient, rational, and comprehensive. Rarely, however, have they been as successful as hoped.

Planning-Programming-Budgeting

In 1961 Secretary of Defense Robert S. McNamara introduced a planning-programming-budgeting (PPB) system into the Pentagon. McNamara brought PPB from the private sector and used it to improve the quality of decision making and budget planning for national security policy. In 1965 President Johnson announced that PPB would be applied to domestic operations as well.

PPB was designed to allow budget decisions to be made by focusing on program goals and on quantitative comparisons of costs and benefits. Once budget officials established priorities among their objectives, they then determined the best expenditure mix in the annual budget to achieve the largest future benefits.

Specifically, PPB had several main characteristics. First, it attempted to improve the planning process before programs were developed and before budget decisions were made. Improving the planning process would allow analysis to be used throughout the budget process and future budget decisions to be based on previously formulated plans.

Second, one of the most important features of PPB was its strong centralization of the budget process. Agencies would base their budget estimates on their objectives and then send the budgets up the hierarchy. This method required strong, centralized control over the composition of executive budget proposals, as well as planning and evaluation of goals.

Third, once each agency identified its goals, it also would have to specify alternative methods for achieving those goals.

Fourth, PPB emphasized cost-benefit analysis. In assessing consequences of policy alternatives, quantitative estimates of costs and benefits were assigned to each alternative. The alternative that produced the greatest benefit at the least cost would be selected. PPB proved to be attractive to budget makers because it appeared logical for the federal government to plan rather than to wander along blindly and wastefully.

By 1971, however, PPB had come into disfavor with executive budget makers. Although many people had looked to PPB to reform budgeting in the executive branch by making it more rational and less "political," PPB failed to gain a permanent place in the budget process for a variety of reasons. It never achieved any great degree of popularity within the departments and agencies in part because it required a very formal structure. One fallacy was the assumption that what worked well in the Defense Department would work well in the entire national government. In reality, comparing alternative defense systems had little resemblance to policy decisions made in, for example, the State Department.

In addition, because the budgeting system largely was forced on BOB from the top down, many BOB staffers lacked commitment to making PPB work. Finally, PPB suffered major resistance from Congress. Advocates of PPB apparently forgot that Congress has an important and jealously guarded role in the budget process. Members of Congress who had spent years building up their contacts and knowledge of agency budgets resented a new budget system that disrupted their channels of influence and information in an effort to make budgeting more rational and less political.

Management by Objective

In the late 1950s, economist Peter Drucker developed a management technique for business called management by objective (MBO). In the early 1970s, OMB adopted the system. Similar to PPB, it was an attempt to make budget decisions more rational. Not quite as ambitious in its comprehensiveness as PPB, MBO simply stated that agencies should specify goals and alternative means of achieving those goals. At each level of the budgeting process objectives would be discussed, agreed upon, and then advanced up the hierarchy. It was a system much less centralized than PPB, with less emphasis on long-range planning, but it still was based on agencies making rational choices about their policy goals.

Despite its simplification, MBO also had a short life in the federal government. By the beginning of Jimmy Carter's administration, it had passed from use.

LeLoup pointed out that many of the problems with PPB remained with MBO. He wrote, "It was difficult to specify and agree on objectives, and to quantify benefits. MBO was not supported at middle and lower levels of agency management because it was still perceived as a system that increased control at the upper levels." [102]

Zero-Base Budgeting

The most recent attempt at presidential control over the national budgeting process is zero-base budgeting (ZBB). Developed in the private sector (like PPB and MBO) by Peter Pyhrr of Texas Instruments, Inc., ZBB was first applied to state governments.

Under Pyhrr's direction, Jimmy Carter first implemented it in Georgia while he was governor. In 1977, several months after he became president, Carter instructed OMB to implement ZBB. Carter promised that "by working together under a ZBB system, we can reduce costs and make the federal government more efficient and effective." [103] ZBB was primarily designed to avoid "incremental" budgeting where some arbitrary percentage is more or less blindly added to the preceding year's budget. Pyhrr has argued that its main goal is to "force us to identify and analyze what we [are] going to do in total, set goals and objectives, make the necessary operating decision, and evaluate changing responsibilities and work loads ... as an integral part of the [budget] process." [104]

ZBB entails three basic steps within each administrative entity. First, agencies must identify "decision units," or the lowest-level entities in a bureaucracy for which budgets are prepared. These may be staffs, branches, programs, functions, or even individual appropriations items. Second, budget makers must formulate "decision packages," a listing of objectives and levels of services and resources needed to provide those services. Decision packages usually suggest estimates of how much service would be provided for various amounts of funding (for example, 80, 90, 100, or 110 percent of current amounts). This type of analysis allows budget makers to evaluate how much an agency would lose if its budget were cut and how much it would gain if it were given an increase. Third, at various stages of the budget process, managers must rank decision packages in order of preference. These rankings may then be revised by higher-level agency officials who consider available funding. The higher-priority packages for which there is funding are then included in the agency's budget request, and the others are dropped.

Like PPB and MBO, the appeal of a comprehensive budgeting program such as ZBB is tremendous, but its success has been limited. Budget scholar Allen Schick has concluded that the effect of ZBB on the budgeting activities of the executive branch has been almost negligible. Most budget items have been funded under ZBB at or slightly above past current services levels.[105] In their evaluation of the success of ZBB, Frank Draper and Bernard Pitsvada suggest that the success of ZBB "has been mixed in the sense that while ZBB involved more people in the budget process, it has tended to overextend itself and evolve away from true zero-base reviews. ... ZBB as a process has not had a major impact on reducing spending, nor did ZBB really change the way agencies budget." [106]

Congressional Response to the President's Budget

Because the presidency traditionally has controlled the compilation and production of the budget, Congress frequently complained that it could get only superficial information from the president on technical budget matters on which it would eventually have to make important decisions. It argued that it did not possess adequate professional staff to evaluate independently the details, proposals, and estimates of the president's budget. Congress had become dependent on OMB and the presidency for all its budgetary information.

Congressional Budget Office

To improve its ability to evaluate the budget, Congress in 1974 created the Congressional Budget Office (CBO) through the Congressional Budget and Impoundment Control Act. CBO was a major innovation for Congress and a major challenge for the presidency. Designed to provide congressional budget committees with a variety of budget and policy information, CBO's professional staff incorporates several functions performed in the executive branch by OMB.

CBO activities fall into five categories. First, CBO prepares an annual report on budget alternatives, including fiscal policy options, levels of tax expenditures, and budget priorities. Second, it issues five-year budget projections for spending and taxation. Third, CBO projects the long-term costs of bills approved by House and Senate committees and sent to the full Congress for consideration. Fourth, CBO performs a "scorekeeping" function by comparing pending and enacted legislation with targets and ceilings specified by Congress. Fifth, CBO provides Congress with special reports on economic and budgetary issues.

CBO's independent data base allows Congress to evaluate presidential budget proposals more effectively. In measuring the success of CBO after its first five years of operation, political scientist Aaron Wildavsky wrote, "The Congressional Budget Office has improved the accuracy of budget numbers by providing a competitive source of expertise, and it has made competent analysis more widely available to those that want it." [107]

This competition in the budget process, however, has irritated more than one president. CBO's economic forecasts usually counter OMB's optimistic and more moderate projections, leading to numerous congressional-presidential confrontations over budget proposals. Shuman notes that in the past, CBO "angered President Carter because it disputed his energy program savings and angered President Reagan by saying that his economic assumptions about inflation, interest rates, and unemployment were unrealistic, overly optimistic, wrong." [108]

Congress and Presidential Lobbying

Since an almost adversarial relationship exists between Congress and the president over development of the budget, presidents must actively lobby Congress for their budget recommendations to become public policy. This difficult task is complicated by the dispersal of congressional budget authority between the House and Senate Appropriations committees and the various standing (ongoing) committees. After the president submits the budget plan, Congress gives different committees jurisdiction over different aspects of it. The House Ways and Means and Senate Finance committees consider revenue proposals. The various standing committees consider proposals for changes in laws that affect the uncontrollable expenses. The Joint Economic Committee studies the fiscal implications of the president's proposals. The House and Senate Budget committees prepare the budget resolution. The House and Senate Appropriations committees consider expenditure requests. Presidents must exert influence on these different committees if their proposals are to become grants of spending authority for their departments and agencies.

Probably the most important committees with which presidents have to deal are the Appropriations committees. These are also the most difficult for presidents to influence because they are among the most powerful and the most isolated from White House control. Appropriations committees have several independent sources of information from which to work when they consider presidential budget requests. They have the figures prepared by OMB, estimates from the substantive committees of possible expenditures from programs under their jurisdiction, program estimates and options prepared by CBO, and tentative spending guidelines prepared by the various budget committees.

In addition to having sources of information besides that prepared by OMB, the Appropriations committees also are free from the political control of the president. Their members enjoy tremendous electoral freedom, especially those in the House. In 1986 98 percent of House members were reelected. Although the percentages are not as large in the Senate, the number of incumbents reelected has been well above the 60 percent range in recent years. Pious has written, "Each committee member can maintain his position in his district through delivery of goods and services and patronage, from agencies eager to please him. The president cannot oust these members from his party, the committee, or the House by purging them if they cross him." [109]

Still, the initiative remains with the president. A determined president, who exerts the full force of the presidency, can overcome many congressional objections. The president represents one view. Congress often speaks with many confused and chaotic partisan voices. It is therefore difficult for Congress to defeat presidential budget initiatives. Consequently, the momentum in the budget proceedings belongs to the presidency, which usually speaks with unanimity. As Shuman has pointed out, because of this consensus the White House can control the debate: the president's "budget and . . . views are the subjects of the lead paragraphs in the early budget stories. Congressional criticism trails as an afterthought at the end of the article." [110] After introducing his first budget in Congress, for example, President Reagan went on the offensive by defending his budget before friendly audiences. Before a joint session of the Iowa legislature, he said, "The budget we have proposed is a line drawn in the dirt. Those who are concerned about the deficits will cross it and work with us on our proposals or their alternatives. Those who are not . . . will stay on the other side and simply continue their theatrics." [111]

Presidential Spending

Although Congress has power over the appropriations process, presidents always have a certain amount of *discretionary power* over spending, that is, they may spend certain funds as they please within broad areas of responsibility. Often Congress delegates discretionary power to the president. In a crisis, for example, especially during wartime, Congress has given the president "lump sum," or very broadly defined, appropriations so that the president and executive branch officials who represent presidential wishes may devote funds as they deem appropriate within the congressional limit. For example, Congress set up the Disaster Relief Fund to be administered by the EOP without restrictions. Although the discretionary power does not give presidents unlimited spending authority, it does give them some budget flexibility and some latitude in the actual spending of funds as well as a final opportunity to make policy. As political scientist Louis Fisher has observed, "What is done by legislators at the appropriations stage can be undone by administrators during budget execution." [112]

Sometimes presidents exercise discretionary spending power that Congress has not delegated specifically by interpreting spending authorizations and appropriations as permissive rather than mandatory. In 1959, for example, President Eisenhower simply did not establish a food stamp program that Congress had passed into law. Presidents also can delay setting up appropriated programs in their efforts to frustrate congressional initiatives. In 1975, after Congress had developed a summer employment program, the Ford administration successfully stymied the program by setting it up so slowly that the appropriated funds could not be spent during the fiscal year. Similarly, OMB can delay funding from the Treasury to an agency in an attempt to eliminate the agency or its programs. In 1975 the Ford administration undermined the Community Services Administration by delaying the agency's funds until after the agency's authority expired.[113]

Confidential Funding

Occasionally, Congress grants the president confidential funding for urgent, highly sensitive, or secretive matters. Presidents have complete discretion over such annually funded budget items. For example, during his 1974 visit to Egypt, President Nixon used a presidential contingency fund to give Anwar Sadat a $3 million helicopter as a gift.

Fisher has reported that several confidential accounts are a matter of public record but are not audited by Congress, including four in the White House, six diplomatic agencies, and one each for atomic energy, space, the Federal Bureau of Investigation (FBI), and the Central Intelligence Agency (CIA).[114] One of the most notorious confidential funds was President Nixon's Special Projects Fund that was used to finance a massive spying and sabotage campaign against Nixon's "political enemies."

Secret Funding

In addition to the various confidential funds, presidents may ask Congress for a general appropriation for secret projects. Secret funds do not require either the appropriation (the amount of money granted by Congress) or the expenditure (the amount of money spent by the executive branch) to be a matter of public record.

Secret funding was used for the Manhattan Project during World War II. The development of the atomic bomb required more than $2 billion, which Congress approved with very little scrutiny of the purpose of the appropriation.

Secret funding also is used for intelligence organizations, such as the CIA. The CIA's expenditures are drawn on requests from the agency's director and are not made public or audited by Congress. CIA activities are financed by secret transfers of funds from the appropriations accounts of other agencies, primarily the Defense Department. This process keeps the CIA budget hidden not only from the public, but also from many members of Congress.

In recent years Congress has attempted to restrict the use of confidential and secret funds and bring existing funds under greater congressional scrutiny. In 1974, after revelations of covert operations overseas, Congress prohibited the CIA from funding operations other than activities intended solely for obtaining necessary intelligence.[115] More recently, there has been a move to make the funding of the CIA and other intelligence agencies a matter of public record. Congress has the power either to control or to limit this type of discretionary power, but so far it has chosen to impose only moderate limitations. As Ippolito has pointed out, "[Congress] can insure, as it has done with respect to the CIA, that more of its members participate in the oversight activities. Congress can also provide for review and audit by the Government Accounting Office to insure that confidential or secret funds are expended in accordance with legislative intent." [116]

Transfers

Another method of bypassing the congressional appropriations process is the transfer and reprogramming of funds. In these cases, presidents attempt to use appropriated funds for purposes other than what Congress originally intended. Such transfers occur when Congress permits the executive to shift funds from one appropriation account to another, allowing officials to use appropriated funds for different purposes. As noted earlier, intelligence agencies frequently are funded with transfer funds. The Central Intelligence Agency Act of 1949 allows the CIA to transfer funds to and from other agencies to perform its functions.

In 1970, the Nixon administration used transfer authority to finance the Cambodian intervention with a $108.9 million transfer from military aid accounts for Greece, Turkey, Taiwan, the Philippines, and South Vietnam. In 1972 Congress prohibited transfers of military aid from one nation to another unless the president gave Congress notice. Yet, despite the Nixon administration's agreements to submit transfers to Congress for approval, the war in Cambodia in 1972 and 1973 was financed by more than $750 million in transfer authority already given the president.

Reprogramming

Presidents may also reprogram funds, that is, move funds within an appropriation account from one budget item to another. In some cases, presidents have used reprogramming to frustrate congressional intent by shifting funds for projects that had been approved to projects that had not been approved.

Presidents most frequently reprogram funds within the Defense budget. The Pentagon often reprograms funds in an attempt to develop new weapons systems after the House and Senate Appropriations committees have cut the Defense budget. In the 1960s, for example, as many as one hundred reprogramming actions moved several billion dollars in a single year. Between 1956 and 1972, average annual reprogramming in the Pentagon totaled $2.6 billion.

In the past, congressional committees allowed departments to reprogram first and inform them afterwards. But because some departments maneuvered around the intent of appropriations measures, Congress now requires at least semiannual notification and, in some cases, prior clearance with the committees.

Impoundment Powers

Until 1974, the most powerful presidential tool in overcoming the congressional funding prerogative was the power of impoundment—the president's refusal to spend funds that Congress has appropriated for a particular purpose. Historically, presidents have claimed both constitutional and statutory authority to impound funds either by treating the funding as permissive, that is, optional, rather than mandatory and rescinding spending authority or by deferring spending to future years. The impoundment power is similar to the veto power in that both are attempts to block or thwart congressional actions.

One of the most famous early examples of a president's use of the impoundment power was Thomas Jefferson's refusal in 1803 to spend a $50,000 appropriation for gunboats on the Mississippi River to protect the western frontier. Jefferson carefully informed Congress that the money should be used for the purchase of more advanced boats the following year. Similarly, President Ulysses S. Grant refused to spend funds that Congress had appropriated for public works projects, arguing that they could be completed for less money than had been appropriated. In both cases Congress eventually accepted the president's power to refuse to spend congressionally appropriated money.

Congress eventually gave impoundment authority a statutory basis by passing the Anti-Deficiency Acts of 1905 and 1906. These laws allowed presidents to withhold funds for a period of time to prevent deficiencies or overspending in an agency. In 1921 the Bureau of the Budget established impoundment authority when its director, Charles Dawes, announced that "the president does not assume ... that the minimum of government expenditures is the amount fixed by Congress in its appropriations." [117]

Under the New Deal, President Roosevelt occasionally used impoundments for budgetary or policy purposes. In some cases, the president acted with at least the implied consent of Congress. During the Great Depression, for example, spending bills were sometimes treated as ceilings, allowing Roosevelt to refuse to spend money that he believed to be unnecessary. During World War II, Roosevelt argued that his war powers gave him the power to cut spending that was not essential to national security. Presidents Truman, Eisenhower, and Kennedy all used impoundments to cut military spending.

President Johnson, however, used impoundments to curtail domestic spending during the Vietnam War. As the war progressed and inflation rose, Johnson impounded funds designated for agriculture, conservation, education, housing, and transportation. These impoundments were usually temporary, and the funds eventually were released. Although Johnson did not use the power of impoundment to cripple congressionally appropriated programs (many of them were his own programs), his actions did set an example of impoundment power being used to combat inflation—a power later adopted and expanded by Nixon.

Both Johnson and Nixon used impoundment to control spending, but Nixon's use was unprecedented in its scope and effects. Whereas Johnson relied on temporary deferrals rather than permanent cuts and worked personally with Congress to soothe tempers, the Nixon administration's impoundments seemed designed to eliminate or to curtail particular programs favored by the Democratic Congress. Between 1969 and 1974 the administration made a determined effort to redistribute the emphasis of governmental services. When Congress overrode Nixon's veto of the Federal Water Pollution Control Act Amendments of 1972, for example, the Nixon administration impounded half of the $18 billion that had been alloted for fiscal years 1973 through 1975, thereby handicapping the program. In addition, the Nixon administration undertook major impoundment reductions in low-rent housing construction, mass transit, food stamps, and medical research programs.

By 1973 Nixon had impounded more than $20 billion, and his budget for fiscal year 1974 contained a list of 109 reductions he wanted to make, 101 of which he said would require no congressional approval. Ippolito concluded, "While administration spokesmen advanced a variety of justifications in support of these impoundments—including precedent, statutory responsibilities, and general executive authority—it was apparent that impoundment was being used to enforce the president's policy preferences and budgetary priorities." [118] More than thirty lower court cases overturned Nixon impoundments. The Supreme Court eventually tackled Nixon's impoundment of funds for water pollution control. In *Train v. City of New York,* the Court ruled that once water pollution control funds had been appropriated by an act of Congress, funds could not be withheld at a later stage by impoundment.[119]

Eventually, public pressure began to build for Congress to do something about Nixon's use of the impoundment power. At first, individual members attempted to intervene personally with the president in an effort to restore funds to certain projects. By 1970 many subcommittees became concerned over the impoundment pattern that was beginning to emerge—a pattern that threatened their control of the policy-making process. In 1973 House and Senate Appropriations committees began holding hearings on the impoundment of funds for low-income housing, and Congress began inserting mandatory language in certain spending bills to eliminate the discretionary authority that had allowed presidential impoundment.

In 1974 Congress adopted the Congressional Budget and Impoundment Control Act. Besides setting up the Congressional Budget Office to improve congressional monitoring and deliberation of the budget, the act also aimed at controlling presidential impoundment. It stipulated two new procedures, *rescissions* and *deferrals,* by which presidents can temporarily override or delay congressional appropriations decisions. If presidents wish to defer (that is, delay) spending, they must tell Congress. If Congress does not agree, it can pass a resolution by a majority vote of both houses requiring immediate spending of the appropriated funds. If presidents wish to rescind (that is, cancel) all or part of the appropriated funds, they also must tell Congress. Unless Congress passes a rescission bill within forty-five days permitting the cancellation of funding, presidents must spend the funds.

Since Nixon resigned in 1974, a few months before the implementation of the impoundment control provisions of the budget act, he never felt the force of the act. The first administration to be confronted with these statutory impoundment limitations was the Ford administration. Of the $9 billion of rescissions requested by President Ford during his term in office, 86 percent of his requests were denied by Congress. Only 24 percent of his deferral requests were rejected, however. This pattern has been followed fairly consistently since the Ford administration. Congress usually grants deferrals; in most years, it allows 90 percent of them. Rescissions are a different matter, however. In recent years, congressional approvals have ranged from 80 percent in 1979 to none in 1980. Usually, Congress approves fewer than half of presidential rescissions.[120]

The President as Chief Law Enforcement Officer

"All is gloom in the eastern states," wrote John Marshall in January of 1787.[121] Farmers, many of them veterans of the American Revolution, sought and were denied legislative or judicial relief from their debt. Under the leadership of Daniel Shays, a former officer of George Washington's army, farmers revolted in Massachusetts. Would, as Marshall plainly worried, the American experiment survive?

It did survive. Shays's Rebellion was suppressed by Massachusetts militia, though not without considerable effort. The national government, such as it existed at the time, was powerless to assist.

Debtors, however, remained resentful, and property owners had become apprehensive. The political leadership of the United States sought a more durable remedy, and a more durable remedy was found.

In February 1787, the thirteen states of the United States were invited by Congress to send delegates to a May convention for the purpose of amending the Articles of Confederation. At the urging of leaders such James Madison and Alexander Hamilton, however, the articles were rejected summarily by the convention as a basis for continued political union among the thirteen states. The convention's new formula for government was proposed by Congress on September 17, 1787, and ratified by the requisite nine states the following year. On June 21, 1788, the U.S. Constitution became the supreme law of the land.

It would be excessive to say that Shays's Rebellion was the singular or even the most significant event leading to the adoption of the Constitution; serious defects in the Articles had been generally known well before the Massachusetts farmers revolted. The contribution of Shays to the Constitution, rather, was to force the political leadership of the various states to do what they already knew had to be done. It aroused "an emotional surge," in favor of a new constitution.[122]

Thus, "We the People of the United States," sought, among other things, to "form a more perfect Union, establish Justice, [and] insure domestic Tranquility."[123] The people would not repeat the mistake of the Confederation; Americans would not render the national government powerless to promote domestic tranquility and justice.

The president, said the Constitution, would "take Care that the Laws be faithfully executed" and would preside as chief executive over what would become a vast law enforcement apparatus. Should such assistance be needed, then the president could invoke the authority of "commander in chief" and deploy the armed forces, including units of state militia, to enforce the law. And, should mercy be a more effective means of promoting domestic tranquility than the sword, then the president would be given extensive clemency authority—the power to grant pardons and reprieves. The president would become chief law enforcement officer of the United States.[124]

Presidential law enforcement power has grown in rough proportion to enlargements in the responsibilities and power of the national government itself. In 1789, the year Washington was inaugurated as the nation's first president, the national government generally restricted itself to activities such as collecting customs taxes, suppressing domestic insurrections, enforcing court orders, and regulating Indian tribes, the mails, and the army and navy. The law enforcement responsibility and power of the national government was potentially great, but actually weak.

This has changed. Congress adds incrementally to the law enforcement responsibility and power of the national government each time it convenes. The process was hastened in the final two decades of the nineteenth century and during the presidential administrations of Theodore Roosevelt, William Howard Taft, and Woodrow Wilson. Increased federal regulatory power was a fundamental element of Franklin D. Roosevelt's New Deal. With the peace following the Second World War came novel and renewed demands for national regulation, demands that have been largely met.

As Congress added to the "police power" of the national government, the power, that is, to regulate the health, safety, morals, and general welfare of the nation, it also increased the enforcement power of the executive branch. It supplemented the authority already vested directly in the president by the Constitution, or prior congressional act, and it gave the president additional resources to exercise these grants more effectively and with more power.

Congress has not relinquished its own considerable power over law enforcement. To the contrary, it has insisted that power in law enforcement be shared between the president and Congress. The role of each actor must be understood, as must be the relationship of each one to the other. So must be the unique contribution of the judicial branch to the power of the president in law enforcement.

Law Enforcement by the U.S. Government

The U.S. Constitution delegates limited power to the government of the United States. This means, essentially, that the U.S. national government possesses only those powers that are specifically granted to it by the Constitution, or those which can be fairly implied from grants that are specifically made and which are not otherwise limited by other constitutional provision. The national government does not possess general law enforcement or police power.

The Constitution itself does not give any branch of the national government explicit authority to regulate the health, safety, morals, or general welfare of the community.[125] Nonetheless, that result has been obtained. Although the Constitution does not make a grant of general police power to the national government, it does grant or enumerate a variety of powers that have been shaped, constitutionally and politically, into what now resembles a general national police power.

Article I, section 8, of the Constitution enumerates a variety of powers that may be exercised by Congress. Congress, to consider only a few such powers, may impose and collect taxes, regulate immigration, print currency and punish counterfeiters, provide postal service, and regulate the armed forces and military bases of the United States. Meriting special mention, Congress also may regulate commerce "among the several States" (the "interstate commerce clause" of the Constitution).

These powers alone may seem neither surprising nor imposing. We would expect Congress to have authority to regulate the collection of taxes, the printing and circulation of a national currency, the operation of a postal service, and trade crossing state lines. These activities, after all, seem national in scope; arguably they are necessary incidents of national power. But alone, these powers do not seem to explain the significant law enforcement power of the national government or, derivatively, of the president.

For an explanation, we must turn to the final clause of Article I, section 8, the "necessary and proper clause" of the Constitution: "The Congress shall have Power . . . To make all Laws which shall be necessary and proper for carrying into Execution the foregoing Powers, and all other Powers vested by this Constitution in the Government of the United States, or in any Department or Officer thereof." If the necessary and proper clause of the Constitution is read to enlarge the enumerated powers of Congress, then we have at least a textual basis in the Constitution for Congress exercising expansive police or regulatory powers.

That is precisely how the necessary and proper clause is read by the U.S. Supreme Court. In the 1819 decision of *McCulloch v. Maryland*,[126] the Court was asked to determine whether the Constitution gave Congress authority to charter a national bank when chartering a national bank was (and is) not among those powers specifically granted Congress. If the national government, the state of Maryland argued, was to be a government of limited, enumerated powers, then the Court must find that Congress had exceeded its authority.

Writing on behalf of a unanimous Court, Chief Justice John Marshall agreed completely with Maryland's contention that Congress is granted only limited regulatory power by the Constitution. He also conceded that chartering a national bank is not listed in Article I, section 8. Marshall was too clever a legal logician, however, and too ardent a supporter of national power to allow congressional regulatory authority to be curbed by such a restricted interpretation of the Constitution.

The constitutional authority of Congress, Marshall wrote, consists of those powers that are expressly granted by the Constitution, plus—here is where he ties the necessary and proper clause to the enumerated powers of Congress—those powers that are necessary and proper to the exercise of its expressly granted powers. If the end (for example, collecting taxes or supporting an army) is legitimate (that is, authorized by an enumerated power), then the means chosen by Congress to promote that end (chartering a national bank) will be upheld judicially, as long as those means are not prohibited by some other constitutional provision.

The attention of the Court was then shifted to giving meaning to the enumerated powers. Granted, Congress is authorized to enact any law which helps it, for example, promote the regulation of interstate commerce, but what exactly does "commerce among the several States" mean? Is the Constitution referring to actual transportation of goods between two or more states? Does the commerce clause imply more?

Again, the antecedents of modern constitutional doctrine were established during the tenure of Marshall.[127] But more than a century of judicial review was required before the modern rule became established: Congress has constitutional authority to regulate anything that *affects* interstate commerce, no matter how slight the effect.[128] Little imagination is required to find an affecting relationship between a specified activity and interstate commerce.[129]

The Supreme Court's expansive interpretation of the Constitution did not mandate a particular national role in law enforcement. It did not in any sense require Congress to exercise its police power to the fullest lawful extent. The Court, rather, conferred constitutional legitimacy on an expansive national police power—if and to the extent Congress chose to exercise that power.

Periodically responding to the perceived need and popular demand for national regulation, Congress has added incrementally to the police power of the federal government. The Interstate Commerce Commission (ICC) Act of 1887 provided for federal regulation of the railroads. This was followed by the Sherman Antitrust Act of 1890, Pure Food and Drug Act of 1906, Federal Reserve Act of 1913, and Federal Trade Commission Act of 1914. The notion of an extensive federal police power, and much of the reality, was firmly in place by the time Franklin Roosevelt was inaugurated president in 1933.

The Great Depression was the singular fact faced by Roosevelt and Congress. Congress deferred to the president, and the president responded with the New Deal, a collection of programs adding directly to the regulatory authority of the federal government. The banking industry became more thoroughly regulated with enactment of the Banking Act of 1933. Enactment of the Securities Acts of 1933 and 1934 placed the sale of stocks under direct federal supervision, as did the National Labor Relations Act of 1935 for labor-management relations, and the Civil Aeronautics Act of 1938 for civilian aviation. Wages and hours of employment became the subject of extensive federal regulation with passage of the Fair Labor Standards Act of 1938.

Roosevelt and Congress had inherited the rudiments of a federal police power in 1933. By the time the New Deal had ended, effectively with the 1941 entry of the United States into the Second World War, the regulatory jurisdiction and power of the federal government had been made even more inclusive, intensive, and extensive. Regulating the health, safety, morals, and general welfare of the nation had become a major preoccupation of the federal government.

This role has been expanded in the years following the conclusion of World War II. The Federal Housing Act of 1949, and multiple amendments, made Washington the principal source of money to finance inner-city public housing construction and urban renewal. Money received from the federal government, whether in the form of loans, grants, or payments for goods and services, is accompanied by a plethora of regulations and contractual obligations. Various pieces of legislation—the most important being the employment, housing, and public accommodations provisions of the Civil Rights Act of 1964—banned discrimination based on race, color, religion, sex, and national origin. Examples of other federal measures enacted during this period are the Federal Aviation Act of 1958, Consumer Credit Policy Act of 1968, National Environmental Protection Act of 1969, Occupational Health and Safety Act of 1970, Consumer Product Safety Act of 1972, and Endangered Species Act of 1973.

This summary points out that the police power of the national government has expanded greatly in the past one hundred years. Still, the summary indicates only some of the ways power has grown. It does not mention, for instance, the many and frequent amendments to the Internal Revenue Code (annual amendments that are sometimes mockingly called "Lawyers and Accounts Relief Acts") or to the criminal code. Nor does it touch on more "traditional" exercises of federal police power: immigration, national security, regulation of Indian tribes, imposition of ethical standards on government employees, import restrictions and taxes, and operation of the postal system.

A policy of selective business "deregulation" initiated by President Jimmy Carter, and supported and furthered by his successor, Ronald Reagan, deserves special mention. Supporters of deregulation argued that it would reduce consumer costs by fostering competition and by reducing the costs of regulation (that is, the costs of record keeping, administrative monitoring, and legal advice) previously borne by the regulated businesses and passed on to consumers.

Deregulation efforts to date have been directed at a limited number of industries—primarily transportation, communications, and commercial credit—and at only selected business practices. Deregulation has reduced but not eliminated the national police power over economic activity. American businesses remain thoroughly regulated by the national government.

After enacting laws, members of Congress do not, of course, pin badges on their chests and act as enforcement officers. Rather, Congress makes the laws of the United States and then delegates enforcement jurisdiction and power to agencies and personnel of the executive branch. These agencies are also the creation of Congress.

Development of the federal civilian bureaucracy, and its power, has almost paralleled these diverse bursts of congressional energy. Civilian personnel employed by the federal government in nondefense capacities numbered 4,279 in 1816. Almost 80 percent of these were postal workers. By 1901, the number of such employees had increased to 186,532. Civilian personnel of the national government employed by nondefense agencies in 1986 totaled 1.9 million.[130]

Not all of these increases can be attributed to the growth of the police power of the national government. Space exploration, agricultural advice, and maintenance of national parks, for example, have little to do with law enforcement. When these demands are combined with the demands created by increasing direct regulation, then it can be seen that much, if not all, of the expansion of the federal civilian work force is associated with the increased law enforcement role of the national government.

As chief executive and chief law enforcement officer of the United States, the president has been the most direct and most frequent beneficiary.

Presidential Law Enforcement Authority and Power

John F. Kennedy exercised the legal power of the president when, in September 1962, he deployed U.S. marshals (and an assortment of other federal civilian law enforcement officers), and then regular army troops to Oxford, Mississippi. Kennedy was acting as chief law enforcement officer of the United States; he was, as Article II, section 3, of the U.S. Constitution requires, "tak[ing] Care that the Laws be faithfully executed."

Enforcing the law, in this case, meant backing a federal court order. In 1961, James Meredith applied for admission to the University of Mississippi ("Ole Miss"). Meredith was a Mississippi citizen, a veteran of the Air Force, and he was black. Ole Miss did not admit blacks at the time.

Denied admission by the university, Meredith appealed to the federal courts for assistance. His complaint was initially dismissed by a federal district court, but this decision was reversed by the U.S. Court of Appeals for the Fifth Circuit. A panel of Fifth Circuit judges found that Meredith had been denied admission to the university solely because of his race, and they ordered his enrollment.

Prolonged negotiations between Ross Barnett, the governor of Mississippi, Kennedy, and Kennedy's lieutenants, principally Attorney General Robert F. Kennedy, failed to produce an agreement for the orderly admission of Meredith. Mississippi, it became clear, would not use its own force to protect Meredith and maintain order on the campus. Protection and the maintenance of law and order, if it was to be supplied at all, would have to come from Washington.

Federal protection was provided initially by a contingent of U.S. marshals. A mob formed, however, and the original federal force had to be reinforced. Additional marshals were sent to Oxford, as were almost any federal law enforcement officer who could be spared—game wardens, border patrol, and prison guards. Even this augmented force was threatened by the persistent and violent mob attacks.

On September 30, 1962, President Kennedy ordered the mob to disperse. He backed his order (and the original court order) with the deployment of regular army troops to the Ole Miss campus. Meredith was registered. *(See box, John F. Kennedy, the Law, and the "Ole Miss" Campaign, pp. 428-429.)*[131]

Kennedy enforced the laws of the United States when he ordered U.S. marshals and troops onto the Ole Miss campus. In doing so, however, he—the president of the United States—also was acting according to law. He was, that is, acting according to and within the limitations set by the U.S. Constitution and Congress.

Presidential law enforcement power may be defined by either or both sources. Article II, section 1, of the Constitution vests in the president the "executive Power" of the United States. Section 2 of the second article designates the president commander in chief of the armed forces, including, when ordered into national service, the National Guard of the various states. It also gives the president almost unlimited authority to appoint the principal officers of the executive and judicial branches.

Finally, Article II, section 3, of the Constitution lays responsibility on the president to "take Care that the Laws be faithfully executed."

The second path is less direct; this path goes from the Constitution, to Congress, and from Congress to the president. Article I, section 8, of the Constitution gives Congress authority to make all laws "necessary and proper" to execute its own enumerated authority as well as any other authority conferred by the Constitution in the government or any branch of the United States. According to this authority, Congress has delegated extensive authority to the president and officers of the executive branch who are subordinate to the president.

The Constitution, for example, grants Congress authority "necessary and proper" to "provide for the Punishment of counterfeiting" the currency of the United States. Congress has used this authority by making counterfeiting a crime, by creating the Secret Service of the Treasury Department, and by giving the Secret Service authority to arrest suspected violators.

Although the Constitution and Congress vest considerable law enforcement authority in the president, both also limit that authority. The Constitution provides generally for shared decision making in many aspects of law enforcement. Presidential appointment of officers of the federal government having major law enforcement responsibilities are often subjected to Senate approval. The president must obtain Senate approval for his or her appointment to the office of attorney general, for instance, as well as the deputy and various assistant attorney generals, director of the FBI, and the U.S. attorney for each judicial district.

Presidential power is also limited by direct restrictions placed on the office by the Constitution or Congress. The president is prohibited by the Constitution from spending money for law enforcement unless an appropriation for that expenditure is first made by Congress.[132] Congress has limited the authority of the president to use military force for law enforcement.

A final characteristic of presidential power must be considered. This is the distinction between *discretionary* and *ministerial* authority.

Discretionary authority involves the exercise of judgment and choice. Ministerial authority does not. It involves, rather, the faithful implementation of decisions made by others.

The Constitution, for example, has given the president authority to nominate and, with Senate consent, to appoint justices to fill vacancies on the U.S. Supreme Court. Whom the president appoints, if anyone, is a matter left constitutionally to the discretion of the president; neither Congress nor the courts may compel the president to nominate a particular person.

Paying the salary of the person eventually appointed, however, is a purely ministerial act (with the constitutional proviso that the salary of a sitting federal judge may not be reduced). Congress sets the salary and authorizes payment; the job of the president (actually a subordinate of the president in the Department of Treasury) is to write the check. Writing the check is a ministerial act.

Where discretionary authority is at issue, the president acts as a policy maker, exercising his or her best judgment about law enforcement. Since this authority is bestowed on the president by the Constitution or Congress, a court cannot compel the president to make a particular decision. The issue is considered political, not legal.[133] A court, for instance, cannot compel the president to grant a pardon to a criminal offender; the decision is entrusted to the discretion of the president.

Much of the law enforcement authority of the president is discretionary. Discretion is assigned the president to set law enforcement priorities and to appoint senior law enforcement officials of the executive branch to implement those priorities. These officials, in turn, have been delegated considerable discretion by Congress and the president to set additional law enforcement policies—what types of offenses merit the greatest attention, what resources shall be allocated, and what cases will be prosecuted.

Merely because a power is discretionary does not mean that external political pressure cannot be brought to bear on the president. A sufficiently aroused public can force the president to be more or less aggressive in enforcing a particular law, as can a sufficiently aroused Congress. Congressional and public dissatisfaction with enforcement of the nation's environmental laws in the early years of the Reagan administration, for example, led eventually to the almost wholesale replacement of the top management of the Environmental Protection Agency. The agency became more aggressive in its enforcement efforts as a result. A disappointed public may turn to a candidate from the opposing party. Congress is equipped to retaliate in a variety of ways, escalating from mere public denouncements, to pubic investigation, to removal by impeachment. The uncompleted impeachment proceedings against President Richard Nixon (who resigned "voluntarily") remain a dramatic reminder of the ultimate measure of retaliation.

A reading of the Constitution reveals four general categories of presidential authority in law enforcement. Three of these make intuitive sense without prior understanding of the Constitution or law. These are the executive, military, and clemency powers of the president.

The fourth category of presidential law enforcement authority stems from the "take care clause" of the Constitution. Intuition is not of great use in comprehending at least the dimensions of the resulting presidential power.

Take Care Power of the President

The U.S. Constitution provides in Article I, section 3, that the president "shall take Care that the Laws be faithfully executed." Two principal interpretations of that clause often may be asserted.

One interpretation holds that the take care clause imposes an obligation on the president. The text itself is imperative in mood; it is a command to the president to obey and enforce the law. No separate and independent grant of authority to the president is stated; none can be implied.

Supreme Court Justice Oliver Wendell Holmes, Jr., urged this interpretation in *Myers v. United States:* "The duty of the President to see that the laws be executed is a duty that does not go beyond the law or require him to achieve more than Congress sees fit to leave within his power." [134] Holmes, it should be noted, was writing in dissent.

No one disputes that the president is obliged to obey the law and to enforce the law with the authority that he or she is granted. Such a view is certainly supported by rulings of the U.S. Supreme Court.[135]

The Court, however, has gone further. It has fashioned a power-granting interpretation of the take care clause, one that does not conform to Holmes's more restrictive interpretation.

The primary ruling resulted from an appeal to the Supreme Court in the case of *In re Neagle.*[136] A deputy U.S. marshal was assigned by the attorney general to guard an associate justice of the Supreme Court, Stephen J. Field. The marshal shot and killed an assailant and was prosecuted for murder by the state of California.

The marshal argued that inasmuch as he was performing official law enforcement duties as an officer of the United States at the time the assailant was shot, he was cloaked with immunity from state prosecution.

California did not dispute that U.S. marshals are generally not answerable in state courts for their official actions. It contended, however, that the marshal could not

John F. Kennedy, the Law ...

U.S. Constitution

The confrontation between President John F. Kennedy and Gov. Ross Barnett is remembered today as an instance in which federal power overwhelmed state resistance to a judicial order. Kennedy faithfully executed the laws of the United States; James Meredith enrolled as a freshman at the University of Mississippi.

But the judicial branch did not just order Meredith's admission to "Ole Miss," and the president did not just enforce that order. The courts and the president acted according to the laws of the United States. Certain of these laws are reproduced here to illustrate how law is connected with the exercise of presidential power.

A number of constitutional provisions were involved in the Ole Miss controversy. These pertained to individual rights, the powers of the president, the powers of Congress, and the power of the national government in general.

Individual Rights. The Fourteenth Amendment, section 1, of the Constitution provides that no state may "deny to any person within its jurisdiction the equal protection of the laws." In 1954 the U.S. Supreme Court interpreted this passage to mean that segregated public educational facilities were constitutionally impermissible.[1] The U.S. Court of Appeals for the Fifth Circuit applied this rule when it ordered the University of Mississippi to admit James Meredith.[2]

Presidential Power. Article II, section 1, of the Constitution vests the "executive Power" of the United States in the president. Section 2 of this article designates the president "Commander in Chief" of the armed forces of the United States and, when called into federal service, of the several state militias. Finally, section 3 of Article II says that the president "shall take Care that the Laws be faithfully executed."

Congressional Power. Congress, under Article I, section 8, of the Constitution, is given power to "make all Laws which shall be necessary and proper for carrying into Execution" its own enumerated constitutional powers "and all other Powers vested by this Constitution in the Government of the United States, or in any Department or Officer thereof." Among the enumerated powers of Congress are the power "To raise and support Armies," "To make Rules for the Government and Regulation of the land and naval Forces," "To provide for calling forth the Militia to execute the Laws of the Union, suppress Insurrection. . . ," and "To provide for organizing, arming, and disciplining the Militia, and for governing such Part of them as may be employed in the Service of the United States. . . ."

National Power. The "Supremacy Clause" of the Constitution provides that the "Constitution, and the laws of the United States which shall be made in Pursuance thereof; . . . shall be the supreme Law of the Land." State and local officials are bound by interpretations of the Constitution made by federal courts.[3]

Congressionally Enacted Legislation

According to its constitutional authority to make all laws "necessary and proper" to carry out the powers of Congress and of the president that are enumerated above, Congress enacted the following laws.

Section 332. Use of militia and armed forces to enforce Federal authority. "Whenever the President considers that unlawful obstructions, combinations, or assemblages, or rebellion against the authority of the United States, make it impracticable to enforce the laws of the United States in any State or Territory by the ordinary course of judicial procedings, he may call into Federal service such of the militia of any State, and use such of the armed forces, as he considers necessary to enforce those laws or to suppress the rebellion."[4]

Section 333. Interference with State and Federal Law. "The President, by using the militia the armed forces, or both, or by any other means, shall take such measures as he considers necessary to suppress, in a State, any insurrection, domestic violence, unlawful combination, or conspiracy, if it—(1) so hinders the execution of the laws of that State, and of the United States within the State, that any part or class of its people is deprived of a right, privilege, immunity, or protection named in the Constitution and secured by law, and the constituted authorities of that State are unable, fail, or refuse to protect that right, privilege, or immunity or to give that protection; or (2) opposes or obstructs the execution of the laws of the United States or impedes the course of justice under those laws. In any situation covered by clause (1), the State shall be considered to have denied the equal protection of the laws secured by the Constitution."[5]

Section 334. Proclamation to disperse. Whenever the President considers it necessary to use the militia, or the armed forces under this chapter, he shall, by proclamation, immediately order

have been acting officially when he was guarding Field since Congress had not expressly given marshals that authority. Without congressional authorization, the marshal was acting merely in the capacity of a private citizen. He was, therefore, subject to the jurisdiction of the California courts.

The Court rejected California's argument and rendered an expansive interpretation of the take care clause in

. . . and the "Ole Miss" Campaign

the insurgents to disperse and retire peaceably to their abodes within a limited time.[6]

Presidential Proclamation and Executive Order

Acting on his constitutional and congressionally delegated authority, President Kennedy ordered federal enforcement of the court desegregation order. First, a force of U.S. marshals and other federal law enforcement personnel were dispatched to the Ole Miss campus. Next, when a mob threatened to overwhelm this force, and when it became apparent that state law enforcement personnel would not assist the beleaguered federal force, the president commanded the secretary of defense to deploy regular army troops to the campus. The following excerpts are from Kennedy's September 30, 1962, proclamation ordering the mob to disperse and from his executive order of the same day, mobilizing the army to enforce the law:

Proclamation 3497
Obstructions of Justice
in the State of Mississippi
By the President of the United States of America
A Proclamation

WHEREAS, the Governor of the State of Mississippi and certain law enforcement officers and other officials of that State, and other persons, individually and in unlawful assemblies, combinations and conspiracies, have been and are willfully opposing and obstructing the enforcement of orders entered by the United States District Court for the Southern District of Mississippi and the United States Court of Appeals for the Fifth Circuit; and

WHEREAS, such unlawful assemblies, combinations and conspiracies oppose and obstruct the execution of the laws of the United States, impede the course of justice under those laws and make it impracticable to enforce those laws in the State of Mississippi by the ordinary course of judicial proceedings; and

WHEREAS, I have expressly called attention of the Governor of Mississippi to the perilous situation that exists and to his duties in the premises, and have requested but have not received from him adequate assurances that the orders of the courts of the United States will be obeyed and that law and order will be maintained:

NOW, THEREFORE, I, JOHN F. KENNEDY, President of the United States, under and by virtue of the authority vested in me by Constitution and laws of the United States, . . . do command all persons engaged in such obstructions of justice to cease and desist therefrom and to disperse and retire peacefully forthwith.[7]

Executive Order 11053
Providing Assistance for the Removal of
Unlawful Obstructions of Justice
in the State of Mississippi

WHEREAS on September 30, 1962, I issued Proclamation No. 3497 reading in part as follows:

[The portions of the proclamation quoted above are reprinted.] and

WHEREAS the commands contained in that proclamation have not been obeyed and obstruction of enforcement of those court orders still exists and threatens to continue:

NOW, THEREFORE, by virture of the authority vested in me by the Constitution and laws of the United States, . . . , it is hereby ordered as follows:

Section 1. The Secretary of Defense is authorized and directed to take all appropriate steps to enforce all orders of the United States District Court for the Southern District of Mississippi and the United States Court of Appeals for the Fifth Circuit and to remove all obstructions of justice in the State of Mississippi.

Section 2. In furtherance of the enforcement of the aforementioned orders of the [specified courts], the Secretary of Defense is authorized to use such of the armed forces of the United States as he may deem necessary.

Section 3. I hereby authorize the Secretary of Defense to call into the active military service of the United States, as he may deem appropriate to carry out the purposes of this order, any or all units of the [national guard] of the State of Mississippi to serve in the active military service of the United States for an indefinite period and until relieved by appropriate orders. In carrying out the provisions of Section 1, the Secretary of Defense is authorized to use the units, and members thereof, ordered into the active military service of the United States pursuant to this section.[8]

1. *Brown v. Board of Education,* 347 U.S. 483 (1954).
2. *Meredith v. Fair,* 306 F2d 374 (5th Cir. 1962)
3. *Cooper v. Aaron,* 358 U.S. 1 (1958).
4. 10 United States Code section 332.
5. 10 United States Code section 333.
6. 10 United States Code section 334.
7. Proclamation 3497, 3 Code of Federal Regulations, 225-226 (1959-1963 compilation).
8. Executive Order 11053, 3 Code of Federal Regulations, pages 645-646 (1959-1963 compilation).

the process. The president's power to enforce the law, wrote Justice Samuel Miller, is not limited to enforcing specific acts of Congress. It also involves enforcing the Constitution and the general peace of the land. California was ordered to release its prisoner.

Another notable Supreme Court interpretation of presidential enforcement authority arose in response to President Grover Cleveland's suppression of the Pullman

Railroad Strike of 1894. Arguing that the strike was interfering with interstate commerce and delivery of the mails, two activities consigned by the Constitution to the national government, the president sought and obtained a federal court injunction ordering the strikers to desist. Federal troops were dispatched to Chicago to enforce the injunction; those resisting were prosecuted for contempt of court.

Both the injunction and the use of military force to enforce the court order were challenged by the defendants. Congress, they argued, had not given the federal court the authority to issue the injunction, nor had it authorized the use of military force by the president to enforce the injunction. Both challenges were rebuffed by the Court.[137]

Neither Supreme Court decision should be read as giving the president power to override or ignore Congress. The take care clause, rather, was invoked in both instances when Congress had been silent.

Executive Powers of the President

Presidents are elected by the people, presumably to make and supervise the implementation of policy. Presidents are not expected to involve themselves in the details of implementation. With few exceptions, they do not.

The same might be said of the attorney general, secretary of the Treasury, or even the director of the Federal Bureau of Investigation or commissioner of the Internal Revenue Service (IRS). Considerable discretion to act is and must be delegated to the men and women who actually enforce the law: special agents of the FBI who witness a violation of federal law, IRS auditors who discover irregularities in tax filings, assistant U.S. attorneys who uncover evidence of criminal activity in the files of investigative reports.

The law enforcement power of the president, therefore, depends substantially upon the president's ability to affect the behavior of subordinates within the executive branch. And the ability of the president to affect the behavior of these subordinates depends, partially at least, on the president's legal authority.

The Constitution says little about presidential authority over officers of the executive branch. The first sentence of Article II, section 1, states that the "executive Power shall be vested in a President of the United States of America." This would seem to give the president great power; however, the Constitution does not give a definition of "executive Power." It may be read as merely descriptive; the powers otherwise mentioned in Article II are vested in the president. It may also be read as conferring authority on the office of president that is otherwise not defined in the Constitution. The latter reading of this abuse is applied by the judicial branch.

Appointment and Removal of Law Enforcement Officers. The executive power of the president embraces authority to appoint senior law enforcement officers of the executive branch and judges of the federal judiciary. *(See also "The Appointment Power," p. 408, in this chapter.)* That authority is conferred by the "appointments clause" of Article II, section 2, of the Constitution. *(See text from Article II, section 2, in box, p. 431, and "Instruments of Presidential Control," p. 398, in this chapter.)* Additional provision is made for temporary appointments during Senate recesses.

The appointment power of the president applies generally to the senior officers of the executive branch charged with law enforcement responsibility. All cabinet members serve by virtue of presidential appointment, as do agency heads and members of the so-called subcabinet: policy-making officers immediately subordinate to the cabinet officer and at the level of under secretary, deputy secretary, and assistant secretary. This means that the president appoints not only the attorney general and the principal officers of the Department of Justice, for example, but also the principal political officers of all federal departments and agencies involved in law enforcement.

These appointees generally serve at the pleasure of the president, which means simply that they may be fired by

Drawn by G.W. Peters from sketch by G.A. Coffin; Library of Congress

President Grover Cleveland's suppression of the Pullman Railroad Strike of 1894 is an example of presidential enforcement authority. Left, a meat train leaves the Chicago stockyards under escort of U.S. Cavalry.

the president—for good reason, bad reason, or no reason at all. Such a move may be costly politically, but it does lie within the legal discretion (that is, authority) of the president, and this discretion may not be curbed by Congress.[138]

Less senior but still high-ranking law enforcement officers may also be subject to presidential appointment. The director of the FBI, commissioner of the IRS, and administrator of the Drug Enforcement Administration (DEA) are examples. Other examples include the U.S. attorney for each judicial district of the United States, the chief U.S. marshal, and the commissioner of the U.S. Customs Service.

Presidential authority to fire these officers varies. Since 1973, the director of the FBI has been appointed to a ten-year term and may not be fired without cause. U.S. attorneys, however, may be removed at the will of the president.

Two other classes of presidential appointees deserve special note: board members and other high-ranking officers of independent regulatory boards and commissions, and federal judges.

Independent regulatory boards and commissions are largely the product of the "good government" movement of the later nineteenth and early twentieth centuries. These boards and commissions are the outgrowth of the notion, naively conceived perhaps, that certain aspects of policy implementation could and should be separated from ordinary partisan politics. If the organization implementing policy is legally separated from politics, then the policy makers in that organization will act faithfully to implement policy created by Congress and will not act to promote the partisan advantage of the incumbent president.

The Interstate Commerce Commission (ICC) was established in 1887 to regulate the nation's growing railroad industry and later was assigned jurisdiction over trucking as well. After establishment of the ICC, other independent boards and commissions were created to regulate the following: business trade practices (Federal Trade Commission, or FTC), labor-management relations (National Labor Relations Board, or NLRB), television and radio broadcasting (Federal Communications Commission, or FCC), sale of stocks and bonds (Securities and Exchange Commission, or SEC), banking (Federal Reserve Board, or FRB), and the nuclear power industry (Nuclear Regulatory Commission, or NRC).

The exact authority of these agencies varies. They generally possess power to make law through what is called "rule making" and to adjudicate disputes about the application of the law through quasi-judicial methods. They also have authority to investigate unlawful conduct and, in some cases, actually to prosecute civil violations. (Criminal violations are prosecuted by the Justice Department.) Their authority may extend to rate setting and licensing of businesses and individuals.

Congress has given the president authority to appoint the principal officers of these agencies. Presidential authority to fire them, however, has been limited to reasons specified by law. These limitations have been challenged but upheld by the U.S. Supreme Court.[139] *(See "The Removal Power," p. 414, in this chapter.)*

Federal judges, including justices of the Supreme Court, are appointed by the president. That ends the president's formal authority over the judicial branch. By explicit constitutional provision, federal judges have life tenure and may not be removed from office except by the impeachment process.[140]

> The President shall be Commander in Chief of the Army and the Navy of the United States, and of the Militia of the several States, when called into the actual Service of the United States. . . .
>
> —from Article II, section 2

Presidential Authority to Command. So far we have considered two variables, appointment and removal authority, affecting presidential power over the behavior of officers of the national government involved in law enforcement. Some relationship is supposed between presidential power over these officers and presidential authority to appoint and, more important, to remove them. A third variable requires consideration: presidential authority to control their official behavior, that is, to command that they perform (or not perform) specified acts.

This authority over federal judges can be described quickly: there is none. Similarly, presidents lack command authority in most instances over officers of independent regulatory boards and commissions. *(See "Regulatory Commissions," p. 396, in this chapter.)*

Command authority over officers of the executive branch who do not enjoy independent status is greater, although still not absolute. If the presidential command is lawful, then failure of a subordinate to obey could constitute neglect or insubordination. The president could remove such an officer and justify the decision to do so.

Presidents themselves, however, are obliged to obey the law, and they have no authority to command their subordinates to commit a violation. What happens, for example, if the president orders the attorney general to have a person's home searched illegally and the attorney general refuses. The attorney general could be fired by the president and have no recourse in court—cabinet members serve at the discretion of the president, and may be fired for good reason, bad reason, or no reason at all.

A third situation is presented when a disagreement exists about what the law requires or prohibits. Laws are often stated ambiguously; two or more competing interpretations of a law or of a set of apparently related laws may be held by reasonable people. May the president fire a subordinate for insubordination when such disagreements are reached?

For cabinet members and other appointed officers who may be removed at the will of the president, the answer is clearly yes. In refusing to comply, the FBI director, however, would be taking a chance that his or her interpretation was correct.

The great majority of federal law enforcement personnel are not appointed by the president. They are, rather, career civil servants, who obtain their positions through a competitive and nonpartisan selection process. *(See The President and the Bureaucracy chapter in Part VI.)* These personnel may be fired only for causes specified by statute or administrative regulation, and only following a neutral and procedurally rigorous judicial-type hearing.

Special agents of the FBI, Secret Service, and Bureau of Alcohol, Tobacco, and Firearms belong to this category. So do deputy U.S. marshals, assistant U.S. attorneys, IRS auditors, and customs inspectors. In fact, just about all investigating and enforcement officers, supporting staff, and many policy-making officers of the executive branch belong to the civil service.

This makes presidential appointment authority especially important to presidential law enforcement power. Civil servants are not obliged to share the same law enforcement goals and priorities as the president. Their goals and priorities, rather, are shaped by their personal values and by their perception of what will promote their own interests. The official behavior of civil servants, therefore, should not be expected to conform in all cases with the goals and priorities of the president.

Civil servants, to be sure, are obliged to obey all lawful commands of the president and of their own bureaucratic superiors. Willful failure to comply will normally constitute legal cause for discipline, including being fired from the job. To be successful, therefore, bureaucratic resistance to the president must be displayed in a less direct, more subtle way. More than a century of accumulated experience has provided civil servants a variety of such methods.

Seasoned bureaucrats know well, for example, the difference between complying with lawful orders and going through the motions of complying. A president might exclaim, "Enough, already!" and direct federal law enforcement agents to be especially aggressive in investigating members of Congress for corruption. Such an order lies within the discretionary power of the president and is entirely lawful.

Most federal agents would comply. That is their job. Other agents, however, may not share the president's enthusiasm for investigating members of Congress. These agents may be concerned that an angry Congress would slice their budgets, or that particularly powerful members of Congress might retaliate in the future by blocking their appointments to high-level agency positions. In such a case, documents will be examined (but not too thoroughly), and leads will be followed (but not too many). All of this will be well documented in reports that pronounce the absence of evidence justifying further investigations. A command was issued, and obeyed.

The chief executive's power over law enforcement, therefore, depends substantially upon the existence of and discretion in exercising three presidential powers: appointment, removal, and command. The appointment power of the president is substantial and even applies to officers of the judicial branch. This is the most comprehensive executive power that can be used by the president to affect law enforcement.

The removal power provides the president a blunt instrument of executive coercion. It is, however, an instrument that can be used unimpeded with only the most senior officers of the executive branch, and then only in certain cases. It does not apply to federal judges at all and can be used against officers of independent regulatory boards and commisioners, certain officers of the executive branch, and civil servants only for reasons specified by Congress.

Command power is tied to removal power. If presidents are to enforce their commands, then they must be capable of removing or otherwise disciplining disobedient or obstructing officials.

The executive power of the president in law enforcement, then, depends substantially on the president's ability to choose trusted appointees who are able to influence the behavior of subordinates. Ideally, subordinates will share the president's values pertaining to law enforcement. Experience shows, however, that at least a degree of bureaucratic resistance may be expected.

Military Power

The significance of the armed forces of the United States to presidential law enforcement power should not be measured by the frequency of their use, which has, especially in this century, been infrequent. The significance, rather, lies in the fact that military coercive power is available to the president to enforce the law when civilian power is unable to do so.

Presidents have used military power to enforce the law in several notable instances. President George Washington used military force to quell the Whiskey Rebellion. His precedent was followed by President Abraham Lincoln, who used a more powerful military force to suppress the southern rebellion. Both presidents were, legally speaking, enforcing the law.

Defiance of court injunctions against labor strikes in the nineteenth century prompted both Rutherford B. Hayes and Grover Cleveland to deploy troops to enforce the law. In the twentieth century, Presidents Dwight D. Eisenhower and John F. Kennedy used force when court desegregation orders were met by local resistance. Lyndon B. Johnson used his military power in 1968 to put down rioting in Detroit.

The military power of the president is derived from the Constitution and Congress.

The U.S. Constitution states in Article II, section 2, that the "President shall be Commander in Chief of the Army and Navy of the United States, and of the Militia of the several States, when called into actual service of the United States." Article IV, section 4, provides that the United States, "on Application of the [state] Legislature, or of the Executive [governor] (when the Legislature cannot be convened)" shall guarantee "against domestic Violence."

The commander-in-chief clause of the Constitution gives the president unquestionable authority to command the men and women of the armed forces. It is authority, however, that is itself shaped by law. The president and Congress share authority over the armed forces of the United States.

Congress, according to its authority to enact laws "necessary and proper" to "make Rules for ... Regulation of the land and naval Forces," and "To provide for calling forth the Militia to execute the Laws of the Union, suppress Insurrections and repel Invasions," has enacted legislation that both authorizes and places limitations on presidential use of the military to enforce the law.[141] *(See box, John F. Kennedy, the Law, and the "Ole Miss" Campaign, pp. 428-429, for a reprinting of these laws.)*

The Constitution does not seriously impede the ability of the president to use military force to assist civil authorities in enforcing the law. To the contrary, wrote Justice David Brewer: "There is no such impotency in the national government.... If the emergency arises, the army of the nation, and all its militia, are at the service of the nation to compel obedience to the laws." [142]

Nor does Congress impede the president in law enforcement. A careful reading of the relevant legislation reveals that although Congress has specified the conditions in which such force may be deployed, it has worded the statute in a way that leaves to the president considerable discretion in deciding if those conditions have been met.

A different situation arises, however, should the president attempt to declare martial law and supplant civil with military authority within the boundaries of the United

States. The Supreme Court has ruled that for such an action to be maintained constitutionally, the situation must be so desperate that the civil courts are closed.[143] The military might of the United States must support, not supplant, the law.

Clemency Power

Article II, section 2, of the U.S. Constitution delegates to the president "Power to grant Reprieves and Pardons for Offenses against the United States, except in Cases of Impeachment." It gives to the president an ability to be merciful as well as vengeful.

But mercy for the sake of being merciful was not necessarily what the Framers had in mind when they included clemency in the enumerated powers of the president. Alexander Hamilton explained in *Federalist* No. 74: "But the principal argument for reposing the power of pardoning . . . in the Chief Magistrate [president] is this: in seasons of insurrection or rebellion, there are often critical moments when a well-timed offer of pardon to the insurgents or rebels may restore the tranquility of the commonwealth." [144] Well-timed offers of pardon helped restore domestic tranquillity to Massachusetts after Shays's Rebellion—a fact specially noted by Hamilton.[145] Allow the president, he urged, the same power.

Shortly after the Constitution was ratified, this power was used. In 1792, President George Washington "most earnestly admonish[ed] and exhort[ed]" whiskey manufacturers of western Pennsylvania to cease their disobedience and obstruction of the law. They were, the president's proclamation continued, not only refusing to pay taxes on the whiskey produced, they were also resisting enforcement of the tax law with violence.[146]

Washington tried demands to end the "Whiskey Rebellion," and he tried force. Law and order in the western counties of Pennsylvania, however, was not restored until the president promised and granted the offenders a full and absolute pardon.[147]

A reprieve reduces a sentence already imposed by a judicial-type tribunal. A person sentenced to death by a U.S. district court or military court martial, for example, may have his or her sentence reduced to a long term of imprisonment by presidential reprieve. The guilt is not wiped out, but the severity of the punishment inflicted on the guilty person may be reduced.

Presidential pardons wipe out both guilt and punishment. They restore the person pardoned to his or her full civil rights, as if the offense had never been committed. President Gerald R. Ford, for example, granted a full and unconditional pardon to his predecessor, Richard Nixon, and relieved the former president of the possibility of being prosecuted for any involvement he may have had in the crimes associated with Watergate.

Reprieves and pardons may be granted to individuals or to classes of people in the form of "amnesties." For example, Presidents Abraham Lincoln and Andrew Johnson signed amnesties for Confederate soldiers and political leaders as did Presidents Gerald Ford and Jimmy Carter for draft evaders during the Vietnam War.

The president may attach conditions to either form of clemency. President Nixon, for instance, pardoned labor leader Jimmy Hoffa but with the condition that Hoffa would never again become involved in union activities.

The clemency authority of the president is extensive. It applies to any federal process or offender, except, by express constitutional language, those persons tried (or being tried) and convicted through congressional impeachment. Moreover, it is one of the few constitutional powers of the president that does not require legislative assent. Congress, in fact, may not interfere with presidential clemency authority in any manner, including, the U.S. Supreme Court has held, the imposition of restrictions on those pardoned.[148]

> [H]e shall have Power to grant Reprieves and Pardons for Offenses against the United States, except in Cases of Impeachment.
>
> —from Article II, section 2

Hamilton's argument in favor of extensive presidential clemency authority received its strongest validation in the events following the Civil War. Harmony among the people of the United States did not occur immediately. In fact, hostility, anger, and resentment on both sides of the conflict made an amicable reunion of the two sides impossible for many decades. Healing took time and the passing of many generations.

The process of healing was nourished, though, by the successful reintegration of Southerners into the American political process. Not only did white Southerners regain the right to vote, they also ascended to high political office. And although no former Confederate soldier or political officer was ever elected president, many later served with distinction in the legislative, executive, and judicial branches of the United States.

Augustus Garland, for example, was appointed attorney general by President Cleveland. President William Howard Taft appointed Edward Douglas White to the position of chief justice of the United States, the titular head of the judicial branch of the nation. Both appointees had previously served the Confederate cause.

The Law Enforcement Bureaucracy

The power of the president in law enforcement has been discussed so far in terms of the legal authority that the U.S. Constitution and Congress give the office. But answering the question, "What does the president command?" is just as important as the question, "By what right?" The president commands a vast law enforcement bureaucracy, comprising scores of departments and agencies.

Perhaps the most familiar element of this bureaucracy is the Federal Bureau of Investigation. Its historical feats (and faults) have been well chronicled. But the FBI is not the national police force of the United States. In fact, the United States has no national police force. Rather, the law enforcement power of the United States is distributed throughout the executive branch.

The FBI is part of the Department of Justice, itself the repository of several other important law enforcement agencies, including the Immigration and Naturalization Service (INS), the U.S. Marshals Service, the Drug Enforcement Administration, and the Criminal Division.

The Justice Department must be considered the lead law enforcement agency at the disposal of the president. The attorney general, statutory head of the department,

Attorneys General of the United States

The attorney general of the United States is the chief legal adviser to the president and is the head of the U.S. Department of Justice. Since virtually every official decision made by the president is governed by law, and since such a large percentage of the work of the federal government is devoted to enforcing the law, the nature of the attorney general's job would almost ensure influence with the president. And indeed it has. The attorney general usually is considered one of the "inside members" of the president's cabinet. It is a position of considerable power.

President George Washington turned to a fellow Virginian, Edmund Jennings Randolph, as his (and the nation's) first attorney general. In Randolph we find two qualities that often have characterized the men (as of January 1989, no woman had been appointed attorney general) who have held that office ever since: talent and controversy.

Before serving with Thomas Jefferson, Alexander Hamilton, and Henry Knox in Washington's first cabinet, Randolph had distinguished himself through his service as military aide to General George Washington, as attorney general and governor of Virginia, as delegate to the Virginia constitutional convention of 1776, as delegate from Virginia to the Continental Congress, and as delegate to the U.S. Constitutional Convention of 1787. Although Randolph refused to sign the product, the U.S. Constitution, because, among other reasons, he opposed vesting the executive power in a single president, he did urge its ratification by Virginia.

When Thomas Jefferson resigned in 1794 as Washington's first secretary of state, Washington picked Randolph to succeed him. Randolph resigned the following year, however, amidst false charges of soliciting bribes and giving secret information to the French government. Although stripped of his public standing by the charges, the capable Randolph led the successful legal defense in the treason trial of Aaron Burr.

Talent and controversy have followed the successors of Randolph. Roger Taney, attorney general to President Andrew Jackson, and Harlan Fiske Stone, attorney general to President Calvin Coolidge, became chief justices of the United States (Stone, after serving sixteen years as associate justice). Other former attorneys general who became Supreme Court justices are Nathan Clifford, Joseph McKenna, James C. McReynolds, Francis W. Murphy, Robert H. Jackson, and Thomas C. Clark.

Harry M. Daugherty was attorney general to President Warren G. Harding and was implicated in the Teapot Dome Scandal. *(See Teapot Dome and Other Scandals," p. 108, in History of the Presidency chapter of Part I.)* Many people thought that Ramsey Clark, the last attorney general to President Lyndon B. Johnson, should have been indicted for treason, but he was not. Clark remains controversial for visiting Hanoi during the Vietnam War after he left office. Two of President Richard Nixon's attorneys general, John N. Mitchell and Richard G. Kleindienst, went to prison after leaving office and being convicted of crimes.

One attorney general, Charles Joseph Bonaparte, had an unusual family history for an American leader. Bonaparte was the grandson of Jerome Bonaparte, king of Westphalia and marshal of France. Jerome, in turn, was the younger brother of Napoleon I, emperor of France. The American Bonaparte first distinguished himself as a leader of the good-government movement of the late nineteenth and early twentieth centuries, serving consecutively as president of the National Civil Service Reform League in 1904 and as president of the National Municipal League in 1905. This commitment appealed to President Theodore Roosevelt, who rewarded Bonaparte with appointments first as secretary of the navy and then as attorney general. *(See Cabinet Members and Other Officials, p. 1455, in the Appendix.)*

commands a variety of important investigatory and enforcement agencies, the FBI being only one. He or she also commands the principal prosecutorial agencies of the national government, the various U.S. attorneys across the United States, and the centralized prosecutorial divisions in Washington. Finally, the attorney general traditionally serves as the principal legal adviser to the president and supervises for the president the selection of nominees for federal judicial posts and clemency. *(See box, Attorneys General of the United States, this page.)*

Law enforcement responsibility and power is divided and allocated even further. It is allocated in significant respects to the Department of Treasury, which contains the Secret Service, Customs Service, and Internal Revenue Service; to the Department of Labor, which enforces laws regulating labor unions, wages, and occupational health and safety; to the Department of Defense, which contains both civilian and military investigative and enforcement agencies; and to various regulatory agencies.

In one respect, applying the term "chief law enforcement officer of the United States" to the president is misleading. Beginning with the Interstate Commerce Commission in 1887, and continuing with the creation of such agencies as the Federal Trade Commission, National Labor Relations Board, and the Securities and Exchange Commission, Congress periodically has allocated various law enforcement powers to independent boards and commissions within the executive branch but outside the supervisory authority of the president. The power of the president over these agencies generally is limited to appointing board members and other important agency officers. These officials may not be fired by the president except for cause, which is defined by Congress.[149]

Categories of Federal Law Enforcement

Agencies of the executive branch are involved in at least eight categories of law enforcement. These categories overlap in many instances and oversimplify a highly complex regulatory scheme, but they do provide an overview of the law enforcement activities of the executive branch.

Economic. Agencies of the executive branch implement a variety of laws seeking to foster economic growth, stability, and competition. Also included in this category are laws designed to advance fairness in business practices and harmonious labor-management relations. The Antitrust Division of the Justice Department, for example, enforces laws promoting fair trade practices and proscribing monopolies. Financial institutions are subjected to regulation by the comptroller of currency and by the IRS of the Treasury Department. Employment is subject to enforcement actions by the Occupational Safety and Health Administration (OSHA) and by the Employment Standards Administration of the Department of Labor. Despite deregulation, substantial regulation of the transportation industry is still administered by the Federal Aviation Administration of the Department of Transportation. Energy, a relative newcomer to the federal regulatory scheme, is under the jurisdiction of the Departments of Energy and of Interior.

Social. Laws have been enacted that can be said to promote a mélange of social goals: equality, fairness, and material comfort. Antidiscrimination laws, such as the equal employment and fair housing provisions of the Civil Rights Act of 1964, the Age Discrimination in Employment Act, and the Civil Rights Restoration Act of 1988 belong to this category. Their enforcement generally is accomplished by the combined efforts of the Civil Rights Division of the Justice Department, the Equal Employment Opportunity Commission, and the Department of Education. Each agency of the federal government also contains offices charged with enforcing internal compliance with these laws, as well as compliance by firms contracting with them. A multitude of retirement, medical care, and educational assistance acts are administered by the Social Security Administration of the Department of Health and Human Services, the Department of Veterans Affairs, and the Department of Education.

Political. Political decisions are made according to a complex system of procedural laws. The often-stated purpose of these laws is to promote fairness and integrity in government. The Voting Rights Act of 1965, for instance, forbids racial discrimination in voting and is enforced by the FBI and Civil Rights Division of the Department of Justice. Bribery of and extortion by federal government officials of all branches also falls under the jurisdiction of the FBI, and violations are prosecuted by the Criminal Division of the Justice Department.

Judicial. Most judicial orders are complied with voluntarily. Judgment is entered against the defendant, and the defendant complies: that is, the defendant makes payment, stops the unlawful activity, or turns himself or herself over to authorities for completion of a jail sentence. Behind every instance of voluntary compliance, however, is at least the implicit backing of armed force. Armed force may also be necessary on occasion to enforce judicial orders and to protect judges, jurors, witnesses, and other participants in a trial. The U.S. Marshals Service of the Justice Department is the agency that usually enforces the authority of the judicial branch. Their power may, in extreme circumstances, be backed by the armed forces of the United States, principally by the army and by Army National Guard units nationalized by presidential order.

Public Health and Safety. The national government oversees many issues of public health and safety. They include transportation safety, a concern of the Federal Aviation Administration (FAA) of the Department of Transportation; occupational safety and health, consigned by Congress to the aptly named Occupational Safety and Health Administration of the Department of Labor; and food purity, which falls under the jurisdiction of the Food and Drug Administration (FDA) of the Department of Health and Human Services; the Environmental Protection Agency; and the Food Safety and Inspection Service of the Department of Agriculture.

Public health and safety activities of the executive branch also entail enforcement of more commonly known criminal laws, such as those prohibiting interstate kidnapping, prostitution, and transportation of stolen property. Finally, federal laws attempting to stem drug and alcohol abuse in the United States are enforced by the FBI, DEA, FDA, Customs Service, Coast Guard, Border Patrol, and Bureau of Alcohol, Tobacco, and Firearms. Prosecutions are the responsibilty of the Criminal Division of the Justice Department and local U.S. attorneys.

National Security. Treason and espionage are crimes, as are assorted other activities that tend to jeopardize the military and diplomatic interests of the United States. Protection of American security is associated most often with the FBI, but the efforts of the FBI constitute only a part of the whole. A number of agencies of the Department of Defense—such as the Defense Investigative Service, the Naval Investigative Service, the Office of Special Investigations (Air Force), and the Intelligence and Security Command (Army)—have law enforcement duties to protect national security, as do the Coast Guard, Border Patrol, Immigration and Naturalization Service, and Office of Security at the Department of State. The Central Intelligence Agency is *not* given domestic law enforcement authority by Congress, but it may pass to the FBI intelligence it gathers abroad about American national security breaches.

Public Resources. The public resources of the national government consist of money, property, and people. Almost every law enforcement agency of the national government is involved in the protection of one or all of these resources. The better known of these agencies are the FBI and the Secret Service. Others include the Postal Inspection Service, Park Police of the Department of Interior, U.S. Marshals Service, and Federal Protective Service of the General Services Administration. Each department and agency of the executive branch contains an internal capability to investigate theft, fraud, and personal security, usually in the form of an Office of Inspector General.

Public Revenue. As Americans, we should appreciate the law enforcement services provided by the national government, for we pay for them, principally through personal and corporate income taxes, estate taxes, excise taxes, and customs duties. Most of us pay our fair share of taxes, that is, the share we are required to pay by law. But some do not. Enforcing the nation's tax laws falls primarily under the jurisdiction of three agencies of the Department of

U.S. Customs Service

Customs agents inspect baggage of all persons entering the United States, searching for illegal possessions such as weapons, drugs, and certain agricultural products.

Treasury: the Bureau of Alcohol, Tobacco, and Firearms (for taxes on alcohol and tobacco products), the Customs Service (for import tariffs and fees), and the Internal Revenue Service (for personal, corporate, and estate taxes). The Tax Division of the Justice Department has been established by Congress to prosecute violations of the various tax laws.

Law Enforcement Functions of the Bureaucracy

The bureaucracy performs four general law enforcement functions: investigation, enforcement, prosecution, and custody.

Investigation. Investigation entails fact finding, that is, a search for facts that may assist an agency in the discharge of its assigned law enforcement responsibilities. The search for facts may be directed toward enactment of new laws or the enforcement of existing laws with more effective strategies, policies, and priorities. Most agencies of the executive branch do this routinely.

For an assortment of reasons—the need for impartiality, prestige, or outside expertise—the president may prefer on occasion that a particular issue in law enforcement be investigated by persons not affiliated with existing agencies. In such instances, the president may appoint a presidential investigatory commission.

The presidential commission normally comprises a bipartisan panel of Americans who may or may not be employed by the federal government but who have distinguished themselves publicly. The commission receives a presidential mandate to answer a question, or a series of questions, and is supported by a professional staff paid for by the president.

The National Advisory Commission on Civil Disorders, better known as the "Kerner Commission" is a good example. In July 1968, Detroit, Michigan, was torn by urban rioting. Unable to control the rioting with state and local forces, including the Michigan National Guard, the governor of Michigan requested the assistance of the president.

The president responded with airborne troops, and order soon was restored. But, as also happened after Shays's Rebellion almost two centuries before, the causes of the rioting presumably remained. And the problem was not confined to Detroit. The president wanted to know the causes, and he wanted to know what could be done to eliminate or control them.

To answer these questions, President Johnson established the Kerner Commission on July 29, 1967.[150] He appointed Otto Kerner, then governor of Illinois, to chair a panel composed of four members of Congress, one mayor, a state official, a local police chief, and a representative each from labor, business, and civil rights.[151] Two advisory panels, a large investigative staff, and outside consultants and witnesses assisted the panel.

The commission's findings followed months of public hearings, statistical analyses, and review of programs, policies, and procedures. Almost all applied and theoretical disciplines of the social sciences influenced the final product: sociology, psychology, political science, economics, criminology, urban planning, and education. Causes were asserted and solutions offered.[152]

Some of the recommendations found their way into national policy; others were talked about but never implemented. The timing of the Detroit riot, and the resulting report, was not good because President Johnson devoted much of his remaining and limited time in the White House to managing the Vietnam War. Richard Nixon, his successor in 1969, was not as receptive to the proposals contained in the report.

The more routine form of law enforcement investigation is directed at enforcing rather than changing policy. This is fact finding aimed at determining whether an unlawful act has been committed, the identity of the perpetrators, and whether evidence can be gathered that is both admissible in court and sufficient to obtain a favorable verdict.

Most enforcement agencies of the executive branch are involved in this phase of law enforcement. The investigation may consist simply of witnessing a crime in progress and interrogating the suspect, in hopes of obtaining a signed confession.

Other investigations take more time, more effort, and considerably more resources. Investigation by the FBI of a national security breach, for example, may require months of investigative work, including surveillance of potential suspects, installation and monitoring of wiretaps, and rigorous background checks.

Certain investigations involve crimes so complex that the resources of multiple agencies from different departments may be mobilized into single task forces. Organized crime falls under this category; agents from the FBI, the IRS, and the DEA often join with their counterparts from state and local police forces and with federal and state prosecutors, to control this persistent problem.

Enforcement. The investigative process is goal directed. In most situations, this goal is the arrest and conviction of a criminal suspect. This is one way in which laws are enforced. Enforcement, however, involves more than arrest and conviction of criminal suspects. It also involves protection of federal resources and execution of judicial orders.

The federal agencies participating in enforcement (most often the same ones that conduct investigations) are too numerous to discuss in this limited space. Nevertheless, a sampling of these agencies are listed and discussed briefly below.

Food Safety and Inspection Service (Agriculture Department). President Theodore Roosevelt is reputed to have been reading Upton Sinclair's *The Jungle* while eating breakfast one morning in the White House. Disturbed by Sinclair's description of the meat-packing industry in Chicago, the president threw his sausage out of the White House window and began working toward enactment of the Pure Food and Drug Act of 1906. Conditions have improved considerably since Roosevelt's day. Meatpacking and other food production and processing industries now are subjected to standards adopted and enforced by the Department of Agriculture. The job of the Food Safety and Inspection Service is to enforce these standards. In fiscal year 1987, this agency employed 8,857 persons and administered a budget of $373 million.[153]

U.S. Department of Defense. By order of the president, units of the armed forces of the United States may be used to suppress domestic violence and to remove obstructions to the enforcement of the law. National Guard units of the states may be "nationalized" for this purpose by presidential order. When they are, they are placed under the operational command of the secretary of defense. The Defense Department, and its component Departments of the Army, Navy, and Air Force, includes a number of internal agencies with law enforcement responsibility and authority. These agencies include both civilian and military personnel and provide protective services to the property and personnel of the department. They also enforce laws pertaining to fraud, corruption, and national security. The Pentagon Procurement Scandal of 1988, for example, was uncovered by investigations conducted by the Naval Investigative Service.

Federal Bureau of Investigation (Justice Department). J. Edgar Hoover, the consummate bureaucratic chief, shaped the FBI into a modern, professional, and semi-autonomous law enforcement agency. Under his almost fifty years of leadership, the bureau gained notoriety in the 1930s by apprehending or killing marauding and overly romanticized criminals, such as John Dillinger. The favorable image Hoover and his agents already enjoyed was only enhanced by the agency's successful apprehension of enemy spies during the Second World War and the ensuing cold war. Always sensitive to public opinion, Hoover insisted that his agents conform to rigid dress and behavioral standards. He also initiated programs cultivating the bureau's reputation for effectiveness—the FBI's "ten most wanted list" is the outstanding example.

The mystique surrounding and protecting the FBI began to decay somewhat in the 1960s. Charges were made that Hoover was insensitive to civil rights issues and refused to commit his resources to the investigation of organized crime. Additional blows to the agency came in the wake of Watergate, when its acting director, L. Patrick Gray, admitted to destroying documents important to the initial investigation and when high bureau officers were convicted of and imprisoned for illegal activities. Under the tutelage of directors Clarence M. Kelley (1973-1978), former police chief of Kansas City, and William H. Webster (1978-1987), former federal appellate judge, the image of the FBI as a professional and competent law enforcement agency has been largely restored. The FBI is the closest thing the United States has to a general police agency in the national government. Its jurisdiciton includes investigation and enforcement of laws pertaining to national security, fraud, corruption, civil rights, elections, kidnapping, and robbery of federally insured banks. In fiscal year 1987, the FBI employed 22,456 persons and had a budget of $1.1 billion.

Peter Main, *Christian Science Monitor*

The U.S. Border Patrol monitors the borders of the United States, detecting and apprehending illegal entrants. Here, U.S. officers pursue illegals into a freight yard in El Paso, Texas.

Gerald R. Ford Library

Secret Service agents surround President Ford and survey the crowd as the president waves from his motorcade. The Secret Service provides security for the president and the first family as well as for past presidents and their families.

Drug Enforcement Administration (Justice Department). Agents of the DEA have perhaps the dirtiest and most dangerous law enforcement job in the federal government: they enforce national drug laws. Most of the work of the DEA is conducted within the boundaries of the United States. Yet, agents may and often do carry their investigations to foreign countries—the drug production, refinement, and transportation centers in Latin America, Europe, Asia, and the Middle East. Here they may advise and exchange intelligence information with their foreign counterparts and, depending on arrangements with their host countries, conduct their own investigations. Although they are subject to reprisals by foreign drug dealers, they are not necessarily authorized to arm themselves. The half-billion dollar budget and 5,680 employees authorized by Congress for the DEA in fiscal year 1987 reflect the agency's importance to federal law enforcement policy.

Border Patrol (Justice Department). The Border Patrol, the uniformed component of the Immigration and Naturalization Service, does just what its name implies: it patrols the borders of the United States. As an agency of the INS, the principal task of the Border Patrol is to detect and apprehend illegal entrants. Performing this task, of course, exposes officers of the Border Patrol to an assortment of other crimes, the most notable of which is drug smuggling across the U.S. border. They have the authority and are expected to make arrests in such circumstances.

U.S. Marshals Service (Justice Department). U.S. marshals have been a law enforcement resource of the president since the administration of President George Washington. In the nineteenth century, marshals acted as the general police force for much of the West; large sections of the American West had not yet achieved statehood and were organized by Congress as territories of the United States. Television has taught us that the U.S. marshal of this period, Wyatt Earp and Matt Dillon being only two, single-handedly stood between the ordinary law-abiding citizen and a host of predators—gunslingers, horse thieves, and the local cattle baron, all aided, apparently, by corrupt local sheriffs, mayors, and judges.

The job of the marshal in contemporary American society is less romantic but still important. Marshals enforce court orders, serve court papers, maintain security and order in courtrooms, protect witnesses, escort federal prisoners, and suppress domestic disturbances. Marshals possess general law enforcement power and are an all-purpose force at the disposal of the president and attorney general. The 1987 budget for the U.S. Marshals Service was comparatively small—$168 million. The service employed 2,729 persons in fiscal year 1987.

Secret Service (Treasury Department). The men and women wearing business suits, sunglasses, and radio earplugs who surround the president on every occasion are the best-known component of the Secret Service. But guarding the president is just one of the duties of this agency of the Treasury Department. It also provides security for the vice president, former presidents, immediate family members of current and former presidents, the president- and vice president-elect, presidential and vice-presidential candidates, and visiting heads of state. A uniformed branch of the Secret Service guards foreign embassies and missions and assists in guarding the White House. The Secret Service also has primary jurisdiction in enforcing laws pertaining to counterfeiting, credit card fraud, and defrauding of federally insured banks. Congress appropriated $334 million for the Secret Service in fiscal year 1987, a large portion of which was used to pay the salaries of the 4,355 men and women it employs.

Internal Revenue Service (Treasury Department). The IRS has an enviable reputation in Washington for efficiency and impartiality, although many Americans view it apprehensively as the nation's tax collector. Consider its assignment from Congress: The IRS not only collects taxes owed the federal government from individuals and corporations but also processes tax returns from almost every American adult, corporation, partnership, and nonprofit organization. It also calculates and returns any amount previously overpaid by the taxpayer. Usually by computer, certain of these returns are selected for audit, a process designed to detect tax fraud and to deter intentional understatement of future tax liabilities. The IRS includes a criminal investigative division, whose agents are authorized to carry firearms, investigate possible criminal violations of the tax code, make arrests, and serve search warrants. In fiscal year 1987, the IRS employed 29,561 persons and was appropriated a budget of $4.4 billion.

Customs Service (Treasury Department). The men and women of the Customs Service are the ones authorized to inspect the baggage of all persons, citizen or visitor, entering the United States. They are searching chiefly for goods subject to federal tax or prohibited by law from being imported into the United States, such as drugs, weapons, and certain agricultural products. Customs agents board and search incoming ships, airplanes, pleasure boats, trucks, buses, and automobiles, as well as their passengers, baggage, and cargo. Although the Customs Service is principally a tax collection and enforcement agency, it has assumed a lead role in the enforcement of the nation's drug laws by intercepting shipments on the borders of the United States. In fiscal year 1987, the Customs Service had 15,610 employees and a budget of $1.1 billion.

Employment Standards Administration (Labor Department). The Fair Labor Standards Act mandates that employees engaged in interstate commerce not otherwise exempted must be paid a minimum hourly wage—$3.35 per hour as of January 1989. The same act also requires that compensation amounting to the employee's usual hourly wage be paid for any work exceeding forty hours in a given work week. Enforcing these laws is the primary responsibility of the Employment Standards Administration (ESA). In fiscal year 1987, the ESA employed 4,100 persons and had a budget of $191 million.

Occupational Safety and Health Administration (Labor Department). Health and safety in the work place are the concerns of OSHA. In accordance with legislation passed by Congress, OSHA has put into effect detailed regulations governing such matters as protective clothing for workers, the handling of hazardous substances, and protective shields on industrial equipment. Inspectors from local OSHA offices inspect work sites and have authority to cite employers who violate or permit violations of the regulations. OSHA employed 2,141 persons in fiscal year 1987 and administered a budget of $226 million.

Federal Aviation Administration (Transportation Department). Americans should appreciate the FAA, for we fly millions of miles each year and are rarely discomforted, much less hurt. Part of the explanation lies in the efforts of the FAA, which administers and enforces laws pertaining to commercial air travel. Its jurisdiction includes pilot licensing, airport safety and security, air traffic control, and airplane safety. It employed 45,266 persons in fiscal year 1987 and administered a budget of $2.3 billion.

Coast Guard (Transportation Department). The Coast Guard traces its origins to the nation's first secretary of the Treasury, Alexander Hamilton, who created a service of revenue cutters (small, armed ships) to help prevent smuggling and the resulting evasion of customs taxes. The Coast Guard still performs this function. It also enforces regulations pertaining to maritime safety, licenses boat captains, patrols waterways for hazards (such as icebergs), and rescues people from sunken or disabled vessels. The Coast Guard has an important role in the current efforts to suppress drug smuggling. During war, operational command of the Coast Guard is transferred to the Navy. In fiscal year 1987, Congress gave the Coast Guard a budget of $1.8 billion, part of which was used to pay its 39,778 uniformed and civilian personnel.

Offices of Inspector General. All federal departments and most federal agencies contain an office of inspector general. The functions vary somewhat by agency but generally include investigations of fraud, abuse, bribery, waste, and personal misconduct within the agency.

U.S. Coast Guard

A Coast Guard crew unloads bails of marijuana seized off the Florida coast.

Prosecution. U.S. attorneys filed 118,237 civil and criminal actions during the 1987 fiscal year. This added to their existing workload of 202,479 docketed cases.[154]

The U.S. attorney is the workhorse of the federal prosecutorial system. Appointed by the president, and located within the Department of Justice, the U.S. attorney assumes the lead responsibility for representing the government in court. One U.S. attorney is appointed for each of the ninety-four judicial districts in the United States and is supported by a professional legal staff.

Although the U.S. attorney represents the government in most cases, there are other prosecutorial resources in the executive branch. The Department of Justice itself comprises different divisions that may, at times, be involved in litigation. Each division is headed by an assistant attorney general. Their jurisdiction is indicated by their division title: Antitrust Division, Civil Division, Civil Rights Division, Criminal Division, Land and Natural Resources Division, and Tax Division.

One other component of the Justice Department is involved in the prosecution phase of law enforcement. This is the Office of Solicitor General. The solicitor general determines which decisions of federal or state appellate courts will be appealed by the United States to the U.S. Supreme Court and represents the government in the appeal. Owing to the considerable influence the Supreme Court has in interpreting the law, including laws allocating power to the president and presidential agencies, this function is particularly critical to the president.

Departments and agencies outside of the Justice Department occasionally are given limited prosecutorial authority and resources by Congress. The solicitor of labor, for instance, has authority to initiate civil actions in federal court to enforce wage-and-hour and occupational health and safety laws.

Custody. Conviction of a crime in federal court may lead to a sentence of imprisonment. When it does, the prisoner is usually remanded to the custody of the Bureau of Prisons for punishment. The Bureau of Prisons is an agency of the Department of Justice and has responsibility for administering the federal prison system. This responsibility includes guarding the inmates (often from one another) as well as supplying them housing, food, recreation, medical care, and rehabilitation services such as education and counseling. The bureau employed 11,257 persons and spent $626 million in fiscal year 1987.

Law Enforcement within the U.S. Political System

Law enforcement responsibility and power are shared in the U.S. political system, first of all by the national government and the fifty states and their units of local government. Responsibility and power for law enforcement are also shared by the three branches of the national government. With the notable exception of the president's constitutional authority to grant reprieves and pardons, all incidents of presidential law enforcement power may be checked by at least one of the two other branches.

Sharing within the Federal System

Federalism refers to a form of political organization whereby at least two levels of government exercise sovereign power over geographically defined and overlapping jurisdictions. The two levels of sovereign government in the United States are the national government and the fifty independent state governments.

Allocation of law enforcement responsibility and power within the U.S. federal system has evolved significantly since George Washington and members of the First Congress took office in 1789. This evolution generally has increased the power and responsibility of the national government at the expense of state power and independence.

National law enforcement responsibility and power were slight in 1789 and remained so until the Civil War. States, however, had significant law enforcement responsibility during this period, and they had power commensurate with that responsibility. Legislating to promote the public's health, safety, morals, and general welfare was the business of the state legislatures, and it was the business of local sheriffs, state militia, and state judges to enforce those laws.

A number of things changed this balance in favor of the national government. First, led by Chief Justice John Marshall, the U.S. Supreme Court handed down rulings in the first decades of the nineteenth century that interpreted expansively the constitutional grants of power to the national government. Congress, the Court ruled, has ample constitutional power to enact any law necessary and proper to carry out its enumerated powers, as long as that law was not proscribed by the Constitution itself.[155] Contrary provisions of state law must yield to laws enacted by Congress in accordance with its constitutional power,[156] and state court interpretations of federal law are susceptible to review and possible reversal by federal courts.[157]

The assumption of significant and broader law enforcement responsibility and power by the national government cannot be attributed to Marshall and his Court; a half-century was to pass before the national government began assuming its modern role and powers. What these early judicial rulings did accomplish, however, was to establish a constitutional doctrine for the assumption when it was to occur.

Marshall and the Supreme Court, then, legitimized an extensive and pervasive national role in law enforcement. Still missing was a workable consensus among the American people and their elected representatives in Congress that such a role ought to be exercised. That consensus was achieved in the latter part of the nineteenth century.

Business in the early decades of the American Republic was largely a local activity and was regulated primarily by state and local governments. By the latter two decades of the nineteenth century, however, it became increasingly apparent that many business activities either could not or would not be regulated effectively by state and local government. The people eventually pressured Washington to assume the burden. Interstate rail transportation came under federal regulatory jurisdiction with enactment of the Interstate Commerce Act of 1887. Today, virtually no business activity is untouched by federal regulation.

The current relationship between the national and the fifty state governments in law enforcement is complex. Some activities are regulated extensively and simultaneously by both levels of government. Retail sales, occupational health and safety, and banking, for example, are subject to a host of national and state laws and regulations.

Other activities tend to be regulated predominantly by either one or the other level of government. The national government exercises a near monopoly in the regulation of interstate and international airline travel, radio and television broadcasting, and nuclear power production. Automobile speed limits, assault and battery, marriage and divorce, and medical licensing are principally matters for state regulation.

The current breakdown of state-national law enforcement responsibility reflects the will of Congress. Congress, without question, is empowered to exert a far wider regulatory reach than it currently exercises. Yet it is content to leave the regulation of most activities to state government. Congress, for example, is quite content to leave the definition and enforcement of many "ordinary" crimes to state governments. Murder, rape, burglary, robbery, and mayhem are offensive to American society. They merit prohibition and punishment throughout the United States. And they are, but not by the federal government (except when a special federal connection exists, such as when the crime is committed by a member of the armed forces and on the premises of a military base). These and other ordinary crimes are generally the object of state, not federal, regulation.

States may already do the job competently, or, in fact, far better than could be expected from the national government. Moreover, Congress understandably wishes to avoid entering additional regulatory fields requiring much additional expense and work—by Congress, as well as the federal executive and judicial branches—and little anticipated benefit.

Consider, for instance, the burden that would be placed on all three branches of the national government should Congress attempt to regulate directly speed limits on federally financed highways. Consider also what, if anything, would be gained.[158]

Congress is susceptible to political pressure as well. When Congress enters a new regulatory field, support for such a move can usually be traced to politically powerful interest groups, or to the American public, or both. Conversely, lack of congressional interest in a regulatory field is understandable when such a move is supported neither by powerful interest groups nor by a significant segment of the American public. This is especially true when a contemplated law is actively opposed.

Little public interest, for example, is aroused by the notion of professional licensing by the national government. But the idea arouses strong opposition from well-organized and assertive interest groups such as national and state bar and medical associations. Attorneys and physicians are licensed by state government.

The relationship between national law enforcement agencies of the executive branch and their counterparts in state and local governments can be characterized most aptly as competitive but cooperative. Federal law enforcement agencies may request, and often receive, investigatory and enforcement assistance from state and local police forces. Such assistance, for instance, may be given to locate and arrest a military deserter, an armed robber of a post office, or a counterfeiter, or it may be given in the form of security for a visiting president or foreign dignitary.

The president and the principal law enforcement officers of the national government will be reluctant to deny a reasonable request from a state governor for law enforcement assistance. The request may be for troops to put down a riot, as occurred when President Lyndon Johnson sent airborne troops to Detriot in the summer of 1967. More commonly, though, it will involve special federal attention to local problems that either are beyond the competence of state and local resources to resolve or can be resolved more effectively and efficiently with federal assistance.

Finally, state and local agencies also receive routine assistance from federal law enforcement agencies. Federal agencies distribute law enforcement assistance grants to state and local governments, offer training in modern law enforcement techniques and technology to state and local enforcement officials, and provide intelligence information about local criminal activity.

Sharing within the National Government

High school civics teaches that laws are made by Congress, enforced by the president, and applied by the courts. It is by this means that tyranny in the United States is averted: political power in the national government is divided and allocated to separate and independent branches. Each branch, therefore, has some check on the goings on (and possible abuses) of the others.

Article I, section 1, of the U.S. Constitution does assign the legislative power to Congress. And Article II vests the executive power of the United States in the president and imposes on the president the obligation to "take Care that the Laws be faithfully executed." Finally, Article III, section 1, delegates the judicial power of the United States to the Supreme Court and to such other courts as Congress chooses to create.

Still, there is more to this arrangement than the division and allocation of power to separate and independent branches. Power is also shared. Congress, the legislative arm of the national government, makes law according to its constitutional grant of power, but is does so subject to presidential approval or veto, and often at the president's urging. Congress also delegates practical law-making power—authority to promulgate binding administrative rules and regulations—to the president and officers of the executive who may or may not report to the president.

The judiciary, if complaints from presidents and members of Congress are any measure, seems to involve itself in functions normally considered legislative or executive. Judges routinely interpret law and by so doing lend their own flavor to its meaning. Occasionally this leads judges to invalidate congressional or executive actions.

Conflicts between the president and Congress or the president and the judiciary attract the attention of the press and, by derivation, of the American public. Intramural conflict is a familiar ingredient of U.S. political life.

Although less attention is drawn to this fact, thus it is less evident to the American people, cooperation also exists among the three branches of American government, more so, perhaps, than conflict. The relationship is not harmonious, nor is it intended to be, but it is generally cooperative.

Congress and Presidential Law Enforcement Power. Article I, section 1, of the Constitution states that "All legislative Powers" of the United States belong to Congress. This power bears directly, extensively, and frequently on the law enforcement obligations and powers of the president. Four categories of power are available to Congress, which, when exercised, may either increase or restrict the law enforcement power of the president. These are law making, investigation, review of presidential appointments, and impeachment.

Congress is, first of all, responsible for defining the laws of the United States. Congress decided that railroads, airlines, and television ought to be regulated by the national government, and Congress determined that national standards ought to apply to production of food and drugs. The expansion of the national police power is the product of congressional action.

The legislative work of Congress does not end with asserting the regulatory power of the national government. A system and a process must be set in place for enforcing the law. Agencies must be created and empowered. They must employ men and women who actually enforce the law, and they must pay them. Finally, law enforcement officers of the executive branch must be granted specific law enforcement authority.

Congress provides the people necessary to staff the president's law enforcement agencies through authorizing legislation, and it provides for payment of their salaries through separate appropriations bills. Through a similar process, it provides enforcement officers the personnel and material support necessary to do a satisfactory job.

Federal law enforcement agencies and personnel receive two principal forms of authority from Congress: jurisdictional and enforcement authority. The former determines the types of laws a given agency is supposed to enforce; the second provides enforcement officers with the specific powers to make their enforcement effective.

Congress, for example, has defined the jurisdiction of the Secret Service to include protection of the current and former presidents and vice presidents of the United States and the members of their immediate families; candidates for the presidency and vice presidency meeting certain conditions; and visiting foreign dignitaries. The Secret Service also has jurisdiction over laws pertaining to currency, enumerated sections of various banking laws, and various forms of electronic and credit card fraud.[159]

Agency jurisdiction occasionally overlaps. The Drug Enforcement Administration has primary jurisdiction over enforcement of the nation's narcotics laws. But that jurisdiction overlaps considerably with the jurisdiction given the FBI, the Customs Service, the Coast Guard, and the Food and Drug Administration. Congress has given all of these agencies, and many more, the authority to enforce various aspects of the nation's drug laws.

Special agents and other FBI personnel have congressional authority to "carry firearms, serve warrants and supoenas issued under the authority of the United States." Congress has also given them authority to "make arrests without warrant for any offense against the United States committed in their presence, or for any felony cognizable under the laws of the United States if they have reasonable grounds to believe that the person to be arrested has committed or is committing such felony."[160]

Congress has made similar grants of authority to U.S. marshals, agents of the Secret Service and Drug Enforcement Administration, and a host of other federal law enforcement personnel.[161]

Congress may limit the authority that it confers on federal law enforcement agencies and personnel. Postal inspectors, for instance, have authority to "make arrests without warrant for offenses against the United States committed in their presence,"[162] but only if the offense is related to the property or use of the Postal Service.[163]

The second way Congress may affect the law enforcement power of the president involves the exercise of its inherent authority to investigate. Investigations may be for the purpose of determining whether new laws are needed, or they may be to determine whether existing laws are being enforced in the manner and with the energy that Congress intends.

Congressional investigations frequently are conducted through the device of a committee hearing. Witnesses give their views on the issue before the committee and subject themselves to questions by commttee members and counsel. The testimony may be given voluntarily or under compulsion (subpoena). In most instances a witness will be placed under oath, subjecting him or her to the possibility of prosecution for giving false testimony intentionally.

Impressive resources are available to Congress to assist in these investigations. These may include personal and committee staff, researchers of the Library of Congress, economists of the Congressional Budget Office, auditors of the General Accounting Office, and analysts of the Office of Technology Assessment. The staffs of each of these congressional agencies have established reputations for objective and competent work.

Television has enhanced the significance of congressional investigations. The specter of organized crime in the United States was revealed starkly in the 1950s televised investigations of the Kefauver Committee (Special Committee to Investigate Organized Crime in Interstate Commerce)—the American people heard, for the first time, mention of the "mafia" and "la cosa nostra" from witnesses who testified to the power and pervasiveness of these organizations in American society.

Of more recent vintage, separate Senate and House committees investigated alleged criminal activities committed during the Nixon administration, after burglars traced to the White House were arrested during a break-in of the Democratic National Committee headquarters at the Watergate complex in Washington, D.C. In 1987, a joint committee of Congress investigated the circumstances surrounding the Iran-contra affair.

Most congressional investigations lack such spectacular quality, but they are important nevertheless. A subcommittee of the House Committee on Interior and Insular Affairs, for instance, conducted an investigation into the enforcement of federal law by the Nuclear Regulatory Commission. Its findings were critical, as is indicated by the title of its report: *"NRC Coziness with Industry: Nuclear Regulatory Commission Fails to Maintain Arms' Length Relationship with the Nuclear Industry."*[164]

Review of Presidential Appointees. The importance of presidential appointment authority to presidential law enforcement power has already been discussed. Congress exercises an important restraint on presidential law enforcement power by saying (within constitutional limitations) which offices are subject to presidential appointment and what limitations are imposed on the presidential authority to remove commissioned appointees.

Congress also influences presidential appointment authority by specifying the appointments that must receive Senate confirmation before the appointees may take office. The only limitation on this legislative check on presidential law enforcement authority is that nominees to the U.S. Supreme Court must be considered and approved by the Senate—that is not a disabling condition.

Presidential appointees to law enforcement and judicial positions are regularly if not routinely approved by the Senate. Generally, the position of the Senate is that appointment, especially of the president's own subordinates in the executive branch, is the president's prerogative. Refusal to confirm must be based on considerations other than partisan or ideological differences. The reasons heard most often for failure of the Senate to confirm are unfitness for office due to questions of ethical or professional competence for the job.

Exceptions occur. In 1985, the Senate refused to confirm William Bradford Reynolds as President Reagan's appointee to associate attorney general. A sufficient number of senators were not satisfied that Reynolds had performed with sufficient vigor in his previous post, assistant attorney general in charge of the civil rights division.

The effect of Senate approval on presidential appointment power, however, cannot be measured solely by reference to the number of times the Senate refuses to confirm. Knowing that appointees must be examined and confirmed by the Senate may well cause the president to moderate appointments, at least on occasion. Moreover, knowing that nominees will be subjected to Senate scrutiny should cause the president to insist that backgrounds be subjected to searching investigation before names are announced and submitted. It does not always work that way.

Finally, Senate examination of presidential nominees, usually done in public hearings, may result in promises being made by the nominee to Congress. A notable instance was when the Senate Judiciary Committee exacted a promise from Elliot Richardson that if confirmed as attorney general, he would not fire the special prosecutor investigating the Watergate improprieties except for misconduct. Richardson was confirmed and kept his promise. He resigned rather than obey President Nixon's order to fire Archibald Cox, the special prosecutor.

Removal from Office through the Impeachment Process. The ultimate congressional check over executive law enforcement power is removal through impeachment. *(See "Impeachment," p. 367, in Removal of the President chapter of Part II.)* Article II, section 4, of the Constitution gives Congress power to remove from office the president, vice president, "and all civil Officers of the United States," upon impeachment for and conviction of "Treason, Bribery, or other high Crimes and Misdemeanors."

The removal process is conducted in two stages: impeachment and trial. The first stage, which is consigned by the Constitution to the House of Representatives, is concerned with whether probable cause exists to believe that misconduct warranting removal has occurred and that the accused is culpable.[165] Acting much like a grand jury in a criminal case, the House considers charges of misconduct, hears evidence concerning the alleged acts of misconduct, makes a preliminary determination of whether the alleged misconduct, if true, warrants removal, and whether the evidence supports the charges. If the House, by a majority vote, considers the allegations of misconduct sufficiently serious to warrant removal, and supported by the evidence, then it reports one or more articles of impeachment to the Senate for trial.

The House functions as a grand jury; the Senate acts much like a trial jury in a criminal case. Its function is to convict or acquit for each article of impeachment, based on evidence heard in a trial conducted in the Senate chambers. Guilt or innocence of the charges contained in the articles of impeachment is determined by a two-thirds vote of the senators present.[166]

Library of Congress

Only one president has been impeached to date—Andrew Johnson in 1868.

"Treason, Bribery, or other high Crimes and Misdemeanors," the constitutionally stated grounds for removal through the impeachment process, do not have a meaning that is agreed upon universally. Alexander Hamilton described the impeachment power as political, for it would be applied to persons committing "injuries done immediately to society itself." [167]

Such injuries, we may safely assume, would include the stated crimes of treason and bribery, as well as such criminal acts as murder, rape, and mayhem. But would they also include, as "high Crimes and Misdemeanors," conduct more in the nature of political misdeeds? Would they include, for example, a violation of the Constitution or a statute not providing criminal penalties? Would they include a *failure* to enforce the law?

Because of a paucity of precedent, no definitive answer can be given. Only one president has been impeached (that is, charged) to date. In 1868, President Andrew Johnson was charged by the House with violating the Tenure of Office Act of 1867.[168] The president was charged with violating his constitutional obligation to take care that the laws are executed faithfully by firing Edwin M. Stanton, his secretary of war, without cause or without prior Senate consent. The Senate, however, failed to muster the two-thirds vote necessary to convict Johnson—by one vote.

The precedent furnished by Johnson's ordeal is primarily negative. A narrow interpretation of the precedent would hold that the Senate merely confirmed that violation of the Tenure of Office Act, a legislative measure of dubious constitutional validity, did not constitute a sufficient basis for removal of the president.[169] A broader reading of the Senate's action would find significant the failure of the Senate to remove a president for what was really political incompatibility.

A more contemporary instance of the impeachment power being used against a president is furnished by the events leading to the resignation of President Nixon in 1974. In 1972, employees of the Committee to Re-elect the President, Nixon's personal campaign organization, were arrested by District of Columbia police during a burglary of the Democratic party headquarters in Washington's Watergate complex.

Investigations by local and federal law enforcement agencies, a federal grand jury, a Senate investigative committee, a special prosecutor, as well as newspaper and broadcast journalists, revealed evidence not only of involvement by high- and mid-level members and former members of the Nixon administration in the burglary but also of various other allegedly unlawful activities. An impeachment bill was introduced on the House floor and referred to the House Committee on the Judiciary.

Following televised hearings, the committee voted to recommend three articles of impeachment to the House. Each one of the three articles charged the president with violating his oath of office and his constitutional obligation to take care that the laws be faithfully executed. The three articles then enumerated specific allegations of misconduct, which, a majority of the committee believed, warranted Nixon's removal: obstruction of justice, abuse of power, abuse of individual rights, misprision (concealment) of felony, and failure to comply with congressional subpoenas.

Nixon was not impeached; that outcome was averted when he resigned from the office on August 9, 1974. Still, the committee action remains a powerful reminder that the removal power of Congress is not entirely dormant. The circumstances warranting its use must be serious, and the charges must be backed by compelling evidence—a "smoking gun" was the phrase often used by some committee members. But the power remains, and it can be used.

The Judiciary and the President. The essential American judicial function is to arbitrate and resolve legal disputes according to the law. In doing this, the judiciary both supports and checks presidential law enforcement authority. It also creates law enforcement opportunities and burdens for the president and makes law through the process of interpreting law.

Presidential law enforcement power is supported by the judiciary when judges lend legitimacy to presidential claims of law enforcement authority by declaring that those claims are in accord with the U.S. Constitution and laws of the United States. Such pronouncements usually settle any immediate disputes between the president and Congress or the states over the existence and extent of specific presidential law enforcement powers, and they offer reassurance to the American people that their president acted within the law.

The judiciary also supports presidential law enforcement power by invalidating efforts by other political actors, usually the Congress and states, to unduly restrict presidential authority.

Americans witnessed the first type of support for presidential power when the U.S. Supreme Court upheld assertions of presidential power to deploy military forces to suppress a domestic insurrection (the Civil War) and to quell strikes inhibiting interstate movement of railroads and delivery of the U.S. mail.[170] Similarly, the Supreme Court upheld presidential discretion to use U.S. marshals to maintain peace in situations neither contemplated nor prohibited by legislation.[171] The Court has protected the president from congressional interference with the power to grant pardons, reprieves, and amnesties.[172]

American judges, however, are an independent lot, constitutionally and in fact. They are not appointed to be mere supporters of the president, and they do not define their own roles in that manner. They have authority to check presidential claims of law enforcement power, and they have the power to make their own authority felt.

Presidential law enforcement authority is checked by the judiciary most often when judges rule against the government in civil or criminal cases. The ruling may be on an important interpretation of law, the admissibility in trial of a critical piece of evidence, or on the facts of the case. An assortment of judicial rulings can lead to the government losing. The result is the same.

When the rulings involve an interpretation of constitutionally or legislatively delegated authority of the president, then the effect may well limit the executive law enforcement capability in future cases as well as in the immediate case. Federal law enforcement agents know well, for example, that a confession obtained through coercion cannot be used as evidence in trial.

Notes

1. Clinton L. Rossiter, *The American Presidency*, 3d ed. (New York: Harcourt Brace Jovanovich, 1963).
2. Woodrow Wilson, *Congressional Government* (1885; reprint, New York: Meridian Books, 1956), 167-168, 170.
3. Peter Woll, *American Bureaucracy*, 2d ed. (New York: W. W. Norton, 1977), 63.
4. Alexander Hamilton, *Federalist* No. 72, in *The Federalist Papers* (New York: Tudor, 1937), 64.
5. Charles T. Goodsell, *The Case for Bureaucracy* (Chatham, N. J.: Chatham House, 1983), 2.
6. H. H. Gerth and C. Wright Mills, *From Max Weber* (New York: Oxford University Press, 1946), 196-199.
7. George J. Gordon, *Public Administration in America*, 2d ed. (New York: St. Martin's Press, 1982), 297.
8. Quoted in Robert Sherrill, *Why They Call It Politics*, 4th ed. (New York: Harcourt Brace Jovanovich, 1984), 260.
9. Michael Nelson, "The Irony of American Bureaucracy," in *Bureaucratic Power, in National Policy Making*, ed. Francis E. Rourke, 4th ed. (Boston: Little, Brown, 1986), 163-187.
10. Ibid., 169.
11. Sherrill, *Why They Call It Politics*, 259.
12. Quoted in ibid.
13. Quoted in Richard Neustadt, *Presidential Power* (New York: Wiley, 1960), 22.
14. Quoted in Mike Causey, "Trying to Activate Bureaucracy," *Washington Post*, May 30, 1972, B-9.
15. Arthur M. Schlesinger, Jr., *The Crisis of Confidence* (Boston: Houghton Mifflin, 1969), 291.
16. Richard M. Pious, *The American Presidency* (New York: Basic Books, 1979), 212.
17. Thomas E. Cronin, *The State of the Presidency*, 2d ed. (Boston: Little, Brown, 1980), 333.
18. Richard Rose, *Managing Presidential Objectives* (New York: Free Press, 1976), 23.
19. Rossiter, *American Presidency*, 129.
20. Stephen Hess, *Organizing the Presidency* (Washington, D.C.: Brookings, 1976), 10.
21. David Truman, *The Governmental Process* (New York: Knopf, 1951); Hess, *Organizing the Presidency*; George Reedy, *The Twilight of the Presidency* (New York: World, 1970).
22. Richard Rose, *Managing Presidential Objectives* (New York: Free Press, 1976), 147.
23. Cronin, *State of the Presidency*, 2d ed., 225.
24. Alexander Hamilton, *Federalist* No. 70, in *The Federalist Papers* (Tudor edition), 49-50.
25. McGeorge Bundy, *The Strength of Government* (Cambridge, Mass.: Harvard University Press, 1968), 37.
26. Woll, *American Bureaucracy*, 2d ed., 241.
27. Ibid., 240.
28. Executive Office of the President, President's Special Review Board 1987, *Report of the President's Special Review Board (Tower Commission Report)* (Washington, D.C.: Government Printing Office, 1987).
29. Anthony Downs, *Inside Bureaucracy* (Boston: Little, Brown, 1967), 116-118.

30. Arthur M. Schlesinger, Jr., *A Thousand Days: John F. Kennedy in the White House* (Boston: Houghton Mifflin, 1965), 683.
31. Cronin, *State of the Presidency,* 226.
32. Louis W. Koenig, *The Chief Executive* (New York: Harcourt Brace and World, 1968), 417.
33. Richard P. Nathan, *The Plot That Failed: Nixon and the Administrative Presidency* (New York: Wiley, 1975), 82.
34. "President Nixon Finds a Real Garbageman to Woo Garbagemen," *Wall Street Journal,* June 21, 1972, 1, 25.
35. Richard P. Nathan, "The Administrative Presidency," in *Bureaucratic Power,* 216. See also Richard P. Nathan, *The Administrative Presidency* (New York: Wiley, 1983.)
36. Dwight D. Eisenhower, *The White House Years: Mandate for Change, 1953-1956* (Garden City, N.Y.: Doubleday, 1963), 114.
37. Hess, *Organizing the Presidency,* 3.
38. Frank Kessler, *The Dilemmas of Presidential Leadership: Of Caretakers and Kings* (Englewood Cliffs, N.J.: Prentice-Hall, 1982), 60.
39. Hess, *Organizing the Presidency,* 3.
40. Quoted in Koenig, *Chief Executive,* 193.
41. Kessler, *Dilemmas of Presidential Leadership,* 72.
42. William Safire, *Before the Fall* (Garden City, N.Y.: Doubleday, 1975); and Henry Kissinger, *The White House Years* (Boston: Little, Brown, 1979).
43. *Congressional Quarterly Weekly Report,* July 21, 1979, 1432.
44. Colin Campbell, *Managing the Presidency: Carter, Reagan, and the Search for Executive Harmony* (Pittsburgh, Pa.: University of Pittsburgh Press, 1986), 61.
45. Kessler, *Dilemma of Presidential Leadership,* 68.
46. Quoted in Campbell, *Managing the Presidency,* 71.
47. Ibid.
48. *Tower Commission Report,* IV-10.
49. Woll, *American Bureaucracy,* 11.
50. Pious, *American Presidency,* 222.
51. Allen Schick, "Politics through Law: Congressional Limitations on Executive Discretion," in *Both Ends of the Avenue: The Presidency, the Executive Branch, and the Congress in the 1980s,* ed. Anthony King (Washington, D.C.: American Enterprise Institute, 1983), 176.
52. Pious, *American Presidency,* 224.
53. Thomas Franck and Edward Weisband, *Foreign Policy by Congress* (New York: Oxford University Press, 1979).
54. Pious, *American Presidency,* 229.
55. *Immigration and Naturalization Service v. Chadha,* 193 S. Ct. 2764 (1983).
56. Executive Office of the President, President's Committee on Administrative Management, *Hoover Commission Report* (Washington, D.C.: Government Printing Office, 1937), 5.
57. Ibid., 6-7.
58. Peri E. Arnold, *Making the Managerial President: Comprehensive Reorganization Planning, 1905-1980* (Princeton, N.J.: Princeton University Press, 1986), 114-115.
59. Commission on the Organization of the Executive Branch of Government, *General Management of the Executive Branch* (Washington, D.C.: Government Printing Office, 1949).
60. Ibid., 34.
61. Arnold, *Making the Managerial Presidency,* 159.
62. Ibid., 177-193.
63. Ibid., 277.
64. Tyrus G. Fain, ed., *Federal Reorganization: The Executive Branch,* Public Document Series (New York: R. R. Bowker, 1977), xxxi.
65. See, for example, Koenig, *Chief Executive,* Chapter 8.
66. James P. Pfiffner, "Strangers in a Strange Land: Orienting New Presidential Appointees," in *The In-and-Outers: Presidential Appointees and Transient Government in Washington,* ed. G. Calvin Mackenzie (Baltimore: Johns Hopkins University Press, 1987), 141. Total number of appointees is based on data from the Center for Excellence in Government, February 1989.
67. Hugh Heclo, *A Government of Strangers: Executive Politics in Washington* (Washington, D.C.: Brookings, 1977), 94.
68. Niccolo Machiavelli, *The Prince* (Harmondsworth, Middlesex, England: Penguin, 1961), 124.
69. Quoted in Schlesinger, *Thousand Days,* 127.
70. Pfiffner, "Strangers in a Strange Land," 142.
71. Richard F. Fenno, Jr., *The President's Cabinet* (New York: Vintage, 1958), 51.
72. G. Calvin Mackenzie, *The Politics of Presidential Appointments* (New York: Free Press, 1981), 6.
73. Cronin, *State of the Presidency,* 164.
74. U.S. Commission on Executive, Legislative, and Judicial Salaries, *Report of the Commission on Executive, Legislative, and Judicial Salaries* (Washington, D.C.: Government Printing Office, 1980), ix and 1.
75. Quoted in Dick Kirschten, "Why Not the Best?" *National Journal,* June 12, 1982, 1064.
76. Mackenzie, *Politics of Presidential Appointments,* 95.
77. Cronin, *State of the Presidency,* 165.
78. Christopher J. Deering, "Damned If You Do and Damned If You Don't: The Senate's Role in the Appointments Process," in *The In-and-Outers,* 119.
79. Ibid., 117.
80. Dom Bonafede, "The White House Personnel Office from Roosevelt to Reagan," in *Presidential Appointees,* 32.
81. John W. Macy, Bruce Adams, and J. Jackson Walter, *America's Unelected Government: Appointing the President's Team* (Cambridge, Mass.: Ballinger, 1983), 32.
82. Quoted in Edward D. Feigenbaum, "Staffing, Organization, and Decision-Making in the Ford and Carter White Houses," *Presidential Studies Quarterly* (Summer 1980): 371.
83. Bonafede, "White House Personnel."
84. Quoted in Ibid., 48.
85. Macy, Adams, and Walter, *America's Unelected Government,* 39.
86. Bonafede, "White House Personnel," 57.
87. *Meyers v. United States,* 272 U.S. 52 (1926).
88. Quoted in Woll, *American Bureaucracy,* 224.
89. *Humphrey's Executor v. United States,* 295 U.S. 602.
90. *Wiener v. United States,* 357 U.S. 349.
91. Pious, *American Presidency,* 256.
92. Lyndon Baines Johnson, *The Vantage Point* (New York: Holt, Rinehart and Winston, 1971), 34.
93. Lance T. LeLoup, "Fiscal Chief: Presidents and the Budgets," in *The Presidency: Studies in Policy Making,* ed. Stephen A. Shull and Lance T. LeLoup (Brunswick, Ohio: Kings Court, 1979), 211.
94. Johnson, *Vantage Point,* 36.
95. Lance T. LeLoup, *Budgetary Politics,* 2d ed. (Brunswick, Ohio: King's Court, 1980), 148.
96. Gerald Ford, "Budget Message of the President," *The Budget of the United States Government, Fiscal Year 1978* (Washington, D.C.: Government Printing Office, 1977), M-3.
97. Dennis S. Ippolito, *The Budget and National Politics* (San Francisco: Freeman, 1978), 40.
98. 42 Stat. 20, sec. 206.
99. Office of Management and Budget, *Preparation and Submission of 1977 "Current Services" Budget Estimates,* Bulletin No. 76-4 (Washington, D.C.: Government Printing Office, 1975), 1.
100. Howard E. Shuman, *Politics and the Budget: The Struggle Between the President and the Congress* (Englewood Cliffs, N.J.: Prentice-Hall, 1984), 225.
101. *Budget of the United States, Fiscal Year 1983: Major Themes and Additional Budget Details* (Washington, D.C.: Government Printing Office, 1982), 37.
102. LeLoup, *Budgetary Politics,* 271.
103. Quoted in Joel Haveman, "Zero-Base Budgeting," *National Journal,* April 2, 1977, 514.
104. Peter A. Pyhrr, *Zero-Base Budgeting: A Practical Management Tool for Evaluating Expenses* (New York: Wiley, 1973), 10.
105. Allen Schick, "The Road from ZBB," in *Contemporary Approaches to Public Budgeting,* ed. Fred A. Kramer (Cambridge, Mass.: Winthrop, 1979), 216.
106. Frank D. Draper and Bernard T. Pitsvada, "ZBB—Looking

Back After Ten Years," *Public Administration Review* 41 (January/February 1981): 77.
107. Aaron Wildavsky in *The Congressional Budget Process After Five Years,* ed. Rudolph G. Penner (Washington, D.C.: American Enterprise Institute, 1981), 99.
108. Shuman, *Politics and the Budget,* 287.
109. Pious, *American Presidency,* 272.
110. Shuman, *Politics and the Budget,* 60.
111. *New York Times,* February 10, 1982, A1.
112. Louis Fisher, *Presidential Spending Power* (Princeton, N.J.: Princeton University Press, 1975), 7.
113. Pious, *American Presidency,* 278.
114. Fisher, *Presidential Spending Power,* 207.
115. 88 Statute 1804, sec. 32 (1974).
116. Ippolito, *Budget and National Politics,* 135.
117. Quoted in Pious, *American Presidency,* 278.
118. Ippolito, *Budget and National Politics,* 138-139.
119. *Train v. City of New York,* 420 U.S. 35.
120. John Ellwood and James Thurber, "The Congressional Budget Process Re-examined," in *Congress Reconsidered,* 2d ed., ed. Lawrence C. Dodd and Bruce I. Oppenheimer (Washington, D.C.: CQ Press, 1981), 266.
121. Letter of John Marshall to James Wilkinson, January 5, 1787, reprinted in *The Papers of John Marshall, 1775-1788,* vol. 1, ed. Herbert A. Johnson (Chapel Hill: University of North Carolina Press, 1974), 200.
122. Samuel Eliot Morison, Henry Steele Commager, and William E. Leuchtenburg, *The Growth of the American Republic,* vol. 1 (New York: Oxford University Press, 1969), 242. See generally this volume, pp. 227-261, for a description of the events immediately preceding and occurring during the Constitutional Convention.
123. U.S. Constitution, preamble.
124. See generally U.S. Constitution, Article II, for an enumeration of presidential powers.
125. The U.S. Constitution does, in Article I, section 8, give Congress authority to "pay the Debts and provide for ... the general Welfare of the United States." This is interpreted as a grant of authority for Congress to *spend money* to promote the general welfare of the nation. It is *not* interpreted as a grant of authority to enact any regulatory scheme it feels will promote the general welfare.
126. *McCulloch v. Maryland,* 17 U.S. (4 Wheat.) 316 (1819).
127. *Gibbons v. Ogden,* 22 U.S. (9 Wheat.) 1 (1824).
128. *Wickard v. Filburn,* 317 U.S. 111 (1942).
129. What, for example, is the relationship between home-grown food for purely household consumption and interstate commerce? The Supreme Court gave its answer in *Wickard v. Filburn*: If a household grows and harvests food on its own land, and for its own use, then it will be less likely to purchase food products on the commercial market. The effects of this isolated instance of self-sufficiency will be felt eventually across state lines.
130. U.S. Department of Commerce, Bureau of Census, *Historical Statistics of the United States: Colonial Times to 1970,* vol. 2 (Washington, D.C.: Government Printing Office, 1975), table Y 308-317, pp. 1102-1103; and U.S. Department of Commerce, Bureau of Census, *Statistical Abstract of the United States,* 108th ed. (Washington, D.C.: Government Printing Office, 1987), table 494, p. 307.
131. Accounts of the "Ole Miss" incident may be found in Schlesinger, *A Thousand Days,* and Theodore C. Sorensen, *Kennedy* (New York: Harper and Row, 1965).
132. U.S. Constitution, Article I, section 9.
133. The most famous discussion of this distinction is found in Chief Justice John Marshall's opinion for the U.S. Supreme Court in *Marbury v. Madison,* 5 U.S. (1 Cranch) 137 (1803).
134. *Myers v. United States,* 272 U.S. 52, 177 (1926).
135. See, for example, *Kendall v. United States,* 37 U.S. (12 Pet.) 524 (1838); *Youngstown Sheet and Tube Co. v. Sawyer,* 343 U.S. 579 (1952) (also known as the *Steel Seizure Case*); and *United States v. Nixon,* 418 U.S. 683 (1974).
136. *In re Neagle,* 135 U.S. 1 (1890).
137. *In re Debs,* 158 U.S. 564 (1895).
138. *Myers v. United States.*
139. *Wiener v. United States,* 357 U.S. 349 (1958); and *Humphrey's Executor v. United States,* 295 U.S. 602 (1935).
140. U.S. Constitution, Article III, section 1.
141. U.S. Constitution, Article I, section 8.
142. *In re Debs,* 158 U.S. 564, 582 (1895).
143. *Ex parte Milligan,* 71 U.S. (4 Wall.) 2 (1866).
144. Alexander Hamilton, *Federalist* No. 74, in *The Federalist Papers* (New York: Mentor, 1961), 449.
145. Ibid., 448.
146. Proclamation of September 15, 1792, George Washington, *Messages and Papers of the Presidents, 1789-1897,* vol. I, ed. James D. Richardson (Washington, D.C.: Government Printing Office, 1897), 124-125.
147. See Proclamation of July 10, 1795, George Washington, in ibid., 181.
148. *Ex parte Garland,* 71 U.S. (4 Wall.) 333 (1866). See generally *Schick v. Reed,* 419 U.S. 256 (1974).
149. *Wiener v. United States* and *Humphrey's Executor v. United States.*
150. Executive Order 11365, July 29, 1967.
151. Kerner was later rewarded by the president with appointment to the U.S. Court of Appeals for the Seventh Circuit. The judge resigned after being indicted and convicted of a felony.
152. Office of the President, National Advisory Commission on Civil Disorders, *Report of the National Advisory Commission on Civil Disorders* (Washington, D.C.: Government Printing Office, 1968).
153. Employment and budget data in this section are taken from Office of the President, Office of Management and Budget, *Appendix: Budget of the U.S. Government—Fiscal Year 1989* (Washington, D.C.: Government Printing Office, 1988).
154. Office of the President, Office of Management and Budget, *Appendix, Budget of the U.S. Government* (Washington, D.C.: Government Printing Office, 1988), I-06.
155. *McCulloch v. Maryland.*
156. *Gibbons v. Ogden,* 22 U.S. (9 Wheat.) 1 (1824).
157. *Martin v. Hunter's Lessee,* 14 U.S. (1 Wheat.) 304 (1816); *Cohens v. Virginia,* 19 U.S. (6 Wheat.) 264 (1821).
158. Congress has constitutional authority, no doubt, to impose a national speed limit on interstate highways. Despite popular impressions to the contrary, it does not do so. Congress, rather, coerces states that receive federal highway assistance to agree to impose and enforce a sixty-five-mile-per-hour limit. The same thing has occurred with respect to the twenty-one-year-old drinking age: if states want federal highway funds, they must agree to a state drinking age of at least twenty-one.
159. 18 United States Code, section 3056 (a) and (b).
160. 18 United States Code, section 3052.
161. See 18 United States Code, section 3053 (U.S. marshals); 18 United States Code, section 3056 (Secret Service); and 21 United States Code, section 878 (Drug Enforcement Administration).
162. 18 United States Code, section 3061 (a) (2).
163. 18 United States Code, section 3061 (b).
164. U.S. Congress, House, Committee on Interior and Insular Affairs, Subcommittee on General Oversight and Investigations, *NRC Coziness with Industry: Nuclear Regulatory Commission Fails to Maintain Arms' Length Relationship with the Nuclear Industry,* Committee Print No. 5, 100th Cong., 1st sess., 1987.
165. U.S. Constitution, Article I, section 2.
166. U.S. Constitution, Article I, section 3.
167. Hamilton, *Federalist* No. 65, in *The Federalist Papers* (Mentor edition), 396.
168. 14 Stat. 430 (1867)
169. Compare *Myers v. United States.*
170. *The Prize Cases,* 67 U.S. (2 Black) 635 (1863); *In re Debs.*
171. *In re Neagle.*
172. *Ex parte Garland.*

Selected Bibliography

Arnold, Peri E. *Making the Managerial President: Comprehensive Reorganization Planning, 1905-1980.* Princeton: Princeton University Press, 1986.

Bundy, McGeorge. *The Strength of Government.* Cambridge: Harvard University Press, 1968.

Campbell, Colin. *Managing the Presidency: Carter, Reagan, and the Search for Executive Harmony.* Pittsburgh: University of Pittsburgh Press, 1986.

Cronin, Thomas E. *The State of the Presidency.* 2d ed. Boston: Little, Brown, 1980.

Dodd, Lawrence C., and Richard L. Schott. *Congress and the Administrative State.* New York: Wiley, 1979.

Fain, Tyrus G., ed. *Federal Reorganization: The Executive Branch.* Public Document Series. New York: Bowker, 1977.

Fenno, Richard F., Jr. *The President's Cabinet.* New York: Vintage, 1958.

Heclo, Hugh. *A Government of Strangers: Executive Politics in Washington.* Washington, D.C.: Brookings, 1977.

Hess, Stephen. *Organizing the Presidency.* Washington, D.C.: Brookings, 1976.

Ippolito, Dennis S. *The Budget and National Politics.* San Francisco: Freeman, 1978.

Koenig, Louis W. *The Chief Executive.* New York: Harcourt Brace and Jovanovich, 1968.

Kramer, Fred A. *Contemporary Approaches to Public Budgeting.* Cambridge: Winthrop, 1979.

LeLoup, Lance T. *Budgetary Politics.* 2d ed. Brunswick, Ohio: King's Court, 1980.

Mackenzie, G. Calvin, ed. *The In-and-Outers: Presidential Appointees and Transient Government in Washington.* Baltimore: Johns Hopkins University Press, 1987.

———. *The Politics of Presidential Appointments.* New York: Free Press, 1981.

Macy, John W., Bruce Adams, and J. Jackson Walter. *America's Unelected Government: Appointing the President's Team.* Cambridge: Ballinger, 1983.

Nathan, Richard P. *The Administrative Presidency.* New York: Wiley, 1983.

Rossiter, Clinton L. *The American Presidency.* 3d ed. New York: Harcourt Brace Jovanovich, 1963.

Rourke, Francis E., ed. *Bureaucratic Power in National Policy Making,* 4th ed. Boston: Little, Brown, 1986.

Legislative Leader

The U.S. constitutional system created by the Framers "blends" power among the three branches of government. The Framers made the legislative branch—the U.S. Congress—dominant in formulating law, for they believed that the legislature most accurately reflects mass opinion. By contrast, they limited the president's ability to influence legislation to two "express" powers: the duty to recommend to Congress any measure deemed "necessary and expedient" (Article II, section 3) and, more important, the power to approve or to veto a bill passed by Congress (Article I, section 7). Presidents also gained the power to negotiate treaties, which become law when "two-thirds of the Senators present concur" (Article II, section 2), and to convene "emergency" sessions of Congress (Article II, section 3). But these are extraordinary events.

The Constitution is remarkably reticent about the president's role in legislating, yet the relationship between Congress and the executive is the most important aspect of the U.S. system of governance. Two hundred years of history have seen an immeasurable and fundamental expansion in the array of resources (such as staff and technical expertise) and powers that presidents can use to influence public policy.

Some of these powers were "implied" in the Constitution, awaiting only time and, perhaps, judicial interpretation as new and unforeseen cases arose. Others were delegated by Congress to meet changing economic or social circumstances, emerging government responsibilities, or new public demands. Still more presidential power has arisen from new technologies, like television, or new international responsibilities for the United States, like the defense of Western Europe since the end of World War II. The formal brevity of the executive's role in legislating thus masks the considerable influence that presidents wield over the congressional agenda and the direction of public policy.

Even with the remarkable expansion in the size and power of the executive branch, a modern president's relationship with Congress remains fluid, ambiguous, and frustrating. Much of what presidents want still requires new laws, congressional appropriations, or senatorial approval of appointees or treaties. The president *needs* Congress, but the legislature so often proves stubbornly independent, uncooperative, or even hostile that residents of the White House rarely can take congressional support for granted.

By Christopher J. Bosso

The Veto

Perhaps the chief legal weapon the president possesses is the veto, the ability to block acts passed by Congress that finds its origins in the 1787 debate over the Constitution.

Constitutional Foundations

Those who wrote the Constitution are revered for their efforts at creating a national government that, above all, sought to safeguard the rights and liberties of both the people and the states. We thus recognize today the enduring importance of the web of checks and balances woven into a system of separate institutions sharing government power, characteristics designed primarily to prevent any single branch (and, by extension, any single individual or group) from wielding potentially tyrannical political power.

Virtually every schoolchild knows well the colonists' complaints against King George III and their subsequent fear of powerful executives. Yet, lost too often in textbook treatments of the Constitution was the Framers' equal dread of unchecked legislative power. After all, Thomas Jefferson's second villain in the Declaration of Independence was the English Parliament, a legislature unobstructed by formal constitutional limits and loathed widely in the colonies for its apparent disregard for due process of law. In addition, the leaders of the new nation met in 1787 expressly because of failures widely seen in the Articles of Confederation (written in 1781), which essentially was a league of friendship among the thirteen states. *(See "Articles of Confederation," p. 1353, in the Appendix.)* Because the national government under the articles largely was a creature of the states, and dependent on them for its powers and funds, it proved unable to promote either national unity or effective government.

Another common concern was that the articles provided for no independent national executive, one strong enough to administer the laws and resist legislative tyranny.[1] State legislatures almost without exception dominated governors and were seen by many delegates at the Constitutional Convention as being as dangerous to liberty as unrestrained monarchs. Jefferson, reflecting on his experiences as governor of Virginia, wrote, "All the powers of government ... result to the legislative body. The con-

> He shall, from time to time, give to the Congress information of the state of the union, and recommend to their consideration such measures as he shall judge necessary and expedient....
>
> —from Article II, section 3

centrating of these in the same hands is precisely the definition of despotic government."[2] These experiences were shared by a number of those present at the convention, and it was clear that the new national executive would need some way to check legislative power.

The concept of a *veto* (Latin for "I forbid") was nothing new to the Framers. Indeed, it was as old as ancient Rome, where it was used by the plebeians to protect the common people against the excesses of a senate dominated by aristocrats. It later emerged in medieval Europe as a royal check on newly developing legislatures. In England, for example, the monarch retained the absolute power to deny acts by Parliament, a weapon that Queen Elizabeth I used quite frequently.[3] Finally, and closer to home, a few state constitutions (such as that of Massachusetts) contained some form of executive veto, but the veto was not a widespread practice.

Thus armed with precedence and spurred on by fear of a rapacious legislature, the Framers moved to include some form of executive check on laws passed by Congress in virtually every plan for the new constitution. The Virginia Plan, for example, called for a "council of revision" made up of members of the executive and the judiciary that would prevent the legislature from drawing "all power into its impetuous vortex."[4] George Mason argued that this type of plural veto would be too weak, since disputes within the council would undermine decisive executive action. Furthermore, Mason continued, the veto should be more than a mere defense against legislative intrusion. Instead, it was necessary to discourage demagogy and prevent "unjust and pernicious" laws.[5] Others attending the convention also were uncomfortable with having judges act on bills before they came up as legal cases, so the veto eventually was confined to the president alone.

Some, including Alexander Hamilton, initially supported an absolute veto, giving Congress no opportunity to respond, but such a weapon seemed too powerful to delegates also worried about unresponsive and capricious executives. After much debate, the Framers instituted a "partial negative" whereby the president could reject bills or joint resolutions passed by Congress (excluding constitutional amendments, concurrent resolutions, or resolutions passed by only one chamber),[6] but which legislature could override by extraordinary majorities of two-thirds of the members present in each chamber.

The veto was destined to be the constitutional core of executive independence. As defended during the battle over ratification by Alexander Hamilton in *Federalist* No. 73, "the primary inducement to confering this power in question upon the executive is to enable him to defend himself; the second one is to increase the chances in favor of the community against the passing of bad laws, through haste, inadvertence, or design."[7] The legislature is not infallible, Hamilton argued, and, unless checked, its love of power would ultimately betray both it and the ability of government to function effectively. Additionally, argued James Madison in *Federalist* No. 48, only by giving each branch some control over the others could power be restrained and rights and liberties protected—a theme he continued in No. 51 with his famous statement, "Ambition must be made to counteract ambition."[8]

Those opposed to the veto included such Anti-Federalists as Thomas Jefferson, who, despite his concerns about potentials for abuse of legislative power, argued ardently that Congress alone represented the people. The veto, Jefferson argued might undermine democratic values by allowing the president to block "good" laws, and opponents viewed the device simply as a means to thwart majority rule. But, Hamilton retorted in *Federalist* No. 73, unrestrained majorities are equally as dangerous as unchecked elites, and "the injury which might possibly be done by defeating a few good laws will be amply compensated by the advantage of preventing a number of bad ones."[9] What is more, allowing the executive to threaten a veto might induce legislative moderation, making actual use of the veto unnecessary.

The Constitution thus gives the president three choices upon being presented with legislation passed by Congress:[10] approve and sign the bill into law; veto the bill by returning it to the chamber where it originated within ten days of passage (Sundays excluded); or, finally, do nothing. If the president does nothing, the bill becomes law after ten days to prevent presidents from killing legislation, and thus thwart the majority will, through simple inaction. The exception to this rule occurs when Congress presents a bill and then adjourns before the required ten days elapse, for any bill not signed by the president when Congress adjourns dies automatically. This procedure is called a *pocket veto*. *(The pocket veto is discussed later in this section on veto power.)*

If the president vetoes a bill, returns it to Congress, and the legislature fails to respond, the bill dies. If two-thirds of the members present *in each house* pass the vetoed bill once again, however, it becomes law despite presidential disapproval.[11] Such overwhelming majorities combine to produce an *override*. Veto overrides are rare (between 1789 and 1988 only 100 of 2,475 presidential vetoes were overridden), because to sustain a veto the president needs to gain only one-third plus one of the votes in either chamber. *(See Table 1.)* Barring an override, Congress either can rewrite the legislation to meet presidential demands (as Hamilton foresaw) or simply can give it up.

Bills vetoed by the president normally are sent back to Congress accompanied by a message stating the reasons for the president's opposition. *(See box, A Veto Message, p. 454.)* Sometimes the reasons given cite constitutional problems, at other times political or issue differences between the branches, but at all times veto messages are aimed at

> Every bill which shall have passed the House of Representatives and the Senate, shall, before it become a law, be presented to the president of the United States; if he approve, he shall sign it, but if not, he shall return it, with his objections, to that house in which it shall have originated who shall ... proceed to reconsider it.
>
> —from Article I, section 7

pressing the president's views on the bills in question. Whatever their other purposes, veto messages are political statements and are directed not only toward Congress but to the public at large. In this sense, then, the messages become additional resources in the president's effort to influence public policy.

Historical Development

Early presidents conformed with the prevailing view that Congress best represented the public will and thus confined vetoes to bills deemed unconstitutional. The notion that a president should veto a bill simply because it was "bad" was not yet widely accepted. Indeed, the first six presidents issued few regular vetoes between 1790 and 1830 and in most instances did so on constitutional grounds.

This narrow interpretation of the president's right (and, perhaps, duty) to use the veto underwent significant redefinition during the tenure of Andrew Jackson (1829-1837)—hero of the War of 1812, keen foe of Eastern business and banking interests, and self-styled "Tribune of the People." Jackson was a strong party loyalist who quickly entered into warfare with his congressional foes, and the veto in his hands became an instrument of political as well as constitutional power. In eight years Jackson issued twelve vetoes, more than his predecessors combined, and none of them was overridden. Perhaps most controversial was his 1832 rejection of a bill rechartering the Bank of the United States, which was opposed bitterly by frontier settlers and farmers hurt by its high interest rates. As political scientist Clinton Rossiter suggested, Jackson "revived the veto and purified it of the niceties that had grown up around it" by making it an overtly political instrument.[12]

Whig presidents after Jackson, while professing allegiance to their party's doctrine of congressional supremacy, also proved surprisingly resolute when challenged by the legislature. John Tyler (1841-1845), for example, vetoed two major bank bills supported by his own party, and his 1843 veto of a controversial tariff measure sparked the first formal attempt in Congress to impeach a president. That effort failed, and Tyler's successors showed equally notable bursts of independence. Even so, only fifty-nine bills were vetoed between 1789 and 1865, more than half of them during the terms of Presidents Jackson, Tyler, and Franklin Pierce (1853-1857).

Table 1 Vetoes and Vetoes Overridden, All Bills, 1789-1988

President	All bills vetoed	Regular vetoes	Pocket vetoes	Vetoes overridden
Washington	2	2	0	0
J. Adams	0	0	0	0
Jefferson	0	0	0	0
Madison	7	5	2	0
Monroe	1	1	0	0
J. Q. Adams	0	0	0	0
Jackson	12	5	7	0
Van Buren	1	0	1	0
W. H. Harrison	0	0	0	0
Tyler	10	6	4	1
Polk	3	2	1	0
Taylor	0	0	0	0
Fillmore	0	0	0	0
Pierce	9	9	0	5
Buchanan	7	4	3	0
Lincoln	7	2	5	0
A. Johnson	29	21	8	15
Grant	93[a]	45	48[a]	4
Hayes	13	12	1	1
Garfield	0	0	0	0
Arthur	12	4	8	1
Cleveland (1st term)	414	304	110	2
B. Harrison	44	19	25	1
Cleveland (2d term)	170	42	128	5
McKinley	42	6	36	0
T. Roosevelt	82	42	40	1
Taft	39	30	9	1
Wilson	44	33	11	6
Harding	6	5	1	0
Coolidge	50	20	30	4
Hoover	37	21	16	3
F. Roosevelt	635	372	263	9
Truman	258	191	67	12
Eisenhower	188	79	109	2
Kennedy	21	12	9	0
L. Johnson	29	18	11	0
Nixon	43	24	19[b]	5
Ford	68	49	19	12
Carter	31	13	18	2
Reagan	68	41	27	8
Total	2,475	1,439	1,036	100

Sources: Guide to Congress, 3d ed. (Washington, D.C.: Congressional Quarterly Inc., 1982), 763; *Congressional Quarterly Weekly Report,* various issues.

a. Veto total listed for Grant does not include a pocket veto of a bill that apparently never was placed before him for his signature.

b. Includes Nixon's pocket veto of a bill during the 1970 congressional Christmas recess later that was ruled invalid by the federal courts.

Post-Civil War Era

Presidents and Congress after Abraham Lincoln (1861-1865) clashed increasingly within a national political arena rife with sharp regional and partisan antagonisms, dramatic social and economic changes, and disputes over the proper role of government. This era, although marked generally by congressional dominance, nonetheless saw stark surges in presidential use of the veto as successive executives attempted to grapple with massive numbers of bills spawned by an often antagonistic Congress. The period between the Civil War and the late 1890s saw some of history's keenest partisan battles, which often spilled over into conflict between the branches of government.

Andrew Johnson (1865-1869), for example, wrestled strenuously with Congress immediately after the Civil War and became the first president whose veto of an important bill was overridden. Among all presidents, Johnson in fact had the greatest percentage of regular vetoes overturned by Congress (fifteen out of twenty-one, or 71 percent). So acrid was the antipathy between the branches that Johnson's refusal to abide by the Tenure of Office Act, a law passed over his veto that forbade presidents from firing political appointees without congressional approval, led directly to his impeachment by the House. Johnson was acquitted in the Senate by only one vote, and the Tenure of Office Act (which many constitutional scholars later viewed as unconstitutional) was repealed in 1887.[13]

Table 2 Private Bills Vetoed, 1789-1988

President	Regular vetoes	Pocket vetoes	Vetoes overridden
Washington	0	0	0
J. Adams	0	0	0
Jefferson	0	0	0
Madison	2	0	0
Monroe	0	0	0
J. Q. Adams	0	0	0
Jackson	0	0	0
Van Buren	0	1	0
W. H. Harrison	0	0	0
Tyler	0	0	0
Polk	0	0	0
Taylor	0	0	0
Fillmore	0	0	0
Pierce	0	0	0
Buchanan	2	0	0
Lincoln	0	1	0
A. Johnson	0	2	0
Grant	29	37	3
Hayes	1	0	0
Garfield	0	0	0
Arthur	1	8	0
Cleveland (1st term)	271	82	1
B. Harrison	5	23	9
Cleveland (2d term)	30	99	2
McKinley	4	32	0
T. Roosevelt	27	31	0
Taft	10	7	0
Wilson	7	2	0
Harding	3	0	0
Coolidge	3	17	0
Hoover	4	6	0
F. Roosevelt	317	180	0
Truman	137	38	1
Eisenhower	43	64	0
Kennedy	8	4	0
L. Johnson	12	4	0
Nixon	0	3	0
Ford	3	2	0
Carter	0	2	0
Reagan	7	5	0
Total	926	650	16

Sources: Guide to Congress, 3d ed. (Washington, D.C.: Congressional Quarterly Inc., 1982), 357; *Congressional Quarterly Weekly Report,* various issues.

Note: The official distinction between public and private bills was rather hazy through the 1930s, although private bills generally were classified as those benefiting a single individual rather than a large segment of society (for example, a private pension bill). Beginning in 1936, however, a Library of Congress publication has listed all private bills.

Johnson's experiences aside, most of the vetoes produced during the rest of the nineteenth century were aimed at "private" bills, actions by Congress that benefited specific individuals, companies, or municipalities. *(See Table 2.)* Most private bills during the late 1800s provided pensions for Civil War veterans, but many were fraudulent or excessive claims that often were passed late in the congressional session. Grover Cleveland (1885-1889, 1893-1897) vetoed 482 private bills during his eight years in office—43 during one three-day period in 1886 alone.[14] Many were through the use of pocket vetoes, and only three of Cleveland's vetoes of private bills were overridden.

Modern Presidents

Franklin D. Roosevelt (1933-1945) used the veto more vigorously than any other president, was the first to use it against major tax legislation, and crafted the threat of the veto into his legislative strategy. Roosevelt in many ways created the modern presidency, and the veto became yet another instrument of executive influence within an environment of expansive government action and power.

His influence on the presidency endures, particularly because contemporary U.S. government so often is marked by split partisan control over the White House and Congress. *(See table, Party Affiliations in Congress and the Presidency, 1789-1989, p. 1453, in the Appendix.)* Vetoes have been used most frequently when such partisan splits occur. Harry S Truman (1945-1953), for example, in 1947 vetoed the controversial Taft-Hartley Labor Act, a bill the Republican-dominated Congress passed to restrain the power of labor unions. Truman subsequently used congressional overrides of this and other vetoes to great political effect in rallying voters to the Democrats in the 1948 presidential and congressional elections.

Republican president Dwight D. Eisenhower (1953-1961) wrestled with a Congress dominated by Democrats during all but two of his eight years in office. He used the veto often to stop liberal social programs and relied heavily on a "conservative coalition" of congressional Republicans and southern Democrats for support against overrides. One notable case occurred in 1959 when Eisenhower squared off against congressional Democrats intent on pushing a new domestic agenda. Eisenhower's veto warnings went unheeded, but the conservative coalition in Congress held fast throughout the year to sustain successive vetoes against new spending for urban housing, rural electrification, and other domestic programs. Threats of further vetoes persuaded Democrats to cut back drastically on their efforts.[15]

Democrats John F. Kennedy (1961-1963) and Lyndon B. Johnson (1963-1969), blessed with friendly majorities in Congress, seldom used the veto, but Republicans Richard Nixon (1969-1974) and Gerald R. Ford (1974-1977) fared differently. Both Nixon and Ford faced off against Democratic Congresses, so the veto by necessity became central to their legislation strategies. Nixon issued several vetoes on major bills he deemed inflationary and even appeared on national television to veto a massive appropriations bill. As when Eisenhower was in office, the conservative coalition in Congress often proved large enough to derail override attempts.

Because the success of the veto is inextricably tied to a president's overall "strength," Nixon's political troubles eventually weakened his national popularity and influence within Congress. In 1973, for example, a resurgent Congress soundly overrode his veto of the War Powers Resolution, an act aimed at limiting presidential ability to commit U.S. armed forces abroad without congressional approval. Congress also overrode Nixon's veto of the 1974 Budget Impoundment and Control Act, which he opposed because it limited presidential ability *not* to spend funds appropriated by Congress. *(See discussion of item veto later in this section on veto power.)*

Ford, who became president after Nixon's resignation

August 9, 1974, used the veto frequently and to great effect. Despite facing a Congress strongly controlled by Democrats, Ford was sustained on all but four of the seventeen vetoes issued in 1975 alone. Ford also used the threat of a veto to derail a consumer protection bill popular in both chambers. His experience showed how the veto can be used to compensate partially for the severe political weakness of being an unelected chief executive succeeding a disgraced president.

Jimmy Carter (1977-1981), like Kennedy and Johnson, relied on the veto less frequently because his fellow Democrats dominated Congress. A notable exception was his rejection of a 1977 energy research bill, a $6 billion authorization measure that Carter successfully opposed because it included funds for a nuclear breeder reactor he thought dangerous and too expensive.[16] Carter was not challenged on that veto, but in 1980 he became the first president since Harry Truman to suffer an override at the hands of his own party.[17] Carter had vetoed a bill to limit the national debt because it contained a provision eliminating import fees on foreign oil. He lost this time, however, because the fees were widely unpopular and, perhaps, because members of Congress were emboldened by the apparent weakening of Carter's public support as the Iran hostage situation dragged on.

The experiences of Ronald Reagan (1981-1989) in many ways mirrored those of Nixon, although Reagan for one term faced a Congress itself split between a Republican Senate and a Democratic House. Like Nixon, Reagan vetoed major spending bills contrary to his program and often warned, "my veto pen is inked up and ready to go," when Congress was on the brink of passing legislation he opposed.[18] Reagan's great popularity with the voters in his first term often was enough to deter congressional action, and his veto of a 1981 continuing appropriations bill proved so potent that Congress reworked the measure to his satisfaction. Reagan found it harder to make veto threats work to his advantage, however, after Democrats regained full control over Congress in the 1986 elections. Indeed, Congress in early 1987 easily overrode his vetoes of major water pollution and highway bills, signaling to many a shift in the president's influence over national policy. *(See box, A Veto Message, p. 454.)*

An Instrument of Presidential Power

James Bryce, the nineteenth-century English observer of U.S. government, argued that the veto "conveys the impression of firmness."[19] Contemporary scholars of the presidency agree with Bryce only to a point, since most view the veto as both a clumsy instrument of executive power and one whose frequent use displays political weakness, not strength.[20] Thomas Cronin, a political scientist who long has studied the presidency, has argued simply that to see the veto as a tool of "strong presidents" is illusory, since presidents historically have used vetoes predominantly against private bills and seldom have vetoed major tax and appropriations measures.[21] Another scholar of the presidency, George Edwards III, added that the veto is a negative instrument, good for stopping unwanted legislation, but once used, it indicates largely that the president has failed to sway Congress from its course.[22] Having a veto overridden underscores a president's relative political weakness, particularly if Congress is dominated by the president's own party.

In discussions of the veto's strength, Ford's frequent use of the device is often mentioned because scholars of the presidency think he was dealt the weakest political hand of any modern president. After succeeding Nixon, he faced a fiercely independent Congress dominated by liberal Democrats. To defend his prerogatives, he used the veto more frequently than any other twentieth-century president because political circumstances gave him no option. That so many of his vetoes were sustained within a largely hostile Congress suggests the raw power of the veto to stop legislation.

The experiences of other presidents buttress this view. Harry Truman's crafty use of the veto as a political weapon against congressional Republicans did not hide the fact that he often lost important override battles. Ronald Reagan's defeat in successive override episodes during early 1987 emphasized his weakening leverage in light of renewed Democratic dominance in Congress and his own troubles over secret arms sales to Iran. In sum, the veto more often than not is the weapon of last resort, to be used when all other attempts at persuasion fail.

When presidents veto legislation, the move may be viewed as a sign of relative weakness; but when they successfully head off unwanted legislation by *threatening* to use the veto, the tactic is seen as an indicator of presidential strength. Veto threats are useful bargaining tools in the hands of a popular and wily executive. Presidential scholars often point to Franklin Roosevelt, who was known to beg his aides to "find something I can veto" as both a lesson and a reminder to Congress of his potential power.[23] The strength of Ronald Reagan's public popularity during his first term more than once allowed him to challenge Congress with the veto and successfully get legislation reworked to his liking. Even Gerald Ford, despite his problems, effectively used the threat of a veto to deter legislation, although he did so when Congress was about to adjourn.

Congress, however, finds ways to undermine vetoes or threats of vetoes made by even popular presidents. Because the president cannot veto parts of a bill, members of Congress many times will load up major legislation with amendments on a completely different subject (known as "riders") or with pet spending programs that they know the president must accept to ensure passage. To make matters more complicated, Congress in recent years has relied on massive omnibus (or "catch-all") bills to pass the budget, to appropriate funds, and to levy new taxes simultaneously. Ronald Reagan several times had to accept omnibus bills containing programs or provisions he detested simply because he needed other spending contained in the same bill. A prime example was the Boland Amendment, a provision restricting U.S. aid to the rebels opposing the Nicaraguan government, which was tacked onto a 1984 appropriations bill.

Congress also tends to wait until late in each session to pass critical spending bills, which narrows the president's range of possible responses because a veto may not be feasible if Congress has adjourned and the funds needed to run the federal government are contained in the legislation.

Finally, a president cannot totally rely on fellow party members in Congress for support on veto threats, or even during override battles, since most members resist being seen by their constituents as mere rubber stamps for the president's wishes. This is true especially when the bill in question benefits a member's district or state, as when Congress overrode Reagan's vetoes on water treatment and

A Veto Message

A bill passed by Congress is formally vetoed when the president returns it to Capitol Hill unsigned and accompanied by a message stating the reasons for executive opposition. Presidents today rarely write their own veto messages. Instead, the messages typically are composed by professional staff assistants in the Executive Office of the President, often with input from experts in the Office and Management and Budget (OMB) or other executive branch agencies. The president may scan the final draft, and on occasion may pen major parts of controversial veto messages, but the overall process of rebuffing Congress on a piece of legislation largely is a collective one.

Whether the reasons given for a veto are constitutional, fiscal, substantive, or "merely" political—or a combination of reasons—a veto message is designed with more than Congress in mind. In today's media-saturated political atmosphere, any message from the White House to Congress is scrutinized closely for its potential political ramifications. Veto messages thus are crafted carefully, designed above all to sell the president's views on a bill to national opinion makers and to the public, not simply to Congress.

Most veto messages are signed in the relative privacy of the Oval Office and sent by courier to Capitol Hill. They then are delivered to the chamber from whence the bills in question originated, which normally takes the lead in any efforts to override the veto. On vetoes of major bills, however, a president may use the opportunity to convene a public ceremony, complete with supporters and members of the national press, to attack the bill and to generate public sentiment against Congress.

In the following excerpt, President Ronald Reagan explained his objections to amendments to the Clean Water Act passed by Congress in January 1987. Despite Reagan's opposition, however, Congress easily overrode the president's veto by large bipartisan majorities.

TO THE HOUSE OF REPRESENTATIVES:

I am returning herewith without my approval HR 1, the "Water Quality Act of 1987." Because all regulatory, research, enforcement, and permit issuance activities are continued under permanent law and current appropriations—including grants to finance the construction of sewage treatment plants—I emphasize that my veto will have no impact whatsoever on the immediate status of any water quality programs.

The cleanup of our nation's rivers, lakes, and estuaries is, and has been for the past 15 years, a national priority of the highest order. This Administration remains committed to the objectives of the Clean Water Act and to continuing the outstanding progress we have made in reducing water pollution. But the issue facing me today does not concern the ensuring of clean water for future generations. The real issue is the Federal deficit—and the pork barrel and spending boondoggles that increase it.

The Clean Water Act construction grant program, which this legislation funds, is a classic example of how well-intentioned, short-term programs balloon into open-ended, long-term commitments costing billions of dollars more than anticipated or needed. Since 1972, the Federal government has helped fund the construction of local sewage treatment facilities. This is a matter that historically and properly was the responsibility of State and local governments. The Federal government's first spending in this area was intended to be a short-term effort to assist in financing the backlog of facilities needed at the time to meet the original Clean Water Act requirements. When the program started, the cost of that commitment to the Federal taxpayer was estimated at $18 billion. Yet to date, $47 billion has been appropriated. HR 1 proposes to put still another $18 billion of taxpayers' money into this program. Despite all this money, only 67 percent of all municipalities have actually completed the construction needed to comply with the Clean Water Act pollution limits. On the other hand, non-municipal treatment systems, which have received no federal funding, have completed 94 percent of the construction needed for compliance with Federal pollution standards. I want a bill that spends only what we need to spend and no more—not a blank check. For these reasons I must disapprove HR 1, a bill virtually identical to S 1128, which I disapproved last November. . . .

HR 1 gave the Congress the opportunity to demonstrate whether or not it is serious about getting Federal spending under control. The Congress should fulfill its responsibility to the American people and support me on these important fiscal issues. Together we can cut the deficit and reduce spending. But by passing such measures as HR 1, the Congress divides our interests and threatens our future.

Ronald Reagan

The White House,
January 30, 1987

highway bills in 1987. So popular were both measures that Republicans abandoned the president in droves, sacrificing his agenda for their constituents' interests.

The veto is a powerful weapon for stopping legislation when all other means have failed. As a tool for crafting policy, however, its utility is limited by a president's popularity, political skills, and timing, not to mention circumstances perhaps beyond the control of the White House.

Pocket Veto

The veto is mentioned specifically in the Constitution, as is the method for congressional override. But, as often is the case with the Founders' handiwork, minor provisions have evolved over time into major constitutional battles between Congress and the presidency. One of the most heated of these battles has been over what has come to be known as the *pocket veto*.

Constitutional Provision

The Constitution gives the president ten days (excluding Sundays) either to sign a bill into law or to return it to Congress with a veto message. A bill not approved by the president becomes law after ten days "unless the Congress by their adjournment prevent its return, in which case it shall not be law" (Article 1, section 7). This provision was intended to ward off last-minute actions by Congress that may prove dangerous or foolhardy. When Congress has left for home after adjournment, the president cannot possibly veto and return bills as prescribed in the Constitution, so the Framers determined that under such circumstances it was better that any bill left unapproved at adjournment simply die.

A *pocket veto* thus results from executive inaction, not anything the president actively does, and the term reflects the notion that the president "pocketed" a bill rather than acted on it.[24] A president technically cannot "issue" a pocket veto; the entire situation occurs simply because Congress has adjourned and the bill cannot be returned with a regular veto message. Even so, not a few presidents have asserted their "right" to use the pocket veto as if it were an active power of the office.

The first president to rely on the pocket veto was James Madison, in 1812, and only twice more did a president use a pocket veto before 1830. The incidence of pocket vetoes increased thereafter, especially against many of the private pension bills passed by Congress in the second half of the nineteenth century. The champion of the pocket veto in absolute numbers is Franklin Roosevelt (263), but Grover Cleveland used the device far more frequently (almost 30 per year in office, compared with Roosevelt's approximately 22 per year) and largely against the many private veterans' pension bills passed in the decades following the Civil War.

Constitutional Issues

The pocket veto is controversial because Congress and the president often disagree over what constitutes congressional adjournment. The Constitution, as so often is the case, is not clear on this point, except for adjournment sine die (Latin for "without a day," meaning "without a day being set for meeting again"). Adjournment sine die marks the end of a two-year Congress. Other circumstances under which a pocket veto is constitutional is a critical question to both branches, since any interpretation narrowing its use to adjournment sine die benefits the legislature. A more expansive definition magnifies executive power over legislation, since presidents might be able to defeat bills through inaction whenever Congress takes a recess, such as between sessions of the same Congress or during holidays occurring within any single session.

This question was not an issue through the nineteenth century, since Congress sat in session, on average, only half a year, and calling members back to Washington could take weeks of travel. But, as Congress began to stay in session almost full time and as new technology made communications to and recall of Congress far easier than the Framers ever envisioned, the issue of when the president legally can use the pocket veto has grown in importance.

The first real shot in this battle came with the 1929 *Pocket Veto Case,* in which the Supreme Court ruled that President Calvin Coolidge could pocket veto an Indian claims bill passed just before a four-month recess.[25] The justices ruled that the term *adjournment* applied to *any* break in the congressional calendar that prevented the return of a bill within the required ten-day period, in this case adjournment between sessions. The ruling, as historian Arthur M. Schlesinger, Jr., noted, "was based in part on the idea that, if Congress was in adjournment, no officer or agent was authorized to receive on behalf of Congress a bill rejected by the President."[26] To close this apparent loophole, particularly as Congress began to convene almost year-round and recess for very short periods, both chambers began to appoint "agents"—usually the clerk of the House and secretary of the Senate—to receive presidential veto messages while members were away, thus theoretically negating a president's rationale for a pocket veto. After all, once Congress returned it could deliberate and perhaps override a presidential veto at any time before adjournment sine die.

Franklin Roosevelt asserted that this strategy was unconstitutional in declaring a pocket veto against a bill passed before Congress went on a three-day recess. In 1938, however, the Supreme Court modified the 1929 ruling and held that pocket vetoes could not occur during brief recesses if agents had been so named.[27] Regular veto procedures, the justices argued, served to give the president time to consider a bill *and* allow Congress the opportunity to respond, so the use of agents to receive presidential veto messages was deemed constitutional. Congress, not surprisingly, made this practice commonplace thereafter.

This issue lay dormant until the early 1970s, when Richard Nixon's application of the pocket veto again sparked controversy about what kind of congressional adjournment "prevents" regular veto procedures. Despite the 1938 ruling, Nixon in 1970 declared that during a six-day congressional holiday recess he would pocket veto the Family Practice of Medicine Act, which provided funds for medical training. Congress had passed the bill unanimously, had appointed agents to receive presidential messages, and arguably would have overridden any regular veto, but Nixon did not give Congress the chance to respond.

Nixon created a furor by asserting that a short holiday was analogous to adjournment sine die. Members of Congress argued that the bill had indeed become law because Nixon could not exercise a pocket veto during a recess, and Sen. Edward M. Kennedy (D-Mass.) subsequently brought suit against the administration.[28] Kennedy's case was upheld by a U.S. court of appeals, which in 1974 ruled that pocket vetoes were disallowed during short recesses so long as Congress established procedures to receive veto messages in its absence.[29]

Kennedy again brought suit after Gerald Ford declared a pocket veto against a bill passed just before the intersession break of the Eighty-eighth Congress. Once again, a federal court of appeals overturned a lower court decision and ruled that pocket vetoes cannot be used except after adjournment sine die so long as both chambers appoint agents.[30] The Ford administration subsequently announced that it would abide by the ruling.[31]

Despite these rulings, Ronald Reagan in 1983 reasserted a more expansive view when he declared a pocket veto against a bill barring aid to El Salvador passed just before the end of the first session of the Ninety-eighth

> If any bill shall not be returned by the president within ten days, (Sundays excepted) after it shall have been presented to him, the same shall be a law, in like manner as if he had signed it, unless the Congress by their adjournment prevent its return, in which case it shall not be a law.
>
> —from Article I, section 7

Congress. As with Nixon, Reagan administration officials argued that the pocket veto should apply to any congressional recess longer than three days. And, just as before, many in Congress declared once again that the device applied only to adjournment sine die. Thirty-three House Democrats subsequently sued the administration, and a U.S. court of appeals in 1984 reversed a lower court decision and reaffirmed the standard set in 1976.[32] The administration appealed the decision to the Supreme Court, which in January 1987 declared the particulars of the case moot (since the dispute over aid to El Salvador had long passed) and upheld the decision of the lower court.[33] Members of Congress and administration officials alike voiced disappointment that the high court had not settled the matter once and for all.

What constitutes constitutional application of the pocket veto thus remains a point of contention between members of Congress eager to protect legislative prerogatives and presidents equally keen to expand their weapons against unwanted legislation. The issue of the pocket veto may not be settled until the Supreme Court acts.

Item Veto

The veto is a blunt tool for executive influence precisely because it is an all or nothing matter. For many who support expansive executive power this is a major flaw, since a president cannot separate items deemed wasteful within a major spending bill. Proposals to give the president the ability to pick and choose among specific appropriations, called an *item veto,* have dotted congressional agendas throughout history; but so far the effort has been thwarted by legislators fearful of even greater executive leverage within their domain.

Forty-three states give their governors some form of item veto. Most of these provisions pertain primarily to spending bills, but others expand the governor's power to substantive laws as well. At least ten states allow governors actually to amend spending bills and send them back to the legislature for reconsideration.[34]

The Framers appear to have given no attention to an item veto during the drafting or ratification of the Constitution, which seems surprising until we recall that even the regular veto proved highly contentious. Granting to Congress full power over appropriations and revenues certainly emphasized the Framers' bias, but the option of allowing the president to excise specific parts of spending bills would arise thereafter. The states of the Confederacy included a clause in their constitution allowing the president to "approve any appropriation and disapprove any other appropriation in the same bill" (Article 1, section 7, clause 2), and efforts to pass a constitutional amendment creating similar executive power in the U.S. Constitution have been commonplace since the 1870s.

A number of presidents through the twentieth century have expressed their support for an item veto, most notably Franklin Roosevelt, Dwight Eisenhower, and Ronald Reagan. Roosevelt came closest to realizing his wishes when the House in 1938 voted to give the president that power, but the effort died in the Senate.[35] In 1985, Sen. Mack Mattingly (R-Ga.) and forty-six cosponsors pushed for a two-year trial run, but, despite President Reagan's enthusiastic endorsement in his 1985 State of the Union address, the proposal was rebuffed both then and a year later. Even if the Senate in 1986 had approved the item veto, it was unlikely that the House, which is highly protective of its power of the purse, would have gone along.

"Quasi-Item Vetoes"

Not a few presidents compensated for the lack of formal item veto power through other means. One mechanism was to "impound"—or *not* spend—money appropriated by Congress for fiscal or administrative reasons. The concept of impoundment is not controversial when presidents can show that the expenditure is no longer needed, as when Thomas Jefferson impounded funds earmarked for naval ships because the hostilities prompting the appropriation no longer existed, or when unforeseen circumstances delay spending. But when presidents try to use impoundment for obvious fiscal or policy reasons, sharp conflict with Congress is guaranteed.

Impoundment was used infrequently until the 1970s, largely because presidents sought to avoid major fights with Congress over control of the purse.[36] Richard Nixon, however, relied openly on impoundment to "veto" specific congressional budgetary allocations, even for entire agencies. These efforts proved so controversial that Congress in 1974 passed the Budget and Impoundment Act (over his veto), which forbade impoundments unless approved by both houses of Congress.

Subsequent presidents have continued to "defer" or "rescind" funds under the auspices of the law, although the actions deemed most controversial have had difficulty getting congressional acquiescence. In 1986, for example, President Reagan attempted to defer $5 billion for housing and urban development programs for fiscal reasons because Congress had appropriated more money than he had requested, but a federal appeals court ruled that his actions violated the intent of the 1974 law.[37]

Presidents also on occasion refuse to abide by specific provisions in laws they sign, or they issue their own interpretations when they think Congress has acted unconstitutionally. In 1959 Eisenhower announced that he would disregard a provision for congressional access to secret documents because it would violate the president's need to protect national security. In 1971 Nixon insisted that he was not bound by a provision requiring the president to state a specific time period for withdrawal from Vietnam.[38] Both presidents effectively undermined the provisions in question, but the constitutionality of such actions has not been tested in court.[39]

The Item Veto Debated

Proponents of the item veto argue that such an instrument would help limit federal spending, allow presidents to excise "wasteful" congressional appropriations, and give chief executives greater opportunities to promote their overall budget priorities. Political commentator George Will called it an "effective instrument of allocation" to help presidents carry out their electoral "mandates" and to strengthen presidential responsibility over both the budget and the general direction of the federal government.[40] The proponents' argument, in sum, is that what is good enough for forty-three governors must be good enough for the president of the United States.

Their critics argue that a presidential item veto simply would not affect federal spending profoundly, particularly since it would not apply to the massive "entitlement" programs (like Social Security) that make up so much of the total budget.[41] Presidents also are seen as being just as responsible for budgetary growth as Congress, since they can use the regular veto to force legislative compliance if they wish. Still others point out that any reference to state item veto provisions negates the very real differences that exist between the powers of state legislatures and those possessed by the U.S. Congress.[42]

Practical questions aside, the debate over the item veto is a debate over power, over which branch will be supreme when it comes to federal spending. Those promoting the item veto favor expanded executive power to control both spending and the direction of national policy. Those opposing the item veto fear the effect of such power on congressional control of the purse and argue that the provision would become yet another way for a president to reward friends, hurt enemies, and dominate the legislative process. Whatever the case, the debate over the item veto promises to sizzle as long as the federal budget deficit continues to be a major political issue.

The President's Program

The president's second express duty is to "from time to time give to the Congress information of the state of the Union, and recommend to their consideration such measures he shall judge necessary and expedient" (Article II, section 3). Unlike the veto, which is a limited and somewhat negative instrument for stopping unwanted legislation, the duty to recommend legislation has over time become the primary mechanism by which chief executives influence the nation's political agenda. Given the presidency's relatively weak array of formal mechanisms for mandating government policy, no other facet of the office today is as critical to presidential success or failure when the nation is not in crisis. This is so because the ability to affect the agenda of government—to decide what is or is not a priority—is in essence the power to influence what government will or will not do.

Determining the agenda of government is no paltry matter. As many a high school debate team member discovers, there are rules for debate—the questions to be discussed and the procedure for discussing them—that participants must follow whether they like it or not. Unlike a scholastic debate competition, however, in the political realm the topics to be discussed and the rules for discourse are not set beforehand by a neutral moderator. Rather, deciding the issues to be debated in the first place is a matter of political power, timing, and, perhaps, luck. As political scientist E. E. Schattschneider long ago concluded, "He who determines what politics is all about runs the country, because the definition of the alternatives is the choice of conflicts, and the choice of conflicts allocates power." [43]

At times, unforeseen crises such as natural disasters, war, or sudden shifts in the economy overwhelm the agenda of government. When that happens, the existing agenda is thrown aside and presidential "success" or "strength" is judged by the pace and suitability of executive response. Franklin Roosevelt's answer to the impending collapse of the banking system in March 1933 often is cited as an example of strong presidential leadership, for within a few days Roosevelt moved Congress to reorganize the system and, equally important, persuaded average Americans to return their savings to the banks. In doing so Roosevelt instilled renewed faith in the financial system and began the road to national economic recovery.

Ronald Reagan, however, reaped a great deal of criticism in October 1987 for his allegedly belated and passive response to a sudden plunge in the stock market, which Wall Street analysts blamed largely on the deadlock between the president and Congress over how to resolve the federal budget deficit. Whether the "crisis" over the budget deficit caused the market crash, or whether Reagan responded inadequately, is hard to say, yet common perceptions that the president had not dealt forcefully with the situation eroded confidence in his leadership.

Crises aside, no single institution in the United States so powerfully influences the national agenda of political debate as the presidency. No other institution is so capable of subjecting Congress to so much pressure in so organized a manner, and no other political figure commands so much attention from the public regardless of the issue. The presidency always has been the focal point of U.S. politics because it is the only political office in the United States chosen through a national election, but its importance has burgeoned since the 1930s. The sheer growth in the scope and influence of the federal government, the emergence of the United States as a world economic and military power (which amplified the president's role as commander in chief), and, perhaps most important, the rise of modern telecommunications technology, all have combined to place the presidency squarely in the public psyche both at home and abroad.

The presidency, as political scientist Bruce Miroff has suggested, commands the "public space" in contemporary U.S. politics, largely forcing other participants in the political process to respond to issues as the president defines them.[44] That reality powerfully influences success or failure on policy initiatives, particularly in issue areas where most Americans have no direct experience. Reagan, for example, consistently portrayed the rebels fighting the Nicaraguan government as "freedom fighters," a picture so compelling to so many citizens that those in opposition were forced continually to refute the president's definition even before they could attack his policies. But, each time they came close to defeating further U.S. aid to the rebels, they discovered anew the president's power to reach out to the nation for support. It may be said, in fact, that Reagan alone carried the rebels along through the sheer power of his office to dominate the agenda of discussion.

The president did not define the national agenda throughout most of the nineteenth century. In those days, Congress dominated government, the White House was populated by a succession of largely forgettable figures, and the technologies of mass communication did not yet exist. Presidents were not expected to formulate legislative agendas, prepare and present executive budgets, or do much else except oversee the executive branch, conduct foreign policy (such as it was when the United States was relatively isolated), and oppose Congress whenever necessary and possible. Nor did the dominant view of government hold that presidents should take active roles in initiating or influencing public policy. Not until Franklin Roosevelt did the presidency become a strong *institution,* one that remained potent regardless of the person sitting in the Oval Office.

Congress and the Presidency: Two Cultures

It is impossible to discuss the president's legislative influence without first recognizing the essential differences between the executive and legislative branches. Not only does the Constitution grant to Congress the sole power to make law, generate revenues, and appropriate funds, but it also established in the national government sets of dynamics and roles that fundamentally set Congress far apart from the presidency. Those differences, which have remained remarkably constant throughout history, are important to understanding why presidents succeed or fail in achieving their legislative goals.[45]

First, presidents and members of Congress reach national office through entirely separate paths. The president is the only political figure elected through a nationwide election. That process, combined with the national responsibilities of the office, inevitably gives the president a broad perspective on issues. Members of Congress, by contrast, come to government through local elections, be they district contests for the House of Representatives or statewide races for the Senate. That fact alone ensures, as former speaker of the House Thomas P. (Tip) O'Neill was fond of saying, that for members of Congress "all politics is local."[46] Those in Congress can and do think in national terms on a wide range of policy questions, but their elective roles force them to tend to their home districts first and foremost. More than one House member or senator has paid a political price for not keeping close tabs on local matters.

What is more, presidents and members of Congress serve different terms of office. A president is elected for four years, but members of the House have only two-year terms, which makes them especially sensitive to momentary pressures and local demands. This also means that, because congressional elections take place in the second year of the president's term, some elections can be construed as public votes of confidence in presidential performance. The president's party almost invariably loses House and Senate seats in midterm elections, and members of Congress from the president's party are keenly aware that public disenchantment with their leader may cause them serious electoral problems. *(See "Party Affiliations in Congress and the Presidency, 1789-1989," p. 1453, in the Appendix.)* The opposition party, for its part, naturally tries to use these contests to its advantage.

In 1980, for example, the Republicans picked up 34 new House seats in the wake of Ronald Reagan's victory over Jimmy Carter.[47] Although House Democrats still outnumbered Republicans by a 243-192 margin, House Republicans in 1981 were able to build alliances with conservative southern Democrats large enough to give the president a working majority and push through his dramatic budget and tax reduction bills. But an economic recession, and Democrats' effective attacks on administration plans to alter the Social Security program, resulted in the Republicans' losing more than two-thirds of those new seats in the 1982 midterm election. The effect on Reagan's influence was palpable: the Democratic majority in the House was larger and more unified, public approval of the president was weaker, and southern conservative Democrats no longer readily joined Republicans against their own party.

The problem for presidents in the Senate is a bit different. Members of the Senate serve for six years, with only one-third of the body up for reelection every second year. Thus, every other Senate term is not affected directly by a presidential election. This gives senators greater freedom to support or oppose presidential initiatives without as much concern about short-term constituent pressures. Additionally, the Senate retains constitutional leverage over the executive through its power to approve presidential nominees to the federal judiciary and to high-level executive branch positions and through its power to approve or reject treaties with other nations. These roles, and the great independence of senators generally, almost guarantees problems for presidents even of the same party. Jimmy Carter failed to obtain Senate approval for the 1978 Strategic Arms Limitation Treaty despite Democratic dominance in the chamber, and Reagan faced the greatest opposition on the 1987 Intermediate Force Missile Treaty from conservative Republicans.

The two branches also possess widely divergent decision-making cultures and processes, variations that emerge from their fundamentally different governing responsibilities. The president, whose primary responsibilities are implementing the laws and defending the nation, is at the top of an executive hierarchy that speaks with one official voice on policy matters. Decisions frequently are dictated to subordinates from the Oval Office, and policy options often stem from the president's overall ideology and political agenda. Loyalty to the president's program is paramount, and dissenting voices find their influence severely limited, if not completely cut off.

Congress, however, speaks with many voices simultaneously, one for each of the 535 members of the House and Senate. Congress is diverse not principally because of inherent failings in the legislature itself, or because members are by nature disputatious (although many are), but because members of Congress must both represent their constituents and make national policy. These dual roles often conflict, since what may be good for any member's constituents (such as new services or public facilities) may bode ill for the nation (in the form of massive budget deficits, for example). Each member of Congress wields but one vote, regardless of seniority or party position, and no member can be expelled from the legislature simply because of voting behavior or personal opinion. Only constituents have the right to "fire" their representatives.

This inherent equality among members forces the institution itself to operate according to relatively nonhierarchical decision-making processes. To do otherwise would appear antidemocratic. Decisions, in the form of legislation, are achieved by building coalitions of members large enough to win committee and floor votes. Consensus becomes a hallowed norm of behavior. Successful legislating depends on knitting together enough diverse interests and demands to overcome opposition, using whatever tactics seem reasonable or necessary. This is true even in the less hierarchical Senate, where the rules of debate and norms of courtesy, reciprocity (trading favors), and consensus allow a single member to obstruct the majority—and the president—until agreement surfaces.

In 1982, for example, Sen. Jesse Helms, a staunchly conservative Republican from North Carolina, singlehandedly held up the Reagan administration's tax bill because he objected to higher levies on tobacco. Throughout the Reagan years Helms stalled appointments to ambassadorial positions because of disagreements with the administration on foreign policy issues. The White House could do little but complain loudly and threaten to withhold favors or federal contracts to firms in his home state, but Helms nonetheless won reelection in 1984.

Presidents usually want to move quickly so they can make the most of their limited opportunities through dramatic and often comprehensive policy initiatives. This is true particularly during the first year, because every president knows that the personal popularity so critical to overcoming the normal inertia of the political system inevitably fades. *(See Ratings, Gallup Poll, Truman-Reagan, p. 1465, in the Appendix.)* But Congress, except in times of crisis or when an issue is especially important, prefers more stately deliberation and a more cautious weighing of the consequences. The needs of each member's constituency must be treated fairly, and coalitions of support must be constructed. These considerations usually are more important to Congress than speed or ideological purity. Many a president, resentful of this glacial pace of deliberation, has chastised Congress publicly for its somewhat messy operating style, but the legislature by design marches to its own drummer.

These fundamental differences all too often produce clashes between presidents theoretically acting on behalf of the national interest and members of Congress promoting constituents' needs. Presidents routinely accuse Congress of waste or inertia, but they also find that cumulative local and state interests often overcome any supposed "national" good. Carter, for example, early in his administration attacked spending for public works projects (such as dams and irrigation canals), but he discovered very quickly that these projects are "sacred cows" to legislators eager to serve their constituents.[48] In 1987 Reagan vetoed a popular reauthorization of the Clean Water Act because he felt that its $20 billion appropriation for water and sewage treatment projects was wasteful, but Congress overrode his veto by overwhelming bipartisan margins.

Contrast these conditions with those common in parliamentary systems, where prime ministers typically are selected by the majority party (or party coalition) in the legislature. There is no separation of powers in the American sense, and strong party cohesion is essential to maintaining control over government. Prime Minister Margaret Thatcher, for example, gained her position as a result of Conservative party dominance in Parliament, a solid majority that allows her to push through major legislation far more easily and quickly than any U.S. president could imagine. In the United States, by contrast, members of Congress can and do go against their party and president when constituent interests are on the line. What the Constitution splits apart, party loyalty cannot easily bind together.[49]

In sum, the relationship between the president and Congress is one determined by the Founders through constitutional provisions on terms, powers, and governing responsibilities. Those who wrote the Constitution were far more concerned with checking the potential abuses of power than with speedy or easy legislating. They *wanted* Congress and the president to be at odds, and they endowed Congress with the ability to withstand executive pressure and, indeed, to dictate public policy if it so willed. Even when dominated by a president's party, Congress as an institution insists on playing its constitutional role according to its own needs and internal dynamics. No president seeking to succeed can forget those realities.

Sen. Jesse Helms (R-N.C.) singlehandedly held up the Reagan administration's tax bill. A single member often can obstruct a congressional majority and the president.

Historical Development

"Whether legislator, opinion-maker, commander, or administrator," argued presidential scholar Clinton Rossiter, "the President molds lasting policy in every sector of American life."[50] Indeed, as political scientist Bertram Gross wrote in 1953, "Except in wartime, Presidents are now judged more by the quality of the legislation they propose or succeed in getting enacted than by their records as executive."[51] The presidency today is seen almost as a third house of Congress, with presidents involved deeply in all aspects of the legislative process and judged by how well they can mobilize support for their programs.

Compare these analyses with the experiences of early presidents, and the contrast is staggering. Rather than expecting the president to formulate a legislative program and lobby for its enactment, Congress, through the late 1800s, almost invariably regarded presidential involvement in policy making as nothing less than unwarranted intrusion.[52] Textbook notions that Congress alone makes the law, which the president then simply administers, were taken seriously, and separation of powers meant that presidents left to Congress the responsibility to initiate public policy. Presidents who forgot this constitutional nicety were quickly reminded of it by members of the legislature always on guard against such presumptuousness.

Whether the Founders actually meant the president to play so passive a role is hotly debated. Certainly, they viewed the presidency as a bulwark against congressional mischief or tyranny. Yet, as Alexander Hamilton argued in *Federalist* No. 70, "energy in the executive is a leading character of good government."[53] *(See "Federalist No. 70," p. 1364, in the Appendix.)* The Founders may have rejected decisively the more monarchical schemes for the executive proposed early on by Hamilton and others, but they also emphatically rejected making the president subordinate to or entirely separate from Congress. The legislature was to make national policy, but the president did receive from the Founders a limited number of instruments for influencing legislation. Bringing those resources to bear, however, would be another question.

Early Presidents

George Washington discovered rather quickly the difficulties of influencing legislation. He was the first—and last—president ever to sit in on Congress during actual floor debate. In line with his early view that oral communications were indispensable to fruitful relations between the branches, on August 22, 1789, Washington personally presented to the Senate the particulars of an Indian treaty and requested that body's advice and consent. The president's proposal was read aloud—twice, since some senators could not hear for the noise coming in off the street—but only awkward silence ensued. Sen. William Maclay of Pennsylvania then rose and called for a reading of the treaty itself and its accompanying papers, and afterward supported a move to refer the entire matter to a committee for further study. Maclay, as he later wrote in his journal, "saw no chance of fair investigation of subjects if the President of the United States sat there, with his Secretary of War, to support his opinions and over-awe the timid and neutral part of the Senate." Washington, wrote Maclay, "started up in a violent fret" at the proposal to refer the matter to committee, exclaiming, "This defeats every purpose of my coming here." The president eventually calmed down and agreed to a two-day delay, but on his return he found many senators still uneasy about his presence. After completing the business at hand, Washington vowed that he would not repeat the experience.[54]

Washington thereafter shied away from face-to-face lobbying, but he nonetheless remained active in influencing legislation, particularly treaties, indirectly. Secretary of the Treasury Alexander Hamilton, however, proved unabashedly aggressive in trying to expand executive policy-making resources. Hamilton's belief in an energetic presidency and his tireless use of his department to initiate and lobby for legislation soon sparked a backlash in Congress. Secretary of State Thomas Jefferson, despite his overall support for Washington, objected strenuously in a letter to the president that Hamilton's "system flowed from principles adverse to liberty, and was calculated to undermine and demolish the republic, by creating an influence of his department over the members of the legislature." [55]

Jefferson, whose Democratic-Republican party in principle glorified the concept of congressional supremacy, eschewed personal lobbying when he became president and went so far as to suspend the fledgling tradition of personally delivering an annual State of the Union message. But Jefferson was no passive chief executive. He carefully maintained the forms of separation of powers and congressional supremacy but relied heavily on cabinet members and his strong party caucus organization, which held the majority in Congress, to initiate and dominate legislative activity. Secretary of the Treasury Albert Gallatin acted as his primary liaison to the party caucus, and Jefferson personally picked his own party floor leaders, who then became known as the president's chief congressional spokespersons. The strength of the party caucus, held together in many ways by Jefferson's own political skills (including innumerable and widely acclaimed dinner parties), produced a style of governing that in many ways paralleled parliamentary systems.

After Jefferson, however, "king caucus" gave way to congressional supremacy. Jefferson's model of party government decayed as splits within the Democratic-Republican caucus eroded its usefulness as a mechanism for executive leverage. Power flowed back to Congress as an institution, and strong leaders such as Henry Clay and John C. Calhoun actively set the agenda of government through the 1820s. House Speaker Clay in particular dominated tariff and public works matters and with his allies would force even James Madison against his will to confront the British in the War of 1812. Congress also began to develop its own institutional mechanisms for sustained policy-making expertise, particularly in the standing committees, which began to evolve into power centers in their own right as presidents came and went.

Andrew Jackson in the 1830s momentarily reinvigorated the role of the Democratic party and its national convention as a means for setting the national agenda. Even more notable, the breadth and strength of his party organization allowed Jackson to become the first president to appeal directly to the public over the heads of Congress on such issues as the National Bank and the tariff.[56] Overall, however, Jackson's legislative strategy was largely negative, relying primarily on the veto to rebuff congressional actions. The idea that the president should actively propose and shepherd legislation through Congress was still controversial, and the increasing power of the standing committees did not allow Jackson to dominate Congress through the party.[57] Nonetheless, and particularly when compared with the series of Whig presidents to follow him, Jackson temporarily reinvigorated executive leadership in national policy making.

A few relatively active presidents aside, and not including Lincoln's emergency actions during the Civil War, nineteenth-century legislating generally was a congressional affair. The president's constitutional responsibilities over the armed forces and foreign policy mattered little, since the United States during most of this century kept resolutely out of international politics and maintained a minimal defense and foreign policy apparatus. On the domestic side, the federal government concerned itself largely with such parochial matters as post offices and other public works projects. Except in times of crisis, government through the late 1800s did relatively little on a national scale, and the presidency by extension played a secondary role in policy formation. Congress never shied from reminding presidents of their "proper" role, and even Abraham Lincoln toward the end of the Civil War was admonished that the president "must confine himself to executive duties—to obey and execute, not make the laws. . . ." [58]

Shift toward Presidential Leadership

These distinctions began to change in the late 1880s as the American economy and society evolved, and as the United States began to play a greater role in international affairs. The industrial revolution brought with it a transition from a self-sufficient farm economy to an urban manufacturing one, from largely localized business concerns to huge national corporations, and, perhaps as a result, a shift from the view that the federal government should do little to calls for it to do more. The issues of the day—interstate commerce, corporate monopoly, child labor, food and drug purity, monetary policy, agricultural research, and transportation, among others—became more national in scope and often overlapped with international trade and diplomacy questions that were growing in importance as the United States became more active in the world.

These trends also altered the prevailing wisdom about government and, by extension, the role of the presidency. Calls for more active executive leadership on legislation began to be heard as Congress increasingly found itself ill-equipped to handle broad national questions. The legislature by nature is better able to deal with issues that can be broken down by congressional districts or state lines, such as allocation of funds for post offices, than it is with issues having no clear constituency boundaries. Moreover, popular perceptions that Congress was not attentive to emerging national and international problems legitimized the notion of an energetic president. The constitutional forms of the two branches in most respects would stay the same, but their dynamics would change subtly as the nation itself entered a new era.

Theodore Roosevelt, who once said the president "can be as big a man as he can," could be called the first exponent of the "new" presidency.[59] Roosevelt was keenly aware that his was the only purely national voice, and he saw the Oval Office as a "bully pulpit" for stimulating public opinion and pushing legislation through Congress. "In theory the Executive has nothing to do with legislation," Roosevelt later wrote in his *Autobiography*.

> In practice, as things are now, the Executive is or ought to be peculiarly representative as a whole. As often as not the action of the Executive offers the only means by which the people can get the legislation they demand and ought to have. Therefore a good executive under the present conditions of American political life must take a very active interest in getting the right kind of legislation, in addition to performing his executive duties with an eye single to the public welfare. [60]

Roosevelt tried to practice what he preached. Largely on the strength of the president's advocacy and wide newspaper publicity, the Pure Food and Drug Act of 1906, a landmark consumer law that established the Food and Drug Administration, was pushed through a Congress dominated by agriculture and business interests. Roosevelt also established the national park system, attacked monopolies, and negotiated the end to a war between Japan and Russia (for which he won the Nobel Peace Prize).

Even more instructive was Roosevelt's decision to send a U.S. naval squadron on a global tour. Congress refused to appropriate money for the "show the flag" exercise, but Roosevelt scraped together enough funds from other naval accounts to send the fleet halfway around the world. He then publicly challenged Congress to provide enough money to bring the ships home. Public opinion so strongly supported Roosevelt that Congress quickly surrendered.

Although Roosevelt was unique in many ways—boundless in energy, aggressively intellectual, eager for public acclaim—his legacy would not disappear. The nation and Congress had been given a taste of energetic presidential leadership, and succeeding chief executives would find both the public and Congress more receptive to their initiatives.

William Howard Taft, Roosevelt's immediate successor and noted advocate of a far less grandiose view of the office, nonetheless was the first president to present draft legislation formally to Congress.[61] Woodrow Wilson in 1913 became the first president since John Adams to deliver his State of the Union message personally before a joint session of Congress. He thereafter used the address as a statement of his legislative agenda and to put into practice his belief that the president should lead government more actively.[62] Wilson also made bold assertions of his right to guide legislation, arguing in a special address to Congress, "I have come to you as the head of the government and the responsible leader of the party in power to urge action now, while there is time to serve the country deliberately, and as we should, in a clear air of common counsel." [63] The object of his speech, the Federal Reserve Act of 1913, was drafted largely in conferences at the White House, with Wilson personally in charge.

The Roosevelt Model

Despite gradual changes in the presidency during the early 1900s, the office remained a largely negative force in opposition to Congress, not the source of initiative and leadership Americans are used to (and demand) today. Theodore Roosevelt or Woodrow Wilson could take the lead in selected instances, particularly when conditions for presidential initiative were most favorable, but the office itself lacked mechanisms for sustained legislative influence. In the 1930s, however, the office underwent major, permanent changes; in many ways the actions of Franklin Roosevelt prefaced the contemporary presidency.

Franklin Roosevelt came to office in 1933 as the nation faced unprecedented economic and social pressures. The Great Depression devastated the national economy, forcing millions into unemployment and crippling public faith in government. Herbert Hoover (1929-1933) had relied on the market system and its leaders to resolve the crisis, but many voters thought this confidence was misplaced and believed that Hoover was to blame for the country's hardships. As a result, Hoover suffered a humiliating defeat in the 1932 presidential election. The emergency required major action and gave Roosevelt the opportunity to take the lead in ways no peacetime president ever had. Congress, which itself had proved unable to resolve the crisis, awaited strong direction. Conditions for redefining the very essence of the presidency were never so ripe.

Roosevelt's immediate attack on the depression would go down in U.S. history as the most sweeping and sustained rearrangement of national domestic policies ever made. During the famous "first Hundred Days" of Roosevelt's first term, Congress in special session gave the new president a blank check to remold the federal government, to introduce new programs, and to do almost anything to turn the economy around. Roosevelt and his battalions of energetic New Dealers took on the task with an almost joyful gusto, pushing major legislation through a willing Congress with unparalleled speed between March 9 and June 15, 1933. *(See box, The First Hundred Days of Franklin D. Roosevelt, p. 462.)* As presidential scholar Clinton Rossiter said of Roosevelt, "In the first Hundred Days he gave Congress a kind of leadership it had not known before and still does not care to have repeated." [64]

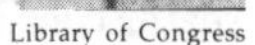

Library of Congress

Library of Congress

President Theodore Roosevelt was an energetic legislative leader, but his cousin Franklin D. Roosevelt went still further. FDR redefined the role of national government through his New Deal legislation and vastly expanded the size of the executive branch.

The First Hundred Days Of Franklin D. Roosevelt

Franklin D. Roosevelt was sworn into office on March 4, 1933, and convened the 73rd Congress into special session on March 9 to consider the Emergency Banking Act, which was passed after eight hours of debate. Roosevelt at first thought about sending Congress back home after passage of the act, but the momentum attained seemed too valuable to waste. As historian Arthur M. Schlesinger, Jr., later wrote, "In the three months after Roosevelt's inauguration, Congress and the country were subjected to a presidential barrage of ideas and programs unlike anything known to American history."[1] The major accomplishments of that first hundred days are:

March 9	Emergency Banking Act: reformed the national banking system
March 20	Economy Act: authorized cuts in federal spending
March 22	Beer and Wine Revenue Act: legalized sale of beer and wine
March 31	Civilian Conservation Corps: created employment for youths in a wide range of conservation efforts
April 19	Abandonment of gold standard: detached value of currency from gold
May 12	Federal Emergency Relief Act: created a national relief system
May 12	Agricultural Adjustment Act: established a national agricultural policy
May 12	Emergency Farm Mortgage Act: refinanced farm mortgages
May 18	Tennessee Valley Authority Act: provided for the unified development of the Tennessee Valley
May 27	Truth in Securities Act: required full disclosure of a firm's financial shape in issuing new securities
June 13	Home Owners' Loan Act: refinanced home mortgages
June 16	National Industrial Recovery Act: created a system of industrial self-regulation under federal supervision and a $3.3 billion public works program
June 16	Glass-Steagall Banking Act: separated commercial and investment banking, guaranteed bank deposits
June 16	Farm Credit Act: reorganized federal farm credit programs
June 16	Emergency Railroad Transportation Act: created greater coordination in national railroad system

1. Arthur M. Schlesinger, Jr., *The Coming of the New Deal* (Boston: Houghton Mifflin, 1959), 20.

Central to Roosevelt's success in 1933 was the link he established between the presidency and the American people, a connection achieved in great part because of his ability to communicate directly over radio. "This nation asks for action, and action now," he said simply in his first inaugural address, which sparked nearly half a million letters of support. "We must act, and act quickly."[65] *(See "Franklin D. Roosevelt's First Inaugural Address," p. 1376, in the Appendix.)* His speeches, the "fireside chats," and the frequent press conferences, all spoke directly to the American people, and indirectly to Congress, about his dreams and priorities. In the process, Roosevelt focused public attention on the presidency.

The New Deal era and Roosevelt's actions during World War II both redefined the role of national government and thoroughly altered the presidency as an institution. By the time Roosevelt died in 1945, the executive branch had exploded in size and in the scope of its responsibilities, and the presidency itself had gained a wider array of resources for influencing legislation, making budgets, and implementing programs. The presidency no longer was a single person but an institution, one that was growing in size and potency as Congress gave the president more staff and more resources to manage the government, initiate public policy, and lead the nation. Congress delegated these responsibilities both because legislators came to realize that the presidency was better situated to lead and, perhaps more important, because Americans demanded it.

When Harry Truman took up Roosevelt's mantle in 1945, he sat at the center of an office completely transformed during the course of twelve years. Under Roosevelt the presidency had become part national cheerleader, and would become even more so with the advent of television to transmit ideas and symbols. It had become part legislative leader, with the president required both to initiate and to shepherd new policies through a potentially recalcitrant Congress. It had become part chief executive officer of a large and busy government organization, with the need to manage and direct the federal bureaucracy toward the common good. It had become part world ambassador, no longer a safe refuge for those ignorant of or unconcerned about international affairs. And, most important, it had become wholly responsible for the nation's successes or failures, for Roosevelt interjected the presidency forcefully into a role traditionally and constitutionally held by Congress. No longer would the presidency remain a passive office, even if its occupant possessed neither Roosevelt's skills nor his vigor.

The Roosevelt Legacy

Roosevelt's legacy has been problematic for contemporary presidents. The office has grown in power and prestige, but perhaps not proportionately with public and congressional expectations about what presidents can deliver. Those in the Oval Office must present and implement broad national programs, but separation of powers ensures that presidents' futures are not necessarily in their own hands. The emergence of the United States as a world power after World War II demands that presidents exercise their commander-in-chief responsibilities more fully and consistently than when the U.S. played virtually no role in international political and military affairs, but these responsibilities frequently do not coincide well with public demands that domestic matters be given top priority. The coming of television brings the world more intimately into every home, and the pace of events has quickened demonstrably; but coalitions of support also seem more fleeting, and governing appears all the more difficult. The world is smaller, and public expectations about government are greater, creating for the presidency a burden of leadership that may, scholars speculate, prove too great to carry.[66]

This is not to argue that presidents have *no* control over their own destinies, but the extent of their control seems at times to depend less on personal intellect and skill than on the social, political, and economic contexts within which they govern. It also depends on the relative quiescence or independence of other governing institutions, particularly Congress.

Lyndon Johnson, for example, was a master of the legislative process, having had a long career as House member, senator, and, later, Senate majority leader. Nonetheless, in 1965 his ability to promote and attain the most sweeping of social programs since Roosevelt's first Hundred Days depended just as much on the trauma of John Kennedy's assassination, a national mood supporting broad social change, and an especially cooperative congressional majority after his sweeping 1964 election victory as it did on his legislative skills. Johnson's successes in 1965, when Congress approved some 69 percent of his requests, was tempered by knowledge that times would soon change.[67] "I have watched the Congress from either the inside or the outside, man and boy, for more than 40 years," Johnson commented early in 1965, "and I've never seen a Congress that didn't eventually take the measure of the president it was dealing with."[68]

Carter discovered that reality acutely very early in his administration when a Congress strongly dominated by his own party proved skeptical of his comprehensive energy plan. Carter's problems in 1977 and later stemmed not only from his relative lack of experience in and even distaste for Washington politics, but from the very changes to have taken place in Congress, and in American politics generally, during the preceding decade. Congress had become far more open, more fragmented, and more independent in the interim, forcing presidents to adapt to new ways of influencing the legislature. Lyndon Johnson had been able to push through his Great Society programs largely on his ability to rally key committee chairs and other congressional leaders, but Carter found it necessary to lobby virtually every member, a decidedly more difficult and frustrating task. Even Reagan, whose masterful rhetorical skills helped him translate his 1980 election victory into early legislative success, found his later efforts frustrated by his inability to induce Congress to follow his lead. Lyndon Johnson's warning is an apt one.

The question of context thus is essential to analyzing a president's ability to set the agenda of government and to persuade Congress to enact those priorities. According to presidential scholar Louis Koenig, Congress most consistently follows presidential leadership in three situations.[69] The first is during crises, when Congress and the nation almost invariably turn to the president for leadership. Roosevelt and the first Hundred Days is the most-cited example, for it is almost impossible to conceive that the New Deal could have been passed under "normal" political conditions.

Second, matters of national security and foreign affairs, where the Constitution gives the presidency primacy, find Congress generally more amenable to presidential initiatives. This was true particularly between World War II and the end of the Vietnam War, when a general view that party "politics ended at the water's edge" gave postwar presidents an unparalleled range of flexibility. The tendency for Congress to accede to presidential demands in defense and foreign policy issues led more than one president to cloak purely domestic programs in the mantle of national security to obtain easier passage. The interstate highway system, federal education programs, and the space program all were defined as essential to national security or pride—highways for easier movement of defense forces, greater education spending to "catch up" to the Soviets after the launch of Sputnik, and the Mercury, Gemini, and Apollo programs to win the "space race." These programs thus won far greater national support than they might have otherwise.

Third, presidents reap benefits from "abnormal" contexts—the combined effects of skilled political leaders, superior partisan dominance in Congress, changing societal values, and, especially, timing. Virtually every newly elected president enjoys a postelection "honeymoon" with Congress, a period during which the new occupant of the White House can push priorities within an atmosphere of general cooperation. Presidents from Roosevelt to the present usually have had their greatest legislative successes in the first six months following their initial election to office. Their success has varied, depending on the president's own abilities, the dominant national mood, and the strength of congressional majorities.

In sum, the ability of any president to dominate the agenda of government, to plan and propose new initiatives, and to lobby successfully on their behalf depends on more than personal skills or intellect. The character of the U.S. political system, the nature of the times, and the types of issues under debate, all affect the extent to which any president can influence the national agenda and the legislative process.

The State of the Union Address

The annual State of the Union Address has become since the 1930s an essential and powerful instrument by which presidents seek to influence the national agenda. It is today the primary means by which presidents review their past accomplishments and outline their future goals, yet this constitutional requirement that presidents give Congress information on the state of the Union has not always played so central a role in presidential strategies. Both George Washington and John Adams appeared personally before Congress to deliver their annual messages, but Thomas Jefferson in 1801 dropped the practice and instead submitted his reports in writing. Jefferson's action appeared to stem from his dislike of a practice that had its roots in the British Parliament, which opened each session with a speech from the king or queen. By eliminating what he saw as a quasi-monarchical rite, historian Arthur M. Schlesinger, Jr., has noted, Jefferson hoped to instill stronger republican values in the still-new American system of government.[70]

Eighteenth century presidents continued Jefferson's practice, and it was not until 1913 that a president appeared again before Congress and personally delivered an address. Woodrow Wilson, who believed that the role of the presidency included strong personal appeals to the nation and to Congress, revived the ritual begun under Washington. In his first personal appearance before Congress for a special messge on finance, Wilson expressed his general

Presidential Appearances before Congress, 1789-1988

President	Number of Appearances	Occasions
Washington	10	8 annual messages (1789-1796); 2 inaugural addresses (1789, 1793—second inaugural before Senate only)
J. Adams	6	4 annual messages (1797-1800), inaugural address (1797); relations with France (1797)
Wilson	26	6 annual messages (1913-1918); tariff reform, bank reform, relations with Mexico (1913); antitrust laws, Panama Canal tolls, relations with Mexico, new tax revenue (1914); impending rail strike (1916); "Peace without Victory" (Senate only), breaking relations with Germany, arming of merchant ships, request for war declaration against Germany (1917); federal takeover of railroads, "14 points" for peace, peace outlook, need for new revenue, request for ratification of women's suffrage amendment (Senate only), armistice (1918); request for approval of Versailles treaty (Senate only), high cost of living (1919)
Harding	7	2 annual messages (1921-1922); federal problems (1921); 2 on the Merchant Marines (1922); coal and railroads (1922); debt (1923)
Coolidge	2	1 annual message (1923); George Washington's birthday (1927)
Roosevelt	16	10 annual messages (1934-1943); 100th anniversary of Lafayette's death (1934); 150th anniversary of First Congress (1939); Neutrality address (1939); national defense (1940); declaration of war (1941); Yalta conference report (1945)
Truman	17	6 State of the Union messages (1947-1952); prosecution of the war (1945); submission of UN charter (Senate only, 1945); congressional Medal of Honor ceremony (1945); universal military training (1945); railroad strike (1946); Greek-Turkish aid policy (1947); aid to Europe (1947); national security and conditions in Europe (1948); 50th anniversary of the liberation of Cuba (1948); inflation, housing, and civil rights (1948); steel industry dispute (1952)
Eisenhower	7	6 State of the Union messages (1953-1954; 1957-1960); Middle East (1957)
Kennedy	3	3 State of the Union messages (1961-1963)
Johnson	8	6 State of the Union messages (1964-1969); assumption of office (1963); voting rights (1965)
Nixon	7	4 State of the Union messages (1970-1972, 1974); Vietnam policy (1969—separate addresses before House and Senate); economic policy (1971); Soviet Union trip (1972)
Ford[1]	6	3 State of the Union messages (1975-1977); assumption of office (1974); inflation (1974); state of the world (1975)
Carter	6	3 State of the Union messages (1978-1980); energy program (1977); Middle East talks at Camp David (1978); SALT II arms control treaty (1979)
Reagan	11	8 State of the Union messages (1981-1988); budget address (1981); Central America (1983); U.S.-Soviet summit (1985)

Sources: Guide to Congress, 3d ed. (Washington, D.C.: Congressional Quarterly Inc., 1982), 767; *Congressional Quarterly Weekly Report* (various issues).

1. On October 17, 1974, President Gerald R. Ford testified before the Subcommittee on Criminal Justice of the House Judiciary Committee on his pardon of former president Richard Nixon for crimes possibly committed during the Watergate affair.

views about spanning the gulf between the branches:

> I am very glad indeed to have the opportunity to address the two houses directly, and to verify for myself the impression that the president of the United States is a person, not a mere department of the government hailing Congress from some isolated island of jealous power, sending messages, and not speaking naturally and with his own voice, that he is a human being trying to cooperate with other human beings in a common service. After this experience I shall feel quite normal in all our dealings with one another.[71]

The annual messages before Wilson's time usually were laborious recitations of department and agency activities. They seldom contained substantive legislative proposals, in line with the prevailing view that Congress alone made law and that the suggestions made by presidents were to be given no greater weight than those of average citizens. The exception to this informal but ironclad rule in many ways emphasized it. When Grover Cleveland deviated from tradition by devoting his entire 1887 message to ideas about tariff reform, he sparked a tremendous debate in the press, divided his own Democratic party, and, as a result, apparently contributed to his defeat in 1888.[72]

Beginning with Woodrow Wilson, however, the State

of the Union address has become a key vehicle for expounding the president's annual legislative agenda and priorities. This use of the annual message grew even more important with the advent of radio and, later, television. Today the president's annual appearance before a joint session of Congress is a major national event. It is a moment of high ceremony, a pageant attended by the members of Congress, department secretaries, the Joint Chiefs of Staff, justices of the Supreme Court, foreign dignitaries, and other special guests. Television cameras pan the House chamber as the president speaks, recording the reactions of particular members of the audience to various presidential statements or proposals. Media commentators and other political experts routinely judge presidential "performance" almost before the president leaves the House chamber. The issues raised by the president get serious consideration in the press, if not always by Congress, and the opposition party almost always feels compelled to ask for equal time to state its own views. *(See box, Presidential Appearances before Congress, 1789-1988, p. 464.)*

The power of the annual address to shape public opinion and spur on Congress should not be underestimated. Kennedy, for example, used it to push successfully for a national effort to put a person on the moon before the end of the 1960s. Johnson passionately promoted his civil rights and Great Society social programs, and Nixon used the opportunity to propose sweeping reorganization of the federal establishment and to defend U.S. actions in Vietnam. Reagan, a master of television speeches, used the annual address to spark national (and congressional) debate on tax reform, on aid to the rebels in Nicaragua, and on his Strategic Defense Initiative. Whatever presidents discuss, the nation discusses—if only for a while. Often, the president's priorities become those of government.

The State of the Union address thus has become an important part of the "conversation" between presidents and Congress, a constant dialogue that may be as formal as the address or as informal as the daily contact among presidents, presidential aides, members of Congress, and Capitol Hill staff.[73] This dialogue can be examined in part by listing the major themes expressed in State of the Union messages of presidents Johnson through Reagan. *(See Table 3.)* A shift in priorities from foreign to domestic policy during the 1970s stands out, as does a shift back in the 1980s. And, as political scientist Charles O. Jones notes, "Many of the domestic requests by Nixon, Ford, and Carter were reform measures seeking to reshape the structure and substance of programs enacted in the 1960s—a shift from issues requiring expansion of government to those demanding consolidation or even contraction of government."[74] All of these come out in the State of the Union address.

The address also is a moment for presidents to proclaim successes, express their grand desires for the future, and engage in a little political theater. Reagan, for example, used his time to praise American "heroes," to chastise Congress for the way it prepares budgets *(see box, State of the Union Address as Political Theater, p. 466)*, and to recruit potential supporters to the Republican party. Using the address for such purposes had its drawbacks, however, particularly when events outstrip plans. In 1986, for example, the Reagan administration intended to make full use of the launch of the space shuttle *Challenger* to praise "teacher in space" Christa McAuliffe as an example of the bright future for the nation. The *Challenger* was launched on the day the speech was scheduled, but the shuttle accident and the deaths of the eight astronauts forced the postponement of the address. President Reagan instead went on television that night to speak of the tragedy and to express his belief that the nation had to go on.

Table 3 Major Themes in Selected State of the Union Addresses

President	Year	Major themes
Kennedy	1961	Economy; social programs
	1962	Getting America moving; economy; military strength
	1963	Cuba; economy; tax reduction
Johnson	1964	JFK legacy; budget
	1965	Great Society domestic programs
	1966	Vietnam, foreign and defense policy
	1967	Maintaining previous momentum
	1968	Vietnam, foreign and defense policy
	1969	Review of achievements
Nixon	1970	Vietnam, foreign and defense policy
	1971	Vietnam; economic and social policy
	1972	Foreign and defense policy; plea for action on previous requests
	1973	Natural resources; economy; social policy
	1974	Energy; economic issues
Ford	1975	Economy; taxes; energy
	1976	Economic and energy issues
	1977	Energy; achievements
Carter	1978	Economic and energy issues
	1979	Inflation; SALT II
	1980	Foreign and defense policy
	1981	Record of progress; budget priorities
Reagan	1982	Economic and budget issues
	1983	Economic and budget issues
	1984	Federal deficit; foreign policy
	1985	Tax reform; government spending
	1986	Foreign policy; welfare reform
	1987	Foreign policy
	1988	Economic and budget issues

Sources: Charles O. Jones, "Presidential Negotiation with Congress," in *Both Ends of the Avenue: The Presidency, the Executive Branch, and Congress in the 1980s,* ed. Anthony King (Washington, D.C.: American Enterprise Institute, 1983), 103; *Congressional Quarterly Weekly Report,* various issues.

The State of the Union message is required by the Constitution, but through statute Congress over time has required the president to make other annual reports as well, the volume of which has skyrocketed since the 1920s. The Budget Act of 1921, for example, requires the president to submit an annual budget message, and the Employment Act of 1946 mandates an annual report on the economy. Hundreds of other reports, messages, and legislative proposals are submitted to Congress annually, all bearing the president's imprint and expressing the White House's views on important policy matters. Each one, particularly the budget and economic reports, has potential political influence.

Preparing Legislation

Setting the national agenda of debate is but the initial stage in successful presidential leadership—if *presidential*

The State of the Union Address as Political Theater

Woodrow Wilson in 1913 revived the earlier tradition of presidents personally delivering the State of the Union address to Congress, but it was not until the advent of radio and, later, television that the annual speech took on powerful symbolic meaning. Widespread public access to radio allowed Franklin D. Roosevelt, for example, to speak directly to the American people and rally the nation out of the depression of the 1930s. Television, however, with its particular capacity to present emotional visual images, elevated the State of the Union address to true public theater, complete with an audience (members of Congress assembled) and critics (network commentators). Televised annual addresses have become less a litany of dry statistics than a panorama of past accomplishments, current endeavors, and future dreams. And, increasingly, the State of the Union address has become the primary fixture in setting the nations' annual agenda for action, with presidents judged on how *well* they delivered their messages. The medium and the message indeed have coalesced.

John F. Kennedy arguably inaugurated the use of television to breathe vibrancy into the annual message, but it was Ronald Reagan, the acknowledged master of visual media, who used the address to its greatest effect thus far. Whether to needle Congress, praise heroes, or express his dreams for America, the State of the Union address in Reagan's hands became an eagerly awaited and heavily analyzed event. Reagan may not have written his own words or dreamed up the various symbolic appeals used—such matters were left to professional speech writers—but he was the bringer of the message to the people. What follows, an excerpt from President Reagan's 1988 State of the Union address, shows how one president transformed this once banal annual accounting into the preeminent national political event.

> . . . Now, it is also time for some plain talk about the most immediate obstacle to controlling federal deficits. The simple but frustrating problem of making expenses match revenues—something American families do and the federal government can't—has caused crisis after crisis in this city. Mr. Speaker, Mr. President, I will say to you tonight what I have said before—and will continue to say: The budget process has broken down; it needs a drastic overhaul. With each ensuing year, the spectacle before the American people is the same as it was this Christmas—budget deadlines delayed or missed completely, monstrous continuing resolutions that pack hundreds of billions of dollars' worth of spending into one bill—and a federal government on the brink of default.
>
> I know I'm echoing what you here in the Congress have said because you suffered so directly—but let's recall that in seven years, of 91 appropriations bills scheduled to arrive on my desk by a certain date, only 10 made it on time. Last year, of the 13 appropriations bills due by October 1st, none of them made it. Instead, we had four continuing resolutions lasting 41 days, then 36 days, and two days, and three days, respectively. And then, along came these behemoths. This is the conference report—1,053-page report weighing 14 pounds. Then this—a reconciliation bill six months late, that was 1,186 pages long, weighing 15 pounds; and the long-term continuing resolution—this one was two months late and it's 1,057 pages long, weighing 14 pounds. That was a total of 43 pounds of paper and ink. You had three hours—yes, three hours, to consider each, and it took 300 people at my Office of Management just to read the bill so the government wouldn't shut down.
>
> Congress shouldn't send another one of these. No—and if you do, I will not sign it.
>
> Let's change all this; instead of a presidential budget that gets discarded and a congressional budget resolution that is not enforced, why not a simple partnership, a joint agreement that sets out the spending priorities within the available revenues? And let's remember our deadline is October 1st, not Christmas; let's get the people's work done in time to avoid a footrace with Santa Claus. And yes, this year—to coin a phrase—a new beginning. Thirteen individual bills, on time and fully reviewed by Congress. . . .

Source: Congressional Quarterly Weekly Report, January 3, 1988, 221.

leadership is defined simply as getting proposals approved by Congress. A president's priorities generally, though not always, require formal congressional consideration if they are to be realized, and in this process presidents through history have relied on a wide array of personnel and resources.

For the president to take an active part in drafting legislation is a departure from strict interpretations of separation of powers, since only Congress has constitutional power to make law. Nonetheless, presidents since Washington have involved themselves directly in this first stage of the legislative process, although early residents of the office usually tried to avoid any appearance of interposing their views in a realm zealously guarded by Congress. George Washington, for example, quietly discussed ideas for new measures with cabinet officials and members of Congress alike, and he secretly lent a hand in composing the odd bill; but he studiously avoided any open and direct role in forming legislation. Instead, he assigned various cabinet members to consult formally with Congress, an activity seen as more legitimate because department heads appeared regularly before congressional committees on routine business. Congress itself validated this strategy by directing Secretary of the Treasury Alexander Hamilton to draft and submit recommendations for a new national bank, a resolution of state debts, and a promotion of manufacturing—tasks the energetic Hamilton took on with such relish that he eventually sparked severe criticism from members of Congress about his dominance over legislating.[75]

Hamilton's chief critic was Secretary of State Thomas Jefferson, but Jefferson proved no less energetic once he became president in 1801. Despite his party's view that Congress alone made public policy, Jefferson secretly composed bills, which he transmitted through his department secretaries to party loyalists in the legislature. Even more important, Jefferson used his cabinet heavily for maximum influence on legislating. He met with department heads regularly to discuss new proposals and to write bills. Afterwards, cabinet members would meet with the relevant congressional committees. Jefferson's strong party caucus—which enjoyed a solid congressional majority—also enabled him to maintain the fiction of his complete separateness from law making even while wielding a strong hand behind the scenes.

Other nineteenth-century presidents continued the pattern of using cabinet officials to craft and lobby for legislation. They had few alternatives. Presidents during the 1800s had very few personal staff members, since Congress did not appropriate funds for clerical assistance until 1857. Nor did they have extensive networks of personal advisers and assistants.[76] Cabinet officials gave presidents valuable access to congressional committees, acted as the chief executive's political eyes and ears, and, as historian James Young has noted, "allowed Presidents to maintain, for what it was worth, the outward appearance of conformity to community norms which decreed social distance between the President and Congress."[77]

This system had its disadvantages, of course. Chief among them was the political reality that department heads frequently were selected to pay off political favors or to accommodate rival factions within the president's own party. Presidents thus never were entirely sure of their department heads' primary loyalties. They always had to guard against the tendency of strong cabinet officials to cultivate their own power bases in Congress. Lincoln, to cite but one example, was plagued constantly by the need to maneuver around such formidable political figures as Secretary of State William Seward and Secretary of the Treasury Salmon P. Chase, who led their own factions within the Republican party and regularly clashed with Lincoln over Civil War policies.

AP

In his 1988 State of the Union address, President Reagan derided Congress's last-minute passage of 3,296 pages' worth of budget reconciliation and governmentwide appropriations.

The Institutional Presidency

The picture of the nineteenth-century presidency generally is one of a lone figure with little reliable assistance. Contemporary presidents, by contrast, reside at the heart of an immense executive institution, aided in their tasks by nearly sixteen hundred special assistants, personal aides, policy experts, and clerical staff distributed among several specialized agencies. *(See Table 4.)* The Executive Office of the President (EOP) is the chief executive's personal bureaucracy, designed expressly to help the president oversee department and agency activities, formulate budgets and monitor spending, craft legislation, lobby Congress, and, above all, ensure that the president's priorities are promoted. *(See chapters on Executive Office of the President in Part V.)*

This support system began to take shape when Congress, in the Budget and Accounting Act of 1921, required the president to coordinate all executive branch spending proposals and present a unified annual budget. These new responsibilities, which grew largely out of the recognition that departments all too often bypassed the chief executive in their pleas for new appropriations, were accompanied by the creation of the Bureau of the Budget (BOB) to assist presidents in their tasks. Thus arose the notion of "central clearance," the use of BOB to monitor all executive branch spending, to judge new funding requests before they went to Capitol Hill, and, especially, to "veto" budget proposals not in line with the president's overall agenda. The president for the first time had a mechanism to coordinate and perhaps even control executive branch activities.[78]

Franklin Roosevelt's New Deal not only spawned a staggering growth in executive branch responsibilities, but also, as a result, strained even the capacity of the presidency to coordinate and control government expenditures and actions. In 1939 the Bureau of the Budget moved to the newly created Executive Office of the President—itself the product of widespread recognition that the president sorely needed sustained personal staff assistance. Roosevelt gradually extended BOB's central clearance functions to include screening bills passed by Congress and recommending to the president whether or not they should be approved.

These central clearance responsibilities were magnified even more during the early 1970s, when Congress transformed BOB into the Office of Management and Budget (OMB) and Richard Nixon made the office into the president's chief instrument of policy advocacy. Subsequent presidents have augmented OMB power and reach even further. Today no legislative proposal generated within the executive branch goes to Congress without OMB approval; no new regulation goes into effect until OMB approves; and no bill passed by Congress hits the president's desk until OMB judges how well it meets the president's policy and budgetary goals and thus should be signed or vetoed. Once a relatively quiet and even neutral accounting department, OMB today is the powerful, parti-

How a Bill . . .

1. Introduction of a Bill. A proposal that will eventually become law must be introduced by a member of Congress. Often when a member introduces a bill he or she will find someone in the other chamber to introduce a "companion bill." Each bill is given a number as it is introduced, and numbering is sequential. House bill numbers start with *HR*, Senate bill numbers start with *S*.

When an executive branch agency or the White House wants Congress to consider a specific proposal they ask a senator or representative to introduce the bill "by request."

2. Referral to Committee. After a bill is introduced it is referred by the parliamentarian to a standing committee. The committee chair then decides which subcommittee will consider the measure.

3. Subcommittee Action. The subcommittee holds hearings on the bill. Testimony may be taken from invited witnesses only, or the committee may issue an open call and hear from anyone who wishes to speak. At this point administration representatives have a chance to urge support for a bill. Subcommittee hearings also provide an opportunity for them to oppose a bill they do not like.

When hearings are completed, the bill is "marked up," that is, rewritten to incorporate the subcommittee's changes. These changes may be designed to strengthen (or weaken) the provisions, or they may be politically inspired to improve (or reduce) a bill's chance of passage. If the president has objections, it is at this point that friendly committee members and White House lobbyists attempt to amend the bill to meet presidential approval. When the subcommittee has finished its work, the bill is sent to the full committee.

4. Full Committee Action. The full committee may ratify the subcommittee's actions, or it may repeat the subcommittee's steps by holding more hearings and marking up the bill a second time. This second markup gives the administration another chance to alter the bill if its effort to make changes at the subcommittee level failed. Whether or not the subcommittee steps are repeated, only the full committee formally reports the bill back to the chamber for floor action; a subcommittee cannot report a measure directly.

5a. House Rules Committee. After the full committee reports the bill, it is placed on a "calendar" and is ready for floor consideration. In the House, controversial or complicated bills are referred to the Rules Committee, which determines the framework for debate and amendment. A special rule written by the Rules Committee specifies how long debate will last, who will control the time, and how many and what type of amendments may be offered.

After the Rules Committee has recommended a rule, the full House votes on whether to accept it. If the rule does not allow amendments that the president favors, or if the legislation contains provisions the president would like to see deleted, the White House may lobby House members to defeat the rule. The White House is seldom successful in defeating a rule; but when it is, that success is a major victory for the president.

5b. House Floor Consideration. If, as usually happens, the House accepts the rule, the next step is debate on the bill. Normal House rules limit each member to one hour during general debate, but often the rule imposes more rigid time limits. Roll call votes may be requested if a certain number of members agree to the request. Roll call votes are taken electronically in the House and usually last fifteen minutes.

If the bill originated in the House, it is referred to the Senate for action after passage *(see solid line)*. If the House is completing consideration of a measure referred from the Senate and the bill has not been amended, it is cleared for presidential action. If the bill is a referral from the Senate and has been substantially amended, it may be referred to a conference committee *(see No. 6)*.

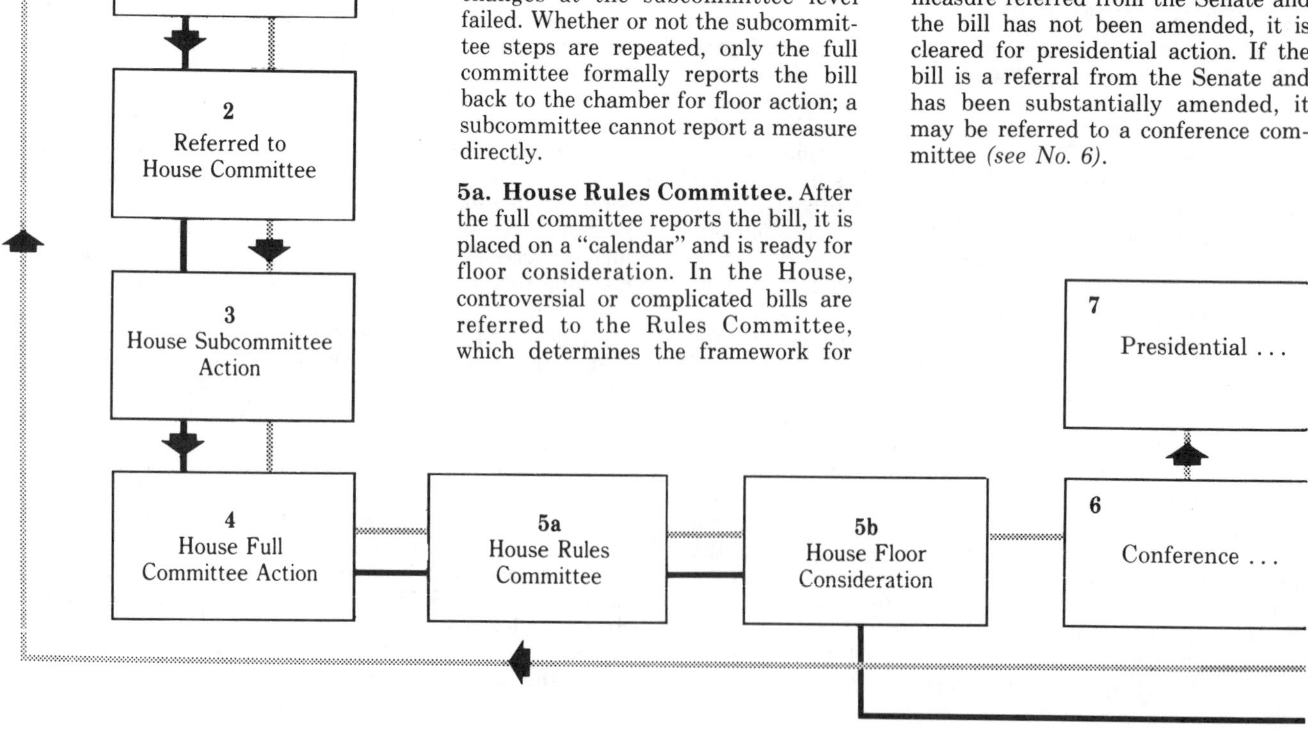

... Becomes a Law

5c. Senate Unanimous Consent. To expedite floor consideration the Senate has developed a procedure, known as the "unanimous consent agreement," similar to the special rules written by the House Rules Committee. A unanimous consent agreement is worked out informally by the majority and minority leaders and by any senator with an interest in the bill under consideration. The agreement specifies how much time will be allotted for debate, what amendments will be considered, and how the time will be divided. Unlike a House rule, however, which needs a simple majority to pass, a unanimous consent agreement must be accepted by all senators on the floor at the time it is proposed. A single objection defeats the agreement.

5d. Senate Floor Consideration. Floor consideration under a unanimous consent agreement in the Senate is similar to action under a rule in the House. If a unanimous consent agreement cannot be worked out, however, the Senate operates under its normal rules, which are much less restrictive than House rules. There is no time limit on debate. Members opposed to a bill under consideration sometimes "filibuster"—that is, hold the floor by speaking for an extended period of time—to delay or kill a bill. A filibuster can be ended only if sixty senators agree to a "cloture" petition to limit debate. As a result floor proceedings in the Senate usually take much longer than in the House. Voting in the Senate is not electronic. The roll is called by a clerk who records each senator's vote.

If the bill under consideration originated in the Senate, it is then referred to the House for action after passage *(see broken line)*. If the Senate is completing consideration of a measure referred from the House and the bill has not been amended, it is cleared for presidential action. If the bill is a referral from the House and has been substantially amended, it may be referred to a conference committee *(see No. 6)*.

6. Conference Action. A bill must be approved by both chambers in identical form before it can be sent to the president. If there are major differences between the versions passed by the House and the Senate, the bill may go to a conference committee, which works out a compromise. The committee usually consists of senior members of the committees that reported the bill. If the president has reservations or objections or prefers the bill passed by one chamber to the version passed by the other, it is in the conference that the White House attempts to influence members to adopt a final version that is acceptable to the administration.

When the conference is completed, the committee files a conference report to which both the House and the Senate must agree. If either rejects the conference agreement, the bill dies. If both agree to the conference report, the measure then goes to the president for final action.

A conference often can be avoided, however. Even if one chamber has amended a bill substantially, it can refer the measure back to the originating chamber, which may accept all the amendments (clearing the bill for the president), accept some and reject others, or even add some amendments of its own (in which case the bill then bounces back to the other chamber for a second time). This back-and-forth can continue until both chambers have agreed to the measure in identical form, thus clearing it for presidential action. In reality, most bills are cleared in this manner, avoiding an official conference.

7. Presidential Action. The president has several options once a bill is received from Congress. The president may sign the bill, making it law immediately; or the president may veto the bill and return it to Congress. Congress may overturn a presidential veto if both chambers vote by a two-thirds majority (of those present and voting) to "override" the veto. If Congress fails to override the veto, the bill dies. Normally, if the president takes no action the bill becomes law after ten days without a signature. An exception may occur at the end of a session of Congress, when the president may "pocket veto" a bill by not signing it within the ten-day limit.

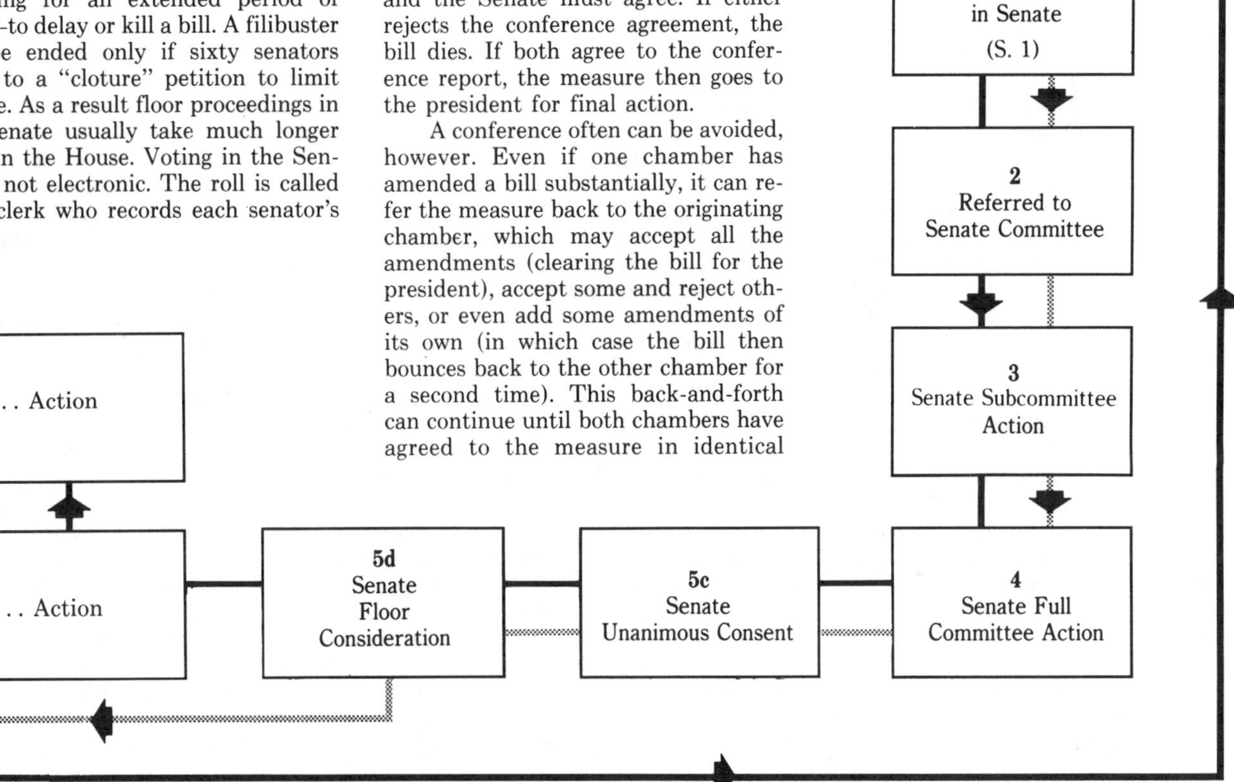

Table 4 Size of Executive Office of the President, Various Offices, 1941-1985

Year	White House Office	Office of Management and Budget	National Security Council [a]
1941	53	305	—
1942	49	459	—
1945	61	565	—
1950	295	520	17
1955	290	444	28
1960	446	434	65
1965	333	524	38
1970	311	633	75
1975	625	673	89
1980	406	616	69
1985	367	566	62

Source: Bureau of the Census, *Statistical Abstract of the United States* (Washington, D.C.: Government Printing Office, various editions).

a. Created in 1947.

san, and often controversial defender of the president's goals and policies.

Other arms within the Executive Office of the President complement OMB's activities, and the EOP as a whole is designed to help occupants of the Oval Office gather information and promote their priorities. The Council of Economic Advisers, normally composed of three noted economists, advises the president on economic matters and how they affect national politics. The National Security Council acts as the president's foreign policy advisory mechanism, designed to transcend the institutional boundaries of the various foreign policy bureaucracies and to give the president a broader view of national security questions.

At the apex of the pyramid sits the White House Office. Home to the president's closest personal aides and special assistants, the White House Office is chiefly responsible for coordinating the executive institution and spearheading the president's agenda.

The contemporary presidency thus is an *institution* with resources and powers that remain potent regardless of the personal traits of individual chief executives. This bureaucracy exists solely because the presidency today is required to design and lobby for legislative proposals, to monitor and coordinate government spending, and to promote an overall national agenda. This is a far cry from the days when presidents crafted legislation in secret or found themselves unable to oversee spending within the various departments.

Ironically, this very institutional capacity to do all these tasks presents presidents with a new dilemma: how to ensure that the Executive Office of the President *itself* can be controlled by the occupant of the Oval Office. Presidents cannot be involved personally with every action that occurs below them and increasingly must rely on subordinates to monitor and guide the behavior of an institution that itself is designed to monitor and guide the behavior of the executive branch as a whole.

If eighteenth-century presidents bemoaned their lack of staff resources, presidents today must wonder how they will be able to make their own vast organization run both well and loyally.

The President's Agenda

Much of the legislation Congress addresses annually originates within the executive branch. No longer do presidents maintain the fiction of separation from the legislative process, and contemporary presidents more often than not are judged by the quality and timing of their annual policy agendas. Congress and the public demand that presidents initiate legislation and criticize severely those who do not. Eisenhower, for example, did not offer a formal legislative agenda during his first year in office, only to receive sharp rebukes from both parties. "Don't expect us to start from scratch on what you people want," said one angry House member to an administration official. "That's not the way we do things here. You draft the bills and we work them over."[79]

A multiplicity of sources provide ideas for the intellectual foundation of the president's program. Before Franklin Roosevelt's administration, presidents could work out their agenda from their personal experiences, since the role of the executive branch was limited and the number of problems requiring presidential attention were relatively few. Theodore Roosevelt's aggressive national park and wildlife conservation policies stemmed at least in part from his background as a western rancher and big-game hunter. Hoover used his experiences as secretary of commerce under Calvin Coolidge (1923-1929) to guide his priorities—until the Great Depression overtook his presidency.

Today, however, as the data compiled by presidential scholar Paul Light suggest, a surprising proportion of a contemporary chief executive's domestic program may come from "outside" sources—Congress, national events, the departments and agencies of the executive branch, and public opinion. *(See Table 5.)* Congress, with its hundreds of members and thousands of staff, is fertile ground for legislative ideas. Many of the formal legislative proposals that come from the White House stem from ideas and proposals that have existed on Capitol Hill for years, waiting to be adopted as the president's own when circumstances permit.[80]

One example of a policy agenda derived from Congress was Kennedy's domestic program, a large portion of which was ideas and options promoted to no avail by liberal congressional Democrats during the Eisenhower years. What Kennedy could not get through Congress, Lyndon Johnson later incorporated into his Great Society program. The same perspective applies to Reagan's vaunted tax reduction bill of 1981, which in many ways was the "offspring" of a Republican tax plan pushed by Rep. Jack Kemp (N.Y.) and Sen. William Roth (Del.) during the late 1970s. Hundreds of policies float about at all times, each awaiting the power of a president to lift it out of the mass of proposals and give it life.[81]

Crises or other events also structure the domestic agenda, probably more than presidents desire or care to admit. This is true particularly as Americans have come to expect government to respond forcefully to new or sudden problems. There is no question, for example, that Hoover's inability to rein in the depression led to his defeat in 1932 and that Franklin Roosevelt attained immortality for his innovative ("try anything") attack on the economic crisis and for his overall leadership during World War II.[82] The 1957 Soviet launch of Sputnik startled Eisenhower into major spending for science education and the space program. The energy crisis of the 1970s, sparked largely by huge hikes in oil prices by producing nations, dominated the fiscal and budgetary agendas of both Ford and Carter.

National concern about the AIDS (Acquired Immune Deficiency Syndrome) epidemic forced the Reagan administration to reverse its policies and to increase research funding to combat that disease. Although presidents enjoy a tremendous institutional capacity to define the agenda of government, many times they are forced to respond to issues or events out of their control.

Executive branch bureaucrats provide another wellspring of policy ideas or options, despite the propensity of presidential candidates to attack the bureaucracy during their election campaigns as bloated and unresponsive. Career civil servants who are deeply dedicated to particular policy realms possess the technical expertise and perspectives that come from long tenure. Their experience can help new presidents initiate new policies or simply avoid repeating the errors of the past.

The degree to which any president adopts ideas generated from within the professional bureaucracy depends in large part on personal ideology and style. The White House staffs of Nixon and Reagan, for example, were highly suspicious of the motives and political leanings of career civil servants and tried whenever possible to draw policy making directly into the White House.[83] Democratic presidents, however, usually seem to share civil servants' fundamental beliefs in the role of government and thus have shown a greater willingness to tap bureaucratic ideas.

Whatever the source of an agenda item, presidents must test its technical, economic, and, particularly, political soundness before sending it off to Congress. Inadequately tested proposals are ripe for disaster. Carter's energy policy, for example, which was hammered out privately by a panel of experts, suffered embarrassing political defeats once it was sent to Congress.

To avoid such problems, presidents ideally seek out a wide range of expertise, but, as they find out, no source is perfect. Professionals within the EOP, for example, are valuable sources of technical expertise or economic analysis, but they may not be attuned to the political climate or understand well the vagaries of Capitol Hill. Personal aides and trusted friends are valued for their political acumen and their ability to say things to the president that others would not dare. Every president has such intimates, be they the Californians making up Reagan's "kitchen cabinet," Carter's "Georgia mafia," or Franklin Roosevelt's "brains trust." But such persons may themselves be new to Washington or blinded to political reality by their loyalty to the president when controversial decisions must be made.

Cabinet secretaries, in contrast to the days when they were the president's primary advisers, today often play a secondary role in judging proposals unless they also enjoy close personal ties to the president or preside over a department particularly important to presidential priorities. Presidents frequently fill the position of attorney general, for example, with a close friend or longtime political ally, who then enjoys ready access to the Oval Office. Kennedy appointed his brother Robert; Nixon looked to friend and former law partner John Mitchell; and Reagan appointed longtime aide Edwin Meese III. Each of these acted as more than a department head; they also were intimates.

By contrast, some cabinet members rarely see the president in private, even when issues central to their departments arise. Department heads often have complained that their phone calls were routed to presidential assistants who they technically outrank. Samuel R. Pierce, Jr., for example, was secretary of the Department of Housing and Urban Development throughout the Reagan presidency, yet he rarely played a central role in policy development because his department was peripheral to the president's agenda. (In fact, as one famous story goes, Reagan even failed to recognize Pierce at a reception for city mayors.) Cabinet members also are regarded with deep suspicion by the president's closest advisers because of their tendency to promote departmental interests over the presidential agenda the longer they stay in office. Cabinet secretaries who "go native" typically find access to the Oval Office cut off and their advice ignored, even when it could prove valuable.

Table 5 Sources of Ideas for the President's Agenda

Source	Respondents mentioning source (percent)
External sources	
Congress	52
Events and crises	51
Executive branch	46
Public opinion	27
Party	11
Interest groups	7
Media	4
Internal sources	
Campaign and platform	20
President	17
Staff	16
Task forces	6

Source: Paul C. Light, *The President's Agenda* (Baltimore: Johns Hopkins University Press, 1983), 118.

Note: Number of respondents: 118. Respondents were past and present White House aides who were asked, "Generally speaking, what would you say were the most important sources of ideas for the domestic agenda?"

Members of Congress may be keenly sensitive to the political feasibility of new proposals—that is, whether or not they can get through the legislature. But, as elected officials in their own right, even those of the president's party may have their own particular agendas to promote. They also may find, given their distinct electoral and governing roles, that their perspectives differ dramatically from the president's. Carter, for example, deeply distrusted members of Congress, whom he felt were largely parochial in their views. He found, to his dismay, that local interests prevailed within the legislature once his proposals went to Capitol Hill. All presidents find this out sooner or later, and most realize that members of Congress must be heard, if only so that they can warn of the potential obstacles that lie ahead.

Career federal bureaucrats know what is feasible technically and economically, but they may have their own policy and institutional goals to consider beyond the president's own. Besides, career bureaucrats will be in their positions long after a particular president is gone from the White House. They generally can wait out an administration hostile to their views until the political winds change or new leaders come to office.

Outside experts such as academics can offer new ideas and perhaps can lend an aura of expertise and legitimacy to controversial issues, but they may not have enough understanding of what is feasible politically. Moreover, there is no guarantee that any recommendations made by panels of experts ever will be more than reams of paper sitting in a file cabinet.

There are, in sum, many possible sources for ideas and expertise available to any president, but only the individual in the White House can decide which information, and which sources, are to be tapped. Some presidents, such as Franklin Roosevelt and Lyndon Johnson, were voracious consumers of advice from a great number of sources. Roosevelt was known to surround himself with assistants who disagreed violently on major issues so that he could get a broader spectrum of opinion. Johnson was famous for his midnight telephone calls to sleepy senators demanding the latest scoop on a piece of legislation. Both had keen political instincts, and for them information was a resource to be used actively in political battles. This style requires tremendous personal energy and intellect and can be overwhelming if the president does not have some way to reduce the deluge of information hitting the Oval Office daily. Presidents who do not adequately delegate tasks to subordinates risk overload.

Other presidents have preferred to let information and policy options "bubble up" through the ranks of advisers and experts surrounding them, using their closest aides to synthesize advice and present a short list of alternative courses of action. Both Eisenhower and Reagan appear to have operated in this manner. Reagan was particularly content to let his assistants parse out competing choices and to withhold his own views until aides presented him with one or two options. The president's role in this approach is far more passive, but it can work well when those who actually weigh the alternatives keep the president's values and priorities firmly in mind. Problems arise when a president's assistants fail to do so or when they keep the president in the dark about their activities.

Presidents' operating styles hinge most on their personal qualities, overall goals, and perspective on the job itself. Carter saw the president's job as one of problem solving, and he insisted on being informed of or involved in virtually every decision—including, as one story goes, the schedule for the White House tennis courts. His problem, critics charged, was that he was so immersed in the minutiae of policy that he failed to discern or convey to the public the broader goals of public policy or of his office. Reagan, by contrast, apparently viewed the presidency as being like chairman of the board; he was content to dictate broad goals and directions while leaving details to his aides. The tendency to remain aloof from the particulars of policy questions often led him to appear uninformed during press conferences, but even Reagan's critics admitted that the strength and passion of his ideals provided his subordinates with clear guidelines by which to judge and select policies.

Presidential Lobbying

Assuming, perhaps wrongly, that legislation is drafted coherently to begin with, presidents next must convince Congress to go along. Presidential scholar Richard Neustadt has argued that the primary power of the presidency is the power to persuade others, but the Constitution is silent about just *how* presidents are to do so.[84] That silence is convenient: presidents seeking little in the way of change can assert that separation of powers does not allow them to influence Congress, but aggressive presidents more often than not regard this silence as justification for any means not expressly forbidden by law or accepted practice. In general, then, the way presidents organize their lobbying activities, and the styles they employ to influence Congress, reflects their policy goals, their knowledge about how government works, and their overall personal skills. It also reflects whether—or how much—Congress is willing to be influenced, a state of receptiveness that always is in doubt.

Presidents through the early 1900s were careful to obey the form, if not the substance, of separation of powers. Their instruments for influencing legislation were few and constrained by prevailing beliefs in congressional supremacy. Party loyalty, favorable newspaper coverage, and politically connected cabinet members were a nineteenth-century president's primary resources, and lobbying tended to be loosely organized and discreet.

This picture changed dramatically by the 1940s, as both government and prevailing public attitudes about presidential leadership underwent fundamental changes. But the evolution of presidential lobbying from the indirect and passive styles of earlier presidents to the open and organized practices of today took decades.

Woodrow Wilson was noted for his strongly personal approach, going so far as to sit in on congressional committee deliberations on trade legislation and pulling party strings to ensure Democratic support; nonetheless, he shied away from a direct lobbying strategy. His chief congressional lobbyist was Postmaster General Albert Burleson, a former House Democrat who used postal positions as inducements for loyalty to the president's program. Wilson also craftily used John Nance Garner, another Texas Democrat, as his confidential lobbyist within the House. Garner, who sat on the influential Ways and Means Committee, each week would enter the White House through a side door and consult with Wilson privately on current congressional news and prospects for the president's legislation.

Less than two decades later Franklin Roosevelt abandoned any pretense of regal noninvolvement and employed a far more open and vigorous lobbying strategy. Many consider Roosevelt the father of contemporary lobbying styles, beginning with his own sustained and overt role in policy formation.

Roosevelt personally goaded Congress through radio addresses to the public and careful cultivation of friendly relations with the press. He also directed personal assistants James Rowe, Thomas Corcoran, and Benjamin Cohen openly to write bills and lobby legislators. Like Wilson, Roosevelt relied heavily on patronage to reward loyalty and to punish deserters; Postmaster General James A. Farley, who was also the national Democratic party chairman, acted as his enforcer. Preferential treatment on public works projects and other New Deal spending programs, funds critical to hard-pressed Democrats during election years, and promises for personal campaign appearances by the wildly popular president also served as inducements. Although Roosevelt's overall influence in Congress waxed and waned with changes in political conditions, he constructed for the presidency a new, more vigorous, and central role in the legislative process.

Formalizing the Process

Although Roosevelt inaugurated or perfected many of the lobbying techniques employed by contemporary presidents, he did not make lobbying a formal process. New

Deal legislation instead was presented and fought for piecemeal; Roosevelt would assign a staff person to lobby for a program only if it got into trouble. Legislative liaison—the practice of having assistants constantly cultivate a receptive environment—remained an informal affair, reflecting in many ways Roosevelt's own more personal approach to politics and his dislike of strongly ordered organizational styles. Roosevelt never established a formal liaison office; instead, he used aides to augment his own considerable skills in swaying legislators.[85]

Dwight Eisenhower adopted the antithesis of Roosevelt's highly personal and avowedly disorganized approach. As political scientist Eric Davis has pointed out, Eisenhower was the first president to formalize the executive lobbying process by creating the Office of Congressional Relations (OCR), a specialized structure reflecting his own hierarchical predispositions and general dislike of direct lobbying. Eisenhower, who was uncomfortable in the rambunctious world of politics, also wanted OCR to act as a buffer between himself and members of Congress, even those from his own party.[86] Heading the office was Bryce Harlow, a longtime House committee staff member who had no other responsibilities but to cultivate cordial relations with Congress and, especially, to keep House and Senate Republicans happy. But Harlow's liaison office seldom took an active role in legislative development, largely because Eisenhower spent more time opposing congressional Democrats than in pushing his own agenda.

John Kennedy, by contrast, planned an aggressive agenda and strengthened the liaison office by appointing a longtime political ally, Lawrence F. O'Brien, as chief lobbyist. O'Brien, for his part, thought it critical that liaison staff not only generate support for specific Kennedy programs but also "create a general climate in favor and receptivity toward the president and the administration among members of Congress, and ... use these positive perceptions as a resource when attempting to obtain support for particular pieces of legislation." [87] O'Brien organized OCR along lines paralleling the structure of Congress by assigning a staff member to interact with virtually every faction and bloc in the legislature. He also constructed cooperative relationships with agency personnel, party leaders, and interest groups—whoever might be useful or necessary to the president's success. Many presidential scholars today consider O'Brien to be the architect of modern legislative liaison practices; the system he established continued through the Carter administration.

Despite O'Brien's efforts, Kennedy generally proved reluctant to push an expansive legislative agenda because conservative Democrats in Congress strongly opposed new social programs and civil rights legislation. Kennedy's narrow victory over Richard Nixon in 1960 did not give him enough leverage in Congress to pressure members for support, even fellow Democrats. Although Kennedy's liaison organization was credited with a handful of notable legislative victories on trade and tax matters, the political climate in Congress was a reality for which no organized lobbying could readily compensate.

Lyndon Johnson, however, fared quite differently. He was successful initially because Kennedy's assassination created in the nation and in Congress a desire to pass some of the slain president's legislation and later because of his own massive 1964 election victory over Barry M. Goldwater. The 1964 election also brought in many new and more liberal House Democrats, thus giving Johnson the necessary political support for his domestic policy agenda.

Dwight D. Eisenhower Library

John F. Kennedy Library

The Eisenhower administration established the first Office of Congressional Relations. Ike appointed Bryce Harlow, an experienced House committee staff member, but Kennedy was more aggressive in his choice of a longtime political ally, Lawrence F. O'Brien.

Johnson retained the liaison office built up by Kennedy to augment his own considerable personal political skills, and he insisted that O'Brien and his liaison staff be consulted closely before initiatives were taken. Congressional scholar Charles O. Jones has characterized Johnson's style of relations with Congress as akin to a majority leader, which Johnson had been in the Senate during the 1950s.[88] Johnson believed that Congress should be consulted regularly on policy initiatives. He knew how to include its members in decision making and how not to overload the system. And he was sensitive to making loyal supporters look good. Above all, in contrast to later presidents, Johnson sought out compromise behind the scenes, going directly to the people only as a last resort, and his liaison staff worked hard to develop and maintain cooperative relationships all over Capitol Hill.[89]

Richard Nixon cared little for domestic political issues; he preferred instead to focus on foreign policy, which required (in his mind) little congressional involvement. He seldom became personally involved in lobbying and rebelled against the sort of bargaining that Johnson had relished. Where Johnson had integrated the liaison office into his overall congressional strategy, Nixon removed it from the policy-making process and instead relied heavily on his close circle of personal aides for legislative advice and strategy. Where Johnson was accessible to many views and representatives, Nixon shielded himself behind a wall of assistants. And where Johnson relied on compromise, Nixon tended to confront and to stick with his course regardless of political considerations—a style not conducive to lobbying when Congress is in the hands of the other party.

Gerald Ford in many ways operated like Johnson, reflecting their shared congressional experiences. Like Johnson, Ford believed in working with members of Congress, and he deployed his legislative liaison team to cultivate friendly relations with both parties. But Ford was a minority president, since the Democrats controlled both houses of Congress. Unlike Johnson, he had to rely heavily on the veto as a central part of his overall strategy, using his staff to build coalitions in support of his vetoes. In this sense at least, Ford was highly effective; but as an unelected president succeeding a president forced to resign, he did not have the political capital to craft and push through a broad domestic agenda.

Unlike the four previous presidents, Jimmy Carter was an outsider who campaigned and won on that appeal. He had less interest in the process of consensus building than in the substance of policy options, was issue-based rather than party-oriented, and had an overall dim view of traditional Washington politics. "Legislative liaison for Carter," Eric Davis suggested, "simply was a matter of convincing members of Congress of the correctness of his positions on the issues." [90] His liaison team, as a result, was organized initially along issue lines, as opposed to the geographical and voting bloc organizational patterns employed since O'Brien. This meant that no single staff assistant could discuss a wide array of issues—or make deals across issues—with any single member of Congress. Also, unlike the days when O'Brien courted members constantly and doled out favors to loyalists and party leaders, the Carter White House initially turned its back on such traditional ways of cultivating support. Carter aides were either so disdainful or so ignorant of the ways of Washington that even House Speaker Thomas P. O'Neill, who Carter later would need desperately to push through his ambitious energy program, was unable to get good seats for his guests at the inaugural gala—a slight O'Neill never forgot.[91]

Carter usually would present his case directly to the public first, believing that his primary task was to persuade citizens to his side on an issue and thereby create a political climate favorable to congressional action. Congressional leaders often were not consulted in advance, and legislative liaison tended toward the exchange of information rather than the building of coalitions.[92]

In his first year Carter bombarded Congress with dozens of bills all at once, thus overloading the legislative process and spreading lobbying resources thin. After a somewhat disappointing first six months—where what victories Carter did win came because of large Democratic majorities in Congress—the White House reorganized the liaison office in line with the O'Brien model and worked harder thereafter to consult with congressional leaders.

Charles O. Jones characterized Carter as a political layman, a label that was true insofar as traditional styles of negotiation were concerned.[93] But Carter encountered a far more complex and frustrating political climate than had Johnson. Public faith in government and willingness to follow political leaders was at a low point after Watergate and Vietnam, and Congress itself had changed dramatically in the interim. Johnson could rely heavily on congressional leaders to carry his banner, since the congressional hierarchy still was strong enough to keep party members in line. But by the time Carter was elected in 1976, that hierarchy had all but dissolved, and Carter needed to construct temporary coalitions among as many members as possible in order to succeed. Negotiating with Congress thus had become a different ballgame by the time Carter arrived, and, in retrospect, his strategy of going directly to the public on important issues in many ways may have been the best possible approach.

Ronald Reagan in fact used that same strategy to great effect during his first year, although it was augmented by an experienced and well-organized legislative liaison staff. House Speaker O'Neill called Reagan's victory on the 1981 budget package "the greatest selling job I've ever seen." Reagan's success came about through a mixture of dramatic public appeals by the president, the work of administration officials sent to generate support in key Democratic constituencies, and a good deal of old-fashioned bargaining.[94] Jones has likened Reagan's lobbying style to that of Franklin Roosevelt, with emphasis placed on communicating views and ideals to the public and generating pressure on Congress to go along.[95]

Trends in Presidential Lobbying

Although there is no single best way for presidents to lobby Congress, certain devices—such as favors, consultation, and personal phone calls—are always useful. Each president's particular style and the manner in which lobbying is organized reflects personal skills, interests, and views about the relationship between the two branches of government. Presidents who see themselves as partners with Congress, such as Johnson, will operate far differently from those, such as Nixon, who see the presidency as essentially independent of the legislature.[96] Each style has its strengths and weaknesses, but neither guarantees success. After all, pushing a legislative agenda also means having to deal with a Congress that sees itself as the energetic center of U.S. government.

Still, even "failed" presidents enjoyed a modicum of success in Congress, if success is measured by the percentage of bills supported by the president that Congress passes into law. *(See "Presidential Support in Congress, 1953-1988," p. 1475, in the Appendix.)* The data show, for example, that Carter, despite his apparent weaknesses, actually enjoyed a great deal of success overall, and that Reagan, for all his popularity and rhetorical skills, on average fared much worse. The reason for this disparity may be simply that Carter faced large and generally friendly Democratic majorities in Congress and that Reagan constantly encountered at least one house dominated by his political foes. One should point out, however, that Reagan's successes came not on the quantity of bills supported in Congress, but on their scope and importance.

Another trend to emerge is the inevitable decline in congressional support throughout the course of any administration despite the equally inevitable sharpening of an administration's lobbying and organizational skills. This paradox perhaps is less mystifying when one compares presidential success in Congress with the president's own popularity. *(See Table 4.)* Both scores drop over time, suggesting how presidential popularity affects legislative success. Members of Congress, George Edwards III points out, "respond to the president's current popularity among their supporters" and thus are reluctant to oppose a popular president.[97] They do not, however, hesitate to vote against one whose public support has weakened, particularly if the president is from the opposing party.

Thus, whether a president succeeds or fails may in fact have less to do with personal attributes or styles than with political conditions at the time. Presidents certainly can influence these conditions, but they cannot control them. Successful presidents, therefore, merely may be those whose particular strengths mesh well with the tenor of the times or with prevailing congressional majorities.

Use of Public Appeals

Every president has found it necessary on occasion to go directly to the people to exert pressure on a recalcitrant Congress. Be it through speeches to the nation on television, "leaks" of information to favored newspaper reporters, or orchestrated public demonstrations of support, presidents find some way to recruit public opinion in their fights with Congress when they believe conditions and issues warrant. *(See Public Opinion chapter in Part IV.)*

Going directly to the people has become far easier and, thus, more desirable as the technology of television has allowed presidents since the 1940s to speak their minds with less worry that their messages will be garbled by intermediaries. The rise of television as the primary means by which most Americans receive their news is a primary factor in the emergence of the contemporary presidency and its power to influence the national agenda. Nonetheless, going directly to the people has its risks, for success hinges largely on the issue in question, a president's own rhetorical skills, and the mood of the public at the moment.

Early Use of Public Appeals

Presidents before the twentieth century neither had the technologies to speak directly to the people nor did they generally conceive of their roles in exactly the same manner as do presidents today. The very earliest presidents were influenced heavily by the Founders' fear of demagogic leaders, which had induced them deliberately to remove presidential election from the popular vote. Congress was meant to represent the people, and Congress generally considered it illegitimate and intrusive for a president to try to pressure members of the legislature on public policy matters.

Even then, however, some presidents did attempt to influence congressional deliberations through indirect, often subtle pressure. Thomas Jefferson, for example, relied heavily on his popular dinner parties to influence key legislators, newspaper reporters, and other important political figures. But it was Andrew Jackson among earlier presidents who began the practice of appealing to the common people for support. Jackson, after all, had come to office as an outsider and a foe of the established ways of doing business, and he used his mass popularity to influence Congress where possible. Jackson in many ways presaged the contemporary presidency by artfully arranging for official documents to be leaked to supportive newspapers, using friendly journalists to convey his views and desires, and relying on his party organization to stir up public support and pressure Congress. "King Andrew," as his enemies came to call him, not surprisingly reaped a great deal of criticism for his unorthodox practices, and most pre-Civil War presidents did not follow his pattern. None had Jackson's popularity with the people, nor his philosophy about the role of the presidency, to continue Jackson's practices.

Abraham Lincoln was almost always on the defensive with Congress over his war policies, but he overcame its opposition by winning public support through the newspapers. Lincoln wrote numerous letters and opinion columns, and friendly publishers, such as Horace Greeley, saw to it they received favorable coverage. Lincoln generated other supportive stories through leaks to reporters. It also was said that Lincoln grew his beard after a supporter remarked that his bare face (and lack of chin) did not look "presidential" enough, and inexpensive lithographs (a new technology) of the newly bearded commander in chief soon graced many a Union household.

Theodore Roosevelt thrived on publicity and made himself easily available to favorite reporters. His love of the press in many ways was reciprocated, for the flamboyant and erudite Roosevelt made for good copy. Roosevelt is credited with creating the official White House press release, which he often issued on Sundays—traditionally the slowest news day—to give newspapers something to print the next day. He also devised off-the-record or "background" press briefings, which he frequently used to float "trial balloons" as one way to assess public and congressional opinion on issues.

Woodrow Wilson, no doubt much to his satisfaction, outdid Roosevelt in going directly to the public by resuming the practice of delivering the State of the Union address personally and by instituting regular and formal press conferences. He was most effective, however, in making direct appeals to people through the newspapers or speeches before Congress. The notable exception was his grueling nationwide tour in 1919 to generate support for the Versailles treaty. The president was followed by a "truth squad" of senators who opposed the treaty, and the journey ruined his health. Wilson's efforts to go to the people went for naught, for the Senate failed to ratify the treaty.

Roosevelt and Radio

Theodore Roosevelt and Woodrow Wilson were, in many ways, masters at generating favorable public opinion through the press, but they lacked the technology to go directly into every citizen's home. Franklin Roosevelt entered the White House as radio entered its heyday, and the ebullient New Yorker made superb use of the new medium.

His public speeches, the twenty-seven "fireside" radio chats, hundreds of formal press conferences, countless informal background sessions with selected reporters, and shrewd use of the newsreels, all constructed a public persona that millions of Americans would recall fondly for decades. So great was the public response to Roosevelt's first inaugural address, in which the president averred that "the only thing we have to fear is fear itself," that humorist Will Rogers wrote, "If he burned down the Capitol, we would cheer and say, 'Well, we at least got a fire started somehow.' "[98]

In his first radio chat to the nation, Roosevelt explained how the banking system worked and why the public should take their money out of their mattresses and put it back into their savings accounts. They did, and Roosevelt was credited with ending the panic. As Arthur M. Schlesinger, Jr., later described the fireside chats, they "conveyed Roosevelt's conception of himself as a man at ease in his own house talking frankly and intimately to neighbors as they sat in their living rooms."[99]

The radio speeches and chats were intended for more than soothing the public: they were meant to move Congress into action on Roosevelt's agenda. According to political scientist Wilfred Binkley, Roosevelt "had only to glance toward a microphone or suggest that he might go on the air again and a whole congressional delegation would surrender. They had no relish for the flood of mail and telegrams they knew would swamp them after another fireside chat to the nation."[100] Roosevelt, particularly after the first year, did not always win when he went to the airwaves, but those in opposition never took his power to move the public for granted.

The Television Presidency

One reason Roosevelt proved so successful with radio was that radio forces listeners to use their imaginations to

Table 6 Television Addresses by Presidents, 1961-1988

President	Year	Topic
Kennedy	1961	Urgent national needs; Berlin Wall
	1962	Racial unrest; quarantine of Cuba
	1963	Civil rights bill; Test ban treaty
Johnson	1963	Kennedy assassination
	1965	Voting rights bill
	1968	Bombing halt/withdrawal from election
Nixon	1969	National unity in Vietnam; Vietnam peace proposals; Vietnam troop reductions
	1970	Vietnam; Cambodia incursion (2); Peace in Indochina
	1971	Withdrawal of troops; economic policy
	1972	Report of trip to the People's Republic of China
	1973	National energy policy
	1974	Resignation
Ford	1974	Post-Nixon resignation speech; inflation
	1975	State of the world
Carter	1977	Energy crisis; energy policy
	1979	Energy crisis; national morale; Soviet troops in Cuba; military spending
	1980	Failure of Iran rescue mission; anti-inflation
	1981	Farewell speech
Reagan	1981	Economic policies and proposals (4)
	1982	Federal budget; Middle East; Lebanon; Arms control
	1983	Strategic Defense Initiative and Central America; Grenada; Lebanon
	1985	Tax reform; U.S.-Soviet summit (Geneva)
	1986	Military spending; aid to contras (2); U.S.-Soviet summit (Iceland); Iran arms sales
	1987	Iran arms sales; economic summit; Iran-contra affair; Bork nomination; U.S.-Soviet summit (Washington)
	1988	Contra aid

Source: Congressional Quarterly Almanac, various issues, and *Congressional Quarterly Weekly Report,* various issues.

Note: Table does not include State of the Union and inaugural addresses, which also are televised; it includes only those addresses that are not part of a ceremonial occasion.

visualize both the speaker and the topic under discussion. He had a powerful voice, creating an image of strength and determination that overcame his own personal disability—stricken with polio at the age of thirty-nine Roosevelt could not walk. Many Americans never knew this because, in a tacit agreement with the press corps, he rarely was photographed below the waist. Those who did know about his disability never seemed to let it detract from the image of strength he projected in his radio addresses. But if Roosevelt had run for the presidency in the age of television—first and foremost a visual medium—he could not have controlled his public image so masterfully. Whether he could have been elected in the first place because of his disability, much less rally a nation through depression and war, is one of the tantalizing "what ifs" of history.

The contemporary presidency in many ways lives—and sometimes dies—by television. Eisenhower was the first president to permit news conferences to be filmed and, later, televised, but he did so only after careful editing by the White House.

John Kennedy, arguably the first president of the television age, was the first to permit live telecasts of his news conferences. For the first time the public saw actual questions and answers as they occurred, with no chance for the president or his aides to edit the president's comments. Kennedy's own ease with television, his intellect, and his humor made television a potent tool for communicating with the American people. His persuasive television appearance was not enough, however, to ensure congressional approval of his programs.

Lyndon Johnson, superb as he was in the art of personal lobbying, proved uneasy with television, although his televised address urging the passage of the 1965 Voting Rights Act did move the nation and Congress. But Johnson discovered how television can be a double-edged sword. Americans absorbed televised images of urban riots and anti-war demonstrations and for the first time could witness the horrors of war by watching the evening news. These televised events frequently appeared to contradict Johnson's own assertions about the pace of social progress at home and the winability of the war in Indochina and therefore shook the nation's confidence in its government. Johnson was particularly wounded by public reaction to a massive North Vietnamese offensive in early 1968, a coordinated assault on south Vietnamese cities that undercut his own statements that the war was winding down, and he decided not to run for reelection. His experience with the powerful impact of television on the American people, one which he could not easily control, was but an early example of how external events can influence a president's own agenda and popularity.

Richard Nixon, who felt that the press had been hostile to his candidacy in 1960 and saw how Johnson had fared with the media, used television extensively to tailor his image and present it directly to the public. His distrust of the Washington press corps, which often proved unwilling to rally around the administration's Vietnam policy, led the president to speak directly to the American people far more often than had his predecessors. In his November 1969 address to the nation on Vietnam, for example, Nixon asserted that a "silent majority" of citizens supported his actions, despite what members of the press wrote.[101] Nixon also held few Washington press conferences, which he felt only offered easy opportunities for his critics to attack him, and instead began to hold press conferences outside the capital, where journalists might be more deferential of his office.

What is more, Nixon used Vice President Spiro Agnew to make vigorous attacks on the news media, a tactic that produced one of the most memorable phrases in American political lore. In a September 1970 speech in San Diego, Agnew railed that the Washington press corps was filled with "nattering nabobs of negativism. They have formed their own 4-H Club—the 'hopeless, hysterical hypochondriacs of history.'"[102] The tactic was clear: discredit the news media and connect the president more directly to the American people.

Nixon also used television successfully to pressure Congress in selected instances, such as his televised veto of a 1970 appropriations bill. The broadcast generated thousands of supportive telegrams to both the White House and

Capitol Hill, and sent the impression of massive popular support for his position. Whether this deluge was spontaneous or orchestrated by Nixon supporters was irrelevant to many members of the House, which upheld the veto.

As with Johnson, however, television played a part in Nixon's downfall. The nation watched in fascination as the daily drama of the 1973 Senate Watergate hearings played out on national television. Nixon's own performances during televised press conferences, and even in speeches to the nation, seemed to many viewers to be the picture of a president trying to deceive the public. Following the emergence of evidence of Nixon's possible complicity in the Watergate coverup, the president resigned in disgrace on August 9, 1974.

His successor, Gerald Ford, worked to reverse the mutual distrust between the White House and the media built up over the previous years. Nixon basked in the trappings of the office, but Ford worked to convey a simpler image; for example, he allowed himself to be photographed while making his own breakfast. Nixon held the rare press conference, but Ford held many—and earned high praise from those in the media for his openness and honesty. Ford did not escape unscathed, however, for his every stumble or slip became grist for the humor mill (an irony, no doubt, for a former football all-American).

Jimmy Carter, given his populist image and belief that Americans had tired of the "imperial presidency," early on cultivated an image as an outsider by holding televised "town meetings" where citizens would call with questions. Carter also tried his own version of Roosevelt's fireside chats, sitting before a fire wearing a cardigan sweater.

But what had worked for Roosevelt in the days of the depression and radio did not work for Carter on television in the post-Watergate era. Too many Americans saw Carter's approach as superficial symbolism, and his efforts to use television to stir the public generally failed. His talk to the nation on the energy crisis, which he called "the moral equivalent of war," evoked no widespread support and even spawned jokes that the acronym for "moral equivalent of war" was MEOW.

Carter's supporters argued that this criticism was unfair, that the president's attempts to rally the American people seemed to come up short less because of Carter's own shortcomings than because the public was far less inclined to follow presidential directions than they may have been before Vietnam and Watergate. Public trust in government had waned measurably in the late 1970s, they noted, making Carter's task all the more difficult. Whatever the cause, Carter's efforts to communicate directly to the public and rally its support frequently fell on deaf ears, and Congress generally went its own way.

Carter's well-known difficulties should not mask his real successes, however. Most notable was the televised signing of the 1979 Camp David Accords, a moment of high drama when Egyptian president Anwar Sadat signed a peace treaty with Israeli prime minister Menachem Begin. Carter, who had been personally instrumental in bringing these longtime adversaries together, used the signing to rally congressional support for significant American aid to both Israel and Egypt.

Generally, however, Carter proved more victim than manipulator of television, particularly after Iranian militants seized and held fifty-three American hostages for over a year. Americans each night witnessed on their television sets the humiliation of the hostage situation and Carter's inability to free the hostages proved instrumental in his loss to Ronald Reagan in 1980.

Reagan, the former movie and television actor, quickly proved a powerful contrast to Carter in his ability to use the media to his political advantage. As radio had been to Franklin Roosevelt, television was to Reagan, and the president relied heavily on his rhetorical talents to whip up massive support for his dramatic budget and tax policy victories in 1981. Of particular potency was Reagan's May 1981 appeal to a joint session of Congress for support on his budget package, his first public appearance since the March 1981 assassination attempt. So powerful was the moment, and so massive was the outpouring of public support for the president, that the Democratic-dominated House passed his package a few days after the speech.

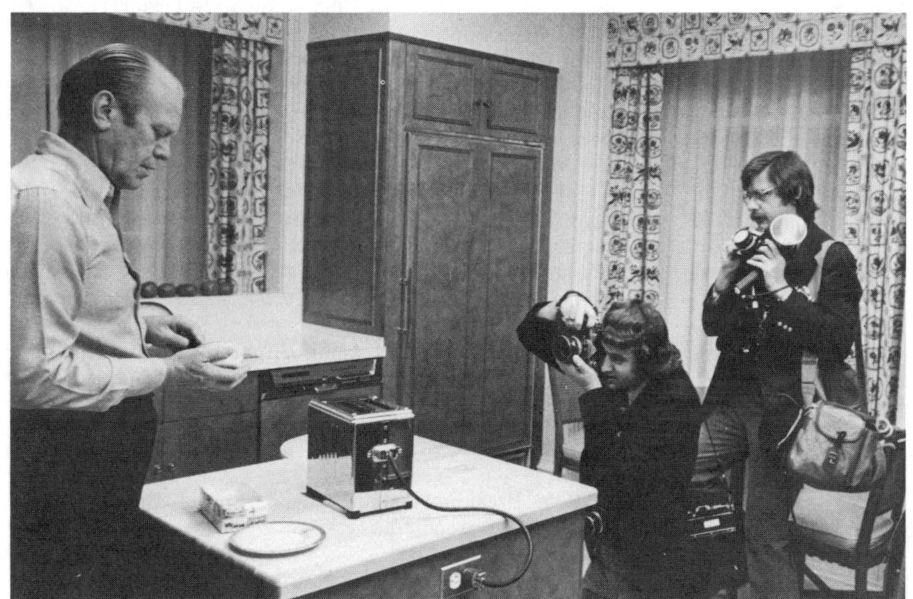

Gerald R. Ford Library

To reverse the mutual distrust between the White House and the media built up during the Nixon administration, Ford worked to convey a simpler image to the press. Here he allows photographers to take pictures as he makes his own breakfast.

No president had used television to establish intimacy with the American people as well as Reagan did. Few could resist the emotional pull of his 1984 speech on the cliffs overlooking Omaha Beach on the fortieth anniversary of the Normandy invasion or of his eulogy for the astronauts who died in the 1986 space shuttle disaster. But even for Reagan the medium had a double-edged effect.

Public responsiveness to televised appeals almost inevitably wanes the more frequently a president relies on them, and Reagan discovered as his time in office went on that the technique has decreasing power. Public confidence in his leadership was eroded by startling revelations about secret arms sales to the Iranian government and their possibly illegal ties to the supply of arms to the contras, or Nicaraguan rebels. Televised congressional hearings on the affair raised broad public concern about Reagan's overall command of his office. By 1988, when the three major networks refused to carry another appeal for aid to the contras because it "was not news," it was apparent that the skills so integral to Reagan's early successes no longer were potent enough to prevail.

The president of the United States has an unparalleled capacity to dominate the national debate because of the office's unique ability to command media attention. Equally important, the president is but one person, whereas Congress is a vast and seemingly disorganized institution. In a battle between the branches, the resident of the White House who possesses good rhetorical skills has a tremendous advantage over the branch of government once given the constitutional mandate to make the law.

Some observers worry that the president's capacity to dominate national debate may drown out many other voices demanding to be heard. Presidents can take credit for ideas that Congress developed, or, conversely, they can blame Congress for their failures. The danger, political scientist Bruce Miroff has concluded, is that presidents could "take over so much of the public space that citizens would perceive the political world chiefly through presidential actions." [103] Should that happen the Framers' fears of a monarchical executive would prove well founded.

Executive Orders

Article II of the Constitution allots to the president the "executive power," one of the least specific but potentially far-reaching phrases in the document. Before 1787, state legislatures generally defined executive power, but the writers of the Constitution (learning from their problems with the Articles of Confederation) shied away from having Congress dictate the boundaries of presidential action. Instead they left the range of such power undefined, open-ended, and ripe for reinterpretation and expansion by later presidents.

Their silence proved critical. When paired with the Article II provision requiring presidents to "take care that the laws be faithfully executed," the executive power clause today provides for a range of "implied" powers whose extent and potency have grown beyond anything the Founders could have foreseen.[104] "Express" powers—those specifically named in the Constitution—like the veto give presidents a limited set of tools for shaping legislation. But powers *implied* in the Constitution, and given substance by years of continuous reinterpretation, are the source of the president's ability to act alone, often without specific congressional statute. Much of U.S. history has involved a struggle between presidents claiming the power to act without clear constitutional mandates and their critics arguing to the contrary.

> The executive power shall be vested in a president of the United States of America.
>
> —from Article II, section 1

On its face, the take care clause directs the president to administer statutes in ways faithful to legislative language and intent. Like so many constitutional provisions, however, it is a clause vague in meaning and elastic in potential ramifications. In 1890, for example, the Supreme Court ruled that the clause pertained not only to statutes but to any "rights, duties, and obligations growing out of the Constitution itself, our international relations, and all the protection implied by the nature of the government under the Constitution." [105]

The 1890 interpretation of the take care clause provided by that decision alone suggests greater discretionary power inherent in the president's roles as chief executive and commander in chief than the Constitution seems to state specifically. This line of reasoning theoretically means that presidents could undertake any actions deemed necessary to carry out their constitutional duties, to provide for the nation's defense, or to protect the common good. To make matters more complex, the Constitution is mute on exactly what the "common good" entails, another one of those "great silences" that makes the potential of implied powers so controversial.

An offspring of the implied powers doctrine is the *executive order.* This critical instrument of active presidential power is nowhere defined in the Constitution but generally is construed as a presidential directive that becomes law without prior congressional approval. It is based either on existing statutes or on the president's other constitutional responsibilities. Executive orders usually pertain specifically to government agencies and officials, but their effects often reach to the average citizen. For example, Lyndon Johnson in 1965 (Executive Order 11246) required firms that win federal government contracts to create programs for hiring more minorities, thus significantly affecting private sector employment practices. For the most part, orders are issued to establish executive branch agencies, to modify bureaucratic rules or actions, to change decision-making procedures, or to give substance and force to statutes.[106] In Executive Order 12298, for example, President Ronald Reagan moved to implement an interstate cooperative agreement authorized by Congress in 1980 by abolishing one coordinating body to make way for a new one. *(See box, An Executive Order, p. 481.)*

There are no specific constitutional procedures for issuing executive orders, and during the first hundred or so years they were issued without any system of publication or

> [The President] shall take care that the laws be faithfully executed. . . .
>
> —from Article II, section 3

recording. The numbering of executive orders began only in 1907, with numbers assigned retroactively to the time of Abraham Lincoln. Almost thirteen thousand executive orders had been recorded as of 1988, although haphazard reporting and record keeping throughout much of U.S. history prompts scholars to estimate that somewhere between fifteen thousand and fifty thousand directives never were recorded.[107] *(See Table 7.)* To respond to growing concerns that these lax conditions created serious problems for governing and democratic accountability, Congress in the Administrative Procedures Act of 1946 mandated that the number and text of all executive orders must be published in the *Federal Register,* the official U.S. government record, published each weekday; of all executive branch announcements, proposals, and regulations. The exception to this rule applies to "classified" executive orders—those pertaining directly to sensitive national security matters, which are entered into the *Register* by number only.[108]

Table 7 Executive Orders, by President, 1789-1989

President	Years in office	Number of orders	Average per year
Washington	8.00	8	1.00
J. Adams	4.00	1	.25
Jefferson	8.00	4	.50
Madison	8.00	1	.13
Monroe	8.00	1	.13
J. Q. Adams	4.00	3	.75
Jackson	8.00	12	1.50
Van Buren	4.00	10	2.50
W. H. Harrison	0.08[a]	0	—
Tyler	4.00	17	4.25
Polk	4.00	18	4.50
Taylor	1.25	5	4.00
Fillmore	2.75	12	4.36
Pierce	4.00	35	8.75
Buchanan	4.00	16	4.00
Lincoln	4.00	48	12.00
A. Johnson	4.00	79	19.75
Grant	8.00	217	27.13
Hayes	4.00	92	23.00
Garfield	0.50	6	—[b]
Arthur	3.25	96	29.50
Cleveland (1st term)	4.00	113	28.25
Harrison	4.00	143	35.75
Cleveland (2d term)	4.00	140	35.00
McKinley	4.75	185	38.95
T. Roosevelt	7.25	1081	149.10
Taft	4.00	724	181.00
Wilson	8.00	1803	225.38
Harding	2.60	522	200.77
Coolidge	5.40	1203	222.77
Hoover	4.00	968	242.00
F. Roosevelt	12.33	3522	285.64
Truman	7.67	897	116.96
Eisenhower	8.00	478	59.75
Kennedy	3.00	228	76.00
L. Johnson	5.00	316	63.20
Nixon	5.60	355	63.39
Ford	2.40	152	63.33
Carter	4.00	311	77.75
Reagan	8.00	409	51.13

Sources: Calculated by the author from Gary King and Lyn Ragsdale, *The Elusive Executive: Discovering Statistical Patterns in the Presidency* (Washington, D.C.: CQ Press, 1988), 160-167; *Code of Federal Regulations.*

Note: Includes both numbered and unnumbered executive orders.

a. W. H. Harrison died after only one month in office.

b. Garfield was assassinated after six months in office, during which he issued six executive orders. At that rate his average would have been twelve per year.

The Discretionary Presidency

Executive orders are critical to the legislative role of the contemporary presidency precisely because Congress frequently finds itself unable or unwilling to respond to complex national problems with highly detailed laws. Instead, Congress copes by legislating in broad language, setting certain goals and instructing executive branch personnel to hammer out technical matters, regulatory procedures, and rules that both meet those goals and carry the force of law. In 1921, for example, Congress directed the president to coordinate all executive branch budget requests and package them together into a single annual budget document. But Congress never said *how* the president should do so, nor what the limits of that authority should be. As a consequence, the Office of Management and Budget (known until 1970 as the Bureau of the Budget) has grown immeasurably in size and power through presidential initiative. In 1981, in Executive Order 12291, to cite but one case, President Reagan dramatically expanded the OMB's role in substantive policy making by requiring that all executive branch agencies submit new rules and regulations for OMB approval before they can go into effect. Congress nowhere specifically transformed OMB's central role, but one president's use of executive discretion in effect redefined the decision-making process in the federal bureaucracy. The impact was seen immediately in such areas as environmental policy, where Environmental Protection Agency personnel increasingly found their directives overruled by the OMB for budget or policy reasons. The overall effect has been to centralize decision making more in the Executive Office of the President, but Congress at no time passed a law to accomplish this fact.[109]

Even when legislative language is precise, as it usually is in tax legislation, there may emerge policy contradictions, unforeseen circumstances, or technical considerations that require executive branch officials to exercise their judgment in administering the programs legislated by Congress. The Tax Reform Act of 1986, for example, spawned approximately forty-two new Internal Revenue Service regulations, sixty-five announcements, thirty-two rulings, and forty-eight new tax forms within the first thirteen months after passage.[110]

Congress also consciously delegates broad discretionary authority in the name of flexibility, effectiveness, or efficiency.[111] The Smoot-Hawley Tariff Act of 1930, for example, ran over 170 pages because Congress tried to codify into law virtually every known type of tariff and trade matter. The 1934 Reciprocal Trade Agreements Act, in contrast, ran but 2 pages; this time Congress simply authorized the president to do whatever was necessary to achieve the law's intent.[112] The rigid Smoot-Hawley tariff schedules had been a spectacular nightmare, and Congress thereafter apparently decided that executive branch personnel were better positioned to act flexibly on issues with

Processing Executive Orders

Proposed executive orders can originate from almost anywhere in the executive branch. A few are composed directly in the White House, but most emanate from the various executive departments and agencies. Some orders, such as those imposing trade sanctions on another nation, may be written at the express instruction of the president. Most, however, are composed by career staff personnel in the departments and agencies to implement federal regulations, propose new rules or procedures, or add technical language to congressional statutes. Whatever the case, executive orders have the force of law, so they are crafted largely by professional legal counsel at the instruction of the president's appointees. Rarely does the president take a direct hand in writing an order's language.

Each proposed executive order must be composed and submitted along procedures laid out in the U.S. Code. It must be prepared in a specific format and style (for example, on certain types of paper, in certain language) and must contain language explaining its nature, purpose, background, and effects, along with an assessment of how it relates to existing law. The proposed order is then sent, with seven copies, to the director of the Office of Management and Budget (OMB), where it is examined for adherence to the administration's overall policy and budgetary goals. If approved, the order and its copies are sent next to the attorney general, whose office scrutinizes it for potential legal problems. Since both the attorney general and the director of the OMB typically are among the president's closest personal advisers, clearance by these offices normally can be assumed to signify presidential approval.

Following these steps, the proposed order is transmitted to the director of the Office of the Federal Register, which is part of the National Archives and Records Services of the General Services administration, the federal government's housekeeping arm. The order is reviewed once more for stylistic and typographical errors, after which it and three copies are submitted to the president for final approval. If signed by the president, the order and two copies go back to the director of the Federal Register for publication in the *Federal Register*. It is only upon the moment of publication in the *Register* that the order takes force.

Not all executive orders follow these precise steps. Those relating to some emergency may bypass much of the review process and go directly to the president for final approval. What is more, the text of an order concerning some aspect of national security may be deemed confidential, in which case only the order's number is published in the *Federal Register*. The overwhelming number of executive orders do not fit into these categories, however, so the process for creating and implementing an order typically follows a pattern set by law.

broad domestic and international effects.

Although administrative actions must conform with legislative intent, the line between "making" and "administering" law often becomes blurred.[113] This uncertain distinction occurs most noticeably in international affairs, executive branch operations, and national security, matters where the Constitution gives the president primary authority. Executive branch agencies thus "make" law continuously by interpreting the intent of the law in ways that belie the fiction that presidents only "administer" the will of Congress.

Some scholars argue that for Congress to delegate broad authority to the president is unwise or illegitimate,[114] but executive orders usually are not controversial when based clearly on existing statutory authority. They do, however, spark disputes when based on vaguely defined implied powers. The first such spat with Congress came in 1793 when George Washington unilaterally declared U.S. neutrality in the war between France and England. Washington justified his action with the argument that his constitutional responsibilities in diplomacy included the implied power to keep the United States out of war, but James Madison retorted that the proclamation was invalid because only Congress could decide issues of war and peace.[115] The dispute has simmered ever since, erupting forcefully whenever presidents take actions that Congress deems unconstitutional intrusions into its domains.

Presidents also court controversy when they base executive orders on "implied" legislative consent; that is, when Congress has not legislated *against* some action. Federal courts tend to judge each case individually, but they usually give presidents the benefit of the doubt when Congress has failed to decide an issue over a prolonged period of time. Making matters still more complex, Congress often gives presidents retroactive authority for their unilateral actions, particularly during emergencies. Congress approved Washington's proclamation of neutrality a year later; this pattern has been repeated enough that presidents often proceed on the assumption that Congress will acquiesce.

Finally, presidents maintain that they have the constitutional authority to act unilaterally because they inherit "war" or "emergency" powers during periods of apparent crisis. *(See "Emergency Powers," p. 486, in this chapter.)*

Growth in Executive Discretion

Alexander Hamilton and other Federalists wanted a national government that "left substantial freedom of action to high officials and kept Congress out of most administrative details."[116] As secretary of the treasury under Washington, Hamilton argued strongly that Congress should legislate and appropriate in broad categories, granting to those in the executive branch wide latitude to administer programs. Washington's years in office in fact witnessed a remarkable degree of deference to presidential authority, particularly in the areas of fiscal policy and trade. This did not deter controversies from arising over Hamilton's aggressive claims to executive branch discretion or Washington's proclamation of neutrality, but Congress generally entrusted the president to get the new nation on its feet.

That deference had eroded by 1800, as Jefferson's Democratic-Republicans took control and asserted their view of legislative dominance. Jefferson and his allies, notes historian Leonard White, "emphasized the responsibility of the executive branch and the administrative system to Congress." During the nineteenth century, Congress usually maintained tight reins over executive branch actions through highly detailed statutes, strict budgetary controls, and reviews of even the most mundane administrative matters.[117] Executive orders during these years most often supplemented acts of Congress to carry out rather minor matters like salary increases for individual employees. With the possible exception of Abraham Lincoln's dramatic assumption of power during the Civil War, presidents and legislators alike tended to accept the view that presidents simply administered the law.

The shift toward greater executive discretion began most forcefully with Theodore Roosevelt. His "stewardship" theory of the presidency hinged on "residual" executive powers implied in the Constitution, and it coincided in the late 1800s with growing federal government responsibilities both in the United States and abroad.[118] Residual powers, he concluded, neither were enumerated in the Constitution nor assigned broadly to a specific branch; instead, they resided simply in concepts, like national sovereignty or the public good. Thus, Roosevelt argued, "my view was that every officer, and above all every executive officer in high position, was a steward of the people. . . . My belief was that it was not only his right but his duty to do anything that the needs of the Nation demanded unless such action was forbidden by the Constitution or by the laws."[119] This view contrasted strongly with the more traditional notion that presidents were mere "clerks" who carried out congressional dictates, for it asserted the responsibility of the president to represent the nation as a whole.

The problem with Roosevelt's position was that the Constitution said little about the powers available for presidential stewardship. Clearly, as political scientist Richard Pious suggested, "to use prerogatives effectively the president must first stake out his claims to them. Like Excalibur's sword, he must wrest his powers from the Constitution before he can wield them."[120] Although Abraham Lincoln and Theodore Roosevelt both carved out new areas for unilateral executive initiative, the specter of the truly discretionary presidency did not gain real shape until the administration of Woodrow Wilson. During World War I Wilson issued almost two thousand executive orders and also wielded expansive emergency powers to direct the war and domestic economic production. The powers Wilson asserted in wartime did not dissolve once hostilities ceased. They endured for the benefit of later presidents in a rachet-like expansion in executive power that was to be repeated thereafter.

Rise of the Discretionary Presidency

Franklin Roosevelt gave permanence to the stewardship view of the presidency during the New Deal and World War II. Elected as depression raged and given wide latitude by Congress and the American people, Roosevelt relied heavily on executive initiatives to attack the economic crisis and rally the nation. He issued 654 executive orders in 1933 alone,[121] including his inaugural day proclamation closing all banks for four days to restructure the crumbling financial system and his creation of administrative mechanisms for implementing New Deal programs.

In most cases Roosevelt won quick and retroactive congressional approval for his actions. Congress during these years also appropriated massive amounts of money to be used at the president's discretion so that Roosevelt could develop and finance a myriad of special New Deal programs quickly and, perhaps, more effectively than Congress thought possible through traditional procedures.[122] The gravity of the crisis called for decisive action, and Roosevelt stretched the boundaries of his constitutional powers to the limit.

Not only did Roosevelt exercise a highly muscular view of presidential discretion, but the sheer growth in federal government activities during the 1930s brought with it an explosion in executive branch responsibility. Congress found it increasingly difficult to grapple with the size and complexity of new national programs and began the widespread delegation of authority that marks contemporary government. Equally important, scholars and politicians alike began to support the idea that broad executive discretion leads to efficient and effective public administration, arguments that redefined the concept of chief executive away from more traditional views of the president as a mere agent of Congress.[123] Delegating broad authority not only made pragmatic sense but also cohered with views that relatively free executive management and administrative discretion offered unalloyed benefits to a fragmented and decentralized system of government. Traits that the Founders deemed essential for safeguarding citizens' rights and liberties now were seen as impediments to sound government. Strong executive leadership was viewed as the only mechanism able to overcome systemic weaknesses in the federal structure of governance.

The approach of World War II accelerated these trends as Roosevelt gained broad authority to prosecute the war and manage the domestic economy. Roosevelt moved unilaterally in many instances without the benefit of even vague statutory authority, basing his actions in-

Executive Order 12298
March 12, 1981
Lake Tahoe Region

By the authority vested in me as President by the Constitution of the United States of America, and in order to eliminate unnecessary and duplicative Federal interference in the responsibilities of the Tahoe Regional Planning Agency (see Public Law 96-351 of December 19, 1980), it is hereby ordered that the Tahoe Federal Coordinating council is terminated and Executive Order No. 12247 of October 15, 1980, is revoked.

Ronald Reagan

The White House,
March 12, 1981.

Source: Office of the Federal Register, *Weekly Compilation of Presidential documents,* March 16, 1981 (Washington, D.C.: Government Printing Office, 1981), 287.

stead on powers allegedly inherent in his constitutional duties as commander in chief and chief executive. In 1941, for example, he ordered the seizure of defense plants, shipyards, and thousands of coal mines to prepare the nation for war. Congress more often than not provided the needed statutory authority afterwards and gave Roosevelt tremendous discretionary spending authority because of the national emergency, but even then there were limits to congressional acquiescence. Roosevelt's tendency to use executive orders to create wartime agencies and then to fund them with money appropriated for other purposes eventually stirred a backlash, and Congress in 1944 barred use of any appropriations for an agency created through executive order unless the funds were authorized specifically for that agency.[124]

Perhaps the most controversial of Roosevelt's actions came in 1942, when his Executive Order 9066 authorized the dislocation of Americans of Japanese ancestry from the West Coast and their confinement to camps in the southwestern desert for the duration of the war. This order later came to be viewed as a gross violation of the civil liberties of U.S. citizens, but at the time it was defended as a safeguard against potential sabotage—although the same logic was not applied to citizens of German or Italian heritage. No citizen of Japanese descent ever was convicted of espionage or sabotage, but the Supreme Court in 1944 ruled that Roosevelt had acted legally to protect the nation during wartime.[125]

National security in fact became the primary justification for unilateral executive action in the postwar era. The "cold war" between the United States and the Soviet Union, additional U.S. commitments around the world, and a consensus on the need for assertive executive leadership prompted Congress through the 1960s to accede to presidential dictates across a wide spectrum of domestic and international policy domains. So generous was congressional delegation of foreign policy making power to the presidency during this era, which stood in sharp contrast to the tight reins the legislature had held on executive discretion before World War II, that many scholars regarded this time as one of relative congressional decline. In its reluctance to hobble presidential flexibility in international affairs, Congress appeared to surrender many of its traditional prerogatives. As political scientist Allen Schick noted, "when Congress controls, it legislates the particulars; when Congress withdraws, it legislates in general terms." [126] If one examines a cross-section of postwar statutes, both in domestic and foreign policy realms, it is striking how far less detailed and constraining they were compared to laws passed before the 1930s.

Postwar presidents relied on executive orders less heavily than did presidents before the war. This trend occurred largely because of the accumulation of a body of administrative law that replaced the need for unilateral presidential action in more routine areas, like personnel administration and regulatory procedures. What is more, of almost two thousand executive orders issued between 1945 and 1965, more than 80 percent were based on existing statutory authority, indicating in part the breadth of the statutory web built up since World War II.[127]

Still, the orders issued by postwar presidents were much broader in scope and were used more frequently to bypass a reluctant Congress. Lyndon Johnson, for example, issued an executive order to create minority hiring guidelines for federal contracts after Congress failed to embody affirmative action in the Civil Rights Act of 1964.[128] Richard Nixon used executive orders to restructure and gain greater control over the executive branch after Congress turned down his reorganization proposals. In 1986 Ronald Reagan preempted possible congressional action in ordering drug testing for federal employees. Thus, while the number of executive orders declined in absolute terms, the tendency of contemporary presidents to use them to bypass Congress made them even more controversial.

Orders as Executive Law Making

Postwar presidents issued executive orders for a wide range of purposes, but three in particular stand out: to combat discrimination, to control executive bureaucracies, and to maintain secrets.

Combating Discrimination

Beginning with Franklin Roosevelt, who directed greater desegregation of defense plants during World War II, presidents have used executive orders to safeguard or promote the civil rights of minorities and women. Many orders were applied to executive branch agencies; others altered federal programs after Congress proved unable or unwilling to act. Harry Truman, for example, in 1948 used Executive Order 9981 to integrate the armed forces, an action that, combined with calls for stronger civil rights protection, split Democrats during the 1948 election. *(See "The Truman Presidency, p. 305, in The Electoral Process chapter of Part II.)* Dwight Eisenhower in 1957 sent federal troops into Little Rock, Arkansas, to enforce Supreme Court decisions forbidding racial segregation in public schools,[129] as did John Kennedy in the early 1960s to protect blacks seeking admission into southern state universities. Kennedy also used Executive Order 11063 in 1963 to bar racial discrimination in federally subsidized housing after finding the legislative route blocked by southern conservatives.

Lyndon Johnson's Executive Order 11246 in 1965 directed that firms contracting with the federal government create minority hiring programs after Congress refused to do so in the Civil Rights Act of 1964.[130] Johnson's creation of affirmative action later was redefined somewhat by Nixon's "Philadelphia Plan," a 1969 executive order setting up racial hiring quotas on federal projects. Nixon was challenged on his order's apparent conflict with the 1964 Civil Rights Act (which forbade quotas of any kind), but he was upheld by a federal court of appeals based partly on the implied power of the president to set federal procurement policies.[131]

Controlling Executive Bureaucracies

The Constitution fails to spell out the relationships between presidents and executive branch employees. Presidents thus have made vigorous use of executive orders to mold and control the activities of bureaucrats, efforts that accelerated sharply as the sheer growth in federal responsibilities brought with it an explosion in executive branch size and complexity. In many ways the contemporary presidency's greatest task is to control the federal establishment, and the executive order has become an instrument for government management.[132]

A major problem for presidents and their political appointees is preventing lower-level career bureaucrats from bypassing their superiors and appealing directly to sympathetic congressional committees. William Howard Taft as early as 1909 (Executive Order 1142) prohibited agency officials from applying to Congress for funds without consent of their cabinet secretaries, but it was Franklin Roosevelt who relied most on executive orders to inaugurate the first great effort to centralize control over agencies and their expenditures. Executive Order 6166 in 1933, for example, transferred all executive budget-making authority from department heads to the Bureau of the Budget. Perhaps more important, Roosevelt in 1939 (Executive Order 8248) moved BOB from the Treasury Department to the newly created Executive Office of the President, thus instituting even greater presidential control over bureaucratic actions.

Richard Nixon directed the next powerful effort to impose stricter presidential control. After Congress in 1970 approved the reorganization of the Bureau of the Budget into the Office of Management and Budget, Nixon in Executive Order 11541 directed the new bureau to monitor agency programs and budgets more forcefully. This order effectively began the transformation of OMB from a low-profile budget office into a powerful and controversial policy-making arm of the presidency.

Ronald Reagan went even further in using OMB to monitor and direct agency actions. His Executive Order 12291 in 1981 prohibited federal agencies from proposing or issuing any new rules until OMB ensured that their benefits exceeded their costs. Even more important, Executive Order 12498 in 1985 extended OMB's reach to agency "pre-rulemaking activities," which were defined as almost any activity that could lead to the *consideration* of the need for a regulation. This order also required OMB to approve an annual "regulatory program" submitted by each agency and prohibited actions not in that program unless cleared by OMB observers.

The cumulative effect of these directives has been to endow OMB with expansive powers to supervise the policy development process in all agencies, stop those deemed in conflict with the president's agenda, and insert the president's own priorities more squarely into the routines of agency life. These actions were criticized for accelerating tendencies toward the "overcentralization" of executive branch power, but most complaints seem to come from those opposing the policies of the respective presidents. Future presidents are unlikely to reverse these trends, since the desire to control bureaucratic action is common to Democratic and Republican presidents alike.

Directing policy making is one thing, but there is far less agreement about presidential efforts to control the personal views or behavior of executive branch employees out of a desire for "loyalty" or "proper" lifestyles. These efforts spark heated debates with those who fear the erosion of civil servants' fundamental rights and liberties. Wilson, for example, used an April 1917 executive order to give agency heads the right to fire employees judged "inimical" to the public welfare. The order was seen as a way of dismissing those holding socialist or other "un-American" views as the nation prepared for World War I. Later, as the nation became caught in the grip of the cold war between the United States and the Soviet Union, Truman's Executive Order 9825 in 1947 instituted loyalty oaths for all federal employees to root out possible Communist sympathizers. This order later was codified into law by the Summary Suspension Act of 1950.[133]

In a different vein, Reagan in September 1986 (Executive Order 12564) ordered all executive branch agencies to establish random drug-testing programs for all personnel in "sensitive" positions. The order was controversial because it was not confined to military or intelligence agencies, which already used such tests, but to all agencies. Most government assertions that public employees do not enjoy privacy at work have been contested hotly in the courts.

Maintaining Secrets

Perhaps most controversial has been the use of executive orders to create a system for classifying government documents or other information in the name of national security. Governments always have pursued secrecy in sensitive diplomatic or military matters, but the idea that the United States should maintain a formal classification system did not take hold until the eve of World War II, when Franklin Roosevelt in March 1940 authorized the classification of military intelligence information. The test of what would constitute secrets worth classifying, Roosevelt said, "is what the Commander in Chief of the Army and Navy thinks would be harmful to the defense of this country to give out."[134]

Later executive orders extended classification beyond its original confines as the war progressed, but the practice did not end once hostilities ceased. The onset of the cold war instead led presidents to expand the category of information deemed essential to national security. Truman in two orders extended classification to *any* executive branch agency when secrecy was deemed essential. Whereas Roosevelt based his 1940 executive order on the vague authority provided by a 1938 statute classifying military charts, Truman's expansion of secrecy was based simply on his assertion that inherent executive powers gave him the responsibility to do whatever was "necessary and proper" to protect the general welfare.[135] Constitutional scholars debated Truman's move but worried even more about the effects of greater secrecy on democratic governance. Agencies could classify almost anything, and there were few mechanisms to guard against the overclassification inevitable when agencies consider information a valuable resource or wish to hide mistakes from public view. As presidential scholar Richard Pious noted, "The new system could be used in the conduct of diplomacy to keep Congress uninformed or misinformed."[136]

Eisenhower in 1953 (Executive Order 10501) also based his action on a general claim of presidential authority when he attempted to streamline the classification system and narrow secrecy to information critical to "national defense." As Arthur M. Schlesinger, Jr., argues, however, Eisenhower's order also gave greater power to the secretive Interagency Committee on Internal Security, a panel composed of security officials from various agencies. These officials, who generally supported extensive classification, thereafter would play decisive roles in narrowing public access to government information.

Kennedy, who did not shy away from using secrecy in military and diplomatic ventures when it suited his purposes, nonetheless fought against bureaucratic tendencies toward blanket classification of all information. His Executive Order 10964 in 1962 set up procedures for declassifying or downgrading the classification of information no longer essential to national security, but his efforts were undermined by bureaucrats and congressional conservatives. In fact, notes Schlesinger, the classification system itself eventually because classified.[137]

Secrecy would expand even further under Nixon. Where Eisenhower, for example, sought to confine classification of information to national defense matters, Nixon in 1972 (Executive Order 11652) stretched the boundaries of "national security" to include any information in "the interest of the national defense or foreign relations of the United States," including domestic intelligence activities. Nixon's order was a reaction to the publication of the *Pentagon Papers,* an internal Pentagon study of how the United States became enmeshed in the Vietnam conflict, and critics charged Nixon with both overexpanding secrecy and strangling freedom of the press. That battle has raged to this day.

Potential for Abuse

Executive orders often are controversial because of their great potential for overuse by presidents who are unwilling to work with Congress, frustrated by opposition, or overeager to impose strict secrecy. The discretionary presidency brings with it fears that presidents have become far less accountable to congressional "oversight" (that is, supervision). Another fear is that use of executive orders to tame the bureaucracy may too easily denigrate professional competence and undermine administrative law.

Potential Threats to Civil Liberties

Besides secrecy, another major controversy since the early 1970s has been the use of executive orders to inaugurate domestic surveillance of persons opposed to presidential foreign policy initiatives. Nixon, for example, in 1971 (Executive Order 11605) created sweeping new authority to investigate Americans and determine if they were threats to national security. Most of the domestic surveillance was aimed at groups opposing U.S. action in Vietnam and included secret wiretapping, breaking into offices, and using informers to infiltrate groups. Details of past activities came to light in the mid-1970s, and the ensuing controversies forced Ford and Carter to narrow the range of permissible domestic surveillance actions and to impose stricter control over federal agents.

Reagan, however, in 1981 loosened up considerably on the restrictions through Executive Order 12333, aimed at combating possible domestic terrorism. Civil libertarians were alarmed because the order sanctioned covert surveillance activities based merely on suspicion that there was "probable cause" to believe that some group might be engaged in terrorist actions, as opposed to the more stringent suspicion of actual crimes applied to criminal law. Even more troubling was that the precise guidelines for initiating and conducting investigations themselves were classified.[138]

Revelations in early 1988 that the Federal Bureau of Investigation (FBI) had relied on this sweeping authority to conduct a large-scale covert surveillance program against groups opposed to U.S. policy in Central America sparked outcries. Particularly troubling to many was the breadth of the investigation, which had spread to religious groups and labor unions, and its basis on information allegedly fabricated by an FBI informant. The episode embarrassed the Reagan administration just as it was seeking to generate greater public support for its Latin American policies. Another round of debate ensued about the use of presidential directives for such sweeping purposes.

Secret Orders

Problems also can arise when an executive order is based on information that *itself* is classified for national security purposes. Although federal law mandates the publication of executive orders and proclamations, it also allows for secret orders in the name of the public interest.[139] For example, Truman's 1952 executive order creating the National Security Agency, the largest and most secretive of the nation's intelligence organizations, itself remains classified almost forty years later.

A notable recent example of the problem is Reagan's secret order of September 1986, which retroactively authorized arms shipments to Iran despite an official U.S. embargo against that nation. Reagan failed to notify congressional intelligence committees of the arms sales, asserting later that notification was "deferred" to prevent leaks of information that might harm hostages being held in Lebanon by groups allied with Iran. Trouble for the president came when news of the arms sales came to light in the foreign press, and Americans reacted with shock and anger over the dealings and their links to financial support for rebels fighting the Nicaraguan government (in apparent violation of a congressional ban on such aid). Whatever the merits of the arms sales, or the use of their profits to aid the rebels, the political damage to the administration grew out of the secrecy surrounding the whole affair and the failure to consult with congressional intelligence committees beforehand.

Inertia and Accountability

Heavy reliance on executive orders can take on a life of its own. Presidents may use them instead of seeking congressional action, for example, simply because executive orders have become the normal way of operating. What is more, political scientist Philip Cooper has argued, "as orders move from administration to administration within any given issue area, they tend to spin off more policy elements more widely distributed across the policy space than their predecessors." [140] The accumulation of orders affecting civil rights and government secrecy over time constructed ever more encompassing policy domains that Congress found increasingly difficult to influence. Equally important, federal courts usually grant legitimacy to such policies because they are the products of long and consistent practice. The result is law making by executive decree, a condition antithetical to those who believe that Congress alone has power to make law.

Whether the policies that result from executive orders are good or bad is immaterial. The real question of government by decree is democratic accountability. Executive orders by nature exclude Congress from the process of decision making, often leaving the legislature to catch up after the fact. Few argue that presidents should not enjoy a degree of discretionary authority to administer the laws and carry out functions of the executive branch. The problem with unilateral presidential actions lies with their tremendous influence, lack of consistent congressional input, and prospects for ever greater centralization of policy making in the executive branch.

Reining in the Discretionary Presidency

The period between the New Deal and the Watergate era (roughly 1933, when Roosevelt was inaugurated, to

The Legislative Veto

Beginning in the 1920s, Congress increasingly legislated in broader language and delegated substantial discretionary authority to executive branch departments and agencies. To cope with the potential danger that federal bureaucrats—or the president—might abuse that authority or engage in decisions contrary to the will of Congress, the legislature also began to attach to these bills provisions allowing Congress to pass judgment on new regulations or other bureaucratic actions. These provisions are known as *legislative vetoes.*

Legislative vetoes typically required that no bureaucratic action could go into effect for a prescribed length of time (such as ninety days). During this period, Congress could vote to disallow the regulation or action through a simple resolution of both houses, one house singly, or even one congressional committee, depending on the provision in question.

Congress saw the legislative veto as a way to restrain the executive branch, but presidents of both parties generally opposed the device as an unconstitutional intrusion by Congress into their prerogatives as chief executive. Worse, from a presidential perspective, there was no response to legislative vetoes because simple resolutions do not go to the president for approval. More than one president during the 1970s vetoed a law passed by Congress because it contained one of these provisions.

Despite presidential opposition, use of legislative vetoes mushroomed during the 1970s, particularly after the bruising battles between Congress and Richard Nixon over war powers and impoundment of appropriated funds. By 1983 more than two hundred separate pieces of legislation contained some form of legislative veto.

In June 1983, however, the Supreme Court, in *Immigration and Naturalization Service v. Chadha,* struck down the legislative veto as unconstitutional.[1] The particulars of the case itself are not so important as the Court's ruling that a legislative veto provision attached to an immigration law violated the constitutional doctrine of separation of powers. If Congress wished to prevent the executive branch from undertaking some action, the majority ruled, it must either legislate in greater detail to begin with or pass a regular bill—subject to presidential review—to redress an action it deems unacceptable.

Although the legislative veto itself is dead, the majority decision in *Chadha* left unanswered whether the laws to which the veto provisions were attached also were null and void. As of 1988 the Court seemed reluctant to go that far, and Congress, for its part, appears to be adapting to life after *Chadha* by using more explicit language in bills. It also increasingly is writing provisions into appropriations bills forbidding funding for some specific bureaucratic or presidential actions—language that provides the functional equivalent of a legislative veto if the president accepts the appropriations bill as a whole. Until the Court rules on this strategy, or until the day that the president gains the item veto, use of appropriations bills to restrain executive actions is likely to grow, suggesting how the branches of government adapt to new legal conditions.

1. 462 U.S. 919 (1983).

1974, when Nixon resigned) marked the apogee of the discretionary presidency. By the early 1970s, however, Congress had begun to seek ways to limit what was perceived widely as a gradual but systematic aggregation of expansive executive power and its apparent abuses in both domestic and foreign policy spheres. The war in Vietnam and the incursion into Cambodia, "excessive" use of impoundment (refusal to spend funds appropriated by Congress) domestic surveillance and other abuses of civil liberties, and Watergate suggested to many a presidency out of control.

During the 1970s Congress enacted a wide range of limitations on executive discretion, including: the 1974 Budget and Impoundment Control Act, increased reliance on legislative vetoes *(see box, The Legislative Veto, this page),* more short-term authorization for federal programs or policies to ensure more frequent reviews of executive agencies as the statutes expire, greater use of provisions in appropriations bills to dictate how funds were to be spent, freedom of information rules, and additional executive branch reporting responsibilities. Congress also dramatically expanded its own institutional capacities for overseeing the executive branch by hiring thousands of additional staff and by creating or expanding congressional support agencies like the General Accounting Office and Congressional Budget Office.

All of these efforts have interposed Congress more forcefully into the routines of federal policy making, but Congress cannot or will not abolish the discretionary presidency. Contemporary government cannot return to congressional government because Congress cannot legislate in the detail necessary to carry out most government functions. There also remains a great reluctance, even by those members of Congress most critical of executive discretion and bureaucratic policy making, to place too many or too strict limitations on the ability of the president to act quickly or flexibly when conditions require.

Tension between Congress and the presidency is nothing new, and it tends to run in cycles. As political scientist Allen Schick has pointed out, "The president and other executive officials try to stretch the authority given them by Congress more broadly than might have been intended. Congress responds by narrowing executive discretion. But the new restrictions hobble executive performance and lead to demands for relaxation." [141]

Neither branch can achieve complete dominance, since the other always retains a range of constitutional and political resources that ensure both independence and a degree of countervailing power.[141] The tension is a dynamic one, and neither presidents nor Congress can dominate for long.

Emergency Powers

In times of crisis presidents often lay claim to extraordinary powers to preserve the nation, to promote the general welfare, or to provide for the common good of the people. Such "emergency" powers neither are granted expressly to the president nor delegated to Congress by the Constitution; instead, they are judged to reside purely in the inherent need for leaders to protect national sovereignty and domestic order. Thus, to many scholars the great silences in the Constitution imply an array of residual powers for each branch to draw on in times of crisis.

The doctrine of emergency powers is a variation of what the Framers knew as the Lockean Prerogative. John Locke, the eighteenth-century English philosopher, believed strongly in a government of laws. But he also argued that, in dire emergencies, "the laws themselves .... give way to the executive power, or rather to this fundamental law of nature and government ... [namely] that, as much as may be, all the members of society are to be preserved." Limited government was the idea; but in emergencies, responsible leaders may have to resort to extraordinary actions because legislatures usually are slow to move, and national self-preservation is superior to legal niceties.

Of equal importance, said Locke, is "the people's permitting their rulers to do several things of their own free choice, where the law is silent, and sometimes, too, against the direct letter of the law, for the public good, and their acquiescing in it when so done." [142] Locke was joined in his views by the French philosopher Jean Jacques Rousseau, who in the 1760s argued simply, "It is advisable not to establish political institutions so strongly as to prevent a possibility of suspending their operation." [143]

The Founders relied on European philosophers such as Locke and Rousseau to supply a great deal of the rationale behind the Constitution, but nowhere in the document did they indicate that government, much less the president, would wield broad emergency powers. The only possible such authority granted to the president in fact was the ability to grant reprieves and pardons (Article II, section 2), which the Founders believed might be useful in resolving domestic insurrections like Shays's Rebellion of 1786-1787 (which had prompted the rewriting of the Articles of Confederation in the first place). The Constitution also provided for suspending writs of *habeas corpus* in cases of rebellion or invasion, which would allow for arrest without due cause, but this provision was enumerated to Congress in Article 1, section 9.[144]

Despite the Constitution's general silence on the subject, the notion of emergency powers arguably remained implicit in the document. Article II mandates, for example, that the president shall "preserve, protect, and defend" the Constitution and uphold its provisions. This duty could require the president to bring to bear the commander-in-chief and chief executive powers from which many implied powers arise. What is more, in *The Federalist Papers* Alexander Hamilton and James Madison both indicated their views that national preservation might be cause for superseding constitutional restrictions.[145] Nonetheless, as Arthur Schlesinger, Jr., argued, they also warned that those claiming emergency powers did so at their own risk and, having acted, must gain support from Congress and the people if constitutional government is to survive.[146]

Philosophic questions aside, the debate over emergency powers also is a highly practical one. The structure of the U.S. system was designed to diffuse political power and safeguard individual rights. As such, it is a system prone to tremendous inertia, even stalemate, since no branch easily or quickly overpowers the others. These conditions might only be maddening to participants in "normal" times, but they could be potentially fatal to the Republic when crisis or war intrudes, particularly in these days of intercontinental ballistic missiles and a highly integrated world economy. That the president alone may be able to act quickly and flexibly when the situation demands speed and dexterity is a reality the Founders recognized when they created the single executive and endowed it with the commander-in-chief and chief executive powers.

The question thus is not who should lead in times of crisis. Rather, the question is how to preserve *both* the nation and the Constitution when crisis threatens the future of the Republic. Abraham Lincoln, in defending his remarkable usurpation of power during the early months of the Civil War, asked simply, "Is there in all republics this inherent and fatal weakness? Must a government of necessity be too *strong* for the liberties of its people, or too *weak* to maintain its own existence?" Or, as Lincoln later asked, "Was it possible to lose the nation and yet preserve the Union?" [147]

Lincoln's experiences during the Civil War were unique, but history is dotted with other moments where this dilemma emerged powerfully. Few doubt the need for presidents to wield extraordinary powers in times of crisis, but debates rage when the "crisis" is not clear to all or when the claims to emergency powers appear overstated. Asserting the powers necessary to defend and preserve the nation under moments of true emergency is one thing, but claiming such powers when the threat is not readily apparent, or when the powers asserted seem disproportionate to the alleged threat, is a far different matter.

That is the dilemma of emergency powers. "Whether intentionally or not," political scientists Erwin Hargrove and Michael Nelson have written, "the Constitution conferred prerogative power in times of emergency on the president. Efforts to define 'emergency' by legislation and thus limit the president in such cases have run up against Locke's warning of the futility of trying to legislate for cases yet unknown." [148]

The history of the nation has been marked by recurrent tensions between presidential claims to extraordinary powers and the right of Congress to impose its will when emergencies occur. It is a struggle yet to be resolved entirely.

Powers in Wartime

The United States has entered into five declared wars, a civil war, and numerous undeclared hostilities in its history. In each instance presidents have relied upon assorted emergency powers to deal with the threat, but as presidential scholar Louis Koenig has argued, they have invoked starkly different justifications of their actions. The "Lincolnian Pattern" asserts an aggressively broad view of the president's inherent war powers, based largely on wedding the presidential oath of office to the commander-in-chief and take care clauses. The "Joint President-Congress Pattern," by contrast, involves broad congressional grants of executive authority to prosecute the war and maintains that presidential powers are statutory as opposed to inherent.[149] Woodrow Wilson and Franklin Roosevelt, during World Wars I and II, respectively, followed this second pattern.

Neither pattern is a pure type, since every president exercises inherent and delegated war powers simultaneously. The difference lies in the fundamental claims presidents make to justify their actions as hostilities loom, distinctions that are increasingly important as the very notion of war itself has changed from the relatively stately styles of the eighteenth century to the short but violent spasms of combat prevalent today.

The Supreme Court through history has upheld presidential claims to *some* extraordinary emergency powers when the nation was involved in hostilities. The earliest important test came during the War of 1812, when several New England governors challenged James Madison's request that their state militias take up specific defense responsibilities. Madison's order was based on authority granted by Congress in the Militia Act of 1795, but the governors' resistance was supported by various state high courts. The Supreme Court, however, in 1827 ruled that Madison could overrule the governors because the president alone could define emergencies when the nation was at war or was faced with imminent hostilities.[150]

The Madison case was the exception to presidential claims of war powers in the years before the Civil War. In most instances, presidents deployed U.S. forces against pirates abroad or Indian uprisings at home to protect American citizens and their property. Their actions usually were based on some specific congressional grant of authority, such as that given to James Monroe to protect merchant ships against pirates. Early presidents, including the headstrong Andrew Jackson, exhibited a great deal of restraint in using their commander-in-chief responsibilities.

Lincoln and Inherent War Powers

Restraint was abandoned during the single greatest threat to national unity yet encountered by the United States. Faced with secession by the Southern states in 1861, Abraham Lincoln claimed numerous emergency war powers to save the Union and in the process became what presidential scholar Clinton Rossiter called a "constitutional dictator."[151] Other scholars saw Rossiter's characterization as unduly harsh, but there is no doubt that Lincoln used remarkable, often unconstitutional, means to quell the rebellion.

Congress was not in session when Fort Sumter fell. With the onset of hostilities, Lincoln unilaterally proclaimed a blockade of Southern ports, mobilized state militias, increased the size of the army and navy, sent weapons to unionists in Virginia (who established the state of West Virginia), authorized construction of ships for the navy, and appropriated funds for purchases of war material.

Lincoln conveniently failed to call Congress back into session for eleven weeks; and when he did, he claimed that his actions were justified by the inherent prerogative powers of the presidency, especially his role as commander in chief. Congress ultimately gave Lincoln retroactive authority for his actions, even though some (such as expanding the army and spending unappropriated funds) clearly were unconstitutional. Legal nuances paled before the emergency at hand, however, and Lincoln continued to assume and exercise independent war powers even with Congress in session.

This same sense of emergency led the courts to sup-

Categories and Examples of Emergency Powers

When emergencies are declared, or during times of crisis, the president has at hand a broad array of potential powers. These emergency powers can be grouped into three categories of actions the president may take:

Powers over Individuals

- Confine individuals seen to be threats to national security
- Restrict travel of Americans to other nations (such as Cuba) or travel of some foreigners to the United States
- Restrict movement of citizens within the United States
- Require persons, because of their backgrounds, associations with certain groups, or ownership of particular articles (such as weapons), to register with government officials
- Restrict certain persons from working in industries critical to national security
- Remove federal employees regarded as threats to national security
- Suspend writs of *habeas corpus*
- Declare martial law
- Assign armed forces to conflicts in foreign nations

Powers over Property

- Order stockpiling of strategic materials (such as uranium)
- Impose restrictions on exports (such as computer equipment)
- Allocate materials in ways necessary to aid national defense
- Require industries to give priority to government contracts and seize industries failing to comply with such orders
- Fix wages and prices

Powers over Communications

- Withhold information from Congress and the public deemed potentially sensitive to national security
- Monitor and censor communications between United States and other nations
- Require foreign representatives to register with U.S. government

Sources: U.S. Congress, House of Representatives, Subcommittee on Administrative Law and Governmental Relations, Committee on the Judiciary, Hearings on H.R. 3884, *National Emergencies Act,* 94th Cong., 1st sess., March 6-April 9, 1975, 22-23; Robert E. DiClerico, *The American President* (Englewood Cliffs, N.J.: Prentice-Hall, 1979), chap. 8.

port many of Lincoln's claims. In the *Prize Cases* (1863), shipowners whose vessels had been seized trying to run the blockade of Southern ports sued on the grounds that the blockade itself was constitutional because Congress had not declared war.[152] This was true technically, but the Supreme Court ruled that the South nonetheless was enemy territory and Lincoln thus was required to deal with the insurrection. As Arthur Schlesinger, Jr., points out, however, the justices endorsed such executive power only in domestic rebellions or invasions, not, as later presidents asserted, to use against sovereign nations overseas.[153]

The Union also faced tremendous dangers behind its own lines. The problems were keenest around Washington, D.C., with secessionist Virginia on one side and Maryland filled with Southern sympathizers on the other. The mayor of Baltimore was decidedly pro-Confederate; mobs attacked federal troops; bridges were sabotaged; and the state legislature was about to convene with the real possibility of voting to secede. Lincoln responded by declaring martial law and suspending writs of *habeas corpus* behind the Northern lines, thus allowing military authorities to arrest without warrants members of the Maryland legislature and other rebel sympathizers. Lincoln also suppressed opposition newspapers and ordered censorship of postal and telegraph communications.

Some of the president's actions provoked clashes with the judiciary. In *Ex parte Merryman* (1861), the Supreme Court ruled that Lincoln had usurped the sole right of Congress to suspend writs of *habeas corpus* during an emergency.[154] Lincoln flagrantly ignored the ruling, and Congress later affirmed his actions in the Habeas Corpus Act of 1863, but the president's continued reliance on preemptive arrests and use of military courts to try civilians set in motion another confrontation.

In *Ex parte Milligan* (1866), the Supreme Court ruled that Lincoln lacked the constitutional authority to use military courts behind Northern lines so long as the civil judicial system remained intact.[155] A civilian, L. P. Milligan, was arrested in Indiana for treason, but the Court ruled that Indiana was not in the "theater of war" and writs of *habeas corpus* thus could not be suspended. The Constitution worked "equally in war and in peace," said the justices, and national preservation was not cause enough to violate its principles.[156]

By the time the Court ruled, however, Lincoln was dead and the Civil War over, so *Milligan* joined a number of judicial decisions that create doubts whether the courts would challenge a sitting president during national crises. These doubts reemerged during World War II when Franklin Roosevelt ordered some 112,000 Japanese-Americans from their homes on the West Coast to internment camps in the southwestern desert. The forced relocation was challenged in the courts but never to any great effect.[157]

World War and Delegated Powers

Unlike Lincoln, who disregarded the Constitution to preserve the nation, both Woodrow Wilson and Franklin Roosevelt fought foreign wars based largely on powers at least broadly delegated to them by Congress. Both Wilson and Roosevelt faced situations in which the nature of war itself had changed. Twentieth-century war was "total war": the lines between combatants and civilians had become blurred; struggles involved not only armies but the entire social, economic, and industrial capacities of nations; and control over national populations was key to success.

Total war thus required swift, massive, and sustained national organization and mobilization, the capacities for which lay most in the executive branch. Congress for its part prepared for war by delegating broad powers to the presidency to carry out military functions and to regulate the domestic economy. The Lever Food and Fuel Control Act of 1917, for example, empowered Wilson to seize defense-related facilities; to regulate food production, manufacturing, and mining; and to fix prices on commodities. The Selective Service Act of 1917 allowed the president to raise an army. The Espionage Act of 1917 gave him the power to restrict exports. The Trading with the Enemy Act of 1917 allowed for regulation and censorship of all extenal communications.

Wilson also received broad authority to monitor the actions of resident aliens, to regulate or operate transportation and communications facilities, and to reorganize executive branch agencies where necessary. In effect, Wilson was granted almost free rein to conduct the war and to maintain the domestic economy—a pattern that recurred two decades later, although on a greater scale, when Congress delegated broad discretionary powers to Franklin Roosevelt.[158]

Moreover, neither Wilson nor Roosevelt overlooked his constitutional prerogatives as commander in chief. Far from it: both claimed the right to create wartime executive agencies, to enforce "voluntary" press censorship, and to coordinate private industry beyond the scope of congressional authorization. Roosevelt in particular claimed emergency powers to sidestep congressional declarations of neutrality as Europe fell into war. In 1939 he declared a "limited" state of emergency, which allowed him to invoke existing statutes and prepare the nation militarily. In early 1941 he declared an "unlimited" state of emergency under which he reorganized the executive branch and prepared to deal with the domestic economy once the U.S. entered into hostilities. In neither instance did Roosevelt obtain previous authorization, although he usually tried to cloak his actions in existing statutory powers.

Once war was declared, however, Roosevelt dropped even the pretense of delegated powers. His seizure of defense plants immediately after Pearl Harbor, for example, was based on claims of authority given to him by the Constitution and "the laws," although he never made clear *which* laws. Perhaps his most intriguing claim came in 1942, when he asked Congress to repeal legislation dealing with farm prices. If Congress did not do so, Roosevelt warned, he would repeal the provisions himself because, he said, "the president has the powers, under the Constitution and under congressional acts, to take measures necessary to avert a disaster which would interfere with the winning of the war." [159] Whether Roosevelt would have acted on his threat was never tested, for Congress quickly gave in.

Truman and the Limits of Emergency Powers

Neither Wilson nor Roosevelt made sweeping claims to *inherent* emergency powers during either world war. Subsequent presidents operated differently, however, as the United States in the late 1940s began a period of prolonged confrontation with the Soviet Union. The nature of war changed again—from total conventional war to indeterminate potential thermonuclear war at one extreme and localized wars of containment at the other. The postwar world, at least the one inhabited by superpowers jockeying for dominance, would be characterized by permanent military establishments and the "imperial presidency." [160] Boundaries between war and peace no longer were clear, and the sheer scope of the meaning of national security (defense, intelligence, economic health, scientific advances—to name a few) gave presidents greater potential power than ever before in virtually every aspect of national affairs. Presidential influence over both civil liberties and congressional authority never seemed so extensive.

The debate about the use of inherent powers exploded first in 1952. Harry Truman had put the nation on emergency war footing in 1950 with the invasion of South Korea and in late 1951 ordered the seizure of strike-threatened steel mills to avoid potential shortages. Truman based his action not on any statutory authority to resolve labor disputes but "on the authority vested in me by the Constitution and laws of the United States, and as President of the United States and Commander in Chief of the armed forces of the United States." [161] When challenged on this rationale, Truman argued simply, "The President has very great inherent powers to meet national emergencies." [162]

Congress did not respond, despite broad antipathy to Truman's action, but the Supreme Court in *Youngstown Sheet and Tube Co. v. Sawyer* (1952) declared the seizure of the steel mills unconstitutional because in the 1947 Taft-Hartley Labor Act Congress had decided *not* to give presidents the right to take over industrial facilities shut down by strikes.[163] What is more, the majority opinion implied that the president did not possess inherent powers in times of emergency, nor did the commander-in-chief role grant special domestic powers. Four out of the five justices concurring in the majority decision, however, did not reject this notion outright. Their concurring opinions suggested that emergency prerogatives may exist when presidents act in accordance with the express or implied will of Congress or in the absence of congressional action. *(See box, Justice Jackson's Test of Presidential Emergency Powers, p. 491.)* Congressional opposition places the presidency in its weakest constitutional position, and Truman's action could not be supported because it so clearly violated congressional intent.

Truman's greatest problem in the *Steel Seizure Case* probably was that he overstated the gravity of the situation. If both Congress and the people had backed Truman as they had Roosevelt in the internment of Japanese-Americans, it is doubtful the Court would have challenged his claims. But, as Rossiter suggests, "the Court's power of judicial review is least useful when most needed," for it is during emergencies that rash actions are likeliest to occur, actions that may indeed violate constitutional safeguards.[164] Many scholars are concerned that the country's ongoing readiness for war and its worldwide commitments have created conditions for unfettered presidential claims to inherent war powers and have increased the potential for rash executive action even in the absence of clear and broadly perceived emergencies.

Powers in Economic Crises

Outside of wartime, presidents also wield emergency powers when the nation's economic system is seriously unstable. In economic crises it appears that such power emanates exclusively from statutes, although presidents have shown ingenuity in stretching the boundaries of that authority.

Procedures for Emergency Orders

The National Emergencies Act of 1976 (PL 94-412) terminated all states of emergency that were in effect until that time but also set in place procedures for declaring and, more important from the view of many in Congress, terminating future states of emergency. As the brief overview below suggests, the provisions of the National Emergencies Act were intended above all to force Congress and the president, acting singly or together, to take action to ensure that any state of emergency does not outlive the conditions upon which it was based.

The president by law cannot declare a state of national emergency without also specifying the provisions of existing law or constitutional provisions under which the proposed action falls. Furthermore, any proclamation of a national emergency must be transmitted immediately to Congress and published in the *Federal Register*.

During any declared national emergency, the president and all relevant executive branch agencies or departments must maintain files on all rules, regulations, executive orders, or any other activities carried out to address the emergency. All of these must be transmitted promptly to Congress. Matters requiring confidentiality are to be handled in a prescribed manner (for example, delivered only to members of the congressional intelligence committees and those staff members with security clearances). All expenditures made by the executive branch to address the emergency also must be reported to Congress within ninety days after each six-month period following the declaration of the emergency.

The law also specifies how states of emergency are to be terminated, either by the president or congress. No later than six months after an emergency is declared, the two houses of Congress by law must meet to consider a concurrent resolution to determine whether the emergency should be terminated. The resolution must go through the normal congressional procedures, but according to a specific schedule to avoid delays. Should Congress be unable or unwilling to terminate the emergency (perhaps because of some disagreement between the House and the Senate), it must consider another such resolution within the next six-month period.

The president can terminate unilaterally any declared state of emergency when it is deemed that the conditions meriting the emergency have passed. But, to avoid another situation where states of emergency endure legally for decades, the law calls for automatic termination of an emergency upon the anniversary of its declaration, unless the president previously notifies Congress (and publishes in the *Federal Register*) of the need to continue the emergency after the anniversary. One way or another, then, states of emergency are to be terminated.

The Trading with the Enemy Act gave Wilson the authority to impose diverse economic measures in times of war or national emergency. This law, passed on the eve of U.S. entry into World War I, was intended as a wartime measure, but its authority was never revoked after the war ended. Later presidents thus discovered, to their delight, the apparent statutory justification for emergency actions to manage a faltering economy.

The best example is the action of the newly inaugurated Franklin Roosevelt in 1933 when faced with the imminent collapse of the nation's financial system. Roosevelt on March 4 declared a national state of emergency and closed the banks, basing his action on the Trading with the Enemy Act. This interpretation of the wartime statute was dubious, but it nonetheless reflected Roosevelt's desire to cloak his action in legal authority. Congress sanctioned his move when it passed the Emergency Banking Act three days later. In the following months it also granted Roosevelt a wide range of new powers to address the economic emergency. In fact, the single greatest outpouring of major legislation in peacetime U.S. history took place between March 9 and June 16.

In 1933 Roosevelt's actions responded to a starkly imminent crisis, but in August 1971 Richard Nixon's declaration of emergency over a growing imbalance in the U.S. balance of payments struck many observers as overly dramatic. Nixon used the emergency to disconnect the value of the dollar from the gold standard, levy a 10 percent surtax on all imports, and freeze all domestic prices for ninety days. The overall effect was to devalue the dollar, drive down the prices of American goods overseas, and halt inflation temporarily. Nixon based his actions on the 1970 Economic Stabilization Act, which authorized the president to "issue such orders as he may deem appropriate to stabilize prices, rents, wages and salaries," although he had signed the law only because it also had contained provisions affecting national defense.[165]

Powers during Domestic Unrest

Presidential emergency powers also include the authority to call out federal troops or take control over state national guards (descendants of the state militias) to quell domestic unrest or to deter violence. Such authority has been used in the United States to put down illegal labor strikes, to ensure delivery of the mail, to impose order during natural disasters and urban riots, and to prevent other volatile situations from exploding.

Before to the 1940s, and particularly during the late nineteenth century, presidents became involved in domestic disorders most often during labor strikes. Until the passage of the Wagner Act of 1933, which ensured the right of collective bargaining and established procedures for negotiations, strikes usually were considered illegal and often resulted in dramatic outbreaks of violence between strikers and company security forces. This was true especially in the mining, steel, railroad, and, later, automobile industries, where relations between management and labor were sharply adversarial in the best of times. Use of troops to break the 1894 Pullman strike in Chicago is but one of several famous examples of a practice that virtually ended by the 1950s.

During the 1950s and 1960s, presidents relied on federal troops or state national guards to ensure calm in situations involving racial desegregation. The first and perhaps most notable case came in 1957, when Dwight Eisenhower sent troops into Little Rock, Arkansas, to enforce desegregation of the public shools in the face of resistance from state officials. John Kennedy confronted state officials when he sent in federal troops to ensure peaceful integration at the University of Alabama in 1963, and later took over (or "federalized") the Mississippi National Guard to do the same in that state. Kennedy, and Lyndon Johnson after him, also used troops to protect civil rights marchers on several occasions.

During the later 1960s, troops were used more frequently to quell urban riots and to control demonstrations against U.S. involvement in Vietnam. Most noteworthy was the unrest following the April 1968 assassination of civil rights leader Martin Luther King, Jr., which sparked widespread rioting throughout more than one hundred cities and forced Lyndon Johnson and various governors to call out some 55,000 troops.[166]

Another case entailed the declaration of a state of national emergency. In March 1970 Nixon responded to a postal strike in New York, which threatened to cripple postal service nationally, by declaring a state of emergency and calling out federal troops to take over the New York postal system and keep mail deliveries flowing. Nixon's use of troops to sort and deliver the mail was unusual, but it shows how presidents can react to potential disturbances.

Powers during Natural Disasters

Presidents by statute also have the authority to declare states of emergency in areas of the country hit by hurricanes, floods, earthquakes, or other natural disasters. By declaring a natural disaster area, the president sets in motion the government machinery that can provide immediate aid, such as food, shelter, police protection. Perhaps more critical, however, the president can ensure longer-term assistance like federally guaranteed home and business loans at interest rates significantly lower than most commercial banks might offer at the time. In doing so, the government ensures that the disaster will be softened some for those able to rebuild more quickly and less expensively.

The Permanent Emergency

Most Americans probably never realized that the United States lived under a state of declared national emergency from 1933 to 1975. In 1952 Truman terminated Roosevelt's pre-World War II emergencies (declared in 1939 and 1941) that had granted the president greater discretion to direct defense preparations, organize the executive branch, and mobilize the nation for potential hostilities. But four other states of emergency were still in force as of 1975: Roosevelt's bank emergency (1933), Truman's mobilization following the invasion of South Korea (1950), Nixon's use of troops to maintain mail deliveries (1970), and Nixon's response to international economic conditions (1971).

In none of these six emergencies had a termination date been specified, nor had Congress written into most of the statutes provisions for terminating the president's emergency authority. Emergency declarations usually are drafted in the White House and rushed through Congress. In 1933, legislators approved the law authorizing Roosevelt's emergency powers to alleviate the bank crisis after

Justice Jackson's Test of Presidential Emergency Powers

Justice Robert Jackson's concurring opinion in *Youngstown Sheet and Tube v. Sawyer* (1952) remains a classic analysis of the conditions under which a president may in fact possess extraordinary powers. More important, Jackson's dispassionate examination suggests when those emergency powers may not exist.

Mr. Justice Jackson, concurring:

The actual art of governing under our Constitution does not and cannot conform to judicial definitions of the power of any of its branches based on isolated clauses or even single Articles torn from context. While the Constitution diffuses power the better to secure liberty, it also contemplates that practice will integrate the dispersed powers into a workable government. It enjoins upon its branches separateness but interdependence, autonomy but reciprocity. Presidential powers are not fixed but fluctuate, depending upon their disjunction or conjunction with those of Congress. We may well begin by a somewhat oversimplified grouping of practical situations in which a President may doubt, or others may challenge, his powers, and by distinguishing roughly the legal consequences of this factor of relativity.

1. When the President acts pursuant to an express or implied authorization of Congress, his authority is at its maximum, for it includes all that he possesses in his own right plus all that Congress can delegate. In these circumstances, and in these only, may he be said (for what it may be worth) to personify the federal sovereignty. If his act is held unconstitutional under these circumstances, it usually means that the Federal Government as an undivided whole lacks power. A seizure executed by the President pursuant to an Act of Congress would be supported by the strongest of presumptions and the widest latitude of judicial interpretation, and the burden of persuasion would rest heavily upon any who might attack it.

2. When the President acts in absence of either a congressional grant or denial of authority, he can only rely upon his own independent powers, but there is a zone of twilight in which he and Congress may have concurrent authority, or in which its distribution is uncertain. Therefore, congressional inertia, indifference or quiescence may sometimes, at least as a practical matter, enable, if not invite, measures on independent presidential responsibility. In this area, any actual test of power is likely to depend on the imperatives of events and contemporary imponderables rather than on abstract theories of law.

3. When the President takes measures incompatible with the expressed or implied will of Congress, his power is at its lowest ebb, for then he can rely only upon his own constitutional powers minus any constitutional powers of Congress over the matter. Courts can sustain exclusive presidential control in such a case only by disabling the Congress from acting upon the subject. Presidential claim to a power at once so conclusive and preclusive must be scrutinized with caution, for what is at stake is the equilibrium established by our constitutional system.

Into which of these classifications does this executive seizure of the steel industry fit? It is eliminated from the first by admission, for it is conceded that no congressional authorization exists for this seizure. That takes away also the support of the many precedents and declarations which were made in relation, and must be confined, to this category.

Can it then be defended under flexible tests available to the second category? It seems clearly eliminated from that class becuase Congress has not left seizure of private property an open field but has covered it by three statutory policies inconsistent with this seizure. In cases where the purpose is to supply needs of the Government itself, two courses are provided: one, seizure of a plant which fails to comply with obligatory orders placed by the Government; another condemnation of facilities, including temporary use under the power of eminent domain. The third is applicable where it is the general economy of the country that is to be protected rather than exclusive governmental interests. None of these were invoked. In choosing a different and inconsistent way of his own, the President cannot claim that it is necessitated or invited by failure of Congress to legislate upon the occasions, grounds, and methods for seizure of industrial properties.

This leaves the current seizure to be justified only by the severe tests under the third grouping, where it can be supported only by any remainder of executive power after subtraction of such powers as Congress may have over the subject. In short, we can sustain the President only by holding that seizure of such strike-bound industries is within his domain and beyond control of Congress. Thus, this court's first review of such seizures occurs under circumstances which leave presidential power most vulnerable to attack and in the least favorable of possible constitutional postures. . . .[1]

1. *Youngstown Sheet and Tube v. Sawyer,* 343 U.S. 579 (1952).

only eight hours of debate.[167] Even more worrisome, these unexpired states of emergency gave the president the technical authority to invoke a wide range of emergency powers, even if no crisis seemed imminent. These powers included the right to seize private property and regulate private enterprise, to organize and control all means of production and transportation, to call up reservists and assign military forces overseas, to institute martial law, and to restrict travel.[168]

The potential gravity of the situation hit home for many in 1972 as a result of friction between Congress and the Nixon administration following the 1970 U.S. incursion into Cambodia. Members of the Senate Foreign Relations Committee asked Secretary of Defense Melvin R. Laird what would happen if Congress cut off funds for continued U.S. involvement. They were surprised when Laird stated that the president could bypass Congress entirely and spend unappropriated funds through emergency authority granted under a 1799 statute. The law was still on the books, and, at least theoretically, so too was the president's emergency power.[169]

Disturbed greatly by this assertion and concerned that other such laws might still apply years after their passage, the Senate created the Special Committee on National Emergencies and Delegated Powers to investigate the possible extent of presidential emergency powers. This committee, through hearings and investigations, discovered approximately 470 statutes dealing with emergency situations still on the books. It also learned that four states of emergency technically remained in effect.[170]

As a result of these findings, and during a period when efforts were made to rein in the "imperial presidency," Congress in 1976 passed the National Emergencies Act terminating, as of 1978, the states of emergency in effect since 1933. The law also terminated the presidential emergency powers stemming from those declarations, established the president's authority to declare future states of national emergency in ways that clearly defined presidential powers during the emergency, provided for congressional review, and mandated that states of emergency will lapse after six months unless renewed.[171] The act does not require the president to consult with Congress before declaring a state of emergency, which everyone realized might be impossible, but it does force the president to specify clearly the nature of the emergency and the statutory powers to be invoked. Congress did not try to legislate for all emergencies; it sought principally to ensure presidential accountability.[172]

In 1977 Congress curbed executive authority to impose economic controls during presidentially declared states of emergency by amending the 1917 Trading with the Enemy Act and by confining the act's broader authority to wartime. The 1977 law also defined economic controls that presidents could employ without calling a state of national emergency, including the ability to regulate foreign currency transactions, to institute embargoes against other nations, and to freeze foreign assets. These powers would be more restricted, however, than might be the case during wartime. This condition was implied in the 1917 law, but presidents beginning with Franklin Roosevelt interpreted it far differently.

Conclusion

There is an understandable tendency to examine the presidency in a context of crisis. Crises, after all, force presidents to act forcefully, and some have done so in ways that expanded presidential power thereafter. Lincoln, for example, claimed for the office a range of inherent war powers that endure today. Roosevelt established the president's capacity to address economic problems, to aid allies in times of trouble, and to prepare the nation for war.

If we study the presidency exclusively through the lens of crisis response, however, we introduce systematic inaccuracies into our understanding of how the institution works and how it relates to the other components of the national government. After all, episodes like the 1962 Cuban missile crisis, the subject of innumerable studies on presidential leadership, remain the exception to the rule. Emergencies are extraordinary times, and to focus on them as the epitome of presidential leadership fosters the impression of greater presidential power than may in reality exist in a system where political authority is shared among separate branches. It also may foster in the White House a view of leadership that may exist only during crises: the need to respond quickly to problems with little or no consultation with Congress, to resort to extraconstitutional or even unconstitutional means to achieve ends, and to function as if the presidency is above the law. Such attitudes—which some observers saw in Nixon's 1970 decision to invade Cambodia and Reagan's efforts to support rebels in Nicaragua—may do the presidency more harm than good since they invite congressional and public backlash. The ultimate lesson of emergency powers is to know when they are appropriate, not merely expedient.

Notes

1. Louis Fisher, *The President and Congress* (New York: Free Press, 1972), 18-21.
2. Thomas Jefferson, "Notes on Virginia," in *The Life and Selected Writings of Thomas Jefferson,* ed. Adrienne Koch and William Peden (New York: Random House, Modern Library, 1944), 237.
3. *Guide to Congress,* 3d ed. (Washington, D.C.: Congressional Quarterly Inc., 1982), 770. The power theoretically exists to this day, although no English sovereign has used the veto since 1707.
4. James Sundquist, *Constitutional Reform and Effective Government* (Washington, D.C.: Brookings, 1986), 30.
5. Ibid., 30-31.
6. The exemption of constitutional amendments from the presidential veto was established by the Supreme Court in *Hollingsworth v. Virginia,* 3 Dall. 378 (1798).
7. Alexander Hamilton, James Madison, and John Jay, *The Federalist Papers,* ed. Clinton Rossiter (New York: New American Library, 1961), 443.
8. Ibid., 322.
9. Ibid., 444.
10. The Constitution gives presidents the authority to approve or veto legislation within ten days after a bill is *presented* to the White House, as opposed to after it is *passed* by Congress. Bills passed by Congress cannot be presented to the president until they have been signed by the Speaker of the House and the president of the Senate (that is, the vice president, although this function is performed normally by the president pro tempore). Therefore, an indefinite gap can occur between passage and presentation. There have been times, in fact, when Congress has delayed presentation of bills because the president has been out of the country. There also have been times when presidents have maneuvered to delay presentation to create opportunities for pocket vetoes. In 1970, for example, Richard Nixon had Vice President Spiro Agnew exercise his authority to sign legislation, which Agnew then delayed in carrying out so that several bills would not be presented to Nixon until just a few days before adjournment. For a discussion of this sort of maneuver, see Eric Redman, *The Dance of Legislation* (New York: Simon and Schuster, Touchstone Books, 1973).
11. As upheld by the Supreme Court in *Missouri Pacific Railway Co. v. United States,* 248 U.S. 277 (1919).
12. Clinton Rossiter, *The American Presidency* (New York: Harcourt Brace and World, 1960), 91.
13. See James Bryce, *The American Commonwealth,* 2d ed., vol. 1 (New York: Macmillan, 1911), 64. The Supreme Court in 1926 ruled that the power to remove political appointees resided with the president alone. See *Myers v. United States,* 272 U.S. 52 (1926).
14. Louis Fisher, *Presidential Spending Power* (Princeton, N.J.: Princeton University Press, 1975), 25.
15. See, for example, Neil MacNeil, *Forge of Democracy: The House of Representatives* (New York: David McKay, 1963), 244-245.
16. Jimmy Carter, *Keeping Faith: The Memoirs of a President* (New York: Bantam Books, 1982), 101.
17. *Guide to Congress,* 771.
18. Robert Pear, "Court Is Asked to Define Power of the Pocket Veto," *New York Times,* November 9, 1986, sec. 4.
19. Bryce, *American Commonwealth,* 59.
20. See Richard E. Neustadt, *Presidential Power: The Politics of Leadership from FDR to Carter* (New York: Wiley, 1980).
21. Thomas Cronin, *The State of the Presidency,* 2d ed. (Boston: Little, Brown, 1980), 81.
22. George C. Edwards III, *Presidential Influence in Congress* (San Francisco: Freeman, 1980), 24.
23. Neustadt, *Presidential Power,* 63.
24. See, for example, Redman, *Dance of Legislation,* 243.
25. *Pocket Veto Case,* 279 U.S. 644 (1929).
26. Arthur M. Schlesinger, Jr., *The Imperial Presidency* (New

York: Popular Library, 1974), 237.
27. *Wright v. United States,* 302 U.S. 583 (1938).
28. See Redman, *Dance of Legislation,* 275-277.
29. *Kennedy v. Sampson,* 511 F.2ds 430 (D.C. Cir. 1974).
30. *Kennedy v. Jones,* Civil Action no. 74-194 (D.D.C.).
31. Pear, "Power of the Pocket Veto," 4.
32. *Barnes v Carmen,* 582 F. Supp. 163 (D.D.C. 1984); *Barnes v. Kline,* 759 F.2d 21 (D.C. Cir. 1985). The lone dissenter was Judge Robert Bork, who argued that members of Congress had no right to sue the president in the first place and the court had no jurisdiction over such issues. Lawyers for Congress argued that the courts have every right to adjudicate disputes between Congress and the executive.
33. *Barnes v. Burke,* 479 U.S., 93 L.Ed. 2d 732, 107 S.Ct. (1987).
34. See Louis Fisher, *The Politics of Shared Power,* 2d ed. (Washington, D.C.: CQ Press, 1987), 210.
35. Ibid., 209.
36. Edwards, *Presidential Influence in Congress,* 20.
37. Stuart Taylor, Jr., "Court Rebuffs Reagan on Deferral of Spending Ordered by Congress," *New York Times,* January 21, 1987, sec. A.
38. Edwards, *Presidential Influence in Congress,* 21.
39. Fisher, *Politics of Shared Power,* 20.
40. George Will, "Power to the President," *Newsweek,* October 12, 1981, 120.
41. Sundquist, *Constitutional Reform,* 209-215.
42. See Fisher, *Politics of Shared Power,* 210-213.
43. E. E.Schattschneider, *The Semi-Sovereign People: A Realist's View of Democracy in America* (Hinsdale, Ill.: Dryden Press, 1975), 66.
44. Bruce Miroff, "Monopolizing the Public Space: The President as a Problem for Democratic Space," in *Rethinking the Presidency,* ed. Thomas E. Cronin (Boston: Little, Brown, 1982), 218-252.
45. For a cogent discussion of the constants of American governance and the effects that they have on presidential leadership, see Bert A. Rockman, *The Leadership Question: The Presidency and the American System* (New York: Praeger, 1984), chap. 3.
46. For an honest defense of this perspective, see Thomas P. O'Neill, Jr., with William Novak, *Man of the House: The Life and Political Memoirs of Speaker Tip O'Neill* (New York: Random House, 1987).
47. Norman J. Ornstein, Thomas E. Mann, and Michael J. Malbin, *Vital Statistics on Congress, 1987-1988* (Washington, D.C.: Congressional Quarterly Inc., 1987), 51.
48. For a president's perspective on this phenomenon, see Carter, *Memoirs of a President,* 83-84.
49. Neustadt, *Presidential Power,* 33.
50. Rossiter, *American Presidency,* 140.
51. Bertram Gross, *The Legislative Struggle: A Study of Social Combat* (New York: McGraw-Hill, 1953), 101.
52. See, for example, James Sundquist, *The Decline and Resurgence of Congress* (Washington, D.C.: Brookings, 1981).
53. Hamilton, Madison, and Jay, *Federalist Papers,* 423.
54. For discussion of Washington's experience, see George M. Haynes, *The Senate of the United States: Its History and Practice,* vol. 1 (Boston: Houghton Mifflin, 1938), 62-63.
55. George B. Galloway, *History of the House of Representatives* (New York: Thomas Crowell, 1969), 12.
56. Edward S. Corwin, *The President: Office and Powers, 1789-1957,* 4th ed. (New York: New York University Press, 1957), 21.
57. Ibid., 23.
58. Galloway, *History of the House,* 245-246.
59. Corwin, *President: Office and Powers,* 28.
60. *Theodore Roosevelt: An Autobiography* (New York: Macmillan, 1913), 282.
61. Sundquist, *Decline and Resurgence of Congress,* 130.
62. Corwin, *President: Office and Powers,* 269.
63. Special address to a joint session of Congress, June 23, 1913. As cited in Corwin, *President: Office and Powers,* 269.
64. Rossiter, *American Presidency,* 140.
65. Arthur M. Schlesinger, Jr., *The Age of Roosevelt: The Coming of the New Deal* (Boston: Houghton Mifflin, 1959), 1.
66. See, for example, Rockman, *Leadership Question.*
67. *Guide to Congress,* 762.
68. Roland Evans and Robert Novak, *Lyndon B. Johnson: The Exercise of Power* (New York: New American Library, 1966), 490.
69. Louis Koenig, *The Chief Executive,* 5th ed. (New York: Harcourt Brace Jovanovich, 1986), 145-146.
70. "Annual Messages of the Presidents: Major Themes of American History," in *The State of the Union Messages of the Presidents, 1790-1966,* ed. Fred L. Israel (New York: Chelsea House, 1966), xiv.
71. *Public Papers of Woodrow Wilson,* vol. 1, 32; as cited in Corwin, *President: Office and Powers,* 269.
72. Fisher, *Shared Power,* 26; see also H. Wayne Morgan, *From Hayes to McKinley* (Syracuse, N.Y.: Syracuse University Press, 1969), 274-319.
73. Charles O. Jones, "Presidential Negotiation with Congress," in *Both Ends of the Avenue: The Presidency, the Executive Branch, and Congress in the 1980s,* ed. Anthony King (Washington, D.C.: American Enterprise Institute, 1983), 99.
74. Ibid., 102.
75. Fisher, *President and Congress,* 52-53.
76. Cronin, *State of the Presidency,* 118.
77. James S. Young, *The Washington Community* (New York: Columbia University Press, 1966), 167.
78. For a superb discussion of the evolution of "central clearance," see Fisher, *Presidential Spending Power.*
79. Richard E. Neustadt, "The Presidency and Legislation: Planning the President's Program," *American Political Science Review* 49 (December 1955): 1015; see also Stephen J. Wayne, *The Legislative Presidency* (New York: Harper and Row, 1979), 19.
80. Paul Light, "Presidents as Domestic Policymakers," in *Rethinking the Presidency,* ed. Thomas E. Cronin (Boston: Little, Brown, 1982), 360.
81. See, for example, John W. Kingdon, *Agendas, Alternatives, and Public Policy* (Boston: Little, Brown, 1984).
82. See William Manchester, *The Glory and the Dream: A Narrative History of America, 1932-1972* (Boston: Little, Brown, 1974), 95.
83. See Joel D. Aberbach and Bert A. Rockman, "Clashing Beliefs within the Executive Branch: The Nixon Administration Bureaucracy," *American Political Science Review* 70 (June 1975): 456-468.
84. Neustadt, *Presidential Power.*
85. Eric L. Davis, "Congressional Liaison: The People and the Institutions," in *Both Ends of the Avenue,* 60.
86. Ibid., 61.
87. Ibid., 62.
88. Jones, "Presidential Negotiation with Congress," 106.
89. See Davis, "Congressional Liaison," 78-79.
90. Ibid., 65.
91. O'Neill, *Man of the House,* 310-311.
92. Davis, "Congressional Liaison," 65.
93. Jones, "Presidential Negotiation," 118.
94. Roger H. Davidson and Walter J. Oleszek, *Congress and Its Members* (Washington, D.C.: CQ Press, 1981), 299. For an insider's view of the 1981 tax and budget battles, see David Stockman, *The Triumph of Politics: The Inside Story of the Reagan Revolution* (New York: Harper and Row, 1986).
95. Jones, "Presidential Negotiation," 126.
96. Ibid., 123-125.
97. Edwards, *Presidential Influence,* 110.
98. As quoted in Manchester, *The Glory and the Dream,* 91.
99. Schlesinger, *New Deal,* 559.
100. Wilfred E. Binkley, *President and Congress* (New York: Vintage Books, 1962), 305.
101. As cited in William Safire, *Safire's Political Dictionary* (New York: Ballantine Books, 1978), 649.
102. Ibid., 444. The phrase "nattering nabobs..." was penned by William Safire, who later became a popular newspaper col-

umnist and expert on the English language. The term *nabob* is Hindi in origin and has come to mean in English a self-important person.
103. Miroff, "Monopolizing the Public Space," 230.
104. Corwin, *President: Office and Powers,* 7; Richard Pious, *The American Presidency* (New York: Basic Books, 1979), 38.
105. *In re Neagle,* 135 U.S. 1(1890). By contrast, see the Court's opinion in *Myers v. United States,* 272 U.S. 52 (1926), where Justice Oliver Wendell Holmes argued, "The duty of the President to see that the laws be executed is a duty that does not go beyond the laws or require him to achieve more than the Congress sees fit to leave within his power." This view of executive discretion is generally superseded by the view propounded in *Neagle.* See Corwin, *President: Office and Powers,* 169, for discussion.
106. *Proclamations,* in contrast to executive orders, are directed specifically at private individuals. Proclamations generally encompass such hortatory matters as Thanksgiving Day or National Black History Month, although some involve substantive issues that carry the force of law. The Supreme Court in *Wolsey v. Chapman,* 101 U.S. 755 (1879), ruled that there is no material difference between proclamations and executive orders, so this section will not make any distinctions between the two. This discussion focuses primarily on executive orders.
107. Phillip J. Cooper, "By Order of the President: Administration by Executive Order and Proclamation," *Administration and Society,* 18 (August 1986): 239.
108. Ibid., 239.
109. See Christopher J. Bosso, *Pesticides and Politics: The Life Cycle of a Public Issue* (Pittsburgh: University of Pittsburgh Press, 1987).
110. *Newsweek,* February 29, 1988, 40.
111. For Supreme Court decisions supporting congressional delegation of authority to the executive branch, see *Field v. Clark,* 143 U.S. 649 (1891); *Butterfield v. Stranahan,* 192 U.S. 471 (1904); *United States v. Grimaud,* 220 U.S. 506 (1911); *Clark Distilling Co. v. West Maryland Railway Co.,* 242 U.S. 311 (1917).
112. Allen Schick, "Politics Through Law: Congressional Limitations on Executive Discretion," in *Both Ends of the Avenue,* 162.
113. See Corwin, *President: Office and Powers,* 126. In the *United States v. Grimaud,* the court made the distinction between "legislative" and "administrative" powers but noted that it was impractical for Congress to provide for every detail or possible occurrence.
114. See, for example, Theodore Lowi's indictment of the practice in *The End of Liberalism,* 2d ed. (New York: W. W. Norton, 1989).
115. Corwin, *President: Office and Powers,* 178-179.
116. Leonard White, *The Federalists* (New York: Macmillan, 1948), 512.
117. Leonard White, *The Jeffersonians* (New York: Macmillan, 1951), 552.
118. Corwin, *President: Office and Powers,* 152.
119. Theodore Roosevelt, *An Autobiography* (New York: Scribners's, 1931), 388.
120. Pious, *American Presidency,* 49.
121. *Executive Orders and Proclamations,* Committee on Government Operations, House of Representatives, 85th Cong., 1st sess., December 1957, 36.
122. See Fisher, *Presidential Spending Power,* 61-64.
123. Schick, "Politics Through Law," 160.
124. Fisher, *Shared Power,* 36.
125. *Korematsu v. United States,* 323 U.S. 214 (1944).
126. Schick, "Politics Through Law," 161.
127. See Ruth Morgan, *The President and Civil Rights* (New York: St. Martin's Press, 1970), 5.
128. Cooper, "By Order of the President," 238.
129. *Brown v. Board of Education of Topeka,* 349 U.S. 483 (1954) and *Brown v. Board of Education of Topeka,* 349 U.S. 294 (1955).
130. Cooper, "By Order of the President," 238.
131. Fisher, *President and Congress,* 51.
132. For a good discussion of these efforts, see Fisher, *Presidential Spending Power.*
133. Corwin, *President: Office and Powers,* 100.
134. Schlesinger, *Imperial Presidency,* 324.
135. Ibid., 325.
136. Pious, *American Presidency,* 348.
137. Schlesinger, *The Imperial Presidency,* 325.
138. *New York Times,* February 13, 1988, 33.
139. See Pious, *American Presidency,* 347.
140. Cooper, "By Order of the President," 254.
141. Schick, "Politics Through Law," 157, 181.
142. John Locke, *The Second Treatise on Government* (Indianapolis: Bobbs-Merrill, 1952), 91-96. See also discussion in Corwin, *President: Office and Powers,* chap. 1; Pious, *American Presidency,* chap. 2; Robert E. DiClerico, *The American President* (Englewood Cliffs, N.J.: Prentice-Hall, 1979), chap. 8; Schlesinger, *Imperial Presidency,* chap. 2.
143. Jean Jacques Rousseau, *The Social Contract* (New York: Hafner Press, 1947), 110.
144. A writ of *habeas corpus* (Latin for "present a body") is a court order requiring that authorities must present a prisoner in court and show cause for that person's detention. The Constitution otherwise generally forbids detention of prisoners without due cause.
145. See *Federalist* No. 28 and No. 41 in *Federalist Papers.*
146. Schlesinger, *Imperial Presidency.*
147. Ibid., 69; Clinton Rossiter, *Constitutional Dictatorship* (Princeton, N.J.: Princeton University Press, 1948), 19.
148. Erwin C. Hargrove and Michael Nelson, *Presidents, Politics, and Policy* (Baltimore: Johns Hopkins University Press, 1984), 26.
149. Koenig, *Chief Executive,* 235-237.
150. *Martin v. Mott,* 12 Wheat. 19, 23-33 (1827).
151. See Rossiter, *Constitutional Dictatorship.*
152. *Prize Cases,* 2 Black 635, 17 L.Ed. 459 (1863)
153. Schlesinger, *Imperial Presidency,* 75.
154. *Ex parte Merryman.*
155. *Ex parte Milligan,* 71 U.S. (4 Wall.) 2, 18 L.Ed. 281 (1866).
156. Schlesinger, *Imperial Presidency,* 78-79.
157. See *Hirabayashi v. United States,* 320 U.S. 81 (1943); *Korematsu v. United States,* 323 U.S. 214 (1944); *Ex parte Endo,* 323 U.S. 284 (1944). In *Hirabayashi,* the Court narrowed, but did not overturn, the ability of military officials to impose special curfews on Japanese-Americans. In both *Korematu* and *Endo* the Court reluctantly upheld the internment itself.
158. Corwin, *President: Office and Powers,* 235-236.
159. See John Roche, "Executive Power and the Domestic Presidency: The Quest for Prerogative," *Western Political Quarterly* 5 (December 1952): 607.
160. See Schlesinger, *The Imperial Presidency.*
161. J. Malcolm Smith and Cornelius Cotter, *Powers of the President During Crises* (Washington, D.C.: Public Affairs Press, 1960), 134.
162. DiClerico, *American President,* 322.
163. *Youngstown Sheet and Tube Co. v. Sawyer,* 343 U.S. 579 (1952).
164. Rossiter, *American Presidency,* 53.
165. William Manchester, *The Glory and the Dream: A Narrative History of America, 1932-1972,* vol. 2 (Boston: Little, Brown, 1974), 1535-1536.
166. Ibid, 1382.
167. See Frank Church, "Ending Emergency Government," *American Bar Association Journal* 63 (February 1977): 198.
168. *Congress and the Nation,* vol. 4 (Washington, D.C.: Congressional Quarterly Inc., 1977), 802.
169. See Fisher, 240, *Presidential Spending Power,* 240.
170. *Congress and the Nation,* vol. 4, 801.
171. P.L. 94-412; see, House Subcommittee on Administrative Law and Governmental Relations, Committee on the Judiciary, Hearings on H.R. 3884, *National Emergency Act,* 94th

Cong., 1st sess., March 6-April 9, 1975.
172. See DiClerico, *American President,* 327-329.

Selected Bibliography

Binkley, Wilfred E. *President and Congress.* New York: Vintage, 1962.

Bryce, James. *The American Commonwealth.* Vol. 1, 2d ed. New York: Macmillan, 1911.

Corwin, Edward S. *The President: Office and Powers.* 4th ed. New York: New York University Press, 1957.

——. *Presidential Power and the Constitution: Essays.* Ed. Richard Loss. Ithaca, N.Y.: Cornell University Press, 1976.

Cronin, Thomas E., *The State of the Presidency.* Boston: Little, Brown, 1980.

Cronin, Thomas E., ed. *Rethinking the Presidency.* Boston: Little, Brown, 1982.

Dodd, Lawrence C., and Bruce I. Oppenheimer, eds. *Congress Reconsidered.* 3d ed. Washington, D.C.. CQ Press, 1985.

Edwards, George C., III. *Presidential Influence in Congress.* San Francisco: Freeman, 1980.

Fenno, Richard F. *The President's Cabinet.* New York: Vintage Books, 1959.

Fisher, Louis. *President and Congress: Power and Policy.* New York: Free Press, 1972.

——. *Presidential Spending Power.* Princeton, N.J.: Princeton University Press, 1975.

——. *The Politics of Shared Power: Congress and the Executive.* 2d ed. Washington, D.C. CQ Press, 1987.

Hamilton, Alexander, James Madison, and John Jay. *The Federalist Papers.* Ed. Clinton Rossiter. New York: New American Library, 1960.

Hargrove, Erwin C. *The Power of the Modern Presidency.* New York: Knopf, 1974.

Hargrove, Erwin C., and Michael Nelson. *Presidents, Politics, and Policy.* Baltimore: Johns Hopkins University Press, 1984.

Heclo, Hugh. *A Government of Strangers: Executive Politics in Washington.* Washington, D.C.. Brookings, 1977.

Hess, Stephen, ed. *Both Ends of the Avenue: The Presidency, the Executive Branch, and Congress in the 1980s.* Washington, D.C.: American Enterprise Institute, 1983.

Koenig, Louis. *The Chief Executive.* 5th ed. New York: Harcourt Brace Jovanovich, 1986.

Mansfield, Harvey C., Sr., ed. *Congress against the President.* New York: Academy of Political Science, 1975.

Nelson, Michael, ed. *The Presidency and the Political System.* 2d ed. Washington, D.C.. CQ Press, 1988.

Neustadt, Richard. *Presidential Power: The Politics of Leadership from FDR to Carter.* New York: Wiley, 1980.

Pious, Richard. *The American Presidency.* New York: Basic Books, 1979.

Polsby, Nelson W. *Congress and the Presidency.* New York: World, 1970.

Polsby, Nelson W., ed. *The Modern Presidency.* Washington, D.C.: University Press of America, 1973.

Rockman, Bert A. *The Leadership Question: The Presidency and the American System.* New York: Praeger, 1984.

Rossiter, Clinton. *Constitutional Dictatorship.* Princeton, N.J.: Princeton University Press, 1948.

——. *The American Presidency.* 2d ed. New York: New American Library, 1960.

Schlesinger, Arthur M., Jr., and Alfred DeGrazia. *Congress and the Presidency: Their Role in Modern Times.* Washington, D.C.: American Enterprise Institute, 1967.

Smith, J. Malcolm, and Cornelius Cotter. *Powers of the President during Crises.* Washington, D.C.: Public Affairs Press, 1960.

Sundquist, James. *Politics and Policy.* Washington, D.C.: Brookings, 1968.

——. *The Decline and Resurgence of Congress.* Washington, D.C.. Brookings, 1986.

Wayne, Stephen J. *The Legislative Presidency.* New York: Harper and Row, 1978.

Young, James S. *The Washington Community.* New York: Columbia University Press, 1966.

Chief Diplomat

John F. Kennedy expressed the importance of foreign affairs to the presidency when he observed, "The big difference [between domestic and foreign policy] is that between a bill being defeated and the country [being] wiped out." [1] Most contemporary presidents would have agreed with Kennedy's appraisal of the importance of foreign affairs. In the nineteenth century when U.S. foreign interests were limited primarily to trade and to disputes about western expansion, presidents often could concentrate on domestic policy. Today the dangers of the international environment and the wide array of U.S. economic, political, and military commitments virtually ensure that presidents will spend at least half of their time on foreign affairs.

Even during periods of relative international calm, foreign policy has remained an area of unique importance to the presidency. Foreign affairs issues usually have offered presidents the greatest freedom to exercise their power and the best opportunity to affect policy personally. Important foreign affairs decisions often have been made by the president alone or during intimate consultations with a few trusted advisers. In contrast, it is more common for domestic policy decisions to originate in the bureaucracy, involve many officials, require less secrecy, be affected by interest group politics, and be subject to strict congressional constraints. In addition, whereas presidents always have expected their domestic policies to be criticized by political opponents and a significant portion of the general public, the desire of political friends and foes alike to project a united front frequently has produced initial support for many foreign policies. Consequently, presidents may choose to retreat to the refuge of foreign affairs where they can exercise their powers most freely and feel like the leader of the nation.

Presidents who are concerned with establishing an enduring place in history often are drawn to foreign affairs. Steadfast wartime leadership, the prevention or resolution of dangerous crises, bold diplomatic initiatives, and historic summit meetings with important foreign leaders can create presidential legends. The most memorable acts of many of the most famous U.S. presidents have involved foreign affairs. George Washington and John Adams kept the United States out of the war between Britain and France; Thomas Jefferson bought Louisiana from France; James Monroe announced the Monroe Doctrine declaring the intention of the United States to resist European intervention in the affairs of independent nations in the Western Hemisphere; Theodore Roosevelt maneuvered to build the Panama Canal; Woodrow Wilson negotiated and unsuccessfully campaigned for the Treaty of Versailles; Franklin D. Roosevelt led the nation through World War II; Harry S Truman ordered the use of the atomic bomb and oversaw the creation of the North Atlantic Treaty Organization (NATO), the United Nations (UN), and the postwar bipolar balance of power; and Kennedy made the Soviets withdraw missiles from Cuba.

The experiences of three recent presidents who upon entering office possessed greater expertise and interest in domestic policy than in foreign policy demonstrated the centrality of foreign affairs to the modern presidency. Lyndon B. Johnson, Jimmy Carter, and Ronald Reagan each found his administration overwhelmed by foreign affairs issues. Johnson's plans for a "Great Society" were undercut by the resource demands of the Vietnam War and the divisions the war created in the American public. Carter, a former governor with little foreign policy experience, became personally absorbed with foreign policy issues such as recognition of the People's Republic of China, arms control, and the Camp David peace process between Egypt and Israel. At the end of his term the Iran hostage crisis dominated his presidency almost as much as the Vietnam War had dominated Johnson's. Reagan, another former governor, did not display Carter's enthusiasm for learning the details of U.S. foreign policy, preferring instead to outline broad policies and to delegate the authority to implement them. Despite Reagan's relative detachment from foreign affairs, his administration probably will be best remembered for its hard-line policies toward Communist countries, its bouts with terrorism, and the scandal surrounding the sale of arms to Iran and the diversion of funds to the Nicaraguan resistance.

Distribution of Foreign Policy Power

The Constitution specifically grants remarkably few foreign affairs powers to the president. It states: "He shall have Power, by and with the Advice and Consent of the Senate, to make Treaties, provided two-thirds of the Sena-

By Daniel C. Diller

> He shall have Power, by and with the Advice and Consent of the Senate, to make Treaties, provided two-thirds of the Senators present concur; and he shall nominate and, by and with the Advice and Consent of the Senate, shall appoint Ambassadors, other public Ministers and Consuls. . . . He shall receive Ambassadors and other public Ministers.
>
> —from Article II, sections 2, 3

tors present concur; and he shall nominate and, by and with the Advice and Consent of the Senate, shall appoint Ambassadors, other public Ministers and Consuls. . . . He shall receive Ambassadors and other public Ministers." The Constitution also bestows upon the president the responsibility to be the commander in chief of the army and navy and to execute the laws of the United States.

The Constitution assigned to Congress the powers "to . . . provide for the common Defence and general Welfare of the United States; . . . to regulate Commerce and foreign Nations; . . . to define and punish Piracies and Felonies committed on the high Seas and Offences against the Law of Nations; to declare War . . . and make Rules concerning Captures on Land and Water; to raise and support Armies; . . . to provide and maintain a Navy; . . . to make all Laws which shall be necessary and proper for carrying into Execution the foregoing Powers. . . ."

At a glance the congressional powers in foreign affairs appear at least as broad as those granted to the president. The president commands the armed forces, but Congress declares war; the president makes treaties, but not without the advice and consent of the Senate; the president appoints ambassadors, but they must be confirmed by the Senate. Only the power to receive ambassadors, a seemingly ceremonial function, was left unchecked by a corresponding congressional power. In contrast, Congress has several specific foreign affairs powers, including the important responsibility of regulating foreign commerce, that are unchallenged by a specific presidential power. More important, the legislative branch's general power to make laws, control appropriations, and "provide for the common defense and general welfare of the United States" gave it broad authority to become involved in any foreign policy decision or action not specifically reserved for the president by the Constitution.[2]

Yet beyond the enumerated foreign affairs powers, the president has other constitutional resources that may be used to shape foreign policy. Since it is impossible clearly to define where policy making stops and policy implementation begins, the executive power gives the president an inherent influence on foreign policy decisions and actions. The veto power supplies the president with another check over Congress's ability to dictate foreign policy. In addition, several presidential foreign affairs powers are implied in the Constitution. As chief of state, negotiator of treaties, and manager of the diplomatic corps, the president is recognized as the official spokesperson of the nation. As commander in chief of the armed forces, presidents can make foreign policy by taking or threatening to take military actions short of declared wars. Finally, the power to send and receive ambassadors is interpreted as implying the president's authority to recognize the legitimacy of other governments.

Still, the affirmative grants of power in the Constitution do not begin to answer all the questions about how foreign policy decisions shall be made and implemented. For example, the Constitution does not say how the president is to receive Senate advice on treaties, whether the president can make international agreements without using the treaty process, who can declare neutrality, whether the president needs congressional approval to sustain military action that might commit the United States to war, or what foreign policy actions the president can take under the general executive authority of the office. The authors of the Constitution formulated a very ambiguous distribution of shared foreign policy powers between the president and Congress, which could be unraveled only by events. In the famous words of presidential scholar Edward S. Corwin, the Constitution is "an invitation to struggle for the privilege of directing American foreign policy." [3]

Presidential Dominance of Foreign Policy

In 1948, addressing members of the Jewish War Veterans, President Truman stated, "I make foreign policy." [4] Most historians and political scientists would agree that although Truman's assessment of presidential power was an exaggeration, it reflects modern presidents' relative autonomy over foreign policy compared with their more limited authority in domestic affairs. Since the beginning of the Republic and especially since World War II presidents have won most of the interbranch struggles for primacy in foreign relations. Although Congress has retained an important role in foreign affairs, its actions almost always have been responses to presidential policies. On many occasions Congress has been able to frustrate, delay, modify, or negate presidential foreign policy when a majority of members has been willing to oppose the chief executive. The president, however, has dominated the formulation and initiation of foreign policy, and the American public and foreign governments expect the president to make decisions and to implement them. Presidents perceived as indecisive or weak in foreign relations quickly lose popularity. It is even common for members of Congress from both parties to criticize a president for failing to provide foreign policy leadership.

Since the constitutional division of foreign affairs powers between the executive and legislative branches is relatively ambiguous, one cannot attribute the establishment of presidential control over foreign relations to the affirmative grants of power in the Constitution. The ambiguity of the document ensured that customs and precedents would be developed that would fill in the gaps left by its brief treatment of the foreign affairs powers. In this vague constitutional environment, the branch most capable of asserting its own interests and demonstrating its ability to make effective foreign policy would likely emerge as the more powerful. This branch proved to be the executive.

Presidential Advantages

Since its creation, the presidency has possessed inherent practical advantages that make it better suited than Congress to the conduct of foreign relations. First, as head of the foreign policy bureaucracy, the diplomatic corps, the intelligence agencies, and the military, the president controls information that is crucial to effective foreign policy decision making. Second, because only 1 person occupies the office of the president, whereas 525 make up the Congress, the president is able to work with speed and secrecy—two capabilities that are indispensable in many diplomatic situations, especially crises that threaten the security of the nation. Third, since it is a responsibility of the presidency to communicate with foreign governments through treaty negotiations and diplomatic channels, the president can most easily formulate policy that is consistent with negotiating positions and official statements. Fourth, as the executor of foreign policy, commander in chief of the armed forces, and appointer of diplomatic personnel, the president and presidential advisers should be in the best position to judge the capacity of the U.S. government to carry out a given foreign policy initiative. Fifth, because presidents are elected every four years, they can provide more continuity to foreign policy than Congress, which must sustain an election every two years. Sixth, because presidents, unlike members of Congress, are elected by a national constituency, they are usually more inclined than Congress to focus on international problems that affect the entire nation. Finally, the president is the most identifiable leader and visible symbol of the nation and is, therefore, the most capable of rallying national support in a crisis.

At various times throughout U.S. history, each of the three branches of government has recognized these inherent practical advantages of the president. The resulting episodes of legislative acquiescence, judicial interpretation in favor of the president, and executive assertiveness have contributed to the president's primacy in foreign affairs.

Precedents Set under Washington

George Washington exercised his foreign affairs power with great restraint by today's standards. He conducted international business through the treaty process rather than through executive agreements between himself and foreign leaders; he consulted with the Senate more closely on treaty matters than subsequent presidents have; he proposed legislation, but thereafter did not attempt to influence congressional debate; and he considered his veto over legislation as a tool to be used only if a resolution were unconstitutional.

Yet Washington and his closest adviser, Secretary of the Treasury Alexander Hamilton, believed the president had the constitutional authority and the practical duty to take the initiative in foreign policy. As a result Washington set several precedents that enlarged the foreign affairs powers of the young presidency beyond a literal reading of the enumerated powers in the Constitution. He established the president's authority to recognize foreign governments, to demand that foreign ambassadors be recalled, to negotiate treaties without congressional involvement, and to withhold from Congress documents pertinent to treaty negotiations. Most important, Washington demonstrated that in foreign affairs the president could use the office's inherent executive power to take actions that were authorized neither by Congress nor by a specific presidential foreign policy power in the Constitution.

Neutrality Proclamation of 1793

Washington set the precedent for unilateral presidential action by keeping the United States neutral in the war that broke out between France and Great Britain in 1793. Although the treaty of alliance with France signed in 1778 was still in effect, and most Americans favored the French, Washington was anxious to avoid involving the United States in the conflict, fearing that it would disrupt the strengthening of the American economy and political institutions.

On April 22, 1793, he issued a proclamation which declared that the United States would be "friendly and impartial" toward the belligerents. The proclamation carefully avoided using the word "neutrality" in deference to Secretary of State Thomas Jefferson, who had opposed the proclamation. Among other objections, Jefferson was not convinced that the president's action was constitutional. Jefferson reasoned that since only the Congress could declare war, the president did not have the power to decide unilaterally that the nation would not fight a war.[5] Although the proclamation was unpopular with many Americans, Congress followed Washington's lead by passing the Neutrality Act of 1794, which endorsed the policy of neutrality already in effect. Washington had shown that the president's executive power could be used to make foreign policy rather than just execute congressional directives.

Hamilton-Madison Debate

Washington's action set off a famous debate between Alexander Hamilton and James Madison—then a member of the House of Representatives from Virginia—on the subject of presidential power. In a series of articles printed in the *Gazette of the United States,* a Federalist newspaper published in Philadelphia, Hamilton defended Washington's authority to issue the proclamation. Writing under the pseudonym "Pacificus," Hamilton argued that the "executive power" granted to the president by the Constitution empowers the president to conduct all facets of foreign policy that do not usurp the powers specifically granted to the Congress. Hamilton reasoned that the president's enumerated powers "ought therefore to be considered, as intended merely to specify the principal articles implied in the definition of executive power; leaving the rest to flow from the general grant of that power, interpreted in conformity with the other parts of the Constitution, and with the principles of free government." [6]

This expansive interpretation of presidential power alarmed the pro-French Democratic-Republicans led by Secretary of State Jefferson. Jefferson had reluctantly agreed to Washington's proclamation, but he wanted to prevent it from establishing a precedent that would greatly enlarge presidential power. Since Jefferson was a member of Washington's cabinet, he felt it would be improper for him publicly to refute Hamilton's article. He therefore urged Madison to respond to Hamilton. Jefferson wrote to Madison, "Nobody answers him and his doctrines are taken for confessed. For God's sake, my dear Sir, take up your pen, select the most striking heresies and cut him to pieces in face of the public." [7]

Writing as "Helvidius," Madison stated that Congress's authority to declare war and its role in the treaty-making process made it the branch of government properly entrusted to formulate foreign policy, including declarations of neutrality. He rejected Hamilton's broad interpretation of the president's executive powers by claiming that "the natural province of the executive magistrate is to execute laws, as that of the legislature is to make laws. All his acts, therefore, properly executive, must presuppose the existence of the laws to be executed." [8] Thus, according to

Supreme Court Cases Related to the President's Foreign Policy Powers

Ware v. Hylton, 3 Dall. 199 (1796). The Court ruled 4-0 that treaties made by the United States overrode any conflicting state laws. The 1783 Treaty of Paris with Britain, which ended the American Revolution, provided that neither Britain nor the United States would block the efforts of the other nation's citizens to secure repayment of debts in the other country. This provision rendered invalid a Virginia law allowing debts owed by Virginians to British creditors to be "paid off" through payments to the state.

Foster v. Neilson, 2 Pet. 253 (1829). By a 5-0 vote, the Court refused to rule on a boundary dispute involving territory east of the Mississippi River claimed by both the United States and Spain. Chief Justice John Marshall described the matter as a "political question," which it was not the business of the judiciary to resolve.

Holmes v. Jennison, 14 Pet. 540 (1840). A fugitive from Canada, detained in Vermont, sought release through a petition for a writ of *habeas corpus*. After the state supreme court denied his petition, he asked the Supreme Court to review that action. The Court dismissed the case for lack of jurisdiction, but Chief Justice Roger B. Taney declared in his own opinion that states were forbidden by the Constitution to take any independent role in foreign affairs, and thus state governors could not surrender a fugitive within their jurisdiction to a foreign country who sought the fugitive's return.

The Prize Cases, 2 Black 635 (1863). These cases involved the capture of four ships seized while trying to run the Union blockade of Confederate ports, which Lincoln instituted in April 1861 and Congress sanctioned in July. By a 5-4 vote, the Court sustained the president's power to proclaim the blockade without a congressional declaration of war. A state of war already existed, the majority said, and the president was obligated "to meet it in the shape it presented itself, without waiting for Congress to baptize it with a name. . . ."

Geofroy v. Riggs, 133 U.S. 258 (1890). The Court ruled 9-0 that it is within the scope of the treaty power of the United States to regulate the inheritance by aliens of land and other property in the United States. The Court declared that the treaty power was unlimited except by the Constitution.

Missouri v. Holland, 252 U.S. 416 (1920). After lower courts ruled an act of Congress protecting migratory birds an unconstitutional invasion of powers reserved to the states, the U.S. government negotiated a treaty with Canada for the protection of the birds. After the Senate approved it, Congress again enacted protective legislation to fulfill the terms of the treaty. The Court sustained this second act by a 7-2 vote. It ruled that in order to implement a treaty, Congress may enact legislation that without a treaty might be an unconstitutional invasion of state sovereignty.

United States v. Curtiss-Wright Export Corp., 299 U.S. 304 (1936). By a 7-1 vote the Court upheld an act of Congress authorizing presidents, at their discretion, to embargo arms shipments to foreign belligerents in a South American war. Justice George Sutherland described the power of the president in foreign affairs as "plenary and exclusive" and called the president "the sole organ of the federal government in . . . international relations."

United States v. Belmont, 310 U.S. 324 (1936). In the executive agreements that established diplomatic relations between the Soviet Union and the United States in 1933, the two nations had agreed that Soviet assets in the United States would be used to pay the claims of U.S. citizens for property seized in the Soviet Union at the time of the Russian revolution. When U.S. government officials tried to recover funds from the accounts of Russian nationals in New York banks, the state maintained that its laws prohibited the action. The Supreme Court, however, ruled that the executive agreements upon which the action was based constituted an international compact that, like a treaty, superseded conflicting state laws.

Goldwater v. Carter, 444 U.S. 996 (1980). In December 1978, President Jimmy Carter announced that the United States would terminate the 1945 Mutual Defense Treaty with the Republic of China (Taiwan) as part of the process of establishing diplomatic relations with communist China. Sen. Barry Goldwater (R-Ariz.) brought a suit to stop the action, maintaining that treaty termination, like treaty ratification, required the prior approval of the Senate. The Court tacitly sided with the president by dismissing the case as a political question outside the realm of judicial review.

Madison, the president's role in foreign affairs was restricted to executing the laws, treaties, and declarations of war made by Congress and performing those duties specifically enumerated in the Constitution.

Over time Hamilton's conception of presidential power has triumphed. Presidents have almost always prevailed when the Constitution is silent on foreign affairs. Indeed, many presidents have behaved as if they had a general, comprehensive power to conduct foreign affairs, while Congress could only participate if it found an opportunity to use one of its specific powers. Congress has enjoyed short periods of ascendancy, but even during these periods, it has usually exercised its influence by reacting to presidential initiatives.

Judicial Endorsement of Presidential Power

Although the Supreme Court has preferred not to rule on disputes between the executive and legislative branches that involve international affairs, when the Court has acted, it has tended to support the president's claims to power. The most important and often cited Supreme Court decision dealing with the president's foreign affairs powers is *U.S. v. Curtiss-Wright,* delivered in 1936. *(See* "U.S. v. Curtiss-Wright," *p. 1378, in the Appendix.)*

In 1934 Congress passed a joint resolution empowering the president to embargo shipments of arms to warring nations. When President Franklin D. Roosevelt imposed an embargo on Bolivia under the resolution, the Curtiss-Wright Export Corporation was prohibited from shipping aircraft armaments to that country. The corporation conspired to send Bolivia arms in spite of the embargo, but its activities were discovered. In court Curtiss-Wright's lawyers argued that Congress's delegation of power to the president was unconstitutional.

With only one dissenting vote, the Supreme Court held that while Congress could not delegate its law-making authority over internal affairs, it could do so with respect to foreign affairs. Justice George Sutherland, delivering the opinion of the Court, explained:

> We are here dealing not alone with an authority vested in the President by an exertion of legislative power, but with such an authority plus the very delicate, plenary, and exclusive power of the president as the sole organ of the federal government in the field of international relations—a power which does not require as a basis for its exercise an act of Congress.... It is quite apparent that if, in the maintenance of our international relations, embarrassment—perhaps serious embarrassment—is to be avoided and success for our aims achieved, congressional legislation which is to be made effective through negotiation and inquiry in the international field must often accord to the President a degree of discretion and freedom from statutory restriction which would not be admissible were domestic affairs alone involved.[9]

U.S. v. Curtiss-Wright was a landmark decision because, as historian Arthur M. Schlesinger, Jr., observed, "the Court thus did in foreign policy what it had been reluctant to do in domestic policy: it affirmed the existence of an inherent, independent and superior presidential power, not derived from the Constitution and not requiring legislation as the basis for its exercise."[10] Sutherland's statements supporting vast presidential foreign affairs powers were contained in the decision's dicta (legal observations not essential to the main issues of the case). Nevertheless, they continue to exercise great influence over conceptions of presidential power in foreign relations.

Congressional Cooperation and Conflict

In spite of the president's advantages in the conduct of foreign policy, the political customs and precedents that favored presidential leadership in foreign affairs, and judicial interpretations that supported the president's claims to authority, presidents have not always controlled U.S. foreign policy. At times Congress has refused to follow the president's leadership and has attempted to legislate its own policy course. Even when presidents have dominated foreign policy, Congress has demonstrated that no chief executive can sustain a foreign policy program for long without its support. Cooperation between the two branches, therefore, has been crucial to establishing effective foreign policies.

Early Cooperation

Congressional majorities often were willing to cooperate with early presidents on foreign affairs matters. Congress passed the Neutrality Act of 1794 a year after President Washington had declared American neutrality in the war between Britain and France, even though many members of Congress had opposed the original proclamation. In 1803, the Senate followed Jefferson's lead by ratifying the treaty with France that transferred the Louisiana Territory into U.S. control.

In 1816 a report by the Senate Foreign Relations Committee demonstrated Congress's recognition of the advantages of presidential leadership in foreign affairs:

> The President is the Constitutional representative of the United States with regard to foreign nations. He manages our concern with foreign nations and must necessarily be most competent to determine when, how, and upon what subject negotiations may be urged with the greatest prospect of success. For his conduct he is responsible to the Constitution. The committee considers this responsibility the surest pledge for the faithful discharge of his duties. They think the interference of the Senate in the direction of foreign negotiations [is] calculated to diminish that responsibility and thereby to impair the best security for the national safety. The nature of transactions with foreign nations, moreover, requires caution and unity of design, and their success frequently depends on secrecy and dispatch.[11]

Nineteenth Century

Presidents during much of the last two-thirds of the nineteenth century exerted less foreign policy leadership than had earlier presidents. The resolution of the slavery question, the development of the American West, and the Reconstruction of the South following the Civil War were the most important political issues of the period. Consequently, presidents spent most of their time on domestic policy. In addition, foreign trade and the acquisition of territory from foreign governments, two matters in which Congress has a large role, were often the primary foreign relations issues. Also, presidents were rarely able to carry out major foreign policy initiatives during this time because they were seldom in office long enough to establish their own foreign policy strategy. From the end of Andrew Jackson's administration in 1837 to the turn of the century, only Ulysses S. Grant served two consecutive four-year terms, and seven presidents served less than one four-year term. Four of these seven died in office, and three of the succeeding vice presidents were not reelected as president.

Congressional power was at its peak during Reconstruction. The executive branch suffered a number of serious setbacks, including the impeachment and near removal of President Andrew Johnson from office and the passage of the Tenure of Office Act in 1867, which gave the

Senate the power to veto a president's decision to remove an appointee from office.[12] The Spanish-American War in 1898 marked a major turn in foreign policy, which Congress strongly supported. Under President William McKinley, the country dropped its traditional policy of nonintervention, went to war to rid Cuba of Spanish rule, and emerged from the conflict with overseas outposts as far distant as the Philippines in the western Pacific.

Theodore Roosevelt's Administration

Following the Spanish-American War presidents expanded their control over foreign affairs. In 1901 McKinley was assassinated, and his vice president, Theodore Roosevelt, succeeded him as president. For the next seven and a half years, Roosevelt frequently ignored or circumvented Congress while using his executive prerogatives aggressively to pursue his perception of U.S. interests abroad. In 1903 he used U.S. naval power to back a small Panamanian revolt against Colombian rule; recognized the state of Panama, which emerged from the revolution; and quickly negotiated a treaty with the new Panamanian government giving the United States the right to dig the Panama Canal. In 1905, Roosevelt implemented an executive agreement with Santo Domingo (now the Dominican Republic) that gave the United States control of that nation's customs in order to guarantee its European debts, even though Congress would not approve the pact. The same year, Roosevelt personally directed mediation efforts between Russia and Japan without consulting Congress. His efforts led to the Portsmouth Conference in New Hampshire, which ended the Russo-Japanese War and won him the Nobel Peace Prize. In 1907 Roosevelt decided to send the U.S. fleet on a world cruise, primarily to impress the Japanese with U.S. naval strength. Congress threatened to deny funding for the mission but relented when Roosevelt declared he had sufficient funds to send the navy to the Pacific—and Congress would be responsible for funding its return.[13]

Roosevelt freely admitted that he had avoided involving Congress in major foreign policy actions. In 1909, while still in office, he wrote: "The biggest matters, such as the Portsmouth peace, the acquisition of Panama, and sending the fleet around the world, I managed without consultation with anyone; for when a matter is of capital importance, it is well to have it handled by one man only." [14]

Versailles to World War II

Presidential disregard for Congress's role in foreign policy reached its height in 1919. Woodrow Wilson traveled to Versailles, France, to participate personally in the negotiation of a peace treaty to end World War I. Under strong pressure from Wilson, the conference agreed to include provisions in the treaty establishing a League of Nations. The president brought the treaty back to the United States and began a vigorous national campaign for Senate approval. During the war, Congress had cooperated with Wilson by granting him unprecedented war powers. Once the threat had passed, however, the Senate was ready to reas-

Theodore Roosevelt Collection, Harvard College Library

Theodore Roosevelt, middle, won the Nobel Peace Prize for his effort in ending the war between Russia and Japan. In 1905, he met with delegates from both sides in Portsmouth, New Hampshire.

sert legislative influence over foreign policy. Many senators resented Wilson's refusal to involve them in the Versailles negotiations or even to inform them of U.S. negotiating positions. In 1919 and 1920, the Senate refused to approve the treaty, thus keeping the country out of the League of Nations. *(See "The Defeat of the League of Nations," p. 106, in History of the Presidency chapter of Part I.)*

The demise of the Versailles treaty signaled a new period of congressional activism in foreign policy. During the next two decades Congress limited U.S. involvement overseas, with little resistance from the executive branch. When war threatened in Asia and Europe in the second half of the 1930s, Congress, reflecting the isolationism of the public, tried to legislate neutrality.[15] But when war finally began, Franklin Roosevelt, like presidents before him in times of crisis, acquired enormous powers through his own assertiveness and Congress's grants of authority, which were motivated by the need for national unity.

Postwar Presidential Power

After World War II ended, however, presidential authority in foreign affairs continued to grow. The period brought many new responsibilities and dangers that seemed to require a chief executive capable of quick, decisive action. The United States had emerged from the war as the most powerful nation on earth and the leader of the non-Communist world. The fear of Communist expansion brought the whole globe into the sphere of U.S. interest. The United States had swung from isolationism in the late 1930s to unprecedented international involvement in the late 1940s, aligning itself with virtually any willing country and sending billions of dollars in economic and military aid overseas.

Dangers to the security of the United States grew along with its commitments. The advancement of missile technology and Soviet development of the atomic bomb in 1949 and the hydrogen bomb in 1953 made a devastating attack on the American homeland a possibility. The fall of China to Communist forces in 1949 reinforced the belief of many Americans that the United States had to be ready to use troops if necessary to stop Communist expansion.

This complex and hostile international environment contributed to a consensus for strong presidential leadership in foreign policy. Congress recognized that only the executive branch had the means to collect and analyze the huge amount of information on foreign policy issues and to act with the speed that seemed necessary to manage U.S. global commitments. In addition, the presidential role of keeper of the nuclear switch magnified the commander in chief's stature as guardian of the free world, thereby enhancing presidential authority in other areas of defense and foreign policy.

Congress repeatedly passed resolutions supporting presidential policy and authorizing the president to use force if necessary to deal with particular international problems. In 1955, Congress authorized the president to use force to defend Formosa (Nationalist China) and the Pescadores Islands if they were attacked by Communist China. An even broader resolution was passed in 1957 that supported the "Eisenhower Doctrine," which announced the intention of the United States to defend Middle Eastern countries "against aggression from any country controlled by international communism." The House and Senate passed resolutions in 1962 declaring their support for any presidential action, including the use of force, that was necessary to defend the rights of the United States in Berlin. The same year Congress adopted similar resolutions pertaining to the Cuban missile crisis.

In August 1964 Congress passed the sweeping Tonkin Gulf resolution with only 2 senators out of 535 members of Congress in opposition. The resolution had been proposed by the Johnson administration in response to cloudy evidence of North Vietnamese torpedo boat attacks on U.S. vessels off the coast of Vietnam.[16] It authorized the president to take "all necessary measures to repel any armed attacks against the forces of the United States and to prevent further aggression." At least two months before the incident, Johnson's National Security Council staff had prepared a draft of a similar resolution supporting presidential freedom to act in Vietnam.[17] Since Johnson never asked Congress for a declaration of war, he used the Tonkin Gulf resolution in subsequent years as evidence of congressional support for his expansion of U.S. involvement in the conflict in Vietnam.

Congressional Rebellion

By the late 1960s, however, Congress began to rebel against what many members considered the aggrandizement of presidential foreign policy power. They objected to the growing tendency of presidents to avoid including Congress in foreign and defense policy issues. Following the Tonkin Gulf resolution, for example, President Johnson never sought congressional approval for any policy or strategy decision about the Vietnam War, except the appropriations bills necessary to continue U.S. military involvement in Southeast Asia. Members of Congress were also unhappy with the increasing use of executive agreements—pacts concluded between the president and other governments that had the force of law but were not subject to congressional approval—to make international commitments.

The Congress was partly responsible for the expansion of executive power between 1945 and 1969. In the interests of national unity and anti-Communism, the legislature had consented to and even encouraged presidential initiative in foreign affairs. Congress became accustomed to following whatever policy direction the president chose and failed to recognize that by granting the president discretion to handle specific foreign affairs problems it enlarged presidential interpretations of executive power.[18] In June 1969, by an overwhelming 70-16 vote, the Senate adopted a "national commitments" resolution, which declared the sense of the Senate that a national commitment by the United States results "only from affirmative action taken by the executive and legislative branches of the United States government by means of a treaty, statute, or concurrent resolution of both houses of Congress specifically providing for such a commitment." In 1969 and 1970, Congress repeatedly attempted to terminate funds for U.S. military activities in Indochina. During that period, Congress also used its investigative powers to probe the extent of U.S. commitments abroad.

In the early 1970s, the revelations of a secret Defense Department study of the decision-making process surrounding the Vietnam War, known as the *Pentagon Papers*, the unwillingness of presidents Johnson and Nixon to include Congress in foreign policy decisions, and the Watergate scandal spurred movements in Congress to recapture foreign affairs power lost to the executive branch. In

1972, Congress passed the Case Act, which established more rigorous requirements for the reporting of international agreements to Congress by the executive branch. The following year Congress passed the War Powers Act over President Nixon's veto. The measure set a sixty-day limit on any presidential commitment of U.S. troops to hostilities abroad, or to situations where hostilities might be imminent, without specific congressional authorization.

In 1974, Congress passed a major trade reform bill only after approving the Jackson-Vanik amendment, which linked trade concessions for Communist countries to their emigration policies. The same year Congress imposed a ban on military aid and arms shipments to Turkey. In 1978, the Senate conducted a long and contentious debate on the Panama Canal treaties and approved them only after adding numerous amendments. During this period Congress also conducted investigations of the intelligence community and began to take a more active interest in the specifics of the Defense Department's budget.

Congressional activism in foreign affairs has continued into the 1980s and appears to have become a permanent feature of U.S. foreign policy. Although Congress often supported President Reagan's actions, many of his foreign policies, such as military assistance to the Nicaraguan resistance and arms sales to moderate Arab nations, were accompanied by tough and sometimes unsuccessful battles for congressional approval. Congress also has routinely submitted alternative plans for weapons acquisition, arms control, and policies on regional problems. In addition, it has passed nonbinding resolutions stating its concerns on a variety of foreign policy issues.

Still, Congress has not superseded the contemporary president's role as formulator, initiator, and negotiator of U.S. foreign policy. Foreign policy remains an area of presidential dominance. Because of Congress's increased willingness and ability to assert itself in foreign affairs, however, congressional support has become more important to the success of a president's foreign policies.

Power of Communication

The Constitution's separation of powers between independent branches created a question that was unique to the United States: Who had the power to receive communications from foreign countries and to speak for the nation? Under the Articles of Confederation, these responsibilities belonged to Congress. The presidency created by the Constitution, however, had strong claims to the communication power. Negotiating treaties and sending and receiving ambassadors, two communicative powers, were specifically assigned to the president. Perhaps more important, communications was a function more suited to an office occupied by a single person with executive power than a large deliberative body composed of many individuals.

Washington was anxious to establish the presidency as the only organ of government empowered to communicate officially with foreign governments. He recognized that if both the president and Congress presumed to speak for the nation, diplomacy would be impossible, and foreign governments might try to exploit the confusion. During the first year of his administration, Washington received a letter from King Louis XVI of France notifying "the President and Members of the General Congress of the United States" that Louis's son had died. Washington told Congress that he had received the letter and that he would send a reply to France. The president informed the king that "by the change which has taken place in the national government of the United States, the honor of receiving and answering your Majesty's letter of the 7th of June to 'the President and Members of Congress' has devolved upon me." [19]

In 1793 Washington's secretary of state, Thomas Jefferson, echoed this assertion when he explained to the French ambassador, Edmond Genêt, that the president is "the only channel of communication between this country and foreign nations, it is from him alone that foreign nations or their agents are to learn what is or has been the will of the nation; and whatever he communicates as such, they have the right, and are bound to consider, as the expression of the nation." [20]

Washington's conception of the president's role as national communicator was accepted without serious challenge. In 1799 John Marshall reaffirmed the president's position as the instrument of communication with foreign governments when as a member of the House of Representatives he declared, "The President is the sole organ of the nation in its external relations, and its sole representative with foreign nations." [21] The same year Congress passed the Logan Act, which prohibited any person other than presidents or their agents from communicating with another country with the intention of affecting its policy toward an issue of contention with the United States.[22] The act has never been enforced against a member of Congress, although it remains in the United States Code. Informal discussions with foreign leaders by members of Congress have become accepted practices, but presumably the Logan Act could be invoked if a senator or representative attempted to usurp the president's power to communicate officially with foreign nations.[23]

Foreign Policy Declarations

The president's authority to communicate with other nations is not merely a ceremonial power. From George Washington to the present, presidents have found they can make foreign policy simply by making a statement. Presidents have used their communications power to make commitments, formalize decisions, or institutionalize broad policy goals.

The president's ability to make foreign policy through declarations derives from the president's position as "the sole representative with foreign nations." Only the president can speak for the United States. Consequently, Congress often is forced to choose between supporting a presidential commitment or decision it had no part in making or undermining that commitment or decision, which the world has accepted as U.S. policy. How a president expresses U.S. interests and intentions, therefore, can shape U.S. foreign policy. Kennedy's famous speech at the Berlin Wall in 1963, for example, encouraged the people of Berlin to expect U.S. protection, thereby committing the United States to its defense. Theodore Roosevelt explained the connection between communication and policy:

> The president carries on the correspondence through the State Department with all foreign countries. He is bound in such correspondence to discuss the proper construction of treaties. He must formulate the foreign policies of our government. He must state our attitude upon questions constantly arising. While strictly he may not bind our

government as a treaty would bind it, to a definition of its rights, still in future discussions foreign secretaries of other countries are wont to look for support of their contentions to the declarations and admissions of our secretaries of state in other controversies as in a sense binding upon us. There is thus much practical framing of our foreign policies in the executive conduct of our foreign relations.[24]

Presidential Doctrines

Presidents have not only made specific commitments through statements and declarations, they have also outlined broad foreign policy themes and strategies that they intended to pursue. The most famous and durable policy statement by a president has been the Monroe Doctrine. In 1823 President Monroe announced during his annual message to Congress that the United States would resist any attempt by a European power to interfere in the affairs of a Western Hemisphere country that was not already a European colony. Monroe did not consult Congress before his announcement, and some of its members believed the president had overstepped his authority. Henry Clay proposed a joint resolution supporting the president's policy, but it never was acted upon. Not until 1899 did the Monroe Doctrine receive a congressional endorsement.[25]

Theodore Roosevelt built upon the Monroe Doctrine in 1904 when he announced what came to be known as the Roosevelt Corollary in his annual message to Congress. Roosevelt claimed for the United States the right to act as the Western Hemisphere's policeman if "chronic wrongdoing or impotence" in a country required U.S. intervention.

Statements of broad foreign policy strategy, or "doctrines," are associated with the administrations of many contemporary presidents. The Truman Doctrine stated that "it must be the policy of the United States to support free peoples who are resisting attempted subjugation by armed minorities or outside pressures."[26] The Eisenhower Doctrine, which was supported by a joint resolution, claimed for the United States the right to intervene militarily in the Middle East to protect legitimate governments from attacks by Communist forces. The Nixon Doctrine (also known as the Guam Doctrine) proposed to continue giving allies military and economic aid while encouraging them to reduce their reliance on U.S. troops. The Carter Doctrine declared the Persian Gulf area to be a vital U.S. interest and warned that the United States would use force to prevent any attempt by an outside power to gain control of it. The Reagan Doctrine declared the Reagan administration's intention to support anti-Communist insurgencies around the world. These broad foreign policy declarations are not always accepted by Congress and do not always last beyond the administration that announces them. Yet, only the president's policy declarations have a chance to become accepted as national policy.

The Treaty Power

The authors of the Constitution used only one clause to explain how treaties were to be made. Article II, section 2, clause 2, declares that the president "shall have the Power, by and with the Advice and Consent of the Senate, to make Treaties, provided two-thirds of the Senators present concur. . . ." This concise statement sets up a classic division of power between the legislative and executive branches. The primary responsibility for conducting treaty negotiations is a presidential duty but the president cannot conclude a treaty without first obtaining the consent of the Senate and probably will be deterred from negotiating a treaty that the Senate is unlikely to approve. The Constitution, therefore, ensures that no formal treaty can be concluded without a strong interbranch consensus.

John F. Kennedy Library

A large crowd gathers as John F. Kennedy delivers his famous "Ich bin ein Berliner" speech at the Berlin Wall in 1963.

Nevertheless, the executive branch has established itself as the dominant branch in treaty making. As the sole organ of communication with foreign countries, commander in chief, and head of the foreign policy bureaucracy, presidents have been equipped with the means necessary to control most phases of the treaty-making process. The president decides what treaties to negotiate, chooses the negotiators, develops the negotiating strategy, and submits completed draft treaties to the Senate for approval. The president, not the Senate as commonly believed, even has the final power of ratification. Once the Senate has approved a treaty, it does not become law until the president ratifies it. If the president decides to ratify a treaty the Senate has approved, an exchange of ratifications occurs between the signatories. Then the treaty is promulgated—that is, officially proclaimed to be law—by the president. At any time the president may stop the treaty-making process, and after a treaty is ratified, the president has the authority to terminate it without Senate consent. Thus, the president has the power of initiative over a treaty from its conception to its ratification and beyond.[27]

Creation of the Treaty Power

In the eighteenth century, treaties were considered to be the primary tool of foreign policy, and the authors of the

Constitution deliberated extensively on how treaties should be made. Under the Articles of Confederation, the treaty power was completely entrusted to Congress. It selected negotiators, wrote and revised their orders, and made the final decision whether a treaty would be accepted or rejected. At the Constitutional Convention, delegates initially assumed that this congressional power would be given to the legislative body created by the new Constitution. After much debate and committee work, however, the convention adopted a proposal on September 8, 1787, to divide the treaty-making power between the executive and legislative branches.

By giving the president the power to make treaties "by and with the advice and consent of the Senate," the authors of the Constitution bolstered the prestige of the office of president, making it possible for future chief executives and their representatives to have the same authority as other world leaders in negotiating treaties. The convention also recognized that the president could conduct treaty negotiations with more speed and secrecy than Congress. John Jay emphasized this consideration in *The Federalist Papers:*

> It seldom happens in the negotiation of treaties, of whatever nature, but that perfect secrecy and immediate dispatch are sometimes requisite. There may be cases where the most useful intelligence may be obtained, if the persons possessing it can be relieved from apprehensions of discovery. Those apprehensions will operate on those persons whether they are actuated by mercenary or friendly motives; and there doubtless are many of both descriptions who would rely on the secrecy of the president, but who would not confide in that of the Senate, and still less in that of a large popular assembly.[28]

The delegates were not willing, however, to place too much treaty-making authority in the hands of the executive. Consequently, they required that two-thirds of the senators voting on a treaty be in favor of it before it could be ratified. The Founders did not unanimously support the two-thirds percentage, but this number, as well as the exclusion of the House of Representatives from the formal treaty approval process, survived several late attempts to change it.

Alexander Hamilton and John Jay defended the exclusion of the House from the treaty-making process in *The Federalist Papers.* Using similar arguments, they contended that the legislative role in treaty making should be limited to the Senate because decisions on treaties would thus be placed in the hands of persons chosen by the "select assemblies" of the states instead of by the rank and file, because the longer and overlapping Senate terms would provide relatively greater continuity, because the smaller size of the Senate would aid "secrecy and dispatch," and because agreement among the president, the Senate, and the House would be more difficult to obtain.[29]

One weakness of the Articles of Confederation that the Constitutional Convention was determined to correct was its dependence on the states to implement treaties. Congress had the power to make treaties with other countries, but it could not force the states to recognize treaty provisions as law. As a result, several states had violated certain articles of the Peace Treaty of 1783 with Great Britain. The convention's answer to this problem was Article VI, clause 2, of the Constitution, which states that "All Treaties made, or which shall be made, under the Authority of the United States, shall be the supreme Law of the Land; and the Judges in every State shall be bound thereby, any Thing in the Constitution or Laws of any State to the Contrary notwithstanding."

Chief Justice John Marshall interpreted this clause in his opinion on *Foster v. Neilson* in 1829. He confirmed that any treaty or portion of a treaty that did not require legislation to fulfill its provisions was binding on the states and had equal force to federal law. Therefore, although Congress may have to enact legislation to carry out acts stipulated by a treaty, any self-executing treaty or part of a treaty automatically attains the status of a law, enforceable by the courts. Provisions of various treaties periodically have been the target of legal challenges, but the Supreme Court has never declared a treaty or provision of a treaty made by the United States to be unconstitutional.[30] *(See "International Compacts," p. 1183, in The President and the Supreme Court chapter of Part VI and "Treaty Making and Executive Agreements, p. 1100, in The President and Congress chapter of Part VI.)*

Presidential Primacy in Treaty Negotiations

The ambiguity of the language in the Constitution that describes the treaty-making power created inevitable questions about how treaties would be made. That both the president and the Senate had a role in treaty making was clear, but the form of the Senate's advice on treaty matters and its influence over negotiations had to be worked out.

President Washington's initial interpretation of the treaty-making clause was that "advice" meant he was to seek Senate opinions in person before his representatives began negotiations. On August 21, 1789, Washington and his secretary of war, Henry Knox, questioned the Senate in its chambers about a treaty to be negotiated with the Creek Indians. After some debate, the Senate decided to postpone its response to Washington's questions until the following week so it could discuss the negotiations further. Washington, who had expected an immediate reply, returned on Monday, August 24, and received answers to his questions, but he was apparently angered by the Senate's indecisiveness and pessimistic that he could rely on that body for timely consultations on treaty matters. He never again attempted to use it as an executive council before treaty negotiations.[31]

It is interesting to speculate whether the history of U.S. foreign policy making would have been different had the Senate given Washington satisfactory answers when he came to consult on the treaty with the Creek Indians. The Senate's role in treaty negotiations would likely have been enhanced had Washington established a presidential precedent of consulting with that body in person. Subsequent presidents, however, agreed with Washington that the advice and consent of the Senate was best obtained from a distance. Several twentieth-century presidents, including Wilson and Truman, went to the Senate to propose or lobby for a treaty, but no president has ever returned to the Senate chamber to seek direct advice on treaty matters.

Washington's handling of the important Jay Treaty of 1794, which avoided war with Great Britain, demonstrated that he had abandoned his initial interpretation of the Constitution's treaty-making clause. During the early years of his presidency, Washington had conscientiously written to the Senate for advice on treaty matters before and during negotiations. He also had routinely submitted the negotiator's instructions to the Senate and kept that body informed of the progress of talks. In preparation for the Jay Treaty negotiations, however, Washington only submitted the appointment of his negotiator, Chief Justice John Jay, to the Senate for approval. He withheld from the Senate Jay's instructions about the sensitive negotiations, and the negotiations were held in London without Senate involvement.

Rather than challenging the president's power to make a treaty independently of the Senate, that body responded by amending the completed Jay Treaty in a manner similar to the method by which it amended legislation. Washington accepted the Senate's authority to do this, and after initial protests, the British ratified the amended treaty. The Jay Treaty established a process of treaty making that subsequent administrations and Senates would emulate. As Corwin observed, "The Senate's function as an executive council was from the very beginning put, and largely by its own election, on the way to absorption into its more usual function as a legislative chamber, and subsequent developments soon placed its decision in this respect beyond all possibility of recall." [32]

Washington's actions established the power of the executive branch to make treaties on its own before submitting them for Senate approval. Today, the right of either house of Congress to offer advice is not questioned, but the advice of the legislative branch is merely persuasive, not compelling. In its landmark decision in the 1936 *Curtiss-Wright* case, the Supreme Court ruled: "The president ... alone negotiates. Into the field of negotiation the Senate cannot intrude, and Congress itself is powerless to invade it." [33]

The degree of congressional participation in negotiations has become entirely a matter of presidential preference. When presidents have cooperated closely with the Senate in the negotiation of a treaty, they usually have been motivated by their recognition that Senate involvement would increase the chances for approval. Thus, the sporadic influence the Senate has retained in treaty negotiations is largely derived from its legislative veto over treaties, rather than from the constitutional provision that the president should consider the Senate's advice when making treaties.

The Treaty-making Process

The first step in making a treaty is negotiating with a foreign power. This stage is controlled by the president and presidential advisers and representatives. During or before this phase Congress may offer advice to the president or express its views on the negotiations individually or collectively. One or both houses of Congress may choose to pass a resolution containing advice on treaty matters. If Congress strongly opposes a treaty under negotiation, a resolution communicating its disapproval may cause the president to change negotiating strategies or abandon a treaty altogether. A supportive resolution, however, may contribute to the executive branch's enthusiasm for a particular treaty. In 1948, for example, the Senate's Vandenberg Resolution, which preceded the development of NATO and other alliance systems, advised the president to negotiate regional security agreements.[34] Regardless of congressional protests or encouragement, the president and representatives of the president cannot be constrained from initiating and conducting treaty negotiations with another country.

Although the executive branch has the power to negotiate a treaty without Congress, many presidents have found that involving individual senators in the negotiating process can be a useful political tool. Such involvement can take several forms. During most treaty negotiations influential senators are at least asked for their opinions on the proceedings, but a president may also ask senators to help select the negotiating team, observe the negotiations, follow the progress of the talks through briefings, or even be negotiators.[35] Up to the end of Madison's administration in 1817, the names of treaty negotiators were referred to the Senate for confirmation. The Senate repeatedly protested subsequent presidents' neglect of that practice, but the Senate never was able to establish firmly its right to confirm negotiators. Presidents seem to have abandoned the practice because of the need for secrecy in employing special agents, whose appointments were recognized as the right of the executive.

On various occasions since Madison's administration, however, presidents have sought Senate confirmation of treaty negotiators. James K. Polk submitted the names of his appointees to negotiate a treaty with Mexico. Grant sought Senate confirmation for the commissioners who negotiated the Treaty of Washington, which settled American claims against Great Britain, which had occasionally violated its neutrality during the Civil War by aiding the Confederacy. Warren G. Harding submitted the names of his appointees to the World War Foreign Debt Commission in 1922, but this submission was required by a provision of the act that created the commission.[36]

The practice of sending the instructions of treaty negotiators to the Senate for review, which Washington had done early in his presidency, proved to be even more temporary than the custom of senatorial confirmation of the negotiators. After Washington's administration, no president asked the Senate to consider the terms of a treaty not yet agreed upon, until Polk submitted the skeleton of a treaty ending the war with Mexico in 1846. Preliminary drafts of treaties were sent to the Senate in a few instances by four other presidents—James Buchanan, Lincoln, Johnson, and Grant. In 1919, the Senate requested a copy of the proposed Treaty of Versailles as presented to the representatives of Germany. The secretary of state replied: "The president feels it would not be in the public interest to communicate to the Senate a text that is provisional and not definite, and finds no precedent for such a procedure." [37]

Wilson's refusal to inform the Senate about the Versailles treaty negotiations contributed to that body's rejection of the treaty. Several of Wilson's successors learned from his mistake and sought to include the Senate at an early stage in controversial treaty negotiations. While World War II was still being fought, Franklin Roosevelt established the Joint Advisory Committee on Postwar Foreign Policy to provide a forum where members of Congress and the executive branch could discuss the composition of an international peace organization. This committee, along with the administration's private consultations with Senate leaders, helped create bipartisan support for the United Nations.[38] When the negotiations on the United Nations Treaty began in 1945, Truman included senators from both parties in the U.S. delegation. The Carter administration also tried to limit Senate objections to the SALT II (Strategic Arms Limitation Talks) treaty it hoped to negotiate with the Soviet Union by encouraging senatorial participation in the treaty-making process. Selected senators were allowed to observe the negotiations, and the administration consulted closely with Senate leaders while the negotiations were in progress. During these consultations senators voiced suggestions and concerns that prompted Carter to instruct his negotiators to modify their position on several issues.[39]

Once U.S. negotiators have agreed upon the terms of a treaty with a foreign government, the president must decide whether to submit the draft to the Senate for consideration. If it appears that Senate opposition to a treaty will make approval unlikely, the president may decide to withdraw the treaty to avoid a political defeat. Also, international events may change the president's mind about the desirability of ratifying a treaty. President Carter came to this conclusion after the Soviet Union invaded Afghanistan in December 1979. He withdrew the SALT II treaty from Senate consideration to protest the Soviet presence in Afghanistan, even though before the invasion he had pressed the Senate to approve the treaty.

If the president does decide to submit a treaty to the Senate for consideration, the Constitution requires that a two-thirds majority of senators voting be in favor of the treaty for it to be approved.

The Senate is not compelled by the Constitution either to approve or to reject a treaty as it has been negotiated by the executive branch. It may attach amendments to a treaty that require the president to renegotiate its terms with the other signatories before the Senate grants its approval. In 1978 Congress added a number of conditions and reservations to the treaty that provided for the transfer of the Panama Canal to Panamanian control after the year 2000. The most notable of these amendments was written by Sen. Dennis DeConcini (D-Ariz.). It claimed for the United States the right to take whatever steps were necessary, including military force, to open the canal if its operations ceased.[40] The Panamanian government agreed to accept the Senate amendments without renegotiation. Such amendments, however, often make agreement between the United States and its negotiating partner impossible.

U.S. presidents have accepted without serious challenge the Senate's power to force renegotiation of parts of a treaty. In effect, when the Senate gives its consent on condition that its amendments are accepted by the negotiating partner of the United States, it is rejecting the treaty while outlining a revision of the treaty to which it grants its consent in advance.[41] Presidents in turn may decide not to renegotiate if they believe the senatorial amendments make the treaty undesirable.

The Senate also has the power to add nonbinding written reservations to a treaty before approving it. This option can be used when the Senate agrees to the basic terms of a treaty but believes it must state its interpretation of the document to dispel ambiguity and to influence the treaty's implementation. Nonbinding resolutions, however, can have a profound effect on the conclusion of a treaty if the foreign government involved disagrees with the resolutions or finds them insulting. Ratification of the 1976 Treaty of Friendship and Cooperation with Spain was delayed several months by Spanish objections to nonbinding Senate resolutions attached to the treaty. The issue was resolved by an agreement between Congress, the Ford administration, and the Spanish government to attach the resolutions to the U.S. instrument of ratification, the document outlining the U.S. understanding of the treaty, but to exclude them from the Spanish instrument of ratification and the treaty ratification document exchanged by the two countries.[42]

After the Senate approves a treaty and the president ratifies it, it may require legislation to fulfill its intent. Such treaties are referred to as "non-self-executing." For example, the Migratory Bird Treaty of 1916 between the United States and Canada pledged the two nations to make and implement laws to protect migratory birds. Therefore, complying with the terms of the treaty required subsequent legislative action by the Congress and the president.[43] Treaties that require the appropriation of funds or the enactment of criminal laws for their implementation would also be non-self-executing, since these tasks can only be accomplished through laws made by the Congress.[44] Consequently, non-self-executing treaties give Congress another chance to pass judgment upon them after ratification. Although Congress rarely has chosen to undermine a treaty by refusing to appropriate funds or enact implementing legislation, its right to do so is well established.[45]

Library of Congress

During the eighteenth and nineteenth centuries, a precedent developed of presidents not traveling outside the United States while in office. Teddy Roosevelt became the first president to break this precedent when he visited Panama in 1906 to inspect the canal under construction.

Treaty Approval

Even though the executive branch often has ignored or minimized the Senate's advisory function, the Senate has approved without changes about 70 percent of the treaties submitted to it.

This apparent Senate acquiescence to the executive branch's will on treaty matters is not as striking as it seems. To avoid a political defeat, presidents often have withdrawn treaties from consideration that were in jeopardy of Senate rejection. Other treaties were neither approved nor

Jimmy Carter Library

On September 7, 1977, President Jimmy Carter and Panamanian leader Brig. Gen. Omar Torrijos Herrera signed the treaty that transferred control of the Panama Canal to Panama after the year 2000. The Senate ratified the treaty the following spring.

rejected by the Senate, but instead left without action in political limbo. For example, the Genocide Treaty, which instructed signers to prevent and punish the crime of genocide, was approved by the Senate in 1986, almost thirty-seven years after Truman submitted it to that body. Many more pacts that could have taken the form of treaties were concluded as less formal executive agreements between the president and a foreign government to avoid the possibility of Senate rejection.

Nevertheless, the Senate seldom has been willing to disapprove of a completed draft treaty without serious cause. The high percentage of Senate approval can be attributed to several political factors. First, because presidents and executive branch officials are mindful that they will eventually need the Senate's approval, they usually take the Senate's concerns into account even when they do not closely consult with that body.

Second, senators, as well as their counterparts in the House, historically have been inclined to follow the president's lead in foreign affairs in the interest of projecting a united front abroad, unless they have serious objections to the administration's course of action. Members of Congress do not wish to be seen as saboteurs of presidential policy, especially when U.S. troops are engaged in hostilities overseas. Since the Vietnam War, however, the Congress has been more willing to challenge the president's leadership in foreign affairs.

Third, when a president concludes a draft treaty with another nation, in the eyes of the international community the United States has made a commitment. Even though the Senate is exercising a constitutionally granted power when it votes to reject a treaty, rejection usually causes both the United States and the president to lose some credibility with other nations. The Senate, therefore, must balance its reservations about a particular treaty against the damage rejection would inflict on international confidence in U.S. ability to make commitments.[46] Finally, the executive-legislative relationship is not purely adversarial. All presidents have their share of allies in the Senate who will work for approval of virtually any treaty the president submits. Furthermore, senators of the president's party often will side with the president on a particular treaty for the sake of the party's welfare and unity even if they have reservations about the agreement. If the president's party happens to be in control of the Senate, obtaining approval for a treaty may require the support of fewer than half of the senators from the opposition party.

Although the Senate's approval record has been overwhelmingly favorable, there have been significant exceptions. The most famous rejection of a draft treaty by the Senate was its refusal in 1919 to approve the Treaty of Versailles, which ended World War I and established the League of Nations. Wilson campaigned vigorously for approval of the treaty after it had been negotiated, but his failure to include the Senate in the treaty-making process contributed to its defeat.

Proposed Changes in Approval Process

The method by which Congress approves treaties has been the target of much criticism. John Hay, secretary of state under McKinley and Roosevelt who fought several losing battles with the Senate over treaty approval, called the power of the Senate to veto treaties the "original mistake of the Constitution."[47] In particular, the constitutional requirement that two-thirds of the senators present must consent to a treaty before it can be ratified has been the subject of proposed changes. After the Senate refused to approve the Versailles treaty, proposals surfaced in both the executive and legislative branches to reduce the fraction of Senate members needed to approve a treaty. Most proposals advocated a simple majority; others suggested lowering the requirement from two-thirds to three-fifths of the senators voting.

None of the proposals has come close to being implemented, but if the requirement for a two-thirds majority were lowered, the effect would be significant. The president probably would be less inclined to substitute executive agreements for treaties on matters that should receive congressional review. Yet, the two-thirds vote requirement has ensured that important treaties requiring a sustained U.S. commitment—such as the treaty that established NATO—have been concluded with strong bipartisan support.[48]

Another periodic reform proposal has been the inclusion of the House of Representatives in the treaty-making process by requiring a majority vote of both houses of Congress before ratification. Madison and James Wilson argued unsuccessfully for this method of treaty approval at the Constitutional Convention in 1787. Several resolutions to make the House a partner in treaty making were introduced in Congress during the 1920s and 1940s, but they met with no more success than the proposals of Madison and Wilson.

A third reform that has been suggested in the twentieth century is to change the Senate's rules of procedure to prevent approval of a treaty from being blocked by inaction or a filibuster. The Senate could eliminate the possibility of a small minority of its members effectively defeating a treaty if it prohibited filibusters in treaty debates and required votes on draft treaties set before it by the president. This proposal would require only the Senate itself to adopt such rules.[49]

Termination of Treaties

Although Article VI, clause 2, of the Constitution declares that treaties are the "supreme Law of the Land," the federal government is not legally constrained from terminating a treaty through agreement with the other party, in response to the other party's violations of the treaty, or for any other reason. It is unclear, however, which branch has the authority to terminate a treaty. The Constitution provides no guidelines as to who determines that a treaty should be revoked and what sort of approval is needed from another branch. Consequently, both the president and Congress at various times have claimed the power to terminate treaties.[50]

In 1979 this issue was brought before the Supreme Court when the Carter administration sought to terminate the 1954 Mutual Defense Treaty with the Republic of China (Taiwan) as part of the process of establishing formal relations with the People's Republic of China (PRC). The treaty had a clause permitting withdrawal, but President Carter took the action without consulting the Senate in advance. Since the president cannot ratify a treaty without Senate consent, his authority to revoke an existing treaty unilaterally was uncertain.

Sen. Barry Goldwater and twenty-three other members of Congress objected to Carter's termination of the treaty and brought suit against the president to prevent it. U.S. District Court Judge Oliver Gasch ruled in October 1979 that treaty termination is a shared power, one that requires the consent of two-thirds of the Senate or a majority of both houses of Congress. He concluded that President Carter's action therefore was unconstitutional on the grounds that it violated the principle of separation of powers.

After a U.S. court of appeals overturned Gasch's decision by a 6-1 vote, Goldwater appealed to the Supreme Court. The Court ruled 7-2 in favor of the president's authority to terminate the treaty on his own. Four justices said that the termination of the treaty was a political issue that the executive and legislative branches would have to resolve themselves.[51]

Executive Agreements

An executive agreement is a pact other than a treaty made by the president or representatives of the president with a foreign leader or government. Presidents have asserted that their power to execute the laws, command the armed forces, and function as the sole organ of foreign policy gives them the legal authority to make these pacts without obtaining the specific approval of the Senate. The executive agreement is a particularly powerful foreign policy tool. The president can make agreements with foreign governments without congressional consent, and these agreements have the force of law. Unlike treaties, they do not supersede U.S. laws with which they conflict, but in every other respect they are binding.

The vast majority of executive agreements are either routine extensions of existing treaties or are based upon broad legislative directives.[52] Agreements made by the president to carry out legislation or treaty obligations are often called "congressional-executive international agreements." Presidents have maintained that their responsibility to execute the laws of the United States gives them the right to make these routine pacts. Other executive agreements have been supported by joint resolutions. Presidents occasionally have chosen to seek the approval of a majority of both houses of Congress for executive agreements when they did not have the support of two-thirds of the Senate but did want some type of specific congressional consent. Although presidents have used joint resolutions to circumvent the formal treaty process, this practice has not elicited strong objections, since it does involve Congress in foreign policy. The small percentage of agreements that do not fall under these categories are the "pure" executive agreements, which are not accompanied by any congressional approval. These are usually the most important and controversial pacts made under the president's authority.

The use of executive agreements has grown dramatically in the twentieth century. During the eighteenth and nineteenth centuries presidents concluded on average only one executive agreement per year.[53] By the 1930s executive agreements had become more common than treaties.[54] Between 1946 and 1973 a mere 6 percent of all international agreements were treaties.[55] Executive agreements not only have grown in number, they also have been used to conduct business once reserved for treaties. Contemporary presidents can accomplish virtually anything through an executive agreement that can be accomplished through a treaty. Trade agreements, the annexation of territory, military commitments, and arms control pacts have all been concluded through executive agreements. *(See Table 4, Treaties and Agreements, 1789-1988, p. 1104.)*

Constitutional Dilemma

The power of the president to make agreements without congressional approval has created much concern and occasionally resentment on Capitol Hill. Although the Constitution does not prohibit executive agreements, the Founders' careful division of the treaty power in the Constitution must be interpreted as an attempt to ensure that Congress has a direct voice in making international commitments. The growing use of executive agreements by presidents and their representatives to avoid the advice and consent of the Senate has been widely regarded by constitutional scholars and members of Congress as a serious deterioration of constitutional checks and balances in the area of foreign policy.

The development of the United States into a world power with security commitments and economic interests in every corner of the world has made some degree of executive flexibility in making executive agreements desirable. Like Jefferson, who was confronted with the irresistible opportunity to buy the Louisiana Territory, contemporary presidents are sometimes faced with an international situation that calls for making commitments with speed and secrecy. Also, executive agreements often provide a simpler method of transacting less important international business that would overload the already tight legislative schedule if treaties were used. Therefore, there are compelling arguments against legislation or constitutional amendments that would seriously limit the president's ability to make executive agreements.

The crux of the problem is that there are important international agreements that should receive Senate approval in accordance with the Constitution, but there are no concrete guidelines to indicate which agreements need Senate consent and which could be handled simply by executive agreement. Presidents may, therefore, use their discretion in deciding how to make a particular agreement. Numerous presidents, faced with the prospect of fighting for two-thirds approval in the Senate, have used executive agreements to skirt the treaty requirements imposed by the Constitution rather than abandon a diplomatic initiative they believed to be good for the nation or important for their own political future. Treaties, therefore, have become an exception to the rule of presidential policy making.

Despite the use of executive agreements to avoid the treaty ratification process, the Supreme Court has repeatedly upheld the president's power to make international agreements without the consent of the Senate. The Court's ruling on *U.S. v. Belmont* in 1936 was particularly significant. At issue was the president's authority to conclude unilaterally several agreements connected with the 1933 recognition of the Soviet Union. In delivering the Court's opinion, Justice George Sutherland wrote:

> The recognition, establishment of diplomatic relations, the assignment, and agreement with respect thereto, were all parts of one transaction, resulting in an international compact between the two governments. That the negotiations, acceptance of the assignment and agreements and understandings in respect thereof were within the competence of the president may not be doubted. Governmental power over internal affairs is distibuted between the national government and the several states. Governmental power over external affairs is not distributed, but is vested exclusively in the national government. And in respect of what was done here, the Executive had the authority to speak as the sole organ of that government.[56]

Justice Sutherland could have based his opinion that the president had the authority to make these agreements on the president's indisputable power to recognize foreign governments. Although he did mention the relevance of this presidential power, he seemed to find authority for the agreements in the president's broader power as the sole organ of foreign policy.[57]

Landmark Executive Agreements

Ironically, Thomas Jefferson, the leader of the Democratic-Republican party, which officially opposed the enhancement of the federal government's power, was the first president to conclude a major international agreement without obtaining the required constitutional approval from the Senate.[58] He agreed to purchase Louisiana from France and delivered the payment before he sent the deal to the Senate for confirmation.

Jefferson acted without the advice and consent of the Senate and against his own political beliefs because he feared that the inevitable delay of a Senate debate would ruin the sale. Napoleon was anxious to sell the territory, and Jefferson did not want to risk the possibilities that Britain might take control of the area or that Napoleon might even sell the land to the British while the Senate debated the purchase. Many future presidents would use executive agreements to avoid lengthy Senate consideration of urgent diplomacy. Since Jefferson eventually did obtain Senate approval, historians generally do not consider the Louisiana Purchase to have been an executive agreement, but it clearly presaged the use of executive agreements by future administrations.[59]

The first major executive agreement concluded between a president and a foreign power was the Rush-Bagot agreement with Great Britain.[60] The pact, which imposed limitations on naval forces on the Great Lakes, was concluded under the supervision of President Monroe in 1817. A year after the agreement was put into operation Monroe decided that he wanted congressional acquiescence to his act of diplomacy. He sent the agreement to the House and Senate and asked if they thought it required the consent of the Senate. The Senate endorsed the "arrangement" with a two-thirds vote but did not consider its action to be an approval of a treaty, and instruments of ratification were never exchanged between the United States and Great Britain.[61]

Although Monroe's executive agreement was significant in establishing a precedent, President John Tyler's annexation of Texas by executive agreement in 1845 was even more important, because it was the first time a president had used an executive agreement to accomplish what could not have been done through the treaty process.[62]

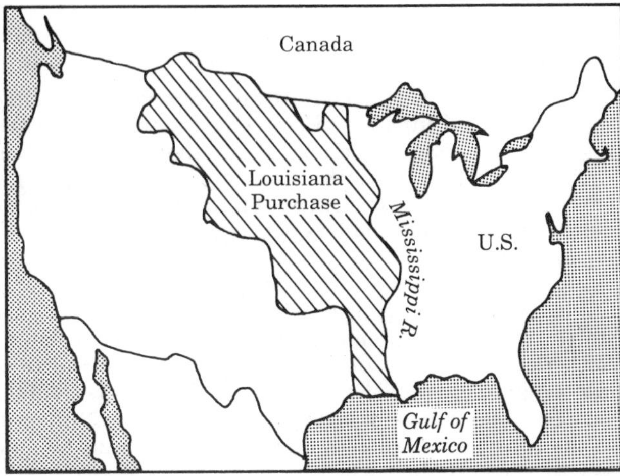

In 1803 President Thomas Jefferson bought the Louisiana territory from France for $15 million, or about four cents an acre, nearly doubling the size of the United States. Jefferson was the first president to conclude a major international agreement without Senate approval.

Tyler wished to bring Texas into the Union to keep it out of foreign hands and to strengthen the slave states, but he was not close to having the necessary two-thirds support in the Senate for conclusion of a treaty of annexation. Late in his term, however, public support in favor of annexation was reflected in Congress, and he called for a joint resolution to bring Texas into the nation. The House easily passed the resolution 120-98, but the Senate gave its approval by only two votes, 27-25, a margin far short of the two-thirds majority that would have been required for Senate approval of a treaty. Armed with this resolution, Tyler invited Texas to become a state. In 1898 McKinley annexed Hawaii as a territory by the same method.[63]

Theodore Roosevelt frequently used his commander-in-chief and executive powers to avoid congressional checks on his authority. Predictably, he was not timid about using executive agreements to accomplish foreign policy objectives that would have been delayed or undermined by the treaty process. One of Roosevelt's most famous executive agreements involved the Caribbean nation of Santo Domingo (now the Dominican Republic). The president wished to block European influence anywhere in the Western Hemisphere. When Santo Domingo fell into heavy debt to European creditors in 1905, Roosevelt oversaw negotiations of an agreement that extended U.S. protection to Santo Domingo and put the United States in control of collecting the country's customs. The United States would turn over a percentage of the revenue to the Dominican government and pay the country's creditors gradually with the rest. Roosevelt hoped that the Senate would consent to the draft treaty, but he immediately implemented it as an executive agreement. When the Senate refused to approve the treaty, Roosevelt continued the arrangement under the executive agreement.[64]

Franklin Roosevelt also used an executive agreement to avoid the treaty process when he provided destroyers to the British in 1940. The United States was still officially neutral at that time, and the persistent isolationist mentality in Congress precluded any possibility that a treaty could be approved to provide Britain with badly needed fighting ships to defend against German submarine attacks. Roosevelt therefore used an executive agreement to trade old U.S. destroyers for the right to lease several British naval bases in the Western Hemisphere. Since the deal was in violation of two statutes and threatened the neutral status of the United States, it was clearly an agreement that should have been accompanied by some sort of congressional approval.[65]

The development of NATO illustrates another use of executive agreements. NATO was established by a short treaty containing only fourteen articles that pledged the signatories to maintain and improve their collective defense capabilities. Upon this foundation, the contracting parties constructed an organization with an integrated command structure, detailed battle plans, extensive transportation and communications facilities, and routinely scheduled multinational maneuvers.

Executive agreements were used to expand the NATO treaty, which had received much bipartisan support. Although the senators who voted for ratification could not have foreseen the enormous development of NATO that would take place through executive agreements, the original treaty did provide the Senate with an opportunity to approve the concept of an alliance with Western European nations.[66]

A dramatic contemporary example of damage that can be caused by a secret informal executive agreement was President Nixon's written assurance to President Nugyen Van Thieu of South Vietnam in 1973 that the United States would "respond with full force," if North Vietnam violated the Paris Peace Agreement, which ended the U.S. military presence in Vietnam. Thieu had consented to the Paris Agreement based on Nixon's personal promise, which was not kept when the North Vietnamese invaded South Vietnam in 1975. Thieu regarded Nixon's pledge as a national commitment, and the United States lost credibility when the promise was not kept.[67]

Nixon's promise, however, was not supported by a corresponding congressional resolution and did not reflect the mood either of Congress or of the American people at the end of the Vietnam War. It is virtually inconceivable that Congress would have consented to a major reescalation of the war by appropriating large sums to fight the North Vietnamese assault that conquered South Vietnam in 1975. Therefore, Nixon's promise, which helped persuade Thieu to accept the Paris agreement, was little more than the optimistic personal promise of a president who almost certainly would not have had the means to keep it, even if he had remained in office.

Attempts to Limit Executive Agreements

Since the end of World War II, Congress has made two major attempts to limit the president's power to make international agreements and commitments without the advice and consent of the Senate. The first was a movement in the 1950s led by Sen. John W. Bricker (R-Ohio), who had proposed a constitutional amendment that would have placed restraints on the president's power to make executive agreements and decreased the effect of the agreements on domestic law. The second occurred in the early 1970s and culminated in the Case Act of 1972, which was intended to compel the executive branch to report all executive agreements to Congress or to selected congressional committees. Except for a clarification of the Case Act passed in 1977, subsequent efforts by Congress to make the executive branch more accountable for its agreements with other nations have been unsuccessful.

Bricker Amendment

Senator Bricker, a conservative Republican, chaired the Foreign and Interstate Commerce Committee. He and his followers were concerned about the implications of Article VI, clause 2, of the Constitution in the postwar environment where the United States was expanding its defense commitments and its participation in international organizations.

The clause provides that treaties made by the United States are the supreme law of the land and binding on the states. The 1936 Supreme Court ruling written by Justice Sutherland in *U.S. v. Belmont* had extended the force of law to "all international compacts and agreements from the very fact that complete power over international affairs is in the national government and is not and cannot be subject to any curtailment or interference on the part of the several states."

The Brickerites believed that the president's broad power to make international agreements that have the force of law over the states threatened the constitutionally guaranteed rights of the American people.[68] In particular, many senators were alarmed by the growing tendency to use executive agreements to implement military alliance pacts and UN programs. In January 1953 Bricker and sixty-three cosponsors introduced an amendment aimed at establishing congressional review of executive agreements and making treaties unenforceable as domestic law without accompanying legislation. The amendment stated:

> 1. A provision of a treaty which denies or abridges any right enumerated in this Constitution shall not be of any force or effect.
> 2. No treaty shall authorize or permit any foreign power or any international organization to supervise, control, or adjudicate rights of citizens of the United States within the United States enumerated in this Constitution or any other matter essentially within the domestic jurisdiction of the United States.
> 3. A treaty shall become effective as internal law in the United States only through the enactment of appropriate legislation by the Congress.
> 4. All executive or other agreements between the President and any international organization, foreign power, or official thereof shall be made only in the manner and to the extent to be precribed by law. Such agreements shall be subject to the limitations imposed on treaties or the making of treaties in this article.
> 5. The Congress shall have power to enforce this article by appropriate legislation.

The third and fourth provisions would have radically altered the way the United States enters into agreements with foreign governments. Every treaty and executive agreement would have required implementing legislation to make them enforceable as domestic laws, and any executive agreement made by a president would be subject to regulation by Congress. As a result, the ability of presidents to make foreign policy through executive agreements and to negotiate treaties without involving Congress would have been severely curtailed. The amendment did not, however, come to a vote by the time Congress adjourned in August. In 1954 a milder version of the Bricker amendment came within one vote of passing the Senate with a two-thirds majority. Thereafter, support for the amendment ebbed, in part because President Dwight D. Eisenhower strongly opposed it.

The Case Act

In the early 1970s a more modest movement surfaced in Congress to restrain the indiscriminate use of executive agreements. The impetus for this effort was a Senate subcommittee's discovery in 1969-1970 that the executive branch had made secret commitments and terms of agreements during the 1960s. The Security Agreements and Commitments Abroad Subcommittee of the Senate Foreign Relations Committee, chaired by Sen. Stuart Symington (D-Mo.), uncovered secret agreements with Ethiopia, Laos, Thailand, South Korea, Spain, the Philippines, and other countries.

The Nixon administration deepened congressional resentment by concluding important executive agreements with Portugal and Bahrain about military bases. The Senate passed a resolution asserting that the agreements should have been made in the form of treaties, which would have required Senate consent.

Congress responded by passing the Case Act in 1972. The act obligates the executive branch to inform Congress of all executive agreements within sixty days after they have been concluded. It also requires the executive branch to inform Congress of all executive agreements in existence at the time the law was signed. Finally, it provides that the House Foreign Affairs Committee and the Senate Foreign Relations Committee be informed of any executive agreements that the president determines need to be kept secret to ensure national security. The Senate passed the bill by a unanimous 81-0 vote and the House by voice vote.[69] Several bills were proposed in the years following passage of the Case Act that were intended to establish a congressional procedure for disapproving executive agreements. In 1974, such a bill introduced by Sen. Sam J. Ervin, Jr. (D-N.C.), passed in the Senate, but the House did not act upon it. Hearings on two similar bills were held in 1975 by the Senate Judiciary Subcommittee on the Separation of Powers, but they did not lead to legislation.

After several years, Congress found that many executive agreements were not being reported under the provisions of the Case Act because executive branch officials did not define them as executive agreements. Congress reacted by passing legislation in 1977 that required Congress to be informed of any verbal or informal understanding made by any representative of the U.S. government that might constitute a commitment.

Although the Case Act and the legislation that followed it do not limit the president's power to make executive agreements, legislators are more likely to be able to check this executive branch power if they know what sort of agreements the president is making. Given that Congress can conduct investigations, issue resolutions, pass legislation, and control appropriations, it does have tools with which it can challenge executive agreements it believes are unwise or improper. This is especially true since many executive agreements depend on supporting legislation.[70]

The Recognition Power

Although the Constitution does not explicitly grant presidents the power to recognize foreign governments, it is generally accepted that they have this power as a consequence of the authority to send and receive ambassadors. Article II, section 2, of the Constitution says the president "shall appoint Ambassadors," and section 3 of the same article grants the president the power to "receive Ambassadors and other public Ministers" of foreign nations. Since the acts of sending an ambassador to a country and receiving its ambassador imply recognition of the legitimacy of the foreign government involved in the exchange, presidents have successfully claimed exclusive authority to decide which foreign governments will be recognized by the United States. Also, given that presidents decide which nations will be recognized, it follows that they have the power to terminate relations with another nation.

This extension of presidential power was not taken for granted at the beginning of the Republic. Madison, writing as Helvidius, argued that the duty to receive ambassadors did not give the president the power to rule on the legitimacy of foreign governments.[71] In *The Federalist Papers,* Hamilton did not appear even to notice the potential connection between the ceremonial power to receive ambassadors and the recognition of nations. Despite his inclination to see many implied executive powers in the Constitution, Madison wrote that the president's power to receive ambassadors "is more a matter of dignity than of authority. It is a circumstance which will be without consequence in the administration of the government; and it was far more convenient that it should be arranged in this manner than that there should be a necessity of convening the legislature, or one of its branches, upon every arrival of a foreign minister." [72]

The first use of the president's power of recognition occurred in 1793 when Washington agreed to receive Edmond Genêt, the ambassador of the new French Republic. Since most of the members of Congress who were inclined to resist the growth of executive power into areas not specifically granted in the Constitution were also supporters of the new republican regime in France, this expansion of the president's power to receive ambassadors was not questioned.[73] All subsequent presidents have assumed the right to make recognition decisions.

Congress has no role in the recognition process other than to approve the president's nominees for ambassadorships. As with treaties, however, Congress can offer its nonbinding advice to the president on matters of recognition. After France was conquered by the Nazis in World War II, for example, the House and Senate passed resolutions supporting the Roosevelt administration's agreement with other nations in the Western Hemisphere not to allow the transfer of the sovereignty of any European colony in the Americas to another European power.[74]

Genêt Affair

Washington's decision to accept Genêt's credentials soon began to cause the president problems. Genêt attempted to exploit the American people's sympathy for revolutionary France by privately enlisting their support against his country's enemies, Great Britain and Spain. He encouraged settlers in Kentucky and other territories in the West to take up arms against the Spanish in Louisiana, and he took steps to outfit French pirates willing to attack British and Spanish shipping from U.S. ports. These activities undercut Washington's Proclamation of Neutrality and threatened to draw the United States into the European hostilities. Washington, therefore, demanded that the French government recall Genêt. The French ordered their ambassador to return home, but retaliated by demanding that Washington recall the U.S. minister to France, Gouverneur Morris, on the grounds that he had supported plots to restore the French monarchy.[75] Washington thus established a second implied presidential power related to sending and receiving ambassadors. He demonstrated that the president could expel a foreign representative whose conduct was judged unacceptable.

Principles of Recognition

Many countries determine whether they will recognize a particular foreign government according to that government's ability to maintain its authority over its people and to meet its international obligations. The ideological system and the moral character of the regime in question are irrelevant under this conception of recognition. In 1913 President Wilson set a precedent by refusing to recognize the Mexican regime of Victoriano Huarta on the grounds that it was immoral and did not represent the will of its people.[76] Since Wilson, the ideology and morality of a foreign regime have become accepted factors in determining whether a government should be recognized. As a result, successive presidents refused to recognize the revolutionary Communist regimes in Russia from 1917 to 1933, and China from 1949 to 1979, even though these regimes were in firm control of their countries long before the United States established diplomatic relations. In the late 1980s, several Communist countries, including Cuba and Vietnam, did not have diplomatic relations with the United States.

A president also can recognize the rights or interests of national or political groups that do not hold political power. In 1978 Jimmy Carter announced a qualified recognition of the interests of the Palestinians living in Israeli occupied territories by saying that any Middle East peace settlement must recognize "the legitimate rights of the Palestinian people" and "enable the Palestinians to participate in the determination of their own future." [77] A president may also deny recognition of a government's legal authority over a part or all of the territory claimed by that government. For example, the United States has continued to refuse to recognize the legitimacy of the Soviet Union's annexation of Latvia, Lithuania, and Estonia, which occurred in 1940.

Recognition as a Policy Statement

A decision to recognize or not to recognize a nation can be a major policy statement that expresses the attitudes and intentions of the United States toward the nation in question, and sometimes toward an entire region. Such policy statements can have profound consequences, including war. In 1836 Andrew Jackson realized that the act of recognizing the Republic of Texas could have the effect of a declaration of war against Mexico, which regarded Texas as a Mexican territory. Although Jackson did not repudiate his authority to recognize Texas or any other nation, he announced his willingness to allow Congress to decide if Texas should be recognized: "It will always be considered consistent with the spirit of the Constitution, and most safe, that it [the recognition power] should be exercised when probably leading to war, with a previous understanding with that body by whom war can alone be declared, and by whom all the provisions for sustaining its perils must be furnished." [78]

Theodore Roosevelt's recognition of Panama in 1903 following its U.S.-backed revolt from Colombia paved the way to a treaty that gave the United States the right to dig the Panama Canal. It also led to a treaty in 1921 between Colombia and the United States that provided for the United States to pay Colombia $25 million in reparations for the loss of its Panamanian territory.

Truman's recognition of Israel on May 15, 1948, was also controversial. A few minutes after Jews in Palestine had proclaimed the state of Israel, Truman rejected the advice of his State Department and made the United States the first nation to recognize the new country. The recognition indicated U.S. support for Israel and effectively blocked a United Nations plan to keep Palestine under a temporary trusteeship.[79]

The president's power to sever diplomatic relations has been used as an ultimate sanction to protest another country's behavior. Severance of relations is usually reserved for situations when the differences between the two nations are so great that there is no hope they may be

U.S. Legal Relationship with Taiwan

The repercussions for U.S. relations with Taiwan from President Carter's recognition of the People's Republic of China (PRC) illustrated the effect a recognition decision can have on U.S. laws and relations with other nations. Successive presidents had refused to recognize the PRC since it was established in 1949. Instead, the United States recognized the Republic of China, the nationalist Chinese government which had fled to Taiwan after its defeat by the Communist Chinese armies. Growing cooperation and friendship between the United States and the PRC in the 1970s, however, made the establishment of diplomatic relations with Beijing a matter of practical importance. In December 1978, the Carter administration announced that it intended to recognize the PRC as the "sole legal government of China" on January 1, 1979.

This recognition could be accomplished only by withdrawing U.S. recognition of the Republic of China as China's legal government. Since many laws and agreements involving commercial, cultural, and security relations with other countries depend on a nation's diplomatic status, the legal framework of the U.S. relationship with Taiwan had to be rebuilt. Without new legislation establishing a special relationship with the Republic of China, the United States could not deal with Taiwan as another nation.

Consequently, Congress passed the Taiwan Relations Act in March 1979. The act was intended to ensure that normal relations would continue between Taiwan and the United States, even though the United States no longer recognized the Republic of China regime that governed the island. The legislation established the American Institute in Taiwan through which the United States would conduct relations with Taiwan. The institute was created as a private, nonprofit corporation that was authorized to enter into, execute, and enforce agreements and other transactions with Taiwan and perform consular functions for U.S. citizens. The act also authorized U.S. government employees, especially Foreign Service officers, to take temporary leaves of absence from their posts in order to work for the institute. While in Taiwan, they would not be considered U.S. government employees, but they would retain their seniority, pensions, and other benefits when they returned to work for the government. Thus, the Taiwan Relations Act created a nonprofit corporation that could do virtually anything done by an embassy.

In addition to creating the American Institute in Taiwan, the act recognized the validity of Taiwan domestic law, contracts entered into under Taiwan law, and all U.S. agreements and treaties with Taiwan except the 1954 mutual defense treaty, which was terminated at the end of 1979. It also authorized the president to grant Taiwan's unofficial representatives in the United States diplomatic privileges and treat Taiwan as a nation with its own immigration quota equal to that of the PRC. These and dozens of other provisions of the Taiwan Relations Act addressed the legal difficulties created by the withdrawal of U.S. recognition of the Republic of China.

resolved through normal diplomatic procedures. It is customary to break diplomatic ties with a country before declaring war against it, but many events short of war have prompted presidents to terminate relations. In 1979, President Carter ended diplomatic relations with Iran in response to the hostage crisis.

Even when relations have been broken with a particular country, communication usually continues. "Interests sections" may be established in each country's capital in the embassies of a third country. For example, U.S. interests in Cuba and Iran are represented by the Swiss embassies in those countries. Foreign nations without diplomatic relations with the United States also have used their representatives to the United Nations to communicate with U.S. officials. Nevertheless, such measures do not accommodate international business between the two countries with the same efficiency as normal diplomatic exchanges. A less drastic method employed by presidents to communicate their displeasure with another nation is the temporary recalling of the U.S. ambassador in that country for "consultations." President Carter used this tactic after the Soviet invasion of Afghanistan, when he recalled Thomas J. Watson, the U.S. ambassador in Moscow, to Washington.

Power to Appoint Diplomatic Personnel

Article II, section 2, of the Constitution states that the president shall, "nominate, and by and with the Advice and Consent of the Senate, shall appoint Ambassadors, other public Ministers and Consuls." Since the president was to be the sole organ of foreign communications, the power to appoint those individuals who would be communicating directly with foreign leaders was properly a presidential duty. The success of a president's foreign policy program depends greatly on the personalities and abilities of the people who fill important diplomatic and advisory posts.

The difficulty of selecting ambassadors and high-level foreign policy officials has increased dramatically for presidents since the early years of the Republic. George Washington and his immediate successors had only a few posts to fill and were able to appoint men whom they knew personally. As the U.S. government grew and expanded its involvement in world affairs, presidents were increasingly forced to delegate responsibility to their advisers for selecting candidates for less important posts.

Although the president appoints officials, the Congress has the constitutional power to create offices. Nevertheless, presidents have used executive orders to create government bodies that required them to make appointments. Kennedy established the Peace Corps in this manner, and Gerald Ford unilaterally created the Committee on Foreign Intelligence and the Intelligence Oversight Board.[80]

Senate confirmation of presidential nominees for diplomatic posts often has been routine, but there have been exceptions. For example, Eisenhower's appointment of Charles E. Bohlen as ambassador to the Soviet Union barely survived the confirmation vote, even though Eisenhower's own party controlled the Senate.[81]

Political Appointees versus the Foreign Service

A question that complicates the diplomatic appointments of contemporary presidents is how to divide ambassadorships and important State Department posts between political appointees and the State Department's own career foreign service officers. Senior foreign service officers can offer a president valuable diplomatic experience that can prevent foreign policy mistakes. Also, since they serve successive presidents, they can provide continuity in foreign policy between administrations.[82] Yet, presidents often have been reluctant to entrust important ambassadorships and assistant secretary posts to foreign service officers, who are less likely than political appointees to be responsive to the president's directives. Because their careers are not dependent on the president but on a self-run promotion system, and because many regard foreign policy as an endeavor that should not be subject to partisan politics, foreign service officers have a greater reputation for resisting presidential policies than do political appointees.

Political appointees can more easily be found who share the president's philosophy, are politically minded, and appreciate how their job fits into the president's comprehensive domestic and foreign policy goals. If an administration favors political appointees, however, the president may gain a measure of diplomatic control at the expense of greater diplomatic expertise at U.S. embassies, the goodwill of the State Department, and the morale of the Foreign Service. An option open to the president is to balance appointments by reserving many ambassadorships for foreign service officers while nominating political appointees to posts crucial to the execution of the president's particular foreign policy goals.[83]

Symbolism and Politics of Appointments

Presidents must take into account more than a candidate's abilities and qualifications when making an appointment. They must consider how the appointment will be perceived. The symbolism of presidential appointments can profoundly affect foreign policy, especially at the beginning of the president's term. Appointments provide the president with an opportunity to indicate to Congress, the American public, and foreign governments the foreign policy goals the new administration intends to pursue. Reagan's appointment of conservative Jeane Kirkpatrick as ambassador to the United Nations reaffirmed his intention to make anti-Communism a foreign policy theme of his administration, just as Carter had underscored his commitment to human rights and third world issues with his appointment of Andrew Young to the same post.

Diplomatic appointments also give presidents certain political opportunities. They may choose to broaden their base of support within their party by appointing people to ambassadorships who originally opposed their nomination. Presidents also can try to build up trust and cohesion within their new administration by giving department and agency heads broad discretion in selecting subordinates.

Presidents sometimes have used appointments to create an atmosphere of bipartisanship. Kennedy believed that by appointing Republicans to senior foreign policy posts in his administration he could disarm potential congressional resistance to his policies. Treasury Secretary Douglas Dillon, Defense Secretary Robert McNamara, national security adviser McGeorge Bundy, director of the Central Intelligence Agency (CIA) Allen Dulles, and disarmament chief John J. McCloy were all Republicans, as were John A. McCone and William C. Poster who eventually replaced Dulles and McCloy, respectively. Other presidents have made appointments with bipartisanship in mind, though no modern president has appointed as many members of the opposing party to such important foreign policy jobs as Kennedy did.[84]

Presidential Envoys

Many presidents have used personal emissaries not subject to Senate confirmation to conduct foreign policy. Often such presidential representatives have been employed to carry out specific diplomatic missions. The use of personal envoys allows presidents to inject their own ideas and proposals directly into negotiations without having to go through the State Department or other official channels through which information may be leaked, misinterpreted, or opposed. The presence of a personal envoy sent by the president sometimes can stimulate stalemated negotiations by lending greater prestige to the talks and demonstrating the president's interest in them. Presidential represen-

Bill Auth

Reagan's appointment of conservative Jeane Kirkpatrick, left, as ambassador to the United Nations reaffirmed his intention to make anti-Communism a foreign policy theme, just as Carter had underscored his commitment to human rights with his appointment of Andrew Young, right, to the same post.

tatives also can provide the president with an additional source of information that is relatively free of institutional biases.

The use of presidential envoys is not specifically allowed or disallowed in the Constitution. The practice contradicts the apparent intention of the Constitution, however, since the president is supposed to appoint ambassadors "with the advice and consent of the Senate." The employment of personal envoys, therefore, is a means by which presidents have circumvented the Senate's check on their diplomatic appointment power.

Washington did not believe that the Constitution prohibited him from using private representatives to conduct diplomacy. In 1791, Gouverneur Morris, who held no public office at the time, carried out important negotiations with the British at Washington's direction. By using a personal representative Washington could explore the possibilities for a treaty without having to involve Congress or deal with the formalities of official treaty negotiations.

The first major controversy over the appointment of diplomats not confirmed by the Senate occurred during Madison's presidency. In 1813, Madison sent a delegation to the negotiations in Europe that produced the Treaty of Ghent, which ended the War of 1812 with Great Britain. The president had dispatched the negotiators without submitting their names for confirmation by the Senate, which was on recess. Madison's critics argued that he could not appoint ministers to offices that had not been authorized by Congress and that the appointments were illegal since the Senate did not have the chance to approve them. The president responded by claiming that it was unnecessary for Congress to create a diplomatic post if the president determined that a need had arisen for one, and the president was free to fill any vacancy that happened to occur during a congressional recess.[85] Since Madison's time, however, Congress has enacted legislation that gives it control over the creation of new ambassadorships.

Many subsequent presidents have found this practice to be useful at some time during their administration. In 1831 Jackson sent unconfirmed representatives to Turkey to conclude a trade and navigation treaty, and in 1893 Cleveland gave his own emissary, J. H. Blount, "paramount authority" over the Senate-approved resident minister in Honolulu at talks on the annexation of Hawaii.[86] Two twentieth-century presidents established the use of personal representatives as a common diplomatic device of the president. Wilson made extensive use of his close friend Col. Edward House to perform diplomatic missions in Europe before and during World War I. Wilson also named House to the U.S. delegation to the peace talks in Paris at the end of the war and sent former secretary of state Elihu Root to Russia in 1917 during World War I to urge the Russian government not to make a separate peace with Germany. Franklin Roosevelt employed Harry Hopkins, a personal aide, as a negotiator in Great Britain and the Soviet Union during World War II. Among other accomplishments, Hopkins helped negotiate and direct the lend-lease agreements under which the United States supplied war materiel to Great Britain and other countries at war with Germany.

Presidents have not felt compelled to submit their appointments of private representatives to the Senate for approval. In addition to the precedent set by Washington, there are strong justifications for this position. Personal envoys of presidents function outside of permanent government positions, do not have their duties enumerated in the Constitution, serve only as long as the president asks them, and often receive no compensation.[87]

Summit Meetings

Presidents are responsible for the conduct of diplomacy. They appoint diplomats, formulate diplomatic policy, and send and receive ambassadors and treaty negotiators. The State Department, the National Security Council (NSC), and other executive branch agencies involved in diplomacy are servants of the president. Yet, despite presidential control over diplomatic activities, presidents themselves rarely met with foreign leaders until World War II. The difficulties of travel, the isolated location of the United States, and the traditional belief that presidents should stay close to their administrative and legislative responsibilities in the capital prevented presidents from acting as their own negotiators.

Today the American public takes for granted meetings between their president and other world leaders. They regard these meetings, which have become known as "summit meetings," as an established and useful tool of presidential foreign policy making. Indeed, if a modern president were to avoid meetings with leaders of foreign governments, the press and public alike would invariably criticize the chief of state as being uninterested in international affairs, or even isolationist. Presidents have found that a highly publicized summit tends to raise their public approval rate. *(See "Presidential Popularity," p. 586, in Chief of State chapter of Part III.)*

Winston Churchill is credited with coining the term *summit*. In 1953 he used the word when he called for a conference between the leaders of the Soviet Union and the Western powers. The media picked up the term and used it to describe the Geneva conference between Soviet and Western leaders in 1955. After Geneva, meetings between national leaders increasingly were referred to as *summits*.[88] The term is used to distinguish between meetings that are actually attended by the recognized leaders of states and meetings between foreign ministers or lower-level officials.

Presidential Diplomacy

Although presidential travel to foreign nations was impractical before the twentieth century, presidents throughout U.S. history have conducted personal diplomacy with foreign leaders through direct exchanges of letters. Personal letters between leaders could accomplish some of the goals of the modern summit meeting. They gave a president the chance to send and receive information, ideas, and proposals without using intermediaries and to establish a personal rapport with a foreign leader. Presidential letters were especially important to early presidents who did not have the benefit of an extensive diplomatic network with representatives in many foreign capitals. President Jefferson, whose years as secretary of state under Washington had provided him with extensive diplomatic experience, had an ongoing correspondence with Czar Alexander I of Russia during the Napoleonic wars.[89]

Early presidents also met with foreign leaders who traveled to the United States. The first high-ranking official of a foreign government to visit the United States was a personal emissary of the ruler of Tunis who came to Amer-

National Archives

FDR made a series of trips overseas to confer with Allied leaders about military strategy and the composition of the postwar world. Left, in February 1945, Roosevelt confers with Winston Churchill and Joseph Stalin at Yalta in the Crimea.

ica in 1805 to discuss the passage of U.S. commercial ships in the Mediterranean. The marquis de Lafayette, who had led colonial troops against the British in the American Revolution, was the first official guest to be invited to the United States by the U.S. government. President Monroe received him in 1824 after he arrived on an American ship that Congress had dispatched to France.[90] During the rest of the nineteenth century visits to the United States by foreign dignitaries were common. Visits by the heads of state of other nations, however, remained rare. Up to the end of World War I, presidents received only about thirty heads of state.[91]

Presidential Travel

During the eighteenth and nineteenth centuries a precedent developed against presidents traveling outside the country during their term. Theodore Roosevelt became the first president to break this precedent when he visited Panama in 1906 to inspect the canal under construction. Presidential travel abroad remained uncommon until World War II when Franklin Roosevelt made a series of trips to Canada and overseas to confer with allied leaders about military strategy and the composition of the postwar world. Truman followed Roosevelt's example by attending the Potsdam Conference in 1945 with Joseph Stalin and Churchill (and, later, Clement R. Attlee).

President Eisenhower, however, institutionalized the role of the president as international diplomat with his foreign trips, including his 22,000-mile "Quest for Peace" tour of eleven nations in 1959. He believed that establishing good will toward the United States in foreign nations was an important presidential function. Accordingly, many of his stops in foreign countries were devoted to ceremony and speech making. After Eisenhower, presidential visits abroad were an accepted part of the president's job and were highly coveted by the leaders of foreign nations.

Eisenhower's successors continued his practice of frequent overseas visits. President Kennedy met with Premier Nikita Khrushchev in Vienna in 1961 and toured Europe in 1963, at which time he delivered his famous *Ich bin ein Berliner* speech in Berlin. President Johnson initially declined taking trips abroad because he had no vice president, but after the election in 1964 he made several overseas trips, including visits to Australia, the Philippines, Vietnam, and Latin America. Nixon embarked on a major European tour in 1969 only a month after he became president. In 1972 he signed the SALT I treaty in Moscow and became the first U.S. president to visit the People's Republic of China. President Ford also went to the Soviet Union, meeting Leonid Brezhnev in Vladivostok in 1974. Carter and Reagan both traveled to numerous foreign countries and met with Soviet leaders overseas.

Constitutional Questions

The Constitution does not specifically sanction the president's authority to meet with other world leaders, but the power to appoint, send, and receive ambassadors and to negotiate treaties clearly establishes the president's right to conduct diplomatic negotiations personally. A more controversial constitutional question about summit meetings was whether a president could properly fulfill the obligations of office while out of the country. The Constitution states that if the president is unable "to discharge the powers and duties of the said office, the same shall devolve on the vice president." The authors of the Constitution did not specify if being absent from the country could render a president incapable of fulfilling the constitutional responsibilities of the office.

No one questioned the constitutionality of Theodore Roosevelt's short trip to Panama in 1906 or Taft's meeting with the Mexican president just across the border in 1909. When President Wilson announced in late 1918 that he planned to go to Europe to attend the peace conference in Versailles, however, numerous critics objected that Wilson's safety could not be ensured and that he would lose touch with the everyday business of running the country during the lengthy Atlantic crossing.[92]

Many of the protests were politically motivated, but some critics sincerely questioned the constitutionality of Wilson's proposed venture. Resolutions were introduced in both houses of Congress that would have declared the presidency vacant and required the vice president to assume the president's powers if Wilson left the country. Former president Taft defended Wilson's plans, however. He argued in an article in the *Washington Post* on December 5, 1918, that the president could properly fulfill the duties of his office while overseas. He wrote: "There is no constitutional inhibition, express or implied, to prevent the president's going abroad to discharge a function clearly given him by the Constitution. That instrument says that he shall make treaties.... It is a curious error to assume that the president himself may not attend a conference to which he can send a delegate." [93] The congressional resolutions against Wilson's trip never got out of committee. Wilson's critics continued to attack the wisdom of his policy, but he went to Europe without a major confrontation over the constitutionality of his trip.[94]

The jet airplane and modern means of communication eliminated any lingering concern that presidential travel could make a chief executive incapable of performing the tasks of office. Modern presidents travel with large staffs and stay in constant touch with administration and congressional officials in Washington, D.C. Although presidents taking a lengthy foreign trip will spend less time on domestic affairs while out of the country, they have the means to carry out virtually any presidential function from any place in the world.

Superpower Summitry

The most famous summit meetings have been those between the U.S. president and the leader of the Soviet Union. U.S. and Soviet leaders have met sporadically since 1943, when Franklin Roosevelt traveled to Tehran for a wartime conference with Stalin and Churchill. Since Roosevelt, every president has met with a Soviet leader at least once. These meetings recently have been associated with arms control negotiations. In some cases, like the summits in Moscow in 1972, Vienna in 1979, and Washington in 1987, the meeting is a culmination of the arms control process where an agreement is signed. In other cases, like the 1985 Geneva Summit and the 1986 Reykjavik Summit, the leaders hoped to stimulate arms control negotiations. The media and public attention that accompanies these meetings between the leaders of the superpowers is inspired by hopes that they can produce an agreement or understanding that will reduce the chances of war and lead to a more cooperative coexistence.

The continuing threat of nuclear war gives the leaders of the superpowers reason to pursue summit meetings despite the mistrust between the two nations. The U.S. president and the leader of the Soviet Union each controls huge arsenals of nuclear weapons targeted on the other super-

In 1972, Richard Nixon became the first U.S. president to visit the People's Republic of China. Here he is greeted by Chinese Communist party chairman Mao Tse-tung.

U.S.-Soviet Summit . . .

Date	Place	Leaders	Topic
July-August 1945	Potsdam	President Harry S Truman, Soviet leader Joseph Stalin, British prime ministers Winston Churchill and Clement R. Attlee	Partition and control of Germany
July 1955	Geneva	President Dwight D. Eisenhower, Soviet leader Nikolai A. Bulganin, British prime minister Anthony Eden, French premier Edgar Fauré	Reunification of Germany, disarmament, European security
September 1959	Camp David, Md.	President Eisenhower, Soviet leader Nikita S. Khrushchev	Berlin problem
May 1960	Paris	President Eisenhower, Soviet leader Khrushchev, French president Charles de Gaulle, British prime minister Harold Macmillan	U-2 incident
June 1961	Vienna	President John F. Kennedy, Soviet leader Khrushchev	Berlin problem
June 1967	Glassboro, N.J.	President Lyndon B. Johnson, Soviet leader Aleksei N. Kosygin	Middle East

power and its allies. Prevention of nuclear war depends in part upon the calculations of these leaders about the behavior of their counterpart. A summit provides the leaders of the two countries with a chance to assess each other and clarify their goals and intentions so the chances of miscalculation are reduced.

Former president Nixon has argued that developing mutual understandings between the superpowers of their respective interests and patterns of behavior should be the primary purpose of a superpower summit. These understandings, which he calls "rules of engagement," do not resolve differences between the two countries or end their adversarial relationship; rather, they reduce the possibility that a crisis will lead to war. He rejects the popular notion that summit meetings are valuable because they create a "spirit" of friendship.[95] Indeed, the superpower summits declared to have created a new spirit of cooperation have been among the least successful at producing substantive progress on major issues: Geneva in 1955, Camp David in 1959, Vienna in 1961, Glassboro in 1967, and Geneva in 1985. Unfounded optimism following a summit can contribute to international disillusionment and hostility if public expectations are inflated beyond what is warranted by progress on tangible diplomatic issues.

Careful preparation is especially important in superpower summits, since the president is dealing with an adversary who is seeking not only an agreement, but also an advantage. The Soviets come to summits with propaganda goals in addition to their bargaining goals. At the Paris summit in 1960, for example, Khrushchev abandoned the opportunity for negotiation in favor of milking the U-2 incident for its propaganda value. The propaganda opportunities of a summit meeting can undermine negotiations if the agenda is not set and if the Soviets have not agreed to measures to ensure serious private negotiations.

The Soviets possess several bargaining advantages that dispose them to be patient negotiators. Unlike the United States, the Soviet Union is under less domestic pressure to conclude an agreement since the government controls the news media. Soviet leaders also do not have to worry about negotiating an agreement that will be acceptable to a legislative body. In addition, if the Soviets are displeased with the negotiating positions of a particular U.S. president, they have the option of waiting until a new one is elected before pursuing an agreement. Summits are most likely to succeed when they are held after the negotiations of lower-level officials who have made substantial progress toward resolving the issues to be discussed at the summit.

Without careful preparation, international pressure and the personal desire to make a diplomatic breakthrough

... Meetings, 1945-1988

Date	Place	Leaders	Topic
May 1972	Moscow	President Richard Nixon, Soviet leader Leonid I. Brezhnev	SALT I, anti-ballistic missile limitations
June 1973	Washington, D.C.	President Nixon, Soviet leader Brezhnev	Détente
June-July 1974	Moscow and Yalta	President Nixon, Soviet leader Brezhnev	Arms control
November 1974	Vladivostok	President Gerald R. Ford, Soviet leader Brezhnev	Arms control
June 1979	Vienna	President Jimmy Carter, Soviet leader Brezhnev	SALT II
November 1985	Geneva	President Ronald Reagan, Soviet leader Mikhail S. Gorbachev	Arms control, U.S.-Soviet relations
October 1986	Reykjavik	President Reagan, Soviet leader Gorbachev	Arms control
December 1987	Washington, D.C.	President Reagan, Soviet leader Gorbachev	INF Treaty, Afghanistan
May-June 1988	Moscow	President Reagan, Soviet leader Gorbachev	Arms control, human rights
December 1988	New York City	President Reagan, Soviet leader Gorbachev	U.S.-Soviet relations

may cause presidents to agree to a proposal they would reject if they were considering it within the framework of the normal diplomatic process. The 1986 "mini-summit" in Reykjavik between Reagan and Mikhail Gorbachev, which was intended as a preparatory meeting to a full summit later in the year, turned into a bargaining session on an extensive arms control agreement. Reagan hastily accepted in principle Soviet proposals to eliminate all ballistic missiles within a decade—a notion from which the administration later distanced itself.

Many U.S. policy makers and foreign policy experts have advocated concluding an agreement with the Soviet Union to hold annual summit meetings. Nixon pointed out three advantages to holding regular summit meetings, in addition to whatever business could be concluded at such meetings. First, regular summits could reduce the risk that a war could be started through a miscalculation, since leaders of both countries would better understand the limits beyond which the other could not be pushed. Second, before regularly scheduled summits, both sides would be inhibited from taking actions that could be perceived as contrary to the interests of the other. Third, regular summits would stimulate movement in the bureaucracies of the Soviet Union and the United States that might lead to further agreement.[96]

Evaluating Summit Diplomacy

Despite its popular appeal, summit diplomacy can be ineffective and even counterproductive. Diplomatic historian Elmer Plischke has pointed out numerous disadvantages and risks of summit meetings compared with conventional diplomacy.

The extensive media attention given summits may distort their substance or lead to popular disillusionment by raising public expectations of improved relations with another country beyond what is warranted. The spontaneity possible at summits may yield agreements that have not received proper scrutiny or that personally commit the president to a policy without allowing for the option to modify it after further review. Summits may also distract presidents from their other responsibilities, place presidents in a location where it is difficult to ensure their safety, and cause physical strain that could threaten the president's health. Because the success of a summit depends on the performance of the president, relations with other countries can be harmed if the president is inexperienced or inadequately prepared. Moreover, if diplomacy with another country is grounded on the personal relationship between a president and that country's leader, relations may suffer when one of them leaves office. Frequent summits may even harm the morale of professional diplomats if they perceive that their talents are being ignored in favor of direct presidential negotiations.[97]

Despite these dangers, a summit meeting has the potential to be a valuable diplomatic tool, if the president and the president's advisers understand the risks and pursue prudent, realizable goals.

Plischke also cites ten advantages of summit meetings that can make them valuable additions to conventional diplomacy. First, by becoming personally acquainted, a president and a foreign leader may reduce tensions, clarify national interests, and establish mutual respect. Second, personal friendship between a president and a foreign statesman may lead to improved relations between the two countries. Third, summits allow presidents to focus national attention on specific issues and to improve public understanding of them. Fourth, presidents engaging in personal diplomacy are more capable than professional diplomats of understanding the domestic policy consequences of a given diplomatic action. Fifth, foreign leaders can be sure that they are dealing with the source of foreign policy power when they negotiate with the president at a summit. Sixth, summit negotiations can yield quick results if desired, since discussions are between leaders with the power of decision rather than between representatives who must receive instructions, make reports, and relay new proposals. Seventh, summit meetings may produce broad agreements that can resolve differences or lead to specific agreements worked out in lower-level forums. Eighth, diplomatic impasses may be overcome at summits by shifts in policy that only the top leaders are empowered to make. Ninth, if presidents desire an international forum for their diplomatic policies, a summit meeting can provide one. Tenth, successful summits can enhance the image of the president and the United States.[98]

As these lists indicate, summit meetings are neither inherently good nor inherently bad. Their advantages and disadvantages are products of the same diplomatic conditions. For example, the potential for a summit to produce a quick breakthrough in stalemated negotiations and the risk that a summit can lead to a hasty, poorly conceived agreement both arise from the president's authority to modify bargaining positions and conclude an agreement on the spot. A summit, therefore, is a special diplomatic environment that offers opportunities but also conceals traps. This environment can be used profitably by skilled, prepared presidents with a firm conception of what they are trying to accomplish and what they are willing to risk; or it can produce a diplomatic disaster if inexperienced or unprepared presidents are influenced by domestic political pressure, media attention, or the desire to make history.

AP/Wide World

President Reagan and Soviet leader Gorbachev discuss arms control and other superpower concerns. The Soviet leader came to Washington, D.C., for three days of summit negotiations in December 1987.

Manager of the Foreign Policy Bureaucracy

The president's management of the foreign policy bureaucracy is less visible than the president's performance as a diplomat, but it is as important to the success of U.S. foreign policy. The "foreign policy bureaucracy" loosely refers to all executive branch personnel whose primary duties pertain to foreign affairs. Almost every department and agency has employees engaged in activities that affect foreign relations, but the State Department, the Defense Department, the intelligence agencies, and the National Security Council staff dominate the foreign policy-making process. Other agencies, such as the Arms Control and Disarmament Agency, the U.S. Information Agency, and the Agency for International Development, deal with specific aspects of foreign policy.

Although the president is responsible for the conduct of foreign affairs, modern foreign policy can not be made by one person. Policy results from a process of consultation and compromise among the president and the president's top foreign affairs advisers. Moreover, the lower levels of the bureaucracy perform functions that are essential to the success of foreign policy. Presidents Kennedy and Nixon preferred to base their decisions on the advice of a small, close-knit group of advisers, but even presidents such as these need a bureaucracy to collect information and intelligence, research policy problems, plan for long-range contingencies, represent the United States abroad, implement presidential directives, and oversee the daily functions of U.S. foreign policy.

Expansion of the Foreign Policy Bureaucracy

During George Washington's administration, the foreign policy bureaucracy consisted of the secretary of state, a small group of clerks, and a few carefully chosen ambassadors to key European states. Although U.S. contacts with other nations expanded during the next hundred years, the foreign policy apparatus of the executive branch remained small. In addition, the low salaries of diplomats and the practice of appointing wealthy campaign contributors and party functionaries to diplomatic posts hindered the development of a professional diplomatic corps.[99] At the end of the nineteenth century the United States began to upgrade the quality and status of its diplomats to correspond with the nation's growing involvement in international trade and politics. Presidents increasingly relied upon the State Department for information, analysis, and staff support.

With the coming of World War II and the emergence of the United States as the most powerful nation on earth, presidents needed greater bureaucratic resources to support their foreign policy decision making. The United States saw itself as an international leader and the protector of the non-Communist world. In the postwar years, it entered into numerous alliances and mutual defense agreements, distributed massive amounts of military and economic aid, hosted the United Nations, and actively participated in most international organizations. This new U.S. involvement in world affairs multiplied the president's foreign policy responsibilities. An expanded bureaucracy was required to administer the growing number of U.S. programs and activities overseas and to provide the president with the information and analysis necessary for constructing effective foreign policies.

As a result, not only did the State Department increase in size, but other departments and agencies were created or expanded to provide military, economic, scientific, and intelligence-gathering expertise that the State Department was not equipped to provide. The State Department thus lost its preeminent role in foreign policy making. It became one player among many in the field of foreign policy. Nevertheless, it has remained the president's primary instrument of negotiation with foreign countries and an important source of information, analysis, and advice on foreign relations.

In 1949, Congress created the Defense Department by unifying the individual armed services. Although the United States rapidly demobilized after World War II, the North Korean invasion of South Korea in 1950 and the growing Soviet threat convinced U.S. leaders that, for the first time in American history, the country needed a large standing military.[100] The size of the unified military budget and the number of people in the armed services ensured that the civilian and military leaders of the new Defense Department would have considerable bureaucratic clout. Moreover, most foreign policy issues had become indistinguishable from national security issues. Containing Soviet expansionism, forming and maintaining an anti-Communist alliance network, and remaining ahead in the nuclear arms race were among the most important international goals for the United States. Defense officials consequently became important players in foreign policy decision making. *(See "Department of Defense," p. 557, in Commander in Chief chapter of Part III.)*

The Central Intelligence Agency (CIA) was created by the National Security Act of 1947 to gather and analyze information from every corner of the globe and to provide the president with a covert operations capability. The CIA along with other intelligence-gathering agencies constitute the intelligence community. The community's members include the Defense Intelligence Agency, the intelligence offices of the individual armed services, the State Department's Bureau of Intelligence and Research, the Federal Bureau of Investigation, and the massive National Security Agency, which intercepts and analyzes communication signals. The director of the CIA was given preeminent status in the intelligence community with primary responsibility for coordinating intelligence activities and advising the president on intelligence matters.

The CIA inherited many of the functions and personnel of the Office of Strategic Services, which had carried out covert operations during World War II. The Japanese sneak attack on Pearl Harbor had impressed the U.S. leadership with the need to have sources of information beyond those provided by U.S. embassies. In addition, Moscow's aggressive use of its intelligence apparatus and the difficulty of extracting information from the closed Soviet society by conventional means seemed to demand a similar intelligence effort by the United States.

Oversight of Intelligence Activities

Because of the requirements of secrecy, the National Security Act of 1947 gave the president nearly exclusive responsibility for oversight of covert intelligence activities. Before the mid-1970s, Congress rarely showed an interest in covert operations, and the president and the intelligence agencies did not willingly offer information about them. Congress routinely approved billions of dollars in funds for the intelligence community with only a few members of its appropriations committees knowing how the money was being spent.

In the mid-1970s, however, numerous revelations of unethical, unauthorized, and illegal activities by the CIA and other intelligence units were uncovered by congressional investigations. Among other abuses, the CIA had helped overthrow the democratically elected government of Socialist president Salvador Allende in Chile. In addition, the FBI and other intelligence agencies were found to have conducted illegal surveillance operations and engaged in other activities that violated the civil liberties of individual Americans.

In response, Congress passed a series of laws that created House and Senate intelligence committees and strengthened congressional oversight of intelligence activities. The Hughes-Ryan Amendment to the 1974 foreign aid bill and the 1980 Intelligence Oversight Act required that the president report all U.S. covert intelligence operations to designated congressional committees in a timely fashion. To complement Congress's actions, Gerald Ford established the Intelligence Oversight Board, a White House three-member panel to oversee intelligence activities and report any questions of illegality to the president through the attorney general.

National Security Council

In addition to creating the CIA, the 1947 National Security Act established the National Security Council

(NSC). The NSC is a presidential advisory body consisting of the president, vice president, and secretaries of Defense and State. In addition to these statutory members, the director of the Central Intelligence Agency and the chairman of the Joint Chiefs of Staff are designated as statutory advisers to the NSC. Presidents were to convene the NSC as often or as seldom as they liked and invite whomever they wanted to attend in addition to its statutory participants.

Although presidents could call cabinet meetings to consider national security matters, the cabinet was a large and unwieldy body that included heads of departments unrelated to national security policy. The NSC gave presidents a forum that was smaller and more focused than the cabinet but would allow them to draw together their top defense, diplomatic, economic, and intelligence advisers to consider broad issues of national security.

The National Security Act stated that the NSC's responsibility was "to advise the President with respect to the integration of domestic, foreign, and military policies relating to the national security so as to enable the military services and other departments and agencies of the government to cooperate more effectively in matters involving the national security." In addition to integrating the efforts of agencies and officials concerned with national security policy, the NSC has performed several other functions. Some presidents have used the NSC as a forum for generating and discussing policy options, while others have made decisions outside the NSC and then asked the council to approve them. The NSC occasionally has been used as a decision-making forum during crises, including the North Korean invasion of South Korea in 1950, the Soviet invasion of Czechoslovakia in 1968, and the *Mayaguez* incident in 1975. At various times the NSC also has been used for less dramatic functions such as policy planning and budget review.[101]

In addition to creating the National Security Council, the National Security Act established an NSC staff, which would be independent of other departments and agencies. *(See "National Security Council," p. 955, in Supporting Organizations chapter of Part V.)* This staff, created to serve the president and the NSC members, has become a major player in foreign policy making. At times it has rivaled or eclipsed the State Department in influence.

The NSC staff is headed by the assistant to the president for national security affairs, a post established by Dwight Eisenhower. Since the Nixon administration, it has commonly been referred to as the "national security adviser." Originally, the national security adviser was supposed to facilitate foreign policy making by coordinating NSC meetings and overseeing the staff that served the NSC, but under Eisenhower's successors the national security adviser often had power equal to cabinet members. As a presidential aide, the national security adviser is not confirmed by the Senate and does not possess the vast legal authority of a cabinet member. Rather, the power of the national security adviser within the administration depends entirely upon the president. The NSC staff has a unique position within the foreign policy bureaucracy. Since the national security adviser and most NSC staffers owe their position and status to the president, they have few competing loyalties. Some NSC staffers who are drawn from other departments and agencies may retain institutional loyalty to their parent organization, but during their tenure on the NSC staff they are responsible only to the president. In addition, the NSC staff is virtually beyond the reach of the legislative branch since it has no statutory responsibility to report to Congress. Presidents therefore can use the NSC staff to fulfill any function they choose. National security advisers such as Henry Kissinger and Zbigniew Brzezinski have served as negotiators, policy advisers, and national security analysts in addition to their duties as manager of the NSC staff. The Iran-contra investigations in 1986 and 1987 revealed that the NSC staff also could be used (in this case unwisely) to implement covert operations.

Foreign Policy-making Process

Although the National Security Council and the executive departments and agencies that deal with foreign affairs are established by law, it is up to the president to create and maintain a responsive and effective foreign policy-making process. Because numerous executive branch units are working on foreign policy, their work must be coordinated to minimize the duplication of their efforts, to avoid institutional conflict, and to ensure that each unit has access to the president. Therefore, as managers of the foreign policy bureaucracy, presidents must establish procedures through executive orders and their personal management style that determine how policy options and information should be presented to them, who should have access to intelligence, how the efforts of various departments and agencies should be coordinated, how the agendas of foreign policy meetings should be set, who should regularly attend these meetings, who should chair these meetings, and who should be responsible for overseeing policy implementation.

Managing the Foreign Policy-making Process

Since World War II, the central question about the process of producing foreign policy has been who should manage that process. The president must ultimately be the referee of the inevitable bureaucratic struggle within the administration for influence, resources, and prestige, but the responsibility of determining the substance of policy leaves the president little time for matters of management. Therefore, some executive branch unit must serve as the facilitator of the foreign policy-making system. The main rivals for this responsibility have been the State Department under the secretary of state and the National Security Council staff under the national security adviser. Since the Kennedy administration, presidents have tended to look to their national security advisers to manage their foreign policy-making system. Critics of this trend have maintained that the oversight, coordination, and leadership of the foreign policy-making system properly belong to the State Department.[102] They argue that the State Department was intended to be preeminent in foreign affairs, and its foreign policy expertise, accountability to Congress, and network of embassies in foreign capitals make it the best choice to run the president's foreign policy-making system.

The State Department, however, has institutional interests like any department that inhibit its ability to be an arbiter between competing departments and agencies. Just as the military mission of the Defense Department or the intelligence mission of the CIA disposes those units to approach foreign affairs from a unique perspective, State's diplomatic mission disposes it to prefer its own foreign policy strategies. Even if State Department officials were able to mediate disputes impartially between other bureaucratic units, those units would never regard State as a neutral department.

Although a foreign policy-making system coordinated by the NSC staff denies the State Department its traditional role as the manager of foreign policy, the NSC has a better chance of succeeding as a referee between competing departments and agencies and ensuring that the president remains in control of foreign policy. This is because the NSC is answerable to the president and has no institutional mission beyond serving the president.

The question of who should lead the foreign policy-making system pertains not only to the NSC staff and the State Department, but to their leaders as well. Some secretaries of state, including John Foster Dulles of the Eisenhower administration and George Marshall and Dean Acheson of the Truman administration, were their presidents' foremost foreign policy advisers. The influence of other secretaries, however, most notably William P. Rogers who served in the Nixon administration, was eclipsed by other officials. Kissinger, Nixon's assistant for national security during his first term, served as the administration's principal foreign policy spokesperson and negotiator. Rogers's activities were confined primarily to ceremonial tasks and administering the State Department. In 1973 Kissinger became secretary of state, thereby occupying the office that traditionally went with the power he already possessed.

The White House

Henry Kissinger served as Nixon's principal foreign policy spokesperson and negotiator. In 1973 he became secretary of state.

Foreign Policy Decision-making Systems

The National Security Act of 1947 established a forum presidents could use as the focus of their foreign policy decision-making system. Presidents were not obliged, however, to convene meetings of the NSC or to regard the meetings that were held as decision-making forums. Congress had mandated the existence of a National Security Council and a staff to support it, but it was up to the president to decide how to use them, if at all. Many presidents have chosen to deemphasize NSC meetings, preferring to rely on ad hoc meetings with small groups of trusted advisers. Others have used the NSC as the formal centerpiece of an extensive web of committees and interagency groups considering foreign policy. Every post-World War II president, however, has brought a unique leadership style to the management of foreign policy decision making.

Harry Truman's suspicion that Congress had created the NSC to check his authority and Truman's strained relationships with his first two secretaries of defense, James Forrestal and Louis Johnson, initially led him to ignore the NSC. He attended only twelve of the first fifty-seven NSC meetings.[103] During the Korean War the NSC developed a more important policy-making role. Truman attended most meetings and the group was used to forge presidential foreign policies. Nevertheless, Truman still emphasized its advisory nature and frequently consulted its individual members or ad hoc groups rather than relying on the entire NSC for policy advice.

Dwight Eisenhower's foreign policy decision-making system reflected his military background. He presided over highly structured weekly meetings of the NSC and created NSC subcommittees to consider specific policy issues. He also established the "Planning Board," a staff body charged with foreign policy planning, and the "Operations Coordinating Board," an interagency committee charged with overseeing implementation of executive decisions.[104] Although Eisenhower's system had the advantages of ensuring that all parties would participate in decision making and the president would not become bogged down in details better left to subordinates, it often has been criticized as being too rigid and formalistic. Meetings were sometimes held because they were routinely scheduled rather than because they were necessary. Eisenhower also insisted that his top advisers reach a consensus on issues. His demand for unanimity led to policy papers that were too general and vague to provide direction to lower-level personnel charged with implementing policy.

John Kennedy replaced Eisenhower's formal committees with a less structured collegial decision-making system. Kennedy's reliance on the advice of departmental experts who had advocated the disastrous U.S.-supported Bay of Pigs invasion of Cuba by Cuban nationals in April 1961 had convinced him that he needed independent sources of national security advice in the White House. As a result, the NSC staff under the direction of the national security adviser, McGeorge Bundy, not only facilitated the decision-making process, it generated and evaluated policy options for the president. Formal NSC meetings also were deemphasized. During the Cuban missile crisis Kennedy relied on an assembly of his closest advisers known as the "Executive Committee." Unlike the NSC, membership in this ad hoc group depended not on statutory requirements, but on the trust and confidence of the president.[105]

Lyndon Johnson made few changes in either Kennedy's national security decision-making system or the personnel who ran it. The number of advisers involved in ad hoc policy-making sessions declined, however, especially when the Vietnam War was the topic. Johnson developed the practice of discussing the war at Tuesday lunch meetings attended by five or six close advisers. NSC meetings were used primarily to announce and discuss decisions that had already been made. In 1966, Johnson created formal interdepartmental groups to develop and coordinate policy proposals that would flow up to the NSC, but the work of these groups was largely confined to peripheral issues unrelated to the war.[106]

Richard Nixon tried to create a foreign policy-making system that incorporated the best aspects of the Eisenhower and Kennedy-Johnson systems. He created a formal interagency committee structure like Eisenhower's to ensure that all departments and agencies would be heard. Unlike Eisenhower's committee system, however, Nixon's was intended to produce several policy options for the president's consideration rather than an interdepartmental consensus. The committees also were designed to make less important decisions, thereby allowing the president and his top advisers to concentrate on the most important issues. Nixon established a strong NSC staff that enabled the president and his national security adviser, Henry Kissinger, to monitor the activities of the committees.

Although most scholars consider Nixon's NSC system to be a well-conceived blueprint for national security decision making, that blueprint was not always followed. His strong interest in national security affairs and the delicate nature of the negotiations to end the Vietnam War and improve relations with the Soviet Union and Communist China led to a centralization of decision making in the hands of Nixon, Kissinger, and the NSC staff that excluded other top advisers and departments. Late in Nixon's presidency, the Watergate scandal dominated the president's time, causing the president to rely even more on Henry Kissinger and a small circle of trusted advisers. [107]

Nixon's successor, Gerald Ford, was able to restore balance to the foreign policy decision-making system. Ford used the NSC staff and national security adviser Brent Scowcroft primarily as coordinators of national security decision making rather than as policy advisers. The president still relied heavily on Kissinger who had become secretary of state in 1973, but the views of other departments and agencies were integrated more often into national security decisions than they had been during the latter years of Nixon's presidency.

Like Richard Nixon, Jimmy Carter leaned heavily on the NSC staff and his national security adviser, Zbigniew Brzezinski. Nevertheless, Carter also tried to encourage a decentralized advisory system that would filter proposals up to his office from the bureaucracy. To ensure that he would not be insulated from a diversity of opinion, he had department and agency leaders report directly to him rather than through a chief of staff or the national security adviser. Carter's system, however, suffered from the frequent disagreements of Brzezinski and Secretary of State Cyrus Vance, who resigned his post in May 1980 after U.S. forces failed to rescue American hostages in Iran.

Ronald Reagan initially announced his intention to give his secretaries of defense and state dominant roles in national security policy making. Nevertheless, Reagan rejected a plan submitted by Secretary of State Alexander Haig to designate the State Department as the manager of foreign policy. The president took a whole year before setting up a formal foreign policy-making system that stressed cabinet predominance.[108] From the beginning of the administration, however, the NSC staff was given a smaller role than it had had under Presidents Nixon, Ford, and Carter. Reagan's first national security adviser, Richard Allen, did not even have direct access to the president. Although subsequent national security advisers William Clark, Robert McFarlane, John Poindexter, Frank Carlucci, and Colin Powell did have daily access to the president, none dominated the policy-making process as Henry Kissinger and Zbigniew Brzezinski had under Nixon and Carter.

The most distinguishing feature of the Reagan foreign policy-making system was the president's hands-off leadership. Ronald Reagan allowed his cabinet secretaries and other subordinates vast discretion in responding to the day-to-day issues affecting their area of foreign policy. He limited his own participation primarily to the articulation of broad themes and the performance of ceremonial duties. Reagan's style of leadership was praised by some observers during his presidency as an example of how presidents should delegate responsibilities to save their energies for the most important decisions and avoid being overwhelmed by the details of foreign policy. The Iran-contra scandal, which was uncovered in 1986, however, demonstrated the dangers of Reagan's detached leadership of the foreign policy-making system. NSC staff member Lt. Col. Oliver North along with national security adviser Vice Adm. John Poindexter and other administration officials attempted to use funds acquired from secret arms sales to Iran to aid the Nicaraguan "contra" rebels, even though Congress had prohibited U.S. government military aid to the contras. The Tower Commission, appointed by the president to review his NSC system in the wake of the affair, commented on Reagan's management style in its 1987 report:

> The President's management style is to put the principal responsibility for policy review and implementation on the shoulders of his advisors. Nevertheless, with such a complex, high-risk operation and so much at stake, the President should have ensured that the NSC system did not fail him. He did not force his policy to undergo the most critical review of which the NSC participants and the process were capable. At no time did he insist upon accountability and performance review. Had the President chosen to drive the NSC system, the outcome could well have been different.

The scandal forced the resignation of several White House officials and led the president to project a more visible role in foreign policy making.

The Bureaucracy as a Source of Presidential Power

The foreign policy bureaucracy can be a great asset to presidents in their struggle with Congress for control of foreign policy and their efforts to provide effective foreign policy leadership. The bureaucracy's most obvious benefit is that it enables presidents and their closest advisers to concentrate on the decisions and initiatives they deem most important while the bureaucracy deals with the many small foreign policy matters the executive branch must handle daily. President Nixon and his national security adviser, Kissinger, spent the vast majority of their foreign policy time during Nixon's first term on three problems: ending the Vietnam War, opening up China, and improving relations with the Soviet Union. Most other foreign policy matters were left to the bureaucracy. Although Nixon and Kissinger certainly neglected other important matters as a result, the extraordinary attention they were able to give these principal issues made progress possible.

The bureaucracy's capacity to supply the president with information and advice is another asset. No institution, including Congress, has information sources in foreign affairs that can compare with the array of channels supplying the president with current intelligence and professional opinions. Most modern presidents have been briefed daily on foreign policy issues by their secretary of state, national security adviser, or other top aides. These officials in turn receive information and proposals that have been distilled and funneled up to them from their respective departments. Presidents also frequently order studies of particular topics. This information and advice make it possible for a president to address foreign policy issues intelligently without being an expert.

In addition to the information available from normal advisory and diplomatic resources, the nation's vast intelligence-gathering capabilities are at the president's service. The director of the CIA coordinates intelligence activities and relays important intelligence directly to the president. Many foreign policy decisions, particularly those that involve the use of force, cannot be made without access to intelligence information. For example, President Kennedy decided to blockade Cuba during the Cuban missile crisis after he and his advisers had carefully analyzed all intelligence information.[109] The president's access to intelligence has provided a rationale for presidential autonomy over foreign policy. Congress's recognition of this presidential advantage contributed to its frequent willingness to accept presidential leadership in foreign affairs following World War II. Since the Vietnam War, however, Congress has more actively sought access to intelligence and has been more reluctant to accept presidential evaluations of international issues.

The professional foreign policy bureaucracy also provides continuity between the policies of successive administrations. When a new president takes office the general policy directives that provide guidance to the bureaucracy change and the political appointees who head the various departments and agencies are new, but the bureaucrats continue to collect intelligence, write reports, and make recommendations. Useful initiatives begun by the previous president have a chance to find a place in the new administration, and foreign governments that are frustrated by the frequent changes in presidential leadership can take comfort in the continuing presence of career officials with whom they have dealt in the past.

The Bureaucracy as an Impediment to Presidential Power

Although presidents have authority over the foreign policy bureaucracy, it does not always serve their purposes. Indeed, since the end of World War II, executive branch departments and agencies often have been a greater obstacle to presidential will in foreign affairs than has Congress. This has occurred because the goals and interests of the bureaucracy often have conflicted with those of the president. Political scientist Richard Neustadt has explained why presidents have found it difficult to control the bureaucracy:

> Everything somehow involves the President. But operating agencies owe their existence least of all to one another—and only in some part to him. Each has a separate statutory base; each has its statutes to administer; each deals with a different set of subcommittees at the Capitol. Each has its own peculiar set of clients, friends, and enemies outside the formal government. Each has a different set of specialized careerists inside its own bailiwick. Our Constitution gives the President the 'take-care' clause and the appointive power. Our statutes give him central budgeting and a degree of personnel control. All agency administrators are responsible to him. But they also are responsible to Congress, to their clients, to their staffs, and to themselves. In short, they have five masters.[110]

The president must, therefore, do more than order bureaucrats to perform a given function. As Neustadt said, the president must "convince such men that what the White House wants of them is what they ought to do for their sake and on their authority." [111]

Such persuasion is not always easy for presidents and their staff. Foreign service officers, military personnel, members of the intelligence community, and other career executive branch employees involved in foreign affairs are neither dependent on the president for their jobs nor necessarily in agreement with presidential goals and policies. Career bureaucrats naturally are concerned with the welfare of their particular department or agency. They usually will fight against policies that could diminish their responsibilities or resources, and they often will resent decisions that show an obvious disregard for their institutional point of view. In addition, foreign policy bureaucrats may regard presidents and their political appointees as temporary invaders of the foreign policy realm whose political goals threaten the permanent interests of the United States.

Members of the foreign policy bureaucracy have several means by which they can resist presidential will in foreign affairs. They can delay or undermine the execution of presidential directives, provide the president only with information and options that do not conflict with their own interpretation of an issue, leak details of a controversial or covert policy to Congress or the media, publicly oppose a policy, or resign in protest. The president may have the constitutional power to order an agency to carry out a particular task, but if that agency drags its feet or otherwise undermines implementation of the order, the president's power can be neutralized.

The most important means available to presidents of controlling the bureaucracy and communicating to it their foreign policy vision is the power to appoint the officials who will head the departments and agencies. These officials serve as department managers as well as members of the inner circle of presidential advisers. In choosing these appointees the president must reconcile, on the one hand, the need to find a qualified person with administrative talent who will be respected by the department he or she heads, with, on the other hand, the president's desire to maintain control over the bureaucracy. Even the most loyal presidential appointee, however, usually will develop a competing loyalty to the department or agency, which may at times conflict with the goals of the president.[112]

Notes

1. Theodore C. Sorensen, *Kennedy* (New York: Bantam, 1966), 573.
2. Louis Henkin, *Foreign Affairs and the Constitution* (New York: Norton, 1972), 76-77.
3. Edward S. Corwin, *The President: Office and Powers 1787-1984,* 5th rev. ed. (New York: New York University Press, 1984), 201.
4. Quoted in Clinton Rossiter, *The American Presidency,* 2d ed. (New York: Time, 1960), 15.
5. Robert F. Jones, "George Washington and the Establishment of Tradition," in *Power and the Presidency,* ed. Philip C. Dolce and George H. Skau (New York: Scribner's, 1976), 19.
6. Alexander Hamilton, *The Gazette of the United States,* June 29, 1793, quoted in Robert S. Hirschenfield, ed., *The Power of the Presidency* (New York: Atherton, 1968), 51.
7. Quoted in Corwin, *The President*, 210.
8. James Madison, *The Gazette of the United States,* August 24, 1793, quoted in Hirschenfield, 57-58.
9. Quoted in Howard Ball, *Constitutional Powers: Cases on the Separation of Powers and Federalism* (St. Paul, Minn.: West, 1980), 176.

10. Arthur M. Schlesinger, Jr., *The Imperial Presidency* (Boston: Houghton Mifflin, 1973), 102-103.
11. Quoted in Arthur Bernon Tourtellot, *The Presidents on the Presidency* (Garden City, N.Y.: Doubleday, 1964), 272.
12. James MacGregor Burns, *Presidential Government: The Crucible of Leadership* (Boston: Houghton Mifflin, 1965), 46-48.
13. Richard Harmond, "Theodore Roosevelt and the Making of the Modern Presidency," in *Power and the Presidency*, ed. Dolce and Skau (New York: Scribner's, 1976), 72-73.
14. Theodore Roosevelt to H. C. Lodge, January 28, 1909, quoted in Schlesinger, *The Imperial Presidency*, 89.
15. Richard M. Pious, *The American Presidency* (New York: Basic Books, 1979), 53.
16. For a discussion of the Tonkin Gulf incident, see Leslie H. Gelb and Richard K. Betts, *The Irony of Vietnam: The System Worked* (Washington, D.C.: Brookings, 1979), 100-104; Eugene Windchy, *Tonkin Gulf* (New York: Doubleday, 1971).
17. Gelb, *The Irony of Vietnam*, 103-104.
18. Robert E. DiClerico, *The American President*, 2d ed. (Englewood Cliffs, N.J.: Prentice-Hall, 1983), 59.
19. Tourtellot, *The Presidents on the Presidency*, 274.
20. Quoted in Pious, *The American Presidency*, 334.
21. Quoted in Corwin, *The President*, 207-208.
22. Henkin, *Foreign Affairs and the Constitution*, 301.
23. Arthur Miller, *Presidential Power in a Nutshell* (St. Paul, Minn.: West, 1977), 134.
24. Quoted in Tourtellot, *The Presidents on the Presidency*, 298.
25. Schlesinger, *The Imperial Presidency*, 27.
26. Ibid., 128.
27. Cecil V. Crabb, Jr., and Pat M. Holt, *Invitation to Struggle: Congress, the President and Foreign Policy* (Washington, D.C.: CQ Press, 1984), 14-15.
28. John Jay, "No. 64," in *The Federalist Papers*, Alexander Hamilton, James Madison, and John Jay (New York: New American Library, 1961), 392-393.
29. George H. Haynes, *The Senate of the United States* (Boston: Houghton Mifflin, 1938), 575.
30. Buel W. Patch, "Treaties and Domestic Law," *Editorial Research Reports*, March 28, 1952, 241.
31. Abraham D. Sofaer, *War, Foreign Affairs and Constitutional Power: The Origins* (Cambridge, Mass.: Ballinger, 1976), 95-96.
32. Corwin, *The President*, 240.
33. Quoted in Ball, *Constitutional Powers*, 175.
34. Joseph E. Kallenbach, *The American Chief Executive: The Presidency and the Governorship* (New York: Harper and Row, 1966), 505.
35. Pious, *The American Presidency*, 336.
36. F. M. Brewer, "Advice and Consent of the Senate," *Editorial Research Reports*, June 1, 1943, 350.
37. Ibid., 352.
38. Louis W. Koenig, *The Chief Executive* (New York: Harcourt Brace and World, 1968), 211-212.
39. DiClerico, *The American President*, 48.
40. Theodor Meron, "The Treaty Power: The International Legal Effect of Changes in Obligations Initiated by the Congress," in *The Tethered Presidency: Congressional Restraints on Executive Power*, ed. Thomas M. Franck (New York: New York University Press, 1981), 116-117.
41. Henkin, *Foreign Affairs and the Constitution*, 134.
42. Meron, in *The Tethered Presidency*, 105-108.
43. Kallenbach, *The American Chief Executive*, 507.
44. Henkin, *Foreign Affairs and the Constitution*, 159.
45. Corwin, *The President*, 205-206.
46. Dorothy Buckton James, *The Contemporary Presidency*, 2d ed. (Indianapolis: Bobbs-Merrill, 1974), 238.
47. Quoted in Henkin, *Foreign Affairs and the Constitution*, 377.
48. Francis O. Wilcox, *Congress, the Executive, and Foreign Policy* (New York: Harper and Row, 1971), 161.
49. Kallenbach, *The American Chief Executive*, 508.
50. Henkin, *Foreign Affairs and the Constitution*, 168-170.
51. Crabb, *Invitation to Struggle*, 15.
52. Loch K. Johnson, *The Making of International Agreements: Congress Confronts the Executive* (New York: New York University Press, 1984), 12. Johnson estimates from his analysis of international agreements made between January 1, 1946, and December 31, 1972, that 87 percent have been made in accordance with treaties or legislation.
53. Lawrence Margolis, *Executive Agreements and Presidential Power in Foreign Policy* (New York: Praeger, 1986), 95.
54. Edward M. Borchard, "Treaties and Executive Agreements," *American Political Science Review* 40 (August 1946): 735.
55. Johnson, *The Making of International Agreements*, 12.
56. Henkin, *Foreign Affairs and the Constitution*, 177-178.
57. Ibid., 178-179.
58. Margolis, *Executive Agreements*, 6-7.
59. Ibid., 6-7.
60. Schlesinger, *The Imperial Presidency*, 86.
61. Ibid., 86-87.
62. Margolis, *Executive Agreements*, 7-9.
63. Ibid., 9.
64. Tourtellot, *The Presidents on the Presidency*, 277.
65. DiClerico, *The American President*, 49.
66. Wilcox, *Congress, the Executive, and Foreign Policy*, 160-161.
67. DiClerico, *The American President*, 51.
68. Johnson, *The Making of International Agreements*, 86-87.
69. *Congressional Quarterly Almanac, 1972* (Washington, D.C.: Congressional Quarterly Inc., 1972), 619.
70. Koenig, *The Chief Executive*, 212.
71. Corwin, *The President*, 212.
72. Alexander Hamilton, "No. 69," in *The Federalist Papers*, 420.
73. Schlesinger, *The Imperial Presidency*, 14.
74. Koenig, *The Chief Executive*, 213.
75. Kallenbach, *The American Chief Executive*, 493.
76. Crabb, *Invitation to Struggle*, 18-19.
77. Seth P. Tillman, *The United States in the Middle East* (Bloomington: Indiana University Press, 1982), 221.
78. Quoted in Tourtellot, *The Presidents on the Presidency*, 291.
79. Pious, *The American Presidency*, 335.
80. Miller, *Presidential Power in a Nutshell*, 37.
81. Koenig, *The Chief Executive*, 213.
82. Robert E. Hunter, *Presidential Control of Foreign Policy: Management or Mishap* (New York: Praeger, 1982), 79-80.
83. Ibid., 84.
84. Koenig, *The Chief Executive*, 217.
85. Corwin, *The President*, 235.
86. Ibid., 236.
87. Henkin, *Foreign Affairs and the Constitution*, 46.
88. Elmer Plischke, *Diplomat in Chief: The President at the Summit* (New York: Praeger, 1986), 13.
89. Kallenbach, *The American Chief Executive*, 498-499.
90. Plischke, *Diplomat in Chief*, 121.
91. Kallenbach, *The American Chief Executive*, 499.
92. James, *The Contemporary Presidency*, 127-128.
93. Quoted in Plischke, *Diplomat in Chief*, 202.
94. Ibid., 200-202.
95. Richard Nixon, "Superpower Summitry," *Foreign Affairs* 64, no. 1 (Fall 1985): 1.
96. Ibid., 9-10.
97. Plischke, *Diplomat in Chief*, 460-473.
98. Ibid., 456-460.
99. Marcus Cunliffe, *American Presidents and the Presidency* (New York: American Heritage, 1972), 286.
100. Amos A. Jordan and William J. Taylor, *American National Security: Policy and Process* (Baltimore: Johns Hopkins University Press, 1984), 64.
101. John E. Endicott, "The National Security Council," in *American Defense Policy*, 5th ed., ed. John F. Reichart and Steven R. Sturm (Baltimore: Johns Hopkins University Press, 1982), 521-522.
102. For an outline of a state-centered foreign policy-making system see I. M. Destler, *Presidents, Bureaucrats, and Foreign Policy* (Princeton, N.J.: Princeton University Press, 1974), 254-294.

103. Endicott, "The National Security Council," 522.
104. Zbigniew Brzezinski, "The NSC's Midlife Crisis," *Foreign Policy* 69 (Winter, 1987-1988): 84-85.
105. Jordan, *American National Security*, 91.
106. Ibid., 91-92.
107. Charles W. Kegley, Jr., and Eugene R. Wittkopf, *American Foreign Policy: Pattern and Process* (New York: St. Martin's Press, 1979), 258-259.
108. Brzezinski, "The NSC's Midlife Crisis," 90.
109. Graham T. Allison, *Essence of Decision* (Boston: Little, Brown, 1971), 46-62.
110. Richard E. Neustadt, *Presidential Power: The Politics of Leadership from FDR to Carter,* 2d ed. (New York: Wiley, 1980), 30-31.
111. Ibid., 26.
112. Hunter, *Presidential Control of Foreign Policy*, 18.

Selected Bibliography

Corwin, Edward S. *The President: Office and Powers 1787-1984.* 5th ed. New York: New York University Press, 1984.

Crabb, Cecil V., and Pat M. Holt. *Invitation to Struggle: Congress, the President and Foreign Policy.* 2d ed. Washington, D.C.: CQ Press, 1984.

Destler, I.M. *Presidents, Bureaucrats, and Foreign Policy.* Princeton, N.J.: Princeton University Press, 1974.

Henkin, Louis. *Foreign Affairs and the Constitution.* New York: Norton, 1975.

Hunter, Robert E. *Presidential Control of Foreign Policy: Management or Mishap.* New York: Praeger, 1982.

Johnson, Loch. *The Making of International Agreements: Congress Confronts the Executive.* New York: New York University Press, 1984.

Kallenbach, Joseph E. *The American Chief Executive: The Presidency and the Governorship.* New York: Harper and Row, 1966.

Margolis, Lawrence. *Executive Agreements and Presidential Power in Foreign Policy.* New York: Praeger, 1986.

Neustadt, Richard E. *Presidential Power.* 2d. ed. New York: Wiley, 1980.

Pious, Richard M. *The American Presidency: The Politics of Power from FDR to Carter,* New York: Basic Books, 1979.

Plischke, Elmer. *Diplomat in Chief: The President at the Summit.* New York: Praeger, 1986.

Schlesinger, Arthur M. *The Imperial Presidency.* Boston: Houghton Mifflin, 1973.

Wilcox, Francis O. *Congress, the Executive, and Foreign Policy.* New York: Harper and Row, 1971.

Commander in Chief

The Framers of the Constitution distrusted both executive and military power and believed the potential for tyranny was great when the two were combined. Among the colonial grievances cited in the Declaration of Independence were the charges that the British monarch had "kept among us, in times of peace, Standing Armies without the Consent of our legislature" and "affected to render the Military independent of and superior to the Civil Power." The document also denounced the quartering of troops in American homes, the impressment of American sailors for British warships, and the unjust war being waged against the colonies. The delegates to the Constitutional Convention were determined to restrain military power to prevent the new government from committing the type of offenses that they believed the British had perpetrated on the colonies. Their main instrument of accomplishing this constitutional goal was the separation of powers. They therefore rejected a proposal to grant the president the authority to declare war and divided the war-making power between the executive and Congress.

Nevertheless, the Founders of the United States were practical people who recognized that they must not cripple their young nation's ability to defend itself, especially against sudden attack, through their efforts to prevent the misuse of military power. While many war powers, including the decision to go to war, could be given to Congress, command of U.S. forces during a conflict necessitated the unified and flexible leadership that only a single person could provide. As Alexander Hamilton noted: "Of all the cares or concerns of government, the direction of war most peculiarly demands those qualities which distinguish the exercise of power by a single hand." [1] The Framers therefore assigned the commander-in-chief power to the presidency and took comfort in the certainty that George Washington would be the first person to hold that office.

Few presidents, however, have been as well suited for the role of commander in chief as George Washington. Many have mismanaged military affairs, and a few have abused their military power. In addition, the dramatic expansion of presidential authority over national security affairs in the decades following World War II led to a confrontation between the executive and legislative branches over the war power that has not been entirely resolved. Yet it is difficult to imagine that the historical record of the United States could have been improved had the Framers separated the role of commander in chief from the presidency. The Civil War, World War I, and World War II demonstrated that a strong president willing to interpret the commander-in-chief power broadly is in the best position to lead the military, unite the American people, and focus the efforts of the nation on victory when war threatens its security. As political scientist Clinton Rossiter wrote: "We have placed a shocking amount of military power in the President's keeping, but where else, we may ask, could it possibly have been placed?" [2]

By Daniel C. Diller

Constitutional Distribution of War-making Power

There was general agreement at the Constitutional Convention that the person who occupied the highest civilian office should also be the commander in chief of the nation's military forces. Article II, section 2, of the Constitution states: "The President shall be Commander in Chief of the Army and Navy of the United States, and of the Militia of the several States, when called into the actual Service of the United States." This statement is all the Constitution says about the president's war-making power. Unlike all other constitutional grants of power to the presidency, the commander-in-chief clause confers an office rather than a function on the president.[3] Since the precise authority of this office was left undefined, presidents have been able to argue that they possess any power or duty traditionally associated with the office of supreme military commander, rather than just the single function of commanding the armed forces. Consequently, virtually any action that improves the nation's defenses in peacetime or helps it prevail over an enemy in wartime without usurping the power of the other branches or violating the law can be justified under a broad interpretation of the commander-in-chief clause.

In addition, foreign policy and chief executive powers give presidents responsibilities in the area of national security that are not specifically enumerated in the commander-in-chief clause. Through their power to negotiate treaties and executive agreements, presidents may establish an alliance or conclude an armistice. As chief executive, commander in chief, and the occupant of the only elected national office that never is out of session, the president is

> The President shall be Commander in Chief of the Army and Navy of the United States, and of the Militia of the several States, when called into the actual Service of the United States.
>
> —from Article II, section 2

also recognized as being responsible for the defense of the nation if it is attacked. This role is reinforced by the presidential oath of office in the Constitution, which pledges the president to "preserve, protect, and defend the Constitution of the United States."

The constitutional authors did not, however, regard war making as a function to be dominated by the executive branch. By giving Congress significant war powers, the Framers hoped to prevent the president from making war alone. In contrast to the single phrase designating the president as commander in chief, the clause outlining Congress's war powers is detailed and specific. Article I, section 8, of the Constitution grants Congress the authority:

> To declare War, grant Letters of Marque and Reprisal, and make Rules concerning Captures on Land and Water; To raise and support Armies. . . ; To provide and maintain a Navy; To make Rules for the Government and Regulation of the land and naval forces; To provide for calling forth the Militia to execute the Laws of the Union, suppress Insurrections and repel Invasions; To provide for organizing, arming and disciplining the Militia, and for governing such Part of them as may be employed in the Service of the United States, reserving to the States respectively, the Appointment of the Officers, and the Authority of training the Militia according to the discipline prescribed by Congress.

As Congress's enumerated war powers indicate, the Framers intended Congress to have authority over the raising, equipping, and organizing of the armed forces, while the president would direct the military in times of war. The two branches would share power over the military, an instrument of government often abused if controlled by a single master. A president seeking to become a military dictator would be hindered by Congress's exclusive authority to raise, equip, and organize an army and navy. Presidents might wish to fight a war, but without Congress's support they would lack the necessary tools to do so. Conversely, Congress's ability to legislate a war would be restricted by the president's command of the military during hostilities and authority to negotiate treaties.

Power to Declare War

Although Congress's power to raise armies and fund wars and the president's command of the military in times of war are unquestioned, the authority over the decision when and where to employ military force has been the subject of conflict between the executive and legislative branches. The Framers' suspicions of executive power ruled out granting the president the exclusive authority to declare war. Yet their decision to give Congress alone the power to declare war is significant, since they could have divided this power between the legislative and executive branches. For example, they could have given the president the power to declare war with the "advice and consent of the Senate" as they had with the treaty power. Instead, the authors of the Constitution deliberately delegated to Congress the entire decision to declare war. Moreover, it is clear from the writings of the Framers that they regarded the act of declaring war as more than a formality. By giving Congress the power to declare war they sought to ensure that the decision to risk American lives in the defense of the United States or in pursuit of its perceived interests would be made by the democratically elected representatives closest to the people who would be called upon to fight and die. James Madison wrote:

> Those who are to conduct a war cannot in the nature of things be proper or safe judges whether a war ought to be commenced, continued, or concluded. They are barred from the latter functions by a great principle in free government, analogous to that which separates the sword from the purse, or the power of executing from the power of enacting laws.[4]

The delegates to the Constitutional Convention, however, did not expect Congress to authorize every use of military force. In an early draft of the Constitution, Congress was given the power to "make war," but Madison and Elbridge Gerry convinced their colleagues to change the phrase to "declare war" so as to give the president the prerogative to repel sudden attacks.[5] The Framers recognized that the speed and secrecy only a single decision maker could provide was essential to the safety of the nation if it came under attack.

Despite this concession to executive power the Framers believed they had sufficiently checked the president's war-making authority. In the *The Federalist Papers*, Hamilton, one of the foremost advocates of a strong chief executive at the Constitutional Convention, narrowly interpreted the commander-in-chief power:

> The president is to be commander-in-chief of the army and navy of the United States. In this respect his authority would be nominally the same with that of the King of Great Britain, but in substance much inferior to it. It would amount to nothing more than the supreme command and direction of the military and naval forces, as first general and admiral of the Confederacy; while that of the British king extends to the *declaring* of war and to the *raising* and *regulating* of fleets and armies—all of which, by the Constitution under consideration, would appertain to the legislature.[6]

The constitutional distribution of authority over the decision to go to war seems clear. Congress decides when to go to war unless the United States is attacked, in which case the president defends the nation. Yet this simple formula is full of ambiguities. How is war to be defined? Are there military missions short of war that the president can order without congressional authorization? Can the president order an attack to preempt an assault from a potential enemy? Can the president order U.S. forces to invade the territory of a neutral nation in pursuit of enemy forces? Can the president incite an attack through actions that are clearly provocative to a potential enemy? The legislative and executive branches were left to battle over these and other war power ambiguities. That Congress has declared war only five times—the War of 1812, the Mexican War, the Spanish-American War, World War I, and World War II—despite U.S. involvement in over one hundred violent military conflicts and incidents illustrates that the Framers' original division of the war power did not address all the situations in which hostilities might be initiated. Because presidents have direct command of military forces and they are charged with defending the nation, they have been in a better position to exploit this ambiguity than Congress. Consequently, when presidents have believed that a war or military action was necessary, they usually have found ways to maneuver the nation into a conflict.

Power to End War or Declare Neutrality

As commander in chief, presidents have the power to order the military to stop fighting or to withdraw from an area of conflict. In addition, their sole authority to negotiate treaties gives them the power to conclude an armistice with an enemy. If Congress has declared war, however, the president cannot unilaterally end the legal state of war that exists. Congress must take some action that supersedes its declaration of war. Usually this action is accomplished through Senate ratification of a treaty negotiated by the president ending the war and establishing peaceful relations with the enemy nation. The Mexican War, the Spanish-American War, and hostilities in the Pacific theater of World War II were officially terminated in this manner. Congress also may formally end a state of war by repealing its declaration of war. This method was used in 1921 after Congress had refused to ratify the Versailles treaty at the end of World War I and in 1951 formally to end war with Nazi Germany.[7]

A more troublesome question is who has the power to declare neutrality. Since only Congress has the authority to declare war, some students of the Constitution have reasoned that only Congress has the power to declare that the nation will not become involved in a war. Secretary of State Thomas Jefferson made this argument in 1793 when President Washington proclaimed that the United States would remain "friendly and impartial" toward the warring British and French.[8] Many Americans wanted to honor the treaty of alliance with France that had been signed during the American Revolution, but Washington believed U.S. involvement in the conflict would disrupt the nation's development. Jefferson supported Washington's proclamation despite his reservations about the constitutionality of the president's declaring neutrality. As a concession to Jefferson, Washington left the word "neutrality" out of his proclamation.

Washington's declaration of neutrality set off a famous debate in the *Gazette of the United States* between Hamilton, who supported Washington's action, and Madison, who opposed this expansion of executive power. Hamilton conceded that the legislature had the exclusive right to declare war but asserted that until war is declared, the executive has the responsibility to maintain peace. Madison saw the declaration of neutrality as a usurpation of Congress's power to declare war. Hamilton and Madison were less concerned with neutrality than with the larger issue of whether a president could declare unilaterally what U.S. foreign policy would be. Over time, Hamilton's view that the president can make U.S. foreign policy has prevailed over Madison's strict interpretation of presidential power. *(See "Hamilton-Madison Debate," p. 499, in Chief Diplomat chapter of Part III.)*

Washington's decision to ask Congress to pass judgment on the proclamation created the precedent that declarations of neutrality were subject to congressional approval. Congress eventually did ratify the president's action by passing the Neutrality Act of 1794.

Subsequently, the custom also developed that Congress would not declare war without a presidential request. Yet on two occasions Congress demonstrated that it could move a president to accept a war even if the president had reservations about the wisdom of doing so. In 1812 a majority of members of Congress convinced President James Madison that war against the British was necessary. In 1898, with public opinion on its side, Congress pressured a reluctant William McKinley to ask for a declaration of war against Spain.

Development of Presidential War Powers

The Constitution's assignment of the office of commander in chief to the president created the basis for presidential war powers, but a more precise outline of these powers had to evolve through events. Most early presidents held a narrow view of their commander-in-chief role that was similar to Hamilton's description of the president as the nation's "first general or admiral." Gradually, however, the commander-in-chief power grew. The Civil War and the two world wars provided the most dramatic boosts to presidential authority.

Presidential war powers expanded during these national security emergencies because the flexibility, secrecy, speed, and unity of command associated with the president were seen as crucial to the preservation and defense of the United States. According to political scientist Edward S. Corwin, "The principal canons of constitutional interpretation are in wartime set aside so far as concerns both the scope of national power and the capacity of the President to gather unto himself all constitutionally available powers in order the more effectively to focus them upon the task of the hour."[9] Presidential actions that would have raised a storm of protest in peacetime were accepted in the name of necessity when the security of the nation was at stake.

This is not to say that when wartime emergencies were over presidents continued to wield exceptional power as if an emergency still existed, but every extension of presidential power set a precedent to which a future president could refer when an emergency of similar gravity appeared. Woodrow Wilson's expansion of presidential war power paved the way for Franklin D. Roosevelt's extraordinary wartime authority, just as Wilson had referred to Lincoln's exercise of power when justifying his own.

Following World War II, the cold war between the United States and the Soviet Union, the development of nuclear weapons, and the U.S. participation in two lengthy undeclared wars in Asia led to a series of national security emergencies. Under these conditions presidential commander-in-chief authority continued to expand until the late 1960s and early 1970s when Congress reacted to executive branch abuses of power by attempting to reassert its role in national security affairs. Although the executive branch still dominates national security policy, Congress has scrutinized national security affairs more closely and has been able to restrict presidential policies on a variety of issues including funding for selected weapons systems and military aid to allied nations and guerrilla organizations.

Ironically, until the latter stages of the Vietnam War the expansion of the president's war powers usually had been accomplished with Congress's approval and often with its active support. Congress validated many of Lincoln's actions, passed legislation delegating sweeping wartime powers to both Woodrow Wilson and Franklin Roosevelt, and acquiesced to the accumulation of power by presidents after World War II. Although the Supreme Court has occasionally ruled against exercises of presidential war power, it seldom has done so when a war was in progress and often has approved presidential actions on the grounds that they are political matters that should be resolved between the executive and legislative branches. Moreover, as the Court's approval of the internment of Americans of Japanese descent during World War II demonstrates, the Court has recognized the authority of the president acting in concert with Congress to take virtually any action in response to a grave national emergency.[10] *(See "Individual Liberty versus Societal Good," p. 1157, in The President and the Supreme Court chapter of Part VI.)*

Early Presidents

Early presidents generally adhered to the principle that Congress was responsible for committing the United States to war. John Adams consulted with Congress in 1798 before allowing U.S. naval forces to attack French vessels that were preying on U.S. commercial shipping. Congress refrained from declaring war but passed legislation that authorized the president to order U.S. military forces to battle the French.[11] Similarly, Jefferson and Madison believed presidents should carefully respect Congress's war-making powers. Yet the events of their administrations demonstrated the desirability of a strong commander in chief when war did come.

Jefferson and the Barbary Pirates

Like Adams, Jefferson faced the problem of a limited naval war. In 1801, American ships in the Mediterranean were being attacked by pirates from Tripoli and the other Barbary Coast states of Algeria, Morocco, and Tunisia. Jefferson wanted to take quick action to resolve the problem, but he also wished to uphold Congress's power to order U.S. troops into hostilities. He therefore dispatched a squadron of ships to the Mediterranean with instructions to offer the rulers of the Barbary Coast states payments to leave U.S. shipping alone. Jefferson anticipated trouble, however, and informed the commodore of the squadron:

> But if you find on your arrival in Gibralter that all the Barbary Powers have declared war against the United States, you will then distribute your forces in such a manner, as your judgment shall direct, so as best to protect our commerce and chastise their insolence—by sinking, burning, or destroying their ships and vessels wherever you shall find them.[12]

Jefferson did not disclose these orders to Congress when he went before that body December 8, 1801, to request approval to take the offensive in the naval war that was already being fought. Rather, he emphasized the constitutional restraints under which the squadron operated:

> I sent a small squadron of frigates into the Mediterranean, with assurance to that power [Tripoli] of our desire to remain in peace, but with orders to protect our commerce against the threatened attack.... One of the Tripolitan cruisers ... was captured, after a heavy slaughter of her men, without the loss of a single one on our part.... Unauthorized by the Constitution, without the sanction of Congress, to go beyond the line of defense, the vessel, being disabled from committing further hostilities, was liberated with its crew.[13]

Congress passed legislation early in 1802 authorizing the naval war that eventually led to a treaty with the Barbary powers. Jefferson had used deception and a *fait accompli* to secure the Mediterranean for U.S. commercial shipping while publicly asserting Congress's right to determine when military force would be used.[14]

Hamilton, however, found Jefferson's consultations with Congress ridiculous. He asserted that the president did not need to ask Congress's permission to turn loose the navy because: "When a foreign nation declares or openly and avowedly makes war upon the United States, they are then by the very fact already at war and any declaration on the part of Congress is nugatory; it is at least unnecessary." [15]

Despite Jefferson's occasional willingness to violate his own principles in pursuit of objectives he considered important, he genuinely believed that the president should not order military operations without congressional approval except in defense of the nation. In 1805 when Spanish subjects in Florida made incursions into the newly acquired Louisiana Territory, Jefferson told Congress: "Considering that Congress alone is constitutionally invested with the power of changing our condition from peace to war, I have thought it my duty to await their authority for using force.... The course to be pursued will require the command of means which it belongs to Congress exclusively to yield or to deny." When Congress chose not to grant Jefferson the authority to attack the Spanish in Florida, he accepted its decision.[16]

The War of 1812

The War of 1812 was the first declared war in U.S. history. Sentiment for the war had been aroused by British captures of American commercial ships and their crews, allegations that the British were supplying hostile Indians on the frontier with arms, and a desire to acquire foreign territory in Canada and Florida. The initial advocates of the war were not President Madison and his close advisers, but members of Congress from the South and the West. These "War Hawks" represented areas that were troubled by Indian attacks and falling agricultural prices. In contrast, the Federalist merchants of the Northeast, who were making large profits on export shipments that avoided capture, were against the war. They feared that war would interfere with their commerce much more than sporadic British seizures of their ships.

Although Madison had tried sincerely to resolve disputes with the British through diplomacy, he was eventually persuaded that the nation must go to war to protect its rights. On June 1, 1812, the president asked Congress for a declaration of war. Madison, like Jefferson, believed strongly that Congress should determine whether the nation should initiate hostilities. In his address to lawmakers asking for a declaration of war Madison called war making a "solemn question which the Constitution wisely confides to the legislative department of the Government." [17] The declaration was passed 79-49 by the House and 19-13 by the Senate. Members of Congress from the South and the West prevailed over their colleagues from the Northeast.

Not only was the nation divided over the war, it was unprepared to fight. The small American navy was hopelessly outmatched, and despite the war's popularity in the South and West the army had difficulty recruiting volunteers. In the Northeast there was talk of secession, and the governors of Massachusetts, Rhode Island, and Connecticut refused to authorize the use of their troops. U.S. forces suffered a string of humiliating defeats including the capture and burning of Washington, D.C., by the British in August 1814.

After the British forces withdrew from the capital, Congress assembled to consider the war effort. Yet, with the army still at only about half its paper strength and enlistments falling off, Congress failed to agree on a conscription bill proposed by James Monroe, Madison's secretary of war and state. Fortunately, the Treaty of Ghent ending the war was signed on Decemeber 24, 1814. Before the news of the treaty reached New Orleans, however, Gen. Andrew Jackson's militia inflicted a stunning defeat on British regulars attacking the city on January 8, 1815. This victory restored some of the nation's pride, but the war had proven that a president's ability to wage a successful war depended not just on the encouragement of Congress but also on public consensus supporting the war.

The Annexation of Texas and the Mexican War

Texas declared its independence from Mexico in 1836 and indicated that it was interested in becoming part of the United States. Although most Americans supported the principle of expansion, the slavery issue made annexation of a new state a tricky political problem for any president. Presidents Andrew Jackson and Martin Van Buren avoided actions on the Texas issue that would anger voters in the North who were opposed to an extension of slavery. John Tyler, who succeeded to the presidency following the death of William Henry Harrison in 1841, however, was a proslavery Virginian who wished to strengthen the slave states and limit English influence over Texas.[18] He began secret negotiations on annexation with Texas and initiated a pro-annexation campaign. The Texans, however, were concerned that if they agreed to annexation they would be invaded by Mexico. They informed Tyler that they would be reluctant to agree to annexation without guarantees that he would protect them with U.S. forces. This created a dilemma for Tyler, whose narrow interpretation of the Constitution had led him to reject presidential authority to use military force without congressional approval except in defense of the nation. In early 1844 Tyler showed that he valued the acquisition of Texas more than his own strict constructionist principles when he ordered the deployment of U.S. forces in Texas and the Gulf of Mexico while the secret negotiations proceeded. When the needed two-thirds of the Senate refused to approve the annexation treaty produced by the negotiations, Tyler sidestepped the Constitution by asking Congress to validate the agreement with a majority vote of both Houses. The joint resolution was passed, thereby establishing a new type of congressionally approved executive agreement.[19]

In the spring of 1846 President Polk ordered Gen. Zachary Taylor to deploy his army in a strip of disputed territory near the Rio Grande that was claimed by Texas but occupied exclusively by Mexicans. Polk had decided to ask Congress for a declaration of war even before Mexican forces attacked Taylor's army, killing a number of American soldiers. The clash ensured the passage of a declaration of war since Polk could claim that Mexico was the aggressor. He told Congress: "Now, after reiterated menaces Mexico has invaded our territory and shed American blood on American soil." [20] On May 13, 1846, Congress recognized "a state of war as existing by act of the Republic of Mexico." Polk's successful maneuvering to place the country in a "defensive" war demonstrated the power of presidents to initiate hostilities through their responsibility to defend the nation.

Library of Congress

U.S. and Mexican forces clash at the Battle of Buena Vista in 1847. In hopes of securing territory occupied by Mexico but claimed by Texas, President Polk maneuvered the country into a "defensive" war after U.S. soldiers were attacked by Mexican forces.

Lincoln and the Civil War

President Lincoln's extraordinary exercise of power during the Civil War demonstrated how far the authority of the presidency could be expanded in wartime. Lincoln believed he faced a choice between preserving the Union and adhering to a strict interpretation of the Constitution. He feared that if he carefully observed the law he would sacrifice the flexibility necessary to prevent the destruction of the nation. In April 1864 he explained his reasoning in a letter to Albert Hodges:

> I did understand, however, that my oath to preserve the Constitution to the best of my ability impressed upon me the duty of preserving by every indispensable means, that government—that nation, of which that Constitution was the organic law. Was it possible to lose the nation and yet preserve the Constitution? By general law, life and limb must be protected, yet often a limb must be amputated to save a life; but a life is never wisely given to save a limb. I felt that measures otherwise unconstitutional might become lawful by becoming indispensable to the preservation of the nation. Right or wrong, I assumed this ground and now avow it.[21]

Lincoln did not come to this conclusion lightly. As a member of the House of Representatives, he had questioned the legality and propriety of President Polk's actions that led to the Mexican War. *(See box, Lincoln's Attack on Presidential War Powers, p. 537)* Lincoln's expansion of his own war-making powers as president, therefore, did not result from a cavalier attitude toward the Constitution but from his recognition of an unprecedented emergency.

Mathew Brady, 1862; Library of Congress

In conducting the Civil War, Lincoln believed he faced a choice between preserving the Union and adhering to the Constitution. "Was it possible to lose the nation and yet preserve the Constitution?" he wrote. "By general law, life and limb must be protected, yet often a limb must be amputated to save a life."

Lincoln's Expanded Powers

On April 12, 1861, the Civil War began when Confederate forces attacked Fort Sumter. Recognizing that strict constructionists in Congress might object to emergency measures he thought necessary to deal with the crisis, Lincoln delayed the convocation of Congress until July 4. He used this three-month period to order a series of executive actions to meet the military emergency.[22]

On May 3, 1861, he called for the mobilization of seventy-five thousand state militia subject to his orders under a 1795 act that authorized the president to issue such a call. Although this action was considered within the powers of the president, most of Lincoln's actions during the early months of the war had no constitutional or congressional sanction. In the same proclamation used to mobilize the militia Lincoln unilaterally increased the size of the regular army by twenty-three thousand troops and the navy by eighteen thousand. In addition he ordered nineteen vessels added to the navy and directed the secretary of the Treasury to advance $2 million to authorized persons to pay for military requisitions. Lincoln also ordered a blockade of Southern ports, suspended the writ of *habeas corpus* (the constitutional guarantee against illegal detention and imprisonment) in the vicinity of routes used by Union forces between Washington, D.C., and Philadelphia, ordered foreign visitors to observe new passport regulations, restricted "treasonable correspondence" from being carried by the Post Office, and directed the military to arrest and detain persons "who were represented to him" as contemplating or participating in "treasonable practices."[23]

When Congress finally convened on July 4, Lincoln asked the members to ratify the actions he had taken in their absence. He maintained that some of his emergency measures "whether strictly legal or not, were ventured upon under what appeared to be a popular demand and a public necessity, trusting then, as now, Congress would readily ratify them." In justifying his suspension of *habeas corpus* Lincoln made the constitutional argument that in spite of the placement of the provision on *habeas corpus* suspension in Article I, the Framers must have intended the president to share with Congress the authority to suspend *habeas corpus* since emergencies requiring such action would not always occur when Congress was in session. Yet Lincoln defended his action on practical grounds as well, asking Congress, "Are all the laws but one to go unexecuted, and the Government itself go to pieces lest that one be violated?" In asking this question Lincoln implied that a national emergency threatening the existence of the nation may empower the president to ignore parts of the Constitution to defend the whole.[24]

During the summer, Congress debated a joint resolution that sanctioned Lincoln's acts. Nagging doubts about the legality of his suspension of *habeas corpus* and blockade of Southern ports prevented a vote on the resolution. Near the end of the session, however, a rider attached to a pay bill for army privates that approved Lincoln's actions was rushed through Congress. On August 6, 1861, Congress passed the bill and its rider, which declared the president's acts pertaining to the militia, the army, the navy, and the volunteers "in all respects legalized and made valid, to the same intent and with the same effect as if they had been issued and done under the previous express authority and direction of Congress." [25]

Throughout the war, Lincoln continued to extend his commander-in-chief power beyond its constitutional limits. In 1862, when voluntary recruitments were not adequately supplying the army's need for additional troops, Lincoln ordered a militia draft. The same year he extended his suspension of the writ of *habeas corpus* to persons throughout the entire nation who were "guilty of any disloyal practice." He also declared that these persons could be tried by military courts. On January 1, 1983, Lincoln issued the Emancipation Proclamation freeing "all persons held as slaves within any State or designated part of a State, the people whereof shall then be in rebellion against the United States." Lincoln maintained that his commander-in-chief power gave him the authority to issue the proclamation, since the liberation of slaves reduced the labor force of the South, thus hindering its ability to carry on the war.[26]

Prize Cases

Although the Supreme Court eventually objected to Lincoln's order that civilians could be tried in military courts, it did sanction his prosecution of a total war against the South. When hostilities began, the president had ordered a blockade of Confederate ports to prevent the South from selling cotton to England and importing supplies. The owners of four vessels seized by the blockade sued for redress on the grounds that the seizures were illegal since Congress had not declared war against the South. They argued that Lincoln's duty to suppress the insurrection was not equivalent to the power to wage war. Therefore, an act of war such as a blockade could not legally be ordered by the president in the absence of a declaration of war.

In 1863 the Supreme Court rejected these arguments in its 5-4 decision on the *Prize Cases.* Writing for the majority Justice Robert C. Grier explained:

> It is not necessary to constitute war, that both parties should be acknowledged as independent nations or sovereign states. A war may exist where one of the belligerents claims sovereign rights as against the other. . . . A civil war is never solemnly declared; it becomes such by its accidents—the number, power, and organization of the persons who originate and carry it on. When the party in rebellion occupy and hold in a hostile manner a certain portion of territory; have declared their independence; have cast off their allegiance; have organized armies; have commenced hostilities against their former sovereign, the world acknowledges them as belligerents, and the contest a *war.*[27]

The decision supported Lincoln's interpretation that the insurrectionist South was without sovereign rights, while the North possessed all rights of a belligerent in wartime. Moreover, the decision gave Lincoln confidence that the Court would not restrict his expansive interpretation of his commander-in-chief powers in the future. Although this case dealt specifically with the president's power to respond to a general insurrection, advocates of a strong presidency have often cited it when arguing in favor of a broad interpretation of presidential war power.[28]

Lincoln's Attack on Presidential War Powers

As president, Abraham Lincoln stretched presidential power until it approached dictatorship. He justified his extraordinary emergency powers under the commander-in-chief clause and his duty "to take Care that the Laws be faithfully executed." Ironically, as a young member of the House of Representatives, Lincoln had argued for a limited interpretation of the president's war-making authority. In a letter to William H. Herndon, his law partner in Illinois, Lincoln asserted his strict view of presidential power:

> Washington, Feb. 15, 1848
>
> Dear William:
>
> . . . Let me first state what I understand to be your position. It is, that if it shall become *necessary, to repel invasion,* the President may, without violation of the Constitution, cross the line, and *invade* the territory of another country; and that whether such *necessity* exists in any given case, the President is to be the *sole* judge.
>
> . . . Allow the President to invade a neighboring nation, whenever *he* shall deem it necessary to repel an invasion, and you allow him to do so, *whenever he may choose to say* he deems it necessary for such purpose—and you allow him to make war at pleasure. Study to see if you can fix *any limit* to his power in this respect, after you have given him so much as you propose. If, to-day, he should choose to say he thinks it necessary to invade Canada, to prevent the British from invading us, how could you stop him? You may say to him, "I see no probability of the British invading us" but he will say to you "be silent; I see it, if you dont."
>
> The provision of the Constitution giving the war-making power to Congress, was dictated, as I understand it, by the following reasons. Kings had always been involving and impoverishing their people in wars, pretending generally, if not always, that the good of the people was the object. This, our Convention understood to be the most oppressive of all Kingly oppressions; and they resolved to so frame the Constitution that *no one man* should hold the power of bringing this oppression upon us. But your view destroys the whole matter, and places our President where kings have always stood. Write soon again.
>
> Yours truly,
> A. Lincoln[1]

1. *The Collected Works of Abraham Lincoln,* ed. Roy P. Basler (New Brunswick, N.J.: Rutgers University Press, 1953), 451-452.

Spanish-American War

The 1895 Cuban rebellion against Spanish rule occurred when the United States was ready to seek a wider role in global affairs. For some Americans the Cuban crisis offered an opportunity to flex American muscle against a European power and extend U.S. influence. Others, aroused by slanted reports in the press of Spanish atrocities in Cuba, wished to rescue the island's inhabitants from Spanish tyranny. This combination of forces resulted in a popular crusade in the United States to aid Cuban independence.

President Grover Cleveland resisted the temptation to satisfy the nation's appetite for war with Spain during the last two years of his term. William McKinley entered office in 1897 similarly determined to avoid war. After the mysterious sinking of the U.S. battleship *Maine* in Havana harbor in February 1898, however, he could no longer stand up to congressional belligerence and public opinion. He asked Congress on April 11, 1898, to approve American armed intervention in Cuba. Spain already had conceded to most American demands for a settlement of the Cuban crisis, but on April 25, Congress passed a declaration of war authorizing the president to use military force to expel Spain from the island. It was adopted by the Senate 42-35 and by the House 310-6.

Although American forces were poorly equipped, trained, and commanded, superior American naval power enabled the United States to oust the Spanish from Cuba, Puerto Rico, and the Philippines. The brevity of the war, the ease with which victory was won, and the popularity of the conflict made McKinley's job as commander in chief an easy one. The issue of what to do with the Philippines, however, was more controversial. McKinley decided to take possession of the islands and, as he later told a group of clergymen, "educate the Philipinos, and uplift and civilize and Christianize them." [29]

On December 10, 1898, Spain signed a treaty relinquishing its control over Cuba and ceding the Philippines along with Puerto Rico and Guam to the United States. Yet many senators had reservations about McKinley's idealistic plans for the Philippines, and the treaty was not assured of ratification. In spite of news that Philippine insurgents had taken up arms against U.S. forces, the Senate approved the treaty after a month of debate by a vote of 57-27, only one vote more than the necessary two-thirds majority. For the first time a president and Congress had acquired territory for the United States outside the North American continent through war.

The World Wars

The first involvement of the United States in an overseas war of massive scale provided the occasion for the most dramatic expansion of presidential powers since the Civil War. The basis for Woodrow Wilson's power differed from Lincoln's, however, in that Lincoln had taken emergency actions independently of Congress, while Wilson was handed most of his expanded war-making authority by statute.[30] Congress gave Wilson not only expanded control of the military and discretion to fight subversion and espionage but also unprecedented control over industries and the allocation of scarce resources. For example, the Lever Food and Fuel Act gave the president "full authority to undertake any steps necessary" for the conservation of food resources. In addition, the Overman Act gave the president complete authority to reorganize the executive branch. Congress was willing to make these broad delegations of power to Wilson because most members believed that the scope and urgency of the war required unified control and direction of all operations and resources related to the the war effort.

Many delegations of authority to the president simply stated their objectives and left Wilson to decide how to achieve them. He commandeered plants and mines, requisitioned supplies, fixed prices, seized and operated the nation's transportation and communications networks, and managed the production and distribution of foodstuffs. The Council of National Defense, an umbrella agency created by Wilson, administered the economy during the war. Wilson created the War Industries Board using his authority as commander in chief. Wall Street broker Bernard Baruch, who had been appointed by Wilson to head the board, became a virtual dictator over American industry. The president also established by executive order the Committee of Public Information, under whose direction a system of voluntary news censorship was instituted and various government publicity services were organized. On April 28, 1917, Wilson imposed strict cable censorship, which later was extended to other forms of communication with foreign countries under authority of the Trading with the Enemy Act of October 6, 1917.

In essence, Congress did not just give Wilson broad discretion in implementing its statutes, it abdicated legislative power to him for the duration of the war. Wilson's confidence in his presidential prerogatives fostered by his wartime authority backfired on him, however, when Congress refused to ratify the Treaty of Versailles after Wilson had ignored lawmakers during its negotiation.[31]

Presidential war power reached its apex during World War II. Constitutional scholar Edward S. Corwin wrote, "The relation . . . of the First World War to the Second as regards constitutional interpretation is that of prologue and rehearsal." [32] Like Wilson during World War I, Franklin Roosevelt was delegated wide powers by Congress to manage the economy and direct the war effort, but Roosevelt went beyond Wilson in asserting his prerogative to take any action he deemed necessary to the war effort.

Overcoming Neutrality

Ironically, Franklin Roosevelt's war powers were tightly restrained during the 1930s by the prevailing mood of isolationism in Congress and among the American people. Congress had enacted a series of laws designed to keep the United States out of the conflicts brewing in Europe and Asia. These laws included the Neutrality Acts of 1935 and 1937, which prohibited shipments of arms, ammunition, or implements of war to any belligerent nation, including those that had been the victims of aggression. Isolationist sentiment was so strong that Roosevelt did not denounce these acts until after Hitler's invasion of Poland in September 1939, which brought Great Britain and France into the war against Nazi Germany.[33] Even after the Nazis' aggressive intentions had become obvious, Roosevelt had to maneuver the country toward active support of Britain and the other allies, whose survival he believed was crucial to U.S. security.

On September 3, 1940, Roosevelt announced that he had concluded an agreement with Great Britain under which that country would receive fifty "overage" destroyers in return for the right to lease certain British territory in the western Atlantic for U.S. naval and air bases. Roosevelt's destroyer deal was accomplished through an executive agreement—a legally binding pact between the president and the British government—rather than a Senate ratified treaty. The trade violated at least two congressional statutes, but Roosevelt's attorney general, Robert Jackson, asserted that the president acted legally under his commander-in-chief authority to "dispose" of the armed forces.

On March 11, 1941, Congress passed the Lend-Lease Act, described by Corwin as the most "sweeping delegation of legislative power" ever given to a president.[34] It authorized the president to manufacture any defense article and to "sell, transfer title to, exchange, lease, lend or otherwise dispose of" the defense articles to the "government of any country whose defense the President deems vital to the defense of the United States." The act gave the president the power to aid the Allied cause as he saw fit by virtually any means short of using the armed forces.

Yet Roosevelt did use the armed forces to aid the Allied cause despite the absence of any congressional sanction for acts of war. After Germany occupied Denmark in April 1941, Roosevelt ordered U.S. troops to be stationed in Greenland. Three months later, American forces occupied Iceland. Both moves were made without consulting Congress, which had forbidden the deployment of U.S. reserves and draftees outside the Western Hemisphere in the Reserves Act of 1940 and the Selective Service Act of 1941.[35] Moreover, by the summer of 1941, U.S. naval vessels under presidential orders were escorting allied convoys across the Atlantic. After the *U.S.S. Greer* exchanged shots with a German submarine on September 4, the president declared that henceforth U.S. warships providing protection to supply convoys bound for Britain would be under orders to attack Axis vessels on sight. Three months before Congress declared war, therefore, Roosevelt had maneuvered the nation into an undeclared naval war in the Atlantic.[36]

Roosevelt's "Dictatorship"

The U.S. entry into World War II was accompanied by the concentration of virtually all war powers in the president's hands. Congress delegated vast authority to the president to prosecute the war as it had during World War I, but it also acquiesced to Roosevelt's many unsanctioned appropriations of power and his broad interpretations of congressional statutes. Although Roosevelt saw the wisdom of obtaining Congress's approval for controversial actions, he was far more assertive than Wilson in using his commander-in-chief power to establish complete control over the war effort. Roosevelt created dozens of executive regulatory agencies that were not based on a specific statute, such as the Office of Emergency Management, Board of Economic Warfare, National War Labor Board, Office of Defense Transportation, and War Production Board. Anything remotely connected to the nation's war effort, including its resources and economic activity, was regulated by these war management agencies, which were responsible to the president rather than to existing departments or independent regulatory agencies. Roosevelt justified their creation by citing general delegations of power from Congress, the powers available to him under his emergency proclamations of 1939 and 1941, and his own prerogatives as commander in chief.[37]

On September 7, 1942, the president demonstrated how far he believed his war powers extended. In a speech to Congress, Roosevelt issued an ultimatum to lawmakers to repeal certain provisions contained in the Emergency Price Control Act of 1942:

> I ask the Congress to take this action by the first of October. Inaction on your part by that date will leave me with an inescapable responsibility to the people of this country to see to it that the war effort is no longer imperiled by threat of economic chaos.
>
> In the event that the Congress should fail to act, and act adequately, I shall accept the responsibility and I will act.
>
> At the same time farm prices are stabilized, wages can and will be stabilized also. This I will do.
>
> The President has the power, under the Constitution and under Congressional acts, to take measures necessary to avert a disaster which would interfere with the winning of the war. . . .
>
> I have given the most thoughtful consideration to meeting this issue without further reference to the Congress. I have determined, however, on this vital matter to consult with Congress. . . .
>
> The American people can be sure that I will use my powers with a full sense of my responsibility to the Constitution and to the country. The American people can also be sure that I shall not hesitate to use every power vested in me to accomplish the defeat of our enemies in any part of the world where our own safety demands such defeat.
>
> When the war is won, the powers under which I act automatically revert to the people—to whom they belong.[38]

With this declaration, Roosevelt claimed, according to Corwin, "the right and power to disregard a statutory provision which he does not deny, and indeed could not possibly deny, that Congress had full constitutional authority to enact, and which, therefore, he was under obligation by the Constitution to 'take care' should be 'faithfully executed.' "[39] Roosevelt was threatening to suspend the Constitution in the interest of national security if Congress did not act. Not even Abraham Lincoln during the Civil War had claimed the power to repeal a specific congressional statute. Many members of Congress were shaken by Roosevelt's ultimatum, and a few denounced it. Republican senator Robert A. Taft of Ohio called the speech "revolutionary and dangerous to the American form of government . . . an assertion that the laws of this country can be made by executive order."[40] The American public, however, supported Roosevelt's position; and with the war raging, there was little desire in Congress to engage the president in a constitutional showdown. Congress therefore amended the law to meet Roosevelt's objections.

Postwar Congressional Acquiescence

After World War II differences between the United States and the Soviet Union brought on the cold war, a state of continuous international tension that contributed to increased presidential control over national security policy. The specter of an aggressive Soviet Union pushing out wherever the West failed to resist made Congress reluctant to impose restrictions on executive action. A consensus developed that since presidents possessed both the capacity to act immediately and access to the most detailed and reliable information, they alone were suited to direct foreign and military policy. Their status as leaders of the free world and caretakers of the U.S. nuclear arsenal, the most devastating military force ever created, contributed to their unchallenged authority.

Korean War

When the North Korean army swept into South Korea on June 24, 1950, Harry S Truman believed he had to act to save South Korea and discourage further Communist aggression. The next day the United States called an emergency session of the United Nations (UN) Security

Council, which passed a resolution condemning the invasion and asking UN members to "render every assistance" to South Korea. By coincidence the Soviets were boycotting the Security Council to protest the exclusion of the new Communist government of China from the UN. Consequently, their representative was not present to veto the resolution. That evening Truman made up his mind to use air and naval forces to defend South Korea. He authorized Gen. Douglas MacArthur to evacuate Americans from South Korea, transport supplies to the South Koreans, and bomb military targets below the thirty-eighth parallel.

On June 27, Truman met with congressional leaders for the first time since the attack. Members of Congress overwhelmingly supported Truman's decision to commit U.S. forces. A few Republicans, however, protested Truman's failure to involve Congress in the decision. Influential Senate Republican Robert Taft announced on June 28 that while he agreed that U.S. forces should be used in Korea, the president had "no legal authority" to send them without the approval of Congress. Truman had indeed asked Secretary of State Dean Acheson and chairman of the Senate Foreign Relations Committee Tom Connally (D-Texas) if his armed reponse to the invasion required a declaration of war or other congressional action. Both men advised Truman that his commander-in-chief power and the UN Security Council resolution gave him ample authority to use the armed forces.

After Truman announced his intention to defend South Korea, the UN Security Council provided an additional justification for armed intervention by passing a second resolution explicitly calling on members to give military assistance to South Korea. By June 30 Truman had authorized MacArthur to use U.S. ground forces and to bomb targets in North Korea, thereby completing the U.S. commitment to defend South Korea.[41]

Truman could easily have secured a congressional resolution approving his use of military forces in Korea, but the president wished to avoid an appearance of dependence on Congress. According to Secreatary of State Acheson, Truman considered the presidency "a sacred and temporary trust, which he was determined to pass on unimpaired by the slightest loss of power or prestige."[42] Throughout American history, presidents had ordered U.S. forces to rescue Americans overseas, intervene in a foreign country, or undertake some other type of limited military mission. The Truman administration cited these precedents in justifying its unilateral actions in Korea.[43] Initially, there was reason to hope that U.S. military involvement in Korea would be short and limited, but soon the United States found itself in an undeclared war without precedent in American history. Although the president's power to use the armed forces for limited missions was unquestioned, presidential authority to commit the nation to a bloody war of undiscernible length involving hundreds of thousands of military personnel was not. By every definition the United States was waging war in Korea, regardless of the Truman administration's restrictions against the use of military force against Chinese territory and its assertions throughout the war that U.S. involvement amounted to participation in a UN "police action."[44]

Congress, however, was not quick to challenge presidential authority. During the fall of 1950, the war remained popular as UN forces were successful in driving the North Koreans up the peninsula. In November General MacArthur's forces had occupied most of North Korea and appeared close to reunifying North and South.[45] In November and December, however, Communist Chinese forces entered the war and drove UN forces back across the thirty-eighth parallel into South Korea.

With Congress already alarmed by the reversal of the war in Korea, Truman announced on December 19 that he planned to send four more divisions to Europe to bolster Allied defenses. Truman's intention to send so many troops abroad without congressional approval triggered a congressional reevaluation of U.S. defense and foreign policy that was known as the "great debate." The debate, which lasted from January to April of 1951, was principally concerned with Truman's deployment of troops to Europe, but it also addressed the issue of the president's authority to involve the nation in the Korean War. In the end the Senate passed two resolutions approving the dispatch of four divisions to Europe. One of the resolutions declared that it was the sense of the Senate that Congress should approve any future deployment of ground troops to Europe.

Truman hailed the resolutions as an endorsement of his policies. Indeed, the great debate had confirmed Congress's unwillingness to challenge the president's power to deploy U.S. forces around the world or send them into battle without congressional approval.

Truman's actions set the stage for a period of unquestioned presidential primacy in foreign and national security policy. Truman did suffer a setback in 1952 when the Supreme Court ruled that he did not have the authority to take over steel mills to prevent a strike that would damage the Korean War effort, but as historian Arthur M. Schlesinger, Jr., wrote: "By bringing the nation into war without congressional authorization and by then successfully defending his exercise of independent presidential initiative, Truman enormously expanded assumptions of presidential prerogative."[46] *(See "Sustaining the War Effort," p. 1188, in The President and the Supreme Court chapter of Part VI.)*

Joint Resolutions

The period following the Korean War was characterized by the passage of congressional resolutions granting presidents the authority to use such force as they deemed necessary to repel armed attacks or threats against designated nations or regions. Between 1955 and 1962 four joint resolutions of this type were passed. The Formosa Resolution, signed into law January 29, 1955, authorized presidents to use U.S. forces to protect Formosa and the Pescadores Islands against attack from Communist China. The Middle East Resolution, signed into law March 9, 1957, proclaimed U.S. intentions to defend Middle East countries "against any country controlled by international communism." The Cuban Resolution, signed into law October 3, 1962, authorized presidents to take whatever steps they believed necessary to defend Latin America against Cuban aggression or subversion and to oppose the deployment of Soviet weapons in Cuba capable of threatening U.S. security. The Berlin Resolution did not have the force of law but expressed the sense of Congress that the United States was determined to defend West Berlin and the access rights of the Western powers to that city.

These resolutions received wide support in Congress, although they did have critics who charged that the resolutions gave too much discretionary power to the president and absolved Congress from any responsibility for national security. Schlesinger described the extent of congressional abdication during this period:

> In the decade after Korea Congress receded not alone from the effort to control the war-making power but

almost from the effort to participate in it, except on occasions when national-security zealots on the Hill condemned the executive branch for inadequate bellicosity. Mesmerized by the supposed need for instant response to constant crisis, overawed by what the Senate Foreign Relations Committee later called "the cult of executive expertise," confused in its own mind as to what wise policy should be, delighted to relinquish responsibility, Congress readily capitulated to what Corwin at the start of the fifties had called "high-flying" theses of presidential prerogative.[47]

Vietnam War

No single president was entirely responsible for U.S. participation in the war in Vietnam. A succession of presidents gradually increased U.S. military involvement in Southeast Asia. In 1954 Vietnamese revolutionary forces defeated the French, who had controlled the region as a colonial power. President Dwight D. Eisenhower had continued the Truman administration's policy of sending aid to the French, but Eisenhower refused to intervene militarily to prevent a French defeat. After the French departed, Vietnam was temporarily partitioned with the Communist government of Ho Chi Minh ruling the North and anti-Communists in Saigon controlling the South. Eisenhower undercut reunification efforts, which he feared would result in Communist control over the entire country, by ignoring the scheduled reunification elections in 1956 and supporting the non-Communist regime in the South. The North Vietnamese and their supporters in the South launched a guerrilla war in an effort to achieve reunification through force. Although Eisenhower stepped up economic and military aid to the Saigon government, which included a small number of advisers, he avoided U.S. military involvement.

President John F. Kennedy, however, fearing the collapse of the Saigon government, responded to South Vietnamese requests for greater assistance by sending additional military advisers and counterinsurgency units to South Vietnam. Before he was assassinated, Kennedy had deployed 16,500 U.S. military personnel in Vietnam.

President Lyndon B. Johnson continued the gradual escalation of U.S. involvement in the widening war. The Gulf of Tonkin incident in August 1964 resulted in a resolution granting the president broad authority to combat North Vietnamese aggression. *(See box, Tonkin Gulf Resolution, p. 542 and "Johnson's Gulf of Tonkin Message," p. 1385, in the Appendix.)* Armed with this congressional sanction and fearing an imminent Communist takeover, Johnson ordered the first regular combat troops to Vietnam in 1965. Their mission was to defend the U.S. airbase at Danang, but soon they were conducting patrols and actively engaging the enemy in combat. Although Johnson believed his commander-in-chief powers and the Tonkin Gulf resolution gave him the authority to send the troops to Vietnam, he nevertheless wanted Congress on record as approving the move. He therefore requested a specific appropriation of $700 million for U.S. military operations in Vietnam. Within two days, both houses had passed the bill with little dissent.[48] By 1968, Johnson had increased U.S. troop strength in Vietnam to 500,000. The Communists' Tet offensive early that year, although militarily unsuccessful, caused Americans including Johnson to begin to lose confidence that the war could be won.

President Richard Nixon began slowly withdrawing U.S. forces from Vietnam in 1969. Nixon's goal was to extricate the United States from the Vietnam quagmire while achieving "peace with honor." In January 1973, the United States and North Vietnam signed a peace accord. The North Vietnamese returned U.S. prisoners of war and allowed the regime of South Vietnamese president Thieu to remain in power. In return the United States withdrew its forces from Vietnam and allowed North Vietnamese army units already in South Vietnam to remain there. Without U.S. support, however, South Vietnam was unable to defend itself against a 1975 North Vietnamese offensive that resulted in the fall of Saigon. Although President Nixon had promised Thieu that the United States would intervene if Communist forces threatened to conquer the South, Nixon had resigned the presidency in 1974, and Congress and the American public were firmly against further involvement in Southeast Asia.

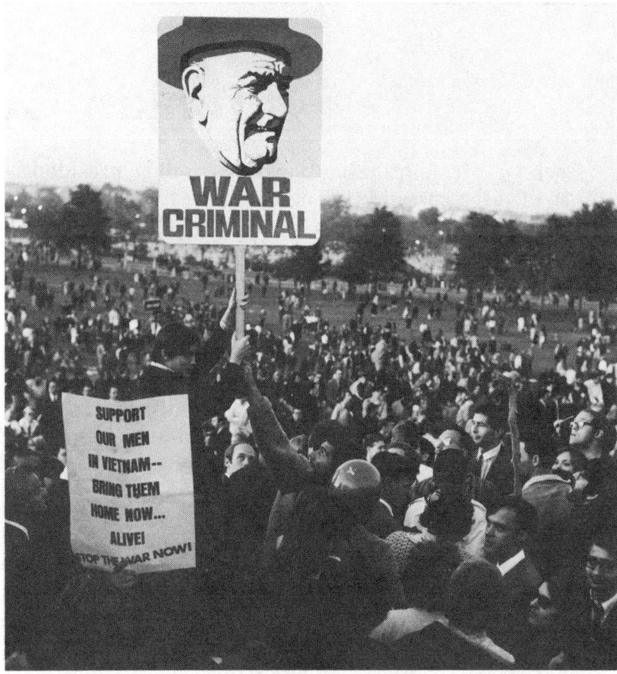

Library of Congress

American citizens protesting the Vietnam War contend that President Johnson, who ordered the first regular combat troops to Vietnam in 1965, is a "War Criminal."

The Vietnam War, like the Korean War, was a presidential war. Decision making about goals and strategy in Vietnam was dominated by the executive branch with little input from Congress. Neither Johnson nor Nixon sought congressional approval for their prosecution of the war after 1965. Nevertheless, the picture of these presidents carrying on military activities in Indochina without congressional consent often was overdrawn by critics of the war. Congress continually voted in favor of military appropriations and the draft, without which Johnson and Nixon could not have carried on the war for long. Once troops and materiel had been committed to battle, most members of Congress believed denying U.S. forces the money and reinforcements they needed to wage the war would be perceived as unpatriotic.

Congressional Resurgence

Not until 1969, when Congress recognized that the growing number of U.S. casualties in Vietnam, the fading

Tonkin Gulf Resolution

Each of the joint resolutions sanctioning presidential use of force passed by Congress between 1955 and 1962 represented a declaration of national policy upon which there was broad agreement. The supporters of these resolutions considered them to be effective tools by which Congress could create a united front behind presidential action. This was the intention of members of Congress when they voted almost unanimously in favor of the Tonkin Gulf resolution in 1964. Unlike the other resolutions, however, the Tonkin Gulf resolution revealed the dangers of congressional willingness to hand the president broad discretion in determining national security policy.

On August 2, 1964, the U.S. destroyer *Maddox*, which the navy contended was on a routine mission in the Tonkin Gulf off the coast of North Vietnam, was attacked by North Vietnamese patrol boats. Two nights later the *Maddox*, which had been joined by another destroyer, the *C. Turner Joy*, reported a second patrol boat attack. Neither ship was damaged. President Lyndon B. Johnson responded to the incidents by ordering U.S. warplanes to bomb North Vietnamese torpedo boat bases.

Johnson informed Congress that U.S. ships had been attacked and asked both houses to pass a resolution empowering him to respond to further North Vietnamese aggression. The administration depicted the incidents as unprovoked acts of belligerence. On August 7, Congress passed the Gulf of Tonkin Resolution by votes of 88-2 in the Senate and 416-0 in the House. The resolution stated that "Congress approves and supports the determination of the President, as Commander-in-Chief, to take all necessary measures to repel any armed attack against the forces of the United States and to prevent further aggression." It also declared that the United States was "prepared, as the President determines, to take all necessary steps, including the use of armed force, to assist any member or protocol state of the Southeast Asia Collective Defense Treaty requesting assistance in defense of its freedom." [1]

Members of Congress understood that the resolution would give the president great authority to prosecute the war. In the debate on the resolution, Sen. John Sherman Cooper (R-Ky.) questioned chairman of the Foreign Relations Committee J. William Fulbright (D-Ark.) on its implications:

> Cooper: In other words, we are now giving the President advance authority to take whatever action he may deem necessary? . . .
>
> Fulbright: I think that is correct.
>
> Cooper: Then, looking ahead, if the President decided that it was necessary to use such force as could lead into war, we will give that authority by this resolution?
>
> Fulbright: That is the way I would interpret it.[2]

By overwhelmingly passing the resolution, Congress was following the practice set during the previous decade of deferring to the president's judgment in national security matters in the name of expediency and unity.

This resolution has often been described as a "blank check" for presidential war making in Southeast Asia. Members of the Johnson administration and the president himself frequently cited the resolution as evidence of congressional authorization of their policies in Vietnam. Although the resolution in combination with U.S. membership in the Southeast Asia Treaty Organization may not have been the "functional equivalent" of a declaration of war, as Under Secretary of State Nicholas Katzenbach had claimed in 1967 during testimony before the Senate Foreign Relations Committee, it did provide a justification for almost any presidential military decision in Vietnam.

Investigations by the Senate Foreign Relations Committee in 1968 revealed that the *Maddox* was actually gathering sensitive intelligence within the territorial waters claimed by the North Vietnamese and that a South Vietnamese naval attack against North Vietnam was taking place near the time and place of the *Maddox* patrol. Furthermore, the investigations showed that the administration anticipated the North Vietnamese attacks. U.S. intelligence had warned that the North Vietnamese navy was under orders to respond to U.S. vessels in the vicinity of the South Vietnamese operation as if they were part of that operation, and U.S. ships had been moved to reinforce the *Maddox* before it was attacked.[3]

The Johnson administration had deceived Congress. Not only had the president permitted the ships to be sent into a situation where they were likely to be attacked, when the attack did occur, he maintained that it was a completely unprovoked act against an American ship on a routine mission in international waters. In addition, although the crews of the *Maddox* and *Turner Joy* did fire at what they believed were enemy vessels, evidence suggested that the second attack may have been the product of nervousness and poor visibility. In 1965, Johnson remarked on the second attack, "For all I know, our Navy was shooting at whales out there." [4] Nevertheless, the second attack was presented to Congress as completely factual.

The 1968 revelations about the Tonkin Gulf incidents and growing congressional discontent with the war led to the repeal of the Tonkin Gulf resolution on December 31, 1970. The repeal provision was added to a foreign military sales bill, which was signed by President Richard Nixon on January 12, 1971. The measure was largely symbolic and had no effect on the continuing prosecution of the war by the Nixon administration, which claimed that the president's commander-in-chief power gave him the authority to carry on the war.

1. Cecil V. Crabb, Jr., and Pat M. Holt, *Invitation to Struggle: Congress, the President and Foreign Policy,* 2d ed. (Washington. D.C.: CQ Press, 1984), 141.
2. Leslie H. Gelb with Richard K. Betts, *The Irony of Vietnam: The System Worked* (Washington, D.C.: Brookings, 1979), 103.
3. Richard M. Pious, *The American Presidency* (New York: Basic Books, 1979), 387.
4. Gelb, *The Irony of Vietnam,* 104.

prospects that the war could be won, and doubts about the morality of U.S. involvement had begun to turn the American public against the war did Congress begin to assert its war powers. In that year the Senate passed the National Commitments Resolution, which stated that a national commitment "results only from affirmative action taken by the legislative and executive branches ... by means of a treaty, statute, or concurrent resolution of both houses of Congress specifically providing for such commitment." Although the resolution only expressed the sense of the Senate and had no force of law, it represented Congress's growing dissatisfaction with its exclusion from national security and foreign policy decisions. Later in the year Congress adopted an amendment supported by President Nixon prohibiting the use of U.S. ground forces in Laos and Thailand. For the first time in three decades, Congress had exercised its authority to limit military activities overseas.[49]

In 1970, even as U.S. forces were being withdrawn from Southeast Asia, President Nixon secretly ordered U.S. forces into Cambodia to attack Communist sanctuaries. When Nixon announced the operation on April 30, 1970, college campuses around the United States erupted in protest against the expansion of the war. Four student demonstrators were killed by National Guard troops at Kent State University in Ohio, and 60,000 to 100,000 protestors marched on Washington. After months of debate, a lame-duck Congress passed an amendment in December 1970 barring the use of U.S. ground forces in Cambodia. This amendment did not lead to a confrontation with the Nixon administration since lawmakers had backed away from prohibiting the use of aircraft over Cambodia and Nixon had withdrawn U.S. ground troops from Cambodia months before the amendment passed. Nevertheless, Congress would not have passed such an amendment several years earlier. Later in December, Congress also repealed the Tonkin Gulf Resolution.

During the early 1970s momentum for legislation that would restore Congress's role in the foreign policy process continued to build in Congress. President Nixon undertook a series of controversial military actions without consulting Congress that underscored the legislative branch's inability to affect policy. He provided air support for South Vietnam's 1971 invasion of Laos, ordered North Vietnam's Haiphong harbor mined in May 1972, and launched massive bombing raids against North Vietnam in December 1972. Furthermore, Nixon's "secret" war in Cambodia in 1970, the publication of the Pentagon Papers in 1971 (which disclosed the deception of the executive branch during the 1960s), and the revelations about secret national security commitments uncovered by a Senate Foreign Relations subcommittee chaired by Stuart Symington (D-Miss.) contributed to the growing perception of lawmakers that executive branch secrecy was out of control. After three years of work and debate, Congress's attempts to construct a bill that would reestablish its foreign policy and national security powers culminated in the passage of the War Powers Act in 1973.

War Powers Act

Implicit in the passage of the War Powers Act (HJ Res. 542, PL 93-148) in November 1973 over President Nixon's veto was an admission by Congress that it had contributed to the debacle in Vietnam by abdicating its war-making responsibilities to the executive branch. The passage of the Tonkin Gulf resolution with only two senators dissenting and Congress's acquiescence to presidential budget and troop requests allowed the Kennedy, Johnson, and Nixon administrations to pursue a costly war that in retrospect had limited strategic significance and questionable chances for success. The results of the Vietnam War had belied the assumption that the executive branch with its superior intelligence resources, its unity of command, and its ability to act quickly should be responsible for determining when and how the nation should go to war. With the passage of the War Powers Act Congress attempted to ensure that it would have a decision-making role on matters of war and peace. The bill's preamble stated that its purpose was:

> To fulfill the intent of the framers of the Constitution of the United States and ensure that the collective judgement of both the Congress and the President will apply to the introduction of U.S. armed forces into hostilities, wherein situations where imminent involvement in hostilities is clearly indicated by the circumstances, and the continued use of such forces in hostilities or in such situations.

The most important and controversial provisions of the legislation outlined the situations under which presidents could commit troops, permitted Congress at any time by concurrent resolution to order the president to disengage troops involved in an undeclared war, and required presidents to withdraw armed forces from a conflict within sixty days—ninety if the president certified that further military action was necessary to disengage U.S. military personnel from a conflict safely—unless Congress specifically authorized its continuation. *(See box, War Powers Provisions, p. 544.)* Other provisions included in the act obligated presidents to report to Congress within forty-eight hours on large troop movements abroad and urged them to consult with Congress "in every possible instance" before ordering U.S. forces into hostilities or a situation where hostilities might be imminent.

Passage of the bill was heralded by its supporters as a major step in reasserting Congress's war-making powers. Republican senator Jacob K. Javits of New York, a chief architect of the Senate version of the legislation declared:

> With the war powers resolution's passage, after 200 years, at least something will have been done about codifying the implementation of the most awesome power in the possession of any sovereignty and giving the broad representation of the people in Congress a voice in it. This is critically important, for we have just learned the hard lesson that wars cannot be successfully fought except with the consent of the people and with their support.[50]

In President Nixon's October 24, 1973, veto message of the war powers bill, he stated that the resolution would impose restrictions on the authority of the president that would be "both unconstitutional and dangerous to the best interests of the nation." [51] Nixon's attempted veto of the legislation was supported by some conservatives in both houses and a small group of liberals who agreed that the measure was unconstitutional, but for different reasons.

The leading liberal opponent of the resolution's final form, Democratic senator Thomas F. Eagleton of Missouri, called the the act "the most dangerous piece of legislation" he had seen in his five years in the Senate.[52] Eagleton and other liberal critics of the War Powers Act charged that while it may force the president to deal with Congress within ninety days after troops are committed, it sanctions

War Powers Provisions

The 1973 War Powers Resolution:

~ stated that the president could commit U.S. armed forces to hostilities or situations where hostilities might be imminent only pursuant to a declaration of war, specific statutory authorization or a national emergency created by an attack upon the United States, its territories or possessions, or its armed forces

~ urged the president "in every possible instance" to consult with Congress before committing U.S. forces to hostilities or to situations where hostilities might be imminent, and to consult Congress regularly after such a commitment

~ required the president to report in writing within forty-eight hours to the Speaker of the House and president pro tempore of the Senate on any commitment or substantial enlargement of U.S. combat forces abroad, except for deployments related solely to supply, replacement, repair or training; required supplementary reports at least every six months while such forces were being engaged

~ authorized the Speaker of the House and the president pro tempore of the Senate to reconvene Congress if it were not in session to consider the president's report

~ required the termination of a troop commitment within sixty days after the president's initial report was submitted, unless Congress declared war, specifically authorized continuation of the commitment, or was physically unable to convene as a result of an armed attack upon the United States; allowed the sixty-day period to be extended for up to thirty days if the president determined and certified to Congress that unavoidable military necessity respecting the safety of U.S. forces required their continued use in bringing about a prompt disengagement

~ allowed Congress at any time U.S. forces were engaged in hostilities without a declaration of war or specific congressional authorization by concurrent resolution to direct the president to disengage such troops

~ set up congressional procedures for consideration of any resolution or bill introduced pursuant to the provisions of the resolution

~ provided that if any provision of the resolution was declared invalid, the remainder of the resolution would not be affected

virtually any use of the military by the president during those ninety days. Eagleton believed that an act that recognized unlimited presidential authority to commit forces to a conflict would enhance rather than restrict presidential war-making power. He warned: "By failing to define the president's powers in legally binding language, the bill provided a legal basis for the president's broad claims of inherent power to initiate a war. Under the formula, Congress would not participate in the warmaking decision until *after* forces had been committed to battle." [53] Although the resolution gave Congress the power to withdraw troops from a conflict, Eagleton believed Congress would rarely have the political will to do so, since such action would be seen by many constituents as unpatriotic or lacking in resolve.

On November 7, the House overrode the president's veto with a vote of 284-135—only four votes over the required two-thirds majority. Later in the day the Senate followed with a 75-18 override vote. The congressional override was made possible, in part, by the Watergate scandal, which had weakened Nixon's support among legislators of his own party.

Presidential Compliance

Since the passage of the War Powers Act, presidents have used military force on a number of occasions. Several of these actions, such as President Gerald R. Ford's evacuation of Saigon, Danang, and Phnom Penh in 1975, were uncontroversial and received the general approval of Congress. In most of the military operations undertaken since 1973, however, presidents have violated the letter or at least the spirit of the law. Presidents Gerald Ford, Jimmy Carter, and Ronald Reagan seldom consulted Congress before using the military, and efforts by Congress to force these presidents to start the sixty-day war powers clock were usually ignored. These operations have underscored the act's inability to control presidential war making in the absence of Congress's determination to assert its authority. They also have demonstrated the president's unrestrained prerogative to use military force during the initial sixty-day period allowed by the act.

Mayaguez Incident

The first major test of the War Powers Act occurred on May 12, 1975, when Cambodian Communist gunboats seized the U.S. merchant ship *Mayaguez* and its crew of thirty-nine off the disputed island of Poulo Wai in the Gulf of Siam. President Ford unilaterally ordered U.S. forces to free the sailors and their ship and to bomb Cambodian targets in retaliation. The rescue attempt succeeded in freeing the *Mayaguez* and its crew but resulted in the deaths of forty-one marines.

In this case, there was general agreement that the president had the authority to commit U.S. troops without receiving congressional authorization. Although Ford complied with the war powers provision that required him to report to Congress within forty-eight hours, some legislators complained that his consultations with selected members of Congress after the order to attack had been issued were inadequate and did not provide an opportunity for meaningful congressional involvement.

Ford, however, defended his decision not to consult with Congress before the operation in his report to that body. He argued: "When a crisis breaks out, it is impossible to draw the Congress in with the decision-making process in an effective way." Ford went on to criticize the resolution itself as "a very serious intrusion on the responsibilities of the President as Commander-in-Chief and the person who formulates and ought to execute foreign policy." [54]

Iran Hostage Rescue Attempt

In April 1980, President Carter sent U.S. forces into Iran in an attempt to rescue forty-nine American embassy personnel held hostage in Tehran. The president ordered the action without any prior consultations with members of Congress except a guarded reference made to Senate Majority Leader Robert Byrd (D-W.Va.) about the rescue attempt the day before it occurred. Equipment failure forced the mission to be aborted after eight commandoes died in a helicopter crash.

Carter justified his decision not to consult with Congress by citing the mission's dependence on secrecy. Many members of Congress agreed with Carter's assertion of the need for absolute secrecy. Sen. John Glenn (D-Ohio) remarked, "If I were on that raid, I wouldn't want it all over Capitol Hill." [55] Carter also maintained that the mission was a "humanitarian" rescue attempt rather than a military action against an enemy nation and therefore fell outside the scope of the act.[56]

Lebanon

In 1982 President Reagan sent U.S. troops to Lebanon as part of a multinational peace-keeping force. Marines initially were introduced into that country on August 24, 1982, with the specific mission of observing the evacuation of Palestine Liberation Organization (PLO) forces from Beirut under an agreement mediated by the United States. The marines left Beirut on September 10, after the PLO withdrawal had been completed. Before this operation, the president held constructive consultations with the foreign relations committees of both houses.[57] Reagan had reported to Congress on the deployment of marines the day before it took place. He nevertheless would not concede the validity of the War Powers Act and stated only that he was reporting to Congress "consistent" with the resolution rather than "under" it.[58]

After the assassination of President Bashir Gemayel of Lebanon on September 14, 1982, and the massacre of Palestinians at the Sabra and Shatila refugee camps by Lebanese Christian militia on September 16, President Reagan ordered twelve hundred U.S. Marines to return to Lebanon. The mission of the peace-keeping force, which arrived on September 29, was to join with Italian, French, and British forces in providing a buffer between warring factions, thereby improving stability in Lebanon and the Middle East in general.

Congress debated whether the marines were in a situation where hostilities were "imminent," but it did not demand that the War Powers clock be started. By the end of the summer of 1983, the marines had become targets of terrorist groups and other combatants in the region. On August 29, 1983, U.S. forces sustained their first casualties. President Reagan authorized the marines to fight back from their positions to defend themselves. On September 8, the president increased U.S. involvement in the conflict by ordering warships in the Mediterranean to shell positions in the hills outside of Beirut from which the marines had been receiving hostile fire.

The obvious escalation of U.S. involvement in Lebanon forced the president to negotiate with Congress on terms for keeping the marines there. On October 12, President Reagan signed a joint resolution empowering him to keep the marines in Lebanon for eighteen months. The compromise resolution stated that the marines had been in a situation of imminent hostilities, since August 29, 1983, and that this legislation was "the necessary specific statutory authorization under the War Powers Resolution for continued participation by United States Armed Forces in the Multinational Force in Lebanon." President Reagan had conceded that the War Powers Act was applicable and agreed to a time limitation that had little possibility of forcing a withdrawal. In return Congress sanctioned his policies in Lebanon. Despite this congressional involvement, the compromise favored the president and demonstrated Congress's reluctance to use the War Powers Act to restrict presidential use of the military.[59]

On October 23, 1983, the suicide terrorist bombing of the marine headquarters in Lebanon killed 241 Americans and weakened public support for the deployment of U.S. troops there. During the winter the chaotic situation in Lebanon failed to stabilize, and the president ordered the marines to withdraw on February 7, 1984.

Grenada

On October 25, 1983, nineteen hundred U.S. troops under President Reagan's orders invaded the small Caribbean island of Grenada. The action, which Reagan referred to as a "rescue mission" was undertaken to overthrow Grenada's pro-Cuban, Marxist government, to restore order to the island, and to ensure the safety of approximately one thousand American citizens living there, most of whom were medical students. U.S. forces were joined by troops from six Caribbean nations belonging to the Organization of East Caribbean States, which had officially asked the United States to intervene.

Both houses of Congress overwhelmingly voted that the sixty-day clock of the War Powers Resolution had begun when U.S. troops invaded Grenada. The United States declared an end to the fighting on November 2, after U.S. troops had evacuated the medical students, overcome light resistance, and secured the island.[60]

Because U.S. troops had quickly achieved their objectives while sustaining few casualties, and the invasion was very popular among the U.S. public, Congress generally supported the Grenada action. The president, however, was sharply criticized by many members of Congress for failing to consult with them meaningfully before the invasion. Reagan had briefed selected congressional leaders about the mission on the evening of October 24, but this briefing was called merely to inform them that troops had already begun their voyage to Grenada. Sen. Charles McC. Mathias (D-Md.) observed after the invasion that the British prime minister was informed of the invasion before top congressional leaders.[61]

Libyan Bombing Raids

On April 14, 1986, President Reagan ordered U.S. warplanes to bomb targets in the Libyan cities of Tripoli and Benghazi. The surprise coordinated air strike resulted in the deaths of two U.S. fliers and, according to the Libyan government, dozens of Libyan military personnel and civilians. The attack was in response to the alleged involvement of Libyan leader Col. Muammar Qaddafi in recent terrorist acts. The operation received broad support from members of Congress of both parties.

Many prominent lawmakers, however, again criticized President Reagan's method of consulting with Congress. Reagan informed twelve congressional leaders of the attack on April 14 when the planes were halfway to their targets. Senate Minority Leader Robert Byrd complained that the meeting amounted to "notification" rather than consultation. Senate Foreign Relations Committee chairman Richard G. Lugar (R-Ind.) disputed Byrd's interpretation, saying the president indicated he would call off the mission if it met with strong congressional objections.[62]

The Libyan bombing highlighted the issue of presidential compliance with the consulting provision of the War Powers Act in cases where the president orders a military strike against terrorists or a nation known to support them. Two approaches to this issue surfaced in Congress in 1986. One advocated early presidential consultation with a designated body of lawmakers before the president ordered a military strike against terrorists. The other sought to exempt counterterrorist military operations from the usual consultation procedures required by the War Powers Act. Neither approach has yet been enacted into law.

Persian Gulf Naval Escorts

Since the war between Iran and Iraq began in 1980, the United States had avoided becoming involved in the conflict. By 1987, however, Iranian attacks on neutral ships threatened to slow the flow of Arab oil through the Persian Gulf. Because Kuwait, a small Persian Gulf state with large oil reserves, supported Iraq in the gulf war, its ships had become a favorite target of Iranian gunboats. In response to Kuwaiti pleas for assistance, President Reagan offered on March 10, 1987, to place tankers owned by Kuwait under the U.S. flag so they could be escorted through the gulf by U.S. warships. The administration's offer to escort the Kuwaiti tankers was intended to ensure the flow of oil through the gulf and to prevent the Soviet Union, which Kuwait also had asked for help, from increasing its influence among moderate Arab nations and its naval presence in the gulf.[63]

On May 17, before the escort operation had begun, the U.S.S. *Stark* was mistakenly attacked by an Iraqi warplane. The ship was struck by a missile that killed thirty-seven crew members. The attack prompted Congress to ask the Reagan administration for a report detailing the risks and objectives of its Persian Gulf policy. Many members of Congress pressed the administration to delay the reflagging operation, but no binding legislation was passed.

On July 24, two days after the escort missions began, a reflagged Kuwaiti tanker was damaged by an Iranian mine. Critics of the administration's Persian Gulf strategy pointed to the incident as evidence that the naval escorts could involve the United States in the gulf war, and many lawmakers called on the president to invoke the War Powers Act. The Reagan administration refused, however, to acknowledge that the escort missions placed U.S. forces into hostilities or an area of imminent hostilities. Several Democratic members of Congress responded by filing suit to force the president to invoke the War Powers Act. In December 1987, a U.S. district court judge dismissed the suit as a political issue that should be settled by the executive and legislative branches.[64]

Legal Questions

The failure of the War Powers Act substantially to change presidential war-making prerogatives is partly due to its questionable constitutionality. Many of its critics and even a few of its supporters have expressed doubts that all of its provisions would stand up to judicial review. President Nixon denounced the war powers bill as unconstitutional when he vetoed it in 1973. The major provisions of the bill, he contended, would "purport to take away, by a mere legislative act, authorities which the president has properly exercised under the Constitution for almost 200 years." They were unconstitutional, he asserted, because "the only way in which the constitutional powers of a branch of the government can be altered is by amending the Constitution—and any attempt to make such alterations by legislation alone is clearly without force." [65]

President Reagan also stated his reservations about the constitutionality of the War Powers Act in 1983 when he signed the resolution that contained the compromise on U.S. military action in Lebanon. He wrote:

> I do not and cannot cede any of the authority vested in me under the Constitution as President and as Commander-in-Chief of the United States Armed Forces. Nor should my signing be viewed as any acknowledgement that the President's constitutional authority can be impermissibly infringed by statute, that congressional authorization would be required if and when the period specified in . . . the War Powers Resolution might be deemed to have been triggered and the period had expired, or that [the 18-month authorization] may be interpreted to revise the President's constitutional authority to deploy United States Armed Forces.[66]

Neither the executive branch nor a majority of members of Congress has appeared anxious to let the Supreme Court decide if the War Powers Act is an unconstitutional legislative intrusion into the commander-in-chief powers of the president. Both branches undoubtedly have preferred to avoid a constitutional clash that could divide the government. It is also likely, however, that both branches have believed they have more to lose than win from such a confrontation. On the one hand, since presidents have been able to ignore the most potent provisions of the War Powers Act, they have had little incentive to seek a decision on the issue in court that might force them to comply more strictly with its provisions. On the other hand, although a Supreme Court ruling that supported the constitutionality of the act would be a major victory for Congress, a decision striking it down would further strengthen the president's authority to use the armed forces. Such a decision would deprive lawmakers of any leverage provided by their threats to invoke the act and would symbolically weaken Congress's claim to a place in the national security decision-making process. In addition, Congress may have been dissuaded from mounting a legal challenge to presidential war making by the Supreme Court's historic tendency to favor the presidency on matters of foreign policy and national security.

Orlando v. Laird and Berk v. Laird

Two 1970 cases tried before district court judges, *Orlando v. Laird* and *Berk v. Laird*, addressed the question of whether the Vietnam War was illegal because Congress had not issued a declaration of war. In independent verdicts two judges ruled that congressional actions short of a formal declaration of war sanctioned U.S. participation in the conflict. The judges cited Congress's continued passage of military appropriations bills to fund the war and its renewal of the Selective Service Act as evidence of congressional support for the war.[67] Indeed, at any time Congress could have withdrawn its support by stopping the draft and refusing to appropriate funds for the war, thereby forcing the executive branch to pull troops out of Vietnam. The rulings did not deny any power to the legislative branch or justify the war on the grounds that presidents possessed inherent authority to use military force whenever they believed it to be in the best interest of the United States. Yet the rulings did indicate that if Congress collaborated with the executive branch in the pursuit of a war through appropriations or other measures, it must be considered to have sanctioned U.S. participation, with or without a declaration of war.

In response to these rulings and the Johnson administration's use of the Tonkin Gulf resolution to justify its expansion of the Vietnam War, Congress included a provision in the War Powers Act denying that a president could infer a congressional sanction for the introduction of troops into hostilities or potentially hostile situations "from any provision of law . . . including any provision contained in any appropriation Act, unless such provision specifically authorizes the introduction of United States Armed Forces into hostilities or into such situations and states that it is intended to constitute specific statutory authorization within the meaning of this resolution." The provision went on to deny the president the authority to infer congressional sanction for presidential war making from a ratified treaty. Thus Congress attempted to restrict to declarations of war and other explicit sanctions of military actions the means through which Congress could be said to have approved presidential war making. Regardless of this provision, however, it is unclear whether the courts would declare a president's use of force illegal on the grounds that Congress had not approved the conflict, if lawmakers had passed specific appropriations bills to pay for military operations as it did during the Vietnam War.

The Chadha Decision

In 1983 the Supreme Court's decision on a case unrelated to the War Powers Act struck down at least one provision of the legislation. The Court ruled 7-2 in *Immigration and Naturalization Service v. Chadha* that legislative vetoes over presidential policy are unconstitutional because they circumvent the president's constitutionally granted executive and veto powers. Legislative vetoes are provisions of laws that give Congress the power to review and rescind executive actions. They had been used by Congress for over fifty years primarily to maintain some control over executive implementation of congressional regulations. Writing for the majority, Chief Justice Warren Burger emphasized, "The hydraulic pressure inherent within each of the separate branches to exceed the outer limits of its power, even to accomplish desirable objectives, must be resisted." [68]

The ruling affected the War Powers Act because that legislation empowered Congress to compel the president to withdraw U.S. forces engaged in hostilities by passing a concurrent resolution. Such a concurrent resolution constitutes a legislative veto over executive action.[69] In addition, the *Chadha* decision casts doubt on the legality of the War Powers provision that requires automatic termination of a military action after sixty or ninety days in the absence of congressional approval. If Congress cannot stop U.S. military involvement in hostilities by a concurrent resolution, it is questionable whether those hostilities could be stopped automatically without any specific congressional action.

The *Chadha* ruling did not affect the reporting and consultation provisions of the War Powers Act or the provision delineating the types of situations under which the president could use the armed forces. Presidents have not, however, considered themselves bound by the latter provision. Independent of *Chadha* they have questioned its constitutionality on the grounds that it places unreasonable restrictions on the president's freedom to defend the nation.[70]

Effect of the War Powers Act

During hearings on the war powers legislation on April 23, 1971, Sen. Barry Goldwater (R-Ariz.) warned a House Foreign Affairs subcommittee:

> The war powers bill is not the correct way to tackle this issue. To my mind, the bill is improper, unwise, and perhaps illegal. It would leave the United States helpless to prevent the annihilation of Israel. It would emasculate NATO. It would unwittingly allow a militant Congress to initiate a nuclear holocaust. And it may incite one of the gravest constitutional crises in American history.[71]

The passage of the war powers bill has not resulted in the dire consequences that Senator Goldwater feared. Although different interpretations of how and when the act should be implemented have at times divided the executive and legislative branches, the act has not proven to be an unreasonable hindrance on the president's ability to protect the United States and its allies.

Since the passage of the War Powers Act in 1973, neither congressional action nor the automatic sixty- to ninety-day time limit has forced a president to disengage U.S. troops from a conflict. Moreover, presidents have appeared undaunted by the act's potential to limit their use of American armed forces. Only once—during President Reagan's deployment of Marines in Lebanon in 1982 and 1983—did the prospect of the invocation of the War Powers Act result in a formal compromise between the legislative and executive branches on the limits of a military operation. Even in this case, the compromise favored the president, and it had little effect on his eventual decision to withdraw the troops. The War Powers Act has remained a potentially powerful congressional tool that for better or worse lawmakers have been unwilling or unable to use.

Nevertheless, world events have never provided a major test for the War Powers Act. It was a product of the Vietnam War, and legislators hoped above all that it would help them prevent a future president from waging another protracted conventional war without congressional approval. The painful experience of Vietnam, however, has created a lingering national aversion to military actions that have the potential to develop into long-term conflicts and to cost the lives of thousands of U.S. military personnel. Presidents have been able to initiate small-scale military operations, usually of short duration, without being seriously challenged by Congress or the public, but every post-Vietnam president has carefully avoided any appearance that the United States might be slipping into a war reminiscent of Vietnam. Even conservative public officials and members of Congress who have argued for a more activist policy against "international Communism" have rarely advocated the use of U.S. forces except for limited missions and the defense of vital, widely agreed upon U.S. interests. Thus, the War Powers Act has never been called into service against the type of presidential war that lead to its passage. Still, one cannot infer from its history that it will never be used by Congress to restrict the deployment of military forces by a future president.

The years since the passage of the War Powers Act have shown that it cannot be a substitute for congressional resolve. Presidents have demonstrated that they will not be automatically restrained by the act if they believe the use of American forces is in the best interest of the United States. Thus, the War Powers Act alone has not and will not reestablish Congress as the branch that decides when to go to war. Like the legislature's power to cut off funding for a particular military action, the effectiveness of the act depends upon the collective will of Congress to challenge presidential leadership. If this collective will exists, Congress has ample means to check the president's war-making power and to expand its role in deciding when and how military force should be used.

President as Military Commander

The commander-in-chief clause gives presidents clear authority to command the military as the nation's first general and admiral. They possess all decision-making powers accorded any supreme military commander under international law. Presidents not only order troops into battle, they are expected to approve major strategic decisions and keep a watchful eye on the progress of any military campaign. Most presidents since World War II have even regarded specific tactical decisions related to certain military operations to be among their commander-in-chief responsibilities.

In making the president the commander in chief the Framers attempted to ensure that civilian authority would always direct the armed forces. Military leaders who might use their authority over the army and navy to accumulate political power or enhance their personal reputation would be subordinate to the president who was elected by the entire country and was responsible for the welfare and security of all the people. Designating the president as commander in chief also aided effective military leadership by establishing a single leader at the top of the military hierarchy who was recognized by all as being the legitimate and indisputable supreme military commander.

Military experience has been common among presidents. Although some presidents who have led the nation during wartime, such as James Madison and Woodrow Wilson, had no military experience, twenty-six of forty chief executives served in the military. A remarkably high number of these were high-ranking officers. Twelve served as generals, and six of these twelve—George Washington, Andrew Jackson, William Harrison, Zachary Taylor, Ulysses S. Grant, and Dwight Eisenhower—attained at least the rank of major general.[72] Three presidents—Grant, Eisenhower, and Carter—graduated from a military academy. Franklin Roosevelt, another wartime president who never entered the military, gained defense-related experience as assistant secretary of the navy. Although few presidents could be classified as military experts, as a group they possessed more knowledge of military affairs than they did of many other policy areas.

Presidential Direction of Military Operations

The degree to which presidents have become involved in the direction of military operations has varied according

Dwight D. Eisenhower Library

Eisenhower was one of twelve generals who served as president. On D-Day—June 6, 1944—he personally encouraged American paratroopers of the 101st Airborne Division before their drop into France as the vanguard of the invasion.

Alexander Gardner; Library of Congress

During the early stages of the Civil War, Abraham Lincoln became deeply involved in battlefield strategy. He occasionally issued direct orders to his generals regarding their troop movements and frequently conferred with them at the front.

to their own military expertise and the circumstances of the military situation. Once troops have been committed to battle, presidents have usually delegated authority for battlefield stategy to their generals and admirals. The Constitution, however, does not prohibit a president from taking direct command of troops in the field. Several delegates to the Constitutional Convention suggested that the president should be prohibited from taking personal command of troops, but the Convention rejected these proposals.[73]

George Washington was regarded as his nation's greatest general, and neither Congress nor the American public would have thought it wrong for him to have led U.S. troops into battle while he was president. In 1794 Washington came close to doing just that when he personally supervised the organization of the militia charged with putting down the Whiskey Rebellion.[74] In 1799 when an undeclared naval war with France threatened to spread to the North American continent, John Adams delegated his authority as commander in chief to George Washington. Adams, who recognized his own lack of military experience and the advantages of enabling the country to rally around a national legend if war came, asked Washington to accept the post of "Lieutenant General and Commander-in-Chief of all the armies raised or to be raised in the United States." Washington agreed on the condition that he would not have to take command of the army unless "it became indispensable by the urgency of circumstances." War with France remained confined to the high seas, and Washington never had to leave his retirement at Mount Vernon to assume active command of U.S. forces.[75]

The poor performance of Union generals during the early stages of the Civil War and the proximity of the fighting to Washington, D.C., caused Abraham Lincoln to become deeply involved in battlefield strategy. He occasionally issued direct orders to his generals regarding their troop movements and frequently conferred with them at the front. Although Lincoln's interference in purely military matters has been criticized by some historians and applauded by others, he did allow his generals broad discretion in their implementation of his orders. After Lincoln had given command of the army to General Grant, in whom he had confidence, the president ceased to involve himself in tactical decisions.[76]

President Wilson, like John Adams, recognized his own lack of military experience and delegated responsibility for strategy and tactics to military leaders. Moreover, the distance between the president and the fighting made personal leadership impractical. He confined his commander-in-chief role during World War I to the domestic war effort and broad military decisions, such as his rejection of a French and British proposal in 1918 to have the U.S. open a major front in Russia to prevent the Germans from transferring troops to the West after the Russians had negotiated a separate peace with Germany.[77]

World War II created conditions that necessitated involvement of the president in strategic decisions. Because the war effort against Germany and Japan depended on the concerted action of the United States, Great Britain, the Soviet Union, and other nations, Allied strategy had to be determined through negotiations between the top leaders of each country. As a result, decisions such as when to launch the invasion of Europe and where to concentrate U.S. forces were decisions that presidents Roosevelt and Truman had to make not just because they were the commander in chief, but also because they were the nation's chief diplomat.

The tendency of presidents to become involved in planning the details of military actions increased with the advent of the nuclear age. Nuclear weapons created an environment of constant danger where any use of U.S. armed forces could escalate into a global nuclear confrontation. Consequently, modern presidents have seldom been willing to order a military operation without personally overseeing its execution. Perhaps the most extreme example of presidential involvement in planning military operations in the nuclear era was Lyndon Johnson's participation in the selection of specific bombing targets in North Vietnam.[78]

Governing Conquered Territory

On many occasions U.S. military forces have occupied enemy territory during hostilities. Presidential authority to administer a recently occupied territory through the armed forces is nearly absolute. Neither the Constitution of the United States nor the former laws of a conquered nation constrain the president. Several hundred Supreme Court cases have upheld the president's authority to function as a dictator over occupied territory subject only to the "laws of war." [1] Presidents and their appointed military representatives may set up new government institutions, make laws by decree, establish a court system, collect taxes, or do anything else they believe necessary to administer the conquered area.

Presidential rule over occupied territory lasts until it is annexed to the United States or a treaty is concluded that transfers power back to a local government. The president may not, however, unilaterally annex acquired territory. Article IV of the Constitution grants Congress the power to "dispose of and make all needful Rules and Regulations respecting the Territory or other Property belonging to the United States." Therefore, Congress must approve a treaty of cession or pass legislation annexing the territory before it can become part of the United States.[2]

1. Clinton Rossiter, *The Supreme Court and the Commander in Chief* (Ithaca, N.Y.: Cornell University Press, 1976), 122-123.
2. Joseph E. Kallenbach, *The American Chief Executive: The Presidency and the Governorship* (New York: Harper and Row, 1966), 541.

Sophisticated communication technologies also have contributed to presidential involvement in military operations by making contact between the president and local military commanders possible. For example, in April 1988, the pilot of a navy aircraft patrolling the Persian Gulf observed Iranian gunboats attacking a set of oil rigs. Because U.S. forces in the Persian Gulf were authorized to respond to attacks only on American aircraft, ships, and facilities, the pilot radioed his aircraft carrier for permission to attack the Iranian vessels. The pilot's request was transmitted up the chain of command from the aircraft carrier commander to the admiral in charge of the naval task force. Then the request was relayed via satellite through the chief of the U.S. Central Command in Florida to the chairman of the Joint Chiefs of Staff and the secretary of defense at the Pentagon who called President Reagan. The president authorized U.S. planes to bomb the Iranian gunboats, and the order was relayed back through the chain of command to navy pilots who moved to attack only three minutes after permission had been requested.[79]

Command of Nuclear Weapons

Despite the absurdity of a modern president ever leading U.S. troops into battle, the realities of nuclear warfare have made the president the nation's "first soldier." The decision to use nuclear weapons or to delegate the authority to use them to local military commanders is entirely the president's. Presidential authority over the nation's nuclear arsenal is derived from the commander-in-chief power and the necessity of making the decision to use nuclear weapons with speed and secrecy. If the Soviet Union were to launch an attack on the United States from their nuclear missile submarines, the president would have no more than ten to twelve minutes to receive positive verification of the attack, decide how to respond, and transmit orders to the military commanders in charge of U.S. nuclear forces. Even if the attack were launched from missile silos in the Soviet Union, the president would have little more than twenty to thirty minutes between the launch of the missiles and their impact.[80] A decision that has to be made this quickly must be assigned to a single individual with indisputable authority. The nature of nuclear weapons, therefore, necessitates presidential control over them.

Theoretically, a first-strike nuclear attack by the United States against another nation would be illegal without a congressional declaration of war, since such an attack would be an initiation of hostilities on an unprecedented scale. Few observers, however, believe there is a significant chance that a U.S. president would purposely order a nuclear strike unless the United States, U.S. forces, or close U.S. allies were under a nuclear or massive conventional attack. Consequently, most scenarios for the use of nuclear weapons by the president without congressional approval can be justified on the grounds that the president is responsible for repelling attacks and defending the United States. Even a presidential order to launch nuclear weapons to preempt a nuclear attack perceived as imminent could probably be justified under the president's power to defend the country, although the ensuing nuclear war would likely diminish the significance of any legal debate.

Regardless of the nuclear decision-making role to which Congress might be entitled under a strict interpretation of the Constitution, the demands of secrecy and speed that accompany crisis decision making in the nuclear age disqualify Congress from taking part in decisions to use nuclear weapons, except through their consultations in advance of potential crises. No president could tentatively make the decision to launch nuclear weapons, then present the plan to Congress for approval. Command over nuclear weapons, therefore, literally gives the president the power to destroy the world. Yet, if a president ordered a surprise nuclear attack during peacetime when no crisis existed, it is likely those orders would be questioned and resisted by civilian and military advisers.

Logistical Limits to Presidential Control

Although presidents alone have the authority to order the use of nuclear weapons, they do not possess perfect central control over them. The U.S. nuclear arsenal consists of thousands of nuclear warheads based throughout the world, delivery vehicles for all types of nuclear missions, and a vast network of personnel, computers, communications equipment, and information and intelligence gathering and processing systems necessary to manage the

Presidential Nuclear Command Procedures

An important component of deterrence is maintaining reliable command procedures for the launch of nuclear weapons. The goal of these procedures is to identify positively that a nuclear attack has been launched against the United States, to characterize the attack for the president and other national leaders, to receive orders from the president based on this characterization, and to transmit these orders to the officers in charge of nuclear weapons.

Because the decision to retaliate with nuclear weapons must be made under conditions of extreme stress, nuclear planners provide the president with the Single Integrated Operational Plan (SIOP). This highly classified document contains the possible U.S. nuclear responses to a variety of attacks. Its purpose is to familiarize the president and other top defense officials with nuclear attack options from which they can quickly choose in a crisis.

If the North American Aerospace Defense Command (NORAD)—the underground post in Colorado charged with processing early warning information—detects evidence of a possible nuclear attack against the United States, NORAD, the Strategic Air Command (SAC), the Pentagon's National Military Command Center, and the Alternate National Military Command Center at Fort Ritchie, Maryland, begin procedural steps to verify the authenticity of the attack. If after a series of conferences, NORAD and the other units determine that the attack is real, the president is informed of the attack and its characteristics. The president then consults with defense leaders and considers SIOP options.[1]

Because the Soviets would almost certainly use submarine-launched nuclear missiles, which would reach their targets in ten to twelve minutes or less, the president would probably have no more than three or four minutes to decide on a response. If a nuclear attack option is chosen, the president transmits the launch codes that unlock the nuclear weapons and assure the officers in charge of the weapons that the launch order is authentic. The launch codes are carried in an ordinary black bag known as the "football" by a military officer who is always near the president. The exact procedures for ordering nuclear forces to launch their weapons are highly classified and probably change depending on the global situation and the incumbent president's preferences.[2]

Before or after a president decides how to respond to a nuclear attack, the president and other top leaders may choose to evacuate Washington, D.C. Underground command posts within range of helicopters were built in the 1950s in Virginia and Pennsylvania from which the president could direct a nuclear war. Since advances in Soviet military technology have made these underground posts vulnerable to nuclear attack, the president may choose instead to rush by helicopter to Andrews Air Force Base ten miles from the White House and take off in one of the National Emergency Airborne Command Posts (NEACP). These aircraft remain on constant alert for the president's use and contain communications equipment that would enable the president to transmit orders to U.S. nuclear forces.[3]

If the president is killed by a nuclear attack or is unable to communicate with nuclear forces, nuclear command devolves upon the president's successors as specified in the Twenty-fifth Amendment and the Presidential Successsion Act of 1947. Presidents, however, may give authority to launch nuclear weapons to specified military leaders rather than depending on the survival of statutory presidential successors. For example, the president may authorize the officers in charge of the Strategic Air Command's airborne command posts, one of which has been aloft every moment since February 3, 1961, to order a nuclear launch if a Soviet strike kills the president and destroys the Washington, D.C., area, where many of the president's successors reside. Such a plan would have the advantage of ensuring that the decision to use nuclear weapons did not fall to a cabinet official completely unfamiliar with nuclear strategy and procedures. It would also decrease the chances that a Soviet nuclear strike would be able to disable U.S. nuclear forces by killing U.S. leaders or interrupting their communications. Yet, bypassing the chain of presidential succession would have the disadvantages of removing nuclear decision making from civilian control and of creating doubts about who was leading the country.[4]

1. Miroslav Nincic, *United States Foreign Policy, Choices and Tradeoffs* (Washington, D.C.: CQ Press, 1988), 265.
2. Walter Slocombe, "Preplanned Operations," in *Managing Nuclear Operations*, ed. Ashton B. Carter, John D. Steinbruner, and Charles A. Zraket (Washington, D.C.: Brookings, 1987), 132.
3. William Sweet, "Civil Defense: Nuclear Debate's New Element," *Editorial Research Reports*, June 4, 1982, 419.
4. Slocombe, "Preplanned Operations," 133.

weapons.[81] Because of the size and complexity of the U.S. nuclear weapons arsenal and the requirements of deterrence, presidents cannot depend on controlling every weapon by simply pushing a button or making a phone call. Their control could be undermined by the failure or destruction of U.S. early warning and communications systems, of personnel who manage the nuclear weapons, or of the weapons themselves.

Presidential control of nuclear weapons has been aided by permissive action links (PALs), or electronic locks that prevent nuclear weapons from being fired without prior presidential authorization. Intercontinental ballistic missiles (ICBMs) based in missile silos and nuclear warheads carried by U.S. strategic bombers are equipped with PALs.[82] The military commanders of certain other types of nuclear weapons, however, have the physical capability,

Table 1 Major Arms Control Agreements

President	Year signed	Agreement	Senate action	Provisions	Parties
Eisenhower	1959	Antarctic Treaty	Ratified	Prohibits all military activity, including deployment of nuclear weapons in Antarctica	Multilateral
Kennedy	1963	Partial Nuclear Test Ban Treaty	Ratified	Prohibits nuclear tests under water, in the atmosphere, and in outer space	Multilateral
Johnson	1967	Outer Space Treaty	Ratified	Prohibits all military activity, including deployment of nuclear weapons in outer space	Multilateral
Johnson	1968	Nuclear Nonproliferation Treaty	Ratified	Prohibits acquisition of nuclear weapons by nations not already possessing them and establishes international safeguards to prevent the spread of nuclear weapons capability	Multilateral
Nixon	1971	Sea Bed Treaty	Ratified	Prohibits deployment of nuclear weapons on the ocean floor	Multilateral
Nixon	1972	SALT I ABM Treaty	Ratified	Limits size and number (two) of antiballistic missile systems in U.S. and Soviet Union. A 1974 executive agreement reduced number of sites permitted to one.	U.S.-Soviet Union
Nixon	1972	SALT I Interim Offensive Arms Agreement	Executive agreement No action	Established a five-year freeze on number of intercontinental ballistic missiles and submarine-launched ballistic missiles deployed by U.S. and Soviet Union	U.S.-Soviet Union
Nixon	1974	Threshold Nuclear Test Ban Treaty	Unratified	Prohibits underground nuclear test explosions greater than 150 kilotons	U.S.-Soviet Union
Ford	1976	Peaceful Nuclear Explosions Treaty	Unratified	Prohibits nuclear explosions greater than 150 kilotons for excavation and other peaceful purposes	U.S.-Soviet Union
Carter	1979	SALT II Offensive Arms Treaty	Unratified	Limits numbers and types of strategic nuclear weapons	U.S.-Soviet Union
Reagan	1987	Intermediate Nuclear Forces Treaty	Ratified	Mandates the removal and destruction of all land-based nuclear missiles with ranges between 300 and 3,400 miles	U.S.-Soviet Union

although not the authority, to launch them without receiving a presidential order. Nuclear missiles deployed in submarines, for example, are not equipped with PALs and therefore could be fired by the officers of a submarine who mistakenly believed that the president had issued a launch order. Since each Trident, the fleet's most modern missile launching submarine, carries twenty-four missiles equipped with eight warheads each, such a mistake would be catastrophic. The navy seeks to minimize the danger of an unauthorized nuclear launch through elaborate launch procedures that require the action of several officers and intensive psychological screening of submarine personnel.

Because of the possibility that the president might be killed or the president's means of communicating with nuclear forces might be destroyed by an enemy nuclear attack, crisis contingency plans exist through which the president could delegate authority to use nuclear weapons to the military commanders in charge of the weapons. Implementation of such a plan during a crisis would require the president's approval, but since "decapitation"—the destruction of the enemy's leadership and communications capabilities—is a central tenet of the nuclear contingency plans of both superpowers, the president may be forced to delegate away the decision to use at least a portion of U.S. nuclear forces.[83] The president could make such a delegation of authority during a crisis as a precaution against a surprise attack, or the president could wait to delegate authority until an enemy launches missiles that threaten the president, secretary of defense, and other leaders in Washington.

When the threat from a potential attack is perceived to be greater than the danger of an accidental or premature launching of nuclear weapons, the president also has the option to put the nuclear missile submarine fleet on a "fail deadly" launch status. Under this arrangement, the submarines receive orders at regular intervals not to launch their missiles, rather than a positive order to launch. If the crews fail to receive an order not to launch, they assume that the president and other top officials have been killed in a nuclear attack, and they fire their missiles. Such a plan is meant to deter an attack by convincing leaders of an enemy nation that their country cannot emerge unscathed from a nuclear war by decapitating the U.S. command and control system.[84]

Nuclear Arms Control

Since the development of atomic weapons, presidents have tried to enhance U.S. security by controlling the nuclear arms race. Arms control agreements have become one of the most important measurements of a president's diplomatic success, and every president since Dwight Eisenhower has concluded some agreement with the Soviet Union or the international community that contributed to the reduction or prevention of the spread of nuclear weapons. *(See Table 1.)*

Arms control has numerous implications beyond its effect on the balance of nuclear forces. It affects U.S. relations with its allies; it can benefit the U.S. economy by reducing the financial burden of defense; it can be the catalyst for the improvement of diplomatic relations with adversaries; and it has become an emotional and moral issue for many groups and individuals. Consequently, arms control is not exclusively a military matter. The president, the official elected by the whole country to oversee the nation's defenses, foreign relations, and economic prosperity, is in the best position to mold a coherent arms control strategy that considers military and diplomatic realities, the nation's economic condition, and the dangers of an unchecked arms race.

As commander in chief and the possessor of the treaty negotiation power, presidents have dominated arms control policy. Although the Senate can exercise negative control over arms control agreements by blocking ratification of a treaty, the president has complete control over the initiation and execution of arms control negotiations. Because arms control agreements are perceived to be among the most important agreements made by the president, they generally have been concluded as treaties. The Senate usually has chosen to approve arms control treaties, but ratification has not been automatic. Three nuclear arms control treaties have remained unratified: the 1974 Threshold Nuclear Test Ban Treaty, the 1976 Peaceful Nuclear Explosions Treaty, and the 1979 Strategic Arms Limitation Treaty (SALT II).

Presidents may choose to avoid the Senate treaty ratification process, however, by concluding arms control accords in the form of executive agreements. In 1972 President Nixon signed the SALT I Interim Offensive Arms Agreement which imposed limitations on the strategic nuclear arsenals of both superpowers, but he did not submit the agreement to the Senate as a treaty. Presidents may also choose to abide by an arms control treaty that the Senate has refused to ratify. President Carter announced in 1980 that the United States would not violate the provisions of the unratified SALT II treaty if the Soviet Union also did not violate it. President Reagan continued Carter's policy of observing SALT II until late 1986 when the administration announced that because of Soviet violations the United States would no longer consider itself bound by the treaty. Even the Senate's treaty ratification power, therefore, may not constrain a president who believes a particular arms control measure is in the interests of national security.

U.S. Navy

A submarine-launched cruise missile is test fired in the Pacific. During the 1980s, the United States deployed hundreds of nuclear-tipped cruise missiles aboard bombers, surface ships, and submarines.

Evolution of Presidential Nuclear Decision Making

Since Franklin Roosevelt directed U.S. scientists to build the atomic bomb, presidents have dominated nuclear weapons policy and the formulation of nuclear strategy. Nuclear age presidents have counted nuclear decision making as among their most important and burdensome responsibilities. Dwight Eisenhower once remarked in a speech:

> When the push of a button may mean obliteration of countless humans, the President of the United States must be forever on guard against any inclination on his part to impetuosity; to arrogance; to headlong action; to expedience; to facile maneuvers; even to the popularity of an action as opposed to the righteousness of an action. . . . He must worry only about the good—the long-term, abiding, permanent good—of all Americans.[85]

U.S. Nuclear Monopoly

Harry Truman asserted that the welfare of Americans had motivated him to use the atomic bomb against Japan. In the summer of 1945, after the war against Nazi Germany had been won, President Truman decided to drop newly manufactured atomic bombs on the Japanese cities of Hiroshima and Nagasaki to bring an end to World War II. Truman officially maintained that using the atomic bombs was the only way to end the war without an invasion of Japan. In a radio address to the American public on August 9, 1945, after both atomic bombs had been dropped, Truman explained that he had ordered the attacks "to shorten the agony of war, in order to save the lives of thousands and thousands of young Americans."[86]

Historical evidence suggests, however, that the decision was not a simple choice between forcing the Japanese to surrender by dropping the bomb and sacrificing tens of thousands of U.S. soldiers in an island assault. Throughout the summer the Japanese had made peace overtures that were not fully explored by the Truman administration. Although Truman may genuinely have been convinced that Japan was unwilling to surrender on acceptable terms without witnessing the power of the atomic bomb, it is also possible he had additional motives for dropping it. Truman wanted to end the war abruptly to prevent the Soviet Union, which was about to enter the war against the Japanese, from having a role in the occupation of Japan. He also may have regarded the bomb as an impressive demonstration of American power that would cause the Soviets to be more conciliatory toward the West.[87]

From the bombing of Hiroshima to the early 1950s, the United States enjoyed a nuclear monopoly. The Soviet Union tested its first atomic bomb in 1949, but it did not have an operational capability for several more years. The U.S. ability to destroy Soviet population centers with atomic weapons served as an effective deterrent against the threat to Western Europe from superior numbers of Soviet conventional forces.[88] Although the U.S. nuclear advantage prevented war with the Soviet Union through the 1940s and 1950s, the Korean War demonstrated the difficulty of using nuclear weapons in limited wars. Truman rejected their use in Korea because allied opinion was squarely against the move, and he believed the limited U.S. nuclear arsenal needed to be conserved to defend against a Soviet attack on Western Europe. A moral prohibition against the use of nuclear weapons also had developed, especially against the citizens of an underdeveloped nation like North Korea who were victims of communist expansion.

U.S. Nuclear Superiority

The small Soviet nuclear arsenal developed in the 1950s was much inferior in number and quality to the U.S. nuclear force. President Eisenhower attempted to use U.S. nuclear superiority to deter Soviet aggression. He believed that maintaining a conventional military force capable of countering the Soviets and their clients anywhere in the world would be disastrous for the federal budget and would not be supported by the American public. In addition, a threat to use nuclear weapons against China had helped end the Korean War. The administration therefore declared in 1954 that the United States would respond to Communist aggression by using nuclear weapons against appropriate targets. These targets were not necessarily to be limited to the region where the Communist aggression was occurring. Thus, the United States threatened to attack the Soviet Union (or China) with nuclear weapons not only in response to a Soviet attack on Western Europe, but also in response to unspecified lesser provocations.[89]

The problem with this strategy, which was known as "massive retaliation," was that it lacked credibility. A U.S. nuclear strike was an inappropriate response to limited acts of Communist aggression such as Soviet-supported guerrilla movements or political subversion. Furthermore, as the Soviet nuclear capability grew during the 1950s, the possibility that the United States could launch a nuclear attack against the Soviet Union without itself and its allies receiving a nuclear counterblow became remote. The successful Soviet launch of the Sputnik satellite in 1957 even engendered false speculation that the gap in military technology that Americans assumed to be in their favor actually favored the Soviets.

John Kennedy sought to bring declared nuclear policy in line with global realities. Upon taking office, he announced a new strategy of "flexible response." Kennedy and his advisers saw that improvements in the Soviet nuclear arsenal had diminished the capacity of U.S. nuclear forces to deter anything but a Soviet nuclear attack or massive invasion of Western Europe. Kennedy also recognized that the United States was faced with many forms of Communist aggression that called for limited responses. Kennedy, therefore, ordered wide-ranging improvements in U.S. military capabilities. Nuclear deterrence remained the centerpiece of U.S. defense, but conventional and counterinsurgency forces also were built up to deal with limited wars.

Soviet placement of medium-range nuclear missiles in Cuba in 1962 precipitated a crisis that pushed the United States to the brink of nuclear war with the Soviet Union. Kennedy refused to accept this alteration of the balance of forces. He ordered a blockade of Cuba to prevent further construction of the Soviet missile sites and demanded that the Soviets withdraw the missiles. After two tense weeks, during which Kennedy estimated the chances of nuclear war at "between one out of three and even," the Soviets agreed to remove their missiles.[90] The Cuban missile crisis highlighted the threat to U.S. security from the growing Soviet nuclear arsenal and stimulated a further modernization of nuclear weaponry.

Like the Korean War, the Vietnam War demonstrated the doubtful utility of nuclear weapons in limited conflicts. Although the Johnson administration found itself committed to a bloody war upon which it had staked its own reputation and the honor of the country, it refused to use nuclear weapons against North Vietnam. The closest the administration came to considering their use was one hypothetical study commissioned in 1967 by Gen. William Westmoreland, the commander of U.S. forces in Vietnam.[91] Johnson refused to employ nuclear weapons because he did not want to risk a wider war with the Soviet Union or China, and he recognized the moral prohibition against their use.

Nuclear Decision Making in the Era of Parity

Presidents Nixon and Ford ascribed to the basic nuclear strategy established by Kennedy and Johnson. The concept of strategic defense—building defensive weapons systems capable of destroying attacking enemy missiles and bombers—had been widely debated during Johnson's presidency. President Nixon, however, concluded a treaty in 1972 with the Soviet Union that placed strict limitations on anti-ballistic missile systems. This formalized the doctrine of "mutual assured destruction" (MAD) that had characterized the nuclear relationship between the superpowers since the Soviets achieved strategic nuclear parity

Presidential Civil Defense Policy

An all-out nuclear war would be a national disaster unrivaled in U.S. history. Tens of millions of civilians would likely be killed, and U.S. governmental structures might cease to exist in many areas of the country. Even a limited nuclear war in which several nuclear weapons exploded on the territory of the United States would create unprecedented medical, communications, transportation, and environmental problems. Because a nuclear war would blur the distinctions between soldiers and civilians and create a civil emergency of enormous magnitude, the commander-in-chief power contributes to the president's authority over civil defense preparations. These preparations are intended to maximize the number of citizens who would survive a nuclear war and provide for the reconstitution of the nation's government and economy.

Rise and Fall of Civil Defense. Civil defense has never been a high priority in the United States. In the first two decades after the Soviet acquisition of the atomic bomb in 1949, the United States pursued a modest civil defense program. Presidential budget requests for civil defense always exceeded the funds appropriated by Congress for that purpose. Because the deliverable Soviet nuclear arsenal was inferior in number and quality to the U.S. arsenal, there was some justification that civil defense preparations could save the lives of many Americans and enable U.S. society to recover more quickly from a nuclear war.

President Kennedy was the strongest advocate of civil defense among presidents of this era. In a televised address delivered on July 25, 1961, he called for an extensive civil defense program that would include marking fallout shelters, stocking them with food, water, and medical supplies, and creating an elaborate nuclear warning system. Congress initially gave Kennedy the money for his civil defense project but within two years, it had cut back civil defense funding.[1]

By the late 1960s, the increase in the numbers and sophistication of Soviet nuclear weapons to a level of rough parity with the U.S. nuclear arsenal convinced most U.S. citizens that regardless of civil defense measures they would be killed in a nuclear war. Given that U.S. strategic doctrine was based on deterring war by maintaining the mutual vulnerability of the populations of the Soviet Union and the United States, the costs of building shelters and developing procedures to warn and relocate citizens in times of crisis seemed unjustified. Moreover, most Americans had a negative attitude toward civil defense planning because these preparations reminded them of nuclear war and seemed to imply that the government accepted its possibility. Civil defense, therefore, remained a low priority during the late 1960s and most of the 1970s.

Civil Defense Revival. In the late 1970s, however, the number of civil defense advocates began to grow. Central Intelligence Agency reports of a $2 billion a year Soviet civil defense program prompted some officials to call for a similar program in the United States. These civil defense advocates feared that the Soviet program, which stressed evacuation of cities, would convince Kremlin leaders that they could protect their population in a nuclear war while the U.S. urban population remained vulnerable. President Carter consolidated civil defense efforts in the new Federal Emergency Management Agency created in 1978 but did not substantially increase civil defense funding, which averaged only about $100 million a year during his term.

With the election of Ronald Reagan, civil defense was thrust into the public spotlight. On March 30, 1982, President Reagan proposed a seven-year, $4.2 billion civil defense program. The plan called for evacuating tens of millions of urban residents to rural areas in the event of a nuclear crisis. Government officials had estimated that a timely evacuation could enable as much as 80 percent of the U.S. population to survive a Soviet nuclear attack. Reagan argued that such a program was needed to counter the extensive Soviet civil defense preparations and to strengthen deterrence by ensuring that a larger portion of American society would survive a nuclear war.[2]

Reagan's civil defense plan was criticized by peace activists who contended that it would make a nuclear war more likely by creating the illusion that death and destruction could be minimized. Several ill-chosen statements by top civil defense officials in the Pentagon brought accusations that the administration believed casualties of a nuclear war could be limited to acceptable numbers. The most notorious statement was made in the fall of 1981 by T. K. Jones, a deputy undersecretary of defense, who stated in an interview that personal fallout shelters constructed by digging a hole in the ground and covering it with a door and three feet of dirt could dramatically reduce deaths caused by a nuclear war. "If there are enough shovels to go around," asserted Jones, "everybody's going to make it." [3]

Congress reacted to the debate by increasing funds for civil defense, but appropriations fell far short of Reagan administration requests. Congress authorized only $152 million out of a requested $252 million for fiscal year 1983, the first year of Reagan's civil defense program.[4] Congress continued to trim the administration's civil defense budget proposals in subsequent years. Although Reagan had succeeded in modestly increasing funding for emergency planning, neither the public nor Congress showed much enthusiasm for significantly expanding the role of civil defense in national security strategy.

1. William Sweet, "Civil Defense: Nuclear Debate's New Element," *Editorial Research Reports*, June 4, 1982, 415-416.
2. Ibid., 411-413.
3. Robert Scheer, *With Enough Shovels: Reagan, Bush and Nuclear War* (New York: Vintage Books, 1983), 18.
4. Pat Towell, "Strategic Arms Top List of Defense Cuts," *Congressional Quarterly Weekly Report*, August 21, 1982, 2059.

in the late 1960s. The MAD doctrine asserted that neither superpower could attack the other with nuclear weapons without its rival launching a devastating counterstrike. Both nations, therefore, would achieve security by holding the populations of the other hostage. It is unclear whether the Soviets accepted the desirability of MAD, but the doctrine did reflect strategic realities.

During the Carter administration, U.S. nuclear war strategy was reevaluated. The result was Presidential Directive 59 (PD-59), which was signed by the president in July 1980. PD-59 stressed that the United States had to be prepared to fight a protracted nuclear war lasting up to sixty days. The directive ordered nuclear planners to develop a wider range of limited nuclear war options and assigned a higher priority to destroying the Soviet's leadership, military capabilities, and economic base if nuclear war occurred. It also called for an improvement of U.S. command, control, and communications to ensure that the president and other top leaders could direct a protracted nuclear war effectively.[92] Critics of PD-59 charged that U.S. officials had made nuclear war more likely by promoting the perceptions that a nuclear war could be fought like any other war and that nuclear destruction could be limited to an acceptable degree. Nevertheless, PD-59 did not represent a movement toward an acceptance of nuclear war by President Carter and the defense establishment. Rather, it was an assertion that preparing to fight a nuclear war was the the best way to deter one.

Ronald Reagan took over the presidency in 1981 vowing to rebuild U.S. defenses, including its nuclear forces. He contended that during the 1970s while the United States observed the letter and spirit of nuclear arms control agreements, the Soviets had continued to build nuclear weapons that would give them an advantage in a nuclear war. Reagan asserted that these developments had created a "window of vulnerability" in the U.S. deterrent that could only be closed by building new U.S. weapons. Most experts discounted Reagan's claims that the U.S. nuclear deterrent was threatened since a large number of nuclear warheads—over 5,000—were deployed at sea aboard nuclear submarines that were invulnerable to Soviet attack. Nevertheless, a consensus had begun to develop during the late stages of the Carter administration that a defense buildup was needed, and much of Reagan's nuclear modernization program was approved.

On March 23, 1983, a proposal by Reagan sparked the most significant change in U.S. nuclear strategy since flexible response. In a nationally televised address he urged the scientific community to develop the technology for a space-based antiballistic missile defense that would someday make nuclear weapons "impotent and obsolete." [93] Implicit in the plan was a rejection of the status quo doctrine of mutual assured destruction. Reagan proposed to achieve security in the future not solely by deterring a Soviet nuclear attack, but also by being able to destroy most incoming Soviet missiles.

Although Reagan's optimistic vision led to an extensive research and development program, many scientists admitted that even if insulating the United States from a Soviet missile attack were possible, it would take decades of research and hundreds of billions of dollars to accomplish. By 1987, budget constraints and growing scientific skepticism that Reagan's "Peace Shield" could be built led to a reorientation of the plan. An authoritative classified document prepared by the Joint Chiefs of Staff called for the development of limited antiballistic missile defenses designed to stop about 30 percent of incoming Soviet warheads.[94] The Reagan administration had abandoned the goal of basing U.S. security on strategic defense and settled for the more attainable goal of using defensive weapons to enhance deterrence.

Library of Congress

Robert S. McNamara, defense secretary from 1961 to 1968, greatly expanded the role of the Office of the Secretary of Defense.

President as Defense Manager

Before World War II the United States maintained a small peacetime defense establishment. The isolation and size of the nation rendered it nearly immune to serious invasions by the armies of Europe. This geographic advantage and the antimilitaristic tradition of the United States worked against the maintenance of large standing armies. When the United States found itself in a war, it mobilized troops and resources until the war was won, after which the armed forces demobilized and the country returned to a state of peace and nonalignment.

After World War II a national consensus developed that the United States should adopt an internationalist defense policy designed to contain the expansion of Communism and limit the coercive potential of Soviet military strength. In pursuit of these regional objectives presidents signed a number of regional alliance treaties that pledged the United States to defend allied nations that came under attack. The most important of these regional alliances was the North Atlantic Treaty Organization (NATO), which committed the United States to the defense of Western Europe. The expanded defense commitments of the United States and its adversarial relationship with the Soviet Union caused the United States to maintain for the first time in its history a huge peacetime military establishment.

Although the Constitution gives Congress the complete authority to raise and equip an army and navy, much of the task of administering the defense bureaucracy and maintaining the nation's defenses in the post-World War II era has been delegated to or assumed by the president and the executive branch. The growth in the size and activities of the military and the perception that nuclear weapons and the Cold War had created a condition of constant emergency combined to legitimize the president's role as defense manager. Presidents functioned not just as the commander in chief in wartime but also as the manager of the routine operations and preparations of the military in peacetime.

Presidents and the Defense Establishment

As commander in chief, the president is positioned at the top of a large and complex defense establishment. The Defense Department is made up of three military services and numerous agencies, offices, and unified multiservice commands all under the leadership of the secretary of defense. During the 1980s the number of active duty military personnel has remained over two million, and in 1987 the Defense Department employed over one million civilians. In addition to the Defense Department, other executive departments and agencies have national security roles. The Central Intelligence Agency (CIA) and State Department provide intelligence about foreign governments and groups; the Federal Bureau of Investigation is responsible for combating espionage; the Energy Department develops, tests, and produces nuclear warheads; the Federal Emergency Management Agency oversees civil defense programs; and the Selective Service System conducts draft registration. The Defense Department, however, is the president's principal means of executing national security policy.

Department of Defense

Before 1947 the War and Navy Departments functioned independently of each other. Both had their own cabinet-level secretary, military command structure, and procurement operations. The National Security Act of 1947 created the post of secretary of defense, but its occupant was not given a staff or significant power over the individual services. The defense secretary functioned as the coordinator between the loose confederation of the Departments of the Army (the old War Department) and Navy, and the new Department of the Air Force. A 1949 amendment to the National Security Act created the Defense Department and recognized the primacy of the defense secretary, but in practice the individual services retained authority over their budgets and were administered autonomously by the service secretaries. The three services were not unified into one military organization because reformers believed such an organization could more easily threaten civilian primacy over the military.

The Department of Defense Reorganization Act of 1958 placed the secretary of defense at the top of the military command structure, second only to the president. The act gave the secretary the means to centralize authority over defense operations and planning within the Office of the Secretary of Defense (OSD). In 1961 Robert S. McNamara became defense secretary with a mandate from President Kennedy to take control of the Defense Department. McNamara greatly expanded the role of OSD and demanded unequivocal support from the military for the administration's programs.[95] McNamara ramained defense secretary until 1968. He established four major roles of the modern defense secretary: principal adviser to the president on defense issues, deputy commander in chief behind the president, director of the Defense Department and its huge military budget, and representative of the Defense Department before Congress and within the executive branch. This enlargement of the role of the secretary of defense gave presidents greater control over the defense establishment and assisted in the integration of defense and foreign policy.

Joint Chiefs of Staff

The Joint Chiefs of Staff (JCS) is the body of military officers responsible for formulating unified military strategy and providing the president with advice on military matters. The JCS consists of a chairman appointed from any of the services, the chiefs of staff of the Army and the air force, the chief of naval operations, and the commandant of the Marine Corps.

All five of the chiefs are appointed by the president with the advice and consent of the Senate. Since 1967, the chairman has been appointed for a two-year term, which can be renewed once by the president. The four service chiefs serve one, nonrenewable, four-year term.

A president can appoint several types of officers to the Joint Chiefs of Staff depending on the president's conception of its advisory role. Most chiefs have been officers nominated by their services and accepted by presidents with little consideration of their political compatibility with the administration. The president may receive the good will of the services for endorsing their choices, but the president will have little political control over these nominees. Presidents also have looked beyond the service's candidates and chosen officers whose professional reputation has come to their attention. These appointments may displease the services, but they allow a president to choose an officer with experience and temperament compatible with the administration. Finally, a few presidents have appointed close associates to the JCS. For example, John Kennedy appointed Gen. Maxwell Taylor chairman of the JCS in 1962. Taylor had earlier been offered the post of director of the CIA in 1961 but had chosen instead to become a special military representative to the White House. When the general was appointed chairman of the JCS he quickly became a member of Kennedy's inner circle of advisers. The military usually dislikes such nominees because their first priority is promoting the policies of the president rather than protecting their service's interests.[96]

Since 1947 when the JCS was created it has been criticized by many observers including influential service chiefs and blue ribbon panels commissioned to study its organization. These critics identified several problems with the JCS. First, the joint chiefs were given the conflicting tasks of being service chiefs responsible for the welfare of their services and members of the JCS responsible for developing unbiased policy plans and proposals for the president. The chiefs have seldom been able to do both and have usually put service interests first. Second, because the entire JCS was considered to be the president's military adviser, the chiefs have been compelled to develop consensus positions. As a result, their advice has consisted of uncontroversial compromise recommendations of little value to the president. Third, although the JCS was supposed to develop military plans, it was outside the military's chain of command. Consequently, JCS budgetary, procurement, and strategy proposals often have been unrelated to the needs of the commanders in chief (CINCs) of the multiservice operational commands in specified geographic areas.[97]

In 1986 President Reagan signed a bill reorganizing the JCS. The intent of the legislation was to improve interservice coordination and to create an organizational framework that would streamline the chain of command and minimize the influence of service parochialism on the military advice given to the president by the JCS.

The reorganization bill sought to accomplish these

Truman and General MacArthur

The most famous clash between a president and a member of the armed forces was Harry Truman's dispute with Gen. Douglas MacArthur during the Korean War. The conflict led to Truman's dramatic firing of MacArthur and tested the principle of presidential control of the military.

Few military leaders in the history of the United States were as respected and revered by the American public as General MacArthur was in the early stages of the Korean War. He had been a decorated hero of World War I, the triumphant commander of U.S. forces in the Pacific in World War II, and the successful military governor of Japan, overseeing that nation's transformation into a modern democratic state. When the Korean War broke out he was made supreme commander of the UN forces in Korea. His landing at Inchon behind North Korean lines in September 1950 reversed the tide of the war and reinforced his reputation as a tactical genius. Many Americans and members of Congress saw MacArthur as indispensable to the success of the Korean War effort. Republican leaders regarded the well-known, eloquent, and handsome general as a potential candidate in a future presidential election.

The conflict between Truman and MacArthur arose over their differing opinions of the goals to be pursued in the Korean War. The United States had sent forces to Korea under the authority of the United Nations in June 1950 after the North Koreans had invaded South Korea. Truman's original intention had been to drive the North Korean forces out of South Korea and reestablish a secure border at the thirty-eighth parallel. By October 1950, U.S. troops had accomplished this goal, but the successful military campaign led Truman and his advisers to order MacArthur to cross into North Korea and attempt to unify the nation.[1] Nevertheless, Truman was concerned about provoking Communist China and prohibited MacArthur from attacking North Korean bases in China.

MacArthur, however, envisioned an Asian strategy in which the United States would seek to overthrow the Communist Chinese by encouraging guerrilla war inside China, bombing Chinese targets, and supporting an invasion of China by hundreds of thousands of Nationalist Chinese troops from Formosa. At the least, MacArthur wanted the latitude to bomb North Korean sanctuaries and supply lines inside China. During the fall of 1950 he openly criticized Truman's policies and encouraged his supporters in Congress to press the administration to give him discretion to widen the war.

In November 1950, with U.S. forces close to crushing the North Korean Army, Communist China entered the war and pushed U.S. forces back across the thirty-eighth parallel. MacArthur blamed his retreat on Truman's constraints. Truman responded with a presidential directive on December 5 that instructed overseas military commanders and diplomats to clear all public statements with Washington, but MacArthur continued to make inflammatory comments. In a March 7 press statement the general characterized Truman's Korean strategy as "Die for [a] Tie." [2]

On March 24, MacArthur interfered with ongoing diplomacy. He undercut Truman's efforts to arrange cease-fire negotiations with the Chinese by issuing a statement that the United Nations might "depart from its tolerant efforts to contain the war to the area of Korea. . . ." [3] MacArthur failed to explain or apologize for the communiqué. On April 5, House Minority Leader Joseph Martin (R-Mass.), a MacArthur ally, read a letter from the general on the floor of the House. It described Korea as the arena where "the communist conspirators have elected to make their play for global conquest," and concluded, ". . . we must win. There is no substitute for victory." Truman could no longer tolerate MacArthur's insubordination. After a week of meetings with his top advisers, the president announced in a 1:00 a.m. news conference on April 11 that he was relieving MacArthur of command.

Truman's public approval ratings, as measured by the Gallup organization, slipped from 28 percent in late March to just 24 percent after he fired MacArthur. Sixty-one percent of Americans disapproved of the way he was doing his job. Impeachment became a common topic of discussion as members of Congress accused the president and his top advisers of appeasing Communism or even being under the influence of Communist agents.[4] MacArthur's welcome home as a war hero intensified the pressure on the Truman administration. The general delivered an emotional farewell address before Congress on April 19 and received a New York City parade attended by an estimated seven million people.

The Truman administration, however, was able to focus attention away from MacArthur's patriotic appeals and denunciations of Truman's policies to the general's insubordination and the constitutional principle of civilian control of the armed forces. At the joint Senate Foreign Relations and Armed Services Committee hearings on MacArthur's firing and Korean War strategy, administration officials united behind the president in denouncing MacArthur's actions and endorsing military restraint in Korea. Most important, Truman received the support of the military. Chairman of the Joint Chiefs of Staff Gen. Omar Bradley told the committees that MacArthur's Korean strategy "would involve us in the wrong war, at the wrong place, at the wrong time, and with the wrong enemy." [5] Talk of impeachment subsided, and Congress took no action against the president. Truman had successfully defended his commander-in-chief authority and reaffirmed the principle of civilian control over the military.

1. John Spanier, *American Foreign Policy Since World War II*, 11th ed. (Washington, D.C.: CQ Press, 1988), 76.
2. James A. Nathan and James K. Oliver, *United States Foreign Policy and World Order*, 2d ed. (Boston: Little, Brown, 1981), 147.
3. R. Gordon Hoxie, *Command Decision and the Presidency* (New York: Reader's Digest Press, 1977), 180.
4. Nathan and Oliver, *United States Foreign Policy*, 149.
5. Hoxie, *Command Decision and the Presidency*, 181.

goals by increasing the authority of the chairman of the JCS. By making the chairman of the JCS the president's supreme military adviser, the bill's advocates theorized that the chairman would be free to develop advice and options independent of service interests. The bill created the post of vice chairman and placed the JCS staff under the direct control of the chairman to bolster the chairman's bureaucratic resources. To ensure that the service chiefs would continue to have an advisory role, the chairman is required to forward their dissenting views to the president and secretary of defense upon the chiefs' request. The bill also enhanced the authority of the CINCs, giving them greater control over the training, supply, organization, and operations of their command.[98]

Presidential Control of the Military

Despite the enhanced authority of the civilian leadership of the Defense Department since 1947, presidents have not dominated the military. Like any government organization, the military has its own organizational objectives and is capable of resisting policies it believes are against its interests. Military leaders have been particularly successful in cultivating friends in Congress who pressure the administration to accept the military's perspective on given issues.

In addition to the military's political clout, presidential control over the armed forces is limited by the president's dependence on the military for evaluations of the nation's military capabilities. Civilian advisers can offer opinions on many military problems, but their assessments must depend on the factual information supplied by the military. Moreover, estimates about the force requirements and prospects for success of a given combat operation can only be supplied by the military.[99] The president may be confident that a particular military operation is justified on moral and political grounds, but the president rarely will order the operation if the military is pessimistic about its chances for success. Presidents also depend on the military to implement their military orders. Whereas presidential initiatives in other areas such as diplomacy can be accomplished through several channels, only the military can carry out a combat operation.

The political leverage of the armed services and their monopoly on military information and resources, therefore, has forced the White House to bargain with the services for cooperation in implementing its programs. Presidents, however, are not always willing and able to compromise with the military. Presidents seeking to reduce their dependence on military sources of defense information and overcome military opposition to their orders and plans can take several steps. They can support defense reorganizations, bring a military officer into the White House as an adviser, rely on the secretary of defense and other civilian advisers for military advice, give the Office of Management and Budget (OMB) greater authority over defense spending, and appoint presidential commissions to study defense problems.[100]

Presidents also can exercise control over the military through their appointments of military officers. Congress establishes the ranks to which officers can be promoted, and the Senate confirms presidential appointees, but the power to assign military officers to posts including the Joint Chiefs of Staff gives presidents the opportunity to shape the leadership of the military. Moreover, one of the most important instruments of presidential control over

Library of Congress

President Truman pins a medal on Gen. Douglas MacArthur at their October 15, 1950, meeting on Wake Island. Truman called the meeting to discuss MacArthur's strategy in Korea. Six months later, Truman would fire MacArthur for insubordination.

the military is the commander in chief's prerogative to dismiss military subordinates in wartime who are incompetent or insubordinate.

Defense Budget

The most frustrating and complicated aspect of presidential defense management is the defense budget. Every year the executive branch must submit a defense budget to Congress, which proposes both defense spending levels and the specific military programs on which funds will be spent. The first question is a highly visible political issue on which most Americans have an opinion and presidential candidates must announce their intentions. The second, however, must be determined through a complex process of conflict and compromise between the president, the Congress, the defense department's civilian leadership, and the individual armed services all under the lobbying pressure of defense contractors and public interest groups.

The amount of money devoted to the defense budget and the manner in which it is spent affect the defense capabilities of the United States by determining what defense programs will be funded. In addition, the defense budget profoundly affects diplomacy. The size and composition of the defense budget create a backdrop for U.S. international relations. Adversaries and allies alike scrutinize it for clues about U.S. global intentions. For example, increases in defense spending, particularly for items such as naval vessels and aircraft, may signal to foreign governments an administration's intention to pursue a more activist foreign policy. Cuts in defense spending may indicate an effort to scale back U.S. defense commitments.

The defense budget also has enormous consequences for the U.S. economy. Even in 1980 before the Reagan administration's military buildup, defense spending accounted for 22.5 percent of all federal expenditures and was equal to 5 percent of the gross national product. By 1986 these figures had climbed to 26.8 and 6.3 percent, respectively.[101]

Defense makes up the largest part of the discretionary budget—the part of the budget that can be cut or shifted from year to year. *(See "The Uncontrollable Budget," p. 654, in Chief Economist chapter of Part III.)* The amount of funds spent on defense, therefore, is a major determinant of the size of the budget deficit or surplus. The sharp increases in the budget deficits that occurred during the 1980s were partially attributable to President Reagan's insistence on dramatically raising defense spending without increasing taxes. Defense spending affects the economy in other ways as well. Although most economists believe that tax cuts have a greater stimulative effect on the economy than increased military expenditures, boosting defense spending can create greater demand for goods and services that can reduce unemployment and lift the country out of a depression or recession. Increases in defense expenditures, however, also may increase inflation by creating excessive competition for the goods and services produced by the economy. Vietnam War expenditures sparked an inflationary spiral that plagued the U.S. economy during much of the late 1960s and 1970s.

Defense Budget Process

The defense budget is a large and complex document that is prepared with the participation of numerous bureaucratic entities including the National Security Council, Office of Management and Budget, and many Defense Department agencies. About a year and a half before a fiscal year begins, the defense secretary issues the Defense Guidance. This document assesses military threats and defines departmental goals and spending priorities. Using this outline the military services develop budget requests. These requests are reviewed and amended by the defense secretary and OMB who reevaluate them in the context of defense and nondefense spending priorities. The resulting comprehensive defense budget is then submitted to Congress.[102]

Presidential participation in the defense budget process is limited by the size and complexity of the budget. Although many presidents have served in the military, few have had executive branch experience with the defense budget. They therefore must rely heavily on career military officers and defense department bureaucrats familiar with the process. Even if a president were a defense expert, the many demands of the presidency would not allow its occupant to become immersed in defense budget details.

Nevertheless, presidents affect the defense budget more than any other individual or group because their assessments of U.S. military capabilities and the threats to U.S. national security create the atmosphere under which the defense budget is formulated. No president can be expected to review every item in the defense budget, but they do determine the approximate level of defense spending, and their defense philosophy affects which types of programs will be emphasized. For example, a president rarely will participate in discussions of budgetary details such as how much to pay privates, but a presidential decision that the military needs to improve the quality of recruits will pervade those discussions.

Besides establishing a national security philosophy, presidents function as the final arbiter of disputes between executive departments and agencies over specific defense budget decisions. OMB and the Defense Department in particular are likely to oppose each other on budget issues since OMB's mission of overseeing spending often clashes with Defense's mission of ensuring national security. Early in his term, Reagan had to choose between the conflicting defense budget recommendations of Defense Secretary Caspar Weinberger, who had been charged with building up the nation's defenses, and OMB Director David Stockman, who had been given the task of reducing the federal deficit despite tax cuts. Reagan sided with Weinberger, thus subordinating budget reduction to the defense buildup.[103]

Since World War II, Congress usually has given presidents most of the funds they requested for defense. Few legislators have wanted to be tagged as "soft on defense," and most of them have defense industries or bases in their states and districts, which their constituents expect them to protect from budget cuts. Nevertheless, Congress has scrutinized the defense budget more carefully since the Vietnam War. The executive branch has retained the initiative over the defense budget, but Congress has challenged the president on funding for individual weapons systems and defense programs such as the MX missile. In addition, the creation of the Congressional Budget Office in 1974 and the expansion of congressional committee staffs that deal with the defense budget have enhanced Congress's ability to detect waste and fraud in the spending programs that are approved.[104]

Weapons Development and Procurement

Presidents and their scientific and military advisers must choose which weapons systems to develop and build from a wide variety of options. Numerous agencies and offices within the Pentagon engage in weapons research, development, and acquisition including the Defense Advanced Research Projects Agency, Defense Logistics Agency, and the offices of Research and Advanced Technology, Research and Engineering, Operational Test and Evaluation, and Spares Program Management. In 1986 Congress enacted laws creating the office of under secretary of defense for acquisition and designating the under secretary as the Pentagon's third-ranking official in an attempt to centralize oversight and direction of the huge procurement bureaucracy.

Weapons procurement decisions seldom are based solely on rational calculations of how a particular weapons system may contribute to national security. The individual services press presidents and top defense officials to adopt various procurement strategies. The development of the U.S. nuclear triad—the policy of deploying some nuclear weapons on land-based missiles, others on bombers, and the rest on submarines and surface ships—resulted in part because the individual services each wanted a nuclear mission. Even groups within the services will maneuver to protect their share of their service's procurement funds.

Technological advances also drive weapons procure-

Presidential Promotion of Weapons Systems

The progress of a weapons system from conception to deployment may depend on the president's ability to create a favorable impression of the program among the American public, Congress, and U.S. allies. The fate of two weapons systems illustrates how major decisions dealing with the development and procurement of weaponry have become public issues that hinge as much on an administration's salesmanship as on the weapon's potential contribution to national security.

Jimmy Carter's plan to produce the neutron bomb, a small nuclear warhead intended for deployment in Europe, was hindered by the negative image of the weapon. The Carter administration argued that the bomb's reduced blast, heat, and fallout would reduce civilian casualties if a tactical nuclear war broke out in Europe, while the bomb's emission of an enhanced wave of neutron radiation would be a more effective weapon against Warsaw Pact tanks built to resist the blast and heat of "regular" nuclear weapons.

These arguments disturbed antinuclear activists in Europe and the United States who mounted a public relations campaign against the weapon. They saw the neutron bomb not as strengthening deterrence, but rather as increasing the chances of nuclear war by making nuclear weapons more usable. The bomb also was criticized as the ultimate capitalistic weapon because it killed people with its enhanced radiation, but its diminished blast left buildings standing. The controversy over the neutron bomb in Europe and the United States and the failure of allies in the North Atlantic Treaty Organization (NATO) to commit themselves firmly to its deployment persuaded Carter in 1978 to abandon his plans to produce the weapon.

In contrast, Ronald Reagan succeeded in harnessing popular opinion for the Strategic Defense Initiative (SDI), a controversial weapons program proposed by Reagan in a dramatic televised speech on March 23, 1983. SDI, which came to be known as "Star Wars," was a research and development project intended to produce a space-based defense against a nuclear ballistic missile attack. That Reagan's vision of a space-based missile defense was possible and desirable was unclear. The scientific community did not reach a consensus on the feasibility of such a defense, and even the most ardent supporters of SDI admitted that a workable system capable of defending the entire United States depended on scientific breakthroughs that were more than a decade away. Moreover, the plan was projected to cost hundreds of billions of dollars, would not solve the problem of defending against Soviet bombers and cruise missiles, and would have unpredictable effects on arms control and the strategic nuclear balance.

Nevertheless, to build public support for the expensive development program the Reagan administration promoted it as a project designed to produce a "Peace Shield" that would free the United States and eventually the world from the threat of nuclear destruction. A majority of Americans agreed with the president that SDI was a worthy goal. Members of Congress responded to their constituents' support of SDI by approving dramatic increases in funding for the project. As with the neutron bomb, popular perceptions of SDI were as important to the decision-making process as the weapons system's strategic value and technical feasibility.

ment. Since the end of World War II the defense establishment has operated under the consensus that the quality of weapons is more important than their quantity. Defense planners have relied on U.S. technological superiority to compensate for the Eastern bloc's advantage in numbers of troops and tanks. This strategy has led defense planners to accept almost any technological improvement in a weapon regardless of its cost.[105] Presidents must serve as a mediator between competing factions in the procurement process and attempt to develop a mix of weapons that best meets the needs of national security at an affordable cost.

Presidents seldom become personally involved in minor procurement matters, but major decisions about purchases of highly visible and expensive items such as ships, missiles, and large numbers of aircraft must ultimately be approved by presidents and often result from their appraisal of the balance of forces. For example, in the early 1980s, Ronald Reagan's determination that U.S. strategic nuclear forces were threatened by a window of vulnerability led to the deployment of the MX missile and a revival of the B-1 bomber project that had been scrapped under Jimmy Carter.

Yet the changes any one president can make on the U.S. arsenal are limited by the length of time required to develop a weapon. Weapons systems often take more than a decade to move from conception to deployment and may be conceived under one president, tested under another, and mass produced under a third. Weapons systems in their early stages of development may not survive once the president who presided over their conception leaves office. At the other end of the process presidents have been reluctant to cancel weapons systems that have reached the production stage because of the time and money that have already been spent on their development. In addition, the longer a weapons program has been in existence, the more likely it will have developed constituencies in the defense bureaucracy and Congress who will resist its cancellation. President Carter's decision not to build the B-1 bomber in 1977 was a rare example of a president cancelling a major weapon after it was completely developed and ready for production.[106]

Ultimately, presidents must secure congressional approval for appropriations to pay for the projects they favor. Not only must presidents contend with members of Congress who do not share their views of procurement priorities, presidents must deal with lawmakers who defend weapons because they happen to be built in their home states and districts.

McNamara Reforms

Robert McNamara became secretary of Defense in 1961 with a mandate from President Kennedy to restructure the budget and procurement process within the Defense Department. McNamara viewed the defense planning and budgeting system that existed during the 1950s as arbitrary and wasteful. Funds were divided among the services, which spent the money according to their parochial conceptions of the nation's defense needs. McNamara sought to centralize budgetary authority within the Office of the Secretary of Defense. By centralizing authority away from the services, he believed he and his staff would be able to make unbiased, cost-effective decisions on budgeting, weapons procurement, and other important resource allocation issues that previously had been decided by the services through a process of conflict and compromise. Although McNamara'a reforms did not eliminate inefficiency and duplication of effort, they did create lasting improvements in the defense budgeting process.

The device McNamara used to centralize power in the OSD was systems analysis. Systems analysis used computer-aided statistical techniques to evaluate the relative costs and effectiveness of alternative defense programs.[107] He instituted a new philosophy of defense management that considered defense programs according to their mission rather than which service would receive funds. His planning, programming, and budgeting system (PPBS) was intended to link budget decisions to overall military strategy and existing force levels. For example, under PPBS the OSD would consider the number and types of forces needed to accomplish the goal of strategic nuclear deterrence given existing U.S. forces, Soviet forces, and budgetary constaints. Then it would determine the most cost-effective method of achieving this goal before allocating funds. Under the old budgeting system an individual service did not consider what weapons the other services possessed or were planning to build before submitting its budget and procurement proposals. Thus, the navy determined how many missile launching submarines it needed without considering how many bombers and missiles the air force had or planned to procure.

The services protested the centralization of authority within the OSD and the domination of defense planning and budgeting by civilian systems analysts. They saw their traditional decision-making role eroding and complained that they were not adequately consulted by OSD. Military leaders also criticized the new system for placing too much emphasis on quantifiable aspects of weapons and programs while devaluing military intuition.[108] McNamara's reforms were implemented, however, with the support of presidents Kennedy and Johnson. McNamara left the Defense Department in 1968, and Johnson left office in 1969, but McNamara's PPBS system, his emphasis on systems analysis, and his conception of a strong defense secretary have survived.

Defense Budget Inefficiency

Despite the introduction of systems analysis in the 1960s, defense department funds continue to be wasted through mismanagement and fraud. Perceptions that the defense budget was out of control were heightened during the Reagan administration. Numerous anecdotes of the defense department buying inexpensive items at ludicrous prices demonstrated the problems with defense procurement and budgeting. For example, the air force purchased a twelve-cent allen wrench for $9,606 and toilet seats for military transport planes for $640. In addition, several major defense contractors were found guilty of price gouging, bribery, and tax fraud. In June 1988 the Justice Department disclosed evidence of a major procurement scandal involving dozens of defense contracts costing tens of billions of dollars that threatened to dwarf all defense budget scandals that had come before it.

Although waste occurs in every government department and agency, several characteristics of the Defense Department have made its problem particularly acute.

First, the enormous size of the defense budget not only creates more opportunities for waste, it makes central control of its details nearly impossible.[109] Neither the president, the secretary of defense, OMB, nor Congress can judge the worthiness of every one of the thousands of line items that make up the defense budget.

Second, the Pentagon's unique buyer-customer relationship with the contractors that supply it with weapons and equipment has led to corruption and waste. The Defense Department has applied the same standards to defense contractors that an average consumer would apply to a manufacturer of consumer goods. The Pentagon often has paid contractors for unexpected expenses incurred in the production of a weapons system rather than letting the company assume the risk of cost overruns. Arms manufacturers also have been given primary responsibility for testing their own products and have not been required to provide warranties for the equipment they sell to the Pentagon.

Third, interservice rivalries still adversely affect the coherence of defense budget planning. Each service and defense agency initially develops its own budget requests. Each service tends to promote its own interests at the expense of the others. Moreover, the services often have failed to consult with one another when developing budget and procurement proposals. They have sought weapons and funding that will enable them independently to perform missions they perceive as traditional and glamorous regardless of the needs of the other services.

It is beyond the capacity of the president to ensure that all defense dollars will be spent efficiently. Yet because the defense budget makes up such a large share of the federal budget and the potential for waste is so great, presidents, as manager of the nation's defenses and economy, must make an effort to promote honest and efficient defense spending practices. This must be done primarily by appointing and supporting the efforts of defense officials who have defense budget experience and are committed to vigorous oversight of defense spending.

Military Personnel Policy

Although the Constitution charges Congress with the responsibility to "make rules for the government and regulation" of the army and navy, the executive branch has substantial authority in military personnel policy. Much of this authority has been delegated to the executive branch by Congress, but authority also has been claimed by presidents under the commander-in-chief power to make regulations that do not conflict with congressional statutes. As a result, the laws passed by Congress governing the armed forces have been supplemented by a body of executive rules and regulations.[110]

Presidents have usually taken the initiative in proposing changes in the size of the armed forces, the methods by which the ranks are filled, and where U.S. forces will be stationed. Ultimate authority for raising an army resides in Congress, but legislators often have accepted presidential actions and recommendations on these issues.

Recruitment and the Draft

Conscription was not used in the United States until the Civil War. The 1863 Enrollment Act set up a draft system run by the War Department and administered by military officers. During World War I Congress again authorized conscription to fulfill troop goals. The 1917 Selective Service Act was challenged in the courts, but the Supreme Court upheld Congress's authority to draft Americans in a series of cases known as the *Selective Draft Law Cases.* Moreover, the Court held that military service was one of a citizen's duties in a "just government."

Not until 1940, however, did Congress pass a draft bill while the nation was at peace. Although the United States had not yet become involved in World War II, President Franklin Roosevelt urged Congress to adopt the measure. In the summer of 1941, with the threat of war looming larger, Roosevelt had a difficult fight before winning enactment of amendments that widened the draft. The measure was passed in the House by just one vote. Whereas earlier drafts had been administered by the War Department, the Selective Training and Service Act of 1940 established an independent Selective Service System, headed by a presidential appointee, to oversee the draft.

In 1947, Congress followed President Truman's recommendation to allow the 1940 draft act to expire. A year later when enlistments failed to meet troop needs, Truman proposed a renewal of the draft and universal military training. Truman's plan would have required all physically and mentally able men to receive one year of military training and serve six months in the reserves. Congress rejected universal military training but passed the Selective Service Act of 1948, which renewed the peacetime draft.

Congress extended the draft several times during the next two and a half decades with the support of a series of presidents. In January 1973 the Paris peace accords were signed ending U.S. involvement in the Vietnam War. Congress followed the recommendation of President Nixon and allowed the draft to expire on July 1 of that year. On April 1, 1975, President Ford announced that eighteen-year-old males no longer had to register for the draft.

The draft's expiration was the first step in establishing an all-volunteer armed forces, which had been under study since 1969. Military pay was raised dramatically to attract volunteers. Since 1973 the armed services have succeeded in meeting their personnel requirements. Although some observers' warnings that the volunteer armed forces would lead to a reduction in the quality of military personnel seemed prophetic in the early years of the volunteer army, during most of the 1980s more than 90 percent of recruits have been high school graduates.

In his State of the Union address on January 23, 1980, Jimmy Carter asked Congress to reinstitute draft registration. Carter was motivated to make the proposal by the international tension created in late 1979 by the takeover of the U.S. embassy in Tehran and the invasion of Afghanistan by the Soviet Union. Draft registration was intended to reduce the time required to bring draftees into the armed services after a mobilization. Congress approved the plan, although it rejected Carter's request to register women. The measure provided only for registration and did not empower the president to draft young men without a further authorization from Congress.[111] Although Reagan opposed draft registration during the 1980 presidential campaign, he ordered its continuation in January 1982.

Peacetime Military Deployments

When U.S. forces become involved in hostilities, presidents have the indisputable authority as commander in chief to determine where those forces will be deployed. In peacetime, however, Congress has occasionally made rules governing the deployment of military personnel. These rules have been justified under Congress's powers to make laws and raise and support the armed forces. Although the commander-in-chief power provides presidents with a justification to determine unilaterally where troops should be deployed even in peacetime, they have generally respected laws limiting their freedom to deploy troops.[112] In 1940 Congress attached a proviso to the Selective Training and Service Act that prohibited troops drafted under the act from being used outside the Western Hemisphere. Franklin Roosevelt accepted this limitation, although he maintained that Iceland was part of the Western Hemisphere and sent troops there in 1941.

A more recent example of a congressional limit on troop deployments occurred in 1982. In that year, Congress attached to a defense appropriations bill an amendment limiting the number of active-duty U.S. military personnel stationed in Europe to 315,000. The Reagan administration argued against the limit, saying that increases in U.S. troop strength in Europe might be required by changes in the military balance between NATO and the Soviet Union and its allies. Despite the administration's objections, Defense Secretary Caspar Weinberger assured Congress that the troop ceiling would be observed. The amendment included a provision that allowed the president to waive the troop limit if the president certified that "overriding national security requirements" made such action necessary. This provision was a recognition by Congress that the purpose of peacetime military deployments is to deter war and that the president as commander in chief should have wide authority to redeploy troops for that purpose.

If a president did refuse to observe limitations Congress placed on peacetime troop deployments, Congress still would have the option of cutting off funds for the base where the troops are stationed or for the supplies needed to sustain the troops. Such action would require a united Congress since presumedly it would have to override a presidential veto of any bill that stopped funds for a troop deployment favored by the president.

Presidential Wartime Emergency Powers

After Thomas Jefferson had left the presidency, in 1810 he wrote:

> A strict observation of the written laws is doubtless one of the higher duties of a good officer, but it is not the highest. The law of necessity, of self-preservation, of saving our country when in danger, are of higher obligation. To lose our country by a scrupulous adherence to written

law would be to lose the law itself, with life, liberty, property . . . thus sacrificing the end to the means.[113]

This argument, that presidents have the authority to violate the Constitution to ensure the security of the nation, has been used by wartime presidents to justify extraordinary exercises of power.

When it is evident that conditions of national peril exist, Congress and the American public have turned to the president for leadership. Under such conditions Lincoln and Franklin Roosevelt stretched, reinterpreted, and in some cases brazenly violated the Constitution in the name of national security. Their claim to an inherent executive power to safeguard the nation was accepted because the American people generally agreed with their assessment of the gravity of the emergency at hand.[114] Presidential claims of an inherent executive power during a doubtful national emergency, however, will likely fail the test of public and judicial scrutiny. President Nixon was not able to convince the American people or the courts that his administration's use of wiretaps and break-ins was in the interest of national security.

Nowhere does the Constitution mention presidential emergency powers, but the courts often have been sympathetic to exercises of emergency power by presidents in wartime, especially when action is taken with the cooperation of Congress. Yet this approval has not been automatic, especially when the rights and property of U.S. citizens is involved. Total war in any age requires sacrifices from civilians and security measures at home, but a wartime emergency does not give the president unrestrained freedom to violate the rights of Americans.

Martial Law and Civil Rights

The most extreme wartime emergency measure a president may take is the declaration of martial law. Under such a declaration, civilian government is temporarily replaced by military rule. Substitution of military for civilian authority may be absolute, or it may involve only the appropriation of a specific civil function by the military. Even cases of limited martial law, however, invariably result in the curbing of individual rights.

The Constitution does not provide for a power to declare martial law, although it does mention the suspension of *habeas corpus* under Article I, which outlines Congress's powers. The declaration of martial law, however, is usually presumed to be a presidential function flowing from the president's powers to command the armed forces and execute the laws. Because there is no specific constitutional basis for martial law, presidents must justify their decision to proclaim it on the grounds that the welfare and security of the nation requires them to govern through military force rather than established laws.

No president has ever declared a condition of absolute martial law that applied to the entire country. Moreover, not since President Lincoln placed several areas of the nation under martial law during the Civil War has any president directly proclaimed martial law on behalf of the national government. Martial law has been declared, however, by presidential agents or military officers often with the explicit or implied approval of the president. For example, Gen. Andrew Jackson declared martial law in New Orleans before his battle with the British there in 1814; the commander of federal troops sent to Idaho in 1899 to quell labor unrest declared martial law with President McKinley's approval; and after the Japanese attack on Pearl Harbor on December 7, 1941, the territorial governor of Hawaii declared martial law on the islands with the support of Franklin Roosevelt.[115]

Although the courts may reject the president's assessment of the necessity of martial law, historically they have done so only after the emergency has passed. In 1866 the Supreme Court ruled in *Ex parte Milligan* that Lincoln's suspension of the the civil court system in Indiana during the civil war was illegal.[116] Similarly, in 1946 the court declared in *Duncan v. Kahanamoku* that the establishment of martial law during World War II in Hawaii by the governor with President Roosevelt's approval had been unlawful.[117] Yet neither decision had any effect on either president's ability to abrogate civil liberties during the wars.

Suspension of Habeas Corpus

The only emergency power mentioned in the Constitution is the suspension of the writ of *habeas corpus*—the right of prisoners to have the legality of their detention reviewed by the courts and to be released upon the court's orders. The Constitution states: "The Privilege of the Writ of Habeas Corpus shall not be suspended, unless when in Cases of Rebellion or Invasion the public Safety may require it." The Framers did not, however, specify who had this power, although their placement of it in Article I has led many legal scholars, judges, and legislators to argue that it was intended as a congressional power.

The issue of presidential suspension of *habeas corpus* arose most dramatically during the Civil War. In response to sabotage by Confederate sympathizers, President Lincoln ordered in the spring of 1861 that *habeas corpus* be suspended along the route between Washington and Philadelphia. Lincoln believed this and other emergency measures were essential to the survival of the Union. On May 25, John Merryman, a prominent Maryland citizen who had been involved in secessionist activities in that state, was arrested by military authorities. Merryman immediately appealed to Chief Justice Roger Taney for a writ of *habeas corpus*. Taney reviewed the case and ordered the army to release Merryman, but Lincoln defiantly refused to permit his release. Taney denounced Lincoln's action and wrote an opinion asserting that the Constitution had conferred authority to suspend the writ on Congress, not the president. Lincoln maintained that since the suspension of *habeas corpus* was an emergency measure and emergencies could occur when Congress was out of session—as it had been in this case—presidents must have authority to suspend the writ unilaterally.

The conflict between the president and the chief justice showed that a president willing to defy legal procedures during a genuine crisis that was widely recognized as such could suspend *habeas corpus* regardless of the president's legal authority to do so. Presidential scholar Clinton Rossiter remarked,

> The one great precedent is what Lincoln did, not what Taney said. Future Presidents will know where to look for historical support. So long as public opinion sustains the President, as a sufficient amount of it sustained Lincoln in his shadowy tilt with Taney and throughout the rest of the war, he has nothing to fear from the displeasure of the courts. . . . The law of the Constitution, as it actually exists, must be considered to read that in a condition of martial necessity the President has the power to suspend the privilege of the writ of habeas corpus.[118]

Trial of Civilians by Military Courts

In addition to suspending *habeas corpus*, President Lincoln also declared that for some crimes civilians could be tried by military courts. On September 24, 1862, he announced that as long as the Civil War continued

> all rebels and insurgents, their aiders and abettors, within the United States, and all persons discouraging volunteer enlistments, resisting militia drafts, or guilty of any disloyal practice affording aid and comfort to rebels against the authority of the United States, shall be subject to martial law and liable to trial and punishment of courts-martial or military commissions.

Lincoln went on to suspend *habeas corpus* for such persons and declared that they could be imprisoned in military facilities. Although Congress had passed legislation approving many of Lincoln's emergency measures, it never approved his subjection of civilians to military courts.[119] *(See "Abraham Lincoln and the Habeas Corpus Controversy," p. 1168, in The President and the Supreme Court chapter of Part VI.)*

Lambdin P. Milligan, a citizen of Indiana, was arrested in 1864 by military authorities who charged him with aiding a Confederate raid into Indiana from across the Ohio River. On May 9, 1865, he was found guilty and sentenced to death. Milligan's case eventually came before the Supreme Court.

The Court held 9-0 in *Ex parte Milligan* that the president did not have the authority to subject civilians to military tribunals in an area where civilian courts were functioning.[120] The Court also ruled 5-4 that even the president and Congress together lacked power to authorize trials of civilians by military courts outside of a war zone. The majority opinion, written by Justice David Davis admitted:

> If, in foreign invasion or civil war, the courts are actually closed, and it is impossible to administer criminal justice according to law, then, in the theatre of active military operations, where war really prevails, there is a necessity to furnish a substitute for the civilian authority, thus overthrown, to preserve the safety of the army and society; and as no power is left but the military, it is allowed to govern by martial rule until the laws can have their free course.

The Court rejected the idea, however, that such conditions existed in Indiana—hundreds of miles from the front—where civilian courts were functioning normally.

Beyond their verdict, the justices used this case to defend the inviolability of the Constitution. Davis wrote:

> The Constitution of the United States is a law for rulers and people, equally in war and in peace, and covers with the shield of its protection all classes of men, at all times, and under all circumstances. No doctrine involving more pernicious consequences was ever invented by the wit of man than that any of its provisions can be suspended during any of the great exigencies of government.

Milligan is regarded as significant by legal scholars for demonstrating that even during the most dire military emergency there are constitutional limits to presidential power.

Korematsu v. United States

When the Supreme Court ruled on *Milligan* in 1866, the war was over and Lincoln was dead. Consequently, the Court was able to strike down a presidential emergency action without confronting an incumbent president during a wartime crisis. Three-quarters of a century later, however, a case involving the violation of individual rights by an exercise of wartime emergency power came before the Court while the emergency still existed.

Following the Japanese attack on Pearl Harbor on December 7, 1941, President Roosevelt ordered several controversial measures to enhance security on the West Coast. These included the imposition of a curfew on persons of Japanese descent and the relocation of 120,000 Japanese Americans to internment camps in the U.S. interior. Both the curfew and the relocation applied to persons of Japanese ancestry regardless of their citizenship or loyalty. Congress subsequently passed legislation validating the president's directives. *(See "Individual Liberty versus Societal Good," p. 1157, in The President and the Supreme Court chapter of Part VI.)*

This wholesale suspension of the rights of American citizens led to several Supreme Court cases. The Court ruled unanimously in *Hirabayashi v. United States* that together the president and Congress had the power to impose the curfew and that the extreme emergency created by Japan's threat to the Pacific Coast made the curfew justifiable.[121] The Court did not reach a consensus, however, on the more severe violation of rights involved in the relocation of Japanese-Americans. In *Korematsu v. United States* it ruled 6-3 that the threat to national security justified the joint action of Congress and the president.[122] Writing for the majority, Justice Hugo Black explained, "Compulsory exclusion of large groups of citizens from their homes, except under circumstances of direct emergency and peril, is inconsistent with our basic governmental institutions. But when under conditions of modern warfare our shores are threatened by hostile forces, the power to protect must be commensurable with the threatened danger." In a bitter dissenting opinion, Justice Francis Murphy rejected the premise of the Court's decision that the emergency on the West Coast warranted the exclusion from the West Coast of all persons of Japanese ancestry. "Such exclusion," he wrote, "goes over 'the very brink of Constitutional power' and falls into the abyss of racism." Although *Korematsu* is now generally regarded as an embarrassing moment in Supreme Court history, it reinforced the prerogative of the president and Congress jointly to take almost any emergency action in time of war, even if that action violates the most basic rights of U.S. citizens.[123]

Seizure of Property

During wartime it sometimes is necessary for a government to seize property of its citizens that is vital to the war effort. Congress has traditionally passed legislation governing the seizure of property belonging to U.S. citizens. Before and during World War I, Congress empowered the president to seize transportation and communications systems if such actions became necessary. President Wilson used these statutes to take over railroad, telephone, and telegraph operations, which were returned to civilian control after the war. Similarly, Franklin Roosevelt was authorized by the War Labor Disputes Act of 1943 to seize industries important to the war effort that were in danger of being shut down by labor disputes.[124]

Presidents have not always waited, however, for Congress to grant them the authority to seize property before they took action. Lincoln personally authorized military units to take possession of telegraph lines during the Civil

War, and Wilson ordered the seizure of a wireless station in 1914 that refused to comply with naval censorship rules. Franklin Roosevelt took control of several strike-threatened industries before Congress authorized such action with the War Labor Disputes Act. Yet unilateral seizures of property by presidents have been exceptions to accepted practice, and the courts generally have rejected the proposition that presidents possess inherent emergency powers that authorize them to seize private property.

The most famous court case dealing with the president's power to seize private property in wartime was *Youngstown Sheet and Tube Co. v. Sawyer,* also known as the *Steel Seizure Case.* In it the Supreme Court ruled that President Truman did not have the authority to seize steel mills about to be closed by strikes despite the ongoing Korean War emergency. United Steel workers threatened to strike on April 9, 1952. Truman believed that the strike would damage the Korean War effort by causing steel shortages. On April 8, he directed Secretary of Commerce Charles Sawyer to seize and operate the steel mills. He justified his seizure of the mills solely on his power as commander in chief and his responsibility to execute the laws. Truman conceded in his report to Congress that it had the authority to countermand his directive, but Congress failed to approve or reject the president's action.

The steel companies brought suit against the government seeking an injunction to stop the president's action. The case quickly reached the Supreme Court, where, by a vote of 6-3, Truman's action was held unconstitutional. The Court claimed that the president had usurped Congress's law-making power. It cited several acts in which Congress had provided procedures for responding to strikes that Truman had ignored. In the debate on one of these laws, the Taft-Hartley Act of 1947, Congress had considered empowering the government to seize an industry to prevent strikes but had refused to include such a provision in the law. Truman, therefore, had not just taken action without congressional authorization, he had taken an action that Congress had rejected.[125]

Although it is unclear whether the Court would have ruled differently had the emergency been more grave or had Congress not rejected the inclusion of property seizure provisions in the Taft-Hartley Act, the decision was a blow to the president's commander-in-chief authority. In a concurring opinion Justice William O. Douglas explained:

> There can be no doubt that the emergency which caused the president to seize these steel plants was one that bore heavily on the country. But the emergency did not create power; it merely marked an occasion when power should be exercised. And the fact that it was necessary that measures be taken to keep steel in production does not mean that the President, rather than the Congress, had the constitutional authority to act.[126]

In an era of rapidly expanding presidential power, the *Steel Seizure Case,* as Clinton Rossiter observed, "revived, for the moment, the notion that Presidents were subject to congressional limitations in foreign affairs." [127]

Armed Forces as a Tool of Presidential Foreign Policy

The armed forces of the United States have assisted presidents in achieving foreign policy goals. A president confronted with an international problem often has the option to use the military to solve that problem. Military strength has enabled presidents to intimidate potential aggressors, impress trading partners, reassure allies, and mediate international disputes. Presidents have been reluctant to deploy armed forces in a crisis, but nearly every twentieth-century president has done so, sometimes with negative results. Beyond the military's potential to use or threaten force in a specific international hotspot, the strength of U.S. armed forces since World War II has allowed presidents to improve relations with other countries by offering them security guarantees and memberships in multinational alliances.

Peacetime Military Missions

From the time the Constitution was ratified until the present, presidents have used the military to accomplish limited missions in peacetime. Presidents have ordered the armed forces to protect settlers from Indians, repel bands of foreign outlaws, punish nations and groups for belligerent or criminal behavior, rescue U.S. citizens abroad, support friendly governments and train their armies, fight pirates and terrorists, warn potential enemies from taking aggressive action, and secure disputed lands. As chief executive, presidents also have used troops to put down domestic insurrections and enforce federal law. The Constitution does not specifically sanction these peacetime military operations, but presidents have justified them under their power to command the military, defend the United States and its citizens, enforce the laws, and conduct foreign policy.

Police Actions and Rescue Missions

Of all peacetime military operations, the most consequential have been police actions and rescue missions ordered by presidents to protect U.S. citizens and interests abroad. The vast majority of these operations have been minor incidents that did not require Congress to declare war. Indeed, many of them were so brief that Congress would not have had time to deliberate on a declaration of war even if the president had asked for one. Presidents have argued that these limited missions require no congressional sanction since they have limited goals and often depend on speed and secrecy. As long as military operations did not threaten to involve the United States in a wider war and casualties remained low, presidential popularity usually has been bolstered by limited uses of force.

Congress and the courts generally have refrained from challenging the president's authority to protect U.S. citizens and property overseas even when military actions taken under presidential orders have been unjust. For example, in 1854 a naval commander acting on the vague but belligerent orders of President Franklin Pierce completely destroyed the Nicaraguan city of Greytown when it refused to pay inflated damage claims filed by a U.S. company. Congress investigated the incident but failed to condemn the Greytown bombardment or make Pierce account for his actions. A U.S. district court dismissed a suit filed by a Greytown property owner against the naval commander on the grounds that the bombardment was a political matter.[128]

Not all presidents have believed the commander-in-chief clause gave them the power to order limited military

Military Responses to Terrorism

Throughout U.S. history, presidents have called on the military to battle not just other nations but also extra-governmental groups that have threatened Americans and their interests. For example, the navy often fought pirates in the eighteenth and nineteenth centuries, and in 1916 President Woodrow Wilson sent Gen. John J. (Blackjack) Pershing and six thousand troops into Mexico in pursuit of the Mexican bandit Pancho Villa after he had raided Columbus, New Mexico.

During the 1970s and 1980s international terrorist groups have threatened the safety of U.S. citizens much as international pirates and bandits did in earlier centuries. Terrorist groups have used violence to gain media attention and strike back at powerful nations they perceive as contributing to their particular plight. Often these terrorist acts have involved attacks on or captures of innocent civilians. Since the mid-1970s the U.S. military has placed greater emphasis on antiterrorist preparations. Intelligence agencies have expanded their efforts to identify terrorists, and elite counterterrorist units have been formed to provide presidents with a more credible military option should they decide to use force against terrorists.

While terrorist groups cannot match the military power of the United States or other industrialized nations, military operations against them have seldom been a practical option. Terrorists have been difficult to identify, and they often have blended into the populace of foreign nations or surrounded themselves with hostages. Presidents who use force indiscriminately risk harming innocent civilians, endangering the lives of hostages, lending credibility to terrorist claims of U.S. injustice, and creating a cavalier image of the United States within the international community. Presidents therefore generally have refrained from using military force against terrorists except when those responsible for a terrorist act could be positively identified and attacked with precision.

Two developments during the Reagan administration increased the likelihood that presidents will use military force against terrorists in the future. First, the administration's popular military operations against terrorists and their sponsors showed that military force could be used to strike back at the roots of terrorism. In October 1985, the president ordered navy fighters to intercept an Egyptian airliner carrying terrorists who had seized a passenger ship and killed a U.S. citizen in the Mediterranean. On April 14, 1986, Reagan directed U.S. warplanes to bomb targets in Libya after U.S. intelligence obtained evidence that Libyan leader Col. Muammar Qaddafi sponsored a terrorist bombing of a Berlin nightclub. The attack set a precedent for U.S. military retaliation against any state proven to sponsor terrorist attacks against U.S. citizens. Regardless of the effectiveness of these operations in deterring terrorism, both satisfied a public impulse to strike back at terrorism and improved President Reagan's standing in public opinion polls. Second, the administration's embarrassing attempt to free U.S. hostages in Lebanon by selling arms to Iran created the perception in government and among the public that negotiating with terrorists will usually be counterproductive.

missions in the absence of congressional approval. For example, Pierce's successor, James Buchanan, claimed that without the consent of Congress he could not "fire a hostile gun in any case except to repel the attacks of an enemy." [129] Most twentieth-century presidents, however, have interpreted the commander-in-chief power broadly to fit the needs and goals of the moment.

No president did more to expand presidential authority to order limited military missions than Theodore Roosevelt. In 1904 he asserted the president's right to exercise an "international police power" in Latin America. In what became known as the Roosevelt Corollary to the Monroe Doctrine he declared that the United States had the right to intervene in Latin America to protect its interests and ensure peace. He justified this position by asserting that those governments in Latin America that were unable to rule justly, maintain order, or meet their international obligations were jeopardizing the security of the hemisphere and violating the rights of the United States. Roosevelt already had acted in the spirit of this proclamation in 1903 when he used military force to protect an American-backed revolt in Panama against Colombian rule. The revolution enabled Roosevelt to conclude a treaty with the new Panamanian government allowing the United States to construct the Panama Canal on favorable terms. In 1905 Roosevelt put his corollary to use when he ordered U.S. forces to seize and operate the custom offices of Santo Domingo, which was failing to pay its foreign debts.

After Roosevelt presidents exercised the "police power" in the Western Hemisphere with little hesitation or consultation with Congress. William Taft, Woodrow Wilson, Calvin Coolidge, John Kennedy, Lyndon Johnson, and Ronald Reagan all used U.S. forces—or foreign troops trained and supplied by the United States—to intervene in the affairs of Latin American nations.[130]

Even if the president's power to order limited military missions is conceded, there is still the problem of defining which missions fall under the president's police and rescue powers and which should be authorized by a congressional sanction if not a declaration of war. Like the prerogative to repel invasions, the police and rescue powers can be manipulated by presidents to justify military actions that Congress might not sanction.

President Johnson sent twelve hundred troops to the Dominican Republic in 1965 in response to a plea by the U.S. ambassador there to protect Americans from the chaos brought by a coup attempt. The goals and size of the intervention soon changed, however, as the president became concerned that the Dominican faction reputed to be controlled by Communists might seize power. Johnson expanded the U.S. military force on the island to twenty thousand troops and ordered its commanders to help establish a provisional government. The troops remained until the following year when elections were held and the candidate favored by the Johnson administration was elected.

Similarly, President Reagan ordered six thousand troops to the tiny Caribbean island of Grenada in 1983 on what he called a "rescue mission." The administration maintained that a pro-Cuban military coup had placed U.S. citizens on the island in danger and threatened to turn Grenada into a Cuban-supported Communist military base. U.S. troops evacuated about one thousand Americans from the island and proceeded to depose Grenada's new leadership.[131]

In both interventions presidents used armed force to accomplish geopolitical goals without the consent of Congress. U.S. actions in the Dominican Republic and Grenada clearly were more than rescue missions or police actions. Nevertheless, the historical precedent supporting the authority of presidents to order military missions and the perceived urgency of the situation at hand have predictably influenced presidents and the U.S. public more often than strict interpretations of the Constitution and of international law.

Military Exercises and Shows of Force

Throughout U.S. history presidents have ordered conspicuous deployments of U.S. military power to dissuade potential aggressors, support allies, and reinforce U.S. diplomatic bargaining positions. Shows of force were initially limited by the weakness of the U.S. military. The demonstrations of force that presidents did order before World War II almost always involved the navy.

Millard Fillmore sent a squadron of ships under Commodore Matthew Perry to Japan in 1853. The Japanese had kept their ports closed to westerners and had abused U.S. seamen shipwrecked off their shores. Perry was instructed to show the Japanese U.S. naval power, demand that U.S. sailors be treated with respect, and propose a commercial relationship between the two countries. Perry's expedition resulted in the Treaty of Kanagawa, which declared friendship between the United States and Japan, opened several Japanese ports to U.S. commercial vessels, and established provisions for the treatment of U.S. citizens shipwrecked off Japan.

Perhaps the most famous show of force by a president was Theodore Roosevelt's dispatch of the U.S. fleet in 1907 on a cruise around the world. The cruise was primarily intended to impress Japan with U.S. naval power. Roosevelt was concerned by indications of Tokyo's belligerence and wished to demonstrate his own resolve to oppose any act of aggression by the Japanese. He believed the "Great White Fleet's" cruise also would be a valuable exercise and would promote respect and good will for the United States throughout the world. The trip went smoothly with the navy observing protocol at each port of call. Roosevelt later asserted, "The most important service that I rendered to peace was the voyage of the battle fleet around the world." [132]

Shows of force may be used to reassure a friendly government as well as warn a belligerent one. On March 17, 1988, President Reagan sent 3,150 additional U.S. troops to Honduras in response to the incursion of Nicaraguan government troops into Honduras. The Nicaraguan forces reportedly crossed the Honduras border to destroy a supply depot of the antigovernment Nicaraguan contra rebels supported by the Reagan administration. Secretary of State George Shultz said of the troops: "They're not near where the fighting is taking place, but they're designed to say to the Government of Honduras that, 'we are your friend and we stand with you, and if you are invaded you can count on the United States.' " [133] The contingent of troops conducted maneuvers in Honduras and withdrew from the country after ten days without engaging in combat.

Training and Advising Foreign Troops

Military advisers have become an established part of the superpowers' struggle for influence. Both the United States and the Communist bloc have sent military personnel into third world countries to instruct the local armed forces in organization, tactics, and the use of weapons. Often these military advisers are sent specifically to teach local troops how to use military equipment that has been given or sold to that nation.

Since U.S. military advisers usually are instructed not to participate in combat, their deployment traditionally has not required congressional approval. Sending military advisers to a foreign country, however, can be controversial. Many Americans see the introduction of U.S. military advisers into a foreign country as a first step toward greater involvement in that country's problems. This perception was created by the gradual escalation of U.S. involvement in the Vietnam War, which began with the deployment of military advisers in that country. Dwight Eisenhower first sent small numbers of advisers to Vietnam. By the end of 1960, 835 U.S. military personnel were training the South Vietnamese Army. Since South Vietnam was fighting a guerrilla war against Communist Vietcong forces in the South, U.S. advisers could not avoid combat entirely. John Kennedy and Lyndon Johnson dramatically increased the number of advisers in Vietnam to meet the growing military threat to the Saigon government. By the end of 1963 over 16,000 advisers were in Vietnam. A year later this number had swelled to 23,210.[134] Beginning with the Kennedy administration, although U.S. forces were still called "advisers," they had active combat roles.

When President Reagan introduced military advisers into El Salvador in 1981, critics of Reagan's policy charged that the U.S. military involvement in Central America could escalate as it had in Vietnam. Reagan promised to limit U.S. military advisers in El Salvador to fifty-five, but the House Foreign Affairs Committee was concerned enough to outline in a report what it considered to be unacceptable activities for U.S. military advisers in all countries. These included accompanying local units into combat, arming or fueling combat aircraft, and delivering weapons and supplies to local troops in combat areas. Although these guidelines did not have the force of law, they did set a standard for the conduct of U.S. military advisers.[135]

United Nations Peace Keeping

Presidents often have promoted UN peace-keeping missions and, when appropriate, have offered the services of the U.S. military to those missions. The advantages that UN peace-keeping missions have over unilateral U.S. action in many regions are that UN peace-keepers are less threatening to local nations, the economic costs to the United States are minimized, and a UN peace-keeping force can promote a spirit of international accountability and cooperation in solving a particular regional problem.

The primary responsibility for the peace and security function of the United Nations resides with the Security Council. The council assesses threats to peace and attempts to use peaceful measures to prevent aggression. If nonmilitary actions fail or are inappropriate, the Security Council may vote to use military force.[136]

A Security Council decision to use military force or to create a detachment of military observers cannot be adopted without the unanimous approval of its members. Since the United States and the Soviet Union are permanent members of the Security Council along with Great Britain, France, and the People's Republic of China, the relevance of the peace-keeping role of the United Nations to conflicts between allies of the superpowers has been limited. UN peace-keeping forces have been used to separate combatants, monitor cease-fire agreements, and protect civilians in places such as the Congo, Cyprus, Indonesia, West New Guinea, and the border between India and Pakistan. The last three included U.S. personnel.

Neither superpower has been willing to allow UN peace-keeping forces to be used against the perceived interests of its clients. Nevertheless, the Security Council has sanctioned limited peace-keeping missions when the interests of the United States and the Soviet Union have converged. During the late 1980s the status of UN-sponsored peace-keeping forces grew as UN peace-keepers were awarded the 1988 Nobel Peace Prize and the Soviet Union and United States both advocated the use of UN peace-keeping troops to monitor negotiated settlements of several regional conflicts. The United Nations created new peace-keeping forces to oversee peace accords in Afghanistan and Angola and between Iran and Iraq.

The most contentious issue in the Senate debate on U.S. membership in the UN was who had the power to commit U.S. forces to Security Council peace-keeping operations. The Senate did not want to hand the executive exclusive authority to provide the United Nations with troops. Such a power would have allowed the president to commit the United States to UN military operations without the congressional consent required by a declaration of war.[137]

The United Nations Participation Act of 1945 outlined the rules under which U.S. forces could be placed at the disposal of the United Nations:

> The President is authorized to negotiate a special agreement or agreements with the Security Council which shall be subject to the approval of the Congress by appropriate Act or joint resolution, providing for the numbers and types of armed forces, their degree of readiness and general location, and the nature of facilities and assistance, including rights of passage, to be made available to the Security Council on its call for the purpose of maintaining international peace and security. . . .

Thus presidents are expressly prohibited by the Participation Act from unilaterally concluding an agreement with the Security Council under their powers to negotiate treaties, execute the laws, or defend the United States. The president cannot legally aid or commit U.S. forces to UN peace-keeping missions without an approving congressional resolution.[138]

The most dramatic use of the UN security function was the Security Council's response to the North Korean invasion of South Korea in 1950. Because the Soviets were boycotting the Security Council to protest the exclusion of Communist China from the council, they were not present to exercise their veto when the council voted to ask UN member nations to aid South Korea.

Section 6 of the United Nations Participation Act required President Truman to secure congressional approval of the agreement between the U.S. and the Security Council that provided for the use of American forces. No such agreement was ever negotiated. Truman based the U.S. intervention in Korea on the Security Council's call to UN member nations to render assistance to South Korea. Truman's consultations with congressional leaders amounted to an information session shortly before he announced to the press that he had ordered U.S. troops into combat.[139]

Not all U.S. peace-keeping missions have been undertaken under UN auspices. For example, as part of the 1979 Camp David Peace accords the United States promised Egypt and Israel that it would organize a peace-keeping force to monitor the withdrawal of Israel from the Sinai Peninsula if the United Nations did not provide such a force. Since the Soviet Union threatened to exercise its Security Council veto to block the creation of any UN peace-keeping force for the Sinai, the United States created a multinational force that included U.S. troops. The United States also sent military forces to Lebanon in 1982 as part of a multinational peace-keeping force. The U.S. contingent of Marines reached 2,000 in 1983 but was withdrawn in February 1984 by President Reagan four months after the terrorist bombing of the Marine barracks in Beirut killed 241 Marines.

Alliances and Mutual Security Agreements

The armed forces have served as a tool of presidential foreign policy not just when presidents have used or threatened force. U.S. military strength since World War II has enabled presidents to offer security commitments and alliance partnerships to countries concerned with their ability to defend themselves. In doing so presidents have improved relations with many other countries, extended U.S. global influence, and strengthened U.S. defenses.

Before World War II, the United States had shunned alliances. Its size and isolated location on the North American continent made it an unattractive target of military adventures. In addition, during most of the nineteenth and early twentieth centuries the military establishments of the great powers of Europe were primarily concerned with defending against threats from their neighbors. Since the security of the United States did not depend on having allies, the American people generally had preferred to remain isolationist. They considered the possibility of becoming imbroiled in a foreign war while honoring an alliance commitment a greater danger than being forced to defend the United States without allies. With the exception of the Franco-American Alliance of 1778, which was effectively voided by George Washington's 1793 neutrality proclamation toward Britain and France, the United States had never participated in a formal peacetime alliance until after World War II.[140] Even when the United States entered World War I against Germany in 1917, U.S. leaders demonstrated the national aversion to alliances by claiming to be only an "associated power" of Britain and France.

World War II shattered the isolationist policies of the United States. The nation emerged from the war not just as a member of the international community, but as a world leader. The growth of Soviet military power and the establishment of Soviet control over Eastern Europe after World War II led many nations to seek the security of an alliance or friendly relationship with the United States. Under Truman and Eisenhower the United States enthusiastically erected a global network of multilateral and bilateral alliances intended to contain Soviet expansionism. The Rio Pact, signed in 1947, reaffirmed the longstanding U.S. commitment to defend the Western Hemisphere. The 1949 North Atlantic Treaty created the North Atlantic Treaty Organization (NATO), an alliance between the United States, Canada, and most Western European democracies that developed into the cornerstone of U.S. containment strategy. The ANZUS alliance was formed between Australia, New Zealand, and the United States in 1951. The United States also joined the Southeast Asia Treaty Organization (SEATO) in 1954 and established ties with, although not membership in, a Middle Eastern alliance known as the Central Treaty Organization (CENTO) in 1956. These multilateral alliances were complemented by bilateral alliances with Japan and the Philippines in 1951, Korea in 1953, Taiwan in 1954, and Iran, Pakistan, and Turkey in 1959.[141]

Although many of these alliances, including SEATO and CENTO, no longer function, maintaining a web of U.S. security relationships has remained a goal of U.S. foriegn policy. In addition to formal alliances, the United States increased its international defense capabilities through agreements on base rights, intelligence sharing, and informal defense cooperation with other countries.

Power to Form Military Alliances

Alliances often can be a contentious political issue because commitments to fight beside alliance partners under attack can draw a nation into a war. Theoretically, participation in an alliance should involve Congress since the Constitution gives it the power to declare war. Although most major alliances have been based on treaties ratified by the Senate, presidents have claimed the authority to make alliances unilaterally by virtue of their commander-in-chief, negotiation, and recognition powers.

Since World War II presidents often have exercised their alliance-making power without formal action by Congress. On August 14, 1941, for example, President Roosevelt signed the Atlantic Charter, which laid the groundwork for an Anglo-American alliance once the United States had entered World War II. Roosevelt then signed the Declaration of United Nations on January 1, 1942, which pledged the United States and, by the end of the war, forty-five other nations to support the Allied war effort and not make a separate peace with the enemy nations.[142] After the war, Presidents Truman and Eisenhower used executive agreements to expand NATO into a unified defense organization with a standing military structure. Although no formal alliance treaty exists between the United States and Israel, presidents since Truman have maintained the extensive U.S. commitment to Israeli security. Even Carter's 1979 declaration that the Persian Gulf was vital to U.S. national security created the potential for de facto alliances with gulf states if their security were threatened.

Presidential Alliance Responsibilities

U.S. membership in an alliance creates additional presidential responsibilities. The most important of these is the president's obligation, as commander in chief and the person who executes the laws, to fulfill the terms of a treaty by coming to the defense of an allied nation that is attacked. This obligation depends on the terms of the alliance agreement and the declared policy of the United States. The NATO treaty states that "an attack on one or more [of the parties] shall be considered as an attack against all of the parties." Advocates of presidential power could argue that by ratifying a treaty with such language Congress has given presidents the same authority to repel an invasion of a NATO country as they have to repel an attack on the United States. An alliance, therefore, can expand the number of situations under which presidents can order troops into battle without a declaration of war by extending their prerogative to repel attacks to alliance partners.[143]

The declared policy of the United States, however, may be even more relevant to the president's authority to defend an alliance partner than the language of a treaty. With over 300,000 troops and many nuclear weapons committed to the defense of Western Europe, no matter how one interprets the language of the NATO treaty and its effect on presidential authority, the president is expected to direct U.S. troops to repel any Soviet attack on NATO. Similarly, presidents have complete authority to respond to attacks on South Korea and Japan, not only because of treaties with those nations, but because many U.S. troops are based there and numerous acts of Congress have recognized and supported U.S. defense commitments in East Asia.

Presidential authority to come to the aid of many other nations with which the United States has less formal mutual security agreements is ambiguous. It is not certain that the president has the legal authority to commit U.S. forces to the defense of Israel, for example, where the United States has no troops and defense cooperation is based on executive agreements rather than a Senate-ratified treaty. Nevertheless, such executive agreements do provide presidents who are determined to defend an ally with a justification for using troops in its defense.

A second presidential alliance responsibility is maintaining alliance cohesion. An alliance that is not unified will likely be ineffective and will contribute little to U.S. security. Therefore, the president is compelled to consider the effect of U.S. foreign and military policy on the cohesion of its alliances and public opinion within the allied countries. For example, since the citizens of the West European allies of United States fear both the arms race and Soviet military strength, modern presidents can neither ignore arms control that would affect Europe nor conclude an agreement that significantly reduces NATO's military capabilities unless such an agreement is supported by allied governments. Even when a foreign policy action does not directly involve an alliance, a president must weigh its effect on alliance countries. The concerns of Presidents Johnson and Nixon that other U.S. allies would see abandonment of South Vietnam as evidence of U.S. inability to fulfill its commitments contributed to their refusal to withdraw American troops from Vietnam without attempting to ensure South Vietnamese security. Membership in an alliance, therefore, can be a powerful restraint on presidential freedom of action.

In addition to being a caretaker of alliance unity, the president is expected to take the lead in developing new alliance policies. In every alliance in which the United States has participated since World War II, it has been the dominant military power. This status gives the president a considerable bargaining advantage over alliance partners but does not enable presidents to dictate alliance policy. Presidents must lobby allied leaders to support their initiatives just as they must lobby members of Congress to support their legislative proposals. To the extent that a president can persuade allies to support U.S. foreign policies, alliances enhance the president's domestic power. When U.S. presidents are able to take strong action with allied support, they increase their prestige and authority over foreign policy at home. Congress is less likely to challenge the foreign policy of a president who is perceived as an effective international leader than one who has not been able to deliver allied support for U.S. programs and actions.

Notes

1. Alexander Hamilton, *Federalist* No. 74, in *The Federalist Papers* (New York: New American Library, 1961), 447.
2. Clinton Rossiter, *The American Presidency*, 2d ed. (New York: Time, 1960), 13.
3. Samuel P. Huntington, *The Soldier and the State* (New York: Vintage, 1964), 178.
4. James Madison, *The Gazette of the United States*, August 24, 1793, quoted in *The Power of the Presidency*, ed. Robert S. Hirschenfield (New York: Atherton, 1968), 59.
5. Arthur M. Schlesinger, Jr., *The Imperial Presidency* (Boston: Houghton Mifflin, 1973), 4.
6. Hamilton, *Federalist* No. 69, 417-418.
7. Joseph E. Kallenbach, *The American Chief Executive: The Presidency and the Governorship* (New York: Harper and Row, 1966), 535-536.
8. Michael P. Riccards, *A Republic, If You Can Keep It: The Foundation of the American Presidency, 1700-1800* (New York: Greenwood Press, 1987), 152-153.
9. Edward S. Corwin, *The President: Office and Powers, 1787-1984*, 5th rev. ed. (New York: New York University Press, 1984), 297.
10. Clinton Rossiter, *The Supreme Court and the Commander in Chief* (Ithaca, N.Y.: Cornell University Press, 1976), 48-52.
11. Robert E. DiClerico, *The American President*, 2d ed. (Englewood Cliffs, N.J.: Prentice-Hall, 1983), 37.
12. Richard M. Pious, *The American Presidency* (New York: Basic Books, 1979), 392.
13. James D. Richardson, *A Compilation of the Messages and Papers of the Presidents, 1789-1910*, (New York: Bureau of National Literature, 1917), 1:314-315.
14. Pious, *The American Presidency*, 392.
15. Quoted in Corwin, *The President*, 229.
16. Schlesinger, *The Imperial Presidency*, 23.
17. Thomas Eagleton, *War and Presidential Power* (New York: Liveright, 1974), 23.
18. Lawrence Margolis, *Executive Agreements and Presidential Power in Foreign Policy* (New York: Praeger, 1986), 9.
19. Schlesinger, *The Imperial Presidency*, 39-41.
20. Wilfred E. Binkley, *The Man in the White House* (Baltimore: Johns Hopkins University Press, 1964), 192.
21. John Nicolay and John Hay, eds., *The Complete Works of Abraham Lincoln* (New York: Francis Tandy, 1891), 10:66.
22. Schlesinger, *The Imperial Presidency*, 58.
23. Corwin, *The President*, 264.
24. Ibid., 265.
25. Carl B. Swisher, *American Constitutional Development*, 2d ed. (Boston: Houghton Mifflin, 1954), 29.
26. Binkley, *The Man in the White House*, 194.
27. *Prize Cases*, 67 U.S. (2 Black), 635, 1863.
28. Rossiter, *Supreme Court*, 71-75.
29. Eagleton, *War and Presidential Power*, 45.
30. Corwin, *The President*, 271-272.
31. Jacob K. Javits, *Who Makes War* (New York: Morrow, 1973), 207-209.
32. Corwin, *The President*, 272.
33. R. Gordon Hoxie, *Command Decision and the Presidency* (New York: Reader's Digest Press, 1977), 11.
34. Corwin, *The President*, 272.
35. Eagleton, *War and Presidential Power*, 64.
36. Javits, *Who Makes War*, 225-226.
37. Schlesinger, *The Imperial Presidency*, 115.
38. Quoted in Corwin, *The President*, 285-286.
39. Edward S. Corwin, *Presidential Power and the Constitution* (Ithaca: Cornell University Press, 1976), 114.
40. Javits, *Who Makes War*, 230.
41. Cecil V. Crabb, Jr., and Pat M. Holt, *Invitation to Struggle: Congress, the President and Foreign Policy*, 2d ed. (Washington, D.C.: CQ Press, 1984), 130-131.
42. Dean Acheson, *Present at the Creation: My Years in the State Department* (New York: Norton, 1969), 415.
43. Schlesinger, *The Imperial Presidency*, 133.
44. James L. Sundquist, *Decline and Resurgence of Congress* (Washington, D.C.: Brookings, 1981), 109.
45. Hoxie, *Command Decision and the Presidency*, 178.
46. Schlesinger, *The Imperial Presidency*, 141.
47. Ibid., 169.
48. Sundquist, *Decline and Resurgence of Congress*, 124-125.
49. Ibid., 249.
50. Quoted in *Congressional Quarterly Almanac 1973* (Washington, D.C.: Congressional Quarterly Inc., 1974), 906.
51. Ibid., 907.
52. Ibid., 906-907.
53. Eagleton, *War and Presidential Power*, 203.
54. Larry Berman, *The New American Presidency* (Boston: Little, Brown, 1987), 75.
55. Ibid., 76.
56. DiClerico, *The American President*, 45.
57. Jacob Javits, "War Powers Reconsidered," *Foreign Affairs* (Fall 1985): 135.
58. Crabb and Holt, *Invitation to Struggle*, 146.
59. Javits, "War Powers Reconsidered," 136.
60. Crabb and Holt, *Invitation to Struggle*, 149-150.
61. Javits, "War Powers Reconsidered," 137.
62. Pat Towell, "After Raid on Libya, New Questions on Hill," *Congressional Quarterly Weekly Report*, April 19, 1986, 839.
63. Mary H. Cooper, "Persian Gulf Oil," *Editorial Research Reports*, October 30, 1987, 567.
64. Pat Towell, "New Gulf Incident Rekindles an Old Debate," *Congressional Quarterly Weekly Report*, April 23, 1988, 1051-1058.
65. Quoted in *Congressional Quarterly Almanac 1973*, 907.
66. Quoted in Crabb and Holt, *Invitation to Struggle*, 147.
67. Schlesinger, *The Imperial Presidency*, 290.
68. *Immigration and Naturalization Service v. Chadha*, 103 U.S. 2764 (1983).
69. *Congressional Quarterly Almanac 1983* (Washington, D.C.: Congressional Quarterly Inc., 1984), 568-569.
70. Pious, *The American Presidency*, 404-405.
71. U.S. Congress, Senate, *Congressional Record*, daily ed., 92d Cong., 1st sess., April 26, 1971, 11914.
72. Kallenbach, *The American Chief Executive*, 531.
73. Charles A. Beard, *The Republic* (New York: Viking Press, 1944), 101.
74. Riccards, *A Republic, If You Can Keep It*, 164-166.
75. Jacob E. Cook, "George Washington," in *The Presidents: A Reference History*, ed. Henry F. Graff (New York: Scribner's, 1984), 24.
76. Corwin, *The President*, 294.
77. Kallenbach, *The American Chief Executive*, 530.
78. Amos A. Jordan and William J. Taylor, Jr., *American National Security: Policy and Process* (Baltimore: Johns Hopkins University Press, 1984), 85.
79. Molly Moore, "Stricken Frigate's Crew Stitched Ship Together," *Washington Post*, April 22, 1988, A1.

80. Jordan and Taylor, *American National Security*, 231.
81. For a detailed description of the U.S. nuclear infrastructure, see William Arkin and Richard W. Fieldhouse, *Nuclear Battlefields* (Cambridge: Ballinger, 1984).
82. For a discussion of permissive action links, see Donald R. Cotter, "Peacetime Operations, Safety and Security," in *Managing Nuclear Operations*, ed. Ashton B. Carter, John D. Steinbruner, and Charles A. Zraket (Washington, D.C.: Brookings, 1987), 46-51.
83. Paul Bracken, *The Command and Control of Nuclear Forces* (New Haven: Yale University Press, 1983), 232-237.
84. Ibid., 229.
85. *Public Papers of the Presidents of the United States, Dwight D. Eisenhower, 1960-1961* (Washington, D.C.: Government Printing Office, 1963), 851.
86. *Public Papers of the Presidents of the United States, Harry S Truman, 1945* (Washington, D.C.: Government Printing Office, 1961), 212.
87. James A. Nathan and James K. Oliver, *United States Foreign Policy and World Order*, 2d ed. (Boston: Little, Brown, 1981), 41-42.
88. Hoxie, *Command Decision and the Presidency*, 13-14.
89. Miroslav Nincic, *United States Foreign Policy: Choices and Tradeoffs* (Washington, D.C.: CQ Press, 1988), 292.
90. Theodore Sorensen, *Kennedy* (New York: Harper and Row, 1965), 705.
91. Leslie H. Gelb with Richard K. Betts, *The Irony of Vietnam: The System Worked* (Washington, D.C.: Brookings, 1979), 264-265.
92. Arkin and Fieldhouse, *Nuclear Battlefields*, 87.
93. For text of speech and further commentary, see *Historic Documents 1983* (Washington, D.C.: Congressional Quarterly Inc., 1984), 305-316.
94. R. Jeffrey Smith, "Pentagon Scales Back SDI Goals," *Washington Post*, March 27, 1988, A1.
95. Lawrence J. Korb, "The Evolving Relationship between the White House and the Department of Defense in the Post-Imperial Presidency," in *The Post-Imperial Presidency*, ed. Vincent Davis (New Brunswick, N.J.: Transaction, 1980), 103.
96. Richard K. Betts, *Soldiers, Statesmen, and Cold War Crises* (Cambridge: Harvard University Press, 1977), 52-68.
97. For discussions of the problems that led to the reform of the JCS, see James Buck, "The Establishment: An Overview," in *Presidential Leadership and National Security: Style, Institutions, and Politics*, ed. Sam C. Sarkesian (Boulder, Colo.: Westview Press, 1984), 59-64, and John G. Kestor, "The Role of the Joint Chiefs of Staff," in *American Defense Policy*, ed. John F. Reichart and Steven R. Sturm (Baltimore: Johns Hopkins University Press, 1982), 527-545.
98. Pat Towell, "Major Pentagon Reorganization Bill Is Cleared," *Congressional Quarterly Weekly Report*, September 20, 1986, 2207-2208.
99. Morton Halperin, "The President and the Military," in *The Presidency in Contemporary Context*, ed. Norman C. Thomas (New York: Dodd, Mead, 1975), 277.
100. Ibid., 280-284.
101. Mary H. Cooper, "The Military Build-Down in the 1990s," *Editorial Research Reports*, April 22, 1988, 211.
102. Alice Maroni, "The Defense Budget," in *Presidential Leadership and National Security*, 194-196.
103. Ibid., 196.
104. Richard Haass, "The Role of the Congress in American Security Policy," in *American Defense Policy*, 558-560.
105. For a discussion of the quality-versus-quantity defense procurement debate, see James Fallows, *National Defense* (New York: Random House, 1981).
106. Jordan and Taylor, *American National Security*, 106.
107. Ibid., 187.
108. Ibid., 192.
109. George F. Brown, Jr., and Lawrence Korb, "The Economic and Political Restraints on Force Planning," in *American Defense Policy*, 583.
110. Kallenbach, *The American Chief Executive*, 543.
111. Marc Leepson, "Draft Registration," *Editorial Research Reports*, June 13, 1980, 427-430.
112. Kallenbach, *The American Chief Executive*, 537.
113. Quoted in Berman, *The New American Presidency*, 57.
114. Robert S. Hirschfield, "The Scope and Limits of Presidential Power," in *Power and the Presidency*, ed. Philip C. Dolce and George H. Skau (New York: Scribner's, 1976), 301-302.
115. Kallenbach, *The American Chief Executive*, 553-554.
116. *Ex parte Milligan*, 4 Wallace 2 (1866).
117. *Duncan v. Kahanamoku*, 327 U.S. 304 (1946).
118. Rossiter, *Supreme Court*, 25.
119. Ibid., 27.
120. *Ex parte Milligan*, 4 Wallace 2 (1866).
121. *Hirabayashi v. United States*, 320 U.S. 81 (1943).
122. *Korematsu v. United States*, 323 U.S. 214 (1944).
123. Rossiter, *Supreme Court*, 54.
124. Kallenbach, *The American Chief Executive*, 557.
125. Corwin, *Presidential Power and the Constitution*, 124-125.
126. *Youngstown Sheet and Tube Co. v. Sawyer*, 343 U.S. 579 (1952).
127. Rossiter, *Supreme Court*, xxi.
128. Javits, *Who Makes War*, 104-115.
129. Quoted in Arthur Bernon Tourtellot, *The Presidents on the Presidency* (Garden City, N.Y.: Doubleday, 1964), 326.
130. Donald L. Robinson, *"To the Best of My Ability"* (New York: Norton, 1987) 224.
131. Nincic, *United States Foreign Policy*, 231-233.
132. Henry R. Pringle, *Theodore Roosevelt* (New York: Harcourt Brace, 1931), 409.
133. Steven V. Roberts, "3,000 G.I.'s and Questions," *New York Times*, March 18, 1988, A1.
134. Timothy J. Lomperis, *The War Everyone Lost and Won* (Washington, D.C.: CQ Press, 1984), 60.
135. Crabb and Holt, *Invitation to Struggle*, 150-151.
136. Corwin, *The President*, 249.
137. Sundquist, *Decline and Resurgence of Congress*, 105-106.
138. Corwin, *The President*, 251.
139. Sundquist, *Decline and Resurgence of Congress*, 108.
140. Hoxie, *Command Decision and the Presidency*, 130.
141. Jordan and Taylor, *American National Security*, 473.
142. Hoxie, *Command Decision and the Presidency*, 40.
143. Pious, *The American Presidency*, 395-396.

Selected Bibliography

Corwin, Edward S. *The President: Office and Powers, 1787-1984*. 5th rev. ed. New York: New York University Press, 1984.

Crabb, Cecil V., Jr., and Pat M. Holt. *Invitation to Struggle: Congress, the President and Foreign Policy*. 2d ed. Washington, D.C.: CQ Press, 1984.

Eagleton, Thomas. *War and Presidential Power*. New York: Liveright, 1974.

Hoxie, R. Gordon. *Command Decision and the Presidency*. New York: Reader's Digest Press, 1977.

Nincic, Miroslav. *United States Foreign Policy: Choices and Tradeoffs*. Washington, D.C.: CQ Press, 1988.

Javits, Jacob K. *Who Makes War*. New York: Morrow, 1973.

Jordon, Amos A., and William J. Taylor, Jr. *American National Security, Policy and Process*. Baltimore: Johns Hopkins University Press, 1984.

Kallenbach, Joseph E. *The American Chief Executive: The Presidency and the Governorship*. New York: Harper and Row, 1966.

Pious, Richard M. *The American Presidency*. New York: Basic Books, 1979.

Rossiter, Clinton. *The Supreme Court and the Commander in Chief*. Ithaca, N.Y.: Cornell University Press, 1976.

Sarkesian, Sam C., ed. *Presidential Leadership and National Security: Style, Institutions, and Politics*. Boulder, Colo.: Westview Press, 1984.

Schlesinger, Arthur M., Jr. *The Imperial Presidency*. Boston: Houghton Mifflin, 1973.

Chief of State

Every government must have a chief of state who presides over ceremonial functions. In many countries this responsibility is fulfilled by a monarch with little governmental authority or an official whose post was created to shelter the chief executive from ceremonial drudgery. In the United States, however, this task has fallen to the chief executive. The ceremonial activities for which presidents are responsible are as diverse as those that monarchs must perform, but presidents also must perform their duties as chief executive, commander in chief, chief diplomat, chief legislator, and head of their party. Presidents, therefore, can devote only a fraction of their time to ceremonial activities.

The chief of state role, however, involves more than presiding over ceremonial functions for which the president must put on a smile and put the business of the nation on hold. Like monarchs, U.S. presidents are, in some ways, the living embodiment of the American people. They symbolize the country's history, liberty, and strength. Presidents can delegate ceremonial functions to their representatives, but while they are in office they cannot escape their chief of state role. At every moment they represent the United States to the international community and to the American people.

Ceremonial Duties and Functions

As chief of state, presidents preside over an endless series of ceremonies that range in tone from the solemnity of the inauguration to the informality of a White House barbecue. They greet foreign ambassadors, dedicate monuments, pin medals on war heroes, buy Easter seals and Girl Scout cookies, visit schools, throw out the first ball on opening day of the baseball season, and hold state dinners for foreign chiefs of state. National ceremonies have much the same purpose for the country as religious rituals have for a church. Ceremonies create shared symbols and emotional sentiments that comfort, motivate, and unify the American congregation.

Although presidents may occasionally find ceremonial events tiresome, they provide presidents with opportunities to dramatize and personalize their presidency. At ceremonial occasions presidents campaign for their reelection, make policy proposals, espouse their political philosophies, underscore the need for unity, create an atmosphere of confidence, and promote patriotism and national pride. Presidents who neglect ceremonial duties may find they have more time to develop policy and run the government, but they are sacrificing a tool of leadership that can be used not only to inspire the nation to greater accomplishments, but also to improve their own popularity.

Constitutional Ceremonial Duties

The Constitution designated several ceremonial duties that presidents are obliged to perform. They are required to take an oath of office, periodically inform Congress of the state of the union, and receive "Ambassadors and other public Ministers." These constitutional ceremonial duties supported the assumption of the chief of state power by George Washington and his successors because they made the president appear as the leader of the whole nation. Both the oath of office ceremony and State of the Union address physically place the president out in front of other government officials and focus the nation's attention on the president's opinions and recommendations. In addition, the president's duty to receive ambassadors implies that foreign governments are to regard the president as the official representative of the United States. Given that the international community sees the president as chief of state, domestic chief of state responsibilities could not be assumed gracefully by anyone but the president.

Oath of Office and Inauguration

Article II, section 1, clause 8, of the Constitution requires the president-elect to recite the following oath before assuming the presidency: "I do solemnly swear (or affirm) that I will faithfully execute the Office of President of the United States, and will to the best of my Ability preserve, protect, and defend the Constitution of the United States." The occasion for this oath taking was not described in the Constitution, but the inaugural ceremony where it is administered has become one of the U.S. government's most important traditions and the president's first chief of state function. *(See "The Inauguration," p.*

By Daniel C. Diller

Constitutional Basis of Presidential Chief of State Role

The Framers of the Constitution did not specifically designate the president as the nation's chief of state, but they created no other office that reasonably could claim the chief of state power. Presidents are the logical possessors of the title of chief of state under the Constitution because they are chosen by a national electorate, are never out of session, and are recognized as the voice of U.S. foreign policy. Consequently, the president can be said to represent the entire nation, is always available to provide ceremonial leadership, and is positioned to perform both international and domestic ceremonial functions.

The Framers never considered establishing a chief of state office separate from the presidency. The creation of a single office that would be filled by one person serving as both the ceremonial and executive leader of the nation, however, was not their only option. The continuing transfer of executive power from the monarch to the prime minister in Great Britain provided the Framers with a model of a political system where the ceremonial and executive functions were separated.[1] Given the objections of many members of the convention to any pretense of royalty in the presidency and the unanimous concern that no president would have the means to become a despot, it is somewhat surprising the Framers accepted the fusion of the two roles without debate.

One can imagine the convention designating a member of Congress such as the Speaker of the House or president pro tempore of the Senate as chief of state, especially since most of the delegates considered the legislature to be the most important branch of government. Such an arrangement would have augmented Congress's power by making it the ceremonial focus of the government, while diminishing the symbolic resources available to any president who sought dictatorial power.

The Framers also could have created an executive council composed of several persons instead of a unitary presidency. The Framers seriously considered this option, but the focus of their debate was on the safety of lodging enormous executive powers in the hands of one person, not on dividing presidential functions between executive officials. The original proposal for a single executive, made by James Wilson of Virginia, was strongly opposed by Benjamin Franklin, Edmund Randolph, George Mason, Roger Sherman, and other prominent members of the convention who feared that having a single executive would lead to despotism or the subordination of the country's interests to the interests of the executive's home region. After several days of debate, however, the Framers decided to reject proposals for a plural executive or an executive advisory committee attached to the presidency in favor of a single executive.[2] Presumably, had the convention opted for an executive committee instead of a single president, the chief of state power would have resided in the entire committee, rather than with one specified member.

According to political scientist Rexford G. Tugwell, an executive committee would not have captured the imagination of the American people the way individual presidents have:

> Since he [the president] would not have been alone in the White House in semi-royal state, with relatives and associates of consuming interest to all his fellow citizens, it would not have been a matter of such consequence whether or not he had an invalid wife and irresponsible children, . . . or whether he possessed social graces as well as wisdom and political talent. He would not, in other words, have been the focus of interest and the symbol of Union for the whole American people, watched with avid curiosity and criticized inevitably by those with standards of conduct differing from his own.[3]

By creating a single executive, the Framers guaranteed that public attention and therefore symbolic power would flow to the president.

1. Erwin C. Hargrove and Michael Nelson, *Presidents, Politics, and Policy* (Baltimore: Johns Hopkins University Press, 1984), 20.
2. Donald L. Robinson, *"To the Best of My Ability"* (New York: Norton, 1987), 69-76.
3. Rexford G. Tugwell, *The Enlargement of the Presidency* (Garden City, N.Y.: Doubleday, 1960), 481.

262, in The Electoral Process chapter of Part II.)

Like a coronation the inaugural ceremony symbolically invests presidents with the power of their office. At the inauguration the president appears before the people not as the manager of one of the three coequal branches of government but as the paternal leader of the nation who swears to "preserve, protect, and defend" the Constitution.

Benjamin Harrison commented on the significance of the oath of office in his 1888 inaugural address:

> . . . from the beginning of the government the people, to whose service the official oath consecrates the officer, have been called to witness the solemn ceremony. The oath taken in the presence of the people becomes a mutual covenant. The officer covenants to serve the whole body of the people by a faithful execution of the laws, so that they may be the unfailing defense and security of those who observe them.

The oath of office also conjures up heroic images of the nation's heritage. The new president's recitation of the same oath that George Washington, Thomas Jefferson, Abraham Lincoln, Woodrow Wilson, Franklin Roosevelt, and every other president has repeated conveys a sense of historic continuity and links the incumbent to the glories of past presidencies.

George Washington established the tradition that presidents should deliver an inaugural address after taking the oath of office. Most presidents have used this speech not to outline specific policy proposals but to restate their political philosophies, establish a mood of optimism, challenge the nation to pursue ambitious goals, and appeal for unity.

Unity is an important and common theme of inaugural addresses because presidential elections tend to divide the nation along party lines.[1] After the bitterly divisive election of 1800, which led outgoing president John Adams to snub Thomas Jefferson's inauguration, Jefferson declared, "We have called by different names brethren of the same principles. We are all Republicans. We are all Federalists." John F. Kennedy called for unity in 1961 after his close election victory over Richard Nixon: "We observe today not a victory of party, but a celebration of freedom." Jimmy Carter opened his inaugural address by praising his 1976 election opponent, Gerald Ford: "For myself and for our nation, I want to thank my predecessor for all he has done to heal our land."

The inauguration and the parades and parties that have usually followed it also provide the first glimpse of the new chief of state's ceremonial style. After the stiff formality and royal pomp observed during the Washington and Adams administrations, Jefferson wanted his inaugural to symbolize the democratic spirit he intended to bring to the presidency. He therefore eschewed a carriage in favor of walking unceremoniously from his boardinghouse to the Capitol to take the oath of office.

Andrew Jackson's election was regarded as a triumph for common people. To symbolize his link with the average person he opened the doors of the White House to anyone who wished to attend his post-inaugural party. Thousands of enthusiastic supporters descended on the White House, thereby destroying furniture, china, glassware, and other household items.

Kennedy's inaugural was a formal affair that reflected the intellectual and cultural sophistication he would bring to his presidency. Kennedy sent 155 special inaugural invitations to noted writers, artists, and scholars, had Robert Frost read a poem at the inaugural ceremony, and decreed that male participants in the ceremony should wear top hats.

Jimmy Carter, like Thomas Jefferson, used his inaugural to project a simpler presidential image. He wore a business suit instead of formal dress and chose to walk in his inaugural parade rather than ride in a limousine.

Pomp came back into style with the election of Ronald Reagan. His 1981 inaugural festivities—the most expensive in history up to that time—included a parade with eight thousand marchers, eight $100-a-ticket balls, and a nationally televised inaugural "gala" that featured many Hollywood celebrities.

State of the Union Address

The Constitution also states that the president "shall from time to time give to the Congress information of the State of the Union, and recommend to their Consideration such Measures as he shall judge necessary and expedient." From this clause developed the ritual of the president's annual message, or "State of the Union address" as it has been known since 1945.

George Washington delivered the first annual message on January 8, 1790. John Adams, who enjoyed royal formalities, followed Washington's precedent, but Thomas Jefferson objected to having presidents deliver their annual messages in person. Like many of his Democratic-Republican colleagues, he thought the custom, which had derived from the British monarch's speech from the throne at the opening of Parliament, had royal pretensions. As part of his effort to "put the ship of state back on its republican tack" he submitted his report to Congress in writing.[2]

Subsequent presidents followed Jefferson's example until 1913 when Woodrow Wilson took the suggestion of journalist Oliver Newman and went before Congress to read his annual message. Wilson saw the change as a way to make the address more personal and dramatic. He explained in the address that he wanted to verify "that the President of the United States is a person, not a mere department of the Government hailing Congress from some isolated island of jealous power, sending messages, not speaking naturally and with his own voice—that he is a human being trying to cooperate with other human beings in a common service." Some members of Congress echoed Jefferson's objections to the practice, but the response to Wilson's speech was generally favorable. Delivering the annual message in person was once again acceptable for presidents. Since Franklin Roosevelt, every president has chosen to deliver the annual message in person.[3]

Like the inauguration, the symbolism of the contemporary State of the Union address reinforces the image of the president as the preeminent leader of the nation, rather than the leader of one of its coequal branches. The Congress, cabinet, and Supreme Court assemble in the House chamber and wait for the president to arrive, like courtiers awaiting a king. After being announced, the president is greeted by a bipartisan standing ovation. Moreover, the event itself implies presidential preeminence, since the president's opinion of the state of the union is the reason for the assemblage. Neither Congress nor the judiciary has a similar opportunity to address the top representatives of the entire government in a formal, ritualistic setting.

The invention of radio and television changed the primary audience of the address from Congress to the American people. Presidents still address Congress, but their remarks are intended primarily for public consumption. Presidents have used this opportunity to put pressure on Congress to vote for their legislative agenda by appealing to the American public for support.

Reception of Ambassadors

The Constitution gives the president the responsibility to "receive Ambassadors and other public Ministers." The authors of the Constitution regarded the reception of foreign visitors as a purely ceremonial responsibility. It was to be given to the president, according to Alexander Hamilton, because Congress could not conveniently perform this function. He wrote in the *Federalist* No. 69 that presidential reception of ambassadors "is more a matter of dignity than of authority. It is a circumstance which will be without consequence in the administration of the government; and it was far more convenient that it should be arranged in this manner than that there should be a necessity of convening the legislature, or one of its branches, upon every arrival of a foreign minister."[4] Subsequently, however, the presidential responsibility to receive ambassadors was used by presidents as a constitutional justification of their authority to recognize or deny recognition to foreign governments. *(See "Recognition Power," p. 513, in Chief*

Robert Frost's Inaugural Poem

Presidents have sometimes attempted to use the celebrity and visibility of their office to promote changes in the lifestyle of the nation. John Kennedy intended to use his position to encourage interest in the fine arts and U.S. culture. He and his wife, Jacqueline, set an example for the nation by frequently patronizing the work of artists, musicians, and writers.

Kennedy began his patronage of the fine arts the day he became president. He asked the famous poet Robert Frost to recite a poem at his inauguration ceremony on January 20, 1961. The eighty-six-year-old Frost planned to read a short introductory verse he had composed for the occasion followed by his poem "The Gift Outright." After Boston's Cardinal Cushing delivered a long invocation, the chairman of the Inaugural Committee, Sen. John Sparkman, introduced Frost. The poet began reading his introductory verse, but the bright sunlight magnified by the glare from the snow that had fallen the day before blinded him. Frost read only three lines before stopping:

Summoning artists to participate
In the august occasions of the state
Seems something artists ought to celebrate.

He said, "I'm not having a good light here at all. I can't see in this light." He tried to continue with the help of Vice President-elect Lyndon B. Johnson, who shaded the poet's manuscript with a top hat, but Frost still could not see. He gave up on the introductory verse, saying, "This was to have been a preface to a poem which I do not have to read." He then recited "The Gift Outright" from memory in a clear voice, changing the last phrase at Kennedy's request from "such as she *would* become" to "such as she *will* become."

The Gift Outright

The land was ours before we were the land's.
She was our land more than a hundred years
Before we were her people. She was ours
In Massachusetts, in Virginia,
But we were England's, still colonials,
Possessing what we still were unpossessed by,
Possessed by what we now no more possessed.
Something we were withholding made us weak
Until we found out that it was ourselves
We were withholding from our land of living,
And forthwith found salvation in surrender.
Such as we were we gave ourselves outright
(The deed of gift was many deeds of war)
To the land vaguely realizing westward,
But still unstoried, artless, unenhanced,
Such as she was, such as she would become.

Diplomat chapter of Part III.)

In the spirit of this constitutional provision, presidents have customarily received the official ambassador of every recognized foreign government. Unfortunately, the growth of the Washington diplomatic corps during the twentieth century and the overcrowded presidential schedule have forced presidents to receive most ambassadors, especially those from smaller countries, in groups at the White House to save time.

Customary Ceremonial Functions

Presidents and their representatives perform numerous chief of state functions that do not have their origins in the Constitution and are not based on a specific legal sanction. Some of these activities have been established as annual events by a succession of presidents. Others are seized upon by individual presidents for their public relations value. Presidents can choose to deemphasize their chief of state role by delegating ceremonial functions to the vice president and others, but they cannot escape many events and practices that the American people have come to regard as part of the president's job. A president who claimed to be too busy to light the national Christmas tree or congratulate the World Series baseball champions would waste valuable opportunities to score political points and would risk being perceived as cold or indifferent to American culture. Like the three ceremonial functions based on the Constitution, these informal chief of state activities emphasize the president's role as the leader of the nation, but in addition, many of them serve to humanize the president and symbolically bridge the gap between the president and the people.

National Voice

The president serves as a ceremonial spokesperson for the nation. A presidential proclamation or dedication is a national stamp of approval for cultural events, national monuments, public works projects, charity drives, and special weeks and days. Such proclamations promote national concern and awareness of worthy organizations and causes by indicating that the president thought the object of the proclamation was important enough to recognize. Often presidents highlight their recognition of a charity, organization, or movement by invitating its leaders to the White House. Such an invitation is a further measure of the group's importance since the president's schedule must be interrupted to accommodate the visit.

Presidential recognition gives an event, cause, group, or monument a place in the national consciousness. It also emphasizes the unity of the United States and can inspire patriotic sentiments. A new hydroelectric dam is said to be not just a source of power for a particular region, but an engineering feat and a symbol of American industrial might and technological ingenuity. The work of a charitable organization such as the American Red Cross is praised as an example of the nation's caring spirit.

Presidential endorsements are constantly in demand by organizations and charities, and the president's staff must choose which will receive presidential time. Many of the causes presidents endorse from year to year are determined by precedent. The United Way, Easter Seals, American Cancer Society, and many others receive annual presidential endorsements. Yet the number and type of causes

UPI/Bettmann Newsphotos

John F. Kennedy's inaugural was a formal affair that reflected the intellectual and cultural sophistication he would bring to his presidency. Robert Frost reads a poem while vice president Lyndon Johnson uses his top hat to block out the sun.

that receive presidential recognition may also reflect the incumbent's political interests or philosophies. For example, Ronald Reagan's frequent endorsement of charities was consistent with his goal of promoting an increase in the nation's charitable giving as a partial alternative to increased government spending on social services.

Conveyor of Awards and Congratulations

In accordance with their role as national spokesperson, presidents are expected to be the conveyors of national awards and congratulations. Presidents routinely invite citizens to the White House, where they congratulate them on their accomplishments and present them with an award or memento of their visit. Presidents also bestow a variety of official awards, the most prominent of which is the Presidential Medal of Freedom.

Congratulating worthy Americans has been used by presidents as a tool of moral and patriotic leadership. When presidents congratulate popular American heroes they make a moral statement by holding up those individuals to the nation as examples to emulate. Presidential congratulations encourage citizens to be as dedicated as a spelling bee champion, as brave as a war hero, as creative as a great artist, or as resilient as a person celebrating a hundredth birthday.

Such congratulations can improve the morale and sense of well-being of the nation. Amidst news reports of war, recession, crime, natural disasters, and other sobering problems, the congratulations of a hero by an appreciative president speaking for the nation can be a reassuring and uplifting event. President Reagan developed presidential congratulations into a political art when he made a practice of weaving the introduction of carefully selected heroic Americans into his upbeat State of the Union addresses. His heroes have included an infantry medic who rescued wounded soldiers in Grenada, a twelve-year-old prodigy of gospel music, a woman about to graduate from West Point despite having escaped to the United States from Vietnam only ten years before with no possessions or knowledge of English, and a seventy-nine-year-old Harlem woman who cared for infants born of mothers addicted to heroin.

Congratulating a famous hero brings obvious political benefits to presidents. For example, members of championship sports teams are now routinely invited to the White House where they will joke with the president and present the chief executive with a jersey, game ball, or other memento of their victory. The president can become identified with their sport, demonstrate good humor, and be photographed with America's current sports idols as they are reduced to wide-eyed excitement by their White House reception. Presidents gain similar public relations benefits from congratulating artists, scientists, heroic members of the armed forces, and others who have performed feats of skill, intelligence, or courage.

First Average American

Alexis de Tocqueville, a French aristocrat and author who traveled widely in the United States during the first half of the nineteenth century, observed that "public officers themselves are well aware that the superiority over their fellow citizens which they derive from their authority they enjoy only on condition of putting themselves on a

Presidential Proclamations

The following list of days, weeks, and months recognized by the Reagan White House during October 1987 demonstrates the variety of causes, charities, groups, and holidays that are promoted during a typical month through presidential proclamations.

National Poison Prevention Week
National Medical Research Day
General Casimir Pulaski Memorial Day
Columbus Day
German-American Day
Polish American Heritage Month
Benign Essential Blepharospasm Awareness Week
Leif Erickson Day
Minority Enterprise Development Week
National Farm-City Week
National Down's Syndrome Month
National School Lunch Week
National Job Skills Week
World Food Day
National Safety Belt Use Day
White Cane Safety Day
National Forest Products Week
National Immigrants Day
National Adult Immunization Week
National Hospice Month

level with the whole community by their manners." [5] Most presidents have understood that although Americans want their president to be an exceptional person who is intelligent, decisive, and inspiring, they also want a leader with common tastes and experiences. Americans want to believe that their president, like the log cabin presidents of the nineteenth century, rose to the top through hard work, moral integrity, and a little ambition. The public values common sense as much as an Ivy League education. The ability to understand the needs and desires of the average American is as important as understanding the most complicated foreign policy or economic problems. In short, they want their president to be an exceptional example of an average American.

Presidents have realized that while the regal trappings of the presidency fortify their power and prestige, they must also project a populist image to satisfy the democratic ideals of the American people. Presidents who appear too urbane or who flaunt the privileges of their office risk alienating many citizens who are attracted to politicians with folksy images. Presidents John Qunicy Adams and Martin Van Buren lost their reelection bids to Andrew Jackson and William Henry Harrison, respectively. The challengers in these two elections successfully contrasted their self-made, populist personas with the stiff and educated styles of the incumbents. Similarly, in the 1952 and 1956 presidential elections Adlai Stevenson's sophisticated image was not much of an asset against Dwight D. Eisenhower, an unpretentious war hero with an engaging smile.

Presidents therefore seek out opportunities to display their common touch. Often this is done simply by publicizing a president's hobbies, habits, and family life. The American public was told that Ronald Reagan chopped his own firewood and snacked on jellybeans, Jimmy Carter played softball and liked Willie Nelson's music, Gerald Ford took a daily swim and cooked his own breakfast. The day after Lyndon B. Johnson's reelection in 1964 he was photographed roping steers on his Texas ranch like any hard-working cowboy. Jimmy Carter made a media event out of his construction of a tree house on the White House grounds for his daughter, Amy.[6]

Presidential appearances at cultural events can reinforce the image of a president as an average person. Presidents attend historical and artistic exhibits, ethnic festivals, and other events where they can display their interest in American life. Presidents have been especially fond of attending sporting contests. Since William Howard Taft threw out the first baseball of the 1910 major league season in Washington, most presidents have observed the tradition. Kennedy wanted to make such a good appearance at the yearly event that he secretly practiced his throwing on the White House grounds.[7] Since the Washington Senators baseball franchise moved to Texas in 1971, presidents who have wished to throw out the first ball have had to travel to other cities. Several presidents, including Kennedy and Nixon, were avid football fans. In December 1969 Nixon attended a highly publicized college football game in Fayetteville, Arkansas, between the Universities of Texas and Arkansas. The president not only was interviewed at halftime in front of a national television audience, he also was filmed visiting both locker rooms after the game.

Observer of Holidays

National holidays reduce societal divisions by emphasizing universal patriotic themes and common traditions. Hundreds of millions of Americans of all races, religions, and regions share the common experience of watching fireworks on the Fourth of July or preparing a banquet on Thanksgiving. On Veterans Day virtually every American citizen will recall someone who served in the military, and on Memorial Day most will remember someone who died in a war. Holidays, therefore, draw a nation together and enhance a citizen's sense of belonging to a single national culture.

As chief of state, presidents usually lead the nation's observation of a holiday. They light the national Christmas tree, deliver a patriotic address on the Fourth of July, and lay a wreath at the Tomb of the Unknown Soldier on Memorial Day. Details of the traditional holiday activities observed by the first family, such as what they ate on Thanksgiving and what gifts they exchanged at Christmas usually are reported to the nation.

Presidents traditionally have issued statements celebrating official holidays such as Memorial Day and Thanksgiving and unofficial holidays like St. Patrick's Day. Presidents, however, cannot proclaim an official federal holiday without an act of Congress. George Washington was the first president to proclaim a national holiday. In response to a congressional recommendation, he declared that a national day of thanksgiving should be observed on Thursday, November 26, 1789.[8] This proclamation contributed to the development of the Thanksgiving holiday now observed in the United States. The most recent holiday

Library of Congress

For years after President William Howard Taft threw out the first baseball of the 1910 major league season in Washington, most presidents observed the tradition.

established by the government was Martin Luther King Day. After initial opposition, Ronald Reagan signed legislation November 2, 1983, declaring the third Monday in January beginning in 1986 to be a legal federal holiday honoring the civil rights leader.

Mourner and Eulogizer

When a prominent American dies the president is expected to lead the nation in mourning. The president routinely issues statements eulogizing Americans who have died. During the first five months of 1983, for example, President Reagan signed statements mourning the deaths of such diverse Americans as Alabama University football coach Paul (Bear) Bryant, entertainer Arthur Godfrey, presidential aide Joseph R. Holmes, three Secret Service agents who were killed in an auto accident, and sixteen Americans who died when the U.S. embassy in Beirut, Lebanon, was bombed by terrorists. Presidential attendance at funerals, however, generally is reserved for former presidents, high government officials, or people who had a close personal or political relationship with the president. When presidents do attend funerals in the United States in their role as chief of state, they usually address the mourners. President Nixon delivered the eulogy at Eisenhower's state funeral at the U.S. Capitol on March 30, 1969.

Presidents also must respond to the deaths of Americans who died while serving their country. Perhaps the most famous of all presidential speeches, Lincoln's Gettysburg Address was delivered during Lincoln's visit to the site of the great battle where thousands of Union and Confederate troops lost their lives. During a war when many soldiers are dying, presidents rarely have time to memorialize individual members of the armed services. In peacetime, however, presidents usually honor any American hero whose death captures the attention of the nation. For example, President Reagan met with the family of Robert Stethem, a Navy diver killed by terrorists who hijacked TWA Flight 847 in 1985. Reagan also addressed the nation on January 31, 1986, at the memorial service for the seven astronauts killed in the *Challenger* space shuttle disaster.

As head of state, presidents receive invitations to the funerals of foreign leaders. Johnson attended Konrad Adenauer's funeral in Cologne in April 1967, and Nixon traveled to Paris to attend Charles de Gaulle's funeral in November 1970. Presidents rarely go to funerals overseas because of the difficulty of postponing other business and arranging security measures on short notice.

If the president does not go to the funeral, a representative is sent in the president's place. The decision of who to send to a foreign funeral depends on the importance of the country to the United States, the current state of diplomatic relations between the two nations, and the deceased leader's political relationship with the United States. The vice president or secretary of state usually represents the president and the nation at the funerals of prominent world leaders. Former presidents who worked closely with a fallen leader also sometimes attend. President Reagan and Vice President Bush did not attend Anwar Sadat's funeral in October 1981 for security reasons, but Reagan asked former presidents Nixon, Ford, and Carter to represent the United States. At the funerals of leaders of countries that had a strained or minimal relationship with the United States, the U.S. ambassador to that country often will represent the president.

American Tourist

George Washington firmly established the precedent that presidents should travel out among the American people. He made two regional tours as president: New England in 1789 and the South in 1791. Washington thought the purpose of these tours of the states was "to become better acquainted with their principle Characters and internal Circumstances, as well as to be more accessible to numbers

George Washington as...

When George Washington became president it was inevitable that the chief of state role would become a prominent aspect of the presidency. His status as a military hero and the leader most identified with the Revolution both in the United States and abroad made him a national symbol even before he became president. Because he had embodied the higher purposes of the Revolution, his acceptance of the presidency brought legitimacy to the Constitution. Presidents since Washington have derived respect and authority from their presidential office and powers. With Washington, however, the flow of benefits was reversed. It was he who brought legitimacy and prominence to an office that had no tradition or established operating procedures and would have been distrusted by the people had he not held it.[1]

Washington believed his primary task as president was to unify the country and establish strong political institutions. In no other presidency were ceremony and symbolism more important to the fulfillment of the president's goals. John Adams saw George Washington as a master of dramatic, symbolic leadership. Many years after Washington's death he commented, "We may say of him, if he was not the greatest President he was the best Actor of the Presidency we have ever had. His address to The States when he left the Army: His solemn Leave taken of Congress when he resigned his Commission: his Farewell Address to the People when he resigned his Presidency. These were all in a strain of Shakespearean and Garrickal excellence in Dramatic Exhibitions." [2]

Washington understood that everything he did as president would set a precedent for future presidents and that even small matters of ceremony could affect the reputation and success of the new government and his office. He wrote: "Many things which appear of little importance in themselves and at the beginning, may have great and durable consequences from their having been established at the commencement of a new and general government. It will be much easier to commence the administration, upon a well adjusted system, built on tenable grounds, than to correct errors or alter inconveniences after they shall have been confirmed by habit." [3]

Washington, therefore, carefully performed ceremonial functions so as to strike a balance between the dignity and accessibility of the presidency. He traveled to his New York inauguration in a carriage, acknowledging the cheers of crowds, but gave a highly formal speech at his inauguration and did not participate in the public revelry surrounding the occasion. Early in his presidency he established a system of formal receptions known as "levees," which allowed him to frequently receive members of government and the public but also to maintain a solemnity that preserved his aura of authority. He also accepted the formal title of "President of the United States" granted by Congress but did not endorse or participate in Vice President John Adams's campaign to have Congress establish the ostentatious presidential title: "His Highness the President of the United States and Protector of the Rights of the Same." [4]

Washington's attention to the details of his chief of state role had significance beyond establishing the proprieties of his office. Washington was also determined to strengthen the common identity of Americans and the primacy of the federal government over the states. The weakness of the federal government and its dependence

of well-informed persons." [9] Since then, presidents have been expected to leave the capital to occasionally reacquaint themselves with the nation's problems and listen to the public's needs and complaints. Franklin Roosevelt explained his own need for such travels: "I have always thought it was part of the duty of the Presidency to keep in touch, personal touch, with the Nation ... now I am going to the Coast ... to have a 'look-see,' to try to tie together in my own mind the problems of the Nation, in order that I may, at first hand, know as much about the questions that affect all the forty-eight states as possible." [10]

Citizens may become apathetic toward politics and government if they perceive that it is a game played in the capital by leaders who do not care what happens in the rest of the country. By traveling out to the people in the "provinces" presidents can show their interest in the culture of particular regions. They can reawaken public interest in their administration's programs and in government in general.

The concerns of citizens that presidents remain in touch with the needs of the whole country were demonstrated by the successful presidential campaigns of Jimmy Carter in 1976 and Ronald Reagan in 1980. As former governors, both men campaigned against the "Washington establishment," which they said had lost touch with the desires of the people. To emphasize his accessibility and interest in local problems, President Carter journeyed to several small towns during his presidency where he answered the questions of citizens at town meetings and stayed overnight with local families.

Chief of State Role and Presidential Power

The chief of state role has received less scholarly attention than other presidential roles. The ceremonial and symbolic aspects of the presidency appear less important than the responsibilities that come with the president's other powers. When presidents veto bills, sign treaties, nominate Supreme Court justices, issue pardons, or order military actions it is obvious that they have exercised presidential power. As chief of state, however, the president acts neither as a commander nor as an administrator. The effects of ceremonial leadership are less observable and impossible to quantify. Consequently, the chief of state duties are seldom described as a "power" and are sometimes denounced as a waste of the president's time.

... the First Chief of State

on the states under the Articles of Confederation had greatly disturbed Washington and had been the motivation behind the establishment of the new government.

Convincing the nation of the primacy of the federal government and inspiring in the American people a sense of common identity was a difficult task. The Constitution clearly gave the federal government legal preeminence over the states. Nevertheless, most Americans felt a greater allegience to their state than to the Union, and state officials naturally tended to resist federal authority as an intrusion into their jurisdictions. The fledgling government lacked tools to implement government policy. In particular, the federal government had no army or navy and only a few federal marshals who could gather information and enforce federal laws. Consequently, Washington had to rely on state governors to provide militia and law enforcement officers to deal with violations of federal statutes.

Washington used his chief of state role to counter impressions that the federal government lacked authority and did not deserve the primary loyalties of the people. Washington traveled to every state to underscore national unity during trips to the northern states in 1789 and the southern states in 1791. He also insisted that foreign governments deal with him, the representative of all the people, rather than with Congress, which was chosen by local constituencies. When Congress voted for a day of thanksgiving in November 1789, Washington issued the proclamation rather than having Congress ask the states to issue it as had been done with similar declarations under the Articles of Confederation.[5]

Even when seemingly trivial matters of protocol were concerned, Washington was careful to assert the primacy of the presidency and the federal government. During his tour of New England in 1789 he asked to dine with John Hancock, the governor of Massachusetts, but indicated that Hancock should call on him first. When Hancock claimed to be too ill to visit the president, Washington canceled dinner and wrote a stiff note to the governor: "The president of the United States presents his best respects to the Governor, and has the honor to inform him that he shall be at home 'till 2 o'clock. The President of the United States need not express the pleasure it will give him to see the Governor; but at the same time, he most earnestly begs that the Governor will not hazard his health on the occasion." [6] Washington scored an important symbolic victory for the presidency and the Constitution when Hancock relented after a two-day standoff. The governor, who continued to profess an illness, was carried to the president's lodgings by several servants.[7]

1. Glenn Phelps, "George Washington and the Founding of the Presidency," *Presidential Studies Quarterly* 17 (Spring 1987): 352.
2. Clinton Rossiter, *The American Presidency*, 2d ed. (New York: Harcourt Brace and World, 1960), 92.
3. James Hart, *The American Presidency in Action 1789* (New York: Macmillan, 1948), 12.
4. Joseph E. Kallenbach, *The American Chief Executive* (New York: Harper and Row, 1966), 274.
5. Phelps, "George Washington and the Founding of the Presidency," 351.
6. Ibid., 351-352.
7. Hart, *The American Presidency in Action 1789*, 20.

Although the president's right to dedicate a monument or congratulate an astronaut may mean little, the symbolism of the chief of state role constitutes a real power because it enhances presidential authority and legitimizes and magnifies other presidential powers. As political scientist Clinton Rossiter explained, "No President can fail to realize that all his powers are invigorated, indeed are given a new dimension of authority, because he is the symbol of our sovereignty, continuity, and grandeur." [11]

The presidency, therefore, is elevated above other offices and institutions not just by its legal authority, but by its symbolic mystique. This mystique has been built up by two centuries of veneration for an office that has been occupied by many of our greatest national heroes. Rossiter wrote:

> Lincoln is the supreme myth, the richest symbol in the American experience. He is, as someone has remarked neither irreverently nor sacrilegiously, the martyred Christ of democracy's passion play. And who, then, can measure the strength that is given to the President because he holds Lincoln's office, lives in Lincoln's house, and walks in Lincoln's way? The final greatness of the Presidency lies in the truth that it is not just an office of incredible power but a breeding ground of indestructible myth.[12]

Symbolic Leadership

Effective government requires more than rational deliberations and actions. Hearts are stirred and ranks are closed more easily by symbols than by reasoned arguments. Consequently, every government that hopes to provide effective leadership must provide symbols that unify, inspire, and reassure the people. The most powerful symbols are human symbols. Journalist Michael Novak, who worked for the Muskie and McGovern campaigns in 1972, wrote of the necessity of human symbols: "Causes, institutions, and administrative processes must be personified before humans can passionately engage them. Humans are flesh and blood, and they understand best what is flesh and blood.... Thus the general law of politics: political movements depend for their general acceptance on the greatness of their leaders." [13] In the United States, the president, as chief of state, is the dominant political symbol for most Americans.

This symbolic stature enables presidents to exercise inspirational leadership from the stage of the White House. Americans want more from a leader than efficiency and honesty. They want a dramatic leader who can articulate their goals, motivate them, and even amuse them. Skillful presidents can use their symbolic assets to build the nation's morale and confidence and call on patriotic sentiments in a crisis. Political scientist Harold J. Laski explained the importance of a symbolic and inspiring leader to the people:

> They must see someone who can say in the grand way what they half-articulately feel. They must have the sense that they are a part of significant events. Dull government can only endure when government is unimportant; a long period of extraordinary prosperity will, as in the Coolidge regime, persuade men that dullness is the same as soundness. But where any significant part of the population is hard pressed, it looks to the president for relief; and it is then urgent that he give the appearance of active intervention on their behalf. A dull president will not last long in a period of crisis. His temptation, just because he is dull, is to throw the burden of responsibility upon the leaders in Congress. He thus ceases to be the symbol of action, and the nation feels deprived of that leadership to which it feels itself entitled.[14]

The chief of state role equips presidents with several symbolic assets through which they can reinforce their executive leadership. Presidents are seen as the symbol of national unity, the symbol of national continuity, and the symbol of the federal government. Although presidents may have varying success at using these assets to further their policies, all presidents possess them. Merely by holding office and exercising presidential powers presidents will represent the nation's unity, continuity, and government to many Americans.

Symbol of National Unity

The Constitution provided for three independent branches of government, but the president, rather than Congress or the courts, has become the symbol of national unity. The presidency's emergence as a unifying symbol was predictable. George Washington, who was a national symbol even before he became president, saw his presidential role primarily as a national unifier who would draw together the citizens of the thirteen states and followers of various political philosophies into one nation. Although no president has been able to remain as nonpartisan as Washington, few presidents have been slaves to their parties and most have worked in some way to reduce national divisions. In addition, presidents are the most identifiable national leaders and the only elected officials (with the exception of vice presidents) who have a national constituency. As such they are seen as the guardian of the interests of the whole nation against the narrow demands of partisan and sectional groups.

The president's status as a symbol of national unity is an especially valuable political asset because much of what the president does as chief executive and party leader divides the nation. Political scientist Thomas E. Cronin has observed that presidents

> necessarily divide when they act as the leaders of their political parties, when they set priorities that advantage certain goals and groups at the expense of others, when they forge and lead political coalitions, when they move out ahead of public opinion and assume the role of national educators, and when they choose one set of advisers over another. A President, as a creative executive leader, cannot help but offend certain interests.[15]

Being a symbol of national unity allows presidents to heal some of the wounds they open while acting in their other roles and to maintain the public's confidence in them as leader of the entire nation. Eisenhower was particularly adept at projecting an image of an amiable unifier while hiding his political side, thereby maximizing the unifying potential of his chief of state role.[16]

The power of the presidency as a unifying symbol is demonstrated by the public's reaction to international crisis. Even when Americans disagree with the president's policies, they have tended to rally around their president when the nation's interests are threatened by a foreign power. Public opinion polls have shown that presidential approval ratings usually improve when the nation becomes involved in a war or other international crisis. For example, President Kennedy's public approval rating jumped 13 percent in 1962 after the Cuban missile crisis. In 1975 Ford's public approval rating shot up eleven points after he ordered marines to rescue the crew of the merchant ship *Mayaguez,* which had been seized by Cambodian forces.

Although presidential approval ratings will improve the most when the public perceives that the president has acted skillfully or boldly to meet an international crisis, even clear foreign policy failures can add to a president's popularity. In May 1960, the Soviets shot down an American U-2 spy plane over Soviet territory. Eisenhower denied the U.S. was conducting intelligence overflights of the Soviet Union, but when Moscow produced the captured pilot, he took responsiblity for the missions. Eisenhower's approval rating jumped 6 percent following the incident, despite heightened East-West tensions and the collapse of a summit meeting in Paris later in the month. Similarly, after the U.S.-sponsored Bay of Pigs invasion of Cuba by exiled Cuban nationals in 1961, Kennedy's approval rating improved eleven points to 83 percent, even though the invasion was universally considered a disaster.[17] The public rallied around Eisenhower and Kennedy in these situations not because they achieved anything, but because they were the symbols of the United States during a time of international confrontation. *(See "Presidential Approval Ratings: Gallup Poll, Truman-Reagan," p. 1465, in the Appendix.)*

White House

Rutherford B. Hayes was the first president to use an eagle as the official presidential seal. In 1903 Theodore Roosevelt added a circular seal around it, bearing the words, and in 1945 Truman changed the eagle's head from one side to the other. He also added two new stars for the two new states.

Symbol of Continuity

Presidents also benefit from occupying an office that is identified with the continuity of the United States and the stability of its political institutions. Before taking office presidents pledge in their oath of office to "preserve, protect, and defend the Constitution of the United States." Lincoln, perhaps the most celebrated U.S. president, is remembered primarily for preserving the Union. The American people see the president as not only the current national leader but also the latest president in a long line of presidents who have guarded the freedom and laws of the United States. Consequently, when political rivals challenge the president they are in the uncomfortable position of confronting the defender of the Constitution and the heir of Washington, Jefferson, Lincoln, and the Roosevelts.

The history of the presidency itself demonstrates the stability of the nation's political institutions. Power has always been transferred peacefully from one president to the next. The unbroken chain of presidents has survived assassinations, civil war, impeachment proceedings, election fraud, and a presidential resignation. Even before the presidency faced any of these trials its continuity impressed Martin Van Buren who wrote, "The President under our system, like the king in a monarchy, never dies." [18]

When presidents leave office they continue to symbolize the United States of a past era and the continuity of the nation's democratic institutions. Although there have been exceptions, retiring presidents customarily attend the inaugural ceremonies of their successors, thereby symbolically demonstrating the strength of the Constitution, which provides for the peaceful and orderly transfer of presidential power.[19] Former presidents also can contribute to an image of stability during crises. At John Kennedy's funeral, Herbert Hoover, Harry Truman, and Dwight Eisenhower sat with Lyndon Johnson in a show of nonpartisan support. Together they constituted a powerful symbol of continuity that reassured a nation not yet recovered from the shock of Kennedy's assassination.[20]

Symbol of Government

As chief of state the president symbolizes not only the nation but also its government. Because the presidency is occupied by a single familiar individual who has broad executive powers including the prerogative to initiate policy, it is the most dynamic and understandable element of the federal government. For many Americans what the president is doing becomes synonymous with what the government is doing. For example, a president unveiling a tax reform proposal to a national television audience is more easily understood than the bargaining and consultations within the executive branch that produced the proposal or the complex political and procedural battles that will be fought over the tax reform issue in Congress. The proposal is not seen as emanating from the Treasury Department or the executive branch, but rather from the president. Policy programs, military conflicts, and economic conditions all become identified with the president who was serving at the time they occurred, even if that president was not primarily responsible for them. The presidency, therefore, is used by many Americans as a "cognitive handle," which personalizes and simplifies the detailed processes of governing the nation.[21]

Being the most visible symbol of government can work against presidents as well as for them. Public expectations of the president tend to be very high and often unreasonable. Since it is easier to blame an individual for society's problems than understand all the complicated factors contributing to them, presidents receive much unjust criticism. Public dissatisfaction with federal government policies or local conditions over which the president has little control may be translated into disapproval of the president.

Yet being a symbol of the entire government upon which the media and public focus attention gives presidents the power to dominate issues. When any significant event occurs, Americans look to the president for an assessment and a response. Michael Novak wrote of the power presidents have because they command the attention of the nation:

> If on television the president says our ships were attacked in the Gulf of Tonkin, then that attack (even if it did not occur) occupies our attention and demands that we refute it or accept it or dismiss it. Whatever we do, there stands the president's assertion, solid until painstakingly disproved. This power over our attention, over our power to structure issues, is so enormous that it dwarfs all others.[22]

Tool of Foreign Policy

As chief of state, the president is the ceremonial representative of the United States before the international community. Presidents make ceremonial visits to foreign countries and greet foreign dignitaries who visit the United States. Whether presidents are receiving visitors in the White House or touring the world, they are expected to fulfill both their diplomatic and ceremonial responsibilities. When U.S. presidents visit Great Britain, for example, they usually have a ceremonial meeting with the reigning monarch and a policy meeting with the prime minister.

The international chief of state role, however, cannot be neatly separated from the president's activities as the architect of U.S. foreign relations. State visits and other international ceremonies and spectacles that the president undertakes as chief of state are tools of foreign policy. They are a means of communicating the intentions and attitudes of the administration and improving the relationships of the United States with foreign governments.

Presidents and their representatives also use international ceremonial appearances and events to lobby for the support of foreign peoples and leaders. The foreign public observes U.S. presidents most often in their chief of state role. When presidents admire landmarks, make speeches, and attend state dinners on their foreign trips, they are trying to increase their popularity overseas and establish a reservoir of good will to benefit U.S. interests. International respect for a president will enhance the image of the United States, the confidence of the U.S. public, and the president's ability to exert leadership in the international arena. President Eisenhower, who made the image of the United States a high priority, wrote near the end of his presidency that he had tried to maintain "a respectable image of American life before the world. Among the qualities American government must exhibit is dignity. In turn the principal governmental spokesman must strive to display it." [23]

The president's international chief of state role also creates unscheduled diplomatic opportunities. Between November 1982 and February 1985, three Soviet general secretaries died—Leonid Brezhnev, Yuri Andropov, and

Library of Congress

In May 1860, President James Buchanan greets Japan's first envoys to the United States.

Konstantin Chernenko. As chief of state of an important nation, President Reagan received invitations to their funerals in accordance with international protocol. These occasions provided Reagan with opportunities to meet face to face with Soviet leaders during a period when poor U.S.-Soviet relations would have made a scheduled meeting difficult, if not impossible to arrange. President Reagan's decisions to send Vice President Bush as the U.S. representative to each funeral rather than attend himself underscored the hard line he was taking toward the Soviet Union at the time. Nevertheless, the funerals allowed the vice president to meet the succeeding Soviet general secretaries and speak to them about U.S. interests.

Greeting Foreign Leaders

Presidents must entertain many visiting chiefs of state, prime ministers, and other foreign dignitaries every year. These visits often include a photo session and a state dinner attended by selected members of Congress, administration officials, and national celebrities.

The manner in which presidents receive a foreign chief of state sends a signal to that leader and other nations about U.S. policy. President Carter's friendly greeting of Chinese Vice Premier Deng Xiaoping in January 1979 was a ceremonial act with profound diplomatic implications. Before, during, and after Deng's visit to the United States, the vice premier had pointedly attacked the leaders of the Soviet Union for pursuing an aggressive foreign policy. The Carter administration's warm reception of Deng and its refusal to condemn his belligerent rhetoric signaled tolerance for the vice premier's views and a clear tilt toward the Chinese in the trilateral relationship.

Presidents also can make a statement about their foreign policy priorities through their invitations to visit the United States. In 1977, for example, Carter wished to emphasize the importance of U.S. relations with its North American neighbors. Consequently, the first two foreign leaders he invited to the White House were President José López Portillo of Mexico and Prime Minister Pierre Trudeau of Canada.

Making International Tours

International tours of presidents and their delegated representatives often consist of more ceremonial activities than policy discussions with foreign leaders. Because U.S. presidents have limited time and ensuring their security is such a difficult and expensive task, a ceremonial visit to a foreign country is a sign of the value the United States attaches to its relations with that country. To be worthwhile, presidential visits do not have to produce a diplomatic breakthrough or even progress in ongoing negotiations. A president may visit a foreign nation solely to reaffirm U.S. interest in that nation or to focus global attention on a particular region or problem.

Before the 1950s, presidential travel to foreign countries was uncommon. When presidents did go abroad they almost always did so to hold negotiations with foreign leaders. Woodrow Wilson went to Europe in 1918 to negotiate the Treaty of Versailles, which ended World War I. Franklin Roosevelt and Harry Truman traveled abroad to confer with Winston Churchill, Joseph Stalin, and other allied leaders during World War II.

Dwight Eisenhower's "Quest for Peace" tour of eleven Asian, European, and Middle Eastern nations in 1959 established the precedent that presidents could go abroad on good-will missions designed primarily to increase foreign support of U.S. policies. Eisenhower traveled twenty-two thousand miles in nineteen days and was met in many cities by enthusiastic crowds numbering in the hundreds of thousands. His trip was almost entirely devoted to ceremonial activities. On December 3, in a televised speech to the nation before his departure, Eisenhower declared he was about to "set forth as your agent to extend once again to millions of people across the seas assurances of America's sincere friendship." [24] Eisenhower conceived of his trip as so purely symbolic that he declined Pakistani president Ayub Khan's request to discuss the contentious issue of the Pakistani-Indian border with Indian prime minister Jawaharlal Nehru unless the prime minister raised the issue first.

Host nations expect a president who is visiting their country to sample their culture and make a pilgrimage to their most cherished landmarks. In 1972, when Nixon made the first trip to the People's Republic of China by a U.S. president, he traveled to the Great Wall and toured the Forbidden City, the ancient home of Chinese emporers. This sightseeing expressed U.S. respect for Chinese culture and symbolized the desire of the administration to widen contacts between the people of the two nations. Given the vast cultural differences and recent animosity between the United States and the People's Republic of China, this symbolism was an important element in establishing a lasting rapprochement. Similarly, President Nixon attended the Bolshoi Ballet and several state dinners during his historic visit to Moscow the same year.

Kennedy's trip to West Berlin in June 1963 demonstrated how the chief of state role could be used to add force to a foreign policy commitment. For several years the Soviet Union had made veiled threats against the city, which existed as a democratic enclave deep within Communist East Germany. In 1961 the Soviet and East German Communist leaders ordered a wall to be built to prevent East Germans from emigrating to West Berlin. The U.S. commitment to defend West Berlin was not new, but the vulnerability of the city to Soviet attack and the great consequences of nuclear war inevitably caused Berliners, as well as other Western Europeans, to question the U.S. commitment to the city. No matter how adamantly U.S. officials insisted that the United States would defend Berlin, establishing the credibility of the commitment was difficult.

While traveling in Europe in 1963 Kennedy delivered a speech at the Berlin Wall in which he declared "Ich bin ein Berliner" (I am a Berliner). The spectacle of the U.S. chief of state standing before the symbol of Communist oppression and declaring to 400,000 Berliners in their own language that he was one of them added a new force to the U.S. commitment. As the commander in chief and manager of U.S. foreign policy, Kennedy had made the decision to reaffirm the standing U.S. policy to defend West Berlin. It was Kennedy's role as chief of state, however, that gave him the opportunity to infuse the U.S. commitment with a dramatic promise that linked the prestige of the United States and his own presidency to the defense of Berlin and Europe.

In 1985 President Reagan planned to make another dramatic presidential trip to West Germany to commemorate the fortieth anniversary of the end of World War II in Europe. To symbolize U.S.-West German reconciliation and friendship that had been accomplished since the war, the president agreed to visit the German military cemetery at Bitburg and lay a wreath at a tomb for German casualties of the war. After the president had made a commitment to visit the cemetery, however, reports revealed that among its dead were members of the infamous Nazi SS, the group that oversaw the execution of millions of Jews in concentration camps before and during the war. Jewish and veterans groups immediately protested Reagan's itinerary. In an attempt to placate the president's domestic critics, the White House added a stop at the site of the Bergen-Belsen concentration camp to his trip. Nevertheless, the protests continued, and Reagan was confronted with the choice of offending significant numbers of American voters or his West German hosts. Reagan chose to absorb the domestic criticism of the cemetery visit to avoid embarrassing West German chancellor Helmut Kohl and undercutting his symbolic message of reconciliation to the German people.

Foreign Chiefs of State

The United States is one of the few developed nations that combine the chief of state and chief executive roles in a single office. The division of these roles between two or more individuals in most Western governments and several Communist nations demonstrates that a nation's top leader does not also need to be its figurehead. In many nations, including Great Britain, Belgium, The Netherlands, Sweden, Denmark, and Norway, a king or queen serves as chief of state even though the monarchy has lost any meaningful executive powers. In these countries the monarchs have become integrative figures who embody the history and ideals of their nations.

In other countries, such as France, Israel, Italy, and West Germany, the chief of state role is assigned to an elected official who serves alongside the head of the government.[1] In many Communist nations there is a triumvirate of leaders: the president, the premier, and the general secretary of the Communist party. The president is the official chief of state, while the premier is formally in charge of the Soviet government. It is the general secretaryship, however, that often is the most powerful post.

Significantly, even when a nation has a full-time chief of state, the official who wields executive power will often perform many chief of state functions. No chief executive can be entirely insulated from ceremonial duties. Even when a chief of state's office is a cherished part of the national culture grounded in centuries of tradition, like the British monarchy, or has retained influence in the government, like the Spanish monarchy,[2] the person who actually wields power will be expected to preside at some ceremonial functions. In particular, chief executives must greet important foreign visitors who want to meet with the most powerful person in the country, not just the reigning figurehead.

1. Merlin Gustafson, "Our Part-Time Chief of State," *Presidential Studies Quarterly* 9 (Spring 1979): 164.
2. William V. Thomas, "World Royalty: Pomp and Circumspection," *Editorial Research Reports*, May 8, 1981, 332-333.

Partisan Politics

When a political system separates the chief of state role from that of the chief executive, the chief of state can transcend partisanship. The British monarch takes no official position in the political struggles between British political parties. Such nonpartisanship is impossible for the U.S. president who must function as the leader of a political party as well as chief of state.

Although the president may genuinely promote a nonpartisan atmosphere on some occasions, presidents frequently exploit their standing as chief of state for partisan purposes. Virtually everything the president does in public as chief of state has political significance. The dignity and status conferred on presidents as the nation's ceremonial and symbolic leader increase their popularity with the American public and their bargaining advantages over other government officials.

The chief of state role also provides presidents with a

Jimmy Carter's Attempt to Depomp the Presidency

During Jimmy Carter's presidential campaign leading up to his 1976 election he perceived correctly that the American people were still disturbed by the Watergate scandal and wanted the next president to reaffirm their trust in government. Carter's emphasis on establishing an honest and unpretentious administration helped propel him to the White House past several better known Democratic candidates and the Republican incumbent Gerald Ford. As president, Carter was determined to eliminate barriers between the presidency and the people.

Carter began his campaign to depomp the presidency on his first day as president. Following Carter's inauguration ceremony he and his family left their limousine and walked up Pennsylvania Avenue to the White House. This gesture symbolized his intention to cut back on the pretentions and privileges surrounding his office as part of his efforts to run a just and open presidency. After Carter's term was over he wrote about his decision to walk back to the White House:

> I began to realize that the symbolism of our leaving the armoured car would be much more far-reaching than simply to promote exercise. I remembered the angry demonstrators who had habitually confronted recent Presidents and Vice Presidents, furious over the Vietnam war and later the revelations of Watergate. I wanted to provide a vivid demonstration of my confidence in the people as far as security was concerned, and I felt a simple walk would be a tangible indication of some reduction in the imperial status of the President and his family.[1]

Thereafter Carter continued his efforts to simplify the imperial presidency. He sold the presidential yacht, carried his own garment bag, donated blood, and ordered the White House thermostat to be set at sixty-five degrees in the winter.[2] In addition, he stopped the practice of having "Hail to the Chief" played when he entered the scene of an official event, delivered an FDR-style fireside chat, and was often photographed in informal clothing.

Carter also attempted to destroy the imperial atmosphere surrounding the presidency by emphasizing his accessibilty. During the first several months of his presidency he held frequent press conferences and question-and-answer sessions with federal employees. He also attended town meetings in rural communities, conducted a phone-in talk show in which members of the public could ask him direct questions, and, when traveling within the country, lodged in the homes of American families.[3] Carter even invited John B. Shanklin, a Washington, D.C., hotel worker, to the White House as he had promised during a 1974 encounter with Mr. Shanklin at the outset of Carter's campaign for the Democratic nomination.

During his first months in office, Carter's openness appealed to the American people, and he enjoyed high public approval ratings. As time passed, however, Carter and his aides suspected that they had gone too far in eliminating pomp from the presidency. As the president's popularity dropped throughout most of his first year and a half in office, it appeared that Carter's accessibility and populist style had made him seem less presidential than past chief executives and had muted the patriotic message contained in presidential symbols. For some people, Carter's actions also seemed to be weakening the office of the president.[4] Carter recalled: "I overreacted at first. We began to receive many complaints that I had gone too far in cutting back the pomp and ceremony, so after a few months I authorized the band to play 'Hail to the Chief' on special occasions. I found it to be impressive and enjoyed it."[5] As his term progressed Carter tried to establish a balance between the regal symbols that contributed to an image of himself as a powerful, decisive president and the populist symbols that had helped him get elected.

Carter had initially misinterpreted what the public wanted following the Watergate scandal. Undoubtedly, they longed for honesty and openness in the White House, but not at the expense of the symbolic trappings that contributed to the presidency's historic and paternal image. Indeed, the "imperial" presidency of Richard Nixon did not end in disgrace because he enjoyed the glamour and ceremonial display of his office, but rather because he had broken the law, cut himself off from everyone but a handful of advisers, and cynically betrayed the trust of the American people. Carter learned that the symbols and privileges of the presidency contribute to presidential power, and no president can reject them without risking an erosion of popular support.

1. Jimmy Carter, *Keeping Faith* (New York: Bantam Books, 1982), 17-18.
2. Larry Berman, *The New American Presidency* (Boston: Little, Brown, 1987), 314.
3. Harold Barger, *The Impossible Presidency* (Scott, Foresman, 1984), 378.
4. Thomas E. Cronin, *The State of the Presidency,* 2d ed. (Boston: Little, Brown, 1980), 159.
5. Jimmy Carter, *Keeping Faith,* 27.

justification to preside over events with obvious public relations appeal. Chief of state activities can be staged to make presidents look patriotic, amiable, concerned, skilled, and noble. Because chief of state activities are built into the president's job description, the role allows presidents to campaign subtly throughout their term without having to appear overly political or self-serving.

Presidential Popularity

One of the most important factors affecting presidents' domestic political power is the public support they receive. When a solid majority of Americans backs the president on a particular issue, other political institutions, including Congress, rarely will challenge the president. The chief of state role is a political asset primarily because it fortifies the president's popularity.

Many Americans will support the office of the presidency because it symbolizes the nation and the government even when they disagree with the incumbent's policies. The popularity of the presidency is demonstrated by the high public approval ratings enjoyed by new presidents. Political scientists Erwin C. Hargrove and Michael Nelson have written that the "honeymoon" period between the American people and new presidents

> is, in a sense, an affirmation of faith in the office. . . . New presidents invariably receive the initial approval of millions of citizens who voted against them; vice presidents who succeed to the office, for whom no one voted, actually fare better. Even after experiencing two highly unpopular presidencies in a row, the second culminating in the near-impeachment and resignation of President Nixon, citizens rallied to the support of President Ford by a margin of 71 percent to 3 percent.[25]

Even the outcome of the Watergate scandal can be viewed as evidence of the presidency's popularity and strength rather than its fragility, since Nixon was not forced to resign until long after the depth of the scandal became known.[26]

Given that the presidency is more consistently popular than any incumbent can hope to be, presidents benefit from chief of state activities because they make them appear "presidential." Formal ceremonies such as the State of the Union address and a state dinner for a foreign head of state appeal to public patriotism and allow the president to look like the nation's leader and guardian. They also underscore the president's links with history and cause people to associate the incumbent with the past glories of the office. Nixon attempted to exploit the history of the presidency by placing a bust of Lincoln on his desk and wearing an American flag pin when he appeared on television during the Watergate scandal to assure the American public that he was innocent of any wrongdoing.[27]

The chief of state role also contributes to presidential popularity by personalizing the president. Less formal ceremonies such as a trip to a sporting event or a White House reception for a civic group make the president appear as an average friendly person who shares the everyday interests and concerns of Americans. Ceremonial activities, therefore, can be used to build the fondness, as well as the respect, the public has for a president.

Finally, many Americans will support an incumbent's foreign policies because the president is seen as the representative and symbol of the United States before the world. Few events make a president look more like a statesman than a summit meeting with a prominent head of state or a reception in a foreign country by hundreds of thousands of cheering foreign citizens hoping to catch a glimpse of the U.S. chief of state. Presidents attempt to maximize the public relations benefits of their chief of state role by dramatizing their foreign tours and staging them for television. President Nixon timed his historic arrival in Beijing in 1972 to coincide with Sunday night prime-time television viewing hours. The president's return to Washington was also timed to coincide with prime time even though this required a nine-hour "refueling stop" in Alaska.[28]

Intragovernmental Relations

Although the public often thinks of presidents as leaders who "run the country," they are far from omnipotent. Congress can block most presidential initiatives, and the courts can declare a presidential action unconstitutional. Even cabinet officers and other members of the executive branch can check presidential power by withholding information, slowing down implementation of presidential directives, leaking details of controversial policies to the media, publicly announcing their opposition to a policy, or resigning to protest a presidential decision. Consequently, presidential power depends not only on the authority of presidents to issue orders and make proposals, but also on their ability to persuade others that those orders and proposals are correct.

The president's status as chief of state strengthens the president's ability to influence other members of the government. Political scientist Richard Neustadt observed:

> Presidential "powers" may be inconclusive when a President commands, but always remain relevant as he persuades. The status and authority inherent in his office reinforce his logic and his charm. . . . few men—and exceedingly few Cabinet officers—are immune to the impulse to say "yes" to the President of the United States. It grows harder to say "no" when they are seated in his oval office at the White House, or in his office on the second floor, where almost tangibly he partakes of the aura of his physical surroundings.[29]

Such presidential lobbying is hard to resist, especially for members of the president's own party who risk political isolation if they do not have a good record of supporting the president. Presidents, therefore, can exploit the symbolic power of their office to pressure an official or member of Congress for support.

Presidents can also use the glamour and social prestige of the White House to influence members of Congress and other public leaders by granting or denying them access to White House meetings and social functions. Officials want to be close to the president not just because they have use for the chief executive's authority, but because they wish to bask in the glow of presidential celebrity. An invitation to a White House dinner or reception can be one of the most sought after "tickets" in Washington. It allows an individual to rub elbows with the most powerful and famous people in the country, and it is a confirmation of the recipient's importance to the nation and the president. Although presidents and their staffs will invite members of the other party to White House events in the name of bipartisanship, political allies of the president obviously will receive more invitations than political enemies. Politicians who engage the president in a particularly bitter political battle or become enmeshed in a scandal may be cut off from the president's presence entirely.[30]

Furthermore when presidents are faced with a stubborn Congress, their status as chief of state contributes to their ability to appeal to the people over the head of the legislative branch. Presidents have done this by presenting their case to the people on an issue and hoping that favorable popular opinion and active public pressure on individual legislators will force Congress to back presidential policy. Franklin Roosevelt had great success with this tactic. His popularity with the American people weakened resistance in Congress to his New Deal programs. Reagan also used this strategy successfully. During his first year in office, he asked the public to pressure Congress to support his efforts to change dramatically the federal government's taxing and spending policies. Despite a solid Democratic majority in the House of Representatives, he was able to pass a large tax cut and sweeping spending reductions totaling over $35 billion.

Other presidents have been less successful at using public opinion. In September 1919 Woodrow Wilson undertook a cross-country crusade to promote U.S. entry into the League of Nations. After making dozens of speeches in twenty-nine cities across the Midwest and West, he became ill and returned to Washington, D.C., where he suffered a stroke on October 2. Despite Wilson's efforts, the public remained skeptical of an activist foreign policy, and the Republican-controlled Senate refused to ratify the Treaty of Versailles, which established the League.

Jimmy Carter saw himself as a Washington outsider who enjoyed a direct relationship to the people that would help him to deal with Congress on contentious issues. Carter discovered, however, that his election victory and initial personal popularity—which exceeded 70 percent during his first months in office—did not translate into public enthusiasm for his programs. His expectations of being able to confront Congress with strong public backing led him to neglect executive-legislative relations and made passage of his programs more difficult.[31]

Extragovernmental Power

The president is indisputably the nation's first celebrity. One 1969-1970 survey found that 98 percent of adult Americans knew who was president, a much higher percentage of recognition than for any other public figure except the vice president, who was known by 87 percent. In contrast, only 57 percent knew the name of one senator from their state, and only 39 percent could identify their representative in the House of Representatives.[32]

Presidents, first ladies, and former occupants of the White House frequently head the list in "most admired person" polls. Most national radio and television news broadcasts will discuss the president's major activity of the day, and few adult Americans would not be able to recite some basic details about the president's personal and political background. Each year almost two million people, many of whom stand in line for more than an hour, visit the White House. Over nine million people tried to call the White House during President Carter's call-in radio press conference in 1977. This constant attention not only contributes to the president's political power it also gives presidents and their families great influence over national culture and attitudes.

Spiritual Leadership

Although one of the most cherished and accepted principles embodied in the U.S. Constitution is the separation between church and state, many Americans look upon presidents as moral and spiritual leaders. Presidents attend church services and national prayer breakfasts, address religious groups, discuss issues with religious leaders, and frequently invoke God in their speeches. Religious influence flows to presidents because they are the nation's foremost celebrities and the symbols of traditional American values. The moral and religious example they set affects the religious climate of the nation during their term.

The president's role as an unofficial spiritual leader was first exercised by George Washington, who said in his first inaugural address that

> it would be improper to omit in this first official act, my fervent supplications to that Almighty Being who rules over the Universe.... No people can be bound to acknowledge and adore the invisible hand, which conducts the Affairs of men, more than the People of the United States. Every step, by which they have advanced to the character of an independent nation, seems to have been distinguished by some token of providential agency.

Since then all presidents have mentioned God in their inaugural addresses.[33] Washington also added the words "so help me God" after the oath of office. Every president has followed Washington's example, thereby making an acknowledgement of God part of the president's first official act.

No self-proclaimed atheist has ever been elected president. Thomas Jefferson, who was accused of being one during the 1800 presidential campaign, asserted his faith in God in his inaugural address. He referred to "that Infinite power which rules the destinies of the universe" and "an overruling Providence."

Although Americans expect their president to profess a belief in God and occasionally participate in religious ceremonies and rituals, they are ambivalent about the president's religious role. The majority of Americans want their president to be a religious person, affirm religious values, and set a moral example, but they do not want the president to govern the country according to a private conception of God's will or to use the presidency to promote a specific religious faith. Carter, who considered himself a "born again" Christian, understood this ambivalence. He openly professed a deep faith in God but denied that he considered himself to be a religious leader.[34]

Above all, presidents are expected to take an ecumenical approach to religion that does not offend any faith with significant numbers of adherents. Eisenhower often professed his faith in God and spoke of the importance of religion in American society, but he was careful not to define God narrowly. In a 1959 speech to the National Council of Churches he stated that the spiritual unity of the West included not only Judeo-Christian traditions but also "the Mohammedans, the Buddhists and the rest; because they too, strongly believe that they achieve a right to human dignity because of their relationship to the Supreme Being." [35] Rather than promoting a particular faith, presidents have generally promoted the concept of religion and the basic values common to most religions.

Style

People want to know the details of the life of presidents and their families. Just as the British scan their newspapers and magazines for information about the royal family, the American public avidly follows the private lives of the first family, the closest American equivalent to royalty.

The national spotlight gives presidents and their families influence to affect the lifestyles and habits of Americans. Presidents will often spark new trends in clothing, foods, hobbies, or athletics even if they do not try to do so. Franklin Roosevelt increased the popularity of cigarette holders and scotty dogs. John Kennedy's preference for rocking chairs, which he favored because of his chronic back ailment, led many Americans to get one for their own home. Lyndon Johnson's taste for Mexican food convinced many Americans to try Mexican cuisine for the first time and stimulated the growth of fast food chains selling Mexican dishes. The company that manufactured Ronald Reagan's favorite kind of jelly bean reported that its sales

Public Reaction to the Death of a President

The reaction of Americans to the death of a president provides dramatic evidence of the American public's emotional attachment to the presidency. The deaths of presidents have produced periods of simultaneous public grief more intense than those caused by any other type of national event. Americans regard the death of an incumbent president not just as the death of their elected leader, but as the death of the symbol of the government, the guarantor of the nation's security and stability, and a person almost as familiar as a family member.

Although no systematic studies were done of public reactions to the deaths of incumbent presidents before John F. Kennedy, anecdotal evidence suggests that Americans have often experienced a traumatizing grief when an incumbent president has died. Hundreds of thousands of people lined the railways to view the train carrying Abraham Lincoln's body from Washington, D.C., to Albany, New York, and west to its grave site in Springfield, Illinois. The massive outpouring of grief for Franklin Roosevelt, who had led the nation through the Great Depression and World War II, demonstrated that not only an assassination but also an imcumbent's death by natural causes could produce a national spasm of emotion.

Nor was it necessary for the president to have been perceived as a great historical figure. After the shooting of James Garfield in 1881, large crowds took to the streets of major cities seeking news of the president's condition. The attack was the main topic of church sermons the following Sunday, and Garfield, who had entered office only four months before as a dark-horse candidate from Ohio, was lionized in the press as a great statesman.[1] Similarly, William McKinley and Warren Harding were mourned deeply by the public despite their unexceptional leadership and relative lack of historical prominence.

Following the assassination of President Kennedy on November 22, 1963, social scientists at the National Opinion Research Center at the University of Chicago hastily constructed a survey designed to probe the American people's feelings in the aftermath of the tragedy. The interviewers asked 1,384 persons a series of questions about their reactions to the assassination. The responses indicated that the president's death had a much stronger effect on people than news of other kinds of disasters such as earthquakes or airline crashes.[2]

Only 19 percent of the respondents said they were able to continue their day "pretty much as usual" after hearing of the assassination. Sixty-eight percent of the respondents reported that at some time during the four-day period between the assassination and the president's funeral they "felt very nervous and tense." Fifty-seven percent said they "felt sort of dazed and numb." Fifty-three percent said they had cried.

The survey showed that the death of President Kennedy produced feelings in the American people usually associated with the death of a relative or close friend. Seventy-nine percent said when they first heard about the assassination, they "felt deeply the loss of someone very close and dear." Seventy-three percent felt anger, and 92 percent felt sorry for Kennedy's wife and children.

Paul B. Sheatsley and Jacob J. Feldman of the National Opinion Research Center observed:

> The presidential assassination seems clearly to have engaged the "gut feelings" of virtually every American. Events of this order are extremely rare. Survey after survey has consistently shown that most people are normally preoccupied with their own health, their own families, their own problems, and those of their friends and neighbors.... The election of an Eisenhower, the defeat of a Stevenson, a revolution in Cuba, the death of a Stalin—the surprise drop of an atomic bomb or the launching of a sputnik—such infrequent events, in contrast to the ordinary run-of-the-mill news, arouse the interest of almost everyone, but even they do not produce the cessation of ordinary activities, the almost complete preoccupation with the event, and the actual physical symptoms we have here described.[3]

1. Charles E. Rosenberg, *The Trial of the Assassin Guiteau* (Chicago: University of Chicago Press, 1968), 7.
2. Paul B. Sheatsley and Jacob J. Feldman, "The Assassination of President Kennedy: A Preliminary Report on Public Reactions and Behavior," *Public Opinion Quarterly* (Summer 1964): 189-215.
3. Ibid., 206.

tripled, and new orders were backlogged for more than a year after the media reported Reagan's fondness for their product in 1981.

First Ladies can have an equally dramatic effect on national trends. Uncounted women, fascinated by the glamorous Jacqueline Kennedy, adopted her hairstyle and clothing tastes. Many Americans disapproved of Nancy Reagan's consultations with an astrologer, but popular interest in astrology increased after knowledge of her hobby was made public.

Some presidents have deliberately tried to influence the lifestyle of the nation. Theodore Roosevelt not only urged Americans to live an active life full of outdoor pursuits, he also set an example for his fellow citizens to emulate. He climbed trees on the White House grounds, swam in the Potomac, played marathon tennis matches, and went for "obstacle walks" in which he would go over or through any obstacle that stood in his way. Roosevelt also promoted vigorous activity by inviting athletes, explorers, cowboys, and other citizens who led a strenuous life to the White House. In addition, Roosevelt waged a campaign to make simplified phonetic spelling acceptable but found that such a controversial cultural reform was beyond even his powers.[36]

John and Jacqueline Kennedy promoted artistic and intellectual pursuits during their years at the White House.

Their patronage of cultural events and recognition of the achievements of writers, artists, and performers awakened American interest in the fine arts. The Kennedys invited famous entertainers and musicians to the White House for "command performances." The president and first lady also promoted interest in science and history. At one famous dinner in 1962 honoring American Nobel Prize winners, the president declared: "This is the most extraordinary collection of talent . . . that has ever been gathered together at the White House—with the possible exception of when Thomas Jefferson dined alone." [37] Mrs. Kennedy, dismayed by the meager White House library, stocked it with 1,780 great works of literature selected by James T. Babb, Yale University's librarian. She also recovered many historical pieces from museums, private collections, and White House storage areas and had the executive mansion redecorated in authentic early nineteenth-century decor.

Chief of State Burdens

One of the justifications of the British monarchy offered by its contemporary proponents is that it shelters the prime minister from many ceremonial duties. Prime ministers can devote their time and energies to formulating policy and dealing with Parliament and foreign governments while the royal family presides at ceremonial functions and absorbs media and public attention. Presidents have no shield against ceremonial activities equivalent to the British monarchy. Although family members, vice presidents, cabinet secretaries, and other presidential associates can lighten the president's ceremonial burden, the president is responsible for innumerable ceremonial functions and never ceases to be chief of state. Between lobbying a member of Congress to support a bill and meeting with the National Security Council to discuss an international hot spot, the president may have to greet Olympic athletes, officials of the United Way, or Miss America. The president's chief of state duties, therefore, may interrupt or even interfere with the president's duties as chief executive.

Calvin Coolidge, who as president refused to overcrowd his schedule, warned:

> The duties of the Presidency are exceedingly heavy. The responsibilities are overwhelming. But it is my opinion that a man of ordinary strength can carry them if he will confine himself very strictly to a performance of the duties that are imposed upon him by the Constitution and the law. If he permits himself to be engaged in all kinds of outside enterprises, in furnishing entertainment and amusement to great numbers of public gatherings, undertaking to be the source of inspiration for every worthy public movement, for all of which he will be earnestly besought with the inference that unless he responds civilization will break down and the sole responsibility will be on him, he will last in office about 90 days.[38]

Few presidents, however, have been able or have wanted to limit their activities the way Coolidge did, and several have driven themselves to exhaustion. Because the chief of state duties increase the presidential workload, one can argue that they are an onerous burden. In addition to the drain on a president's time and energy, the chief of state role can make the president more vulnerable to assassination attempts, reinforce unreasonable public expectations of the president, and contribute to an atmosphere of deference that may warp the president's judgment. In response to these problems some observers of the presidency have suggested that the office be reformed so that the president, like the British prime minister, is free of ceremonial responsibilities.

Demands on Time

Presidential time is a scarce resource. Presidents are ultimately responsible for everything that the executive branch does. They must have time to preside over policy meetings, review the work of their staff and cabinet, establish working relationships with members of Congress, read intelligence reports, study new policy proposals, hold press conferences, make decisions, and perform numerous other functions necessary to the operation of the government and their administration. In addition, they must find time for political campaigning, personal relaxation, and ceremonial functions.

No chief executive can begin to satisfy all the requests for presidential attention. Woodrow Wilson and Franklin Roosevelt, two presidents with a hands-on managerial style, complained of the burdens of their office. Wilson called the presidential workload "preposterous," and Roosevelt claimed to work fifteen-hour days.[39] Lyndon Johnson related in his memoirs: "Of all the 1,886 nights I was President, there were not many when I got to sleep before 1 or 2 a.m., and there were few mornings when I didn't wake up by 6 or 6:30." [40] Even presidents like Eisenhower and Reagan, who were noted for their willingness to delegate responsibility and authority to their subordinates, faced daily decisions about which activities would have to be sacrificed to the pressures of time.

Although presidential responsibilities have expanded greatly in the twentieth century, eighteenth- and nineteenth-century presidents also had more work than time in which to do it. George Washington found himself overwhelmed by the number of visitors he had to receive and civic functions he had to attend. He complained: "From the time I had done breakfast and thence till dinner and afterwards till bedtime I could not get relieved from ceremony of one visit before I had to attend to another." [41] Washington approached the problem in his typical manner—by asking the advice of colleagues he trusted. He solicited the opinions of Alexander Hamilton, John Jay, James Madison, and John Adams. After hearing their recommendations, Washington decided to limit his public entertaining to a dinner every Thursday at four o'clock for government officials and their families, a public levee on Tuesday afternoons for men, and a public tea party on Friday evenings for men and women.[42]

The enormity of presidential responsibilities received a judicial validation in 1807. Chief Justice John Marshall subpoenaed President Thomas Jefferson to appear before the grand jury in Richmond considering former vice president Aaron Burr's indictment for treason. Jefferson refused to appear. He justified his decision in part by explaining that a president's duties as chief executive should not be set aside for an appearance at a trial: "The Constitution enjoins his constant agency in the concerns of six millions of people. Is the law paramount to this, which calls on him on behalf of a single one?" [43] The court accepted Jefferson's refusal to appear and withdrew its request for his testimony. The president cooperated fully with the investigation and offered to give a deposition, but the court never asked him for one.

George Tames, *New York Times*

This candid photo of JFK in the Oval Office has come to signify the heavy burden of the presidency.

Numerous other nineteenth-century presidents commented on the burdens of their office. James Monroe wrote to Congress just before his second term expired that the higher duties of the presidency, consisting primarily of legislative and administrative tasks, were "sufficient to employ the whole mind, and unceasing labors of any individual." [44] James Polk, who died less than four months after he left office, complained in his diary that his presidential duties left him "almost prostrated by fatigue." [45]

Of all presidential activities, ceremonial functions are usually regarded as the most expendable and are frequently delegated to other individuals. Each year the White House turns down hundreds of requests for the president's time from groups and organizations seeking to publicize their cause through an appointment with the president. When a crisis erupts, ceremonial functions that have been scheduled are sometimes cut to accommodate time constraints. Despite the White House's ability to trim the president's ceremonial schedule, chief of state functions still occupy blocks of the president's time. Many ceremonies over which presidents preside are trivial when compared with the weighty affairs of state. For example, in spite of tradition, appearing at the annual White House Easter egg outing is a questionable use of the president's time considering the unending procession of problems that require the president's attention.

There is evidence, however, that although international ceremonial functions occupy much presidential time, the demands of the domestic chief of state role are less than one might expect. A study of the years 1952 and 1960 from the presidencies of Harry Truman and Dwight Eisenhower revealed that they spent only about one hundred hours per year, or about two hours per week, on domestic ceremonial functions. Sample surveys of the appointment calendars of Herbert Hoover, Franklin Roosevelt, Lyndon Johnson, Gerald Ford, and Jimmy Carter indicated that these presidents spent about the same amount of time as Truman and Eisenhower in their domestic chief of state role.[46]

International chief of state duties, however, took up a much greater percentage of presidential time. For example, Eisenhower spent 376 hours in 1960—the equivalent of 47 eight-hour days—on foreign trips or in meetings in Washington with other heads of state.[47] Taken together, therefore, the international and domestic chief of state responsibilities constitute a significant drain on the president's time and may cause unwanted interruptions in the president's workday.

Risks to the President's Health

Scholars and presidents generally have agreed that the presidency is a tremendous physical burden.[48] The pressures of the presidency can weaken the health of even the strongest person. Presidents usually work long hours, must occasionally take extended trips that require physical and mental stamina, and must endure enormous emotional stress rising out of the responsibilities of their job. Presidents seldom look as vigorous when they leave office as when they entered it.

One study of presidential longevity has shown that most presidents have failed to reach the age to which they were expected to live at the time of their election. Excluding the four presidents who were assassinated, twenty-two of the thirty-two presidents who have died of natural causes failed to reach their life expectancy. As the nation and presidential responsibilities have expanded, so has the tendency of presidents to die prematurely. Only four deceased presidents who were elected after 1836 reached their life expectancy.[49]

Illnesses can and have inhibited the execution of presidential duties. Four presidents—William Henry Harrison, Zachary Taylor, Warren Harding, and Franklin Roosevelt—died of natural causes before their terms expired. Several other presidents, including Wilson and Eisenhower, were incapacitated by illness during their incumbency.[50]

Given the consequences of presidents becoming ill, reducing their workload without diminishing their effectiveness is a worthwhile goal of reform. Since common practice has demonstrated that many of the president's ceremonial duties can be delegated, these duties seem to be the logical starting place of efforts to trim the president's schedule.

George Reedy, who served as press secretary under Lyndon Johnson, has argued that even if ceremonial functions do take up valuable presidential time, the primary source of strain on presidents is not long workdays but the knowledge of the consequences of their actions.[51] From war to welfare reform, presidential policies can have life and death consequences. For presidents who have served during the atomic age, the knowledge of their responsibility as the person who must decide to use nuclear weapons can be particularly stressful. Lyndon Johnson wrote that he felt relief after hearing Richard Nixon complete the oath of office in part because "I would not have to face the decision any more of taking any step, in the Middle East or elsewhere, that might lead to world conflagration—the nightmare of my having to be the man who pressed the button to start World War III was passing." [52]

Reedy maintains, as others have, that chief of state duties can provide a psychological release to presidents from the overwhelming responsibilities of their office.[53] These ceremonial events allow presidents to get away from the strains of decision making, and since ceremonies are an accepted presidential responsibility, presidents are unlikely to feel as if they are neglecting their duties.

The effect of the chief of state role on a president's mental and physical health may depend on that individual's personality. For those presidents who revel in the spotlight of national attention, or are stimulated by an affirmation of public affection, like Theodore Roosevelt, Franklin Roosevelt, or Ronald Reagan, chief of state duties can be the most enjoyable and rejuvenating aspect of the presidency. Those presidents, however, who are uncomfortable with the public attention showered upon them, like William Howard Taft and Herbert Hoover, or who feel like they are wasting time when they avert their attention from policy matters, like James Polk, will likely regard chief of state duties as a burden rather than a release.

Risks to the President's Safety

The assassination of a president is an even greater national disaster than the death of a president by natural causes. There may be time to prepare for the transfer of power to the vice president when a president dies from an illness, but an assassination usually does not allow for a period of administrative or emotional preparation. An assassination not only can cause governmental confusion, it can send the country into shock because people perceive an attack upon the president, the symbol of the United States, as an attack upon the nation itself.

Assassination attempts against presidents have not been uncommon. Lincoln, Garfield, McKinley, and Kennedy were killed by their assailants. Jackson, Truman, Ford, and Reagan, who was wounded, each survived attempts on their lives. In addition, president-elect Franklin Roosevelt was attacked three weeks before his first inauguration; and three presidential candidates, Theodore Roosevelt, Robert F. Kennedy, and George Wallace, all were shot—with Kennedy being killed. In all, presidents, presidents-elect, and presidential candidates have been attacked thirteen times. All but three of these attacks have occurred in the twentieth century. Moreover, threats against the president's life and attempts by individuals to enter the White House grounds illegally have become increasingly frequent.[54]

The most dangerous presidential activities are those that require the president to appear before a large crowd outside the White House grounds.[55] Since the chief of state role often involves such appearances, it contributes to the danger of assassination. The symbolic goal of many chief of state events is to bridge the gap between the government and the people. This goal is difficult to accomplish from inside a bullet-proof limousine or behind a wall of Secret Service agents. Consequently, presidents, especially those running for reelection, still occasionally seek personal contact with unscreened gatherings of voters while nervous Secret Service agents scan the crowd for possible danger. Yet the benefits of a ceremonial event or symbolic gesture in a location where the president's safety cannot be absolutely guaranteed must always be weighed against the risk of an assassination attempt.

The threat of assassination and the cumbersome security measures necessary to ensure the president's safety have forced changes in the way presidents perform their chief of state role. The days when presidents were expected to wade unprotected into a crowd of citizens to shake hands are gone. Just before leaving office Ronald Reagan commented that he would have liked to have gone to see a college football game between Army and Navy as many other presidents had done, but he did not because "nobody wants to run 75,000 people through a magnetometer." Reagan even justified his lack of church attendance, a traditional ceremonial activity of the president, on the grounds that security measures necessary to ensure his safety would disrupt the congregation. Orchestrated events in front of carefully screened groups and televised speeches and press conferences have become the usual methods by which presidents communicate with the American people. This development has contributed to the isolation of presidents. Now, when they spontaneously place themselves before a crowd, as Carter did when he left his limousine and walked up Pennsylvania Avenue after his inauguration in 1977, it is considered a brave and confident gesture.

Excessive Public Expectations

For better or worse, the presidency is an idealized and romanticized office of which the American people have high expectations. With each election the public hopes for a president who will combine the best qualities of past presidents. They want a president with the confidence of Franklin Roosevelt, the international popularity of Dwight Eisenhower, the charisma of John Kennedy, and the legislative skill of Lyndon Johnson. Few individuals can ever live up to such expectations

Moreover, the American people do not want just a president who will combine the skills and insight of past presidents; they want a leader who will satisfy requirements that are often contradictory. Political scientist Thomas Cronin has identified several paradoxes of the presidency that make the president's job nearly impossible. For example, the president must be gentle and decent but also forceful and decisive; a crusader with an agenda and a pragmatic compromiser; a leader able to inspire the nation but one who does not make unrealistic promises; and a common person who understands the American people but a leader of exceptional intellect and sophistication.[56]

Political scientist Godfrey Hodgson has agreed that the expectations of the American people are not easily reconciled:

> The things "the people" want are mutually inconsistent. They want lower taxes *and* higher benefits. They want to be sure of the supply of gasoline, *and* they do not want to pay higher prices for it. They want national security *and* disarmament. They do not want American boys to be sent abroad to be killed, *and* they want the United States to be respected and feared in Vietnam and Ethiopia and Iran.[57]

The public disillusionment created when presidents fail to meet the public's contradictory demands can lead to declining public approval over the course of a president's term. Public opinion polls have shown that presidential popularity usually peaks shortly after the president takes office. It then tends to fall steadily before reaching its nadir late in the second half of the four-year term. After hitting bottom the president's popularity may rise somewhat, but it never reaches the levels enjoyed during the president's first months in office. Although the exact causes of this pattern are uncertain, the public's unrealistic expectations work against presidential popularity.[58]

The chief of state role contributes to high public expectations of the presidency by causing the public to believe presidents have more power than they actually do. As chief of state and the official who represents the entire country, the president is the personification of the nation and the closest American equivalent to royalty. The president's familiarity and symbolic status cause the media and the public to focus their hopes and expectations upon the president. Political scientist Merlin Gustafson wrote, "When one person exercises both symbolic and political authority his public image tends to become distorted. A substantial portion of the public may be led to identify the presidential person with the governmental process, and assume that he alone determines national policy or 'runs the country.' "[59]

The public tends to blame and praise presidents for virtually everything that occurs during their terms regardless of their actual responsibility for conditions. For example, the public holds presidents responsible for economic prosperity even though the natural swings of the business cycle, foreign economic conditions, and economic shocks such as droughts and oil embargoes guarantee that even the best presidential economic policies will not yield economic growth all the time.

When judging presidents, the public often ignores that the Constitution was designed to prevent any one person from completely dominating the government. Presidents must work with a Congress that may be controlled by the opposing party and is always composed of members primarily concerned with serving their home states and districts. Presidents also must avoid unconstitutional actions and motivate their executive branch subordinates who are capable of undermining presidential policies and initiatives. Presidents who cannot get their bills passed or programs implemented often are accused of being weak leaders or poor compromisers. In short, even though presidents are constrained by the Constitution, they are expected to be as effective as if they were absolute monarchs.

The danger of high public expectations and their negative effect on presidential approval ratings is that presidents may become obsessed with maintaining their popularity. This can cause presidents to take actions that are popular but that are not in the public's interest. In the worst case, presidents may be tempted to skirt legal constraints in pursuit of effective leadership. Cronin has commented: "Our expectations of, and demands on, the office are frequently so paradoxical as to invite two-faced behavior by our presidents. We seem to want so much so fast that a President, whose powers are often simply not as great as many of us believe, gets condemned as ineffectual. Or a president often will overreach or resort to unfair play while trying to live up to our demands." [60] Even if a president is willing to sacrifice public approval to do what is right, the decline in popularity will make the president's task of leading the nation more difficult.

Dangers of Deference

Because presidents are partisan political leaders they are routinely attacked by their political opponents and scrutinized by a combative press. Yet because they are the chief of state, the symbol of the unity and majesty of the United States, they are also treated with deference.

Presidents are provided with a mansion, guards, aircraft, and custom-made automobiles and are waited upon by a host of servants. They are addressed as "Mr. President" even by close friends they have known for many years. The strains of "Hail to the Chief" greet them when they enter the scene of an important occasion. An omnipresent contingent of reporters seeks their thoughts on any subject, no matter how mundane or irrelevant to national policy. Despite the democratic origins of the presidency, the president enjoys the luxury and veneration usually reserved for monarchs.

The intoxicating effects of the deference given to presidents is reinforced by the historic significance of the presidency and the White House. Newly elected presidents become members of an elite and celebrated club. No matter how ordinary their political career might have been before their succession or election, as soon as they take the oath of office they become a major historical figure. They know historians will be rate them on lists with Lincoln, Washington, and other immortal presidents. Election to the presidency ensures that many books will be written about their lives. When they have left office politicians and journalists will continue to seek their opinions as elder statesmen. A presidential library will be constructed to hold their official papers, and when they die their graves will become national landmarks.

Presidents are daily reminded of their place in history as they live in a house that is one of the nation's most cherished monuments and was occupied by every president except George Washington. In the White House they are surrounded by the artifacts of past administrations. They can view the portrait of George Washington that was rescued by first lady Dolley Madison in 1814 when the British burned the capital, or they can write at the desk given to President Rutherford B. Hayes by Queen Victoria in 1880 and used by many presidents since.

Outside the White House presidents can take a walk through the gardens past the magnolia tree planted by Andrew Jackson in memory of his wife, Rachel, or the Rose Garden originally planted by Ellen Wilson and redesigned under John Kennedy. George Reedy, who served as Lyndon Johnson's press secretary has observed:

> The atmosphere of the White House is calculated to instill in any man a sense of destiny. He literally walks in the footsteps of hallowed figures—of Jefferson, of Jackson, of Lincoln. The almost sanctified relics of a distant, semimythical past surround him as ordinary household objects to be used by his family. From the moment he enters the halls he is made aware that he has become enshrined in a pantheon of semidivine mortals who have shaken the world, and that he has taken from their hands the heritage of American dreams and aspirations.[61]

The deference shown presidents because they are chief of state and the mythic atmosphere created by presidential privileges and the regal White House environment may enoble some presidents by giving them a sense of destiny or historic duty, but the royal trappings of the office also can have damaging effects. During the Nixon administration, the well-being of the president and the presidency became more important than the law. The respect given to Nixon as chief of state and the privileges of the presidency, which he relished, undoubtedly enabled Nixon and his staff to justify more easily to themselves violations of the law and unethical political tactics.

In addition, if the deference shown presidents causes them to believe they are always right and above criticism, meaningful debate on presidential policies may be squelched. Presidents who become overconfident of their own judgment may feel resentment toward staff members who disagree with their opinions. Such an attitude will likely cause subordinates to avoid expressing negative opinions to preserve their own influence with the president. Political scientist Robert DiClerico has written:

> Presidents have a tendency to become intoxicated by the deference and veneration shown to the Office they hold. They begin to see themselves as deserving of praise and come to view challenge and disagreement as an affront.... The isolation of presidents from the disquieting advice of staff members was especially pronounced in the Johnson and Nixon administrations. Both men were lacking in a sense of security, and consequently they were especially susceptible to the arrogance generated by the intoxicating atmosphere of the Presidency.[62]

Presidents accustomed to being treated like monarchs inside the White House grounds may also develop a deep resentment of criticism coming from outside the White House. This may cause a president to rely exclusively on a small group of loyal advisers. Even if the president permits disagreement and frank discussion within this group, an isolated decision-making process will deprive the president of valuable sources of insight and information.

Proposals for Change

Given the problems inherent in having a president who is both the nation's chief executive and chief of state, observers of the presidency have occasionally put forward proposals to reform the chief of state role. Change could be accomplished in two ways: through executive orders or practices that formalize the delegation of most chief of state duties away from the president or through a constitutional amendment that assigns ceremonial duties to some other official or creates a new office of chief of state separate from the presidency. More sweeping reforms of the presidency, such as the creation of a plural executive or the incorporation of parliamentary elements into the American political system, also would affect the chief of state role.

Altering the president's chief of state role has not been a major concern of presidents and their advisers. The most prominent executive branch study of the issue was done by Eisenhower's Advisory Committee on Government Organization, also known as the Rockefeller Committee. The committee, which functioned throughout Eisenhower's tenure in office and studied the organization of the entire executive branch, recommended merely that the vice president perform many ceremonial duties to lighten the president's chief of state burden.[63] Presidents have commonly delegated ceremonial duties to the vice president and other individuals, but no president has set up formal rules concerning which officials would preside at which events. Even if such rules were implemented, the succeeding president might overturn whatever precedent had been set.

Most proposals for changing the president's chief of state power by amending the Constitution have come from scholars and public officials who have speculated on ways to make the presidency more efficient while acknowledging the difficulty of convincing the American people that such reforms are desirable.

One such proposal was a constitutional amendment introduced by Rep. Henry S. Reuss (D-Wis.) in 1975. It would have created an office of "Chief of State of the United States" separate from the presidency. The office as conceived by Reuss would be a purely ceremonial position. The president would nominate a candidate for chief of state who would be confirmed by a majority vote of both houses of Congress. To promote the office's nonpartisanship, the chief of state's four-year term would begin two years into the president's term and last two years into the next administration. There would be no limit on the number of terms a chief of state could serve. The amendment designated the chief of state as "the ceremonial head of the United States" and "the sole officer of the United States to receive ambassadors and other public ministers." In addition the chief of state would carry out ceremonial duties "as recommended by the president." The chief of state was to be paid a salary identical to the president and be subject to the same impeachment provisions.

When introducing the amendment, Reuss acknowledged that tinkering with the Constitution was controversial. He maintained, however, that the demands of the chief of state role on the president's time and the dangers of the "symbolic deification of the president" warranted amending the Constitution.[64]

Neither Congress nor the American people showed much interest in Reuss's amendment. Most Americans are not eager to alter an institution to which they are accustomed and with which they associate many of the nation's foremost heroes. Since Abraham Lincoln, Franklin Roosevelt, and other great presidents were able to use the power of the presidency to meet the nation's great crises, they reason, the solution to the nation's problems will not be found by changing the presidency but by electing leaders who can make it work.

Delegation of Chief of State Functions

Since George Washington, presidents have sought ways to control the number of ceremonial events over which they must preside. There are always more worthy causes to recognize and important events that deserve presidential attention than the president can attend. Presidents have managed to bridge part of this gap by delegating ceremonial tasks to family members, the vice president, cabinet officers, close associates, and staff members. Like representatives sent to negotiate with foreign governments, these substitute chiefs of state have authority because they either occupy an important office within the administration or have a personal relationship with the president. Because they do not possess the power of the presidency, their presence does not have the symbolic force of a presidential appearance, but they are substitutes that most groups readily accept.

First Lady and Family

Presidents have often delegated ceremonial functions to their spouses. First ladies are fitting presidential representatives because they are nearly as well-known as the president and are themselves recognized symbols of American history and culture. When a first lady addresses an organization or presides over a ceremonial event, the audience understands that the president is being represented by an intimate confidant and adviser.

Eleanor Roosevelt's ceremonial activism set the standard for modern first ladies. Franklin Roosevelt, who was crippled by polio, frequently sent his wife to the scene of strikes, disasters, and centers of poverty as his personal representative. She also traveled to England, South America, and the South Pacific during World War II to encourage U.S. troops and allies. Most succeeding first ladies also performed chief of state duties. Pat Nixon traveled widely with her husband and on her own. In 1972 she toured West Africa after representing the United States at the inauguration of the president of Liberia. Rosalynn Carter made an ambitious good-will tour of Latin America in 1977 in which she carried out diplomatic as well as ceremonial missions. Nancy Reagan visited several foreign countries as her husband's representative, including Great Britain in 1981 for the wedding of Prince Charles and Lady Diana, Monaco in 1982 for the funeral of Princess Grace, and Mexico in 1985 to express concern for the victims of an earthquake.

First ladies not only have served as substitute chiefs of state for their husbands, they also have performed their own traditional ceremonial roles. First ladies are expected to serve as hostesses at state dinners and other White House social functions. In addition, during international trips, while presidents have met with foreign leaders, their wives have often taken part in ceremonies or visited local sights where the international press can photograph them admiring an example of the host country's culture. For example, Pat Nixon visited the Moscow circus and the GUM department store while her husband met with Soviet leaders in 1972. First ladies have also entertained the wives of foreign leaders who have visited the United States. *(See "The First Lady," p. 865, in Daily Life of the President chapter of Part V.)*

Other first family members also have been used as ceremonial representatives by presidents. Julie Nixon Eisenhower and Maureen Reagan both occasionally represented their fathers before civic groups. Jimmy Carter's son Chip was employed by the president as his personal roving emissary. The president explained Chip's role in response to a question asked on his famous nationally broadcast radio talk show in 1977: "When we have a special problem anywhere in the nation, and I want the people there to know how deeply concerned I am about it, I would like to have the opportunity to use members of my family to go and represent me personally, along with professionals who serve in the government." [65] Chip's travels included trips to Buffalo to express concern over a severe winter storm, to China as the president's representative in a congressional delegation, to Great Britain to participate in a ceremonial event with the royal family, and to the Middle East as part of a delegation seeking Arab approval for the Camp David peace accords. President Carter's mother, Lillian, also represented him at ceremonial occasions, including the funeral of the president of India in February 1977. *(See "Family and Friends of the President," p. 895, in Daily Life of the President chapter of Part V.)*

Vice President

During John Adams's tenure as the first U.S. vice president he remarked, "My country has in its wisdom contrived for me the most insignificant office that ever the invention of man contrived or his imagination conceived." Many of the vice presidents who followed Adams agreed with his appraisal of the office. The Constitution had given the vice president no formal policy-making or administrative powers other than to preside over the Senate and break tie votes in that body. Vice-presidential involvement in governing the country depended on the president's inclination to include the vice president in the policy-making process. Few vice presidents of the nineteenth and early twentieth centuries had a significant role within their administrations. Although post-World War II vice presidents have become more involved in policy making, the office has remained one that takes on many ceremonial functions.

Vice presidents are well-positioned to act as substitute chiefs of state not only because they have the time to do it, but also because their office is associated with the presidency. Vice presidents run on the same ticket as their presidential running mates and are the only officials besides presidents who are elected by the entire nation. In addition, although their office may at times seem trivial, vice presidents are first in line for the presidency. Fourteen vice presidents have become president, including eight who succeeded to the presidency when the incumbent died in office and one when the incumbent resigned. The political and historic link between the two offices makes the vice president an appropriate stand-in for the president at ceremonial functions.

Since the advent of the jet airplane, presidents have frequently sent their vice presidents on ceremonial missions overseas. Occasionally these missions have included serious negotiations with leaders of important nations, but often their purpose was more symbolic than substantive. Hubert Humphrey explained the vice president's diplo-

Nixon Project, National Archives

Henry Kissinger became the most recognized symbol of President Richard Nixon's foreign policy. Originally national security adviser, he became secretary of state in 1973.

matic role: "He can perform assignments that the President feels would be unwise for him to take on himself, but for which an official lower than Vice President would be unsuitable." [66]

These assignments have included representing the United States and the president at inaugurations, coronations, and funerals of foreign leaders and major world figures. George Bush, who traveled more than one million miles and visited more than seventy countries as vice president, frequently took President Reagan's place at ceremonial functions overseas. Bush's attendance at the funerals of foreign dignitaries became so common he joked that his motto should be: "I'm George Bush. You die, I fly." [67] Vice presidents generally welcome any overseas trip regardless of its importance because foreign travel makes them appear busy and brings them more press attention than their usually undramatic domestic policy role.[68]

Presidents can enhance the symbolic effect of a vice-presidential trip by demonstrating their interest in it and designating the vice president as their personal envoy. John Kennedy would usually hold a publicized meeting with Lyndon Johnson before the vice president left on a foreign mission. Immediately after entering office, Jimmy Carter sent Walter Mondale on a tour of Europe and Japan to demonstrate the importance of close allied cooperation to the Carter administration. In a South Lawn ceremony President Carter bolstered his vice president's status by declaring: "Vice President Mondale has my complete confidence. He is a personal representative of mine, and I'm sure that his consultation with the leaders of these nations will make it much easier for our country to deal directly with them on substantive matters in the future." [69]

Sending vice presidents on foreign tours not only relieves presidents of their international ceremonial burdens, it gives the president's "understudy" foreign policy experience. Vice presidents whose previous work in Congress or as governor of a state may not have given them extensive foreign policy experience can become better acquainted with world leaders and the process of international diplomacy in case they should have to assume the presidency. Most foreign leaders welcome a vice-presidential visit and recognize that the vice president one day could become president.

Cabinet Members and Personal Advisers

Cabinet members often operate as assistant chiefs of state within the area of their department's concern. For example, the education secretary makes ceremonial visits to public schools; the housing and urban development secretary tours inner-city housing projects; the commerce secretary speaks to business groups; the interior secretary addresses environmentalist groups; and the defense secretary inspects military installations and presides at ceremonies honoring war heroes and veterans. These events symbolize the administration's concern with a particular issue or group. In addition, cabinet members often use ceremonial occasions or symbolic settings to make speeches that unveil a new program or announce a policy decision affecting their department.

The secretary of state has a special ceremonial role. After the president and vice president, the secretary of state is the nation's highest diplomatic and ceremonial representative. The secretary receives foreign ministers who visit the United States and often heads U.S. delegations at funerals, inaugurations, and other special ceremonies overseas that are not attended by the president or vice president. In matters of protocol the secretary of state also is considered to be the highest ranking cabinet officer. This unofficial rank is reinforced by the Succession Act of 1947, which designates the secretary of state as the first cabinet officer in line for the presidency and the fourth government official after the vice president, Speaker of the House, and president pro tempore of the Senate.

Presidents occasionally have used close friends and White House advisers to perform chief of state duties. Unlike cabinet members these chief of state stand-ins derive their legitimacy not from an office, but from their close political or personal relationship with the president. Woodrow Wilson sent his friend and confidant Col. Edward House, who held no government office, on five diplomatic missions to Europe. Franklin Roosevelt used Harry Hopkins, who carried the title "special assistant to the president," as his personal emissary to allied leaders during World War II. Although both of these men functioned primarily as diplomatic operatives rather than as presidential representatives at ceremonial functions, they became so closely identified with Wilson and Roosevelt that they not only spoke for their presidents when they met foreign leaders, they symbolized the presidency.

During the Nixon administration, National Security Adviser Henry Kissinger transformed his post from a behind-the-scenes presidential aide into a rival of the secretary of state for the diplomatic spotlight. The force of

Kissinger's personality, his close relationship to President Nixon, and his celebrated diplomatic missions to the People's Republic of China and the Soviet Union made him the most recognized symbol of Nixon's foreign policy. During Kissinger's second trip to the People's Republic in October 1971, he performed ceremonial activities including visits to the Great Wall of China and other Chinese landmarks. Kissinger also was constantly at the president's side during the historic 1972 summit meetings in Beijing and Moscow. Kissinger's activities resembled those of the secretary of state so much that he was criticized by some defenders of the State Department for having usurped the role of the secretary. After Secretary of State William Rodgers resigned, Kissinger assumed the post in September 1973.

Notes

1. Karlyn Kohrs Campbell and Kathleen Hall Jamieson, "Inaugurating the President," *Presidential Studies Quarterly* 15 (Spring 1985): 396-397.
2. Arthur M. Schlesinger, Jr., "Annual Messages of the Presidents: Major Themes of American History," in *The State of the Union Messages of the Presidents 1790-1966,* vol. 1 (New York: Chelsea House, 1966), xiv.
3. Ibid., xvi.
4. Alexander Hamilton, *Federalist* No. 69, in *The Federalist Papers,* Alexander Hamilton, James Madison, and John Jay (New York: New American Library, 1961), 420.
5. Cited in Richard Pious, *The American Presidency* (New York: Basic Books, 1979), 5.
6. Harold M. Barger, *The Impossible Presidency* (Glenview, Ill.: Scott, Foresman, 1984), 382.
7. Theodore C. Sorensen, *Kennedy* (New York: Harper and Row, 1965), 368.
8. James Hart, *The American Presidency in Action 1789* (New York: Macmillan, 1948), 24-25.
9. Ibid., 17.
10. *Public Papers of the Presidents of the United States, Franklin Roosevelt, Containing the Public Messages, Speeches, and Statements of the President, 1937* (Washington, D.C.: Government Printing Office, 1938), 379.
11. Clinton Rossiter, *The American Presidency,* 2d ed. (New York: Harcourt Brace and World, 1960), 18.
12. Ibid., 102-103.
13. Michael Novak, *Choosing Our King* (New York: Macmillan, 1974), 8.
14. Harold J. Laski, *The American Presidency, An Interpretation* (New York: Harper and Brothers, 1940), 38.
15. Thomas E. Cronin, "The Presidency and Its Paradoxes," in *The Presidency Reappraised,* 2d ed., ed. Thomas E. Cronin and Rexford G. Tugwell (New York: Praeger, 1977), 79.
16. Fred I. Greenstein, *The Hidden-Hand Presidency: Eisenhower as Leader* (New York: Basic Books, 1982), 5.
17. Erwin C. Hargrove and Michael Nelson, *Presidents, Politics, and Policy* (Baltimore: Johns Hopkins University Press, 1984), 23.
18. Quoted in Arthur Bernon Tourtellot, *The Presidents on the Presidency* (Garden City, N.Y.: Doubleday, 1964), 36.
19. Four presidents who finished their terms chose not to attend the inaugural ceremonies of their successor: John Adams, John Quincy Adams, Martin Van Buren, and Andrew Johnson.
20. Pious, *The American Presidency,* 7.
21. Dale Vinyard, *The Presidency* (New York: Scribner's, 1971), 5.
22. Novak, *Choosing Our King,* 5.
23. Cited in Greenstein, *The Hidden-Hand Presidency,* 240.
24. *Public Papers of the Presidents of the United States, Dwight Eisenhower, Containing the Public Messages, Speeches and Statements of the President, 1959* (Washington, D.C.: Government Printing Office, 1960), 799.
25. Hargrove and Nelson, *Presidents, Politics, and Policy,* 21.
26. Pious, *The American Presidency,* 8-9.
27. Barger, *The Impossible Presidency,* 377.
28. Robert E. DiClerico, *The American President* (Englewood Cliffs, N.J.: Prentice-Hall, 1979), 171.
29. Richard E. Neustadt, *Presidential Power: The Politics of Leadership From FDR to Carter,* 2d ed. (New York: Wiley, 1980), 27.
30. Herman Finer, *The Presidency: Crisis and Regeneration, an Essay in Possibilities* (Chicago: University of Chicago Press, 1960), 103.
31. Larry Berman, *The New American Presidency* (Boston: Little, Brown, 1987), 314-317.
32. Fred Greenstein, "What the President Means to Americans," in *Choosing the President,* ed. James David Barber (Englewood Cliffs, N.J.: Prentice-Hall, 1974), 125.
33. James David Fairbanks, "The Priestly Functions of the Presidency: A Discussion of the Literature on Civil Religion and Its Implications for the Study of Presidential Leadership," *Presidential Studies Quarterly* 11 (Spring 1981): 225.
34. Arthur J. Hughes, " 'Amazin' Jimmy and 'A Mighty Fortress Was Our Teddy': Theodore Roosevelt and Jimmy Carter, the Religious Link," *Presidential Studies Quarterly* 9 (Winter 1979): 80-81.
35. Quoted in James David Fairbanks, "Religious Dimensions of Presidential Leadership: The Case of Dwight Eisenhower," *Presidential Studies Quarterly* 12 (Spring 1982): 264.
36. Joseph E. Kallenbach, *The American Chief Executive* (New York: Harper and Row, 1966), 280.
37. Sorensen, *Kennedy,* 384.
38. Quoted in Tourtellot, *The Presidents on the Presidency,* 366.
39. Ibid., 365 and 369.
40. Lyndon Johnson, *The Vantage Point* (New York: Holt, Rinehart and Winston, 1971), 425.
41. Michael P. Riccards, *A Republic, If You Can Keep It: The Foundation of the American Presidency* (New York, Greenwood Press, 1987), 87.
42. Ibid., 88.
43. Hart, *The American Presidency in Action 1789,* 46.
44. U.S. Congress, House, *Congressional Record,* daily ed., 94th Cong., 1st sess., July 21, 1975, 23717.
45. Emmet John Hughes, *The Living Presidency* (Baltimore: Penguin Books, 1972), 86.
46. Merlin Gustafson, "Our Part-time Chief of State," *Presidential Studies Quarterly* 9 (Spring 1979): 166-167.
47. Ibid., 167.
48. Robert E. Gilbert, "Personality, Stress and Achievement: Keys to Presidential Longevity," *Presidential Studies Quarterly* 15 (Winter 1985): 33.
49. Ibid., 35.
50. Louis W. Koenig, *The Chief Executive,* 4th ed. (New York: Harcourt Brace Jovanovich, 1981), 81-84.
51. George E. Reedy, *The Twilight of the Presidency* (New York: New American Library, 1970), 24.
52. Johnson, *The Vantage Point,* 566.
53. Reedy, *The Twilight of the Presidency,* 24-25. See also Gustafson, "Our Part-Time Chief of State," 167; and Thomas E. Cronin, *The State of the Presidency,* 2d ed. (Boston: Little, Brown, 1980), 158.
54. Frederick M. Kaiser, "Presidential Assassinations and Assaults: Characteristics and Impact on Protective Procedures," *Presidential Studies Quarterly* 11 (Fall 1981): 545-548.
55. In seven of the nine attacks on incumbent presidents, the assailants assaulted the president with a handgun while the president was near a crowd. The exceptions were the attack in 1950 by two men with automatic weapons on Blair House in Washington, D.C., where Harry Truman was staying while the White House was being renovated, and the fatal shooting of John F. Kennedy by Lee Harvey Oswald, who used a high-powered rifle to kill the president as Kennedy traveled through Dallas in a motorcade in 1963.
56. Cronin, "The Presidency and Its Paradoxes."
57. Godfrey Hodgson, *All Things to All Men, The False Promise*

of the Modern American Presidency (New York: Simon and Schuster, 1980), 241.
58. Cronin, "The Presidency and Its Paradoxes," 81.
59. Gustafson, "Our Part-Time Chief of State," 169.
60. Cronin, "The Presidency and Its Paradoxes," 69.
61. Reedy, *The Twilight of the Presidency,* 15.
62. DiClerico, *The American President,* 221.
63. Gustafson, "Our Part-Time Chief of State," 164.
64. *Congressional Record,* July 21, 1975, 23716-23719.
65. *Public Papers of the Presidents of the United States, Jimmy Carter, Containing the Public Messages, Speeches, and Statements of the President, 1977,* Book 1 (Washington, D.C.: Government Printing Office, 1977), 295.
66. Cited in Joel K. Goldstein, *The Modern American Vice Presidency* (Princeton, N.J.: Princeton University Press, 1982), 160.
67. David S. Cloud, "Loyal Lieutenant Bush Seeks Job at the Top," *Congressional Quarterly Weekly Report,* August 6, 1988, 2176.
68. Goldstein, *The Modern American Vice Presidency,* 160.
69. *Public Papers of the Presidents of the United States, Jimmy Carter 1977,* Book 1, 11.

Selected Bibliography

Barger, Harold M. *The Impossible Presidency.* Glenview, Ill.: Scott, Foresman, 1984.

Campbell, Karlyn Kohrs, and Kathleen Hall Jamieson. "Inaugurating the President." *Presidential Studies Quarterly* 15 (Spring 1985): 395-411.

Cronin, Thomas E., and Rexford G. Tugwell, eds. *The Presidency Reappraised.* 2d ed. New York: Praeger, 1977.

Greenstein, Fred I. *The Hidden-Hand Presidency: Eisenhower as Leader.* New York: Basic Books, 1982.

Gustafson, Merlin. "Our Part-time Chief of State." *Presidential Studies Quarterly* 9 (Spring 1979): 163-171.

Hargrove, Erwin C., and Michael Nelson. *Presidents, Politics, and Policy.* Baltimore: Johns Hopkins University Press, 1984.

Hart, James. *The American Presidency in Action 1789.* New York: Macmillan, 1948.

Kallenbach, Joseph E. *The American Chief Executive.* New York: Harper and Row, 1966.

Novak, Michael. *Choosing Our King.* New York: Macmillan, 1974.

Phelps, Glenn. "George Washington and the Founding of the Presidency." *Presidential Studies Quarterly* 17 (Spring 1987): 345-363.

Pious, Richard. *The American Presidency.* New York: Basic Books, 1979.

Reedy, George E. *The Twilight of the Presidency.* New York: New American Library, 1970.

Riccards, Michael P. *A Republic, If You Can Keep It: The Foundation of the American Presidency.* New York: Greenwood Press, 1987.

Rossiter, Clinton. *The American Presidency.* 2d ed. New York: Harcourt Brace and World, 1960.

Chief of Party

Presidential leadership involves role playing. In Harry S Truman's apt analogy, the president wears many hats: chief executive, chief of state, commander in chief, chief diplomat, chief economic manager, legislative leader, and chief of party. Presidential role playing, or hat wearing, is simultaneous, however, rather than sequential. A president does not doff one hat and replace it with another but wears several at a time.

This recognition is especially meaningful in considering the presidential role of party chief. Rarely will a president act solely as party leader. It is equally rare that other roles will be performed without regard for party leadership.

Paradox pervades the presidential role of party leader. Party chieftainship both stands apart from and connects diverse presidential roles. It is simultaneously on the periphery yet at the center of presidential leadership. It clearly divides, and yet more subtly and significantly, it complements and integrates. It is not so much a power as an opportunity; yet under certain conditions, it becomes an obstacle.

The Constitution does not authorize party leadership. It developed outside the framework formed by the constitutionally enumerated presidential powers. Moreover, the assignment of presidential leadership responsibilities over a specific part of the public conflicts with the general expectation that as head of state the president presides over the entire nation.

Yet, because political parties play significant linkage roles in politics, party leadership also is situated at the hub of the varied array of presidential responsibilities. Through the party, the president establishes and maintains connections with other elements in the political order, both inside and outside the government. These connections produce cohesion rather than division.

The exercise of presidential party leadership is often shrouded because of perceived presidential role conflicts and public antagonism toward the concept of partisanship. Given the structure and character of the United States political order, however, turn-of-the-century political scientist Woodrow Wilson's observation remains pertinent: the president's responsibility as chief of party is virtually inescapable.[1]

Party chieftainship calls for particular leadership skills. Political scientist James MacGregor Burns has conducted a general study of leadership in which he identifies two basic types: transactional and transforming. Transactional leadership operates within the framework of exchange. It features bargaining and negotiation. The more complex and potent transforming leadership has an elevating, even moralistic quality. Burns places party leadership in the transactional category.[2] And yet, certain exercises of party leadership are surely transformational.

The generally accepted concept of party in the United States embraces three analytically separate structural elements of party membership: the party in the electorate, the party organization, and the party in office (sometimes referred to as "the party in the government"). The party in the electorate is those voters who with varying degrees of intensity support the party's candidates and causes. The party organization consists of the variably linked network of activists who hold membership and leadership positions in party headquarters throughout the country. The party in office comprises the public officials who hold their positions under the banner of the party along with those who aspire to do so. This group includes both elected officials and those appointed under partisan auspices. According to political scientist Frank Sorauf, the president is chief among the officeholders who have "captured the symbols of the party and speak for it in public authority." [3]

By Harold F. Bass, Jr.

Origins of Presidential Party Leadership

The presidential role of party leader emerged outside the constitutional framework of expectations and powers established in 1787. The reason is simple. In 1787, political parties were not a part of the existing political order. Moreover, to the extent that the Founders' generation contemplated the prospect of political parties, it was generally antagonistic toward them. It is significant that George Washington, the first president, stood second to no one in upholding this position.

Looking from a distance at the Whig and Tory parliamentary factions in Great Britain, the Framers perceived them as divisive and detrimental to national unity. In contrast, the appropriate model of executive leadership appeared in the concept of a patriot king provided a half-century earlier by the British author and statesman Lord

Bolingbroke. Such an ideal figure stood above party and faction and ruled benevolently in the public interest.

Nevertheless, almost immediately following the onset of the new government, political parties appeared on the scene. At least in part, their origins can be found in an increasingly acute division within the newly-formed cabinet of President Washington. This division pitted the secretary of the Treasury, Alexander Hamilton, against the secretary of state, Thomas Jefferson.

Their conflict had roots in ambition, interest, and ideology. Each saw himself as heir to President Washington. Moreover, each realized that the new constitutional order provided a skeletal framework for development that would inevitably need to be fleshed out; and their respective visions of what the new nation should become were in conflict.

Hamilton glorified the urban areas and their resident merchants and financiers; Jefferson idealized the rural setting and saw the real America embodied in the hard-working farmer. Hamilton perceived the need for strong, dynamic national government; Jefferson professed not to be the friend of energetic central government. During the early years of the Washington administration, conflict between these two principals rocked the cabinet. Among the issues of controversy were those of assumption of the state debts, establishment of a bank of the United States, and the protective tariff. Subsequently, foreign policy differences arose that intensified the cleavage.

In the federal framework created by the Constitution, with its decentralized separation of powers, these disputes could not be contained within the national executive branch. Inevitably, they extended beyond its bounds into the Congress and the states.

Consequently, organization of the respective Hamiltonian and Jeffersonian interests took place. The Hamiltonians took the name Federalists; Jefferson's followers were variously titled Republicans or Democratic-Republicans. *(See box, When and Why Did Parties Begin? p. 159.)* In contrast to Hamilton, Jefferson himself was not especially visible in the early stages of this process. Rather, his longstanding ally James Madison, a member of the House of Representatives, propelled their common cause and opposed Hamilton's measures in Congress.

George Washington

President Washington viewed these developments with alarm and despair, in keeping with his virulent antipathy toward party. He implored Hamilton and Jefferson to mute their differences, and he steadfastly insisted on holding himself above the emerging partisan battles dividing the government and indeed the entire political community. The president could not remain oblivious, however, to the disputes over policy that were occurring. Indeed, his office forced him to take a stand. Regularly, he opted for the Hamiltonian alternative, even as he denied the legitimacy of partisan conflict. Washington's legacy to presidential party leadership thus emphatically rejects its propriety while very tentatively embracing its inevitability.

John Adams

Washington's successor as president, John Adams, found himself in an exceedingly awkward position in the ongoing party conflict, which was not of his making. In contrast to Washington, Adams viewed parties as natural and inevitable in a free society. However, his theory of government was built on a similar foundation of disinterested executive leadership. He viewed the executive as the balance wheel in a political order featuring a bicameral legislature that represented distinct class interests.

During the Washington administration, Adams generally had supported Hamilton's public policies while maintaining his distance from the latter's organizational maneuvers. Personally, he was far closer to Jefferson than to Hamilton. Adams's occupancy of the vice-presidential office made him the logical successor when Washington chose to retire; and the Federalists readily embraced his candidacy in 1796, claiming him as their own. Nevertheless, he had not played any significant organizational role within the party—this was indisputably Hamilton's domain. Meanwhile, Jefferson was thrust forward as a candidate by Madison and other Democratic-Republican partisans. Adams won a narrow electoral vote victory in the first presidential election conducted along partisan lines. *(See "Election of 1796," p. 267, in the Electoral Process chapter of Part II.)*

In the presidency, Adams's claims to party leadership foundered on his own theoretical objections to the president's assumption of the role and on Hamilton's ongoing claims. The tension between Adams and his supporters on the one hand and Hamilton and his followers on the other grew until by the end of Adams's term, the Federalist party clearly had split into two wings. Thus, President Adams can be said to have been the leader of, at most, a party faction.

Thomas Jefferson

The third president, Thomas Jefferson, is truly the father of presidential party leadership.[4] By the time Jefferson ascended to the presidency, partisan institutions had begun to take shape. Within the executive, appointments to federal positions were being made with partisan affiliation in mind. Inside the legislature, assemblies or caucuses of like-minded partisans were meeting, not only to plot legislative strategy but also to nominate party candidates for president. Finally, at the state and local level, electoral organizations had formed to secure the selection of partisan candidates to public offices.

The Democratic-Republican partisans looked unequivocally to Jefferson for leadership. While sharing many of his predecessors' prejudices against presidential party leadership, he nevertheless exercised it in a pioneering and exemplary fashion that established high expectations of his successors.

Early on in Washington's presidency, Jefferson acknowledged partisan division as natural but nevertheless deplored its presence. In the ensuing years, he came to defend and justify party activity on grounds of expediency and even honor. Confronted with the realities of Hamilton's initiatives, and disagreeing profoundly with so many of them, he increasingly saw party organization as an exigent and appropriate response. He did not retreat from his antiparty position so much as he superimposed on it a temporary acceptance of party.

For Jefferson, republicanism, or representative government, was the preferable alternative to monarchism, which he associated with arbitrary, hereditary government.

Republicanism derived governmental authority from popular sovereignty and held public officials accountable to popular control. As such, it had distinctly democratic implications, although Jefferson was not an advocate of direct democracy. Thus, the Jeffersonian party promoting this cause was labeled "Republican" or "Democratic-Republican." *(See box, Origins of Party Labels, p. 687.)*

It is important to note that Jefferson did not clearly endorse the notion of institutionalized party competition. He was never really willing to accord legitimacy to those who opposed him and the republican cause he associated with his party. Furthermore, he demonstrated no abiding commitment to the concept of the Democratic-Republican party. Instead, he viewed the party as dispensable once it had accomplished the restorative tasks for which it had been formed.

Executive-Legislative Relations

Jefferson's party leadership had its chief influence on executive-legislative relations. For Jefferson, presidential party leadership enabled him to overcome an ideological restraint well-established in republican thought: an antipathy toward executive power and a corresponding preference for legislative autonomy. While it is accurate to say that Jefferson never embraced this position with the enthusiasm and extremism of some of his fellow partisans, still he honored it.

For him, the problem was how to exercise positive presidential leadership in the face of republican ideological objections. Here, the presence of party provided a convenient façade facilitating leadership on his part without compromising a fundamental position of his republican followers. He could justify actions taken under the protection of party that, according to republican ideology, might be considered inappropriate under purely executive auspices. In this sense, from his followers' perspectives, Jefferson the party leader had more legitimacy than Jefferson the chief executive. Thus, in adding party leadership to the president's powers, he substantially increased the president's strength in the political arena.

The tactics and techniques Jefferson developed in using party leadership in legislative relations remain the standard in this area. He participated in recruiting candidates. He enlisted members of the legislature as his agents and worked through them in pursuit of his objectives. He deployed the executive department secretaries who constituted his cabinet as emissaries on Capitol Hill.

Not content to rely exclusively on surrogates, Jefferson sought to establish personal relations with rank-and-file legislators. He corresponded extensively with members of Congress. He also regularly scheduled dinner parties in which the guest lists were limited to small groups of legislators who shared his partisan affiliation.

Further, the president sought to generate cooperation and good will with Democratic-Republican legislators through patronage. Although departmental secretaries and state and local officials also were involved in this process, he consistently solicited recommendations and evaluations from individual legislators for prospective appointees.

Jefferson did not choose to continue the practice inaugurated by his predecessors of personally delivering an annual message to Congress. Instead, he tended to work informally, behind the scenes, and through his agents. From this vantage point, however, he was quite willing to make suggestions about details of proposed legislation. Indeed, he often provided trusted legislators with drafts of actual bills for them to introduce according to prescribed procedures, accompanying these communications with admonitions of secrecy and disavowals of meddling.

During his presidency, the opposition Federalist press alleged that Jefferson met with and oversaw the deliberations of the Democratic-Republican party caucus. *Caucus* was the term used to refer to the meetings of the partisan legislators. One well-documented practice was the quadrennial meeting to nominate party candidates for the presidential ticket. In addition, numerous reports make reference to informal assemblies of sizable numbers of legislators to plot legislative strategy and tactics. Unfortunately, the historical record cannot clearly establish the nature and extent of the president's relationship with this early partisan institution.

In exercising party leadership through these various processes, President Jefferson based his partisan appeals for support on four main foundations. The first was principle. His correspondence is replete with references to the promotion of common republican principles. The mirror image of this appeal was one that invoked the specter of the Federalist opposition. Often nothing produces unity as well as a common adversary, and Jefferson frequently sought to keep his followers together by denouncing the other party. Third, Jefferson traded on the immense personal regard in which he was held by his fellow Democratic-Republicans. Finally, as president, he tried to make legislators see that his preferences were in their own self-interests.

Effect of Parties on the Presidency

By the end of Jefferson's presidency, some twenty years into the constitutional era, the unforeseen emergence of political parties had transformed the character of the presidency and indeed the U.S. political system in several respects. Their assertion and assumption of nominating responsibilities for the presidential ticket necessitated a formal change in the balloting arrangements of the electoral college. Originally, the Constitution required presidential electors to cast a single ballot with the names of two presidential candidates listed on it. After the counting of the assembled ballots, the candidate with the most votes, provided that number was a majority, was elected president. The candidate with the next largest number of votes became vice president.

Under this procedure, the election of 1800 produced a tie. The Democratic-Republican party objective before the election was to secure the selection of presidential electors committed to the slate of Jefferson for president and Aaron Burr for vice president. It did so to ensure that as president, Jefferson might not be bedeviled by the presence of a Federalist adversary in the secondary slot, as he himself had acted in quiet opposition to President Adams.

The party effort was too successful. Every elector who voted for Jefferson also voted for Burr, and vice versa; and more electors voted for Jefferson and Burr than for any other contenders. The electoral college tie sent the presidential election to the House of Representatives, where the lame-duck Federalist majority eventually consented to the choice of Jefferson.

Before the next presidential election in 1804, Congress

proposed and the state legislatures ratified the Twelfth Amendment. The change separated the ballots for president and vice president, thus allowing presidential electors effectively to vote for party tickets. This amendment fundamentally altered the status of the electors. They quickly lost the independent agent status envisioned by the Framers. Instead, they became instruments of party will.

Moreover, the parties' monopoly over presidential selection had the result of adding a new, extraconstitutional presidential eligibility requirement above and beyond those enumerated in the Constitution: a party nomination. The expectations and requirements for presidential candidates, heretofore considerable public service and esteem, came to include not only party affiliation but also party nomination.

In turn, the presence of a party's candidate for president at the head of the party ticket for elective public offices conferred on that individual the status of party leader. Once elected, that figure could presume to be something more than the head of the executive branch. Indeed, there was now a basis for claiming government chieftainship, with the idea and organization of party unifying separated national institutions under the leadership of the president.[5]

Evolving President-Party Relationship

Although aspects of presidential party leadership as developed by Thomas Jefferson endure to this day, the president-party relationship has not been static since the first decade of the nineteenth century. Rather, the relationship has gone through a number of changes. Few of these changes have been sudden and dramatic. Instead, they have been mostly gradual and evolutionary, occurring over several presidencies with their essences emerging in clear form only in retrospect.

After Jefferson's retirement in 1809, the congressional party caucus that had responded in a generally positive fashion to his leadership proved to be less accommodating to his immediate successors. Indeed, the caucus came to perceive its role in nominating and, in effect, electing presidents as subordinating the president to congressional authority.

By 1828, however, the caucus was in disarray; and the new president, Andrew Jackson, presided over important transformations in the president-party relationship. Two developments in particular were taking form at this time: the growth of national party organization and the emergence of a mass party—ordinary citizens who identified with a political party and provided electoral support for a party's candidates. *(See Political Parties as President-Public Link chapter in Part IV.)*

These developments significantly enhanced the president's party leadership role. The presidency became linked with a national party organization that in turn connected state and local party organizations throughout the country. This came about with the advent of the national party convention as the nominator of the president. Further, the presidency became directly tied to the citizenry of the Republic. With Jackson, a general and a popular hero, paving the way, the presidency became the focus of popular attention and representation. Meanwhile, under the astute direction of Jackson's vice president and successor in the White House, Martin Van Buren, presidential patronage assisted the creation and strengthening of the party organizational machinery.

The next important shift in the character of president-party relations occurred in the immediate aftermath of the Civil War. The congressional Republicans reacted against President Lincoln's assertive wartime leadership by restraining his successors. Also, party leaders at the state and local levels—fortified by patronage resources and strong party identifications and loyalties in the electorate—increased in stature and significance in national politics in the latter part of the nineteenth century. They came to dominate the presidential nomination process, and the presidential nominee was usually beholden to the party organization sponsors.

After the turn of the twentieth century, the balance of power began to shift in favor of the president. Strong, assertive occupants of the White House such as Theodore Roosevelt and Woodrow Wilson invigorated the office of the presidency by dint of personality. An increasing world role for the United States enhanced the visibility and power of the presidential offices. Further, advancing communications technology focused more popular attention on the president. In keeping with these developments, the president's party leadership position gradually became more commanding.

Franklin Roosevelt ushered in the modern era in president-party relations with his long presidential tenure, 1933-1945. In responding to the Great Depression and World War II, Roosevelt effected a dramatic increase in the size and scope of the federal executive. This had important implications for party relations, because Roosevelt came to rely on executive branch personnel to perform many of the political and social service roles that had traditionally been the province of the political party.

Since then, further advancements in communications technology, especially television, served to connect the president even more directly with the public. This weakened the party's traditional position as intermediary between the two. In addition, and indeed in response, party identification in the electorate began to decline. Party reforms reduced the power of the party organization in the nomination of the president.

Thus, the president-party relationship has gone through a number of twists and turns over the years. Jefferson's legacy persists, but it has been augmented by numerous additional trends. The present status of the relationship has been shaped by and remains rooted in these various and conflicting patterns. Further changes, no doubt, will be forthcoming.

The President and the National Party Organization

Within a quarter-century of Jefferson's retirement from the presidency in 1809, a new arena of presidential party leadership opened up with the establishment of national party organizations.[6] This institution arose after the collapse of the congressional party caucus as a nominating device. Beginning in the 1790s, congressional party caucuses had assumed responsibility for nominating the parties' presidential tickets. The gradual demise of the Federalist party following Jefferson and the Democratic-Republicans' electoral success in 1800 left the Democratic-

Republican caucus in effect as the designator of the president, with the electoral college eventually ratifying its choice.

The caucus effected reasonably smooth party leadership transitions from Jefferson to James Madison in 1808-1809, and from Madison to James Monroe in 1816-1817. The culmination of the Virginia dynasty following Monroe's retirement from the White House in 1824 left the party caucus without an obvious consensus choice. Internal division ensued. The decline of interparty competition had served eventually to heighten intraparty competition for the presidential nomination that was tantamount to election.

Further, the very concept of the caucus came under attack from various outside sources. States and congressional districts not in the hands of the dominant Democratic-Republican party had no voice in the caucus proceedings. These areas found themselves excluded from meaningful participation in presidential selection.

In 1824, the supporters of Andrew Jackson's presidential candidacy assaulted the caucus procedure as too elitist. Embracing values of popular participation and reflecting the interests of outsiders in the political order, Jackson's cause did not draw much support from the members of the Washington-based caucus.

Alternatively, others perceived the caucus to be a de facto denial of the constitutional principle of separation of powers, since it allowed a congressional majority to choose the president. Under the weight of these onslaughts, the caucus as a nominating device virtually disintegrated in the mid-1820s, although for a brief time state legislative party caucuses engaged in nominating activities.

The controversy over the caucus was part of a larger issue, the growing division within the dominant Democratic-Republican party. Jackson's 1824 candidacy, followed by his successful run for the presidency in 1828, clearly split the party into two irreconcilable wings. Before the 1832 presidential election, with the caucus discredited and inoperative, a new format for presidential nominations came into being.

The Jackson faction, now styling itself the Democrats, along with the anti-Jackson elements, calling themselves National Republicans, and a third group, the Anti-Masons, separately convened to name their presidential tickets. These conventions, the first in U.S. history, brought together delegations from state parties, thus opening up participation in the nomination process to representatives of the rank-and-file party members. The concept took hold, and since then the quadrennial conventions have been the standard feature of the presidential nominating process.

In 1848, the Democratic national convention inaugurated the practice whereby that body authorized and established a national party committee consisting of leaders of state parties to conduct presidential campaigns and to guide the national party's fortunes between elections. Traditionally, the national committees comprise representatives designated by the state party organizations and ratified by the national conventions. These committees chose individuals to head them, thus creating the office of national party chair.

During the 1920s, national party chairs began staffing national party headquarters on a permanent basis. These national organizations formed the apex of a hierarchical party organization pyramid, atop the similarly constituted state and local party organizations. These, then, are the elements of the national party organization: the convention, the committee, the chair, and the headquarters staff.

Changing Patterns of Interaction

The traditional patterns of interaction between president and national party organization emerged out of mutual needs. A presidential aspirant needed the party nomination to legitimize the candidacy. Further, a nominee needed the resources of the party organization to conduct the general election campaign. Following a successful effort to elect its nominee, the party organization could then justifiably claim the fruits of federal patronage distributed through the executive to its loyal laborers.

Over the past half-century, three important developments have altered the traditional nature of the relationship between the president and the national party organization: changes in the structure of the presidential campaign organization, the emergence of the civil service, and the establishment and expansion of the White House Office.

The critical question in the structure of the presidential campaign organization is the status of the national party organization. A century ago, the contemporary expectation was that it would be peripheral.

Vast patronage resources once awaited the victorious party assuming control of the executive branch, but the expansive coverage of civil service has reduced drastically the quantity of political appointments. The remaining appointments are at such high and specialized levels that the party organization is less often able to provide qualified candidates.

Finally, the establishment and expansion of the White House Office has provided the president with an in-house assemblage of loyalists willing and able to do the sorts of political chores previously delegated to the national party organization. Their presence, and the president's reliance on them, render the party organization less meaningful in presidential politics. *(See White House Office chapter in Part V.)*

Forms of Interaction

The president and the national party organization interact in selecting and deploying the party chair, managing party headquarters, establishing financial and organizational plans, arranging and running the convention, and managing the nomination and election campaigns.

Selection of the Party Chair

The party chair sits at the hub of the relationship between the president and the national party organization. The national party committee formally names its chair.

The national party committee traditionally represents the state parties. The Republican National Committee is organized according to the principle of state equality, with each state party designating a national committeeman, national committeewoman, and state chair. In addition, the District of Columbia and the territories of Guam, Puerto Rico, and the Virgin Islands receive similar representation.

The Democratic National Committee is over twice as large as its Republican counterpart, and its representational basis is much more complicated. In addition to state and territory party representatives and officers, proportionally represented, ex officio membership is granted to representatives of the party's governors, mayors, county officials, members of Congress, and headquarters officials. Provision is also made for at-large members.

The committee organizes and conducts the national convention, and it asserts responsibility for the conduct of national election campaigns. Normally, its most significant collective action is to elect its chair.

More than a century of custom and practice provide, however, that immediately following the nominating convention, the presidential nominee recommends a candidate for the party chair. The national committee then ratifies that choice. This procedure developed to unify the presidential campaign with the party effort. It carries over to the victor's incumbency, making the national party chair of the president's party in effect a presidential appointee.

The average tenure for post-World War II national chairs of the party controlling the White House is approximately two and one-half years. Thus, virtually all presidents have the opportunity to interact with the national party in selection of the national chair. Among modern presidents, only Lyndon Johnson never exercised the opportunity to choose a party chair. *(See "Lyndon B. Johnson," p. 631, in this chapter.)*

Customarily, when a vacancy exists, perhaps at the instigation of the president, the national committee sends a delegation of its members to call on the president at the White House to be informed of the president's choice. The national committee then convenes to elect that person. Having done so, the national committee's subsequent interaction with the president typically is limited to occasional presidential addresses and receptions scheduled in conjunction with regular meetings of the committee.

Traditionally, the eligibility requirements for the position of national party chair have been very loose, affording the president discretion. As often as not, the chair has not been a member of the committee at the time of selection. Under rules established in the 1970s, both major parties now require that the chair's position be full-time. In 1982, however, the requirement was relaxed when President Ronald Reagan wanted to designate Sen. Paul Laxalt of Nevada to succeed Richard Richards as party chair. The Republican National Committee obliged the president by creating a new unsalaried position of general chair of the Republican party especially for Laxalt. In that role, Laxalt became nominally responsible for coordinating Republican party political operations on Capitol Hill, at party headquarters, at the White House, and in the forthcoming presidential campaign. In addition, to conform with party rules, the national committee elected Frank Fahrenkopf, a Laxalt associate and former Nevada state GOP chair, as its titular salaried chair with responsibility for party headquarters management.

Most observers of this development assumed that Laxalt would be the dominant partner in a tandem arrangement. Over the years, however, it became increasingly clear that Laxalt's title was honorary, and Fahrenkopf emerged as a relatively strong party chair. After Laxalt declined to run for reelection to the Senate in 1986, he quietly abandoned his title as general chair, and the position was not filled. Meanwhile, Fahrenkopf remained as party chair through the end of the Reagan administration.

As the top leadership position in the party organization hierarchy, the position of party chair unquestionably has high symbolic value, especially to the activists who make up the party organization at all levels. Its high visibility makes it something of a plum for persons and factions within the party. Its substantive significance varies considerably according to the expectations of the nominee or president and the orientations of the designated chair.

Looking at decisions made by nonincumbent presidential nominees, some generalizations can be made about patterns of recruitment for the party chair. In recognition of services on the nominee's behalf, the position is often awarded to a personal loyalist from the preconvention campaign organization or to a state organizational leader who has delivered crucial delegate support. *(See Table 1.)*

Examples of personal loyalists serving nominees include Democrat James A. Farley (chosen by Franklin D. Roosevelt in 1932), Republican Herbert Brownell (by Thomas E. Dewey in 1944), Democrat Stephen A. Mitchell (by Adlai E. Stevenson in 1952), Republican Dean Burch (by Barry Goldwater in 1964), and Democrat Lawrence F. O'Brien (by Hubert H. Humphrey in 1968). All were recruited from the preconvention personal organization of the nominee. Loyalty and personal sponsorship brought them to their position. With the exception of O'Brien, each had come from the same state as the nominee and had worked in previous campaigns on the nominee's behalf. In selecting a personal loyalist as party chair, the nominee rewards a trusted associate, takes steps to ensure the responsiveness of the party machinery, and stamps a personal imprint on it.

In past instances of closely contested nominations, the position of party chair became a bargaining gambit for delegate support. Traditionally, the key units of bargaining have been state delegations under the control of powerful state party chieftains. In 1948, Dewey was obligated to the Pennsylvania delegation for its vital support. He reciprocated by naming as party chair a then obscure member of that delegation, Rep. Hugh D. Scott, Jr. In 1952, the national chair was Michigan party leader Arthur Summerfield's prize for declaring for Dwight D. Eisenhower at a crucial moment.

The nominee may use the prerogative of naming the party chair to cultivate or mollify important party and electoral constituencies. Symbolic demographic variables such as region, religion, and sex have come into play here. For example, nominees have used the position of party chair to reinforce the geographical distribution of party power (as they do by balancing the ticket with the vice-presidential nomination) or to recognize a regional center of party power. Summerfield's selection gave representation to the traditional heartland of the Republican party. In 1960, Sen. Henry Jackson, hailing from Washington in the Pacific Northwest, complemented a balanced Democratic ticket composed of a northeasterner, John F. Kennedy, for president and a southwesterner, Lyndon B. Johnson, for vice president.

For more than three decades, from 1928 to 1960, every national chair of the Democratic party was an Irish Catholic. This tradition recognized the influence of that powerful constituency within the party organization. It also compensated for the absence, except for the ill-fated Al Smith, of a Roman Catholic among the party's presidential nominees. Since the 1960 nomination of John Kennedy, the relevance of this consideration has receded.

Democratic nominee George S. McGovern's 1972 selection of Jean Westwood, the first woman to chair a national party committee, reflected two important new developments in nominating politics. The first was the growing clout of women in party affairs. The second was the emergence of new bargaining units at the convention transcending the state party delegations, caucuses that represented pressure groups in the larger political order.

Similar symbolic considerations have turned the party

Table 1 Campaign Party Chairs Chosen by Nonincumbent Presidential Nominees, 1948-1989

Name, Party, Years of Service	Chosen by	State	Age	Religion	Political background
Hugh D. Scott, Jr. (R, 1948-1952)	Dewey	Pennsylvania	47	Episcopalian	U.S. representative
Arthur Summerfield (R, 1952-1953)	Eisenhower	Michigan	53	—	State organization leader
Stephen Mitchell (D, 1952-1955)	Stevenson	Illinois [a]	49	Catholic	Personal associate of nominee
Paul Butler (D, 1955-1960)	Stevenson [b]	Indiana	50	Catholic	State organization leader
Thruston B. Morton (R, 1959-1961)	Nixon [b]	Kentucky	52	Episcopalian	U.S. senator
Henry M. Jackson (D, 1960-1961)	Kennedy	Washington	48	Presbyterian	U.S. senator
Dean Burch (D, 1964-1965)	Goldwater	Arizona [a]	37	—	Personal associate of nominee
Ray Bliss (D, 1966-1969)	Nixon [b]	Ohio	58	Episcopalian	State organization leader
Lawrence F. O'Brien (D, 1968-1969)	Humphrey	Massachusetts	51	Catholic	Federal executive
Jean Westwood (D, 1972)	McGovern	Utah	49	Mormon	State organization leader
Robert Strauss (D, 1972-1977)	Carter [b]	Texas	55	Jewish	State organization leader
William E. Brock III (R, 1977-1981)	Reagan [b]	Tennessee	46	Presbyterian	Former U.S. senator
Charles Manatt (D, 1981-1985)	Mondale [b]	California	48	Methodist	State organization leader
Paul Kirk (D, 1985-1989)	Dukakis [b]	Massachusetts	50	Catholic	National party official
Frank Fahrenkopf (R, 1983-1989)	Bush [b]	Nevada	48	Catholic	State organization leader

Source: From Harold F. Bass, Jr., "The President and the National Party Organization," in *Presidents and Their Parties: Leadership or Neglect?* ed. Robert Harmel (New York: Praeger, 1983), 63.

Note: Dash (—) means no religious affiliation.

a. Nominees chose party chair from home state.

b. Nominees chose to retain the incumbent party chair.

chair into a potential consolation prize to an unsuccessful aspirant for a spot on the presidential ticket. At the 1960 Democratic convention, nominee John Kennedy offered the vice-presidential nomination to his defeated rival, Lyndon Johnson. After opposition to Johnson's proposed nomination quickly developed among certain elements within the liberal wing of the party, Robert F. Kennedy, his brother's campaign manager, informed Johnson that should he wish to withdraw, he could be named party chair instead. Johnson declined and accepted the initial offer. The position of party chair then went to Henry Jackson, who had been a leading contender for the vice-presidential nomination.

On numerous occasions, presidential nominees have elected to forgo their prerogatives of designating the party chair in favor of retaining the incumbent. In performing their responsibilities, party chairs can develop strong and vocal personal followings, which provide pressures and incentives for their retention, in recognition of jobs well done and in the interests of party unity. Between 1948 and 1988, eight party chairs were retained by nonincumbent presidential nominees: Democrat Paul Butler was kept on by Stevenson in 1956; Republican Thruston Morton by Nixon in 1960; Republican Ray Bliss by Nixon in 1968; Democrat Robert Strauss by Carter in 1976; Republican William Brock by Reagan in 1980; Democrat Charles Manatt by Mondale in 1984; Democrat Paul Kirk by Dukakis in 1988; and Republican Frank Fahrenkopf by Bush, also in 1988.

A final consideration taken into account by the nominee about the selection of the party chair is the primary role the chair is expected to play in the upcoming general election campaign. Traditionally, that role was one of management, concentrating energies and talents on problems of campaign organization and strategy. A recently emerging role is that of spokesperson and campaigner, highly visible but largely separated from the centers of campaign decision making.

Presidents-elect and incumbent presidents exercise selection prerogatives when vacancies exist in the position of party chair. From an examination of such selections in the years since World War II, certain patterns emerge. *(See Table 2.)*

Chairs have been recruited from diverse political backgrounds, with state organization leaders and legislators predominating. All have been identified with the political causes and campaigns of their presidents, but relatively few can be considered close associates. Geographically, most of these chairs have come from the East and Midwest. Two came from the same state as their presidential sponsors, six from the same region, and nine from different regions. Most of the Democratic chairs have been Catholics, while Methodists and Episcopalians have predominated among Republicans. Their average age at election has approached fifty. Gerald Ford chose the only woman, Mary Louise Smith (1974).

Vacancies between the quadrennial nominating conventions come about for a variety of reasons. On several occasions, presidential promotions of chairs to high-level government positions have created openings. Truman made Sen. Howard McGrath attorney general; Richard Nixon chose Rep. Rogers C. B. Morton to head the Interior Department; and Ford sent George Bush to the People's Republic of China to head the United States Liaison Office.

Several chairs have left for personal reasons or to pursue their own political interests. Although presidential dissatisfaction has not loomed particularly large in the departures of party chairs, press speculation has addressed this possibility; and scandal tainted the resignations of both Democrat William Boyle (1951) and Republican Wesley Roberts (1953).

A brief review of presidential decisions about party chairs since World War II illustrates some of the dynamics of the selection process. When Harry Truman became president on the death of Franklin Roosevelt in 1945, the Democratic party chair was Robert Hannegan, an old Missouri friend and ally of the new president. When Hannegan resigned in poor health in 1947, President Truman named Senator McGrath to succeed him.

Table 2 National Chairs, President's Party, 1944-1989

Name, Party, Years of Service	Chosen by	State	Age	Religion	Political background
Robert Hannegan (D, 1944-1947)	Roosevelt	Missouri	41	Catholic	State organization leader, federal executive
J. Howard McGrath (D, 1947-1949)	Truman	Rhode Island	44	Catholic	U.S. senator
William Boyle (D, 1949-1951)	Truman	Missouri	47	Catholic	Presidential associate, national party official
Frank McKinney (D, 1951-1952)	Truman	Indiana	47	Catholic	State organization leader
C. Wesley Roberts (R, 1953)	Eisenhower	Kansas	49	Methodist	State organization leader
Leonard W. Hall (R, 1953-1957)	Eisenhower	New York	53	Episcopalian	Former U.S. representative
H. Meade Alcorn (R, 1957-1959)	Eisenhower	Connecticut	50	Congregationalist	State organization leader
Thruston B. Morton (R, 1959-1961)	Eisenhower	Kentucky	51	Episcopalian	U.S. senator
John Bailey (D, 1961-1968)	Kennedy	Connecticut	57	Catholic	State organization leader
Rogers C. B. Morton (R, 1969-1971)	Nixon	Maryland	55	Episcopalian	U.S. representative
Robert J. Dole (R, 1971-1973)	Nixon	Kansas	48	Methodist	U.S. senator
George Bush (R, 1973-1974)	Nixon	Texas	49	Episcopalian	Former U.S. representative, federal executive
Mary Louise Smith (R, 1974-1976)	Ford	Iowa	59	Protestant	State organization leader, national party official
Kenneth M. Curtis (D, 1977-1978)	Carter	Maine	45	Protestant	Former governor
John White (D, 1978-1981)	Carter	Texas	54	Baptist	Federal executive
Richard Richards (R, 1981-1983)	Reagan	Utah	49	Presbyterian	State organization leader
Paul D. Laxalt (R, 1983-1986) [a]	Reagan	Nevada	60	Catholic	U.S. senator
Frank Fahrenkopf (R, 1983-1989)	Reagan	Nevada	43	Catholic	State organization leader
Lee Atwater (R, 1989-)	Bush	South Carolina	37	Methodist	Political consultant

Source: From Harold F. Bass, Jr., "The President and the National Party Organization," in *Presidents and Their Parties: Leadership or Neglect?*, ed. Robert Harmel (New York: Praeger, 1983), 74.

a. General chair

Ten months after the 1948 election, Truman moved Senator McGrath into the executive branch as attorney general and elevated William Boyle, the executive vice chair of the Democratic National Committee, to the position of chair. Boyle was an old family friend of the Trumans and a longstanding political ally who had been very active in the 1948 presidential campaign. Boyle's tenure concluded in 1951, ostensibly because of his health. Allegations of his involvement in an influence-peddling scandal, however, were circulating at the time of his resignation.

Truman's choice as his successor was Frank McKinney, a state party leader in Indiana. McKinney served through the 1952 national convention, after which he stepped aside in favor of Stephen Mitchell, the choice of presidential nominee Adlai Stevenson.

After winning the 1952 presidential election, Dwight Eisenhower brought his choice as campaign party chair, Arthur Summerfield, into his cabinet as postmaster general. To fill the vacancy in the party chair, the president chose a longtime party organization leader from his home state of Kansas, Wesley Roberts. Roberts had worked at the national party headquarters during the presidential campaign as organization director, where he coordinated the party's role in the presidential campaign with that of the Citizens for Eisenhower. He had served only two months as chair when he resigned amid charges of influence peddling back in Kansas.

Eisenhower's choice to fill the position was representative Leonard W. Hall of New York. Hall had previously chaired the Republican congressional campaign committee and had traveled with the Eisenhower campaign, providing liaison with the Republican National Committee. Hall served for the remainder of Eisenhower's first term. After directing the successful reelection campaign, he resigned to pursue his own political objectives in New York.

Hall's successor was H. Meade Alcorn of Connecticut. Long active in state and local party politics, Alcorn had supported Eisenhower's candidacy in 1952 and had been a member of the national committee since 1953. He stepped down as chair in 1959, after the party's poor showing in the midterm congressional elections.

Eisenhower chose Sen. Thruston Morton of Kentucky to replace Alcorn. A member of a prominent Kentucky family, Morton was a former member of Congress who also had served in the Eisenhower administration as the State Department's legislative liaison before his election to the Senate. Morton remained party chair through the 1960 nomination and general election campaigns. He resigned midway through 1961, in preparation for his successful senatorial reelection campaign in 1962.

After receiving the 1960 Democratic nomination, John Kennedy designated Sen. Henry M. Jackson of Washington as a party chair for the duration of the campaign. Jackson, passed over for the vice presidential nomination in favor of Lyndon Johnson, received public visibility and performed a valuable service as a campaign spokesman throughout the fall contest. After the election, Jackson resigned to devote full attention to his senatorial responsibilities. Jackson's departure freed Kennedy to install Connecticut party leader John Bailey, a long-time supporter, as national party chair.

When Lyndon Johnson became president after Kennedy's assassination, he kept Bailey on as party chair, although he inserted his own loyalists at the party headquarters. Bailey stayed on as party chair through the 1968 national convention. Afterward, deferring to the wish of nominee Hubert H. Humphrey, he gave up the position to Lawrence F. O'Brien, manager of Hubert H. Humphrey's successful nomination campaign. Serving for seven and one-half years, Bailey has the longest tenure among the post-World War II national party chairs.

After winning the Republican nomination in 1968, Nixon responded to strong party organization support for the retention of incumbent party chair Ray Bliss by keeping Bliss in that position until after the victory in the November election.

At that time, Bliss resigned with Nixon's blessing, enabling the president to install someone of his own choosing. The new president indicated his preference for Rep. Rogers Morton of Maryland (brother of Thruston Morton) to take the reins of the party organization. Morton served for two years. Shortly after the 1970 congressional elections, Nixon appointed him secretary of interior, and he resigned as party chair.

Nixon chose Sen. Robert Dole of Kansas to succeed Morton. Dole served through the 1972 reelection campaign and dutifully resigned, in response to the president's expectation, to be replaced by George Bush, a Texas political figure fresh from a tour of duty as ambassador to the United Nations. Bush stayed in office for the rest of Nixon's tenure. After Nixon resigned in 1974, the new president, Gerald Ford, named Bush to head the U.S. Liaison Office in the People's Republic of China. Ford then elevated the vice chair Mary Louise Smith of Iowa to the position, where she remained through the conclusion of Ford's term.

When Jimmy Carter won the Democratic presidential nomination in 1976, he chose to keep on incumbent party chair Robert Strauss through the election campaign. After the election, Carter appointed Strauss and named former Maine governor Kenneth Curtis to be party chair. Within a year, Curtis resigned amid reports of persistent squabbling between the White House and the party headquarters. Carter then named Texas politico John White as his choice for the party chair. White continued in office until after the party's defeat in the 1980 presidential election.

In 1980 Ronald Reagan's nomination as the Republican candidate resulted in the temporary retention of William Brock as party chair. After the election victory, Brock moved into the same administration position that Strauss had occupied. On Reagan's recommendation, the party chair went to Utah party leader Richard Richards. Richards resigned following the 1982 midterm congressional elections because of longstanding rumors of White House dissatisfaction with his performance.

Existing party rules required that the position of party chair be full time, which seemed to preclude the choice of an incumbent legislator. President Reagan arranged, however, for Sen. Paul Laxalt of Nevada to assume the specially created position of general chair of the Republican party. This position was superimposed on the traditional national committee chair, which went to Frank Fahrenkopf, one of Laxalt's associates in the Nevada Republican party.

When Laxalt retired from the Senate after the 1986 elections, he also took leave of his position as general chair and was not replaced. Fahrenkopf remained as chair to the end of the Reagan presidency. His replacement, the choice of president-elect George Bush, was campaign manager Lee Atwater.

In sum, the selection of the national party chair is a presidential prerogative, although it is usually exercised in a fashion mindful of pressures within the party and the larger body politic. Presidents and presidential nominees can reward trusted loyalists, repay political debts incurred, or reach out to new party constituencies.

Deployment of the Party Chair

Installed in office by the president, and serving at the president's pleasure, national chairs encounter their party leaders in circumstances that vary considerably in both frequency and substantive significance. The tendency is toward infrequent meetings in rather formal, ceremonial

Lyndon B. Johnson Library

President Lyndon Johnson talks with Democratic party chair John Bailey in the Oval Office in 1968. Serving for seven and one-half years, Bailey has the longest tenure among the post-World War II national party chairs.

settings. To be sure, President Truman had a standing appointment every Wednesday afternoon with the Democratic national chair to discuss party politics. Somewhat similarly, President Eisenhower genuinely expected his party chair to be the "political expert" in his delegation of administrative responsibilities.

Still, a facetious anecdote shared by Sen. Robert Dole about his tenure as party chair captures well the contemporary character of the relationship. Dole tells of receiving a telephone call from the White House, informing him that his longstanding request to see President Nixon was about to be granted. All he had to do was to turn his television set to the proper channel to receive the president's scheduled campaign address.[7]

Cabinet Meetings. Although no one has served simultaneously as party chair and as a cabinet secretary since 1947, several party chairs have made individual arrangements to attend cabinet meetings either regularly or intermittently. At these sessions, party chairs can be kept informed of the administration's public policy proposals, can assess their partisan ramifications, and can seek to present the party's perspective on them. In addition, cabinet meetings can provide the chair with opportunities to request and establish clearance procedures for political appointments. In general, while the party chair's physical presence at cabinet meetings undoubtedly affords an avenue of access to the president, the value is more symbolic than substantive.

Congressional Leadership Meetings. The inclination of some modern presidents to name incumbent legislators as party chair has introduced a new arena for interaction—the weekly congressional leadership meetings. Although none of these chairs has been a ranking member of the party congressional hierarchy, several of them (along with chairs who are not members of Congress) have requested that they be present at sessions where legislative strategy is planned and progress is monitored. Here, the presence of the party chair enables coordination of legislative activities with the party's organs of party policy and publicity and provides a forum to bring the chair's point of view directly to the president.

Headquarters Management

Another form of interaction between the White House and the national committee is the management of the national party headquarters. Ostensibly, headquarters management would appear to be the primary responsibility of the chair, but few chairs have devoted much personal attention to this task. Other responsibilities with higher priority and other institutional and professional affiliations typically conflict with that of administrator. The accepted procedure is for the chair to exercise discretion in delegating managerial authority to a chosen subordinate. The chair then remains free in varying degrees to engage in other activities.

On several occasions in recent years, the president or White House aides have deployed at party headquarters a presidential agent with managerial authority. Typically, these instances have occurred when a legislator has been named chair and by definition serves part-time. Such a situation developed during the Truman presidency with the assignment of Truman's old Missouri political assistant William Boyle to a management position at the Democratic National Committee then headed by Sen. Howard McGrath.

In his first months in office, Nixon sought to establish an analogous arrangement at the Republican National Committee. According to journalists Rowland Evans and Robert Novak, he promised a position there to longtime associate Murray Chotiner. Their apparent understanding was that Chotiner would have responsibility for running the headquarters operation with an appropriate title under a figurehead chair. When the designated chair, Rep. Rogers Morton, refused to go along with the plan, it fell through. Subsequently, however, Nixon succeeded with a similar arrangement, using Thomas Evans at the outset of the tenure of Morton's successor, Sen. Robert Dole.[8]

Even chairs who are not members of Congress receive this treatment. While retaining Kennedy-designate John Bailey as party chair, President Lyndon Johnson sent his Texas operative Clifton Carter to the Democratic National Committee headquarters to represent the president's interests there. President Jimmy Carter originally installed fellow-Georgian Phil Wise as Chairman Ken Curtis's executive director.

Financial and Organizational Collaboration

The national party organization engages in a great deal of congenial accommodation on behalf of the White House. Routinely, the White House relies on the financial and organizational structures of the national committee to sponsor what are really White House programs. For example, the White House bills the national committee for travel and living expenses incurred by the president while attending to party leadership responsibilities. Such situations include personal campaigning, campaigning for other party candidates, and appearances at party-sponsored affairs such as fund-raisers, rallies, and the national convention. Occasionally, the national committee can be prevailed upon to carry on its payroll individuals who actually work at the White House.

The national committee staff and the White House also interact in the preparation of publications that serve as publicity for the administration. The White House staff is in a position to furnish the party headquarters with data and inside information to make the publication attractive, relevant, and substantive. Typically, the party headquarters both seeks and welcomes such assistance.

Convention Arrangements and Management

An impending national nominating convention provides the setting for a great deal of interaction between the White House and the national party organization. Although the national committee has responsibility for arranging and conducting the convention, it does so under the close supervision of the incumbent president, even when the incumbent is not a candidate for the presidential nomination.

When the party is out of power, the national committee is supposed to be neutral toward competing candidacies for the nomination. When an incumbent president is seeking the nomination, however, the party headquarters usually strongly supports that candidacy.

When the incumbent is not a candidate for the nomination, concern and interest about the party's choice abound. Typically, the retiring president's aides will monitor convention arrangements and become deeply involved in maneuverings during the proceedings. In past years, these agents have afforded the outgoing president considerable influence at the convention.

The national committee formally establishes the site of the convention, but the president's preference, if not volunteered, is routinely solicited and accepted. *(See "National Party Conventions," p. 220, in the Electoral Process chapter in Part II.)* According to Nixon campaign aide Jeb Magruder, for personal and political reasons Nixon insisted that the 1972 Republican national convention meet in San Diego, California. The White House sent Magruder, an official at the Committee for the Reelection of the President, to Denver, Colorado, in July 1971, to monitor the meeting of the Republican national committee's site selection committee. The committee was not inclined to choose San Diego, but party chair Robert Dole informed the members that "if the president wanted the convention in San Diego, it would just have to be in San Diego." [9] Although the committee obediently selected San Diego, the convention site subsequently had to be shifted to Miami Beach, Florida. The change took place amid concerns about inadequate hotel facilities in San Diego and fears that security arrangements there would be inadequate to deal with the expected onslaught of anti-Vietnam War demonstrators at the convention site.

Similarly, the convention date can be manipulated to the benefit of the incumbent. It is no coincidence that modern conventions expected to nominate incumbent presidents all have been scheduled relatively late in the summer, after those of the opposition party. *(See Table 3.)* The 1964 and 1968 Democratic national conventions occurred the week of President Lyndon Johnson's birthday. In the former instance, the convention schedule afforded time for a birthday celebration. For a unified party led by an incumbent president, a late convention builds momentum for the upcoming general election campaign.

When the president is a candidate, considerable White House input is usually evident in the preparation of the party platform. Such participation ensures that the president's policies receive party endorsement, equates the party's stance on issues with that of the president, and precludes significant divergence toward an independent position. Even when the president is not a candidate, the presidential presence is likely to hover over platform deliberations. Beyond party policy, recent presidents and White House staffs have concerned themselves with administrative details of convention management, to the point of preparing minute-by-minute scenarios.

Traditionally, the national party has convened only in connection with the nomination of the presidential ticket. In 1974, however, the out-of-power Democrats met in Kansas City for an issues conference midway through the presidential term. Four years later, with Democrat Jimmy Carter in the White House, a similar conference was held in Memphis, which provided an unprecedented opportunity for interaction between the White House and the national committee.

On this occasion, encountering substantial anti-Carter sentiment in the ranks of the delegates, the White House and presidential agents at the national party headquarters designed and controlled the agenda. They mounted a monitoring operation on the floor of the conference to ensure that the administration's positions would prevail against intraparty challenges. The effort duplicated the typical pattern of White House surveillance and supervision repeatedly demonstrated at the nominating conventions. Neither party has held a midterm convention since 1982.

Table 3 National Party Convention Sites, Dates, and Nominees, 1944-1988

Year	President	Democrats	Republicans
1944	Roosevelt (D)	Chicago July 19-21 Roosevelt [a]	Chicago June 26-28 Dewey
1948	Truman (D)	Philadelphia July 12-14 Truman [a]	Philadelphia June 21-25 Dewey
1952	Truman (D)	Chicago July 21-26 Stevenson	Chicago July 7-11 Eisenhower [a]
1956	Eisenhower (R)	Chicago August 13-17 Stevenson	San Francisco August 20-23 Eisenhower [a]
1960	Eisenhower (R)	Los Angeles July 11-15 Kennedy [a]	Chicago July 25-28 Nixon
1964	Johnson (D)	Atlantic City August 24-27 Johnson [a]	San Francisco July 13-16 Goldwater
1968	Johnson (D)	Chicago August 26-29 Humphrey	Miami Beach August 5-8 Nixon [a]
1972	Nixon (R)	Miami Beach July 10-13 McGovern	Miami Beach August 21-23 Nixon [a]
1976	Ford (R)	New York July 12-15 Carter [a]	Kansas City August 16-19 Ford
1980	Carter (D)	New York August 11-14 Carter	Detroit July 14-17 Reagan [a]
1984	Reagan (R)	San Francisco July 16-19 Mondale	Dallas August 20-23 Reagan [a]
1988	Reagan (R)	Atlanta July 18-21 Dukakis	New Orleans August 15-18 Bush [a]

a. Won election.

Presidential exercises of convention leadership have produced a long string of successes for presidents who wanted to be renominated. Not since Chester A. Arthur in 1884 has an incumbent president who sought his party's nomination been denied it. Indeed, most of Arthur's successors have been nominated with ease. Although both Truman and Johnson were constitutionally eligible to seek another presidential term, both chose not to in the face of growing opposition.

In 1976 and 1980, strong nomination challenges were mounted against the Republican and the Democratic incumbents, respectively. Reagan's contest against President Ford and Sen. Edward Kennedy's against President Carter suggest that post-1968 reforms in the methods of selecting convention delegates may offset partially the incumbent's traditional advantages. These reforms drastically reduced the state party organizations' control over delegate selection and increased popular participation in that process.

Customarily, an incumbent president seeking the nomination could count on the support of the state party leaders. They had been the beneficiaries of presidential favors and attention and would fear presidential reprisal should support be withheld. Thus, even an unpopular president could be quite secure in the face of a nomination challenge. Party reforms deprive modern presidents of this bulwark of potential sustenance, however, leaving them potentially more vulnerable to intraparty challengers able to capitalize on popular disenchantment.

The immediate postconvention task of selecting the party chair assumed by nonincumbent presidential nominees has less relevance for incumbents. Incumbents usually retain the current chair at least through the general election. Put differently, incumbent presidents expecting renomination have installed their choices as party chairs well in advance of the nominating convention.

Presidential Election Campaigns

Journalist Theodore H. White observed that a presidential campaign "starts with a candidate, a handful of men, a theme and a plan. By November of election year it has enlisted hundreds of thousands of volunteers, politicians, state staffs, national staffs, media specialists and has become an enterprise."[10] A key question is, what is the relationship of the national party organization to the presidential campaign?

Traditionally, that role was central. National party committees came into being in the mid-nineteenth century to provide direction to the presidential campaign. Party chairs customarily served as campaign managers. Indeed, the practice of allowing the presidential nominee to name the party chair developed to facilitate integration of the presidential campaign with the party effort.

The campaign manager and a handful of key associates would set up shop at the headquarters of the national party. The party organization provided the nominee with the potent party symbol legitimizing the candidacy. Further, it made available the personnel necessary for the labor-intensive campaign that had to be waged.

More recently, however, presidential nominees have tended instead to establish autonomous campaign organizations, headquartered separately from the national party. A number of factors account for this development. Strategic considerations can turn a campaign away from the party organizations. A nominee representing the minority party in the electorate, for example, might prefer to maintain some distance between the candidacy and the party effort in hopes of attracting broader support. Republican Richard Nixon's 1960 and 1968 campaigns took this approach.

On the Democratic side, the relative autonomy of Adlai Stevenson's 1952 campaign resulted in part from his ongoing status as governor of Illinois, necessitating the establishment of campaign headquarters in Springfield, the state capital. The Stevenson campaign also wanted to distance itself symbolically from the "mess in Washington," the home base of Democratic president Harry Truman and the national party headquarters.

Modern presidential nominees seek to appeal to an electorate that is decreasingly dependent on partisan sources and structures for political information, economic employment, and social services. As a result, the electorate appears decreasingly inclined to make durable partisan attachments. Thus, the nominees are wary and disinclined to rely primarily on the party organization to carry them to victory.

Modern communications and transportation also have altered the character of election campaigns. Television brings a candidate into living rooms throughout the country. Jet airplanes allow an office seeker to cross the country both rapidly and comfortably. Candidates now can wage far more individualistic efforts than they could previously, and with far less need to rely on the party.

From a different standpoint, changes in the rules governing presidential nominations and elections have contributed to this shift toward more autonomous campaigns. The expansion of presidential primaries has made the coveted presidential nomination increasingly attainable through an appeal to the party electorate rather than the party organization. Indeed, recent nominating conventions have served less as decision-making bodies than as ratification conventions for the party's nominee, already chosen in the fragmented and decentralized delegate selection contests.

This development contributes to autonomy in the campaign organization, since candidates must assemble an effective campaign staff well before the nominating convention in order to run in the primaries. During the preconvention period, unless an incumbent president is seeking the nomination, the party organization is expected to be neutral toward competing candidacies, which precludes integration of the party and the campaign staffs. Yet after the convention, the tested campaign vehicle of the victor remains intact. This both complicates integration and makes it relatively unnecessary.

Finally, federal election laws enacted in the 1970s require a separate campaign organization for a candidate to qualify for public funds. Thus, the likelihood of the traditional sort of integrated campaign, conducted under the auspices of the party apparatus, is virtually nil.

All in all, no longer does the presidential campaign provide the context for interaction initiating the president-to-be's leadership relationship with the national party organization. The other traditions on which the relationship was based—political operations and patronage—also have eroded. Thus, the national party organization has become increasingly superfluous in presidential politics.

Presidential Party Leadership within the Executive

Presidential party leadership within the executive branch has undergone dramatic structural changes since the 1930s. White House aides have taken over party management responsibilities once assigned to members of the cabinet, particularly the postmaster general. Appointments once provided the president as party chief with party-building resources, but the decline in the quantity and elevation in the quality of presidential patronage have diminished drastically this party leadership consideration. Although partisanship is still a part of presidential appointments, it remains significant primarily as an indicator of policy responsiveness and has become largely divorced from party-building concerns.

The Constitution authorizes the president to act as chief executive, that is, as head of the executive branch. Party leadership augments executive authority in presidential relations with the administration and the bureaucracy.

In the context of party leadership in the executive, three conceptual distinctions should be made. First, the word *presidency* refers to the office of the president, those elements within the executive branch most directly under the control of the chief executive. Second, *administration* applies to a particular president and the surrounding team of appointed aides, advisers, and managers within the upper echelons of the executive branch. Third, the *bureaucracy* is the permanent government, the men and women who are essentially full-time governmental employees more removed from the president's direct supervision.

Party Management in the Executive Branch

The president's exercise of party leadership has long featured the establishment of organizational bases within the executive branch for oversight of party affairs. Traditionally, the president's cabinet, composed of the executive department heads, included one or more key political advisers who were deeply involved in party management.

The Post Office and Party Politics

For more than a century, the post office provided the customary haven for a political adviser and party manager. Since it was established as a cabinet office during President Andrew Jackson's administration, the position of postmaster general often went to a leading party strategist. Before the Civil War new presidents frequently named their campaign managers as postmasters general. In that position, this person's political acumen could be put to fruitful use. The primary task was to allocate the considerable resources of federal patronage available through the post office.

With the strengthening of party organization in the latter half of the nineteenth century, the postmaster generalship regularly went to a prominent party politician. After the turn of the century, it became established practice to place the national party chair in that position.

George Cortelyou (R, appointed in 1905), Frank Hitchcock (R, 1909), Will Hays (R, 1921), James Farley (D, 1933), Robert Hannegan (D, 1945), and Arthur Summerfield (R, 1953) were all incumbent party chairs who became postmasters general. Democrat Frank Walker (D, 1943) reversed the process when, while serving as postmaster general, he became the party chair in 1943. Hitchcock and Summerfield resigned their position as party chair on assuming their responsibilities at the post office; the others held the two positions simultaneously, at least for a time.

The alliance was one of convenience, and the keystone was government patronage, dispensed by the post office to recipients authorized by the party organization. This practice also gave formal representation to the party organization in the inner circles of presidential politics. Thus, President Truman could refer to Hannegan as the "political representative of the Democratic party in the cabinet of the president." [11] No party chair since Hannegan, however, has held the two offices at the same time; and no party chair since Summerfield has been named to head the post office.

Nevertheless, through the 1960s, the head of the post office continued to be associated with party politics and political operations. Lyndon Johnson named White House political aide Lawrence O'Brien postmaster general in 1965. O'Brien went on to chair the Democratic National Committee on two occasions, 1968-1969 and 1970-1972. After O'Brien resigned in 1968 to direct Sen. Robert Kennedy's presidential campaign, Johnson appointed another White House political assistant, appointments secretary Marvin Watson, a former Texas state Democratic party chair, as postmaster general. Richard Nixon's choice for that position was Winton Blount, an Alabaman prominent

Courtesy of St. Louis Post-Dispatch; Harry S. Truman Library

Robert Hannegan simultaneously served as postmaster general and Democratic party chair. His good friend President Harry Truman referred to Hannegan as the "political representative of the Democratic party in the cabinet of the president."

in the growth of the Republican party in the South and a visible symbol of Nixon's southern strategy, an effort to expand his personal and partisan base in that region.

During the Nixon presidency, administrative reform changed the structure of the post office, removing it from the cabinet and reconstituting it as a government corporation, the U.S. Postal Service. This development ended the historic connection between the post office, party management, and the party chair.

Three important factors brought about this change. First, after World War II the post office had severe financial problems, which required the exercise of active and effective management at the top. The traditional assumption that the department essentially would run itself, leaving the postmaster general free to tend to partisan politics, had to be discarded. Thus began a trend toward placing business and public administration executives in this traditional sanctuary of party managers.

Second, presidents began to realize that the major justification for placing a party manager in the post office no longer applied. Even before World War II, the increasing proportion of executive branch positions under civil service protection had greatly depreciated the value of the post office as a strategic operating base for dispensing federal patronage. The civil service classification of the positions of postmasters, the basic patronage commodity, was virtually complete by 1938, although a residual degree of discretion lingered. Moreover, the Hatch Act of 1939 prohibited overtly partisan political activity of government employees. This law thereby restricted the maintenance of an ongoing political organization through a network of post office activists.

In her 1943 study of the political significance of the postmaster generalship, Dorothy G. Fowler made a prediction that became an epitaph: "Shorn of his patronage weapon, his employees forbidden to participate in party management or be assessed for campaign funds, the postmaster general may become, like his British counterpart, merely the head of a large business organization rather than the political adviser of the president." [12]

Finally, considerations of "good government" contributed to the separation of the post office from party politics. In the years immediately following World War II, influential public administration specialists decried the official coupling of the political and administrative responsibilities. The Hoover Commission officially recommended that the postmaster general "should not be an official of a political party, such as chairman of a national committee." [13]

Presidents often find it politically expedient and beneficial to appear nonpartisan. The separation of the post office from party politics provided an appropriate opportunity to do so.

The Justice Department and Party Politics

In a 1959 study, political scientist Richard Fenno observed, "If a party politician lands in the cabinet at some other position [than postmaster general], it is likely to be that of attorney general." [14]

Warren G. Harding appointed his 1920 presidential campaign manager Harry Daugherty to that position. Homer Cummings, a former chair of the Democratic National Committee, became Franklin Roosevelt's first attorney general in 1933. Soon after election in his own right in 1948, Truman moved campaign party chair Howard McGrath over to head the Justice Department. Similarly, in 1953 Dwight Eisenhower named former GOP national chair and key campaign strategist Herbert Brownell to this position.

Subsequently, John Kennedy appointed his 1960 presidential campaign manager, brother Robert Kennedy, attorney general. Nixon did the same for his 1968 campaign manager, John Mitchell. When Mitchell resigned early in 1972 to head up Nixon's reelection effort, his successor was his deputy, Richard G. Kleindienst, an old hand in Republican presidential campaigns.

Thus, by the early 1970s, the designation of a leading campaign official as attorney general had become a standard feature of the postwar presidency. When the Watergate scandal enveloped both Mitchell and Kleindienst in criminal prosecutions that resulted in convictions, this particular recruitment pattern came under serious attack.

Presidential candidate Jimmy Carter was one of the leading critics of the modern tendency to politicize the Justice Department. Nevertheless, his choice for attorney general, Griffin B. Bell, was an old political ally, adviser, and friend. Indeed, Bell was the only figure with such a background to be named to the cabinet. In the Reagan administration, the attorney generalship went first to his California associate William French Smith. Following Smith's resignation, Edwin Meese III, an even closer political aide and adviser, took over the office.

The Justice Department always has been politically sensitive and significant. Presidents have long recognized that the office of attorney general is one that can occupy profitably the talents of a key political adviser.

Several prestigious political appointments are channelled through the Justice Department, including U.S. attorneys, assistant U.S. attorneys, and federal marshals. The department also makes important recommendations about presidential nominations of federal judges, including justices of the Supreme Court.

The increasing tendency of interest groups to resort to litigation as a means of achieving their objectives has heightened the political sensitivity of the Justice Department. The increasing extent of government regulation of the economy places the Justice Department in the midst of significant government decisions about benefits and penalties. Key political constituencies can be cultivated and managed by lending support and by exercising discretionary aspects of its law enforcement and prosecutorial powers.

It behooves a president to place a politically astute ally in this crucial post. Moreover, the position itself is a very attractive one. Compared with that of postmaster general, it is more prestigious and substantive. For a lawyer, the attorney generalship is a distinct professional as well as political honor. It is also sometimes a steppingstone to a seat on the Supreme Court.

Thus, after World War II, the attorney generalship supplanted the position of postmaster general as the office within the cabinet to be occupied by a key political adviser. Still, the attorney general is less affected by explicit party politics than was the postmaster general. The party thus lost an institutional identity within the cabinet.

White House Office

Because of the creation and growth of the White House Office, White House staff assistants today have the major responsibility for the conduct of political operations and the management of party affairs.

The White House Office was established in 1939 during Franklin Roosevelt's administration. Previous presidents had received clerical support from a handful of secretaries and personal aides, but the growing size of and demands on the federal government in the New Deal era led a 1937 presidential commission on administrative management to report that "the president needs help." [15] Congress responded by passing a governmental reorganization act creating the White House Office as part of the Executive Office of the President and authorizing the president to hire additional administrative assistants. Since then, White House staff has expanded tremendously. In 1987, near the end of the Reagan presidency, the *U.S. Government Manual* listed eighty-four titled assistants under the heading "White House Office."

These aides usually have come from the campaign organizations of incoming presidents. They typically exhibit a strong personal loyalty to the president and an organizational responsibility to the presidential office. Although recruits almost always come from the president's political party, their political experience often is limited to efforts on behalf of their candidate. Only a very few former elected officials and party warhorses appear on the rosters of the White House staff. Thus, the political interests of the president dominate the personal and organizational perspectives of the members of the White House staff.

With this enlarged staff, Truman and all subsequent presidents have chosen to set up political operations inside the White House. White House staff assistants now handle many of the political chores once assigned to the national party organization. Further, such assistants have become the principal instruments through which the president exercises party leadership.

Two ongoing practices have produced this turn of events. The first is the designation of staff assistants as the president's personal contacts with party and political leaders throughout the country, including the national party organization and the congressional party. The second is the employment of personnel and the establishment of an apparatus at the White House for handling political appointments.

Staff Liaison. As liaison, a presidential staff assistant ostensibly serves merely as a conduit in a two-way flow of advice and information, requests and demands, between the president and representatives of the political party. In speaking and acting for the president in party matters, however, a White House aide inevitably supersedes and supplants the party chair in that central linkage role.

To be sure, the president's primacy as party leader has always made the White House the focus of attention for party representatives. Still, the establishment of a sizable White House staff, sufficient and willing to meet expectations, has enhanced this tendency greatly. In the process of conveying messages, power gravitates to the conveyer, at the expense of those who once dealt with the president directly and now do so through a presidential assistant.

Every White House staff since Truman's has included at least one such figure. This modern pattern of White House staff management of president-party relations first emerged in Matthew Connelly, Truman's appointments secretary. During most of the Eisenhower years, chief of staff Sherman Adams filled this role. For Kennedy, it was Kenneth O'Donnell. Walter Jenkins and then Marvin Watson served Johnson in this crucial capacity. Nixon used H.R. ("Bob") Haldeman to direct a team of political operators. Ford relied on Donald Rumsfeld and later Richard Cheney. Hamilton Jordan was Carter's chief political agent. During the Reagan years, the White House chief of staff had overall responsibility for political operations, while subordinates Lyn Nofziger and later Edward Rollins and Mitchell Daniels were primarily in charge of Reagan's interaction with the Republican party.

In recommending the establishment of the White House office, FDR's Commission on Administrative Management envisioned presidential assistants operating with a passion for anonymity. Instead, these political operators have become very visible and powerful presidential party managers.

Personnel Management. In the White House, as in any other office, expansion in size has been accompanied by increased division of labor and specialization. Another characteristic feature of White House staff organization has been the assignment of a presidential assistant to operate an in-house personnel office managing presidential appointments. In the late 1940s, Truman administrative assistant Donald Dawson set up such an office as a clearinghouse for information on jobs available and potential candidates to fill them. In subsequent administrations, this administrative apparatus and function has been maintained and has become institutionalized.

This organizational development has placed White House aides at the center of what was once a major responsibility of the national party organization. Since partisanship continues to be a major factor in presidential appointments, this element within the White House Office also serves as a major component of presidential party management.

Partisanship and Political Appointments

Political appointments constitute a chief means by which presidents exercise leadership within the executive branch. The Constitution confers on the president a broad appointing power. Article II, section 2, provides that the president "shall nominate, and by and with the Advice and Consent of the Senate, shall appoint ... Officers of the United States, whose Appointments are not herein otherwise provided for, and which shall be established by Law." In addition, it authorizes the Congress to "vest the Appointment of such inferior Officers, as they think proper, in the President alone."

What is the significance of partisanship in presidential appointments and the influence of party in the making of those appointments? Generally, the president's primary concern in making executive appointments is policy responsiveness. Partisanship and party influence are less ends in themselves than instruments for achieving that purpose.

Development of the Spoils System

As the first president, George Washington had the initial responsibility of filling subordinate positions within the executive branch. Ostensibly, partisanship played no role in his decisions; for at the outset of his administration, political parties had yet to appear on the scene. Washington deplored even the idea of partisan division and put forward instead the criterion of fitness of character for consideration as a presidential appointee. Nevertheless, the great majority of the fit characters receiving presidential appointments during his administration turned out to be followers of the policies advocated by Alexander Hamilton.

Thus, by the time Thomas Jefferson entered the presidential office in 1801, the executive branch was filled with his partisan adversaries. For the most part, Jefferson did not so much clean house as make new and replacement appointments with partisan considerations in mind. Andrew Jackson, the seventh president, joyfully embraced what came to be called the *spoils system* (from the old Roman saying, "to the victor belong the spoils"). Under the spoils system appointive positions within the federal executive were viewed as rewards of electoral victory, to be doled out to the supporters of the winning presidential candidate. Thus, after a half-century under the Constitution, the principle of partisanship as a criterion for a presidential appointment had become well-established.

Presidents needed assistance in making the appointments available. If partisanship was to be a major expectation, who better than the party could provide that help? The emerging national party organizations of the post-Jacksonian era quickly asserted claims on the distribution of federal patronage. They had assembled and directed the campaign support essential to electoral victory, and patronage was the means by which they could reward the party faithful. Within the federal government, the post office offered a harvest of available jobs, establishing the longstanding connection between the post office and party politics detailed earlier. Presidents usually retained personal control over the high-level appointments in the executive branch, but they customarily delegated responsibility for the vast number of lower-level appointments to the party managers.

The operation of the spoils system in the mid-nineteenth century produced extensive partisanship and party control over presidential appointments. Further, it enhanced policy responsiveness within the executive branch. It also was associated, however, with allegations of incompetence and scandal. Increasingly, reformers called for its abolition in favor of a system of civil service based on merit.

Rise of the Merit Principle

The 1881 assassination of President James A. Garfield by Charles Guiteau, who was angry at not being appointed U.S. consul to Paris, led Congress in 1883 to pass the Pendleton Act, also known as the Civil Service Reform Act. This landmark legislation sought to replace partisanship with merit as the essential standard for lower-level positions within the executive branch. It established a nonpartisan Civil Service Commission with authority over certain classes of executive positions.

Initially, only a small minority, about 10 percent, of the total number of executive branch positions came under the coverage of the Civil Service Commission. The majority remained in the hands of the president and continued to be allocated through the party as spoils. Gradually, however, the number and proportion of civil service positions increased. By the turn of the century, more than 40 percent were classified. Under President Theodore Roosevelt (1901-1909), a reformer and former Civil Service commissioner, civil service covered more than 50 percent of the positions within the executive branch.

In the 1910s, classification extended to 60 and then 70 percent of the positions and hovered around 80 percent by 1930. The percentage declined to 67 percent during the presidency of Franklin Roosevelt, when the absolute numbers of federal positions increased dramatically as the federal government responded to the crises of the Great Depression and World War II. The percentage rose into the mid-eighties shortly after the war and remained relatively constant at that level for over two decades.[16] In the late 1980s it hovered at slightly more than 90 percent, a rough reversal of the percentage distribution at the outset a century earlier.

Partisan considerations dominated this expansion of civil service coverage. Under the "good government" guise of civil service reform, presidents would extend classification to large groups of their appointees, who had been awarded jobs because of their party affiliations. In turn, subsequent presidents would find their discretion in making appointments severely limited by the actions of their predecessors.

Establishment of the White House personnel offices further changed the procedures for allocating presidential appointments. Partisanship remained important, but the role of the party organization was reduced.

Critical Developments: Roosevelt to Eisenhower

Several critical developments encompassing the presidencies of Franklin Roosevelt and Dwight Eisenhower illustrate these patterns.

After Roosevelt's election in 1932, national party chairman Jim Farley took on the assignment of patronage distribution. Besieged by job seekers during the depression-ridden early days of the New Deal, Farley allocated government positions by the thousands to "deserving Democrats." According to his own testimony, he gave special favor to those members of the F.R.B.C. club (For Roosevelt Before Chicago, the site of the nominating convention). He discussed major appointments directly with the president and other high government figures, but he had considerable leeway in making the lower-level appointments. He intended to deal with applicants at national party headquarters. He soon found their numbers so great, however, that he moved to the more spacious post office building. Serving as both party chairman and postmaster general, he easily could make this shift.[17]

In making political appointments, Roosevelt and Farley benefited from New Deal legislation creating several new executive organizations to administer the expansive New Deal social and economic programs. Initially, positions in these new entities were not covered by the civil service. Thus, they could be and indeed were awarded to loyal Democrats. Presidents Roosevelt and Truman later extended civil service protection over many of the positions.

Recognizing the partisan character of the executive branch under Roosevelt, Congress passed another landmark law affecting the civil service, the Hatch Act of 1939. It prohibited partisan political activity by federal government workers. A second Hatch Act a year later extended this prohibition to state and local government employees engaged in programs supported by federal funds. Political scientist Herbert Kaufman has observed, "While the Civil Service Act sought to keep political workers out of the government service, the Hatch Acts operated to keep government workers out of the parties." [18]

Meanwhile, within the Roosevelt administration, Jim Farley's stature diminished considerably after the 1936 reelection campaign. In retirement some years later, Farley attempted to analyze the circumstances surrounding his fall from grace.

> Almost before I knew it, I was no longer called to the White House for morning bedside conferences. My phone no longer brought the familiar voice in mellifluous tones. Months dragged by between White House luncheon conferences. Soon I found I was no longer being consulted on appointments, even in my own state.... White House confidence on politics and policy went to a small band of zealots, who mocked at party loyalty and knew no devotion except unswerving obedience to their leader.[19]

Farley's fate reflects institutional as well as personal considerations. The emerging White House Office was beginning to have an influence on presidential politics, to the detriment of the traditional party organization representatives. As noted earlier, during the Truman administration, White House aide Donald Dawson set up a personnel office to serve as a clearinghouse for information on jobs available and potential candidates to fill them.

Dawson toiled in relative obscurity at the White House, while the public spotlight continued to focus on the party chair as the administration's patronage dispenser. Indeed, the party headquarters continued to play a significant patronage role. It was by no means ignored or completely supplanted by the White House personnel office. Yet an administrative structure, inside the White House and apart from the party, had begun to handle presidential appointments.

During the Eisenhower years, the changing patterns of patronage availability and allocation came sharply into focus. The 1952 presidential election returned the presidency to the Republicans for the first time in twenty years. The hopes of party regulars clamoring for jobs climbed then quickly plummeted into disillusionment as they discovered to their dismay that patronage of the variety they remembered and expected simply no longer existed. Indeed, the expansion of civil service coverage had had the effect of classifying jobs held by Democratic partisans.

Moreover, their standard-bearer was neither attuned nor sympathetic to the idea of using patronage as a tool for party building. Within the White House, Eisenhower assigned responsibilities for managing political appointments to Charles Willis, one of Chief of Staff Sherman Adams's assistants. An energetic young businessman, Willis was an amateur in politics who had cofounded and directed Citizens for Eisenhower, an amalgamation of independents and "discerning" Democrats, enthusiastically committed to the Eisenhower presidential candidacy but distinctly uncomfortable with the regular Republican party organization. The selection of Willis at the outset reflected the new president's organizational and philosophical disposition to keep presidential appointments out of the realm of party politics.

The Republican national organization, under the capable direction of party chairman Leonard Hall, sought to assert its traditional prerogatives in the appointments process. Hall was able to institute a procedure whereby the party headquarters was to be informed of any job openings and was entitled to make recommendations. For a time Willis formally routed employment applications through the Republican National Committee. When press reports publicly exposed this program a few months after its inception, however, considerable criticism ensued from proponents of a depoliticized civil service; and the Eisenhower administration quietly abandoned it.

Franklin D. Roosevelt Library

National party chairman Jim Farley, right, speaks to President Franklin Roosevelt. Using new executive organizations created by New Deal legislation, these two collaborated to award jobs to loyal Democrats.

Thus, over the years, two clear patterns developed. The first was the reduction of the political appointments available to the president. The second was the shift of influence over the appointment-making process from the national party organization to the White House. These patterns continued in the subsequent presidencies.

Diminishing Patronage Categories and Party Role

The decline in patronage has coincided with a significant alteration in the general categories of available patronage. The classification process over time [virtually] "blanketed in" the types of jobs, such as postmaster, that the political party was best able to fill from the ranks of its qualified activists. Since the New Deal era, low-level jobs for deserving partisans have been in exceedingly short supply; and the old-style patronage, associated with party chairs such as Jim Farley, is nearly obsolete.

Today, executive branch presidential patronage applies primarily to the relatively small number of political appointments to upper-level, executive positions in the departments and agencies that the president is authorized to fill. To be sure, party affiliation continues to be an important consideration in presidential appointments. Democratic presidents tend to appoint Democratic partisans; Republican presidents appoint Republicans. But the shift in primary organizational responsibility for handling presidential appointments from the national party to the White House means that patronage has become much less oriented toward party building than was true in the past.

Table 4 Partisanship and Presidential Appointments, 1961-1984

President	Number of appointees	From president's party (%)	Party affiliated (%)	Non-party (%)
Kennedy	430	63	73	27
Johnson	524	47	58	42
Nixon	737	65	73	27
Ford	293	56	64	36
Carter (1977-78)[a]	402	58	65	35
Reagan (1981-84)[a]	524	82	85	15

Sources: Roger G. Brown, "Party and Bureaucracy: From Kennedy to Reagan," *Political Science Quarterly* 97 (Summer 1982): 283; updated by Brown, in James W. Davis, *The American Presidency: A New Perspective* (New York: Harper and Row, 1987), 296.

a. Data for 1979-1980 were not comparable to data for other years and so were not included.

The party organization's role has become peripheral rather than central. Although it may be called on to make recommendations or to provide political clearances, these requests occur at the discretion of the White House. *(See Table 4.)*

Policy responsiveness has always been a primary presidential objective in presidential appointments. In years past, however, it usually went hand in hand with party building. Consider the case of a Democratic president, for example, doling out jobs to deserving partisans. The very act of placing party loyalists in positions charged with enforcing policies provided both (1) the expectation that implementation would occur according to the president's designs and (2) a significant reward for services rendered the party. Prospects of such rewards constituted important incentives for partisan involvement. Further, the holders of these positions could be expected to look out for the interests of the party from their strategic vantage points. This has become much less the case in the post-World War II era. The two have become separated.

The staffing practices developed by the Reagan White House illustrate well this altered emphasis in managing presidential appointments. Control over appointments was centralized tightly in the White House, under the supervision of personnel officer E. Pendleton James. Ideological compatibility with the president emerged as the chief standard in making appointments. Indeed, for this reason President Reagan, compared with his predecessors, was able to effect noteworthy success in ensuring responsiveness from his appointees in the executive branch.

Civil Service Classification and Policy Responsiveness

The extension of civil service classification has generated new problems for policy responsiveness. A bureaucracy designed to enhance expertise may well sacrifice accountability in the process. Modern presidents have grown increasingly frustrated with the perceived unresponsiveness of the permanent bureaucracy.

In 1978 President Carter promoted the cause of civil service reform to increase presidential control. In that year, Congress enacted the Civil Service Reform Act, which had two important features.

First, it created the Senior Executive Service, a group comprising mostly high-level career civil servants. From the president's perspective, this innovation was designed to increase the flexibility of the White House in dealing with the upper echelons of the bureaucracy and to increase the responsiveness of the bureaucracy to the White House. The experience of Presidents Carter and Reagan with the Senior Executive Service, however, has not altered existing patterns significantly.

Second, the 1978 Civil Service Reform Act abolished the Civil Service Commission, that bipartisan body created in 1883 to oversee the establishment of the merit principle in the federal bureaucracy. Congress created the Office of Personnel Management (OPM). Headed by a single presidential appointee, OPM seeks to increase presidential direction of the civil service. Still, while the president wants a responsive bureaucracy, OPM's concerns are not specifically partisan, thus widening the breech between policy responsiveness and party building. *(See "Office of Personnel Management," p. 1050, in Independent Agencies chapter of Part V.)*

Presidential Party Leadership in Congress

Presidential party leadership within the executive branch augments the executive authority the Constitution provides for the president. Such constitutional authority is largely lacking when the chief executive confronts the Congress. Rather, the constitutional principle of separation of powers positions the president as an outsider in dealing with the legislature. Moreover, legislative leadership is not a constitutional responsibility. Rather, it emerges out of the presidents' ambitions and the expectations of their followers.

Presidents seeking to lead the Congress in the enactment of presidential initiatives must do so without formal command authority. Persuasion becomes the key.

With the conspicuous exception of Thomas Jefferson, and to a lesser extent Andrew Jackson, nineteenth-century presidents did not seek much in the way of legislative initiatives, nor was Congress disposed to look to the president for legislative leadership. In the first half of the twentieth century, however, such pivotal presidents as Theodore Roosevelt, Woodrow Wilson, and Franklin Roosevelt, by dint of their expansive conceptions of the presidential office and in response to new situations and demands, succeeded in altering the political environment, placing the presidency in a much more activist legislative posture. *(See "Historical Development," p. 459, in Legislative Leader chapter of Part III.)*

In the separated institutional environment, party emerges as an important unifying force. Presidents can employ their standing as party leaders to secure cooperation from party members in Congress. In theory, the idea and the organization of party can bridge the constitutionally separated institutions under the leadership of the president. Thus, from the presidential perspective, party leadership provides the foundation for legislative leadership.

This leadership is, however, extremely problematic. Its success is dependent on numerous structural and stylistic factors. Indeed, relatively few U.S. presidents have been able to unlock the party key to legislative leadership.

The Congressional Party

Political parties had no formal standing in 1787 when the Constitution organized and defined the powers of Congress. But today, we speak of the congressional party, or the party in Congress, a concept founded on the fact that virtually all members of Congress have long been elected as nominees of political parties. Collectively, the party nominees elected to Congress make up the congressional parties. In addition, the partisans in each chamber constitute separate units. Thus, today we observe four congressional parties: House Democrats, House Republicans, Senate Democrats, and Senate Republicans.

Further, partisanship provides the basis for the leadership and organization of Congress. The purpose of congressional party leaders and organizations is to heighten the significance of the party cue in congressional behavior. In each chamber, House and Senate, the members of the congressional parties constitute the party caucuses, or, as the Republicans style themselves, the party conferences. At the outset of each session of Congress, the party caucuses meet to select their party leaders.

Party Leaders

Congressional party leadership includes the constitutional leadership positions within the Congress: the Speaker of the House and the president pro tempore of the Senate. When Congress formally convenes, House members uniformly vote according to party lines for their parties' candidates for the leadership position of Speaker. The senatorial counterpart is also elected on party lines. The incumbent does not stand for reelection at the outset of each Congress, however, as does the Speaker. Rather, the incumbent remains in office so long as the party retains its majority. Thus, changes will occur with (1) the departure of the incumbent from the Senate or (2) a change in party power. Thus, the majority party in each chamber is able to elect its nominee to the constitutional leadership position.

The parties choose other leaders as well. In the House, each party caucus elects a leader. The leader of the majority party becomes the Speaker. The caucus also designates a deputy to fill the position of majority leader, and the House will confirm this action. In turn, the candidate of the minority party for Speaker becomes the minority leader. The majority and minority leaders are also called "floor leaders."

In addition, both party caucuses select party whips to assist their leaders in maintaining two-way communication with the party members, especially about party positions and expectations on pending legislation. Both parties have established whip organizations, consisting of deputy and regional whips. The whips extend the congressional party leadership well into the rank and file.

The Constitution names the vice president of the United States as the president of the Senate, or presiding officer, who votes only to break a tie. The Constitution also authorizes the designation of a president pro tempore to preside in the absence of the vice president. In the nineteenth century, vice presidents routinely attended to their presiding responsibilities. In their occasional absences, presidents pro tempore were elected ad hoc to serve until the return of the vice president.

Beginning in 1980, the position became much more stable, with the incumbent now serving until the Senate otherwise orders. Twentieth-century vice presidents have virtually abandoned their senatorial presiding duties, so opportunities for the president pro tempore have increased. Since 1945, the position of president pro tempore customarily has gone to the member of the majority party who has served the longest. Junior members of the majority typically assume much of the daily burdens of presiding.

Despite its constitutional authorization and the status of its incumbent as the senior majority party member, the position of president pro tempore has not emerged as a significant party leadership position as has the House Speakership. Rather, it is much more an honorific office.

The main party leaders in the Senate are the majority and minority leaders, chosen by the party caucuses. As in the House, each floor leader is assisted by a whip. Because of the smaller size and less formal operating procedures that differentiate the Senate from the House, however, much less elaborate whip organizations have evolved in the upper chamber.

Party Organizations

Congressional party leadership positions operate within the context of partisan organizations within each body. The caucuses have already been introduced. While traditionally, their responsibilities have been limited to presession preparation, they have occasionally maintained a presence throughout the session.

During the Jeffersonian era, the Democratic-Republican caucus reportedly met frequently during the course of congressional sessions. More recently, among House Democrats, noteworthy instances of ongoing caucus meetings occurred during the early years of the presidencies of both Woodrow Wilson and Franklin Roosevelt, and again in the mid-1970s when the Republicans Richard Nixon and Gerald Ford occupied the White House. For the House Republicans, regular meetings of the conference were a standard feature in the 1940s and 1950s.

In addition, in the twentieth century, both congressional parties have established "steering" and "policy" committees to work with the leadership on scheduling and strategy. Further, both have created ad hoc groups to recommend committee assignments. These various tasks have frequently been combined in single bodies.

The congressional parties play central roles in the committees of Congress. The party caucuses authorize procedures and ratify decisions for the assignments of party members to the committees. Further, the majority party in each chamber controls the chairs of all the committees in that chamber, with positions on all committees distributed roughly proportionally between the parties: the larger a party's majority within the chamber that term, the larger its majority on each committee. For example, the 1964 elections increased the Democratic majority in the 435-member House by 37, up 8.5 percent from 258 to 195. When the eighty-ninth Congress convened in 1965, Democratic representation on the 50-member Appropriations Committee went up 8 percent, from 30 to 34.

Within the congressional committees in the twentieth century, leadership typically has been established and maintained according to the *seniority system,* a custom whereby the position of committee chair goes to the member of the majority party with the most years of continuous service on the committee.

Additional party organizations in Congress include the diverse array of specific party interests that have proliferated in recent years. These interests typically are based on

Table 5 Presidential Support by Party, House of Representatives, 1953-1988

Year	President	Democrats (%)	Republicans (%)
1953	Eisenhower (R)	49	74
1954	Eisenhower	45	71
1955	Eisenhower	53	60
1956	Eisenhower	52	72
1957	Eisenhower	50	54
1958	Eisenhower	55	58
1959	Eisenhower	40	68
1960	Eisenhower	44	59
	Eisenhower average	49	65
1961	Kennedy (D)	73	37
1962	Kennedy	72	42
1963	Kennedy	73	32
	Kennedy average	73	37
1964	Johnson (D)	74	38
1965	Johnson	74	42
1966	Johnson	64	38
1967	Johnson	69	46
1968	Johnson	64	51
	Johnson average	77	43
1969	Nixon (R)	48	57
1970	Nixon	53	66
1971	Nixon	47	72
1972	Nixon	47	64
1973	Nixon	36	61
1974	Nixon/Ford (R)	44	57
	Nixon average	46	63
1975	Ford (R)	38	63
1976	Ford	32	63
	Ford Average	35	63
1977	Carter (D)	63	42
1978	Carter	60	36
1979	Carter	64	34
1980	Carter	63	40
	Carter average	63	38
1981	Reagan (R)	42	68
1982	Reagan	39	64
1983	Reagan	28	70
1984	Reagan	34	60
1985	Reagan	30	67
1986	Reagan	25	65
1987	Reagan	24	62
1988	Reagan	25	57
	Reagan average	31	64

Source: Congressional Quarterly Almanac (Washington, D.C.: Congressional Quarterly Inc., various issues).

the members' ideology, region, or entry "class" (the election or Congress in which the members initially took office). Examples include the Democratic Study Group, the Republican Study Committee, the California Democratic Congressional Delegation, and the Ninety-ninth New Members Caucus (Democratic).

Finally, since the Civil War, congressional parties have maintained their own campaign committees. These committees assist the election campaigns of party candidates to Congress. Thus, the congressional party as a concept embraces a wide variety of specific groups and organizations.

Congressional Party Voting and Presidential Support

Empirical research on congressional behavior shows that party is the major influence on roll call voting and that party is the foundation of presidential support in Congress. Yet other factors also affect members' voting decisions. It is therefore difficult to know exactly how much influence the parties have.

It is entirely correct to observe, for example, that Democrats tend to vote with other Democrats, and Republicans with other Republicans. Similarly, presidents receive stronger support from their partisans in Congress than from the opposition. Yet disquieting questions emerge when we try to draw conclusions from these findings. Do Democrats vote with other Democrats simply because they belong to the same party? Common policy preferences, constituency pressures, or the personal influence of other members may be the reasons; party affiliation may be merely coincidental. Similar questions surround ostensibly partisan support for presidential initiatives.

Still, these questions notwithstanding, party remains a key to presidential support in Congress. The president's challenge as party leader is to mobilize this base of support, to heighten the significance of the party cue. *(See Tables 5 and 6.)*

The President and the Congressional Party

How does the president as party leader exercise influence? Thomas Jefferson's pioneering exercise of presidential party leadership extended to designating floor leaders and even, according to contemporaneous although inadequately substantiated Federalist reports, meeting with and presiding over the caucus.

Jefferson's successors have fallen far short of these alleged accomplishments. By and large, the congressional party organizes itself and selects its leadership without regard to the president's needs and interests. It does so in keeping with the principle of separation of powers and with the institutional need to protect itself against outside, presidential domination.

No direct presidential participation in the congressional party caucuses has even been alleged in the post-Jeffersonian era. Activist presidents such as Woodrow Wilson and Franklin Roosevelt, however, have conveyed messages to the caucuses informing the members of presidential concerns.

Leadership Selection

Respectful of congressional sentiments, wary of the consequences of unsuccessful initiatives, and aware that hierarchical succession is often the norm, presidents usually are loath to intervene in congressional party leadership contests. A noteworthy exception occurred in 1937, when, following the death of Senate Majority Leader Joseph T. Robinson, President Roosevelt did not hide his clear preference that the successor be Alben W. Barkley of Kentucky rather than B. Patton (Pat) Harrison of Mississippi. Barkley won a narrow victory.

Much more typically, presidents view the party leadership contests as internal congressional matters and are content to work with the leaders thus chosen. Similarly, in the committees, the seniority system insulates leadership positions from presidential influence.

This hands-off approach can invest congressional party leadership in individuals antagonistic toward the president and presidential objectives. The death of Senate Republican majority leader Robert A. Taft in 1953, early in President Eisenhower's first term, resulted in the elevation of Republican senator William F. Knowland of California. Knowland frequently opposed Eisenhower's legislative objectives. Democratic representative John W. McCormack, who succeeded Sam Rayburn in the Speaker's chair after Rayburn's death in 1961, represented a faction in Massachusetts politics that sometimes conflicted with that of the president, John Kennedy. In each case, however, the presidents had no effective say in the determination of the congressional party.

Meetings with Congressional Party Leadership

Franklin Roosevelt and the presidents who have succeeded him have set up regular meetings with the congressional party leadership. Typically, these sessions have occurred on a weekly basis when Congress is in session. They provide regular opportunities to trace the course of the president's program in Congress, to establish priorities, and to develop and coordinate strategies and tactics.

Depending on the president's style and schedule, these sessions may take place in the early morning over coffee and doughnuts or perhaps in the late afternoon accompanied by bourbon and branch water. Should the president's party be in the minority in a congressional chamber, then the opposition party leadership may well be invited to participate in such sessions.

In addition to regular meetings with the party leadership, presidents can and do meet with committee chieftains and individual members and groups of the party rank-and-file in pursuit of their legislative objectives. The frequency with which a president does so depends very much on considerations of personal style. Lyndon Johnson did so often; Jimmy Carter, less so.

White House Legislative Liaison

The determination of the Brownlow Commission that "the president needs help" has had an institutional influence on the presidential conduct of legislative leadership. With the expansion of the White House Office, specific presidential assignments to White House aides of responsibilities for congressional relations have followed.

During the Eisenhower administration, the structure of a legislative liaison office took formal shape under Wilton B. ("Jerry") Persons, a deputy to Chief of Staff Sherman Adams. When Persons replaced Adams as chief of staff in 1958, Bryce Harlow took charge of the liaison office.

These staffers and a handful of associates had the task of establishing and maintaining a presidential presence on Capitol Hill. In a word, they became the president's official lobbyists.

In the ensuing years, this office has grown in size and stature. It has become a vital part of the president's conduct of legislative leadership. It has partisan significance in that it usually is staffed by members of the president's party and it works more closely with the leaders and members of the president's party than with the opposition.

Table 6 Presidential Support by Party, Senate, 1953-1988

Year	President	Democrats (%)	Republicans (%)
1953	Eisenhower (R)	47	67
1954	Eisenhower	40	71
1955	Eisenhower	56	72
1956	Eisenhower	39	72
1957	Eisenhower	52	69
1958	Eisenhower	45	67
1959	Eisenhower	38	72
1960	Eisenhower	42	65
	Eisenhower average	45	69
1961	Kennedy (D)	65	37
1962	Kennedy	63	40
1963	Kennedy	73	44
	Kennedy average	67	40
1964	Johnson (D)	62	45
1965	Johnson	65	48
1966	Johnson	57	43
1967	Johnson	61	53
1968	Johnson	48	47
	Johnson average	59	47
1969	Nixon (R)	47	66
1970	Nixon	45	62
1971	Nixon	41	65
1972	Nixon	44	67
1973	Nixon	37	61
1974	Nixon/Ford (R)	39	56
	Nixon average	42	63
1975	Ford (R)	47	68
1976	Ford	39	63
	Ford average	43	66
1977	Carter (D)	70	52
1978	Carter	66	41
1979	Carter	68	47
1980	Carter	62	45
	Carter average	67	46
1981	Reagan (R)	49	80
1982	Reagan	43	74
1983	Reagan	42	73
1984	Reagan	41	76
1985	Reagan	35	75
1986	Reagan	37	78
1987	Reagan	36	64
1988	Reagan	47	68
	Reagan average	41	73

Source: Congressional Quarterly Almanac (Washington, D.C.: Congressional Quarterly Inc., various issues).

Presidential Appeals

Personally, and with the assistance of legislative liaison assistants, presidents put forward a variety of appeals to their fellow partisans in encouraging them to support the president's legislative initiatives. In many respects, they merely overlap with and build upon the foundations established at the outset by Thomas Jefferson. In a study of presidential influence in Congress that casts doubt on the ultimate value of these appeals, political scientist George C. Edwards III details a number of these diverse approaches.[20]

These appeals may be purely partisan, focusing on the centrality of the measure in question to the party program, and calling for support on the basis of party loyalty. Oftentimes, this invocation itself is sufficient. Themselves elected on the party ticket, members of the president's party typically are sympathetic to rallies to the party banner that call forth their own emotional commitments to the party, its programs, and its leader.

More specific approaches aimed primarily at the partisan audience include patronage and campaign assistance. As noted earlier, the quantity of political appointments the president can bestow has declined markedly in the twentieth century, but party is an important consideration for presidents in making such appointments as remain. These can be used to entice or reward supportive members of Congress—who tend to be vitally interested in presidential appointments in their states and districts—by designating individuals recommended by the members. At the outset of the Kennedy administration, the White House staff functions of patronage distribution and legislative liaison were combined in a single office under the direction of Lawrence F. O'Brien. This ensured that the congressional party interest in patronage would be addressed.

Another service the president as party leader can provide for fellow partisans in the legislature is campaign assistance. The president can agree to campaign on behalf of members running a close race, honoring them and their constituencies with the presidential presence and establishing a credit balance for future dealings. The president also may influence the national party organization in deciding whether to offer its financial and organizational resources to a particular legislator's campaign.

Supplementing partisan appeals are those directed at members without regard to partisan affiliation. Among these bipartisan efforts are some of a more personal nature, in which presidents solicit backing as a personal favor. Lyndon Johnson could call on old congressional and senatorial colleagues of decades-long standing, pleading with them on the basis of friendship to support him on a critical issue. Ronald Reagan's background lacked congressional experience and familiarity with congressional personages. Nevertheless, he would resort to his experience as a Hollywood actor, imploring members of Congress to "win one for the Gipper."

Members of Congress are often quite susceptible to such entreaties, for they invoke the prestige of the presidential office and entail direct access to the president, either over the telephone or in person. Further, they are typically linked with an overarching national interest transcending the party one. Among recent presidents, Lyndon Johnson was particularly prone to invoke nationalistic themes in appealing for congressional support. While he clearly did so in a calculating fashion, he was also unquestionably sincere and emotional in his personal patriotism.

Similarly, presidents can use the numerous amenities at their disposal to curry favor with members of Congress and thus reinforce these personal appeals. These include visits to the White House, photo opportunities with the president, cruises down the Potomac River on the presidential yacht, flights on *Air Force One,* and the like. The president's desk in the Oval Office is filled with souvenirs bearing the presidential seal, such as cuff links, matches, ash trays, and golf balls. Visitors to the presidential retreat at Camp David are provided with windbreakers similarly labeled. Members of Congress are far from immune to such blandishments.

Conversely, presidents can make themselves available to members of Congress at the members' initiatives. Lyndon Johnson and Gerald Ford took care to return promptly telephone calls from members of Congress. Richard Nixon and Jimmy Carter were much less attentive. The accessibility of the president looms large in congressional responses to and evaluations of presidential legislative leadership.

Presidents also can resort to bargaining in pursuit of their legislative objectives. Here, presidents provide favors to members of Congress in return for legislative support. In the congressional vernacular, this is called "logrolling"—you scratch my back and I'll scratch yours.

Edwards has documented several examples. He reported that President Kennedy was attempting with little success to persuade Sen. Robert Kerr of Oklahoma, an influential member of the Finance Committee, to support an investment tax credit bill that was languishing in committee. In turn, Kerr expressed his dissatisfaction with the administration's unwillingness to back an Arkansas River project he was pushing. Kerr proposed a trade, to which Kennedy responded, "You know, Bob, I never really understood that Arkansas River bill before today." Thus, the deal was done, to the mutual satisfaction of president and senator.[21] Although the president or presidential aides occasionally may initiate bargaining, members of Congress are perhaps more likely to do so as this anecdote suggests, in response to a presidential request for help.

Presidents have at their disposal a variety of services that can be useful to members of Congress. Making these services available builds good will and potential support. Although job-related patronage has long been in decline, another brand of patronage continues to flourish—pork barrel patronage, the allocation of federal projects among the states and congressional districts. As Senator Kerr's behavior indicates, pork barrel patronage provides the president with a potential device to encourage cooperation on the part of members.

As head of the executive branch, the president is in a position to make available the resources and assistance of the executive branch on behalf of a member's special legislative interests. The president also can provide assistance to a member's constituents as an incentive for legislative support. Both presidents Kennedy and Johnson instructed their legislative liaison offices to solicit from members of Congress such opportunities to provide assistance.

All of the above are carrots offered by the president or presidential agents as incentives for support. In contrast, the president has relatively few sticks available to use if Congress chooses not to cooperate. About all the president alone can do in the way of pressure is to threaten to withhold the available incentives. This can be effective for members of Congress who are accustomed to them and reliant on them. For more independent members who are willing and able to do without presidential support, the president's threats often can be disregarded.

During the Johnson presidency, Sen. J. William Fulbright, an Arkansas Democrat, chaired the powerful Senate Foreign Relations Committee. After Fulbright began expressing reservations about the administration's Vietnam War policies, he found that his once warm relationship with the president began to cool noticeably. Indeed, where invitations to White House state dinners for visiting foreign dignitaries had once been commonplace, befitting Fulbright's leadership position, they were no longer forthcoming. Fulbright ignored the obvious slights and continued his opposition.

Alternatively, presidents can seek to pressure members of Congress through the use of outside strategies, employing and relying on interest groups and public opinion to encourage or intimidate members to support presidential initiatives. This approach is akin to a bank shot in billiards. The president appeals directly to interest groups and the public, and they in turn exert pressure on the members of Congress. *(See Interest Groups chapter in Part IV.)*

For example, a president seeking to influence members of Congress from industrial states to support a presidential program might encourage allies in the labor unions to lobby those members on behalf of the president. Alternatively, in reaching out to members from farming states, the president could deploy supporters from among agricultural interest groups. In the television age, the president has the opportunity to go public with pleas to citizens across the nation to write their representatives and senators.

Shifting the perspective from individual members to the Congress as a whole, the Constitution does authorize a presidential veto of legislation unacceptable to the chief executive. Its utilization is thus indicative of unsuccessful legislative leadership. In this fashion, the veto stands as a dramatic negative form of legislative leadership. Interestingly, the president who resorted most often to the veto was Franklin Roosevelt, routinely acknowledged as a masterful legislative party leader. He did so on more than six hundred occasions. *(See "The Veto," p. 449, in Legislative Leader chapter of Part III.)*

Limitations on Presidential Party Leadership in Congress

For generations, political scientists have spoken with appreciation of a responsible party government model. This model contains several components. Initially, parties develop programs to which they commit themselves. Then, they nominate candidates for public office who share those programmatic commitments. Competing parties provide voters with clear policy alternatives. Voters choose between or among the competing parties and authorize one to govern. Then, the governmental representatives of the party so authorized demonstrate sufficient discipline and cohesion to enact the party's promises as public policies, thus fulfilling its commitments to the voters.

The British party system has long been viewed as an excellent working illustration of responsible parties. American parties, however, have been roundly criticized for falling well short of the mark, particularly with regard to the behavior of the party in the government.

As noted earlier, party does provide the central cue for congressional voting behavior and the primary foundation for presidential support. Still, the members of the congressional party exhibit an independence from the party program and the party leadership in both the Congress and the White House that is striking when compared with their European counterparts. Why are the party leaders and members in Congress often disinclined to respond positively to presidential leadership? The initial answers may be found in the Constitution.

Separation of Powers

The Constitution does not provide for political parties, nor does it authorize party leadership. Further, the separation of powers principle places the president outside the legislative arena. This is in distinct contrast to a parliamentary model as in Britain that officially combines executive and legislative authority, establishing the leader of the majority party in the legislature as the chief executive.

The presence of party competition within the context of separation of powers makes possible divided party government, again impossible under the classic parliamentary system. Should the president encounter an entire Congress or a chamber controlled by the opposition party, the limitations of party leadership are obvious. A president hardly can be expected to pursue legislative objectives primarily on partisan grounds when the party constitutes a legislative minority. *(See table, Political Party Affiliations in Congress and the Presidency: 1789-1989, p. 1453, in the appendix.)*

This awkward situation has confronted all of the Republican presidents in the post-World War II era. Eisenhower had to deal with Democratic majorities in both houses for six of his eight years in office. Nixon and Ford faced opposition party control throughout their presidencies. During the Reagan years, the Democrats prevailed throughout in the House and for the last two years in the Senate. Among the postwar Democratic presidents, only Truman from 1946 to 1948 had to deal with opposition party control of the Congress.

As an offshoot of separation of powers, the constitutional principle of checks and balances consciously breeds antagonism between the two separated branches. In James Madison's view, protections against concentration of power, leading toward tyranny, necessitated not merely separating the executive and the legislature, but also pitting the two against each other, providing "constitutional means and personal motives to resist encroachments.... Ambition must be made to counteract ambition." [22]

Bicameralism further divides the congressional party into House and Senate bodies. Institutionally, the members of each chamber are conditioned to preserve and protect their particular prerogatives, against each other as well as the president.

Federalism

The other great organizing constitutional principle is federalism, the division of governmental power between the central government and those of the states. The federal principle inhibits the president's party leadership in Congress from several vantage points. First, it works to decentralize party organization in the United States. Party organization parallels government organization at each level: national, state, and local, separating national parties from their state and local counterparts.

Party nominating power for congressional offices clearly rests with the local party organizations. Further, the advent of the direct primary method of party nomination places control over the nominations in the hands of party voters in the states and districts, far removed from the president's party leadership. Thus, the national party and the president as party leader have minimal say over who receives party nominations for seats in the legislature. Indeed, those nominations could go even to individuals openly antagonistic toward the president and the party program.

Second, the federal principle provides for different electoral constituencies—national for the president, state and local for senators and representatives. Diverse constituencies undermine the unifying potential of party. In the heterogeneous American culture, regional variations persist. Massachusetts Democrats and Arkansas Democrats can be two distinctive breeds, as can Pennsylvania and California Republicans.

Staggered Elections

In addition, the Constitution staggers electoral terms and schedules. Presidents serve four-year terms, representatives two, and senators six. In the context of any given presidential election, all the representatives and one-third of the senators will be elected simultaneously. Two years later, however, all the representatives and another third of the senators will be elected apart from the president. These disjointed elections also undermine the unity that party can bring to the political order by partially separating presidential and congressional elections.

Moreover, the midterm congressional elections almost invariably produce a decline in the numbers of the president's party in Congress. This development weakens the influence of the president on the legislature. It undermines the base of party support and encourages the opposition.

In large measure because of these constitutional features of separation of powers, federalism, and staggered elections, political parties in the United States have not developed the discipline and responsibility demonstrated by their counterparts in parliamentary systems. Many of the limitations on party leadership by the president also hold true for the congressional party leadership. Take, for example, regional differences enhanced by the federal system. Democratic president Jimmy Carter lacked rapport with many northern liberals in the congressional party; some southern conservative Democrats viewed House Speaker Thomas P. (Tip) O'Neill with suspicion because of his Massachusetts background. Neither Carter nor O'Neill, both representing central, national party leadership, had much say over who the voters in the 435 congressional districts and the 50 states sent to Congress. Of course, should congressional party leaders be antagonistic toward the president, presidential problems intensify.

Political Culture

The political culture in the United States—that is, the widely held attitudes and beliefs about politics and the political order—is another limitation on presidential leadership in Congress. In the United States, the general public has long viewed political parties with considerable disfavor. In part, this negative view can be traced to the antiparty position of the Framers in the late eighteenth century. It was reinforced about a century later by the intellectual assault on parties brought forth by the progressive era reformers.

Further, the American political culture is an individualistic one. We expect our political representatives to look out for us and not to subordinate our needs and interests on the altar of party. Thus, we effectively discourage members of Congress from the fundamental commitment to party loyalty as a behavioral cue.

Presidential Influence on the Partisan Composition of Congress

All these specific and general limitations notwithstanding, the fact remains that members of the president's party in Congress are relatively more inclined to support presidential legislative initiatives than are the partisan opposition. Therefore, among the most potentially effective exercises of presidential party leadership are those that influence the election of fellow partisans to Congress. Presidential coattails, midterm campaigning, and party purges are three ways presidents have tried to affect the partisan composition of Congress.

Presidential Coattails

Presidential coattails is the voting phenomenon by which voters attracted to a presidential candidacy are inclined to cast their ballots for the nominees of the president's party for seats in Congress. In a classic sense, the coattails theory is usually based on the presumption that voters cast straight party votes; therefore, the more popular the presidential nominee at the head of the ticket, the more likely the election of congressional party nominees. A variation holds that presidential coattails are generated not so much by normally straight party ticket voters as by ticket splitters who, having voted for the presidential nominee of the opposition party, proceed to support congressional nominees of the president's party.

For generations, observers of presidential elections noted a generally positive relationship between the two votes, one that could not be explained purely in terms of straight party ticket voting. In other words, the popular appeal of a presidential candidate was held to increase the electoral support for the party's congressional nominees resulting in the election of more of them to Congress.

In turn, the coattails effect presumably translated into increased presidential support in Congress. Since shared party affiliation produces a predisposition to support the president, a swelling of the ranks of the congressional partisans should increase presidential support. Further, the members who have ridden into office on the president's coattails should be particularly grateful to their benefactor and thus inclined to be particularly supportive. *(See Table 7.)*

This theory of presidential coattails as an influence on Congress is, however, both riddled with holes and difficult to test. In the first place, not all presidents have "coattails." In the post-World War II presidential elections, several presidents appear to have been associated with minimal changes in the size of the congressional parties. Moreover, there is also the possibility of reverse coattails. In such an instance, the presidential nominee would run behind the congressional party nominees in their states and districts.

For example, in 1960, Democratic presidential nominee John Kennedy, a Massachusetts Catholic, ran behind the party's congressional and senatorial nominees throughout the South. Conversely, in 1976, the party's presidential nominee, Jimmy Carter of Georgia, trailed the party ticket in many northern states and districts.

The Democratic party's domination of Congress in the post-World War II era also complicates the theory of a coattails effect. The Democrats seized control of both houses of Congress in the election of 1948, when Harry Truman won by a narrow margin. They relinquished it in 1952 when Dwight Eisenhower won the presidency. Only two years later, however, the Democrats reestablished majority control and have maintained it ever since in the House. After a twenty-six year drought, the Republicans gained control of the Senate in 1980 when Ronald Reagan won the presidency. Six years later, the Democrats returned to power in the Senate, once again giving them majorities in both chambers.

Thus only Presidents Truman and Eisenhower can be associated with shifting party control of both chambers; Reagan, with shifting party control of only one. The gains and losses of the president's party in the remaining presidential elections affected the size of existing party majorities, to be sure, but not the majorities themselves. *(See Table 16, Coattail Victories, House Elections, p. 1133.)* From an empirical examination of the coattails effect in the House, political scientist George Edwards identified specific coattails victories.[23] He concluded that "the coattail effect on congressional elections has been minimal for some time" and attributes this result primarily to decreasing competitiveness of congressional districts.[24] In other words, safe seats have become pervasive in Congress and severely reduce presidential opportunities to influence electoral outcomes. He sees the explanation for this phenomenon in the heightened congressional responsiveness to the voters.

The decline of the coattails effect hinders the president's ability to exercise party leadership in Congress. If the president is unable to carry partisan supporters into office on the strength of popular appeal at the head of the party ticket, then presidents have lost a key incentive in winning congressional support.

Table 7 Gains and Losses in House and Senate in Presidential Election Years, 1944-1988

Presidential Election Year	Winner of Presidential Race	Party	House	Senate
1944	Roosevelt	Dem.	−50	−12
1948	Truman	Dem.	+75	+9
1952	Eisenhower	Rep.	+22	+1
1956	Eisenhower	Rep.	−3	0
1960	Kennedy	Dem.	−21	+1
1964	Johnson	Dem.	+37	+1
1968	Nixon	Rep.	+5	+7
1972	Nixon	Rep.	+12	−2
1976	Carter	Dem.	+1	+1
1980	Reagan	Rep.	+33	+12
1984	Reagan	Rep.	+14	−2
1988	Bush	Rep.	−3	−1

Midterm Campaigning

Midway through the president's term, the Constitution mandates elections for the entire House and one-third of the Senate. By campaigning for party nominees for seats in Congress, the president may influence the partisan composition of Congress.

Midterm campaigning is one of the most visible manifestations of presidential party leadership. Here the president departs from an above-partisanship stance to assume openly the mantle of party chief. Among the forms this activity can take are public speeches, general statements and gestures of support for the party ticket, appearances throughout the country on behalf of the selected party congressional nominees, mobilization and deployment of administrative personnel such as cabinet members, access to the organizational resources of the national party, and fund-raising.

As a dimension of presidential party leadership, midterm campaigning has emerged relatively recently. Political scientist Roger Brown points to President Woodrow Wilson as the inaugurator of the practice in 1918.[25] In that year, Wilson put forward an unprecedented plea to the electorate to vote Democratic to demonstrate support for and to protect the integrity of his foreign policy objectives.

More recently, the allegedly nonpolitical Dwight Eisenhower can be credited with extending presidential involvement in midterm campaigns. Indeed, his participation in the 1954 and 1958 campaigns went well beyond the precedents already established. In 1962, President John Kennedy exceeded his predecessor's pace. In the ensuing years, presidential midterm campaigning has become an important component of the expectations and responsibilities of presidential party leadership.

Thus, in 1966 when President Lyndon Johnson cut short his projected campaign activities and appearances, party figures reacted very negatively. They did so in the face of public opinion polls indicating low popularity for the president and reservations expressed by some party candidates about the possible harm of presidential campaigning. Since then, the presidential presence in midterm elections has been generally high. *(See Party Affiliations in Congress and the Presidency, p. 1453, in the Appendix.)*

These exercises of presidential party leadership cannot be associated with conspicuous success. Indeed, one of the abiding truisms of electoral politics in the United States is that the president's party loses seats in the House at the midterm elections. The record in the Senate is less clear, but significant gains have not been the norm.

Efforts to explain this phenomenon point in a variety of directions. Although some analysts view the president as a central actor in accounting for election outcomes, others focus attention elsewhere, alternatively contending that different electorates are present in presidential and midterm elections, that economic conditions have significant influence, and that incumbency is the critical variable.

Whatever the explanation, midterm campaigning appears more an effort to minimize losses than to maximize gains. One of the most visible exercises of presidential party leadership therefore appears, at least on the surface, to be one of the least productive.

When one party controls the presidency and another controls at least one house of Congress, midterm campaigning responsibilities carry with them potentially severe disadvantages for presidential legislative leadership. Midterm campaigning can inflame partisan opposition, making the president's subsequent bipartisan appeals less effective. Further, some presidents have found members of the opposition party to be more consistently supportive than their own partisans. They have thus been reluctant to campaign against those members.

For this and other reasons, presidents occasionally delegate certain of their midterm campaign chores to their vice presidents. Most notably, President Eisenhower asked Nixon to campaign in 1954 and 1958, and President Nixon assigned campaign tasks to Spiro Agnew in 1970. In the 1958 and 1970 elections, a Republican president confronted a Congress controlled by Democratic majorities

The presidential placement of the vice president in the forefront of the party effort in midterm congressional campaigns can be interpreted as an attempt to fulfill party leadership responsibilities while avoiding direct personal involvement that might antagonize the leaders and members of the opposition party and impair presidential stakes in the upcoming Congress.

Party Purges

In the decentralized parties, presidents are usually far removed from the selection of party senatorial and congressional nominees. This is the task of the voters in party primaries in the states and districts. Further, one of the fundamental norms of U.S. party politics is that the party organization should be neutral toward competing candidacies for a nomination, and then it should willingly support whoever secures that nomination. Departures from this norm, when they do occur, strongly benefit incumbents against challengers.

Nevertheless, on rare occasions, presidents facing members of the party in Congress who consistently oppose them and their policy initiatives have undertaken efforts to secure the defeat of those persons in nominating contests. The most well known and widespread of these efforts occurred in 1938 when President Roosevelt openly sought the defeat of several congressional party incumbents who had voted against key New Deal legislation. According to political scientist Sidney Milkis, "In the dozen states within which the president acted against entrenched incumbents, he was successful in only two of them." [26] Thus, the blatant purge effort must be judged a failure.

In the 1970 general election, the Nixon administration undertook to purge a single Republican senator by supporting the candidacy of Conservative party nominee James L. Buckley (N.Y.) over the incumbent Republican Charles E. Goodell (N.Y.). Although President Nixon stopped short of an endorsement of Buckley, confining himself to a statement of appreciation, vice president Agnew was openly critical of Goodell as a betrayer of party interests. Aided by administration support, Buckley succeeded in his campaign to unseat Goodell.

This incident notwithstanding, presidents are unlikely to exercise party leadership by seeking the removal from Congress of antagonistic partisans. When attempted, party purges are rarely successful and therefore are not a very realistic option available to the president.

President, Party, and Judiciary

The federal judiciary consists of the Supreme Court of the United States, explicitly provided for in the Constitution, and inferior courts, established by Congress under constitutional authorization. The system of inferior courts consists of district courts and courts of appeals, or circuit courts.

The constitutional principles of separation of powers and checks and balances frame the relationship beween the executive and judicial branches of the federal government. The chief presidential check is the president's responsibility for nominating federal judges. The judiciary's check on the presidency is its capacity to exercise *judicial review,* which holds the president's actions accountable to the Supreme Court's interpretation of presidential power under the Constitution.

Partisan considerations rarely surface directly in treatments of the federal judiciary. Unlike the chief executive and members of Congress, federal judges are not elected in the wake of party nominations. Rather, they are appointed. Moreover, unlike the legislature, the judiciary is not organized along partisan lines, with majority and minority institutions. Judges do not take action as overt partisans. Indeed, the judicial role ostensibly requires a nonpartisan stance.

One should not assume, however, that partisan considerations and presidential party leadership have no relevance in the federal judiciary. They do, but in an indirect and often shrouded fashion. In the judicial arena, partisanship manifests itself perhaps most clearly in the appointment of judges.

Appointment in turn is a two-stage process consisting of nomination and confirmation. Article III of the Constitution specifically empowers the president to nominate justices of the Supreme Court. The appointment occurs by and with the advice and consent, or confirmation, of the Senate to the president's nomination. The appointment process for lower federal judges also consists of presidential nomination and senatorial confirmation.

Partisanship and Supreme Court Appointments

According to the Constitution, Congress determines the size of the Supreme Court. Over the years, the number of justices has fluctuated between five and ten. Since 1869, the number has been set at nine.

In making nominations to the Supreme Court when vacancies occur, the president normally considers several factors. Partisanship looms large among these. Certainly, the record of appointments to date indicates that presidents are strongly inclined to name persons who share their party affiliation. Political scientist Henry Abraham found that presidents do so approximately 85 percent of the time. From his examination of the 105 presidential appointees who actually served on the Court since Washington's day, he was able to identify only thirteen or fourteen instances when a president crossed partisan lines in the appointment process.[27] *(See Table 8.)*

Thus, the question is not whether partisanship is associated with presidential nominations to the Supreme Court, but why partisanship is important. Do Supreme Court nominations constitute a presidential party leadership opportunity?

The answer is a qualified yes. In the words of President Theodore Roosevelt,

> In the ordinary and low sense which we attach to the words "partisan" and "politician," a judge of the Supreme Court should be neither. But in the highest sense, in the proper sense, he is not in my judgment fitted for the position unless he is a party man, a constructive statesman constantly keeping in mind his adherence to the principles and policies under which this nation has been built up and in accordance with which it must go on.[28]

Supreme Court nominations are probably the highest form of presidential patronage. They can be used to reward persons for previous services rendered to the president and the party. Several presidents, for example, have elevated members of their cabinets to the court, with the attorney generalship in particular being a steppingstone. In the twentieth century, five attorneys general have been named to the high court: James C. McReynolds (1914), Harlan Fiske Stone (1925), Frank Murphy (1940), Robert H. Jackson (1941), and Thomas C. Clark (1949).

From a slightly different and more symbolic perspective, Supreme Court nominations provide presidents as party leaders with opportunities to reward supportive groups or to broaden the party coalition by reaching out to new groups within the electorate. Here persons appointed can be identified with larger groups of which they are a part. Consider the longstanding customs of maintaining geographical, Catholic, and Jewish seats on the Court, along with the more recent appointments of a black and a woman.

In 1967, in an era featuring dramatic advances in federal civil rights policies, President Johnson nominated noted black civil rights lawyer Thurgood Marshall to a Court seat. In 1981, with women's groups becoming increasingly visible and assertive in the political process, President Reagan named Sandra Day O'Connor to fill a Court vacancy. In each instance, the president recognized an important political constituency and achieved a historic first by choosing a member of a previously unrepresented group.

Notwithstanding presidential initiatives, these interests can and do put pressure on the president for representation on the Court. Similarly, party managers encourage the president to be attentive to party interests in making Supreme Court nominations. In 1969, with two vacancies on the Court confronting President Nixon, national party chairman Rogers Morton encouraged the president to "think Republican." He added, "That's the name of the game. This is our opportunity and we ought to take it." [29]

Party leadership considerations alone, however, are not the primary motivations underlying Supreme Court nominations. Rather, as in the executive branch, presidents first seek policy responsiveness. The stakes are much higher in appointing Supreme Court nominees because of their tenure. Executive appointees serve at the pleasure of the president, but justices, according to the Constitution, hold office during good behavior, which is tantamount to a lifetime term. Thus, presidential nominees on the Court can influence the course of public policy long after the departure of the president.

From this vantage point, partisanship takes on significance as an indicator of policy orientation. Ideological compatibility emerges as the overriding presidential expectation, with party-building considerations occupying a slot of secondary importance.

Republican president Theodore Roosevelt illustrated his endorsement of this distinction in an observation to Henry Cabot Lodge about the prospect of nominating Democrat Horace H. Lurton: "The nominal politics of the man has nothing to do with his actions on the bench. His real politics are all important." [30]

Partisan considerations can reinforce ideological ones in the senatorial confirmation process for presidential appointees. In 1969-1970, the Democrat-controlled Senate rejected two of Republican president Nixon's nominations. More recently, the return of the Democrats to majority status in the Senate in the 1986 elections set the stage for the Senate's 1987 rejection of Republican president Reagan's nominee Robert H. Bork.

Table 8 Nonpartisan Presidential Supreme Court Nominations

Year	President	President's Party	Nominee	Nominee's Party
1845	Tyler	Whig	Samuel Nelson	Dem.
1863	Lincoln	Rep.	Stephen J. Field	Dem.
1893	B. Harrison	Rep.	Howell E. Jackson	Dem.
1909	Taft	Rep.	Horace H. Lurton	Dem.
1910	Taft	Rep.	Edward D. White [a]	Dem.
1910	Taft	Rep.	Joseph R. Lamar	Dem.
1916	Wilson	Dem.	Louis D. Brandeis	Rep.
1922	Harding	Rep.	Pierce Butler	Dem.
1932	Hoover	Rep.	Benjamin N. Cardozo	Dem.
1939	F. Roosevelt	Dem.	Felix Frankfurter	Ind.
1941	F. Roosevelt	Dem.	Harlan F. Stone [a]	Rep.
1945	Truman	Dem.	Harold H. Burton	Rep.
1956	Eisenhower	Rep.	William J. Brennan, Jr.	Dem.
1971	Nixon	Rep.	Lewis F. Powell, Jr.	Dem.

Source: Henry J. Abraham, *The Judicial Process*, 5th ed. (New York: Oxford University Press, 1986), 68.

a. Elevated from Associate Justice to Chief Justice

Partisanship and Lower Federal Court Appointments

As of 1985, the lower federal court system comprised ninety-four U.S. district courts, with 576 judges, and thirteen U.S. courts of appeals, with 168 judges. The formal appointments process for judges on lower federal courts is the same as for justices on the Supreme Court: presidential nomination and senatorial approval. The president tends to be much less involved, however, owing to the larger number of appointments. Typically, the attorney general and Justice Department associates play a critical role in the recruitment process.

The longstanding practice known as senatorial courtesy also comes into play in these judicial nominations. Under this tradition, senators of the president's party from the state in which the nominee is to serve have effective veto power over that nomination. Thus, presidents or their agents usually consult the relevant senators before making the nomination.

Further, presidents may well encourage recommendations from these senators, or the senators may volunteer candidates. In practice, senators' recommendations for district court judges carry more weight than those for the appeals courts.

Should a judicial vacancy occur in a state where the president's party is not represented in the Senate, the senatorial role remains important. The opposition senators normally are at least consulted. In this case, bipartisan consensus or perhaps allocation of nominations between the senators and the president may occur.

State and local party leaders can play significant roles in these presidential nominations. In addition, members of the state delegation in the House of Representatives who share the president's party affiliation may assume and assert influence over presidential nominations. Their participation is not institutionalized in the fashion of senatorial courtesy; there is no guarantee they will be consulted. Rather, their influence depends on such considerations as power relationships, friendships, and favors owed and claimed. State party leaders sometimes mediate disagreements within the state's senatorial delegation over judicial appointments. Alternatively, if the state delegation in the Congress does not include a member of the president's party, the state party leader may play a significant role.

Other persons and groups who may influence judicial nominations include the American Bar Association, sitting

Table 9 Federal Judicial Appointments from the President's Party, 1884-1985 (percentages)

President	Party	Percentage
Cleveland	Democratic	97.3
B. Harrison	Republican	87.9
McKinley	Republican	95.7
T. Roosevelt	Republican	95.8
Taft	Republican	82.2
Wilson	Democratic	98.6
Harding	Republican	97.7
Coolidge	Republican	94.1
Hoover	Republican	85.7
F. Roosevelt	Democratic	96.4
Truman	Democratic	93.1
Eisenhower	Republican	95.1
Kennedy	Democratic	90.9
L. Johnson	Democratic	95.2
Nixon	Republican	93.7
Ford	Republican	81.2
Carter	Democratic	94.8
Reagan (1985)	Republican	98.0

Source: Henry J. Abraham, *The Judicial Process,* 5th ed. (New York: Oxford University Press, 1986), 75.

judges, and interest groups. In these cases, partisan and party leadership considerations recede in importance.

Lower federal court judges share the president's party affiliation in even higher percentages than do Supreme Court justices—about 90 percent of the time, in Abraham's study. *(See Table 9.)* As with Supreme Court nominations, policy responsiveness remains the overriding consideration. Ideological compatibility also transcends partisanship. Party leadership considerations receive greater weight in staffing the lower federal courts, however, simply because of the vast number of positions, the key role of the senatorial party, and the pressure from state party leaders.

Because members of the Senate are more directly involved in the recruitment of lower court judges, the confirmation process itself is rarely controversial or overtly partisan. The Judiciary Committee receives the nomination, typically holds brief hearings, and then recommends the nomination to the entire Senate. On the Senate floor, lower federal court nominations ordinarily pass by voice votes.

President, Party, and the Electorate

This section examines the relations between the president and the party in the electorate. The concept of the party in the electorate refers to people who are qualified to vote and who identify with the party, its causes, and its candidates.

Party Identification in the U.S. Electorate

Party identification is a psychological attachment a person feels toward a political party. It is ascertained by self classification and manifests itself most significantly in electoral behavior, especially voting.

Survey research over the past half-century indicates that most Americans do develop partisan attachments. These attachments are relatively persistent for individual voters and, in the aggregate, are stable over time. Since the 1930s, for example, the percentage of American adults identifying with the Democratic party has fluctuated some fourteen points between 37 and 51 percent. Republican identifiers have varied about sixteen points, between 22 and 38 percent of the population.[31]

Party identification develops through the process of political socialization, the acquisition of political information and attitudes. Students of political socialization have learned that party loyalties emerge relatively early in a person's life; they are usually in place by the elementary school years. This finding points to the family as a primary agent for determining a person's party identity. Further, surveys of elementary school children indicate that while they may know little else about politics, children are fully aware of the identity of the president and generally associate the president with a political party.[32]

The president's extremely high public visibility and name recognition, and the inevitable association with the president's political party, combine to make the president's status as party leader perhaps most clear from the perspective of the party in the electorate. Here, there is no real appreciation for the conflicts, rivalries, and tensions that can beset exercises of presidential party leadership over the party organization or the congressional party. Rather, the president's party leadership is readily and uncritically acknowledged.

Partisanship and Presidential Support

Partisanship in the electorate influences evaluations of the president by providing filters or screens through which people see the chief executive. As Gallup poll surveys show, voters who identify with the president's party are inclined to be supportive, and opposition party identifiers are not so inclined. *(See Table 10.)*

In addition, evidence indicates that members of the president's party associate themselves and the president with similar policy positions. On the one hand, they tend to assign to the president their stances. On the other, they may alter theirs to conform to the president's.[33]

Forging the Link

This link between the president and the party in the electorate emerged during the presidency of Andrew Jackson. It was not a part of Thomas Jefferson's pioneering presidential party leadership. In Jefferson's day, voter eligibility was restricted by state law to white male property holders.

Moreover, the Constitution had placed presidential selection in the hands of electors, themselves chosen by methods determined by the state legislatures. At the outset, the state legislatures divided between those making the choice of electors themselves and those authorizing the popular vote to do so. More opted for the former than the latter.

Gradually, however, more democratic norms and practices began to prevail. Over the next three decades, revised state constitutions eliminated property requirements for voting, and the constitutions of the new states entering the Union omitted them. Also, the state legislatures that initially had retained control over selection of presidential electors passed that power to the voters. Thus, by the Jackson presidency, the country was more democratic than it was at the founding. A connection between president and mass party had been established.

In turn, Jackson was a popular hero who seized this opportunity unavailable to his predecessors to forge the link. In doing so, he dramatically increased the power of the president in the U.S. political system. Henceforth, the president could claim to have been chosen by the majority of the people and derive power from their sovereignty.

Twentieth-century Technology

Twentieth-century innovations in the realm of communications technology enhanced this popular connection. First radio and then television brought the president into the living rooms of partisan supporters throughout the nation, heightening the sense of identification. In this fashion, the president emerges as the embodiment of the party in the eyes of the voters.

An intriguing question arises about a president's capacity to influence and even induce party identification within the electorate. Most studies of the distribution of party loyalties point toward social class, region, religion, race, and gender as controlling factors. They see individual personalities, and issues also, as having short-term importance in explaining departures from party loyalty.

Thus, in the 1950s, millions of Americans could like Ike (Dwight Eisenhower) without abandoning their traditional Democratic loyalties. Similarly, in the 1980s, even though the Democrats continued to hold the professed allegiance of more voters than did the Republicans, Reagan could attract droves of Democratic voters in his sweeping electoral victories.

Still, fundamental realignments of party loyalties have taken place in years past and have elevated new parties into positions of dominance. Environmental factors, especially economic ones producing depressions, remain an important explanation of these phenomena. But we cannot ignore the potential contribution of presidential party leadership.

One of the major challenges of presidential party leadership becomes establishing or maintaining the party in the dominant position. By this standard, Franklin Roosevelt was eminently successful, and Dwight Eisenhower fell short.

Party identification in the electorate appears to have declined in recent years. This decline can be seen first in a weakening of the commitments of the professed party identifiers and second in the corresponding rise in split-ticket voting. Third, the number of declared independents is on the rise. This trend could undermine the significance of party and of party leadership in presidential relationships with the electorate.

Table 10 Partisanship and Public Approval of the President, 1953-1980

Year	President's party	Partisan group approval (%)		
		Democrats	Republicans	Independents
1953	Rep.	56	87	67
1954	Rep.	49	87	69
1955	Rep.	56	91	74
1956	Rep.	56	93	75
1957	Rep.	47	86	66
1958	Rep.	36	82	56
1959	Rep.	48	88	66
1960	Rep.	44	87	64
1961	Dem.	87	58	72
1962	Dem.	86	49	69
1963	Dem.	79	44	62
1964	Dem.	84	62	69
1965	Dem.	79	49	69
1966	Dem.	65	31	64
1967	Dem.	59	26	38
1968	Dem.	58	27	36
1969	Rep.	50	83	61
1970	Rep.	42	83	57
1971	Rep.	36	79	49
1972	Rep.	41	86	67
1973	Rep.	26	71	43
1974	Rep.	25	60	35
1975	Rep.	33	66	45
1976	Rep.	36	71	51
1977	Dem.	73	46	60
1978	Dem.	56	28	42
1979	Dem.	47	25	35
1980	Dem.	54	26	36

Source: Gallup poll; George C. Edwards III, *The Public Presidency* (New York: St. Martin's Press, 1983), 214.

Parties as Coalitions

Students of voting behavior routinely observe that individual voters can be viewed as members of groups within the population. Political parties can be described as shifting coalitions of diverse electoral interests. For example, we speak of the New Deal or of the Roosevelt coalition assembled by Franklin Roosevelt under the banner of the Democratic party in the 1930s. The party embraced disparate groups such as southerners, farmers, blue-collar workers, and racial minorities, who provided the party with electoral support for years to come.

To speak of the party in the electorate is to recognize that the electorate is divided into many different groups. Parties seek to enlist the support of these groups on behalf of their nominees. In turn, appealing nominees can point voters in these groups toward their parties. In the electorate a president's personal and party leadership interests converge in an effort to maintain and expand the party's electoral coalition.

In the context of presidential campaigns, candidates make specific overtures to various groups in seeking their support. The most common approach takes the form of an issue or policy stance proposed to gain favor with the group. A candidate seeking to appeal to Jewish voters, for example, might emphasize a commitment to aid for Israel. In 1980, Ronald Reagan called the business community home to the Republican party with a strong advocacy of deregulation.

Political parties assemble platforms, or wide-ranging statements of issue positions, and present them to voters as promises in return for support. The party's presidential nominee usually has a significant role in the development of the platform. The positions that presidential nominees and incumbent presidents take inevitably are attributed to the nominating party.

Presidential Patronage

Patronage provides presidents with opportunities to develop and maintain support from interest groups. Appointments to positions in the executive and judicial branches, particularly those with high visibility, enable the president to recognize and to reward representatives of key interest groups in the electoral coalition. Also, presidents can reach out to new constituencies through an astute use of the appointing power.

As mentioned earlier, President Lyndon Johnson's 1967 nomination of Thurgood Marshall, a black, to a seat on the Supreme Court had immense symbolic value. It recognized the contribution of black voters to the electoral successes of the president and the Democratic party. Further, it demonstrated the abiding commitment of the Johnson administration to the cause of black civil rights.

Political scientist Nelson Polsby identifies "clientele representation" as one of three strategies presidents use in forming cabinets. Presidents acknowledge that many cabinet departments serve as advocates for major interests, and they appoint as departmental secretaries leaders who reflect these interests.[34] Two of President Carter's designations clearly fit this pattern. He selected Cecil Andrus, a former governor of Idaho with close ties to environmentalist groups, to head the Department of Interior. He also named Bob Bergland as secretary of agriculture. Bergland brought to the assignment a lifelong background in agricultural concerns.

Public Liaison

In addition to electoral and symbolic appeals to distinct groups, presidents since Franklin Roosevelt have made the White House a point of direct access for representatives of supportive interest groups. Previous presidents, of course, had to be attentive to the groups that composed the party coalitions. However, the modern presidency has developed an organizational machinery to work directly with a variety of interests, which evolved into the White House Office of Public Liaison.

As with any organization, the expansion of the White House Office has been accompanied by division of labor and specialization. Early on, in the Truman White House, one task of presidential assistant David Niles was to maintain relations with representatives of minority groups. Subsequent presidents built on this foundation and broadened it by designating specific aides as liaisons with specific interest groups. For example, inside the Eisenhower White House, Frederick Morrow, the first black appointed to the White House staff, served as a contact point for the black community on issues pertaining to civil rights. Through designated staff assistants, Lyndon Johnson reached out to Jews and Catholics.

During the Nixon years, plans to organize and give more official standing to this activity took shape. Ford established the Office of Public Liaison, with a director and a staff, in the White House. The office has continued under Ford's successors, and it appears to be established firmly as part of the White House Office. *(See White House Office chapter in Part V.)*

Public liaison aides play an intermediary role. On the one hand, they communicate to the president the needs and interests of the various groups. On the other, they seek to build support for the president and presidential policies within and among the groups.

In institutionalizing this liaison function in the White House Office, in one sense presidents have advanced the cause of presidential party leadership. Because of the clear identification in the public mind between president and party, the party can benefit from the president's successful efforts to call forth support from interest groups.

In another sense, however, this establishment of direct presidential communications with interest groups can work to the detriment of the political party. Historically, parties served as intermediary associations connecting the electorate with the government. The development and maintenance of direct ties between interest groups and the presidency largely bypass the party as an intermediary. To the extent that the president can assemble interest groups into a coalition of supporters, they themselves constitute a party, in a manner of speaking.

This aggregation must then be linked up in an enduring fashion with the existing party organization. The capacity to do so constitutes a measure of considerable success in presidential party leadership. Failure, in turn, intensifies separation between president and party.

FDR to Reagan, Party Leadership Portraits

Presidential style is an elusive concept. As used in this section, it refers to the distinctive behavior of the president as party leader. The presidency is an extremely personal office that takes on the character of its immediate occupant. In a study of presidential character, political scientist James David Barber focused attention on the significance of the personal dimensions of the presidency.[35]

At the same time, presidents exercise leadership within a structural framework that provides opportunities in some situations and constraints in others. An assessment of individual presidents as party leaders therefore must consider both personal and structural factors.

The background and experiences of the president, particularly as they pertain to party politics, are highly relevant. Structurally balancing these characteristics are the distribution and significance of partisanship in both the electorate and Congress during the president's tenure, along with the vitality of the party organization. Linking the two are the assistance the party is able to provide toward the achievement of the president's political objectives and the personal contributions of the president to the structure of party competition.

Political scientist Ralph Goldman has developed a useful categorization for assessing presidents as party leaders. He classifies presidents as nonpartisan, subpartisan, transpartisan, or partisan. Nonpartisans largely lack experience in party politics and try to remain above the party battle. Subpartisans tend to be seen and to act as representatives of factions within the party. Transpartisans exhibit weak party identities and cross party lines in their own political careers. Finally, partisans openly identify with their parties and engage in party management and party-building activities.[36] *(See Table 11.)*

In assessing the recent presidents, Goldman describes most of them as partisan. His exceptions are Eisenhower, whom he classifies as nonpartisan, and Carter, viewed as a subpartisan.

Political scientists Roger Brown and David Welborn have categorized presidents as party leaders another way, using two characteristics. The first is party leadership, which they define as "the encouragement and development of party organization and . . . the active solicitation of public support for a party's objectives and candidates." The second is partisanship, the presidents' attitudes toward their parties "in the affective and symbolic sense," that is emotionally and associationally. From their descriptions of presidents as either "weak" or "strong" in these two characteristics, Brown and Welborn created a four-part grid.[37]

Presidents classified as "strong" with reference to party leadership were seen as relatively attentive to the needs and interests of the party organization. For example, in making presidential appointments and relating positively to its ranking officials as enthusiastic about rallying the public to the causes of the party through midterm campaigning. "Weak" party leadership presidents were viewed as inattentive and even antagonistic toward the party organization and less willing to invest their own political capital on behalf of the party.

The "partisanship" dimension refers to the president's personal identification with the party, a function of background and experiences. "Strong" partisans have a well-established association with the party label, while their "weak" counterparts lack, in relative terms, this connection. *(See Figure 1.)*

Table 11 Types of Presidential Party Leadership

Nonpartisan	Subpartisan	Transpartisan	Partisan
Washington	J. Adams	Tyler	Jefferson
J. Q. Adams	Pierce	Fillmore	Madison
W. H. Harrison	Buchanan	Lincoln (1865)	Monroe
Taylor	Hayes	A. Johnson	Jackson
Grant	Arthur	Cleveland (1893)	Van Buren
Eisenhower	Taft	T. Roosevelt	Polk
	Harding		Garfield
	Carter		Cleveland (1885)
			B. Harrison
			McKinley
			Wilson
			Coolidge
			Hoover
			F. D. Roosevelt
			Truman
			Kennedy
			L. B. Johnson
			Nixon
			Ford
			Reagan

Source: Ralph M. Goldman, "The American President as Party Leader: A Synoptic History," in *Presidents and Their Parties: Leadership or Neglect?* ed. Robert Harmel (New York: Praeger, 1983), 21.

Franklin D. Roosevelt

Franklin D. Roosevelt was a transitional figure in the history of the presidency. He presided over the emergence of the modern presidency. His actions as party leader prefigured some developments and patterns that have become standard features for his successors. Roosevelt was an enthusiastic partisan who was instrumental in remaking the Democratic party.

Roosevelt came from a distinguished New York family. His branch of Roosevelts settled in Hyde Park, where they were known as the Democratic Roosevelts. This label distinguished them from their Oyster Bay cousins, led by Theodore, who were Republican to the core.

While still in his twenties, Franklin Roosevelt entered party politics and ran successfully for a seat in the state Senate. He supported Woodrow Wilson's presidential candidacy in 1912. After Wilson was elected, he named Roosevelt assistant secretary of the navy. Roosevelt held this position until the end of the Wilson administration. The Democratic party nominated him for the vice presidency and James M. Cox for the presidency in 1920.

Unsuccessful in that quest, he retired to private life and underwent a debilitating bout with polio. He labored in behalf of fellow Democrat Al Smith in Smith's campaigns for the Democratic presidential nomination in 1924 and 1928. Following Smith's nomination in 1928, Roosevelt received the state party nomination to succeed Smith as governor. Elected in 1928 and reelected in 1930, he sought his party's presidential nomination in 1932 with a clear and longstanding identity as a Democrat.

His successful nomination campaign was spearheaded by party chieftain James A. Farley, who traveled the country lining up support among key party activists. For the general election campaign, he named Farley as party chair and emphasized his party affiliation. His electoral victory accompanied Democratic successes in the congressional elections.

Thus, Roosevelt entered the White House as an unabashed partisan with comfortable party majorities in Congress. Not surprisingly, he openly grasped the mantle of party leadership. The Democrats in Congress responded positively by enacting a broad social and economic program commonly called the "New Deal."

Roosevelt's relations with congressional Democrats also featured considerable conflict, however. Not only did the president fail dramatically in his effort to gain legislative approval to add justices to the Supreme Court (the "court-packing" plan), he also vetoed a record number of congressional bills.

Both inside and outside Congress, Roosevelt sought to remake the Democratic party in a modified image that would alter its structure and its ideological orientation. This effort entailed bringing new groups and forces into the Democratic electoral coalition. It also meant moving the party in a more liberal direction ideologically. This required extraordinary efforts to influence the composition of the party in office by openly campaigning against recalcitrant incumbents in congressional party primaries.

Finally, he sought to relocate control within the party away from the traditional party bosses in the states and localities, replacing them as leaders with his agents in positions of responsibility within the ranks of the federal government. It was partly this development that led to a widely publicized falling-out between Roosevelt and party chairman Farley.

Although he fell short of full achievement of these ambitious party leadership objectives, Roosevelt nonethe-

Figure 1 Strength of Partisanship and Party Leadership in Recent Presidencies

Party Leadership	Partisanship: STRONG	Partisanship: WEAK
STRONG	Kennedy Ford	
WEAK	Nixon	Johnson Carter

Source: Roger G. Brown and David M. Welborn, "Presidents and Their Parties: Performance and Prospects," *Presidential Studies Quarterly* 12 (Summer 1982): 305.

less enjoyed conspicuous success in his exercise of presidential party leadership. Further, his extraordinarily long tenure, spanning both the Great Depression and World War II, established him as the exemplar of the modern presidency. Thus, subsequent presidents are evaluated as party leaders against Roosevelt's benchmark.

Harry S Truman

On Roosevelt's death in 1945, Vice President Harry S Truman succeeded to the presidency. In his rise to the vice presidency, Truman developed an intimate association with Democratic party politics. Indeed, he began his political career in his native Missouri toiling on behalf of the Pendergast machine in the Kansas City area, renowned for its strength and its corruption. He served as county judge and received the party nomination for the United States Senate in return for his loyalty to and services in behalf of the party organization. Party loyalty marked his senatorial career, placing him in position to receive the vice-presidential nomination in 1944. He held that office less than three months before Roosevelt's death.

A vice president elevated to the presidency through a vacancy inherits certain constitutionally based roles and responsibilities. The presidential role of party leader, however, operates outside the specific constitutional framework. Thus, Truman's exercise of party leadership as an accidental president illlustrates a variation from the normal pattern whereby the party nomination initially confers leadership status that is confirmed by the victory in the general election.

Truman became party leader without the legitimacy of nomination and election. Nevertheless, he benefited from Robert Hannegan's presence in the national party chair. Hannegan was an old Missouri political ally who held that position in part because of Senator Truman's earlier recommendation. In turn, Hannegan had been instrumental in pushing for Truman's selection as Roosevelt's vice-presidential running mate in 1944.

Thus, the relationship between the president and the party organization began on a positive note. Following Hannegan's departure, Truman did not hesitate to exercise his presidential prerogative in recommending a successor to the national committee. His choice, Sen. J. Howard McGrath of Rhode Island, quickly received committee approval.

Truman began his presidential tenure with Democratic party majorities in both houses of Congress. The foreign and defense policy tasks of concluding World War II and preparing for peace in the postwar world precluded, however, any major domestic policy initiatives at the outset. In the 1946 midterm congressional elections, the Republicans won majorities in both houses. The president pursued a combative strategy in dealing with the Republican congressional leadership for the next two years of his presidency.

In 1948, Truman won an upset victory over his Republican challenger, Gov. Thomas E. Dewey of New York. The Democrats also regained control of Congress and maintained it for the duration of Truman's presidency. During these years, Truman sought without noteworthy success to secure the enactment of his domestic policy agenda, the Fair Deal.

One major problem Truman faced in his party relations was the developing strains in the Democratic party coalition. A major controversy over the party's commitment to civil rights split the 1948 national convention, resulting in a walkout by several southern delegations and the subsequent formation of the Dixiecrat party for the general election. The party also experienced ideological conflict that led to the departure of a portion of its left wing that year under the banner of former vice president Henry Wallace and the Progressive party.

In sum, Truman followed Roosevelt in openly and enthusiastically embracing partisanship. He was a partisan Democrat to the core, fully comfortable with the mantle of party leadership in spite of the extraordinary conditions surrounding his accession. Yet his presidential party leadership did not demonstrate the transformational character of his predecessor's.

Dwight D. Eisenhower

Dwight D. Eisenhower entered national politics at the presidential level following his distinguished military career. He lacked any background or experience in party politics. Courted by representatives of both major parties, he cast his lot with the Republicans when they had not won a presidential election in more than two decades and when they held the allegiance of a distinct minority of the electorate.

Eisenhower's presidential candidacy attracted an abundance of enthusiastic amateurs under the organizational umbrella Citizens for Eisenhower. In the years to come, the president labored without noteworthy success to integrate this element into the regular party organization. In that effort, he encountered resistance from both amateurs and party regulars.

As president, he exhibited a leadership style that political scientist Fred Greenstein has characterized as "hidden hand." [38] He self-consciously and systematically sought to obscure his political activities. While all presidents are aware of the political benefits to be derived from a nonpolitical posture, Eisenhower appreciated this reality more than most.

He was acutely aware of his lack of formal authority over the Republican party. This is clearly evident in his comments at two press conferences about midway through his tenure. In the first, weeks away from his 1956 reelection victory, he observed:

> Now, let's remember, there are no national parties in the United States. There are forty-eight state parties, then they are the ones that determine the people that belong to those parties.
>
> There is nothing I can do to say that one is not a Republican. The most I can say is that in many things they do not agree with me. We have got to remember that these are state organizations, and there is nothing I can do to say so-and-so is a Republican and so-and-so is not a Republican.[39]

In the second statement, less than six months into his second term, he noted: "He, the president, is the leader not of the, you might say, hierarchy of control in any political party. What he is is the leader who translates the platform into a legislative program in collaboration with his own executive departments and with the legislative leaders." [40]

He regularly bemoaned his inability to move the party in the direction of the "modern Republicanism" he espoused. In turn, party activists often viewed him as inattentive to their interests. Certainly, he demonstrated little concern with or enthusiasm for the exercise of patronage power as a party-building device.

His administrative style featured extensive delegation of authority, and he tended to view "politics" as the special province of the party chair. Thus, the party chairs who served during his presidency found themselves generally more within the presidential circle than has been typical since World War II. His 1956 reelection campaign, under the general direction of party chairman Leonard Hall, featured extensive integration with the national party effort.

In Congress, the Republican party gained a majority of the seats in both houses in the 1952 elections that brought Eisenhower to the White House. The party lost control of Congress in the midterm 1954 elections, however, and remained in the minority for the remainder of his presidency. This development forced Eisenhower to look beyond the party ranks in seeking support for his policy initiatives and further muted his partisanship.

Thus, for Eisenhower, personal and structural factors combined to diminish the emphasis on presidential partisanship in comparison with the Roosevelt and Truman years. He was not personally comfortable with its exercise. Neither did the political climate encourage it. Indeed, Eisenhower perceived political benefits in denying it. Further, such efforts as he made to reshape the Republican party and make it over as a majority party failed. Still, he remained a revered and unifying figure in the eyes of most of his fellow Republicans.

John F. Kennedy

In contrast with his predecessor, John F. Kennedy ardently embraced partisanship. His family was closely identified with the Democratic party, and successful congressional and senatorial contests under the party banner had preceded his race for the presidency. In the early days of his presidential candidacy, he proclaimed his leadership responsibilities in the party arena.

> No president, it seems to me, can escape politics. He has not only been chosen by the nation—he has been chosen by his party. And if he insists that he is "president of all the people" and should, therefore, offend none of them—if he blurs the issues and differences between the parties—if he neglects the party machinery and avoids his party's leadership—then he has not only weakened the political party . . . he has dealt a blow to the democratic process itself.[41]

Kennedy installed his long-time political ally, Connecticut party chairman John Bailey, in the national chair. There, Bailey lacked direct access to the president. White House appointments secretary Kenneth P. O'Donnell provided primary liaison between the party organization and the president.

In Congress, Democratic majorities controlled both chambers during the Kennedy administration, but a large portion of the party and committee leadership consisted of southern conservatives, who were not especially keen on his policy initiatives. As a result, the Kennedy administration had failed to achieve noteworthy legislative successes at the time of the president's assassination.

As party leader, President Kennedy reverted to the Roosevelt-Truman pattern of unabashed partisanship in his rhetoric. His substantive accomplishments in this realm were not particularly noteworthy. Any evaluation of his presidency must take into account, however, his short tenure in office.

Lyndon B. Johnson

Although clearly identified as a Democrat, Lyndon B. Johnson sought consensus throughout his political career. He came to Washington from a background in the one-party politics of his native Texas, where party organization was notoriously weak. In his rise to the presidency he served consecutively as congressional assistant, New Deal bureaucrat, congressman, senator, and vice president.

On assuming the presidency following the assassination of John Kennedy, Johnson inherited the party management team assembled by his predecessor. He retained them, in the interest of party unity and also because he needed their expertise in his upcoming quest for a presidential term on his own. Still, he felt he could not fully trust the Kennedy loyalists to act in his behalf.

Johnson interspersed his own group of trusted associates amid the Kennedy holdovers. In the realm of party relations, the main responsibilities initially were assigned to Walter Jenkins at the White House and Clifton Carter, who went to the national committee as the president's untitled representative. Subsequently, Marvin Watson took over the White House end, and John Criswell succeeded Carter at the national headquarters. Having established this structure, Johnson generally was inattentive and occasionally even antagonistic toward the needs and interests of the party organization.

In Johnson's 1964 campaign for president, his agents supervised the convention proceedings closely. The national party headquarters, however, was much less visible within the campaign organization than its counterpart had been during President Eisenhower's 1956 reelection campaign. After the Republicans nominated Barry Goldwater, a strong ideological conservative, Johnson was able to draw support from disaffected Republicans. In doing so, he blurred his own partisanship and undertook a nonpartisan effort. The result was a landslide victory of historic proportions.

The 1964 elections also brought impressive Democratic majorities to both houses of Congress, giving Johnson a strengthened partisan base on which to seek the enactment of his party's legislative program. He was much more successful than his predecessor not only because of the improved arithmetic, but also because of his considerable skill as a legislative leader. He clearly appealed to party loyalty and unity, but he also worked closely and cooperatively with the opposition leadership, particularly on civil rights legislation, to offset southern Democratic opposition and to promote national unity.

As his term wore on, Johnson faced increasing opposition within the ranks of his own party to both his domestic initiatives and his foreign policies. The Vietnam War was especially divisive. At the beginning of the 1968 presidential campaign season, Sen. Eugene McCarthy of Minnesota announced his challenge to Johnson's expected renomination. McCarthy's impressive early showing in the New Hampshire primary encouraged Sen. Robert F. Kennedy of New York to join the race. In a dramatic nationally televised address on March 31, 1968, President Johnson announced that he would neither seek nor accept the party's presidential nomination. For the remainder of his term, Johnson affected a nonpartisan stance, although his agents were very visible at that summer's Democratic national convention.

President Johnson never appeared fully comfortable in his role as party leader. His consensus style did not allow the exclusion of significant elements of Congress or the electorate from his domain.

During his retirement years, the vehement opposition he had engendered within the ranks of the party lingered, precluding his assumption of a role as party elder statesman. Indeed, at the 1972 national convention, he received none of the accolades customarily accorded a former nominee and president. He died in 1973.

Richard Nixon

Richard Nixon began his campaign for the White House in 1968 with a well-deserved reputation as a slashing Republican partisan. He had earned this designation during his years as a member of the U.S. House and Senate from 1946 through 1952. He reinforced it as Eisenhower's vice president from 1953 to 1961. As vice president he assumed many of the responsibilities of party leadership with which Eisenhower was uncomfortable. He gained the enduring gratitude of the Republican activists for his extensive party-building efforts. His scathing attacks on Democratic personalities and programs simultaneously generated emotional public support and antagonism. In his successful 1968 presidential campaign, however, Nixon labored to appear above partisanship and called for a lowering of voices and an end to divisiveness.

In the Oval Office, President Nixon frequently disappointed party regulars with his general disregard and occasional animosity toward the party organization. He assembled a team of personal loyalists in the White House who demonstrated a low regard for the needs and interests of the party organization. Three national party chairmen—Rep. Rogers Morton, Sen. Robert Dole, and George Bush—found themselves largely excluded from the conduct of presidential party leadership.

In Congress, Nixon encountered Democratic party majorities in both houses. This reality forced on him a nominal posture of bipartisanship, although the opposition Democrats were not inclined to support his policy initiatives.

When the time came to organize his 1972 reelection effort, Nixon chose virtually to ignore the Republican National Committee in favor of the Committee to Re-elect the President, a personal electoral vehicle. The presidential effort went forward with little attention to the needs of other Republicans on the party ticket. In seeking reelection, Nixon did give rhetorical support to the concept of a "new American majority" that would realign the party coalitions.

In June 1972, agents of the president's campaign organization were arrested on charges of breaking and entering the headquarters of the Democratic National Committee at the Watergate office building. The scandal that ensued, known as "Watergate," had little effect on the election. President Nixon won an overwhelming victory.

Eventually, however, Watergate and related scandals drove the president from office. By the time he resigned on August 9, 1974, he had lost the support of large numbers of party activists and officeholders whom he had treated so cavalierly throughout his presidency. Further, the Republican party inevitably was tainted by the scandal. Like his predecessor Lyndon Johnson, Nixon was viewed as a pariah in party circles in the years immediately following his departure.

As president, Nixon backed away from the extreme partisanship that had characterized his political career. Indeed, his attitudes and behavior toward the Republican party were surprisingly hostile. In part, this shift can be attributed to his conception of the presidential office as above the party battle. Moreover, his position as a minority party president mitigated against emphasis on partisanship. This was true both for Congress and the electorate. Thus, Nixon's party leadership experience was unsatisfactory in several respects.

Gerald R. Ford

Gerald R. Ford became president on August 9, 1974. His background was in Congress, where he had toiled from 1949 until 1973 in behalf of the Republican party. He served as minority leader from 1965 until his elevation to the vice presidency in 1973.

The unique circumstances that produced his accession, and his struggle to maintain his incumbency in the face of vigorous nomination and general election challenges that dominated his tenure, elevated the significance of party leadership considerations. Ford was not only the first president to come to office via the resignation of his predecessor; he was also the first person to become vice president through the procedures of the Twenty-fifth Amendment—nomination by the president and confirmation by majority vote of both houses of Congress.

In his interaction with the national party organization, Ford was unlike any of his "accidental" predecessors in that he had come to both the vice presidency and the presidency under the procedures of the Twenty-fifth Amendment. In no way had the national party legitimized his incumbency.

In certain respects, the pattern of Ford's dealings with the national party organization did not differ significantly from Nixon's. A vacancy in the party chair occurred when Ford sent George Bush to head the U.S. Liaison Office in China. The incumbent vice chair, Mary Louise Smith, received the president's blessing as Bush's successor. She became the first woman to chair the Republican National Committee. Meanwhile, White House political advisers provided liaison with the party headquarters.

The initial expectation that Ford might be a caretaker president and not seek the 1976 presidential nomination for himself, and the subsequent prospect and presence of a serious nomination challenge from Ronald Reagan, produced an unusual relationship between the party chair and the president. Although Smith publicly supported Ford, she did not overtly forestall or hinder the Reagan challenge in a manner comparable to previous party chairs favoring incumbent presidents.

Ford's postnomination choice of Sen. Robert Dole as his vice-presidential running mate signaled his intention to assume an above-the-battle, presidential stance in the upcoming general election campaign. A former party chair, Dole spiritedly took on the tasks of partisan attacks on the Democratic opposition.

Ford's dealings with the Democratic-controlled Congress were more congenial (if no less partisan) than Nixon's had been during the latter years of his presidency. During Ford's long years of service in the House of Representatives, he had established comfortable social and working relationships with the Democratic party leaders in the Congress. Executive-legislative relations during his presidency, however, suffered not only from conflicts over policy and ideology but also from the legislators' desires to assert themselves against a presidency weakened by the ravages of Vietnam and Watergate.

As party leader, President Ford openly and willingly embraced his party. He asserted his presidential prerogatives in party affairs despite his unique status as an accidental president. He strove with some success to restore the party's credibility in the aftermath of Watergate. As is true of John Kennedy, his brief tenure as president makes evaluation inconclusive.

Lyndon B. Johnson Library

One of the most influential presidential lobbyists was Lyndon B. Johnson, shown here with Senate Majority Leader Mike Mansfield, left, and Minority Leader Everett McKinley Dirksen.

Jimmy Carter

In 1976, former Georgia governor Jimmy Carter came out of obscurity to win the Democratic presidential nomination and then to defeat President Ford in the general election. He assumed the reins of party leadership as an outsider unfamiliar with national party politics.

In his dealings with the national party organization, he followed closely in the pattern of his recent predecessors. After receiving the party nomination, he retained the incumbent party chair, Robert Strauss, for the duration of the campaign while keeping intact and relying on his personal campaign organization for the conduct of the general election campaign. After the election, he brought Strauss into the administration and designated former Maine governor Ken Curtis as the party chair.

Meanwhile, political operations were controlled by the White House. Indeed, the national committee became so outraged by the unwillingness of the White House to address the needs and interests of the party organization, especially in the realm of patronage, that it formally rebuked the president for his neglect.

One year into his presidency, Carter attempted to make amends. He replaced Curtis as party chair with Texas politico John C. White and pledged increased accommodation and sensitivity in the future. For the remainder of his presidency, the national committee operation supported the president without incidents. This support was an important factor in the president's successful effort to thwart a major challenge to his renomination mounted by Massachusetts senator Edward M. Kennedy.

In dealing with the Congress, Carter had the benefit of comfortable party majorities in both houses. Still, he achieved little success for his legislative initiatives. His difficulties stemmed from several sources. First, his electoral victory had been narrow, and he had run behind Democratic senatorial and congressional victors in most districts and states. Thus, he could not claim that his coattails had secured the positions of many legislators. Second, his ideological leanings were moderate, placing him at odds with many of his fellow partisans of a more liberal bent. As an outsider, he was unfamiliar with the norms and procedures of the Congress. Finally, he appeared uncomfortable with expectations of many legislators that presidents seeking their support shower them with personal attention and engage in lengthy bargaining sessions.

President Carter was never comfortable with the cloak of party leadership. His approach to presidential leadership was more administrative and technical than political. His antiestablishment campaign placed him at odds with both the party organization and the congressional party.

Ronald Reagan

Ronald Reagan came to Republican party politics relatively late in life. After a lengthy career as a Hollywood actor, during most of which he claimed a Democratic party affiliation, he gradually shifted allegiance during the 1950s. In 1960, he openly supported Nixon's presidential candidacy; and in 1964, he was highly visible in behalf of Barry Goldwater. By this time, he clearly identified with the ideological conservatives of the Republican party's right wing and served as one of that faction's chief spokespersons.

Reagan successfully sought the Republican nomination for the governorship of California in 1966, and he went on to win in the general election. In 1968, he conducted a very tentative campaign for the GOP presidential nomination that failed to ignite. He won reelection as governor in 1970, retiring at the end of his second term in 1974. In 1976, he challenged incumbent president Gerald Ford for the party's presidential nomination and came close to success. In 1980, he won a comfortable nomination victory, followed by his election in November over President Jimmy Carter.

Although late blooming, Reagan's Republican party loyalty had become extremely strong over the previous two decades. He willingly accepted the responsibilities of party leadership. Structurally, the relationship between the Reagan White House and the Republican National Committee developed along the lines of his presidential predecessors, with White House aides assuming responsibility for political operations, including party liaison. Rumors of White House dissatisfaction with his performance accompanied the resignation of Richard Richards as national party chair after two years in office.

Nevertheless, the spirit of the relationship between the party chair and the White House was much more positive than it had been during the Johnson, Nixon, and Carter presidencies. Cooperation and good will prevailed as President Reagan provided strong support and encouragement for the party-building efforts undertaken by the national headquarters.

In dealing with the Congress, Reagan benefited from the 1980 senatorial elections that placed the Republican party in a majority position for the first time in a quarter-century. He worked closely and cooperatively with the congressional party leadership in pursuit of economic policy objectives.

His relations with the House of Representatives, still controlled by the Democrats, were more antagonistic. He tried to expand the boundaries of his secure party base by enlisting the support of conservative House Democrats. In that respect, he emphasized ideology over partisanship.

In 1984, Reagan won a massive reelection victory over Democratic challenger Walter F. Mondale. The party majorities in the House and Senate remained stable. In 1986, however, the Democrats recaptured control of the Senate, preventing the president from relying primarily on the party symbol in pursuing his policy objectives there. Increasingly, he resorted to threats of presidential vetoes in congressional relations.

Reagan's record of party leadership may be regarded as among the most successful in the modern era. He was a committed partisan who established and maintained congenial relations with the congressional party and the party organization.

Moreover, his electoral successes attracted new groups of voters to the Republican ranks. Whether they stay in this camp remains to be seen. Nevertheless, he restored a positive aura to the presidential role of party leader following a sequence of negative experiences.

As this review has indicated, the experiences of the modern presidents as party leaders have differed in numerous and significant ways, yet some common features also have emerged. The variations appear to be threefold. They pertain first to the presidents' personal orientations toward partisanship, generally positive or negative; second to the tone of president-party relations, relatively congenial or hostile; and third to the political circumstances confronted by the incumbents, either favorable or unfavorable for the exercise of party leadership.

These factors can either inform and reinforce one another or diverge for particular presidents.

Among modern presidents, Roosevelt, Truman, Kennedy, Ford and Reagan viewed partisanship in generally positive fashions. Eisenhower, Johnson, Nixon, and Carter were less affirmatively disposed. Party relations were relatively congenial for presidents Roosevelt, Truman, Eisenhower, Kennedy, and Reagan, while they were more hostile for presidents Johnson, Nixon, and Carter.

Political circumstances relate primarily to party competition in the electorate and in the government. Since the Great Depression, the Democratic party has consistently claimed more professed loyalists than its Republican opposition, measured by public opinion surveys and voter registration totals.

Further, the Democratic party has controlled Congress the great majority of the time. The only exceptions were 1947-1949, 1953-1955, and 1981-1987. On the first two occasions, the GOP held both houses; on the third, only the Senate came under Republican domination. Thus, in general, for the time period considered, Democratic presidents would appear to be better positioned to exercise party leadership in the political arena than their Republican counterparts.

Roosevelt, Eisenhower, Johnson, Nixon (1972), and Reagan all won comfortable, if not landslide, electoral victories. Truman, Kennedy, Nixon (1968), and Carter had much narrower winning margins. Ford was an unelected president throughout his brief tenure. The general expectation is that a generous margin of electoral victory should enhance the prospects for presidential party leadership.

Taking these factors together, Roosevelt more clearly combined personal partisan commitment, positive party relations, and a favorable political context for the exercise of presidential party leadership. Truman, Kennedy, Ford, and Reagan generally shared his positive orientations and congenial relations amid less favorable political circumstances.

Alternatively, while Eisenhower's party relations were relatively congenial, he lacked partisan commitment and confronted a political setting that inhibited party leadership. Johnson, Nixon and Carter faced very different political circumstances—Johnson's positive and the others less so. All not only appeared personally uncomfortable with party leadership, they also experienced and contributed to generally antagonistic relations with the parties they nominally led.

Party Leadership and Presidential Power

This section addresses the relationship of party leadership to presidential power by examining the relationship between party chief and other presidential roles.

In a constitutional sense, party leadership conveys no power. The president derives no legal power from it, and within the party, the president lacks command authority. Rather, party leadership operates within the domains of bargaining and negotiation.

Party leadership ordinarily is intertwined with other leadership roles and responsibilities. The reason other elements in the party—elected and appointed public officials, party organization officials and activists, and party supporters in the electorate—look to the president for leadership has less to do with party power per se than with power coming from other sources, such as the Constitution and the laws, or public support.

The exercise of party leadership often enables the president to perform successfully in other roles. Policy responsiveness is an important presidential expectation in making executive appointments. Although partisanship is not an absolute requirement for policy responsiveness, it serves as a convenient indicator. Presidents' effectiveness as chief executive turns in part on their success as party leader.

Similarly, by acting as party leader the president can be an effective legislative leader, another presidential role that has no constitutional authority. The party connection can unite the separated executive and legislative branches under presidential leadership. In a divided party government, however, where opposing parties control the White House and Congress, presidential party leadership turns into an obstacle rather than an opportunity.

Party leadership is relevant to the president's powers and responsibilities as chief economic manager because the general public identifies the president with the party. The president's success in the economic arena can influence the electoral fortunes of the party's nominees, including the president.

Further, presidential approaches to economic management can reflect ideological positions associated with the party. For example, the more ideologically conservative Republican presidents have tended to view monetary policy as more appropriate than fiscal policy. The more liberal Democratic presidents have tended to prefer fiscal to monetary policy.

Presidential party leadership has less obvious relevance for the president's responsibilities in the diplomatic and military arenas of foreign affairs. The United States has a long heritage of foreign policy bipartisanship. Nevertheless, the electoral and ideological considerations mentioned above can come into play here also, along with those elements of partisanship associated with political appointments.

The presidential role of chief of state surely has the least relevance for party leadership. In symbolizing the nation undivided, the president ostensibly puts partisanship aside. The problem here is that presidential roles cannot simply be discarded like hats. The basic contradiction between these two roles produces tension for the president and confusion throughout the political system.

President Nixon's attempts to deal with allegations concerning his involvement in the Watergate scandal while pursuing his ongoing presidential responsibilities illustrate this situation. In his January 1974 State of the Union message, he bemoaned that "One year of Watergate is enough," and he asserted that in responding to congressional demands, he would never do "anything that weakens the office of the president of the United States or impairs the ability of the presidents of the future to make the great decisions that are so essential to this nation and to the world." [42]

A few weeks later, during a March 19 question-and-answer session before the National Association of Broadcasters, the president urged the House Judiciary Committee considering the issue of presidential impeachment to resolve the question quickly, asserting that "dragging out Watergate drags down America." [43]

The paradoxes of the president's role as party chief will remain unresolved. The president of all the people is the champion of a specific part and the antagonist of another. Yet, in acknowledging the divisiveness inherent in presidential party leadership, we also must credit it with providing the means for presidential leadership in other roles. Without embodying specific powers, it nevertheless enhances the president's power position in the political order.

Notes

1. Woodrow Wilson, *Constitutional Government in the United States* (New York: Columbia University Press, 1980), 67.
2. James MacGregor Burns, *Leadership* (New York: Harper and Row, 1978), 4.
3. Frank J. Sorauf, *Party Politics in America* (Boston: Little, Brown, 1968), 11-12.
4. This section draws on Harold F. Bass, Jr., "Thomas Jefferson's Presidential Party Leadership" (Paper presented at the 1987 annual meeting of the American Political Science Association, Chicago, September 3-6, 1987).
5. Robert V. Remini, "The Emergence of Political Parties and Their Effect on the Presidency," in *Power and the Presidency,* ed. Philip C. Dolce and George H. Skau (New York: Scribner's, 1976), 30-32.
6. This section draws on Harold F. Bass, Jr., "The President and the National Party Organization," in *Presidents and Their Parties: Leadership or Neglect?* ed. Robert Harmel (New York: Praeger, 1983), 59-89.
7. Theodore H. White, *The Making of the President 1972* (New York: Atheneum, 1973), 61.
8. Rowland Evans and Robert Novak, *Nixon in the White House: The Frustration of Power* (New York: New American Library, 1968) 71-74, 364.
9. Jeb S. Magruder, *An American Life: One Man's Road to Watergate* (New York: Atheneum, 1975), 178.
10. Theodore H. White, *Breach of Faith: The Fall of Richard Nixon* (New York: Atheneum, 1975), 97.
11. Harry S Truman, "The President's News Conference of October 31, 1945," *Public Papers of the Presidents of the United States, Harry S Truman, 1945* (Washington, D.C.: Government Printing Office, 1953), 456.
12. Dorothy G. Fowler, *The Cabinet Politician: The Postmaster General, 1829-1909* (New York: Columbia University Press, 1943), 302.
13. Hoover Commission, *Report on Organization of the Executive Branch of Government* (New York: McGraw-Hill, 1949), 224-225.
14. Richard Fenno, *The President's Cabinet: An Analysis in the Period from Wilson to Eisenhower* (Cambridge: Harvard University Press, 1959), 70.

15. President's Committee on Administrative Management, *Administrative Management of the Government of the United States* (Washington, D.C.: Government Printing Office, 1937), 5.
16. Herbert Kaufman, "The Growth of the Federal Personnel System," in *The Federal Government Service,* 2d ed., ed. Wallace S. Sayre (Englewood Cliffs, N.J.: Prentice-Hall, 1965), 40-53.
17. James A. Farley, *Behind the Ballot: The Personal History of a Politician* (New York: Harcourt, Brace, 1938), 223-238.
18. Kaufman, "Growth of the Federal Personnel System," 55.
19. James A. Farley, *Jim Farley's Story: The Roosevelt Years* (New York: Whittlesey House, 1948), 68.
20. George C. Edwards III, *Presidential Influence in Congress* (San Francisco: Freeman, 1980), 125-188 passim.
21. Ibid., 129, citing Harry McPherson, *A Political Education* (Boston: Little, Brown, 1972), 197; and Russell D. Renka, "Legislative Leadership and Marginal Vote-Gaining Strategies in the Kennedy and Johnson Presidencies" (Paper delivered at the annual meeting of the Southwestern Political Science Association, Houston, Texas, April, 1978, 26-27).
22. James Madison, *Federalist* No. 51, in *The Federalist Papers,* Alexander Hamilton, James Madison, and John Jay (New York: Bantam, 1982), 262.
23. George C. Edwards III, *The Public President: The Pursuit of Public Support* (New York: St. Martin's Press, 1983), 83-88.
24. Edwards, *Presidential Influence in Congress,* 77.
25. Roger G. Brown, "Presidents and Midterm Campaigners," in *Presidents and Their Parties,* ed. Harmel, 127.
26. Sidney M. Milkis, "Presidents and Party Purges: With Special Emphasis on the Lessons of 1938," in *Presidents and Their Parties,* ed. Harmel, 167.
27. Henry J. Abraham, *The Judicial Process: An Introductory Analysis of the Courts of the United States, England, and France,* 5th ed. (New York: Oxford University Press, 1986), 68.
28. Walter F. Murphy and C. Herman Pritchett, *Courts, Judges, and Politics: An Introduction to the Judicial Process,* 4th ed. (New York: Random House, 1986), 150; citing Henry Cabot Lodge, *Selections from the Correspondence of Theodore Roosevelt and Henry Cabot Lodge, 1894-1918* (New York: Scribner's, 1925), vol. 1, 517-519.
29. Abraham, *The Judicial Process,* 74; citing *New York Times,* May 17, 1969, 1.
30. Ibid., 76; citing Lodge, *Correspondence of Theodore Roosevelt and Henry Cabot Lodge,* vol. 2, 228.
31. William H. Flanigan and Nancy H. Zingale, *Political Behavior of the American Electorate,* 4th ed. (Boston: Allyn and Bacon, 1979), 54; Frank J. Sorauf and Paul Allen Beck, *Party Politics in America,* 6th ed. (Glenwood, Ill.: Scott, Foresman, 1988), 167.
32. See Fred I. Greenstein, *Children and Politics* (New Haven: Yale University Press, 1965); Robert D. Hess and Judith V. Torney, *The Development of Political Attitudes in Children* (Chicago: Aldine, 1967).
33. Edwards, *The Public Presidency,* 213.
34. Nelson W. Polsby, "Presidential Cabinet Making: Lessons for the Political System," *Political Science Quarterly* 93 (Spring 1978): 19.
35. James David Barber, *The Presidential Character: Predicting Performance in the White House,* 2d ed. (New York: Prentice-Hall, 1977).
36. Ralph M. Goldman, "The American President as Party Leader: A Synoptic History," in *Presidents and Their Parties,* ed. Harmel, 20-22; Goldman, "Titular Leadership of Presidential Parties," in *The Presidency,* ed. Aaron Wildavsky (Boston: Little, Brown, 1969), 384-410.
37. Roger G. Brown and David M. Welborn, "Presidents and Their Parties: Performance and Prospects," *Presidential Studies Quarterly* 12 (Summer 1982): 304-305.
38. Fred I. Greenstein, *The Hidden Hand Presidency: Eisenhower as Leader* (New York: Basic Books, 1982).
39. Dwight D. Eisenhower, "The President's Press Conference of October 11, 1956," *Public Papers of the Presidents, Dwight D. Eisenhower, 1956,* (Washington, D.C.: Government Printing Office, 1956), 891.
40. Ibid., 1957, "The President's News Conference of June 5, 1957," 435.
41. *New York Times,* January 15, 1960, 14.
42. Congressional Quarterly, *Watergate: Chronology of a Crisis,* vol. 2 (Washington, Congressional Quarterly, 1974), 228.
43. Ibid., 286.

Selected Bibliography

Brown, Roger G. "Party and Bureaucracy: From Kennedy to Reagan." *Political Science Quarterly* 97 (Summer 1982): 279-294.

——. "The Presidency and the Political Parties." In *The Presidency and the Political System,* ed. Michael Nelson. Washington, D.C.: CQ Press, 1985.

——, and David M. Welborn. "Presidents and Their Parties: Performance and Prospects." *Presidential Studies Quarterly* 12 (Summer 1982): 302-316.

Cotter, Cornelius P. "Eisenhower as Party Leader." *Political Science Quarterly* 98 (Summer 1983): 255-284.

Cronin, Thomas E. "The Presidency and the Parties." In *Party Renewal in America,* ed. Gerald M. Pomper. New York: Praeger, 1980.

Goldman, Ralph M. "Titular Leadership of Presidential Parties." In *The Presidency,* ed. Aaron Wildavsky. Boston: Little, Brown, 1969.

Harmel, Robert, ed. *Presidents and Their Parties: Leadership or Neglect?* New York: Praeger, 1983.

Kessell, John H. *Presidential Parties.* Homewood, Ill.: Dorsey, 1984.

Ketchum, Ralph. *Presidents above Party: The First American Presidency, 1789-1829.* Chapel Hill: University of North Carolina Press, 1984.

Milkis, Sidney M. "The Presidency and the Political Parties." In *The Presidency and the Political System,* ed. Michael Nelson. 2d ed. Washington, D.C.: CQ Press, 1988.

Odegard, Peter H. "Presidential Leadership and Party Responsibility. *Annals of the American Academy of Political and Social Science* 307 (September 1956): 66-81.

Parker, Joseph, and Edward N. Kearny. "The President and Political Parties." In *Dimensions of the Modern Presidency,* ed. Edward N. Kearny. St. Louis: Forum Press, 1981.

Ranney, Austin. "The President and His Party." In *Both Ends of the Avenue: The Presidency, the Executive Branch, and Congress in the 1980s,* ed. Anthony King. Washington, D.C.: American Enterprise Institute, 1983.

Seligman, Lester. "The Presidential Office and the President as Party Leader (with a Postscript on the Kennedy-Nixon Era)." In *Parties and Elections in an Antiparty Age,* ed. Jeff Fishel. Bloomington: Indiana University Press, 1978.

Chief Economist

The authors of the Constitution clearly intended Congress to be the branch of government most concerned with the economic affairs of the nation. Article I, section 8, of the Constitution grants Congress numerous economic powers, including the authority to:

> lay and collect taxes, duties, imposts and excises, to pay the debts and provide for the common defense and general welfare of the United States . . . ; borrow money on the credit of the United States . . . ; regulate commerce with foreign nations, and among the several states . . . ; and coin money, regulate the value thereof, and of foreign coin. . . .

In contrast, the Constitution grants the president no specific economic powers. Nevertheless, the Framers expected presidents to have significant influence over the economy. They would, after all, oversee the implementation of Congress's spending and taxing decisions, suggest economic legislation in their State of the Union address and other communications to Congress, negotiate commercial treaties with foreign nations, and have the power to veto legislation on economic matters.

Presidential economic power, however, has developed beyond these constitutional powers. Presidents have effectively used their visibility and their prerogatives over the execution of policy to promote their own economic programs. In addition, as management of the economy has grown more complex during the twentieth century, Congress has given presidents greater economic power through statutes.

Because the American people associate the presidency—the nation's most powerful and identifiable political office—with the performance of the federal government, they have come to expect presidents to produce economic prosperity for the United States just as presidents are expected to enforce its laws and ensure its security. As political scientist Clinton Rossiter observed near the end of the Eisenhower administration:

> The people of this country are no longer content to let disaster fall upon them unopposed. They now expect their government, under the direct leadership of the President, to prevent a depression or panic and not simply wait until one has developed before putting it to rout. Thus the President has a new function which is still taking shape, that of Manager of Prosperity.[1]

By Daniel C. Diller and Dean J. Peterson

Limitations on Presidential Power over the Economy

Despite the expectations of the American public and the president's pivotal role in economic policy making, the president's ability to influence economic conditions does not measure up to presidential responsibility for them. All presidents would like to be able to adjust the economy from a central switch in the White House, but no absolutely reliable controls exist.

When unemployment, inflation, and budget deficits rise, presidents receive most of the blame. Herbert C. Hoover, Gerald R. Ford, and Jimmy Carter lost their reelection bids, in part because of the poor economic conditions that prevailed during their presidencies. The president's party also may suffer in midterm congressional elections if the economy is in a recession.

Presidents themselves are partially responsible for high public expectations of their economic management. As candidates, future presidents usually have overestimated their ability to improve the economy.[2] Presidential candidates never promise just to "prevent economic decline" or "do the best they can." To get elected, presidents must promise to produce economic growth with low inflation, and balanced budgets, even if their predecessors have left them with serious economic problems that cannot be quickly or easily corrected.

This relationship between presidential popularity and the economy, however, also may work to a president's advantage. Presidents are quick to take credit for economic growth, price stability, and low unemployment. Presidential candidate Ronald Reagan capitalized on poor economic conditions in 1980 by asking voters, "Are you better off now than you were four years ago?" Voters responded "no" and elected Reagan to succeed Jimmy Carter. Four years later, however, when the economy was in the midst of a strong expansion after the recession of 1981-1982, Reagan repeated the question, and the American people reelected him in a landslide.

Four factors combine to limit the president's control over the U.S. economy. First, the chief executive must share power with other individuals and government bodies. As the enumeration of congressional economic powers shows, Congress has the constitutional authority to frus-

Economic Terms

Classical economic theory: a body of theory developed during the late eighteenth and early nineteenth centuries maintaining that economies naturally tend to achieve full employment and that government intervention in economic matters should be limited.

Contractionary policy: restrictive fiscal or monetary policy designed to decrease demand thereby reducing inflation.

Expansionary policy: stimulative fiscal or monetary policy designed to increase demand thereby decreasing unemployment and promoting economic growth.

Federal Reserve System: the central bank of the United States; oversees the nation's banking system and controls monetary policy.

Fiscal policy: the manipulation of government spending and tax rates for the purpose of altering the levels of unemployment, inflation, and economic growth.

Gross national product: the value of goods and services produced by an economy in a given year; the principal measure of economic growth.

Inflation: a sustained increase in prices.

Keynesian theory: the body of economic theory developed by British economist John Maynard Keynes that advocates government intervention in the economy to stimulate or dampen demand as a way to deal with high unemployment or inflation.

Laissez faire: an approach to economic policy that advocates a limited government role in the economy in favor of a reliance upon free-market forces.

Monetarism: an approach to economic policy making that emphasizes the role of the money supply in determining inflation, unemployment, and economic growth.

Monetary policy: the manipulation of the money supply for the purpose of altering the levels of unemployment, inflation, and economic growth.

Price stability: the absence of inflation.

Protectionism: an attempt by a government to protect the domestic markets of its industries from foreign competition by erecting trade barriers.

Recession: a prolonged downturn in the economy during which investment, incomes, and employment all decline.

Stabilization policy: monetary and fiscal policies designed to smooth undesirable fluctuations in inflation, unemployment, and the rate of economic growth.

Stagflation: simultaneous high inflation and unemployment.

Supply-side theory: an economic theory that focuses on the role played by incentives in achieving economic growth; supply-siders generally favor lower tax rates and government efforts to stimulate investments.

Tariff: a tax on imports or exports.

Trade barriers: protectionist devices such as tariffs or import quotas that make it more difficult for foreign companies to sell their goods and services in a given country.

Trade deficit: condition when a nation's imports exceed its exports.

trate virtually any presidential economic initiative. Most important, the president cannot levy taxes or appropriate money without the consent of Congress.

Executive branch organizations also cut into presidential economic power. The independent Federal Reserve Board, which sets monetary policy, is not obliged to cooperate with the president. *(See "Monetary Policy," p. 658, in this chapter.)* Spending and taxing policies adopted by presidents to achieve one economic result may be undercut by the monetary policies of the Federal Reserve Board designed to achieve a conflicting result. The president's own economic advisers also can check presidential power by unenthusiastically implementing the chief executive's directives or refusing to join a policy consensus.

Each economic advisory organization has a different mission that disposes it to concentrate on a particular economic problem rather than the entire economic situation. The Office of Management and Budget (OMB) looks to trim the budget; the president's Council of Economic Advisers (CEA) focuses on lowering unemployment and inflation and promoting economic expansion; the Treasury Department oversees the national debt and develops international monetary policy; and the heads of other departments and agencies seek to protect funding for projects within their jurisdictions. These missions often conflict, making agreement on policy goals difficult and creating rivalries within an administration.

A second factor limiting presidential control of the economy is the highly complex and theoretical nature of the science of economics. Presidents with little formal training in economics may feel overwhelmed, as did Warren Harding who once confided to an associate:

> I don't know what to do or where to turn on this taxation matter. Somewhere there must be a book that tells all about it, where I could go to straighten it out in my mind. But I don't know where the book is, and maybe I couldn't read it if I found it. There must be a man in the country somewhere who could weigh both sides and know the truth. Probably he is in some college or other. But I don't know where to find him, I don't know who he is and I don't know how to get him.[3]

Even if presidents do trust the judgment of their economic advisers, there is little consensus among economists about which economic theory or theories should guide economic policy.

A third factor limiting presidential economic control is the imprecision of economic information. When presidents attempt to adjust the economy, they assume that they have accurate and timely information about how the economy is performing. Economic statistics and indicators do not, however, measure the immediate conditions of the economy, but rather the conditions that prevailed between one and four months ago, depending on the particular economic statistic. Consequently, presidents who take action on the basis of incoming economic information may be reacting to a problem that no longer exists or is much worse than believed. In such cases presidential economic policies may destabilize the economy. A president's attempts to manage the economy, therefore, are only as good as the information upon which they are based.

When government figures indicate that unemployment is rising and consumer demand is falling the president may wish to enact spending increases or a tax cut. If, however, the unemployment figures are misleading or the estimate of consumer demand is outdated, such antirecession measures could cause an inflationary spiral. In 1977 President Carter was forced to abandon his tax rebate proposal and initiate an anti-inflation program because the economy had already begun to pull out of the recession he had intended to correct.[4]

Similarly, an anti-inflation strategy based on inaccurate information can deepen a recession. At the beginning of 1980 the inflation rate reached 18 percent. Although many economists had predicted that a recession would occur during the first half of that year, mixed economic indicators suggested that the economy was still expanding. In March Carter and his advisers decided to impose credit controls designed to lower inflation. Later in the year, however, as more complete economic statistics about the first quarter became available, it was apparent that the recession predicted by economists was already under way when Carter initiated his anti-inflationary policies. The second quarter saw the sharpest decline in gross national product (GNP) in a single three-month period since World War II. Unemployment rose from 6.3 percent in March to 7.5 percent in June. Economic statistics had provided Carter with an incomplete economic picture that induced him to take measures that exacerbated the economy's troubles.[5]

Finally, presidential control over the economy is limited by forces outside the reach of the federal government. The economic policies of state and local governments may undercut those of the federal government; international factors such as the price of oil or foreign trade policies may exacerbate U.S. economic problems; bad weather may limit agricultural production; public expectations may make certain economic options such as large cuts in Social Security and Medicare politically impossible; and large corporations may make business decisions that adversely affect unemployment, inflation, the trade deficit, and other economic problems. A president making all the right decisions will not, therefore, necessarily produce a thriving economy; nor will an economically inexperienced or inept president inevitably bring on a national economic disaster or even a recession.

Yet in spite of these limitations, no single force has more influence over the U.S. economy than the president. As chief executive the president oversees the government's economic and regulatory functions and appoints cabinet and Federal Reserve Board members who make many economic decisions; as chief legislator the president proposes spending, tax, and other economic-related legislation and can use the veto to influence what legislation becomes law; as commander in chief the president oversees the multibillion-dollar purchases of the Defense Department; as chief diplomat the president negotiates with foreign governments about trade and currency issues; and as chief of state the president affects the morale, attitudes, and expectations of the American people.

Early Presidential Economic Management

From the beginning of the Republic presidents understood that promoting the nation's prosperity was as much a part of their job as ensuring its security and enforcing its laws. Presidents did not, however, attempt to affect the performance of the economy through spending and taxing decisions until the Great Depression of the 1930s. Before then, the classical theory of economics, associated with the writings of Adam Smith, the eighteenth-century British economist, prevailed. This theory held that a laissez-faire approach to government economic activity—one that allowed farmers, merchants, and manufacturers to operate unencumbered by government intervention and regulation—would result in the most prosperous economic conditions. Consequently, if the economy were running smoothly, the president's economic responsibilities were limited primarily to executing the spending and revenue measures passed by Congress, promoting a balanced budget, and working with business leaders and foreign governments to expand industrial development and trade.

The U.S. economy did not always run smoothly, however. As it became increasingly industrialized in the late nineteenth and early twentieth centuries, fluctuations in employment became more frequent and severe. The growth of industry also created new demands on the nation's financial system and forced the government to protect consumers and workers from the power of monopolies. Society came to believe that government should work to prevent crises and create a stable and fair business environment. Consequently, presidents in the late nineteenth and early twentieth centuries occasionally abandoned their laissez-faire stance and proposed or supported solutions to obvious economic problems. The public increasingly looked to the president, the symbol of government and the leader of the party, for economic innovation and direction. By the time the Great Depression struck, laissez-faire attitudes toward the executive's economic role had already given way to more activist conceptions of governmental and presidential power.

Financial Foundations of the New Nation

George Washington ensured that economic affairs would have a central place in his administration when he appointed Alexander Hamilton, his closest adviser, as secretary of the Treasury. Hamilton often worked independently of Washington, who seldom intervened in his treasury secretary's unfinished projects. Hamilton recognized that the international reputation of the United States and its ability to command respect among its own citizens—many of whom felt stronger loyalties to their home state than to the new federal government—depended on the government's financial stability and the vibrancy of the American economy. Hamilton, therefore, aggressively promoted the interests of merchants and manufacturers and tried to create an atmosphere of confidence through measures that included the assumption of state debts by the national government and the establishment of a national bank.

Debt Assumption

Both the federal government and the states had gone heavily into debt to finance the Revolutionary War. Congress and the states had borrowed money from virtually anyone who would lend it. The United States owed money to the French government, Dutch bankers, state treasuries, and individual holders of bonds and promissory notes. A comprehensive plan was needed that would allow the government to pay back the debts without imposing burdensome taxes on its citizens, establish good international credit, and reconcile the competing interests of its domestic creditors.

Ten days after Hamilton assumed the office of secretary of the Treasury, the House of Representatives asked him to draft a plan for the "adequate support of the public credit." Hamilton used this simple mandate to construct an ambitious plan to resolve the debt situation and bring fiscal stability to the federal government.[6]

The scope and intricacy of Hamilton's plan surprised Congress when he presented it to that body on January 14, 1790. It called for federal assumption of the $25 million in debts incurred by the states during the Revolutionary War and refunding of the national debt through various bonds and securities. Existing tariffs, which Congress eventually continued at Hamilton's urging, would provide the primary source of revenues to gradually retire the debt.

The most politically divisive aspect of the debt question was how and to what degree the federal government would assume the debts of states. Predictably, the states that had paid their wartime debts, including Virginia, Maryland, North Carolina, and Georgia were against having the federal government take over the financial burden of the states with a large debt, while the latter, including Massachusetts, Connecticut, and South Carolina, pressed for full assumption.

Division over the assumption question initially led to rejection of Hamilton's plan by a slim margin in both houses of Congress. With Thomas Jefferson's help, however, a compromise was reached whereby the debt assumption bill was linked to a measure moving the capital from New York to Philadelphia for ten years and then to what would become Washington, D.C. This act placated a few southern members of Congress who changed their votes, and the bill was passed. President Washington signed it on August 4, 1790.[7]

Establishment of the National Bank

In addition to the assumption of debts by the federal government the other component of Hamilton's plan to bring financial credibility and stability to the new nation was the establishment of a national bank. Hamilton outlined his bank proposal to Congress in December 1790. He asked Congress to charter a national bank to assist in the financial operations of the United States. It was to be run primarily by private directors and funded by private capital. Of the bank's original $10 million capitalization, only $2 million were to come from the Treasury, while the rest would be provided by individual investors.

Opponents and supporters of the bank saw that it would provide the president with added power over the economy and would serve as a symbol of the preeminence of the federal government. Many of the bank's detractors opposed it because they feared granting more influence to the federal government. Others, including James Madison, argued that the bank was unconstitutional since the Constitution did not explicitly give the government the power to charter a bank.[8] Legislators in favor of the bill prevailed, however, and the legislation passed both houses by February 1791.

George Washington solicited the opinions of his cabinet on whether to sign the bill. Two members of his cabinet, Secretary of State Thomas Jefferson and Attorney General Edmund Randolph concurred with Madison, their fellow Virginian. They saw the bank as a violation of the yet unratified Tenth Amendment which, in their view, prohibited the federal government from exercising authority not granted to it by the Constitution.[9]

Washington, who conceived of the president's veto as a tool to prevent the passage of unconstitutional legislation, was concerned about these charges against the bank. Although he favored the establishment of the bank as a practical step toward a stronger U.S. economy he was prepared to veto the bill if he became convinced of its unconstitutionality. On February 16, 1791, he asked Hamilton for an assessment of the objections of Madison, Jefferson, and Randolph. Hamilton responded with his "Defense of the Constitutionality of an Act to Establish a Bank." The paper artfully refuted the Virginians' claim that the bank would be unconstitutional by emphasizing the necessity of a broad interpretation of the government's economic powers. On February 25, Washington signed the bill chartering the bank.[10]

The First Bank of the United States functioned well for 20 years, but Congress refused to recharter it in 1811 by one vote. Because the bank was the brainchild of Federalist Alexander Hamilton, many members of the Democratic-Republican Party, which dominated U.S. politics in the early nineteenth century, tended to be against renewing its charter. Some party members agreed with Democratic-Republican Party leaders Thomas Jefferson and James Madison that the bank was unconstitutional. This inherent opposition to the bank, combined with the lobbying efforts of commercial banks that competed for business with the national bank, led to its demise.[11]

Development of Presidential Involvement in the Economy

The election of Thomas Jefferson in 1800 ushered in an economic era in the United States that was dominated by agrarian interests. Jefferson and his successors, most notably Andrew Jackson, rejected the Hamiltonian economic approach of concentrating the federal government's activities on the promotion and protection of industry and business.[12] Most economic regulatory activity and responsibility for internal improvements that benefited commerce, such as the construction of roads, bridges, and railroads, were left to the states. Even central banking came to be considered outside the government's proper domain. After refusing to recharter the national bank in 1811, Congress chartered the Second Bank of the United States in 1816 after experiencing difficulties with national finance during the War of 1812. Andrew Jackson, however, vetoed the bill that would have rechartered the second bank of the United States and its charter expired in 1836. The United States went without a central bank until 1914 when the

Federal Reserve System was established.[13]

Nevertheless, the federal government did not entirely abandon business promotion. It maintained tariffs to protect industries from foreign competition, provided systems of money and patents, and in 1817 gave U.S. ships a monopoly on East Coast trade. Yet until the Civil War, the United States remained essentially an agrarian society with the proponents of agrarianism dominating national politics.[14]

The Civil War brought greater industrialization and the political division of northern and southern agrarian interests. The Republican presidents of the second half of the nineteenth century were generally conservative men who favored federal promotion of business affairs, but not federal regulation. These presidents in cooperation with Congress aided manufacturing and commercial interests by raising protective tariffs to new highs, giving land to railroads, and continuing to rely on regressive taxes.[15]

As the American business community grew, however, the need for regulation became more apparent. By the 1880s the power of major corporations had begun to alarm many members of the public. State governments no longer were adequate to control companies that operated in many states and functioned as monopolies. The federal government gradually responded to growing demands for regulation.

In the 1890s Congress passed the Sherman Antitrust Act and other laws which gave the president and the executive branch the power to break up monopolies and otherwise regulate business activity. Presidents Theodore Roosevelt and William Howard Taft sharply increased government prosecutions of antitrust cases and expanded other regulation activities, setting the stage for further economic reforms that would widen presidential authority over the economy.

Establishment of Income Tax

During the eighteenth and nineteenth centuries the federal government had financed its activities through excise taxes, sales of the vast national lands that stretched to the Pacific, and most importantly, tariffs. Tariffs were simple to administer but were not always an adequate source of income. In wartime, when the government required increased revenue, tariff receipts would fall as trade with other countries was disrupted.[16]

During the Civil War, Congress had levied a tax on incomes to help make up the gap between peacetime revenue sources and wartime expenses. The tax expired in 1872, and there was no attempt to revive it until 1894 when Congress levied a 2 percent tax on personal incomes over $3,000. In 1895, however, the Supreme Court declared income tax unconstitutional in *Pollock v. Farmers' Loan & Trust Co.* The Court held that an income tax was an example of a direct tax that violated Section 9, Clause 4 of the Constitution which prohibited direct taxes unless each state paid a share in proportion to its population.

With the support of President Taft this obstacle was overcome on February 23, 1913, when the 16th Amendment was ratified. It stated: "The Congress shall have power to lay and collect taxes on incomes from whatever source derived, without apportionment among the several states, and without regard to any census or enumeration." Although Congress passed a 1 percent income tax in 1913, the power of income tax as a source of revenue was not demonstrated until World War I when an expanded income tax generated the revenues necessary for U.S. participation in the war.

Thereafter income taxes grew in importance. In 1915 custom duties and excise taxes provided eighty-five percent of federal revenues. By 1930 income taxes were providing over half of the funds coming into the treasury, while the share from customs and excises had fallen below thirty percent.[17]

Although the 16th amendment had given Congress the power to levy income taxes, the amendment greatly expanded presidential power by providing a source of revenue that could finance presidential foreign policy and domestic initiatives. As political scientist Emmet J. Hughes noted, the income tax was "ready for lavish use by future Presidents to meet future needs or crises. And without such a reservoir of funds, there hardly could have followed any grand dreams of Presidential programs in the realms of welfare, education, health, housing, and transport."[18] The tax also enhanced the president's ability to make fiscal policy. Increasing and decreasing income taxes would become one of the methods most commonly used by presidents and Congress to combat inflation and recession.

Budget and Accounting Act of 1921

During the eighteenth and nineteenth centuries presidents had no formal responsibility to submit a budget to Congress or even conduct a comprehensive review of executive branch spending proposals. Executive departments and agencies submitted budget requests directly to Congress in a "Book of Estimates." A number of presidents, such as John Quincy Adams, Van Buren, Tyler, Polk, Buchanan, Grant, and Cleveland did insist on revising budget estimates, but the budgeting process continued to be dominated by Congress and individual executive departments and agencies.[19]

During the budget process, there was no means by which Congress could balance expenditures with revenues or evaluate alternative spending programs. As a result, the overlapping or extravagant spending proposals submitted by executive departments and agencies could not be weeded out of the budget. Moreover, the lack of central coordination made the use of the budget as an instrument of fiscal policy impossible.[20]

With the 1921 Budget and Accounting Act, Congress sought to reform the financial machinery of the executive branch. The nation had incurred a series of budget deficits before and during World War I that created a debt problem and led Congress to set up new procedures and organizations to provide more central coordination of the budget process.[21] The 1921 act established two important offices—the Bureau of the Budget (which became the Office of Management and Budget in 1970) and the General Accounting Office. The former was created to centralize fiscal management of the executive branch directly under the president; the latter was designed to strengthen congressional oversight of spending.

The act ended the practice of allowing executive departments and agencies to address their annual budget proposals directly to Congress. The Budget Bureau, originally a subdivision of the Treasury Department, but later placed under the direct control of the president, became a central clearinghouse for all budget requests. The Budget Bureau evaluated these requests, adjusted them to fit the president's goals, and consolidated them into a single executive branch budget for the consideration of Congress.

Consequently, the Budget Act of 1921 transformed budget making from a random and fragmented process over which presidents had little control into a tool through which presidents could advance their social, economic, and defense priorities.

Presidential Economic Stabilization Policy

Every president has been concerned with the U.S. economy, but close presidential supervision of its performance is a relatively recent historical development. Before the Great Depression of the 1930s, Americans generally believed that extensive government intervention in the economy was counterproductive. The human suffering of the depression, however, convinced the American public and its leaders that the government should intervene to relieve and prevent periods of economic trauma. Moreover, by the time World War II ended, a national consensus had developed that the government, and especially the president, should use every means available to produce the best economic conditions possible even if the economy were not depressed. The president had become not just a guardian against economic disaster, but an economic manager whose popularity usually depended on a strong and stable economy.

Post-depression presidents have attempted to create the best economic conditions possible through their *stabilization policies.* The U.S. economy, like all capitalist economies, experiences cyclical patterns of expansion and contraction in which the levels of inflation, unemployment, and economic growth vary. During contractionary periods businesses lose sales, investment decreases, unemployment grows, and prices tend to increase at a slower rate or even fall. During expansionary periods consumers spend more, investment increases, unemployment declines, and prices tend to increase at a faster rate. The objective of stabilization policy is to smooth out the natural swings in the economy so unemployment does not become too severe during contractionary periods and inflation does not get out of control during expansionary periods. Ideally, an administration should achieve these goals while maintaining a steady rate of economic growth and balancing the federal budget, or at least running manageable deficits that can be corrected during periods of prosperity.

The tools presidents use to stabilize the economy are *fiscal policy* and *monetary policy.* Fiscal policy refers to the government's taxing and spending decisions. Presidents make fiscal policy in cooperation with Congress, which passes spending and tax bills. Monetary policy refers to decisions about the supply of money. Although presidents do not have legal control over monetary policy, which is determined by the independent Federal Reserve Board, they do exercise much informal influence over it.

As the history of stabilization policy shows, it has been one of the most frustrating aspects of the president's job. No single economic theory has explained the behavior of the economy or held the key to prosperity for long. As theories have been tested in the laboratory of national economic stabilization policy, their limitations have surfaced. Few national leaders or economists would call themselves pure *Keynesians, monetarists, or supply-siders.* Economists who once stridently espoused a single theory have been forced to add broad qualifications to their insights and incorporate other theories into their economic thought. As a result, presidents have been left without a clear economic orthodoxy.

The New Deal and the Emergence of Keynesian Theory

Before the Great Depression most economists believed that the president could best contribute to the health of the economy by working for a balanced federal budget and not overregulating business activity. Deficit spending by the federal government was regarded as an imprudent and irresponsible practice that eroded business confidence in the monetary system and produced inflation.[22]

This conservative economic orthodoxy handcuffed President Herbert Hoover when the stock market crashed and the depression began to unfold in 1929. All of Hoover's efforts to turn the economy around proved ineffectual, and by 1933 unemployment had reached a staggering 25 percent. Like presidents before him, Hoover believed in the conventional wisdom that public debt could undermine the economic health of the nation just as private debt could undermine a person's financial well-being. He therefore was suspicious of deficit spending programs that would have reduced the severity of the depression. Nevertheless, in his search for an answer to the country's economic troubles Hoover did try a variety of measures, including a tax reduction, intended to put more money into the hands of the public. He quickly gave up on this approach, however, when it appeared not to be working and returned to a conservative strategy of cutting expenditures in an effort to balance the budget.[23] This policy, combined with the Federal Reserve Board's failure to expand the money supply, deepened the depression.[24] In fact, many modern economists believe the depression would have been limited to a severe recession had the president and the Federal Reserve Board not exacerbated the problem.

While campaigning for the presidency in 1932 Franklin D. Roosevelt did not advocate revolutionary fiscal policies. Like Hoover before him, he promised to cut expenditures and balance the budget. Indeed, during the campaign he had attacked Hoover for failing to achieve a balanced budget.

Roosevelt, however, was a pragmatic leader who believed that the government should take emergency measures to fight the depression. Once in office he initiated "New Deal" policies, which created government construction and relief programs that threw the federal budget into deficit. The deficit spending, however, was not a fiscal strategy designed to stimulate the economy but a byproduct of the president's decision to spend the money necessary to reduce the suffering of the poor, the elderly, and the unemployed and to begin putting Americans back to work.[25] Most New Deal initiatives were to be phased out as economic conditions improved, and indeed some were terminated within a few years. Other programs, however, including Social Security and federal credit assistance to home buyers, small businesses, and farmers, became permanent government activities.

While the United States and the world struggled through the depression, the theories of the British economist John Maynard Keynes became widely known. Keynes outlined his theories in *The General Theory of Employment, Interest and Money,* published in 1936. Keynes's thought focused on unemployment. He argued that recessions occurred when industrial, consumer, or government demand for goods and services fell. This caused unsold inventories to mount, industries to scale back their operations, and unemployment to rise.

Keynes posited that the government could counteract a recession by cutting taxes or increasing its expenditures. Lower taxes would put more money into the hands of consumers, thereby stimulating demand for goods and services. Tax cuts given to industry would create new jobs by boosting firms' investment in their productive facilities. Greater government expenditures would create jobs and prime the economy through a "multiplier effect." According to Keynes, each dollar spent by the government could stimulate private economic transactions equaling much more than the original dollar. Keynes's recession remedy of having the government put money into the hands of its citizens contradicted the conservative economic goal of balancing the budget. It nevertheless quickly gained a following among economists.

In May 1937, after the U.S. economy had achieved a partial recovery, a new recession confronted Roosevelt. This recession was caused in part by the Federal Reserve Board, which had again contracted the money supply in its concern to prevent inflation.[26] The president initially ignored the advice of converted Keynesians in his administration and attempted to cut spending in an effort to balance the budget. Roosevelt's strategy deepened the recession and solidified a consensus among his advisers in favor of government spending designed to stimulate demand. By April 1938 the president himself was convinced that greater government expenditures were needed to combat the depression. Roosevelt continued to pay lip service to a balanced budget, but he worked to increase expenditures and accepted growing budget deficits as a necessary evil in a difficult economic period.[27] Unemployment gradually declined from its 1933 high of 25 percent to under 15 percent in 1940.

World War II ultimately brought massive government expenditures financed by borrowing that woke the U.S. economy from the nightmare of the 1930s. The war effort required a total mobilization of the U.S. productive resources, which ended unemployment.[28] In 1944 unemployment stood at just 1.2 percent. Most economists saw the economic results of New Deal and wartime expenditures as a validation of Keynesian theory.

Keynesianism as Orthodox Theory

By Franklin Roosevelt's last term in office Keynesianism had become the dominant economic theory both in policy-making and in academic circles. Some conservative economists and politicians clung to theories about balancing the budget, but even they recognized that Keynes had provided a good explanation of the economic conditions during the depression and World War II.

Following the war, Congress debated the role government should play in the economy given the success of Keynesian policies. Many members of Congress believed that since Keynesian economic theory had provided the federal government with a tool through which it seemingly could hold down the level of joblessness, the government should be obliged to use that tool to promote full employment. In 1945 the Full Employment Bill was introduced into the Senate. It mandated that full employment should be a national goal and the government should run budget deficits when necessary to provide the investment and expenditures required to achieve it.

The bill alarmed many business leaders and economic conservatives, however, who saw the law as a first step toward budget deficits, inflation, and excessive regulation

Table 1 Inflation and Unemployment, 1929-1987 (percent)

Year	Inflation, all items [a]	Unemployment
1929	0.0	3.2
1933	−5.1	24.9
1939	−1.4	17.2
1940	1.0	14.6
1941	5.0	9.9
1942	10.7	4.7
1943	6.1	1.9
1944	1.7	1.2
1945	2.3	1.9
1946	8.5	3.9
1947	14.4	3.9
1948	7.8	3.8
1949	−1.0	5.9
1950	1.0	5.3
1951	7.9	3.3
1952	2.2	3.0
1953	0.8	2.9
1954	0.5	5.5
1955	−0.4	4.4
1956	1.5	4.1
1957	3.6	4.3
1958	2.7	6.8
1959	0.8	5.5
1960	1.6	5.5
1961	1.0	6.7
1962	1.1	5.5
1963	1.2	5.7
1964	1.3	5.2
1965	1.7	4.5
1966	2.9	3.8
1967	2.9	3.8
1968	4.2	3.6
1969	5.4	3.5
1970	5.9	4.9
1971	4.3	5.9
1972	3.3	5.6
1973	6.2	4.9
1974	11.0	5.6
1975	9.1	8.5
1976	5.8	7.7
1977	6.5	7.1
1978	7.7	6.1
1979	11.3	5.8
1980	13.5	7.1
1981	10.4	7.6
1982	6.1	9.7
1983	3.2	9.6
1984	4.3	7.5
1985	3.6	7.2
1986	1.9	7.0
1987	3.7	6.2

Sources: Labor Department, Council of Economic Advisers.

a. Pecentage change in consumer price index year to year.

of the economy. Despite President Harry S Truman's support for the Full Employment Act, the House promoted a more modest version, which eventually was passed by both chambers.[29]

The final version of the act was called the Employment Act of 1946. It stated that the government should work for "maximum employment, production and purchasing power," rather than "full" employment, and references to budget deficits as the tool that would be used to achieve high employment were deleted. A statement also was added that measures taken to implement the act must be consistent with the free enterprise system. Economist Herbert Stein wrote of the revision of the bill:

> Given the experience of the 1930s, it was inconceivable that the government would fail to commit itself to maintaining high employment.... But the form that commitment took in the United States, as embodied in the Employment Act of 1946, could hardly have been more satisfactory to conservatives. That is, after a major national discussion the Congress rejected an overly ambitious, inflationary definition of the goal, rejected exclusive reliance on deficit financing as the means, and reaffirmed its devotion to the free enterprise system.[30]

Although the original Full Employment Act had been watered down, the Employment Act of 1946 nevertheless demonstrated the new national consensus that government leaders should deeply involve themselves in the management of the economy. Beyond stating the government's responsibility to work for low unemployment, the act reinforced the president's role as the public official primarily responsible for managing the economy. Although the legislation did not provide presidents with new economic powers, it did require them to report annually to Congress on the state of the economy, and created the Council of Economic Advisers, which gave presidents an economic advisory body answerable only to them.[31] These measures encouraged Congress, the business community, and the American public to continue to look to presidents for economic leadership as they had done during the depression.

Despite the demise of the original Full Employment Bill, Keynesian theory continued to gain adherents. The strong postwar economy convinced people that the structure of the economy was sound and major economic reforms were unnecessary to prevent a return to depression. What was needed was steering between the problems of inflation and unemployment. Keynesian theory implicitly held that there was an inverse relationship between inflation and unemployment. Presidents could expect higher inflation when they attempted to reduce unemployment by stimulating demand through spending increases or tax cuts. Conversely, tax increases and budget cuts would reduce demand, bringing price stability at the cost of greater unemployment. Until the 1970s this trade-off between inflation and unemployment governed presidential stabilization policy. Presidents and their economic advisers generally believed that if inflation or unemployment became severe, they could use Keynesian fiscal policies to reestablish a balance.

Truman Administration

When Harry Truman succeeded to the presidency following Franklin Roosevelt's death in April 1945, the U.S. economy was booming. Federal expenditures had grown from just $8.8 billion in 1939 to $92.7 billion in 1945, and unemployment was virtually nonexistent. Many Americans feared that the economic sluggishness of the 1930s would return when the war ended, but the years following the war saw continued expansion and a relatively smooth transition from a wartime to a peacetime footing. Many women and elderly workers who had entered the work force during the war because labor was in short supply retired when the war ended, thus making room in the work force for returning soldiers. The influx of GIs also created greater demand for housing and consumer goods that partially offset the decrease in demand caused by reduced government spending for defense.

Inflation was a more serious problem. Although Truman had enthusiastically supported the original version of the Employment Act, which mandated measures to achieve full employment, as president he followed a pragmatic course that often made fighting inflation the highest economic priority. After the war, inflation was fueled by consumers who demanded goods that had been in short supply during the conflict. Moreover, wartime controls had held the prices of many goods below their true value. As these price controls were lifted in 1946 and 1947, prices inevitably rose dramatically to correct the artificial imbalance. Inflation, which had been just 2.3 percent in 1945, rose to 8.5 percent in 1946 and 14.4 percent in 1947. Truman, who had vetoed one price control removal bill but reluctantly signed a second in July 1946, urged labor groups to resist price and wage hikes and sent an anti-inflation program to Congress in October 1947 that included consumer credit controls, rent controls, price ceilings on selected products and controls over the allocation of some scarce commodities. The Republican Congress put off most of the program until the following year and then enacted only a part of it.[32] Inflation, however, peaked in 1947, falling to 7.8 percent in 1948 and then disappearing entirely in 1949 while the economy endured a recession.

In 1947 and 1948 Congress tried to force a tax cut on the president, which, it maintained, would reverse the tax and spend policies of Truman and of Roosevelt before him. Truman vetoed three such bills on the grounds that they would lead to budget deficits and greater inflation. Congress, however, overrode the last of Truman's vetoes in April 1948. The tax cut was timely, since the economy fell into a mild recession later in the year. The extra money in the hands of consumers stimulated demand, thereby reducing the recession's severity.

The Korean War, which began on June 24, 1950, when North Korea invaded South Korea, rekindled inflationary pressures that had eased after the post-World War II price acceleration. Growing military expenditures on the war effort stimulated industrial demand. Demand for consumer goods also increased as consumers bought many items in anticipation of wartime shortages. In 1951 inflation shot back up to 7.8 percent. Congress reluctantly granted part of Truman's tax increase request and agreed to wage, price, and credit controls, which succeeded in holding inflation below 1 percent during 1952 and 1953.

Eisenhower Administration

In spite of the prominence of Keynesian thought among economists, President Dwight D. Eisenhower entered office skeptical of its utility. He emphasized the traditional conservative economic priorities of balancing the federal budget, limiting government interference in the economy, and, most important, fighting inflation.[33] During Eisenhower's eight years in office, he produced three budget surpluses—a significant achievement given that since 1961 only the 1969 budget has been in surplus.

Throughout his presidency, Eisenhower was willing to accept higher rates of unemployment than his Keynesian critics thought necessary. In response to a recession in 1953 and early 1954, the administration did accept some minor tax increases and sped up government expenditures. Although the administration took credit for helping the recovery with "speedy and massive actions," the modest antirecession measures of 1954 were an exception to Eisenhower's rule of nonintervention.[34]

During his second term Eisenhower pursued an anti-inflationary strategy in defiance not only of his critics but also of several of his own advisers who urged him to support a tax cut. Unemployment averaged a post-depression high of 6.8 percent during the 1958 recession, but Eisenhower remained true to his noninterventionist principles. Moreover, he vetoed a number of spending bills during his last two years in office in pursuit of a balanced budget and low inflation.[35] As a result unemployment averaged 5.5 percent in 1959 and 1960 when it could have been significantly lower.

When signs of a recession appeared in the spring of 1960, Eisenhower's vice president, Richard Nixon, who was running for president that year, advocated following CEA chairman Arthur Burns's advice to increase defense expenditures and loosen credit. Eisenhower, however, sided with other administration economic advisers who rejected the proposal because they did not believe the recession, if there was one, would be of sufficient magnitude to warrant government intervention.[36] Nixon undoubtedly lost votes because of the economic slump.

Although Eisenhower's stiff resistance to antirecession measures appears old-fashioned by today's standards, he was successful in holding down consumer prices, which never climbed more than 4 percent in any year of his presidency.

Kennedy Administration

With the election of John F. Kennedy to the presidency in 1960, Democrats believed they could change the economic goals of the nation. During the Eisenhower years price stability and balanced budgets had been the highest economic priorities. In contrast, Kennedy and his advisers were determined to achieve full employment and sustained economic expansion through fiscal stimulation. They hoped to be able not just to correct the swings of the business cycle but to stimulate the economy to greater growth and productivity. They were motivated by their desire to alleviate poverty and to improve medical care, education, and other social services and by their concern over the apparent rapid growth of the Soviet economy and its military expenditures.

Kennedy also came into office with a more aggressive attitude toward the president's role in ensuring the nation's prosperity than his predecessor. Whereas Eisenhower believed that the U.S. economy would perform best if it were left alone and was willing to accept a significant degree of unemployment, Kennedy believed the economy never would create jobs for everyone without government stimulation. He and his advisers were confident they could direct the economy to greater prosperity. For the first time the Keynesian views of professional economists were fully applied to the political situation.[37]

In the opening months of Kennedy's term, the economy was pulling itself out of the recession that had begun in 1960. Since the budget was in deficit and inflation was a concern, Kennedy hoped that he would not have to use fiscal stimulation to achieve his employment and expansion goals. By early 1962, however, the economy had begun to slow. Kennedy agreed with his advisers that the economy should be stimulated through increased government spending. They believed such a policy would help low-income people and be less controversial than a tax cut at a time when budget deficits persisted. Congress, however, resisted Kennedy's spending plans. Kennedy responded in late 1962 by proposing a tax cut.

The president and his economic advisers attempted to sell the tax cut by promoting the concept of the "full employment budget." The administration argued that although the government was currently running budget deficits, the greater tax revenues produced by an economy operating at full employment would result in budget surpluses. Therefore, if a tax cut could produce full employment and sustained economic expansion, it would increase government revenues rather than decrease them.[38] Kennedy lobbied Congress to pass the tax cut during 1963, but before he could persuade lawmakers to pass it, he was assassinated in November.

Johnson Administration

Following Kennedy's death, President Lyndon B. Johnson delivered an emotional speech to Congress on November 27, 1963. He asked lawmakers to honor Kennedy by passing his civil rights bill and asserted: "No act of ours could more fittingly continue the work of President Kennedy than the early passage of the tax bill for which he fought all this long year." Johnson used his legendary lobbying skills and Congress's feelings for the slain president to push the tax cut through Congress quickly. Johnson signed the Revenue Act of 1964 on February 26. It was the largest tax cut in U.S. history up to that time. The act reduced personal income taxes for 1964 and 1965 by about 20 percent and corporate taxes by 4 percent.[39]

The 1964 tax cut was a milestone in the history of U.S. stabilization policy. It was the first time the president and Congress had intentionally stimulated the economy through a tax cut while the economy was expanding. Unemployment fell from 5.7 percent in 1963 to 4.5 percent in 1965. Despite the reduction in tax rates, revenue rose beyond what inflation and normal economic growth would have been expected to produce had the tax cut not been enacted.[40] The impressive results of the tax cut generated enthusiasm and confidence among President Johnson's economic advisers. They believed they could "fine tune" the economy through Keynesian stabilization policies.

The Vietnam War, however, forced Johnson to reconsider his economic priorities. By 1966 expenditures on the war and "Great Society" social programs had caused a growing budget deficit and rising inflation. Johnson's advisers urged him to correct the overstimulation of the economy caused by the deficit spending through an excise tax or increase in income taxes. Congress, however, showed no enthusiasm for a tax hike, and Johnson feared that higher taxes would erode public support for the Vietnam War.[41] Consequently, Johnson did not push for an income tax increase, and the task of fighting inflation was left to the Federal Reserve Board's monetary policy.

The following year, however, Johnson recognized that he had to slow inflation and reduce the deficit. He pro-

UPI/Bettmann Newsphotos

On January 26, 1964, President Lyndon Johnson signs the Revenue Act of 1964 in the presence of congressional leaders. To that point, it was the largest tax cut in history.

posed new taxes, but Congress did not react to Johnson's 1967 tax hike proposal until the summer of 1968. In that year inflation had risen to 4.2 percent from just 1.7 percent in 1965, and the deficit had expanded to $25.2 billion from only $1.6 billion in 1965. This deficit disappeared in 1969, when Johnson's 10 percent tax increase and Johnson's successor's efforts to cut government spending led to the first budget surplus since 1960. This belated fiscal restraint failed, however, to eliminate the long-term inflationary pressures that had been built into the economy or the rising unemployment that was left for Johnson's successor, Richard Nixon, to combat.

Retreat from Keynesianism and the Emergence of Monetarism

Walter Heller, who served as chairman of the Council of Economic Advisers under Kennedy, declared in 1967 that "Economics has come of age in the 1960s."[42] Heller and many of his colleagues believed that the combination of Keynesian economic theory, computer technology, and enlightened leaders had made it possible for the government successfully to promote prosperity through stabilization policy. The economic conditions of the the mid-1960s with its low unemployment and inflation demonstrated that Heller's optimism was not unfounded.[43] Yet his remark contrasts sharply with the loss of confidence by economists during the 1970s that the economy could be fine tuned.

The main problem with applying Keynesian theory to the management of the economy was that the political process made the Keynesian solution to inflation—cutting spending and raising taxes—difficult to enact. Politicians were predictably unwilling to adopt measures to control inflation because high taxes and cuts in government programs were unpopular with their constituents. Even if an administration were willing to propose a tax increase to combat inflation, it would seldom be able to persuade Congress to risk a recession, especially in election years.[44] Keynesian theory, therefore, offered presidents a politically practicable response only to recession. Some other means had to be found to control inflation.

The theory to which many national leaders turned was *monetarism.* The monetarists, led by economist Milton Friedman, argue that inflation occurs when the money supply is allowed to grow faster than the economy, because a greater number of dollars is available to chase the goods and services produced. The best way to control inflation, the monetarists believe, is to reduce the amount of money in circulation.

Economists had acknowledged since the late 1950s that monetary policy had a role in stablizing the economy. The political problems involved in reducing inflation through fiscal policy during the late 1960s, however, gave monetarism a new attractiveness. The appointees of the Federal Reserve Board who were responsible for regulating the money supply could cool down the economy without having to worry, as members of Congress and the president did, that their actions would cost them the next election. The solution to inflation would, therefore, be removed from the political atmosphere that made the Keynesian response unusable. When inflation was under control, the Federal Reserve Board carefully could relax its tight monetary policy to allow for greater economic growth.

The inflation dilemma became particularly acute in the 1970s when rising prices seemed beyond the control of presidents and Congress. Not only did national leaders find it difficult to muster the political will to fight inflation, when they did cut government spending and raise taxes, inflation did not fall as expected. The inverse relationship between inflation and unemployment (increases in one had been accompanied by decreases in the other) implicit in Keynesian policies appeared to have disintegrated. Policy makers could no longer be confident that tolerance for a period of higher unemployment would result in lower inflation. Nor could acceptance of higher inflation be relied upon to bring decreased unemloyment. The prevailing conditions of high inflation and unemployment, which came to be known as *stagflation*, defied Keynesian logic and caused presidents to lean heavily on monetary policy.

Nixon Administration

Richard Nixon entered office intending to fight inflation through small spending cuts coordinated with a tight monetary policy. He hoped his incremental stategy would reduce inflation while holding unemployment near 4 percent.[45] Nixon submitted a budget to Congress for fiscal 1970 that would have yielded a small budget surplus. Congress did trim some spending but refused to go along with Nixon's cuts, many of which targeted social programs. The relationship between Nixon and the Democratic Congress became increasingly confrontational as the president vetoed a number of appropriations bills and resorted to impounding appropriated funds.[46] *(See "Impoundment Powers," p. 423, in Chief Executive chapter of Part III.)*

Despite Nixon's budget cutting efforts and the Federal Reserve Board's tight monetary policy, inflation continued to rise. By 1970 inflation had reached 6 percent. Moreover, the increase in inflation was not accompanied by a corresponding decrease in unemployment, which had risen from 3.6 percent in 1968 to 4.9 percent in 1970. The worsening unemployment situation was exacerbated by the deescalation of the Vietnam War, which brought hundreds of thousands of troops back into the civilian work force.

Congress responded to the bleak economic conditions by passing the Economic Stabilization Act of 1970. Under this act, Congress gave the president the authority to combat inflation through wage and price controls. Nixon signed the act but renounced the use of such controls, saying on June 17, 1970: "I will not take this nation down the road of wage and price controls, however politically expedient they may seem." Nixon objected to wage and price controls because he believed they were an incursion on the rights of Americans and would only postpone a burst of inflation.

In 1971, with his reelection bid less than two years away, Nixon was unwilling to fight inflation by allowing a recession as Eisenhower might have done. Early that year he had abandoned his attempts to achieve a balanced budget and had initiated stimulative fiscal policies to combat rising unemployment that averaged 5.9 percent for the year. Nixon, like John Kennedy, justified deficit spending by arguing that the budget would be balanced if the economy were operating at full employment and output. Nixon admitted to an interviewer in January 1971, "I am now a Keynesian in economics."[47]

Inflation, however, was the more troubling economic problem. The president received pressure from Congress, the public, and even prominent leaders of his party to take dramatic action against inflation. On August 15, 1971, President Nixon announced that, owing to the economic crisis, he was using the authority granted to him by Congress to impose a wage and price control policy.

His "New Economic Policy" had several phases. Phase I froze wages, prices, and rents for ninety days. Phase II created a pay board and price commission that acted to limit inflation to 3 percent and wage increases to 5.5 percent per year. In January 1973 Phase III relaxed the controls, and in July of that year Phase IV replaced controls with commitments from businesses to limit price increases for a year. In April 1974 all wage and price control activity ended when Congress refused to extend President Nixon's wage and price control authority.[48]

Initially the controls were successful and popular. Consumer prices rose 4.3 percent in 1971 but just 3.3 percent in 1972. Unemployment fell from 5.9 percent in 1971 to 5.6 percent in 1972 and 4.9 percent in 1973. The brightening economic picture helped Nixon easily win a second term as president in the November 1972 elections.

As Nixon had feared, however, the problems with wage and price controls began to surface during his second term. Shortages of some goods occurred when many manufacturers began exporting a greater share of their products overseas where prices were higher. In addition, the numerous exemptions from the controls program that had been granted to various industries caused economic distortions. For example, grain prices had been exempted from controls while meat prices remained fixed. Consequently, high feed costs forced many meat producers to slaughter their stock causing immediate meat shortages and meat price increases later in the decade.

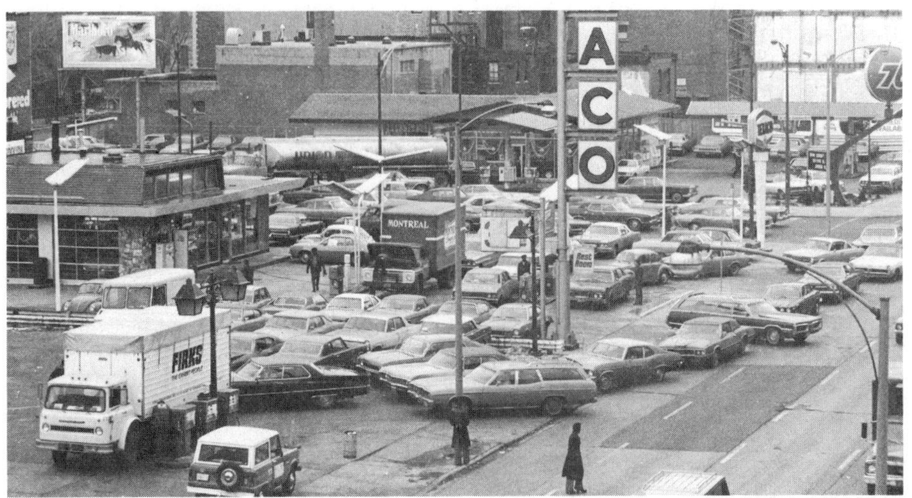

UPI/Bettmann Newsphotos

In January 1974, cars line up at gas stations, causing traffic jams in Chicago, left, and across the country. In October 1973, the Arab oil-producing states had imposed an embargo on the United States for its support of Israel during the Yom Kippur War.

More important, the wage and price controls proved to be only a temporary remedy for inflation. In 1972 the growing number of exemptions weakened the controls, and the consumer price index began rising again in the second half of the year. Then in October 1973 the economy received a severe shock when the Arab oil-producing states imposed an embargo on the United States for its support of Israel during the Yom Kippur War of 1973. The price of a barrel of oil rose from under $3 in early 1973 to between $10 and $14 in 1974. Rising oil prices, a poor 1973 harvest, and the phasing out of price controls begun in 1973 and completed in 1974 led to a dramatic jump in inflation. Prices increased 6.2 percent in 1973 and a painful 11.0 percent in 1974. That year the Nixon administration attempted to fight inflation with more restrictive fiscal and monetary policies, but the Watergate scandal made any cooperation with Congress difficult. On August 9, Nixon resigned to avoid impeachment for his part in the Watergate affair.

Ford Administration

Like Richard Nixon, Gerald Ford assumed the presidency intending to fight inflation through a policy of moderate fiscal restraint supported by a tight monetary policy. The inflationary effects of the 1973 Arab oil embargo and the removal of the wage and price freeze remained strong after Ford took office. He asked Congress for a 5 percent tax surcharge on corporations and the upperclass and for selected spending cuts and deferrals.

A minor part of Ford's economic program, however, received the most attention. He encouraged Americans to fight inflation voluntarily by saving more, conserving energy, increasing charitable contributions, and resisting price and wage increases. The voluntary measures were to be symbolized by "WIN" buttons, which stood for "Whip Inflation Now." The buttons were ridiculed as a symbol of the ineffectuality of the administration's policies.[49]

Ford, however, was forced to abandon his anti-inflationary strategy in early 1975. Statistics showed that the economy had fallen into a deep recession in 1974 before he took office, partly as a result of the sharp rise in oil prices, which forced businesses to cut back their operations. Unemployment reached 9 percent late in the year.

He responded in January by asking Congress for a $16 billion tax cut and new investment tax credits for business to stimulate the economy. Congress and the president compromised with a $23 billion tax cut bill that favored the lower class. The tax cut, however, was enacted in March 1975 when the recession began to ease. Consequently, by the time the benefits of the cut reached Americans the economy was already growing.[50]

Despite the persistently high rates of inflation, many Democrats in Congress pressed the president to make low unemployment the nation's first economic priority. During the rest of 1975 and early 1976 Ford battled Congress over economic policy, repeatedly vetoing spending measures he considered inflationary. Nevertheless, Ford compromised on several appropriations bills, which, coupled with large unemployment compensation and welfare payments caused by the recession, increased federal deficits to new highs of $53 billion in 1975 and $74 billion in 1976.

In early 1976 inflation leveled off, and the economy appeared to be improving just in time for Ford's reelection bid. Inflation had fallen from 11 percent in 1974 to 9 percent in 1975 and just 5.8 percent in 1976. Meanwhile, unemployment averaged 7.7 percent in 1976, which was an encouraging improvement after 8.5 percent in 1975. The country, however, voted for Jimmy Carter to replace Ford in the White House, as the incumbent could not overcome the recent tough economic times and the legacy of Richard Nixon.

Carter Administration

Jimmy Carter took over an economy that had improved slightly during the last year of the Ford administration. The Federal Reserve Board's tight monetary policies had brought down inflation to 5.8 percent for 1976, and Carter entered office intending to work on lowering unemployment.

Despite this slight economic improvement, Carter was taking over the economy in an era that would be dominated by forces outside his control. During the late 1960s and 1970s, several factors had combined to produce an increasingly difficult economic environment where astute stabilization policy could not necessarily be relied upon to produce prosperity. The inflationary pressures built up during the Vietnam War had not yet dissipated. In addition, OPEC engineered the second major oil price hike of the decade in 1979. Oil prices increased from under $15 a barrel in 1979 to almost $40 a barrel in 1981. Also, the growth of regulation during the 1970s in areas such as environmental protection, job safety, and consumer protection increased the cost of producing goods and contributed to inflation. Simultaneous with these inflationary pressures the economy was also experiencing a continued decline in productivity relative to foreign competitors that had begun in the 1960s. Finally, the maturation of federal benefit programs had decreased the controllable portion of the budget that could be cut from year to year, nearly ensuring budget deficits in the absence of a tax increase or substantial spending cuts.[51] Although Carter was not responsible for the underlying economic conditions he faced as president, his policies did little to help the situation.

Carter entered office hoping to focus his economic policy on reducing unemployment. He proposed a stimulative program that included a $50 tax rebate. Carter withdrew the rebate proposal when economic statistics showed that unexpectedly strong economic growth threatened to spark a renewed surge of inflation, but much of the rest of his plan, including increased spending for jobs programs and public works, was enacted. Until late 1979, Carter gave priority to reducing unemployment. From 1977 to 1979 he encouraged a stimulative monetary policy that brought the biggest expansion of the money supply of any three-year period since World War II.[52] As a result, the economy continued the expansion that had begun in late 1975.

During this period, however, the public became increasingly concerned about inflation. Consumer prices had risen 7.7 percent in 1978, up from 5.8 percent in 1976. The OPEC price hike of 1979 triggered a jump in inflation, which rose 11.5 percent for the year. Carter recognized that inflation had become the nation's foremost economic problem.

One of Carter's most fateful economic decisions was the appointment of Paul Volcker as chairman of the Federal Reserve Board in 1979 after William Miller had resigned. On October 6, 1979, Volcker indicated that he would use monetary policy vigorously to fight inflation. Although in the long run, Volcker's contractions of the money supply were effective in bringing down inflation, the consumer price index did not respond to the tight monetary policy in 1979 and 1980. Consequently, interest rates soared without an accompanying drop in inflation. In 1979, prices increased 13.5 percent, real per capita income declined 0.7 percent, and the prime lending rate of banks stood at a whopping 15.25 percent. Carter complemented Volcker's tough stand with fiscal restraint designed to combat inflation and lower the budget deficit. Just as the demands of economic management had induced a conservative Richard Nixon to adopt the very liberal tool of wage and price controls, Carter had abandoned his liberal goal of achieving low levels of unemployment and had adopted the traditionally conservative strategy of fighting inflation with monetary and fiscal policy while pursuing a balanced budget.[53]

For the first time since presidents began submitting an annual economic report thirty years before, Carter's 1980 report forecasted a recession. In the second quarter of that year the recession came as predicted, while double-digit inflation remained. During that year, Republican presidential nominee Ronald Reagan attacked Carter for producing a "misery index" (the combined total of the inflation and unemployment rates) over 20. In August 1980 a CBS News/*New York Times* poll found that only 19 percent of those polled approved of Carter's "handling of the economy." [54] With the public convinced of the president's inability to manage economic affairs, Reagan defeated Carter in a landslide.

Supply-Side Theory

During the late 1970s, a theory outside mainstream economics began to gain influential supporters. *Supply-side economic theory* was based on the premise that economic growth and low unemployment could best be achieved by promoting investment and productivity. Supply-side theorists advocated using tax policy to encourage individuals and businesses to invest more and be more productive. The supply-siders asserted that income tax rates affect people's choice between work and leisure and between saving and consumption. The more individuals are taxed, the less incentive they have to work and save. Similarly, the more businesses are taxed, the less money they have to invest in new plants and equipment that would raise their productivity.

By cutting taxes the theorists believed the government could increase personal and corporate productivity and investment thereby increasing the amount of goods and services produced. Thus, whereas Keynesian economic strategists sought to promote economic growth by stimulating demand for goods and services, a strategy that often led to inflation, supply-siders focused on increasing the supply of goods and services. Since supply-siders claimed to be able to stimulate the economy without increasing inflation, their theory seemed to provide a promising solution to the economic condition that plagued the 1970s—simultaneous high inflation and unemployment.

Supply-side theory was also attractive because many of its advocates asserted that tax cuts would not create larger budget deficits. They predicted that the expansion of the economy brought on by a supply-side strategy would generate enough revenue to decrease deficits even though tax rates were lower. This principle was illustrated by the Laffer Curve, developed by Arthur B. Laffer of the University of Southern California. Laffer posited that government revenues rise as tax rates rise until they reach a point at which the increases in revenue brought by higher rates are less than the loss of revenue caused by the public's reduced incentive to work. Laffer and his adherents challenged the assumptions of most professional economists by arguing that the tax rates in force under the Carter administration were above this optimal level. Therefore, they believed tax revenues could be increased not by raising rates, which would intensify the disincentives to produce, but by lowering the rates so that they would be closer to the optimal rate of taxation.[55]

Ironically, in 1963 President Kennedy also had argued that his proposed tax cut would ultimately result in greater revenue. Kennedy's reasoning was based on Keynesian theory rather than supply-side theory, and his tax cut occurred when economic conditions were very different from the late 1970s, but some supply-siders pointed to the increase in tax revenue following Kennedy's tax cut as evidence of the validity of the Laffer Curve.[56]

Although few professional economists supported a supply-side approach to the economic problems of the late 1970s, the theory was adopted by several members of Congress. Its most visible proponent in government was Rep. Jack F. Kemp (R-N.Y.), who with the cooperation of Sen. William V. Roth, Jr., (R-Del.), had constructed an income tax reduction plan in 1977 based on supply-side theory. With the nomination in 1980 of Ronald Reagan as the Republican presidential candidate, however, supply-side theory was thrust into the political limelight. Reagan had become a believer in supply-side economic theory, including Laffer's controversial assertions about deficit reduction, during the late 1970s as he prepared to run for the Republican presidential nomination. Reagan had been defeated for the nomination in 1976 by incumbent Gerald Ford in part because he had advocated an austere policy of budget cuts with tax relief being conditioned on the success of deficit reduction.[57] Supply-side theory gave Reagan a justification for moving away from painful economic prescriptions without abandoning his conservative philosophies about balancing the budget.

Reagan campaigned on his plan to cut taxes while balancing the budget through domestic budget cuts and increases in revenue, which he hoped would be produced by the tax cut. Reagan's plan held out the promise of achieving general prosperity without increased budget deficits and inflation. During Reagan's campaign for the nomination his Republican opponent and eventual vice president, George Bush, reflected the skepticism of many economists and politicians when he labeled Reagan's supply-side strategy "voodoo economics." The American public, however, elected Reagan in a landslide over incumbent Jimmy Carter, setting the stage for a test of supply-side theory.

Reagan Tax Cut

Ronald Reagan's first economic policy priority was passing the largest spending and tax cuts in U.S. history. His landslide victory enabled him to claim a mandate for his plan to cut personal income taxes by 30 percent, introduce new tax incentives for businesses, and sharply cut nondefense expenditures. Opponents of Reagan's strategy warned that it could be inflationary if the public did not save an adequate percentage of their tax savings.

Some Democrats in Congress also attacked the plan as a disguised attempt to lighten the tax burden of the wealthy while cutting back on government aid to the poor, another feature of Reagan's economic program. Reagan and his advisers admitted that their tax cut was structured to benefit upper-income individuals most but argued that these were precisely the people who would be best able to invest their tax break, thus fueling the economic expansion for everyone. Reagan's critics called this reasoning a return to a predepression, Republican, "trickle down" strategy in which benefits for the rich were justified on the grounds that the poor eventually would benefit from a stronger economy.

Although many Americans perceived Reagan's taxing and spending strategy as inequitable, a strong majority of Americans supported it, and his congressional allies were able to push most of the plan through Congress despite the solid Democratic majority in the House. The president signed the Economic Recovery Tax Act of 1981 in August. It reduced individual tax rates 25 percent—5 percent less than Reagan had wanted—over thirty-three months. In addition, the bill indexed the tax system for the first time ever to keep inflation from forcing taxpayers into higher brackets as their incomes kept pace with prices. Reagan was also successful in pushing $35 billion in 1982 nondefense spending cuts through Congress.

Budget Dilemma

Reagan had hoped that his tax cut would create an economic boom that would bring increases in tax revenues. These increased revenues along with reduced domestic spending would reduce the federal budget deficit until the budget was balanced. In 1980, while running for the presidency, Reagan had attacked Carter and the Democratic-controlled Congress for their deficit spending and promised to balance the budget by 1983.[58] By late 1981, however, economic statistics showed that the country was entering a recession. This recession, the deepest since the depression, lasted through 1982. It widened the budget deficit because tax revenues were depressed by declining industrial output and personal income, while government spending on unemployment insurance and welfare increased.

In addition, after the initial wave of spending cuts, Reagan's budget cutting lost momentum as the administration and Congress refused to make major concessions to the priorities of the other. In November 1981, after less than a year in office, Reagan conceded that he probably could not balance the budget in one term. In 1982, despite his position against taxes, Reagan agreed to a tax increase that reduced the 1981 tax cut by about a quarter, with most of the restored revenue coming out of corporate tax reductions.[59]

When the economy recovered from the recession in 1983, the budget deficit, contrary to the administration's predictions, continued to grow. In 1983 the deficit reached $195 billion. Against the recommendation of several advisers, including CEA chairman Martin Feldstein and budget director David Stockman, Reagan refused to consider a further tax increase as a remedy to the deficit. He maintained that higher taxes would threaten economic growth and would not substantially reduce the budget deficit because Congress would find a way to spend most of the additional revenue.[60] Reagan's firm stand against raising taxes was popular with the public, but it ignored the growing deficit problem.

In addition, the president fought against cuts in defense spending. Reagan had charged that Carter had allowed the nation's defenses to deteriorate while the Soviet Union continued to pursue a massive military buildup. According to Reagan, the growing Soviet advantage in military capability threatened the security of the United States and its allies. During the early 1980s public support for a military buildup and tensions between the United States and the Soviet Union led Congress to accept many of Reagan's defense spending proposals. Military expenditures rose from 5.0 percent of GNP in 1980 to 6.2 percent in 1987.

However necessary increased defense spending was to U.S. national security, the president and Congress were unable to spend more on defense without deepening the deficit problem. They did not have the political will to cut Social Security and other popular entitlements to offset the increase in defense spending; nor had Reagan's supply-side tax cutting strategy proven to be a realistic cure for the growth of the federal deficit.

Economic Recovery

The recovery of 1983 became a sustained period of economic growth accompanied by low inflation that lasted through Reagan's second term, with unemployment falling below 6 percent in 1988. Reagan proudly pointed to the growth as a vindication of his policies. Many economists, however, believed that Reagan took too much credit for the expansion. The collapse of the oil cartel of the Organization of Petroleum Exporting Countries (OPEC) in the early 1980s produced falling oil prices that helped reduce inflation and spur economic growth; the restrictive monetary policies of Federal Reserve Board chairman Paul Volcker, a Carter appointee, had wrung inflation out of the economy by 1982, setting up a period when the president could concentrate on stimulating the economy with little worry that significant inflation would return; the Reagan administration's tolerance of a high dollar had contributed to the development of a large trade deficit, which exceeded $100 billion by 1984; and the Reagan administration's unprecedented tax cut pumped money into the American economy and created jobs—but at the expense of creating an intractable debt problem. Ironically, Ronald Reagan, who had repudiated Keynesian economics had presided over a period in which prosperity was achieved in part through peacetime deficit spending by the government, the classic Keynesian prescription for combating a recession.[61]

Unprecedented budget deficits loomed over the otherwise prosperous economic conditions of the mid-1980s. The budget deficit widened sharply from $79 billion in 1981 to $221 billion in 1986. Annual payments to finance the national debt had risen from $69 billion to $136 billion during the same period.

By 1985 the enormous budget deficit led legislators to pass the Gramm-Rudman-Hollings Deficit Reduction Act with the support of President Reagan. *(See "Presidents and the Budget," p. 652, in this chapter.)* It was intended to force spending cuts aimed at balancing the budget by 1991. Despite cuts in defense spending and other deficit reduction measures, however, the budget deficit was still $150 billion in 1987. Over the course of the Reagan administration the national debt had nearly tripled from $914.3 billion in 1980 to a projected $2.825 trillion in 1989. Cutting the deficit was widely regarded as the most pressing and difficult problem facing the incoming administration of George Bush.

Fiscal Policy

Fiscal policy is the body of spending and taxing decisions made by the government in pursuit of economic stabilization. The government can choose to combat unemployment and stagnant economic growth by stimulating the economy through tax cuts or increased spending. It can choose to fight inflation by contracting the economy through tax increases or reduced spending. Although Congress must pass legislation approving every taxation and spending decision, presidents and their advisers initiate most fiscal policy proposals and greatly influence congressional deliberations. Congress, however, rarely has rubber-stamped presidential fiscal policies. Consequently, any president hoping to exercise control over fiscal policy must persuade Congress to accept the substance of the executive branch initiatives.

The Politics of Fiscal Policy

Fiscal policy is not made by a group of economists in Washington who gather information, weigh all their options, consider the long-term and short-term needs of the country, and decide on a policy they believe will produce the best economic outcome. Rather, it is produced through an unwieldy political process of negotiation and compromise between the legislative and executive branches.

When presidents formulate economic policy, they must consider not only what is theoretically optimal but also what is politically feasible. A president's fiscal policies depend as much on the chief executive's ability to present them to the American people and bargain with Congress as on the ability of the president's economic team to understand the economic situation and formulate effective fiscal responses. The most insightful fiscal strategies are meaningless if they are objectionable to major interest groups or if a president is unable to sell them to Congress. In addition, presidents must consider the effects of their fiscal policies on their own reelection chances and the fate of their party at the polls.

Election Cycle

The performance of the economy during a president's term affects the incumbent's chances for reelection as much as any other issue. In times of peace many Americans will "vote their pocket books," by basing their vote on whether the American economy has given them the opportunity to meet their own economic expectations. Moreover, an economy that improves during the year before an election can erase voters' memories of a longer period of economic stagnation or inflation.

Even second-term or newly elected presidents who are not immediately concerned with their own reelection chances understand that economic conditions will affect the outcome of midterm elections, which will determine the strength of their party in Congress. Since the entire House and one-third of the Senate face an election every other year, significant turnover in congressional membership is possible. If an administration loses too many congressional allies its programs may be threatened, and the president's reelection chances in two years may be weakened. Fiscal policy, therefore, is never completely free from the influence of electoral politics and in an election year may be dominated by it.

The connection between economic conditions and the political success of presidents is a powerful incentive for an incumbent administration to try to create short-term improvements in the economy before an election. Economist Edward R. Tufte has identified several economic trends that correspond to the U.S. election cycle. His studies of the economy from 1948 to 1976 have shown that the unemployment rate on presidential election days tends to be significantly lower than twelve to eighteen months before and after an election.[62]

The elections that occurred during Eisenhower's presidency are notable exceptions to this trend. Eisenhower believed that Americans were more concerned with achieving a balanced budget and low inflation than low unemployment and economic growth. He therefore opposed short-term stimulations of the economy for political purposes. The Republican losses in Congress in 1954 and 1958 and John Kennedy's victory over Richard Nixon in 1960, all of which occurred during economic slumps, provide evidence that Eisenhower may have been wrong.[63] After his 1960 defeat, Nixon wrote:

> The bottom of the 1960 dip did come in October and the economy started to move up in November—after it was too late to affect the election returns. In October, usually a month of rising employment, the jobless roles increased by 452,000. All the speeches, television broadcasts, and precinct work in the world could not counteract that one hard fact.[64]

Tufte also found that increases in Social Security payments—the most direct way to put more money into the hands of voters—usually were enacted with the president's approval in even-numbered years during the ten months preceding an election. Since increases in payroll taxes required to pay for the higher Social Security payments start at the beginning of a year for administrative reasons, the price of Social Security increases was not felt by taxpayers until after the election.[65] In 1975, however, Social Security benefits were indexed so recipients receive annual cost-of-living increases to offset inflation, thereby weakening the justification for politically motivated benefit increases.

In addition to stimulative fiscal policies and increased transfer payments, other presidential economic policies have been affected by electoral politics. Lyndon Johnson did not press Congress for a tax hike in 1966 partly because he did not wish to focus attention on the growing costs of the Vietnam War before the midterm congressional elections.[66] Despite Nixon's personal distaste for severe government economic intervention, he imposed wage and price controls on the nation in August 1971 because the deteriorating economic situation threatened his upcoming 1972 reelection bid.[67]

Presidential efforts to manipulate the economy for political purposes are seldom in the best interests of the nation's long-term economic health. Although some politicians may argue that election year economic stimulations are attentive political responses to the desires of voters, the public pays a price for these short-term boosts. Presidents and Congresses do not always have the political will to take away pre-election benefits and tax cuts after the election. Consequently, electoral pressures on economic policy contribute to budget deficits and inflation. Even when the president and law-makers do agree on measures to offset their election year generosity, there is evidence that short-term decreases in unemployment brought about by election year tax cuts and spending hikes may be more transitory than the increases in inflation that usually accompany them.[68]

Beyond the inflationary and budgetary costs of pandering to voters' short-term economic desires, this practice makes coherent economic policy making difficult. Tufte has concluded:

> The electoral-economic cycle breeds a lurching, stop-and-go economy the world over. Governments fool around with transfer payments, making an election-year prank out of the social security system and the payroll tax. There is a bias toward policies with immediate, highly visible benefits and deferred, hidden costs—myopic policies for myopic voters.[69]

Legislative Requirement

In addition to the distortions caused by electoral politics, fiscal policy is complicated by the requirement that it be enacted through the legislative process. Having 535 members of Congress examine, debate, and vote on a fiscal policy proposal ensures that the American people, through their elected representatives, will have a say over the government's taxing and spending decisions. This democratic necessity reduces, however, the effectiveness of fiscal policy as a presidential economic stabilization tool.

Even when no election is imminent, the legislative process required to enact fiscal policy may take so long that by the time the policy takes effect it may be irrelevant or counterproductive to the needs of the economy. This "lag" between the time a policy is needed and the time it can be enacted is a major weakness of fiscal policy.[70] Taxing and spending legislation usually takes months and may take more than a year to weave its way through committees and emerge in a form acceptable to a majority of both houses of Congress. Consequently, fiscal policy is often unresponsive to the most recent economic information. The democratic process guarantees that legislation will get a fair hearing, but in the case of fiscal policy, the fair hearing may render the legislation irrelevant.

Fiscal policy is also weakened by the narrow economic focus of many members of Congress. Individual senators and representatives are seldom held responsible for a general economic decline by their constituents. If they are members of the same party as the president, they may suffer from an antiparty vote when the economy is performing badly, but usually they are judged according to how well they serve the interests of their district or state. Although many members of Congress do have a national perspective on some economic issues, few will put the economic interests of the nation ahead of the local economic interests of their constituency. Fiscal legislation that costs jobs in a particular district will almost always be opposed by that district's representative. Thus, the American democratic political system encourages a narrow focus by members of Congress that contributes to the difficulty of making rational fiscal policy.

Interest Groups

Presidents are chosen by a national electorate and therefore do not have to worry about promoting prosperity in a particular state or congressional district as members of Congress do. Nevertheless, presidents are not immune to the pressures interest groups can exert on taxing and spending decisions. Labor unions, trade associations, business and agricultural interests, the financial community, ethnic groups, senior citizens organizations, and many other interest groups seek to affect fiscal policy.[71] These groups have political clout because they are able to offer campaign contributions, to mobilize blocs of voters, and to publicize their opinions in an effort to support candidates who work for causes important to their members. They can also use the same tools to seek the defeat of candidates whom they consider hostile to their interests.

No single decision to yield to the requests of an interest group is likely to undermine a president's fiscal policy, but if the president gives in to too many groups, the cumulative effect may inflate the president's budget. President Carter faced this problem when he was beset by groups who expected a Democratic president to deliver policies favorable to their interests. Organized labor, farmers, and a variety of groups advocating traditional Democratic social policies lobbied the White House to address their budgetary concerns. Carter was forced to compromise with many of these groups whose support was crucial to his presidency. As a result many budget items received more funds than Carter had intended. This failure to restrain spending contributed to the budget deficit and inflation.[72]

Despite their susceptibility to interest group pressures, presidents are in the best position to rise above politics and provide impartial economic leadership. This is because the American people ultimately will hold them responsible if the economy falters during their presidency. The support of certain interest groups will mean little to a president's popularity and chances for reelection if the public is unsatisfied with the current levels of inflation and unemployment and other economic factors.

Presidents and the Budget

The budget is the most important annual document produced by the Executive Office of the Presidency. It not only spells out the funding decisions of the president and his advisers, it is an important fiscal policy tool that can be used to influence the levels of inflation, unemployment, and economic growth. Moreover, as Gerald R. Ford has said, "The budget reflects the President's sense of priorities. It reflects his best judgment of how we must choose among competing interests."[73] It is therefore a document that affects presidential political and social programs as much as it affects fiscal policy.

As previously noted, the president had little effect on the budget-making process until Congress enacted the 1921 Budget and Accounting Act, which required the chief executive to submit a comprehensive executive budget to Congress. Since then presidents have exercised varying influence on the budget, depending on their relationship with Congress and their interest in budget details. Some presidents such as Jimmy Carter and Gerald Ford have chosen to immerse themselves in budget management. Others such as Richard Nixon and Ronald Reagan showed interest only in broad budgetary decisions that could not be easily delegated to someone else.[74]

Regardless of their interest in the budget, presidents are ultimately responsible for the executive branch's spending proposals and can greatly influence Congress's consideration of them. The political, social, and economic priorities of presidents provide guidelines to OMB officials and others involved in constructing the budget. Presidents also must arbitrate disputes between agencies and hear last-minute appeals from agency heads who feel a cherished program has been shortchanged.[75]

Since the late 1960s, the budget-making process has been a struggle to limit budget deficits despite erratic economic growth and dramatic increases in funding for entitlements, social programs, and defense. The American people consistently indicate in surveys that they believe government spending should be reduced. They also predictably say they do not want higher taxes. Yet this desire for less government spending is not accompanied by a willingness to sacrifice funding for specific programs. The public believes the government spends too much in only a few policy areas such as foreign aid, welfare, and space exploration.[76] Thus the budget is one of the most persistent political dilemmas facing presidents. They must try to reduce overall spending (or convince the electorate that they are trying to reduce it) while funding the programs that the American public has come to expect.

Presidential Impoundment of Appropriations

The Constitution did not spell out whether presidents were required to promptly spend funds appropriated by Congress or whether they could make independent judgments on the timing and even the necessity of putting appropriated funds to use. Many presidents during the nineteenth century took advantage of this constitutional ambiguity to impound appropriated funds they believed unnecessary or wasteful. In effect, the impoundment "power" gave presidents a second veto over appropriations since they could withhold funds Congress intended to be spent.

After World War II presidents increasingly used impoundments as a fiscal policy tool. Presidents Truman, Eisenhower, and Kennedy all clashed with Congress over their withholding of appropriations for defense projects. In 1966 Lyndon Johnson impounded $5.3 billion in domestic appropriations to slow inflationary trends brought on by the Vietnam War.

Presidential impoundments reached their zenith under Richard Nixon, who impounded billions of dollars of appropriations during the first five years of his presidency. He argued that he was withholding funds only as a financial management technique designed to slow inflation. Democratic leaders in Congress, however, charged that Nixon used impoundments to overturn Congress's spending decisions and further his own social goals. The conflict between Nixon and Congress over impoundments led to the passage of an act that restricted presidential use of impoundments.

Congressional Budget and Impoundment Control Act of 1974

The 1974 Congressional Budget and Impoundment Control Act created new procedures designed to prevent a president from impounding appropriations against the will of Congress. Under the act presidents must notify Congress when they decide to permanently impound appropriated funds. Congress has forty-five days in which to signal its disapproval of these permanent impoundments, known as rescissions, by a majority vote of both houses. After forty-five days, if Congress has not acted, presidents may make their proposed rescissions.[77] The law also allows presidents to defer spending appropriated funds by notifying Congress they are doing so. The funds can be held until Congress passes an act directing the president to spend the funds.

The rules governing impoundments, however, were only a small part of the Congressional Budget and Impoundment Control Act. It was an attempt by Congress to revitalize the entire budget process and link congressional deliberations on spending and revenue legislation. The act created a timetable designed to force action on the budget, moved the start of the fiscal year from July 1 to the following October 1 to give Congress more time to consider budgetary details, and established measures intended to aid Congress in evaluating the budget as a whole rather than as a group of unconnected spending bills. The act created the House and Senate Budget committees to centralize congressional budget making and the Congressional Budget Office to provide Congress with an expert staff to analyze the budget.[78]

Although many members of Congress lauded the new process, it did not achieve its two primary goals: bringing more order to the budget process and reducing the federal deficit. Deficits continued to grow after 1974, and Congress struggled, often unsuccessfully, to meet the budgetary deadlines set down in the act.[79]

The potential of the 1974 Budget Act as an executive tool, however, was not realized until 1981. At that time Ronald Reagan used the process to push his dramatic fiscal program of increased defense spending, decreased domestic spending, and a large tax cut through Congress. The new centralized budget-making process in Congress allowed him to negotiate with congressional leaders on the substance of his entire budget plan rather than being forced to bargain on a dozen or more appropriations bills, each of which might have been opposed by a different congressional bloc. To get his budget approved, Reagan used his public popularity to build a conservative coalition in the House of Representatives despite the Democratic majority.

Political scientist Louis Fisher explained why the new process favored the president:

> Whereas the politics of incrementalism under the old process had operated as a brake on radical changes, the Budget Act of 1974 strengthened Reagan's hand by requiring Congress to vote on an overall budget policy. . . . Although the administration did not get everything it wanted, the omnibus measure was more of an advantage to the executive branch than to Congress. By packaging all the cuts in a single bill, the White House was able to build a majority for final passage. Members could announce that they objected to specific cuts but supported the bill "on balance."[80]

After Reagan's dramatic 1981 budget victory, however, Congress regrouped and became more resistant to his domestic budget-cutting proposals.

Federal Budget Deficits

Budget deficits are not a phenomenon unique to the 1970s and 1980s. The federal government often has been forced to run deficits during wars and other national emergencies, including the depression. Yet not until the 1970s did budget deficits become a persistent peacetime economic problem. Between 1792 and 1946 the federal government had produced 93 budget surpluses and 61 budget deficits. From 1947 to 1969, a period during which two wars

Table 2 U.S. Federal Debt, Interest Payments, and Budget Deficits, 1971-1987 (billions of dollars)

Fiscal year	Total federal debt	Budget deficit	Interest payments
1971	409.5	−23.0	14.8
1972	437.3	−23.4	15.5
1973	468.4	−14.9	17.3
1974	486.2	−6.1	21.4
1975	544.1	−53.2	23.2
1976	631.9	−73.7	26.7
1977	709.1	−53.6	29.9
1978	780.4	−59.2	35.4
1979	833.8	−40.2	42.6
1980	914.3	−73.8	52.5
1981	1,003.9	−78.9	68.7
1982	1,147.0	−127.9	85.0
1983	1,381.9	−207.7	89.8
1984	1,576.7	−185.3	111.1
1985	1,827.5	−212.3	129.4
1986	2,130.0	−221.2	136.0
1987	2,355.3	−150.4	138.6

Source: Office of Management and Budget, 1988.

were fought, the government produced 8 surpluses and 15 deficits; but since 1970 the budget has been in deficit every year.[81]

The size of deficits since the Vietnam War has been especially troubling. In the past, periods of deficit spending were followed by years of surplus or at least balanced budgets. From 1975 to 1988, however, budget deficits have exceeded $45 billion every year except 1979, despite the absence of a war or significant military conflict. Moreover, the deficit widened dramatically under Ronald Reagan, surpassing $200 billion in 1983, 1985, and 1986. These deficits alarmed most economists and common citizens and forced the president and Congress to search for ways to get the budget under control.

Large budget deficits have several negative effects on the economy. First, they limit the government's flexibility to fight a recession through tax cuts and deficit spending because the president and Congress must be concerned about exacerbating the debt problem. Since tax revenues fall during a recession and unemployment insurance and welfare payments rise, the budget would be under further strain precisely when deficit spending would be needed to pull the economy out of recession.

Second, large deficits reduce the amount of funds available for achieving the nation's social and defense goals because interest must be paid on the national debt. As larger budget deficits have pushed the national debt toward $3 trillion, interest payments have taken up an increasing share of the federal budget. In 1987 interest payments on the federal debt totaled $138.6 billion, or almost 14 percent of federal goverment spending. This was more money than the government spent on any other budget category except defense and Social Security and came close to equaling the deficit itself.

Third, large budgets can threaten the economy by "crowding out" corporate and private borrowers from the credit market. Because the government must borrow heavily to finance its deficit, it competes with businesses and individuals also seeking to borrow funds. This increased competition forces interest rates higher causing loans to become more expensive. As a result, businesses can afford to purchase less plant and equipment to expand and modernize their operations, and fewer consumers can afford to finance purchases of expensive items such as houses and cars. The resulting reduction in demand may threaten economic growth.

Finally, budget deficits of the 1980s have become so large that domestic savings no longer can provide enough capital to service the debt. Consequently the government must borrow from foreign sources to make up the difference. This makes the United States dependent on foreign investors and raises the small possibility of a "stabilization crisis," which can occur if foreign investors lose confidence in the dollar and liquidate their U.S. investments. Such a crisis could cause the dollar to plummet and interest rates and inflation to rapidly accelerate.[82]

The Uncontrollable Budget

Presidents hoping to limit budget deficits must face the fiscal difficulties brought by the spending items that are reqired from year to year by existing law. These are known as uncontrollable or mandatory budgetary items. Although the term "uncontrollable" is somewhat misleading since these programs can be changed by an act of Congress, it does accurately describe the lack of power presidents have over these items in any given year.

Before the depression, most of the federal budget was devoted to the costs of running the government and, in times of war, the costs of defense. With the establishment of Social Security in the 1930s, however, the government began making large-scale payments directly to people who qualified for them. These transfer payment programs, which now include Medicare, Medicaid, welfare, job training assistance, student loan guarantees, food stamps, subsidized school lunches, unemployment compensation, and federal retirement benefits are intended to alleviate suffering and poverty, promote the health and advancement of individuals, and provide a safety net for those members of society who cannot provide for themselves because of economic recession, poverty, old age, or physical infirmity. Some of these transfer payment programs, such as welfare and unemployment insurance, also act as automatic economic stabilizers, since they increase the amount of money in the hands of the public when the economy goes into recession.[83]

These payments have consciously been expanded by Congress and several presidents, most notably Franklin Roosevelt and Lyndon Johnson, in an effort to use the wealth generated by the U.S. economy to promote social welfare and care for the less fortunate. Many federal transfer payment programs were established or substantially enlarged during the 1960s when the strong American economy seemed capable of providing funds for virtually any worthy purpose. This goal has become an accepted role of the government from which there appears to be no retreat. Even Ronald Reagan, who denounced the growth of the federal government and advocated deep cuts in domestic spending, did not propose dramatic reductions in funds for established entitlement programs such as Social Security that make up society's "safety net."

Transfer payments pose a special problem for presidents and their advisers who must be concerned with balancing the budget because the payments are not based on a yearly congressional appropriation or the government's ability to pay for them in a given year. They continue from year to year unless a law is passed that supersedes the measure which created them. Moreover, in 1974 Congress established cost-of-living increases for Social Security payments, thereby ensuring that these benefits would not be reduced by the eroding effects of inflation.[84]

Predictably, presidents and Congress have seldom been willing to assume the political risk of significantly reducing entitlement programs, subsidies, and other payments as the capacity of the government to pay for them has fallen. The growth of transfer payments has been accompanied by an increase in the activities of interest groups who attempt to protect these payments from cutbacks. Lobbyist organizations representing senior citizens, veterans, farmers, and other groups can pressure the president or a member of Congress to protect benefits to their constituents by offering or withholding campaign contributions, threatening them with negative publicity, and mobilizing blocs of voters that can make or break their candidacies. The activities of these lobbyists and the negative public reaction to cuts in transfer payments received by tens of millions of Americans have made large sections of the budget politically untouchable.

Consequently, the ability of presidents to propose significant cuts in the budget from year to year has been reduced as federal transfer payments have claimed a greater portion of the budget. In 1962 transfer payments stood at $29.5 billion, or less than one-third of the budget. By fiscal year 1983 they had reached $362 billion, or almost half of the budget.

In addition to transfer payments, other items in the budget are also outside the control of the president and Congress. Interest payments on the national debt are determined by the size of the debt and prevailing interest rates and must be subtracted from the incoming revenue. Also, the federal government is obligated to pay for items that it has ordered in previous years. For example, large weapon systems such as a new fighter plane or nuclear missile must be paid for over a span of years. Consequently, funds committed in the past to such items cannot be cut from a current budget without breaking contracts and wasting the funds spent on the items in past years. Expenditures for many other items in the budget, such as defense and the costs of operating the government, can be trimmed but not eliminated entirely.

Presidents seeking to reduce government spending, therefore, can search for cuts in only a fraction of the budget. The Office of Management and Budget estimated that in 1967 59 percent of the budget was uncontrollable. During the 1980s uncontrollable spending has climbed above 75 percent. According to political scientists Kim Hill and John Plumlee, this trend has diminished presidential budgetary power: "Presidential budgetary discretion has been significantly eroded. . . . The President in fact must propose and defend a budget much of which is determined elsewhere and in prior years."[85]

Gramm-Rudman-Hollings Deficit Reduction Act

In response to popular concern about growing budget deficits, Congress passed in 1985 the Gramm-Rudman-Hollings Deficit Reduction Act with President Reagan's approval. The bill was an acknowledgment that Congress and the president needed to be forced to make the tough budget-cutting decisions necessary to reduce the deficit. The legislation required $36-billion decreases in the deficit for five years. To ensure that these budget cuts were made, the law mandated "across the board" cuts known as "sequesters" to meet the deficit reduction targets if the projected deficit for a fiscal year exceeded the targeted amount by more than 10 billion dollars. The authors of the bill reasoned that since nobody would want these indiscriminate cuts—half of which were to come from defense and half from domestic spending—to occur, Congress and the president would meet the deficit reduction targets through normal budget procedures.

Critics of Gramm-Rudman-Hollings charged that it reduced the government's flexibility and encouraged the use of accounting techniques that would disguise rather

UPI/Bettmann Newsphotos

Congress responded to growing budget deficits by passing a landmark deficit reductions act in 1985. Sponsored by Senators Warren Rudman, Phil Gramm, and Ernest Hollings, the law required "across the board" cuts if deficit reduction targets were not met.

than lower the budget deficit. Some critics also claimed that the bill was unconstitutional because the president and Congress would be abdicating their budget-making responsibilities if the automatic cuts were used. The Supreme Court objected to a more limited and technical aspect of the law. The Court ruled on July 7, 1986, that because the law assigned to the comptroller general the final responsibility for determining the size of the budget cuts and for executing the automatic cuts, the bill was unconstitutional; only the president and the executive branch are empowered to execute the laws. The comptroller general heads the General Accounting Office, considered part of the legislative branch.[86] Congress responded to the Court's ruling in September 1987 by passing an amendment that gave the Office of Management and Budget—an executive branch agency—the final authority to determine the magnitude of cuts necessary to meet the deficit reduction goals. The amendment also substantially eased the deficit reduction targets, which were recognized as unrealistic. Under the revised Gramm-Rudman-Hollings the federal budget did not have to be balanced until 1993.

Apart from the law's constitutional problems, many critics of the plan doubted that the deep cuts mandated by the law would be carried out. In 1987 Congress and the president reached their deficit reduction target after an extended period of negotiation. The adopted 1988 and 1989 budgets were within minimum Gramm-Rudman-Hollings guidelines but depended on optimistic OMB forecasts of economic growth. Meeting the targets for 1990 and subsequent years, however, appeared to be difficult without a tax increase, which President-elect George Bush had promised not to accept, or substantial cuts in Social Security and Medicare, which were opposed by a solid block in Congress. This increased the possibility that the government might be forced to accept automatic spending cuts or again amend the Gramm-Rudman-Hollings law.[87]

Balanced Budget Amendment Proposals

The sharp growth of federal budget deficits during the 1970s and 1980s convinced many government officials and common citizens that the only way to control deficit spending was through a balanced budget amendment. Such an amendment was seen by its supporters as the best way to ensure that the president and Congress would only spend what revenues they took in, since they would be required to do so by the highest law of the land. Under the pressure provided by the amendment Congress and the president would be more capable of making the politically difficult budgeting decisions necessary to balance the budget.

Critics of a balanced budget amendment argued that the amendment would be hard to enforce. Would the president and Congress be penalized for failing to balance the budget? If so, critics asked, who would be responsible for enforcing such penalties? In addition, since the precise amount of spending and revenues for the following year is affected by the size of transfer payments, tax revenues, and other variables unknown to budget makers, a balanced budget amendment would depend on highly imprecise forecasts of spending and revenues that would be subject to dispute.[88] For example, the budget forecasts of the Congressional Budget Office, a congressional agency, routinely differ from the estimates of the president's Office of Management and Budget. A balanced budget amendment would require one set of budget estimates that is recognized as official.

Perhaps the most important criticism of the balanced budget amendment, however, was its effect on fiscal policy as a stabilization tool. If the government did live up to budget-balancing requirements, it would no longer be able to use fiscal policy to stabilize the economy. Since tax receipts fall and transfer payments rise during a recession, balancing the budget would require additional spending cuts or higher taxes that would likely deepen the recession. During expansionary periods budget balancing would risk spurring inflation, because tax revenues would rise, requiring the government to spend more or cut taxes to dispose of the surplus.[89]

The balanced budget amendment found a strong proponent in Ronald Reagan. He advocated its passage during his campaign in 1980 and during the early days of his presidency. Some observers believed the amendment had a chance to become part of the Constitution since it was supported by a popular president. When Ronald Reagan entered office in 1981 thirty-two states already had voted in favor of a constitutional convention to consider a balanced budget amendment. In 1982 the Senate voted 69-31, two votes more than the necessary two-thirds majority, for a constitutional amendment that would have required a balanced budget. The same year, the House voted 236-187 for a similar amendment, falling 46 votes short of the necessary two-thirds. By 1983 growing skepticism that current budget deficits could be quickly reduced deflated the balanced budget amendment movement. Even the president's budget projections did not envision achieving a balanced budget within five years. Consequently, an amendment that would force the government to balance the budget when no acceptable means existed for doing so in the near future was unrealistic.[90] Ronald Reagan continued to pay lip service to the concept of a balanced budget amendment, but it became an idea to be reconsidered in the future when budget deficits were under control.

Line-Item Veto

Another proposal designed to control the federal government's deficit spending is to give the president a line-item veto. Currently, presidents only may sign an appropriations bill or veto it. A line-item veto would give presidents the third option of vetoing specific spending items within a bill while approving the balance of the legislation. Proponents of such a veto argue that it could be used by presidents to guard against wasteful and unnecessary spending items that become law only because they are attached to worthy appropriations bills.

Although many presidents have supported a line-item veto, Ronald Reagan was a particularly vocal advocate of the device. He repeatedly called on Congress in major speeches to enact legislation giving him and future presidents this power. In his last State of the Union address in 1988, Reagan asked Congress to

> help ensure our future of prosperity by giving the President a tool that—though I will not get to use it—is one I know future presidents of either party must have. Give the president the same authority that forty-three governors use in their states, the right to reach into massive appropriations bills, pare away the waste, and enforce budget discipline. Let's approve the line item veto.

As described by President Reagan, the line-item veto appeared to be a simple and effective way to control government spending. In reality, although it might help presidents make some cuts in the budget, it is a highly controversial tool that could have several negative effects. If the president were armed with the line-item veto, Congress would be tempted to pass many pork barrel spending items to satisfy their constituents while relying on the president to make the politically difficult choices about which items to cut. Even if the president were to veto a substantial number of these items, the budget might still contain more fat than if Congress had not been given a way out of its legislative responsibilities. The line-item veto also might make budgetary restraint more difficult because a president would be able to threaten a member of Congress with a line-item veto of a program that would benefit that member's state or district unless that member agreed to vote for a bill supported by the administration. Even if the line-item veto did result in less budget waste, it could cause a dramatic shift of legislative power to the president that would violate traditional American principles of separated powers.[91]

Some opponents of a line-item veto have also argued that its supporters have overestimated its effectiveness in reducing budget deficits. A line-item veto would have no effect on entitlements, interest payments on the national debt, and other parts of the budget that cannot be controlled from year to year. Moreover, contrary to popular perceptions, few spending bills contain significant line items that could be cut with a line-item veto. Spending details are often found in the reports of congressional committees and agency budget justification documents, while the legislation funding the activities of a particular unit of an agency or department only mentions the lump sum allocated to it.[92] Given these limitations, the line-item veto is not the answer to huge deficits. At best it would allow the president to make minor cuts in the controllable budget.

Tax Policy

Traditionally, presidents have exerted less influence over tax policy than over spending matters. Whereas presidents are required to submit an executive budget to Congress outlining their spending proposals each year, tax laws do not require the executive to make major annual revisions. In addition, legislators, especially members of the powerful House Ways and Means Committee, have historically regarded tax policy as a special province of Congress.

Nevertheless, presidential influence over tax policy is significant and has grown since World War II. This increase in influence has been furthered by the growth in presidential responsibility for economic policy in general.[93] As Congress and the nation have become used to looking to the president for economic initiatives, the chief executive has taken over much of the burden of proposing and campaigning for changes in the tax code.

In addition to proposing tax legislation, presidents influence tax policy by standing ready to veto tax bills passed by Congress that they believe are unfair, excessive, or harmful to the economy. Presidents after World War II rarely have had to veto tax bills, since the threat to veto them usually has been enough to stop congressional tax initiatives opposed by the president. Ronald Reagan's success at preventing tax increases during his second term despite huge budget deficits demonstrates the president's power over tax policy. Presidents may not be able to get their tax measures passed by Congress, but they will usually be able to stop or at least force the modification of any tax bill they do not like.

Congress, however, has similar power to negate the president's tax proposals. Political scientist John Witte has written: "Although the earlier notion that presidents should set only general revenue targets has been replaced by more detailed, almost annual tax proposals, the majority of the tax agenda is still set by Congress. Furthermore, there is no doubt that when presidential requests run counter to legislative momentum or the short-term mood of Congress, they can and are summarily dismissed by congressional actions."[94]

Within the executive branch, the Treasury Department has primary responsibility for tax policy. Its Office of the Tax Legislative Council drafts tax legislation and reviews tax regulations. The Office of Tax Analysis estimates the effect tax changes have on revenues. In addition, the Treasury Department's Internal Revenue Service is responsible for collecting taxes and enforcing the tax laws passed by Congress.[95] Other officials in the administration, particularly the director of the Office of Management and Budget, also are involved in formulating tax strategies.

Although tax policy and expenditure policy are the two components of fiscal policy, they are rarely coordinated. When formulating the budget, presidents and lawmakers generally have anticipated revenue to be the amount of funds current taxes will produce. Tax cuts and increases only occasionally have been direct responses to expected revenue shortfalls.[96]

All presidents face the dilemma of taxation. While taxes are unpopular, the operation of the government requires revenue. The American public has come to expect many government services, but they also expect that their taxes will be kept to a minimum. Consequently, presidents must back taxes that will raise sufficient revenue to run the government while avoiding responsibility for any tax increases.

Partly because of the political dangers inherent in this dilemma and partly because of the complicated and tedious nature of tax policy, few presidents have placed tax changes or reforms at the top of their domestic policy. Presidents Kennedy and Reagan were two exceptions. Both pressed Congress for major tax cuts to stimulate the economy. Kennedy's tax cut, enacted in 1964 after his death, was smaller than Reagan's, but more successful in promoting economic growth.[97] The growing budget deficit forced Reagan to reclaim part of his 1981 tax cut through "revenue enhancers" enacted in 1982.

Reagan also supported the bipartisan Tax Reform Act of 1986. It was a sweeping attempt to simplify the tax code and eliminate loopholes without increasing or decreasing tax revenues. The bill reduced the number of tax brackets from fourteen to just two. It cut the top individual tax rate from 50 to 28 percent and taxed 85 percent of taxpayers at the bottom rate of 15 percent. President Reagan hailed the law as "the best anti-poverty bill, the best pro-family measure, and the best job-creation program ever to come out of the Congress of the United States." The bill received a favorable reception from the American public although many taxpayers did not believe paying their federal income taxes had been made any easier. In addition government figures indicated in 1988 that the revised tax codes had produced less revenue than the old tax codes would have yielded.

Using tax policy as a tool of fiscal policy is complicated by the government's need for revenue. Although some tax cuts have generated greater revenues, most notably the Kennedy tax cut of 1964, tax cuts usually result in less revenue and higher deficits than would have resulted had they not been enacted. The supply-side economic theory that cutting tax rates would result in higher revenues became popular in the early 1980s, but the budget deficits that followed Ronald Reagan's 1981 tax cut diminished public and professional enthusiasm for this concept. *(See "Supply-side Theory," p. 649, in this chapter.)* A tax cut meant to stimulate the economy may succeed, but policy makers risk higher budget deficits. Conversely, raising taxes may increase revenues in the short term but also contract the economy, resulting in higher unemployment.

Tax cuts are a popular fiscal policy tool because they directly increase net personal income. Tax cuts have often been used successfully to stimulate the economy. The unpopularity of tax increases, however, has made them difficult to enact with the speed that is necessary if they are to be an effective fiscal policy tool. Political scientist Godfrey Hodgson has written of Lyndon Johnson's experience with this problem:

> Even a timely shift in the direction of tax policy for macroeconomic reasons is generally beyond the capacity of. . .congressional procedures. Lyndon Johnson found this to his cost in 1965-68, when he tried to raise tax revenues to pay for the Vietnam War. His inability to do so may have cost him the presidency. Certainly it spelled the end for his great society programs and gave a sharp new impetus to the inflation combined with economic stagnation that has troubled the economy ever since.[98]

The wave of antitax sentiment that hit the United States during the late 1970s and 1980s further diminished the relevancy of anti-inflationary tax measures. Presidential candidates during this period who did advocate a tax increase, such as 1984 Democratic nominee Walter Mondale and 1988 Democratic contender Bruce Babbitt, were praised by many observers for their realism but fared poorly with voters. Mondale won only thirteen electoral votes in his election battle with Reagan, and Babbitt bowed out of the 1988 Demcratic nomination race after receiving meager support in the early primaries.

One proposal that has been offered by proponents of a more efficient fiscal policy process is giving the president the authority to manipulate tax rates to stabilize the economy the way the Federal Reserve Board can manipulate the supply of money. This reform would require a constitutional amendment, since it would shift much taxation power from the Congress to the president.

Under such an amendment the president would be empowered to make small adjustments in personal and corporate income tax rates to stimulate or contract the economy. These adjustments would not require the approval of Congress but would be subject to congressional review and veto. The change in tax rates could have a limited duration, and their size could be constrained to a certain percentage of existing rates, such as 5 or 10 percent. This authority would provide the president with a way to act swiftly to stabilize the economy without having to depend on the time-consuming legislative process that often delivers tax measures too late to be effective as stabilization tools. The danger of such an amendment, however, is that it would disrupt the balance of economic power between the president and Congress and make fiscal policy less democratic.[99] Since Congress would object vigorously to the transfer of power inherent in the amendment and the public would probably fear that it would lead to higher taxes, it is highly unlikely that such an amendment could ever be ratified.

Monetary Policy

Monetary policy, like fiscal policy, is a tool with which the government attempts to stabilize the economy. It is based on the relationship of the supply of money in circulation to the performance of the economy. Since changes in the rate of growth of the money supply profoundly affect unemployment, inflation, and interest rates, the government can regulate economic activity by controlling the supply of money. Increasing the rate of growth of the money supply will stimulate the economy; decreasing it will contract the economy and combat inflation.

The Mechanics of Monetary Policy

In contrast to fiscal policy, which is made through a slow public process of conflict and compromise between the president, Congress, and executive departments, monetary policy is determined within the Federal Reserve System, known as the "Fed." The Fed consists of twelve regional banks, several advisory bodies, and a Board of Governors. *(See "Federal Reserve System," p. 1041, in Independent Agencies chapter of Part V.)* The members of the Board of Governors, who are appointed by the president, are responsible for setting monetary policy and overseeing the operations of the Federal Reserve System.

Between 1836 when the charter of the Second Bank of the United States was allowed to expire, and 1914, the United States did not have a central bank. The nation had experienced several banking panics between 1873 and 1907 that prompted Congress to establish the National Monetary Commission to study the American banking system and its problems. In 1912 the commission recommended that the country needed a central bank to regulate credit conditions and provide stability to the U.S. banking system. With these goals in mind, Congress passed the Federal Reserve Act in 1914, which created the Fed.[100] Unlike the First and Second Banks of the United States, Congress gave the Federal Reserve System a permanent charter to avoid the type of political fight that prevented the first two national banks from being rechartered. The Federal Reserve Act does not mention a stabilization policy role for the Federal Reserve System. This role evolved gradually after the Great Depression until stabilization of the economy through monetary policy became its primary function.

The Fed studies the economy and constructs economic forecasts that it uses to determine its monetary policy. Like fiscal policy, the goals of monetary policy include low inflation, low unemployment, and strong economic growth. Fighting inflation, however, has traditionally been the Fed's first priority.

Managing the Money Supply

The Fed has several means through which it can change the rate of growth of the supply of money. First, it can require commercial banks to keep a greater or smaller proportion of deposits on reserve. If this reserve requirement is lowered, banks have more money to lend, and the money supply grows faster. If the reserve requirement is raised, banks have fewer funds to loan, and the growth of the supply of money slows. Second, the Fed can slow or accelerate the growth of the money supply by decreasing or increasing the rate at which banks may borrow funds from the Federal Reserve System. When this rate, known as the *discount rate,* increases, banks can afford to borrow less from the Fed and therefore will have less money to loan. A lower discount rate will put more money in the hands of banks by making it cheaper for them to borrow from the Fed. Finally, the Fed can alter the growth of the money supply by buying and selling U.S. securities. This process, known as *open market operations,* is by far the most commonly used method for affecting the money supply. When the Fed buys securities, it pumps money into the banking system. Selling securities to banks brings money into the Fed that banks could have loaned, thereby slowing the growth of the money supply.[101]

The Fed's manipulations of the money supply affect the performance of the economy through their impact on interest rates. If the Fed increases the money supply, interest rates fall because banks have more funds available to loan. The lower interest rates induce firms to borrow more money to invest in the expansion and modernization of their operations. This increase in investment causes the economy to expand. Consumers also find borrowing cheaper, so they are able to finance the purchase of expensive items such as homes and cars more easily. If the Fed slows the growth of the money supply, banks have fewer funds to loan, and the competition for these limited funds forces interest rates up. Firms and consumers respond to more expensive rates of interest by borrowing less money for investment and purchases, so the economy contracts.

Monetary Policy as a Stabilization Tool

Monetary policy is an attractive policy tool because it is less constrained by politics than is fiscal policy. Since the monetary policy-making structure created by Congress was intended to be nonpolitical, politicians usually have tried to avoid the appearance of interfering in the Fed's business. In addition, the complexity of monetary policy discourages many potential critics from looking over the Fed's shoulder. Monetary policy also has a less visible and immediate effect on the economic welfare of the American public than a major spending or tax decision and therefore will draw less public protest.[102]

Monetary policy's primary role in stabilization policy has been to fight inflation. Monetary policy has two advantages over fiscal policy as an inflation-fighting tool. First, the time required to decide on and execute a strategy is much shorter for monetary policy than for fiscal policy. After an economic problem has been recognized, the Fed can reach a monetary policy decision within days. In contrast, the president may not be able to develop a fiscal policy program and secure congressional approval for many months, if at all. Although monetary policy, once implemented, takes longer to affect the economy than fiscal policy, this delay is usually shorter than the delay caused by the fiscal policy process.[103] Second, the Fed's relative insulation from politics makes its fight against inflation simpler than the president's. Fiscal policy remedies for inflation—tax increases and expenditure cuts—are seldom popular with voters. Since the members of the Fed are not elected, they do not have to worry that growing unemployment or declining economic growth brought on by anti-inflationary monetary policy may anger constituents or cause them to lose an election.[104]

Despite these advantages, monetary policy, like fiscal policy, has its limitations. Although a tight monetary policy can be used to control inflation when the economy is growing too fast, during a period of stagflation when both unemployment and inflation are rising, restrictive monetary policies are likely to deepen the recession.[105] The restrictive monetary policies of Fed Chairman Paul Volcker during the late 1970s and early 1980s succeeded in dramatically lowering inflation, but they also contributed to the severe recession of 1981-1982. Although Volcker deserves much credit for making the tough policy choices necessary to relieve the high inflation that had plagued the U.S. economy since the Vietnam War, the Fed can become too concerned with inflation. The Fed's relative political independence and banking orientation may dispose it to emphasize low inflation at the expense of other economic goals. Specifically, the Fed may at times tolerate unacceptably high unemployment in its pursuit of low inflation.[106]

Presidential Influence over Monetary Policy

The Federal Reserve System is relatively free of formal congressional or executive control. Although there are other independent agencies, none serves such an important and politically sensitive function as formulating monetary policy. The Fed ultimately is answerable to Congress, but the only formal power Congress has over the Fed is the authority to restrict or revise the Fed's powers through legislation. Congress can neither pass judgment on nor veto Fed policies. Since the Fed is self-financing, Congress also cannot gain leverage by threatening to withhold appropriations.

The Fed's independent control of monetary policy is a potent restriction on presidential control of the economy. Except for their power to appoint Federal Reserve Board officials, presidents have no formal means through which they can influence monetary policy. Yet presidents will receive most of the blame or the praise for changes in the economy brought on by monetary policy. Given this situation, presidents naturally try to exert as much informal influence over Fed decisions as possible.

Presidential influence over Fed policy is derived primarily from the president's status as the nation's chief economic manager. Board members recognize a practical need to coordinate fiscal and monetary policy and, despite some prominent exceptions, have usually cooperated with presidential efforts to do so. The Fed also has been mindful that the president is the elected representative of the people who, theoretically, embodies the policy directions preferred by the American electorate.

Although the independence of the Fed is a restraint on presidential control of the economy, it does enable presidents to rely on the Board of Governors to make politically unpopular economic decisions that take some public pressure off the White House. For example, in 1965 President Johnson's advisers urged him to propose a tax increase to cool down the economy, which was beginning to produce inflation. Johnson, however, refused to propose higher taxes, thus forcing the Fed to bear the responsibility for fighting inflation. When the Fed raised the discount rate, Johnson told reporters, "The Federal Reserve Board is an independent agency. Its decision was an independent action. I regret, as do most Americans, any action that raises the cost of credit, particularly for homes, schools, hospitals, and factories." As political scientist Richard Pious has noted, "Had Johnson fought for the politically unpopular

Economic Advisers...

As presidential economic responsibilities increased during the twentieth century, the fulfillment of those responsibilities became increasingly institutionalized. Congress created new organizations, and presidents expanded existing organizations to increase the executive branch's capacity to analyze, coordinate, and manage the American economy and economic relations with other countries. Although White House political advisers and virtually all cabinet secretaries have some influence on economic policy, three executive branch units dominate economic policy making. These are the Treasury Department, the Council of Economic Advisers, and the Office of Management and Budget. The leaders of these three units function as the president's chief economic advisers and meet frequently with one another to coordinate economic policy. Recent presidents have established working groups beneath the three leaders with representatives from various departments to develop and analyze economic policies.

Department of the Treasury

The Treasury Department, one of the original cabinet departments created in 1789 by an act of Congress, was the first executive branch unit to be responsible for advising the president on economic policy and has remained an important participant in economic policy making throughout U.S. history. The department has a variety of economic responsibilities, including collecting taxes and customs, managing the nation's currency and debt, developing tax legislation, and working with foreign governments to adjust the value of the dollar relative to other currencies. Because the Treasury oversees the financing of the debt, the department traditionally has advocated taxes that will bring balanced budgets and monetary policies that yield low interest rates.

The Treasury secretary's position as head of a large cabinet department lends status to the post relative to other top presidential economic advisers. The Treasury secretary's influence on presidential economic decision making, however, may be constrained in some administrations by the time the secretary spends overseeing the many operational responsibilities of the department. As the world's economies have become more interdependent, the Treasury secretary's international economic policy activities have become increasingly important. James A. Baker III, Treasury secretary during Ronald Reagan's second term, spent much of his time formulating exchange rate policies and developing a plan to reschedule Latin American debt payments to the United States.

Council of Economic Advisers

The Council of Economic Advisers (CEA) is a three-member body appointed by the president and subject to Senate confirmation. It is headed by a chair who oversees the operations of the council's small staff, reports to the president, and represents the CEA before the rest of the executive branch and Congress.

The primary function of the CEA is to provide the president with expert economic advice and analysis. The Employment Act of 1946, which established the CEA as a unit in the Executive Office of the President, states that each member of the council "shall be a person who, as a result of his training, experience and attainments is ex-

but necessary tax increase, there would have been no need to blame the board for its action."[107]

Presidential Appointment of Board Members

The most obvious source of influence presidents have over monetary policy is their power to appoint the members of the Fed's Board of Governors. The Federal Reserve Board of Governors consists of a chair appointed by the president to a four-year term with the approval of the Senate and six members appointed to fourteen-year terms, also subject to Senate confirmation. The members' terms are staggered so that one of their terms expires at the end of January in each even-numbered year. Barring deaths or resignations by board members, a president will appoint two members and a chair during a four-year term.

The chair's term, which is renewable, does not coincide with the president's term. Consequently, during the first part of their time in office first-term presidents must work with a chair appointed by their predecessor. These appointment rules are designed to ensure the independence of the Fed's Board of Governors and to prevent any president from dominating its policies by packing the board with administration supporters. The expectations of the financial and scholarly communities that presidents will appoint board members with high academic credentials and relatively nonpartisan backgrounds also serve as a check against overly political appointments.

The chances that the Fed will cooperate with the president, however, are increased greatly if the Fed chair is a recent appointee of the incumbent president. In 1977, President Carter's expansionary fiscal policy was countered by the anti-inflationary monetary policy of Fed chair Arthur Burns, the conservative appointee of Richard Nixon. When Burns's term expired in 1978, Carter replaced him with G. William Miller, a Carter associate who worked closely with the president's economic team.[108]

Coordination of Fiscal and Monetary Policy

Although the organization of the Fed is designed to insulate it from outside influence, monetary policy is most effective when it is coordinated with the administration's fiscal policy. Both tools are seeking to promote economic stability and prosperity, but the effects of one may cancel, blunt, or distort the intended effects of the other if the president and the Fed do not cooperate. For example, the president may ask Congress to stimulate the economy by spending more than the government receives in revenues.

... to the President

ceptionally qualified to analyze and interpret economic developments, to appraise programs and activities of the government ... and to formulate and recommend national economic policy." Because the council does not represent a large bureaucratic body and has no responsibilities in operating the government other than preparing the president's annual economic report, Congress hoped that the CEA would have the time and independence to provide presidents with long-term, nonpartisan advice on economic policy and professional analysis of economic conditions. Traditionally, the CEA has been most concerned with promoting growth and managing the trade-off between inflation and unemployment.

The CEA's influence depends entirely on the president. If the president values its advice and involves it in decision making, the CEA can have considerable power because its three members and small staff of professional economists usually possess the greatest amount of economic expertise within an administration. Because of this expertise, however, CEA members can be vulnerable to charges from other economic advisers that they approach the realities of economic policy making from a perspective that is too theoretical. CEA members must, therefore, be careful to pay adequate attention to the president's political needs if they wish to retain their influence.

Office of Management and Budget

In 1921 Congress created the Bureau of the Budget to coordinate and modify the budget estimates of the executive departments. It was originally located within the Treasury Department but was placed under the newly created Executive Office of the President in 1939. In 1970 Richard Nixon expanded its staff and duties and renamed it the Office of Management and Budget (OMB).

OMB's primary function is to formulate an executive branch budget for the president that considers how much revenue the government is likely to raise through taxes and how much each federal agency and program should receive. OMB, therefore, continually analyzes the merits of budget requests and makes recommendations to the president on what funding should be cut, preserved, or expanded. The office is also responsible for budget forecasts that estimate the size of the budget deficit or surplus. The institutional bias of OMB has been to limit spending. This tendency is a result of OMB's role as the central budgetary control within the administration that must pare down the budget requests of department and agency heads who usually will seek as much funding as is politically possible for their unit.

The post of budget director has become highly politicized since the Nixon administration. Budget directors frequently testify before Congress and are involved in shaping and promoting the president's social agenda through their budget recommendations. David Stockman, budget director under Ronald Reagan from 1981 to 1985, epitomized the budget director's new role. President Reagan gave him a broad mandate to cut items from the budget in pursuit of smaller budget deficits. In the first six months of the Reagan administration he became not only the dominant presidential adviser on the budget within the administration, but also a symbol of Reagan's domestic budget cuts and social agenda that emphasized a more limited role for the federal government.

This requires the government to borrow funds, which increases competition for loans, thereby driving up interest rates. The higher interest rates, however, may offset the stimulative effects of the government's spending increases unless the Federal Reserve Board accommodates the president's fiscal policy by increasing the money supply.

The Fed has sometimes "leaned against the wind" to counter administration policies it considered wrong. In 1957, the Fed kept a tight reign on the money supply while the Eisenhower administration was pursuing a moderately expansionary fiscal policy. Similarly, the Fed fought inflation during the late 1960s while spending on the Vietnam War and Lyndon Johnson's Great Society social programs stimulated the economy.

The Fed may even use public pressure to attempt to change administration policies. In 1977 Fed chairman Arthur Burns testified against Jimmy Carter's tax cut proposals, raising the possibility that if the tax cuts were passed, the Fed would use monetary policy to offset their stimulative effect.[109] Fed chairman Alan Greenspan warned the incoming Bush administration through testimony before Congress on January 24, 1989, that the Fed would not tolerate an acceleration of inflation. George Bush and his economic advisers had placed a high priority on continued strong economic growth, but Greenspan indicated the Fed might slow growth in the near future to combat inflation, saying, "The Federal Reserve policy at this juncture might be well advised to err more on the side of restrictiveness than stimulus."

Presidents, therefore, generally try to coordinate their fiscal policies with the Fed to produce the best economic results and limit political friction between economic policy makers. Coordination is accomplished through informal meetings between the Fed chair and the president's top economic advisers. The Fed chair, the Treasury secretary, the budget director, and the chair of the CEA—a group known as the "quadriad"—usually will meet at least once a month to discuss coordination of fiscal and monetary policy. Any agreements forged out of these discussions, however, are nonbinding, and the Fed may pursue a monetary policy at odds with the administration's goals.

Proponents of greater executive control over monetary policy have proposed several reforms. The most radical would be to place the Federal Reserve under executive control and allow presidents and their advisers to set monetary policy in addition to performing their other economic functions. This reform would result in the greatest degree of coordination possible between fiscal and monetary policy, since the incumbent administration would be making both. It would, however, allow presidents to use monetary policy for political purposes. For example, presidents could quietly stimulate the economy through monetary policy in an election year to improve their chances of being reelected.

A more modest reform that has been considered by Congress but never passed is to make the term of the Fed chair coincide with the president's term of office. This would improve coordination since the president would presumably enter office with a like-minded Fed chair. The chair, however, would retain independent control over monetary policy.[110]

International Economic Policy

The president's international economic powers have become increasingly important as nations have become more economically interdependent. Because of high volumes of trade, integrated financial markets, multinational corporations, and other factors that bind the world's economies, prosperous conditions in the United States cannot be sustained if other large economies, especially those of Western Europe and Japan, are ailing. Specific economic problems in other countries can be transferred to and from the U.S. economy. For example, inflation caused by one economic power's expansionary conditions can contribute to inflation in other countries because consumers faced with domestic inflation may increase their purchases of less expensive imports. This increased demand for foreign goods puts pressure on prices outside the inflationary country that contributes to worldwide inflation. Similarly, a recession in one country can contribute to slower economic growth in other countries because consumers in the country experiencing a recession will have to cut back on their purchases of imports.

Because of this shared economic destiny between industrial nations, presidents must function not just as national economic managers, but also as international economic coordinators. They dispatch the U.S. trade representative to international negotiations aimed at reducing trade barriers, oversee the Treasury Department's negotiations with other finance ministries about the value of major currencies, and announce U.S. economic policies to the international community.

Since 1975 presidents also have attended annual economic summits where the leaders of the major industrial nations have met to confer on broad issues of economic policy. These meetings, which are attended by the leaders of the United States, Japan, West Germany, France, Great Britain, Italy, and Canada (known collectively as the Group of Seven or G-7) have greatly increased international economic coordination. The summits have focused attention on the international component of economic policy, forced politicians to develop a better understanding of international economic issues, created a justification for frequent meetings between finance ministers and other economic officials, and provided a forum where economic matters can be discussed in the broader context of allied relations. Because the annual meetings compel the G-7 leaders to face one another, they have had a positive influence on free trade. The leader of a country that has erected protectionist trade barriers or taken other measures contrary to the interests of the group must justify those measures to the other leaders and face their collective pressure to reverse the action.

Trade Policy

President Ronald Reagan noted in his 1983 State of the Union address that "one out of every five jobs in our country depends on trade. We export over 20 percent of our industrial production, and 40 percent of our farmland produces for export." Given the importance of trade to the U.S. economy, one of the most important international economic goals of presidents has been to maximize U.S. access to foreign markets.

Because the Constitution gives Congress the power "to regulate Commerce with foreign Nations," the rules governing foreign trade are set by legislation. Since the depression, however, trade legislation has contained broad grants of power to the president to implement the laws through international negotiations and the implementation of tariffs and other trade barriers designed to force other countries to open up their markets to American products.

Congress has granted the executive broad trade powers because only the president has the authority to negotiate with foreign governments. Therefore, when Congress adopted the strategy of pursuing mutual reductions in tariffs through international negotiations in 1934, it had to turn to the president to carry out those negotiations. In addition, Congress wanted to isolate U.S. trade policy from pressures for protectionism from specific industries. Since individual members of Congress have to be concerned with the economic conditions in their states and districts, protectionist sentiments have tended to be stronger in Congress than in the executive branch. If a single industry such as agriculture or steel predominates in a congressional district, that district's representative often will be disposed to support protectionist measures for that industry. Political scientist Erwin Hargrove explained that by delegating power to the president Congress is able to respond to the local interests of its constituents without undermining the free trade position of the nation:

> Congress would rather not have responsibility for setting specific tariff levels because the flood of demands for individual industrial areas would be far too intense. Therefore, it has allowed the Executive to set such levels within parameters set by Congress. This permits members of Congress to make their requests in behalf of constituency interests and still permit the President to do what is needed for a national position on international trade.[111]

Throughout much of its history the U.S. economy has benefited from trade surpluses. In 1981, however, the U.S. trade position began to decline rapidly as U.S. exports failed to keep pace with imports. The following year the U.S. current account, a measure of the net flow of goods and services traded with other countries, dropped into deficit. By 1987 the current account deficit reached $154 billion. The large current account deficit cost the U.S. economy good jobs because Americans were buying so many products manufactured overseas. In addition, because the U.S. had to borrow to finance the trade imbalance, the current account deficit was increasing the U.S. dependence on foreign credit and adding to the debts of the nation.

These problems focused public attention on the trade deficit and increased pressure on Congress to pass legislation to protect American industries from foreign competition. In response to the mounting U.S. trade deficit, Congress enacted the Omnibus Trade Act in 1988, which mandated retaliatory responses to unfair foreign trade practices. President Reagan's firm support of free trade prevented Congress from enacting a more protectionist trade bill, but the persistence of the current account deficit, which improved to only about $140 billion in 1988 despite a decrease in the value of the dollar, sustained protectionist sentiments in Congress and among the American people. *(See box, 1988 Omnibus Trade Act, p. 664.)*

Protectionism

The primary question that trade policy must decide is whether to pursue free trade or whether to erect barriers that protect U.S. industries but ultimately risk reducing the overall flow of trade. Few economists or politicians would argue that the ideal trade environment for enhancing international prosperity is one in which nations can trade goods and services without trade barriers such as tariffs, import quotas, embargoes, and strict licensing procedures for importing goods. Yet even the most ardent free trade advocates recognize that the threat of protectionism is the most effective negotiating tool the government has to convince other nations to end their unfair trading practices. Appeals for protection from specific industries often have diverted national policy from the ideal of free trade. Nevertheless, since 1934, even when Congress has enacted bills to protect specific industries or to pry open foreign markets, policy makers have maintained the consensus that the U.S. economy will benefit from free trade.

Throughout U.S. history, tariffs have been a contentious political issue. The nation's first Treasury secretary, Alexander Hamilton, supported high tariffs, which he hoped would nurture the infant industries of the Northeast. Although the tariffs enacted during the Federalist era were not swept away when Thomas Jefferson took power in 1800, the pro-agrarian Democratic-Republicans favored trade policies that enhanced the ability of farmers to sell their products overseas.

During most of the nineteenth century the industrial and commercial interests of the North contended with the agricultural interests of the South over national tariff policy. Because the South was dependent on foreign markets for its agricultural products, it opposed tariffs that could trigger a retaliatory response from its foreign customers. In addition, tariffs raised the price of many goods the South needed to buy from foreign countries. The intersectional tensions over trade policy led to the nullification crisis in South Carolina in 1832. After Congress passed a high-tariff bill in 1832, the South Carolina state legislature passed an ordinance declaring the tariff void in that state. President Andrew Jackson, determined to assert federal authority, threatened to enforce the law in South Carolina with federal troops. Hostilities were averted when Jackson and South Carolina leaders accepted a compromise tariff. Tensions caused by the tariff issue remained, however, and eventually contributed to the secession of southern states in 1861 that brought on the Civil War.

For the rest of the nineteenth century, tariffs remained high as American industries desirous of protection grew and the protariff Republican party dominated national politics. Average U.S. tariff rates generally ranged from 35 to 50 percent of the cost of imports subject to tariffs. With the election of President Wilson in 1913, tariff policy was reversed. That year, with President Wilson's strong support, Congress enacted the Underwood-Simmons Tariff Act, which sharply cut tariffs. Wilson saw tariff reduction as a way to help American consumers, limit the influence of powerful probusiness lobbyists, and stimulate competition.

Table 3 Current Account Surplus or Deficit, 1950-1987 (billions of dollars)

Year	Current account surplus or deficit (−) a
1950	−1.8
1951	0.9
1952	0.6
1953	−1.3
1954	0.2
1955	0.4
1956	2.7
1957	4.8
1958	0.8
1959	−1.3
1960	2.8
1961	3.8
1962	3.4
1963	4.4
1964	6.8
1965	5.4
1966	3.0
1967	2.6
1968	0.6
1969	0.4
1970	2.3
1971	−1.4
1972	−5.8
1973	7.1
1974	2.0
1975	18.1
1976	4.2
1977	−14.5
1978	−15.4
1979	−1.0
1980	1.9
1981	6.3
1982	−8.7
1983	−46.2
1984	−107.0
1985	−116.4
1986	−141.4
1987	−154.0

Sources: Office of Management and Budget, Commerce Department, Treasury Department, 1988.

a. Net total of U.S. international trade in merchandise, services, and investments.

America's participation in World War I rekindled "America first" sentiments in the United States that led to a return of high tariffs. The Tariff Act of 1921 and the Fordney-McCumber Act of 1922, both supported by Republican president Warren Harding, returned tariffs roughly to their pre-1913 levels.

When the depression struck in 1929, the governments of the major industrialized nations reacted by erecting trade barriers to protect their domestic industries. In 1930 Congress passed the Smoot-Hawley Act, which established the highest tariffs the United States had ever erected. The trade war of the early 1930s strangled trade between nations until it was a small fraction of what it had been. Protectionist measures left the world to dig out of the depression without the benefits of international trade.[112]

1988 Omnibus Trade Act

On August 23, 1988, President Reagan signed the Omnibus Trade and Competitiveness Act of 1988. The act signaled Congress's determination to take a more activist role in trade policy and mandated a limited but significant change in the staunchly free trade policies of the Reagan administration.

Sentiment in Congress for an overhaul of trade legislation developed during the early 1980s as trade deficits grew and the Reagan administration refused to intervene in currency markets to push the dollar lower or take a discernibly tougher position toward other nations' unfair trade practices. In 1985, members of Congress began work on the trade bill, which proceeded slowly because of other economic priorities, the bill's broad scope, and administration resistance to some of its proposed provisions. Although the act evolved considerably from its inception, its major intent from the beginning was to increase the use of retaliatory trade measures and give Congress more control over trade policy. By strengthening the retaliatory measures already a part of U.S. trade law, Congress hoped to pry open foreign markets to ailing domestic industries by using the threat of restricting access to U.S. markets.

In 1987 both chambers passed separate trade bills with many protectionist features. Lawmakers realized, however, that they had to make the bill acceptable to the Reagan administration or their efforts would be nullified by a presidential veto they would have little hope of overriding. Negotiations between the two houses and the administration to produce a single bill resulted in a trade bill that was much less protectionist than its earlier versions. In particular, a highly publicized proposal by Rep. Richard Gephardt that would have required cuts in U.S. imports from countries that had trade surpluses with the United States and refused to moderate unfair trade practices was abandoned. Congress also gave the administration a five-year extension of the president's authority to negotiate trade agreements, a power delegated to the executive branch almost continuously since the 1930s.

Despite compromises made by Congress, President Reagan vetoed the bill on May 24, 1988, citing provisions requiring advanced notice of plant closings and restrictions on Alaskan oil exports. Congress passed an identical trade bill, minus the provisions cited by the president in July. The bill became law when President Reagan signed it in August.

The act's most significant provisions for U.S. trade were its mandating of retaliatory steps against violations of trade agreements or other "unjustifiable" trade practices by foreign countries and its shifting of much authority over trade policy from the president to the U.S. trade representative, a cabinet-level official appointed by the president who has functioned as the main U.S. negotiator at trade talks. Congress transferred the authority to decide whether a foreign trade practice was unfair and how to respond from the president to the trade representative.

Since the trade representative would still be a member of the president's administration, however, it was unlikely that the trade representative would seriously diverge from administration policy. In addition, although Congress required the trade representative to retaliate against unfair trade practices, the president retained the authority to block retaliation by issuing a waiver on one of several grounds. These included an agreement by the foreign government in question to stop its unfair practice or a determination by the president that the retaliatory measure could harm U.S. national security.

Nevertheless, Congress hoped that the shift of power would make retaliation more likely because the trade representative, who is required to testify before Congress and consult with legislators on trade matters, would be more accountable to Congress and more likely to implement tough responses to unfair trading practices. Ultimately, the direction of U.S. trade policy depended less on who possessed authority to develop it than on how voters saw foreign trade practices affecting the trade deficit and the domestic economy. If the American public came to perceive that foreign governments were to blame for U.S. economic problems, the pressures for retaliation and protectionism would be difficult for even the most strident advocates of free trade in Congress and the executive branch to resist.

International Trade Negotiations

As with many other areas of economic policy, the depression forced Congress and the president to reconsider the country's position on trade. Franklin Roosevelt proposed to stimulate trade and thereby the depressed American economy by negotiating mutual reductions in tariffs with U.S. trading partners. With the enthusiastic support of his secretary of state, Cordell Hull, Roosevelt asked the Democrat-controlled Congress to delegate him the authority to reduce U.S. tariffs up to 50 percent in return for equal tariff concessions by other nations. Despite nearly unanimous Republican opposition, Congress passed the Trade Agreements Act of 1934, which delegated this power to the president. Armed with new authority the Roosevelt administration negotiated bilateral agreements with many nations that cut tariffs and increased the flow of trade. The increased access to foreign markets that resulted helped stimulate the U.S. economy. After the initial success of Roosevelt's negotiations, congressional grants of authority to the president to negotiate mutual tariff reductions became a regular feature of U.S. trade policy.

After World War II, President Truman sought to establish more sweeping arrangements to reduce international protectionism. At the urging of the United States, 23 nations signed the General Agreement on Tariffs and Trade (GATT) in 1947. Since then most noncommunist nations have signed the agreement. Under GATT, mutilateral negotiations aimed at reducing trade barriers were to be held at regular intervals. The signatories also agreed to the "most-favored-nation" principle, which committed each nation to apply tariff rates equally to all the other GATT participants. In addition, the agreement prohibited certain restrictive trade practices such as import quotas and set up procedures to mediate trade disputes and implement sanctions against violators of the agreement.

Since 1947 GATT signatories have held eight multinational trade negotiation rounds. The first five rounds produced small but significant tariff reductions. In 1962 Congress passed the Trade Expansion Act with the strong support of the Kennedy administration. The act gave the president the broad authority to reduce or eliminate U.S. import duties in return for similar trade concessions from other countries. The sixth round of GATT, known as the "Kennedy Round," resulted in sharp mutual cuts in tariffs. Fifty-three nations agreed to cuts in tariffs on industrial products averaging more than 35 percent.[113] When the round ended in 1967, however, many industries in the United States and in other countries lobbied against further cuts in tariffs because they feared increased foreign competition.

Following the end of the Kennedy Round in 1967, dozens of bills with protectionist provisions were introduced in Congress. Few were passed, but the apex of trade barrier reduction clearly had been reached. Congress did not renew the president's authority to participate in multilateral trade negotiations, which had expired in 1967, until it passed the Trade Act of 1974 after the next GATT round was already under way.[114] Although this act extended the president's authority to negotiate reductions of trade barriers, it placed more restrictions on the president's power and reflected the growing pressures from U.S. domestic industries to retaliate against foreign unfair trading practices. The seventh round of GATT (Tokyo Round) and the present Uruguay Round have been far less successful in reducing tariff barriers than the Kennedy Round, although they have made some progress on eliminating nontariff barriers.

International Monetary Relations

When one nation imports goods from another, it usually must pay for those goods with the seller's currency. Consequently, the buyer must purchase the seller's currency at the prevailing exchange rate. Exchange rates affect a country's ability to export its goods because the higher its currency is valued on international markets, the more expensive its goods will be for foreign buyers. Since a dollar that is worth less relative to foreign currencies will make U.S. goods cheaper for foreigners to buy, intervention to lower the value of the dollar is the primary tool presidents have used to fight trade deficits.

Bretton Woods Agreement

After World War II the United States led the world in setting up an international monetary system that established stable exchange rates conducive to free trade. Forty-four nations signed an agreement at Bretton Woods, New Hampshire, in 1944 that made gold the standard by which currencies were valued. The Bretton Woods agreement established the International Monetary Fund (IMF) to oversee adjustments in exchange rates and the World Bank to provide loans for postwar reconstruction. The intention of the United States was to build a predictable international currency system that would prevent destabilizing fluctuations in exchange rates and deliberate currency devaluations that could threaten free trade.

Each member of the IMF was required to declare a "par" value for its currency in relation to the U.S. dollar, which was pegged to gold at $35 dollars per troy ounce. Official exchange rates of the world's currencies were not allowed to fluctuate more than 1 percent from their par value. Because the United States held most of the world's gold reserves and the U.S. dollar's value was backed by the government's pledge to convert dollars into gold, nations used the dollar as an international trading currency and as a reserve of wealth just like gold. In effect, the United States functioned as banker to the world.[115]

The Bretton Woods arrangement functioned well during the 1940s, 1950s, and early 1960s. The stability it produced brought an enormous increase in world trade and the resurgence of economies devastated by World War II. By the mid-1960s, however, the dollar's role as an international reserve currency was causing the United States economic problems. Because other nations wanted to hold dollars to trade and back up their own currencies, dollars flowed overseas but failed to return. The result was a growing U.S. balance-of-payments deficit that weakened international confidence in the dollar and led many foreign investors to exchange their dollars for gold. U.S. gold reserves fell from more than $23 billion in 1949 to just $10 billion in 1971.

In response to this problem, on August 15, 1971, Richard Nixon stunned the world by announcing that the U.S. Treasury would no longer convert dollars into gold. The dollar's value would be allowed to "float" to a level determined by international currency markets. Since other currencies depended on the dollar, they, too, would have to float. The dollar, which had been overvalued, declined against other currencies, making U.S. goods cheaper overseas.[116]

Nixon's decision ushered in a new era of international monetary relations that required a higher degree of coordination between governments. Although several countries proposed plans to salvage the Bretton Woods system, by 1973 all major currencies were floating. Nations found that currency values could not be left entirely to market forces because the markets produced sharp fluctuations in exchange rates as investors shifted large amounts of money from currency to currency in search of higher earnings. Moreover, the market forces did not always push exchange rates in the direction that was needed to prevent trade imbalances. Thus, between 1981 and 1985, despite a growing U.S. trade deficit that would have been slowed by a weaker dollar, the dollar's value increased as foreign investors converted their money to dollars to take advantage of the high interest rates, low inflation, and political stability to be found in the United States.

Managing the Value of the Dollar

Under the post-Bretton Woods system of floating exchange rates, governments may attempt to adjust the value of their currency through intervention in the currency markets. The United States and other governments intervene in currency markets through their central banks. If U.S. policy makers decide that the value of the dollar is too high they can lower its value by selling dollars on the open

Bill Fitz-Patrick, The White House

In June 1988 in Toronto, President Reagan attended his eighth economic summit. Next to him, clockwise, are Canadian prime minister Mulroney; French president Mitterrand; West German chancellor Kohl; Italian premier de Mita; ECC president Delors; Japanese premier Takeshita; and British prime minister Thatcher.

market. Conversely, a weak dollar can be strengthened by having the central bank shrink the supply by buying dollars on the open market.

Technically, the president has no role in intervention. It is the U.S. central bank—the Federal Reserve System—which makes the currency transactions that affect the value of the dollar. Yet it is difficult for even the Fed with its massive reserves to alter the value of the dollar without cooperation from the central banks of the other industrialized powers. Consequently, coordination of exchange rate policies between the major industrialized countries is necessary to control currency values effectively. The president, as chief economic manager and the official charged with negotiating with foreign countries, must oversee this coordination.

Negotiations with other nations on currency levels are usually led by the Treasury secretary and attended by representatives of the Federal Reserve Board of Governors. Currency levels are also frequently discussed by the president and the leaders of the G-7 nations at their annual economic summits. Negotiations between governments often have resulted in informal agreements to take concerted action to adjust exchange rates. In January 1989, for example, the major industrial nations agreed to slow the rise of the dollar, which was being pushed up near a previously agreed upon secret limit by rising interest rates in the United States that were attracting foreign capital. At the same time, West Germany wanted its currency to be held up because of fears in that country that a weaker mark would lead to inflation by increasing the costs of imports. The world's major central banks responded by buying marks with dollars, thereby holding down the dollar's rise and propping up the mark.[117]

The importance of currency intervention was illustrated dramatically in the early 1980s. The strong dollar had encouraged American consumers to buy foreign goods and made American goods too expensive overseas to compete with comparable foreign products, thus contributing to the growing U.S. trade deficit. During Ronald Reagan's first term the administration largely had ignored the dollar's value. The president maintained early in his term that the strong dollar was a sign that his policies had restored international confidence in the U.S. economy.[118] Perhaps this was true, but with the current account deficit jumping from $46 billion in 1983 to $107 billion in 1984 the Reagan administration concluded that it had to act to bring down the value of the dollar. It therefore announced in January 1985, shortly after James Baker had taken over as Treasury secretary, that the U.S. would intervene in the currency markets to bring down the value of the dollar. U.S. intervention, sometimes with the cooperation of other central banks, succeeded in dramatically lowering the value of the dollar from the peak reached in February 1985. Although the lower dollar did not produce a reduction in the U.S. current account deficit until 1988, the U.S. trade problem would have been much worse without intervention.

Notes

1. Clinton Rossiter, *The American Presidency* (New York: Harcourt Brace, 1956), 21.
2. Harold M. Barger, *The Impossible Presidency: Illusions and Realities of Executive Power* (Glenview, Ill.: Scott, Foresman, 1984), 320.
3. Francis Russell, *The Shadow of Blooming Grove* (New York: McGraw-Hill, 1968), 559.
4. Richard Pious, *The American Presidency* (New York: Basic Books, 1979), 305.
5. Rudiger Dornbusch and Stanley Fischer, eds., *Macroeconomics*, 4th ed. (New York: McGraw-Hill, 1987), 450-451.
6. Michael P. Riccards, *A Republic, If You Can Keep It: The Foundation of the American Presidency, 1700-1800* (New York: Greenwood Press, 1987), 90.
7. Ibid., 91-97.
8. Jonathan Hughes, *American Economic History*, 2d ed. (Glenview, Ill.: Scott, Foresman, 1987), 195.
9. Riccards, *A Republic, If You Can Keep It*, 100-101.
10. Ibid., 101.
11. Hughes, *American Economic History*, 199.
12. James E. Anderson, *Politics and the Economy* (Boston: Little, Brown, 1966), 9.
13. Hughes, *American Economic History*, 195.

14. Anderson, *Politics and the Economy,* 9-10.
15. Ibid., 11-12.
16. Arthur M. Johnson, *The American Economy* (New York: Free Press, 1974), 52.
17. John F. Witte, "The President vs. Congress on Tax Policy," in *The President and Economic Policy,* ed. James P. Pfiffner (Philadelphia: Institute for the Study of Human Issues, 1986), 166.
18. Emmet John Hughes, *The Living Presidency* (Baltimore: Penguin Books, 1974), 216-217.
19. Louis Fisher, *The Politics of Shared Power: Congress and the Executive,* 2d ed. (Washington, D.C.: CQ Press, 1987), 192.
20. Anderson, *Politics and the Economy,* 123.
21. George C. Edwards III and Stephen J. Wayne, *Presidential Leadership, Politics and Policy Making* (New York: St. Martin's Press, 1985), 262.
22. Richard A. Watson and Norman C. Thomas, *The Politics of the Presidency,* 2d ed. (Washington, D.C.: CQ Press, 1988), 400.
23. Herbert Stein, *Presidential Economics* (New York: Simon and Schuster, 1984), 32-33.
24. Anthony S. Campagna, *U.S. National Economic Policy 1917-1985* (New York: Praeger, 1987), 101.
25. Pious, *The American Presidency,* 295.
26. Campagna, *U.S. National Economic Policy,* 131.
27. Ibid., 141.
28. Watson and Thomas, *Politics of the Presidency,* 405.
29. Campagna, *U.S. National Economic Policy,* 196.
30. Stein, *Presidential Economics,* 77.
31. Dorothy Buckton James, *The Contemporary Presidency,* 2d ed. (Indianapolis: Bobbs-Merrill, 1974), 94.
32. Campagna, *U.S. National Economic Policy,* 210-211.
33. Charles E. Jacob, "Macroeconomic Policy Choices of Postwar Presidents," in *The President and Economic Policy,* 65.
34. Campagna, *U.S. National Economic Policy,* 238-243.
35. Jacob, "Macroeconomic Policy Choices," 67.
36. Richard Nixon, *Six Crises* (New York: Doubleday, 1962), 309-310.
37. Jacob, "Macroeconomic Policy Choices," 67.
38. Stein, *Presidential Economics,* 102-106.
39. Campagna, *U.S. National Economic Policy,* 306-307.
40. Stein, *Presidential Economics,* 112.
41. Watson and Thomas, *Politics of the Presidency,* 405.
42. Pious, *The American Presidency,* 297.
43. Jacob, "Macroeconomic Policy Choices," 69.
44. James, *The Contemporary Presidency,* 96.
45. Campagna, *U.S. National Economic Policy,* 351.
46. James, *The Contemporary Presidency,* 103.
47. Ibid., 106.
48. Watson and Thomas, *Politics of the Presidency,* 407.
49. Stein, *Presidential Economics,* 213-214.
50. Campagna, *U.S. National Economic Policy,* 401-402.
51. Jacob, "Macroeconomic Policy Choices," 75.
52. Stein, *Presidential Economics,* 218.
53. Ibid., 231-232.
54. Jacob, "Macroeconomic Policy Choices," 74.
55. Campagna, *U.S. National Economic Policy,* 485-488.
56. Ibid., 486.
57. Stein, *Presidential Economics,* 255-256.
58. Mary H. Cooper, "Federal Budget Deficit," *Editorial Research Reports,* January 20, 1984, 50.
59. James P. Pfiffner, "The Crisis of Confidence in U.S. Economic Policy," in *The President and Economic Policy,* 10.
60. Cooper, "Federal Budget Deficit," 50-51.
61. The U.S. current account, the net total of international transactions including merchandise, services, and investments, plunged from a $6-billion surplus in 1981 to a $107-billion deficit in 1984. Despite the Reagan administration's support for a lower dollar in 1985, which improved trade figures by raising the cost of imports for Americans and making U.S. exports cheaper for foreign consumers, the current account deficit reached $154 billion in 1987 and had improved only to about $140 billion in 1988.
62. Edward R. Tufte, *Political Control of the Economy* (Princeton, N.J.: Princeton University Press, 1978), 19-21.
63. Tufte, *Political Control of the Economy,* 7-9.
64. Nixon, *Six Crises,* 310-311.
65. Tufte, *Political Control of the Economy,* 29-33.
66. Watson and Thomas, *Politics of the Presidency,* 405.
67. James, *The Contemporary Presidency,* 106.
68. William R. Keech, "Elections and Macroeconomic Policy Optimization," *American Journal of Political Science* 24 (1980): 345-367.
69. Tufte, *Political Control of the Economy,* 143.
70. Dornbusch and Fischer, *Macroeconomics,* 442-443.
71. Watson and Thomas, *Politics of the Presidency,* 413-416.
72. Erwin C. Hargrove and Michael Nelson, *Presidents, Politics and Policy* (Baltimore: Johns Hopkins University Press, 1984), 190.
73. Kim Quaile Hill and John Patrick Plumlee, "Presidential Success in Budgetary Policymaking: A Longitudinal Analysis," *Presidential Studies Quarterly* 12 (Spring 1982): 174.
74. Edwards and Wayne, *Presidential Leadership,* 268.
75. Hill and Plumlee, "Presidential Success in Budgetary Policymaking," 175.
76. Pfiffner, "The Crisis of Confidence in U.S. Economic Policy," 2.
77. Joseph A. Pechman, *Federal Tax Policy* (Washington, D.C.: Brookings, 1983), 56-57.
78. Pious, *The American Presidency,* 322-324.
79. Fisher, *The Politics of Shared Power,* 199-201.
80. Ibid., 204-205.
81. Cooper, "Federal Budget Deficit," 48-52.
82. Ibid., 56.
83. Anderson, *Politics and the Economy,* 113.
84. Edwards and Wayne, *Presidential Leadership,* 263.
85. Hill and Plumlee, "Presidential Success in Budgetary Policymaking," 179.
86. Donald L. Robinson, *"To the Best of My Ability"* (New York: Norton, 1987), 210-211.
87. David Rapp,"Is Anyone Really Trying to Balance the Budget?" *Congressional Quarterly Weekly Report,* November 26, 1988, 3387.
88. Campagna, *U.S. National Economic Policy,* 471.
89. Ibid., 472.
90. Stein, *Presidential Economics,* 311-312.
91. Fisher, *The Politics of Shared Power,* 213.
92. Ibid., 212-213.
93. Witte, "The President vs. Congress on Tax Policy," 180.
94. Ibid., 180.
95. Pechman, *Federal Tax Policy,* 39.
96. Paul Peretz, "The Politics of Fiscal and Monetary Policy," in *The Politics of American Economic Policy Making,* ed. Paul Peretz (Armonk, N.Y.: Sharpe, 1987), 145.
97. Peretz, "Politics of Fiscal and Monetary Policy," 145-146.
98. Godfrey Hodgson, *All Things to All Men* (New York: Simon and Schuster, 1980), 227.
99. Neil H. Jacoby, "The President, the Constitution, and the Economist in Economic Stabilization," *History of Political Economy* 3 (Fall 1971): 411-412.
100. William J. Baumol and Alan S. Blinder, *Economics, Principles and Policy* (New York: Harcourt Brace Jovanovich, 1979), 218.
101. Alberta Sbragia, "Monetary Policy and Monetary Theory: The Poverty of Choice," in *The President and Economic Policy,* 222.
102. Peretz, "Politics of Fiscal and Monetary Policy," 149.
103. Dornbusch and Fischer, *Macroeconomics,* 439-446.
104. Peretz, "Politics of Fiscal and Monetary Policy," 149.
105. Edwards and Wayne, *Presidential Leadership,* 279.
106. Peretz, "Politics of Fiscal and Monetary Policy," 148.
107. Pious, *The American Presidency,* 315.
108. Michael Bradley, *Economics* (Glenview, Ill.: Scott, Foresman, 1980), 576-577.
109. Pious, *The American Presidency,* 313.

110. Jonas Prager, *Fundamentals of Money, Banking and Financial Institutions* (New York: Harper and Row, 1982), 297.
111. Erwin C. Hargrove, *The Power of the Modern Presidency* (Philadelphia: Temple University Press, 1974), 159.
112. Miroslav Nincic, *United States Foreign Policy, Choices and Trade-offs* (Washington, D.C.: CQ Press, 1988), 334-335.
113. I.M. Destler, *Making Foreign Economic Policy* (Washington, D.C.: Brookings, 1980), 134.
114. Charles W. Kegley and Eugene R. Wittkopf, *American Foreign Policy, Pattern and Process* (New York: St. Martin's Press, 1979), 146-147.
115. Nincic, *United States Foreign Policy*, 337-338.
116. James, *The Contemporary Presidency*, 117-118.
117. Walter S. Mossberg, "Dollar Selling Aimed at Curbing Its Rise," *Wall Street Journal*, January 12, 1989, A2.
118. Mary H. Cooper, "Dollar Diplomacy," *Editorial Research Reports*, March 13, 1987, 118.

Selected Bibliography

Anderson, James E. *Politics and the Economy*. Boston: Little, Brown, 1966.

Barger, Harold M. *The Impossible Presidency: Illusions and Realities of Executive Power*. Glenview, Ill: Scott, Foresman, 1984.

Campagna, Anthony S. *U.S. National Economic Policy 1917-1985*. New York: Praeger, 1987.

Dornbusch, Rudiger, and Stanley Fischer, eds. *Macroeconomics*. 4th ed. New York: McGraw-Hill, 1987.

Fisher, Louis. *The Politics of Shared Power: Congress and the Executive*. 2d ed. Washington, D.C.: CQ Press, 1987.

Hughes, Jonathan. *American Economic History*. 2d ed. Glenview, Ill.: Scott, Foresman, 1987.

Pechman, Joseph A. *Federal Tax Policy*. Washington, D.C.: Brookings, 1983.

Peretz, Paul, ed. *The Politics of American Economic Policy Making*. Armonk, N.Y.: Sharpe, 1987.

Pfiffner, James P., ed. *The President and Economic Policy*. Philadelphia: Institute for the Study of Human Issues, 1986.

Pious, Richard. *The American Presidency*. New York: Basic Books, 1979.

Stein, Herbert. *Presidential Economics*. New York: Simon and Schuster, 1984.

Tufte, Edward R. *Political Control of the Economy*. Princeton, New Jersey: Princeton University Press, 1978.

Watson, Richard A., and Norman C. Thomas. *The Politics of the Presidency*. 2d ed. Washington, D.C.: CQ Press, 1988.

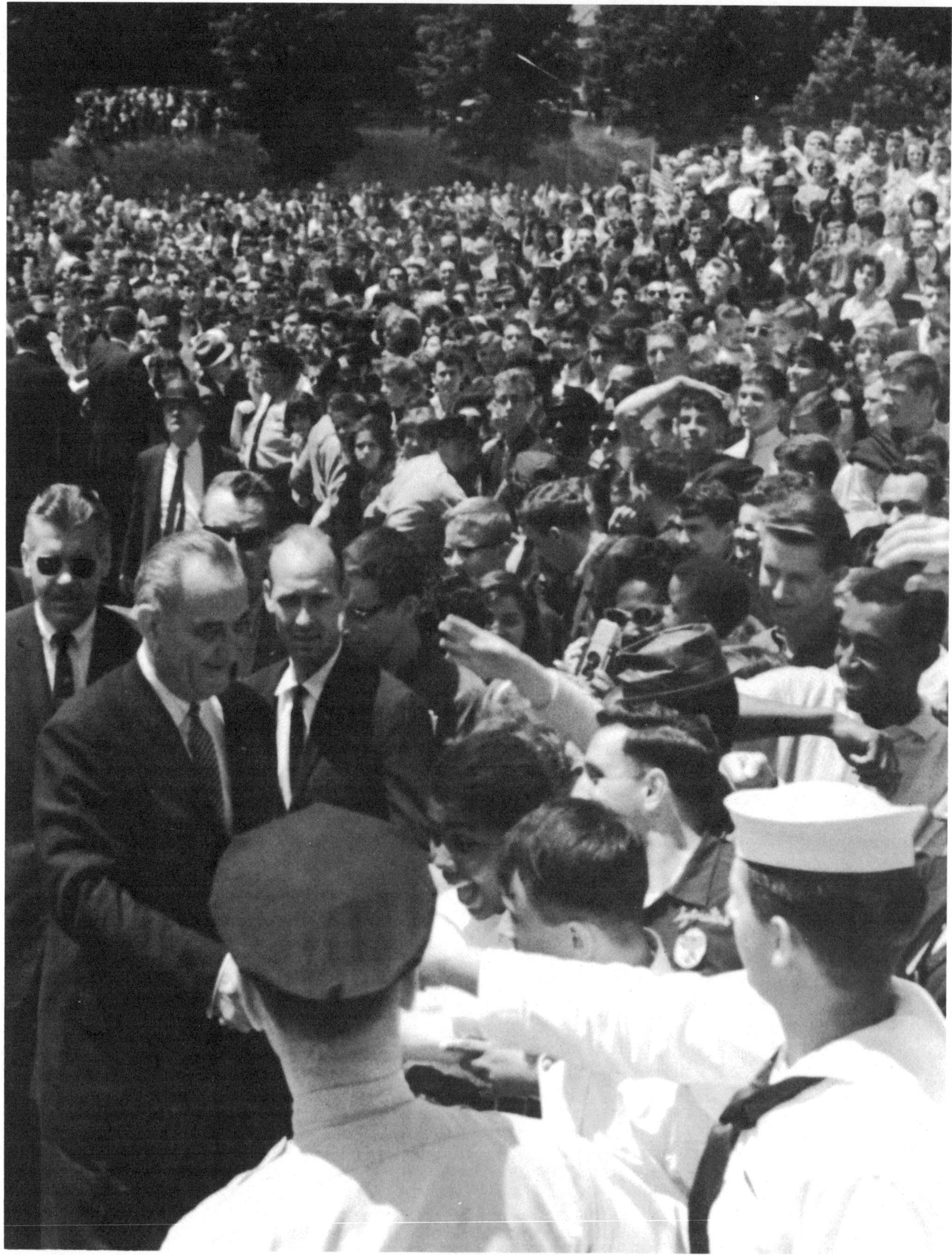

Lyndon B. Johnson Library

President Johnson shakes hands as Secret Service agents look on.

Part IV

The President and the Public

The President and the Public

It has long been recognized that presidential success rests largely on favorable public opinion. "Public sentiment is everything," Abraham Lincoln declared. "With public sentiment nothing can fail, without it nothing can succeed." [1]

The precursor of the modern president was Theodore Roosevelt, who expanded the role of the chief executive to include that of chief legislator and leader of public opinion. He converted the presidency into a "bully pulpit" from which he spoke out against industrial trusts and in behalf of conservationist causes. He was the first president fully to appreciate the value of public communications in enlisting the electorate's support for his programs and policies. TR (he was the first president identified by his initials) maintained that "publicity, publicity, publicity" was the most effective way to keep government responsive to the will of the people.

For the most part, as exemplified in the presidency of John F. Kennedy, the success and popularity of presidents is determined not just by legislation won and lost but also by their ability to set a political tone and direction, to instill trust and confidence, to offer a vision of the future, and to create a national consensus. As political scientist Richard E. Neustadt has stated, the power of the presidency is in the power to persuade.[2] That they must do through the various channels of communication available to them if they hope to influence Congress, retain control of their party, and win reelection. Summarizing the relationship between the president and the public, media specialist Doris A. Graber concluded that "the president's relations with the public are important to him in three major contexts: they affect his personal political survival; they are crucial to his ability to do his job well; and they are important for establishing his historical image." [3]

In dealing with the public, presidents have many advantages and resources: the deference accorded the office; the historical aura and stately trappings of the institution; an overshadowing political presence; a huge corps of aides who advise chief executives, plan their schedules, and handle public relations; and recognition that the Constitution states "the executive Power shall be vested in *a* President of the United States of America." These advantages set the president apart in the eyes of the public, yet none of them guarantees public support, without which a president cannot govern effectively.

The presidency forms the cornerstone of the U.S. political structure and is the most conspicuous symbol of the nation. The dependency of the office on public appeal was recognized by Woodrow Wilson, who, before becoming president, underscored the bigger-than-life presence of the president in national affairs: "Let him once win the admiration and confidence of the country, and no other single force can withstand him, no combination of forces will easily overpower him. His position takes the imagination of the country. He is the representative of no constituency, but of the whole people. When he speaks in his true character, he speaks for no special interest. If he rightly interpret the national thought and boldly insist upon it, he is irresistible; and the country never feels the zest for action so much as when its president is of such insight and calibre." [4]

A comparison of the British parliamentary system with the American system provides a clearer understanding of the American presidency and of its need for public support. In the British system the prime minister and the cabinet, collectively responsible for government decisions, rise and fall together. In the U.S. system, however, final authority in the executive branch is vested in one person. Furthermore, the American president is neither served by an extensive party organization nor tied institutionally to the national legislative body.

The eminent British writer C. P. Snow emphasized the differences between the American and British systems in a series of novels grouped under the title *Strangers and Brothers*. Snow pointed out that the British system produces "brothers" at the top of government who have served in their respective parties for years and have gained extensive experience in national administration. In contrast, newly elected presidents frequently appoint to high positions people they barely know. The administration may well be led by people who are strangers to one another and who have little experience with the federal bureaucracy or the complexities of managing a central government. The president alone is the cohesive element and as such is dependent on public support to make the system work.

The Public's Need for Presidential Leadership

Lacking a monarchy with its resplendent reminders of history and traditions, the American people look to the

By Dom Bonafede

president as the unifying symbol of the country. Presidential scholar Clinton Rossiter noted that "the president is the American people's one authentic trumpet, and he has no higher duty than to give a clear and certain sound." [5]

The imprint of the presidency is graphically etched on the American psyche. Historical time is measured by presidential clockwork: Americans speak of "the Jacksonian era," "the Hoover depression," "FDR's New Deal," "Lyndon Johnson's Great Society." When a crisis threatens the nation's security and welfare, Americans look to and rally around the president. The White House itself—said by Thomas Jefferson to be "big enough for two emperors, one Pope and the Grand Lama"—is revered as a national shrine.

Political scientist Robert S. Hirschfield has written, "The office is truly a mirror of our national life, reflecting accurately the events that have made our history, the men we have chosen, for better or worse, to deal with those events, and our own willingness to entrust them with enormous authority over the nation's destiny." [6]

The emotional attachment of Americans to their presidents is evident when a president dies in office. The psychic impact of the death is reflected in the increase in public esteem and affection for the fallen president. This phenomenon is especially evident in the martyrdom of Lincoln and Kennedy and the nationwide mourning at the death of Franklin Roosevelt near the close of World War II.

As the chief representative of the most venerable democracy in history, the president looms as a sort of mythic superhero. Yet, ironically, the American presidency is riddled with anomalies and contradictions. The holder of the office is variously perceived as having too much power or too little power, as being too strong or too weak. The office has a physical presence, embodied in the White House and the legions of aides who surround the president; yet it has an almost spiritual aura as well.

In *The State of the Presidency* political scientist Thomas E. Cronin wrote, "Our expectations of, and demands on, the office are frequently so paradoxical as to invite two-faced behavior by our presidents." [7] Americans want their presidents to be compassionate, but tough enough to deal with the country's foes, as did John Kennedy in the 1962 Cuban missile crisis. Presidents should be religious, but not wear their piety on their sleeve, as some observers felt Jimmy Carter did. The country wants inspirational leaders, but not those who promise more than they can deliver, as did Lyndon Johnson in the Vietnam War. And Americans generally want an ordinary person who will give a seemingly extraordinary performance, as did Harry S Truman.

Virtually every move the president makes and every word uttered is transmitted to the public, especially in an age of mass communications. An archivist records to the second the president's comings and goings; the identity of visitors to the White House and the length of their stay; the papers read, documents signed, meetings attended, and speeches delivered. Even the president's choice of food at meals, hour of rising and retiring, and moments of relaxation alone or with family are chronicled for the public and posterity. No person is so public and yet so alone in carrying out official decision-making responsibilities, all of which adds to the mystique that envelops the presidency.

Political scientist Grant McConnell has proposed that the mystique of the presidency is part of what endows the office with informal, unstated power. Despite the intense scrutiny and criticism the president endures, "the aura of grandeur remains ... no exposure of pettiness or human fallibility can destroy it. Indeed, the attention that hangs upon his every word and all the criticisms are signs that the president combines the symbolic role of chief of state with the substantive one of head of government. Every expectation proclaims that he is a man of power, and at every point the expectation is itself a source of power." [8]

Perhaps no president combined mystique, power, and public appeal more effecively than FDR. As one scholar wrote: "Voters knew that his legs were crippled by polio, but it seemed impossible that one who sounded so vigorous could be seriously handicapped. Careful, defensive management of the 'visual' helps to explain why. The White House discouraged the publication of photographs showing FDR from the waist down—and few such photographs appeared in print. Roosevelt's patrician artifices—the pince-nez and the cigarette holder—helped to make him look supremely self-confident. In our pictures of Roosevelt, we see a man so sure of himself that his vitality bursts out of the frame. The props help: that so-called fighting jaw, the angle of the cigarette holder, the rumpled hat. Roosevelt was our modern presidential salesman, the man who knew how to flatter and cajole."

Packaging and Selling Presidents and Policies

The advent of television, refinements in the "packaging" of candidates and the marketing of issues, the scientific canvassing of public opinion, and the sophisticated use of mass communications have radically changed electoral politics and the politics of governing.

To win election, lead the nation, deal with Congress, and negotiate with foreign governments, presidents must be able to strike a popular chord and gain the endorsement of the electorate. Their principal means of winning public support is through the mass media (chiefly network television and the national press) and other means of communication, including formal speeches, official proclamations, televised news conferences, press releases, nonattributable backgrounders, statements by designated spokespersons, domestic and foreign travel, and private talks with members of Congress, journalists, special interest advocates, financiers, and world leaders. Presidents learn this lesson long before entering the White House, for favorable public opinion is as important in winning an election as it is in governing the nation.

Selling the Candidate

The day after his defeat in the 1984 presidential election, Walter Mondale, the Democratic candidate, commented on the pervasive influence of the news media—particularly television—on campaign politics:

> Modern politics requires television. I think you know I've never really warmed up to television; in fairness to television, it's never really warmed up to me.... I like to look someone in the eye.... I don't believe it's possible any more to run for president without the capacity to build confidence and communications every night.[9]

As Mondale's remarks suggest, the changes in mass communications have radically altered the way politics is conducted. Candidates are tutored on how to deal with the media; their appearances are timed for maximum media exposure; and their speeches are written with the media in mind—for a thirty- or sixty-second "bite" that television producers can easily fit in their newscasts.

Almost all national candidates have media consultants who, along with the pollsters, professional campaign strategists, political advertising producers, and direct-mail specialists, make up the new political elite.

Author Theodore White observed in 1972, "Television *is* the political process: it's the playing field of politics. Today, the action is in the studio, not in the back rooms." [10] The influence of television has shifted emphasis from substance to style, and issues often are turned into slogans. Whereas television once covered news, news is now produced for television. An indistinguishable line exists between reality and imagery.

Modern presidential campaigns, therefore, center on "media events"—elaborately choreographed public appearances. The purpose of the careful planning and strategic scheduling behind such events is to draw press attention to the candidate for transmission to the voting public. Often, the size of the press contingent at a campaign affair and the stature of the news organizations they represent is more important than the number of people in the audience.

To a great extent, the press itself is recognized as a constituency. Solely for the benefit of the news media, campaign officials set up "press opportunities" in which reporters can talk with the candidates and photographers can take pictures. "Walking tours" are scheduled during which the candidate, followed by reporters, photographers, and television crews, visits potential supporters. Campaign staff also regularly set up press conferences, select interviews, and background briefings. Sometimes, brief, informal interviews are arranged between the press and the candidate on the campaign plane, in a hotel room, even in the candidate's rented limousine.

To political candidates, mass media coverage entails both "free" coverage provided by news organizations and "paid" coverage—television and radio commercials—supplied and paid for by them or their supporting campaign organizations. Although candidates attempt to manipulate free coverage, they cannot directly control it. For viewers, free coverage is more credible than paid commercials.

Another reason for presidential candidates to seek media exposure is the high cost of campaigning, particularly in an era when a thirty-second campaign commercial on prime-time network television may cost $150,000. It is a basic principle of politics that the candidate who garners media attention has a better chance of receiving public acceptance and raising campaign funds.

The Citizens' Research Foundation, a private group that studies campaign financing, reported that spending on national, state, and local political campaigns reached a record high of almost $2 billion in the presidential election year of 1988. Of that total, an estimated $500 million was spent by presidential candidates. It is generally acknowledged that from 50 to 75 percent of most candidates' campaign budgets is spent on political advertising, the vast proportion on television.

Selling the President

The first president to use public opinion surveys as they are known today was Franklin Roosevelt. From time to time Hadley Cantril, a Princeton University professor sometimes referred to as "the father of polling," and George Gallup conducted surveys for FDR. But not until the 1960s, when John Kennedy retained Louis Harris, did polls became an accepted tool of the White House to gain outside perspectives on presidential actions and to learn the concerns of the public.

In his book *The Selling of the President,* an inside account of Richard Nixon's 1968 presidential campaign, Joe McGinniss disclosed the critical role of professional media advisers and the way politics are shaped by contrived imagery, manipulation of the news media, and exploitative campaign advertising—in sum, how candidates often try to deceive voters with illusions. McGinniss noted that Eisenhower had used the New York advertising firm of Batton, Barton, Durstine and Osborn while in the White House and in his reelection campaign. Eisenhower also relied on actor Robert Montgomery to advise him on how to use the new medium of television.

McGinniss quoted Leonard Hall, the national Republican chairman in 1956, saying, "You sell your candidates and your programs the way a business sells its products." McGinniss concluded, "It is not surprising then that politicians and advertising men should have discovered one another. And, once they recognized that the citizen did not so much vote for a candidate as make a psychological purchase of him, not surprising that they began to work together. The voter, as reluctant to face political reality as any other kind, was hardly an unwilling victim." [11]

Jimmy Carter was the first president to include his pollster, Patrick H. Caddell, as a regular member of the White House staff—a sign in itself of the rising importance of public opinion surveys in the presidential decision-making process. Gerald Rafshoon, an Atlanta advertising executive and member of Carter's band of loyal Georgian aides, was teamed with Caddell, and together they provided public opinion research and marketing services for the president's policies. By this time it was recognized that "selling the president" was no longer so simple as promoting brand-name soap; rather, it involved computer science, socioeconomic data, and psychological analyses to plumb the motivational and behavioral aspects of public attitudes. Subsequently, Richard B. Wirthlin, a California-based public opinion specialist, performed a similar function for Ronald Reagan. Thus the president's pollster became an accepted part of the White House staff.

Presidents do not, however, blindly follow the findings of their pollsters or of those outside the White House. Caddell reported that Carter often questioned the polls; instead of being led by them, he used poll results to govern in keeping with his own convictions and instincts. Also, Reagan continued to push for U.S. aid to the contra rebels in Nicaragua despite public opinion polls that showed the majority of Americans to be against such help. In such instances, presidents can portray themselves courageously adhering to their principles rather than abandoning them to the caprices of public opinion or the demands of special interests.

A National Theater

The camera's eye focuses on the stately double doors. There is a long moment of silence. Suddenly, as if by magic, the two panels open and the president of the United States appears, standing tall and impeccably tailored. He is smiling slightly, and exuding confidence. As the camera pans in on him he strides briskly down the long East Wing corridor. With jaunty self-assurance, he hops on the platform and, flanked by the U.S. and presidential flags, looks into the face of America. It is the opening of one of Ronald Reagan's news conferences—a simple yet highly polished scene, minutely scripted and carefully orchestrated by his media advisers. What he says afterwards may well be of secondary importance; for in television, as Richard Nixon once noted regretfully, it often seems that it is looks that count.

The presidency is a form of national theater in which the chief executive is the most visible and important actor on the American stage. Presidents have recognized this since the Republic's beginning.

George Washington once a week held an afternoon reception, a "levee," at which he met with members of the public. Aware of the importance of the president's appearance, Washington saw to it that when he went riding, his horse's "hoofs were meticuloulsy blacked, its mouth washed out, its teeth picked and cleaned, its hide curried to a satin sheen."

Several years after Washington's death, John Adams offered an assessment of the first president's proclivity for the dramatic: "If he was not the greatest President he was the best Actor of the Presidency we have ever had. His Address to the States when he left the Army; his solemn Leave taken of Congress ... his Farewell Address to the People when he resigned his Presidency. These were all in a strain of Shakespearean and Garrickal excellence in Dramatic Exhibitions." [12]

Almost a century and a half later Herbert Hoover, commenting on the same theme, sadly observed in his *Memoirs,* "I was convinced that efficient, honest administration of the vast machine of the Federal government would appeal to all citizens. I have since learned that efficient government does not interest the people as much as dramatics." [13]

As Hoover realized, modern presidents often must couch their ideas and proposals in melodrama to attract public attention and win support.

Looking to Peoria

Nixon's domestic policy adviser, John Ehrlichman, popularized the phrase "Will it play in Peoria?" The question, a common criterion at the highest levels of government, is asked to determine whether people throughout the United States—beyond Washington's political community—will endorse a particular presidential decision or administration policy proposal. Within that context, Peoria is a metaphor for "Middle America."

Before leaving on June 2, 1982, for a series of consultations with Western European leaders, President Reagan commented, "I know that what we've been doing doesn't read well in the *Washington Post* or the *New York Times,* but believe me, it reads well in Peoria." In so saying, Reagan was underscoring his support among the many Americans uninfluenced by Washington's intense political climate and Eastern establishment press.

Probably more than anyone else, politicians and government officials are cognizant of the relationship between public opinion and public policy. They know that the perceptions that most people have of events and public figures are filtered through the press and that much of the power of the press lies in its selectivity—which stories make the news and how much emphasis is given to them. Recognition of the news media's influence on public opinion, in turn, often determines how the decision makers propose and promote presidential initiatives.

In a book on his White House years, John Ehrlichman provides a case in point:

> I would estimate that Richard Nixon spent half of his working time on the nonsubstantive aspects of the presidency, and probably 40 percent of that half dealing with the problems of communication. I have watched Nixon spend a morning designing Walter Cronkite's lead story for that evening and then send Ron Ziegler, Henry Kissinger or me out to a press briefing to deliver it in such a way that Cronkite couldn't ignore it. [14]

By all accounts, most contemporary presidents have operated in the same fashion.

Going Public

According to political scientist Samuel Kernell, "the frequency with which presidents in the past half century have communicated directly with the American public shows that the more recent the president, the more often he goes public." [15] Kernell contends that new communications technology and modes of transportation have enabled contemporary presidents to adopt an innovative strategy of going public to solicit popular support, thus substantially replacing political bargaining as a means to achieve their objectives.

He notes that since the early 1960s presidents have steadily increased their prime-time TV exposure. In 1981 Ronald Reagan delivered eight major televised addresses, setting a first-year record for any president.

Between the 1940s and the late 1980s, the annual number of minor public addresses by presidents increased fivefold. Foreign and domestic presidential travel also increased significantly, often solely in search of favorable publicity.

One of the compensations that presidents enjoy when fighting for their policies and programs or seeking reelection is constant media exposure. They are the prime news subject in the country, and they receive worldwide media coverage. No political rival can match the president as a publicity attraction. Also at the president's disposal is a vast publicity machine with a reach that encircles the globe.

The president has access to a fleet of the most modern aircraft and the services of U.S. Army Signal Corps specialists. The White House is equipped with its own television and radio broadcast facilities. A large staff of communications and public relations experts choreograph activities to ensure that the chief executive looks presidential. White House photographers are almost always present to record moments large and small in the president's daily routine. A highly structured White House press office deals with the constant demands of the news media. Speechwriters draft and polish the president's messages.

Today, it is acknowledged that continual publicity is a critical aspect of presidential politics. As former journalist and White House aide Douglass Cater observed, publicity is as essential to the orderly functioning of modern American government "as the power to levy taxes and pass laws." [16]

Patterns of Public Opinion toward Presidents

President James A. Garfield complained that he was "the last person in the world to know what the people really want and think." Today, with the development of the mass media and the refinement of opinion survey techniques, it is unlikely that a president would utter the same complaint.

David B. Truman, an American government scholar, defines public opinion as "the expression of an attitude on an issue or proposition." There are, however, a number of publics, divided, for example, by race, religion, cultural background, political affiliation, social beliefs, occupational pursuits, and financial income. To enhance their leverage and promote their interests, they may band together into organizations, such as the American Bankers Association, Veterans of Foreign Wars, U.S. Chamber of Commerce, or National Wildlife Federation.

Public opinion, however, can change dramatically over time or through a revised perspective on an issue. The American public had been staunchly opposed, for example, to the recognition of Communist China; but Nixon's celebrated trip to the People's Republic in 1972 led to a policy of accommodation, and many Americans, following the president's leadership, reversed their position.

Because presidents are constantly in the public eye, they are particularly vulnerable to the subtle and sometimes tempestuous shifts in the winds of popular sentiment. No matter what they do, their public standing fluctuates erratically since they seldom can fully satisfy the expectations their supporters had when they entered office. Even as President Reagan achieved consistently high popularity ratings, many of his followers on the far right expressed displeasure because they felt he had not gone far enough in following the conservative credo.

Occasionally, the public turns on a president even when the White House is not fully the cause of what went wrong. As a case in point, President Carter bore the brunt of public displeasure in 1979 when OPEC (Organization of Petroleum Exporting Countries) policies led to a hike in U.S. gasoline prices. Yet the public is just as likely to rally around the president during periods of national peril, even those that administration policies may have created. For example, Americans supported President Kennedy in the 1961 Bay of Pigs fiasco when U.S.-backed Cuban exile forces failed in an effort to invade the island and overthrow Fidel Castro.

Minute scrutiny by the national news media further intensifies the ebb and flow of presidential public opinion. Harry Truman, who disdained presidential pandering to public opinion surveys and was subject to wild swings in popularity, said the experience was "like riding a tiger."

Public Opinion Cycles

Students of government almost universally agree that presidents begin their tenure in office with a high level of popular support and a willingness, even an eagerness, by the public to accord them a full measure of trust and goodwill. A subliminal sense exists that the public and the president are joined in the hope that the new administration can bring peace and prosperity to the nation. This period of good feeling, roughly the first few months of a presidency, is referred to as the "honeymoon."

Although there are risks of misreading the events of an administration's early days, the period does offer a convenient opportunity to take the measure of the new president and project what may be expected throughout the term. During that brief spell, presidential character begins to form, working habits are set, and the changing of the guard is nearly completed. Following FDR's first one hundred days, Walter Lippmann wrote, "We became again an organized nation confident of our power to provide for our own security and to control our destiny." [17]

The fickleness of public opinion toward a president is reflected in President Gerald R. Ford's experience. The euphoric spirit in which his administration began was promptly deflated by his pardon of Nixon and offer of conditional amnesty for Vietnam draft evaders and war deserters. He also incurred criticism because he appeared unwilling—or unable—to get out from under the shadow of his predecessor, particularly in his insistence on keeping Nixon holdovers on the White House staff and his reluctance to reorganize the cabinet. After one hundred days, the Ford White House still lacked its own distinctive character, other than that of a benign stewardship—a trait that plagued his entire presidency.

Reagan's early days were widely perceived as a personal success, marked by the release of the American hostages from Iran at the same time that he was taking the oath of office. A "second honeymoon" followed the assassination attempt on March 30, 1981. There was, however, less effusion in many quarters over Reagan's supply-side economic plan and the retraction of his pledge to balance the budget by 1983. Moreover, each of his introductory overtures in foreign affairs prompted controversy—the elevation of the El Salvador conflict to a test of U.S.-Soviet relations, the lifting of the Soviet grain embargo, and the proposed sale of AWACS (Airborne Warning and Control System) surveillance planes to Saudi Arabia.

In the next stage of the opinion cycle, as presidents push their programs, the gloss begins to wear thin. Their proposals inevitably antagonize certain interest groups, and their popularity, predictably, begins to decline. Their public rating may erode further in a third stage if unemployment increases, the president becomes engaged in partisan politics during the midterm elections, or a military operation goes sour. In 1980, for example, many people viewed President Carter's aborted attempt to rescue the American hostages in Iran as an example of his inability to take decisive action at the opportune moment. In November 1980 he lost his bid for reelection.

Since Truman, every president except Eisenhower, Kennedy, and Reagan has left office less popular than when he entered. Throughout the term, however, the presidents' popularity rose and fell in response to numerous unforeseen influences. Truman is said to have been the most and least popular U.S. president, fluctuating between an extraordinarily high rating of 87 percent shortly after he became president and a low of slightly more than 20 percent at one point in his second term. Reagan, recognized as the most effective public relations president since FDR, received only a 37 percent approval rating at the midpoint of his first term, lower than any of the four preceding presidents at that stage of their administrations. But he left office with a 63 percent approval rating—the highest since FDR's 66 percent.

Lyndon Johnson reversed the traditional pattern, receiving low marks for his foreign policy decisions—those pertaining to the Vietnam War—and high marks for his Great Society domestic policies at the start of his presidency. By the end of his administration, his popularity had dropped measurably because of mounting Vietnam War casualties and suspicions that he had lied to the people about the conduct of the war, creating what became known as his "credibility gap."

Traditionally, public evaluation of presidential leadership hinges more on performance than on personal qualities. In this regard, domestic policy issues invariably provoke sharply divided public responses because of the involvement of deeply felt political and personal interests. Big business, for example, reacted unfavorably when President Kennedy forced a roll back in steel price rises in 1962, as did many southerners when the White House enforced the 1954 Supreme Court school desegregation decision.

International events, meanwhile, can cut both ways. As political scientists Richard A. Watson and Norman C. Thomas have noted, dramatic events involving national and presidential prestige—such as Reagan's 1983 Grenada invasion and his air strikes against Libya in 1986—produce a "rally-round-the-flag" phenomenon, with Americans generally supporting their president. However, long-term wars that inflict a heavy toll in casualties, such as those in Korea and Vietnam, can cost the president public support. [18]

How the Public Judges Presidents

Scholars are generally at pains to determine what influences presidential popularity and why. Steven A. Shull, a political scientist, observed, "It seems to be affected by events, the economy, media, the type policy involved, and the style of the president." [19]

The public, not unnaturally, assesses presidents largely from a personal perspective. Favorable opinion may be based on ideological compatibility or simply on whether, as Ronald Reagan suggested, the country seems to be better off than it was under the previous administration.

Among the qualities Americans look for in their presidents is leadership. Americans want chief executives who are steadfast in their convictions—not mired in self-doubts, like Warren Harding, who asked, "Am I a big enough man?" The public clearly prefers activist presidents who perform seemingly superhuman acts of courage and who, for the good of the country, extend their powers to the outermost limits when confronted with war or economic depressions, as did FDR. Americans respect as well the strength of character Truman displayed during the Korean War, particularly in his recalling of Gen. Douglas MacArthur, and during the tensions of the cold war.

Presidential personality, style, and image—that is, how presidents comport themselves and exemplify national values—also are important to the country. Wit counts, too. John Kennedy received high marks both at home and abroad when, during his first official trip to Paris, he introduced himself as the husband of Jacqueline Kennedy, rather than as the president of the United States.

Unfair as it is, presidents susceptible to physical mishaps or clumsiness become victims of public embarrassment. Ford is the most glaring example. Despite his background as a college athlete, he earned a reputation as a bumbler when photographed falling while skiing, hitting his head exiting *Air Force One,* and tumbling down the ramp on arriving in Salzburg, Austria, in June 1975. In his presidential memoirs, Ford wrote that "every time I stumbled or bumped my head or fell in the snow, reporters zeroed in on that to the exclusion of almost everything else." [20] Carter suffered a similar indignity when he was forced to drop out of a long-distance run because of exhaustion.

To succeed, presidents must exhibit rhetorical prowess—the ability to lift the spirits of people with words and ideas and crystallize a vision for the nation. FDR boosted the country's flagging morale during the Great Depression when he asserted in his 1933 inaugural address, "The only thing we have to fear is fear itself." Kennedy's call to service in his inaugural address in 1961 has become part of the national lore: "Ask not what your country can do for you—ask what you can do for your country."

Americans are most likely to view presidents favorably when they are seen performing ceremonial duties or are projected as personal embodiments of the nation's constitutional and moral values. Such activities include signing legislation, greeting heads of state, welcoming home members of the military wounded in hostile action, or delivering a televised speech dealing with an issue vital to the national well-being. Presidents also invoke a favorable public impression when they are portrayed as family men or pictured in situations common to most Americans, as was Ford in the photograph of him toasting his own English muffins for breakfast.

Eventually, all presidents discover that public opinion can be overpowering. Woodrow Wilson's dream of a League of Nations was destroyed on the shoals of dissenting public opinion. In 1945-1946, after the end of World War II, public pressure to "bring the boys back home" and to demobilize the armed forces was irresistible despite diplomatic imperatives for maintaining a strong military force in Europe. Johnson decided against seeking reelection when it became painfully clear that most Americans were opposed to the Vietnam War. Once the tide of public opinion swept against him at the height of the Watergate scandal, Richard Nixon became the first U.S. president to resign from office. Sometimes, White House public relations plans go awry, as did Ford's anti-inflation campaign featuring buttons labeled "WIN"—whip inflation now. And public impatience to win the release of the American hostages in Iran perceptibly diminished Carter's popular standing and contibuted significantly to his defeat in 1980.

Avenues of Communication

Historically, the most significant link between presidents and the American public has been the press. But presidents also have other means of seeking and measuring support for themselves and their policies. Political parties (although more significant in the past than today), the president's own pollsters and public liaison staff, interest groups, and personal appearances both in the United States and abroad are among the other ways the president communicates with the public.

Political Parties

Political organizations first took shape in the 1790s, but not until the election of Andrew Jackson in 1828 did public participation in the parties become widespread. National politics polarized around Jackson and his opposition, and Jackson turned to the public for support. As Bruce Buchanan wrote, "Jackson used his charismatic personality to arouse the consciousness of [the middle] class and focus its attention on the presidency as the instrument for protecting and furthering its interests. In the process, he showed that a president backed strongly by the mass public had the leverage to impose his leadership and make the constitutional system work.... The Jackson presidency was the first great historical demonstration of the contribution made by public support to presidential effectiveness." [21]

By the early twentieth century, throngs of immigrants had moved into the cities, and political machines were held together largely by patronage. Local party organizations, to gain converts and ensure votes, acted as welfare agents, providing jobs, food, loans, and clothes and steering these new Americans through the coils of bureaucratic red tape. Although these functions of the parties changed in the 1930s when the government, under Roosevelt's New Deal, took over many of these tasks, parties remained the principal instrument for selecting and electing presidents until the late 1960s. Because of deep dissension at its 1968 convention, the Democratic party undertook a series of reforms that changed the presidential nominating system and, in a larger context, altered the face of American politics. The party "opened up" the nominating process by augmenting the number of rank-and-file party members as delegates to the national conventions and by accelerating the growth of binding state primaries. The number of primaries grew to 23 in 1972, 30 in 1976, and 38 in 1980, severely limiting the ability of party leaders to handpick delegates. Although Republican party leaders were under less pressure from within to change the rules than were their Democratic counterparts, they too were prompted by state laws to institute reforms that opened the party's nominating process more to rank-and-file voters.

As the parties declined, the role of the media in American politics vastly expanded. Today, it is mainly the media that assess the candidates and, to a degree, select the issues—functions that formerly belonged almost exclusively to the parties. Moreover, the public's impressions of candidates and issues are mostly transmitted through the prism of the news media. Because candidates are less reliant on and less beholden to their party, they run campaigns that are virtually independent of the party but that are quite dependent on the media to project their persona. The media have become the main forum in which the political process is played out.

Critics insist that party reforms have led to unfavorable consequences. Some Democrats assert that under the old system neither George McGovern, Jimmy Carter, nor Michael Dukakis could have been nominated and that the party would not have suffered the damage it did by their political defeats. They additionally stress that the accountability of the new political amateurs and the media representatives is not commensurate with the power of their enlarged roles.

Critics further maintain that national party conventions have evolved into synthetic, made-for-television productions, their outcomes foreordained in the extended primaries. Political scientists William Crotty and Gary Jacobson observed, "The role of the political party in campaigns has given way to the technology of television-centered campaigns built on polls and run by media and public relations experts." [22] For the most part, the conventions have become ceremonial investitures, an amalgam of politics and show business.

Defenders argue that the reforms tended to democratize the process by opening it to citizen activists and independents, creating new political coalitions. And as Byron E. Shafer has pointed out, the reforms could be seen not only in the identity of the candidates themselves, but "in a shift from party careerists to political insurgents, from insiders to outsiders. [23]

As a consequence of the restructured political process, which diminished the power of machine bosses, the news media became the principal intermediary in the public's relationship with candidates and government officials.

News Media

In 1980 James David Barber described national political journalists as the "new kingmakers" or the "new power brokers." He contends that "journalism took over where the parties left off." Another writer, Stephen Hess, has suggested that the nation is moving "from party democracy to media democracy."

With ample justification, the United States has been called "the first media state." Network television and the national press are no longer simply observers or instant chroniclers of events. Because they interpret as well as report on public affairs, government policy, and popular attitudes, the media have become an integral part of the political process.

The media emerged from the Vietnam War and Watergate more confident—arrogant, in the view of their critics—and freer than ever of some of their self-imposed restraints. Since the war, news organizations have become bigger, more diverse, more influential, and more controversial. In fact, they have become such a participatory ingredient in political life that policy makers and the public alike have a sense that many events do not really take place unless they are witnessed and reported by television and the newspapers or news magazines.

Most presidents enter the White House promising an "open administration" and frequent news conferences. Then, after a relatively brief honeymoon, the president becomes convinced that the media, because of their criticism, are intent on undermining the administration. The media are equally persuaded that the White House in its self-interest is withholding or distorting potentially embarrassing information and seeking to cover up mistakes, errors in judgment, and poorly conceived and executed policies.

Carter's presidency serves as an example. Shortly before his inauguration, Carter said, "If I can stay close to the people of this country ... I think I have a chance to be a great president." He pledged to hold press conferences every other week. On alternate weeks, as part of the White House's media liaison program, out-of-town editors and broadcasters were invited to Washington to hear administration executives and to meet with the president. Nonetheless, by the end of his administration Carter was holding press conferences less than once a month. Later, he asserted that one of his deepest disappointments as president was "the irresponsibility of the press." [24]

Acknowledging the predictability of relations between the White House and the media, Tom C. Korologos, a congressional lobbyist in the Nixon White House and a transition planner for Reagan, said, "His [Reagan's] relations with the press will be like all presidents. You can put it on a graph. They all start out great, and then one day the White House press secretary comes in and throws his briefcase at the wall. The press thrives on controversy and, in effect, constitutes the opposition government." [25]

Inevitably, what starts out on a harmonious note deteriorates into an adversary relationship. Presidential press conferences occur less frequently. The White House permits only selective interviews with proadministration journalists and cultivates the news media outside of Washington. Finally, the White House circumvents the Washington media by relying more heavily on carefully scheduled presidential speeches and personal appearances, appeals to interest groups, extensive travel, information by news release, and public statements by faithful surrogates.

Television, above all, has changed the relationship between the press and the presidency.

Modern presidents and their advisers are keenly aware that television has increasingly become the medium through which the great majority of voters get their news and form their impressions of public figures. It has allowed presidents to virtually monopolize the political limelight and convey to the American people the impression that they can effectively cope with the problems and crises facing the country.

It has become part of political lore that television enhanced the candidacy of John F. Kennedy in his quest for the White House against Richard Nixon, contributed to Lyndon Johnson's downfall, provided Jimmy Carter with national exposure, and made Ronald Reagan one of the most popular presidents of the twentieth century.

In the pretelevision era, it would have been almost impossible for an outsider from the Deep South with no national identity, such as Jimmy Carter, to suddenly gain the recognition needed to win the presidency. But, as William Lee Miller noted, Carter perceived "the increased importance of the instant, visual, mass communications of signs, signals, and images." [26]

On the negative side, television has significantly altered the political environment in which presidents toil and it can conceivably affect their potential for leadership. Their mental and and physical mishaps are recorded for posterity. Critical coverage can provoke questions about their competence and ability to lead the nation in times of crises, as well as raise doubts about their sincerity and motives. Finally, the constant pressure of being under intense scrutiny and forced to forfeit their privacy serves to sap their energy and consume their time.

Recognizing the positive and negative aspects of the televised presidency, Kenneth W. Thompson, director of the University of Virginia's White Burkett Miller Center of Public Affairs, has stressed that although the power of the media is manifested in every sector of public life "voices continue to be raised asking what its impact will be for good or ill.... Only strong institutions and strong leaders can survive the brunt of the media's thrust. A Franklin D. Roosevelt harnessed the media to his ends, a Lyndon B. Johnson or Richard M. Nixon was destroyed. Those who would live in the television age must master it, not be ruled by it." [27]

Measures of Public Support

Presidents are constantly trying to find out what the people are thinking. "What I want," Lincoln once exclaimed, "is to get done what the people desire to have done, and the question for me is how to find that out exactly."

Public opinion can be fickle and is often a source of consternation to public officials. Before the advent of scientific public opinion research in the 1930s, presidents had to rely on crowd reactions, popular sentiment as reflected in White House mail, comments from visitors, editorial positions of the nation's newspapers, observations of friends, and trends in election results. Today, public opinion surveys—conceded to be as much art as science—are part of the political orthodoxy. Refinements in methodology, canvassing techniques, and survey analysis have made polls an indispensable element of campaigning for office and governing once in office.

As defined by veteran public opinion specialist Louis Harris, "Polling is a systematic way of providing intelligence." Others describe it as the best way to make campaign decisions in the most rational way.

Measuring who is ahead and who is behind—the horserace aspect of a campaign—is the most elementary way political polls are used. More specifically, they are used to appraise voter attitudes, identify cutting national issues, help draft campaign strategy, monitor the candidate's strength among the various constituencies, and help determine how the campaign's financial and political resources are to be committed.

Poll findings further provide clues as to where candidates should go to shore up support, what issues they should address, where and how they should run media commercials, what themes they should emphasize to distinguish themselves from the pack.

Richard Wirthlin, President Reagan's pollster, reported that polls help candidates locate opportunities among the sundry constituencies. In 1980, for example, Reagan acted on his survey findings and broke the traditional Democratic coalition by pursuing the votes of blue-collar workers.

Two days before the election, Wirthlin took a poll to measure the probable political consequences should the American hostages be released by Iran before the balloting began. "We found . . . it would have had very little effect on either candidate," he reported. "Knowing that, we kept our campaign very much on [the same] track."

After Reagan took office, Wirthlin's surveys indicated widespread displeasure with administration environmental policies, underscored by controversy involving improper practices within the Environmental Protection Agency (EPA). As a result, to restore credibility and stature to the agency, Reagan appointed the highly regarded William D. Ruckelshaus as EPA director.

Notwithstanding the increased prominence of political polls, no one, including practitioners themselves, contends they are infallible. Indeed, as they proliferate and become more sophisticated, there seems to be more room for miscues and misunderstandings. The margin for error in conducting public opinion surveys is broad and deep: the way the questions are worded, the context in which they are asked, the timing of the poll, whether the sample is large enough to provide a valid reading, whether the findings are correctly analyzed and presented.

Realists recognize that polls are only a snapshot in time and that usually the most beneficial information gained is in spotting movements in public opinion. Even then, polls may be overtaken by events. The *New York Times*/CBS News Poll in February 1984 showed that Democratic presidential candidate Walter Mondale "now holds the most commanding lead ever recorded this early in a presidential campaign by a nonincumbent." That same day, Gary Hart scored an upset victory over Mondale in the New Hampshire primary, overnight turning the contest, at least temporarily, into a two-man race.

While polling is accepted as an essential element of politics, there is suspicion that some politicians depend too much on them and not enough on other sources of information or their own knowledge, experience, and instincts. They may change not only their policy positions, style, and strategy but, in some instances, their political philosophy.

Most successful politicians want to know what public opinion is on any given issue, but will go with their judgment and instinct notwithstanding; they know it is but one of a multitude of factors that envelop most political issues.

George McGovern, the losing Democratic presidential nominee in 1972, who made an unsuccessful bid for the 1984 nomination, offered this view of campaign pollsters: "If you are not careful, they can run the campaign. They have too much influence on some candidates. It's too easy for a candidate to back away from difficult questions based on the findings of his pollster. In that way, they are a threat to a candidate's convictions."

Presidents, for the most part, are attentive to the polls, not simply to secure public affection and boost their popularity, as significant as that may be, but rather to discover opportunities for gain in specific policy areas and detect possible slippage in government performance, thereby allowing them to take remedial action.

Interest Groups

In a speech to the graduating class of Rollins College in 1936, President Franklin Roosevelt declared, "There are . . . groups to which almost every man and woman is tied, connected in some way. They are connected with some form of association—the church, the social circle, the club, the lodge, the labor organization, the neighboring farmers, the political party. Even business and commerce are almost wholly made up of groups. It is the problem of government to harmonize the interests of these groups which are often divergent and opposing. The science of politics, indeed, may be said to be in large part the science of the adjustment of conflicting group interests."

Thus Roosevelt acknowledged the interaction between the presidency and the myriad interest groups throughout the United States. He recognized that appeals to the public and Congress are most effective when there is evidence of substantial support from interest groups, many of which have large memberships and are nationally organized and well financed.

Since the Roosevelt era, the number of interest groups has multiplied tremendously. With each emerging concern—arms control, abortion, equal rights, a balanced federal budget, sex and violence on television, noise pollution, the dumping of toxic wastes, consumer protection—new constituencies form organizations to promote, defend, or defeat proposals that would affect their interests.

By the late 1980s, approximately 10,000 professional representatives—or lobbyists—were working in Washington, 7,600 of whom were registered with the clerk of the House, compared with 365 who were registered in 1960. (The statute, which is widely criticized as more loophole than law, allows some special-interest representatives to avoid registration and thus does not indicate the true number of Washington lobbyists.) Among those registered were officers of 1,600 trade and professional associations and labor unions; agents of some 4,000 individual corporations; lawyers and consultants who registered as lobbyists or foreign agents with the Justice Department; and spokespersons for virtually every state and large U.S. city, as well as for many universities and most religious groups. The most recent development is the proliferation of public relations firms in the nation's capital, most of which include lobbyists and special-issue lawyers.

Beginning in the Nixon administration, the White House institutionalized its relationships with interest groups through the establishment of the Office of Public Liaison. The office was formed as a response to the withering of the party system and the collateral emergence of single-issue pressure groups. Presidents recognize that they can no longer rely on traditional political alignments in the promotion of their legislative agenda and executive programs and must seek, issue by issue, the endorsement of floating coalitions.

A critical part of the office's function is regularly to invite various interest group leaders from across the United States to the White House where they are royally treated and briefed on administration policies by top government officials, including White House aides, cabinet members, and the president. Although the White House describes the work of the Office of Public Liaison as an "educational program," it is in effect a lobbying effort based on the expectation that the guests will return home and spread the administration's message, thereby increasing pressure on Congress on behalf of the president's programs. On their part, the interest group participants generally feel they have been given the chance to have their voice heard at the highest level of government.

Presidential Appearances

In the ceremonial role of chief of state, presidents are portrayed as the embodiment of the national interest. Simply the appearance of the president—with the display of the presidential seal and the playing of "Hail to the Chief"—strikes an emotional chord and taps patriotic sentiments among Americans. Whether they voted Republican or Democrat, Americans generally perceive the president as the living symbol of the nation. The chief of state is, further, the country's most familiar and most notable celebrity.

When presidents deliver a major speech, as they do frequently, to national business, labor, veterans, minority, religious, and professional organizations, they are expressing interest in the concerns of these groups, while also addressing the rest of the country. Breakthroughs in transportation and communications technology have offered presidents increased opportunities for going public and for capturing the attention of the electorate. Nixon's trip to China, Carter's town hall meetings and his trip to Panama, Reagan's presence at highly publicized summit meetings with Soviet leader Mikhail Gorbachev and his participation in the glittering centennial celebration of the Statue of Liberty, and George Bush's visit to China shortly after his inauguration all present strong and memorable visual images. The ceremonial presidency plays to a mass audience and is ensured television coverage and front-page headlines. The symbolism and rhetorical flourishes invariably enhance the president's popularity.

The marvel of presidential travel is in the planning and coordination and the assurances taken so that everything goes according to schedule. While the paramount concern is the president's safety and comfort, the objective is to achieve maximum political effect. Stage-managed appearances by the president emphasize the atmosphere and allow the White House to control events, which are avidly televised and reported.

Not infrequently, even the crowd that gathers to greet presidents as they disembark from *Air Force One* is programmed. When Reagan returned from a European trip in June 1982, for example, 50,000 special tickets were distributed to administration officials, federal workers, and employees of the Republican National Committee to guarantee a large welcoming crowd when *Air Force One* landed at Andrews Air Force Base outside of Washington. Although the White House denied any pressure was being applied, "point people" were designated at the various agencies to oversee the turnout. Buses were provided and color-coded tickets printed—yellow for important political figures, green for senior government executives, and white for civil servants and the general public.

Jet travel permits presidents unlimited opportunities to journey to distant capitals and to star in diplomatic dramas, as the world follows each move on the television screen and through the printed press. For the Republic's first 117 years, however, U.S. presidents were expected to remain on American soil to ensure national leadership. Theodore Roosevelt was the first president to venture abroad, sailing to Panama aboard an American ship and, except for a few hours, remaining within U.S. waters. Woodrow Wilson became the first president to cross the seas when he attended the Paris Peace Conference following World War I. He was was severely criticized for his extended absence from the seat of government and the withdrawal of physical protection provided at home. Sen. Lawrence Y. Sherman of Illinois introduced a resolution to declare the presidency vacant whenever the occupant left American soil, but the proposal lacked congressional support.

Wilson's lengthy trip overseas is blamed for his inability to stay in touch with national sentiment concerning the proposed League of Nations and with public attitudes on domestic issues. Not for nearly a quarter of a century did a U.S. president again venture abroad: in 1943 Franklin Roosevelt journeyed to Casablanca aboard a Pan American plane to meet with British Prime Minister Winston Churchill for a wartime conference.

Truman was the first president to popularize domestic air travel but mostly for brief vacation trips to his home in Independence, Missouri. Eisenhower's 1959 "good will" tour around the world generally is recognized as the first presidential trip where favorable publicity appeared to be the primary objective.

Foreign Publics

Under the Constitution, the president has the duties of commander in chief of the armed forces, the power to make treaties and appoint ambassadors with the advice and consent of the Senate, and the authority to deal with other nations. In addition to these formal powers, other factors contribute to the president's preeminence in foreign affairs, including the symbolic nature of the office as a unifying national force, jurisdiction over a huge and highly specialized federal bureaucracy, and high visibility and access to the news media as a means of influencing the public to support White House initiatives.

Presidential supremacy in foreign policy was reinforced with the outbreak of World War II and throughout the ensuing postwar period when the United States abandoned its traditional isolationism and assumed the role of a world power. During the so-called cold war, the United States began massive foreign aid and economic development programs, developed an elaborate network of overseas military bases, and became a leading party to a series of international commitments and collective security pacts.

As it became increasingly evident after World War II that the conduct of U.S. foreign policy affected domestic policy, the nation's economy, the level of U.S. military strength, international trade, and human rights around the world, the president's role as chief diplomat and commander in chief was enhanced. The policies, decisions, and personality of the president, more than of any other single figure, clearly determine the image and credibility of the United States within the international community of nations.

As advances in mass communications and public relations techniques took hold in American society, foreign policy turned more on an enlightened public opinion. "The major decisions in our foreign policy since [World War II] have been made on the basis of an informed public opinion and overwhelming public support," Truman acknowledged.

This trend in a sense had been in motion for several decades. The evolution from secret to open diplomacy following World War I underlined the significance of public opinion in the international arena. In the first of his famous Fourteen Points proposed at the Paris Peace Conference, President Wilson called for "open covenants of peace, openly arrived at, after which there shall be no private international understandings of any kind, but diplomacy shall proceed always frankly and in the public view." Clarifying what he meant by *open diplomacy,* Wilson said, "I meant, not that there should be no private discussions of delicate matters, but that no secret agreements should be entered upon, and that all international relations, when fixed, should be open, aboveboard, and explicit."

Another development that has changed the way sovereign nations deal with one another is "media diplomacy"—the manipulation of the news media and the application of sophisticated public relations to sway international opinion and constituents at home. Formerly, diplomacy was dependent on quiet consultation and private negotiations, but since the 1970s government leaders commonly speak to one another through the media rather than through traditional channels. Television, with its immediate impact, compels heads of government to make quick decisions, often without sufficient mediation and consultation.

Also, with the rise to power of Soviet leader Mikhail S. Gorbachev in 1985 and his policy of *glasnost,* or "openness," the Soviet Union adopted Western-style news and public relations techniques, which sharpened competition between the two global powers for world opinion.

Among the key U.S. institutions involved in this competition is the United States Information Agency (USIA), which falls under the umbrella of the State Department but has its own mandate as the principal voice of the United States abroad. Created in 1953, its essential mission is to portray American values and culture to other countries and explain U.S. government policies and actions. In addition to carrying out a wide variety of cultural and educational programs, USIA advises the president and U.S. representatives abroad on foreign opinion regarding American policies and practices and on other public affairs issues. The agency has branches in 128 countries and lists an estimated 9,000 employees in Washington and overseas.

Operating virtually autonomously within USIA, the Voice of America (VOA) broadcasts news around the world in forty-two languages, with a worldwide audience of at least 120 million. Each week it beams more than 980 hours of news reports and analyses, feature programs, seminar discussions, music, and editorials. In 1985 Radio Marti was launched as a special part of VOA for broadcasting programs scripted solely for audiences in Cuba.

These and the other developments reaching back to Woodrow Wilson and the early movement toward open diplomacy vastly increased the number of players in the formulation, adaptation, and execution of foreign policy. To gain support for their foreign policy programs, modern presidents must now deal not only with Congress but with special interest groups, lobbyists and other representatives of foreign governments, international business and trade corporations, private economic and foreign affairs groups, foreign opposition leaders, U.S. and foreign news media, academic specialists, and social-cultural organizations. Presidents must appreciate that television and other news media are a vital tool in governing and be skilled in their use to win the endorsements of foreign publics.

Notes

1. George C. Edwards III, *The Public Presidency* (New York: St. Martin's Press, 1983).
2. Richard E. Neustadt, *Presidential Power* (New York: Wiley, 1976).
3. Doris A. Graber, ed., *The President and the Public* (Philadelphia: Institute for the Study of Human Issues, 1982).
4. Quoted in Thomas E. Cronin, *The State of the Presidency,* 2d ed. (Boston: Little, Brown, 1980).
5. Clinton Rossiter, *The American Presidency,* rev. ed. (New York: New American Library, 1962).
6. Philip C. Dolce and George H. Skau, ed., *Power and the Presidency* (New York: Scribner's, 1976).
7. Thomas F. Cronin, *The State of the Presidency* (Boston: Little, Brown, 1975).
8. Grant McConnell, *The Modern Presidency,* 2d ed. (New York. St. Martin's Press, 1976).
9. *Washington Post,* November 8, 1984.
10. *Washington Journalism Review* (Fall 1980).
11. Joe McGinniss, *The Selling of the President 1968* (New York: Trident Press, 1969).
12. Emmet John Hughes, *The Living Presidency* (Baltimore: Penguin, 1972), 89.
13. Ibid., 99.
14. John Ehrlichman, *Witness to Power: The Nixon Years* (New York: Simon and Schuster, 1982).
15. Samuel Kernell, *Going Public: New Strategies of Presidential Leadership* (Washington, D.C.: CQ Press, 1986).
16. Douglass Cater, *The Fourth Branch of Government* (New York: Vintage Books, 1965).
17. Quoted in Arthur M. Schlesinger, Jr., *The Coming of the New Deal,* 2d ed. (New York: Houghton Mifflin, 1958).
18. Richard A. Watson and Norman C. Thomas, *The Politics of the Presidency,* 2d ed. (Washington, D.C.: CQ Press, 1987).
19. Steven A. Shull, *Presidential Policy Making* (Brunswick, Ohio: King's Court, 1979).
20. Gerald R. Ford, *A Time to Heal* (New York: Harper and Row, 1979).
21. Bruce Buchanan, *The Citizen's Presidency* (Washington, D.C.: CQ Press, 1987).
22. William J. Crotty and Gary C. Jacobson, *American Parties in Decline* (Boston: Little, Brown, 1980).
23. Byron E. Shafer, *Quiet Revolution* (New York: Russell Sage Foundation, 1983).
24. Jimmy Carter, *Keeping Faith: Memoirs of a President* (New York: Bantam, 1982).
25. Tom C. Korologos, interview with the author.
26. William Lee Miller, *Yankee from Georgia* (New York: Times Books, 1978).
27. Kenneth W. Thompson, ed., *The Media: The Credibility of Institutions, Policies and Leadership,* vol. 5 (Lanham, Md.: University Press of America, 1985).

Political Parties as President-Public Link

Political parties serve by default as links between the president and the people. The Framers of the Constitution did not design a clear president-public connection. They established instead an office of chief executive that was remote from popular influence. Political parties did not exist at the time of the constitutional founding and the Framers envisioned the presidency in nonpartisan terms, so it is not surprising that they did not provide a formal role for political factions.

Parties quickly emerged, however. They became central features of presidential politics and, indeed, the whole of American politics. Their critical functions of linkage or intermediation were exercised primarily in the electoral arena.

Parties linked citizens with rulers. A shared party affiliation could connect the most humble, ordinary citizen with political luminaries such as governors, members of Congress, and even the president of the United States. Parties became the principal channels for participation in the political process. As such they encouraged and facilitated increasingly democratic government in the United States.

Parties also served as vehicles for linking these various public officeholders within the separated-powers system that dispersed them into different branches and levels of government and further positioned them as rivals. The party idea and organization could provide common ground for cooperation among the president, Congress, and, to a lesser extent, the federal judiciary, and even between national and state governments.

Finally, parties connected officeholders with private elites—notable nongovernmental political actors who sought to influence public policy. Largely through campaign contributions, such forces relied on parties to make known their views in the counsels of government.

In the process of presidential selection, political parties serve as gatekeepers, authorizing candidacies through nominations. Without the party nomination, a presidential candidate lacks legitimacy. Conversely, party control over nominations constrains the public's role in the process.

A contemporary assessment of the party-presidency relationship confronts an interesting paradox: the parties persist despite their indisputable loss of influence over campaigns and elections.

By Harold F. Bass, Jr.

Parties do not appear to have the claim on the allegiances of the electorate they once had. Presidents and public can now interact more directly, through institutions such as the communications media, public opinion polls, and pressure groups, with less reliance on political parties. *(See Media, Public Opinion, and Interest Group chapters elsewhere in Part IV.)*

The organizational connections between presidency and parties have eroded substantially. This can be attributed to changes in presidential selection procedures and practices, the structure of the presidential office, and the decline of patronage.

Despite their general decline in electoral identification and allegiance, the parties organizationally are renewed and in ascendancy. This can be seen in the establishment and maintenance of permanent headquarters, full-time officers, and the performance of a variety of service functions by both of the national parties and by a growing number of state parties. Presidential aspirants still seek the party nomination to authorize their candidacies, and they run for office under the party label and the symbolism it evokes. Once elected, the president, more than any other individual, embodies the political party in the eyes of the general public, which in large part still identifies with the parties. For all the changes in the president-party relationship, the two remain fundamentally linked.

Historical Perspectives on Parties and the Presidency

The emergence of political parties had a profound and transforming effect on the executive office. The constitutional principle of separation of powers produced a clearly divided governmental structure with three distinct branches: executive, legislative, and judicial. Checks and balances, while blurring these divisions, nevertheless were intended to inhibit cooperation by encouraging rivalries among the branches.

The appearance of national political parties altered this setting. They provided a foundation for coordination, cooperation, and unity. The presidential nominee's position at the head of the party's electoral ticket carried with it, in title at least, the status of party leader. This elevated the chief executive position from that of head of one of

AP

Democratic vice-presidential candidate Lloyd Bentsen, left, and presidential candidate Michael Dukakis acknowledge their nomination at the Democratic National Convention July 22, 1988.

three separate and equal branches to that, in theory, of government leader, through the institution of the political party.

Initially, in the 1790s, American political parties were governmental factions. By 1800, however, they were developing organizational means to appeal to the electorate to support the parties' candidates for public offices. Party organization was taking shape, primarily in the form of loosely linked campaign committees, complemented by the partisan press.

In reaching out to the citizenry, and thus positioning themselves as intermediary institutions linking citizens and government, political parties recognized that the constitutional order rested in part on a foundation of popular sovereignty. By the standards of the day, the states' suffrage requirements were liberal and becoming more so, making it easier for the rank-and-file to vote. Religious tests had been abandoned in the revolutionary era, and property requirements were largely eliminated in the decade of the 1820s. Further, the voters' authority in presidential selection was enhanced by post-1800 changes in the operation of the electoral college.

The establishment of the citizen-government link dramatically increased the president's power position in the political order. By virtue of the selection process, nationwide in scope and increasingly popular in operation, the president could claim a national, popular constituency above and beyond that of any governmental rival. The "people connection" allowed the president to tap into the wellsprings of popular sovereignty that nourished the exercise of political authority in an increasingly democratic society. As "tribune of the people," the president could claim a prerogative not specifically enumerated in the constitutional allocation of governmental power.

These critical transformations began in large measure during the administrations of two early nineteenth-century presidents: Thomas Jefferson and Andrew Jackson.

Jefferson merits credit for originating the presidential role of party leader. He led the Democratic-Republican party before his presidential election in 1800, and he carried this leadership responsibility with him to the White House. As president, Jefferson relied extensively on partisan connections to elicit cooperation from like-minded allies in Congress.

Jackson was a genuine popular hero. Before he entered presidential politics, he had attained widespread acclaim by his military accomplishments in the War of 1812 and the Indian conflicts that followed. In his pursuit of the presidency in 1824 and 1828, he emphasized his appeal to the masses. His party took advantage of this situation by mobilizing supporters under the party banner.

However, these new perspectives on the presidency did not gain widespread acceptance until much later, in the twentieth century, when presidents in general began to reap the political benefits of these developments.

From a different standpoint, the formation of two political parties within a decade of the constitutional founding affected the Framer's design for choosing presidents. In seeking the selection of presidential electors committed to a party ticket, the parties necessitated a constitutional change in the electoral college balloting arrangement. The Constitution originally called for each elector to cast a single ballot. On it were to be placed two names, with only one coming from the elector's state. The name that received the most votes, providing that number composed a majority, would be elected president. The name receiving the next most votes would become vice president. If a tie resulted, or if no name received a majority of votes, the House would decide the election.

The first two presidential elections took place absent partisan competition, indeed without any competition. In each instance, George Washington's name appeared on every ballot, while John Adams's name appeared the next most times. Thus, Washington became president and the vice presidency went to Adams. In the election of 1796, there was a contest between Adams, supported by the Federalists, and Thomas Jefferson, running under the banner of the Democratic-Republicans. Adams won a narrow victory, so Jefferson succeeded him as vice president. *(See "Early Experience, 1789-1828," p. 155, in the Electoral Process chapter of Part II.)*

The presidential contest of 1800 provided a rematch. This time, Jefferson's partisan supporters openly sought the selection of electors committed not only to Jefferson's presidential candidacy, but also to that of running mate Aaron Burr for vice president. In a sense, the Democratic-Republicans were almost too successful. Every elector who voted for Jefferson also voted for Burr, and more voted for Jefferson and Burr than for any other choices. With Jefferson and Burr receiving the same number of votes, the House had to decide which one would be president. Ultimately it chose Jefferson. In the aftermath, Jefferson's partisan supporters in Congress quickly proposed the Twelfth Amendment, ratified in 1804. It called for electors to cast two ballots, clearly differentiating the presidential from the vice presidential vote.

This reform allowed, indeed encouraged, electors to vote for party tickets. As such, it transformed the role of the presidential electors. The Framers had envisioned them as trustees: disinterested, public-spirited elites exercising independent wisdom and judgment. After 1800 the electors acted instead primarily as agents, chosen on party tickets and consistently following the instructions of the victorious party in their state.[1]

The Constitution authorizes each state legislature to determine how that state's electors are designated. At first there was a rough balance between those that opted for legislative selection and those preferring popular election. Increasingly, popular election on party tickets became the norm. By 1836 only South Carolina remained committed to legislative selection, a position it held until after the Civil War. This virtually universal acceptance of popular election of presidential electors enhanced both the connection between the president and the public and the intermediary position of political parties.

The public now had a clear role to play in presidential selection and presidential contenders were dependent on the votes of ordinary citizens. The party, in designating electors committed to the presidential nominee and to be chosen by the voters on that basis, now clearly linked the two.

Virtually from the outset, political parties focused their attentions on election of the president, which contributed strongly to their establishment of national bases. This coordinated and united the diverse factions in the several states.

Thus, the parties transformed American political conflict. At first it was a fight mainly among states. But these rivalries came to be supplanted by party competition, which promoted consensus by reducing the potential for fragmentation from among thirteen states to between two parties.

Origins of Party Labels

Our understanding of political party development in the United States is complicated by considerable confusion surrounding the names of the parties. Contemporary Democrats trace their partisan ancestry back to Thomas Jefferson. In Jefferson's day, however, the party went by two different names, either Republican or Democratic-Republican. By 1830 the dominant wing of a divided Democratic-Republican party, led by President Andrew Jackson, abandoned the "Republican" portion of their label, leaving "Democratic" standing alone ever since.

A quarter-century later, in 1854, antislavery sympathizers forming a new party appropriated the name "Republican." Today's Republicans are their descendants.

The term "Democrat" comes from the Greek word "democratia," a combination of "demos," meaning "common people," and the suffix "-kratia," denoting "strength, power." Thus, "democratia" means "power to the people," or "the people rule."

The term "Republican" derives from the Latin phrase "res publica." It literally means "public thing," or "public affair," and it connotes a government in which citizens participate.

Both party names thus suggest the Democrats' and Republicans' common belief in popular government, conducted by representatives of the people and accountable to them.

The Presidency and Two-Party Competition

A distinctive feature of party competition in the United States is that it is dualistic. In other words, contests ordinarily pit two parties against each other. This is in contrast to the multi-party competition prevalent in many European countries, and the absence of party competition in Communist countries and many of the nation-states of the developing world.

In seeking to explain this phenomenon, scholars have pointed to diverse factors such as tradition, culture, and electoral arrangements. Early on, the political conflicts in America divided the participants into pairs: patriots versus loyalists, Federalists versus Anti-Federalists, Federalists versus Democratic-Republicans. Thus, a tradition of two-party competition developed that hindered the emergence of alternatives.

The American political culture has been cited as a factor in the dominance of the two-party system because it is supportive of accommodation and compromise. This allows diverse interests to ally under a party banner despite significant differences. Absent this spirit of concession, the various groups would form their own, separate political organizations, and a multi-party system would prevail.

Finally, electoral arrangements are critical to an understanding of the two-party system. American elections are for the most part organized on the principle of single-member district, winner take all. Electoral units designate a single individual—the one who receives the most votes—to occupy a public office. The winner-take-all provision frustrates minor parties that, while perhaps capable of assembling sizable numerical minorities, cannot realistically aspire to triumphing in an absolute sense over the two entrenched major parties.

The presidency can be viewed as a special case of, and credited with a critical contribution to, the electoral-arrangements explanation. The constitutional standard of an electoral college majority to elect the president discourages competition from parties that cannot hope to attain the high level of support necessary for victory. As such, it supports the maintenance of the two-party system.

In the early years of the Republic, party competition matched the Federalists led by Alexander Hamilton against the Democratic-Republican followers of Thomas Jefferson. In the wake of the Federalists' demise—caused by Jefferson's conclusive triumphs in 1800 and 1804 and reinforced by the victories of his lieutenant, James Madison, in 1808 and 1812—a brief period of one-party rule ensued. Jeffersonian heir James Monroe presided over this so-called "Era of Good Feelings."

By the mid-1820s, however, intraparty conflict had resulted in the emergence of two rival Democratic-Republican factions. These factions reflected personal ambitions and rivalries in the party leadership, pitting Andrew Jackson and his advocates against an alliance of John Quincy Adams, Henry Clay, and their combined supporters. The Jackson faction represented the emergent claims of the growing southwestern region in party and national politics, as well as those of the lower classes, including immigrants; while Adams in particular spoke for the more traditional regional and socioeconomic elements within the party coalition.

As the Democrats and the Whigs, these erstwhile factions became partisan adversaries in the 1830s. About the time the Whigs died out in the 1850s, a new party, the Republicans, appeared on the scene to challenge the Democrats. Their competition has endured ever since.

Two-party competition has typically taken the form of sustained periods of dominance by one party, measured in terms of control of the presidency. From 1800 to 1860, the Democratic party, in its Jeffersonian and Jacksonian incarnations, ordinarily prevailed in presidential elections. Amid the upheaval of the Civil War, this pattern gave way to one of Republican ascendancy. The rise of the Republican party can be attributed initially to the demise of the Whigs and the self-destruction of the Democrats, both precipitated in large part by the slavery controversy. The ultimately successful prosecution of the Civil War under Republican auspices allowed the party to seize the banner of patriotism, while the Democratic opposition was stained by its Southern roots. Increasingly in the postwar years, the Republican party developed lasting ties with business interests that provided it with solid financial support. The Republican era endured, with few exceptions, until 1932, when it was undermined by the Great Depression. That year marked the beginning of a new Democratic era that clearly lasted two decades.

The presidential elections from 1952 until 1988 departed from the previous patterns in that no party was able to sustain its hold on the White House for more than eight years. Thus, if two-party competition is measured in terms of alternation in the occupancy of the White House, these years constituted an unprecedented era of competitiveness. In 1988 Republican nominee George Bush's quest to succeed retiring incumbent Ronald Reagan met with electoral approval, guaranteeing the Republicans at least three consecutive four-year terms in control of the White House and suggesting the presence of a new era of Republican dominance in presidential politics.

Parties as Coalitions

Political parties appeal to interest groups, or collections of individuals who share common backgrounds and concerns. Indeed, parties can be seen as broad coalitions of diverse interests: geographic, social, economic, ethnic, and issue. Particularly in presidential elections, parties seek to achieve victory by attracting sufficient electoral support from voters who are members of these groups.

Presidential leadership is part and parcel of the linkages between president and public, and between parties and groups. For example, during the decade of the 1930s, under the New Deal policies of President Franklin D. Roosevelt, the Democratic party assembled under its umbrella a formidable electoral coalition that generally included the South, racial minorities, blue-collar laborers, farmers, and middle-class elements brought low by the ravages of the Great Depression. This party coalition successfully supported Roosevelt's presidential candidacies an unprecedented four separate times. It remained sufficiently intact in 1948 to bring victory to his successor, Harry S Truman. Lingering vestiges of the Roosevelt coalition could be observed in the electoral support for the victorious 1976 Democratic presidential nominee, Jimmy Carter.

Republican responses to this era of Democratic domination entailed successful presidential campaigns by Dwight Eisenhower, Richard Nixon, and Ronald Reagan that appealed to traditionally Democratic voters. The Eisenhower and Reagan appeals in particular were personalistic. Both of these individuals enjoyed popularity that transcended partisanship. In addition, all three benefited from public dissatisfaction with the performance of the Democratic incumbents who preceded them. In each instance, it was fueled by foreign policy problems besetting Democratic administrations: Korea in 1952, Vietnam in 1968, and Iran in 1980.

As presidents, they followed up with efforts to reshape electoral alignments into a new winning coalition of interests under the party banner. Over the years, they achieved significant defections to the GOP in the white South, the middle class, and among blue-collar workers.

Linkage Patterns and Changes

As political parties developed institutionally during the nineteenth century, their intermediary role took on diverse dimensions. In the electoral arena, they structured the vote, providing the voters with alternative choices. Indeed, they effectively controlled the voters' options as well as the routes to public office through their nominations. Without a party nomination, a candidacy lacked credibility and legitimacy.

Their symbols labeled candidates for the benefit of the voters. In an era when literacy rates were much lower than now, and when voters lacked access to much specific personal information about particular candidates, this contribution was critical. The Republican elephant and the Democratic donkey gave voters crucial decision cues regarding the qualities of candidates.

Political parties also provided economic employment and social services for their constituencies. The former occurred through the mechanism of patronage, or appointment to government jobs according to partisan political criteria. Following an election, loyal adherents of the victorious party could claim government positions as spoils.

Significantly, the rise of the "spoils system" occurred in part as a systematic attempt to link the president with the public through the political party. President Andrew Jackson bemoaned the established practice he encountered of elitist careerism in public service. He tried to open public employment to the ranks of ordinary citizens, who provided the foundation of his political support.

As the government grew in size and function, widespread patronage resources gave citizens incentives to establish and maintain party ties. In 1841, for example, the available federal government positions numbered some 23,700. By the 1880s, when the abused and maligned spoils system was reformed, the number of positions had increased about fivefold.[2]

In the nineteenth-century heyday of patronage, practitioners recognized its significance for political parties and enthusiastically defended it in the name of the public good. One of the more flamboyant of the patronage politicians around the turn of the century, George Washington Plunkitt, of New York City's Tammany Hall, perceived the connections as follows:

> First, this great and glorious country of ours was built up by political parties; second, parties can't hold together if their workers don't get the offices when they win; third, if the parties go to pieces, the government they built up must go to pieces, too; fourth, then there'll be h--- to pay.[3]

The social service role assumed by the parties in the latter part of the nineteenth century was exercised primarily by the urban party machines that responded to the needs of the teeming masses of immigrants arriving and residing there. Until the New Deal of the 1930s and the Great Society of the 1960s, neither the federal government nor its state counterparts provided citizens much in the way of help to the needy. The individualistic political culture viewed what has come to be called "welfare" as beyond the pale of the public sector. Such assistance, if any, typically came from private sources such as churches, the Salvation Army, and philanthropists.

Thus, political parties moved into a public void of sorts when they at times directly delivered primary social services: food, clothing, and shelter. More generally, they enabled newcomers to take part in the political process and solicit governmental responses to their needs and interests. It was to the parties that they looked when problems arose that involved the government. Local party leaders pulled strings and provided favors.

As such, political parties served as a channel for social advancement integrating outsiders into the mainstream of society. They attracted constituents who came to rely on the party in meeting daily needs and aspirations for the future and who reciprocated with their loyalties and electoral support.

Within this context, parties came to occupy a central and critical position in the political process. Citizens developed enduring attachments that were manifested primarily by voting for the parties' candidates and otherwise supporting the parties' causes with their energies and resources.

The presidency was significant in these developments. As the most visible party officeholder, the president personified the party in the eyes of the general public. Further, as chief executive, the president authorized the allocation of federal patronage, the bulk of which was distributed through the cabinet-level Post Office Department, a vast operation that extended to virtually every city, town, and village throughout the United States.

Rather quickly, then, in the nineteenth century a system of mutual benefits developed between president and party. A presidential aspirant looked to the party to authorize the candidacy through nomination and depended on its organizational support for victory. Further, an incumbent president looked to the party to promote support for presidential policies.

Besides making available to the party the federal government's patronage resources, the president could be expected to promote the party's fortunes by campaigning for its nominees for other elective offices, shouldering some fund-raising responsibilities, and pushing for enactment of laws to implement the party's public policies. Thus, the presidency provided a critical contribution to the development of the parties as intermediaries.

Party Identification

Voters appear to develop psychological attachments over time to political parties in response to a number of factors.[4] One of those is the success or failure of the president and the presidency in winning adherents to the party cause. *(See Chief of Party chapter in Part III.)*

Traditionally, party identifications seem to have taken place relatively early in individuals' lives. Indeed, they have emerged in childhood and in the absence of much specific information about politics. This suggests that political socialization, or the process of learning political and social roles in society, is an important force in the development of party identification.

This early gravitation to one party or another focuses attention on the family as a primary agent in the process. In other words, citizens can acquire party identification by inheritance. This process rarely involves systematic indoctrination on the part of family members. It is normally much more informal and subtle. Children hear parents discussing candidates and issues, and they often come to identify with and share their parents' preferences. Initial, familial influence can be reinforced by a relatively homogeneous environment largely controlled by the family. A focus on inheritance as the foundation for party identification begs the question of why one's ancestors originally developed a party tie. Thus, looking for additional factors associated with party identification, many commentators consider social class, or socioeconomic status, as a major influence.

Social class is a complicated concept. It has both objective and subjective elements. Objectively, class can be defined in terms of wealth, occupation, education, and heritage. Subjectively, class is a function of how one views oneself, and how that individual is viewed, with respect to a relative position within a hierarchical society. According to this perspective, voters are attracted to parties, and parties appeal to voters, on the basis of class interests.

The relationship between class and party in the

Table 1 Social Characteristics and Party Identification: 1984

	Democrats		Independents leaning		Independents leaning	Republicans		Party	No. of
	Strong	Weak	Democratic	Independents	Republican	Weak	Strong	difference	cases
Education									
No high school	27%	18%	9%	14%	8%	12%	10%	23%	494
High school graduate	15	22	12	13	14	14	10	13	775
College	13	20	11	8	14	17	16	0	918
Income									
Lower third	24	21	13	13	10	11	9	25	635
Middle third	17	20	12	10	14	15	12	10	690
Upper third	12	19	9	8	27	18	16	−3	623
Occupation									
Service	25	26	12	12	8	10	7	34	264
Blue collar	19	20	12	12	14	12	10	17	744
White collar	17	21	8	10	16	14	14	10	293
Professional	13	18	10	9	14	19	18	−6	629
Farm	10	17	7	18	12	18	16	−7	98
Religion									
Jews	29	31	14	8	10	4	6	50	52
Catholics	19	23	10	14	12	11	10	21	571
Protestants	16	19	9	9	13	18	14	3	1,355
Race									
Blacks	33	32	14	11	6	1	3	61	242
Whites	15	19	11	11	14	17	14	3	1,900
Region									
South	21	23	9	14	11	11	9	24	740
Non-South	15	19	12	10	13	17	14	3	1,473
Sex									
Female	18	22	10	10	11	15	12	13	1,256
Male	16	17	13	12	14	15	13	5	980
Subjective Class									
Working	19	23	12	12	12	13	8	21	1,082
Middle	15	18	10	9	13	17	17	−1	1,043

Source: Center for Political Studies, University of Michigan; data made available by the Inter-University Consortium for Political and Social Research. Cited in Frank J. Sorauf and Paul Allen Beck, *Party Politics in America,* 6th ed. (Glenview, Ill.: Scott, Foresman, 1988), 175.

Note: Totals cumulate horizontally to 100 percent, minus apoliticals. Party difference is calculated by subtracting the percentage of strong and weak Republicans from the percentage of strong and weak Democrats. Negative numbers indicate a Republican advantage in the group.

United States is complex and inconclusive. In comparison with European societies, class consciousness is relatively weak; class mobility is relatively high. There have always been substantial cross-cutting cleavages along class and party lines. Nevertheless, it is fair to say that today's Democratic party is identified with and appeals to the poor and working-class elements of American society to a greater extent than is the case for the Republican party. The converse is also true, with the Republican party drawing greater support from and reflecting the interests of the upper echelons of society.

Tables 1 through 4 provide data regarding party identification in the American electorate. In nationwide polls, members of the public were asked about their social characteristics, their party identification, and their voting behavior. The poll results indicate, for example, that in 1984 27 percent of those surveyed who lack a high school education identified themselves as strong Democrats, while only 13 percent of college graduates did so. In contrast, while only 10 percent of the respondents who lacked a high school education considered themselves strong Republicans, 16 percent of the college graduates did so. Thus, one can demonstrate a positive relationship between level of education and party identification, warranting the assertion that the Democrats draw more support than do Republicans from the less-educated elements of American society. *(See Table 1, Social Characteristics and Party Identification, 1984, this page.)*

Demographic factors such as region, religion, race, and sex also influence party identification. Among these, regionalism appears in decline. Years ago, the Democratic party received unquestioning support from most southerners. At least at the presidential level, this is no longer the case. In 1984 only 44 percent of those southerners surveyed identified themselves as Democrats. Even more tellingly, only once between 1964 and 1988 had a Democratic presi-

Table 2 Party Identification of American Adults: 1952-1984

	1952	1956	1960	1964	1968	1972	1976	1980	1984
Democrats									
Strong	22%	21%	20%	27%	20%	15%	15%	18%	17%
Weak	25	23	25	25	25	26	25	23	20
Independents closer to Democrats	10	6	6	9	10	11	12	11	11
Independents	6	9	10	8	10	13	14	13	11
Independents closer to Republicans	7	8	7	6	9	10	10	10	12
Republicans									
Weak	14	14	14	13	14	13	14	14	15
Strong	13	15	15	11	10	10	9	8	12
Others	4	4	3	2	2	2	1	3	2
	101%	100%	100%	101%	101%	100%	100%	100%	100%

Source: Center for Political Studies, University of Michigan; data made available through the Inter-University Consortium for Political and Social Research. Cited in Frank J. Sorauf and Paul Alan Beck, *Party Politics in America*, 6th ed. (Glenview, Ill.: Scott, Foresman, 1988), 167.

Note: Percentages are based on surveys of the national electorate conducted in October of each presidential election year.

dential nominee won the once-solid South, and that was favorite son Jimmy Carter in 1976. Similarly, the Republicans' traditional midwestern base has experienced erosion.

Clear racial and religious distinctions can be seen among partisans. Oftentimes, however, these may stem mostly from underlying class and regional differences. For example, the Democratic party receives disproportionate support from racial minorities, as evidenced by the report that 65 percent of the blacks polled in 1984 considered themselves Democrats, but only 4 percent styled themselves Republicans. Since this racial group tends to be located at the lower end of the social-class ladder, however, it is not always clear whether minority or class status is the determining factor.

Similarly, Catholics and Jews have historically supported the Democrats, while nonsouthern Protestants have leaned in the Republican direction. But at least some of these differences can be attributed more directly to class. This was traditionally the case for Democratic-disposed immigrant Catholics and Southern Baptists. Among the latter, the class factor reinforced an even stronger and more fundamental regional one.

In recent years, students of voting behavior have discerned the presence of a "gender gap," a divergence in the partisan tendencies of men and women. Women currently appear more likely than men to support the Democratic party.

Ideology and issues also help shape party attachments. Voters who consider themselves more liberal tend to gravitate in the Democratic direction, while conservatives lean toward Republicanism. In taking issue positions, political parties seek to elicit support from like-minded groups and individuals. For example, an antiabortion party platform plank invites opponents of abortion to flock to the party banner.

Attractive nominees on the party ticket, especially at the presidential level, can lead voters to identify with a party. For post-World War II Republicans dispirited by a long series of defeats, their hope for the future was expressed in the slogan, "I Like Ike," a reference to the personal popularity of their 1952 presidential nominee, Dwight Eisenhower. More recently, the popularity of two-term winner Ronald Reagan often overcame the pull of party allegiance. The term "Reagan Democrats" described his appeal to working-class individuals who normally would not vote for a Republican candidate.

The successful candidates' performance in public office, again especially at the presidential level, looms as an important consideration. Public approval of President Franklin Roosevelt's leadership through the travails of the Great Depression and World War II catapulted the Democratic party into an enduring position of dominance. Conversely, President Richard Nixon's involvement in the Watergate scandal had a detrimental influence on the support levels enjoyed by the Republican party.

A series of empirical voting studies in the 1950s demonstrated a high degree and substantial significance of party identification and party loyalty in electoral behavior. More recently, studies consistently show that this psychological identification with party is waning. Where straight-ticket voting once prevailed, voters demonstrate increasing inclinations to split their tickets.[5]

Indeed, these tendencies toward weakening party identification and increased ticket-splitting help explain why recent Republican presidential nominees generally have been successful despite apparently greater popular support for the Democratic party. In particular, white southerners are prone to retain their traditional party identification and vote Democratic in congressional, state, and local elections and yet vote Republican at the presidential level.

Party Decline

Party decline can be attributed to a number of important developments.[6] One is the explosion of mass media of communication that brings an abundance of information about politics and politicians to an increasing literate electorate. Thus fortified, voters become much less dependent on the party symbol as a guide in choosing among candidates.

Another is the decline of patronage, diminishing a once-potent motivation for party loyalty. The spoils system institutionalized in the early nineteenth century came under increasing attack after the Civil War. Sentiment for the merit principle for government service grew steadily. It found expression in the 1883 Civil Service Reform Act that

Table 3 Presidential Voting among Party Identifiers: 1952-1984

	1952	1956	1960	1964	1968	1972	1976	1980	1984
Democrats									
Strong	84%	85%	90%	95%	85%	73%	91%	86%	87%
Weak	62	62	72	82	58	48	74	60	67
Independents closer to Democrats	60	68	88	90	52	60	72	45	79
Independents	—	—	—	—	—	—	—	—	—
Independents closer to Republicans	93	94	87	75	82	86	83	76	92
Republicans									
Weak	94	93	87	56	82	90	77	86	93
Strong	98	100	98	90	96	97	96	92	96

Source: Center for Political Studies, University of Michigan; data made available by the Inter-University Consortium for Political and Social Research. Cited in Frank J. Sorauf and Paul Allen Beck, *Party Politics in America*, 6th ed. (Glenview, Ill.: Scott, Foresman, 1988), 199.

Note: The table shows the percentages of each category of partisans who reported a vote for their party's candidate for president. To find the percentage voting for the opposing party's candidate or some other candidate, subtract the entry from 100 percent. Individuals who did not vote or did not vote for president are excluded.

resulted in some 10 percent of federal government employees being classified under merit coverage.

From this small base, the classification coverage grew steadily to its current level of more than 90 percent. But while the percentage of civil service positions gradually increased, more patronage positions became available as the federal government grew. Still, in a century's time, the percentages of patronage versus classified positions in the federal executive have reversed. State and local governments have tended to follow suit. As a result, as Tammany Hall's Plunkitt feared, no longer could the party establish and maintain ties with citizens by holding out prospects of jobs and the status they entailed.

Yet another factor is the advent of the welfare state. Traditionally, the public sector, or government, affected a laissez-faire, or hands-off, posture in the realm of social services. Since the New Deal of the 1930s, however, government in general and the federal government in particular has assumed widespread responsibilities in this area. In doing so, it has supplanted the urban political machines that had built enduring commitments to party through the delivery of social services formerly unavailable from the public sector.

Another pertinent element is change in the methods by which political parties nominate candidates. For much of the nineteenth century, the party organization exercised tight control over this process. It served as a gatekeeper, commanding the route to public office. Thus aspirants had to receive the endorsement of the party organization to achieve their ambitions.

In the name of democratic reform, however, the Progressive movement around the turn of the twentieth century advocated broader popular participation in the nomination process. The Progressives' preferred method was the direct primary, a party election whereby voters chose the party's nominee to contest the general election.

The Progressives proved successful. The primary has become the standard method of party nominations, with the notable exception of the presidential contest. Even here, the Progressive influence can be seen in the early twentieth-century appearance of presidential primaries in a handful of states and in their dramatic proliferation since 1968.

By enhancing popular participation, presidential primaries strengthen the relationship between the president and the public. On the other hand, primaries open the party's nomination to candidates not necessarily approved by the party organization, and perhaps even antagonistic toward it. They deprive the organization of a traditional responsibility—one that provided a major foundation for the power of the party. Thus, many commentators view the party primary as destructive of the organization and a major factor in the decline of party as an intermediary between president and public.

Party Organization

The formal machinery of the party parallels government organization in the United States. At every level of government in our federal system—national, state, and local—there is a corresponding unit of party organization. Throughout, the lower levels of the organization generally designate membership for the higher levels.

Traditionally, most party power rested with the state and local organizations. They dominated the national parties, which were essentially holding companies. In recent years, this balance has shifted, centralizing power at the national level. This centralization has been made formal, especially by the Democrats, through a codification of national party responsibilities in the party's rules and procedures.

The institutions of party organization are the convention, the committee, the chair, and the headquarters staff. The first three typically exist at all levels, with the fourth appearing only occasionally in localities.

National Level

National party organization activity traditionally centered on the presidency. It had relatively little control over the operations of the state and local entities. More recently, it has become increasingly superfluous to presidential politics and removed from them. However, it has assumed increasing supervision over the lower levels. In the wake of these historic shifts, national party organization today appears stronger and more vital in many respects than ever before, though less relevant to the presidency.

Table 4 Straight-ticket Voting among Party Identifiers: 1952-1984

	1952	1956	1960	1964	1968	1972	1976	1980	1984
Democrats									
Strong	86%	84%	87%	80%	72%	66%	—	62%	69%
Weak	69	72	74	53	43	38	—	39	46
Independents closer to Democrats	56	58	56	37	32	28	—	23	38
Independents	56	43	65	53	24	28	—	21	25
Independents closer to Republicans	65	56	51	33	43	30	—	28	33
Republicans									
Weak	72	69	68	44	49	40	—	35	41
Strong	85	83	79	71	74	60	—	61	59

Source: Center for Political Studies, University of Michigan; data made available by the Inter-University Consortium for Political and Social Research. Cited in Frank J. Sorauf and Paul Allen Beck, *Party Politics in America*, 6th ed. (Glenview, Ill.: Scott, Foresman, 1988), 201.

Note: The table shows the percentages of each category of partisans who reported voting a straight ticket in state and local elections. To find the percentage splitting their tickets, subtract the entry from 100 percent. Individuals who did not vote or did not vote in state and local elections are excluded. The question was not asked in 1976.

Convention

Party organization at the national level dates back to the Jacksonian era, when the nominating convention appeared on the scene. Replacing the discredited congressional caucus as a nominating device, the quadrennial convention brought together state delegations to name the party's presidential ticket.[7]

The convention delegates also agreed upon a statement of party principles and issue stances, or platform, on which the party's nominees could run in the upcoming election. The gathering served as a massive party rally, where rival factions could be conciliated and unified, and enthusiasm generated, in preparation for the general election campaign. The convention provided a national institutional identity, serving as the party's voice and authority.

In the nineteenth century, state representation at the national convention followed the electoral college formula, itself an extension of the Constitutional Convention's Great Compromise on congressional apportionment. In the bicameral Congress, the House of Representatives was apportioned according to population, and the Senate according to state equality, two senators for each state. Under this arrangement, delegate seats at the nominating convention were allocated in proportion to the states' representation in Congress: a mixture of population plus state equality.

In the twentieth century, both major parties adopted formulas that weight representation according to the states' previous electoral support for the party. In other words, a positive record of support for the party's nominees produces bonus representation at the convention.

For example, for the Republicans in the 1980s, each state had a core of delegates assigned as a multiple of the size of its congressional delegation. Each received a specified number of at-large delegates. Each state got additional delegates if it had Republican governors, senators, and a party majority in its congressional delegation. A final bonus provision gave the state more representation if its electoral votes had gone to the GOP nominee in the previous presidential election. Nonstate units (District of Columbia, Puerto Rico, Virgin Islands, and Guam) received varying at-large delegates.

The Democrats in recent years have moved beyond the bonus system to embrace two alternative representational principles. First, they have systematically sought through affirmative action to give representation to a variety of population groups. These include women, racial minorities, and age cohorts. Second, they have seated ex officio "superdelegates," party officeholders chosen apart from the normal delegate-selection processes.

Over the years, the conventions have grown dramatically. Early conventions drew fewer than 300 delegates. In contrast, contemporary Democratic conventions bring together more than 4,000, and today's Republicans assemble more than 2,000. Twenty cities have been the convention sites through 1988, some more than once. *(See Table 3, National Party Convention Sites, Dates, and Nominees, p. 609.)*

In the nineteenth century state party organizations tightly controlled the selection of convention delegates. Around the turn of the century, the Progressive movement pushed for popular selection of delegates through a party primary. While a few state parties adopted this mechanism, most kept the party organization in charge.

However, some epochal reforms within the Democratic party after 1968 lodged far more effective party authority at the national level than had been the case and dramatically increased the number of state parties electing delegates through primaries. These reforms also, along with other coinciding trends, transformed the character of convention decision making. Party voters essentially choose the nominee in primaries and caucuses, leaving the convention little to do except ratify the voters' choice.

As a result every major party convention since 1952 has resulted in a first-ballot victory. In 1988 Republican George Bush and Democrat Michael S. Dukakis wrapped up convention majorities through delegate-selection contests in the states well in advance of the convention. For them and their parties, the convention's nominating role was a mere formality.

Increasingly, the modern convention has become a media event, heightening its traditional party rally function. The target of attention has shifted, however, from the party activists in the hall to the vast television audience viewing the prime-time proceedings. The convention gives the nominee a forum to kick off the general election campaign by demonstrating presidential leadership qualities to

In 1972, when Democratic vice-presidential nominee Thomas Eagleton, left, withdrew from the ticket, the Democratic National Committee formally nominated a replacement, Sargent Shriver.

both party and public. This can be achieved through actions such as the choice of a running mate, acceptance of the nomination with a forceful speech, and general management by the nominee and the campaign staff of the events of the convention week.

The national convention endures as the formal/legal nominator of the presidential ticket and as the apex of authority within the party. It remains a quadrennial event, though the Democrats experimented with midterm conventions in 1974, 1978, and 1982. These meetings were designed to stimulate discussion and development of party positions on issues. The party now has abandoned this experiment, restoring the traditional four-year gap between conventions.

Committee

An institution convening for a few days every four years can hardly exercise power and authority within a political party. Early on, in the 1840s, the Democratic national convention established a national committee to oversee the conduct of the presidential campaign and to guide the party's fortunes between conventions. Subsequently, when the Republican party formed a few years later, it adopted a similar organizational arrangement.[8]

These national committees consisted of representatives of the state and local parties. At the outset, the principle of state equality was established: one member from each state party. In the 1920s both parties expanded committee membership to two representatives from each state—one male and one female. This revision clearly responded to the Nineteenth Amendment that denied states the power to discriminate according to sex in establishing voter qualifications.

In 1952 the Republican party departed from the historical commitment to state equality as a representational principle. That year, its national convention voted to give ex officio national committee membership to party chairs from states that (1) supported the Republican nominee for president, (2) selected a majority of Republican House members and senators, or (3) selected a Republican governor. This reform gave added weight to those states that consistently voted Republican. Subsequently, the GOP returned to the principle of state equality by designating all state party chairs as committee members. Additionally, the District of Columbia, Guam, Puerto Rico, and the Virgin Islands came to be treated like states for representational purposes.

In the early 1970s the Democratic party abandoned state equality by adopting weighted representation and dramatically expanding the committee's membership. Table 5 indicates the current composition of the national committees.

While the convention formally designates the national committee, in practice it ratifies state-level decisions regarding membership. State parties utilize a variety of means for choosing their representatives, usually according to their own rules and/or state laws. In most states, the state convention selects them. Alternatively, the state committee, the national convention delegation, or the party voters through a primary may be authorized to do so. Members serve a four-year term beginning with adjournment of the national convention and ending with adjournment of the following convention.

Party rules require the Democratic National Committee to meet at least once a year, while the Republican National Committee is supposed to meet at least twice a year. Typically, the party chair calls meetings, but each party provides for alternative avenues whereby meetings can be called, such as by the executive committee or a stipulated percentage of the membership.

The committee's major collective function is the election of officers, chief of which is the party chair. Beyond formally designating its leadership, the committee as a collective body has little to do. Most of its assigned functions are undertaken by the chair and headquarters staff, with the committee customarily authorizing and ratifying these decisions.

One noteworthy assignment was to fill vacancies that occur before the election in the nominations for president and vice president. If a convention's nomination is vacated for any reason, legally it falls to the national committee to meet and fill it. Thus, in 1972, when Democratic vice-presidential nominee Thomas Eagleton withdrew, the Democratic National Committee, on the recommendation of presidential nominee George McGovern, formally nominated R. Sargent Shriver for the second spot on the ticket. A somewhat similar situation had developed for the Democrats in 1860, when their vice presidential nominee declined the nomination and the national committee replaced him.

Chair

The position of national party chair has high visibility and significance within the party organization. To the general public, its occupant stands as a symbol and spokesperson for the party. To the president, the chair is a top-level presidential appointee who links White House and party and through whom the president traditionally has exercised considerable party leadership.[9]

Selection. The national committee formally elects its top officer, traditionally at a meeting immediately following the national convention. This established the presumption that the term of office was four years. In practice, few national party chairs have served that long. Within-term vacancies have been exceedingly common, especially in the chair of the party that lost the presidential election.

The Democrats continue to elect their party chair after

the convention. In the 1980s the Republicans decided to elect the chair in January of each odd-numbered year, thus reducing the term of office to two years and somewhat isolating chair selection from the contest for the party's presidential nomination.

By custom and practice of a century's standing, the national committee has deferred to the party's presidential nominee in electing its chair. The usual procedure has been for a delegation from the committee to call on the nominee to solicit a recommendation. The committee would then convene to ratify that choice. This practice initially developed to tie the nominee's campaign with the national party effort. It had the effect of placing the party leadership under the nominee's authority.

After the election, the president-elect can continue to claim that prerogative. Thus, for the party whose nominee occupies the White House, the position of chair remains in effect a presidential appointment. Its incumbent serves at the pleasure of the president, with the national committee compliantly endorsing the president's choice.

Thus, in practice, the only times the national committee has acted on its own in choosing its chair have been in cases of vacancies occurring between nominating conventions when the party does not control the presidency. Even here, the influence of former or potential nominees, along with congressional party leaders, cannot be discounted.

The significance of the Republican party's realignment and limitation of the term of the party chair is not yet clear. However, it is doubtful that it will fundamentally reorient established patterns and practices.

For much of its existence, the chair has been a part-time position, with no definite eligibility requirements. But in most cases the incumbent has been a state party leader, a member or former member of Congress, a political associate of the presidential nominee, or a combination of the three. George Bush, a former House member who headed the GOP in the last two years of the Nixon administration, is the only national chair who went on to become president. *(See Table 6, National Party Chairs, p. 696, and box, The Party Chair as Candidate for National Office, p. 697.)*

In the 1970s both major parties began requiring that the chair position be full time and salaried. This action appears to have been in response to an increasing tendency to place legislators, parttime by definition, in that office. It relates to the increasing institutionalization of the national organization, whose members consider themselves ill-served by part-time leaders with primary loyalties to other elements within the party. Moreover, with the increasing amount of responsibility and activity located at the national level, the party headquarters requires full-time leadership.

Table 5 Composition of the National Party Committees: 1989

	Number of members
Democratic National Committee	
National committee officers	9
Chair and highest-ranking officer of opposite sex from each state, District of Columbia, and Puerto Rico	104
Chair and highest-ranking officer of opposite sex, national committeeman and national committeewoman from Guam, Virgin Islands, and American Samoa	12
Cochairs and highest-ranking officers of opposite sex, national committeemen and national committeewomen of Democrats Abroad	8
Members apportioned to states and equivalent units on basis of current national convention apportionment formula	200
Auxiliaries	
Democratic Governors Association (3)	
Congressional Parties (4)	
Democratic Mayors Conference (3)	
Young Democrats (3)	
National Federation of Democratic Women (3)	
Democratic County Officials Conference (3)	
Democratic State Legislative Leaders Association (3)	
National Democratic Municipal Officials Conference (3)	25
Additional Members	45
Total	403
Republican National Committee	
National committeeman, national committeewoman, and a chair from each state and from the District of Columbia, Guam, Puerto Rico, and the Virgin Islands	162
Total	162

Source: The Charter and the Bylaws of the Democratic Party of the United States, and *The Rules of the Republican Party.*

Backgrounds. The early chairs were often men of considerable wealth. While sizable personal fortunes have not been a disqualification in recent years, they are no longer quite so common. Since World War I, the following chairs have come from the ranks of state party leaders, most of whom were state chairs: Republicans Will Hays, Hubert Work, Claudius Huston, John Hamilton, Harrison Spangler, Arthur Summerfield, Wesley Roberts, Ray Bliss, Mary Louise Smith, Richard Richards, and Frank Fahrenkopf; Democrats James Farley, Ed Flynn, Robert Hannegan, Howard McGrath, Frank McKinney, Jean Westwood, and Charles Manatt.

A congressional connection can be found for a number of national chairs. In the twentieth century, national chairs with congressional experience before, during, and/or after their party organization leadership are Republicans Mark Hanna, Henry Payne, Harry New, Simeon Fess, Everett Sanders, Joseph Martin, Carroll Reece, Hugh Scott, Leonard Hall, Thruston Morton, William Miller, Rogers Morton, Robert Dole, George Bush, William Brock, and general chair Paul Laxalt; Democrats James Jones, Thomas Taggart, George White, Cordell Hull, Howard McGrath, Henry Jackson, and Fred Harris.

Apart from Congress, the national-level political office from which the most chairs have been associated has been that of postmaster general. The list of chairs who had served previously, subsequently, or simultaneously as head of the Post Office consists of Democrats James Farley, Frank Walker, Robert Hannegan, and Lawrence O'Brien, and Republicans Marshall Jewell, Henry Payne, George Cortelyou, Harry New, Frank Hitchcock, Will Hays, and Arthur Summerfield.

Table 6 National Party Chairs

Name	State	Years of service
Democratic party		
B. F. Hallett	Massachusetts	1848-1852
Robert McLane	Maryland	1852-1856
David A. Smalley	Virginia	1856-1860
August Belmont	New York	1860-1872
Augustus Schell	New York	1972-1876
Abram S. Hewitt	New York	1876-1877
William H. Barnum	Connecticut	1877-1889
Calvin S. Brice	Ohio	1889-1892
William F. Hartity	Pennsylvania	1892-1896
James K. Jones	Arkansas	1896-1904
Thomas Taggart	Indiana	1904-1908
Norman E. Mack	New York	1908-1912
William F. McCombs	New York	1912-1916
Vance C. McCormick	Pennsylvania	1916-1919
Homer S. Cummings	Connecticut	1919-1920
George White	Ohio	1920-1921
Cordell Hull	Tennessee	1921-1924
Clem Shaver	West Virginia	1924-1928
John J. Raskob	Maryland	1928-1932
James A. Farley	New York	1932-1940
Edward J. Flynn	New York	1940-1943
Frank C. Walker	Pennsylvania	1943-1944
Robert E. Hannegan	Missouri	1944-1947
J. Howard McGrath	Rhode Island	1947-1949
William M. Boyle, Jr.	Missouri	1949-1951
Frank E. McKinney	Indiana	1951-1952
Stephen A. Mitchell	Illinois	1952-1954
Paul M. Butler	Indiana	1955-1960
Henry M. Jackson	Washington	1960-1961
John M. Bailey	Connecticut	1961-1968
Lawrence F. O'Brien	Massachusetts	1968-1969
Fred Harris	Oklahoma	1969-1970
Lawrence F. O'Brien	Massachusetts	1970-1972
Jean Westwood	Utah	1972
Robert Strauss	Texas	1972-1977
Kenneth Curtis	Maine	1977-1978
John White	Texas	1978-1981
Charles Manatt	California	1981-1985
Paul Kirk	Massachusetts	1985-1989
Ronald H. Brown	Washington, D.C.	1989-
Republican party		
Edwin D. Morgan	New York	1856-1864
Henry J. Morgan	New York	1864-1866
Marcus L. Ward	New Jersey	1866-1868
William Claflin	Massachusetts	1868-1872
Edwin D. Morgan	New York	1872-1876
Zachariah Chandler	Michigan	1987-1879
Republican party (continued)		
J. Donald Cameron	Pennsylvania	1879-1880
Marshall Jewell	Connecticut	1880-1883
D. M. Sabin	Minnesota	1883-1884
B. F. Jones	Pennsylvania	1884-1888
Matthew S. Quay	Pennsylvania	1888-1891
James S. Clarkson	Iowa	1891-1892
Thomas H. Carter	Montana	1892-1896
Mark A. Hanna	Ohio	1896-1904
Henry C. Payne	Wisconsin	1904
George B. Cortelyou	New York	1904-1907
Harry S. New	Indiana	1907-1908
Frank H. Hitchcock	Massachusetts	1908-1909
John F. Hill	Maine	1909-1912
Victor Rosewater	Nebraska	1912
Charles D. Hilles	New York	1912-1916
William R. Wilcox	New York	1916-1918
Will Hays	Indiana	1918-1921
John T. Adams	Iowa	1921-1924
William M. Butler	Massachusetts	1924-1928
Hubert Work	Colorado	1928-1929
Claudius H. Huston	Tennessee	1929-1930
Simeon D. Fess	Ohio	1930-1932
Everett Sanders	Indiana	1932-1934
Henry P. Fletcher	Pennsylvania	1934-1936
John Hamilton	Kansas	1936-1940
Joseph W. Martin, Jr.	Massachusetts	1940-1942
Harrison E. Spangler	Iowa	1942-1944
Herbert Brownell, Jr.	New York	1944-1946
B. Carroll Reece	Tennessee	1946-1948
Hugh D. Scott, Jr.	Pennsylvania	1948-1949
Guy George Gabrielson	New Jersey	1949-1952
Arthur E. Summerfield	Michigan	1952-1953
C. Wesley Roberts	Kansas	1953
Leonard W. Hall	New York	1953-1957
H. Meade Alcorn, Jr.	Connecticut	1957-1959
Thruston B. Morton	Kentucky	1959-1961
William E. Miller	New York	1961-1964
Dean Burch	Arizona	1964-1965
Ray C. Bliss	Ohio	1965-1969
Rogers C. B. Morton	Maryland	1969-1971
Robert Dole	Kansas	1971-1973
George Bush	Texas	1973-1974
Mary Louise Smith	Iowa	1974-1977
William Brock	Tennessee	1977-1981
Richard Richards	Utah	1981-1983
Paul Laxalt (general chair)	Nevada	1983-1986
Frank Fahrenkopf	Nevada	1983-1989
Lee Atwater	South Carolina	1989-

Source: Hugh A. Bone, *Party Committees and National Politics* (Seattle: University of Washington Press, 1958), 241-243; updated by author.

Gubernatorial linkages are slightly less frequent. In the nineteenth century, three incumbent governors simultaneously served as national party chairs: Republicans Edwin Morgan, Marcus Ward, and William Claflin. Five former governors later occupied the party chair: Republicans Marshall Jewell, John Hill, and Paul Laxalt; Democrats Howard McGrath and Kenneth Curtis. Two former party chairs went on to serve as governors: Democrats Robert McLane and George White.

Until the 1970s the party chair was exclusively the province of white males. Democrat Jean Westwood broke this pattern in 1972, followed by Republican Mary Louise Smith in 1974. The Democrats shattered precedent in 1989 and chose a black, Ronald Brown, as chair. The GOP also avoided stereotypes, choosing as chair Lee Atwater, 37, a former rock 'n' roll guitarist.

The Party Chair as Candidate for National Office

Traditionally, the national party chair performed in the arena of organizational politics and eschewed personal participation in electoral politics at the presidential level. Democratic national chair James A. Farley's candidacy for the 1940 presidential nomination constituted a major and singular departure from established practice. Since 1960, however, the incumbent national party chair frequently has figured in speculation surrounding the composition of the party's presidential ticket. This connection has taken three forms: (1) the chair's availability for the vice-presidential nomination; (2) consideration of the party chair position as a consolation prize for a loser in the vice-presidential sweepstakes; (3) the presence of former party chairs in the field of contenders for the party's presidential nomination.

These modern patterns first emerged in 1960, when Sen. Thruston B. Morton of Kentucky, the Republican national chairman, was a finalist on nominee Richard Nixon's list of vice-presidential prospects. Passed over in favor of Henry Cabot Lodge, Morton retained the chairmanship.

On the Democratic side in 1960, nominee John F. Kennedy placed Sen. Henry M. Jackson of Washington on his short list of potential running mates. After he opted for Lyndon B. Johnson, Kennedy tapped Jackson for the DNC chairmanship for the duration of the campaign. When his nomination met with vocal opposition at the convention, Johnson received word from the Kennedy camp that should he decline the offer, he could have the party chairmanship.

In 1964 Republican nominee Barry M. Goldwater named as his running mate the incumbent national party chair, Rep. William E. Miller of New York. As of 1989 Miller remained the only incumbent chair ever named to a major party ticket.

The year 1968 marked the return of Richard Nixon to the Republicans' presidential ticket. Nixon seriously considered Rep. Rogers C. B. Morton of Maryland, younger brother of Thruston, as his vice-presidential partner, before settling on Spiro T. Agnew. When a vacancy occurred in the chairmanship following the general election, Nixon recommended Morton for the post.

In the Democratic contest that year, Sen. Fred Harris of Oklahoma lost out to Edmund S. Muskie as Hubert H. Humphrey's choice of running mate. Harris then unsuccessfully sought the party chairmanship that on Humphrey's suggestion went to Lawrence F. O'Brien. Harris's persistence paid off when he was named chair in January 1969 amid speculation that he was positioning himself for a future presidential bid.

In 1972 O'Brien figured prominently in convention-week speculation for the vice-presidential spot that went to Sen. Thomas Eagleton of Missouri. When Eagleton resigned the nomination shortly afterward, O'Brien again was mentioned as a possible choice, though the slot eventually went to R. Sargent Shriver.

When Richard Nixon resigned in 1974, Gerald R. Ford became president, creating a vacancy in the vice presidency. Ford considered appointing George Bush, then the incumbent Republican national chair, but instead he chose Nelson Rockefeller. Ford dumped Rockefeller from the ticket at the 1976 convention, replacing him with a former national chair, Sen. Robert Dole of Kansas. One of the individuals Ford passed over, John B. Connally, was offered the party chairmanship as a consolation prize, but Connally reportedly rejected the offer. The Democratic presidential field that year included former party chair Harris.

The 1980 Republican nomination contest featured the candidacies of two former party chairs, Bush and Dole. After both lost out to Ronald Reagan and Bush became Reagan's running mate, the ticket's victory made Bush the first former party chair to be elected vice president.

In 1988, with Reagan's second term due to expire, Bush and Dole resumed their presidential rivalry. Early in the campaign season rumors had former senator Paul Laxalt of Nevada, who held the position of general chair of the Republican party from 1982 through 1986, as a possible contender; but Laxalt never entered the fray. Bush prevailed, and his November victory made him also the first former party chair to be elected president.

From the late 1950s through the mid-1970s, several House and Senate members were national party chairs. The visibility of the office made it attractive to electoral figures who sought the role of party spokesman. But the decision by both parties in the 1970s to make the chair a full-time position was likely to diminish this connection in the future.

Other Officers. Besides designating a chair, the national committee selects a number of other officers. The Democrats elect three vice chairs (two of whom are of the opposite sex of the chair), a treasurer, a finance chair, a secretary, and other appropriate officers as they deem necessary. The full committee is also empowered to choose an executive committee, determining its size, composition, and term of office.

The Republicans choose a cochair of the opposite sex, along with eight vice chairs—a male and a female from each of four different regional state associations: West, Midwest, Northeast, and South. They also select a secretary, treasurer, and such other officers as they desire. Other collective leadership structures include the chair's executive council and the executive committee, with party rules stipulating procedures for selection and responsibilities.

Activities. There is a distinction between the status and activities of the national chair whose party nominee occupies the White House and the one whose party is out. The in-party's chairs serve under the party leadership of the president. Out-party chairs have no obvious party superior, yet they occupy ambiguous positions with respect to the congressional party leadership.

The role of the in-party chair has undergone major changes over the past fifty years. Once, the national chair was a central actor in presidential politics. By and large, this is no longer the case. Both in-party and out-party chairs today are far more involved in directing party-building endeavors—national, state, and local—than was previously typical. This has come about because of changes in both the presidency and the political parties.

In the past the national chair customarily directed the party campaign, of which the presidential race was the central feature. The expectation of tying together the overall party effort and the specifically presidential campaign underlay the development of the custom whereby the national committee began soliciting the presidential nominee's recommendation for its chair. Operating out of party headquarters, the president's choice would direct the campaign.

More recently, the presidential nominees have instead developed and relied on personal campaign organizations. The reasons include strategic considerations related to declining party identification in the electorate, federal election laws effectively mandating the establishment of separate organizations, and, most important, changes in the nature of nomination campaigns.

Years ago, nomination campaigns were low-key efforts designed to elicit the support of a relative handful of party chieftains, who in turn controlled state delegations at the convention. With the advent of primary contests to select delegates, prospective nominees must develop full-scale campaign organizations well in advance of the convention.

The road to the convention nomination now proceeds through delegate-selection primaries in well over thirty states, where campaign organizations are tried and tested. The eventual winner normally will be inclined to continue to operate through that organizational vehicle in the general election campaign that follows.

This development relegates the national organization to the periphery of the campaign effort. It similarly places the chair outside the inner circle of campaign decision makers. Thus, a major role traditionally performed by the party chair has been rendered negligible.

At the outset, national chairs had important patronage responsibilities. The chair claimed the spoils of electoral victory for the party loyalists. The traditional association between the chair and the postmaster generalship pertained directly to this task, because the Post Office provided an abundance of government jobs to be distributed among the party faithful. By the time of the Nixon administration, the Post Office's patronage position had long since been decimated by civil service expansion. In 1971 the department was restructured as the Postal Service, a government corporation, removing it from both the cabinet and party politics.

Throughout the government, the establishment and expansion of the merit system has drastically reduced the available patronage. Moreover, the types of positions now available tend to be less appropriate for party organization claimants. Thus, the role of the party chair as patronage dispenser has become passé.

Party chairs in days gone by also served their presidents as key political advisers. They kept chief executives in touch with the perspectives of their counterparts in statehouses and city halls.

Modern presidents have perceived much less need for such advice. They now have a sizable personal staff of aides they can rely on as advisers and intermediaries with other political leaders. Polling organizations provide presidents with an abundance of data about the public pulse. Here again, the traditional role of the chair has been supplanted.

Developments within the party organization also have worked to distance the chair from the presidential inner circle. Party chairs have always operated under a norm of neutrality toward competing candidacies for the presidential nomination. Usually, this norm was conveniently ignored by in-party chairs serving as presidential appointees and pursuing the interests of their sponsors. As the parties have come to be more bureaucratic and institutional, the expectations regarding neutrality are growing stronger. Federal election laws reinforce the pressure for the chair to remain neutral.[10] Thus, modern party chairs are less likely to occupy the traditional role of key presidential adviser.

The chair's role of fund raiser endures today, but in vastly altered form and more removed from presidential politics. Nineteenth-century chairs tended to be wealthy individuals who made major personal contributions to the presidential campaign, bankrolled a limited party operation that supplemented the campaign, and prevailed upon their similarly disposed friends and associates to do likewise.

The growing costs of presidential campaigns have placed financing them beyond the means of a relative handful of individuals, even those of immense personal wealth. Further, federal election laws limit the financial contributions of individuals. They also provide for public funding of presidential campaigns.

National party headquarters operations have also grown beyond the capacity of the chair personally to subsidize them. Thus, while contemporary chairs continue to perform a significant fund-raising function, they do so in an altered fashion that is oriented toward party building and somewhat distanced from the presidential arena.

Both national committees have for many years established finance committees and designated individuals to chair them. The Republicans began doing so in the 1930s, and the Democrats followed suit some two decades later. These individuals, while under the authority of the chair, nevertheless operate separately and thus relieve the chair of many traditional fund-raising responsibilities.

As these traditional roles have diminished in importance, other time-honored functions have endured and even increased. Three identified by political scientists Cornelius Cotter and Bernard Hennessy are those of *image-maker*, *hell-raiser*, and *administrator*.[11]

Public relations has always been a major responsibility of the party chair. In the nineteenth century, many national chairs came from newspaper backgrounds. While this has been much less the case since World War I, a sensitivity to and a flair for public relations continue to be expected of the chair.

The chair seeks to promote a positive public image for the party, to position its actions and objectives in the best possible light. This can be done by personally assuming the role of party spokesperson. Such a chair will regularly make the rounds of the network television interview shows such as "Meet the Press" and "Face the Nation" and will be readily available for interviews and comments to reporters. In addition, the chair acts as a good-will ambassador for party unity and expansion. Chairs uncomfortable with personal appearances will nonetheless sponsor similar efforts by other voices for the party.

The chair as hell-raiser is the partisan's partisan. Such a figure will seek to satisfy the expectations of the party faithful by flailing away at the opposition party and righteously defending the party against detractors' assaults. Presidents often rely on their party chairs to emphasize this party leadership role. Doing so enables presidents to appear above partisan battles. However, it also reduces the party's significance as a link between president and public.

As administrators, party chairs supervise the activities of the national headquarters—a role that has grown with the headquarters' expansion. The current requirement that the chair's position be full time and salaried also serves to emphasize the administrative aspects of the job.

Headquarters

In the nineteenth century, party operations were conducted largely within the context of the convention and the presidential campaign.[12] The chief responsibilities of the committee and its chair were to prepare and conduct the quadrennial nominating convention and direct the ensuing presidential campaign. Once the nominations were completed, headquarters would be established, usually in New York City, and the campaign led by the party chair. After the election, the organization would be largely disbanded. The committee would meet perhaps once a year; at other times the national party would exist in the person of the chair. The pace would pick up again when plans had to be made for the forthcoming convention.

In the 1920s both national parties established year-round headquarters operations with paid staff. The Republicans took the lead here. In the ensuing years, they would continue to emphasize organizational development more than their Democratic counterparts. Initially, both parties rented office space in Washington, D.C. During the Nixon administration, the Republicans moved into their own building adjacent to the House Office Buildings on Capitol Hill. In the 1980s the Democrats did the same, opening their permanent offices just a few blocks away.

Both parties have expanded their staffs and scope of operations, which swell temporarily before presidential elections. In the intervening years, the staff size remains relatively high. Political scientists Cornelius Cotter and John Bibby have assembled figures indicating that since 1950 the Republicans have never had fewer than eighty paid employees, and the Democrats, never fewer than forty. Further, off-year staffing for both parties has averaged in excess of seventy.[13]

With this increased staff capacity, the national party has been shifting its emphases away from its traditional responsibilities toward party-building activities. But tasks related to the planning and conduct of the convention persist. The committee issues the convention call, which stipulates procedures for delegate apportionment and selection, along with temporary convention rules. It designates the membership and leadership of preconvention committees and designates key convention presiders and speakers. It establishes the site, date, and order of business, though with in-party committees the White House normally has a significant say in these determinations.

The national headquarters retains some presidential campaign responsibilities. The Democratic party charter formally authorizes it to conduct that campaign.[14] The nominee's own campaign organization, however, typically assumes the brunt of the campaign effort, relegating the party organization to the periphery. Nevertheless, operations of a contemporary presidential campaign are sufficiently broad that there is plenty of activity to occupy the time and energy of an expanded national committee staff throughout the fall campaign.

It is outside the arena of presidential politics, however, that party headquarters are making increasingly significant contributions, primarily in campaign assistance and other services to the state and local parties. The national parties are now actively engaged in candidate recruitment. They offer training sessions and make available a wide variety of information and expertise for the benefit of the parties' nominees. These include research, polling, data processing, direct mail, consultants, and money in vast quantities.[15]

Here again, the Republicans were the pioneers, initially under the leadership of Ray Bliss, party chair from 1965 to 1969. The same approach was emphasized by William Brock, chair from 1977 to 1981. The Democrats have followed suit since the late 1970s.

State and Local Levels

There are of course substantial variations among the fifty state and countless county and subcounty units of the political parties. Their structural components typically replicate the national pattern: convention, committee, chair, and, in recent years, headquarters staff.[16] At the lower levels, the pattern persists, though with the omission of headquarters staffs.

State Conventions

State conventions ordinarily meet once every two years, preceding the scheduled elections. They bring together representatives of the lower-level party units and vary in size. Most draw under a thousand delegates, but several exceed this total. In 1978 more than 7,300 delegates assembled for the Virginia Republican convention.

The advent and acceptance of the direct primary in this century has almost completely taken from these bodies what was originally one of their primary responsibilities—nominating candidates for statewide offices. Contemporary conventions may elect party officers and adopt a party platform. During presidential election years, the state conventions traditionally played an important role in the selection of the state parties' delegates to the nominating convention. Party reforms have substantially reduced this role.

State Committees

State party committees also vary in size, from under fifty to more than five hundred. California, the biggest, assembles more than 800 members. As is the case at the national level, the state committees are charged with leadership selection and guiding the party's fortunes between conventions. By and large, these tasks are delegated to chairs and headquarters staffs. Many state party committees also designate executive committees to act for them.

State Chairs

State party chairs can be categorized into in-party and out-party groups, depending on whether the party's nominee holds the governorship. In-party chairs can be further subdivided into those who act as political agents of their governors and those who act independently. In many state parties, the convention or the committee defers in selecting

How States Allocated Democratic Delegates in 1988

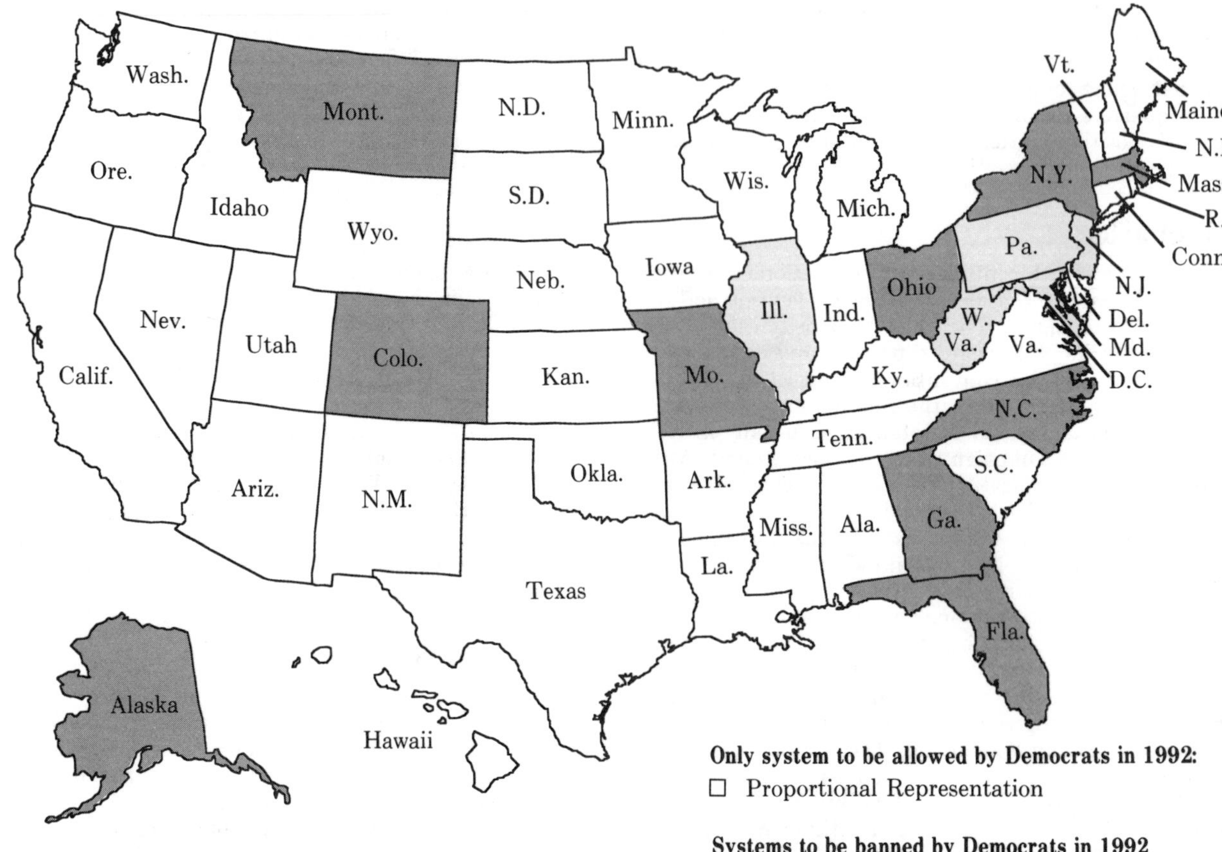

Only system to be allowed by Democrats in 1992:
☐ Proportional Representation

Systems to be banned by Democrats in 1992
☐ Direct Election
■ Bonus

The Democratic national convention at Altanta in 1988 approved rules changes to ensure that the party's presidential delegates in 1992 would be elected to more closely reflect one-person, one-vote.

One change would reduce the number of uncommitted "superdelegates," who had moved overwhelmingly in mid-1988 to the eventual nominee, Massachusetts Gov. Michael S. Dukakis. Another would require delegates to be divided among candidates to reflect their share of a state's primary or caucus vote. Banned would be delegate-allocation systems used in 1988 that gave an extra reward to the winner.

Those systems benefited Dukakis in a number of states. He won four of the five states that held direct election primaries (where voters balloted directly for district delegates and winner-take-all was possible). And he won six of ten states with bonus systems (where the winner in each district won one delegate before the rest were divided proportionally).

In 1988 Democrats in most of the megastates used one of these two systems of awarding delegates, but in 1992 they must join the rest of the country in allocating their delegates proportionally to reflect the primary or caucus vote.

The table below compares the percentage of the primary vote that Dukakis and Jesse L. Jackson received in 1988 with the share of delegates they won under the various systems of delegate allocation. Each candidate's delegate total is based on the number he won as a result of primary voting and does not include delegates gained after other candidates or from the uncommitted ranks.

Maryland had a hybrid system, electing district delegates by direct election and statewide delegates by proportional representation. (Puerto Rico's direct election primary results are included in the tabulations.)

Primary Results in 1988 (percent)

Primaries	Dukakis		Jackson	
	Primary vote	Delegates	Primary vote	Delegates
Direct election	46	56	29	12
Bonus	43	54	28	30
Proportional representation	40	43	30	34

a chair to the wishes of the governor or the gubernatorial nominee. Party building is a primary concern of state party chairs, who also are involved in fund-raising and campaign-related activities.

State Headquarters

Contemporary state party chairs usually operate out of year-round party headquarters occupied by small but full-time, paid staff. This development is relatively recent, dating back to the early 1960s. Political scientist Robert Huckshorn attributes this phenomenon to four factors. One is the increase in party competition at the state level, especially in the South. Another is the growth of technology that has inspired state parties to take advantage of new methods and approaches in electoral politics.

A third factor is pressure from the national parties and government. Reforms in the selection of delegates to the national convention have imposed procedural guidelines on the state parties that require considerable attention to detail. Federal campaign finance legislation also has imposed stringent reporting guidelines.

Finally, Huckshorn contends that increased communication among the state chairs in recent years, taking the form of meetings under formal organizational auspices, has encouraged chairs lacking headquarters facilities to emulate those who do. The result is an increased bureaucratization of the state parties.

Local Party Organization

At the local level, the components of convention, committee, and chair exist amid vast variations. The legendary urban party machines are essentially extinct. Nevertheless, some retain a residual and relative strength. In Chicago, for example, remnants of the once-powerful Daley organization linger. Elsewhere, some local parties are but organizational shells, with positions unoccupied and handfuls of officials quietly tending to procedural regularities. Here as at the other levels, election campaigns provide the primary arena for party activity. A recent comparative study found few signs of organizational decline among local parties.[17]

State and Local Parties and Presidential Politics

More so than today, the past relationship between state and local party organization and the presidency centered on presidential selection. After the national convention became the nominating vehicle in the 1830s, and until recently, state and local party leaders tightly controlled the selection of convention delegates and effectively instructed their delegations in voting on nominees. Thus, astute presidential candidates sought the support of these grass-roots political leaders.

The preconvention presidential campaign typically consisted of relatively low-key efforts by candidates and managers to line up commitments from the party bosses. In turn, the bosses had options such as jumping aboard a bandwagon, backing favorite sons, or remaining uncommitted in hopes of ultimately tipping the balance at a divided convention.

Conventions in those days featured "smoke-filled rooms" where the party leaders gathered to wheel and deal for the presidential nomination. Thus, the victor would be beholden to the bosses who had authorized the outcome. Around the turn of the century, Ohio's Mark Hanna epitomized power brokers of this type.

In the years immediately preceding World War II, Frank Hague of New Jersey and Boss Crump of Memphis, Tennessee, represented the breed. As late as the 1960s, Mayor Richard Daley of Chicago still embodied the traditional pattern.

In campaigns of this era the presidential nominee relied heavily on personnel resources that the state party leaders could mobilize. Old-time campaigns were much more labor-intensive than they are today. Until about 1960 the state party leaders were able to provide the necessary campaign workers.

Following the campaign, the victorious party's bosses would claim the federal patronage as a reward for their workers. Thus, through the spoils system, the presidential-selection process clearly linked the state and local parties with the presidency.

Fundamental changes have altered this traditional linkage process. Party reforms beginning in the Progressive Era around the turn of the century, and picking up steam after 1968, have drastically diminished the role of state party leaders in designating and controlling delegations to the national convention. Delegates formerly hand-picked by party leaders now are mostly chosen through primaries and participatory caucuses.

In presidential primaries, party voters sometimes vote directly for convention delegates. In many states, they do so in conjunction with a vote for the presidential candidate of their choice. Convention delegates slots usually go to supporters of the various presidential candidates in proportion to their electoral support.

In the caucuses, local party activists gather at specified locations in voting precincts to register their support for particular presidential candidates. Each precinct will send representatives to a county-level assembly in proportion to the initial division of support for the various contenders. At the county level, candidate supporters will be selected, again proportionally, to attend congressional district and finally state conventions. There the national convention delegates will be chosen from among the survivors of the earlier trials. The state parties also provide for at-large representatives to be chosen at the state level. *(See box, How Caucuses Work, p. 169.)*

Thus, presidential candidates are considerably less likely to rely on the state leaders' support. Instead, they will emphasize appeals to pressure group leaders and party activists in the electorate who, through presidential primaries and participatory caucuses, have the controlling say in delegate selection. The delegations so chosen will be more under the direction of candidate and pressure group organizations, lessening the state party leaders' influence on the convention's choice.

Modern presidential campaigns are capital and technology intensive. Where once party workers rang doorbells to solicit support, today through television candidates themselves appear in living rooms throughout the land.

The expansion of civil service and consequent reduction of patronage resources also has helped to disengage state and party leaders from the presidency. This is not to say that the state and local parties have declined organizationally. Indeed, there is considerable evidence to the contrary.[18] But their organizational activity no longer relates so clearly to the presidency as it once did.

Strom Thurmond, left, ran for president under the Dixiecrat party label in 1948. Twenty years later, George Wallace ran under the American Independent party banner.

National-State Party Relations

National parties of the past were weak and lacking in resources compared with the state and local political organizations, primarily because the federal system decentralized power in general and party power in particular.[19] In recent years, a dramatic "nationalization" has taken place as the national parties expanded authority and influence over their state counterparts. The two parties have taken different paths to similar ends. The Democrats have reformed party rules that primarily address delegate-selection procedures for the national convention. The Republican approach has been less legalistic, concentrating instead on making the state parties more reliant on the national party for needed services.[20]

The Democrats' altered course began in the late 1940s in the context of uncertainty about the loyalty of certain southern state parties toward the national ticket and platform. Twice in a twenty-year period, sizable elements of the southern Democratic party bolted to follow a regional favorite son.

In 1948 several southern delegations walked out of the national convention following the passage of a controversial platform plank supporting black civil rights. After the convention, several southern state parties held a rump assembly and nominated South Carolina governor Strom Thurmond to head a "Dixiecrat" ticket in the presidential election. Thurmond won four states and thirty-nine electoral votes.

In 1968 Alabama governor George Wallace mounted a presidential bid under the American Independent party label. He carried five states and won forty-six electoral votes.

During the two decades of conflict over the loyalty issue, the national party demanded that the state units guarantee support for the convention's decisions. To put teeth in this demand it threatened not to seat noncomplying state delegations at subsequent conventions.

Initially, this controversy was closely associated with the issue of civil rights for blacks. The 1964 Democratic national convention resolved to prohibit racial discrimination in delegate selection to the 1968 convention. This constituted a historic assertion of national authority over what had previously been the state parties' exclusive prerogative. It also authorized the national chair to appoint a committee to assist the state parties in complying with this new guideline.

This committee and the 1968 convention, along with a new group established by the latter, the Commission on Party Structure and Delegate Selection, broadened the issue beyond that of black civil rights to embrace more generally popular participation in delegate selection and other party activities. These various proposals were accepted by the Democratic National Committee and the party's 1972 convention. They culminated at the 1974 midterm convention in the adoption of a charter that clearly subordinates the state parties to their national counterpart. As amended, this charter and accompanying bylaws remain in force as the party's "constitution."

The nationalization of the Republican party has placed much less emphasis on formal rules. Where the national Democrats have mandated reform in delegate selection, the Republicans have merely recommended it. In practice, however, many of the Democratic party guidelines have been incorporated by state legislatures into laws, so that they are similarly binding on the state Republican parties.

The national Republican party has amassed a formidable financial foundation that allows it to bestow "favors," such as monetary assistance and campaign and party-building expertise, that bind state and local parties to the national organization. Therefore, while the Republicans have not formally altered their party structure, they too have positioned the national organization in the dominant position.

Notes

1. Nine isolated instances of "faithless electors," or those who did not follow partisan instructions, have been identified since 1796. The most recent occurred in 1988. Congressional Quarterly, *Presidential Elections Since 1789,* 4th ed. (Washington: Congressional Quarterly Inc., 1987), 147.
2. Herbert Kaufman, "The Growth of the Federal Personnel System," in Wallace Sayre, ed. *The Federal Government Service,* 2d ed. (Englewood Cliffs, N.J.: The American Assembly, Prentice-Hall, 1965), 41-43, provides a table, "Extension of Competitive Civil Service, 1884-1963," which sets the total number of federal government employees in 1884 at 131,208. His source was the Commission on Organization of the Executive Branch of Government, *Report on Organization of the Executive Branch of Government* (February, 1955), 97-98.
3. William A. Riordan, *Plunkitt of Tammany Hall* (New York: Dutton Paperback, 1963), 13.
4. This discussion follows the outline of the presentation by Frank J. Sorauf and Paul Allen Beck, *Party Politics in America,* 6th ed. (Glenview, Ill.: Scott, Foresman, 1988), 167-187.
5. The most important single statement of the concept and significance of party identification is found in Angus Campbell et al., *The American Voter* (New York: Wiley, 1960), ch. 5-7. For a general consideration of more recent findings attaching less significance to party identification, see Norman H. Nie, Sidney Verba, and John R. Petrocik, *The Changing American Voter* (Cambridge, Mass.: Harvard University Press, 1976). On the phenomenon of ticket-splitting, see Walter DeVries and Lance Tarrance, Jr., *The Ticket-Splitter: A New Force in American Politics* (Grand Rapids, Mich.: Eerdmans, 1972).
6. The party-decline thesis finds expression in Walter Dean Burnham, *Critical Elections and the Mainsprings of American Politics* (New York: Norton, 1970); Gerald M. Pomper,

"The Decline of the Party in American Elections," *Political Science Quarterly* 92 (Spring 1977): 21-41; William J. Crotty and Gary C. Jacobson, *American Parties in Decline* (Boston: Little, Brown, 1980); and Martin P. Wattenberg, *The Decline of American Political Parties* (Cambridge, Mass.: Harvard University Press, 1984).

7. The traditional role and status of the national party convention is developed at length in Paul T. David, Ralph M. Goldman, and Richard C. Bain, *The Politics of National Party Conventions* (Washington: Brookings Institution, 1960).
8. Two classic works on the national party committees are Hugh A. Bone, *Party Committees and National Politics* (Seattle: University of Washington Press, 1958); and Cornelius P. Cotter and Bernard C. Hennessy, *Politics Without Power: The National Party Committees* (New York: Atherton, 1964). Also see *The Charter and the Bylaws of the Democratic Party of the United States* (Washington, D.C.: Democratic National Committee, 1987); and *The Rules of the Republican Party* (Washington, D.C.: Republican National Committee, 1984).
9. Generally, see Cotter and Hennessy, *Politics Without Power*, chs. 4-5, for a consideration of the traditional role and status of the national party chair.
10. Cornelius P. Cotter and John F. Bibby, "Institutional Development of Parties and the Thesis of Party Decline," *Political Science Quarterly* 95 (Spring 1980): 6-7.
11. Cotter and Hennessy, *Politics Without Power*, 67-71, 78-80.
12. See Bone, *Party Committees and National Politics*, ch. 2; Cotter and Hennessy, *Politics Without Power*, ch. 6-9; Cotter and Bibby, "Institutional Development of Parties," 2-9.
13. Cotter 14. *The Charter and Bylaws of the Democratic Party*, 3.
14. *The Charter and Bylaws of the Democratic Party*, 3.
15. Sorauf and Beck, *Party Politics in America*, 144.
16. Sources for this discussion include Malcolm E. Jewell and David Olson, *American State Parties and Elections*, rev. ed. (Homewood, Ill.: Dorsey, 1982), ch. 3; Robert J. Huckshorn, *Party Leadership in the States* (Amherst: University of Massachusetts Press, 1976); and Cornelius P. Cotter et al., *Party Organizations in American Politics* (New York: Praeger, 1984).
17. Cotter et al., *Party Organizations in American Politics*, ch. 2.
18. Ibid., passim.
19. See E. E. Schattschneider, *Party Government* (New York: Rinehart, 1942), 129-133; Morton Grodzins, "American Political Parties and the American System," Western Political Quarterly (December 1960): 974-998.
20. Cotter and Bibby, "Institutional Development of Parties," 13-20; Charles Longley, "Party Reform and Party Nationalization: The Case of the Democrats," in *The Party Symbol: Readings on Political Parties*, ed. William Crotty (San Francisco: Freeman, 1980), 359-378; John F. Bibby, "Party Renewal in the National Republican Party," in *Party Renewal in America*, ed. Gerald Pomper (New York: Praeger, 1981), 102-115.

Selected Bibliography

Bibby, John F. "Political Parties and Federalism: The Republican National Committee." *Publius* (Winter 1979): 229-36.

———. "Party Renewal in the National Republican Party." In *Party Renewal in America*, 102-115. Edited by Gerald M. Pomper. New York: Praeger, 1981.

Bone, Hugh A. *Party Committees and National Politics*. Seattle: University of Washington Press, 1958.

Burnham, Walter Dean. *Critical Elections and the Mainsprings of American Politics*. New York: Norton, 1970.

Campbell, Angus, Philip E. Converse, Warren E. Miller, and Donald E. Stokes. *The American Voter*. New York: Wiley, 1960.

Cotter, Cornelius P., and John F. Bibby. "Institutional Development of Parties and the Thesis of Party Decline." *Political Science Quarterly* 95 (Spring 1980): 1-27.

———, James L. Gibson, John F. Bibby, and Robert J. Huckshorn. *Party Organizations in American Politics*. New York: Praeger, 1984.

———, and Bernard D. Hennessy. *Politics Without Power: The National Party Committees*. New York: Atherton, 1964.

Crotty, William J., and Gary C. Jacobson. *American Parties in Decline*. Boston: Little, Brown, 1980.

David, Paul T., Ralph M. Goldman, and Richard C. Bain. *The Politics of National Party Conventions*. Washington: Brookings Institution, 1960.

Flanigan, William H., and Nancy H. Zingale. *Political Behavior of the American Electorate*, 6th ed. Dubuque, Iowa: William C. Brown, 1987.

Huckshorn, Robert J. *Party Leadership in the States*. Amherst: University of Massachusetts Press, 1976.

Jewell, Malcolm E., and David M. Olson. *American State Parties and Elections*, rev. ed. Homewood, Ill.: Dorsey, 1982.

Longley, Charles. "Party Reform and Party Nationalization: The Case of the Democrats." In *The Party Symbol: Readings on Political Parties*, 359-378. Edited by William J. Crotty. San Francisco: Freeman, 1980.

Polsby, Nelson W. *Consequences of Party Reform*. New York: Oxford University Press, 1983.

Pomper, Gerald M. "The Decline of the Party in American Elections." *Political Science Quarterly* 92 (Spring 1977): 21-41.

Price, David E. *Bringing Back the Parties*. Washington, D.C.: CQ Press, 1984.

Wattenberg, Martin P. *The Decline of American Political Parties, 1952-1980*. Cambridge, Mass.: Harvard University Press, 1984.

Wekkin, Gary D. "National-State Party Relations: The Democrats' New Federal Structure." *Political Science Quarterly* 99 (Spring 1984): 45-72.

Presidents and the News Media

In the various roles of chief of state, head of government, commander in chief, and party leader, modern American presidents must be effective communicators. To promote their programs and policies, they must be able to forge a bond with the electorate and earn its trust and confidence. This presidents do largely by "going public" and by managing the news media. As a former White House aide noted, "presidential power is communications power." [1]

Communication has become an integral part of politics and the governing process to the extent that its use has become institutionalized. Because of the revolution in mass communications, presidents have been persuaded to change their political styles and governing procedures. Television, especially, has enhanced their ability to project their message and mobilize public sentiment. Correspondingly, television subjects them to microscopic scrutiny and tends to magnify their defects, hence diminishing some of the mystique of the office. In the main, however, it provides them with a marked advantage over their critics and rivals.

Today, an incumbent president enjoys constant media exposure. The president's voice is the most distinct in public affairs, the president's face the most familiar. The chief executive is the prime news personality in the country; each official act and most of the president's personal activities are reported and photographed by the news media and disseminated around the world. No other celebrated figure can match the president as a national attraction, thus ensuring that the electorate will listen and frequently heed what the White House has to say about public policy.

In a sense, the presidency has evolved into a form of theater in which the chief executive is the most visible and compelling actor on the American stage. Accordingly, one student of the presidency has observed, "The whole of the White House is an institution for communicating on behalf of the President." [2]

Specifically, political scientist Doris Graber has noted, the news media perform four basic functions for presidents. They keep them informed about breaking events, including developments in other parts of the government; they keep presidents attuned to the major concerns of the American people; they enable presidents and their staffs to "convey their messages to the general public as well as to political elites within and outside of government"; and they allow chief executives to "remain in full public view on the political stage," thereby ensuring that their human qualities and professional skills are thoroughly displayed.[3]

Thus, the media age has contributed toward the making of a more visible and personalized presidency.

By Dom Bonafede

Historical Background

The tradition of a free press in the United States is almost as old as the nation itself. It has become part of the national heritage, protected by the Constitution and woven in the country's social fabric.

From the early colonial years, the press—primitive by today's standards and politically partisan—was recognized as a force in the affairs of the citizens and their governmental representatives. James Madison perceived a free press as an essential pillar of democracy. "Whatever facilitates a general intercourse of sentiments," he wrote, "as good roads, domestic commerce, a free press, and particularly a circulation of newspapers through the entire body of the people ... is favorable to liberty." [4]

Madison, along with Alexander Hamilton and John Jay, wrote *The Federalist Papers* to enlist support for the new Constitution. Thomas Paine vigorously promoted separation from the crown in his provocative pamphlets, such as *Common Sense*. He also penned the *Crisis* papers, one of which contained the memorable line, "These are the times that try men's souls."

Universal acceptance of the notion that a free society cannot endure without a free exchange of ideas and information was not achieved easily. The struggle dates back at least to 1690 when the first colonial newsletter, *Publick Occurrences Both Foreign and Domestick*, was published in Boston by Benjamin Harris, who had fled to the New World after being pilloried in London for printing anticrown pamphlets. His small, three-page publication lasted only one issue because he had neglected to obtain the "countenance of authority" required by the royal governor of Massachusetts. Harris further offended the governor, as well as Puritan officials in Boston, by offering an account of the corruption of Indians by colonists and suggesting that the king of France had an affair with his son's wife.

During this period, the British crown viewed the press

and the spread of knowledge as a threat to its rule and discouraged the dissemination of public prints. This autocratic attitude was reflected in remarks by his majesty's governor in Virginia: "I thank God we have no free schools nor printing, and I hope we shall not have these hundred years. For learning has brought disobedience and heresy and sects into the world, and printing has divulged them and libels against the government. God keep us from both."[5]

In 1704 the *Boston News-Letter,* put out by John Campbell, the local postmaster, appeared under the notice that it was being "published by authority." The imprimatur, of course, meant that the paper was allowed to exist only with the benevolence of the royal governor. Accordingly, the paper was exceedingly dull and cautious in its reports, which consisted mainly of old news, death notices, summaries of church sermons, and notices of ship arrivals and departures.

To Campbell, the paper had been merely a sideline. In 1719 he lost his job as postmaster and his successor promptly began a new paper, the *Boston Gazette.* Incensed by the competition, Campbell wrote of the rival paper, "I pity [its] readers. Its sheets smell stronger of beer than of midnight oil."[6]

The incident thus served as a preface to the circulation wars that would mark the newspaper business in the late nineteenth and and early twentieth centuries. It was not until 1721, with the publication of the *New England Courant* by James Franklin, that criticism of the reigning authority began to seep into the American press. Franklin dared to publish without the approval of the colonial authorities and because of his temerity was thrown into prison and later prohibited from publishing a newspaper without prior sanction. He evaded the restriction by appointing his younger brother Benjamin as publisher. Young Ben had been an apprentice printer at twelve, and, though he was still little more than a boy, his intellect, unceasing curiosity, and grasp of public affairs, as well as his deft way with words, served to make the paper a success. He and his brother had a falling out, however, and Ben moved to Philadelphia, where at twenty-three he began the *Pennsylvania Gazette.*

Benjamin Franklin's colorful personality and prominent role in the birth of the new nation have tended to overshadow his accomplishments as a creative journalist. He published one of the first American magazines, launched the first newspaper chain, and founded the first American foreign-language papers. Franklin additionally was one of the first advertising copywriters. One of his newspaper ads, which in those days looked similar in print to the news items, plugged a product called "Super Fine Crown Soap": "It cleanses fine Linens, Muslins, Laces, Chinces, Cambricks, with Ease and Expedition, which often suffer more from the long and hard rubbing of the Washer, through the ill qualities of the soap than the wearing." Interestingly, the soap was made by his brothers John and Peter.

Above all a patriot, Benjamin Franklin urged his fellow colonialists to join in a confederation and in 1754 drew and published what is considered the first American editorial cartoon: a reptile divided in separate parts, each representing one of the colonial states, over the caption, "Join, or Die."

By the early 1700s printing was an established, honorable craft; Ben Franklin demonstrated that journalism could be a respectable calling.

Evolution of Press Freedom

In a landmark case that exemplified the tension between the Colonies and crown, John Peter Zenger, publisher of the *New York Weekly Journal,* noted for its outspoken criticism of the British-born royal governor of New York, was charged with seditious libel in 1734. His attorney, Andrew Hamilton, argued that contrary to Brit-

Library of Congress

In 1754 Benjamin Franklin drew what is considered the first American editorial cartoon. In his *Pennsylvania Gazette,* Franklin published the drawing of a reptile divided into separate parts, each representing one of the colonial states.

ish law—which held "the greater the truth the greater the libel"—truth could be used as a defense against libel and that a jury, not a royal magistrate, should decide questions of libel. The jury agreed, thereby striking a symbolic blow for press freedom.

Even so, a philosophical doctrine espousing freedom to exchange ideas and express views different from those of governing authorities developed more slowly among the public than the press. By the mid-eighteenth century more than a dozen independent weekly newspapers, necessarily small because of poor transportation and the need to set type laboriously by hand, had been established, mostly in port towns. Published mainly by printers and postmasters, they were directed at the educated, well-off urban classes and the political and commercial elites, who could afford the relatively high subscription rates. The "news" generally consisted of shipping and mercantile announcements, the promotion of special interests supported by the publisher, and information culled from old British newspapers brought in by ship.

But as the conflict between the Tories and patriots became more intense, the papers grew in numbers and circulation, and the press began assuming more of a significant role in the changing social and political realm. The papers were basically political, some siding with the Colonies and others with the crown, and all openly endorsing a particular faction, cause, party, or personality.

Their contents were distinctly editorial in tone, with a good deal of opinion. Personal attacks and biased information were common fare. No effort was made to disclose the closed-door deliberations of government bodies, yet editors of the early press risked imprisonment with their heavily caustic and bitterly critical editorials. By the time of the Revolutionary War, publishers were recognized as influential public figures, and newspapers went to an estimated 40,000 colonial homes.[7]

As rebellious fervor against British rule gathered momentum, many of the colonial papers, though divided on numerous issues, openly opposed stringent impositions by the crown, notably the 1765 Stamp Act, which was intended to replenish the royal coffers depleted by the war against France. The act levied a penny tax per issue upon each newspaper. The colonial publishers angrily denounced the tax as an infringement on their freedom and an example of taxation without representation. The opposition voices were so forceful that within a year Parliament repealed the act.

With the beginning of the revolutionary war in 1775, the colonial press, comprising about thirty-seven papers, remained polarized between the crown and the revolutionists, with most favoring the latter. Several new papers sprang up while others went out of business; by the war's end in 1783 about thirty-five papers were being published regularly.[8] That same year the *Pennsylvania Evening Post and Daily Advertiser* was converted from a weekly to become the first American daily newspaper.

Party Newspapers

Following the Revolutionary War, newspapers in the new nation transferred their partisan leanings to the debate and controversy over the powers of the central government, manifested in the struggle between the Federalists under the banner of Alexander Hamilton, Washington's chief lieutenant, and the antifederalist Democratic-Republicans led by Thomas Jefferson. In essence, the Federalists favored a strong national government and the Democratic-Republicans, a league of more or less independent states.

The Founders by now were aware of the usefulness of the press and found expression of their views in the "party press"—newspapers and journals that sided with them and served their political purposes in mobilizing public opinion.

In his campaign to promote the Federalists' cause, Hamilton established the *Gazette of the United States.* Not to be outdone, Jefferson recruited Philip Freneau, "The Poet of the Revolution," ostensibly to act as a paid "translator" but in reality to publish a party newspaper, the *National Gazette.* Name-calling and vitriolic language were not uncommon in the pages of these and other papers of the time.

It is highly unlikely, however, that the Founders ever envisioned that the press would attain the lofty prominence it has or that it would become the "Fourth Branch of Government." The struggle for press freedom in the early years of the Republic, as reflected in the press duels between Hamilton and Jefferson, was part of a more ambitious struggle to form a constitutional government and a manifestation of the self-interests of the men who participated in the fight.

Furthermore, even those patriots who advocated press freedom also insisted on press responsibility. They were convinced that the press should be free to publish without prior restraint but should not be immune from sanctions for publishing false and malicious calumnies against the government.

In his defense of Zenger, attorney Andrew Hamilton told the jury that "Nothing ought to excuse a man who raises a false charge or accusation, even against a private person, and that no matter of allowance ought to be made to him who does so against a public magistrate."[9]

Benjamin Franklin himself declared in reference to journalists guilty of libeling government officials, "We should, in moderation, content ourselves with tarring and feathering and tossing them in a blanket."[10]

Testing the Limits

In 1798 the press became embroiled in the dispute between the Federalists and Jeffersonian Democratic-Republicans when, at a time when war with France appeared imminent, Congress passed the Sedition Act. Endorsed by the Federalist administration of John Adams, the legislation, notwithstanding the First Amendment, provided penalties of up to two years in prison and a fine of $2,000 for writing, printing, or uttering "false, scandalous and malicious" statements against the government or Congress. To the Democratic-Republicans, the act was an attempt by the Federalists to create a one-party press and one-party government. Over the next two years ten editors of Republican newspapers were convicted of violating the law. It expired in March 1801 when Jefferson assumed the presidency and pardoned all those prosecuted under its provisions.

As American government scholar James Q. Wilson observed,

> The debate over the Sedition Act was the first effort by the new republic to define the acceptable limits of public criticism of government. The Federalist position was that the First Amendment, while it prohibited censorship (such as the government preventing a newspaper from publishing a story), did not prohibit punishing a newspaper for having printed a false and malicious story. Just as individual citizens had the right to sue a newspa-

per for publishing a libelous story about them, so also the government had the right to sue a newspaper for libeling it.[11]

Jeffersonians did not contend that the press should be immune from any government controls. Rather they argued that the First Amendment did not authorize the federal government to punish the press for seditious libel. Jefferson claimed that punishment for "the overwhelming torrent of slander" in the press was "the exclusionary right" of the states. Thus, as Wilson observed, "The first major debate over the meaning of the constitutional freedoms conferred on those who wrote and spoke was in large measure a debate over states' rights." [12]

The Supreme Court never reviewed the convictions under the Sedition Act; the issue of criminal libel remained mired in confusion, and the scope of the First Amendment was left undetermined.

While Jefferson perceived the press as performing an educational function necessary for self-government and regarded free expression as one of man's inalienable natural rights, he also appreciated its pragmatic capabilities. In an effort to counter the *Gazette of the United States*, established by Alexander Hamilton to promote the Federalists' cause, Jefferson recruited Philip Freneau, "The Poet of the Revolution," to create *The National Gazette*, which became the voice of the Anti-Federalists and Washington's strongest critic.

After becoming president, Jefferson persuaded a young printer, Samuel Harrison Smith, to start up the *National Intelligencer*, as his administration's party organ, subsidizing him with government printing contracts.

Newspapers continued to grow as the country entered the new century. By 1800 there were more than 230 newspapers in the United States, and most large cities had at least one daily newspaper.

Library of Congress

Horace Greeley used his newspaper for crusades and causes. His *New York Tribune* was the first major paper to endorse the abolition of slavery and the first to introduce a separate editorial page.

Throughout the nineteenth and twentieth centuries, the press expanded beyond the most fertile imagination into the mass media, largely because of advanced technology, the imperatives of public policy and private enterprise, and the recognition that communications had become a vital social, political, and cultural force as the world assumed the proportions of a "global village."

Rise of New Forms of Media

Historically, American journalism has passed through a succession of epochal cycles. The first of these saw fundamental changes in the print media, which for centuries had served throughout the world as the public's main sources of news and information. In the twentieth century, the advent of electronic journalism brought Americans even closer to their government and its leaders.

Mass-Circulation Newspapers

Advocacy journals of the colonial era served as a vehicle for narrowly defined political interests. "News" was primarily something on which to tie editorial opinions.

Then, with the birth of Jacksonian democracy in 1833, the party press began to wane and the penny press, aimed at the mass of the American populace, emerged. Its appearance resulted from a fortunate combination of factors: the development of high-speed presses that enabled publishers to print thousands of copies of a newspaper cheaply and quickly, an increase in the level of literacy, and the rise of self-supporting urban workers. Also, the invention of the telegraph in 1844 meant that news could be disseminated almost immediately; in 1790 it took more than ten days for news of an event in Boston to be published in Philadelphia.

These changes gave rise to mass circulations and increased advertising, hence publishers did not have to rely so much on political subsidies for operating revenues. Also, in the period from Jackson to Lincoln, presidents were generally unskilled in mastering the press as a political vehicle.

The end of the party press was sealed in 1860, when the Government Printing Office was established, thereby terminating their profitable printing contracts. The growth of professional Washington news bureaus and the realization by editors that their influence did not depend on party affiliation gave the coup de grace to the party press in the United States.

Forerunner of the penny press was Benjamin H. Day's *New York Sun*, which cost one cent compared with six cents for most other dailies. Penny papers that followed included James Gordon Bennett's *New York Herald* and Horace Greeley's *New York Tribune*. The country's first popular, commercialized newspapers, they played up human interest, crime, and social injustice and enticed an untapped audience from among the middle levels of society. By cutting across social class and political party lines, they attracted advertisers who relied on a broadly based clientele. They further expanded the scope of the news, with firsthand reports of national and foreign events, thus shaping a journalistic concept that would become an enduring element of the American press.

Aside from their common characteristics, each paper and publisher was distinctly individualistic.

The *Sun* specialized in short, breezy items about local

people and domestic occurrences. One of the paper's most popular features, called "Police Office," carried reports of local people arrested for drunkenness and boisterous behavior.

Bennett, who viewed himself as a reformer, pursued an aggressive editorial policy and broadened the *Herald* to include financial news and sports reporting.

Greeley preferred to use his newspaper for crusades and causes. He called the *Tribune* "the great moral organ" and, using it as such, he exposed slum conditions in New York, advocated women's rights, and opposed capital punishment, alcohol, and tobacco. Greeley's *Tribune* was the first major paper to endorse the abolition of slavery and the first to introduce a separate editorial page. As romanticized in legend, Greeley advocated the western expansion of the country.

Within a decade after the emergence of the penny press, the combined circulation of all U.S. dailies climbed from 78,000 to an estimated 300,000. It was during this period that news reporting acquired special characteristics as a vocation. Interviewing became an integral tool of news gathering. Bennett's *New York Herald* created a sensation when it published an interview with the madam of a "fancy house" where a murder had occurred. As a result of the *Herald*'s stories, a young suspect was released by the police.

During this period, worldwide news agencies were formed—the Associated Press in 1848 and Reuters, the British wire service, the following year.

As the number of newspapers increased, editors relied more on the wire services for news beyond their local community and range of coverage. But since the wire services served numerous client newspapers of various editorial viewpoints, they confined themselves to reporting news in a straight, impartial manner, without commentary or opinion. This emphasis on objectivity soon became a sacred tenet of American journalism.

Civil War Coverage. Perhaps more than any other single event, the Civil War prompted sweeping changes in journalistic practices. The overwhelming demand for news sent newspaper sales soaring, and editors began trying to gain exclusive news and satisfy a popular appetite for the latest happenings.

Reporting of wars and foreign affairs up to the mid-nineteenth century was largely haphazard. Editors simply plagiarized war news from foreign newspapers. English papers employed junior military officers at the front to send letters, which more often than not were slanted and full of self-aggrandizement.

Accorded the honor of being recognized as one of the first notable war correspondents was William Howard Russell, of the *Times* of London. His account of the charge of the Light Cavalry Brigade during the Crimean War in 1854 remains memorable in the annals of journalism-"... In diminished ranks, with a halo of steel above their heads, and with a cheer which was many a noble fellow's death cry, they flew into the smoke of the batteries...." [13]

As noted by Phillip Knightley, author of *The First Casualty*, "Russell's coverage of the Crimean War marked the beginning of an organized effort to report a war to the civilian population at home using the services of a civilian reporter." [14]

The American Civil War shortly afterward afforded the opportunity to report a massive conflict on a grand scale, helped by the fact that during the early 1860s there were an estimated 50,000 miles of telegraph lines throughout the eastern part of the country.

Mathew Brady was the foremost pioneer of modern photography. His photographs offered a vivid visual account of the Civil War and served as an example for succeeding generations of photojournalists.

Library of Congress

Some 500 correspondents covered the war for the North alone; the *New York Herald* reportedly put more than sixty correspondents in the field and spent nearly $1 million on the coverage. The *New York Tribune* and *New York Times* each dispatched at least twenty reporters to the fighting zone. Many British and European newspapers devoted almost as much space to the war as the American press.

Modern photography also came into being during the war. Mathew Brady followed the Northern armies and took thousands of photographs, although unfortunately the newspapers were unable to print them because they lacked the equipment and technique. Yet, Brady's photographs offered a vivid visual account of the war and served as an example for succeeding generations of photojournalists.

But because of a confluence of factors—erratic mail service and interrupted telegraph transmissions, heavy-handed censorship, the inexperience of many reporters, and the unethical conduct of others—the reporting of the war was often biased, inaccurate, sensationalist, and propagandistic. Nevertheless, it established war correspondence as a distinct brand of reporting and vastly expanded journalism's horizons.

Pulitzer and Hearst. With the burgeoning of the industrial revolution and the growth of the United States as a fledgling world power, the mass-circulation journals of Joseph Pulitzer and William Randolph Hearst, pandering to blatant sensationalism and chauvinistic sentiments, flourished during the late nineteenth century and early decades of the twentieth century. Massive tides of immigrants were entering the United States and editors designed their newspapers to meet changing social conditions and boost readership. They provided glaring headlines, splashy "reform" crusades, circulation stunts, large doses of cheap melodrama, and lurid tales of sin and sex.

As powerful "press lords," Hearst and Pulitzer extended their influence deep into politics and government by appealing to a mass audience.

Pulitzer promoted his *New York World* as the "people's champion" and its editorial pages, reflecting the paper's independence and crusading spirit, endorsed income and inheritance taxes and regulary sided with labor unions in strike situations. It was a leading voice against industrial monopolies and political bossism. An exposé by the *World* in 1905 of corruption and embezzlement by "money interests" in the life insurance industry led to regulatory legislation in New York State. In foreign affairs, the paper opposed the annexation of the Philippines and U.S. imperialism in the Caribbean. Pulitzer himself was elected to Congress in 1884 but resigned after a few months because service in Washington kept him away from overseeing his beloved *World*.[15]

Espousing programs and policies even more radical than those of Pulitzer, his chief competitor, Hearst and his *New York Journal* attacked the "criminal trusts" and came out in favor of the nationalization of coal mines, railroads, and telegraph lines. He supported a graduated income tax, election of U.S. senators by popular vote rather than by state legislatures, and improvement of the public school system. He endorsed William Jennings Bryan for president in 1896 and 1900. When President McKinley was assassinated by an anarchist in 1901 with a copy of the *Journal* in his pocket, the public was reminded of the paper's vitriolic assaults against McKinley, and Hearst judiciously changed the name of the paper to the *American*.

A man of monumental ego, Hearst frequently sought elective office and in 1904 made a vigorous drive for the Democratic presidential nomination on an antitrust platform. He narrowly lost the nomination when some of his delegates were denied credentials. He served two terms in Congress but was defeated in elections for New York governor and mayor of New York City.

The popular fervor whipped up by Hearst against Spanish colonial rule in Cuba prompted journalism scholar Frank Luther Mott to write that it was highly probable, "If Hearst had not challenged Pulitzer to a circulation contest at the time of the Cuban insurrection, there would have been no Spanish-American War."[16]

Before World War I, Hearst's papers sought to keep America out of the conflict. They harassed President Wilson's policies with slogans such as "America First" and "No Entangling Alliances." According to one biographer, John K. Winkler, the publicity campaigns Hearst fashioned around the slogans "possibly postponed for many months our entry into the war." Winkler further observed that after the war Hearst "used every atom of his influence to rally sentiment against the League of Nations and Woodrow Wilson saw his hope for outlawing war go down into dust."[17]

In 1932, near the end of his flamboyant career, Hearst was instrumental in the selection of Franklin Roosevelt as the Democratic presidential nominee. Hearst originally supported John Nance Garner of Texas for the nomination. When it became apparent that the Chicago convention was deadlocked, Hearst, who was at his palatial home at San Simeon, California, was persuaded by FDR's campaign manager, James A. Farley, to call Garner and have him release his California and Texas delegates to Roosevelt. On the fourth ballot, California cast its forty-four votes for FDR. "Hearst had named a President," one writer observed, and Garner agreed to be FDR's running mate.[18]

Pulitzer, who abandoned the excesses of sensationalism in the last years of his life, apologetically acknowledged that if a newspaper were to have "any influence, to accomplish anything worthwhile, it was necessary to have a great circulation." To Pulitzer, his *World* was a force for good. He maintained, "The *World* should be more powerful than the President. He is fettered by partisanship and has only a four years' term."[19]

Occupying a special niche in the archives of American journalism is the account of Hearst's sending illustrator Frederic Remington to Cuba to cover the Spanish-American War. Remington cabled: "Everything is quiet. There is no trouble here. There will be no war. Wish to return." Hearst, according to legend, wired back, "Please remain. You furnish the pictures and I'll furnish the war."

Whether fact or fable, the story reflects the flavor of "yellow journalism." More important, it presaged the expanding influence of the press in public policy affairs, as well as its own sense of self-importance.

To a large degree, Hearst and Pulitzer were mythmakers with a thirst for power and wealth. They were giants in their field, for they more than anyone else understood and foresaw the awesome potential of mass circulation newspapers. For good or ill, they set the pattern for modern American newspapers with dramatic exposés of public abuses and the graphic use of headlines, illustrations, color printing, and, later, photographs. Their papers were self-portrayed as champions of the people. The formula suited a time of national consciousness, and circulations skyrocketed. After turning the *St. Louis Post-Dispatch* into a highly respected newspaper, Pulitzer brought the *New York World* in 1883 for $346,000; by 1886 its circulation topped 250,000, making it the most widely read newspaper in the city, and before long it was reputed to be worth $10 million.

Hearst, after successfully running the *San Francisco Examiner*, bought the *New York Journal* and immediately engaged in a newspaper war with Pulitzer, hiring away some of the *World*'s best writers and illustrators. Within two years, the *Journal* surpassed the *World*'s circulation.

Ironically, this period of racy journalism also marked the beginning of the ascendancy of the *New York Times* as one of the premier newspapers in the country. Begun in 1851 on an investment of $51,000, the paper gained a reputation for thoughtful, objective journalism under its legendary early editor, Henry Raymond. On the brink of bankruptcy in 1896, the *Times* was bought by Adolph Ochs, who would launch a dynasty that would make the paper a social and political force and a model of journalistic excellence.

Heyday of the Tabloids. As early as 1897 the muckraking journalist Lincoln Steffens concluded after surveying the American press that "Journalism today is a business."[20]

With advances in newspaper photography and the bold use of editorial cartoons and illustrations, tabloids became the rage in New York during the jazz era of the 1920s. World War I secured the U.S. dominance in international affairs, the country was entering a decade of prosperity, and its attention was captured by the movies, "flapper" girls, airplanes, gangsters, sports heroes, and Prohibition. In the forefront of the tabloids during the "Roaring Twenties" were the *Daily News*, *Daily Graphic*, and Hearst's *Daily Mirror*. They offered the readers a pastiche of gossip, inside tidbits about the rich and famous, sex and crime stories, advice to the lovelorn, horoscopes, and sports. The writing was short, simple, and explicit, and the compact size made tabloids easy for people to handle while on the subway or bus.

They read about the party hosted by a Broadway producer at which a nude dancing girl cavorted in a bathtub full of champagne; of the Hall-Mills murder trial in New Jersey, in which a minister's widow was accused of slaying her husband and his choirsinger paramour; of the superhuman athletic feats of Babe Ruth, Jack Dempsey,

Bill Tilden, and Gertrude Ederle; of how a corset salesman by the name of Judd Gray conspired with Ruth Snyder in disposing of the unwanted Mr. Snyder.

Writing about "the war of the tabloids" in *The Press in America*, Edwin Emery reported that when Charles Eliot, former Harvard University president, and Rudolph Valentino, "the Sheik" of Hollywood fame, died in August 1926, the *Daily News* gave Valentino six pages of space and Eliot a single paragraph. Blared one tabloid headline: "Valentino Dies With Smile as Lips Touch Priest's Crucifix." [21]

The Gray-Snyder murder trial particularly exemplified the unrestrained "jazz journalism." Following their conviction, one of the tabloids published an artist's conception of what the pair would look like strapped in the electric chair. The *Graphic* promoted an exclusive about the condemned Ruth Snyder that remains a classic example of journalistic bad taste: "Don't fail to read tomorrow's *Graphic*. An installment that thrills and stuns! A story that fairly pierces the heart and reveals Ruth Snyder's last thoughts on earth; that pulses the blood as it discloses her final letters. Think of it! A woman's final thoughts just before she is clutched in the deadly snare that sears and burns and FRIES and KILLS! Her very last words! Exclusively in tomorrow's *Graphic!*"

Photographs were forbidden of the actual execution, but the *Daily News*, in what many critics condemn as one of the most infamous episodes in American journalism, had a photographer strap a tiny camera to his ankle and take a picture an instant after the current was turned on. The enlarged photo took up the entire front page of the January 14, 1928, *Daily News*. As Emery noted, the paper "sold 250,000 extra copies, and then had to run off 750,000 additional pages later."

The preoccupation of the tabloid press with sex, crime, and entertainment in the Roaring Twenties extended to politics. The papers played up the Teapot Dome oil lease scandal that plagued the administration of Warren G. Harding, the first newspaper publisher to become president. Calvin Coolidge was painted in the press as "Silent Cal" because of his New England taciturnity, and Herbert Hoover was voted into office amid the constant reminder that the Republican party had promised two chickens in every pot and two cars in every garage.

The 1920s were made to order for journalistic sensationalism, which reflected the spirit of the times. The country's cry was "back to normalcy"; people wanted to forget the war years and concentrate on "living." Political conservatism and laissez-faire policies prevailed throughout the nation.

Competitive Media. During this same period, new claims were staked on the U.S. news audience with the rising popularity of radio and the creation of *Time* magazine in 1923 by Henry Luce and Briton Hadden, two young Yale graduates who felt there was a need to condense and provide focus to the news.

Politicians were quick to seize on radio as a useful tool to further their objectives. In 1920 station KDKA of Pittsburgh broadcast the returns of the Harding-Cox presidential election. By 1922 there were some 600 stations on the air and three million sets were available to listeners by the time of the 1924 presidential election. Presidential contests would forever be changed. Presidents henceforth would need to be skilled practitioners of the new medium to gain office and effectively govern.

By the end of the decade, tabloid journalism went into decline. Largely because of the intense competition, the rising costs of distributing a large number of daily editions, and the new technology, the tabloid papers were not highly profitable. The Wall Street crash of 1929 and the onset of the Great Depression that left millions unemployed changed the national atmosphere. This was evident in the rise of interpretive reporting during the 1930s and 1940s, partly in response to FDR's revolutionary New Deal legislation. Americans needed to understand the meaning and significance of events and developments. Roosevelt was keenly aware of this and relied on the press to deliver his message and gain public support.

It was a period of transition in both politics and journalism. In 1933 the American Newspaper Guild was established, changing forever the labor-management relationship between owner-publishers and working journalists.

During World War II, Edward R. Murrow showed how radio news could be shifted from the studio to the scene of the event and became a role model for succeeding generations of electronic newscasters.

Following the war, the arrival of television, coupled with the counterculture revolution of the 1960s, ushered in a new mode of journalism in which inhibitions on the press were markedly relaxed. Emphasis was on the intimacies of private lives, on personal style, and on imagery and symbolism. Anecdotal, "fly-on-the-wall" reporting, popularized by author-journalist Theodore H. White in his "Making of the President" series, revolutionized political reporting. Objectivity, once a sacred sacrament of American journalism, gave way to a more personalized, opinionated advocacy reporting.

Murrow, one of broadcasting's legendary figures, revolutionized radio journalism with his personalized live reports from bomb-ravaged London during World War II. Afterward, his radio documentary series, "Hear It Now," subsequently transformed with the growth of television to "See It Now," and his highly popular "Person to Person" interview program probed national issues and served to underscore the potential influence of the electronic medium on public policy. In a March 9, 1954, broadcast of "See It Now," Murrow openly condemned the witch-hunting tactics of Sen. Joseph R. McCarthy, R-Wis. (1947-1957), thus initiating his downfall. The broadcast, one of the most controversial in broadcast history, changed the course of American journalism, as well as the national political scene.

Up to that point, the press had generally published with traditional journalistic objectivity McCarthy's unsubstantiated charges that certain Americans in and out of government were engaged in subversive activities. Objectivity, or the simple recitation of facts, had long been rooted in American journalism. Beginning in the last half of the nineteenth century, the major newspapers endorsed the concept to gain a broad spectrum of readers and not offend any faction with partisan opinion or bias. The wire services particularly were strong advocates of objectivity since they sought to solicit clients of all stripes. Adherence to the standard was based as much or more on economics than on professional idealism.

The "New Journalism," employing a highly impressionistic style of writing and other literary devices such as reconstructed dialogue and the writer's own perceptions, became the vogue. At the same time, tabloid journalism was revived and renamed "supermarket journalism." Tabloids, such as the *National Enquirer* and *National Star*, highlighting "intimate secrets" of celebrities, were popularly sold at supermarket checkout counters.

Meanwhile, the role of the news media and the organizational structure of the journalistic community underwent vast changes. The press's persuasive impact in the Vietnam War and the Watergate scandal made the public aware of its influence on popular opinion and public policy. The advent of television and changes in social patterns and work habits led to the demise of numerous newspapers, especially afternoon dailies. Within a decade, the number of daily circulation papers dropped from 1,764 in 1978 to 1,654 in 1989, and 97 percent of U.S. cities were being served by only one daily newspaper.

Total daily newspaper circulation slipped from 63.3 million in 1984 to 62.5 million in 1986. Advertisers, however, continued to spend more with newspapers than with television—$27.0 billion on newspapers in 1986 compared with $22.4 billion on TV.

The News Conglomerates. Most surviving newspapers enjoyed unprecedented profits, leading to a wave of newspaper purchases by major news organizations and corporate investors, thus reducing the number of independent, individual owners and family-owned news properties. By 1988 an estimated 70 percent of U.S. dailies were owned by large chains and big-name news organizations, such as Rupert Murdoch's News Corporation Ltd., Gannett, Knight-Ridder, Hearst, Cox, Scripps-Howard, *New York Times*, *Los Angeles Times*, and *Washington Post*.

Inevitably, the emergence of media conglomerates raised disturbing questions as to whether the diversity of American journalism, acknowledged as the basis of its strength, was being diluted by a concentration of ownership. The American press has experienced radical changes from the colonial era to the nuclear age, but the recognition that a free flow of information is vital to the sustenance of a democratic society remains constant.

No relationship in presidential life is more ambiguous, more unpredictable and volatile, or more serious in consequences. The American concept of freedom of the press owes more to Thomas Jefferson than any other public figure, yet while defending the principle he was at the same time a severe critic of the press, maintaining that "advertisements . . . contain the only truths to be relied on in a newspaper." A century and a half later, Dwight D. Eisenhower, scarcely disguising his disdain for the press by cautioning his cabinet members not to believe everything they read in the newspapers, nevertheless defended their First Amendment rights. He publicly proclaimed, "I . . . will die for the freedom of the press."[22]

The built-in tension between presidents and media representatives is muted by mutual recognition that neither can perform their assigned functions without the assistance of the other. Presidents must communicate with the public to garner popular support for their programs and policies; the press must receive the cooperation of the White House to accurately report and assess events and developments at the highest level of government.

Wire Services

In the tradition of the wire service reporter, there is a "deadline every minute." The wire services—known also as news agencies or press associations—are wholesale purveyors of news, photographs, and features. The world—including city halls, state legislatures, Washington, Wall Street, Hollywood, and distant foreign capitals—is their beat. Their clients are mainly newspapers, news magazines, and broadcast stations, of which not even the richest and biggest have the resources to completely cover the globe.

Because their media clients operate under various time zones, and because of the intense competition between them, the wire services are under constant pressure to be first with the news. Some editor, somewhere, is rushing to meet a deadline and needs the most recent news development to provide a well-balanced, up-to-the-minute account of what is happening in the world.

The two major news agencies in the United States are the Associated Press (AP), the nation's largest news-gathering organization, and United Press International (UPI); together they provide much of the news offered by the print and electronic media. Even the giant news organizations, with their own corps of domestic and foreign correspondents, rely on the wire services to achieve thorough coverage.

Founded in 1848 when several New York newspapers decided to pool their manpower to reduce the costs of covering ships coming in from Europe, the AP expanded into a nonprofit cooperative of subscribing publications and broadcast stations. Under AP bylaws, members are obligated to share their news with the AP for possible distribution to other members. Each member pays AP for the service, based on its size and circulation and amount of editorial material provided; thus, a large newspaper such as the *New York Times* will pay more for the service than a small-town paper.

In 1907 newspaper chain owner E. W. Scripps began operating the United Press, and two years later Hearst founded the International News Service (INS). In 1958 United Press absorbed the International News Service and changed its name to United Press International.

UPI, unlike AP, is a privately owned company that sells its news services on a contract basis according to a formula similar to its chief competitor's. While AP has been the foremost wire service for many years, UPI gained a reputation for journalistic aggressiveness. It was the first to recognize the potential market among broadcast stations.

Both AP and UPI utilize a large network of domestic and foreign bureaus, many of which operate around the clock. AP, which has been increasing its lead over the financially ailing UPI since the mid-1970s, employs an estimated 1,600 reporters, editors, and photographers stationed at some 100 regional domestic bureaus and 60 foreign bureaus. It serves about 1,500 U.S. newspapers and more than 6,000 radio and television stations. Overall, it files a reported three million words a day, reaching one billion people worldwide through 15,000 news outlets. Its Washington bureau alone is said to transmit an average of 200,000 words and 300 photographs each day.[23]

Besides their general news wire, the press associations have special wires for sports, financial, and regional news, as well as a radio-TV wire written in broadcast style for easy delivery on the air.

Wire service reporters follow certain rules in writing straight news stories. They are principally concerned with communicating facts and are instructed to be as accurate and concise as possible and to separate news from opinion. Since their readers and listeners have varying interests and span the ideological spectrum, they place a high value on objectivity and impartiality. Analysis and interpretation are avoided—unless clearly labeled as such.

Because the AP and UPI reporters are writing for a broad audience, they usually delete local references or generalize about them. They must get to the heart of the story almost immediately to grasp the attention of fast-acting editors and to tell the story in a minimum number of words in inverted pyramid style (with the most important information at the top) so that it can be cut from the bottom if necessary. In keeping with newspaper trends, however, the wire services in recent years have placed greater emphasis on enterprise reporting and made more of an effort to offer in-depth reports.

In line with long-established practice, AP and UPI transmit separate stories on the same topic for morning and afternoon papers on A.M. and P.M. cycles to ensure that they are not duplicated and are updated with fresh leads and new information.

Several major newspapers and chains have formed syndicates of their own to sell their stories and services to other press organizations, among them the *New York Times*, *Los Angeles Times-Washington Post*, *Copley*, and *Knight-Ridder*. They do not try to compete with the wires on "spot" stories, but rather offer background, analytical, and feature material. Some chains, such as Gannett, operate internal news services that send editorial material to all member papers.

Two foreign news services, Reuters, the British press agency, and Agence France-Presse, the French wire service, are comparable to AP and UPI and even have some U.S. clients. Numerous other countries have national news services, such as the Soviet Union's Tass and the People's Republic of China's Hsinhua news agency. National wire services are often government controlled and sometimes used for propagandistic purposes.

For years U.S. news agencies transmitted their stories over leased telegraph circuits to domestic subscribers who received them on teleprinter machines. Satellite technology, however, has vastly speeded up the transmission process; where teleprinter machines typed out 66 words a minute, computer-based equipment can print more than 1,200 words a minute.

UPI has had at least three changes in ownership since merging with INS in 1958, during which it experienced a turnover in editorial leadership and a constriction in operations. It further suffered a loss of some of its clients, leading to speculation that it might fold or revamp its editorial services.

Magazines

Magazines have served as a supplemental form of information to newspapers since colonial times. In 1741 Andrew Bradford published *American Magazine*, the first publication of this type to appear in the Colonies, beating Benjamin Franklin's *General Magazine and Historical Chronicle* by a few days. Both publications, however, soon folded because of financial difficulties.

For the next century and a half, numerous successors, mainly monthlies, emerged, but most failed to survive because of a lack of advertising and a limited editorial vision devoted principally to literature and contemporary social manners. Some few, nevertheless, made their mark by expanding their appeal and coverage to include questions of public policy, among them *Graham's Magazine*, under the direction of Edgar Allan Poe, the *Saturday Evening Post*, and *Godey's Lady's Book*, a pioneer for women's rights, which by 1850 had a circulation of more than 150,000.[24]

During the mid-1800s the *Nation*, *Atlantic*, and *Harper's Weekly*, which in 1863 published reproductions of Mathew Brady's Civil War photographs, came into prominence. In 1870 *Harper's*, with the help of Thomas Nast's searing editorial cartoons, contributed toward the downfall of the "Tammany Hall" political machine controlled by William "Boss" Tweed.

In 1879 Congress lowered postal rates for periodicals, thus stimulating broader distribution of newspapers and magazines. Shortly afterward, publishers ushered in the era of mass-circulation magazines by restructuring editorial content to bring the publications into harmony with the popular tastes and interests of the rising American middle class. Designed to appeal to a broad audience, magazines were easier to read, more entertaining, and, significantly, cheaper to buy than the restricted circulation magazines. S. S. McClure founded *McClure's* in 1893 and charged fifteen cents a copy, about half the regular magazine rate at that time. The same year Frank Munsey dropped the price of his magazine, *Munsey's*, to ten cents. Munsey, in the tradition of the yellow journalists of that day, was primarily interested in making a profit. Then, in 1897, Cyrus H. K. Curtis bought the *Saturday Evening Post* for $1,000 and began to sell it at five cents a copy.

Soon after the turn of the century, the *Ladies' Home Journal* became the first magazine to reach a circulation of one million. By 1912 circulation of the *Saturday Evening Post* soared to nearly two million.[25]

During this period, "muckraking" journalism—a term coined by President Theodore Roosevelt—reached its zenith. Published in national magazines of opinion, muckraking journalists specialized in essay-type, in-depth revelations of political corruption, social injustice, industrial abuses, and other ills accompanying the meteoric economic and population growth of the country. In contrast to the sensation-seeking "crusading" press of the time, they were motivated by a keen sense of morality and a rising social consciousness. Among the muckraking exposés, published in *McClure's*, were Ida M. Tarbell's "History of the Standard Oil Company" and Lincoln Steffens's "The Shame of the Cities."

During the first half of the twentieth century, magazine sales boomed, notwithstanding the introduction of movies, radio and television programs, and paperback books. Following World War I news magazines, pictorial magazines, and digests, such as the *Reader's Digest*, sprang up. *Newsweek* and *U.S. News*, copying a format inaugurated by *Time*, appeared in 1933. Publishers were now shifting the emphasis on sales from subscriptions to newsstands.

In 1936, following the successful debut of *Time* thirteen years earlier, Henry Luce launched *Life*, a dazzling, innovative pictorial magazine that was to revolutionize the visual media. Luce perceived *Life* as offering a "window on the world." The magazine led to a new journalistic genre—photojournalism—and enhanced the professional stature of news photographers. Inspired by *Life*, *Look* magazine appeared in 1937.

But by the early 1970s both *Life* and *Look* would cease weekly publication, killed by a medley of factors, including high production costs, the competition from television, and the trend toward specialized magazines appealing to specific audiences. The latter included magazines such as women's—*Cosmopolitan*, *Ms.*, *Glamour*, and *Good Housekeeping*; men's—*Playboy*; celebrity and personality—*People* and *Us*; science—*Scientific American* and *New En-*

gland Journal of Medicine; history and culture—*National Geographic* and *Smithsonian*; family living—*Better Homes and Gardens.*

By the late 1980s there were more than 100 magazines dealing with farming alone and at least 2,500 devoted to business, including *Business Week*, *Fortune*, *Nation's Business*, and *Forbes.* At the same time, an increasing public awareness of politics and public affairs sustained the popularity of magazines such as the *New Republic*, the *Nation*, and *National Review*, as well as those dealing in factual accounts and objective analyses, such as *Congressional Quarterly* and *National Journal.* There were also about 150 city magazines.

Although many mass-circulation magazines, such as *Collier's*, folded, the magazine industry has generally enjoyed economic prosperity. In 1986 more than 320 million copies of magazines were printed per issue in the United States and three magazines—*Reader's Digest*, *TV Guide*, and *National Geographic*—each topped ten million in circulation.

Radio

In 1920 Pittsburgh station KDKA went on the air to report the election returns of the presidential race in which Warren G. Harding defeated James M. Cox. It marked the first time that radio news of a significant event was broadcast. From then on the airwaves would serve as the foremost instant chronicler of events and rituals and forever change the way people perceive the world beyond their immediate reach. Over succeeding decades radio would stir the imagination and provide news and entertainment for a vast majority of Americans.

At first radio was largely conceived as a fad; indeed, many thought of it as an extension of the telephone. Only a half-million radio sets were sold in 1924. The next year some two million sets were purchased. Throughout these early years, sales of radio equipment formed the most lucrative aspect of broadcasting; the principal promoters were less visionaries than commercial investors.

But with the formation in 1926 of the National Broadcasting Company (NBC), a wholly owned subsidiary of the Radio Corporation of America (RCA), and the network that in 1927 became known as the Columbia Broadcasting System (CBS), a vast communications structure linking stations for simultaneous broadcasts began to take shape. By 1934—the same year the Mutual Broadcasting System was established—radio had evolved into an advertising medium. A half-century later there were roughly a half-billion working radio sets in the United States and about ten thousand radio stations in operation.

The American Broadcasting Company (ABC) was established when NBC, which dominated national radio, was forced by the Federal Communications Commission (FCC) to give up one of its two networks, the Red or the Blue. NBC sold the Blue Network in 1943 to Edward J. Noble, who renamed it the American Broadcasting Company in 1945.

Radio had several pioneering fathers: Guglielmo Marconi, who developed a wireless transmitter in 1901; Lee de Forest, the inventor of a vacuum tube that amplified voice and music transmissions; David Sarnoff, one of the first to recognize radio's potential and a dominant figure in the growth of RCA; and William Paley, scion of a cigar company fortune, under whose direction CBS became a powerful communications empire.

As a new communications vehicle, radio required a new style of writing. Radio scriptwriters wrote for the ear, newspaper reporters for the eye. Radio writing was conversational in tone, with short, direct sentences in the active tense, minus complex explanations and literary flourishes.

Entering directly into the living room, radio cultivated an intimate bond between speaker and listener; the two shared a common interest. People had to schedule their time to conform with radio's schedule; hence, at a given hour, millions of listeners gave their attention to the same program, making radio a universal communications medium.

Another major difference is that broadcasting uses the public airwaves and, as a result, is subject to government licensing and regulation through the FCC—in contrast to newspapers and magazines, which are virtually unregulated because of First Amendment freedoms. An FCC radio license is renewable every seven years (and every five years for television). Created by Congress in 1934 as an outgrowth of the 1927 Federal Radio Commission, the FCC stipulated that broadcasting stations must "serve the public interest, convenience and necessity." *(See "Federal Communications Commission," p. 1037, in the Government Agencies and Corporations chapter in Part V.)*

In one of its most significant policy actions, the FCC instituted the "fairness doctrine," requiring broadcasters to present a variety of viewpoints on controversial issues of public importance. Opponents favoring a deregulation of the broadcast industry maintained that the doctrine served to stifle the very democratic debate it was designed to promote and that the intense competition among the large number of stations precluded the necessity to mandate fairness. After years of controversy, the FCC on August 4, 1987, voted unanimously to abolish the fairness doctrine on the grounds that it restricted the free speech rights of broadcast journalists. Earlier, a congressional majority, led by Sen. Ernest F. Hollings, D-S.C., sought to enact the doctrine into law, but President Reagan on June 20, 1987, vetoed the measure. "In any other medium besides broadcasting, such federal policing of the editorial judgment of journalists would be unthinkable," Reagan said in rejecting the legislation.

Supporters of the proposal maintained that radio and television rely on a limited public resource—the electromagnetic spectrum—and that the doctrine was necessary to ensure that minority viewpoints were aired. Reagan and other opponents argued that because of advancements in communications technology the public had a large number of alternative information sources available—including more than 10,000 radio stations, about 1,600 television stations, and an estimated 7,700 cable TV systems.[26]

Left standing was the equal-time rule, which required broadcasters who sell air time to one political candidate to sell equal time to the candidate's opponent. The FCC, incidentally, does not regulate the networks because they do not use the airwaves but instead use privately leased lines to relay programs to individual stations.

The "golden age of radio" is measured from the mid-1920s to the end of the 1940s. During that quarter of a century mystery and action-adventure shows such as "Gangbusters" and "Ellery Queen" were among the most popular programs. Radio also had soap operas, such as "Our Gal Sunday," and, for young listeners, "Jack Armstrong, the All-American Boy." The first successful radio situation comedy, "Amos 'n' Andy," went on the air in 1930.

President Calvin Coolidge's inauguration in 1925 was heard coast to coast on a twenty-one-station hookup. In 1933 President Roosevelt spoke directly to the American electorate and solicited its support in the first of his radio fireside chats.

And in one of the most memorable incidents in the annals of radio, on October 30, 1938, Orson Welles triggered a panic with a production of H. G. Wells's play *War of the Worlds*. Although a fictional account, it made many listeners believe that alien creatures from Mars were invading the United States, causing wholesale confusion and traffic jams in New Jersey by people fleeing their homes. Above all, the show demonstrated the power of radio.

Included in the pantheon of early radio celebrities, whose names were familiar to most U.S. households, were news broadcasters Lowell Thomas, H. V. Kaltenborn, Floyd Gibbons, Gabriel Heatter, Elmer Davis, Walter Winchell, and Edwin C. Hill, as well as Graham McNamee and Ted Husing, who were best known as sportscasters. Perhaps the greatest was Edward R. Murrow, whose vivid, eyewitness accounts of the Battle of Britain during World War II brought the war home to millions of Americans and continue to stand as classic examples of radio reporting. Murrow's economy of language and ability to evoke drama in unfolding events remain unmatched.[27]

Murrow was personally responsible for arranging the first radio world news roundup on March 13, 1938, while war hovered over Europe, with live pickups from London, Paris, Berlin, Rome, and Vienna for relay to New York. In his memoirs, William L. Shirer, who was hired by Murrow to help cover the war for CBS, wrote that the breakthrough "helped radio news broadcasting abruptly come of age.... From that hasty development sprang the principal format of broadcast news—first over the radio, then over television—as we have known it ever since."[28]

The explosive emergence of television dimmed the golden age of radio. Many media observers predicted that radio would soon become an anachronism. But while radio lost massive advertising revenues to television, it continued to thrive, mainly on news reports, talk shows, and music played by disc jockeys, many of whom became the medium's new celebrities. The development of miniature transistors and the proliferation of automobile radios further contributed to its enduring popularity.

Television

Television, the most glamorous and extravagant medium, ironically lacks a rich early history to match its pervasive presence in contemporary American society. Following experimentation in the 1920s and 1930s, commercial television burst on the scene in the late 1940s without difficult birth pangs. Radio provided an already established network and station structure, as well as news and entertainment formulas that television would adopt. The star system had earlier been introduced by movies and radio. Advertisers, conditioned by radio, were lined up. Even the appropriate government regulatory agency, the FCC, was ensconced and prepared to deal with the new medium.

Television's principal contribution was its technical competence. By 1938 David Sarnoff was able to announce that home television was "now technically feasible." The following year, NBC, owned by RCA, offered a public demonstration of television at the New York World's Fair.

But the technological advancements that made home TV possible were developed long before its public unveiling. Two scientists credited with the development of television were Vladimir Zworykin, who perfected a primitive television tube, the idonoscope, in 1932, and Philo Farnsworth, who invented the electric camera in 1930.

The FCC received its first application for a commercial TV license from a Milwaukee newspaper in 1939. The permit was granted in 1941, along with licenses for nine other stations. At the time, radio was riding a crest of popularity and the public consensus was that TV could never replace radio. Many thought of it as a toy. Filmmakers did not take it seriously. During the new invention's infancy, performers had to wear heavy, green makeup to appear "normal" to the TV camera and take salt tablets because of the heat from the blazing lights.

World War II interrupted TV's development, but by January 1948 the nation had 102,000 television sets and by April the number more than doubled. Ten years later, four out of five American homes had TV sets. By the 1980s there was no part of the United States that could not receive some TV signal. An estimated 98 percent of all American homes had at least one TV set and nearly half had two or more sets. There were more TV sets in the country than telephones or bathtubs.

FCC regulations limit the number of broadcast enterprises that one owner may hold to twelve AM radio stations, twelve FM stations, and twelve television stations. The TV stations, however, cannot cover more than 25 percent of the country's TV households.[29]

The FCC further prohibits the cross-ownership of a TV station and a daily newspaper in the same market. The intent of the rules was to encourage decentralized or local ownership and preclude a concentration of media ownership. Critics, however, contended that the regulations were counterproductive and not necessary to preserve diversity of media ownership and that they further raised questions concerning protection of free speech under the First Amendment. It was additionally argued that the cross-membership prohibition contributed to the decline of competing dailies in large markets.

Networks and Ratings. In the forefront of the television era were the three national networks—ABC, CBS, and NBC—which focused primarily on entertainment to draw large audiences and attract advertisers. Essentially, the networks are program distribution companies that buy shows from television production companies, such as Music Corporation of America, Disney, Universal, and 20th Century Fox. They then distribute the programs to the independently owned local stations across the country with which they are affiliated. Advertisers pay the networks to include commercial announcements with the programs. In turn, the networks pay the stations a portion of their advertising fees for running the programs and commercials. The local stations can further sell time between programs to local advertisers. With apparent justification, local TV stations are sometimes referred to as "moneymaking machines."

Central to the marriage of television with advertising is the ratings systems, because the larger the audience the higher the advertising income. Shows with high ratings charge more for commercials than shows with low ratings. In 1986 total advertising revenue for television amounted to $22.4 billion (compared with $27.0 billion for newspapers, $7.0 billion for radio, and $5.4 billion for magazines).[30]

The cost of a TV commercial varies widely from station to station. The average thirty-second network commercial in prime time costs about $150,000, but the price can go to twice that figure for a top-rated show. For a thirty-second spot during a Superbowl championship football game, the cost can even be more than a half-million dollars.

Audience feedback, which determines ratings, is monitored by two major marketing research firms, A. C. Nielsen and Arbitron. Basically, each surveys a representative sample of households nationwide. Viewers, broken down demographically, keep diaries to indicate their viewing habits. To enhance the precision of the findings, researchers in 1987 began experimenting with "peoplemeters," hand-held electronic devices that viewers punch to record the channel being watched.

Like radio, TV had its "golden age." The decade of the 1950s was a period of rapid expansion and daring innovation, during which some of the medium's most celebrated stars reigned on the TV screen in vaudeville-like variety shows. They included Ed Sullivan's "Toast of the Town," "Arthur Godfrey's Talent Scouts," and "Texaco Star Theater," featuring Milton Berle, who became known as "Mr. Television." Popular dramas were performed live on programs such as "Studio One," "Robert Montgomery Presents," and "Kraft Television Theater," inasmuch as videotape would not be invented until near the end of the decade. A new genre, the "adult western," attracted a loyal following, and among the favorites were "Gunsmoke," "Wagon Train," and "Maverick."

In 1951 Murrow premiered "See It Now," a program that explored controversial issues of the day. Murrow also narrated a memorable CBS documentary, "Harvest of Shame," which focused on the tragic condition of American migrant farm workers. The first successful big-money TV quiz show, "The $64,000 Question," went on the air in 1955. Four years later, scandal swept the television industry when it was disclosed that the quiz show was rigged; as a result, the networks became more aware of their ethical responsibilities.

Public Affairs vs. Entertainment. Almost from its beginning, television has exerted a powerful influence in public affairs, especially at the presidential level. Madison Avenue advertising techniques were adopted to fashion Eisenhower's TV commercials in the 1952 campaign. That same year Richard Nixon, Eisenhower's running mate, paid NBC $75,000 for network time to defend himself—in what became famous as his "Checkers" speech—against charges that he had misused campaign contributions. (Checkers was his pet dog, given to him as a gift and which he said he would keep notwithstanding his critics.) The televised speech is generally credited with saving Nixon's political career.

In 1956 the networks extensively covered the Eisenhower-Stevenson campaign. And in 1960 Kennedy and Nixon engaged in the first TV presidential debate.

Congress, on the other hand, was slow in grasping the importance of television as a political instrument, with the result that it was less able to compete as a coequal with the executive branch.

The Senate allowed broadcast coverage of committee hearings in the early 1950s and among the early examples were the 1950-1951 Kefauver hearings on organized crime and the 1954 Army-McCarthy hearings. In 1966 Sen. J. William Fulbright, D-Ark. (1945-1974), chairman of the Foreign Relations Committee, held televised hearings to inquire into White House policy on the Vietnam War. The House first permitted television coverage of a committee hearing in 1974. For fifty-four days the nation watched as the House Judiciary Committee heard testimony on impeachment charges against President Nixon.

Although the House trailed the Senate in opening committee hearings to live broadcast coverage, it was the first to authorize coverage of its actual sessions. After many years of internal debate, the House in 1979 set up a closed-circuit television system that permits cable subscribers in many communities to see gavel-to-gavel coverage on the C-SPAN cable network. The Senate followed suit several years later.[31]

Television by the late 1950s and early 1960s was acknowledged as a highly popular and effective caterer of news. Many network newscasters became household names, notably Walter Cronkite, Eric Sevareid, Chet Huntley, David Brinkley, John Chancellor, Howard K. Smith, and Harry Reasoner.

In a sense, television was both a style-setter and a reflection of the incumbent American life style. Beginning in the early 1970s adult comedies such as "All in the Family" and "M*A*S*H*" ventured into areas previously off-limits, such as abortion, homosexuality, premarital sex, drug addiction, and racial prejudice. Next, the networks offered "Dallas" and other prime-time soap operas that typically dealt with rich and powerful families and were spiced with sex scenes. Situation comedies, drawing on popular predecessors such as "I Love Lucy" and "The Honeymooners," were revived in the 1980s, among them "The Bill Cosby Show" and "Family Ties." Action-adventure programs also made a comeback in contemporary settings, including "Hill Street Blues" and later "Miami Vice," which was aimed at a young, aware audience.

As an ubiquitous visual medium, television stirs the imagination of viewers and adds to their knowledge by providing a window on places and events. The unparalleled sensation of watching man walk on the moon, the poignant drama surrounding President Kennedy's assassination, and the heartsick anguish felt in viewing the *Challenger* space shuttle explosion remain indelible in the minds of Americans. Television brought the Vietnam War into living rooms and raised viewers' consciousness over the issue. The televised Watergate hearings in 1973 and the Iran-contra hearings in 1987 served as a public education into shadowy operations of government. And Mikhail Gorbachev's 1987-1988 meetings with President Reagan in Washington and Moscow, as viewed through the prism of television, offered a rare glimpse of a new type of Soviet leader.

For all that, the limitations of television are as exceptional as its benefits. It is a transitory medium, concerned almost exclusively with the moment as it rushes from one story to another; hence, there is little continuity or coherent perspective in the march of events. Television speaks in captions and turns issues into slogans and converts complexities into bite-sized superficialities. With television, everything is magnified; every news item is front-page news because there are no back pages on the screen or different sizes of headlines to suggest the significance of a story. In contrast to the print medium, which attempts to impose a kind of order out of chaos, television creates an emotional impact. Spurred by the craving for high ratings, television allows sensations to dominate, rather than reflection and reason. By the late 1980s the average American household had its TV set on for about seven hours a day. It remained uncertain, however, how long viewers were actually watching and whether they fully absorbed what they were seeing and hearing.

Nevertheless, television broadens viewers' horizons and changes their way of seeing things and their concept of reality. Its impact on American culture, politics, and government is universally recognized, if unclear as to degree and quality.

Cable and Public TV. Advances in electronic technology, notably the satellite transmission of video signals, provide alternate systems of news, educational, and entertainment programs for home viewers who pay for the service. Cable TV, or CATV (community antenna television), began as a means to bring commercial TV signals into isolated communities. It soon became apparent, however, that the coaxial cable had the capability of using numerous channels for a variety of specialized programs, including sports, news, movies, shopping tips, educational instruction, and government information.

In 1956 only about 400,000 U.S. homes had cable TV; in 1967 the number grew to three million, and by 1988 more than half of the nation's TV households were linked to cable systems. Cable TV broke the near-monopoly enjoyed by the broadcasting networks, which by 1989 had lost nearly 20 percent of their prime-television audience because of the competition. Among the popular cable systems were CNN (Cable News Network), offering round-the-clock news, and C-SPAN (Cable Satellite Public Affairs Network), specializing in public service programs, including gavel-to-gavel coverage of Congress. Each of the cable networks devoted more air time to the 1988 national presidential conventions than any of the three major commercial networks, thus in a sense preempting the latter's traditional role.

Another development in the broadening use of television was Congress's creation in 1967 of the Corporation for Public Broadcasting. As set up, public, or noncommercial, television and radio are nonprofit and depend on a mixture of public and private financing. A separate Public Broadcasting Service, a cooperative association of local stations, produces TV programs, often in collaboration with foreign broadcast systems, and acts as sort of a network for distributing TV programs. Among public television's biggest hits were "Sesame Street," "Civilisation," and "The Forsythe Saga." Popular programs from British television included "Upstairs, Downstairs" and "The Adams Chronicles."

In radio, the stations are linked by the National Public Radio system, which produces and distributes programs.

Public broadcasting system members in 1987 included 394 noncommercial television stations and 296 noncommercial FM radio stations.[32] Overall the hallmark of public broadcasting is its emphasis on cultural affairs, classical drama, experimental programs, academic discussions, political analysis, documentaries, and minority-oriented shows.

White House Press Corps— Early Years

Presidents since George Washington have had relations with the press of one kind or another, ranging at various times from mutual cordiality to tense adversary relationship. From the colonial era until now there has been no break in the relationship, which has evolved into one unlike that of any other head of state in the world. Nowhere else is the press literally quartered in the same house as the nation's chief executive, thus symbolizing the importance of communications and public opinion to democratic government.

As former presidential aide Douglass Cater observed, "No monarch in history has had a retinue like that which gathers about the American President and calls itself the White House press corps. The reporters hang about his antechamber with the indolence of courtiers at some feudal court keeping those who pass in and out—Governors, Cabinet members, Senators, Ambassadors—under constant surveillance and interrogation. They dog the President's every step and turn his most casual public conversation into a mass meeting. They follow him wherever he goes." [33]

In keeping with his aloof nature, Washington had little direct contact with the partisan press of the day and occasionally voiced criticism of it. "Newspaper paragraphs unsupported by other testimony, are often contradictory and bewildering," he once maintained.[34]

On another occasion, he declared, "We have some infamous Papers, calculated for disturbing if not absolutely intended to disturb, the peace of the community." [35]

Notwithstanding his wary view of the press, Washington knew the importance of an informed public opinion; he sensed its role in deciding the fate of the proposed new Constitution and he advocated favorable postal rates for newspapers. He was a regular reader and often used the press for personal advertisements, including one that read: "A COOK—Is wanted for the family of the President of the United States. No one need apply who is not perfect in the business, and can bring indubitable testimonials of sobriety, honesty, and attention to the duties of the station." [36]

Inevitably, the adulation bestowed upon Washington as the new nation's revolutionary war hero and first president soon was tempered by sharp criticism and bitter innuendoes by partisan journals. He was accused of unlawfully appropriating land belonging to his friend, Lord Fairfax. In papers such as the *Aurora*, published by Benjamin Bache, the New York *Argus*, Boston *Chronicle*, Richmond *Examiner*, *Kentucky Herald*, and *Carolina Gazette*, Washington was censured for "stately journeying through the American continent in search of personal incense," putting on royal airs, hosting "court-like levees" in "queenly drawing-rooms," and preferring the seclusion of a monk. Tom Paine, who had fallen on hard times, accused him in print of being "treacherous in private friendship . . . and a hypocrite in public life."

Noting Washington's irritation with such press accounts during a cabinet meeting, Thomas Jefferson wrote:

> The President was much inflamed, got into one of those passions when he cannot command himself, ran on much on the personal abuse which had been bestowed on him, defied any man on earth to produce one single act of his since he had been in govmt which was not done on the purest motives . . . that by gold he had rather be in his grave than in his present situation. That he had rather be on his farm than to be made emperor of the world and yet they were charging him with wanting to be king.[37]

Hence, a pattern was set in which succeeding presidents recognized the necessity of dealing with the press, even at their own peril, to ensure an informed national constituency and mobilize popular support.

From Printers to Professionals

The development of the news media, from print to radio and thence to television, has become one of the determinant factors in how presidents and their initiatives are presented and promoted. And just as the political process has changed, so have the journalists who cover Washington and the White House.

During the early years of the Republic, newspapers were mainly subsidized, highly partisan political organs published by printers who were more accomplished in mechanical than intellectual matters.

In his travels throughout America in 1831, Alexis de Tocqueville was admittedly impressed that almost every hamlet had a newspaper. But he noted that their publishers were "generally in very humble position with a scanty education and vulgar turn of mind." He further remarked on the papers' "open and coarse appeals to the passions of the readers." [38]

The early publishers, for the most part, were accorded little social and professional status. Most began as printer apprentices. They were unskilled as writers. Reporting, as subsequently defined to mean the collecting and disseminating of news and information, was unknown. Newspaper producers largely relied on letters, travelers, ship crews, other papers, and official sources for their material.

Oddly, newspapers then showed meager interest in chronicling events involving the new government. When the nation's capital was transferred from Philadelphia to Washington in 1800 there were no correspondents on hand. Gradually, the genesis of a Washington press corps began to take shape in the form of editors who visited the backwater town while Congress was in session. Their reports were sent back to their papers as letters, which more often than not reflected their personal bias and were printed under pseudonyms.

Efforts had previously been taken to establish newspapers in Washington but none succeeded, although nearby Georgetown and Alexandria each boasted a journal. Within weeks after the seat of government moved to Washington, several newspapers appeared, the most important being the *National Intelligencer*, which became the official organ of the Democratic-Republicans led by Jefferson.

The paper's young editor, Samuel Harrison Smith, who had moved from Philadelphia where he published the *Universal Gazette*, sought permission to report the proceedings of Congress. The request was initially denied but later approved, and reporters were allowed to attend the legislative sessions. Indeed, for some time, Smith's stenographic reports were the only printed records of congressional proceedings and were the ancestor of today's official *Congressional Record.*

During the War of 1812 the offices of the *National Intelligencer*, now under new ownership, were sacked and burned by the British. After a few days' inconvenience, the paper resumed publication.

Credited with being one of the first Washington correspondents according to modern terms was Nathaniel Carter, a senior editor of the New York *Statesman and Evening Advertiser.* He went to Washington in 1822 to provide what he described as "the latest intelligence of every description which can be obtained at the seat of government." [39]

The same year, Elias Kingman arrived in Washington from Rhode Island and for the next forty years operated a news bureau from which he served newspapers all over the country. Shortly thereafter, Col. Samuel L. Kapp, of the *Boston Galaxy*, appeared in the capital and began to furnish news to his paper and others.

Many of their journalistic contemporaries wrote under pseudonyms, including Matthew J. Davis, who appeared in print as "The Spy in Washington," and Nathan Sargent, whose pen name was "Oliver Oldchild." [40]

Still, for the first several decades of the nineteenth century, newspapers were written for the classes rather than the masses; they published less domestic than foreign news and were not sold on the streets. Many journals appeared to promote a particular political interest or public figure and just as suddenly disappeared. Among them was the *Atlantic World*, which was established in 1807 to support the political ambitions of Aaron Burr but survived only a few months.

Also, many New York papers of that day relied mainly on written accounts by members of Congress for coverage of legislative activities in Washington. The notion of regularly paying reporters to serve as a paper's staff observer and chronicler did not emerge until the mid-1820s. About that time, a Congressional Press Gallery was established, presaging a profound change in press-government relations. The lawmakers' action recognized the blossoming influence of the press in public affairs.

Even so, the growth of professional journalism and the creation of a Washington press corps as recognized today were slow and erratic. Newspapers favored by Washington administrations received government printing contracts and other patronage. Reporting was considered a seasonal occupation and its practitioners were often hired by the month at wages ranging from twelve to twenty dollars, including food and lodging. Sometimes, they were paid space rates—that is, according to how many column inches of their copy was published. Frequently, they left the provincial capital city on the Potomac mudflats as soon as Congress adjourned.

Shortly after his assumption of the presidency, Andrew Jackson and a group of his friends launched the Washington *Globe* as the voice of the new administration under the editorial direction of Amos Kendall, publisher of the Kentucky *Argus.* Kendall soon became a principal adviser to Old Hickory. One incensed House member of that period said of Kendall, "He was the president's thinking machine, his writing machine—aye, and his lying machine." [41]

Popularized News

A member of the pioneer Washington press corps at the time was James Gordon Bennett, who later became a legendary figure in American journalism as founder and editor of the New York *Herald.* Bennett's specialty, which became a characteristic element of the penny press, was writing lively accounts of Washington society and intimate details about the lives of well-known people. He is credited with popularizing the news and liberating the press from party control.

In 1841 Bennett, after becoming head of the *Herald*, set up the first Washington newspaper bureau with regular courier service to New York. Before long, Benjamin Day's New York *Sun* and Horace Greeley's *Tribune* followed his lead.

The period just before and during the Civil War gave impetus to the formation of an institutionalized Washington press corps and changed the course of American journalism. The bitterly contested 1824 presidential campaign between John Quincy Adams and Andrew Jackson focused news attention on Washington. Personal journalism supplanted the partisan press. The first telegraphic news dispatch, sent from Washington to the Baltimore *Patriot* on May 25, 1844, revolutionized press operations.

Above all, the press was designed to appeal to a mass audience, rather than a select segment of society, and this audience wanted to read more about important political figures. For the first time a reporter was assigned full time to cover a president-elect, a step that led to the creation of the modern White House correspondent. The reporter was Henry Villard, of the Associated Press, who in 1865 accompanied Lincoln from Springfield, Illinois, to Washington.

The Civil War created an insatiable demand for news and prompted sweeping changes in journalistic practices. In his 1975 book *The First Casualty* Phillip Knightley described the massive effort to cover the fighting:

> Some 500 [correspondents] went off to report the war for the North alone. The New York Herald put sixty-three men into the field and spent nearly one million dollars in covering the war. The *New York Tribune* and the *New York Times* each had at least twenty correspondents, and smaller papers, in such places as Cincinnati and Boston, all had their own men at the front. European war correspondents, such as William Howard Russell of *The Times* of London and Georges Clemenceau of *Le Temps*, were there, and many European newspapers devoted almost as much space to the war as did the American press.[42]

Several correspondents earned their reputations covering the war, among them H. Whitelaw Reid, of the *Cincinnati Gazette*, who later became publisher of the *New York Tribune*; John Russell Young, who marched with the Army of the Potomac; Sylvanus Cadwallader, of the *New York Herald*, who was present when Lee surrendered to Grant at Appomattox; George Smalley, of the *New York Tribune*, who wrote a stirring account of the Battle of Antietam; and Henry Villard, who voiced his opinion to Lincoln about what he felt was wrong with the Union Army.

The poet Walt Whitman, while serving as a nurse with the Union Army, also filed dispatches for the *New York Times*. In the main, however, the competent correspondents were vastly outnumbered by those in their ranks who were ill-trained, unethical, or dishonest. Most made no pretense at maintaining objectivity and were given to hyperbole and chauvinistic exaggeration: skirmishes were reported as glorious victories and retreats as strategic withdrawals before an enemy force vastly superior in numbers.

According to one study, "Sensationalism and exaggeration, outright lies, puffery, slander, faked eye-witness accounts, and conjectures built on pure imagination cheapened much that passed in the North for news." [43]

Gen. William Tecumseh Sherman particularly viewed the press as a pariah and on occasion threatened to treat correspondents as spies. In their defense, the correspondents contended they were hampered by poor communications, strict censorship, and uncooperative military officers.

Nevertheless, the war underscored to newspaper publishers that enterprise reporting and getting the news ahead of the competition was a way to build up circulation. Correspondingly, the war elevated journalism to a position of importance. By war's end reporters were solidly ensconced as part of the institutional scene in Washington.

In "Recollections of a Washington Newspaper Correspondent," Francis A. Richardson noted how cabinet officials, members of Congress, and government executives now sought out reporters of the major newspapers at their favorite retreats along Washington's Newspaper Row.[44]

Illinois State Historical Library

The first reporter ever assigned to cover a president-elect full time, Henry Villard followed Abraham Lincoln in 1865, thus becoming a forerunner of the modern White House correspondent.

Emblematic of journalism's elevated stature, President Andrew Johnson agreed to an interview with J. B. McCullagh, of the *St. Louis Globe-Democrat*, and permitted the reporter to quote him directly—the first time a president agreed to be formally interviewed for a newspaper story.

How Presidents Dealt with the Press

Presidents, who are constantly reminded of their power and prestigious rank, become exasperated because they cannot control the news media, even though they can to a large degree set the news agenda. This inability exposes their vulnerability and tends to mock the grandeur of their office.

All presidents, at some time or another, become frustrated at what they perceive as unfair treatment by the press, even while acknowledging its vital function in a free society. This sensitivity, often resulting in a strained relationship between the two institutions, is part of the baggage of the presidency and dates back to its beginnings.

How presidents respond when they feel mistreated by the press varies according to their personal temperaments, their relationship with members of the news media, their interpretation of the role of the press, and the particular state in their presidency. The period when they serve also has a bearing: early-nineteenth-century presidents, for example, could simply avoid personal contact with the press, an obvious impossibility in the television age. Among the various reactions of recent presidents beleaguered by the press, Nixon compiled an "enemies list," Kennedy canceled the White House subscription to the *New York Herald Tribune*, and Reagan rarely held formal press conferences toward the end of his presidency.

Propaganda Tool

Early presidents—including George Washington, John Adams, Thomas Jefferson, and later Andrew Jackson—felt unfairly abused and slandered by opposition journals. They sought to circumvent the daily litany of lies and vitriol by favoring their own partisan newspapers, which were equally biased, as the dominant source of presidential news.

The press, it should be stressed, was largely a propaganda tool at that time. The notion of the press as an independent news medium had not yet been developed. Essentially, newspapers were vehicles designed to advance the interests of the various political factions. Nonetheless, contemporaries recalled that the colonial newspapers had been a potent weapon in the fight for freedom from British rule and were keenly aware of their force and influence on public opinion.

Up to the Jacksonian era, U.S. presidents had little or no association with the press as direct sources of news. All, however, were conscious of the importance of informed public opinion and eagerly endorsed party newspapers supporting their administrations. John Adams briefly toyed with the idea of establishing a government gazette, as was the common practice among European governments.

While some of the early presidents, such as Adams and Madison, frequently contributed articles and essays to favorite newspapers, Jefferson vigorously refused to offer his writing to the public prints. He cautioned recipients of his letters not to make their contents public and occasionally boasted that he did not read the papers—yet he always seemed to know what was being printed in them.

Washington was an avid newspaper reader and the partisan excesses of the press offended his sense of decorum and nationalistic zeal, provoking him to complain that the "calumnies" against his administration were "outrages on common decency." [45] His antagonism toward the press, however, was mainly confined to personal correspondence and private conversation. Throughout his public life, he was the particular target of bitter criticism in the *Aurora*, published by Benjamin Franklin Bache, known as "Lightning Rod Junior" in reference to his illustrious grandfather. In one notable incident, Bache printed in detail the provisions of a treaty that John Jay negotiated with the British in 1795.

Bache denounced the secret pact in a separate pamphlet and accused President Washington of having "violated the Constitution and made a treaty with a nation abhorred by our people. . . ." [46]

In the original draft of his Farewell Address, Washington attacked the press, but he deleted the criticism at the urging of Alexander Hamilton. He did, however, remark on the significance of an informed public, stating, "In proportion as the structure of a government gives force to public opinion, it is essential that public opinion should be enlightened."

Washington personally arranged that his Farewell Address be exclusively published on September 19, 1796, in the *Pennsylvania Packet and Daily Advertiser*, cited by historians as the nation's first daily newspaper.

John Adams felt so maligned by the colonial press that he signed into law the notorious Alien and Sedition acts, which served as a gag law on the press and led to the imprisonment of several editors. Highly unpopular and clearly unconstitutional, the legislation, which was subsequently overturned, helped hasten the demise of the Federalist party.

Jefferson exalted freedom of the press as "one of the great bulwarks of liberty," but he was not above using the press for political purposes. It was while serving as Washington's secretary of state that Jefferson was instrumental in enlisting the poet-journalist Philip Freneau to act as a paid "clerk for foreign languages" in his office. This was a charade for Freneau's real mission, which was to establish the *National Gazette* as an editorial voice in opposition to the Federalist party of Washington and Hamilton.

After becoming president, Jefferson induced Samuel Harrison Smith to set up the *National Intelligencer* as an organ of his administration. It remained the preeminent newspaper in the country for more than a decade, serving the Jefferson Republican cause well and faithfully.

Another future president, James Madison, was a coauthor of the *Federalist* papers. The persuasive essays he, Hamilton, and Jay wrote contributed greatly to the adoption of the new government. Renowned as the "father" of the Constitution, Madison deserves equal credit for his advocacy of the Bill of Rights. He was a defender of a free press and one of the first public men to perceive the value of bipartisan reporting and commentary.[47]

Andrew Jackson used the press aggressively for partisan purposes. As a vital element of his restructuring of the party system and the presidency, he surrounded himself with a coterie of friends and advisers, which became known as the "Kitchen Cabinet." Included were Amos Kendall and another established editor, Francis P. Blair. Midway in Jackson's first term, his friends began the Washington *Globe*, with Kendall and Blair the guiding spirits. The paper promptly received lucrative government printing contracts, federal officeholders with salaries of $1,000 or more a year were expected to subscribe, and before long it changed from a semiweekly to a daily.

It was widely recognized that the voice of the *Globe* was that of Jackson, the head that of Blair, and the ideas those of Kendall. One of Blair's ploys was to reprint favorable articles that Jackson allies were suspected of planting in rural journals. And at one point fifty-seven journalists were reported to have been on the government payroll during Jackson's administration.

Even before the end of Jackson's term, the *Globe* began promoting his heir apparent, Vice President Martin Van Buren. Alongside the dynamic, forceful, and strong-willed Jackson—"Old Hickory"—Van Buren came across as a dandified political opportunist whose career was promoted by the Albany *Argus*, in which he had a personal financial interest.

Although Van Buren had the support of several leading newspapers, few presidents have been so bitterly assailed by the press, at least in part because of his aristocratic pretensions. Like today's new media, the press examined Van Buren's past with a fine-tooth comb—once it became apparent that he would succeed Jackson. The story was revived that he was the natural son of Aaron Burr. The New York *American* warned of "the great and menacing evil, the blighting disgrace of placing Martin Van Buren, illiterate, sycophant, and politically corrupt, at the head of this great republic." Davy Crockett, the frontiersman and Alamo defender who became a member of Congress, wrote,

> Van Buren is as opposite to General Jackson as dung is to a diamond. . . . When he enters the Senate chamber in the morning, he struts and swaggers like a crow in a gutter. He is laced up in corsets, such as women in a town wear, and, if possible, tighter than the best of them. It would be difficult to say from his personal appearance, whether he was man or woman, but for his large red and gray whiskers.[48]

During his presidency, Van Buren broke tradition by receiving and talking with a few reporters, including James Gordon Bennett. But the meetings were perceived more as audiences than as news interviews, as currently defined.

The 1840 presidential campaign offered a glimpse of the future with its emphasis on imagery and slogans. Whig candidates William Henry Harrison, hero of an 1811 battle against Tecumseh, and John Tyler ran under the war cry of "Tippecanoe and Tyler, too." Their campaign emblem was the log cabin, a readily recognized symbol of the young nation's vision, virility, and pioneering spirit. In reality, however, Harrison was neither born in a log cabin, nor was his home built of logs, except for one section.

James K. Polk, the first dark-horse candidate to become president, preferred to remain out of the public eye and was little known to the national electorate except through the news journals. Although he mistrusted the press, he was cognizant of its influence, and like his predecessors he used a favorite newspaper, in this case the Washington *Union*, as a platform for his administration.

Commenting in his diary on an editor who had broken a confidentiality, Polk wrote, "He meant no harm, I am satisfied. It is a constitutional infirmity with him, I believe, that he cannot keep a secret: all he knows, though given him in confidence, he is almost certain to put into his newspaper. . . ." That, in essence, reflected his convictions about journalists.

Franklin Pierce, in acknowledgment of the increasing role of the press in public affairs, supplied newspapers with advance copies of his December 1854 message to Congress—a customary practice today.

The last president to rely on a special newspaper as an official administration voice was James Buchanan. The party press had been withering since the Polk regime and its demise was inevitable. Among the contributing factors was the invention of the telegraph, which led to formation of the wire services and the growth of Washington news bureaus staffed by enterprising journalists. "Objective reporting" began to take root as a professional standard. Another factor was the increased use of the press for advertising, which provided newspapers with financial revenue independent of the patronage of presidential administrations. Finally, in 1860 the Government Printing Office was established, eliminating the profitable printing contracts on which many papers subsisted.

Civil War and Reconstruction

Abraham Lincoln rarely sought publicity for the sake of self-aggrandizement but he was acutely aware of the importance of public opinion and the forces that shaped it. He was a faithful newspaper reader and an occasional contributor to local journals early in his career. Throughout his public life, he developed a cordial relationship with the press and often corresponded with journalists and sometimes sought their counsel, although he did not speak directly to them for publication. Prominent among the journalists with whom he frequently dealt were Horace Greeley, of the New York *Tribune*, who often tried the president's patience; Col. John W. Forney, publisher of the Washington *Chronicle* and Philadelphia *Press*, a friend and confidant; and Henry J. Raymond, editor of the New York *Times*.

Lincoln further believed, however, that he had to go beyond the press to measure public aspirations and find out what the people were feeling and saying. Hence, twice a week he held open White House receptions where ordinary citizens could meet him, express their sentiments, and air their grievances. "I call these receptions my public-opinion baths," he said, ". . . and, though they may not be pleasant in all particulars, the effect as a whole is renovating and invigorating to my perceptions of responsibility and duty. It would never do for a President to have guards with drawn sabres at his door, as if he fancied he were, or were trying to be, or were assuming to be, an emperor." [49]

Lincoln's paramount concern was the salvation of the Union. During the Civil War he permitted censorship and suppression of the press on a scale not seen since the founding of the Republic. Editors of antiwar papers—"Copperheads," as opponents of the war were called—were sometimes thrown in jail without formal charges against them. Telegraph companies were monitored, and Union generals were allowed to control the activities, movements, and access of correspondents on their own initiative. In the white-hot passions of the time, mobs occasionally destroyed the offices of antiwar newspapers and tarred and feathered their editors.

While recognizing the need to curb press activities that might aid and comfort the enemy, including news dispatches revealing troop movements and other details that endangered the lives of Union soldiers, Lincoln frequently displayed moderation in his attitude toward the press. On one occasion, General Sherman, whose antipathy toward the press was well known, arrested a *Tribune* correspondent and would have had him shot as a spy if the president had not intervened. In another instance, Gen. Ambrose E. Burnside ordered the suspension of the Chicago *Times* because of its Copperhead sentiments and its undisguised enmity toward Lincoln, but at Lincoln's suggestion the suspension was lifted.

With the country divided, Lincoln's press critics assailed him on a scale unsurpassed for its violence and vitriol. He was abused in print as "the Illinois ape . . . a baboon . . . a monster." One New York newspaper accused him of taking his presidential pay in gold, while rebel president Jefferson Davis was taking his in Confederate money, worth about a fourth of its face value. Yet, though he had no formal method of dealing with the press, Lincoln fully understood its role and dealt with newspapers and journalists on a more intimate basis than any of his predecessors.

As Lincoln's successor, Andrew Johnson was at a distinct disadvantage because of comparison with the Great Emancipator. Moreover, his public image suffered under the accusation that he was given to excessive drinking. The allegation—unfair, as it turned out—stemmed from his inauguration as vice president when because of an illness he drank some whiskey and water, which caused him to speak incoherently and act strangely.

During his presidency Johnson was constantly embroiled in controversy over his Reconstruction policies and efforts to remove him by impeachment. His practice of granting exclusive newspaper interviews was a means to reach out to the people. As part of an interview with Col. A. K. McClure of the *Franklin Repository*, Johnson was quoted as saying he wanted the South back "with all of its manhood," even though he was aware it might lead to "a sad breach between the President and the Congress." [50]

The Senate acquitted Johnson of wrongdoing by one vote—a fact etched in history—but to American journalists he is remembered for establishing presidential interviews as a regular practice.

Gen. Ulysses S. Grant was a hero to the nation because of his triumphant military campaigns in the Civil War, but as a president he was a failure, who because of his generous nature and political naiveté presided over an administration riddled with corruption. Newspapers for the first time engaged in what became known as investigative reporting, prompting Grant to declare he was "the subject of abuse and slander scarcely ever equaled in political history."

During his two terms in office, Grant had virtually no direct dealings with the press, partly because he was uncommunicative by nature and partly because of bad advice from aides and allies. This contributed to the poor press he received, giving vent to the haze of scandal that clouded his tenure as president.

The Press as Watchdog

By the time William McKinley was elected, the press had assumed its role as the people's watchdog over governmental affairs. McKinley allowed reporters to wait in an anteroom for interviews with visitors following important White House meetings. Also, his staff routinely gave reporters the president's speaking schedule and advance copies of his speeches. However, McKinley himself remained distant from the press and any direct contact was left largely to chance.

The first American president to fully appreciate the influence of the press in society and public affairs and to cultivate journalits for personal and political purposes was Theodore Roosevelt. The genesis of the White House press corps took shape during his administration. He courted publicity and reaped political currency by casting himself as a "trustbuster." But when crusading journals sought to expose the monopolistic and unprincipled activities of some of these same trusts, he branded them as "muckrakers"—a term intended as derogatory but which came to be descriptive of a respected journalistic function.

TR's dynamic personality, rhetorical flair, sense of the dramatic, and instinctive gravitation toward the camera made him a favorite subject of the press. He was an unswerving advocate of an unfettered press, but he frequently took issue with newspaper accounts and was sensitive to criticism. Above all, he insisted that the relationship should be on his own terms.

On his first day as president, he called in a group of wire service reporters and laid down a set of ground rules that would give them unprecedented access to the White House but leave him in control of what was published. He demanded that information given in confidence remain in confidence. Anyone who broke the rule would be barred from the White House and denied access to legitimate news. "If you ever hint where you got [the story]," he warned, "I'll say you are a damn liar." [51]

Roosevelt arbitrarily divided reporters between insiders and outsiders, the former comprised of those whose stories reflected favorably on his administration. He was able to impose such a dictum because the idea of professional journalistic standards was still in its infancy and the adversary relationship between press and government had not yet evolved. Nevertheless, he was responsible for bringing White House press relations into the modern era.

But it was not until Woodrow Wilson that the ad hoc interrelationship between the press and the president settled into an institutionalized format. Continuing Theodore Roosevelt's custom of frequent meetings with the press, Wilson opened them to all reporters and initiated the first formal news conferences, at which reporters were required to submit their questions in written form.

Wilson's relations with the press soon deteriorated, however, because of what he considered excessive prying into his private life and a breach of confidence by some reporters concerning an "off-the-record" account by the president on conditions in Mexico. Soon thereafter, the White House Correspondents Association was formed to set guidelines for presidential news conferences and establish standards of professional conduct. Following World War I Wilson embarked on a publicity campaign to gain public support for his "Fourteen Points" treaty proposals, but he failed in the attempt.

Franklin Roosevelt, through the force of his personality, his keen sense of what made news, and his profound appreciation of the value of public opinion, exerted a great impact on White House press relations. During his record tenure as president, he was the central figure in a national economic recovery effort and a global war, providing him with a stage from which he dominated the news.

In his initial meeting with the press as president, he announced he was dispensing with written questions and introducing a new working relationship with White House correspondents. Labeling his sessions with reporters as "delightful family conferences," he said White House information would be presented in any of four different categories: (1) occasional direct quotations permitted only through written authorization from the White House; (2) press conference comments attributed to the president "without direct quotations"; (3) background information to be used in stories without reference to the White House; (4) off-the-record remarks not to be repeated. He additionally appointed the White House's first official press secretary, Stephen T. Early.[52]

During his more than twelve years in office, FDR invited reporters into the Oval Office for news conferences on 998 occasions, usually on Tuesdays and Fridays. They met in an informal setting, with the president seated behind his desk encircled by members of the White House press corps. Almost always he seemed eager to take on his inquisitors, was well informed and lavish in his comments. Seldom did the reporters leave without a story. Though generally good-humored, he would not infrequently chastise reporters whom he felt had inaccurately or unjustly misrepresented the administration's position. Once he suggested that a reporter stand in the corner with a dunce cap on his head. No matter what the situation, he was always in command.

FDR was equally a master at speaking over the radio to inform the American people of his policies and decisions and to appeal to them for support. His "fireside chats"—as they were called—became a familiar part of the American scene and, as such, have never been quite duplicated in terms of national interest.

The Television Era

The emergence of mass communications technology in the post-Roosevelt era, with its emphasis on imagery and symbolism and the new refinements in public relations techniques, further compelled presidents to be skillful communicators and establish an effective relationship with an increasingly pervasive media. As a visual medium, television created instant impressions and required presidents to operate more in the open. As they soon learned, this could be both a curse and a blessing.

Mainly because of his popularity as a war hero, few presidents enjoyed more favorable treatment at the hands of the press than General Eisenhower. While it was generally believed that "Ike" was indifferent to publicity and his relations with the news media, revisionist studies indicate that he was intensely preoccupied with public relations. In personal letters, he noted that his public image helped him carry out his role as a military leader.

Prominent among the network of businessmen who gathered around Eisenhower and persuaded him to run for president in 1952 were several professional public relations consultants. During his campaign they served as his media advisers and developed his political commercials. Among them was actor and television producer Robert Montgomery, who instructed Eisenhower on the mechanics of delivering speeches and how to perform on television.[53]

In 1960 the nation was stunned when it was disclosed that the Soviets had shot down a U.S. reconnaissance plane manned by Francis Gary Powers. At first, the Eisenhower White House reported that the plane was on a weather surveillance mission. But when the Soviets announced they had captured Powers and that the airplane was virtually intact, the White House changed its story and admitted that the U-2 was a "spy plane" on an espionage mission. Media critic A. J. Liebling contended the exposure marked the "beginning of wisdom" in the media's attitude toward the government.

Eisenhower was the first president to hold a televised news conference, but before the film was shown to the public it was edited by his press secretary, James C. Hagerty, to delete segments that might reflect unfavorably on the president or be confusing to viewers because of his garbled syntax in speaking.

The first "live" TV presidential news conference was held by his successor, Kennedy, whose youth, good looks, and disarming wit were ideally adaptable to television. Kennedy was generally popular with the White House press. He had briefly worked as a reporter before turning to politics and counted some well-established Washington journalists as his friends and confidants, including columnist Charles Bartlett and Benjamin C. Bradlee, who became executive editor of the *Washington Post.*

Before the 1961 Bay of Pigs assault in Cuba by U.S.-backed anti-Castro forces, Kennedy took the unusual step of prevailing upon the *New York Times* to tone down a story on the imminent invasion for the sake of national security. Following the ill-fated attack, Kennedy expressed regret he had persuaded the *Times* to modify its story, because advance disclosure of the operation might have spared the country a disaster.

Among modern presidents, few experienced worse press relations than Richard Nixon. His evident distaste of the "establishment" press, and its distrust of him, permeated his administration and nurtured a conspiratorial state of mind among his aides. This mind-set incited the Nixon White House to include several journalists on its "enemies' list." The blackballing further contributed to the Watergate coverup, for which ten presidential aides were convicted and jailed after the groundbreaking work of reporters such as the *Washington Post*'s Bob Woodward and Carl Bernstein.

Notwithstanding his grasp of politics, his knowledge and understanding of foreign policy, and his familiarity with governmental affairs, Nixon was an anomaly in the

Franklin D. Roosevelt Library

The forceful FDR transformed presidential press relations. He held 998 Oval Office news conferences during his twelve years in office.

Wide World Photos; Dwight D. Eisenhower Library

Eisenhower was the first president to hold a televised news conference. But before the film was shown to the public, it was edited by his press secretary.

new media age. He became president when a high premium was being placed on charisma, yet his public image was that of a stiff, plastic figure. Television tended to underline his personal defects. Yet, possibly because of this incompatibility with the media, he was particularly conscious of its effect on public opinion. He consequently sought to remedy the situation through organizational initiatives. During his presidency, the White House's press/public relations operation was vastly enlarged. A White House communications office was established to deal with reporters and broadcasters outside of Washington; an office of public liaison was set up to deal with interest groups; and a news summary unit was created to monitor the print and electronic media.

The hostility between the Washington press and the Nixon White House reached a peak in the Watergate scandal, ultimately ending in the president's resignation and his replacement by Gerald R. Ford.

Seldom has a president taken office on such cordial terms with the news media as Ford. In his inaugural address, he pledged that his would be an administration of "openness and candor." Because of his constant contact with the press during his quarter of a century in Congress, Ford knew many journalists by name and enjoyed a personal association with many of them. His rapport with the news media was strengthened when he appointed Jerald F. terHorst, Washington bureau chief of the *Detroit News*, as White House press secretary.

Ford's "honeymoon" with the press ended abruptly, however, one month after he took office and pardoned former president Nixon, sparing him any trial in connection with Watergate. Ford's credibility additionally came into question because he had earlier indicated that he was opposed to a pardon for the time being.

The unexpected pardon also prompted terHorst to resign, because, as he said, he disagreed in principle with the action and was not informed of it in advance. From that point on, Ford's relations with the Washington news media proceeded along conventional lines.

Jimmy Carter, who rose to the presidency as a virtually unknown former governor of Georgia, was in a large measure indebted to the national news media for the highly favorable treatment he received during his 1976 campaign. Early in his administration, he indicated a deep appreciation of the balance between the press and the president and their respective roles, stating, "If I can stay close to the people of this country and not disappoint them, I think I have a chance to be a great president." [54]

His walk down Pennsylvania Avenue hand-in-hand with his wife as they returned to the White House following his inauguration caught the spirit of his campaign, as did his decision to wear a sweater during one of his first televised talks to the nation.

Generally, Carter's attitude toward the press was one of correctness and cordiality. There was none of the cloying affection sometimes displayed by Lyndon Johnson or, at the other extreme, any of the embittered antipathy inherent in Nixon's relations with the press. Early on, Carter pledged to hold press conferences every other week. And on alternate weeks, out-of-town editors and broadcasters were invited to the White House. Carter also employed a number of unconventional techniques to communicate with the electorate, including fireside chats, participation in town meetings, overnight stays at the homes of private citizens, and a regional televised question-and-answer session with Southern California residents.

Before the end of his first year in the White House, however, Carter's relations with the press began to cool, mainly because of his persistent defense of his good friend Bert Lance, director of the Office of Management and Budget, whose private banking practices were being questioned and who subsequently resigned under a cloud. Presumably disillusioned by the course of events, Carter became noticeably more reserved toward the press and with time his news conferences became less frequent.

The "Great Communicator"

Ronald Reagan's ascendancy to the White House was largely viewed as the natural culmination of the dominance of American politics by image-makers, television consultants, pollsters, speech writers, and other specialists who transformed campaigning into a form of media theater. No president in modern history, other than perhaps Franklin Roosevelt, was more successful in the presentation of himself than Reagan, a former Hollywood actor and television host. His long career before the cameras, his buoyant personality, and affable temperament ideally equipped him for the on-stage existence that contemporary presidents must endure.

Referred to as the "Great Communicator," Reagan had a natural knack for synthesizing and clearly defining complex issues, as well as leavening weighty topics with humor. After being wounded in a 1981 assassination attempt, he quipped to his wife, Nancy, "I forgot to duck."

The high priority given to public relations and press communications in the Reagan White House was reflected in its hierarchical structure. Among the senior advisers were Michael K. Deaver, longtime friend and professional public relations executive who served as deputy White House chief of staff, David R. Gergen, assistant to the president for communications, and Richard Wirthlin, the president's special pollster and public opinion analyst.

Reagan's press and public relations advisers were especially adept at orchestrating media events and staging the president in highly visible situations, while at the same time protecting him from inquisitive reporters. "Photo opportunities" were routinely available, but formal press conferences were few and far between.

Ironically, even as he was being perceived as the Great Communicator, Reagan's administration was intent on rigid management of the news and stemming the free flow of information. Measures to regulate government information included the widespread use of lie detector tests to trace news leaks by government employees and contractors with high-level security clearance; discretionary upgrading of classified information by federal agencies for an indefinite period, as well as the reclassification of information already in the public domain; a requirement that government officials possessing top security clearance sign statements forcing them for the rest of their lives to submit for official, prepublication review all articles and books they write for public consumption; a tightening of exemptions allowed under the Freedom of Information Act; and vigorous enforcement of the 1952 McCarran-Walter Act, prohibiting writers, artists, and political figures from entering the United States because of their views and associations.

Reagan enjoyed a fairly high level of popularity during most of his two terms in office. A crack in his credibility developed, however, with the disclosure in 1987 of the Iran arms sales/contra funding affair. Reagan insisted the secret operation was conducted without his knowledge or approval and blamed the news media for sensationalizing the incident.

Presidential Attitudes toward the News Media

As John F. Kennedy neatly phrased it when he said that he was reading the press more and enjoying it less, all presidents inevitably become frustrated in their dealings with the Fourth Estate.

Thomas Jefferson complained that "newspapers, for the most part, present only the caricature of disaffected minds. Indeed, the abuses of freedom of the press have been carried to a length never before known or borne by any civilized nation." These harsh comments underscore presidential ambivalence toward the press, for earlier it was Jefferson who had written that "were it left to me to decide whether we should have a government without newspapers or newspapers without a government, I should not hesitate to prefer the latter." [55]

It was said of Abraham Lincoln that "in his dealings with the press he knew how to be as wise as a serpent and as gentle as a dove, yet it cannot be said that he truckled to it, collectively or individually." [56]

Lincoln's skill in dealing with the press and his awareness of public opinion was evident in a letter he wrote to

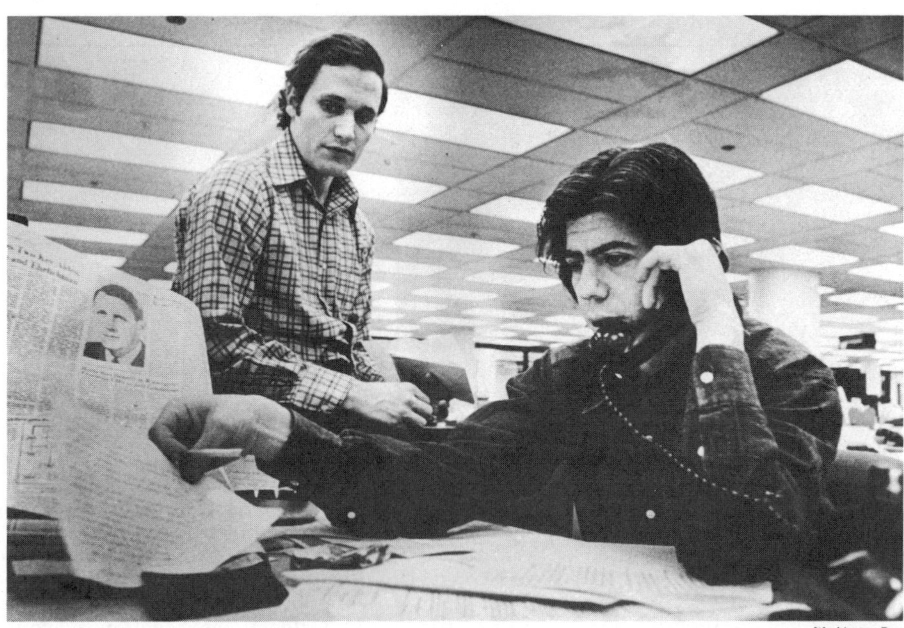

Washington Post

The *Washington Post's* Bob Woodward, left, and Carl Bernstein, right, broke many of the Watergate stories that led to President Nixon's eventual resignation.

New York Tribune editor Horace Greeley, an early advocate of emancipation, in which the president stated, "My paramount object in this struggle is to save the Union, and it is not either to save or destroy slavery. If I could save the Union without freeing any slave, I would do it; and if I could save it by freeing some and leaving others alone, I would also do that. What I do about slavery and the colored race, I do because I believe it helps to save the Union. . . ."[57]

Actually, Lincoln had long been thinking about freeing the slaves but wanted a military triumph to make the emancipation effective. On September 19, 1862, following the battle of Antietam, he issued his famous proclamation.

Ironically, the newspapers virtually ignored Lincoln's epic address at Gettysburg in favor of a lengthy speech by Edward Everett, an eminent orator of the time. The *Cincinnati Gazette* published Everett's speech in full, while noting, "President Lincoln made a few remarks. . . ." *(See "The Emancipation Proclamation," p. 1370, and "The Gettysburg Address," p. 1371, in the Appendix.)*

Ulysses S. Grant, who rode to the White House on his heroic exploits in the Civil War, proved to be a better soldier than politician. Because of his political naiveté and trusting manner, his two terms as president were marked by wholesale corruption at the highest levels of government. During this same period, the press began to develop its investigative function, thus shedding light on the unethical and illegal practices that plagued Grant's tenure in the White House.

The newspapers, with great relish, disclosed that he had appointed forty-eight of his relatives to government positions, that he was the beneficiary of lavish gifts—including three houses—from his wealthy friends, and that his sister's husband was involved in a conspiracy to rig the gold market.

With rare exceptions Grant had no official relations with the press. In his second inaugural address he declared that he had been "the subject of abuse and slander scarcely ever equaled in political history."

During Grant's second term it was learned that high administration officials had accepted stock for helping dishonest promoters of the Union Pacific Railway. The War Department was rocked by a scandal, involving the president's own brother Orvil, in which bribes had been taken by political appointees. Subsequently, the *St. Louis Democrat* exposed a conspiracy of revenue officials to defraud the government of tax money in what became known as the "Whiskey Ring" scandal. By the time he left office Grant was a broken and disillusioned man. He lived only long enough to write a widely acclaimed autobiography.

"Keyhole Journalism"

Grover Cleveland's relations with the press were tense and often stormy throughout his years in the White House. He particularly resented what he contended were misrepresentations and sensationalist innuendos and consequently kept reporters at a distance.

The course was set soon after his nomination in July 1884 when the *Buffalo Telegraph* reported that Cleveland was the father of an illegitimate son, then ten years old. His political opponents thereupon took up the cry:

Ma, Ma, Where's my pa?
Gone to the White House
Ha, Ha, Ha

Upon assuming the presidency in March 1885, Cleveland mostly dealt with White House correspondents through his secretaries. His marriage to the young Frances Folsom fifteen months later further distanced Cleveland from reporters who practiced the so-called "keyhole journalism." *(See box, A President's Wedding, p. 728.)*

Another incident in Cleveland's presidency is significant because it was the precursor of attempts by succeeding presidents to conceal or disguise actions and developments that they believed might be detrimental to their administration and the national welfare. Shortly into his second term, a malignant growth was found in the president's mouth. In an effort to avert a panic over the president's health in view of mounting economic instability, an operation was secretly performed aboard a friend's yacht.

UPI/Bettmann Newsphotos

Like FDR and JFK, Ronald Reagan was extremely adept at presenting himself through the media. His long career before the cameras and his affable temperament ideally equipped him for the on-stage existence that contemporary presidents must endure.

Most of Cleveland's upper left jaw was removed, incapacitating him for a period of time. But it was two months before the press learned the bare outlines of the story and twenty years before the complete facts were disclosed.

Theodore Roosevelt, who created the modern model of White House press relations and was probably the most prolific writer among U.S. presidents, offered his views on the responsibilities and functions of the press in an address before the Milwaukee Press Club in September 1910.

> The newspaper men—publishers, editors, reporters—are just as much public servants as are the men in the government service themselves, whether those men be elected or appointed officers.
>
> The highest type of newspaper man ought to try to put his business above all other business. The editor, who stands as a judge in a community, should be one of the men to whom you would expect to look up, because his function as an editor makes him a more important man than the average merchant, the average business man, the average professional man can be. He wields great influence; and he cannot escape the responsibility of it. If he wields it well, honor is his beyond the honor that comes to the average man who does well; if he wields ill, shame should be his beyond the shame that comes to the average man who does ill. . . .

Because Roosevelt understood the role of the press in public affairs, he was especially sensitive to it. He harbored a bitter antipathy toward Joseph Pulitzer's *New York World* ever since one of its correspondents, famed author Stephen Crane, wrote an unflattering account of his celebrated charge up San Juan Hill during the Spanish-American War. And when the *World* in 1908 exposed the involvement of several of his associates in the financing of the Panama Canal, Roosevelt tried to get Pulitzer indicted and thrown in jail.[58]

Woodrow Wilson set out in his presidency to establish a working relationship with the press, and at one of his early news conferences more than two hundred reporters crowded the Oval Office. But he soon became irritated with White House reporters for what he felt was an unjustified intrusion into his personal life and private family affairs, notably those involving his three daughters. An academic by training, he tended to give the impression that journalists were beneath his intellectual level.

As David Lawrence, one of the few Washington correspondents to gain Wilson's confidence, observed, "Mr. Wilson's quarrel with the press was not personal but impersonal. He disagreed with the methods of American journalism. . . ."[59]

"Making News and Being News"

While Franklin D. Roosevelt is acclaimed as a nonpareil in dealing with the press, he sometimes displayed an overbearing self-confidence in his attitude toward reporters. Often, he would tell them in an apparent attempt to influence their reports, "If I were writing this story, here is how I would write it," or, "If I were writing the heading on this story, here is how I would headline it."[60]

On more than one occasion, FDR complained directly to newspaper publishers about reporters whom he felt had misrepresented his views and even sought to have them transferred, among them Arthur Krock, Washington bureau chief of the *New York Times* and one of the most eminent journalists in Washington. "I am all in favor of chloroforming for certain newspaper men," he wrote a friend. As a mark of displeasure, he once presented a *New York Daily News* reporter with a German Iron Cross.[61]

In a reference to *Time* cofounder Henry R. Luce, Roosevelt declared, "Beginning with the first number of *Time*, I discovered that one secret of their financial success is a deliberate policy of either exaggeration or distortion. Pay no attention to them—I don't."[62]

However, as historian Arthur M. Schlesinger, Jr., noted, "By the brilliant but simple trick of making news and being news, Roosevelt outwitted the general hostility of the publishers and converted the press into one of the most effective channels of his public leadership."[63]

The end of World War II marked the beginning of a new era in relations between the White House and the press. Television and jet air travel allowed presidents to engage in frequent, direct communication with the American public, and thus they were less dependent on the Washington press corps to convey their views.

At the same time, however, the advent of the mass media brought with it a raised consciousness among journalists concerning their responsibilities and professional standards. Hence, the adversary relationship between the White House and the press became more intense and more public. Furthermore, the new technology and the growth of the Washington press corps produced a new breed of journalist less concerned with custom and tradition.

Harry S Truman became president upon FDR's death and announced he would continue his predecessor's press policies. Truman, however, possessed neither the skill nor the personality to match Roosevelt, and before long his feisty, occasionally irascible nature worked its way into his dealings with the press. He once said he was "saving up four or five good, hard punches on the nose" for reporters who, he felt, had been unfair to him. On another occasion, when White House reporters complained about an exclusive interview he had given to *New York Times* correspondent Arthur Krock, Truman replied, "I'll give interviews to anybody I damn please."

In a display of paternal outrage, the feisty Missourian sent off an angry letter to Paul Hume, music critic of the *Washington Post*, for his "lousy review" of a concert given by the president's daughter, Margaret, in December 1950. The president declared that Hume sounded "like a frustrated old man who never made a success" and that if he ever met Hume the critic would need "a new nose and plenty of beefsteak."[64]

Later, President Kennedy, in a fit of pique over stories critical of his administration, canceled his subscription to the *New York Herald Tribune*. Lyndon B. Johnson, called by Walter Lippmann "a pathologically secretive man," was appalled by what he considered the perfidy of the press and took every criticism of his administration as a personal blow. He once exclaimed, "You guys. All you guys in the media. All of politics has changed because of you. You've broken all the machines and the ties between us and Congress and the city machines. You've given us a new kind of people . . . Teddy, Tunney [Sen. Edward M. Kennedy, D-Mass., and John V. Tunney, D-Calif., House 1965-1971, Senate 1971-1977]. They're your creatures, your puppets. . . . They're all yours. Your product."[65]

Richard Nixon's perennial war with the news media was evident in personal White House files made available to the public in 1987 by the National Archives. In a series of memorandums to his chief of staff, H. R. Haldeman, and his press secretary, Ronald L. Ziegler, Nixon ordered that

A President's Wedding

The already-tense relations between Grover Cleveland and the press worsened early in his presidency when it became known that he was planning to marry Frances Folsom, the young and comely daughter of his late law partner. With unprecedented vigor the newspapers pursued the betrothal story, embellishing the smallest detail, some more imaginative than factual. At one point Cleveland, who wanted a quiet wedding, declared, "I regret that the President of the United States does not have the same rights and privileges as an ordinary citizen." [1]

Critics condemned the press for resorting to "keyhole journalism" because of the aggressively intrusive manner in which it covered the presidential wedding and honeymoon. Although such reporting would later become commonplace and be perceived as part of the burden of being president, Cleveland and his bride were victims of an emerging type of journalism, characterized by its assertiveness and penchant for intimate detail.

Speaking at the 250th anniversary celebration of Harvard College in 1886, about five months after the June 2 wedding, President Cleveland emotionally criticized newspapers that had engaged in this practice:

> No public officer should desire to check the utmost freedom of criticism as to all official acts; but every right-thinking man must concede that the President of the United States should not be put beyond the protection which American love of fair play and decency accords to every American citizen. This trait of our national character would not encourage, if their extent were fully appreciated, the silly mean and cowardly lies that every day are found in the columns of certain newspapers, which violate every instinct of American manliness, and in ghoulish glee desecrate every sacred relation of public life. . . .[2]

1. James E. Pollard, *The Presidents and the Press* (New York: Octagon Books, 1973), 504.
2. Ibid., 512.

certain reporters and columnists who had written unfavorable stories about him be cut off from White House access and their calls not be returned.

He noted in a June 1, 1971, memo that he had attended the annual White House Correspondents Dinner at Ziegler's suggestion, only to find at his next press conference that "The reporters were considerably more bad-mannered and vicious than usual. This bears out my theory that treating them with considerably more contempt is in the long run a more productive policy."

Shortly after the press conference and memo, Nixon, who had been angered by the *New York Times*' publication of the Pentagon Papers, the secret government history of the Vietnam War, directed Haldeman to see to it that "under absolutely no circumstances is anyone on the White House staff, on any subject, to respond to an inquiry from the *New York Times* unless and until I give express permission—and I do not expect to give such permission in the foreseeable future." [66]

Yet, notwithstanding Nixon's distrust of the press, he seemed, as his White House domestic policy adviser, John Ehrlichman, observed, "to believe there was no national issue that was not susceptible to public relations treatment."

In his White House memoirs, Ehrlichman wrote that "During the years I worked for him, Nixon was usually capable of a passionless and penetrating analysis of his press opportunities. He was a talented media manipulator. I often watched him successfully plan how he or his spokesmen would dominate the evening news, capture the headlines and right-side columns of the front page of *The Washington Post* or the lead story in *Time* or *Newsweek*. Richard Nixon could think like an editor." [67] Yet, it would be the news media that would eventually help bring down the Nixon presidency because of its Watergate-related transgressions.

Throughout his single term as president, Jimmy Carter's relationship with the Washington press was one of strained formality: neither side seemed to fully accept the other and consequently each kept its guard up. Carter's attitude was implicit in a remark he made in a memorable interview with *Playboy* magazine (November 1976) during his first presidential campaign: "Issues? The local media are interested, all right, but the national news media have absolutely no interest in issues at all. . . . What they're looking for is a 47-second argument between me and another candidate, or something like that. There's absolutely nobody in the back of this plane [the press section] who would ask an issue question unless he thought he could trick me into some crazy statement."

After leaving office, Carter maintained that his two greatest disappointments as president were the inertia of Congress and the "irresponsibility" of the press. He also referred to the national news media as "one of the blights of most presidents' existences, including to a high degree my own." [68]

Ronald Reagan, the first president to serve two full terms since Eisenhower, generally received benign treatment at the hands of the press. It is widely believed that his conviviality and jaunty optimism, as well as his actor's sense of the right gesture and his personal popularity, blunted the news media's innate skepticism. The press regularly reported his misstatements and verbal gaffes, but these reports made no dent in the president's popular standing.

Beneath the picture of congeniality and openness that he publicly presented, Reagan preferred to deal with the press in elaborately controlled settings. There was none of the give-and-take that characterized FDR's regular meetings with reporters. Despite his famous communications skills, Reagan held infrequent news conferences, fewer than any of his recent predecessors. *(See Table 2.)*

Instead, his media advisers arranged "photo opportunities," allowing constricted access to the president while showing him in a theatrical setting. Furthermore, background briefings with White House aides were carefully monitored and news leaks, a particular obsession with Reagan, severely condemned. Accordingly, imagery and the artful use of public relations reached unprecedented heights in the Reagan White House.

Emergence of Modern White House Press Corps

Theodore Roosevelt's generosity in allowing reporters to set up working quarters in the White House symbolized the emergence of the press as an institution in government affairs. Journalists have been based at the White House ever since, observing, reporting, analyzing, photographing, and eventually televising virtually every action as well as many private moments involving the occupant.

With the growth of the so-called "imperial presidency" and the introduction of television, members of the modern White House press corps have become, in effect, an elite subspecies of Washington journalism. They are, notwithstanding the traditional independence of the press, part of the monarchical white House entourage. They work within the heady environment of the White House—their creature comforts catered to and their professional prerequisites swiftly satisfied. They travel (at their employers' expense), occasionally play tennis with, and generally socialize with the presidential household.

In a speech at the 1975 White House Correspondents' Association dinner, President Ford embraced the members as part of the "White House family." He said,

> We work together. We laugh together. We exchange ideas, facts and speculation. We interact. We cannot function without each other. This is the stuff that families are made of. And like all families, we have disagreements. We take in and assimilate individual attitudes, concerns, information, interests. Then, we shine the spotlight of our unique perceptions on each problem, each new challenge.[69]

Once but a handful—all could comfortably stand alongside FDR's desk in the Oval Office—the White House reporters have multiplied into a sizable legion. The increase in their numbers supports the perception of innate power. In 1955, when President Eisenhower left for a vacation in Denver, he was accompanied by twenty-two reporters. Thirty years later, more than one hundred fifty members of the news media trailed along whenever President Reagan left on a trip outside of Washington. Almost two thousand applied for press accreditation when Reagan traveled to Moscow in May 1988 for the fourth summit meeting with Soviet leader Mikhail Gorbachev.

From fewer than a hundred correspondents in the 1860s, the Washington press corps has grown to more than 2,500 newspaper, 1,025 magazine, and 2,400 radio-television reporters accredited in 1989 to the congressional media galleries.[70]

"Regulars" and Part-timers

The nucleus of the White House press corps is comprised of sixty to seventy-five journalists, referred to as the "regulars." They cover the White House and the activities of the president on a day-to-day basis. Their members represent just about every form of the mass media—major dailies, television and cable networks, wire services, national news magazines, specialized journals, trade publications, and foreign news organizations.

The regulars, for the most part, are confined to the West Wing press area. Each is provided with a private working cubicle in the basement operations section.

In addition, there are numerous "irregulars" who cover the White House only part time or whose interests are on particular issues or institutional aspects of the presidency. All must obtain Secret Service security clearance to receive a White House press card.

The White House "beat" is generally considered to be a coveted assignment because of its high visibility. Print reporters are ensured almost daily, bylined stories, and television correspondents are consistently seen on the evening newscasts. Surveys show that an average of four items on the nightly news shows deal directly or indirectly with the White House. Journalistic careers thus can be enhanced by this assignment.

Not unexpectedly, the various news organizations adopt their own internal systems in assigning reporters to the White House. Some newspapers simply allow the reporter who covered the victorious candidate in the campaign to follow the new president to the White House. Others replace their White House correspondents from time to time in search of a fresh perspective. Still others change their White House reporters with each new administration. Some, like United Press International, may leave them there indefinitely.

Overall, White House regulars are made up of a motley cast of journalists, differing widely in talent, personality, background, audience, and professional objectives. While there is inevitable turnover among them, there is also a hard core of veterans who provide continuity and institutional memory extending from one administration to another.

Regardless, all are subject to the flow of news, the rhythm of the White House operations, and the sitting president's attitude toward the news media. Accordingly, political scientists Michael B. Grossman and Martha J. Kumar, in their study of presidential press relations, refer to White House reporters as members of "Milton's Army," from the line in John Milton's *On His Blindness* that states, "They also serve who only stand and waite."[71]

Presidents and their aides must also deal with other members of the Washington press community, many of whom are highly vocal and nationally known and, hence, influential in varying degrees. Notable among them are syndicated columnists, television news anchors and commentators, and Washington bureau chiefs.

Once considered journalism's royal elite, columnists still enjoy an exalted position, but in recent years their status has somewhat declined because of competition from nonprofessionals, technical experts, and academics who have access to expanded editorial pages in the major newspapers. No longer perceived as "Renaissance men" in an increasingly complex world, the most prominent among them are recognized as specialists in particular areas or the voice of a distinct ideology. Television, however, has elevated many columnists to national stardom.

Playing to the Cameras

TV anchors and network commentators exercise an inordinate impact on public opinion because of their visibility and celebrity status. The bitter confrontation that ensued when CBS anchorman Dan Rather pressed Vice President George Bush concerning his role in the Iran-contra affair was considered one of the signal events of the 1988 presidential campaign.

Contemporary White House press aides openly acknowledge that their primary concern is television coverage of the president and his administration. In his White House memoirs, Donald T. Regan emphasized the role of Michael Deaver, President Reagan's public relations adviser and deputy chief of staff:

> It was Deaver's job to advise the President on image, and image was what he talked about nearly all the time. It was Deaver who identified the story of the day at the eight o'clock staff meeting and coordinated the plans for dealing with it, Deaver who created and approved photo opportunities, Deaver who alerted the President to the snares being laid by the press that day. Deaver was a master of his craft. He saw—designed—each Presidential action as a one-minute or two-minute spot on the evening network news, or a picture on page one of the *Washington Post* or the *New York Times*, and conceived every Presidential appearance in terms of camera angles.[72]

Noting the dramatic change in routine White House coverage because of the importance and physical presence of television operations, former *Time* magazine White House correspondent Laurence I. Barrett observed that

> Not a single television camera was present in the Oval Office when Lyndon Johnson held his first "impromptu" press conference soon after Kennedy's death. Today at least five TV camera crews and twelve to fifteen broadcast correspondents are present whenever the President is in the White House. The appetite for footage adaptable for evening news spots of 60 to 120 seconds or longer pieces on the morning shows is insatiable. The competition among network correspondents when they do their "standups" on the White House lawn is keener than the rivalry among soccer teams in Latin countries.[73]

The editorial decisions of Washington bureau chiefs and other media executives are of paramount interest to the White House because they determine what stories will be covered, who will cover them, and the extent of the play given them. The bureau chiefs further speak for their news organizations and are frequently called on to deal with officials on matters such as the establishment of reporter "pools," negotiating arrangements for travel with government executives, settling on media facilities at certain events such as national political conventions, and providing air time for presidential press conferences and speeches.

In sum, columnists, TV news personalities, and bureau chiefs are important to the White House because of the space and air time they can provide, the size and caliber of the audience they reach, their capacity to help frame the news agenda, their explanations of why particular events occurred, and their interpretations of the issues. Above all, the modern White House is aware that public impressions are largely filtered through the media. In another sense, the media act as the intermediary between the public and the government.

Daily Routine

The high point of the White House reporter's normal day is the prenoon briefing at which the presidential press secretary, sometimes assisted by other administration officials—and on rare occasions the president personally—delivers announcements and takes questions. The raw material for most of the day's White House stories are gleaned here.

Earlier in the morning, at about nine o'clock, the press secretary will have met with a select group of twenty or so regulars to update the previous days' stories and review the president's schedule, so that the media will be alerted as to what to anticipate. This early meeting sets the press direction for the rest of the day—barring unexpected developments. Also, information released at that time is sent out by the wire services and provides the basis for the day's first stories on radio and television.

More often than not the 11:30 briefing, which attracts a larger audience of regulars and other journalists, turns into a highly charged sparring match, as the reporters try to goad the press secretary, standing on a dais at one end of the press room, into saying more than the secretary is able or willing to say.

Information offered by the presidential assistants—involving, for example, the president's position on a policy issue, a new appointment, a scheduled trip, the White House's response to congressional action—generally provides White House reporters with the gist of their news stories for that day. Only rarely are the daily briefings televised. Invariably, they cover a broad range of subjects from the trivial to the highly complex. Increasingly, the tenor of the questions has centered on the personal life of the president and his family. When Donald Regan disclosed in his book, *For the Record*, that Nancy Reagan, the president's wife, used the services of an astrologer to help guide her husband in making decisions, reporters responded with seventy questions on the disclosure at a single briefing.

It is widely contended that White House reporters are the object of excessive indulgence. During the Ford years, author-journalist Richard Reeves characterized the White House press operations as "an adult day-care center" run by a press secretary whose job was to keep the reporters "occupied, dumb and happy." Indeed, on any major issue, an abundance of information is made available to reporters through briefings, interviews, press releases, special backgrounders, and possibly a session with the president. This is referred to as "handout journalism" by critics.

Good reporters, some of the best of whom are assigned to the White House, go beyond what they are given and seek other sources to flesh out their stories and offer a balanced picture.

A tableau of the White House press room during the LBJ era was offered by press secretary George Christian:

> The reporters who covered Johnson on a regular basis were as much a part of the White House as the employees who worked there. The White House was their office, even if only a cubbyhole in the crowded press room off the West Lobby. Many of them never went to their own bureaus except to pick up their paychecks. From nine o'clock or so in the morning until the press secretary told them the business of the day was finished—which might be four-thirty in the evening or midnight—they lived in the environs of the West Lobby. Some had the habit of napping on the stuffed chairs and sofas in the lobby, which was the main entrance to the working West Wing of the White House. On occasion, the lobby took on the appearance of a genteel flop house.[74]

Since then, changes wrought by the Vietnam War and the Watergate scandal have sharpened the adversary relationship between the press and government. White House press/public relations operations have been significantly enlarged and refined in an attempt to exert greater management of the news. Members of the news media are physically quartered in the White House, but for all intents and purposes they are hermetically sealed off from the rest of the building. Vital decisions may be made only a few feet from the press room without its occupants being remotely aware of them.

Emblematic of the change in the relationship was the refurbishing of the White House press room. Early in the Reagan administration, rows of theater seats were installed in the open area of the press room. Metal plaques engraved with the names of the news organizations were attached to the seats, reserving them for their reporters during briefings. White House aides maintained that the purpose was to inject some order into the sometimes chaotic briefing sessions.

Be that as it may, the informal, if sometimes unruly yet democratic exchange that previously existed gave way to a regimented forum that permitted White House press aides to exercise greater control over the proceedings. Few, if any, of the White House regulars criticized the change; they were, after all, guaranteed reserved seats at the briefings. And the appropriately engraved metal plaque was recognized as a new status symbol.

The President's Press Secretary

Next to the president, the White House press secretary is one of the most visible officials in the U.S. government. With the growth of the presidency and big government, the advent of mass communications techniques, and the focal position of the United States in world affairs, the White House press secretary has become a household name, better known than most cabinet secretaries and all but a few members of Congress. The press secretary is never far from the president's side, is privy to most White House decisions, and is mentioned in the media virtually every day. Thus, modern presidential press secretaries have themselves become figures of national standing. *(See Table 3.)*

Among the roles the press secretary plays, other than that of principal conduit of news and messages from the president and major administration agencies to the press, are that of creator and protector of the presidential image, caterer to representatives of the print and broadcast media, and adviser in the art of communications, as, for example, the timing of the release of information, who should release it, and the form in which it is presented. The secretary is also administrator of the White House press-public relations section and coordinator of the administration's entire public affairs operations.

Still another less recognized function: because of the job's closeness to members of the news media, the secretary is able to pick up public opinion trends and issues of paramount concern to various constituencies. Far more than any other subordinate, the press secretary speaks publicly for the president, to the extent that anyone can. As George E. Reedy, onetime press secretary to President Johnson observed, "The press secretary is an echo of the president." [75]

Practically every word the press secretary utters is heard around the world and instantly dissected for its meaning and significance regarding administration policies and intentions. Hence, as noted by Larry Speakes, former press spokesman for President Reagan, "U.S. policy is . . . made from my podium." [76]

Every White House press secretary is fully aware, and is constantly reminded, that the first and overriding obligation is not to the press but to the president, at whose pleasure the secretary serves. The chief task of the press aide is to illuminate the presidency in the best possible light and attract popular support for the president's policies and programs. Accordingly, truth becomes less of a moral imperative than a commodity in the political marketplace.

In a real sense, a press secretary complements and is an extension of the president. Some have been so closely identified with a president that they seemed to be bodily projections of him, such as James C. Hagerty and Dwight Eisenhower, Pierre Salinger and John Kennedy, Ronald L. Ziegler and Richard Nixon, Jody Powell and Jimmy Carter. Press secretaries are never wholly their own persons. To serve effectively, they must assume the president's principles and philosophy.

Describing his role, Ronald H. Nessen, President Ford's press secretary, said, ". . . I always try to answer a question as the president would answer it if he were there. I think that is the most valuable service that a press secretary can perform—to be an accurate reflector of the president's own views." [77]

In addition, presidential press secretaries are burdened with administrative and personnel duties. Depending on their closeness to the president, they may participate in policy decisions.

Informal Press Relations

During the nineteenth century, several presidents sought advice on press relations in an informal, unstructured manner from friends and aides. The novelist Nathaniel Hawthorne, for example, performed such a service for his friend, President Franklin Pierce.[78]

Throughout Abraham Lincoln's presidency, his private secretary, John G. Nicolay, acted as his liaison with the press. Ever protective of the president, the faithful and tenacious Nicolay was an innovator in attempts to influence the press. He sent letters to newspapers complaining of what he considered unfair treatment of the president. On one occasion, he personally dressed down Horace Greeley, of the *New York Tribune*, for a "villainous, unfair, and untrue" editorial. The rebuked Greeley allowed Nicolay space in his newspaper to respond.

Since it was impossible for the president, whose time was monopolized by the war, to review the newspapers himself, Nicolay, along with another young White House aide, John Hay, began drafting brief summaries of important news stories—a practice that survives to this day. (Hay, in his early twenties at the time, would later become a leading novelist and outstanding secretary of state under Presidents McKinley and Theodore Roosevelt.)

As one writer noted, "Lincoln was no more immune to newspaper criticism than any other president, and he came to rely on Nicolay as his watchdog of the press." [79]

Subsequent presidents retained aides who served in a nonprescribed capacity as their contacts with the press. Grover Cleveland enlisted the services of Daniel Lamont, an Albany, New York, newspaper editor, and later Theodore Roosevelt relied on William Loeb, Jr., his secretary who became a role model for future White House chiefs of staff, to handle his press relations. Loeb employed a carrot-and-stick approach in dealing with reporters: those who wrote stories about the president perceived to be "fair" were given full cooperation of the White House, those critical of the administration were denied access and banished to outer darkness.

The evolution of presidential press relations made rapid strides with the dawn of the twentieth century. Joseph P. Tumulty, a secretary who had been with Woodrow Wilson since his days as New Jersey governor, coordinated the president's schedule and doubled as his adviser on press matters. Tumulty, who is credited with being one of the first presidential aides to appreciate the use of public relations in governmental affairs, often was obliged to smooth things with reporters when Wilson would express his distrust of them. During his first year in the White House, Wilson gave serious thought to creating a federal "publicity bureau" whose primary purpose would be to release "real facts" about the government to counter false impressions in the press. The idea, however, never got beyond the talking stage.[80]

Succeeding presidents Harding and Coolidge generally dealt with the press through an assistant who had other duties. Although radio had become a popular medium in the 1920s, the print journals were still the dominant purveyor of news and formulator of public opinion. The usual practice extending through the Hoover era was to require White House reporters to submit their questions in writing.

Modern Concept of the Office

The first White House aide formally designated as "press secretary" with the full-time job of handling reporters was George Akerson, one of three new presidential secretaries authorized by Congress when Herbert Hoover entered office.[81]

A popular man-about-town, Akerson had to abdicate some of his turf to another Hoover aide, Lawrence Richey. A mysterious presence in the Hoover White House, Richey served in various roles as the president's bodyguard, troubleshooter, plugger of news leaks, and reporters' nemesis. Richey reportedly prepared a "black list" of journalists who had "turned against" the Hoover administration—a device duplicated forty years later with Nixon's "enemies list." Akerson resigned before the end of Hoover's term.

The modern concept of the presidential press secretary dates from President Franklin Roosevelt's appointment of Stephen T. Early. A longtime Associated Press reporter, he is generally considered the first such aide to have a sense of presidential press relations. It was during his tenure that the press secretary function became permanently established.

Early would usually hold an informal briefing session with FDR to review the day's news developments before the president met with reporters at his 10:30 A.M. press conferences. The press secretary would then escort the reporters into the Oval Office where FDR would hold court. Marvin H. McIntyre, the president's appointments secretary, generally sat in on the sessions.

Early and McIntyre enjoyed the confidence of the press corps, but there was never any doubt that FDR was the supreme master at orchestrating White House media relations. He eliminated the awkward practice of having reporters submit questions in advance, and his use of radio to reach millions of Americans opened up a new chapter in presidential public relations.

Although always in FDR's shadow, Early was the first White House press secretary whose name became familiar to the public. Columnist Raymond Clapper once described him as "one of the most important voices in Government."[82]

In the course of his presidency, Truman was served by three press secretaries—Charles Ross, Joseph Short, and Roger Tubby. Each of the three men came from a journalistic background, solidifying a tradition of appointing professional journalists as White House press secretary.

The pattern for modern White House media operations was set by James C. Hagerty, former *New York Times* political reporter who served as press secretary throughout President Eisenhower's eight years in office—a period that coincided with the development of television as a political tool. Hagerty, who enjoyed Eisenhower's confidence and the respect of members of the press, was highly effective. His organizational and operational techniques established a prototype for succeeding White House press secretaries.

Hagerty's total effort as Eisenhower's press secretary was to protect the president and discourage the publication or broadcast of any views contrary to administration policy. He not only supervised White House press operations but also coordinated the executive agencies' news releases and counseled cabinet secretaries concerning their public relations. As a former reporter, he was adept at anticipating the needs of the working press. In this regard, one writer observed,

> Ninety percent of a Press Secretary's job is concerned not with policy but with endless routine: seeing that speeches and press releases are issued well in advance; arranging the press corps' travel plans on presidential trips; finding out what the President gave the First Lady for Christmas, and so forth. On such things, Hagerty was unbeatable.... Hagerty knows just what makes a good still picture, the exact amount of lighting for television, exactly when to break up a press conference in order to make deadlines for home editions on the East Coast.[83]

Hagerty's talent was particulary evident on the three occasions Eisenhower became ill, in 1955 when he suffered a heart attack in Denver, the following year when he underwent an ileitis operation, and in 1957 when he had a stroke. Hagerty's candor and penchant for detail set an example that future White House press secretaries would follow in releasing news and information about presidential illnesses.

Under Hagerty's direction, Eisenhower became the first president to allow edited telecasts of his news conferences. The natural progression of full-dress, live presidential press conferences occurred shortly afterward in the Kennedy administration. Pierre Salinger, Kennedy's press secretary and former reporter for the *San Francisco Chronicle* and *Collier's* magazine, was a firm believer that the job required extensive journalistic experience. Equally important in Salinger's case was his gregarious nature and ability to get along with reporters while maintaining his loyalty to the president. Salinger's personality ideally complemented the natural charm and dry wit of President Kennedy.

With the increasing emphasis on media politics, the White House press/public relations operations has burgeoned into one of the largest divisions of the presidential complex. The number of people in the White House press office alone rose from a mere handful in the Kennedy era to almost fifty in the Nixon years and in each succeeding administration.

In addition to the press office, the modern White House includes an Office of Communications, which deals with overall media relations; a news summary unit that monitors the print and electronic media for stories of interest to the White House; a pollster to measure public opinion and popular attitudes; a press advance detail that handles the logistics for members of the media during presidential trips; special radio-TV advisers and technicians; a photography staff; and an Office of Media Liaison that serves as the White House contact for news organizations outside of Washington. Working closely with the press operations is the White House Office of Public Liaison, which deals with special interest groups. Also, some of the various units of the Executive Office of the President have their own press relations officers, including the Office of Management and Budget, Council of Economic Advisers, and the National Security Council.

Dealing with Crises

During President Kennedy's relatively brief but eventful period of office, Pierre Salinger had to deal with the Bay of Pigs operation, the Berlin crisis of 1961, the Cuban missile crisis, and numerous domestic civil rights demonstrations, including the Birmingham riots of 1963.

Lyndon Johnson's obsessiveness with news coverage and his public image, as well as his demanding personality, created incessant problems for each of the three press secretaries who served under him—George Reedy, Bill Moyers, and George Christian. Johnson never fully understood the adversary role of the press, a conviction reaffirmed in his view by the Vietnam War coverage. Contemporary observers contended that Johnson, who kept three TV monitors in his office, attempted to be his own press secretary. His depictions of events were often at cross purposes with press reports, serving to further impair his relationship with the news media.

Throughout much of his political career, Richard Nixon's relations with the media were marred by barely concealed antagonism. Upon gaining the presidency, he restructured and expanded the press operations with the intent of centralizing the dissemination of White House news and controlling the flow of information. Appointed as presidential press secretary was Ronald Ziegler, who had joined the Nixon campaign from a Los Angeles advertising firm. Herbert Klein, a longtime Nixon political aide, was named director of the newly created Office of Communications, which was designed to circumvent the Washington press corps and deal directly with editors and broadcasters outside the capital.

From the beginning, it was apparent that Ziegler, who initially held the second-rank title of "press assistant," was not part of the senior Nixon staff and stood "outside the loop" of the White House decision-making apparatus, thus severely diminishing his effectiveness.

Eventually, the Watergate scandal strained Nixon's relationship with the press to the breaking point. A poisoned atmosphere permeated the White House press room as Ziegler and reporters clashed in inflammatory exchanges. Ziegler's occasional references to previous White House statements and explanations as being "inoperative" added to the hostility and he gradually relinquished the daily press briefings to the assistant press secretary, Gerald L. Warren. Several years after he left the White House, Ziegler conceded at a press symposium that much of the information that he gave about Watergate was incorrect "because I was not told what the facts were." [84] *(See "Watergate Investigations," p. 374, in Removal of the President chapter of Part II.)*

Table 1 Presidential Press Secretaries, 1929-1989

Press secretary	President	Years	Background
George Akerson	Hoover	1929-31	reporter
Theodore G. Joslin	Hoover	1931-33	AP reporter
Stephen T. Early	Roosevelt	1933-45	AP, UPI reporter
Charles Ross	Truman	1945-50	reporter
Joseph H. Short	Truman	1950-52	reporter
Roger Tubby	Truman	1952-53	journalist
James C. Hagerty	Eisenhower	1953-61	reporter
Pierre E. Salinger	Kennedy	1961-63	investigative writer
Pierre E. Salinger	Johnson	1963-64	investigative writer
George Reedy	Johnson	1964-65	UPI reporter
Bill Moyers	Johnson	1965-67	associate director of Peace Corps
George Christian	Johnson	1967-69	reporter
Ronald L. Ziegler	Nixon	1969-74	advertising
Jerald F. terHorst	Ford	1974	bureau chief, newspaper
Ron H. Nessen	Ford	1974-77	journalist
Jody L. Powell	Carter	1977-81	advertising
James Brady[a]	Reagan	1981-89	Reagan campaign aide
Larry Speakes	Reagan	1981-87	reporter
Marlin Fitzwater	Reagan	1987-89	government information aide
Marlin Fitzwater	Bush	1989-	government information aide

a. Although Brady was severely wounded in the 1981 presidential assassination attempt, his title remained press secretary until 1989. Speakes's title was assistant to the president and principal deputy press secretary, while Fitzwater's was assistant to the president for press relations. He became White House press secretary in the Bush administration.

President Ford's selection of Jerald terHorst as his press secretary temporarily restored peace in the White House press room. But after terHorst resigned in protest of the Nixon pardon, his successor, Nessen, experienced credibility problems. Reporters suspected that Nessen, a former NBC correspondent, was not privy to the White House inner councils.

Jimmy Carter's press secretary, Jody Powell, was perfectly suited for the position. A fellow Georgian, he had been a confidant, aide, and adviser to Carter for about ten years. White House reporters were keenly aware that Powell had the complete confidence of the president and that he had unrestricted access to Carter and accurately reflected his views. While Powell's easy manner and sense of humor made him popular with members of the press, they also recognized his unswerving partisanship as a Carter loyalist. As a result, he was seen as much as the president's chief salesman, image maker, and public defender as his official voice.

Powell was put to his most severe test during the 444 days of the Iranian hostage crisis, which dominated the final months of the Carter administration. With each evening TV newscast the networks played a drumbeat on the

Jimmy Carter Library

Jody Powell, left, fell within the tradition of press secretaries who reflected their president's personalities. A fellow Georgian, Powell had been a confidant, aide, and adviser to Jimmy Carter for about ten years.

increasing number of days that the fifty-two hostages had been held, keeping the issue alive in the public's mind. Seldom a day passed that Powell was not asked about the situation.

Because of the need for secrecy to protect the lives of the hostages, Powell was forced to grapple with a question that inevitably confronts most presidential spokesmen: should the government lie when national security is at stake? Powell concurred with Pentagon spokesman Arthur Sylvester's declaration in 1963 that under certain circumstances "government does have the right to lie." In his White House memoirs Powell wrote that when the welfare of the nation requires it, "government has not only the right but a positive obligation to lie." [85]

Powell was directly faced with the issue when asked by Jack Nelson, Washington bureau chief of the *Los Angeles Times*, whether the Carter administration was planning a military operation to rescue the hostages. Powell had been informed by the president himself that such an attempt was imminent. Yet, he denied there were any rescue mission plans, stressing instead the White House's "cover" story that it was considering a naval blockade or the mining of Iranian harbors—options that had already been ruled out.

Two days later, the hostage rescue attempt ended in disaster. Although troubled by the moral dilemma, Powell observed, "It is ludicrous to argue that soliders may be sent off to fight and die, but a spokesman may not, under any circumstances, be asked to lie to make sure that the casualties are fewer and not in vain." [86]

In Carter's own words, the hostage crisis had "cast a pall" over his administration, raising questions of his leadership and eventually contributing to his reelection defeat in 1980.[87]

Larry Speakes was propelled into the position of President Reagan's chief spokesman through a tragic accident of history. On March 30, 1981, slightly more than two months after his inauguration, Reagan was seriously wounded by bullets fired by John W. Hinckley, Jr., a troubled young man. White House press secretary James Brady, a member of the presidential party leaving a Washington hotel following a Reagan speech, was also hit, suffering a severe head wound. Brady in the ensuing confusion was at first reported to have been killed. He eventually recovered but, while retaining the title of White House press secretary, never actively resumed the duties.

Speakes, a public relations consultant who had worked as a White House press aide in the Nixon and Ford administrations, was immediately thrust into the job. For almost the next six months, he served as Reagan's chief spokesman with the title of principal deputy press secretary.

For most of his time in the position, Speakes, at his own admission, "was excluded from a number of key meetings" and not until the near end of his tenure was he admitted as a member of the White House inner circle.[88]

Speakes's exclusion from the inner circle resulted in an embarrassment for him in October 1983 when CBS White House correspondent Bill Plante asked about a report that U.S. forces were poised to invade the Caribbean island of Grenada, where a bloody military coup was taking place. Speakes replied he would check on it and passed the inquiry on to Rear Adm. John M. Poindexter, deputy director of the National Security Council and later a central figure in the clandestine Iran-contra affair. "Preposterous," Poindexter replied—the exact word Speakes used when he got back to Plante. Twelve hours later, U.S. military forces attacked Grenada.[89]

Ironically, Speakes received his greatest amount of national publicity after he left the White House. In *Speaking Out*, a book on his White House experience, he acknowledged that on at least two occasions he fabricated quotes attributed to the president—once in September 1983 following the Soviet Union's shooting down of Korean Air Lines Flight 007, killing 269 people, and in November 1985 during the Geneva summit between Reagan and Soviet leader Mikhail Gorbachev. In the latter instance, Speakes reported to the press that the president had said to Gorbachev, "There is much that divides us, but I believe the world breathes easier because we are talking here together."

The comment was picked up by the U.S. and international media and heard around the world—yet Reagan had never made such a statement. The disclosure by Speakes in his book more than two years later created a furor in the press and at the White House, where his successor, Marlin Fitzwater, denounced the improvisation as a "damn outrage." Shortly afterward, Speakes was forced to resign from his job as a vice president for communications with a New York brokerage firm.

Presidents' Techniques of Managing the News

The success of modern-day presidents depends in a large measure on the artful use of persuasion and their skills as communicators to mobilize a national coalition and gain popular support. Just as the press needs the White House to carry out its function as the collector, relayer, and interpreter of news and information, so the White House needs the press to spread its message.

Not unexpectedly, presidents want news of their administration presented in a favorable light and editorial opinions and commentaries couched in terms compatible with official policy lines. This helps account for the elaborately orchestrated attempts by incumbent administrations to manage the news and shape its content.

To an immeasurable degree—for good and bad—the business of government is public relations. Seeded throughout the federal landscape, from the White House to the gargantuan cabinet departments to the mini-agencies cloistered in bureaucratic depths, is a huge, amorphous network of employees whose chief mission is to package and dispense information about government policies, services, and programs at one level and to promote them on another. The former is essentially an educational function; the latter is primarily political in nature. It is this dichotomy that has traditionally bred confusion and suspicion about federal public affairs operations.

At least part of the problem is that the line between the need to inform as a public service and the desire to solicit public support for political objectives has never been satisfactorily delineated. Moreover, it has never been established as to how many federal employees are engaged in what is broadly construed as government public relations—preferably referred to in the bureaucracy as public affairs or public information—or what the total costs are, mainly because of misleading job titles and budgets that camouflage the outlays.

Unofficial estimates place the number of government employees involved in some facet of public relations in excess of 25,000 and the cost at about a billion dollars a year. Indeed, no governmental warren is too small to have a public affairs officer, including the U.S. Marine Band.

Each day this vast, interlocking federal information machine spews forth millions of words, pictures, statistics, magazines, advisories, books, and films. It arranges tours, sets up exhibits, sponsors aerial events, schedules speakers, offers press interviews and news briefings, transmits radio programs around the world, and produces telecasts beamed abroad by orbiting satellites. The objective, simply put, is the selling of the government.

It is generally conceded, particularly in an age of mass communications and sophisticated image making, that the flow and quality of information that emanates from Washington are vital ingredients in the democratic process. As amply documented, the government can withhold information, classify it, distort it, or, on occasion, even lie. But more important is what the government chooses to report and reveal and the manner in which it is done.

For the most part, presidents assess communications in terms of helping or hindering them in the pursuit of their goals. Prohibited by the First Amendment from controlling or censoring the press, they seek to manage and manipulate it, or circumvent it through resources at their command.

At times, in their zeal to protect their administrations, they have resorted to untruths, half-truths, and deceptions, including the Eisenhower administration's misleading account of the U-2 incident, the attempt by the Johnson administration to conceal the escalation of U.S. military involvement in the Vietnam War, the Nixon White House's blatant efforts to cover up and delude the public and press throughout the Watergate scandal, and the secrecy imposed by Reagan administration officials in the Iran arms sale/contra aid episode.

Bill Fitz-Patrick, The White House

Marlin Fitzwater succeeded Larry Speakes as head of press relations in 1987. When Speakes later published memoirs disclosing White House operations, Fitzwater denounced the book's revelations as a "damn outrage."

Such questionable tactics are aberrations in the affairs of government. In the main, the White House attempts to manage the news by utilizing conventional techniques that have evolved over the years and are constantly being refined in step with advancements in communications technology.

Prominent among these techniques are daily press briefings, background briefings, formal televised press conferences, exclusive interviews, the issuance of news releases and handouts, photo opportunities, impromptu question-and-answer sessions, and public announcements.

The Daily Briefing

The most common and possibly the most effective tactic in White House news management involves the daily briefing conducted by the presidential press secretary. The customary practice among modern press secretaries has been to hold a news briefing each day, shortly before noon, thereby giving the television correspondents plenty of time to film "visuals" and put together their stories for the evening newscasts.

Almost always, the press secretary, standing at a podium in the White House press room before rows of seated reporters, opens the briefing with a series of announcements concerning the president and the administration. The announcements, for example, may concern the president's position on pending legislation, an innovative policy proposal, the introduction of a new administration program, a high-level government appointment, or a planned presidential trip. In so doing, the White House, in effect, sets the news agenda for the day because of presidents' dominance in American politics and the insatiable demand for news about them and their activities. As a result, news organizations are virtually compelled to publish and broadcast what the press secretary reports at the daily briefing. In a sense, members of the press are "captive" to the White House.

When it suits its objectives, the White House may provide special "backgrounder" briefings for reporters, generally to explain and elaborate on administration initiatives. These sessions may take any one of several forms. They may be: "on the record," meaning that the remarks may be quoted and the source identified; "on background," in which the source cannot be identified, except by status, as, for example, "an administration official"; on "deep background," under which attribution of any sort is prohibited; and "off the record," in which information given to reporters may not be included in their stories and is mainly provided for their guidance. Briefing sources may range from the president personally, to cabinet secretaries, White House aides, press officers, and policy specialists.

Regularly scheduled daily briefings are also held by the State Department and at least twice weekly by the Defense Department. Other departments and agencies hold them in response to events and developments or as the need requires.

While backgrounders may furnish reporters with useful information, they are especially beneficial to the administration. By evading direct quotation, officials may speak out on sensitive policy issues without being directly accountable for their words. It ensures them greater flexibility in getting their message across to the public or, if the case may be, to special constituencies, Congress, and foreign governments.

Backgrounders may also be used to send up "trial balloons" to gauge public reaction to prospective administration proposals, to mute speculation about presidential plans, to disseminate self-serving propaganda or "disinformation," to inflate the administration's public image, and to scotch rumors. As an example of the latter, President Carter once invited the Washington bureau chiefs of the *New York Times* and *Los Angeles Times* to his office to deny published reports that Vice President Walter F. Mondale was being excluded from his inner circle of advisers.[90]

Reporters are aware that they are being "used" in such instances, but are usually willing to go along with protecting the identities of their sources since they receive more information complying with the system than they would without it. It is the White House, however, that determines in line with its own self interest what information will be released, when, how, and to whom.

Programmed Events

Stage-managing, using the tricks and techniques of the theater, have become a staple of the White House. President Reagan, a former actor and TV show host, was particularly adept at such presentations under the direction of aide Michael Deaver, the former California public relations consultant and longtime friend and confidant of the Reagans. There were widely publicized scenes scripted by Deaver of President Reagan delivering a speech high above the steep cliffs of Pointe du Hoc, France, on the fortieth anniversary of the Normandy invasion as veterans of the historic assault looked on, and of Reagan, standing at the Korean Demilitarized Zone, dramatically peering through field glasses into Communist North Korea. In such scenes, conceived for their visual impact, members of the press are cast as extras in a public relations spectacle.

Sometimes in an attempt to convert an illusion out of reality, the White House will try to put a "spin" on what actually occurred. As a notable example, following the breakdown of the October 1986 Reykjavík summit between Reagan and Soviet leader Mikhail Gorbachev, White House chief of staff Donald Regan told the president's advisers, "This summit must not be seen or portrayed as a defeat. We've got to turn any such perception around, starting now." [91]

Shortly afterward Regan told a *New York Times* reporter that "Some of us are like a shovel brigade that follow a parade down Main street cleaning up. We took Reykjavík and turned what was really a sour situation into something that turned out pretty well." [92]

Access to the president and principal aides, other than through programmed media events, is a White House reporter's ultimate objective. During the Eisenhower administration almost all news and information was channeled through the White House press office. Subsequent administrations loosened the system, making White House officials sometimes available to the press—but always under the control of the president and staff. Because reporters do not have easy access to the presidential inner circle, they are more often than not compelled to go along with the official account of events.

Because of the expanding role of the media, modern presidents have increasingly granted exclusive interviews to selective reporters, usually those from major news organizations and those known to be sympathetic toward the administration. It has further become customary for presidents to grant private interviews to Washington-based foreign correspondents from countries they are scheduled to visit. In so doing, they set the stage for their visits and define their objectives and expectations on their own terms.

White House officials have come to appreciate that small, private sessions with members of the media allow them to have more influence over the tone and content of stories than they do in heavily attended press conferences. Furthermore, they find that it is a way to build media support.

As might be expected, however, those reporters excluded from private meetings with the president are likely to vent their displeasure. This occurred when Franklin Roosevelt granted his exclusive interview to the *New York Times'* Arthur Krock. FDR pledged to an angry White House press corps that he would never do it again—and he did not.

The granting of exclusive interviews is widely recognized as the president's privilege, and though there may be costs involved they are usually less than the benefits received, because the president almost always holds some trump cards in relations with the press.

Managing the news has reached such a stage of refinement that Reagan White House staff aides would meet each morning and decide what they wanted to be "the story of the day" to advance the president's interests. As one television correspondent observed, "Then they let the press in at presidential appointments or gatherings that lend themselves to that 'story' and keep the press away from those that don't. This forces television into a choice of airing the pictures and words they let us see and hear or not having any White House pictures that day. We can always put on a story without them, but pictures are our main commodity—and the [White House] staff knows it." [93]

Means of Evasion

A classic example of how the White House can mislead the press occurred in 1985 when President Reagan, who had only recently undergone intestinal surgery, appeared with a small bandage on the side of his nose. Press Secretary Larry Speakes was asked by reporters if a biopsy had been performed to check for cancer. Evading their questions, Speakes simply reported that a patch of skin had been scraped for testing. Later that day, the White House released a statement saying that a small area of skin on the right side of the president's nose had been "aggravated by the adhesive tape used while the president was in the hospital. It was submitted for routine studies for infection, and it was determined no further treatment was necessary."

However, it was soon learned that a biopsy had been performed and that it showed the president had skin cancer, which was correctable by mild surgery. Mrs. Reagan, nonetheless, ordered that the news be constricted and that the word "cancer" not be used in the press releases. A few days later, President Reagan himself publicly revealed the whole truth.

A relatively recent development in White House media operations is the "photo opportunity." Formalized in the Carter White House, a photo opportunity, as implied, is simply giving photographers a few minutes to take pictures at a special White House event, or, as more often the case, at the beginning of a meeting between the president and a distinguished visitor. The undisguised purpose is to provide the White House with visual exposure in a controlled environment.

Reporters, however, began to accompany the photographers and took advantage of the chance to ask the president questions, often unrelated to the event. Because of several embarrassing misstatements by President Reagan on such occasions, the White House moved to limit the practice by permitting only a representative "pool" of reporters to attend photo opportunities.

Recent administrations have further employed rather disingenuous methods of managing the press. It became the customary practice, for example, of the Reagan White House to discourage reporters from shouting questions to the president as he left for his Camp David retreat by having the pilot turn up the motors of the presidential helicopter. Frequently, Reagan would indicate to the reporters that he could not hear them above the roar of the engines. That saved the president from engaging in risky dialogue with the media, leaving them merely with pictures of him waving as he boarded the helicopter.

Another White House technique involves "stonewalling" by the president's press secretary or other administration officials. The term applies to the refusal to satisfy inquiries, generally by responding with "no comment," or by giving misleading answers, or by clouding the issue through obfuscation. It came into common political usage during the Watergate scandal as a tactic employed by Nixon press secretary Ronald Ziegler and others in the administration.

It is not unusual for a White House press secretary to avoid making mistakes, or lying, or having to plead ignorance by sidestepping reporters' questions with "no comment." In his book on the Reagan White House, Larry Speakes declared, "There are 10,000 ways of saying 'no comment.' "[94]

White House press managers also routinely release bad news on late Friday nights when media organizations are minimally staffed. Another advantage is that the news is likely to draw less public attention over the weekend. Still another ploy is to have someone other than the president announce bad news, thus separating him from public reaction.

With the increasing popularity of TV talk shows and public service programs, White House press officers have become casting directors or booking agents. They deliberately pursue a strategy of carefully selecting—or rejecting—administration officials who will appear on the shows. This ensures them a measure of control over the television outlets. They may further impose certain conditions: that the administration representative will be guaranteed a set amount of air time, for example, or they may exact a promise that no unfriendly opponent will appear on the same program.

Presidents, meanwhile, have additional resources at their command to circumvent the news media and get their message across without its being filtered through reporters. These include speeches to organized interest groups; national television appearances in connection with critical events; regularly scheduled radio addresses; constitutionally mandated reports, such as those on the State of the Union and the nation's economy; and the public release of administration documents and publications.

Presidential Showcase: the Televised News Conference

With the possible exception of the presidential debates, the televised news conference affords Americans the best opportunity to see their president in the act of thinking and speaking. It takes viewers onto the scene, where they can assess the performance and derive a sense of where the chief executive hopes to lead the country.

Traditionally, press conferences have been a mutually beneficial device employed by presidents to disclose their plans and policies and explain their decisions, and by reporters to gain information and insights into governmental decision making—and the person in charge of that process.

Students of government further note that the question-and-answer sessions are analogous to the British parliamentary system in which the prime minister regularly faces interrogation by members of the House of Commons, and thus they offer one of the few institutionalized opportunities to hold the president accountable.

As observed in a 1975 National News Council study, "Presidents aren't compelled to explain themselves to anybody—not to their own party, nor to the opposition (as in Great Britain), nor least of all to the press." Yet, presidential news conferences have become such an ingrained part of the political process that they almost seem to be "as much a part of government as voting . . . one of the few visible examples of democracy in action."[95]

Though they are unmentioned in the Constitution and not required by statute, any move by a president to abandon them would be taken at great political risk.

Presidential press conferences, as currently conceived, began their genesis in Woodrow Wilson's administration. At the outset of his presidency he held weekly question-and-answer sessions open to all correspondents. Before long, however, Wilson, who maintained a condescending attitude toward reporters, became disenchanted with what he viewed as breaches by the press. In one instance, an off-the-record account he had given of conditions in Mexico appeared on the first page of several newspapers. Eventually, his weekly press sessions were dropped.

Since Wilson, presidents have used news conference techniques in their own way, according to the manner most comfortable to them and in conformity with their attitudes toward the press and their communications skills. Warren Harding, Calvin Coolidge, and Herbert Hoover each insisted that reporters' questions be written and submitted in advance. The practice began when Harding, unprepared for a question concerning a diplomatic treaty, gave an erroneous interpretation of it.

Coolidge added new stringencies: reporters were not only prohibited from quoting him, but they could not even say that they saw the president or report any White House news as coming from an official. Upon taking office, Hoover announced that he was liberalizing press regulations. But none of the promised reforms were instituted. Instead, Hoover further exacerbated White House press relations when he repeatedly refused to answer a great majority of the questions and began favoring sympathetic reporters with choice stories.

It was not until the presidency of Franklin Roosevelt that reporters were allowed to ask spontaneous questions and the news conference became an institutionalized part of the White House public affairs operations. Roosevelt had a particular knack of preparing reporters for controversial decisions by educating them in advance with confidential background information, thus averting unnecessary surprises and gaining their endorsement because they understood the reasons behind his actions.

Harry Truman and Dwight Eisenhower held regular news conferences, but neither was able to master the process. Truman tended to give snappy, off-the-cuff answers and seemed unable to envision how his words would look in print or how they might be interpreted.[96]

Eisenhower usually gave the impression that news conferences were a presidential burden that had to be tolerated. His natural inclination to garble syntax and use tortuous sentence structures was a constant vexation for White House reporters. But Eisenhower relaxed the rule against direct presidential quotation, and he was the first president to permit his press conferences to be taped and edited for TV viewing.

His successor, John Kennedy, introduced live, televised news conferences. His youth, good looks, and comfortable rapport with members of the news media were ideally suited for television. At the first live telecast of a presidential news conference, in January 1961, Kennedy attracted 418 correspondents and an extraordinarily large audience of 65 million viewers.

Where Kennedy's polished persona came across perfectly on television, Lyndon Johnson's mercurial personality, so effective in face-to-face encounters, seemed wooden on the screen. He disliked formal TV press conferences, preferring impromptu meetings with reporters in his office or in rambling walks around the White House Rose Garden. Yet, he continued to hold regular news conferences because he recognized that a president had an obligation to the public to be seen and heard.

Richard Nixon, whose relationship with the press throughout his political career was marked by overt and mutual hostility, held an average of less than one press conference every two months during his presidency. He and his White House aides were more intent on staging events that would appear on prime-time network television than on exposing him to the reporters' sharp-edged questions.

Although Nixon did not come across well on television, he did have a firm grasp of policy and governmental issues—in contrast to Reagan, who projected a likable image but was not effective at communicating issues. It was universally agreed that Reagan was considerably more adept at delivering prepared messages and speeches than at impromptu responding to reporters' questions at formal press conferences.

Gerald Ford, like Lyndon Johnson, preferred informal news conferences that were announced briefly in advance of the meetings—the advantage being that reporters had less time to prepare difficult questions.

Upon taking office, Jimmy Carter pledged to hold press conferences twice a month. But by the time he left the White House Carter, like other modern presidents, was holding them only about once every two months. For all of his use of symbolic gestures, Carter always kept the press at arm's length, leaving the impression that to him it was one more entrenched Washington interest group with which he had to deal.

The President's Advantages

Basically, the president controls the press conferences, notwithstanding the sometimes persecutorial tone of the reporters' questions. "It's his news conference, not the media's," observed George Reedy, President Johnson's former press secretary.[97]

The president decides when a press conference will be held, he sets the ground rules, he selects the reporters who will ask questions, and he alone decides what information will be divulged. In an extreme case, during the 1973-1974 Watergate investigation, Nixon went five months without a press conference and, at one stretch, fourteen months without a televised meeting with reporters.

Toward the close of his presidency, Eisenhower was asked by a reporter if he felt that the press had been fair to him in their questions. Hinting at the decided advantage that presidents hold in their relationship with the press, Eisenhower replied, "Well, when you come down to it, I don't see what [*sic*] a reporter could do much to a president, do you?"[98]

Sometimes, presidents may evade a question by making a quip or pleading inability to reply on grounds of national security. They may simply decline to answer some questions without giving a reason, or they may abruptly change the tone and direction of the questioning by calling on a reporter with a reputation for asking soft questions. Prior to a press conference, the president studies the conference room's seating arrangements to know where certain reporters will be located.

Reedy additionally noted that "the aura of the presidency" tends to inhibit reporters from becoming too aggressive, even though the unembellished directness of some questions may indicate otherwise. "Most [reporters] are not going to be disrespectful to the president," Reedy said. "After all, he symbolizes the United States."[99]

There are still other invisible advantages that the presidents enjoy. By scheduling long intervals between news conferences they can ensure a supply of superficial questions, because the reporters will have so much to cover. And when there is a major development, most questions center on it, which means little else is covered.

The vastly increased size of the press corps itself has had an impact on presidential news conferences. When White House reporters were able to gather around FDR's desk in an informal exchange on issues of the day, they were able to deeply explore his thinking and discover the reasons he made certain decisions. Members of today's massive press corps are fortunate if they are able to ask even one question, let alone delve deeply into the president's reasoning.

The ritualistic formula followed at press conferences also gives the president an edge. TV press conferences almost always last but one half-hour. Some presidents, such as Lyndon Johnson, invariably consume a good portion of that time with announcements at the start of the press conference, leaving reporters with less time to ask questions.

Moreover, some reporters are accorded special recognition. Tradition requires that the senior wire service reporter asks the first question. Almost always, the president then calls on easily recognizable TV correspondents who are in the front-row seats. Only an average of eighteen questions can be asked in a half-hour, which means most of the print press reporters are denied an opportunity to ask a question.

Formerly, reporters were allowed to ask only one question; but the Reagan White House, with the concurrence of the news media, instituted a new system that permitted reporters to ask a follow-up question. That, of course, took up additional time, further reducing reporters' chances of being allowed to query the president.

On cue, the wire service reporter who began the questioning ends the press conference with the familiar expression, "Thank you, Mr. President."

The biggest danger to presidents is that they will issue a misstatement or inadvertently report an untruth or make a mistake. They must be meticulous and cautious, yet informative and affable. A single word, an inflection of voice, or a raised eyebrow can send tremors throughout the world.

Truman, for example, committed a verbal gaffe when asked about the possible use of atomic weapons in the Korean War. His reply that such action was always under consideration served to alarm many foreign governments, including U.S. allies.

Similarly, President Reagan erred during a press conference when he said that no third country had been involved in clandestine U.S. arms sales to Iran. Within minutes afterward the White House issued a news release acknowledging that Israel had been involved in the transaction.

The Reporters' Role

For members of the news media, presidential press conferences offer a chance to assert themselves as the fourth branch of government under the limelight of national television. In the past, members of the media were recognized only as the supporting cast at these sessions. But Washington reporters today seek and have been accorded almost equal billing with the president within the theatrics of the news conferences. Their performance and the tenor of their questions hold nearly as much interest as the president's utterances from the spectators' view. At times, the two sides engage in a war of words, or a battle of semantics and a search for nuance.

Until recently most reporters were not identified when they stood to ask a question of the president, because the TV crews covering the conference could not know the faces of all the reporters in the room. But the networks have largely solved this problem, and the reporter's name is usually flashed on the screen, giving him or her a measure of star treatment. Ironically, in an earlier era, print reporters resented being involuntary participants in the television conferences. But before long they began vying to be seen on TV while asking the president a question. It afforded the mostly anonymous print reporters national TV exposure and was valued by many as a career boost.

Overall, the press's role at these events is rife with ambiguity. On the one hand, reporters are faulted for asking soft questions that presidents can exploit to their advantage; on the other hand, the journalists are accused of being rude and unnecessarily hostile.

Defenders of the press maintain that asking the president to explain, justify, and defend his policies is a critical function in a democracy. In recent years, however, the news conferences' format and function have radically changed, and there is a sense that they have declined in significance. With the increased use of television and other forms of mass communications, as well as jet travel, presidents are less dependent on the press to convey their views.

The new breed of TV correspondents is mainly interested in headline news and fifteen-second sound bites, completely revising the nature of what constitutes news. Furthermore, the news conferences have become elaborately staged events in which the visual image has become equally as important as the substance of the president's statements. For modern presidents, they have become an opportune vehicle for self-promotion, diverting criticism, and soothing political supporters.

Presidential press conferences, in essence, have become more confrontational than informational, more choreography and theater than legitimate news, more of an egocentric exhibition than an opportunity to probe presidents' intentions and assess their leadership.

Against that background, Larry Speakes, press secretary for President Reagan, declared,

> The press conference in its present form may have outlived its usefulness, its usefulness to the presidency, its usefulness to the press and to the public.... What's wrong? The press conference is a theater. They're scripted. Reporters ask written questions to which a president gives a rehearsed answer. The spontaneity is lost. The press is not looking for information, they're out to

Table 2 Presidential News Conferences with White House Correspondents, 1929-1988

President	Average number of press conferences per month	Total press conferences
Hoover (1929-1933)	5.6	268
Roosevelt (1933-1945)	6.9	998
Truman (1945-1953)	3.4	334
Eisenhower (1953-1961)	2.0	193
Kennedy (1961-1963)	1.9	64
Johnson (1963-1969)	2.2	135
Nixon (1969-1974)	0.5	37
Ford (1974-1977)	1.3	39
Carter (1977-1981)	1.2	59
Reagan (1981-1988)	0.4	46

Source: Harold W. Stanley and Richard G. Niemi, *Vital Statistics on American Politics* (Washington, D.C.: CQ Press, 1988), 50.

make news. An "I gotcha" syndrome prevails. There is an attempt to entrap a president. How can we get him to say what he doesn't want to say? [100]

Speakes, nonetheless, conceded that the press conferences play "an important role in the relationship between the president and the press." In a real sense, they combine the most powerful office in the nation with the most powerful medium, providing the best chance for most Americans to see and hear the person at the helm of government.

Governmental Efforts to Control Information

With the growing recognition that information is power, the struggle between the news media and the government over the free flow of information and opinion has become a critical issue of the communications age.

Tension between the two institutions is endemic, largely because of their conflicting roles. The press is conditioned to challenge authority and act as a buffer against extraconstitutional and questionable governmental activities; the government, on the other hand, seeks to put its best face forward by controlling the terms of public debate. In furthering its objectives, the government may take measures to tighten control over the release of information about what it is doing or planning, often under the guise of national security.

On occasion, the government may attempt to delude the press through secrecy or deception or try to circumvent it entirely. Inevitably, the two institutions clash over the extent of the public's right to know what is being done in its name.

While presidential administrations have always sought to justify and embellish their actions through ingenious fabrications, the nation as a whole first became conscious of such tactics in the tumultuous decade of the 1960s—a period of social unrest at home and military adventures abroad.

Americans, it has been said, lost their innocence in 1960 when a United States U-2 spy plane was shot down over the Soviet Union. Its penetration of Soviet air space was a clear violation of national sovereignty, which the Eisenhower White House at first dismissed as a weather reconnaissance mission. In swift succession other incidents occurred in the realm of foreign affairs, a policy area where the president can act with minimal constraints. The disastrous 1961 Bay of Pigs invasion was feebly portrayed by the Kennedy administration as a unilateral expedition by rebel Cuban exiles. President Johnson asserted that U.S. Marines were sent into the Dominican Republic in April 1965 to save American lives, but it was widely suspected that the real reason was fear of a Communist takeover. As one author-journalist wrote, "Within days more than 24,000 U.S. troops had invaded the small Caribbean country; the President spent hours personally attempting to convince newsmen that this was justified because 'fifteen hundred innocent people were murdered and shot, and their heads cut off,' which turned out later to be pure myth." [101] Later U.S. military incursions in Vietnam, Laos, and Cambodia were shrouded in secrecy and subterfuge.

Distortions and misleading accounts by President Johnson concerning the escalation of the Vietnam War created what became known as LBJ's "credibility gap." A White House reporter wrote, "The credibility gap has left scars on the institution of the Presidency. It has impaired the image of the American government. It has been a factor in serious foreign policy failures. The problem of credibility, in its broadest sense, will remain after Lyndon Johnson leaves the White House." [102]

Not long afterward, an attempt by President Nixon to block release of the Pentagon Papers, which detailed the genesis of the Vietnam War, was widely viewed as a ploy to intimidate and control the press.

The faith of many Americans in their government was further shaken by the abuse of power and coverup revealed in the Watergate scandal leading to President Nixon's resignation, and later by the high-level deception and deceit that masked the Iran arms sales/contra funding affair in President Reagan's second term.

As early as 1973, an observer of the Washington scene contended,

> The American system is based not only upon formal checks and balances among the three branches of government, it depends also, and perhaps more importantly, on a delicate balance of confidence between the people and government. That balance of trust has been altered.
>
> By 1972 the politics of lying had changed the politics of America. In place of trust, there was widespread mistrust; in place of confidence, there was disbelief and doubt in the system and its leaders.[103]

During this same period, television was emerging as a pervasive purveyor of news and commentary; it graphically underscored high-level duplicities and exacerbated the adversary relationship between press and government. Thus, several related of issues were brought into play, including free speech guaranteed under the First Amendment, the media's role and responsibility, the need to ensure the nation's security, occasional conflicts between civil liberties and ideology, and the people's right to know as a basic element in the shaping of official policy in a democractic society.

Reagan Administration Actions

Ironically, although Ronald Reagan was universally hailed as the "Great Communicator," he presided over an administration that was criticized as being intent on stemming the free flow of information and muzzling the national news media.

From the beginning, the Reagan administration assumed an unprecedented narrow view of the First Amendment rights involving free speech and the unfettered flow of information. Accordingly, it consistently invoked measures to regulate the dissemination of government information, including:

~ The prohibition of a large number of foreign writers, artists, and political figures from entering the United States under the 1952 McCarran-Walter Act. Among them were Nobel Laureate Gabriel Garcia Marquez, the widow of former Chilean president Salvador Allende, and Canadian nature writer Farley Mowat.

~ A requirement that all government employees and contractors who had or had sought high-level security clearance, including political appointees but not elected officials, submit to lie detector tests. The purported purpose of the polygraphs was to guard against infiltration by spies and to trace leaks of information to the press.

~ An executive order signed by the president expanding the discretion of federal agencies to classify information for an indefinite period. The order additionally provided authority to reclassify information already in the public domain.

~ A decree under the Foreign Agents Registration Act that certain foreign documentary films—mainly those considered ideologically inconsistent with U.S. policy—be required to carry notices that they were "political propaganda" when shown in the United States. Among the targeted films were several involving nuclear war and acid rain, including three from Canada: the Academy Award-winning documentary, *If You Love This Planet*, as well as *Peace—A Conscious Choice* and *In Our Backyards—Uranimum Mining in the United States.*

~ A mandate that all government officials with access to high-level classified information sign statements requiring them during their lifetime to submit for official, prepublication review all articles and books they wrote for public consumption. A book by former CIA director Stansfield Turner, *Secrecy and Democracy, the CIA in Transition*, was delayed eighteen months before being cleared by censors who insisted on almost one hundred deletions on security grounds.

~ A directive that required two million civil servants to sign secrecy pledges not to reveal "classifiable information." Opponents, including federal employee unions and several members of Congress, challenged the order, maintaining it would have a chilling effect on the flow of information to Congress and the public. In related litigation, a federal district judge ruled that the use of the word "classifiable" without a clear definition was unconstitutional.

Other stratagems designed to constrict government information: CIA director William J. Casey, in an apparent attempt to inhibit the media, threatened to prosecute news organizations should they disclose classified data involving national security; the Justice Department subpoenaed video and audio tapes made by members of the news media of the June 1985 terrorist hijacking of TWA Flight 847 and the seventeen-day hostage crisis in Beirut; the National Aeronautics and Space Administration imposed a news blackout of the March 1986 explosion of the *Challenger* space shuttle; a pornography commission headed by Attorney General Edwin Meese III warned bookstores, drugstore chains, and other retailers they would be placed on a "blacklist" if they continued to sell "adult magazines"—action that a federal court subsequently held to be a violation of the First Amendment.

The 1983 Grenada invasion provoked one of the most highly publicized and contentious incidents involving the press and government. Reagan indicated that the purpose was to forestall "another Cuba" in the Caribbean by local, Cuban-trained Marxists who had earlier staged a military coup and executed the prime minister. The president further expressed concern about the several hundred American medical students studying there and contended that the United States was in fact responding to a formal request by the Organization of Eastern Caribbean States to help restore order and democracy on the island. Whether the latter reasons were valid or were designed to legitimize the neutralization of Grenada has become a matter of debate.

Breaking a long tradition dating back to the Civil War, reporters were barred from accompanying the assault troops and a news blackout was imposed. Coverage of the initial stages of the operation was selectively provided by the Defense Department's own news services, whose reports were marred by glaring omissions and serious inaccuracies. American military planes threatened to shoot any U.S. reporters who tried to reach the island on their own, even though some foreign newsmen were allowed to cover the invasion.

At the time, Reagan administration officials, discounting military precedent, said they were primarily concerned for the safety of the journalists. Later, Defense Secretary Caspar W. Weinberger defended their action as a means to maintain secrecy and help ensure the operation's success. Secretary of State George P. Shultz claimed the action was taken because "reporters are always against us, and so they're always seeking to report something that's going to screw things up." [104]

In the view of one journalist, "The administration seemed to want a news monopoly until it could shape public attitudes." [105]

At first, public opinion supported the news blackout. But by December, with disclosures of military foul-ups—including the bombing of a hospital—and the difficult time the U.S. forces had in overcoming a small band of Cuban defenders, public opinion polls showed that most Americans felt that the administration had erred in not letting reporters accompany the troops into Grenada. As a result of the furor, a joint military-press commission was set up, which proposed that a press pool go along on future military operations.

A "Right" to Lie?

Whether the government has the right to lie and resort to deception to camouflage its actions and decisions has long been an issue of ongoing debate. The debate went public in 1963 when Pentagon spokesman Arthur Sylvester declared in response to a reporter's question, "Yes, under certain circumstances I think government does have the right to lie."

In his White House memoirs Jody Powell, President Carter's press secretary, admitted that he had deceived the press on matters less serious than the Iran hostage rescue mission discussed earlier. He maintained that "... government has a legitimate right to secrecy in certain matters because the welfare of the nation requires it. In other cases, individuals, even public figures, have a certain right to privacy because common decency demands it." [106]

Powell admitted that on one occasion he "lied" in reply to a reporter's question about the personal life of a White House colleague and his family to avert "great pain and embarrassment for a number of perfectly innocent people. Beyond that, I could see no reason why the matter should be of public interest."

Occasionally, administration press relations officers are purposely kept in the dark about high-level plans and decisions. As Larry Speakes subsequently explained about his deception of reporters concerning the Grenada invasion plans: "I had been lied to, not the one who had been the liar." [107]

Carter press secretary Powell agreed with the Reagan administration's decision to deceive journalists rather than risk disclosing the Grenada invasion plans. In his book he quoted Britain's World War II prime minister, Winston Churchill, as saying in 1943 that " 'In wartime, truth is so precious that she should be attended by a bodyguard of lies.' "[108]

In some instances, presumably rare, the government has resorted to "dirty tricks" not to save lives but to promote its policies. It was disclosed in October 1986 that President Reagan approved a strategy of "disinformation" aimed at Libyan leader Muammar Qaddafi. A memo drafted by Poindexter, then Reagan's national security adviser, and obtained by the *Washington Post*, proposed that false information be leaked to the press with the objective of bringing down Qaddafi. It advocated a propaganda campaign that "combines real and illusionary events—through a disinformation program—with the basic goal of making Qaddafi think that there is a high degree of internal opposition to him within Libya, that his key trusted aides are disloyal, that the U.S. is about to move against him militarily."[109]

Earlier, as the recipient of an apparent leak, the *Wall Street Journal* reported on August 25 that Qaddafi "has begun new terrorist attacks" and that "the U.S. and Libya are on a collision course again."[110]

The disclosure stunned many Americans because "disinformation" was invariably associated with Soviet techniques for planting false information. Further, it exposed a side of the U.S. government that was seldom seen—one that it was not generally thought capable of heeding.

Poindexter asserted that the disinformation was not intended to mislead the American news media, but to keep Qaddafi off balance. Nevertheless, much of the U.S. press felt that the administration had sought to use and manipulate it by creating a phony crisis in the furtherance of its foreign policy vis-à-vis Qaddafi.

Freedom of Information Act

Acting quietly but effectively, the Reagan administration was able to tighten accessibility to government information by constrictions applied to the Freedom of Information Act. Passed by Congress in 1968, and amended in 1986, the FOIA was designed to make all but the most secret government documents available to the public, press, and academicians. Critics, including constitutional lawyers, journalists, scholars, and public interest advocates, maintained, however, that the administration subverted the act's intent.

It severely limited the scope of the act through several devices, including restrictions on the type and amount of government material made available, delaying responses to requests beyond the designated time limit, charging exorbitant fees for copies of documents, deleting—or blacking out—all but the most innocuous information, denying fee waivers for academic researchers and sometimes forcing them to pay tens of thousands of dollars for documents, thus compromising scholarly investigations.

Also, staff reductions in FOIA offices at the various federal departments and offices further made the procedure more cumbersome, discouraging use of the act. Even acknowledgment of requests filed under the act could take a year or more. And some documents dating back three decades or more have yet to be declassified.

In still another attempt at controlling information, recent administrations have taken increasingly harsh steps to plug news leaks, by requiring federal employees to take lie detector tests, threatening to fire "leakers," and reassigning them to less meaningful jobs. Ironically, incumbent administrations may themselves engage in authorized leaking—to promote their own interests—but inevitably they oppose leaks that serve to question their policies and decisions.

As a classic example, the Justice Department in 1985 prosecuted Samuel L. Morison, a Navy Department intelligence analyst, for selling satellite photos of a Soviet shipyard to the British magazine *Jane's Defense Weekly*. Morison was convicted of violating the Espionage Act of 1917—a rarely invoked law that had previously been used to prosecute people for aiding a foreign enemy, but not for leaking to the Western press. One study showed that at least 42 percent of senior federal officials had participated in leaks to reporters.[111]

Stages in White House-Press Relationship

Every modern president enters office promising to preside over an "open" administration, to offer all information necessary for the public to assess the administration's policies and performance, to make the chief executive accessible to the news media, and to hold frequent news conferences.

Following his 1968 election victory, Richard Nixon proclaimed that his administration would be "open to new ideas . . . open to the critics as well as those who support us." Jimmy Carter pledged "more accessibility to the press and public." He even considered opening cabinet meetings to the press.

George Bush promised to meet with members of the media more often than Ronald Reagan, who held fewer news conferences than any modern president. In the first week of his presidency, Bush invited two reporters (from the *New York Times* and the *Houston Post*) into the Oval Office for a brief interview and held a forty-three-minute news conference with the White House press corps.

Inevitably, however, promises remain unfulfilled, proposed policies are revised or rejected, presidential decisions are criticized, and the relationship between the White House and the news media evolves from early acceptance and cooperation to mutual tolerance, and, finally, to suspicion and thinly cloaked hostility.

As an example, Carter made a commitment to hold two news conferences a month. With time, however, he cut back on them, and by the end of his term he held them about once every six weeks. After leaving the White House, Carter recalled that he had been warned by knowledgeable Washington insiders that he "could not win a war with the press."[112]

At the heart of this predictable pattern is the media's natural tendency to want to know virtually everything that is going on inside the White House, and the White House's predisposition to manage the news and release only selective information—that which is favorable to the president and the administration.

In their study of the White House and the news media, political scientists Michael B. Grossman and Martha J. Kumar refer to the traditional stages in the relationship between the two institutions as "alliance," "competition," and "detachment."[113]

The initial phase coincides with the incoming president's so-called "honeymoon." During this brief period of good feelings, there are high expectations and a willingness to cooperate. Appropriately, the new president's first 100 days coincide with spring, a time of hope and rejuvenation in a confluence of politics and nature.

It is additionally a period when news flows from the White House in abundance concerning new appointments, fresh policies, and dramatic decisions. In that short spell, presidential character is defined, working habits are set, and the tone and direction of the administration are fixed. The changing of the guard is completed, and the president settles into his job and new home. Thus, the news media's thirst for news is gratified.

Sometimes, however, these euphoric early months are disrupted by unexpected developments, creating tension between the press and the president. Before the end of his first 100 days in office, tremors from the Bay of Pigs disaster shattered John Kennedy's "honeymoon." Gerald Ford's pardon of Richard Nixon, only thirty days days after succeeding him, cast a shadow over the remainder of his presidency. Similarly, the publicity generated during Carter's first year in office over alleged banking improprieties by Bert Lance, the president's good friend and budget director, before he had come to Washington inflicted inestimable damage on the new administration. As Jody Powell, Carter's press secretary, remarked, "There never was a honeymoon with the press, just a one-night stand."

At the other extreme, President Reagan, because of his personal popularity, was able to deflect media criticism throughout most of his two terms, except for doubts raised concerning his role in the Iran arms sales/contra funding episode. Ironically, during his first year in office he enjoyed a "second honeymoon" beginning March 30, 1981, when he survived an assassin's bullets. His good humor and courage, amplified by the real-life drama, made him a hero in the eyes of many Americans and served to disarm much of the press.

Normally, during the initial phase of a new presidency, White House aides, seeking maximum exposure, are readily accessible and are on friendly terms with reporters, eager for stories about the incoming administration. This is a time when the symbiotic relationship between the two sides is particularly evident. The president is likely to hold regularly scheduled news conferences, administration officials make themselves available for interviews, and news stories are more likely to be favorable to the administration.

Also, presidents tend to be more amenable to media requests and to give more private interviews in the beginning of their terms than in the latter stages. President Johnson, for example, met with reporters thirty-five times during his first thirteen months in office, while holding only sixteen press conferences during his second full year in the White House.

Not unnaturally, the second or "competitive" phase in president-press relations begins with political conflicts over issues and policies. Administration opponents openly voice their disenchantment and leak adverse information to the news media. Interest groups seek out the press to make known their displeasure with administration priorities.

The "free ride" or soft treatment given the president by the news media may change perceptibly. In retaliation, the White House closes regular avenues to press access and becomes more manipulative in its handling of news and information. Reporters deemed to be overly critical may find themselves cut off from administration sources.

During this period the adversary relationship blooms in full flower. Tempers often flare at the White House press secretary's daily news briefing. On one such occasion, Ron Nessen, President Ford's press secretary, deplored what he called the "poisoned atmosphere" in the White House press room. By now, the lines have been drawn between the White House and the news media, and each side warily eyes the other even as they are obliged to work side by side.

The detachment phase occurs at varying times among administrations but usually in the autumnal years of a presidential term. White House media advisers, convinced that press criticism subverts presidential decisions, try to keep reporters at arm's length. Press conferences are few and far apart. Requests for interviews are carefully reviewed, and frequently the White House insists on controlling which administration officials appear on TV talk shows.

Unlike the early months of the administration, the relationship is much more formal and structured. During the latter period of the Reagan presidency, reporters mostly had contact with him at "photo opportunities," when they would seize the moment to shout questions at him.

More and more, the president uses controlled channels to get his message across, including TV-radio addresses, news releases, public speeches to carefully selected groups, highly publicized trips, and meetings with other world leaders.

Notwithstanding the influence and pervasivess of the American news media, it is generally conceded that the president—especially if he is a skilled communicator—enjoys the upper hand in dealing with the press. As Clinton Rossiter observed, "The President is the American people's one authentic trumpet, and he has no higher duty than to give a clear and certain sound." [114]

Notes

1. Bradley H. Patterson, Jr., *The Ring of Power* (New York: Basic Books, 1988).
2. Richard Rose, *The Postmodern President* (Chatham, N.J.: Chatham House, 1988).
3. Doris A. Graber, *Mass Media and American Politics,* 3d ed. (Washington, D.C.: CQ Press, 1989), 237-238.
4. *Responsibility and Freedom in the Press,* Report of Citizen's Choice, National Commission on Free and Responsible Media, 1985, 1.
5. Donald H. Johnston, *Journalism and the Media* (New York: Barnes & Noble Books, 1979), 45.
6. Joseph R. Dominick, *The Dynamics of Mass Communication,* 2d ed. (New York: Random House, 1987).
7. David L. Lange, Robert K. Baker, Sandra J. Ball, *Violence and the Media,* vol. xi, *A Report to the National Commission on the Causes and Prevention of Violence* (Washington, D.C.: Government Printing Office, 1969), 16.
8. Dominick, *Dynamics of Mass Communication.*
9. Leonard W. Levy, *Emergence of a Free Press* (New York: Oxford University Press, 1985), as quoted in the *Washington Times,* August 26, 1985.
10. Ibid.
11. James Q. Wilson, *American Government: Institutions and Policies* (Lexington, Mass.: D. C. Heath, 1986), 502.
12. Ibid.
13. Phillip Knightley, *The First Casualty: From the Crimea to Vietnam: The War Correspondent as Hero, Propagandist,*

and Myth Maker (New York: Harcourt Brace Jovanovich, 1975).
14. Ibid.
15. Edwin Emery and Michael Emery, *The Press and America: An Interpretive History of the Mass Media,* 4th ed. (New York: Prentice-Hall, 1978), 264-265.
16. Frank Luther Mott, *American Journalism* (New York: Macmillan, 1950), 519.
17. John K. Winkler, *W. R. Hearst: An American Phenomenon* (New York: Simon and Schuster, 1928).
18. W. A. Swanberg, *Citizen Hearst* (New York: Charles Scribner's Sons, 1961).
19. J. Herbert Altschull, *Agents of Power: The Role of the News Media in Human Affairs* (New York: Longman, 1984), 55.
20. Lange et al., *Violence and the Media,* 25.
21. Emery, *The Press and America,* 514-516.
22. Emmet John Hughes, *The Living Presidency* (New York: Coward, McCann, & Geohegan, 1972), 157.
23. Bruce D. Itule and Douglas A. Anderson, *News Writing and Reporting for Today's Media* (New York: Random House, 1987), 6.
24. Dominick, *Dynamics of Mass Communication,* 87.
25. Edward Jay Whetmore, *Mediamerica,* updated 3d ed. (Belmont, Calif.: Wadsworth Publishing, 1987).
26. Associated Press, "Permanent 'Fairness Doctrine' Vetoed," *Washington Post,* June 21, 1987.
27. Edward Bliss, Jr., and John M. Patterson, eds., *Writing News for Broadcast,* rev. 2d ed. (New York: Columbia University Press, 1978).
28. William L. Shirer, *Twentieth Century Journey: The Nightmare Years 1930-1940* (Boston: Little, Brown, 1984), 303.
29. Graber, *Mass Media and American Politics,* 44.
30. Michael Schrage, "Advertising on Software Could Be Coming to a PC Near You," *Washington Post,* March 9, 1987.
31. Sydney W. Head and Christopher H. Sterling, *Broadcasting in America,* 4th ed. (Boston: Houghton Mifflin, 1982), 532-537.
32. Graber, *Mass Media and American Politics,* 39.
33. Douglass Cater, *The Fourth Branch of Government* (New York: Vintage Books, 1965), 22.
34. James E. Pollard, *The Presidents and the Press* (New York: Octagon Books, 1973), 3.
35. Ibid., 16.
36. Ibid., 7.
37. Ibid., 15.
38. David H. Weaver and G. Cleveland Wilhoit, *The American Journalist* (Bloomington: Indiana University Press, 1986), 2.
39. Cater, *Fourth Branch of Government,* 78.
40. Federal Writers' Project of the Works Progress Administration, *Washington—City and Capital* (Washington, D.C.: Government Printing Ofice, 1937), 177.
41. Cater, *Fourth Branch of Government,* 76.
42. Knightley, *First Casualty,* 20.
43. J. Cutler Andrews, *The North Reports the Civil War* (Pittsburgh: University of Pittsburgh Press, 1955), as quoted in Knightley, *First Casualty,* 21.
44. Federal Writers' Project, *Washington—City and Capital,* 176.
45. Pollard, *Presidents and the Press,* 14.
46. Philip C. Dolce and George H. Skau, eds., *Power and the Presidency* (New York: Charles Scribner's Sons, 1976), 238.
47. Pollard, *Presidents and the Press,* 113.
48. Ibid., 187.
49. Arthur M. Schlesinger, Jr., *The Cycles of American History* (Boston: Houghton Mifflin, 1986), 333.
50. Pollard, *Presidents and the Press,* 414.
51. George Juergens, *News from the White House* (Chicago: University of Chicago Press, 1981), 17.
52. Samuel Kernell, *Going Public: New Strategies of Presidential Leadership* (Washington, D.C.: CQ Press, 1986), 63-64.
53. Fred I. Greenstein, *The Hidden-Hand Presidency* (New York: Basic Books, 1982).
54. Edward Walsh, "Carter Sees Chance to Be Great President," *Washington Post,* January 20, 1977, A24.
55. George C. Edwards III, *The Public Presidency: The Pursuit of Popular Support* (New York: St. Martin's Press, 1983), 106.
56. Pollard, *Presidents and the Press,* 390.
57. Ibid., *Presidents and the Press,* 355.
58. John W. Tebbel in Dolce and Skau, *Power and the Presidency,* 242.
59. Pollard, *Presidents and the Press,* 690.
60. Arthur Krock, *Memoirs—Sixty Years on the Firing Line* (New York: Funk and Wagnalls, 1968), 182.
61. Ted Morgan, *FDR: A Biography* (New York: Simon and Schuster, 1985), 561.
62. Arthur M. Schlesinger, Jr., *The Coming of the New Deal* (Boston: Houghton Mifflin, 1958), 565.
63. Ibid., 566.
64. James E. Pollard, *The Presidents and the Press: Truman to Johnson* (Washington, D.C.: Public Affairs Press, 1964), 38.
65. David Halbertstam, *The Powers that Be* (New York: Knopf, 1979), 6.
66. "Nixon's Notes Tell of an Early Distrust of the Press," *New York Times,* May 31, 1987.
67. John Ehrlichman, *Witness to Power: The Nixon Years* (New York: Simon and Schuster, 1982), 263-264.
68. Jimmy Carter, speech delivered at a presidential colloquium, Southern Methodist University, March 26, 1984.
69. *Public Papers of the Presidents, Gerald R. Ford, 1975, Book 1* (Washington, D.C.: Government Printing Office, 1977), 237-238.
70. According to superintendents of the House and Senate press, periodical, and radio-television galleries.
71. Michael B. Grossman and Martha J. Kumar, *Portraying the President: The White House and the News Media* (Baltimore: Johns Hopkins University Press, 1981), 36.
72. Donald T. Regan, *For the Record: From Wall Street to Washington* (New York: Harcourt Brace Jovanovich, 1988), 247-248.
73. Laurence I. Barrett, *Gambling With History: Reagan in the White House* (New York: Doubleday, 1983), 437.
74. George Christian, *The President Steps Down* (New York: Macmillan, 1970), 190.
75. Dom Bonafede, "Powell and the Press—A New Mood in the White House," *National Journal,* June 22, 1977, 980.
76. Larry Speakes with Robert Pack, *Speaking Out: The Reagan Presidency from Inside the White House* (New York: Charles Scribner's Sons, 1988), 168.
77. Dom Bonafede, "White House Report: Nessen Still Seeks 'Separate Peace' With Press," *National Journal,* October 11, 1975, 1411.
78. William C. Spragens, *From Spokesman to Press Secretary: White House Media Operations* (Lanham, Md.: University Press of America, 1980), 5, 34.
79. Michael Medved, *The Shadow Presidents* (New York: Times Books, 1979), 21.
80. Pollard, *Presidents and the Press,* 640.
81. Spragens, *From Spokesman to Press Secretary,* 88.
82. Pollard, *Presidents and the Press,* 784.
83. Patrick Anderson, *The President's Men* (New York: Doubleday, 1968).
84. Ronald L. Ziegler, remarks at the Presidential Press Secretaries' Forum, Gonzaga University, April 1, 1978.
85. Jody Powell, *The Other Side of the Story* (New York: William Morrow, 1984), 223.
86. Ibid., 233.
87. Jimmy Carter, *Keeping Faith: Memoirs of a President* (New York: Bantam Books, 1982), 4, 569.
88. Speakes, *Speaking Out,* 151, 168.
89. Ibid., 152.
90. Grossman and Kumar, *Portraying the President,* 168.
91. Regan, *For the Record,* 354.
92. Ibid., 336.
93. Sam Donaldson, *Hold On, Mr. President!* (New York: Ballantine Books, 1987), 158.

94. Speakes, *Speaking Out,* 156.
95. Lewis W. Wolfson, *A Report on the State of the Presidential Press Conference* (Washington, D.C.: National News Council, 1975), 5.
96. Richard A. Watson and Norman C. Thomas, *The Politics of the Presidency,* 2d ed. (Washington, D.C.: CQ Press, 1988), 173.
97. Dom Bonafede, "Thank You, Mr. President," *National Journal,* May 5, 1987, 1070.
98. Text of Eisenhower's January 18, 1961, news conference, his last as president, *Congressional Quarterly Weekly Report,* January 20, 1961, 101.
99. Bonafede, "Thank You, Mr. President," 1070.
100. Speech at National Press Club, Washington, D.C., January 30, 1987.
101. Godfrey Hodgson, *All Things to All Men* (New York: Simon and Schuster, 1980), 188-189.
102. James Deakin, *Lyndon Johnson's Credibility Gap* (Washington, D.C.: Public Affairs Press, 1968), 14.
103. David Wise, *The Politics of Lying* (New York: Random House, 1973), 18.
104. Hedrick Smith, *The Power Game: How Washington Works* (New York: Random House, 1988), 435.
105. Ibid.
106. Powell, *Other Side of the Story,* 223.
107. Speakes, *Speaking Out,* 153.
108. Powell, *Other Side of the Story,* 233.
109. Smith, *Power Game,* 447
110. Ibid.
111. Martin Linsky, *Impact: How the Press Affects Federal Policymaking* (New York: W. W. Norton, 1986), 172, 238.
112. Carter, *Keeping Faith,* 117.
113. Grossman and Kumar, *Portraying the President,* 273-274.
114. Clinton Rossiter, *The American Presidency,* rev. ed. (New York: New American Library, 1962).

Selected Bibliography

Cater, Douglass. *The Fourth Branch of Government.* New York: Vintage Books, 1965.

Dominick, Joseph R. *The Dynamics of Mass Communication.* 2d ed. New York: Random House, 1987.

Edwards, George C. III. *The Public Presidency: The Pursuit of Popular Support.* New York: St. Martin's Press, 1983.

Graber, Doris A. *Mass Media and American Politics.* 3d ed. Washington, D.C.: CQ Press, 1989.

Grossman, Michael B., and Martha J. Kumar. *Portraying the President: The White House and the News Media.* Baltimore: Johns Hopkins University Press, 1981.

Halberstam, David. *The Powers That Be.* New York: Knopf, 1979.

Hertsgaard, Mark. *On Bended Knee: Ronald Reagan and the Taming of the Press.* New York: Farrar, Straus, & Giroux, 1988.

Hughes, Emmet John. *The Living Presidency.* New York: Coward, McCann, & Geohegan, 1972.

Kalb, Marvin, and Frederick Mayer. *Reviving the Presidential News Conference: Report of the Harvard Commission on the Presidential News Conference.* Cambridge: Joan Shorenstein Barone Center on the Press, Politics, and Public Policy, John F. Kennedy School of Government, Harvard University, 1988.

Kernell, Samuel. *Going Public: New Strategies of Presidential Leadership.* Washington, D.C.: CQ Press, 1986.

Knightley. Phillip. *The First Casualty: From the Crimea to Vietnam: The War Correspondent as Hero, Propagandist, and Myth Maker.* New York: Harcourt Brace Jovanovich, 1975.

Patterson, Bradley H., Jr. *The Ring of Power.* New York: Basic Books, 1988.

Pollard, James E. *The Presidents and the Press.* New York: Octagon Books, 1973.

———. *The Presidents and the Press: Truman to Johnson.* Washington, D.C.: Public Affairs Press, 1964.

Rose, Richard. *The Postmodern President.* Chatham, N.J.: Chatham House, 1988.

Smith, Hedrick. *The Power Game: How Washington Works.* New York: Random House, 1988.

Speakes, Larry, with Robert Pack. *Speaking Out: The Reagan Presidency from Inside the White House.* New York: Charles Scribner's Sons, 1988.

Spear, Joseph C. *Presidents and the Press: The Nixon Legacy.* Cambridge: MIT Press, 1984.

Spragens, William C. *From Spokesman to Press Secretary: White House Media Operations.* Lanham, Md.: University Press of America, 1980.

Whetmore, Edward Jay. *Mediamerica.* Updated 3d ed. Belmont, Calif.: Wadsworth Publishing, 1987.

Wolfson, Lewis W. *A Report on the State of the Presidential Press Conference.* Washington, D.C.: National News Council, 1975.

Public Support and Opinion

Democratic processes—with their emphasis on measurement of popular support—have always been just one element of U.S. politics. Politics also involve bargaining among elite groups, negotiating with foreign countries, struggling over legal definitions, controlling public institutions such as schools and utilities, and managing major economic institutions.

Although public support is just one element of political strategy, it is an important one. As political scientist E. E. Schattschneider has argued, politicians always have tried to bolster their positions by claiming support from ever expanding segments of the population.[1] Since the nation's suffrage expanded to almost all citizens, politicians have turned to other ways to widen the "sphere" of politics. Public opinion polls offer one way to bolster claims of support. Demonstrations, letters, telegrams, telephone calls, and feedback from key party leaders, elected officials, and interest groups also indicate support.

Understanding the role of public opinion in the presidency requires first understanding the fundamental levels and sources of support for the presidency as an office, then determining the way specific presidents work with that support. All presidents enjoy a basic reserve of support because of the public's near-reverence of the office. But individual presidents experience a complex, constantly changing level of support for their programs and style of leadership.

The President's Relationship with the Public

The American public has deep psychological bonds to all of its presidents. Those bonds often strain as a result of specific events and the conflicting interests of the population, but they are a foundation for the president's oscillating relationship with the public.[2]

Schools, media, economic enterprises, voluntary associations, cultural events, and even religious institutions all teach Americans to respect and even revere the presidency, even when they find fault with the specific president on important issues. This fundamental support for the presidency creates a basic reserve of popular support for the occupants of the White House to develop backing for their specific programs and actions.

By Charles C. Euchner

The presidency is revered largely because the chief executive is the most visible single figure in American life. All but a tiny segment of the population knows who the president is at a given moment—98 percent, according to one study, compared with 57 percent for one senator, 39 percent for the House member, and 31 percent for both senators. The president is well-known throughout the world. In a 1972 British poll, the president tied for first place among most-admired world political figures.[3]

As the only government official who represents the entire population, the president is unique in American politics. Other elected officials—members of Congress, governors, and local government officials—have parochial outlooks. The Supreme Court has a national constituency, but its members are appointed, and its role in American politics is obscure and usually limited to narrow legal argumentation. The president is the only person who can profess to speak for the "national interest" or the "general will" of the people.

The prestige of the presidency is enhanced by the president's role as head of state as well as the top government official. Other nations, such as Great Britain and Japan, give symbolic functions to a king or emperor, and leave the job of governing to someone else. But the president is the embodiment of the state in the United States. The emotional attachment that Americans give to the nation as a whole, therefore, is transferred also to the president.

The first political figure that children ever learn about is the president, and the president is depicted to the child as a uniquely benevolent, intelligent, and even-handed person. Early impressions are important. Although people grow up to be more skeptical of specific presidents, they retain the early lesson that the presidency is a special, important, stabilizing office usually deserving of awe.[4]

The "legacy of juvenile learning," to use the term of political scientist Fred I. Greenstein, is evident in the different attitudes of adults to the office of the presidency and the specific president in office. It is common for the president's backers in difficult times to ask for public support by referring to "the president" rather than the specific name of the president. Richard Nixon's 1972 campaign slogan was "Reelect the President" rather than "Reelect Richard Nixon."

The childhood lesson that the president is benign and

patriotic comes to the surface any time the nation faces a crisis. A military attack such as Pearl Harbor, a technological challenge such as the *Sputnik* launch, or national grieving over tragedies such as the assassination of John F. Kennedy cause the public to offer the president unquestioned, almost paternal loyalty for at least a short period.

Because the average citizen knows little about politics, the president is a symbol of the government. The president is covered in the media as a personality as well as a government official, so citizens develop a vicarious relationship with the president. Citizens identify with the president's personality as a shortcut to dealing with the complexities of the government. If citizens can develop "trust" for the president's personality, they can feel safe leaving the complexities of governing to the president.

Political scientist Murray Edelman, a leading student of the political uses of symbols and language, has written:

> Because it is apparently intolerable for men to admit the key role of accident, or ignorance, and of unplanned processes in their affairs, the leader serves a vital function by personifying or reifying the processes. As an individual, he can be blamed and given "responsibility" in a way that processes cannot. Incumbents of high public office therefore become objects of acclaim for the satisfied, scapegoats for the unsatisfied, and symbols of aspiration or of whatever is opposed.[5]

National Archives

The single most visible figure in American life, the president is covered by the media as both personality and government official.

The public has a tendency to "project" its own desires on the president—in other words, to interpret the president's actions to fit with the way it would like the president to be. Psychologists speak of citizens reducing "cognitive dissonance," or avoiding unpleasant facts or interpretations that might undercut a preferred view of the world. The citizen's desire to believe in the strength and stability of the system causes this identification with the president. This process becomes evident when the president uses vague language to appeal to groups with different goals. Even when the president's actions have clear winners and losers, both groups often interpret those actions in a way that makes them coincide with their own desires.

Psychological needs for strong leadership contribute to a steady base of presidential support. A study has confirmed the following proposition: "Persons having great needs for strong guidance, regimen, and a well-ordered society will probably score more highly on measures of general support for the president than individuals who do not have such needs."[6]

The president not only has a basic reserve of support based on widespread respect for the office. The president also can rely on the makeup of public opinion remaining somewhat constant in terms of social class, region, race, education, and residence in urban or rural areas. Since the president operates in a federal system, putting together majorities of support across the country is less important than putting together coalitions of support from the nation's different regions and groups.

The president usually can count on the South and West to be more conservative than the rest of the country, and city-dwellers to be more liberal than suburbanites or residents of rural areas. Educated people tend to be among the more independent citizens, with a "show me" attitude toward politicians on the day's leading issues. Paradoxically, many educated people take cues more readily from political parties. Ethnic and religious groups also display consistency in the way they approach certain issues.

Americans tend to be less ideological and more pragmatic than citizens of other countries. Surveys show that most Americans place themselves in the "moderate" middle part of the political spectrum. The U.S. system has a great deal of consensus on issues ranging from individual rights to the most preferable economic system. Presidents and other public officials who veer too far away from the American mainstream do so at their own risk.[7]

Measuring Support before Polls

In the years before polling became a regular part of politics and government, the measures of public support were rough and sporadic. The unscientific nature of public support fits with the original desires of the Founders. The drafters of the Constitution were wary of the constant pressures that public sentiments would have on the government's operation. The Constitution thereby contains limits to the influence of public opinion, such as indirect election of the president and Senate, the "checks and balances" between branches of government, a divided legislature, an independent judiciary appointed for life, and a federal system of national and state governments.

Institutions usually mediated public opinion in the nation's first century. As former corporate executive Chester Barnard has noted, to gauge public opinion nineteenth-century legislators "read the local newspapers, toured their districts, and talked with voters, received letters from the home state, and entertained delegations which claimed to speak for large and important blocks of voters." [8]

Party and Other Organizations

Until about World War II, state and local party organizations provided the most regular and reliable information about political attitudes. Party leaders were in touch with voters about issues ranging from trade to internal improvements. Attitudes about political matters were revealed by local party meetings, as well as by outside efforts of reform organizations and petition drives. If the issue persisted, officials at higher levels often began to pay attention.

Much of the reform impulse in national politics around the turn of the century came from the activities of parties and reform organizations in states and cities.

As states and localities passed reform legislation for the organization of city government and the regulation of business, national leaders began to shift their way of doing business. Woodrow Wilson's legislative program can be seen as a response to the demands of reform organizations in the states. Franklin D. Roosevelt kept a regular watch on party organizations in cities such as New York, Chicago, Philadelphia, and Detroit.

Party organizations not only offered a rough barometer of popular opinion but also stabilized opinion. Political figures could be more certain of their popular standing with active citizens since party membership demanded some commitment. Polls measure the opinions of uncommitted as well as committed citizens. As political scientist Theodore J. Lowi has written: "The moorings of the voters are now so loose that, regardless of any partisan consistency displayed in local elections (which is lessening too), their relationship to the presidency is highly personal." [9]

The rise of third parties in the pre-polling years offered a dramatic demonstration of changes in public opinion. When the two major parties did not address developing political issues, additional parties developed to give voice to those concerns. Public opinion found expression in third parties on issues such as slavery, agriculture policy, monetary policy, women's rights, and labor relations.

Interest groups and other elected officials have long been vehicles for transmitting opinion information to the president. The Kennedy administration kept a finger on the pulse of the civil rights movement through contacts with leaders of the National Association for the Advancement of Colored People and other organizations. Presidents regularly visit economic leaders in groups such as the Chamber of Commerce and the Business Roundtable.

Public Demonstrations

Public events—such as demonstrations, parades, and riots—have always provided the president and other government leaders with dramatic expressions of public opinion. With the development of more regular and "scientific" means for measuring public opinion, public spectacles have declined in importance.[10]

Protests and demonstrations have served as a means of expressing public opinion throughout U.S. history on issues such as slavery, tariffs, women's rights, ethnic and religious divisions, Prohibition, wars, abuses of monopolies, capital-labor disputes, problems of agriculture, the death penalty, civil rights, welfare rights, school busing, abortion, education, and drug abuse. Despite the dominance of polls as expressions of public opinion, demonstrations have been used since the 1960s to express opinions on civil rights, abortion, and involvement in war.

Demonstrations expressed public opinion most vividly during the 1880s and 1890s when farmers, workers, and owners of small businesses took to the streets to demand government regulation of corporations and basic protections and assistance programs. The protest movements of that period were instrumental in forming populist organizations and campaigns as well as in structuring the countermovements of the progressives and conservatives.[11]

Protest is a way of expressing opinions more for people who either do not have the ballot or find the ballot to be an empty gesture. Political scientist Benjamin Ginsberg has found that nations with regular voting procedures do not experience demonstrations when economic conditions change for the worse; the citizens of nations with more sporadic voting procedures, such as Latin American countries, must take to the streets to express their opinions.[12] The findings suggest that formal procedures for expressing opinion preclude spontaneous development and expression of opinion.

Studies show that lower-income people are more likely to take part in demonstrations than they are to vote. Underrepresented in voting booths and many surveys, these people go to the streets to express their opinions about a wide range of issues.[13]

Newspapers

Until the Civil War, newspapers were partisan sheets designed not so much to deliver news as to persuade or agitate a fiercely partisan audience. The fortunes of a newspaper—especially the size of its circulation, advertising, and the reaction it got from elites and the general public—provided a rough barometer of the public mood. Newspapers also indicated party strength since they depended on the parties for advertising and readership. The newspapers' indications of party strength provided clues about the popularity of presidents. Newspapers were important in shaping as well as measuring public opinion. James Bryce, the noted British analyst of American politics, wrote of readers' acceptance of partisan newspaper versions of events: "They could not be at the trouble of sifting the evidence." [14]

With the newspaper boom of the late nineteenth century, newspapers dropped their blatant partisan ties. Readership of the New York *World,* the nation's first mass-circulation newpaper, rose from 15,000 to 1.5 million between 1883 and 1898.[15] Because newspapers were cheap and geared toward the general public, they reached every class of people. Many cities had a dozen or more newspapers with distinct readerships. The news pages, letter columns, and advertising space all provided clues about the tenor and trend of popular opinion.

Letter Writing

One of the more regular forms of expression is to write letters to the president and other public officials.[16]

In the nation's early years, letter writing was a practice used mostly by economic and educational elites. As the nation expanded its notion of democracy, and as the government extended its reach during times of crisis, the letter-writing population grew to include not only elites but the whole literate public. Then, with the growth of mass communications, the letter became a regular tool of instantaneous public opinion pressure.

The first major letter-writing campaign persuaded George Washington to seek a second term as president in 1792.

Like other forms of political activity, letter-writing booms during periods of national crisis. During periods of "normalcy" before the New Deal, the number of letters written per 10,000 literate adults ranged from 4.7 in 1900 during William McKinley's administration to 11.8 during Herbert C. Hoover's administration before the 1929 economic crash. The letter-writing rate increased during the crises of the Civil War (44 letters per 10,000 literate adults) and World War I (47). A major—and permanent—change came with the public presidency of Franklin D. Roosevelt. Roosevelt's mail rate reached 160 during the Great Depression and fell to 111 during the calm of the late 1930s.

Letter writing still influences both large- and small-scale policy initiatives. As might be expected, however, letter writing has been part of the larger process of technologically sophisticated politics. Computers have become a large part of this once intimate form of communication.

Until recent years, most letters were the work of persons acting on their own initiative. According to one study, less than 10 percent of Franklin Roosevelt's third-term mail could be linked to interest groups: "Mail is very often a means through which unorganized and transitory interests make themselves heard." [17]

Headline events are most likely to spur letter writing. State of the Union addresses, presidential speeches on television, press conferences, congressional hearings, wars and other military events, major appointments, Supreme Court decisions, international summits or meetings, and political scandals spark mass letter writing. The top letter-writing events in recent years include the Vietnam War, the Watergate scandal, the energy crisis, the Iran-contra affair, the appointment of Robert H. Bork to the Supreme Court, events in the Middle East, relations with the Soviet Union, and the testimony of White House aide Lt. Col. Oliver North before a congressional committee.

Many letter-writing campaigns result from the public urging of prominent officials during controversial political events. Sen. Joseph R. McCarthy of Wisconsin, for example, initiated a deluge of letters to President Dwight D. Eisenhower urging that the United States cut ties with countries doing business with the People's Republic of China. Members of Congress who regularly correspond with voters urge constituents to write letters to the president on key issues.

The president, too, sometimes calls for letters to the White House and to Congress to indicate support for presidential policies. Full-time White House staffers read and keep track of letters the president receives to determine the general flow of opinion.

Interest groups have begun to play a more prominent role in spurring letter writing. National organizations and grass-roots organizations often circulate postcards and letters on specific issues for supporters to sign and send to the White House and Congress. Interest groups also print advertisements in newspapers urging a barrage of letters to elected officials. Interest groups with vast memberships are capable of managing letter-writing blitzkriegs to the president, to members of Congress, and to state officials. Those letters often get brief consideration because it is easy for the recipients to see that they are not spontaneous. But they do reinforce the sense of vulnerability of some elected officials.

Even though polls have replaced letters as the regular means for assessing public opinion, letters can provide clues about concerns that are submerged in the restricted format of surveys. In 1954, for example, the Democratic National Committee received a number of letters from people concerned about the effects of inflation on pensions. It was the first indication that inflation was a prime concern among the elderly. Letters can draw attention to issues that pollsters do not include in their surveys.

Besides giving the president a means of measuring public opinion, letter writing provides a way of pressuring other politicians in Washington. The power of letters was vividly underscored when both President Reagan and Rep. Daniel Rostenkowski (D-Ill.) appealed to television audiences to write to them about tax reform issues. The president and congressional leaders both used letters to bolster their arguments during the tax reform procedures.

Telephone Calls and Telegrams

For immediate reaction to political events, telephone calls and telegrams have replaced letters and augmented the increasing use of overnight polls.

Telegrams provide a tangible if biased indication of support. White House officials refer to the volume of positive telegrams to bolster their credibility during crises such as Watergate, Vietnam, the explosion of the space shuttle *Challenger,* and the congressional hearings over the Reagan administration's secret dealings with Iran.

Richard Nixon survived a major crisis as a candidate for vice president in 1952 when he appealed on television for telegrams expressing support. Nixon's "Checkers speech" produced, according to Nixon's own reckoning, between one million and two million telegrams and permitted him to stay on the Republican ticket despite the controversy over the propriety of a fund for his personal expenses.

During the Iran-contra affair in 1987, White House officials and backers pointed to the thousands of telegrams sent to fired National Security Council aide Oliver North as a sign of outward support. North brought bags of the telegrams to the congressional hearings, giving both himself and the White House a boost during the administration's greatest crisis.

During the Iran-contra affair, Reagan referred to the deluge of supportive telephone calls he received. "After my speech, some 84 percent of those people who called in supported me," Reagan said. "It was the biggest outpouring of calls they've ever had. The letters coming in are in my favor." [18]

Development of Formal Surveys and Polling

Presidents and other political figures have used surveys since the early nineteenth century, but only since the development of sophisticated systems of communications and analysis have surveys and polls become a major part of White House efforts to measure and shape public opinion.

Polling data are often sketchy and contradictory, but they at least reduce the uncertainty under which the president operates. As President Reagan's pollster, Richard Wirthlin, suggested, polling is "the science of ABC—almost being certain." [19]

The first poll in the United States was a straw poll of presidential candidates John Quincy Adams and Andrew Jackson that appeared in the *Harrisburg Pennsylvanian* in 1824. With the rise of mass circulation newspapers in the 1880s, polls became regular features. Papers such as the *New York Herald Tribune, Los Angeles Times,* and *St. Louis Republic* all published regular poll results. A 1936 survey of *Literary Digest* readers, which predicted that Alfred Landon would defeat Franklin Roosevelt for the presidency, both damaged polling's credibility and helped pave the way for more sophisticated surveys. The *Digest*'s huge mistake—Roosevelt won by a landslide—could be attributed to the built-in bias of the magazine's predominantly Republican, well-to-do readership.

The founder of modern polling was George Gallup, whose surveys helped his mother-in-law win election as secretary of state in Iowa in 1932. Gallup wrote a doctoral thesis on sampling techniques and in 1935, with Elmo Roper and Archibald Crossley, founded the independent Gallup Poll, which was the leader in scientific polling for decades. Gallup was a key figure in giving polling its scientific credentials by using large, representative sample sizes and carefully worded questions.

Franklin Roosevelt was the first president to use polling data regularly to interpret the public's reactions to the political and policy actions of the administration. As U.S. involvement in World War II became more likely in the late 1930s, Roosevelt got advice from Gallup on how to frame his rhetoric on possible U.S. involvement. Around the same time, Princeton University professor Hadley Cantril conducted surveys to determine the supply and demand of housing and consumer goods as well as public attitudes about the war. Cantril later polled members of the military about their housing and supply conditions during the war.

In 1946, New York lawyer and congressional candidate Jacob K. Javits was believed to be the first candidate for a public office to commission a private political poll.[20] Harry S Truman in 1948 and Dwight Eisenhower in 1952 used polls to develop campaign appeals. With regular information about voter attitudes, elections and governing became more and more intertwined. John F. Kennedy hired pollster Louis Harris two years before his successful 1960 presidential campaign to gauge support and develop strategy.

Polls gradually developed into a daily part of government action and the flow of news and academic analysis. Dozens of newspapers and magazines, television and radio stations, government agencies, business firms, universities, and private organizations commission surveys of political and social attitudes and habits. Surveys are so pervasive that pollsters now ask survey questions about polling itself.[21]

By 1962, virtually all gubernatorial candidates, two-thirds of all Senate candidates, and half the winning candidates for the House of Representatives commissioned polls sometime during their campaigns.

Lyndon B. Johnson was the first president to hire a pollster to the White House staff, Hadley Cantril's son Albert. The administration also consulted the pollster Oliver Quayle regularly. Throughout his term, Johnson kept a steady stream of polling data from every state. Academics working at Johnson's presidential library in Austin have found dozens of memorandums and poll results among Johnson's papers.

When faced with growing opposition to the Vietnam War, Johnson constantly referred to polls that suggested a majority of Americans favoring the administration's war policies. Johnson rejected arguments that most of the nation was uninformed and that those who were knowledgable about the war opposed it. When polls showed a majority of Americans opposing the war effort, Johnson moved toward a decision against seeking a second full term.

Nixon's public-relations campaigns were based on the idea of the "silent majority," which the president claimed backed his administration's policies on Vietnam, civil rights, crime, regulation, social programs and budget priorities, and the Watergate affair. The lack of widespread opposition to his policies, Nixon argued, could be interpreted to be approval. Nixon's argument, in effect, gave as much weight to people with no strong feelings or knowledge as those with well-informed, strong views.

Nixon regularly used polls to formulate policy statements to go over the heads of Congress and interest groups. When polls showed that he was personally popular with blue-collar workers, Nixon decided to ignore the opposition of labor union leadership on issues such as wage and price controls.

Current Public Opinion Efforts

Polls became pervasive in U.S. politics in the 1970s. In 1972, no newspapers conducted their own polls; they relied on private polling organizations. By the end of the decade, most major news organizations conducted their own regular surveys, which became an important part of determining which stories were "news." Polling also became a permanent part of the White House staff with the elections of Jimmy Carter in 1976 and Ronald Reagan in 1980.

Carter's Use of Polls

Carter became president with no Washington experience and an uncertain ideology; he therefore did not have a strong sense of his role in the government. His campaign was successful partly because of the work of Patrick Caddell, a pollster who was one of the top architects of the campaign agenda. Caddell gave Carter regular advice in the White House.[22] Polling data were a regular part of decision making in the Carter White House. Carter often relied on polls to tell him what an ideological "compass" told presidents such as Ronald Reagan.

Perhaps the most significant moment of Carter's presidency was the nationally televised speech he delivered about the country's moral lassitude. During a gas shortage in the summer of 1979, Carter planned to deliver a speech to promote a variety of energy conservation and development initiatives. While working on the address, however, he decided that it would fail to move a public that had already heard four such speeches. Caddell gave Carter polling data and a memorandum recommending a shift in emphasis. Carter's decision to act on the data was one of his presidency's fateful moments.

Caddell's data suggested that the public would react

cynically to another call for new energy conservation. The memorandum said that the public had become "completely inured" to warnings about the energy crisis, and would not make sacrifices because of cynicism about both the government and the oil industry.[23] Caddell argued that the breakdown of faith in U.S. institutions could be overcome only with a dramatic call for common cause and sacrifice. Caddell had made that argument to Carter at least since the 1976 campaign.[24]

Carter's speech—which analyzed a "crisis of confidence" in the American public—originally was well received. But a series of cabinet firings, which Carter acknowledged handling "very poorly," created an atmosphere of crisis not in the nation as much as in the administration.[25] The "malaise" speech, as it came to be known, became a source of ridicule rather than national unity.

Reagan's Use of Polls

Despite widespread criticism of Carter's reliance on polls, Reagan brought campaign pollster Richard Wirthlin with him to the White House in 1981. Reagan was able to have the best of both worlds with in-house polling. While consistently touching on a wide range of common themes, he steered specific public debates according to information supplied by specific polling data. Richard Beal, an associate of Wirthlin, was given a White House job sifting through polling data. White House communications director David Gergen, a founder of the magazine *Public Opinion,* was another influential aide. Annual funding from the Republican National Committee (RNC) of about $900,000 allowed Wirthlin's firm, Decision Making Information, to conduct the most extensive and expensive polls ever undertaken on behalf of a president. Wirthlin was a paid staffer, and in the early Reagan years his firm got paid separately by the RNC for conducting research.

Wirthlin's surveys and regular "tracking" polls—in which changes in a sample of opinion are followed daily—affected administration policy in several areas. Reagan's "honeymoon" poll results persuaded the president to seek dramatic tax and budget legislation in early 1981. Later data, as well as an outcry from legislative leaders and interest groups, persuaded Reagan to drop plans for wholesale changes in Social Security. When the 1982 economic slump threatened big midterm election losses, polling data showed widespread support for giving the administration's tax policies a chance but disturbing declines in support from blue-collar voters. In 1982, Reagan agreed to budget and tax compromises with Congress when polls revealed big drops in the percentage of the public urging the administration to "continue as is."[26] Polling data also guided administration actions on the nomination of Sandra Day O'Connor to the Supreme Court, U.S. involvement in the Lebanese civil war, Reagan's visit to the Bitburg cemetery in West Germany, and tax reform.

Wirthlin's most extensive polling took place in early 1987, when the administration struggled to control the effects of disclosures that the White House had secretly sold arms to Iran in exchange for help in releasing American hostages in Lebanon and that profits from these sales went to help rebels against the government of Nicaragua. During the first six or seven weeks of the year, Wirthlin conducted constant rounds of interviews with a total of twenty-five thousand people—more than most pollsters interview in an entire year.[27]

The Reagan administration, attentive every day to poll results, orchestrated a number of dramatic events that provided surges of support. Foreign summits, Oval Office speeches, military attacks on Libya and Grenada, emotional public appearances after such tragedies as the truck-bombing of the marine barracks in Lebanon and the space shuttle *Challenger* explosion, and strongly worded statements after terrorist attacks and the Soviet attack on the Korean Air Lines plane all provided "rally points" for Reagan.

No president uses polls to determine major policy stances. But polls give the president information about what issues to highlight and downplay. Polls showing public alarm over the truck-bombing of the marine barracks in Lebanon in 1983, for example, alerted the administration

Pete Souza, The White House

Despite criticism of Carter's reliance on polls, Reagan brought campaign pollster Richard Wirthlin with him to the White House in 1981. Wirthlin's surveys and regular tracking polls affected administration policy in several areas.

to the need to shore up public support. Many critics also charge that the U.S. invasion of the tiny island of Grenada two days after the Lebanon bombing was designed to divert public attention from the disaster. As a result of the poll data, Reagan also gave a major television address to increase his support.

Political scientist Philip Converse puts the use of polls into perspective:

> Acquiring relevent public opinion data is not unlike the riverboat captain buying the latest mapping of sandbar configurations before embarking on a voyage. Few politicians consult poll data to find out what they should be thinking on the issues, or to carry out errands. But they have very little interest in flouting the will of their constituency in any tendentious, head-on way. Such data give them a sense of what postures to emphasize and avoid.[28]

Cycles of Presidential Popularity

Presidential popularity tends to decline throughout the four-year term in office, with temporary increases after important international events and at the beginning of a reelection campaign or at the end of the term.

Since 1945, the Gallup Poll has surveyed Americans about once a month to determine popular support for the president. The identical question—"Do you approve or disapprove of the way [the incumbent] is handling his job as president?"—has produced a unique series of data about presidents' relations with the public. The data suggest the limits of presidential leadership via appeals to public opinion.

Every president enjoys a honeymoon period in which the nation gives the new chief executive broad, general support.[29] The administration's early days are considered the best time for a president to pass difficult legislation, such as Carter's energy program or Reagan's tax- and budget-cutting packages. Presidential popularity averages about 69 percent in the first year in office. The approval ratings are much higher early in the year. After their third month in office, Truman received a rating of 89 percent, and Kennedy received a rating of 83 percent. Lyndon Johnson had a rating of 80 percent after his second month, and Gerald R. Ford and Carter had early 71 percent ratings.[30]

Political scientist Samuel Kernell has argued that a president's popularity throughout his term is partly determined by the results of previous polls.[31] Poll results do not vary much from month to month—mostly because only a small segment of the population is likely to veer very far from its orientations, but also because of the public's inertia and use of previous polls to judge the president. Presidents therefore have a strong base of support at the beginning of their term. The key question for the president is how quickly the support will decline.

Since the beginning of the Gallup survey, public approval of the president has ranged from a low of 14 percent under Carter to a high of 87 percent under Truman.[32] The approval rating for Nixon during the final days of perhaps the greatest crisis of the modern presidency—the Watergate affair, which led to Nixon's resignation August 9, 1974—was 23 percent.

The oscillation of support within an administration was greatest during the Truman presidency. Truman's support varied by as much as 64 percentage points, from a low of 23 percent to a high of 87 percent. Eisenhower had the most consistent support. In his first term, approval scores were almost always between 60 and 80 percent, and in the second term the scores were almost always between 50 and 70 percent.

The average level of support for presidents has varied widely, too. Kennedy received the highest average rate of support, 70.5 percent, during his shortened presidency. Other average levels of support are: Eisenhower (64.8), Johnson (56.3), Nixon (48.7), Ford (46.8), Carter (50.1), and Reagan (52.7).

Patterns of Support

Studies by political scientists John E. Mueller and James A. Stimson suggest that public support of the president follows regular patterns, no matter who is president and what policies the president pursues. Mueller argues that the president's popularity declines steadily, in a straight line, after the first several months in office.[33] Stimson argues that popularity ratings follow the form of a parabola, a curve that slowly declines before flattening out and then rising slightly late in the term.[34] Stimson writes: "The president, in this theory, is largely a passive observer of his downsliding popularity."[35]

Both Mueller and Stimson agree that the trend is interrupted—but only temporarily—by "rally points" such as U.S. military involvement overseas, the release of economic news, assassination attempts, and campaign activities. Such events can give a president a spurt of approval above the point on the overall line of decline. But even if a president benefits from public attention to highly visible news, the basic trend of decline is immutable.[36]

Mueller simply states that after an average approval rating of 69 percent early in the term, the president's rating will fall about 6 percentage points each year. Because of a "coalition of minorities" effect—in which groups aggrieved by administration policies slowly but steadily build an antiadministration coalition—presidential popularity ratings form a line in steady decline on a chart. Different presidents decline in popularity at different rates.

Stimson disagrees with Mueller mainly about the dynamic aspects of public opinion. A president's popularity at a given point cannot be considered an isolated judgment of the president, Stimson argues. Instead, one month's approval rating feeds into and influences the next. Rather than simply reflecting accumulation of grievances, as Mueller argues, the decline in popularity is the result of the public's psychological relationship with the president.

Because the public is usually inattentive to politics, it does not know much about presidents. But in the media excitement and soaring rhetoric of a new president, the public develops high expectations of the president. The two factors—inattentiveness and high expectations—are a dangerous combination for presidents. Political scientist Thomas Cronin has written:

> The significance of the textbook presidency is that the whole is greater than the sum of the parts. It presents a cumulative presidential image, a legacy of past glories and impressive performances ... which endows the White House with a singular mystique and almost magical qualities. According to this image ... only men of the caliber of Lincoln, the Roosevelts, or Wilson can seize the chalice of opportunity, create the vision, and rally the American public around that vision.[37]

The public, in effect, wants the president to reach the promised land but it does not appreciate the rockiness of the terrain.

The public's response, Stimson argues, is not just a steady decline of support but a deep disappointment. That deep disappointment is reflected in a fast decline of support. The decline then bottoms out and rises slightly at the end of the term, both because of the public's desire to correct its overreaction and the president's return to more simplistic rhetoric as the reelection campaign approaches.

President Reagan's first-term surge in popularity was unusual. After approval ratings similar to Carter's and Nixon's, Reagan's support surged in his third and fourth years. A January 1983 poll put Reagan's popularity at 35 percent; by his second inauguration, it was almost 62 percent. Scholars attribute the surge to favorable economic trends, such as lower inflation and interest rates, and to adept use of public events to rally the nation around the president's leadership. Another cause also might be the nation's desire for a leader in which it could place faith. After the assassination of President Kennedy and the failed presidencies of Johnson, Nixon, Ford, and Carter, the public may have decided to believe in Reagan's leadership just to give the nation stability it had lacked since the 1950s.

Second-term presidents are generally less popular than first-term presidents. Eisenhower, Johnson, Nixon, and Reagan all had lower support scores after their second inauguration. Johnson and Nixon were driven from the White House at least partly by depressed opinion scores.[38]

The second-term decline has several explanations. First, the president is a "lame duck," without the prospect of a bold reelection campaign to inspire supporters. The public, Congress, and key bureaucrats expect to be involved with national politics after the president's departure, which makes the president's position on long-term issues less and less relevent. Second, problems are more difficult to explain away with reference to the mistakes of the previous president. Reagan constantly referred to the "mess" left him by Carter, but the public was less willing to blame Carter the longer Reagan was in office. Third, the best members of the administration often leave office soon after the president's reelection, creating the aura of a provisional and "second-string" team less deserving of respect. The president also loses top political operatives as they go to work for other politicians who will be involved in public life after the president leaves office. Finally, other politicians, who want to develop an independent base and perhaps succeed the president, try to develop their own political messages distinct from that of the president, reducing the reinforcement that the president's message receives.

Steadiness during the Cycles

Throughout the cycles of presidential approval, the public offers a steady level of support and opposition to the president. Many groups are constantly for or against the president, while "swing" groups fluctuate greatly and cause the ups and downs of presidential approval.

Different segments of the population react to public events according to their education, income, gender, and political involvement.

The president usually can depend on support from citizens who are members of the same party and opposition from members of the opposing party. The groups expressing support for the Vietnam War switched with Republican Richard Nixon's move into the White House and Lyndon Johnson's move out, that is, Republicans generally opposed the war under Johnson but supported it under Nixon. Unless the president deeply offends the basic tenets of party, he usually can count on party identifiers for support. Many of those people actually will be registered with the party, and others will just "lean" toward the party—and rely on the party for cues—on most issues.[39]

Besides these "partisans," the president must also deal with a set of "believers," a small minority of the population with fully developed ideological stances on a wide range of economic, social, and political issues. Believers are committed to a cause, such as the security of Israel, free-market values, or a U.S. struggle to "contain" Soviet geopolitical threats. They also have "psychological predispositions" on issues ranging from military activity to community values. Presidents can count on consistent behavior by believers, just as they can count on consistent behavior by partisans. But the consistency depends on the issue rather than the political affiliation.

Another group—the "followers"—is willing to follow the president's lead on a wide range of issues, especially foreign affairs, simply because the president is the president. This group often associates its support for the president with patriotism—a "my president, right or wrong" attitude.

The battle for public opinion, then, centers on the opinions of the less aligned, more independent citizens. The opinions of people with greater status and involvement fluctuate and polarize more than those of the rest of the population. If they identify with a party, these citizens react to the "cues" of party politics and current events more than people of lower status. But if they are part of the growing number of independents, they react primarily to the constantly shifting set of news events. Because better educated people tend to read newspapers more regularly, they respond to the fluctuations of news more than the rest of the population. If they know that a president is struggling with Congress or the Soviets, for example, a better-informed citizen may alter previously positive feelings about the president. The better-informed citizen has constantly changing "good" and "bad" political news that she or he uses to judge the president.[40]

Why Support Declines

No matter whether the Mueller or Stimson models best depict the trends of approval, it is clear that presidential approval usually declines throughout a term of office. There are several explanations for the decline:

~ Inevitable disappointment after high expectations. Presidential campaigns are exercises in popular education and excitement. As the nation prepares to select its next leader, the candidates attempt to depict the positive changes that would occur in their administration as dramatically as possible.[41]

The public—usually inattentive to politics—gradually gets to know prospective presidents and develops personal attachments to the personalities of the leading contenders. As the media explore the candidates' personal background, voters get an intimate view of the persons who might lead the next government.

When the president takes office, the public has unrealistic expectations of what might be accomplished. When the public begins to see the president's weaknesses, it views the president less and less favorably. Even when it supports the president's stances and policies on specific issues, the public might be critical because of the president's inability to achieve all that was promised. Even when the president is able to deliver on a specific program, support among certain groups might decline because the program yields less impressive results than were expected.

~ Accumulation of grievances. When taking the oath of office for the first time, the president has not yet damaged the material fortunes of any segment of society. Even the most skeptical observers—such as business leaders under a Democratic administration or labor leaders under a Republican administration—are willing to suspend judgment of the new chief executive. Their hope is that their skepticism can be used to move the president closer to their own way of thinking.

As the president submits federal budgets, adopts legislative programs, and uses the "bully pulpit" to promote various social causes, different groups develop specific grievances with the administration. Any public policy decision helps some groups at the expense of others. Even defense and economic policies—which, the president argues, benefit all members of society—have clear winners and losers.

As the president builds a record, some groups develop into consistent winners and others into consistent losers. As the president becomes involved in more and more policy areas, the number of groups affected negatively by policy decisions increases. Even if a group receives some benefits as well as losses because of the administration's policies, the group's support for the president likely will decline because of unhappiness with the losses.

Mueller calls the accumulation of grievances the "coalition of minorities effect." The premise of Mueller's study is that groups that are dissatisfied with government policy are more likely to organize than groups that are satisfied with the government.[42]

Political scientist Richard A. Brody has linked presidential popularity to the amount of "good" and "bad" news the public receives in the media. Brody's model posits that the public keeps a running score of the news about politics and the economy and rewards presidents who have presided over periods full of good news—regardless of their role in creating that news.[43] Still, presidential popularity will decline.

~ Manipulation of the political calendar for electoral advantage. When first taking office, the president has one overriding goal: creating the best possible circumstances for a reelection campaign four years later. Secondary goals include passage of important policies and improvement of the president's party strength in Congress and state governments.

These goals demand different kinds of presidential popularity at different points in the nation's electoral cycles. The president will try to time the administration's policies and pronouncements to produce the support necessary for the crucial electoral and policy-making decisions.

Most presidents, for example, are willing to see their popularity decline after the first year in office. The first year is usually the best time for achieving budgetary and other legislative goals, which require high levels of popularity. After a couple years of lower levels of support—during which the White House might pursue policy goals through regulation and more modest or bipartisan legislative action—the president seeks to boost public support in time for the reelection campaign.

~ Persisting problems. Major national problems—many of which give the president broad support when first exposed publicly—develop into liabilities for the president if they are not resolved quickly.

The Korean War, Vietnam War, Watergate, Iran hostage crisis, fears about drug trafficking and abuse, and American involvement in the Lebanese civil war all gained the president broad public support when they first came to the public's attention. But after those problems remained unsolved for one or more years, the public became disenchanted and turned against the president.

Jimmy Carter's experience with Iran is a dramatic example. When Iranian students stormed the American embassy in Tehran and took fifty-two Americans hostage on November 4, 1979, Carter's popularity jumped dramatically. Carter's approval rating was 14 percent on October 30; the approval rating was 38 percent on November 13, and almost 58 percent the next January 22. As the crisis dragged into the summer months, Carter's popularity ratings dipped into the low 30s.

~ Evidence of a breach of faith. Because of their highly personal relationship with the president, Americans are more likely to lose confidence in the chief executive over a personal moral failing, such as lying, than over ineffective, dangerous, or even immoral policies.

President Nixon's slide in public opinion did not come with revelations that his administration had undertaken questionable activities, such as illegally bombing Cambodia during the Vietnam War, destabilizing the Marxist regime of Chilean leader Salvador Allende, and presiding over a number of unethical campaign practices. The slide came instead with revelations that he had consistently covered up such activities.

Controversial Reagan administration policies in Central America, the Middle East, Iran, and South Africa did not cause Reagan as much trouble as the public's concern that he may have lied about his activities. When former White House aide Oliver North acknowledged and even bragged about breaking the law (shredding government documents, lying to Congress, diverting government funds to Nicaraguan rebels), the White House experienced a surge of support.

Issues Affecting Presidential Popularity

The relative importance of foreign affairs and domestic politics to presidential popularity is difficult to determine. In foreign affairs, the public is quick to unite behind the president because the source of concern is external. But domestic policy usually involves internal divisions, so public support is less monolithic.

Domestic Affairs

Referring to the election adage that people vote according to "pocketbook issues," some students of public opinion maintain that a president is only as popular as the economic conditions allow. During periods of high unemployment or high inflation, the president's popularity is bound to suffer. As the nation's most visible public figure, the president bears the brunt of voter anxiety about the economic health of the country. Likewise, presidents benefit when economic conditions are bright.

The experience of twentieth-century presidents lends some support to the pocketbook interpretation of presidential popularity. The most dramatic example of a president suffering from poor economic conditions was Herbert Hoover, president when the Great Crash of October 1929 plunged the nation into its most severe depression. The popularity of Hoover's successor, Franklin Roosevelt, appeared to decline at the end of his second term when the nation experienced another economic downturn. Historian David Green has argued that the failure of the New Deal to produce prosperity forced Roosevelt to shift political tactics by 1938. To distract the nation from the economic slump, Roosevelt launched public campaigns against "reactionaries" at home and fascists abroad.[44]

Eisenhower's popularity ratings—the steadiest ever recorded for a president—declined when the nation entered a deep recession in 1958. The first poll of the year gave Eisenhower a 60 percent approval rate; by the time of the midterm congressional elections, it was down to 52 percent. Eisenhower also had the highest disapproval scores of his two terms during 1958—as high as 36 percent. More important, Eisenhower's Republicans were thrashed in the congressional campaign, losing forty-seven House seats and fifteen Senate seats.

The 1970s were a particularly difficult time for the U.S. economy, with, at various times, double-digit inflation and unemployment rates, a trebling of energy prices, high interest rates, and unprecedented trade and budget deficits. The conditions led one president, Richard Nixon, to make drastic changes in the U.S. and world monetary systems and to impose wage and price controls for the first time in peacetime.

The presidents during the economic stagnation struggled to maintain a moderate level of popularity. Johnson, Nixon, Ford, Carter, and Reagan all suffered in the polls during perilous economic times. As political scientist Kristen R. Monroe has argued, economic factors such as unemployment and inflation may have both an immediate and a cumulative effect. The public has a "lagged response" to inflation. A single monthly increase in inflation will have a political effect for as many as eleven months. Monroe has written: "The lagged impact suggests that the public has a long memory. The public is not easily distracted by sudden declines in inflation which directly precede an election."[45]

Pocketbook issues besides the nation's economic condition also affect presidential popularity. Tax rates, the strength of social welfare programs, and perceptions of government efficiency all affect the public's sense of economic well-being and, perhaps, its view of the president's performance. Studies show that economic problems are more likely to damage a president's popularity than economic well-being is likely to boost the president's standing.[46]

Other domestic events affect presidential popularity as well. Domestic disturbances such as the urban riots of the 1960s, controversial issues like busing and abortion, protests over the deployment of nuclear weapons, presidential appointments, and domestic scandals all tend to damage the president's popularity.

Political scientist Theodore J. Lowi has argued that "pocketbook" and other domestic issues do not provide the popularity boost that most presidents seek. Instead, a series of foreign policy events often is the only thing that can help a president regain popularity.[47] For example, most analysts attribute President Reagan's strong rebound from low poll ratings during his first term to improvements in the economy. One study states that the rise in Reagan's approval rating from 35 percent to 61 percent "seems to have been caused almost entirely by changes in economic conditions in the country."[48]

Lowi maintains, however, that the economic improvements took place too gradually and affected people in too minor a way to produce Reagan's dramatic turnaround. Indeed, Reagan's ratings on specific economic issues—such as inflation, budget deficits, and efforts to get the country out of the recession and to help groups in economic distress—were very negative. Lowi points to other evidence against the pocketbook explanation for presidential popularity. Economic conditions improved in both 1968 and 1976 but did not help Presidents Johnson and Ford, whose high negative ratings and intense public opposition prevented both from winning reelection.

The Foreign Policy Explanation

Reagan experienced impressive improvements in his approval rating after foreign policy events with which he associated publicly, such as the bombing of the U.S. embassy in Lebanon, the Soviet attack on the Korean Air Lines plane, the redeployment of marines in Lebanon, changes of leadership in the Soviet Union, and the invasion of Grenada.

As Lowi has suggested, foreign policy events of short duration help a president's public standing, even if the event was not considered a "success" for the president. Domestic politics have a less certain effect on ratings. Economic news is considered the most useful domestic event for a president, but many experts question how much it can help a president's overall standing. Other domestic events are more divisive, since they almost always produce clear losers as well as winners.

That president's tendency to get more involved with foreign policy as the term progresses may be an indicator of the public's inclination to "rally 'round the flag." Other reasons for greater presidential involvement in foreign policy exist, such as the greater experience and expertise that the administration acquires over time. But the steady decline in approval ratings gives the president reason to take actions that provide at least temporary surges of support.

The public's willingness to back a president in times of international crisis is almost complete. President John Kennedy marveled at his public support after an event that he acknowledged to be a complete failure, the aborted invasion of Cuba and attempted overthrow of Fidel Castro at the Bay of Pigs. Kennedy's public approval rating jumped from 73 to 83 percent after the disaster, with only 5 percent giving negative views. A Democratic fund raiser in Chicago produced an overwhelming show of support for Kennedy.

Kennedy and other presidents have experienced surges of support after other major foreign policy events, whether or not they could be considered "successes." Kennedy's own foreign policy crises included the Cuban missile crisis, the construction of the Berlin Wall to separate the eastern and western parts of Berlin, the Kennedy-Khrushchev showdown at Vienna, and the assassination of South Vietnamese president Ngo Dinh Diem, as well as the Bay of Pigs disaster.

Incidents producing gains in the president's approval rating include: the Gulf of Tonkin crisis (Johnson); early bombing of North Vietnam and Cambodia (Nixon); the *Mayaguez* incident and the fall of Saigon (Ford); the tak-

Table 1 Effect of Foreign Policy Events on Presidential Popularity, 1939-1975

Date and type of event	Incumbent	Specific event	Popularity Before	Popularity After	Change	Duration in months
Wars and military crises						
1941/12	Roosevelt	Pearl Harbor	72	84	+12	8
1962/10	Kennedy	Cuban missile crisis	61	73	+12	8
1975/5	Ford	*Mayaguez* incident	40	51	+11	8
1950/6	Truman	North Korea invades South Korea	37	46	+9	5
1961/7	Kennedy	Berlin crisis	71	79	+8	12
1966/6	Johnson	Extension of bombing, Hanoi	48	56	+8	2
1967/6	Johnson	War in the Middle East	44	52	+8	1
1958/7	Eisenhower	Troops sent to Lebanon	52	58	+6	3
1965/4	Johnson	Troops to Dominican Republic	64	70	+6	3
1939/8	Roosevelt	War starts in Europe	57	61	+4	—
1970/4	Nixon	Troops to Cambodia	56	59	+3	2
1948/4	Truman	Berlin blockade	36	39	+3	1
1965/2	Johnson	Bombing North Vietnam	68	69	+1	1
1971/1	Nixon	Expansion of war to Laos	56	49	−7	14
Peace and reconciliations						
1973/2	Nixon	Vietnam settlement	51	67	+16	2
1954/7	Eisenhower	Indochina truce signed	64	75	+11	2
1951/6	Truman	Korean talk begins	25	29	+4	5
1968/4	Johnson	Partial bombing halt	42	46	+4	5
1953/7	Eisenhower	Korean truce signed	71	74	+3	2
1974/5	Nixon	Middle East ceasefire	25	28	+3	1
1963/10	Kennedy	Test ban treaty signed	56	58	+2	1
1968/10	Johnson	Full bombing halt	42	43	+1	1
Summit conferences						
1959/12	Eisenhower	Good-will tour to Europe	67	76	+9	1
1972/5	Nixon	Trip to Russia	53	62	+9	2
1970/10	Nixon	Trip to Europe	51	58	+7	2
1959/9	Eisenhower	Camp David	61	66	+5	7
1975/11	Ford	Trip to China	41	46	+5	1
1955/7	Eisenhower	Geneva summit	72	76	+4	2
1972/2	Nixon	Trip to China	52	56	+4	1
1973/6	Nixon	Brezhnev visit	44	43	−1	1
1974/7	Nixon	Trip to Russia	26	24	−2	1
1961/6	Kennedy	Summit with Khrushchev	74	71	−3	1
Policy initiatives						
1947/3	Truman	Truman Doctrine announced	48	60	+12	9
1969/10	Nixon	Vietnamization speech	56	67	+11	1
1953/11	Eisenhower	UN speech on atom	58	66	+8	6
1961/2	Kennedy	Peace Corps	72	78	+6	6
1948/4	Truman	Marshall Plan announced	36	39	+3	1
1941/6	Roosevelt	Lend-lease program	73	73	0	0
International setbacks						
1973/12	Nixon	Vietnam talks break off	59	51	−8	1
1968/1	Johnson	Tet offensive-*Pueblo*	48	41	−7	5
1975/4	Ford	Cambodia falls	44	39	−5	2
1951/4	Truman	MacArthur recalled	28	24	−4	2
1960/5	Eisenhower	Japan trip canceled	65	61	−4	1
1950/11	Truman	China intervenes	39	36	−3	7
1951/8	Truman	Korean talks break off	31	30	−1	1
1957/10	Eisenhower	*Sputnik* launched	57	60	+3	1
1960/5	Eisenhower	U-2 incident	62	65	+3	1

Source: Jong R. Lee, "Rallying around the Flag: Foreign Policy Events and Presidential Popularity," *Presidential Studies Quarterly* 7 (Fall 1977): 254-255; and Center for the Study of the Presidency, New York, N.Y.

The Great Communicator: Reagan after Grenada, 1983

Reagan was falling in public esteem immediately after the deaths of 241 marines in Beirut on October 23, 1983, and the invasion of the Caribbean island of Grenada on October 25. His response, on October 27, came in the form of a masterful television address to the nation that immediately boosted his ratings and had a chilling effect on critics. (These findings are from national *Washington Post/ABC News* opinion polls the evening before and the evening after the address.)

Q: Would you say the United States is trying to do too much with its armed forces overseas, or not?

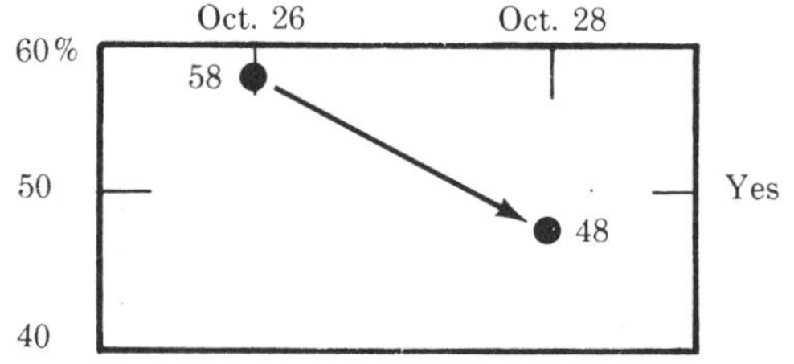

Q: Do you approve of the way Reagan is handling the situation in Lebanon?

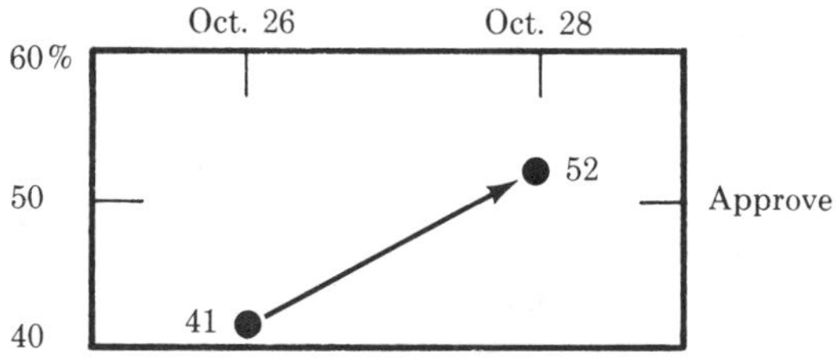

Q: Would you say you approve or disapprove of the invasion of Grenada by U.S. troops?

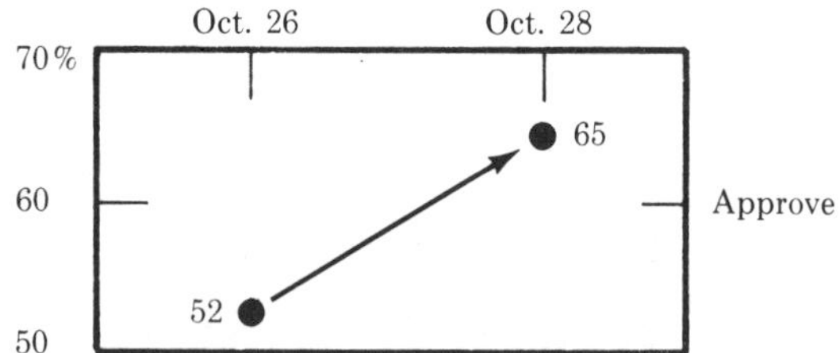

Q: Do you approve or disapprove of the way Ronald Reagan is handling his job as president?

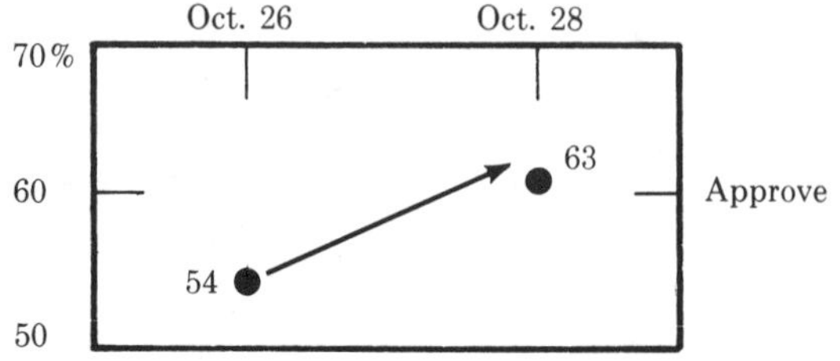

Source: Barry Sussman, *What Americans Really Think* (New York: Pantheon, 1988), 70.

ing of American hostages at the U.S. embassy in Iran and the Soviet invasion of Afghanistan (Carter); and the bombing of a discotheque in Berlin, terrorist attacks in Europe, the attack on a Korean Air Lines plane that strayed into Soviet territory, the Grenada invasion, the U.S. bombing of Libya, and the U.S. response to crises in the Philippines and Haiti (Reagan).[49]

It might be incorrect to ascribe paramount importance to either domestic or foreign policy issues for presidential popularity; both policy areas can increase or decrease the president's range of options. Domestic concerns perhaps provide a more durable base of popularity. Foreign policy events, by contrast, provide a dramatic but fleeting opportunity for the president to build popularity.

Effects of Opinion on Public Debate

Especially since the dawn of the media age, the president's popularity has been an important tool for attaining public policy goals. Presidents use information about their level of public support to persuade Congress to go along with their proposals for foreign and domestic policies.

Especially on issues on which the public has not formed strong opinions, presidents can shape public opinion simply by speaking out on an issue. The public's deep-seated desire to support its president gives the president opportunities for moving the population. A number of surveys have determined that the public is more willing to support an initiative if it knows the president proposed or backed the measure. One researcher, Corey Rosen, for example, found different samples showing different levels of support for proposals when respondents are either told or not told that the president backs the proposals.[50] The identification of the proposal with the president served to "personify" the policy and brought support in line with public approval of the president.

Political scientist Lee Sigelman used one sample to determine that public support for the policy rises when respondents are told of the president's position. Sigelman found the public less willing to go along with the president's policies as the president's position became more "radical."[51] The latter finding suggests that the president's prestige depends to a great extent on a strong base of public respect for the president's office. That respect is one of the nation's fundamental values. As presidents move away from the nation's other fundamental values with "radical" proposals, they might lose the public's automatic support.

History offers additional evidence for the academic findings of Rosen and Sigelman. Public support for President Truman's proposed aid to Greece and Turkey—which was not a prominent issue at the time—rose dramatically after Truman's speech of 1947 on the matter.[52] Support for bombing Hanoi and Haiphong increased from 50 to 80 percent after the bombing there began in 1966.[53] Before Lyndon Johnson announced a halt to bombing of North Vietnam on March 31, 1968, only 40 percent of the public opposed bombing the enemy. In early April, polls showed that 64 percent approved the bombing halt.

Samuel Kernell has argued that "going public" has at least partly replaced negotiation with other powerful actors in Washington as a means of achieving policy goals. By referring to the public's general support for the president and its support for specific policies, the White House takes the initiative away from Congress. Congress is given the choice of supporting the president's agenda or facing the wrath of voters back home.[54] Congress almost always gives the president the initiative, especially on foreign policy.[55]

Influencing Capitol Hill

The link between presidential approval ratings and support of the White House on Capitol Hill is not clear. Political scientist Richard E. Neustadt has argued that high approval ratings and poll support for specific policies help the president persuade Congress to support key policy proposals.[56] But the record of postwar presidents suggests that the link is indirect and that other factors enter into the calculation of Congress and other actors to follow the president.

One reason Congress pays attention to presidential popularity is that many members of Congress have no other regular barometer of the public mood. The president is the dominant figure in national politics, and when the public reacts to administration stands, members of Congress gain a sense of public opinion. Another reason is that the public generally expects Congress to cooperate with the president.[57]

Political scientist George C. Edwards III analyzed the president-Congress link with a statistical analysis of congressional roll-call votes and presidential popularity polls. Constituents expect their representatives to cooperate with the president, and Congress members respond to the general desires of their major supporters back home. "In effect, congressmen choose which groups within their constituencies they will represent. These groups will generally be part of their successful electoral coalitions. In addition, it is these groups with whom the congressmen are likely to communicate most frequently." [58]

Edwards found that congressional support for the president was strongest with "secure" Congress members and on foreign policy issues. Not surprisingly, Edwards found, partisanship played a role in the responses of both the Congress members and their constituents. Edwards argued that the president should "attempt to influence congressmen indirectly by strengthening his support among the American people." [59] Such a strategy, however, is limited by partisan and other considerations.

Statistical analysis by political scientist Harvey G. Zeidenstein concluded that a president's public support affects the willingness of Congress to go along with the president on key votes. Of all the congressional votes on which presidents from Eisenhower to Carter expressed a preference, 27 percent can be explained by the president's public approval ratings. The explanatory power of presidential ratings increases to 46 percent when the Eisenhower administration is removed from the sample.[60]

Eisenhower's popularity, unlike that of his successors, did not greatly influence congressional action. The Eisenhower exception helps to explain the limits of the link between presidential popularity and congressional support. Other factors were clearly more important in Eisenhower's congressional support, such as his rocky relations with his own party in Congress, an absence of divisive public issues, moderate legislative proposals, and a willingness to allow Congress to act without presidential prodding.[61]

If a president decides to use high approval ratings as a tool in working with Congress, the result could be greater acceptance of White House initiatives. Eisenhower apparently was not as inclined as other presidents to risk his personal support on specific programs. Eisenhower might have been concerned that identifying with one side in a controversial matter would give the other side reason to reduce its support for him.

There are many examples of the link of popularity and congressional action. Congress went along with President Reagan's budget, tax, and military policies during the height of his popularity but started to distance itself from Reagan when he struggled. Congress cut off funds for the Vietnam War as President Nixon's popularity plunged.

Public Opinion

The regularity of polling operations on every conceivable issue gives the president and other political figures the opportunity to shape public opinion and react to it.

Pollsters gather information daily about the ways all kinds of citizens think on a variety of issues, including many hypothetical situations. Polling data include combinations of conditions to which the polling subject can respond. The president can anticipate the way the population—and specific groups of the population—will react to large and small initiatives on any issue imaginable. By analyzing polling data, the president can know, for example, what the Jewish population thinks about the administration's policies in Lebanon and other parts of the Middle East and what it thinks about different approaches to the broad problems as well as the minor elements of the situation.

With the inevitable decline in popularity, the president is inclined to take dramatic, public actions to improve poll ratings. Presidential leadership then "tilts" toward dramatic actions designed to bolster approval ratings rather than concerted effort and cooperation with other government officials to deal with complex problems.

George Gallup relates the public's desire for strong leadership to the president's sometimes feverish activity to boost ratings:

> I would say that any sharp drop in popularity is likely to come from the president's inaction in the face of an important crisis. Inaction hurts a president more than anything else. A president can take some action, even a wrong one, and not lose his popularity.... People tend to judge a man by his goals, what he's trying to do, and not necessarily by what he accomplishes or how well he succeeds. People used to tell us over and over again about all the things that Roosevelt did wrong and then they would say, "I'm all for him, though, because his heart is in the right place; he's trying." [62]

Recent events appear to support Gallup's statement: Nixon's trips to the Soviet Union and China in 1974 during the height of the Watergate controversy, Ford's military action against Cambodia after the attack on the *Mayaguez,* Carter's dramatic actions after the Soviet invasion of Afghanistan and the Iranian seizure of hostages, and Reagan's Grenada and Libya attacks.

Implications of Polling

Changes in public opinion measurement have produced a fundamental alteration in the way groups press political demands and political leaders respond to those problems. Scholars have disagreed about whether a system with constant polling promotes or damages democracy.

Some argue that regular polling makes political leaders responsive to the wishes of the electorate more than infrequent elections ever could. Gallup, one of the pioneers of modern polling, maintains that elected officials can be expected to do a better job if they have "an accurate measure of the wishes, aspirations, and needs of different groups within the general public."[63] Behavior in office that is influenced by polls is a kind of rolling election campaign, with officials constantly on the lookout for ways to please and avoid displeasing the public.

Proponents of polling stress the "scientific" nature of findings and the increasingly sophisticated views of the political landscape that well-done polls offer. If gathered comprehensively, proponents say, polls can offer a more complete picture of politics than any other single tool.

Others disagree. Political scientist Benjamin Ginsberg argues that polls have the effect of stifling public expressions rather than measuring them in a neutral manner for voter-conscious political leaders.

The regular assessment of a wide variety of public attitudes—where a diverse range of issues is assessed according to the many demographic characteristics of survey respondents—enables the government to "manage" demands rather than dealing with the complex problems that produce political demands. By determining which groups in society would object to certain governmental actions, the government is able to adapt its policies and presentation of those policies to avoid conflict. Many issues, then, never receive the full public discussion that they might if the public pulse were not so regularly tested.

Ginsberg cites a federal conservation program that surveys found to have aroused opposition in southern communities. Rather than canceling the program or negotiating with citizens, administrators used polling data to pinpoint the public's most nagging concerns and use propaganda to dispell those concerns.

> Opinion surveys provided officials with more or less reliable information about current popular sentiment, offered a guide to the character of the public relations efforts that might usefully be made, and served as means of measuring the effect of "information programs" on a target population. In essence, polling allowed officials a better opportunity to anticipate, regulate, and manipulate popular attitudes.[64]

Presidents Carter and Reagan employed full-time White House pollsters who monitored the vagaries of public opinion among all imaginable demographic groups. Other parts of the federal government—from executive departments and agencies to Congress—also use polls regularly to monitor and shape public opinion. To the extent that such polling allows public officials to head off a full discussion of major issues, critics argue, democracy is thwarted.

Ginsberg also is concerned about the way polling shapes the expression of public opinion. He has argued that poll data channel political expression into formulations provided by the pollster that discourage group political action. Besides allowing government officials to manage public opinion, polls have four possible negative effects on democratic expression.

First, polling eliminates the cost of expressing an opinion, which reduces the influence of the people most concerned and knowledgable about various issues. Polls tally the preferences of cross-sections of the population that include people who do not know or care about issues. The respondent's knowledge and the issue's salience are usually ignored. "Polls, in effect, submerge individuals with strongly held views in a more apathetic mass public."[65]

Second, polls shift the concern of public debate from behavior to attitudes. Where expressions of opinion previously took the form of demonstrations that required some kind of public interaction, polls simply tally the isolated responses of survey subjects. Polls give the government the opportunity to shape opinion before it can enjoy full debate, thereby reducing public engagement.

Third, polls shift politics from the group to the individual. Before polls, citizens needed to band together to express their desires and demands. Such a requirement served to build political institutions such as parties, unions, neighborhood groups, and farmer cooperatives. Active involvement in such groups has declined as public officials have turned to polls for information about public opinion.

Fourth, polls shift political expression from assertions to responses. Survey subjects can react only to the agenda of the poll-taker; they rarely make an independent assertion. The subjects that respondents—and therefore, the public—can discuss is thereby limited to the interests of pollsters.

Notes

1. E. E. Schattschneider, *The Semisovereign People* (New York: Holt, Rinehart, and Winston, 1960).
2. This discussion relies mostly on the following studies by Fred I. Greenstein: "Popular Images of the President," *American Journal of Psychiatry* 122, no. 5 (November 1965): 523-529; "The Benevolent Leader: Children's Images of Presidential Authority," *American Political Science Review* 54 (December 1960): 934-943; "College Student Reactions to the Assassination of President Kennedy," in *Communication in Crisis*, ed. B. Greenberg and E. Parker (Stanford, Calif.: Stanford University Press, 1965); and "What the President Means to Americans," in *Choosing the President*, ed. James David Barber (Englewood Cliffs, N.J.: Prentice-Hall, 1974), 121-147. See also Roberta S. Sigel, "Image of the American Presidency, Part II of An Exploration into Popular Views of Presidential Power," *Midwest Journal of Political Science* 10 (February 1966): 123-137.
3. Greenstein, "What the President Means to Americans," 125, 128-129.
4. The respect for the presidency is not uniformly strong. Groups that are left out of the mainstream of economic and political life, such as blacks and Appalachian whites, respond less favorably to mention of the presidency and specific presidents.
5. Murray Edelman, *The Symbolic Uses of Politics* (Urbana: University of Illinois Press, 1985), 78.
6. Samuel Kernell, Peter W. Sperlich, and Aaron Wildavsky, "Public Support for Presidents," in *Perspectives on the Presidency*, ed. Aaron Wildavsky (Boston: Little, Brown, 1975), 150, 158-164.
7. For examinations of consensus in U.S. politics, see Louis Hartz, *The Liberal Tradition in America* (New York: Harcourt, Brace, Jovanovich, 1955); Daniel Boorstin, *The Genius of American Democracy* (Chicago: University of Chicago Press, 1958); Daniel Bell, *The End of Ideology* (Glencoe, Ill.: Free Press, 1960); and Samuel H. Beer, "In Search of a New Political Philosophy," in *The New American Political System*, ed. Anthony King (Washington, D.C.: American Enterprise Institute, 1978), 5-44.
8. Benjamin Ginsberg, *The Captive Public* (New York: Basic Books, 1986), 61.

9. Theodore J. Lowi, *The End of Liberalism* (New York: Norton, 1979), 91.
10. Michael Lipsky, "Protest as a Political Resource," *American Political Science Review* 62 (December 1968): 1144-1158.
11. Richard A. Cloward and Frances Fox Piven, "Toward a Class-Based Realignment of American Politics: A Movement Strategy," *Social Policy* (Winter 1983): 8.
12. Ginsberg, *Captive Public*, 56-57.
13. See Frances Fox Piven and Richard A. Cloward, *Regulating the Poor* (New York: Random House, 1972), and *Poor People's Movements* (New York: Random House, 1979).
14. Quoted in Michael E. McGerr, *The Decline of Popular Politics* (New York: Oxford University Press, 1986), 22.
15. Daniel Boorstin, *The Americans: The Democratic Experience* (New York: Random House, 1973), 403.
16. Leila Sussman, "Dear Mr. President," in *Readings in American Public Opinion*, ed. Edward E. Walker et al. (New York: American Book Company, 1968).
17. Barry Sussman, *What Americans Really Think* (New York: Pantheon Books, 1988), 336.
18. Ibid., 226.
19. James R. Beniger and Robert J. Guiffra, Jr., "Public Opinion Polling: Command and Control in Presidential Campaigns," in *Presidential Selection*, ed. Alexander Heard and Michael Nelson (Durham, N.C.: Duke University Press, 1987), 189.
20. Larry J. Sabato, *The Rise of Political Consultants* (New York: Basic Books, 1981), 105.
21. Herbert Asher, *Polling and the Public* (Washington, D.C.: CQ Press, 1988), 13.
22. For a critique of Caddell's conception of politics and polling, see Sidney Blumenthal, "Mr. Smith Goes to Washington," *The New Republic*, February 6, 1984, 17-20.
23. Jimmy Carter, *Keeping Faith* (New York: Bantam Books, 1982), 114.
24. Sabato, *Rise of Political Consultants*, 74-75.
25. Carter, *Keeping Faith*, 123.
26. Laurence I. Barrett, *Gambling with History* (New York: Doubleday, 1983), 351-352.
27. Sussman, *What Americans Really Think*, 35-36.
28. Philip E. Converse, "Changing Conceptions of Public Opinion in the Political Process," *Public Opinion Quarterly* 51 (1987): 22.
29. Some scholars argue that the honeymoon is no longer something a new president can rely upon. See Karen S. Johnson, "The Honeymoon Period: Fact or Fiction," *Journalism Quarterly* 62 (Winter 1985): 869-876.
30. Gary King and Lyn Ragsdale, *The Elusive Executive: Discovering Statistical Patterns in the Presidency* (Washington, D.C.: CQ Press, 1988), 295-307.
31. Political scientist Theodore J. Lowi has argued that the honeymoon, the period in which presidents try "sincerely to succeed according to their oath and their promises," is the only opportunity for the president to achieve major policy gains—and that period is shortening. See Lowi, *The Personal President*, (Ithaca, N.Y.: Cornell University Press, 1985), 7-11.
32. King and Ragsdale, *The Elusive Executive*, 292-293.
33. See John E. Mueller, *War, Presidents, and Public Opinion* (New York: Wiley, 1973). Mueller's shorter works include "Presidential Popularity from Truman to Johnson," *American Political Science Review* 64 (March 1970): 18-34; and "Trends in Popular Support for the Wars in Korea and Vietnam," *American Political Science Review* 65 (June 1971): 358-375.
34. James A. Stimson, "Public Support for American Presidents: A Cyclical Model," *Public Opinion Quarterly* 40 (Spring 1976): 1-21.
35. Ibid., 10.
36. See the works by Mueller and Jong R. Lee, "Rallying Around the Flag: Foreign-Policy Events and Presidential Popularity," *Presidential Studies Quarterly* 7 (Fall 1977): 252-256.
37. Thomas E. Cronin, *The State of the Presidency* (Boston: Little, Brown, 1980), 84.
38. King and Ragsdale, 296-307.
39. This discussion relies on John E. Mueller, "Public Opinion and the President," in *The Presidency Reappraised*, ed. Rexford G. Tugwell and Thomas E. Cronin (New York: Praeger, 1974), 133-147. It should be emphasized that the categories overlap; for example, a citizen can have elements of both the partisan and the follower.
40. See ibid. and Richard A. Brody and Benjamin I. Page, "The Impact of Events on Presidential Popularity: The Johnson and Nixon Administrations," in *Perspectives on the Presidency*, ed. Wildavsky, esp. 145: "Foreign events reach people through news reports, [while] some domestic events, like real personal income, may be perceived without mediation."
41. Eric B. Herzik and Mary L. Dodson have suggested that the "climate of expectations" has more to do with the president's personal appeal than with programmatic plans ("The President and Public Expectations: A Research Note," *Presidential Studies Quarterly* 12 [Spring 1982], 168-173).
42. Mueller, "Presidential Popularity," 20-21.
43. Richard A. Brody, "Public Evaluations and Expectations and the Future of the Presidency," in *Problems and Prospects of Presidential Leadership in the 1980's*, ed. James Sterling Young (New York: University Press of America, 1982), 45-49. See also Stanley Kelley, *Interpreting Elections* (Princeton, N.J.: Princeton University Press, 1983), for a similar view of how voters make judgments.
44. David Green, *Shaping Political Consciousness* (New York: Oxford University Press, 1988), 126-134.
45. Kristen R. Monroe, "Inflation and Presidential Popularity," *Presidential Studies Quarterly* 9 (Summer 1979): 339. See also Kristen R. Monroe, "Economic Influences on Presidential Popularity," *Public Opinion Quarterly* (1978): 360-370. Kim Ezra Sheinbaum and Ervin Sheinbaum, "Public Perceptions of Presidential Economic Performance: From Johnson to Carter," *Presidential Studies Quarterly* 12 (Summer 1982): 421-427, find a strong link between prosperity and popularity. Henry C. Kenski, in "The Impact of Economic Conditions on Presidential Popularity," *Journal of Politics* 39 (1977): 764-773, argues that high unemployment and inflation rates affect Republican and Democratic presidents differently.
46. Henry C. Kenski, "The Impact of Unemployment on Presidential Popularity from Eisenhower to Nixon," *Presidential Studies Quarterly* 7 (Spring-Summer 1977): 114-126.
47. Lowi's analysis of the spurts in presidential popularity is part of his overall critique of the public presidency. See Lowi, *The Personal President*.
48. Thomas Ferguson and Joel Rogers, *Right Turn* (New York: Hill and Wang, 1986), 26.
49. See Mueller, *War, Presidents, and Public Opinion*.
50. Corey Rosen, "A Test of Presidential Leadership of Public Opinion: The Split Ballot Technique," *Polity* 6 (1972): 282-290.
51. Lee Sigelman, "Gauging the Public Response to Presidential Leadership," *Presidential Studies Quarterly* 10 (Summer 1980): 427-433.
52. Samuel Kernell, "The Truman Doctrine Speech: A Case Study of the Dynamics of Presidential Opinion Leadership," *Social Science History* 1 (Fall 1976): 20-45.
53. See Mueller, *War, Presidents, and Public Opinion*.
54. Samuel Kernell, *Going Public: New Strategies of Presidential Leadership* (Washington, D.C.: CQ Press, 1986).
55. Mueller, "Public Opinion and the President," 141.
56. Richard E. Neustadt, *Presidential Power* (New York: Wiley, 1980), 64-73.
57. See George C. Edwards III, "Presidential Influence in the House: Presidential Prestige as a Source of Presidential Power," *American Political Science Review* 70 (March 1976): 101-113.
58. Edwards, "Presidential Influence in the House, " 107.
59. Ibid., 113.
60. Harvey G. Zeidenstein, "Presidential Popularity and Presidential Support in Congress: Eisenhower to Carter," *Presidential Studies Quarterly* 10 (Spring 1980): 227.
61. Ibid., 227-230. See also Harvey G. Zeidenstein, "Varying Relationships between Presidents' Popularity and Their Legisla-

tive Success," *Presidential Studies Quarterly* 13 (Fall 1983): 530-548.
62. Quoted in Edelman, *Symbolic Uses of Politics*, 78.
63. Quoted in Ginsberg, *Captive Public*, 237.
64. Ibid., 85.
65. Ibid., 65.

Selected Bibliography

Asher, Herbert. *Polling and the Public*. Washington, D.C.: CQ Press, 1988.

Edelman, Murray. *The Symbolic Uses of Politics* (Urbana: University of Illinois Press, 1985).

Ginsberg, Benjamin. *The Captive Public*. New York: Basic Books, 1986.

King, Gary, and Lyn Ragsdale. *The Elusive Executive: Discovering Statistical Patterns in the Presidency*. Washington, D.C.: CQ Press, 1988.

Lowi, Theodore, J. *The Personal President*. Ithaca, N.Y.: Cornell University Press, 1985.

Mueller, John E. *War, Presidents, and Public Opinion*. New York: Wiley, 1973.

The Presidency and Interest Groups

Balancing the demands of organized interests always has been a major part of the president's job. Observers of U.S. politics have noted Americans' distinctive tendency to form private associations to pursue their political ends, as well as the president's difficulty controlling such groups.

An interest group may be defined as a set of people who form associations to promote ideals or material benefits. Groups usually know in advance what ends they want to pursue, but their goals and tactics evolve according to their relationship with other forces in society. Because interest groups usually seek assistance available only from the public, they often go to the government with their claims.

In U.S. politics, the president has played a greater role in interest group activity in the years following the New Deal and World War II.[1]

Constitutional Debate about "Factions"

Debate over the U.S. Constitution framed the major issues of interest group politics that occupy students of U.S. government today. After the completion of the Constitution in Philadelphia in 1787, Federalists and Anti-Federalists debated about the best way to achieve adequate "energy" in the federal government and the presidency without stifling free debate and competition among social groups, which are central to a democratic society. The debate's basic tension has persisted to the modern day.

James Madison presented what has come to be the main justification for interest group politics.[2] In *Federalist* No. 10, Madison argued that separate, competing interests were inevitable in a free society and that trying to snuff out this competition would require the drastic step of curbing free thought and action. The goal of government should not be to ban interest groups, Madison argued, but to control them by competition. In *Federalist* No. 10, Madison wrote:

> As long as the reason of man continues fallible, and he is at liberty to exercise it, different opinions will be formed.... From the protection of different and unequal faculties of acquiring property, the possession of different degrees and kinds of property immediately results; and from the influence of these on the sentiments and views of the respective proprietors ensues a division of the society into different interests and parties.[3]

Alexis de Tocqueville, a nineteenth-century French aristocrat, argued in his classic study *Democracy in America* that the "equality of conditions" and the lack of a feudal tradition in the United States gave Americans the freedom to pursue their interests by using large and small associations. Tocqueville wrote:

> Americans of all ages, all conditions, and all dispositions, constantly form associations. They have not only commercial and manufacturing companies, but associations of a thousand other kinds—religious, moral, serious, futile, general or restricted, enormous or diminutive.... Wherever, at the head of some new undertaking, you see the government in France, or a man of rank in England, in the United States you will be sure to find an association.[4]

Tocqueville argued that the American condition was a double-edged sword. He feared that the United States could develop into a "tyranny of the majority" because equality would undermine citizens' willingness to be tolerant of people who express unpopular ideas or have different characteristics. But he said equality and freedom of expression also enabled a variety of institutions—newspapers, the legal profession, and interest groups—to brake the tendency of majorities to impose their will on the entire population.

When Tocqueville published his work in 1835 and 1840, interest groups were established mainly at the local level. State and local governments had control over most matters of public life, including property laws, banking and commerce, morals, education, use of land and resources, and criminal procedures. The states and localities also played an important part in developing "internal improvements," such as roads, canals, railroads, schools, hospitals, and agricultural enterprises.[5]

John C. Calhoun, one of the South's great champions in the nineteenth century, developed another doctrine of interest groups that had a profound effect on U.S. history. Calhoun's theory of "concurrent majorities" asserts that the legitimacy of national government action depends on the acquiescence of the interests affected by the action. The distinct interests of the states, Calhoun said, deserved protection from the larger interests of the nation. Calhoun argued that a state could "nullify," or veto, federal actions

By Charles C. Euchner

that usurp state independence.

Calhoun's home state of South Carolina invoked the doctrine of nullification after enactment of a tariff bill in 1828 that state officials considered discriminatory against the South. President Andrew Jackson responded by sending warships to the harbor of Charleston, and the state legislature soon revoked the act of nullification.

Even though Jackson defeated the most extreme form of concurrent majorities, the theory remained a part of U.S. politics. The notion that states' rights have priority over the national interest led to the Civil War. After the war, the states' rights view held considerable sway in national political debate. In the compromise over the 1876 presidential election, the national government ceded considerable autonomy to the states over issues of basic civil rights and commerce. *(See "The Compromise of 1876," p. 286, in The Electoral Process chapter of Part II.)*

When the states' rights view crumbled as the national government's rise gained strength in the twentieth century, a doctrine similar in many ways to Calhoun's theory arose. Especially since the Great Society of the 1960s, a practice that might be called "representational democracy" has guided policy making in national politics. This practice encourages or requires the government to gain the consent of groups affected by legislation or regulations before it implements such policies.

The "Two Republics" of U.S. History

As political scientist Theodore J. Lowi has argued, the United States has progressed into two distinct styles of government which he calls the first and second "republics." The national government in the early years of the United States was a "patronage state" based on the demands for internal improvements by governments and businesses at the state and local level.[6] The national party system, with the president at its apex, played an important role in the process of internal development. That process remained fundamentally parochial—congressional and party leaders from the states merely vied for a fair share of patronage—until Franklin D. Roosevelt's New Deal programs of the 1930s.

National politics developed cohesion in the nineteenth century at least partly because of the development of presidential leadership. Regional politics have always been important because the different demands for internal improvements stem from the needs of the distinctive geographic, economic, and social makeups of different areas. But since national party alliances developed around presidential elections, the president has always been an important part of the system of development.

Starting with the administrations of Theodore Roosevelt and Woodrow Wilson, and developing full strength during Franklin Roosevelt's New Deal, the federal government took on more and more general regulation of the economy. Rather than simply dole out resources to discrete states and constituencies, the government began to play an important role in the management of almost all aspects of political and economic life.

In time, the federal government regulated the everyday activities of a wide range of enterprises, such as banking, labor relations, transportation systems, the media, mining and development of natural resources, manufacturing, product safety, farming, the environment, and civil rights. These enterprises therefore saw a greater need for a regular presence in Washington. Rather than simply seeking direct material rewards from the government—and then using those rewards as they saw fit—a wide variety of enterprises saw even the most mundane business practices regulated by the government. The government continued to offer material rewards, but those rewards had strings attached. Enterprises therefore saw a greater need to establish a permanent presence in Washington to influence the federal agencies and committees that controlled those strings. As the government's regulation of all aspects of economic and social life increased, interest groups sprung up to influence the way the government controlled their affairs.

Library of Congress

President Calvin Coolidge meets with members of the Sioux Indian Republican Club in March 1925.

Modern Interest Group Politics

Interest group politics boomed with the New Deal of Franklin Roosevelt. Today, interest groups are one of the most important parts of national politics. Estimates of the number of interest groups in operation are not entirely reliable, but they are suggestive. A 1929 study estimated that five hundred interest groups were at work in Washington at the time. A 1977 study estimated thirteen hundred interest groups in the nation's capital, and a 1980 study found seventeen hundred. Another indication of the interest group explosion is a survey that found that 30 percent of all groups active in 1980 organized in the previous twenty years. Of 200 groups surveyed in 1980, two-fifths had offices in Washington just since 1970 and three-fifths since 1960.[7]

Those figures underestimate the amount of interest group activity because of the even more extensive activity of national organizations at the state and local level. For example, the Chamber of Commerce and the American Federation of Labor-Congress of Industrial Organizations (AFL-CIO) each count as one interest group in the Washington surveys, but they have many subdivisions across the nation. The chamber, for example, has seventy thousand firms and individuals as members, along with twenty-five hundred state and local chapters. The AFL-CIO includes some fourteen million dues-paying members in more than one hundred affiliates.[8]

Political action committees (PACs) boomed in the 1970s and 1980s after election finance laws were changed in 1974.[9] PACs are essentially checkbook organizations that depend on sophisticated direct mail techniques to raise money for election campaigns, lobbying, and research. They do not have the active membership programs and tangible benefits that other groups like the AFL-CIO have. PACs have become a major contributor to federal and statewide campaigns. In November 1975, just 722 PACs were in business; by 1982, the figure was 3,400.[10]

Interest groups have increased their role in national politics partly because of the decline of political parties, the fragmentation of Congress, the rise of regulatory politics, the greater complexity of many government issues, and changes in the style of campaigning. Interest groups represent the politics of specialization, whereas the political style in the United States previously was generalist.

Modern Theories of Interest Groups

Since the rise of the modern bureaucratic state, scholars have developed theories to justify or explain the place of interest groups in politics. One of the predominant theories of U.S politics uses a market model to justify the role of interest groups in policy making. Sociologist Arthur Bentley argued in 1908 that pursuit of the public interest is misguided; the sum total of government, he argued, was the result of groups competing for position and favor.[11] Interest groups, Bentley maintained, had a "representative quality" that ensured a degree of democratic activity as groups competed for influence.

Political scientist David Truman argued in 1951 that the result of interest group competition and bargaining was a consensus on the public interest.[12] Truman's model resembles the economic model of Adam Smith, which holds that an "invisible hand" guides self-interested competition among firms toward the public interest. According to Truman, the interaction of groups enables a variety of viewpoints and material interests to get a public hearing. The result is a democratic contest over policy at all levels. Political scientist Robert A. Dahl reached similar conclusions in a 1961 study of community power.[13]

Later students of interest groups have disputed the cheery view of pluralists such as Bentley, Truman, and Dahl. Political scientist E. E. Schattschneider and sociologists C. Wright Mills and Floyd Hunter have argued that the interests of economically disadvantaged groups do not receive adequate representation simply because they do not have the resources to press their causes.[14] These scholars maintain that the makeup of the interest group "universe" has an elite bias.[15]

In perhaps the most influential work to question the assumption that citizens easily form groups to represent their interests, economist Mancur Olson argued that many groups with a definite stake in government actions have difficulty organizing because of limited resources and limited incentives for individuals to join the cause.[16] Group formation is most likely when groups can offer material incentives or even can coerce prospective members. Labor unions with automatic deduction of dues from workers' checks are a form of membership coercion. Because the less advantaged groups in society have a smaller "surplus" to spend on political action, they lose out in the competition for influence over the government.

Another critique of interest group politics stresses the "overload" of modern bureaucratic politics. Sociologist Daniel Bell has argued that economic forces have displaced their conflicts to the federal government, asking it to provide entitlements to paper over fundamental contradictions, such as the management—labor and business—environmentalist schisms. "One large question that the American system now confronts is whether it can find a way to resolve these conflicts. Lacking rules to mediate claims, the system will be under severe strains." [17]

A growing danger is erosion of government authority and legitimacy. Rather than integrating citizens into a process of mutual accommodation with a goal of the public interest, interest groups often isolate citizens from one another. The common purpose that is the hallmark of republican theory is lost to self-interested competition that does not recognize common social destiny.[18]

The autonomy given to many interest groups removes many policies from democratic deliberation and reduces the maneuvering room on issues that are on the public agenda. For example, the control given farmers over prices and land cultivation removes agriculture policy from the general debate about how society should allocate resources. Because they are often non-negotiable, policies on agriculture, Social Security, Medicare, job training, and military spending reduce the options for the president and Congress on a wide variety of budget and social issues.

In Theodore Lowi's view, by giving groups autonomy over parts of public policy, the public loses control over the wide range of interrelated issues. The system is inflexible; options for policy are closed.[19]

How the President Deals with Interest Groups

Most students of U.S. national politics conclude that interest group activity is concentrated on the specific bureaucratic agencies and congressional committees that address the particular concerns of organized interests—not on the White House. For example, farmers deal with the Department of Agriculture and the congressional committees that allocate money to farm programs.

Interest groups do not concentrate on the White House for a number of reasons. First, the schedule of the president and top presidential aides is tight, so it is difficult even to get the president's time and attention. It is much easier to get the attention of a member of Congress or of a civil servant. One aide to President Johnson explained: "There are 535 opportunities in Congress and only one in the White House. You get an hour to present your case before each representative, and only fifteen minutes once a year with the president. Where would you put your effort?" [20]

Second, the president's tenure in office is short compared to the terms of key bureaucrats and members of Congress. Postwar presidents have served an average of only five and a half years. Much of the president's time is spent learning the ropes or struggling with "lame duck" status.

Even when presidents are at full strength, they usually devote their time to a few top priorities—and those priorities are shaped by previous alliances. Only occasionally can an interest group alter a president's set agenda. Finally, the president is the nation's most public political figure, and interest groups usually operate best out of the glare of public attention where they can promote their interests through small legislative and regulatory means. Seeking a shift in important duties, for example, is a matter best addressed by Commerce Department bureaucrats, not by the president.

Even if interest groups favor the predictability of agencies and committees, many have a relationship with the presidency. Since World War II, the presidency has developed regular channels for interest groups to make and receive appeals. The size of the White House staff has increased greatly, with many officials assigned in some way to keep track of interest groups. The most formal mechanism for dealing with interest groups is the Office of Public Liaison, created in the administrations of Richard Nixon and Gerald R. Ford. *(See "A Greater White House Role," p. 769, in this chapter.)*

Political scientist Robert Salisbury has noted that interest groups often "tend to gravitate toward the effective centers of power in a given political system." As the White House has become the initiator of national politics, it has become the focus for at least some policy areas such as economic and security policy, and even minor matters such as prayer in schools—even if the bulk of policies are better tended in the bureaucracy and congressional committees. The White House may not be the focus of all interest group activity, but neither is it a place of last resort for groups.[21]

Some authorities maintain that the president has an advantage in dealing with lobbies. The White House "is less likely to be besieged at its most vulnerable points because lobbyists are less likely to know where those points are," according to political scientists Michael Baruch Grossman and Martha Joynt Kumar.[22]

Although interest groups have difficulty finding a point of entry into the White House, they do know their way around the executive bureaucracy. The White House must then struggle to get control over the huge and complex bureaucracy.

The White House and Interest Groups

The ongoing calculations of interest group politics at the White House depend on a number of factors. Perhaps the most important consideration is which interests have supported the president during previous political campaigns and government initiatives. As when dealing with public opinion, the president must maintain the steady backing of a basic core of supporters and bring independents and opposition figures into alliances for different issues. For example, when campaigning for his tax-cutting initiative in 1981, President Reagan could count on the support of large organized business interests. To secure passage of the legislation, Reagan worked to bring other groups such as labor unions and small businesses into his alliance.

Interest group alliances shift from issue to issue. Most groups do not get involved in legislative or regulatory activity outside their direct interests; groups become active when they see a possible gain or threat in government initiatives. Large-scale policy making entails a wider array of competing groups than "incrementalist" policy making. As a result, presidents must consider the extent to which their initiatives will activate interest groups. Business and organized labor often switch sides depending on the issue. The two groups often work together on issues such as construction projects, banking regulation, and other legislation affecting economic "growth." They oppose each other on issues affecting the organization of the workplace, such as "common site" picketing (picketing of a workplace by workers not directly involved in the dispute), "right to work" (restrictions on union organizing), and workplace safety legislation.

Another factor in the shifting interest group calculations is the salience of issues and the timing of events. As economist Anthony Downs has noted, issues have a cycle of attention.[23] After a period of high publicity, most issues tend to fade from public consciousness. The president can bring attention to issues, but the public and interest groups still react according to their own priorities at the time. The president must respond to issues put on the public agenda by concerted interest group efforts.

The president must take into account—and influence, if possible—just how much attention the public is giving an issue and how groups are responding to that attention. Ronald Reagan, long a critic of federal coercion of states, signed legislation in 1984 to penalize states that did not increase the mandatory drinking age to twenty-one after a lengthy campaign by Mothers Against Drunk Driving (MADD) and other citizen's groups produced high public awareness of the problem. At a different time, Reagan probably would have resisted such legislation.

A final factor in the calculations is the relative strength of different interest groups. The membership, wealth, and status of various advocacy organizations varies greatly. Most interest groups have just a few hundred members and budgets in the hundreds of thousands of dollars. Others have multimillion-dollar-budgets, a large membership that can be deployed swiftly on various campaigns, and professional staffs and consultants to advise them. Many are connected with corporations that they can use for overhead expenses, expert advise, technology, and membership lists.

The White House examines the balance of power

Pete Souza, The White House

During his presidency, Ronald Reagan frequently criticized federal coercion of states. In 1984, however, he signed legislation to penalize states that did not increase the mandatory drinking age to twenty-one after a lengthy campaign by Mothers Against Drunk Driving.

among interest groups on specific issues before it plans strategy. That is not to say that the president decides which side of the issue to take based on this balance of power, only whether to attempt to influence the issue and if so, what tactics to use. Jimmy Carter decided to withdraw the second Strategic Arms Limitation Talks (SALT) treaty from the Senate in 1980 after the Soviet Union's invasion of Afghanistan dramatically altered public opinion and the alignment of interest groups.[24] President Reagan decided to pursue "omnibus" budget-cutting reconciliation legislation in 1981 when a wide range of interest groups appeared ready to defeat the administration, issue by issue, in congressional committees. The package cut $130.6 billion from the federal budget over four years.[25]

The president's relationship with interest groups usually develops issue by issue. The president can rely on certain groups always to be supportive and others always to offer opposition; the president usually must seek the support of many fence-straddling groups. Groups traditionally aligning with Republican presidents include business, oil companies, conservative social groups, and some farm groups. Traditional Democratic allies include many multinational firms, labor, environmental groups, blacks, and developers.

Sometimes the president is so concerned about the appearance of interest group activity that the White House will ask supporters to lobby discreetly or not at all. The Reagan administration kept a distance from Teamsters officials, for example, when they were under indictment for corruption in the mid-1980s. In the 1980s, responding to criticism that the Democrats are a party of special interests, Democratic leaders have sought to create an image of independence from supporters such as blacks and Hispanics, feminists, gays, and teachers. After the 1984 campaign, Paul Kirk, chairman of the Democratic National Committee, withdrew party recognition of seven party caucuses for specific groups.[26]

Inevitably, interest groups that supported the president during campaigns become disenchanted with the administration's performance. Organized labor, civil rights groups, mayors, social workers, and advocates of a national health system were disappointed with President Carter's policies—particularly after his budget and defense priorities shifted in the second half of his term. This disappointment led many to urge Sen. Edward M. Kennedy (D-Mass.) to challenge Carter for the 1980 nomination. The "New Right" groups that supported Reagan's candidacy in 1980 later were upset that Reagan was not more vigorous in promoting their agenda, such as prayer in the schools, tuition tax credits for private schools, and an antiabortion constitutional amendment.

Influencing the Interest Group Balance of Power

Even if presidents are limited in their dealings with interest groups on particular issues, they influence the balance of power among competing interest groups. Presidential use of public opinion, budget priorities, and White House staff can enhance some groups and undercut others. In this way, the president can "set the table" for later political conflicts.

Political scientists Martin Shefter and Benjamin Ginsberg have identified three strategies for a president to shape the makeup of the interest group universe.[27] First, the president can try to transform the identities of established and nascent groups. Second, the president can "divide and conquer" existing alliances of groups and attempt to bring fragments of the old alliance under White House influence. Third, the president can attempt to bring estranged groups together on an issue in a movement where they find common interest.

Franklin Roosevelt provides a textbook example of presidential influence over interest group alignment. Roosevelt gave a number of groups—such as the elderly, labor, and the "third of a nation" that was poor—a positive new identity that led to their involvement in Democratic politics. The New Deal offered a wide range of incentives to certain businesses to support the president, thereby chipping them away from a strong business alliance that had been hostile to previous liberal initiatives. Finally, by stressing the common desire for economic security, Roosevelt forged an alliance of ethnic groups in similarly vulnerable economic positions.[28]

Postwar presidencies steadily expanded the number of interest groups involved in national politics. The expansion of federal regulation over civil rights, workplace safety, consumer products, the environment, trade requirements, energy production and prices, air travel, and home building continued through the Carter administration, regardless of the president's party. That regulatory expansion, added to the hundreds of federal programs and studies, increased the stake of interest groups in the federal government.

Lyndon Johnson's Great Society led to the creation of many new interest groups. Domestic initiatives in housing, community development, job training, education, and health care included specific instructions to involve the communities and interests involved in the programs. The most famous example is the Economic Opportunity Act, which requires some urban programs to be "developed, conducted, and administered with the maximum feasible participation of residents of the areas and members of the groups served." The "maximum feasible participation" provision was among the most controversial 1960s programs. Proponents maintained that the provision allowed poor people to develop self-esteem and political skills so they could become self-sufficient members of society. Opponents argued that it simply gave antagonistic groups resources to undermine the government's efforts.[29]

A president's program does not need an explicit demand for participation to promote interest groups. In fact, such provisions have a minor effect compared with the way a president's budget priorities provide the resources and incentives for interest groups. Robert Reischauer, an official of the Urban League, has explained:

> In each area of federal involvement a powerful network of interest groups developed. First there were the representatives of the recipient governments. These included not only interest groups representing governors, mayors, city managers, county executives, state legislators, and the like, but also recipient agency organizations such as chief state school officers, public welfare directors, and highway commissioners. All told, some seventy-two groups of this sort existed. A second element of the network consisted of the general providers of the services provided by the grants—organized teachers, builders of public housing, and so forth. The recipients of the services also formed an element in this network—ranging from welfare recipients to P.T.A. organizations to automobile clubs. Private-sector suppliers of the inputs needed to provide the services also joined the effort. These organizations might represent the producers of library shelves, manufacturers of school buses, book publishers, or asphalt suppliers. The academics and private-sector consulting firms that made a living evaluating existing programs and planning and designing new programs also formed an element in the support group for the grants strategy.[30]

The Reagan administration skillfully transformed the interest group balance of power.[31] First, the president gave greater visibility to many groups. Reagan attracted the support of southern white conservative groups by appealing not to past racial issues but to the moral concerns of their evangelical churches and organizations. The network of churches throughout the South served as a base for organizing on issues ranging from school prayer to nuclear arms policy. Reagan also helped shift the focus of many blue-collar workers to stress their patriotism and devotion to family issues such as opposition to abortion. The president appealed to middle-class voters not on the basis of federal programs—which they favored and he wanted to cut—but as overburdened taxpayers.

Reagan's policies also unified many groups long at odds. Protestants and Catholics came together with common concerns about abortion and other "moral" issues pertaining to personal values. Corporations and small domestic businesses—long antagonistic on tariff, trade, and tax issues—united on environmental, consumer, and other regulatory concerns. Middle-class professionals, who often had sided with Democrats and liberals on social issues, were drawn to the Reagan camp with tax cuts.

Many alliances split over Reagan administration initiatives—business and labor on issues of regulation, college-educated professionals over taxes, and beneficiaries of federal programs over tax and budget cuts. Business and labor, which previously allied on many regulatory issues, for example, split in the late 1970s and early 1980s as deregulation led to the rise of nonunion firms that undersold unionized firms. Consumer groups also opposed former allies in business and labor.

Reagan's approach to interest groups extended beyond the federal government. With the budget cuts of 1981 and with his celebration of voluntarism and state and local government Reagan shifted the focus of interest group activity. Reagan's emphasis on nonfederal programs for addressing social problems increased the work of interest groups at the state level. The increased reliance on "public-private partnerships" and voluntarism limited the notion of public responsibility for social problems. The president's task force on private sector initiatives was dominated by business people. Even though Reagan's tax policies reduced incentives for corporate giving, and even though Reagan argued that he was not seeking to replace vital services with private action, his celebration of voluntary action took some of the political pressure off the administration for its budget cuts.[32]

Reagan came to Washington determined to "defund" what he considered to be irresponsible liberal interest groups. Many groups such as environmentalists and legal advocates depended on the federal government for some support, but Reagan cut that support in 1981.

Any president's policies are bound to rouse interest groups that oppose the administration. Many groups develop or improve their organization in response to threats they perceive from the White House. President Nixon's grain export policies led to the creation of the American Agriculture Movement.[33] Independent oil companies organized on a large scale for the first time when President Carter pushed a windfall profits tax.[34] Labor, environmental, women's rights, Social Security, civil rights, and public interest groups improved their membership and fund-raising efforts in response to Reagan policies. Those groups used the negative images of officials such as Interior Secretary James G. Watt, Attorney General Edwin Meese III, and Judge Robert H. Bork as part of their direct mail fund-raising appeals and rallies. The Sierra Club's membership almost doubled from 180,000 to 300,000 during Watt's tenure at the Department of Interior.[35]

A number of grass-roots organizations developed sophisticated operations and national bases in their campaigns against Reagan's policies on Central America, nuclear arms, South Africa, and the environment. Some fifty thousand canvassers knocked on doors every night in the early 1980s with petitions and requests for donations.[36]

The President's Staff and Interest Groups

Since the nation's earliest years, the president has assigned staff members to monitor important interest groups. Andrew Jackson's aides, for example, carefully gauged the activities and strength of bankers and businesses opposed to the administration. Franklin Roosevelt's New Deal initiated government growth that gave hundreds of new groups reason to have a regular relationship with Washington politicians, including the president. Today, interest groups are so important to the presidency that the White House has an office devoted exclusively to liaison with them, the Office of Pubic Liaison. *(See "A Greater White House Role," this page.)* The president and top aides continue to play an important role in monitoring and cajoling interest groups.

The president's relations with interest groups have not always been so direct as they are today. Before the expansion of the White House staff in the postwar era, the cabinet served as the main link between interest groups and the administration. Cabinet officials tended to have strong ties to the groups whose affairs their departments oversaw, and over the years they developed an appreciation for the concerns of interest groups. The administration also developed relations with interest groups through political parties and campaign organizations.

Many of the cabinet-level departments were designed to serve the interests of specific groups. The Departments of Agriculture, Commerce, and Labor resulted from years of lobbying by farmers, business leaders, and unions. At first designed to be research centers, the departments later gave their clients authority over a wide range of programs. Other federal agencies created at the urging of interest groups include the Interstate Commerce Commission, the Federal Reserve Board, and Federal Trade Commission. Agencies even helped create organizations for interest groups, as when the Department of Commerce helped to organize the U.S. Chamber of Commerce.

Departments develop strong ties to interest groups even if they were not created specifically to serve those groups. Political scientists have used images of "iron triangles" and "issue networks" to express the common outlooks and interests that develop with agencies and the groups they regulate.[37] Even the most independent administration appointees develop protective views toward their agencies and the interest groups they work with. They "marry the natives," to use the common argot.

To the extent that presidents need advice on issues, they rely on the information provided by the departments as well as the advice of a small staff in the White House and informal advisers. The interest-dominated departments were the incubators of presidential legislative initiatives. Bureaucrats interested in improving the status of their agencies developed programs that enlarged their involvement with interest groups.

Appointing interest group representatives to the administration always has been an important way to gain support. Less than 1 percent of the federal bureaucracy today is filled with presidential appointees, but strategic use of those posts can improve presidential relations with the groups. The president appoints interest group representatives for a number of reasons: to gain insight into constituent groups or leverage in bargaining, to co-opt groups by giving them formal involvement in policy discussions, and simply to establish a common ground for dealing with those groups.

In some agencies, interest groups have almost absolute authority over presidential appointments. The Justice Department must consider the likely rating of judicial appointments by the American Bar Association, for example. Appointments for the Federal Reserve Board, the Treasury Department, the Central Intelligence Agency (CIA), and the Defense Department must meet the approval of their interest group establishments—bankers, contractors, academic experts, and businesses. President Carter dropped his nomination of Theodore C. Sorensen as CIA director after the intelligence community and conservative activists criticized it strongly.

Democratic presidents must get the blessing of blacks, women's groups, environmental activists, consumer groups, real estate developers, multinationals, social workers, and organized labor for its major appointments, since those groups are an important part of the Democratic coalition. Republican presidents must satisfy developers of natural resources, multinational and small business concerns, financial and insurance interests, conservative social groups, and defense contractors. President Reagan consulted Moral Majority leader Jerry Falwell before appointing Sandra Day O'Connor to the Supreme Court because he was concerned that Falwell might oppose O'Connor over her vote as an Arizona state legislator for funding abortions. President Carter withdrew his nomination of John Dunlop for secretary of labor in 1976 because of opposition from black and women's groups.[38]

Who does not get important cabinet positions is often as revealing as who gets the posts. Some Republican presidents have reached out to groups outside their coalition by appointing moderates to the Environmental Protection Agency and the Labor, Interior, and Energy departments. Reagan, however, rebuffed those agencies' key clients by making appointments antagonistic to their concerns. Reagan's first secretary of interior, James G. Watt, had been a lawyer for a firm strongly opposed to restrictions to development of natural resources. (Watt himself was associated with the Mountain States Legal Foundation, an interest group for developers and oil concerns.) Reagan's first energy chief, James B. Edwards, had no experience in the field and was told to do all he could to close down the department.

A Greater White House Role

As the government extended its reach over more economic and social policy areas, conflicts between departments and agencies developed that required White House arbitration. The sheer size and the inertia of the bureaucracy created difficulties for presidents trying to exert "top-down" control.

In response to a growing feeling that the departments and interest groups were impossible to control without extra help, postwar presidents have increased the size of the White House staff. The staff developed an often antagonistic relationship with the departments as it tried to develop and implement a program consistent with the president's wishes. The president ceased to rely on the departments for key legislative proposals.

Interest groups still had considerable reason to maintain regular contacts with federal departments, but the White House increasingly dominated the formation of legislative proposals and regulatory change. For the White House, contact with important interest groups became an important part of the president's strategy for mobilizing support on specific issues. First lady Eleanor Roosevelt was one of Franklin Roosevelt's most important emissaries to interest groups such as blacks and labor. Roosevelt also appointed White House aides James A. Farley, Harry Hop-

Franklin D. Roosevelt Library

First lady Eleanor Roosevelt was one of Franklin Roosevelt's most important emissaries to interest groups such as blacks and labor. Here she speaks to members of the CIO, AFL, and unaffiliated unions in West Park, New York.

kins, Louis Howe, Adolph Berle, Raymond Moley, and Phillip Nash to stay in contact with interest groups as part of their jobs. Both Roosevelt and his successor, Harry S Truman, expressed discomfort with assigning aides strictly to work with interest groups. Roosevelt informed his advisers that he did not want a formal White House apparatus "on the theory that it brought in people with vested interests," according to political scientist Richard Neustadt.[39]

Roosevelt and Truman recognized the need to deal with interest groups but wanted to work through the Democratic National Committee. Interest groups were considered parts of the electoral coalition rather than a governing coalition.

Despite the lack of a large or formal White House apparatus, presidents have always constructed ad hoc coalitions of interest groups to pursue policies on specific issues. The Truman administration formed a coalition of business, labor, religious, and charitable groups to promote the Marshall Plan. Representatives of these interest groups met with administration officials to help develop the plan and to sell the plan to Congress and the public.

Interest groups also are represented on a major scale on advisory committees, ad hoc groups formed to advise the president on specific policies. The New Deal expanded the ad hoc use of commissions; by 1939, eighty-two advisory committees advised the government. During World War II, some one thousand committees advised the Office of Price Administration. Three thousand committees were in operation in the late 1960s according to one survey.[40]

Recent presidential lobbying includes many examples of building coalitions of interest groups. John F. Kennedy assembled a coalition of interest groups to promote the Trade Expansion Act. Nixon assigned aide Charles Colson to head a campaign to enlist interest group support for the 1969 antiballistic missile treaty with the Soviet Union. Nixon also put together coalitions for his "New Federalism" system of intergovernmental relations, for his economic programs, and for his two doomed Supreme Court nominations.

Nixon planned to create a White House office to oversee contacts with interest groups, but the Watergate scandal distracted him. Nixon's successor, Gerald R. Ford, created the Office of Public Liaison (OPL) in 1976. The new office supplemented the ad hoc efforts of the rest of the White House to stay in regular contact with key groups.

OPL has had an uneven history. The first full-time director was the Carter administration's Margaret Costanza. Costanza made public her differences with the president as she courted "outsider" groups such as blacks, women, and gays. Her most publicized differences with Carter concerned abortion: Carter opposed the use of federal funds for abortion, and Costanza openly favored federal support. Under Costanza, the office was more oriented toward advocacy than toward building coalitions for the president's policies.

After Carter replaced Costanza with Anne Wexler, the office became an effective instrument for White House lobbying. Costanza had complained that the office was strictly an outlet for meaningless public relations, but Wexler involved OPL in the policy formation and lobbying operations of the rest of the White House. The office participated in drafting legislation from the beginning.

One member of Carter's legislative liaison staff said of Wexler's OPL: "The public liaison folks have a pretty sophisticated operation for pinpointing potential interest group allies. When they pulled together a coalition, it could be pretty valuable on the Hill. I guess they had about 30,000 names and contacts on their computer for mobilization."[41]

Even with a sophisticated public liaison office, the president still usually entrusts the most important interest group assignments to specific staff members. Late in the Carter administration, even as OPL gained stature, the president called on Chief of Staff Hamilton Jordan to set up task forces to promote the administration's policy. Those task forces gradually won the administration praise from political professionals, but they came too late to promote much of Carter's agenda. White House attention shifted to the 1980 election just as it developed an effective way to build coalitions.

In addition to OPL and Jordan's task forces, the Carter administration relied on a number of interest group representatives on the White House staff and in agencies to reach out to interest groups. Carter appointed people affiliated with teachers' unions, Ralph Nader advocacy groups, Jewish groups, alternate energy developers, environmentalists, and social work veterans to the administration. Women's groups, blacks, Hispanics, and labor leaders were consulted and given greater representation on courts and agencies.

Good interest group relations give the White House a public relations machine that reaches into every corner of the country. "The realtors can send out half a million Mailgrams within 24 hours," one observer noted. "If they have a hundred target congressmen, they can get out 100,000 Mailgrams targeted by district."[42] The Chamber of Commerce, Moral Majority, AFL-CIO, American Federation of State, County, and Municipal Employees, National Education Association, and American Medical Association all can mobilize their many chapters and members within days. In many ways, the interest groups can be considered the new political machines of U.S. politics.

Carter both wooed and excoriated interest groups throughout his presidency, which created public confusion about his competence. For example, in 1979 Carter created a cabinet-level Department of Education to fulfill a promise to the National Education Association, the teachers' union that endorsed him in 1976 and 1980. Carter also made well-publicized efforts to promote groups such as evangelicals, organized labor, banks, some energy producers, and blacks.

As a result, Carter was criticized for "pandering" to interest groups. But Carter himself expressed frustration with interest group politics. In his 1979 "crisis of confidence" speech and in his farewell address, Carter decried the effects of interest groups on national policy development. In his farewell address, he said:

> We are increasingly drawn to single-issue groups and special-interest organizations to ensure that whatever else happens our own personal views and our own personal interests are protected. This is a disturbing factor in American political life. It tends to distort our purposes. Because of the fragmented pressures of these special interests, it's very important that the office of the president be a strong one.[43]

Interest Groups in the 1980s

Interest group politics have continued to grow and change with the inclusion of new groups in the political process. In the 1980s a proliferation of groups on both the right and left presented a new challenge to leaders of both parties. Especially pronounced was the challenge from the right, since its forces were better financed.

Jimmy Carter and Ronald Reagan had no national political experience and won the presidency without much help from the party organizations, so they reached out for interest groups outside the Washington establishment. Their interest group ties did not always bind them to Congress and the bureaucracy. Political scientist Joseph Pika wrote: "In this way, presidents may have weakened political parties just at the time they were most needed as mechanisms to organize effective coalitions to pass legislative initiatives."[44]

An important part of Reagan's electoral strategy in 1980 was the so-called New Right, a wide range of groups that promoted an agenda including tax cuts, reduced federal regulation, an end to legal abortions, a return to prayer in the schools, federal tax breaks for parochial schools, restricted gay rights, and a more rigid interpretation of civil rights. Reagan provided hortatory leadership, submitted legislation on these issues, and involved Christian organizations in drafting tuition-tax credit legislation. But the New Right agenda was a low priority in Reagan's first term. Reagan held on to the groups' support, however, because they had nowhere else to go.

Presidents Carter and Reagan found themselves fighting large and small interest groups when their administrations tried to cut the budget. Social Security recipients, western water interests, military contractors, farmers, hospitals, and state and local governments all resisted the two administrations' budget axe. Carter expended great political capital early in his fights with western water interests, the nuclear power industry, oil companies, and many liberal groups who found his programs on welfare and health care stingy.

Reagan's budget-cutters were forced to look for relatively small savings—but were frustrated even there. The administration once proposed that the Coast Guard charge commercial vessels and pleasure yachts for the $1 billion worth of services they receive at sea. The administration plan would have brought in $400 million. The proposal was roundly criticized and, whittled down, produced only $8 million in new revenues. When Secretary of Education William J. Bennett proposed restrictions on college loans to prevent fraud, a wide range of university and student groups protested.[45]

The size of the White House staff increased from a few dozen under Franklin Roosevelt to 550 under Richard Nixon. After falling to 488 under President Carter, the staff increased again under Reagan to 575. The Executive Office of the President was at its largest—five thousand—in the 1970s.[46]

Tasks of the White House Staff

Political scientists Martha Joynt Kumar and Michael Baruch Grossman have argued that the presidency's relationship with interest groups involves four basic roles.[47] Many of the roles overlap, but they represent distinct tasks for the administration. The administration usually must deal with all four tasks at the same time to enact its policies.

The "marker" keeps track of the president's debts to particular groups and attempts to help those groups. The "communicant" gathers information about current interest group concerns. The "constructor" builds coalitions for specific policy initiatives. The "broker" helps the administration and groups with different interests negotiate their differences to give the president broad enough backing for policy initiatives.

The Reagan administration's action on its tax cuts in 1981 illustrates all four roles. Partly to repay the business community for its support in the 1980 election, the administration proposed and shepherded legislation in Congress that would reduce the marginal tax rates on individuals by 30 percent over three years. The original decision to push the legislation illustrates the "marker" role.

Before and after taking up the legislation, the White House acted as a communicant, sounding out diverse groups on tax and other issues. The White House gathered information about which groups were likely to support and oppose the legislation, and how strong and reliable they were. White House constructors helped to build a coalition to back the legislation in Congress. A wide variety of groups joined the coalition, including the U.S. Chamber of Commerce, the Business Roundtable, the National Small Business Association, the Moral Majority, and the National Conservative Political Action Committee. Wayne Valis, a special assistant to the president, oversaw the coordination of interest group efforts.

Finally, the administration served as a broker to settle differences between the administration, congressional leaders, and interest groups. One result of the bargaining was a reduction of the cut from 30 to 25 percent and a delay of the legislation's implementation.

Interest group relations with the White House are most routine—and important—on budgetary matters. Interest groups develop relationships with bureaucrats in federal agencies throughout the year, and those agencies develop budget proposals in the last three months of the calendar year. Those proposals work their way up the system to the cabinet secretaries and the president.

As it has grown in size, the White House staff has played a greater role in overseeing budget recommendations. The White House often distrusts department recommendations and wants to create coherent domestic and foreign programs that often are impossible without top-down control. Departments and agencies often conflict over budget and program authorities, and only the president and the White House staff can settle the differences.

In the Reagan administration, the Office of Management and Budget (OMB) played an important role not only in arbitrating budget claims but also in developing new federal regulations. Under a presidential order, OMB must study the impact of new regulations before they can go into effect. White House and OMB purview over the budget and regulations means a reduced role for interest groups. Before, the most public action on regulations was publication of comments in the *Federal Register;* under Reagan, regulations must enter the realm of the generalists at OMB. The close relationship that the groups enjoy with specific agencies is not enough for their wishes to prevail.

Criticism of these developments turns on the lack of expertise that the White House staff and OMB officials have on many complex matters under agency jurisdiction. The White House staff is made up of political operatives, and OMB is made up of political professionals and accountants—few of whom know much if anything about the chemical issues involved in environmental regulations, for example, or the complex interrelationship between different components of tax and welfare policy.

The Interest Group Universe Today

The interest groups active in national politics are in many ways the "dead weight of the past." Today's active interest groups are the offspring of past political and economic movements, and their survival and involvement in politics is one of the constraints on the activities of the president, the executive bureaucracy, and Congress. But the interest groups are not just constraints. They offer politicians the means for mobilizing political activity.

Interest groups represent every conceivable group in the United States: big and small business, domestic and multinational manufacturers, banks and insurance companies, real estate developers, teachers, miners, lawyers, blue-collar workers, opponents of unions, the elderly, "peaceniks," military contractors, consumers, evangelicals, Jews, Arabs, guardians of different notions of the "public interest," states and cities, government workers, secretaries, custodians, athletes, actors, environmentalists, developers of natural resources—the list goes on and on.

The interest group universe is so large that it contains innumerable internal contradictions. Within the set of interest groups concerned about military affairs, for example, there is often keen competition. When President Carter signed the SALT II treaty in Moscow in 1978, military-related interest groups lined up on both sides of the issue.

To understand interest groups, it is important to understand their different goals and functions, resources, everyday activities, and long-term strategies.

Goals and Functions

Interest groups form to protect a group's material interests in budget, tax, and regulatory proceedings in Washington, to express a group's ideology and desires, or to provide a forum, services, and standards to a group.

The U.S. Chamber of Commerce is an umbrella organization for seventy thousand firms and individuals, twenty-five hundred state and local chapters, and one thousand trade and professional associations. The chamber's annual $16-million budget allows extensive lobbying of both the federal and state governments. The chamber is dedicated to one overriding goal: improving the conditions for business expansion. It has been active in issues such as tax legislation, labor laws, and regulatory relief. The group has a definite ideology, but it is interested primarily in material concerns.

The chamber is the largest business organization. Other active business groups, designed strictly to produce better conditions for economic activity, include the Business Roundtable, oil lobbies, and the National Small Business Association.

The American Federation of Labor-Congress of Industrial Organizations (AFL-CIO) is also designed to further the material benefits of its members. The AFL-CIO has fourteen million dues-paying members in more than one hundred affiliates, including the Teamsters, the United Auto Workers, the United Mine Workers, and American Federation of Teachers. The AFL-CIO's job is simple: bargain for the best wages, benefits, and working conditions possible, and make organizing workers as easy and efficient as possible.

The Chamber of Commerce and the AFL-CIO are interested mainly in material benefits for their members; other interest groups have a more "expressive" agenda. Rather than simply seeking a share of federal largesse, they exist to promote their ideological or cultural values. Many of the evangelical and conservative groups that fall under the New Right umbrella were founded to promote values rather than material interests.

Frustrated with what they perceive to be a decline in the moral values of the family, groups like the Moral Majority, the National Right to Life Committee, and National Conservative Political Action Committee contributed generously to political campaigns and lobbied hard in the White House and on Capitol Hill. They promoted an anti-abortion amendment to the Constitution, prayer in the schools, and tuition-tax credits for private schools. They also spoke out on foreign policy issues such as the war in Nicaragua and arms control. Other important ideologically oriented organizations include the Americans for Democratic Action, the American Civil Liberties Union, Americans for Constitutional Action, the Eagle Forum, and People for the American Way.

Professional organizations take on both material and expressive functions. The American Bar Association, the American Medical Association (AMA), and the American Association of State Colleges and Universities serve as protectors of professional standards and ideals, but they also want to defend the privileges of their members. The AMA, for example, is among the biggest contributors to political campaigns and actively defends the profession's material interests whenever Congress considers issues such as Medicare or hospital cost-containment legislation.

Many professional organizations, such as the American Political Science Association and the Modern Language Association, are primarily dispensers of information.

Since the 1970s, there has been a boom in "public interest" lobbies. These groups do not promote the interests of any single sector but instead promote their vision of the general interest of all society. The members of these groups themselves do not stand to receive special material benefits if their ideals are realized, but the policies they promote would help some groups at the expense of others.

Prominent public interest groups include Common Cause, People for the American Way, the League of Women Voters, the U.S. Public Interest Research Group and other organizations set up by consumer activist Ralph Nader, the Consumer Federation of America, Americans for Constitutional Action, and the American Civil Liberties Union.

Resources and Everyday Activities

The influence of interest groups differs according to their resources. Money, size of membership, technological sophistication (such as computers, direct mail operations, telephone banks, polling operations), expertise on issues, familiarity with the political process, political reputation and contacts, motivation, and leadership are the important factors defining an organization's strength.[48]

Most lobbies' everyday activities consist of unglamorous work such as monitoring legislation on Capitol Hill and regulatory action in agencies, researching issues, fund raising, surveying and responding to the concerns of membership, and staying in touch with congressional staff members.

Most interest groups have a legislative agenda that they would like to pursue, but they rarely have the opportunity to press specific proposals at the White House or Capitol Hill. Usually they must form alliances with other groups on specific issues that the president, Congress, or federal departments are considering. An interest group's agenda, then, is pursued bit by bit rather than as a whole. This helps explain why interest groups become disenchanted with an administration that considers itself an ally: the interest group considers its program to be the president's program, but presidents also must serve other, often conflicting groups.

Long-term Strategies

Because of the slow pace of legislative action in Washington, lobbies must be content to pursue "incremental" change most of the time. Groups must do what they can to develop a wide range of large and small initiatives, however, so they are able to act when opportunities for exerting influence arise.

Interest groups must decide whether they are going to use "insider" or "outsider" strategies to influence the president and the rest of the Washington establishment.[49] Insiders establish ties with a number of White House, agency, and congressional staffers and, depending on the administration, can play a role in writing legislation and regulations that affect their interests. Outsiders attempt to pressure the administration by putting the public spotlight on the issues they consider important.

Interest groups often move from outsider to insider roles with a change in adminstration. Before Ronald Reagan was elected president, the Moral Majority and other conservative groups relied on public relations campaigns and insurgent candidates. After Reagan became president, however, the White House consulted these groups on many social initiatives. They actually helped to write tuition-tax credit legislation. Likewise, many consumer protection and environmental protection groups moved from the outside to the inside with the election of Jimmy Carter in 1976. Carter appointed many "Naderites"—disciples of activist Ralph Nader—to top agency positions.

White House Efforts to Rouse Interest Group Support

Presidents' interest group strategies fit somewhere between their attempts to control the huge bureaucracy and to appeal to the public at large. Interest groups have many of the open characteristics involved in public appeals, but groups also become intricately involved with the everyday machinery of hundreds of agencies that develop and execute federal policy.

The president needs to line up interest group support for difficult policy battles to mobilize both the public and the elites who are important players in the complex negotiations of congressional and bureaucratic politics.

Whether a president can persuade Congress to adopt the administration's policy proposals depends on how much pressure interest groups bring to an issue. Interest groups offer the president important tools to prod Congress:

- Expertise and legitimacy. An organization that includes respected analysts of a political problem not only serves as a school for the president and the White House staff but also puts the reputation of the experts behind the White House.

~ Membership and organization. Most interest groups do not have a large, active membership, but many have access to mailing lists and expertise in mobilizing the important participants in a political battle.

~ Money for media campaigns. Even the most skeletal organizations often have financial resources for a media campaign. Recent battles over issues such as the Panama Canal treaties, the tax cuts of 1981, and the nomination of Robert H. Bork to the Supreme Court have involved extensive broadcast and newspaper advertising to sway public opinion.

~ A system of balancing political concerns. The participation of many interest groups enables the president and members of Congress to engage in extensive bartering that goes far beyond the specific controversy. Votes for highly visible initiatives are won by promising members of Congress support on other, unrelated matters.

~ Leadership. Interest groups include not only many nationally recognized names—such as Lane Kirkland of the AFL-CIO, Phyllis Schlafly of the Eagle Forum, Norman Lear of People for the American Way, and Jerry Falwell of the Moral Majority—but also sophisticated organizational operators. These groups can offer the kind of leadership that mobilizes whole segments of the population on issues important to the president.

Political battles tend to develop into battles between two sets of interest groups and their White House and congressional allies. Interest group activity determines the extent of the propaganda battle and the intricacy and duration of the maneuvering between the president and key members of Congress.

Reagan Confronts Domestic Groups

President Reagan's budget-cutting victory in the summer of 1981 was a classic contest between two sets of interest groups. The outcome of the struggle was determined by bartering, public appeals, strong presidential leadership, and the organizational strength of interest groups.

The prospect of more that $160 billion in budget cuts over Reagan's first term in office activated a wide range of interest groups involved with domestic policy. The usual strategy of such groups is to work with the staff members of congressional committees and the federal agencies to restore proposed cuts, piece by piece, to the budget. This "micro" activity was to be supplemented by a publicity campaign that would show low public support and put both the president and Congress on the defensive. The groups responding to the budget cut proposals included the AFL-CIO, the National Association for the Advancement of Colored People, the Urban League, the U.S. Conference of Mayors, the Children's Defense Fund, the U.S. Public Interest Research Group, the National Organization for Women, Operation PUSH, and the American Association of Retired Persons.

President Reagan and his lieutenants thwarted the two-prong interest group attack, however. First, it reduced the chances for micro response to the cuts by asking Republican Senate leaders for a consideration of the cuts as a single budget package; that is, Congress would have one up-or-down vote on all the cuts. The all-or-nothing legislation reduced the possibilities for interest groups to appeal to friendly members of congressional committees. One observer noted: "Many hundreds of lobbying groups that had built strong relationships over the years with authorizing with appropriations committee members and aides have found themselves not so much without a sympathetic ear as without a way to leverage that sympathy to get more money." [50]

Second, by including authorizing legislation as well as spending legislation—that is, legislation that allowed funding as well as legislation that actually funded the programs—Reagan forced Congress to deal with otherwise protected entitlement programs. If the authorization for a program were cut, it could not be funded later in that budget year. Third, the administration led supportive interest groups in its own public offensive in favor of the cuts.

The groups Reagan brought into its alliance included the Chamber of Commerce, the National Association of Manufacturers, the National Conservative Political Action Committee, the Moral Majority, the National Jaycees, the National Federation of Small Business, and the American Medical Association. The White House managed the interest groups' campaign. It selected key congressional districts where the administration might find support and instructed the interest groups to pressure House members from those districts. Lee Atwater, the president's assistant political director, explained:

> The way we operate, within forty-eight hours any Congressman will know that he has had a major strike in his district. All of a sudden, Vice President Bush is in your district, Congressman Jack Kemp is in your district. Ten of your top contributors are calling you, the head of the local AMA, the head of the local realtors' group, local officials. Twenty letters come in. Within forty-eight hours, you're hit by paid media, free media, mail, phone, all asking you to support the president.[51]

The interest group politics of the budget cuts had an elaborate system of rewards and punishments. As Reagan sought congressional approval, he co-opted the United Auto Workers union by going along with import relief on Japanese automobiles. The president also punished two of his biggest Democratic foes, House Speaker Thomas P. (Tip) O'Neill, Jr., and Sen. Edward M. Kennedy, by lifting duties on Taiwan and Korea—a move that hurt the shoemaking industry in their home state of Massachusetts.[52]

Under such a system of lobbying, the president depends on interest groups when bartering with reluctant budget-cutters in Congress. The cozy system of back-room bargaining between the White House staff and key congressional figures is not replaced, but it is supplemented by the mobilization of interest groups for the district pressure campaigns.

Reagan was not the only practitioner of interest group politics, just one of the more successful. Carter was considered a failure in congressional relations, but he succeeded in getting Senate approval of the Panama Canal treaties because of his ability to assemble a broad coalition of interest groups and his willingness to barter for the final crucial votes.

Treaty opponents were led by former California governor Ronald Reagan, who had found the issue to be potent in the 1976 presidential campaign. Groups fighting the treaty included the American Conservative Union, the Liberty Lobby, the National States' Rights Party, and the John Birch Society. Some fifteen hundred State Department officials led the fight for the treaty, backed by Common Cause, the National Education Association, the AFL-CIO, the National Jaycees, and business leaders. The interest groups were troops in a battle for public opinion to sway skeptical senators. At the beginning, only 8 percent of the public supported "giving up" the canal; by the time of the Senate vote, a majority favored the treaties. The emotional debate eventually worked to Carter's detriment, however. Leaders of the New Right later said the canal issue was the catalyst for the activism in the 1980 election campaign for Reagan and against Carter. The issue strengthened New Right groups' membership, treasuries, organization, and technological sophistication.

Early Interest Group Politics

Some of the great twentieth-century drives for enactment of legislation resulted from presidential management of interest-group lobbying, including: adoption of the constitutional amendment granting suffrage to women, the amendments for Prohibition and repeal of Prohibition, the Truman administration's aid to Greece and Turkey and the subsequent Marshall Plan for postwar European economic recovery, civil rights legislation of the 1950s and 1960s, Carter's energy package, and Franklin Roosevelt's attempt to gain control of the U.S. Supreme Court by increasing its size.

Even when presidents are at odds with major interest groups, they must at least pay their respects to them, usually with appearances at annual conventions of the organizations. Occasional appearances and meetings are necessary expressions of good faith for the president who wishes to stand as a symbol for the whole nation.

The number of presidential appearances before groups has increased steadily in the postwar era. President Ford attended meetings to deliver "minor" speeches an average of thirty-five times a year; President Carter delivered twenty-one annually; President Reagan twenty. Speeches to interest groups in Washington are far more numerous: Ford, Carter, and Reagan averaged about fifteen each month.[53]

The president often appears before interest groups to appeal for support on specific issues. Johnson appealed to leaders of civil rights organizations to keep the pressure on Congress for passage of the landmark Civil Rights Act of 1964. Reagan asked veterans' and Latin American groups to support the "contra" war against Nicaraguan government.

Presidential appearances before interest groups also can be pure symbolism—the head of state going before unfriendly groups to urge national unity. Reagan's appearances before the NAACP, Carter's speech before the Veterans of Foreign Wars, and Nixon's speech before the AFL-CIO are all examples.

The Use of the "Ad-hocracy"

When the White House faces a crisis or a seemingly intractable problem, the president often appoints representatives of interest groups to a commission to study the problem. Commissions have proved an effective way to use interest group representatives to overcome the difficulties of public wrangling by interest groups.

"Ad-hocracy," as the temporary commission has been called, offers several advantages to a president facing intransigent interest group politics.[54] First, the president can co-opt the interest groups by naming selected representatives to the panel. The president can often ensure favorable policy recommendations by "stacking" the panel. Second, the commission can stifle partisan debate by including members from both parties. Third, the commission can work in almost complete secrecy, thereby bypassing debilitating debate on each major issue that it faces. Fourth, ad-hocracy can offer all-or-nothing proposals that preclude endless public bargaining after the report's release.

President Reagan appointed ad-hocracies for problems including Social Security funding, the deployment strategy of the MX missile, the investigation of the Iran-contra affair, and the health crisis over Acquired Immune Deficiency Syndrome (AIDS). All of these issues proved too difficult for the normal public process of interest group bargaining—or at least the president thought he could defuse public controversy with a panel.

Social Security, for example, was in perilous financial shape, but efforts to trim benefits or raise taxes encountered well-orchestrated opposition campaigns. Democratic candidates campaigned emotionally and effectively against administration reform proposals in 1982. Reagan's 1983 commission helped build support for more taxes.

The debate over the MX missile presented a different problem for the administration. Reagan was committed to the mobile missile program, but Republican supporters in the West were reluctant to see the missiles based in their home states. Commission recommendations skirted the most difficult turf issues.

Even though a commission can cause problems for the president if it recommends actions that antagonize the administration's supporters, a commission's chief virtue is that it is a low-risk venture. President Reagan was pleasantly surprised by the favorable publicity that his National Commission on Excellence in Education created. Reagan initially maintained that the commission was Education Secretary Terrel H. Bell's panel, not his. When the report got rave reviews, Reagan adopted the commission and education issue as his own. Reagan may have been the most successful in his use of commissions, but he was not the first to try them.

John Kennedy, a skeptic of bureaucratic routines, appointed a number of commissions to bypass the usual method of policy development by departments. The Kennedy efforts foundered, however, when the makeup of the commissions received criticism and possible proposals were leaked.

Lyndon Johnson used task forces to develop much of his Great Society domestic legislation. Johnson's panels were more secretive and included fewer intellectuals and more members of the affected groups.

Task forces enabled Johnson and his special assistant, Joseph A. Califano, to maintain tight control of domestic policy. As an official in the U.S. Office of Education acknowledged, "much policy development in education has moved from here to the White House."[55] Johnson's 1964 task forces were ad-hoc efforts to develop a quick legislative package. In later years, the task forces were more entrenched. Fifty task forces worked on domestic programs in 1967. Most of the task forces recommended "incremental," or small-scale, adjustments to already existing policies and programs. But the task forces also proposed major initiatives.

The makeup of the Johnson task forces varied. Some contained a large number of officials from the White House and bureaucracy; others had strong interest group representation.

Public Efforts by Interest Groups

Textbooks of U.S. politics stress the "cozy" behind-the-scenes relationships between interest groups and agencies and committees of government. But many groups are not part of the secure federal establishment and must orchestrate large public demonstrations to influence the president and other parts of the government.

Outstanding examples of interest group efforts to influence the president and the rest of the government by "going public" include: the civil rights movement starting in the 1950s; the protests against the Vietnam War; the movements for and against ratification of the Equal Rights Amendment; the pro- and antiabortion movements; expressions of support and opposition to the Reagan administration's policies in Central America, particularly the activities of Lt. Col. Oliver North; protests by farmers vulnerable to foreclosure; antidrug rallies; protests against Reagan's nuclear weapons policies; and gay rights marches.

The most sustained recent public protests were over civil rights and the Vietnam War. When black organizations confronted the limits of the legal strategies of the NAACP and the state-by-state action to protect rights, a series of protests helped to put the issue on the national agenda. Demonstrations and other "outsider" efforts by civil rights organizations forced Presidents Eisenhower, Kennedy, and Johnson to deal with the issue. The most dramatic demonstration was the 1963 march on Washington, capped by Martin Luther King's "I Have a Dream" speech and civil rights leaders' visit to the White House.

President Johnson first dismissed Vietnam War protests as unrepresentative of public opinion, but the protests drew attention to moral and tactical questions about the war in elite circles such as the media and universities. Extensive war coverage following protests helped to shift public opinion against the war and persuade Johnson to halt bombing in 1968.

Many protests fail to move the president, at least in any direct way. President Reagan stood by his nuclear arms policies—including the decision to base Pershing missiles in Europe—despite massive demonstrations in West Germany, Great Britain, and the United States. Reagan dismissed the protests, including a gathering of several hundred thousand people at New York's Central Park, as inspired and organized in part by Soviet agents. Reagan's aggressive activity on arms control in his second term, however, suggests that the "peace" movement might have had an effect on him after all.

Scholars Frances Fox Piven and Richard Cloward have argued that public protest and disruption have historically been necessary for poor people to obtain benefits from the federal government and the states. Protests develop when economic conditions decline, resulting in government provision of social welfare programs to serve as a "safety net." When the economy improves, and public pressure declines, the government adopts restrictions on benefits.[56]

Public protest opens or narrows the space for political discussion and negotiation. Demonstrations have brought new issues to public debate and thereby opened up debate on matters such as civil rights, the Vietnam War, gay rights, military spending, abortion, and environmental pro-

Frequently, groups not part of the federal establishment feel the need to orchestrate large public demonstrations to influence the president. In August 1976, a group in favor of the Equal Rights Amendment marches in front of the White House.

tection. Debates about Social Security, however, were restricted by the climate created by public lobbying against cuts in benefits.

Protest sometimes blunts the edge of a movement. Groups that mobilize followers for rallies have difficulty translating their activism to sustained research and lobbying on Capitol Hill. Followers mistake their expression of opinion to be adequate political action.

Campaign Promises and Debts

Despite the cynical view that candidates forget campaign promises as soon as they enter public office, studies have found that presidents at least attempt to honor their pledges. Presidents usually target those pledges to specific interest groups, so interest group influence on the White House can be understood to begin before a president even takes office.[57]

An analysis of Carter's 1976 campaign promises and subsequent policies shows that he pursued the policies he promised in seven of ten policy areas. Carter's ambitious and legislative agenda did not lead to success on many major issues, so Carter often was under attack from interest groups even though he pursued many of his promises. The issues in which Carter tried to honor pledges included: creation of a cabinet-level Department of Education (a promise to the National Education Association), creation of a consumer protection agency (Ralph Nader organizations), common-site picketing legislation (AFL-CIO), amnesty for Vietnam War draft dodgers (peace groups), deregulation of businesses such as the airline industry (business and labor groups), expansion of environmental regulations (the Wilderness Society and other environmental groups), and a new public works program (AFL-CIO and big-city mayors).

Other presidents have had similar records honoring campaign pledges. John Kennedy faced a Congress as reluctant to enact his programs as did Carter. Kennedy, however, tried to honor campaign promises and succeeded—most frequently when policy changes did not require legislation to be passed. Kennedy's successes included the Peace Corps, minimum wage legislation, job training, trade expansion, regional development, arms control, the Alliance for Progress, and civil rights protections. Presidents Nixon and Reagan followed up on a number of campaign themes, such as a devolution of power to states and localities, a stronger U.S. military posture, free trade policies, cuts in domestic programs, and reduced federal regulation of business and the environment. Nixon departed from his promises to some interest groups, however, by supporting détente and strict regulation of the economy.

Despite dedication to the campaign agenda, interest groups complain that the president should do better. White House officials complain that interest groups do not understand the limits of political bargaining. One Carter official said of organized labor's impatience:

> The basic issue is not whether we support most of the things labor supports. We do! We had to make decisions about how much of our agenda could be dominated by labor-demanded bills in the first two years. Our decision to go with comprehensive welfare reform meant that health insurance had to wait. Not forever, but just intelligently delayed.... We're using a lot of credit in the Senate on the labor bill. But we get no thanks from them [labor organizations].[58]

Regulation of Lobbying

Lobbying is protected by First Amendment guarantees of the freedom of speech, but Congress has acted several times to monitor and regulate the kinds of contacts that interest groups make with the president and Congress.

Concern about conflicts of interest in the White House and the bureaucracy caused Congress to pass restrictions on the lobbying activities of former administration officials. Under the Ethics in Government Act of 1978, administration officials are not permitted to lobby for a year after they leave the government.

Two top Reagan advisers—Lyn Nofziger and Michael K. Deaver—were indicted for illegally contacting their former Reagan administration colleagues on behalf of clients after the two men had become lobbyists. Nofziger was convicted of illegal lobbying for a military contractor, and Deaver was convicted on three counts of perjury in connection with his lobbying work for the Canadian government.

The history of regulating lobbies has been spotty. Congress and the president have faced intense interest group resistance to any regulation of their activities. The legislation that has passed is either so vaguely defined or restricted that lobbies' activities are barely controlled.

The Revenue Act of 1934 denied tax-exempt status to groups that devote a "substantial part" of their activities to influencing legislation. The provision enumerated vague definitions and no sanctions, and courts applied the law inconsistently. The Foreign Agents Registration Act of 1938 requires representatives of foreign governments and organizations to register with the U.S. government. The act was the source of controversy when President Carter's brother Billy was hired by the Libyan government as a U.S. representative.

The Revenue Acts of 1938 and 1939 deny tax exemptions to corporations devoting a "substantial part" of their activities to propaganda and lobbying. The acts also state that citizens' donations to such corporations are not tax deductible. The Federal Regulation of Lobbying Act of 1946, the most comprehensive legislation at the time, requires registration of anyone who is hired by someone else to lobby Congress. The act requires quarterly reports from registered lobbyists.

Notes

1. For a comparative perspective on interest groups, see Frances Millard, *Pressure Politics in Industrial Societies* (London: Macmillan, 1986).
2. *Federalist* No. 10 was largely ignored by historians and theorists of American democracy until the early twentieth century. See David Rodgers, *Contested Truths* (New York: Basic Books, 1987), 185.
3. Clinton Rossiter, ed., *The Federalist Papers* (New York: New American Library, 1961), 78.
4. Alexis de Tocqueville, *Democracy in America* (New York: New American Library, 1956), 198.
5. Theodore J. Lowi, *The Personal President* (Ithaca, N.Y.: Cornell University Press, 1985), 22-41.

6. Theodore J. Lowi, *The End of Liberalism* (New York: Norton, 1979), 3-63.
7. Jack L. Walker, "The Origins and Maintenance of Interest Groups in America," *American Political Science Review* 77 (June 1983): 394-395; Harold Wolman and Fred Teitelbaum, "Interest Groups and the Reagan Presidency," in *The Reagan Presidency and the Governing of America,* ed. Lester M. Salamon and Michael S. Lund (Washington, D.C.: Urban Institute, 1984), 302.
8. Norman J. Ornstein and Shirley Elder, *Interest Groups, Lobbying, and Policymaking* (Washington, D.C.: CQ Press, 1978), 37, 24.
9. The Federal Election Campaign Act amendments of 1974 limit donations to individual candidates to $1,000 and donations to groups to $5,000. This provision encourages donors to give to PACs rather than candidates. *(See "The Campaign Finance System," p. 182, in The Electoral Process chapter of Part II.)*
10. Jeffrey Berry, *The Interest Group Society* (Boston: Little, Brown, 1984), 160. Congressional PAC spending increased from $23 million in 1976 to $80 million in 1982. See also Martha Joynt Kumar and Michael Baruch Grossman, "The President and Interest Groups," in *The Presidency and the Political System,* ed. Michael Nelson (Washington, D.C.: CQ Press, 1984), 288.
11. Arthur F. Bentley, *The Process of Government* (San Antonio: Principia Press, 1949).
12. David Truman, *The Governmental Process* (New York: Knopf, 1951).
13. Robert A. Dahl, *Who Governs?* (New Haven, Conn.: Yale University Press, 1961).
14. E. E. Schattschneider, *The Semisovereign People* (New York: Holt, Rinehart, and Winston, 1960); C. Wright Mills, *The Power Elite* (New York: Oxford University Press, 1959); Floyd Hunter, *Community Power Structure* (Chapel Hill: University of North Carolina Press, 1953).
15. For a concise examination of the bias of interest group representation, see Kay Lehman Schlozman, "What Accent the Heavenly Chorus? Political Equality and the American Pressure System," in *Journal of Politics* 46 (1984): 1006-1031.
16. Mancur Olson, *The Logic of Collective Action* (Cambridge, Mass.: Harvard University Press, 1965).
17. Daniel Bell, "The Revolution of Rising Entitlements," in *Fortune,* April 1975, 99.
18. For a recent critique of the breakdown of a civic ethic due to individualist and interest-group liberalism, see Benjamin Barber, *Strong Democracy* (Berkeley: University of California Press, 1984), esp. 3-114. For a conservative statement of similar concerns, see Robert Nisbet, *The Twilight of Authority* (New York: Oxford University Press, 1975).
19. Lowi, *End of Liberalism,* 62.
20. Paul Light, *The President's Agenda* (Baltimore: Johns Hopkins University Press, 1982), 94.
21. Joseph A. Pika, "Interest Groups and the Executive: Presidential Intervention," in *Interest Group Politics,* ed. Allen J. Cigler and Burdett A. Loomis (Washington, D.C.: CQ Press, 1983), 312.
22. Grossman and Kumar, "President and Interest Groups," 289.
23. Anthony Downs, "Up and Down with Ecology—The Issue Attention Cycle," *Public Interest* 28 (Summer 1972): 38-50.
24. The Carter and Reagan administrations observed the terms of the arms treaty, but Carter decided that a public battle for ratification would be damaging politically. Carter, therefore, did not reap the usual public relations benefits of a major foreign policy event.
25. Reagan's reconciliation budget-cutting strategy is discussed in Allen Schick, *Reconciliation and the Congressional Budget Process* (Washington, D.C.: American Enterprise Institute, 1981).
26. Larry J. Sabato, *The Party's Just Begun* (Glenview, Ill.: Scott Foresman, 1988).
27. The following discussion relies on Benjamin Ginsberg and Martin Shefter, "The Presidency and the Organization of Interests," in *The Presidency and the Political System,* ed. Michael Nelson (Washington, D.C.: CQ Press, 1988), 311-330.
28. Ibid., 311-333.
29. Maximum feasible participation never played as important a role as its promoters and detractors argued. Most organizations created by the provision eventually came under the control of local governments and other more conservative groups such as local businesses. But the principles behind the program—that interest groups can be created to promote policies and that interested parties should be consulted before policies affecting them are implemented—have remained part of American politics. Perhaps most important, the provision led to the development of a wide range of interest groups and trained a generation of government and interest group leaders. See Dennis R. Judd, *The Politics of American Cities: Power and Public Policy,* 2d ed. (Boston: Little, Brown, 1984), 311; Daniel Patrick Moynihan, *Maximum Feasible Misunderstanding* (New York: Free Press, 1970).
30. Robert D. Reischauer, "Fiscal Federalism in the 1980's: Dismantling or Rationalizing the Great Society," in *The Great Society and Its Legacy,* ed. Marshall Kaplan and Peggy Cuciti (Durham, N.C.: Duke University Press, 1986), 187-188.
31. Ginsberg and Shefter, "The Presidency and the Organization of Interests," 313-327.
32. Marc Bendick, Jr., and Phyllis M. Levinson, "Private-Sector Initiatives or Public-Private Partnerships," in *The Reagan Presidency,* 455-479.
33. Allan J. Cigler, "From Protest Group to Interest Group: The Making of American Agriculture Movement, Inc.," in *Interest Group Politics,* ed. Allan J. Cigler and Burdett A. Loomis (Washington, D.C.: CQ Press, 1988), 46-69.
34. Thomas Byrne Edsall, *The New Politics of Inequality* (New York: Norton, 1984), 99-103.
35. Jeff Fishel, *Presidents and Promises* (Washington, D.C.: CQ Press, 1985), 168.
36. John Herbers, "Grass-Roots Groups Go National," *New York Times Magazine,* September 4, 1983, 22-23, 42, 46, 48.
37. Thomas Cronin, *The State of the Presidency* (Boston: Little, Brown, 1980), 84.
38. Nelson W. Polsby, "Interest Groups and the Presidency: Trends in Political Intermediation in America," in *American Politics and Public Policy,* ed. Walter Dean Burnham and Martha Wagner Weinberg (Cambridge, Mass.: MIT Press, 1978), 46.
39. Grossman and Kumar, "President and Interest Groups," 284.
40. Joseph A. Pika, "Interest Groups and the Executive," 307-308.
41. Light, *President's Agenda,* 95.
42. Grossman and Kumar, "President and Interest Groups," 309.
43. "President Carter's Farewell Address," *Congressional Quarterly Weekly Report,* January 17, 1981, 156.
44. Pika, "Interest Groups and the Executive," 301.
45. Alfred A. Malabre, Jr., *Beyond Our Means* (New York: Vintage Books, 1987), 111-114.
46. Lowi, *Personal President,* 141-142.
47. See Grossman and Kumar, "President and Interest Groups," 290-307.
48. Ornstein and Elder, *Interest Groups, Lobbying, and Policymaking,* 69-79.
49. Ibid., 82-93.
50. Wolman and Teitelbaum, "Interest Groups and the Reagan Presidency," 308.
51. Hedrick Smith, "The President as Coalition Builder: Reagan's First Year," in *Rethinking the Presidency,* ed. Thomas E. Cronin (Boston: Little, Brown, 1982), 280.
52. Ibid., 281.
53. Gary King and Lyn Ragsdale, *The Elusive Executive: Discovering Statistical Patterns in the Presidency* (Washington, D.C.: CQ Press, 1988), 254-259.
54. Francis E. Rourke, *Bureaucracy, Politics, and Public Policy* (Boston: Little, Brown, 1984), 150.
55. Norman C. Thomas and Harold L. Wolman, "Policy Formulation in the Institutionalized Presidency," in *The Presidential Advisory System,* ed. Thomas E. Cronin and Sanford D. Greenberg (New York: Harper and Row, 1969), 127. See also

Daniel Bell, "Government by Commission," in the same volume, 117-123.

56. Frances Fox Piven and and Richard Cloward, *Regulating the Poor: The Functions of Public Relief* (New York: Random House, 1972).
57. See Fishel, *Presidents and Promises.*
58. Ibid., 93.

Selected Bibliography

Berry, Jeffrey. *The Interest Group Society*. Boston: Little, Brown, 1984.

Cigler, Allan J., and Burdett A. Loomis. *Interest Group Politics.* 2d ed. Washington, D.C.: CQ Press, 1988.

Heclo, Hugh. "Issue Networks and the Executive Establishment." In *The New American Political System*, ed. Anthony King. Washington, D.C.: American Enterprise Institute, 1978.

Lowi, Theodore J. *The End of Liberalism.* New York: Norton, 1979.

Ornstein, Norman J., and Shirley Elder. *Interest Groups, Lobbying, and Policymaking.* Washington, D.C.: CQ Press, 1978.

Schlozman, Kay Lehman. "What Accent the Heavenly Chorus: Political Equality and the American Pressure System." *Journal of Politics* 46 (1984): 1006-1031.

Presidential Appearances

Presidents always work at a distance from the American public. Public opinion polls, interest groups, the media, and relations with Congress and the bureaucracy give presidents indirect access to the public. Speaking directly to the population helps presidents create at least the illusion of a direct relationship, but it does not help them develop the relationships needed to assemble coalitions and to govern. As presidents attempt to build a coalition, they appeal to the many separate groups, or separate publics, within the population as much as to the public at large. Presidents' constant public appeals have made the presidency an extension of electoral campaigns.

The President as Public Figure

The president occupies the most prominent position in American politics, largely because the United States has no other nationally elected leader. One reason for the president's prominence is the ability to use what Theodore Roosevelt called the "bully pulpit." The president's unique ability to promote a national vision and to influence actors in both the public and private spheres has been crucial in disproving the predictions of some observers of early America that the presidency would play a minor role in national government.

In the twentieth century, the president's prominence in American politics has increased not only with a growing involvement in domestic policy and the rise of the United States to international leadership, but also with an expansion of the president's role as the major preacher in American politics.[1] With words and images as well as the actions of the administration, the president plays a major role in setting the terms of debate for the entire political system.

Public speaking is one of the most important ties between the president and the public. For many citizens, the firmest memory of the president is the president delivering a speech.[2] Between 1945 and 1975, public speeches by presidents increased by about 500 percent. A 1972 report estimated that "a half million words annually flow out of the White House in a torrent of paper ink." [3] Not only presidents' words but also their appearances are important in communicating with the public. Academic studies conclude that nonverbal signs, such as appearances, have four to ten times the effect of verbal signs on "impression formation." [4]

By Charles C. Euchner

Political scientist Richard E. Neustadt has argued that the president can exert influence only rarely by command. A more important tool of power is the "power to persuade." [5] Neustadt concentrated on the president's power to persuade other members of the Washington establishment, but the breakdown of many stable institutions has moved presidents to use their persuasive abilities more and more on the public. Even when presidents do not speak out, the threat of "going public" is an important tool.[6]

Communications expert Roderick P. Hart has argued that ubiquitous presidential speech has transformed not only the president and the rest of the national government but the way people perceive politics. The president dominates the public sphere. Working within a "matrix of countervailing forces," the president must maneuver with speech. "Virtually every activity in the modern White House is designed to shape or reshape something that the president has said or will say." [7]

Even when urging change, the president's themes are basically conservative. Philip Abbott has written: "President after president, whether advocating reform or retrenchment, attempt[s] to justify policy by calling America back to its origins, restating its basic values, applying them to current problems by seeking to establish an underlying unity amidst current conflict through a call to rededication and sacrifice." [8]

The development of a voluble presidency stems from changes in the U.S. political system as well as from advances in communications and transportation technologies. The president is now the premier figure in American politics and cannot depend on traditional bases of support such as Congress, party organizations, the print media, or the bureaucracy. Without those mediators of public policy, presidents increasingly must rely on their ability to move people with words.

The connection between presidential speech and the absence of institutional bases was underscored by the Nixon administration's handling of the Watergate scandal. As President Nixon lost support in Congress, in public opinion polls, and among interest groups, he depended increasingly on his rhetorical powers. Nixon's last year in office was dominated by behind-the-scenes strategy sessions on how to respond to charges of lawbreaking and the carefully crafted release of information and public statements.[9]

The disparate parts of the American federal system—from states and localities to the wide variety of economic and social groups—regularly turn to the president for rhetorical as well as administrative and legislative leadership. As political scientist E. E. Schattschneider has noted, battles that originate in a restricted setting often move to higher and higher levels as the combatants seek to attract powerful allies.[10] The president exerts rhetorical force on almost every possible political and economic issue that Americans face, even if the president plays no direct role in the issue.

The president has a variety of ways to use rhetoric in politics. The chief executive regularly meets with reporters and other media representatives, gives speeches on television and radio, addresses large crowds and groups, holds informal meetings with leaders of interest groups, travels abroad to meet foreign leaders, meets and speaks by telephone with members of Congress and other elected officials, and attends events that feature celebrities. The president also has command of large research and public relations operations in the White House and federal agencies. Presidential appointees also promote the administration's policies.

What presidents say is often less important than how they say it. The potency of presidential remarks lies not in their content but in the ceremonial way they are delivered. Deference to the president is the norm. As Hart has noted: "Precious few of these ten thousand texts [presidential addresses from Eisenhower to Reagan] were remembered by listeners even a day after their delivery. But what was recalled was the speech event itself—the crowds and the color and the dramaturgy and the physical presence of the chief executive." [11]

As theorists of public rhetoric have noted, the setting for speeches can be even more important than the words uttered. Few spectators of all but the most important presidential speeches can remember much of the arguments in the speech, but most retain a memory of the ceremonial or otherwise symbolic backdrop. When the substance of the speech is remembered, it is usually restricted to a few key phrases or ideas.

Pete Souza, the White House

The setting for a president's speech can be even more important than the words uttered. President Reagan's speech at the Statue of Liberty celebration on July 3, 1986, is a prime example.

Political scientist Murray Edelman has argued that the stage on which presidents appear can provide a rhetorical advantage because the stage removes the audience from its daily routine. "Massiveness, ornateness, and formality are the most common notes struck in the design of these scenes, and they are presented upon a scale which focuses constant attention on the difference between everyday life and the special occasion," Edelman writes. Such backgrounds make for heightened sensitivity and easier conviction in onlookers, for the framed actions are taken on their own terms. They are not qualified by inconsistent facts in the environment.[12]

Presidents bask in the regal splendor of the presidency whenever they make a public appearance. The podium usually holds a seal of the president on the front, and flags usually hang somewhere within the audience's frame of vision. Standing alongside the president is usually a line of dignitaries who look on with respect and even reverance. The distance between the president and the audience increases the sense of the president's "untouchable" status.

When presidents give a State of the Union message, they face a rare assemblage of both houses of Congress, the Supreme Court, and the cabinet; the vice president and Speaker of the House are seated behind the president, and a huge flag hangs in the background. When presidents visit military officials, they stand before impressive-looking equipment such as a navy ship, or before highly disciplined officers and troops, or a military band. When they visit a foreign country, they are treated to welcomes from dignitaries and bands as well as formal dinners and presentations. When they welcome the winners of the World Series or Super Bowl, they are surrounded by the team's banners and other trappings of the sport.

Even in the most unceremonial situations, the president evokes strong national sentiment by the setting. After the truck-bombing of marine barracks in Lebanon in 1985, President Reagan stood in the drizzling rain with his wife and somberly read a statement of tribute to the murdered men and a warning to the forces responsible for the attack. After President Kennedy was assassinated in 1963, Lyndon Johnson took the oath of office on an airplane to emphasize the suddenness of the tragedy and the swift assumption of power.

Although the major television networks occasionally refuse to broadcast an address, presidents almost always have the prestige to gain a wide electronic audience for their speeches and informal discussions. Radio stations always will agree to broadcast short speeches and special events, like Jimmy Carter's call-in show. The importance of televised speeches has increased since the 1960s as the number of press conferences has declined. The more formal talks give the president greater control over the agenda and tempo than the give-and-take of press conferences.

Historical Background

Even though the president has always been the preeminent single figure in American politics, it has been only since the rise of an activist national government and vast systems of communications and transportation that the

Mezzotint by H. S. Sadd, 1849 after T. H. Matteson; Library of Congress

George Washington delivers his inaugural address, April 30, 1789, in New York's old City Hall.

president has been at the center of constant, partisan, policy-oriented rhetoric. In the early days of the Republic, presidents usually confined their public appeals to written messages and addressed only matters of broad national interest. Presidential messages, at least until Woodrow Wilson's administration (1913-1921), took on the quality of a national civics lesson in constitutional government rather than open appeals for political support.

The nation's history of presidential rhetoric can be roughly divided into three periods: the age of the Founders, the age of economic expansion and reform, and the age of presidential leadership.

The Age of the Founders and Early Expansion

The president's role in the nation's rhetoric was set by George Washington (1789-1797) and the rest of the "Virginia Dynasty" that ruled the young nation from 1789 to 1829. Everything Washington did was a conscious precedent for later presidents. Washington's successors—John Adams, Thomas Jefferson, James Madison, James Monroe, and John Quincy Adams—all had direct ties to the nation's founding. They all experienced the same fears about the dangers of democratic or "mob" rule and the importance for national leadership to avoid rhetorical excess. The same impulse that led the Founders to set limits on democratic rule also led the first presidents to set limits on presidential rhetoric to avoid demagogy.

The sense of rhetorical limits that guided presidential rhetoric for its first century began with Washington's first inaugural address. After hearing recommendations from his advisors, Washington discarded plans to include a seventy-three page set of policy recommendations in his inaugural speech. Instead he used the occasion to deliver a more general lecture on virtue and the need for guidance from the Constitution and from God. Washington was the only president to deliver his inaugural address to a select crowd of members of Congress and other dignitaries rather than the people at large. As was true throughout his presidency, Washington tried to offer leadership by example rather than by argumentation. Washington feared that the regal ceremony might give later presidents dangerous dreams of monarchy, so at his second inaugural he issued a simple two-paragraph address.[13]

With the exception of John Adams (1797-1801), subsequent presidents until Abraham Lincoln (1861-1865) used the inaugural address to explain and extoll the principles of republican government, complete with warnings about the potential excesses of democracy. Discussion of specific policy matters was infrequent and always linked directly to the president's conception of American constitutional values. Of the early presidents, James K. Polk (1845-1849) was the most explicit on policy questions; he pushed for lower tariffs and annexation of Texas and Oregon and opposed creation of a third national bank.

The president also issued a variety of proclamations, mostly written. Those proclamations rarely argued any points; they usually stated government policies, from the institution of Thanksgiving Day to the emancipation of black Southerners from slavery during the Civil War. As political scientist Jeffrey K. Tulis has noted, the proclamations derive their force not from argumentation but from appeals to the Constitution, the nation's sacred document.[14]

The most outstanding example of argumentation in a proclamation was Andrew Jackson's statement denying states the right to "nullify," or declare invalid, laws passed by the national government. Jackson's style was more like that of a Supreme Court decision, explaining the rationale for an irrevocable decision rather than seeking to persuade people to join a coalition.

Perhaps the most ceremonious speech presidents regularly deliver today is the State of the Union address. Until Woodrow Wilson, however, presidents since Thomas Jefferson had met the constitutional requirement to address the nation's affairs with a written report. Congressional leaders followed up the written report with a response to each of the president's points. The State of the Union address, then, was just the beginning of a formal dialogue about government policies based on constitutional and republican principles.

The nation's early years saw some presidential appeals to the people, but the rhetoric was restrained and the audience limited. Below the level of presidential politics, however, debate could be bitter and divisive. As historian Michael E. McGerr has noted, political debate took place as a public spectacle: "Through participation in torchlight parades, mass rallies, and campaign clubs and marching companies, men gave expression to the partisan outlook of the [fiercely partisan] newspaper press." [15] Debates in Congress, for example, often took violent turns. City politics were organized by the gangs and political machines that operated in the streets. Mass demonstrations over slavery, labor, and U.S. involvement in wars were a regular part of the American landscape in the nineteenth century. Political discussions in speeches, pamphlets, and newspapers could be personal and invective. People who worked for presidential campaigns often resorted to caustic language and threats. Through it all, however, the president himself stood above the fray, speaking little publicly about some of the most important issues of the day.

The Founders resisted unbridled democracy, and their rhetoric sought to dampen whatever political passions might exist at the time. The Constitution includes many mechanisms for blocking democratic processes, such as a federalist system, an independent executive, a bicameral legislature, indirect election of presidents and (until 1913) senators, and an independent and tenured judiciary. The ideal political leader was not the man of the people, but rather the statesman who could guide the nation. Alexander Hamilton expressed this ideal in *Federalist* No. 71:

> The republican principle demands that the deliberative sense of the community should guide the conduct of those to whom they entrust the management of their affairs; but it does not require an unqualified complaisance to every sudden breeze of passion, or to every transient impulse which the people may receive from the arts of men, who flatter their prejudices to betray their interests.... [W]hen occasions present themselves in which the interests of the people are at variance with their inclinations, it is the duty of the persons whom they have appointed to be the guardians of those interests to withstand the temporary delusion in order to give them time and opportunity for more sedate reflection.[16]

The president was expected to account for his actions with public, but not necessarily popular, messages. Written messages explaining vetoes and the "state of the union" would be available to Congress and anyone else educated and interested enough to seek them out, but presidents would not aggressively seek public support.

From the administration of George Washington through that of Herbert C. Hoover (1929-1933), the president spent several hours a week at the White House shaking hands with any citizen interested in glimpsing him. The "open house," usually held on Sundays after church services, did not communicate anything of substance, but it conveyed the message that the president would not be monarchical and removed from the people. After the sounding of trumpets and bands and the announcement that the president was on his way to meet the people, single-file queues would move rapidly through the public room of the Executive Mansion. Presidents often tried to calculate just how many hands they would shake in an afternoon, as well as the handshake-per-minute rate. The conversation consisted of little more than greetings and best wishes, although some citizens occasionally tried to convey an opinion about a pressing policy question.[17]

The change in presidential rhetoric is marked by the way biographers have treated presidents before and after 1930. Later biographers express puzzlement that the earlier presidents did not turn to rhetoric as a tool of leadership. But earlier biographers underscore the value of the "custom" of limiting public remarks since such remarks would "sacrifice [the president's] dignity to beg in person for their support." [18]

George G. Bain; Library of Congress

Up through the administration of Herbert Hoover, presidents spent several hours a week at the White House shaking hands with citizens. Above, the general public is admitted for a New Year's Day reception.

Political scientist Jeffrey Tulis found evidence of some one thousand presidential speeches before the twentieth century. Of the twenty-four presidents who served during that period, only four attempted to defend or attack a specific piece of legislation, and only three—Van Buren, Johnson, and Cleveland—made partisan speeches. Only Lincoln addressed the war in which the nation was engaged; Madison and Polk did not. Only nine presidents indicated the general policy directions of the nation in popular speeches. Eighty percent of the speeches were brief.[19]

Throughout this period, presidential rhetoric was circumscribed by the mores that Washington established. Those mores changed—policy issues crept into presidential speeches, even if they were tethered to constitutional principles—but they remained strongly in force. Just how strong those mores remained was underscored by the miserable failure of President Andrew Johnson (1865-1869) in his attempt to rally the public through a national speech-making tour in the early years of Reconstruction.

Washington was the nation's greatest public figure, a symbol of the new nation's unity. Washington made several public tours in which he put himself on display, but the purpose of the excursions was limited. Washington toured to gather information, ease tensions, and simply show himself to the people. Washington treated the tours "as auxiliary to the president's narrow executive function of carrying out the law and preserving tranquility, rather than his legislative responsibility to initiate new policies."[20]

Washington set an important precedent by insisting on written replies to the remarks of others after speeches.[21] Washington's farewell address was a more scholarly document, open for careful analysis but not grand rhetorical movements.

The second president, John Adams, occasionally met with small groups but did not make public tours. Some historians suggest that Adams lost his chance to improve his public standing on issues, particularly foreign affairs, because of his public reticence. Thomas Jefferson (1801-1805), considered the most democratic theorist of early America, limited his public statements to a few meetings with American Indians and his formal, written messages to Congress. Despite a difficult war with Great Britain, James Madison (1809-1817) continued the practice of presidential communication by proclamation rather than speech.

James Monroe (1817-1825) reinstituted Washington's practice of the national tour, but otherwise stayed within the limits of unity appeals and limited speech. Despite his background as a teacher of rhetoric at Harvard College, John Quincy Adams (1825-1829) refused to do more than put himself "on display" in public gatherings. His public remarks were simple statements of greetings and congratulations. Adams almost never even referred to the public issues of the day before popular audiences.

Following the bitter controversy over the 1824 election of John Quincy Adams over Andrew Jackson (1829-1837), the nation experienced major pushes to expand the idea of democratic rule. Suffrage barriers pertaining to property fell during this period as the nation moved westward and politicians from different regions competed for control over the nation's development. Political parties, which put forth radically different views of development and protection, gained legitimacy for the first time and created a regular public clash of ideas. The sectional tensions finally led to the bloody Civil War of 1861 to 1865.

Jackson rarely gave speeches. He enjoyed popular discourse, but once elected president he limited the number of appearances and contained his argumentation within the limits set by his predecessors. Jackson's most public campaigns—against the National Bank and the doctrine of nullification—were quite limited. His public appeals were mediated—that is to say, he spoke to the public through the formal channels of official documents and proclamations. Jackson's annual messages and the nullification proclamation to Congress were all written appeals.

Jackson's successors were also reluctant to speak. Martin Van Buren faced a boycott of councils in three New York towns after he delivered a slightly partisan remark, then abandoned any more such rhetoric. John Tyler (1841-1845) delivered no public addresses. James Polk took one public tour but considered other public appearances a nuisance and therefore avoided them. Zachary Taylor took one tour but avoided being seen; the journey was a fact-finding tour more than a public relations effort.

Millard Fillmore (1850-1853) was the first president since Washington to discuss policy in public when he defended the Compromise of 1850 in a series of short speeches. But these speeches took place after policy had been determined; they were not intended to sway action during the policy-making process. Franklin Pierce (1853-1857) expanded presidential rhetoric, discussing the role of tariffs and federalism. As a lame-duck president just before the Civil War, James Buchanan (1857-1861) discussed the nominating process of the Democratic party and the role of property and popular rule in the states.

Abraham Lincoln appeared before a number of groups but averred that he could not speak about policy except in a more appropriate place. Tulis has outlined five reasons for Lincoln's infrequent public rhetoric: modesty about his own "wisdom" before his inauguration, a desire to let problems sort themselves out, the need for flexibility, the dramatic effect that his statements might have, and a desire to lend greater authority to the few public pronouncements he eventually would make.[22]

Still, some of Lincoln's addresses were important to his governing. As Abbott has noted, all of Lincoln's speeches were rooted in specific political problems, such as the lynching of an abolitionist journalist and the economic aspects of slavery.[23]

Lincoln's successor, Andrew Johnson, was the exceptional case of the voluble president. As a Southern Democrat who rose to the presidency through assassination, Johnson had no real base of power in Washington. He found himself under attack from all sides and fought back with words. But his rhetorical thrusts further undermined his position.[24]

The Age of Economic Growth and Reform

As the nation recovered from the Civil War, economic growth resumed on a scale previously unimagined. Transportation and communications networks stretched across the nation, and businesses grew in size and geographic importance. The national government played an important role in the expansion but did not address the more negative consequences of rapid industrialization and urbanization. The national government responded to the economy's swings of boom and bust, but its role was limited by the constrained rhetoric and vision of public action. As politicians recognized the need for more concerted national action, both the rhetoric and the vision expanded.

Woodcut in J. T. Trowbridge, *A Picture of Desolated States*, 1868; Library of Congress

Seeking to build his political strength, President Andrew Johnson made a speaking tour of the country in 1866.

In many ways, the dilemmas that Andrew Johnson faced after succeeding President Lincoln resembled the situation of modern presidents. Bereft of a strong party organization, dealing with an independent-minded Congress, facing deep sectional divisions, and lacking control over patronage, Johnson desperately needed a way to build his political strength. Like presidents in the late twentieth century, Johnson sought that strength by appealing over the heads of political elites to the power of public opinion. Because the system was not accustomed to such appeals, Johnson's attempt to go public failed. He was the only president in history to be impeached, and one of the counts against him actually concerned the style of his "intemperate" rhetoric. Johnson committed the most important rhetorical "crimes" while trying to rally public support for his policies for the defeated states of the Confederacy. Tulis has described Johnson's rhetorical style:

> Like contemporary electoral campaigns, Johnson had one rough outline, carried in his head, on which he rendered variations for particular audiences. In the typical speech, Johnson would begin by disclaiming any intention to speak, proceed to invoke the spirits of Washington and Jackson, claim his own devotion to the principles of Union, deny that he was a traitor as others alleged, attack some part of the audience (depending on the kind of heckles he received), defend his use of the veto, attack Congress as a body and single out particular congressmen (occasionally denouncing them as traitors for not supporting his policies), compare himself to Christ and offer himself as a martyr, and finally conclude by declaring his closeness to the people and appealing for their support.[25]

Johnson's tour, which received bad notices in the Republican-dominated press, was avoided even by Johnson's cabinet and aides. When on February 24, 1868, the House of Representatives resolved to impeach Johnson, the tenth and last article concerned Johnson's bad rhetoric. The Senate acquitted Johnson (by one vote), but no major political figure disagreed with the notion that his public appeals were improper. *(See "Impeachment of Andrew Johnson," p. 369, in Removal of the President chapter of Part II.)* The lessons from Johnson's bitter experience were clear: politics are a dirty game, and presidents who become involved in the nasty rhetoric put themselves in danger of getting tarred in the process.

Ulysses S. Grant (1869-1877) and Rutherford B. Hayes (1877-1881), the two presidents immediately after Johnson, limited their public speechmaking to official greetings and plaudits to veterans and other groups. Both presidents refused to campaign for the White House and issued written statements to indicate policy preferences. Hayes delivered more than one hundred speeches, but they were limited to greetings to groups. This real but unsubstantive expansion of presidential speech might be attributed to the need to shore up national confidence because of the controversy surrounding Hayes's election by the House. *(See "The Compromise of 1876," p. 286, in the Electoral Process chapter of Part II.)* Hayes also took several tours and delivered speeches that addressed policy within the larger philosophical framework of republicanism.

James A. Garfield (1881) campaigned for the White House but did not speak on policy as president. His successor, Chester A. Arthur (1881-1885), also limited his talks to symbolic statements at public ceremonies. Grover Cleveland (1885-1889, 1893-1897) discussed taxes, civil service, and labor during his presidential campaigns but made few public remarks as president. He also wrote extensively on many issues. Benjamin Harrison (1889-1893) broke with tradition when he discussed policy issues such as the railroads and postal service during his public tours; still, he was reluctant to go too far. He told a Kingston, New York, crowd, for example: "You ask for a speech. It is not very easy to know what one can talk about on such an occasion as this. Those topics that are most familiar to me, because I am in daily contact with them, namely, public affairs, are in some measure prohibited to me."[26]

William McKinley (1897-1901) vowed to talk on a wide range of issues, but his speeches were formal and philosophical in character like those of the nineteenth-century presidents. McKinley did not make any speeches on the Spanish-American War, the sinking of the battleship *Maine*, the Philippines, or southern race laws.

Theodore Roosevelt (1901-1909), the feisty former New York governor who assumed the presidency upon McKinley's assassination, was the first president to go over the head of Congress since Andrew Johnson, but Roosevelt did not overturn the longtime balance of power between the two branches of government. As political scientist Elmer Cornwell has noted, Roosevelt's tours on behalf of specific policies began and ended before Congress took up the matter.[27]

Roosevelt's handpicked successor, William Howard Taft (1909-1913), increased presidential leadership of public opinion. Taft regularly issued lists of legislative initiatives he favored. He was more adept as an administrator than as a rhetorician, however. Although his antitrust and environmental policies were in line with Roosevelt's, his hortatory deficiencies were one of the reasons Roosevelt opposed him in the 1912 election.

Woodrow Wilson (1913-1921) was a crucial figure in the transformation of the national government from a congressional to a presidential system. He argued for a more unified system of government with the president as the leader, overcoming the fragmented, plodding committees in Congress. Moving public policy from the darkness of the committee meeting to the bright light of public debate was central to Wilson's system. He argued that the public could judge the president's character; if the public could find a leader to trust, the president could be entrusted with a wide grant of power. Wilson wrote: "Men can scarcely be orators without the force of character, that readiness of resource, that clearness of vision, that earnestness of purpose and that instinct and capacity for leadership which are the eight horses that draw the triumphal chariot of every leader and ruler of free men. We could not object to being ruled by such men." [28]

Wilson's ambitious domestic programs and involvement in World War I and the Versailles peace conference put the presidency in the middle of the nation's rhetorical battles. As historian David Green has argued, Wilson's public comments on the European war left room open for eventual U.S. involvement in the war. Wilson promised to keep the United States out of war but contrasted American "liberty" with German "authoritarianism." [29]

Once the United States entered the war and the Allied powers won, Wilson took an active public role. Wilson's depiction of the war as the "war to end all wars" helped to overcome many of the deep internal divisions within the United States based on the nationalities of U.S. immigrant citizens. Wilson's 1919 trip to Versailles and his subsequent parade through the streets of Paris was a rare foreign trip. The height of this public role was his U.S. tour to build support for U.S. membership in the League of Nations. Wilson's moralistic campaign ended when he collapsed with a stroke, and the Senate rejected the treaty.

The presidents who succeeded Wilson—Warren G. Harding (1921-1923), Calvin Coolidge (1923-1929), and Herbert C. Hoover (1929-1933)—were less active rhetorically. Harding, elected president because of a back-room bargain at the Republican convention in 1920, limited his public appearances and statements and instituted a written-questions-only policy for questions from the media. He died of a heart attack two years into his term. Coolidge—"Silent Cal"—was best known for his taciturn manner. In his press conferences, Coolidge continued Harding's policy of written press questions. Hoover was the first president to use radio extensively, but the audience was too small and Hoover's speaking style too formal for a strong president-public relationship to develop around his speeches.

The Age of Presidential Leadership

During the Great Depression, which began in 1929, the nation turned to Franklin D. Roosevelt (1933-1945) for presidential leadership. Roosevelt was tireless in his efforts to expand the government's involvement in both domestic and international politics.

Both Roosevelt's programs and rhetoric emphasized the need for strong central direction that only a president could provide. For the first time, the government in Washington moved from its traditional role as patronage state to a regulatory state.[30] As the government became involved in all aspects of everyday life, the need for strong executive direction increased. Sophisticated systems of communication also tightened the bond between the president and the public. From the administration of Franklin Roosevelt through that of Ronald Reagan (1981-1989), the president became more of a rhetorical leader on a wide range of issues rather than an executive on a limited set of fundamentally national concerns.

By the time FDR took office, millions of American homes were tied together by the airwaves of radio broadcasting. Politics moved from the crowds to the smaller units of a radio-listening audience. Political speeches, once bombastic, became more conversational and intimate. As communications expert Kathleen Hall Jamieson has noted, this shift was reflected in the metaphors used to describe human relations. Warlike words such as *armed*, *forceful*, *take*, *hold*, *yield*, *marshal*, *battle*, *weapons*, and *onslaught* once described political debates; with the dawn of the media age came warm, electrical words like *wavelength*, *relayed*, *channeled*, *transformed*, *turned on*, *fused*, and *defused*.[31]

Roosevelt was the perfect president to begin the new style of debate. He delivered a series of "fireside chats" to the nation over the radio that identified him with everyday concerns. Roosevelt's secretary of labor, Frances Perkins, described the talks:

> When he talked on the radio, he saw them gathered in the little parlor, listening with their neighbors. He was conscious of their faces and hands, their clothes and homes. His voice and his facial expression as he spoke were those of an intimate friend.... I have seen men and women gathered around the radio, even those who didn't like him or who were opposed to him politically, listening with a pleasant, happy feeling of association and friendship. The exchange between them and him through the medium of the radio was very real. I have seen tears coming to their eyes as he told them of some tragic episode, of the sufferings of the persecuted people in Europe, of the poverty during unemployment, of the sufferings of the homeless, of the sufferings of the people whose sons had died during the war, and they were tears of sincerity and recognition and sympathy.[32]

Since the end of World War II, presidents have spoken in public more than ten thousand times—an average of one speech every working day.[33]

Harry Truman used rhetoric as a tool in his relations with Congress, but it was always directed toward specific policy aims. Truman relied on rhetoric to promote his

Table 1 Level of Public Activities of Presidents, 1949-1984

President	Total activities	Yearly average	Monthly average
Truman	520	130	10.8
Eisenhower, I	330	83	6.9
Eisenhower, II	338	85	7.0
Kennedy	658	219	18.8
Johnson [a]	1,463	293	24.0
Nixon, I	634	159	13.2
Nixon, II	204	113	10.2
Ford	756	344	26.0
Carter	1,047	262	22.0
Reagan [b]	1,194	299	24.9

Source: Gary King and Lyn Ragsdale, *The Elusive Executive: Discovering Statistical Patterns in the Presidency* (Washington, D.C.: CQ Press, 1988), 275.

Note: Public activities are defined as including all domestic public appearances by a president, including major speeches, news conferences, minor speeches, Washington appearances, and U.S. appearances but not political appearances.

a. Includes full term from November 1963 to January 1969.

b. Figures for Reagan through first term only.

policies on European redevelopment, relations with the Soviet Union, aid to Greece and Turkey, and civil rights. Truman's 1948 election campaign was a marathon of public speaking, a whistlestop excoriation of Congress and a call for public support. Perhaps the Truman administration's most important legacy was its rhetoric about the Soviet Union. Truman acknowledged overstating the Soviet threat to arouse the public during the Greece-Turkey crisis, after a congressional leader advised him to "scare the hell out of the country." [34] Harsh anti-Soviet rhetoric since the Truman administration may be responsible for the bitterness of U.S.-Soviet relations and the costly nuclear arms race.

Because of improved air transportation, modern presidents have traveled regularly, both within the United States and around the world. Presidents through Dwight D. Eisenhower felt obliged to justify their trips abroad, but international travel has become a regular, expected, and even desired part of the office.

The president's expanded role in national politics has other causes besides advanced systems of transportation and communication, including: the decline of party strength, the development of populist nomination systems, the rise of political consultants, the fragmentation of Congress, and the "nationalization" of politics and policy.

Modern Presidential Appearances and Rhetoric

Presidential rhetoric in the postwar years shifted fundamentally with the ascension of John F. Kennedy to the White House. Harry Truman and Dwight Eisenhower used public speech almost solely in pursuit of a specific policy initiative, but later presidents have spoken out regularly on a wide range of matters. Speech has become a daily fact of life for presidents.

Modern presidents appear willing and even compelled to talk about every possible aspect of political and social issues—even those about which they are ignorant. Presidents also speak before a greater variety of groups.[35]

Presidential speech is more personal today than it ever has been. Whereas previous presidents spoke formally about issues of great national importance, modern presidents talk in a conversational, intimate way.[36] The shift to the informal style was gradual. Eisenhower spoke formally, but, generally, presidents after Roosevelt at least tried to connect with the public in a casual way.

The number of self references a president makes increases throughout the term of office. Typical are the following statements by Jimmy Carter: "I've always been proud of the fact that when I came to Virginia to begin my campaign a couple years ago and didn't have very many friends, I went to Henry Howell's home, and he and Betty were nice enough to. . . ." "I would like very much to tell my grandchildren that I slept in the same bed that was used by the governor of Virginia." [37]

Perhaps the most famous example of intimate discourse—which went beyond the bounds of personal reflection because it tied personal and policy issues too closely—was President Carter's discussion of his daughter Amy's fear of nuclear war during his debate with Ronald Reagan in the 1980 campaign. Personal statements must show the president to be intimate, but citizens expect the president to move from this deep personal concern to tough-minded action.

The Kennedy Style

John Kennedy may be considered the founder of modern presidential speechmaking. Kennedy rose to the presidency partly because of his good television appearance during the 1960 election debates with Richard Nixon. Kennedy took advantage of his ease with television once he occupied the White House. Kennedy used his humor and his ease on camera and in group settings to disarm opponents.

Kennedy was the first president to make regular appearances year-round. Previous presidents and politicians appeared publicly during elections and campaigns for specific policies, but Kennedy stayed in public view even during the slow months of summer. Television—which by the early 1960s was in 90 percent of all American households—presented a powerful new opportunity for speaking directly to Americans.

President Kennedy used the presidential news conference to appear on television more frequently than previous presidents. The conferences usually took place during the day because White House aides worried about overexposure and the effect that mistakes would have on the president's public standing. Despite this reluctance, Kennedy was aware of the way the Oval Office occupant intrigued the public, and he moved to exploit that interest. Kennedy's wit was a central part of the press meetings.

Beyond the development of a personal relationship with the public, speeches were at the center of the most important policy developments of the Kennedy years. The Bay of Pigs invasion, the Cuban missile crisis, the visit to the Berlin Wall, the decision to accelerate the space program, relations with the Soviet Union, and the civil rights movement, all were marked by important addresses. Unlike the addresses of later presidents, the Kennedy speeches remain important events today for their content as much as

John F. Kennedy Library

President John F. Kennedy developed a personal relationship with the public by pioneering the frequent use of televised press conferences.

for the atmosphere in which they were delivered.

The Kennedy inaugural address was one of the most memorable in history because it was a new expression of national purpose and energy. Kennedy won the presidency in 1960 with the narrowest margin of victory ever, and he needed a rallying cry to establish his leadership. Congress was skeptical and moved slowly throughout Kennedy's presidency, making the president's stirring calls to action all the more important.

The speech after the failed invasion of Cuba is a classic statement of presidential responsibility for failed policy. The invasion, planned by the Central Intelligence Agency during the Eisenhower administration and designed to topple Cuban leader Fidel Castro, was one of Kennedy's first tests as a world leader. When it failed, Kennedy pulled American troops out quickly and reported to the nation. The report itself was viewed as an important test of the young president's ability to persevere and learn from mistakes.

In a nationally televised speech, Kennedy told the nation: "There is an old saying that victory has a hundred fathers and defeat is an orphan. . . . I am the responsible officer of government and that is quite obvious." [38] After the speech, Kennedy's poll support increased by 10 percentage points. Other presidents—most notably, Ronald Reagan—have copied the technique of accepting responsibility for a failed undertaking, thereby diffusing difficult political situations.

President Kennedy used his television address on the Cuban missile crisis as a negotiating tool with the Soviet Union. Kennedy's selective use of information about the stalemate over Soviet placement of nuclear missiles in Cuba gave him flexibility in his private negotiations with Soviet leader Nikita Khrushchev. Later presidents all used dramatic television speeches as levers in their international bargaining. Nixon's speeches on the Vietnam War and Reagan's speeches on arms control are important examples.

The tension over the status of Berlin—a city in the middle of East Germany that was occupied by the four World War II Allied nations—produced two important kinds of public speech. As part of their own strategy of public diplomacy, Soviet leaders had threatened the status of the city's "free" sectors. Kennedy responded with a threatening television speech. The speech was not an ultimatum, but it evoked the possibility of nuclear war and even discussed the advisability of Americans building bomb shelters. One critic called it "one of the most alarming speeches by an American president in the whole, nerve-wracking course of the cold war." [39] The speech was impetus for Congress to mobilize and was a stark warning to the Soviets.

In June 1963, Kennedy visited Berlin. The famous "Ich bin ein Berliner" speech at the Berlin Wall was a classic statement to foreign publics and a warning to U.S. adversaries. The speech spoke through symbols in a very personal way about major world politics. President Kennedy stood at the wall the Soviets constructed to halt the free movement of citizens in the city and declared himself and the rest of the Western world citizens of the troubled city.

President Kennedy's speech at American University the same month helped to establish a framework for the later policy of U.S.-Soviet détente. Few presidential speeches have helped to chart major changes in policy as much as that address at the Washington, D.C., university.

Johnson and Nixon

Lyndon Johnson was a less graceful speaker, but he spoke even more frequently than Kennedy. Johnson's appearance before a joint session of Congress after Kennedy's assassination was crucial in restoring confidence and stability in the government. After winning election as president on his own, Johnson used a State of the Union address to outline his ambitious "Great Society" domestic programs.

Johnson also increased the number of domestic ceremonies, which already had quadrupled from the Eisenhower to the Kennedy administrations. Johnson made a ceremony of the activities of every conceivable group that could be identified with the nation. Like later presidents, Johnson took refuge in ceremony especially when polls

Table 2 Minor Presidential Speeches by Year, 1949-1984

Truman		Nixon, I	
1949	8	1969	5
1950	13	1970	6
1951	9	1971	10
1952	9	1972	4
Total	39	Total	25
Eisenhower, I			
1953	5	Nixon, II	
1954	2	1973	12
1955	2	1974	10
1956	2	Total	22
Total	11		
		Ford	
Eisenhower, II		1974	5
1957	5	1975	36
1958	7	1976	36
1959	2	Total	77
1960	4		
Total	18		
		Carter	
Kennedy		1977	21
1961	6	1978	15
1962	7	1979	22
1963	17	1980	24
Total	30	Total	82
Johnson			
1963-64	11	Reagan [a]	
1965	9	1981	11
1966	11	1982	27
1967	4	1983	19
1968	14	1984	21
Total	49	Total	78

Source: Gary King and Lyn Ragsdale, *The Elusive Executive: Discovering Statistical Patterns in the Presidency* (Washington, D.C.: CQ Press, 1988), 271.

a. Figures for Reagan through first term only.

showed low levels of public support.

Richard Nixon ran his public relations campaign on two tracks—national television, where he gave regular addresses and press conferences, and local communities and White House meetings, where he appeared before groups likely to support him. On the three issues that occupied Nixon the most—foreign policy (especially the Vietnam War), the economy, and Watergate—Nixon's strategy was closely tied to the way he presented himself to the public. From the time of his successful 1968 campaign, Nixon used public relations to bypass the Washington "establishment." Nixon's presidency was plebiscitary in that he sought public approval after acting on important issues.

Nixon was adept at using foreign travels to build public support. His 1972 trips to the Soviet Union and the People's Republic of China attracted unprecedented television and print coverage and established him as an epoch-making world leader.

Toward the end of his presidency, Nixon's public support fell badly—he had the approval of just 23 percent of the public before his resignation—and he tried to revive his fortunes with carefully orchestrated trips to small, friendly communities. Domestic trips to places like Nashville's Grand Ole Opry gave the president a chance to get away from the insistent questioning of the national press corps. This strategy was lampooned in the newspaper comic strip "Doonesbury," which showed a fictional town called Critters, Alabama, awaiting a presidential motorcade.

Despite his reputation as a cold and even devious politician, Nixon often showed an emotional side to the public and to his staff. The emotional displays were at least partly responsible for many citizens' intense loyalty to the president. In his farewell talk to White House staff after his resignation, Nixon recalled his mother's guidance—he called her a "saint"—and his own setbacks as a politician. With tears streaming down his face, he spoke of how Theodore Roosevelt fought to rebuild his life after the death of his first wife, implying that he would do the same. Nixon's staff—and the television audience—were profoundly moved by the speech.

Ford and Carter

When Gerald R. Ford inherited the presidency after Nixon and Vice President Spiro Agnew resigned, his main job was to restore faith in the badly bruised presidency. In his first address to the nation, Ford declared that "our long national nightmare is over." Ford's relaxed style won him broad public support, but his popularity fell badly when he pardoned former president Nixon. Ford was unable to recover because of a lack of support in Congress and an inability to stir the nation with his words.

Ford was the nation's most voluble president, even if his speaking did not win him public support. Ford made public remarks on 1,236 occasions in less than two and a half years in office.[40] None of his speeches (except his first) was considered memorable, but that was not very important for Ford's immediate purpose of wrapping himself in the prestige of the presidency. The most memorable Ford statements were "gaffes," such as his declaration that Eastern Europeans did not consider themselves to be dominated by the Soviet Union. Ford's aborted public campaign to "Whip Inflation Now" also met with derision.

Jimmy Carter's rise to the presidency stemmed in part from his intimate statements during the 1976 campaign. Carter's presidency was filled with symbolic events and addresses to the nation; for example, he wore a cardigan sweater in his televised address asking the nation to make energy sacrifices. The crucial moment of the Carter term occurred when, after a ten-day consultation with leaders in various fields at Camp David, the president spoke on television about a "crisis of confidence" in the nation.

Carter was a tireless public performer and was sometimes very effective. Especially in small groups, Carter's grasp of facts and quiet manner were rhetorically impressive, but his halting speech and southern drawl did not serve him well on television and before larger groups. Moreover, the public did not always receive well his often gloomy assessments of world affairs, such as his descriptions of American moral decay, environmental dangers, human rights abuses, the Vietnam War's legacy, and nuclear war.

The Reagan Approach

Ronald Reagan presented a rosier picture of the future than Carter. Reagan's training as a movie actor, host of a

Table 3 President Carter's Minor Addresses, October 1977

Date	Location	Audience	Subject
October 4	United Nations	General Assembly	Controlling nuclear proliferation
October 4	United Nations	U.S. delegation	Thanks for fine job, importance of the U.N.
October 5	United Nations	not stated	Remarks on signing international covenants on human rights
October 5	United Nations	Foreign ministers, heads of delegations	Changing international relationships
October 7	Washington Hilton Hotel	Democratic National Committee	Political support for Panama Canal treaties
October 19	State Department	Conference for International Nuclear Fuel Cycle Evaluation	Provisions for adequate power sources
October 21	Des Moines, Iowa	not stated	Importance of Iowa farm bill
October 21	Des Moines, Iowa	Democratic party dinner	New farm legislation, energy issues
October 22	Denver, Colorado	Western states governors	Western water policy
October 22	Denver, Colorado	Citizens from Rocky Mountain West	Panama Canal
October 22	Los Angeles, California	Democratic National Committee dinner	Human rights, peace in the Middle East, energy issues

Source: Samuel Kernell, *Going Public: New Strategies of Presidential Leadership* (Washington, D.C.: CQ Press, 1986), 92.

television show, and speaker on the "mashed potato circuit" for General Electric served him well as a speaker both on television and before large and small crowds. Reagan's optimism gained credibility with his jovial reaction to events such as the attempt on his life. After the 1981 shooting, Reagan told his wife, "Honey, I forgot to duck"—a line from an old Hollywood boxing movie.

President Reagan's reputation as the "Great Communicator" underscored a growing separation between the president and the message. All of Reagan's addresses were drafted by professional speechwriters, and even some of his apparently extemporaneous remarks, such as greetings to specific people and jokes, were scripted. Reagan held the fewest press conferences of any modern president because White House aides questioned his grasp of many policy issues and his ability to make statements that were not written out beforehand.

A number of embarrassing extemporaneous remarks seemed to suggest Reagan was ill-informed about many subjects he addressed, such as the role of Americans in the Spanish Civil War, the effects of budget and tax cuts, weapon systems, the makeup of the nuclear "freeze" movement, American Indians, monetary policy, Central American politics, and Soviet politics.

Still, Reagan succeeded in promoting his policies because of his apparently deep and consistent convictions and his comfort with public speaking. With the possible exception of Kennedy, Reagan was the first president to have a well-developed affinity for the electronic media. That affinity carried over to live events because audiences in the media age are comfortable with public performances that resemble television appearances.

Reagan restored the pomp and ceremony stripped from the presidency in the reaction to Nixon's "imperial" administration. A hallmark of his appearances was the grand celebration of American icons, from the Statue of Liberty to ordinary citizens whom Reagan hailed as "heroes" during State of the Union addresses. Reagan basked unabashedly in hearing "Hail to the Chief" before his speeches, and his rhetoric about liberty and opportunity in America and the need to confront the Soviet Union in world politics was inspirational to many Americans weary of the apparent decline the United States suffered in the 1970s.

As Kathleen Hall Jamieson has argued, Reagan's speech was in line with the more intimate manner of public addresses of the media age.[41] His discussions of first-hand experiences and concrete events were lucid, while his remarks about more abstract policy matters often was disjointed. Previous presidents used first-person accounts, but Reagan's personal remarks were effective because they used humor and modesty to portray him as a likable, stable figure. After brief periods in the hospital, Johnson and Nixon used personal anecdotes to attempt to connect with the public. Johnson's words were cold, Nixon's competitive.

United Press International Photo

Jimmy Carter's presidency was filled with symbolic addresses to the nation. Here he wears a cardigan sweater in his televised address asking the nation to make energy sacrifices.

Reagan's presidency, by contrast, was a string of self-deflating cracks and yarns about his experiences in Hollywood and politics.[42]

Kinds of Presidential Speeches

The president has different ways and reasons to communicate with the public. How widely the president's remarks will be circulated is the main consideration for the tone and content of a speech. The group's role in the president's past and future political battles is another consideration. Still another is the president's present political standing with the public and with various interest groups.

The deadlock of U.S. domestic politics may explain a shift in the content of televised speeches from foreign to domestic affairs. Presidents Carter and Reagan were more likely to devote air time to domestic affairs than were their predecessors. Both sought to overcome interest group alignments on issues like energy, taxes, and budgetary matters with appeals to the public at large.[43]

The effect of presidential speechmaking is complex. In one respect, the greater emphasis on rhetoric centers the whole political system on the presidency; the other parts of the system, such as parties, interest groups, and regions, become subordinate to the White House. But as political scientist Samuel Kernell has argued, presidential speeches are neither a plebiscitary nor a leveling force in U.S. politics. Presidents "go public," in Kernell's words, to assemble temporary coalitions of many different groups on specific policies.[44] Indeed, the explosion in minor addresses supports Kernell's contention that the system remains complex despite the president's primacy.

It is useful to break down presidential communications according to the audience, mode of communication, the purpose of the address, and political situation at the time of the speech. There are six basic categories of presidential addresses: ceremonial speeches, official state speeches, general persuasive speeches, hortatory or moralistic speeches, crisis speeches, and addresses to specific groups. Some of the speeches fit more than one category.

Ceremonial Speeches

As the symbolic embodiment of the nation, the president represents the United States in international affairs and in events designed to underscore the country's unity and progress. The president receives foreign dignitaries at home and abroad. The president also sets the tone for a number of domestic events, such as presentation of awards, space shuttle launchings, and hortatory efforts such as the fight against drug abuse. *(See "Ceremonial Duties and Functions," p. 573, in Chief of State chapter of Part III.)*

As Roderick Hart has noted, the increase in presidential speechmaking since World War II is largely attributable to ceremonial events. The average number of monthly ceremonial speeches has increased from 2.4 under Truman and 3.4 under Eisenhower to 15.2 under Ford and 10.7 under Carter.[45] The number of Reagan ceremonies—7.85—was not so high as that of his predecessors, but it was still significant. Reagan also made ceremonies out of more business-like events, like the State of the Union address and policy and interest group speeches. The pomp surrounding Reagan's addresses restored the ceremony stripped from the presidency in the 1970s.

The chief of state role strengthens the president's efforts to build widespread support for policies and ideas that are part of the president's political program. Hart has noted: "To stand in this spotlight is to risk comparatively little, for in such situations listeners' defenses are down, the press is prohibited by cultural mandate from being excessively cynical, and the institution of the presidency—its traditions and its emotional trappings—insulate the chief executive from partisan attack." [46]

Hart has identified four kinds of presidential ceremonies.[47] *Initiating ceremonies* mark major transitions—signing legislation or treaties and swearing in government officials. *Honorific ceremonies* bestow some formal recognition of achievement. Testimonial dinners, awards of medals, university commencements all fit this category. *Celebrative ceremonies* pay tribute to important national events or values. They include eulogies, dinners for foreign dignitaries, patriotic remembrances, and building dedications. The Statue of Liberty celebration in New York in 1986 was a prime example. *Greeting and departure ceremonies* mark the important travels of presidents and foreign dignitaries.

Inaugural addresses are the premier ceremonies of the presidency. A president sets the tone for the administration at the inauguration. Traditionally delivered at the steps of the Capitol building right after the swearing-in, the inaugural address provides the most important hint of the kind of moral leadership the president wants to provide. The president uses the inaugural to unite a nation that has just undergone a partisan election campaign. The president asks the opposition for help and asserts that the nation's factions have common purposes despite disagreements about how to achieve goals.

The content of most inaugural addresses is usually forgotten soon after the event. Some addresses are so eloquent or poignant, however, that they have become part of the nation's "civic religion." Thomas Jefferson's first inaugural argued that the nation shared a common purpose despite the bitter battles of the Federalists and the Anti-Federalists. Andrew Jackson asserted the power of the common man in his inaugural. Abraham Lincoln's second inaugural was an eloquent appeal for national healing in the midst of the horrors of the Civil War. *(See Presidential Documents in the Appendix for text of these addresses.)*

Other famous inaugural addresses include Franklin Roosevelt's 1933 admonition that "there is nothing to fear but fear itself" and John Kennedy's 1961 call for national sacrifice. Kennedy urged: "Ask not what your country can do for you; ask what you can do for your country." Kennedy also pledged to "friend and foe alike" that the United States would be an activist force in international affairs. *(See Presidential Documents in the Appendix for text of these addresses.)*

Farewell addresses are another important ceremonial speech. What the president says upon leaving office can help set the tone for the next administration and, more likely, help to shape the nation's memory and assessment of the outgoing executive. The farewell can be an emotional time for the president and the public and the president's closest political allies.

When moving from active leader to historical figure, presidents are not subject to the same political pressures as they were while in office, nor are they able to muster the same clout. The farewell address can exert great force over time but is not likely to have much of an effect on immediate politics. The purpose is more to leave the nation with a lasting statement of principles from an elder statesman to which it can refer. George Washington's farewell set substantive policy and etiquette for future presidents. Other important farewell addresses were delivered by Jackson, Cleveland, Eisenhower, Nixon, and Carter.

Official State Speeches

The Constitution requires the president to make a statement on the "state of the nation" every year, and since Woodrow Wilson the president has addressed a joint session of Congress to propose policies and to assess the nation's problems and achievements. (Thomas Jefferson discontinued the practice of personal, oral delivery of State of the Union addresses, which George Washington had begun.)

Once presented in writing, the State of the Union address has become a major event in presidential leadership and congressional relations. Delivered before a joint session of Congress, the Supreme Court, and the cabinet, these addresses survey the range of budgetary and other policies the administration plans to pursue in the coming year. Even if the administration has not completed the design of its programs, presidents announce their major initiatives in the address.

Lyndon Johnson's Great Society and Vietnam initiatives; Richard Nixon's Vietnam, "New Federalism," and economic programs; Jimmy Carter's energy, civil service, welfare and tax reform, and foreign affairs initiatives; and Ronald Reagan's tax, budget, regulatory, and military programs were all outlined in State of the Union addresses.

Because many programs are announced without thorough planning, there is a danger that the State of the Union address could create false expectations and eventual disappointment. Many of Johnson's Great Society programs, for example, were in their nascent stages when announced. The combination of warlike rhetoric and fragmented program designs contributed to the eventual disappointment with many of the programs, such as the Community Action program, which had been designed to "empower" the urban poor.

Other state speeches include addresses to foreign bodies such as the British Parliament and the United Nations General Assembly.

General Persuasive Speeches

Most presidential addresses seek to develop a favorable environment for a wide variety of policies, but less than half of the president's speeches try to persuade the public to adopt specific policies and directions.

Reagan successfully urged passage of his tax and budget packages in 1981. On February 5, Reagan told a national television audience that the nation faced the "worst economic mess since the Great Depression." Less than two weeks later, Reagan told a television audience about his plans to deal with the problem. After an assassination attempt boosted his popularity, Reagan in late April 1981 addressed an enthusiastic joint session of Congress. In July, he returned to national television and asked viewers to pressure Congress to support administration policies. Reagan's appeal generated fifteen million more letters than Congress normally receives in a session.[48]

Woodrow Wilson's national campaign after World War I for Senate acceptance of the Versailles treaty and the League of Nations was perhaps the most dramatic example of persuasive oratory in U.S. history. Unwilling to bargain with the Republican leaders on the treaty, Wilson traveled eight thousand miles over a month starting September 3, 1919. He delivered thirty-seven speeches and attended even more public events during which he urged the treaty's passage. Wilson's tour ended when he collapsed of a stroke. The Senate defeated the treaty.

Recent examples of major persuasive speeches include Reagan's tax and budget speeches; Carter's energy and economic speeches; Ford's addresses on the economy and his pardon of Nixon; Nixon's speeches on Vietnam, the economy, and Watergate; Johnson's addresses on Vietnam, social problems, and domestic disorder; and Kennedy's addresses on civil rights and economics.

Hortatory or Moralistic Speeches

The president attempts to persuade the public to set aside personal, selfish aims and seek a more general public interest. Like a high school football coach, the president also attempts to infuse the public with confidence and zeal for tasks that may seem difficult.

Presidential speechmaking in the nation's first century usually was confined to educational or moralistic messages. On their tours of the expanding nation, presidents discussed constitutional and republican principles, federalism, economic policies, and the place of American values in world politics.

Twentieth-century president Jimmy Carter spoke frequently on the energy crisis—so frequently that he began to worry that Americans were "inured" to the major problems that the issue presented. To confront the public's blasé attitude, Carter delivered—after a ten-day retreat to Camp David—a speech about what he called the nation's "crisis of confidence." That speech—a choppy text—failed to offer a plan of action that matched the spiritual crisis Carter described. Although delivered in an atmosphere of crisis, the address was quickly dismissed. Republican opponents in 1980 revived the speech as evidence of Carter's leadership failures. *(See "Jimmy Carter's 'Crisis of Confidence' Speech," p. 1393, in the Appendix.)*

Crisis Speeches

The president is the focal point of the nation during times of crisis. The public turns to the president for leadership during difficult times, partly out of practical considerations—the president is the political figure most familiar to most Americans—and partly out of a psychological need for the reassurance that strong leadership can provide.

The president's speech in times of crisis can mobilize the nation almost instantly. Franklin Roosevelt's call for war on the Axis powers in World War II after the bombing of Pearl Harbor, for example, dramatically changed the public's mood and willingness to get involved in a foreign war. Before the dramatic address to a joint session of Congress, the public and Congress were reluctant to enter the war; after the speech, public opinion favored all-out involvement.

John Kennedy's addresses on the failed invasion of the Bay of Pigs, confrontations with the Soviet Union over the status of Berlin, and the Cuban missile crisis were among the most dramatic speeches in modern history. Each suggested the possibility of apocalyptic confrontations. The youthful Kennedy was able to use the speeches to build confidence in his own leadership, even on occasions when his administration had failed, as at the Bay of Pigs.

Lyndon Johnson's first presidential address is another example of a major crisis speech. Both the traumatized Congress and the public watched the address not only for clues of Johnson's policy intentions but also for signs of the stability of the government five days after President Kennedy's assassination. Johnson and his aides worked on the speech almost without interruption throughout those five days and produced an address that reassured the nation of the government's stability and Johnson's own vigor. Johnson was able to outline his own legislative program while paying homage to the martyred Kennedy. "Let us continue," Johnson said, a reference to Kennedy's "Let us begin."[49]

Richard Nixon delivered a number of addresses on the Vietnam War and the Watergate affair, with mixed success. Nixon slowly developed a national consensus on the war and blunted opposition to his bombings of Laos and Cambodia.[50] Nixon was unable to convince the nation of his credibility on the Watergate affair, however. His many television speeches on the campaign scandal in fact produced more questions and criticisms than they answered.

Carter's "crisis of confidence" speech may fit in this category as well as the hortatory category. Other crisis speeches Carter delivered included his address on the Soviet invasion of Afghanistan, on the discovery of Soviet troops in Cuba, and on the American hostages in Iran.

The wide latitude that the public gives presidents during a crisis invites possible abuse of the crisis speech. President Johnson reported that North Vietnam had attacked U.S. ships without provocation in the Gulf of Tonkin and quickly won congressional approval of a resolution that granted him almost unlimited war powers. The evidence for the North Vietnamese attack, however, was questionable at best, as Johnson privately acknowledged. The crisis atmosphere created by Johnson's speech might have been the most important element in the growing U.S. involvement in the war.

The existence of a crisis gives the president an opportunity for rhetorical leadership but does not guarantee it.

Lyndon B. Johnson Library

Just five days after Kennedy's assassination, President Lyndon Johnson delivers a painstakingly worded speech to Congress. The address succeeded in reassuring the nation of its government's stability during a time of crisis.

President Carter's address after the Soviet invasion of Afghanistan eventually fueled the arguments of critics on both the left and the right that Carter was too naive and inexperienced to continue as president. Carter stated that the invasion fundamentally changed his perception of the nature of the Soviet Union.

Failure to give an address during a major crisis can undermine the president's support. Herbert Hoover's unpopularity after the Great Crash of 1929 is attributable not so much to his policies as his inability to convey a sense of national purpose and sympathy for the victims of the economic depression.

Addresses to Specific Groups

As the government has become more complex, and more interest groups have developed permanent ties to the government, the president has spent more time addressing specific groups. The purpose of such addresses often is nothing more than flattery. Whether delivered to faithful supporters or skeptical adversaries, such addresses are designed to create a feeling of awe with the presidency. These addresses often have some kind of appeal that is designed for media coverage.

The advantage of appearing before specific constituency groups is that remarks can be tailored to the group, and the president's words will be transmitted to the larger group membership for weeks after the speech. By merely accepting an invitation to address a particular group, a president tells the group that it is important.

Appearances before constituencies also enable the president to see how the group might behave during the "bargaining" process of budgetary, tax, and other current legislative matters. The president can then fine tune the White House approach on those issues. The National Association for the Advancement of Colored People (NAACP) provided presidents from Franklin Roosevelt on with strong signals about the civil rights initiatives it would find meaningful.

Perhaps more important, the president also can use interest group appearances to line up support for policy initiatives. Presidents frequently appear before business and labor groups to seek backing for their economic programs. Carter tried to build support for his energy program and Panama Canal treaties with appearances before interest groups, but he was opposed by a well-financed cadre of conservatives.[51]

Business organizations are perhaps the most constantly courted in the constellation of interest groups. Presidents of both parties need support from business to pursue their economic and social policies. Some presidents—such as Franklin Roosevelt, Harry Truman, and John Kennedy—have publicly attacked business but eventually had to build support among business people.

Other groups to be courted depend on the president's base of support. Almost half of all presidential speeches by postwar presidents were minor, "targeted" appeals to specific constituencies. Most of these appeals take place in or around Washington, D.C., where national organizations are housed. Groups ranging from the AFL-CIO to the Moral Majority attract the sporadic attention of the president.

Government workers are one of the most important interest groups the president addresses. Especially when morale is low in departments, the president's words can provide a big lift. Speaking before government groups also enables the president to lay out policy positions in the sanctified arena of officialdom. Because the president's words are usually reported widely, the government audience provides an opportunity to talk not just about specific policies but about other issues as well. Jimmy Carter spoke to government workers on the morality of couples living together outside marriage.

As the leader of the national party, the president also delivers a number of partisan addresses. These appeals usually take place during important election campaigns. President Reagan, for example, was tireless in campaigning for Republican congressional and gubernatorial candidates in the 1980s. If a president is not popular, he is not asked to participate in other campaigns. Democratic candidates studiously avoided Carter in the 1980 campaign.

Appearances before groups also can distract them so the administration can pursue other priorities. Reagan used rhetoric to allay the concern of New Right organizations—who wanted immediate action on abortion, school prayer, and other social issues—during his tax and budget initiatives of 1981 and 1982. Reagan promoted state education reforms in a series of speeches in 1983 and 1984, diffusing pressure for national initiatives and spending increases.

Presidents often appear before skeptical groups to coopt whatever opposition they might present and to portray themselves as leader of all the people. Good examples are Carter's appearances before the Veterans of Foreign Wars, and Reagan's speeches to the NAACP. Presidents sometimes deliberately even antagonize interest groups to solidify the alliances that have developed in opposition to those groups.[52]

The Imperative to Speak

Because the presidency is central to American politics, presidents are expected to offer authoritative opinions even on subjects about which they are ignorant or uncertain about an appropriate position. As presidents move past the first year or so of their term, the imperative to speak grows because they must shore up political standing after an inevitable decline.

Speech is an important strategic weapon for the president. The president usually enjoys a honeymoon period of six months to a year when Congress and the public are inclined to yield to presidential leadership on many important questions. Lyndon Johnson's Great Society legislation of 1965 and Ronald Reagan's budget- and tax-cutting initiatives of 1981 are notable examples.

After the initial period of good will, however, presidents begin to lose their initial appeal. The president is better known and develops disputes with more groups as the term progresses.

The president also must accept responsibility for many of the nation's problems previously blamed on Congress or a former president. Political scientist John E. Mueller has asserted that the longer the president is in office, the more a "coalition of minorities" develops grievances that cut the president's base of support.[53]

Presidents tend to increase their speechmaking considerably from the first to second years in office. For example, Carter delivered 282 speeches in his first year and 323 in his second year; Reagan delivered 211 in his first year and 344 in his second. As the reelection campaign nears, presidents give even more speeches. Ford increased the number of his speeches from 392 to 682 in the year of his reelection bid; the figures for Carter were 272 and 436; for Reagan, 384 and 421.[54]

Because presidents cannot count on party machinery or congressional leadership for support, they turn to the public. Several presidents have appealed to the public "over the heads of Congress" when Congress has shown reluctance to go along with legislative initiatives. Carter's public statements on western water projects, the Panama Canal treaty, the nation's energy problems, relations with the Soviet Union, and economic problems all were intended to overcome resistance on Capitol Hill to unpopular programs.

The psychological demands of the presidency probably contribute to the tendency to speak often, as political scientist Bruce Buchanan has suggested. The combination of stress, deference from underlings, and the search for clear signs of success combine to push the president toward dramatic rhetoric.

Frustrated presidents search for scapegoats to pummel in public and improve their own relative standing and leverage over the political process.

The imperative to speak is self-generating. "Presidents have developed a rhetorical reflex, a tendency to resort to public suasion as an initial response to a political situation," Hart has written. Carter displayed the built-in push toward presidential speech. "Always he spoke, and the speaking justified its own continuance: if the coverage were favorable, it stood to reason that more speaking would generate even more flattering responses from the media; if the press disparaged him, more speaking would set matters right."[55]

If presidents need to go public to promote their political agendas, that does not mean they speak all the time about important policy issues. Much of the president's time is occupied with noncontroversial, almost trivial appearances, such as presentation of awards and proclamations of special days. Even if these talks appear trivial, they strengthen the president's public standing and symbolic hold on the nation and its different "publics."[56]

One of the reasons the president turns to rhetoric is the institutionalization of speech writing and public relations efforts in the White House. The president has a growing corps of aides who analyze the political situation and develop public campaigns for improving it.

The emergence of a public presidency presents dangers as well as opportunities for the chief executive. If the president is blamed by the media or the voters for problems, making regular appearances can aggravate rather than improve the president's position. The regular presence can serve as a constant reminder of the administration's failings.

Jimmy Carter suffered politically in 1980 because voters associated him with the Iranian hostage crisis, "stagflation," tense relations with the Soviet Union, and divided leadership in Washington. When Carter appeared on television or before groups, he struck many as tired and ineffectual.

The problem of "overexposure" did not begin with Carter. Both John Kennedy and Lyndon Johnson were criticized for speaking too much.

Presidents are in many ways trapped by their public utterances. Because the media record every public word, presidents must carefully weigh the effect of their statements and take care not to get caught in a tangle of contradictory remarks.

Critics of the "Rhetorical Presidency"

Critics of the new rhetorical style argue that it has led to confusion on the part of both the president and the public about the difference between political action and political speech. The president's dominance in politics also "crowds out" other legitimate actors and issues.[57]

When a presidential address or "photo opportunity" is treated as a meaningful political event, attention is diverted from the complicated process of policy making and implementation that is the substance of politics. Not only the public, but also the president, can be deceived about the state of government activity. Media coverage of speeches reinforces the notion that speech is tantamount to substantive action.

As political scientist Bruce Miroff has argued, the president's dominance in U.S. politics starves the political actors and issues not in the president's orbit. The president's "monopolization of public space," as Miroff put it, makes it difficult for citizens interested in an issue to pursue it. The president's public monopoly simplifies issues and distances politics from the average citizen; politics become a spectator sport. The citizen's "vicarious" relationship to important policy issues also reduces important policy decisions to a game. The suspense over Jimmy Carter's decision on whether to produce the B-1 bomber, for example, concerned the game-like political maneuvering and not the merits of the superbomber.[58]

Theodore J. Lowi has argued that the movement toward a rhetorical presidency has led to an "oversell" of specific policies that breeds disappointment. "Such are the president's channels of mass communication that he must simplify and dramatize his appeals, whether the communication deals with foreign policy, domestic policy, or something else again. Almost every initiative is given a public relations name. Every initiative has to be 'new and improved.' "[59] Simplifying and dramatizing policies removes them from their natural state of uncertainty and complexity—and produces frustration and cynicism when major improvements do not result.

Presidents have taken to more frequent speech partly to improve the chances of their legislative and other initiatives, but the link between the two has proved tenuous at best. Legislative success is no greater in the modern age of presidential talk than it was in previous periods of limited speech. Presidents Eisenhower, Kennedy, Johnson, and Nixon won close to three-quarters of their major tests in Congress while giving an average of 150 policy speeches a year between 1957 and 1972. Presidents Nixon, Ford, and Carter won less than 60 percent of the key issues between 1972 and 1979 while speaking more than 200 times a year.[60]

Increased presidential communications—not only speech but also written material—do not appear to have increased the understanding between the leaders and the led. Americans exhibit continued ignorance of most public policy issues despite the ubiquitous media and "teaching" of the president. Even more revealing, Americans tell pollsters that they feel increasingly ignored. Voters sense that politicians talk to them but do not listen.[61]

Presidential speechmaking also reduces the president's control over the job. Because presidents speak so often, they cannot possibly write or even contribute significantly to the drafting of speeches. The White House speechwriting corps drafts all the president's words. If presidents do not have to work on the complex ideas they present to the public, they are less likely to have a thorough and nuanced understanding of issues.

One authority has argued that the "scripted presidency" might have contributed to Reagan's decision to trade arms to Iran in exchange for the release of American hostages in Lebanon. "President Reagan's reliance on speechwriters and before them [movie] scriptwriters played a role in his disposition to accept information about the Iran/Contra dealings uncritically and to trust his aides to act in his best interest."[62]

Proponents of constant presidential talk say it brings the political process into the open. Because presidents are such compelling figures, what they say attracts wide attention and makes politics a more open affair. But presidents must be cautious because their remarks are so thoroughly covered. That caution can drain public politics of any meaningful content. The effect, ironically, is that open, public politics can drive important policy discussions underground. The tendency to "go public" is one result of the decline of party strength in Congress. Since World War II, the president and Congress have been from different parties under Eisenhower, Nixon, Ford, and Reagan. Even when the president's party controls Congress, support for specific policies must be developed issue by issue. Public support has therefore become a crucial tool to prod Congress.

The President and the Foreign Policy Debate

Every president since Theodore Roosevelt has traveled to foreign countries, but only since the Eisenhower administration have such trips become a regular part of the president's routine. Many of the trips have been related to diplomatic events, such as treaty negotiations, but most trips have been more for public relations.

The trips usually give the president a temporary lift in public opinion polls.[63] Longer trips—such as President Nixon's trip to China and President Reagan's trip to the Soviet Union—have a more permanent effect on the president's standing. More important than the brief surge in popularity, however, is the presentation of an image of the president as a statesman in charge of world affairs.

Presidential travel once was considered a risky proposition with the voters. When President Eisenhower embarked on his first foreign trip, he felt obliged to explain the necessity for the trip in almost apologetic terms:

> Now, manifestly, there are many difficulties in the way of a president going abroad for a period, particularly while Congress is in session. He has many constitutional duties; he must be here to perform them. I am able to go on the trip only because of the generous cooperation of the political leaders in Congress of both political parties who have arranged their work so that my absence for a period will not interfere with the business of the government. On my part, I promised them that by a week from Sunday, on July 24th, I shall be back here ready to carry on my accustomed duties.[64]

The surges in public approval that followed Eisenhower's trip led him—and later presidents—to make travel a regular part of the job.[65]

The Importance of Foreign Policy Rhetoric

Control of foreign policy events has always been an important political "card" for the president. Especially since the United States became a world economic and military power at the turn of the century, presidents have been able to increase their prestige with military and diplomatic action. The public often defers to authorities because of its scant knowledge of foreign affairs, so presidents receive a boost in public support even when the action concerns an obscure nation or issue.

Presidents have been able to depend on foreign affairs to enhance their political stock even more than economic or social events because they are able to supersede temporarily the divisions engendered by the domestic struggle over "who gets what, when, and how." On foreign policy issues, the president acts for the nation as a whole, creating a situation in which "we" are acting, but domestic actions always create internal divisions. The president can argue that foreign policy involves outside threats to the security of all of the people and therefore requires a unified response.

The boost that the president gets from foreign policy is usually short-lived. Still, the president can use a series of foreign events and rhetoric about foreign policy to develop a general disposition among the public to defer to presidential leadership.

Foreign policy action can be a double-edged sword, however. If presidents do not appear to assert control over crises after the initial period of emergency, the public might develop suspicions about presidential expertise and control. Presidents also can lose on foreign policy if their actions create or aggravate internal divisions—usually by asking for difficult sacrifices of important domestic constituencies.

Presidents appeal not only to domestic audiences with foreign policy appearances and actions but to foreign audiences as well. By bolstering their prestige with foreign leaders and the foreign public, presidents can develop the kind of leeway necessary to conduct themselves in a wide variety of situations. Federal agencies such as the U.S. Information Agency and the Voice of America can be useful in the long-term propaganda battle with other nations.

Finally, the administration is able to exert a great deal of control over the foreign policy agenda with its control over information held in the federal bureaucracy. The president benefits from the huge operations of the public relations offices of the Pentagon, State Department, and Central Intelligence Agency. Through the power of classification, the president also can exert control over how much information journalists, scholars, and political activists have at their disposal.

Scholars have raised concerns about the effects of the executive's control over information. A constant tension exists between the democratic value of openness and the strategic value of secrecy. As the president speaks more and more in public, the president and government also hold more matters in secrecy. This development may be attributed to the need for different strategies to overcome and control a growing bureaucracy. Political scientist Francis E. Rourke has written:

> To be sure, the bureaucracy did not invent secrecy in American government. The Founding Fathers found it expedient to conduct the deliberations of the Constitutional Convention at Philadelphia in 1787 in private [and] presidents have, through the development of "executive

National Archives

Presidents have often appealed to foreign publics and their leaders to increase their political capital. In December 1918, Woodrow Wilson made a successful European tour to promote his postwar foreign policy agenda.

> privilege," contributed a great deal to the secrecy surrounding executive activities.... But it remains true that the growth of bureaucracy in American government has brought about an enormous expansion in the secretiveness with which policy is made.[66]

The erection of a "national security state," critics have argued, gives the president almost dictatorial power over foreign affairs and even many areas of domestic policy. Presidents always can assert that "national security" requires withholding information.

Presidents clearly enjoy an important advantage in deciding what information they want released and how they want to do it. President Nixon's "secret" bombing of Cambodia in 1970 and his handling of the Watergate affair were both justified on the grounds of national-security requirements. The Reagan administration's refusal to allow reporters to witness the invasion of Grenada was based on similar claims. Perhaps more important is the routine information that presidents can keep secret.

Reaching Foreign Publics

American presidents have taken to public speech not only to speak over the heads of their own government, but also to speak directly to foreign publics. Presidents sometimes speak directly to other nations' populations to strengthen their negotiating positions with those nations' leaders. More often, presidents simply try to foster a more general good will abroad with their public appeals.

Some of the boldest appeals to foreign audiences took place during President Reagan's 1988 visit to Moscow. Reagan spoke to Soviet citizens on television during his trip and later met crowds with Soviet leader Mikhail Gorbachev at Red Square, an event televised to millions of homes in both the United States and the Soviet Union. Reagan was most outspoken at the University of Moscow. Standing before a huge Soviet flag and portrait of V. I. Lenin, Reagan challenged the nation to restructure political and economic institutions and praised the U.S. system.

Reagan spoke several times about the protests over the placement of American nuclear missiles on European soil. The U.S. missiles were strongly opposed by peace activists in Great Britain and West Germany, and Reagan alternately sought to win over opponents of the missiles and to undercut their legitimacy.

A speech at Normandy, France, commemorating the fortieth anniversary of the 1945 U.S. invasion was a dramatic statement of solidarity among Western nations and values. President Reagan spoke movingly of the soldiers who died in the invasion and their families and of the need for nations to avoid another world war.

Reagan's foreign appeals sometimes backfired. His trip to Bitburg, West Germany, in 1985 was intended to symbolize the development of ties between former World War II foes the United States and Germany. The visit was controversial from the time of its scheduling, however. The discovery that former officers of an elite Nazi brigade were buried in the Bitburg cemetery insulted Jews and others who had fought the Nazis. Reagan defended the trip by saying that German soldiers "were victims, just as surely as the victims in the concentration camps." [67] Despite calls for him to cancel the trip, Reagan went.

Presidential statements to foreign publics often take the form of threats. Presidents often talk about other nations' weapons buildups, terrorist actions, human rights problems, military actions, and trade policies. Although such statements often are intended for domestic consumption, they also offer flexible ways to communicate with other governments outside the normal channels of diplomacy. The president gives addresses to foreign bodies such as the United Nations (UN) and Organization of American States. These meetings are well-covered by media across the world, so they offer opportunities to address foreign publics. Because many nations practice censorship, presidents often try to embed their true message in larger statements that will be reported.

Even Reagan, who sharply criticized the UN, took advantage of the platform of the international body. His farewell speech in 1988 attempted to promote internal Soviet political reforms and arms control agreements. Reagan and his UN ambassadors used the body to criticize the Soviet Union, Nicaragua, and third world countries.

The president leads the world with words in other ways also. At summit meetings and economic conferences with foreign leaders, the president speaks for the nation on a wide variety of issues. The "news" from most conferences is that the leaders will try to cooperate in pursuit of common goals. But if a president can visibly "take charge," it helps to provide the authority the president needs in world affairs.

Presidents do not speak to other nations only through their own appearances and statements. The U.S. government includes a number of agencies designed to appeal to the "hearts and minds" of foreign peoples. The president's appointments for these agencies can put a distinctive mark on the way the rest of the world sees the United States.

The U.S. Information Agency promotes U.S. foreign policy through a variety of media, libraries, speakers, and programs. With 204 posts in 127 countries, the nation's chief propaganda agency operates a radio service called Voice of America (VOA). The VOA broadcasts 1,003 hours of news and other programs in forty-two languages each week. The State Department and Central Intelligence Agency also disseminate information to foreign nations.

An administration's policy on government information—what documents and information should be classified (that is, made secret) or made public—can have a profound effect on the nation's foreign policy.

Because the president is the commander in chief and controls a huge national security apparatus, the president has access to information about foreign affairs that people outside the government lack.

The president enjoys a huge advantage in the sheer size of the public relations operations of the government. The public information office of the Pentagon, for example, spends more money each year than the major news services. Especially considering that the wire services devote only a small part of their operations to foreign affairs, the Pentagon's public relations work gives the government an awesome advantage in communicating its point of view.

The Terms of Presidential Discourse

Besides dominating the political stage and tilting the balance of many specific public issues, the president's rhetoric has been important in shaping the way political issues are discussed. The president's prominence is crucial in establishing the terms of debate for other participants in the political system.

Many linguistic experts have argued that shaping the political vocabulary is the most important element in gaining public support for a wide range of policies. The president is perhaps the most important political figure in defining and creating a context for widely used terms such as *conservative, progress, liberalism, economic growth, national security,* and *free trade.* The meanings of such terms change over time, sometimes helping and sometimes hurting the presidents' ability to promote their agenda.

Even the most fundamental ideas in American political discourse are constantly changing. The rise and fall of terms like *people* and *interests* closely parallel the historical development of the nation and the evolution of the presidency. The regular public use of the word *interests,* for example, in the nation's early years was tied to the decline of notions of public virtue and the development of more competitive ideals of politics and society. Theodore Roosevelt and Woodrow Wilson, leaders of the national Progressive movement, used the rhetoric of interests both to decry what Roosevelt called "the ferocious, scrambling rush of an unregulated and purely individualistic industrialism" and to propose government remedies. The upshot was the "pluralistic" idea that a clash of interests managed by popular government would redound to the national interest.[68]

Political scientist Murray Edelman has argued that such words always have contradictory meanings. But because people have contradictory interests and beliefs, they need catch-all words that cover up the contradictions. These words help overcome "cognitive dissonance"—the unsettling feeling that comes with the realization that one's thoughts are contradictory. These words also provide enough "signposts," or guides, for people to get along in life without constantly having to assess their situations and alternatives.

An example of a self-contradictory word is *conservative,* which in U.S. politics is used to denote both stability (family, neighborhoods, local control) and turbulence (economic growth, mobility, exploration, and research). President William McKinley described his "Open Door" policy, which reduced trade and cultural barriers among nations, as conservative; although the policy augured unprecedented changes in world trade activities, it also was said to be the surest policy for maintaining traditional American values. President Reagan wove together the contradictory meanings of conservatism. His rhetoric and policies for "unleashing" the dynamic forces of capitalism contradicted his denunciations of the decay of traditional "values" and practices regarding religion, family life, sexual mores, and authority.

The complex and changing definitions of political words mean that presidents have wide latitude in shaping the way people talk about political issues at all levels of society. Presidents not only have a "bully pulpit" from which to promote their choices in important policies, as Theodore Roosevelt asserted, but also the ability to shape the way the population thinks about what those choices are in the first place.

David Green has chronicled the way twentieth-century presidents have used labels to give themselves a privileged position in policy debates. According to Green, presidents have attempted to use words like *progressive, liberal, isolationist,* and *conservative* to give their own actions greater legitimacy and to undercut the legitimacy of their opponents.

Franklin Roosevelt's presidency is a thorough case study of adapting, avoiding, and switching labels. Roosevelt avoided using the label *progressive* because it had connotations of confiscation for many members of the older generation. Roosevelt labeled his policies "liberal" and fended off attacks that his policies were "fascist," "socialist," and "communist." The liberal label connoted openness, generosity, and popular support. Roosevelt branded his opponents "conservative" and "reactionary." When it became apparent that the New Deal policies were not ending the Great Depression, Roosevelt stepped up his attacks on opponents, particularly business interests and the wealthy whom he called "economic royalists." Roosevelt went beyond the debate over domestic and economic policy with a move into international affairs. As the United States inched toward involvement in World War II, Roosevelt branded war opponents "isolationists," "appeaser fifth columnists," and "propagandists of fear" and linked those terms to his broader argument about reactionaries. Critics who questioned the war or specific tactics found themselves undercut.[69]

What goes around usually comes around in rhetoric. By the 1970s and 1980s, the word *liberal* was poison. President Reagan's constant labeling of Democrats as "tax and spend liberals" helped to make *liberal* the scarlet letter of politics in the 1980s. Politicians were so scared to identify themselves as liberal, because of the word's negative connotations, that pundits took to calling it the "L-word" as if it were profanity.

Twentieth-century presidents have tended to use catch-all phrases to describe their policy programs. Among the phrases are Square Deal (Theodore Roosevelt), New Freedom (Wilson), New Deal (Franklin Roosevelt), Fair Deal (Truman), New Frontier (Kennedy), Great Society (Johnson), New Foundation (Carter), and New Federalism (Nixon and Reagan). Such phrases can give the president's program a sense of coherence and completeness but also can create false expectations about what the president's policies can accomplish. Johnson's Great Society, for example, was a collection of relatively small and uncoordinated programs—many of which had no viable support system in the state and local governments where they were to be administered. The policies were prepared hurriedly, and funding was restricted before many of the programs were fully implemented.

David Zarefsky maintains that the potent rhetorical force of the Great Society label left the domestic programs vulnerable to attack: "The very choices of symbolism and argument which had aided the adoption of the program were instrumental in undermining its implementation and in weakening public support for its basic philosophy."[70]

Theodore Lowi has argued that the use of vague slogans and "sentiments" rather than precisely worded programs has corroded the entire U.S. political system.[71] The growth of national involvement in all areas of public life, and the need for the president to lead national efforts, not only breeds constant disappointment with the programs' results but also undermines the president's efforts to gain control of the federal leviathan. According to Lowi, the use of ringing slogans clearly has profound consequences for the government.

Speeches of Departing Presidents

Among the most prominent speeches of any presidency are the addresses delivered at the end of the administration. The farewell addresses of many presidents are remembered long after other speeches have been lost in the bog of presidential rhetoric. Speeches that former presidents deliver also gain prominence because they are so infrequent and because they depict politicians jousting to help determine their place in history.

George Washington delivered the first and most famous farewell address. *(See "Washington's Farewell Address," p. 1365, in the Appendix.)* Washington's most lasting advice to the country was to avoid becoming entangled in European alliances, which he predicted would sap the strength and resources from the young nation. Much of the speech was written by Alexander Hamilton, but Washington himself took an active hand in its drafting. Experts agree that it reflects his values and character.

The most influential modern farewell address was Dwight Eisenhower's valedictory of 1961. *(See "Eisenhower's Farewell Address," p. 1381, in the Appendix.)* He warned the nation against a "military-industrial complex" that he argued was starting to dominate the American system and could endanger democratic processes and liberties. Eisenhower said:

> We must never let the weight of this combination endanger our liberties or democratic processes. We should take nothing for granted. Only an alert and knowledgeable citizenry can compel the proper meshing of the huge industrial and military machinery of defense with our peaceful methods and goals, so that security and liberty may prosper together.[72]

Notes

1. Along with the explosion in presidential speechmaking is an explosion of research about the development. See Theodore Otto Windt, Jr., "Presidential Rhetoric: Definition of a Field of Study," *Presidential Studies Quarterly* 16 (Winter 1986): 102-116.
2. Roderick P. Hart, *The Sound of Leadership* (Chicago: University of Chicago Press, 1988), 1.
3. Kathleen Hall Jamieson, *Eloquence in an Electronic Age* (New York: Oxford University Press, 1988), 212-213.
4. Lloyd Grove, "Dukakis: If He Only Had a Heart," *Washington Post*, October 9, 1988, D1.
5. Richard E. Neustadt, *Presidential Power* (New York: Wiley, 1976).
6. Samuel Kernell, *Going Public: New Strategies of Presidential Leadership* (Washington, D.C.: CQ Press, 1986), 37.
7. Hart, *The Sound of Leadership*, 2.
8. Philip Abbott, "Do Presidents Talk Too Much? The Rhetorical Presidency and Its Alternative," *Presidential Studies Quarterly* 18 (Spring 1988): 335.
9. Hart, *The Sound of Leadership*, 5.
10. E. E. Schattschneider, *The Semisovereign People* (Hinsdale, Ill.: Dryden Press, 1975).
11. Hart, *The Sound of Leadership*, xix.
12. Murray Edelman, *The Symbolic Uses of Politics* (Urbana: University of Illinois Press, 1985), 96.
13. Jeffrey K. Tulis, *The Rhetorical Presidency* (Princeton, N.J.: Princeton University Press, 1987), 47-49.
14. Tulis, *The Rhetorical Presidency*, 51-55.
15. Michael E. McGerr, *The Decline of Popular Politics* (New York: Oxford University Press, 1986), 22-23.
16. Alexander Hamilton, *Federalist* No. 71, in *The Federalist Papers*, quoted in Tulis, *The Rhetorical Presidency*, 39.
17. Calvin Coolidge once commented on this practice: "At twelve thirty, the doors were opened and a long line passed by who wished merely to shake hands with the president. On one occasion, I shook hands with nineteen hundred in thirty-four minutes" (quoted in Gary King and Lyn Ragsdale, *The Elusive Executive: Discovering Statistical Patterns in the Presidency* [Washington, D.C.: CQ Press, 1988], 249).
18. Tulis, *The Rhetorical Presidency*, 63.
19. Ibid., 67, 64-65.
20. Ibid., 69.
21. Ibid., 67-68.
22. Ibid., 79-83.
23. Abbott, "Do Presidents Talk Too Much?" 333-334.
24. Tulis, *The Rhetorical Presidency*, 87-93.
25. Ibid., 88.
26. Ibid., 86.
27. Elmer Cornwell, *Presidential Leadership of Public Opinion* (Bloomington: Indiana University Press, 1965), 24-25.
28. Quoted in Tulis, *The Rhetorical Presidency*, 131.
29. David Green, *Shaping Political Consciousness* (Ithaca, N.Y.: Cornell University Press, 1987), 81.
30. Theodore J. Lowi, *The Personal President* (Ithaca, N.Y.: Cornell University Press, 1985), 22-66.
31. Jamieson, *Eloquence in an Electronic Age*, 45-53.
32. Daniel J. Boorstin, *The Americans: The Democratic Experience* (New York: Random House, 1973), 475.
33. Hart, *The Sound of Leadership*, xix.
34. Kernell, *Going Public*, 22.
35. Hart, *The Sound of Leadership*, 11.
36. Ibid., 12-14; see also Jamieson, *Eloquence in an Electronic Age*, 165-201.
37. Hart, *The Sound of Leadership*, 36.
38. Theodore C. Sorensen, *Kennedy* (New York: Harper and Row, 1965), 346.
39. Herbert S. Parmet, *JFK: The Presidency of John F. Kennedy* (New York: Dial Press, 1983), 197.
40. Hart, *The Sound of Leadership*, 8. In calculating the total number of Ford's speeches, Hart counted all public occasions at which the president made remarks, including press conferences, dinners, and welcoming ceremonies.
41. Jamieson, *Eloquence in an Electronic Age*, 182-200.
42. Kathleen Hall Jamieson contrasts the more awkward style of Johnson and Nixon with the casual, modest style of Reagan (ibid., 186-187). The media critic Mark Crispin Miller makes the same point: "Reagan is unfailingly attractive, not at all like a predator, nor, in fact, like anything other than what he seems—'a nice guy,' pure and simple.... We, too, should appreciate the spectacle, after all the bad performances we've suffered through for years: LBJ, abusing his dogs and exposing his belly; Richard Nixon, hunched and glistening like a cornered toad; Jimmy Carter, with his maudlin twang and interminable kin. While each of these men, appallingly, kept lunging at us from behind the mask of power, Reagan's face and mask are as one" (Mark Crispin Miller, *Boxed In* [Evanston, Ill: Northwestern University Press, 1988], 82).
43. Kernell, *Going Public*, 87.
44. Ibid., 91.
45. Hart, *The Sound of Leadership*, 51.
46. Ibid., 50.
47. Ibid., 219-220.
48. Kernell, *Going Public*, 121.
49. Patricia D. Witherspoon, "'Let Us Continue': The Rhetorical Initiation of Lyndon Johnson's Presidency," *Presidential Studies Quarterly* 17 (Summer 1987): 531-540.
50. Kernell, *Going Public*, 83.
51. Craig Allen Smith, "Leadership, Orientation, and Rhetorical Vision: Jimmy Carter, The 'New Right,' and the Panama Canal," *Presidential Studies Quarterly* 16 (Spring 1986): 317-328.

52. King and Ragsdale, *The Elusive Executive*, 255.
53. John E. Mueller, *War, Presidents, and Public Opinion* (New York: Wiley, 1973); Lowi, *The Personal President*, 11.
54. Hart, *The Sound of Leadership*, 8.
55. Ibid., 33.
56. Ibid., 19.
57. A good overview of the criticism of the trend is James W. Ceaser, Glen E. Thurow, Jeffrey Tulis, and Joseph M. Bessette, "The Rise of the Rhetorical Presidency," *Presidential Studies Quarterly* 11 (Spring 1981): 158-171. For a response, see Abbott, "Do Presidents Talk Too Much?"
58. Bruce Miroff, "Monopolizing the Public Space: The President as a Problem for Democratic Politics," in *Rethinking the Presidency*, ed. Thomas E. Cronin (Boston: Little, Brown, 1982), 226. See also Richard Sennett, *The Fall of Public Man* (New York: Vintage, 1974), 150-194, for an analysis of the way politics dominated by personalities affect discussion of complex issues.
59. Lowi, *The Personal President*, 170.
60. Hart, *The Sound of Leadership*, 32.
61. Ibid., 30.
62. Jamieson, *Eloquence in an Electronic Age*, 220-222.
63. Robert E. Darcy and Alvin Richman, "Presidential Travel and Public Opinion," *Presidential Studies Quarterly* 18 (Winter 1988): 85-90.
64. Hart, *The Sound of Leadership*, 58.
65. Kernell, *Going Public*, 97.
66. Francis E. Rourke, *Bureaucracy, Politics, and Public Policy* (Boston: Little, Brown, 1984), 155.
67. David I. Kertzer, *Ritual, Politics, and Power* (New Haven, Conn.: Yale University Press, 1988), 94.
68. Daniel T. Rodgers, *Contested Truths* (New York: Basic Books, 1987), 182.
69. Green, *Shaping Political Consciousness*, 119-163.
70. Quoted in Tulis, *The Rhetorical Presidency*, 172.
71. Theodore J. Lowi, *The End of Liberalism* (New York: Norton, 1979).
72. Dwight D. Eisenhower, "Farewell Address to the American People," in *Great Issues in American History: From Reconstruction to the Present Day, 1864-1969*, ed. Richard Hofstadter (New York: Vintage, 1969), 451.

Selected Bibliography

Green, David. *Shaping Political Consciousness*. Ithaca, N.Y.: Cornell University Press, 1987.

Hart, Roderick D. *The Sound of Leadership*. Chicago: University of Chicago Press, 1988.

Jamieson, Kathleen Hall. *Eloquence in an Electronic Age*. New York: Oxford University Press, 1988.

Kernell, Samuel. *Going Public: New Strategies of Presidential Leadership*. Washington, D.C.: CQ Press, 1986.

King, Gary, and Lyn Ragsdale. *The Elusive Executive: Discovering Statistical Patterns in the Presidency*. Washington, D.C.: CQ Press, 1988.

Tulis, Jeffrey. *The Rhetorical Presidency*. Princeton, N.J.: Princeton University Press, 1984.

Windt, Theodore Otto, Jr. "Presidential Rhetoric: Definition of a Field of Study." *Presidential Studies Quarterly* 16 (Winter 1986): 102-116.

Wide World Photos

South side of the White House, distinguished by the Truman balcony

Part V

The White House and the Executive Branch

Housing of the Executive Branch

The best-known executive branch structure is surely the White House, the official residence of the best-known U.S. government employee. But the executive branch employs five million other people as well. They work in fourteen cabinet-level departments and sixty-two independent agencies in a vast network of buildings around the world. U.S. military installations, embassies and consulates, Social Security offices, and post offices all house executive branch employees. Approximately five hundred executive branch buildings, including the headquarters of the departments and agencies, are in the Washington, D.C., area alone.

Managing these properties is largely the job of the General Services Administration (GSA). In particular, GSA's Public Buildings Service (PBS) operates as the owner, developer, and manager of properties for all three branches of the government. It provides space for government employees by constructing new buildings, buying existing ones, and leasing space in others. PBS manages 227 million square feet of work space in approximately seven thousand office buildings ranging in size from the Social Security office in Monticello, Arkansas, with 1,339 square feet, to the Pentagon, with 3.8 million square feet. Since 1982 PBS has allowed some thirty departments and agencies to operate and maintain their own headquarters in the Washington area.

The White House

Along the East Coast of the United States, guides at historic sites often claim that "George Washington slept here." Although there is much uncertainty about just where the nation's first president did lodge, historians are sure about one thing—Washington never spent a night in the White House. In fact, Washington is the only president who never lived in the building known around the world as the symbol of the U.S. presidency. *(See box, Where Did President Washington Live? p. 806.)*

Early History

Although he never lived there, the nation's first president was instrumental in determining the location and appearance of the White House. Under Washington's direction, French engineer and architect Pierre Charles L'Enfant mapped out the new capital city. Together, they selected the site for the presidential residence.

Washington appointed three commissioners to oversee development of the federal city and its buildings, and in 1792 they conducted a public contest to choose the design for the house. Thomas Jefferson, under the pseudonym "A.Z.," submitted a plan, as did many others. The winner was James Hoban, a self-taught, Irish-born master builder who, in addition to the honor of becoming the architect of the "President's House," as Washington called it, received a $500 gold medal and a plot of land for his personal use. *(See box, What's in a Name? p. 814.)* The commissioners subsequently hired Hoban as general supervisor of construction.

Hoban designed a simple, three-story, boxlike structure that incorporated the harmonious proportions of late eighteenth-century Georgian architecture. The plan called for balustrading, a hipped roof, and columns at the main entrance. Symmetrical, rectangular windows would provide the main exterior ornamentation: windows on the first floor would be tall, with alternating arched and triangular pediments.

Hoban's interior design included a large entrance hall with a spacious ceremonial room on the east end of the building (today's East Room) balanced by a formal dining room on the west end (the State Dining Room). Three smaller drawing rooms (the Green Room, the Blue Room, and the Red Room) would line the transverse corridor joining the East Room and the State Dining Room. Hoban's plan for these rooms on the first floor (also called the "state floor") has not been changed significantly since he designed them.

Master stonemason Collen Williamson laid the cornerstone of the President's House on October 13, 1792, eleven months before George Washington laid the cornerstone of the Capitol. The White House is thus the oldest federal building in the District of Columbia.

The building is made of white-painted sandstone from the Aquia Creek Quarry in Virginia. The quarry, on an island in the Potomac about forty miles south of Washington, supplied the stone for many public buildings in the new capital from 1791 to 1837.

Money was in short supply from the beginning, and Congress held the purse strings tightly. To cut costs, Washington instructed Hoban to eliminate the third floor. (This floor eventually was added in 1927.) Major construction

By Margaret Seawell Benjaminson

Where Did President Washington Live?

The only chief executive who never lived in the White House—or the "President's House," as he called it—was the nation's first president, George Washington.

When he was sworn into office on April 30, 1789, New York was the capital of the United States. The president and Martha Washington lived first in a residence on Cherry Street and later in a house on Broadway. An official residence for the president was under construction in New York when the government moved in 1790 to Philadelphia, named as the temporary capital until the new federal city could be finished.

In Philadelphia, President and Mrs. Washington lived at 190 High Street in a house owned by financier Robert Morris. Washington described the house as "the best *single* House in the City.... There are good Stables ... and a Coach House which will hold all my Carriages."[1] Philadelphia, too, planned an official residence, but it was not finished in time for Washington to live there.

When his term ended in March 1797, Washington left Philadelphia to return to his home at Mount Vernon, Virginia. On the way he stopped in the city of Washington for a banquet in his honor and a visit to the White House, still under construction. Expecting the general, a crowd had gathered at the residence and cheered wildly for the first president. James Hoban directed the Washington Artillery Company in a sixteen-gun salute. Washington never attended another White House ceremony, for he died on December 14, 1799, eleven months before President John Adams moved into the President's House.[2]

1. Kenneth W. Leish, *The White House* (New York: Newsweek, 1972), 15.
2. William Seale, *The President's House*, vol. 1 (Washington, D.C.: White House Historical Association, 1986), 74-75.

took eight years and cost approximately $240,000; but much work remained to be done when President John Adams (1797-1801) and his wife, Abigail, became the first residents of the President's House in November 1800.[1] In fact, only six rooms in the house were usable. "Not a chamber is finished of the whole," wrote Abigail Adams of her new home. There was little firewood to warm the large, drafty rooms and no indoor bathrooms. Plaster was still wet, the main staircase was unfinished, and water had to be carried to the house from a park five blocks away.

Still, Mrs. Adams made the best of things in her four-month stay. She used the vast, unfinished East Room as a place to hang her laundry, and each week she and President Adams held large, formal receptions—then called "levees"—in the Oval Room (known today as the Blue Room).

Thomas Jefferson (1801-1809) introduced a different style of living when he succeeded Adams as president. Instead of large receptions, he held small dinner parties where he seated no one by precedence. Instead of bowing to his guests, as had his predecessors, the new president preferred the more democratic gesture of shaking hands.

Jefferson worked with his architect, Benjamin Henry Latrobe, to complete and add to the President's House. Latrobe replaced the leaking roof and built pavilions on the building's east and west ends. He also proposed a semicircular portico for the south side and a "porte cochere," or carriage porch, for the north. The South Portico was not finished until 1824; the North Portico, 1830. Both included elements of Hoban's original design.

James Madison (1809-1817) and his wife, Dolley, a well-known hostess, followed Jefferson to the President's House. Congress appropriated $14,000 for household furnishings and $12,000 for repairs when Madison took office. Dolley Madison redecorated, under the direction of Latrobe, who designed Greek Revival furniture for the Oval Room. In 1813 Elbridge Gerry, Jr., son of the vice president, described the finished room as "immense and magnificent."[2] But the splendor was not to last.

In 1814, during the War of 1812, the British invaded Washington and burned the Capitol, the departmental buildings, the Navy Yard, and the White House. Through a spyglass from the White House roof, Dolley Madison watched British troops approach. Just before leaving the house, she demanded that the Gilbert Stuart portrait of George Washington be saved. She wrote to her sister:

> Our kind friend, Mr. Carroll, has come to hasten my departure and is in a very bad humor with me because I insist on waiting until the large picture of General Washington is secured: and it requires to be unscrewed from the wall. This process was found too tedious for these perilous moments; I have ordered the frame to be broken and the canvas taken out; it is done, and the precious portrait placed in the hands of two gentlemen of New York for safe keeping....[3]

Fire gutted the interior. Only the sandstone exterior walls, blackened from smoke and flames, were left standing.

The Madisons finished out their term first in Octagon House, an elegant New York Avenue mansion owned by Col. John Tayloe, and later in a smaller house at the corner of Nineteenth Street and Pennsylvania Avenue.

Renovations and Refurbishings

The White House has been hollowed out and its interior rebuilt twice in its history—after the fire of 1814 and from 1949 to 1952 during the administration of Harry S Truman, when the building was found to be structurally unsound. Major, but less encompassing, structural renovation took place during Theodore Roosevelt's administration in 1902 and during Calvin Coolidge's administration in 1927. Between 1817 and 1902, however, the White House underwent only minor changes in its structure, although every first family engaged in some degree of redecorating, depending on the generosity of Congress.

Hoban Returns

One could say that James Hoban built the White House twice. After supervising its initial construction, he returned to rebuild the mansion after the fire of 1814.

Library of Congress

In 1792 master builder James Hoban won the competition for architect of the White House with this design.

Beginning in March 1815 with only a burned and roofless shell, Hoban hired workers and acquired the materials necessary for reconstruction. Carpenters and stonecutters worked long days, and the President's House, which had taken almost ten years to build originally, was reconstructed in just under three at a cost of $247,000.[4] By September 1817 the house was ready for the new president, James Monroe (1817-1825), who had been inaugurated in March.

Congress appropriated $20,000 for refurbishing the mansion, and Monroe proved more than equal to the task of spending it. He purchased for the White House furniture of high quality from the French Empire period and sold to the government many of his personal furnishings collected while he was U.S. ambassador to France. Items from the Monroe administration—particularly pieces made by French cabinetmaker Pierre-Antoine Bellangé—form the core of the White House's historic collection. The only item of greater historic significance is the portrait of Washington, rescued by Dolley Madison in 1814, which has belonged to the White House since 1800.

In 1824, during Monroe's second term, Hoban built the semicircular South Portico with Ionic columns two stories tall. (One hundred twenty-four years later, President Truman would object to the height of these columns and build a balcony on the second floor.) In 1829 Hoban began work on the North Portico, finishing it the following year.

Modernization and Popular Taste

Andrew Jackson (1829-1837) was the "people's president," and hundreds of newly enfranchised voters came to the White House to celebrate his inauguration. In the process, the East Room suffered mightily as rowdy supporters destroyed furniture and broke dishes and glassware. Jackson finally escaped the crowd and spent his first night as president at Gadsby's Hotel.

The new president made up for the damage by decorating the East Room lavishly; he spent one-fifth of his $50,000 furnishings allowance on that room alone.[5] He ordered from Pittsburgh a shipment of glassware that included twelve dozen tumblers and eighteen dozen wineglasses for $1,452 and bought a French porcelain 440-piece dinner service and 412-piece dessert set for $2,500.[6]

In 1833, during Jackson's first term, iron pipes were installed, which brought running water into the White House for the first time. Shortly thereafter, lines for the first sewer were laid.

Martin Van Buren (1837-1841), Jackson's successor, installed a furnace in 1840 to augment the twelve fireplaces Hoban had added in 1817. Although he spent less than Jackson on White House furnishings, Van Buren's purchases took on unusual political significance. In April 1840 Rep. Charles Ogle, a Whig from Pennsylvania, delivered a three-day oration criticizing what he called the "princely lifestyle" of the Democratic president. He proclaimed that Van Buren was living in "a palace as splendid as that of the Caesars" while the rest of the nation was suffering from a financial panic and economic depression. The speech—itself excessive and inaccurate in many respects—was delivered seven months before the 1840 election with the intention of swaying public opinion in favor of Ogle's preference for president, the simple "hard cider man," Gen. William Henry Harrison. Certainly Ogle alone did not decide the president's fate; but after the election of 1840, it was Harrison, not Van Buren, who called the White House home.

Harrison died of pneumonia after one month in office, and his successor, John Tyler (1841-1845), had a difficult time securing funds from Congress to refurbish an increasingly shabby executive mansion.

James K. Polk (1845-1849) received an appropriation of $14,900 for redecorating the White House, which had seen little improvement since Jackson's administration.[7] Polk was the first president to enjoy central heating (installed in 1845-1846) and gas lighting (installed in 1848).[8] He also purchased an icebox in 1845 for $25.

In 1850 Millard Fillmore (1850-1853) improved the kitchen further by adding a stove. Previously, food had been prepared in open fireplaces. Fillmore's wife, Abigail, saw to it that Congress appropriated $5,000 for a small White House library. When the former schoolteacher

Library of Congress

President Ulysses S. Grant and his wife made extensive changes in the White House. They referred to the new style of the East Room, above, as "Greek," but their critics called it "steamboat Gothic."

moved into the executive mansion, she had been surprised to find no books—not even a Bible or a dictionary.[9]

Fillmore's successor, Franklin Pierce (1853-1857), was the first president to have a bathroom with hot and cold running water in the second-floor family quarters.[10]

President James Buchanan (1857-1861) replaced much of the White House furniture after auctioning off numerous old pieces (including some of the Monroe collection, which would later find its way back to the White House). He also built the first of several conservatories, which supplied plants and flowers for the White House until the administration of Theodore Roosevelt.

Abraham Lincoln (1861-1865), who presided over the White House during the Civil War, was scrupulous about expenditures, but his wife was not. Mary Todd Lincoln purchased rosewood furniture and expensive upholstery, exceeding a congressional appropriation by $6,700. The angry president responded: "It would stink in the nostrils of the American people to have it said that the President of the United States had approved a bill overrunning an appropriation of $20,000 for *flub dubs* for this damned old house, when the soldiers cannot have blankets." [11]

Lincoln said he would make up the difference out of his own pocket, but Congress approved funds to cover the first lady's expenses. The president opened his house to the army and at one point quartered Union soldiers in the East Room.

After Lincoln's assassination, his grief-stricken widow remained cloistered for six weeks in a bedroom overlooking the North Portico. Meanwhile, souvenir-seekers, who had free access to the house, looted the state rooms, cutting swatches from draperies and upholstery and carrying off the china and silver.

Although Congress impeached President Andrew Johnson (1865-1869), it did give him funds to begin redecorating the executive mansion, left in poor condition after the Civil War. But it was Ulysses S. Grant (1869-1877) who in 1873 oversaw the most extensive refurbishing in decades. Although ceilings had cracked and settled (one had even collapsed), President and Mrs. Grant focused not on structural improvements but on redecoration of the mansion in an ostentatious style typical of the Gilded Age. In the East Room, for example, they installed ornamental beams and pillars, massive cut-glass chandeliers, and floral wall-to-wall carpet. The first family said their decorating scheme followed "the Greek style," but their critics called it "steamboat Gothic."

Rutherford B. Hayes (1877-1881) and his wife, known as "Lemonade Lucy" for serving only nonalcoholic beverages at parties, led modest lives and made few changes during their White House tenure. One notable improvement, however, was the installation of a telephone in 1879.

Chester A. Arthur (1881-1885), nicknamed "Elegant Arthur" for his sophisticated tastes, became president when James A. Garfield was assassinated. He refused to move into the White House until extensive renovations took place, which he began by auctioning off twenty-four wagonloads of furnishings he considered worn or outmoded. (Almost another quarter-century would pass before first families would value historic use or ownership over the current fashion in furnishing the White House.) Arthur expanded the conservatories, installed an elevator, and engaged New York artist Louis Comfort Tiffany to redecorate the state rooms. Expenses for Arthur's refurbishing ran to $110,000 ($80,000 over budget), the most that had been spent on the building since its reconstruction after the fire of 1814.

Throughout the nineteenth century, the greater part of the White House had served for the official duties of the president. Job-seekers, politicians, lobbyists, and sightseers milled about in droves on the first and second floors, leaving the first family little privacy. A mere eight rooms were available as family living quarters during Grant's presidency, and Benjamin Harrison (1889-1893) had to accommodate his family of eleven in only five bedrooms.

Caroline Harrison, the president's wife, devised three proposals for expanding the White House. One of the plans would have moved the family quarters to a separate residence on Sixteenth Street; the others added large wings to the mansion. Congress refused to fund any of the plans, and Mrs. Harrison was able to improve the house only by having rotting floorboards replaced and the kitchen modernized. Her hobby of painting china led her to begin the White House China Collection, which today contains pieces from almost every administration. The landmark improvement of the Harrison administration was the installation of electricity in 1891.

Presidents Grover Cleveland (1885-1889, 1893-1897) and William McKinley (1897-1901) also had plans to expand the White House that were never carried out. Not until the next administration did a major renovation take place.

Restoration and a Sense of History

Although he had a very large family, President Theodore Roosevelt (1901-1909) had no intention of abandoning the White House for another residence. Instead, he chose to take the offices out of the White House and expand the

Library of Congress

In contrast to Grant's changes, Theodore Roosevelt's renovation of the White House restored its classical interior. This is the East Room largely as it appears today.

living quarters on the second floor. He hired architects William R. Mead, Charles F. McKim, and Stanford White of New York, who were known for their work in the historic style called "colonial" (referring to the early days of the Republic). Roosevelt assigned them the following five goals: make the White House structurally sound; move the offices out of the main building; provide for smoother handling of guests at large, official receptions; enlarge the State Dining Room; and remove the conservatories (or, as the exuberant president ordered, "Smash the glass houses!").[12]

Roosevelt received congressional approval in June 1902 and demanded that the work in the new office be finished in October of that year. The first family moved to a house on Lafayette Square as work got under way. The floors were rebuilt, and modern plumbing, heating, and wiring were installed.

On schedule, Roosevelt moved his offices to the new, white brick West Wing, which also included work and meeting space for the cabinet and the press. A colonnade connecting the offices to the residence was built on the foundations of Jefferson's original west terrace, discovered when the greenhouses were removed.

To accommodate crowds, the architects built an East Wing containing cloakrooms, restrooms, a porte cochere that could shelter three carriages, and a portico that could hold five hundred guests.

Inside the White House, McKim redecorated the state floor, removing all the Victorian furnishings of Roosevelt's predecessors. Hoban's original grand staircase, which had led from the west end of the transverse corridor to the executive offices on the second floor, was removed to allow more space for an expanded State Dining Room.

By December, when the renovation was complete, costs had reached $65,000 for the West Wing and $475,000 for the rest of the house. Since 1902, presidents and first ladies who have redecorated the White House have followed Roosevelt's example and conscientiously furnished the state rooms in a style appropriate to the early days of the Republic.

No renovation matched in scope that of the 1902 work until the Truman reconstruction of 1949-1952. Still, intervening presidents continued to make changes.

Ellen Axson Wilson, first wife of Woodrow Wilson (1913-1921), added guest rooms to the attic. During Calvin Coolidge's administration (1923-1929), a study by the Army Corps of Engineers revealed that the roof was in danger of collapse because the beams were rotten. President Coolidge, known for his frugality, responded that "there were plenty others who would be willing to take the risk" of living under that roof. Nonetheless, in 1927 the Coolidges moved to a mansion on Dupont Circle owned by the Patterson family, and the roof was replaced.

At this time the third story—eliminated from Hoban's 1792 design—finally was added to the White House, giving the mansion an additional eighteen rooms for guests, servants, and storage. A sun room, which Grace Coolidge called the "sky parlor," was built on the South Portico roof. Hidden from view from the ground by the balustrade, it affords both privacy and splendid views of the Mall.

Grace Coolidge also took an interest in furnishing the White House with antique or historic furniture and urged Congress to pass legislation authorizing presidents to accept such donations from the American public. A joint resolution of Congress, passed in February 1925, marked the first legal recognition of the White House as a museum. A committee established to evaluate the gifts remained in operation through the Eisenhower administration.

Franklin D. Roosevelt (1933-1945) was the next president to make permanent changes in the White House, although his alterations were largely utilitarian. The president and first lady of a nation in the midst of the Great Depression and then World War II had no interest in decoration for its own sake. Instead, they wanted the White House to be a comfortable and practical home for their large family.

The West Wing, which had been damaged by a fire in 1929 and was proving short of office space for the New Deal president, was rebuilt in 1934 and given new underground work space. Also added were three stories of office space to the East Wing and an underground bomb shelter in the basement of the Treasury Department, connected by passageway to the White House. Eleanor Roosevelt had the servants' quarters and the kitchen improved and enlarged. In 1933 the Roosevelts added an indoor swimming pool—paid for by private funds, largely in small donations from the people of New York—so that the polio-stricken president could take regular exercise.[13]

Harry S Truman (1945-1953) left his mark on both the outside and the inside of the White House. In 1948 he had a second-floor balcony built over the South Portico, which cost $10,000 and earned him much criticism. But Truman stuck by his conviction that the balcony was both an aesthetic improvement (to divide the two-story columns, which he thought looked awkward) and a practical one (to shade the Blue Room, since there was no air conditioning, and to provide a cool place for the first family to relax in summer).

Later in 1948 engineers' reports concluded that the rest of the White House was structurally unsound. Although the first floor had been reinforced with steel in 1902, as had the third floor in 1927, the remaining walls and beams were largely those of the 1814-1817 reconstruction. They had been cut into many times to accommodate plumbing, wiring, and heating ducts and consequently were standing "purely by habit," as the commissioner of public buildings put it.[14] There was also visible evidence of the engineers' reports. In 1948 a leg of Margaret Truman's grand piano punctured the floor of her bedroom, causing portions of the ceiling in the room below to collapse. And chandeliers in the East Room often swayed—for reasons only the building itself fully knew.

The president had three options. First, he could move to a new presidential residence and have the White House designated a museum. Second, the entire White House could be razed and a replica reconstructed. Third, the exterior walls could be left intact, and the interior torn out and rebuilt.[15] The third—and most expensive—option was chosen, and in 1949 Congress appropriated $5.4 million for the work.[16]

The Trumans moved across the street to Blair House in November 1948 as architects and engineers began planning the reconstruction. Starting in December 1949, workers took apart the interior, setting aside mantelpieces and fixtures, labeling decorative moldings, and tagging paneling—all to be carefully reinstalled. Pieces that could not be reused—the walls and floors themselves—were demolished, except for small quantities of wood, brick, and stone that

White House Historical Association

During the Truman renovation of 1949-1952, only the exterior walls were left intact. Here, beneath steel scaffolding, a bulldozer excavates a new basement.

were sold as "relic kits." [17] By mid-1950, apart from supportive scaffolding, the entire White House, basement to roof, was hollow.

In twenty-seven months of rebuilding, fifty subcontractors and hundreds of workers (all of whom had to have security clearances) gave the President's House new foundations, two newly excavated basements, a new steel frame, fireproofing, and air conditioning. Interior details were faithfully restored.

Shortly after his return to the White House on March 27, 1952, President Truman conducted a televised tour of the mansion with Walter Cronkite. His was the first such tour, but not the most famous. Ten years later, on February 14, 1962, Jacqueline Kennedy would conduct another tour of the White House to a television audience of forty-six million.

In 1961 the wife of John F. Kennedy (1961-1963) created the Fine Arts Committee for the White House and the Special Committee on Paintings. She planned to furnish the White House with authentic American antiques and paintings of the eighteenth and nineteenth centuries and to dispose of the reproduction pieces, many of which were mediocre in quality and irrelevant to U.S. history. No public funds were available, so all contributions came from private donors. Before President Kennedy's death, Jacqueline Kennedy's Fine Arts Committee restored the state rooms on the first floor and several historic rooms on the second floor.

In September 1961 Congress passed legislation stating that White House acquisitions of "historic or artistic interest" would become part of the permanent White House collection. When not in use, they would be stored at the Smithsonian Institution. No longer would it be possible simply to lose track of historic pieces, as had happened so often in the past, or for furnishings to be sold to the highest bidder, as President Arthur had done when he moved into the White House in 1881.

On March 7, 1964, Lyndon B. Johnson (1963-1969) signed Executive Order 11145 establishing the Committee for the Preservation of the White House and the permanent office of White House curator. Still operating today, the committee advises the first family on the selection and use of furnishings for the executive mansion.

Throughout Richard Nixon's tenure in the White House (1969-1974), Patricia Nixon oversaw renovation of the main rooms on the ground and state floors. Nearly a decade of heavy use since the Kennedy refurbishing had left much of the furniture nearly threadbare. Under the guidance of curator Clement E. Conger, the Nixons continued the program of antiques collection begun by Jacqueline Kennedy. The swimming pool in the West Wing was boarded over to make more room for the fifteen hundred reporters accredited to the White House.

Gerald R. Ford (1974-1977) and Jimmy Carter (1977-1981) collected paintings rather than furniture during their terms of office. Ford acquired twenty-six works, including a small wax portrait of James Hoban, the only known likeness of the architect.[18] Carter added thirty-four paintings to the White House collection.[19]

Ronald Reagan (1981-1989) raised more than $1 million in private funds to redecorate the second and third floors. Since the Truman renovation, efforts to furnish the White House had focused entirely on the historic rooms of the ground and first floors, leaving for the family quarters and other second-floor rooms whatever furniture presidents chose to bring with them or could find in White House warehouses. Many pieces of nineteenth-century American furniture were retrieved from storage, refurbished, and returned to use in the executive mansion. As a parting gift, President and Mrs. Reagan had a $49,625 handmade carpet installed in the Oval Office in 1988.[20]

Plans for major improvements to the building itself proceeded under the Reagan administration. In 1980 workers began the slow process of chemically removing 175 years' buildup of whitewash and paint from the exterior walls and repairing the delicate sandstone carvings beneath. When cleaned, some sections, under as many as thirty-two layers of paint, revealed the black scorch marks from the burning of the mansion in the War of 1812. In the fall of 1988 the north façade was a study in contrasts—the east side stripped to the grey sandstone, the west side still white before treatment. As of September 1988 the project had cost $2.4 million and was scheduled for completion in 1992, the bicentennial of the laying of the cornerstone.[21]

The White House Today

The White House contains 132 rooms, including 32 bathrooms. The residence, which is 170 feet long and 85 feet wide, comprises four floors (referred to as the ground, first, second, and third floors) and two basements; the West and East wings each have three floors. The ground floor, opening onto the South Portico, is visible only from the south side of the house. The five state rooms open for tours are on the first floor, which contains the main, North Portico entrance facing Pennsylvania Avenue. The second floor contains seven historic rooms and the principal living quarters. On the third floor are additional rooms for the first family, the solarium, guest bedrooms, and storage areas.

The Committee for the Preservation of the White House works closely with the White House Historical Association, a nonprofit organization, to acquire furniture, paintings, and decorative objects through private donations. At the beginning of each presidential term since 1925, Congress has appropriated $50,000 for the president to paint and decorate the family living quarters.

The East Wing and the Ground Floor

The public tour of the White House begins in the *East Wing Lobby*, a wood-paneled hall decorated with portraits of first ladies. The East Wing, built in 1902 during Theodore Roosevelt's administration, was rebuilt and enlarged in 1934 by Franklin Roosevelt. It contains the visitors' office and the offices of the first lady's staff, the president's military aides, the White House congressional liaison staff, and the Uniformed Division of the Secret Service. In 1942 Roosevelt added the East Wing Lobby and converted the cloakroom—known as the "Hat Box"—into a movie theater, still in use today. Adjacent to the lobby is the bright, informal *Garden Room*, which overlooks the Jacqueline Kennedy Garden. Visitors proceed through a glass-enclosed colonnade, built on the foundations of Thomas Jefferson's east pavilion, to the ground floor of the White House. Before the renovation of 1902, the *Ground Floor Corridor* (the only area open to the public on this floor) and adjacent rooms served as work and storage areas. The Truman renovation restored the clean lines of Hoban's groined arches and covered the walls and floors with marble. Portaits of first ladies hang in the hall.

Plan of the White House

West Wing, Ground Floor, East Wing

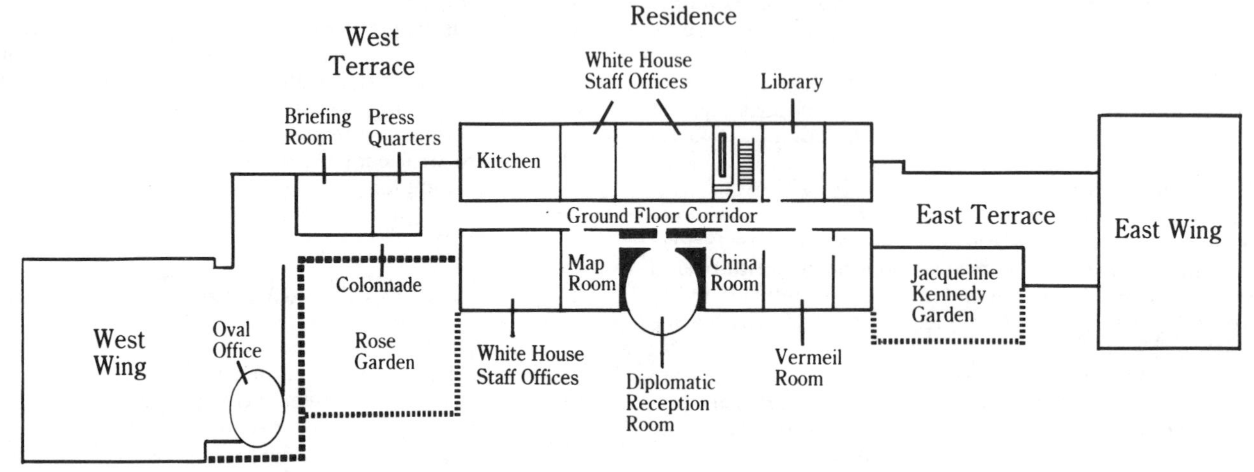

First, or State, Floor

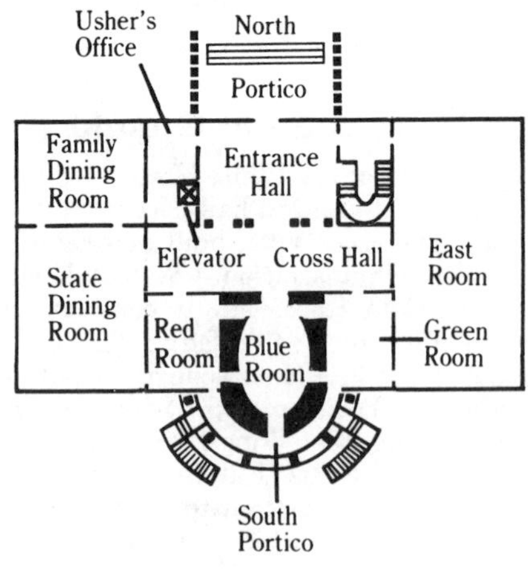

Second Floor

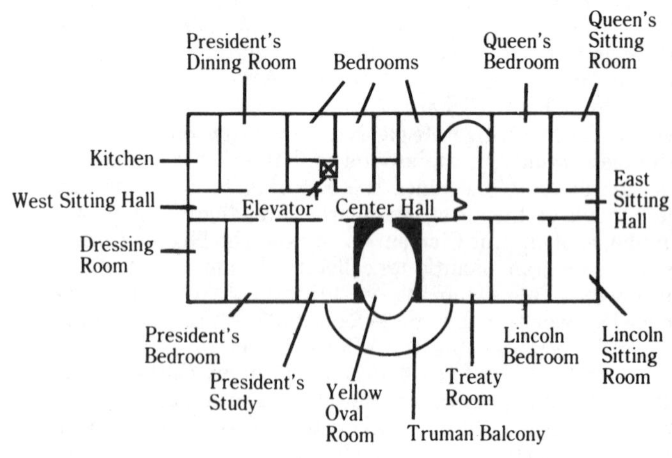

Note: Drawings are not to scale.

The first room on the south side of the corridor is the *Vermeil Room* (also called the "Gold Room"), which contains a collection of gilded silver, given to the White House in 1956 by Margaret Thompson Biddle. Hanging on the south wall is Douglas Chandor's 1949 portrait of Eleanor Roosevelt, who, not liking to sit for portraits, wrote in one corner of the canvas, "A trial made pleasant by the painter." Above the fireplace on the west wall is Claude Monet's "Morning on the Seine," the painting the Kennedy family gave to the White House in 1963 in memory of President Kennedy. This display room also is used as a women's sitting room on formal occasions; a powder room is adjacent.

The second room on the south side of the corridor is the *China Room*, so named in 1917 by Edith Bolling Wilson, Woodrow Wilson's second wife, to display the china collection begun by Caroline Harrison in 1889. Almost every presidential administration is represented. The white, red, and gold state china service commissioned by Nancy Reagan was donated to the White House in 1982. Howard Chandler Christy's 1924 portrait of Grace Coolidge wearing a red dress determined the red and white color scheme of this room.

Portraits of the most recent first ladies hang on either side of the door to the *Diplomatic Reception Room*. Opening onto the South Portico, the Diplomatic Reception Room contains the south entrance to the White House, used by the first family and foreign dignitaries on informal occasions. (For state dinners, heads of state enter through the North Portico on the first floor; all other guests pass through security checks in the East Wing.) Franklin Roosevelt broadcast his fireside chats from this room in the 1930s and 1940s. In 1961 Jacqueline Kennedy redecorated the room with historic furnishings. "Scenic America," a wallpaper printed in 1834, forms a panorama of American scenes along the curved walls, one of Hoban's three oval rooms.

For President Roosevelt during World War II, the *Map Room*, next-door to the Diplomatic Reception Room, served as a communications center where he tracked the movement of troops and ships. Today, the president and first lady use the room for private meetings and small receptions.

On the north side of the Ground Floor corridor is the *Library*. Used for storage in 1801, later as a laundry room, and in Theodore Roosevelt's day as a "Gentlemen's anteroom," the Library assumed its present use in 1937. Old timbers removed from the house during the Truman restoration were made into wood paneling for the room, now painted a soft grey after the fashion of "painted" rooms in the early 1800s. On the west wall are the original architectural drawings James Hoban and Thomas Jefferson submitted in the 1792 competition for White House architect. In 1961 a committee was formed to select books on American subjects for the Library. The collection for the Library and for the family living quarters continues to grow with presidential biographies and papers and with quadrennial gifts of 250 to 300 titles from the American Booksellers Association.

Also on the ground floor are the main kitchen, the florist's workshop, and offices of the curator, the housekeeper, the president's physician, and the auditor.

The First Floor

The rooms on the first, or state, floor are those viewed by the public on morning tours and used by the president for official entertaining at other times. The five state rooms—the East Room, Green Room, Blue Room, Red Room, and State Dining Room—are the most historic and the most used parts of the White House. Consequently, they undergo the most refurbishing.

Library of Congress

Just before fleeing the White House as British troops invaded Washington in August 1814, Dolley Madison demanded that this Gilbert Stuart portrait of George Washington be cut out of its frame so she could take it with her.

The *North Entrance Hall*, opening onto the North Portico, and the *Cross Hall*, connecting the East Room and the State Dining Room, were part of Hoban's original design. The only major change since Hoban's time took place in 1902 when the main staircase at the west end of the Cross Hall was removed and a new one was installed across from the Green Room. During the Truman restoration, the staircase was repositioned so that it now descends into the Entrance Hall. Also between 1949 and 1952, marble was added to the floors and walls of the Cross Hall, where portraits of recent presidents hang.

The elegant but sparsely furnished *East Room* is probably the most famous room in the White House, for it is here that most White House press conferences are held. Decorated in the classical style of the late eighteenth century, the East Room appears today much as it did after the

What's in a Name?

French engineer and architect Pierre Charles L'Enfant, chosen by George Washington to plan the new capital city on the Potomac, insisted on calling the presidential residence the "President's Palace." But Washington preferred a less regal term and called the residence simply the "President's House." Others spoke of it as the "Executive Mansion."

Once the house was completed its appearance determined its name, for the painted white sandstone stood in sharp contrast to the brick and frame buildings surrounding it. In November 1810 a reporter for the *Baltimore Whig* first referred to the house in print as the "white house." [1] By the end of the Madison administration in 1817, the term had gained full currency.

Not until 1901, however, did the name become official. In that year Theodore Roosevelt issued an executive order changing the official name from the "Executive Mansion" to the "White House." [2] Today, the president's letterhead reads simply:

The White House
Washington

1. Amy La Follette Jensen, *The White House and Its Thirty-three Families* (New York: McGraw-Hill, 1962), 21.
2. William Seale, *The President's House*, 2 vols. (Washington, D.C.: White House Historical Association, 1986), 1088, 654.

1902 renovation by the architectural firm McKim, Mead, and White. It is eighty feet long by forty feet wide, with ceilings twenty-two feet in height. The walls are paneled in wood, intricately carved, and painted white. Three Bohemian cut-glass chandeliers hang above an oak floor of Fontainebleu parquetry. The principal article of furniture is a Steinway grand piano with gilded legs in the shape of American eagles, which the Steinway Company donated to the White House in 1938. On the wall is the full-length Gilbert Stuart portrait of George Washington that Dolley Madison saved from the fire of 1814.

In addition to news conferences, the East Room is used for large gatherings on many sorts of occasions—bill signings, receptions, dances, concerts, after-dinner entertainment, weddings, and funerals. It was here that Abigail Adams hung her laundry in 1801; James Madison met with his cabinet in 1812; and Abraham Lincoln dreamed he saw his catafalque surrounded by mourners in 1865—which, but a few days later, it was. President Grover Cleveland married Frances Folsom in the East Room in 1886 (the only White House wedding of a president); Theodore Roosevelt's children roller skated in the early 1900s; and cellist Pablo Casals performed for Kennedy guests in 1961. Seven presidents have lain in state in the East Room: W. H. Harrison in 1841, Lincoln in 1865, Garfield in 1881, McKinley in 1901, Warren G. Harding in 1923, Franklin Roosevelt in 1945, and Kennedy in 1963.

On the tour, visitors enter the East Room from the Cross Hall and exit through a door to the *Green Room.* Hoban called this room the "Common Dining Room," but only Thomas Jefferson used it regularly for meals. For James Madison, it was a sitting room; for James Monroe, a card room. John Quincy Adams called it the "Green Drawing Room," establishing both its color and its function for future presidents. In the Green Room today small receptions and teas are held and occasionally a small formal dinner.

The room is furnished with Sheraton pieces from the Federal period (1800-1815), many from the New York workshop of cabinetmaker Duncan Phyfe. The walls are covered in green watered-silk, a fabric originally chosen by Jacqueline Kennedy in 1961 and matched and replaced by Patricia Nixon in 1971. The carpet in the Green Room, a large, multicolored Turkish Hereke, is unusual for its green field. On the walls are portraits of presidents and other paintings by well-known American artists.

Hoban designed three oval rooms for the White House, one on each floor at the midpoint of the south side of the house. The *Blue Room,* which Hoban called the "elliptic saloon," is the most historic of the three. Thomas Jefferson first decorated the room in blue, which for most of its history has been used for formal receptions. (The Blue Room is also where the White House Christmas tree is put up each year.) After the fire of 1814, President Monroe decorated the room with French Empire furnishings, largely with pieces made by Pierre Antoine Bellangé. Items from Monroe's collection that were lost or sold at auction in the nineteenth century gradually have been located or reproduced in the twentieth. Refurbishings of 1902, 1962, and 1972 have fully restored the French Empire style of the room.

The fourth state room open to the public, and the third of the three parlors on the first floor, is the *Red Room.* Decorated in the American Empire style (1810-1830) with red damask upholstery and wallpaper of red twill satin, the room has been used as a parlor since Jefferson's day. Earlier, it was John Adams's breakfast room. Dolley Madison held her glittering Wednesday night receptions here, and Eleanor Roosevelt held press conferences in this room for women reporters, who were not allowed to attend her husband's meetings with the press. The Red Room gained political fame in 1877 as the place where Rutherford B. Hayes secretly was sworn into office during a party hosted by retiring president Grant. Because of a close race and a final decision challenged by Hayes's opponent, Grant was eager to ensure a smooth transition of government. *(See "The Compromise of 1876," p. 286, in The Electoral Process chapter of Part II.)*

The last of the five state rooms on the public tour is the *State Dining Room.* First given this name by Andrew Jackson, the room earlier served as a drawing room, cabinet room, and office. The 1902 renovation enlarged the room by extending the north wall and removing the grand stairway at the end of the Cross Hall. The State Dining Room today can seat 140.

Similar to the spacious white and gold East Room, the State Dining Room has wood paneling painted in several shades of antique ivory to highlight the delicately carved Corinthian pilasters and neoclassical frieze. Golden silk damask draperies frame the floor-to-ceiling windows. The mantel over the fireplace is a 1962 reproduction of the bison-head mantel from Theodore Roosevelt's administration. In 1952 Truman replaced the Roosevelt mantel with a simpler molding and declared the original "surplus"; the original mantel today is in the Truman presidential library. The face of the mantel is inscribed with the following passage from a letter John Adams wrote to his wife on his second night in the White House:

> I Pray to Heaven to Bestow
> the Best of Blessings on
> THIS HOUSE
> and on All that shall hereafter
> Inhabit it. May none but Honest
> and Wise Men ever rule under this Roof.

Adjacent to the State Dining Room, in the northwest corner of the first floor, is the smaller *Family Dining Room.* Although President Monroe gave his state dinners here and called it the "Public Dining Room," the room usually has served as the formal dining room for the president's family or for official entertaining of a small number of guests. During formal dinners in the State Dining Room, the staff drape the furniture and use this room as a pantry to lessen the inconvenience of having the kitchen and dining room on separate floors. The Family Dining Room appears today much as it did after the 1902 renovation, when its white vaulted ceiling and classical frieze were installed. The walls are painted a light yellow, and the furniture is from the Federal period.

The Second and Third Floors

The east half of the second floor contains historic areas—the Queen's Suite, the Lincoln Suite, the Treaty Room, and the Yellow Oval Room. The west half contains several rooms of the family living quarters. The third floor comprises additional family rooms as well as sitting rooms and bedrooms for guests. None of these rooms is open to the public, but it has not always been so.

The Historic Areas. "All sorts of people come upon all sorts of errands," wrote an assistant to Abraham Lincoln about the crowds milling about in the second-floor hall near the president's office. Throughout the nineteenth century, before offices were moved to the West Wing, the public was free to come and go—and wait—in what is now the *East Sitting Hall.* The room today is a small parlor, furnished largely with antiques from the White House collection, including a seventeenth-century armchair used by George Washington in his rented presidential residence in Philadelphia. Filling the east wall of the hall, overlooking the East Wing and the Treasury Building, is Hoban's original double-arched window.

To the north of the East Sitting Room is the *Queens' Suite,* comprising a small sitting room and a bedroom furnished in the American Federal style. The bed in the *Queens' Bedroom* is believed to have belonged to Andrew Jackson. The *Queens' Sitting Room* appears today much as it did during the Kennedy administration. Wallcovering, draperies, and upholstery are made from a French fabric with ivory, neoclassical medallions on a blue field. The room is furnished with antiques from the American and French Empire periods held in the White House collection. Among the guests who have occupied the Queens' Suite are: Queen Elizabeth, wife of Great Britain's King George VI, and her daughter Queen Elizabeth II; and Queen Wilhelmina of the Netherlands and Queen Juliana, her daughter.

On the south side of the East Sitting Hall is the *Lincoln Suite,* comprising the *Lincoln Bedroom* and the *Lincoln Sitting Room.* Used today as a guest room for friends of the president, the bedroom once was Lincoln's office and cabinet room. It was there that he signed the Emancipation Proclamation on January 1, 1863.

President Truman decorated the room with American Victorian furnishings from the period 1850-1870. Notable are a desk that Lincoln used and a rosewood bed—eight

Frank Leslie's Illustrated Newspaper, April 7, 1877; Library of Congress

Nineteenth-century office seekers gather in the White House awaiting an interview with the president. Before Theodore Roosevelt built the West Wing offices, visitors milled about on the first and second floors of the White House, leaving the first family little privacy.

feet long and six feet wide—thought to have been purchased by Mary Todd Lincoln in 1861. Although Lincoln probably never used the bed, other presidents did, including Theodore Roosevelt and Woodrow Wilson. It is known that Lincoln was particularly fond of the portrait of Andrew Jackson that hangs in the room.

The Lincoln Sitting Room is a small room with a fireplace on the southeast corner of the second floor. Throughout much of the nineteenth century it served as office space for presidential assistants, although English novelist Charles Dickens recorded on his visit to the White House during John Tyler's administration (1841-1845) that this room was the president's office. The Reagans decorated the sitting room with red carpet and upholstery and a patterned wallpaper that complement the Victorian furnishings of the Lincoln Bedroom. The room contains four rosewood chairs purchased by Mrs. Lincoln and a small mahogany desk built by White House architect James Hoban.

Also on the south side of the building, beside the Lincoln Bedroom, is the *Treaty Room*, so named during the Kennedy administration. The Treaty Room served as the cabinet room from 1865 to 1902 and as a sitting room from 1902 to 1961. Since 1961 presidents have signed several important documents here, including U.S. instruments of ratification for the 1963 test ban treaty and the 1972 antiballistic missile treaty.

The furnishings in this room mirror the style popular during the Grant administration. The maroon draperies and dark green wallpaper are copies of Victorian patterns. In 1869 President Grant purchased the large Victorian walnut table in the center of the room, which contains locking drawers for each of his eight cabinet members. On March 26, 1979, President Jimmy Carter had this table moved outdoors for the signing of the Egyptian-Israeli peace treaty.

Adjacent to the Treaty Room is the *Yellow Oval Room*, the third in the tier of Hoban's elliptical rooms. Today the room serves as a formal drawing room for the first family and as a reception room where the president greets foreign dignitaries before state luncheons and dinners. Throughout its history, the room has seen many other uses as well. President John Adams held the first White House reception here on January 1, 1801. It has been a bedroom, a family room, and an office, and Abigail Fillmore set up the first White House library here. Franklin Roosevelt and Harry Truman called the room their "oval study" and used it as a less formal working space than the Oval Office.

Dolley Madison decorated the room in yellow damask in 1809, and Jacqueline Kennedy chose a yellow color scheme again in 1961 when she added furnishings in the neoclassical style of Louis XVI. The Yellow Oval Room contains the works of several important American artists, such as William Merritt Chase and Albert Bierstadt.

The Yellow Oval Room opens onto the Truman balcony, built in 1948, where first families occasionally dine, entertain guests, and on July 4 watch fireworks on the Mall.

The yellow and white *Center Hall* is today a large drawing room for the president's family and for foreign guests waiting to be received in the Yellow Oval Room. During the Truman administration, a cornice and bookshelves were installed. The hall is furnished with late eighteenth- and early nineteenth-century antiques from the White House collection and, like the Yellow Oval Room, is decorated with works of American artists.

The Family Living Quarters. With each first family, both the decor and the number of rooms used as the family living quarters change, for they become the Washington home of the person elected president. These rooms constitute a private home within a very public house; comfort and familiarity, not the historical record, govern their use and appearance.[22]

This part of the White House has been changing constantly, as President Truman discovered when he asked Chief Usher J. B. West whether his family's plan for the living quarters would be "tampering with history too much." West replied:

> The President may use the house any way he wishes. . . . It's always been so. Actually, the room that Mrs. Truman has chosen for her sitting room was probably where Lincoln slept. The Coolidges kept the Lincoln furniture there, and President and Mrs. Coolidge slept in the room together. The Hoovers slept in the same room, but they moved the Lincoln furniture across the hall. . . . You could just as easily move it down the hall over the East Room, because that was the Lincoln Cabinet Room.

To this convoluted history lesson Truman replied, "Now I know why they say Lincoln's ghost walks around up here all night. He's just looking for his bed!"[23]

The West Sitting Hall, opening off the Center Hall, is the first family's private living room, which, with each new administration, is decorated with personal items from the family's former home. Like the East Sitting Hall, one end of the room is dominated by Hoban's double-arched window, which overlooks the West Wing and the Old Executive Office Building. Before the 1902 renovation, this hall was little more than a stair landing. During the Truman renovation, the hall became a room when it was enclosed with solid partitions.

Jacqueline Kennedy disliked the Family Dining Room on the first floor and wanted a smaller, more intimate dining room for her family in their living quarters. So in 1961 she converted one of the Eisenhowers' sitting rooms on the north side of the West Sitting Hall into the President's Dining Room. Early in the century, this space had served as a bedroom, and Alice Roosevelt Longworth, daughter of Theodore Roosevelt, remembered having her appendix removed here.

The President's Dining Room is furnished largely with American Federal pieces donated to the White House in 1961 and 1962 through Jacqueline Kennedy's Fine Arts Committee. The mahogany sideboard was once owned by Daniel Webster; it still bears his initials. James Madison's portable, walnut medicine chest on display here was taken from the house by a British soldier just before troops burned the mansion in 1814. A Canadian descendant of the soldier donated the chest to the White House in 1939.[24] The wallpaper, called "The War of Independence," is a panorama of scenes from the American Revolution—some accurate in their details, some merely imagined by the artist.

The first family's private kitchen, also built in 1961, is adjacent to the dining room on the northwest corner of the second floor. This was not, however, the first private kitchen in the family living quarters. Franklin Roosevelt did not like the food his wife's cook prepared, so in 1938 he had a kitchen built on the third floor and brought in his own cook from his Hyde Park home. Thereafter he took many of his meals with friends or staff in his second-floor study (now the Yellow Oval Room).

Like many presidents before him, President Reagan used a private, second-floor study in addition to the West Wing Oval Office. This room, adjoining the Yellow Oval Room on the south side of the house, had been the bedroom of presidents Franklin Roosevelt through Nixon. President Ford used this room as a sitting room, as did President Carter, who had a wall of mahogany bookcases built.[25] On the side of the mantelpiece is a small plaque that Jacqueline Kennedy had installed after her husband's assassination; it reads: "This room was occupied by John Fitzgerald Kennedy during the two years, ten months and two days he was President of the United States. January 20, 1961-November 22, 1963."

President and Mrs. Reagan shared the bedroom adjacent to the president's study, as did the Fords and the Carters. In earlier administrations, Mamie Eisenhower, Jacqueline Kennedy, Lady Bird Johnson, and Patricia Nixon made this room their bedroom. First families since the Eisenhowers have used the small adjoining room in the southwest corner of the second floor as a dressing room.

A small room just above the North Portico entrance served as Nancy Reagan's private study. She converted another room in the living quarters into an exercise room. Family quarters extend to the third floor, although not all first families have used these rooms regularly. The Third Floor Center Sitting Hall, lined with bookshelves, follows the decorating style of the Central Hall on the second floor. Various parlors and guest bedrooms open onto the hall. The Solarium—or "sky parlor," as Grace Coolidge called it—has been a favorite retreat of first families since 1927. It served, for example, as a schoolroom for Caroline Kennedy, an entertaining room for Luci and Lynda Johnson (who had a soda fountain installed there), and a family room for the Carters. Octagonal in shape with three walls of glass, the room overlooks the south lawn of the White House and the Mall. Outside the Solarium, hidden behind the balustrade, is a space large enough for sunbathing.

National Park Service

The *Resolute* desk, a gift from Queen Victoria to President Rutherford B. Hayes in 1880, was made famous in this photograph of John F. Kennedy, Jr., peeking out from behind the panel FDR had installed to conceal his leg braces.

The West Wing

The West Wing of the White House is where the chief executive conducts the official business of the presidency. Built during the Roosevelt renovation of 1902 as temporary offices, the wing has since become a permanent addition to the White House. It was doubled in size in 1909 and enlarged again in 1927 and 1934. The structure was rebuilt in 1930 after a fire on Christmas Eve, 1929.

In 1969 President Nixon remodeled the West Wing. A north portico and driveway were added to the front of the building, and the swimming pool along the colonnade joining the West Wing and the mansion was boarded over to make more room for the press. The old press lobby, in use since 1902 on the north side of the wing, was converted to the *West Wing Reception Room* and is used today as an appointments lobby.

High-level staff meetings and conferences are held in the *Roosevelt Room*, which President Nixon named for both Theodore and Franklin Roosevelt, in honor of their contributions to the construction and expansion of the West Wing. Service flags from the army, navy, air force, Marine Corps, and Coast Guard stand at one end of the large conference table, which dominates the room. On one wall is the medal presented to Theodore Roosevelt in 1906 when he won the Nobel Peace Prize for his role in settling the Russo-Japanese War. Today the room is decorated with presidential portraits and American landscape paintings, but during Franklin Roosevelt's administration it looked quite different. The New Deal president installed an aquarium and filled the room with mementoes of his fishing trips, so the staff called it the "Fish Room." The tradition continued through the Kennedy administration when JFK mounted a sailfish on the wall.

In the *Cabinet Room*, added to the West Wing in 1909, the president meets with the cabinet, the National Security Council, and members of Congress and occasionally conducts award ceremonies. An oval, mahogany conference table seating twenty, purchased by President Nixon in 1970, fills the room. The president's chair is two inches taller than the others. Overlooking the Rose Garden, the Cabinet Room contains likenesses of former presidents and statesmen—the choice reflecting the preferences of the current chief executive. President Reagan selected busts of Washington and Benjamin Franklin and portraits of Jefferson, Lincoln, Taft, Coolidge, and Eisenhower.

The *Oval Office* is the president's formal office, where meetings with heads of government and chiefs of state are held. The first Oval Office was built in 1909 in the center of the West Wing; in 1934 it was moved to its current location on the southeast corner of the wing, overlooking the Rose Garden. Each president has decorated the Oval Office to suit his tastes. The only features that remain constant are the presidential seal in the ceiling medallion and the two flags behind the president's desk—the U.S. flag and the president's flag.

For their Oval Office desk, Presidents Reagan and George Bush used the one Queen Victoria gave to President Hayes in 1880, made from timbers of the H.M.S. *Resolute*. In 1855 American whalers had rescued the ship trapped in Arctic ice, and the United States returned it to the British government. Later, when the *Resolute* was broken up, Queen Victoria had the desk made for the U.S. president in a gesture of appreciation. Truman used the desk, as did FDR, who installed a front panel to conceal his leg braces. Kennedy also used the *Resolute* desk, but it was John F. Kennedy, Jr., who made the desk famous in a photograph of the boy peeking out from behind the central panel while his father worked above.

White House Grounds

The eighteen acres surrounding the White House have changed a great deal since John and Abigail Adams's time. In November 1800 the grounds were muddy and littered with the shacks and supplies of workers still building the mansion.

Methods of groundskeeping have changed as well. The grass, for example, is no longer kept short by grazing sheep, as it was as recently as Woodrow Wilson's administration, or by William Howard Taft's cow, Pauline Wayne. Today, the National Park Service takes care of the house and grounds. Still, touches of the past remain.

Thomas Jefferson was an avid gardener and landscaped what he called the "President's Park." John Quincy Adams devoted much time to the gardens, and a massive American elm that he planted on the south lawn stands today as a monument to his efforts. Growing tall beside the South Portico, the southern magnolias that Andrew Jackson planted in memory of his wife nearly conceal the windows of the president's bedroom on the second floor. Since the Wilson administration, every president has planted trees on the White House grounds. Twice a year, in the spring and fall, the grounds are open for public tour.

Special Gardens

The *Rose Garden* is one of three special gardens on the grounds of the White House. Situated between the West Wing and the residence, the Rose Garden is planted in the style of a traditional eighteenth-century American garden. From early spring until the first frost, flowers and trees provide seasonal color within the rectangular frame of boxwood and osmanthus hedges.

Until 1902 conservatories and greenhouses covered the ground where the West Wing and Rose Garden now are. Theodore Roosevelt had them removed. Ellen Axson Wilson first planted roses here in 1913, and the garden remained largely unchanged until 1962 when President Kennedy asked Rachel Lambert Mellon to redesign it.[26]

The president receives special guests in the Rose Garden, such as foreign dignitaries, Medal of Honor winners, and U.S. astronauts. Occasionally, the president will host a state dinner in the garden. In June 1971 the first outdoor White House wedding took place there, when Tricia Nixon married Edward Cox.

The *Jacqueline Kennedy Garden* is to the first lady what the Rose Garden is to the president. Located beside the East Wing of the White House, the garden is a setting for the first lady's informal receptions. Shaded by rows of lindens, the garden contains ornamental flowering trees and shrubs around a rectangular lawn. Lady Bird Johnson named the garden for her predecessor in 1965, but Patricia Nixon called it "the east garden." Today, it again bears Mrs. Kennedy's name.

On January 18, 1969, Lady Bird Johnson established a third special garden, this one in honor of the young children associated with the White House. Plaques bearing the handprints and footprints of the Johnson grandchildren and two Carter grandchildren decorate the garden.

Recreational Facilities

Presidents through the years have set up their own sports facilities on the White House grounds. Hayes played croquet, Harding played medicine ball, Hoover played golf (and trained his Airedale to retrieve the balls), and Truman played horseshoes. Ford installed the first outdoor swimming pool, and presidents since Theodore Roosevelt have enjoyed the tennis court on the south lawn.

Children, too, have had their fun outdoors at the White House. Benjamin Harrison's grandson, Baby McKee, rode around the grounds in a cart pulled by His Whiskers—the boy's pet goat. Eleanor Roosevelt had a jungle gym and a sandbox built for her grandchildren and resisted the advice of groundskeepers against hanging an old-fashioned swing from a tree limb.[27] Theodore Roosevelt's son Quentin rode his pony Algonquin on the south lawn, and Caroline Kennedy riding Macaroni was a favorite subject for photographers in the early 1960s.

An annual public treat for children begun in 1879 is the Easter Monday egg-rolling. Children are invited to bring their eggs to the party and compare their artistic and egg-rolling skills. In 1986, thirty-five thousand people attended the event.

Security and Communications

The Secret Service is tight-lipped about White House security procedures, reasoning that the more that is known about its practices the better equipped a potential assassin could be.[28] Yet the Secret Service is keenly aware that the White House is a national monument and an important symbol to the American people. Consequently, the White House—even on a tour of its interior—appears remarkably accessible. It is not.

Round-the-clock protection of the president and the mansion is the duty of plainclothes Secret Service agents (the ones dressed in business suits with small white lapel pins) and of the White House Branch of the Uniformed Division of the Secret Service. *(See also "Protecting the President: The Secret Service," p. 905, in Daily Life of the President chapter of Part V.)* The agents, working in eight-hour shifts, are stationed throughout the residence and in the East and West wings. Officers of the Uniformed Division are positioned on the grounds of the residence, at the guardhouses, and at selected posts inside, such as the hallways and entrances to the Oval Office. Two main duties of the Uniformed Division are to police the grounds of the White House and to conduct and monitor visitors' tours.

The White House is surrounded by a black iron fence six and one-half feet tall. Two uniformed guards usually staff each of the small white guardhouses along the perimeter of the grounds, one standing outside, the other watching over surveillance devices inside. Entrance gates to the White House were reinforced in the late 1970s after two gate-crashing incidents.

Electronic sensors and video equipment ensure thorough protection of the grounds. Buried seismic sensors can detect even the lightest footsteps. Television cameras disguised as lanterns or concealed in plantings provide visual surveillance. Uniformed guards regularly check the grounds from observation points on the roof of the White House and the Treasury Building next door. Foot and vehicular patrols (on small motorcycles) cover the grounds and the streets around the White House. A canine unit, trained in attacking and scouting, is used primarily to check the buildings and grounds for explosives.

In 1983 security of the house and grounds was stepped up significantly, prompted by several incidents: a bombing at the U.S. Capitol, the receipt of intelligence reports about possible terrorist attacks on the White House, and bombings of the U.S. Embassy and the Marine barracks in Lebanon. At a cost of $6.9 million, East Executive Avenue was closed and made into a park.[29] A wall of concrete barriers, installed in 1983, was replaced in 1988 by 274 barrel-shaped cement posts linked by heavy chains; they cost $670,000.[30] The posts, thirty-eight inches high and four feet apart, are placed so that only slow-moving vehicles can approach and enter the White House gate.

The Secret Service also must guard the airspace above the White House. It uses monitoring systems to identify aircraft approaching nearby National Airport and shoulder-fired Redeye antiaircraft missiles as a last resort should a plane refuse warnings and approach the President's House. One such incident occurred during the Nixon administration when a discontented twenty-year-old soldier buzzed the White House in a stolen helicopter. Gunfire forced the chopper to land, and the soldier was arrested. He explained that he had not intended to harm the president but "was just kissing off. I wanted to buzz everything that was popular." [31] Further steps to secure White House airspace were taken in 1983 with the installation of fixed-base ground-to-air missiles.[32]

The Uniformed Division also carefully monitors White House tours. Visitors enter through the East Wing and, as at airports, pass through a magnetometer, which checks for concealed metal. Still more sensitive are the devices for detecting radioactive materials. In 1986 two women on a White House tour were questioned by the Secret Service when they set off these alarms. Several days before their White House visit, each had had a radioisotope scan for heart disease, and small amounts of radioactivity remained in their bodies.[33]

The uniformed guards inspect all handbags and packages and ask visitors to leave behind all newspapers, which conceivably could hide a weapon. Guards watch the tourists on closed-circuit television as they make their way through the five rooms and two hallways that are open to the public. Plainclothes Secret Service agents mingle with the visitors, watching and listening for signs of threatening behavior.

Careful security procedures extend well beyond the monitoring of tourists. Electronic sensing devices, embedded in the floors, ceilings, and walls, track all movement in the house. Secret Service agents know at all times exactly where the president is within the White House so that they can maintain a "protective ring" around the chief executive. All visitors and aides, even the president's closest advisers, must wear a visible security badge. Transparent bullet-proof shields cover the windows in the Oval Office, even though the office is not visible from the street. The president has the added security of a knee-high "panic button" located beneath the Oval Office desk. The president can push the button while appearing simply to shift position. Occasionally, the chief executive pushes the button by accident and is startled when a cadre of arms-wielding agents bursts into the office.

The Secret Service inspects all incoming packages and takes no chances with gifts of food—none ever reaches the president. The White House also is equipped with highly sensitive air and water filtration systems for detecting poisonous gas and bacteria. To ensure that no one tampers with the president's food, all food suppliers for the White House are cleared by the Secret Service. Even so, White House kitchen staff hand select many food items at random.

One of the most secure—and seldom discussed—areas of the White House is the Situation Room, the presidential communications nerve center. Located under the Oval Office in the basement of the West Wing, the Situation Room is run by a twenty-five person duty staff of communications experts from the U.S. Army Signal Corps. Twenty-four hours a day they operate the Signal Board, which links the White House with the Pentagon, the State Department, the Central Intelligency Agency, and other military and intelligence facilities. The Situation Room receives some three thousand messages daily.[34] Contrary to popular assumptions, the Washington-Moscow "hotline" is not in the White House; rather, it is part of the National Military Command Center at the Pentagon. *(See "Department of Defense," p. 822, in this chapter.)*

For the president and members of the first family, the White House telephone system provides immediate connections with virtually any place in the world. Without dialing or looking up numbers, they have only to pick up the telephone and tell switchboard operators who and where they want to call.[35]

When presidents travel, they remain in constant, secure telephone contact not only with the Situation Room but with U.S. military facilities throughout the world. The president's plane, *Air Force One*, is outfitted with a special switchboard that keeps the chief executive in constant touch while airborne. Always near the president is a military aide assigned to the White House Communications Agency (WHCA, pronounced "Whocka"). This staffer carries the "presidential emergency satchel," called the "football," containing the authentication codes and emergency declarations to be used in the event of war.[36]

WHCA also provides communications for the Secret Service. Former Secret Service agent Rufus W. Youngblood has described WHCA procedures:

> Wherever the Secret Service went, WHCA went. Whenever agents went out to do the advance work for a Presidential trip, WHCA men went with them. Whether our assignment was in Washington . . . or on a South Sea island, WHCA's job was to see to the installation and operation of telephones, radios, teletypes, and highly classified cryptographic equipment, as the occasion demanded. If it became necessary for me to talk to an agent in Paris while we were aboard . . . [a] cruiser on a lake in Texas, WHCA would establish a circuit through phone patches, switchboards, keying lines, relays, and all I had to do was flick the switch on my . . . walkie-talkie and start talking.[37]

Naval Observatory

In 1974 Congress designated the home of the chief of naval operations at the Naval Observatory as the official residence of the vice president.

Whether traveling by plane, car, or ship, walking at Camp David, attending a concert at the Kennedy Center, or visiting a foreign head of state, the president is said to be never more than thirty seconds away from the communications link to the White House command post.[38]

The Vice President's Residence

On the grounds of the Naval Observatory on Massachusetts Avenue, N.W., barely visible from the road, stands the official home of the vice president. Although the president has had an official Washington residence since 1800, not until July 1974 did Congress give the vice president a permanent home. Costs of securing and protecting the house of each new vice president had become greater than the cost of establishing and maintaining a single residence.

Formerly known as the Admiral's House, the residence served as the home of the superintendent of the Naval Observatory until 1928 and of the chief of naval operations until 1974. Adm. Elmo R. Zumwalt was the last military resident of the house.

Designed by Washington architect Leon E. Dessez and completed in 1893, the white brick Queen Anne-style house comprises a basement and three floors—twelve rooms plus service areas and six bathrooms (four full and two half-baths). On the first floor an entrance hall, dining room, living room, sitting room, and sunroom provide space for entertaining. Because the dining room can accommodate only thirty persons, vice presidents often have entertained large numbers of guests outdoors. A bedroom, sitting room, and bath form the master suite on the second floor, which also contains an office and a guest bedroom. Another bedroom and three smaller rooms (once maids' rooms) are on the third floor. The kitchen, laundry, and quarters for the staff are in the basement. A back staircase runs from the butler's pantry on the first floor to the third story, through a back hall on each floor.

Outside, a pillared porte cochere forms the main entrance. A wide veranda extends from the right of the entrance along the front of the house and curves around the three-story Romanesque tower on the south, forming a porch on three sides. The steep roof of grey slate contains the three dormer windows of the third floor. The house is situated on twelve acres, landscaped in the style of an English park.

When Congress claimed the Admiral's House for the vice president in 1974, it appropriated $315,000 for renovation and installation of security devices. At that time the roof leaked, the floors sagged, the six fireplaces did not work, the wiring was unsafe, and the house was air-conditioned with twenty-two window units (since replaced with central air-conditioning). In the late 1980s the annual appropriation for operating the residence was $258,000, which included $75,000 for entertaining. The navy, which still owns and maintains the house, also supplies staff for the vice president's residence, including six enlistees who serve as stewards.

Although the house has been available to five vice presidents, only three have lived there. Mrs. Gerald Ford began plans for decorating but had time to do little more than select china and crystal before her husband became president in August 1975. Vice President and Mrs. Nelson Rockefeller (1975-1977) continued to live in their home on Foxhall Road in Washington, but they supervised the renovation and contributed several pieces of their own artwork and furnishings to the house. One controversial Rockefeller donation was a $35,000 bed by Surrealist artist Max Ernst, titled "Cage Bed with Screen." The bed eventually left the residence, but an Adams-style dining room table that had belonged to the Rockefeller family remains.

Vice President and Mrs. Walter F. Mondale (1977-1981) and their three children were the first full-time residents. Mrs. Mondale, an art historian, used the house as a showcase for works of contemporary American artists. The Mondales also established a household library of works by and about vice presidents.

Vice President and Mrs. George Bush (1981-1989) discovered the limitations of the initial $315,000 appropriation when the roof began to leak again, mortar between bricks began crumbling, and damp streaks appeared on the living room walls. As a result, the navy spent more than $240,000 for repairs. The Bushes redecorated the house through approximately $200,000 in private donations and restored the interior by adding their personal furnishings and paintings borrowed from art museums in Washington and Houston.

Vice President and Mrs. Dan Quayle moved into the mansion in January 1989.

Executive Office of the President

The Old Executive Office Building (OEOB), formerly the State, War, and Navy Building, may be the government's most maligned structure. Mark Twain called it "the ugliest building in America." Utah senator Reed Smoot said it was "covered with gimcracks and spizzerinktums." Herbert Hoover declared that it was "an architectural absurdity," and Harry Truman described it as "the greatest monstrosity in America." Excessive or engaging, the French Second Empire structure, now a historic landmark, remains a monument to the architectural enthusiasm of a victorious government after the Civil War.

Supervising Architect of the Treasury Alfred Bult Mullett designed the building, constructed from 1871 to 1888, for the State, War, and Navy departments. The State Department's south wing was completed in 1875; the Navy's east wing in 1879; and the War Department's north, west, and center wings in 1888. But these departments continued to grow, and by 1947 each had vacated the building for larger quarters. In 1939 the White House began moving some of its offices into the building, and in 1949 the State, War, and Navy Building was given over entirely to the Executive Office of the President (EOP). Today the building houses the White House Office, the National Security Council, the Office of Management and Budget, the Council of Economic Advisers, and the vice president's office.

The OEOB comprises 440,250 square feet—including 553 rooms, two miles of black-and-white-tiled corridors, and ten acres of floor space. When completed the OEOB was the largest office building in Washington and among the largest in the world. It is still one of the largest granite buildings, with four and one-half-foot exterior walls and many eighteen-foot ceilings. Construction costs totaled $10.1 million.

The French Second Empire styling makes the OEOB architecturally unique in Washington. Some say its seven floors with tier upon tier of columns (some nine hundred in all) look like a wedding cake. Its elaborate dormer windows, mansard roof of light green copper, and more than two dozen chimneys topped with oversize chimney pots make it a curious companion to the Georgian-style White House next door.

In 1934 and 1944 Congress approved plans to give the OEOB a Greek Revival façade to match its neighbor to the east of the White House, the Treasury Building. In 1957 a commission appointed by President Eisenhower recommended its demolition. But funds ran short after each proposal, and the OEOB remained untouched. Although John Kennedy's Commission on Fine Arts recommended preservation of the building, full-scale restoration did not get under way until 1981, under President Reagan's Office of Administration.

When the carpeting, partitions, and dropped ceilings

The White House

The OEOB, formerly the State, War, and Navy Building, today houses most of the vice president's staff and various offices of the Executive Office of the President. Harry Truman once characterized the controversial building as "the greatest monstrosity in America."

were removed, the three-story White House Law Library, formerly the War Department Library, revealed its colorful Minton tile floor and the delicate cast-iron tracery of its balcony railings. Also restored was the four-story State Department Library, which now serves as the White House Library and Research Center. Both libraries were constructed entirely of cast iron to reduce the danger of fire. The Indian Treaty Room, with its tile floor and coffered ceiling, is used for receptions and award ceremonies.

Five presidents worked in the OEOB before becoming chief executive, and more than one thousand treaties have been signed within its walls. It was in this building on December 7, 1941, that Secretary of State Cordell Hull confronted the two Japanese envoys who pretended to negotiate peace in the Pacific as Japanese warplanes bombed Pearl Harbor.

Less than twenty-five years after moving into the OEOB, the Executive Office of the President again needed more space. The solution became known as the New Executive Office Building, a ten-story structure completed in 1968, one block from the OEOB at Seventeenth and H streets, N.W. Designed by John Carl Warnecke, the contemporary red-brick building contains 307,000 square feet of office space and approximately nine hundred EOP employees.

The Departmental Headquarters

When the federal government moved from Philadelphia to Washington, D.C., in 1800, the executive branch consisted of four departments—State, Treasury, War, and Navy. By 1820 each had its own brick building within short walking distance of the president's office in the White House. The entire executive branch was neatly contained within two city blocks. Today, there are fourteen departments and more than five hundred executive branch buildings in the Washington, D.C., area.

Only the Treasury Department is located on appoximately its original site. Like its neighbors the White House and the Old Executive Office Building, it is a historic landmark, as designated by the interior secretary's National Park System Advisory Board.

Other departmental buildings are unusual for their history, their artwork (the Justice and Interior buildings contain exceptional examples of American art of the 1930s), or, simply, their size. Several were considered to be the largest office building in the world when completed. Today, it is said that the Pentagon holds that distinction.

Department of Agriculture

The Department of Agriculture headquarters on Fourteenth Street, S.W., is contained in two structures—the Administration Building facing the Mall and the South Building facing Independence Avenue. The two are joined by two third-floor archways over Independence Avenue and an underground tunnel.

The neoclassical Administration Building, designed by Rankin, Kellogg, and Crane of Philadelphia, was built in three sections, largely of marble. The four-story, L-shaped east and west wings, constructed from 1904 to 1908, set the precedent for a four hundred-foot setback from the center line of the Mall. The five-story center section, with its imposing Corinthian colonnade, connects the east and west wings. It was built from 1928 to 1930. The Administration Building contains a gross floor area of 380,000 square feet, with 280,000 square feet of offices and other work areas. The secretary of agriculture's office is in this part of the departmental headquarters.

The seven-story South Building, with nearly six times as much office space as the Administration Building, was designed in the office of the Supervising Architect of the Treasury and constructed from 1930 to 1937. It contains seven miles of corridors and 1.5 million square feet of office space, divided into more than four thousand rooms. Its seven wings and six interior courtyards cover three city blocks. The exterior of the building is neoclassical, but less ornamented than the Administration Building. The Twelfth and Fourteenth Street wings are finished in limestone; the rest of the exterior, in variegated tan brick and terra-cotta.

Approximately ten thousand people work in the headquarters building, which contains all but two bureaus of the Agriculture Department. Agriculture has field offices in every state and most major cities throughout the United States, including more than seventy Extension Service locations and approximately fifty offices of the Farmers Home Administration.

Department of Commerce

The Herbert Clark Hoover Building, named in 1982 for the former president (1929-1933) and commerce secretary (1921-1918), was the largest office building in the world when completed in 1932. The building encompasses 1.1 million square feet of work space, covers eight acres, contains 3,311 rooms, and houses approximately forty-two hundred employees.

Construction of the seven-story building, designed by the New York architectural firm of York and Sawyer, began in 1927 on swampland the government purchased in 1910 for $2.5 million. The Commerce building sits atop Tiber Creek, and sections of the basement floor are three feet thick to withstand pressure from the water flowing underneath.

The building comprises three large rectangular sections joined by accordion-like expansion joints. Because these joints expand in the heat and contract in the cold, the Hoover Building may be three inches longer in July than it is in January. Filling three city blocks, Commerce forms the western side of Federal Triangle and is bounded by Fourteenth and Fifteenth Streets, N.W., on the east and west and by D Street and Constitution Avenue on the north and south. It cost $17.5 million to build.

Two unusual features of the building are on view to the public. A census "clock" digitally records births and deaths in the United States, showing an American born every eight seconds and dying every fifteen seconds (for a population growth rate of 0.9 percent). A basement aquarium displays more than one thousand fish from around the world.

Department of Defense

The Pentagon—headquarters of the Department of Defense (DOD)—is located in Arlington, Virginia, just across the Potomac River from Washington, D.C. Said to

U.S. Air Force

Often called the world's largest office building, the Pentagon, headquarters of the Department of Defense, contains 3.7 million square feet of work space and seventeen and one-half miles of corridors.

be the world's largest office building, it is the only departmental headquarters outside the District of Columbia.

Gen. Brehon B. Somervell's 1941 plan to house the nation's military establishment under one roof aroused controversy, but pressures of impending war hastened congressional approval of new headquarters for what later became the Defense Department. The government already owned more than half of the 583 acres needed for the proposed building, and it bought the rest—mostly swamps, dumps, and dilapidated buildings—for $2.2 million. Starting in August 1941, thirteen thousand laborers worked in shifts around the clock and completed construction in January 1943—a mere seventeen months later. The building itself cost $49.6 million; the total project, including outside facilities, $83.0 million.

With a gross floor area of 6.5 million square feet (3.7 million of which is work space), the Pentagon contains three times the floor space of the Empire State Building. Its other statistics also are impressive. The building covers twenty-nine acres and contains 150 stairways, nineteen escalators, thirteen elevators, 280 restrooms, 7,748 windows, and fifteen thousand light fixtures. The parking lot covers sixty-seven acres and has space for almost ten thousand cars. Twenty-six thousand military and civilian employees use the stores, restaurants, theaters, barbershop, post office, education centers, and libraries within the building. Each day, the Pentagon post office handles 130,000 pieces of mail, while the building's 22,500 telephones accommodate 200,000 calls.

Architects George E. Bergstrom and David J. Whitmer designed the five-sided steel and concrete structure to fit its site, which is bounded by five roads. The number five recurs throughout the building's design. Besides having five sides, the Pentagon contains five concentric rings; that is, the exterior ring surrounds four progressively smaller pentagons, each with five floors. A center courtyard with grass and trees covers five acres.

The total length of Pentagon hallways is seventeen and one-half miles, but because ten spoke-like corridors connect the five rings, it takes no more than seven minutes to walk from any one point to another.

Armed forces guides at the Pentagon take visitors through displays of model ships, art depicting scenes from World War II, and memorials to military heroes. Two such exhibits are the Hall of Heroes, commemorating the four thousand Medal of Honor winners, and the corridor honoring the twenty-four hundred Americans listed as Prisoners of War/Missing in Action in the Vietnam War.

Also at the Pentagon but not on view to the public is the Washington-Moscow Direct Communications Link, better known as the "hot line." It was set up in 1963 in response to the Cuban missile crisis and is located in the National Military Command Center.

Vast though the Pentagon is, less than 1 percent of the Defense Department's 3.2 million employees work there. (Defense employs 1.1 million civilian and 2.1 million military personnel.) Approximately 150,000 people work at more than twenty-five other Defense facilities in the Washington area—workplaces as diverse as the Walter Reed Army Medical Center, the Naval Observatory, and the National War College. DOD comprises 871 military installations in the United States and 393 abroad.

Department of Education

The Education headquarters, at 400 Maryland Avenue, S.W., is housed in Federal Office Building (FOB) No. 6, one of several modern, numbered office structures commissioned in the late 1950s in southwest Washington to accommodate the growing executive branch bureaucracy. FOB 6, designed by two Washington, D.C., firms—Faulkner, Kingsbury, and Stenhouse; and Chatelain, Gauger, and Holan—was built between 1959 and 1961 at a cost of $13.3 million. Its several hundred tall, narrow windows on the second through the sixth floors give an impression of greater height to the eight-story limestone building.

FOB 6 contains 401,544 square feet of office space and houses fifteen hundred workers; approximately nine hundred work for Education, the remainder for the National Aeronautics and Space Administration. Education staffers work in two other buildings in Washington and in ten regional offices throughout the country.

Department of Energy

The Department of Energy moved into the James Forrestal Building at 1000 Independence Avenue, S.W., in 1977, the year the department was established. For its first seven years the building had housed employees of the Defense Department. In December 1963 Congress appropriated $33.7 million for the structure known as FOB (Federal Office Building) No. 5 until it was named for former secretary of defense Forrestal. The contemporary-styled building of precast concrete was under construction from September 1965 to April 1970 and was designed by the architectural firms of Curtis and Davis, Fordyce and Hanby Associates, Frank Grad and Sons.

The Forrestal Building is a sprawling, three-part structure with 1.1 million square feet of occupiable space in floors above and below ground. The South Building has eight floors above ground; the North Building has four; the West Building, two. Each building is constructed of architectural concrete with recessed window pockets one story tall. The three wings are connected by two floors of office space underground. The Forrestal Building houses forty-five hundred employees and all divisions of the Energy Department, except for the Federal Energy Regulatory Commission offices, which are on Capitol Hill.

Department of Health and Human Services

The Hubert H. Humphrey Building, headquarters of the Department of Health and Human Services (HHS) at 200 Independence Avenue, S.W., is one of two departmental headquarters buildings designed by architect Marcel Breuer. Under construction from 1971 to 1975, the contemporary steel and concrete structure is heavily fenestrated with hundreds of convex trapezoidal windows cantilevered over the first floor. The walls of windows break off at each corner, leaving recesses for shafts, discreetly incorporated into the building's design, to vent exhaust fumes from the freeway tunnel that passes underneath.

The twelve-story building houses appoximately 1,800 HHS staffers in 328,490 square feet of office space. The remaining 22,100 HHS employees in the Washington, D.C., area are scattered among fifty-nine other buildings, including the Parklawn Building in Rockville, Maryland, housing approximately 6,000 staffers. HHS employs more than 125,000 people throughout the United States in regional and field offices of the Social Security Administration, the Public Health Service, and other HHS agencies.

Department of Housing and Urban Development

The Housing and Urban Development (HUD) building, at Seventh and D streets, S.W., was the first of two departmental headquarters that the federal government commissioned from architect Marcel Breuer. Similar in design to Breuer's UNESCO headquarters in Paris, HUD is unique among Washington buildings for its curvilinear shape: from above, it looks like two *Y*'s joined at their base. The American Institute of Architects awarded Breuer its 1968 gold medal for this design and other work.

Built between 1965 and 1968 at a cost of $22.5 million, HUD was the first federal structure made of precast concrete, a mark of the International style. The sculptural effects of precast concrete are apparent in the 1,585 recessed window units, each weighing ten tons, that form the curve of the walls. The building's ten stories rest on dozens of *pilotis*, or pillars, creating a 5.5-acre courtyard instead of a first floor at ground level.

Unlike the straight, seemingly endless hallways of the Pentagon (875 feet) and other government buildings, the longest corridor at HUD (180 feet) seems even shorter because the curving walls create an optical illusion that gives the building a more human scale. The building contains 543,000 square feet of office space for the forty-two hundred employees working there.

HUD has eighty-one regional and field offices throughout the United States. All of its Washington bureaus are housed within the headquarters building.

Department of the Interior

The Department of the Interior building, at Eighteenth and C streets, N.W., three blocks southwest of the White House, was the first project undertaken by the Public Works Administration (PWA) to provide work for the unemployed during the New Deal era. Constructed in only sixteen months, August 1935 to December 1936, the eight-story granite and limestone building contains sixteen acres of floor space and two miles of corridors, housing twenty-nine hundred employees.

President Franklin D. Roosevelt laid the cornerstone in 1936 with the same trowel George Washington had used to lay the Capitol cornerstone in 1793.

The building, designed by Waddy B. Wood, is utilitarian and plain on the outside but has an elaborately decorated interior containing more New Deal art than any other government structure. Bas-reliefs and murals by Heinz Warneke and Louis Bouché, among others, depict the themes and work of the department. Notable among Interior's murals is Henry Varnum Poor's nine-by-forty-two-foot work showing the origins of the conservation movement in the United States.

Harold Ickes, interior secretary from 1933 to 1946 and head of PWA, took a keen interest not only in the building but in a state-of-the-art museum with exhibits of the department's programs. Today, one still can see the museum's original dioramas portraying each bureau's history as well as artifacts, documents, photographs, and crafts. An Indian arts and crafts shop and many areas of the building containing artwork are open to the public. Other Interior Department offices in the Washington area are the Bureau of Mines and the U.S. Geological Survey.

Department of Justice

The Department of Justice had numerous homes before Congress appropriated $12 million for its permanent headquarters in downtown Washington. Under construction from 1931 to 1935, the Justice building fills the block of Federal Triangle between Ninth and Tenth streets,

N.W., and Constitution and Pennsylvania avenues.

The seven-story limestone structure comprises a gross floor area of 1.2 million square feet, including 1,712 rooms, eighty-seven stairways, almost four miles of corridors, and underground parking for 150 cars. More than twenty-five hundred employees occupy the building.

Principal architects Clarence Zantzinger and Charles L. Borie, Jr., made wide use of aluminum, an uncommon construction material for that period. The exterior doors (each twenty feet tall), frames for the 1,908 windows, all door trim, stair railings, and much ornamentation are aluminum. One observer remarked that the designers used enough aluminum to make "not only forks and spoons but pots and pans for a whole city." [39]

Although the exterior of the Justice headquarters, like many federal buildings, is classical revival in style, many of its decorative elements reflect the Art Deco influence of the 1920s and 1930s. Notable Art Deco features include the nine exterior doors and aluminum torchiers as well as John Joseph Earley's striking mosaic ceilings, the first made of American materials.

All sculptural work was designed by C. Paul Jennewein, who consulted philosophy professor Hartley B. Alexander in rendering a unified theme for the numerous exterior relief panels depicting the role of a justice department in a constitutional democracy. Still, his work aroused controversy. The president's Commission on Fine Arts objected to three nude male figures proposed for a six-by-fourteen-foot exterior relief panel and, in a letter to Jennewein, asked, "Do you think it would be possible to adopt the fig leaf for these figures?" Jennewein conceded and offered a second design. The commissioners again objected: "The fig leaves are not quite large enough," they wrote.[40] Today, the larger fig leaves may be seen in the pediment above the Constitution Avenue entrance.

Throughout the building, vast murals by noted New Deal artists Boardman Robinson, George Biddle, and John Steuart Curry depict themes of justice. The murals took six years to complete (1935-1941) and cost $68,000.

Other offices of the Justice Department include the Federal Bureau of Investigation and the Immigration and Naturalization Service in Washington and the U.S. Marshals Service in McLean, Virginia.

Department of Labor

The modern Department of Labor building, which occupies two city blocks at 200 Constitution Avenue, N.W., was dedicated by President Gerald R. Ford upon its completion in 1974. Six years later President Jimmy Carter named the building for Franklin D. Roosevelt's labor secretary, Frances Perkins, on the centennial of her birth, April 10, 1980.

The six-story steel and limestone building, designed by two Texas architectural firms—Brooks, Barr, Graeber, and White of Austin, and Pitts, Mebane, Phelps, and White of Houston—comprises one million square feet of office space and two and one-half miles of corridors. It cost $95 million to build and houses forty-seven hundred employees. Like Health and Human Services, the Labor headquarters was built above a freeway tunnel, so the architects had to incorporate exhaust shafts into the building's design.

To commemorate the country's bicentennial in 1976, the General Services Administration commissioned New York artist Jack Beal to paint four murals for the building. Called "The History of Labor in America," the work continues the tradition of Social Realist art exemplified by the New Deal artists in other government buildings in Washington.

The Labor Department also occupies two other buildings in Washington and numerous regional and field offices, including eight regional offices of the Bureau of Labor Statistics and ten of the Occupational Safety and Health Administration.

Department of State

Until 1947 the State Department shared quarters with the War and Navy departments in the State, War, and Navy Building (now called the Old Executive Office Building) next-door to the White House. When the department needed more space, it moved to its current location at Twenty-first and D streets, N.W. The eight-story, neoclassical limestone building was designed by Gilbert S. Underwood and William Dewey Foster; Louis A. Simon served as supervising architect.

The department continued to grow, however, and by the mid-1950s—less than a decade after it moved—it occupied more than twenty-five annexes in addition to its main building. Congress approved funding for an extension, which was built from 1957 to 1961 under direction of the architectural firm of Graham, Anderson, Probst, and White.

The State Department building today covers 11.8 acres—the two blocks between Twenty-first and Twenty-third streets on the east and west and C and D streets on the south and north. The building contains approximately 2.5 million square feet of gross floor space and houses the Agency for International Development (AID) and the Arms Control and Disarmament Agency in addition to State Department staff, approximately seven thousand employees altogether. Other AID and State employees staff approximately 250 U.S. embassies, consulates, and missions in 155 countries around the world.

At the C Street entrance of the contemporary-styled addition is the three-story Diplomatic Lobby. Television reporters covering the State Department often broadcast from this room, where the national flags of countries that have diplomatic relations with the United States form a colorful backdrop. At each end of the lobby is a plaque commemorating more than 150 State Department employees who have died "under heroic or tragic circumstances in foreign service." More than seventy-five names have been added since 1965. The Exhibition Hall on the first floor displays the Great Seal of the United States, in use since 1782 to seal instruments of ratification of treaties and the commissions of cabinet officers, ambassadors, and Foreign Service officers.

In 1961 the State Department's Fine Arts Committee began the Americana Project to remodel and redecorate—entirely through private funds—the sixteen diplomatic reception rooms on the eighth floor and the office of the secretary. The refurnished rooms, a showcase of the country's cultural heritage, contain museum-quality furniture, rugs, paintings, and silver from the classical period of American design, 1740-1825. Senior government officials, including the president and secretary of state, use the rooms for official functions.

National Archives

The Treasury Building is the oldest federal government departmental headquarters. Here, columns are erected as the early construction of the building begins.

Department of Transportation

The Nassif Building, which contains the principal offices of the Transportation Department, is the only departmental headquarters not built and owned by the federal government. The General Services Administration, the federal government's property manager, leases 1.6 million square feet of the building, bounded by D, E, Sixth, and Seventh streets, S.W., for $8.6 million a year.

Edward Durell Stone, architect of the Kennedy Center and the National Geographic Society building in Washington, designed the modern ten-story structure for Boston real estate developer David Nassif. When completed in 1969 it was the largest private office building in Washington. The one-inch white marble exterior veneer comes from quarries in Carrara, Italy, like the marble in the Kennedy Center.

The only major change or addition since Transportation first occupied the building in 1970 was the construction of a 22,873-square-foot computer room in 1983. Approximately fifty-five hundred of the department's more than eleven thousand employees work in the Nassif Building. Other Transportation offices in Washington include the headquarters of the Federal Aviation Administration and the Coast Guard.

Department of the Treasury

The Treasury building is the oldest federal government departmental headquarters. The five-story granite structure in the Greek Revival style set a precedent for the design of many other government buildings in Washington. Constructed in stages from 1836 through 1869, it is Treasury's third home on this site. The first Treasury building was burned by the British in 1814; the second, by arsonists in 1833.

Treasury's five wings fill two city blocks at Fifteenth Street and Pennsylvania Avenue, N.W., just east of the White House. Legend has it that President Andrew Jackson, annoyed at the protracted controversy over the exact location of the building, one day walked over from the White House, planted his cane in the ground, and declared, "Right here is where I want the cornerstone." Unfortunately, the building spoiled the clear view along Pennsylvania Avenue between the White House and Capitol. Treasury served as a barracks for Union soldiers during the Civil War and provided a temporary office for President Andrew Johnson while he waited six weeks for Mary Todd Lincoln to leave the White House after her husband's assassination.

Robert Mills, architect of the Washington Monument, designed the east and center wings (1836-1842). The most impressive feature of Mills's design is the east front colonnade—thirty Ionic columns, each thirty-six feet (three stories) tall, carved from a single block of granite. Thomas Ustick Walter, architect of the Capitol dome, did the preliminary design of the west and south wings (1855-1864). Ammi B. Young and Isaiah Rogers completed the plans, incorporating ornate details of late nineteenth-century tastes in their interior designs.

The architect of the north wing (1867-1869) was Alfred Bult Mullett, designer of the State, War, and Navy Building. *(See "Executive Office of the President," p. 821, in this chapter.)* In the north wing is the Cash Room, a two-story hall finished in nine varieties of marble. The seventy-two by thirty-two foot room was opened in 1869, in time to serve as the site of President Ulysses S. Grant's inaugural ball March 4 of that year.

At 450,000 square feet (290,000 of which is office space), Treasury was one of the largest office buildings in the world when it was finished. Today the headquarters houses only 6 percent of the department's twenty thousand Washington-area employees. Others work in the Treasury Annex, connected to the main building by a tunnel under Pennsylvania Avenue, and in buildings housing the various bureaus of the department, including the Bureau of Printing and Engraving and the Internal Revenue Service. Treasury has field organizations in every state and offices in most major U.S. cities.

Department of Veterans Affairs

The goal of consolidating under one roof all Washington employees handling veterans affairs has eluded the federal government throughout most of the twentieth century. In the early 1900s the department's predecessor, the Bureau of War Risk Insurance, operated out of seventeen different buildings. In late 1988, when the Veterans Administration gained cabinet-level status, the new Department of Veterans Affairs (DVA) occupied eight buildings in the Washington metropolitan area. The main building, containing the office of the secretary, is at 810 Vermont Avenue, N.W.

The eleven-story structure in the classical revival style was designed by the architectural firm of Wyatt and Nolting to be a hotel. In 1918, however, the government bought the site and foundation for $1 million, redesigned the exterior, and modified the interior to accommodate offices rather than hotel rooms. Construction of the War Risk Building, as it then was called, was completed in 1918 at a cost of $3.6 million. It comprises 442,000 square feet of office space. Today the building houses approximately twenty-nine hundred out of seven thousand DVA employees in the Washington area.

Notes

1. The figure for the cost of construction was obtained from the White House Office of the Curator.
2. *The White House: An Historic Guide,* 16th ed. (Washington, D.C.: White House Historical Association, 1987), 114.
3. Joseph Nathan Kane, *Facts about the Presidents: A Compilation of Biographical and Historical Material* (New York: Wilson, 1981), 39.
4. According to White House historian William Seale, one reason the rebuilding proceeded so quickly was that Hoban substituted timber for brick in some of the interior partitions. Although he saved time, Hoban created a weaker structure than the original—one that would necessitate the interior reconstruction of 1949-1952 (William Seale, *The President's House,* [Washington, D.C.: White House Historical Association, 1986], 2 vols. 2: 142-143). The figure for the cost of reconstruction was obtained from the White House Office of the Curator.
5. Kenneth W. Leish, *The White House* (New York: Newsweek, 1972), 39.
6. *The White House,* 119.
7. Seale, *The President's House,* 1: 265.
8. Ibid., 268.
9. Amy La Follette Jensen, *The White House and Its Thirty-three Families* (New York: McGraw-Hill, 1962), 72.
10. Seale, *The President's House,* 1: 316.
11. *The White House,* 128.
12. Ibid., 140.
13. Seale, *The President's House,* 2: 923.
14. Leish, *The White House,* 116.
15. Ibid.
16. Seale, *The President's House,* 2: 1028.
17. Ibid., 1035.
18. Ibid.
19. *The White House,* 153.
20. Judith Havemann, "Adding Up the Reagan Renovations," *Washington Post,* September 7, 1988, A1.
21. White House Office of the Curator.
22. The number of rooms used by the first family in their living quarters changes with each family, depending on how many of the president's children live in the White House and how many guest rooms the family needs. Although none of Franklin and Eleanor Roosevelt's children lived in the White House, the couple used every available room for their constant stream of guests—both state visitors and personal friends. According to White House curator and former chief usher Rex Scouten, the Reagans used seven rooms for their living quarters. The Reagans' redecorating of the second and third floors is described and illustrated in "Architectural Digest Visits: President and Mrs. Reagan at the White House," *Architectural Digest,* December 1981, 104-121.
23. J. B. West, with Mary Lynn Kotz, *Upstairs at the White House: My Life with the First Ladies* (New York: Coward, McCann, and Geoghegan, 1973), 61-62.
24. Leish, *The White House,* 29.
25. Rosalynn Carter, *First Lady from Plains* (Boston: Houghton Mifflin, 1984), 147.
26. Rachel Lambert Mellon, "President Kennedy's Rose Garden," *White House History* 1:1 (1983): 5-11.
27. Leish, *The White House,* 107.
28. Except where noted, details of Secret Service protection of the White House are from Philip H. Melanson, *The Politics of Protection: The U.S. Secret Service in the Terrorist Age* (New York: Praeger, 1984).
29. Havemann, "Adding Up the Reagan Renovations," A1.
30. "White House Eyesore," *New York Times,* March 29, 1988, B6.
31. Harry Edward Neal, *The Secret Service in Action* (New York: Elsevier/Nelson Books, 1980), 125.
32. "House Guards," *Time,* December 19, 1983, 21.
33. Christine Russell, "Tourists' Telltale Hearts," *Washington Post,* September 25, 1986.
34. Bradley H. Patterson, Jr., *The Ring of Power: The White House Staff and Its Expanding Role in Government* (New York: Basic Books, 1988), 49.
35. Carter, *First Lady from Plains,* 161.
36. Patterson, *The Ring of Power,* 322.
37. Rufus W. Youngblood, *Twenty Years in the Secret Service: My Life with Five Presidents* (New York: Simon and Schuster, 1973), 214-215.
38. Elmer Plischke, *Diplomat in Chief* (New York: Praeger, 1986), 56.
39. Lois Craig, "Hidden Treasures of a Walled City," *American Institute of Architects Journal* 67 (June 1978): 21.
40. Antonio Vasaio and the Justice Management Division, *The Fiftieth Anniversary of the U.S. Department of Justice Building, 1934-1984* (Washington, D.C.: Government Printing Office, 1984), 26.

Selected Bibliography

Executive Office of the President, Office of Administration. *The Old Executive Office Building: A Victorian Masterpiece.* Washington, D.C.: Government Printing Office, 1984.

Jensen, Amy La Follette. *The White House and Its Thirty-three Families.* New York: McGraw-Hill, 1962.

Leish, Kenneth W. *The White House.* New York: Newsweek, 1972.

The Living White House. 7th rev. ed. Washington, D.C.: White House Historical Association, 1982.

Look, David W., and Carole L. Perrault. *The Interior Building and Its Architecture and Its Art.* Washington, D.C.: Government Printing Office, 1986.

Melanson, Philip H. *The Politics of Protection: The U.S. Secret Service in the Terrorist Age.* New York: Praeger, 1984.

Oulahan, Richard. "Capital's Doughty Dowager Becomes a New Cinderella." *Smithsonian.* March 1986. 84-94.

Seale, William. *The President's House.* 2 vols. Washington, D.C.: White House Historical Association, 1986.

Vasaio, Antonio, and the Justice Management Division. *The Fiftieth Anniversary of the U.S. Department of Justice Building, 1934-1984.* Washington, D.C.: Government Printing Office, 1984.

West, J. B., with Mary Lynn Kotz. *Upstairs at the White House: My Life with the First Ladies.* New York: Coward, McCann, and Geoghegan, 1973.

The White House: An Historic Guide. 16th ed. Washington, D.C.: White House Historical Association, 1987.

Executive Branch Pay and Perquisites

The national executive branch is staffed by approximately 3 million civilian employees. At the top of the federal hierarchy sits the president, the vice president, and the White House staff. The entire executive branch, however, has a quite diverse workforce. Executive branch employees include cabinet members, White House aides, national security advisers, Secret Service agents, Federal Bureau of Investigation agents, Foreign Service officers, policy analysts, computer programmers, engineers, physicians, forest rangers, and people from hundreds of other occupations in the federal government.

An important feature of the executive branch is that most of its employees are hired under the requirements of civil service, ensuring that most executive branch jobs are filled on the basis of merit and that employees are not fired for political reasons. Along with this political protection, civil service employees are compensated according to a uniform federal salary scale.

Some executive branch positions remain political appointments, specifically those occupied by policy advisers to the president. Although most of the political positions do not pay as much as their occupants might make in similar positions in private business, they carry with them a number of perquisites that make them attractive to many potential appointees. The job of president itself has a modest salary (considering its importance), but over the years many perquisites of the office have evolved. Other executive branch positions, including the vice presidency, also carry with them a growing number of fringe benefits and extra courtesies that have become part of their official status. Because of its complexity and enormous number of positions, the executive branch contains a maze of compensation standards.

The President

The material rewards of the presidency are substantial. While the president's annual salary of $200,000 is large by most standards, it pales in comparison to the value of the perquisites and other tangible benefits of the office itself. The worth of all the privileges and fringe benefits that go with the job of president of the United States would amount to an annual income of millions of dollars, if the president were a private citizen.

Along with the special burdens and responsibilities of the office come the rewards. The president and the first family live in an environment of comfort and grandeur in the White House, a mansion provided by the government at public expense. Utilities and maintenance for the White House, which cost more than $2 million a year, are free to the president. The White House staff of approximately one hundred has a combined salary exceeding $1 million a year, also completely free to the president. In addition, the government maintains a vacation home for the president at Camp David, Maryland. Several limousines, airplanes, and helicopters stand ready to transport the chief executive any time, anywhere. These amenities come with round-the-clock protection of the president and first family from 1,650 Secret Service agents, which costs U.S. taxpayers about $100 million a year.

Many of these perquisites are necessary to ensure the smooth functioning of a complex office. For example, when the chief executive needs to be in Europe, the president's own plane can accommodate staff and the press, can avoid scheduling problems, and can ensure the president's security in ways commercial airlines cannot. Moreover, while many perquisites add to the prestige of the job and facilitate the president's many tasks, they also create and maintain an aura of majesty around the presidency. Most Americans want to look to the president (and the office of the president) with pride; the president represents the American people to others and to Americans themselves, embodying the idealism of American life. In this sense the salary and perquisites of the presidency are an object of interest and pride to Americans.

How much does all of this presidential pomp and circumstance cost U.S. taxpayers? Because many of these expenses are merged within the budgets of various departments, it is impossible to determine the exact cost. Undoubtedly, however, the cost is high. In the mid-1970s Dan Cordtz, writing on the excesses of the Nixon administration estimated it to be more than $100 million a year. In the mid-1980s, Robert Sherrill estimated the cost to run around $150 million.[1]

By W. Craig Bledsoe

Table 1 Growth of Presidential Salary and Allowances

September 24, 1789	$ 25,000 salary
March 3, 1873	$ 50,000 salary
June 23, 1906	$ 50,000 salary 25,000 travel allowance
March 4, 1909	$ 75,000 salary 25,000 travel allowance
June 25, 1948	$ 75,000 salary 40,000 travel allowance
January 19, 1949	$100,000 salary 50,000 expense account[a]
January 17, 1969	$200,000 salary 100,000 travel allowance 12,000 entertainment allowance

a. Includes travel allowance.

Presidential Salary

Presidential salaries are determined by Congress. Article II, section 1, of the Constitution makes the following provisions for the president's salary: "The President shall, at stated Times, receive for his Services, a Compensation, which shall neither be increased nor diminished during the period for which he shall have been elected, and he shall not receive within that Period any other Emolument from the United States, or any of them." Consequently, on September 24, 1789, the First Congress set the salary for the president of the United States at $25,000 a year.

The issue of actually paying the president caused some controversy at the Constitutional Convention. The delegates were quite concerned that their president not become their king, and there was some discussion about making the office of the president one with no or little pay. Benjamin Franklin suggested that the chief executive of the new nation not be paid any salary at all. Franklin argued that the love of money was the root of all political evil, and he proposed to allow the president to receive "no salary, stipend, fee or reward" above what was necessary to defray the expenses of office.[2]

Franklin's proposal was postponed and conveniently forgotten, but his goal of making the presidency largely an office of honor and not of profit was achieved when George Washington declined any share of personal compensation to which he was constitutionally entitled, proclaiming in his inaugural address: "I must decline as inapplicable to myself any share of the personal emoluments which may be indispensably included in a permanent provision for the executive department, and must accordingly pray that the pecuniary estimates for the station in which I am placed may during my continuance in it be limited to such actual expenditures as the public good may be thought to require."

With changing times and with the increased importance in the office of the presidency, the president's salary has gradually been adjusted upward. Not until after the Civil War, when Ulysses S. Grant became president, did Congress pass the first increase in the president's salary, however. From the beginning, the salaries of all public officials in the United States were low when compared with those of other nations. In 1873, in an effort to keep top public officials from drawing on their own private resources, Congress voted to increase the salaries of some of the major federal government positions, including those of Congress, the president, and other executive branch officials. At this time the president's salary was doubled to $50,000 a year. *(See Table 1.)*

Even though most of the country viewed these increases in pay as justifiable, much resentment was created when Congress decided to vote its own pay raises retroactive to 1871. This action aroused so much resentment among the public that it became known as "the salary grab." Eventually, Congress repealed the retroactive pay. Public indignation continued to be so great, however, that the members of Congress finally reduced their own salaries back to their former levels but left the president's raise untouched. Since Congress initially had approved the increase on March 3, 1873, a day before Grant's second term, Grant served his first term at half of what he was paid for his second term.

As a result of political pressure against raising the salaries of public officials, subsequent presidential pay increases have not come frequently. Congress voted for a second pay raise for the president in 1909, increasing the annual salary to $75,000. President William Howard Taft was the first to benefit from this increase in salary.

In 1949 Congress raised the salary of the president to $100,000 a year. It also decided that the president henceforth would be paid monthly rather than quarterly, as previous presidents had been paid. In addition, Congress for the first time recognized the need to assist the president in defraying the expenses of official presidential duties. President Harry S Truman was the first president to receive the $100,000 yearly salary and a $50,000 yearly tax-free expense account. In the Revenue Act of 1951, however, Congress reversed itself and subjected the president's expense account, as well as the expense accounts of members of Congress, to income taxes.

The most recent presidential pay raise occurred on January 20, 1969. Acting upon a recommendation by President Lyndon B. Johnson, Congress voted to double the president's salary. Less than a week later Richard Nixon became the first president to receive a yearly salary of $200,000. Congress also voted to give the president a $100,000 travel allowance and a $12,000 entertainment allowance, both tax free.

The president's salary—at $200,000 a year, plus the $50,000 a year expense account—is roughly equal to that of a corporate chief executive. Many presidents have been wealthy in their own right, but only one president besides Washington ever indicated that he would be willing to take a cut in salary. Recent presidents, such as John F. Kennedy, Johnson, Nixon, Jimmy Carter, and Ronald Reagan, have all been millionaires. But only President Kennedy returned his entire salary to the U.S. Treasury.[3]

Presidential pay does not tell the whole story, however. In addition to the $250,000 annual taxable salary and expense account, presidents receive many more tangible benefits from being in office. It would be impossible to put a price tag on some of the presidential perquisites. Cordtz has remarked that some of the best rewards of the office, such as the top consideration in air traffic given *Air Force One* or the priority the president's car takes over other traffic, are invaluable. Perquisites make the job worth a great deal more than the annual salary of the officeholder.

Perquisites of Office

Concerned about the prospects for a burgeoning monarchy in the new American nation, Patrick Henry warned,

"Your president may easily become king." [4] *The Federalist Papers,* written to ease the concerns of citizens in New York about the coming constitution, pointed to the fears that the presidency would become too powerful and would resemble the British monarchy. Alexander Hamilton in defending the constitutional provisions for the presidency argued that no similarities existed between the new American presidency and the British monarchy. He derided those who saw the president with "imperial purple flowing in his train . . . seated on a throne surrounded with minions and mistresses, giving audience to the envoys of foreign potentates in all the supercilious pomp and majesty . . . decorated with attributes superior in dignity and splendor to those of the king of Great Britain." [5]

The presidency has not become a monarchy in the sense of the eighteenth-century British monarchy. Yet, over the years the president's world has developed not only a regal style but a lavish splendor. Much of the pomp and circumstance that Hamilton refused to believe would accompany the growth of the presidency now exists. In fact, the perquisites of the presidency led President Nixon to remark candidly about his life in the White House, "We're roughing it pretty nicely." [6]

Early Perquisites

When George Washington became president, he attempted to establish a protocol of behavior in office for future presidents to follow. As an aristocrat, he believed that the presidency should be honored and esteemed on a level above the other branches of the federal government. In 1789, when Washington traveled from Mount Vernon, in Virginia, to New York City for his inauguration, his journey was punctuated by tolling bells, booming cannons, and shouting citizens. Once in office Washington presented a demeanor of grandeur. When he traveled among the citizenry, he did so in a stately cream-and-gilt coach drawn by six matched horses, the best in the United States. When he went out on horseback, he rode a white stallion covered with a leopard-skin blanket; the horse's hooves were painstakingly blackened, and its teeth were cleaned. Given to much formality, Washington refused to accept private invitations but dispensed his own social invitations to political leaders and prominent individuals to attend elegant receptions and ceremonial affairs. Receiving his guests with a bow rather than a handshake, Washington gave the appearance of a strong and dignified leader.

When Thomas Jefferson, the nation's third president, took the oath of office in 1801, he shunned the ornate horse-drawn coaches of Washington and John Adams and simply walked from his boardinghouse to the Capitol to give his inaugural address to members of Congress. He then walked back to his lodgings for dinner. The story is told that upon arriving at the common dinner table the new president found all of the chairs occupied. At first Jefferson was ignored. But eventually one woman recognized him and offered him her seat. Jefferson refused, however, and waited until others had finished their meal before taking his seat at the table.

Jefferson's presidential style reflected his approach to American democracy. He spurned the brilliant display of the two previous Federalist administrations and tried to create an atmosphere of egalitarianism. Most presidents after Jefferson tended to follow his example. It was considered far more important to be born in a log cabin than to exhibit aristocratic tendencies in office. Consequently, for political as well as financial reasons, most early presidents lived a much more Spartan existence than had Washington.

Washington, Jefferson, and the other early presidents did not enjoy the large expense accounts of modern presidents. For example, until the presidency of Calvin Coolidge, presidents had to pay for all the food consumed in the White House, including food at state dinners. During his eight years in office, Jefferson recorded that he spent $10,855.90 on wine alone. With these types of expenses, and a salary of only $25,000 a year, Jefferson left office $20,000 in debt. Presidents still pay for all the food they and their families consume privately at the White House, but in the 1920s U.S. taxpayers began paying for most of the expenses of state dinners.

Some of the nation's first presidents actually endured physical hardships while in office. John Adams, the first president to live in the White House, found life there not very comfortable. Mrs. Adams said that the unfinished mansion did not offer many of the "luxuries" of her old home. She dried her washing in the partially finished audience hall (now the East Room) and suffered the indignity of an outdoor privy. On the night Franklin Pierce moved into the White House in 1853, the mansion had little furniture and no lights. Pierce could find only a single candle to illuminate his way to a mattress on the floor of his bedroom. Congress did allocate $25,000, however, for Pierce to refurbish the White House—at that time the largest sum ever set aside for improvements to the president's home. Pierce installed the White House's first furnace and had the presidential residence painted inside and out. Yet, Congress balked at providing funding for someone to tend the new furnace. Some presidents brought their own furniture to the White House and took it with them when they left. Others, such as James Monroe, left their furniture for future occupants. Transportation was usually furnished by private individuals or companies to the presidents and their families. Occasionally, someone gave the president a horse or carriage to use, and the railroads allowed the president and the first family to travel free on their lines. But until the presidency of Taft, no funds were available for official travel expenses.

Retirement from office brought little in the way of financial rewards to the first chief executives. Most found themselves without pensions and with few benefits. Thomas Jefferson retired to Monticello at the age of sixty-five. Even though he was a prolific writer, a creative inventor, and an expert architect, musician, and lawyer, he found himself in almost immediate financial crisis. Heavily in debt from his days in the presidency, Jefferson had to accept a gift of $16,500 to save himself from bankruptcy. When James Monroe left office at sixty-six, he retired to private life in his home in Oak Hill, Virginia. Forced to sell his home to help pay his debts, he later moved to New York City. At his death, seven years after his retirement, he left an estate drained of funds. In 1880, after Ulysses S. Grant tried unsuccessfully for a third term in the White House, he set up an investment firm in New York that eventually went bankrupt. Things got so bad for Grant that even his swords and presidential souvenirs were eventually sold. Before his death of throat cancer, however, he published a two-volume personal memoir that left his family nearly $500,000. *(See Former Presidents chapter in Part V.)*

Modern-Day Perquisites

Presidential lifestyles gradually became easier and more enjoyable. The White House switched from animal

UPI/Bettmann Newsphotos

President Nixon is noted for having made the royal style of life part of the American presidency. Here, White House guards display the ceremonial uniforms that he ordered.

transportation to the automobile during Theodore Roosevelt's administration, and Congress established a travel allowance for the president; Taft was the first to receive it. Woodrow Wilson was the first to travel in a yacht; Franklin Roosevelt was the first to use airplanes, and Dwight D. Eisenhower added the first helicopter squadron to the president's means of transportation. In the 1920s Congress allocated an entertainment allowance for the president's official functions, and during President Truman's administration it put meals for servants under the federal budget.

From these rather modest beginnings presidential living evolved impressively to the point of the "imperial" presidential lifestyle of Richard Nixon, whom many Americans believed abused the perquisites available to a president by spending almost $10 million in government funds to upgrade his two private homes. Nixon is noted for making the royal style of life part of the American presidency. Bill Gulley, who served in the White House under Presidents Johnson, Nixon, Ford, and Carter as director of the Military Office, has written: "The buzz word around the Nixon White House for projecting the proper image was 'Presidential.' If a thing or place wasn't dignified enough . . . , then it wasn't 'Presidential.' And that meant money had to be spent on it." [7]

To a large extent the perquisites a president enjoys have been the result of the president's style. Thus, the rewards of office vary from time to time and from administration to administration. In an effort to back away from the image of the imperial presidency of Nixon, President Carter took many symbolic measures to deflate the image of excessive White House perquisites. Within a few weeks of his inauguration, Carter sold off two presidential yachts and reduced the motor pool by 40 percent. In addition, he removed three hundred television sets and two hundred AM-FM radios from the White House and the Executive Office Building. Even with these reductions in presidential perquisites, few would argue that the quality of life was bad at the White House during the Carter years.

President Reagan restored many of the ceremonial touches that Carter had removed. Carter had ended the practice of a Marine band playing "Ruffles and Flourishes" and "Hail to the Chief" at major social events. Reagan reinstated both and stationed a Marine in full dress uniform at the entrance of the West Lobby of the White House just to salute and open the door. Military aides escorted each member of the official guest party at state dinners, and a color guard preceded the Reagans and their guests of honor. Fringe benefits for the presidential staff also improved under Reagan. Among other things, Reagan expanded the White House motor pool to allow senior staff members to use limousines for their business around town.

Just how many rewards of office do Americans want their chief executive to enjoy? The question is difficult to answer. Presidential scholar James David Barber has noted that Americans are apparently ambivalent on the issue: "We want our President to be plain and fancy at the same time, up there with all the other monarchs and yet be Abraham Lincoln, too." [8] Perhaps there is even a need for some Americans to experience a little regality in their president. But no matter how Americans may feel about the benefits of the office, the perquisites of the presidency, whether because of necessity or personal style, are considerable.

Residences. One of the luxuries that presidents and their families enjoy is the rent-free White House mansion. The full-time staff of about one hundred includes butlers, cooks, stewards, gardeners, plumbers, electricians,

Bill Fitz-Patrick, The White House

President Reagan and his wife, Nancy, walk through the grounds of Camp David. With them is James Broaddus, the camp's commanding officer.

Camp David

About fifty miles northwest of the nation's capital, nestled away in nearly 6,000 rolling acres of Catoctin Mountain National Park, lies one of the most popular presidential perquisites, Camp David. Since 1942 presidents have used this 180-acre Appalachian Mountain retreat for solitude, relaxation, and important diplomatic negotiations. For most recent presidents, Camp David has served as a place where, burdened with the day-to-day demands of the office, they could "escape" and come a bit closer to normal life. For most Americans, however, it has remained hidden and something of a mystery.

In the spring of 1942, the federal government, at the request of Franklin Roosevelt, set up the beginnings of the Camp David compound on the highest land in Catoctin Mountain Park. President Roosevelt wanted a secluded retreat that was closer to Washington than his home in Hyde Park, New York. Roosevelt's doctor wanted him to be able to get away to a place that was cool and at least 2,000 feet above sea level. The camp, located in a hardwood forest of oaks, hickories, hemlocks, tulip trees, and sugar maples, met his doctor's criteria. Roosevelt named the camp Shangri-La. Originally, the compound was rugged, composed of a large cottage made by moving together three log cabins built by the Civilian Conservation Corps during the 1930s. It contained a kitchen, a butler's pantry, a combined living and dining room, four bedrooms, and two bathrooms. Over the years Camp David matured. During the Reagan administration, the retreat consisted of ten cabins, plus a dining lodge. The president has a separate cabin with a valley view, a stone patio, and a swimming pool. There are also tennis and basketball courts, a bowling alley, and a trampoline.

Because the retreat received little publicity, Roosevelt could slip away to the mountains and escape the hectic pace of Washington. He could relax at Shangri-La, where he worked on his stamp collection and played poker with his secretary, Grace Tully, and other friends. He entertained a variety of guests there, including Prime Minister Winston Churchill. Most Americans did not know until after Roosevelt's death that Shangri-La existed.

The retreat experienced a decline in importance during the Truman years. Preferring the sea, the Trumans found Shangri-La rather dull. Eisenhower, however, enjoyed the Maryland retreat at least as much as Roosevelt had. He spent almost every other weekend there, and after suffering a heart attack, he convalesced there for several months. Eisenhower eventually renamed the compound *Camp David* after his grandson.

President Kennedy preferred Cape Cod to Camp David, but he made the compound available to his staff. President Johnson and his family used the camp regularly, frequently inviting guests for the weekend. President Nixon liked Camp David so much that he spent almost every other weekend there in 1972 and regularly made it available to his staff. President Ford used Camp David as a family retreat and took advantage of the pool and tennis courts to keep in shape. President Carter enjoyed some of the best trout fishing in Maryland in sparkling Big Hunting Creek. And the Reagans regularly helicoptered to Camp David with many of their aides. President Reagan enjoyed horseback riding, swimming, and hiking the many trails throughout the camp.

Over the years Camp David has proven to be more than a recreational retreat, however. It often has served as a secluded getaway where presidents have conducted sensitive negotiations with foreign dignitaries. In 1959, Eisenhower invited Soviet Premier Nikita Khrushchev to Camp David for informal discussions of foreign affairs. Out of this meeting the media coined the phrase "the spirit of Camp David," indicating a spirit of serious negotiation and compromise. Probably the most notable diplomatic negotiations at Camp David occurred in September 1978 when Carter met with Egyptian President Anwar Sadat and Israeli Prime Minister Menachem Begin. This meeting, embodying the spirit of Camp David, produced the Camp David Accord for peace in the Middle East.

maids, and other assistants. Almost every imaginable convenience is available to the president within the White House complex and the adjoining Executive Office Building, including a theater, a swimming pool, a gymnasium, tennis courts, a bowling alley, a putting green, and a library regularly supplied by the publishing industry. With all these amenities at the personal disposal of the president, the operating cost of the White House has risen considerably. The annual cost of $13,800 to run and maintain the mansion a century ago seems meager with today's costs of more than $2 million a year.

Almost every new chief executive has the desire to refurbish the White House. Some of the cost of the president's remodeling has been at public expense. President Kennedy, concerned about the public's perception of his wealthy background, refused to use public money to pay for redecorating. When Kennedy's father commissioned a mural to brighten up the White House swimming pool area, an overzealous aide ordered the General Services Administration to install better lighting to highlight the mural. When the president found out about it, he insisted that he be billed for the $56,000 expense. Jacqueline Kennedy began the practice of making souvenir books available to White House tourists to help offset the costs of remodeling. Recently, presidents mostly have used donated funds to cover refurbishing expenses. When Gerald Ford became president, the government made plans to build a $500,000 pool and fitness center to replace the pool that Nixon had covered over to make a press room. Later, however, these plans were modified and privately donated funds were used to build a $55,000 outdoor pool. President Carter did very little redecorating, but President Reagan raised more than $1 million in privately donated money to refurbish the family living quarters of the mansion.

Nixon's "Second" Homes

Former president Richard Nixon maintained two controversial residences other than his official White House address. Both houses, one in Key Biscayne, Florida, and the other in San Clemente, California, required extensive repairs and renovations to make them sufficiently secure and comfortable for a president. Nixon purchased both of the residences with his own money, but various agencies of the federal government—including the Secret Service, General Services Administration, and the Defense Department—paid for most of the renovations on the estates since the improvements were necessary to protect the president and maintain the properties.

Among the improvements necessary to make both Key Biscayne and San Clemente suitable for a president were helicopter pads to transport the president to *Air Force One* and office complexes for himself and his staff. In addition, both homes were inherently hard to protect. The Key Biscayne property, for example, fronted on busy Biscayne Bay. To screen it off, neighboring houses had to be leased and the Coast Guard continuously had to patrol the waters near the house. Nonrecurring construction and equipment expenses came to over $1.3 million—just for Key Biscayne. At San Clemente, bullet-proof glass was installed in all the windows and in a screen that shielded the swimming pool from seaborne attackers and cold Pacific breezes. Some renovations, however, involved more than security and the normal overhead of maintaining the residence.

In 1973, the congressional Joint Committee on Internal Revenue Taxation, an investigatory and policy recommending committee, came to the conclusion that a number of repairs to Nixon's Key Biscayne and San Clemente homes served more to enrich the value of the estates than to provide increased security. Questionable expenditures on the Nixon homes included: $18,494 for a forced-air heating system, $621.50 for an ice-cube-making machine, $1,600 for four picture windows facing the ocean, $388.78 for an exhaust fan for a fireplace, $4,981.50 for a gazebo, and $2,329 for a flagpole. The committee found that many of these improvements had little to do with protecting the president or maintaining him in a reasonable manner.

Camp David, hidden away in Maryland's Catoctin Mountains, serves as the president's second official residence, or weekend retreat. Franklin Roosevelt built this 180-acre estate and called it "Shangri-La." Renamed "Camp David" by Eisenhower in honor of his grandson, the estate has become a posh recreational park. Presidents and their guests can enjoy a number of recreational facilities, including a heated, free-form pool, a bowling alley, archery and skeet ranges, tennis courts, a small golf course, a movie theater, and many miles of nature trails. *(See box, Camp David, p. 833.)*

As commander in chief of the armed forces, the president also has access to the best accommodations available on any one of the nation's widespread military bases. Since some of these bases are located in exotic places, they have provided presidents some very good lodgings. The president may choose either the VIP quarters, which are usually staffed and well maintained, or the quarters of the commanding officer. The cost to the taxpayer is small since military bases usually provide good security and communications facilities and would require less expense to bring them up to security standards. Truman occasionally took vacations in the sun at the naval base in Key West, Florida, and Eisenhower from time to time visited the base at Newport, Rhode Island. Most recent presidents, however, have not taken advantage of this fringe benefit.

Finally, many presidents prefer to have their own "private" residences, which serve as hideaways from the hustle and bustle of Washington life. Johnson frequently withdrew to his 400-acre LBJ Ranch in Texas; Nixon regularly visited his two homes, in Key Biscayne, Florida, and San Clemente, California; Carter often returned to his farm in Plains, Georgia; and Reagan frequently flew home to his ranch in California. Even though these were private residences, public money often had to be spent on them to ensure the president's safety. An estimated $10 million of public funds was spent on renovating and bringing up to security standards Nixon's private homes. *(See box, Nixon's "Second" Homes, this page.)*

Transportation. Perhaps the most misleading presidential expense account is the $75,000 annual travel allowance. This sum does not begin to cover even the annual salary of just the crew of *Air Force One,* a cost actually borne by the Department of Defense and not considered part of the president's travel allowance. The total costs of transporting the president and the president's family and staff have become one of the largest expenditures of the office.

Presidents' use of automobiles has increased tremendously since President Taft used the first official limousine provided at public expense. Today, a dozen limousines are available for the president's use, including a $500,000, armor-plated Lincoln. The Secret Service provides drivers for the presidents' automobiles and additional automobiles for others in the presidential party. No one would dispute the need for presidents to have their own carefully protected cars. Yet, over the years, various presidents have been accused of abusing their limousine privileges. President Nixon was criticized for giving his Irish setter, King Timahoe, a solitary ride to Camp David in an official automobile. Ordinarily only the most senior White House staffers are given limousine privileges, but these privileges sometimes have been exploited. Cordtz has reported that Nixon's press secretary, Ron Ziegler, while in Key Biscayne, Florida, would take his tennis partners to the courts in a Continental Mark IV rented by the government. President Carter objected to some staff members' using limousines to commute from home to work, so he cut back on the number of limousines available to staffers.

Only relatively recently have presidents begun to make many long-distance trips. In fact, before World War II, only two presidents traveled outside the country while in office. Theodore Roosevelt made a quick boat trip to Panama, and Wilson ventured to Europe at the end of World War I to attend the Paris Peace Conference. By the next world war, however, long-distance presidential travel had become more of a necessity. In January 1943, Franklin

UPI/Bettmann Newsphotos

***Air Force One* is the centerpiece of the presidential air fleet. Here it flies over George Washington's home, Mount Vernon, in Virginia.**

Roosevelt became the first president to fly overseas when he went to Casablanca, Morocco, to meet with British prime minister Winston Churchill and Allied commanders to plan the D-Day invasion. (Only after the trip did the rest of the world learn of the historic flight.) Roosevelt made the trip in a commercial airplane that had been pressed into wartime service. Compared with the amenities of contemporary presidential air travel, Roosevelt's trip would appear arduous.

Today, the best, and certainly the most expensive, travel benefit for the president is the air fleet maintained by the Air Force for the president's official use. At the president's disposal are a half-dozen jets, each outfitted with a bedroom and an office, and several sound-proofed helicopters for short trips. The president also has access to several Lockheed Jet Stars stationed at Andrews Air Force Base, which serve as courier planes to transport mail and staff when the president is out of Washington. The presidential air fleet was created primarily for the use of the president and the vice president. In recent years, however, some presidents have made the jets available to members of their immediate families for personal trips. They have felt justified in doing so for security reasons, since hijackings have increased and threats of violence against presidents and their families have multiplied. Because of increasing communications and security demands, air travel constitutes one of the largest expenditures on behalf of the president. Each weekend trip the Reagans took to their family ranch in southern California cost the federal government approximately $100,000.[9]

The centerpiece of the presidential air fleet is *Air Force One.* (Technically, the designation *Air Force One* is reserved for whatever plane the president is flying on at the time.) Equipped with the latest technology, *Air Force One* is a quick and comfortable means of transportation that allows the president to keep in constant contact with Washington and the rest of the world through an extensive communications center. On any presidential trip at least two large jets—a back-up plane and a communications plane—accompany *Air Force One.* And sometimes a large cargo plane carrying the chief executive's bullet-proof limousine will precede the presidential entourage. The Secret Service tries to keep secret most of the communications facilities aboard *Air Force One,* but President Reagan once boasted that he could place a telephone call to anywhere in the world and speak freely on a "secure" line (a telephone line supposedly safe from being tapped).[10] Also, somewhere aboard *Air Force One* is a compartment for the "black box," which contains the secret codes for the president in case of a military crisis.

For more than twenty-five years, U.S. presidents used Boeing 707s for *Air Force One.* New Boeing 747-200Bs were ordered for 1989. The new jets are larger, faster, more comfortable, and more self-sufficient than the 707s, providing many more of the conveniences of a flying White House. They also have more sophisticated communications systems and greater range (at least twice that of the 707s). The two new planes together cost more than $300 million, including crew training, the ground crew, and spare parts. Secret Service officials, White House aides, and aviation experts argued that by the 1990s the Boeing 707s would be nearly obsolete; factory parts would be hard to obtain and engine noise too loud for flight rules. Also, aviation experts and the Secret Service expressed a desire to provide the president with the biggest and the best that the United States could offer. In an effort to get the Air Force to consider the new planes, one former *Air Force One* pilot said, "The president should be able to take off in Washington and turn right or left and get there on one tank of gas—Moscow or Peking." [11]

The new *Air Force One* has enough room for seventy passengers and twenty-three crew members. The president's bedroom, furnished with a vanity, closets, a lavatory, and a shower-tub is in the nose of the aircraft. The plane also contains an office for the president, a conference room, a staff room, several working stations with computers, a guest area, space for members of the media and their telex equipment, and medical facilities. Communications equip-

Air Force One

When presidents first became airborne, the Army Air Corps (Air Force) took its rightful place as air chauffeur to the commander in chief and has been in charge of selecting and piloting presidential planes ever since. The first official plane used by a president was a U.S. Air Corps Douglas C-54 Skymaster, dubbed the *Sacred Cow* by the press. Shortly before his death in 1945, Franklin D. Roosevelt first used the plane on one trip. Harry S Truman, who thoroughly enjoyed flying, used the *Sacred Cow* often for presidential trips. By the summer of 1947, the official presidential plane was upgraded to a state-of-the-art Douglas Aircraft DC-6. Named the *Independence* after Truman's hometown in Missouri, the plane was equipped with weather radar, long-range capability, and a teletype system that allowed the president to stay in touch with Washington even when he was 3,000 miles away. The *Independence* served him throughout his administration.

Dwight D. Eisenhower enjoyed flying even more than Truman. Although he did not pilot the planes himself, he did possess a pilot's license. President Eisenhower's first official plane was a Lockheed Constellation 749. Named *Columbine II,* after his personal military craft during World War II and the state flower of his wife's home state of Colorado, the model was a personal favorite of his. Because of rapidly advancing aviation technology, the plane was replaced in 1954 by *Columbine III,* a Lockheed 1049C Super-Constellation, which remained Eisenhower's official plane throughout his administration. On a whirlwind, eighteen-day tour of eleven countries in Europe, Africa, and Asia in 1959, Eisenhower chose not to use the propeller-driven *Columbine III* and became the first president to travel by jet.

The distinction of becoming the first president to travel regularly by jet, however, belonged to John F. Kennedy. Assigned a propeller Douglas VC-118A by the Air Force, Kennedy preferred the much faster Boeing jets. In fact, he used his assigned plane only for travel to airports at which the runways were not long enough for the jets to land. In 1962, as a result of the increased demands for faster presidential travel, a Boeing 707 was delivered to Kennedy and became officially known as *26000* and designated *Air Force One,* as is any plane the president might be riding in. Previous planes had been military in appearance, but designer Raymond Loewy, along with Jacqueline Kennedy, created a new exterior that is still used today. Among the changes, "United States Air Force" was replaced with "Air Force One" on the body of the craft. And Mrs. Kennedy added a number of amenities for which the plane became famous. President Kennedy was not able to enjoy *Air Force One* for very long, however. On the day of his assassination, November 22, 1963, Kennedy's body was flown from Dallas to Washington in the plane he had used for just over thirteen months. Nine years later, the plane Kennedy had first used became the backup to a newer version of the Boeing 707. These two planes remained the "president's planes" for more than twenty-five years.

ment and the crew are upstairs. Other special touches include fresh flowers and embossed memo pads, napkins, playing cards, cigarette packages, and matches with the presidential seal and the words "Aboard Air Force One."

Designers wanted to produce a plane that would provide not only luxury but also the greatest possible security. In addition to a gourmet kitchen, numerous televisions, a stereo system, and movie facilities, the plane has several important security features; for example, it has been hardened against electromagnetic pulse from a possible nuclear explosion. When the plane lands, it can become a total communications center for the president and the staff. Also, the president has extra security and a public relations advantage by being able to watch welcoming crowds on television screens as the plane taxis up the runway.

Entertainment. Like many of the other perquisites of the presidential office, the amount of money and staff resources expended on entertainment depends significantly on the person holding the office. Even though protocol requires all presidents to do some entertaining of foreign heads of state and foreign and U.S. governmental notables, the social pace at the White House largely depends on the inclination of the president. The Trumans, for example, seldom entertained, but other presidents and their families have taken advantage of the many entertainment opportunities the White House affords. The Kennedys, Johnsons, Fords, and Nixons all enjoyed a busy social calendar. The Carters cut back on White House social events, but the Reagans stepped up the presidential social pace, delighting in state dinners, congressional breakfasts, political teas, luncheons, barbecues, receptions, and various command performances. In 1984, *U.S. News & World Report* found that President Reagan had entertained 222,758 persons during just his first three years in office.[12] *(See box, An Evening at the Reagan White House, p. 838.)*

Even though the president receives an entertainment allowance of $12,000 a year, most entertainment expenses are not paid out of the White House budget. The State Department pays for all state banquets and functions. Periodically, various entertainers are asked to come to the White House and perform for the president and White House guests. The distinction of performing at a White House function is so great that celebrities do so without charge. In fact, many even will cancel previously scheduled appearances to accommodate the president. At most White House affairs, the army, navy, air force, or marine bands continuously play for the pleasure of the president and White House guests. Smaller groups, such as the Army Chorus, the Air Force Strolling Strings, and the Navy Sea Chanters, may also perform. Since these are military groups, the Defense Department bears the costs of their performances. Also, a number of White House functions are paid for by the organizations that benefit from them.

During the Reagan administration, the Republican National Committee picked up the tab for several fetes for Republicans.

In addition to White House entertaining, from time to time presidents will entertain dignitaries while abroad. Several presidents have gone to extremes to carry the pageantry and glamour of a White House dinner to other countries. It was not uncommon for Johnson and Nixon to take with them White House china and crystal for entertaining government officials in the countries they visited. In 1984, President and Mrs. Reagan hosted 600 Chinese and American guests in the banquet facilities of Beijing's Great Wall Hotel—one of the largest state dinners ever held outside the United States. The Reagans treated their guests to a "typical American meal" of turkey and dressing. To accommodate the large crowd with the best possible meal, forty frozen turkeys were flown in from California, and a professor from the Peking Agricultural College was asked to oversee the selection of vegetables to make sure they were garden fresh. Some of the vegetables came from the hotel's own greenhouse. Canned cranberries were flown in from Hong Kong. The amount of food required for the dinner was massive: 176 pounds of beef for consommé; 440 pounds of prawns, scallops, Mandarin fish, and turbot for the seafood mousse appetizer; 132 pounds of hearts of palm for the salad; and 22 pounds of almonds, 600 eggs, 36 quarts of cream, and 3 bottles of Grand Marnier for the praline ice cream dessert. The Reagans selected three types of California wine for the event. Seventy-six chefs and 120 staffers were required to assist in the preparation. Special arrangements were made with the hotel to provide place settings of German chinaware, Irish linen, and French crystal, candelabra, and silverware. A twelve-piece Chinese orchestra played music chosen by the Reagans, including works by Irving Berlin, George Gershwin, and Rodgers and Hammerstein.[13]

For four decades, presidents had the use of a 105-foot yacht, the *Sequoia*, for entertaining friends and dignitaries. In 1976, however, President Carter sold it for $286,000, a symbolic sacrifice in the interest of cutting back on presidential pomp. Upon the urging of several friends and advisers—among them former House Speaker Thomas P. (Tip) O'Neill—the Reagan administration tried to replace the yacht. Many felt it had served a useful purpose in the past by allowing the president to get away from the hectic atmosphere of the White House to a more intimate environment for official entertaining and lobbying. The cost of replacing it proved prohibitive, however.

Protection. Most presidents have viewed the Secret Service as a mixed blessing. Probably the most necessary and important presidential perquisite, it is also the most annoying. Since the assassination of President Kennedy and the failed, but close, attempts on presidents Ford and Reagan, the growing need for greater security has dictated an increase in Secret Service protection and a decrease in the personal freedoms of the chief executives. Almost every week someone, whether dangerous or merely annoying, makes some attempt to get to the president.

Every month almost six thousand new pieces of information concerning possible threats to the president pour into Secret Service headquarters. Sometimes the information may be just a report of a malicious statement, such as someone in a bar saying, "That jerk in the White House ought to be shot." Or a woman might report that her next-door neighbor blames the president for losing her job. Even though all tips are taken seriously, some are viewed with the utmost urgency. In November 1981, intelligence sources warned that Libya's Col. Muammar Qaddafi had sent assassination teams to murder top-ranking government officials, including President Reagan. Even though nothing came of the threat, the Secret Service put the tightest possible security measures in place. As of 1982, the Secret Service had computerized files on some 26,000 individuals who had threatened the president or other government officials at some time, or who had done something to make the Secret Service suspicious and concerned. Of these, 250 to 450 were on the "hot" list of those the agency was most concerned about.[14]

Ironically, Abraham Lincoln was the first president to

John F. Kennedy Library

The social pace of the White House largely depends on the inclination of the president. John Kennedy hosted cellist Pablo Casals and many other leading artists in the East Room.

An Evening at the Reagan White House

President and Mrs. Reagan restored to White House social events much of the European-like glitter and elegance that had been missing since the days of the Kennedys. Anyone invited to an evening of dinner and entertainment at the White House found an elaborate meal amidst much ceremony. The Reagans, given to a certain amount of pomp and show, always seemed to host affairs that were considered elegant and enjoyable. This created an even greater demand for the coveted White House invitation.

Nancy Reagan always devoted much time and attention to the guest list of a typical White House event. Taking suggestions from top White House aides and the State Department, she was careful to choose guests who would be compatible. Usually, the guest list included a number of old friends, such as Hollywood stars Dinah Shore, Gregory Peck, Burt Reynolds, Jimmy Stewart, Bob Hope, and Charlton Heston, as well as Washington notables and foreign dignitaries.

Once the guest list was completed, White House calligraphers would prepare and mail out the invitations five weeks before the event. Mrs. Reagan would then spend hours studying the list, arranging the seating so that people from different backgrounds, but with common interests, would be near one another. Mrs. Reagan, acclaimed as a gracious hostess, gave special attention to a variety of small details; for example, in order for the evening to be as pleasant and comfortable as possible for single women, they often were offered a military escort to the event.

Great care and attention also was given to dinner. Choosing menus with the guest of honor's likes and dislikes was always important. Mrs. Reagan often would have sample meals prepared for her to try the day before, and it was not unusual for her to make some modifications in the planned meal after her sampling. A typical dinner would include smoked mountain trout, roast supreme of duckling a l'orange with wild rice and raisins, watercress and mushroom salad, brie and chèvre cheeses, and melon glacé en surprise. The Reagans always served California wines. Their favorite was Schramsberg Blanc de blanc, a sparkling wine served with dessert. And there was usually an after-dinner toast.

Musical entertainment often followed the dinner. Entertainers, such as violinist Isaac Stern, pianist Byron Janis, singer Sergio Franchi, the cast of "A Chorus Line," members of the Harlem Ballet, and the Juilliard String Quartet, performed at the request of the president. After the entertainment, the Reagans would lead everyone in dancing to a military band playing popular music, such as Cole Porter show tunes. As the night wound down and the guest of honor departed, the Reagans would remain and continue to dance and mingle with the lingering guests.

Source: U.S. News & World Report, June 1, 1981, p. 43.

have bodyguards, paid for by the state of Ohio. After the assassination of William McKinley in 1901, the Treasury Department's Secret Service, which had primarily investigated counterfeiting, was charged with the protection of the president. Florence Harding was the first first lady to appropriate the services of her own Secret Service agent, and during Calvin Coolidge's administration, Secret Service protection was extended to the president's immediate family. Even though the Secret Service undertakes other activities, such as detecting and arresting counterfeiters and offering and paying rewards for information contributing to the arrest of criminals, the majority of its budget goes to protecting the president of the United States. At the time of the Kennedy assassination, the Secret Service had 389 agents and a budget of $8 million. In the late 1980s, the number of agents had grown to more than 1,600, and the budget of the Secret Service was more than $300 million. *(See "Protecting the President: The Secret Service," p. 905, in Daily Life of the President chapter of Part V.)*

No longer can a president take a casual stroll through the streets of Washington, as Truman frequently did. Kennedy used to elude his Secret Service agents and visit friends in Georgetown. And Johnson used to take a walk around the grounds of the White House without any Secret Service protection. But those days are long gone. Reagan became a virtual prisoner of the White House after he was wounded in an assassination attempt in 1981. Before the shooting, the Reagans occasionally went to church. After the attempt on the president's life, however, the Reagans decided to quit attending services altogether because members of any church they visited would have been subjected to checks by metal detectors and other security-related annoyances. Because of Secret Service protection, Nancy Reagan could not even go shopping without disrupting a store's normal business. Instead, she ordered from catalogs and asked her secretary to shop for her.[15]

Even in the White House itself, the president and the first family are restricted in their activities by security requirements. They live on the second and third floors in approximately 13 of the 132 rooms of the White House. The rest of the rooms are used for offices or for the president's official duties. The Secret Service makes sure that the White House is one of the most secure places on earth. At every exit and throughout the White House, security guards and the Secret Service stand a careful watch. When the president entertains, guests must be approved in advance by the Secret Service before they can even enter the White House. Any presents given to the president or to family members must be opened by someone else. And as a routine security measure, the Secret Service confiscates all varieties of food that arrive at the White House by mail. The agents constantly monitor, using hidden television cameras and electronic sensors, the almost nineteen acres of White House grounds and routinely test the air for poisonous gases and bacteria. As groups tour the mansion, Secret Service agents discreetly mingle with the crowd.

Occasionally, threats against presidents and their families will force the Secret Service to take extraordinary measures of protection. After the attempted assassination of Reagan, the 1983 bombings of the U.S. Marines' barracks in Beirut and of a corridor in the U.S. Capitol, and several specific threats against Reagan's life, Secret Service agents decided to blockade the entrances to the White House. Protected by police vans and dirt-filled dump trucks, the White House came to resemble an outpost of a battle zone. These steps were in addition to the steel gates and sensors already in place at the entrances and on the grounds of the White House. Eventually, the Secret Service replaced these vehicles with the more attractive, permanent concrete barriers standing three feet high.

Safety precautions are not confined to possible ground assaults. In the Old Executive Office Building next-door to the White House, a command and control center closely monitors all aircraft using National Airport, a mere 3 miles from the White House. Ground-to-air missiles are hidden near the White House, but security is so tight the Secret Service has refused to disclose either the location or the type of missiles that would be used. Should a suspicious aircraft stray from an established flight pattern, security officers have less than a minute to decide whether or not to fire on it.[16]

When the president makes a public appearance, the Secret Service takes special precautions. Wherever the president is scheduled to speak, the Secret Service works with local law enforcement officials to make sure any risk is minimal. Security officers carefully check the motorcade route to the president's destination for any places where an assassin would have an open shot. They look for possible sniper posts and inspect utility holes and bridges for bombs. In case of an emergency, the Secret Service selects alternative routes and designates certain hospitals to have a ready supply of the president's blood type. Moreover, in every city or town where a public appearance is scheduled, agents search local files to see if there are people in the area who could pose a threat to the president. Anyone considered suspicious is interrogated and put under constant surveillance.

When *Air Force One* arrives at the airport, the Secret Service quickly escorts the chief executive from the airplane into the armored presidential limousine, fitted with bullet-proof tires and windows. An agent drives the limousine, and a second agent rides in the back with the president. Twenty or so agents jog alongside the car or follow in cars complete with a supply of Israeli-made submachine guns, tear gas, emergency tools, and medical supplies. As the motorcade passes through the streets, sharpshooters with high-powered binoculars and rifles watch warily from the rooftops. Other agents with .357-magnum pistols watch the motorcade from strategic locations along the way. Some agents closely observe onlookers for anything suspicious. At the destination, the president will speak in a "secured" room, that is, one that has been thoroughly checked by Secret Service agents. Before sealing off the room, agents use specially trained dogs to sniff out bombs. And as people enter the room, they pass through metal detectors and have their bags or purses inspected. Although the Secret Service prefers that the president speak in a secure auditorium, the president will sometimes address an audience outdoors. Since the Secret Service cannot screen everyone in the crowd, it places an extra burden on them. They must station agents on the rooftops of nearby buildings and place extra agents in the crowd.

Protecting presidents when they travel or go on vacation often entails elaborate measures. When President Eisenhower took golfing vacations, he usually was followed around the golf course by an athletic-looking twosome with high-powered rifles in their golf bags. When President Ford vacationed in Vail, Secret Service agents would ski alongside him. And when President Reagan visited his ranch, agents adept at horseback riding would accompany him on trail rides.

Sometimes, especially when a president visits other countries, the Secret Service takes what may seem to be ludicrous precautions. When President Reagan visited Costa Rica in December 1982, he arrived with a C-5 cargo plane carrying three bullet-proof Lincoln Continentals and an entourage of three hundred Secret Service agents. Costa Ricans were amused at these protective measures in their peaceful, democratic country, for the Costa Rican president can walk about in public without security guards.[17] But, understandably, the Secret Service would rather err on the side of caution.

Retirement. Few executive officers of major corporations enjoy the generous retirement benefits that former presidents of the United States have today. Yet, until 1958 neither presidents nor their families received any pension after retirement from the highest public office in the country. Calvin Coolidge moved from the White House into a $36-a-month rented duplex. And the Trumans paid their own train fares back to Independence, Missouri. The first annual presidential pension of $25,000 was given to Truman in 1958. Since then the costs of maintaining retired presidents have risen considerably. In 1984 alone, the federal government spent more than $29 million on pensions and other retirement benefits for the three living ex-presidents (Nixon, Ford, and Carter).

When Truman left the White House and went back to Missouri, he did so empty handed. All presidents who preceded him also left office without any retirement benefits. During his retirement years, Truman refused to accept any job that might take advantage of his former occupation as president. Because he was not independently wealthy and spent much of his time answering large quantities of mail, he faced real financial hardship just a few short years after retiring. To help Truman and to rectify past negligence, Congress passed the Former Presidents Act of 1958, which gave Truman his pension and provided him with an additional $50,000 a year for office and staff. Since then, Congress has steadily increased these pensions and allowances.

As of January 1989, every ex-president received an annual pension equal to the salary of a cabinet secretary ($99,500 in 1988). A president's widow receives $20,000 a year. In addition, the retired president also receives $150,000 annually for a staff for the first thirty months out of office and a $96,000 annual allowance thereafter. But there are other retirement benefits as well. The government provides each ex-president with unlimited postage for nonpolitical correspondence and a furnished office. Ex-presidents receive these benefits in addition to the $1 million budgeted to ease the transition from president to former president and help the president and vice president wind up their official affairs.

The most expensive presidential retirement perquisite for the federal government is the operational budget for the increasing number of presidential libraries. American taxpayers paid almost $15 million to operate presidential libraries in 1984. Six deceased presidents (Herbert Hoover, Roosevelt, Truman, Eisenhower, Kennedy, and Johnson) and two living presidents (Ford and Carter) have libraries that house their presidential papers and related memorabilia. *(See box, Presidential Libraries, p. 841.)* As of January 1989, Presidents Nixon and Reagan had libraries either under construction or in the planning stage. These facilities were originally paid for by funds raised through private donations, but since 1955 the federal government has picked up the expense of maintaining them. Although the libraries were built mainly for research, the National Archives, which maintains them, estimates that the number of researchers looking at presidential documents is a fraction of 1 percent of the total number of tourists. Most visitors to the libraries are more interested in the presidential museums, which are usually housed in the same buildings, than in presidential papers. In recent years many members of Congress have felt that these libraries serve more as monuments than research centers and have proposed limits on the size of new presidential libraries.[18]

The cost of Secret Service protection for ex-presidents ranks close behind the cost of maintaining presidential libraries. In 1962, shortly before President Kennedy was assassinated, Congress ordered the Secret Service to begin protecting ex-presidents and to continue to do so for a "reasonable time." Then, in 1965, Congress approved lifetime protection for all retired chief executives, their spouses, and their children under the age of sixteen. Lawmakers also granted a president's widow Secret Service protection as long as she did not remarry. When Amy Carter turned sixteen, she lost her Secret Service protection, as did Jacqueline Kennedy when she remarried. Occasionally, a president will decline some allowable protection. In 1984, Nixon dropped Secret Service protection for his wife, Pat, who had suffered a stroke and thereafter rarely traveled.

The General Services Administration (GSA) controls presidential retirement funds and keeps an eye on how former presidents make use of public money. The GSA approves most requests for funds for office allowances and other items. Some of the more interesting items that ex-presidents have requested, and received, include: Nixon's subscriptions to a variety of newspapers and magazines, including the *Wall Street Journal,* the *New York Times,* the *Washington Post, Foreign Affairs, Fortune, New Republic, Facts on File, Time,* and *U.S. News & World Report;* Ford's cable television service; and Carter's computer equipment complete with service contract. The GSA rejects items it feels breach the bounds of propriety. Shortly after leaving the presidency, Carter began to set up his new office in Atlanta. Initially, he asked GSA for an appropriation of $15,000 for a wool rug for his office and $3,500 for two chandeliers. The GSA refused, and Carter had to "settle" for buying the rug with government funds under list price for $12,600 and for installing chandeliers that cost only $1,850. The GSA also rejected Carter's request for funds to pay for photographs of Amy Carter to be sent to children writing her and asking for pictures.

Much controversy surrounds the upkeep of former presidents. Under heavy pressure to slash the federal budget, in the 1980s members of Congress introduced several bills to curtail the steady surge in the amount of money allocated to former presidents. Sen. Lawton Chiles (D-Fla.) introduced bills in 1980 and 1981 that would have limited the size of presidential libraries that the government would pay to maintain. The bills also would have limited Secret Service protection to eight years. The secretary of the Treasury could have extended the service two more years, if it was deemed necessary. And Secret Service protection for widows would have been cut off six months after the husband's death. Another provision of the bills would have cut back on the practice of using federally funded staffs to help prepare presidential memoirs. Chiles would have preferred for a president's staff to be able to help only if the book was to be published by the federal government and the profits were to go to the federal government. While Chiles's bills never became law, the debate continued into the late 1980s.

Critics argue that too much federal money is used to support and protect persons who hardly need it. Today, ex-presidents are millionaires. Former presidents remain in the public spotlight, and they take advantage of the lingering interest in their tenure at the White House. As a result, they become marketable and coveted commodities. Through speaking engagements, serving as consultants, serving on corporate boards, and writing books, former chief executives can use their previous position to profit handsomely. On the one hand, critics contend that the public should not be asked to subsidize this wealth any more than is absolutely necessary. On the other hand, some Americans believe that the government should help pay the bill for all the fringe benefits that go with presidential retirement. Defenders contend that ex-presidents still have public responsibilities and should be financially supported in their activities.

The Vice President

The trappings of political office have always been important to vice presidents. Yet, they have never shared in the pomp and grandeur of the office of the president. Neither the pay nor the perquisites of office have been as substantial as those of the presidency. In fact, until relatively recently the vice presidency was an insignificant office, not only in terms of its power and functions but also in terms of the privileges and honor of the position. Because most presidents did not give meaning to the vice president's role, the job failed to win meaningful fringe benefits. Since the mid-1970s, vice presidents have enjoyed a wider range of benefits, and they certainly have lived in a style that many Americans would envy. The splendor of their perquisites, however, does not approach that of the president's.

Vice-Presidential Salary

On September 24, 1789, when Congress first fixed the president's salary at $25,000 a year, it placed the annual salary of the vice president at $5,000. When Congress doubled the president's salary in 1873, it also doubled the vice president's. No more consideration was given to the vice president's salary until 1906, when Congress raised it from $10,000 to $12,000 annually. This amount was well below the $75,000 a year that the president was given, and it reflected the relative unimportance of the job to most Americans.

However, since the late 1940s the vice president's salary has increased substantially. The Legislative Reorganization Act of 1946 contained a measure that provided for a $20,000 salary for the vice president. In 1949 Congress

Presidential Libraries

Recent presidents have established libraries to house their presidential papers and memorabilia, as well as films, tapes, and clippings relating to their administrations. These libraries were built by private funds but are maintained by the federal government. The following is a list of these libraries, their locations, and the date each was dedicated.

The Herbert Hoover Presidential Library
Parkside Drive
West Branch, Iowa 52358
Phone: (319) 643-5301
Dedicated: August 10, 1972

The Franklin D. Roosevelt Library
Albany Post Road
Hyde Park, New York 12538
Phone: (914) 229-8114
Dedicated: July 4, 1940

The Harry S. Truman Library
U.S. Highway 24 and Delaware Street
Independence, Missouri 64050
Phone: (816) 833-1400
Dedicated: July 6, 1957

The Dwight D. Eisenhower Library
Southeast Fourth Street
Abilene, Kansas 67410
Phone: (913) 263-4571
Dedicated: May 1, 1972

The John F. Kennedy Library
Morrissey Boulevard
Columbia Point
Boston, Massachusetts 02125
Phone: (617) 929-4500
Dedicated: October 20, 1979

The Lyndon B. Johnson Library
2313 Red River Street
Austin, Texas 78705
Phone: (512) 482-5137
Dedicated: May 22, 1971

The Gerald R. Ford Library
1000 Beal Avenue
Ann Arbor, Michigan 48109
Phone: (313) 668-2218
Dedicated: April 27, 1981

The Jimmy Carter Library
One Copenhill Avenue
Atlanta, Georgia 30307
Phone: (404) 331-3942
Dedicated: October 1, 1986

raised the vice-presidential salary from $20,000 to $30,000 a year and added an annual tax-free expense account of $10,000. Twelve years later Congress voted the vice president a $5,000 raise. The Federal Employee Act of 1964 again raised the compensation, from $35,000 to $43,000 a year; and in 1969, when Congress increased the president's salary to $200,000, it raised the vice president's salary to $62,500. The vice president received several raises after 1969 and in 1988 earned $115,000 in salary and was given an expense account of $10,000 a year, all of which was taxable.

Vice-Presidential Perquisites

In the George Gershwin musical comedy *Of Thee I Sing,* Alexander Throttlebottom felt so mistreated as vice president that he complained that he had to take the public tour even to get into the White House. Many vice presidents have felt that they were excluded not only from administration policy making but also from White House perquisites. Although Gershwin's characterization of vice-presidential prestige was extreme, it does represent the historical lack of White House fringe benefits for vice presidents.

Vice-presidential perquisites can be measured in a manner different from those of the president. Although most vice presidents always have enjoyed a certain amount of fringe benefits of the job itself, the actual importance of a specific vice president's job often can be seen in the tangible rewards granted to the vice president by the president. A vice president's job and responsibilities are dependent upon the president. If a president recognizes the importance of the vice presidency and uses the vice president for things other than receiving visiting delegations of Boy Scouts, then the vice president will likely share in many of the trappings of the presidential office. Historically, vice presidents have found themselves enjoying the perquisites of office when their presidents have recognized their importance.

It was the lack of importance in the vice presidency that prompted Franklin Roosevelt's first vice president, John N. ("Cactus Jack") Garner, to tell Lyndon Johnson that the office "ain't worth a cup of warm spit." Until the Carter and Reagan administrations, most presidents seemed to ignore their vice presidents, giving them few responsibilities or privileges and little recognition. Political scientist Paul C. Light notes that for vice presidents Walter Mondale and George Bush, the proximity of the West Wing office, the vice president's increased staff, and the extension of other perquisites gave them advantages most earlier vice presidents, such as Johnson, Hubert Humphrey, Spiro Agnew, and Ford, did not have.[19] Of recent vice presidents, Johnson, Humphrey, and Agnew seemed almost to disappear in office. Their presidents seldom recognized their importance or sought their advice.[20] A former Humphrey assistant noted the reality of vice-presidential privileges: "It used to take an act of Congress to get us into the White House. We had to get cleared in by somebody because we didn't have White House passes.... We were treated like little children, allowed to look but not to touch.... We didn't have any symbols of power and that was currency in the White House." [21] In contrast, both Mondale and Bush found that their counsel was consistently sought and their positions recognized through the granting of White House fringe benefits.

Although the relation between perquisites and power is uncertain, the advancement of vice-presidential perquisites does reflect the rise in the vice president's position. Instead of having their main office in the Old Executive Office Building across the street from the White House, both Mondale and Bush were allowed an office in the West Wing of the White House and greater access to the president than their predecessors had. In addition, their staffs were granted greater access to the White House and given more privileges than earlier vice-presidential staffs. Simply having White House mess privileges meant that the vice president's staff rubbed elbows with the president's staff, allowing greater contact and accessibility.

The location of the vice president's office is one of the most important perquisites for the second in command. The formal office of the vice president, in the Old Executive Office Building, contains all the amenities befitting a vice president. A Mondale aide once described it in glowing terms: "That EOB office is nothing less than magnificent. Royal blue carpeting. Two entrances, both protected by huge mahogany doors. Great view of the White House and monuments. Good location. Balcony. High ceilings." [22] But for all the splendor of that office, the real perquisite is to be located in the West Wing of the White House. The West Wing vice-presidential office is small, and not nearly as grand—but it provides the vice president with greater access to the president. As another former Mondale aide remarked: "The West Wing Office is really quite grubby. It is cramped and closed in. There's a lot of traffic and the view isn't so hot out the back window. It's got lots of advantages if you want to be a player, but it isn't that great if you're into offices." [23] Today, the vice-presidential office in the Old Executive Office Building is used mostly for ceremonial functions. The vice president also maintains an office on Capitol Hill to serve the constitutional function as the presiding officer of the Senate.

Over the past thirty years, the vice president's staff has grown tremendously, indicating the increased importance of the position. The size of the vice president's staff again represents increased influence. In 1959, when Nixon was vice president, the staff of the vice president was fewer than twenty. By the time Bush served in the office, it had increased to more than seventy. In fact, the vice president's office staff today is almost a replica of the president's staff. The vice president has a national security adviser, a press secretary, an issues staff, a counsel's office, a chief of staff, a scheduling team, an appointments secretary, and an advance team. An enlarged staff not only increased the ability of vice presidents to stay abreast of the issues, it gives them the appearance of importance and the intangible perquisite of clout.

Recent years have seen an increase in other tangible vice-presidential fringe benefits, such as improved airplanes, more limousines, and an official residence. Until the Carter administration, vice-presidential air travel paled in comparison to the president's *Air Force One.* Humphrey had to travel in a small jet with just enough room for ten or twelve persons, which prevented the media from going along. Agnew moved up a bit to an Air Force transport without windows. Often called "Air Force Thirteen" by Agnew's staff, it resembled a flying coffin. Vice President Ford's air travel accommodations were hardly much better. He traveled in *Air Force Two,* an aging turboprop Convair that "creaked and groaned its way through the skies." [24] By the time Mondale became vice president, vice-presidential air travel had improved markedly. He always had one plane on standby and two or three others at his disposal. During the 1980 presidential campaign, his aircraft was equipped to carry representatives from the media. As one of his long-time aides gratefully remarked, "We had two or three planes that could not be moved without our permission. And they were decent airplanes. Windows, engines, wheels, the whole package." [25]

Only recently have vice presidents even been given an official residence. *(See "Vice President's Residence," p. 820, in Housing chapter of Part V.)* On April 9, 1966, Congress authorized the planning, design, construction, furnishing, and maintenance of an official vice-presidential residence to be built on the site of the United States Naval Observatory in Washington, D.C. However, it never appropriated any money for the project. Finally, on July 12, 1974, Congress selected the Admiral's House—a building almost a century old on a twelve-acre section of the seventy-two-acre observatory property—as the official residence of the vice president. This time, Congress also authorized expenditures for its repair. On January 20, 1977, Mondale became the first vice president to occupy the renovated building.

White House Staff and Executive Agencies

Establishing salaries for members of the top echelon of presidential aides and the executive branch has always posed special problems for lawmakers. On the one hand, there is the belief that top members of the executive branch should be the brightest and the best people available and that salaries for executive positions should be high enough to attract such people. On the other hand, many Americans are uneasy when their public servants earn more than they do. This is complicated by the fact that the issue of federal executive compensation often becomes a political football. As John W. Macy, Bruce Adams, and J. Jackson Walter observed in their study on appointing presidential aides, "Much as they may desire to set government salaries high enough to attract talented people into the public service, members of Congress are profoundly sensitive to the electoral backlash that federal pay policies can inspire." [26] As a consequence, the salaries of top-level executive branch staff are lower than the salaries of their private-sector counterparts; most key presidential aides could earn much more in private life.

When President Washington established his cabinet, salaries were based upon the perceived difficulty of the position. The first three cabinet officers Washington selected were Secretary of State John Jay, Secretary of War Henry Knox, and Secretary of the Treasury Alexander Hamilton. The annual salary for the secretary of war was $3,000; for the two other cabinet secretaries, $3,500 each.

Later, the attorney general and the postmaster general became members of Washington's cabinet at $1,500 a year. Finally, the secretary of the navy was added as a sixth cabinet member at an annual salary of $3,000. Compared with Washington's $25,000 annual salary, cabinet officers' salaries were quite low.

The Postal Revenue and Federal Salary Act of 1967 set up the system by which federal executive salaries are determined today. One purpose of the act was to keep salaries from being a political issue by creating the nine-member Commission on Executive, Legislative, and Judicial Salaries. The president appoints three members of the commission, and the president pro tempore of the Senate (the presiding officer of the Senate in the absence of the vice president), the Speaker of the House, and the chief justice each appoint two members. Known as the Quadrennial Commission because it is set up during the last year of each presidential term, the commission reviews the salaries of members of Congress, federal judges, and top officers of the executive branch covered under the Executive Schedule and makes recommendations to the president. Once the commission makes its recommendations, the president may revise them or submit them unchanged in the annual budget message to Congress. Under the provisions of the 1967 act, the president's recommendations become law automatically within thirty days unless both houses of Congress disapprove them or Congress submits its own salary structure. In 1975, Congress enacted the Executive Salary Cost-of-Living Adjustment Act, which supplemented the Quadrennial Commission's work by providing cost-of-living adjustments during the interim period.

This process was originally designed to keep executive compensation from falling so far below comparable private sector salaries that qualified candidates would not apply for high-ranking positions. The system has not been very successful, however, in keeping executive branch salaries competitive. Regardless of the recommendations of the Quadrennial Commission and cost-of-living adjustments, Congress has been reluctant to increase federal executive pay. Much of the problem results from the practice begun in 1969 of linking salaries of executive officials to those of members of Congress. As a result, executive salary decisions depend on congressional salary decisions. Macy, Adams, and Walter wrote,

> Members of Congress always find it difficult to raise their own salaries, especially if an election is approaching. Nothing more clearly reflects this difficulty than the fact that congressional pay has been increased less than a dozen times in this century. As long as the linkage of executive and congressional salaries remains in effect, there appears little likelihood of establishing an executive compensation system that is objective and consistent.[27]

Federal executives received only a 5 percent raise from 1969 to 1976, and that came in 1975. In 1978, upon the recommendation of President Carter, Congress froze executive pay.

Even though White House aides and cabinet officers have received small increases in pay since 1978, their salaries have not kept up with the cost of living. In late 1986, the Quadrennial Commission reported that the cost of living for the average citizen had risen more than 225 percent since 1969, resulting in a 40 percent decline in real earnings for senior government officials. The head of the National Aeronautics and Space Administration, for example, earned $77,400 in 1986. In 1969, the same position paid $42,500. Adjusted for inflation over the past eighteen years, that salary would have been worth $133,531 in 1986. In 1969 dollars, the 1986 salary had a value of only $25,236.[28]

Table 2 Executive Branch Salaries, 1988

Position	1987 compensation	Quadrennial Commission recommendation	Actual
Executive Level I	$88,000	$155,000	$99,500
Executive Level II	77,400	135,000	89,500
Executive Level III	75,800	125,000	82,500
Executive Level IV	74,500	120,000	80,700
Executive Level V	70,800	115,000	75,500

Source: Quadrennial Commission on Executive, Legislative, and Judicial Salaries; Karen Riley, "Large Salary Increases Are Urged for Congress, Judges, Cabinet Officers," *Washington Times,* December 16, 1986; Barbara Vobejda, "Citizens Celebrate as Raise Collapses," *Washington Post,* February 8, 1989.

Note: Executive Level I comprises cabinet secretaries; Executive Level II, deputy secretaries and heads of offices and agencies; Executive Level III, undersecretaries and chairs of regulatory commissions; Executive Level IV, assistant secretaries, members of regulatory commissions; Executive Level V, directors of major bureaus of the cabinet.

In general, chief presidential aides, cabinet officers, and agency heads are divided into five pay and responsibility classifications. Executive Level I consists of cabinet secretaries. Executive Level II includes deputy cabinet secretaries and heads of offices and agencies. Executive Level III comprises undersecretaries of the cabinet and chairs of regulatory commissions. Executive Level IV is made up of assistant secretaries of the cabinet, members of regulatory commissions, and general counsels. And Executive Level V includes the directors of the major bureaus of the cabinet. Top White House staff members are paid at Executive Levels III to V.

In 1987, based on the 1986 Quadrennial Commission's report, President Reagan recommended to Congress that it raise salaries for his staff and other top officials in his administration, as well as for federal legislators and judges. Although Reagan's recommended raises were much lower than the commission's, they did constitute significant increases for top officials in all three branches. In December 1986, the commission had recommended that top employees in all three branches of the federal government receive raises by as much as 60 to 80 percent. The commission argued that these increases were necessary to offset the prolonged erosion of top executives' earning power. In response to the report, President Reagan approved raises that ranged from 2 to 16 percent. Even though Congress attempted to kill the raises, they became law after the required thirty-day period. Salaries of cabinet secretaries increased from $88,800 to $99,500; those of deputy cabinet secretaries and heads of government agencies increased from $81,100 to $89,500; and those of other top-level executives increased at comparable amounts. *(See Table 2.)*

These raises met stiff opposition not only from Congress but from some consumer groups as well. In response to the raises, consumer advocate Ralph Nader wrote President Reagan and urged him to reconsider: "Nothing is more absurd in this perennial debate than the assertion by legislators, judges, and other government officials that they can't get by at salary plus benefit levels five times greater than what the average American worker receives." [29] In fact, the Office of Management and Budget estimated that each 10 percent increase in top officials' pay in all three branches of government would cost American taxpayers $100 million, when increased life insurance, pensions, Social Security, and the costs of severance pay were considered.

Before leaving office in January 1989 President Reagan accepted the Quadrennial Commission's recommendations that executive, legislative, and judicial salaries be raised by 51 percent to make up for the cost of inflation since 1969. Since raising top executive branch salaries was once again tied to raising those of lawmakers, the increase was voted down in the eleventh hour by both houses of Congress. Consumer activist Ralph Nader led citizens from around the country in protesting the recommendations of the commission. Some lawmakers predicted an end to the Quadrennial Commission. Rep. Jim Slattery (D-Kan.) argued that relying on the commission was an "abdication by Congress" of the responsibility for setting executive, legislative, and judicial salaries.[30] The commission has made recommendations for pay raises six times in twenty years with increases going into effect three times.

Most White House aides and top executive branch officials indeed could make more money in private business, but there are other incentives for them to stay in public service. The fringe benefits of working in the White House are considerable. Chief White House aides rarely have to worry about fitting their travel plans to airline schedules. If the trip is considered important enough, there are several presidential planes always available. Often, presidential aides, cabinet members, and other top officials may be allowed to accompany the president on *Air Force One.* Most aides have limousine service and are delivered door to door, often in cars that have the presidential seal on their doors. White House staffers eat in the White House mess, which resembles a dining room in an exclusive men's club. Many carry beepers that allow the White House switchboard to get in touch with them at all times. Most carry business cards with "The White House" inscribed on them. And many may be called "The Honorable. . . ."

The distribution of perquisites to White House aides and top executive officials is uneven. That is, which White House officials get what perquisites is left up to the president and, therefore, varies from administration to administration. At the discretion of the president, the Military Office at the White House controls access to perquisites such as *Air Force One,* the Marine Corps Helicopter Squadron, Camp David, the presidential yachts (before Carter), the White House garage with its fleet of cars, the White House stewards, and the White House mess. Although these fringe benefits were meant for the comfort and convenience of the president, many staffers also have enjoyed these perquisites. Bill Gulley, former director of the Military Office, wrote, "The Military Office holds the White House perks, the status symbols, and staff members, high and low, devote more time and ingenuity to trying to get access to them than they do to high affairs of state. Literally. They impress the hell out of themselves and each other by getting the use of a White House car or a ride on *Air Force One.*" [31]

The demand for White House perquisites always has been high, and often abused. For example, not only did Nixon White House and executive branch officials enjoy the comfort and convenience of *Air Force One* on trips to San Clemente and Key Biscayne, but many Nixon staffers were able to arrange for their wives and children also to have access to *Air Force One* on these trips. During the Ford administration, Sheila Weidenfeld, press secretary for the first lady, continually badgered the Military Office for some of the same perquisites that the president's press secretary, Ron Nessen, enjoyed. These included a chauffeur-driven limousine and a ticker-tape machine.

Although most staffers seek them, presidents differ in their generosity in allocating White House perquisites. In the Nixon White House, Chief of Staff H. R. Haldeman played favorites, allowing certain staff members to enjoy perquisites that others could not. President Johnson enjoyed keeping a tight reign on White House perquisites. His administration kept a violation sheet to keep track of staff violations of the use of presidential planes, automobiles, Camp David, the yacht, the White House mess, and special telephones and radios. Once Secretary of Health, Education, and Welfare Joseph Califano had his driver drop his wife at the beauty shop. He was promptly called in and threatened with loss of his car privilege.

President Carter also was dedicated to not allowing his staff to take advantage of government-funded perquisites of office. When Carter's secretary of state, Cyrus Vance, was working abroad on peace negotiations between Israel and Egypt, he wanted to fly back to the United States for his son's college graduation. When it was suggested that it would be easier and quicker to fly Vance back by military aircraft, Carter said no and made him fly back by commercial airline. Still, there is some evidence Carter allowed a double standard to exist in his administration. According to Gulley, "Family, or those close to it, were allowed advantages others weren't. During the transition, before Carter was even inaugurated, his son Chip and wife Caron, and their dog, lived in a government owned house in Lafayette Square, across from the White House." [32]

Even though presidential perquisites have sometimes been abused by staff and family members, many of them are legitimate and serve the best interests of the president and the country. For example, presidents must carry certain aides on cross-country trips and, as a matter of expediency, these staff members get to enjoy the luxury and comfort of *Air Force One.*

The most important perquisite that comes from working with the president has not been mentioned. Not only are White House aides and executive-level staffers provided with the perquisites that go along with the presidency, but by their association with the president they also have the biggest psychological fringe benefit of all—clout.

The Federal Civil Service

The way presidents fill positions in the federal government has been a volatile issue throughout much of U.S. history. In the nineteenth century, most federal jobs were filled through *patronage*; that is, presidents awarded jobs to their supporters. Patronage, however, was a power shared with Congress. Although it had no constitutional mandate, Congress by the end of the nineteenth century was able to exert tremendous influence on presidential appointments.

Under the patronage system a widespread turnover in jobs occurred after almost every presidential election. Employees who were qualified for specific jobs but were not of the president's political party had trouble finding positions with the government. Today, however, only a small percentage of federal employees—usually top-ranking policy makers—are replaced with each new administration. Most jobs in the federal government are filled through the *competitive civil service* and are awarded according to the competence of the applicant.

By any standard, the federal government has grown extremely large and complex since its early days. As the United States matured and expanded, the executive branch in general—and the presidency in particular—also grew. As the presidency itself expanded, the president's role in dispensing federal jobs for political loyalty became increasingly controversial. The civil service has evolved in an attempt to place executive branch employees under a *merit system* of appointment, making the federal government less susceptible to political manipulation.

Growth in the number of federal employees remained low and relatively stable until the early part of the twentieth century. The population of the United States at the time of George Washington's presidency was about three and a half million, just a little more than the number of civilian federal employees in the late 1980s. At the beginning of Washington's administration, there were only nine federal employees in the State Department, fewer than 100 in the War Department, and only about 350 throughout the entire federal government. The largest department was the Post Office, with seventy-five offices throughout the new nation. At the beginning of the nineteenth century, the number of federal employees had increased to about 2,100. By the time of the Civil War the federal government employed approximately 49,000 people, or about two-tenths of the population of 31 million. By 1900 the federal civil service comprised only 208,000 employees, or less than 0.3 percent of the population.

When World War I broke out, however, the number of employees on the federal payroll began to expand more rapidly, reaching 515,000 by 1923. The years of the New Deal immediately following the Great Depression saw a tremendous amount of growth in federal employees, from 572,000 in 1933 to 920,000 in 1939. Federal workers constituted 0.7 percent of the population of 130 million in 1939. By the end of World War II the number of employees in the federal civil service reached an all-time high of 3.75 million. Even after the massive war effort ended and federal employment declined, the number of federal workers remained high. In fact, social scientist Bruce D. Porter has argued that it is precisely because of American involvement in World Wars I and II and in the Korean and Vietnam wars that the bureaucracy has expanded:

> The principal cause of the expansion of the United States government has been the nation's involvement in four foreign wars in the twentieth century. This is true for the entire executive branch, not just for the defense related sectors of the bureaucracy. Modern warfare requires national economic mobilization, and the non-defense bureaucracy must be enlarged to accomplish this task.... Following the wartime expansion of the bureaucracy, a "ratchet" effect comes into play and the bureaucracy retains much of its growth despite postwar layoffs. This "ratchet" effect occurs because Congress lacks the political will to force deep cutbacks.... Wartime gains in federal employment that are not trimmed within five years will generally become permanent.[33]

In 1988 the federal government comprised almost 3.1 million civilian employees, most working under some type of merit protection. *(See Table 3)*

The Growth of Merit

Under the present civil service system most jobs are awarded according to the abilities of the applicants. Throughout much of U.S. history, however, the president (with the influence of Congress) had wide latitude in deciding which job seeker received which job. Many positions were awarded through patronage, the decisions based on the "spoils system" (from the maxim "To the victor belong the spoils"). In other words, until relatively recently, most presidents were able to offer federal government jobs as a reward for loyalty. From the beginning, however, Congress increasingly has exerted its influence in the appointment process. It was impossible for presidential administrations to know all office seekers. Consequently, as early as John Adams's administration it was accepted practice to consult with Congress on federal appointments.

In his book *Democracy and the Public Service,* Frederick C. Mosher divides the history of the growth of the merit system into six distinct stages. Each of these stages reflects the values held by both the public and the president during the evolution of the federal civil service.[34]

Government by Gentlemen, 1789-1829

When George Washington became president in 1789, he had the opportunity to build an entirely new executive structure. The federal government under the Articles of Confederation had been small, and many government employees returned to private life when the new government was established. Washington was unique among U.S. presidents in that he had the chance to appoint a fresh slate of civil servants. Not surprisingly, many people attempted to influence his selection of employees. From the beginning of the nation's history, therefore, people seeking office for themselves or their friends tried to force their interests on the president.

In setting an early standard, Washington sought to nominate individuals to office on grounds of "fitness of character." He refused appointment even to many veterans of the Revolutionary War, arguing that such distinguished service did not outweigh the need for excellence in the job. Washington's primary consideration was competence. He did not allow kinship to be a reason for appointment.

Washington's idea of competence was not necessarily job related, however; that is, he did not always look for a person who possessed specific qualifications for a certain job. Instead, he was interested in the honesty and integrity of his appointees and in the loyalty of the individual to the new federal government. Technical expertise mattered much less than reputation. (Moreover, during this period of civil service history, few jobs required technical or specialized knowledge.) In creating this early form of merit, Washington also attempted to be conscious of equitable representation; that is, he made sure his principal appointments came from all regions of the country. Nonetheless, Washington appointed those who strongly supported the new federal form of government, creating a civil service that came from the elite of society—the well educated, well to do, and well respected.

As the first political parties began to develop in the

1790s, Washington began to make more partisan appointments. Early in his administration he had offered government positions to some Anti-Federalists (members of the opposition party); but as the parties grew stronger, he came under increasing pressure to appoint members of his own political party, the Federalists. Nonetheless, there is general agreement among historians that Washington took great effort to appoint a federal executive work force that exhibited a high degree of competence.

Adams's administration constituted a further step toward partisanship in the use of presidential appointments. Although Adams's conscience and personal honesty prevented him from using his patronage powers fully, his Federalist administration began increasingly to manipulate political appointments to maintain its partisan advantage. Civil service historian Paul P. Van Riper has written, "Adams normally tried to be above partisanship, but caught in the dilemma of conflict policies, his actions did not always match his ideals.... The trend was fairly clear. Appointments were more factional than under Washington."[35]

When Thomas Jefferson came into office, many expected him to expand the base of political appointments because Jefferson, as a Democratic-Republican, had a sincere commitment to broadening the democratic foundation of government. Upon assuming office he found that Federalists held nearly every government position. In a letter to a friend Jefferson complained: "If a due participation of office is a matter of right, how are vacancies to be obtained? Those by death are few; by resignation none. Can any other mode than that of removal be proposed?"[36] Believing that his presidential election victory in 1800 was a mandate for change, Jefferson set out to achieve what political scientist Herbert Kaufman describes as a "balance between Republicans and Federalists in the civil service corresponding to their proportionate shares in the general population, which, once achieved, would allow him to make appointments purely on the basis of honesty, ability, and loyalty to the constitution."[37]

Jefferson used a great deal of prudence in replacing employees. Although he did turn out some of the early Federalist appointees, he retained many more than he fired. During the course of his administration, however, Jefferson took the opportunity to fill many positions with Democratic-Republicans by either removing existing Federalist appointees or through attrition. By the end of his administration he had replaced almost half of the Senate-approved Federalist appointees. Significantly, he continued to fill vacancies in his administration with the elite of society.

During the twenty years after Jefferson's presidency the pattern of executive personnel appointments changed very little. Because presidents James Madison and James Monroe came from the same political party as Jefferson (the Democratic-Republicans), they found little reason to replace existing employees. And as a matter of integrity and conscience, the sixth president, John Quincy Adams, did not significantly alter the civil service. As a result, from 1803 to 1828 the makeup of the civil service changed little.

In this forty-year period most government employees were hired from a "patronage of the elite." They were generally white, male, and from the upper class. This system of political appointment was initiated by Washington and practiced by both the Federalists and the Democratic-Republicans. It became the standard for this period—a pattern of filling positions on the basis of both character and competence.

Table 3 Civilian Employees, Executive Branch, 1818-1988

Year	Number of employees	Year	Number of employees
1818	4,837	1959	2,382,804
1821	6,914	1960	2,398,704
1831	11,491	1961	2,435,804
1841	18,038	1962	2,514,197
1851	26,274	1963	2,527,960
1861	36,672	1964	2,500,503
1871	51,020	1965	2,527,915
1881	100,020	1966	2,759,019
1891	157,442	1967	3,002,461
1901	239,476	1968	3,055,212
1911	395,905	1969	3,076,414
1921	561,142	1970	2,981,574
1931	609,746	1971	2,860,000
1941	1,437,682	1972	2,815,000
1942	2,296,384	1973	2,788,000
1943	3,299,414	1974	2,866,000
1944	3,332,356	1975	2,857,000
1945	3,816,310	1976	2,842,000
1946	2,696,529	1977	2,848,000
1947	2,111,011	1978	2,855,000
1948	2,071,009	1979	2,869,000
1949	2,102,109	1980	2,847,000
1950	1,960,708	1981	2,800,000
1951	2,482,666	1982	2,760,000
1952	2,600,612	1983	2,722,000
1953	2,558,416	1984	2,758,000
1954	2,407,676	1985	2,775,000
1955	2,397,309	1986	2,785,000
1956	2,398,736	1987	3,017,967
1957	2,417,565	1988	3,054,378
1958	2,382,491		

Source: Historical Statistics, Colonial Times to 1970 (Washington, D.C.: Census Bureau, 1976); *Statistical Abstract of the United States* (Washington, D.C.: Census Bureau, 1981); *Budget of the United States, FY 86;* Office of Personnel Management, 1987, 1988.

Government by the Common Man, 1829-1883

Andrew Jackson's inauguration as president in 1829 pushed the civil service into a new era. Although many people attribute the spoils system and its bleak consequences to Jackson, it is probably more accurate to say that Jackson's actions reflected his desire to democratize the American public service rather than a lack of commitment to the merit system. Whatever his intentions, he nonetheless was one of the most outspoken early American defenders of the spoils system.

In running for the presidency in 1828, Jackson appealed to many propertyless voters who recently had won the vote when property ownership was abolished as a voting requirement. Jackson promised civil service "reform" and stated that he would appoint "men whose diligence and talents will insure in their respective stations able and faithful cooperation."[38] And in his inaugural address, Jackson defended the practice of rotating federal employees in government jobs because, he said, the duties of public offices did not require any special abilities. Furthermore, he argued that no one had any intrinsic right to an official position.

Since Jackson had campaigned on a theme of reform, he felt the American people had voted for change when they elected him, and he did not intend to disappoint them. He instituted a large-scale system of spoils. Those who came from his own political party were awarded jobs. In this respect, Jackson's concern for competence was not as strong as his concern for loyalty.

Jackson is identified with the spoils system more because of what he said than what he did. The term *spoils system* did get its name during Jackson's administration, but not from Jackson. Sen. William L. Marcy of New York popularized the term in 1932 when he remarked that politicians "see nothing wrong in the rule, that to the victor belong the spoils of the enemy." Yet Jackson, under his method of dispensing spoils, removed only a few more persons from office than his predecessors had. He replaced 90 percent of the previous administration's top executive officers; Jefferson had replaced 80 percent. During his full eight years in office Jackson removed from the entire federal work force only about one employee in five.

Just as Washington's initial system of hiring the competent elite had set a pattern for other administrations to follow, so did Jackson's egalitarian philosophy. Jackson's public advocacy of the spoils system made it easier for subsequent presidents to manipulate patronage to strengthen their political parties and gain congressional support for their programs. By appointing the friends and patrons of various members of Congress, presidents were able to trade patronage for congressional votes. Even though the opposition party Whigs were extremely critical of the way Jackson and his successor, Martin Van Buren, used the appointment power, they nonetheless employed the same tactics—although not to the same degree. Whig party workers wanted political jobs just as much as the Jacksonian Democrats had. When William Henry Harrison, a Whig, assumed office in 1841, he faced the demands of an estimated thirty to forty thousand office seekers. However, in the Harrison administration fewer of the old employees were removed, and more of the new employees were from the upper class.

This pattern of removal and appointment of federal employees continued under succeeding presidents. As Kaufman has noted, up to the mid-1850s "every four years, with the regularity of tides, the civil service was swept nearly bare and restaffed." [39] The spoils system reached its peak during Abraham Lincoln's presidency. In 1861 in an effort to consolidate the federal government behind his program and the war effort, Lincoln made a more thorough house cleaning of federal employees than any president before him. In the higher levels of his administration, he replaced the employees in nearly every position with members of his party. Lincoln's use of patronage was not without purpose, however, for through it he skillfully won cooperation and concessions from a predominantly Republican Congress in managing the Civil War.

Although Jackson's open support of the spoils system had drawn widespread public attention, the subsequent problems and misbehavior of patronage appointees in the administrations of Andrew Johnson and Ulysses S. Grant attracted even more attention to the procedure. There is no real evidence that corruption in the civil service increased during and following Jackson's presidency, but the press certainly began to pay more attention to corruption and to the problems of the spoils system by the late 1860s. Van Riper has suggested that reform of the patronage system became part of a larger reform movement: "Not until the late eighteen sixties did reform become more than a dream. Then the powerful energies and ideals of the Anti-Slavery Society and similar organizations of the forties and fifties took up the cudgels. As the sixties moved into the seventies, civil service reform and its new generation of champions, along with other reform movements involving such things as money and the tariff, slowly but surely came to occupy a prominent place among the current political issue." [40] Consequently, civil service reform became a popular concern among legislators and critics.

By the time Ulysses S. Grant became president in 1869, a great deal of public disapproval surrounded the spoils system. In fact, the corrupt Grant administration did much to contribute to this public dissatisfaction. During Grant's presidency several top officials were found to be involved in various scandals, including kickbacks, land speculation, fraud, embezzlement, and tax evasion. Reformers argued that all of these problems could be traced directly to the spoils system. True or not, this argument gave conviction and determination to the reform movement beginning to take shape.

Ironically, one of the first attempts at reforming the spoils system occurred during the Grant administration. In 1871, President Grant sought relief from continuing and increasing pressure to appoint more of his supporters and successfully pushed Congress to pass a "rider" (a nongermane amendment) to an appropriations bill that would establish a system to promote efficiency and to determine the fitness of candidates for public service. Under the authority of this law, Grant appointed the first U.S. Civil Service Commission, consisting of seven members, three of which were full-time federal employees. In 1872, the Civil Service Commission conducted the first competitive examinations for entry into the federal work force. In the following year, however, because President Grant continued to give in to the pressure of patronage and ignored the work of his own creation, Congress refused to continue funding the commission's work, and this first effort at reform was aborted in 1875.

Calls for civil service reform continued to be heard in Washington. President Rutherford B. Hayes, who succeeded Grant in 1877 and had campaigned on a reform in government Republican party platform, also tried to promote a system of merit appointment. But because of opposition from the more conservative elements in his own party he, too, was unsuccessful. Hayes, like Grant, continued to use civil service appointments as a means of rewarding those who had helped him reach the presidency. By the late 1870s, several civil service reform associations had sprung up throughout the country. The first of these was the New York Civil Service Reform Association, founded in 1877. By 1881 the thirteen existing state reform associations merged to form the National Civil Service Reform League. Carefully judging the climate of opinion as not favorable to massive changes, the league pushed for very modest goals. The reformers were interested primarily in instituting minimal examinations for entry into some federal clerical jobs, limiting the president's ability to remove officeholders for political reasons, and prohibiting the custom of assessing party contributions on officeholders. Reformers remained unsuccessful in reaching any of these goals until Congress and the public were convinced that they were needed.

One small triumph for the reformers resulted from an

assistant noted the reality of vice-presidential privileges: "It used to take an act of Congress to get us into the White House. We had to get cleared in by somebody because we didn't have White House passes.... We were treated like little children, allowed to look but not to touch.... We didn't have any symbols of power and that was currency in the White House." [21] In contrast, both Mondale and Bush found that their counsel was consistently sought and their positions recognized through the granting of White House fringe benefits.

The Garfield Assassination. Significant civil service reform did not occur, however, until after the assassination of President James A. Garfield. As a member of the House of Representatives, Garfield had supported civil service reform, so when he became president in 1881, reformers had high expectations that he would quickly institute meaningful changes in the system. But Garfield did not initiate reform immediately; the new president instead spent much of his time trying to satisfy literally thousands of demands for federal jobs by party workers who had helped him in the election. It is estimated that for every appointment Garfield was able to make, twenty office seekers were turned down. Among those who did not receive an appointment was Charles J. Guiteau who on July 2, 1881, shot Garfield in a Washington railroad station. After suffering for eleven weeks, Garfield died on September 19, 1881. Many saw the spoils system as the cause of his death. In 1880, Guiteau, a member of the Stalwart faction of the Republican party, had supported the nomination of Grant to a third presidential term. When the nomination went instead to Garfield, the Republicans nominated Arthur, a Stalwart, for the vice presidency. Guiteau switched allegiances, worked for Garfield's election, and after the election moved to Washington expecting a position in Garfield's administration. Looking for an appointment as a consul to Paris, Guiteau waited around the halls of the State Department and the White House and sent numerous letters to Garfield. Finally, in May 1881, he was met in the hall of the White House by Secretary of State James G. Blaine who told Guiteau never to bother him again about the Paris consulship. Depressed and unemployed, Guiteau decided to remove Garfield from the presidency and make way for Vice President Arthur to become president. When seized after shooting Garfield, Guiteau shouted, "I am a Stalwart; now Arthur is president!" The implication was that, with a member of his faction of the party in the White House, he would now get a federal job. At his trial Guiteau requested that all who had benefited politically from Garfield's assassination contribute to his defense fund.

Garfield's death provided the final impetus for civil service reform. Newspapers ran numerous editorials deploring Guiteau's actions and the spoils system in general. President Arthur himself began to support reform measures. Ironically, Garfield's greatest achievement as president may have been the results of his death. His assassination shocked the nation into taking action to eliminate abuses in the federal hiring system. As political scientist Robert S. Lorch has observed, "The bullet that killed Garfield also killed the federal spoils system." [41]

Civil Service Act of 1883. Meaningful civil service reform finally came on January 16, 1883, when President Arthur signed into law the Civil Service Act of 1883 (the Pendleton Act). *(See box, The Civil Service Act of 1883, p. 850)*. This act had been introduced in Congress by Sen. George H. Pendleton in 1880, but it was not until after Garfield's death that it finally gained enough momentum to become law. Inspired by the British civil service system, the reformers believed that power to make political appointments had to be transferred from the president to a nonpolitical, neutral agency. Entitled "An Act to Regulate and Improve the Civil Service of the United States," the Pendleton Act created a bipartisan commission of three members to help the president make rules for filling government positions. The act required that government employees be chosen "from among those graded highest" in competitive examinations. In addition, it prohibited assessments of federal employees for money to help party candidates.

Even though the Civil Service Act created a new system of appointing federal officeholders based on an equal chance for all to compete in job-related skills, the act did not immediately end the massive turnover of personnel at the end of each presidential administration. In fact, the act initially affected only about fourteen thousand positions, or about 10.5 percent of federal employees. Under the provisions of the act, however, the president could issue an executive order extending the coverage to other appointees. As succeeding presidents exercised their option to extend merit coverage, almost all federal employees eventually came under a merit system.

Government by the Good, 1883-1906

The passage of the Civil Service Act in 1883 brought about a new era in the administration of civil service jobs. It did not effect a complete change in the way that presidential appointments were made, but it did signal the beginning of a change in direction. The Civil Service Act actually built upon the tradition of egalitarianism and equal opportunity that prevailed during the earlier period of public employment. In other words, the authors of the act did not abandon the Jacksonian belief in widespread access to jobs in the federal administrative structure. Instead, they provided for "practical" entrance tests that would ensure that the applicants would be able to do their jobs. The framers of the act had no intention of filling federal positions with an "administrative class" educated to administer the government permanently.

The Civil Service Act placed the Civil Service Commission within the executive branch. Specifically, the act allowed the president to use the commission to make rules and regulations governing the selection of personnel to fill executive positions. The president, with the advice and consent of the Senate, appointed the three-member commission. Not more than two members of the commission could be from the same political party. This rule ensured a certain amount of neutrality on the Civil Service Commission, although it was a part of the executive branch. The effect of the act, Kaufman maintains, was "to substitute the Commission for Congressional and party officials in providing appointment advice to the President and his department heads." [42] The act did not eliminate presidential influence on appointments covered by the Civil Service Act altogether. The presidents had influence on the commission itself just by their power to appoint and remove commission members. It was hoped, though, that the members of the commission would raise a loud enough public cry to embarrass any president who tried to bypass their efforts.

Although the framers of the act were sincere in their

Frank Leslie's Illustrated Newspaper, July 16, 1881; Library of Congress

Charles Guiteau, a disgruntled office seeker, is arrested on July 2, 1881, after shooting President Garfield. As one political scientist has observed, "The bullet that killed Garfield also killed the federal spoils system."

desire to provide an effective mechanism for civil service reform, they initially failed to provide sufficient funding for the commission. They gave very little consideration to funding a staff for the three commissioners apart from the secretary, stenographer, messenger, and chief examiner provided for in the act. By omitting provisions for any further staffing, the act implied that employees of other federal agencies would perform many of the duties of the commission. Through the years this dependency on other agencies threatened to compromise the commission's neutrality. By 1890, the commission, dissatisfied with its lack of personnel, began to submit requests for an expanded staff.

The merit system under the new Civil Service Commission experienced slow but steady growth. In an effort to reduce the remaining effects of patronage, reformers put pressure on presidents and Congress to bring as many federal employees as possible under the jurisdiction of the commission. Although they faced a real challenge in increasing the number of employees in the competitive system, the reformers were generally successful. A major obstacle was persuading presidents to increase equitably the number of employees in the "classified civil service," that is, federal jobs that can be entered only by competitive examinations. The Pendleton Act originally placed only clerical and technical employees under the protection of the civil service. As subsequent presidents increased the number of positions to be classified as civil service positions, they tended not only to increase the number of clerical positions under civil service but also to place more and more policy-making positions under civil service shortly before they left office. Since only new appointees had to take examinations, these presidents were able to "blanket in" their supporters.

When Grover Cleveland became president he attempted to change the balance of federal workers to favor Democrats by firing Republicans, but made no effort to jeopardize the 10 percent of federal positions that were already classified. Only upon leaving office did he extend classification to positions that had not been competitive previously. This extension not only broadened the merit system but also blanketed in Cleveland's political appointments, ensuring that whole agencies would be staffed with Democrats for some time to come. Cleveland's appointees were political; that is, they had not been required to take competitive examinations. Their successors, however, would have to take examinations.

When Benjamin Harrison assumed the presidency, he followed Cleveland's pattern by firing many opposition party federal workers, hiring members of his own party, and blanketing in many of his party before leaving office. He dismissed more than thirty-five thousand employees in the first year of his administration alone, appointing replacements from the Republican party.

In 1893, when Cleveland became president for the second time, he once again appointed mostly partisans to fill executive offices. In 1896, at the end of his administration, he again blanketed in a large number of his appointees by increasing the classified civil service, this time by a full one-third. This extension brought to 85,000 the total number of competitive positions out of 205,000 in the entire civil service. Cleveland and Harrison had established a pattern of increasing the classified civil service, but at the same time protecting their own political employees. Patronage and merit had merged.

Even though many political employees were protected in their jobs through classification, the number of positions under the merit system increased through this process. By 1897, the newly inaugurated president, William McKinley, had the smallest percentage of patronage jobs to offer of any president before or since. Some Republicans suggested that positions placed under the merit system by Cleveland be made political appointments again. Many new, unclassified jobs became available, however, because of an enlarged federal civil service that developed to conduct the Spanish-American War. This increase allowed McKinley to make many political appointments without taking many positions out of the classified category. McKinley's complaint

The Civil Service Act of 1883

With the passage of the Civil Service Act of 1883 (Pendleton Act), the executive branch experienced its most dramatic restructuring since George Washington set up the first federal bureaucracy. Known as the Magna Carta of civil service reform, the act is the basis of the federal personnel system today. The Pendleton Act comprised seven main provisions:

1. It created a bipartisan Civil Service Commission of three members appointed by the president with the consent of the Senate. Members were subject to removal by the president at any time.
2. It created the Civil Service Commission to help the president by preparing rules for the management of the competitive civil service, consisting of those federal employees who were under the rules and regulations of the commission.
3. It allowed the president by executive order to bring positions into the competitive service that had previously been outside. It also allowed the president to remove any positions at any time from the competitive service.
4. It based entrance into the merit system on competitive examination.
5. It provided that examinations should test the practical skills required to do the job.
6. It allowed applicants, regardless of age, to enter into the competitive civil service at any rank or grade for which they were qualified.
7. It provided that competitive civil service employees could not be removed for refusing to contribute money or services to a political party.

that too many jobs had been classified during Cleveland's tenure led the Senate to conduct an investigation, after which it recommended that a substantial number of jobs be unclassified. Consequently, political pressures forced McKinley to remove more than nine thousand from the competitive service in 1899.

Several important civil service advances occurred during this period. McKinley strengthened the position of the competitive services by weakening the potential for political removals. He ordered that classified employees not be removed from office unless they had been given sufficient written notice of the charges against them and a chance to respond in writing to the accusations. In addition, McKinley, bowing to partisan Republican pressures for jobs, increased the number of competitive employees by blanketing in over nineteen thousand positions. This increase brought the total number of federal employees covered by civil service to 41 percent. McKinley also extended the merit system to the newly acquired territories. "In the contest between spoils and merit," Kaufman has stated, "merit pushed steadily ahead." [43]

Theodore Roosevelt played a significant role in the growth of the merit system during this period. President Harrison's appointment of Roosevelt as chairman of the Civil Service Commission in 1889 began a period of innovation and expansion for the merit service during which Roosevelt made major changes. He introduced a promotion system based on the efficiency records of the individual employee, instituted a program that systematized the hiring of workers in the Navy yards, and successfully classified the Indian service, which had suffered through many patronage-related scandals.

After he became president in 1901, Roosevelt continued to be a friend to the merit system. He blanketed into the classified services an additional thirty-five thousand jobs while he was president, making almost 64 percent of federal jobs merit positions. And since he was a Republican who succeeded a Republican, he felt no need to remove vast numbers of federal employees from office because of their political affiliations. Roosevelt therefore was able to effect many civil service improvements without the pressure and demands of patronage. In addition, he made procedural reforms that further strengthened the Civil Service Commission and its overall position within the federal system. Specifically, he defined the principles of removal by specifying the reasons for which an employee might be fired.

The main emphasis during this period was neutrality. The framers of the Civil Service Act and civil service reformers believed that the proper administration of government lay outside the sphere of politics. They felt that the administration of public duties should be apolitical; that is, it should not be manipulated by the partisan politics of either the White House or Congress. Consequently, reformers desired that the Civil Service Commission be politically independent of both. At first, the commission did little more than screen applicants. Later, especially under the presidency of Roosevelt and with the advantage of greater funding, it began to play an increasingly important role in a broader range of personnel policy decisions. The main concern of the commission was to end corruption in the hiring practices of federal agencies. The power of political appointment—previously a common practice among presidents—came to be equated with corruption.

At all levels of government, morality became an increasingly important consideration in appointments for public service, and state and local governments came to regard the Civil Service Commission as a model of political neutrality for the management of personnel. The commission provided the buffer between the politics of the White House and of Congress and the appointment of federal employees. One way it did so was through its use of the "rule of three." Originally established under the Pendleton Act, the rule required that the commission provide a list of the three best-qualified candidates for a job and that the executive branch appoint one of these three. Because the commission could not make the actual choices but only offered advice in the form of a list of candidates, the rule ensured the commission's neutrality. The rule of three was passed on to state and local civil service organizations and became accepted practice to ensure the independence of their commissions as well.

Government by the Efficient, 1906-1937

Neutrality and morality were important considerations also during the fourth period of personnel administration, but efficiency became a significant concern as well. The principle of the separation of politics and personnel administration continued to be of primary importance, but a desire on the part of reformers to make government as efficient as possible exerted increasing influence. This desire stemmed mainly from developments in business administration, dominated during this period by the scientific management school. The main value of scientific management was efficiency, or doing the job with the least resources. According to political scientist Nicholas Henry, during this period efficiency became sufficiently integrated with the concept of neutrality to produce "a somewhat inconsistent but soothing amalgam of beliefs ... that packed goodness, merit, morality, neutrality, and science into one conceptual lump." [44]

Specifically, during this stage in the development of the federal merit system the Civil Service Commission concentrated on classifying jobs that had a logical relationship to one another and on developing job descriptions for each position. In 1923, Congress passed the Classification Act, which guaranteed the principle of equal pay for equal work. This act allowed jobs to be defined by the responsibilities and qualifications necessary to carry them out. Also, the classification of positions made it possible for examinations to measure objectively the qualifications for a particular position. Merit was no longer based on the qualifications of honesty and general education but on an applicant's ability to perform a set of tasks well.

The overall effect of scientific management theory during this period was to depersonalize the civil service. Examinations were more objective as were several other aspects of the federal personnel system. Training personnel in the specific knowledge and skills of a set of job classifications became an important function of the civil service. Also, efficiency ratings came into use as a better way to supervise and promote workers objectively. Central to all of these advancements was the new system of classifying jobs according to content and requirements, which made it possible to be more objective about examining, training, and rating the performance of employees. This method of classification significantly reduced the president's direct influence in naming specific persons to federal jobs. And as succeeding presidents placed more and more jobs under the protection of civil service, partisan patronage continued to diminish.

Generally, presidents during this period treated the classified civil service favorably. Republican presidents had controlled the office for twelve years by the time another Republican, William Howard Taft, succeeded Theodore Roosevelt in 1909. He therefore was not inclined to effect large-scale turnover in positions that had not yet been classified. He added thirty-nine thousand positions to the classified service and vetoed a bill to limit the amount of time one could spend in the civil service to seven years. This bill would have reduced the overall level of experience in the civil service.

When Democratic president Woodrow Wilson took office in 1913 after sixteen years of Republican control, he faced tremendous pressure to clean house. The Democratic party pushed for opportunities for patronage, and Wilson's supporters descended on Washington much as other job seekers had in previous years. Wilson acceded to some of the demands and exempted eight thousand internal revenue deputy collectors from the classified service. But he opposed other attempts to increase patronage and actually contributed to the growth of the merit system. Before his election Wilson had been an enthusiastic supporter of civil service reform, serving as vice president of the National Civil Service Reform Association. As president he introduced several reform measures to make the civil service more objective. Perhaps his greatest contribution was withstanding pressure from his party to take partisan advantage of World War I. As the war began to occupy more of the federal government's resources and energy, new agencies developed, and the number of federal employees increased. Resisting pressure to make these patronage positions, Wilson placed most of the new positions in the competitive service.

Warren G. Harding, a Republican, confronted many of the same pressures Wilson had faced in succeeding a president of the opposing party. The Republicans were as hungry for patronage after eight years of Democratic party control of the White House as the Democrats had been after the Republicans' sixteen years. Harding, however, was in a much more difficult position than Wilson. As the war machinery demobilized and there was no longer the need for as large a federal civil service, it became extremely difficult to satisfy Republican party office seekers. As a result, Harding reversed some of the earlier reforms, exercising a small measure of patronage by dismissing some employees for rather peculiar reasons. In early 1922, for example, President Harding by executive order dismissed thirty-one employees in the Bureau of Printing and Engraving for reasons "of the service" and even abolished the positions themselves, later creating new positions and filling them with his own appointees.[45] Kaufman concluded that "the merit system did well to hold its own ground in this period." [46]

Presidents Calvin Coolidge and Herbert Hoover treated the merit system more favorably. Together they classified about thirteen thousand positions during their tenures in office. More significantly, they were both committed to the concept of a competent and efficiently run government and thus did not allow the reduction of the federal work force caused by the end of World War I to be accompanied by a corresponding reduction of the classified civil service. As a result, the percentage of classified jobs in relation to the entire number of federal jobs amounted to about 80 percent by 1924. Even though the civil service began to grow again by the end of the 1920s, enough of the new positions had been classified that by the end of Hoover's administration the percentage of merit employees remained approximately the same.

When Franklin D. Roosevelt became president in 1933, he faced some of the same demands for patronage as earlier presidents had. Once again Democrats were eager for patronage jobs after twelve years of Republican control of the White House. This time the Depression compounded the pressure for political appointments. With the unusual lack of private sector jobs, the prospect of public employment was especially appealing to Democratic party loyalists. The stability of the merit system, and what were regarded as outstanding benefits, such as sick leave, retirement pensions, and paid vacations, made it especially attractive to those seeking employment of any kind. In the face of this challenge, the future of the merit system seemed uncertain.

But as before when under pressure, the merit system survived the demands placed upon it. Confronted with the economic disasters of the depression, Roosevelt inaugurated the most extensive peacetime program of public employment the country had ever known. Countless agencies, all needing staff, were created to handle the problems of the depression. Through these agencies Roosevelt was able to undertake programs he judged indispensable for the well-being of the nation. At the same time, by not placing these new jobs under the authority of the Civil Service Commission, he was able to provide patronage positions to Democratic party workers, an opportunity he would not have had otherwise. Without removing positions from the classified service, he satisfied the pressure from his party for patronage. Because the federal government expanded dramatically, the percentage of jobs in the classified civil service was reduced temporarily to less than 61 percent in 1936. But this expansion laid the foundation for further growth in the merit system during the later years of the Roosevelt administration when many of these new positions were eventually classified under civil service.

Government by Administrators, 1937-1955

By 1937 the civil service had noticeably shifted its emphasis from efficiency to what Mosher labels "administration." This shift resulted from the depression and from Roosevelt's attempts to solve the resulting problems of society and the economy. As the government grew larger in its efforts to solve these problems, there was more need for a strong and active administration. And as government assumed a more active role, public administrators (that is, civil servants) found themselves more involved in establishing policy. Proper management of federal programs became a political objective in that many felt that the purposes of the programs were political. No longer was efficiency the primary consideration. Many now viewed politics as an essential element of the administration of the New Deal programs. Mosher has written, "More important than efficiency in carrying out given tasks were initiative, imagination, and energy in the pursuit of public purposes." Furthermore, those purposes were viewed as political, and "administrators charged with responsibility for them ... had to be politically sensitive and knowledgeable."[47]

Two major reports prepared for two different presidents mark the beginning and end of this period. The first was the Brownlow Report, named after Louis Brownlow, chairman of President Roosevelt's Committee on Administrative Management. The second was prepared for President Dwight D. Eisenhower.

In 1937 the Brownlow Commission called on the president to accept greater responsibility and authority in conducting the affairs of the executive branch. The commission interpreted executive power to include administrative power, which meant that the president should be involved in both the discharging of existing policies and the initiative for creating new policies. Specifically, the commission called for the extension of the merit system "upward, outward, and downward." And it was critical of the Civil Service Commission's policy of encouraging a narrow, specialized federal work force; it called instead for the hiring of administrators with broad, general skills. Overall, the aim of the Brownlow Report was to centralize the powers and responsibilities of the president, blurring the distinction between politics and administration that had previously been established by reformers most concerned with efficiency and the elimination of patronage.

President Roosevelt responded to the Brownlow Report in several ways. He began to take a more active role in the day-to-day administration of the federal bureaucracy, personally attending to such matters as directing the bureaucracy and defining more precisely the lines of authority. The effect of these reforms was to show that the administration of executive personnel was a function of the president's responsibility as chief administrator. Ultimately, the effect was to blend politics and administration through the president's personal involvement.

The classified service continued to grow from 1937 to 1945. After President Roosevelt's initial problems of providing patronage to his Democratic supporters, the number of classified positions in the merit system soared to new heights. It became apparent to Roosevelt's administration that the complete success of New Deal programs depended upon their efficient administration. As the public began to rely more and more on relief programs, it also became concerned with their administration. As a result, interest in civil service reform increased. During World War II the whole federal government had to mobilize, so figures from this period are distorted; but by 1948, 83.7 percent of all civil service employees were in classified positions. Roosevelt's extension of merit had a twofold purpose, however. Not only did he attempt to increase the efficient administration of New Deal programs by putting a large number of positions in the protected category, but by doing so, he also intentionally blanketed in thousands of Democrats who had been placed in their jobs through patronage. Roosevelt's moves caused Republicans a great deal of concern. If they opposed him, they would open themselves to the charge of opposing the merit system itself. Their only option was to wait for a new Republican administration and face the problem then.

As more FDR Democrats were blanketed in, many reformers began to be concerned that the principle of political neutrality would be violated. Since the majority of those who worked in federal agencies owed their jobs to FDR and the Democratic party, it seemed normal for them to campaign for the Democratic party. And most Democrats did not object. In the election of 1938, however, a coalition of Republicans and conservative Democrats seized control of Congress and passed the Political Activities Act of 1939, known as the Hatch Act.

The original Hatch Act prohibited federal workers from taking an active role in the political management of campaigns. Federal workers could vote, attend political rallies, and talk privately about politics. But they were prohibited from participating in partisan voter registration drives, endorsing candidates, or working for or against a candidate in any way. In addition, the Hatch Act makes illegal the use of rank to force federal employees to support certain candidates or to make political contributions. The courts resisted attempts to weaken the Hatch Act, reaffirming the desire to have a nonpartisan federal civil service. Many government employees and legislators believed, however, that restrictions on political activity by federal employees could be eased without undermining the protections against using force or coercion by supervisors. In late 1987, Congress passed legislation that lifted restrictions on political activities by federal employees. Federal employees can now use their off-duty hours to run for office, manage campaigns, and solicit contributions.

When Truman became president in 1948, he faced very little demand for patronage jobs; the Democrats had been in control of the executive branch since 1933. Between 1946 and 1951 Truman blanketed in another thirty-five thousand jobs, bringing the percentage of the classified service to 87 percent. Even though the percentage went down during the Korean War as emergency agencies were created to handle the pressures of the war, it once again climbed to the pre-war figure as more wartime related jobs were classified.

Not surprisingly, Republican president Dwight D. Eisenhower also faced patronage problems when he took office in 1953, for the presidency had been controlled by Democrats since 1933. No president since McKinley had as few patronage positions to distribute as he did, and never before had so many workers from the opposition party been locked into their jobs. Many Republicans wanted government jobs, yet very few jobs were available. Eisenhower ultimately resorted to a technique used many times by presidents before him. He declassified a large number of jobs that had originally been filled on a noncompetitive basis and put under merit protection. Since previous Democratic administrations had blanketed in so many positions that only about 15,000 positions were immediately open to removal for political purposes, the Eisenhower administration felt justified in declassifying some. On March 31, 1953, Eisenhower canceled removal protection for 134,000 full-time positions. Half of this number, however, retained removal protection through the Veteran's Preference Act of 1944, and 68,000 were positions overseas not usually subject to patronage. Van Riper estimated that all in all only about 30,000 positions were affected.[48] Although he did not engage in a wholesale housecleaning, Eisenhower's declassifications were a setback for the merit system and caused debate among reformers.

The second major report of this period was prepared by President Eisenhower's Commission on Organization of the Executive Branch of Government, chaired by former president Hoover and known as the Hoover Commission. This commission was to look at administrative problems unique to the transition of presidential power from Truman to Eisenhower. The federal government had grown tremendously between 1933—when Hoover, the last Republican president, left office—and 1953, the year Eisenhower was inaugurated. After twenty years of Democratic domination, few Republicans had experience in federal government.

Further confusing matters for Republicans was that Democrats held many of the important policy positions, and they were protected from dismissal by civil service regulations on neutrality. Thus, Eisenhower's transition to power was complicated by the problem of making a largely Democratic federal bureaucracy responsive to the policies of a new Republican administration. Conflicts existed between political appointees and career employees, or those whose activities the new political appointees would oversee. Many newcomers doubted that career officers would change their goals for the new administration. Mosher writes, "Some feared, and may have even experienced, sabotage in the carrying out of the changed policies." The administration recognized that "some protected civil servants were in positions which could influence effective public policy."[49]

In an early attempt to ensure that the bureaucracy's goals were the same as those of his administration, Eisenhower created a section of the federal service called "Schedule C" by executive order on March 31, 1953. Schedule C was composed of fifteen hundred confidential or policy-determining positions, which for political reasons Eisenhower and the Civil Service Commission felt should be exempt from merit testing and qualifications and made subject to direct appointment by the president. Since 1953, when top-level aides and assistants and the confidential secretaries to these officials were exempted, the House Post Office and Civil Service Committee occasionally has published a listing of Schedule C appointments, known among Washingtonians as the "plum book." Although the move was controversial because it involved Eisenhower's attempt to gain control of the federal bureaucracy by staffing it with his own appointees, it nonetheless was considered a reasonable effort at defining the relationship between an administration's chief policy makers and career bureaucrats.

In 1955, after two years of deliberation, the Hoover Commission delivered its report, including a sweeping analysis of the relations between political appointees and career administrators. One of the specific recommendations for smoothing relations between these two groups was the creation of a "Senior Civil Service." The Senior Civil Service would comprise politically neutral employees with particular skills and competencies who could be transferred to similar jobs in different agencies. The creation of a Senior Civil Service would place more importance on ability than on the specific requirements of a position. Although this recommendation was not incorporated into the civil service, the Hoover Commission did spawn the modern idea that civil service employees should be capable of being transferred from one agency to another. In addition, the commission's suggestion of a Senior Civil Service generally endorsed the distinction between career bureaucrats and political employees made by the Eisenhower administration's creation of Schedule C.

Schedule C epitomized this period. It answered the complaints of the Eisenhower administration about executive control of the bureaucracy. As the Brownlow Report and the Hoover Report pointed out, the need existed for presidents to exert more control over the bureaucracy. Consequently, administration became a more important part of the chief executive's duties. Thus, centralization of power in the president and the emergence of a new genre of civil servants were trademarks of this period. Both innovations allowed the president to take a more active role in managing the federal bureaucracy.

Government by Professionals, 1955 to the Present

In 1955 the civil service started requiring applicants to take the Federal Service Entrance Exam (FSEE). This exam had several important objectives. First, it served as a single point of entry to the civil service system. Applicants could take a standard examination that could be used as a core of information for personnel decisions. Second, the common entrance examination made it easier to move employees from one agency to another. As long as each agency had its own entrance qualifications and examinations, it was difficult to foster an environment where broad, general skills were encouraged. Third, the FSEE made recruiting more efficient. Recruiters from the Civil Service Commission could visit college and university campuses and offer potential applicants a standardized examination that required no special skills to take.

By placing a premium on professional skills, the FSEE marked another change in emphasis in the federal civil service. Professionalism became a major concern among reformers who desired that the civil service be run as effectively as possible. As professionalism increased in the business community, so too did it grow in the federal government. Consequently, since 1955 the federal government has hired more professionally trained personnel than ever before—military officers who have entered the civil service, those who have trained to become Foreign Service officers, civil engineers, physicians, educators, lawyers, foresters, and scientists from almost all disciplines.

In addition, several new professions centered on government service have developed during this period, including penologists, recreation specialists, environmental specialists, public health professionals, and employment security officers.

Professionalism has had broad implications for the civil service. According to political scientist George J. Gordon, it has caused the civil service to shift its emphasis from the job itself to the people filling the job.

Previously, reformers expended much effort to create a system of administrative positions classified into categories of functions and responsibilities, which were logically related to one another and to develop the mechanisms—such as competitive examinations—necessary to fill those jobs through merit (that is, through job competence). Since 1955, professionalism, and its emphasis on the career needs of people filling government positions, challenges the egalitarian tradition of the merit system.[50]

Professionalism nurtures a career-oriented system that tends to be elitist since it places a greater emphasis on the person than on the position. Henry has drawn a distinction between the civil service system and the "career system": "where what one does in a job is of paramount importance in the civil service system, how one does it is of major significance in the career system." Furthermore, "where neutral and autonomous control of the entire public personnel system is valued by the civil service system, planned and autonomous control of the individual professional is the concern of the career system."[51] This means that, as of the 1980s, the traditional position-oriented civil service was being challenged by a growing trend among federal government employers that emphasized professional methods and standards of behavior over merit and autonomy. In other words, the trend among federal employees is to look not at the civil service job but at the specific profession of the employee. For example, since the 1960s federal agencies have increasingly begun to rely on graduates from exclusively governmental programs in higher education, such as criminal justice and public administration, to fill such jobs as police, assessors, penologists, and purchasing experts.

As a result the civil service has had to readjust its thinking. The creation in 1974 of the Professional and Administrative Career Examination (PACE) to replace the FSEE reflected the continued growth of professionalism in the civil service. Rather than measuring only the general education and background of applicants, PACE was designed to assess the professional training of prospective employees. Accessible to college graduates who majored in almost any field, PACE examined applicants for federal government careers rather than for specific jobs. (In 1981 the Office of Personnel Management dropped PACE as an examination for administrative generalists because minority group advocates argued that it tended to institutionalize racism by stressing education that only middle class whites would possess. Also, since the mid-1970s, in an effort to reflect the demand for professional training, the Civil Service Commission and OPM have officially exempted more than ninety professions from its oversight and have established separate salary schedules in designated personnel grades for certain professionals.

In addition to the growth of professionalism, the history of the civil service during the 1960s, 1970s, and 1980s reflects a desire on the part of presidents and reformers both to make the civil service responsive to presidential prerogatives and to continue it as a true merit system. The schizophrenic function of the Civil Service Commission, as both manager and watchdog of civil servants, led many reformers to demand that the functions of the commission be split into two separate agencies. Chief among the reformers was Sen. Joseph Clark who introduced a bill in the early 1960s to transfer most of the commission's staff and functions to an office of personnel management in the Executive Office of the President. This would leave the Civil Service Commission to function only as a watchdog of the merit system. Even though it received widespread support from political scientists and public administrators, Congress refused to pass the Clark bill.

During this period opportunities for patronage have continued to decline. In 1969, President Richard Nixon issued an executive order that placed about 70,000 postmasters and rural letter carriers under the protection of the federal merit system. These positions were considered the "last great pool of patronage." Since Nixon's action, presidents have had comparatively little patronage to dispense. In 1970 the Postal Reorganization Act removed more than 700,000 employees from the auspices of the Civil Service Commission and placed them under their own civil service system administered by the new United States Postal Service. As was true under the federal Civil Service Commission, political influence in appointments to the postal civil service is prohibited. Today, presidents still have approximately thirty-five hundred high-level policy positions, such as cabinet and subcabinet jobs, agency heads, and Executive Office of the President appointments, they can fill through patronage, but they do not have the large number of administrative patronage posts earlier presidents had.

As patronage has declined, presidents have tried to make the civil service more responsive to the goals of their administrations. Presidents John F. Kennedy and Nixon both provide examples. Kennedy tried to become involved in the day-to-day direction and control of his administration by communicating his objectives to his top-level administrators. Frustrated by a continued lack of responsiveness among career bureaucrats, Kennedy finally remarked that dealing with bureaucracies was like trying to nail jelly to the wall.

Nixon attempted to make his administration more responsive by devising ways of circumventing the merit system. Through the White House Personnel Office, Nixon directed that each department set up a special assistant to the secretary who would write a job description for job openings within the department. In order to circumvent civil service requirements, these job descriptions were written to fit particular persons the Nixon administration wanted in the position. In the *Federal Political Personnel Manual*, or the Malek Report, produced as an unofficial political "textbook" for Nixon personnel offices, Nixon loyalists were told how to fake job descriptions and manipulate selection procedures to gain positions or promotions.

Although other presidents from time to time had been guilty of some of the same intrigues, no other president had violated civil service regulations so boldly and on such a wide scale. This scheme initially gave Nixon some control over the civil service, but the Watergate scandal eventually loosened his grip. After Nixon resigned, the Civil Service Commission gave documented information to the House Committee on Post Office and Civil Service, which led to a House investigation of Nixon's civil service practices. The commission eventually pressured Nixon's successor, Gerald Ford, to strengthen merit procedures.

The Civil Service System Today

President Jimmy Carter oversaw the most sweeping reform of the civil service since 1883. Legislation passed in 1978 established the Office of Personnel Management (OPM), the Merit Systems Protection Board, and new procedures for classifying jobs, recruiting personnel, and compensating employees.

Civil Service Reform Act of 1978

The Civil Service Reform Act of 1978, primarily the work of Alan K. Campbell, head of the Civil Service Commission during the Carter administration, abolished the ninety-five-year-old commission. In its place the act set up the Office of Personnel Management and the Merit Systems Protection Board. Similar to Senator Clark's earlier bill, the Civil Service Reform Act of 1978 recognized the conflict between the dual functions of personnel management and protection of employees against merit violations by setting up new administrative machinery to carry out these functions.

Office of Personnel Management

Civil service restructuring became effective January 1, 1979. The Office of Personnel Management was made an independent executive agency and made responsible for administering examinations, training, and salary and other benefits. It was made accountable for approximately 2.1 million out of 2.8 million federal civil service employees. The director of OPM is appointed by the president, with the confirmation of the Senate. Primarily, OPM advises the president and agency managers on personnel policies, and it is generally responsible for the direction of human resources in the federal civil service. Its principal functions are the classification of positions, recruitment of personnel, administration of examinations, and disbursement of compensation.

'Go through this door, take a left, then a right, then a left, a right, a left, another left, a right . . .'

Classification. Each federal agency is responsible for classifying its own positions, but it follows specific OPM guidelines to maintain consistency in classifications from one agency to another. Many positions in different agencies entail similar duties and responsibilities, so these jobs are grouped into the same classification. This standardization allows the federal civil service to maintain a coherent personnel system for most of the executive branch and to follow uniform procedures for recruitment, examination, and pay.

OPM ensures this uniformity by classifying positions for most of the civil service within the General Schedule (GS). Positions are ranked according to their difficulty and are assigned a specific GS grade. Generally, GS-1 through GS-6 comprise lower-grade positions; GS-7 through GS-12, middle grade; GS-13 through GS-18, higher grade. Although many federal agencies have set up their own classification systems, they usually have based them on OPM's General Schedule. OPM also administers the Wage Grade for blue-collar positions. These standardized systems allow applicants to be sent to an agency that requires a job with skills that fit the applicants and salaries to be awarded by the standard of "equal pay for equal work."

Recruitment. OPM acts as a recruiting agency for the federal bureaucracy. Its primary tools for recruitment are the Federal Job Information Centers (FJICs) located throughout the country. The sole purpose of the FJICs is to provide information and application forms to anyone seeking federal employment. The centers also send out information about federal jobs to college and university placement offices to recruit students for federal employment. When a job opens up in a federal agency, OPM applies the "rule of three" and refers a list of three eligible candidates to the agency. The agency has to hire someone from this list.

Examination. Almost 62 percent of all appointed federal officials are part of the competitive service. In other words, they have been appointed after they have satisfied the requirements of a written exam administered by OPM or have met certain selection criteria formulated by the hiring agency and approved by OPM. Most examinations are written and are designed to measure both aptitude and competence. Occasionally, consideration is given to education and experience, which sometimes substitute for taking an exam. For example, entry into the mid-level grades of the federal service (GS-9 through GS-12) is usually based upon the applicant's background and qualifications. An applicant's acceptance, however, into the civil service most often is based upon a combination of written and oral examinations and education and experience. OPM also uses a system of veteran's preference in which disabled veterans and certain members of their families may receive up to ten extra points on their examination scores; honorably discharged veterans receive five additional points. These additional points make it possible for a veteran to score as high as 110 on an exam.

The remaining 38 percent of the federal work force constitute the excepted service, or those who do not come under the authority of OPM or under qualifications designed or approved by OPM. They have been excepted either by order of OPM or by federal statute. They include Post Office employees, agents of the Federal Bureau of Investigation, Foreign Service officers in the State Department, and Secret Service agents. Most of these positions are nonpartisan and are filled through merit systems independent of OPM. There are basically no differences in the excepted service and the competitive service in terms of salaries and personnel regulations. Less than 3 percent of the excepted employees are appointed on a basis other than, or in addition to, merit. These include presidential appointments (such as cabinet officers, judges, and ambassadors), Schedule C positions (policy-making positions), and noncareer executive assignments (high-ranking members of the civil service who are involved in high-level policy making, such as subcabinet positions). These three groups constitute the president's remaining patronage.

An additional part of the examination process is a personal investigation conducted by OPM of the reputation, character, and loyalty to the United States of those who apply for appointment to government positions. These investigations help OPM to enforce civil service regulations and, by evaluating qualifications, help to determine the suitability of applicants for positions that affect national security or entail professional skills. (If the job is a highly sensitive national security position, such as one on the National Security Council staff, the FBI may conduct the investigation.) In addition, new civil service employees must swear or affirm their allegiance to the Constitution of the United States and swear not to participate in a strike against the federal government or any agency of the government.

Compensation. About half of all federal government workers are under the General Schedule for white-collar positions. These include administrative, technical, and clerical employees. Within this schedule, there are eighteen grades, or levels, and ten steps within each grade. *(See Table 4.)* Each October the president may change the pay rate, corresponding to rate changes in the private sector for comparable jobs. Most federal employees not under the General Schedule fall under the Wage Grade schedule. These workers are paid the prevailing wage in their geographical location for the type of work they are doing. Most of these positions are skilled labor positions such as electricians, machinists, toolmakers, masons, welders, and painters. OPM periodically surveys standard rates for typical work in each geographic region.

Federal government employees at the GS-13, GS-14, or GS-15 level may be rewarded for meritorious service under the Merit Pay System. The amount of the salary increases for these grades depends entirely on performance appraisals. Unlike employees at lower grades, those at the GS-13 level and above do not advance through the grades on the basis of length of service and continued adequate performance. If performance appraisals are high enough, employees may receive raises that exceed those on the regular GS scale.

Table 4 GS Ratings and Their Respective Minimum Salaries, 1988

Rating	1988 Salary	Rating	1988 Salary
GS-1	$ 9,811	GS-10	$25,226
GS-2	$11,032	GS-11	$27,716
GS-3	$12,038	GS-12	$33,218
GS-4	$13,513	GS-13	$39,501
GS-5	$15,118	GS-14	$46,679
GS-6	$16,851	GS-15	$54,907
GS-7	$18,726	GS-16	$64,397
GS-8	$20,739	GS-17	$73,958[a]
GS-9	$22,907	GS-18	$86,682[a]

Source: Current Salary Schedules of Federal Officers and Employees (Washington, D.C.: U.S. Government Printing Office, 1988).

a. These rates are applicable to the "super grade" officers but have been limited by Congress to $70,800.

Merit Systems Protection Board

Separate from OPM under the 1978 reform is the Merit Systems Protection Board. This is an independent quasi-judicial agency, which is really the successor agency to the Civil Service Commission. It comprises three members, serving nonrenewable, three-year terms. As with the old Civil Service Commission, no more than two of its members may be from the same political party. They are appointed by the president and confirmed by the Senate. MSPB has responsibility for hearing and adjudicating appeals of personnel actions taken by OPM. These cases may include removals, suspensions, demotions, denials of periodic pay raises, and merit system violations. In addition, MSPB has the authority to review rules and regulations issued by OPM to see if they meet merit system standards.

MSPB was given authority for protecting employee rights and interests and for enforcing provisions of the act that forbade certain personnel practices, including reprisals against "whistle blowers" (civil servants who expose possible wrongdoing). Within MSPB, the Office of the Special Counsel receives and investigates allegations of prohibited personnel practices and recommends corrective action if there is evidence of a violation. These provisions put new force into the concept of a federal merit system and, simultaneously, reduced the conflict in the old Civil Service Commission over its roles.

Senior Executive Service

In addition to dividing the functions of the Civil Service Commission, the Civil Service Act of 1978 provided another important reform: it classified about eight thousand positions as the Senior Executive Service (SES). The second Hoover Commission originally had proposed this reform with the hopes of creating a large pool of professionally mobile, all-purpose senior executives, ideally to serve two functions. First, these executives could be transferred with no loss of rank to agencies requiring their managerial skills. Second, top political executives who wanted to assemble their own management teams would have a pool of talent from which to choose.

SES was designed in part after the British civil service system, which traditionally has stressed general training and mobility over technical specialization. Senior executives who choose to join SES have less job security and are susceptible to being transferred from one organization to another. As a reward, however, they are eligible for substantial cash bonuses for superior service instead of automatic pay raises awarded for length of service. Theoretically, the federal administrators constituting SES will be more responsive and responsible to the president because the president will have more discretion in rewarding or removing them. Of those eligible to join SES (mostly administrators at the GS-16 through GS-18 levels), well over 90 percent have joined. Apparently, the enticement of financial rewards for merit performance has outweighed job security.

Bonuses for SES merit performance take several forms. Originally, as many as 50 percent of SES executives were eligible to earn performance bonuses of up to 20 percent of their base pay in the regular bonus system. Congress reduced that number to 25 percent of SES members, but the bonus system remains in effect today. In addition, SES members are eligible for two "presidential ranks": up to 1 percent of SES executives may earn the rank of Distinguished Executive, providing a $20,000 bonus; up to 5 percent may be awarded the rank of Meritorious Executive, which carries a $10,000 award.

Notes

1. Dan Cordtz, "The Imperial Lifestyle of the U.S. President," *Fortune,* October 1973, 144; Robert Sherrill, *Why They Call It Politics,* 4th ed. (New York: Harcourt Brace Jovanovich, 1984), 14.
2. Quoted in Joseph E. Kallenbach, *The American Chief Executive: The Presidency and the Governorship* (New York: Harper and Row, 1966), 196.
3. Sherrill, *Why They Call It Politics,* 14.
4. Quoted in Norine Dickson, *Patrick Henry: Patriot and Statesman* (Old Greenwich, Conn.: Devin-Adair, 1969), 345.
5. Alexander Hamilton, *Federalist* No. 67, in *The Federalist,* introduction by Edward Gaylord Bourne (New York: Tudor, 1937), ii, 30.
6. Quoted in Sherrill, *Why They Call It Politics,* 13.
7. Bill Gulley, with Mary Ellen Reese, *Breaking Cover* (New York: Simon and Schuster, 1980), 147.
8. Quoted in Tom Morganthau and Eleanor Clift, "Hail, Hail to the Chief," *Newsweek,* May 25, 1981, 44.
9. Michael Kilian and Arnold Sawislak, *Who Runs Washington?* (New York: St. Martin's Press, 1982), 85.
10. Jack Messmer and Ellen Messmer, "All the President's Planes," *Popular Mechanics,* February 1986, 164.
11. Quoted in Hugh Sidey, "The Loftiest Chariot," *Time,* July 21, 1986, 25.
12. Patricia A. Avery, "Reagan White House Steps Up Social Pace," *U.S. News & World Report,* January 23, 1984, 54.
13. J. Frank Diggs and Patricia A. Avery, "Reagan White House—Glitter and Grace," *U.S. News & World Report,* June 1, 1981, 43.
14. Carl T. Rowan and David M. Mazie, "Shield against Assassins: The Secret Service," *Reader's Digest,* April 1982, 144.
15. Quoted in Sara Fritz and Patricia A. Avery, "Why They Call the White House a 'Gilded Cage,'" *U.S. News & World Report,* February 15, 1982, 50.
16. "House Guards," *Time,* December 21, 1983, 21.
17. Sherrill, *Why They Call It Politics,* 16-17.
18. "When Uncle Sam Turns Librarian," *U.S. News & World Report,* May 2, 1983, 24.
19. Paul C. Light, *Vice-Presidential Power: Advice and Influence in the White House* (Baltimore: Johns Hopkins University Press, 1984), 123, 162-164.
20. Unlike his predecessors, President Ford showed a willingness to listen to Vice President Nelson Rockefeller. This elevated Rockefeller to a position of importance that other vice presidents to this time had not enjoyed. Political scientist Paul C. Light has written, "Much of Ford's willingness came from circumstances surrounding Watergate. Rockefeller had a considerable store of political and policy resources, but he also brought legitimacy to an administration already weakened by the Nixon pardon" (Light, *Vice-Presidential Power,* 162).
21. Ibid., 74-75.
22. Ibid., 122.
23. Ibid.
24. Gerald Ford, "On the Threshold of the White House," *Atlantic Monthly,* July 1974, 63.
25. Light, *Vice-Presidential Power,* 74.
26. John W. Macy, Bruce Adams, J. Jackson Walter, *America's Unelected Government: Appointing the President's Team* (Cambridge: Ballinger, 1983), 76.
27. Ibid., 80.
28. Bill Whalen, "Congress Figures a Pay Raise's Cost," *Insight/Washington Times,* February 2, 1987.
29. Judith Havemann, "Top Salary of $135,000 Proposed," *Washington Post,* December 14, 1986.
30. Tom Kenworthy, "Pay Raise Debacle Poses Challenges for Congress," *Washington Post,* February 9, 1989, A21.
31. Gulley, *Breaking Cover,* 159.
32. Ibid., 276.
33. Bruce D. Porter, "Parkinson's Law Revisited: War and Growth of American Government," *Public Trust* (Summer 1980): 44.
34. Frederick C. Mosher, *Democracy and the Public Service,* 2d ed. (New York: Oxford University Press, 1982), chaps. 3, 4.
35. Paul P. Van Riper, *History of the United States Civil Service* (Evanston, Ill.: Row, Peterson, 1958), 21.
36. Letter in Saul K. Padover, *The Complete Jefferson* (New York: Tudor, 1943), 518.
37. Herbert Kaufman, "The Growth of the Federal Personnel System," in *The Federal Government Service: Character, Prestige, and Problems* (New York: Columbia University, 1954), 23.
38. James D. Richardson, *Messages and Papers of the Presidents,* vol. 2 (Washington, D.C.: Bureau of National Literature and Art, 1903), 438.
39. Kaufman, "Growth of the Federal Personnel System," 27.
40. Van Riper, *History of the Civil Service,* 63.
41. Robert S. Lorch, *Public Administration* (St. Paul, Minn.: West, 1978), 94.
42. Kaufman, "Growth of the Federal Personnel System," 35-37.
43. Ibid., 38.
44. Nicholas Henry, *Public Administration and Public Affairs* (Englewood Cliffs, N.J.: Prentice-Hall, 1975), 191.
45. Van Riper, *History of the Civil Service,* 207.
46. Kaufman, "Growth of the Federal Personnel System," 38.
47. Mosher, *Democracy and the Public Service,* 79-80.
48. Van Riper, *History of the Civil Service,* 497.
49. Mosher, *Democracy and the Public Service,* 85-86.
50. George J. Gordon, *Public Administration in America,* 2d ed. (New York: St. Martin's Press, 1982), 307.
51. Henry, *Public Administration and Public Affairs,* 197.

Selected Bibliography

Albertazzie, Ralph, and Jerald F. terHorst. *The Flying White House: The Story of Air Force One.* New York: Coward, McCann and Geoghegan, 1979.

Avery, Patricia A. "Reagan White House Steps Up Social Pace," *U.S. News & World Report.* January 23, 1984.

Collins, Herbert R. *Presidents on Wheels: The Complete Collection of Carriages and Automobiles Used by Our American Presidents.* Washington, D.C.: Acropolis Books, 1971.

Cordtz, Dan. "The Imperial Lifestyle of the U.S. President." *Fortune.* October 1973.

Dickson, Norine. *Patrick Henry: Patriot and Statesman.* Old Greenwich, Conn.: Devin-Adair, 1969.

Diggs, J. Frank, and Patricia A. Avery. "Reagan White House—Glitter and Grace." *U.S. News & World Report.* June 1, 1981.

Ford, Gerald. "On the Threshold of the White House." *Atlantic Monthly.* July 1974.

Fritz, Sara, and Patricia A. Avery. "Why They Call the White House a 'Gilded Cage.'" *U.S. News & World Report.* February 15, 1982.

Gordon, George J. *Public Administration in America.* 2d ed. New York: St. Martin's Press, 1982.

Gulley, Bill, with Mary Ellen Reese. *Breaking Cover.* New York: Simon and Schuster, 1980.

Hamilton, Alexander, John Jay, and James Madison. *The Federalist.* Introduction by Edward Gaylord Bourne. New York: Tudor, 1937.

Harvey, Donald R. *The Civil Service Commission.* New York: Praeger, 1970.

Henry, Nicholas. *Public Administration and Public Affairs.* Englewood Cliffs, N.J.: Prentice-Hall, 1975.

Havemann, Judith. "Top Salary of $135,000 Proposed." *Washington Post.* December 14, 1986.

"House Guards." *Time.* December 21, 1983.

Kaiser, Frederick M. *Presidential Protection: Assassinations, Assaults, and Secret Service Protective Procedures.* Washington, D.C.: Congressional Research Service, 1981.

Kallenbach, Joseph E. *The American Chief Executive: The Presidency and the Governorship.* New York: Harper and Row, 1966.

Kaufman, Herbert. "The Growth of the Federal Personnel System." In *The Federal Government Service: Character, Prestige, and Problems.* New York: Columbia University, 1954.

Kilian, Michael, and Arnold Sawislak. *Who Runs Washington?* New York: St. Martin's Press, 1982.

Lawford, Valentine. "The Presidential Yacht U.S.S. *Sequoia.*" *Architectural Digest.* January 1983.

Light, Paul C. *Vice-Presidential Power: Advice and Influence in the White House.* Baltimore: Johns Hopkins University Press, 1984.

Lorch, Robert S. *Public Administration.* St. Paul, Minn.: West, 1978.

Macy, John W., Bruce Adams, J. Jackson Walter. *America's Unelected Government: Appointing the President's Team.* Cambridge: Ballinger, 1983.

Messmer, Jack, and Ellen Messmer. "All the President's Planes." *Popular Mechanics.* February 1986.

Morganthau, Tom, and Eleanor Clift. "Hail, Hail to the Chief." *Newsweek.* May 25, 1981.

Mosher, Frederick C. *Democracy and the Public Service.* 2d ed. New York: Oxford University Press, 1982.

Parker, Nancy W. *The President's Car.* New York: Crowell, 1981.

Richardson, James D. *Messages and Papers of the Presidents.* 2 vols. Washington, D.C.: Bureau of National Literature and Art, 1903.

Rowan, Carl T., and David M. Mazie. "Shield against Assassins: The Secret Service." *Reader's Digest.* April 1982.

Sherrill, Robert. *Why They Call It Politics.* 4th ed. New York: Harcourt Brace Jovanovich, 1984.

Sidey, Hugh. "The Loftiest Chariot." *Time.* July 21, 1986.

Whalen, Bill. "Congress Figures a Pay Raise's Cost." *Insight/Washington Times.* February 2, 1987.

"When Uncle Sam Turns Librarian." *U.S. News & World Report.* May 2, 1983.

Daily Life of the President

Although in theory just another citizen, the president does not live like one. The first family occupies the White House, a fully staffed, 132-room structure that combines personal living quarters and an office complex. Located at 1600 Pennsylvania Avenue in Washington, D.C., the Executive Mansion sits on an immaculate eighteen-acre estate, which is maintained by the National Park Service. Within its walls are thousands of beautiful items of furniture, art, china, and antiques, many of which are very valuable. Should the president or first lady not like the paintings on the walls, for example, the National Gallery of Art will provide new ones.

White House Life

A newly elected president receives $50,000 to be spent on redecorating the White House, which is repainted every four years at no extra charge. Because the redecorating allowance does not go very far, some presidents and first ladies, most recently the Reagans, have conducted campaigns to raise private funds and material donations for the mansion.

In addition to offices and the first family's living quarters, the Executive Mansion houses exercise rooms and recreational facilities for the president, who may invite guests or staff to use them as well. On the ground floor is an office for the president's physician and a small clinic with a staff of thirteen that is adequate for routine medical care (major or specialized treatment is available at one of Washington's hospitals). There is also a dental clinic, a barbershop, a tailor's shop, a cafeteria, laundry rooms, a carpenter's shop, a machine shop, a painter's shop, and a bomb shelter.

Presidential Expenses

Since 1969 the president has drawn annually a salary of $200,000, a taxable expense account of $50,000, and a travel allowance of $75,000. But in reality, because the president travels almost exclusively on government transportation, the cost of which is covered by government agencies such as the Department of Defense, most of the president's travel allowance is available for other uses.

The president has access to over a dozen limousines and cars—including an armor-plated one with a detachable roof—which are leased by the manufacturer to the government at a small fee. Family members and designated staff on official business may use the cars as well. The president also may use a Marine Corps helicopter for short trips such as to the presidential retreat, Camp David, in Maryland. For longer journeys, a small fleet of airplanes is available, including *Air Force One,* the primary jet. A modified Boeing 747 that can carry eighty passengers, *Air Force One* has a special crew of twenty-three, comfortable compartments with desks, sofas, and beds, medical and food service facilities, and communications equipment for constant access to the rest of the world. The president's family and invited guests also may fly on these official aircraft; however, unless they are on official business, they must pay their own way. By custom of the White House military office, which operates the aircraft, the fare is calculated at the first-class rate plus one dollar.

Security and communications considerations dictate that the president use government transportation almost exclusively. The president's guardians, the Secret Service, have discouraged the use of private transportation by the president since the Truman administration. When President Harry S Truman's mother-in-law died, Truman, seeking privacy, wanted to return to his Missouri home on a commercial train, but the service refused to allow it.

The expenses incurred in operating the White House itself are paid by the government. For example, the electric bills, which can total more than $180,000 per year, are paid by the federal treasury. Similarly, the White House telephone service, which operates through an in-house switchboard and is among the best in the world, is provided at no charge to the president. In 1986 utilities, supplies, equipment, and other services for the White House cost the government a total of $847,000.

Despite the lavish accommodations and generous perks that presidents receive, the many items that the government does not pay for can be a serious drain on the president's personal resources. As a general rule personal items—toiletries, clothing, laundry, games, and so on—must be purchased by the president. The president also must absorb the cost of the food served the first family and their personal guests, as well as the maintenance of personal items such as appliances and furniture that the first

By Stephen L. Robertson

family brought to the White House.

A similar distinction exists in White House entertainment. The government will pay for official entertaining; the tab for a state dinner, for example, will be picked up by the State Department. And for any strictly political functions the president's political party may help defray expenses. The cost of any other entertaining, however, such as receptions, dinners, recitals, or parties that are not directly connected to business on behalf of the U.S. government, is covered by the president. For example, a White House reception honoring a Nobel laureate or a party for thirty members of Congress would be a private expense. While there is always a military band available, and while many entertainers and performers gladly donate their time to the White House, the expense of entertaining easily can become quite high. During the administration of Lyndon B. Johnson, for example, entertainment bills were sometimes as much as $10,000 a month.[1]

Despite the size of the president's salary and benefits, living in the White House is far from inexpensive, as first families learn to their dismay. Rosalynn Carter wrote of her shock when the food bill for her first ten days in the White House in 1977 came to $600.[2] Other first ladies have expressed similar feelings. Thus, they look for ways to economize: Bess Truman scrutinized every line of the budget, and Mamie Eisenhower searched newspaper advertisements for bargains. Lady Bird Johnson's cook sometimes made the round of supermarkets looking for specials. And when Mrs. Johnson's daughter Luci once asked for a second dress to wear to a festival, the first lady, citing the budget, refused to buy it. Although most were fairly wealthy, each first lady has echoed Jacqueline Kennedy's orders to her staff: "I want you to run this place just like you'd run it for the chinchiest president who ever lived." [3]

Some presidents take their desire to save money even further. For example, Lyndon Johnson constantly harassed staff and family alike to turn off the lights in the White House when not needed, even though he personally did not pay the electric bill. The harassment continued until finally Johnson came home one night to a blacked-out White House; the only light in the entire mansion was a single candle on the table where his brother, Sam Houston Johnson, was writing.

Purchases for the White House, including many of the president's personal wants, are made by the staff. For example, the first family's food is bought wholesale from selected stores (limited in number due partly to security). After the White House menu is fixed, government trucks visit the stores, where White House staff members and carefully screened store employees collect the food. Such purchases are paid with the president's personal check. Other types of purchases are made in a similar way.

It is rarely if ever possible for the president or the first lady to go on public shopping trips. As late as the 1920s Grace Coolidge shopped virtually unnoticed; on one such trip she even encountered another customer who told her that she resembled the first lady. Such informality rapidly disappeared, however. In 1945, Bess Truman drove herself around Washington, but she soon began to cause traffic jams and had to stop. More recently, in 1977, Rosalynn Carter tried to fly quietly on a commercial airliner to New York City to buy some clothes, only to find a mob of journalists waiting for her when she left the store. And in 1981 Ronald Reagan created pandemonium when he tried to go to a store to buy his wife a valentine.

The Executive Mansion is fully staffed. The White House domestic staff consists mainly of permanent, full-time employees who remain from president to president and whose primary loyalty is to the presidency itself. Although this staff is not protected by civil service status, staffers are fired infrequently. Moreover, because jobs within the White House have a certain prestige, turnover is low. Accounts indicate that the staff takes great pride in serving the president. For example, when Lady Bird Johnson, aware of her husband's erratic working hours, encouraged the White House butlers to go home early, they refused to hear of it.

The most important member of the White House domestic staff is the chief usher. Responsible for the general operation of the White House, the chief usher manages the mansion's budget; hires, directs, and dismisses personnel; and oversees the various White House activities under way. Should the president or the first family want something done around the White House, they seek out the chief usher. Chief ushers have been charged with coordinating the mansion's redecoration, organizing a president's last-minute reception for hundreds of people, supervising a president's funeral, and even acquiring animals for the president's children. *(See box, Chief Usher of the White House, p. 861.)*

Below the chief usher is the large permanent White House work force. In 1986 the permanent domestic staff consisted of ninety-three people. They included butlers, maids, cooks, operating engineers, electricians, carpenters, plumbers, painters, floral designers, and a seamstress. Staff salaries totaled $2.7 million. The staff is sufficiently diversified to handle most problems internally. On occasion in the past other government employees have been drafted to supplement the domestic staff. For example, when President Johnson, at the end of the period of mourning for President John F. Kennedy, decided suddenly to invite the entire Congress to the White House for a Christmas party, additional government personnel had to be brought in to assist with the preparations. Such short-term borrowing is rare, however.

The first family is permitted to place a small number of personal servants on the government payroll. These employees, although paid temporarily by the government, are in fact distinct from the rest of the domestic staff. They are employed by the president and first lady and leave with them. Their pay is generally on a par with that of the permanent staff; some, however, may live in the White House itself and therefore may draw a smaller salary. Included among such employees would be the president's valet(s), personal cook, and barber, and the first lady's personal secretary and maids.

The President's Workday

The work load of the president has changed a great deal during the twentieth century. While it is probably true, as George Reedy, LBJ's press secretary, has said, that no president has ever died from overwork, the load certainly seems to have been much heavier after 1930 than before.

Before 1930 most presidents had a fairly light work load. The Congress dominated American government, and the president was expected to do little. Indeed, the federal government as a whole was not expected to do much, for most government activities were at the state and local levels. In general, people expected the government to take a hands-off attitude about most problems.

Consequently, presidents did not have to work very long or hard. In 1890 a schedule such as Benjamin Harrison's was typical: arrive at the office around nine in the morning, work for two or three hours, and take the rest of the day off. Later, in 1905, Theodore Roosevelt disposed of government in the morning and devoted his afternoons to exercise and his evenings to reading. Calvin Coolidge spent fairly little time in his office from 1923 to 1929 because he felt the government should do nothing. There were exceptions—James K. Polk (1845-1849) worked so long and hard that he ruined his health and died at age fifty-three —but most presidents did not find the job terribly taxing. Fighting off the would-be officeholders was more demanding.

The work load began to change in 1930, however, when problems arose that were beyond the capacities of the states. The Great Depression, followed by World War II, led to new expectations of the federal government. It thus increased its role in society and the economy with each passing year. Concurrently, people began to look to the president more than to Congress for direction and solutions. Just as the federal government was expected to solve the nation's problems, so the president was expected to lead the government.

Longer presidential workdays were therefore inevitable. Herbert Hoover (1929-1933) spent many more hours in the Oval Office than most of his predecessors, and his successor, Franklin D. Roosevelt (1933-1945), spent all day at work, with brainstorming sessions often held over meals. Harry Truman (1945-1953) arose at 5:30 in the morning, had breakfast at 8:00, and went straight to work. Although he did not labor under the pressures of Roosevelt, he worked a full day.

By 1952 the public viewed the presidency as a full-time job. Many Americans therefore found Dwight D. Eisenhower's approach to the job somewhat disconcerting. Relying on his extensive staff, Eisenhower (1953-1961) tried to return to the old work patterns; he concentrated his work into the mornings and tried to take afternoons off as much as possible. And unlike Roosevelt and Truman, Eisenhower avoided working on weekends. He argued that a rested president made better decisions than an overworked one, but not everyone agreed. He was criticized for the amount of time he spent playing golf, and a bumper sticker appeared, which read: "Ben Hogan for President. If We're Going to Have a Golfer, Let's Have a Good One."

For the most part John F. Kennedy (1961-1963) was not a long worker either. As a senator he had had a reputation as a four-day legislator; as president he consistently took his weekends off. Kennedy worked through the morning, paused in the afternoon for a swim, lunch, and a nap, and then returned to the office for a time in the late afternoon.

Life under Lyndon Johnson (1963-1969) was not so relaxed. A driven man who possessed almost superhuman energy, Johnson wanted to accomplish more than any other president and drove himself, and everyone else, accordingly. He arose early and held bedroom meetings with selected staff members; he then spent the morning in his office. After lunch he took a nap, on doctor's orders, from two to four. Thus refreshed, he started the day all over again, frequently working late into the night. It was not at all unusual for LBJ to hold staff meetings at nine or ten in the evening and to work until after midnight. He drove his staff as hard as himself, demanding that they be available at all times of the night and day.

Chief Usher of the White House

The chief usher of the White House has one of the most varied jobs anywhere in the government, as seen in the following job description taken from the U.S. Civil Service Commission's position description form:

> Subject only to the general direction of the President of the United States, serves as "Chief Usher" of the White House. As such is the general manager of the Executive Mansion, and is delegated full responsibility for directing the administrative, fiscal, and personnel functions involved in the management and operation of the Executive Mansion and grounds, including construction, maintenance, and remodeling of the Executive Mansion.
>
> Is responsible for the preparation and justification of budget estimates covering administrative and operating expenses, and for the construction and maintenance projects of the Executive Mansion . . . , as well as for the allotment, control, and proper expenditure of funds appropriated for these purposes.
>
> Is responsible for the direction and supervision of the activities of approximately one hundred employees of the President's household including their selection, appointment, placement, promotion, separation, disciplinary action, etc. In addition, exercises responsibility over the mechanical and maintenance forces in connection with the maintenance and repair of buildings and grounds.
>
> Serves as the receptionist at the White House, and as such is responsible for receiving and caring for all personal and official guests calling on the President or the First Lady. These guests include, among others, members of the Congress and their families, members of the Judicial Branch, governors, foreign dignitaries, and heads of state. Is responsible for arranging for accommodations for house guests, their comfort, their acquaintance with customs of the household, etc. Is responsible and arranges for all personal and official entertainments, receptions, dinners, etc., in the Executive Mansion, which frequently include the heads of the sovereign states, and several hundred persons. Is responsible for the procurement of all food consumed by the President's family and their guests. Makes personal appointments for the President and other members of his official family.
>
> Is responsible for answering a large volume of correspondence regarding the Executive Mansion, its history and furnishings, historical subjects, sightseeing, Congressional requests with regard to the Mansion and Grounds, State function, etc.
>
> Is completely responsible for the efficient operation, cleanliness, and maintenance of the 132 rooms of the Executive Mansion containing 1,600,000 cubic feet; $2,000,000 of mechanical and airconditioning equipment.[1]

1. J. B. West, *Upstairs at the White House: My Life With the First Ladies* (New York: Coward, McCann, and Geohegan, 1973), 10-11.

Although Richard Nixon (1969-1974) was not as frantic as Johnson, he too worked long hours. He generally arose at 7:30 a.m. and was at his office by 8:30. Meetings began at nine and lasted throughout the morning. After a brief lunch, Nixon would resume work until early evening. A workday of ten to eleven hours, with perhaps an hour out for lunch, was common. At times, Nixon would return to his office around nine in the evening to read and work another hour or two. He generally went to bed between midnight and one in the morning.

The habit of presidents working long days continued with Gerald R. Ford (1974-1977) and Jimmy Carter (1977-1981), both of whom put in full days and not a few nights. By then it was believed that the president had to work twelve-hour days because the burdens of government were so great. One of Carter's commercials during his 1980 reelection campaign illustrated and played on that belief; it pictured a dark White House late at night, with a solitary light where Carter worked alone.

Ronald Reagan (1981-1989), in contrast, was more of a nine-to-five president, and he took frequent vacations. Like Eisenhower, he did not care to immerse himself in details and thought he worked better with less work. But the public had become accustomed to more workaholic presidents, and there was criticism of Reagan from many quarters about his "banker's hours" approach to the presidency. It is worth noting, however, that even though Reagan had a shorter workday than his immediate predecessors, he labored longer than most presidents before 1930. *(See box, A President's Work Schedule, p. 863.)*

The President's Recreation

With its long hours and psychological burden the modern presidency is a stressful job. Consequently, rest and relaxation are important to the well-being of the president.

Among the recreational facilities available at the White House is a heated outdoor swimming pool, built with private funds by Gerald Ford. The original White House swimming pool was built in 1933 with publicly donated funds for Franklin Roosevelt, who used it frequently, at least during his early years in office. Truman, Kennedy, and Johnson also used the pool often, but Eisenhower did not. Nixon later eliminated the pool to make space for a press room.

The White House also contains a small gymnasium, a tennis court which was built originally for Theodore Roosevelt, and a one-lane bowling alley which was particularly popular with Nixon. In the movie theater the first family and their guests can watch their favorite movies; presidential requests for new movies are filled quickly by the film studios. The White House library regularly receives new books from publishing houses, who send titles that match each president's interests. For example, when the Eisenhowers moved in the White House the library was flooded with western and romance titles, which were the favorites of the president and first lady.

Presidents have managed to relax in a variety of ways. When he wanted to relax, Benjamin Harrison took walks or used the billiard table in the basement of the White House. In fact, the entire Harrison family played the game, despite the terrible condition of the basement in the 1890s.

Harrison's successor (and predecessor), Grover Cleveland (1885-1889, 1893-1897), also tried to relax at the billiard table, and he enjoyed taking carriage rides through the city as well. Although Cleveland spent more time at his desk than many previous presidents, he still got away for hunting and fishing.

Because of the time he spent caring for his frail, epileptic wife, William McKinley (1897-1901) was unable to indulge in many recreational activities. He took walks and, like Cleveland, enjoyed an occasional carriage ride. He also enjoyed visits from his friends and an infrequent game of cards. His greatest pleasure, however, was the cigar that was his constant companion. It was perhaps the one indulgence he permitted himself as he was devoted to caring for his wife, Ida.

A "man's man," Theodore Roosevelt walked and hiked regularly, jogged often, excelled at horsemanship, hunted, swam in the Potomac, and played tennis on the White House courts with invited guests. Roosevelt's tennis guests were members of Congress, diplomats, cabinet members, and other political figures. An invitation to play tennis with Roosevelt was a privilege, and only those who played well were invited back. Roosevelt also enjoyed fencing, boxing, and wrestling, and he might devote an entire afternoon to any one of them. He even practiced the martial arts and once set up a contest between American wrestling and Japanese jujitsu to see which was superior. Yet he loved to read as well and frequently devoted his evenings to a book or the latest magazines. The entire Roosevelt household read with him.

William Howard Taft (1909-1913), not being a fan of the strenuous life, preferred less-demanding recreation. Taft took walks and occasional automobile rides, and he enjoyed reading the newspapers and having massages. A baseball fan, Taft was the first president to open a season by tossing out the first pitch. He also played golf often.

For Woodrow Wilson (1913-1921) golf was never more than an amusement; he never tried to be good at it. Rides in his car, billiards, solitaire, particularly Canfield, and the theater were among his other favorite pastimes.

Warren G. Harding (1921-1923) played golf and walked a little for exercise, but he preferred spending his spare time playing cards, poker and bridge, with old cronies from Ohio.

Calvin Coolidge relaxed by taking walks and working jigsaw puzzles. One of his Secret Service agents taught him to fish and he became an avid angler, although all he did was hold the rod; his agents baited the hook and removed the fish for him. One day, when he noticed someone catching fish from the stream in front of his South Dakota vacation house, he sent the Secret Service to confiscate them and tell the trespassers, "They are my fish." His favorite relaxation, however, was sleeping. Coolidge slept at least eleven hours a day, getting nine hours a night and taking two- to four-hour naps each afternoon.

Herbert Hoover, who spent his 1929-1933 term grappling unsuccessfully with the Great Depression, seems to have relaxed very little in the White House. Irwin Hood (Ike) Hoover, then chief usher at the White House, noted that the president "labored practically all his waking hours and never spent any time with his family."[4] Hoover worked out with a medicine ball in the mornings, however, and read often. It was his complaint about being unable to find adequate reading material in the White House that led to publishers' donations. And the Hoovers apparently enjoyed dinner companions; in fact they rarely ate alone.

Franklin Roosevelt's inability to walk because of polio

A President's Work Schedule

The president of the United States is a very busy person, who may work from the dawn's early light to the twilight's last gleaming, and well beyond. The schedule that follows is a day (June 23, 1981) in the life of President Ronald Reagan. The fact that Reagan was viewed as having a very leisurely presidency gives some indication of the hours that presidents perceived to be more energetic have kept.

4:30 a.m. The president, having trouble sleeping, gets up and does some paper work. Goes back to bed about 6.

8:00 a.m. Reagan receives wake-up call from White House switchboard.

8:41 a.m. Senior aides James Baker, Edwin Meese, and Michael Deaver join the president in the family quarters to discuss the day's schedule.

9:08 a.m. Reagan walks from second floor residence down to the State Dining Room for breakfast with 38 Democratic lawmakers who backed his budget cuts.

10:15 a.m. The president goes to the Oval Office for the daily national-security briefing. Among those attending are Vice President Bush and National Security Adviser Richard Allen. Meeting concludes at 10:34.

10:37 a.m. At his desk, Reagan is briefed on the day's developments by aides Baker, Meese, Deaver, Max Friedersdorf, David Gergen, and Larry Speakes. At 10:46, the meeting ends.

10:50 a.m. *U.S. News & World Report* editors interview the president.

11:09 a.m. White House advisers Melvin Bradley and Thaddeus Gerrett enter Oval Office to prepare Reagan for meeting with NAACP officials Benjamin Hooks and Margaret Bush Wilson.

11:13 a.m. Hooks and Wilson begin discussions with the president. Also present are Vice President Bush and White House aide Elizabeth Dole. Meeting ends at 11:50.

12:01 p.m. Reagan poses for photographs in Oval Office with new U.S. Ambassadors Arthur Burns, Maxwell Rabb, and Ernest Preeg and their families.

12:15 p.m. Ocean explorer Jacques Cousteau enters for lunch with Reagan, Deaver, and White House aide Richard Darman on patio outside the Oval Office.

1:31 p.m. Treasury Secretary Donald Regan briefs the president in the Oval Office on tax developments in Congress.

1:39 p.m. Reagan walks across the hall to the Roosevelt Room to meet with 11 Republican members of the Senate Finance Committee. Meeting ends at 2:01.

2:08 p.m. The president enters the Cabinet Room for meeting with the cabinet council on commerce and trade. Session ends at 2:27.

2:34 p.m. The Chief Executive convenes a meeting of the entire cabinet. It concludes at 3:38.

3:46 p.m. The president goes to the State Dining Room for meeting with the Presidential Advisory Committee on Federalism. Session ends at 4:24 and Reagan returns to the Oval Office.

4:33 p.m. Personnel Adviser E. Pendleton James enters Oval Office to discuss presidential appointments.

4:48 p.m. CIA Director William Casey enters for meeting with the president.

5:09 p.m. Reagan goes to Rose Garden reception for 175 teenage Republicans.

5:16 p.m. Reagan enters the East Room for a reception in honor of 190 House Republicans.

6:12 p.m. The president goes back to the family quarters, has dinner alone, telephones Mrs. Reagan in California, catches up on some reading and retires at 11:15 p.m.[1]

1. "9 Hours Inside the Oval Office," *U.S. News & World Report,* July 6, 1981, 16-17.

limited the forms of recreation he could enjoy. At first, Roosevelt swam frequently in the White House swimming pool, but as the cares of his office mounted, he used the pool less and less; he had largely abandoned it by 1945. In the way of hobbies Roosevelt was a skilled bird-watcher, and he liked to collect stamps, books, and models of sailing ships. His White House study in fact was filled with these things, much to the dismay of the housekeeping staff.[5] Roosevelt relaxed as well by taking weekend trips to his mountain hideaway, Shangri-La (now Camp David), in the Maryland countryside. He also frequently enjoyed the quiet and privacy of long automobile rides in the country, and he liked to fish from the presidential yacht. Roosevelt's yacht was one of several vessels that had been maintained by the navy and made available to presidents since the Theodore Roosevelt administration. President Carter sold the last of these boats during his administration, and as of 1989 there was no presidential yacht.

Harry Truman used an exercise regime while in the White House. He began the day with an hour's brisk walk at six, followed by a swim in the pool, a workout on the rowing and exercise machines, some calisthenics, and another dip in the pool. From 1949 to 1951 part of the well-publicized daily walks were devoted to viewing the renovation of the White House, which had to be almost totally rebuilt due to accumulated structural problems. (During the renovation, the Trumans lived at Blair House, which is situated across Pennsylvania Avenue from the White House.) The walks stopped after an aborted assassination attempt on Truman in 1950. Truman also relaxed by playing the piano during quiet evenings with his family.

Believing that proper rest was vital to effective work, Dwight Eisenhower carefully guarded his leisure time while president. An avid golfer, he had a putting green installed outside the Oval Office—he even threatened to shoot the squirrels that kept burying nuts there—and practiced his swing on the South Lawn. He played golf often at the Burning Tree Country Club in Bethesda, Maryland. The president also enjoyed painting and set up a studio in the White House. He liked to watch movies, particularly westerns; preferred to read westerns, mysteries, and cookbooks; and was the first president to spend much time watching television.

John Kennedy relaxed by leaving Washington. Almost

every weekend Kennedy was off to his family's property in Massachusetts or Florida, a friend's home in rural Virginia, or Camp David. Many of these holidays were taken without his wife, who often vacationed separately. While at the White House itself, Kennedy used the White House pool; he would take a nude swim in the afternoon, return to his room for a nap, go back to work, and then return to the pool afterward. J. B. West, chief usher at the White House from 1957 to 1969, wrote that Kennedy followed this routine every day that he was at the mansion.[6] Because the president had a chronically bad back that hampered his physical activity, he exercised regularly to strengthen it, and he kept a rocking chair in the Oval Office for relief from his chronic back pain. But despite his ailment, Kennedy enjoyed sailing and was a good golfer.

Lyndon Johnson was a human dynamo who never seemed to need rest. For Johnson, a man always on the move, work itself seemed to be a form of relaxation. When he sought some other form of activity, he swam in the pool, played an occasional game of dominoes, and sometimes watched a movie. The president also enjoyed dancing; at parties he took turns dancing with different partners and often danced with his daughters, Luci and Lynda. Because Johnson liked a good massage, when he left the White House he arranged to have his masseur, a navy officer, transferred to Bergstrom Air Force Base near his Texas ranch.

Dwight D. Eisenhower Library

Eisenhower plays golf at a club in Newport, Rhode Island, while onlookers watch and take pictures.

The more sedate Richard Nixon, who rarely swam, had the pool filled in. Nixon did, however, watch an occasional movie, sometimes played golf, and used the White House bowling alley. Moreover, he went out frequently on the White House yacht. Nixon also often read for relaxation and seemed to find comfort in the White House fireplaces, which were used even in the summer; the air-conditioning was turned up to compensate. In the way of spectator sports, Nixon liked baseball and greatly enjoyed football. In fact, he was an avid fan of the Washington Redskins and followed the team closely when he could. He even suggested plays to the Redskins' coaching staff. According to Dennis V. N. McCarthy, a member of Nixon's Secret Service detail, one evening after a game Nixon came outside and sat on the porch with him "just like two guys getting together over a couple of beers to discuss the game, except there was no beer."[7]

Gerald Ford was a former football player who enjoyed watching the game, but he also liked more active recreation. An outdoor swimming pool was built during Ford's term, and the president lifted weights and rode an exercise bicycle. Ford's greatest pleasure, however, was golf. He played whenever he could and unfortunately developed a reputation as a rather erratic player after hitting a spectator or two with his golf shots.

Like many of his predecessors, Jimmy Carter relaxed with a swim. He jogged on the White House grounds, bowled in the bowling alley, and played tennis on the mansion's courts. The Carter family particularly enjoyed the movie theater, which by Mrs. Carter's account became one of their favorite places to escape. The family frequently retreated there with popcorn or an entire meal to watch movies, including to-be-released titles with the director or an actor as a guest. Carter enjoyed classical and some pop music, and, as a speed reader who could read two thousand words per minute with 95 percent retention, he could read three or four books a week.

Ronald Reagan regularly followed an exercise routine that actually increased his muscular strength while he was president. Evenings with friends were a favorite pastime; he was an excellent storyteller who loved a good joke. Reagan also enjoyed the outdoors, particularly riding horses and working at his California ranch in the Santa Yaez Mountains.

Alternatives to the White House

When the pressures of the presidency become too great, it may not be enough to retreat to the movie theater or the swimming pool. Presidents often feel the need to leave the White House altogether to put their problems behind them. For that purpose the government maintains a presidential retreat in the mountains of Maryland, known as Camp David.

Originally named Shangri-La, Camp David was built for Franklin Roosevelt, who traveled there frequently. Eisenhower renamed it Camp David in honor of his grandson, Dwight David Eisenhower II, and made it his weekend home for the early part of his administration. Subsequent presidents, particularly since Johnson, have found it an invaluable source of solitude for self-renewal. It also has been a place where presidents can retreat to meditate on problems, design programs, and write speeches. For example, it was at Camp David that FDR plotted much of the strategy for the Normandy invasion of World War II. The retreat even has been used for international diplomacy. In 1978 Carter hosted an important summit meeting there between Egyptian president Anwar Sadat and Israeli prime minister Menachem Begin.

When first used in 1942, the buildings at Camp David looked unfinished and were filled with furniture from the White House attic. But the modern Camp David complex, which is far from rustic, is designed to let the president relax in comfort. It has a four-bedroom, air-conditioned lodge and additional guest cabins. Conference rooms are provided as well. Like the White House, Camp David has a swimming pool, bowling alley, and tennis court. For presidents who like to fish, there is a stream stocked with trout; for shooting, there is an archery and skeet-shooting range; and for playing golf, there is a par-three hole. The camp's riding stables were particularly appreciated by Jacqueline Kennedy, a skilled rider.

Most important, Camp David is also private. It is thirty minutes by helicopter from the White House, but it contains adequate communications equipment to keep in touch with the rest of the world. The grounds are surrounded by a chain link fence, topped with barbed wire, and are patrolled by marine guards. No one enters without an invitation from the first family; even the omnipresent White House press corps is left outside the compound. As President Reagan has noted, Camp David is one of the few places where a president can just step outside and go for a walk. The cost of maintaining this retreat has been estimated at more than $1 million a year.[8]

Even with the availability of Camp David, most presidents like the alternative of a private home for rest and relaxation. Such homes, popularly known, for example, as the western or Georgia White House, are equipped with communications and security facilities at public expense. Whereas Camp David is used frequently for weekend escapes, a president generally will use the alternate White House for extended vacations.

Every recent president has had at least one such retreat. FDR withdrew to his family estate in Hyde Park, New York, or to Warm Springs, Georgia, where he could undergo physical therapy. Truman went home to Independence, Missouri, or traveled to the Key West naval base when he took a vacation. Eisenhower sometimes vacationed in Denver, Colorado, near his wife's family; he was there when he suffered a heart attack in 1955. During his term, Eisenhower had a Gettysburg farmhouse that he had purchased remodeled, and before he left office it had become his weekend and vacation retreat.

Kennedy used several retreats. Originally avoiding Camp David because he was sure he would not like it if the Eisenhowers had, he vacationed instead at his family's compound at Cape Cod, Massachusetts, his father's house in Palm Beach, Florida, or at a friend's house, leased for his use, at Glen Ora, Virginia. After leaving the Glen Ora home the Kennedys decided to build their own retreat, and it was virtually finished when they decided they liked Camp David after all. Kennedy and his wife made news with their separate vacations; Mrs. Kennedy traveled alone to India, Italy, and the Mediterranean.

Johnson retreated to the LBJ Ranch on the Pedernales River in the Texas hill country. He loved to oversee the operation of his spread, speeding around it in his car and showing it off to visitors. The president also enjoyed hosting barbecues, sometimes on the spur of the moment. He challenged his Secret Service detail to speedboat races on the ranch's lake; the service always let him win the races so that secretly they could keep the fastest boat.

President Nixon had two retreats: a home in Key Biscayne, Florida, and one in San Clemente, California. The Nixon homes became involved in the Watergate controversy, when it was charged that improper funds were used in their purchase. Other critics claimed that the remodeling of the Nixon homes, done in the name of security, in fact increased their resale value at the taxpayer's expense.

President Ford maintained only one retreat, a home in California, and President Carter went back to his longtime home in Plains, Georgia, for a break from Washington. Ronald Reagan enjoyed his California ranch while president and vacationed there frequently. In fact, Reagan enjoyed his ranch so much that he was criticized for taking too many vacations.

The First Lady

As the president's wife the first lady is one of the most prominent women in the country. Many first ladies have had little to distinguish themselves except the position they have held by marriage, but others have achieved distinction on their own. Particularly since 1900 the first lady has been increasingly active politically and visible to the public. She is now among the best-known figures in American politics, more well known in fact than members of Congress and cabinet secretaries, and often even the vice president. *(See first lady biographies, p. 871.)*

The term "first lady" was not applied to the president's wife until after the Civil War. In its early days the Republic, uncertain of how much respect was due its leader's wife, tried several titles without success. Among them were Lady Washington, Mrs. President, presidentress, and Republican (or Democratic) queen. Sometimes no title was used. The title of first lady was first applied to Julia Grant in 1870, but it did not gain wide acceptance until Lucy Hayes held the position from 1877 to 1881.[9]

The modern first lady has a varied, demanding role. She acts as the manager of the White House, as well as the gracious hostess at receptions, parties, and formal dinners. She also is expected to play a political role and participate in social causes on behalf of her husband's administration, while fulfilling her responsibilities as wife and mother. Yet she holds no official position—the Constitution does not mention her—and earns no salary; her modern importance stems from history and changing customs.

The First Lady as Hostess

It has long been accepted that the primary responsibility of the first lady is to act as hostess at White House social events. Since the first presidential administration in the late eighteenth century, the public has expected the president to act as leader of Washington society. At the same time presidents have viewed the social calendar as a political tool. George Washington personally arranged for the first social season to serve political aims, and, similarly, more than a century and a half later Lyndon Johnson used White House functions to persuade people to adopt his point of view.

Custom demands that the president's wife organize and preside at social events. The first lady is supposed to arrange any teas, receptions, banquets, coffees, and state dinners that the president may have. And although she has both a personal and the White House domestic staff to assist her, the basic responsibility is still hers, even on those occasions when she does not have to act as hostess. Most first ladies have carefully selected the menus, entertainment, decorations, and even chairs for social events. For example, Mamie Eisenhower (1953-1961) replaced all the banquet chairs in the mansion after she decided the old ones were much too small.

Not all first ladies have been willing to accept the social role generally expected of them. Some, such as Dolley Madison (1809-1817) and Julia Tyler (1844-1845), seemed to relish company and loved to entertain at the White House. For others, such as Helen Taft (1909-1913) and Eleanor Roosevelt (1933-1945) it was largely a necessary formality. Still others avoided it altogether; for example, Letitia Tyler (1841-1842), Margaret Taylor (1849-1850), and Abigail Fillmore (1850-1853) made few, if any, social appearances, leaving relatives to act as hostess.

In her social role the first lady frequently can use parties and other social events to soothe ruffled feathers and charm the uncommitted, thereby helping the president. Perhaps the best first lady at this was Dolley Madison, famous for her glorious parties. Mrs. Madison's charm and ability to put people at ease won numerous friends for her aloof husband, James Madison, who was once described by American writer Washington Irving as a "withered little apple-john." [10]

The First Lady as Manager

Besides organizing parties, the first lady is expected to be the traditional homemaker. When one's home is the White House, that may be a rather large order. The first lady acts as the general supervisor of the White House, much like the mistress of a large estate. She oversees food selection, decorations, furnishings, cleaning, and other household duties.

Again, some first ladies have been much more concerned with these duties than others. Eleanor Roosevelt had little or no interest in how well the White House was kept up—she had no time for it. One visitor to the White House, having soiled her gloves on the banisters, wrote that Mrs. Roosevelt should spend less time traveling and more time cleaning the house.[11] In contrast, her successor, Bess Truman, was quite concerned with the general dirtiness of the mansion and had a running battle with the housekeepers to improve their cleaning in general and dusting in particular. Mamie Eisenhower, who succeeded Mrs. Truman, was a demanding mistress and was particularly choosy about the carpets, insisting that they be vacuumed several times each day so as not to show footprints. Mrs. Eisenhower was used to running a tight ship; one of her first demands was that all menus be approved by her alone.

Despite the best managerial efforts of the first lady, however, the White House is not always readily responsive. The large permanent staff has a natural inertia, which leads it to resist the first lady even as it tries to serve her. Thus, a new first lady who suddenly wants previously neglected corners made spotless may find the housekeepers slow to respond to her demands and the corners dirty. For the first lady and the staff, there is a process of mutual accommodation, where she adjusts to their established ways as they adjust to her desires.

The First Lady as Public Figure

The first lady has always had a social role to play; receptions and dinners have long been part of Washington life. Similarly, the duties of household manager are not new. The letters of first lady Abigail Adams, wife of President John Adams (1797-1801), reveal her continual concern with her budget and her home, and subsequent first ladies have had the same worries in managing the White House. The modern first lady differs from her predecessors, however, in the extent of her public activity. Rarely have first ladies been as visible as they are today; moreover, the public expectations of the first lady are higher than ever before.

Early first ladies were not expected to play any political role at all. Being the gracious hostess at social functions was the norm, and more than that was frowned upon. The established model for women was that of passive purity; placed on a pedestal, they were thought to be both above and unsuited for the dirty world of politics. A woman had her place, and the first lady, like any other woman, was expected to remain there.

As a result early first ladies were apolitical and often relegated to the background. For most of these first ladies life in the White House was very restrictive, for it was imperative that the president's wife display only "proper" behavior. Martha Washington (1789-1797) declared herself to be a virtual prisoner as first lady. Elizabeth Monroe (1817-1825) avoided Washington life altogether, and Louisa Adams (1825-1829) played the part of social lady but never assumed any other public role. Dolley Madison (1809-1817), however, was much more prominent and became the grande dame of Washington, but her fame was limited strictly to her social role; she indicated no political views.

The limits on first ladies were seen most clearly during the tenure of the nation's second first lady, Abigail Adams. A very intelligent woman with an excellent sense of judgment, she took a keen interest in politics and political figures. Her husband, John Adams, frequently sought her advice on issues of the day and privately acknowledged her importance as an adviser. Yet all of her political activity was strictly behind the scenes; when she displayed her political leanings in public, she was roundly criticized for inappropriate and unladylike behavior. Her strong political views and clear influence on John Adams were offensive to many.

During the first half of the nineteenth century the White House was occupied by a series of first ladies who maintained almost no profile, in keeping with the accepted image of the day, which depicted women as fragile creatures who easily became ill. Several first ladies thus avoided a public role on the grounds of ill health or personal tragedy. Letitia Tyler (1841-1842), Margaret Taylor (1849-1850), Abigail Fillmore (1850-1853), Jane Pierce (1855-1857), and Eliza Johnson (1865-1869) were among those who so abdicated a public role.

The exceptions to this trend were John Tyler's young second wife, Julia (1844-1845), and Mary Lincoln (1861-1865). Julia Tyler never lacked for flair. She had scandalized polite society by appearing in advertisements when a teenager; as first lady she hired a press agent and received

Franklin D. Roosevelt Library

From 1933 to 1945 Eleanor Roosevelt redefined the role of the first lady, constantly plunging into political activities and humanitarian projects. Here she holds a press conference for women journalists.

guests while seated on a raised platform. Mary Lincoln also was very visible but in a less appealing manner. She was compulsive and neurotic, and her mental instability and erratic behavior drew widespread public attention and negative publicity. Although both first ladies were more prominent than their predecessors, neither was politically active.

Throughout the nineteenth century the ideal of a demure, polite, proper first lady persisted and most first ladies remained obscure. In the second half of the century, however, public interest in first ladies grew. The growth of literacy, especially among women, along with an increase in the amount of reading material available meant that Julia Grant (1869-1877), Lucy Hayes (1877-1881), and particularly glamorous Frances Cleveland (1886-1889, 1893-1897) were better known to the public than most of their predecessors. Nevertheless, the activist first lady had to wait until the twentieth century.

The first step in the creation of the modern first lady was the development of mass communication, particularly the invention of the linotype press in 1885. The spread of mass-circulation newspapers and magazines helped stimulate curiosity about the president's family and increased coverage of its activities. First ladies naturally became celebrities. Historian Betty Boyd Caroli has argued that there were several reasons for the growing media interest in first ladies: "The absence of any clearly defined role for presidential wives, the possibility that they exercised some private influence on their husbands, and their place as symbols of how women ought to behave made them the object of the same kind of media attention that surrounded actresses, sports figures, and society women." [12] The mass media first lady began emerging with the publicity that surrounded the wedding of Frances Folsom and Grover Cleveland on June 2, 1886, which was the first presidential wedding to take place in the White House itself (President Tyler's wedding was held in New York). It has continued ever since.

The second important step was a gradual change in the nation's attitudes toward women and public life. The traditional view of women as passive, delicate creatures began to fade in the 1870s with the growing pressure for greater equality for women. Much of this trend was symbolized in the drive for women's suffrage, which took root in 1890. Only after fifty years, however, would this trend directly affect the role of first lady.

Edith Roosevelt (1901-1909), the twentieth century's first first lady and the second wife of Theodore Roosevelt, began to take advantage of the revised public outlook toward women. Realizing the importance of the news media and the public interest in her boisterous family of six children, Mrs. Roosevelt carefully managed the news coming from the White House. While she was not active politically, it was well known that her husband sought and listened to her advice, and, unlike Abigail Adams, she was not criticized for it. Under Edith Roosevelt, the first lady emerged as the leader of Washington society. Her meetings with the cabinet wives and her regular evening musicales helped insure a new prestige for the first lady.

Edith Roosevelt also began the process of institutionalizing the office of the first lady. She hired a social secretary to assist with her growing load of mail and to deal with press releases and reporters' questions. This marked the beginning of a permanent staff for the first lady, independent from that of the president, to handle the first lady's business. As such, it was a major step in the evolution of the modern first lady.

The first ladies who followed Edith Roosevelt contributed in different ways to the emerging modern first lady. Helen Taft (1909-1913), for example, began to alter the notion that first ladies were to be politically seen but not heard. It was widely known that William Howard Taft never would have become president had it not been for the driving ambitions of his wife. It also was known that Mrs. Taft participated in her husband's politics; only a stroke kept her from being an important if unofficial player in the Taft administration. Woodrow Wilson's first wife, Ellen (1913-1914), was the first first lady to support publicly social legislation (a housing bill) pending before Congress. His second wife, Edith (1915-1921), was perceived to be running the country after the president's stroke in 1919. Neither Grace Coolidge (1923-1929) nor Lou Hoover (1929-1933) were involved in politics, but both were very visible and had an interest in social causes.

The increasing attention of the media to the first lady, the changing attitudes toward women's roles, and the development of the first lady's office came together with Eleanor Roosevelt, who from 1933 to 1945 redefined the role of the first lady. She expanded the initiatives of her predecessors, reaching into areas previously untouched by a first lady. She gave the office her unique stamp and changed its place in American politics.

Mrs. Roosevelt realized the potential of her position for publicity, and she exploited it to the hilt. She regularly granted interviews and routinely held her own press conferences, which were open to women journalists only. In 1933 journalistic coverage of the president was almost exclusively a man's job; Mrs. Roosevelt hoped her press conferences would stimulate opportunities for women in journalism. And early on she mastered the art of posing publicly for staged photographs with children or working people—what in later days would be known as "photo ops." In fact, she became so good at managing the media that she was constantly in the newspapers and newsreels.

Of course, to be in the news she had to do something, and here she again broke new ground. Her level of activity was incredible and unprecedented for a first lady; she was always in motion. Projects followed one another in rapid succession. She visited the rural poor, miners, prisoners, soldiers in their foxholes, hospitals, and "New Deal" programs. She seemed everywhere. Sometimes she traveled for the president, other times for herself. Her constant movement was the subject of jokes and cartoons as well as of admiration.

Mrs. Roosevelt also was politically active to a unprecedented degree. She took up social causes publicly; for example, she pushed openly for an end to racial segregation. She drew attention to the plight of the poor in the slums, the unemployed, and the war veterans who had lost pensions. She advocated equality for women. During World War II she served as deputy director of the Office of Civilian Defense. She scrutinized various New Deal programs, offering suggestions when possible, and kept close watch over her favorites. In an effort to push her programs she frequently pressured President Roosevelt, sometimes to the point that he would have to leave the room. If FDR avoided someone his wife thought he should see, she might invite that person to dinner. Her political clout was thought to be extensive, and she became a kind of liaison for the general public.

She also answered thousands of letters herself, gave speeches and lectures, had her own radio program, and wrote a syndicated newspaper column, "My Day," and numerous magazine articles. She even wrote a best-selling autobiography, *This Is My Story.* Although most of the money from her writing was given to charity, she enjoyed the satisfaction of having her own source of income.

When Eleanor Roosevelt left the White House in 1945 the role of first lady had been changed drastically and permanently. She had established it as something separate from the presidency, and with her outspokenness, activity, and visibility had made it independent from, although linked to, the Oval Office. She also changed forever the public's expectations of the first lady. After her, the public would begin to look for an active woman in the White House; the passive, retiring first lady was gone for good.

Mrs. Roosevelt's immediate successors, Bess Truman (1945-1953) and Mamie Eisenhower (1953-1961), were more retiring than she. Mrs. Truman regarded the White House as the "Great White Jail" and, noting that "we are not any of us happy to be where we are," said that she "most definitely" would not have become first lady of her own choice.[13] Although she shrank from publicity and refused to grant interviews, it was well known that Bess Truman was very influential with her husband and gave him considerable, if general, political advice. Truman himself acknowledged her help and claimed that she was frequently objective when he was not.

Despite her weak heart and chronic inner ear problems, Mrs. Eisenhower was more visible than Mrs. Truman. She was widely admired, and her bangs, her clothes, her favorite pastels of pink and green, and even her cooking recipes were copied by thousands of women across the country. Although Mrs. Truman and Mrs. Eisenhower did not take center stage as first ladies, neither did they retreat to the extent of earlier first lady Jane Pierce (1853-1857) who, burdened by the death of her son, simply withdrew from the position.

The next first lady, Jacqueline Kennedy (1961-1963), elevated the position to a glamour spot. Young, attractive, cosmopolitan, and fluent in French, Mrs. Kennedy became a media star and largely gave the Kennedy White House its image. She was not interested in politics; instead, she focused on art and culture. She worked to bring historical antiques to the White House, and entertainment under Mrs. Kennedy featured some of the finest talent from the opera and the classical concert stage. Although in many ways the most private of people, Jacqueline Kennedy renewed the first lady's office as a grand public stage; her cultured charm and poise, seen best in her televised tour of the White House in 1962, left her successors with a high-profile position to fill.

Lady Bird Johnson (1963-1969) may have lacked some of Mrs. Kennedy's style, but she did resurrect the political possibilities of the first lady. She used her position to help achieve policy goals and as a platform to speak to the public and push for action. Believing that improved surroundings meant a better quality of life, Mrs. Johnson traveled thousands of miles across the country to support her beautification program and lobbied Congress in behalf of the Highway Beautification Act of 1965. In fact, her repeated emphasis of the nation's natural beauty helped fuel the ecological movement. She worked as well to improve conditions in Washington's slums. Mrs. Johnson even took the unprecedented step of actively campaigning for her husband, touring the South by herself to gather support. In essence, she became an unnamed presidential aide, and in doing so she raised the level of the first lady's political involvement.

Hampered by her own retiring nature and her husband's political difficulties, Pat Nixon (1969-1974) was able to add little to the first lady's role, although she was one of the most widely traveled first ladies and the first to represent the president abroad in peacetime. Betty Ford (1974-1977), however, was active in a variety of social causes. A former dancer, she encouraged the fine arts whenever possible. She worked in behalf of the poor, elderly, and handicapped, and became perhaps the most visible spokesperson for women's rights in general and the Equal Rights Amendment (ERA) in particular. She even personally called Illinois legislators to try to win support for the ERA. Her "pillow talks" with her husband over issues became common knowledge. She also proved to be one of the most candid of first ladies; she was willing to discuss everything, including controversial issues, such as abortion and premarital sex, and personal difficulties, such as her own breast cancer. Mrs. Ford thus increased the social concerns and the visibility of the first lady, but she also made the first lady a sort of Everywoman, to whom everyone could relate.

Rosalynn Carter (1977-1981) pushed her office to its limits during her four years in the White House. She testified before a congressional committee in support of legislation promoting mental health, one of her major interests, thereby becoming only the second first lady (after Eleanor Roosevelt) to appear before Congress. She also advocated improved programs for the elderly and supported the ERA. What distinguished Rosalynn Carter was the extent of her political involvement, which went far beyond what had been seen before. She was essentially an equal partner in her husband's presidency. Mrs. Carter sat in on cabinet meetings; she traveled abroad and met heads of state as her husband's representative; and she held regular working luncheons with the president. She effectively functioned as a presidential adviser, and her influence with President Carter was extensive and openly acknowledged by both. In fact, she seemed to be involved in almost everything, which led to widespread criticism. Certainly no first lady, except perhaps Eleanor Roosevelt, had explored the possibilities of her position more than Rosalynn Carter. One could argue in fact that she took the position further than the public was willing to see it go.

Nancy Reagan (1981-1989) pulled back from the extreme exposure of Mrs. Carter. Her public political activity was slight, and her influence, while extensive, was exercised behind the scenes. She was interested in restoring elegance to the White House. Like other recent first ladies, she also had a social cause to champion—drug abuse—and she traveled widely and hosted conferences in an effort to reduce drug abuse in the United States. She promoted as well the Foster Grandparents program.

The first lady's position in American politics has changed dramatically since 1789. Once, the first lady was seen and not heard (and sometimes not even seen). She was expected to be passive and retiring, to be a proper hostess, and to refrain from action or even opinion on political and social problems. The modern first lady is a part of her husband's team. She takes positions, works for causes, makes public appearances and speeches, and is often an important figure in her own right.

First ladies now may take a much more active role in electoral politics as well. Once the idea of a woman campaigning was inconceivable, and even an otherwise irrepressible Eleanor Roosevelt did not campaign separately for her husband. This, however, has changed. Lady Bird Johnson led the way by campaigning alone in the South for her husband's reelection in 1964.

At the same time the expectations of the first lady have changed. She is no longer expected to be a shrinking violet. The legacy of Eleanor Roosevelt and her activist successors is that Americans now anticipate that the first lady will take up some social problem as her own and work for its solution. When Betty Ford became first lady, the first question she was asked was "What is your program going to be?" And as Nancy Reagan discovered, the consequences of having no program can be serious. When she moved into the White House in 1981, Mrs. Reagan announced that she was not interested in public social work; her husband was her project, she said. The public no longer accepted such a limited role for the first lady, however, and Mrs. Reagan's public image suffered. She did not begin to gain wide public favor until she initiated her work on preventing drug abuse.

Over the years changing social attitudes and the efforts of a succession of women have caused the first lady's office to take its present form. The modern first lady has her own staff and set of offices in the East Wing of the White House. *(See "The First Lady's Staff," p. 871.)* She remains responsible for the social functions and management of the mansion, but she is also a political activist with her own special issues, a distinct political figure in her own right, and an integral part of the president's administration. The wife of the president can largely shape the role of the first lady to her needs and desires, yet it is clear that a set of imprecise yet definite expectations about her role has emerged. The first lady must satisfy them if she is to be a success and an asset to the president.

Similar opportunities and pressures will exist for any future presidential spouse. When a woman occupies the Oval Office, there may be a "first gentleman" who will have the opportunity to expand the office while meeting public expectations that he serve as an asset to his wife.

The First Lady as Asset and Liability

How and what the first lady does can be very important to the president. If she plays her role well, it may strengthen his support, but if she carries out her duties poorly, it can hurt his political standing. First ladies have proven to be both assets and detriments to their presidents.

Some first ladies, such as Dolley Madison, were assets to their husbands through their social roles. Although he was a brilliant and privately charming man, James Madison was cool and aloof in public. Mrs. Madison's grace, compassion, and sunny disposition more than offset her husband's weaknesses. By her own admission she was primarily interested in people, and she had a great ability for making them relax and feel at ease. When a young guest spilled his drink at one of her receptions and became flustered and embarrassed, she reassured him with the smiling remark that in such great crowds, accidents were unavoidable. She had a remarkable memory for names and faces and seemed to have a genuine concern for everyone. Her entertaining made her the star of Washington. Her courage and composure also were renowned. When the British burned the White House during the War of 1812, it was Dolley Madison who stayed behind until the last possible minute to rescue papers and the portrait of George Washington by Gilbert Stuart. So popular was she that James G. Blaine, who tried for the presidency himself in the 1870s and 1880s, wrote that "she saved the administration of her husband.... But for her, DeWitt Clinton would have been chosen president in 1812." [14]

Seventy years after Dolley Madison left the White House, another woman arrived who proved to be a similar asset to her husband. Frances Cleveland married into the

White House on June 2, 1886, and her youth, beauty, and grace made her instantly and immensely popular—quite in contrast to dour and grumpy Grover Cleveland, who sometimes ignored visitors altogether. She stood in reception lines shaking hands for so long that her arms required a massage afterward. The president's new wife also became a trendsetter in fashion; if Mrs. Cleveland wore it, so did everyone else. Merchants even began using her unauthorized likeness in their advertisements. She was so popular that one Republican official lamented, "It will be so much harder for us to win against both Mr. and Mrs. Cleveland." [15] In the election of 1888, which Cleveland lost to Benjamin Harrison, Mrs. Cleveland was a focal point of the campaign. The Democrats put her picture above that of the president on their campaign posters, while the Republicans circulated rumors that Cleveland beat his wife.

The first lady who in many ways was the biggest asset to her husband was Eleanor Roosevelt. Mrs. Roosevelt's assistance to her husband went beyond a transfer of popularity, for although she was widely admired and respected, she was also intensely disliked by many. Her real importance to the president lay elsewhere. Crippled by polio, the president relied on his wife to be his eyes and ears, to go to places where he could not and report back to him. She became his link to the public, keeping him informed on what the people wanted, how New Deal programs were working, and what kinds of new projects were needed.

Her well-publicized independence from the president proved a tremendous asset as well. Eleanor frequently took positions on issues such as desegregation and women's rights that were well beyond those of FDR himself. When she did so, the praise she won went in part to him by association as her husband, and thus he was able to broaden his base of support through her. To those she offended he could say, "That's my wife" and "I can't do a thing with her." Her separate identity let him have it both ways. Eleanor's daily newspaper column, "My Day," which began as a diary but soon was discussing issues of the day, also helped the president; he sometimes used it to send up trial balloons, and politicians read it in an effort to anticipate the president's intentions.[16]

Two recent first ladies whose popularity rubbed off on their husbands were Jacqueline Kennedy and Betty Ford. Beautiful and stylish, Mrs. Kennedy emerged as the star of the Kennedy administration. She became immensely popular, and even her hairstyle and clothing were copied—everyone wanted the "Jackie look." She was as well the subject of constant media attention and drew big crowds when she made public appearances. When she traveled with President Kennedy, crowds would call for her more than him. The president, realizing what an asset she was, took advantage of it, and he would introduce himself (as he did on a trip to France) as "the man who accompanied Jacqueline Kennedy."

Similarly, Mrs. Ford was more popular than her husband, Gerald, who jokingly wished that "I could just get my ratings up to hers." Mrs. Ford's courage and candor won her thousands of admirers, and she became one of the world's most popular women. She even publicly discussed her bout with breast cancer. While her support for the ERA and her remarks about the possibilities of drug use or premarital affairs by her children angered some people, they also won great support from many others. By 1976 she was so popular that buttons began to appear saying, "Betty's Husband for President" and "Keep Betty in the White House." She continued to gain admirers after leaving the White House by speaking openly of her successful struggle to overcome an addiction to alcohol and prescription painkillers.

Other first ladies have been helpful to their husbands in different ways. Mrs. Coolidge's cheerful personality proved a welcome contrast to "Silent Cal," and Mrs. Truman advised her husband and kept his famous temper under control. Mrs. Johnson's campaigning won votes for Lyndon. Mrs. Carter's open assistance of her husband was so great that it aroused animosity in many citizens, who felt an unelected first lady had no business doing as much as she did.[17]

Not every first lady has been an asset to the president, of course, especially during the 1800s. For example, Elizabeth Monroe, aristocratic and reserved, refused to participate in the expected social round; the sharp contrast with

Gerald R. Ford Library

Betty Ford was one of the most popular first ladies. By the time of the 1976 campaign, buttons began to appear saying, "Betty's Husband for President" and "Keep Betty in the White House."

her predecessor, Dolley Madison, brought much ill will toward James Monroe. Likewise, Jane Pierce contributed little to her husband, Franklin. She had poor health, was morbidly religious and frequently depressed, and acutely disliked her husband's political career. She was burdened as well by the death of her son. Thus the White House, far from being a cheerful place to win friends for the president, was shrouded in gloom for four years.

Mary Lincoln, the first lady who was perhaps the biggest liability to her husband, was emotionally unstable. She meddled in appointments, bought clothes compulsively, and was prone to irrational jealousy and emotional outbursts. Mrs. Lincoln was the target of vicious criticism on all sides, with charges ranging from poor taste to treason. In the presidential campaign of 1864 she became a major issue, and newspapers attacked her as much as or more than Lincoln himself. As the pressure increased, her behavior deteriorated. Far from helping, the first lady was a political and personal millstone to a husband trying to deal with the Civil War.

The First Lady's Staff

The permanent staff that assists the modern first lady in her duties is completely separate from the White House domestic staff that she also oversees (on a flow chart the domestic staff appears under the chief usher's office).

Prior to 1900 there was no staff for the first lady, and few first ladies had any reason to need one. They did little except to entertain in season, which did not necessarily constitute an excessive amount of work, and most remained quietly within the White House, with the occasional exception such as Julia Tyler, who had a press agent. At a time when the president needed little or no staff, there was certainly no reason for the first lady to have any.

In 1901 the first step toward establishing an East Wing staff was taken by Edith Roosevelt. The growth of literacy and of the media had created a greater interest in the White House and an increase in mail to and press coverage of the first family. Aware of the need to satisfy public curiosity, yet wanting to protect her family's privacy, Mrs. Roosevelt hired Belle Hagner as her secretary. Hagner became an all-purpose aide to the first lady; she released photographs and news stories about the Roosevelts, helped answer the mail, and helped supervise the operation of the White House. The secretary's position became a permanent one, passed down to the first ladies who followed.

There was now a permanent staff for the first lady, but for about fifty years it remained quite small: one or two people, as well as an occasional person on loan from some government agency. Even Eleanor Roosevelt, who received some 300,000 letters in 1933 alone, had only one full-time person working under her; she had to borrow help from the president's staff. The staff only began to grow when Mamie Eisenhower entered the White House in 1953 and it accelerated after her. Including all the "borrowed" help, Mrs. Kennedy's social secretary, Letitia Baldridge, claimed to have as many as forty people working for the first lady.

The staff acquired more diversification and structure under Lady Bird Johnson, who formally separated the press and social functions of her staff. Bess Abell, her social secretary, was responsible for arranging parties, banquets, and receptions, and Elizabeth S. (Liz) Carpenter was press secretary and overall staff supervisor. The staff was divided by functions and organized as well or better than the president's own. Later first ladies continued this trend.

The size of the staff has varied with each first lady. In recent years the permanent staff has numbered between twenty-one and twenty-six, with some allowance made for borrowing from other sources when needed. Even so, the first lady often is pressed for help. Rosalynn Carter, for instance, pleaded repeatedly with Jimmy for more staff, but she never got it. He also refused to let her borrow staff from other agencies.[18]

The organization and duties of the staff also have varied with each first lady. Like the president, the first lady can use staffers as she sees fit, and in fact her smaller staff gives her more flexibility that way. Most staffs, however, are now divided into social, press, and policy sections. The press secretary handles media inquiries; the social office plans events and compiles invitation lists; and policy advisers inform the first lady on policy questions that interest her. In addition, the staff has a director of scheduling to ensure that the first lady's travels are properly coordinated and a correspondence office to deal with her mail. There is also a calligrapher's office to take care of any engraving, such as on invitations, that may be needed. (The calligrapher's office also holds the presidential seal and grants permission for its use.)

The organization of Mrs. Johnson's staff was typical: six people handled media relations, four organized social functions, four answered correspondence, and two dealt with the "beautification" question.[19] While the numbers change, the basic divisions remain.

Biographies of the First Ladies

An important but sometimes overlooked part of the presidency is the spouse who comes to the White House with the president. The women who have served as first lady have acted as hostesses, political activists, and presidential advisers. They represent a range of personalities: some have been quiet and withdrawn, figures in the shadows; others have been colorful, visible, and even controversial. The story of some is one of success; of others, tragedy. But all contributed to the success of their president and to the development of the office of the first lady.

National Portrait Gallery

Martha Washington

Born: June 21, 1731;[20] New Kent County, Virginia
Parents: Col. John and Frances Jones Dandridge

Spouses: Col. Daniel Parke Custis; June 1749; New Kent County
George Washington; January 6, 1759; New Kent County
Children: By Daniel Parke Custis: John Parke (1754-1781); Martha (Patsy) Parke (1756-1773)
Died: May 22, 1802; Mount Vernon, Virginia

The early years of Martha Dandridge Custis Washington are not well documented. Her father was a small plantation owner, who, although not well-to-do, was part of the Virginia aristocracy. Martha was well trained in the social graces but apparently had little schooling, as her erratic spelling attests.

In 1749 Martha met and married Col. Daniel Parke Custis, son of a wealthy Virginia plantation owner. Custis, by whom Martha had four children (two died in infancy), was twice her age. The elder Custis left his son his considerable estate when he died in November 1749. Thus, when Daniel died of heart failure on July 8, 1757, the estate passed on to Martha, making her a very wealthy widow at the age of twenty-six.

George Washington probably had met Martha before her husband's death, and shortly afterward he came to pay his respects to the widow. Courtship followed, and although many historians have argued that Martha was not Washington's first love, the pair married in 1759. The addition of Martha's estate to George's plantation, Mount Vernon, where the Washingtons lived, made the couple wealthy, and the years until 1775 were spent tending to the plantation. But this period was punctuated by two sorrows: Martha's failure to have more children and the 1773 death of her daughter, Patsy, from an epileptic seizure.

With the onset of the American Revolution in 1775, George left Mount Vernon to lead the American army. Martha spent the summers of the war at Mount Vernon, but each winter, when the armies paused in their struggle, she joined her husband in camp, endeavoring to cheer him and his troops. When the war drew to a successful conclusion in 1781, Martha looked forward to a quiet retirement with George, but instead he became the nation's first president on April 30, 1789.

Martha did not join George in New York, the temporary capital of the new nation, until May 1789. She found being first lady (although not called such then) to be somewhat restrictive: "I live a very dull life here . . . I think I am more like a state prisoner than anything else." Martha may not have been well read, but she was a pleasant and engaging hostess who generally enjoyed entertaining. Her Mount Vernon home rarely had been empty. As the initial first lady, she set patterns for her successors, such as the regular Friday afternoon parties for ladies and the custom of opening the White House to all visitors on New Year's Day. The latter custom remained in effect until it was discontinued by the Hoovers in 1931.

George and Martha retired to Mount Vernon in 1797. The time left was not easy; financial worries nagged them, for the plantation had not been very profitable in recent years, and Martha's health had begun to deteriorate. "Lady Washington" lived quietly at her home until her death in 1802. She was buried on the plantation's grounds next to George, who had died two years earlier.

Library of Congress

Abigail Adams

Born: November 11, 1744; Weymouth, Massachusetts
Parents: Rev. William and Elizabeth Quincy Smith
Spouse: John Adams; October 25, 1764; Weymouth
Children: Abigail Amelia (1765-1813); John Quincy (1767-1848); Susanna (1768-1770); Charles (1770-1800), Thomas Boylston (1772-1832)
Died: October 28, 1818; Quincy, Massachusetts

Outspoken Abigail Smith Adams was the second of four children born to a New England minister and his wife. Abigail was sickly as a child, and she had no formal schooling, yet she acquired a considerable education in the private library of her family. Her intelligence, sharp wit, and willingness to speak out impressed those people who knew her. One such person was John Adams, who made his first reference to Abigail in his diary when she was only fourteen. After overcoming the objections of her parents, who did not consider him to be in her social class, John and Abigail married in 1764.

Abigail quickly proved to be an adept manager of their household. She ran their family farm efficiently, prosperously, and largely on her own while John was pursuing his legal and political careers and serving as an American diplomat abroad. She also helped educate their children, teaching them Latin after first teaching herself. In 1784, after a six-year separation, she sailed to London and rejoined John, who was then the first American minister to England. She spent four years in London and Paris, not entirely approving of the customs there, before returning to the United States in 1788 when John became vice president.

Abigail became first lady when John was elected president in 1796. In many ways the four years that she spent as first lady were difficult for her. The expense of entertaining was a strain on the president's salary, and the demands upon her left her with almost no time of her own. Although she managed to save some money and find some private time, she complained bitterly (but privately) about both problems. John was not a popular president and was subjected to constant vilification in the press, which angered Abigail greatly. In 1800 Abigail supervised the move from Philadelphia to the new presidential mansion on the Potomac. Unfortunately, it was far from finished when she arrived; only a few rooms were habitable and many facilities were lacking. But as a practical New Englander she hung laundry in the East Room. The new nation's capital, Washington, was in no better condition with its collection of mud roads and half-built buildings, and Abigail was privately unhappy at having left Philadelphia for it. Nevertheless, she spent her time there laying the foundations of a proper social life for the capital.

Abigail was a prolific letter writer (over two thousand of her letters still exist) and from them it is clear that, unlike most other first ladies for years to come, she took an active interest in politics and did not hesitate to express her views on the issues and personalities of the day. For example, Abigail had urged John in 1775 to support independence and later to back more education for women and the abolition of slavery. As a pioneering feminist, Abigail repeatedly urged her husband to "remember the ladies" in forming the new government. Moreover, she attacked his political enemies such as Alexander Hamilton, who opposed Adams's nomination for a second term and whom she called "the very devil."

Her husband had a very high regard for her judgment and intelligence, and her influence and political involvement were clear to her contemporaries. Many of them, however, took exception to both as unbecoming a woman. The extent of her political activism, while perhaps not as great as that of some modern first ladies, would be unmatched for years to come.

Roundly disliked by Federalists for refusing to go to war with France and by the Republicans for being a "monarchist," John Adams served only one term as president before retiring to Massachusetts. Abigail lived there for seventeen years, her health gradually deteriorating but her mind remaining alert, before she died of typhoid fever at the age of seventy-four. She was buried in Quincy. John, who outlived her by six years, was buried later next to her. Shortly before his death, John wrote of the love and admiration that he had always had for his wife and spoke of his gratitude for her "never-failing support" during his political career.

Library of Congress

Dolley Madison

Born: May 20, 1768; New Garden, North Carolina
Parents: John and Mary Coles Payne
Spouses: John Todd; January 7, 1790; Philadelphia, Pennsylvania
James Madison; September 15, 1794; Harewood, Jefferson County, Virginia
Children: By John Todd: John Payne (1792-1852); William Temple (1793)
Died: July 12, 1849; Washington, D.C.

Perhaps the most popular of the early first ladies, the elegant Dorothea (Dolley) Payne Todd Madison was born into a Quaker family of nine children.[21] Her family lived on a Virginia plantation until she was five, when her father freed their slaves and moved to Philadelphia. There, in 1789, Dolley met a young Quaker lawyer, John Todd, whom she married a year later. They had been married for three years when a yellow fever epidemic struck Philadelphia and claimed Dolley's husband and younger son.

Shortly after Todd's death Dolley met James Madison and within a year married him. For the indiscretion of marrying outside her faith, she was expelled from the Friends, but this only seemed to allow her true self to shine through. She discarded her plain grey Quaker garments for bright clothing and elegant turbans. Dolley loved entertaining and delighted in giving large, formal dinner parties. In fact, she was greatly admired as a hostess, particularly because of her memory for names and her remarkable ability to put everyone at ease. In this, she was a particular asset to Madison's political career, for he was generally withdrawn and cool around crowds.

With Dolley as first lady the White House became a festive place. Although she occasionally had served as hostess for the widowed Thomas Jefferson, Dolley came into her own when Madison was elected president in 1808. Her weekly receptions were always lively and gay. And she paid all the expected social calls, knowing that they would help her husband. So popular was Dolley that even her habit of taking snuff, which was considered very unladylike, was overlooked.

Although Dolley greatly loved social life and company, she was not one-dimensional. As a Quaker, she was a well-educated woman for her time, and her managerial skills were good as well. But she downplayed her intelligence and strong will to help her husband. During the War of 1812 when the British threatened Washington, she displayed her courage by staying behind in the White House to supervise the removal of documents. She remained there until the last possible moment, taking the portrait of George Washington by American portraitist Gilbert Stuart as her last act before leaving the White House. (Contrary to popular legend, the painting was not cut down. Dolley had its frame broken, and it was rolled up.)

When Madison's term expired in 1817 he and Dolley retired to their Virginia estate, Montpelier. Life was not easy in retirement; Dolley still entertained, but financial woes plagued them, aggravated by the wastefulness of her son, John Payne. After Madison died in 1836 Dolley was reduced to near poverty and had to sell first his well-known papers on the Constitutional Convention and then Montpelier to pay her debts.

Finally, she returned to Washington and spent the rest of her life there. Even as she grew older, she remained the center of Washington society, admired by every president through James K. Polk. She was even granted a lifetime seat on the floor of the House of Representatives. In 1849 her funeral was attended by every dignitary the capital could muster. She was buried in Washington but later was removed to rest beside Madison at Montpelier.

Library of Congress

Elizabeth Monroe

Born: July 30, 1768; New York City
Parents: Capt. Lawrence and Hannah Aspinwall Kortright
Spouse: James Monroe; February 16, 1786; New York City
Children: Eliza Kortright (1786-1835); James Spence (1799-1801); Maria Hester (1803-1850)
Died: September 23, 1830; Oak Hill, Virginia

Elizabeth Kortright Monroe, who brought a new touch of aristocracy to the White House, was born into one of New York's premier families. Not much is known of her younger years. She met James Monroe in 1785, and although her family and friends disapproved of both his politics and his social status, she married him the next year.

The Monroes moved from New York to Virginia in 1789. James was elected to the U.S. Senate in 1790, and from 1794 to 1796 he served as ambassador to France. While in France, Elizabeth, upon learning that Madame Lafayette was facing execution, boldly drove to the prison to speak with her publicly—a gesture that earned her release. James later served on other diplomatic missions to Europe (1803-1807), and Elizabeth spent much of that time in Paris, where she found the environment convivial. While in Europe, the Monroes adopted European formality, believing that it helped them deal with Europeans.

That formality was carried into the White House when James became president in 1817, for the Monroes believed it to be appropriate to the presidential office. The contrast between the haughty Elizabeth Monroe and her predecessor, the vivacious Dolley Madison, was dramatic and, so far as social Washington was concerned, very unfavorable for Elizabeth. Quiet and somewhat aloof, she refused to follow the accepted Washington custom of paying social calls. Her many critics decried her as too aristocratic and French, and for a time they boycotted her receptions. Her elder daughter, Eliza, angered many with her arrogant behavior, and Elizabeth angered them further when she refused to extend mass invitations to younger daughter Maria's wedding, the first in the White House.

Bothered by chronically weak health and disliking much of her role as first lady, Elizabeth nonetheless continued her entertaining until she left the White House in 1825. Her last years were spent at the Monroe mansion, Oak Hill, in Virginia, but they were clouded by financial difficulties. She died in 1830 and was buried at Oak Hill. Monroe died in New York a year later and was buried next to her.

Library of Congress

Louisa Adams

Born: February 12, 1775; London, England
Parents: Joshua and Catherine Nuth Johnson
Spouse: John Quincy Adams; July 26, 1797; London
Children: George Washington (1801-1829); John (1803-1834); Charles Francis (1807-1886); Louisa Catherine (1811-1812)
Died: May 15, 1852; Washington, D.C.

Louisa Catherine Johnson Adams did not see the United States until she was twenty-six. She was born in 1775 in England, where her father represented an American tobacco firm, but her family moved shortly to France and lived there until 1790. In 1790 they returned to England. There, in 1795, she met John Quincy Adams, who was on a diplomatic mission from the United States. Two years later they married. Because their personalities were quite different in many ways, the early years of their marriage were somewhat strained. They grew much closer in later years, however.

Louisa's time abroad has led some to call her "the most travelled woman of her time." From England she went to Berlin, where John Quincy was the American minister to Prussia during the administration of his father, John Adams (1797-1801). When Jefferson became president in 1801, John Quincy was recalled, and Louisa saw the United States for the first time and met her in-laws, who received her with reservations. From 1803 to 1808 she lived in Massachusetts while John Quincy served in the U.S. Senate. In 1809 President James Madison appointed him minister to Russia. Leaving her two oldest sons behind with their grandmother, Louisa accompanied her husband to St. Petersburg.

The time in Russia was difficult for Louisa. The harsh weather adversely affected her health, and her only daughter died after living less than a year. Moreover, she was frequently lonely, particularly after John Quincy left for Belgium in 1814 to negotiate the treaty ending the War of 1812. Early in 1815 he sent word to her that his mission in Russia was finished and that she should join him in France. After packing their goods, she set out with her young son in the dead of the Russian winter for Paris; only her courage and resourcefulness got them through the perilous two thousand-mile journey.

An intelligent and talented woman, Louisa spoke French fluently and enjoyed sketching and playing the harp and piano. Yet she seems to have had virtually no effect on John Quincy's political career. By her own admission, "no woman certainly had interfered less in [politics] than I have." For his part, John Quincy deliberately shared none of his professional life with her.

President James Monroe appointed John Quincy secretary of state in 1817, and in 1825 he became president. Louisa's time as first lady was not a pleasant one, however. The regular receptions that she held were a strain on her and, although well attended, were not thought exciting. She suffered from poor health in the form of recurrent migraine headaches and fainting spells, and she was hurt by the vicious criticism that was aimed at her husband, particularly after his controversial victory over Andrew Jackson in 1824. No doubt she was pleased to return to Massachusetts in 1829 when his term expired.

Louisa came back to Washington when John Quincy was elected to the House of Representatives in 1830. There she lived quietly the rest of her life, generally apart from Washington society. In 1848 John Quincy suffered a stroke on the floor of the House and died without regaining consciousness. Despite the strains their marriage had endured in earlier times, Louisa's letters indicate her anguish at losing her husband of fifty years so abruptly. She died four years later and was buried next to him in Quincy, Massachusetts.

Anna Harrison

Library of Congress

Born: July 25, 1775; Walpack Township, New Jersey
Parents: John and Anna Tuthill Symmes
Spouse: William Henry Harrison; November 25, 1795; North Bend, Ohio
Children: Elizabeth Bassett (1796-1846); John Cleves Symmes (1798-1830); Lucy Singleton (1800-1826); William Henry, Jr. (1802-1838); John Scott (1804-1878); Benjamin (1806-1840); Mary Symmes (1809-1842); Carter Bassett (1811-1839); Anna Tuthill (1813-1845); James Findlay (1814-1817)
Died: February 25, 1864; North Bend

Almost a footnote in White House history, Anna Symmes Harrison never saw the executive mansion that she was supposed to run. Anna's father was a New Jersey farmer and an army officer. She was educated at some of the better schools for girls in the young nation and is the first first lady for whom there is a definite record of her schooling. In 1795 Anna's father took her to the new Ohio settlement of North Bend, where she met William Henry Harrison, a military officer who was stationed there. The two eloped the same year over the objections of Anna's father, who did not believe that an army man could adequately support his daughter.

The life Anna adopted was that of an army officer's wife. She traveled with her husband until her family became too large. The couple lived primarily in a substantial log cabin in North Bend during their marriage, but they did spend a few years in Vincennes when Harrison was governor of the Indiana Territory. There Anna managed to care for her large family, frequently without any help from her absent husband.

Anna was intelligent and much better educated than most frontier women, and she was a devout Presbyterian. The years on the frontier were hard, however, on her health. The Harrisons rarely had any excess money, particularly after they were forced to assume the debts of their eldest son, who owed the government $12,000 when he died.

When the country went wild over "Tippecanoe and Tyler Too" in 1840 (Tippecanoe was Harrison's nickname), Anna was far less enthusiastic. Her husband had been content in retirement, and she thought he should stay there. She was concerned about her ability to be a satisfactory hostess—although she had proved able to entertain capably when necessary—and about her reception in Washington. When William Henry left for the capital in February 1841, Anna was too ill to accompany him; she decided to wait for spring before going herself. But Harrison died after only a month in office, and Anna never left Ohio.

Anna Harrison lived for nearly twenty-three more years in North Bend. In fact, she outlived all but two of her children. After her own home burned down, she spent her final years in the home of her last surviving son, John, and there she died in 1864. Despite being the wife of one president and the grandmother of another (Benjamin Harrison), Anna never saw Washington. She was buried next to her husband and her father in North Bend.

Letitia Tyler

Library of Congress

Born: November 12, 1790; Cedar Grove, New Kent County, Virginia
Parents: Col. Robert and Mary Brown Christian
Spouse: John Tyler; March 29, 1813; Cedar Grove
Children: Mary (1815-1848); Robert (1816-1877); John, Jr. (1819-1896); Letitia (1821-1907); Elizabeth (1823-1850); Anne Contesse (1825); Alice (1827-1854); Tazewell (1830-1874)
Died: September 10, 1842; Washington, D.C.

Letitia Christian Tyler was born into a wealthy Virginia plantation family; her father was a friend of President George Washington. Although Letitia apparently had no formal education, she learned at home the skills needed to be the mistress of a southern plantation. Modest and reserved, she had many friends. Letitia met John Tyler in 1808, and after a five-year courtship in part imposed by her parents, they married.

Letitia's skills as a manager were needed quickly, for John's law practice and budding political career—he had been elected to the Virginia House of Delegates in 1811—kept him away from home frequently. Apparently, Letitia was an excellent manager and ran the growing Tyler plantation very effectively. She refused to go to Washington when John was elected senator from Virginia in 1826, both because she was needed on the plantation and because she disliked the unpleasant conditions then found in the capital. She also was a quiet woman who was devoted to her family and preferred to remain in her husband's shadow.

By the time John became president upon William Henry Harrison's death in 1841, Letitia's health had deteriorated dramatically. She had suffered a serious stroke in 1839 and had only partially recovered. Although she could still oversee the plantation, she was largely homebound. Letitia finally came to the White House, but she took no part in the mansion's public life. During her time as first lady, her daughter Letitia managed the White House, and her daughter-in-law Priscilla served as hostess. Her only public appearance was at daughter Elizabeth's White House wedding in January 1842. Otherwise, she remained out of sight, a semi-invalid, content to read her Bible and prayer book.

On September 9, 1842, Letitia suffered another stroke. She died one day later, becoming the first president's wife to die in the White House. The depressed president ordered the White House hung in black for an extended period of mourning. Letitia was buried in Virginia on her father's estate, Cedar Grove.

Library of Congress

Julia Tyler

Born: May 4, 1820; Gardiners Island, New York
Parents: David and Juliana McLachlan Gardiner
Spouse: John Tyler; June 26, 1844; New York City
Children: David Gardiner (1846-1927); John Alexander (1848-1883); Julia Gardiner (1849-1871); Lachlan (1851-1902); Lyon Gardiner (1853-1935); Robert Fitzwalter (1856-1927); Pearl (1860-1947)
Died: July 10, 1889; Richmond, Virginia

Vivacious Julia Gardiner Tyler, who brought cheer back to the Tyler White House, was a dark-haired beauty from a wealthy New York family. She was educated at an elite New York finishing school, and she was very popular in New York society. Somewhat impetuous and daring, at age nineteen Julia scandalized her family by posing for a department store advertisement, which polite ladies did not do in 1839. Her family promptly took her to Europe to avoid more embarrassments.

Julia first met President Tyler at a reception in 1842 while her family was visiting Washington, but he did not take much notice of her until after the death of his wife, Letitia. Julia refused his first marriage proposal in early February 1843, but she changed her mind after her father was killed in an accident on board a U.S. Navy frigate a year later. In June 1844 the couple was wed in a secret ceremony in New York. The wedding was so secret in fact that even Tyler's children were not told in advance. As a result relations between several of them and Julia were strained for years. Julia produced seven additional Tyler offspring during her marriage, the youngest when Tyler was seventy.

The energetic Julia's time in the White House was brief, but she enjoyed it enormously. She established her own court, despite the ridicule of the press, and entertained lavishly. She was the first first lady to have her own press agent (although she hardly needed it), and she initiated the custom of playing "Hail to the Chief" for the president.

The Tylers left the White House in 1845 for their Virginia plantation. Conservative and defensive of her husband's politics, Julia became increasingly pro-southern, and by the time of the Civil War, both she and John wholeheartedly supported the Confederacy.

The years after John's death in 1862 were very difficult for her. The Civil War and Reconstruction destroyed most of the Tyler estate, and Julia had very little money. Moreover, she was plagued by legal battles over her property and her share of her mother's estate, contested by estranged members of her family. When she petitioned Congress for a pension, the pleas of the widow of the traitor Tyler were not favorably received for some years. Much of what she did have was lost in an economic panic in the early 1870s.

Not until the late 1870s was Julia able to begin rebuilding her estate. In 1882 Congress included her in a pension it extended to widowed ex-first ladies, enabling her to be more comfortable in her last years. In July 1889 Julia Tyler died of a stroke in the same Richmond hotel in which John had died twenty-seven years earlier. She was buried next to him in Richmond.

Library of Congress

Sarah Polk

Born: September 4, 1803; Murfreesboro, Tennessee
Parents: Capt. Joel and Elizabeth Whitsitt Childress
Spouse: James K. Polk; January 1, 1824; Murfreesboro
Children: None
Died: August 14, 1891; Nashville, Tennessee

One of the most politically minded of the first ladies, Sarah Childress Polk was born on her father's plantation in Rutherford County, Tennessee. She was educated at a private school in Nashville and spent one year at the Moravian Female Academy in North Carolina, one of the best schools of its kind in the South, before her father's death forced her to return home. In 1819 she began a courtship with James K. Polk, who was a clerk in the Tennessee Senate. They married in 1824.

Intelligent and strong-willed, Sarah began to play an important role in her husband's career. Far from being a reluctant partner, she shared and actively encouraged his political ambitions, and, unlike other politicians' wives in those days, she routinely assisted her husband in his political activities. For example, she served as his personal secretary, reading and marking papers important for him to read, and kept him informed about political matters when he was absent and provided advice on questions of the day. Her high profile led many observers to conclude that Polk was under her thumb, but she insisted that she was helping because of his delicate health.

During the presidential campaign of 1844 Sarah let it be known that she had no intention of churning butter and keeping house if she became first lady, and she kept her word. Impatient with social functions, she preferred to spend time with her husband on political matters and often did so until late at night. The Polks worked together without a vacation for four years. While she dutifully carried out her social responsibilities as first lady, Sarah, a devout Presbyterian, dismayed Washington society by banning drinking and dancing at the White House.

Worn out by his exertions in the White House, James died a few months after his term ended in 1849, and for the rest of her life Sarah always wore a bit of black. Showing great business skill, she operated profitably the Mississippi plantation that James had acquired while president until—perhaps anticipating the changes coming to the South—she sold it in 1860. She continued to live alone at Polk Place in Nashville—from which she had run the plantation—until her death in 1891. The southern woman who said that she belonged to the entire nation remained respected and admired by all, even during the turmoil of the Civil War. She and James are buried on the grounds of the Tennessee capital building in Nashville.

Margaret Taylor*

Born: September 21, 1788; Calvert County, Maryland
Parents: Walter and Ann Mackall Smith
Spouse: Zachary Taylor; June 21, 1810; Jefferson County, Kentucky
Children: Ann Mackall (1811-1875); Sarah Knox (1814-1835); Octavia Pannel (1816-1820); Margaret Smith (1819-1820); Mary Elizabeth (Betty) (1824-1909); Richard (1826-1879)
Died: August 18, 1852; Pascagoula, Mississippi

* No portrait known

One of the most obscure of first ladies, Margaret Mackall Smith Taylor was born into a prosperous Maryland family, but very little record of her early years has survived. It is known, however, that she attended a New York finishing school and that she met Zachary Taylor in 1809 while visiting her sister in Kentucky. She and Taylor married a year later.

For the better part of the next thirty years Margaret led the life of a military wife, following her husband to various posts from Wisconsin and Minnesota to Louisiana and throughout the South. She was unable to make a truly permanent home until 1840, when Zachary became southwestern commander and was assigned to Baton Rouge, Louisiana. Even then, he had to leave her to fight in the Mexican War. The constant moving took a toll on Margaret's health and her family. A malaria outbreak in Louisiana in 1820 claimed two of her daughters and almost killed her.

By 1848 Margaret Taylor was a semi-invalid who wanted only to live peacefully with her husband. She was appalled at Zachary's nomination and election to the presidency in that year, regarding it as a plot to deprive her of his company. Thus, she came to Washington very reluctantly, and once there she completely abdicated her duties as first lady in favor of her youngest daughter, Betty. Because her time in the White House was spent upstairs as a semirecluse, wild rumors soon spread through Washington that she was a pipe-smoking simpleton. But in fact she was quite articulate with the few old friends she saw, and tobacco smoke made her acutely ill. So withdrawn was she that many people did not know until Zachary died that there even was a Mrs. Taylor.

Devastated by President Taylor's sudden death in July 1850, Margaret left the White House and went to live with her son in Mississippi. Two years later she died there, without ever referring to her days as first lady. No portrait or photograph of her remains, and her obituary in the *New York Times* failed to give her Christian name. She was buried next to Zachary near Louisville, Kentucky.

Library of Congress

Abigail Fillmore

Born: March 13, 1798; Stillwater, New York
Parents: Rev. Lemuel and Abigail Newland Powers
Spouse: Millard Fillmore; February 5, 1826; Moravia, New York
Children: Millard Powers (1828-1889); Mary Abigail (1832-1854)
Died: March 30, 1853; Washington, D.C.

Growing up on the frontier, Abigail Powers Fillmore had little formal education. Yet she was able to educate herself well from the large library left by her father, who died when she was two. By sixteen, Abigail was a teacher in New Hope, New York, where she met Millard Fillmore, who was one of her students, although only two years younger than she. After a seven-year romance, the couple overcame the objections of her family and married.

For the first two years of their marriage Abigail continued to teach, which was unusual at a time when married women rarely worked. She did not cease working until Millard's election to the New York State legislature in 1828. She continued to educate herself, however, learning French and the piano as an adult. Intelligent and well informed, Abigail took an active interest in her husband's political career, and she was able to join in political discussions with friends. Her political sense was keen, and she advised Millard frequently throughout his career. He acknowledged that he consulted her on any important matter. Yet despite her private importance in Millard's life, she felt a public role for herself was inappropriate and refused public speaking opportunities.

Abigail remained in New York when Millard became vice president in 1848 and did not arrive in Washington until October 1850, after he had become president upon the death of Zachary Taylor. As first lady, Abigail turned much of the formal entertaining over to her daughter, generally limiting herself to more casual evening receptions and musicales. In part this was due to an old ankle injury which made prolonged standing difficult for her, but she also had little interest in Washington social life. She preferred a quiet evening with a book to a party and thought that social Washington would find her dull. Thus, she generally stayed in the background. Appalled at not finding one book in the White House, Abigail sought and received a congressional appropriation to start the mansion's first library.

In March 1853 Abigail insisted on attending the outdoor inauguration of Millard's successor, Franklin Pierce, despite her poor health and the bad weather. A chill then turned into pneumonia, and Abigail Fillmore died less than a month later in Washington. She and Millard, who died twenty-one years later, were buried in Buffalo.

Library of Congress

Jane Pierce

Born: March 12, 1806; Hampton, New Hampshire
Parents: Rev. Jesse and Elizabeth Means Appleton
Spouse: Franklin Pierce; November 19, 1834; Amherst, Massachusetts
Children: Franklin (1836); Frank Robert (1839-1843); Benjamin (1841-1853)
Died: December 2, 1863; Andover, Massachusetts

Jane Means Appleton Pierce was born in 1806 to a Congregationalist minister and his wife, who hailed from a wealthy New England family. Jane's father, the excessively hard-working president of Bowdoin College in Brunswick, Maine, died in 1819. Under her parents' strict Calvinist influence, Jane became a very religious yet almost morbid young woman, possessed of delicate health and a fragile beauty that she hid in her simple dress. Although she had little formal schooling, it is likely that she gained a reasonable education from her father and various tutors.

Jane met Franklin Pierce, a graduate of Bowdoin, at her widowed mother's house in Amherst around 1826. Because of resistance from Jane's family, they did not marry until 1834. Upon their marriage they moved to Washington, D.C., as Franklin was then a member of Congress from New Hampshire. Jane, however, passionately hated both Washington and politics. Thus, she stayed away from the capital as much as possible and tried to convince Franklin to leave politics for his law practice. In 1842, surrendered to her pleas and resigned his seat in the U.S. Senate.

But the quiet, happy life that Jane wanted in New Hampshire was not to be. Her first child lived only three days; her second died of typhoid fever at the age of four. These tragedies accented her tendency toward depression and nervous tension so much that Franklin had to refuse an appointment as U.S. attorney general. He did, however, volunteer for the Mexican War. He also maneuvered himself into the Democratic presidential nomination in 1852, despite assuring Jane he would not do so. When Jane discovered his deception, her trust in him was shattered. She prayed for his defeat in the presidential election of

1852 and was greatly depressed when he was elected. In January 1853 the Pierce family was involved in a train wreck in Massachusetts. Franklin and Jane were unhurt, but their remaining son, Bennie, was killed before his mother's eyes.

Jane never really recovered from this disaster. She believed Bennie's death to be some sort of divine judgment of Franklin's election. She did not come to Washington until after the inauguration of her husband, and when she did arrive, she stayed upstairs in the White House and wrote letters to her dead son. She did not make an appearance as first lady until New Year's Day, 1855. Her sense of duty led her to carry out her social responsibilities for the rest of Franklin's term, but she had no enthusiasm for them. Throughout her stay in Washington she was considered an invalid, and the White House was regarded as a gloomy place.

An admittedly sick woman by 1857, Jane left the White House to travel abroad for her health. The cure was ineffective, however, and she returned to Massachusetts, depressed and ill. She died of tuberculosis in 1863 and was buried beside her children (and eventually her husband) in Concord, New Hampshire.

Library of Congress

Mary Lincoln

Born: December 13, 1818; Lexington, Kentucky
Parents: Robert and Elizabeth Parker Todd
Spouse: Abraham Lincoln; November 4, 1842; Springfield, Illinois
Children: Robert Todd (1843-1926); Edward Baker (1846-1850); William Wallace (1850-1862); Thomas (Tad) (1853-1871)
Died: July 16, 1882; Springfield

Perhaps the most controversial of the first ladies, Mary Todd Lincoln was one of fifteen children born to a prominent Lexington, Kentucky, businessman and his wife. Her parents provided her with a good education; Mary spoke French and studied dance and music. By age twenty-one she had gone to live with a sister in Springfield, Illinois. Mary was attractive, intelligent, and witty, but she was troubled by severe insecurity and a mercurial temperament that would worsen as she grew older.

While in Springfield, she met Abraham Lincoln, whom she married when she was twenty-four. The motive for her decision to marry Lincoln, as with so many of Mary's actions, is not clear. Some scholars believe that she claimed to see a future president in the man she chose above other suitors, but their early marriage was hardly presidential. They lived in near poverty for the first year, and, although circumstances improved as Lincoln served in Congress and then was a Springfield lawyer, Mary still lacked the luxury she had known as a girl.

Mary's belief in her husband was justified when he was elected president in 1860, but her dream of being first lady was to become a nightmare. The difficulties of her young married life, including the death of her eldest son at age four, had combined with her moody temperament to leave her emotionally unstable. Lincoln called her his "child wife," and often he had to treat her as one. By the time she became first lady, she was extremely nervous and prone to blinding headaches. Her moods swung erratically and violently, making her extremely impetuous and unpredictable. Her insecurity often showed as well, frequently in displays of irrational jealousy. Her instability made her a burden on a president trying to deal with war.

During Mary's stay at the White House she was the target of unceasing criticism. With the Civil War on, she fought with Congress for more money to renovate the White House. Her family's ties to the Confederacy led many to call her a traitor, and she was even investigated by a congressional committee. When she held White House receptions, she was criticized for her inappropriate frivolity during a national crisis. If she chose not to host social functions, she was attacked for "adding to the gloom" of the day. When her son Willie died of typhoid in 1862, her unrestrained grief was condemned as excessive in a time of national tragedy.

The constant pressure and criticism intensified Mary's emotional problems, and her behavior became even more extreme. Her grief at Willie's death was "uncontrolled"; Lincoln had to treat her like a "sick child." She refused to ever again enter the rooms where the boy died and was embalmed. She also banned flowers and music from the White House (for which she was criticized as well) and conducted séances with his spirit. Driven by her insecurity and the pressures of living in the White House, Mary compulsively bought clothes without Lincoln's knowledge, and her clothing bills soon exceeded his yearly salary. She fearfully awaited the returns of the 1864 elections, knowing that a loss would force her to face creditors she could not pay. When Lincoln won, she bought more clothes.

Mary was forty-seven when Lincoln was assassinated in 1865. She did not attend his funeral and stayed in mourning in the White House for five weeks. Her behavior after leaving the White House became increasingly erratic. She developed an obsession that she was impoverished, although Lincoln's estate left her $35,000 after settling debts. Mary petitioned Congress for a pension, but she was so clumsy in her appeals that she alienated most members of Congress as well as the public. To escape the criticism she went with her favorite son, Tad, to Europe and did not return until Congress gave her a small pension in 1870. But when Tad died of typhoid in 1871 she developed symptoms of paranoia and kept her money and securities sewed into her coat. Her behavior became so erratic that in May 1875 her remaining son, Robert, had her committed to a mental hospital.

After one of her sisters arranged her release from the sanitarium a few months later, Mary moved to France and lived there alone until she fell and badly injured her back in 1879. Sick and unhappy, estranged from her only remaining son, and largely forgotten, Mary went back to Springfield and died there of a stroke in 1882. She was buried next to her husband and children in Springfield.

Library of Congress

Eliza Johnson

Born: October 4, 1810; Leesburg, Tennessee
Parents: John and Sarah Phillips McCardle
Spouse: Andrew Johnson; May 17, 1827; Greeneville, Tennessee
Children: Martha (1828-1901); Charles (1830-1863); Mary (1832-1883); Robert (1834-1869); Andrew, Jr. (1852-1879)
Died: January 15, 1876; Greeneville

Eliza McCardle Johnson was born a few miles from Greeneville in east Tennessee. Her father was a shoemaker, who died when she was still very young, but her mother was able to support herself and her daughter by weaving, and Eliza managed to acquire a basic education. She met Andrew Johnson, a tailor newly arrived in Greeneville, in 1826; within a year they married.

While the Johnsons lived frugally on Andrew's income as a tailor, Eliza taught him to write and otherwise improved his education. In 1828, two years after arriving in Greeneville, Andrew's political career began when he was elected town alderman. That career would take him to the U.S. House of Representatives, the Tennessee governorship, the U.S. Senate, and the vice presidency. But throughout his career Eliza shunned the attendant social life, preferring instead to focus on the efficient operation of her home.

With Andrew's work and Eliza's management the family prospered, but Eliza's health did not. She suffered from a form of tuberculosis, and by 1853 the disease had already progressed so far that she felt unable to move to Nashville when Andrew became governor. She was forced from her east Tennessee home during the Civil War by the Confederate army, but she returned when the troops left and stayed there even when Andrew was elected vice president in 1864.

Lincoln's assassination in April 1865, which elevated Andrew to the presidency, changed her plans, and she arrived in Washington in August of that year. Although Eliza lived in the White House during her husband's turbulent administration, she took very little part in it. By then largely an invalid, she usually stayed in an upstairs room overlooking the front lawn, making only two public appearances during her time as first lady. Her daughter Martha served as White House hostess and supervised the renovation of the mansion after the Civil War. Although Eliza had no influence on Andrew's politics, her support for him never wavered. When told of his acquittal on impeachment charges, she said that she had known he would be.

With the expiration of Johnson's term in March 1869, Eliza returned to east Tennessee, where she lived for the next seven years. She died at the age of sixty-five, six months after her husband's death, and was buried next to him in Greeneville.

Library of Congress

Julia Grant

Born: January 26, 1826; St. Louis, Missouri
Parents: Col. Frederick and Ellen Wrenshall Dent
Spouse: Ulysses S. Grant; August 22, 1848; St. Louis
Children: Frederick Dent (1850-1912); Ulysses Simpson, Jr. (1852-1929); Ellen (Nellie) Wrenshall (1855-1922); Jesse Root (1858-1934)
Died: December 14, 1902; Washington, D.C.

Julia Boggs Dent Grant was born at White Haven, her father's large farm about five miles west of St. Louis, Missouri. From ages ten to seventeen she attended a private school in St. Louis. In 1843 she met Ulysses S. Grant, an army officer stationed in St. Louis, who had been a classmate of her brother at the U.S. Military Academy. The pair soon decided to marry, but opposition from Julia's father and the outbreak of the Mexican War delayed them for five years.

The first twelve years of their marriage were not always easy ones for Julia. Ulysses's army career led to several moves and then a long separation when he was transferred to the Pacific coast. In 1854 he left the army and returned to civilian life, but his attempts at farming and business were dismal failures. Julia, who had been brought up in a slave-owning family, struggled to raise four children and manage her household largely on her own and on very little income. She also had to deal with Ulysses's tendency to drink excessively.

The Civil War gave Ulysses the chance to escape oblivion. By its end his battlefield success had made him the most popular man in the United States, except perhaps for

President Abraham Lincoln. Ulysses was easily elected president in 1868. As first lady, the engaging Julia was a striking contrast to her immediate predecessors. At great expense she refurbished the White House, and she entertained lavishly—formal banquets had as many as twenty-nine courses. The country loved her style and her lively family. Politics was admittedly of no interest to her, but no one expected it; her society was sufficient. She was so prominent that, according to one historian, she was the first first lady to become a truly "national" figure.

After eight years in the White House the Grants toured the world and then settled in New York City. Another bad business deal left them penniless, but Grant's memoirs, written while he was dying of cancer, brought Julia an adequate income. She lived for seventeen years after his death in 1885 and wrote her own autobiography—the first president's wife to do so. It remained unpublished, however, until 1975. The woman who was the first to be called the "first lady of the land" died in Washington, D.C., and was buried next to her husband in New York City.

Library of Congress

Lucy Hayes

Born: August 28, 1831; Chillicothe, Ohio
Parents: Dr. James and Maria Cook Webb
Spouse: Rutherford B. Hayes; December 30, 1852; Cincinnati, Ohio
Children: Birchard Austin (1853-1926); James Webb Cook (1856-1934); Rutherford Platt (1858-1927); Joseph Thompson (1861-1863); George Crook (1864-1866); Fanny (1867-1950); Scott Russell (1871-1923); Manning Force (1873-1874)
Died: June 25, 1889; Fremont, Ohio

Lucy Ware Webb Hayes was the daughter of an Ohio doctor, who died in 1833 while on a trip to Kentucky to free his family's slaves. From her parents Lucy acquired a strong opposition to slavery. She was educated in private schools in Chillicothe and graduated from Wesleyan Women's College in Cincinnati in 1850, the first first lady to have a college degree. Lucy met Rutherford B. Hayes in 1847, before entering college. He subsequently set up a law practice in Cincinnati and eventually proposed to her, in 1851.

Lucy was a serious, intelligent woman, who took an active interest in her husband's military and political careers. During his service in the Civil War she traveled regularly to the camps where he stayed, and once brought him to Ohio to recuperate after being wounded. She was very interested in politics and kept abreast of the issues of the day. It was Lucy's persuasion that helped turn Rutherford against slavery, and at least in her early days she displayed feminist leanings. Her compassion for people showed in her kindness toward wounded soldiers and her concern for orphans and the poor while Rutherford was governor of Ohio.

Lucy became first lady in 1877. Her simplicity and frugality marked a dramatic change from the extravagance characteristic of the Grant administration. Devoutly religious and a teetotaler, Lucy instituted daily morning worship in the White House and banned alcohol from White House functions. The latter act, which earned her the derisive nickname of "Lemonade Lucy," was in fact as much a political as a moral gesture, for temperance was a burning issue of the day. Beyond this issue, however, she displayed no political leanings while first lady. She was a popular national figure who received letters from women throughout the country asking for help and advice. She initiated the custom of the children's Easter egg roll on the White House lawn.

After one term as president Hayes retired to Fremont, Ohio, in 1881. Lucy spent the next few years busy with her family and various charitable activities. On June 21, 1889, she suffered a severe stroke and died four days later. She was buried in Fremont, where Rutherford was laid to rest in 1893.

Library of Congress

Lucretia Garfield

Born: April 19, 1832; Hiram, Ohio
Parents: Zebulon and Arabella Mason Rudolph
Spouse: James A. Garfield; November 11, 1858; Hiram
Children: Elizabeth Arabella (1860-1863); Harry Augustus (1863-1942); James Rudolph (1865-1950); Mary (Molly) (1867-1947); Irvin McDowell (1870-1951); Abram (1872-1958); Edward (1874-1876)
Died: March 14, 1918; South Pasadena, California

Lucretia Rudolph Garfield was born to parents who strongly believed in education. Her father was one of the founders of what became known as Hiram College in Hiram, Ohio. With the encouragement of her parents,

Lucretia grew into a studious, thoughtful young woman, who attended the school her father had founded. There her intelligence impressed many.

While at Hiram, Lucretia came to know James A. Garfield, who was both a student and a teacher at the school. Although James admired Lucretia's intellect, he initially found her "dull." The romance that developed between them was an off-and-on affair that lasted nine years before their marriage, in part because Lucretia was reluctant to surrender her independence and in part because James mistrusted what he saw as her feminist leanings. Initially, their marriage was a strained one, aggravated by frequent separations during its first four years. A close bond did not begin to develop between them until after the death of their first child in 1863, as James was on his way to Congress.

As the wife of a member of Congress, Lucretia had little impact on Washington society. She preferred to spend time at the Library of Congress, which was near her home, and joined the Washington Literary Society. She also took a hand in her children's education in the classics and advised her husband when needed. She had become a political wife.

James became president in 1881, but Lucretia's time as first lady was very brief. She was making plans to redecorate the White House in an historical manner, and undertaking research for accuracy, when she was stricken with malaria in May 1881. She then left Washington to recuperate. James was on his way to visit her when he was shot in July; he died on September 19. Lucretia's stoic courage through his ordeal won her the admiration of the country. Unlike any previous first lady, she both organized his funeral and appeared publicly at it.

Lucretia Garfield lived for thirty-six more years, avoiding publicity while living briefly in Europe and then in Ohio. She died at her winter home in California and was buried next to James in Cleveland, Ohio.

Library of Congress

Frances Cleveland

Born: July 21, 1864; Buffalo, New York
Parents: Oscar and Emma Harmon Folsom
Spouses: Grover Cleveland; June 2, 1886; Washington, D.C.
Thomas J. Preston, Jr.; February 10, 1913; Princeton, New Jersey
Children: Ruth (1891-1904); Esther (1893-1980); Marion (1895-1977); Richard Folsom (1897-1974); Francis Grover (1903-)
Died: October 29, 1947; Baltimore, Maryland

Frances Folsom Cleveland, the daughter of a Buffalo, New York, attorney, was born in 1864. One of the first people to see the infant Frances was her father's close friend Grover Cleveland, who became her de facto guardian after Oscar Folsom was killed in an accident in 1875. Frances was educated in public schools in Buffalo and attended Wells College in Aurora, New York. She grew into a lively and attractive young woman, who maintained close ties with her friend Grover Cleveland.

In 1884 Cleveland became the first bachelor elected to the presidency since James Buchanan. For two years rumors about potential romances surrounded him—including one linking him with Frances's mother—until the White House announced his engagement to Frances in May 1886. Their wedding, the first of a president to be held in the White House itself, was small and yet a public sensation.

Frances Cleveland was admired widely. Her hairstyle and clothing became national fads, and her picture was used without her permission in various advertisements. Numerous causes solicited her endorsement without success. She held public receptions on evenings and Saturdays so that working women could come, and thousands did so. At one such reception nine thousand people came through her receiving line, and Frances's arms had to be massaged afterward. Her formal parties were just as popular. Frances's charm and beauty served as a valuable contrast to Grover, who could be rude and boorish. In fact, the public curiosity about her was so great that the Clevelands rented a second residence in Washington to use as living quarters, and Grover commuted to the White House.

Frances's six years as first lady were interrupted by the term of Benjamin Harrison (1889-1893). During the campaign of 1888, she became a campaign issue as the Republicans accused the president of beating his wife; Frances had to refute the charges publicly. Her picture eventually appeared on Democratic campaign posters, the first time a politician's wife had been displayed as such. When Frances returned to the White House in 1893 she reduced her social schedule to accommodate her growing family. Her second daughter, Esther, was the first child to be born in the White House.

In 1897 the Clevelands retired to Princeton, New Jersey. Eleven years later Grover died. Frances remained in Princeton and eventually married Thomas J. Preston, Jr., an archaeology professor who later taught at Princeton University. She remained active in social and charity work and was a key figure in distributing clothes to the poor during the depression.

On October 29, 1947, Frances died suddenly while visiting her son Richard in Baltimore. She was buried in Princeton next to her first husband, Grover.

Library of Congress

Caroline Harrison

Born: October 1, 1832; Oxford, Ohio
Parents: Rev. John and Mary Neal Scott
Spouse: Benjamin Harrison; October 20, 1853; Oxford
Children: Russell Benjamin (1854-1936); Mary Scott (1858-1930)
Died: October 25, 1892; Washington, D.C.

Caroline Lavinia Scott Harrison was the second of three children born to one of the "most illustrious educators of the early West." Because her parents believed in education for women Caroline was well taught; she displayed outstanding artistic and musical talents as well. Caroline first met Benjamin Harrison in 1848 while he was a student at Farmer's College in Cincinnati, Ohio, where the Reverend Scott was teaching. In 1849 the Reverend Scott took his family back to Oxford, Ohio, Caroline's birthplace, to establish the Oxford Female Institute, and in 1850 Benjamin transferred to Miami University in Oxford. Both Benjamin and Caroline were serious and intelligent and attracted to one another. Thus, in 1853 they married.

Within a year they settled in Indianapolis, Indiana, where they remained largely until 1881. Benjamin became a successful lawyer, and in 1881 he was elected by the Indiana legislature to the U.S. Senate. For her part, Caroline never completely developed her artistic abilities. Spurred perhaps by the needs of her husband's career, she concentrated on civic work and was active in her church. As a lively, cheerful person who made guests welcome, in contrast to her aloof husband, Caroline spent much time teaching art, music, and needlepoint to others.

Benjamin was elected president in 1888. Caroline came to the White House with the hope of not just refurbishing the mansion but also structurally changing or rebuilding it. She had three different plans for major changes drawn up. Congress refused to approve any of them, however, and she was left with a more modest remodeling that included repairing the furniture, redoing the floors and plumbing, repainting, exterminating the mice and insects, and adding bathrooms (an important consideration, since the Harrisons had several relatives staying with them). Electricity was also installed in the White House while Caroline was first lady, but she was so fearful of it that she would never touch the switches. Caroline designed her own china pattern and started the White House china collection by gathering pieces from previous administrations. Outside the White House she played an important role in making the new Johns Hopkins medical school coeducational.

Caroline's health became a growing problem as her term as first lady wore on. She had been seriously ill in 1883 and in 1886, but she recovered. By 1892, however, she was again so sick with tuberculosis that Benjamin refused to campaign actively in his reelection bid (his opponent, Grover Cleveland, also refrained from campaigning). Caroline continued to deteriorate through the summer and died two weeks before the election that turned her husband out of the White House. She was buried in Indianapolis, where Benjamin was buried as well six years later.

Library of Congress

Ida McKinley

Born: June 8, 1847; Canton, Ohio
Parents: James and Catherine Dewalt Saxton
Spouse: William McKinley; January 25, 1871; Canton
Children: Katherine (1871-1875); Ida (1873)
Died: May 26, 1907; Canton

Ida Saxton McKinley was one of three children born to a wealthy Canton, Ohio, banker from a prominent family. Active and headstrong as a young woman, she attended Brook Hall Seminary in Media, Pennsylvania, and worked in her father's bank for the pleasure of it, something rare for a woman in the 1860s. While working, she met William McKinley, a Civil War veteran and Canton lawyer, whom she married within a year.

For a brief time things went well for Ida. The family lived comfortably in Canton, and their first child was born within a year of their marriage. Then in early 1873 Ida's mother died. Shortly thereafter her second daughter was born, but the sickly infant lived only a few months. And less than two years later the McKinleys' other child, Katy, also died.

Ida never recovered physically or emotionally from these successive shocks. She developed a form of epilepsy and was subject to frequent seizures. She also suffered from severe headaches and phlebitis, and she was frequently depressed and irritable. For the rest of her life Ida remained an invalid, who made extreme demands on the time and patience of her husband. Yet William remained devoted to her, tending carefully to her needs despite his flourishing political career which led him to the presidency in 1896. Ida returned his devotion with a love that was almost worship.

Unlike previous first ladies who had been ill, Ida refused to remain in the background. She insisted on playing her role as White House hostess, and on attending all the social functions, despite the difficulties caused by her health. Special arrangements had to be made for every event to deal with the possibility of her becoming acutely ill. The president even changed the seating at formal dinners to place Ida next to him. If a minor seizure struck in the presence of guests, he would calmly cover her face with his handkerchief until it had passed and she could rejoin the conversation. Quick exits followed a major seizure. She also insisted on traveling with him, even though she was often too weak to do more than just be seen. Ida was not even able to manage the White House.

William McKinley developed a reputation as a saint for his care of his wife, and his foremost concern upon being shot in 1901 was for her. Ida, however, displayed surprising strength during his decline, death, and funeral, despite the anguish recorded in her diary. She returned to Canton to live, sick and lonely, for six more years. At first, she prayed daily to die, but later she decided that she wanted to live until completion of the McKinley mausoleum. She died four days before its dedication and was buried in Canton next to William and her two long-dead daughters.

Library of Congress

Edith Roosevelt

Born: August 6, 1861; Norwich, Connecticut
Parents: Charles and Gertrude Tyler Carow
Spouse: Theodore Roosevelt; December 2, 1886; London, England
Children: Theodore, Jr. (1887-1944); Kermit (1889-1943); Ethel Carow (1891-1977); Archibald Bulloch (1894-1979); Quentin (1897-1918)
Died: September 30, 1948; Oyster Bay, New York

Edith Kermit Carow Roosevelt was a childhood acquaintance of her future husband. They grew up in the same neighborhood, where she was a close friend of his younger sister. Although Edith did not attend college, she was a voracious reader and was considered well educated.

Edith was not Theodore's first love; his first wife had died in 1884 after a four-year marriage. A year later Theodore renewed his long association with Edith, and in 1886 they married.

Edith was intelligent and serious, and she possessed a detached serenity that served her well in managing the boisterous Roosevelt household. She had five children of her own, a stepdaughter, Alice, from Theodore's first marriage, and Theodore himself, whom she often seemed to regard as another child. She also was politically astute, and Theodore, who respected her intelligence, frequently looked to her for advice. Her stepdaughter, Alice, noted that the afternoon walks that Edith and Theodore took regularly seemed to have a "calming" effect on him.

Edith's organizational skills were valuable to her as first lady. To eliminate friction and control expenses she held weekly meetings of cabinet wives to coordinate entertainment. And in running the White House, she used caterers for formal entertaining and a personal secretary to help handle correspondence. Edith introduced other innovations as well. She began carrying bouquets of flowers to avoid having to shake hundreds of hands during receptions, and she initiated a portrait gallery so that there would be a permanent memorial to each first lady. A music lover, Edith replaced the customary White House socials with musicales.

Edith also worked to ensure that her family had some measure of privacy in the fishbowl of the White House. Realizing that public curiosity about the president's family would have to be satisfied, she released posed photographs and managed stories to produce more, instead of less, privacy. To the same end, she arranged to have the first family's living quarters separated distinctly from the White House offices and placed off-limits when the White House was remodeled. She also controlled the publicity surrounding Alice's elaborate White House wedding in 1906.

Public opinion was very favorable about Edith when she left the White House in 1909 to retire with Theodore to Oyster Bay. After his death in 1919, Edith traveled widely throughout the world, engaged in charity work, and continued her ties with the Republican party—she actively opposed Franklin Roosevelt's presidential bid in 1932. Her last years were spent quietly at Oyster Bay, and she was buried there next to Theodore.

Library of Congress

Helen Taft

Born: June 2, 1861; Cincinnati, Ohio
Parents: John and Harriet Collins Herron
Spouse: William Howard Taft; June 19, 1886; Cincinnati
Children: Robert Alphonso (1889-1953); Helen Herron (1891-1987); Charles Phelps (1897-1983)
Died: May 22, 1943; Washington, D.C.

Helen Herron Taft was the eldest daughter of the eleven children born to a Cincinnati judge and his wife. During a quiet childhood, she attended private schools and became a skilled pianist. Later she taught school for a few years and was part of a group of the city's young people who met frequently to discuss ideas. Although the Herrons knew the Tafts well, Helen did not meet William Howard until she was eighteen. Over the next seven years a romance gradually developed between the two, and they married in 1886.

Ambitious and discontented with a quiet life in Ohio, Helen prodded her less-driven husband in his career. She had visited the White House in 1888 and greatly wanted to return to it as its mistress. Although Taft was content with a place on the federal bench in Ohio, Helen pushed him to accept nationally important positions, first as U.S. solicitor general, then as governor of the Philippines (1901-1904), and finally as Theodore Roosevelt's secretary of war. Her objections twice led him to refuse a possible appointment to the U.S. Supreme Court during the Roosevelt administration. In 1908, despite his reluctance, Helen encouraged him to run for the presidency. It was known quickly that without her push, he never would have made the effort.

In the inaugural parade of 1909 Helen broke precedent by riding next to her husband. The symbolism was appropriate, for she was intimately involved in his political decisions and frequently assisted and advised him on political matters. Her influence over him was obvious. She had little patience for social events and tried to downplay them as much as possible to remain where important things happened. She even complained that when traveling with the president, she was often shunted to some idle social frivolity while he was engaged in important meetings.

Helen's drive for William's success strained her health. During her stay in the Philippines, she had been forced to go to Europe for treatment for nervous exhaustion. After two months as first lady she suffered a severe stroke that temporarily impaired her speech. She was away from the public for over eighteen months. Typically, she found the forced absence from the political councils far more aggravating than missed social duties.

Taft served only one term as president, and Helen left the White House bitter toward Roosevelt, whom she believed had ruined her husband's chance at reelection. The Tafts then moved to New Haven, Connecticut, where William taught at Yale Law School. In 1921 they returned to Washington when he was appointed chief justice of the Supreme Court. No longer politically active, Helen remained in Washington after William's death in 1930, until her death in 1943. She is the only first lady to be buried in Arlington National Cemetery. Helen Taft left at least one enduring legacy: Washington's famed cherry trees were planted at her request.

Library of Congress

Ellen Wilson

Born: May 15, 1860; Savannah, Georgia
Parents: Rev. Samuel and Margaret Hoyt Axson
Spouse: Woodrow Wilson; June 24, 1885; Savannah
Children: Margaret Woodrow (1886-1944); Jessie Woodrow (1887-1933); Eleanor Randolph (1889-1967)
Died: August 6, 1914; Washington, D.C.

Ellen Louise Axson Wilson was born into a family of Presbyterian ministers. She was an intelligent woman whose father once declared to be "entirely too much inclined" to make her own decisions. She attended Rome Female College in Georgia, and, as a talented artist, she spent a year taking art classes in New York City. Ellen continued to paint throughout her life and maintained a studio on the third floor of the White House while she was first lady. She was a member of what is now the National Association of Women Artists, and her work was publicly displayed at a one-woman exhibition in 1913.

In 1883, while still at home in Georgia, she met Woodrow Wilson, who was visiting Rome on legal business. He was immediately attracted to her and proposed within five months. Ellen returned his affection, but their marriage had to wait for two years; because her mother was dead and her father was emotionally unstable, Ellen felt that she had to remain at home to care for her younger siblings. Her father's sudden death in 1884 provided her with the freedom and money to pursue her interest in art and then to marry Woodrow.

Woodrow's academic career took the Wilsons to Bryn Mawr College in Pennsylvania, Wesleyan University in Connecticut, and Princeton University in New Jersey, where he became the university's president. Ellen was an immense asset to him. By tending to the daily household details he disliked, Ellen freed Woodrow for his work. More facile in language than he, she learned German to help translate materials he needed. Her calm disposition provided stability for her intense husband. When Woodrow left Princeton to become governor of New Jersey in 1910, Ellen again proved invaluable; her incisive intellect and her intuitive understanding of people and politics made her one of his most trusted advisers.

Throughout their years together the Wilsons maintained a special relationship. Although there is no evidence that Woodrow ever had an affair, he did prefer the company of attractive women, yet Ellen never displayed any jealousy. Because the Wilsons were frequently apart for various reasons, they maintained a constant correspondence that eventually totaled about fourteen hundred letters, in which their devotion to each other is obvious.

As first lady, Ellen maintained a hectic schedule of entertainment and social concerns. Perhaps because of her three career-oriented daughters, two of whom had White House weddings, Ellen became interested in women's suffrage. She supported the vote for women long before Woodrow did but never advocated it publicly. Instead, she took an interest in charitable work; for example, the revenue from her 1913 art exhibition went to a school for the underprivileged. She became interested in the problem of substandard housing in Washington and, after touring the capital's ghettos, openly pushed for legislation to improve the decrepit black neighborhoods. When a housing bill eventually passed in 1914, it was popularly known as "Ellen Wilson's bill." (The Supreme Court later declared the law unconstitutional, however.)

Ellen Wilson did not live to enjoy her legislative success. She was terminally ill with Bright's disease, a kidney ailment, and her health had been failing rapidly since late 1913. She was on her deathbed when her legislation was passed. Ellen died a few days before World War I began and was buried in Rome, Georgia, next to her parents.

Library of Congress

Edith Wilson

Born: October 15, 1872; Wytheville, Virginia
Parents: William and Sallie White Bolling
Spouses: Norman Galt; 1896; Washington, D.C.
Woodrow Wilson; December 18, 1915; Washington, D.C.
Children: None
Died: December 28, 1961; Washington, D.C.

Born into a family of eleven children, Edith Bolling Galt Wilson received most of her education at home and had only a few years of formal schooling. At age twenty-four she married Norman Galt, an older man who was a Washington, D.C., jeweler. But in 1908 Galt died suddenly and left his store to his wife. Edith continued to manage the business and she lived well, dressing fashionably and often making trips to Europe.

In March 1915 Edith was introduced to Woodrow Wilson by Wilson's cousin, Helen Bones, who was helping him manage the White House after Ellen Wilson's death. Edith and Woodrow were immediately attracted to one another and a romance developed rapidly. After hesitating briefly because of the possible political consequences of Woodrow marrying too soon after Ellen's death, they wed quietly at Edith's home. Despite the fears of his aides, Wilson suffered no political fallout, and he was reelected president in 1916.

Self-assured and decisive, the new Mrs. Wilson brought life and entertainment back to the White House. She also proved to be an important assistant to the president, working as his personal secretary and helping with his papers. Her primary interest was her husband; she was not particularly interested in politics and denounced the women's suffrage movement as unladylike. When the United States entered World War I, Edith tried to set an example for the country by observing the various meatless and gasless days, sewing items for the Red Cross, curtailing entertainment, and using sheep to keep the White House lawn trimmed (she donated their wool to the war effort).

While battling the Senate for ratification of the Treaty of Versailles after the war, Wilson's health broke down. By October 1919 a stroke had largely paralyzed him. Edith immediately stepped in to protect and shield her husband. She screened all papers, business, and visitors, keeping as much as possible away from him while he recovered. For a time, almost no one saw Wilson except her. Exactly how much power she wielded and how long she held it has never been determined conclusively. Critics then and now have argued that she was actually the acting president and essentially ran the country for the balance of Wilson's term. Edith herself claimed that her "regency" lasted but a few weeks and that Woodrow always made the important political decisions.

Sick and disillusioned, Woodrow Wilson lived only three years after leaving the White House. Edith survived him by almost thirty-eight years. During that time she traveled widely, participated in Democratic politics, wrote her memoirs, and served as a director of the Woodrow Wilson Foundation. She died of heart disease in 1961 and was buried with Woodrow in Washington's National Cathedral. Their house on S Street in Washington is now a museum.

Library of Congress

Florence Harding

Born: August 15, 1860; Marion, Ohio
Parents: Amos and Louisa Bouton Kling

Spouses: Henry A. DeWolfe; 1880; Marion
Warren G. Harding; July 8, 1891; Marion
Children: By Henry DeWolfe: Eugene Marshall (1880-1915)
Died: November 21, 1924; Marion

Florence Kling DeWolfe Harding was born into one of the wealthiest families in Marion, Ohio. She was educated at the local schools and then attended the Cincinnati Conservatory of Music. Willful and tenacious, Florence fought repeatedly with her domineering father. In 1880 she eloped with Henry DeWolfe, the son of a local coal dealer, and six months later had her only child. A man who liked to drink and hated to work, DeWolfe proved unreliable and abandoned Florence in 1882; she divorced him in 1886. She then allowed her parents to adopt her son, and she eked out a living giving piano lessons.

In 1890 she met Warren G. Harding, then a Marion newspaperman, and married him a year later over the violent objections of her father. Strong and demanding where Warren was weak and pliable, Florence quickly became the dominant force in the Harding household. She took charge of his newspaper, the *Marion Star,* and made it into an effective business, thereby freeing him for politics. She also pushed his political career, helping him into the U.S. Senate in 1914 and into the presidency in 1920. Because she believed in astrology, Florence at first hesitated to urge Warren to seek the presidency because a fortune-teller had predicted that although Warren would win the office, he would also die there.

Florence's personal life was not so successful. Health problems deprived her of the limited beauty she had had, and she knew that Warren, who was quite handsome, was having affairs. Her shrill voice and domineering manner led to further difficulties between them. Unflatteringly, Warren once had nicknamed her "Duchess." Their relationship continued to be strained during his presidency.

As first lady, Florence showed no interest in running the White House; she preferred to meet people. She entertained constantly, if not lavishly, opened the White House to the public, and shook hands for hours. And she frequently visited wounded war veterans. She also tried to control the news coming from the White House, partly to conceal the continued indiscretions of Warren and their unhappy marriage, and partly to downplay his unsteady health. Her own health was poor, for the one kidney she had (the other had been lost in 1905) was frequently infected. In fact, she almost died in 1922. Assertive and demanding, Florence apparently strongly influenced her husband, but she later destroyed most of the papers that could have indicated her exact role.

As scandals began to break over the Harding administration in 1923, the president traveled to the West Coast, where he died suddenly on August 2. His death was so unexpected—the true state of his health had been well hidden—that rumors circulated that Florence had poisoned him. She coldly ignored them. The night before his state funeral she sat for hours with his body, speaking to it as a mother would speak to a child.

Florence then returned to Marion, where Warren was buried. Based again on astrological forecasts, she believed that she had only a short time left to live. In fact, her diseased kidney continued to weaken, and she died fifteen months after leaving the White House. Ironically, one of the songs sung at her funeral was "The End of a Perfect Day." She was buried next to her husband.

Library of Congress

Grace Coolidge

Born: January 3, 1879; Burlington, Vermont
Parents: Andrew and Lemira Barrett Goodhue
Spouse: Calvin Coolidge; October 4, 1905; Burlington
Children: John (1906-); Calvin, Jr. (1908-1924)
Died: July 8, 1957; Northampton, Vermont

An only child, Grace Anna Goodhue Coolidge was born to parents from old New England families. She attended public high school and graduated from the University of Vermont in 1902, thereby becoming the first president's wife to have attended a coeducational university. After graduation from college, she spent three years teaching at the Clarke Institute for the Deaf in Northampton, Vermont. She remained interested in the hearing impaired throughout her life.

In 1903, while teaching at Clarke, Grace met Calvin Coolidge. Looking up from her gardening one morning, she noticed a man standing by the window shaving while wearing only a felt hat and his underwear. The sight struck her as ludicrous, and she burst out laughing. The man was Coolidge, who heard her laughter and arranged to meet her. A romance developed between the two (which many friends, then and later, found hard to understand because Grace and Calvin seemed so different), and they married two years later.

Calvin's political career led him to the White House upon Harding's death in 1923; he was elected to the presidency in his own right in 1924. Along the way Grace was a great asset to her husband. She was never involved politically (Calvin refused to allow it nor would he permit her to be interviewed), and there is no indication she ever gave him any political advice; she learned that he was not running for reelection in 1928 from reporters. But her outgoing personality and her remarkable memory for names and faces were a great contrast to tight-lipped Calvin's dour disposition, and she often won friends for him.

As first lady, Grace's good-natured cheerfulness made her extremely popular. Many thought that her cheerful vitality epitomized the twenties. She was charming, friendly, and colorful, and was seen frequently with children or her pet animals. Her passion for baseball made her popular with men. Moreover, she loved music and the theater and brought notables in both fields to entertain at the White House. When the White House was renovated in 1927 Grace campaigned to have authentic period furniture donated to the mansion, but few people gave any. Grace's stay at the White House was marred by one tragedy: the death of her younger son in 1924 from blood poisoning contracted from a blister on his toe.

Calvin Coolidge died four years after leaving the White House, but Grace lived and remained active for twenty-four more years. As first lady, she had helped raise $2 million for the Clarke School, and she spent much of her retirement trying to help meet the needs of the hearing impaired. During World War II she worked with the Red Cross and civil defense programs. In her last years her health slowly failed, and she died in 1957. Grace was buried next to her husband and younger son in Plymouth Notch, Vermont.

Library of Congress

Lou Hoover

Born: March 29, 1874; Waterloo, Iowa
Parents: Charles and Florence Weed Henry
Spouse: Herbert Hoover; February 10, 1899; Monterey, California
Children: Herbert, Jr. (1903-1969); Allan Henry (1907-)
Died: January 7, 1944; New York City

The best educated of any first lady, Lou Henry Hoover was born in 1874 about one hundred miles from the birthplace of Herbert Hoover, West Branch, Iowa. She lived in Waterloo, Iowa, attending public schools, until 1884, when, because of Mrs. Henry's poor health, her family moved to California. A public lecture on geology that she heard in Pacific Grove, California, led her to enroll at Stanford University in 1894, where she became the first woman to major in geology. She met Herbert, also a Stanford geology student, the same year.

In 1898 Lou graduated from Stanford and accepted a marriage proposal from Herbert, who wired it from his job site in Australia. In 1899 he returned to California to marry her, and a week later they set out for China, where he had accepted a position with a mining firm. Thus began a global odyssey that would make Lou Hoover the most-traveled first lady in a century.

In China the Hoovers found themselves in the middle of the Boxer Rebellion, and Lou tried to assist people wounded in the conflict. From China they went to Great Britain and were there when World War I began in 1914. Lou helped Herbert's relief efforts, working with the needy in England and traveling in the United States and abroad in search of donations of food, clothes, and money to aid war victims. For her work Belgium's King Leopold awarded her the Cross of Chevalier, one of the country's highest honors. Herbert then entered domestic politics when he became secretary of commerce in 1921. In 1929 Lou Hoover became first lady.

Lou was an intelligent woman who spoke five languages—she conversed with Herbert in Mandarin when they wanted to speak privately in a crowd. She even translated a sixteenth-century mining treatise from Latin into English. As first lady, Lou preferred a more active public role than earlier cabinet wives and recent first ladies. She supported social causes, advocated better social status for women, and was national president of the Girl Scouts of America.

When Lou became mistress of the White House, she found it drab and spent some of her private funds to refurbish it. The Hoovers entertained constantly but on a small scale. The Hoover administration was barely eight months old when the collapse of the stock market triggered the Great Depression. Touched by the suffering, Lou donated generously to charity and publicly urged others to do the same. But the Hoovers' formal and reserved manner, combined with Herbert's inability to resolve the crisis, led to the perception that they were cold and uncaring. Even the White House staff, which was kept at arm's length (staff members were instructed to stay out of sight when the president or first lady passed), shared this feeling. The staff was also bothered by the frequent and often impulsive entertainment carried out in the Hoover White House.

Overwhelmed by the depression, Herbert Hoover was defeated for reelection in 1932. Lou, however, remained active in social causes after leaving the White House, particularly the Girl Scouts. With the outbreak of World War II she began organizing efforts to provide necessities for war refugees. She was still at work when she suffered a heart attack and died in her New York apartment in 1944. So carefully had she guarded her privacy that even her husband did not realize how many people she had helped until he examined her papers after her death. She was buried in Palo Alto, California; her body was later moved to West Branch, Iowa, and placed next to Herbert's.

Library of Congress

Eleanor Roosevelt

Born: October 11, 1884; New York City
Parents: Elliott and Anna Hall Roosevelt
Spouse: Franklin D. Roosevelt; March 17, 1905; New York City
Children: Anna Eleanor (1906-1975); James (1907-); Franklin (1909); Elliott (1910-); Franklin Delano, Jr. (1914-1988); John Aspinwall (1916-1981)
Died: November 7, 1962; New York City

Anna Eleanor Roosevelt Roosevelt, the most dynamic of all the first ladies, was born into a distinguished New York family. Her mother died of diptheria when she was eight; her father, of whom she was very fond, was an alcoholic who died when she was ten. An unhappy girl, Eleanor was raised by a strict great aunt and taught by tutors. Her formal education consisted of three years at Allenwood School in London between ages fifteen and eighteen. In 1902 Eleanor met Franklin Delano Roosevelt, a distant cousin, and married him two years later. Their wedding date was set for the convenience of Eleanor's uncle, President Theodore Roosevelt, who gave the bride away.

Oddly enough, one of the most prominent first ladies was very shy and insecure as a youngster. She was a plain girl, in contrast to her beautiful mother, and she felt the difference keenly. So serious was her disposition that her own mother nicknamed her "Granny." Things only grew worse when she married. Franklin's witty and urbane friends made her feel inadequate, and her mother-in-law, Sara Delano Roosevelt, was a dominating personality who largely ran Eleanor's household. Eleanor was even intimidated by the nursemaids who looked after her children. Not until she was in her thirties did she begin to emerge from her shell. A series of events—including a move away from Sara to Washington, exposure to the capital's politics, the discovery of her husband's affair with her social secretary, and finally Franklin's polio attack in 1921—combined to bring her into public life. Knowing that Franklin's political career depended upon having an active wife, she learned to make public appearances and to participate in New York politics. Her new energy spilled over into other aspects of her life. She began teaching history, English, and drama; writing; and lecturing; and she opened a furniture factory with two other women.

Her whirlwind of activity continued when she became first lady in 1933. Although she had to give up her teaching job at Todhunter, a private school for girls, she made it clear that she did not intend to surrender any of her other activities. She continued to earn her own income from her writing, primarily for the satisfaction of doing so, but she donated most of her money to various charities. As President Roosevelt's eyes and ears she was everywhere. She traveled throughout the country, visiting coal mines and impoverished Appalachian farms. During World War II she regularly traveled abroad to cheer American troops. She was the first first lady to fly and advocated air travel when most Americans were afraid of it.

Refusing to be a quiet helpmate as first lady, Eleanor adopted a variety of causes and fought openly for them all. She called for programs to assist the young and the rural poor. An advocate of women's rights (although not of an equal rights amendment), she was influential in the selection of the first female cabinet member, Secretary of Labor Frances Perkins, and helped expand government employment opportunities for women. She was an outspoken critic of racial discrimination, symbolized in her public resignation from the Daughters of the American Revolution because of the group's racist policies, and she pushed for better job opportunities for blacks. Her activism made many criticize her harshly, but only her concern with Franklin's reelection kept her from being more vocal than she was. While she publicly denied influencing the president, privately she regularly, and often passionately, discussed her views on policy and legislation with him and clearly was an important factor in many decisions.

No first lady has been more visible than Eleanor Roosevelt. She was active in the National Youth Administration and acted as cochairwoman of the Office of Civilian Defense. In addition to her travels and political activism, she, like Franklin, held regular news conferences, but she invited only women reporters, since only men attended his. She made frequent radio broadcasts, continued writing magazine articles and giving public lectures, and began her own daily newspaper column. She also kept up a steady correspondence, personally answering most of the thousands of letters she received, and did it all with only a tiny staff to help her. Her tremendous energy allowed her to work eighteen-hour days regularly.

Eleanor's term as first lady ended abruptly when Franklin Roosevelt died on April 12, 1945, but she did not fade away. Named as a delegate to the infant United Nations in 1946, she was instrumental in writing the Universal Declaration of Human Rights. She actively supported Adlai E. Stevenson's presidential bids in 1952 and 1956 and continued to speak and write in favor of more equality in American society. Her last public appointment came at the age of seventy-seven when in 1961 she was selected to chair the President's Commission on the Status of Women.

Because she was seriously ill with bone marrow tuberculosis, Eleanor Roosevelt's health deteriorated rapidly as the summer and autumn of 1962 passed. The woman who was called "first lady of the world" died in November 1962 at her New York home. She was buried next to her husband on their Hyde Park estate.

Library of Congress

Bess Truman

Born: February 13, 1885; Independence, Missouri
Parents: David and Madge Gates Wallace
Spouse: Harry S Truman; June 28, 1919; Independence
Children: Mary Margaret (1924-)
Died: October 18, 1982; Independence

Elizabeth Virginia (Bess) Wallace Truman was one of four children born into a prominent family in Independence, Missouri. Besides attending school, Bess was something of a tomboy, who enjoyed baseball, basketball, tennis, and fencing, as well as throwing the shot put. Her father committed suicide when she was eighteen, leaving her to help her mother with her younger siblings. The trauma of this event, according to her daughter, Margaret, largely led to her later insistence on privacy for her own family. Her relationship with Harry S Truman, whom she had known since a child, developed slowly over some eighteen years before they were married in 1919 after he returned from World War I.

As her husband went into the very public career of politics, Bess, who argued that publicity was unbecoming to a lady, carefully remained in the background. She was far from insignificant in Harry's career, however. A calm and practical woman, she exerted an enormous influence over Harry. She was essentially his partner, reviewing his speeches, working on his correspondence and papers, and moderating his hot temper. She was so important to Harry that he put her on his Senate staff, arguing that "I need her there. . . . I never make a report or deliver a speech without her editing it."

The same pattern held when Bess became first lady in 1945, for she was determined not to be changed by the White House and actually became annoyed if old acquaintances treated her differently than before. Harry consulted her on every problem, including major ones such as the Marshall Plan and the Korean intervention, claiming that "her judgment [is] always good." She continued to restrain Harry's impulsive anger, and her admonishing "you didn't have to say that" was legendary among the White House staff. She insisted on remaining private, generally refusing to take stands on issues or make public statements, except for appeals for charities or on the question of repairing the White House (which by then badly needed it). Unlike Eleanor Roosevelt, Bess did not hold regular press conferences; in fact she spoke with the press very reluctantly. So successful was she at remaining in the background that, despite her importance in Harry's decisions, she was a virtual unknown. In 1949 the news media dubbed her a "riddle," and many of the "facts" reported about her were wrong. Throughout, however, the Trumans remained one of the closest families ever to occupy the White House.

Harry and Bess retired to Independence in 1953. Although he had been unpopular when he left Washington, Harry gradually acquired a reputation as a sort of folk hero, while Bess was considered one of the grand ladies of America. She went on living as quietly as ever, however, until her death from heart failure at the age of ninety-seven. She was buried next to Harry, who had died a decade earlier, in Independence.

Library of Congress

Mamie Eisenhower

Born: November 14, 1896; Boone, Iowa
Parents: John and Elivera Carlson Doud
Spouse: Dwight D. Eisenhower; July 1, 1916; Denver, Colorado
Children: Doud Dwight (1917-1921); John Sheldon Doud (1922-)
Died: November 1, 1979; Washington, D.C.

Marie (Mamie) Geneva Doud Eisenhower, the last first lady whose birth date was in the nineteenth century, was born in Iowa of well-to-do Scandinavian parents. When Mamie was seven her mother's poor health prompted the family to move to Colorado, where Mamie attended high school and finishing school. The Douds later bought a winter home in San Antonio, Texas. There, in 1915, Mamie met Dwight D. Eisenhower, an army officer assigned to a nearby base. They married less than a year later.

For the next thirty-five years Mamie moved constantly as Dwight went from one military assignment to another. They moved in fact twenty-eight times, and they did not have a permanent home until they bought a farm in Gettysburg, Pennsylvania, in 1950. The longest time spent in one place prior to retirement was the Eisenhowers' eight-year occupancy of the White House. Throughout these years Mamie suffered from poor health, becoming critically ill in 1937. She was bothered by a weak heart, which apparently was a hereditary problem that had killed her sister as a young woman. She also suffered from Ménière's disease, a chronic inner ear condition that interfered with her balance and often caused her to stumble and bump into things. This condition led to groundless rumors that she was an alcoholic. Because of another illness she was unable to care for her first son when he contracted scarlet fever in 1921; his death from the disease was a devastating blow to the Eisenhowers.

As first lady, Mamie brought frills and lace to the White House and became the nation's model for femininity. While more visible than Bess Truman, she took no interest at all in politics, preferring to concentrate on her managerial and social duties. She claimed to enjoy entertaining, and she worked diligently at being a good hostess. Mamie became very popular all over the country. Women copied her clothes, her bangs, and even her recipe for fudge. Her health continued to be a problem, however, and many of her friends feared she would not survive a second Eisenhower term. Yet despite her apparent delicacy, she was a strong and demanding woman who ran the White House with a firm hand, often conducting white glove inspections.

The Eisenhowers left the White House and retired to Gettysburg in 1961. When Dwight suffered a series of heart attacks in 1968-1969, he spent almost eleven months in the hospital with Mamie at his side. She lived quietly after his death in 1969, until she had a stroke in September 1979. She never recovered and died two months later. Her birthplace in Iowa is now a national museum. Abigail Adams is the only other first lady so honored.

Library of Congress

Jacqueline Kennedy

Born: July 28, 1929; Southampton, New York
Parents: John and Janet Lee Bouvier III
Spouses: John F. Kennedy; September 12, 1953; Newport, Rhode Island
Aristotle Onassis; October 20, 1968; Skorpios, Greece
Children: Caroline Bouvier (1957-); John Fitzgerald, Jr. (1960-); Patrick Bouvier (1963)

One of the most glamorous of the first ladies, Jacqueline (Jackie) Lee Bouvier Kennedy was the daughter of a New York stockbroker. Her parents divorced in 1940, however, and her mother later married the very wealthy Hugh Auchincloss. Intelligent and strikingly attractive, Jackie grew up in high social circles. In fact, she was noted in the society columns at age two. She attended private schools and then Vassar, the Sorbonne (Paris), and George Washington University, graduating in 1951 with a degree in art. She worked as a writer for a time on the *Washington Times-Herald* and had a daily column in the newspaper with her own by-line.

Jackie met Sen. John F. Kennedy (D-Mass.) at a dinner party in 1951 and, after an off-and-on romance, married him two years later. She found being a political wife sometimes trying, for she had little interest in politics and had to learn to temper her wit for public consumption.

With her beauty, intelligence, and youth—she was thirty-one when Jack became president in 1961—Jackie cut a much higher profile as first lady than her immediate predecessors. She made the White House a center for promoting culture and the arts, and she worked to obtain authentic antiques to furnish the mansion. As part of these efforts she led a televised tour of the White House in February 1962, which enhanced her popularity. Women throughout the country found her glamorous and began copying her fashions (particularly her fondness for pillbox hats) and hairstyle, much as they had done with Mamie Eisenhower. Unlike Mamie, however, Jackie refused to remain cheerfully subservient. Citing the needs of her small children, she stubbornly insisted on a restricted social schedule. Her independent streak also showed when she took vacations separately from the president.

Despite its fairy tale appearance, life was not always easy for Jackie. Childbirth proved traumatic: her first child was stillborn, the next two were difficult Caesarean births, and her last child, Patrick, died after only two days. Moreover, shadowing her marriage were the extramarital affairs of her husband, which were hushed up at the time. Finally, in 1963, on one of the infrequent political trips that she took with Jack, he was assassinated as she rode next to him through the streets of Dallas, Texas. En route to Washington later the same day she witnessed the swearing-in of Vice President Lyndon B. Johnson while still wearing a pink suit stained with her husband's blood. And back in Washington, she largely planned her husband's funeral.

After leaving the White House Jackie tried to maintain a more private life, despite constant pressure by inquisitive outsiders. In 1968 she married Aristotle Onassis, a wealthy Greek shipping tycoon, but his death in 1975 left her a widow for a second time. Her interest in the arts then led her to pursue a career in publishing, and she accepted a position as a senior editor for a major New York book company.

Lyndon B. Johnson Library

Lady Bird Johnson

Born: December 22, 1912; Karnack, Texas
Parents: Thomas and Minnie Pattillo Taylor
Spouse: Lyndon B. Johnson; November 17, 1934; San Antonio, Texas
Children: Lynda Bird (1944-); Luci (originally Lucy) Baines (1947-)

Her given name was Claudia Alta Taylor, but a nursemaid nicknamed her "Lady Bird" while she was still an infant. Her father was a successful farmer and merchant, but her mother, who suffered from health problems, died from a fall when Lady Bird was five. Thus, the young Texan was raised mostly by a maternal aunt. Lady Bird graduated from high school in Marshall County, Texas, at age fifteen, spent two years at St. Mary's School for Girls in Dallas, and then attended the University of Texas, where she finished in the top ten of her class with degrees in liberal arts and journalism. She earned a teaching certificate as well. In 1934 she met Lyndon B. Johnson, then a secretary to a member of Congress, and married him after a courtship of only two months.

A skillful and frugal homemaker, Lady Bird handled all of the family's financial and domestic matters. She also proved to be an astute businesswoman. In 1942 she borrowed from her inheritance to purchase a nearly bankrupt Austin radio station. Under her supervision the station expanded into a multimillion-dollar broadcasting empire known as the Texas Broadcasting Corporation. Although the extent of her active management of the corporation varied over the years, she always maintained some involvement in its operation.

Lady Bird had virtually no experience in politics, but

she quickly became a capable political wife. She learned to entertain numerous guests on short notice and became adept at remembering names, faces, and places. She borrowed from her inheritance to provide money for Lyndon's first race for Congress in 1937, and when he volunteered for active duty at the beginning of World War II, she even ran his congressional office by herself for a few months. She was so capable that, according to some observers, she could have won elected office herself, although she never showed any interest in doing so. During her time as the vice president's wife (1961-1963), she substituted for the first lady at several formal events when Jacqueline Kennedy, who zealously guarded her time, refused to appear.

Lady Bird became first lady when President John F. Kennedy was assassinated in 1963. When her husband sought election to the presidency in 1964, he faced serious opposition in the South because of his support for civil rights legislation. Thus, Lady Bird campaigned there for him. She made forty-seven speeches and gained votes from people who would have refused to listen to the president himself. With Lyndon elected, she turned her attention to her national "beautification" project, which she saw as symbolic for improving the quality of life in both urban and rural areas. She and her staff rallied public and private support for her program. Lady Bird also traveled 200,000 miles to make speeches in its behalf and personally lobbied Congress for passage of the Highway Beautification Act of 1965. She took an interest in education policy as well. In all, despite her attempt to avoid controversial policy issues such as the Vietnam War, she was the most active first lady since Eleanor Roosevelt. She also was an excellent manager. Observers have claimed that she ran her wing of the White House much better than the president ran his.

President Johnson's decision not to run for reelection in 1968—which was as much of a surprise to Lady Bird as everyone else—led to their retirement to their Texas ranch. After Lyndon's death in 1973 Lady Bird largely withdrew from public life. She continued to manage her business interests successfully and pursue her interests in natural resources, including publishing the book *Wildflowers Across America* in 1988.

Library of Congress

Pat Nixon

Born: March 16, 1912; Ely, Nevada
Parents: William and Katharine Bender Ryan
Spouse: Richard Nixon; June 21, 1940; Riverside, California
Children: Patricia (1946-); Julie (1948-)

Thelma Catherine Ryan Nixon was the daughter of an Irish miner, who nicknamed her "Pat" because her birthday was so close to St. Patrick's Day. Her father took up farming in Artesia, California, when she was two. In 1925 her mother died, leaving Pat to take care of the house. When her father died four years later after a lengthy illness, she went to New York to work. In 1932 Pat returned to California and entered the University of Southern California. After graduating cum laude she took a teaching job in Whittier and there met Richard Nixon at a local theater production in which both were playing. He proposed to her on the night of their first meeting. Startled, Pat at first refused, but she eventually changed her mind and they married two years later.

Richard became successful as a small-town lawyer, but he sought more and entered politics after World War II. For Pat, the decision proved to be a trying one. She did not relish the constant public exposure, and as Richard sought higher offices and the campaigns became more intense and vicious, she came to dislike politics. In September 1952 rumors about financial misconduct forced Richard to make his famed Checkers speech in a successful effort to save his vice-presidential candidacy. While for him it was a great triumph, for Pat it was a public humiliation as the family finances became common knowledge. As early as 1950 she extracted a pledge from Richard not to seek office again, but he broke it repeatedly. Dutifully, Pat learned to be a proper political wife, but her lively personality was replaced by a stiff, formal, almost "doll-like" demeanor, at least in public.

The years between 1960 and 1968 were spent in private life, much to Pat's satisfaction, but Richard Nixon became president in 1969. As first lady, Pat sought authentic antiques to refurnish the White House, and she tried to make the mansion more accessible to the public. Pat was also the most traveled of first ladies, having visited eighty-three countries.

Because she knew that public expectations of first ladies had changed and required more social activism, Pat attempted to embrace various social projects, but her efforts largely failed. As a result, of the modern first ladies she was the least active. This stemmed in part from her own difficulties in dealing with the public and in part from the White House staff's insistence that she maintain a low profile. She seemed to have little influence on her husband's political business and was left out of many important decisions, including his decision to run for president in 1968.

As the Watergate scandal broke over Richard Nixon in 1973, Pat urged him to destroy the White House tapes, arguing that they were a private diary and not public fare. Her husband chose to ignore her warning, however. He resigned from the presidency in 1974. The Nixons retired to San Clemente, California, and moved to New York City in 1979 and to Saddle River, New Jersey, in 1981. In 1976, while at home in California, Pat suffered a stroke and had to undergo several months of physical therapy; she had a second but milder stroke in 1983. She now devotes much of her time to gardening.

Library of Congress

Betty Ford

Born: April 8, 1918; Chicago, Illinois
Parents: William and Hortense Neahr Bloomer
Spouses: William C. Warren; 1942; Grand Rapids, Michigan
Gerald R. Ford; October 15, 1948; Grand Rapids
Children: Michael Gerald (1950-); John Gardner (1952-); Steven Meigs (1956-); Susan Elizabeth (1957-)

Elizabeth (Betty) Bloomer Warren Ford was the daughter of a Chicago salesman, who moved to Grand Rapids, Michigan, when she was three. As a young girl, Betty decided to become a dancer. Thus, in 1935 she graduated from the Calla Travis Dance Studio and then spent time at the Bennington School of Dance in Bennington, Vermont. From 1939 to 1941 she worked in New York City as a dancer and model. After returning to Grand Rapids, she married William Warren, a local salesman, in 1942, but their marriage ended after five years. Betty met Gerald R. Ford in 1947 and married him the next year.

Three weeks after their wedding Jerry Ford was elected to Congress for the first time, and Betty took on the role of political wife. She joined the organizations expected of the wife of a rising member of Congress, and, because her husband frequently was away on speaking trips or campaigning for fellow House Republicans, she took a major role in raising their four children. The demands upon her were great, and the strain finally forced her to seek psychiatric counseling in 1970. As a result, she was learning stress management and had fixed a date with Jerry for his retirement from politics, when he was named Richard Nixon's vice president in 1973, replacing Spiro T. Agnew who had resigned.

Richard Nixon resigned from the presidency on August 9, 1974, and Betty Ford found herself first lady. Her outspoken honesty quickly brought her considerable attention. She strongly endorsed the Equal Rights Amendment, which was faltering in its drive for ratification, and personally lobbied state legislators for its passage. Although ratification eventually failed, she worked to increase the number of women in high government positions and pushed unsuccessfully for a woman on the Supreme Court. She also supported more assistance for the arts, the handicapped, and the mentally retarded.

Some of her statements proved to be controversial, however. Her endorsement of the Supreme Court's abortion decision, discussion of a hypothetical affair by her daughter, and comments on her children's experimentation with drugs all created a storm of protest. The courage and openness she displayed in her bout with breast cancer, which ended in a radical mastectomy, won her admirers and helped focus public attention on that problem. Her influence on President Ford was considerable. He acknowledged the value he placed on her opinions, while she referred to the importance of the "pillow talk" she had with him over issues.

Betty Ford left the White House in 1977 and retired with Gerald to Palm Springs, California. By the time she left she had become one of the most outspoken, and one of the more popular and respected, of the first ladies. She was praised when she acknowledged publicly her dependency on drugs and alcohol (caused by pain from an inoperable pinched nerve and arthritis together with the emotional stress of being a political wife) and told of her struggle to overcome it. She received awards for her work in behalf of women's rights and against cancer, and she helped establish the Betty Ford Center for Drug and Alcohol Rehabilitation in Rancho Mirage, California.

Jimmy Carter Library

Rosalynn Carter

Born: August 18, 1927; Plains, Georgia
Parents: Wilburn and Frances (Allie) Murray Smith
Spouse: Jimmy Carter; July 7, 1946; Plains
Children: John William (1947-); James Earl (Chip) III (1950-); Donnel Jeffrey (1952-); Amy Lynn (1967-)

Rosalynn Smith Carter was born and grew up about three miles from the Plains, Georgia, home of her future husband, Jimmy Carter. Her father died of leukemia when she was thirteen, leaving her to help her mother with the family. After serving as valedictorian of her high school class, Rosalynn attended Georgia Southwestern Junior College in Americus so that she could remain near home. She had known Jimmy for some time, but her first date with him was not until she was seventeen. She married him a year later.

Jimmy was a navy officer at the time of their marriage, and for the first time Rosalynn moved away from Plains, spending time in California, Pennsylvania, Hawaii, Virginia, and Connecticut. She enjoyed her new independence and the opportunities it offered. When her father-in-law died in 1953 and Jimmy decided to resign his commission to run the family peanut business, Rosalynn reluctantly returned to Plains. She soon began to like her life there, however. She helped with the business and became active in local organizations. Rosalynn even overcame an acute fear of public speaking so that she could help Jimmy when he ran unsuccessfully for governor of Georgia in 1966 and then successfully in 1970. When he decided to run for the presidency in 1976, Rosalynn set off alone to campaign for him, touring hundreds of miles to give speeches in his behalf.

Few first ladies have achieved the prominence that Rosalynn Carter attained between 1977 and 1981. She was frequently compared to Eleanor Roosevelt, even by her husband. She was constantly active. It has been noted that "in her first two years as first lady, she made 248 speeches or public comments, gave 154 press interviews, attended 641 briefings, and visited 36 foreign countries." She fought for better treatment of the mentally ill and appeared before congressional subcommittees to support her views. Problems of the aged, refugee camps in Thailand, and equality for women were all causes she took up. Rosalynn also traveled abroad on the president's behalf, most notably to Latin America in 1977. She frequently sat in on cabinet meetings and even participated in President Carter's Camp David negotiations between Egyptian president Anwar Sadat and Israeli prime minister Menachem Begin. Rosalynn was thus Jimmy's alter ego; she discussed policy matters and appointments with him daily. Their partnership in policy making was so openly equal that Rosalynn Carter has been called one of the most influential of all the first ladies. In fact, in a poll of historians she was rated more effective as first lady than her husband was as president.

Burdened by an economic downturn and his failure to obtain the release of American diplomats being held hostage in Iran, Jimmy Carter was defeated in his bid for reelection in 1980. He and Rosalynn retired to Plains where they wrote separate accounts of their years in the White House.

Library of Congress

Nancy Reagan

Born: July 6, 1923;[22] New York City
Parents: Kenneth and Edith Luckett Robbins
Spouse: Ronald Reagan; March 4, 1952; Riverside, California
Children: Patricia Ann (1952-); Ronald Prescott (1958-)

Nancy Reagan was the daughter of an auto salesman and a stage actress. Her father left the family shortly after she was born, and her mother, determined to pursue a stage career, left young Nancy with relatives. Born Anne Frances Robbins, Nancy, as she was nicknamed, lived until age six with an aunt in Washington, D.C. In 1929 her mother married a Chicago physician, and Nancy went to live with them. She was legally adopted at age fourteen and became Nancy Davis. Later, Nancy attended a private high school in Chicago and Smith College in Massachusetts. While attending Smith, she had a brief romance with a Princeton student, who was accidentally struck by a train and killed.

Like her mother, Nancy decided to pursue an acting career. She had been in theatrical productions in high school and had majored in drama at Smith. In 1943 Nancy began her stage career, and in 1949 she moved to Hollywood to break into movies. There she met Ronald Reagan, then president of the Screen Actors Guild, who cleared her of a baseless charge of Communist associations. After the couple married in 1952, Nancy largely abandoned her acting career to be a homemaker, returning to the screen only for very brief intervals when financially necessary. She made her last movie in 1954. She returned to the public eye, however, when Ronald entered politics and became governor of California in 1966 and president in 1980.

Initially as first lady, Nancy argued that her only concern was taking care of her husband. She thus attempted to remain out of sight. Her first two years in the White House were stormy ones, however. She was criticized sharply for her fashionable wardrobe, her rich friends, and the general image of luxury that she projected while the president called upon the nation for austerity. Particularly attacked were her $900,000 remodeling of the White House and the $200,000 china set she ordered (although most of the money used for both was from private donations).

By 1982 Nancy was making determined efforts to improve her public image and to establish better relations with the news media. Among other things, she became active in drug abuse programs, a longtime concern, and supported antidrug efforts, both domestically and internationally. By 1985 Nancy had gone from being one of the most disliked first ladies to being more popular than the president.

Beyond these efforts, she also was a great influence on the president himself. Fiercely protective of her family, she displayed an iron will in protecting the interests of the more easy-going Ronald. Nancy kept abreast of current events, but she was more interested in personalities. Even the president acknowledged that she was very perceptive in personnel matters. Her behind-the-scenes influence, particularly on personnel, was strong. Several White House insiders even attested to her power to remove people she thought a liability to her husband.

In 1989, after two terms in the White House, the Reagans retired to Los Angeles, California. Nancy, the only first lady to publish an autobiography before entering the White House, planned to write a memoir of her years there.

White House

Barbara Bush

Born: June 8, 1925; Rye, New York
Parents: Marvin and Pauline Robinson Pierce
Spouse: George Bush; January 6, 1945; Rye, New York
Children: George Walker (1946-); Robin (1949-1953); John Ellis (1953-); Neil Mellon (1954-); Marvin Pierce (1956-); Dorothy Walker (1959-)

Barbara Pierce Bush was born in Rye, New York, a suburb of New York City. Her father was the publisher of *McCall's* magazine; her mother was the daughter of an Ohio Supreme Court justice. Her family was well-to-do, and she attended school at prestigious Ashley Hall in South Carolina. She met George Bush at a Christmas dance in 1942 and became engaged to him a year later. Their marriage was delayed, however, while George served in the U.S. Navy. In 1945 Barbara dropped out of school after two years in Smith College to marry him.

After George graduated from Yale University in 1948, the Bushes moved to Odessa, Texas, where George entered the oil business. That was the beginning of an odyssey that included twenty-eight homes in seventeen cities. After succeeding in oil, George became active in politics, serving as a member of Congress from Texas, U.S. ambassador to the United Nations, chairman of the Republican National Committee, U.S. representative to China, director of the Central Intelligence Agency, and finally vice president and president. In the midst of traveling around the country and the world, Barbara had six children, the second of which, Robin, died of leukemia just before her fourth birthday.

A strong believer in volunteerism, Barbara Bush has donated much of her own time to helping the less fortunate. She has been honorary chair of the Leukemia Society of America and has been concerned about the plight of the homeless and of poor, single parents. Her primary concern, however, has been illiteracy in the United States. She has been actively involved in programs to improve literacy and donated the entire proceeds of over $65,000 from her book *C. Fred's Story* (a collection of anecdotes about the Bush family told from the point of view of their cocker spaniel, C. Fred Bush) to major literacy organizations. She won the Distinguished American Woman Award in 1987 and, after becoming first lady in 1989, continued to be involved in community affairs.

George and Barbara Bush have homes in Houston, Texas, and Kennebunkport, Maine. She enjoys reading, needlepoint, gardening, and spending time with her family, which includes eleven grandchildren.

Family and Friends of the President

While the presidency may be "the loneliest job in the world," presidents rarely have been completely alone in the White House. There have been wives, children, and other family members who were close to the president. Indeed, family and the presidency have gone hand in hand; only two bachelors, James Buchanan and Grover Cleveland, have ever been elected president, and one of them, Cleveland, married during his term. Most presidents have been so-called family men.

Given the burdens of the office, one might suppose that an unmarried person, who would not have to deal with family worries, would be better suited for the job. In fact, those burdens may increase the importance of a family for the president. The first family provides a support system for the president, a refuge where the problems of the nation can be put aside. For many people, the president's family is important because it indicates that the president is a stable, healthy, and mature individual who is capable of handling the responsibilities of adulthood and the presidency. Politically, the family symbolizes traditional American values and therefore becomes invaluable to the man or woman who would be president.[23]

Presidential families have come in considerable variations. They have been large and small, close-knit and distant. Some family members have been quiet, and others have been colorful. Some have proven to be real assets to a president, others have been liabilities. With the increasing attention focused on the White House, the president's family has become a prominent part of the presidency.

Children in the White House

Several presidents have had older children who had already left home when they entered office, but others have brought their children, some young, into the White House. Abraham Lincoln had two young sons when he was president, and Ulysses S. Grant brought a ten-year-old son to the White House. Benjamin Harrison brought such a large family to the White House that the mansion was not really large enough to accommodate it. But perhaps the most famous White House family was that of Theodore Roosevelt.

Roosevelt arrived in Washington in 1901 with six children, ages four to fourteen. Like their father, they were boisterous and active and often made their presence known, even on official activities. When Roosevelt had been governor of New York, they had kept a small zoo of their own in the basement of the governor's mansion, and at least one official dinner had been cut short when the aroma of their animals drifted through the open windows.

Having established a reputation in New York, the Roosevelt children quickly became the delight of Washington. They came to the White House just as press coverage of—and interest in—the president's family was beginning to grow, and although their mother carefully controlled the news about them, their exploits were soon the talk of the entire country.

The White House was just a "bully" playhouse for Roosevelt's brood. They crawled into the spaces between the ceilings and the floors, explored the out-of-the-way

Library of Congress

While living in the White House, Theodore Roosevelt's six children were boisterous and active, often disrupting their father's meetings and social events. Here, two of his sons pose with White House guards.

corners of the attic and the basement, and poked into all sorts of other places where people had not been for years. They slid down the banisters, rode bicycles and roller-skated on all the hardwood floors, walked on stilts in every room, climbed the trees, swam in the fountains, and used the furniture for leapfrog games. They kept pets everywhere and produced them for visitors at the slightest invitation; their pony got rides on the White House elevator. Once, son Quentin Roosevelt used mirrors to flash light into the government offices, thus disrupting all work there.

Far from restricting his children, the president seemed to encourage their activities and often took part in their games. To a visitor who suggested that he do something about his irrepressible daughter Alice, who was interrupting a meeting by repeatedly rushing into the Oval Office, he replied, "I can do one of two things. I can be president of the United States or I can control Alice. I cannot possibly do both." He also once said that no one had had more fun in the White House than he, and an observer noted that "you must remember that the president is about six." [24] Edith Roosevelt herself frequently seemed to treat him as a big child. When he cut his chin with a hatchet, she complained that he was spoiling the rugs by bleeding all over the house.

Roosevelt's boisterous family proved to be a great asset for him. Their antics drew attention to the president and "reinforced the image of a vibrant, energetic man in the White House." [25]

Over half a century later another family with young children came into the White House. When John Kennedy moved into the mansion in 1961, his daughter, Caroline, was three years old and his son, John, was only an infant. Like Theodore Roosevelt's children, Caroline and "John-John" were the subject of much curiosity, and they were constantly photographed and written about. Strongly wanting them to have a "normal" childhood, Jacqueline Kennedy carefully protected them and managed the publicity about them. She even went so far as to have holly trees and rhododendrons planted to block the view of the White House from the street, a move that greatly annoyed the White House police.

A playground with a tree house, slide, tunnel, sunken trampoline, and swing was built outside the president's office for the children, and there they frequently played within sight of Kennedy as he worked. There was also a small zoo with rabbits, guinea pigs, dogs, lambs, ducks, and ponies. (The ducks eventually were removed—they ate the flowers, and the dogs ate them.) There was an effort as well to get Irish deer and peacocks for the children, but none ever came to the South Lawn. Mrs. Kennedy insisted on keeping her afternoons free for her children and skipped several social functions in their behalf; she and the children took regular walks around the White House driveway.

On the third floor of the White House a nursery school was built for Caroline and was equipped with books, a sandbox, goldfish, toys, and plants. Mother and daughter slipped in at night to play in the sand. Nine other children shared the school with her. After Kennedy's assassination in 1963 the school remained for the rest of that semester before being dismantled, and little Caroline was driven to the White House every day for school.[26]

While the Kennedy children were not as publicly rambunctious as the Roosevelt clan, they remain the most photographed of any White House family. Images of the pair are part of American lore: running to meet their father, walking with their mother, dancing in the Oval Office, Caroline holding her mother's hand at her father's funeral as John-John salutes his coffin. The public attention continued to follow them as adults; Caroline had to give up a job as a photojournalist because she became the focus of attention wherever she went.

The charm of younger children has proven an asset to presidents. Jimmy Carter came to the White House with a nine-year-old daughter, still young enough to be a symbolic help to him. Amy Carter showed up as a Typical Girl: strawberry blonde with freckles and glasses, a good stu-

Historians' Ranking of First Ladies

In 1982 Thomas Kelly and Douglas Lonnstrom of the Siena Research Institute, Loudonville, New York, conducted a poll of history professors to rank the first ladies. The poll included White House hostesses but did not include presidents' wives who did not live in the White House. Because the poll was taken early in the Reagan administration, it may not reflect accurately Nancy Reagan's later rating.

Ranking		Score
1	Eleanor Roosevelt	93.3
2	Abigail Adams	84.6
3	Lady Bird Johnson	77.5
4	Dolley Madison	75.4
5	Rosalynn Carter	73.8
6	Betty Ford	73.4
7	Edith Wilson	71.8
8	Jacqueline Kennedy	69.5
9	Martha Washington	67.5
10	Edith Roosevelt	65.4
11	Lou Hoover	63.5
12	Lucy Hayes	63.1
13	Frances Cleveland	62.3
14	Louisa Adams	62.0
15	Bess Truman	61.7
16	Ellen Wilson	61.5
17	Grace Coolidge	61.3
18	Martha Jefferson Randolph (daughter of Thomas Jefferson)	61.0
19	Helen Taft	61.0
20	Julia Grant	60.7
21	Eliza Johnson	60.7
22	Sarah Polk	60.5
23	Anna Harrison	60.1
24	Elizabeth Monroe	60.1
25	Mary Arthur McElroy (sister of Chester A. Arthur)	60.1
26	Emily Donelson (niece of Andrew Jackson)	60.0
27	Julia Tyler	59.9
28	Abigail Fillmore	59.8
29	Harriet Lane (niece of James Buchanan)	59.8
30	Lucretia Garfield	59.8
31	Mamie Eisenhower	59.7
32	Martha Patterson (daughter of Andrew Johnson)	59.6
33	Margaret Taylor	59.4
34	Caroline Harrison	59.4
35	Letitia Tyler	59.3
36	Angelica Van Buren (daughter-in-law of Martin Van Buren)	59.3
37	Pat Nixon	58.5
38	Jane Pierce	57.6
39	Nancy Reagan	57.4
40	Ida McKinley	57.0
41	Florence Harding	55.8
42	Mary Lincoln	52.9

Source: Betty Boyd Caroli, *First Ladies* (New York: Oxford University Press, 1987), 385-386.

dent, lonely when her parents were out campaigning, and not at all eager to leave her friends in Plains. As such, she became someone everyone could identify with, and she was a popular public figure well before Carter was elected in 1976.

Her parents wanted her to have a "normal childhood" while living in the White House. Amy caused a sensation by attending public school in Washington; on her first day of class, members of the news media turned out in droves to cover the event. She had parties for her friends in the White House movie theater and in the tree house her father built on the South Lawn. She also learned to play the violin, studied astronomy from the mansion's roof, and received as presents an elephant from Sri Lanka and reindeer from Finland (they went to the National Zoo). Although Amy knew little of Washington behavior when she arrived—she showed up for her first state dinner with a book in her hand—she soon learned and she appeared at several public receptions, such as that held for the Energy Department's youth conservation program.

For younger children, living in the White House is not a problem. Since most of their families are well-to-do, the large house and numerous servants may seem normal. A greater adjustment is required of older children, who may find the mansion a restriction as much as a pleasure.

One major problem is the glare of publicity that surrounds the president and the first family. The children's faces become almost as well known as the president's own, which makes going out such a difficult prospect. It is now rare that a president's child can pass unnoticed in public. Incidents such as the one in which Lyndon Johnson's daughter Lynda was approached by a fellow student at the University of Texas and told that "the president's daughter was a student on campus somewhere" are infrequent. More likely, every move they make is subject to public scrutiny. Thus, the public learned all about Susan Ford's eighteenth birthday, her senior prom, how much she charged for babysitting (one dollar per hour), and the rides she rode at Disney World. While some may enjoy such publicity, it is hard on others; quiet Tricia Nixon shrank from all the attention and remained so reclusive that her sister once referred to her as "the Howard Hughes of the White House."

A second problem, related to the first, is that it is not easy for a teenager to have much of a social or romantic life in the White House. The constant public watchfulness makes it as difficult to have a quiet date as to go for pizza with the gang. Then too the omnipresent Secret Service

White House Hostesses: . . .

Over the life-span of the American presidency, particularly between 1828 and 1868, several presidents' wives have refused or have been unable, usually for health reasons, to fulfill the social duties of first lady. Other presidents simply had no wife. Thus, substitutes have carried out the social responsibilities of the first lady when the wife of the president has not been available.

Hostesses Serving Widower or Bachelor Presidents

Six presidents had no wife to act as first lady: four presidents entered the White House as widowers, and two others were bachelors, one at least for a time.

Martha Jefferson Randolph. The need for a surrogate first lady first occurred during the term of Thomas Jefferson, who had been a widower for eighteen years when he became president in 1801. Although Jefferson did less formal entertaining than President John Adams, the Jefferson White House was still the center of much social activity. Dolley Madison, wife of Secretary of State James Madison, and Jefferson's daughter, Martha Jefferson Randolph, frequently filled the role of first lady for Jefferson.

Martha Randolph was the eldest of Jefferson's six children and one of only two to live to maturity. She was born in 1772 at Monticello, her father's home in Virginia. After her mother died in 1782, Martha went to a boarding school in Philadelphia. In 1784, when Jefferson became U.S. minister to France, Martha went with him. She attended an elite convent school in Paris for five years, until her decision to become a nun prompted her father to remove her from the school and hire tutors instead. Martha's girlhood letters indicate a great interest in her studies and her personal habits and appearance.

After returning to the United States in 1789, Martha married her cousin Thomas Mann Randolph in 1790 and had the first of her five children in 1791. The demands of her family prevented her from acting regularly as White House hostess. Her only extended stays at the mansion were during the winters of 1802-1803 and 1805-1806. An intelligent and very practical woman, Martha skillfully managed the White House and later Monticello.

After the deaths of her father in 1826 and her husband in 1828, Martha was forced to sell the Virginia estate to settle debts. Her last appearance in Washington society was during Andrew Jackson's administration when Secretary of State Martin Van Buren, needing a hostess for a state dinner, turned to Martha. She died of apoplexy in 1836.

Emily Donelson. Andrew Jackson came to the presidency in 1829 newly widowed; his wife, Rachel, died in the interval between his election and the inauguration. For much of his time in office the role of first lady was played by his niece Emily Donelson, who was born in 1808 in Davidson County, Tennessee. Emily was educated at the Old Academy in Nashville and at age sixteen married a cousin who served as Jackson's secretary. She had four children. Rachel Jackson, who was uncomfortable in Washington society, already had asked Emily after the election to handle many of the social functions of the White House. Despite her relative lack of sophistication and education, Emily was charming, gracious, and very popular in Washington society. She remained hostess until shortly before her death in 1836 from tuberculosis.

Angelica Singleton Van Buren. Martin Van Buren's wife, Hannah, died nineteen years before he reached the White House in 1837. His daughter-in-law, Angelica Singleton Van Buren, thus served as the mansion's hostess during his administration. The daughter of a wealthy South Carolina planter, Angelica was related to several powerful southern families and was a distant relative of Dolley Madison. She met President Van Buren's eldest son, Abraham, at a state dinner in March 1838 and married him eight months later. President Van Buren, who until that time had had no White House hostess and had done little entertaining, asked Angelica to take charge of the mansion's social life. Her first social function was the New Year's reception of 1839. For the remainder of Van Buren's term in office, Angelica enlivened the White House.

Harriet Lane. Because James Buchanan never married, his niece Harriet Lane served as hostess during his administration (1857-1861). Born in 1831, Harriet was orphaned at age nine, and her guardianship passed to Buchanan. He found homes with relatives for her siblings but chose to raise Harriet as his own daughter. She was sent to the best schools, concluding with two years at an elite Georgetown convent school. In 1853, when Buchanan became minister to England, he took Harriet with him.

Few women have come to the White House as well prepared for their social duties as the lively and attractive Harriet Lane. In fact, Buchanan's term was judged by many contemporaries to be the "gayest administration" because of her skill as a hostess. As with other immensely popular first ladies, fashions changed in response to her preferences, and the lower necklines she favored suddenly became the rage. Yet Harriet was more than just a capable hostess. Having been exposed for years to political discussions at Buchanan's table, she was well informed, and it is likely that the president listened to her opinions on many questions. She also was seen as an intermediary by those with problems and therefore received many appeals for help from the general public.

Buchanan served just one term. In 1866 Harriet married Henry Johnston and then had two sons, neither of whom lived beyond age fourteen. When Buchanan died in 1869, he left his estate to Harriet, and she lived there until her husband died in 1884. Harriet's remaining years were spent in Washington and abroad. Her extensive art collection formed the basis of the National Gallery of Art's collection, which was opened to the public in 1941. She died in 1903.

. . . Surrogate First Ladies

Other Surrogate First Ladies

From 1828 to 1868 several presidents whose wives were living prevailed upon other family members to act as first lady, usually because they were in poor health.

Jane Irwin Harrison. The first of these presidents was William Henry Harrison, whose widowed daughter-in-law, Jane Irwin Harrison, agreed to assist as White House hostess. Harrison's term lasted only a month after his inauguration in 1841, however, and thus Jane was left as a footnote in White House history.

Priscilla Cooper Tyler. When John Tyler succeeded Harrison in 1841, his first wife, Letitia, who had suffered a stroke, was a semi-invalid. His daughter-in-law, Priscilla Cooper Tyler, acted as his hostess. Born in 1816, Priscilla was one of the nine children of actor Robert Cooper. She performed on stage herself for a time as a young woman, but she lived in severe financial straits. In 1837 she met Tyler's son Robert after he saw her perform as Desdemona in Shakespeare's *Othello*. They were married in September 1839. Priscilla served as hostess until Tyler's marriage to Julia Gardiner in 1844. Her letters convey both her devotion to the president and her wonder at being acting first lady. She died in 1889 in Montgomery, Alabama.

Mary Elizabeth Taylor. When Zachary Taylor came to the White House in 1849, his wife, Margaret, lacked the health or the desire to act as first lady. That role was played by her youngest daughter, Mary Elizabeth (Betty).

Betty Taylor was born in 1824 in Jefferson County, Kentucky. Although her father had little formal education, he was concerned with that of his children, and Betty was sent to boarding school in Philadelphia. She married Maj. William Bliss, her father's adjutant, in 1848. After his death she married Philip Pendleton Dandridge in 1858. Contemporaries have noted that she was charming, gracious, and lovely, and a popular hostess while in the White House, particularly in contrast to the more austere Sarah Polk, her predecessor. Betty died in 1909 in Winchester, Virginia.

Mary Abigail Fillmore. Abigail Fillmore, who followed Margaret Taylor into the White House, also lacked the interest or health to play the social game and thus let her daughter take her place. Mary Abigail Fillmore was born in 1832 in Buffalo, New York, and was educated in schools in Massachusetts and New York. She taught school for a time before coming to Washington in 1850 when her father became president. A talented young woman, Mary spoke five languages and played the guitar, piano, and harp. At age twenty-two, less than two years after Millard Fillmore left the presidency, she contracted cholera and died in Aurora, New York.

Abby Kent Means. For the first two years of Franklin Pierce's presidency (1853-1857) his wife, Jane, crushed by the tragic death of her only child, refused to participate in White House society. Mrs. Abby Kent Means, a longtime friend of Jane Pierce and the second wife of Jane's uncle, thus filled in as first lady. With the help of Varina Davis, wife of Secretary of War Jefferson Davis, Abby attempted to maintain pleasantry in a melancholy White House and held receptions twice a week. But despite her efforts, the White House was a gloomy place, even after Jane Pierce assumed her duties.

Martha Johnson Patterson. Andrew Johnson's wife, Eliza, suffered from tuberculosis when she became first lady, and her daughter, Martha Johnson Patterson, became hostess instead. Martha was born in Greeneville, Tennessee, in 1828 and married David Patterson in 1855. When her father became president in 1865, she was both White House hostess and wife of a U.S. senator. Proclaiming herself to be "plain folks from Tennessee," Martha put cows on the White House lawn to provide milk and butter. She also supervised the redecoration of the mansion, which had been damaged in the aftermath of Lincoln's assassination. Her simplicity and calm dignity earned her respect and admiration during the turbulent Johnson years. She died in Greeneville in 1901.

Mary Arthur McElroy. When Chester A. Arthur succeeded James A. Garfield as president in 1881, his wife, Ellen, had been dead for about eighteen months. Although Arthur personally took a great interest in White House entertainment, the official hostess in his administration was his younger sister, Mary Arthur McElroy. Mary was born in Greenwich, New York, in 1842 and was educated in private schools, concluding with Mrs. Willard's Female Seminary in Troy, New York. She married John McElroy in 1861. While White House hostess, Mary continued to live in Albany, New York, traveling to Washington for the social season each year. Although Mary was popular as a hostess, she also was careful to protect the privacy of both the president and her family. She died in 1917.

Rose Cleveland. Grover Cleveland (1885-1889) was the second bachelor president to reside in the White House. He eventually married while president, but until then his sister Rose served as White House hostess.

The youngest child in the family, Rose Cleveland was born in Fayetteville, New York, in 1846. Rose was an intelligent and well-educated woman; she taught at Houghton Seminary and gained a favorable reputation as a college lecturer. She knew several languages and published scholarly studies on literature. Although a sparkling conversationalist and a gracious hostess, she sometimes intimidated visitors with her intellect. At times, she was bored with her social duties. Finding receiving lines dull, Rose would occupy herself by silently conjugating Greek verbs. After Cleveland married Frances Folsom in 1886, Rose returned to her scholarly work and lived in Europe for a time before her death in 1918.

Presidents' Wives . . .

Often overlooked in discussions of first ladies are the four women who died before their husbands reached the White House: Martha Jefferson, Rachel Jackson, Hannah Van Buren, and Ellen Arthur.

Martha Jefferson. Martha Wayles Skelton Jefferson was born October 19, 1748, in Charles City County, Virginia. Her parents were John and Martha Eppes Wayles. When she was seventeen, Martha married Bathhurst Skelton, a lawyer and landowner, by whom she had one son. Skelton died in 1768, and four years later, on January 1, 1772, she married Thomas Jefferson. She and Jefferson had six more children, but only two—daughters Martha Washington and Maria—lived more than two years.

Relatively little is known of Martha Jefferson. Few references to her remain, and none of her correspondence still exists. Although there are no portraits of her, she was apparently a very attractive woman who had considerable talent on the piano and harpsichord, as well as the practical ability to keep accounts for the Jeffersons' Virginia plantation, Monticello. Moreover, her inheritance made her fairly wealthy.

Never very strong, Martha's health was weakened by her repeated burdens of childbearing and a flight through the snow and freezing weather from British troops in 1780. The birth of her last child, in May 1782, proved too much for her, and she died on September 6, 1782, at Monticello. Jefferson was so distraught at her death that he refused to leave his room for three weeks. He never remarried.

Rachael Jackson. Rachel Donelson Robards Jackson hailed from a pioneering family. Her parents, John and Rachel Stockley Donelson, were among the first settlers of Nashville, Tennessee. Rachel was born on June 15, 1767, in Halifax County, Virginia; she moved with her family to Tennessee in 1780. She had little formal education.

In 1784 Rachel married Lewis Robards, a Kentucky landowner, and moved to Kentucky with him. Robards, however, proved to be insanely jealous and abusive. Fearing physical harm, Rachel fled back to Nashville. She returned once to Robards, but shortly afterward left again in the company of Andrew Jackson, who had been sent to her aid by her family.

To protect her from Robards, Jackson took her on to Natchez, Mississippi. In 1791, on receiving word that Robards had been granted a divorce, Andrew and Rachel married. But the information was wrong. Robards only had been given permission to seek the divorce in Kentucky, and the actual divorce did not occur until 1793. When the Jacksons were informed, they immediately remarried on January 17, 1794, but the damage was done. The fact that Rachel was technically an adulteress would haunt her for the rest of her life, and Andrew fought several duels to protect her honor.

Rachel stayed on the Jackson estate in Nashville for much of her married life. She wanted only to remain quietly at home with her husband, but his ambition frequently took him away for long intervals. Although she moved to Washington after he became a senator, she was generally reclusive. Short, stout, and interested only in friends, family, and church, she favorably impressed some visitors with her unassuming ways, but others thought her to be detrimental to Jackson's career.

Rachel accepted Jackson's election to the presidency in 1828 with great reluctance, saying that she "would

agent that accompanies every president's child impedes the development of intimate relationships. Although agents maintain as discreet a distance as circumstances permit, knowledge of their presence may be inhibiting. The president's children therefore often wish to lose their protective detail and occasionally have tried. Early in her White House days Luci Johnson would jump in her car and drive away before the agents were ready to go; they eventually stopped her by confiscating her car keys.

Older presidential offspring are much more aware of the political fallout from the actions of the president. They may suffer from guilt by association, or they may be the target of criticism. Like it or not, they frequently are in the center of the storm. Julie Nixon, for example, often encountered hostility while a student at Smith College during the Vietnam War. Her husband, David Eisenhower, skipped his commencement exercises at Amherst College because of tensions on the campus.

Despite the drawbacks, most children of presidents have seemed to enjoy life at the White House. Perhaps one cannot go out as much, but there are many opportunities for entertaining, as well as resources that cannot be had elsewhere.

Presidential Relatives as Assets

The president's relatives have become much more prominent in recent years. As media coverage of the first family has increased, attention has expanded from just the president to the first lady and then the children and the extended family. Prior to World War II it was very unusual to hear much about the president's extended family. While occasionally some relative would be newsworthy, most kin remained in the background. Easily the most prominent relative of a president was Eleanor Roosevelt, who was a niece of Theodore Roosevelt.

The visibility and importance of a president's relatives began to change after 1945. Public curiosity about the president spread to his family until today everyone remotely connected to the president gets at least some attention. Some relatives naturally have proven more interesting and important than others. Many, in fact, have been quite valuable to the president.

Several family members have served as advisers to the president, either formally or informally. For example, Milton Eisenhower, the younger brother of President Eisenhower, never held any official position in the Eisenhower

. . . Who Were Not First Ladies

rather be a doorkeeper in the house of God than live in that palace in Washington." She feared that she was unsuited to be first lady. During the campaign, Jackson's opponents had viciously resurrected the story of Rachel's "adultery." The details, however, were kept from her until, in Nashville to be fitted for an inaugural gown, she overheard some women discussing them disparagingly. Friends found her weeping hysterically. Rachel suffered a heart attack a few days later and died on December 22, 1828, at the Jackson estate, Hermitage. She was buried there in the gown that had been made for the inaugural ball. Jackson never remarried.

Hannah Van Buren. The first president's wife to be born an American citizen, Hannah Hoes Van Buren entered the world on March 8, 1783, at Kinderhook, New York. Her parents, Johannes and Maria Quackenboss Hoes, were Dutch, and Hannah grew up speaking that language. She knew Martin Van Buren as a child, and by age eighteen the couple was engaged. Because Martin wanted to study law and gain admittance to the bar before they wed, the actual wedding did not take place until February 21, 1807, in Catskill, New York.

Shortly after their marriage Martin began his political career. He was a New York state senator from 1812 to 1820 and state attorney general from 1816 to 1819. From 1808 to 1817 Hannah spent much of her time in their home in Hudson, New York, raising their new family. They had four children: Abraham (1807-1873), John (1810-1866), Martin (1812-1855), and Smith (1817-1876). In 1817 she moved the family to Albany, where the weather proved bad for her health. She contracted tuberculosis and gradually declined. She never left her home after September 1818 and died on February 5, 1819, at the age of thirty-five.

Very little is written about Hannah Van Buren. She left no correspondence or writing of her own, and her husband's autobiography, so descriptive of public matters, says virtually nothing about his wife of twelve years. Apparently she was an attractive although shy woman, who was religious and very concerned with the poor and the needy. She was buried in Albany, and Martin later had her reburied in Kinderhook.

Ellen Arthur. Ellen Lewis Herndon Arthur, the daughter of William and Frances Hansbrough Herndon, was born on August 30, 1837, at Fredricksburg, Virginia. After her father, a naval officer, died at sea in 1857, she and her mother moved to New York City. There she met Chester A. Arthur, a young lawyer, in 1858, and they married on October 25, 1859.

Chester's law practice proved very successful, and he entered New York State politics. The Arthurs continued to live in New York City, where Ellen cared for their three children: Billy (1860-1863), Chester, Jr. (1864-1937), and Ellen (1871-1915). A gifted singer, Ellen was active in the Mendelssohn Glee Club and performed publicly several times. She was also active in charity work. Her musical and charitable work helped Chester's developing political career.

In early January 1880 Ellen became ill after waiting outside in the cold for a carriage. Her illness was not considered serious at first, but she worsened abruptly and died of pneumonia on January 12. She was buried in Albany. Chester never remarried; he placed flowers before her portrait every day and kept her room in their home as she had left it.

---

administration, but he was a close confidant of the president. Because Milton had made his career in government, he had an understanding of its workings and nuances that his brother, a career military officer, lacked. More important was the relationship that existed between the brothers; they were close enough that the president was able to try out ideas on his brother and get honest advice in return. As Milton Eisenhower put it:

> President Eisenhower found it helpful to reveal his innermost thoughts and plans to one who was not subservient to him, was not an advocate of special interests, had no selfish purpose to serve, and would raise questions and facts solely to help the president think through his problems without pressing for a particular decision.[27]

Milton Eisenhower's role was so important that some observers considered him to be the most helpful person, official or unofficial, around President Eisenhower.

There is little doubt that the most important adviser to John Kennedy was his brother Robert. Unlike Milton Eisenhower, however, Robert F. Kennedy had an official position in his brother's administration. Risking charges of nepotism, the president named his brother attorney general, despite his extremely limited experience in the law profession. In fact, Robert Kennedy's title meant little, for although he did spearhead an assault on organized crime, his real importance lay in his ties to his brother.

Robert Kennedy was almost an alter ego to the president. He ran John Kennedy's Senate campaign in 1952 and his presidential race in 1960 and gradually developed a strong bond with him. The two brothers complemented each other well. Passionate where John was detached, a stern and demanding taskmaster where John was easygoing, Robert provided a driving force that both accomplished things and took the heat for his brother. The two even began to think alike, so much in tune that they could communicate without talking. Robert Kennedy's closeness and unquestionable loyalty to his brother allowed him to make suggestions and criticisms that no one else could.

The best illustration of Robert's importance was the 1962 Cuban missile crisis. While his formal position indicated that he should not have been involved at all, the attorney general not only sat in on the deliberations of the Executive Committee that was convened to decide the American response to the crisis, but also was a central actor. When President Kennedy removed himself from the

ExCom's deliberations to promote freer debate, it was Robert Kennedy who took charge, aggressively probing and questioning the other members of the committee to obtain the best decision possible.

While other presidents may have sought advice from relatives, Milton Eisenhower and Robert Kennedy are the most prominent examples of presidential relatives who served as advisers. In other administrations relatives have been an asset to the president without being an adviser. For example, Mary McElroy, sister of widowed Chester A. Arthur, and Rose Cleveland, sister of Grover Cleveland, both won favor for their respective brothers with their work as White House hostesses.

A president's family also can prove an asset in times of trouble. While strong support by family members may not make the problem disappear, it can be both politically and personally advantageous to the president. For example, Richard Nixon's younger daughter, Julie Eisenhower, rallied to his defense during the Watergate affair. In 1973-1974, as the Watergate scandal consumed Nixon's presidency, both Pat Nixon and older daughter Tricia Cox gradually faded into the background; sunny and outgoing Julie stepped forward in his defense. In 1968 and 1972 she had campaigned for Nixon. Then in 1973, as the rest of the family withdrew, Julie made numerous public appearances, granted interviews, and met the press in her father's behalf. The most famous of her public appearances was a televised Saturday morning press conference with her husband in May 1974 in which she vigorously defended her father. She became the family spokesperson and one of her father's closest confidants. Her courage and her spirited, dogged defense of Nixon won the respect of many observers and put her on the list of most admired women. Although she could not save Nixon's presidency, her constant support may have been critical to his emotional survival.[28]

A different sort of asset was President Carter's mother, Lillian, who gave new meaning to the term first mother. Other presidents' mothers who have survived to see their sons take office have had such a low profile as to be almost invisible. Lillian Carter, however, was a star in her own right. She was lively and intelligent, outspoken, and down to earth. And courageously, she welcomed blacks into her south Georgia home long before it was acceptable to do so. In 1966 at age sixty-eight, she joined the Peace Corps and went to India. When Jimmy Carter became president in 1977, she became his goodwill ambassador. She toured drought-stricken East Africa, represented the president at state funerals in India and Israel, and made other trips on his behalf. She also traveled around the country to gather support for Carter among Democrats. In 1977 the Synagogue Council of America gave "Miss Lillian" the Covenant of Peace award for aiding "international justice, understanding, and peace." Her style and substance drew public support to an otherwise beleaguered president.

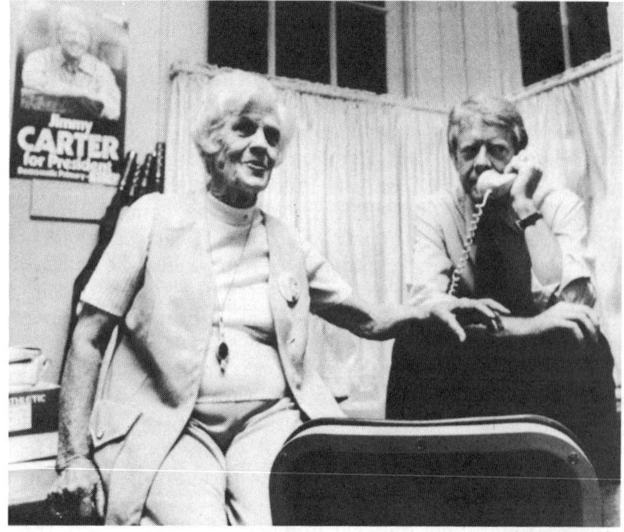

Wide World Photos

Lillian Carter, mother of Jimmy Carter, traveled around the country campaigning for her son in the 1976 election. She was an asset as well after he won the White House.

The efforts of the president's extended family also can prove useful in campaigning. The Kennedy clan pioneered in this area; before them, presidential family members rarely participated publicly in campaigns, but Kennedy's races in 1952 and 1960 were family affairs. His brother Robert served as campaign manager on both occasions, and his brother Edward had responsibility for producing votes in the western states for JFK in 1960. Joseph P. Kennedy, JFK's father, was a driving force as well, especially in the early campaigns. He pushed his son John into politics and dominated his campaigns so much that only Robert proved able to cope with him. The elder Kennedy also provided abundant money and contacts for his son. JFK himself would joke about charges that his father was "buying elections" for him. Referring to the West Virginia primary in 1960, he remarked, "I got a wire from my father: Dear Jack. Don't buy one more vote than is necessary. I'll be damned if I'll pay for a landslide." His mother, Rose Kennedy, and his sisters—Eunice Shriver, Pat Lawford, and Jean Smith—stumped the country, ringing doorbells and attending receptions and banquets on a carefully orchestrated schedule aimed at maximizing exposure. In particular, Rose Kennedy proved a natural politician, plugging her son to everyone she met and turning every situation to his advantage. Even his brother-in-law Stephen Smith played an important administrative role in the campaign. This family effort was critical to JFK's run for the White House; he would not have been nominated and elected without it.[29]

Presidential Relatives as Liabilities

Many relatives of presidents have been perceived as liabilities. Some presidential relatives have come under direct public criticism; others, because the president believed that they would in some way foster negative publicity, have been kept out of sight. For example, JFK's mentally disabled sister, Rosemary, who eventually had to be institutionalized, was carefully excluded from public view. In a media-dominated era in which relatives have become a factor, only those who help the president's image are welcome; others are shunted aside.

Sam Houston Johnson, Lyndon Johnson's younger brother, was apparently seen as a liability by LBJ, although the reasons are not entirely clear. Once referred to as his primary political adviser by Lyndon Johnson himself, Sam Houston was relegated to obscurity when his brother reached the White House. He seemed to be dominated by the president and totally dependent on him both before and during LBJ's term; he had no home of his own and no steady job. Moreover, Sam Houston was in poor health and struggled with alcoholism. Apprehensive about the image his brother projected, the president put him under virtual house arrest; during LBJ's term Sam Houston lived on the third floor of the White House, unable to do anything without the president's prior approval. The primary job of the Secret Service agent assigned to Sam Houston was to keep track of everywhere he went and everyone he spoke with. His contact with the outside world was restricted to the White House domestic staff, and he was mentioned in the press only four times in the five years of the Johnson administration.[30]

One of Richard Nixon's younger brothers, Donald, who was struggling to make a business venture succeed in the 1950s, borrowed money from Howard Hughes, a major manufacturer of defense equipment. The loan, however, was never repaid and became an issue in the 1960 presidential campaign, with Nixon's opponents making charges of influence buying, and again in the California gubernatorial campaign of 1962. Nixon thus became seriously concerned that this and other of his brother's financial dealings (none of which were illegal) might be embarrassing to him as president. After Richard Nixon became president, Donald Nixon was kept under wraps; his telephone was tapped, he was placed under physical surveillance, and a report on his activities was prepared for Nixon's aides.

A more public problem was caused by Jimmy Carter's younger brother, Billy. In the early days of the Carter administration (1977-1981), Billy was actually an asset to the president; his folksy, down-home, beer-drinking, country boy image made cool Jimmy seem a bit more accessible. Billy Carter became an instant celebrity. He appeared on television talk shows, made paid public appearances, and had his own beer marketed. The press loved him and even commented upon his shrewd business sense.

Unfortunately, by 1979 most of the good feeling toward Billy had been replaced by public criticism and ridicule. Some of his escapades and comments received extremely unfavorable publicity: once he urinated outdoors at an Atlanta airport, and another time he made remarks that were widely interpreted as being anti-Semitic. Allegations of financial irregularities, including the diversion of a business loan to his brother's campaign, were made but never proven. Moreover, Bill was castigated for the tour he cohosted for Libyan officials and a free trip he had taken to that country. In 1980 it was learned that Billy had accepted over $200,000 in "loans" from Libya and also was apparently in technical violation of a law requiring him to register as a Libyan agent. These disclosures led to a Senate investigation later that year of Billy Carter's affairs. The president's brother argued that the Libyan money had been needed for living expenses; so much of the family business had been put into a blind trust during President Carter's term that Billy Carter had been forced to sell his own share and had been left without income.

Although the congressional hearings into "Billygate" produced no evidence of anything beyond poor judgment, Billy Carter remained a liability to his brother. Republicans seized on the lingering claims of his financial improprieties to challenge President Carter's integrity in the 1980 elections. Moreover, people believed that the president should somehow muzzle his brother, who was seen as a national embarrassment. When the president would not or could not keep Billy Carter under control, it reinforced the public perception of a weak president. Certainly, the poor image Billy Carter had acquired damaged the president's hopes for reelection in 1980.

Relatives can sometimes pose difficulties for the president even if they are not alcoholics or in financial hot water. Just as the American public expects the first lady to be the epitome of womanhood, so it expects the first family to be the essence of harmonious family life, with the implication that something is wrong if it is not. Such expectations can bedevil presidents who have tensions within their families. Ronald Reagan, for example, had to deal with such problems. When his first term began, there were strained relations between his older children, Maureen and Michael, and their stepmother, Nancy. When Maureen ran for the U.S. Senate in 1981 the Reagans gave her no help, and Michael complained publicly in 1985 that the president had never seen his two-year-old granddaughter because of Nancy Reagan's "jealousy." The rifts were patched over successfully, but such familial stresses could be damaging to presidents with less popular appeal than Reagan.

Presidential Friends

Over the years several friends and close associates of the president have been important, if informal, players on the political scene. The reason for this is simple: because presidents are surrounded every day by people who expect something from them or who have a cause to endorse or a personal interest to protect, they naturally look for those who ask for nothing. As Franklin Roosevelt noted, the president needs someone "who asks for nothing except to serve [the president]." Such people are usually found among old friends.

Herein lies the origin of the so-called kitchen cabinet. Many members of the president's official cabinet are appointed for reasons other than friendship or compatibility; they may have expertise in the subject area of the cabinet department, or the appointment may be made in light of political necessities. Once named, cabinet appointees frequently develop a loyalty to the department in which they serve that overrides their loyalty to the president. In the words of John Ehrlichman, one of President Nixon's aides, "They go off and marry the natives and we never see them again."[31] Presidents look to old friends to provide the unbiased advice that the cabinet may not give.

Presidents consult old friends to gain a fresh perspective. Old friends usually are not caught inside the Washington Beltway; they look at politics from the outside in. Most presidents have had one or two, and sometimes several, such advisers.

The kitchen cabinet was created by President Andrew Jackson (1829-1837). Jackson's first official cabinet was a relatively weak body, several of whose members had been appointed to satisfy factions within the Democratic party, most notably one led by Vice President John C. Calhoun. Jackson thus tended to rely on his unofficial advisers much more than his official ones. Most members of the kitchen cabinet had been important in Jackson's 1828 presidential campaign. Some were old Tennessee associates, such as Maj. John H. Eaton and Andrew J. Donelson; others such as Amos Kendall, Issac Hill, and Frances P. Blair were important newspapermen. Finally, there were political figures such as Roger B. Taney and Martin Van Buren. Several of these men remained in the background, but others occupied important places in the government: Eaton was secretary of war (1829-1831), Taney became attorney general (1831-1836) and then chief justice of the Supreme Court (1836-1864), and Van Buren was first secretary of

Culver Pictures

On matters both personal and political, Col. Edward M. House was Wilson's closest confidant throughout much of his presidency.

state (1829-1831) and then vice president (1833-1837). The kitchen cabinet never dominated Jackson, but it was a significant source of advice, particularly between 1829 and 1831.

Not every kitchen cabinet has been composed of six or seven persons. From 1913 to 1920 Woodrow Wilson had a one-man advisory board, Col. Edward M. House. A wealthy man who entered politics for the excitement of it, Colonel House met Wilson in 1911 and became his closest confidant throughout much of his presidency. Ike Hoover, chief usher at the White House in the Wilson years, noted that Wilson was in constant contact with House and "there was nothing too big, too important, too secret, or too sacred to discuss with Colonel House." [32]

Wilson sought House's advice on various aspects of public policy, and even on personal matters such as the details of his wedding to Edith Galt. The colonel also became the president's emissary, representing him in Europe in efforts to mediate World War I. Later, House helped lay the foundations of the Paris peace conference that ended the war. He was recognized as being so close to Wilson that people came to him to get their ideas before the president. Although House and Wilson eventually had a falling out and never spoke after 1919, their relationship has become the symbol of closeness between president and adviser.

Another president who had a particularly close relationship with his unofficial advisers was Franklin Roosevelt. While Roosevelt had some men of notable ability in his cabinet, he drew on many sources for information. One of the most important in the early days of the New Deal was the brains trust, a group of academicians led by Rexford G. Tugwell, Raymond Moley, and Adolph A. Berle, Jr. Each held minor posts in government but were instrumental in stimulating ideas on dealing with the depression.

Of greater importance was the influence of two longtime associates, Louis McHenry Howe and Harry Hopkins. Howe, a "wizened gnome," was a newspaperman who recognized Roosevelt's potential while FDR was still in the New York State legislature. He was Roosevelt's closest political adviser throughout the early years of the New Deal, and he strongly encouraged Eleanor Roosevelt to become involved in politics. Perhaps the most intimate of Roosevelt's advisers and blessed with acute political instincts, Howe was particularly important in pointing out errors to the president and was the only man who could speak bluntly to him and get away with it. Harry Hopkins, who lived at the White House, had been part of FDR's New York State administration. He was a major adviser during World War II and served as an important figure in Roosevelt's operation of the war effort.

While presidential friends and cronies often have been valuable sources of advice to the president, some friends of presidents have embarrassed and injured them by dishonesty and corruption. For example, Ulysses S. Grant came to the White House in 1869 as a career army officer with no experience in politics. To fill the various offices in his administration, Grant turned to his old friends and appointed so many of them that Sen. Charles Sumner (R-Mass.) declared it to be a case of "dropsical nepotism swollen to elephantitis." [33] Unfortunately, many of Grant's old friends and associates were dishonest, and Grant, although honest himself, was reluctant to crack down on them.

The result was one of the most scandal-plagued administrations in history. In 1875 it was learned that Grant's personal secretary, Gen. Orville E. Babcock, was involved first in a questionable scheme to annex Santo Domingo and later in the Whiskey Ring, which defrauded the government of millions of dollars in taxes. In 1876 Secretary of War William W. Belknap was impeached by the House of Representatives for selling licenses for the sale of goods to the Indians; he avoided conviction in the Senate because he resigned first. Grant was slow to respond to these and other scandals—not until the very end of his second term did he begin to acknowledge them—and they have severely damaged his historical reputation.

In 1920 Warren G. Harding was elected president, a position for which he was unsuited in many ways. Although Harding was a personable and attractive man, he was of but moderate intelligence, and he knew it. He was a trusting person, who seemed unable to see misconduct in his close associates. A contemporary joke was that George Washington could not tell a lie, but Harding could not tell a liar. He was very weak and pliable as well. His father once noted that if his son had been a girl, he would "have always been in a family way."

Harding was simply one of the boys, and he brought his cronies to Washington with him. Upstairs in the White House, Harding and friends such as Albert B. Fall and Harry H. Daugherty would play cards and drink from the president's private bar, even though Prohibition was then in force. Soon, however, scandals began breaking around Harding. The head of the Veterans' Bureau was indicted for graft, and shortly thereafter the Teapot Dome scandal, involving the illegal sale of oil leases in the western states, erupted. Fall eventually went to prison for his part in the latter; Daugherty was implicated in several crimes, but he was never convicted for lack of evidence. The emerging accounts of corruption were devastating to Harding, who complained bitterly about his "goddamned friends." Already in uncertain health, he was put under great stress by the misdeeds of his pals, which contributed to his sudden death from pneumonia and coronary thrombosis in 1923.

Other presidents have suffered as well from the misdealings of their associates, although few to the extent of Grant and Harding. In 1945 President Truman brought to Washington a number of his old Missouri cronies, some of whom turned out to be associated with an influence-peddling scandal, thereby helping undercut his chances to run in 1952. The allegations of financial wrongdoing that surrounded President Carter's old friend and budget director Bert Lance also helped undercut the Carter administration in its early days.

Protecting the President: The Secret Service

One of the major benefits provided presidents is the full-time personal protection of them and their families. While the bulk of the president's security is provided by the U.S. Secret Service, other government agencies also contribute to the effort to protect the president.[34] The Federal Bureau of Investigation (FBI) points out to the Secret Service those people within the United States who might pose a threat to the president, and the Central Intelligence Agency (CIA) provides information on potential assassins in other countries, a source of increasing concern to the service. Because the personnel of the service is insufficient to fill all the human resource demands of protecting the president, local and foreign police may be used, depending on where the president travels. The air force provides a fighter escort for *Air Force One;* the navy furnishes backup in case an emergency develops while the president flies over the ocean; the army provides communication equipment; and the Marine Corps posts a detachment to guard Camp David. Finally, the General Services Administration (GSA) arranges for any renovations needed to improve security at a presidential residence.

While all of these agencies contribute to the president's safety, the central agency is the Secret Service, which coordinates their activities. Any measures taken by GSA, for example, are at the request of the service, and it is the service that provides the human shield needed to protect the president.

Origins of the Secret Service

What is now known as the Secret Service was created in July 1865 to reduce the wholesale counterfeiting of U.S. currency. This crime had reached such proportions that as many as one-third of all bills in circulation may have been bogus. Thus in one of the last official acts of his life, President Abraham Lincoln agreed to the creation of a unit within the Treasury Department that would have the permanent task of catching forgers and counterfeiters. Indeed, the Secret Service Division proved quite successful at this task; over its first few years it captured over two hundred counterfeiters a year.

Because then the service was the only federal government agency that acted as a general law enforcement body, it found that its role rapidly expanded. By 1874 it was investigating fraud, peonage, and slavery cases, as well as the Ku Klux Klan. The service also began to acquire the form and structure of a bureaucratic institution and, unfortunately, a reputation for unsavory tactics. Thus, in 1874 a distrustful Congress stripped it of all but its original functions.

The Secret Service languished until 1898 and the Spanish-American War, when President William McKinley, needing an intelligence agency to gather information about the Spanish, asked for its help. During the war the service operated as both a military espionage body and a domestic counterintelligence body, and by the end of the war it had established itself as one of the best such units of the time. After the war the intelligence role was de-emphasized but was restored during World War I. Although the Secret Service worked well with the State Department during the conflict, it found itself out of the spy game by World War II; the growth of the FBI and military intelligence rendered the service's activities in that area superfluous.

The service's quite active anticounterfeiting operations remained intact throughout this period, however. In 1917 alone it obtained over a thousand arrests and convictions and seized nearly $300,000 in fraudulent money. It also conducted investigations into official misconduct and played a major part in uncovering the Teapot Dome scandal during the Harding administration.

Protection of the president was not part of the service's original function. For many years presidents who wanted bodyguards had to hire them themselves, and most did without. Confronted with a would-be assassin in 1835, President Andrew Jackson himself attacked his assailant and drove him off. On the night he was killed, President Lincoln was guarded by a single District of Columbia policeman; the guard had wandered off when assailant John Wilkes Booth arrived. Secret Service agents were nearby when Presidents Garfield and McKinley were shot, but none of them were responsible for protecting the president. In McKinley's case there were three agents next to him, but their only job was crowd control. Indeed, early efforts by the service to protect the president were rebuffed by Congress, and it was not until 1906 that the first presidential detail was authorized.

The coverage given by the service gradually expanded over the years, and with the decline in its intelligence role, protection became its second major function. In 1940 the service survived a threat to that function from the FBI, which had taken on the job of protecting the vice president from 1929 to 1932, when a proposed relocation of the service into the Justice Department failed. In fact, the Secret Service was only permanently granted the job of presidential protection in 1951; until that time its authorization had to be renewed annually.

Organization and Personnel

In keeping with its original anticounterfeiting role the Secret Service is an arm of the Treasury Department, which administers the service with a very light touch. The director of the Secret Service is not a political appointee; he or she is selected by the secretary of the Treasury from the ranks of the experienced agents. There are approximately 36,000 employees in the agency, of whom about 1,800 are special agents, the elite who handle personal protection or counterfeiting cases. The remaining employees consist of the Uniformed Division and the support staff. A very small but growing number of female special agents have been assigned to every aspect of the service's work, including the presidential detail. The annual budget of the service is about $180 million, but budgeting can be difficult because it is hard to know in advance exactly how much protection may be needed. The total varies with the changing number of protectees and the activities in which they engage.

Structurally, the service has five divisions (or offices) under the director and deputy director. The most important of these are the Office of Investigations, the Office of Protective Research, and the Office of Protective Operations. *(See Figure 1.)*

The Office of Investigations is responsible for forgery and counterfeiting cases. Its experts investigate, analyze documents, and provide evidence in forgery cases. The office also conducts background checks on government employees and investigates threats against service protectees—but not actual assassination attempts, which is the responsibility of the FBI. Finally, it maintains control of the Treasury Security Force, which protects the Treasury building itself. Because the agency's regional offices normally deal with forgery and counterfeiting cases, those offices are supervised by the Office of Investigations.

The Office of Protective Research compiles data on individuals who, for whatever reason, have come to the service's attention as potential threats to its protectees. Its files contain over forty thousand people, about 1 percent of whom are on a "watch list" as a serious threat. Others are singled out depending on the president's travel plans. In addition to identifying dangerous persons to be monitored, the Office of Protective Research also conducts searches to ensure that any environment the president will occupy is safe and secure, without dangerous objects such as explosives or surveillance devices.

The agents who actually protect the president are in the Office of Protective Operations. Each of its divisions is responsible for a particular protectee. The division for the president contains the White House detail; other divisions are responsible for the vice president, each of the living former presidents, and any widowed first ladies. Thus, Jimmy Carter and Lady Bird Johnson have their own divisions within the Secret Service's Protective Operations Office. Should a protectee die or decline coverage, his or her division is disbanded. The service is also responsible for protecting announced presidential candidates and foreign heads of state, but the Candidate/Nominee Protective Division and the Dignitary Protective Division are basically skeletal and only staffed as needed.

Also within Protective Operations is the Uniformed Division, which originally was part of the District of Columbia Police Department, but President Harding, who wanted better control over it, removed it from the department in 1922. In 1930, after a stranger walked unchallenged into President Hoover's dining room one evening, the Secret Service was given authority over the division. The Uniformed Division is responsible for the White House security guards, and since 1970 it also has provided protection for foreign embassies in Washington. When the service provides protection for an embassy, it protects only that; guards do not leave the grounds and take action only if someone trespasses onto the property.

Most Secret Service employees have demanding jobs, and the training for special agents is particularly arduous. To be a special agent an applicant must be between twenty-one and thirty-five years of age and able to pass a physical exam, the Treasury Enforcement Agent Exam, an extensive interview, and a security check. Candidates who pass the initial screening undergo an intensive training program to prepare them for both parts of the service's mission. They are first sent to the Federal Law Enforcement Facility in Brunswick, Georgia, to learn to deal with forgery and counterfeiting. Then they move on to the service's 420-acre school in Beltsville, Maryland, to learn the details of investigation and protection.

A superb training ground, the Beltsville facility has classrooms and laboratories in which sophisticated methods for detecting forgeries are taught. To prepare for their protective role, prospective agents are taught emergency medical principles, abnormal psychology, hand-to-hand combat, investigative techniques, and evasive driving tactics. They also become firearms experts. They study movies of previous assassination attempts and engage in simulations in which their own responses are videotaped and studied. Using full-size mock-ups of the White House and of a city street, new agents can refine their skills.

The pay for special agents begins at $25,000 per year and may increase to $40,000 within the first eight years. Agents start in a field office, move to a protective detail after a few years if they are good enough, and after a few more years go back to a field office and eventually an administrative job. For people on protective details, particularly the president's, the stress can be extreme; thus agents tend to be rotated regularly. Moreover, the hours can be long and irregular; agents even may find themselves on duty for sixteen hours and more. Because an agent can be called on duty on short notice and sent anywhere around the world, a normal family and personal life is often unachievable. Indications of this are found in the fact that the average age of an agent is only thirty-five, and that the service teaches its agents the warning signs of psychological disorders and alcoholism.[35]

The Roles of the Secret Service

With its roles of defender of the nation's currency and protector of the president, the Secret Service is in a sense two agencies in one: a criminal investigation unit and a bodyguard service. Unfortunately, the two roles do not always fit together very well, and some agents are not equally comfortable in both. The skills required to crack a counterfeiting ring are not the same as those needed to foil an assassination attempt. The service thinks the juxtaposition is useful, but not everyone agrees.

Since relatively few agents regularly participate in the protective role, the major task for most agents is the prevention of counterfeiting and forgery. In 1987 the service closed over 120,000 cases of these two crimes, arresting 8,900 people and confiscating over $62 million in counterfeit currency. It obtained convictions in 99 percent of the cases it prosecuted. The service attempts to break counter-

Figure 1 Organization of the U.S. Secret Service

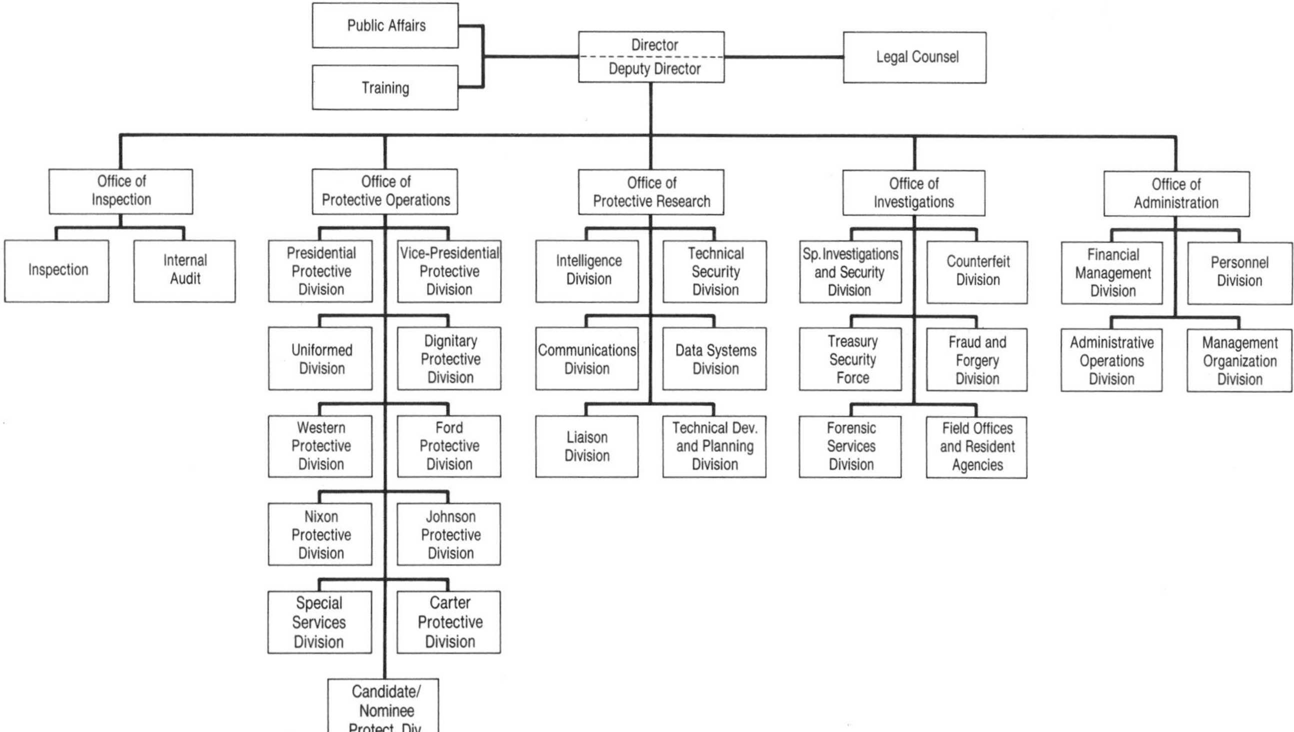

Source: U.S. Secret Service

feiting rings before the bogus bills go into service, targeting the big distributors. It also investigates cases of forged checks and documents and has recently investigated food stamp fraud. Of particular interest are cases involving stolen government checks and bonds. The service tries to combine public awareness with the latest technology to control these crimes.

The better-known part of the service's mission is protection of the president. That role has expanded considerably since its inception. The first White House detail, assigned to Theodore Roosevelt in 1901, had only two agents; it had expanded to ten by 1918 and to thirty-seven by 1940. In 1989 it numbered seventy. The protection has broadened as well. Originally, it included just the president, but in 1908 it was extended to the president-elect. In 1962 the vice president came under the agency's full-time protection (previously, protection of the vice president was on a request-only basis). Further additions to the service's work load were made in 1965, when retired presidents, widows of presidents, and their children under age sixteen were protected. In 1968 presidential candidates were covered, in 1971 foreign heads of state, and in 1976 candidates' wives (limited coverage). Additionally, in 1971 the president was granted the right to request protection for anyone thought to need it, as Jimmy Carter did for Edward Kennedy in 1980 before the senator became an official presidential candidate.

Although any of these people can refuse Secret Service protection, few do. Combined with greater travel and activity by public figures, the demand for protection results in a considerable load for the service, particularly in election years when it may be forced to borrow from elsewhere in the Treasury Department to meet its obligations. This is true even though it normally protects only those candidates who can raise enough campaign funds to warrant matching funds from the federal treasury.

Occasionally, the service finds itself with other tasks as well. During the Second World War, for example, it was responsible for protecting the original Constitution and the Declaration of Independence. Similarly, when Leonardo da Vinci's painting *Mona Lisa* toured the United States in 1962, it was guarded by the service.

Protecting the President: Tactics and Problems

All of the training undertaken by agents in the Secret Service's operations divisions is aimed at keeping the president alive and well. The service has adopted numerous tactics to insure the president's continued safety in a world filled with dangers.

The service prefers, of course, that the president remain in the White House, where there are numerous safeguards and a more carefully controlled environment. Although the service is not eager to reveal any details, it is clear that White House security arrangements are elaborate. Anyone entering the mansion on business is checked; anyone working there, including presidential aides, must wear a photo badge. All incoming packages and visitors are carefully monitored as well, and armed guards and plainclothes agents keep watch around the premises. The grounds are protected by reinforced fences, guardhouses, television cameras, and electronic sensors. There is even a bomb shelter and antiaircraft weapons. Finally, should the president need help, there is a "panic button" under the desk in the Oval Office which can unobtrusively summon agents at any time. *(See "Security and Communications," p. 818, in Housing of the Executive Branch chapter of Part V.)*

Despite the trained agents and equipment, the system still fails. In 1977, for example, a visitor was able to walk up to the windows outside the Oval Office and speak directly to President Carter. In 1981 a man with a history of mental illness gained access to the White House grounds and was there unchallenged for ten minutes; he made it to the mansion itself before he was stopped.[36]

When the president travels, the challenges for the service are greater because the variables that can be easily controlled are fewer. The White House detail and the field offices in the areas where the president plans to travel must make extensive security arrangements. Working with the local police, they secure the airport where the president will arrive and depart. They carefully plan and survey the routes to be traveled, secure the buildings in which the president will appear, and arrange that rooftops and other overlooks be patrolled. Procedures for screening onlookers are introduced. The service's files are checked for any people known to be a possible threat to the president; some of them may be watched during the visit. Preparations even extend to identifying a hospital to use in case of emergency and ensuring that it has adequate supplies of the president's blood type.

In recent years security arrangements have not permitted publicity of the president's travel plans. Once it was customary—to insure the largest crowds possible—to publicize the president's travel route. For example, President Kennedy's exact route through Dallas on November 22, 1963, was available to anyone who picked up a Dallas newspaper. This is no longer true, however. When the president travels today the arrival and departure times and travel details are not public knowledge.

The most visible part of the presidential protection effort to an outsider is the cordon of agents that surrounds the president. These agents are with the president at almost all times, even in the White House, except the family quarters. They stand guard both inside and outside of every room occupied by the president. When the president leaves the White House, the agents form (as best they can) a human shield around the chief executive. The service tries to maintain what it calls a "safe zone" or clear space around the president, so that the agents have a better chance to spot a potential assailant. Their efforts to keep a safe zone have sometimes led to criticism of their tactics.

Because these agents represent the last line of defense for the president, they are under enormous pressure. Beyond watching for any known dangerous people who may be around, agents scan the crowds in search of unusual or threatening behavior: a man wearing an overcoat on a warm day, a person carrying a newspaper in a strange way, a woman too eager to get close to the president, or even a face that keeps reappearing in different places. Because the goal of the service is prevention, not retribution, agents must develop a sixth sense to anticipate trouble. An instinct for danger and quick reactions are critical to keeping the president safe.

Should an attack occur, agents shield the president first, then subdue the assailant, and finally, once the president is safely removed, secure the area and assist any injured bystanders. Agents are trained to become a human shield for the president. As he watched agents stand to practice with firearms, President Reagan commented that they made a very large target that way; he was told that that was the point. In Dallas in 1963 agent Rufus W. Youngblood covered Vice President Lyndon Johnson with his own body when the presidential motorcade came under attack. Videotapes of the 1981 assassination attempt on President Reagan show agent Timothy J. McCarthy, with arms and legs spread wide, walking directly toward the assailant, John W. Hinckley, Jr., thus blocking his view of the president (McCarthy was shot, but he recovered).

The service has encountered several serious difficulties in its efforts to keep presidents alive, and several of these have had to do with presidents themselves. Some presidents have been quite cooperative with the service, but others have tended to balk at its requests, generally for two reasons.

One is strictly political. Most presidents like crowds, and even if they do not, it is simply good politics for them to be seen mingling with their adoring supporters. Thus, while the service probably would prefer that presidents spent their days in one room in the White House, political realities dictate that they get out and "press the flesh." The more presidents do that, the harder it is for the service. President Johnson, for example, loved to dive into crowds much to his bodyguards' dismay. On that fateful day in Dallas in 1963 Kennedy had the protective cover removed from his limousine so that the crowds could see him better.

Even a president like Nixon, who was something of a loner and thus easy to protect, was a problem for political reasons. Nixon's staff constantly wanted to show how much Nixon was loved by the people and looked for close public contacts to prove it. Thus, the staff consistently fought the service over security arrangements, which it regarded as too restrictive for its aims. One argument over where the crowd restraining line was to be was so bitter that the chief of Nixon's protective detail threatened to arrest Chief of Staff H. R. Haldeman because of his interference.

If politics makes life difficult for the service, so may presidents' reactions to their bodyguards. Agents are a constant intrusive presence in the president's life, which may lead to presidential resentment and resistance. President Johnson complained that the service would not hesitate to occupy his bedroom, and when he was at his ranch, he would often try to lose his detail by jumping in the car and ordering his driver to drive as fast as possible. Presidents want some privacy and to think they can still do as they like, but the service restricts them. As a result, many try to avoid their agents from time to time and in other ways be uncooperative.

The Secret Service, however, has ways to get around presidents and first ladies, who may find their protection particularly burdensome. Eleanor Roosevelt, for example, flatly refused to accept her protective detail. Finally, the service worked out a deal: if she would carry and learn to fire a handgun, the service would stop tailing her. But in fact the gun stayed in her dresser drawer, and the service put undercover agents at her every stop. Early in his term Harry Truman liked to walk to the bank, but the service did not like how long he waited on street corners for the lights to change. Their solution? They fixed all the traffic lights on his route so that they would turn red in all directions at once and Truman would never have to wait on a corner again—he soon caught on, however, and ordered the service to stop.[37] Pat Nixon tried to keep the number of agents with her on trips around Washington smaller than the service wanted, but her wishes were ignored. When one day she noticed the second car of agents that was accompanying her, she was reassured that it was only there in case her car had engine trouble.[38]

Presidents also tend to be fatalistic, further complicating the service's job. Many presidents in fact begin to feel that personal risk is part of the job. The feeling expressed by Lyndon Johnson that "all a man needs is a willingness to trade his life for mine" seems common to most presidents. This sense that "no amount of protection is enough" in the face of a determined assassin makes the service's job more difficult, for it leads presidents to be less cautious than their guardians would like. Not all presidents are fatalistic to the same degree, but those who are prove quite difficult for the service. Indeed, one of the most fatalistic of presidents, John Kennedy, was also one of the hardest to protect.

Another problem the service faces is trying to identify a potential assassin, a critical step in preventing an attack on the president. The master files maintained by the service of anyone who may pose a risk to the president—for example, people who have made threats, mentally disturbed and violent people, or members of political extremist groups—are updated constantly and sorted by degree of threat. Before the president moves from the White House, a watch list is put together of anyone in the files who resides where the president is going, and the agents in charge account for everyone they can and keep special watch for the rest.

In practice, however, this system has several flaws. First, the service has to rely on the FBI for much of the information that goes into its files, and communication between the two agencies sometimes fails. It also must rely on local police for information about individuals, and the quality of the data obtained may vary. Second, the service, which is a rather small agency, lacks the human resources to evaluate reports more carefully. Thus, the watch list is limited to about four hundred people primarily because the agents cannot handle much more. After the attempt on President Reagan in 1981, some critics argued that John Hinckley's arrest for trying to carry a gun onto an airplane in 1980 should have put him on the watch list. But unfortunately the agency lacked the people necessary to investigate the case and determine that.

The major problem, however, is that there is no consistent way to identify an assassin, either in the files or among the public at large. Despite its best efforts, the service has never managed to develop any statistical or psychological techniques that would allow it to distinguish unerringly a real assassin from all the false alarms in its own files, nor does it have any sure way to spot one in a crowd. In fact,

> despite the impressive progress in the fields of computer technology and psychiatry, the Service has few clues as to how to look for potential assassins. Without a reliable set of profiles or indices that can be used to identify those who are actually dangerous, as opposed to potentially dangerous, neither the agents nor their computers can derive much benefit from increased quantities of intelligence data.[39]

Such profiles simply do not exist, however. Thus, compilation of a watch list becomes a matter of subjective judgment by the agents in charge, as does the determination of which reports warrant inclusion in the master files. Without some foolproof guide to help evaluate information, truly dangerous people can be and are overlooked. In fact, of the people who have allegedly shot at service protectees since 1960—Lee Harvey Oswald (President Kennedy, 1963), Sirhan Sirhan (Robert Kennedy, 1968), Arthur Bremer (Gov. George Wallace, 1972), Lynette Alice Fromme (President Ford, 1975), Sara Jane Moore (President Ford, 1975), and John Hinckley (President Reagan, 1981)—none were in the agency's files at the time.

Complicating the service's mission further is the increased threat of foreign terrorist activity against the president. While such a threat may be mostly hypothetical, the service cannot take chances and must treat it seriously. Thus, in late 1981 it spent two months in a state of constant alert because of reports that Libya's Muammar Qaddafi had sent a "hit team" to kill President Reagan. Rumors flew about the nature and location of the team. In the end, however, nothing happened and the hit squad may in fact never have existed. This case indicates the additional burden thrown upon the service in an era of international terrorism. Given the agency's limited resources, such a threat spreads the service thin and makes its job even more difficult.

Notes

1. J. B. West, *Upstairs at the White House: My Life With the First Ladies* (New York: Coward, McCann, and Geohegan, 1973), 342.
2. Rosalynn Carter, *First Lady from Plains* (Boston: Houghton Mifflin, 1984), 144.
3. West, *Upstairs at the White House,* 209.
4. Irwin Hood Hoover, *Forty-Two Years in the White House* (Boston: Houghton Mifflin, 1934), 267.
5. West, *Upstairs at the White House,* 20.
6. Ibid., 204-205.
7. Dennis V. N. McCarthy, *Protecting the President: The Inside Story of a Secret Service Agent* (New York: Morrow, 1985), 195.
8. "Why It Will Be Hard to Stay 'Just Plain Folks,' " *U.S. News & World Report,* January 24, 1977, 24-25.
9. Betty Boyd Caroli, *First Ladies* (New York: Oxford University Press, 1987), xv.
10. Quoted in ibid., 14.
11. Paul F. Boller, Jr., *Presidential Wives* (New York: Oxford University Press, 1988), 296.
12. Lewis L. Gould, "First Ladies," *American Scholar* (Autumn 1986): 528-535.
13. Boller, *Presidential Wives,* 319-320.
14. Ibid., 46.
15. Ibid., 169.
16. Ibid., 296.
17. Gould, "First Ladies," 534.
18. Carter, *First Lady from Plains,* 158-159.
19. Caroli, *First Ladies,* 241-242.
20. Scholars disagree about Martha Washington's actual birth date. June 21, 1731, is the date most commonly used, but several others also have been mentioned.

A number of sources were used to prepare the biographies of the first ladies. The major ones were: Caroli, *First Ladies*; Sol Barzman, *The First Ladies* (New York: Cowles, 1970); William A. De Gregorio, *The Complete Book of the Presidents* (New York: Dembner Books, 1984); Joseph Nathan Kane, *Facts about the Presidents* (New York: Wilson, 1985); and Tim Taylor, *The Book of Presidents* (New York: Arno Press, 1972).

21. Dolley Madison's given name is not clear. Some scholars have declared that "Dorothea" was her given name and "Dolley" a nickname. Others have insisted that "Dolley" was her real name.
22. The birth records for Nancy Reagan have been lost, but school records indicate that she was born in 1921. Mrs. Reagan claims that she was born in 1923.
23. Barbara Kellerman, *All the President's Kin* (New York: Free Press, 1981), 26.
24. Paul F. Boller, Jr., *Presidential Anecdotes* (New York: Oxford University Press, 1981), 206.
25. Caroli, *First Ladies,* 120.
26. See West, *Upstairs at the White House,* 216-220.
27. Kellerman, *All the President's Kin,* 4.
28. Ibid., chap. 6.
29. Ibid., 8-10.
30. Ibid., 215-219.
31. Quoted in Stephen J. Wayne, *The Legislative Presidency* (New York: Harper and Row, 1978), 49.
32. Hoover, *Forty-Two Years in the White House,* 87.
33. Boller, *Presidential Anecdotes,* 157.
34. The discussion of the Secret Service that follows relies heavily upon Philip K. Melanson's *The Politics of Protection: The U.S. Secret Service in the Terrorist Age* (New York: Praeger, 1984), an excellent study of the origins and operations of the service.
35. For a firsthand account of the stress of a service job, see McCarthy, *Protecting the President,* especially chap. 5.
36. Melanson, *The Politics of Protection,* 92.
37. Ibid., 128.
38. McCarthy, *Protecting the President,* 172.
39. Melanson, *The Politics of Protection,* 115.

Selected Bibliography

Akers, Charles W. *Abigail Adams: An American Woman.* Boston: Little, Brown, 1980.

Baker, Jean H. *Mary Todd Lincoln: A Biography.* New York: Norton, 1987.

Barzman, Sol. *The First Ladies.* New York: Cowles, 1970.

Boller, Paul F., Jr. *Presidential Wives.* New York: Oxford University Press, 1988.

Caroli, Betty Boyd. *First Ladies.* New York: Oxford University Press, 1987.

Carter, Rosalynn. *First Lady From Plains.* Boston: Houghton Mifflin, 1984.

Furman, Bess. *White House Profile: A Social History of the White House, Its Occupants and Its Festivities.* Indianapolis: Bobbs-Merrill, 1954.

Gould, Lewis L. "First Ladies." *American Scholar* (Autumn 1986): 528-535.

Hofstadtler, Beatrice K. "How to be First Lady." *American Heritage* 34 (August-September 1983): 98-100.

Hoover, Irwin Hood. *Forty-Two Years in the White House.* Boston: Houghton Mifflin, 1934.

Johnson, Lady Bird. *A White House Diary.* New York: Holt, Rinehart, and Winston, 1970.

Kellerman, Barbara. *All the President's Kin.* New York: Free Press, 1981.

Levin, Phillys Lee. *Abigail Adams: A Biography.* New York: St. Martin's Press, 1987.

McCarthy, Dennis V. N. *Protecting the President: The Inside Story of a Secret Service Agent.* New York: Morrow, 1985.

Melanson, Philip K. *The Politics of Protection: The U.S. Secret Service in the Terrorist Age.* New York: Praeger, 1984.

"Nine Hours Inside the Oval Office." *U.S. News & World Report,* July 6, 1981, 14-20.

"Presidential Offspring: How They're Faring Today." *U.S. News & World Report,* August 13, 1984, 50-52.

"Safeguarding the President's Life: Where the Money Goes." *U.S. News & World Report,* August 13, 1973, 24-26.

Thomas, Helen. *Dateline: White House.* New York: Macmillan, 1975.

West, J. B. *Upstairs at the White House: My Life With the First Ladies.* New York: Coward, McCann, and Geohegan, 1973.

Whitton, Mary Ormsbee. *First First Ladies, 1789-1865.* New York: Hastings House, 1948.

"Why It Will Be Hard to Stay 'Just Plain Folks.' " *U.S. News & World Report,* January 24, 1977, 23-26.

Youngblood, Rufus W. *Twenty Years in the Secret Service: My Life With Five Presidents.* New York: Simon and Schuster, 1973.

Youngs, William T. *Eleanor Roosevelt: A Personal and Public Life.* Boston: Little, Brown, 1984.

Office of the Vice President

The constitutional and statutory responsibilities of the vice presidency are few and unimportant—legally, it is a weak office. To a large extent, the roles and resources that the vice president does enjoy are delegated—and can be revoked—at the discretion of the president. "The president can bestow assignments and authority and can remove that authority and power at will," wrote Hubert H. Humphrey, who served as vice president with President Lyndon B. Johnson. "I used to call this Humphrey's Law—'He who giveth can taketh away and often does.' " [1] Accordingly, the activities and influence of individual vice presidents vary considerably from administration to administration.

During the twentieth century, however, the office of the vice president has been enhanced in enduring ways, especially since the end of World War II, when a cluster of events took place that aroused public concern about the vice presidency. In April 1945, after President Franklin D. Roosevelt died, Vice President Harry S Truman succeeded to the presidency in virtual ignorance of both the administration's plans for the postwar period and the existence of the atomic bomb. Within a year, the United States had entered into an ongoing "cold war" with the Soviet Union, a conflict that was heightened by both nations' possession of nuclear weapons and the technological capacity to launch them with intercontinental ballistic missiles. The real possiblity of a virtually instantaneous war of unprecedented destruction led many Americans to insist that the vice president be sufficiently competent and informed so that, if the need for a presidential succession should arise, no lapse in national leadership would occur.

In response to this concern, most modern nominees for president, wishing to satisfy the voters, have examined the talents and abilities of the candidates they have considered as vice-presidential running mates before making a choice and, once in office, have kept the vice president informed and in the public eye. Some of the tasks with which presidents have entrusted their vice presidents, such as foreign travel and the right to give political and policy advice in weekly private meetings, have involved real responsibility; what is more, precedents have been created that subsequent vice presidents have been able to follow. To help carry out these new responsibilities, vice presidents have won additional resources for their office—perhaps most important, a larger and more professional staff. As a result, the vice presidency has become institutionalized, both in the narrow sense that it is organizationally larger and more complex than it used to be and in the broader sense that certain kinds of vice-presidential activities now are taken for granted.

By Michael Nelson

Evolving Roles

The myriad roles that modern vice presidents perform can be grouped into four categories: constitutional, statutory, advisory, and representative. The resources that vice presidents now have available to fulfill these responsibliities are discussed in the next section.

Constitutional Roles

The original Constitution assigned two roles to the vice president: to serve as president of the Senate, voting only to break ties, and to succeed to the presidency in the event of a presidential death, resignation, removal, or disability. In 1967, the Twenty-fifth Amendment clarified the vice president's responsibilities as presidential successor and as acting president during periods of presidential disability. The amendment also made the vice president the central figure in determining whether a president is disabled.

President of the Senate

In the early years of the Republic, when the Senate was small and relatively informal, the vice presidency's role as president of the Senate allowed vice presidents to influence the Senate's agenda, steer debate, name the members of its committees, and cast relatively frequent tie-breaking votes. Vice Presidents John Adams and John C. Calhoun, for example, decided twenty-nine and twenty-eight tie votes, respectively. *(See History of the Vice Presidency chapter in Part I.)*

In contrast, modern vice presidents spend little time performing their constitutional role in the Senate. Because the Senate has become more institutionalized, the powers of the presiding officer are circumscribed and largely ceremonial—the vice president is expected to follow the advice of the Senate's parliamentarian, not to lead independently. Because the Senate is larger today than it was when Adams and Calhoun presided, tie votes are highly infrequent. Vice

President Lyndon Johnson cast no tie-breaking votes; Vice President Spiro T. Agnew, two; Vice President Walter F. Mondale, one; and Vice President George Bush, eight. Equally important, the vice presidency has come to be associated more closely with the presidency than with Congress in recent years. Vice President Richard Nixon estimated that he spent 90 percent of his time on executive tasks and only 10 percent fulfilling his Senate responsibilities.[2] Vice President Mondale presided over the Senate on only nineteen occasions one year, for a total of eighteen hours.

Successor

The language of the original Constitution was unclear about the vice president's responsiblities as presidential successor. Was the vice president to assume the office of the president itself or merely its powers and duties? Was the succession to last until the end of the departed president's four-year term or only until a special election could be called? When President William Henry Harrison died in 1841, Vice President John Tyler set the pattern for future successions by claiming the office for the balance of Harrison's unexpired term. In 1967, the Twenty-fifth Amendment codified this precedent by declaring that "in case of the removal of the President from office or of his death or resignation, the Vice President shall become President." Nine vice presidents—Tyler, Millard Fillmore, Andrew Johnson, Chester A. Arthur, Theodore Roosevelt, Calvin Coolidge, Truman, Lyndon Johnson, and Gerald R. Ford—have become president by succession. *(See Selection by Succession chapter in Part II.)*

In one sense, the vice president's role as presidential successor resembles what physicists call a "potential" energy: it is dormant unless triggered by a vacancy in the presidency. But, as noted above, since World War II, concern about the vice president's successor role has prompted presidents to entrust the vice presidency with other responsibilities in order to assure the nation that the vice president will be prepared, literally at a moment's notice, to step into the presidency if needed.

Codeterminer of Presidential Disability

The original Constitution listed presidential disability as one of the situations that would prompt a vice-presidential succession but created no procedure for determining when a disability existed. The Twenty-fifth Amendment empowers presidents to declare themselves disabled. It also provides for situations in which a disabled president is unable or unwilling to make such a declaration. In such situations, the amendment requires that both the vice president and a majority of the heads of the departments (commonly referred to as the "cabinet") agree that the president is unable to fulfill the powers and duties of the office. Clearly, however, the vice president is, constitutionally, the more important figure in this decision: although the amendment authorizes Congress to replace the cabinet with some other body in disability determinations, it cannot replace the vice president.

The one occasion when a vice president nearly exercised the new power, however, suggests that it may be more a burden than a blessing to individual vice presidents. In 1981, shortly after President Ronald Reagan was shot and taken into surgery, White House counsel Fred Fielding prepared documents that would guide the vice president and cabinet in deciding whether to declare the president disabled and to transfer temporarily the powers and duties of the presidency to Vice President Bush. Other presidential aides, especially Richard Darman, the deputy assistant to the president, headed Fielding off for fear of confusing the nation and making the president look weak. Vice President Bush, anxious that the White House staff not regard him as an interloper, remained silent.[3]

Acting President

The Twenty-fifth Amendment also provides that while a president is disabled, whether by self-declaration or by determination of the vice president and the cabinet, "the Vice President shall immediately assume the powers and duties of the office as Acting President" and shall wield them until the president is once again able to resume office or until the term expires, whichever comes first. This, too, clarifies an ambiguity in the original Constitution, which seemed to imply that a vice-presidential succession in response to a presidential disability was to be treated in the same way as a succession after a president's death, resignation, or removal.

As with the vice president's role in determining whether a president is disabled, however, this new power may be at best a mixed blessing for the vice presidency. In 1985, in anticipation of extensive cancer surgery, President Reagan reluctantly signed over the powers and duties of the presidency to Vice President Bush, reclaiming them soon afterward. Eager not to offend the president or his aides with even the slightest hint of activity, Bush played tennis and chatted with friends at the vice-presidential residence during his eight hours as acting president. Even this self-effacing behavior did not satisfy White House chief of staff Donald Regan, who would have preferred that Bush stay at his vacation home in Maine.

Statutory Roles

In contrast to the presidency, to which numerous responsibilities have been assigned by law, the vice presidency has only two statutory roles: member of the National Security Council (NSC) and member of the Board of Regents of the Smithsonian Institution. The latter role is inconsequential—an aide to Vice President Mondale described it as "a dinosaur that will be with the vice presidency forever."[4] Membership on the NSC seems important, but it is less so than meets the eye.

The vice president was added to the NSC by Congress in 1949, partly at the behest of President Truman. As the only council member whom the president cannot command or remove from office, the vice president is entitled to attend all NSC meetings for the entire term. It is a prestigious post and, for Vice President Nixon—the one vice president whose president, Dwight D. Eisenhower, relied heavily on the formal advisory structures of the executive branch—NSC membership really did provide an important channel of influence.

But few presidents have wanted to feel obligated to involve the vice president in important foreign policy deliberations. As a result, most either have called a limited number of NSC meetings or used the meetings as forums to announce, rather than make, policy. During the Cuban missile crisis, for example, President Kennedy ignored the NSC, creating instead an ad hoc Executive Committee of the National Security Council to deal with the crisis. The "Excom" included not only all the NSC members except Vice President Johnson, but others, such as the attorney general and some White House aides. President Reagan relied on the NSC staff in his efforts to negotiate with the government of Iran in 1985 and 1986, but not on the council itself, which included Vice President Bush. (For discussion of NSC and NSC staff, see *"The National Security Council" p. 955, in Supporting Organizations chapter of Part V.)*

Advisory Roles

Vice presidents perform two sets of roles that are informal—that is, not grounded in the law or the Constitution. These informal roles originated and have evolved during the twentieth century. They were created by presidents for their vice presidents, reflecting the vice presidency's ever closer identification with the executive rather than the legislative branch. One set of roles, discussed in the next section, involves representing the president and the administration to foreign, intragovernmental, and public audiences. The other set of roles is advisory to the president, whether as cabinet member, commission chair, or senior adviser.

Cabinet Member

Every vice president since John Nance Garner has attended cabinet meetings at the invitation of the president. Vice President Garner was invited to meet regularly with the cabinet by President Franklin Roosevelt, who, as a candidate for vice president in 1920, had written an article urging that vice presidents be included.[5] (So had cousin Theodore Roosevelt in an 1896 article, but, as president, he did not practice what he preached with his own vice president, Charles W. Fairbanks.)[6]

Garner was not the first vice president to sit with the cabinet. A few earlier presidents had invited their vice presidents to cabinet meetings, notably President George Washington to Vice President John Adams and President Woodrow Wilson to Vice President Thomas R. Marshall, but only in exceptional cases. Nor was Franklin Roosevelt the first president who wanted to establish the practice of vice-presidential membership in the cabinet. In 1921, President Warren G. Harding tried to set a precedent by inviting Vice President Coolidge "to arrange to be present on all such meetings," on the grounds "that the second official of the Republic could add materially to the fullness of his service in this way." Coolidge accepted, writing later that the vice president "should be in the Cabinet because he might become President and ought to be informed on the policies of the Administration." As president, however, Coolidge was turned down even before he could offer cabinet membership to his own vice president, Charles G. Dawes. Dawes argued after his and Coolidge's election in 1924 that future presidents should not feel bound by a precedent that would force them to include vice presidents they did not want at cabinet meetings.[7] Coolidge's successor as president, Herbert Hoover, did not invite Vice President Charles Curtis to join the cabinet. *(See History of the Vice Presidency chapter of Part I.)*

For all its symbolic value, cabinet membership seldom has been a position of real influence for the vice president. (The exceptions were Vice Presidents Garner and, especially, Nixon, who presided over nineteen cabinet meetings during President Eisenhower's various illnesses.) One reason is that cabinet meetings themselves have become less important in recent years. *(See Cabinet chapter in Part V.)* In addition, most vice presidents have felt bound to sit in near silence at such meetings, listening to the discussions of presidents, department heads, and others who are responsible for administering the executive branch.

Commission Chair

Eisenhower was the first president to appoint a vice president to chair a presidential commission, a practice that most of his successors have followed. Vice President Nixon was charged to monitor and end racial discrimination in federal contracting as head of the newly created government contracts commission in 1953; later he chaired the Cabinet Committee on Price Stability for Economic Growth. President Kennedy named Vice President Johnson as chair of both the President's Committee on Equal Employment Opportunity, a more powerful successor to Nixon's government contracts commission, and the National Aeronautics and Space Council. As president, Johnson assigned numerous commissions to Vice President Humphrey, such as youth opportunity, Native American opportunity, recreation and natural beauty, and tourism. But when civil rights became a major part of the administration's agenda, Johnson stripped Humphrey of responsibility for the equal employment opportunity commission and assigned it to members of his own staff.

For ideological reasons, President Nixon abolished most of the commissions Vice President Humphrey had headed, but made his own vice president, Spiro Agnew, chair of a new commission on intergovernmental relations. Agnew's successor, Gerald Ford, headed only a commission on privacy during his brief vice presidency. After succeeding to the presidency, however, Ford appointed Vice President Nelson A. Rockefeller to chair several commissions, including the National Commission on Productivity and Work Quality, the President's Panel on Federal Compensation, the National Commission on Water Quality, and a commission to investigate abuses by the Central Intelligence Agency (CIA).

Far from being a boon to the vice presidency, most commission assignments have been burdensome. Typically, presidents have created commissions to symbolize their concern for an issue or constituency; they have named their vice presidents as chairs because the vice presidency is a visible and prestigious office and because they have wanted to convince the public that the vice president is actively involved in the business of government. Seldom, however, do presidents entrust vice-presidential commissions with substantive powers and responsibilities. *(See Presidential Commissions chapter in Part V.)*

After Mondale's election as vice president in 1976, he asked President Jimmy Carter to spare him commission duties so that he could be free to serve the president as general adviser and troubleshooter. (In doing so, Mondale was following the advice of Humphrey and Rockefeller, the two vice presidents who, to their regret, had been most active as commission chairs.) Mondale argued that commissions inevitably rouse the ire of the agencies of the bureaucracy whose activities they study, that neither commissions nor the vice president have any authority to enact any goals, that commission assignments demean the vice presidency by wasting the vice president's time, and that the vice president lacks the staff to do an effective job as commission chair. Carter granted Mondale's request.

No vice president has enjoyed chairing commissions (Vice President Nixon does not even mention his assignments in his memoirs), and all have regarded the task as a distraction from other, potentially more useful, roles. The Mondale precedent may help future vice presidents avoid or at least minimize commission activity. Still, some vice presidents may feel compelled to chair one or more commissions in order to establish credibility within their administrations. During his first year in office, for example, Vice President Bush was still too much the outsider in the Reagan White House to pass up any opportunity to demonstrate his loyalty. In one case, to head off a major struggle that was developing among the president's major foreign policy advisers about responsibilty in times of international crisis, the vice president was asked to head a newly formed Special Situations Group for crisis management. Bush agreed, which pleased the president and his aides, but shrewdly downplayed the assignment, placating the secretary of state, the head of the CIA, and the president's national security adviser.

Senior Adviser

Throughout history, some vice presidents have been sought out by the president, at least occasionally, for advice and counsel. But, until recently, these vice presidents were very much the exception. Before President Franklin Roosevelt won for presidential candidates the right to name their own running mates, party leaders invariably used the vice-presidential nomination as a means to unite the party, usually by pairing the nominee for president with a vice-presidential nominee from an opposing faction. Thus, presidents typically took office with little personal trust in their vice presidents, much less a willingness to rely upon them for political or policy advice.

Since 1940, the year of President Roosevelt's convention coup, presidential candidates have been able to name political leaders they trust as running mates. Since 1945, the year President Roosevelt died, leaving Truman to serve out the term during wartime, they have had every political incentive to choose vice-presidential candidates who are talented and accomplished in their own right. Not surprisingly, then, most recent presidents have turned to their vice presidents after the inauguration for advice on matters about which they are knowledgeable or experienced. President Eisenhower respected Vice President Nixon's judgments about Congress and the Republican party; President Ford valued the expertise of his vice president, former New York governor Rockefeller, on domestic policy; President Reagan made good use in foreign policy of Vice President Bush's experience as director of the CIA, ambassador to the United Nations, and chief U.S. diplomat in China.

Vice President Mondale extended the vice president's role as presidential adviser beyond all previous (or subsequent) limits. He had an unusually strong relationship with President Carter, who had selected him with great care and who, as a former governor, valued his experience as a Washington politician. After the 1976 election, Mondale wrote a memorandum to Carter arguing that the vice presidency is, by nature, a nationally elected office unburdened by specific constitutional responsibilities and that these qualities suited it best for the role of senior adviser to the president. Mondale further urged that to perform this role, he would need full access to all the information that the president received, the right to require other administration officals to meet his requests for facts and assistance, a staff of his own, a close relationship with the White House staff, the right to participate in all important administration policy groups, access to the president whenever necessary, and freedom from specific ongoing assignments. Carter approved Mondale's recommendations and added to them an office for the vice president in the West Wing of the White House.[8]

Mondale's proposed arrangement worked out in practice for the entire four years of Carter's term because the vice president gave the president consistently sound advice and gave it discreetly. As Mondale later counseled his successor, Vice President Bush,

> Advise the president confidentially. The only reason to state publicly what you have told the president is to take credit for his success and to try to escape blame for failure. Either way there is no quicker way to undermine your relationship with the president and lose your effectiveness.... Don't wear a president down.... Give your advice once and give it well. You have a right to be heard, not obeyed.... The vice president should remember the importance of personal compatability. He should complement the president's skills....[9]

Representative Roles

In recent years, presidents have called upon vice presidents to represent their administrations to a variety of constituencies. Within the government, the modern vice president serves as a liaison from the president to Congress. Vice presidents also are used as envoys to foreign governments. Finally, the vice president publicly defends the president to a variety of domestic audiences.

Legislative Liaison

Even as the Senate responsiblities of the vice presidency have declined in importance and its affiliation with the executive branch has grown, vice presidents have developed a new role on Capitol Hill, as legislative liaison. Since 1933, ten of thirteen vice presidents—Garner, Truman, Alben W. Barkley, Nixon, Johnson, Humphrey, Ford, Mondale, Bush, and Dan Quayle—have had experience as members of Congress. (Henry A. Wallace, Agnew, and Rockefeller are the only modern vice presidents who have not.) Five of them—Vice Presidents Garner, Truman, Nixon, Mondale, and Bush—served presidents who lacked legislative experience themselves, often with great skill. Not surprisingly, then, vice presidents are frequently used to pass information and advice between representatives and senators on one end of Pennsylvania Avenue and the president on the other, working in conjunction with the White House staff's team of legislative lobbyists. The vice president's suite in the Capitol building, which was assigned many years ago in recognition of the office's constitutional role as Senate president, provides a convenient setting for such discussions and "head counts" on pending legislation.

Not all vice presidents are skillful legislative liaisons, and blunders born of inexperience can backfire on both the vice president and the president. When Vice President Agnew wandered onto the Senate floor in 1969 to ask Sen. Len Jordan, a fellow Republican, if the administration could count on his vote for a tax bill, Jordan barked, "You had it until now," then vowed to oppose any bill that Agnew asked him to support.[10] Even Lyndon Johnson, arguably the most effective Senate leader in history before his election as vice president in 1960, was rebuffed by Senate Democrats when he asked to be allowed to continue presiding over meetings of the Senate Democratic conference at the start of his term in 1961. As Sen. Clinton Anderson, who had been one of Johnson's closest political allies, protested, Johnson no longer was a member of the legislative branch.[11]

Special Envoy

Garner was the first vice president to make an official trip abroad. After attending, as a representative of the Senate, the installation of the first president of the Philippines, Garner undertook a goodwill mission to Mexico at the behest of President Franklin Roosevelt. Vice President Nixon established the precedent of extensive vice-presidential travel as a special envoy of the president, making seven trips to fifty-four countries during his eight years in office. (Two of these missions were especially memorable—the trip to the Soviet Union in which Nixon conducted an impromptu "kitchen debate" with the Soviet leader, Nikita Khrushchev, and the trip to South America in which he was attacked and spat upon by leftist rioters.) Johnson took ten trips as vice president, Humphrey twelve, Agnew seven, Ford one, Rockefeller six, Mondale fourteen, and Bush twenty during the first term alone.[12] Quayle was sent on a mission to South America during his first month in office.

Many, perhaps most, special envoy assignments have been almost entirely symbolic in nature—the president simply wished to demonstrate the good will of the United States toward the visited country without having to undertake a trip personally. "I go to funerals," lamented Vice President Rockefeller. "I go to earthquakes." [13] But sometimes the vice president has carried an important message to a foreign government, affirmed U.S. support for a beleaguered regime, or negotiated on a small diplomatic matter. And even relatively inconsequential trips are of political value to vice presidents, who gain greater-than-usual press coverage while they are abroad and reinforce their image among voters as knowledgeable world leaders.

Administration Defender

Modern vice presidents are most frequently seen in their role as defender of the president's leadership, policies, and party to a variety of public audiences, including interest groups, the news media, state and local party organizations, and the general public. The role of administration defender is one that the vice president must perform vigorously, enthusiastically, and with unquestioned loyalty, lest the wrath of the president's supporters—both inside the administration and in the nation at large—be aroused. Journalists, White House staffers, and politicians are constantly on the watch for any sign of disagreement between the president and the vice president.

The role of administration defender offers significant political benefits to the vice president who performs it well. It builds trust for the vice president with the president and the White House staff, endears the vice president to the party faithful, and increases the vice president's political visibility. Taken together, these benefits usually give the vice president the inside track for a subsequent presidential nomination. Vice Presidents Nixon, Humphrey, Mondale, and Bush stepped directly from the vice presidency into their party's nomination for president, and even Vice President Agnew was the early favorite for a Republican presidential nomination.

But the administration defender role can be dangerous to the vice president as well. Vice presidents may appear to be narrow, divisive figures, especially when defending the administration involves attacking its critics, as Vice Presidents Nixon and Agnew did with great fervor. Slashing partisan rhetoric may alienate the general electorate even as it gratifies the party faithful. (Despite their success in winning presidential nominations, no incumbent vice president was elected president from 1836 until 1988, when Bush accomplished the feat. In addition, vice presidents may come to seem weak and parrot-like, always defending

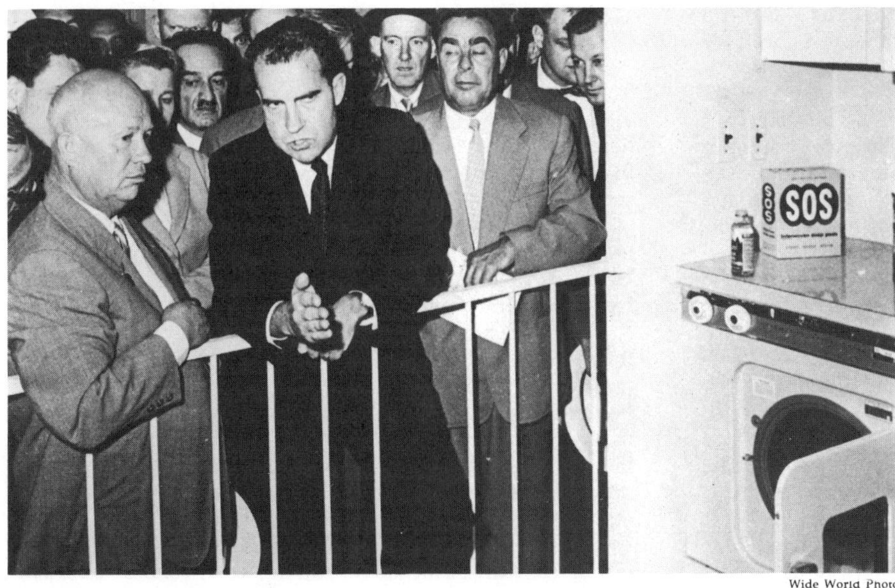

Wide World Photos

Vice President Richard Nixon conducts an impromptu "kitchen debate" with Soviet leader Nikita Khrushchev, left, during their tour of an American exhibition in Moscow in 1959.

Library of Congress White House

The old vice-presidential seal, left, created in 1948, seemed to many people to portray the low esteem in which the office was held. In 1975 Vice President Nelson A. Rockefeller ordered the design of a more imposing seal, still in use.

the ideas of another while submerging their own thoughts and expertise. Vice President Bush, for example, was excoriated as a "wimp" and "lap dog" by political columnists and cartoonists. Finally, vice presidents may feel compelled to defend administration policies with which they profoundly disagree, as Vice President Nixon frequently did.[14]

Institutional Resources

Historically, the institutional resources of the vice presidency have been meager, consisting mainly of a suite of offices in the Capitol building and a small staff paid for by Congress's own budget. In recent years, the development of new vice-presidential roles has been a wellspring of added resources, as has the vice presidency's closer affiliation with the executive branch. The enhanced resources of the vice presidency have enabled it, in turn, both to assume new roles and to fulfill traditional roles more effectively.

Growing Resources

The 1960s and 1970s were marked by substantial gains in the resources of the vice presidency that the 1980s did not undo. In 1961, Vice President Lyndon Johnson won for the office an impressive suite in the Executive Office Building, adjacent to the White House. At the beginning of Vice President Agnew's term in 1969, he requested and received a line item in the budget of the executive branch to supplement the traditional congressional appropriation. Taken together, these two developments freed vice presidents from their earlier dependence on Congress for office space and operating funds. In 1972, the vice presidency was listed for the first time as a part of the Executive Office of the President in the *United States Government Organization Manual.*

Even more substantial institutional advances were registered by Vice Presidents Ford and Rockefeller during the mid-1970s. Ford received President Nixon's consent both to name his own staff members, rather than rely on White House-approved appointees, and to increase the size of the vice president's staff. Ford and his successor, Vice President Rockefeller, then reorganized the staff to make it resemble more closely the White House staff, including a press secretary, counsel, and national security adviser. This additional staff freed the vice president's political and policy specialists from administrative and other distractions and fostered better communications and working relationships between members of the presidential and vice-presidential staffs. From 1974 to 1977, the vice president and high-ranking staff members also received certain perquisites that enhanced the prestige of the office within the status-conscious Washington community. New vice-presidential perquisites included an official residence (the Admiral's House at the Naval Observatory), a better airplane for *Air Force Two,* and an impressive new seal of office, showing a star-shrouded, arrow-clutching eagle at full wingspread. New privileges for the vice president's staff included use of the White House mess and official automobiles. *(See "The Vice President's Residence," p. 820, in Housing of the Executive Branch chapter of Part V.)*

One reason that vice presidents Ford and Rockefeller were able to secure these resources for their office is that, for political reasons, the presidents who invited them to become vice president very much needed their assent. Both were appointed—not elected—vice presidents, the first to be selected under the Twenty-fifth Amendment. After Vice President Agnew resigned in 1973, President Nixon, who was embroiled in the Watergate affair, chose Ford because, as the minority leader of the House of Representatives, he was well liked and certain to be confirmed by Congress. When Ford became president after Nixon's 1974 resignation, he urgently wanted Rockefeller to become vice president because of the stature the former New York governor and presidential candidate could bring to the administration. As part of his agreement to serve, Rockefeller won the right to a weekly private meeting with the president.

Vice President Mondale, whom President Carter had selected out of respect for his talents, experience, and loyalty, consolidated the institutional gains his predecessors had made and added more, notably an office in the West Wing of the White House near the president's Oval Office, full access to the White House paper flow, freedom from commission and other trivial assignments, and the right to attend all presidential meetings. Although neither Bush nor Quayle was an administration insider at the start of his term as vice president, they, too, were able to reap the gains their predecessors had made.

Relation of Roles and Resources

The roles and institutional resources of the modern vice presidency are linked in a synergistic way. Resources help to shape traditional roles. The vice president's office in the Capitol has made participation in legislative liaison sensible; the president's own liaison staff often uses the office as a headquarters while involving the vice president in the ongoing business of congressional relations. Similarly, the availability of free time has left vice presidents free to tour the country as administration defenders.

New resources also have paved the way for new roles for the vice presidency. The vice president's ability to serve usefully as a senior adviser is greater than it used to be because the creation in 1969 of a vice-presidential line item in the executive budget allowed vice presidents to hire talented staff. In 1977, the granting of a West Wing office put the vice president literally in the middle of the informal policy flow that surrounds the Oval Office.

Finally, new roles have generated new institutional resources. Almost all of the gains Vice President Mondale was able to make for the vice presidency flowed from his success in convincing President Carter that his main role in the administration should be that of general adviser. Mondale argued successfully that he could not fulfill this role unless he had full access to the president, the White House staff, and the documents that flowed back and forth between them.

Notes

1. Hubert H. Humphrey, "Changes in the Vice Presidency," *Current History* 67, no. 396 (August 1974): 59.
2. "Nixon's Own Story of 7 Years in the Vice Presidency," *U.S. News & World Report,* May 16, 1960, 98.
3. Lawrence I. Barrett, *Gambling with History: Ronald Reagan in the White House* (Garden City, N.Y.: Doubleday, 1983), chap. 7.
4. Quoted in Paul C. Light, *Vice-Presidential Power: Advice and Influence in the White House* (Baltimore: Johns Hopkins University Press, 1984), 34.
5. Franklin D. Roosevelt, "Can the Vice Presidency Be Useful?" *Saturday Evening Post,* October 16, 1920, 8.
6. Theodore Roosevelt, "The Three Vice-Presidential Candidates and What They Represent," *Review of Reviews,* September 1896, 289.
7. Irving G. Williams, *The Rise of the Vice Presidency* (Washington, D.C.: Public Affairs Press, 1956), 122-123, 134-135.
8. Light, *Vice-Presidential Power,* 201-202.
9. Quoted in Thomas E. Cronin, "Rethinking the Vice Presidency," in *Rethinking the Presidency,* ed. Thomas E. Cronin (Boston: Little, Brown, 1982), 339-340.
10. Quoted in Light, *Vice-Presidential Power,* 43-44.
11. Rowland Evans and Robert Novak, *Lyndon B. Johnson: The Exercise of Power* (New York: New American Library, 1966), 305-307.
12. Joseph Pika, "A New Vice Presidency?" in *The Presidency and the Political System,* 2d ed., ed. Michael Nelson (Washington, D.C.: CQ Press, 1988), 474.
13. Quoted in Joseph E. Persico, *The Imperial Rockefeller* (New York: Simon and Schuster, 1982), 262.
14. Stephen E. Ambrose, *Nixon: The Education of a Politician, 1913-1962* (New York: Simon and Schuster, 1987), chaps. 15-27.

Selected Bibliography

Cronin, Thomas E. "Rethinking the Vice Presidency." In *Rethinking the Presidency*, Thomas Cronin, ed. Boston: Little, Brown, 1982.

Light, Paul C. *Vice-Presidential Power: Advice and Influence in the White House.* Baltimore: Johns Hopkins University Press, 1984.

Nelson, Michael. *A Heartbeat Away.* New York: Unwin Hyman, 1988.

Pika, Joseph. "A New Vice Presidency?" In *The Presidency and the Political System*, 2d ed., ed. Michael Nelson. Washington, D.C.: CQ Press, 1988.

Williams, Irving G. *The Rise of the Vice Presidency.* Washington, D.C.: Public Affairs Press, 1956.

Executive Office of the President: White House Office

In contrast to the early days of the presidency, when presidents had little or no staff to help them, the modern presidential establishment is a bureaucracy with thousands of employees, all of whom work for the president. The Executive Office of the President (EOP) is the president's tool for coping with Congress and the far-flung executive branch.

In no real sense is the EOP an "office"; rather, it is a collection of agencies whose only tie is their direct responsibility to the president. The components of the EOP have changed many times over the years as the needs of the presidency have changed. Today some of the major elements of the EOP are the National Security Council, Office of Management and Budget, Council of Economic Advisers, Office of Science and Technology Policy, Office of the Special Representative for Trade Negotiations, and White House Office.

Of these, perhaps the most important and surely the closest to the president is the White House Office. While all of the EOP does the president's business, the White House Office consists of the president's most intimate and trusted advisers. Of the entire presidential establishment, the White House Office is the most loyal to the president and has his or her particular interests most at heart.

A White House staff who knows the president's needs and desires and has political savvy can be a tremendous asset. They can advance the administration's programs to fruition and avoid the potential pitfalls that undermine a president's credibility. Indeed, much of a president's success depends on the ability of the White House staff, while many of a president's failures result from the staff's failures.

Examples of the importance of the White House staff abound. On the one hand, the vision and skill of President John F. Kennedy's staff were very important to his legislative success. The same was true in the early days of Lyndon B. Johnson's administration; the ability of Johnson's staff to deal with Congress was crucial in implementing the "Great Society." The disorganization and inexperience of President Jimmy Carter's staff, on the other hand, undermined his chances of achieving much in Congress. And it was the staff's failure to anticipate problems adequately and protect the president's interests that led to Watergate, which destroyed the presidency of Richard Nixon, and to the Iran-contra affair, which haunted and weakened Ronald Reagan's second term.

Although the White House staff is important to the president, there is no set pattern for its selection or organization. In fact, the office itself has been in existence for only just over a half century.

By Stephen L. Robertson

Origins and Development of the White House Office

The problem of how to count the White House Office staff is a factor in any discussion of its growth. No universally accepted figures exist on the precise size of the White House staff, and published estimates vary considerably depending on who is counting and how. There are several reasons for this discrepancy: short-term fluctuations in staff size, placement of White House people elsewhere in government, use of detailees, and hiring of staff out of the discretionary funds (such as the Special Projects account) that are available to the president. Consequently, the figures that follow should be treated with caution; they are indicators of trends but are not necessarily exact.[1]

The existence of a large presidential staff is a relatively recent development. Early presidents had little or no staff to assist them, and what staff did exist was strictly clerical. There were no specialized or resident policy advisers, speechwriters, or liaison personnel. Believing that presidents should take care of their own business, Congress did not specifically appropriate funds for staff until 1857, when it provided an allowance for a presidential secretary.

Presidents who wanted more help were forced to hire it themselves and to pay for it out of their own pockets. George Washington hired his nephew to assist him in 1792 and paid him $300 a year from his own salary. Several later presidents followed Washington's lead and retained relatives or cronies in the White House. For most of those employed, however, the pay remained low and the jobs menial. Staff duties consisted almost exclusively of clerical work and scheduling the president's appointments.

Over the years the common practices of nepotism and cronyism resulted in the appointment of several advisers and presidential secretaries who proved hopelessly inadequate. For example, Andrew Johnson appointed his son Robert as secretary to the president even though the younger man was a womanizer and an alcoholic. Ulysses S. Grant's secretary, Gen. Orville E. Babcock, was a corrupt power-grabber who was involved in the Whiskey Ring, a group of liquor producers who were illegally avoiding federal liquor taxes. He eventually was indicted for fraud. And Rutherford B. Hayes chose William K. Rogers, an old classmate who had failed in three careers, as his secretary. Rogers proved inept at that job, too.

Given the limitations of the presidential pockets, as well as the small size of the government as a whole, the White House staff necessarily remained quite small throughout the nineteenth century. Presidents rarely could afford much staff, and they generally made more use of their cabinet as advisers than is true today. Benjamin Harrison was able to house his entire staff next to his living quarters on the second floor of the White House. Herbert Hoover doubled the number of his administrative assistants, increasing them from two to four (which caused a minor sensation). Besides them, Hoover had only military and naval attachés and about forty clerks and typists.

To some extent the small size of these staffs is misleading. Historically, presidents have resorted to "detailing," or borrowing, personnel from the executive departments to carry out various tasks. Thus, a president who needs assistance might requisition an aide or two from the War or State Department. Some presidents placed trusted advisers in positions within the executive branch to keep them available. Andrew Jackson named his close friend Amos Kendall as fourth auditor of the Treasury Department, but Kendall in fact did little work there, instead spending his time assisting Jackson. To keep his brains trust around him, Franklin D. Roosevelt appointed them not to his staff (which was still the size of Hoover's) but to posts in other departments: Raymond Moley became an assistant secretary of state, Rexford G. Tugwell was named assistant secretary of agriculture, and Adolph A. Berle, Jr., was appointed as counsel to the Reconstruction Finance Commission. They did almost no work for their departments, however.

Although the use of detailees was a great asset to presidents, the growing demands of the office meant that presidents needed more in-house advisers who were not encumbered by even minimal jobs elsewhere. As the nation and its government grew in the early twentieth century, the need for a larger presidential staff increased.

The potential value of a larger staff was indicated by the work of some of the presidential secretaries. Daniel G. Rollings, who was secretary to Chester A. Arthur, assisted the president in writing speeches and legislative proposals for Congress. Daniel Lamont was an able administrator, campaign manager, and public relations man for Grover Cleveland (who definitely needed the latter). Joseph P. Tumulty, secretary to Woodrow Wilson, was an all-purpose aide who "functioned as an appointments secretary, political adviser, administrative manager, and public relations aide" as well as a White House doorkeeper.[2] Calvin Coolidge's secretary, C. Bascom Slemp, proved to be an important liaison between the president and the Congress, as well as between the president and his own party. And Louis McHenry Howe was a highly important influence on Franklin Roosevelt until Howe's death in 1935.

Even more significant was the work of aides George B. Cortelyou and William Loeb, Jr. Cortelyou, who later became the first secretary of the Department of Commerce and Labor, was presidential secretary under William McKinley and Theodore Roosevelt. As secretary, particularly to McKinley, he drafted speeches and messages, scheduled appointments, organized trips, ran the White House clerical staff, and tended to First Lady Ida McKinley, who suffered from poor health. He was also politically adept, working to defeat a possible move against Roosevelt as the vice-presidential nominee in the Republican national convention of 1900 and serving as the de facto president in the immediate aftermath of McKinley's assassination while greatly easing the transition for the vice president.

Loeb followed Cortelyou and was just as valuable while serving under Roosevelt. He too kept the White House and its occupants running smoothly. Loeb also served as the president's sounding board and had no small influence on Roosevelt and his policies. As a political operative, he was instrumental in pulling together support for William Howard Taft in the Republican national convention of 1908.

In the hands of aides such as Cortelyou and Loeb the position of secretary to the president was the crucial one on the presidential staff; indeed, to a large extent it *was* the staff. The presidential secretary was a jack-of-all-trades: legislative drafter, congressional liaison, press and public relations coordinator, appointments and junket scheduler, political manipulator, and White House manager. He was in fact a chief of staff with a very limited kingdom. By the 1930s, however, the responsibilities of the position had outstripped the abilities of any one person to fill them. When Franklin Roosevelt appointed Howe as his secretary in 1933, he also appointed Stephen T. Early as press secretary and Marvin H. McIntyre as appointments secretary. But when Howe died, the position died with him. Roosevelt never filled it, and its responsibilities were distributed eventually throughout a growing White House bureaucracy.

FDR: Beginning of the Present Staff System

The present staff system began during the administration of Franklin Roosevelt (1933-1945). The White House staff had been growing slowly for several years, but it still remained quite small. Like his predecessors, Roosevelt regularly borrowed help from elsewhere in the executive branch, using at least a hundred detailees in each year from 1934 to 1945. Unlike his predecessors, however, he concluded that such arrangements were hopelessly inadequate, and, as an activist president faced with an unprecedented economic crisis, he decided to change them. In his mind, dealing with the nation's problems required a larger permanent staff that worked solely for him. He was not alone in his belief; at least nine proposals for reorganizing the executive branch appeared between 1918 and 1937, and all recognized the need for more executive efficiency and planning capability.[3]

Roosevelt found the justification for his larger staff in the work of the Committee on Administrative Management, more popularly known as the Brownlow Committee. Created on March 20, 1936, the committee—consisting of Louis Brownlow, chairman, and members Charles Merriam and Luther Gulick—was directed to study the staffing needs of the presidency. Declaring that "the American Executive must be regarded as one of the very greatest contributions by our Nation to the development of modern democracy," the committee concluded that "the President needs help . . . in dealing with managerial agencies and administrative departments of the Government" and recommended the creation of additional staff to assist him. The committee also recommended that

> these assistants . . . not be interposed between the president and the heads of his departments. They would not be assistant presidents in any sense. Their function would be . . . to assist [the president] in obtaining quickly and without delay all pertinent information possessed by any of the executive departments so as to guide him in making his responsible decisions; and then when decisions have been made, to assist him in seeing to it that every administrative department and agency affected is properly informed. . . . They would remain in the background, issue no orders, make no decisions, emit no public statements. . . . They should be men in whom the president has personal confidence and whose attitude and character are such that they would not attempt to exercise power on their own account. They should be possessed of high competence, great vigor, and a passion of anonymity. They should be installed in the White House itself, directly accessible to the president.[4]

The Brownlow Committee report was submitted to the president in January 1937. Immediately endorsing its findings, with which he completely agreed and over which he had had significant influence, Roosevelt quickly forwarded the report to Congress for authorization to implement the committee's recommendations. The Congress, however, was angry over Roosevelt's ill-fated attempt to pack the Supreme Court, and it refused to act upon the report. Not until April 1939 did Congress agree to most of the Brownlow proposals. *(See Executive Office of the President: Supporting Organizations chapter in Part V.)*

Under the congressional authorization the president was allowed to hire six new administrative assistants, although Roosevelt initially hired only three. Congress also permitted the president to undertake a partial reorganization of the executive branch. On September 8, 1939, Roosevelt issued Executive Order 8248, creating the Executive Office of the President and transferring the Bureau of the Budget (renamed the Office of Management and Budget in 1972) into it from the Treasury Department. The president intended the EOP to be a more permanent and professional support staff than that of the White House. The White House staff was seen as the president's personal assistants; the EOP was the institutionalized infrastructure of the presidency.

Executive Order 8248 represents the birth of the modern presidency, including the modern White House Office staff. Roosevelt did not greatly increase the size of the staff, however. He preferred and was able to manage with a staff small enough to allow him to interact with all of his aides equally. Thus, the number of presidential aides never exceeded twelve, and the total number of full-time White House employees was fewer than sixty-five.[5] The latter figure stayed relatively low despite a huge increase in mail to the White House, which required hiring more clerical staff to handle it.

Roosevelt's staff remained not only small but also rather unstructured. Disliking flow charts and rigid hierarchies, the president preferred to work on an ad hoc basis, distributing assignments to whoever was then available. Few of his aides had specific titles. Aside from Press Secretary Early and Appointments Secretary McIntyre, only Harry L. Hopkins, who bore the title of special assistant to the president, and Samuel I. Rosenman, who was the counsel to the president, had special designations. Nevertheless, the first steps toward the differentiated structures maintained by other presidents were taken under Roosevelt. Hopkins, who had extensive influence over foreign affairs during the war years, was another forerunner of the chief of staff who would appear in later administrations. Rosenman's position was created just for him on the grounds that the president required an in-house legal adviser.

Thus, by the end of the Roosevelt administration the need for a larger staff had been recognized, and its expansion and differentiation had begun. The increasing role of the national government, both domestically and internationally, would fuel further staff growth over the next decades.

Franklin D. Roosevelt Library

Although FDR's staff remained small, unstructured, and free of specific titles, Harry Hopkins, left, a special assistant to the president, was a forerunner of today's White House chief of staff.

The Truman Staff: The Beginnings of Growth

Roosevelt's White House staff had swelled to meet the demands of the war years. Distrusting the larger staff and fearing that it would impede his interaction with his cabinet and the rest of the government, President Harry S Truman (1945-1953) initially planned to return his staff to its prewar size. He quickly found that this was impossible, however. With Europe in ruins, the United States was the leader in the international community. At home the difficulties of restoring the economy to a peacetime status and repairing the dislocations caused by war created economic and political tensions for the federal government. The result was increasing pressure upon the Truman White House for action, which inevitably led to a staff size that exceeded that of the Roosevelt years. Furthermore, where Roosevelt had maintained a fairly small permanent staff and used a large number of detailees, by 1947 Truman had reversed that trend, employing an in-house staff of two hundred or more while detailing only a handful of other aides. The earlier practice of storing advisers in various government posts also came to an end. After Truman, presidents simply brought whatever advisers they wished into the White House, creating new positions for them if necessary.

The staff evolved in structure as well as size during the Truman years. When he became president, Truman inherited Roosevelt's relatively unstructured staffing system, which provided access to the president and allowed Roosevelt to play his advisers against one another. Truman valued the accessibility the open system allowed, but he found the intrastaff competition it fostered too chaotic and soon called for more structure.

To this end, Truman created the position of assistant to the president in 1946 and named John Roy Steelman to fill it. One of Steelman's duties was to serve as a link with the domestic agencies and to resolve many of their problems and disputes. As such, he too was a direct forerunner of the chief of staff who would emerge in later administrations. Unfortunately, Steelman was not very successful at keeping problems from the president; he was reluctant to bruise feelings, and Truman was unable to distance himself from the everyday problems of his administration.

Besides Steelman, Truman's staff consisted of a press secretary, an appointments secretary, a personnel director, a special counsel, a legislative drafter, a military aide and a naval aide, a special assistant, a minority liaison, a few speechwriters (who also doubled as general assistants), and the more institutionalized position of budget director. Clerical and subordinate aides made up the remaining staff.

During the Truman years Congress created two other bodies within EOP to assist the president. The National Security Act of 1946 established the National Security Council (NSC) to help the president deal with foreign policy problems. The NSC membership (as amended in 1949) consisted of the president, the vice president, the secretaries of state and defense, and anyone else the president wished to invite. The NSC was designed to insure coordination among the foreign policy agencies so that the president would be given the necessary facts and options about a problem quickly and efficiently.

Skeptical of a body that had been thrust upon him, Truman made little use of the NSC before the Korean War. Indeed, the decision to intervene in Korea was made without formally consulting the NSC at all. During the war Truman found ways to use the NSC to his advantage and met with it more frequently, but the importance of the NSC as a personal staff remained minor.

The second body created to assist Truman was the three-member Council of Economic Advisers (CEA), intended to be the president's primary source of economic information and advice. As with the NSC, Truman rarely used the CEA at first, in part because under chairman Edwin G. Nourse it provided abstract advice devoid of any political considerations. It was only when Leon Keyserling replaced Nourse as chairman in 1949 that the CEA emerged as an important body. *(See Executive Office of the President: Supporting Organizations chapter in Part V.)*

The Truman administration also saw the emergence of staffers as policy advocates. Truman's special counsel, Clark M. Clifford, was a key figure in advocating liberal positions before the president. Such a role defied the original vision of the Brownlow Committee, which had proposed that aides be neutral facilitators of policy decisions; policy advocacy was to be left to the cabinet. Clifford's role of policy advocate represented a potentially major change in the role of the White House staff, but its extent would not be realized until later.

Thus, under Truman the White House staff increased in size and took on a more formal structure. Differentiation increased as particular staff members were assigned specific areas of responsibility, and White House staffers began to acquire small staffs of their own. In addition, Congress added two new bodies to the White House to assist the president. Finally, policy advocacy began to move into the White House and out of the cabinet where it theoretically belonged.

Despite these important developments, however, the Truman White House did not wield much power overall. With the exception of Clifford and W. Averell Harriman, who was in the administration only briefly, no major names or dominant personalities stood out on Truman's staff. Moreover, Truman preferred to use his cabinet as policy advisers; his staff was not allowed to gain much influence. The makings of a powerful staff were there but were not realized until later administrations.

Eisenhower and the Formalized Staff

Under Dwight D. Eisenhower (1953-1961) the staff grew in both size and complexity. As a former general and a career military officer, Eisenhower recognized the benefits of a properly structured staff. A well-organized staff could handle the simple problems and minor tactical details at the lower levels, allowing the commander to concentrate on the major problems and questions. Reacting to what he saw as confusion within the Roosevelt and Truman administrations, Eisenhower preached that organization could provide a more efficient, high-quality government. His message resulted in the most highly structured and diversified staff seen to that time in the White House.

Eisenhower's staff included many of the elements found in the Truman White House. His press secretary, James C. Hagerty, won a considerable reputation for his skillful handling of the position. Other staff members were an appointments secretary, a special counsel, and, of course, the much-needed clerks, typists, and messengers.

Several new positions were created as well. The Congressional Relations Office was established to facilitate interaction between the White House and Congress. The liaison aide was responsible for conveying the president's wishes to Congress, lobbying there for the president's programs, and relaying congressional feedback. This was not a completely new position; Matthew Connelly had fulfilled the same functions without the title under Truman, while others had acted in the same capacity for Roosevelt (including the president himself). Still, Eisenhower was the first to operate openly a congressional liaison office and to give it a formal place in the White House.

To improve the flow of paperwork through the channels of the administration, Eisenhower created the positions of staff secretary and secretary to the cabinet. In particular, the cabinet secretary's job was to improve the cabinet's ability to advise the president by coordinating meetings and facilitating communications between the two.

Eisenhower also used the position of special adviser to the president to bring in his own experts as needed. For example, he responded to the Soviet launching of *Sputnik* in 1957 by naming a science adviser. Many of these special advisers made a significant contribution to the Eisenhower administration. The president's Open Skies proposal of 1955, for example, which called for surveillance flights to allow each super power to monitor the other's military installations, was devised by Nelson A. Rockefeller, who was then serving as a special adviser.

All these additions, made in the name of efficiency, naturally swelled the White House staff. The number of professionals appointed by the president in the White House increased from 32 in 1953 to 50 by 1960.[6] Overall, the size of the permanent staff increased by some 90 people, to 355, during the same period.

Eisenhower also made important changes in the way some existing personnel were used. One major change concerned the National Security Council. Truman rarely met with the NSC before the outbreak of the Korean War in 1950 and never gave it much structure. To Eisenhower, however, the NSC appeared much more useful. He created an extensive apparatus that could examine problems and produce analyses and options for him. Under Eisenhower the NSC became an important element in the foreign policy process, although certainly not the dominant one. The lead in U.S. foreign policy remained with John Foster Dulles and the State Department. The president also created the post of national security adviser. This new adviser served as the administrative head of the NSC and as the president's personal aide in foreign policy matters. For Eisenhower, the national security adviser had the important job of coordinating America's foreign policy apparatus and providing him with timely information.

In one other major staff change Eisenhower elevated the role of the assistant to the president, which under Truman had not been very important. Believing in hierarchy and not wanting to be bothered with unnecessary details, Eisenhower sought an aide to manage the White House, much as his chief of staff had managed his headquarters staff in the army. In filling this post, Eisenhower's assistant, Sherman Adams, became the gatekeeper to the president during Eisenhower's first six years in office.

As presidential chief of staff, Adams was perceived as possessing enormous power; anyone wishing to do business with the president had to pass through Adams first. Given Eisenhower's distaste for routine matters, it seemed certain that a great many decisions were being made by Adams, not Eisenhower. Commentators described Adams as an "assistant president," particularly in domestic affairs in which Eisenhower had less interest. Indeed, some saw Adams as running domestic policy during his stint as assistant to the president. One contemporary observer noted that

> Adams has handled a considerable amount of the work that in past administrations has been done by the president himself.... While it has not been an inflexible rule, it has been the general practice that almost everything of importance in the White House bearing on domestic and political policy clears through Adams.... He is the channel through which many of the most important projects in domestic affairs reach the president ... [and] by the time [they] have reached the president they have already been shaped in part by Adams himself. Time and again when a caller or official springs an idea on Eisenhower, the president will tell him, "Take it up with Sherman." [7]

In reality, Adams probably did not have that much power. Witnesses within the administration have recalled that while Adams had great influence over administrative matters in the White House, he rarely was involved in policy discussions. Others remember considerable interaction among staff members, despite the staff hierarchy. In any case it is certain that Adams, in his role of official presidential choke point, possessed a degree of influence that was unprecedented for a White House staffer. It would pave the way for powerful staffs in the future.

Eisenhower thus introduced many changes in the White House staff; he increased its numbers, formalized its structure, and built a fairly strict operational hierarchy. With the exception of Adams, however, his staff remained largely anonymous and relatively uninfluential. Eisenhower believed that his staff should be subordinate to the cabinet and remain in the background, and he tried to operate his administration along those lines. To him, the staff was supposed to move information and help policy makers, not make policy itself.

Kennedy and Johnson: The Birth of the Activist Staff

John F. Kennedy (1961-1963) came to the presidency determined to eliminate the elaborate mechanisms that Eisenhower had created in the White House. Convinced that Eisenhower's staff structure was too restrictive and left the president too removed from his own administration, Kennedy deliberately attempted a return to a staff more akin to that of Franklin Roosevelt. He replaced the committees and secretariats that had supported the cabinet and the NSC under Eisenhower with a few senior aides who had distinct yet overlapping responsibilities. The overlap occurred because the staff structure was fluid, and because Kennedy tended to hand out assignments as they arose to whoever was available rather than channeling them to a predesignated individual.

Kennedy's staff included several of the now-established White House positions: press secretary, special counsel, appointments secretary, congressional liaison, and national security adviser. He had no formal chief of staff. Appointments secretary Kenneth P. O'Donnell doubled as White House administrator, while Kennedy himself controlled the paper flow, personally receiving reports from subordinates. He also had no designated speechwriters; as with Roosevelt, speech-writing duties were spread among his aides, most notably his special counsel, Theodore C. Sorensen.

In spite of the dismantling of Eisenhower's staff system, the Kennedy White House did not decrease in size. Under Kennedy the regular White House employees numbered between 300 and 350, which was less than during Eisenhower's second term (but not his first). Kennedy used far more detailees than Eisenhower, however. His White House employed between 429 and 476 full-time personnel—figures unmatched by any previous administration.

The continual growth of the White House staff reflected the increasing tendency of the public to look to Washington, and particularly the White House, for solutions to the nation's problems. This tendency was only accelerated by events such as the Berlin controversy and the Cuban missile crisis. As one scholar noted:

> The White House was allowed to keep growing because there was no resistance to growth. Indeed, creating another White House office was often the easiest way to solve a personnel or constituent problem, a conferring of high status with little effort. The White House was the only place in government where the president could totally control expenditures and was free to move personnel and establish units at will.[8]

The ease with which the White House staff could be expanded made such expansion irresistible.

The most significant development in the staff during the Kennedy years was not the increase in its size but in its responsibilities and influence. As a group, Kennedy's senior aides had far more influence than any previously. They meshed well with one another and with the boss. Because they thought along the same lines as Kennedy and often could anticipate him, they were readily able to speak for the president. This gave them a good deal of clout in Washington.

Beyond this, the influence of Kennedy's staff was increased by the governing style of the president himself. Kennedy was an activist president who wanted to get things done and to fulfill his campaign promise to get the country moving again. He sought actions and results. Inevitably, perhaps, he became frustrated with the permanent government, which was filled with elaborate standing routines and career bureaucrats who shared neither his goals nor his sense of urgency. He quickly came to regard the bureaucracy as "an institutional resistance movement . . . a force against innovation with an inexhaustible capacity to dilute, delay, and obstruct presidential purpose."[9] To prod and even avoid the bureaucracy, he turned to his staff, and, being activists also, they were eager to respond. *(See the Bureaucracy chapter in Part VI.)*

Like other presidents, Kennedy came into office intending to rely on his cabinet for policy innovations and advice. He quickly discovered, however, that cabinet meetings were dull and unproductive (he soon discontinued them) and that the loyalty of many of his department heads was open to question. He thus turned to other resources.

As a result, Kennedy's staff became involved in policy making to an unprecedented degree. Previous presidents had, with exceptions, prevented the White House staff from crossing the line that separated facilitating decisions from making decisions. The staff aided but rarely advised. Kennedy's senior staff became advisers and advocates more than aides. They were involved directly in many policy decisions, and as their importance swelled accordingly, they began acquiring larger staffs to assist them. Kennedy was in fact beginning to pull policy making, and thus power, out of the executive departments and concentrate it within the White House.

Kennedy's "New Frontier" was devised and advocated by his staff, largely under Sorensen's direction, not by the bureaucracy. Many other programs were handled similarly. Perhaps the staff's greatest influence lay in foreign policy. Having destroyed Eisenhower's elaborate NSC apparatus, and highly frustrated by the State Department, Kennedy turned to his national security adviser, McGeorge Bundy, and gave him a central role in the formulation and conduct of his foreign policy.

Kennedy's staff lacked that "passion for anonymity" that the Brownlow Committee had advocated. As the "president's men," they clearly stood apart from the rest of the government and were more visible than previous staffs. And while it was probably not anyone's conscious intent—for in theory the staff was still just a link between the president and the bureaucracy—the White House staff began to take on the characteristics of a shadow government, parallel to the bureaucracy.

When he became president on November 22, 1963, Lyndon B. Johnson inherited Kennedy's staff and its organization, which for various reasons he found acceptable and so left intact. Like Kennedy, he intended to follow the example of Franklin Roosevelt, and the fluid nature of Kennedy's staff suited him.

The White House staff continued to grow in influence during the Johnson administration (1963-1969). Johnson too was an activist president who wanted rapid access to the information and ideas needed to help him formulate new policies. He also wanted his staff to have sufficient authority to supervise policy implementation. LBJ found the cabinet departments to be too slow and ponderous to be truly useful, but he continued to hold cabinet meetings merely to obtain endorsement of his plans. This concentration of power in the White House was reinforced by Johnson's dominant personality, which led him to extend his control as much as possible. Later, the public outcry against his conduct of the Vietnam War caused him to withdraw into the sanctuary of the White House, relying on his staff even more.

Initially, Johnson kept Kennedy's people and staff arrangements, but as they gradually left he began clarifying the areas of responsibility within his staff. He maintained the usual press secretary, appointments secretary, special counsel (and deputy counsels), and congressional liaison offices. The latter received particular attention under Johnson, who had an extensive background in Congress. Speechwriters generally were drawn from other positions. Johnson also used his aides as links to groups outside the White House such as business, labor, and various religious and ethnic organizations. He was in fact operating a public liaison staff, although no formal structure or title was ever devised.

The major structural development of the Johnson administration was the creation of a domestic policy staff within the White House. The notion of a domestic policy adviser was not new; although he had had the title special counsel, Theodore Sorensen had performed a similar function for Kennedy. Johnson established the role as a separate position placed in the hands of Joseph A. Califano, Jr., and a small staff of assistants. Califano was responsible for isolating domestic problems, producing proposals for possible solutions, and assisting with the production of Johnson's legislative programs.

Although the president's activism and desire for control caused more authority to be vested in the White House staff, the staff's visibility decreased somewhat. Johnson preferred the public limelight for himself, particularly during the early days of his administration, and he downplayed his staff.

Overall, the White House staff increased in size and authority during the Johnson administration. Because the president used many detailees, his White House staff always numbered over four hundred, and in 1967 there were almost five hundred. The demands of his office and his own personality caused Johnson to concentrate more power within the White House than any previous president. Thus, the White House staff that Johnson passed on to Nixon was both the largest and most influential in history.

The Imperial White House: The Nixon Staff

By 1969 two major trends characterized the development of the White House staff. The first was a continuing trend toward increased size and complexity. The second was a tendency for presidents to consolidate resources and hence power within the White House. Eisenhower had demonstrated the virtues of a large and structured staff; Kennedy and Johnson had developed the staff to promote policy. These trends and characteristics came together in the Nixon administration (1969-1974).

The White House Office of Richard Nixon had by far the most elaborate structure seen to that time. As vice president during the Eisenhower administration, Nixon had observed firsthand the benefits of Eisenhower's staff hierarchy. Like Eisenhower, Nixon felt that he as president should deal with the broad policies, not the trivial details. He was also a private man who valued his time alone and preferred to make decisions solitarily, working from briefing papers. The staff he installed was designed to operate smoothly and to protect him from the outside distractions he disliked.

As originally constructed, Nixon's White House Office had four areas of operations: foreign policy, domestic affairs, congressional relations, and White House operations. *(See Figure 1.)* Each was headed by an administrative assistant responsible for its coordination and operation, assisted by a large number of specialists in various policy areas. The system was designed to channel expertise to the president and to facilitate the implementation of his decisions.

Nixon maintained the traditional offices of press secretary, appointments secretary, and special counsel, as well as a personnel office for staff selection and a small political operations staff. He also gathered a stable of designated speechwriters, something Kennedy and Johnson had abandoned.

Specialization was common on the Nixon staff. In his speech-writing operation, for example, Nixon had three primary speechwriters: Patrick J. Buchanan, William Safire,

Figure 1 Organization of the Nixon White House, 1972

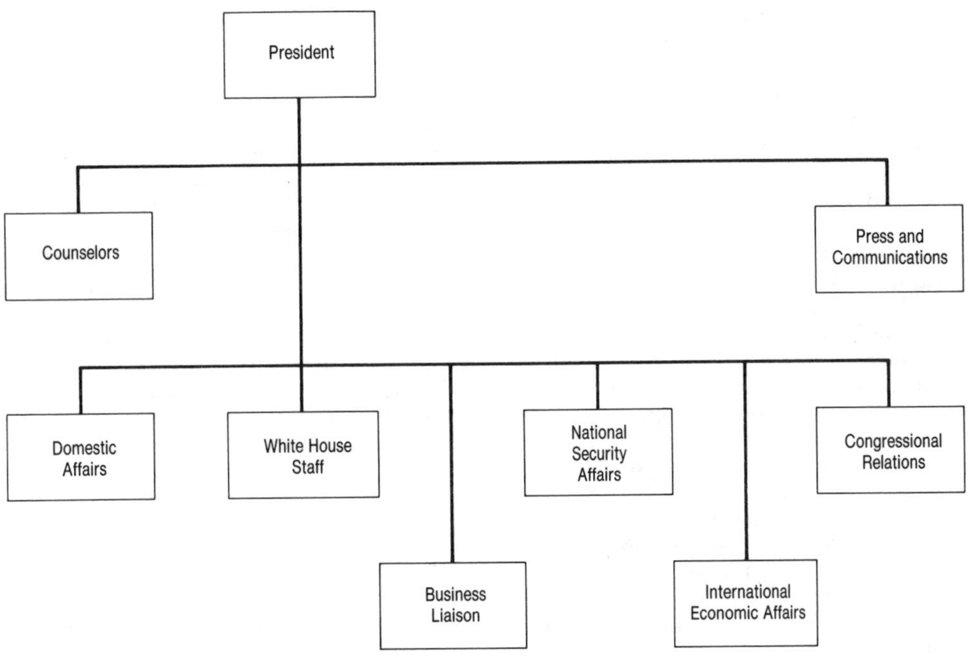

Source: Stephen J. Wayne, *The Legislative Presidency* (New York: Harper and Row, 1978), 48.

and Raymond Price, who represented, respectively, the right, center, and left of the Republican party. Nixon never combined the talents of these men; rather, he used them selectively, depending on the nature of the speech he was to deliver. It was a highly specialized arrangement.[10]

The cornerstone of the structure was the chief of staff, a position Nixon resurrected and gave to H. R. Haldeman. Haldeman's task was to shield the president from unwanted paperwork, problems, or visitors, and to see that the business of the White House was carried out efficiently. He proved to be ruthlessly effective in his job. As the president's gatekeeper, he had as much or more authority than any staffer had ever possessed.

Staff innovations during the Nixon administration included a formalized Domestic Council. Unlike Kennedy and Johnson, who had maintained an untitled domestic adviser on their staffs (Sorensen and Califano, respectively), Nixon originally had two domestic advisory staffs, one under Daniel Patrick Moynihan and the other under Arthur F. Burns. Because Moynihan and Burns generally took opposing sides on policy questions, Nixon found himself being an arbitrator, a role he acutely disliked. Thus, he began using his special counsel, John D. Ehrlichman, as an intermediary.

Eventually, Ehrlichman replaced both Burns and Moynihan, and in November 1969 he was officially named as assistant to the president for domestic affairs. Eight months later Nixon established the Domestic Council, a counterpart to the NSC, and Ehrlichman became its director. The Domestic Council was supposed to coordinate the domestic policy-making apparatus, isolating and analyzing problems and providing possible solutions to the president. Several presidents had attempted to improve the domestic policy machinery, but the council was the most formal attempt to do so.

Nixon also originated the White House Communications Office, which essentially was a public relations arm of the White House. Other presidents such as Kennedy had been concerned with public relations, but they had left it to the press secretary's office, which rarely had much time for it. To Nixon, public relations was far more important; as much as one-fifth of his entire staff was dealing with press and public relations.[11] The Communications Office became a separate operation, a sister to the press secretary's office, and it continued to operate separately even after Nixon's press secretary, Ronald Ziegler, also became communications director.

This specialized structure naturally demanded still more personnel within the White House. In fact, Nixon had the largest White House staff in history. The number of detailees dropped dramatically after 1970, but the decrease was matched by an increase in permanent staff. In all, the Nixon White House never employed fewer than five hundred people, and in 1970 the number of staffers exceeded six hundred.

During the Nixon administration the White House Office became a small bureaucracy. The patterns of growth and formalization that had been developing for years culminated under Nixon, resulting in a largely depersonalized staff that was out of contact with the president it served. Franklin Roosevelt had worked closely with all his aides; in the Nixon White House there were assistants to the president who rarely, if ever, saw him. Nixon could not hope to supervise his staff; the staff had to control itself.

At the same time Nixon's staff had an enormous amount of power, to the extent that the White House largely became the government, rendering much of the regular government to a role of secondary importance. Problems were identified, options evaluated, and decisions made and implemented with minimal, if any, help from the traditional bureaucratic agencies. An increasing number of decisions and details formerly left to the executive departments were taken over by the White House staff. The White House bureaucracy mirrored and then overshadowed the permanent bureaucracy. Those who had problems learned to go not to the bureaucracy but to the appropriate official in the White House where the real power was. Interest groups, members of Congress, and even executive department officials had to take their business to the White House if they hoped to get decisions and actions. Sen. Ernest F. Hollings (D-S.C.) complained:

> It used to be that if I had a problem with food stamps, I went to see the secretary of agriculture, whose department had jurisdiction over that problem. Not anymore. Now, if I want to learn the policy, I must go to the White House to consult with John Price. If I want the latest in textiles, I won't get it from the secretary of commerce, who has the authority and responsibility. No, I am forced to go to the White House and see Mr. Peter Flanigan. I shouldn't feel too badly. Secretary [of Commerce Maurice] Stans has to do the same thing.[12]

For its part the staff frequently screened callers as it saw fit. To an unprecedented degree the White House staff was actually running the government's agencies.

The extent of the staff's power was seen most clearly in the role of the National Security Council under Henry A. Kissinger. The NSC structure resembled that of the State Department, with "desks" for the various world regions. All of the important foreign policy decisions originated in the NSC, which also played a key role in implementing them. For example, Nixon's China initiative was conducted without the knowledge of the State Department. Similarly, overtures toward the Soviet Union and Vietnam, among others, were largely devised and executed by the White House. The State Department generally was bypassed and the secretary of state reduced to a figurehead. At one point the world was treated to the spectacle of Secretary of State William P. Rogers publicly insisting that he really *did* have some role in the administration's foreign policy process.

While all the power amassed in the Nixon White House and the EOP allowed the presidency to operate the government almost autonomously, the same organization, having been designed to serve the president, was unable to distinguish between his best interests and those of the country. The staff's power, its zeal in serving Nixon, and its lack of outside supervision contributed to the political and legal excesses known collectively as Watergate. Watergate would cost many staffers, including Haldeman and Ehrlichman, their positions and eventually would drive Nixon from the White House. It also arrested, or at least slowed, the steady trend toward a larger and more powerful White House staff.

Ford, Carter, and Reagan: Trends in White House Staffing

The perceived power of Nixon's staff, with its tight shielding of the president, and the abuses stemming from its blind loyalty led to protests about the increasing authority gathered within the White House. Partly in response, both Gerald R. Ford (1974-1977) and Jimmy Carter

Figure 2 Organization of the Ford White House, 1976

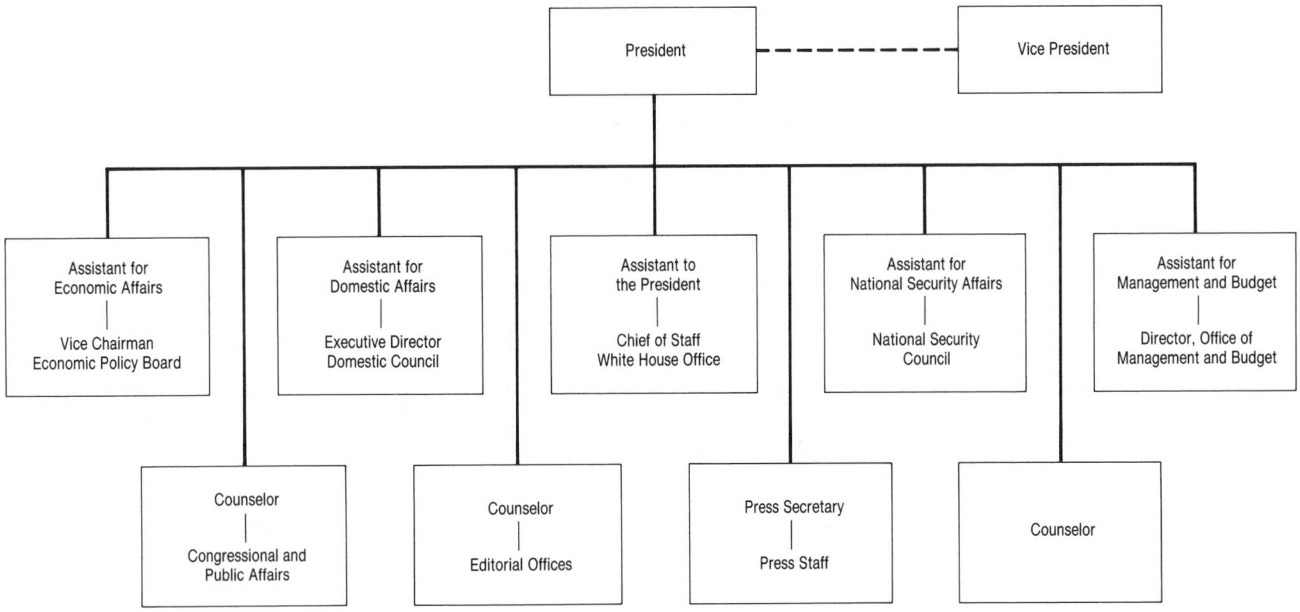

President — Vice President

- Assistant for Economic Affairs
  - Vice Chairman Economic Policy Board
- Counselor
  - Congressional and Public Affairs
- Assistant for Domestic Affairs
  - Executive Director Domestic Council
- Counselor
  - Editorial Offices
- Assistant to the President
  - Chief of Staff White House Office
- Press Secretary
  - Press Staff
- Assistant for National Security Affairs
  - National Security Council
- Counselor
- Assistant for Management and Budget
  - Director, Office of Management and Budget

Source: Stephen J. Wayne, *The Legislative Presidency* (New York: Harper and Row, 1978), 53.

(1977-1981) tried to create staff structures that avoided the excesses of the Nixon White House.

On paper, Ford's staff was structured much like the Nixon staff he had inherited, with its characteristic hierarchy and specialization. *(See Figure 2.)* Ford wanted more openness, however, and so he increased the number of advisers who had ready access to him. Whereas hardly anyone beyond Haldeman, Ehrlichman, and Kissinger had had easy access to Nixon, all of Ford's senior aides could see him at any time. In fact, Ford soon discovered that he had become too available and began to restrict access to better use his time.

Carter attempted a return to the Roosevelt-Kennedy models of White House staffing. Ford had tried to downplay the role of the chief of staff; Carter tried to eliminate it altogether. He wanted an informal structure in which a number of aides would have ready access to him, and he would be staff coordinator. The Nixon hierarchy was abandoned.

Like Ford, Carter found this arrangement unworkable. By 1976 the White House had become so large and complex that some hierarchical structure was essential. *(See Figure 3.)* Both Ford and Carter became bogged down in details and problems that swallowed up the time they needed for more important matters. They also found themselves settling turf disputes among their aides. Eventually, both turned to a chief of staff and reimposed hierarchy upon the White House.

Neither president was able to reduce the staff's influence as much as he wanted. Both sang the praises of cabinet government, but both found that it was confusing and ineffective. In what had become a very large and diversified White House, both Ford and Carter maintained the basic offices of press secretary, special counsel, appointments secretary, speechwriters, congressional liaison, cabinet secretary, staff secretary, public liaison, and domestic and national security advisers. Many of these offices had become rather large. For example, under Ford's press secretary, Ron Nessen, there were two deputy press secretaries, eight assistant secretaries (including ones for domestic affairs, foreign affairs, and administration), a personal photographer to the president, and the necessary clerical workers.

White House growth also reflected the rise of special-interest groups in American politics. Between 1975 and 1979 White House liaison offices were established for business and trade associations, minorities, Hispanics, civil rights, consumer affairs, youth, women, and senior citizens. There was also an assistant for human resources and a director of White House conferences.

Such specialization meant that the staff remained large, despite the efforts of Ford and Carter to reduce it. Ford's total staff remained at between 500 and 550, but Carter was able to reduce his staff to about 460 by 1978. By the end of his administration, however, it had returned to about 500.

By 1980 the White House had developed to such a size and complexity that major staff reductions had become difficult, if not impossible, to make. It also was impossible to operate the staff without a chief of staff and clear lines of authority. To structure the staff in the Rooseveltian manner would mean a loss of efficiency and control.

Figure 3 Organization of the Carter White House, 1980

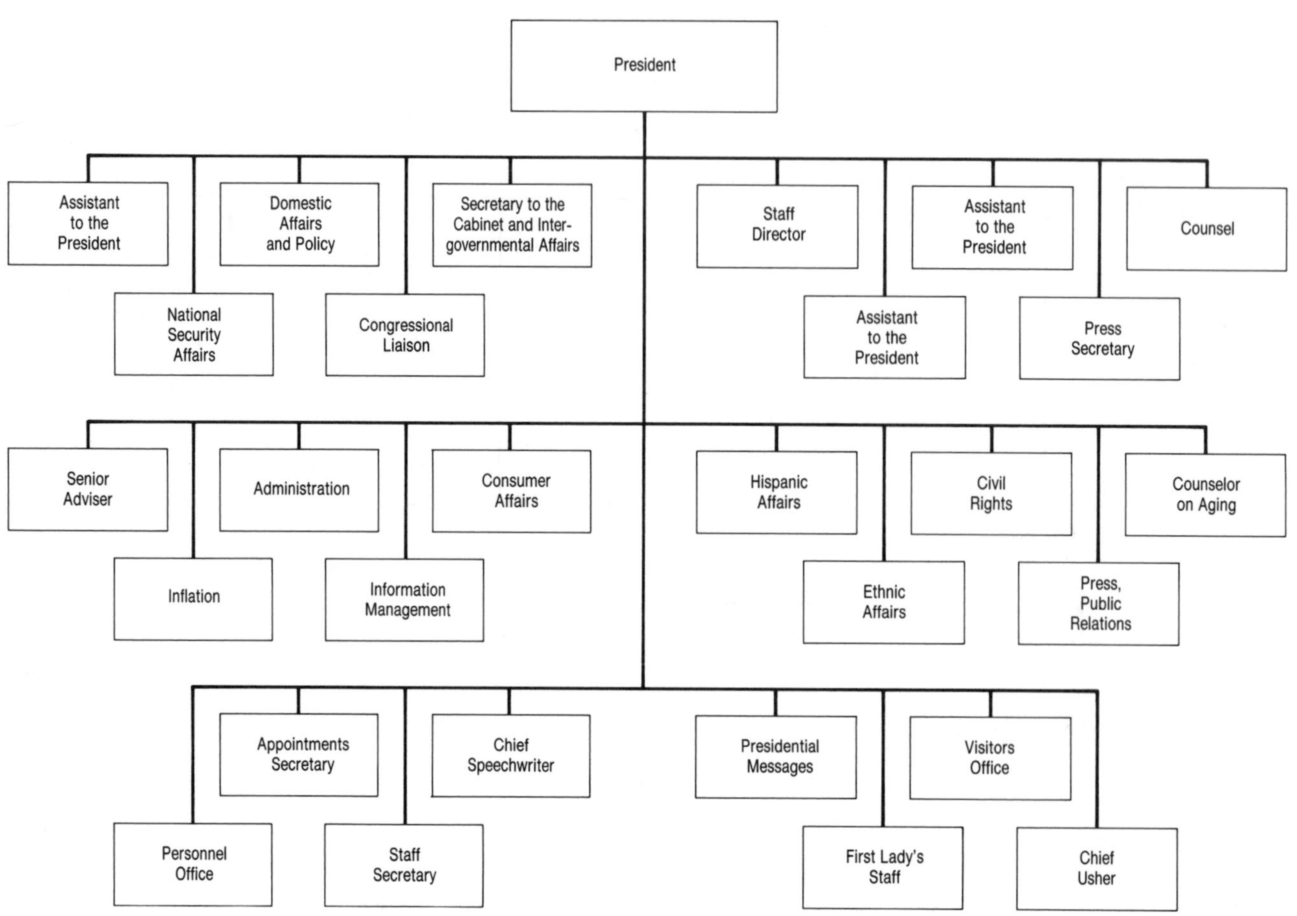

Source: Hugh Heclo and Lester M. Salamon, eds., *The Illusion of Presidential Government* (Boulder, Colo: Westview Press, 1981), 314.

Just as Ford and Carter organized their staffs in partial reaction to the Nixon experience, the Reagan administration (1981-1989) built a staff with one eye on the problems faced by its immediate predecessors. Moreover, Ronald Reagan saw no reason to tie himself up with technical details, preferring to concentrate instead on general strategies and broad policies as well as political leadership. In response to Carter's perceived obsession with details, President Reagan removed himself from the minutiae of governing perhaps more than any president in the modern era.

Thus, the Reagan staff was designed to implement the president's desire to avoid unnecessary details. It was carefully structured to work out policy specifics at lower levels; only the most important questions and broad outlines of policy were taken to the president. The staff was sufficiently specialized and hierarchical to ensure that Reagan could focus on his role as the "Great Communicator." He retained most of the offices that had become an institutionalized part of the White House, including a chief of staff, a special counsel, and a new position, counsellor to the president, which was created for Reagan's close adviser Edwin Meese III. *(See Figure 4.)*

One innovation in the Reagan White House was the Office of Planning and Evaluation (OPE), which coordinated the development of Reagan's policies with the public mood. The OPE used data from public opinion surveys to gauge public receptiveness to Reagan's programs and made long-range plans for their form and nature accordingly. This office represented the most sophisticated use of pollsters to date by the White House. While all presidents since FDR had used polling data, only Carter had a pollster as even an informal staffer, and none had institutionalized public opinion studies like the Reagan White House.[13]

Other innovations in the Reagan White House included the creation of a cabinet secretariat to coordinate interaction between the White House and the cabinet departments and an office of political affairs to work with political elements outside the White House such as the Republican party.

The Reagan staff was also original in its initial structure. As first created, the staff was subdivided to split policy formulation from political action. Separate units were charged with formulating administration policy and implementing it. A third section of the staff handled administrative details for the White House. The White House

Figure 4 Organization of the Reagan White House, 1981

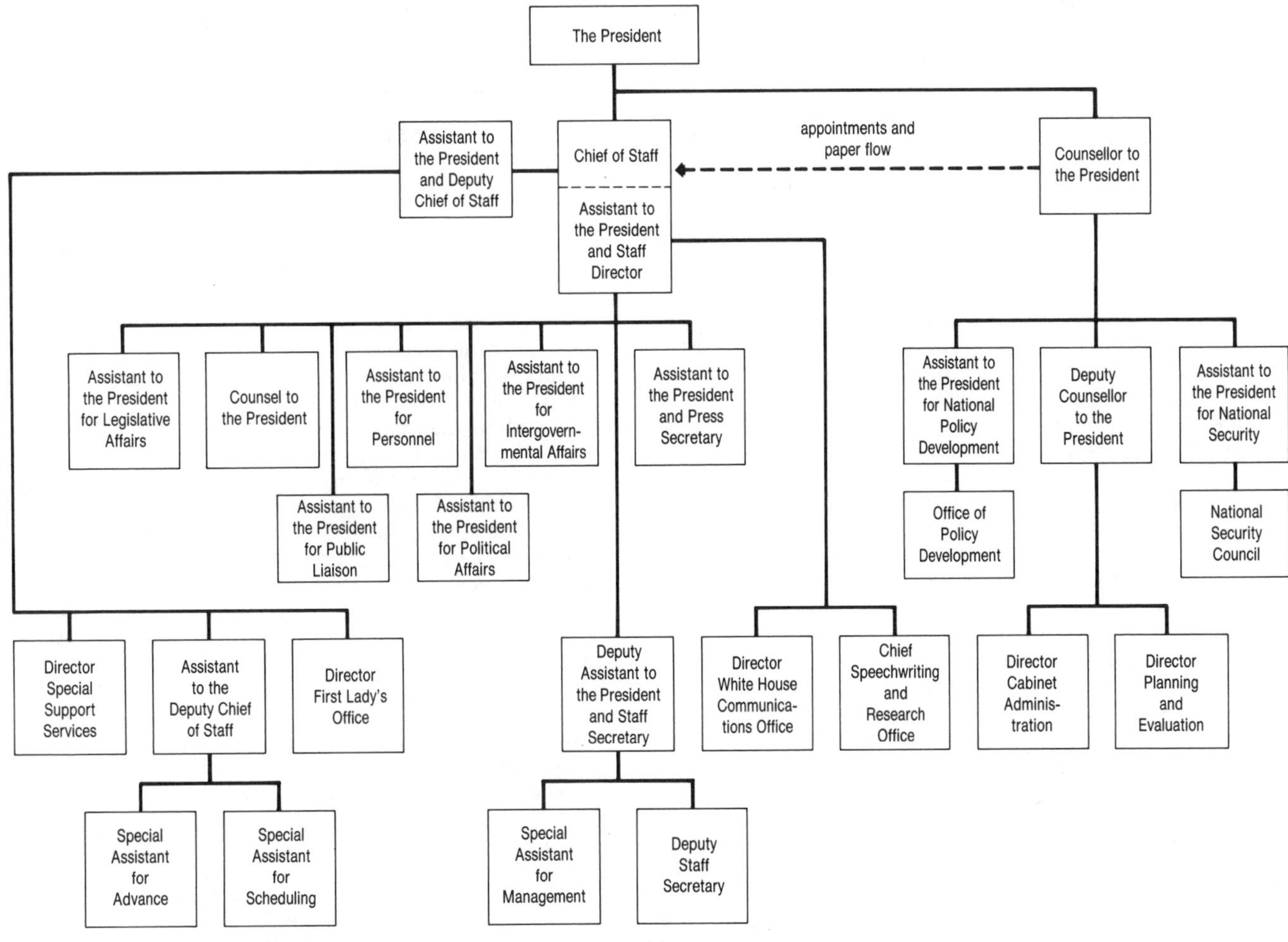

Source: Samuel Kernell and Samuel L. Popkin, eds., *Chief of Staff: Twenty-five Years of Managing the Presidency* (Berkeley: University of California Press, 1986), 202.

staff had for many years been engaged in both policy development and policy advocacy, but an institutionalized division between the two functions was unique in the evolution of the White House Office.

The Reagan White House remained large and specialized. President Reagan entered office declaring his love of cabinet government, but like Ford and Carter, he found that goal unattainable. Thus, his staff numbers did not greatly decline; he began with about 450 permanent employees and a budget of $21 million, and there was some minimal reduction.[14] The decline in size may have been largely an illusion, however. Presidential scholar Thomas E. Cronin has argued that the staff reduction was achieved on paper by moving the Office of Administration and the Office of Policy Development from the White House Office into the EOP, where they performed the same duties as before.[15]

Within the staff there was a shift as the roles of its most influential members—the national security and domestic advisers—were de-emphasized and the role of budget director was upgraded. Yet overall, despite another president's original desire to return to cabinet government, the White House staff remained an influential force in the federal government.

The Modern White House Staff

By 1989 the White House had evolved into an institutionalized bureaucracy with several hundred employees (several thousand if the EOP is included) and a multimillion-dollar budget, all of which exists solely to assist the president. Its influence remains formidable; even under Carter and Reagan, who sought to de-emphasize their staffs, the White House dominated the policy apparatus and monitored the bureaucracy. And it still had the ability to conduct operations on its own, as the Iran-contra affair indicated. It remains "the directing force of the presidential branch."[16]

Successive presidents have sought with little success to reduce the power and size of the White House, but today the White House bureaucracy has become a permanent fixture of American politics. Presidential scholars have noted several reasons for this. Perhaps the major reason is the public's tendency, in an era of ongoing crises, to expect the president to solve every problem from national defense and economic recession to drug addiction and AIDS. The president can respond only by appointing more staff to deal with all these expectations.

More presidential staff are also needed to coordinate

policy within the executive branch. Problems and the policies to deal with them now often spill across neat departmental divisions; farm policy, for example, may be the province of not only the Department of Agriculture but also the Departments of Treasury, Commerce, Labor, and even State. Coordination of all these agencies requires some direction from the top—and therefore more staff.

A correlation between the level of presidential skepticism about the performance of the permanent bureaucracy and the size of the White House staff is also evident. Either because they become impatient with the snail's pace maintained by the executive departments (Kennedy and Johnson), or because they see a bureaucracy filled with personnel left over from previous administrations and perhaps unsympathetic to their programs (Nixon), presidents often try to control within the White House as much of the development and implementation of their programs as possible. And the more activist presidents have the largest staffs. *(See Bureaucracy chapter in Part VI.)*

The growth of the White House staff also parallels the growth of the congressional staff. In an effort to offset the capabilities of the executive departments, Congress has increased the size of both its personal and committee staffs over the last thirty years. In 1955 the total congressional staff (personal, committee, and support staff) was 5,585. By 1982 the number of total staff had swollen to 18,761, and either chamber had more staff than the entire Congress of 1955: the Senate staff numbered 6,800, while the staff of the House of Representatives numbered 11,961.[17] Since most of the contact between the president and Congress takes place at the staff level, an increase in congressional staff almost inevitably leads to a corresponding increase in presidential staff.

White House staff growth also has been prompted by the inclusion of special-interest representation within the White House. Since the Truman administration, presidential aides have been designated, at first unofficially but then more formally, as liaisons to certain groups in society such as labor or religious groups. The trickle of recognition has gradually grown into a torrent as literally dozens of groups have gained a voice within the White House. Cronin has noted that

> a partial listing of staff specializations that have been grafted onto the White House in recent years . . . [forms] a veritable index of American society: budget and management, national security, economics, congressional matters, science and technology, drug abuse prevention, telecommunications, consumers, national goals, intergovernmental relations, environment, domestic policy, international economics, military affairs, civil rights, disarmament, labor relations, District of Columbia, cultural affairs, education, foreign trade and tariffs, the aged, health and nutrition, physical fitness, volunteerism, intellectuals, Blacks, youth, women, Wall Street, governors, mayors, "ethnics," regulatory agencies and related industry, state party chairmen.[18]

The multitude of interests with ties to the White House and the larger staff needed to deal with them helps explain the growth not only of the White House Office but also of the entire EOP.

A final factor in the growth of the White House staff is its increased concern with the president's public image. Every president has wanted to put forward the best image possible, but this concern took on greater sophistication beginning with the Nixon administration. The modern White House maintains considerable staff to manage the news and to handle public relations in an effort to "sell" the president and presidential programs to the people. Even pollsters have become a part of the presidential staff.

Structure of the White House Staff

As the president's personal staff, members of the White House organization provide the president with the advice and information needed to make decisions and try to ensure that presidential decisions are carried out. Their loyalty is to the president whose best interests are always in mind. Within the government the White House Office is the president's only exclusive domain.

Unlike other parts of the Executive Office of the President, the White House staff is not institutionalized and can change in size and form to suit a president's managerial style. Congress has been careful not to impose any structure upon it. Members of the White House staff are appointed solely by the president and are not subject to congressional confirmation. Staffers have no government status and no tenure in their position; they serve at the president's discretion and can be dismissed at any time for any reason.

While staffers may have enormous influence, that influence depends entirely upon their relationship with the president. With no independent power base, staff members may find that their influence will wax and wane according to their intimacy with the boss. Staffers with offices near the Oval Office, or those who have ready access to the president, are likely to be very powerful. Those who are stuck in the White House basement and see the president only by appointment are much less influential. Within the White House staff, proximity is everything. Thus, allotment of offices and the right to be the first or last to see the president each day become vital matters.

The following description of units within the White House staff must be prefaced with a caveat. In simple terms there is nothing fixed about the White House. Presidents can create, abolish, or reorganize its offices as they choose. Indeed, presidents are free to eliminate the entire staff if they wish. Similarly, the functions assigned to a given office may vary from one administration to another, and sometimes even within an administration. Presidents are free to change the job description of any office at any time, whether it is an office passed down from a previous administration or one of their own invention. Thus, titles do not always accurately indicate who does what in the White House.

Nor do titles always reveal whom the president consults on important matters. Presidents tend to seek advice from those assistants with whom they feel the most comfortable, regardless of the staffer's position or the subject matter. For example, President Carter consulted his special counsel, Lloyd N. Cutler, for advice on a variety of questions that were well outside Cutler's theoretical area of responsibility.

Chief of Staff

The most important position in the present-day White House is chief of staff. This person is responsible for the smooth operation of the White House, which is no small task. Materials must be made available to the president in a timely manner, and the president's requests and directives must be acted upon and implemented quickly. The swift and accurate flow of business is a primary goal.

The chief also acts as head gatekeeper to the president, and by reviewing all papers and visitors he or she funnels as many as possible around the president. Sherman Adams in the Eisenhower administration and H. R. Haldeman in the Nixon administration were very effective in this role. The gatekeeping function provides the chiefs of staff with a great deal of influence, since anyone wishing to bring an issue before the president must meet their approval.

Although most chiefs of staff have denied a role in policy making, the position has acquired a policy function as well. The close working relationship that most chiefs have with presidents means that it is only natural for presidents to seek and heed their opinions. Hamilton Jordan, who served as Carter's chief of staff, was an important voice in the administration, and James A. Baker III was an adviser as well as a political operative under Reagan. George Bush acknowledged even before taking office that his chief of staff, John H. Sununu, would be an administrator and a policy adviser. *(See Table 1.)*

Another important function of the chief is presidential hatchet wielder. All presidents have had jobs that they wanted to avoid, confrontations that they wished to dodge. Haldeman once noted that "every president needs his son-of-a-bitch" to do the dirty work.[19] The chief of staff is that person. Adams reprimanded or dismissed people to save Eisenhower the unpleasantness of doing it himself. Haldeman did the same for Nixon: after the 1972 election Nixon called a staff meeting and thanked everyone for their efforts in his behalf. Then, just before leaving, he turned the meeting over to Haldeman, who without preface immediately demanded everyone's resignation. The demand was really Nixon's and everyone knew it, but Haldeman had the task of carrying it out.

Finally, the chief often shoulders the blame for the president. Performing unpleasant jobs such as dismissals, which may have political significance, and taking credit for misstatements or other errors in fact made by the president are two cases in which the chief may act as presidential shield. Or the chief may act as a lightning rod to draw criticism away from the president. This function will not be found in any job description, but the possibility of being a scapegoat for the president is part of the job, and most chiefs know it.

Table 1 Chiefs of Staff, 1932-1989

President	Chief of Staff	Years
Roosevelt	—	—
Truman	John R. Stedman[a]	1946-1952
Eisenhower	Sherman Adams[a]	1953-1958
	Wilton Persons[a]	1958-1961
Kennedy	—	—
Johnson	—	—
Nixon	H. R. Haldeman	1969-1973
	Alexander M. Haig	1973-1974
Ford	Donald Rumsfeld	1974-1975
	Richard B. Cheney	1975-1977
Carter	Hamilton Jordan	1979-1980
	Jack Watson	1980-1981
Reagan	James A. Baker III	1981-1985
	Donald T. Regan	1985-1987
	Howard H. Baker Jr.	1987-1988
	Kenneth Duberstein	1988-1989
Bush	John H. Sununu	1989-

Sources: Presidential libraries and the White House, 1989.

Note: The Roosevelt, Kennedy, and Johnson presidential libraries each reported that there was no chief of staff or even a presidential assistant who served in that role.

a. These aides carried the title of "assistant" rather than "chief of staff."

Special Counsel

The position of special counsel has varied in importance over the years. In creating the position, Franklin Roosevelt argued that the White House needed its own lawyer because the attorney general, the nation's chief law officer and the government's first lawyer, was too busy to give the White House the necessary time. In reality, he envisioned a bigger role for his counsel.

The special counsel is the White House's private lawyer. This staff member provides legal advice on an assortment of topics, reviews legislation before it is sent to Congress, and may even check potential treaties for legal problems. The president also may seek the counsel's advice on the legality of certain actions. The counsel's office is concerned as well with "overseeing security clearances for presidential appointees, supervising the selection of new federal judges, maintaining liaison with the Justice Department and the legal counsels in the other federal departments, and monitoring internal conflict-of-interest guidelines for employees" of the EOP.[20] Since Watergate, the special counsel's office also has been responsible for insuring the proper behavior of the presidential staff.

Beyond these duties the office has often served presidents as a place to put valuable aides. Franklin Roosevelt named a special counsel primarily to create a place for Samuel Rosenman, who served him as an adviser and a speechwriter. Clark Clifford filled a similar function while occupying the same post under Truman. Kennedy named Theodore Sorensen special counsel and used him as a speechwriter and domestic policy adviser. Under Carter, the office was used in two different ways: Robert J. Lipshutz confined himself to legal matters; his successor, Lloyd Cutler, advised the president on a wide range of issues, both foreign and domestic.

National Security and Domestic Advisers

The national security adviser is the president's primary adviser on foreign policy. Created originally as a largely administrative post, the national security adviser was responsible for overseeing the functioning of the National Security Council and coordinating the various elements of the foreign policy establishment, such as the State Department, Defense Department, and Central Intelligence Agency. Over the years the position has retained these administrative functions, and the Reagan administration, at least in its initial days, tried to reemphasize them. *(See Executive Office of the President: Supporting Organizations chapter in Part V.)*

Given the central location of the national security

adviser in the policy process, it was natural that presidents began turning to them for advice as well as coordination. National security advisers became important policy-making figures; men such as Bundy, Kissinger, and Zbigniew Brzezinski (under Carter) were major players, if not the crucial figures, in the development of their administration's foreign policy. Under these advisers the role of foreign policy designer began to overshadow that of administrator.

The prominence of the national security adviser has led to an occasional controversy about the position. The possibility that a national security adviser could dominate the execution of U.S. foreign policy has led to calls for congressional confirmation of appointees to the post. Demands for congressional approval have been particularly strident when evidence has surfaced of uncontrolled or excessive NSC activity, such as the Iran-contra affair.

The domestic policy adviser has existed under different names in several administrations. Some scholars have contended that Adams was a de facto domestic adviser under Eisenhower. Sorensen served as one under Kennedy. The title was first given to Califano in the Johnson administration, and the Domestic Council was formalized under Ehrlichman in the Nixon years. Carter rechristened it the Domestic Policy Staff, and Reagan renamed it yet again, designating it the Office of Policy Development. *(See Executive Office of the President: Supporting Organizations chapter in Part V.)*

By whatever name, the office of the domestic policy adviser has responsibilities that parallel those of the office of the national security adviser. The domestic adviser coordinates domestic policy making and acts as a policy adviser. The adviser's office settles disputes between domestic agencies and uses input from them to formulate legislative proposals. The president may also turn to the domestic adviser for advice on domestic problems.

The domestic adviser has not been as influential or as effective a coordinator as the national security adviser. This stems from the larger number of agencies and constituencies in the domestic adviser's domain, many of which are powerful and active. Thus, the domestic adviser cannot exercise the same degree of control as his or her foreign counterpart.

White House Liaison Offices

Several offices in the modern White House are concerned with its links with the world outside its gates. The oldest of these is the office of the press secretary. The press secretary manages the administration's relations with the news media. News summaries and daily briefings issued by the secretary for journalists provide information on the president's activities and decisions. The press secretary is regarded as the spokesperson for the administration, and his or her words often are taken to be the president's position.

Because of their proximity to the president, press secretaries may also become policy advisers. Hagerty functioned in that dual capacity for Eisenhower, as did the Nixon administration's Ronald Ziegler, who eventually was named as an assistant to the president as well.

Closely related to the press secretary is the Communications Office. The two offices were actually one through the Johnson administration, with the press secretary handling all press relations, but the increasing work load caused by the government's growth and the electronic era necessitated a division of labor. The Communications Office was separated from the press secretary's office by President Nixon in 1969, and it has remained a separate entity since.

Like the press secretary's office, the Communications Office is concerned with the news media, but it is more involved in managing the news. The communications director responds to reporters' inquiries, provides information and briefings, and arranges interviews. The director also tries to get the administration's point of view across, using press releases, interviews, mailings, and other techniques to promote the president's side of a story. During the Nixon presidency, for example, the Communications Office sent out summaries of administration accomplishments to some five thousand journalists and commentators. During Watergate, it acted as a liaison between the White House and various groups opposing a possible Nixon impeachment.[21] The Communications Office functions as well as an advertising department and the public relations agency for the White House.

The White House also maintains offices to facilitate communication with important groups. One of the most important of these is the congressional liaison office, known under Reagan as the Office of Legislative Affairs. Used to control the interaction between the president and Congress, this office was formally established during the Eisenhower administration—previous presidents had unofficial liaison personnel, however. Subsequently, it has grown as Congress has grown.

The congressional liaison staff, with its components for the House and the Senate, tries to maintain a two-way flow of communication between the White House and the Congress. Staff members present the president's positions to Congress and sell presidential programs there. They also nurture good relationships with individual members of Congress who might support the administration on various bills. Information and materials are provided as well to help the administration's congressional friends persuade others in Congress and defend themselves back home.

In facilitating communications from Congress to the White House, the liaison staff relays and tries to resolve problems that members of Congress may be having with the administration. It is a channel through which Congress can talk to the president. The liaison staff also keeps the president informed on the mood in Congress and the chances of success there.

For specific bills the liaison staff must work with the president's congressional supporters to help determine when a bill should be introduced, how it should be worded, how it should be pushed and modified, and when it should be brought to a vote. Staff members also must keep accurate counts of the number of votes available to the president for a bill. They then know exactly who is wavering, and either can be won over or must be reinforced, and what incentives are needed to gain a member's vote. The staff also must know when and to what degree direct presidential involvement is needed to save a bill. Any slip-up may mean losing a salvageable bill or wasting valuable presidential resources.

The public liaison office was established during the Nixon administration, and it has remained a White House fixture. Its goal is to build support for the administration's policies within the general public. Liaison staffers contact constituency groups and try to educate them about the administration's goals and actions. One of President Carter's assistants for public liaison, Anne Wexler, invited influential groups to the White House to hear administration officials, including the president, explain the administration's positions on particular issues. Her goal was increased public support for the president. Other White House liaison offices maintain ties with various specific constituency groups.

The White House also has a staff of presidential speechwriters. Unlike earlier staffs, recent staffs have had distinct speechwriter positions. Presidential speechwriters are the administration's wordsmiths: they compose the addresses, statements, and messages that the president delivers to Congress and the general public, both at home and overseas. Much of President Kennedy's famed inaugural address, for example, was actually written by Theodore Sorensen. Many phrases that have defined an administration were created by speechwriters, not the president who spoke them. Because words define policy, speechwriters also may have a role in policy making. Indeed, in the Roosevelt, Truman, and Kennedy administrations speechwriters were policy advisers as well.

Personnel Office

Throughout every administration numerous vacancies occur in the executive branch, and all presidents' staffs maintain a personnel office to find people to fill them. This office locates potential officeholders, checks on qualifications and conducts interviews, and along with the special counsel's office arranges for background checks, often by the Federal Bureau of Investigation. If all is in order, the office presents the nominee to the president for approval and submission to the Senate, if necessary. It also might brief the appointee on the questions he or she may face from that body. The rigor with which the personnel office does its business varies from administration to administration, ranging from using computer data banks to informal queries.[22]

Recruiting the White House Staff

Because the success or failure of an administration may depend largely upon the abilities of the White House staff, the problem of how to find good people is of major concern to presidents. Unfortunately, few studies have examined critically how presidents choose their staffs and what factors determine how and why staffers are selected.

Recent presidents have had both an inner and outer staff. In a bureaucracy that includes hundreds if not thousands of people (depending on whether one includes the EOP), not everyone can have the ear of the president. The inner staff refers to those senior aides who are close to the president and can reasonably expect admission to the Oval Office when needed. The outer staff refers to the other members of the presidential establishment who perform specialized functions in the lower echelons of the White House but see the president rarely, if ever. The distinction between the two staffs is of some importance, for presidents may choose personnel for each in different ways.

Historically, the senior inner staff is chosen from among the president's close friends and cronies. To fill these staff positions, presidents usually look to the people with whom they have worked closely in the past, tending to select campaign workers or old friends to take the top staff positions. In 1968, for example, President Nixon chose his campaign manager as his White House chief of staff. Technical qualifications thus may not matter as much as a good relationship with the president.

Presidents often bring their inner staff to Washington with them. Truman appointed a number of old cronies from Missouri to various staff positions. Kennedy had his "Irish Mafia," staffed by men from Harvard and the Northeast; Carter's Mafia was drawn from his native Georgia. Johnson brought old Texas associates such as Jack Valenti and Bill Moyers, while Reagan brought William P. Clark, Edwin Meese III, and Michael K. Deaver from California to serve in his new administration.

Presidents tend to choose their inner staff from close friends and associates for good reasons. In the first place, these people are nearby when a new president starts forming the White House team. In the crush of a presidential transition period the new president has a multitude of details to worry about, and a serious search to fill staff appointments is often not really possible. Indeed, because a new president needs help immediately after the election, the only way to get that help is to call on friends and associates to fill staff positions.

More important, the president usually chooses the inner staff from among close associates because these are the people the president can trust when seeking political or personal advice. The need for trustworthy confidants is particularly keen for a president. For example, when FDR's Republican opponent in the 1940 election, Wendell L. Willkie, asked Roosevelt why he continued to keep assistant Harry Hopkins, he replied that

> I can understand that you wonder why I need that half man around me. But someday you may be sitting here where I am now as president of the United States. And when you are, you'll be looking through that door over there and knowing that practically everybody who walks through it wants something out of you. You'll learn what a lonely job this is, and you'll discover the need for somebody like Harry Hopkins who asks for nothing except to serve you.[23]

Although most members of the inner staff are chosen from the president's friends and former aides, presidents sometimes choose senior aides primarily on the basis of reputation, and close working relationships may follow. For example, President Nixon selected Henry Kissinger as his national security adviser after just one meeting with him. The selection was based on Kissinger's writings on foreign policy and international politics. Only later did Kissinger have a good working relationship with Nixon. Similarly, James Baker was far from a close confidant of President Reagan when he was selected to fill the position of chief of staff. Thus, while special knowledge or qualifications may become important in filling high-profile senior posts such as budget director or national security adviser, new presidents continue to select most senior aides on the basis of old ties.

Lower White House personnel, who fill more specialized roles, may be appointed on the basis of either connections or merit. Depending on the desires of the president, such staffers are selected in a systematic screening process similar to that used for other executive branch personnel. Potential staff who meet the criteria of agreement with the president's program and competence may be subjected to background checks (to prevent something embarrassing to the administration from surfacing later) before taking their positions. White House staff appointments do not require congressional confirmation.

Every recent administration has had a White House personnel office responsible for finding and screening potential appointees. The care with which such searches are undertaken, however, varies from one administration to another. Under Lyndon Johnson, for example, a computerized file was set up to keep records on possible appointees; whenever a position became available, Johnson's personnel staff could scan the computer banks and find people qualified for the job. Other presidents have employed less advanced methods. After President Nixon's election in 1968 his staff tried to find personnel by soliciting recommendations from everyone in *Who's Who in America* (which included such political notables as Casey Stengel and Elvis Presley; a letter also was sent to Nixon himself).[24]

What seems to be more common than computers and systematic searches is the BOGSAT method of appointing personnel: a bunch of guys sitting around a table saying, Who do you know? Frequently, White House staff selection appears to be based on connections; it is a matter of knowing a person who knows a person who knows the president. Like Franklin Roosevelt, many presidents have chosen a large part of their staff by drawing upon friends, colleagues, campaign workers, the "old boys' network," and party operatives to fill posts both in the White House and in the administration at large. While most administrations worked this way, the Johnson, Carter, and Reagan administrations, who were more systematic than most in their selection of executive personnel, avoided it to some degree.

Profiles of White House aides over the years are strikingly consistent—no doubt partly because of the way in which they are chosen. From 1948 through 1974 the staff was almost exclusively white men: 98 percent were white and 98 percent were male. Eighty-six percent had college educations. Of these, 57 percent had undertaken some advanced graduate work, particularly in law. Sixty-nine percent of the staffers were between the ages of thirty and fifty, and the average age has tended to decline over the years. The private sector has produced 60 percent of the White House staffers, with the predominant fields being law (16 percent), business (15 percent), journalism (13 percent), and education (11 percent). Nonelected government positions produced 29 percent of the staff, while 4 percent were former elected officials and 6 percent were former military men.[25]

Styles of Organization of the White House Office

No hard or fast rules govern the way presidents shape their staffs; the only variables are their preferences and work habits. At the same time certain patterns of organization have recurred over the years, leading scholars to discern two types of patterns: pyramidal and circular.

As the name suggests, pyramidal staffs are structured as a hierarchy with the president occupying the top position. Immediately under the president is usually a chief of staff who has a few key assistants who are close to the president; some may have direct access to the Oval Office. Arranged in order of importance below these close aides are the other assistants, increasing in number as their relative importance decreases.

This structure is designed to insure a clear chain of command and provide precise channels of communication for information going up and directives coming down. It permits specialization at the lower levels and control at the top. In theory, those higher up in the system are able to provide the president with more accurate information in a timely manner, while filtering out and eliminating unnecessary information. President Eisenhower argued that "a president who doesn't know how to decentralize will be weighted down with details and won't have time to deal with the big issues."[26] A pyramidal staff arrangement provides this decentralization.

Critics of the pyramidal staff have contended that the structure may distort information and problems. Highly complex problems may resist compression into the one-page memoranda preferred by presidents Eisenhower and Reagan; information and policy alternatives that the president should have may be lost or discarded at the lower staff levels.

A staff pyramid also may malfunction and isolate the president. By acting as a screen the staff may keep from the president not only unnecessary but also just unpleasant information. What staff member wants to be the bearer of bad news? Critics charge that pyramidal staffs can cause the president to lose contact with reality. Indeed, it may happen that the staff is controlling the president more than the president is controlling the staff.

In the circular or "spokes of the wheel" method of organizing the White House, the president also acts as chief of staff. Surrounded by a number of trusted advisers, all of whom have approximately equal access to the Oval Office, the president makes assignments, receives reports, and largely determines how presidential time is allotted among staffers. Essentially, the president sits in the middle of a ring of advisers who funnel information to and are in equal contact with the Oval Office, much like the hub of a wheel.

The circular approach to staff organization permits the president to obtain information from a variety of sources. Properly pursued, this approach reduces the possibility that dissenting voices are lost in the shuffle and never reach the president. Because not all details are worked out at the lower staff levels, the president can have more input in the specifics of the administration's policies, thereby ensuring that an important idea is not lost in the evolution of a brief policy memo. As some scholars have noted, activist presidents who want an exchange of ideas at the highest levels have tended to prefer this approach.

The circular staff arrangement may permit too much access to the president, however. Given the size of the modern White House staff, a president who does not have someone else to control the flow of people and paper to the Oval Office is at serious risk of being inundated and swept away. There is simply not enough of the president to go around. H. R. Haldeman once observed that "if everyone who wanted to see [the president] got in, nobody would get in because there wouldn't be room."[27] And as President Ford noted,

> because power in Washington is measured by how much access a person has to the president, almost everyone wanted more access than I had access to give. I wanted to have an "open" door, but it was very difficult; my working day grew longer and longer, and the demands on my time were hindering my effectiveness. Someone ... had to be responsible for scheduling appointments, coordinating the paper flow, following up on decisions I had made....[28]

Circular staffing arrangements also have been criticized as stimulating unhealthy friction between staffers, who may find themselves competing for the president's attention. Most (but not all) presidents have found such jealousies disruptive to peak staff performance. But, if internal bickering is not a factor, a circular staff could easily become excessively collegial and lose its critical perspective, thus developing what is referred to as "groupthink."[29]

Roosevelt and the Competitive Staff

Some presidential scholars have drawn a distinction between the circular model employed by Franklin Roosevelt and those of other presidents. The Rooseveltian model has been characterized as a "competitive" one in which members of the president's staff are set on conflicting assignments. Out of the competition between staffers to win the president's favor, the president can get a better array of options and data, more forcefully argued. Other presidents with circular staffs have used a "collegial" approach, intended to facilitate staff cooperation and to promote more harmony and efficiency.

Roosevelt surrounded himself with a small staff of about a half dozen administrative assistants, most of whom were simply "special assistants," or generalists, able to handle whatever problems emerged. Formal staff meetings were rare or nonexistent, as the president preferred informal gatherings with any assistant who needed to see him. There were no experts on particular policy areas, no special-interest liaisons, and no rigid lines of authority; aides moved across policy areas as the president saw fit.

The president served as his own chief of staff and handed out assignments himself on a seemingly random basis, often selecting the aide most readily available. He could be so capricious in his assignments because he had created a staff that could move readily from one problem to another. Roosevelt expected his aides to take on whatever assignment that he might give them, resulting in a very fluid staff structure.

Roosevelt also received all of the staff's reports personally. In his constant search for more information about problems and issues, Roosevelt tapped numerous sources, both within and outside of his immediate staff, for facts and advice. For Roosevelt, a separate chief of staff to sort out incoming information would have been an unwelcome obstruction. A master politician and manipulator, he wanted all the facts to come directly to him so that he personally could evaluate and use them.

Roosevelt's staff, which in most ways was a prototypical circular arrangement, was unique in the extent to which he turned it upon itself. Most presidents have disliked internal staff competition and infighting, but Roosevelt seemed to thrive upon it. Instead of trying to discourage intrastaff competition, he promoted it. Instead of worrying about stress and struggles within his staff, he encouraged them. In fact, Roosevelt often gave the same assignment to more than one assistant, thus setting them potentially in conflict. Yet he always maintained control of the competition; unlike most presidents he did not even feel the need to maintain a facade of internal staff harmony.

For Roosevelt, operating a staff by the principle of competition had several distinct advantages. The president reasoned that putting aides in competition would stimulate them to work faster, dig harder for needed information and critical insights, and devise more creative solutions to national problems. This was something Roosevelt was constantly seeking, particularly in his early years. He also was better able to evaluate his personnel and their ideas. And the conflict itself apparently appealed to Roosevelt; as Kennedy adviser Richard E. Neustadt has noted, he encouraged his staff to jostle and "evidently got a kick out of bruised egos."[30]

To an outsider, Roosevelt's staff operation seemed chaotic, strife-ridden, and often wasteful of time and resources. It appeared that too many people were duplicating efforts and there was no organization or planning. For Roosevelt, however, the open staff system provided what he wanted: a flow of ideas. For that, the lack of order was a fair trade-off. Then too the small size of the staff and Roosevelt's manipulative skills made it possible for him to retain sufficient control over the operation. His staff arrangement remains unique; no other president has been willing or able to operate with the somewhat acrimonious confusion in which Roosevelt thrived.

President Truman certainly was not willing to adopt the Rooseveltian style and set out to alter it soon after becoming president. While he maintained a basically open and circular staff, he took steps to provide more order and reduce the intrastaff competition that had been so dear to his predecessor. Assignments were more functional; overlap was reduced. Still, Truman preferred to remain at the center of the staff wheel.

Kennedy, Johnson, and the Collegial Staff

Two later Democratic presidents also operated circular staffs. Indeed, President Kennedy's staff is often cited as a prototype of the collegial staff system.

When he organized his White House staff, Kennedy made a conscious decision to return to the informal staffing arrangements once employed by Roosevelt. In this decision, which was encouraged by advisers such as Neustadt, he was reacting to the Eisenhower administration. Kennedy believed that Eisenhower's staff was too rigid in its structure and that it stifled creativity and debate. His staff was designed to avoid this rigidity.

Like Roosevelt, Kennedy created an open, circular staff structure in which he was accessible to all of his advisers equally. Because the president made assignments and received papers personally, the business of his government moved through him. There was no chief of staff to censor the flow of papers and advisers.

As an activist president, Kennedy thought that his circular staff would be more creative in dealing with problems and devising policy. The bureaucracies were too slow in their operation and too traditional in their thinking to suit him; he wanted more originality and faster action, and he set up an interactive staff to produce it.

The president's tendency toward an informal staff structure was no doubt reinforced by the number of crises that arose during his administration. In foreign affairs, particularly, Kennedy had to confront such problems as the Bay of Pigs fiasco, the Berlin crisis, and the Cuban missile crisis. Crisis management is necessarily improvised, and the frequency of the crises confronting Kennedy's administration strengthened the president's belief in fluid staff patterns.[31]

The Kennedy staff was very fluid in structure. On

paper there was more organization than had existed under Roosevelt, but in practice the dividing lines were not often observed. Like Roosevelt, Kennedy wanted a staff of generalists; he wanted every aide to be able to assume whatever duties were called for at a given moment. The staff was composed of equals, all of whom were free to interact with the president or one another.

The Kennedy staff was notable for its harmony. Most presidents have encountered jealousies among staffers, sometimes to the extent of disrupting staff performance, but an unusual degree of collegial spirit existed in the Kennedy White House, perhaps because the president's staff perceived itself to be on the cutting edge of the New Frontier, distinct from the rest of the Washington establishment. This camaraderie helped Kennedy's circular staff structure function effectively.

In the aftermath of Kennedy's assassination on November 22, 1963, Johnson tried to keep most of his predecessor's advisers around him, believing that he needed the expertise and the legitimacy that their presence would provide. At the same time, he began to bring in his own people gradually, often without dislodging the Kennedy staff. Thus, Johnson ran a dual staff for a time, overlapping former Kennedy staffers with his own personnel.

The circular staffing structures that Kennedy had employed appealed to the new president. A great admirer of Franklin Roosevelt, Johnson was a very active president, eager to create a Great Society of social programs to help the nation's poor and disadvantaged. In doing this, he wanted to emulate Roosevelt and perhaps overshadow Kennedy. He was eager for new ideas and programs and sought any pertinent facts aggressively, particularly in the early days of his administration before the Vietnam quagmire engulfed him.

Thus, the Johnson White House was very idiosyncratic and loosely structured to fit the whims of an energetic and mercurial president. It was so unstructured in fact that anyone who asked for its organization chart was told that there was no such thing. Aides declared that drawing up one would simply be a waste of time, as no one would follow it anyway.

Unlike the Kennedy staff, Johnson's aides were in constant competition for the president's ear. Preferring informal arrangements and one-on-one encounters, Johnson avoided large staff meetings. He particularly liked to meet with selected staffers in his bedroom, either first thing in the morning or last thing at night, and aides who were admitted to such meetings were viewed as very influential.

Although the structure of Johnson's staff was similar to Kennedy's, the atmosphere was quite different. A man with incredible energy, Johnson drove his staff mercilessly to keep up. The president's energy was legendary. He would work from seven o'clock in the morning until two in the afternoon, when he would stop for lunch, a short nap (on his doctor's orders; he already had had a heart attack), a shower, and a change of clothes. Then from four until nine o'clock or later he would resume working as furiously as ever. Aides were supposed to be available at any time, night or day; no excuses were acceptable (when Joseph Califano failed one day to answer a presidential phone call because he was in the bathroom, Johnson ordered him to put an extension in there). The pace and pressure under Johnson thus were such that he simply wore his staff down. The collegiality that had marked the Kennedy staff was much less present under Johnson.

Eisenhower, Nixon, and the Staff Pyramid

The Eisenhower staff was the first attempt at a more formal, hierarchical staff structure. An orderly person, Eisenhower was repelled by the chaos of the Roosevelt staff, even after it had been somewhat refined by Truman. His military experience had taught him the benefits of organization, and the result was a degree of differentiation and specialization previously unseen in the White House.

Eisenhower's staff was the traditional pyramid, with none of the fluid and shifting assignments that Roosevelt had used. Everyone had specific areas of responsibility and knew what they were. Eisenhower was more interested in good management than spontaneity; specialization was the name of the game. This arrangement allowed the president to know exactly where to go for information or action.

The desire for specific areas of responsibility among the staff naturally led to a bigger staff, which, for better organization, was divided into subunits. One example of this was the National Security Council staff. The first president to give much organization to the NSC, Eisenhower created a rather elaborate system of working groups to analyze particular problems and to produce studies and recommendations. The NSC operation was criticized by opponents as a useless paper mill, but it typified the organization and specialization that Eisenhower wanted of his staff.

Unlike Roosevelt, Eisenhower did not want to be involved in every detail of operation or policy; he believed that presidents were supposed to make big decisions and leave little ones to subordinates. His attitude is captured in his remarks to Defense Secretary Charles E. Wilson, who repeatedly came to him with minor problems early in the administration: "Charlie, you have to run Defense. We can't both run it. And I won't run it." [32]

To ensure that problems found their appropriate level, Eisenhower created a chain of command to control the paper flow through the staff. Problems and papers came up from the lower levels until they reached a point of decision (which in most cases was below the president), and then orders went back down. Eisenhower was thus relieved of the need to bother with most problems at all, while at the same time ensuring that they were being dealt with systematically.

At the top of the pyramid was the president, but because Eisenhower preferred to distance himself from everyday business, the most important operations figure was the chief of staff. From 1953 to 1958 that person was Sherman Adams, followed by Maj. Gen. Wilton B. (Jerry) Persons. Simply put, the chief of staff managed the operation of the staff, making sure that it ran smoothly and efficiently, and kept unimportant matters and people away from the president. Adams in particular acted as gatekeeper and arbiter for Eisenhower, restricting access to the Oval Office and forcing decisions, whenever possible, to be made somewhere else. "We must not bother the president with this" was his watchword.[33]

Adams's authority over the president's business and Eisenhower's distance from daily events, particularly in domestic affairs, led to the perception that the chief of staff, with his extensive power, was some sort of an "assistant president." Adams was seen as being so influential that a joke began to make the rounds: "Wouldn't it be awful if Eisenhower died and Nixon became president?

Library of Congress

Unlike FDR and Truman, Eisenhower ran a structured and diversified staff. Sherman Adams became the gatekeeper to the president during Ike's first six years in office.

Yes, but what if Adams died and Eisenhower became president?" In fact, if Adams had so much authority as presidential gatekeeper, it was because the president wanted it that way.

Beneath Adams the Eisenhower staff was the prototypical hierarchy. At least at the top, however, it was not completely rigid in its organization. There were lines of command, but they were not irrevocable; Eisenhower's staff structure was meant to control staff interaction, not necessarily eliminate it. Senior staff had access to the president and participated in policy discussions whenever appropriate.

The hierarchic staff, abandoned after Eisenhower, was resurrected by Nixon in 1969. Having served as Eisenhower's vice president, Nixon knew the organizational merits of a more formal staff structure. It also well served his personal needs. A man who preferred to work alone, making decisions in solitude from the many briefing papers he received, Nixon used his staff to insulate himself from the rest of the world and provide the isolation he sought.

In the Nixon White House with its pyramidal structure, information and options were passed up the chain of command from specialists at the lower staff levels, and decisions and requests were returned down the ladder from the top. Much more information made its way to the top, however, than during the Eisenhower years. Unlike Eisenhower, who wanted one-page policy summaries and oral briefings, Nixon wanted detail and read extensively.

Nixon used the staff as a buffer even more than Eisenhower did. Senior staff members contended that no unreasonable restrictions were placed on the flow of traffic through the Oval Office, but complaints from outsiders about the difficulties encountered in seeing the president were numerous. Transportation Secretary John Volpe, frustrated over lack of access to the president, once pulled a list of problems out of his pocket while greeting Nixon in a church reception line.

At its peak, the Nixon staff was a model of efficiency. Everyone knew their roles; everyone knew the chain of command. As one staffer noted, "The place had a structure, had a way of doing things, had a flow and a follow-up system that was beyond belief. Things happened." There was relentless pressure from the top to get work done quickly and thoroughly. The staffer who was late or sloppy in his assignments was immediately brought into line. Nixon aide John W. Dean remembered that

> I spent too much time preparing my answers to a few action memoranda, let the due dates slide by, and discovered the consequences. First a secretary in the staff secretary's office called my secretary, asking where the answer was, and when the explanation was found unsatisfactory, a very bitchy Larry Higby called to say, "What's the matter, Dean, can't you meet a deadline? Do you think you're somebody special?" When I explained I was working on the response, Higby snapped, "Work a little faster." Higby was chewed out by Haldeman when the paper did not flow as the chief of staff wanted, so he leaned on others.[34]

The man who ran this machine with a firm hand was chief of staff H. R. Haldeman. Haldeman performed many of the same functions that Sherman Adams had performed for Eisenhower, and in fact once acknowledged himself that he was more like Adams than any other past staffer. But where Eisenhower had placed Adams alone at the top of the pyramid, Nixon included more specialists at the lower levels and broadened the top, making his chief of staff first among equals instead of a majordomo. In reality, although Haldeman remained the major figure on the staff, two other members also had ready access to the president: John Ehrlichman, who was first counsel to the president and later domestic adviser, and Henry Kissinger, the national security adviser. Increasingly, Haldeman, Ehrlichman, and Kissinger were the filter through which the outside world, including cabinet secretaries, had to pass to see the president. Furthermore, because Nixon's distrust of the permanent bureaucracy led him to concentrate more authority within the White House, the influence wielded by the "Big Three" became formidable indeed.

To meet his desire for organization and concentration of authority over the government within the White House, Nixon devised a new plan for structuring his staff. In July 1973 he unveiled a supercabinet proposal, in which the various executive departments were grouped into three blocks, each of which was to report to a presidential counsellor who doubled as a department head. The counsellors in turn reported to Ehrlichman, who was to oversee the entire operation. The goal was greater efficiency and better organization. How well it might have worked will never be known. No sooner had it been introduced than the Watergate controversy began to overwhelm the Nixon administration. After the resignations of Haldeman and Ehrlichman in early 1974, the system was dismantled.

Because staff arrangements are a reflection of the president and the president's needs, the Nixon White House did not change greatly in structure with the replacement of Haldeman by Gen. Alexander M. Haig, Jr. Haig continued to sit atop the White House bureaucracy, controlling the flow of business to the president. Although he tried to coordinate the administration's domestic programs, the increasing disarray of the staff and the growing congressional hostility made his task difficult. His efforts to expand the circle of White House advisers was for naught when the embattled Nixon, always a private man, increasingly withdrew into himself as Watergate destroyed his presidency. By the end of his administration, Nixon was seeing few people besides Haig, Kissinger, and Press Secretary Ziegler.

Reacting to Watergate: Ford and Carter

The pattern of staff organization used in the White House has reflected not only each president's personality, but also their desire to avoid the errors of their predecessors. Thus, Kennedy adopted a circular staff in part because of the perception of overcentralization on Eisenhower's staff, and Nixon returned to a centralized staff because of the disarray he perceived in Johnson's staff. Similarly, Gerald Ford and Jimmy Carter tried to incorporate more openness into their staffs in response to what they saw as the excessive authority of the "Prussian guards" under Nixon. Neither was completely successful.

President Ford inherited his staff from the departing Nixon. Desiring continuity, Ford kept many of the Nixon staffers for a time, particularly at the lower and middle levels of the White House bureaucracy; most higher-level staffers were replaced early in the Ford administration. He set out quickly, however, to modify Nixon's staff structure. Ford's desire to open the Nixon structure stemmed in part from the apparent excesses of the Watergate period and in part from his long congressional experience, which led him to prefer personal interaction.

Ford therefore changed the Nixon pyramid into a rectangle. Each of nine senior aides was given specific areas of responsibility, a small staff, and equal access (at least in theory) to the president. The chief of staff position was abolished. Donald Rumsfeld was put in charge of White House operations, the traditional chief of staff duty, but Ford insisted carefully that there was no real chief. Ford did not entirely abandon hierarchy, however. His staff design was supposed to delineate clearly staff responsibilities and thus maintain more order than a circular staff, while also providing more accessibility and more channels of communication than the traditional pyramid.

In practice, the staff rectangle failed to operate as Ford had hoped. Despite his preference for receiving information orally and having personal contact, the president found that his staff arrangements permitted too many people to have access to him and too many demands on his time. Eventually, Ford was forced to have someone control the flow of traffic to and from his office. He thus appointed Richard B. Cheney chief of staff, in fact if not in title. The rectangle had become a pyramid again.

President Carter came into office seeking to re-create the circular staff system used by his illustrious Democratic predecessors, Roosevelt and Kennedy. Carter wanted to serve as his own chief of staff, sitting in the middle of a circle of advisers who would keep him in touch with the events of his administration. Like the presidents he was emulating, Carter wanted innovation and valued new ideas, and he thought that a circular staff system would encourage them.

No doubt Carter thought that he could manage a circular staff, even a large one, because of his ability to handle facts and details. Like Ford, however, he soon found that there was not enough of him to go around. With no gatekeeper, too many people brought too many problems to his attention, and Carter was soon handling such trivial matters as the allocation of parking spaces in the White House garage. It was no wonder that he quickly was overwhelmed by the volume of demands on his time. Overall policy and long-range goals were lost as he tried to cope with the mass of visitors and papers that descended upon him.

In the end, Carter was forced to capitulate to the reality of the modern White House. In 1979, attempting to shake off the "great malaise," he reorganized his staff into a more pyramidal form. He appointed a chief of staff (originally Hamilton Jordan, who was Carter's closest aide, and later Jack H. Watson, Jr.) to control the president's business. Formal staff meetings replaced small informal gatherings. Although he never became so structured as Nixon or Eisenhower, Carter necessarily adopted a more systematic approach to his staff.

Reagan and the Triumvirate Staff

The most unusual staff arrangement of any president was that employed by President Reagan during his first term in office. Although it resembled the traditional pyramid structure in the concentration of power at the top, Reagan did not use a single chief of staff to guard the door to the Oval Office. Instead, the president divided his staff into separate units, each headed by a senior staff member who had direct access to him. The senior staff linked the president to the lower staff. One can visualize the staff as a set of columns supporting the president.

Initially, the Reagan staff was broken down into three divisions which addressed (1) policy development, (2) the political problems of promoting the president's programs, and (3) the actual operation of the White House. A fourth division was added later when William P. Clark arrived as national security adviser. This division of the staff by functions was unique in the history of the White House staff.

Policy development was handled by a staff supervised by presidential counsel Edwin Meese. Staff units under Meese included the Office of Policy Development, the Office of Planning and Evaluation, and initially the National Security Council. This portion of the White House staff was supposed to formulate policy options and proposals for the president to consider.

The task of organizing political support for President Reagan's programs and pushing them through Congress and into action was given to a staff unit headed by chief of staff James Baker. Baker supervised the White House liaison units such as those for Congress, the public, other government agencies, and political organizations, as well as the press secretary's office, the Communications Office, and the speechwriters.

Operation of the White House was supervised by the deputy chief of staff, Michael Deaver. Deaver's staff handled the support services, travel arrangements, and scheduling for the president. Deaver's influence was much greater than his title or nominal duties might indicate, however. An old confidant of the president, he was closely involved in many presidential decisions and was important to the smooth operation of the staff. Indeed, another staff member referred to Deaver as "the glue that holds this [staff] together." [35]

A few months into the Reagan administration, the triumvirate of Meese, Baker, and Deaver was joined by

William Clark, who replaced Richard Allen as national security adviser. Although Clark knew little about foreign affairs, he was an old friend of the president and so was included immediately in the inner circle. Clark envisioned himself as the honest broker in the foreign policy process and supported the consensus view of the foreign policy establishment.

Together, the foursome of Baker, Clark, Deaver, and Meese were the cornerstones of the Reagan staff. They operated as equal partners, working together to insure coordination and to facilitate the transmission of information from below and directions from above. The president met with them regularly, and they in turn worked with their section of the White House staff. Responsibilities were assigned by mutual decision among them.

That the four-pillar staff functioned at all is perhaps remarkable. As Deaver once noted, the staff arrangement worked "in spite of the fact that it probably shouldn't have worked. . . . You see you are supposed to have a chief of staff, but in fact what you have are three or four different systems that are all working here."[36] Yet despite the potential for discord and infighting, always present in the White House bureaucracy, and some tension, the Reagan staff managed to operate relatively harmoniously and effectively. The impressive string of political successes rung up by President Reagan during his first term testifies to the efforts of his senior staff to make his unique staffing arrangement work.

Unique and effective as it seemed to be, the original Reagan staff plan did not survive into his second term. Each of the four key staffers who made it function had left the White House by early 1985. Meese moved from his position as counsel to the president to that of attorney general. Clark first became secretary of the interior and then went home to California. Deaver resigned his position to go into private business. And Baker, in a rather unusual move, swapped jobs with Donald T. Regan: he became secretary of the Treasury, while Regan took over as White House chief of staff.

By the beginning of Reagan's second term the pillar-and-platform structure that had characterized his White House staff had collapsed into the traditional pyramid. Essentially, new chief of staff Regan was replacing four top staffers. A successful businessman and powerful chief executive officer with little political experience, Regan preferred to operate the White House much like a business. Seeing himself as the White House CEO, he tried to draw all the staff's business through him and to have a hand in all aspects of the White House operations.

The staff Regan created was perhaps the most centralized of any ever found in the White House, equaling or exceeding that of Sherman Adams or H. R. Haldeman. He also was among the most visible of White House chiefs; in the aftermath of the 1985 Reykjavik summit, for example, Regan gave fifty-three media interviews. A man who was used to being prominent, he did not shrink from public view, nor from asserting the extent of his authority.

Unfortunately for Regan, his highly centralized staff failed to achieve the successes of the first Reagan term (although some of the reasons for that were beyond his control), and his high profile made him a natural target when the Iran-contra controversy erupted in late 1986. Having claimed to have control over all aspects of the White House, Regan became the focus of criticism when the staff went awry. He resigned under pressure in February 1987 after the Tower Commission's report blamed him for failing to control his subordinates and to protect the president's interests.

The basic staff structure remained the same under Regan's successor, former U.S. senator Howard H. Baker, Jr. (R-Tenn). The staff pyramid was left in place, but the new chief was not seen as being as aloof and domineering as Regan. The structure remained the same because that was the way the president wanted it, which, of course, is the final determinant of how the White House Office is organized.

Criticism of the White House Staff

The steady growth of the White House Office over the past fifty years has given presidents more resources to handle problems and the personnel needed to deal with the increasing demands on their time and energy. Given the size of the government and the active role it plays in American society, the president could not hope to keep up with either the sprawling executive branch or a growing and diverse Congress without the assistance of a large White House staff, which has become a permanent fixture of the presidential establishment.

Despite this, or perhaps because of it, the enlarged White House has been subjected to serious criticism by a number of scholars, all related to its increased size and prominence. Some of this criticism has been echoed by White House insiders as well.

One major fault pointed out by critics is that the White House staff simply has grown too large to be supervised and managed adequately. Instead of being an efficient personal staff, the White House Office is a small bureaucracy that is often unwieldly and inefficient. Complaints about the excessive size of the staff are not limited to scholars; recent White House chiefs of staff have agreed that it has grown too much and should be reduced as much as possible.[37] Despite this, none have had significant success at reducing the staff while in office themselves.

One problem arising from a swollen White House staff is that the larger the staff, the greater the possibility that needed information may be distorted or lost as it passes through different hands on its way to the president. This problem inevitably stems from the pyramidal organization needed to manage a large staff. It is complicated by staffers who try to shield the president from what they see as unnecessary or unpleasant information. Delays in implementation of presidential directives as the directives work their way back down the chain of command are also a problem.[38]

Members of an oversized staff who are underemployed and undersupervised may look for their own (generally unauthorized) projects to pursue and may wind up embarrassing the president. The Iran-contra affair was largely such a project and indicates the managerial problems that large staffs pose for the president.

Critics also have contended that the size of the White House staff has passed the point of diminishing returns for the president. The overly large staff can provide more information than a president with a limited supply of time and attention to devote to solving problems can hope to use. Thus, much of the staff is superfluous, if not actually counterproductive. Political scientist Aaron B. Wildavsky has argued that "after a while, the addition of new staff just multiplies [the president's] managerial problems without giving him valuable service in return. Forcing a president to 'count hands' all the time, by making him consider endless strings of alternatives, is a good way of rendering him useless."[39]

A second major criticism leveled at the modern White House is that the president's staff has entirely too much influence on policy. Presidential assistants have always had a political role, but their input into the policy-making process is a recent development. The Brownlow Committee report issued during Franklin Roosevelt's administration envisioned a staff of neutral aides who would provide the president with objective information and options; policy advocacy or formation was not part of the staff's role. For reasons put forth elsewhere in this chapter, over the years that ideal has been lost.

According to the critics, the modern White House staff now operates as a policy-making organism, often in unequal competition with the federal bureaucracy. Indeed, the staff frequently leaves the established departments with a secondary role in policy making. While the staff rarely dominates the bureaucracy to the extent it did in the Nixon administration, it still tends to be the primary actor in the policy-making process. *(See the Bureaucracy chapter in Part VI.)*

The problem with this, critics argue, is twofold. First, the staff has too narrow a focus: it tends to see everything through the limited perspective of the president's needs. Unlike the bureaucracy, the staff has no institutional memory and may easily overlook the problems of implementing a policy. The result may be policy that is idiosyncratic and lacks long-term perspectives on what is feasible and effective.[40] Second, there is something disturbing about major policy decisions in a constitutional democracy being made by the presidential staff, whose members are unelected and are responsible to no one except the president (if the president can supervise them) and one another.

A further criticism of the enlarged presidential staff is that the presence of so many special interests pleading for the president's attention is not in the president's best interests. Over the years liaison aides for different social groups have been added to the White House, and, although a few were dropped by the Reagan administration, the majority remain.

As the staff grows, it also increasingly isolates the president from the rest of the government. As a consequence, depending on the personality of the president, the large and influential staff may only reinforce the natural doubts that the president may have about the bureaucracy's loyalty and efficiency. In any event, the president is at serious risk of becoming a prisoner of the staff, dependent upon it alone for information and options and able to be no more effective and to make no better decisions than the staff's abilities will allow.

Notes

1. A good discussion of this problem is found in John Hart, *The Presidential Branch* (New York: Pergamon Press, 1987), 96-109. Unless noted otherwise, the figures on staff size used in this chapter are from Stephen J. Wayne, *The Legislative Presidency* (New York: Harper and Row, 1978), 220-221.
2. George Edwards and Stephen J. Wayne, *Presidential Leadership: Politics and Policy Making* (New York: St. Martin's Press, 1985), 181.
3. Edward H. Hobbs, "An Historical Review of Plans for Presidential Staffing," *Law and Contemporary Problems* 21 (August 1956): 666-675.
4. The President's Committee on Administrative Management, *Report of the Committee* (Washington, D.C.: Government Printing Office, 1937), 5.
5. The figures cited are taken from U.S. Congress, House, *Congressional Record,* daily ed., 92d Cong., 2d sess., June 20, 1972, H21512; and from Wayne, *The Legislative Presidency,* 220.
6. Stephen Hess, *Organizing the Presidency* (Washington, D.C.: Brookings, 1976), 74.
7. Quoted in Patrick Anderson, *The President's Men: White House Assistants of Franklin D. Roosevelt, Harry S Truman, Dwight D. Eisenhower, John F. Kennedy, and Lyndon B. Johnson* (Garden City, N.Y.: Doubleday, 1968), 152-153.
8. Hess, *Organizing the Presidency,* 88.
9. Ibid., 87.
10. Ibid., 118-119.
11. Dom Bonafede, "Dual Capacity Brings Power to Ronald Ziegler," *National Journal,* March 2, 1974, 325.
12. Quoted by Thomas E. Cronin in "The Swelling of the Presidency," *Saturday Review of the Society* 1 (August 1973): 33.
13. Dom Bonafede, "As Pollster to the President, Wirthlin Is Where the Action Is," *National Journal,* December 12, 1981, 2184-2188.
14. Dick Kirschten, "The White House Office: Where the Power Resides," *National Journal,* April 25, 1981, 678.
15. Thomas E. Cronin, "The Swelling of the Presidency: Can Anyone Reverse the Tide?" in *American Government: Readings and Cases,* 9th ed., ed. Peter Woll (Boston: Little, Brown, 1987), 336.
16. Hart, *The Presidential Branch,* 94.
17. Congressional staff figures are taken from *Guide to Congress,* 3d ed. (Washington, D.C.: Congressional Quarterly Inc., 1982), 583.
18. Cronin, "The Swelling of the Presidency," in Woll, *American Government,* 346-347.
19. Dan Rather and Gary Paul Gates, *The Palace Guard* (New York: Harper and Row, 1974), 240.
20. Dom Bonafede, "There's More to the Counsel's Job than Just Giving Legal Advice, *National Journal,* December 22, 1979, 2139.
21. Dom Bonafede, "President Still Seeks to Restore Staff Efficiency, Morale," *National Journal,* January 5, 1974, 1-6.
22. For more on the selection process for the executive branch, see John W. Macy, Bruce Adams, and J. Jackson Walter, *America's Unelected Government: Appointing the President's Team* (Cambridge, Mass.: Ballinger, 1983).
23. Anderson, *The President's Men,* 7.
24. More details of presidential appointment practices can be found in Matthew B. Coffey, "A Death at the White House: The Short Life of the New Patronage," *Public Administration Review* 34 (September 1974): 440-444; and in Macy, *America's Unelected Government,* especially chapters 2 and 3.
25. Figures are from Patricia S. Florestano, "The Characteristics of White House Staff Appointees from Truman to Nixon," *Presidential Studies Quarterly* 7 (Fall 1977): 186.
26. Quoted in Anderson, *The President's Men,* 135.
27. Rather and Gates, *The Palace Guard,* 239.
28. Quoted in Edwards and Wayne, *Presidential Leadership,* 203.
29. Ibid., 188.
30. Quoted in Wayne, *The Legislative Presidency,* 32.
31. Hess, *Organizing the Presidency,* 88.
32. Quoted in Richard T. Johnson, *Managing the White House: An Intimate Study of the Presidency* (New York: Harper and Row, 1974), 84.
33. Quoted in Anderson, *The President's Men,* 152.
34. Both quotations in this paragraph are from Wayne, *The Legislative Presidency,* 47.
35. Quoted in John H. Kessel, "The Structures of the Reagan

White House," *American Journal of Political Science* 28 (May 1984): 253.
36. Ibid., 251.
37. Samuel Kernell and Samuel L. Popkin, eds. *Chief of Staff: Twenty-five Years of Managing the Presidency* (Berkeley: University of California Press, 1986), 199.
38. Hess, *Organizing the Presidency,* 9.
39. Aaron B. Wildavsky, "Salvation by Staff: Reform of the Presidential Office," in *The Presidency,* ed. Aaron B. Wildavsky (Boston: Little, Brown, 1969), 697.
40. Hess, *Organizing the Presidency,* 9.

Selected Bibliography

Anderson, Patrick. *The President's Men: White House Assistants of Franklin D. Roosevelt, Harry S. Truman, Dwight D. Eisenhower, John F. Kennedy, and Lyndon B. Johnson.* Garden City, N.Y.: Doubleday, 1968.

Cronin, Thomas E. "The Swelling of the Presidency: Can Anyone Reverse the Tide." In *American Government: Readings and Cases,* ed. Peter Woll. 9th. ed. Boston: Little, Brown, 1987.

Cronin, Thomas E., and Sanford D. Greenberg. *The Presidential Advisory System.* New York: Harper and Row, 1969.

Hess, Stephen. *Organizing the Presidency.* Washington, D.C.: Brookings, 1976.

Johnson, Richard T. *Managing the White House: An Intimate Study of the Presidency.* New York: Harper and Row, 1974.

Kernell, Samuel, and Samuel L. Popkin, eds. *Chief of Staff: Twenty-five Years of Managing the Presidency.* Berkeley: University of California Press, 1986.

Koenig, Louis W. *The Invisible Presidency.* New York: Holt, Rinehart, and Winston, 1960.

Macy, John W., Bruce Adams, and J. Jackson Walter. *America's Unelected Government: Appointing the President's Team.* Cambridge, Mass.: Ballinger, 1983.

Patterson, Bradley H., Jr. *The Ring of Power: The White House Staff and Its Expanding Role in Government.* New York: Basic Books, 1988.

Redford, Emmette S., and Richard T. McCulley. *White House Operations: The Johnson Presidency.* Austin: University of Texas Press, 1986.

Wayne, Stephen J. *The Legislative Presidency.* New York: Harper and Row, 1978.

Wildavsky, Aaron B. "Salvation by Staff: Reform of the Presidential Office." In *The Presidency,* ed. Aaron B. Wildavsky. Boston: Little, Brown, 1969.

Executive Office of the President: Supporting Organizations

Beyond the president's inner circle of White House Office aides lies an outer circle of presidential advisers who head the supporting organizations of the presidency. These organizations, together with the White House Office, form the Executive Office of the President (EOP). Most of these offices are housed adjacent to the White House in both the new and old Executive Office buildings.

While EOP organizations perform services directly for the president, their staff members may or may not have daily access to the Oval Office. The heads of EOP organizations, like the president's closest White House advisers, are appointed by the president. Unlike the president's personal staff, however, the top positions in the EOP are subject to Senate approval.

Only recent presidents have enjoyed the increased management and control that the EOP provides. Based on the recommendations of the Brownlow Committee on Administrative Management, and with congressional authorization, President Franklin D. Roosevelt established the Executive Office of the President in 1939 to help him manage the burgeoning bureaucracy resulting from his "New Deal" programs. At that time the EOP consisted of five units, the most important of which were the Bureau of the Budget and the White House Office. As federal programs proliferated and the ensuing bureaucracy grew even larger, the EOP became the more specialized and complex organization needed to coordinate federal activities.

Styles and Methods of Appointment

The composition and organization of the EOP have changed many times since its inception. Over the last fifty years, forty-six different boards, offices, and councils have been established within the EOP. Congress created some of these, but many others were created by executive order. During Reagan's second term (1985-1989) the EOP consisted of nine units: White House Office, Office of Management and Budget, National Security Council, Office of Policy Development, Council of Economic Advisers, Office of the U.S. Trade Representative, Office of Science and Technology Policy, Council on Environmental Quality, and Office of Administration. Some of these organizations are so large that they may be considered small bureaucracies themselves. *(See figure 1.)*

Even though the components of the EOP have changed from one administration to the next, the functions of the EOP have continued to fall into several general categories. According to presidential scholar Richard M. Pious, four functions traditionally have been carried out by EOP organizations. First, organizations such as the Office of Economic Opportunity (1964-1975) gained autonomous "presidential status" but really performed departmental functions. Second, offices such as those for consumer affairs (1971-1973), science and technology (1962-1973), and drug abuse policy (1976-1978) represented the interests of various constituencies. Third, EOP units such as the National Security Council (1947 to present) and the Council of Economic Advisers (1946 to present) develop policy. And finally, offices such as the Office of Management and Budget (1970 to present) perform management functions.[1]

The organization and structure of EOP have changed considerably over the years, but this change has not occurred systematically. Most presidents have altered the composition of EOP based upon their needs and problems, resulting in its rather piecemeal development. Recent presidents have attempted, nevertheless, to centralize and streamline the operations of EOP to make it more responsive to their programs and objectives.

Appointment Process

While most federal jobs are filled by appointment procedures designed to ensure that selections are made on the basis of qualifications and without political influence, the president is responsible for appointing staff to certain federal positions. The legal authority for making such appointments is derived from two sources: the Constitution and the various statutes that created the federal agencies requiring presidential appointments. Article II of the Constitution empowers the president to make many federal appointments with "the advice and consent of the Senate." While there occasionally has been some dispute over which executive officers require confirmation by the Senate, it

By W. Craig Bledsoe, Margaret C. Thompson, and Harrison Donnelly

generally is recognized that the very top positions in the supporting organizations of the EOP are subject to such review. In fact, Congress has absolute power to make any officer of the EOP subject to Senate confirmation.

No consistent legal principle clearly defines, however, which middle-level jobs in the EOP are appointed by the president and confirmed by the Senate and which jobs are appointed by an office head. Some scholars have suggested that the rules of appointment stem from whatever presidential-legislative relations exist at the time a particular component of the EOP is created.[2] Thus, while the president is responsible for appointing staff to the top-level positions in the EOP, a presidential subordinate may appoint staff to many other positions, including high-level ones.

A president-elect must fill vacancies in the EOP during the period of transition (about seventy-five days) from the old to the new administration. Unfortunately, it is during this period that the new president is least prepared to make the best choices. According to presidential scholar Stephen Hess, just three weeks after his election John F. Kennedy reacted to the difficulty he had in finding qualified people by saying, "People, people, people! I don't know any people. I only know voters."[3]

Public relations considerations further complicate the EOP staffing procedure. A president's first appointments indicate the tone and style of the new administration. The kind of individuals the president has chosen to fill EOP positions and the policy direction the new administration appears to be taking will be of keen interest to both the media and the public. Political party activists and other supporters will wonder whether the initial presidential appointments to EOP will reflect the president's campaign goals.

The president also has the political problem of appointing people who agree with the administration's policy positions and who will be loyal to the administration and its objectives. According to the authors of *America's Unelected Government:*

> [The president] will want to build teams that can work together when they share jurisdiction over critical issues like the economy or national security. He will want to pick appointees who can command the respect of the career civil servants and of foreign governments. And, of course, he will want people whose ability to do their jobs effectively is beyond doubt.[4]

The president is not always successful in appointing qualified people, however. Pressures from congressional supporters will influence some appointments; in fact, the number of congressional recommendations for executive office vacancies is quite large. Frederic V. Malek, President Richard Nixon's personnel director, claimed that during his tenure the White House received five hundred letters each month from Congress requesting executive positions. Frank Moore, head of President Jimmy Carter's congressional liaison office, estimated that during Carter's first month in office the administration received over a thousand requests for jobs from legislators.

The demands of political party patronage will influence appointments as well. Shortly after Dwight D. Eisenhower's election to the presidency, Sen. Robert A. Taft of Ohio, the Republican leader in the Senate, led a delegation of Republicans to the president-elect's headquarters. They complained that Eisenhower and his staff were ignoring traditional patronage considerations and trying to depoliticize the executive recruitment process. As a result of political party pressure, Eisenhower acquiesced and instructed his staff to make more staffing decisions on the basis of patronage.

Although the president may pay off political debts by filling some positions with appointees who may or may not be competent to fill them, other positions will be filled by people with whom the president has had little or no personal contact but who are eminently qualified to work in the EOP. As a result, some EOP officeholders feel a strong sense of loyalty to the president's programs, while others do not and may be publicly at odds with them.

Staffing of the EOP does not end with the close of the presidential transition period. Normal appointment intervals and the turnover that occurs during any presidential administration require presidents to continue to make major personnel decisions throughout their tenure in office. Often the factors and conditions that govern these in-term decisions are different from those that prevail during the transition period. Since most electoral debts have been paid off, presidential attention turns to finding people who will best help accomplish administration goals. Presidential appointment scholar G. Calvin Mackenzie found that in-term appointment decisions usually are based on two very practical questions: Will the quality and character of the executive appointment have a strong impact on the president's ability to control and direct the government? And will the appointee improve the president's relation with Congress?[5] In-term appointments therefore usually reflect presidential concerns in dealing with the bureaucracy and Congress, and they thus become a central part of an administration's political and administrative strategy.

Some presidents have struggled to remedy the initial and ongoing helter-skelter EOP staffing process, and make it more responsive to the administration's needs, by use of a transition appointments staff. But throughout their administrations presidents face a flood of personnel decisions that would benefit from some kind of centralized personnel management. Recent presidents have attempted to handle ongoing staffing problems by incorporating full-time personnel managers into their administrations.

The Changing Styles and Methods of EOP Appointments

Presidents, with their different needs and policy objectives, have used a variety of styles and methods for filling positions in the Executive Office of the President. While presidents have relied generally on the traditional methods of presidential appointments—such as appointing friends and colleagues—the expanded size of the modern EOP is making such methods increasingly impractical. Indeed, presidents have had to make innovations in the appointment process, including establishment of a staffing agency in the White House to locate talented administrators who also exhibit loyalty to the president's programs.

The Early Years

As the EOP began to expand in the early 1940s, President Franklin Roosevelt recognized the need for greater presidential control over the appointment process. When initially staffing the EOP, Roosevelt, like earlier presidents, relied on old friends and colleagues: those who had served in his New York gubernatorial administration, some

Figure 1 Executive Office of the President, Reagan Administration

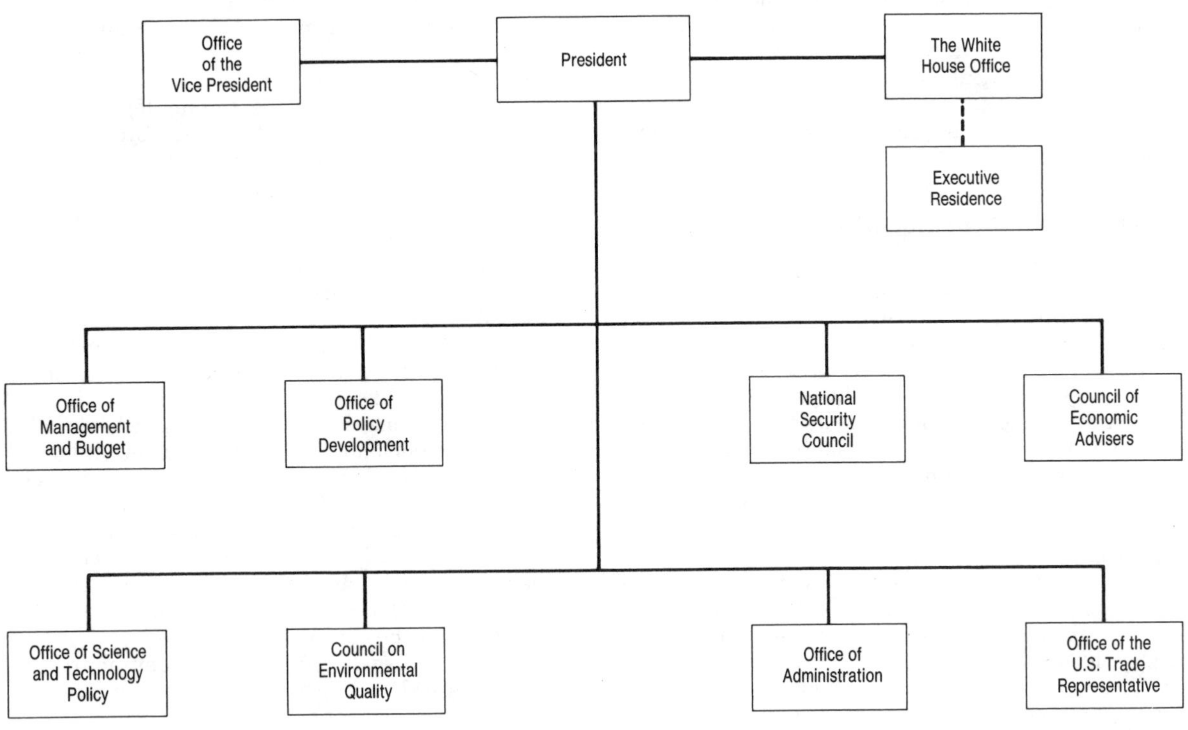

Source: U.S. Government Manual (Washington, D.C. : Government Printing Office, 1988), 88.

of his 1932 campaign workers, people from the "old boys' network," and Democratic party activists. His method of appointment lacked coordination and control. As one presidential scholar noted: "Roosevelt's staffing practices were primarily a haphazard blend of fortuity, friendship, obligation, and pressure, as were those of presidents who followed him. He was luckier than most and his network of acquaintances was larger than most." [6]

In 1939 Roosevelt designated a personnel manager to coordinate his EOP staffing procedure. Partisan politics played a significant role, however, in even this attempt at appointment coordination. As Roosevelt's administration evolved, it became obvious that the primary responsibility of the president's personnel manager was to serve as the presidential liaison to the Democratic National Committee and to certify potential appointees' Democratic credentials. Thus, by removing much of the control of the appointment process from the president and placing it squarely in the hands of the Democratic party leadership, the administration increased the Democratic party's influence over the process.

Presidents Harry S Truman and Dwight Eisenhower viewed the appointment of their White House staffs and the top positions in the supporting organizations of the EOP as an important way to control their presidencies, but they usually left mid- and lower-level appointments to the office heads. Truman took a more active role than Eisenhower, however, as he enjoyed dealing with people directly by calling them to the White House for personal interviews. Because Truman assumed office upon the death of Roosevelt, he faced an EOP made up of Roosevelt loyalists. He was determined, however, that his appointees would be loyal to him and his administration's goals, and he wasted little time in actively replacing carryover officials who could not give their allegiance to him. Not sharing in Truman's enthusiasm for the day-to-day routine of dealing with possible appointees, Eisenhower decentralized the appointment process by allowing many heads of offices to make the initial recommendations for staff selection. The president, however, always reserved the right to make the final decision.

Eisenhower had little choice in delegating most of his appointment authority. The size of the ever-expanding EOP made his personal involvement in every personnel decision increasingly difficult. Thus, early in his first term Eisenhower created the position of special assistant for executive appointments. Although the special assistant, Charles F. Willis, Jr., was responsible for managing the appointment process for the administration's executive offices, he did not choose the president's appointees. Instead, he managed the paperwork and served as the president's liaison with the Republican National Committee and members of Congress who solicited appointments for their political allies. The special assistant and his staff then weeded through the various lists of nominees presented to the president and identified the strongest candidates with the fewest political drawbacks.

Eisenhower had two major criteria for selecting personnel to fill executive posts: loyalty and demonstrated success. Presiding over the first Republican administration in twenty years, he wanted a federal government bureaucracy that was responsive to his programs. In addition, according to Hess, "Eisenhower believed that a successful person, someone who had already proven that he could run something big, would be best able to tame a government department." [7]

The Kennedy Administration

Shortly after his election in 1960, President-elect Kennedy set up a loosely organized staff, known as "Talent Hunt," to sift through the possible appointees to his administration. Composed of some of his best campaign aides, Talent Hunt was designed to reward people who had helped Kennedy win the presidency by giving them jobs in his administration and to identify the most important jobs in the administration and the best-qualified persons to fill them. After the transition a more permanent staffing operation was established in the White House. Headed by Dan Fenn, Jr., this operation reached out beyond the traditional political channels and established a "contact network" as a source of potential appointees. By drawing on contacts at the Brookings Institution and other "think tanks," Fenn was able to make a list of several hundred national leaders in industry, labor, state government, academia, and other sectors. These "contacts" then either suggested potential appointees or served as references for appointees suggested by others.

The Kennedy administration used this list of contacts to circumvent normal political channels. Kennedy did not intend to depoliticize the appointment process, however. Rather, he wanted a personnel operation that would allow him to triumph in the political conflict among his administration, his political party, and Congress over executive office positions. According to presidential scholars John W. Macy, Bruce Adams, and J. Jackson Walter, "With an independent recruiting capability the president could often find better qualified candidates than those recommended to him by his party, by members of Congress, and by the leaders of interest groups." [8] Kennedy could also expect a higher degree of loyalty and responsiveness from his own nominees than from patronage appointees.

Kennedy's appointments to EOP generally reflected what presidential historian William Manchester has called his "generational chauvinism." Kennedy felt more comfortable with people with whom he had something in common. Among the factors he considered in his appointments to the EOP were age, military service, quality of education, and participation in his campaign for the presidency. As a result, the three original members of the Council of Economic Advisers were relatively young at forty-five, forty-four, and forty-two, very close to Kennedy's age of forty-three. Moreover, the educational backgrounds of Kennedy's appointees were impressive; fifteen Rhodes scholars served in his administration. And many of his top EOP appointees had been members of his campaign team since 1956.[9]

The Johnson Administration

When Lyndon B. Johnson suddenly became president in 1963 after Kennedy's assassination he moved very slowly in replacing Kennedy appointees with his own. To Johnson, the nation's need for stability was greater than his need for his own loyal appointees—a decision he later regretted. After six months, however, President Johnson found himself filling many EOP positions and taking a strong personal interest in appointment decisions. Johnson was even more concerned than Kennedy about outside influence on these decisions; to him, loyalty was essential. Political scientists Emmette S. Redford and Richard T. McCulley have noted that in making new appointments "Johnson was extremely cautious in selecting people to meet his qualifications for executive performance and especially careful to assure their loyalty to his objectives and to him personally. Even when responding to political influence in appointments, he normally sought assurance of loyalty." [10]

Like Kennedy, Johnson set up a systematized personnel office in the White House for help in making appointments, but unlike Kennedy, he relied on it much more frequently. Johnson eventually appointed John W. Macy as head of his personnel selection operation. While the selection of Macy was unusual, since he also served as chairman of the Civil Service Commission, it helped Johnson distance his appointments from political pressures. In fact, Johnson often used Macy's civil service position to dissuade potential job seekers and their patrons on the grounds that Macy insisted that all appointments be based on merit and thus he, Macy, had a well-qualified candidate of his own. This relieved President Johnson from having to rely excessively on appointments that appeared to fulfill some political obligation.

Macy introduced a more systematic approach to the presidential appointment process to replace the BOGSAT ("a bunch of guys sitting around a table") method of political recruitment used previously. The computer system he designed, known as the White House Executive Biographic Index, provided the president with quick and accurate information about a pool of potential appointees. By the end of the Johnson administration, almost thirty thousand names were in the index. When a position opened up, Macy sent Johnson names from the talent bank for his consideration. Johnson then chose the nominee and sent the name back to Macy, who had the nominee's background checked by the Federal Bureau of Investigation.

Curiously, Johnson's appointees to second-echelon slots tended to come up through the civil service, because he found it difficult to attract qualified outsiders to his administration. During President Johnson's first eighteen months in office, career civil servants filled almost half of the major appointments, and the political turmoil characterizing the last part of his administration prolonged the president's difficulty in attracting quality people from outside government. Even though Johnson looked for loyalty in his appointees, his inability to find many staffers beyond the confines of the civil service limited his staff's devotion to his programs. Former Kennedy staffer and presidential scholar Theodore C. Sorensen reported, "Lyndon Johnson complained privately that too many of his policy positions went by default to career civil servants who were willing, available, and technically competent but had no 'fire in their bellies.' " [11] They lacked the drive and devotion to administration programs that Johnson desired.

The Nixon Administration

Early in his administration, President Richard Nixon asserted that ability, not loyalty, would be the standard for appointment. Beyond his top White House aides and cabinet members, however, Nixon expressed little interest in personally choosing members of the EOP, and most of the time he delegated responsibility for making appointments to members of his White House staff. When he did express an interest, it was usually to approve or reject a candidate selected by his staff.

In the transition period and early stages of the Nixon administration the appointment process was slow and awkward; no systematic appointment procedure was in place. Macy, Adams, and Walter noted that because of this lack of control over the appointment process and Nixon's early lack of interest in staffing, "the management needs of the president were often a low-level consideration in appointment decisions, and far too many appointees were people who did not agree with the president on important substantive matters." [12] Nixon eventually recognized the need to tie personnel to his management needs, however, and his administration developed a more sophisticated staffing system.

By 1971 Nixon and his senior White House staff members had recognized the important relationship between loyalty and talent in selecting people to fill executive positions. Consequently, Nixon hired Frederic Malek to take over the personnel staffing operation. Based on his experience as a student of scientific management and a former manager in the Department of Health, Education, and Welfare, Malek implemented a personnel system that aggressively pursued Nixon's policies by appointing loyal and skilled executives. Under the direction of Malek the practice of achieving White House policy objectives by appointing officials who were loyal to the president soon became official White House procedure.

In the process of linking personnel to policy objectives, Malek created the White House Personnel Operation (WHPO) to bring professional executive practices to the EOP appointee search procedure. WHPO was composed largely of private sector "headhunters." Following models established by the Kennedy and Johnson administrations, WHPO rated potential appointees and recommended those who expressed loyalty to Nixon's objectives. Primarily, Nixon wanted to exert control over almost all noncareer appointments in the federal government.

By developing the largest and most systematic evaluation system ever found in the executive branch, the Nixon administration effectively tied its management objectives to its appointments. Following Malek's departure in 1972 to direct the Office of Management and Budget, however, the Nixon personnel operation took on a life of its own. WHPO tried to push its influence beyond the scope of its original conception, and some of its members attempted to influence the appointment of civil service assignments, generating a damaging controversy in the press and in Congress.

The question of loyalty continued to be the most important consideration in choosing personnel for the EOP throughout Nixon's tenure in office. During his first term the White House produced the *Federal Personnel Manual,* which advised the appointment of only those persons who held the same partisan beliefs as the administration. As a guideline for appointments the *Manual* argued that policy control depended on political control of appointees:

> The record is quite replete with instances of the failures of the program, policy, and management goals because of sabotage by employees of the Executive Branch who engage in frustration of those efforts because of their political persuasion and their loyalty to the majority party of Congress rather than the Executive that supervises them.[13]

Moreover, according to G. Calvin Mackenzie,

> Eventually, perhaps inevitably, the territorial aggressiveness of the postelection WHPO began to get out of control. Political criteria were applied to appointments to competitive positions in the civil service. A variety of ingenious ways to circumvent the merit system were developed and employed.... Subsequent investigations by congressional committees, journalists, and grand juries uncovered abundant evidence of agency, departmental, and White House efforts to subvert civil service merit hiring procedures for political purposes.[14]

The Ford Administration

Because of the political situation that triggered his rise to the presidency, Gerald R. Ford moved into the White House with little planning for staffing his Executive Office. From the beginning, however, Ford played an active role in the appointment process. He initially appointed a four-member transition team composed of some of his closest friends and colleagues: Donald Rumsfeld, Rogers C. B. Morton, William W. Scranton, and John O. Marsh, Jr. In the aftermath of Watergate, and faced with a possibly brief tenure in the White House, the administration and its transition team had to go to extra lengths to attract talented and loyal personnel from outside government. Ford's participation in the appointment process, however, facilitated the recruitment of appointees.

While Ford tried to follow the recommendations of his transition team by replacing all Nixon appointees, he did not succeed as quickly as he would have liked. Early in his administration the EOP largely was made up of both Nixon and Ford appointees. This resulted in a lack of staff loyalty to Ford's programs and objectives, and Ford thus began appointing those with whom he felt comfortable; his early appointments reflected his reliance on old friends and colleagues.

According to presidential scholar Edward D. Feigenbaum, the appointments made by Ford during his administration originated from four groups: the "old boys' network," including colleagues from the House of Representatives and some of Ford's congressional aides; the Grand Rapids crowd, or those from his Michigan past; the New York set, or colleagues of Vice President Nelson A. Rockefeller, a former New York governor (they were appointed primarily to the Domestic Council); and the "New Wave" group, who were primarily young and energetic and were appointed to highly responsible positions.[15]

The Carter Administration

When Jimmy Carter became president in 1976, he already had a personnel selection system in place. In the summer before the national election and a possible transition to the presidency, he had set up a small staff in Atlanta, known as the Policy Planning Office (PPO). Under the direction of Jack H. Watson, Jr., this group identified important positions in the new administration and people qualified to fill them. After the election the PPO became known as Talent Inventory Program (TIP) and was firmly established in the White House. Like similar programs before it, TIP provided a comprehensive inventory of potential candidates for the EOP and other positions.

The good intentions of TIP were upset, however, by

Vicissitudes of the . . .

Since its creation by Franklin D. Roosevelt in 1939, the Executive Office of the President (EOP) has been a constantly changing, fluid entity. The strength and composition of a particular EOP office in the final analysis have depended on its relationship to the president. Some chief executives have preferred a formal organization; others have opted for informality. Some have relied on a small inner circle of advisers; others have drawn on a larger pool of talent. The distinction between a White House office or advisory body and an EOP office often has been blurred. Moreover, some offices were created first in the EOP and then transferred to the White House, or vice versa.

As presidential scholar Stephen Hess has noted, EOP offices frequently experience conflicting pulls between their mandate to serve the institution of the presidency as "objective" advisers and their loyalty toward a particular president and administration policies. At times Congress has tried to impose its view on the kind of advice a president needs by creating offices that an administration might not want. (Presidents, however, always can ignore such statutory advisers.)

President Franklin Roosevelt relied on an informal coterie of close White House advisers, as well as a large group of perhaps more than a hundred outside advisory bodies. At the same time, he established many new offices within the executive branch (primarily interdepartmental), the proliferation of which led to chaos. To address this problem the Brownlow Committee on Administrative Management, which was convened in 1937, recommended changes in the White House staff and the creation of the Executive Office of the President. When the office finally came into being in 1939, the Bureau of the Budget (the predecessor of the Office of Management and Budget) and the National Resources Committee (renamed the National Resources Planning Board or NRPB) were added to it. The NRPB consisted of three part-time advisers who were responsible for planning long-range public works, assisting state and local governments, and informing the president of economic trends. The board was not very effective, however, and Congress abolished it in 1943. Another agency transferred to EOP in 1939 was the Office of Government Reports (a public information clearinghouse that became part of the Office of War Information in 1942). Roosevelt also established the Office of War Mobilization in 1939 as part of the Executive Office. The Committee for Congested Production Areas (1943-1944) and the War Refugee Board (1944-1945) were added later.[1]

During the presidency of Harry S Truman the Council of Economic Advisers (CEA), the National Security Council, and the Office of Defense Mobilization, among others, were added to EOP. The mission of the latter was to direct and coordinate federal agency activities during the Korean War. "Possibly no other legal act of either the Congress or the President ever came so close to the actual creation of an Assistant President," wrote John R. Steelman and H. Dewayne Kreager of the office's wide-ranging powers.[2] In 1951 the Office of Director for Mutual Security was established to provide military, economic, and technical aid to other nations. In 1953 its functions were transferred to the Foreign Operations Administration.

Eisenhower's EOP staff, like his cabinet, was composed primarily of business leaders, not politicians, and pragmatic "doers," rather than strictly conservative theoreticians. In contrast to Roosevelt's informal and some-

political infighting within the Carter administration. While Watson intended to make personnel selection a nonpolitical undertaking, the Georgia politicians who had managed Carter's campaign wanted some political control of the process. Macy, Adams, and Walter reported that as a result "no central coordinating mechanism emerged to manage the appointment process, and much of the work done by TIP was simply disregarded." Even though a personnel organization eventually emerged in the White House, "its ability to control the appointment process was undermined by a confused mandate."[16]

The confusion surrounding appointments arose from two conflicting concerns. Like most presidents, Carter wanted a responsive administration, staffed by appointees who were not only qualified but also loyal and free of conflicts of interest. At the same time, however, Carter came into office committed to a cabinet administration in which departments would run their own show, including selection of their own personnel. While these concerns little affected the selection of EOP members, they fostered in the Carter administration a conflict and ensuing paralysis that frustrated the filling of many EOP appointments. Many of the positions in Carter's executive branch went unfilled until the spring of his first year in office.

At first, Carter took an active interest in the appointment process. As time went on, however, he lost his enthusiasm for filling executive positions, and the task of filling most of the major vacancies became one of the primary responsibilities of Hamilton Jordan. One of Carter's top assistants from his home state of Georgia, Jordan was fiercely loyal to Carter. And in seeking similar loyalty in Carter appointees, Jordan made the appointment process a decidedly political affair. This set up a power struggle between Jordan and Watson over the control of appointments, which Jordan eventually won because of his close relationship to President Carter.

Carter's appointment process throughout his administration largely reflected the conflict of styles exhibited by Watson and Jordan. Major appointments were made either by department and agency heads or by Carter's staff through the "old boys' network." Consequently, there was little consistency in their quality and character.

One of Carter's most important EOP appointments indicates the problems the Carter administration faced in staffing. In nominating Bert Lance, a Carter supporter from Georgia, for director of the Office of Management and Budget, Carter's staff either failed to identify or ignored important information. Carter demanded a rather rigorous

. . . Executive Office of the President

what haphazard methods of seeking advice, Eisenhower—drawing on his military background—established an ordered chain of command and was not averse to delegating authority. He relied heavily on the National Security Council and CEA and was the first president to appoint a special assistant for national security affairs. During Eisenhower's tenure the directors of the Bureau of the Budget and Defense Mobilization, as well as the mutual security administrator, regularly attended the weekly cabinet meetings.

The White House EOP complex expanded considerably under President John F. Kennedy, with establishment of the Office of the Special Representative for Trade Negotiations, the Office of the Food for Peace Program, and others. Lyndon B. Johnson's "Great Society" programs resulted in a further expansion of EOP, including addition of the Office of Consumer Affairs and the Office of Economic Opportunity.

Richard Nixon also established a number of EOP offices during his presidency. Among them were the cabinet-level Council for Urban Affairs (precursor of the Domestic Council), the Office of Intergovernmental Relations, the Council on Environmental Quality, the Council for Rural Affairs, the Council on International Economic Policy, the Special Action Office for Drug Abuse Prevention, and the Office of Telecommunications Policy, which dealt with highly technical questions. At the same time Nixon abolished a number of offices, including the Space Council and Office of Economic Opportunity. He shifted the advisory functions of the Office of Science and Technology to the National Science Foundation and transferred the duties of the Office of Emergency Preparedness to other agencies.

During his brief tenure in the White House, President Gerald R. Ford did little restructuring in the EOP except to replace Nixon's Special Action Office for Drug Abuse Prevention with the Office of Drug Abuse Policy. Most of Ford's organizational changes took place within the White House Office, which he reorganized to insure an open administration and accessibility to the president.

President Jimmy Carter reduced the White House office staff by 28 percent and the total EOP staff by 15 percent. His Reorganization Plan 1, which was implemented in April 1978, eliminated seven of the seventeen units in the Executive Office: the Office of Drug Abuse Policy, the Office of Telecommunications Policy, the Council on International Economic Policy, the Federal Property Council, the Energy Resources Council, the Economic Opportunity Council, and the Domestic Council (the latter, however, was reorganized). Congressional criticism of the plan focused primarily on the elimination of the Office of Drug Abuse Policy. Critics complained that the office had been created by Congress less than a year before and had not been given time to prove itself.

President Ronald Reagan further streamlined the Executive Office, particularly where its functions were related to support for cabinet councils, which he reduced in number during his second term.

1. Stephen Hess, *Organizing the Presidency* (Washington, D.C.: Brookings, 1976), 38.
2. John R. Steelman and H. Dewayne Kreager, "The Executive Office as Administrative Coordinator," *Law and Contemporary Problems,* 21 (Autumn 1956): 704.

security and conflict-of-interest check on each appointee, but the system broke down in the case of Lance. Facing political pressures for appointment, the administration overlooked evidence that Lance may have been involved in questionable banking practices and campaign conduct. After several press revelations to this effect, Lance was forced to resign in September 1977.

The Reagan Administration

Ronald Reagan, like Carter, set up a presidential staffing organization during the 1980 presidential campaign that was carried over into the new administration. Headed by E. Pendleton James, a professional headhunter who had worked in the Nixon administration, this organization attempted to increase the president's control over his administration by tying policy objectives to executive appointments. Appointees not only had to have the qualifications and talent necessary to carry through on policies, but they also had to agree with Reagan's objectives. Reagan's chief advisers believed that only then could the administration be confident that the president's programs would be implemented.

Unlike the Carter administration, the Reagan administration showed consistency in its appointments, and the appointment procedure worked well under James. While there was much internal debate over various nominees, almost always agreement was reached on the criteria for appointment and the objectives to be sought in potential appointees. The Reagan administration's stated criteria for appointment to the EOP were fairly straightforward: "Support for Reagan's objectives, integrity, competence, teamwork, toughness, and a commitment to change." [17]

During the transition period and the first year of his administration, Reagan consistently displayed an active interest in the appointment process. Reportedly, he made all the important staffing decisions. This helped reduce congressional influence on administration appointments because congressional leaders did not attempt to exert as much influence on Reagan as they might have if they believed his staff was making the final decisions.

Political party influence over the appointment process also declined during the Reagan administration. In the past, political parties had served as clearinghouses for patronage requests and had put pressure on the White House to make certain appointments for political reasons. During the Reagan administration, however, potential appointees went directly to the president and his staff to apply for

EOP jobs. This situation relieved some of the pressure on the president to appoint candidates who may not have been his choice, but it also created something of a logistical problem. It placed a tremendous burden on Reagan's personnel staff at a time when the staff was not in the best position to handle it, during the transition and the early stages of the new administration.

Further complicating the selection procedure for Reagan (and future presidents) were the increasingly rigorous ethical and conflict-of-interest considerations mandated by Congress after the Watergate scandals. This increased scrutiny not only delayed the appointment process by requiring much more complicated investigation and disclosure procedures, but it also made recruiting much more difficult by raising the stakes for public employment. Potential EOP officeholders had to endure a thorough and considerable background check. And in many cases they had to give up control of their financial holdings by putting them into some form of financial trust to avoid potential conflicts of interest. Such measures caused many to think more than once about leaving a lucrative private endeavor to serve the federal government.

Office of Management and Budget

The history of the Office of Management and Budget (OMB), previously known as the Bureau of the Budget (BOB), is inextricably linked to the development of the president's Executive Office, which was established in 1939. The budget office, created in 1921, was one of several offices to be reconstituted in the EOP where it joined the National Security Council and Domestic Policy Council as one of the three primary Executive Office advisory organizations. Indeed, the budget office has considered itself "first among equals" in the Executive Office, according to many observers.

The Office of Management and Budget, as it has been known since 1970, has far-reaching influence over not only how much the federal government spends but also how it spends and how the states disburse what they are allocated. The office is the final arbiter of the budgets that the cabinet departments and other agencies propose to send to the president and Congress for authorization and appropriation. It is a principal broker in distributing the taxpayers' dollars.

As OMB has described its own role:

> The actions of OMB touch the lives of all Americans. Nowhere are those actions more directly and broadly felt in society than in OMB's preparation of the budget.... The budget is essentially a resource allocation plan for the vast amount of federal funds and staff involved in activities that range from agriculture to zoology and cover locations that range from a lone fire lookout tower in Idaho to a housing project in the heart of New York City, from research in the Antarctic to a Peace Corps office in Ecuador, from salaries for all government employees to school lunch subsidies, and from the operating budget of the Supreme Court to funds for the launch of a spacecraft.[18]

Throughout its long existence the president's budget office has been a steadfast accountant of federal expenditures. It also has played a major role in fashioning government policy by virtue of its recommendations, its director's access to the president, and periodic self-reappraisals of its own functional efficacy and organization.

Shifts in the office's influence on presidential—and subsequent congressional—decisions have been caused largely by each director's relations with the president and Congress, each director's perception of the role of the budget office, and, more indirectly, changes in overall relations between the executive branch and Capitol Hill. But OMB is the president's right-hand adviser on what federal spending and revenue should be. The president, in close consultation with the budget office, approves or modifies the proposals made by OMB. Thus, it is the president's budget that is sent to Congress, which then deals with the spending and revenue program as it sees fit.

Projections for the vast spending of the federal bureaucracy (amounting to three-quarters of a trillion dollars, or about 20 percent of the nation's gross national product) are contained in several volumes produced by a rather small budget office staff (numbering 533 in 1987). These volumes are compiled from submissions by federal agencies on a timetable that allows little latitude for further extensive revision by those agencies. What the administration proposes to spend in the forthcoming fiscal year, beginning October 1, is presented by the president in a January message to Congress. This major document is supplemented by a thick appendix that details the presidential plans (and frequently through its expenditure breakdowns gives a sharp insight into an agency's overall goals), by a less technical hundred-page "Budget in Brief," and by other analytical documents on special topics. Congress then decides item by item, through the relevant authorization and appropriation committees and subcommittees and finally on the floor, which parts of the president's program it will accept, modify, or reject. The budget office plays a central role throughout the process.

Since 1974 the president's budget office has had something of an analytical counterpoint on Capitol Hill. In enacting the Congressional Budget and Impoundment Control Act (PL 93-344), Congress established a Congressional Budget Office to oversee deadlines on clearing appropriations bills and to make its own recommendations on government spending. Another check on the federal government's expenditures is the General Accounting Office (GAO), which was established in 1921 by the same act that created the Bureau of the Budget. But while GAO's initial mandate and activities essentially have remained unchanged (a congressional arm for overseeing and auditing federal spending), the executive branch budget office has expanded its role, increasingly injecting itself into areas that some critics have viewed as being beyond the bounds of its initial mandate of providing objective accounting and analysis. The budget office's history provides much evidence of the push and pull between a perception of its role as a nonpartisan "factual" adviser and its role as a premier executive office with an obligation to promote the office of the presidency, if not always the policies of a particular president.

Origins and Development of the Budget Office

Before 1921 no system existed in the executive branch for unified consideration or control of fiscal policy. The secretary of the Treasury did no more than compile the estimates of the various departments before forwarding them to Congress for approval. No coordination, analysis, or recommendation was attempted, and it became increasingly apparent that the procedure was inadequate.

In 1911 President William Howard Taft appointed a Commission on Economy and Efficiency to review the budget process. The panel recommended creation of a central office, but this measure was not enacted for several years, largely owing to the involvement of Taft's successor, Woodrow Wilson, in World War I and its aftermath. The next president, Warren G. Harding, refocused attention on the idea, however, and in 1921 Congress enacted the Budget and Accounting Act, thereby ending the right of federal departments and agencies to decide for themselves what appropriations levels to seek. The act established the Bureau of the Budget to serve as a central clearinghouse for the president's budget requests; the office, however, initially was placed in the Department of the Treasury. The bill authorized BOB "to assemble, correlate, revise, reduce or increase the requests for appropriations of the several departments or establishments." The bureau also was authorized to develop "plans for the organization, coordination and management of the Executive Branch of the Government with a view to efficient and economical services." The act further required the new office, at the request of any congressional committee having jurisdiction over revenue or appropriations, to provide that panel with the assistance or information it requested.

Budget Circular 49, approved by President Harding on December 19, 1921, called for all agency proposals for appropriations to be submitted to the president before they were sent to Congress. The proposals were to be reviewed for their relationship to "the president's financial program" and were to be forwarded to Capitol Hill only if the president approved them.

Early Directors of BOB

Much depended on the personality and capabilities of the first budget director, as well as his relationship with the president. Gen. Charles G. Dawes, a former chief of supply procurement for the U.S. Army in France and later vice president (1925-1929) under Calvin Coolidge, was selected by President Harding for the post. Hard working and enthusiastic, Dawes established a close working relationship with the president, who allowed him frequent access to cabinet officials. Although Dawes set out to develop long-range tasks, his major emphasis was on efficiency and economy in government agency programs, including his own bureau's operations.

Dawes believed, moreover, that Treasury was not the place for BOB because it should be independent of any agency influence and answerable solely to the president. He was a strict constructionist, however, concerning his organization's role as policy maker, firmly believing that BOB should be impartial and nonpolitical. According to the 1945 budget bureau *Staff Orientation Manual,* "Dawes had not prepared the bureau for the assumption of functions more typical of a general administrative staff agency. The broader aspects of administrative management, outside the province of economical conduct of business transactions, had not received the attention they deserved." [19]

The three succeeding bureau directors, including Franklin D. Roosevelt's first appointment, Lewis W. Douglas, had similar views about BOB's role. As a result, the agency's staff remained relatively small given its broad statutory mandate, and its effectiveness was curtailed. Douglas disagreed with Roosevelt's burgeoning New Deal projects and their hefty expenditures, and he resigned in 1934. He was succeeded by a Treasury Department staffer, Daniel Bell, who served as acting BOB director for the next five years. Although relations between Bell and the president were not close, a number of changes effected during the period enhanced the bureau's standing.

An Expanded Role and New Home

In 1935 President Roosevelt broadened the budget office's clearinghouse function to include other legislation as well as appropriations requests, saying that he had been "quite horrified—not once but a dozen times—by reading in the paper that some department or agency was after this, that or the other without my knowledge." [20] According to political scientist Richard E. Neustadt, Roosevelt's actions were not merely designed to extend the budget process. "On the contrary ... this was Roosevelt's creation, intended to protect not just his budget, but his prerogatives, his freedom of action, and his choice of policies in an era of fast-growing government and of determined presidential leadership." [21]

In 1939 Roosevelt heeded the recommendations of his Committee on Administrative Management—chaired by Louis Brownlow and appointed to study the organization of the executive branch—by issuing the first reorganization plan in the nation's history. Approved by Congress, it created the Executive Office of the President, of which BOB was a major part. A second reorganization plan established divisions of the Executive Office and gave more power to BOB to improve and coordinate statistical services. *(See box, Presidential Reorganization Authority, p. 990.)*

The budget office expanded considerably under the direction of Harold Smith, who served as its director from 1939 to 1946, the longest tenure of any budget director. Growing from a staff of forty to more than six hundred in 1944, BOB retained its position as the central budget review agency and increased its powers in the areas of legislative clearance and administrative management. While before it had been empowered to send departmental legislative requests to the president—and, with presidential approval, to Congress—only if they had fiscal implications, BOB was given oversight authority during Smith's tenure for all proposed legislation, executive orders and proclamations, and recommendations for reorganization plans. According to presidential scholar Stephen Hess, under Smith BOB attracted competent young professionals who recommended far-reaching management changes in federal departments.[22]

During World War II the budget office played a central role in managing the defense and war effort. According to Roger Jones, a former BOB official, "There was rapid acceleration of attention to the Budget Bureau's role as an organization and management planner for the President and as a sorter out of fiscal priorities and possibilities." [23]

Smith was succeeded by James E. Webb, a little-known bureaucrat from Texas, who proved to be an effective manager. "While Harold Smith was responsible for creating the modern BOB, James Webb was instrumental in redirecting bureau staff work into the program development process," wrote Larry Berman in his history of OMB. "Many observers viewed the Webb period as the golden age of the Bureau of the Budget." [24] Under Webb's direction the bureau assumed responsibility for drafting complex legislation such as the 1946 Employment Act (which created the Council of Economic Advisers) and the Taft-Hartley Labor-Management Relations Act of 1947. BOB's relations with Congress also expanded; congressional committees increasingly requested the bureau's opinion on pending legislation.

Hiatus and Reorganization

Because of BOB's added responsibilities it soon became apparent that a restructuring was needed to bring more efficiency and coordination to the budget office's operations. Although postponed by Webb's resignation in 1948, a major overhaul of BOB was carried out in 1952. Budgetary, fiscal analysis, and administrative management were divided along functional lines, and five operating divisions were established to work directly with government agencies on program, budgetary, economic, and management issues.

Although streamlined, the bureau during the first years of Dwight D. Eisenhower's two-term presidency became less central to policy making. Two of the BOB directors were bankers and two were accountants; none had experience in public administration. The president, wrote Berman, viewed the budget office primarily as "his agent for obtaining control of spending trends." [25] Yet Eisenhower's initial appointment as budget director, Joseph M. Dodge (who served from January 1953 until April 1954), was the first to hold cabinet rank. Later, in 1958, when the president named deputy director Maurice Stans to head the office, a senior budget official said it was "like opening up all the curtains in the building and letting the sun shine in. There was confidence, there was leadership, everything turned around. . . ." [26]

Despite that assessment, others expressed the view that BOB had lost some initiative, flexibility, and creativity. Outside pressure for reform was growing as well. In 1957 the President's Advisory Committee on Government Organization, chaired by Nelson A. Rockefeller, proposed an overhaul of BOB that would establish an Office of Administration reporting directly to the president. The recommendation was opposed by Stans, who suggested instead reorganizing and upgrading the bureau into an Office of Executive Management. In 1959, while these proposals were pending, the budget office initiated its own internal review of operations.

In 1960 President-elect John F. Kennedy asked the Brookings Institution (a private research organization) to study the role of the Bureau of the Budget. The Brookings report recommended that the BOB director possess "sensitivity to political and administrative as well as financial and organizational matters." [27] In fact, the political emphasis dominated during Kennedy's three years in office. BOB directors David E. Bell and Kermit Gordon were program oriented and served as close personal advisers to the president. But in doing so, oversight of the day-to-day management of the office fell by the wayside, and the bureau's operations suffered.

The Great Society and the Bureau

Questions about BOB's role, organization, purpose, and efficiency deepened during the presidency of Lyndon B. Johnson with the advent of his complex and financially burdensome "Great Society" programs. The numerous task forces established advocated new welfare and other proposals with little attention paid to their cost or how they would work together. As a result, the focus of the budget office shifted from its primary institutional mandate as budget overseer to that of coordinator of interagency activities.

The problem BOB confronted by the end of the Johnson presidency in 1969 is reflected in the figures. In 1949 the bureau employed 534 employees to oversee federal expenditures of $40 billion. By 1969, 503 staffers had to contend with a budget of $193 billion, involving scores of innovative programs, conflicting agency priorities, and uncoordinated activities.

Dissatisfaction with the bureau's performance was apparent both within and outside the office. A task force established in 1965 by Budget Director Charles L. Schultze concluded that BOB needed to "develop a clear definition of its role and of its organization and staff requirements under the pressure of new federal programs and responsibilities." [28] According to an internal staff survey, the bureau's prestige was at an all-time low because of too much attention to detail, personnel problems, lack of internal management (the director spent too much time advising the president and too little time attending to the agency's organization), a rapidly growing work load, lack of feedback on what was wanted, and inadequate skills for dealing with current problems. A number of outside studies also were highly critical of BOB's management of the Great Society programs.

From BOB to OMB

Like Kennedy, President-elect Richard Nixon established a task force to study government organization. The panel gave top priority to revising the structure of the Executive Office and White House staff and to renewing the president's expired authority to make organizational changes. Congress granted the authority in March 1969, and in April Nixon established an advisory council, headed by industrialist Roy L. Ash, to study the issues confronting the establishment of more effective executive branch operations. The Ash panel recommended creation of an Office of Executive Management and a Domestic Policy Council. The primary responsibility of the Office of Executive Management (which would include a substantially revised budget bureau) was to manage programs, while the Domestic Policy Council would make forecasts, analyze alternative policies, and suggest program revisions. *(See "Office of Policy Development," p. 957.)*

After renaming the Office of Executive Management the Office of Management and Budget (and dropping "Policy" from the Domestic Policy Council), Nixon sent Reorganization Plan 2 to Congress on March 12, 1970. It was accompanied by a message:

> The Domestic Council will be primarily concerned with what we do; the Office of Management and Budget will be primarily concerned with how we do it, and how well we do it. . . . The creation of the Office of Management and Budget represents far more than a mere change of name for the Bureau of the Budget. It represents a basic change in concept and emphasis, reflecting the broader management needs of the Office of the President.[29]

The House Subcommittee on Executive and Legislative Reorganization approved a resolution of disapproval. Some top staffers at BOB also opposed the reorganization, but the House of Representatives approved the measure on

May 13, 1970 (after strenuous Ash committee lobbying), and the Senate followed suit on May 16. On July 1, 1970, by means of Executive Order 11541, the Bureau of the Budget was officially redesignated the Office of Management and Budget.

This redesignation did not downgrade the budgeting function of the office; rather, it amplified it. The budget office's existing responsibilities were expanded, and greater emphasis was placed on organization and management systems, development of executive talent and a broader career staff, better dissemination of information, and appropriate use of modern techniques and equipment. All these changes were intended to enhance the capability of the executive branch to coordinate, evaluate, and improve the efficiency of government programs. Thus in one major new role, OMB was to help implement major legislation, such as bills to preserve the environment, under which several agencies would share responsibility for action.

Another major new task assigned OMB was coordination of the complex system of federal grants. This often involved more than one federal agency as well as agencies and government entities at the state and local levels.

Finally, OMB was asked to evaluate the cost-effectiveness of particular programs and the relative priority of the needs they were designed to meet.

Some observers have speculated that OMB was established to strengthen the budget planners' hand in questioning the expenditure requests of the Department of Defense. This task had fallen into disarray as Pentagon budgets skyrocketed and became almost uncontrollable.

George P. Shultz, OMB director from 1970 to 1972, established himself as a principal adviser in domestic affairs. Under his leadership career officers were replaced by noncareer officers who served as assistant directors and dealt with policy decisions. The career officers then retained responsibility for day-to-day OMB operations.

During the Watergate crisis, when the president was under seige and his domestic policy adviser, John D. Ehrlichman, and several others on the White House staff were under investigation, OMB assumed de facto responsibility for day-to-day management of the government. Yet according to observers, OMB, even with its expanded role, did not fare well under the Nixon presidency. "The Office of Management and Budget was a major casualty of the Nixon presidency, in part for what it did, but also for what it appeared to be doing," wrote Berman. "By responding to the partisan needs of the president, OMB depleted valuable credibility with its other clients—leading many observers to maintain that OMB could not serve the long-range needs of the presidency." [30]

Controversies over the Role and Directors of OMB

Partly in reaction to what was perceived as OMB's partisan role, Congress enacted legislation in 1973 that required Senate approval of the office's director and deputy director. James Lynn, who served under Nixon's vice president and successor, Gerald R. Ford, was the first head of OMB to be subject to confirmation. He did much to repair the agency's "overly politicized" image.

Thomas Bertram Lance was appointed OMB director by President Jimmy Carter, who succeeded Ford in 1977. Lance followed Lynn's philosophy of reestablishing the agency's image as an objective assistant to the presidency, rather than a partisan political adviser. He was one of Carter's closest confidants, however. Lance resigned after less than a year in office when faced with accusations of unethical banking practices during his years as a Georgia bank president. He was succeeded by James T. McIntyre, Jr., who was serving as deputy director of OMB.

During President Ronald Reagan's first term in office (1981-1985), OMB found itself the center of political attention with Reagan's appointment of David A. Stockman, a two-term Republican representative from Michigan, to the director's post. Reagan selected Stockman to lead his revolutionary campaign to cut both government spending and taxes after Stockman caught the presidential candidate's eye in 1980 while playing the role of independent candidate John B. Anderson in a practice debate. Stockman began his career in Washington in 1970 as a legislative assistant to Anderson.

Reagan was particularly impressed with Stockman's knowledge of economics. And Stockman's November 1980 "manifesto" on how the new Republican administration could avoid an "economic Dunkirk" seemed to seal his fate as Reagan's chief economic adviser. In fact, Stockman has been credited with being the main architect of the massive 1981 tax and budget cuts that he and others in the administration said would lower inflation, spur economic growth, and eventually eliminate the deficit.

Instead, the economy began to sour, and in the December 1981 issue of the *Atlantic Monthly* Stockman conceded that the tax cutting went too far and defense spending should have been restrained. He revealed other doubts as well about the administration's economic policy, saying, "None of us really understands what's going on with all these numbers."

Publication of the article, it was thought, would mean the end of Stockman's time in office. He offered his resignation, but instead of accepting it, Reagan took Stockman to the "woodshed" for a verbal beating. Afterward, Stockman's impact was primarily in behind-the-scenes negotiations on the budget. During the following three years he was credited with using his knowledge of the minutiae of the federal budget to help steer through Congress several deficit-reduction measures that cut spending and raised taxes.

Nonetheless, during his latter days in office Stockman's growing exclusion from the inner circle in the administration cost him influence on Capitol Hill, according to members of Congress. Frustrated by his inability to bring down the deficit, Stockman resigned in July 1985.

"He was an extraordinarily talented and capable person," said House Budget Committee Democrat Thomas J. Downey (N.Y.), who often disagreed with Stockman on policy. "He had a tenacity and ability to frame the issues politically. Those qualities will be missed." [31] Stockman was succeeded by James C. Miller III, then chairman of the Federal Trade Commission and former administrator of OMB's Office of Information and Regulatory Affairs.

Organization and Functions of OMB

The organization and functions of the president's budget agency have changed often through the years. The scope of its purview has reflected the growth of the economy and federal budget, each president's political inclinations and perception of what the office should do, changing relations within the executive branch and with Congress, and the office's own perception of its mission. Internal organizational realignments usually have accompanied such changes.

Organization of OMB

OMB is headed by a director who is assisted by a deputy director. Both are appointed by the president and confirmed by the Senate.

The office, which had 533 employees in 1987, is broken down into budget and management divisions, as well as an administrative and support staff. The budget staff is grouped into program areas: national security and international affairs; human resources, veterans, and labor; economics and government; and natural resources, energy, and science. These staff members are responsible for preparing agency funding requests, supervising spending authorized by Congress, and formulating economic and financial analyses and forecasts. Special studies groups within the division conduct in-depth reviews of selected programs. The work of the budget analysts is compiled by the Budget Review Division, which looks at the programs in light of overall federal spending. The division also is responsible for developing better management techniques for formulating and presenting the budget.

The management staff—subdivided into a management improvement and evaluation division, an intergovernmental affairs division, and a financial management division—oversees government procurement and management. In doing this, the staff evaluates the efficiency of programs and proposes methods for improving interagency coordination (state and local as well as federal). The Office of Federal Procurement Policy develops and monitors government-wide purchasing policies.

Functions of OMB

In 1970 OMB was designated "the President's principal arm for the exercise of his managerial functions." This responsibility grew in 1974 with enactment of the Congressional Budget and Impoundment Control Act; it added oversight of congressional budget reporting deadlines to the office's work load, among other tasks. The same year, Congress established a forty-person Office of Federal Procurement within OMB to handle procurement and contracting policy development. In 1980 the Office of Information and Regulatory Affairs (OIRA) was created in OMB to coordinate the administration's efforts to cut down on federal regulations and paperwork.

By 1987 OMB's responsibilities included:

~ advising the president on the nation's fiscal and economic policies

~ preparing the budget and formulating the government's fiscal program

~ supervising execution of the executive branch budget

~ reviewing the organizational structures and management procedures of the executive branch

~ evaluating the performance of federal programs

~ encouraging interagency and intergovernmental cooperation and coordination

~ coordinating and clearing with the president departmental recommendations for proposed legislation to be sent to Congress and for presidential action on bills passed by Congress

~ assisting the relevant departments and the White House in the consideration, clearance, and preparation of executive orders and proclamations

~ keeping the president advised of activities proposed, actually initiated, and completed by federal agencies, and coordinating interagency activities to ensure that funds appropriated by Congress were spent with the least possible overlap.[32]

By far the most important of OMB's functions is its central role in the federal budget process. The administration's budget proposes specific levels of new spending authority for appropriations, as well as outlays (amounts to be spent for the fiscal year) for all government agencies and functions. The budget presents as well a detailed account of the administration's program. *(See Table 2, Budget Timetable in the Executive Branch and Congress, p. 418.)*

Controversial New Role: OIRA and Regulation

President Reagan entered office in 1981 determined to cut down on the number of federal regulations and amount of paperwork that the private sector must contend with in doing business. The 1980 Paperwork Reduction Act (PL 96-511) established the Office of Information and Regulatory Affairs as a principal unit of OMB. Its task is to oversee and review the actions of all major regulatory agencies to determine whether they meet administrative guidelines for studying the costs and benefits of proposed and existing regulations.

All of Reagan's top economic advisers favored regulatory reform and deregulation wherever it seemed possible, and plans for the attack were developed before Reagan was inaugurated. Incoming OMB director Stockman called for an "orchestrated series of unilateral administrative actions to defer, revise, or rescind existing and pending regulations where clear legal authority exists." [33]

On February 17, 1981, Reagan issued Executive Order 12291, which required executive branch agencies to prepare a regulatory impact analysis for all new and existing major regulations. OMB's regulatory office was authorized to issue criteria for deciding when a regulation was needed and to order an agency to perform a regulatory impact analysis that would assess the potential benefits, costs, and net benefits of a regulation.

A second executive order (12498), issued in January 1985, required agencies to give OMB their agendas for each year, including activities such as studies that might lead to regulation. The order gave OMB authority to determine whether agency plans met administration objectives and guidelines.

The zeal with which OIRA assumed its role, however, came under attack by outside experts, regulators, and Congress. Congressional critics of the expanded OMB function argued that the office had become a regulatory czar and that department and other federal agency personnel—not the budget office staff—should have final authority over rules needed to implement laws passed by Congress. According to a May 1986 report by the Senate Environment and Public Works Committee, "OMB's ability to ... substantively influence agency regulations and to delay their promulgation is inappropriate encroachment upon congressional legislative authority and upon agency independence and expertise. ..." [34]

In February 1986 that position was upheld by a federal district court in Washington, D.C. The court ruled (*Environmental Defense Fund* v. *Thomas*) that OMB's ability to delay or force changes in agency regulations was "incompatible with the will of Congress and cannot be sustained as a valid exercise of the president's Article II powers" (Article II of the Constitution delineates the president's powers as chief executive).[35]

The result of congressional ire over OMB's new regulatory authority was a 1986 attempt to eliminate funding for the OIRA. Although that effort failed and a compromise authorized the office through 1989, the authorizing bill required that future administrators of OIRA be presidential appointees, subject to Senate confirmation. The bill also restricted OMB's regulatory oversight functions to reviewing requests for information contained in proposed rules or regulations.

In addition to OMB's regulatory authority, which was a source of contention during the Reagan administration, Congress scrutinized the entire structure of the federal government's budgetary procedures. In June 1986 the Senate Governmental Affairs Committee approved a sweeping bill that would create within OMB an Office of Financial Management, two deputy director positions, and an executive deputy director position. Although the bill died that year and was not reintroduced in 1987, its introduction and testimony on the legislation indicated that, as stated by Governmental Affairs Chairman William V. Roth, Jr. (R-Del.), "We're dissatisfied with the 'M' [in OMB]." [36]

Indeed, over its long history the president's budget office has assumed a variety of functions and responsibilities so vast that it has not been difficult to find some critics of aspects of its work. Yet the overall consensus has appeared to be that OMB is dedicated to performing its functions well and that, although some internal restructuring might be needed, the agency has a secure place in the Executive Office structure.

National Security Council

In the decades following World War II the Executive Office of the President assumed an increasingly important role in all aspects of the management of foreign and defense policy. A key vehicle used by most presidents in seeking to expand their authority in these areas has been the National Security Council (NSC).

Formally, the NSC is composed of the president, the vice president, and the secretaries of state and defense, with the director of central intelligence and the chairman of the Joint Chiefs of Staff serving as advisers. It is the highest-level advisory body to the president on military and diplomatic issues.

The National Security Council was established in 1947 to help the president coordinate the actions of government agencies into a single cohesive policy for dealing with other nations. Many members of Congress also saw the new panel as another institutional check on President Harry S Truman's power in the areas of foreign affairs and defense. The council has acted as a true decision-making body on only a few important occasions. In 1956, for example, members of the NSC helped formulate President Dwight D. Eisenhower's response to the Soviet invasion of Hungary.

Instead, the prime significance of the NSC has stemmed from the development of its staff into an apparatus used by presidents to implement their personal visions of U.S. foreign policy. The NSC staff is made up of policy experts who analyze foreign policy issues and make recommendations to the president. They are distinct from the formal members of the council. Presidents have turned to the NSC because it is subject to little effective control from Congress and is without the independent institutional loyalties frequently evident in the State, Defense, and other departments.

The role of the NSC has varied greatly over the years, usually depending on the personal influence of the president's national security adviser, who heads the NSC staff. When the national security adviser has been a relatively weak figure within the government, the NSC staff has been merely a bureaucratic shell with little power. At other times, however, it has been the dominant institutional force in the setting of foreign policy; this occurred under President Richard Nixon's national security adviser, Henry A. Kissinger.

During the Reagan administration NSC staffers played key roles in carrying out secret plans to sell arms to Iran and to divert the proceeds to guerrillas fighting the leftist government of Nicaragua. The so-called Iran-contra affair was a major political embarrassment for President Ronald Reagan during his second term.

Since Kissinger's term as national security adviser, considerable debate has raged over how much independent authority the NSC staff should exercise. Many experts in the organization of foreign policy argue that the NSC staff should be limited to managing the flow of information and policy options from the departments to the president. But some former national security advisers argue that their office and the NSC staff in general should have considerable authority to define the president's overall policy and to control the departments to ensure that this policy is carried out.

Origins and Development of NSC

The NSC represents the first institutional attempt in U.S. history to foster coordination and cooperation among the organizations contributing to a U.S. national security policy. Before the end of World War II the president was essentially the only person able to impose harmony on the often opposing positions and actions of the State and War departments and other agencies.

The conflicts and lack of coordination among the military services and civilian agencies during World War II convinced many government officials that a fundamental reorganization of the national security structure was needed. This realization led in 1947 to passage of the National Security Act, landmark legislation that created the Defense Department out of the old War (Army) and Navy departments. The act also established the Central Intelligence Agency (CIA).

Passage of the National Security Act was marked by bitter debate in Congress and in the services over the creation of a single military command system. But the law's provisions establishing the NSC as a permanent agency for policy coordination enjoyed broad support. According to the act, the purpose of the NSC was to "advise the president with respect to the integration of domestic, foreign, and military policies relating to the national security. . . ." [37]

The role played by the NSC in the decades that followed was generally the product of the attitudes of succeeding presidents toward it. As a 1978 Congressional Research Service study of the NSC observed, "The NSC was a malleable organization, to be used as each President saw fit. Thus, its use, internal substructure and ultimate effect would be directly dependent on the style and wishes of the President." [38]

In its early years under President Truman, the NSC was not a major factor in the formulation of foreign and defense policy. Truman viewed the council as only an advisory body and rarely attended its meetings. President Eisenhower, by contrast, carried out a major expansion and institutionalization of the NSC. Perhaps most important, he appointed an assistant to the president for national security affairs—a position not mentioned in the 1947 act—to head the council staff. He frequently attended NSC meetings, moreover, and relied on its advice during times of international crisis.

Eisenhower's heavy reliance on the NSC led to complaints from the Senate Government Operations Committee and others that the council had become "overinstitutionalized." President John F. Kennedy came into office thus determined to rely more on a small group of personal advisers than on the NSC bureaucracy. Although Kennedy worked closely with his national security adviser, McGeorge Bundy, he ordered a substantial reduction in the staff size and responsibilities of the NSC. President Lyndon B. Johnson followed a pattern similar to Kennedy's. Although the NSC system as a whole was not a major factor in determining policy, Walt W. Rostow, who became national security adviser in 1966, played an important role in encouraging Johnson to order a major escalation of the Vietnam War.

The role of the NSC underwent a radical change under Nixon and his national security adviser, Kissinger. The NSC staff tripled in size, to about fifty high-level professional experts, and it wielded unprecedented power within the Washington bureaucracy. Kissinger himself became the coarchitect of Nixon's key foreign policy moves, including the negotiated end to the Vietnam War, the opening to Communist China, and the onset of détente with the Soviet Union.

Kissinger enlarged the power of his office in two major ways. One was a shift from the strictly advisory role played by his predecessors to an active involvement in diplomatic negotiations. Beginning in 1969, for example, he engaged in secret diplomacy with the North Vietnamese, holding private talks with enemy leaders in Paris that eventually led to a peace settlement. Even more dramatic was his secret trip to China in 1971. At that point, Nixon and Kissinger were ready to end the decades-old hostility of the United States toward the Communist Chinese regime, but they were unwilling to reveal their intentions to the world. On a trip to Pakistan, Kissinger eluded the press and observers and flew unnoticed to Peking, where he met with Communist leaders. Upon returning to the West, Kissinger made an announcement that shook world power diplomacy: the potential alliance of the United States and China against the Soviet Union.

Kissinger also succeeded in completely overshadowing Nixon's secretary of state, William P. Rogers. He worked to exclude Rogers from key information and negotiations, resulting in a strong personal and institutional antagonism that has continued to affect relations between subsequent national security advisers and secretaries of state. In his memoirs, Kissinger revealed the bitter strains between the two men. Rogers was an "insensitive neophyte," Kissinger wrote, while acknowledging that Rogers viewed him as an "egotistical nitpicker." [39]

The conflict between the national security adviser and the secretary of state ended in 1973 when Kissinger assumed the latter post while retaining the former. Tensions continued at a relatively low level under the administration of Gerald R. Ford, who became president following Nixon's resignation in 1974. In November 1975 Kissinger relinquished his position as Ford's national security adviser to Lieut. Gen. Brent Scowcroft. Scowcroft viewed his responsibilities primarily in terms of coordinating and overseeing foreign policy actions; he did not attempt to challenge Kissinger's primacy in determining foreign policy.

President Jimmy Carter came into office proclaiming his intention to place more responsibility in the departments and agencies while reducing the policy-making role of the NSC. Almost from the start, however, there were sharp conflicts between National Security Adviser Zbigniew Brzezinski and Secretary of State Cyrus R. Vance. Not content with being a mere facilitator of the policy views of others, Brzezinski was determined to assert his own views, which centered around a policy of hard-line confrontation with the Soviet Union. Carter did not indicate whether he agreed with Brzezinski or with Vance, who stressed mutual cooperation and arms control agreements with the Soviets. As a result, the public and foreign governments frequently were left in confusion about which man truly reflected U.S. foreign policy. Finally, however, Vance resigned in protest against the unsuccessful 1980 attempt to conduct a military rescue of American hostages held in Iran, leaving Brzezinski with more influence over foreign policy during the last year of Carter's presidency.

Ronald Reagan assumed the presidency affirming cabinet government as his model. Although Reagan was somewhat more willing than his immediate predecessors to hold formal NSC meetings with the vice president and secretaries of state and defense, he de-emphasized the role of the NSC staff and dismantled much of the existing elaborate system of NSC staff committees that analyzed and formulated policy. He did not move to establish a formal NSC structure until 1982. At the same time, he designated the secretary of state as his principal foreign policy adviser.

During his first six years in office, Reagan had four national security advisers, who were viewed in Washington as relatively weak figures, lacking either strong foreign policy experience or close ties to the president. They were virtually unknown to the public. Behind the scenes, however, two of the advisers and their staffs were directing operations of pivotal importance to Reagan's presidency. Investigations of the Iran-contra affair revealed that Robert C. McFarlane and Vice Adm. John M. Poindexter masterminded the secret plan to sell arms to Iran in exchange for the release of American hostages held in Lebanon. Moreover, NSC staffer Lieut. Col. Oliver L. North, with Poindexter's approval, arranged for the allegedly illegal transfer of proceeds from the sales to Iran to the "contra" guerrillas in Nicaragua. In carrying out these activities, McFarlane, Poindexter, and North became involved in the operational side of foreign policy at a level far beyond that achieved by Kissinger even at his most active. In the wake of disclosures in late 1986 about the secret transactions, Reagan replaced Poindexter with Frank C. Carlucci, who moved to scale back the power of the NSC staff.

Organization and Functions of NSC

The organizational structure of the NSC over the years has been as fluid as the roles to which different presidents have assigned it. Other than the presence, since Eisenhower's presidency, of a national security adviser as head of the NSC staff, there has been little consistency in either the organization of the NSC staff hierarchy or in the large number of interagency working groups and oversight committees established within the NSC structure. Nor has the number of NSC employees remained constant. Reaching a total of three hundred or so under Kissinger, the number of employees at all levels within the NSC structure fell to perhaps a quarter of that under Brzezinski and rose again to 180 by the end of Reagan's first term.

One theme has been consistent over time, however: the high degree of independence of the NSC from outside control. Like other parts of the Executive Office of the President, the NSC is institutionally responsible only to the chief executive. Thus over the years, presidents have relied increasingly on the council's staff because of their confidence that it could be held accountable only to them. Presidents frequently have questioned the loyalty of staff members of the State and Defense departments, the CIA, and other agencies, who may have long-term institutional commitments that are at odds with the president's personal agenda. That concern usually does not apply to NSC staffers, however, as they are dependent on the president alone.

Presidents also have acted to strengthen the loyalty of NSC staffers to themselves alone. Originally, the staff was thought to be a nonpolitical group of experts, who, like many of the fiscal experts at the Office of Management and Budget, might hold their positions over the course of several administrations. Beginning with President Kennedy, however, new presidents have purged the ranks of the NSC upon taking office, substituting their own allies for those of the outgoing presidents.

The president selects a national security adviser without fear of congressional questioning or rejection. The position is not subject to Senate confirmation, which, according to a long-standing Washington tradition, means that the officeholder cannot be compelled to testify before Congress. It was not until 1980 that a national security adviser made his first formal appearance before a congressional committee, and subsequent appearances have been rare.

Another factor that increases the autonomy of the NSC is the relative lack of congressional controls over its budget. Although Congress sets the NSC's budget, council officials are able to exceed that limit by having staffers detailed, or lent, by other agencies. At the end of 1986 about half of the 180 NSC staff members were detailed from other agencies.

As the history of the council and its staff shows, views about how the NSC should function have changed many times over the years. Many foreign policy scholars argue that the NSC staff should not be a strong, independent force in decision making. According to this viewpoint, national security advisers and their staffs should be facilitators rather than policy makers, "honest brokers" who present the views of different departments to the president without prejudice and monitor the departments' actions to make sure presidential policies are being followed. National security advisers should not contest the secretary of state's role as chief foreign policy spokesperson for the administration, nor should they assume a direct role in international negotiations and the management of covert operations.[40]

Surprisingly, this view came to be held even by Kissinger, the foremost example of NSC power. "Though I did not think so at the time, I have become convinced that a President should make the secretary of state his principal adviser and use the national security adviser primarily as a senior administrator and coordinator to make certain that each significant point of view is heard," wrote Kissinger in his memoirs. "If the security adviser becomes active in the development and articulation of policy he must inevitably diminish the Secretary of State and reduce his effectiveness."[41]

Other experts argue, however, that the NSC needs the authority to strive for unity and cohesiveness among the competing forces in an administration. Even some of those who were most critical of the NSC staff's moves into covert action in the Reagan administration complained that the council as an institution did not have the strength to insure agreement within the administration on key issues. Critics frequently found foreign policy disarray within the administration—for example, the continuing differences between the State and Defense departments over arms control negotiations with the Soviet Union—and some attributed this disarray to the weakness of the NSC. Past national security adviser Brzezinski thought that the system would work best if "the practical coordination and definition of the strategic direction would originate from [the president's assistant for national security affairs], who would then tightly coordinate and control the secretary of state, the secretary of defense, the chairman of the joint chiefs, and the director of central intelligence as a team, with them knowing that he was doing so on the president's behalf."[42]

Office of Policy Development

Established in 1977 as the Domestic Policy Staff, the Office of Policy Development (OPD, redesignated as such in 1981) supports the coordination and implementation of policy for the White House Domestic and Economic Policy councils. It is unique among Executive Office agencies in that *all* staff members (including nonprofessionals) are political appointees. Its history is therefore closely tied to that of the White House staff (its head serves as a special assistant to the president), and it has one client: the president.

Origins and Development of OPD

In 1970 President Richard Nixon established the first formalized office for domestic policy; his predecessors had relied on ad hoc arrangements for advice on domestic policy making. For example, with the growth of the presidency as an institution under Franklin D. Roosevelt, domestic planning was centralized in the White House. There was no organized staff structure, however. Instead, Roosevelt—to assure his control over policy making—established a web of overlapping responsibilities for his advisers.

President Harry S Truman depended on a small core of advisers headed by his special counsel, Clark M. Clifford. During the Truman presidency, however, as George Washington University political scientist Stephen J. Wayne observed, "policy initiative clearly rested with the individual department secretaries."[43]

The same kind of informal system was used by Dwight

D. Eisenhower, whose chief of staff, Sherman Adams, coordinated domestic policy. Under John F. Kennedy, policy planning was further centralized in the White House. Kennedy's top domestic aide, special counsel Theodore C. Sorensen, assumed an active role in the "New Frontier" legislation.

The seeds of an institutional domestic policy staff were planted during the presidency of Lyndon B. Johnson. His chief of White House staff, Joseph A. Califano, Jr., formed a cadre of aides who played a key role in drafting Johnson's Great Society domestic programs. The idea of establishing a formal domestic policy council to strengthen the president's capacities for fomulating policy arose as early as 1964, when White House staffer Richard Goodwin wrote Johnson: "I suggest the establishment of a Domestic Policy Planning [Council]. There is such a staff on foreign policy ... yet the need is far more obvious in the field of domestic policy.... This would be a full-time council of experienced people—scholars, government people, etc. Its director would be on your staff. It could be attached to the Bureau of the Budget or operate independently and report directly to you." [44]

Nixon's Reorganization

It was not until Richard Nixon entered the White House that the idea caught hold. As a president-elect who wanted to streamline and formalize policy-making procedures, Nixon appointed an advisory panel on executive organization, chaired by industrialist Roy L. Ash, to propose solutions. The Ash panel recommended redesigning the Bureau of the Budget to form an Office of Management and Budget (OMB) and creating a Domestic Council. Acting on the panel's advice, Nixon sent Congress Reorganization Plan 2 in March 1970, proposing these changes. While OMB's function was conceived as primarily budgetary and managerial oversight, the Domestic Council was to serve in a broader policy-making capacity. *(See "Office of Management and Budget," p. 950, in this chapter.)*

Under the reorganization plan, the new Domestic Council would be composed of the president (who would act as chairman), the vice president, and the attorney general. It also would include the secretaries of the Treasury; Interior; Agriculture; Commerce; Labor; Health, Education, and Welfare; Housing and Urban Development; and Transportation. The president could designate others to serve on the council as the relevant issue arose. The staff of the council, located in the Executive Office, would be headed by an executive director who would act as an assistant to the president.

"The staff of the Domestic Council formalized the development over the last decade of a substantial policy group in the White House," observed political scientist Peri E. Arnold. "The Domestic Council staff would greatly increase the president's support system for developing policy proposals at the same time that it removed that system from the White House, thus appearing to fulfill the Nixon pledge for a lean White House." [45]

According to the president, the creation of a council had two assets. First, it placed those responsible for domestic policy making in the forefront of the effort. A second, more important asset was suggested by Nixon in his message transmitting the reorganization plan to Congress:

> The Council will be supported by a staff.... Like the National Security Council staff, this staff will work in close coordination with the President's personal staff but will have its own institutional identity. By being established on a permanent, institutional basis, it will be designed to develop and employ the "institutional memory" so essential if continuity is to be maintained, and if experience is to play its proper role in the policy-making process.[46]

Some members of Congress were troubled by Nixon's concept of the proposed staff. During hearings on the reorganization plan—at which Ash and Dwight A. Ink, Jr., assistant director of management for the budget bureau, appeared—Rep. Chester E. Holifield (D-Calif.) queried the meaning of "institutional memory," noting that the staff would be "a political organization headed by a political appointee, none of whom have civil service tenure, and the director, of course, not being confirmed by the Senate." Ink admitted that would be the case, but he said the staff would be heterogeneous: "It is not expected that they have tenure," he declared. He then added that "institutional memory" should not be "interpreted as necessarily going from administration to administration," to which Holifield responded that it must be "a four-year institutional memory." [47]

The problem of relations with OMB also threatened congressional acceptance of the reorganization plan. The Domestic Council was charged with developing domestic policy; yet the budget director was not a statutory member. Moreover, the council was to have a large, expert staff, implying that the new OMB was in fact being demoted. The administration denied that was the case, but Budget Director Robert P. Mayo testified, "The Budget Bureau makes policy recommendations to the President.... This will continue as far as I know...." [48] Another troubling point was the first section of the reorganization plan. It stated: "There are hereby transferred to the President ... all functions vested by law ... in the Bureau of the Budget or the Director of the Budget." This implied that the statutory functions of the bureau could be placed anywhere at the president's discretion.

Despite these misgivings and the fact that the head of the Domestic Council staff, like the new OMB director, was not subject to Senate confirmation (and therefore was not required to testify on Capitol Hill), Congress approved the plan.

Like OMB, the Domestic Council "never quite fulfilled the expectations of the Ash Council," wrote Arnold. "Far from becoming a mechanism for policy formulation, the Domestic Council became a large staff for presidential errands, admittedly increasing presidential reach, but providing little analytic or formulative capacity over policy." [49] During Nixon's tenure the cabinet-level council and its subcommittees met infrequently.

The president had described the Domestic Council as "a domestic counterpart to the National Security Council" (NSC), which was established in 1947.[50] Although the two agencies had been conceived as cabinet-level advisory groups, during the Nixon years both became White House offices whose heads—Henry A. Kissinger of the NSC and John D. Ehrlichman of the Domestic Council—were among the president's closest advisers. Ehrlichman and OMB Director George P. Shultz (the latter gained influence with Nixon as Watergate consumed the presidency and led to Ehrlichman's downfall) were the "czars" of domestic policy and agency budgets. "Traditionally, Cabinet officers ... had the right of appeal to the President when negotiating their budgets; now this right was to be denied them," wrote presidential scholar Stephen Hess. "Shultz and Ehrlichman became the final arbiters."[51] Although the stated function of the council was coordination, under Ehrlichman its major activity was to overrule departmental agencies, who complained that they in fact had less access to the president than before. The staff under Ehrlichman was viewed as "high handed"; during the Watergate crisis, however, the council ceased to play much of a role in domestic policy making, while the role of OMB grew.[52]

During Nixon's tenure the Domestic Council staff became highly professional, according to political scientist John H. Kessel.[53] Of its twenty-one professional members, twelve had law degrees, seven had Ph.D. degrees, and two had degrees in business administration. Each of the six assistant directors covered a policy field (transportation and crime; energy, environment, and agriculture; and so forth). In addition, ad hoc working groups were formed to address specific policy areas. Such a group might consist of representatives of the Domestic Council and OMB staffs and assistant secretaries from each of the concerned departments.

Changes under Ford and Carter

President Gerald R. Ford gave his vice president, Nelson A. Rockefeller, control of the Domestic Council. Rockefeller then installed a longtime colleague, James M. Cannon, as associate director. The staff did not jell, however, largely because of their varied allegiances (some were holdovers from the Nixon presidency). Moreover, the austerity-minded president gave the council and its staff little to do.

In February 1977 President Jimmy Carter, in an effort to streamline White House operations, sought—and subsequently was granted—legislation to restore presidential reorganization authority, which had expired in 1973. He then submitted Reorganization Plan 1, which abolished the Domestic Council and reorganized it into the Domestic Policy Staff. Georgia lawyer Stuart E. Eizenstat, who headed the redesignated office, soon was described as "one of the most powerful men in Washington."[54] Under his purview the Domestic Policy Staff launched a host of varied and important legislative initiatives, among them a tax on oil windfall profits, hospital cost-control proposals, criminal code revisions, and a Social Security overhaul. The staff steadily gained influence as well, overseeing the framing of legislation and resolving interagency conflicts. "Often, it has the last word on the shape of an administration bill before it is sent to Capitol Hill," wrote reporter Larry Light in 1979.[55] Eizenstat did point out, however, that the staff did not initiate legislation. "Rather, we coordinate it," he said.[56]

The staff also served as a principal adviser to the president. "I give personal advice to the president himself, telling him what I think he should do," noted Eizenstat.[57] Carter's domestic adviser was a member, moreover, of the Economic Policy Group, composed of government officials concerned with fiscal policy. And during Eizenstat's tenure a close working relationship with OMB was developed.

The Domestic Policy Staff included twenty-seven professionals, generally young and highly educated, who won high praise from Congress. The total staff numbered eighty, however, even though President Carter sought a leaner White House and Executive Office. Under the director there were ten associate directors, each responsible for an "issues cluster" such as economics or government reorganization; the remainder of the staff worked in one of those clusters.

The staff played a central role in formulating the domestic legislative agenda and maintained close ties with White House lobbyists on Capitol Hill. Although the Domestic Policy Staff itself did not lobby, it briefed members of Congress on legislative issues. Much of its stature resulted from Eizenstat's personal influence with the president and Congress.

Organization and Functions of OPD in the 1980s

Soon after entering office in 1981 Ronald Reagan restructured the Domestic Policy Staff, renaming it the Office of Policy Development. At first, the House of Representatives refused to fund the office because the administration declined to send anyone to testify on its behalf. To explain that reasoning, White House counsel Fred F. Fielding wrote Rep. Edward R. Roybal (D-Calif.), chairman of the House Appropriations Subcommittee on the Treasury-Postal Service: "The President is not subject to questioning as to the manner in which he formulates executive policy." And, according to Fielding, the principle applied equally to senior members of the president's staff.[58] The Senate, however, restored the $3 million requested for the office, and the funds cleared Congress.

Reagan's Office of Policy Development proved to be a leaner version of its predecessor. Its staff was reduced (numbering forty-one in 1981), as were professional titles (under Carter, almost all professional staff members were associate or assistant directors). Reagan's first appointment as domestic policy adviser (assistant to the president for policy development) was Martin C. Anderson, an economist who made his name as a critic of welfare and urban renewal. During Anderson's tenure the policy development staff was organized around seven cabinet councils (commerce and trade, economic affairs, food and agriculture, human resources, legal policy, management and administration, and natural resources and the environment). A senior member of the policy development staff served as executive secretary to each, while a second member of the staff served as OPD's representative on the "staff secretariat."

The cabinet council system collapsed under its own weight, however, and in an April 11, 1985, statement Reagan announced the consolidation of the seven councils into a Domestic Policy Council and an Economic Policy Council. The former was composed of the attorney general (who served as chairman pro tempore); the secretaries of the Interior, Health and Human Services, Housing and Urban Development, Transportation, Energy, and Education; and the director of OMB. The heads of nonmember departments were invited to participate in the council's deliberations whenever matters affecting their organizations were on the agenda. The vice president and chief of staff served as ex officio members of both councils.[59] "Under Reagan, the White House domestic staff concept has come nearly full circle to the idea originally put forth by the Ash council: a White House support mechanism designed to facilitate discussion and decision making by the Cabinet itself," wrote reporter Dick Kirchten.[60]

By 1987 there had been four assistants to the president for policy development in the Reagan administration. Among the staff the turnover rate was high. The organization of the office (always extremely fluid) consisted then of a director, three assistant directors, and several special assistants. They served both the Domestic and Economic Policy councils. Total staff numbered thirty-nine—all political appointees.

The major functions of the OPD were threefold: (1) to provide the president with an early warning of important domestic issues likely to arise, (2) to produce an independent evaluation of policies, and (3) to oversee implementation and follow-up of initiatives in domestic legislation. Two major areas of OPD activity in 1986-1987 concerned drug abuse programs and welfare reform.[61]

Perhaps because of its political nature, the domestic policy staff—whatever its name—had not by 1987 evolved into a lasting, "institutional" center of power and influence. One reason might be that, as Kirchten observed, no administration had been willing to commit itself to a "permanent" staff with an "institutional memory." [62] In any event, the domestic policy staff continued to be overshadowed by the firmly entrenched budget office.

Council of Economic Advisers

Twenty-five years after Congress established the Bureau of the Budget (renamed the Office of Management and Budget—OMB—in 1970), another organization was authorized to help president handle the economy. The Council of Economic Advisers (CEA) was a central part of the 1946 Employment Act, which created a three-member committee to advise the president on wide-ranging issues confronting the nation's economic future. The president had therefore a source of ammunition for documenting problems and their solutions.

The position of the CEA in the Executive Office of the President (EOP) is unique. Unlike other presidential offices of its stature, the council acts independently, advising the president instead of rigidly adhering to administration policy pronouncements. Throughout its existence the CEA has viewed its mission as strictly professional—that of an adviser to the president to point out trends in the economy. Yet there is an unstated conflict in its role as an "objective observer" for the president: the council naturally wants to point out measures the president should take to adjust economic assumptions and actions in light of its own analyses. Because the president appoints—and the Senate confirms—all three members of the council, the CEA has become an important presidential policy-making tool.

According to professor of public administration Edward S. Flash, Jr., in an opinion shared by many observers, "The Council of Economic Advisers, originally characterized as a source of objective and politically neutral expertise, has instead emerged as an active and frequently influential font of knowledge and ideas, which often provides a foundation for the President's economic policy." [63]

This relationship has continued to characterize the status of the CEA within the Executive Office structure. Its small staff, supplemented by a large number of consultants, works closely with the White House, OMB, and congressional committees to advocate the administration's view of economic trends and policies, to identify the trouble spots and opportunities that lie ahead, and to suggest what the federal government might do to avoid or promote them.

Although slight fluctuations in staff size and some reorganization have occurred during the existence of the CEA, its functions and character "have remained remarkably consistent," noted Roger Porter in his 1983 study of the CEA.[64] Its members and staff have come primarily from academe, usually "on loan" for two to three years. Political party affiliation is of little importance in selection of staff, and institutional loyalty to the council is not strong. The CEA, noted Porter, is primarily an advocate, not a policy broker. "It has no 'constituency'; rather, it has a 'client,' the president." [65]

Origins and Development of the CEA

According to political scientist David Naveh, "The creation of the President's Council of Economic Advisers was a landmark in transforming the science of economics into a policy-making tool." [66] The CEA was an integral part of the 1946 Employment Act—post-World War II legislation that was born of the recognition that a laissez-faire economic policy would be inadequate for dealing with the transition from a wartime, high-production environment to a civilian economy. Transition aids and new economic goals were needed.[67] In general, the 1946 legislation was intended to provide employment opportunities for those returning to a civilian economy who were willing and able to work and to promote maximum employment, production, and purchasing power for the nation as a whole. At the same time the act emphasized the government's continued commitment to a free enterprise system.

To assist the administration in carrying out the mandate of the act, Congress, in a bipartisan effort, established the CEA. It was a unique undertaking: never before had an independent, professional council (instead of a single adviser) been established to provide the president with an objective overview of where the economy was headed. Moreover, the bill's requirement that the three members of the CEA be confirmed by the Senate also was unique at the time. The Capitol Hill initiative was viewed by many observers as an attempt to reassert congressional control over economic policy making, which had been conducted rather haphazardly during Franklin D. Roosevelt's presidency. Congress also established the Joint Committee on the Economic Report (later renamed the Joint Economic Committee), composed of House and Senate members, to prepare its own annual analysis of the economy and to critique the CEA findings.

Section 4 (a) of the Employment Act set out the qualifications for the three-member CEA panel, "each of whom shall be a person who, as a result of his training, experience and attainment, is exceptionally qualified to analyze and interpret economic developments, to appraise programs and activities of the Government . . . and to recommend national economic policy to promote employment, production and purchasing power under free competitive enterprise." Each council member was to receive $15,000, and the total council budget was not to exceed $345,000.

The CEA's initial mandate—which has changed little over the years—was fivefold:

1. To assist and advise the president in the preparation of the president's annual Economic Report to Congress in January and to submit an annual report to the president during the previous December.

2. To gather, analyze, and interpret information on economic developments and trends.

3. To assess federal government programs in light of how well they are satisfying the president's goals and those of the Employment Act.

4. To provide ongoing studies and advice to the president on the state of the economy.

5. To provide additional studies and reports to the president as requested or on its own initiative.

Early Years of the CEA

Like the other EOP offices, from the beginning the CEA and its stature have been highly dependent upon the chairman's (and the president's) perception of its mission. The relationship of the council members—particularly the chairman—to the president, as well as to Congress, also has been important. Perhaps the most decisive factor in the status of the council has been whether the CEA chairman has viewed his role as primarily that of an economic analyst or that of a major voice in economic policy making.[68]

President Harry S Truman did not propose creation of the CEA. It was first proposed by the House Committee on Executive Expenditures. Congress overwhelmingly passed the measure, and in signing the bill on February 20, 1946, the president hailed it as "a commitment to take any and all measures necessary for a healthy economy." [69] The act did not specify whether the "exceptionally qualified" members of the CEA should come from academe. The president therefore received hundreds of applications from people of varied backgrounds. Even congressional supporters of the legislation were divided about whether the council's members should have solid academic credentials or practical experience—in either government or business. The former attribute prevailed.

Truman nominated Edwin G. Nourse to serve as the first chairman of the CEA. Vice president of the Brookings Institution, Nourse was a highly regarded moderate conservative with a background in academics and agricultural policy. According to Erwin C. Hargrove and Samuel A. Morley in their oral history of the CEA, this appointment was seen as an "indication of [Truman's] desire to appoint a person of professional standing rather than partisan loyalty." [70] Truman named as vice chairman, however, an experienced government professional, Leon Keyserling, who was a firm advocate of Roosevelt's New Deal policies and a principal drafter of the 1946 Employment Act. The third CEA member, John D. Clark, also was a liberal.

Differences soon emerged in the members' interpretations of the CEA's mission. Nourse, for example, did not wholeheartedly embrace the administration's economic policies, and he was firmly convinced that the economic advisers should assume a "scientifically objective" view without injecting themselves into policy making. Perhaps because he hailed from academe, Nourse found it difficult to adapt to the quick decision making and policy formulation that were facts of life for anyone with influence in Washington (although several succeeding "academic" CEA chairmen adjusted to the atmosphere quite well). In any event, relations between Nourse and Truman were not close. Looking back on the situation some years later, Gerhard Colm, a CEA staff member during Nourse's term, observed that the president might have felt uncomfortable in dealing with the CEA chairman because Truman "did not feel equal to discussing economics with a man whom he respected as a great scholar and authority." [71] Nourse himself recognized the difficulties in his relations with the president:

> After the lapse of a little more than a year, it can be said that there has been no single case when he [Truman] has called upon us in any specific situation for counsel in his study of any matter of national economic policy. While he has accepted the material which we have presented to him for use in the Economic Report and passed it on without material change . . . there is no clear evidence that at any juncture we had any tangible influence on the formation of policy. . . .[72]

In an article written in 1948, Nourse emphasized that the council's function was to assist the president in a strictly advisory manner.[73] But the chairman soon found himself outvoted on a controversial issue—whether CEA members should testify on Capitol Hill before the Joint Committee on the Economic Report. Nourse refused to appear on the grounds that doing so would jeopardize the CEA's tradition of confidentiality with the president and that the council's economic policy role was to advise, not advocate. (The Employment Act did not require CEA congressional testimony, nor did it mandate council accountability to the joint committee.)

Nourse thus viewed the CEA's role as somewhat like that of a top administrator in a large corporation—primarily advisory, with policy decisions and implementation left in the hands of professional executives.[74] During his tenure the CEA expanded its research capabilities, drawing on a coterie of outside specialists for consultation. Professionalism, not politics, was the trademark of Nourse's council.

With the 1948 presidential elections approaching, Keyserling and Clark expressed their wish to be helpful by testifying in behalf of the administration's economic programs. Truman encouraged such activity, and the two CEA members complied, thereby fueling dissension within the council's ranks. In 1948 a midyear CEA economic review contained a minority statement written by Chairman Nourse. A few months earlier the Hoover Commission on the Organization of the Executive Branch had recommended ending the ambiguity in relations between the CEA chairman and members by forming an Office of Economic Adviser with a single head. Although a version of this recommendation was to take effect later, no action was taken at the time.

Nourse resigned in November 1949 and was succeeded by Keyserling, who almost immediately set about redefining the CEA's philosophy and position. Although he played a more active role as chairman than Nourse, Keyserling condoned statements of disagreement by his colleagues. He was more interested than his predecessor in organization of the staff, and he encouraged outside contacts and informality. Keyserling also established a number of interagency committees chaired by council staff, thereby affording a greater role for the CEA in developing government programs. He continued, however, like Nourse, to hire staff analysts who were familiar with government bureaucracy and legislative procedures.

"Unlike Nourse, Keyserling perceived the CEA as trustee for the president's economic programs in Congress," wrote Hargrove and Morley. "He rejected Nourse's claims to objectivity and nonpartisanship, claiming instead that the Council was part of the administration and should act accordingly." [75] The result was a closer relationship with the president and White House staff. Keyserling contributed to drafts of presidential speeches, used the media to publicize the CEA's work, and was made a de facto member of the cabinet and National Security Council. Indeed, he viewed the CEA's role as equivalent to that of a cabinet office, which included appearances before Congress to explain and defend presidential economic proposals. Keyserling himself became increasingly active in Democratic party politics. Partly for this reason, he clashed with the Republican-controlled Joint Committee on the Economic Report, which issued a brittle critique of the CEA's Economic Report as overly political and paving a path to a controlled economy.

Nonetheless, according to presidential scholar Stephen Hess, the CEA under Keyserling

> became a serious contending force in the formulation of administration policy. . . . [F]reed of operating responsibility (with the exception of preparing the Economic Report) and located in close proximity to the President, the CEA had ample opportunity to develop and to expound its judgments within the higher reaches of the administration. . . .
>
> Congress was wrong in its belief that it could direct the president to accept economic advice; the experience under Nourse graphically proved otherwise. But it was right in believing that the quantity and quality of economic advice might be force-fed. The presence of a group of professional economists in the White House resulted in additional sources of information and analysis, which the President absorbed, often through his personal staff, sometimes by osmosis.[76]

Changes Under Eisenhower

By the time Dwight D. Eisenhower entered office, the CEA's existence was in jeopardy. The Republicans in Congress had taken issue with the council's role and activities under Keyserling. Thus, in considering a bill providing continuing appropriations for the council, Congress was uncertain whether to grant supplemental funding to continue the existing CEA or to pass new legislation restructuring it. Congress finally decided to provide monies for the rest of the fiscal year, but for only one economic adviser. Shortly after his inauguration, however, Eisenhower decided to continue the CEA, but in its previous form as a strictly professional, nonpolitical body whose primary mission was to provide factual advice. He asked his White House staff to seek out 'the best man in the country on the ups and downs of business." [77] On the advice of Gabriel Hauge, Eisenhower's assistant on economic matters, the president selected Arthur F. Burns, a highly respected economist, to assume the post. Burns, a "Democrat for Eisenhower," had impressive academic credentials as a professor of economics at Columbia University and the director of the National Bureau of Economic Research. He also was well known for his study of business cycles. "The CEA survived its crucial transition in administrations because of the increased stake of the President in the behavior of the economy, because the council members and their staff were congenial to the President, and because they provided the President with information that he considered immediately useful," concluded Hess.[78]

In August 1953, shortly after assuming office, Eisenhower issued Reorganization Plan 9, which effected far-reaching changes in the CEA's structure. Much of the rearrangement had been suggested by Burns. The major change of the brief reorganization order was to make the chairman—not the three-person council—the linchpin of CEA contacts with the president. The post of CEA vice chairman was eliminated. In a letter accompanying the reorganization plan, Eisenhower declared that its purpose was "to take the appropriate actions to reinvigorate and make more effective the operations of the CEA."

Burns, a newcomer to the Washington scene, soon made his mark on the CEA. Not only was he the preeminent member of the council as spokesman to the president, but as CEA chairman he also had the sole authority for employing staff, specialists, and consultants. Only three members of the staff had remained on board from the Keyserling era, and Burns set about filling the vacancies with a substantial number of academic economists. He felt more comfortable working with colleagues from academe, and he viewed their presence as "a means to depoliticize the CEA and establish its professional credibility." [79]

Like Nourse, Burns viewed his role as independent, but he was less objective. Hargrove and Morley observed that "if the Burns Council was determined to stay out of the political spotlight, it nevertheless took an active role in policy formation that extended beyond the scientific expertise and neutral competency that Edwin Nourse had sought during his tenure." [80] Adhering to the policies of the first CEA chairman, Burns refused to appear before the Joint Economic Committee in public hearings (a decision that severely strained his relations with Congress), yet he made numerous public appearances to defend the president's programs. "While Keyserling had encouraged policy considerations by the staff, Burns felt the staff's role was simply to advise him, providing him with whatever information he needed to make the necessary policy decisions," wrote Hargrove and Morley. "He wanted a completely objective support staff." [81] Burns controlled all staff contacts with administration agencies (the staff totaled thirty full-time and part-time professionals as well as consultants), and under his stewardship, the CEA no longer authored the annual reports it prepared.

During his tenure as council chairman, Burns developed close contact with the president, and he regularly advised the cabinet. In 1953 he was designated chairman of the new Advisory Board on Economic Growth and Stability, an economic subcabinet. Task forces and interagency groups abounded under Burns.

Burns resigned in December 1956 and was replaced by CEA member Raymond J. Saulnier, who, like his predecessor, viewed the council's mission as that of an objective adviser. Saulnier, however, was more inclined to delegate responsibility to his colleagues on the council. Although his relationship with the president was not as close as that enjoyed by Burns, the CEA chairman continued to attend all cabinet meetings, and he helped draft speeches and legislation. The council was in fact an active participant in policy making.

That role was spurred in part by Treasury Secretary Robert B. Anderson, who in 1957 suggested that he, Saulnier, Federal Reserve chairman William McChesney Martin, Jr., and presidential economic adviser Hauge consult regularly on economic issues and trends. The group, known as the "little four" or "financial committee," was a consultative, not policy-making, body. It was the precursor of President John F. Kennedy's Troika and Quadriad. *(See following section, "The CEA in the 1960s.")*

The CEA in the 1960s

The tendency to appoint academics to CEA positions intensified during President Kennedy's three years in office, beginning in 1961. Kennedy nominated Walter W. Heller, a well-respected economics professor from the University of Minnesota, to chair the council, and he selected professors James Tobin of Yale University and Kermit Gordon of Williams College as the remaining members. When the president approached Tobin with the offer of the position, the professor hesitated, remarking, "I'm afraid I am only an ivory tower economist." Kennedy responded, "That is the best kind. I am only an ivory tower president." [82] All three council members, however, had extensive Washington experience.

As before, staff vacancies were filled primarily by academicians. Most were young and lacking government experience, but they were eager to apply their knowledge to the many challenges of the New Frontier.[83] "They were, in short, 'action intellectuals,' " wrote Hess. "They knew the proper way to lecture the President, and a CEA memorandum reached Kennedy's desk on the average of once every third day. Before long, CEA members were taking on the sort of programmatic assignments that had been unknown to prior councils, such as developing legislative proposals regarding poverty and transportation." [84]

One of the president's close personal advisers, Heller was an active chairman, concerned more with policy than economic theory. According to Hargrove and Morley, "He saw nothing wrong with the CEA publicly advocating the policies it felt to be economically wise and educating the public in the 'New Economics' espoused by himself and his colleagues." [85] President Kennedy was a bit more conservative, but he encouraged Heller and his colleagues to expound their views in public congressional testimony, speeches, and articles.

As chairman of the CEA, Heller established the Quadriad—composed of the heads of the CEA, Federal Reserve Bank, OMB, and Treasury—which met regularly. (The Troika was composed of the heads of the CEA, OMB, and Treasury.) The CEA assumed an active role in wage-price stabilization policy in 1961 and began work on poverty programs. This role continued under President Lyndon B. Johnson (1963-1968), who wholeheartedly embraced the War on Poverty and continued the wage-price guideposts.

Heller resigned in November 1964 and was succeeded by Gardner Ackley, a professor of economics at the University of Michigan, who had served as a CEA member since 1962. Ackley made few policy changes. The council's staff remained small (sixteen professional economists), but the chairman retained full access to the president. Ackley was succeeded for a brief period by Arthur M. Okun (1968-1969), the youngest chairman in the council's history (he was thirty-nine), who had been responsible for the CEA's economic forecasts. Under both Ackley and Okun the CEA gained influence as the Vietnam War impinged on the economy and the president became increasingly preoccupied with the conflict, leaving much of domestic policy making to others.

The Nixon and Carter Eras

Shortly after his Republican victory in 1968 President-elect Richard Nixon announced that Paul W. McCracken, a member of the CEA under Eisenhower, would become its new chairman. Characterized as a "centrist," the new CEA chairman believed that fiscal policies (which determine the amount of taxing and spending) and monetary policies (which determine the amount of currency and credit in the country) were equally important in establishing the nation's long-term economic goals.

Although Nixon retained the Troika and Quadriad, the Troika worked more closely with the White House staff than with the president, while the Quadriad assumed a larger role in macroeconomic policy making. The CEA also participated in the cabinet's Council on Economic Policy as well as White House working groups on economic matters convened by John D. Ehrlichman, the president's domestic policy adviser. Although the council was represented in daily White House staff meetings, Nixon's establishment of the Domestic Council under Ehrlichman and reorganization of the Bureau of the Budget into the Office of Management and Budget cut into the CEA's influence on economic policy.

The major economic problem confronting the administration during Nixon's first term was inflation. McCracken was a principal force in the president's decision to impose wage and price controls in 1971. He served as chairman of the Executive Policy Committee of the Cost of Living Council (CLC), which was established to monitor the freeze. The policy committee was responsible for interpreting existing policies and recommending new ones to the CLC.

In January 1972 Herbert Stein, a council member and senior fellow at the Brookings Institution, became chairman of the CEA, serving until September 1974. Although Stein was "perhaps the most ardent free-marketer and opponent of economic controls within the Nixon administration," [86] by the time he assumed the CEA leadership he had come to believe in the necessity of wage and price controls. During his tenure the CEA continued to be represented on the CLC, the Council on Economic Policy, the Domestic Council, and the Council on International Economic Policy, but its influence diminished as that of Treasury Secretary John B. Connally and that of his successor, George P. Shultz, grew.

That situation was reversed with the accession of Nixon's vice president, Gerald R. Ford, to the presidency following Nixon's resignation in 1974. The new CEA chairman, Alan Greenspan, had in fact been recruited by Nixon. Unlike previous heads of the CEA, Greenspan came from the business community, where he was a consultant. He was a critic of government intervention in the economy and an advocate of reduced government spending to achieve a balanced budget. Greenspan's "sound reputation as a forecaster and his plans for restoring the CEA to an advisory role easily won him the support of the profession," wrote Hargrove and Morley. "Although he was perhaps the most conservative chairman in the council's history, even the more liberal past chairmen affirmed their respect for his abilities as an economist. He announced intentions to 'depoliticize' the CEA and avoid a public role." [87] According to Greenspan, he did this by assuming a low profile as CEA chairman, making few speeches, reducing congressional contacts, and cancelling monthly press briefings. And during his tenure the Troika and Quadriad all but faded from view.

President Jimmy Carter entered the White House in 1977 as unemployment was running at 6-7 percent, the budget deficit was rising, and inflation was pegged at 5-6 percent. Carter's new CEA chairman, Charles L. Schultze, came from the Brookings Institution; he also had served in the CEA and OMB. Much of Schultze's preinaugural package of programs to stimulate the economy (returning to full employment without inflation) was adopted by the Carter administration. "It is difficult to imagine a selection for the CEA chairmanship who could have won more respect or have been more in the mainstream of pragmatic, liberal approaches to economic policy," wrote Hargrove and Morley.[88] Schultze has been described as a liberal Democrat and a Keynesian economist who believed that government could actively influence the economy through fiscal policy to insure healthy expansion. But he also was known as a hard-headed skeptic when it came to assessing the value of government spending programs.

Congress adopted Schultze's plan to stimulate the economy quickly through tax refunds that would generate business and consumer confidence. Testifying before the House Budget Committee in January 1977, the CEA chairman noted, "This package has been designed to tread prudently between the twin risks of over- and under-stimulation." [89]

Regulatory reform was another concern of the president and his economic adviser. As chairman of both the CEA and the Regulatory Analysis Review Group, Schultze focused attention on the inflationary consequences of many proposed regulations and favored in some cases the use of taxation, rather than specific standard setting, as a cost-effective approach to compliance. Regulatory reform became even more of a major issue during Ronald Reagan's presidency, but primary responsibility for it was lodged in OMB. *(See "Office of Management and Budget," p. 950, in this chapter.)*

The CEA Under Reagan

Reagan's first appointment to the CEA leadership, Murray Weidenbaum, reflected the president's view that one of the major tasks of his administration was to cut down on federal regulations. Weidenbaum, a former assistant secretary of the Treasury and head of the Center for the Study of American Business at Washington University in St. Louis, was a conservative who advocated a cost-benefit analysis approach to weeding out unnecessary government rules.

It soon became apparent, however, that Weidenbaum's talents would be better used in a position in which he had a decisive role in the mission to prune federal regulations—and that position had been created in the OMB's new Office of Information and Regulatory Affairs. Weidenbaum also had come under attack for his 1981 congressional testimony that played down the importance of deficits, appearing to contradict years of Republican rhetoric. Even though White House spokespersons later denied that the remarks reflected administration policy, stunned Senate Republicans denounced the CEA comments as "incredible," "disheartening," and "foolish." [90]

Weidenbaum was succeeded by Martin S. Feldstein, a professor at Harvard University and president of the National Bureau of Economic Research. Feldstein served as CEA chairman for almost two years (from October 1982 to July 1984), but, ironically, his outspoken calls for deficit reduction above all issues—including the need to increase defense spending—angered other administration officials.

Feldstein's replacement was an undersecretary of the Treasury, Beryl W. Sprinkel, who was confirmed in April 1985. Sprinkel, a former Chicago bank executive and economics professor, had close personal ties to Donald T. Regan, the president's chief of staff. Although Sprinkel had direct contacts with the president, Treasury Secretary James A. Baker III was the Reagan administration's chief economic spokesperson. Sprinkel's first economic forecast, envisioning strong economic growth, was attacked as excessively rosy by members of Congress when it was presented to them in February 1986. Other economists appearing before the Joint Economic Committee were equally skeptical about the CEA's projected economic growth rate.

The controversy continued in 1987. In presenting the annual Economic Report to Congress, Sprinkel observed that "the U.S. economy demonstrates continued strength as it moves into the fifth year of the current economic expansion, but ... important sectoral and structural problems remain." Those problems, discussed in the report, included the large and persistent budget and trade deficits.[91]

Organization and Functions of the CEA

The activities of the president's Council of Economic Advisers include:

- Briefing the president on overall economic policy objectives and what programs needed to be implemented.
- Preparing an annual economic report to the president and an Economic Report of the President for submission to Congress in January.
- Informing the president on a continuing basis of major policy issues, including international economic issues.
- Chairing an interagency forecasting group that included the Treasury and OMB for developing economic projections.
- Participating in the cabinet-level Council on Economic Policy to discuss the economic effects of tax reform, trade and balance-of-payments issues, international policy coordination, and budget reform. The CEA participated as well in the cabinet-level Domestic Policy Council and dealt with such issues as agricultural problems, regulatory and antitrust reforms, catastrophic health insurance, welfare reform, energy policy, transportation and communications regulation, and tax policy.

The CEA chairman also headed the economic policy committee of the twenty-five-nation Organization for Economic Cooperation and Development (OECD) and other OECD committees as well. Moreover, the CEA chairman was particularly active in U.S.-Japan meetings to discuss trade issues.

In 1986 the professional staff of the three-member council consisted of a special assistant, a senior statistician, twelve senior staff economists, two staff economists, four junior economists, and one research assistant. There were eleven support staff members.

Most CEA heads and staff members have been outspoken in their belief that the council's staff should remain small and transitory (most have tenured positions elsewhere). Indeed, the small size of the staff, and its transitory nature, have been considered advantages. The party affiliations of staff members remain of little importance.

The CEA has continued to avoid operational responsibility for programs, serving instead as an adviser to the president to forecast economic trends and provide analyses of issues. The CEA's position on administration economic policy making has always depended upon three factors: the quality of its advice, the chairman's perception of CEA's role, and the relation between the president and the council (particularly the chairman). But these factors have their nuances. "The CEA was created by Congress in 1946 to force presidents to accept economic advice in a particular form. Yet they have chosen to use or not use the CEA largely on the basis of whether they preferred working with an individual council chairman to receiving economic advice from other sources," wrote Hess.[92] According to former CEA chairman Arthur Okun,

> When the President's economists decide to go on public record, they cannot serve two masters. They cannot speak for both the President and for the [economics] profession. And they cannot speak for the Profession publicly and still maintain confidence and rapport internally with the President. The choice should be clear. It is far more important for society and for the Profession to have economists who maintain rapport with the President and thus have the greatest influence on the inside.[93]

Office of the U.S. Trade Representative

The Office of the Special Representative for Trade Negotiations was established in 1963 and redesignated the Office of the U.S. Trade Representative in 1980. The original office was created in response to a perception that a presidential spokesperson was needed to deal with the increasingly complex issues facing the nation in its economic contacts with foreign nations. Almost twenty-five years later that perception remained unaltered, but the circumstances were drastically reversed. In 1962 the government's trade philosophy—both in Congress and within the Kennedy administration—advocated opening the doors to international transactions and promoting free trade. By 1987, faced with spiraling balance-of-payments deficits—brought on primarily by imports from Japan and the other fast-growing economies of Singapore, South Korea, and Taiwan—the United States confronted a crisis situation. The Reagan administration U.S. trade representative, Clayton K. Yeutter, found himself in the eye of a cyclone, with a mandate to fend off congressional demands for retaliation, advance the administration's commitment to fair and free trade, and retain the good will of the major trading partners of the United States, while trying to persuade them to modify their own protectionist practices.

Origins and Development of the Trade Office

The removal of barriers to the free flow of international trade was a principal goal of American foreign policy for more than two decades following World War II.[94] With little variation, presidents Harry S Truman, Dwight D. Eisenhower, John F. Kennedy, and Lyndon B. Johnson held that a liberal trade policy, no less than foreign aid, was an essential means of establishing a more secure and prosperous world. Each was forced to do battle, however, with an array of protectionist interests whose pressures on Congress complemented a historic legislative view that tariffs were a domestic matter, not to be subordinated to foreign policy objectives.

By 1962 there were new and compelling reasons for the United States to champion the free flow of trade. Although exports and imports remained small in relation to a gross national product of more than $500 billion, they occupied an increasingly important role in an economy beset by a slow rate of growth. Moreover, despite its substantial and continuing surplus of exports over imports, the United States was experiencing severe deficits in its total international accounts because of heavy expenditures abroad for military and other purposes. Of the several alternatives for bringing the payments deficit under control, rapid expansion of exports was in many ways the most desirable.

Creation of the Trade Office

The expansion of exports depended, however, upon reversal of a new trend toward protectionism abroad, as evidenced in the common tariff wall constructed by the six-member European Community (EC or Common Market) in 1957. In 1962 the large economic stake of the United States in the freest possible access to world markets, as well as the overriding political interest of the United States in building a strong and interdependent free world, led Congress to authorize President Kennedy to take a new initiative in behalf of trade leberalization. Even though some U.S. industries were unable or unwilling to compete with the products of other nations, the Trade Expansion Act of 1962 reflected the majority view that freer trade was no longer a choice but a necessity for the United States.

In a special message sent to Capitol Hill on January 25, 1962, Kennedy asked Congress for unprecedented authority to negotiate with the Common Market for reciprocal tariff concessions. With the help of strong bipartisan support in the business community and concessions to potentially obstructive interests, Kennedy finally got substantially all that he wanted in the Trade Expansion Act of 1962 (PL 88-794). The act granted the president far-reaching tariff-cutting authority and provided safeguards against damage to American industry and agriculture. The act further authorized the formation of a cabinet-level Interagency Trade Organization and the establishment of the post of special representative for trade negotiations, who would act as the chief U.S. spokesperson in trade talks. On January 15, 1963, Kennedy appointed Christian A. Herter, secretary of state under Eisenhower, to the new post. According to a former trade negotiator, Herter "had supported the purposes of the bill from the outset and had the courage to resist any efforts of special interest groups to divert him from achieving them."[95] Herter was the chief U.S. negotiator for the "Kennedy Round" of tariff-cutting talks (1963-1967), undertaken under the auspices of the General Agreement on Tariffs and Trade (GATT, formed in 1947, had a membership of about one hundred nations in 1987).

1974 Trade Act

By the late 1960s and early 1970s competition for world markets was growing, the U.S. share of world trade was in persistent decline, and protectionist sentiment was on the rise. Like his predecessors, however, President Richard Nixon remained committed to free trade, although conflicts with the EC and Japan, in particular, over trade reciprocity and quotas were occurring more frequently. In late 1969 the president sent Congress legislation that would have permitted him to retain his tariff-cutting authority while increasing assistance to U.S. businesses harmed by imports. But the protectionist mood on Capitol Hill was strong, and by the end of 1970 the administration's bill had been altered severely by the House of Representatives. The measure never reached the president's desk.

In 1973 Nixon resubmitted proposals for new trade-negotiating authority, largely in response to growing trade deficits and as the major industrial nations were preparing for another series of trade negotiations (known as the Tokyo Round). In December 1974, after a year's delay, Congress passed the 1974 Trade Act (PL 93-618) which authorized U.S. participation in the tariff negotiations and established a cabinet-level special trade representative's office within the Executive Office of the President. The office was given the powers and responsibilities needed to coordinate trade policy.

Carter Reorganization

The Tokyo Round of negotiations on reducing nontariff barriers to trade was completed in 1979. Submitted by President Jimmy Carter that same year and quickly approved by Congress, the bill (PL 96-39) implementing the agreement consolidated and coordinated U.S. trade policy making.[96] Carter effected the consolidation and coordination by Executive Order 12188 in January 1980. Under this act, the U.S. trade representative was designated as the nation's chief trade negotiator and U.S. representative in the major international trade organizations. The act also transferred domestic oversight of most trade programs from the Treasury to the Department of Commerce, including responsiblitiy for determining whether countervailing tariffs or antidumping duties should be imposed against what were considered unfair trade practices or excessive foreign imports. Carter's final trade reorganization plan was close to House proposals but fell short of demands made by the Senate for a separate trade department.

Reagan's Trade Representatives

President Ronald Reagan continued his predecessors' commitment to free trade, despite the deepening trade deficit, mounting concern over the competitiveness of U.S. products abroad, and growing criticism about the restrictiveness of other nations' markets. All three issues applied primarily to Japan. Reagan's first trade representative, William E. Brock III, remained an advocate of free trade, As he noted in January 1983: "In recent years four out of five of the new U.S. jobs in manufacturing have been created by international trade. One out of every three acres planted by American farmers is producing crops for export internationally and the potential for growth is unlimited." [97] But Brock also summarized the ironies and difficult choices in the free protectionism versus trade debates. "Everyone is against protectionism in the abstract," he said in 1983. "That is easy. It is another matter to make the hard, courageous choices when it is your industry or your business that appears to be hurt by foreign competition." [98]

Brock was succeeded in June 1985 by Clayton Yeutter, who was head of the Chicago Mercantile Exchange when nominated. Yeutter had served as deputy special trade representative during the administration of Gerald R. Ford and as assistant secretary for agriculture under Nixon. In his confirmation hearings Yeutter said he was prepared to take a more aggressive approach to dealing with trade pressures. He pledged to step up enforcement of existing statutes, including provisions that protected U.S. business from foreign products sold in the United States at unfairly low prices. And he emphasized the need for international trade talks, identifying the biggest problem as that of convincing other nations to lower nontariff barriers, such as foreign government purchasing programs, that discriminated against U.S. exports. To set the agenda for trade talks, Yeutter planned to consult actively with Congress and the business community. He also indicated that he was prepared to take a pragmatic approach to trade.[99]

Organization and Functions of the Trade Office

The trade office is headed by the U.S. trade representative (USTR), a cabinet-level official with the rank of ambassador, who is directly responsible to the president and Congress.[100] The representative is confirmed by the Senate and thus testifies before congressional committees. Of the three deputy representatives, who also have ambassadorial rank, two are located in Washington, D.C., and one is in Geneva, Switzerland (GATT headquarters).

The USTR is the president's chief adviser on international trade policy and is responsible for developing this policy and coordinating its implementation. The holder of this position also acts as the nation's chief negotiator for international trade agreements. The USTR also chairs the cabinet-level Trade Policy Committee and three interagency committees: the Trade Policy Review Group, the Trade Negotiations Committee, and the Trade Policy Staff Committee (which has forty-four subcommittees). The USTR serves as an ex officio member of the boards of directors of the Export-Inport Bank and the Overseas Private Investment Corporation and sits on the National Advisory Council for International Monetary and Financial Policy.

With the advice of the cabinet-level Economic Policy Council of which it is a member, the USTR office is responsible for policy guidance on issues related to international trade, including the expansion of U.S. exports; matters concerning GATT; overall U.S. trade policy on unfair trade practices, to the extent permitted by law; international trade issues involving energy; and direct investment matters, to the extent they are trade related.

As the principal trade negotiator for the United States, the U.S. trade representative is the chief U.S. representative at international negotiations. These include all activities of GATT; discussions, meetings, and negotiations within the Organization for Economic Cooperation and Development (OECD) on matters affecting trade and commodity issues; meetings of the United Nations Conference on Trade and Development (UNCTAD) and other multilateral institutions dealing with trade and commodity issues; and other bilateral and multilateral negotiations where trade, including East-West trade or commodities, is the primary issue.

The deputy USTR in Geneva is the U.S. representative to GATT and is responsible for negotiations on commerce and trade under UNCTAD. One of the deputy trade representatives located in Washington, D.C., oversees trade policy coordination and bilateral and multilateral negotiations outside GATT and UNCTAD. This official is also responsible for USTR's offices for trade policy and anslysis, trade policy coordination, and bilateral trade negotiations, as well as its region-specific offices (Canada/Mexico, Japan/China, Latin America/Caribbean/Africa, Asia and the Pacific). The second deputy located in Washington is responsible for sectoral and external affairs and management, including industry and services, agriculture and commodities, congressional affairs, public affairs and private sector liaison, management, and computer operations. The chief textile negotiator, who also has ambassadorial rank, has primary responsibility for negotiating textile agreements and representing the government in matters related to textile trade.

Finally, the USTR office includes a general counsel and a counselor to the trade representative who provides advice on trade policy and represents the United States on the OECD trade committee. In 1987 the staff of the office of the U.S. Trade Representative numbered 146.

Outlook for the Trade Office in the Late 1980s

During Reagan's second term in office, trade policy became a central concern. One principal area of contention was U.S.-Japan trade relations. In May 1987, in response to what it perceived as unfair trading practices, particularly on the part of Japan, the House of Representatives passed comprehensive legislation designed to toughen U.S. actions against unfair trading practices abroad while improving U.S. competitiveness at home. Although Yeutter and others criticized the House bill, they shied away from threatening a presidential veto. In a March 16, 1987, speech to the National Grain and Feed Association, the trade representative cautioned against "get tough" actions that might provoke retaliation.[101] Three days earlier in an address to the Heritage Foundation, Yeutter had asserted that the administration had confronted unfair foreign trade practices "more aggressively than has any administration in history," was negotiating stronger international trade agreements that will provide more opportunities for American exporters to compete in foreign markets, and was striving "to improve the international economic climate for exports by cutting our own budget deficit."[102] Finally, in an April 7 address at the University of Chicago, Yeutter declared that the Uruguay Round of tariff negotiations, then underway, was "the most significant multilateral trade undertaking in 40 years. A successful conclusion of the Uruguay Round will strengthen GATT and create new rules in areas of critical importance to the United States, including trade in agriculture and services, intellectual property protection and investment."[103]

In August 1988 the Senate gave final approval to a sweeping revision of U.S. trade law, which Reagan subsequently signed. The bill for the first time defined trade policy comprehensively, reaching well beyond traditional remedies of tariffs and quotas to include such matters as currency imbalances and third world debt, patent law, and education. The legislation had received bipartisan support from its origins in 1985, when congressional anger over accelerating trade deficits and currency imbalances, and at administration reluctance to intervene, was at its height.

But for all its bipartisan support, the trade bill moved only fitfully through Congress. Although a similar bill was approved by both chambers in April 1988, President Reagan vetoed it primarily because the legislation included a controversial requirement that certain industries give workers sixty days notice of plant closings and mass layoffs. In June Democratic leaders reintroduced the bill without the plant closing requirement, which was introduced in separate legislation. Reagan signed both measures. "This [trade bill] is not going to solve all problems," said Democratic vice-presidential nominee and Senate Finance Committee chairman Lloyd Bentsen (D-Texas). "It's not going to turn the trade deficit around, but it's a plus."[104]

Office of Science and Technology Policy

Although it was formally established in 1976, the president's Office of Science and Technology Policy (OSTP) has had a longer history that began during World War II, when the government recognized that science and technology were vital to the nation's military capabilities.

According to the National Science and Technology Policy, Organizations, and Priorities Act of 1976 (PL 94-282), OSTP provides "a source of scientific and technological analysis and judgment for the president with respect to major policies, plans and programs of the federal government." Its mission became even more central to the government during the late 1970s and 1980s as scientific and technological breakthroughs in other parts of the world challenged America's leadership. The urgency of the situation was addressed in stark terms by the OSTP in its 1983-1984 biennial report:

> A quarter century ago, U.S. industry had few worries about competition. The United States dominated essentially all industrial technologies and had always been able to develop and introduce them at its own pace. Today we must use our technological resources much more aggressively.
>
> In the decades after World War II, the United States built the world's largest research and development capability, primarily through investment of Federal money.... Industry was strongly stimulated by and benefited from this Federal role. But the commercial market for technology has expanded tremendously in the past decade.... Non-Federal spending for research and development reached that of the Federal Government in 1978 and has been rising ever since.
>
> Today, Federal research and development [R & D] spending is about 46 percent of the national total. It is industry, not Government, that is pushing hardest at technological frontiers in many areas.[105]

Although OSTP has tried to encourage the government to participate in a wide range of R & D efforts, the science counselors in the Executive Office of the President (EOP), like the academicians who generally compose the Council of Economic Advisers, have found it often difficult to make their voices heard in the highly political and bureaucratic environment of the nation's capital.

Origins and Development of OSTP

During World War II a number of White House advisory panels were created, primarily to serve the war effort. In 1950 President Harry S Truman signed a bill establishing the National Science Foundation (NSF); a year later he appointed a Science Advisory Committee in the Office of Defense Mobilization. That panel was a forerunner of President Dwight D. Eisenhower's Presidential Science Advisory Committee (PSAC). According to Lee A. Dubridge, President Richard Nixon's science adviser, "PSAC and the science adviser were regarded as the capstone of the government's scientific advisory structure...." The president, said Dubridge, "found it very helpful to have an unbiased, broadly-based and distinguished scientific group helping him to unravel the many technical problems which he faced in defense, space, and various civilian enterprises." Under Eisenhower, concluded Dubridge, "PSAC developed some extraordinarily penetrating and far-reaching recommendations." [106]

The need to upgrade U.S. scientific efforts was perceived as even more urgent after the Soviet Union launched the *Sputnik I* satellite in 1957. Americans, who generally had prided their country for being in the forefront of scientific and technological know-how, were shocked that their major adversary appeared to be taking the lead in space efforts. In light of that concern PSAC recommended creation of the National Aeronautics and Space Administration (NASA).

According to James R. Killian, Jr., science adviser to Eisenhower and chairman of PSAC (after *Sputnik I,* he was given the title of special assistant to the president for science and technology), PSAC worked very closely with the president, the National Security Council, and the budget bureau. Most PSAC members were nonpartisan, with no political ambitions (sometimes they were criticized for being too conservative and unimaginative). "They were motivated primarily by a feeling of obligation to make their specialized learning and skills available to the government in time of need," said Killian.[107]

After John F. Kennedy's election to the presidency in 1960, the position of science adviser was further upgraded. Jerome B. Wiesner, Kennedy's science adviser and chairman of PSAC, found the president extremely receptive to science advice. Indeed, according to Wiesner's successor, Donald F. Hornig, the science adviser "became the White House contact point for the entire governmental science apparatus." [108]

Reorganization Plan 2, implemented in 1962, institutionalized the Office of Science and Technology (OST) in the Executive Office of the President, with its own budget and staff. Its director also served as an official special science adviser to the president, which gave the office more statutory responsibility. Wiesner and PSAC members were apprehensive that the move from the White House Office to EOP might downgrade their access to and influence with the president. Yet, under Kennedy OST took on greater responsibility for energy, environment, and natural resource policies, as well as other civilian technology concerns. At the same time the science office continued to be involved in arms control, defense, and space issues.

Wiesner's apprehensions were perhaps well founded, not so much because of the reorganization, but because President Lyndon B. Johnson, unlike Kennedy, was not particularly comfortable with scientists and academicians. Although OST grew during Johnson's presidency (the staff numbered about twenty professionals, and the office employed between two hundred and three hundred consultants), federal sponsorship of research and development was drastically reduced. Hornig, who served as director during that period, noted that his relationship to the president could be described as "friendly but arms-length." According to Hornig, Johnson "used the talents of PSAC, the OST staff, and the Science Adviser and was happy to hear from them, but one never had the feeling that he depended on them to shape his views." [109] The president's growing preoccupation with the Vietnam War made him even less accessible to his domestic advisers. OST had more contact with members of Congress—and in fact was required to appear before its committees—but it spent less time advising the president.

The science adviser's influence in the White House was further eroded with the accession of Richard Nixon to the presidency in 1969. Under Nixon, White House staff members placed themselves between the science adviser and the president; at the same time, PSAC began openly to criticize the president's policies. The result was Nixon's decision to abolish OST, PSAC, and the position of science adviser. According to one observer, Nixon's science adviser, Dubridge, "lacked toughness" and was unable to develop a close personal rapport with the president. His opposition to presidential policies, including the development of the supersonic transport (SST) aircraft, also distanced him from the White House.[110]

President Gerald R. Ford was more comfortable with and interested in science policy. In June 1975 he introduced legislation that established the Office of Science and Technology Policy (OSTP) within the Executive Office; it was enacted in 1976. The director was chief policy adviser to the president on science and technology for major national policies, programs, and issues. OSTP was authorized to examine the adequacy of federal programs, the utilization of new ideas and discoveries, and the coordination of government scientific activities. Ford was "receptive and interested" in science advice, commented the OSTP's first director, H. Guyford Stever.[111] Vice President Nelson A. Rockefeller further promoted the science advisory role; under the Ford administration, the government's R & D budget began to grow, and initiatives were undertaken in basic research.

The 1976 act had assigned OSTP the responsibility for producing a five-year outlook and annual reports to the president and Congress. But in 1977 these reporting responsibilities were transferred to the National Science Foundation (they were later assumed by the National Academy of Sciences), because of a general feeling that OSTP was overly taxed with reports to Congress and that its prime function was to serve as adviser to the president. (Subsequently, OSTP was asked to submit a biennial report.)

The position of OSTP under President Jimmy Carter was somewhat ambiguous. Frank Press (who served as presidential science adviser from 1977 until 1981 and who later became president of the National Academy of Sciences) maintained a low profile. He was well respected, however, by the president, the scientific community, government departments, and the Office of Management and Budget (OMB), which was important because OSTP had to work closely with OMB. Under the Carter presidency more emphasis was placed on the role of the science office in encouraging R & D, but according to presidential scholar James Everett Katz, OSTP's role under Carter was nevertheless "greatly diminished." [112] The staff was proscribed from taking policy initiatives, particularly in the areas of defense, natural resources, and energy. "The vision of a vigorous, politically significant science policy office was snuffed out, largely because the President's top advisers recognized that many areas of science and technology were politically sensitive and hence should be handled at the political level," wrote Katz.[113] Press reduced the office's already small staff by 30 percent.

Press was succeeded by G. A. Keyworth II, who served as President Ronald Reagan's first appointee to the post (Benjamin Huberman was acting science adviser from January to August 1981). On January 1, 1986, John P. McTague, incumbent deputy director, became acting science adviser and acting OSTP director until May of that year. Between May and October, Richard G. Johnson served as acting OSTP director, until William R. Graham was appointed science adviser and OSTP director.

Organization and Functions of OSTP

The director of OSTP, who is appointed by the president and confirmed by the Senate, also serves as the president's science adviser. In this capacity the director advises the president on how science and technology will affect, for example, the nation's economy, national security, foreign relations, health, energy, environment, and resources. The OSTP head also assists the president in coordinating the government's R & D programs and evaluates existing government science and technology efforts as a basis for recommending appropriate action. Finally, the director advises the president on science and technology considerations in the federal budget and works with OMB on the review and analysis of research and development items in the budgets of all federal agencies.[114]

The National Security Council seeks advice from the director on matters related to science and technology. Moreover, he or she works closely with the Council of Economic Advisers and the Council on Environmental Quality, as well as with other government agencies.

The two associate directors are nominated by the president as well, subject to Senate confirmation. Five assistant directors, appointed by the director, work on areas of current concern, and a small group of policy analysts deal with specialized policy fields. Finally, the executive director manages the OSTP office.

Most of OSTP's coordination tasks are carried out through special committees that address such topics as ocean pollution, radiation policy, solar-terrestrial research, supercomputers, federal laboratories, and food/agriculture/forestry research.

According to OSTP's 1983-1984 *Biennial Science and Technology Report to Congress*, "The U.S. science and technology enterprise still leads the world." [115] Prepared by OSTP with assistance from the National Science Foundation, the report estimated that total U.S. expenditures for research and development in 1983 and 1984 were $86.6 billion and $95.9 billion, respectively (more than the total spent by the United Kingdom, Japan, West Germany, and France); private industry contributed slightly more than 50 percent. "It is industry, not Government, that is pushing hardest at technological frontiers in many areas," noted the report.[116] During the Reagan administration OSTP emphasized basic research, instead of the applied research and development stressed during the late 1970s. Some of the subjects addressed by OSTP activities during the Reagan administration were a national aeronautics policy, agricultural research (including a new competitive awards program in plant science), Arctic research, health issues surrounding the use of the defoliant "Agent Orange" during the Vietnam War, biotechnology, basic research in defense and space policy, and the nation's scientific and technological competitiveness with the Soviet Union in national security matters. During the Reagan years OSTP also tackled emergency preparedness planning, energy policy issues (focusing on nuclear and electric), and international scientific cooperation (particularly between the United States and the People's Republic of China, Brazil, and Japan). Animal rights and the protection of human subjects in experimentation were subjects of OSTP policy statements and monitoring. OSTP sponsored, moreover, a report intended to be a framework for regulatory agencies in assessing cancer risks from chemicals and, with the cooperation of an informal policy group, the office took the lead in establishing an interagency research program to study the climatic effects of a nuclear war, known as the "nuclear winter" phenomenon.

Overall Position of OSTP

"The most effective science advisers were those with clear understanding of the government, and how to make it work," observed David Z. Robinson, who served on the science adviser's staff in the 1960s.

> Technical skill is available outside the government, and a science adviser can find technical help. The help needed to accomplish goals is harder to find. Successful advisers had long experience with government agencies. They knew how far to push things.... They knew how to form alliances, both with the agencies and with key parts of the Executive Office.... In summary, they were first-rate politicians.[117]

William G. Wells, Jr., former staff director of the House Subcommittee on Science, Resources, and Technology, agreed:

> There should be at least a general political rapport between a president and his science adviser. This is not to argue that the post of science adviser should be strictly a political appointment.... Yet, there is no escaping the reality that the White House is a political place, that the problems of the public sector are primarily political, and that a science advisory apparatus—especially the president's science adviser—must be able to function in an intensely political environment.[118]

Katz has noted the problems inherent in OSTP's umbrella function.[119] On many issues it serves as the lead agency, assembling and chairing interagency panels, often tapping outside resources for human resources, money, and administrative support. Yet the office's regular outreach program to draw in private sector experts entails a potential conflict in relying on private organizations to contribute to public policy work. OSTP has been spread even thinner by involvement in a growing "user" group—state and local governments—as well as coordination problems with other executive agencies. "The massive workloads combined with this high rate of dispersal of the tasks to various agencies and organizations have led to problems of coordination for the OSTP," wrote Katz. "It is difficult for the director and the second-rung assistant directors to know what is going on in each division and the information problem is magnified for those lower down in the hierarchy. In the past the lack of communication has led to inefficiency and overlapping responsibilities within OSTP." [120]

"The need for balance and diplomacy means that there is no simple recipe for a science adviser's effectiveness," concluded Katz. "Each science adviser must carve out his own niche within the flow of the dynamic and powerful forces surrounding the central position in the U.S. political system, or be swept away by them." [121]

Council On Environmental Quality

Like the Office of Science and Technology Policy (OSTP), where the director acts in a dual capacity as OSTP head and science adviser to the president, the chair of the Council on Environmental Quality (CEQ) also serves as director of the Office of Environmental Quality (OEQ), whose staff acts as backup for the council. The council was established by the National Environmental Policy Act of 1969 (PL 91-190). The three members of the council are appointed by the president, subject to Senate confirmation, and the president designates one member as chair. Although the chair interacts with the cabinet, cabinet rank does not accompany the position. The chair does serve, however, on the cabinet's Council on Natural Resources and Environment.

The 1970 Environmental Quality Improvement Act (PL 91-224) established the OEQ in the Executive Office of the President "to provide the professional and administrative staff for the Council." Although the council received permanent authorization, periodic reauthorization is required for the OEQ.[122]

In submitting its 719-page annual report on environmental policy for fiscal year 1984, the council noted that the initiatives undertaken marked

> another milestone in the development of a unified national environmental policy. That development has not been easy. For the past 15 years, numerous statutes dealing with environmental quality and natural resources have been enacted, with each new law designed to solve some specific pollution or resource problem, rather than to advance environmental quality as a whole. Thus, they provided little flexibility for resolving difficulties arising when the "solution" to one problem caused or exacerbated another. The task of blending these diverse laws into a more unified environmental policy, and of structuring the environmental agencies accordingly, is a difficult one.[123]

Because the oversight responsibility of the council and the office is extremely broad, they have been selective in choosing areas of study. These areas have depended in turn on the priorities of a varied constituency, which includes their own members and staff, Congress, the president, the American public, and the international community. Their relations with federal agencies, state and local governments, and private interests have made it even more difficult for the council and office to preside over the formulation of a unified national environmental policy.

Origins and Development of CEQ and OEQ

Both CEQ and OEQ were created in response to the nation's increasing concern about declining air and water quality and a general deterioration of the environment. The dramatic blowout of an oil well in the channel off the coast of Santa Barbara, California, in late January 1969, focused public attention on the seriousness of environmental problems. Miles of beaches were covered with oil, and thousands of fish and wildfowl were killed.

On June 3, 1969, four months after the Santa Barbara incident, President Richard Nixon established by executive order the cabinet-level Environmental Quality Council. Congress was not satisfied, however, calling the formation of the council a patchwork approach to environmental problems. In December 1969 Congress passed the National Environmental Policy Act (NEPA), which made environmental protection a matter of national policy. The act required all federal agencies to submit environmental impact statements for all proposed actions and created the Council on Environmental Quality to replace the Environmental Quality Council. NEPA was denounced by many industry groups, but conservation organizations such as the Sierra Club hailed it as "an environmental Magna Carta."[124]

During its early days the Nixon administration was criticized widely for not displaying a strong commitment to environmental protection. In 1970, as the pressure for corrective action mounted, the president submitted to Congress a plan to consolidate the federal government's widespread environmental efforts into a single Environmental Protection Agency (EPA). There was little congressional opposition, and on December 2, 1970, the EPA was created by executive order as an independent agency within the executive branch. The Council on Environmental Quality continued to exist as an advisory and policy-making body. While EPA was charged with setting and enforcing pollution control standards, CEQ focused on broad environmental policies and coordination of the federal government's activities in that area.

Organization and Functions of CEQ and OEQ

For budget planning purposes CEQ and OEQ divided its responsibilities into three categories: analysis and development of environmental policy, interagency coordination of environmental quality programs, and acquisition and assessment of environmental data.[125]

The environmental policy analysis and development functions are a primary responsibility of the CEQ chair and the two council members, who provide the president with expert opinion and policy advice on environmental issues. The council chair participates in discussions of the Domestic Policy Council when matters concerning the environment arise, while the other members of the CEQ serve on two White House subcabinet working groups on environmental policy.

A primary function of the council is preparation of a lengthy annual Environmental Quality Report, which details how activities of the federal, state, and local governments, as well as private enterprise, are affecting the environment. This report is based on CEQ's own research, work with other federal agencies, the findings of the OEQ staff, and contract studies. The council also publishes reports on specific topics.

The second major responsibility of CEQ and OEQ—interagency coordination of environmental quality programs—includes the promulgation and implementation of regulations related to the National Environmental Policy Act, coordination of federal environmental programs, and participation in the review process conducted by the Office of Management and Budget (OMB) for proposed legislation related to environmental quality. A principal effort of CEQ and OEQ in the mid-1980s was participation in an interagency task force on acid rain, chaired by a council member. The CEQ has coordinated other studies as well. Prominent among them was a study of hazardous waste cleanup, carried out with other groups such as EPA, the National Institute for Environmental Health Sciences, the National Science Foundation, and the congressional Office of Technology Assessment. CEQ members also regularly testify before Congress on the administration's environmental policies.

The role of CEQ and OEQ in the acquisition and

assessment of environmental data has been directed toward coordinating an interagency effort to update information about environmental data sources. For example, the council's chair joined the EPA administrator in heading an Interagency Toxic Substances Data Committee. In 1985 a management fund was established to support OEQ participation in interagency environmental policy studies by allowing it to enlist outside expertise.

One of CEQ's major functions has been monitoring federal compliance with provisions of the NEPA. This act required CEQ to prepare detailed statements (environmental impact statements) on proposed legislation and other major federal actions that would significantly affect the quality of the human environment. CEQ revised the guidelines for its purview in 1971 and 1973, but they were advisory, not binding. As CEQ chairman and OEQ director A. Alan Hill testified on April 9, 1987, "By the mid-1970s significant problems had become associated with the NEPA process. As the number of court cases increased, so too, the number of pages in [environmental impact statements] doubled and tripled, and complaints about the paperwork and delay associated with the process were frequently heard." [126] In 1977, in response to this problem, President Jimmy Carter issued Executive Order 11991, which provided CEQ with the legal authority to issue regulations to federal agencies for implementing the procedural provisions of the NEPA. The order also established a referral process to CEQ for any conflicts among agencies about NEPA implementation. The executive order directed that the regulations "be designed to make the environmental impact statement more useful to decisionmakers and the public," thereby reducing the paperwork involved and turning the attention to the "real environmental issues and alternatives." After soliciting reviews and comments, CEQ issued the NEPA regulations in November 1978; they became effective for all federal agencies in 1979.

With the accession of Ronald Reagan to the presidency in 1981 the NEPA regulations were reviewed and approved by his newly created Task Force on Regulatory Reform, chaired by Vice President George Bush. CEQ later amended the regulations, however, to deal with cases of incomplete or inadequate information on environmental impact. The new rules, which went into effect in May 1986, required federal agencies to point out in the statements that accompanied and documented their material any inadequacy in or lack of information.

The CEQ is also active in international environmental conferences and in the resolution of issues that go beyond national boundaries. For example, in 1981 the CEQ chair headed the Global Issues Working Group, which was established at President Reagan's request. Composed of senior policy representatives from eighteen major federal agencies, the group was convened to coordinate the administration's policies on international issues dealing with environmental protection, population, and the utilization and protection of natural resources. In 1986 and 1987 the council participated in the World Commission on Environment and Development, an independent group which had its origins in a United Nations General Assembly resolution calling for preparation of an "environmental perspective to the year 2000 and beyond." The commission examined a wide range of topics, including air, water, and ocean pollution; hazardous and nuclear waste; deforestation and soil erosion; human shelter; land tenure; and industrial and environmental controls.

Other CEQ and OEQ projects undertaken during the Reagan administration included studies of depletion of the ozone layer and related issues of climatic change stemming from the "greenhouse effect"; participation in an international conference on the assessment processes for environmental impacts held in Nairobi, Kenya, in June 1987; and participation in bilateral environmental agreements with the Soviet Union and Japan.[127]

Considering its broad responsibilities, the Office of Environmental Quality had a small staff of ten in 1987, a few of whom were detailed temporarily to the OEQ from various federal agencies. Nonetheless, its mission was almost overwhelming, as the office itself noted in its 1984 annual report:

> The scope of the tasks defined under current environmental and natural resources policies is massive; the federal government is charged with managing the whole economy as it impacts upon environmental or natural resource questions, which increasingly means almost every activity by almost everyone in society. . . . [The CEQ report] describes an active search for ways to address environmental quality and resource conservation problems in new and innovative ways. Clearly, these efforts are important. However, it is also important to note that this administration along with the vast majority of all Americans continues to support the environmental agenda. Possibly no other national goal retains such strong public support from such a broad base of the population. In a very real sense, all Americans are now environmentalists. The disagreements that have arisen and are likely to continue to arise concern the selection of policies viewed as best able to advance environmental objectives. All answers are not yet available. [128]

Office of Administration

As the scope and activities of the Executive Office of the President (EOP) expanded over the years following its establishment in 1939, it became apparent that the support functions of all EOP offices needed to be centralized in a single agency. Reorganization Plan 1 of 1977 (implemented by Executive Order 12028, issued on December 12, 1977) established the Office of Administration within EOP. The director of the office, who was appointed by and is directly responsible to the president, has the task of "ensuring that the Office of Administration provides units within the Executive Office of the President common administrative support and services" (Section 2, Executive Order 12028).

The office provides administrative support services to all EOP offices in the White House. These services include personnel management; financial management; data processing; library services, record-keeping, and information services; and office services and operations, including mail handling (except for presidential mail), messenger service, printing and duplication, graphics, word processing, procurement, and supply.

In 1987 the Office of Administration consisted of 165 full-time and 35 temporary and part-time employees. These employees were divided into five sections: personnel, financial, library and informational services, automated systems, and administrative operations. The two printing plants of the office prepare the Budget Message and other documents for distribution. (For large print quantities, the type is set by the Office of Administration and sent to the Government Printing Office, which either prints and binds the publication itself or seeks an outside printer and binder.) For all EOP offices the Administration Office maintains accounts, recruits employees (with the exception of the Office of Policy Development and White House staff, all of whom are political appointees), and maintains official records, including those of the White House. In 1987 the Office of Administration provided support services for the 1,495 men and women who served in the Executive Office. It also provided services to the Commission on the Bicentennial of the Constitution (not officially part of the EOP). Three libraries (not open to the general public) come under its oversight as well: a general reference library located in the New Executive Office Building and reference and law libraries in the Old Executive Office Building.

Since its inception the Office of Administration has developed a sophisticated computer system, which responds to the ever-growing and increasingly complex needs of the White House and the EOP.

Notes

1. Richard M. Pious, *The American Presidency* (New York: Basic Books, 1979), 253.
2. John W. Macy, Bruce Adams, and J. Jackson Walter, *America's Unelected Government: Appointing the President's Team* (Cambridge, Mass.: Ballinger, 1983), 4.
3. Stephen Hess, *Organizing the Presidency* (Washington, D.C.: Brookings, 1976), 14.
4. Macy, Adams, and Walter, *America's Unelected Government,* 7.
5. G. Calvin Mackenzie, *The Politics of Presidential Appointments* (New York: Free Press, 1981), 8-9.
6. Hess, *Organizing the Presidency,* 29.
7. Ibid., 62.
8. Macy, Adams, and Walter, *America's Unelected Government,* 30.
9. Hess, *Organizing the Presidency,* 79-80.
10. Emmette S. Redford and Richard T. McCulley, *White House Operations: The Johnson Presidency* (Austin: University of Texas Press, 1986), 137.
11. Theodore C. Sorensen, *Watchmen in the Night* (Cambridge, Mass.: MIT Press, 1973), 36.
12. Macy, Adams, and Walter, *America's Unelected Government,* 33.
13. Quote found in Stephen J. Wayne, *The Legislative Presidency* (New York: Harper and Row, 1978), 187.
14. Mackenzie, *The Politics of Presidential Appointments,* 54-55.
15. Edward D. Feigenbaum, "Staffing, Organization, and Decision-making in the Ford and Carter White Houses," *Presidential Studies Quarterly* 10 (Summer 1980): 366-367.
16. Macy, Adams, and Walter, *America's Unelected Government,* 37.
17. Ibid., 49.
18. Office of Management and Budget, "The Work of the Office of Management and Budget," mimeographed (Washington, D.C.: OMB, 1987).
19. Bureau of the Budget, *Staff Orientation Manual* (Washington, D.C.: Government Printing Office, 1945), 38.
20. Quoted in *Congress and the Nation, 1969-1972* (Washington, D.C.: Congressional Quarterly Inc., 1973), 3:73.
21. Richard E. Neustadt, "Presidency and Legislation: The Growth of Central Clearance," *American Political Science Review* 48 (September 1954): 641-671.
22. For a discussion of this period, see the chapter on Franklin D. Roosevelt in Hess, *Organizing the Presidency.*
23. Quoted in Larry Berman, *The Office of Management and Budget and the Presidency, 1921-1979* (Princeton, N.J.: Princeton University Press, 1979), 28.
24. Ibid., 42.
25. Ibid., 52.
26. Ibid., 55.
27. Brookings Institution, *Study of the 1960-61 Presidential Transition: The White House and the Executive Office of the President* (Washington, D.C.: Brookings, 1960), 33.
28. "Task Force Report on Intergovernmental Program Coordination: The Bureau of the Budget During the Administration of Lyndon Baines Johnson," mimeographed (Washington, D.C.: U.S. Executive Office of the President, Bureau of the Budget, November 14, 1968).
29. *Presidential Documents,* March 16, 1970 (Washington, D.C.: Government Printing Office, 1970), 355-357.
30. Berman, *The Office of Management and Budget and the Presidency,* 125.
31. *Congressional Quarterly Weekly Report,* July 13, 1985, 1356.
32. See Office of Management and Budget, "The Work of the Office of Management and Budget," 5.
33. *Federal Regulatory Directory, 1983-84* (Washington, D.C.: Congressional Quarterly Inc., 1983), 66.
34. Julie Rovner, "OMB's Activities Draw Fire in Congress, Courts," *Congressional Quarterly Weekly Report,* June 14, 1986, 1341.
35. See *Congressional Quarterly Weekly Report,* June 14, 1986, 1340.
36. Quoted in Dave Kaplan, "Senate Committee Approves OMB Overhaul," *Congressional Quarterly Weekly Report,* June 28, 1986, 1488.
37. From Title I, "Coordination for National Security," of the National Security Act, PL 80-253. See *Congress and the Nation, 1945-1964* (Washington, D.C.: Congressional Quarterly Inc., 1965), 1:247.
38. From Mark M. Lowenthal, "The National Security Council: Organizational History," Congressional Research Service, Washington, D.C., June 27, 1978.
39. From Henry A. Kissinger, *White House Years* (Boston: Little, Brown, 1979), 31.
40. For a description of this "conventional wisdom" on the NSC, see I. M. Destler, "National Security Management: What Presidents Have Wrought," *Political Science Quarterly* 95 (Winter 1980): 81.
41. Kissinger, *White House Years,* 30.
42. From Allen Weinstein and Michael R. Beschloss, "The Best National Security System: An Interview with Zbigniew Brzezinski," *Washington Quarterly* (Winter 1982): 74.
43. Larry Light, "White House Domestic Policy Staff Plays an Important Role in Formulating Legislation," *Congressional Quarterly Weekly Report,* October 6, 1979, 2202.
44. Quoted in Peri E. Arnold, *Making the Managerial Presidency: Comprehensive Reorganization Planning 1905-1980* (Princeton, N.J.: Princeton University Press, 1986), 285.
45. Ibid., 284-285.
46. *Public Papers of the Presidents of the United States, Richard Nixon, 1970* (Washington, D.C.: Government Printing Office, 1971), 257.
47. House Committee on Government Organization, *Hearings, Reorganization Plan No. 2 of 1970,* 91st Cong., 2d Sess., 1970, 55-56.
48. Ibid., 23.
49. Arnold, *Making the Managerial Presidency,* 298.
50. Quoted in Hess, *Organizing the Presidency,* 131.
51. Ibid., 132.
52. Dick Kirchten, "Policy Development Office: A Scaled-down Operation," *National Journal,* April 25, 1981, 684.
53. John H. Kessel, *The Domestic Presidency: Decision-Making in the White House* (Boston, Mass.: Duxbury Press, 1975), 29.
54. Light, "White House Domestic Policy Staff," 2199.
55. Ibid., 2199.
56. Ibid., 2200.
57. Ibid.
58. *Congressional Quarterly Almanac: 1981* (Washington, D.C.: Congressional Quarterly Inc., 1982), 356. The letter was dated July 8, 1981.

59. Text of announcement in *Congressional Quarterly Weekly Report,* April 20, 1985, 757.
60. Kirchten, "Policy Development Office," 684.
61. The organization and functions of the OPD were provided by special assistant Michael Driggs in a May 19, 1987, interview.
62. Kirchten, "Policy Development Office," 684.
63. Edward S. Flash, Jr., "The Broadening Scope of the President's Economic Advisers," *The George Washington Law Review* 35, no. 2 (December 1966): 286.
64. Roger Porter, "Economic Advice to the President from Eisenhower to Reagan," *Political Science Quarterly* (Fall 1983): 404.
65. Ibid., 405.
66. David Naveh, "The Political Role of Academic Advisers: The Case of the U.S. President's Council of Economic Advisers, 1946-76," *Presidential Studies Quarterly* 11 (Fall 1981): 492.
67. The origins and politics of the act have been well documented by Stephen K. Bailey in *Congress Makes a Law* (New York: Columbia University Press, 1950).
68. For a good discussion of this issue, see E. Ray Canterbury, *The President's Council of Economic Advisers* (New York: Exposition Press, 1961).
69. Edwin G. Nourse and Bertram M. Gross, "The Role of the Council of Economic Advisers," *American Political Science Review* (April 1948).
70. Erwin C. Hargrove and Samuel A. Morley, eds., *The President and the Council of Economic Advisers: Interviews with CEA Chairmen* (Boulder, Colo.: Westview Press, 1984), 47.
71. Gerhard Colm, "The Executive Office and Fiscal and Economic Policy," *Law and Contemporary Problems* 21 (Autumn 1956): 716.
72. Edwin G. Nourse, *Economics in the Public Service* (New York: Harcourt Brace, 1953), 380.
73. Nourse and Gross, "The Role of the Council of Economic Advisers."
74. Edwin G. Nourse, "The Employment Act and the Economic Future," *Vital Speeches XII* (January 1, 1946).
75. Hargrove and Morley, *The President and the Council of Economic Advisers,* 50.
76. Hess, *Organizing the Presidency,* 55.
77. Hugh S. Norton, *The Council of Economic Advisers: Three Periods of Influence* (Columbia, S.C.: Bureau of Business and Economic Research, 1973), 23.
78. Hess, *Organizing the Presidency,* 75.
79. Naveh, "The Political Role of Academic Advisers," 497.
80. Hargrove and Morley, *The President and the Council of Economic Advisers,* 91.
81. Ibid., 90.
82. Arthur M. Schlesinger, Jr., *A Thousand Days: John F. Kennedy in the White House* (Boston: Houghton Mifflin, 1965), 137.
83. Edward S. Flash, Jr., *Economic Advice and Presidential Leadership* (New York: Columbia University Press, 1965), 209.
84. Hess, *Organizing the Presidency,* 90.
85. Hargrove and Morley, *The President and the Council of Economic Advisers,* 163.
86. Ibid., 359.
87. Ibid., 409.
88. Ibid., 459.
89. *Congress and the Nation, 1977-1980* (Washington, D.C.: Congressional Quarterly Inc., 1981), 5:233.
90. *Congressional Quarterly Almanac: 1981* (Washington, D.C.: Congressional Quarterly Inc., 1982), 270.
91. Council of Economic Advisers, *Economic Report of the President* (Washington, D.C.: Government Printing Office, January 1987).
92. Hess, *Organizing the Presidency,* 167.
93. Quoted in Naveh, "The Political Role of Academic Advisers," 501.
94. For a general history of U.S. trade policy, see *Trade: U.S. Policy Since 1945* (Washington, D.C.: Congressional Quarterly Inc., 1984).
95. John W. Evans, *The Kennedy Round in American Trade Policy: The Twilight of the GATT?* (Cambridge, Mass.: Harvard University Press, 1971), 156.
96. See, among other sources, *Congress and the Nation, 1977-1980,* 5:273.
97. *Trade,* 2.
98. Clyde M. Farnsworth, "William Brock: Our Man for Trade," *New York Times Magazine,* November 13, 1983.
99. *Congressional Quarterly Weekly Report,* June 29, 1985, 1303.
100. Information on the organization and functions of the USTR was supplied by interviews with staff members and a mimeographed article produced by the office.
101. *Congressional Quarterly Weekly Report,* March 28, 1987, 555.
102. Office of the U.S. Trade Representative, mimeographed copy of an address by Clayton K. Yeutter to the Heritage Foundation, Washington, D.C., March 13, 1987.
103. A mimeographed copy of the April 7, 1987, address by Clayton K. Yeutter to the Graduate School of Business, University of Chicago, was provided by the Office of the U.S. Trade Representative.
104. Elizabeth Wehr, "Senate Clears Trade Bill by Lopsided Vote," *Congressional Quarterly Weekly Report,* August 6, 1988, 2215.
105. Office of Science and Technology Policy (in cooperation with the National Science Foundation), *Biennial Science and Technology Report to the Congress: 1983-1984* (Washington, D.C.: Government Printing Office, 1985), 4. This report summarizes OSTP's wide-ranging activities. See also a mimeographed fact sheet by OSTP, available from that office.
106. Lee A. Dubridge, "Science Advice to the President: Important and Difficult," in *Science Advice to the President,* ed. George Bugliarello and A. George Schillinger, a special issue of *Technology and Society* (New York: Pergamon Press, 1980), 2:11. These volumes provide invaluable articles by former presidential science advisers, observers, and legislative experts on the evolution of the science advisory role.
107. James R. Killian, Jr., "The Origins and Uses of a Scientific Presence in the White House," in *Science Advice,* 31.
108. Donald F. Hornig, "The President's Need for Science Advice: Past and Future," in *Science Advice,* 42.
109. Ibid., 47.
110. William G. Wells, Jr., "Science Advice and the Presidency," in *Science Advice,* 214. Wells served as staff director of the House Subcommittee on Science, Resources, and Technology at the time.
111. H. Guyford Stever, "Science Advice—Out of and Back to the White House," in *Science Advice,* 74.
112. James Everett Katz, "Organizational Structure and Advisory Effectiveness," in *Science Advice,* 230.
113. Ibid.
114. For greater detail, see Office of Science and Technology Policy, *Biennial Science and Technology Report.*
115. Ibid., 3.
116. Ibid., 4.
117. David Z. Robinson, "Politics in the Science Advising Process," in *Science Advice,* 163.
118. Wells, "Science Advice and the Presidency," 214.
119. Katz, "Organizational Structure." Katz himself noted, "Conventional wisdom dictates that the science advisor's usefulness is predicated entirely on his personal rapport with the president" (p. 243).
120. Ibid., 233.
121. Ibid., 243.
122. To learn the full relevant statutory authority at the time, see Executive Office of the President, Council on Environmental Quality, *Regulations for Implementing the Procedural Provisions of the National Environmental Policy Act* (Washington, D.C.: Government Printing Office, November 1978), reprint 43FR 55978-56007.
123. Executive Office of the President, Council on Environmental Quality, *Environmental Quality,* Fifteenth Annual Report (Washington, D.C.: Government Printing Office, 1985), 1.

124. For background, see *Federal Regulatory Directory, 1983-84,* 113.
125. A succinct summary of the council's activities was given by CEQ chairman A. Alan Hill in a statement before the House Merchant Marine and Fisheries Subcommittee on Fisheries and Wildlife, Conservation and the Environment, April 9, 1987.
126. Ibid., 8.
127. For summaries of CEQ and OEQ activities, see the annual reports of the Council on Environmental Quality, particularly the eleventh and fifteenth reports (Washington, D.C.: Government Printing Office, 1981). Other reports of particular interest are: *Report of an Expert Meeting on Research Needs and Opportunities at Federally-supervised Hazardous Waste Site Clean-ups* (Washington, D.C.: Executive Office of the President, Council on Environmental Quality, October 20, 1986); *Report on Long-term Environmental Research and Development* (Washington, D.C.: Executive Office of the President, Council on Environmental Quality, Office of Environmental Quality, March 1985).
128. Council on Environmental Quality, Fifteenth Annual Report, 6, 8.

Selected Bibliography

Arnold, Peri E. *Making the Managerial Presidency: Comprehensive Reorganization Planning 1905-1980.* Princeton, N.J.: Princeton University Press, 1986.

Bailey, Stephen. *Congress Makes a Law.* New York: Columbia University Press, 1950.

Berman, Larry. *The Office of Management and Budget and the Presidency, 1921-1979.* Princeton, N.J.: Princeton University Press, 1979.

Bugliarello, George, and A. George Schillinger, eds. *Science Advice to the President,* a special issue of *Technology in Society,* Vol. 2, Nos. 1 and 2. New York: Pergamon Press, 1980.

Feigenbaum, Edward D. "Staffing, Organization, and Decision-making in the Ford and Carter White Houses." *Presidential Studies Quarterly* 10 (Summer 1980): 364-377.

Hargrove, Erwin C., and Samuel A. Morley, eds. *The President and the Council of Economic Advisers: Interviews with CEA Chairmen.* Boulder, Colo.: Westview Press, 1984.

Hess, Stephen. *Organizing the Presidency.* Washington, D.C.: Brookings, 1976.

King, Anthony. *Both Ends of the Avenue: The Presidency, the Executive Branch, and Congress in the 1980s.* Washington, D.C.: American Enterprise Institute, 1983.

Light, Larry. "White House Domestic Policy Staff Plays an Important Role in Formulating Legislation." *Congressional Quarterly Weekly Report,* October 6, 1979, 2199-2204.

Macy, John W., Bruce Adams, and J. Jackson Walter. *America's Unelected Government: Appointing the President's Team.* Cambridge, Mass.: Ballinger, 1983.

Mosher, Frederick C. *A Tale of Two Agencies: A Comparative Analysis of the General Accounting Office and the Office of Management and Budget.* Baton Rouge: Louisiana State University Press, 1984.

Naveh, David. "The Political Role of Academic Advisers: The Case of the U.S. President's Council of Economic Advisers, 1946-76." *Presidential Studies Quarterly* 11 (Fall 1981).

Pious, Richard M. *The American Presidency.* New York: Basic Books, 1979.

Redford, Emmette S., and Richard T. McCulley. *White House Operations: The Johnson Presidency.* Austin: University of Texas Press, 1986.

Sorensen, Theodore C. *Watchmen in the Night.* Cambridge, Mass.: MIT Press, 1973.

Trade: U.S. Policy Since 1945. Washington, D.C.: Congressional Quarterly Inc., 1984.

Wayne, Stephen. *The Legislative Presidency.* New York: Harper and Row, 1978.

Cabinet

The cabinet is one of the most unusual institutions of the presidency. Although not specifically mentioned in the Constitution or specifically provided for in statutory law, the cabinet has become an institutionalized part of the presidency. The country's first president, George Washington, initiated the practice of meeting with the secretaries of state, Treasury, and war as well as his attorney general, to seek their advice on domestic and foreign policy. The modern presidential cabinet consists of the president, vice president, heads of the fourteen executive departments, and any other officials the president might wish to invite, such as the head of the Office of Management and Budget and the ambassador to the United Nations. While some presidents have attempted to use their cabinets regularly, recognizing that a presidency that effectively utilizes its cabinet is still considered ideal, presidential cabinets have for the most part been the stepchildren of the presidency. In fact, because cabinet members usually become advocates of their departments, they contribute little to presidential decision making unless the decisions involve matters that concern their respective bailiwicks. As a result, most presidents have viewed their cabinets as more of a burden than a help.

Origin and Development of the Cabinet

The idea of some kind of advisory council for the president was discussed at the Constitutional Convention. Gouverneur Morris and Charles Cotesworth Pinckney, the first delegates to use the term "cabinet" at the convention, proposed creation of a council of state, composed of the executive department heads, to advise the president. This proposal failed to win adoption, but advocates of a cabinet kept the idea alive throughout most of the convention. Indeed, less than two weeks before finalization of the Constitution, Benjamin Franklin continued to insist that a council of state "would not only be a check on a bad president but be a relief to a good one." [1]

The cabinet concept eventually failed to win enough support among the convention's delegates, however. The majority of the Founders apparently feared that the presidency might become too overburdened with unnecessary advisory councils. Alexander Hamilton explained the Founders' concerns in the *Federalist* No. 70: "A council to a magistrate, who is himself responsible for what he does, are generally nothing better than a clog upon his good intentions; are often the instruments and accomplices of his bad, and are almost always a cloak to his faults." [2] Consequently, when the Committee on Style finished drafting the Constitution, all that remained of the idea was the authorization that the president "require the Opinion, in writing, of the principal Officer in each of the executive Departments, upon any Subject relating to the duties of their respective Offices" (Article II, section 2).

Having no constitutional or statutory mandate for the institution of a cabinet, presidents have relied on the constitutional mandate that allows them to seek the advice of their principal executive branch officers. Under the Articles of Confederation, several executive departments already existed. Thus, in reality Washington's first cabinet merely evolved out of an already established executive pattern that began in the early 1780s. President Washington understood that the constitutional language about the responsibility of the departments was ambiguous. His biographer, James Thomas Flexner, has written: "Whether what was defined as 'the heads of the great departments' were to be under the jurisdiction of the president was not stated: the president was merely empowered to require their opinions relating to their duties." [3] When Washington was inaugurated in 1789, he consulted with Alexander Hamilton, James Madison, and others on the powers and duties of the presidency and permanently settled the matter by instituting the foundation of the modern cabinet. Early in his administration, Washington took the view that department heads should be assistants to the president and not to Congress.

Seeking both administrative and advisory help in his new administration, Washington asked Congress to create three executive departments to oversee, respectively, foreign affairs, military affairs, and fiscal concerns. During the months before the executive branch was firmly in place, Washington relied on the services of those who had served in the same areas under the Articles of Confederation. John Jay continued temporarily as secretary of foreign affairs, Henry Knox remained at the secretary of war post, and the old Treasury Board continued to manage fiscal concerns.

By W. Craig Bledsoe

For more than two months Congress debated the proper establishment of these three executive departments. Primarily concerned with the relationship of each department to Congress and believing that not all departments should be alike in these relationships, most members of Congress preferred that the departments concerned with foreign affairs and war be primarily under the control of the executive. The Treasury, however, had some legislative purposes and thus should fall more under the control of Congress. The statutes setting up these departments reflected these preferences. On July 27, 1789, Congress established the Department of Foreign Affairs. The secretary of foreign affairs was given the responsibility of performing duties assigned by the president. (Two months later Congress changed the name to the Department of State.) Similarly, the statutory language setting up the War Department placed it squarely under the control of the president. Unlike the Departments of State and War, the Treasury Department was not designated by Congress as an "executive department." Instead, the secretary of the Treasury was directed to report fiscal matters directly to Congress. Part of the rationale for this special status was the constitutional requirement that revenue bills originate in the House of Representatives.

Alexander Hamilton did much to increase the prestige and independence of the cabinet. Early in his administration Washington asked Hamilton to head the Treasury, and there is some evidence that the secretary contributed greatly to the drafting of the Treasury Act. Hamilton, who had served as Washington's chief adviser during the organization of the new government, virtually assumed the role of prime minister after his confirmation as secretary of the Treasury on September 11, 1789. In addition to his abilities and his special relationship with Washington, Hamilton's ascension to a position of such unofficial prominence was assisted by the relative statutory importance of the Treasury Department. He assumed an office that Congress had intended as an extension of its own authority and made it a stronghold of executive power. According to presidential scholar R. Gordon Hoxie, "With his admiration of the British model and his high regard for Washington, Hamilton conceived of executive power as generated through a cabinet of department heads, administered by a judicious executive head. In such a system, by the sheer vent of his energies and genius, Hamilton came to be Washington's dominant adviser." [4]

Washington's use of the cabinet soon resulted in an institution that the Framers of the Constitution had failed to include. The president eventually appointed Henry Knox as secretary of war (September 12, 1789) and Thomas Jefferson, who had been serving as minister to France, as secretary of state (March 22, 1790). In addition, Edmund Randolph was named attorney general, although there was no Department of Justice until 1870.

Washington initially believed that the Senate would fill the role of an advisory council, but that hope faded in August 1790 when Washington, accompanied by Knox, went to the Senate floor to get advice on an Indian treaty. The senators made it clear that they were uncomfortable meeting with the president and that they would not serve in the capacity of an advisory council. As a result, Washington gradually began to rely on the advice of his department heads, the attorney general, Vice President John Adams, and Chief Justice John Jay.

At first Washington consulted with each individually, both in person and in writing. Later, in 1791, when he was preparing to leave the capital for a few days, he authorized his vice president, the chief justice, and the secretaries of Treasury, state, and war to meet and discuss government matters during his absence. In the following year the president conferred frequently with his department heads and attorney general, omitting the vice president and the chief justice. These meetings occurred even more often during the undeclared naval war with France. By 1793 James Madison was applying the term "cabinet" to these conferences. The name stuck, and the cabinet became a permanent addition to the executive branch.

Library of Congress

Although the Treasury secretary was not part of the original cabinet, Alexander Hamilton made the department a stronghold of executive power and became Washington's dominant adviser.

Like many presidents after him, Washington had hoped that his advisers would consult with one another and work together harmoniously. Early cabinet meetings, however, were marred by a growing rift between Jefferson and Hamilton, who detested each other and differed on a number of important policy positions. Although Washington tried to get them to work together, they quarreled continuously. Jefferson finally resigned in the summer of 1793. Less than two years later Hamilton retired from government service to return to his lucrative law practice, yet Washington continued to write him for advice during his remaining two years in office. In fact, the president apparently abandoned his hopes of his cabinet serving as an advisory board.

When Washington replaced Jefferson and Hamilton in his cabinet, he chose men of cooler heads but lesser talents, and evidently he did not value their advice as much as that from his first cabinet. Flexner wrote: "Unlike their predecessors they were not consulted concerning executive decisions; they were limited to the routines of their departments." [5] This disillusionment and uncertainty surrounding the proper role of the cabinet has afflicted almost every administration since Washington's.

President John Adams, who retained all of Washington's cabinet members, was even more disillusioned with his cabinet than his predecessor. Early in his administration important differences of opinion developed between Adams and his department heads. Indeed, his cabinet members were more loyal to Hamilton than to him. And because the president was often away from the capital, cabinet members began to advise each other and to seek Hamilton's advice. In the final year of his administration Adams removed two cabinet members. Yet during his administration the formal cabinet remained the president's principal official advisory unit.

The role of the cabinet under Washington and Adams

thus established a pattern of ambiguity that has endured throughout the history of the presidency. According to R. Gordon Hoxie,

> The twelve Federalist years had established the joint consultation between the president and the department heads as a body, but it was clear that the president was bound neither to consult nor to accept the advice received. Nor was the cabinet an administrative body. The business of government was carried out throughout the executive departments.[6]

Nineteenth-Century Cabinets

The first part of the nineteenth century witnessed a gradual decline in the importance of the cabinet. Few cabinets got along all that well, and few presidents relied on their cabinets as advisory groups. Because the selection of cabinet members became more and more dictated by political and geographic considerations, presidents increasingly appointed cabinet members whom they did not know personally or necessarily trust. Indeed, many times presidents had to struggle to maintain control over their cabinets. If because of a lack of interest in using the cabinet a president declined to prepare an agenda for a cabinet meeting, the secretaries would take the initiative.

Appointments to earlier cabinets were based primarily on the appointee's abilities. Beginning with President James Madison's administration (1809-1817), however, political and geographic factors often took precedence over ability or loyalty. For example, the Senate strongly opposed Madison's selection of Albert Gallatin, Jefferson's secretary of the Treasury, to succeed Madison as secretary of state. Instead, several senators forced the president to appoint Robert Smith, the brother of an influential senator, to the position. For the first time the president was no longer in complete control of the cabinet selection process.

Because of these pressures, as well as his own personality, Andrew Jackson (1829-1837) was the first president to largely ignore his collective cabinet. During his first two years in office, he did not even meet with his cabinet, and he convened it only sixteen times during his entire eight years as president. Jackson preferred the intimacy of his "kitchen cabinet," a group of close personal advisers (many of whom were newspapermen who kept him in touch with public opinion), over the formality of his official cabinet. Throughout his administration, he steadfastly refused to use his formal cabinet to help him make final decisions. As he explained: "I have accustomed myself to receive with respect the opinions of others, but always take the responsibility for deciding for myself." [7]

Abraham Lincoln (1861-1865) appointed strong political leaders, many of them his political antagonists, to his cabinet. In fact, some of his cabinet members believed themselves superior to Lincoln. This resulted not only in several overly ambitious cabinet members but also in some rather bitter relationships between cabinet members and the president. Cabinet officers during the Lincoln administration were known for their intrigues. Secretary of State William H. Seward, for example, considered himself Lincoln's prime minister. Salmon P. Chase, secretary of the Treasury, schemed with a few members of the Senate to remove Seward and increase his own influence. Lincoln's strong leadership, however, allowed him to retain control of his cabinet and use it for his own ends. Indeed, as the story goes, when seeking advice on one critical decision, Lincoln polled his entire cabinet, only to be overwhelmingly outvoted. He then proclaimed: "Seven nays and one aye, the ayes have it." The critical decisions, such as the Emancipation Proclamation, were his alone, although he usually sought cabinet endorsement. Hoxie wrote: "Just as he was the strongest nineteenth-century president, he had the strongest cabinet members, who worked strenuously in their respective departments, although as a body they were subordinated to him." [8]

During the latter part of the nineteenth century an attempt was made to move responsibility for the cabinet from the White House to Congress, thereby giving Congress considerable access to information on the executive branch. Chief among the members of Congress introducing legislation to accomplish this goal was George Hunt Pendleton (D-Ohio), who in 1864 proposed a bill that would allow secretaries of executive departments to occupy seats on the House floor. Supported strongly by others in Congress (including future president James A. Garfield), the bill came up for debate in 1865 and several times thereafter. The proposal was never voted into law.

Twentieth-Century Cabinets

Early in the twentieth century the cabinet grew in size but continued to play only a modest role as an advisory body. As the federal government became more complex and the power of the presidency began to expand, the size of the cabinet expanded as well. In 1913, during Woodrow Wilson's administration (1913-1921), the cabinet swelled to ten members. President Wilson, however, rarely met with his cabinet. Even during World War I Wilson did not consult with his cabinet about the 1915 sinking of the *Lusitania* or his 1917 call for Congress to declare war. Instead, he relied for advice on his Council of National Defense, which was created in 1916 and composed of the secretaries of war, navy, interior, agriculture, commerce, and labor. As one department secretary complained, "Nothing talked of at Cabinet that would interest a nation, a family, or a child. No talk of the war." [9]

Under Franklin D. Roosevelt (1933-1945) cabinet meetings continued to be more of a forum for discussion than a decision-making body. Roosevelt even downplayed the importance of the cabinet. During cabinet meetings he customarily went around the table and asked each cabinet member what was on his or her mind. His secretary of the interior, Harold L. Ickes, summarized Roosevelt's attitude: "The cold fact is that on important matters we are seldom called upon for advice. We never discuss exhaustively any policy of government or question of political strategy. . . . Our cabinet meetings are pleasant affairs, but we only skim the surface of routine affairs." [10] In addition, Roosevelt often interceded in the activities of his cabinet members. According to Hoxie,

> Roosevelt constantly interposed in the executive departments both in domestic and foreign policy. He became, in essence, his own secretary of state, war, and navy. Secretary of State Cordell Hull and Secretary of War [Henry L.] Stimson both voiced their unhappiness. So did Roosevelt's new vice-president, Harry S Truman, who was neither consulted nor informed of what was going on.[11]

President Truman (1945-1953) boasted that he had "revived the cabinet system," believing that it should be similar to a board of directors. Indeed, Truman called for a

Harry S Truman Library

Truman called for a strong, active cabinet, yet not once did he convene his cabinet to discuss the North Korean invasion of South Korea.

strong, active cabinet: "The cabinet is not merely a collection of executives administering different governmental functions. It is a body whose combined judgment the president uses to formulate the fundamental policies of the administration." [12] Unlike Roosevelt, Truman actually asked his cabinet to vote on some major issues. Toward the end of his administration, however, he backed away from the board of directors approach. For example, when North Korea attacked South Korea in 1950 Truman never once convened his cabinet to discuss the matter. He relied instead on an informal group—consisting of the secretaries of defense and state, the Joint Chiefs of Staff, and some of his closest aides—to advise him on the entry of the United States into the war. Throughout his administration Truman reserved the most difficult decisions for himself. Presidential scholar Stephen Hess has written: "Over the years he [Truman] drew back from the board of directors concept; powers delegated could be powers lost, and Truman, while modest about himself as president, was zealous in protecting those prerogatives that he felt were inherent in the presidency." [13]

Dwight D. Eisenhower (1953-1961) took his cabinet more seriously than any other twentieth-century president. He established a cabinet secretariat (one of the cabinet secretaries set the agenda and served as liaison with the president), and he charged his cabinet with both advising him on major issues and seeing that every decision was carried out.

Eisenhower expanded cabinet meetings to include not only department secretaries but also important aides such as the U.S. ambassador to the United Nations, the budget director, the White House chief of staff, as well as the national security affairs assistant and other top White House advisers. Vice presidents have served on cabinets since Franklin Roosevelt's first administration, but Eisenhower was the first president to effectively use his vice president in the cabinet. He made the vice president chairman of several cabinet committees and his acting chairman of the cabinet if he was unable to attend a meeting. Eisenhower's cabinet, which usually numbered around twenty or more, held regularly scheduled, weekly meetings which often lasted three or more hours.

Although Eisenhower accepted responsibility for final decisions, he attempted to make the cabinet more than just a body of advisers by including wide-ranging, important issues on the cabinet agenda. According to noted presidential scholar Thomas E. Cronin,

> [Eisenhower] did, within certain limits, encourage his cabinet members to take an independent line of their own and argue it out within the cabinet session. Eisenhower fully appreciated the limits of a cabinet system but seemed motivated to use the cabinet sessions both as a means to keep himself informed and as a way to prevent the personality conflicts, throat-cutting, and end-running that had characterized the history of past administrations.[14]

In his relationship with his cabinet, John F. Kennedy (1961-1963) did not follow the example set by President Eisenhower. Although he spent time with his department heads individually, President Kennedy held cabinet meetings as seldom as possible. Historian Arthur M. Schlesinger, Jr., has quoted Kennedy as saying, "Cabinet meetings are simply useless. Why should the Postmaster General sit here and listen to a discussion of the problems of Laos?" [15] Because he believed that few subjects warranted discussion by the entire cabinet, Kennedy preferred to spend his time with the aides and secretaries most concerned with a specific issue. Eisenhower was highly tolerant of meetings because of his long military experience, but Kennedy wanted to avoid them. Hess wrote: "Kennedy was too restless to sit for long periods, too impatient with long-winded speakers, and too mentally agile to accept repetitious, circuitous Cabinet-NSC discussions as a tolerable method for receiving information." [16]

Although Lyndon B. Johnson (1963-1969) used his cabinet much more than Kennedy, cabinet meetings were mostly for show and contained little in the way of substantive discussion. Johnson, in fact, used cabinet meetings to create the impression of consensus within his administration. According to Johnson's press secretary George Reedy, "Cabinet meetings were held with considerable regularity, with fully predetermined agendas and fully prewritten statements. In general, they consisted of briefings by cabinet members followed by a later release of the statements to the press. It was regarded by all participants except the president as a painful experience." [17] Johnson thus gave little credit to the cabinet as a consultative body, keeping many of his cabinet officers at a distance. His use of his cabinet to dispense information and to promote the appearance that a substantive debate was taking place led one of his cabinet officers to complain: "Cabinet meetings under L.B.J. were really perfunctory. They served two purposes: to let Dean Rusk brief us on the state of foreign affairs and let the president give us some occasional new political or personnel marching orders." [18]

Prior to his election in 1968 Richard Nixon (1969-1974) seemed to be calling for a powerful cabinet in his administration: "I don't want a government of yes-men.... [I want] a cabinet made up of the ablest men in America, leaders in their own right and not merely by virtue of appointment ... men who will command the public's respect and the president's attention by the power of their intellect and the force of their ideas." [19] After his election Nixon took the unprecedented step of introducing his soon-to-be appointed cabinet on national television.

Despite his announced intention to use a cabinet system, President Nixon held few cabinet meetings and relegated the cabinet to a position of lesser importance than that of most of his White House staff. At one point Secretary of the Interior Walter J. Hickel, complaining that he had had only two or three private meetings with the president, advised Nixon: "Permit me to suggest that you consider meeting, on an individual and conversational basis, with members of your cabinet. Perhaps through such conversations we can gain greater insight into the problems confronting us all, into solutions of these problems." [20] Because of his disdain for his original cabinet, Nixon had a totally new one in place five years later. Only the Watergate revelations forced him to promise to deal regularly and openly with his cabinet, but his eventual resignation prevented him from making good on that promise.

Both Gerald R. Ford (1974-1977) and Jimmy Carter (1977-1981) pledged to use their cabinets as decision-making bodies. Although both held regular cabinet meetings at the beginning of their administrations, only President Ford came close to making his cabinet a meaningful advisory group. Convinced that Watergate resulted from Nixon's carelessness in allowing his personal aides to gain too much power at the expense of his cabinet, Ford restored the cabinet secretariat established by Eisenhower but abandoned by subsequent presidents. Like Eisenhower, he asked a cabinet secretary to draw up formal agendas for cabinet meetings, which often were used to gauge the views of his department heads on different issues. Hoxie noted: "More than any other president in the period from 1916 to 1981, he [Ford] restored the cabinet as a deliberative, meaningful advisory and administrative body." [21]

Jimmy Carter, in contrast, failed to achieve his goal of revitalizing the cabinet. Early in his administration President Carter made this promise: "There will never be an instance while I am in office where the members of the White House staff dominate or act in a superior position to the members of the cabinet." [22] In fact, regular use of his cabinet became less of a concern as his administration elapsed, resulting in fewer and fewer cabinet meetings. Carter met with his cabinet weekly during the first year of his administration; biweekly during the second year; monthly during the third year; and only sporadically during his last year in office.[23] Early on, the Carter White House became embroiled in a controversy over the cabinet's status. Aide Jack Watson advocated a strong cabinet, but close Carter adviser Hamilton Jordan preferred that major decisions be made by high-level White House staffers. Jordan finally won, and Carter's cabinet lost any hope of achieving much prominence in presidential decision making.

Similarly, Ronald Reagan (1981-1989) met less frequently with his cabinet as his term in office progressed. His administration was much more successful, however, in utilizing the cabinet as an advisory group. Reagan divided the cabinet into seven councils, each of which addressed a specific substantive area: economic affairs, commerce and trade, food and agriculture, human resources, natural resources, legal policy, and management and administration. Under this system, cabinet members could concentrate on matters germane only to them and not to the cabinet as a whole. Indeed, in some respects this system restored the advisory function that the cabinet enjoyed during the Eisenhower administration.

Nixon fired Interior Secretary Walter J. Hickel, who, it turned out, was an outspoken opponent of some of the Nixon administration's programs.

Nixon Project, National Archives

Role and Function of the Cabinet

Most presidents have come to expect little from their cabinets except the opportunity to exchange information. At best, the cabinet may serve as a source of advice for the president, but this use of the cabinet has been rare. Even when presidents, such as Nixon and Carter, emphasized the importance of their cabinets early in their administrations, commitment to a strong cabinet soon diminished. As administrations mature, daily administrative matters and domestic and international crises often take more and more of a president's time. Moreover, presidential programs and goals become fixed, and cabinet secretaries, as heads of their departments, may find themselves competing for scarce resources. Cabinet meetings thus become less frequent, less enthusiastic, and less cordial, as well as a burden for both the department secretary and the president. Indeed, some department secretaries see cabinet meetings as nothing more than opportunities for their peers to take potshots at their departments' programs. Seeking to protect their administrative turf and hoping to avoid excessive and detrimental departmental sniping, many secretaries intentionally exercise restraint in cabinet meetings. Jesse H. Jones, Franklin Roosevelt's secretary of commerce, declared: "My principal reason for not having a great deal to say at cabinet meetings was that there was no one at the table who could be of help to me except the president, and when I needed to consult him, I did not choose a cabinet meeting to do so." [24]

Cabinets as Advisers

Although many presidents have intentionally avoided placing their cabinets in an advisory role, such a role is still considered the ideal one for the presidential cabinet. In 1940 the leading British scholar on the presidency, Harold J. Laski, offered this description of what a good cabinet should do for an American president:

> A good cabinet ought to be a place where the large outlines of policy can be hammered out in common, where the essential strategy is decided upon, where the president knows that he will hear, both in affirmation and in doubt, even in negation, most of what can be said about the direction he proposes to follow.[25]

No American presidential cabinet has lived up to Laski's model, however, and some presidents—Jackson, Wilson, and Kennedy, for example—have even gone to great lengths to avoid taking advice from their cabinets. Only Eisenhower came close to the model suggested by Laski, and even his cabinet procedures came up lacking.

Historical experience suggests that cabinets can serve presidents as an advisory group in one of three ways. First, in the cabinet meetings of some past presidents, department heads discussed issues and problems informally, primarily to exchange information. This custom was generally followed by Roosevelt, Truman, Kennedy, Johnson, and Nixon. Second, the Eisenhower cabinet regularly considered specific issues, using papers authored by cabinet members and circulated prior to meetings. Both the president and the cabinet were aided by agendas, concise records, and a small secretariat. And third, under both Eisenhower and Truman the National Security Council provided summit discussions of issue papers that earlier had been subjected to a thorough interdepartmental review, with dissidents identified and alternative language proposed. No president has ever utilized a cabinet in this manner, however.[26]

Why then do most presidents avoid using their cabinets as advisory groups? Primarily, presidents are rarely willing to delegate the decision-making power needed to make the cabinet an effective advisory board. Many presidents feel that doing so might challenge their power. Moreover, a strong, institutionalized cabinet with its own staff might put the president at a disadvantage in the control of resources and information. Few presidents want to feel that they are not in control of the flow of information in the White House. According to presidential scholar Richard M. Pious, "A collective cabinet with its own staff could become a competitor for 'The Executive Power' and come to function as a 'council of state'—the system rejected at the Constitutional Convention." [27] Consequently, presidents have tended to downgrade the importance of their cabinets.

The presidential reluctance to use cabinets as advisory groups also stems from situations in which presidents are forced to choose cabinet appointees who may be weak or who may not represent the goals of their administrations. Schlesinger has contended that "genuinely strong presidents are not afraid to surround themselves with genuinely strong men [in the cabinet]." [28] Past presidents, however, have rarely had more than one or two notable departmental secretaries at one time. Most of the time cabinet selections are influenced heavily by political considerations. Hess has written:

> Historically, presidents have selected their cabinets on the basis of traditions, trade-offs, and obligations.... Once the obligations were fitted into the appropriate slots, balances had to be made.... The end result was often that a new president found himself surrounded with some people of less than inspiring ability, personalities that were incompatible, and even some cabinet members of questionable loyalty.[29]

Because past presidents seldom have been closely associated with their cabinet officers, they have tended to rely on their White House staffs for advice. Since the establishment of the Executive Office of the President and the White House staff in 1939, the White House staff has acted as a threat to the cabinet's role as a policy-making institution. With their closer proximity to the Oval Office, White House staffers have more access to the president than the cabinet. Moreover, these staffers often are longtime personal friends of the president, and they exhibit loyalty not necessarily found among members of the cabinet. Both Presidents Nixon and Carter reduced the influence of their cabinets in favor of the personal loyalties of certain members of their staffs. Indeed, both presidents asked their cabinets to resign en masse to allow them to appoint new "loyal" cabinet members and to rely more closely on their personal staffs. Specifically, cabinet advice gave way to Nixon's reliance on his trusted aide John Ehrlichman and Carter's close connections with aide Hamilton Jordan and press secretary Jody Powell. Writing about this tendency for presidents to rely on advice from their staffs rather than their cabinets, British author Godfrey Hodgson noted:

> The cabinet has been losing ground to the White House staff for a long time now.... Where successive presidents ... have all come to rely more and more on their own staff and less and less on their cabinet members, where, moreover, two such different presidents as Richard Nixon and Jimmy Carter have both turned to their staff for help after an initial, apparently sincere effort to reverse the trend and give more authority to cabinet members, it is tempting to come to the conclusion that the decline of the cabinet is inevitable.[30]

The result is that the stronger and more assertive presidents attempt to be, the less likely they are to use their cabinets as vital advisory bodies. Thus, to protect their powers and to guard against a vigorous cabinet system that may be more of a threat than a help, presidents may use cabinet meetings more as devices for generating enthusiasm or displaying cabinet unity than as devices for a thorough discussion of problems facing the nation. Most presidents want advice when they ask for it, but they also want to reserve the right to either disregard it or not even seek it. A strong cabinet system that imposes advice upon them is then something to be resisted.

Inner Cabinet

Although presidents may shun their collective cabinets as sources of information for decision-making purposes, individual cabinet members may serve as important sources of experience and advice. According to political scientist Frank Kessler, "Seasoned political veterans in the cabinet can provide a president one thing that the most dedicated and informed White House staffer often cannot, and that is a sense of perspective gained from years of experience and political savvy."[31]

Certain cabinet members, by virtue of either their close relationship with the president or the department they head, find themselves with greater access to the president and often the opportunity to influence the administration's policy. In fact, every cabinet usually has one or two members who have dominant personalities and who form close relationships with the president. In the Truman administration, for example, Secretary of State Dean Acheson and George C. Marshall, who served at different times as secretary of state and secretary of defense, overshadowed the rest of the cabinet. With his strong and outspoken foreign policy positions, Secretary of State John Foster Dulles dominated the Eisenhower cabinet. As defense secretary during the cold war and the Vietnam war, Robert S. McNamara enjoyed close ties with both Presidents Kennedy and Johnson. Most of these cabinet members also had a significant influence on presidential decision making based upon their personal friendships with the president. Acheson's friendship with Truman, for example, allowed him to greatly influence the president. These were, however, personal relationships based upon intimate friendships and confidences; they were never transferred to colleagues or successors.

Access to the president is often determined by the amount of importance that the president places on a particular department. Because departments of defense and state receive much attention from presidents, their secretaries usually have a more cordial relationship with their presidents based on the frequency of their contacts. On occasion some departments, and thus their secretaries, might actually increase in importance in the eyes of the president. For example, the Department of Health, Education and Welfare (HEW) took on more significance as the number and size of social programs increased during the 1960s. John W. Gardner, secretary of HEW, gained status within the cabinet as he began the significant task of managing the Johnson administration's major education and health programs. Usually, however, presidents devote most of their time and attention to national security and foreign policy matters. Consequently, some staff members, particularly heads of agencies such as the Central Intelligence Agency (CIA), may have more access to the president than most cabinet members.

Composition of the Inner Cabinet

Not all cabinet members are treated equally. Cronin has suggested that contemporary presidential cabinets can be divided into inner and outer cabinets.[32] Based on extensive interviews with White House aides and cabinet officers about their views of the departments and their access to the president, Cronin found that the inner cabinet generally includes the secretaries of state, defense, and Treasury, and the attorney general (a body analogous to President Washington's first cabinet). Because of the importance of their departments to the making of public policy, these cabinet members have been the most successful in influencing presidential decisions in a broad range of policy areas. The departments that deal almost exclusively with domestic policy and commerce form the outer cabinet. Their secretaries usually are more concerned with advocacy for their constituent groups than with advising the president on policy issues.

Because presidents usually are very selective in filling appointments to inner cabinet positions, the views of these cabinet members are likely to mirror those of their chief executive. In addition, these appointees are often Washington veterans such as John Foster Dulles, Cyrus R. Vance (Carter's secretary of state), and George P. Shultz (Reagan's secretary of state). Significant responsibility and visibility accompany these cabinet positions, and the officials holding them are usually in contact with the president on a daily basis. In addition to the top four cabinet positions, the inner cabinet frequently includes White House aides who have a close counseling relationship with the president.

The inner cabinet is generally divided into two subgroups, the first of which Cronin labeled the national security cabinet. This group is composed of the two cabinet members responsible for national security policy, the secretaries of state and defense. During the French crisis of 1793 President Washington met with his cabinet almost every day. Similarly, recent presidents have met at least weekly with their national security cabinets and have maintained telephone contact with them daily. One Johnson aide believed that President Johnson trusted just two of his cabinet members, Secretary of State Dean Rusk and Secretary of Defense Robert McNamara. Likewise, Secretary of State Cyrus Vance and Secretary of Defense Harold Brown were probably Carter's closest cabinet counselors.[33]

In addition to the national security cabinet, presidents rely heavily on the legal and economic counsel that they receive from their attorneys general and secretaries of the Treasury—the second inner cabinet subgroup. In recent years the Justice Department has been headed by close friends—or relatives—of the president. John Kennedy, for example, appointed his brother Robert, and Richard Nixon appointed his law partner and trusted friend John N. Mitchell. Jimmy Carter named his close friend Griffin B. Bell, and Ronald Reagan, during his second term in office, appointed one of his longtime California advisers and friends, Edwin Meese III. Because the attorney general usually serves as the president's attorney, the head of the Justice Department has a special responsibility that brings about close, personal contact with the president.

The secretary of the Treasury has been an important presidential adviser since the days of the Washington administration when Alexander Hamilton first occupied the office. Although the formal responsibility of the Treasury Department may have been somewhat diminished with its loss of the Bureau of the Budget and the creation of the Council of Economic Advisers as an independent presidential advisory board, the secretary of the Treasury continues to play a significant role in domestic monetary and fiscal matters, as well as international commerce and currency. The latter area brings the Treasury secretary into the inner cabinet of foreign policy counselors. Cronin has suggested that the importance of the Treasury secretary as a member of the inner circle is to some degree a function of the intelligence and personality of the secretary. President Eisenhower said of his Treasury secretary George M. Humphrey: "In cabinet meetings, I always wait for George Humphrey to speak. I sit back and listen to the others talk while he doesn't say anything. But I know that when he speaks, he will say just what I was thinking."[34]

One curious feature of the inner cabinet is that its members tend to be more noticeably interchangeable than the members of the outer cabinet. Henry L. Stimson, for example, served as William Howard Taft's secretary of war,

Herbert C. Hoover's secretary of state, and Franklin Roosevelt's secretary of war. Dean Acheson was undersecretary of the Treasury under Roosevelt and secretary of state under Truman. Eisenhower's attorney general William P. Rogers later became Nixon's first secretary of state. Elliot L. Richardson served as undersecretary of state, secretary of health, education and welfare, defense secretary, and attorney general. George Shultz, another versatile cabinet member, served as Nixon's secretary of the Treasury and later as Reagan's secretary of state. When Kennedy was trying to attract McNamara to the cabinet, he reportedly offered him his choice of either the defense post or the Treasury post. There has been some movement between the inner and outer cabinets, but most position shifts have remained in the inner cabinet.

Although outsiders are brought into the inner cabinet by all presidents, why is there so much movement within that cabinet? Why are presidents reluctant to go beyond those few cabinet members who served in an earlier inner cabinet? Cronin has suggested simply that presidents look for appointees with whom they feel comfortable for these positions.

> This interchangeability may result from the broad-ranging interests of the inner-cabinet positions, from the counseling style and relationships that develop in the course of an inner-cabinet secretary's tenure, or from the already close personal friendship that has often existed with the president. It may be easier for inner-cabinet than for outer-cabinet secretaries to maintain the presidential perspective; presidents certainly try to choose men they know and respect for these intimate positions.[35]

Cabinets as Advocates: The Outer Cabinet

The outer cabinet deals with more highly organized and specialized clientele than the inner cabinet. While inner cabinet members are selected more on the basis of personal friendships and loyalty, outer cabinet members are selected more on the basis of geographical, ethnic, or political representation. And because they have fewer loyalties to the president, they often adopt an advocacy position for their departments.

The secretaries of interior, agriculture, commerce, labor, health and human services, housing and urban development, transportation, energy, education, and veterans affairs form the outer cabinet. Because their interests are so specialized, these secretaries are under extreme pressure from their clientele groups and political parties to serve specific interests. According to Cronin, "Whereas three of the four inner cabinet departments preside over policies that usually, though often imprudently, are perceived to be largely nonpartisan or bipartisan—national security, foreign policy, and the economy—the domestic departments almost always are subject to intense crossfire between partisan and domestic interest groups."[36]

Department secretaries are torn between loyalty to their presidents and loyalty to the departments they represent. Almost all secretaries go through what political scientist Richard P. Nathan has called "the ritualistic courting and mating process with the bureaucracy."[37] Because most outer cabinet members have only limited loyalty to the president, they usually are "captured" by the permanent bureaucracies. In fact, it is often in the best interest of secretaries to "go native" by adopting the concerns of the departments they administer, thereby gaining the confidence of the career bureaucrats who work daily to further the pursuits of the department. Political scientist Hugh Heclo wrote: "Fighting your counterparts in other departments creates confidence and support beneath you.... Less politically effective executives may be personally admired by civil servants but have little to offer in return for bureaucratic support."[38] Not surprisingly, the tendency of cabinet secretaries to assume an advocacy role for their respective departments increases over the term of an administration. As they see their influence with the president diminishing, department secretaries try to build their political base of support within their own bureaucracies by forging good will with their bureaucrats.

Cabinet members who adopt an advocacy position contrary to their president's may find life in Washington difficult. The history of the presidency is full of examples of department secretaries who were "fired" by their presidents for not publicly supporting the president's programs. Truman fired Henry Wallace, his secretary of commerce, for criticizing his foreign policy, and Eisenhower fired Secretary of Labor Martin P. Durkin. In appointing Durkin, former head of the AFL Plumbers and Pipe Fitters Union, Eisenhower was seeking to broaden the perspective of his cabinet. Durkin apparently proved to be more of a spokesperson for labor than Eisenhower had expected. Later, Nixon fired Secretary of the Interior Walter J. Hickel, who, it turned out, was an outspoken opponent of some of the Nixon administration's programs. In fact, few cabinet members stay the length of a president's administration. In recent years the average tenure of a cabinet member has been forty months. In the first five years of his administration Nixon replaced his entire cabinet with a total of thirty appointments, making the average tenure of a cabinet member in the Nixon administration about eighteen months. Over a single year and a half period Nixon had five attorneys general.[39]

Relations between presidents and their cabinet members—sometimes even members of the inner cabinet—deteriorate rapidly after the inauguration. For example, scarcely one and a half years after being sworn into office, Secretary of State Alexander M. Haig, Jr., left the Reagan administration when he failed to gain the confidence of the president and his aides. More often than not, however, friction develops between presidents and their cabinet members because cabinet secretaries adopt the view of the bureaucracies and constituencies they represent, whether that view represents that of the president. Further complicating the problem, department secretaries—who have the political power and skill needed to achieve their leadership positions in their own right—are usually not afraid to stand up to the president on policy positions they believe are correct.

As a cabinet secretary assumes a larger advocacy role, the relationship between president and cabinet member becomes more strained. Cabinet meetings become increasingly confrontational, and the cabinet becomes less useful to the president as an effective advisory body. If cabinet secretaries carefully build their bases of support, they can effectively frustrate a president's policy-making initiatives. Franklin Roosevelt often complained about the difficulty he had in dealing with the bureaucracies:

> The Treasury is so large and so far-flung and ingrained in its practices that I find it almost impossible to get the action and results that I want even with Henry [Morgenthau] there. But, Treasury is nothing compared with the

Cabinet Holdovers

When President-elect Herbert C. Hoover sent his list of cabinet nominations to the Senate for approval in 1929, he failed to mention that his predecessor's controversial Treasury secretary, Andrew W. Mellon, would be staying on the job. "He wanted to minimize the fight" by shielding Mellon from a confirmation battle, said Senate historian Richard A. Baker. Mellon had already been confirmed once when President Warren G. Harding tapped him for the Treasury post in 1921. And he had held the job throughout Calvin Coolidge's 1923-1929 presidency as well.

Hoover's decision to keep Mellon on drew howls of protest from liberal and progressive lawmakers who opposed Mellon's economic policies. But the president-elect had ample precedent for his move.

From the time of John Adams's presidency, cabinet members appointed by one administration had been passed to the next without having to wait for Senate approval. In fact, holdovers were quite common. John Adams retained five members of George Washington's cabinet. Between then and 1929, 110 cabinet appointees served in consecutive administrations. The majority of those, however, were retained between terms of the same president. From Washington's time to the present, only 42 appointees have been held over from one administration to the next when there was a clear change of power.

In 1989 George Bush followed in Hoover's footsteps. Three of his cabinet appointments—Treasury Secretary Nicholas F. Brady, Education Secretary Lauro F. Cavazos, and Attorney General Dick Thornburgh—were holdovers from the Reagan administration. None had to be reconfirmed.

In the years between Hoover and Bush, many presidents have retained their closest advisers from one term to the next. When a president died in office, his successor often kept the cabinet team intact. In fact, when Lyndon B. Johnson was elected in his own right in 1964, he held onto eight cabinet members originally appointed by John F. Kennedy.

The Bush cabinet, however, marks the first time since Hoover took over from Coolidge that a completely new administration has retained department heads named by a former president. In part, that is because it is the first time since 1929 that there has been a "friendly takeover" at the White House, with the incoming president belonging to the same party as his predecessor. "Obviously when a new party comes in, they'll want new cabinet members," Baker said.

Bush was on firm legal ground when he asserted that his holdovers did not need to be reconfirmed. "Nowhere in the Constitution is there a specific termination date" for cabinet secretaries, a Senate legal adviser explained. "They are appointed for an indefinite period of time, and unless they are dismissed by the president [or resign], they are not subject to reconfirmation."

Cavazos and Thornburgh submitted letters of resignation in compliance with President Reagan's efforts to clear the way for Bush. But Reagan did not accept those letters once Bush made his choices public. Brady was writing his letter when Bush asked him to stay on the job November 15. He never finished it.

Source: Excerpted from Macon Morehouse, "Cabinet Holdovers Need No Senate Approval," *Congressional Quarterly Weekly Report*, November 26, 1988, 3390.

> State Department. You should go through the experience of trying to get any changes in thinking, policy, and action of the career diplomats and then you'd know what a real problem was.[40]

Close presidential advisers usually view outer cabinet members as more of a burden than a help to presidential decision making. Over the years, many high-level White House staffers have performed cabinet-level roles for the president. Some actually found themselves attending presidential cabinet meetings. Eisenhower, for example, designated aide Sherman Adams to serve as an ex officio member of his cabinet. Other presidents have simply trusted and confided in their close aides more than their cabinets. For example, for his important decisions, Kennedy preferred the advice of aides Theodore C. Sorensen and McGeorge Bundy over that of his cabinet members. Such White House advisers believe that they have the president's best interests in mind. In their view, most outer cabinet members neglect the president's interests for those of their own clientele. One close Carter aide explained: "Nobody expects Ray Marshall at Labor to be a spokesman for anything other than big labor. You just have to live with this. . . ."[41] The White House does not view advocacy as anything positive.

Advocacy alienates outer cabinet members even more than they already are. For example, in response to pressure from western Republicans, Richard Nixon appointed Walter Hickel, a former governor of Alaska, to head the Department of the Interior, instead of his first choice, Rogers C. B. Morton from Maryland. At first feared by environmentalists, Hickel turned out to be an opponent of big oil's plans to route the Alaskan pipeline through some northern wilderness lands. Hickel's opposition to the Nixon administration's programs and his tendency to be outspoken quickly got him into hot water with the president, who then considered Hickel an adversary. Hickel explained:

> Initially I considered it a compliment because, to me, an adversary in an organization is a valuable asset. It was only after the president had used the term many times and with a disapproving inflection that I realized he considered an adversary an enemy. I could not understand why he would consider me an enemy.
>
> As I sensed that the conversation was about to end, I asked, "Mr. President, do you want me to leave the administration?"
>
> He jumped from his chair, very hurried and agitated. He said, "That's one option we hadn't considered." He called in Ehrlichman and said: "John, I want you to

> handle this. Wally asked whether he should leave. That's one option we hadn't considered."[42]

A week later Hickel was fired. Although extreme, Hickel's case is typical of what most outer cabinet members face when they consider their relationships with their presidents.

In reality, presidents rarely fire cabinet members; cabinet members usually anticipate presidential dissatisfaction and resign. Hickel's case was an exception, as he forced Nixon to ask him to leave. Cabinet members sometimes become so disenchanted with presidential programs and policies that they decide to leave on their own accord. For example, after becoming increasingly concerned about the direction of U.S. foreign policy during the late 1970s, Secretary of State Cyrus Vance finally decided to part company with the Carter administration over the attempted Iranian hostage rescue mission. Although he disagreed privately with many of Carter's foreign policy decisions during his tenure, Vance did not make his concerns public until three weeks after his resignation.

Cabinet Alternatives

Has the presidential cabinet outived its usefulness? Presidents continue to seek the advice of their inner cabinets, but rarely in the history of the presidency have collective cabinet meetings been meaningful. Many scholars believe that as long as presidents are subject to political pressures to appoint certain cabinet members who are not personally loyal to them and as long as cabinet secretaries are captured by the interests of their departments, the collective cabinet will remain useless as an advisory group.

This is not to say, however, that presidents and presidential scholars have ignored alternatives to the present cabinet system. Many, in fact, have sought ways to utilize individual cabinet members. Most presidents have used task forces composed of several cabinet or subcabinet members and White House aides to help them study specific problems. President Kennedy, for example, used many such task forces to study national security problems, chaired invariably by his brother, Attorney General Robert F. Kennedy. Kennedy required these study groups to produce both majority and minority reports.

Although task forces produce some meaningful and innovative policy analysis, they have had some problems. Typical of the Kennedy task forces was the executive committee he created to handle the Cuban missile crisis in 1962. It was composed of the president, Vice President Lyndon Johnson, Secretary of State Dean Rusk, Secretary of Defense Robert McNamara, Secretary of the Treasury C. Douglas Dillon, Attorney General Robert Kennedy, Special Foreign Affairs Assistant McGeorge Bundy, Chairman of the Joint Chiefs of Staff Gen. Maxwell Taylor, White House aide Theodore Sorensen, CIA Director John McCone, and Paul Nitze, George W. Ball, and Llewellyn Thompson, all from outside the executive branch. Kennedy ordered the task force to put any other duties they might have aside. The system worked well for the missile crisis, but would it have worked if there had been anything else pressing the administration for attention? According to Frank Kessler, "Presidential task forces and White House staff-created options provided a certain creative chaos to the Kennedy system for gathering foreign policy ideas. The arrangements proved useful in moving from crisis to crisis but left much to be desired in heading off crises before they reached the flash point. Long-range policy making suffered. . . ."[43]

Some scholars such as Stephen Hess have maintained that the cabinet should be strengthened and made more collegial. Hess has argued for a presidency in which responsibility is shared by the president and the cabinet:

> Effective presidential leadership in the immediate future is likely to result only from creating more nearly collegial administrations in which presidents rely on the cabinet officers as the principal sources of advice and hold them personally accountable—in the British sense of "the doctrine of ministerial responsibility"—for the operations of the different segments of government.[44]

Benjamin V. Cohen, one of Franklin Roosevelt's chief advisers during the 1930s, suggested a similar idea in a 1974 lecture at the University of California. Cohen called for creation of an executive council composed of five to eight distinguished citizens appointed by the president. The council would have staff, access to information, and the power to monitor and coordinate government activities. The president would be obliged to consult with this group before acting on critical decisions.[45]

President Nixon apparently considered introducing a "supercabinet" in his second term. In his 1971 State of the Union address he proposed merging the eight existing domestic departments into four new superagencies: resources, human resources, economic affairs, and community development. Although Congress proved uncooperative and refused to approve his plan, Nixon proceeded to name four cabinet members (the secretaries of Treasury, agriculture, HEW, and HUD) as presidential counselors. As White House aides as well as cabinet members, they assumed functional responsibility over the areas served by the proposed superagencies. Nixon's efforts in this area were soon sidetracked, however, as he became engulfed in the Watergate scandal.

Some presidents have formed cabinet councils in an attempt to integrate the advice of department secretaries and White House advisers on important policy decisions. Organized on the basis of broad policy areas, such councils function much like Eisenhower's full cabinet; they deliberate policy recommendations, develop administration positions, and coordinate presidential decisions. Nominally in charge of each council, the president usually designates one of the department heads as chair. Because the White House provides staff support, the councils are able to act fairly independently.

Both Presidents Ford and Reagan, who tended to delegate much of their authority, used cabinet councils. Reagan usually designated one of his cabinet members or White House aides to chair a council in its initial stages of discussion. During the final sessions the president presided. Patterned after the National Security Council, Reagan's cabinet councils were designed to make cabinet members part of the presidential decision-making process by centralizing policy discussions. During the first eighteen months of the Reagan administration, the councils considered approximately two hundred issues. There appeared to be some danger, however, that the councils would do just the opposite of what they were intended to do. Critics have argued that instead of decentralizing the presidential advisory system, cabinet councils actually centralize decision making in the White House or in an even smaller group similar to the inner cabinet.

Notes

1. See Richard F. Fenno, Jr., *The President's Cabinet* (New York: Vintage Books, 1959), 12.
2. Alexander Hamilton, John Jay, and James Madison, *The Federalist,* Intro. by Edward Gaylord Bourne (New York: Tudor, 1937), ii, 57.
3. James Thomas Flexner, *Washington: The Indispensable Man* (Boston: Little, Brown, 1974), 220.
4. R. Gordon Hoxie, "Cabinet," in *Encyclopedia of American Political History: Studies of the Principal Movements and Ideas,* 3 vols., ed. Jack P. Greene (New York: Scribner's, 1984), 1:149.
5. Flexner, *Washington: The Indispensable Man,* 326.
6. Hoxie, "Cabinet," 152.
7. Quoted in Emmet John Hughes, *The Living Presidency: The Resources and Dilemmas of the American Presidential Office* (Baltimore, Md.: Penguin, 1973), 147.
8. Hoxie, "Cabinet," 156.
9. Quoted in Fenno, *The President's Cabinet,* 123.
10. Quoted in ibid., 125.
11. Hoxie, "Cabinet," 158-159.
12. Quoted in Thomas E. Cronin, *The State of the Presidency,* 2d ed. (Boston: Little, Brown, 1980), 263.
13. Stephen Hess, *Organizing the Presidency* (Washington, D.C.: Brookings, 1976), 46.
14. Cronin, *The State of the Presidency,* 271.
15. Arthur M. Schlesinger, Jr., *A Thousand Days* (New York: Fawcett, 1967), 632.
16. Hess, *Organizing the Presidency,* 84.
17. George Reedy, *The Twilight of the Presidency* (New York: New American Library, 1970), 74.
18. Quoted in Cronin, *The State of the Presidency,* 266.
19. Excerpted from a radio address dated September 19, 1968, in Robert Hirschfield, ed., *Power of the Modern Presidency,* 2d ed. (Chicago: Aldine, 1973), 165-166.
20. *New York Times,* May 7, 1970, C18.
21. Hoxie, "Cabinet," 161.
22. Quoted in Edward D. Feigenbaum, "Staffing, Organization, and Decision-Making in the Ford and Carter White Houses," *Presidential Studies Quarterly* 10 (Summer 1980): 371.
23. George C. Edwards III and Stephen J. Wayne, *Presidential Leadership* (New York: St. Martin's Press, 1985), 173.
24. Quoted in Robert J. Sickels, *Presidential Transactions* (Englewood Cliffs, N.J.: Prentice-Hall, 1974), 31.
25. Harold J. Laski, *The American Presidency: An Interpretation* (New York: Harper, 1940), 257-258.
26. Bradley H. Patterson, Jr., *The President's Cabinet: Issues and Questions* (Washington, D.C.: American Society for Public Administration, 1976), 113.
27. Richard M. Pious, *The American Presidency* (New York: Basic Books, 1979), 241.
28. Arthur M. Schlesinger, Jr., "Presidential War," *New York Times Magazine,* January 7, 1973, 28.
29. Hess, *Organizing the Presidency,* 180.
30. Godfrey Hodgson, *All Things to All Men: The False Promise of the Modern American Presidency* (New York: Simon and Schuster, 1980), 109-112.
31. Frank Kessler, *The Dilemmas of Presidential Leadership: Of Caretakers and Kings* (Englewood Cliffs, N.J.: Prentice-Hall, 1982), 92.
32. Cronin, *The State of the Presidency,* 276-293.
33. Ibid., 278.
34. Quoted in ibid., 280.
35. Ibid., 282.
36. Ibid., 283.
37. Richard P. Nathan, *The Plot That Failed* (New York: Wiley, 1975), 40.
38. Hugh Heclo, *A Government of Strangers* (Washington, D.C.: Brookings, 1977), 196.
39. Pious, *The American Presidency,* 238.
40. Quoted in Kessler, *The Dilemmas of Presidential Leadership,* 93.
41. Quoted in Cronin, *The State of the Presidency,* 283.
42. Walter J. Hickel, *Who Owns America?* (Englewood Cliffs, N.J.: Prentice-Hall, 1971), 259.
43. Kessler, *The Dilemmas of Presidential Leadership,* 106.
44. Hess, *Organizing the Presidency,* 154.
45. Benjamin V. Cohen, "Presidential Responsibility and American Democracy," Royer Lecture, University of California, Berkeley, May 23, 1974; quoted in Cronin, *The State of the Presidency,* 361-362.

Selected Bibliography

Cronin, Thomas E. *The State of the Presidency.* Boston: Little, Brown, 1975.

Edwards, George C., III, and Stephen J. Wayne. *Presidential Leadership.* New York: St. Martin's Press, 1985.

Feigenbaum, Edward D. "Staffing, Organization, and Decision-Making in the Ford and Carter White Houses." *Presidential Studies Quarterly* 10 (Summer 1980): 364-377.

Fenno, Richard F., Jr. *The President's Cabinet.* New York: Vintage, 1959.

Flexner, James Thomas. *Washington: The Indispensable Man.* Boston: Little, Brown, 1974.

Hamilton, Alexander, John Jay, and James Madison. *The Federalist.* Intro. by Edward Gaylord Bourne. New York: Tudor, 1937.

Heclo, Hugh. *A Government of Strangers.* Washington, D.C.: Brookings, 1977.

Hess, Stephen. *Organizing the Presidency.* Washington, D.C.: Brookings, 1976.

Hickel, Walter J. *Who Owns America?* Englewood Cliffs, N.J.: Prentice-Hall, 1971.

Hirschfield, Robert, ed. *Power of the Modern Presidency,* 2d ed. Chicago: Aldine, 1973.

Hodgson, Godfrey. *All Things to All Men: The False Promise of the Modern American Presidency.* New York: Simon and Schuster, 1980.

Hoxie, R. Gordon. "Cabinet." In *Encyclopedia of American Political History: Studies of the Principal Movements and Ideas,* Vol. 1, ed. Jack P. Greene. New York: Scribner's, 1984.

Hughes, Emmet John. *The Living Presidency: The Resources and Dilemmas of the American Presidential Office.* Baltimore, Md.: Penguin, 1973.

Kessler, Frank. *The Dilemmas of Presidential Leadership: Of Caretakers and Kings.* Englewood Cliffs, N.J.: Prentice-Hall, 1982.

Laski, Harold J. *The American Presidency: An Interpretation.* New York: Harper, 1940.

Nathan, Richard P. *The Plot That Failed.* New York: Wiley, 1975.

Patterson, Bradley H., Jr. *The President's Cabinet: Issues and Questions.* Washington, D.C.: American Society for Public Administration, 1976.

Pious, Richard M. *The American Presidency.* New York: Basic Books, 1979.

Reedy, George. *The Twilight of the Presidency.* New York: New American Library, 1970.

Schlesinger, Arthur M., Jr. *A Thousand Days.* New York: Fawcett, 1967.

____. "Presidential War." *New York Times Magazine.* January 7, 1973, 28.

Sickels, Robert J. *Presidential Transactions.* Englewood Cliffs, N.J.: Prentice-Hall, 1974.

Executive Departments

Executive departments are the largest units of the federal executive branch. Each department covers broad areas of responsibility. As of 1989, there were fourteen cabinet departments: Agriculture, Commerce, Defense, Education, Energy, Health and Human Services, Housing and Urban Development, Interior, Justice, Labor, State, Transportation, Treasury, and Veterans Affairs.

Styles and Methods of Appointment

Selection of the department secretaries, who also serve as members of the cabinet, is a crucial presidential decision because the cabinet is the most prominent feature of the president's team. Although the number of appointments each president makes is small when compared to the size of the departments themselves, appointments to the cabinet and subcabinet (the more than one thousand deputy secretaries, undersecretaries, assistant secretaries, and deputy assistant secretaries who staff the departments) indicate both the policy direction and credibility of a new administration. *(See Table 1.)* Consequently, most new presidents face intense public scrutiny of their cabinet appointments. In fact, after the 1980 election the public interest was so great that in the two and a half months between the election and Ronald Reagan's inauguration the *New York Times* printed one hundred articles and editorials on the new administration's cabinet appointments. Twenty-one of these articles appeared on the front page.[1]

Beyond their symbolic importance, however, cabinet appointments provide presidents with their best early opportunity to show their leadership. Moreover, the first step toward a successful administration is in all likelihood the wise and prudent selection of a new cabinet.

The cabinet secretary's job is by any standard a difficult one. The relationship that secretaries maintain with the president and their individual departments has an important bearing on the success of an administration. Presidential scholar Richard M. Pious has pointed out that department secretaries "must manage their departments and set priorities; represent constituencies to the president and the president to constituencies; help make administration policy and propose new policy initiatives; offer advice to the president."[2]

Ideally, cabinet appointees should be able to demonstrate that they are uniquely qualified to head one of the major departments of the federal government, and presidents should be able to make appointments to cabinet positions based upon the administrative qualifications of the nominee. In practice, however, presidents rarely make appointments based solely on administrative ability. Instead, they consider such factors as personal loyalty, political party loyalty, ideological compatibility, acceptability to Congress, geographic representation, constituent group representation, reputation, expertise, and prior government experience.

Different presidents use different strategies for filling cabinet positions. Although no president has ever adhered to a single appointment strategy, political scientist Nelson W. Polsby found that most recent presidents have used at least one of three major approaches.[3] First, some presidents base appointments on constituent concerns. They enter into coalitions with certain clientele groups by finding appointees who already have strong connections or political associations with groups served by the department. While such an arrangement may serve the department and certain constituent groups well in some respects, it also may prove to be divisive to the function of the department as a whole because very few departmental secretaries will be acceptable to all clientele groups. For example, conservationists might welcome a particular secretary of the interior, while miners might find the appointee to be completely unsympathetic to their concerns.

Second, for some presidents expertise in the subject area served by the department is the primary criterion for appointment. In practice, however, secretaries appointed on the basis of their technical mastery of the substantive concerns of the departments are concerned primarily with the performance and impact of their departments, and they are often oblivious to the political goals of the president's administration.

A third approach used by presidents is the appointment of generalists to cabinet positions. Such secretaries are not connected to the constituent groups served by the department, nor do they have expertise in the substantive interests of the department. They are sought instead for their loyalty to the president. Thus in theory, appointees are able to focus on implementing the president's programs

By W. Craig Bledsoe and Margaret C. Thompson

Table 1 Number of Employees and Political Appointments in Cabinet Departments, 1989

Department	Total number of employees	Schedule C appts.	Total number of appts.[a]
Agriculture	124,706	226	308
Commerce	44,347	107	190
Defense	1,057,842[b]	119	248
Education	4,602	125	348
Energy	17,316	68	108
Health and Human Services	125,331	79	152
Housing and Urban Development	13,436	91	135
Interior	77,994	54	111
Justice	75,605	59	281
Labor	18,480	72	107
State	26,272	162	1,053
Transportation	63,386	73	136
Treasury	164,541	43	93
Veterans Affairs	246,529	9	190
Total	2,060,387	1,287	3,460

Sources: Office of Personnel Management; Center for Excellence in Government.

a. Includes noncareer employees in the Senior Executive Service and public law positions, such as State Department Foreign Service officers.

b. Total civilian employees.

and not on a narrow set of policies advocated by constituents or the department. Polsby contends, however, that the generalist's loyalty to the president can become pathological. For example, departmental officers not obligated by the charter of the department or ties to clientele groups would be much more likely to oblige a president who asks them to do things that are illegal or immoral to further the president's political cause.

After electoral debts have been paid off with the initial cabinet selections and the media attention has begun to fade, presidents often turn to appointees who will help them accomplish their objectives. Competence and loyalty become the most important criteria for selection. Presidents need competent and loyal cabinet officers to help them deal with the federal bureaucracy and with Congress. According to presidential appointments scholar G. Calvin Mackenzie, "It is characteristic of in-term selection decisions to reflect the president's concerns in dealing with the executive establishment and with Congress.... In-term personnel selections ... often become a central part of an administration's political and administrative strategies for accomplishing its policy objectives." [4]

While the criteria that presidents use in filling cabinet positions often call for certain selections, the appointment process itself can impose additional restrictions on their ability to choose the best possible cabinet. Unlike some presidential appointments, cabinet appointments must be submitted to the Senate for majority confirmation. Some nominees, however, are unwilling to submit to the scrutiny that accompanies the Senate confirmation procedure. And this procedure can be quite long and demanding. After a particularly exhausting confirmation hearing in the summer of 1975, Gov. Stanley K. Hathaway of Wyoming, President Gerald R. Ford's appointee for secretary of the interior, suffered a nervous breakdown. Although this type of confirmation hearing is hardly the rule, it indicates the potential hazards of a tough Senate confirmation procedure.

Other nominees may not be willing to make the financial sacrifice necessary to enter public service. In their study of the presidential appointment process, John W. Macy, Bruce Adams, and J. Jackson Walter found that almost all executives in the private sector are better paid than those holding positions at similar levels of responsibility in the public sector.[5] Consequently, presidential appointees recruited from the private sector usually take a cut in salary to work for the federal government. It is conceivable that a cabinet appointee might give up a $300,000 annual salary for a cabinet post that pays $99,000 a year. Similarly, the rigors of financial disclosure are a disincentive to some nominees. Some conflict-of-interest regulations, such as those imposed on President Jimmy Carter's appointees, contain very precise demands. From his nominees Carter required full financial disclosure of their net worth, a promise not to return to Washington to lobby for pay for at least one year after leaving federal employment, and a commitment to shed all financial holdings that might be affected by a later official decision.

Those who decide to accept the challenges of the confirmation process and the terms of presidential appointment now face higher standards for appointment to public office, as well as the increased expectations of the American public. Thus, cabinet officers must have the management skills necessary to administer a large public bureaucracy, as well as some knowledge of the subject area under the purview of their departments. The personal lives of appointees are subject to higher standards as well. Former Texas senator John Tower, President George Bush's nominee for secretary of defense in 1989, saw his nomination defeated on the Senate floor following allegations of drunkenness and other improprieties.

How well do cabinet officers meet these public demands? A 1967 Brookings Institution study analyzed the background, tenure, and later occupations of those in high executive positions, including cabinet posts, from 1933 through April 1965. It found that most high federal officeholders had high levels of education and substantial federal administrative experience; generally they were well prepared for their positions. But the study also suggested that with their short tenure, top executives rarely had enough time to learn the issues and personalities of the job.[6]

A comparable study conducted by the National Academy of Public Administration (NAPA) in 1987 found that political executives of the past twenty years were very similar to those in the Brookings Institution study. Using data on federal political executives for the period 1964-1984, the NAPA study reported very little difference in these appointees and those holding office fifty years ago. Executive-level appointees remain predominantly elites. They are mostly white, middle-aged males with degrees from prestigious universities. While the number of women and members of racial minorities in cabinet positions has increased in recent years, their proportions in no way reflect their representation in the general population.[7]

The NAPA survey also pointed out a few significant changes in the characteristics of executive appointees. For example, career public servants increasingly are filling executive-level appointments. As a result, fewer people are being recruited (or are willing to be recruited) from business, professional, and academic careers, and more appointees are coming from public service "professions" such as state and local governments, congressional staffs, and other noncareer and career federal appointments. The NAPA study found as well that more appointees are going into private business after leaving the federal government. Apparently, executive appointees are benefitting from their federal offices. Nearly half of the NAPA survey respondents believed that their public service had increased their earning power.[8]

In general, presidents replace cabinet members frequently, leading the critics to argue that cabinet members are not in their positions long enough to learn all the important aspects of their jobs. How long does a typical cabinet member stay in office? The 1967 Brookings study found that cabinet secretaries remained in office a median of 3.3 years, while the more recent NAPA study found that the length of tenure of cabinet secretaries had dropped significantly, to a median of 1.9 years. The authors of the Brookings study argued, however, that length of tenure in a particular office is not as important as length of tenure in the federal government. The NAPA survey discovered that cabinet secretaries have a median of four years of general federal experience, indicating that many have come from public service with several years of experience.

Nominees to cabinet or subcabinet and undersecretary positions often view their appointment as a ticket to a later position in private business. In the NAPA twenty-year survey almost 93 percent of those questioned decided to leave public service for the private sector, a much higher percentage than that for appointees leaving the private sector for the public sector. The Department of Defense has suffered the most from this public service drain. Two-thirds of its top political appointees later found their way into business positions.

Some presidents have come into office determined to control the staffing of the over one thousand high-level department positions directly below those of the department secretaries. In seeking to accomplish their programs and goals, presidents want the loyalty of these high-ranking department executives. The Reagan administration, for example, sought to keep the appointment of these subcabinet officials squarely within the control of the White House, allowing little counsel from the department secretaries. Richard Nixon and Jimmy Carter, in contrast, invited their department secretaries to make their own senior departmental appointments. Both presidents wanted their cabinets to be independent of the White House. Later, however, these administrations spent a great deal of energy trying to bring this decision-making power under their control to maintain some degree of loyalty to administration objectives.

Recent Presidential Appointments

No president is ever really free to make the cabinet or subcabinet appointment of choice. Political parties, special-interest groups, members of Congress, and constituent concerns all play a role in the selection process. Their role is not constant, however; sometimes one factor has been more important than others, and at other times presidents have ignored some or all of these factors. A look at recent cabinet selection decisions may illustrate more adequately how presidents select cabinet appointees.

Franklin D. Roosevelt

In the general staffing of his administration Roosevelt usually relied on five sources: friends and colleagues from his younger years, participants in his New York gubernatorial administration, his 1932 presidential campaigners, the "old boys' network" (or people-who-knew-people-who-knew-Roosevelt), and the rank and file of the Democratic party.[9] As a result, his selection of nominees for cabinet positions outwardly showed no underlying purpose or consistency. For example, apparently Frances Perkins was appointed secretary of labor because Roosevelt wanted a woman in his cabinet. He appointed Harold L. Ickes, a nominal Republican, as secretary of the interior, Henry A. Wallace, a noted agricultural economist and also a nominal Republican, as secretary of agriculture, and Daniel C. Roper, an old friend who was not well known in public life, as secretary of commerce.

Presidential scholar Stephen Hess contends that in reality Roosevelt had two principles that dictated his cabinet appointment strategy. First, early in his administration Roosevelt sought to appoint only cabinet members who would not overshadow him or threaten him politically. The only appointee of any real national prominence was Secretary of State Cordell Hull. As World War II approached, however, Roosevelt appointed cabinet members, such as Henry L. Stimson and Frank Knox, who had more of a national stature. This early strategy of appointing relative unknowns to the cabinet was designed to make sure that the public perceived the administration to be distinctively Rooseveltian.

Second, Roosevelt embarked on a deliberate strategy of appointing opposites to his cabinet; he revelled in the give and take of opposing opinions. For example, by appointing both fiscal conservatives, such as Secretary of the Treasury William H. Woodin, and fiscal liberals, such as Secretary of Commerce Harry L. Hopkins, to the cabinet, Roosevelt was able to play each side against the other and hear both sides of an issue. He once told Frances Perkins, "A little rivalry is stimulating. . . . It keeps everybody going to prove he is a better fellow than the next man. It keeps them honest too."[10]

Similarly, Roosevelt insisted on being involved in the appointments to lower-level cabinet positions, and he succeeded in appointing superior-quality subcabinet members. These young intellectuals and academics, who had little experience in politics but shared Roosevelt's ideological beliefs, included such qualified undersecretaries and subcabinet members as Dean G. Acheson, Jerome Frank, and

Frances Perkins was FDR's secretary of labor, the first woman ever appointed to the cabinet.

Presidential Reorganization Authority

For several decades presidents had the authority to reorganize the executive branch by shifting duties from one department to another, shifting responsibilities from one agency within a department to another, and creating new departments and agencies. The Reorganization Act of 1949 permitted presidents to make a wide range of organizational changes. The act provided that presidents did not have to seek congressional approval for organizational changes, but it did permit Congress to veto them. If either house of Congress passed a resolution disapproving the restructuring within sixty days of the presidential order, it took place automatically.

Before the Reorganization Act of 1949, twentieth-century executive reorganization was carried out with the specific approval of Congress. The first general authority to reorganize, the Overman Act of 1918, gave the president power to coordinate and consolidate government agencies to make them more efficient during World War I, but this authority lasted only through the end of the war. President Franklin D. Roosevelt received limited reorganization authority through the Reorganization Act of 1939. Under the provisions of this act, which expired on January 20, 1941, Roosevelt submitted five reorganization plans, none of which were blocked by Congress.

The Reorganization Act of 1949 grew out of recommendations made by the first Hoover Commission and gave presidents much greater latitude than earlier legislation. It eliminated exemptions for specific agencies and for the first time permitted presidents to create cabinet-level departments. Nevertheless, Congress continued to exercise influence over reorganization by occasionally using their legislative veto to block presidential plans. Because authority for reorganization expired periodically and had to be extended, it was not unusual for Congress to allow temporary lapses in executive reorganization authority.

In 1983 these longstanding reorganization procedures were dealt a blow by the Supreme Court. In *Immigration and Naturalization Service v. Chadha,* the Court declared that legislative vetoes such as the one used by Congress to pass judgment on presidential reorganization plans, were unconstitutional. Since the Reorganization Act's legislative veto provision was invalid, Congress refused to renew the act, which had expired in 1981. Consequently, reorganizations of the government can now be achieved only through laws passed by both houses of Congress and signed by the president.

James Landis. Although Roosevelt's cabinet secretaries may not have approved of this selection process, they nevertheless yielded to the president's selections.

Harry S Truman

Upon Roosevelt's death in 1945, Harry Truman at first encouraged his inherited cabinet to remain in the new administration. Within three months, however, he had replaced six of Roosevelt's ten department heads, as he found that he did not enjoy the conflicting policy advice offered by Roosevelt's diverse cabinet. Truman thus quickly began to replace Roosevelt's appointees with personal acquaintances and others whom he felt were qualified as well as personally loyal to him.

Because he wanted to have his own team in place in 1945, the president gladly accepted the resignations of Roosevelt loyalists. Their replacement by appointees loyal to Truman's programs and goals became a major task of his administration.

To show his keen interest in the selection of his new cabinet, Truman invited nominees to the White House to inform them personally of their nomination. For Truman, loyalty and experience in government were the two major criteria for appointment to his cabinet. Thus, in an attempt to justify the nomination of Lewis B. Schwellenbach (a former senator from Washington) as secretary of labor, Truman argued that he and Schwellenbach "saw right down the same alley on policy." [11] As for the criterion of experience in government, four of Truman's first six cabinet appointments were former members of Congress. He also chose more members of his administration from the ranks of the federal government than did any of his successors. Truman believed that success in government could be transferred to the political arena of the presidential cabinet. He wrote:

> I consider political experience absolutely necessary, because a man who understands politics understands free government. Our government is by the consent of the people, and you have to convince a majority of the people that what you are trying to do is right and in their interest. If you are not a politician, you cannot do it.[12]

For the most part Truman chose highly qualified, experienced cabinet appointees, especially in areas dealing with foreign affairs. His most celebrated cabinet appointments included Secretaries of State George C. Marshall and Dean Acheson, Secretaries of Defense James V. Forrestal and Robert A. Lovett, and Secretary of War Robert P. Patterson. Although some Truman appointments were members of America's governing elite, who went to the most prestigious schools and belonged to the American upper class, the president generally appointed those with whom he had the most in common and knew the best—government employees.

Dwight D. Eisenhower

As the first Republican president in twenty years, Dwight Eisenhower had to look beyond the Democratic-controlled federal government for cabinet appointees. And unlike Truman, he was not involved personally in most of these decisions. Even though Republican leaders were extremely interested in the new administration's choices for these positions, Eisenhower did not seek their advice in selecting his cabinet. The job of filling new government positions, including those of the cabinet, went to two friends, Herbert Brownell, Jr., a New York attorney, and Gen. Lucius Clay, chairman of the board of Continental Can Company. While Brownell and Clay made the initial selections for the cabinet, the choice of a subcabinet was left to the cabinet secretaries themselves.

Eisenhower strongly disliked the role that patronage played in the appointment process. Expressing the "profound hope" that he would not have to become too involved in the distribution of federal patronage, Eisenhower wrote in his diary: "Having been fairly successful in late years learning to keep a rigid check on my temper, I do not want to encounter complete defeat at this late date." [13]

With his distaste for patronage and a management style that sought to delegate as much administrative responsibility as possible, Eisenhower found himself with a cabinet made up almost entirely of strangers and Republican party unknowns. Only two of Eisenhower's ten initial choices, Attorney General Brownell and Postmaster General Arthur E. Summerfield, had played a major role in his presidential campaign.

The lack of conservative Republican party notables particularly offended party leaders. Although Eisenhower had appointed primarily Republicans to his cabinet, most were from the moderate faction of the party. When Sen. Robert A. Taft (R-Ohio), the Republican leader in the Senate, took exception to being excluded from the cabinet selection process, Eisenhower agreed to allow members of Congress to advise the departments in their selection of subcabinet-level appointees. Known as the "Commodore Agreement," this compromise did not entirely please congressional leaders. It succeeded in making Eisenhower aware, however, of the importance of political considerations in making cabinet selections.

The *New Republic* described Eisenhower's first cabinet as "eight millionaires and one plumber." The millionaires not only had money, but they also were successful in their professions. According to Stephen Hess, "Eisenhower believed that a successful person, someone who had already proven that he could run something big, would be best able to tame a government department." [14] Only three members of his cabinet did not have backgrounds in management. Secretary of State John Foster Dulles and Brownell were attorneys. Secretary of Labor Martin P. Durkin was the most notable exception. The nomination of Durkin, head of the AFL Plumbers and Pipe Fitters Union and an Adlai Stevenson supporter, surprised many observers. Apparently, Eisenhower wanted to appease the unions and broaden the perspective of the cabinet. Out of harmony with the rest of the Eisenhower administration, Durkin resigned within the first year.

John F. Kennedy

John Kennedy was elected to the presidency in 1960 by one of the narrowest margins in history. This factor, probably more than any other, dictated the selection of the Kennedy cabinet. Although Kennedy expressed a desire to choose men and women of superior quality, he was restricted by a number of political factors. Kennedy viewed the appointment of department secretaries primarily as an opportunity to consolidate various political factions and to enlarge his popular base of support. Consequently, he appointed representatives of both political parties, all sections of the country, a variety of religious backgrounds, and a wide range of professions as his first ten cabinet members. They included a corporation president, Robert S. McNamara, as secretary of defense, and a Republican who had contributed heavily to Richard Nixon's campaign, C. Douglas Dillon, as secretary of the Treasury.

Like his predecessors, President Kennedy wanted to make the federal government responsive to his programs and direction. He therefore sought cabinet members who would support his agenda and carry out his directives. After eight years of Republican control of the bureaucracy, Kennedy expressed the real fear that the departments had developed a life of their own. As G. Calvin Mackenzie noted, Kennedy did not want his department heads to be "simply the instruments or mouthpieces of the organizations they were appointed to lead." [15] He wanted a cabinet on whom he could rely to pursue his goals vigorously in the departments; otherwise, his task as president would be much more difficult.

From this perspective then it was not surprising that Kennedy appointed his younger brother, Robert, as his attorney general. While Robert F. Kennedy had limited judicial experience, he was close to the president and could be counted on to carry out the president's program in the Department of Justice.

Some of Kennedy's other appointments, however, were surprising. Both McNamara and Secretary of State Dean Rusk were unknown to Kennedy. They were the products of an informal network of talent hunters that produced much of Kennedy's cabinet and personal staff. To screen candidates personally for his cabinet, Kennedy called upon friends and acquaintances across the country to help him assess the qualifications or abilities of potential appointees. He then interviewed candidates himself, and he made the final decisions on appointments. This informal network and Kennedy's personal interest helped him recruit quality individuals from the U.S. business, professional, and university communities.

Robert McNamara, president of Ford Motor Company and a nonpolitical Republican, impressed Kennedy from the beginning. McNamara's management abilities meant that Kennedy would not have to worry about the day-to-day business of the Defense Department. Dean Rusk, an assistant secretary of state during the Truman administration, understood the folkways of the State Department. Kennedy expected this to be helpful in accomplishing his goal of moving the primary responsibility for foreign policy decision making from the National Security Council to the State Department. Rusk proved not to be assertive enough, however, in pushing for Kennedy's goals of diplomacy. Hess wrote: "In constructing a national security triumvirate of Rusk-McNamara-Bundy [McGeorge Bundy was Kennedy's national security adviser], the President put the most diffident in the post that required the most assertive." [16]

Early in his administration Kennedy also focused his attention on appointments to secondary cabinet positions, primarily in the State Department. Kennedy's lower-level appointments in the State Department, many of whom were named before he nominated the secretary, were more qualified than Rusk to be head of the department. They included Adlai E. Stevenson, W. Averell Harriman, and Chester Bowles. Although Kennedy apparently was attempting to spread talent and diversity throughout the State Department, he soon found the task of naming subcabinet appointees wearisome. Thus, he eventually gave McNamara an almost free hand in naming his top subordinates in the Pentagon. As a result, most of McNamara's appointees remained in the Defense Department for the duration of his tenure. In contrast, top-level State Department personnel left the department on average after about fourteen months.

Lyndon B. Johnson

Feeling the need to maintain stability in the government, Lyndon Johnson made no changes in the Kennedy cabinet until thirteen months after President Kennedy's assassination. After the 1964 election, however, Johnson decided to put his own stamp on the administration. Thus, during his term in office, fifteen of the twenty-five men who served in his cabinet he selected himself; the others he inherited from John Kennedy.

Even though Johnson relied heavily on a personnel staff to help him make his cabinet decisions, he participated in almost every step of the selection process. In fact, probably no other recent president has maintained the continuing interest that Johnson exhibited in the selection of all of his executive personnel. While he usually followed his personnel staff's recommendations, he always reserved the final decision for himself.

Johnson applied to his cabinet selections very explicit criteria, which included not only intelligence and ability but also some important political considerations. For example, because he wished to increase the number of minorities in the federal government, in 1965 Johnson appointed Robert C. Weaver, the first black cabinet member, as secretary of housing and urban development (HUD).

Johnson also considered loyalty to be of prime importance. At first he appeared to pay little attention to political party affiliation. He boasted, for example, that he was unaware that John W. Gardner was a Republican until shortly before he announced Gardner's nomination as secretary of health, education and welfare (HEW). Loyalty to his programs soon became very important, however. As Johnson's presidency matured and friction developed between some of his advisers and the remaining Kennedy staffers, it became increasingly clear that he needed to have his own team in place in the cabinet. According to journalist David Halberstam, Johnson, when discussing loyalty among his cabinet members, said: "If you ask those boys in the cabinet to run through a buzz saw for their president, Bob McNamara would be the first to go through it. And I don't have to worry about Rusk either. Rusk's all right. I never have to worry about those two fellows quitting on me." [17]

Nevertheless, Johnson soon began to confuse loyalty with blind allegiance to his Vietnam policies. G. Calvin Mackenzie observed that this made it increasingly difficult for Johnson to find people for all of his executive positions. "The more criticism the war engendered, the more concerned Johnson became that his appointees support his war policies. The effect of his concern was to narrow the range of people from which executive selections were made." [18] Johnson thus began to turn increasingly to people who already held major positions in his administration, and his cabinet was a good example of Johnson's bias toward appointing those who already had experience in government. Of the fifteen cabinet members he appointed, only four came from outside government. The others were internal promotions, such as Wilbur J. Cohen's appointment as Johnson's last HEW secretary; Cohen had spent most of his career at the Social Security Administration. The Johnson cabinet thus tended to well represent the clientele of the agencies, but it also did not have much political independence from the president.

LBJ appointed Robert C. Weaver, the first black cabinet member, as secretary of HUD.

Library of Congress

Richard Nixon

Soon after his election in 1968 Nixon turned over direction of the effort to select a cabinet to his law partner John N. Mitchell and a Wall Street banker named Peter M. Flanigan. On December 11, 1968, after a "crash program" of selection lasting five weeks, Nixon went before a national television audience to introduce twelve men of "extra dimension" who were to form his first cabinet.

In choosing a cabinet that proved more diverse than the Eisenhower counterpart, Nixon relied on some of the traditional sources of recruitment: personal friends (John Mitchell as attorney general, Robert H. Finch as secretary of HEW, and William P. Rogers as secretary of state); Republican governors (Walter J. Hickel as secretary of the interior, George W. Romney as secretary of housing and urban development, and John A. Volpe as secretary of transportation); academics (Clifford M. Hardin as secretary of agriculture and George P. Shultz as secretary of labor); members of Congress (Melvin R. Laird [R-Wis.] as secretary of defense); and business people (Winton M. Blount as postmaster general, David M. Kennedy as secretary of the Treasury, and Maurice H. Stans as secretary of commerce). And he followed the traditional patterns of constituency representation: he chose a westerner for Interior, a banker for Treasury, and a midwesterner with an agricultural background for Agriculture. Even though Nixon appointed a number of millionaires, they were generally self-made wealthy men who had meager beginnings.

In many ways Nixon chose an nontraditional cabinet, and he made a number of noticeable omissions. For example, traditionally presidents have appointed at least one member of the defeated party; there were no Democrats on Nixon's cabinet. Nixon ignored other prominent groups as well by not including any labor union members, blacks, Jews, or women. And because Republicans had gained little top-level federal experience over the last eight years, Nixon's cabinet was somewhat short on Washington executive experience. According to Mackenzie, "The selection process [for Nixon's cabinet] seems to have been guided by little more than the desire to follow convention, to pay off some personal and electoral debts, and to surround the new President with people who seemed to share his political outlook." [19] Historian Arthur M. Schlesinger, Jr., publicly criticized Nixon's cabinet appointments for a lack of independence, asking, "Who in President Nixon's cabinet will talk back to him?" [20]

Early in 1969 President Nixon told his cabinet that

they would have the primary responsibility for filling subcabinet positions. Specifying that the selection process should be based on ability first and loyalty second, Nixon thus delegated to his cabinet the authority for determining the responsiveness of the federal government to his programs. Mackenzie wrote: "Nixon recognized almost immediately that in granting this discretion he had made an error in judgment. As he left the cabinet room after the meeting, he is reported to have said to an aide, 'I just made a big mistake.' "[21]

After Nixon delegated subcabinet appointment power to his department heads, the White House personnel staff found it difficult to exert much control over these appointments. The White House therefore spent a great deal of time trying to reconfirm its right to approve nominations made by department heads.

By 1970 Nixon had realized that he needed to install in the White House a selection process that would ensure that high-level departmental appointees were loyal enough and bold enough to carry out his programs. As a result, Frederic V. Malek, deputy undersecretary of HEW, was put in charge of studying the White House personnel operation. When Malek recommended that the centralization of all personnel decisions be placed in a new White House Personnel Operation (WHPO), Nixon agreed and asked him to run the operation.

By centralizing the appointment procedure in the WHPO, the Nixon White House hoped to protect the president's nominations from outside influences, thereby making it easier to limit appointments to those well in line with Nixon's policies. For all its good intentions, however, the WHPO was not entirely successful. Nixon continued to remain aloof from the nominating process. He even often refrained from meeting his subcabinet nominees when they joined the administration. This overall lack of interest, as well as the lack of presidential control over the selection process, made it difficult for the Nixon administration to instill loyalty to Nixon's policies and goals in its cabinet officers.

Gerald R. Ford

After Nixon's resignation Gerald Ford came into office facing many of the same problems that Johnson confronted after Kennedy's assassination. Primarily, he faced the need to place his own mark on the federal government. Ford entered the presidency with Nixon's cabinet and not much preparation for his new job. Thus, several months passed before his administration began to take shape. When he finally found himself in a position to make changes, he encountered many potential nominees who were hesitant to take executive positions in his administration because of the possible short tenure in office.

Ford sought geographical balance and group representation in all of his appointments by nominating women, minorities, and young people to his administration. Because of the Watergate scandal, which had forced Nixon's resignation, Ford asked his personnel staff to be particularly sensitive to political considerations; he sought nominees who shared his political beliefs and reflected his administration's goals. He was, however, less strenuous about political compatibility than many of his predecessors, and he thus appointed several cabinet members who were not responsive to Republican party demands: Secretary of Transportation William T. Coleman, Jr.; Secretary of Housing and Urban Development Carla A. Hills; Secretary of Labor John T. Dunlop; Secretary of Health, Education and Welfare F. David Mathews; and Attorney General Edward H. Levi. Most were not Republicans, and many represented minorities.

Gail S. Rebhan

Wide World Photos

Although Carter's goal for his cabinet was to choose new faces, he ended up with Washington insiders. Cyrus Vance, left, held the post of secretary of state; Zbigniew Brzezinski, right, headed the National Security Council.

Jimmy Carter

Even though Jimmy Carter won the 1976 election by a slim margin, his cabinet selections did not reflect any obligations that he might have had to the groups that helped put him over the top. He came into office believing that he owed little to anyone, except blacks, and promising that his administration would appoint new leaders to key posts based on merit and well-balanced geographical representation. In an oft-quoted comment, Carter's closest adviser, Hamilton Jordan, stated during the transition period: "If, after the inauguration, you find a Cy Vance as Secretary of State and Zbigniew Brzezinski as head of national security, then I would say we failed. And I'd quit. But that's not going to happen. You're going to see new faces, new ideas. The government is going to be run by people you have never heard of."[22]

Promises of this kind set up many unfulfilled expectations. Initial cabinet and other executive position selections did little to satisfy either traditional Democratic party supporters or those hoping for new leadership. Democratic legislators expressed dismay when their suggestions were not heeded. Minority groups and women, who felt they had contributed significantly to Carter's election, were disappointed in his selections.

And in an unprecedented move the National Democratic Committee adopted a resolution criticizing the Carter administration for failing to confer with Democratic state officials in making federal appointments. Carter in fact was attempting to take firm control of the nomination process, and in doing so he sacrificed many traditional Democratic ties. Mackenzie wrote: "By failing to recognize some legitimate political claims and by promising a good deal more than it could deliver, the Carter administration failed to capitalize fully on the political opportunities the selection process provides, especially in the initial stages of a new administration."[23]

No president had started as early as Carter in finding personnel for his administration. In the summer of 1976, even before the election, Carter established a Policy Planning Office (PPO). Headed by Jack H. Watson, Jr., the PPO was charged with finding qualified nominees and giving the new administration a head start on the selection process during the transition. The early start in appointing executives to the new administration did little to speed up the cabinet selection process, however. Carter took longer in selecting his cabinet than had any of his postwar predecessors. Although all cabinet members were sworn in within a week of the inauguration, many subcabinet positions remained unfilled for several months. The deliberateness of the selection process and the exceptional security and conflict-of-interest checks contributed to the uncommon slowness of the appointment process.

Carter insisted on direct participation in the selection of his department heads, and he preferred to pick all appointees in a specific department before moving on to another. Because he was concerned about compatibility among his top advisers, Carter tried to ascertain the quality and compatibility of potential nominees by holding joint meetings with candidates in the same policy area. So many candidates were involved in these meetings that it was difficult to keep them out of the public eye. This had the advantage, however, of giving Carter feedback from observers who might have an interest in the nomination.

Carter compiled a list of potential cabinet nominees by soliciting suggestions countrywide from experts in foreign policy, domestic affairs, defense, economics, education, and other areas covered by cabinet appointments. He then turned his list of names over to Hamilton Jordan, who undertook a thorough analysis of each candidate. Before making his final decision, Carter talked to the individuals being considered.

This firm control of nominations occurred only at the department head level, however. Initially, President Carter invited his department secretaries to make their own senior departmental appointments, as he wanted to establish an independent cabinet. But this freedom of selection set up a power struggle between Jordan, who retained overall responsibility for personnel selection, and the department heads. According to presidential scholar R. Gordon Hoxie, "During the first year a warfare erupted between departmental personnel and White House staff over control of the turf and the action. The staff rationale was that *their* coordination, their orchestration, was required in all matters." [24] Eventually, because of his closeness to the president, Jordan and the White House staff won, and the process of selecting subcabinet personnel became concentrated in the White House.

Ronald Reagan

Following Carter's example, Ronald Reagan started the process of selecting cabinet members and other executive personnel well before the transition period ever began. E. Pendleton James, a professional executive recruiter, headed the overall personnel selection process. James believed it important that the president exercise his appointment power in a manner that would insure his control over his administration. Thus, the president had to appoint not only people who were loyal to him and shared in his objectives, but also those who were committed to implementing them.

Unlike the Carter administration, however, the Reagan administration initially succeeded in keeping the appointment process firmly within the White House under the control of James. Reagan supported the process and actively participated in it. During the transition, Reagan made the final decisions on all important appointments, especially cabinet selections. This made it difficult for the departments and agencies—and even for members of Congress—to exert much influence on the selection process in general.

Like Carter, Reagan required an excessive amount of time to get his administration fully in place. Ironically then, the two presidents who started the earliest to select executive appointees took the longest to fully staff their administrations. As in the Carter administration, post-Watergate-mandated security checks and conflict-of-interest disclosures contributed to the delay in the Reagan appointments. The diminished role that political parties played in Reagan's appointment process slowed the process as well. By the Reagan presidency, political parties no longer served as clearinghouses for political appointments. Instead, applications went directly to the White House, generating something of an administrative logjam. Appointment experts Macy, Adams, and Walter noted that "this creates an enormous and politically delicate logistical problem at a time when a new administration is unlikely to be well equipped to handle it." [25]

Another problem facing the Reagan administration was the growing conflict between differing ideologies and political philosophies. Senate confirmation hearings thus became even more difficult. For example, Reagan appointee Warren Richardson, nominated for assistant secretary of health and human services, withdrew his name from consideration when members of the Senate Labor and Human Resources Committee objected to his conservative political views. In another incident, Sen. Jesse Helms (R-N.C.) and a group of other conservative senators effectively delayed the nomination of twenty-nine State Department appointees before receiving assurances from Secretary of State George P. Shultz that six conservative employees of the State Department would not be fired. Faced with this kind of ideological tightrope, Reagan had difficulty finding acceptable cabinet appointees.

Reagan's initial cabinet nevertheless reflected many traditional political considerations. It was a combination of political cronies and strangers and well-known politicians and obscure state officials. Political scientist Ross K. Baker divided members of Reagan's cabinet into "mailmen" (management-oriented moderates) and "Grail seekers" (conservative advocates). The mailmen in Reagan's first cabinet were Treasury Secretary Donald T. Regan, Secretary of Housing and Urban Development Samuel R. Pierce, Jr., Secretary of Commerce Malcolm Baldrige, Secretary of Labor Raymond J. Donovan, and Secretary of Transportation Drew Lewis. His Grail seekers included Secretary of the Interior James G. Watt, Secretary of Energy James B. Edwards, and Secretary of Agriculture John R. Block.[26] More than anything else, Reagan's cabinet represented his electoral constituencies. Groups that did not support Reagan (liberals, environmentalists, and liberal labor unions) were not represented in his cabinet, while groups that helped give him his electoral majority (farmers, developers, and big business) were well represented.

Department of Agriculture

The U.S. Department of Agriculture (USDA) was established in 1862 and elevated to cabinet status in 1889. In

1987 it employed more than one hundred thousand people, with about ten thousand of them in Washington, D.C.

USDA assists the nation's farmers through a variety of programs, among them, subsidies, credit, and rural development (through loans for improved water systems, recreation areas, electrification, telephone service, and housing). USDA also oversees the nation's food quality through inspections of processing plants, and it establishes quality standards for every major agricultural commodity. It provides nutrition education programs as well. USDA's research facilities are investigating animal production, plant and animal diseases, pest controls, crop production, marketing and the use of agricultural products, food safety, and forestry. Moreover, the department supports environmental protection through its energy, soil, water, and forest resource conservation programs. Other responsibilities of the department include administering school lunch, food stamp, food-for-the-needy, and overseas distribution programs; managing the nation's 188 million acres of national forests and parklands; and helping developing nations improve food production.

Despite the importance of USDA, in 1971 President Richard Nixon proposed abolishing the department, and in 1977 President Jimmy Carter suggested transferring a number of USDA's functions to other agencies. Neither happened.

From Small Beginnings . . .

The idea of establishing an agricultural agency in the federal government surfaced in 1776, when farmers made up 90 percent of the nation's population, and virtually all exports were farm products. President George Washington recommended creating such an agency in 1796, but it was not until 1839 that Congress appropriated $1,000 for collecting agricultural statistics, conducting agricultural investigations, and distributing seeds. These functions were assigned at first to the Patent Office because Henry L. Ellsworth, commissioner of patents, had initiated the seed distribution idea.

The pressure to establish a federal agricultural agency mounted, led by the U.S. Agricultural Society, which was organized in 1852. The society found an ally in the Republican party, which pledged in 1860 to enact agrarian reforms. The law authorizing the department in 1862 instructed it "to acquire and to diffuse . . . useful information on subjects connected with agriculture in the most general and comprehensive sense of the word." In carrying out this mandate, the commissioner of agriculture was to conduct experiments, collect statistics, and "procure, propagate, and distribute among the people new and valuable seeds and plants."

The first commissioner of the department was Isaac Newton, a Pennsylvania dairy farmer and personal friend of President Abraham Lincoln. He had a staff of four clerks and a gardener as well as an annual budget of about $50,000. In his 1862 annual report the commissioner proposed a research and information program that was to become the basis of the department's activities over the next several years. The agency published statistical and research reports and dispatched scientists overseas to study other nations' agricultural practices.

Newton's successor, Norman J. Coleman, became the first secretary of agriculture in 1889, although he served in that capacity for only three weeks. A lawyer and lieutenant governor of Missouri, Coleman was active in state, regional, and national agricultural organizations. He played a key role in the passage of the 1887 Hatch Agricultural Experiment Stations Act, which authorized the establishment of such stations, under the direction of the land-grant colleges, in each state and territory.

Coleman's successor, Jeremiah M. Rusk, who was appointed by incoming President Benjamin Harrison, reorganized the department and inaugurated publication of farmers' bulletins. He created USDA's first assistant secretary post—to oversee the department's scientific work—and he named Edwin Williams to head the office.

Expansion of Functions

A new era for the department began in 1897 with the appointment of James ("Tama Jim") Wilson as secretary. Wilson, who served sixteen years—twice as long as any secretary before or since—had been director of the Iowa state agricultural experiment station and had served three terms in the House of Representatives. During his tenure the department became known as one of the great agricultural research institutions of the world. Wilson established new bureaus which operated autonomously under the leadership of well-known aggressive scientists. The Forest Service was established in 1905, as oversight of the national forests was transferred from the Department of the Interior to USDA. USDA was given additional regulatory authority as well, including responsibility for administering the 1906 Meat Inspection and Food and Drugs acts (the latter was transferred to the Food and Drug Administration in 1940). By 1912 the number of employees (13,858) and the department's budget were nearly seven times what they had been in 1897.

Under the leadership of David F. Houston (1913-1920), the department focused its efforts increasingly on the farmers' social and economic plight. Houston also made significant organizational changes, centralizing the department and establishing the Office of Markets and the Office of Information. Passage of the Smith-Lever Agricultural Extension Act in 1914 allowed the department and land-grant colleges, under formal cooperative agreements, to carry research directly to farmers. This arrangement resulted in creation of the Cooperative Extension Service, which served as a model for similar programs abroad.

In 1916 the department became active in establishing standards and grades for grain and cotton. Subsequently, standards were established for other products. The 1921 Packers and Stockyards Act barred unfair, deceptive, discriminatory, and monopolistic practices in livestock, poultry, and meat marketing.

The World War I years were accompanied by a surge in farm production and speculation. At the same time, farmers confronted declining prices for their products and high mortgage indebtedness. By the 1920s agriculture was swept into the general economic decline that was to culminate in the Great Depression. To help farmers meet market needs, the Bureau of Agricultural Economics was established in 1922 to foster statistical and economic research. During the depression Congress responded to the farmers' plight by passing a number of significant laws, among them the 1933 Agricultural Adjustment Act (AAA), which provided for production adjustment to be achieved principally through direct USDA payments to farmers. The Farm Credit Act, passed the same year, consolidated all farm credit programs under the Farm Credit Administration. The Soil Conservation Service was established in 1935, as were the Resettlement Administration (which later became the Farm Security Administration and Farmers Home Administration) and the Rural Electrification Administration. In 1936 the Supreme Court declared the AAA unconstitutional; it was replaced by Soil Conservation and Domestic Allotment Act.

In addition to assisting farmers during the depression, USDA joined the welfare agencies in aiding the poor in rural and urban areas through programs designed to distribute surpluses to the needy.

Postwar Farm Policy

Responding to overseas food needs following World War II, USDA urged U.S. farmers to expand their productive capacity. By the time the Korean War ended in 1953, however, the policy of emphasizing capacity production had resulted in surpluses and falling farm prices. Faced with that problem, President Dwight D. Eisenhower's secretary of agriculture, Ezra Taft Benson, chose to institute programs to expand markets rather than establish high price supports. A Soil Bank Program was put into place nevertheless, whereby farmers were paid to take farmland out of cultivation. The Rural Development Program was inaugurated in 1955 to help low-income farmers. That program was greatly expanded under Benson's successor, Orville L. Freeman (1961-1969). Passage of the Food Stamp Program, and expansion of the school lunch, school milk, and other food donation programs during this period, not only provided food aid to low-income families, but also reduced farm surpluses to more manageable levels. At the same time, "Food for Peace" activities were increased. More than 100 million people in 115 counries received U.S. food surpluses.

Clifford M. Hardin took over as USDA secretary in 1969 and was succeeded by Earl L. Butz in 1971. Butz, a controversial appointee, was forced to resign in 1976.

Fifty years after the federal government first paid farmers to plow under crops and slaughter surplus livestock, the Reagan administration launched a drive to end many depression-era farm programs and eliminate the assumption that the federal government is directly responsible for farmers' well-being. Reagan's first USDA secretary, John R. Block (an Illinois farmer), and others—including portions of the farm community—argued that earlier programs had in fact destabilized American agriculture and had to be changed radically.

During his tenure Block was alternately praised and criticized as a well-intentioned but often ineffectual director of the president's free-market philosophy for agriculture. Block came into office hoping to free farmers from relying so heavily on government programs, yet the crisis in agriculture—high interest rates and declining agricultural exports caused by the strength of the dollar—only deepened each year he was in office, despite unprecedented tax expenditures for price supports and income subsidies. Although Block lasted longer than all but three of Reagan's original cabinet officials, his influence on Capitol Hill waned considerably; he resigned in February 1986.

To replace Block, Reagan chose longtime associate Richard E. Lyng, an agriculture consultant and lobbyist and a former California seed company executive with wide experience in government. He was known to be Reagan's original choice for the cabinet post following the 1980 election, but congressional pressure then led Reagan to pick Block because he was a "working farmer" from the midwestern state of Illinois. Lyng then took the number-two job in the department. He remained in that position through Reagan's first term, overseeing day-to-day operations and often acting as point man on Capitol Hill for the administration's more controversial farm policies.

Organization

USDA has been reorganized a number of times in response to an emphasis on different problems and the gradual addition of functions. The only major organizational change made after the 1930s was the 1953 move to increase the number of assistant secretaries from one to five. In 1988 USDA was headed by a secretary, deputy secretary, two undersecretaries (one for international affairs and commodity programs, and the other for small community and rural development), and seven assistant secretaries (administration, economics, food and consumer services, governmental and public affairs, marketing and inspection services, natural resources and environment, and science and education). The offices of budget and program analysis, the general counsel, the judicial officer, and the inspector general report directly to the secretary.

Department of Commerce

Between 1850 and 1900 the nation's rapid economic growth fueled demands for business representation at the highest levels of government. The Panic of 1893 and the ensuing depression led the newly formed National Association of Manufacturers to lobby strenuously for formation of a department of commerce and industry that would include the Department of Labor (which had been established as a noncabinet-rank department in 1888). Congress responded by authorizing a U.S. industrial commission to study commercial problems.

In 1901, in his first state-of-the-union message, President Theodore Roosevelt proposed a combined department of commerce and labor. Labor representatives argued that workers needed a separate department, but business interests were willing to compromise. In the end the latter prevailed, and the Department of Commerce and Labor came into being in 1903. The new department was one of the largest and most complicated in the federal government; within five months its employees numbered 10,125. Its responsibilities included foreign and domestic commerce; mining, manufacturing, shipping, and fishery industries; labor interests; and transportation.

As the nation's manufactured exports continued to expand and workers moved from farms to industry, pressures built up on both sides to separate labor and commerce into independent departments. As a result a March 4, 1913, law gave labor cabinet status and the Department of Commerce was born.

Expansion of the Department

President William Howard Taft signed the bill on his last day in office. His Democratic successor, Woodrow Wilson, appointed the first commerce secretary, William C. Redfield, a manufacturing executive and politician. Despite the constraints of a $60,000 budget and elimination of funding for collecting domestic statistics, Redfield established a cadre of bilingual commercial attachés with business experience, opened branch offices in eight cities, and sent specialists overseas to study foreign markets.

Commerce came into the limelight during Herbert Hoover's tenure as its secretary (1921-1928). Hoover was determined to make Commerce the most powerful department in the government. His primary interest was to expand trade, and, indeed, by 1925 U.S. exports had increased by one-third over the figure recorded in 1913. During Hoover's stewardship, Commerce acquired a Building and Housing Division (1922), the Bureau of Mines and the Patent Office (both were transferred from Interior in 1925), an Aeronautics Division (1926; it was the forerunner of the Federal Aviation Administration), and a Radio Division (1927; it later became part of the Federal Communications Commission).

Keenly interested in revitalizing the department's statistical functions, Hoover instituted in 1921 a program of balance-of-payments reporting, publishing the data in the first *Survey of Current Business.* The department also developed safety codes for industry and transportation (including assistance in developing traffic signals and air and road safety standards, as well as expansion of its previous responsibility for safe ocean travel). In tandem with its increased responsibilities was the growth in the department's budget, from $860,000 in 1920 to more than $38 million in 1928.

Hoover left Commerce in 1928 to become president at the beginning of the Great Depression. The national income declined drastically, and U.S. exports fell below their 1913 levels. Franklin D. Roosevelt, who defeated Hoover in the 1932 election, slashed Commerce's budget and reduced its activities. There was even some thought of abolishing the department.

World War II and the years that followed ushered in a new role for Commerce. The National Bureau of Standards gained importance in its efforts to insure interchangeability of weapons parts, while the Civil Aeronautics Administration significantly expanded its pilot training programs. The Bureau of Public Roads and the Maritime Administration were moved to Commerce in 1949 and 1950, respectively. Until the Department of Transportation was established in 1967, Commerce was the principal overseer of transportation programs.

Although Commerce has remained an important source of economic information, its responsibilities in international economics have been taken over increasingly by special presidential advisers, the Treasury, and the Office of the U.S. Trade Representative.

Organization and Functions

In the Department of Commerce the general counsel, inspector general, Office of Business Liaison, and Office of Public Affairs report directly to the secretary and the deputy secretary. Four undersecretaries are responsible for oceans and atmosphere, international trade, economic affairs, and travel and tourism. The department has assistant secretaries for congressional and intergovernmental affairs, administration, patents and trademarks, communications and information, and economic development. A number of key offices are administered by directors. Commerce has offices in major U.S. cities and more than one hundred posts overseas. The department is organized according to the following functions.

Trade

The International Trade Administration (ITA) is the agency most closely associated with the department's mandate "to foster, promote and develop the commerce and industry of the United States." Congress authorized establishment of ITA in 1980 to help deal with soaring U.S. merchandise trade deficits. ITA helps formulate foreign trade and economic policies, works with the U.S. Trade Representative and other agencies, and administers legislation to counter unfair foreign trade practices.

The Bureau of Export Administration, established in 1987, formulates U.S. policy for the control of high-technology exports and monitors such exports. This program is designed to prevent the loss of commodities and technologies that would harm the nation's security and advance the military capabilities of adversaries. ITA originally had jurisdiction over this function.

The National Tourism Policy Act of 1981 replaced the U.S. Travel Service, established in 1961 to address a $1.2 billion balance-of-payments deficit in tourism, with the U.S. Travel and Tourism Administration (USTTA).

Economics

Created by President John F. Kennedy in 1961 to coordinate the formulation of economic policy, the Office of Economic Affairs provides foreign and domestic economic data, analyses, and forecasts, based on information provided by its two bureaus, Economic Analysis and Census. The Constitution stipulates that censuses are to be taken, but it was not until 1902 that Congress enacted legislation making the Census Bureau a permanent organization.

The Office of Productivity, Technology and Innovation was established in 1962 to spur U.S. competitiveness abroad by fostering government and private partnerships to stimulate the spread of innovative technologies.

The department's National Technical Information Service (NTIS) serves as a clearinghouse for scientific, technical, and engineering information and analysis. It is self-supporting through its sales of information products and services.

Sciences

In 1970 Congress authorized establishment of the National Oceanic and Atmospheric Administration (NOAA) in response to the presidentially commissioned report "Our Nation and the Sea," which called for bringing several existing agencies into a unified program. In 1987 NOAA employed thirteen thousand people and was the largest agency in Commerce. It predicts the weather, charts the seas and the skies, protects ocean resources, and collects data on the oceans, atmosphere, space, and sun.

The National Bureau of Standards was created in 1901, when the United States was the only major commercial nation without a standards laboratory. The new bureau—first located in Treasury and transferred to Commerce and Labor in 1903—was charged with custody, comparison, and, when needed, establishment of standards.

In 1978 an executive order merged the Office of Telecommunications in the Executive Office with the Office of Telecommunications in Commerce. The product of this merger was the National Telecommunications and Information Administration. Its mandate is to develop policies on the advancement and use of new technologies in common carrier, telephone, broadcast, and satellite communications systems.

The Patent Office, one of the oldest federal agencies, was authorized by Article I, section 8, of the Constitution. In 1802 a full-time Patent Office was established in the State Department; the office was transferred to Commerce in 1925. The Patent Office began registering trademarks in 1870. In 1975, one year after the one millionth trademark was registered, the office's name was changed officially to the Patent and Trademark Office.

Development

Authorized in 1965, the Economic Development Administration (EDA) works to generate and preserve private sector jobs in economically depressed areas by utilizing public works funds, business loans, loan guarantees, technical assistance, long-range economic planning, and economic research.

The Minority Business Development Agency was created in 1969 to promote minority businesses by generating private capital—and, later, by providing federal contracts and grants.

The Office of Business Liaison (1981) is a central source of information for people interested in doing business overseas or with the federal government.

Department of Defense

"The role of a Defense Secretary is to rein in the disparate interests in the defense establishment and shape a military program to suit the overall goals of himself and his administration," wrote Richard A. Stubbing, a defense analyst at the Office of Management and Budget for twenty years. "Given his limited time and political resources, the task is enormous, in some ways impossible, but the performance of the Defense Secretary is vitally important to the overall effectiveness and efficiency of the defense program." [27]

The Department of Defense (DOD) officially became part of the cabinet only in 1949, but in terms of human resources and money it is the largest of the fourteen departments that make up the cabinet. Providing the umbrella for the army, navy, Marine Corps, and air force, DOD is composed of about 2.2 million men and women on active duty. Of these, some 525,000—including about 72,000 on ships at sea—serve outside the United States. They are backed, in case of emergency, by the 1.7 million members of the reserve components. In addition, about 1.2 million civilian employees work for the Defense Department. The Reagan administration's defense budget request for fiscal year 1989 totaled $328.3 billion.

Creation of the National Military Establishment

Before the twentieth century there was little need for a centralized defense establishment; the army fought on land and the navy fought at sea. The acquisition of overseas territories and the growing U.S. role in international affairs, however, led many observers to conclude that a more coordinated national security system was needed—an observation that proved to be all the more true with the advent of air power in the period between World Wars I and II. The Air Corps, as the air force was then called, lobbied for equality with the other branches; although it was nominally a part of the army, it in fact operated independently.

Between 1921 and 1945 at least fifty bills aimed at unifying the armed forces were introduced in Congress. But the major argument for unification also acted as the stumbling block to an interservice agreement. The army's Air Corps sought separate status—a goal that was practicable only within a framework that provided some degree of unified direction at the top. To the navy, however, the logic of separate services for land, sea, and air represented the potential loss of naval aviation to the air force and the Marine Corps to the army.

Despite the navy's opposition, Congress passed the National Security Act of 1947 (PL 80-253) on July 25. This act provided "a comprehensive program for the future security of the United States" and gave the three services "authoritative coordination and unified direction under civilian control" without merging them. The law thus created a national military establishment, to be headed by the secretary of defense and to consist of the Departments of the Army, Navy, and Air Force. The secretary was designated "the principal assistant to the President in all matters relating to the national security." At the same time, however, the three service departments were to be "administered as individual executive departments by their respective Secretaries," who retained the right to present "to the President or to the Director of the Budget ... any report or recommendations relating to his department which he may deem necessary." The secretary of defense was not allowed to establish a military staff and was restricted to three civilian assistants. The Joint Chiefs of Staff (JCS), including a chief of staff, were given statutory authority as "the principal military advisers to the President and the Secretary of Defense," with authority to prepare strategic plans, "establish unified commands," and "review major material and personnel requirements of the military forces."

President Harry S Truman signed the law on July 26, 1947, and immediately named Navy Secretary James V. Forrestal as the first secretary of defense.

1949 Amendments

Concern over the high cost of national defense—not its adequacy—was the major factor that persuaded Congress to amend the National Security Act in 1949. The report of the Hoover Commission on Organization of the Executive Branch had recommended (1) giving the secretary of defense complete statutory authority over the three services, (2) eliminating the three military departments and demoting the service secretaries to undersecretaries of defense, and (3) appointing a chairman of the JCS responsible to the secretary. Truman essentially adopted the proposals and sent them to Congress.

As enacted, the National Security Act Amendments of 1949 converted the national military establishment into an executive cabinet-level Department of Defense. The amended act incorporated the military departments of the three services and stipulated that each was to be "separately administered" by a secretary under the "direction, authority, and control" of the secretary of defense. The secretary was barred, however, from acting to transfer, abolish, or consolidate any of the services' combatant functions. Moreover, nothing was to "prevent a Secretary of a military department or a member of the Joint Chiefs of Staff from presenting to the Congress, on his own initiative, . . . any recommendations relating to the Department of Defense that he may deem proper."

The law also provided for a deputy secretary of defense, three assistant secretaries, and a nonvoting chairman of the Joint Chiefs of Staff (to replace the chief of staff to the president), who was to rank first but hold no command. Finally, provision was made for adding comptrollers to the Defense Department and the three military departments and for instituting uniform accounting and budgetary procedures.

Dwight D. Eisenhower assumed the presidency committed to the same general foreign policy and security objectives as his predecessor, yet he pledged to bring about a sharp reduction in defense spending and a reorganization of DOD. For civilian leadership in the Pentagon, Eisenhower turned to the business world, selecting Charles E. Wilson, president of General Motors Corporation, as defense secretary. The deputy secretary and secretaries of the army, navy, and air force also came from the business community.

Like World War II, the Korean War pointed out the organizational shortcomings of the military complex. President Eisenhower thus asked a group of prominent citizens to propose changes in the Defense Department, and their recommendations were embodied in a reorganization plan that the president submitted to Congress. Although there were some objections from legislators, the plan was adopted, providing for six additional assistant secretary positions and giving the secretary the power to select the director of the joint staff of the Joint Chiefs of Staff.

Between 1953 and 1957 Eisenhower and Wilson were largely successful in holding down attempts to increase defense spending to levels unacceptable to them. But in the aftermath of the 1958 Soviet launch of the first unmanned satellite, *Sputnik I,* the administration found itself under attack from Republicans as well as Democrats, who called for major changes in the defense program. These changes included a reorganization of the Defense Department to speed decision making in the development of new weapons systems and to curtail waste and duplication of effort by the three services.

The administration reluctantly agreed to go along with some of the proposed changes. The Department of Defense Reorganization Act of 1958 authorized the secretary to consolidate common supply and service functions and to assign responsibility for the development and operation of new weapons systems. It also authorized the secretary to transfer, reassign, abolish, or consolidate existing combatant functions of the three services, subject to congressional veto. The act established the position of director of defense research and engineering as the principal adviser to the secretary for all scientific and technological matters. An administration proposal to appropriate all defense funds to the secretary—rather than to the military departments—to "remove all doubts" about the secretary's authority was dropped because of strong Republican as well as Democratic criticism.

McNamara, Laird, and Brown

Within six months of taking office, President John F. Kennedy had increased his predecessor's defense requests for fiscal year 1962 by almost $6 billion, initiating a sharp acceleration of strategic programs and a major expansion of conventional forces. In moving to a higher level of defense spending, however, the president and Defense Secretary Robert S. McNamara did not abandon all considerations of cost. On the contrary, McNamara continued and strengthened the policy of cutting back, terminating, or postponing programs of marginal or dubious effectiveness.

McNamara, president of the Ford Motor Company when Kennedy nominated him as secretary, quickly gained a reputation as a highly intelligent and forceful "boss" of the Pentagon. The new secretary asserted the full authority of his office under the 1958 reorganization act, achieving a greater degree of centralization and control over the services than had ever existed. In the field of management, he introduced a planning-programming-budgeting process that attempted to tie together, in terms of national objectives, the requirements and projected activities of all elements of the military establishment.

Richard Nixon's choice of Melvin R. Laird as secretary of defense was considered widely to be an astute one. Laird, an eight-term Republican representative from Wisconsin (1953-1969), was the first member of Congress to serve as DOD secretary. A professional politician who had served on committees dealing with defense, Laird had a reputation as a "mover and shaker" in Congress. He recognized his relative lack of managerial experience, however, and he chose David Packard, a highly successful industrialist, as his deputy to run the day-to-day business of the department. The two established a close working relationship.

Laird believed strongly in the power of appointments for both civilian and military posts; he personally selected the three service secretaries and met separately with them each week. He also held weekly meetings with his assistant secretaries. Despite major budget and force cutbacks and an end to the draft, Laird was popular among military personnel, and he developed a close rapport with Gen. Earle G. Wheeler, chairman of the Joint Chiefs of Staff.

Laird left Defense in 1973 to assume the position of presidential assistant for domestic affairs, which had been vacated by John D. Ehrlichman in the wake of the Watergate scandal. He was replaced in January 1973 by Elliot L. Richardson, who was reassigned the following May to Justice as attorney general. Richardson's tenure as defense secretary was the briefest in the twenty-six-year history of the office.

Nixon's third selection as DOD secretary was James R. Schlesinger, who had just been named director of the Central Intelligence Agency in January. Although Schlesinger was viewed as an intellectual, his approach to defense issues was pragmatic, and, unlike McNamara, whose emphasis on cost-effectiveness Schlesinger had criticized, he was willing to negotiate. Nonetheless, management suffered during Schlesinger's tenure; he did not get along well with President Gerald R. Ford, who fired the secretary in 1975 over policy disagreements.

In contrast to the musical chairs of the Nixon administration, Harold Brown's tenure as defense secretary lasted throughout the administration of Jimmy Carter. A physicist and former McNamara protege, Brown was secretary of the air force from 1965 to 1969 before becoming president of the California Institute of Technology. Brown brought with him a thorough knowledge of defense programs and a sterling reputation. He was, above all, a scientist and administrator, not a politician. As secretary, he utilized a more centralized management style than that favored by Laird or Schlesinger, and he took a more active role in making budget and program decisions.

During his first year in office Brown ordered a comprehensive review of DOD's organization. As a result, fewer people reported directly to the secretary, and a number of headquarters activities were consolidated. A General Accounting Office report concluded that no substantial economies had been effected, however. "Defense recently completed a Harold Brown ordered economy movement that resulted in almost no economy and even less movement," commented the *Washington Post* on October 7, 1978.[28]

One of Brown's major difficulties in asserting his role as secretary was Carter's personal involvement in defense issues, even small ones. Brown was unwilling to challenge the president and generally was overshadowed by him.

Buildup under Reagan

Caspar W. Weinberger was Ronald Reagan's choice as secretary of defense when the Republican administration entered office in 1981. A longtime friend of the president, Weinberger had a distinguished career in public service and private business. When he was nominated to be DOD secretary, however, opponents criticized Weinberger's lack of background in defense policy and feared that he would manage the Pentagon's budget too tightly. But he quickly established himself as a relentless advocate of a rapid military buildup.

After Reagan's first few years in office, Congress became less willing to back the defense buildup at the pace sought by the president and Weinberger. There was a growing sense that Pentagon funds were utilized poorly. Weinberger was hesitant to override the budget requests of the services and gave them a relatively free hand in setting military priorities and making program decisions. The secretary's "hands-off" approach and his inattention to management resulted therefore in strained relations with Congress, not helped by the increasingly perfunctory character of the secretary's dealings with Capitol Hill. Defense committees asked him for advice on where to find budget cuts, but Weinberger insisted that his requests were the minimum required for the nation's safety. Hardliners applauded his tenacity, but many congressional defense specialists contended that by refusing to bargain, he dealt himself out of the process.

Citing personal reasons, Weinberger resigned in November 1987. He was replaced by his longtime associate Frank C. Carlucci, who had established a reputation as a shrewd operator of the machinery of government.

Organization and Functions

DOD is structured around four principal elements: the office of the secretary, the military departments, the Joint Chiefs of Staff, and the unified and specified commands. The secretary's line of command is direct to both the staff and fighting forces. Nonetheless, "the responsibilities of the job [of DOD secretary] are not matched by corresponding powers," wrote John G. Kester, former special assistant to Defense Secretary Harold Brown. "The Secretary is an official whose position is impinged upon from many directions, and who often must feel that he is sitting on top of a centrifuge. Without a lot of pulling at the center, the Defense Department tends to fly off in all directions."[29]

The office of the secretary includes the offices of the deputy secretary, executive secretary, assistant to the secretary, undersecretary for acquisition, undersecretary for policy, comptroller, general counsel, inspector general, and directors of defense research and engineering, operational testing and evaluation, and program analysis and evaluation. Three deputy undersecretaries oversee policy, trade security policy, and planning and resources. In addition, in 1987 there were nine assistant secretaries: command, control, communications, and intelligence; health affairs; legislative affairs; force management and personnel; international security affairs; international security policy; public affairs; reserve affairs; and intelligence oversight.

Reporting to the office of the secretary are the following agencies: communications, mapping, legal services, contract audit, security assistance, national security, investigative service, logistics, advanced research projects, and intelligence. In January 1984, under Reagan's directive, the Strategic Defense Initiative Organization was established as a Defense agency reporting directly to the secretary of defense.

The Joint Chiefs of Staff—consisting of the chairman; chief of staff, U.S. Army; chief of naval operations; chief of staff, U.S. Air Force; and commandant of the Marine Corps—constitute the immediate military staff of the defense secretary. Other members of the JCS are the senior military officers of their respective services, the National Security Council (NSC), and the secretary of defense. The JCS is served by the joint staff, which is composed of not more than four hundred officers selected in approximately equal numbers from the army, navy (including the Marine Corps), and air force.

Each military department is organized separately under its own secretary, who is responsible to the secretary of defense. In addition, there are a number of unified and specified commands. A "unified command" is a force under a single commander that is engaged in a broad, continuing mission, assisted by assigned personnel from two or more services. The unified commands are the European, Atlantic, Central, Pacific, Southern, Transportation, Special Operations, and Space. A "specified command" is similar but normally represents only one service. In 1988 there were three such commands: Strategic Air Command, Military Airlift Command, and Forces Command.

Outside the functional organization structure is the Armed Forces Policy Council (AFPC), which advises the secretary of defense on matters of broad policy relating to the armed forces and such other matters as the secretary, who serves as its chair, may direct. Members of the council are the deputy secretary of defense, the secretaries of the military departments, the JCS chairman, the undersecretaries of defense, the chief of naval operations, and the army chief of staff, the air force chief of staff, and the commandant of the Marine Corps.

Department of Education

President Jimmy Carter entered office in 1977 with one much-publicized legislative priority in the area of education. During the 1976 presidential election campaign, he had vowed to establish a cabinet-level department to oversee education. In return, he received the endorsement of the 1.7 million members of the National Education Association, the first campaign endorsement given in the organization's history. Congress passed legislation creating the Department of Education in 1979.

Predecessors of the Department

Unlike many other countries for whom a centralized educational system was a vital component of nation building, the United States traditionally has avoided a strong federal role in education. It was not until 1867 that President Andrew Johnson called for the creation of an education department "for the purpose of collecting such statistics and facts as shall show the condition and progress of education in the several States and Territories, and of diffusing such information respecting the organization and management of schools and school systems, and methods of teaching. . . ." The new department had a staff of four: Commissioner of Education Henry Barnard and three clerks. Their total annual salary was $7,800.

The first Department of Education was downgraded quickly to the status of a bureau in the Interior Department. For the next seventy years it limped along as a small recordkeeping office, collecting information on the modest federal education efforts. Proposals for a separate department surfaced periodically, but they went nowhere. In 1939 the renamed Office of Education was transferred to the Federal Security Agency, which became the Department of Health, Education and Welfare (HEW) in 1953.

With the tremendous expansion of federal education programs in the postwar period, arguments for a separate department grew more persuasive. During the 1960s several studies recommended establishment of a separate department, as well as related reorganization proposals. In 1972 Congress established within HEW an Education Division, headed by an assistant secretary for education. It included the existing Office of Education.

Controversy Over Its Creation

One of the main arguments for a separate education department was the confusing and contradictory structure of the existing federal educational administration. In 1978 the hundreds of existing federal educational programs were located in more than forty different agencies.

Lumping all these programs in one department, however, proved to be very difficult politically. For every program going into the department, some other department would have to lose power and money. Agencies and interest groups fought against giving up long, established relationships for an uncertain future in the Education Department. The bill creating the new department also was opposed by a coalition of labor and civil rights groups, who feared that their influence would be reduced in a department dominated by professional educators. The strongest supporters of the new department were those in elementary and secondary education. Higher education organizations were basically neutral on the question.

At first it appeared that the bill would clear Congress easily despite some bitter struggles among administration officials, interest groups, and members of Congress over exactly what should be in the new department. But, faced with dilatory tactics, House leaders decided to shelve the bill in 1978. Opposition was vigorous when the legislation came before Congress again in 1979, but effective lobbying by the agency's supporters—including President Carter—and the addition of some safeguards against federal domination provided the margin needed for creation of the department. Congress completed action on the bill on September 27, and Carter signed it on October 17. Some 152 federal education-related programs were consolidated in the new agency, which at its creation was the fifth largest department handling the eighth largest budget.

Shirley M. Hufstedler, the first secretary of education, took office on December 6. A member of the U.S. Court of Appeals for the Ninth Circuit since 1969, Hufstedler brought no professional education credentials to her new job other than her experience as a member of the boards of trustees of three California institutions of higher education. That lack of experience caused some concern in the education community. Defenders of Carter's appointment argued, however, that Hufstedler's lack of experience and close connection with one or another of the sectors of the education community was a virtue. They said she would bring a fresh perspective to the deep-seated problems of the nation's public education system.

The new department formally opened its doors on May 7, 1980. By 1987 its budget totaled $19.5 billion, and its staff numbered 4,500. The department is constrained in its authority, however, by the long-standing tradition in the United States that education be primarily a state and local function. Congress restated that commitment to decentralized control when it declared in the act that created the department that "the establishment of the Department of Education shall not . . . diminish the responsibility for education which is reserved to the states and the local school systems and other instrumentalities of the state." It is they who make policies on such matters as the length of the school day and year, textbook selection, teacher certification, high school graduation requirements, grading scales, and other instructional and administrative policies.

The Department of Education distributes most of its program funds directly to the states as formula grants. The amounts are based on the number of students in various special categories, and the states then distribute the money to local districts under Education-approved plans.

The existence of the department was precarious during its first years. Ronald Reagan, riding a wave of voter dissatisfaction with what was seen as widespread federal intervention into local affairs, promised during the 1980 election campaign to dismantle the young agency and reduce Washington's role in education programs. His selection of Terrel H. Bell as secretary of education was viewed, however, as an indication that the president would abandon, or at least scale back, his campaign pledge to abolish the department. Bell had been U.S. commissioner of education from 1974 to 1976 and Utah commissioner of higher education since 1976. Education groups were pleased by the selection of a fellow educator with long experience. Bell had supported creating the department, and he stated during his confirmation hearings that he did not want to see a return to the days when education was a low-status unit of the massive Department of Health, Education and Welfare.

After 1981 Reagan made little progress in his efforts to reduce spending and restructure federal involvement in education. Although in 1982 he proposed abolishing Education, Congress ignored the suggestion, and the proposal gradually faded from view.

Bell fought within the administration to moderate proposals to curb education spending, and as a result, he was criticized frequently by conservatives. He resigned as secretary at the end of 1984 and was succeeded in February 1985 by William J. Bennett, former chairman of the National Endowment for the Humanities. When Bennett resigned in 1988, Reagan named Lauro F. Cavazos to the post, making him the nation's first Hispanic cabinet member. When George Bush became president in 1989, he retained Cavazos as secretary.

Organization and Functions

The Department of Education is headed by a secretary who serves as the president's chief adviser on education and supervises the department's staff. The secretary also performs certain functions related to four federally aided corporations: American Printing House for the Blind in Lexington, Kentucky; Gallaudet University (for assisting the deaf) in Washington, D.C.; Howard University in Washington, D.C.; and National Technical Institute for the Deaf (part of Rochester Institute of Technology in New York State). The secretary is assisted by an undersecretary, general counsel, inspector general, three deputy undersecretaries, and eight assistant secretaries.

The deputy undersecretaries are in charge of the Office of Management; Office of Planning, Budget, and Evaluation; and Office of Intergovernmental and Interagency Affairs, which serves as the liaison between the department and its ten regional offices, state and local governments, and other federal agencies.

The Office of Elementary and Secondary Education provides state and local education agencies with the financial assistance needed to help improve preschool, elementary, and secondary education—both public and private. Its largest program, authorized under Title I of the 1965 Elementary and Secondary Education Act, is aimed at disadvantaged children. The office also administers funds provided by the Indian Education Act. It oversees voluntary and court-ordered school desegregation programs, provides assistance to school districts affected by federal activities that overburden local tax sources (impact aid), and helps districts struck by natural disasters.

The Office of Special Education and Rehabilitative Services assists in the education of handicapped children and in the rehabilitation of disabled adults. Many of the numerous children whose native languages are not English are aided by the Office of Bilingual Education and Minority Languages Affairs. Under programs administered by the office, children are instructed in their own languages as they are taught English.

The Office of Postsecondary Education supports financially needy young people who want to go to college or a vocational training school after high school. The office also supports programs for institutional development, student services, housing and facilities, veterans' affairs, cooperative education, international education, graduate education, historically black colleges, foreign language and area studies, innovative teaching methods and practices, and other subjects related to the improvement of postsecondary education.

The Office of Vocational and Adult Education helps states and communities provide specialized vocational education to young people and adults so that they can acquire marketable skills, or so that they can obtain a high school diploma or its equivalent.

Research and demonstration projects designed to improve education at all grade levels—preschool through graduate school—are funded by the Office of Educational Research and Improvement. The office also deals with libraries, museums, and educational programming by the media.

The Center for Statistics gathers, evaluates, and then disseminates information on the characteristics of U.S. education, while the Office for Civil Rights is responsible for seeing that educational institutions comply with four federal statutes that prohibit discrimination in programs and activities receiving federal financial assistance from the department.

Department of Energy

The 1973-1974 Arab oil embargo brought with it dramatic evidence that the U.S. government needed to formulate a more coherent and comprehensive energy policy to centralize its energy-related programs, which then were scattered among various federal agencies. The initial federal response to this need was creation in 1974 of the Energy Research and Development Administration (ERDA) and the Federal Energy Administration (FEA) to administer federal policy for energy planning and regulation. It soon was recognized, however, that additional steps were needed. Thus, on August 4, 1977, President Jimmy Carter signed into law a bill (PL 95-91) that created a cabinet-level Department of Energy (DOE). The new department came into existence on October 1, 1977.

The first new cabinet department since creation of the Department of Transportation in 1966, DOE assumed the powers and functions of FEA, ERDA, the Federal Power Commission (FPC), and the four regional power commissions. DOE also absorbed energy-related programs formerly administered by the Departments of the Interior, Defense, Commerce, and Housing and Urban Development, and the Interstate Commerce Commission. The department assumed as well the role of consultant to the Department of Transportation and the Rural Electrification Administration.

The first secretary of energy was James R. Schlesinger, President Carter's chief energy adviser during the early months of the administration. Although Schlesinger had a long record of government service, he drew vigorous criticism for his lack of administrative skill in putting the new department into working order; he resigned in mid-1979. Carter replaced him with Charles W. Duncan, Jr., deputy secretary of defense since 1977, who won high marks for his management of the new department.

DOE initially employed almost twenty thousand people—transferees from the existing energy programs in other departments and agencies. Its fiscal year 1978 budget was $10.6 billion.

Response to the Energy Crisis

President Richard Nixon was the first president to suggest that the federal agencies dealing with energy be reorganized and consolidated. In 1971 he proposed creation of a Department of Natural Resources, based upon the

Department of the Interior, but including such energy-related programs as those run by the Atomic Energy Commission. Congress greeted Nixon's proposal with yawns, and it progressed no further than the hearing stage. In 1973 Nixon resubmitted his proposal. Once again, it went nowhere on Capitol Hill. As the energy crisis became a fact of life, however, Congress responded in 1974 to Nixon administration requests to create FEA and ERDA.

One of President Gerald R. Ford's final official actions was submittal of a plan to Congress for reorganizing the energy bureaucracy into a Department of Energy. Congress had requested such a plan when it passed legislation in 1976 extending the life of the FEA. Ford's plan was in many respects similar to that proposed by Carter a few months later. "Nowhere is the need for reorganization and consolidation greater than in energy policy," Carter said in a March 1, 1977, message to Congress unveiling his reorganization plan. "All but two of the executive branch's Cabinet departments now have some responsibility for energy policy, but no agency . . . has the broad authority needed to deal with our energy problems in a comprehensive way."

The bill that finally reached Carter's desk for his signature differed in only one major respect from his original proposal. Carter and Congress disagreed over who in the new energy structure should have the power to set prices for natural gas, oil, and electricity. Carter would have given this power to the secretary, but the sentiment of the majority in both chambers of Congress was opposed on the ground that it was unwise to give such power to a single person who served at the pleasure of the president. To shield such sensitive and far-reaching economic decisions from political pressure, Congress included in the DOE legislation language that created an independent Federal Energy Regulatory Commission (FERC) that would set energy prices. If the president found that a national emergency required quick action on such matters, however, the secretary could circumvent the commission on the question of oil prices.

Declining Interest in Energy

During Ronald Reagan's administration, Congress all but forgot the national energy problems that it had spent the previous decade trying to solve. Indeed, by 1985 the stormy political debates over the energy policy of the 1970s had lost their thunder. With no crisis to raise an alarm, members of Congress who were still concerned about the adequacy of the nation's long-term fuel supplies could generate little political momentum for challenging Reagan's determination to scale back federal control over U.S. energy markets.

During the 1980 presidential campaign, Reagan had contended that federal actions had caused, rather than alleviated, the nation's energy problems. Declaring that "America must get to work producing more energy," he pledged to keep the government from interfering with marketplace supply-and-demand incentives that would encourage domestic fuel development. Reagan also vowed to abolish DOE; conservatives viewed the department as an unneeded instrument for federal meddling in energy matters. Congress refused to comply, but Reagan's first-term energy secretaries—former South Carolina governor James B. Edwards (an oral surgeon) and Donald P. Hodel (former deputy secretary of the interior)—de-emphasized the department's programs to promote conservation, encourage solar and other alternative technologies, and develop new ways to burn fossil fuels.

Edwards had little experience in dealing with energy issues. As South Carolina's governor, however, he had been an unabashed advocate of developing nuclear power. Environmental groups were dismayed by his strong backing of the commercial reprocessing of spent nuclear fuel into fresh fuel, plutonium, and liquid wastes. As energy secretary, Edwards continued to back nuclear research and development as offering the best long-term solution to U.S. energy needs.

In selecting Hodel to replace Edwards, the administration ignored environmental groups' criticism of Hodel's close ties to Interior Secretary James G. Watt and his record of supporting nuclear power. Hodel was able, however, to improve the morale of DOE employees by playing down talk of abolishing the department. He also won praise from some members of Congress, even Democrats who opposed his policies. While Edwards and Hodel gave DOE a low profile, Watt, as chairman of Reagan's cabinet Council on Natural Resources and the Environment, took the lead in shaping the administration's agenda for easing federal regulatory restraints on the U.S. energy industry.

In January 1985 Reagan nominated John S. Herrington, then an assistant to the president for personnel, to replace Hodel, who was nominated to be secretary of the interior after the controversial Watt was forced to resign. The announcement came amid new rumors that Reagan would seek to abolish DOE and merge its functions into the Interior Department. But Herrington played down this possibility in an appearance before the Senate Energy and Natural Resources Committee, saying, "The president has nominated me to be a full-time secretary of energy, not a caretaker." The Senate confirmed both nominations in February. The idea of a merger then faded, and as of 1988 the two departments retained their separate identities. In 1989 President George Bush appointed as secretary James D. Watkins, a former nuclear submarine skipper and chief of naval operations. It was hoped that Watkins's expertise in nuclear energy would lead to solutions for the nation's problem-plagued weapons reactor complex.

Organization and Functions

DOE is responsible for the long-term, high-risk research and development of energy technology, the marketing of federal power, energy conservation, a nuclear weapons program, energy regulatory programs, and a central energy data collection and analysis program.

The department is organized around five broad groups of activities. The largest includes programs dealing with energy research, development, and demonstration activities. The next largest is the department's defense program—nuclear weapons development, production, and surveillance activities. The remaining three major programs are under the purview of DOE's Economic Regulatory Administration, which oversees most price, supply, and allocation activities; the Federal Energy Regulatory Commission, which controls the prices and the interstate transmission of natural gas, oil, and electricity; and the Energy Information Administration, which collects and analyzes energy data.

The secretary and deputy secretary are responsible for the overall planning, direction, and control of DOE activities. The undersecretary has the primary responsibility for developing the department's policies on energy conservation and renewable energy technology.

The assistant secretary for defense programs manages and directs DOE's programs for nuclear weapons research, development, testing, production, and surveillance. In addition, the office is responsible for the Nuclear Materials Production Program and the Defense Waste and Transportation Management Program.

The assistant secretary for nuclear energy is responsible for the administration of advanced technology programs and projects for nuclear fission power generation and fuel technology; the evaluation of alternative reactor fuel cycle concepts, including nonproliferation considerations; the development of space nuclear generator systems; the development of naval nuclear propulsion plants and reactor cores; uranium enrichment activities; and remedial actions and nuclear waste technology. Much of the nuclear energy effort is directed toward technology and engineering development programs.

The assistant secretary for international affairs and energy emergencies develops and directs international energy policy and coordinates energy emergency preparedness planning operations (excluding nuclear incidents and accidents). The deputy assistant secretary for international affairs develops and implements international energy policy; monitors world energy markets and trade, price/supply trends, and technological developments; and assesses energy supply vulnerability and the international implications of U.S. contingency plans.

The Office of Conservation and Renewable Energy, headed by an assistant secretary, formulates and directs programs for long-term, high-risk research and development on renewable and conservation technologies. The office also has responsibility for administering statutorily mandated, conservation-oriented assistance programs which operate through state and local governments.

The Nuclear Waste Policy Act of 1982 established within DOE an Office of Civilian Radioactive Waste Management to focus on research and development leading to the siting, construction, and operation of geologic repositories for the disposal of civilian and defense high-level radioactive wastes and spent nuclear fuel.

The director of energy research advises the secretary on DOE physical research programs, the department's overall energy research and development programs, and university-based education and training activities.

The mission of the Office of Fossil Energy, headed by an assistant secretary, is to develop technologies designed to increase domestic production of oil and gas and to permit the United States to shift from less abundant fuels to more abundant coal.

Other offices in DOE are: Management and Administration; General Counsel; Inspector General; Board of Contract Appeals; Minority Economic Impact; Small and Disadvantaged Business Utilization; Congressional, Intergovernmental and Public Affairs; and Environment, Safety and Health. Finally, DOE has an extensive network of field organizations.

Department of Health and Human Services

The Department of Health and Human Services (HHS) was established in 1979 as the successor to the Department of Health, Education and Welfare (HEW). The second largest federal agency (after defense), HHS is the cabinet department most involved with U.S. citizens. In fact, in one way or another—whether it is mailing out Social Security checks or making health services more widely available—HHS touches the lives of more Americans than any other federal agency. Its budget is second only to that of the Defense Department; President Ronald Reagan requested $273.3 billion in new budget authority for HHS in fiscal year 1989 ($81.9 billion of which is for Social Security), compared with $328.3 billion for defense.

Product of Reorganization

HEW evolved in a series of presidential reorganization plans and laws that became effective between 1939 and 1953. In 1939 President Franklin D. Roosevelt sent Congress his first presidential reorganization plan, creating a new federal office, the Federal Security Agency (FSA), to be headed by an administrator. The plan transferred a number of existing agencies to FSA, among them the Public Health Service (PHS) from Treasury, the Social Security Board (established in 1935 as an independent agency), and the Office of Education from Interior. A 1940 reorganization plan transferred additional units to FSA; among them, the most important was the Food and Drug Administration (FDA) from Agriculture. The 1943 Barden-LaFolette Act authorized an expanded federal-state vocational rehabilitation program, which led to the creation of a separate office of vocational rehabilitation in FSA.

A 1946 reorganization plan transferred the Children's Bureau to FSA (from Labor) and the Office of Vital Statistics to PHS (from the Census Bureau in Commerce). The Social Security Board was abolished and its functions handed over to the FSA administrator, who subsequently created a Social Security Administration (SSA) to oversee the program. In 1948 management of the Federal Credit Union Act of 1934 was shifted from the Federal Deposit Insurance Corporation to FSA, where a bureau of federal credit unions was established. One year later the Bureau of Employment Security (responsible for unemployment compensation) was transferred from Labor to FSA.

On March 12, 1953, President Dwight D. Eisenhower submitted to Congress a reorganization plan that transformed FSA into a cabinet-level Department of Health, Education and Welfare. There was little opposition in either party to the substance of the plan, which took effect April 11. Republicans and many southern Democrats, who had opposed similar efforts by President Harry S Truman in 1949-1950, supported Eisenhower's initiative, as did the American Medical Association, which also had criticized the Truman proposals. Objections to the earlier plans had stemmed largely from fears that creation of a new department would enhance the power of Oscar R. Ewing, then FSA administrator and a staunch advocate of compulsory national health insurance. Ewing was expected to be the president's choice as secretary, and in that capacity he was expected to help the Truman administration put across its national health insurance proposals. Republicans also had resisted the earlier plans on the grounds that they would submerge education and health matters in a welfare-oriented agency and subject decisions on health matters to "nonprofessional" bureaucratic control.

Later in 1953 those fears were obviated by several factors. First, Oveta Culp Hobby, a strong opponent of national health insurance, was to be the new secretary rather than Ewing. Second, the 1953 plan did not vest all departmental powers directly in the new secretary; it left the functions of the PHS and Office of Education the responsibility of those two agencies, which were to be subordinate units of the new department operating under the secretary's general supervision (the existing setup under FSA). Finally, the plan provided for the creation of a new post of special assistant to the secretary for health and medical affairs. The special assistant, to be appointed by the president, was to be a person of wide nongovernmental experience in that field (but not necessarily a physician). The plan also gave the new secretary the power to administer Social Security and welfare programs (as it had been vested in the FSA administrator since 1946), but it provided for the presidential appointment of a commissioner of Social Security, subject to Senate confirmation, to carry out whatever duties in connection with those programs that might be assigned by the secretary.

Expansion of Responsibilities

During the next few years the responsibilities of HEW increased significantly. In 1954 far-reaching changes were made in the Old Age and Survivors Insurance (OASI) program, greatly extending coverage. In 1956 OASI was changed to OASDI to include disability insurance. Also that year, Congress authorized the PHS to create a National Library of Medicine (its initial stock consisted of the existing Armed Forces Medical Library), which subsequently became one of the world's largest specialized libraries.

The department's purview continued to expand under presidents John F. Kennedy and Lyndon B. Johnson. One of the most enduring legacies of the Johnson administration was the wide range of innovative social programs initiated under the banner of the "Great Society." Certainly the most dramatic development was enactment of the Medicare program in 1965 to provide hospital insurance for the elderly, financed through the Social Security system. Also in 1965 a Medicaid program of aid to the poor for medical expenses was enacted. Existing programs were broadened, including community mental health and retardation as well as aid to education for doctors, nurses, and other health specialists. Social Security was revised, with retirement benefits raised and eligibility requirements eased.

Despite Richard Nixon's desire to shift power and funding from the federal government to the states and localities, entitlement programs—among them, Social Security—continued to grow.

President Jimmy Carter's first HEW secretary, Joseph A. Califano, Jr., wasted little time in pushing forward internal reorganization at HEW in an attempt to manage more effectively one of the government's largest bureaucracies, a task that had stymied many before him. Califano made changes in both the policies and procedures of his department. In March 1977 he announced a restructuring of the bureaucracy that he said was expected to save $2 billion a year in the long run. He consolidated administration of the Medicare and Medicaid programs in a new Health Care Financing Administration (HCFA). In July he announced a reorganization of the department's regional offices, and in September he pledged a thorough review of the department's voluminous regulations—six thousand pages in thirteen volumes. The overhaul was labeled "Operation Common Sense."

A much more dramatic reorganization occurred in 1979 when Congress voted to consolidate the education functions of HEW and several other cabinet departments in a separate Department of Education, with the remaining HEW responsibilities vested in the renamed Department of Health and Human Services.

Organization and Functions

HHS has nine offices: Inspector General, General Counsel, Civil Rights, Consumer Affairs, Management and Budget, Legislation, Personnel Administration, Public Affairs, and Planning and Evaluation. The latter five are headed by assistant secretaries. The Office of Consumer Affairs is located within HHS but reports directly to the president. The department has five operating divisions.

Office of Human Development Services

The Office of Human Development Services (HDS) oversees programs for the elderly, children and youth, families, Native Americans, rural dwellers, the handicapped, and public assistance recipients.

Within HDS, the administration on aging is designated the principal office for carrying out the provisions of the 1965 Older Americans Act. It advises the secretary and other federal departments on the characteristics and needs of older people and develops programs designed to promote their welfare. The administration for children, youth, and families manages the adoption opportunities program and discretionary grant programs providing Head Start preschool services and runaway youth facilities. The office also manages provisions of the Child Abuse Prevention and Treatment Act. The administration for Native Americans develops policies and legislation and administers grant programs designed to enhance the social and economic development of American Indians, Native Alaskans, and Native Hawaiians; it also serves as a departmental liaison with other federal agencies on issues concerning Native Americans. The administration on developmental disabilities helps states increase the provision of quality services to people with developmental disabilities through a grants program, development of standards and guidelines, technical assistance, and policy initiation.

Public Health Service

The PHS had its origin in a July 16, 1798, act which authorized a Marine Hospital Service for the care of American merchant sailors. Subsequent legislation vastly broadened the scope of its activities, and it was renamed the Public Health Service in 1912. The Public Health Service Act of July 1944 consolidated and revised substantially all existing legislation related to PHS. The service's basic responsibilities have been expanded many times since then.

PHS now administers grants to states for health services, financial assistance to educational institutions for the health professions, and national health surveys; grants to state and local agencies for comprehensive health planning; health services for American Indians and Native Alaskans; and funds for research in improving the delivery of health services. The PHS National Center for Health Services Research and Health Care Technology Assessment plans, develops, and administers a program of health services research, evaluation, research training, and related grant- and contract-supported research on the financing, organization, quality, and utilization of health services.

Within PHS, the Alcohol, Drug Abuse, and Mental Health Administration oversees the National Institute on Alcohol Abuse and Alcoholism, the National Institute on Drug Abuse, and the National Institute of Mental Health. Established by the HEW secretary in 1973, the Centers for Disease Control (CDC), based in Atlanta, Georgia, administers national programs for the prevention and control of communicable and vector-borne diseases and other preventable conditions.

The National Center for Health Statistics collects, analyzes, and disseminates health statistics, and conducts basic and applied research on health data systems and statistical methodology. The activities of the Agency for Toxic Substances and Disease Registry, established in 1983, are designed to protect both public health and worker safety and health from exposure to and the adverse effects of hazardous waste sites and hazardous substances released in fires, explosions, or transportation accidents.

The Food and Drug Administration was first established in the Agriculture Department in 1931, although similar law enforcement functions had been in existence under different organizational titles since 1907, when the 1906 Food and Drug Act became effective. The activities of FDA are directed toward protecting the health of the nation from impure and unsafe foods, drugs, and cosmetics, as well as other potential hazards. Within FDA are centers for drugs and biologics, food safety and applied nutrition, veterinary medicine, and radiological health.

The Health Resources and Service Administration develops health care and maintenance systems that are adequately financed, comprehensive, interrelated, and responsive to the public's needs. It is composed of bureaus of health care delivery and assistance, health professions, resources development, and the Indian health service.

The mission of the National Institutes of Health (NIH) is to improve the health of the American people by conducting and supporting biomedical research into the causes, prevention, and cure of diseases; supporting research training and the development of research resources; and communicating biomedical information.

Health Care Financing Administration

The HCFA was established by an internal HEW reorganization in 1977, which placed under one administration oversight of the Medicare and Medicaid programs and related federal medical care quality control staffs.

Social Security Administration

The SSA administers the national program of contributory social insurance whereby employees, employers, and the self-employed pay contributions that are pooled in special trust funds. When earnings stop or are reduced because the worker retires, dies, or becomes disabled, monthly cash benefits are paid to replace partially the earnings the family has lost. Part of the contributions go into a separate hospital insurance trust fund for Medicare. SSA also administers certain aspects of the black lung benefits provisions of the 1969 Coal Mine Health and Safety Act.

The principal SSA programs are OASDI (Old Age and Survivors Disability Insurance) and the supplemental security income (SSI) program for the aged, blind, and disabled (funds for SSI come out of general revenues rather than a special trust fund). Within SSA are ten regional offices, six program service centers, and more than thirteen hundred local offices.

Family Support Administration

The Family Support Administration (FSA) advises the HHS secretary on programs to assist children and families, especially low-income families. It recommends actions and strategies designed to improve coordination of family support programs among HHS programs, other federal agencies, state and local governments, and private sector organizations.

Department of Housing and Urban Development

After four years of lobbying by presidents John F. Kennedy and Lyndon B. Johnson, Congress elevated the federal government's role in housing to cabinet-level importance in 1965 by establishing the Department of Housing and Urban Development (HUD). This move was viewed as a response to the urgent problems arising from a situation in which more than 70 percent of the U.S. population lived in the cities and suburbs—and that percentage was growing rapidly. Programs intended to deal with the problems of urban and suburban living—housing shortages, pollution, lack of mass transit, urban renewal, inadequate roads—were in disarray, scattered among federal, state, and local governments. The results of this disarray were often illogical: a new public housing project or hospital might be located far from public transportation, while slums might be replaced by parking lots or new high-rent dwellings.

HUD is principally responsible for some 115 federal housing and urban development programs affecting the development and preservation of communities and the provision of equal housing opportunities. These programs include Federal Housing Administration (FHA) mortgage insurance programs that help families become homeowners and facilitate the construction and rehabilitation of rental units; rental assistance programs for lower-income families who otherwise are unable to afford decent housing; the Government National Mortgage Association (GNMA) mortgage-backed securities that help insure an adequate supply of mortgage credit; programs to combat housing discrimination and promote fair housing; assistance to community and neighborhood development and preservation; and programs that protect the home buyer in the marketplace.

When Ronald Reagan took office in 1981, about one of every three poor families who were renting lived in subsidized housing. HUD programs supported more than 3 million rental units—or about 11 percent of all the occupied apartments in the country. Of these, about 1.2 million units were public housing; the rest were under various federally subsidized housing programs.

Establishment of HUD was one of two major housing bills that became law in 1965. The first bill, which passed Congress on August 10, authorized rent supplements for poor persons unable to pay for decent housing from their own incomes. The bill establishing HUD soon followed and was signed into law on September 9. Accompanying legislation, passed between 1965 and 1968, gave the department additional, and controversial, responsibilities: administering rent supplements to help the poor who could not afford decent housing, a model cities program intended to pump extra federal funds into needy cities, and a program to promote home ownership by the poor.

Creation of HUD

The idea of establishing a department of housing was controversial from the time of its initial proposal by Kennedy in 1961. He promised to make House and Home Finance Agency (HHFA) Director Robert C. Weaver, a black, secretary of the new department. In the Senate, however, a leadership head count found almost solid southern Democratic and Republican opposition, ensuring defeat. Using his reorganization authority, Kennedy then submitted a plan to create a housing and urban development department, but the House disapproved the resolution to put the plan into effect.

On March 2, 1965, in his "Message on the Cities," Lyndon Johnson called for a department of housing and urban development "to give greater force and effectiveness to our effort in the cities." The president's proposal had rough sledding, however: on Senate and House roll calls, a majority of Republicans and southern Democrats voted against the bill, which nonetheless passed the House on June 16 by a 217-184 vote. The Senate concurred on August 11, with much less contention.

As signed by the president on September 9, 1965, the HUD bill (PL 89-174) basically upgraded the existing HHFA to cabinet-level status. The HHFA then consisted of the Office of the Administrator and five operating units: the Federal Housing Administration, the Public Housing Administration, and the Federal National Mortgage Association—all three of which had specific authorization in law—as well as the Community Facilities Administration and the Urban Renewal Administration—both of which were created administratively within the HHFA.

The new department was not given authority to administer all federal programs related to cities and urban problems. One section of the bill, however, required a study of the functions of other agencies to determine if any should be transferred to HUD. The bill did not attempt to define an urban area or to limit the size of communities that could benefit from a HUD program. Both small towns and villages as well as large cities were thus within the department's scope.

HUD became the eleventh cabinet-level department at midnight on November 8, under provisions of the bill ordering it created no later than sixty days after the president approved the legislation. Johnson, however, postponed HUD's actual establishment until a special study group completed a report on the government's role in solving urban problems. On January 13, 1966, he appointed HHFA Director Weaver as HUD secretary.

Development of HUD's Programs

The young department was thrust immediately into the fray of administering several major controversial and extremely complex housing laws. Rent supplements and the model cities program, as well as a program to promote home ownership by the poor, immediately came under HUD's purview. By the time Johnson left office in 1969, these programs were reasonably well established and were expected to survive. Even after the precariously close votes on enactment of the basic authorization, however, Congress threatened several times to deny implementing funds.

By the late 1970s the federal government was providing a wide range of housing assistance, including direct mortgage and rent subsidies and government-insured mortgages, loans, secondary market programs, and programs designed to help special-risk homeowners and renters. In addition to HUD, the Veterans Administration and the Department of Agriculture's Farmers Home Administration participated in these programs.

During the presidency of Jimmy Carter, attention turned to revising community development programs intended to improve the nation's cities and counties. In 1977 the administration introduced a new urban development program—Urban Development Action Grants (UDAG)—which was an immediate success among the nation's cities. Aimed at urban areas with the most severe problems, UDAG used federal funds to spur private investment. But a year later, Congress decided to take away some of HUD's authority to regulate community development projects. HUD Secretary Patricia Harris had wanted to require cities to spend 75 percent of federal community development funds for projects benefiting low- and moderate-income persons. After strenuous objection from House Banking Committee members, however, HUD retreated from the proposal and required instead that at least 51 percent of the block grant funds (federal money given to state and local governments to fund a group—or "block"— of programs) be set aside for low- and middle-income projects. In addition, the final legislation allowed the House and Senate banking committees to review all proposed regulations and delay their effective date for ninety days.

By 1980 the fights over allocating community development funds had subsided. The Reagan administration, however, proposed a fundamental shift in federal housing and urban policies in the early 1980s. Blight, housing shortages, and economic decline, Reagan said, represented the failure of past federal social programs. He consistently sought to reduce the federal role in solving urban problems, while increasing incentives for a larger role by the private sector. Although the president persuaded Congress to accept substantial reductions in federal housing programs, lawmakers resisted his attempts to eliminate or sharply curtail community development and other projects.

Reagan continued his effort to cut the housing budget in 1988, proposing a $13.8 billion reduction in HUD's budget, which would kill urban development action grants, rental development grants, economic development assistance grants, and loans for redevelopment and rehabilitation assistance. Early in the year the administration was the subject of congressional criticism when it came to light that HUD Secretary Samuel R. Pierce, Jr., had not testified before any of the agency's three oversight committees for almost three years.

Organization and Functions

The HUD secretary is assisted by an undersecretary and two deputy undersecretaries (intergovernmental relations and field coordination). The office of the secretary also contains five staff offices with department-wide responsibility in specialized functional areas: Indian and Alaskan Native programs, small and disadvantaged business utilization, labor relations, international affairs, administrative and judicial proceedings, and contract appeals.

In addition to the general counsel and inspector general offices, there are eight assistant secretaries, who are responsible for public affairs, legislation and congressional relations, administration, community planning and development, fair housing and equal opportunity, housing-federal housing, public and Indian housing, and policy development and research. HUD also maintains numerous regional and field offices.

The GNMA, a government corporation within the department, administers support programs for government-sponsored mortgages through its mortgage-backed securities programs. The latter are designed to increase liquidity in the secondary mortgage market and attract new sources of financing for residential loans.

Department of the Interior

As the nation's principal conservation agency, the U.S. Department of the Interior is responsible for more than 549 million acres of public lands, or about 28 percent of the total U.S. land area. The Department of Agriculture oversees the nation's forests.

During the nation's early years, functions that would be carried out by an "interior," "home," or "internal affairs" department were apportioned by Congress among other agencies. To streamline these activities, proposals to establish a home office were made as early as 1789, but to no avail.

Shortly before the War of 1812 a House committee appointed to study the operations and organization of the Patent Office revived the idea of setting up a separate home department. And in 1816, after the war, a cabinet report recommended that a new home department be established to supervise territorial governments, construction of federal highways and canals, and the Post Office, Patent Office, and Indian Office. President James Madison endorsed the report, and a bill was introduced in the Senate in 1817, but again no action was taken.

Interest in creating a home department lagged during the next decade. Various efforts to establish one were made between 1827 and 1849, but none proved successful until 1848 and the administration of James K. Polk. In December of that year Secretary of the Treasury Robert J. Walker sent Congress a proposal to create a Department of the Interior. Before becoming Treasury secretary, Walker had served in the Senate (D-Miss.) and chaired its Committee on Public Lands. During the 1830s he had advocated selling public lands solely to settlers to discourage land speculation. That policy served as the basis of his plan to establish a new executive department.

By the late 1840s the Treasury Department had become burdened by increasing fiscal duties, and Walker did not wish to become involved in managing the vast domain acquired from the Louisiana Purchase of 1803, the Mexican War of 1846-1848, and the 1848 treaty with Great Britain by which the United States acquired the Oregon Territory. The nation's expansion, he argued, had made the responsibilities of the Treasury greater than it could handle.

Congressional Struggle over Interior

On February 12, 1849, the House Ways and Means Committee reported out a bill to establish a Department of the Interior. Samuel F. Vinton, an Ohio Whig and chairman of the committee, was a key figure in securing enactment of the legislation. The House passed the bill three days later with only minimal debate. The Senate Finance Committee reported out the bill on March 3, the last day of the Thirtieth Congress. That night, in a dramatic session, the full Senate chamber approved the measure by a margin of only six votes, 31-25.

"The bill to establish the Home Department has become law, having passed the Senate after a long, arduous and rather stormy debate; and a new and valuable Department has thus been added to the Government," noted the Washington, D.C., *Daily National Intelligencer* on March 5, 1849.

Almost one hundred years later, Harold L. Ickes, a longtime secretary of the interior (1933-1946) and one of the most famous of its chiefs, speculated that the long delay in establishing the department resulted primarily from "States' rights and the ever occurring problem of expenditures in government."

Congress transferred to the new Interior Department the General Land Office from the Treasury Department, the Patent Office from the State Department, and the Bureau of Indian Affairs and Pension Office from the War Department. Other responsibilities assigned to the department included supervision of the commissioner of public buildings, the Board of Inspectors, the Warden of the Penitentiary of the District of Columbia, and the Census of the United States, as well as the accounts of marshals and other officers of the U.S. courts and the accounts of lead and other kinds of mines in the United States.

Evolution of the Department's Policy

For a long time Interior's policy mirrored the more general public sentiment that natural resources were the limitless foundation on which a powerful nation could be built. As a result, public policy on their exploitation was extremely permissive.

Gradually, however, Americans realized that their natural resources were not inexhaustible. The environmental movement of the 1960s and 1970s resulted in the establishment of a Council on Environmental Quality and the Environmental Protection Agency, which share responsibility for overseeing natural resources with Interior. The Energy Department, created in 1977 in response to growing awareness of the need to conserve fuel resources, also plays a role in establishing environmental policy.

Throughout most of the 1960s environmentalists found an ally in Interior Secretary Stewart L. Udall, a former representative (D-Ariz.), who was appointed to the position by President John F. Kennedy. Udall had been a well-known supporter of conservation, reclamation, and national park improvement during his tenure in the House. As interior secretary, he added significantly to the department's role in water planning, outdoor recreation, and national parks programs.

The federal government's philosophy underwent an abrupt turnaround with Richard Nixon's selection of Walter J. Hickel to succeed Udall. Hickel's nomination became controversial after conservation groups questioned his dedication to natural preservation and others criticized his ties with oil companies. At a December 1968 news conference he stated that he was opposed to "conservation for conservation's sake" and that the high national standards for clean water "might even hinder industrial development."

Hickel was criticized for his opposition, as governor of Alaska, to plans to create a foreign trade subzone for oil at Machiasport, Maine, which would result in cheaper fuel for New England. Another complaint concerned his opposition, as governor, to an Interior Department freeze on the status of Alaskan public lands until Congress settled pending claims to the land by Native Alaskans.

Despite the controversy the Senate confirmed Hickel's nomination. The Alaskan claims, giving natives 40 million acres of land and $962.5 million, were cleared in 1971, but Hickel's ideology and outspokenness led to his downfall; the president fired him in November 1970.

The environmental movement waned during the early 1970s, but President Jimmy Carter's appointment of conservationist Idaho governor Cecil D. Andrus as interior secretary brought praise from environmentalists and criticism from mining, logging, and other development interests. While Interior was headed by Andrus (1977-1981), major legislation was enacted to control strip mining, protect millions of acres of wilderness in Alaska, and clean up chemical contamination.

Although conservationists generally found an ally in the interior secretary, President Ronald Reagan's first appointee to the post, James G. Watt, aroused considerable controversy when he attempted to instigate broad changes in the department's programs and personnel. Although he was generally considered an able administrator, Watt's rhetoric was occasionally abrasive. Moreover, his philosophy of emphasizing private use of resources in the public domain and of returning to the states more control over government lands did not sit well with environmentalists.

Initially, Reagan stood by his secretary, but Watt was forced to resign in October 1983. He was succeeded by William P. Clark, who took over temporarily and was followed in 1985 by Donald P. Hodel, who had been secretary of energy and previously had served as undersecretary of interior under Watt.

Organization and Functions

The Interior Department consists of some thirty major bureaus and offices. The secretary is responsible for meshing departmental activities with the assistance of an undersecretary and five assistant secretaries (fish and wildlife and parks, Indian affairs, land and minerals management, territorial and international affairs, and water and science). An assistant secretary for policy, budget, and administration serves as principal policy adviser to the secretary. The department is divided into functional offices, which are responsible for a wide variety of managerial, regulatory, promotional, planning, and research activities.

The Bureau of Mines is primarily a research and statistics-gathering agency. It also frequently produces special studies on subjects of particular national interest, such as the effects of potential economic, technological, or legal developments on resource availability.

The U.S. Geological Survey (USGS) was established in 1879 to provide a permanent federal agency to conduct the systematic and scientific "classification of the public lands, and examination of the geological structure, mineral resources, and products of the national domain." USGS is the federal government's largest earth science research agency, the nation's largest civilian mapmaking agency, the primary source of data on the nation's surface water and groundwater resources, and the employer of the largest number of professional earth scientists.

The Bureau of Indian Affairs (BIA) is the federal agency with primary responsibility for working with Indian tribal governments and the village communities of Native Alaskans. Other federal agencies may deal with Indians or Native Alaskans as members of an ethnic group or simply as individuals, but the BIA is distinctive in that it deals with them as governments in a government-to-government relationship. For one of its principal programs, BIA administers and manages some 52 million acres of land held in trust by the United States for Indians.

The mandate of the U.S. Fish and Wildlife Service is to conserve, protect, and enhance fish, wildlife, and their habitats. Its primary focus is on migratory birds, endangered species, freshwater and anadromous fisheries, and certain marine mammals. Headquartered in Washington, D.C., the service has seven regional offices and numerous field units, including national wildlife refuges, national fish hatcheries, research laboratories, and a nationwide network of law enforcement agents.

Established in 1946, the Bureau of Land Management oversees about 300 million acres of public lands, located primarily in the West and in Alaska and comprising about one-eighth of the total U.S. land area. Day-to-day management of these lands and related resources is decentralized into twelve state offices.

The 1977 Surface Mining Control and Reclamation Act established the Office of Surface Mining to collect funds from coal companies and provide disbursements for reclamation of coal lands mined before August 1977. The office also establishes and enforces standards and regulations ensuring that current and future mining will be environmentally sound.

The Bureau of Reclamation was chartered in 1902 to reclaim the arid lands of the western United States for farming by providing a secure, year-round supply of water for irrigation. Among its most notable projects were the Grand Coulee Dam on the Columbia River and Hoover Dam on the Colorado River. In addition to irrigation, the bureau's responsibilities include hydroelectric power generation, municipal and industrial water supplies, river regulation and flood control, outdoor recreation, enhancement of fish and wildlife habitats, and research.

The Minerals Management Service, created in 1982, is responsible for establishing an effective means of collecting revenues generated from mineral leases offshore (including the outer continental shelf) and on federal and Indian lands. It is also charged with the orderly development of offshore energy and mineral resources while safeguarding the environment. These funds, the largest federal source of revenue outside the Treasury Department, are distributed in turn to Indian tribes and the appropriate states, the Land and Water Conservation Fund, the Historic Preservation Fund, and the U.S. Treasury.

The National Park Service, established in 1916, administers the National Park System, which comprises more than 330 parks, monuments, historic sites, battlefields, seashores and lakeshores, and recreation areas. The service also directs programs that assist states, other federal agencies, local governments, and individuals in the protection of historical, natural, architectural, engineering, and archeological resources that lie outside the National Park System. It maintains the National Register of Historic Places and a registry of natural sites.

The office of the assistant secretary for territorial and international affairs is responsible for coordinating federal policy in the territories of American Samoa, Guam, the Virgin Islands, the Commonwealth of the Northern Mariana Islands, and the Trust Territory of the Pacific. The office also oversees and coordinates various international activities of the Interior Department.

Department of Justice

The U.S. attorney general was one of the first positions to be established, with cabinet rank, in the federal government. The Judiciary Act of September 24, 1789, made the attorney general the chief legal officer of the federal government. At the time, the nation's top law officer was assisted by one clerk. The Department of Justice itself was established in 1870, with the attorney general as its head. Through its thousands of lawyers, investigators, and agents, the department investigates violations of federal law (ranging from income tax evasion to criminal syndicates), supervises the custody of those accused or convicted of federal crimes, oversees legal and illegal aliens, and directs U.S. domestic security when the nation is threatened by foreign or internal subversion. Moreover, Justice polices narcotics trafficking; helps state and local governments increase their numbers of police departments, courts, and correctional institutions (through federal aid); advises the president and other government agencies on legal matters; and drafts legislation. The Justice Department also conducts all suits in the Supreme Court to which the U.S. government is a party. The attorney general supervises and directs these activities, as well as those of the U.S. attorneys and U.S. marshals in the nation's ninety-four judicial districts.

Despite its staggering number of lawyers (the department employs about five thousand attorneys), Justice is one of the smallest cabinet departments. Writer Richard Harris has noted that "the federal government has only a small fraction of the manpower that is required to combat crime nationally," largely because the Constitution gives the policing power to the states. Nonetheless, Harris observed, "Limited as the federal role is . . . it can be critically significant. . . . [I]t provides a model for every lesser jurisdiction, and the federal government's overall approach . . . will probably determine whether or not the nation's traditional freedoms are preserved." [30]

Evolution of the Department in the 1950s and 1960s

Before the 1960s the department's mission was perceived as primarily one of prosecuting violations of the Internal Revenue Code, instituting some antitrust suits, and keeping watch over "subversives" and "public enemies." In the 1960s, however, Justice became intimately involved with major domestic issues—racial violence, mass demonstrations, riots, draft resistance to the Vietnam War, and rising crime rates, among others. To cope with its increased responsibilities the department created a number of new divisions, and by 1970 Justice had 208 units.

Crime as a national political issue became the most emotionally charged, and perhaps the most crucial, of all domestic concerns in the 1968 elections. President Lyndon B. Johnson's attorney general, Ramsey Clark, was keenly interested in civil rights, but it was his approach to crime that brought him the greatest criticism and made him an issue in the 1968 presidential campaign. An uncompromising opponent of efforts to maintain order at the expense of due process, Clark became a natural target of those who advocated a "get tough" policy on crime. "If we are going to restore order and respect for law in this country, there's one place we're going to begin; we're going to have a new attorney general of the United States of America," stated Richard Nixon on accepting the Republican presidential nomination.

Nixon's "War on Crime" and Watergate

Crime was increasing at a frightening pace when Nixon was sworn in for his first term in 1969, elected on a tough "law and order" platform. But five years and billions of dollars later, with stringent new federal anticrime laws in place, the crime rate was still climbing. Late in 1974, plain-spoken attorney general William B. Saxbe declared the war on crime a "dismal failure." But even before Nixon left office in 1974, national opinion polls showed that the public's attention had shifted away from concern with street crime to economic problems, the energy crisis, and Watergate.

Climbing even more swiftly than the crime rate during the Nixon/Ford years was the amount of federal dollars spent on law enforcement. In fiscal year 1971 the Justice Department had its first billion dollar budget. In fiscal year 1975 its budget hit $2 billion. Justice spending levelled off just above the $2 billion mark in fiscal year 1976.

It was a peculiar twist on the "law and order" theme of the Nixon administration: the crimes that drew national attention in its last years were those committed by or charged against some of its highest officials, including the president himself. Among the Nixon administration officials accused of crimes during this period was Attorney General John N. Mitchell. Mitchell was convicted in early 1975 of conspiracy and obstruction of justice for his participation in the effort to cover up White House involvement in the Watergate break-in at Democratic National Headquarters in June 1972. The attorney general, who was also Nixon's campaign manager, was aloof, blunt, and a product of Wall Street. Unlike Clark, Mitchell stated that he believed Justice "was an institution for law enforcement, not social improvement." [31]

In 1972 Mitchell was replaced by Richard G. Kleindienst, who pleaded guilty in May 1974 to charges that he did not testify fully before the Senate Judiciary Committee when it was investigating charges that political pressure had figured in the settlement of the government's case against the International Telephone and Telegraph Corporation. After Kleindienst was forced to leave office in 1973, Secretary of Defense Elliott L. Richardson took over. He resigned on October 10, 1973, however, rather than obey the president's order to fire special Watergate prosecutor Archibald Cox. Nixon then selected William Saxbe as attorney general.

Justice Under Ford, Carter, and Reagan

With the accession of Gerald R. Ford to the presidency, the tone of the administration's anticrime effort changed markedly. Emphasizing that law enforcement should focus more upon the needs of the victims of crime than upon the criminal, Ford asked Congress to authorize financial aid for the victims of crime, to approve a revised criminal code, to provide mandatory minimum sentencing for certain crimes, to provide for more consistency in sentences, and to enact a mild control on gun ownership.

Crime was not a top priority in the White House or on Capitol Hill from 1977 to 1980. Access to justice, rather than a war on crime, was the theme of the Carter administration's law enforcement program. That emphasis was explicable in light of the fact that the top two law enforcement officials in the administration—Attorney General Griffin B. Bell and Federal Bureau of Investigation Director William Webster—had served a total of more than twenty years on the federal bench before moving to the executive branch posts. In the Justice Department, Bell set up a new entity, the Office for Improvements in the Administration of Justice. Out of that office came proposals to expand the powers of federal magistrates—a measure that was passed in 1979.

For the most part, crime was mentioned little during Ronald Reagan's first years in office, even though the nation appeared more concerned about this issue than it had been during Carter's administration. The Federal Bureau of Investigation (FBI) nevertheless became a billion dollar operation for the first time in fiscal year 1984, spending more than the entire federal court system, whose funding rose from $631 million in fiscal year 1981 to $977.9 million in fiscal year 1985.

William French Smith, once Reagan's personal lawyer, served as attorney general throughout Reagan's first term, but he resigned in January 1984 to return to his law practice. Reagan then announced the nomination of White House counselor Edwin Meese III, one of his closest advisers, to succeed Smith. Questions about Meese's personal finances, however, led to a prolonged investigation that delayed Senate confirmation until 1985. As attorney general, Meese was criticized for his failure to conduct a thorough investigation of the Iran arms sales and contra aid scandal when it became public in November 1986. He also was probed for connections with individuals tied to a New York defense contractor, the Bronx-based Wedtech Corporation, which was the subject of federal investigations of fraud and bribery of public officials. In 1987 independent counsel James C. McKay was appointed to investigate Meese's personal finances, his involvement with Wedtech, and several other instances of alleged wrongdoing. After a fourteen-month investigation, McKay concluded in an 814-page report made public July 18, 1988, that although he would not indict Meese for criminal wrongdoing, the attorney general had "probably violated" the law. Before the report's release, Meese had announced on July 5 that he intended to resign in August. He left Justice on August 12, and Reagan appointed Dick Thornburgh to replace him.

Organization and Functions

The office of the attorney general provides overall policy and program direction for the offices, divisions, bureaus, and boards of the department. The office represents the United States in legal matters generally; it also makes recommendations to the president about appointments to federal judicial positions.

The attorney general is assisted by a deputy attorney general and associate attorney general, who are the principal agents for managing the department. In addition to offices, the department consists of seven divisions: offices and services, antitrust, civil, civil rights, criminal, land and natural resources, and tax—all of which are headed by assistant attorneys general.

Divisions

In the *Offices and Services Division,* the Solicitor General's Office supervises and conducts government litigation in the Supreme Court. Such litigation comprises about two-thirds of all cases decided by the Court each year. The Solicitor General, often called the "tenth justice" of the Court, determines for which cases the government will seek Supreme Court review as well as the position the government will take in the Court. Another function of the office is to decide which cases, of those lost before the lower courts, the United States should appeal.

The assistant attorney general in charge of the Office of Legal Counsel drafts the formal opinions of the attorney general and provides his or her own written opinion and informal advice in response to requests. The staff frequently prepares and delivers testimony to Congress on a variety of legal issues, particularly constitutional matters such as legislative vetoes, executive privilege, and the power of the president to enter into executive agreements.

Established in early 1981, the Office of Legal Policy is a strategic legal "think tank," which serves as the attorney general's principal policy development staff. The Office of Intelligence Policy and Review provides legal advice and recommendations on national security matters. It reviews executive orders, directives, and procedures related to the intelligence community and approves certain intelligence-gathering activities.

The Office of the Pardon Attorney receives and reviews all petitions for executive clemency, initiates the necessary investigations, and recommends to the president which form of executive clemency—including pardon, commutation of sentence, remission of fine, and reprieve—it finds appropriate.

The assistant attorney general in charge of the Office of Legislative Affairs is responsible for liaison between the department and Congress.

The Community Relations Service (CRS), created by Title X of the Civil Rights Act of 1964, falls under the general authority of the attorney general and is headed by a director, who is appointed by the president with the advice and consent of the Senate. The CRS helps resolve disputes through its field staff of mediators and conciliators, who work out of ten regional offices. It also is charged with integration into the United States of the almost 180,000 Cubans and Haitians who have entered the country since 1980 without documentation or imminent prospects of returning to their homelands.

Under the direction of the assistant attorney general for administration, the Justice Management Division assists senior management officials with matters related to basic department policy for selected management operations and provides direct administrative services to offices, boards, and divisions of the department.

The Office of Professional Responsibility, which reports directly to the attorney general, oversees investigations of allegations of criminal or ethical misconduct by employees of the department.

The Office of Liaison Services represents the department in dealings with other governments and with nongovernmental organizations—both foreign and domestic—interested in the justice field.

Under the supervision of the deputy attorney general, the Executive Office for United States Attorneys provides the ninety-four offices of U.S. attorneys with general executive assistance and nonlitigative oversight, and it publishes the *United States Attorneys' Manual* and the *United States Attorneys' Bulletin.*

U.S. trustees insure compliance with the federal bankruptcy laws and supervise the administration of cases and trustees in cases filed under Title I of the 1978 Bankruptcy Code. Formerly established as a pilot program with limited jurisdiction, the U.S. trustee program—under the Bankruptcy Judges, United States Trustees, and Family Farmer Bankruptcy Act of 1986—is a permanent, nationwide system for the administration of bankruptcy cases.

U.S. marshals serve as executive officers of the federal courts and agents of the Department of Justice. They and their staffs are located in each of the ninety-four federal judicial districts encompassing the fifty states, Guam, Puerto Rico, the Virgin Islands, and the Northern Mariana Islands. The director of the service provides overall supervision.

As a law enforcement agency, the *Antitrust Division* prosecutes criminal and civil antitrust cases, primarily under the Sherman and Clayton Antitrust acts. The division also appears as a competition advocate before congressional committees and federal regulatory agencies.

The *Civil Division* is known as the "government's lawyer." This is sometimes a complicated role, because in every case there are two clients: the agency concerned and the people of the United States. The division's clients include more than a hundred federal agencies and commissions, individual federal employees acting in their official capacities, and, in some instances, members of Congress and the federal judiciary. The division's litigation is organized into six areas: commercial litigation, federal programs, torts, appellate staff, immigration litigation, and consumer litigation.

Established in 1957, the *Civil Rights Division* enforces the nation's laws and executive orders related to civil rights. The division works primarily on litigation and connected matters. Except for criminal law enforcement work, where cases normally are tried before a jury, suits filed by the division are in equity, usually before a single judge and seeking injunctive relief.

The assistant attorney general in charge of the *Criminal Division* formulates criminal law enforcement policies and enforces and generally supervises all federal criminal laws except those specifically assigned to the other divisions. This division—by far the most active of the principal Justice divisions—also supervises certain civil litigation related to federal law enforcement activities (such as federal liquor, narcotics, counterfeiting, gambling, firearms, customs, agriculture, and immigration laws). It supervises as well litigation resulting from petitions for writs of habeas corpus by members of the armed forces, actions brought by or on behalf of federal prisoners, alleged investigative misconduct, and legal actions related to national security issues.

The *Land and Natural Resources Division* represents the United States in litigation involving public lands and natural resources, environmental quality, Indian lands and claims, and wildlife resources. The fastest growing area of its responsibility involves civil and criminal enforcement of environmental statutes.

In all courts except the U.S. Tax Court, the *Tax Division* represents the United States and its officers in civil and criminal litigation involving federal, state, and local taxes. The Internal Revenue Service (IRS) is the division's principal client. For IRS, the division collects federal revenues by instituting many types of actions at the request of IRS and defends tax refund and other suits brought by taxpayers.

Bureaus

Established in 1908, the Federal Bureau of Investigation is the principal investigative arm of the department. It is charged with gathering and reporting facts, locating witnesses, and compiling evidence in cases involving federal jurisdiction.

The Federal Bureau of Prisons is responsible for the care and custody of persons convicted of federal crimes and sentenced by the courts to incarceration in a federal penal institution. The bureau operates a nationwide system of maximum, medium, and minimum security prisons and community program offices.

The International Criminal Police Organization-United States National Central Bureau (INTERPOL-USNCB) was created to promote mutual assistance between all law enforcement authorities in the prevention and suppression of international crime. Established in 1923 and reorganized in 1946, INTERPOL has grown from an organization composed of a few European countries to a worldwide consortium of 142 member countries. In 1977 Justice and Treasury officials were given dual authority in administering INTERPOL-USNCB.

The Immigration and Naturalization Service, established in 1891, has four major areas of responsibility: (1) aliens entering the United States (controlling entry into the country, facilitating the entry of qualified persons, and denying admission to illegal aliens); (2) aliens within the United States (providing immigration benefits, maintaining information on alien status, and deporting illegal aliens); (3) naturalization and citizenship; and (4) aliens who enter illegally or whose authorized stay in the United States has expired (apprehending and removing such individuals).

The Drug Enforcement Administration (DEA) is the lead federal agency in enforcing the laws and regulations governing narcotics and controlled substances. Created in 1973, DEA concentrates on high-level narcotics smuggling and distribution organizations in the United States and abroad, working closely with such agencies as the Customs Service, the Internal Revenue Service, and the Coast Guard.

The Justice Assistance Act of 1984 restructured the criminal justice research and statistics units of the department and established a program of financial and technical assistance to state and local governments. The act also established the Office of Justice Programs, headed by an assistant attorney general, to coordinate the activities of some existing offices (such as statistics and juvenile justice and delinquency prevention) and to oversee a new program designed to locate and recover missing children.

Boards

Seven boards are associated with the Justice Department. They are the Executive Office for Immigration Review, Board of Immigration Appeals, Office of the Chief Immigration Judge, Office of the Immigration Judge, Office of the Chief Administrative Hearing Officer, United States Parole Commission, and Foreign Claims Settlement Commission of the United States.

Department of Labor

On March 4, 1913, President William Howard Taft signed a bill that established a cabinet-level department "to foster, promote, and develop the welfare of the wage earners of the United States, to improve their working conditions, and to advance their opportunities for profitable employment." Although the beginnings of the Department of Labor were rather small and somewhat inauspicious, the department was enforcing more than 140 laws by the 1980s. They deal with wide-ranging and significant areas of workers' well-being, including unemployment insurance and workers' compensation, minimum wages and overtime pay, occupational health and safety, antidiscrimination in employment, protection of pension rights, job training, and strengthening free collective bargaining. The department compiles statistics on prices, employment, and other appropriate subjects and strives to solve the job market problems of minorities, youth, older workers, women, and disadvantaged and disabled groups.

Background

As labor unions grew in strength, pressures increased after the Civil War to create a federal office that represented workers. This effort was led by William Sylvis, a well-known labor leader, who contended that existing federal departments were closely tied to wealthy businesses, and there was no federal agency that had as its "sole object the care and protection of labor." Sylvis and others lobbied President Andrew Johnson to support a secretary of labor, with cabinet status, to be selected from labor's ranks. According to labor historian Jonathan Grossman, more than one hundred bills and resolutions to create a labor department were introduced in Congress between 1864 and 1900.[32]

In 1884 Congress passed and President Chester A. Arthur signed a bill that established a Bureau of Labor in the Interior Department. The bureau was to gather information pertaining to workers and devise a "means of promoting their material, social, intellectual, and moral prosperity."

It took some time for Arthur to name the first commissioner of labor. The unions had expected that he would appoint Terence Powderly, leader of the Knights of Labor union, but the president apparently found Powderly too radical. Instead, he appointed Carroll D. Wright of the Massachusetts Bureau of Labor Statistics. Under Wright's leadership the new bureau flourished.

Arthur's successor, Grover Cleveland, pressed for enlarging the bureau and empowering it to investigate and arbitrate labor disputes. The Knights of Labor lobbied for creation of a cabinet-level department and succeeded in having a bill introduced in 1888. The legislation was watered down, however; the bill that emerged, with little debate, established an independent Department of Labor, without cabinet status. Cleveland signed the legislation on March 21 and chose Wright to head the new agency.

Over the next few years the department gained in stature as the most important federal statistics-gathering agency and as author of significant reports on such subjects as labor legislation, compulsory insurance, housing, railroad labor, and the status of women in the work force. In 1895, it began publishing the *Bulletin of Labor* (today called the *Monthly Labor Review*).

Merger, then Independence

On becoming president after William McKinley's assassination, Theodore Roosevelt suggested appointing a secretary of commerce and industries, with cabinet status. "It should be his province to deal with commerce in its broadest sense, including among many other things whatever concerns labor and all matters affecting the great business corporations. . . ." Legislation reflecting this view was introduced in the Fifty-seventh Congress. It was opposed vigorously by Democrats, who argued that mutual distrust between business and labor would paralyze the department and that the powers of the existing independent Department of Labor would in fact be weakened. But Republicans, who were in the majority, responded that the two groups had mutual interests and that a new department would be more efficient in obtaining and synthesizing economic information scattered through existing departments. Their position predominated; legislation creating the new department, its name changed to the Department of Commerce and Labor, was signed into law in February 1903.

Democrats won control of the House in 1910, and fifteen union members were elected to Congress. Rep. William Sulzer (D-N.Y.) introduced a Department of Labor bill in 1912; it cleared both chambers and was signed into law on March 4, 1913. Although President Taft opposed the bill, a veto was fruitless: President-elect Woodrow Wilson had already selected William B. Wilson, a trade unionist and member of the House (D-Pa.), to be his secretary of labor.

During its early years the fledgling department faced rough going: businesses distrusted it, and conservative members of Congress slashed at its funds and functions. For many years Labor was the smallest and least influential cabinet department. But under President Franklin D. Roosevelt's labor secretary, Frances Perkins (the first woman named to the cabinet), the department's authority and stature grew considerably. Thereafter, other functions and responsibilities were added to the department's purview with the passage of significant labor relations legislation and Supreme Court decisions upholding these acts and workers' rights in general.

From the viewpoint of organized labor, the administration of Lyndon B. Johnson produced one of the most fruitful legislative periods in American history with the enactment of Johnson's "Great Society" programs. Congress also cleared an administration measure for far-reaching extension of minimum wage coverge and increases in the pay floor. Business interests and their allies emerged victorious, however, over both the labor unions and the administration when Congress refused to enact laws expanding unemployment compensation and lifting restrictions on construction site picketing by striking unions. Overseeing labor's interests during these years was secretary W. Willard Wirtz, who had served under the administration of John F. Kennedy and remained through the Johnson presidency. He figured in several critical labor-management confrontations.

Labor interests did not fare so well under Richard Nixon's presidency, when the administration was bent on cutting back on domestic social programs. Jimmy Carter's administration began optimistically enough—labor interests had hoped to take advantage of a labor-supported president and Congress—but those hopes quickly faded. Although Congress enacted traditional labor legislation measures such as an increase in the minimum wage, it rejected or qualified a number of items on labor's agenda. This happened despite the efforts of Carter's labor secretary, F. Ray Marshall, whose nomination had broad appeal to key elements of Carter's coalition: unions, civil rights groups, and the South. Marshall brought with him a distinguished career in economics—his work focused on employment problems of blacks and rural human resource and poverty issues.

Labor Secretaries in the 1980s

The influence of organized labor declined during the Reagan presidency. Moreover, the voice of labor's representative in the cabinet was weakened when Reagan's first labor secretary, Raymond J. Donovan, resigned his post March 15, 1985. Donovan was the last member of Reagan's original cabinet to win Senate approval because his confirmation was held up by the Senate Labor and Human Resources Committee. It was investigating charges, made by a Federal Bureau of Investigation informer, that Donovan and Schiavone Construction Company, a New Jersey firm Donovan had worked for since 1958, had provided illegal payoffs to corrupt union officials to maintain "labor peace." Other informants said the company had close ties with organized crime. Although the Senate did confirm the appointment, with only Democrats dissenting, a special prosecutor was appointed in December 1981 to investigate the charges, and in October 1984 a grand jury named Donovan in a 137-count indictment. Donovan pleaded not guilty, but he asked for a leave of absence. He resigned after a New York Supreme Court judge refused to dismiss larceny and fraud charges against him. On May 25, 1987, he was acquitted.

Reagan's choice of U.S. Trade Representative William E. Brock III to succeed Donovan drew praise from organized labor. "While we have not always agreed [with Brock], he has earned our respect," said AFL-CIO President Lane Kirkland.[33] Throughout Donovan's tenure, Labor's budget cuts and allegedly lax enforcement of labor laws had come under steady criticism from union officials, most of whom opposed Reagan's reelection in 1984.

Brock resigned in November 1987, and Reagan named Ann Dore McLaughlin to succeed him. McLaughlin, whose specialty was public affairs, had not worked in the Labor Department but had held ranking posts in Treasury and Interior. She was handily confirmed on December 11, 1987. McLaughlin had three goals: (1) ensure enforcement of the existing labor statutes; (2) use changes in the work force—largely the growing proportion of women—as an opportunity to galvanize labor and management to solve problems such as child care; and (3) along with the Education and Commerce departments, move quickly to develop retraining and education for workers in the fast-changing economy.

Organization and Functions

The secretary of labor is assisted by a deputy secretary and deputy undersecretaries for international affairs and for labor management relations and cooperative programs. The department has four assistant secretaries in charge of congressional affairs, public and intergovernmental affairs, administration and management, and policy. The secretary's office includes the Women's Bureau, an inspector general, a solicitor, the Benefits Review Board, the Employees' Compensation Appeals Board, the Office of Administrative Law Judges, and the Wage Appeals Board.

In addition to the commissioner of labor statistics, there are seven assistant secretaries responsible for the following areas: occupational safety and health, employment and training, labor management standards, mine safety and health, pension and welfare benefit programs, veterans' employment and training services, and employment standards.

The department's functions that most affect the lives of American workers include those administered by the Employment and Training Office, which is responsible for employment services, work experience, work training, and unemployment insurance. This office operates a Job Training Partnership Program, in which more than a million people (more than 40 percent are youths) participate. It also runs summer youth programs and a program to assist dislocated workers (primarily those affected by plant closings), and it oversees an employment and training program for Native Americans. The Job Corps provides a wide range of training, educational, and support services for disadvantaged youths aged sixteen to twenty-one. The Senior Community Service Employment Program helps older Americans obtain employment. The office administers as well apprenticeship programs and claims for unemployment benefits.

The Labor-Management Office assists collective bargaining negotiators, protects veterans' reemployment rights, oversees labor organizations through the Labor Management Reporting and Disclosure Act, and aids employees and unions in meeting problems caused by technological change.

The Employment Standards Office deals with minimum wage and overtime standards through its wage and hour division and attempts to achieve nondiscrimination in employment by federal contractors through the Office of Federal Contract Compliance Programs. Federal workers' compensation programs also are under the purview of this office.

Worker safety and health concerns are the responsibility of the Occupational Safety and Health Administration, which formulates safety and health standards for the workplace, and the Mine Safety and Health Administration, which operates in all types of mines.

The Bureau of Labor Statistics is the principal fact-finding agency for data on labor requirements, labor force, employment, unemployment, hours of work, wages and employee compensation, productivity, technological developments, and general economic trends. It publishes the *Monthly Labor Review, Consumer Price Index, Employ-*

ment and Earnings, Current Wage Developments, Producer Prices and Price Indexes, and *Occupational Outlook Quarterly,* among numerous other publications.

Department of State

Although it has far-flung responsibilities, the State Department—the senior executive department of the U.S. government—has remained one of the smallest departments in the cabinet. About one-third of its approximately nineteen thousand employees serve domestically; of the two-thirds serving abroad, slightly more than one-third are American citizens, and the rest are foreign nationals. Of the cabinet departments, State has the smallest budget even though it includes U.S. contributions to seventy-five multinational organizations and their affiliates. Americans employed by the department are members of either the Civil Service or the Foreign Service. Those in the Civil Service generally do not serve abroad, while Foreign Service personnel spend approximately 60 percent of their years of service in foreign countries.

History of the Department

The present-day Department of State had its beginnings in 1781, when Congress established a Department of Foreign Affairs, redesignated the Department of State in September 1789. During Secretary Thomas Jefferson's tenure (1789-1793), the department consisted of five clerks, two messengers, and a part-time translator of French. It maintained legations in London and Paris, a diplomatic agency in The Hague, and two consular missions. Only ten persons were added to the staff in the ensuing thirty years.

The department was reorganized by Secretary Louis McLane (1833-1834) into seven bureaus dealing with diplomatic, consular, internal, and servicing functions. That arrangement continued until 1870, when Secretary Hamilton Fish (1869-1877) split the diplomatic and consular bureaus into two geographically oriented units. In the early 1900s secretaries Elihu Root (1905-1909) and Philander C. Knox (1909-1913) reorganized the department into regional divisions, the basis for the contemporary structure. The 1924 Rogers Act combined the diplomatic and consular services in a single Foreign Service.

Throughout the 1920s and 1930s most of the State Department's work was carried out by its geographical divisions, which formulated policy and drafted instructions. Because of the small size of the divisions, it was relatively easy to conduct the nation's foreign policy. World War II, however, thrust the United States into the unambiguous position of world leader. Responding to the expansion of State's activities, Secretary Cordell Hull (1933-1944) regrouped related functions under individual assistant secretaries and established eleven coordinating offices.

According to author Martin Mayer, "The modern State Department is essentially the creation of George C. Marshall [1947-1949], who . . . immediately saw what was wrong. No staff . . . no planning: no real sense of who the other actors were, domestically."[34] Marshall put the undersecretary (who was Dean G. Acheson at the time) in charge of the daily operations of the department; staff wishing access to the secretary had to be cleared by him first. Marshall also established a Policy Planning Staff, with George F. Kennan (later U.S. ambassador to the Soviet Union) in charge. Marshall's reorganization and the strength of the Policy Planning Staff (subsequently renamed the Policy Planning Council) gave the State Department preeminence in foreign policy making.

After the Hoover Commission on government reorganization recommended a thorough overhaul of the department in 1949, Secretary Acheson (1949-1953) rearranged the existing eighteen offices into five bureaus (four geographic and a Bureau of United Nations Affairs), as well as units dealing with economic, intelligence, public, and press affairs. The budgetary, personnel, and operating facilities were assigned to a deputy undersecretary. Eventually, there were six substantive and eight functional agencies.

During Dwight D. Eisenhower's first term the information service and foreign aid programs were taken away from State, and Congress reinstated the Foreign Agricultural Service in the Department of Agriculture. By 1953-1954, Sen. Joseph R. McCarthy's (R-Wis.) virulent accusations of communist penetration of the State Department had severely weakened its stature; recruitment into the Foreign Service came to a halt. In response, Secretary of State John Foster Dulles appointed a commission to examine the department's organization and personnel procedures. The commission recommended a sizeable expansion of the Foreign Service, achieved primarily by giving Foreign Service officer status to the department's Civil Service employees.

Another major reorganization occurred in 1970, following a period of intensive internal review by several task forces. Secretary William P. Rogers (1969-1973) phased in a number of managerial changes that strengthened the policy formulation process and assigned decision-making and managerial responsibilities to the secretary and assistant secretaries. Nonetheless, complaints continued to abound over what were considered an excessive number of meetings and the huge quantity of paperwork (including more than two million words of cable traffic a day) generated by the department.

Secretary's Position

The secretary of state, along with the secretaries of defense, Treasury, and justice, is generally considered a member of the president's inner cabinet, although the influence of the department has varied according to personalities and circumstances. President Harry S Truman, for example, relied heavily on the advice of Secretary Marshall in the postwar reconstruction of Europe. In the following years of mounting international tension, presidents continued to look to their secretaries for principal foreign policy leadership: Acheson under Truman, Dulles under Eisenhower, Dean Rusk (1961-1969) under presidents John F. Kennedy and Lyndon B. Johnson, and Henry A. Kissinger under Richard Nixon.

Before 1968, according to Mayer, "Presidents usually spent considerable time with their Secretaries of State—Dean Rusk estimated that he saw Kennedy more than two thousand times in the thousand days. Recently, and unfortunately, both President and Secretary have become too busy, and too tightly cosseted by their staffs."[35]

Recent secretaries have had their ups and downs in relations with the president. Jimmy Carter's first secretary of state, Cyrus R. Vance (1977-1980), brought to the administration broad experience in foreign policy and crisis management. He offered to foreign governments the reassurance of a well-known and widely respected figure in charge of U.S. diplomacy. It was primarily the president himself, however, who assumed the foreign policy initiative in reaching the major foreign policy achievement of his administration: the 1979 Camp David Peace Accords between Israel and Egypt.

Ronald Reagan's first secretary of state was Alexander M. Haig, Jr., a former army general and NATO commander known for his loyal service as President Nixon's White House chief of staff during the Watergate period. Haig remained controversial during his year and a half in office, declaring himself Reagan's foreign policy "vicar" and engaging in jealous turf fights over policy formulation with other administration figures. He suddenly resigned in June 1982, later saying that his departure was not entirely voluntary.

George P. Shultz—a former economics professor, corporate executive, and Nixon cabinet officer—succeeded Haig. Shultz changed both the style and substance of U.S. foreign policy, using a less aggressive posture and more quiet diplomacy.

Organization and Functions

The secretary of state is responsible for the overall direction, coordination, and supervision of U.S. foreign relations and for the interdepartmental activities of the U.S. government overseas. The secretary is the first-ranking member of the cabinet and a member of the National Security Council.

The secretary is assisted by a deputy secretary and four undersecretaries (security assistance, science, and technology; political affairs; economic and agricultural affairs; and management). The department's counselor is a principal officer, serving the secretary as a consultant on major foreign policy problems. The counselor conducts special international negotiations and consultations as directed by the secretary and provides guidance to the appropriate bureaus on such matters.

Also attached to the secretary's office are the U.S. ambassador to the United Nations, several ambassadors-at-large who undertake special missions, the chief of protocol, the special assistant for press relations, the executive secretariat, and the Policy Planning Council.

Regional Bureaus

Primary substantive responsibility in the department rests with the five regional bureaus (European and Canadian Affairs, African Affairs, East Asian and Pacific Affairs, Inter-American Affairs, and Near Eastern and South Asian Affairs), which are headed by assistant secretaries. These bureaus advise the secretary on the formulation of U.S. policies toward countries within their regional jurisdiction and guide the operations of the U.S. diplomatic establishments in those countries.

The Bureau of International Organization Affairs manages U.S. participation in the United Nations and its system of programs and agencies. The bureau also deals with international problems such as food production, air traffic safety, communications, health, human rights, education, and the environment. In addition, the bureau is responsible for U.S. participation in more than nine hundred international conferences, some hosted by the United States.

Functional Bureaus

The legal office is the principal adviser to the secretary, and through the secretary to the president, on all matters of international law arising in the conduct of U.S. foreign policy.

The remaining bureaus are divided by function. The Bureau of Administration provides supply, procurement, and administrative services for the department and for more than $3 billion worth of U.S. government-owned real estate in 240 cities abroad. Its security officers guard the department, protect visiting foreign dignitaries, and supervise security—provided by Marine security guards (numbering about 1,500) and about 150 State Department security agents—at U.S. embassies and consulates.

The Bureau of Economic and Business Affairs deals with international energy policy, international monetary developments, trade policy, assistance to U.S. business overseas, aviation, shipping, telecommunications, foreign investment, patents, trademarks, technology transfers, commodity matters, and other international economic concerns.

The Bureau of Intelligence and Research has three principal functions. First, it prepares current and long-range intelligence analyses for the department, overseas missions, and other government agencies. Second, it serves as the department's coordinator with other members of the U.S. intelligence community to assure conformity of their programs with U.S. foreign policy. And, third, the bureau manages the department's program of external research, which provides foreign policy expertise from outside the government.

The Bureau of Public Affairs, headed by an assistant secretary who also serves as spokesperson of the department, advises other bureaus in State on public opinion and arranges continuing contacts between department officials and the public through conferences, briefings, and speaking and media engagements. It produces and distributes publications (including the encyclopedic series, *The Foreign Relations of the United States*), films, and other information and educational materials on U.S. foreign policy.

The Bureau of Consular Affairs, under the direction of an assistant secretary, assists Americans who travel or live abroad. Its Passport Services office issues more than five million passports a year. Through 250 U.S. diplomatic and consular posts abroad, its Overseas Citizens Services assists Americans, ranging from distribution of federal benefits checks to help when sudden illness or death strikes. The Visa Services division oversees U.S. consular officers who interview foreign nationals applying to come to the United States to settle, work, study, or visit; they issue some six million nonimmigrant and some 300,000 immigrant visas annually.

The Politico-Military Affairs Bureau originates and develops policy guidance and provides general direction within the department on issues that affect U.S. security policies, military assistance, nuclear nonproliferation and conventional arms transfer policy, and arms control matters.

Established by Congress in 1974, the Bureau of Oceans and International Environmental and Scientific Affairs ensures that scientific, technological, and environmental developments are taken into account in the formulation and execution of U.S. foreign policy.

The Bureau of Human Rights and Humanitarian Affairs is concerned with human rights, asylum requests, and other humanitarian subjects, while the Bureau for Refugee

Programs administers refugee relief, care, and maintenance programs overseas and initial refugee reception programs within the United States.

Foreign Service

The United States has diplomatic relations with 155 countries. In some smaller countries where the United States does not maintain a mission, official contacts are channeled through embassies in neighboring countries or the United Nations. As of January 31, 1987, diplomatic and consular missions abroad included 141 embassies, eleven missions, seventy-three consulates general, twenty-nine consulates, one branch office, and forty consular agencies. Ambassadors are the personal representatives of the president as well as representatives of the Department of State and all other federal agencies. They have full responsibility for the implementation of U.S. foreign policy by all U.S. government personnel within their country of assignment, except those under military commands.

As chiefs of mission, each ambassador heads a "country team" which typically includes a deputy chief of mission; heads of political, economic, consular, and administrative sections; defense, agricultural, and foreign commercial service attachés; a public affairs officer; the director of the Agency for International Development (AID) mission; and, as needed, representatives of other agencies of the U.S. government.

Department of Transportation

Development of a coordinated national transportation policy—long a goal of Congress and the executive branch—eluded lawmakers in the early 1960s. Instead, Congress was, for the most part, content to extend existing programs, which President John F. Kennedy had described as "a chaotic patchwork of inconsistent and often obsolete legislation [evolving] from a history of specific actions addressed to specific problems of specific industries at specific times."

The search for integrated programs that would lead to a diversified transportation system was complicated by the fact that each mode of transportation had some vested interest in existing policies, regulations, and legislation—and each had its own spokespersons in the administration and Congress. They tended to oppose any changes that would alter these advantages, while often advocating changes designed to improve their own situations.

Kennedy's successor, Lyndon B. Johnson, nonetheless pursued the idea of establishing a transportation department, and Congress acceded to his wishes in 1966. As the president requested, Congress excluded from the new Department of Transportation (DOT) all economic regulatory and rate-setting activities conducted by existing federal agencies. The urban mass transportation programs administered by the Department of Housing and Urban Development (HUD) also were excluded pending further study of their logical place in the executive branch (they later were transferred to DOT). The final legislation substantially weakened the powers proposed for the secretary of transportation, effectively denying the secretary independent authority to coordinate or revise existing federal transportation policies and programs. This stemmed partly from the desire of Congress to retain direct influence over transportation activities and partly from the desire of various private transportation groups to preserve their relationships, built up over many years, with existing federal agencies.

The bill creating DOT established a National Transportation Safety Board—independent of the secretary and other units—to oversee accident investigations, determine the cause of accidents, and review license and certificate appeals. The existing separation of aviation safety functions was continued by transferring the Federal Aviation Agency's safety duties to the new Federal Aviation Administrator, whose decisions would be administratively final. The Civil Aeronautics Board's responsibilities, which included accident investigations, probable cause determination, and review of appeals, were given to the safety board. On other safety matters, the secretary was directed to enforce the 1966 auto and highway safety laws; the Federal Railroad and Federal Highway administrators (not the secretary) were given statutory authority over the safety functions transferred to them from the Interstate Commerce Commission; and the U.S. Coast Guard was to continue to enforce maritime safety.

Johnson named Alan S. Boyd, undersecretary of commerce for transportation, the first DOT secretary. Earlier, Boyd had been a member of the Civil Aeronautics Board, serving as chairman from 1961 to 1965. The Senate confirmed his appointment on January 12, 1967, and the department officially began operation on April 1.

The First Two Decades

With its inception, DOT assumed responsibility for administering the High Speed Ground Transportation Program transferred from the Department of Commerce. In July 1967 the Urban Mass Transportation Administration was shifted from HUD to DOT. During 1967 DOT issued the first thirteen national highway safety standards under the Highway Safety Act, and the first set of federal motor vehicle standards became effective that year.

In 1970 DOT and the Department of Defense announced their cooperation in a project called Military Assistance for Safety in Traffic. The 1970 Airport and Airways Development Act provided for a long-term airport/airway development project under the auspices of DOT but strictly supervised by Congress.

During the administration of Jimmy Carter, Congress enacted legislation to deregulate the airlines, railroads, and trucking. The new laws, for which DOT was the major overseer, pared away years of federal regulations that threatened the health of the industries and, in some cases, resulted in higher consumer costs. As for other major actions, in 1978 Congress provided nearly $54 million in aid for highway and mass transit programs administered by DOT. The controversial Chrysler Corporation Loan Guarantee Act of 1979 directed the secretary of transportation to prepare an assessment of the long-term viability of the corporation. Another hotly debated measure was the department's promulgation of final rules requiring recipients of DOT financial aid to make their facilities accessible to the handicapped. That was followed in 1979 by a ruling that all buses purchased after September 1, 1979, had to be accessible to the elderly and handicapped.

Other transportation highlights included passage of the 1980 Aviation Safety and Noise Abatement Act; passage in 1980 of the Staggers Rail Act, giving railroads more freedom in rate making and service options; authorization in 1981 of the Northeast Corridor Rail Improvement Project under the Federal Railroad Administration, and establishment in 1984 of the Office of Commercial Space Transportation.

Deregulation continued under Ronald Reagan with the sale of Conrail (the freight rail system). The president proposed cutting federal subsidies for Amtrak passenger service, phasing out mass transit subsidies, and returning responsibility for most roads, including the interstate system, to state and local governments. By the mid-1980s, however, DOT was focusing on combating terrorism and drug trafficking.

Organization and Functions

The secretary of transportation, assisted by a deputy secretary, oversees the nine operating administrations that compose the department, eight of which are concerned with a specific form of transportation. The secretary's office also develops and updates national transportation policy, prepares transportation legislation, issues licenses for commercial expendable space launch vehicle operations, and helps negotiate international transportation agreements. Reporting to the secretary are the Office of Civil Rights, the Contract Appeals Board, the Office of Small and Disadvantaged Business Utilization, the Office of Commercial Space Transportation, the general counsel, and the inspector general. Five assistant secretaries are assigned, respectively, to policy and international affairs, budget and programs, government affairs, administration, and public affairs.

Nine Operating Administrations

Created by Secretary of the Treasury Alexander Hamilton in 1790 to combat smugglers, the U.S. Coast Guard has seen its role and mission expand tremendously over the years. Coast Guard personnel go out on some seventy thousand search and rescue missions each year. They investigate and clean up oil spills, regulate operation of the U.S. merchant fleet, enforce U.S. maritime laws, operate the nation's only fleet of icebreakers, and help in the search for drug smugglers and illegal aliens. The Coast Guard maintains more than 45,000 navigational aids, which include buoys, lighthouses, and offshore towers. As one of the nation's five military services, the Coast Guard protects U.S. ports from sabotage, and it has participated in U.S. military conflicts abroad.

The principal mission of the Federal Aviation Administration (FAA) is to promote aviation safety while insuring efficient use of the nation's navigable airspace. The administration is responsible for issuing and enforcing safety rules and regulations; certifying aircraft, their quotas, aircraft components, air agencies, and airports; conducting aviation safety-related research and development; and managing and operating the national airspace system. FAA oversees approximately 710,000 licensed pilots, 274,000 mechanics, 14,000 air traffic controllers, and 43,000 flight engineers. It operates and maintains 24 air route traffic control centers, 400 airport traffic control towers, 316 flight service stations, 4 international flight service stations, 109 air route surveillance radars, 200 airport surveillance radars, and 851 instrument landing systems.

The Federal Highway Administration (FHWA) is responsible for administering the federal aid program for highways, which, including the interstate system, make up a network of some 900,000 miles and carry about two-thirds of the nation's motor vehicle traffic. The FHWA also regulates and enforces federal requirements on the safety of trucks and buses engaged in interstate or foreign commerce, as well as the transport of hazardous cargoes.

The principal duties of the Federal Railroad Administration (FRA) are to issue standards and regulations designed to improve rail safety. It also provides policy guidance on legislative matters affecting rail transportation—such as the sale of Conrail, rail deregulation, and Amtrak (the passenger system)—and oversees the development of the northeast high-speed rail corridor between Washington, D.C., and Boston.

Created by Congress in 1966, the National Highway Traffic Safety Administration is authorized to issue motor vehicle safety standards and to investigate possible safety defects. In recent years the agency has waged a campaign against drunk drivers and for use of safety belts.

The Urban Mass Transportation Administration (UMTA) provides financial and planning assistance to the nation's public transit systems, including buses, subways, trolleys, commuter trains, and ferry boats. Although the federal government's involvement in mass transportation began in 1961, the existing $3 billion transit program started with passage of the 1964 Urban Mass Transportation Act. Between 1964 and 1987 the federal government invested more than $43 billion in the nation's transit systems.

Created by legislation in 1954, the St. Lawrence Seaway Development Corporation constructed the U.S. facilities of the St. Lawrence Seaway navigation project, operated jointly by the United States and Canada. The corporation continues to operate and maintain that part of the seaway between Montreal and Lake Erie, within the territorial limits of the United States, and it is responsible for developing the full seaway system from the western tip of Lake Superior to the Atlantic Ocean—a distance of twenty-three hundred miles.

The Maritime Administration (MARAD), which initially was excluded from DOT's purview, became part of the department in 1981. Like its predecessor agencies dating back to the creation of the United States Shipping Board in 1916, MARAD is responsible for developing and maintaining a merchant marine capable of meeting the nation's requirements for both commercial trade and national defense. The agency administers financial and technical programs, develops promotional and marketing programs, trains ships' officers at the U.S. Merchant Marine Academy at Kings Point, New York, negotiates bilateral maritime agreements, and maintains the National Defense Reserve Fleet.

In contrast to DOT's eight other administrations which focus on a single transportation sector, the purview of the Research and Special Programs Administration (RSPA) extends to all transportation modes. Established in 1977 by combining the functions of other offices, RSPA consists of an Office of Hazardous Materials Transportation and an Office of Pipeline Safety. Its Transportation Safety Institute designs and conducts training programs, and the Transportation Systems Center plans, develops, and manages programs in all fields of transportation research and development. RSPA is also responsible for ensuring that the nation's civil transportation system will continue to operate effectively during an emergency.

Department of the Treasury

Management of the monetary resources of the United States is the primary function of the Department of the Treasury. Among other responsibilities, it regulates national banks, assesses and collects income taxes and customs duties, manufactures coins and bills, determines international economic policy, reports the federal government's financial transactions, conducts international and domestic economic research, enforces tax and tariff laws, directs anticounterfeiting operations, and provides executive protection.

One of the oldest cabinet departments, Treasury was established by the first session of Congress on September 2, 1789. Yet many of its functions were carried out even before the signing of the Declaration of Independence; the Continental Congress issued paper money to finance the revolutionary war and appointed joint treasurers to oversee the effort.

The new republic's finances, however, remained in disarray until September 1789 when President George Washington appointed Alexander Hamilton to be the first secretary of the Treasury. Hamilton's shrewd financial policies resulted in renewed confidence in the Bank of the United States, which issued money in the government's name. As Treasury's first secretary, Hamilton established a precedent for the position's power in advising the president, as well as the controversy surrounding many of its holders. The department is not only intrinsically influential; its secretaries also have numbered among the president's closest advisers.

Bureau of Engraving

The Bureau of Engraving and Printing began operating in 1862, when the government started printing "greenback" currency to finance the Civil War. Today it issues annually more than 40 billion security documents, such as paper currency, postage stamps, and Treasury bonds.

Almost 150 years later, President Dwight D. Eisenhower was quoted as saying of his Treasury secretary: "In Cabinet meetings, I always wait for George Humphrey to speak. I sit back and listen to the others talk while he doesn't say anything. But I know that when he speaks, he will say just what I was thinking."

Evolution of the Department

Treasury's authority expanded considerably during the Civil War. The loss of customs revenues from the seceded southern states led to establishment of the Bureau of Internal Revenue, as well as the printing of paper currency and the institution of a national banking system. The growth of international trade following World Wars I and II resulted in a central role for Treasury in the 1944 Bretton Woods Conference, which established the International Monetary Fund and the postwar monetary system.

Many federal functions that originally resided in Treasury have been transferred over the years to other departments. For example, Treasury administered the Postal Service until 1829. The General Land Office, which was the core of the Interior Department, was part of Treasury from 1812 to 1849. Business activities were under Treasury's purview until the Department of Commerce and Labor was established in 1903. The functions of the Office of the Supervising Architect of the Treasury were transferred to the General Services Administration in 1949. The Coast Guard, the oldest seagoing armed service in the United States, was part of Treasury until its transfer to the Department of Transportation in 1967. Other marine interests initially administered by Treasury were passed on to other departments. The Bureau of the Budget was transferred from Treasury to the Executive Office in 1939.

Organization and Functions

Treasury is divided into two major components: the office of the secretary and the operating bureaus. The secretary, who is officially the second-ranking cabinet officer, has primary responsibility for formulating and recommending domestic and international financial, economic, and tax policy; participating in the preparation of broad fiscal policies that have general significance for the economy; and managing the public debt. As chief financial officer of the government, the secretary serves as chair of the cabinet Council on Economic Affairs and Senior Interagency Group on International Economic Policy and as U.S. governor of the International Monetary Fund, International Bank for Reconstruction and Development, Inter-American Development Bank, Asian Development Bank, and African Development Bank. The Treasury secretary is required by law to submit periodic reports to Congress on the government's fiscal operations, including an annual report.

The secretary is assisted by a deputy secretary, an undersecretary for finance, a general counsel, and an inspector general. Nine assistant secretaries are responsible for the following areas: economic policy, international affairs, fiscal operations and activities (including the Financial Management Service and the Bureau of the Public Debt), domestic finance, legislative affairs, management, tax policy, public affairs and public liaison, and enforcement (which oversees enforcement activities of the U.S.

Customs Service, Internal Revenue Service, U.S. Secret Service, Bureau of Alcohol, Tobacco and Firearms, Federal Law Enforcement Training Center, and Office of Foreign Assets Control).

The Office of the Treasurer of the United States was established September 6, 1777. Initially, the treasurer was responsible for the receipt and custody of government funds. Over the years, however, these duties have been dispersed throughout various Treasury bureaus. In 1981 the treasurer was assigned oversight of the Bureau of Engraving and Printing, the United States Mint, and the U.S. Savings Bond Division.

The Office of the Comptroller of the Currency, created February 25, 1863, is an integral part of the national banking system. The comptroller oversees the execution of laws related to nationally chartered banks (including trust activities and overseas operations) and promulgates rules and regulations governing their operations.

The Bureau of Alcohol, Tobacco and Firearms (ATF) was established on July 1, 1972, as successor to the Alcohol Tax Unit of the Bureau of Internal Revenue. ATF enforces federal laws that require excise taxes on alcoholic substances, control of firearms and explosives, and regulation of the tobacco industry.

In 1927 the Bureau of Customs was established as a separate agency within Treasury; in August 1973 it was redesignated the U.S. Customs Service. The Customs Service collects revenue from imports and enforces customs and related laws. Customs also administers the 1930 Tariff Act. As the principal border enforcement agency, the service's mission has been extended over the years to cover the administration and enforcement of some four hundred provisions of wide-ranging safety standards on behalf of more than forty federal agencies. In the seven customs regions and forty-four subordinate district or area offices in the fifty states, Virgin Islands, and Puerto Rico, there are approximately 240 ports of entry into the United States.

The Bureau of Engraving and Printing began operations in July 1862, when the government started printing "greenback" currency to finance the Civil War. It designs, prints, and finishes a large variety of security products, including all paper currency; U.S. postage, customs, and revenue stamps; Treasury bills, notes, and bonds; permits; and certificates of award. It is the largest printer of security documents in the world, issuing more than 40 billion security documents annually.

Responsibility for the government's cash management, credit management, debt collection programs, and central reporting and accounting systems originally rested with the Register of the Treasury. In 1920 those functions were transferred to the newly created Office of the Commissioner of Accounts and Deposits, which was renamed the Bureau of Government Financial Operations in 1974 and became the Financial Management Service (FMS) in 1984. FMS issues approximately 500 million Treasury checks and close to 250 million electronic fund transfer payments annually for federal salaries and wages, payments to suppliers of goods and services to the government, income tax refunds, and payments under major government programs such as Social Security and veterans' benefits.

The Bureau of Internal Revenue came into existence on July 4, 1862, to collect new income taxes—money that was used to pay for the Civil War. The Supreme Court declared the national income tax unconstitutional in 1894, but it was reinstated in 1913. Reorganized in 1953, the bureau was renamed the Internal Revenue Service (IRS). The largest of Treasury bureaus, IRS employs more than ninety thousand persons in its Washington headquarters, seven regional offices, and sixty-two districts.

Congress created the Mint of the United States on April 2, 1792, and placed it in the State Department. In 1799 the Mint was made an independent agency, and in 1873 it became part of the Treasury as the Bureau of the Mint. It was placed under the supervision of the treasurer of the United States in 1981, and its name was changed to the United States Mint in 1984. The Mint's principal function is to produce coins and medals; it also has custody over Treasury gold and silver bullion.

Management of the national debt was consolidated from several departments into the Public Debt Service in 1920; it became a bureau in 1940. The primary responsibilities of the Bureau of the Public Debt include overseeing the management of the public debt, issuing U.S. securities, and managing receipts and expenditures. The department's Savings Bond Division was authorized in 1945 as successor to a number of World War II agencies. The division promotes and directs the sale and holding of U.S. savings bonds and notes. The U.S. treasurer administers the division and serves as its national director.

The U.S. Secret Service was created in 1865 to halt counterfeiting operations. It continues to pursue this goal, but its more well-known function is executive protection, which it assumed after the assassination of President William McKinley in 1901. *(See "Protecting the President: The Secret Service," p. 905 in Daily Life chapter of Part V.)*

Established in March 1970, the Federal Law Enforcement Training Center, located in Georgia, is an interagency training facility serving sixty federal law enforcement organizations, including the Secret Service, Customs, and Bureau of Alcohol, Tobacco and Firearms, as well as the Federal Bureau of Investigation and other non-Treasury agencies.

Department of Veterans Affairs

Bills to elevate the Veterans Administration (VA) to cabinet-level status had been introduced in at least seventeen successive Congresses, but finally, fifty-eight years after it was created, legislation establishing the VA as the Department of Veterans Affairs (DVA) was signed into law October 25, 1988. Perhaps somewhat ironically, Ronald Reagan, who signed the authorizing legislation (PL 100-527), had stated as a presidential candidate that he would view his election "as a mandate to reduce the size of government. . . ." [36] He also had advocated abolishing the Departments of Education and Energy, both of which were still in place at the end of his tenure. Reagan, however, in November 1987 had endorsed putting the VA—an agency with enormous political clout—in the cabinet.

The DVA came into being on March 15, 1989, making it the fourteenth executive department and the fifth to be created since 1953. President George Bush named Edward J. Derwinski, a twelve-term member of the House of Representatives, to the post of secretary.

Size and Functions

The VA was the largest of all federal independent agencies, providing the most comprehensive assistance and care for veterans of any nation. With more than 240,000 employees, the VA ranked in size below only the Defense Department and the U.S. Postal Service. Its budget, totaling more than $27.6 billion in fiscal year 1988, exceeded those of the Departments of Energy, the Interior, Justice, State, and Commerce combined and was the fifth largest among federal departments and agencies.

The functions the DVA assumed from the VA were essentially unchanged. They include administration of the following programs for veterans: disability compensation and pensions, education and training, medical care, medical research, home loan assistance, insurance, and national cemeteries. Under the DVA's purview is the largest health care system in the free world. Transferred to the DVA were 172 VA hospitals, 231 outpatient clinics, 58 regional offices, 117 nursing homes, 27 domiciliaries, and 189 "outreach" centers for Vietnam-era veterans. Its GI education programs have interacted with nearly every institution of higher education in the nation. The DVA operates 111 national cemeteries. The department also has significant ties to the U.S. housing and banking industries. In fiscal year 1987, the VA guaranteed 474,400 home loans for veterans, worth $34.7 billion.

History of the VA

Following the English precedent, the American colonies as early as 1636 enacted laws providing that returning disabled soldiers should be "maintained competently" by the colonies for the rest of their lives.[37] The Continental Congress, in an effort to encourage enlistment during the American Revolution, continued that policy, and, in fact, benefits were paid to veterans of the revolutionary war and their dependents until 1911.

In the meantime, Congress in 1789 passed a pension law that initially was administered by Congress and was subsequently transferred in 1818 to the secretary of war. In 1849, the Office of Pensions was moved from the War Department to the newly created Interior Department. During the Civil War, Congress authorized benefits for federal volunteers on the same basis as those already provided for the regular army. In his second inaugural address in March 1865, President Abraham Lincoln called upon Congress and the American people "to care for him who shall have borne the battle and for his widow, and his orphan" (the phrase subsequently became the VA's motto).

Early veterans legislation emphasized pensions, with direct medical and hospital care provided by states and localities. It was not until 1811 that Congress authorized the first medical facility for veterans, the U.S. Naval Home in Philadelphia, as a "permanent asylum for disabled and decrepit Navy officers, seamen and Marines." During the nineteenth century, other homes were established—among them the U.S. Soldiers Home—to provide care for the indigent and disabled veterans of the Civil War, Indian Wars, Spanish-American War, and Mexican War, and the discharged regular members of the armed forces. An honorable discharge from military service was one of the requirements for admission.

Congress greatly expanded veterans benefits after the United States entered World War I in 1917, establishing disability compensation, insurance for servicemen and veterans, a family allotment program for servicemen, and vocational rehabilitation for the disabled. With the exception of the latter, these programs were administered by the Bureau of War Risk Insurance, which had been created in 1914. At the same time, another agency, the Public Health Service, also provided medical and hospital care.

Divided responsibilities for veterans among various departments and agencies proved unwieldy. Responding to the recommendations of a presidential study commission to consolidate functions in a single agency, Congress in 1921 established the United States Veterans' Bureau. Nonetheless, two other agencies also continued to administer veterans benefits: the Bureau of Pensions in the Interior Department and the National Homes for Disabled Volunteer Soldiers.

In 1930, Congress authorized the president further to "consolidate and coordinate government activities affecting war veterans." The three existing agencies became bureaus within the new Veterans Administration. Brig. Gen. Frank T. Hines, then head of the Veterans' Bureau, was named the first administrator of veterans affairs, a post he held until 1945.[38] Given its wide-ranging responsibilities, the new agency had a relatively small staff of 31,600.

The VA served about 4.7 million veterans during its first year; by the end of World War II, their numbers had swelled to almost 19 million. To deal with this challenge, VA facilities were substantially enlarged, and significant new programs, such as the GI bill (signed into law June 22, 1944), were established. Other new programs included vocational rehabilitation legislation (1943, expanded in 1980), establishment of a VA Department of Medicine and Surgery (1946), the Korean Conflict GI Bill (1952), creation of the Department of Veterans Benefits (1953), a new GI bill for veterans with service between 1955 and 1977 (1966), and a Veterans Educational Assistance Program for post-Vietnam-era veterans.

Debate over Establishing the DVA

Only a week after Reagan announced his support for a DVA, the House of Representatives on November 17, 1987, overwhelmingly passed its version of implementing legislation, and the Senate followed suit in July 1988. The action came despite a nonpartisan, congressionally mandated report that found "little evidence" such a move would improve government services for veterans. The report, by the National Academy of Public Administration (NAPA), concluded that "there is no compelling reason why the VA . . . should be elevated to cabinet status." But at a March 15 Senate Governmental Affairs Committee hearing, during which the NAPA report was made public, Chairman John Glenn (D-Ohio) said if cabinet status for the VA was accompanied by management improvements at the agency, "then the case for elevation becomes very, very strong."

The NAPA report said the creation of a cabinet-level department would not "significantly improve access to the president, affect the adequacy of necessary resources or improve the organization, management and delivery of high-quality services and benefits." The NAPA report projected only "marginal" improvements in VA operations if the legislation were to become law. Furthermore, the report pointed out that an enlarged cabinet tended to "reduce its value to the president" and added that VA elevation could strengthen the argument for upgrading other federal agencies, such as the Social Security Administration. But NAPA stopped short of recommending against a Department of Veterans Affairs.

A second evaluation, also released at the March 15

hearing, criticized VA officials for "management inattention." The report, by the General Accounting Office, criticized the decentralized organization of VA services and said high-level VA managers "have not exercised enough oversight of the field facilities that deliver benefit and medical services to veterans."[39]

Proponents of placing the VA in the cabinet pointed out that the work of the agency reached far beyond the 27.4 million veterans in the United States. The VA also served millions of dependents and survivors of veterans. Altogether, they amounted to about one-third of the nation's population. Giving the agency a seat at the cabinet table would enhance its access to the president and improve its ability to defend itself during budget decisions, supporters maintained. They argued that giving the VA cabinet status would also allow better coordination of policy with other departments. "Veterans will no longer have to go through the back door of the White House" to focus the president's attention on their problems, said Rep. G. V. (Sonny) Montgomery (D-Miss.), chairman of the House Veterans Affairs Committee and a champion of cabinet status for the VA.[40]

During floor debate on the bill, however, Senate Veterans Affairs Committee chairman Alan Cranston (D-Calif.), said that Reagan, through executive order and without legislative action, could have had his VA chiefs attend cabinet sessions, as had occurred during the administration of his Democratic predecessor, Jimmy Carter.

Organization

Replacing the position of VA administrator is the secretary of the DVA, who is assisted by a deputy secretary. Before the establishment of the DVA, the VA's programs were administered by three separate departments—Veterans Benefits, Medicine and Surgery, and Memorial Affairs, which varied greatly in number of employees and budget. These departments were continued under the DVA.

The functions of the Department of Memorial Affairs were delegated to an assistant secretary. The Department of Medicine and Surgery was redesignated the Veterans Health Services Administration, headed by a chief medical director, and the Department of Veterans Benefits was renamed the Veterans Benefits Administration under a chief benefits director, who must be a medical doctor. Both directors are intended to be nonpolitical appointments but subject to Senate confirmation. The two officers are appointed for four years, and the president is required to notify Congress if either is removed from office before expiration of the four-year term. The existing Board of Contract Appeals continues to operate unchanged. Shortly after passing the DVA bill, however, Congress cleared legislation that would make the existing VA Board of Veterans' Appeals somewhat more independent by requiring the chair to be appointed by the president and confirmed by the Senate, among other changes.

Functions assigned to the associate deputy administrators were delegated to DVA assistant secretaries. They include budget and finance; personnel management; labor relations; planning; studies and evaluations; oversight; advisory functions regarding management; productivity and logistic support; information management; supervision of capital facilities and real property programs; equal opportunity; employment discrimination; procurement; and congressional, intergovernmental, public and consumer information and affairs. The responsibilities of the VA's Office of General Counsel and the Office of Inspector General (IG) were unchanged under the new oganization. The Senate had wanted to add 150-200 new IGs to the approximately 380 existing positions (the VA had the second smallest IG staff in the federal government), but the House opposed the increase. The final compromise would phase in 40 new IGs over fiscal years 1990-1991.

Notes

1. James D. King and James W. Riddlesperger, Jr., "Presidential Cabinet Appointments: The Partisan Factor," *Presidential Studies Quarterly* 14 (Spring 1984): 231.
2. Richard M. Pious, *The American Presidency* (New York: Basic Books, 1979), 936.
3. Nelson W. Polsby, "Presidential Cabinet Making: Lessons for the Political System," *Political Science Quarterly* 93 (Spring 1978): 19-20.
4. G. Calvin Mackenzie, *The Politics of Presidential Appointments* (New York: Free Press, 1981), 9.
5. John W. Macy, Bruce Adams, and J. Jackson Walter, *America's Unelected Government: Appointing the President's Team* (Cambridge, Mass.: Ballinger, 1983), 76-82.
6. David T. Stanley, Dean E. Mann, and Jameson W. Doig, *Men Who Govern: A Biographical Profile of Federal Executives* (Washington, D.C.: Brookings, 1967).
7. Linda Fisher, "Fifty Years of Presidential Appointments," in *The In-and-Outers: Presidential Appointees and Transient Government in Washington,* ed. G. Calvin Mackenzie (Baltimore: Johns Hopkins University Press, 1987), 28.
8. Ibid.
9. Stephen Hess, *Organizing the Presidency* (Washington, D.C.: Brookings, 1976), 28.
10. Ibid., 30.
11. Mackenzie, *The Politics of Presidential Appointments,* 12.
12. Harry S Truman, *1945, Year of Decisions* (New York: Signet, 1955), 364.
13. Dwight D. Eisenhower, *Mandate for Change* (New York: Signet, 1963), 137.
14. Hess, *Organizing the Presidency,* 62.
15. Mackenzie, *The Politics of Presidential Appointments,* 22.
16. Hess, *Organizing the Presidency,* 82.
17. David Halberstam, *The Best and the Brightest* (New York: Random House, 1972), 434.
18. Mackenzie, *The Politics of Presidential Appointments,* 39.
19. Ibid., 41.
20. Arthur M. Schlesinger, Jr., "Presidential War," *New York Times Magazine,* January 7, 1974, 28.
21. Mackenzie, *The Politics of Presidential Appointments,* 45.
22. Quoted in Dom Bonafede, "Cabinet Comment," *National Journal,* vol. 8 (December 11, 1976), 1784.
23. Mackenzie, *The Politics of Presidential Appointments,* 64.
24. R. Gordon Hoxie, "Staffing the Ford and Carter Presidencies," *Presidential Studies Quarterly* 10 (Spring 1984): 393.
25. Macy, Adams, and Walter, *America's Unelected Government,* 40.
26. Ross K. Baker, "Outlook for the Reagan Administration," in *The Election of 1980: Reports and Interpretations,* ed. Gerald Pomper (Chatham, N.J.: Chatham House, 1981), 164.
27. Richard A. Stubbing, with Richard A. Mendel, *The Defense Game* (New York: Harper and Row, 1986), 259-260.
28. *Washington Post,* October 7, 1978.
29. John G. Kester, "Thoughtless JCS Change Is Worse Than None," *Armed Forces Journal International* (November 1984): 113.
30. Richard Harris, *Justice: The Crisis of Law, Order, and Freedom in America* (New York: Dutton, 1970), 33-34.
31. Ibid., 161.
32. Jonathan Grossman, "The Origin of the Department of Labor," *Monthly Labor Review,* March 1973.

33. Janet Hook, "Brock Selected to Replace Donovan at Labor," *Congressional Quarterly Weekly Report,* March 23, 1985, 549.
34. Martin Mayer, *The Diplomats* (New York: Doubleday, 1983), 211.
35. Ibid., 240.
36. Quoted in *Congressional Quarterly Weekly Report,* October 19, 1988, A-21.
37. From *VA History in Brief* (Washington, D.C.: Government Printing Office, 1986).
38. Like the earlier Veterans' Bureau, the Veterans Administration originally used the apostrophe (Veterans' Administration), but the apostrophe eventually was dropped from the name.
39. The above quotations in this section come from Richard Cowan, "VA-Cabinet Plan Questioned, But Not Slowed," *Congressional Quarterly Weekly Report,* March 19, 1988, 749-750.
40. Quoted in Ben A. Franklin, "Congress Votes to Make the VA a Cabinet-Level Department," *New York Times,* October 19, 1988.

Selected Bibliography

Baker, Ross K. "Outlook for the Reagan Administration." In *The Election of 1980: Reports and Interpretations,* ed. Gerald Pomper. Chatham, N.J.: Chatham House, 1981.

Bonafede, Dom. "Cabinet Comment." *National Journal* Vol. 8 (December 11, 1976), 1784.

Eisenhower, Dwight D. *Mandate for Change.* New York: Signet, 1963.

Fisher, Linda. "Fifty Years of Presidential Appointments." In *The In-and-Outers: Presidential Appointees and Transient Government in Washington,* ed. G. Calvin Mackenzie. Baltimore: Johns Hopkins University Press, 1987.

Halberstam, David. *The Best and the Brightest.* New York: Random House, 1972.

Hess, Stephen. *Organizing the Presidency.* Washington, D.C.: Brookings, 1976.

Hoxie, R. Gordon. "Staffing the Ford and Carter Presidencies." *Presidential Studies Quarterly* 10 (Spring 1980): 378-401.

King, James D., and James W. Riddlesperger, Jr. "Presidential Cabinet Appointments: The Partisan Factor." *Presidential Studies Quarterly* 14 (Spring 1984): 231-237.

Mackenzie, G. Calvin. *The Politics of Presidential Appointments.* New York: The Free Press, 1981.

Macy, John W., Bruce Adams, and J. Jackson Walter. *America's Unelected Government: Appointing the President's Team.* Cambridge, Mass.: Ballinger, 1983.

Pious, Richard M. *The American Presidency.* New York: Basic Books, 1979.

Polsby, Nelson W. "Presidential Cabinet Making: Lessons for the Political System." *Political Science Quarterly* 93 (Spring 1978): 16-24.

Schlesinger, Arthur M., Jr. "Presidential War." *New York Times Magazine,* January 7, 1974, 28.

Stanley, David T., Dean E. Mann, and Jameson W. Doig. *Men Who Govern: A Biographical Profile of Federal Executives.* Washington, D.C.: Brookings, 1967.

Truman, Harry S. *1945, Year of Decisions.* New York: Signet, 1955.

Government Agencies and Corporations

In addition to the fourteen cabinet departments the president is directly responsible for several other kinds of federal government agencies. Some of these agencies are autonomous and not part of any cabinet department, while others are part of the cabinet hierarchy but with significant power to operate largely as separate entities. No matter what kind of organizational relationship these agencies have to the rest of the executive branch, however, the president has direct legal responsibility for them—and often in fact exerts considerable control over them. Independent agencies are autonomous mainly because they are separated organizationally from the presidency.

These agencies have different objectives, powers, methods of determining their members, and organizations. Any similarity is derived from their existence largely outside the traditional lines of authority of the executive departments. Their independent or semi-independent structure results from either the desire of Congress to remove their operations from the control of the presidential hierarchy or presidential attempts to show concern for specific problems that could best be solved in an environment lacking political pressure. These agencies can be divided into three general categories: regulatory agencies, independent executive agencies, and government corporations.

Regulatory Agencies

Regulatory agencies and commissions regulate various aspects of the economy and, more recently, consumer affairs. The commerce clause of the Constitution (Article I, section 8) gives the federal government the legal authority "to regulate Commerce with foreign Nations, and among the several States. . . ." Although there is no universally agreed-upon definition of federal regulation, in 1977 the Senate Governmental Affairs Committee (then named the Government Operations Committee) defined a federal regulatory agency as "one which (1) has decision-making authority, (2) establishes standards or guidelines conferring benefits and imposing restrictions on business conduct, (3) operates principally in the sphere of domestic business activity, (4) has its head and/or members appointed by the president . . . and (5) has its legal procedures generally governed by the Administrative Procedure Act." [1]

Regulatory agencies are either organizationally independent or part of an existing executive department. Independent regulatory agencies are governed by bipartisan commissions of five or more members. These commissioners usually serve lengthy, fixed terms, and they cannot be removed by the president. Among the major independent regulatory agencies are the Interstate Commerce Commission (ICC), Federal Reserve Board (FRB), National Labor Relations Board (NLRB), Federal Communications Commission (FCC), Federal Trade Commission (FTC), Civil Aeronautics Board (CAB), and Securities and Exchange Commission (SEC).

Agencies within an executive branch department serve under the authority of the department in which they are located. Heads of these agencies are subject not only to presidential appointment but also to presidential dismissal. Presidents may appoint and dismiss these agency heads either personally or through their department secretaries. Agencies within executive branch departments include the Food and Drug Administration (FDA), located in the Department of Health and Human Services, and the Occupational Safety and Health Administration (OSHA), located in the Department of Labor.

Although regulatory agencies oversee a variety of activities, they share certain jurisdictional and organizational characteristics. For example, all of these agencies have substantial federal authority to carry out various regulatory functions. Sometimes called quasi-agencies because they are empowered legally to perform quasi-legislative, quasi-executive, and quasi-judicial functions, they can issue rules that govern certain sections of the economy, oversee implementation of those rules, and adjudicate disputes over interpretation of the rules.

In creating these organizations Congress has attempted to protect their independence. For example, commissioners, who are appointed by the president, serve overlapping fixed terms, usually four to seven years. Even though they are political appointees, presidents cannot simply fire them. In 1935 the Supreme Court ruled that President Franklin D. Roosevelt unconstitutionally fired a member of the FTC. In *Humphrey's Executor v. United States* the Court held that presidents cannot remove regulatory commission members for ruling in ways that might displease the president or members of Congress. In a further attempt to ensure political independence from the president, Congress made these commissions bipartisan

By W. Craig Bledsoe and Richard A. Karno

with limits placed on the number of appointees from any single political party. Generally, neither political party may have a majority of more than one. This organizational design makes these agencies and commissions independent of other executive organizations and places responsibility for the execution of their policies with the commissioners rather than the president.

Presumably, appointees to regulatory commissions should be not only experts in the policy area in which they have been chosen to oversee but also objective parties who would not favor one side over another in a policy dispute. In practice, however, regulatory agencies tend to develop reciprocal relationships with the interests they are supposed to regulate. Political scientist Samuel Huntington has suggested that regulatory agencies are inevitably "captured" by the interest groups they are supposed to be regulating.[2] Thus, the ICC would look out for the interests of the trucking industry, the FDA for the interests of drug manufacturers, and the Nuclear Regulatory Commission (NRC) for the interests of the nuclear industry.

Some regulatory agencies go through an inevitable life cycle. Regulatory agency scholar Marver H. Bernstein has argued that agencies are most aggressive when they are new. Over the years, however, they gradually lose their stamina and become captives of the interests they are supposed to regulate, or they become dormant. As public attention moves from the initial problem that prompted the regulation, the regulatory agency, out of public scrutiny, might become free to operate as it wishes.[3] Even if a regulatory life cycle exists, however, some agencies have been spurred on to new innovative action by the public. In the 1950s and 1960s, for example, the FDA became much more aggressive about drug testing after the public expressed concern about unsafe drugs.

While the original mandate of regulatory activity was primarily economic regulation, modern regulatory agencies undertake regulation that goes beyond the traditional economic motives, moving more and more into the area of social concerns. Although these social concerns usually are related to economic activities, their scope is different from traditional regulation in that they touch upon issues that are of importance to individual consumers. For this reason regulatory activity is divided into economic regulation and social regulation.

Economic Regulation

In 1887 the federal government undertook its first major regulation of a private sector of the economy when Congress, exercising its constitutional right to regulate interstate commerce, created the Interstate Commerce Commission. According to political scientist Robert E. Cushman, "The Interstate Commerce Commission was an innovation not because it was endowed with a new type of power, but because it represented a new location of power in the federal system."[4]

Ironically, Congress initially did not intend to make the Interstate Commerce Commission independent of the control of the executive branch. During the original congressional debate on creation of the ICC, matters of independence and presidential control were never considered. Congress first placed the ICC in the Interior Department, which subjected its budget, staff, and internal management to control by an executive department. Two years later, Congress gave the ICC control over its own affairs.

It was only several years after it achieved independence that the ICC gained any real measure of power. Initially, it lacked the power to do anything more than issue cease-and-desist orders to stop railroads from violating provisions of the Interstate Commerce Act of 1887. It had neither the authority to set or adjust railroad shipping rates nor any coercive power to enforce its rulings. Moreover, in the early years the courts conscientiously reviewed ICC orders, often substituting their own judgments favoring the railroads for those of the commission. It soon became obvious to the railroads that they could circumvent the ICC by appealing judgments to the courts.

Gradually the ICC became politically and organizationally independent. In 1906 Congress passed the Hepburn Act, which gave the commission final rate-making powers and the authority to adjust rates that the ICC deemed unreasonable or unfair. And in 1910, with the passage of the Mann-Elkins Act, Congress strengthened the commission's enforcement ability by authorizing it to suspend and investigate new rate proposals and to set original rates.

Abandoning the idea that the ICC might be able to handle the regulation of all commerce, Congress created a network of new regulatory agencies patterned after the ICC. In 1913, for example, the Federal Reserve System began to govern banking and regulate the supply of money. The following year saw creation of the Federal Trade Commission to regulate business practices and control monopolistic behavior. Between 1915 and 1933, the beginning of Franklin Roosevelt's administration, Congress set up seven other regulatory agencies, including the Tariff Commission (1916), Commodities Exchange Authority (1922), Customs Service (1927), and Federal Power Commission (1930).

After the Great Depression and beginning with Roosevelt's "New Deal," an extraordinary flood of regulatory programs passed Congress. Between 1932 and 1938 eight major regulatory agencies were set up to handle problems created by the economic crisis of the depression. These included several agencies that have become mainstays in the American way of life. For example, the Federal Home

Sue Klemens

The Interstate Commerce Commission, the nation's oldest regulatory agency, regulates interstate surface transportation within the United States.

Loan Bank Board (FHLBB) was set up in 1932 to regulate federally chartered savings and loan associations; they were a source of private funds for building and buying homes. The Federal Deposit Insurance Corporation (FDIC) was created by the Banking Act of 1933 to regulate state-chartered, insured banks that were not members of the Federal Reserve System and to provide federally guaranteed insurance for bank deposits. And the Securities and Exchange Commission was founded in 1934 to protect the public against fraud and deception in securities and financial markets. Finally, the Wagner Act of 1935 created the National Labor Relations Board to prevent "unfair labor practices" and to protect the right of collective bargaining.

Social Regulation

While the New Deal was the true beginning of large-scale federal regulation of the economy, it also provided the foundation for the many social regulatory agencies that characterized the 1960s and 1970s. As New Deal programs expanded the scope of the federal government, use of the federal government to solve the nation's economic and social problems became accepted. By the mid-1960s the federal government was providing medical care, educational aid, nutritional help, urban renewal, and job training, among other services. And by the mid-1970s social activism had grown to such an extent that many consumer and environmental groups had called for a new wave of regulation intended to achieve certain social goals such as clean air and consumer protection. Congressional Quarterly's *Federal Regulatory Directory* divides these social regulatory agencies into four areas of concern: regulations to protect consumers, environmental protection, workplace safety, and energy regulation.[5]

By the early 1970s the well-defined consumer movement had begun to have a significant impact on American life. Consumers were very vocal in their cries for protection against false advertising and faulty products. Organized groups were demanding safer and better products and lower prices for food, fuel, and medical care. Earlier, in 1965, Ralph Nader had more or less launched consumerism as a political movement with the publication of his book *Unsafe at Any Speed,* which attacked the automobile industry's poor safety record. Through Nader's efforts and those of other consumer advocates interested in automobile safety, the National Highway Traffic Safety Administration (NHTSA) was created within the Department of Transportation in 1970. With its authority to set automobile safety and fuel efficiency standards, the agency represents one of the early efforts at consumer legislation. The Consumer Product Safety Commission (CPSC) represents an independent consumer protection agency. With its passage of the Consumer Product Safety Act in 1972, Congress gave the commission the task of protecting consumers against unreasonable risks of injury from hazardous products.

Advocates of a cleaner environment were also part of the consumer movement; the creation of the Environmental Protection Agency (EPA) in 1970 stemmed directly from their efforts. Set up as an independent regulatory agency, EPA was charged with supervising and protecting the nation's environment, including its air, water, land, and noise. In its short history EPA has become one of the most controversial of all federal agencies, largely because of its wide-ranging responsibilities and the costs of the programs that it advocates to clean up the environment.

Workplace safety was another concern of the consumer movement. Consumers wanted to minimize hazards in the workplace by establishing guidelines for improving safety and health on the job. Established as an agency within the Labor Department in 1970, the Occupational Safety and Health Administration was charged with promulgating and enforcing worker safety and health standards. It is authorized to conduct unannounced on-site inspections and to require employers to keep detailed records on worker injuries and illnesses. OSHA thus has considerable regulatory power that it can wield in carrying out its quasi-legislative, quasi-executive, and quasi-judicial functions.

By the 1970s the United States found itself repeatedly confronted with the dual problems of a dwindling energy supply and the rising costs of energy. In an attempt to protect consumers from growing energy problems, Congress created a number of agencies designed to alleviate some of the difficulties. In 1973 it established the Federal Energy Administration (FEA) to control short-term fuel shortages, and in 1974 the Energy Research and Development Administration (ERDA) with the mandate to develop nuclear power and new energy sources. Also in 1974 Congress created the Nuclear Regulatory Commission to regulate nuclear safety. All of these agencies, except the NRC, were abolished in 1977 when their functions were moved to the newly created Department of Energy.

Methods of Regulation

Regulatory agencies use a variety of techniques to carry out their mandates. In fact, the method that each agency uses may be limited by the legislation that created the agency in the first place. For example, Congress may find an issue of such importance that it tells the agency exactly how to regulate the area of concern. For issues of lesser importance, Congress may give the agency a free hand to use whatever regulatory methods it believes appropriate.

One of the most common methods of regulation is the required disclosure of consumer information. For example, the Food and Drug Administration requires manufacturers of a variety of food products to list the ingredients of their product, and often the product's nutritional value. In 1977, in an extreme form of public disclosure, the Consumer Product Safety Commission banned Tris, a flame retardant used in children's sleepwear, because the product contained carcinogens. In less severe action, the agency might require labels on some products warning consumers of the risks attached to product use. Health warnings on cigarette packages and containers of artificially sweetened soft drinks are some of the best-known examples.

The most extreme form of regulation is mandatory licensing—that is, specific professions and businesses must obtain licenses to practice their trade, to take certain actions, or own certain goods. In most cases failure to obtain the license results in civil or criminal action. Licenses usually are required when the consumer is unable to determine the qualifications of the individuals offering their services. Various federal agencies and commissions license everything from radio and television stations to nuclear power plants. Licensing requires a massive amount of red tape, but for successful applicants it provides some economic benefit in that it allows them to practice their trade or provide their service while protecting their interests by keeping the unqualified out.

When information about certain products cannot be conveniently provided to consumers or the potential harm of a product is very high, agencies often will set standards to which the company must comply. Failure to maintain the standards could result in legal penalties. Agencies can impose two kinds of standards. Performance standards require simply that minimum goals be met, but no guidelines are given on the method or methods to be used. Thus, EPA could require a specific city to meet minimum air pollution standards without reference to how that city achieves those standards. Specification standards, in contrast, spell out exactly how certain requirements are to be met. EPA would tell a city exactly what kind of equipment to use to reduce pollution.

Standards are only as effective as the agency's ability to enforce them. One method of enforcing regulatory rules or standards is taxation—historically a tool of regulation. Higher taxes often are imposed on companies or persons who refuse to comply with the rules. The tariffs placed on imported goods to protect American manufacturers were early examples of a regulatory tax. More recently taxes have been imposed on automobiles that use fuel less efficiently than others.

Other economic incentives are used by regulatory agencies to encourage certain types of behavior. Tax credits, for example, frequently are offered to firms to encourage investment in capital equipment. Colleges and universities receive research grants to conduct needed agricultural research. Farmers receive price supports to encourage them to grow particular crops. In each case, the government regulates by giving or withholding economic benefits.

Some agencies have the power to recall consumer products that could harm their users. *Consumer Reports* estimates that between 1973 and 1980 the Consumer Product Safety Commission recalled more than 120 million products in more than twenty-six hundred separate actions, resulting in about eighty recalls a week. From the time automobile recalls began in 1966 to 1980 over eighty-six million automobiles, trucks, vans, and other vehicles were recalled. Recalls do not always result, however, in effective regulation. Whether the product is corrected is usually left up to the consumer.

Florida Department of Commerce

NASA is a civilian agency that controls U.S. aeronautical and space activities. In 1958 the first American satellite went into orbit, and eleven years later, *Apollo II* completed the first successful manned flight to the moon.

Independent Executive Agencies

Independent executive agencies are similar to independent regulatory agencies in that they are not part of a specific cabinet department. But unlike regulatory agencies, they are normally considered to be part of the presidential hierarchy and report to the president. The most important examples of these agencies are the National Aeronautics and Space Administration (NASA) and the General Services Administration (GSA).

Many of these agencies were created in an effort to avoid bureaucratic inertia, often resulting from the failure of existing agencies to accomplish their objectives. In 1964, for example, the Johnson administration created the Office of Economic Opportunity (OEO) to help implement its "Great Society" programs. By locating OEO in the Executive Office of the President and not in a specific department, the White House was able to exert more control over its operation and ensure that the administration's antipoverty objectives were carried out. Similarly, NASA was located outside the control of a specific department to help expedite its formation and operation, free from the traditional demands of departmental control. In addition, it was set up apart from the Defense Department to demonstrate that the U.S. space program would be controlled by civilians rather than the military.

Often independent agencies are born out of vested interests. Members of Congress and interest groups want to guarantee that these agencies are responsible to their wishes. In addition, presidents and Congress often want these agencies free from the traditional constraints and methods of old-line departments. For example, in an effort to challenge directly actions detrimental to the environment, Congress made the EPA independent of old-line departments that might have traditional environmental interests.

With some degree of independence from hierarchical executive control, independent executive agencies can maneuver more openly in ways that will maximize their objectives. This kind of freedom, however, often means that independent agencies will have few allies in the executive branch, possibly diminishing their overall influence on the development of executive policy. Some agencies have been quite successful in their independent status by developing new coalitions with groups not traditionally represented by executive departments. For example, the Civil Rights Commission, established in 1957 as a bipartisan, six-member independent agency, used its autonomous organizational status to become a constructive critic of federal civil rights policies. Between 1959 and 1970, by successfully forging coalitions outside the executive branch, the commission was able to get over two-thirds of its recommendations either enacted into law or included in executive orders.

Executive independence can result, however, in overlapping jurisdictions and conflicts between the independent agencies and existing executive organizations. Until it was replaced by the Office of Personnel Management in 1978, the Civil Service Commission's independence made it an easy target for groups seeking to influence particular aspects of federal personnel policy. An interviewee in a Brookings Institution report noted the difficulty of placing responsibility within the commission: "Well, we think it works first for its congressional committees, second for the status of employees, third for the American Legion in support of veterans' preference laws, fourth for the civil service employees' unions, and possibly fifth for the President." [6] The attempt to remove politics from the federal personnel selection process therefore resulted in just the opposite; politics became a primary factor in determining federal job selection.

Government Corporations

A third type of agency, which operates either autonomously or semiautonomously of the regular departmental structure, is the governmental corporation. Even though investors in them cannot buy stock and collect dividends, these organizations operate much like a private corporation that sells a service. Government corporations usually provide a service for a public need that the private sector has found too expensive or unprofitable to undertake.

Three of the best-known government corporations are the Tennessee Valley Authority (TVA), created in 1933 to develop electric power and navigation in the Tennessee Valley region; the National Railroad Passenger Corporation, or Amtrak, the nation's passenger train service; and the U.S. Postal Service. Several successful government corporations have been based on the TVA model. Comsat, for example, is a modern government corporation which sells time-sharing on NASA satellites. The Postal Service became a government corporation only recently. Originally created in 1775 by the Continental Congress with Benjamin Franklin as its postmaster general, this longtime cabinet department assumed its corporate status in 1970. In urging reorganization of the Postal Service, President Richard Nixon argued that by freeing the agency from the direct control of the president and Congress, and the resulting bipartisan pressure, it could operate more efficiently.

By giving them a corporate charter Congress has given these corporations greater latitude in their day-to-day operations than that given other agencies. As corporations, federal agencies can acquire, develop, and sell real estate and other kinds of property, acting in the name of the corporation rather than the federal government. They have the power as well to bring a lawsuit on behalf of the corporation, and they can be sued. Also like private corporations, these agencies are headed by a bipartisan board of directors or board of commissioners. Often a corporation such as the Postal Service will have a single head who is supplemented by a board. Corporation heads and members are appointed by the president and approved by the Senate. They serve long, staggered terms to prevent any one president from controlling the corporation.

Government corporations are not dependent on annual appropriations as are other executive departments and agencies. Their earnings may be retained by them and deposited directly back into their operations. Consequently, they are less subject to financial control by the president or Congress, and they are free of the annual process of defending their estimates for the fiscal year before the Office of Management and Budget (OMB), the president, and Congress. Even so, their operations are reviewed annually by all three, using a review process that tends to be less demanding since they are not requesting appropriations. Because some government corporations have difficulty operating in the black, Congress is committed to providing long-term appropriations for their operations. For example, Congress has promised the Postal Service a fifteen-year funding program.

Government corporations also are free to provide some of their own financing. The Postal Service not only uses revenues that it generates from its own activities, but it is also empowered to borrow money by issuing bonds.

Compared to their modern counterparts, the original government corporations had more independence, as well as much more fiscal freedom than other agencies and departments so that they could realize their goals. Almost unheard of until the New Deal, government corporations became particularly important during World War II as a means of accomplishing specific tasks such as developing raw materials. They operated almost identically to private corporations. Initially, Congress gave them independent funding, which they sustained through their revenues.

In 1945, however, Congress passed the Government Corporation Control Act, which sought to make these agencies more accountable to the president and Congress. While preserving some of the previous independence of government corporations, the act attempted to control them in unique ways. It provided that Congress must first authorize the corporate form of organization, specifying what the corporation may and may not do. Congress may modify the authority or responsibilities of the corporation, or even dissolve it. And if it chooses Congress may withhold working capital.

Sometimes the federal government takes over an ailing corporation in an effort to insure its survival. Amtrak, the nation's railway service, is a prime example. Although Amtrak is a losing proposition in terms of its multibillion dollar federal subsidy, Congress decided that the survival of passenger train service in the United States is in the public interest.

Styles and Methods of Appointment

Almost all independent and semi-independent agency heads and commissioners are selected according to Article II, section 2, of the Constitution, which states that the president "shall nominate, and by and with the advice and consent of the Senate, shall appoint Ambassadors, other public Ministers and Consuls, Judges of the Supreme Court and all other Officers of the United States. . . ." The Founders decided, however, to permit the president or heads of the departments to appoint such "inferior officers" as they thought proper. Thus, the heads of a few regulatory agencies within the departments, such as the Food and Drug Administration, are not appointed by the president but by the secretary of the department in which the agency resides. In either case appointees must be approved by the Senate. Once the Senate has confirmed a nominee, it may not reconsider the nomination.

The president has the power to remove for any reason the heads of agencies within the executive branch, but independent agency heads and commissioners usually may be removed only for inefficiency, neglect of duty, or misconduct. Even though removal is rare, it occasionally occurs. In 1975 President Nixon removed the chairman of the Civil Aeronautics Board, Robert D. Trimm, for "incompetence." Trimm resigned involuntarily out of respect for the office of the president. If he had chosen to fight his removal, the Nixon administration would have had to submit proof of Trimm's incompetence.

Although the Constitution does not specify qualifications for agency heads and commissioners, Congress has required statutorily that appointees to certain agencies meet certain criteria. For example, the act creating the Federal Reserve Board requires its members to be a fair representation of financial, agricultural, industrial, commercial and geographical interests. Similarly, appointments to the Federal Aviation Administration must be not only qualified administrators but also civilians with aviation experience.

One of the requirements for most agencies, especially regulatory, is that they have no more than a simple majority of commissioners from the same political party. Ironically, then administrations pay more attention to nominees from the opposition party than from their own. According to executive branch scholar William E. Brigman, "By careful scrutiny every administration has managed to find members of the opposition party, or registered independents, who are supportive of administration goals." [7] By choosing members of the opposition party who agree with their views, presidents are able to bypass the intent of bipartisanship. Richard Nixon, for example, once attempted to nominate the Tennessee leader of "Democrats for Nixon" to a Democratic slot on a commission. When the Democratic-controlled Senate refused to confirm the nominee, Nixon successfully appointed him as an independent. Although bipartisan representation may exist in terms of numbers, rarely does a true minority party view exist in an agency or commission.

Because presidents are authorized to name the heads of most agencies and commissions, they usually take this opportunity to appoint someone from their own party. Presidents may decide to replace existing chairs. If they name one of the sitting commissioners as the new commission head, the retiring chair does not have to leave the commission until his or her term of appointment has expired. Many, however, decide to leave anyway. The terms of most heads of agencies and commissions are fixed. For example, the chair of the Federal Reserve Board serves a four-year term, while a new chair of the Civil Aeronautics Board is named each year.

Selection and Nomination

Appointees to independent agencies and regulatory commissions represent 20.3 percent of all major executive appointments made by the president. Thus, the task of selecting these personnel is one of the president's most important jobs.[8]

As for most presidential appointments, the president relies heavily on others—such as advisers or a formal personnel office—to help search for, screen, and recommend potential appointees. Presidents are presented then with several choices, and they often make the final decision themselves; however, this may mean simply affirming the selection of their advisers.

Few presidents have played active roles in the process of selecting and nominating appointees to independent agencies and regulatory commissions, but President Gerald R. Ford paid attention to almost every such appointment. Yet even Ford did not meet with the nominees. That privilege was reserved for the nominated chairs.

Even though presidents take very little time with the appointment of commissioners, their selection and nomination is one of the most important sources of influence that presidents have over independent agencies and regulatory commissions. Despite the organizational independence of these agencies, every administration has sought to control them. The process of influence appears to be a simple matter of appointing ideologically pure partisans, but factors other than political philosophy must be considered because of the difficulty encountered in measuring partisan purity and loyalty in potential nominees.

Traditionally, most presidents have viewed agency seats as important political rewards and have instructed their advisers to use them as such. Agency vacancies thus have become an important way to pay political debts and not necessarily the best way to influence policy.

Few people are nominated who are not politically acceptable to the White House. Although a potential appointee's educational background, geographical representation, and party loyalty are all important, political connections may be the most important presidential consideration. Congressional sponsorship has been particularly useful to appointees. In a study of thirty-eight appointments to four regulatory agencies over a fifteen-year period, the Senate Governmental Affairs Committee found that congressional sponsorship most often determined selection of the nominee.[9] And very few administrations do not first consult with members of Congress and special-interest groups to obtain some type of informal clearance for the nominee.

Whether regulatory commissioners should come from the industries that they are supposed to regulate is one of the more controversial questions confronting the appointment process. The most logical place to turn for experts on the interest to be controlled is that interest itself. But appointing someone who has such an association leaves the commissioner open to a conflict-of-interest charge.

Most presidents, however, at least check with the interests to be regulated, whether they be traditional interest groups or consumer groups. Political scientist Louis Kohlmeier, Jr., has argued that every recent president has run some kind of check with the regulated interest before appointing a regulator. "Almost no president has ever sent up for Senate confirmation a name to which industry takes vigorous exception. . . . All presidents have run checks with industry before picking regulators, fundamentally because all have looked upon regulation more or less as industry's preserve." [10] Yet there are often pressures in the other direction as well. Because presidents want to avoid confirmation fights, they usually have their aides consult with key public-interest groups. According to presidential appointments scholar G. Calvin Mackenzie, "The appointment of regulatory commissioners . . . rarely aroused much interest or controversy before 1970. But the growing political prominence of a number of self-declared public interest

U.S. Postal Service

The Postal Service was created in 1775 with Benjamin Franklin as the first postmaster general. In 1987 postal workers handled 154 billion pieces of mail.

groups sharply increased the conflict engendered by these appointments in the decade that followed.... The likely effect ... is that the president's freedom of choice will be circumscribed." [11]

Presidential Use of Appointments

Recent presidents have looked upon the appointment of a strong and loyal agency or commission chair as the most effective method for influencing agency policies. Consequently, presidents pay close attention to the selection of commission chairs. Since 1969, when President Richard Nixon finally gained control over the last holdout, the president has had the power to name the agency or commission chair. With the exception of the Federal Communications Commission and the Interstate Commerce Commission, which have resisted attempts at consolidating power within their chairs, there are very few collegial decisions within the agencies and commissions. Chairs have power over budgets and personnel, and they have more information than the other commissioners. They therefore wield substantial powers in the direction and control of their agencies. Brigman wrote: "Realizing that a strong chairman can accomplish the administration's goals without explicit intervention, thereby preserving the fiction of regulatory independence, the White House pays much more attention to the selection of chairmen than it does to ordinary commissioners." [12]

The desire of presidents to control a regulatory commission often stems from their philosophy of regulation and the role of government in general. By appointing agency heads and commissioners that share their philosophical views, presidents are best able to leave their imprint on the government. Regulation itself represents the expanding role of government in an individual's life. The presidencies of Jimmy Carter and Ronald Reagan point to two different views of the role of regulation, reflected in their desire to control the philosophy of the regulatory agencies and commissions through the appointment process.

Even though President Carter expressed an interest in reducing regulation through several of his appointments to executive branch and regulatory posts, he still appointed a significant number of "activists" to head agencies concerned with consumer protection and health and safety standards. For example, he appointed Michael Pertschuk, who had been instrumental in developing the Consumer Product Safety Commission, as chairman of the Federal Trade Commission. Pertschuk pushed the FTC into an activist position on the issues of television advertising directed at children and automobile advertisements that promoted more driving during periods of gas shortages. Carter also named Joan Claybrook, former director of Ralph Nader's public-interest group Congress Watch, as director of the National Highway Traffic Safety Administration. During her tenure, NHTSA proposed the mandatory installation of automatically inflating airbags in automobiles. In addition, Carter appointed to CPSC some of its most activist commissioners, making that commission the most energetic in its history.

President Reagan, in contrast, made extensive use of the appointment process to promote his policy of attacking the expanding role of the federal government. Many of his appointments to executive branch regulatory agencies and independent agencies and commissions were nominees who shared his philosophy of hostility to governmental regulations and controls. By appointing Thorne Auchter to head the Occupational Safety and Health Administration, Reagan instilled in OSHA a philosophy sympathetic to businesses who complained of high regulatory costs. Reagan's appointment of Raymond Peck as NHTSA's administrator created in that agency a philosophy of deregulation of the automobile industry, reversing the support for mandatory airbags expressed during the Carter administration. And his appointment of S. R. Shad, a vice president of E. F. Hutton and Company, to head the Securities and Exchange Commission narrowed the SEC's view of its role in the regulation of the marketing of new securities. This contrasted greatly with an agency that had an independent and aggressive staff that traditionally had sought tough enforcement of disclosure requirements and antifraud provisions.

Agency Profiles

The following agency profiles describe the sixty-three independent establishments, government corporations, and quasi-official agencies, as defined in the *U.S. Government Manual,* in existence as of January 1989. Unless stated otherwise the following rules apply to each agency: the agencies do not have a bipartisanship requirement of its governing body; a new president can replace the agency head at the beginning of a new administration; and the governing body serves at the discretion of the president.

ACTION

Established in 1971 by executive order, ACTION is the center for federal volunteer programs, resources, and initiatives. The organization is headed by a director and a deputy director who are appointed by the president with Senate confirmation, as is an associate director for Domestic and Anti-Poverty Operations. Terms of office are not fixed, and appointees serve at the discretion of the president and may be replaced by an incoming president.

ACTION is headquartered in Washington, D.C., and maintains nine regional offices and forty-eight state or district offices. ACTION programs are carried out in all fifty states, Puerto Rico, the Virgin Islands, and the District of Columbia. Programs supported by ACTION involve more than 397,000 volunteers who serve full time or part time for up to two years. Some volunteers receive stipends; others receive no remuneration.

Volunteers in Service to America (VISTA) is the oldest program in ACTION. VISTA's goal is to alleviate poverty in the United States. Volunteers serve on a full-time basis and work through locally sponsored community projects. ACTION provides VISTA volunteers with a basic subsistence allowance for housing, food, and incidentals. More than half of VISTA's programs are designed to serve young people.

In the Foster Grandparents Program, low-income volunteers sixty years old and over provide companionship and guidance to mentally, physically, or emotionally handicapped children and those in the juvenile justice system. In 1987, more than twenty-three thousand seniors participated in the Foster Grandparent Program. The Retired Senior Volunteer Program (RSVP) is the largest ACTION program, with 365,000 volunteers. RSVP places retirees aged sixty and over with nonprofit organizations and public agencies in need of volunteer services. Funding and technical assistance are provided by ACTION and local communities. The Senior Companion Program was established in 1974 under the Domestic Volunteer Service Act. Under the program, low-income persons aged sixty or over provide care and companionship to other adults, particularly the homebound elderly.

ACTION also operates the National Center for Service Learning, a student volunteer program. The center provides free training, resource materials, and on-site consultation to high school, college, and community staff personnel who direct, plan, and develop student volunteer programs. Young Volunteers in Action consists of volunteers aged fourteen to twenty-two, who participate in projects such as tutoring homebound students, serving in parks and recreation centers, assisting in hospitals, and aiding disaster-relief efforts. Volunteers may be eligible for academic credit for their work. The Office of Voluntarism Initiatives administers programs that support local self-reliance through volunteer initiatives and that encourage citizen participation in volunteer projects.

ACTION has primary responsibility for carrying out the federal drug abuse prevention effort through its Drug Prevention Program. The program sponsors drug-use education and prevention efforts and disseminates information on the health effects of drugs and on various prevention methods.

Administrative Conference of the United States

The Administrative Conference of the United States is a permanent, independent federal agency that recommends improvements in the administration of regulatory, benefit, and other government programs. Established by the Administrative Conference Act of 1964, the Administrative Conference is headed by a chair who is appointed to a five-year term by the president, with Senate confirmation. A council, which acts as an executive board, consists of the chair and ten other members appointed by the president for three-year terms. Additional members numbering not fewer than sixty-four or more than eighty are drawn from government and the private sector to serve two-year terms. Members representing the private sector are appointed by the chair, with council approval.

The Administrative Conference provides a forum for agency officials, private lawyers, university professors, and other experts in administrative law and government to study procedural problems and to develop improvements. The entire membership meets at least once each year. Membership is divided into six standing committees: adjudication, administration, governmental processes, judicial review, regulation, and rule making. The committees study subjects selected by either the chair, the council, or the assembly. The assembly has authority to approve, reject, or amend any recommendations presented by the committees. Although the final recommendations of the Administrative Conference are nonbinding, the chair is authorized to encourage departments and agencies to adopt the proposed changes.

African Development Foundation

The African Development Foundation (ADF) is an independent public corporation created by Congress to provide development assistance to indigenous nongovernmental African groups and individuals. Congress authorized ADF in 1980 as a complement to U.S. foreign aid programs; its aim is to deliver economic assistance directly to African communities and grass-roots organizations. Aid is awarded primarily for farming, education, husbandry, manufacturing, and water management projects. In the legislation that created ADF, Congress required that the corporation's beneficiaries design and implement their own projects. Since 1984 ADF has funded more than one hundred projects in nineteen countries. The foundation is governed by a seven-member board of directors appointed by the president with Senate confirmation. Board members serve staggered terms ranging from two to six years. By law five members are chosen from the private sector and two are from the government.

The goal of ADF is to make local communities responsible for their own development through programs appropriate for their needs and to give priority to objectives established by the community. ADF also seeks to demonstrate the value of local or traditional methods, so as to avoid social and economic disruption caused by the introduction of new equipment or production systems.

Because its purpose is to provide grass-roots assistance, ADF requires that a basic level of community organization be in place at the time a request is made. In addition, a proposed project must involve the community at large, and the community must comprehend the responsibilities of implementing the project and its recurring costs. Communities requesting ADF aid also must demonstrate the skill and capacity to manage project funds effectively.

In addition to funding grass-roots development activities, ADF supports applied research conceived and executed by Africans. ADF's field staff includes African Regional Liaison Officers (RLOs) who serve as liaisons between ADF and applicants in each of ADF's five African regions. RLOs provide technical support, assist ADF in monitoring projects, and provide information about funding procedures. Country Resource Facilitators provide the same support in those countries in which they are resident.

American Battle Monuments Commission

The American Battle Monuments Commission (ABMC) is responsible for commemorating the services of American armed forces where they have served since the United States entered into World War I on April 6, 1917. A small independent agency, ABMC oversees the design, construction, operation, and maintenance of permanent U.S. military burial grounds in foreign countries. ABMC also controls the design and construction of U.S. military monuments and markers in foreign countries by U.S. citizens and organizations both public and private.

Created by Congress in 1923, ABMC administers, operates, and maintains twenty-four permanent U.S. military burial grounds, twelve separate monuments, and four memorials in twelve countries worldwide. The policy-making body of the commission comprises eleven members who are appointed by the president for an indefinite term and serve without pay. The board members and their elected chair serve at the pleasure of the president. New appointments can immediately be made by an incoming president. A professional staff of full-time civilian employees consists of U.S. citizens and foreign nationals from countries where ABMC installations are located. Field offices in Paris and Rome supervise operations in Europe and the Mediterranean. The superintendents of the cemeteries in Mexico City, Corozal, Panama, and Manila report directly to the Washington office.

The commission provides assistance in locating grave and memorial sites and general information on travel and accommodations for visitors. For immediate family traveling overseas specifically to visit a grave or memorial site, the commission provides letters authorizing "non-fee" passports and other services at the grave site.

Appalachian Regional Commission

The Appalachian Regional Commission (ARC) administers a comprehensive program for the economic development of the Appalachian region. Created by the Appalachian Regional Development Act of 1965, the commission consists of fourteen members, including the thirteen sitting governors of states within the Appalachian region and a federal chair, appointed by the president and subject to Senate confirmation. A cochair also is appointed. The federal cochair serves at the pleasure of the president. Members' terms run concurrent with their terms as governor.

The Appalachian region, as defined by the Appalachian Regional Development Act as amended, includes all of West Virginia and parts of New York, Pennsylvania, Maryland, Virginia, Ohio, Kentucky, Tennessee, North Carolina, South Carolina, Georgia, Alabama, and Mississippi. It incorporates 397 counties, covers a total of 195,000 square miles, and has a current population of more than twenty million.

Federal efforts to revitalize the economy of the Appalachian region had been considered as early as 1902. The region had been poor and underdeveloped even though it is rich in resources. By 1964 per capita income in many areas of the region was less than half the national average, and education levels in the region were far below the national average.

Board for International Broadcasting

The Board for International Broadcasting (BIB) is an independent federal agency chartered to oversee the operations of the nonprofit radio corporation Radio Free Europe/Radio Liberty (RFE/RL). Radio Liberty broadcasts to the Soviet Union, and Radio Free Europe broadcasts to Poland, Romania, Czechoslovakia, Hungary, Bulgaria, and the Baltic states. Both programs operated as separate entities from the early 1950s until 1976, when they merged to create Radio Free Europe/Radio Liberty, Inc. RFE/RL has a statutory mission to further the open communication of information and ideas in Eastern Europe and the Soviet Union. In terms of broadcast hours, it is the leading external broadcaster to those areas.

The main function of BIB is to "assess the quality, effectiveness, and professional integrity" of RFE/RL's broadcasts "within the context of the broad foreign policy objectives of the United States." Established in 1973, the board is composed of nine members including a chair, who are appointed by the president with Senate confirmation. No more than five members may be from the same political party, and members serve three-year terms. The chief operating executive of RFE/RL is chosen by the board and becomes an ex officio, nonvoting member of BIB. All members of the board serve at the pleasure of the president.

In addition to its oversight responsibilities, the board develops long-range strategies for REF/RL and conducts studies to determine the most efficient allocation of resources. The board administers grants awarded to REF/RL and procures specialized electronic equipment for the company. Under the board's guidance, REF/RL provides news, political analysis, and cultural programs in twenty-two languages, using five transmitter relay stations. In 1985, Radio Free Afghanistan, a new service of Radio Liberty, went on the air. The service broadcasts seven hours a week to Afghanistan in that country's principal language, Dari.

Central Intelligence Agency

The Central Intelligence Agency (CIA) is an independent agency established by the National Security Act of 1947 to coordinate the nation's intelligence activities and to correlate, evaluate, and disseminate intelligence that affects national security. The CIA is responsible for the production of political, military, economic, biographical, sociological, and scientific and technical intelligence to meet the needs of national policy makers.

The CIA is headed by a director and a deputy director who are appointed to an indefinite term by the president with Senate confirmation and serve at the discretion of the president. The director of the CIA is designated as the director of central intelligence (DCI). In addition to heading the CIA, the DCI heads the intelligence community and is the primary adviser to the president and the National Security Council on national foreign intelligence matters. The director of the CIA is not a cabinet-level position. One exception, however, was William Casey, who was appointed by President Ronald Reagan, and designated as a cabinet officer.

In addition to the DCI's office staff, the intelligence community consists of the CIA, the National Security Agency, the Defense Intelligence Agency, the offices within the Department of Defense responsible for collection of specialized national foreign intelligence, the Bureau of Intelligence and Research of the Department of State, and the intelligence elements of the military services, the Federal Bureau of Investigation, and the Departments of Treasury and Energy.

In 1949 the National Security Act was amended by the Central Intelligence Agency Act. The legislation permits the CIA to use confidential fiscal and administrative procedures, and it exempted the agency from certain limitations on expenditure of federal funds. The act allows CIA funds to be included in the budgets of other agencies and then transferred to the CIA without regard to the restrictions placed on the initial appropriation. The amount of CIA funds held by other agencies is classified. The 1949 act also exempted the CIA from having to disclose its organization, functions, number of personnel, and the names, titles, and salaries of its employees.

The CIA conducts covert activities abroad in support of U.S. foreign policy objectives. These actions are executed so that the role of the U.S. government is not apparent or acknowledged publicly. Only the president can authorize covert actions upon the recommendation of the National Security Council. Upon initiating a covert action, the DCI must notify the intelligence oversight committees of Congress.

The agency has no law enforcement or security functions either at home or abroad. The CIA is expressly prohibited by presidential executive order from routinely engaging in the domestic use of electronic, mail, or physical surveillance, monitoring devices, or unconsented physical search. These restrictions can be lifted only under the most extraordinary conditions of concern for the national welfare and only with the approval of the U.S. attorney general.

Oversight of the CIA is conducted by the Intelligence Oversight Board. The board consists of three voluntary members appointed by the president from the public sector. Board members serve indefinite terms at the discretion of the president. The chair of the board is also a member of the president's Foreign Intelligence Advisory Board.

Commission of Fine Arts

The Commission of Fine Arts was established by Congress in 1910 to advise the government on matters pertaining to the arts and the architectural development of Washington, D.C. The commission, comprising seven members including a director who are appointed by the president for four-year terms, was initially authorized to advise on statues, fountains, and monuments within the District of Columbia. Subsequent executive orders and acts of Congress have greatly expanded the commission's duties to include the preservation of places of national interest and approval of architectural designs of government buildings.

The commission also reviews plans for private structures within the district and advises on building height limits and architectural standards in the Old Georgetown and Shipstead-Luce areas. Land to be acquired as parkland in the District of Columbia, Maryland, and Virginia also falls under commission responsibility.

The commission's members advise on matters of art and architectural development when requested to do so by the president or by a member of Congress. Contracting officers of the federal and district governments also are directed to call for the commission's advice on such matters. Among the more significant reviews by the commission are the Mall, the Lincoln Memorial, the Federal Triangle, the National Gallery of Art, and the Vietnam Veterans Memorial. The commission is not required by law to be bipartisan, and members serve at the pleasure of the president.

Commission on the Bicentennial of the U.S. Constitution

Established by Congress in July 1985, the Commission on the Bicentennial of the U.S. Constitution promotes and coordinates activities to commemorate the Constitution, adopted at the Constitutional Convention on September 17, 1787. Through national, state, and local events, it seeks to increase awareness and understanding of the country's founding document.

The commission comprises twenty-three members, twenty of whom are appointed by the president. The chief justice of the United States, the president pro tempore of the Senate, and the Speaker of the House of Representatives, or their designees, are also members. Commission members, including the chair, serve for the life of the commission. Senate confirmation of the chair was not required. A staff director manages the commission. The commission receives funds from corporate sponsors as well as from the federal government.

Nationwide bicentennial activities included a high school essay contest; a traveling exhibition of the Constitution, Magna Carta, and other historic documents; and distribution of more than 300 million copies of the Constitution. The commission recognized cities, towns, and counties—termed "Designated Bicentennial Communities"—that formed a body to plan local events celebrating the Constitution. Before it disbands in December 1991, the commission also will mark bicentennials of the Bill of Rights, the formation of the first federal government, and the first Congress.

Commission on Civil Rights

Established by the Civil Rights Act of 1957, the Commission on Civil Rights is an independent, fact-finding agency that monitors developments in civil rights under the Constitution. The Civil Rights Act of 1983 increased the commission's membership from six to eight commissioners, four of whom are appointed by the president and four by Congress. Not more than four members may be of the same party. With the approval of a majority of the commission, the president designates a chair and a vice chair from among its members.

Commissioners serve either six- or three-year-terms and can be removed by the president only for neglect of duty or malfeasance in office. A full-time staff director oversees the day-to-day activities of the commission. The chair is appointed by the president with the commission's approval and serves at the pleasure of the president. An incoming president can appoint a new chair at any time.

The commission assesses the laws and policies of the federal government to determine the nature and extent of denial of equal protection under the law on the basis of race, color, religion, sex, national origin, age, or handicap, and it submits reports to the president and to Congress. Areas of study include employment, voting rights, education, and housing.

In its fact-finding capacity, the commission may hold hearings and issue subpoenas for the production of documents and the attendance of witnesses at such hearings. Subpoenas may be issued in the state in which the hearing is being held and within a fifty-mile radius of the site. The commission maintains advisory committees and consults with representatives of federal, state, and local governments and private organizations. The commission lacks direct enforcement powers but refers complaints to appropriate government agencies for action.

Advisory committees are located in each state and in the District of Columbia. Each committee comprises citizens familiar with local and state civil rights issues. The members serve without compensation and assist the commission with its fact-finding, investigative, and information dissemination functions. Three regional offices coordinate the commission's regional operations and assist the state advisory committees in their activities. The offices are staffed by a director, equal opportunity specialists, researchers, attorneys, and other administrative personnel.

The commission maintains a library that serves as a national clearinghouse for civil rights information and conducts studies of discrimination against certain groups, including women, blacks, Hispanics, eastern and southern Europeans, and Asian and Pacific island Americans.

Commodity Futures Trading Commission

The Commodity Futures Trading Commission (CFTC) is an independent regulatory agency established in 1975 to administer the Commodity Exchange Act of 1936. Congressional legislation established the CFTC in 1974 for four years. This mandate was renewed in 1978, 1982, and 1986.

The purpose of the commission is to ensure that futures markets function smoothly. Oversight regulation is needed to guard against manipulation, abusive trade practices, and fraud. Specific responsibilities of the commission include regulating commodities exchanges, approving futures contracts, registering commodities traders, protecting customers, and monitoring information. The commission has three major operating units: the Divisions of Economic Analysis, Enforcement, and Trading and Markets. The CFTC serves as a disseminator of knowledge about commodities markets. It publishes weekly commodity reports, *Monthly Commitments of Traders* reports, and relevant books and pamphlets. It also provides training courses to people in the field.

The CFTC is headed by five commissioners who are appointed by the president with the consent of the Senate. They serve staggered five-year terms, and no more than three commissioners can be of the same political party. The president designates one commissioner as chair. A majority vote by the commissioners is required for major policy decisions and committee actions.

In 1981, the CFTC registered the National Futures Association (NFA) as an industrywide self-regulatory organization. The NFA safeguards the interests of public and commercial users of futures markets by establishing codes of conduct and offering advice. If a dispute arises between customers and sellers, the NFA can provide arbitration. In 1982, Congress passed a law requiring the NFA and the CFTC to begin actively sharing regulatory responsibilities.

Consumer Product Safety Commission

The Consumer Product Safety Commission (CPSC) is an independent regulatory agency established by Congress to protect consumers from unreasonable risks of injury associated with consumer products. Created by the 1972 Consumer Product Safety Act (CPSA), in response to the consumer movement, the CPSC comprises five commissioners, not more than three of whom may be members of the same political party. Commissioners are appointed to seven-year terms by the president, with Senate confirmation. The president also designates one of the commissioners to serve as chair. The chair and commissioners can be removed by the president for neglect of duty or malfeasance, but for no other reason. A newly elected president, however, can appoint a new chair.

In addition to the Consumer Product Safety Act, the CPSC administers the Flammable Fabrics Act, the Federal Hazardous Substances Act, the Poison Prevention Packaging Act of 1970, and the Refrigerator Safety Act. The commission's statutory mandate provides a broad range of regulatory authority over consumer products. CPSC responsibilities include development of uniform safety standards, bans on unsafe products, safety test methods and testing devices, and development of consumer and industry education programs. Consumer products not regulated by the CPSA include boats, cars, planes, food, drugs, cosmetics, pesticides, medical devices, alcohol, tobacco, and firearms. Standards set by the CPSC preempt any differing state or local law; however, states and localities may set different standards that produce a greater degree of consumer protection without undue burden on interstate commerce.

The CPSC currently uses two advisory bodies to implement its legislative mandate. The Toxicological Advisory Board is composed of members qualified in scientific disciplines relating to toxicology. The board gives the commission scientific and technical advice on precautionary labeling for hazardous substances.

The commission also can create a Chronic Hazard Advisory Panel to advise the commission about the risk of cancer, birth defects, or gene mutations associated with consumer products. The panels, formed when the commission perceives a need, consist of seven members appointed from a list of scientists nominated by the president of the National Academy of Sciences.

Responsibility for correcting potentially hazardous products belongs primarily to manufacturers, who are required to certify that the consumer products they produce meet all applicable safety standards issued under the CPSA. They must allow the CPSC to test products for compliance and inspect and investigate their factories. If a manufacturer fails to comply with a standard or certification requirement, charges may be brought against the company by the Justice Department of the commission in U.S. district court.

Environmental Protection Agency

The Environmental Protection Agency (EPA) is an independent regulatory agency responsible for implementing the federal laws designed to protect the environment. EPA was created in 1970 through an executive reorganization plan that consolidated components of five executive departments and independent agencies into a single regulatory agency.

The agency is directed by an administrator and a deputy administrator appointed by the president with Senate confirmation. Nine assistant administrators manage specific environmental programs or direct other EPA functions. The agency's general counsel and its inspector general also are named by the president with Senate confirmation. The agency has ten regional administrators across the country. All governing members of EPA are appointed to no fixed term and serve at the pleasure of the president.

EPA administers nine comprehensive environmental protection laws that authorize the agency to protect the public health and welfare from harmful effects of pollutants and toxic substances. The Clean Water Act authorizes EPA to restore and maintain the "chemical, physical, and biological integrity of the Nation's waters." Under the Safe Drinking Water Act of 1974, EPA establishes national standards for drinking water from both surface and ground water sources. The fundamental objective of the Clean Air Act is the protection of the public health and welfare from harmful effects of air pollution. Regulation of current and future waste management and disposal practices was authorized by the Resource Conservation and Recovery Act. In 1980 Congress passed the Comprehensive Environmental Response, Compensation, and Liability Act, also called the "Superfund." The Superfund program provides EPA with a trust fund of $8.5 billion to respond to conditions or sites that pose a danger to human health or the environment.

EPA's Office of Pesticide Programs administers two statutes regulating pesticides. The Federal Insecticide, Fungicide, and Rodenticide Act governs the licensing or registration of pesticide residue levels in food or feed crops. The Toxic Substances Control Act authorizes EPA to identify and control chemicals that pose an unreasonable risk to human health or the environment. In addition, EPA administers the Marine Protection, Research, and Sanctuaries Act and the Uranium Mill Tailings Radiation Control Act.

The agency maintains a research office that provides data in six major research areas: engineering and technology, environmental processes and effects, monitoring systems and quality assurance, health effects, health and environmental assessment, and exploratory research. For technical advice and review, EPA relies on its Science Advisory Board, consisting of eminent non-EPA scientists. Congress created the board to advise the agency on scientific issues and to review the quality of EPA scientific research.

Enforcement of EPA regulations is supported by state agencies and the agency's National Enforcement Investigation Center in Denver, Colorado. The agency also maintains a criminal investigation unit with specialized training in criminal law enforcement techniques. The agency enforces its regulations through compliance promotion, administrative money penalties, negotiated compliance schedules, and judicial enforcement entailing criminal proceedings.

Equal Employment Opportunity Commission

The Equal Employment Opportunity Commission (EEOC) is an independent agency established in 1965 to eliminate employment discrimination based on race, color, religion, sex, or national origin. EEOC is composed of five commissioners, not more than three of whom may be of the same political party. The commissioners are appointed by the president and confirmed by the Senate for staggered five-year terms. The president designates one member to serve as chair and another to serve as vice-chair. The general counsel also is nominated by the president and confirmed by the Senate for a four-year term. The chair is responsible for the administration of the commission. The five-member commission decides equal employment opportunity policy and approves all litigation undertaken by the commission. The general counsel is responsible for conducting all commission litigation. All appointees to EEOC serve at the pleasure of the president.

The commission was created by Title VII of the Civil Rights Act of 1964. The Equal Employment Opportunity Act of 1972 extended the commission's jurisdiction to include state and local governments, public and private educational institutions, public and private employment agencies, and private businesses that ship or receive goods across state lines and employ fifteen or more persons. EEOC jurisdiction also covers labor unions with fifteen or more members and joint labor-management committees for apprenticeships and training.

The commission has authority to investigate, conciliate, and litigate charges of discrimination in employment. It also has the authority to issue guidelines, rules, and regulations and to require employers, unions, and others covered by Title VII to report regularly the race, ethnic origin, and sex of their employees and members. In cases where a charge of discrimination cannot be conciliated, EEOC has the authority to file a lawsuit in federal district court to force compliance with Title VII.

In addition to administering Title VII, EEOC enforces the Equal Pay Act of 1963, which requires equal pay for equal work, and the Age Discrimination in Employment Act of 1967. In 1978, the Pregnancy Discrimination Act amended the Civil Rights Act of 1964 to prohibit discrimination on the basis of pregnancy, childbirth, or related medical conditions.

EEOC also administers Executive Order 12067, which requires oversight and coordination of all federal equal employment opportunity regulations, practices, and policies. Responsibility regarding handicap discrimination in federal employment was transferred to the commission from the former Civil Service Commission. Employees of the U.S. Congress are not under the protection of the EEOC because the Congress exempted itself from the provisions of Title VII.

Export-Import Bank of the United States

The Export-Import Bank (Eximbank) is an independent, corporate agency that stimulates foreign trade by supporting export financing of U.S. goods and services. Founded in 1934, Eximbank was intended to increase foreign trade during the Great Depression. The agency's first loan in 1935 financed the Cuban government's purchase of silver from U.S. mines. Eximbank also financed construction of the Burma Road in the late 1930s and the Pan American Highway through Latin America in the 1940s. After World War II, Eximbank helped U.S. companies participate in the reconstruction of Europe and Asia. Eximbank supports U.S. exports by neutralizing the effect of export credit subsidies from other governments and absorbing risks the private sector will not accept.

Eximbank's board of directors consists of five full-time members appointed for four-year terms by the president with Senate confirmation. One member is appointed by the president to serve as chair. All members of the board serve at the discretion of the president. In addition, the secretary of commerce and the U.S. trade representative serve as ex officio, nonvoting members. The board is responsible for Eximbank's activities and policies and approves support for individual transactions.

The bank is organized into two main operating divisions. The International Lending Division manages, administers, and coordinates Eximbank's medium-term and long-term international lending and guarantee activities. Eximbank's loans provide competitive fixed-interest-rate financing for U.S. exports facing foreign competition that is backed with subsidized official financing. Evidence of foreign competition is not required for exports produced by small businesses where the loan amount is $2.5 million or less. Eximbank extends direct loans to foreign buyers of U.S. exports and intermediary loans to fund parties that lend to foreign buyers.

The Insurance and Banking Division is divided into a United States division and an insurance division. The U.S. division is responsible for loans and guarantees to U.S. borrowers, specifically the Working Capital Guarantee Program, which helps small companies obtain pre-export financing from commercial lenders. In addition, Eximbank provides loans and guarantees to American companies competing for domestic sales against foreign firms backed by unfairly subsidized financing from a foreign export credit agency.

The insurance division is responsible for Eximbank's export credit insurance programs. The agency's Foreign Credit Insurance Association provides credit insurance policies for nonpayment on export credit transactions that cover political and commercial risks. Political risks include war, cancellation of an existing export or import license, expropriation, confiscation of or intervention in the buyer's business, and transfer risk (failure of foreign government authorities to transfer the foreign currency deposit into dollars). Commercial risks cover nonpayment for reasons other than specified political risks.

Eximbank's policies are coordinated with overall U.S. government foreign and economic policies and do not normally support sales to Communist countries. To be eligible for Eximbank support, 50 percent of goods or services exported must be of U.S. manufacture.

Farm Credit Administration

The Farm Credit Administration (FCA) is an independent financial regulatory agency established in 1933 to oversee the Farm Credit System. FCA was created in response to the need for increased lending to rural farmers unable to obtain credit from bankers headquartered in large U.S. cities.

FCA is administered by a three-member, full-time board of directors appointed by the president with Senate confirmation. The directors serve staggered terms of two, four, and six years, and not more than two members can be of the same political party. The president also selects one member to serve as chair and as the agency's chief executive officer. Board members can be removed for neglect of duty or malfeasance, but for no other reason. New appointments including the chair can be made immediately by an incoming president. As head of FCA, the board provides for the examination and regulation of and reporting by institutions within the Farm Credit System, a nationwide network of agricultural lending institutions and their service organizations. The Farm Credit System comprises three types of banks: the Federal Land Banks, the Federal Intermediate Credit Banks, and the Banks for Cooperatives. In addition to the FCA board, the agency is organized under offices of Examination, General Counsel, Internal Audit, Congressional and Public Affairs, Analysis and Supervision, and Administration.

In 1916 Congress passed the Federal Farm Loan Act, which divided the country into twelve farm credit districts and created and funded a Federal Land Bank in each of them. The land banks make long-term farm mortgage loans through local Federal Land Bank Associations. Loans can be made to farmers, ranchers, commercial fishers, rural homeowners, and people operating farm-related businesses and legal entities. Federal Land Banks hold more than 40 percent of all outstanding farm real estate debt in the United States.

In 1923 Congress passed the Agricultural Credits Act, establishing and funding twelve Federal Intermediate Credit Banks. The banks provide short- and intermediate-term loan funds to Production Credit Associations and other financing institutions serving agricultural producers.

The Production Credit Associations, established in 1933 by the Farm Credit Act, also provide short- and intermediate-term loans. Loans are made to farmers, ranchers, rural homeowners, producers and harvesters of aquatic products, and to people operating certain farm-related businesses. Most loans are for operating purposes and mature within a year. The associations also grant intermediate-term loans of up to ten years to agricultural producers and up to fifteen years for commercial fishers.

The Farm Credit Act also established thirteen Banks for Cooperatives to provide financing for agricultural cooperatives. The banks participate with the district banks on loans that exceed their individual lending capacities. They also participate in international lending activities that benefit U.S. cooperatives.

In its regulatory capacity, the FCA has a broad range of authority, including the power to issue cease-and-desist orders, levy civil money penalties, and remove officers and directors of system institutions. The FCA also is responsible for direct examination of the Federal Land Bank Associations and the Production Credit Association. Although it is a federal agency, the expenses of the FCA are paid by the Farm Credit Banks.

Federal Communications Commission

The Federal Communications Commission (FCC) is an independent regulatory agency charged with regulating interstate and international communications by radio, television, wire, satellite, and cable. Established by the Communications Act of 1934, the FCC assumed regulatory authority previously exercised by the Federal Radio Commission (which was abolished), the secretary of commerce, and the Interstate Commerce Commission. FCC jurisdiction covers the fifty states, the District of Columbia, and the possessions of the United States.

The FCC is composed of five commissioners, not more than three of whom may be members of the same political party. The commissioners are nominated by the president and confirmed by the Senate for staggered seven-year terms. The terms are arranged so that no two expire in the same year. The president also designates one of the members to serve as chair. The chair can be removed for neglect of duty or malfeasance, but for no other reason unless replaced by an incoming president.

The commissioners supervise all FCC activities, delegating responsibilities to staff units, bureaus, and committees. The FCC allocates bands of frequencies to nongovernment communications services and assigns frequencies to individual stations. The commission also licenses and regulates stations and operators. It regulates the technical aspects and equal employment practices of cable systems and monitors competition in the cable industry.

The FCC does not regulate the broadcast networks or programming practices of individual stations, but it does have rules governing obscenity, slander, and political broadcasts. The FCC has no authority over government communication or other forms of communications media, including movies, newspapers, and books.

The four bureaus that conduct most FCC regulatory activities are Mass Media, Common Carrier, Private Radio, and Field Operations. The Mass Media bureau regulates AM, FM, and television broadcast stations and related facilities. The bureau also administers and enforces cable television rules and licenses private microwave radio facilities used by cable systems. The Common Carrier bureau regulates common carriers of wire and radio communications including telephone, telegraph, and satellite companies. The Private Radio bureau regulates radio stations providing communications services to businesses, individuals, nonprofit organizations, and state and local governments. Field Operations detects violations of radio regulations, monitors transmissions, inspects stations, investigates complaints of radio interference, and issues violation notices.

The FCC maintains a chief scientist and general counsel to act on international matters and to assist in regulatory functions. The chief scientist advises the commission on technical, engineering, and scientific matters. The general counsel advises the commission on legal issues, coordinates its legislative program, and represents the commission in court.

Federal Deposit Insurance Corporation

The Federal Deposit Insurance Corporation (FDIC) is an independent agency that provides insurance to bank depositors and serves as the federal regulator and supervisor of insured state banks that are not members of the Federal Reserve System. The FDIC was established by the Banking Act of 1933 to provide protection against mounting bank failures that followed the stock market crash of October 1929. The corporation insures funds of bank depositors up to $100,000. Separate $100,000 coverage is provided to holders of Keogh Plan Retirement Accounts and Individual Retirement Accounts.

Management of the corporation is carried out by a three-member board of directors, two of whom are appointed by the president with Senate confirmation for six-year terms. One of these appointed directors is designated by the president to be chair. Board members can be removed for neglect of duty or malfeasance but for no other reason, although the president may appoint another director as chair at any time. The comptroller of the currency, who serves ex officio as the board's third member, also is appointed by the president with Senate confirmation for a five-year term. Only two members of the board may be members of the same political party.

Many states require state-chartered banks that are not members of the Federal Reserve System to apply to the FDIC for federal insurance coverage. The FDIC examines banks to determine the adequacy of their capital structure, prospects for future earnings, the general character of each bank's management, and the needs of the community in which each bank is located. National banks and state banks that are members of the Federal Reserve System receive FDIC insurance with their charters and do not require investigation by the corporation.

At year-end 1985, the FDIC employed 1,542 bank examiners at 105 offices throughout the nation. Corporation examiners conduct about ten thousand bank examinations and investigations each year and issue reports on their findings. Each examination report outlines any unacceptable banking practices or violations of law and suggests corrective steps. Usually, the FDIC then attempts to work with the bank management informally by obtaining its approval of a corrective agreement or by privately issuing a proposed notice of charges and a proposed cease-and-desist order. If, after a meeting with the bank and the appropriate state supervisory authority, the bank does not consent to comply with the proposed order, the FDIC will initiate formal proceedings by publicly issuing the notice of charges and holding a hearing before an administrative law judge.

The FDIC also can terminate a bank's insurance if it finds the bank has been conducting its affairs in an unsound and unsafe manner. When insurance is terminated, existing deposits, less subsequent withdrawals, continue to be insured by the FDIC for two years. If a bank becomes insolvent, the FDIC attempts to arrange a deposit assumption, in which another bank takes over many of the assets of the failed bank and assumes both insured and uninsured deposits. If such a transaction cannot be arranged, the FDIC pays off all depositors to the insured maximum limit.

The FDIC receives no annual appropriations from Congress. Funding is provided from assessments on deposits held by insured banks and from interest on the required investment of its surplus funds in government securities. The FDIC can withdraw up to $3 billion from the Treasury to augment its Deposit Insurance Fund, but this option never has been exercised. Depositors in failed FDIC-insured banks have recovered about 99.4 percent of their total deposits from January 1, 1934 through December 31, 1984.

Federal Election Commission

The Federal Election Commission (FEC) is an independent regulatory agency created in 1975 to administer and enforce the provisions of the Federal Election Campaign Act of 1971. The commission comprises six members appointed by the president and confirmed by the Senate. The commissioners serve staggered six-year terms, and no more than three commissioners may be members of the same political party. The chair and vice-chair must be members of different political parties and are elected annually by their fellow commissioners. The chair can be removed only by impeachment and cannot be replaced by the president until the chair's term expires. The clerk of the House of Representatives and the secretary of the Senate serve as nonvoting members of the commission.

There were several attempts to reform campaign financing before the Federal Election Campaign Act of 1971. As early as 1907, Theodore Roosevelt recommended public financing of federal elections and a ban on private contributions, with little success. The Corrupt Practices Act of 1925 attempted to force public disclosure of campaign finances; but, because, it was not specific and inclusive, it was difficult to enforce.

The Federal Election Campaign Act of 1971, as amended, requires the disclosure of sources and uses of funds in campaigns for any federal office, limits the size of individual contributions, and provides for partial public financing of presidential elections. The act was amended in 1974 and 1976 to establish public financing of presidential primary elections, limits on campaign contributions, and an independent body to oversee the campaign finance law.

Any candidate for federal office and any political group or committee formed to support a candidate must register with the FEC and file periodic reports on campaign financing. Individuals and committees making expenditures on behalf of a candidate must also file reports.

Contributions from national banks, corporations, labor organizations, government contractors, and nonresident foreign nationals are prohibited. Also prohibited are contributions of cash in excess of $100, contributions from one person given in the name of another, and contributions exceeding legal limits.

FEC staff members review the reports for omissions, and, if any are found, they request additional information from the candidate or committee. If the missing information is not supplied, the FEC has the authority to seek a conciliation agreement, to impose a fine, or to sue for the information in U.S. district court. These procedures also apply to cases in which the FEC discovers a violation of campaign finance law. If any matter involves willful violations, the commission may refer the case to the Justice Department.

The commission also administers provisions of the law covering the public financing of presidential primaries and general elections.

Federal Emergency Management Agency

The Federal Emergency Management Agency (FEMA) is an independent agency responsible for the federal government's civil emergency preparedness, mitigation, and response activities in both peace and war. The agency headquarters are in Washington, D.C. The director of FEMA is appointed by the president with consent of the Senate and serves at the pleasure of the president.

In 1979 a presidential directive consolidated five federal agencies to form FEMA and transferred closely allied functions from other departments to the new agency. The former federal agencies that make up FEMA are: the Defense Civil Preparedness Agency, the Federal Disaster Assistance Administration, the Federal Preparedness Agency, the Federal Insurance Administration, and the United States Fire Administration. Other programs transferred to FEMA include the community preparedness for weather emergencies, Earthquake Hazard Reduction, dam safety coordination, and oversight of the Federal Emergency Broadcast System. In addition, two new functions were added to the agency's responsibilities—coordination of emergency warnings and federal response to consequences of terrorist incidents.

FEMA's National Preparedness Directorate develops and coordinates federal programs to ensure that government at all levels is able to respond to and recover from national emergencies. Its responsibilities include arrangements for succession to office and emergency organization of departments and agencies. The agency assesses national mobilization capabilities and develops programs for resource management during national and civil emergencies.

The State and Local Programs and Support Directorate provides funding, technical assistance, supplies, equipment, and training for state and local emergency programs. The directorate administers the President's Disaster Relief Program, which provides supplemental federal assistance when the president declares an emergency or major disaster. Requests for assistance under this program are made by the governor of the affected state and are directed to the president before being sent to the FEMA regional director. FEMA then evaluates the damage and assistance requirements and makes recommendations to the president. Direct disaster assistance can be extended to state and local governments and to individual victims and their families.

FEMA's National Flood Insurance Program provides insurance coverage to participating communities and works with local government officials to reduce future flood damage through floodplain management. FEMA also administers the National Earthquake Hazards Reduction program, which publishes seismic resistance design codes and construction methods. The United States Fire Administration seeks through education and research programs to lower loss of life and property because of fire. FEMA maintains the National Emergency Training Center in Emmitsburg, Maryland, which conducts education programs in hazard mitigation, emergency preparedness, fire prevention and control, disaster response, and long-term disaster recovery. There are ten FEMA regional offices nationwide. Each office is headed by a regional director who reports to the FEMA director and is responsible for all FEMA programs in the region.

Federal Home Loan Bank Board

The Federal Home Loan Bank board is an independent agency responsible for all federal regulation of the thrift industry. The board is one of three components of the Federal Home Loan Bank System and adopts the policies and regulations that guide the system. The other elements of the bank system are the twelve regional (district) federal home loan banks and the individual savings institutions that make up the thrift industry.

The bank system originated with the Federal Home Loan Bank Act passed by Congress in 1932. The act was a response to the Great Depression, which had undermined the nation's banking system and created a need for a reserve credit system to ensure the availability of funds for home financing.

The bank board comprises a governing panel that makes policy and an independent federal agency that carries out board policy in regulating, monitoring, and supervising the bank system. The board panel is composed of three members appointed by the president and confirmed by the Senate to four-year terms. The president designates one member of the panel as chair. Board members serve at the discretion of the president, and no more than two board members may belong to the same political party. An incoming president can appoint a new chair at any time.

The board members meet in formal session as often as necessary and adopt or amend regulations affecting the thrift industry and individual thrift institutions. The board also decides when to close or merge failing institutions, directs the policy of the Federal Savings and Loan Insurance Corporation (FSLIC), and regulates the twelve district banks. The bank board also governs the Federal Home Loan Mortgage Corporation, which operates a secondary or resale market for conventional home mortgages or mortgages not insured by a federal agency.

The agency is self-supporting, and its operating costs are paid from a U.S. Treasury account funded by assessments on the twelve district banks and by assessments on the FSLIC. The board creates new savings institutions by granting federal charters, grants new FSLIC deposit insurance, directs how associations must keep their books, and invests assets.

The district banks operate within guidelines established by the bank board and assist in carrying out the board's responsibilities. Each district bank is wholly owned by the member thrift institutions in its area. The banks are located throughout the United States and provide thrifts with additional funds and services. Certain district bank employees are empowered by the bank board to act as the board's agents, examining thrift institutions and supervising corrective measures when problems are found.

The bank system's third component consists of its member thrift institutions, which number more than three thousand. The majority of these institutions are savings and loan associations, and one-half of these are federally chartered and thus subject to all bank board regulations. State-chartered thrift institutions that carry FSLIC insurance are subject to some regulation by the bank board in addition to state regulations. Other bank board regulations apply to all members of the bank system.

Federal Labor Relations Authority

The Federal Labor Relations Authority (FLRA) is an independent agency established to administer Title VII of the Civil Service Reform Act of 1978. The FLRA is chartered to serve as a neutral third party in the resolution of labor-management disputes arising among unions, employees, and federal agencies. The FLRA is charged with resolution of labor-managements disputes among all employees, both U.S. citizens and foreign nationals of the Panama Canal area.

The authority comprises three full-time members appointed by the president with Senate confirmation and removable only for cause. Not more than two members may be of the same political party, and one member is designated by the president to serve as chair. Members serve staggered five-year terms, and an incoming president can appoint a new chair. The president also appoints a general counsel to a term of five years. The general counsel has direct responsibility for the investigation of alleged unfair labor practices and the filing and prosecuting of complaints.

The Federal Service Impasses Panel is an entity within the FLRA whose function is to assist in resolving negotiation impasses between agencies and unions. If the parties are unable to reach a settlement after assistance from the panel, the panel may hold hearings and take whatever action it deems necessary to resolve the impasse. The panel consists of a chairman and six other members appointed by the president. The panel is not bipartisan by law, and members serve five-year terms.

Specifically, the FLRA is empowered to determine the appropriateness of organizations representing federal employees. The authority supervises or conducts elections of labor organizations by employees and sets criteria for representation of national federal labor organizations. The authority also conducts hearings to resolve complaints of unfair labor practices and exceptions to awards granted by federal arbitrators.

Federal Maritime Commission

The Federal Maritime Commission (FMC) is an independent regulatory agency established by executive order in 1961 to replace the Federal Maritime Board as regulator of the ocean commerce of the United States. The order abolished the board and transferred its responsibility for promoting the nation's merchant marine to the Transportation Department's Maritime Administration.

The FMC has five members who are appointed by the president with Senate confirmation. No more than three of the commissioners may be members of the same political party. The president designates one of the commissioners to serve as chair at the president's discretion. Members serve five-year terms.

The FMC consists of six offices directly responsible to the chair: the offices of the managing director, the secretary, equal employment opportunity, policy planning and international affairs, the general counsel, and administrative law judges. Six bureaus report to the director of programs and are responsible for trade monitoring, domestic regulation, economic analysis, hearing investigations, and administration.

As required by the Shipping Acts of 1916 and 1984, the commission regulates the rates charged for shipping in domestic commerce, monitors the rates in foreign commerce, and licenses ocean freight forwarders. The commission also regulates the formation by shipping companies of rate-setting cartels (conferences) that would otherwise be in violation of antitrust statutes (the ocean carrier conferences were exempted from antitrust laws by both acts).

Other responsibilities of the FMC include review of rates filed by common carriers and investigation of charges of discriminatory practices in ocean commerce. The commission does not have the authority to approve or disapprove general rate increases or individual commodity rates in U.S. foreign commerce except for certain foreign government-owned carriers. Charges of discriminatory treatment are investigated and resolved by administrative proceedings conducted by FMC staff.

Federal Mediation and Conciliation Service

The Federal Mediation and Conciliation Service (FMCS) is an independent federal agency created to prevent and to minimize labor-management disputes having a significant effect on interstate commerce or national defense. Created by the Labor-Management Relations Act of 1947 (also known as the Taft-Hartley Act), FMCS is headed by a director who is appointed by the president with Senate confirmation. The director serves an indefinite term at the discretion of the president. An incoming president can appoint a new director at any time.

The FMCS objective is to prevent or minimize work stoppages by providing free mediation to labor-management disputes in both the public and private sectors of the economy. Collective bargaining, mediation, and voluntary arbitration are the processes encouraged by FMCS mediations for settling labor-management issues. FMCS does not mediate labor-management disputes in the railroad and airline industries, which fall under the jurisdiction of the National Mediation Board.

The Labor-Management Relations Act requires parties to notify FMCS thirty days before a contract termination or modification date so that mediation services may be proffered. If, in the opinion of the president, a threatened or actual strike may imperil the national health or safety, a board of inquiry, appointed from an agency list of arbitrators, may be appointed to submit a report on the dispute. After receiving the report, the president can seek to enjoin the strike for not more than eighty days.

FMCS offers five types of technical assistance programs: Labor Management Committees, training, Relationship by Objectives, consultation/liaison, and conferences and seminars. Labor Management Committees are cooperative efforts by disputing parties directed at improving specific work site problems, including safety and health, organization of work quality, productivity, and absenteeism. The committees also address common issues such as worker training and retraining and introduction of new technology.

Relationship by Objectives programs are usually implemented only when labor-management relations have deteriorated to the point that negotiators face difficulty proceeding. In these programs FMCS mediators attempt to analyze and restructure existing labor-management relationships and determine objectives agreeable to both parties.

Parties having disputes under collective bargaining agreements fall under the responsibility of the FMCS Division of Arbitration Services. FMCS maintains a roster of qualified private citizens experienced in the collective bargaining process. Upon request, FMCS will furnish a panel of these arbitrators from which the parties select the one most mutually acceptable to hear and provide a final decision on their particular dispute. In most cases a panel of arbitrators is provided only on joint request of the disputing parties.

To encourage cooperation among disputing parties FMCS regulations provide that information obtained by mediators in the course of the duties shall not be subsequently revealed in judicial, arbitrable, or administrative hearings. The Labor-Management Cooperation Act of 1978 empowered FMCS to provide financial assistance to eligible applicants for the establishment and operation of labor-management committees. The committees focus on such issues as enhancing labor relations, improving economic development, and increasing productivity.

Federal Reserve System

The Federal Reserve System (the "Fed") is an independent regulatory and monetary policy-making agency established by the Federal Reserve Act in 1913. The Fed is the nation's central bank and is charged with making and administering policy for the nation's credit and monetary affairs. It also has supervisory and regulatory power over banking in general and over state-chartered banks that are members of the system.

By buying and selling government securities, it influences the supply of credit and the level of interest rates, in turn strongly affecting the pace of economic activity and the overall price level. The Fed also regulates credit activities, collects economic data, and oversees the activities of bank holding companies.

The Fed consists of five major parts: the board of Governors, the Federal Open Market Committee, the twelve Federal Reserve banks, the Federal Advisory Council, and the member banks of the system. The Fed is administered by a board of seven governors who are nominated by the president and confirmed by the Senate. Governors are appointed to a single fourteen-year term. One member is designated by the president to serve as chair for a four-year term and can be reappointed. All appointees serve at the pleasure of the president.

The board's primary function is the formulation of monetary policy. It has authority to approve proposed changes in the discount rate, to change reserve requirements, to set margin requirements for financing of securities traded on national security exchanges, and to set maximum interest rates on time and savings deposits of its member banks.

The Federal Open Market Committee (FMOC) is composed of seven board members plus the president of the New York Reserve Bank. Four other voting positions rotate among the eleven remaining Reserve bank presidents. The committee establishes the extent to which the Fed buys and sells government and other securities. Purchases and sales of securities in the open market are undertaken to supply the credit and money needed for long-term economic growth, to offset cyclical economic swings, and to accommodate seasonal demands of businesses and consumers for money and credit. The committee also oversees the system's operations in foreign exchange markets.

The operations of the Fed are conducted through a nationwide network of twelve Federal Reserve banks and twenty-five branches. Each Reserve bank is an incorporated institution with its own board of directors. Under supervision of the Board of Governors, they determine interest rates the bank may charge on short-term collateral loans to member banks and on any loans extended to nonmember institutions.

The Federal Advisory Council consists of one member from each of the Federal Reserve districts. The council meets in Washington, D.C., at least four times a year. It confers with the Board of Governors on economic and banking matters and makes recommendations regarding the affairs of the system.

The Fed receives no funding from Congress. Interest

paid on government securities purchased by the Fed constitutes about 94 percent of the Fed's earnings. In addition, the Fed earns money from the fees it charges for its services, from interest on its discount window loans, and from its foreign currency operations.

Federal Retirement Thrift Investment Board

The Federal Retirement Thrift Investment Board is an independent agency responsible for establishing policies for the investments, management, and administration of the Thrift Savings Plan (TSP) for federal employees. Created by the Federal Employees' Retirement System Act of 1986, the board consists of five part-time members who are appointed by the president with consent of the Senate. The president designates one member as chair. A sixth member is appointed by the board as executive director, responsible for the management of the agency and TSP.

The board operates TSP solely for the benefit of the participants and their beneficiaries. Investments in the plan and earnings on those investments cannot be used for any other purpose. The plan is a tax-deferred retirement savings and investment plan chartered by Congress to provide federal employees with the same savings and tax benefits that many private corporations offer their employees. Because TSP is a defined contribution plan, the amount employees and their agencies may contribute to an account is established by law. Plan benefits are determined by the amount contributed and the earnings on the contributions. TSP is one of the three parts of the Federal Employees' Retirement System (FERS). FERS employees may invest up to 10 percent of their salary and are eligible for up to 5 percent in employer matching contributions.

The plan began operation on April 1, 1987, with $148 million invested in retirement savings accounts for 563,000 federal and postal employees. As of September 1988 thrift savings fund investments totaled $2.2 billion with 1.3 million participants.

Federal Trade Commission

The Federal Trade Commission (FTC) is an independent agency created to regulate interstate commerce in the United States. The FTC is headed by five commissioners who are nominated by the president and confirmed by the Senate for seven-year terms. One commissioner is designated chair by the president, and no more than three of the commissioners may be members of the same political party. Commissioners are removable only for cause. The chair serves at the discretion of the president but remains a commissioner if removed as head of the commission. An incoming president can appoint a new chair at any time.

Established in 1914 by the Federal Trade Commission Act, the FTC was created to act as the federal government's chief trustbuster. That same year, Congress passed the Clayton Antitrust Act, giving the FTC broad powers to define and prohibit unfair methods of competition and specific business activities tending to lessen competition or create monopolies. Consumer protection was added to the FTC's responsibilities in 1938 through passage of the Wheeler-Lea Amendment to the original FTC act.

In 1974, the Magnuson-Moss Warranty/Federal Trade Commission Improvement Act empowered the FTC to issue trade regulation rules (TRR). TRRs have the force of law and can apply to an entire industry or only to industries in a specific geographical region. The Bureau of Competition handles investigations and actions related to anticompetitive behavior. The Bureau of Consumer Protection handles consumer issues and problems.

Once the FTC determines that a company has engaged in illegal activities, it either negotiates an agreement with the company voluntarily to stop the practice, or it initiates adjudicative proceedings to order the practice stopped. The FTC also can order violators to make restitution to consumers harmed by their actions.

At the request of a business or an individual, the FTC may issue an advisory opinion on whether a practice violates FTC restrictions. The opinions define the limits of the law as they relate to that particular business practice. Advisory opinions may be overturned by the commission, which then must give the individual or business originally affected by the opinion a reasonable amount of time to alter practices to conform to the new ruling.

In complaints alleging anticompetitive or anti-consumer practices, the FTC initiates adjudicative proceedings. Before beginning a proceeding, the FTC conducts an investigation to determine whether charges of illegal behavior should be brought. The party charged is notified and given thirty days to respond to the complaint. If the respondent decides not to dispute the charge, the illegal practice must be stopped. The respondent also may dispute the charge in a hearing before an administrative law judge. If a respondent fails to comply with an FTC cease-and-desist order or TRR, the commission can obtain a court order imposing a penalty of $10,000 a day for each rule or order the respondent ignores. Further failure to comply can result in contempt-of-court charges.

The FTC operates an outreach program to apprise businesses of laws and regulations. The commission also publishes pamphlets and other materials for consumers to warn them of fraudulent practices and to inform them of their rights under the law.

General Services Administration

The General Services Administration (GSA) is an independent central management agency responsible for federal procurement, property, and telecommunications services. Established in 1949, GSA, with more than twenty-four thousand employees nationwide, services congressional, judicial, and executive agencies and many of their international facilities. GSA's principle components are the Federal Supply Service (FSS), the Federal Property Resources Service (FPRS), the Public Buildings Service (PBS), and the Office of Information Resources Management (OIRM). The director of GSA is appointed by and serves at the pleasure of the president.

The Federal Supply Service purchases and distributes goods and services for government use. Goods include office supplies, industrial items, and scientific and medical equipment. Services supplied by GSA include use of prenegotiated contracts for freight and household moves and for maintenance and repair of government items. FSS controls a fleet management system consisting of eleven centralized, computerized maintenance and repair control centers across the country. The system oversees GSA's motor pool of eighty-five thousand vehicles and manages the government's federal travel program.

The Federal Property Resources Service sells surplus government land, buildings, and other materials or distributes those items between federal agencies. Unneeded real property can be donated to state and local governments. FRPS also controls the emergency stockpiles of strategic and critical materials. GSA manages the stockpile under the policy guidance of the Federal Emergency Management Agency.

Federal workspace is controlled by the Public Buildings Service, which functions as owner, developer, and property manager of federal work sites, including office buildings, laboratories, and warehouses. PBS provides space by constructing new buildings, purchasing existing buildings, or leasing workspace.

The Office of Information Resources Management combines several previously separate GSA organizations. OIRM provides federal agencies with products and services covering telecommunications, data processing, office automation, and information management. The GSA-run Federal Telecommunications System is the largest private phone system in the world.

GSA also assists other federal agencies in developing acquisition policies. In conjunction with the Department of Defense and the National Aeronautics and Space Administration, GSA developed the Federal Acquisition Regulation, the primary regulation used by all executive agencies for procuring supplies and services.

GSA also issues the Federal Information Resources Management Regulations governing telecommunications, automated data processing, and records management. GSA operates Business Services Centers in twelve major cities across the country to provide information to anyone interested in doing business with the federal government. Public inquiries are handled by GSA Federal Information Centers. Federal publications are promoted and distributed to the public by the GSA's Consumer Information Center in Pueblo, Colorado.

Inter-American Foundation

The Inter-American Foundation (IAF) is an independent government corporation established to promote assistance programs in Latin America and the Caribbean. Created in 1969, the IAF was granted authority to conduct its affairs independently of other U.S. foreign policy agencies. The IAF is based in Rosslyn, Virginia, and is governed by a nine-member board of directors appointed by the president and confirmed by the Senate. Six members of the board are drawn from the private sector and three from the government. The president appoints one member as chair. All members of the board can be removed for neglect of duty or malfeasance but for no other reason.

The IAF supports local and private development efforts through grants and educational programs. The majority of IAF grants go to grass-roots organizations such as agricultural cooperatives, community associations, and small urban enterprises. Other grants are awarded to large organizations that work with local groups, providing credit, technical assistance, training, and marketing services. Funding comes from congressional appropriations and the Social Progress Trust Fund administered by the Inter-American Development Bank.

The IAF awards fellowships to doctoral and masters degree candidates at U.S. universities to conduct field work on grass-roots development issues. Fellowships also are awarded to scholars from Latin America and the Caribbean wishing to study development issues at U.S. universities. In 1986 the IAF inaugurated an Office of Learning and Dissemination to document and evaluate projects conducted through IAF grants. The office's findings are made available through seminars and conferences. In addition, the IAF publishes a quarterly journal in three languages, which reports on projects and issues affecting IAF countries.

Interstate Commerce Commission

The Interstate Commerce Commission (ICC) is an independent federal agency responsible for regulating interstate surface transportation within the United States. Established by the Interstate Commerce Act of 1887, the ICC is the nation's oldest independent regulatory agency. The ICC was created to regulate the rapidly expanding railroad industry and in the ensuing years assumed responsibility for the burgeoning trucking industry.

During the 1970s and early 1980s Congress passed legislation aimed at deregulating the transportation industry. The new legislation greatly reduced the budget and responsibilities of the commission and the number of commissioners was reduced from seven to five. The commissioners are appointed by the president with Senate confirmation to five-year terms. No more than three commissioners can be of the same political party. The chair, who is designated by the president and serves at the pleasure of the president, coordinates and organizes the commission's work and acts as its representative in legislative matters.

The ICC maintains jurisdiction over for-hire companies providing surface transportation in the United States. Companies regulated by the ICC include interstate railroads, trucks, buses, household movers, some inland water carriers, freight forwarders, transportation brokers, and commodity pipelines that carry resources other than oil, water, or natural gas. Not falling under ICC jurisdiction are domestic and international air traffic, ships in international trade, oil and gas pipelines, and transportation companies that operate entirely within a single state.

The ICC has authority to settle controversies over rates and charges among competing and similar modes of transportation and shippers and receivers of freight. In addition, the ICC rules upon applications for mergers, consolidations, and acquisitions and approves the sale of carriers.

Businesses entering interstate transportation must obtain operating authority from the ICC specifying routes that may be served and types of freight to be handled. Authority is granted on a temporary or permanent basis depending on need. A carrier may apply to purchase existing authority from another carrier.

Carriers operating under ICC authority are required to file with the commission a tariff schedule, or lists of rates and charges, which must be adhered to by law. The ICC cannot set rates charged by carriers but can approve or disapprove rate schedules filed by companies. If rates are challenged, or if the ICC on its own determines they are unfair, it can suspend their effectiveness pending an investigation and hearing. If for any reason the rates are found to be unlawful, the commission can order them canceled. If a carrier fails to comply, the commission may ask for a court order enforcing the rulings. Further failure to comply may result in civil or criminal penalties.

Cases requiring a formal proceeding are heard by ICC administrative law judges. Upon completion of formal hearings and arguments the administrative law judge may issue an initial report, which may be appealed to the commission. Informal cases or "modified procedures" are those with limited or no opposition and are presided over by the ICC's Office of Proceedings. Decisions of the Office of Proceedings may be appealed to the commission.

The ICC has special responsibilities in several fields of transportation. The agency's Rail Services Planning Office oversees the restructuring of sections of the railroad network and allows railroads greater flexibility in adjusting their rates. In addition, the agency sets guidelines and rules to ensure that fair prices are charged by household movers and that customers are aware of legal protections.

Legal Services Corporation

The Legal Services Corporation (LSC) is a nonprofit, independent organization established by Congress to provide financial support for legal assistance in noncriminal matters to persons unable to afford such assistance. Established by the Legal Services Corporation Act of 1974, the LSC assumed responsibility for the nation's legal services program from the Office of Economic Opportunity. The creation of the LSC was an attempt by Congress to depoliticize the provision of legal services. LSC was chartered as a private corporation with a bipartisan board and with restrictions on lobbying and political advocacy. Funding for LSC is provided by Congress and by outside sources, such as interest earned on participating lawyers' trust accounts.

In keeping with its independent status, LSC officers and employees are not considered officers and employees of the federal government. LSC financial statements are audited by an independent firm of certified public accountants and included in the corporation's annual report, which is submitted to Congress. The LSC is governed by an eleven-member board of directors appointed by the president with Senate confirmation. Board members serve three-year terms and can be removed only for cause. By law no more that six members may be of the same political party. The board selects a chair from among its members by a vote of seven or more directors.

The board is authorized to provide financial assistance to qualified programs furnishing legal assistance to eligible clients. The maximum income level prescribed by the corporation for eligible clients is 125 percent of the official poverty threshold. Each program's board of directors, taking local living costs into account, sets its own financial eligibility standards for clients and cannot go beyond the corporation level without LSC approval. Eligibility is determined primarily by family income, fixed debts and obligations, medical bills, child care expenses, liquid and nonliquid assets, and seasonal income variations.

The corporation is responsible for ensuring that recipient programs provide services efficiently and effectively and that all recipients comply with the Legal Services Corporation Act, the terms of appropriations bills, and all rules and regulations issued by the corporation. Oversight of recipient programs is provided by advisory councils established in each state. Each state's advisory council consists of nine members appointed by the governor from among the attorneys admitted to practice in the state. The advisory council is charged with notifying the LSC of any apparent violation of the provisions of the LSC act.

Merit Systems Protection Board

The Merit Systems Protection Board (MSPB) is an independent quasi-judicial agency created to safeguard against partisan politics in federal merit systems and to protect employees against unlawful abuses by agency management. The board was established in 1979 by the Civil Service Reform Act of 1978. The act abolished the Civil Service Commission and divided its responsibilities among the MSPB, the Office of Personnel Management (OPM), and the Federal Labor Relations Authority. In addition to its Washington, D.C., headquarters, the board maintains regional offices in eleven major cities around the country.

Operating under bipartisan leadership, the board consists of a chair, a vice-chair, and one other member. No more than two of its three members may be from the same political party. Board members are appointed by the president with Senate confirmation and serve overlapping, nonrenewable, seven-year terms. An independent special counsel to the board is also appointed by the president with Senate confirmation to a five-year term. Both the special counsel and the board members may be removed only for inefficiency, neglect of duty, or malfeasance in office. The chair can be removed by the president without cause but remains a board member unless cause for dismissal is shown.

The Reform Act established merit system principles for federal employment that include the selection and promotion of employees based on merit, through fair, open competition and equal pay for work of equal value in the private sector. In addition, the principles guarantee employee constitutional rights, protection for whistle-blowers, and rights of privacy. The Reform Act also outlines a number of prohibited personnel practices, including discrimination and coercion of an employee to participate in political activities.

The board hears and decides appeals brought by employees concerning agency actions and reviews cases of discrimination. The board also reviews employment regulations established by OPM to determine if they conflict with established personnel principles and cases brought by the special counsel, who investigates prohibited personnel practices such as reprisals against whistle-blowers and violations of the Freedom of Information Act. Discrimination complaints that do not involve adverse actions, such as removal, demotion, or suspension of more than fourteen days, go to the Equal Employment Opportunity Commission. Cases involving examination ratings and classification decisions are reviewed by the Office of Personnel Management.

The board conducts special studies of particular merit systems to measure compliance with established principles. If the board finds an agency in violation of the Reform Act the agency has fifteen days to show evidence of compliance, a schedule for full compliance, and a statement of actions completed, in progress, or remaining.

National Aeronautics and Space Administration

After the Soviet Union launched Sputnik I, the world's first artificial satellite, on October 4, 1957, Congress and the administration of President Dwight D. Eisenhower agreed to combine the government's existing individual space efforts into one agency, which would manage the national space program. The National Aeronautics and Space Act of 1958 created the National Aeronautics and Space Administration (NASA), a civilian agency chartered to exercise control over U.S. aeronautical and space activities.

NASA is headed by an administrator who is charged with responsibility for all functions and authorities assigned to the agency. The administrator is appointed by the president with Senate confirmation to an indefinite term and serves at the pleasure of the president. The NASA Advisory Council advises the NASA administrator on the agency's aeronautics and space plans, programs, and issues. Council members are chosen by the administrator from the scientific community to serve at the pleasure of the administrator.

The problem of launch vehicles occupied much attention in NASA's first years, and on January 31, 1958, the first American satellite, *Explorer 1,* went into orbit. On April 12, 1961, however, the Soviet Union achieved the first successful manned space mission. NASA responded on May 5, 1961, with the *Freedom 7* Mercury spacecraft. On May 25, 1961, President John F. Kennedy addressed a joint session of Congress and called for a national goal of "landing a man on the moon and returning him safely to Earth" within a decade. The U.S. manned space program continued with the Gemini series in 1965-1966, and on July 20, 1969, *Apollo 11* completed the first successful manned flight to the moon.

In addition to space flight, NASA is responsible for many other scientific research programs, including studies in the fields of space science, aeronautics, solar system and planetary science, astrophysics, life science, and earth science. NASA employs more than twenty-two thousand people in fourteen space flight centers, research centers, and other installations throughout the United States.

The agency's Washington, D.C., headquarters determines programs and projects, establishes management policies, procedures, and performance criteria, evaluates progress, and reviews and analyzes the agency's aerospace program.

Following the explosion of the space shuttle *Challenger,* a presidential committee organized to study the accident issued a report recommending nine changes in the agency's organization and operations. The recommendations included creating an office of Safety, Reliability, Maintainability and Quality Assurance, which would report directly to the administrator. Three separate committees of the National Research Council were organized to provide oversight of space shuttle redesign efforts, including redesign and testing of the shuttle's booster rocket O-rings, whose failure was determined to be the cause of the *Challenger* explosion.

National Archives and Records Administration

The National Archives and Records Administration is responsible for identifying, preserving, and making available to the federal government and to the people of the United States all forms of government records not restricted by law that have been determined to have sufficient historical, informational, or evidential value to warrant being preserved.

The National Archives was first established as an independent agency in 1934. In 1949 the archives was incorporated into the newly established General Services Administration and renamed the National Archives and Records Service. In 1984 Congress once again established the archives as an independent agency renaming it the National Archives and Records Administration.

The archives is headed by the archivist of the United States, who is appointed by the president with Senate confirmation to no fixed term. The archivist can be removed only for cause. In addition to the agency's regular staff, the archives' major organizational elements are the offices of Management and Administration, the National Archives, Public Programs, Records Administration, Federal Register, Presidential Libraries, and Federal Records Centers.

Daily operations of the archives are managed by the office of Management and Administration. The office's responsibilities include the agency's budget, property, personnel, and security and safety management.

The office of the National Archives oversees the reference and maintenance of permanently valuable records in the National Archives in Washington, D.C., and eleven field branches throughout the country.

The Public Programs office oversees public outreach programs that include distribution of audiovisual materials, workshops, lectures, exhibitions, volunteers, ceremonial events, and publications such as *Prologue,* the quarterly journal of the National Archives.

The office of Records Administration determines the appropriate disposition of all federal records including those produced by federal agencies. These records include microforms, maps, charts, drawings, photographs, motion pictures, sound recordings, and electronic and paper records. The office reviews the retention periods proposed by each agency for its documents and determines how documents will be handled once they are no longer held by the agencies.

The Records Administration office also indentifies records of continuing value to be preserved in the National Archives. These records may document the organization, policies, and activities of the federal government or contain information of high research value.

The office of the Federal Register publishes the official text of laws, administrative regulations, and presidential documents. It publishes the daily *Federal Register,* the *Code of Federal Regulations,* the *United States Government Manual,* the *Weekly Compilation of Presidential Documents,* the *Public Papers of the Presidents,* and the *Codification of the Presidential Proclamations and Executive Orders.* The office also is responsible for publication of slip laws, the *United States Statutes at Large,* and the *Privacy Act Compilation,* and it ensures the accuracy of the official count of electoral college votes for president and vice president.

As of 1988, the office of Presidential Libraries maintained nine presidential libraries and museums dedicated to preserving and displaying records of presidents Herbert C. Hoover, Franklin D. Roosevelt, Harry S Truman, Dwight D. Eisenhower, John F. Kennedy, Lyndon B. Johnson, Richard Nixon, Gerald R. Ford, and Jimmy Carter.

The current estimate of the holdings in the National Archives is 1.5 million cubic feet of records, not including records held by the presidential libraries. Archive records include 3 billion paper documents, 91 million feet of motion pictures, 5.2 million still photographs, 1.6 million maps, 173,000 video and sound recordings, 9.7 million aerial photographs, and 3,600 reels of computer tape.

National Capital Planning Commission

The National Capital Planning Commission (NCPC) is the central development planning agency for the federal government in the Washington area. Established in 1924 as a park planning agency, NCPC's role was expanded under the National Capital Planning Act of 1952 to include central planning for the federal and District of Columbia governments. In 1973, the National Capital Planning Act was amended by the D.C. Home Rule Act, which made the mayor of the District of Columbia the chief planner for the District.

NCPC prepares the federal components of the Comprehensive Plan for the National Capital (the District of Columbia and federal property within the region), which is a statement of goals, policies, and guidelines for the future development of the national capital. In addition to work facilities for federal employees, historic preservation, and parks within the region, NCPC is responsible for reviewing plans for all new federal buildings in the area. NCPC also prepares and submits annually to the Office of Management and Budget a five-year Federal Capital Improvements Program that contains land acquisitions and development proposals from all federal agencies. NCPC planning activities cover the national capital region, which includes the District of Columbia and Prince George's and Montgomery counties in Maryland, and Arlington, Fairfax, Prince William, and Loudoun counties in Virginia.

The commission consists of five appointed and seven ex officio members. Three citizen members are appointed by the president and two by the mayor of the District of Columbia. Presidential appointees include one resident from Maryland and Virginia and one from anywhere in the United States. The two mayoral appointees must be District residents. Ex officio members include the secretaries of defense and interior, administrator of the General Services Administration, the D.C. mayor, chair of the D.C. city council, chair of the Senate Committee on Governmental Affairs, and chair of the House Committee on the District of Columbia. The president designates a chair from among the twelve members.

National Credit Union Administration

The National Credit Union Administration (NCUA) is an independent agency created to regulate the nation's federal credit unions. NCUA approves or disapproves applications for federal credit union charters and examines federal credit unions to determine their financial condition. NCUA issues charters to credit unions whose applications are approved and supervises credit union activities.

Established by a 1970 amendment to the Federal Credit Union Act of 1934, NCUA is based in Washington, D.C., and maintains six regional offices nationwide. Before 1970, administration of the original Federal Credit Union Act was shifted among several federal agencies. The Financial Institutions Regulatory and Interest Rate Control Act of 1978 reorganized NCUA and replaced the agency's single administrator with a three-member governing board. Board members are appointed by the president with Senate confirmation to six-year terms. The president designates one member to serve as chair, and not more than two members may be of the same political party. Board members can be removed only for cause. An incoming president may, however, appoint another member as chair.

A credit union is a cooperative association designed to promote thrift among its members. Membership in a credit union is limited to persons having a common bond of occupation or association and to groups within a well-defined neighborhood, community, or rural district. The credit union accumulates a fund from savings to make loans to members for useful purposes at reasonable interest rates. Credit unions are managed by a board of directors and committees made up of members of the credit union. After expenses and legal reserve requirements are met, most of the earnings of a credit union are returned to the members in the form of dividends on share holdings. There are two types of credit unions: federal credit unions, chartered by NCUA, and state credit unions, chartered by state agencies. In 1987 the federal credit union system consisted of 9,566 credit unions with total assets of $104 billion.

Federal credit unions pay an annual operating fee to NCUA and provide the agency with financial reports at least annually. NCUA also regulates the operations of the Central Liquidity Facility (the central bank for loans) and administers the National Credit Union Share Insurance Fund (NCUSIF). All federally chartered credit unions are insured by NCUSIF, which was authorized in 1970. Insurance coverage for member accounts was increased from $40,000 to $100,000 in 1980. The fund also insures member accounts in 60 percent of state-chartered credit unions.

National Foundation on the Arts and Humanities

The National Foundation on the Arts and the Humanities is an independent agency established by Congress in 1965 to promote progress and scholarship in the humanities and the arts in the United States. The foundation consists of the National Endowment for the Arts, the National Endowment for the Humanities, the Federal Council on the Arts and the Humanities, and the Institute of Museum Services.

Each endowment is itself an independent agency and is governed by its own council comprising a chair and twenty-six members who are appointed to four-year terms by the president with Senate confirmation. Council members, chosen for their expertise in the arts or humanities, advise the chair on policies and procedures and review applications for financial support. Members can be removed only for cause.

The National Endowment for the Arts was created to support American arts and artists. The endowment awards matching grants to nonprofit, tax-exempt arts organizations of outstanding quality and both matching and nonmatching fellowships to artists of exceptional talent. By law, the agency also provides a minimum of 20 percent of its program funds in matching grants to state arts agencies and to regional arts organizations. Programs receiving endowment funds include dance, design arts, folk arts, literature, media arts, music, opera-musical theater, theater, and visual arts. Funding of endowment programs is guided by advisory panels of private citizens who are artists or recognized experts in their particular field. The council reviews the panel decisions and makes final recommendations on grants and policy to the chair. The endowment budget for fiscal year 1987 was more than $165 million.

The National Endowment for the Humanities was created to support research, education, and public programs in the humanities. According to the legislation that created the endowment, the term *humanities* includes, but is not limited to, the study of history, philosophy, languages, linguistics, literature, archaeology, jurisprudence, comparative religion, ethics, the social sciences that employ historical or philosophical methods, and the history, criticism, and theory of arts. The endowment provides grants through five divisions—Education Programs, Fellowships and Seminars, General Programs, Research Programs, and State Programs—and two offices, the Office of Challenge Grants and Office of Preservation. The 1986 budget for the National Endowment for the Humanities was $134.7 million.

The Federal Council on the Arts and Humanities consists of twenty members, including the two endowment chairs and the director of the Institute of Museum Services. Membership is made up of heads of federal agencies whose service with the council is determined by their agency position. The council is designed to coordinate the activities of the two endowments and related programs of other federal agencies. The Institute of Museum Services is an independent agency established by Congress in 1976 to assist museums in maintaining, increasing, and improving their services to the public. The institute makes grants to museums subject to policy directives and priorities set by the National Museum Services Board. The board comprises fifteen nonvoting members appointed by the president with Senate confirmation to indefinite terms, and four ex officio, nonvoting members. Members serve at the discretion of the president.

National Labor Relations Board

The National Labor Relations Board (NLRB) is an independent federal agency created in 1935 to administer the National Labor Relations Act (the Wagner act), the nation's principal labor relations law. NLRB has five board members including a chair who are appointed by the president, with Senate confirmation, to staggered five-year terms. The board also has a general counsel who is appointed to a four-year term. By law the board is bipartisan, and the president can reappoint or remove members for neglect of duty or malfeasance in office, but for no other cause.

As chief administrator of the National Labor Relations Act, NLRB seeks to reduce interruptions in commerce caused by industrial strife. In its statutory assignment, NLRB determines and implements, through secret-ballot elections, the choice of employees whether to be represented by a union and, if so, by which one. The act also is intended to prevent unfair labor practices by either employers or unions. It outlaws practices such as interference with employees' freedom to organize and bargain collectively, domination of unions, antiunion discrimination, and refusal to bargain. In 1947, the Taft-Hartley Act added prohibitions against various union practices such as intimidation of employees and restraint or coercion of neutral employers. In 1959, the act was again amended, and steps were taken to eliminate gaps between federal and state jurisdiction in labor relations disputes.

The five-member board acts primarily as a quasi-judicial body in deciding cases brought before it by one of its thirty-three regional offices or sixteen field offices throughout the country. The general counsel is responsible for the investigations and prosecution of charges of violations of the act. NLRB does not bring action on its own but responds to charges or petitions filed by employees or employers.

Charges are initially investigated by regional or field office staff who then determine whether formal proceedings are warranted. If so, the parties involved are encouraged to reach a voluntary settlement. If the case cannot be settled, a formal complaint is issued and the case is heard before an NLRB administrative law judge. The administrative law judge's decision may be appealed to the board; if left unchallenged, it becomes the order of the board. In cases of representation disputes, the thirty-three regional directors are authorized to process all petitions, rule on contested issues, and direct elections or dismiss the request. Actions of the regional directors are subject to review by the board on limited grounds.

Since its establishment, NLRB has processed more than 350,000 cases alleging unfair labor practices and has conducted more than 250,000 secret-ballot employee self-determination elections.

National Mediation Board

The National Mediation Board (NMB) is an independent agency that governs collective bargaining and representation disputes in the airlines and railroads as prescribed by the Railway Labor Act of 1926. Established in 1934, the NMB comprises three members appointed by the president with Senate confirmation. Members serve staggered three-year terms, and not more than two members may be of the same political party. The position of chair, which is decided by the board, rotates annually among the three members. Board members serve at the pleasure of the president.

The NMB administers the Railway Labor Act, the oldest extant labor relations statute in the United States. The act is intended to maintain a free flow of commerce in the railroad and airline industries and to ensure the right of employees to organize and bargain collectively through representatives of their own choosing. Originally enacted to cover only the railroad industry, the act was extended in 1936 to include the nation's airlines.

The NMB is the only federal labor relations agency authorized to handle both mediation and representation disputes. Since its inception the board has resolved more than fifty-five hundred representation issues and nearly twelve thousand rail and air mediation cases. The board mediates contract disputes between employees and the carriers over wages, rules, and working conditions. These are known as "major disputes." When negotiations reach a stalemate, either party may request mediation by the board, or the board may intervene in negotiations at its own initiative. Once the NMB becomes involved in a dispute, the status quo must be maintained until the board decides to release the parties from negotiations. If the NMB is unsuccessful in its mediation efforts, the disputing parties are urged to submit to voluntary arbitration for final and binding settlement. If arbitration is rejected by either party, a thirty-day "cooling-off" period begins during which the parties must continue to maintain the status quo and refrain from self help. If the dispute continues and threatens to interrupt interstate commerce and deprive sections of the country of essential transportation services, the NMB can notify the president who may then appoint an emergency board. The president's board has thirty days to investigate the dispute and report its findings, which are nonbinding. If either side rejects the findings, neither party may act, except to reach an agreement, for thirty more days. If after that time an agreement still has not been reached, the parties are then legally free to act.

Representation disputes involving labor organizations and railroad or airline employees also fall under NMB jurisdiction. The board is authorized to determine the appropriate crafts or classes of rail or airline employees and to designate an employee representative through secret ballot among the employees or through other appropriate methods.

The National Railroad Adjustment Board in Chicago is authorized by the NMB to mediate "minor disputes," which are disagreements over the interpretation and applications of existing contracts between individual carriers and employees.

National Railroad Passenger Corporation (Amtrak)

The National Railroad Passenger Corporation (Amtrak) is an operating railroad corporation whose capital assets are owned by the U.S. government through the Department of Transportation. In 1986 Amtrak carried 20.3 million travelers over more than five billion passenger miles. Created in 1970 by the Rail Passenger Service Act, Amtrak began operation on May 1, 1971, with a $40 million appropriation from Congress. At that time, railroads carried less than 7 percent of the intercity passenger traffic in the United States with less than 450 trains in operation. Before the creation of Amtrak, highway and air transportation systems in the United States were beginning to be overwhelmed by the growing need for transportation between the nation's major population centers. With thousands of miles of existing tracks and rights-of-way into major population centers, the nation's rail facilities were viewed by some as an economical form of transportation when compared with the costs of constructing new highways and airports.

The new corporation inherited, however, an antiquated system of locomotives, passenger cars, and other railroad assets. The Amtrak fleet consisted of twenty- to thirty-year-old steam-heated cars, and the average age of Amtrak's locomotives was seventeen years. For the first two years of operation, Amtrak was almost totally dependent on private railroads from which they leased equipment and facilities. When created, Amtrak assumed responsibility for managing intercity passenger train service over twenty-three thousand route miles connecting twenty-one major population centers. In 1973 Amtrak received its first new equipment, and in 1976 the corporation acquired a major portion of the busy 455-mile Northeast Corridor between Washington, D.C., and Boston, as well as two important feeder lines. Also in 1976, Congress passed the Railroad Revitalization and Regulatory Reform Act, which authorized spending $2.5 billion to rebuild the Northwest Corridor. The corporation continued to upgrade its facilities, and by 1982 all fifteen hundred of Amtrak's cars were new or rebuilt.

Management of Amtrak was assigned to a board comprising nine members. They include the president of Amtrak, who is appointed by the board, and the secretary of transportation. Three members are appointed by the president of the United States with Senate confirmation: one of the three is selected from a list recommended by the Railway Labor Executives Association; one is selected from among the governors of the states with an interest in rail transportation; and one is selected as a representative of business connected with rail transportation. Two additional members are selected by the president from a list recommended by commuter agencies that provide service over the Amtrak-owned Northeast Corridor; and two members are selected annually by the Department of Transportation, which is the preferred stockholder of the corporation. Board members serve staggered one- to two-year terms and can be removed only for cause. The board of directors meets ten times each year at Amtrak's Washington, D.C., headquarters. Meetings consist of a closed session for the discussion of personnel and proprietary matters and a session open to the media and interested persons.

National Science Foundation

The National Science Foundation (NSF) is an independent federal agency established to promote and advance scientific progress in the United States. Created by the National Science Foundation Act of 1950, the NSF was an outgrowth of the important contributions made by science and technology during World War II. Since its inception the NSF has provided financial and other support for research, education, and related activities in science, mathematics, and engineering. The NSF is headed by a director, who is appointed by the president, and a twenty-four-member governing board; all are appointed for indefinite terms and serve at the pleasure of the president. Board members include scientists, engineers, educators, and industry officials.

Each year the NSF receives thousands of proposals for research and graduate fellowships from academic institutions, private research firms, industrial laboratories, and major research facilities and centers. The NSF staff is divided into grant-making divisions covering various disciplines and fields of science and engineering. Outside advisers from the scientific community serve on formal committees or as ad hoc reviewers of the proposals. Applicants receive verbatim, unsigned copies of reviews of their proposals and can appeal final decisions, which are made by NSF staff members. Awardees are wholly responsible for doing their research and preparing the results for publication. The NSF does not assume responsibility for research findings or their interpretation.

Specific fields of research funded by the NSF are the mathematical and physical sciences, all fields of engineering, biological and environmental sciences, the social sciences and economics, behavioral and neural sciences, computer and information science, atmospheric, earth, and ocean sciences, and engineering education. The NSF does not support projects in clinical medicine, the arts and humanities, commerce, or social work.

The NSF does not conduct research itself but funds large-scale cooperative facilities for scientists and engineers. National and regional facilities supported by the NSF include research centers for physics, astronomy and atmospheric sciences, supercomputer centers, oceanographic vessels, and Materials Research Laboratories. In addition, the NSF manages a long-term U.S. scientific research program in Antarctica.

Other NSF programs include funding of cooperative research efforts between industry, government, and academics and outreach programs with state government and private organizations. The NSF also monitors resources for science and engineering and publishes analyses and statistical studies on the supply and demand for personnel and funding in those fields. In 1985, the NSF sponsored the first National Science and Technology Week. The annual event includes science fairs, competitions, and public access to research facilities, lectures, and other activities.

National Transportation Safety Board

The National Transportation Safety Board (NTSB) is an independent agency authorized to investigate transportation accidents and to formulate safety recommendations. Established by the Department of Transportation Act of 1966, the NTSB was made entirely independent of the Department of Transportation by the Independent Safety Board Act of 1974.

The safety board is composed of five members appointed by the president with Senate confirmation. Members serve five-year terms, and the president designates two members to serve as chair and vice-chair for two-year terms. No more than three members can be of the same political party, and all serve at the pleasure of the president.

The board is authorized to investigate and determine the probable cause of air, rail, highway, and marine accidents. The board also investigates pipeline accidents involving a fatality or substantial property damage. The NTSB assembles investigative teams, or "Go-Teams," that are dispatched to accident scenes. The Go-Teams consist of board personnel skilled in various types of accident investigation and may include a board member. The Go-Team gathers data from the accident or through interviews with witnesses. For accident investigations requiring off-site engineering studies or laboratory tests, the board operates its own technical laboratory. The laboratory has the capability to read out "black boxes" containing aircraft cockpit voice recorders and flight data recorders. The laboratory's metallurgists can determine whether failures resulted from a design flaw, from overloading, or from deterioration in static strength through fatigue or corrosion.

Following an accident, the board may hold a public hearing to collect additional information. A board member presides over the hearings, and witnesses testify under oath. Upon completion of the fact-finding phase, the data is reviewed at NTSB headquarters where the "probable cause" of the accident is determined. The final accident report is then presented to the full five-member board for discussion and approval at a public meeting in Washington.

To increase safety, the board makes a safety recommendation as soon as a problem is identified, without necessarily waiting until an investigation is completed and the probable cause of an accident determined. Each recommendation designates the person or party expected to take action, describes the action the board expects, and clearly states the safety need to be satisfied. The Department of Transportation is required to respond to each board recommendation within ninety days. The board also is empowered to conduct special studies that go beyond examination of a single accident to broader transportation and safety problems.

Nuclear Regulatory Commission

The Nuclear Regulatory Commission (NRC) was established by the Energy Reorganization Act of 1974 to regulate the civilian uses of nuclear materials in the United States. When President Gerald R. Ford signed the legislation creating the NRC in 1975 the commission formally took over the nuclear regulatory and licensing functions of the Atomic Energy Commission (AEC), which was abolished.

The NRC is headed by five commissioners appointed by the president and confirmed by the Senate. No more than three commissioners may be of the same political party. Commissioners serve five-year terms with one commissioner appointed by the president to serve as chair. The chair directs the day-to-day operations of the agency and is responsible for the commission's response to nuclear emergencies. Commission members can be removed only for cause.

The NRC's Office of Nuclear Reactor Regulation licenses nuclear reactors used for testing, research, and power generation. A construction permit must be granted before construction can begin on a nuclear facility, and an operating license must be issued before fuel can be loaded and the reactor started. The office reviews license applications to determine what effect the proposed facility will have on the environment and whether it can be built and operated without undue risk to public safety and health. Applicants are investigated to determine whether they are properly insured against accidents. No application to construct a new nuclear plant has been filed since 1979.

Public hearings on applications for construction permits are mandatory. Hearings are conducted by the Atomic Safety and Licensing Board in communities near proposed nuclear facilities. Notices of these hearings are published in the *Federal Register* and the local newspaper and are posted in the nearest public document room. Interested parties can petition for the right to participate in the public hearings.

The Office of Nuclear Material Safety and Safeguards ensures that public health and safety, national security, and environmental factors are considered in the licensing and regulation of nuclear facilities. Safeguards also are reviewed and assessed against possible threats, thefts, and sabotage. The Office of Nuclear Regulatory Research administers the commission's research program. In 1980 it merged with the Office of Standards Development. Their combined functions include developing and recommending nuclear safety standards in the construction of nuclear power plants and preparing standards for the preparation of environmental impact statements. The Office of Inspection and Enforcement inspects nuclear facilities to determine whether they are constructed and operated in compliance with license provisions and NRC regulations. Analysis of operating data, enforcement of NRC regulations, and special projects are controlled by separate offices within the agency.

After the accident at Pennsylvania's Three Mile Island nuclear power plant on March 28, 1979, President Jimmy Carter appointed a commission to study government and industry safety practices in nuclear energy. The conclusions of the commission led to a reorganization of the NRC in 1980, in which greater responsibility for directing the commission's response to nuclear emergencies was transferred to the office of the chair.

The new plan also provided that the executive director

for operations for the agency report directly to the chair. Formerly, supervision of the operating staff was left to the collective commission.

Occupational Safety and Health Review Commission

The Occupational Safety and Health Review Commission (OSHRC) is an independent, quasi-judicial agency created to review contests of citations or penalties prescribed by the Occupational Safety and Health Administration (OSHA). Established in 1971 by the Occupational Safety and Health Act of 1970, the review commission is based in Washington, D.C., and is independent of OSHA and the Department of Labor. The commission comprises three members who are appointed by the president, with Senate confirmation, and their administrative staff. Members are appointed for staggered six-year terms.

After the issuance of citations or penalties by OSHA, the employer is notified in writing and a period of time is allocated to correct the violation. The employer then has fifteen days to contest the assessment. If the employer does not contest the citations or penalties, they become the final order of the commission. If a citation is contested, the review commission usually holds a hearing before an OSHRC administrative law judge. The judge's decision becomes final thirty days after the commission receives it, unless a petition for discretionary review is filed. Decisions also can be reviewed at the discretion of one or more commission members. Penalties imposed by the commission range from fines up to $1,000 for "other than serious violations" to $10,000 and/or imprisonment for up to six months for willful violation resulting in the death of an employee.

In fiscal year 1985, the review commission received 1,360 cases of which 1,165 were resolved without a hearing. In addition to the Washington, D.C., office, review commission judges are stationed in four regional offices.

Office of Personnel Management

The Office of Personnel Management (OPM) is an independent agency that sets and carries out personnel policies for the federal work force. OPM was created by the Civil Service Reform Act of 1978, replacing the U.S. Civil Service Commission, which had been established in 1883 by the Pendleton Act. The Reform Act also established the Office of Government Ethics within OPM to direct executive branch policies toward preventing conflicts of interest by executive branch personnel.

Headquartered in Washington, D.C., OPM has approximately 6,500 permanent employees and maintains ten regional offices nationwide. In 1986, OPM personnel policies covered a work force of 2.1 million federal employees. The director of OPM is appointed by the president with Senate confirmation and serves as chief adviser on personnel policies governing civilian employment in executive branch agencies and some legislative and judicial agencies. The director is appointed to a four-year term and can be removed only for cause. An incoming president can appoint a new director at any time.

As the U.S. government's central personnel agency, OPM is responsible for recruiting and examining federal employees, providing development and training programs, classifying jobs, investigating personnel to support its selection and appointment processes, evaluation of agency personnel programs, and overseeing pay administration. Positions covered by OPM include the federal civil service from General Schedule grades one through fifteen and Wage Grade (blue-collar) positions. The agency also administers the Qualifications Review Board examining process for career Senior Executive Service appointments.

OPM oversees federal employee retirement and insurance programs and enforces government policies on labor relations and affirmative action. OPM is chartered to administer federal employment under a merit system based on knowledge and skills through the Merit Systems Protection Board.

OPM's Incentive Awards program gives cash and honors to employees who provide suggestions that improve government operations and whose performance is judged superior. OPM also administers the Presidential Rank Awards program for recognition of sustained high-quality accomplishment of career members of the Senior Executive Service.

Panama Canal Commission

The Panama Canal Commission manages, operates, and maintains the Panama Canal under the Panama Canal Treaty of 1977. The treaty abolished the former canal organization—the Panama Canal Company and the Canal Zone Government. Two years later Congress passed the Panama Canal Act of 1979, which established the commission as the managing agency of the Panama Canal until the year 2000 when the treaty expires. At that time the entire facility will be turned over to the government of Panama, which is committed to keeping the canal open and efficient to international marine traffic.

The commission is supervised by a nine-member board. Five members are U.S. nationals appointed by the president with Senate confirmation. Four members are Panamanian nationals proposed by their government for appointment by the U.S. president. The commission administrator is a U.S. citizen, and the deputy administrator is a Panamanian citizen. Beginning in 1990, the positions will be reversed. The U.S. administrator serves at the pleasure of the president.

The canal is approximately fifty-one miles long and runs across the Isthmus of Panama connecting the Pacific and Atlantic oceans. In 1987, 677,521 vessels, of which more than 80 percent were oceangoing commercial class, transited the canal. A canal on the Isthmus of Panama was first proposed by King Charles I of Spain in 1534. In 1880 the French under Count Ferdinand de Lesseps, the builder of the Suez Canal, began work on the Panama Canal; but disease and financial problems ended the French effort almost twenty years later. In 1903, shortly after Panama's independence from Colombia, Panama and the United States signed a treaty by which the United States, under President Theodore Roosevelt's administration, undertook to construct the canal. The project was completed eleven years later at a cost of $387 million.

Peace Corps

The Peace Corps is an independent agency created by executive order in 1961 to help developing countries meet their basic needs for health care, food, shelter, and education. The corps trains volunteers to participate in its programs in Latin America, Africa, Asia, and the Pacific. Peace Corps volunteers offer skills in a variety of fields including education, health, nutrition, agriculture, forestry, and rural development. The goals of the Peace Corps as set by Congress are: to help developing countries to meet their needs for trained workers, to help promote a better understanding of Americans on the part of the peoples served, and to help promote a better understanding of other peoples on the part of Americans.

The corps is headed by a director who is appointed by the president with Senate confirmation. There is no fixed term, and the director serves at the discretion of the president.

The Peace Corps's overseas operations are administered through three regions comprising twenty-five nations in sub-Saharan Africa, nineteen countries in Central and South America and the Caribbean, and nineteen nations in North Africa, the Near East, Asia, and the Pacific. Africa is the Peace Corps's largest area of operations; almost half of the corps' volunteers are stationed there. In 1986 the Peace Corps had nearly six thousand volunteers in programs worldwide. The average age of the volunteers was twenty-nine years old, and almost 10 percent of the volunteers were fifty years of age or older.

The idea of the Peace Corps originated in 1960 when Sen. Hubert H. Humphrey (D-Minn.) introduced a bill calling for establishment of a "Peace Corps." Although Congress defeated the bill, less than four months later in a campaign speech at the University of Michigan, presidential candidate John F. Kennedy questioned his audience whether they would be willing to volunteer their services overseas as representatives of the United States. The idea became a presidential directive soon after Kennedy's election and was funded out of the White House. In 1961 Congress approved funds and legislation formally establishing the Peace Corps with the mandate to "promote world peace and friendship."

In 1971 President Nixon created ACTION to incorporate various federal voluntary organizations, including the Peace Corps, under one umbrella agency. After complaints from the corps' leadership that the corps had lost its identity, President Carter in 1979 signed legislation granting the Peace Corps special independence within ACTION.

Volunteers must be U.S. citizens, at least eighteen years old, and medically qualified. There is no upper age limit. If married, an applicant must serve with his or her spouse. Although they participate in a U.S. agency program, Peace Corps volunteers are not officials of the U.S. government and have no diplomatic privileges. All volunteers receive intensive, short-term technical and language training. They also are offered cultural studies of the history, customs, and the social and political systems of the host country. The normal tour of duty is twenty-four months following three months of training. Volunteers receive a monthly allowance for rent, food, travel, and all medical needs. A readjustment allowance of $175 a month is set aside, payable on completion of service.

Pennsylvania Avenue Development Corporation

The Pennsylvania Avenue Development Corporation (PADC) was established by Congress in 1972 to plan the development and use of the area adjacent to Pennsylvania Avenue between the U.S. Capitol and the White House. The legislation that created the PADC charged the corporation with creating a plan for developing and administering the area in a manner "suitable to its ceremonial, physical and historic relationship to the legislative and executive branches of the federal government." The corporation's Pennsylvania Avenue Plan includes oversight responsibilities of the government buildings, monuments, memorials, and parks in and around the area.

A board of directors comprising fifteen voting members and seven nonvoting members heads the PADC. Eight of the voting members are appointed by the president to serve six-year terms. Seven other voting members representing specific public interests include heads of federal agencies, the mayor of the District of Columbia, and the city council chair (or designees of the mayor and council chair). All voting members can be removed only for cause. The seven nonvoting members are advisory officials expert in or responsible for cultural, historic, or planning activities in the District. The chair of the corporation is appointed by the president.

The PADC maintains three operating committees: Cultural Affairs, Design, and Affirmative Action. The legislation that created the PADC provides for various powers, including review and approval authority over public and private development. The corporation also has authority to construct and to rehabilitate buildings, to manage property, and to establish restrictions, standards, and other requirements that ensure conformance to the plan. According to the PADC plan, by 1992 the area will contain 8.3 million square feet of office space, 825,000 square feet of retail space, 2,500 hotel rooms, and 1,200-1,500 residential units.

Pension Benefit Guaranty Corporation

The Pension Benefit Guaranty Corporation (PBGC) was created by Title IV of the Employee Retirement Income Security Act of 1974. PBGC ensures that participants in the pension plans it insures will receive their benefits in the event that the plan does not have sufficient funds to pay. PBGC also may force a plan to terminate if the agency determines that the pension fund is in trouble. In 1988, nearly forty million workers participated in more than 112,000 covered plans.

PBGC is a nonprofit corporation wholly owned by the federal government. It is financed by premiums levied against covered pension plans, the assets of plans it places into trusteeship, and investment income. The corporation is administered by a board of directors and an executive director. The board comprises the secretaries of labor, commerce, and the Treasury; the labor secretary serves as chair. A seven-member advisory committee made up of two labor representatives, two business representatives, and three public members advises the corporation.

PBGC coverage is mandatory for single-employer, private defined pension plans—plans whose benefits are determined by using a formula including factors such as age, length of service, and salary. The agency also protects the pension benefits of the approximately eight million participants in multiemployer pension plans. Multiemployer plans are based on collective bargaining agreements involving a union and two or more employers.

Postal Rate Commission

The Postal Rate Commission (PRC) is an independent regulatory agency established to consider proposed changes in postal rates, fees, and mail classifications and to issue recommended decisions to the governors of the Postal Service. The PRC was created by the Postal Reorganization Act of 1970, which also changed the old Post Office Department into the U.S. Postal Service.

The commission consists of five members appointed by the president and confirmed by the Senate and can be removed only for cause. Members serve six-year terms, and no more than three may be members of the same political party. The president designates one of the commissioners as chair. A vice-chair is elected annually by the commissioners. An incoming president can appoint a new chair.

In addition to reviewing proposed changes in rates and classifications, the PRC considers changes in the nature of available postal service and customers' appeals of Postal Service decisions to close or consolidate post offices. The PRC also investigates complaints concerning postal rates, fees, and mail classifications or services.

After receiving a rate proposal and supporting testimony from the Postal Service, the PRC issues public notice of the filing and appoints an officer of the commission, who is a staff member of the PRC's Office of the Consumer Advocate, to represent the interest of the general public before the commission. After a discovery period and public hearings, during which the commission receives oral and written testimony, the PRC issues a written recommendation, which is then forwarded to the Postal Service governors. The governors may either accept the decision, in which case the proposed rate is implemented, or reject the decision and return it for reconsideration by the commission. The governors also may allow the commission's recommendation to stand, but under protest. In this case the rate proposal will be implemented under protest, while the decision either undergoes judicial review by the Postal Service or is returned for reconsideration. Decisions on mail classifications (which are official definitions of the different services available from the Postal Service) and proposed changes in postal services undergo similar reviews by both the PRC and the Postal Service governors.

Railroad Retirement Board

The Railroad Retirement Board (RRB) is an independent agency created to administer retirement and unemployment programs for the nation's railroad employees. The board, which is based in Chicago, is made up of three members who are appointed by the president with Senate confirmation. Members serve staggered five-year terms. By law, one member is appointed upon recommendations made by railroad labor organizations, one upon recommendations of railroad employers, and the third member, the chair, is in effect independent of the employees and employers and represents the public interest. The president also appoints an inspector general for the board who reports directly to the chair. Board members serve five-year terms and can be removed only for cause.

The function of the board is to determine and pay benefits under the retirement-survivor and unemployment-sickness programs. The board maintains lifetime earnings records for covered employees, a network of field offices to handle claims, and examiners to adjudicate the claims.

The railroad retirement system is based on three federal laws: the Railroad Retirement Act, the Railroad Unemployment Insurance Act, and the Railroad Retirement Tax Act. The original Railroad Retirement Act of 1934 set up the first retirement system for nongovernment workers to be administered by the federal government before being declared unconstitutional. A federal district court held that neither employees nor their employers could be compelled to pay railroad retirement taxes. However, the act evolved into the Railroad Retirement Carriers' Taxing Acts of 1935, and the RRB began awarding annuities in 1936. The act was further amended in 1937 to establish the railroad retirement system. In 1946 and 1951 the act was again amended to coordinate in certain areas with the Social Security system. In 1974 Congress adopted a two-tier system of benefits that would provide amounts equal to Social Security benefits and other industrial pension systems. The system was designed to phase out dual railroad retirement/Social Security benefits being collected by railroad employees. With several modifications the two-tier system remains intact today.

From 1936 when the board first began issuing benefits, through September 1986, benefits under the railroad retirement system have been awarded to 1.6 million retired employees, and 2.9 million survivors. During the same period, over $89 billion was paid in benefits of all types.

Securities and Exchange Commission

The Securities and Exchange Commission (SEC) is an independent, quasi-judicial regulatory agency created in 1934 to administer federal securities laws. The commission is composed of five members, not more than three of whom may be of the same political party. The commissioners are nominated by the president and confirmed by the Senate for staggered five-year terms. The president also designates one of the members to serve as chair. A general counsel serves as the chief legal officer for the commission. Commission members serve five-year terms at the discretion of the president.

The origins of the SEC may be traced to the stock market crash of October 29, 1929. The crash and the ensuing economic depression focused public attention on reported stock manipulations and unscrupulous trading during the 1920s. A Senate investigation of securities trading eventually prompted the passage of the Securities Act of 1933, also known as the "truth-in-securities" bill. The act required anyone offering securities for sale in interstate commerce or through the mails to file information with the Federal Trade Commission (FTC) on the financial condition of the issuing company. The following year Congress passed the Securities Exchange Act of 1934, which created the SEC and transferred to it the functions that had been assigned to the FTC under the 1933 law. The 1934 act required companies whose securities were traded on national exchanges to file periodic financial reports. The measure also required that exchanges and over-the-counter dealers and brokers conduct business in line with principles of fair and equitable trade.

The SEC maintains four divisions with specific areas of responsibility for various segments of the federal securities laws. The Division of Corporation Finance has the overall responsibility of ensuring that disclosure requirements are met by publicly held companies registered with the commission.

The Securities Exchange Act requires the registration of "national securities exchanges" (those have a substantial trading volume) and of brokers and dealers who conduct an over-the-counter securities business in interstate commerce. Exchanges establish their own self-regulatory rules, although the commission, through its Division of Market Regulation, may alter or supplement them if it finds that the rules fail to protect investors. The division also examines applications from brokers and dealers to determine if they conform to business practices and standards prescribed by the commission.

Since 1934, Congress has passed three additional securities measures, including the Public Utility Holding Company Act of 1935, the Investment Company Act of 1940, and the Investment Advisers Act of 1940. Administration of these acts is the primary responsibility of the commission's Division of Investment Management.

Investigation and enforcement of securities laws is the primary responsibility of the commission's Division of Enforcement. Although most investigations are conducted through informal inquiry, the commission has the authority to issue subpoenas requiring sworn testimony and the production of books, records, and other documents pertinent to the subject under investigation. If the investigations show possible fraud or other violation, the securities laws provide several courses of action or remedies. The commission may apply for a civil injunction enjoining those acts or practices alleged to violate the law or commission rules. If fraud or other willful violation is indicated, the commission may refer the facts to the Department of Justice with a recommendation for criminal prosecution. The commission also may, after a hearing, issue orders that suspend or expel members from exchanges, censure firms or individuals, or bar individuals from employment with a registered firm.

Selective Service System

The Selective Service System is an independent agency that provides personnel to the armed forces in emergencies and administers the alternative service program for conscientious objectors. The legislation under which the agency operates is the Military Selective Service Act. The Selective Service was originally mandated by the Selective Service Act of 1948, which ordered that men be selected for the draft on a fair and equitable basis consistent with the maintenance of an effective national economy. The act replaced the expired Selective Training and Service Act of 1940, which was the first peacetime draft in U.S. history.

The last draft calls were issued in 1972, and the president's authority to conscript men into the armed forces expired on July 1, 1973. Mandatory registration continued until 1975 when it was suspended; it was reinstated in the summer of 1980 by the Military Selective Service Act. The act states that male U.S. citizens and male aliens residing in the United States, who are between the ages of eighteen and twenty-six are required to register with the Selective Service within thirty days of their eighteenth birthday. Failure to register or otherwise comply with the act is, upon conviction, punishable by a fine or imprisonment, or both. According to the act, a person who knowingly counsels, aids, or abets another to fail to comply with the act is subject to the same penalties.

The director of the Selective Service is appointed by the president and confirmed by the Senate. The director is appointed to an indefinite term and serves at the discretion of the president. The staff of 270 full-time employees is composed of civilians and active duty military officers. Approximately 725 National Guard and Reserve officers conduct monthly drills under the jurisdiction of the Selective Service System and could be called up to active duty in an emergency.

The Selective Service System headquarters is in Washington, D.C. The agency maintains six regional headquarters throughout the country in addition to offices in each state. Additional offices are in New York City, the District of Columbia, Guam, Puerto Rico, the Virgin Islands, and the Northern Mariana Islands. Local boards are allocated to counties or corresponding political subdivisions.

The local boards make judgments about registrant claims for deferment or exemption from military service if a draft is resumed. The local board members are the only officials permitted to make initial decisions about claims of conscientious objections, hardship, or religious ministry. The local board also can review claims denied by the area office for other classifications or student postponements if a registrant requests a review.

District appeal boards are maintained in areas corresponding to federal judicial districts. The boards review and affirm or change any decision appealed to it from any local board in its area. Members of both the local boards and the district appeal boards are civilians appointed by the president, who serve without pay. If a claim for classification is denied by the district appeal board by less than a unanimous vote, the registrant can appeal to the president through the National Selective Service Appeal Board. Decisions of the National Appeal Board are final.

Small Business Administration

The Small Business Administration (SBA) is an independent federal agency that provides both new and established small businesses with financial assistance, management counseling, and training. Created by the Small Business Act of 1953, the authority of SBA was expanded by the Small Business Investment Act of 1958. The act authorized SBA to aid, counsel, and assist the interests of small businesses in order to promote free, competitive enterprise. The agency's Office of Advocacy works to ensure that a fair proportion of the total purchases and contracts for supplies and services for the government be placed with small business enterprises.

SBA is headed by an administrator and a deputy administrator. The administrator, the agency's chief counsel for advocacy, and its inspector general are appointed by the president with Senate confirmation. The deputy administrator is appointed by the administrator. The appointees serve at the discretion of the president under no fixed term.

Most SBA aid is in the form of guarantees of loans made by banks. In particular, loans are provided to assist small businesses that have sustained substantial economic injury from sources such as: major natural disasters; urban renewal or highway construction programs; construction programs conducted with federal, state or local funds; and the closing or reduction in operation of major federal military installations. SBA also makes loans to businesses to assist them in meeting requirements imposed by federal laws and by federal air and water pollution standards. In addition, loans are provided to homeowners who have suffered economic injury as a result of natural disasters. Special programs expand and promote ownership of businesses by women and minorities.

SBA licenses, regulates, and lends to small business investment companies (SBICs). These companies provide venture capital to small businesses in the form of equity financing, long-term loans, and management services. SBA determines SBIC loan requirements, approves SBIC charters and articles of incorporation, reviews specific terms of financing and interest rates to be charged, and enforces regulations and penalties regarding investments.

Two pieces of legislation affecting SBA were signed into law in 1980. Both acts are intended to aid small businesses that cannot absorb the costs of regulation compliance. The Regulatory Flexibility Act requires the federal government to anticipate and reduce the impact of federal regulations on small business. The Small Business Investment Incentive Act exempts certain small- and medium-sized businesses from the registration requirements of securities laws.

Smithsonian Institution

The Smithsonian Institution, which encompasses the world's largest museum complex, is an independent trust establishment devoted to public education, research, and national service in the arts, sciences, and history. The Smithsonian complex comprises the National Zoological Park and fourteen museums and galleries—thirteen in Washington, D.C., and one in New York City. Nine of the museums are on the National Mall between the U.S. Capitol and the Washington Monument. The institution also maintains research facilities in nine states and the Republic of Panama.

The institution is governed by a board of regents, which is composed of the vice president of the United States, the chief justice of the United States, three members of the Senate, three members of the House of Representatives, and nine citizen members, nominated by the board and approved by Congress in a joint resolution signed by the president. The chief justice traditionally has served as chancellor of the institution, and the chief executive officer is the secretary, who is appointed by the board.

In 1829, James Smithson, a British scientist, drew up his will naming his nephew, Henry James Hungerford, as beneficiary. The will stipulated that should Hungerford die without heirs (as he did in 1835), the estate would go to the United States "to found at Washington, under the name of the Smithsonian Institution, an establishment for the increase and diffusion of knowledge among men." Smithson's fortune—105 bags containing approximately 100,000 gold sovereigns worth more than $500,000—was brought to the United States in 1838. Eight years later, on August 10, 1846, an act of Congress signed by President James K. Polk established the Smithsonian Institution. James Smithson never visited the United States. He died in Genoa, Italy, in 1829 where he was buried in a small English cemetery. In 1904, when the burial ground was to be displaced by the enlargement of a quarry, his tomb and remains were escorted to the United States by Alexander Graham Bell, and reinterred in the original Smithsonian building.

The original building, commonly known as "the Castle," was completed in 1855 and today houses the institution's administrative offices and the Visitor Information and Associates Reception Center. The Castle also serves as headquarters for the affiliated Woodrow Wilson International Center for Scholars. Other Smithsonian facilities include the Arts and Industries Building, which serves as a showplace for items from the institution's collections in the fields of history, technology, and air and space; the Arthur M. Sackler Gallery, which is the museum of Near Eastern and Asian art; the Freer Gallery of Art; the Hirshhorn Museum and Sculpture Garden, which is devoted to the exhibition, interpretation, and study of modern and contemporary art; the National Air and Space Museum; the National Museum of African Art; the National Museum of American History; the National Museum of Natural History; and the Cooper-Hewitt Museum in New York City, which is the only museum in the United States devoted exclusively to the study and exhibition of historical and contemporary design.

Smithsonian research facilities include the Archives of American Art, the international Environmental Science Program, the Smithsonian Astrophysical Observatory, the Environmental Research Center, and the Tropical Research Institute. In addition to the Smithsonian trust funds, which include endowments, donations, and other revenues, the Institution receives an annual appropriation from Congress.

State Justice Institute

The State Justice Institute is a private, nonprofit corporation created to further the development and improvement of the administration of justice in the state courts. Established by the State Justice Institute Act of 1984, the institute is based in Alexandria, Virginia. It is administered by a board of directors consisting of eleven members appointed by the president, with consent of the Senate, to three-year terms. By law the board membership comprises six judges, a state court administrator, and four members of the public, of whom no more than two may be of the same political party. The board may remove its own members only for cause.

The board of directors selects a chair from among its membership to act as governor of the institute's quarterly meetings. The board also selects an executive director, an ex officio member who manages the daily business of the institute.

The institute's statute contains fourteen broad areas of interest including education for judges and support personnel of state court systems, access to a fair and effective judicial system, and coordination and cooperation of the state courts with the federal judiciary. The institute provides grants and funds cooperative agreements with individuals or organizations interested in carrying out innovative programs. All funding for the institute and its programs is authorized by Congress. Interested parties submit concept papers to the institute for review. Those chosen by the board of directors may receive grants from the institute of up to $300,000, although grants of more than $200,000 are unusual. In 1987, the institute awarded eighty-two grants totaling $8.6 million.

Tennessee Valley Authority

The Tennessee Valley Authority (TVA) is an independent corporate agency of the federal government, charged with responsibility for developing the resources of the Tennessee Valley region. Established by Congress in 1933, TVA serves ninety-one thousand square miles in the southeast United States comprising parts of seven states—Tennessee, Alabama, Mississippi, Kentucky, Virginia, North Carolina, and Georgia. TVA is responsible for providing for flood control and improving navigation on the Tennessee River, producing electric power, and promoting agricultural, economic, and industrial development.

TVA is headed by a three-member board of directors appointed by the president with Senate confirmation. Directors serve staggered, nine-year terms, and one director is designated as chair by the president. The daily affairs of TVA are administered by a general manager, who is responsible to the board of directors.

The three major administrative offices of TVA are in Muscle Shoals, Alabama, and Knoxville and Chattanooga, Tennessee. A small liaison staff is in Washington, D.C., and seven district offices are located throughout the Tennessee Valley region. Day-to-day operations of TVA are conducted by three divisions: Power and Engineering, Natural Resources and Economic Development, and Agricultural and Chemical Development.

The Office of Power and Engineering is responsible for the overall electrical supply program in the TVA area. The office oversees the design, construction, and daily operation and maintenance of the TVA power system, the nation's largest. The TVA electric power system serves more than seven million consumers through 160 municipal and cooperative power distributors. The power system is self-supporting from revenues from power sales. Other TVA programs, such as fertilizer development and flood control, are funded by Congress.

The Office of Natural Resources and Economic Development manages programs designed to use and protect the natural resources of the Tennessee Valley area. Programs include reservoir land use, aquatic plant control, and water conservation, development, and management.

Through TVA facilities, the Office of Agricultural and Chemical Development researches and develops new fertilizers and fertilizer manufacturing processes. The office is chartered to improve and preserve agricultural resources and to encourage soil conservation in the Tennessee Valley area.

United States Arms Control and Disarmament Agency

The United States Arms Control and Disarmament Agency (ACDA) is an independent government agency mandated by Congress to formulate, implement, and support arms control and disarmament policies. The agency has four main tasks: to prepare for and manage U.S. participation in negotiations on disarmament and arms control, to conduct research, to participate in verifying compliance with existing agreements, and to disseminate information on arms control and disarmament to the public.

ACDA is headed by a director and deputy director who are appointed by the president with Senate confirmation. The appointees serve an unspecified term at the discretion of the president. The offices of director and deputy director advise the president, the National Security Council, the secretary of state, and other senior government officials on arms control and disarmament matters.

Before ACDA was created, disarmament negotiations usually were handled by the State Department's Office of United Nations Affairs. While campaigning for president, John F. Kennedy proposed the establishment of the U.S. Arms Control Research Institute. The new agency, which was renamed as a result of a compromise between the Kennedy administration, the Senate, and the House, was signed into law in 1961.

ACDA maintains four bureaus and four offices. The Strategic Programs Bureau (SP) develops, for presidential approval, arms control policy, strategy, tactics, and language for ongoing arms limitation talks with the Soviet Union. The bureau provides analysis and support for negotiations on the U.S. Strategic Defense Initiative. SP also provides agency representatives and advisers for delegations to negotiations for the Strategic Arms Reduction Talks and the Defense and Space Talks.

The Multilateral Affairs Bureau develops arms control policy, strategy, tactics, and language for ongoing multilateral arms limitations negotiations and provides organizational support, delegation staffing, and advice for multilateral negotiations.

The Bureau of Verification and Intelligence is responsible for policies and studies dealing with the verifiability of provisions of current and projected arms control agreements. The bureau also provides operations analysis, intelligence, and computer support for all ACDA's activities.

The Bureau of Nuclear Weapons Control performs ACDA work on nuclear nonproliferation issues, arms and technology transfers, arms control impact studies, defense economics and economics of arms control, military expenditure recording and analysis, and weapons analyses.

The Office of General Counsel is responsible for all matters of domestic and international law relevant to ACDA's work and provides advice and assistance in drafting and negotiating arms control treaties and agreements. Other ACDA offices include the Office of Public Affairs, which coordinates the agency's dissemination of public information; the Office of Congressional Affairs, which coordinates ACDA's contacts with Congress on all matters relating to arms control; and the Office of Administration, which has responsibility for the daily operation of the agency and its negotiating staffs in Geneva, Stockholm, and Vienna.

United States Information Agency

The United States Information Agency (USIA) is an independent agency responsible for the U.S. government's overseas information, educational exchange, and cultural programs. Its director reports to the president and receives policy guidance from the secretary of state. The director, deputy director, and four associate directors are appointed by the president with Senate confirmation and serve at the discretion of the president.

USIA originated as the Voice of America (VOA) in 1942 during World War II. The Smith-Mundt Act established the information program as a long-term, integral part of U.S. foreign policy in 1948, and in 1953 Congress created USIA. The State Department retained control over educational and cultural affairs until 1978.

In 1988 USIA had 204 posts in 127 countries. Overseas posts are maintained at U.S. diplomatic missions and are grouped in five geographical areas: Africa; Europe; East Asia and the Pacfic; the American Republics; and North Africa, the Near East, and South Asia. Each post reports to an area office in the agency's Washington, D.C., headquarters. USIA officers overseas engage in political advocacy of American foreign policy objectives. In addition to its radio service, the Voice of America, the agency uses personal contacts with foreign leaders and films, videotapes, magazines, and direct satellite to carry out its mission. USIA also maintains a library open to the public in many of its overseas posts.

The chief of the agency's program in any country is the public affairs officer (PAO), who usually has the diplomatic designation of counselor of the embassy for public affairs. PAOs advise U.S. ambassadors on issues of public affairs diplomacy and the public articulation of U.S. policies.

Program direction and administrative responsibilities of USIA are held by the agency's Washington office. U.S.-based personnel conduct the broadcasting operations of the Voice of America and the Television and Film Service and produce agency publications, films, exhibits, and other support materials for field posts. USIA's Washington office is also responsible for advising the president and others in the official foreign affairs community on the implications of foreign opinion for the United States. USIA provides opinion analyses on international issues as well as daily summaries of foreign media treatment of U.S. actions and policies.

The Voice of America is the global radio network of USIA. It broadcasts 1,003 hours each week in forty-two languages and is heard by more than 100 million adults at least once a week. USIA's WORLDNET is an interactive international television service that provides direct communication on international issues between U.S. spokespersons and foreign leaders and journalists. USIA also sponsors educational exchange programs including the Fulbright Program, which operates in 120 countries and awards more than 3,500 scholarships each year.

United States Institute of Peace

The United States Institute of Peace is an independent, federal, nonprofit corporation created to develop and disseminate knowledge about the peaceful resolution of international conflict. Established in 1984, the institute is governed by a bipartisan fifteen-member board of directors. Board members are appointed by the president with Senate confirmation and serve at the discretion of the president. Members of the board include the director of the U.S. Arms Control and Disarmament Agency, the assistant secretary of state for human rights and humanitarian affairs, the president of the National Defense University, and the assistant secretary of defense for international security policy. The president of the board is the only nonvoting member.

The institute maintains a program of grants to nonprofit organizations and to public institutions and individuals researching the nature and processes of peace, war, and international conflict management. The institute also administers an internal research and studies program and a fellowship program for scholars and practitioners of conflict management. Other activities include an education and public information program and a research library program. The institute produces a biennial report to Congress and the president and the *United States Institute of Peace Journal.* All funding for the institute and its activities is appropriated by Congress.

United States International Development Cooperation Agency

The United States International Development Cooperation Agency (IDCA) was established by Congress in 1979 to plan and coordinate U.S. policy on economic issues affecting developing countries. The director of IDCA is intended to serve as principal international development adviser to the president and to the secretary of state. The agency's mission requires that the director of IDCA and senior agency staff participate in a wide range of interagency activities.

IDCA incorporates the Agency for International Development, the Trade and Development Program, and the Overseas Private Investment Corporation. Responsibility for U.S. participation in multilateral development banks is shared by the director of IDCA and the secretary of the Treasury. The director of IDCA also shares policy responsibility for the Food for Peace Program with the Department of Agriculture. The agency guides U.S. participation in certain programs of the United Nations (UN) and the Organization of American States (OAS), including the UN Development Program, the UN Children's Fund, the World Food Program, and the OAS Technical Assistance Funds.

As head of the primary policy-making agency for U.S. assistance programs, the director of IDCA is a member of the National Advisory Committee on International and Monetary Affairs, the Trade Policy Committee, and the Advisory Committee on Agricultural Assistance. The director also chairs the Development Coordination Committee, a broad interagency body that coordinates development and development-related policies and programs.

United States International Trade Commission

The United States International Trade Commission is an independent, quasi-judicial agency that investigates the effect of U.S. foreign trade on domestic production, employment, and consumption. Created by Congress in 1916 as the United States Tariff Commission, the agency acquired its present title under the Trade Act of 1974.

The commission comprises six members appointed by the president, with Senate confirmation for terms of nine years, unless appointed to fill an unexpired term. A commissioner who has served for more than five years is not eligible for reappointment. No more than three commissioners may be of the same political party. The chair is designated by the president and serves a two-year term. No chair may be of the same political party as the preceding chair. The chair and vice-chair also must belong to different parties.

As a fact-finding agency, the commission has broad powers to study and investigate all aspects of U.S. foreign trade, the competitiveness of U.S. products, and foreign and domestic customs laws. It does not set policy, although its technical advice forms a basis for economic policy decisions on U.S. international trade. The commission conducts three types of investigations. It examines whether increasing imports cause serious injury to U.S. industry and whether importers are infringing on U.S. patents, copyrights, or trademarks. The commission may initiate an investigation or arrange one after receiving a complaint.

After receiving a petition from an industry representative or from the Commerce Department, the commission also investigates whether there are reasonable indications that U.S. industries are threatened or materially injured by imports that are subsidized or sold in the United States at prices lower than foreigners would charge in their home market (a practice known as "dumping"). At the same time, the Commerce Department examines whether those subsidies or pricing practices are unfair. If both preliminary investigations are affirmed, the commission must conduct a final investigation to determine whether a U.S. industry is being materially injured or threatened by unfairly priced imports. If the commission finds that such harm is occurring, the Commerce Department must order that a duty be placed on the imports equal to the amount of the unfair subsidy or price. That duty cannot be lifted by the president.

United States Postal Service

Established on July 26, 1777, at the meeting of the Second Continental Congress in Philadelphia, the United States Postal Service (USPS) is the second oldest department or agency of the U.S. government. By 1780 the new Post Office Department consisted only of a postmaster general, a secretary/comptroller, three surveyors, one inspector of dead letters, and twenty-six post riders. When the seat of government and postal headquarters were moved to Washington, D.C., in 1880, officials were able to carry all postal records, furniture, and supplies in two wagons. In 1987 the U.S. Postal Service employed more than 750,000 people and handled 154 billion pieces of mail. In that year USPS had operating revenues exceeding $31 billion and more than 29,000 post offices nationwide.

The growth of the USPS during its long history reflects the rapid expansion of the nation and has been marked by both great successes and great difficulties. Benjamin Franklin was appointed the first postmaster general of the new nation, and the methods and organization of mail delivery that he created remained intact for almost two hundred years. By 1966, however, years of financial neglect and lack of centralized control had left the Post Office Department unable to deal efficiently with the increasing demands of the modern era.

The problems led Winton M. Blount, postmaster general under President Richard Nixon, to propose in 1969 a reorganization of the Post Office Department. Reforms passed by Congress less than a year later failed to rectify the situation, however, and on March 16, 1970, approximately 152,000 postal employees in 671 postal locations began a work stoppage. The department and leaders of the seven unions representing the postal employees met to try to agree on a plan for reorganization. That plan was submitted to Congress, and on August 12, 1970, President Nixon signed into law the most comprehensive postal legislation since the founding of the Republic.

The new organization, renamed the United States Postal Service, began operating on July 1, 1971, under the vested authority of a board of governors. The board comprises eleven members, nine of whom are appointed by the president on a bipartisan basis with advice and consent of the Senate. The nine members in turn appoint a tenth member of the board, the postmaster general, who serves as the chief executive officer of the Postal Service. The nine members and the postmaster general appoint the deputy postmaster general, who serves as the eleventh member of the board. The new legislation also established an independent postal rate commission of five members, appointed by the president, to recommend postal rates and classifications for adoption by the board of governors. *(See "Postal Rate Commission," p. 1052, in this chapter.)*

Notes

1. *Federal Regulatory Directory, 1983-1984* (Washington, D.C.: Congressional Quarterly Inc., 1983), 3.
2. Samuel Huntington, "The Marasmus of the ICC," *Yale Law Journal* 61 (April 1952): 467-509.
3. Marver H. Bernstein, *Regulating Business by Independent Commission* (Princeton, N.J.: Princeton University Press, 1955).
4. Robert E. Cushman, *The Independent Regulatory Commissions* (New York: Oxford University Press, 1941), 19.
5. *Federal Regulatory Directory, 1983-1984,* 16-20.
6. Marver H. Bernstein, *The Job of the Federal Executive* (Washington, D.C.: Brookings, 1958), 172.
7. William E. Brigman, "The Executive Branch and the Independent Regulatory Agencies," *Presidential Studies Quarterly* 11 (Spring 1981): 251.
8. Linda Fisher, "Fifty Years of Presidential Appointments," in *The In-and-Outers: Presidential Appointees and Transient Government in Washington,* ed. G. Calvin Mackenzie (Baltimore: Johns Hopkins University Press, 1987), 4.
9. *Federal Regulatory Directory, 1983-1984,* 37.
10. Louis Kohlmeier, Jr., *The Regulators: Watchdog Agencies and the Public Interest* (New York: Harper and Row, 1969).
11. G. Calvin Mackenzie, *The Politics of Presidential Appointments* (New York: Free Press, 1981), 82-83.
12. Brigman, "The Executive Branch," 249.

Selected Bibliography

Bernstein, Marver H. *Regulating Business by Independent Commission.* Princeton, N.J.: Princeton University Press, 1955.

_____. *The Job of the Federal Executive.* Washington, D.C.: Brookings, 1958.

Brigman, William E. "The Executive Branch and the Independent Regulatory Agencies." *Presidential Studies Quarterly* 11 (Spring 1981): 244-261.

Cushman, Robert E. *The Independent Regulatory Commissions.* New York: Oxford University Press, 1941.

Federal Regulatory Directory, 1983-1984. Washington, D.C.: Congressional Quarterly Inc., 1983.

Fisher, Linda. "Fifty Years of Presidential Appointments." In *The In-and-Outers: Presidential Appointees and Transient Government in Washington,* ed. G. Calvin Mackenzie. Baltimore: Johns Hopkins University Press, 1987.

Huntington, Samuel. "The Marasmus of the ICC." *Yale Law Journal* 61 (April 1952): 467-509.

Kohlmeier, Louis, Jr. *The Regulators: Watchdog Agencies and the Public Interest.* New York: Harper and Row, 1969.

Mackenzie, G. Calvin. *The Politics of Presidential Appointments.* New York: Free Press, 1981.

Presidential Commissions

Since the birth of this nation, presidents have been appointing commissions to probe subjects that normally are beyond the daily scope of presidential advisory organizations. Twentieth-century presidents have relied on commissions to gather information and to focus public attention on specific problems.

Although commissions can be created either by the president or by Congress, they are usually placed within the executive office. Carl Marcy, an early scholar of presidential commissions, has noted that commissions "grow out of the inadequacies in the executive departments or in Congress, or, in some instances, they develop because of the unusual nature of the problem to be met." [1] In recent years the number and variety of presidential commissions have increased tremendously. Yet often they have been ridiculed by presidential scholars and the press for their sometimes meaningless objectives and empty conclusions. In truth, not all presidential commissions have worked well; some, however, have proven valuable and important.

Presidents have no specific constitutional grant of authority to appoint commissions. They usually justify such a step, however, by pointing to the general grant of authority in the Constitution that directs the president to "take care that the laws be faithfully executed" and "from time to time give to the Congress information on the State of the Union, and recommend to their consideration such measures as he shall judge necessary and expedient" (Article II, section 3). President John Tyler (1841-1845), in naming a presidential commission to investigate corruption in the New York City Customhouse, was the first president to justify such action by pointing to his constitutional authority to do so. Tyler asserted that the information collected by the commission was for his use as president, but that it probably would find its way to Congress in the form of proposed legislation. He argued: "The expediency, if not the necessity, of inquiries into the transactions of our customs houses, especially in cases where abuses and malpractices are alleged, must be obvious to Congress." [2] His constitutional justification of presidential commissions has stood up over the years.

Although it is generally recognized that presidents have the power to establish presidential commissions, they often seek congressional approval anyway. One reason may be the funds required to operate and staff a presidential commission. Presidents often seek public funds for financing commission activities through legislation, which Congress routinely passes. Some presidential commissions, however, are created by an executive order of the president and are financed by emergency, executive, or special projects funds, which are spent at the president's discretion. President Herbert C. Hoover (1929-1933), who significantly expanded the use of presidential commissions by appointing sixty-two during his first sixteen months in office, reportedly raised at least $2 million in private funds to finance them.

Presidential commissions date back to the administration of George Washington (1789-1797), who appointed a commission to investigate the Whiskey Rebellion. In this incident a group of liquor distillers in western Pennsylvania threatened the nation with civil disorder over the federal liquor tax. Washington, perplexed over a situation potentially divisive to the young nation, took the problem to a group of distinguished citizens; he clearly had confidence in their findings. In his sixth annual address to the Congress, Washington flatly stated: "The report of the commissioners marks their firmness and abilities, and must unite all virtuous men." [3]

Most nineteenth-century presidents used commissions to meet the specific needs of their administrations. President Martin Van Buren (1837-1841), for example, appointed a commission to examine the European postal systems. Strong presidents have used commissions freely. Andrew Jackson (1829-1837) appointed two commissions just to check up on the actions of the Navy.

The use of presidential commissions is nevertheless primarily a twentieth-century phenomenon. The first serious study of commissions found that some one hundred commissions had been appointed up to 1940.[4] A more recent study indicated that another forty-four were appointed between 1945 and 1970.[5] Since 1970 their numbers have increased greatly. In the late 1980s the White House Personnel Office listed about 250 commissions or special committees.[6] These commissions ranged from the President's Council on Physical Fitness and Sports to the President's Committee on the Arts and Humanities to the Presidential Commission on the Human Immunodeficiency Virus Epidemic (AIDS Commission).

Over the years presidential commissions have played significant roles in many policy areas. Recent commissions have investigated business regulation, tariffs, government waste, defense spending, the space program, Social Security,

By W. Craig Bledsoe

Although presidential commissions are largely a twentieth-century phenomenon, they date back to George Washington's administration, when he appointed a commission to investigate the Whiskey Rebellion.

Library of Congress

the Iran-contra affair, and government reorganization. Theodore Roosevelt (1901-1909) introduced the use of commissions for substantive policy advice to the president. Inspired by the royal commissions used extensively in Great Britain to investigate policy questions, Roosevelt appointed a number of commissions during his administration, including the Aldrich Commission, whose recommendations led to establishment of the Federal Reserve System. Herbert Hoover himself, after his retirement from the presidency, headed two important commissions on government reorganization appointed by Presidents Harry S Truman and Dwight D. Eisenhower, respectively. Presidential commissions also have been sent overseas to supervise national elections and investigate the stability of foreign governments. In 1917, for example, after the overthrow of Czar Nicholas II, President Woodrow Wilson sent a special commission to Russia to find out how democratic the regime of Aleksandr Fyodorovich Kerensky would be.

Although the objectives of presidential commissions have varied, most have been important to presidential decision making, and many have contributed significantly to the development of government policy. For example, Franklin D. Roosevelt's most notable commission, the President's Committee on Administrative Management (Brownlow Committee), developed the blueprint for the Executive Office of the President. *(See White House Office chapter in Part V.)*

Types of Presidential Commissions

Presidential commissions fall into three broad categories: permanent federal advisory organizations, ad hoc or blue ribbon commissions, and White House conferences.

Permanent Federal Advisory Organizations

When presidents want advice from sources outside the White House staff and the cabinet, they often establish a permanent advisory organization—committee, commission, council, board, or task force—within the executive branch. These organizations formulate and coordinate recommendations for the president on specific policy issues over an indefinite period of time. A permanent advisory organization is either given independent status, placed in the Executive Office of the President (EOP), or placed in the department to which it is most germane. *(See Table 1.)* For example, the Advisory Committee for Trade Negotiations, the Presidential Board of Advisors on Private Sector Initiatives, and the President's Committee on the Arts and Humanities are officially located in EOP. Both the National Advisory Committee on Oceans and Atmosphere and the President's Export Council are located in the Department of Commerce. The Advisory Committee on Federal Pay has independent organizational status.

Permanent advisory organizations usually have the right to review and question presidential initiatives and programs. Congress may give these organizations large grants of authority, and it usually specifies membership qualifications and the terms of office for members. Because permanent advisory organizations often are set up in response to interest group pressure, their composition is likely to reflect the respective groups. Normally, qualifications for advisory organization membership are couched in language open to broad interpretation, but statutory provisions usually make interest group representation mandatory. The Federal Council on the Aging, for example, must have members representative of older Americans and national organizations that have an interest in the aging.

Although permanent advisory organizations are designed to facilitate presidential decision making, presidents sometimes view them as an uninvited burden. For example, the National Council on Marine Resources and Engineering Development (1966-1971), established to develop a comprehensive program of marine science exploration, was forced upon Lyndon B. Johnson's administration by interest groups trying to protect their industry. Both Presidents Johnson and Richard Nixon often clashed with the council. Thus, when Nixon took office he dismantled the group by moving its functions into existing departments. Presidential scholar Richard M. Pious has described the effects of these organizations: "The president has little time to consider their proposals and may wall himself off from officials who run them. He may become impatient with long-range planning and irritated at lack of consideration for his political problems." [7]

Ad Hoc Commissions

Ad hoc commissions investigate particular issues or related policy questions. They consist of three or more members, who are appointed directly by the president for a specified period of time. A commission is considered ad hoc

Library of Congress

President Hoover significantly expanded the use of presidential commissions, appointing sixty-two during his first sixteen months in office.

Table 1 Presidential Advisory Organizations, 1987

Organization [a]	Location
Advisory Committee on Federal Pay	Independent
Advisory Committee for Radio Broadcasting to Cuba	EOP
Advisory Committee for Trade Negotiations	EOP
Advisory Council on Dependents Education	DOD
Advisory Council on Education Statistics	DED
Advisory Council on Historic Preservation	EOP
Commission of Fine Arts	Independent
Commission on Presidential Scholars	DED
Employee Retirement Income Security Act Advisory Council (ERISA)	DOL
Federal Council on the Aging	HHS
Federal Council on the Arts and Humanities	EOP
Intergovernmental Advisory Council on Education	DED
Missing Children's Advisory Board	DOJ
National Advisory Committee on Oceans and Atmosphere	DOC/NOAA
National Advisory Council on Adult Education	DED
National Advisory Council on Child Nutrition	USDA
National Advisory Council on Continuing Education	DED
National Advisory Council on Indian Education	DED
National Advisory Council on Maternal, Infant and Fetal Nutrition	USDA
National Advisory Council on Women's Educational Programs	DED
National Agricultural Research and Extension Users Advisory Board	USDA
National Cancer Advisory Board	HHS
National Commission for Employment Policy	DOL
National Council on Educational Research	DED
National Council on Vocational Education	DED
National Highway Safety Advisory Committee	DOT
National Volunteer Advisory Council	EOP
Presidential Academic Fitness Program	DED
Presidential Advisory Commission on Small and Minority Business	SBA
President's Advisory Council on Mediation and Conciliation	FMCS
President's Board of Advisors on Private Sector Initiatives	EOP
President's Cancer Panel	HHS
President's Commission on Americans Outdoors	DOI
President's Commission on Executive Exchange	EOP
President's Commission on White House Fellowships	EOP
President's Committee on the Arts and the Humanities	EOP
President's Committee on Employment of the Handicapped	DOL
President's Committee on Mental Retardation	HHS
President's Committee on the National Medal of Science	EOP
President's Council on Integrity and Efficiency	EOP
President's Council on Physical Fitness and Sports	HHS
President's Economic Policy Advisory Board	EOP
President's Export Council	DOC
President's Foreign Intelligence Advisory Board	EOP
President's National Security Telecommunications Advisory Committee	EOP
President's Physical Evaluation Board	Army
President's Task Force on Legal Equity for Women	EOP
South Florida Task Force and National Narcotics Border Interdiction System	EOP
U.S. Arms Control General Advisory Committee	USACDA
U.S. Sentencing Commission	DOJ
United States Advisory Commission on Public Diplomacy	USIA

Source: Charles B. Brownson and Anna L. Brownson, eds., *1987 Federal Staff Directory* (Mt. Vernon, Va: Congressional Staff Directory, Ltd., 1987), 46-47.

Note: DED-Department of Education; DOC-Department of Commerce; DOD-Department of Defense; DOI-Department of the Interior; DOJ-Department of Justice; DOL-Department of Labor; DOT-Department of Transportation; EOP-Executive Office of the President; FMCS-Federal Mediation and Conciliation Service; HHS-Department of Health and Human Services; NOAA-National Oceanic and Atmospheric Administration; SBA-Small Business Administration; USACDA-U.S. Arms Control and Disarmament Agency; USDA-U.S. Department of Agriculture; USIA-U.S. Information Agency.

a. Active as of 1987.

when it has a termination and reporting date not more than three years after its creation. Created either by executive order, by congressional legislation, or by joint action, ad hoc commissions are purely advisory with no power to implement their findings or recommendations, which are published and made available to the public. At least one member of an ad hoc commission must not be from the executive branch. Members, however, may be from Congress, the federal judiciary, or state or local governments, or they may be private citizens. Many ad hoc commissions have been composed entirely of private citizens.[8]

Ad hoc commissions are sometimes called blue ribbon commissions when their members have distinguished records in the public or private sector. Thus, in this way national leaders in business, agriculture, science, technology, and other important fields, who otherwise might not accept permanent positions in the federal government or might not make a suitable permanent adviser, are able to serve in a temporary but official advisory capacity to the president. A 1979 study of the effect of ad hoc commissions on presidential policy making found that of the thirteen hundred commissioners studied "over 60 percent were prestigious members of some national elite at the time of their appointment."[9]

Ad hoc commissions usually are asked to examine a particular problem and to offer advice on how to deal reasonably with that problem. According to political scientist David Flitner, Jr., such commissions are either procedure oriented, situation oriented, or crisis oriented.[10] Procedure-oriented commissions examine the operating procedures of existing agencies before recommending improvements in their efficiency or making judgments about their overall utility. These commissions have examined, among other things, postal procedures, criminal code reform, and general government operations. For example, the 1980 Grace Commission on More Effective Government examined the efficiency of virtually all federal government operations in the United States.

Situation-oriented commissions investigate broad areas of vital concern to large sectors of the population. These commissions include the Commission on Law Enforcement and the Administration of Justice (Katzenbach Commission), the Commission on Obscenity and Pornography (Lockhart Commission), the Commission on Population Growth and the American Future (Rockefeller Commission), and the National Commission on Marijuana and Drug Abuse (Shafer Commission).

As their name implies, crisis-oriented commissions arise from a particular event or crisis. Such a commission may or may not investigate the more fundamental cause underlying the crisis. Examples of crisis-oriented commissions include the President's Commission on the Assassination of President Kennedy (Warren Commission), the National Advisory Commission on Civil Disorders (Kerner Commission), the National Commission on the Causes and Prevention of Violence (Eisenhower Commission), the President's Commission on Campus Unrest (Scranton Commission), and the AIDS Commission.

White House Conferences

The White House conference is another means of going beyond the traditional executive branch advisory bodies. Invitees to such a conference (often as many as several hundred attend) usually meet for several days to discuss a specific topic. Like ad hoc commissions, White House conferences are temporary and must report back to the president on the subject of their investigation.

Customarily, a small organizational committee is convened first to prepare an agenda for the conference itself. The 1980 White House Conference on Families, for example, followed the administrative work of the National Advisory Committee to the White House Conference on Families, which was established in June 1979 to guide and assist the chair of the conference.

Most conferences meet only once or in a series of panels or committees that make recommendations to the entire conference. Another small committee usually writes the report of the conference.[11]

The White House Conference on International Cooperation, held in late 1965, was typical of this kind of conference. Called in recognition of the International Year of Cooperation, designated by the United Nations, the conference was designed to promote a dialogue between private citizens and government officials on international problems and prospects for world peace. A National Citizen's Commission on International Cooperation, composed of 230 members working in thirty separate committees, was convened to lay the groundwork for the conference. In addition to these committees, other government and private experts were added as the committees went about their deliberations. All together more than a thousand persons from various areas of expertise took part in the overall discussions before the final conference was held in December 1965. Although all the committees did not come together until the final conference, each put in many hours in their separate meetings. For example, the Committee on Culture and Intellectual Exchange divided itself into twelve committees and held six meetings of the full committee, and the Arms Control and Disarmament Committee held four full committee meetings with many of its members meeting regularly in smaller groups. The final conference produced a report entitled "Blueprint for Peace," which contained over four hundred recommendations.[12]

Paul Hosefros, *New York Times*

The 1987 three-member Tower Commission investigated the White House's involvement in the Iran-contra affair. From left: Sen. John Tower, President Ronald Reagan, Edmund Muskie, and Gen. Brent Scowcroft.

The Commissioners

Although White House conferences tend to be large affairs, most presidential commissions are relatively small, with between fifteen and twenty-five members. The size of a commission usually depends on its scope and possible political impact. For example, one of the smallest recent ad hoc commissions was the three-member President's Special Review Board, or Tower Commission, which in 1987 investigated the White House's involvement in the Iran-contra affair. One of the largest was the twenty-four-member Commission on Population Growth and the American Future, established during the early 1970s to study the effects of population growth on the United States. The more narrowly defined the commission's topic, the more likely it is that the commission will be small. The 1970 President's Commission on Campus Unrest, founded to study disorder and violence on college and university campuses, had only nine members. The larger commissions usually are given more time to conduct their operations. *(See Table 2.)*

The appointment of commissioners is related to how the commission was established. If a president establishes a commission by executive order, the president is responsible for appointing all members of the commission. If Congress at the request of the president or through its own initiative establishes a commission through statutory law within the presidency, appointment power is divided among several sources with the president having the majority of appointments. The two Hoover-chaired Commissions on the Organization of the Executive Branch of Government of 1949 and 1955 are good examples of presidential commissions established by statutory law with appointment power divided among different sources. Both commissions were set up by a unanimous vote of Congress. Each commission had twelve members—four appointed by the president, four by the vice president, and four by the Speaker of the House. Of these, at least two members had to come from the private sector and two from the public sector. Moreover, appointments had to be based on proportional partisan representation. The first Hoover Commission comprised six Democrats and six Republicans; the second, five Democrats and seven Republicans. The Commission on Population Growth and the American Future had a congressionally mandated membership composed as follows:

> (1) two members of the Senate who shall be members of different political parties and who shall be appointed by the President of the Senate;
> (2) two members of the House of Representatives who shall be members of different political parties and shall be appointed by the Speaker of the House of Representatives; and
> (3) not to exceed twenty members appointed by the President.[13]

Most commissions represent a number of constituencies. According to Frank Popper, a scholar of presidential commissions, "A commission generally includes at least one businessman, labor leader, lawyer, educator, editor, farmer, woman, Negro, Protestant, Catholic, Jew, Easterner, Midwesterner, Southerner, Westerner, federal government official, congressman, member of a previous administration, enlightened amateur, and friend of the president." [14] Even though many of these constituencies may be represented by one person, most major sectors of American society will be represented on a single commission. Presidents customarily attempt to maintain bipartisanship on commissions; to do otherwise would completely discredit the results of the commission's investigation.

Table 2 Number of Commissioners on Recent Presidential Commissions

Commission	Number of commissioners
President's Commission on the Assassination of President Kennedy	7
President's Commission on Law Enforcement and the Administration of Justice	19
National Advisory Commission on Civil Disorders	11
National Commission on the Causes and Prevention of Violence	13
Commission on Obscenity and Pornography	18
President's Commission on Campus Unrest	9
Commission on Population Growth and the American Future	24
National Commission on Marijuana and Drug Abuse	13

Source: David Flitner, Jr., *The Politics of Presidential Commissions* (Dobbs Ferry, N.Y.: Transnational Publishers, 1986), 45-46.

Commission appointments usually are not considered political plums, but most commissioners tend to be well known, with outstanding records in either public or private service. Representatives of the private sector are primarily attorneys, college professors, and other professionals. *(See Table 3.)*

Some scholars see the elite nature of commissions as a positive characteristic that allows them to forge a consensus among various elite interests. Daniel Bell, a member of the National Commission on Technology, Automation, and Economic Progress (1964-1965) has written: "The distinctive virtue of the government commission arrangement is that there is a specific effort to involve the full range of elite or organized opinion in order to see if a real consensus can be achieved." [15] Popper has noted that most commissioners are more like each other than like their constituents.

> [Commission members] know, or know of, each other. They are primarily administrators, and they are used to working in committees. They have already succeeded in their careers, and their commission service is an honor rather than a steppingstone. They do not really need the nominal payment they get for their commission service. Some have national power, and all share what may be called the conservatism of personal success.[16]

Although elites are represented on commissions, leaders of some interest groups are not. And because of the nature of elite representation, representatives of most minority groups are seldom on the rosters of commissions. For example, of the 114 members of the commissions listed in Tables 2 and 3, only 12 were women.[17] *(See Tables 2 and 3.)*

Any group that is out of the mainstream of American politics is not represented at all. Political scientists

Thomas E. Cronin and Sanford E. Greenberg noted that during the Eisenhower, Kennedy, and Johnson administrations, presidential commissions were "extraordinarily skewed in composition in favor of the best educated and the professionally well established." [18]

Elite participation on commissions is so complete that often the same names appear on commission rosters again and again. In seeking bipartisanship, both Democratic and Republican presidents often appoint the same people. And ad hoc commissions have been especially popular ways for former government officials to return to the policy-making process. From 1950 to 1970 seven individuals served on three commissions each and twenty-five on two commissions each.[19] Over the years Milton Eisenhower, President Eisenhower's brother, served on some twenty commissions. Among those officials who served on more than one commission during the Reagan administration (1981-1989) were former senator John G. Tower (R-Texas) and former secretary of state Edmund S. Muskie (National Commission on the Public Service and the President's Special Review Board), retired Air Force lieutenant general Brent Scowcroft (Commission on Defense Management and President's Special Review Board), former astronaut Neil Armstrong (*Challenger* Commission and National Commission on Space), former Virginia governor Charles S. Robb (National Commission on the Public Service and National Bipartisan Commission on Central America), and business executive J. Peter Grace (President's Private Sector Survey on Cost Control, Peace Corps Advisory Council, and Presidential Commission on World Hunger).

Table 3 Number of Commissioners by Profession

Profession	Number of commissioners
Attorney	15
Professor	14
U.S. representative	10
U.S. senator	10
Clergy	7
Medical	6
University president or dean	5
Business	4
Federal judge	4
Police	3
State government (not governor)	3
Cabinet member or official	2
Former governor	2
Housewife	2
Labor leader	2
Newspaper publisher or editor	2
Political action group	2
Private foundation official	2
Race relations group	2
Research, research institute	2
State judge	2
Student	2
Governor	1
Civic leader	1
Author	1
Mayor	1
University fellow	1
Cannot be determined	5

Source: David Flitner, Jr., *The Politics of Presidential Commissions* (Dobbs Ferry, N.Y.: Transnational Publishers, 1986), 46.

The tendency to appoint former government officials to commissions has created an "established class of commissioners who are tapped repeatedly for service." [20] A Johnson aide explained:

> There is a problem that the same damn names turn up time after time. It is as hard as the devil to find new people. There was a lot of talk about finding that bright young man in Iowa in the Kennedy Administration. They didn't find him. There is really a sort of a liberal house establishment. The same people keep turning up on the same problems. You have a deuce of a time trying to reach out to get outside of the major cities.

This situation results in what presidential commission critic Thomas R. Wolanin has described as a "ho-hum-those-guys-again" attitude from the public, which reduces the effectiveness and persuasiveness of a commission's work.[21]

Selection Process for Commission Members

Shortly after the decision has been made to establish a commission, a presidential aide usually is put in charge of developing a list of potential nominees. Political considerations almost always are part of the deliberations that go into formulating a list of members. One Johnson aide described the process:

> After we had a topic, we'd make up a list of the general skills and areas we wanted represented, but no names. The lists were a lot alike. We'd check with the appropriate departments, the Budget Bureau, and the Civil Service Commission. They'd suggest specific names which would go to the president. He would add, subtract, or substitute names or categories. He'd add the people we wanted for general wisdom-at-large delegates. When he didn't like a list, he'd say things like "That guy's been on everything lately," or "Everyone's from New York and Texas. See if you can spread it out a little." [22]

Most administrations have maintained lists of people who were recommended for appointment to various federal positions, or who came to the attention of the White House because of their distinguished accomplishments. In addition to consulting these files, presidential aides also consult various constituent groups. Sometimes people in these groups themselves volunteer, or groups submit names for consideration. Certain groups will be asked to submit names, especially if their support is crucial to the successful operation of the commission. The Kennedy administration, for example, wanted the support of both political parties for an investigation into the increasing costs of campaign financing. It thus asked the Republican National Committee to submit a list of names for the President's Commission on Campaign Costs (1961-1962). In addition, former cabinet members and other former presidential appointees frequently turn up on commissions because nominees often are chosen from lists of people who have served on previous commissions, who held positions in past administrations, or who testified at congressional hearings in the relevant area.[23]

Once the list of potential appointees has been narrowed, it is given to the president for final approval. As in most presidential appointments the amount of interest that individual presidents show in the final selection process varies. President Johnson, for example, paid meticulous attention to his commission appointments. Other presidents have given little attention to final decisions on commission personnel, especially if the commission is of minor importance. If the commission is politically important, however, presidents may intervene just before the final selection is made by deleting or adding names for personal or political reasons. For example, at the final selection point President John F. Kennedy added one of his personal friends to the list of nominees for the President's Commission on Campaign Costs. One of Kennedy's assistants explained, "He was conservative as hell but the president respected him. Kennedy had served in the House with him and may have served on the same committee with him."[24]

Selection Process for Commission Chairs

Because the chairs of commissions serve as the public symbols of their groups (their names may even be used as a shorthand way of referring to a commission), selection of the chair is an important presidential decision. The most famous example of this is probably the President's Commission on the Assassination of President Kennedy, which became known as the Warren Commission after its chairman, Chief Justice Earl Warren. Similarly, the Kerner Commission (named after former Illinois governor Otto Kerner) and the Grace Commission (named after industrialist Peter Grace) both represent commissions that became better known by the names of their chairs. The heads of commissions assume most of the responsibility for the operation of their groups. They publicize their commission's work by testifying before congressional committees, giving speeches, making television appearances, and writing articles about the commission's investigation. Presidents also may ask chairs to play a role in the selection of other commission members.

Most important, however, commission heads are responsible for leading their commissions to a consensus and producing a report with specific recommendations at the conclusion of their investigations. The chair sets the tone for the commission and its success or failure. Because chairs preside at meetings, they are in a distinctive position to provide the commission with leadership. Indeed, as Wolanin has noted, they can exercise social leadership and facilitate the process of producing the commission's report: "The role of the chairman is most often primarily political, producing agreement, and administrative, producing a report, rather than substantive."[25] Lloyd M. Cutler, executive director of the 1968-1969 National Commission on the Causes and Prevention of Violence (also known as the Eisenhower Commission on Violence), has described the importance of an effective chair:

> Our chairman was Dr. Milton Eisenhower, an able and devoted man who ... was the key to the success of the entire commission. Dr. Eisenhower was a man with whom all of the commissioners were ready to agree even though they might disagree a great deal with one another. It was his presence and his continuing force on the commission that I think led to the largely unanimous reports that were filed. He is also quite a draftsman in his own right and ... every word in this report was at least reviewed and edited by Dr. Eisenhower and a very large number of those words were written in the first instance by him.[26]

Commission chairs should have multidimensional qualities. According to Flitner, "The chairman must, ideally, exhibit the integrity and fairness of a judge, the administrative skills of an executive, and the intellectual abilities of a scholar."[27] President Johnson had to make a very thoughtful decision about his selection of a chair for the Commission on the Assassination of President Kennedy. In his memoirs Johnson commented on the politically sensitive appointment and his choice for the post:

> The Commission had to be bipartisan, and I felt that we needed a Republican chairman whose judicial ability and fairness were unquestioned. I don't believe that I ever considered anyone but Chief Justice Earl Warren for chairman. I was not an intimate of the Chief Justice. We had never spent ten minutes alone together, but to me he was the personification of justice and fairness in this country.... We had to bring the nation through that bloody tragedy, and Warren's personal integrity was a key element in assuring that all the facts would be unearthed and that the conclusions would be credible.[28]

The most important characteristics sought in a commission chair are national prominence and a reputation for fairness.

Although few potential nominees eventually refuse to chair a commission, presidents may have difficulty persuading some of their selections to serve. When Johnson asked Milton Eisenhower to chair the Commission on Violence, for example, Eisenhower proved somewhat reluctant. Johnson "persuaded" him by pointing out that a press conference already was scheduled for that day to announce the appointments to the commission. Most potential appointees end up agreeing to serve as chair because, as one commission member put it, "You just don't say no to the President of the United States."[29]

Commission Staff

One of the first and most important responsibilities of a commission chair is selection of the commission's staff. The staff provides the support services necessary to carry out the commission's mandate and does most of the commission's work. This includes collecting data, preparing briefings, coordinating meetings, and working out differences of opinion among commission members. Staffers usually are younger and not as well known as commissioners. They tend to be lawyers or academics, and they often come from federal agencies working in the commission's area of interest. Staffers not recruited from federal agencies most often come from universities, private industries, research firms, and private law practices.

Generally, a commission's staff is divided into four components: executive director, subordinate staff, consultants, and general counsel.

Executive Director

Although presidents may designate a commission's executive director, most often this task is left to the newly appointed commission chair, who may confer with the president or with other commission members. Most executive directors are known by someone in the White House or the federal agency that advocated creation of the commission. The executive director, perhaps with the assistance of the commission chair, is generally responsible for recruiting other staff members. If the staff is large, the higher-level staff members may recruit their own staff. In almost all cases, however, recruitment of staff members occupies a major portion of the executive director's initial time and efforts. Recruitment is especially difficult for executive directors of short-lived ad hoc commissions. Few potential staffers are willing to leave their permanent jobs for positions that will last no longer than a few months. Lloyd Cutler, executive director of the Eisenhower Commission on Violence, reportedly spent ten weeks of the eighteen-month commission lining up thirty-one staff members.[30]

In addition to hiring staff the executive director serves as mediator between the staff and the commission. According to political commentator Elizabeth Drew, the relationship between the commission and the staff is usually one of mutual contempt.

> The staff is often composed of young, less experienced people who still think that the world can and should be changed; the commissioners know better.... [In addition] the commissioners, being important people, are not very interested in chewing things over with a lot of young staff members.... So the policy alternatives go up from the staff, and the policy directives come down from the commission, and seldom do the twain meet, except in the person of the exhausted, whipsawed executive director.[31]

Executive directors thus serve not only as administrators but also as diplomats who must motivate and fashion the work of the commission. Popper observed that executive directors

> must prevent commissioners from taking the commission in contradictory or irrelevant directions. He has the nearly impossible task of making commissioners and staff members regard the commission as a cohesive group, and not as a fragmented and temporary collection of individuals. But above all, he must infuse the commissioners and staff with a sense of urgency.[32]

Executive directors are responsible as well for overseeing and coordinating the entire operation of their commissions. They are, above all, administrators, and they devote much of their time to activities that have little to do with the substance of the commission's work. The rest of the staff researches and writes the report. Drew noted that much of the job of an executive director is

> begging for money from executive agencies, which have their own problems,... cutting through civil service regulations so that the staff can be hired before the commission expires; arguing with the General Services Administration over office space and typewriters and with the Government Printing Office over how long it will take to print the report.[33]

Subordinate Staff

Past commission staffs have ranged in size from just a few staffers to well over a hundred. To some extent the size of the staff depends on the scope of the investigation—the narrower the scope, the smaller the staff. The Warren Commission, which conducted a very narrow investigation using the resources of the Federal Bureau of Investigation, had a relatively small staff of only 27. The Kerner Commission on Civil Disorders had a much broader scope and a staff of 115. No hard and fast rule can be applied to staff size, however. The most important determinant of the size of a commission's staff is the commission's operational budget, and that frequently is a political consideration. Popper has written:

> The fact that some technical commissions have a small staff often means that the president does not really want much substantive advice from them; he is doing little more than showing concern for a specialized group. If he had wanted more from them, he would have given them more money to hire larger staffs. Such funds are given to the small, highly publicized commissions from which he expects broad political impact.[34]

Not all commissions have the same positions. Staff titles may include: deputy or associate director, administrative officer, editorial officer, public affairs officer, and director of research.[35] Staff members usually are chosen for their competence in the areas relevant to the work of the commission. The staff director also tries not to rely too heavily on any one source of staff, thereby promoting the objectivity and independence of the staff in the eyes of the public. Finally, to establish political credibility staff appointees often have ties to important constituencies with which the commission must deal.[36]

Consultants

Commissions often use outside consultants and researchers—individuals, consulting firms, or "think tanks"—to supplement the work of the permanent staff. The 1967 President's Commission on Postal Organization relied on Arthur D. Little, Inc., a consulting firm in Cambridge, Massachusetts, for most of its research, and the Eisenhower Commission on Violence (1968-1969) hired the Louis Harris organization to take several polls. Consultants write most of the technical supplements that accompany a commission's final report, and they are free to disagree with the overall findings of the commission.[37] At least two ad hoc commissions used consulting organizations exclusively: the National Advisory Commission on Libraries (1969-1970) used nine private firms, and the President's Commission on an All-Volunteer Armed Force (1969-1970), three outside firms.[38]

Although consultants provide commissions with a variety of talents, commissioners and staffers often question their work. But, in fact, faced with time constraints, many consultants feel rushed and uncomfortable with their own efforts. Nevertheless, their work is an important part of a commission's effort. According to Popper, "The consultant's work, regardless of its quality and its pertinence to the report, is fundamentally valuable to a commission, not for its intellectual merits or policy proposals, but because it involves the appropriate academic, professional, and technical communities in the work of the commission." [39]

General Counsel

The complexity of the legal issues encountered by most commissions requires the services of legal counsel. Commissions having a large number of attorneys on staff may not appoint a general counsel, but this is the exception rather than the rule. Depending on the nature of a commission's investigation, its general counsel may consist of only one attorney or an entire legal staff. The Warren Commission, for example, had in addition to its regular staff of twenty-seven a fourteen-member legal team to investigate the assassination of President Kennedy. The general counsel is usually consulted on any legal questions that arise during the commission's investigation.

How Commissions Operate

Permanent commissions operate much like any federal agency; they carry out their investigations and business on an ongoing basis, funded by annual congressional appropriations. Ad hoc commissions, in contrast, operate under quite different circumstances because of the money and time constraints arising from their temporary status.

Ad hoc commissions must work toward a deadline. President Johnson called on the Kerner Commission, for example, to produce a preliminary report in March 1968, just seven months after the commission was established. Thus, as sociologist Amitai Etzioni has observed, "More than anything else, commissions are part of government by fire-brigade." [40] After forming, commissions spend much of their time hiring staff. They then organize to distribute the workload, investigate their area of concern, and report their findings, and they finally disband without any means of implementing their findings or recommendations. Whether good or bad, temporary ad hoc commissions are a stopgap method of solving problems. James F. Campbell, general counsel to the Eisenhower Commission on Violence, viewed the fast pace of ad hoc commissions in a positive light.

> It's a very hectic pace ... but at least one is thinking, deliberating, researching, and so on. You have the same kind of pace in the executive branch to "put out fires," and to meet budget deadlines, and to get something up to the Hill. The pace is just as fast there and there's no time for thinking or deliberating or writing or researching.... At least with commissions one is "hectically thinking." [41]

Commissions have varied in how often they meet. The Kerner Commission, for example, had a reputation for hard work and met a total of forty-four days over its lifetime of seven months. The mid-1960s President's Commission on Law Enforcement and the Administration of Justice had a more typical pace of only nineteen days over seventeen months. Meetings usually are held on weekends for the convenience of the participants and rarely take place more than once a month. Attendance also varies from commission to commission. Small, highly publicized commissions might have a normal attendance as high as 80 percent. Some commissions, however, rarely have more than 50 percent of their commissioners at a given meeting.[42] Wolanin found that most commissioners and staff members did not find poor attendance to be a problem; in fact, they found attendance at commission meetings adequate for exercising commission responsibilities. Although attendance at subcommittee meetings and hearings also tends to vary from commission to commission, it generally is considered good.[43]

Some passive members may attend commission meetings but not participate actively in commission proceedings. Most commissioners who attend meetings, however, participate in the debates and deliberations of the commission. Popper has reported that the commissioners who make the most useful contributions have the greatest sense of urgency about the commission's topic.[44] Just their appointment to the commission indicates that most commissioners have a generally high interest and involvement in the subject of the commission and therefore the commission's work. The impact of this active involvement is reflected in the writing of the report. According to one staff member of the National Commission on Technology, Automation, and Economic Progress, "The report went through fourteen bloody drafts, and I mean bloody. You couldn't recognize the relation between the first two drafts and the final report. This indicates the impact that the commissioners had." [45]

Wolanin has divided the approaches of commissioners to their work into two categories: the commissioner as statesman or stateswoman and the commissioner as constituency representative. Commissioners with the first perspective view the problem under investigation in terms of the public interest; those representing constituencies view their work primarily in terms of its impact on their clientele. As one labor leader explained, "When I serve [on a commission], I do so as an individual citizen, but always with the thought of labor's viewpoint, of course.... I just sit as a member and discuss the report, in particular how it affects the workers." [46]

Most commissioners are statesmen or stateswomen because of their initial objectivity, which usually figures in their selection for the commission, or because of their growth during the commission's investigation. Commissioners apparently undergo a period of learning which leads to their advocacy of positions that they ordinarily might oppose. Flitner called this phenomenon "collegial intellectual growth among commissioners," reflecting an exposure to facts that dispel the commissioner's preconceptions. He quoted Milton Eisenhower, whose Commission on Violence made eighty-one nearly unanimous recommendations: "It was a revelation to me.... We freed our minds of all preconceptions. When we started we couldn't agree on anything." [47]

Commissions carry out their investigations differently. Some commissions divide themselves into study groups or task forces that investigate specific areas within the broader scope of the commission. The 1967 Commission on Pornography, for example, had four study groups: (1) legal, (2) traffic and distribution, (3) effects, and (4) positive approaches. Each area was assigned commissioners, staff, consultants, and advisers. Some commissions do not use task forces at all. The Eisenhower Commission on Violence, for example, did not assign its commissioners to task forces. Instead, it allowed its staff the freedom to work on task force problems, and the commission then reviewed the staff's work.[48]

In addition to their private meetings and deliberations, commissions often hold hearings. With the exception of the final report, hearings are the most visible activity of a commission, and they allow commissioners to become better acquainted with their subject. Hearings may be open or closed. Closed hearings are primarily for informational purposes. The Warren Commission heard direct testimony from 94 witnesses in closed testimony. Its legal staff heard testimony from 395 others and received sixty-one sworn affidavits. These witnesses provided commissioners and staffers with a wealth of information from a variety of perspectives otherwise unavailable. Hearings generally allow a commission to be more thorough and impartial. According to Popper, "There is a general agreement, even among commissioners, that hearings inform commissioners so that, by the time the report is being written, their knowledge of the commission's subject is often comparable to the staff's." [49]

Public hearings also allow commissions to establish legitimacy and to generate publicity. Political scientist Martha Derthick found that members of the President's Commission on Campus Unrest "knew that by making hearings public, whatever value they might have as sources of information would be lost." The commission held public hearings anyway, however, "to demonstrate that it would listen to diverse opinions." [50] Howard Shuman, executive director of the National Commission on Urban Problems (1967-1968), has pointed out the dramatic effect of its public hearings:

> Among the best things the Commission did was to hold hearings in the ghettos of the major cities of the country.... The best testimony received was from the ordinary citizens. It had a fire and a spirit which was unmatched by the experts we heard.... The hearings and inspections provided a common experience for the members of our commission and united them as no other action could have done. [51]

Most presidential commission hearings receive more publicity than their congressional counterparts. For example, in investigating the ghetto racial riots of the summer of 1967, the Senate Permanent Subcommittee on Investigations, chaired by Democratic senator John L. McClellan of Arkansas, found the possible causes of the riots to be conspiracies, the involvement of antipoverty workers, and the moral degeneracy of the rioters. Public hearings conducted by the National Advisory Commission on Civil Disorders, an ad hoc presidential commission created to investigate the same problem, found no evidence of conspiracy, no misconduct on the part of antipoverty workers, and no evidence of the moral degeneracy of the rioters. Although the two investigations came to different conclusions, the Commission on Civil Disorders received greater publicity than McClellan's Senate investigation and its report became more widely accepted.[52]

For any commission, all of the staff work, investigations, public and private hearings, subcommittee meetings, and full commission deliberations are conducted with the goal of the final report in sight. Reports have varied in length from the three-page letter to the president produced by the President's Commission on the World's Fair (1959) to the six-volume report produced by the National Commission on Higher Education (1946-1947). Reports often include appendices of technical reports, subcommittee studies, and hearing transcripts.

Wolanin found that commissions generally use one of three methods in producing a report.[53] According to the most common method, subcommittees of commissioners review the data, and the staff for each group then produces position papers. After reviewing these papers, the subcommittees make recommendations to the full committee. The full commission then reviews the subcommittees' reports and recommendations, making revisions and producing a mutually acceptable final report. The second method frequently used by commissions is similar to the first, except that the subcommittees do not make detailed reports and recommendations to the full commission. Instead, all the subcommittees meet together acting as a committee of the whole, which undertakes all revisions, itself. This method is generally used by smaller commissions with narrowly defined mandates. According to the third and least used method, the commission makes policy decisions and then directs the writing of the report to conform to its decisions.

As the writing of the final report looms ever larger on the commission's agenda, tensions rise among the staff and the commissioners. Reports often go through draft after draft with certain commissioners seemingly impossible to satisfy. Some chapters of the final report of the Warren Commission reportedly went through twenty drafts. Staffers often spend day and night working on the final report and endure endless criticism from all sides. In describing this growing tension among the staff and commissioners, Popper recalled the words of a journalist who worked with several commissions:

> All the strands of activity and hostility always come together in the writing. The first few commission meetings haven't done anything more than introduce the commissioners to each other. They size up each other. Then in the next few meetings, attendance drops off and the staff begins to show its strength. Then the staff trots out its early drafts, and all of a sudden the swing members, the ones with open minds and without ideological preconceptions, assert themselves. They make worthwhile, influential suggestions about the drafts. Apparently vulnerable people like women and clergymen can pull a lot of weight here. Finally, in the last few meetings, the staff produces drafts all over the place, the homework swamps the commissioners, and the staff sneaks in everything they think they can get away with. They get away with a lot, because by this time the commissioners have fourteen chapters to read in two days, and it's too late to change anything anyway.[54]

In their final reports, however, commissions seek accommodations and compromise. Efforts also are made to ensure that relations among commissioners and staffers do not fragment beyond repair. A strong, competent chair is likely to intervene and call for more temperate rhetoric from commissioners. For example, Nicholas Katzenbach, chair of the President's Commission on Law Enforcement and the Administration of Justice, helped produce a unified report through his ability to negotiate compromise positions when serious conflicts developed among staffers and commissioners.[55]

Commissions often seek unanimity in their reports because they believe that it instills more legitimacy in their work. According to Martha Derthick, this goal leads to inaccuracies in reports. "Commissions frequently decide that it would be best not to confuse the nation with divided counsel. Since the commissioners usually are divided on important issues, this guarantees that a large number of these issues will be fudged." [56]

Although dissenting footnotes could be added to the final report, they usually do not appear. Instead, commissions seek consensus, and "consensus can nearly always be made to cover up differences." [57] For example, the Warren Commission was divided on whether President Kennedy and Texas governor John B. Connally were hit by the same bullet. Three commissioners believed that both men had been hit by the same bullet, while three others believed that the men were hit by different bullets.

In seeking a unanimous report, the commission entered into a debate over adjectives. One commissioner wanted the report to state that there was "compelling" evidence that the same bullet had hit both Kennedy and Connally. The commission finally compromised on the adjective "persuasive." The issue was never really settled by the commission.

Functions of Commissions

Although ostensibly used to supplement standard presidential advisory procedures, presidential commissions serve a variety of functions. Some scholars have argued that commissions serve no useful purposes and should not be a part of the presidential advisory system. Others have argued, somewhat skeptically, that presidents use commissions for their own purposes—that is, either to generate support for existing policies or to postpone effective action by passing the problem off on a presidential commission. Elizabeth Drew has listed eight rather cynical reasons for appointing a commission:

1. To obtain the blessing of distinguished men for something you want to do anyway.
2. To postpone action, yet be justified in insisting that you are working on the problem.
3. To act as a lightning rod, drawing political heat away from the White House.
4. To conduct an extensive study of something you do need to know more about before you act, in case you do.
5. To investigate, lay to rest rumors, and convince the public of the validity of one particular set of facts.
6. To educate the commissioners, or get them aboard on something you want to do.
7. Because you can't think of anything else to do.
8. To change the hearts and minds of men.[58]

Another factor further complicates trust in the efficacy of commission work: once a commission's report is written, presidents can choose either to follow or to ignore the report's recommendations. They sometimes choose to ignore them, fueling the fires of the critics. Sen. Edward M. Kennedy (D-Mass.) has characterized commissions as "so many Jiminy Crickets chirping in the ears of deaf presidents, deaf officials, deaf congressmen, and perhaps a deaf public." [59]

What functions do commissions actually serve? The conventional wisdom is that presidents appoint commissions to avoid confronting an issue, to delay action, or to divert public attention. Yet research indicates that most presidents heed and act favorably on the reports they receive from their commissions.[60] Commissions serve a variety of other purposes, however, besides merely providing presidents with advice. Several scholars have identified these functions, and political scientist George T. Sulzner has classified them into two general categories. Functions in the first category generally relate to solving problems. They include investigating, defining, and recommending action on specific problems and generating public demands for such action. Functions in the second category relate to presidential management of conflict. They include consensus building and pacifying political groups.[61] Each use of presidential commissions may go beyond the purely advisory function for which the commission was nominally created. Presidents may, and often do, use commissions to manage conflict during their administrations.

The first and most obvious function of commissions is to provide presidents with the information needed to make informed decisions. Although some scholars have inpugned this motive, most presidents appoint commissions to facilitate the fact-finding activities of the executive branch. According to Wolanin, "Most commissions are formed because the president wants to act but is not sure how, or is not sure that important segments of public opinion, congressional leadership, or executive branch agencies are ready to support him." [62] In fact, commission recommendations are usually accepted and often implemented. For example, President Truman's response to the growing demand for action against the outbreak of black lynchings in the fall of 1946 was appointment of the President's Committee on Civil Rights in late 1946 to look into civil rights violations across the nation. In his memoirs, Truman explained that he took this action "because of repeated antiminority incidents immediately after the war in which homes were invaded, property was destroyed, and a number of innocent lives were taken. I wanted to get the facts behind these incidents of disregard for individual and group rights which were reported in the news with alarming regularity. . . ." [63] The final report of the commission eventually forced congressional consideration and implementation of its various proposals.

Presidents often turn to presidential commissions to obtain information about a problem that regular presidential advisory mechanisms are unable to handle. Flitner has reported that a primary function of commissions is "surmounting the pathologies of organizational complexity: for avoiding duplication of effort and circumventing bureaucratic obstacles." [64] Some presidential commissions are able to bring together resources, skills, and information in a way that is unachievable by other advisory agencies of the executive branch. For example, the President's Private Sector Survey on Cost Control (1982-1983), or the Grace Commission, was composed entirely of private sector appointees, who were charged with recommending where the government could spend its money more efficiently. The 170 members of the Grace Commission issued a report that proposed 2,478 cost-cutting measures, which in theory would have saved the government $425 billion. Judging from the bureaucratic and congressional debate that ensued over the proposals, it is doubtful that any other executive branch advisory mechanism could have produced such a report. Four years after the report was issued only about thirteen hundred of its recommendations were in place, reportedly saving the government almost $39 million.

In addition to their advisory function, presidential commissions allow presidents to manage conflict by building a consensus for their programs. As many critics have charged, presidents use commissions to sell their programs to the country. Political commentator Harlan Cleveland has observed that "Commissions can . . . help the president build support for what he has already decided to do." [65] And according to Daniel Bell, the ability of presidents to use commissions to build consensus has become so pronounced that there is a danger that presidents may use commissions primarily to manipulate public opinion.[66] Other observers believe, however, that presidents can use commissions to focus the nation's attention on problems that otherwise would not gain legitimacy.

The very presence of "blue ribbon" commissioners, who represent a variety of interests, lends credibility to a commission's work. As an example, Etzioni pointed to the composition of the National Commission on the Causes and Prevention of Violence, which refocused the national dialogue on the causes and prevention of violent behavior: "If ten wise men drawn from such a cross-section of the nation support a set of conclusions, the country is more likely to go along with them than if these conclusions are advocated by ten experts." [67] Similarly, the National Bipartisan Commission on Central America (1984) gave the Reagan administration a report that essentially upheld the administration policy of increased military assistance to El

Salvador and continued aid to the Nicaraguan rebels. Because of its distinguished commissioners, headed by former secretary of state Henry Kissinger, and its bipartisan character, including former Democratic National Committee chairman Robert Strauss, criticism of the final report was muted.

Increasingly, however, the blue ribbon nature of some commissions has been questioned, leaving some final commission reports suspect. For example, the composition of the 1988 Presidential Commission on the Human Immunodeficiency Virus Epidemic (AIDS Commission) apparently offended both ends of the political spectrum. The Reagan administration nominated appointees representing various interests in the AIDS crisis. Liberals, however, were offended by the participation of such conservatives as state representative Penny Pullen of Illinois, who authored a mandatory AIDS testing bill, and conservatives were outraged by the inclusion of an avowed homosexual, New York geneticist Dr. Frank Lily. The medical community complained, as well, noting that not enough medical personnel were represented. As a result, the commission's final report did not receive the widespread support enjoyed by most other commission reports.

The symbolic functions of commissions can be the most useful to presidents in managing conflict. The very creation of a commission sends signals to various groups and individuals that the administration is concerned about a specific problem. According to Flitner,

> By their existence, commissions symbolize the highest cognizance and concern over a situation. Commissions communicate that the president is aware of a situation and will begin a process of directing attention to it. This implies a search for facts and answers and willingness to give the disaffected members of society a "fair hearing." . . . In short, commissions represent the fact that the president is at least doing something.[68]

In many respects the creation of the AIDS Commission was a symbolic response of the Reagan administration to the growing AIDS crisis. Similarly, in late 1987 in response to demands by public service groups, President Reagan appointed the National Commission on the Public Service to conduct a two-year study of the morale of federal bureaucrats.

Some critics charge that the symbolic function of commissions undermines effective policy making by allowing presidents to delay action. Cleveland has contended: "On the whole, presidential commissions are probably better adapted to smothering problems with well-publicized inaction than to paving the way for novel action."[69] This assessment may have been true in some cases, but overall it does not seem to be the motivation behind most presidential commissions.

Delay does occur, however. Sulzner has suggested that the delay that results from the appointment of commissions is an integral part of the policy-making process by which government adapts to emerging social problems. It promotes political pacification through a cooling-off period. "Frequently, commissions hold public hearings where they solicit representative testimony from diverse sources, and these hearings can serve as outlets for the airing of grievances. Moreover, the opportunity for expression may have cathartic effects for the interests involved that may be as rewarding to them as the provision of concrete remedies."[70]

Over the years some commissions have been abused or ignored in their efforts. Commission recommendations often do not become policy; somethimes they do. The final report of the Commission on Law Enforcement and the Administration of Justice is generally credited with having prompted the passage of the Safe Streets Act of 1968, for example. But more than just making policy recommendations, commissions have served other important, although often symbolic, functions. According to Flitner,

> They have affected the attitudinal atmosphere of society. They have helped demythologize subjects such as the conspiracy theory or riot origins and the assumption that increasing population growth is necessarily advantageous. Commissions have helped lower the emotional content of certain issues, such as marijuana use. . . . Commissions have altered the terms in which issues are discussed and, although they have by no means either reached or convinced everyone of their findings, they have spread awareness to all levels of society, a not undesirable function in a democracy.[71]

Notes

1. Carl Marcy, *Presidential Commissions* (New York: King's Crown Press, 1945), 97.
2. Ibid., 8.
3. Quoted in Elizabeth B. Drew, "On Giving Oneself a Hotfoot: Government by Commission," *Atlantic Monthly,* May 1968, 45.
4. Marcy, *Presidential Commissions,* 8.
5. Frank Popper, *The President's Commissions* (New York: Twentieth Century Fund, 1970), 66-67.
6. Bill Whalen, "Commissions: The Mixed Ones Often Are More Productive," *Washington Times,* October 6, 1987.
7. Richard M. Pious, *The American Presidency* (New York: Basic Books, 1979), 164.
8. Alan L. Dean, "Ad Hoc Commissions for Policy Formulation," in *The Presidential Advisory System,* ed. Thomas E. Cronin and Sanford E. Greenberg (New York: Harper and Row, 1969), 101-102.
9. Terrence R. Tutchings, *Rhetoric and Reality: Presidential Commissions and the Making of Public Policy* (Boulder, Colo.: Westview, 1979), 12.
10. David Flitner, Jr., *The Politics of Presidential Commissions* (Dobbs Ferry, N.Y.: Transnational Publishers, 1986), 28-29.
11. Thomas R. Wolanin, *Presidential Advisory Commissions: Truman to Nixon* (Madison, Wis.: University of Wisconsin Press, 1975), 10.
12. Henry Fairlie, "Government by White House Conference: Two Views," in Cronin and Greenberg, *The Presidential Advisory System,* 144-149.
13. Flitner, *The Politics of Presidential Commissions,* 45.
14. Popper, *The President's Commissions,* 15.
15. Daniel Bell, "Government by Commission," in Cronin and Greenberg, *The Presidential Advisory System,* 121.
16. Popper, *The President's Commissions,* 18.
17. Flitner, *The Politics of Presidential Commissions,* 46.
18. Cronin and Greenberg, *The Presidential Advisory Commission,* xix.
19. Popper, *The President's Commissions,* 17.
20. "The Commission: How to Create a Blue Chip Consensus," *Time,* January 19, 1970, 20.
21. Quoted in Wolanin, *Presidential Advisory Commissions,* 85.
22. Quoted in Popper, *The President's Commissions,* 20.
23. Wolanin, *Presidential Advisory Commissions,* 82-83.
24. Quoted in ibid., 83.
25. Ibid., 123.
26. Quoted in Flitner, *The Politics of Presidential Commissions,* 50-51.
27. Ibid., 50.

28. Lyndon Baines Johnson, *The Vantage Point—Perspectives on the Presidency, 1963-1969* (New York: Popular Library, 1971), 26.
29. Wolanin, *Presidential Advisory Commissions,* 84.
30. Popper, *The President's Commissions,* 22.
31. Drew, "On Giving Oneself a Hotfoot," 48.
32. Popper, *The President's Commissions,* 24.
33. Drew, "On Giving Oneself a Hotfoot," 48.
34. Popper, *The President's Commissions,* 22.
35. Flitner, *The Politics of Presidential Commissions,* 59.
36. Wolanin, *Presidential Advisory Commissions,* 108.
37. Popper, *The President's Commissions,* 24.
38. Tutchings, *Rhetoric and Reality,* 27.
39. Popper, *The President's Commissions,* 26.
40. Amitai Etzioni, "Why Task Force Studies Go Wrong," *Wall Street Journal,* July 9, 1968, 18.
41. Quoted in Flitner, *The Politics of Presidential Commissions,* 63.
42. Popper, *The President's Commissions,* 27.
43. Wolanin, *Presidential Advisory Commissions,* 112.
44. Popper, *The President's Commissions,* 28.
45. Quoted in Wolanin, *Presidential Advisory Commissions,* 113.
46. Ibid., 121.
47. Flitner, *The Politics of Presidential Commissions,* 79-80; quote on p. 80.
48. Ibid., 65-66.
49. Popper, *The President's Commissions,* 37.
50. Martha Derthick, "On Commissionship—Presidential Variety," Brookings Reprint No. 245 (Washington, D.C.: Brookings, 1972), 627, 636.
51. Quoted in Flitner, *The Politics of Presidential Commissions,* 77.
52. Popper, *The President's Commissions,* 36-37.
53. Wolanin, *Presidential Advisory Commissions,* 110-111.
54. Popper, *The President's Commissions,* 31-32.
55. Flitner, *The Politics of Presidential Commissions,* 87.
56. Derthick, "On Commissionship," 629.
57. Popper, *The President's Commissions,* 33.
58. See Drew, "On Giving Oneself a Hotfoot," 45-47.
59. Quoted in Flitner, *The Politics of Presidential Commissions,* 2.
60. Thomas E. Cronin, "On the Separation of Brain and State: Implications for the Presidency," in *Modern Presidents and the Presidency,* ed. Marc Landy (Lexington, Mass.: Lexington Books, 1985), 60-61.
61. George T. Sulzner, "The Policy Process and the Uses of National Governmental Study Commissions," in *Perspectives on the Presidency: A Collection,* ed. Stanley Bach and George T. Sulzner (Lexington, Mass.: D. C. Heath, 1974), 207.
62. Wolanin, *Presidential Advisory Commissions,* 193.
63. Harry S Truman, *Memoirs* (Garden City, N.J.: Doubleday, 1955-1956), 2: 180.
64. Flitner, *The Politics of Presidential Commissions,* 180.
65. Harlan Cleveland, "Inquiry into Presidential Inquirers," in *The Dynamics of the American Presidency,* ed. Donald B. Johnson and Jack L. Walker (New York: Wiley, 1964), 292.
66. Bell, "Government by Commission," 121.
67. Etzioni, "Why Task Force Studies Go Wrong," 18.
68. Flitner, *The Politics of Presidential Commissions,* 180.
69. Cleveland, "Inquiry into Presidential Inquirers," 292.
70. Sulzner, "The Policy Process," 216.
71. Flitner, *The Politics of Presidential Commissions,* 180-181.

Selected Bibliography

Bach, Stanley, and George T. Sulzner, eds. *Perspectives on the Presidency: A Collection.* Lexington, Mass.: D. C. Heath, 1974.

Bell, Daniel. "Government by Commission." In *The Presidential Advisory System,* ed. Thomas E. Cronin and Sanford E. Greenberg, 117-123. New York: Harper and Row, 1969.

Cleveland, Harlan. "Inquiry into Presidential Inquirers." In *The Dynamics of the American Presidency,* ed. Donald B. Johnson and Jack L. Walker, 291-294. New York: Wiley, 1964.

Cronin, Thomas E. "On the Separation of Brain and State: Implications for the Presidency." In *Modern Presidents and the Presidency,* ed. Marc Landy, 51-63. Lexington, Mass.: Lexington Books, 1985.

Cronin, Thomas E., and Sanford E. Greenberg, eds. *The Presidential Advisory Commission.* New York: Harper and Row, 1969.

Dean, Alan L. "Ad Hoc Commissions for Policy Formulation." In *The Presidential Advisory System,* ed. Thomas E. Cronin and Sanford E. Greenberg, 101-116. New York: Harper and Row, 1969.

Derthick, Martha. "On Commissionship—Presidential Variety." Brookings Reprint No. 245. Washington, D.C.: Brookings, 1972.

Drew, Elizabeth B. "On Giving Oneself a Hotfoot: Government by Commission." *Atlantic Monthly,* May 1968, 45-49.

Etzioni, Amitai. "Why Task Force Studies Go Wrong." *Wall Street Journal,* July 9, 1968, 18.

Fairlie, Henry. "Government by White House Conference: Two Views." In *The Presidential Advisory System,* ed. Thomas E. Cronin and Sanford E. Greenberg, 144-149. New York: Harper and Row, 1969.

Flitner, David, Jr., *The Politics of Presidential Commissions.* Dobbs Ferry, N.Y.: Transnational Publishers, 1986.

Johnson, Donald B., and Jack L. Walker, eds. *The Dynamics of the American Presidency.* New York: Wiley, 1964.

Landy, Marc, ed. *Modern Presidents and the Presidency.* Lexington, Mass.: Lexington Books, 1985.

Marcy, Carl. *Presidential Commissions.* New York: King's Crown Press, 1945.

Popper, Frank. *The President's Commissions.* New York: Twentieth Century Fund, 1970.

Sulzner, George T. "The Policy Process and the Uses of National Government Study Commissions." In *Perspectives on the Presidency: A Collection,* ed. Stanley Bach and George T. Sulzner, 206-218. Lexington, Mass.: D. C. Heath, 1974.

"The Commission: How to Create a Blue Chip Consensus." *Time,* January 19, 1970, 20.

Tutchings, Terrence R. *Rhetoric and Reality: Presidential Commissions and the Making of Public Policy.* Boulder, Colo.: Westview, 1979.

Whalen, Bill. "Commissions: The Mixed Ones Often Are More Productive." *Washington Times,* October 6, 1987.

Wolanin, Thomas R. *Presidential Advisory Commissions: Truman to Nixon.* Madison, Wis.: University of Wisconsin Press, 1975.

Former Presidents

When the Framers of the Constitution rejected a proposal by Alexander Hamilton that the president be elected to a lifetime term, they unwittingly created an unofficial office: the ex-presidency. At noon on January 20, 1989, Ronald Reagan became the nation's thirty-second former president. (Seven presidents died while still in office.) Collectively, Reagan's thirty-one predecessors had lived more than three hundred years, including three—Richard Nixon, Gerald R. Ford, and Jimmy Carter—who were former presidents during the entire Reagan presidency. *(See Table 1.)* Only once before 1989 had more former presidents been alive at the same time: five—Martin Van Buren, John Tyler, Franklin Pierce, Millard Fillmore, and James Buchanan—all were living between March 4, 1861, when Buchanan left office, and January 18, 1862, when Tyler died. On four occasions—all of them in the early or mid-nineteenth century—the nation had four living ex-presidents: March 4, 1825-July 4, 1826 (John Adams, Thomas Jefferson, James Madison, and James Monroe); March 1, 1845-June 8, 1845 (John Quincy Adams, Andrew Jackson, Van Buren, and Tyler); March 4, 1857-March 4, 1861 (Van Buren, Tyler, Fillmore, and Pierce); and January 18, 1862-July 24, 1862 (Van Buren, Fillmore, Pierce, and Buchanan). On five occasions there have been no living ex-presidents at all: for two years after George Washington died (1799-1801), for two years after Andrew Johnson died (1875-1877), for two years after Grover Cleveland died (1908-1909), and from January 22, 1973, when Lyndon B. Johnson died, until August 9, 1974, when Nixon resigned.

"[F]ormer presidents," observed the political scientist Alan Evan Schenker, "are a mixed bag, older and younger, Democrat and Republican, willing and unwilling retirees, healthy and ill, rich and poor, loved and hated." [1] Some former presidents were young when they left office: Theodore Roosevelt, Pierce, Fillmore, and James K. Polk were all in their early fifties. (Indeed, Schenker has noted, the majority of post-presidential years have been lived by men in their fifties and sixties.) Others were old at the time of their retirement: Dwight D. Eisenhower was seventy, Buchanan and Jackson were sixty-nine, and Truman was sixty-eight. Reagan, the oldest person ever to be elected to the presidency, was also the oldest ever to leave it: he turned seventy-eight on February 6, 1989.

Former presidents have left office under a variety of circumstances. Some were retired against their will: Pierce, Harry S Truman, and Lyndon Johnson were among those who, in effect, were denied renomination by their parties to run for another term; Cleveland, William Howard Taft, Herbert C. Hoover, Ford, and Carter were renominated but were defeated in the general election; Nixon resigned from the presidency to avoid impeachment; and Eisenhower and Reagan were denied the opportunity to run for a third term by the Twenty-second Amendment (1951), which imposed a two-term limit on presidents who were elected to the office.

Washington, in contrast, yearned for "the shade of retirement" (a phrase he used in his Farewell Address) and stepped down willingly after the end of his second term. Jefferson, Madison, and Monroe followed suit. Four former presidents actively sought another term—Van Buren as the candidate of the Free Soil party in 1848, Fillmore as the nominee of the American party in 1856, Cleveland as the Democratic nominee in 1892, and Theodore Roosevelt, who ran as the Progressive (or Bull Moose) nominee in 1912 after failing to win the Republican nomination. Only Cleveland was successful.

Some former presidents lived long lives after exiting the White House, including Hoover (almost thirty-two years), John Adams (twenty-five years), and Fillmore (twenty-one years). Polk and Chester A. Arthur, both of them young, lived only three months and two years, respectively, after their terms expired.

Almost from the beginning, former presidents have been uncertain about what they should and should not do after leaving the White House. (Taft suggested that the former president should be chloroformed and cremated in order to "fix his place in history and enable the public to pass on to new measures and new men." [2]) Some have remained in politics, including not just the four who sought a return to the presidency, but also three who were elected to Congress (John Quincy Adams, Andrew Johnson, and, in the Confederate congress, Tyler), and one (Taft) who became chief justice of the United States. Others have left the political arena almost entirely; still others (notably Hoover) have served the federal government in one or more special assignments. Whether politically active or not, however, "nearly every president has been critical of his successor," according to author James Clark. "Even George Washington criticized John Adams for spending too much time away from his office." [3]

Some former presidents, such as Ulysses S. Grant and Ford, have traded on their status in an effort to become

By Michael Nelson

Table 1 Former Presidents: Length of Life after Leaving Office

President	Date left office	Date of death	Length of life after leaving office
1. Washington	March 4, 1797	Dec. 14, 1799	2 years, 285 days
2. J. Adams	March 4, 1801	July 4, 1826	25 years, 122 days
3. Jefferson	March 4, 1809	July 4, 1826	17 years, 122 days
4. Madison	March 4, 1817	June 28, 1836	19 years, 116 days
5. Monroe	March 4, 1825	July 4, 1831	6 years, 122 days
6. J. Q. Adams	March 4, 1829	Feb. 23, 1848	18 years, 356 days
7. Jackson	March 4, 1837	June 8, 1845	8 years, 96 days
8. Van Buren	March 4, 1841	July 24, 1862	21 years, 142 days
9. Tyler	March 4, 1845	Jan. 18, 1862	16 years, 320 days
10. Polk	March 4, 1849	June 15, 1849	103 days
11. Fillmore	March 4, 1853	March 8, 1874	21 years, 4 days
12. Pierce	March 4, 1857	Oct. 8, 1869	12 years, 218 days
13. Buchanan	March 4, 1861	June 1, 1868	7 years, 89 days
14. A. Johnson	March 4, 1869	July 31, 1875	6 years, 149 days
15. Grant	March 4, 1877	July 23, 1885	8 years, 141 days
16. Hayes	March 4, 1881	Jan. 17, 1893	11 years, 319 days
17. Arthur	March 4, 1885	Nov. 18, 1886	1 year, 260 days
18. Cleveland[a]	March 4, 1889	June 24, 1908	15 years, 112 days
19. B. Harrison	March 4, 1893	March 13, 1901	8 years, 9 days
20. T. Roosevelt	March 4, 1909	Jan. 6, 1919	9 years, 309 days
21. Taft	March 4, 1913	March 8, 1930	17 years, 4 days
22. Wilson	March 4, 1921	Feb. 3, 1924	2 years, 337 days
23. Coolidge	March 4, 1929	Jan. 5, 1933	3 years, 308 days
24. Hoover	March 4, 1933	Oct. 20, 1964	31 years, 231 days
25. Truman	Jan. 20, 1953	Dec. 26, 1972	19 years, 340 days
26. Eisenhower	Jan. 20, 1961	Mar. 28, 1969	8 years, 67 days
27. L. Johnson	Jan. 20, 1969	Jan. 22, 1973	4 years, 2 days
28. Nixon	August 9, 1974	—	—
29. Ford	Jan. 20, 1977	—	—
30. Carter	Jan. 20, 1981	—	—
31. Reagan	Jan. 20, 1989	—	—

Source: Congressional Research Service.

a. Even though Grover Cleveland was elected to the presidency two different times (not in succession), he is counted only once as a former president.

wealthy. (Grant was disastrously unsuccessful; Ford, as ex-president, became a multimillionaire for the first time in his life.) Others (including Jefferson, Madison, Monroe, and several other nineteenth-century presidents) have ended their lives heavily in debt. Until recently, no pension or expense money was provided to former presidents or their widows, a situation that was remedied by the passage of the Former Presidents Act of 1958 and later legislation. Since the 1970s, some critics have argued that presidents now are provided for too generously after they leave the White House.

The longer the time that passes after a former president leaves office, the more appreciative historians usually become. Hoover ranked twentieth of twenty-nine presidents in a 1948 survey of historians by Arthur M. Schlesinger, Sr.; in a 1981 survey by Robert K. Murray and Tim H. Blessing, he ranked twenty-first of thirty-six. Franklin D. Roosevelt rose from third in 1948 to second in 1981. Harry Truman, in a 1962 Schlesinger-sponsored survey of historians, scored ninth of thirty-one presidents; by 1981 he was eighth of thirty-six. Eisenhower registered the most impressive gain of all, from twenty-second (the bottom third) in 1962 to eleventh (the top third) in 1981. Of the more recent former presidents, the reputations of Nixon (ranked thirty-fourth in 1981) and Carter (ranked twenty-fifth) already seem to be on the rise. John F. Kennedy, however, was so admired by historians after he was assassinated in 1963 that his standing seems likely to fall.[4] *(See Ranking the Presidents chapter in Part I.)*

Just as former presidents are to some degree uncertain about what is expected of them, Americans seem ambivalent about the ex-presidency as an institution. The titles of recent articles on the subject mirror the range of feelings Americans have: from respect ("Presidents Emeritus") to resentment ("Caring for Ex-Presidents Can Cost a Bundle") to bewilderment ("What Shall We Do with Our Ex-Presidents?").[5]

Evolution of the Ex-Presidency

Former presidents were not thought of as a group—nor was the ex-presidency regarded as even an unofficial office—until recently. "The evolution of the ex-presidency has been rather haphazard," observed the historian John

Whiteclay Chambers II in 1979. "For most of its history the nation has left the former presidents to fend for themselves and to work out their own post-executive careers. But in the last thirty years, the quasi-public 'Office of the Ex-President' has emerged with quite well-defined perquisites, and some of the trappings of power." [6]

The evolution of the ex-presidency may be divided into three main periods. The first period began with the first former president, George Washington, and ended during the post-presidential career of Grant. Although Washington established some precedents for later ex-presidents to follow, great uncertainty prevailed for many years about what the proper role of a departed chief executive should be. The 1870s until the mid-1950s (Rutherford B. Hayes to Harry Truman) constitute a second era in the evolution of the ex-presidency, one in which active concern was expressed about what former presidents should do and how they should be supported. The third period has witnessed the development of what Chambers called the "Office of Ex-President," with a panoply of institutional roles and resources.

George Washington to Ulysses S. Grant

Washington is most admired by historians for the precedents he set for future presidents. Less remarked are the precedents he set for future former presidents. First—and, perhaps, foremost—Washington eschewed the opportunity to remain in office (probably, for life, if he had chosen to stand for reelection every four years) and voluntarily became a former president at the end of his second term on March 4, 1797. Equally important, in deciding to return to his plantation in Virginia, Washington departed from the seat of government instead of remaining behind as an active or potential rival to his successor as president. Finally, as former president, Washington accepted a call of duty that later was issued. When the nation faced war with France in 1798, Washington accepted President John Adams's request to serve as commanding officer of the army.

Adams was the first president to be defeated for reelection. He also was one of the longest lived former presidents, surviving for twenty-five years after leaving office at age sixty-five. Initially, Adams was bitter at his defeat and avoided politics. Eventually, however, he entered into one of the most fabled and friendly correspondences in U.S. history with Thomas Jefferson, his erstwhile political rival and the man who had beaten him in the election of 1800. In 1820, at the age of eighty-five, Adams served as a delegate to the Massachusetts constitutional convention. (He also served his home town of Quincy, Mass., as a surveyor of roads, a selectman, and an assessor.) Four years later, in 1824, Adams became the only former president to witness the election of his son (John Quincy Adams) as president. On July 4, 1826, the fiftieth anniversary of the signing of the Declaration of Independence, Adams and Jefferson both died.

Jefferson was the first president to leave office after two terms as a matter of principle. *(See "Twenty-second Amendment," p. 47, in Constitutional Beginnings chapter of Part I.)* Sixty-six at the time, Jefferson's final years were financially disastrous, partly because he was untalented as a farmer, but also because he "was one of America's major attractions, and it appeared that every visitor to America made a point of breaking his journey at Jefferson's lovely home" (Monticello) near Charlottesville, Virginia.[7] Jefferson died more than $100,000 in debt.

Several of Jefferson's successors as former president also suffered the consecutive burdens of neglecting their own financial affairs while serving in the White House (at an annual salary of $25,000), then of bearing the responsibility of entertainment, correspondence, and the other obligations of fame when out of office. Former presidents received no pension (nor did their widows) or expense money. Three of the four presidents who followed Jefferson—Madison, Monroe, and Jackson—endured considerable financial distress in retirement. Monroe actually had to leave his home state of Virginia to live with a daughter and son-in-law in New York, where he died. In 1841, Congress did vote to give $25,000 (one year's presidential salary) to the widow of William Henry Harrison, who was the first president to die in office. More grudgingly, Congress in 1870 approved a small annual pension for the unpopular Mary Todd Lincoln, whose husband Abraham Lincoln was assassinated in 1865.

In contrast, the post-presidential career of John

The Bettmann Archive

After his presidency, John Quincy Adams served eighteen years in the House of Representatives. Adams is the earliest president of whom there is a photograph; this daguerrotype was made shortly before his death in 1848.

Quincy Adams, who was chosen as president in the disputed election of 1824 and roundly defeated by Jackson four years later, was happier than his presidency ("the four most miserable years of my life," Adams later said).[8] In 1830, Adams was asked by voters in Quincy, Massachusetts, if he would consider election to the U.S. House of Representatives to be degrading. "No person could be degraded by serving the people as a representative," Adams replied. "Nor, in my opinion, would an ex-president be degraded by serving as a selectman of his town, if elected thereto by the people." [9] Adams served eighteen years in Congress until his death at age eighty. His most famous victory came in 1844, when he secured the repeal of the House's 1836 "gag resolution," under which antislavery petitions were tabled without consideration.

For a time, most of Adams's successors as former president followed his precedent of active involvement in politics. Van Buren unsuccessfully sought the Democratic presidential nomination in 1844 and accepted the nomination of the Free Soil party in 1848. (He received 10 percent of the popular vote but no electoral votes.) Fillmore was nominated for president by the American party (the Know Nothings) in 1856: he won 21.5 percent of the popular vote and eight electoral votes. In 1861, the Virginian Tyler presided over the Peace Conference that sought vainly to avert civil war, then was elected to the lower house of the congress of the Confederate States of America. (He died before taking his seat.) After being impeached, almost convicted, and denied renomination to run for president in 1868, Andrew Johnson won a vindication of sorts when, on his third effort, the Tennessee legislature narrowly elected him to the U.S. Senate in 1874.

Few of the early former presidents did much writing of consequence after leaving office. One exception was James Buchanan, who wrote a labored defense of his generally unsuccessful presidency called *Mr. Buchanan's Administration on the Eve of the Rebellion.* Buchanan waited until 1866 to publish his book so that it would not be regarded as an effort to embarrass President Lincoln. It sold only five thousand copies. Grant was much more successful as an author. His two-volume *Memoirs* of his service as general during the Civil War earned $440,000 for his estate. (Grant died of cancer three days after completing the work.) Grant's memoirs said nothing of his presidency.

Unfortunately, Grant also traded on his status as a former president to engage in some tarnished business dealings. He and his son joined with an unscrupulous speculator to form a Wall Street investment house called Grant and Ward. The firm went bankrupt in 1884, destroying the savings of thousands of investors who, in many cases, had been attracted to the firm by Grant's reputation.

Grant's business affairs seemed especially notorious because in 1873, at the start of his second term as president, Congress had voted to double the president's salary to $50,000. The reason for doing so, explained the House Judiciary Committee in the report that recommended the legislation, was that while no law prevented "an ex-president of the United States from engaging in the business pursuits of life for the purpose of acquiring property, . . . custom and public sentiment" were "decided against such a course." The committee felt that a former president "ought to have a sufficient provision while in office to enable him when he leaves it to retire from all active, or at least all money making, pursuits." [10]

Library of Congress

After the bankruptcy of his investment house in 1884, Ulysses S. Grant wrote his memoirs to make ends meet. This photograph was taken at Grant's New York cottage in 1885, the year of his death.

Rutherford B. Hayes to Harry S Truman

Grant's financial indiscretions notwithstanding, the belief grew over the years that business was an unsuitable career for former presidents—not because private enterprise was regarded as inherently bad, but because a company's motive in hiring a former president presumably would be to trade on the prestige of the office. Calvin Coolidge expressed the attitude of many of his colleagues in rejecting an offer that would have paid him much more than he ever had been paid as president. "These people are trying to hire not Calvin Coolidge, but a former president of the United States," he argued. "I can't do anything that might take away from the presidency any of its dignity, or any of the faith the people have in it." Truman later echoed this sentiment: "I could never lend myself to any transaction, however respectable, that would commercialize on the prestige and dignity of the presidency." [11]

Congress periodically raised the president's salary—to $75,000 in 1909 and $100,000 in 1949—in order that presidents would be able to save for their retirement and so not need to pursue commercial careers.[12] The industrialist Andrew Carnegie's 1912 offer—evidently benign in origin—to fund personally an annual pension of $25,000 a year to former presidents was rejected by former presidents Taft and Theodore Roosevelt as unnecessary and was disapproved of as unseemly by many members of Congress.

A quiet retirement was one choice available to former presidents, assuming they had accumulated sufficient savings before or during their tenure in the White House to be able to afford to retire. At age fifty-seven, Coolidge and his wife returned to Northampton, Massachusetts, and resumed residency in their modest duplex. (Tourists annoyed them so much that they eventually moved to a larger home on the outskirts of town.) Truman bought train tickets for himself and his wife and rode from Washington to their modest family home in Independence, Missouri.

Most former presidents (including Truman) pursued one or more active roles in retirement that were widely regarded as appropriate to their status. Among these were: law, writing, service in temporary public assignments, testimony before congressional committees, and, in ways more restricted than for the early presidents, politics.

Law

For a time, beginning in the late nineteenth century, several former presidents (notably, Cleveland, Benjamin Harrison, and Taft) resumed legal careers of one sort or another. (Fillmore had rejected such a career for himself as improper for a former president.) Harrison actually argued cases before Supreme Court justices whom he had appointed. Cleveland declined to appear in court but wrote legal briefs for clients. Taft, shortly after leaving the presidency in 1909, became the Kent professor of law at Yale University.

Writing

Eighteen former presidents, including Reagan, have devoted a substantial portion of their time to writing memoirs and other books.[13] In contrast, John Quincy Adams (the sole president to become a published poet), Van Buren, and Buchanan were the only early presidents to write extensively for publication after leaving office.

Grant established writing as the norm for former presidents. Grant wrote a series of articles (at a rate of $500 each) for *Century Magazine* about his Civil War experiences and later expanded them into his critically and commercially successful *Memoirs.* Cleveland wrote numerous magazine articles and books on subjects as diverse as the presidency (*Presidential Problems*) and hunting and fishing (*Fishing and Hunting Sketches*). Theodore Roosevelt averaged one book per year in the decade after his term as president ended, along with hundreds of magazine articles and newspaper editorials. Taft also wrote frequently for magazines and newspapers, as did Coolidge. Hoover compiled collections of his speeches for publication in a series of books called *Addresses Along the American Road* and wrote other books as well, including his *Memoirs* and *The Ordeal of Woodrow Wilson.* (Theodore Roosevelt and Coolidge each published books called *Autobiography.*) Truman's two-volume *Memoirs* and a later book about his retirement (*Mr. Citizen*) sold very well and provided his main source of income.

Temporary Service in Government

Although Rutherford B. Hayes served in no official capacity after leaving the presidency, he stated the simple creed that has guided most ex-presidents ever since: "Let him, like every good American citizen, be willing and prompt to bear his part in every useful work that will promote the welfare and happiness of his family, his town, his state, and his country." [14]

Most former presidents have accepted temporary assignments of one sort or another from the federal government. For example:

~ Grant served as U.S. Commissioner to Mexico in 1882 to negotiate a commercial treaty.

~ Benjamin Harrison accepted an appointment to the Permanent Court of Arbitration.

~ At the request of President Theodore Roosevelt, Cleveland headed a study commission during the coal strike of 1902.

~ Theodore Roosevelt was the U.S. delegate to the funeral of Great Britain's King Edward VII in 1910.

~ During World War I, Taft was cochair of the National War Labor Board and served as a member of several war commissions.

No president has taken on more temporary assignments than Hoover, especially during the Truman administration. He headed the Famine Emergency Committee in 1946, which helped to save millions of lives by documenting the need for food relief after the end of World War II. In anticipation of the Marshall Plan for postwar economic aid to Europe, Hoover led the President's Economic Mission to Germany and Austria in 1947. In 1947 and 1953 he directed the first and second "Hoover commissions" (Commission on Organization of the Executive Branch of the Government) and recommended numerous reorganization plans for the federal bureaucracy, several of which were adopted.

Testimony before Congress

John Tyler was the first and only former president in the nineteenth century to appear before a congressional committee.[15] (Tyler was subpoenaed in 1846 to shed light on accusations—groundless, as it turned out—that had been made against former secretary of state Daniel Webster.) Of the twentieth-century former presidents, Theodore Roosevelt, Taft, Hoover, Truman, and Ford testified to Congress on several occasions. In some cases, their testimony bore on decisions that had been made while they were president. Roosevelt, for example, was called upon to defend both an antitrust decision and his 1904 campaign fund-raising practices. At other times, the testimony of the former president related to policy issues about which he had a particular concern (Taft on budgeting, Truman on repeal of the two-term limit on presidents.) A former president's service in a temporary assignment often was the occasion of congressional testimony. Hoover's record-setting twenty appearances mainly concerned his work on famine relief and the first and second Hoover commissions.

All of the twentieth-century appearances of former presidents before congressional committees have been voluntary, none by subpoena. Indeed, when the House Committee on Un-American Activities sent a subpoena to Truman in 1953 to testify about the promotion of alleged communists in his administration, he refused by claiming the same immunity (on grounds of separation of powers and executive privilege) that the incumbent president traditionally had enjoyed.[16]

Politics

In contrast to several of their predecessors, former presidents since Grant have not pursued or accepted other offices after leaving the White House. Some, however, have tried to return to the presidency, and one, Grover Cleveland, succeeded. (Cleveland defeated Benjamin Harrison, who had defeated him four years earlier, in 1892.) Among

Henry Miller; Library of Congress

Having yearned to head the Supreme Court, even over the presidency, William Howard Taft finally got his wish. He was appointed chief justice by President Warren Harding in 1921.

those who were less successful was Theodore Roosevelt, who, after failing to wrest the Republican nomination from President Taft in 1912, ran for president on the Progressive "Bull Moose" party ticket. (He finished second—ahead of Taft—to the Democratic nominee, Woodrow Wilson, with 27.4 percent of the popular vote and eighty-eight electoral votes.) Despite the scandals that tainted the Grant administration and the physical disability that crippled Woodrow Wilson, each seems to have hoped that he would be drafted by his party to run for another presidential term.

Taft was perhaps history's happiest former president. He always would have preferred to have been chief justice of the United States rather than president. When Chief Justice Edward D. Whate died in 1921, Taft was elevated to that position by President Warren G. Harding. "Next to my wife and children, the Court is the nearest thing to my heart in life," Taft declared on one occasion. In 1925, he wrote blissfully: "The truth is that in my present life I don't remember that I ever was president." [17]

The "Office of the Ex-President"

Since the 1950s, the "ex-presidency" has taken on many of the trappings of a government institution—"a form of public office," in the words of the historian John Whiteclay Chambers. "This has not been the result of any coherent, deliberate policy," Chambers has written; "developments have often been fortuitously related to other events. Nevertheless, more codification has taken place in the last thirty years than in the first 150 years of the Republic." [18] Indeed, the ex-presidency to some degree has become institutionalized in both senses of the word—its size and complexity are greater than in the past, and new expectations exist of its incumbents.

Chronologically, the ex-presidency has developed in four main stages: the generally successful assertion by former president Truman of a right for former presidents to make constitutional claims of executive privilege *(see "Testimony before Congress," p. 1077, in this chapter)*; the passage of the Presidential Libraries Act of 1955, which funded the maintenance of libraries and museums for each recent former president; the passage of the Former Presidents Act of 1958 and later legislation, which provided each former president with a pension, protection by the Secret Service, and money for office, staff, and other expenses; and the granting to former presidents of the right to address the Senate.

Since the mid-1970s, these developments have triggered a reaction against what critics sometimes call the "imperial ex-presidency." [19] The ex-presidency has become an expensive office *(see Table 2)*—taken together, the cost to the Treasury of presidential libraries, pensions, and other expenses rose from nothing in 1954 to $147,000 in 1958 to $28 million in 1987 (roughly two-thirds of that amount to maintain presidential libraries).[20] Former presidents also are largely unaccountable. As Chambers has noted, "despite the growth of the office and of the sums of public funds spent on its maintenance, a former chief executive is under virtually no obligation to do, or not to do, anything at all." [21]

Presidential Libraries

Among the precedents George Washington established as a former president was the right to claim private ownership of his presidential papers. During the nineteenth century, several groups of presidential papers were purchased from former presidents or their estates by the federal government and stored at the State Department. In 1903, the Library of Congress began taking possession of the papers that the government had purchased. Still, significant collections of the papers of the first twenty-nine presidents remain scattered about the country. Some former presidents gave parts of their papers away as souvenirs; others burned their papers or mutilated them.

During his second term, President Franklin Roosevelt conceived the idea of creating a Roosevelt presidential library, and organized a private committee to fund and construct one in his home town, Hyde Park, New York. Roosevelt asked Congress to authorize the National Archives to receive the library and his papers as a gift, agreeing in turn to see to it that the library's operation and maintenance were publicly financed. In 1939, Congress consented to do so. The Roosevelt Library opened in 1948.

Encouraged to make similar arrangements by committees that were planning libraries for former presidents Truman and Eisenhower, Congress passed the Presidential Libraries Act in 1955. The Harry S Truman Library opened in Independence, Missouri, in 1957; the Dwight D. Eisenhower Library in Abilene, Kansas, in 1962; the Herbert Hoover Library in West Branch, Iowa, in 1962; the Lyndon B. Johnson Library in Austin, Texas, in 1971; the John F. Kennedy Library in Boston, Massachusetts, in 1979; the Gerald R. Ford Library in Ann Arbor, Michigan, in 1980; and the Jimmy Carter Library in Atlanta, Georgia, in 1984. Libraries for Richard Nixon and Ronald Reagan, both to be located in California, also are planned.

Funding policies, as well as the traditional policy of individual presidential control over the papers of their administrations, have been limited by laws passed in 1974, 1978, and 1986. *(See "Official Reactions," p. 1082, in this chapter.)*

Support and Protection

Until 1958, former presidents were virtually the only officials or employees of the federal government who were not covered by some sort of retirement plan. Congress briefly included former presidents in a 1942 pension act that was mainly intended to cover its own members, but public outcry against congressional avarice during wartime prompted the act's quick repeal. After World War II ended, Congress enacted another pension program but did not include the president in its coverage.

In 1955, however, the financial plight of former president Truman led members of both houses of Congress to introduce legislation to provide office and staff assistance to former presidents and pensions for both them and their widows. Truman had complained to Speaker of the House Sam Rayburn that it cost him $30,000 a year just to answer mail and fulfill requests for speeches and public appearances. He had turned down numerous business offers as improper activities for a former president, Truman added, but if federal assistance was not provided, he would be forced to "go ahead with some contracts to keep ahead of the hounds." [22] Herbert Hoover, the only other living ex-president in 1955, indicated formally to Congress that he did not want a pension.[23]

Debate on the proposed legislation extended over three years. Speaking for its proponents, House Majority Leader John W. McCormack urged passage on grounds that "a former president is considered a dedicated statesman, available, if desired, for service to our country; his responsibility does not end when his term of office has ended; and a former president is not expected to engage in any business or occupation which would demean the office he once held." Republicans on the House Committee on Post Office and Civil Service argued publicly that the law would create in effect a new office: a "separate entity" for former presidents, with "an aura of official standing yet a wholly undefined relationship to the constitutional functions of the federal government." Privately, Republicans grumbled that they were being asked to subsidize Truman's attacks on their party.[24]

The Former Presidents Act was passed in 1958. It provided all presidents who left office (unless by impeachment and conviction) with a pension of $25,000 per year (roughly comparable to the salary then paid to members of Congress), a generous allowance to hire a staff, office space and furnishings in a federal building of their choice, franking (that is, free mailing) privileges for nonpolitical mail, and a pension of $10,000 per year for their widows. Hoover and Truman were the first beneficiaries of the new pension; Mrs. Franklin D. Roosevelt and Mrs. Woodrow Wilson were the first to receive the widows' pension.

Several additional benefits were added to the ex-presidency during the 1960s.

In 1962, Congress extended Secret Service protection to former presidents for a period of six months after they left office. The following year, after President Kennedy was assassinated, such protection was granted to his widow and children. In 1965, after testimony by a Treasury Department official that former presidents and their families are subject to "annoyance by the idly curious" and remain possible targets of the "mentally deranged," Congress passed a law to grant lifetime Secret Service protection to presidents and their spouses, as well as to the widows of former presidents until they remarry and to their children until they reach the age of sixteen.[25]

Table 2 Cost of Former Presidents, 1987

	(dollars in millions)
Secret Service protection	$ 9.3[a]
Pensions	0.3[b]
Staff	0.3
Office (rent, telephones, travel, postage, etc.)	0.4
Total	$ 10.3

Source: General Accounting Office.

Note: Table does not include costs of presidential libraries.

a. For Mrs. Lyndon B. Johnson, Mr. and Mrs. Jimmy Carter, and Mr. and Mrs. Gerald R. Ford.

b. For Ford, Carter, Mrs. Johnson, and Richard Nixon.

With two exceptions, every former president and his family have accepted the protection of the Secret Service: Patricia and Richard Nixon decided to rely instead on private security guards beginning in 1984 and 1985, respectively. The attitude of former president Carter was more typical: he said that the Secret Service is "very necessary because wherever a former president goes, crowds gather and it's comforting to know they are around." [26] In some cases, however, Secret Service agents have acted more as servants and staff than as guardians. After the death of President Eisenhower, for example, Mamie Eisenhower relied on her Secret Service agents mainly to take her to church and to run errands.

The Presidential Transition Act of 1963 provided outgoing presidents with $300,000 to cover the costs of leaving office, mainly office rental and staff assistance during their first six months out of office. During this period, the office and staff provisions of the Former Presidents Act do not apply. In 1976, Congress raised the amount of the transition subsidy to the outgoing president to $1 million. (The incoming administration receives $2 million under the act.)

In 1969, a historic Victorian townhouse in Washington was designated as the Former Presidents' Residence and made available for the use of former presidents when they are visiting the capital. The approximately two-thousand-square-foot house, at 716 Jackson Place, N.W. (about one block from the White House), was first used in 1977 by former president Ford and has been used an average of six times per year since 1980, mostly by Ford.

Congress attached an escalator clause to the presidential pension in 1970, setting it as equal to the annual salary of department heads. It also raised the widow's pension to $20,000 a year.

Senate Privileges

Over the years, the most frequently offered suggestion to involve former presidents formally in the activities of the federal government has been to make them nonvoting members of the Senate. President Rutherford B. Hayes opposed the idea as "inconsistent with the principles of popular government" when it was debated in Congress in

Three Living Former Presidents: . . .

Richard Nixon

Richard Nixon was the first president to resign from office. He stepped down on August 9, 1974, to avoid impeachment and conviction by Congress. A pardon from President Gerald R. Ford one month later spared Nixon the threat of criminal prosecution for his involvement in the Watergate affair, but Ford's requirement that he publicly accept the pardon was humiliating for the former president. Severe health and financial problems followed in short order; Nixon nearly died from phlebitis. Books on Watergate appeared, portraying Nixon variously as an evil genius, a foul-mouthed drunk, and a maudlin incompetent. The General Services Administration (GSA) considered denying Nixon the pension and other benefits due him under the Former Presidents Act because he had resigned before completing his term. (The Justice Department told GSA that the law excluded only an impeached and convicted president.)

Warner Books soon mitigated Nixon's financial problems with a $2.5 million advance contract for his memoirs. He nonetheless felt compelled to sell his homes in San Clemente, California, and Key Biscayne, Florida, and to do a series of grueling but financially rewarding television interviews with journalist David Frost.

Publicly, Nixon's reemergence was slow but generally successful. The government of China, grateful for the relationship Nixon had forged with it as president, invited him to visit in early 1976. His first domestic public appearance was in the small town of Hayden, Kentucky, which decided in 1978 to dedicate its new recreation center to him. He began giving occasional interviews to journalists and made himself available for private consultations with Republican politicians. In 1984, Nixon received a standing ovation at an appearance before the American Newspaper Publishers Association. Not long after, he was asked to arbitrate a labor dispute that threatened to disrupt the World Series. Books that Nixon wrote on foreign affairs—*The Real War; Leaders; Real Peace; No More Vietnams;* and *1999*—were published every few years. His book of memoirs (*RN, The Memoirs of Richard Nixon*) was a best seller.

Nixon's "rehabilitation" may never be complete. Neither his presence nor invocations of his name have been welcome at Republican national conventions. Historians continue to judge him harshly. But the Reagan administration saw fit to consult Nixon frequently on political and foreign affairs. "As far as this White House is concerned, his rehabilitation is complete," a senior Reagan aide told *Newsweek* magazine. A Gallup poll taken for *Newsweek*'s May 19, 1986, issue reported that 54 percent thought Ford had been right to pardon Nixon, compared with 35 percent in 1976. Thirty-nine percent said they would like to see Nixon in a public role, such as ambassador.

Gerald R. Ford

Gerald Ford was appointed to the vice presidency after Vice President Spiro T. Agnew resigned in October 1973; he then became president in August 1974 after Nixon resigned. Defeated just twenty-seven months later in his bid for a full term as president, Ford met in the White House with Hollywood agent Norman Brokaw to plan his future. Ford, who had never been wealthy, wanted to make money without foreclosing a possible political comeback. He initially resisted business offers in favor of a Brokaw-negotiated, million-dollar publishing contract for himself and his wife, Betty Ford, along with public consulting roles with the American Enterprise Institute and the NBC television network.

In 1978, Ford campaigned heavily for Republican congressional candidates. While eschewing an active presidential bid in 1980, he made known his availability for a draft. None was forthcoming, and on March

1879, as did President Taft three decades later. Truman, however (with the endorsement of former president Hoover), sought to persuade Congress to revive the nonvoting senator proposal after he left office. In 1963, the Senate relented in part by modifying its rules to read: "Former presidents of the United States shall be entitled to address the Senate upon appropriate notice to the presiding officer who shall thereupon make the necessary arrangements." Truman made some bantering remarks on the occasion of his eightieth birthday in 1964, but no former president has used the Senate as a forum to make a formal address.

Executive Privilege

Several former presidents have testified voluntarily before congressional committees *(see "Testimony before Congress," p. 1077, in this chapter)*, but, until 1953, only Tyler was ordered to do so under a subpoena. (He complied.) In 1953, former president Truman rejected a subpoena from the House Committee on Un-American Activities to provide information about the promotion to a higher government position of an alleged Communist during his administration by asserting the same rights of executive privilege that presidents historically had claimed while in office. *(See "Presidential Privileges and Immunities," p. 1176, in The President and the Supreme Court chapter of Part VI.)*

Constitutional scholars disagreed over the legitimacy of Truman's assertion, but the committee backed down. Citing this precedent, former president Nixon refused in 1977 to testify before a House subcommittee that was investigating his administration's negotiations with North Vietnam. "If the doctrine of separation of powers and the independence of the presidency is to have any validity at all," Nixon argued, "it must be equally applicable to a president after his term of office has expired when he is sought to be examined with respect to any act occurring

. . . Nixon, Ford, and Carter

15, 1980, Ford announced his withdrawal from presidential politics. Ronald Reagan, who was nominated by the Republican party in 1980, made an effort to woo Ford onto the ticket as his vice-presidential running mate. After trying unsuccessfully to negotiate an arrangement that would enable him, as vice president, to exercise some of the president's powers in office, Ford declined Reagan's offer.

Freed from any concern about the political effects of bad publicity, Ford (who had never worked in business) accepted numerous lucrative offers to serve on corporate boards of directors and as a business consultant. Corporations like Santa Fe International, whose board Ford joined twelve days after withdrawing from the presidential race in 1980, G. K. Technologies, which he joined six weeks later as board member and consultant, and Shearson Loeb Rhoades, which he joined eight days after that (again as board member and consultant), appreciated the prestige and publicity that the presence of a former president on the board brought. According to an article in the February 15, 1987, issue of the *Los Angeles Times Magazine,* in 1986 Ford earned at least $541,300 from companies he was affiliated with, along with more than a quarter million dollars from lecture fees, a substantial stipend from the American Enterprise Institute, and more than $150,000 in congressional and presidential pensions.

Ford was severely criticized in 1978 when he endorsed a commercially produced series of presidential medals. The *New York Times* lamented in an editorial, "We wish he could earn his way without dragging the presidency into it." An investment company Ford formed with Leonard Firestone (called Fordstone) became controversial when environmental groups opposed a real estate development project it was financing in California.

No former president since Ulysses S. Grant has been involved in business to the extent that Ford has.

Jimmy Carter

Jimmy Carter, like Herbert Hoover, was a politically unsuccessful president who conducted himself as former president in ways that brought almost universal applause. In contrast to Nixon (a Californian who settled in New York City, then moved to its New Jersey suburbs) and Ford (a lifelong resident of Michigan who moved to California after leaving the White House), Carter returned to his modest home in Plains, Georgia, along with his wife, Rosalynn Carter. Like most recent former presidents, Carter worked to raise money to construct a presidential library, in his case on the campus of Emory University in Atlanta. But in designing the library, Carter emphasized the importance of attaching a conference center that could be used to address important topics of public policy.

Carter eschewed business endeavors and abandoned any political ambitions in order to pursue activities he considered more interesting and worthwhile. He wrote his critically and publicly well-received memoirs (*Keeping Faith: Memoirs of a President*) and followed it with books on the Middle East, retirement, and hunting and fishing. Carter lent his talents as a carpenter to the Christian organization Habitat for Humanity, which builds and repairs houses for poor people in the United States and abroad. He continued to teach Sunday School at his Baptist church in Plains.

Carter has risen in scholarly and public esteem since he left office. A June 24, 1988, article in the *Wall Street Journal* found strong evidence of "Carter revisionism" among political scientists and historians, who now concede that he handled the unusually difficult problems of his time courageously. A *Wall Street Journal*/NBC poll found that 32 percent of the American people now think more of Carter's performance as president than they did while he was in office, compared with 19 percent who think less of him. A plurality now feel that Carter was a successful president.

---

while he is president." Although Nixon agreed to speak informally on the telephone with a few subcommittee members, Congress's acquiescence to his initial refusal seemed to affirm the acceptability of Truman's assertion.

For all the newfound privileges of their position, former presidents in the modern era are not completely unlike their predecessors. All have spent the major portion of their first years out of office writing memoirs, usually after negotiating a large advance payment from a book publisher and always with the help of research assistants. Eisenhower wrote two books about his presidency—*Mandate for Change: The White House Years, 1953-1956* (1963), which covered his first term as president, and *Waging Peace: The White House Years, 1956-1961* (1965), which treated his second term. Johnson wrote *The Vantage Point: Perspectives on the Presidency, 1963-1969* (1971). Nixon, who resigned from office in disgrace and desperately needed the income a publisher could offer, was obliged to write a somewhat franker and, regarding Watergate at least, more confessional memoir, *RN, The Memoirs of a President* (1978). Most presidential memoirs, however, are extended defenses of their authors' actions in office, a pattern that was restored with Ford's *A Time To Heal: The Autobiography of Gerald R. Ford* (1979) and Carter's *Keeping Faith: Memoirs of a President* (1982). Reagan began the task of writing his memoirs shortly after leaving office in 1989.

Several recent former presidents, like some of their predecessors, also have written books on subjects other than themselves. Nixon has written extensively on international affairs, including *The Real War* (1980), *Leaders* (1982), *No More Vietnams* (1985), *Real Peace* (1985) and *1999* (1988). Carter has written books on topics as varied as the Middle East (*The Blood of Abraham,* 1985), retirement (*Everything to Gain: Making the Most of the Rest of Your Life,* 1987, written with his wife, Rosalynn Carter), and camping and fishing (*An Outdoor Journal,* 1988).

Election

One generally overlooked aspect of the Reagan legacy is that the former president has laid to rest the myth of "Tecumseh's Curse."

According to the curse, each president who is elected in a year ending in a zero is destined to die in office. It supposedly originated with the great Shawnee chief Tecumseh, who was defeated in a battle during the War of 1812 by Gen. William Henry Harrison. However implausible the story (what would have prompted an enraged Tecumseh to utter such an oddly detailed curse?), Harrison, who was elected president in 1840, died in office. So did the presidents who subsequently were elected in 1860 (Abraham Lincoln), 1880 (James A. Garfield), 1900 (William McKinley), 1920 (Warren G. Harding), 1940 (Franklin D. Roosevelt), and 1960 (John F. Kennedy).

Adherents of Tecumseh's Curse must have felt especially confident when Ronald Reagan was elected in 1980. Reagan supplanted Harrison (by one year) as the oldest person ever to be elected president: he turned sixty-nine on February 6, 1980. Two weeks after leaving office, hale and hearty, Reagan turned seventy-eight, eight years older than any other former president. And he took the curse with him.

Each of the three most recent first ladies also has written one or more books. Betty Ford, with Chris Chase as coauthor, wrote *The Times of My Life* (1978); she and Chase later recounted her struggles with drugs and alcohol in *Betty: A Glad Awakening* (1987). Critics found Rosalynn Carter's *First Lady from Plains* (1984), a memoir of her years in the White House, to be more insightful in some ways than Jimmy Carter's book. Before her husband's second term ended, Nancy Reagan declared her intention to write a book about her service as first lady.

In addition to writing books, recent former presidents have emulated their predecessors' willingness to provide confidential advice to and accept temporary assignments from the president. In 1981, for example, Reagan dispatched all three living former presidents—Nixon, Ford, and Carter—to represent the United States at the funeral of assassinated Egyptian leader Anwar Sadat. Each also has commented on public policy issues and, except for Nixon, sometimes participated in political campaigns.

Critics

During the 1970s and 1980s, the "office of ex-president" came under severe criticism from some quarters. A 1979 *Washington Monthly* article that assailed "The Imperial Ex-Presidency" was typical of many such writings.[27] Bills were introduced in Congress to reduce the privileges, benefits, and, consequently, the cost of supporting former presidents. A bill sponsored by Rep. Andrew Jacobs, Jr., (D-Ind.) was called the "Former Presidents Enough Is Enough and Taxpayers' Relief Act." The historian Arthur Schlesinger, Jr., in a 1981 issue of *Parade* magazine, reflected the tone of much of the recent criticism: "Ex-Presidents, like other old folk, tend to live in the past, preoccupied with the issues, remedies, and self-justifications of another time.... We recognize all this in the private sector. When presidents retire from corporations or from universities, no one wants them offering advice."[28] Schlesinger cautioned against succumbing to what he called "the patriarchal illusion. If our three living ex-presidents [Nixon, Ford, and Carter] are really all that wise, they would surely have been better presidents."

To some degree, the backlash against the ex-presidency resulted from the changed roster of former presidents. In the late 1960s and early 1970s, Truman, Eisenhower, and Hoover died and were replaced by Johnson and Nixon, each of whom had been forced to withdraw from office, then Ford and Carter, both of whom were defeated in their bids for reelection as president. Criticism also was born of the growing cost to the Treasury of supporting former presidents with pensions, offices, staff, Secret Service protection, and maintenance of their libraries. "They can make a million dollars or so a year going around and being ornaments and making dull speeches," charged Representative Jacobs. "Let them pay their own office rent and let them pay for their own secretaries."[29] Jacobs, Democratic senator Lawton M. Chiles, Jr., of Florida, and other critics seemed particularly offended by the money-making activities of former president Ford, who earned hundreds of thousands of dollars annually from serving on corporate boards, consulting for corporations, and giving speeches mainly to business groups. *(See box, Three Living Former Presidents: Nixon, Ford, and Carter, p. 1080.)*

Official Reactions

Critics of the ex-presidency won several victories for their cause, some legislative, some legal, and some administrative.

In response to the various Watergate investigations that were going on at the time, Congress passed the Presidential Recordings and Materials Preservation Act of 1974, which deprived Nixon of control over his papers and tape recordings. (Nixon's secret tape recordings of White House conversations provided vital evidence of administration wrongdoing.) Under the act, the administrator of the General Services Administration (GSA) was enjoined to obtain "complete possession of all papers, documents, memorandums, transcripts, and other objects and materials which constitute the presidential historical materials of Richard M. Nixon."

Four years later, the Presidential Records Act of 1978 broadened the requirements of the 1974 act by granting the government complete ownership and control of all presidential records, beginning with the next president. (Ronald Reagan, who was elected in 1980, was the first to be covered.) Former presidents were permitted, however, to restrict access to some of their papers for up to twelve years.

In 1986, Congress passed a law to reduce the government's responsibility for future presidential libraries. Previously, such libraries had been constructed with privately raised funds but maintained at the expense of the National Archives. The new law required that endowments be created by the organizations that built the libraries to help pay for their maintenance. President Reagan's request for an exemption from this requirement was granted, but future presidential libraries will be covered.

A federal court ruled in 1976 that a former president could be held accountable for personal misconduct in office. The judge found former president Nixon personally liable for damages to Morton Halperin, a former Nixon aide, because of an illegal wiretap that Nixon had authorized to be placed on Halperin's telephone. The principle was more important than the damages, however, which were set at one dollar.

The GSA, which is charged to administer the benefits former presidents receive, became harsher in its discretionary judgments. (The law on office space and furnishings, for example, is vague, requiring only that the GSA administrator should provide "suitable office space appropriately equipped with furniture, furnishings, office machines and equipment, and office supplies, as determined by the administrator.") Nixon was enjoined to accept an office in New York in a federal building rather than (at triple the expense) in the Chrysler Building. Carter was told to buy a less expensive Persian rug than the one he had in mind for his office.

Additional Proposals

Critics of the modern ex-presidency still object to many aspects of the largely informal institution. Some would further restrict the cost of the benefits provided to former presidents, notably Secret Service protection, office and staff expenses, and libraries. Others fret that the laws governing benefits for former presidents are too vague—someone who held the office of president for even one day would be fully eligible, for example.

Legislation was introduced in Congress in 1985 (but not passed) to limit Secret Service protection to a former president to five years, to the widow of a former president for six months, and to the former president's children only when they are with the former president. (These limits could be extended at the discretion of the secretary of the Treasury.) Proponents argued that the danger to former presidents and their families does not justify the expense—with the exception of Theodore Roosevelt, who was running for president in 1912, no assassination attempt has ever been made against a former president or any member of a former president's family. Yet each former president requires twenty-four agents, eight per eight-hour shift. Extensions of Secret Service protection to family members have raised the annual cost of such protection from $50,000 in 1968 to nearly $10 million in 1988, even though the same number (three) of former presidents was alive in each year. In the face of a wave of international terrorism, however, Congress was reluctant to reduce security of any kind.

The General Services Administration has urged Congress to establish specific guidelines for former presidents' office furniture, travel expenses, and office size and location. In 1985, the House of Representatives (but not the Senate) passed a bill that would have placed ceilings on the amount of government funds former presidents could spend for office and staff. These ceilings would decrease every year that the president was out of office.

Critics of presidential libraries have charged that their dispersed geographical locations make them difficult for researchers to use. (Indeed, all but a few visitors to presidential libraries are tourists visiting the in-most-cases adjoining museums.[30]) One proposed remedy is to create a central depository for the papers of all former presidents. Another would microcopy all presidential papers and store the copies in one place.

Notes

1. Alan Evan Schenker, "Former Presidents: Suggestions for the Study of an Often Neglected Resource," *Presidential Studies Quarterly* 12 (Fall 1982): 545.
2. John Whiteclay Chambers II, "Presidents Emeritus," *American Heritage* 30 (June 1979): 16. When the question of "What shall we do with our former presidents?" was broached in a Chicago meeting at which Grover Cleveland spoke, Cleveland said he opposed a newspaper editor's suggestion that they be taken out in "a five acre field and shot." He explained: "In the first place, a five acre lot seems needlessly large, and in the second place, an ex-president has already suffered enough." (Lowell H. Harrison, "Presidents in Retirement," *American History Illustrated* 8 [December 1973]: 41).
3. James C. Clark, *Faded Glory: Presidents Out of Power* (New York: Praeger, 1985), v.
4. Arthur M. Schlesinger, Sr., "The U.S. Presidents," *Life*, November 1, 1948, 67-74; Schlesinger, "Our Presidents: A Rating by 75 Historians," *New York Times Magazine*, July 29, 1962, 12-13, 40-43; and Robert K. Murray and Tim H. Blessing, "The Presidential Performance Study: A Progress Report," *Journal of American History* (December 1983): 535-555.
5. Chambers, "Presidents Emeritus"; Dom Bonafede, "Life after the White House: Caring for Ex-Presidents Can Cost a Bundle," *National Journal*, August 31, 1985, 1943-1947; and Milton S. Mayer, "What Shall We Do with Our Ex-Presidents?" *Forum* 89 (March 1933): 185-189.
6. Chambers, "Presidents Emeritus," 17.
7. Harrison, "Presidents in Retirement," 37.
8. Ibid., 34.
9. Ibid., 35.
10. Quoted in Stephanie Smith, *Federal Benefits to Former Presidents and Their Widows*, CRS Report 85-173 GOV (Washington, D.C.: Library of Congress, Congressional Research Service, August 19, 1985), 12-13.
11. Chambers, "Presidents Emeritus," 18. Harrison, "Presidents in Retirement," 37. In his memoirs, Truman described a number of lucrative offers he received after leaving office. (He rejected all the offers):

    > A chain of clothing stores wanted me to be its vice president at an annual salary in six figures. A sewing machine company wanted me to be its chairman of the board, also at a salary in six figures but with no work to do except appear in public ceremonies for the company. The chief executive of a motion picture company called on me to try and interest me in a merger of several producing companies, saying that the deal could be consummated only if I agreed to join and head it up. He offered a fabulous salary and added that I could name my own terms. Several oil companies thought I would be a good man to have around. One proposal of an eight-year contract, requiring only an hour's "work," guaranteed over a half million dollars.

12. In 1913, Taft told President-elect Woodrow Wilson that he had saved nearly $100,000 from his salary as president. "Congress is very generous to the president," he told Wilson. The only expenses a president has are "those of furnishing food to a large boarding house of servants and to your family, and your own personal expenses of clothing, etc." (Smith, "Federal Benefits to Former Presidents," 12).
13. Ibid., 3.
14. Harrison, "Presidents in Retirement," 37. Hayes was no hypocrite: He worked hard in the service of a number of private charities and causes.

15. This section is based on Stephen W. Stathis, "Former Presidents as Congressional Witnesses," *Presidential Studies Quarterly* 13 (Summer 1983): 458-481.
16. Unaware of his predecessors' many appearances before congressional committees, Truman told reporters after voluntarily testifying to the Senate Foreign Relations Committee in 1955: "I think I made history yesterday in being the first president to allow himself to be questioned by a legislative committee." Ibid., 458.
17. Harrison, "Presidents in Retirement," 35.
18. Chambers, "Presidents Emeritus," 21.
19. Teresa Riordan, "The Imperial Ex-Presidency," *The Washington Monthly*, April 1983, 24-28.
20. Stephanie Smith, "Federal Expenditures for Former Presidents," CRS Issue Brief (Washington, D.C.: Library of Congress, Congressional Research Service, January 12, 1988), 1.
21. Chambers, "Presidents Emeritus," 17.
22. Marie B. Hecht, *Beyond the Presidency* (New York: Macmillan, 1976), 187.
23. Nonetheless, Hoover accepted the pension and other benefits that subsequently were offered to former presidents by law.
24. Smith, "Federal Benefits to Former Presidents," 15.
25. Ibid., 33.
26. Ibid., 34.
27. Riordan, "The Imperial Ex-Presidency."
28. Arthur M. Schlesinger, Jr., *Parade*, June 21, 1981.
29. Bonafede, "Life after the Oval Office," 1946.
30. The Ford library is on the campus of the University of Michigan in Ann Arbor. The university required that the museum be elsewhere, however, and it was built in Grand Rapids, Michigan.

Selected Bibliography

Chambers, John Whiteclay, II. "President Emeritus." *American Heritage* 30 (June 1979).

Clark, James C. *Faded Glory: Presidents Out of Power.* New York: Praeger, 1985.

Harrison, Lowell H. "Presidents in Retirement." *American History Illustrated 8* (December 1973): 41.

Hecht, Marie B. *Beyond the Presidency.* New York: Macmillan, 1976.

Schenker, Alan Evan. "Former Presidents: Suggestions for the Study of an Often Neglected Resource." *Presidential Studies Quarterly* 12 (Fall 1982).

Smith, Stephanie. *Federal Benefits to Former Presidents and Their Widows.* CRS Report 85-173 GOV. Washington, D.C.: Library of Congress, Congressional Research Service. August 19, 1985.

——. "Federal Expenditures for Former Presidents." Washington, D.C.: Library of Congress, Congressional Research Service. January 12, 1988.

Stathis, Stephen W. "Former Presidents as Congressional Witnessess." *Presidential Studies Quarterly* 13 (Summer 1983).

Air Photographics

Aerial view of Capitol Hill with the Supreme Court behind the Capitol

Part VI

The Chief Executive and the Federal Government

The President and Congress

In framing a government which is to be administered by men over men, the great difficulty lies in this: you must first enable the government to control the governed; and in the next place oblige it to control itself.

—James Madison
Federalist No. 51

The constitutional convention of 1787 is supposed to have created a government of "separated powers." It did nothing of the sort. Rather, it created a government of separated institutions sharing *powers.*

—Richard E. Neustadt
Presidential Power

I have been told I was on the road to Hell, but I had no idea that it was just a mile down the road with a dome on it.

—Abraham Lincoln

The Framers of the Constitution who convened in Philadelphia in the summer of 1787 disagreed about much when it came to the size, nature, and functions of the national government. They were in substantial agreement, however, that the American government should consist of three branches—legislative, executive, and judicial. This agreement stemmed from both the colonial experience and the failure of the Articles of Confederation. Each colony had established some version of a three-branch governing system. When the first national government set up under the articles deviated from this pattern by establishing a legislature-centered system, its failings were attributed in part to the absence of separate, coequal branches. In particular, the absence of a strong executive was felt keenly, as many believed that an executive was essential to provide some measure of leadership and to serve as well as a check on legislative excesses.

The arrangement implemented by the Founders—separation of powers—was designed to ensure that each of the three branches of government would perform different governing functions. At the same time, however, the Founders introduced checks and balances, whereby each branch needed the cooperation of the others to perform most important aspects of governing. This complex relationship was summarized by political scientist Richard E. Neustadt, who is quoted at the beginning of this chapter, as a system of "separated institutions *sharing* powers." To understand this relationship, characterized by patterns of conflict and cooperation, is to understand much about the relationship between the president and the Congress.

By Robert J. Spitzer

"Separated Institutions"

Most Americans take for granted the division in the Constitution of governing responsibilities into three separate, if interrelated, categories. Yet for the Framers, this decision represented a major change from the pattern of government followed at the time by most other nations.

Constitutional Provisions

The Constitution treats the legislative and executive branches separately. Article I describes in considerable detail the powers and responsibilities assigned to Congress, and states that, in concept, Congress has the sole power to legislate. According to Article I, "All legislative Powers herein granted shall be vested in a Congress of the United States. . . ." The power to enforce the law is reserved to the president, as specified in Article II: "The executive Power shall be vested in a President of the United States of America."

The distinction between the branches is seen partly in the separate selection of the members of each branch. Members of the House of Representatives are elected for two-year terms from districts within each state. Senators serve staggered six-year terms, with two elected from each state. Under the original Constitution, senators were elected by the state legislatures; this was changed by the Seventeenth Amendment, ratified in 1913, which provided for direct election of senators. The president, in contrast, is elected every four years by the electoral college, which in turn is selected by popular vote on a state-by-state basis according to the outcome of the presidential contest in each state.[1]

This election cycle has an important effect on the president's political relations with Congress. Since the entire membership of the House and one-third of the Senate

Painting by Howard Chandler Christy; Library of Congress

After many initial disagreements over the size and function of the national government, on September 17, 1787, the Framers signed the Constitution, providing for three separate but equal branches and a strong executive.

is up for reelection every two years, members of Congress face reelection during midterm elections when the presidency is not up for grabs. During presidential election years the victorious presidential candidate may succeed in helping to elect members of his or her political party seeking election for congressional or other offices (called the "coattail effect"). But during midterm elections the president's political party almost always loses seats in the Congress, resulting in a weakening of the president's influence over legislators. By incorporating an electoral cycle of midterm elections, the Founders were helping ensure that coordination between the two branches of government would not be too close.[2] *(See Party Affiliations in Congress and the Presidency, 1789-1989, p. 1453.)*

The Constitution also stipulates in Article I, section 6, that individuals may not serve in more than one branch at the same time (such as a member of Congress serving simultaneously in the president's cabinet); this is the norm in parliamentary cabinet government systems such as that found in Great Britain. As James Madison noted in the *Federalist* No. 51, this division was constructed carefully "to render [the branches of government], by different modes of election and different principles of action, as little connected with each other as the nature of their common functions and their common dependence on the society will admit." The president is further protected from improper congressional influence by the provision in Article II, section 1, that the president's salary, which is approved by Congress, "shall neither be increased nor diminished during the Period for which he shall have been elected. . . ." Thus, the two branches are separated by structure and selection procedures.

Reform?

Although this separation has been an integral component of the relationship between the legislative and executive branches, many critics have proposed that the terms for members of the House be extended to four years, coterminous with the president's election, and that senatorial terms be lengthened similarly to eight years. This presumably would lead to a greater likelihood that the same political party would control both branches at the same time, thus minimizing the oft-heard complaint that modern governing is typified by deadlock, paralysis, and gridlock rather than decisive leadership.

The prevalence of divided party control is evident in the period from 1952 to 1988; during that time, the presidency and both houses of Congress were controlled by the same political party for only twelve years. From 1968 to 1988 same-party control existed for only four years. As a 1950 report critical of the current system noted, "If the elections for these offices always coincide, recurrent emphasis upon national issues would promote legislative-executive party solidarity." [3]

The idea of a four-year term for members of the House was not considered at the Constitutional Convention of 1787; at that time, representatives in state legislatures served one-year terms.[4] At one point, however, the convention approved a three-year term for House members. The question of how long legislators should serve has been the subject of longstanding contention. In fact, a proposal to change term lengths was advanced with renewed vigor during the 1987 bicentennial celebration of the Constitution. As one critic observed, "The midterm election cannot result in a clearly defined change in governmental direction. . . . All it can do is deadlock the government. . . ." [5] The coterminous term proposal was advanced in other important writings during the bicentennial as well.[6]

Custom and Tradition

The ambiguity of constitutional wording has meant that the actual separation between the legislative and executive branches has varied according to historical circumstance and the predilections of the leaders of both branches. For example, writing in the 1830s, Supreme Court Justice Joseph Story observed that the president was "compelled to resort to secret and unseen influences, to private interviews, and private arrangements, to accomplish his own appropriate purposes instead of proposing and sustaining his own duties and measures by a bold and manly appeal to the nation in the face of its representatives."[7] Story was reflecting the dominant view of the time that presidents ought to respect scrupulously the preeminence of Congress over law making. Yet by modern standards such appeals by the president to the Congress and the nation are considered integral to the president's involvement in the legislative process.

This concern for the proper boundary between executive and legislative powers was evident in the early 1800s in debates over the propriety and constitutionality of public threats by presidents to use the veto power. Although presidential veto power over legislation was clearly stated in the Constitution, there was a strong sense that a publicly issued threat to use the veto represented an improper and even unconstitutional presidential intrusion into the legislative process. *(See "Veto Power," p. 1107, in this chapter.)*

President James Monroe provoked considerable dissent in Congress when he announced his intention to veto internal transport improvement legislation in 1817. Although Monroe used the veto only once in his eight years as president, this statement prompted the House to set up a special committee to review his views. The committee concluded that if the president's threat had any impact on congressional deliberations, it would amount to stripping Congress of its duly authorized preeminence over law making. President Andrew Jackson relied more heavily on veto threats, provoking anguished howls from congressional critics that he was intruding unconstitutionally into the legislative sphere. By the middle of the nineteenth century, however, such intrusions had become an accepted norm.[8] Indeed, today no one would question the constitutionality of a presidential veto threat.

Executive Privilege

The separation between the branches has been cloudy as well in the area of executive privilege. Under this privilege the president and other executive officials have the right to withhold sensitive documents and information from Congress or the courts. Presidents have argued that executive privilege is necessary to safeguard certain information in the public interest, including secret negotiations, without fear of interrupting the flow of legitimate government business. In short, presidents have argued that executive privilege is an important component of executive power.

In rebuttal, Congress has argued that it has an equally legitimate "right to know" about executive business, especially as it relates to congressional oversight of administrative matters. In the overwhelming majority of cases, congressional requests for sensitive executive documents have been granted eventually.

Uncertainty over the extent and nature of this privilege dates back to President George Washington, when he refused to give information to the House of Representatives about the Jay Treaty. Most presidents have had similar confrontations with Congress (although the term "executive privilege" was coined only during the Eisenhower administration), but differences generally have been resolved through accommodation and compromise. Even so, presidents are in general free to define what communications are and are not covered, especially in the area of national security.

Arguments about executive privilege came to a head during the administration of Richard M. Nixon. The special prosecutor appointed to investigate the Watergate crimes subpoenaed tape recordings of conversations between the president and his aides as part of the evidence being compiled in a criminal prosecution. Nixon refused to turn the tapes over, however, arguing that the communications were protected by executive privilege. The case was taken to the Supreme Court, which ruled unanimously in 1974 that Nixon had to comply with the subpoena. Although the Court ruled against Nixon in *United States v. Nixon,* it recognized the concept of executive privilege for the first time.[9] Speaking for the Court, Chief Justice Warren E. Burger recognized the need for such privilege as it applied to the president's "need for complete candor and objectivity from advisers" and "to protect military, diplomatic, or sensitive national security secrets." As with many Court rulings the question of executive privilege was by no means resolved in 1974, and the nature, legitimacy, and limitations of the concept continue to be debated hotly.[10]

Ambiguous Role of the Vice President

The United States is almost the only nation in the Western world to have formally created a "standby" executive. Most other nations fill chief executive vacancies with a caretaker or through a special election until a new executive is selected. This anomaly is compounded by the fact that the vice president is granted only two significant powers in the Constitution—one executive and the other legislative. *(See Office of the Vice President chapter in Part V.)*

According to Article II, section 1, the vice president becomes the chief executive in case of the death, resignation, or disability of the president. The vice president also serves as president of the Senate—clearly a legislative function. Both of these powers reflect the longstanding truism that the vice presidency is a position of little real power or importance during the normal course of events. Vice-presidential succession to the presidency rarely occurs through the normal election process. Of the thirteen vice presidents who became president before 1981, only four were elected on their own. The other nine ascended to the presidency owing to the death or resignation of the previous president. *(See Table 1.)*

Similarly, the vice president's position as president of the Senate is a rather unimportant job during normal times. The position takes on real significance only when a tie vote occurs on the floor of the Senate. The vice president may then cast the tie-breaking vote, an occurrence that arises on average only once every few years.

The position of president of the Senate is, and has always been, considered primarily ceremonial, even when the vice president came from the Senate. For example, Lyndon B. Johnson had served as Senate majority leader for eight years prior to his selection as John F. Kennedy's running mate in 1960. After the presidential election, Johnson proposed that he be allowed to serve as presiding

Table 1 Vice-Presidential Successors to the Presidency

Successor	Date of vacancy	Time left in term		
		Years	Months	Days
John Tyler	4/4/1841	3	11	0
Millard Fillmore	7/9/1850	2	7	23
Andrew Johnson	4/15/1865	3	10	17
Chester A. Arthur	9/19/1881	3	5	13
Theodore Roosevelt	9/14/1901	3	5	18
Calvin Coolidge	8/2/1923	1	7	2
Harry S Truman	4/12/1945	3	9	8
Lyndon B. Johnson	11/22/1963	1	1	29
Gerald R. Ford	8/9/1974	2	5	11
Total		26	4	1

Source: Joel K. Goldstein, *The Modern American Vice Presidency: The Transformation of a Political Institution* (Princeton, N.J.: Princeton University Press, 1982), 10. Reprinted by permission of the publisher.

officer over the Senate Democrats, but this proposal was rebuffed sharply by Senate leaders. In arguing against such an idea an otherwise sympathetic senator said that to grant Johnson such a position "would violate the spirit of separation of powers." [11]

The ambiguity of the vice presidency stems from several concerns of the Framers of the Constitution when creating that office. First, some of the Founders believed it important that the presiding officer of the Senate be selected from outside the body, so that no Senator would have to lose his vote by serving in this position. (Originally the Senate was composed of only twenty-six members. The same problem did not exist for the larger House of Representatives.)

Second, the Founders followed many of the provisions of the New York State constitution, which provided for a lieutenant governor. Thus, the principle of vice-presidential succession is based on similar provisions in that constitution.

Third, the Founders were looking for a means of facilitating the election and enhancing the legitimacy of the president. By specifying that the president and the vice president "shall not be an Inhabitant of the same State"—thereby ensuring that at least two states would be represented on the national ticket—the Constitution's Framers were hoping to minimize the state rivalries that might prevail in presidential elections. A situation in which candidates hailed from the same state was especially likely to occur under the original system in which the vice presidency went to the presidential candidate who received the second-highest number of electoral votes. In changing this system, the Twelfth Amendment provided for a ticket composed of a presidential and a separately designated vice-presidential candidate.[12] With the rise of national political parties and improved communications and transportation, the presidential race became "nationalized."

The lack of a lengthier and more detailed constitutional charge for the vice president, combined with a vice president's political dependence on the president for meaningful work and a political identity, has resulted in an institution that has remained mostly in the shadows. Yet in recent years the growth of the institutional presidency has helped prod the growth of an institutional vice presidency. Recent vice presidents—notably Walter F. Mondale and George Bush—have participated actively in advisory and policy-shaping roles. If this trend continues, the vice president's dilemma of sharing both executive and legislative functions may be resolved through the expanded involvement of the vice president in the affairs of the executive branch.[13]

"Sharing Powers"

Just as the constitutional system consists of three separate branches, it is equally true that, under most circumstances, no one branch can operate without the other two. This reality especially applies to the relationship between the president and Congress. The familiar list of constitutionally granted powers makes it clear that most powers cannot be carried out without some degree of mutual cooperation between the two branches.

Constitutionally Shared Powers

Congress passes laws, but they cannot be enacted until they cross the president's desk for a signature or veto. If vetoed, they are returned to the congressional house of origin for a possible override vote. A bill is enacted over a veto if two-thirds majorities are mustered in both houses. When a bill is vetoed after Congress adjourns, it is considered "pocket vetoed" and it dies. *(See "Veto Power," p. 1107, in this chapter.)*

As for other constitutionally shared powers in Article II, section 3, the president is charged with giving the Congress "Information of the State of the Union" and recommending for its consideration "such Measures as he shall judge necessary and expedient." The president also can call special sessions of Congress. Presidential nominations to important administrative and judicial positions must be approved by the Senate, and treaties with other nations negotiated by the president must be ratified by a two-thirds Senate vote. The president holds commander-in-chief powers over the military, but Congress declares war and regulates the armed forces.

In the case of misconduct ("high crimes and misdemeanors") the president is subject to impeachment and removal from office by Congress. In such an eventuality articles of impeachment are voted by the House, and an impeachment trial is held in the Senate. In 1868 President Andrew Johnson actually was impeached by the House (that is, charges were brought); in the Senate trial Johnson avoided conviction by a single vote. In 1974 the House Judiciary Committee voted three articles of impeachment against President Richard Nixon. In the face of mounting political opposition and a likely Senate trial, Nixon resigned.

Even in the case of a presidential election Congress may play a role. If no presidential candidate receives an absolute majority of electoral college votes, the presidential election is thrown into the House of Representatives, which then ballots with each state casting one vote until one candidate receives a majority of state votes. The vice president is selected separately by the Senate. Although this procedure has been used only once since 1824 (when the Senate selected a vice president in 1836), it illustrates one additional way the branches may interact.

Sharing Powers by Legal Delegation

One of the key sources of presidential authority has arisen from concerted efforts by Congress to delegate some of its authority by statute to the president and other executive officials. (In a challenge to the Judiciary Act of 1789, Chief Justice John Marshall observed that Congress could in fact delegate certain powers to either of the other two branches.) This delegation of powers is based on several considerations. First, until this century Congress typically was in session for only a few months out of the year. Thus, Congress found it necessary to delegate certain of its powers to the executive branch to ensure the smooth functioning of government programs while it was not in session.

Second, the need for flexibility in the timing of legislative policy often has resulted in delegation. In 1799, for example, Congress voted to renew commercial restrictions against France, but it allowed the president the option of ending them "if he shall deem it expedient and consistent with the interest of the United States." [14]

Third, delegation of power to the president is based on the long-practiced tradition that presidents act as channels for communication with foreign nations. For example, an 1822 law barred British West Indies ports from shipping to America unless the president received satisfactory information that American ships could enter the British ports.

Fourth, the president has long been considered the one representative of the American people. Thus, many powers have been delegated to the executive by Congress to avoid the political fragmentation and controversy that often attend congressional decision making. This was seen, for example, in attempts to delegate tariff powers to the executive in the early twentieth century.

A fifth consideration underlying delegation of powers is the president's responsibility for fact-finding and coordination. This is especially true when intervention in the economy is necessary; measures designed to stimulate or otherwise direct the economy depend directly on the quality and timeliness of information. Because the executive branch gathers and generates much of this information, it often has proven to be the logical source of timely action. The Federal Pay Comparability Act of 1970 was enacted to ensure that federal pay levels remained roughly comparable with those for similar jobs in the private sector. Such assessments depend on data supplied by several federal bureaus. Based on these data the president makes recommendations to Congress.

Finally, national emergencies have been a reason for delegating power to the president. During times of war and economic crisis, the desire for speed and flexibility, and respect for presidential expertise, contribute to congressional willingness to give broad powers to the president.[15]

The delegation of congressional powers to the executive is a practice that extends back to the beginning of the country. Over the last two centuries Congress has delegated authority in hundreds, perhaps even thousands, of instances. An excellent example of the nature and impact of congressional delegation of authority to the president is illustrated by the evolution of budgetary authority.

Federal Budgetary Authority

Before 1921 Congress was vested with the sole budget-making authority. Many presidents and Treasury secretaries played important roles in formulating national spending priorities, but Congress bore principal responsibility for the budget, and it had relatively little difficulty in formulating annual spending priorities up to the time of the Civil War. The magnitude of wartime spending placed a great strain on the legislative committee structure, however, and Congress responded by dispersing budgetary authority among several committees, including the newly created Appropriations Committee, and separating authority over the appropriation and revenue components of budget making.

In the latter part of the nineteenth century the increasing fragmentation of budget authority to more congressional committees encouraged railroad interests, land speculators, other business interests, and many individuals seeking government pensions to obtain lucrative concessions in the budget. The fiscal consequence was more extravagant use of public funds. The only public figure to stand up consistently against this abuse was the president. President Grover Cleveland in particular gained a reputation as "protector of the purse" by his prolific use of the veto. In his first term alone he vetoed 304 bills—almost three times as many as all of his predecessors combined. Of those, 241 were aimed at private and general pension bills.

From the early 1900s on the swell of reformers' cries (including many in Congress) called for giving greater budgetary authority to the president. In 1921 Congress enacted the Budget and Accounting Act, which provided for an executive Bureau of the Budget (BOB) and allowed the presidential appointment of a budget director. For the first time the BOB would formulate and submit to Congress a comprehensive budget document. In 1933 Congress passed the Economy Act, which centralized and reorganized various budgetary authorities within the executive. And in 1939 President Franklin D. Roosevelt used the reorganization authority granted by Congress to bring BOB into the newly created Executive Office of the President. *(See Table 2.)*

In 1970 President Nixon issued an executive order based on reorganization authority granted by Congress that broadened the mandate of BOB from simply preparing the budget to assessing and evaluating existing programs. The name of the bureau was changed to the Office of Management and Budget to reflect its enhanced authority. In 1974, however, in reaction to the excesses of the Nixon administration, including expanded use of impoundment power (refusing to spend funds duly appropriated by Congress), Congress passed the Budget and Impoundment Control Act. This act reasserted some congressional control over the budget and ended the practice of presidential impoundment of funds.[16]

This case illustrates how congressional authority over the budget was delegated to the president, resulting in a significant increase in presidential authority. The progressively greater scope of that authority was challenged only when the institutions concerned came into sharp political dispute over claims that the executive had abused its authority. The increase in the president's budget power could not have occurred without congressional willingness to delegate its authority to the executive.

Challenges to Delegation

Legal challenges to congressional delegation of power to the executive have arisen periodically. The thrust of court decisions addressing the question generally has included an assertion that Congress cannot delegate its

Table 2 Budget Receipts and Outlays, 1789-1987 (millions of dollars)

Fiscal year	Budget receipts	Budget outlays	Budget surplus or deficit (−)
1789-1849	1,160	1,090	70
1850-1900	14,462	15,453	−991
1901	588	525	63
1902	562	485	77
1903	562	517	45
1904	541	584	−43
1905	544	567	−23
1906	595	570	25
1907	666	579	87
1908	602	659	−57
1909	604	694	−89
1910	676	694	−18
1911	702	691	11
1912	693	690	3
1913	714	715	a
1914	725	726	a
1915	683	746	−63
1916	761	713	48
1917	1,101	1,954	−853
1918	3,645	12,677	−9,032
1919	5,130	18,493	−13,363
1920	6,649	6,358	291
1921	5,571	5,062	509
1922	4,026	3,289	736
1923	3,853	3,140	713
1924	3,871	2,908	963
1925	3,641	2,924	717
1926	3,795	2,930	865
1927	4,013	2,857	1,155
1928	3,900	2,961	939
1929	3,862	3,127	734
1930	4,058	3,320	738
1931	3,116	3,577	−462
1932	1,924	4,659	−2,735
1933	1,997	4,598	−2,602
1934	2,955	6,541	−3,586
1935	3,609	6,412	−2,803
1936	3,923	8,228	−4,304
1937	5,387	7,580	−2,193
1938	6,751	6,840	−89
1939	6,295	9,141	−2,846
1940	6,548	9,468	−2,920
1941	8,712	13,653	−4,941
1942	14,634	35,137	−20,503
1943	24,001	78,555	−54,554
1944	43,747	91,304	−47,557
1945	45,159	92,712	−47,553
1946	39,296	55,232	−15,936
1947	38,514	34,496	4,018
1948	41,560	29,764	11,796
1949	39,415	38,835	580
1950	39,443	42,562	−3,119
1951	51,616	45,514	6,102
1952	66,167	67,686	−1,519
1953	69,608	76,101	−6,493
1954	69,701	70,855	−1,154
1955	66,451	68,444	−2,993
1956	74,587	70,640	3,947
1957	79,990	76,578	3,412
1958	79,636	82,405	−2,769
1959	79,249	92,098	−12,849
1960	92,492	92,191	301
1961	94,388	97,723	−3,335
1962	99,676	106,821	−7,146
1963	106,560	111,316	−4,756
1964	112,613	118,528	−5,915
1965	116,817	118,228	−1,411
1966	130,835	134,532	−3,698
1967	148,822	157,464	−8,643
1968	152,973	178,134	−25,161
1969	186,882	183,640	3,242
1970	192,807	195,649	−2,842
1971	187,139	210,172	−23,033
1972	207,309	230,681	−23,373
1973	230,799	245,707	−14,908
1974	263,224	269,359	−6,135
1975	279,090	332,332	−53,242
1976	298,060	371,779	−73,719
TQ[b]	81,232	95,973	−14,741
1977	355,559	409,203	−53,644
1978	399,561	458,729	−59,168
1979	463,302	503,464	−40,162
1980	517,112	590,920	−73,808
1981	599,272	678,209	−78,936
1982	617,766	745,706	−127,940
1983	600,562	808,327	−207,746
1984	666,457	851,781	−185,324
1985	734,057	946,316	−212,260
1986	769,091	990,258	−221,167
1987	854,143	1,004,586	−150,444

Source: Office of Management and Budget, 1988.

Note: Data for 1789-1933 are for the administrative budget; data for 1934 and all following years are for the unified budget. Beginning in 1937, table includes amounts for social security trust funds that are off-budget.

a. $500,000 or less.

b. In calendar year 1976, the federal fiscal year was converted from a July 1-June 30 basis to an Oct. 1-Sept. 30 basis. "TQ" refers to the transition quarter from July 1 to Sept. 30, 1976.

power (or can do so only within certain limits). At the same time, however, the courts have ruled in favor of the delegations raised in particular cases. This pattern has appeared in several Supreme Court cases, including *Wayman v. Southart,*[17] *Field v. Clark,*[18] and *S. W. Hampton, Jr. & Co. v. United States.*[19] The Court has recognized nonetheless that limits on congressional delegation to the president are greater in the area of foreign policy than in domestic policy. This position was laid out clearly in *United States v. Curtiss-Wright Export Corporation.*[20] *(See "United States v. Curtiss-Wright Export Corporation," p. 1378, in the Appendix.)*

In another important case, *Schechter Poultry Corp. v. United States,*[21] the Court invalidated a provision of the National Industrial Recovery Act on the grounds that the delegation of legislative power to the president was too broad. As Justice Benjamin N. Cardozo observed, "This is delegation run riot." [22] Although *Schechter* has not been overturned, it has been neglected as precedent. Some observers have argued that the *Schechter* principle should be reexamined as a means of limiting the extent to which Congress can delegate its authority.[23]

The Politics of Shared Powers

Louis Fisher, a keen observer of relations between the executive and legislative branches, has noted that separation of powers and a system of checks and balances are by no means contradictory, even though the first calls for separation and the second for intermixing. "Far from being contradictory, they complement and support one another. An institution cannot check unless it has some measure of independence; it cannot retain that independence without the power to check." [24] Without a doubt, powers are shared, yet each branch retains sole domain over certain actions. Both the Congress and the president can claim ties to popular sovereignty, as the members of each branch are elected popularly. Yet differing bases of representation may result in the two branches holding very different views of what the American people want their government to do. These differences are visible in several areas where the branches interact.

Foreign Affairs

The relationship between the Congress and the presidency in the area of foreign affairs is marked in general by the historic dominance of the president over the Congress. The president's ascendance in foreign affairs is such that one analyst has concluded that there are actually "two presidencies"—one for domestic policy and the other for foreign policy. Despite variations according to historical era and area, presidents generally have realized more of their objectives in foreign affairs than in domestic politics.[25]

Despite presidential ascendance the Constitution is by no means one-sided in favoring one branch over the other. In Article II, section 2, the president is empowered to serve as "Commander in Chief of the Army and Navy of the United States, and of the Militia of the several States, when called into the actual Service of the United States. . . ." The president also has the power to "make Treaties," with two-thirds concurrence of the Senate, and to nominate "Ambassadors, other public Ministers and Consuls" subject to Senate approval. Other presidential responsibilities are receiving ambassadors and ensuring that the laws are "faithfully executed." Some analysts believe that presidential influence over foreign affairs also stems from Article II, section 1, which vests "executive power" in the president. Finally, the presidential oath of office requires that the executive "preserve, protect and defend the Constitution of the United States."

Congress is charged with several responsibilities in Article I, section 8. Among these are providing for "the common Defence and general Welfare of the United States" and regulating commerce with other nations. Congress punishes crimes on the high seas and settles "Offenses against the Law of Nations." It also has the power to "declare War, grant Letters of Marque and Reprisal, and make Rules concerning Captures on Land and Water." Other congressional responsibilities are raising and supporting an army, providing for a navy, making the rules that govern both, calling up and regulating the militia, and making all laws considered "necessary and proper" to carry out its other responsibilities.

Despite what appears to be a rough balance in powers and responsibilities between the executive and legislative branches, from the beginning presidents have taken the lead in determining foreign policy. The first five presidents all provided forceful leadership in this area. In 1793, for example, President George Washington issued a Proclamation of Neutrality in the war between France and Britain. Pro-French Americans, led by Thomas Jefferson, criticized the proclamation, however, arguing that Washington was usurping congressional authority. Alexander Hamilton then defended Washington's action, saying that the conduct of foreign relations was an executive function. This dispute was aired in a series of articles published in a Philadelphia newspaper and written by Hamilton and James Madison, who defended the Jeffersonian position. Hamilton wrote under the name "Pacificus" and Madison under the name "Helvidius."

Other factors have contributed as well to presidential ascendance in foreign policy. First, Congress by its nature is more likely to be drawn to concerns that are close, substantively and geographically, to the hearts of its constituents. Thus, service by members of Congress on the Agriculture or Public Works committees, for example, is likely to be of greater interest to constituents for the immediate impact those committees may have on representatives' home districts than service on the Foreign Affairs or Foreign Relations committees. Similarly, as the only political leader elected at the national level, the president often is viewed as a purely national leader, who is more likely to receive political credit for, and thus benefit from, foreign policy initiatives.

Second, the president benefits from the unitary nature of the position. Although the modern presidency incorporates a large administrative apparatus, the president can act authoritatively as a single individual. Especially in times of emergency and crisis, presidential measures can be taken with decisiveness, secrecy, and dispatch. Even presidential critics acknowledge the necessity that a country speak with a single voice to the rest of the world. The president is the obvious leader to fulfill such a role.

Third, presidents are always on hand. Because up until about the middle of this century Congress held session for only part of the year, many responsibilities fell on presidential shoulders out of simple necessity, including many pertaining to foreign affairs.

Fourth, strong presidents set precedent. Although the history of presidential-congressional relations is marked by periods in which each has held some degree of ascendance, the cumulative impact of unilateral presidential actions in areas that include war making, diplomacy, and intelligence has buttressed arguments that presidential assertiveness in these areas is appropriate, if not obviously constitutional. (Particular examples are considered in succeeding sections.)

Finally, court decisions generally have supported an expansive interpretation of the presidential prerogative in foreign affairs. The courts largely have avoided constitutional challenges to presidential initiatives abroad (often

Major U.S. Military . . .

The following are major instances of U.S. military intervention since World War II (not including participation in multinational peace keeping forces):

July-August 1946. President Harry S Truman sends U.S. naval units to Trieste, near the Italian-Yugoslav border, anticipating an attack from Yugoslav-Soviet forces. After U.S. Army transport planes are shot down, reinforcements arrive in Italy.

August 1946. To counter Soviet threat to Turkish control of Bosporus Straits, President Truman dispatches powerful carrier force as a display of resolve.

September 1946. One U.S. carrier is stationed off Greece during attempted communist takeover.

January 1948. Marine reinforcements sent to the Mediterranean are seen as a warning to Yugoslavia to stay away from the five thousand U.S. Army troops in Trieste.

July 1948. During the Arab-Israeli War a consular guard is detached from the U.S.S. *Kearsarge* and sent to Jerusalem to protect the U.S. consul general. Two Marines are later wounded.

April 1948-November 1949. U.S. Marines are sent to Nanking and Shanghai to protect the U.S. embassy and to aid evacuation of American nationals in wake of communist takeover of China.

June 1950-July 1953. Korean War.

July 1954-Febraury 1955. Five U.S. carriers arrive at the Tachen Islands north of Taiwan to evacuate American and Taiwanese civilians and military personnel threatened by Chinese communist bombing.

November 1956. During the Suez crisis one Marine battalion evacuates fifteen hundred people, most of them Americans, from Alexandria, Egypt.

February 1957. Marines stationed 550 miles northeast of Sumatra are poised to intervene for protection of Americans during revolt in Indonesia.

July 1957. Four U.S. carriers are sent to defend Taiwan during Chinese communist shelling of Kinmen Island (Quemoy).

January 1958. When mob violence breaks out in Caracas, Venezuela, the U.S.S. *Des Moines,* with one company of U.S. Marines on board, is stationed nearby.

March 1958. A Marine company, attack squadron, and helicopter squadron are deployed with the Seventh Fleet off Indonesia to protect U.S. citizens.

July-October 1958. Following civil unrest in Beirut, President Dwight D. Eisenhower sends five thousand Marines to Lebanon to "protect American lives" and to "assist Lebanon in preserving its political independence." Eventually, fourteen thousand U.S. soldiers and Marines occupy areas in Lebanon. The last U.S. forces withdraw in late October.

July 1959-April 1975. Vietnam era. Sent as troop trainers, the first U.S. military are killed in South Vietnam in July 1959. In October 1961 President John F. Kennedy decides to send Green Beret "military advisers." In August 1964 Congress passes Gulf of Tonkin Resolution. In March 1973 last U.S. troops withdraw. At the end of April 1975 last Americans are evacuated from Saigon.

November 1959-February 1960. A Marine Ground Task Force is deployed to protect U.S. nationals

arguing that such questions are "political" and thus not justiciable.) In a few cases, however, the courts have spoken to presidential power. Perhaps the strongest statement favoring presidential authority in foreign affairs came in the Supreme Court case of *United States v. Curtiss-Wright Export Corp.* Speaking for the majority, Justice George Sutherland referred to "the very delicate, plenary and exclusive power of the President as the sole organ of the federal government in the field of international relations. . . ."[26]

Two reasons can be offered for the courts' apparent deference and infrequency of ruling in such cases. First, the wording of Article II of the Constitution is less clear than that of Article I. Thus, presidents possess more leeway to interpret the wording so that it fits their political goals. Second, and related to the first reason, an aura of nearly monarchical dimensions has surrounded the office of the president for most of the country's history. Phrases such as "Sun King complex," "textbook presidency," "cult of the presidency," and "American monarchy" refer to enduring popular images of the president as moral leader, problem solver, and benevolent, omniscient parent figure. The enduring popular support emanating from these images has been a vital basis for the growth of presidential power.[27] The fundamental recognition of popular support for presidential actions that might be otherwise subject to constitutional challenge has contributed to the discouragement of such challenges, or the recognition that the political consensus behind presidential actions may be more potent than seemingly narrow constitutional interpretation.

War Powers and Use of Military Force

Although ambiguity surrounds many of the Founders' deliberations, little uncertainty exists about the construction of war powers. The power to initiate war was vested in the Congress. In a draft of the Constitution circulated to the convention members on August 6, 1787, the legislature was to have the power "to make war." In subsequent debate this phrase was changed to "declare war." As Madison's notes revealed, he and Elbridge Gerry "moved to insert '*declare*,' striking out '*make*' war; leaving to the Executive the power to repel sudden attacks."[28] Thus, the purpose of the change was not to enhance the president's power; rather, it was to permit the president to take actions "to repel sudden attacks." Only one delegate to the convention, Pierce Butler, proposed giving the president war-making powers, but his proposal found no support. Both Madison and James Wilson assured the convention that the power of war and peace was a legislative, not an executive function.

In addition to repelling sudden attacks on the United

. . . Interventions, 1946-1983

in Cuba during the revolution.

November 1961. U.S. Navy planes and ships arrive off the Dominican Republic as show of force to discourage members of Trujillo family from attempting to retake the government they lost when dictator Rafael Trujillo was assassinated the previous May.

May-July 1962. A Marine expeditionary unit of five thousand lands in Thailand to support the government against threat of outside communist pressure. Marines depart nine weeks later.

October-December 1962. Challenging a Soviet introduction of missiles into Cuba, President Kennedy orders 180 U.S. Navy ships and a B-52 bomber force carrying A-bombs into the Caribbean to effect a quarantine. Troop carrier squadrons of the U.S. Air Force Reserve are being recalled to active duty when Soviet premier Nikita Khrushchev agrees to withdraw the missiles.

May 1963. A U.S. Marine battalion is positioned off the coast of Haiti in the wake of domestic protest against the Duvalier regime and a threat of intervention by the neighboring Dominican Republic.

November 1964. U.S. transport aircraft in the Congo carry Belgian paratroopers in an operation to rescue civilians, among them sixty Americans held hostage by antigovernment rebels near Stanleyville.

May 1964-January 1973. Beginning as retaliation for the downing of American reconnaissance planes flying over Laos, U.S. Navy jets attack Pathet Lao communist strongholds. Air attacks on Laos continue into the 1970s.

April 1965. Following a communist-leaning revolt in the Dominican Republic, President Lyndon B. Johnson dispatches 21,500 U.S. troops to protect Americans and to offer supplies and military assistance to locals. By fall, constitutional government is restored.

June 1967. During the Arab-Israeli War, President Johnson sends the U.S. Sixth Fleet within fifty miles of the Syrian coast as a warning to the Soviet Union against entering the conflict.

July-December 1967. Responding to an appeal from Congolese president Joseph-Désiré Mobutu, President Johnson sends three C-130 transport planes with crews to aid government forces battling white mercenaries and Katangese rebels.

April-June 1970. U.S. ground troops attack communist sanctuaries in Cambodia.

May 1975. President Gerald R. Ford sends combined force of navy, Marine, and air force to rescue crew of thirty-nine from the U.S. merchant ship *Mayaguez,* which had been captured by Cambodian communists.

April 1980. Ninety-man U.S. commando team in Iran aborts effort to rescue American hostages beld in the U.S. embassy in Tehran. Eight die in collision between transport plane and helicopter.

October 1983. U.S. Marines and troops from neighboring eastern Caribbean nations invade the island of Grenada.

Source: Congressional Quarterly Weekly Report, October 29, 1983, p. 2222.

States, it also was understood that the president would direct and lead the armed forces and put them to any use specified by Congress, as the president was dependent on, and responsible to, final legislative authority. Jefferson summarized the thinking of many when he wrote to Madison in 1789: "We have already given in example one effectual check to the Dog of war by transferring the power of letting him loose from the Executive to the Legislative body, from those who are to spend to those who are to pay." [29]

As with many shared powers the practice of war making and deployment of troops was shaped by necessity, ambition, and enterprise. During the nineteenth century, American armed forces were used by presidents on their own authority to suppress piracy and the slave trade, to pursue criminals across frontiers, and to protect American lives and property in primitive or backward areas. Some presidents, such as James K. Polk, Ulysses S. Grant, and William McKinley, interpreted the commander-in-chief powers more broadly, while others, such as George Washington, Thomas Jefferson, James Buchanan, and Grover Cleveland, were more deferential to the war powers of Congress. Regardless of these differences, however, the dominant view of the time was that the president could deploy the military outside of U.S. borders as long as the military was not used to commit an "act of war" (using military force against a sovereign nation without that nation having declared war on or used force against the United States).[30]

This pattern changed in the twentieth century. Presidents from Theodore Roosevelt on began to use the military against sovereign nations without congressional authorization. Roosevelt, for example, directed the U.S. Navy against Colombia to prevent the latter from suppressing the Panamanian insurrection. Presidents William Howard Taft and Woodrow Wilson both used American troops freely in Central America and the Caribbean without congressional authorization. And President Franklin Roosevelt exercised even greater discretion over use of American troops abroad prior to the start of World War II.[31] *(See box, Major U.S. Military Interventions, above.)*

After the war America emerged for the first time from its predominantly isolationist posture in world affairs, assuming instead an assertive internationalist and interventionist role. This trend opened the door to a more active military role, with military initiatives arising from presidential initiative and congressional acquiescence.

President Harry S Truman committed American troops to Korea in 1950 without congressional authorization. Truman himself offered no explanation for declining to seek congressional assent (although he did consult with congressional leaders after the initial commitment of troops), but a State Department bulletin asserted that "the President, as Commander in Chief of the Armed Forces of the United States, has full control over the use thereof." [32] The following year Secretary of State Dean Acheson defended Truman's actions before a congressional hearing by asserting that the president had acted properly by carrying out American foreign policy and that Congress could not interfere.

President Dwight D. Eisenhower, in contrast, took care to seek congressional authorization in the case of the Formosa Resolution of 1954, which empowered the president to employ American forces to defend the island of Formosa. But in subsequent resolutions, including the Middle East Resolution of 1957, the Cuba Resolution of 1962 (under President John F. Kennedy), and the Gulf of Tonkin Resolution of 1964 (under President Lyndon B. Johnson), the concept of seeking congressional authorization was dropped. Rather, the terminology used implied acceptance of the idea that the president already had the power to use the armed forces in the ways mentioned in the resolutions.

Presidents from Eisenhower through Nixon all asserted unrestricted executive authority to commit American forces without prior congressional consent. With some minor exceptions Congress acquiesced in this arrangement until 1973.

The War Powers Resolution

The 1960s and 1970s saw American engagement in the longest war in American history. Although the scale of American involvement was less than that of World War II, for example, the length of the war and the growing doubts about its justification and its progressively greater human and material costs fanned the flames of discontent nationwide. Congressional leaders pressed for means to curtail the president's relatively free hand, which in turn sparked renewed interest in reinvigorating congressional influence over war making. This pressure culminated in the passage of the War Powers Resolution in 1973. Although vetoed by President Richard Nixon, the bill was enacted over the veto.

The resolution incorporates three key provisions. First, the president must consult with Congress "in every possible instance" before introducing U.S. forces into hostilities. Second, the president must submit a written report to Congress within forty-eight hours of the introduction of American forces into hostilities. And third, the president must withdraw forces within sixty-to-ninety days unless Congress provides appropriate authorization. Congress may direct the president to withdraw forces at any time by passage of a concurrent resolution. The sixty-to-ninety-day period does not begin, however, until the president submits a written report. *(See box, War Powers Provisions, p. 544.)*

Despite what initially was considered a successful attempt to involve Congress more meaningfully in war making, the War Powers Resolution has been the subject of much criticism and debate. Some critics have argued that it attempts improperly to tie the president's hands, while others view it as an invitation for the president to conduct war freely for sixty days.[33] In any case, no president from Gerald R. Ford to Ronald Reagan has complied fully with its terms (and all have questioned the act's constitutionality, mostly on the grounds that the act improperly infringes on the president's constitutional prerogatives). This has raised the added objection that the act lacks any mechanism to force the president to comply with it (aside from the concurrent resolution provision), as it provides no means of impelling the president to submit an initial report or even to consult with Congress.

In 1975 the War Powers Resolution was invoked on four occasions. The first three occurred in April and involved the evacuation of refugee U.S. citizens from Vietnam and Cambodia in the waning days of the Vietnam War. In these cases, "consultation" with Congress occurred, but the rescue attempts were concluded quickly.

The fourth instance occurred in May, when an American vessel, the *Mayaguez,* was captured by a Cambodian gunboat. President Ford then ordered air strikes against Cambodia and called up the Marines, who launched a costly invasion of Koh Tang Island in the erroneous belief that the *Mayaguez* crew was being held there. Despite problems with the military operation the crew was returned two days later (although apparently not as a result of the military assaults), and Ford's actions prompted euphoria at a time when the country was still feeling the sting of Vietnam. In this instance Ford did not consult with Congress, but he did inform some members of Congress of the operation as it was being carried out.

When President Jimmy Carter launched an unsuccessful military effort in April 1980 to rescue American hostages being held in Iran, he did not consult with Congress, citing the need for secrecy. He submitted a brief report to Congress, however, but he argued that the War Powers Resolution did not apply as the mission was a humanitarian effort.

Lebanon. The presidency of Ronald Reagan saw several clashes between the executive and legislative branches over the deployment of American troops abroad. In August 1982 Reagan sent Marines to Lebanon to serve as part of an international force, which included French and Italian (and later British) troops deployed to help bring peace to that war-torn nation. Despite agreement that a state of hostilities existed, Reagan submitted a report to Congress that was consistent with the War Powers Resolution rather than under its terms. Thus, he did not set in motion the sixty-to-ninety-day limit the resolution imposes.

The continued presence of American troops in Lebanon in what was considered an untenable military situation raised doubts about the mission.[34] Such doubts were aggravated when Marines were killed in several bombing incidents. On October 23, 1983, 241 Marines were killed when a Moslem fundamentalist drove a truck full of explosives into Marine headquarters.

In the absence of the automatic triggering of the War Powers clock, Congress moved to direct the president to withdraw the troops. Protracted negotiations between the administration and congressional leaders ensued, spanning many months. Congress passed and President Reagan signed a bill giving him authority to keep troops in Lebanon for eighteen months. Despite uneasiness over the length of this period, many in Congress felt it politically prudent to see that this period extended past the 1984 elections. They also believed that Reagan would acknowledge the legitimacy of the War Powers framework. Instead, the president made it clear that he did not consider himself bound by the act, and that he would consider keeping troops in Lebanon past the eighteen-month deadline.[35]

By early 1984 the military situation was deteriorating steadily. On February 7, 1984, Reagan ordered the Marines withdrawn to American ships.

Grenada. On October 25, 1983, President Reagan launched an invasion of the tiny Caribbean island of Grenada (population, about 110,000). The operation utilized almost ten thousand soldiers from all service branches.

In 1979 the ruling government of Prime Minister Eric Gairy was overthrown in a coup led by Maurice Bishop. In October 1983 Bishop was overthrown. The Reagan administration had viewed the Bishop regime with suspicion, and it feared a new regime more sympathetic to Cuba. Moreover, approximately one thousand Americans were living on the island at the time, six hundred of whom were medical students.

Reagan briefed congressional leaders the night before the invasion and submitted a report on the day of the invasion. Despite their overwhelming military superiority, U.S. forces took about a week to win control of the island. Nineteen U.S. soldiers were killed and 116 were wounded; 24 Cubans were killed, as were 45 Grenadians (27 were killed accidentally when U.S. forces bombed a mental hospital). By the end of October both houses of Congress had taken steps to begin the sixty-day War Powers clock, but by December only about three hundred American personnel were still on the island.

Critics of the invasion questioned whether the Americans on Grenada were in fact in danger, and, if so, whether an armed invasion was the appropriate response. They also criticized the fact that news reporters were not allowed to accompany the invading U.S. troops, as had been the practice in previous wars. The Defense Department claimed that reporters were excluded for their own safety, but after the invasion the department announced that a few reporters would be allowed to cover future similar military actions.[36]

Gulf of Sidra. On April 14, 1986, President Reagan ordered air strikes against port and military installations in Libya, in response to Libya's widely reputed support of terrorism. The air strike was prompted by two particular incidents: the terrorist bombing of a nightclub in West Germany frequented by U.S. soldiers, and U.S. naval maneuvers in the Gulf of Sidra. Libya claimed all of the gulf as its territorial waters, but the Reagan administration ordered maneuvers to be conducted there nevertheless.

President Reagan summoned congressional leaders to the White House for a late afternoon briefing after American F-111 bombers had already left their bases in Great Britain (they were joined in the raid by carrier-based aircraft). After the mission the Reagan administration admitted that the naval maneuvers held inside the gulf were designed to provoke Libya's leader, Muammar Quaddafi, into military action to provide a basis for a U.S. response. The air strikes also were an attempt to assassinate Quaddafi, who narrowly escaped death when planes bombed his residence.

Persian Gulf. When the Iran-Iraq war of the 1980s spilled over into the Persian Gulf, a central shipping lane for oil, oil tankers became targets of raids by both countries. Although American ships already had been patrolling the gulf and the Indian Ocean, patrols were stepped up in 1986 in response to requests by Kuwait that its oil tankers be "reflagged" under U.S. registry to provide a basis for armed U.S. protection. American ships and personnel were involved in several skirmishes. In one instance an Iraqi Exocet missile hit the frigate U.S.S. *Stark*, killing thirty-seven crew members, and injuring twenty-one. Although the attack was a mistake and Iraq immediately apologized, it underscored the vulnerability of American vessels to harm from missiles, mines, and small attack speedboats.

As with the situation in Lebanon, many in Congress and the country were concerned that the American purpose and mission were ill-defined. Despite the fact that the Persian Gulf was considered "the most dangerous body of water in the world for shipping," and that U.S. soldiers were given "imminent danger" pay, the Reagan administration argued that the War Powers Resolution did not apply.[37] In response, 112 members of Congress filed suit in federal court to force the president to comply.[38] In early 1988 the Reagan administration announced that it was cutting back on the American presence in the gulf.

Presidential War Making

Despite the attempt by Congress to reinsert itself in the war-making process, it is evident that presidents who wish to project U.S. military strength still have considerable ability to do so. Several reasons help explain this persisting trend.

First, even when taken at face value the War Powers Resolution contains a number of loopholes for presidents with predilections to military action. The resolution says, for example, that "Nothing in this joint resolution . . . is intended to alter the constitutional authority of the . . . president. . . ." Other loopholes and ambiguities, such as concern that the sixty- to ninety-day period provides the president with an open invitation to make war for that period, are highlighted by the cases summarized above. Presidents also have argued that parts of the act are simply impractical. In discussing the *Mayaguez* incident, President Ford noted later that many key legislators were out of town, making consultation difficult. He also observed that legislators have other concerns that minimize the attention they can give to a single problem; that the need to gain a congressional consensus may inhibit speed of action, and that information may leak from Congress.[39]

Second, the historical record indicates that presidents usually benefit politically when they engage in foreign military operations. Most foreign policy crises and operations, especially when brief, boost a president's popularity ratings.[40] More to the point, Congress is less likely to challenge the president if it perceives that the public supports the president's actions.

Third, an apparently successful military action invariably outweighs seemingly mundane constitutional and legal questions. The military necessity of both the *Mayaguez* and Grenada incidents was questioned, for example; yet such questions were far outshadowed by national feelings of euphoria. Moreover, although members of Congress recognized in the *Mayaguez* incident that President Ford had not followed the law, they muted their criticism because of the positive reaction to the president's actions.[41]

Fourth, Congress has by no means been unified in opposing presidential military initiatives. Many in Congress support presidential actions for ideological or partisan reasons, and many believe that the president indeed has the constitutional prerogative. Some would just as soon let the president take the lead, given the political risks of military adventures that fail. And once a military operation has begun, members of Congress invariably are reluctant to interfere in a way that might be interpreted later as having contributed to the defeat of, or harm to, U.S. soldiers. This was a key consideration in the reluctance of Congress to force Reagan's hand in Lebanon.

Admittedly, congressional attempts to limit unilateral presidential actions, or to involve members of Congress more meaningfully, have met with limited success. Still, the War Powers Resolution has served as a focal point for the debate on war making.

Treaty Making and Executive Agreements

Treaty making is treated succinctly in Article II, section 2, of the Constitution, which gives the president the power "to make Treaties, provided two-thirds of the Senators present concur. . . ." The House of Representatives clearly is excluded from the treaty process, yet it becomes involved when appropriations or enabling legislation is required.

Treaty-making power was discussed frequently at the Constitutional Convention. Initially, the Founders proposed that power over treaties remain solely in the hands of the legislature, as had been the case under the Articles of Confederation. But late in the convention the Founders yielded to the argument that the president should "make treaties." The exclusion of the House was defended by Alexander Hamilton and John Jay in *The Federalist Papers* when they argued that the Senate's smaller size and institutional continuity (attributable to senators' longer terms of office and staggered election cycle) would facilitate secrecy and dispatch in the treaty process.

The Founders envisioned that the president actually would consult with the Senate while treaty formulation was under way. But when President Washington attempted such a process with an Indian treaty in 1789, it proved entirely unsatisfactory and was abandoned. From that time to the present the Senate has played more of a "consent" role than an "advice" role.[42] In fact, the Senate (and Congress as a whole) has been more active in peace-related matters than war-related matters. According to one study an inverse relationship exists between the active involvement of Congress and the presence of military hostilities in a situation. Stated another way, the greater the specter of armed conflict, the less likely it is that Congress will play a key role.[43]

Although the Senate as an institution typically enters the treaty-making process when a treaty is presented to the Senate by the president, individual senators often have participated in negotiations with other countries. As early as 1814, for example, President Madison appointed two members of Congress to negotiate a peace treaty with Great Britain. More recently, in 1945, the United Nations Charter received key input from senators Arthur H. Vandenberg (R-Mich.) and Thomas T. Connally (D-Texas). And President Kennedy's negotiations with the Soviet Union over the nuclear test ban treaty of 1963 occurred with Senate members present. Many observers argue that the absence of senators during Wilson administration negotiations on the League of Nations agreement at the end of World War I contributed to the treaty's defeat by the Senate in 1919. After Woodrow Wilson's experience, senators were often appointed to important international conferences, especially by presidents Warren G. Harding, Herbert C. Hoover, Franklin Roosevelt, and Harry Truman.[44]

The relationship between the Senate and the president in the treaty process often is viewed as one of conflict, characterized by presidential defeat, especially in light of the two-thirds approval requirement. Examples that seem to support this proposition are the defeat of the League of Nations treaty by the Senate in 1919, the withdrawal of the SALT II Treaty by President Carter in 1980 in the face of vocal Senate opposition, and Carter's protracted battle to win ratification of the Panama Canal Treaty in 1978. Yet from 1789 to 1983 only sixteen treaties (about 1 percent) were voted down by the Senate. About 15 percent were accepted by the Senate after alteration. *(See Table 3.)*

The very nature of treaty making has provided the president with an immediate advantage in dealing with the Senate. Since the process of negotiating treaties falls clearly (although not necessarily exclusively) to the president, the White House staff is associated closely with the construction of the treaty document. (The president may invite members of Congress to participate or may permit key legislators to have a say in the selection of the negotiating team.) Thus, the administration is likely to have control over, if not a monopoly on, information about the content and political process leading up to finalization of an agreement. The proposed treaty is presented to the Senate as the president's document, carrying the weight and prestige of the chief executive. Since the president also is recognized as the nation's chief spokesperson, the political initiative rests with the president in a way that it does not with routine legislation, especially since Senate involvement in the negotiations process is likely to occur only at the invitation of the president.[45]

The treaty-making process actually incorporates three stages. First, the president's representatives, usually including the secretary of state, engage in negotiations with the governments of other nations, the end result of which is a treaty. As was the case with the Panama Canal Treaty, such negotiations often span decades and several administrations. Congress may offer advice and opinions about negotiations, but legally they carry no special weight. Second, the document is transmitted to the Senate, which has several options. It can approve the treaty, reject it, amend it (in which case it may have to go back to the foreign country for reapproval), or attach reservations and understandings designed to clarify treaty provisions and language. Third, at the conclusion of the Senate's deliberations the treaty must be "proclaimed," or accepted, by the president.[46] As this sequence reveals, the president retains the political initiative throughout, but Senate involvement at every stage is by no means precluded. At any stage other than ratification, however, such involvement must be at the president's request, however.

Although the treaty process favors the president's political predilections, the chief executive cannot take Senate support for granted. Presidents must lay careful political groundwork to improve the chances of ratification, even when substantial support for proposed treaties already exists.

Ending Treaties

The Constitution is silent on the question of treaty termination. Scholar Louis Fisher has noted that Article V of the Constitution vests federal statutes and treaties with the same status, yielding the conclusion that Congress possesses the power to end a treaty by the normal legislative process.[47] Other scholars have argued that, since the Senate must ratify treaties, it follows that Senate consent is neces-

Table 3 Treaties Killed by the Senate (as of June 1988)

Date of vote	Country	Vote Yea	Vote Nay	Subject
March 9, 1825	Colombia	0	40	Suppression of African slave trade
June 11, 1836	Switzerland	14	23	Personal and property rights
June 8, 1844	Texas	16	35	Annexation
June 15, 1844	German Zollverein	26	18	Reciprocity
May 31, 1860	Mexico	18	27	Transit and commercial rights
June 27, 1860	Spain	26	17	Cuban Claims Commission
April 13, 1869	Great Britain	1	54	Arbitration of claims
June 1, 1870	Hawaii	20	19	Reciprocity
June 30, 1870	Dominican Republic	28	28	Annexation
January 29, 1885	Nicaragua	32	23	Interoceanic canal
April 20, 1886	Mexico	32	26	Mining claims
August 21, 1888	Great Britain	27	30	Fishing rights
February 1, 1889	Great Britain	15	38	Extradition
May 5, 1897	Great Britain	43	26	Arbitration
March 19, 1920	Multilateral	49	35	Treaty of Versailles
January 18, 1927	Turkey	50	34	Commercial rights
March 14, 1934	Canada	46	42	St. Lawrence Seaway
January 29, 1935	Multilateral	52	36	World Court
May 26, 1960	Multilateral	49	30	Law of the Sea Convention
March 8, 1983	Multilateral	50	42	Montreal Aviation Protocol

Source: Congress A to Z (Washington, D.C.: Congressional Quarterly Inc., 1988), 501.

Note: Two-thirds majority vote is required for Senate consent to the ratification of treaties. In many cases treaties were blocked in committee or withdrawn before ever coming to a vote in the Senate.

sary to terminate a treaty. At the same time several presidents have claimed for themselves the power to end treaties. President Franklin D. Roosevelt, for example, ended a commerce and friendship treaty with Japan two years before the United States entered World War II.

More recently a political and legal challenge was raised against President Carter's termination of treaties with the Republic of China (Taiwan) as a prelude to full recognition of the People's Republic of China (mainland China). Contention centered around the Mutual Defense Treaty of 1954, which allowed either party to end the treaty on a year's notice. Carter announced the termination of the treaty in December 1978, while Congress was out of session. Senator Barry Goldwater (R-Ariz.) then filed suit in federal court to block Carter's action. And although a federal district court sided with Goldwater, the federal court of appeals ruled that the president possessed the power to terminate the treaty. In the case of *Goldwater v. Carter,* a divided Supreme Court upheld the lower court ruling.[48]

The ruling in the *Goldwater* case also clarified an important point about recognition of foreign governments. Termination of the treaty with Taiwan was a necessary step to the full recognition of the Beijing government, which was the goal of Carter's actions. (Supreme Court Justice William J. Brennan, Jr., noted in his opinion: "Our cases firmly establish that the Constitution commits to the President alone the power to recognize, and withdraw recognition from, foreign regimes."

Treaty-making Success: Panama Canal Treaties

Since the American-inspired Panamanian revolution in 1903, a ten-mile wide strip of land running through the middle of Panama has been controlled by the United States. This arrangement allowed the United States to construct the Panama Canal and maintain complete control over its operation. The terms of the agreement granting American control "in perpetuity" were so favorable to the United States that, despite treaty renegotiations in 1936 and 1955, Panamanians grew increasingly resentful of continued U.S. domination. In contrast, most U.S. leaders felt little need to alter significantly the terms of the relationship, as it had been very advantageous to this country.

In the early 1960s riots broke out in Panama and the U.S.-controlled Canal Zone. Although the immediate cause of the riots was whether the Panamanian flag would be flown along with the American flag in the zone, the riots were symptomatic of growing resentment in Panama over continued U.S. domination.

In the spring of 1964 treaty negotiations began again; they did not conclude until 1977. During the long negotiations, some in Congress—especially the House Merchant Marine and Fisheries Committee and its subcommittee on the Panama Canal—kept a watchful eye on their development. Both the full committee and its subcommittee were sources of opposition to changes that might arise from a new treaty, and in 1975 the House passed an amendment that barred any use of federal funds in relinquishing U.S. rights to the Canal Zone. This measure failed in the Senate, but it was reintroduced in the House in 1976 and 1977.

Treaty negotiations ended during the summer of 1977, and two treaties were transmitted to the Senate on September 16. The first, the Panama Canal Treaty, superseded the 1903 treaty and abolished the Canal Zone. The United States maintained the right to manage, maintain, and operate the canal through a new administrative apparatus (that would include Panamanians) until the end of 1999, when complete control of the canal would pass to Panama. At that time the United States would relinquish some of its control over administration of the canal and would increase payments to Panama for continued favored treatment of the United States. The other treaty, the Neutrality Treaty, asserted that the canal would operate under a permanent state of neutrality, and that Panama alone would operate the canal after 1999. As a special concession to the United States, U.S. warships were to be allowed expeditious transit through the canal.

From the beginning, treaty ratification was an open question. The polls showed a large number of undecided senators. Many citizens and government officials simply had assumed that the canal properly belonged to the United States. Indeed, public opinion surveys revealed majority opposition to treaty ratification, although those citizens better informed about the treaties were more likely to support them.[49] Part of the suspicion surrounding the treaties arose from concern that relinquishment of legal control would result in a compromise of U.S. security.[50]

Thus, when President Carter tackled the task of winning treaty ratification in the Senate, he faced several political obstacles. He began to lay the political groundwork in the spring of 1977 by apprising key members of the Senate of treaty developments and soliciting their views. In addition to rallying public opinion, Carter had to satisfy members of his own administration and a Congress that had maintained a long-term interest in the affairs of the Panama Canal. According to scholar William L. Furlong, "Few foreign policy issues in the history of the United States have involved the Congress more than negotiations and relations regarding the Panama Canal."[51] Although this involvement is not typical of congressional interest in foreign affairs, the Panama case reveals much about how the president and Congress interact during the formulation and ratification of treaties.

House ratification is not needed for treaties, but the House had made its political weight felt in previous attempts to influence funding affecting the canal. During the ratification process for the two canal treaties, the House served as an important forum for generating both support for and opposition to the treaties. In particular, three House committees held hearings on the canal and the treaties: Merchant Marine and Fisheries, International Relations, and Armed Services.

In the Senate, hearings were conducted by the Judiciary, Armed Services, and Foreign Relations committees. Those of the Foreign Relations Committee were the lengthiest and the most extensive. In addition, no fewer than forty-two of the Senate's one hundred members traveled to Panama, as did many members of the House. On the floor of the Senate the debate continued for thirty-eight days and was the second longest treaty debate in the Senate's history—only the Treaty of Versailles debate was longer. No fewer than eighty-eight changes were proposed and voted on. Of these, over twenty reservations, understandings, and conditions were added.

Most of the senators who visited Panama did so to gather information, but some actually negotiated directly with the Panamanian leadership. Such negotiations, after finalization of the terms of the treaty by the heads of government, were highly unusual and represented a degree of Senate involvement not seen since consideration of the Treaty of Versailles in 1919. President Carter responded to the specific concerns of undecided senators. In one key incident a first-term senator—Dennis W. DeConcini (D-Ariz.)—succeeded in attaching an amendment to the treaty (with Carter's consent) that allowed the United States to use military force to keep the canal open after the year 2000. The addition infuriated the Panamanians, and some last-minute bargaining was necessary to satisfy both the Senate, including DeConcini, and Panama. Carter's concession on the DeConcini amendment was obviously a move to win his support, yet it nearly collapsed the treaty process.

DeConcini's pivotal influence illustrates a larger point about ratification. Senators who remained undecided found themselves in the best political position to influence the terms of the treaty, and also to extract concessions (often unrelated to the treaty issue) from the president in exchange for their support. Indeed, some senators who initially had committed themselves to the treaty backed off in an attempt to gain some leverage with the White House.[52]

After months of intense investigation, bargaining, and debate, the Senate approved the Neutrality Treaty on March 16, 1978, and the Panama Canal Treaty the following April 18. Both passed by the same 68-32 margin—one vote more than the necessary two-thirds.

Treaty-making Failure: SALT II Treaty

Since 1968, the United States has engaged in systematic talks with the Soviet Union, designed to control aspects of the nuclear arms race. For the Nixon, Ford, and Carter administrations these talks were known by the acronym SALT (Strategic Arms Limitation Talks). The two most important treaties emerging from this process were SALT I, completed and ratified in 1972, and SALT II, completed in 1979 but withdrawn from the Senate shortly after completion because it was clear that it could not achieve the necessary two-thirds affirmative vote.[53]

SALT II negotiations had begun in November 1972 and had stretched on for seven years, spanning three presidential administrations. The treaty dealt with a variety of complex issues, but in general it set limits on how many of the vehicles (including missiles and bombers) used to deliver nuclear warheads each side could have. It also included a three-year "protocol" that addressed the controversial issues dividing the two nations and a statement that addressed President Carter's "deep cuts" proposal, which called for significant reductions in weapons numbers set out in prior agreements. The negotiations process stretched on during Carter's first two years in office because of disagreements about how to deal with particular weapons systems, such as the cruise missile and the Soviet Backfire bomber.

As with the Panama Canal treaties the president had to deal domestically not only with the Senate, but also with the House, his own administration, and public opinion. In Congress, key members had been vocal about the negotiations process since the early 1970s. Certain House members had been influential in shaping the SALT debate nationally, and various attempts had been made to influence the nature and direction of the treaty through control of funding. (Members of Congress were excluded from actual negotiations.)

In fact, Carter made good on his campaign promise to involve key legislators by appointing a group of thirty senators and fourteen House members as advisers to, and participants in, the SALT negotiations. The views of some Senate hardliners were sought as well by the Carter administration as a means of ultimately winning their support. These efforts prompted Senate Minority Leader Howard H. Baker, Jr., (R-Tenn.) to praise Carter for his bipartisan approach. In addition, prevailing congressional sentiment often was used as a bargaining chip with the Soviets, as the U.S. negotiators would sometimes argue for or against a certain proposed provision based on predictions about what the Senate would or would not accept.

Despite all these careful steps, SALT II encountered a series of roadblocks. Many in Congress, for example, sought to link the SALT agreement to other issues not related to the nuclear balance in an attempt to alter Soviet policy in these areas. Others were concerned that some of Carter's negotiators, such as Arms Control and Disarmament Agency head Paul Warnke, would not be sufficiently tough. And still others believed that the treaty gave away too much, or that some provisions would be difficult to verify. These and related criticisms were presented forcefully at a time when Congress was moving to assert itself generally in policy making, and the presidency was still suffering from the aftermath of Vietnam and Watergate.

The final provisions of the treaty were worked out in May 1979, and the agreement was signed on June 14. By the time the treaty was sent to the Senate the public SALT debate had been going on for several years. Thus, the major issues were well known to the principals. The Senate Foreign Relations Committee held four months of both open and closed hearings on the treaty. Consideration of the military consequences of the treaty was undertaken by the Armed Services Committee.

After narrowly averting several attempts to kill the treaty, the Senate Foreign Relations Committee agreed to send the treaty to the full Senate by a lukewarm vote of 9-6. In addition, it attached twenty-three conditions to the ratification resolution. It thus became clear that the treaty would not be approved without changes, and yet Carter was unwilling to renegotiate the treaty. Also in 1979 congressional critics were noting with alarm the presence of Cuban troops in Africa and the taking of American hostages in Iran in November. Shortly thereafter, a group of nineteen senators urged Carter to put off a vote on the treaty. Finally, Carter asked the Senate to postpone consideration of the treaty in the aftermath of the Soviet invasion of Afghanistan in December. The treaty was never brought back to the Senate, although its terms were followed generally by both sides throughout the 1980s.

The withdrawal of SALT II was facilitated by external events, but also by persistent divisions within the government over the goals and purposes of the SALT process. Some observers have suggested that the substantial involvement of Congress was instrumental to SALT's demise. Yet it was the exclusion of key legislators from the negotiations for SALT I that did much to energize congressional opposition to the SALT process that followed.

Treaties, the President, and Congress

The Panama Canal treaties and the SALT II Treaty were both high-visibility treaty efforts involving a single presidency—that of Jimmy Carter. They nevertheless reveal much about the politics of treaty making. First, the rise of congressional assertiveness in the 1970s reinvigorated the role of Congress. Thus, the president now must take greater care when laying the political groundwork for approval of major or controversial treaties.

Second, the president cannot ignore the House. Through the appropriations process, committee investigations, and the ability to gain public attention, the House (especially through key committees) can have a profound impact on the treaty process.

Third, the door is clearly open for greater direct involvement by members of Congress in the actual process of formulating treaties, despite the possible pitfall of involving too many hands in the negotiations process. In many respects this is consistent with the intent of the Framers of the Constitution. Moreover, political circumstances make such involvement desirable.

Fourth, political bargaining occurs over treaty support just as it does over more mundane domestic political issues. The two-thirds requirement means that thirty-four senators can veto a treaty. This extraordinary majority requirement therefore gives a relatively small number of legislators a disproportionately great influence. Most treaties are relatively noncontroversial and deal with minor matters, but those treaties that are likely to raise questions invite senators to use the two-thirds threshold as a lever to extract concessions (whether related or unrelated to the treaty issue at hand) from the president. While one might question the trading of a vote for an important treaty in exchange for funding an unrelated pet project in a senator's home state, such processes are part of the currency of presidential-congressional relations.

Fifth, organizationally the modern Congress is more decentralized than it used to be. Party and chamber leaders possess less control over the behavior of members, and committees and committee chairs are extremely influential. Thus, a president needing to win two-thirds support in the Senate must be sensitive to the concerns of a variety of influential senators, including party leaders, committee leaders, ideological leaders, and regional leaders.

Finally, treaties belong, in a political sense, primarily to the president. It is the job of the chief executive to build coalition support by any available means. Given the historical record it is clear that presidents have carried this burden with considerable success. Yet in recent years presidents increasingly have avoided the treaty route altogether in favor of a means of reaching international agreements without involving Senate ratification.

Executive Agreements

Agreements with other countries are achieved not only by treaties, but also by executive agreements. An executive agreement is an understanding reached between heads of state or their designees. It can be oral or written and may require either prior congressional authorization or later congressional approval. An executive agreement, however, does not go to the Senate for ratification. It has nevertheless the force of law and, compared with a treaty, possesses "a similar dignity." [54]

Many executive agreements involve routine matters, from fishing rights to postal agreements. Yet some important international agreements have been concluded through the executive agreement route, including the 1940 exchange of fifty American destroyers for some British military bases undertaken by President Franklin Roosevelt and British prime minister Winston Churchill, and a series of agreements in the 1950s and 1960s between the White House and South Vietnamese leaders promising military and other assistance.

Executive agreements date back to the founding of the country. In 1792, for example, the postmaster general initiated an agreement on international postal arrangements. Executive agreements have been used frequently since then, but since World War II the number of executive agreements has skyrocketed. In fact, about 95 percent of all international understandings since the war have taken the form of executive agreements. *(See Table 4.)*

This rise in executive agreements is attributable partly to the greater role of the United States in international military, political, and economic affairs since World War II. But it also represents presidential efforts to make foreign policy commitments without having to go through the laborious treaty process. This trend is based in part on the president's increased political influence, congressional willingness to allow the president wide latitude in this area, and the fundamental legal ambiguity in deciding when an understanding should be treated as a treaty and when it can be handled as an executive agreement.

As a result, an international understanding is likely to be handled as an executive agreement, unless it deals with a politically important subject and Congress expresses sufficient objections to avoidance of the treaty route. Presidents often test the political waters by suggesting that an understanding might be treated as an executive agreement. President Carter did exactly this with both the Panama Canal treaties and the SALT II agreement. In both cases, however, congressional objections were sufficiently strenuous that he decided to deal with them as treaties.

Congressional dissatisfaction with the president's more frequent use of executive agreements—including some agreements arrived at secretly without the knowledge of Congress—culminated in the passage of the Case Act of 1972. Congress was not informed, for example, of important executive agreements reached between the president and Ethiopia in 1960, Laos in 1963, Thailand in 1964 and 1967, and Korea in 1966.[55] The Case Act directs the president to transmit all executive agreements to Congress within sixty days of their completion, including secret agreements (although access to information about secret agreements is restricted).

Some critics have found the Case Act too weak. Because the act does not define executive agreements, presidents have applied their own definitions, which have excluded understandings that many in Congress believed were agreements. President Nixon, for example, promised South Vietnamese president Nguyen Van Thieu that the United States would "respond with full force" if North Vietnam violated the Paris Peace Agreement, but he did not inform Congress of this promise. The pledge proved to be an embarrassment in 1975 when South Vietnam was overrun, and Congress declined to provide assistance. One member of Congress estimated in 1975 that from 1972 (when the Case Act was enacted) until then, presidents had entered into from four hundred to six hundred understandings with other governments that had not been reported to Congress.[56]

Table 4 Treaties and Executive Agreements, 1789-1988

Years	Treaties	Executive agreements
1789-1839	60	27
1839-1889	215	238
1889-1929	382	763
1930-1939	142	144
1940-1949	116	919
1950-1959	138	2,229
1960-1969	114	2,324
1970-1979	173	3,040
1980-1988	136	3,094
Total	1,476	12,778

Source: Guide to Congress, 3d ed. (Washington, D.C.: Congressional Quarterly Inc., 1982), 291; Department of State, Treaty Affairs Staff, Office of the Legal Adviser.

Other Aspects of Foreign Affairs

For about the first twenty years after World War II, U.S. foreign policy was characterized by relatively strong bipartisanship. Republicans and Democrats alike in the Congress and the White House shared a deep antipathy toward communism and the Soviet Union. During this Cold War era, arms sales, foreign aid programs, and direct military efforts usually focused on some aspect of anticommunism. The president provided the principal leadership, and Congress generally followed step.

During the mid-1960s, however, dissent began to rise in Congress and throughout the country over conduct of the Vietnam War. Although conduct of the war was in many respects consistent with past policies, many onlookers began to question the monolithic view of communism that had been the basis of U.S. policy up to that time. This questioning then manifested itself in the growing division between the executive and legislative branches of government. American involvement in the Vietnam War began with the approval and support of Congress, but it soon became identified with the two presidents most heavily committed to waging the war—Johnson and Nixon. As the institutional rift between the branches widened, so too did presidential-congressional differences over other aspects of foreign policy.

The immediate evidence of this rift was repeated congressional efforts to end or otherwise limit American involvement in Vietnam. But evidence surfaced in other areas as well, such as the handling of arms sales.

In 1974, for example, an amendment passed by Congress required the president to report arms sales of over $5,000 to Congress (although multiple sales under that amount did not have to be reported), and it provided a mechanism whereby Congress could move to block some arms sales. This act helped prod Congress to challenge proposed presidential arms sales. In 1978 members of Congress fought unsuccessfully to block the sale of fighter jets to Egypt and Saudi Arabia. Congress succeeded, however, in stalling or forcing the withdrawal of proposed arms sales to Turkey, Chile, Argentina, Libya, Iraq, and other nations.[57]

Saudi Arms Deal

The Reagan administration tried to exert greater presidential prerogative, but Reagan too encountered opposition to proposed major arms sales. In 1985, for example, Reagan had planned to propose the sale of a billion dollar arms package to Saudi Arabia, including F-15 Jet fighters, M-1 tanks, helicopter gunships, and other equipment. This plan was scratched before it was formally proposed, however, because of informal but overwhelming Senate opposition that would have ensured defeat of the package. This sentiment stemmed partly from an experience with Iran in 1979, when billions of dollars in recent-vintage American military and other hardware sold to the Shah of Iran fell into the hands of the unfriendly Khomeini regime during that country's revolution.[58]

In the spring of 1986 the Reagan administration proposed a scaled down $354 million missile package for Saudi Arabia that included air-to-sea Harpoon missiles, air-to-air Sidewinder missiles, and ground-to-air, shoulder-held Stinger missiles. Congressional resistance to even this modified package was stiff because of Saudi support for Syria and the Palestine Liberation Organization (PLO), Saudi refusal to support Egypt and Jordan in the peace process, and the continued belligerence of Saudi Arabia toward Israel.

Congress had fifty days in which to block the sale, and both the Republican-controlled Senate and the Democratic-controlled House did so. President Reagan then vetoed the disapproval on May 21. The relatively rapid and lopsided vote against the arms sale was partly a function of the administration's decision to prevent the negative vote by presidential veto, rather than by efforts at the outset to block the initial vote.

Congressional critics decried the use of arms sales as a primary means of diplomacy and lamented in particular the inclusion of Stinger missiles in the package. One persistent concern was that given the volatility of the Middle East, such weapons might find their way into the hands of terrorists (the Stinger was referred to as a "terrorist's delight").

The White House argued that Saudi Arabia had remained a friend of the United States, was a key source of oil, and was a moderate voice in the Arab world. It also argued that the package was needed to counter Soviet and Iranian influence in the region. Then in a significant concession the president eliminated the Stingers from the package. White House pressure to uphold the Reagan veto was facilitated by a recurring argument—namely, the president's ability to conduct foreign policy could be impaired if his wishes were denied by Congress. At least one senator changed his vote in favor of the president in response to this argument. Then after last-minute pressure from the White House, the veto was upheld in the Senate by the exact margin required.

Foreign Aid

Presidential-congressional relations with respect to foreign aid have followed a similar path in recent years. In the 1970s Congress began to press the president to tie foreign assistance to progress on human rights. And in 1973 Congress enacted the Foreign Assistance Act, in which it inserted two provisions expressing the opinion or "sense" of Congress that the president should deny foreign aid to any country that practiced incarceration of its citizens for political purposes. One provision stated this as a general principle; the other provision specifically addressed the government of Chile, which recently had undergone a coup (with the covert assistance of the U.S. Central Intelligence Agency) that deposed its elected president, Salvador Allende, and replaced him with a harsh military regime. The human rights abuses of Chile's new Pinochet regime provoked Congress into tying U.S. aid to human rights practices. Similar human rights-related restrictions were tied to aid packages for Argentina, Cambodia, El Salvador, Guatemala, Haiti, Mexico, Nicaragua, South Africa, South Korea, and Uganda.

Two members of Congress, Rep. Charles A. Vanik (D-Ohio) and Sen. Henry M. Jackson (D-Wash.), spearheaded an effort to link U.S. trade relations with the Soviet Union to Soviet human rights practices. They were especially eager to encourage more liberal emigration policies for Soviet dissidents, Jews, and others. Despite resistance by the White House, which felt that quiet diplomacy could accomplish more, the policy was enacted. Some critics of this policy have argued that it actually resulted in a constriction of emigration from the Soviet Union.[59]

From 1976 to 1980, Congress strengthened the legal language tying foreign aid to human rights practices. This effort was facilitated by the Carter administration, which elevated concern for human rights to a policy goal, applying not just to foreign aid but also to the overall conduct of foreign policy (including policy toward the Soviet Union). Congress worked progressively to apply rigorous standards for human rights in security assistance and multilateral aid programs, but it was less rigorous in programs aimed at development assistance and food aid, since the latter programs were targeted at more fundamental human needs.

Struggle between Congress and the White House intensified during the Reagan administration, which sought a more conciliatory policy toward nations with records of human rights abuses such as South Africa, El Salvador, Chile, and the Philippines under President Ferdinand Marcos. The thinking of the Reagan administration, as articulated, for example, by United Nations Representative Jeane Kirkpatrick was that the United States should continue to aid its allies even if human rights problems exist, because such nations support the United States, do not violate human rights to the same degree as other nations, and will likely improve their human rights practices.[60] Others in Congress and elsewhere argued that the United States was in the best position to influence the human rights practices of these nations.[61]

In general, for foreign aid the political pattern of presidential-congressional relations follows closely that noted for war making and other foreign policy areas. The president continues to be the dominant actor, even when Congress attempts to reassert its role in various foreign policy areas. Political initiative typically belongs to the president, but Congress can meaningfully affect the course of policy when it wishes.

"Intermestic" Issues

Cheap and plentiful gas and oil supplies were taken for granted in the United States until 1973, when the Arab nations imposed an oil embargo on the nations that supported Israel during the Arab-Israeli War of that year. For the first time Americans recognized their interdependence and the relationship between gasoline prices in the United States and events across the globe. This is an example of an "intermestic" issue (one with both international and domestic effects), and it is an area in which the political pattern of presidential-congressional relations resembles that of conventional domestic politics.

One longstanding intermestic policy has been the use

of food. Since 1954 the Food for Peace program (also known as PL 480) has provided food for humanitarian, diplomatic, and political purposes abroad and a means of disposing of domestic agricultural surpluses. The program has expanded in high-surplus years and contracted when surpluses were small. In high-surplus years the program has provided American farmers with a major subsidy.

The Food for Peace program has grown steadily over the years, largely because of domestic political pressure and support from the Foreign Agricultural Service of the U.S. Department of Agriculture, the relevant agriculture commodity subcommittees, farmers' groups, and shipping interests. Although the program has served an important foreign policy objective, its political impetus lies in conventional interest group politics.

In the 1970s an executive-legislative dispute arose over administrations' increasing tendency to use the Food for Peace program abroad to reward political allies and coax other nations into greater cooperation with the United States. Many members of Congress opposed this use of the program, arguing that its purpose should be fundamentally humanitarian. Even though this debate persists—strategic considerations continue to influence the distribution of food abroad—the program continued to thrive throughout the 1980s (despite budget cutbacks in other foreign aid programs) largely because of its solid domestic support.[62]

Domestic political forces also play an important role in trade and tariff policies. American steel and auto manufacturers, and the unions representing workers in these areas, take a keen interest in policies that affect the import of foreign-made steel and cars. With American jobs apparently at stake, these groups lobby Congress and the president to see that they are not driven out of business by foreign competition. In this way vital domestic concerns expressed through conventional domestic political means may shape foreign policy.

Not all intermestic issues involve jobs and the economy. Jewish organizations take a strong interest in U.S. policy toward Israel. Greek-Americans and Turkish-Americans are represented by groups who work to influence U.S. policy toward those traditionally antagonistic nations. Opponents of abortion have pressed Congress and the president to cut family planning aid to Third World nations that include abortion as a means of limiting population. In all of these intermestic issues domestic political forces substantially affect political foreign policy as it is shaped by the president and Congress.

Control over Intelligence Agencies

Control over sensitive information pertaining to national security and intelligence matters is a key source of presidential ascendancy. Virtually all of the intelligence gathering is conducted through executive agencies. In 1981, Executive Order 12333 (issued by President Reagan) listed thirteen agencies as composing the intelligence community. Six of these were affiliated with the Department of Defense and the rest with the Executive Office of the President or a cabinet agency. In theory Congress plays the same role in relation to intelligence agencies that it plays with other government agencies: It provides the legal basis for such agencies and oversees agency actions. In reality, however, Congress had little impact on government intelligence efforts until the 1970s. *(See box, Intelligence Community, p. 1107.)*

The need for intelligence has always existed, but the executive appetite for information accelerated with America's expanded role in international affairs after World War II. In 1947 Congress passed the National Security Act, which created the Central Intelligence Agency (CIA); its forerunner was the Office of Strategic Services, formed to gather intelligence during the war. Yet Congress paid little attention to the agency or its activities. Other intelligence agencies such as the Defense Intelligence Agency and the National Security Agency were created by executive order. Because funds for these agencies were included in lump sum appropriations, members of Congress were unaware of the purposes of the funds and the actual amounts budgeted. Congressional interest in intelligence was aroused only when embarrassing problems arose, such as when an American U-2 spy plane was caught flying over the Soviet Union in 1960, and when the Bay of Pigs invasion (a CIA-sponsored invasion of Cuba by anti-Castro Cuban exiles) failed. The few members of Congress informed of intelligence activities rarely questioned executive priorities. As the chair of one "watchdog" committee, Sen. John C. Stennis (D-Miss.), said, "You have to make up your mind that you are going to have an intelligence agency and protect it as such and shut your eyes and take what is coming."

Congress was finally emboldened to involve itself more actively in intelligence-related matters when it was revealed that both the CIA and the Federal Bureau of Investigation had been involved in illegal surveillance and investigation of Americans (mostly anti-Vietnam War protesters) in the late 1960s and early 1970s at the behest of the Nixon administration, and that the CIA had played an active role in the violent overthrow of the popularly elected Allende regime in Chile. Several important congressional investigations helped bring these activities to light, especially the investigation headed by Sen. Frank F. Church (D-Idaho) in 1975 and 1976. Executive branch authorization of such activities at home and abroad raised fundamental questions about control over and misuse of the American intelligence establishment.

In 1974 Congress passed the Hughes-Ryan Amendment, which required that covert actions of the CIA (that is, operations designed to do more than gather information) be reported to the appropriate congressional committees. The act did not have dramatic consequences, as the executive was to report "in a timely fashion," and the CIA and the president interpreted this to mean after the conclusion of an operation.

In 1975 President Ford created a special commission to examine CIA activities. Based on the commission's findings, Ford directed the CIA to refrain from engaging in further assassination plots. This action followed revelations that the CIA had plotted to assassinate Fidel Castro and other heads of government deemed unfriendly.

As a result of these revelations each house of Congress created a permanent Select Committee on Intelligence. Although the jurisdiction of each committee is slightly different, both are designed to provide some meaningful oversight. Each committee has a substantial staff and the power to compel testimony, demand information, and review reports. In addition, these committees control budgetary authorizations (that is, grant legal permission to spend appropriated money) for intelligence agencies. For the sake of secrecy neither committee operates with the openness characteristic of other congressional committees. And despite fears that Congress cannot keep secrets, both committees have favorable records of not disclosing national security information.

To help ensure that the committees would engage in meaningful oversight and would not be coopted by the intelligence agencies, as had happened in the past, a limit was put on the number of terms a member could serve on the committees, and their leadership is rotated. In 1980 Congress passed the Accountability for Intelligence Activities Act.

This act stipulated that the two intelligence committees would be the sole funnels for information about covert activities, and it required the committees to be fully informed of all intelligence activities. It also terminated the Hughes-Ryan Amendment. Finally, despite wording designed to strengthen and clarify the role of Congress, the act granted the president wide discretion and freedom of action in covert operations.

Although Congress assumed a more active role in intelligence activities, controversial covert operations continued. Beginning in 1981, for example, the Reagan administration engaged in a large-scale covert program to aid rebels (called contras) fighting against the Sandinista regime in Nicaragua. In December the administration informed the intelligence committees of its support for the contras.

In 1982 Congress enacted for the first time an amendment aimed at curtailing Reagan's support for the contras. Successively stronger amendments were enacted in 1983, 1984, and 1985, and were attached to authorization and appropriation bills. These amendments were known collectively as the Boland Amendment, named after Rep. Edward P. Boland (D-Mass.), their prime sponsor. *(See box, Attempts by Congress to Restrict Aid to the Nicaraguan Contras, pp. 1110-1111.)* The strongest measure, enacted in 1984, barred all military and covert-related assistance to the contras during fiscal year 1985.

In 1985 and 1986 the administration succeeded in gaining congressional permission to expand support for the contras. Yet in 1986, Reagan's national security advisers and other members of the administration were implicated in an "off the books" operation to fund the contras covertly by selling arms to Iran and using the profits to purchase weapons for the contras. This operation was designed to maintain funding for the contras despite the congressional ban. Throughout the summer of 1987 a joint Senate-House committee chaired by Sen. Daniel P. Inouye (D-Hawaii), a former Senate Intelligence Committee chair, conducted hearings to investigate the Iran-contra affair.

The committee's majority report concluded that members of the National Security Council (NSC) and others (including private business people) had consciously attempted to circumvent the law through private means. The political sting accompanying these revelations was heightened by the scheme to sell arms to Iran, an avowed enemy of the United States. Iran was in the market for weapons to help in its protracted war with Iraq.

The Iran-contra affair dramatized how difficult Congress found it to influence the conduct of covert operations and an intelligence process that is structured to serve the president. Despite renewed congressional efforts in the 1970s and 1980s, Congress continues to be handicapped because of its lack of involvement with, and influence over, the National Security Council, which has acquired principal control over the formulation and coordination of national security matters. Some analysts have suggested that nominees for the national security adviser position be subject to congressional ratification. *(See White House Office chapter in Part V.)*

Intelligence Community

The agencies and bureaus that collect and analyze information on foreign affairs for the executive branch are collectively known as the *intelligence community.* As specified in Executive Order 12333, issued by President Ronald Reagan on December 4, 1981, the intelligence community consists of the Central Intelligence Agency; the National Security Agency; the Bureau of Intelligence and Research in the Department of State; the Defense Intelligence Agency and the intelligence offices of the army, navy, air force, and marine corps in the Department of Defense; the Federal Bureau of Investigation; intelligence offices in the Department of Energy and the Department of the Treasury; and staff elements of the director of central intelligence.

Intelligence is only a minor part of the overall activities of some of these agencies. Nevertheless, the intelligence collected is important in terms of national security and the total flow of information to the U.S. government.

Source: Cecil V. Crabb, Jr., and Pat M. Holt, *Invitation to Struggle: Congress, the President and Foreign Policy*, 3d ed. (Washington, D.C.: CQ Press, 1989), 25.

Veto Power

The presidential veto is one of the cornerstone powers in the Constitution, tying the president to the legislative process. Veto power was included as a presidential power from the beginning of the Constitutional Convention—it was included in the Virginia Plan—even though use of the veto by British monarchs and colonial governors had been a key source of irritation for the colonists. Despite the opinions of Alexander Hamilton and James Wilson at the convention that the president's veto should be absolute (that is, no provision for an override vote by both houses of Congress), as was that of the British monarchs, the veto remained qualified. Initially, the Founders agreed to a three-fourths override vote for vetoes, but they eventually settled on a two-thirds override.

The first six presidents used the veto sparingly—only ten times. George Washington was the first president to exercise the power when he vetoed a congressional reapportionment bill on April 5, 1792. President Andrew Jackson drew heavy political fire for using the veto twelve times in eight years for plainly political reasons. President John Tyler used the veto ten times in his single term of office, and he was even subject to a vote of impeachment in the House for one of his vetoes. The loud congressional outcry that followed these early vetoes—especially those of Jackson and Tyler—was founded partly in political opposition, but also in the belief that the veto should only be used against bills of questionable constitutionality. (Although the Constitution places no restrictions on veto use, this was the principal charge used against Tyler.) Also, many felt

An Iran-Contra Guide: . . .

1981. President Reagan signs a "finding" authorizing a covert Central Intelligence Agency (CIA) operation to support the contras.

December 21, 1982. The first Boland Amendment, barring use of federal money to overthrow the government of Nicaragua, becomes law.

December 12, 1983. Truck bombs explode at American and French embassies in Kuwait. Relatives of seventeen convicted in the attack decide the best way to free the prisoners is to seize American hostages.

February 21, 1984. Robert C. McFarlane, the national security adviser, warns President Reagan that the CIA operation will have to be curtailed unless new money is found.

March 16. William Buckley, CIA station chief in Beirut, is kidnapped by pro-Iranian extremists in Lebanon.

May. McFarlane meets with Saudi Arabia's ambassador to Washington, Prince Bandar, who agrees to keep the contras alive with a contribution of $1 million a month.

May 8. The Rev. Benjamin Weir is kidnapped.

October 12. President Reagan signs measure containing new Boland Amendment banning military aid to the contras.

December 3. Another American, Peter Kilburn, is kidnapped in Beirut.

January 8, 1985. The Rev. Lawrence M. Jenco is kidnapped in Beirut.

March 16. Terry A. Anderson of the Associated Press is kidnapped, in Beirut.

May 28. David P. Jacobsen of the American University Hospital in Beirut is kidnapped.

June 3. Buckley reportedly dies.

June 9. Thomas M. Sutherland is kidnapped.

Early July. David Kimche, director general of the Israeli foreign ministry, tells McFarlane that Iran wants to open a "political discourse" with the United States.

Mid-July. President Reagan approves "in principle" sale of TOW anti-tank missiles to Iran, subject to review.

August 20. Israel sends ninety-six TOW missiles to Iran. On September 14 Israel sends 408 more TOWs to Iran. Weir is released that day.

December 5. President Reagan signs a "finding" retroactively authorizing the Iran operation. Later, Vice Admiral John M. Poindexter testifies that he tore up this document a year later because he feared it would embarrass Reagan. At about the same time, McFarlane resigns as national security adviser and his deputy, Admiral Poindexter, is appointed his successor.

January 17, 1986. President Reagan signs an order authorizing arms shipments to Iran. On February 17 the United States sends five hundred TOW missiles to Israel for shipment to Iran. No hostages are freed.

February 27. Another five hundred TOW missiles are sent to Israel, once again for Iran. Again no hostages are freed.

April 4. In a memorandum, Lieutenant Colonel Oliver L. North of the National Security Council (NSC) staff outlines a plan to have $12 million in profits from the Iran sales diverted to the contras.

April 17. Kilburn's body is found.

that frequent use of the veto was simply inappropriate and reminiscent of the abuses of British monarchs. By the mid-nineteenth century, however, these objections had subsided. *(See Table 5.)*

After the Civil War the veto was used more frequently, with the significant increase attributable to greater presidential involvement in legislative affairs and to a flood of private pension bills (many of them of questionable justification) stemming from war-related claims. The veto allowed presidents to exert greater influence over the legislative process in the nineteenth century, first through the veto itself, then through the presidential threat to use the veto, and finally through anticipation of the president's legislative preferences as a means of avoiding the veto.

The veto continues to be an important weapon in the president's dealings with Congress; about 93 percent of all vetoes subject to override have been sustained. When broken down by public and private bills, presidential vetoes of public bills have been upheld about 81 percent of the time; vetoes of private bills have been upheld over 99 percent of the time. A public bill affects the people as a whole and relates to individuals only by classification or category. In contrast, a private bill names the individual or entity who will receive some form of relief—such as payment of a claim or pension—from the federal government.

Several factors help to explain why presidents veto, or are more likely to veto, legislation. When the presidency and Congress are controlled by different political parties, presidential vetoes occur more often. Presidents also are more likely to veto when they have little or no prior service in Congress (stemming from a presumed lack of sensitivity to congressional nuance), when they are in their second and fourth years of their term (resulting from greater congressional independence in an election year), when the role of government expands, and when public support for the president sags. Congress is more likely to override a veto

... What Happened and When

May 23-24. 508 TOW missiles and 240 spare parts for Hawk missiles are shipped to Israel.

May 25. McFarlane, Colonel North, and other Americans fly to Iran, trying in vain to win American hostages' release.

June 26. Congress approves $100 million in aid for the contras beginning October 1.

July 26. Jenco is freed.

August 4. The United States sends Iran spare parts for Hawk missiles.

August 6. Colonel North meets with members of Congress and denies raising money for the contras or offering them military advice. Later, he testifies that he lied.

September 9. Frank Herbert Reed is kidnapped. New Iranian intermediaries are flown to Washington for meetings with Colonel North.

September 12. Another American, Joseph James Cicippio, is seized. Then, on October 21, Edward Austin Tracy is kidnapped.

October 28. Another five hundred TOW missiles are sent from Israel to Iran.

November 2. Jacobsen is released.

November 3. A Lebanese magazine, *Al Shiraa,* discloses that the United States sent arms to Iran and that McFarlane visited Tehran.

November 12-19. Colonel North and White House officials prepare inaccurate chronologies of events.

November 19. President Reagan, in a news conference, makes errors in numbers of weapons sent and countries involved.

November 21. William P. Casey, the director of central intelligence, appears before the House and Senate intelligence committees after a major battle inside the administration over what he will say about the CIA's role in the November 1985 arms shipment. Attorney General Edwin Meese III suggests that the president have him conduct an inquiry. Colonel North begins shredding documents.

November 23. Colonel North tells Meese that money was diverted to the contras but misstates other aspects of deal.

November 24. Meese tells the president of the diversion.

November 25. Meese publicly announces diversion. President announces Admiral Poindexter's resignation and Colonel North's dismissal.

January 6-7, 1987. Senate and House committees are set up to investigate the affair.

February 26. A commission set up to study NSC operations issues its report.

May 5. Public testimony begins before the Senate and House committees. On August 3 the hearings end.

November 18. The congressional committees issue report.

Source: New York Times, March 17, 1988, D26. Copyright © 1988 by the New York Times Company. Reprinted by permission.

when party control is split between the branches, when the president's political standing is low, and in times of economic crisis.[66]

The veto poses a paradox for presidents who contemplate its use. With the exception of private bill vetoes in the twentieth century, frequent use of the veto by presidents invariably tends to erode their reservoir of political resources. This occurs because Congress becomes more resentful and confrontational when its measures are vetoed too frequently. Moreover, even though the Founders viewed the veto as a creative, positive tool (it was often called the "revisionary power") that could be used to mold better legislation in concert with Congress, today the veto is predominantly viewed as a negative power used by presidents to frustrate and block. A president who uses the veto in the latter fashion in the twentieth century faces a significant political obstacle in dealing with Congress.

Indeed, more frequent use of the veto usually means that presidents have not succeeded in establishing a pattern of positive leadership based on the president's legislative program. Presidents who establish such leadership usually are able to avoid numerous vetoes either by winning passage of their important programs or by obtaining a favorable compromise with congressional leaders. Thus, presidents who most need the veto are those who lack other sources of power to compensate, while presidents needing the veto least exert greater influence over Congress and have more sources of power, such as a high standing in the eyes of the public[67].

President Franklin Roosevelt was the most prolific veto user of all the presidents (although his per year veto average was second to that of President Grover Cleveland). Unlike most frequent veto users, however, Roosevelt faced a sympathetic Congress during his thirteen years in office. His frequent use of the veto indicated his willingness to use all of the tools at his disposal in dealing with Congress, as

Attempts by Congress to Restrict Aid . . .

In December 1981 Reagan administration officials told members of the House and Senate intelligence committees about the president's secret decision to channel funds and weapons to the contras through the Central Intelligence Agency (CIA). Some members expressed concern over this policy and attempted to restrict aid to the Nicaraguan contras by attaching limiting provisions to the following laws:

Intelligence Authorization Bill for FY 1983. (The exact wording of the bill was classified, known only to members of the congressional intelligence committees and members of the administration). This was the first legislative attempt by Congress to restrict the nature and quantity of aid to the contras, who were fighting to overthrow the Nicaraguan regime. In the early 1980s aid to the contras was still "covert," although Nicaragua and other nations already were aware of the support given by the CIA and the Department of Defense (DOD). (PL 97-269, signed Sept. 27, 1982)

Continuing Appropriations Bill for FY 1983. For the first time a law passed by Congress included a provision designed to curtail President Reagan's efforts to support the contras: "None of the funds provided in this Act may be used by the Central Intelligence Agency or the Department of Defense to furnish military equipment, military training or advice, or other support for military activities, to any group or individual, not part of a country's armed forces, for the purpose of overthrowing the Government of Nicaragua or provoking a military exchange between Nicaragua and Honduras." This wording was essentially the same that appeared in PL 97-269. At this point Congress was responding to Reagan's refusal to alter his contra policy. Congress was unaware of the financing being conducted out of the White House—the act refers only to the CIA and DOD.

This effort was spearheaded by Rep. Edward P. Boland (D-Mass.). Boland did not seek to renew this wording the following year because the Senate (then controlled by Republicans) would not accept it.

The provision quoted above imposed two restrictions: (1) military aid must be used solely to interdict arms shipments from Nicaragua to leftist rebels in El Salvador, and (2) aid must not be used to overthrow the existing Nicaraguan government or to provoke conflict between Nicaragua and Honduras. (PL 97-377, signed Dec. 21, 1982)

DOD Appropriations Bill for FY 1984. This provision placed a $24 million cap on U.S. aid for military/paramilitary operations in Nicaragua. House Intelligence Committee Chair Boland, who led the opposition to covert aid, attempted to eliminate all such aid. Reagan had hoped to obtain from $35 million to $50 million in aid, so the $24 million figure represented a compromise. (PL 98-212, signed Dec. 8, 1983)

Authorization for Intelligence Activities for FY 1984. Same as PL 98-212. During 1983 Reagan launched a major public campaign to buoy his efforts to aid the contras. By removing the cloak of secrecy, Reagan hoped to rally public support. It had the opposite effect, however. (PL 98-215, signed Dec. 9, 1983)

Continuing Appropriations Bill for FY 1985. In this provision Congress agreed to allow the president to spend $14 million on contra guerrilla military operations after February 28, 1985, provided that both houses of Congress agreed. For the first time in eight years Congress had called a halt to a "covert" CIA activity. The key section said: "During fiscal year 1985, no funds available to the Central Intelligence Agency, the Department of Defense, or any other agency or entity of the United

indicated by his well-known "send me a bill I can veto" attitude. More to the point, however, the vast majority of Roosevelt's vetoes were of private bills or other matters that garnered little attention and less interest. Although Roosevelt believed that the veto was a key presidential power, it received relatively little attention during a time when more attention was focused on the depression, the "New Deal," and World War II.

Roosevelt's successor also valued the veto as a presidential tool. Facing a more hostile Congress, Harry Truman and his vetoes attracted more attention. His most best-known veto was that of the Taft-Hartley Labor-Management Relations Act of 1947, which was enacted into law over his veto. Truman took pride in the claim that he gave his veto messages careful personal attention, and he used them to set forth administration policy. Of the veto, he said that it was "one of the most important instruments of his authority." [68]

Dwight Eisenhower faced a Congress controlled by the opposition party for six of his eight years in office, and thus the veto was an important tool. Eisenhower did not use the veto lightly, but he did rely on it more heavily later on in his term, especially as a device to "subdue" the overwhelmingly Democratic Congress of 1958-1959.

During the presidencies of Democrats John Kennedy and Lyndon Johnson, the Democratic party controlled the executive and legislative branches. Both presidents were relatively influential over congressional actions (Johnson more so), and neither needed to rely on the veto as a major weapon. Nevertheless, occasional vetos were viewed as useful, even therapeutic, for interbranch relations. As an aide to Johnson later noted, "It is inevitable that the President will use the veto at some point. It's the best method to show the Congress he means business." [69] When Kennedy and Johnson did use the veto, they were careful to avoid a successful override, and none of their vetoes were overridden.

Appreciating the negative consequences of frequent

. . . to the Nicaraguan Contras, 1982-1986

States involved in intelligence activities may be obligated or expended for the purpose or which would have the effect of supporting, directly or indirectly, military or paramilitary operations in Nicaragua by any nation, group, organization, movement, or individual." During 1984 Reagan continued to try to rally public support. (PL 98-473, signed Oct. 11, 1984)

Authorization Bill for Intelligence-related Activities for FY 1985. The wording of this bill was essentially the same as that of PL 98-473. It also applied to any unexpended funds allocated in PL 98-215. (PL 98-618, signed Nov. 8, 1984)

International Security and Development Co-operation Act of 1985. The relevant provision barred the expenditure of any money for military support of the contras, but it did provide a mechanism whereby the president could request such money from Congress at a later date. The provision provided $27 million in "humanitarian assistance" (through March 31, 1986), but neither the CIA nor DOD could be involved in administering the assistance. (PL 99-83, signed Aug. 8, 1985)

Supplemental Appropriations for FY 1985. Replicated the provisions of PL 99-83. Questions concerning the disposition and use of this humanitarian aid were raised. Questions also were raised, starting in 1985, about the possible unlawful diversion of U.S. oreign aid designated for other countries. For example, in fiscal years 1984 and 1985, U.S. arms aid to Honduras was $77 million and $61 million respectively. Yet the Honduras total military budget for each year was only about $50 million. (PL 99-88, signed Aug. 15, 1985)

Intelligence Authorization Act for FY 1986. The relevant provision barred the CIA from using its contingency funds to resume covert military aid to the contras. It also broadened the definition of "humanitarian" to include such items as radios and trucks. (PL 99-169, signed Dec. 4, 1985)

Continuing Appropriation Resolution for FY 1986. Appropriations must conform to the stipulations laid out in PL 99-169. (PL 99-190, signed Dec. 19, 1985)

Intelligence Authorization Act for FY 1987. This provision approved Reagan's request for $100 million in aid to the contras, including $70 million for military aid and $30 million for nonmilitary assistance. The CIA and DOD could resume their involvement, but they and other government intelligence agencies were barred from using contingency funds to give the contras aid above the $100 million total. (PL 99-569, signed Oct. 27, 1986)

Appropriations Act for FY 1987. This provision followed the terms of PL 99-569. The passage of the $100 million aid package represented a significant political victory for Reagan and was the culmination of a protracted political struggle that lasted most of the summer. (PL 99-591, signed Oct. 30, 1986)

On August 14, 1987, news reports revealed that President Reagan planned to ask Congress for additional military aid for the contras should peace talks falter. The following day, however, spokespersons said that the request would be delayed. Revelations emanating from the Iran-contra investigations continued to hamper Reagan's drive to fund the contras.

Source: Compiled by the author.

veto use, Richard Nixon used the veto rarely in his first three years in office. This pattern changed, however, when he vetoed seventeen bills over a six-month period in 1972 after concluding that a broad attack on congressional spending was needed. Nixon's aides also recognized that minimal effort can be devoted to upholding a veto, since all that is needed is the support of one-third plus one of the membership of one house of Congress. It was understood, nevertheless, that the veto was a substitute for compromise with the legislature.

The veto power was a vital tool for the brief administration of Gerald Ford. Ford's political position was weak from the start by virtue of how he became president (appointed vice president by a president who himself later resigned). Moreover, he had little opportunity to formulate his own legislative program after becoming president. This left Republican Ford few options beyond reacting to the initiatives of the Democratic-controlled Congress. As the first post-Watergate president, he faced a strong anti-Republican, anti-"imperial presidency" backlash. Ford hoped to gain initiative by winning the 1976 election, but instead he was defeated by Jimmy Carter. During his two and one-half years in office, Ford vetoed sixty-six bills; of these, fifty-four were sustained. Insofar as the veto was a cornerstone of his legislative relations, his presidency was the only one in this century to adopt a true veto strategy. Ford's aides recognized the adverse effects of the numerous vetoes, but they believed that they had few other options.

Jimmy Carter's administration saw a return to sparing use of the veto on a par with that of the Kennedy and Johnson years. Despite Democrat Carter's reputed difficulties with the Democratic-controlled Congress, he found relatively little need to resort to the veto. Unlike Ford, Carter established a substantial legislative agenda from the start of his presidency, which impelled Congress to react to him rather than the opposite. Most of Carter's thirty-one vetoes aroused little interest in Congress.

The presidential veto played an important role in the

Table 5 Fates of Veto-Threatened Bills

President	Total threatened bills	Congress backs down; bill dies	Compromise	President backs down; bill enacted	Bill passed as is and vetoed	Vetoes overridden
John F. Kennedy	0	0	0	0	0	0
Lyndon B. Johnson	0	0	0	0	0	0
Richard Nixon	5	0	0	0	5	1
Gerald R. Ford	10	2	0	0	8	1
Jimmy Carter	12	3	5	2	2	1
Ronald Reagan (1981-1986)	29	8	11	1	9	2

Sources: New York Times Annual Index, 1961-86; Robert J. Spitzer, *The Presidential Veto* (Albany: State University of New York Press, 1988), 103. Copyright © 1988 by State University of New York Press. Reprinted by permission of the publisher.

Note: The numbers of veto threats listed above are not considered definitive. Threats may have been delivered by presidents Kennedy and Johnson, for example, but not reported in the newspapers. There is no doubt, however, that presidents with larger numbers of threats used these more, as the potency of threats depends largely on the extent to which they are widely known.

administration of Republican Ronald Reagan, but not in the way that it had for Ford. During Reagan's first seven years in office, he averaged less than ten vetoes per year, most of which concerned relatively noncontroversial measures. This is explained partly by his legislative successes (despite Democratic party control of the House and Republican control of the Senate for only six years). Yet, veto rhetoric played a large role in his administration. He often challenged Congress to send him bills that exceeded his spending guidelines, even using a well-known line from a Clint Eastwood movie in daring Congress to "make my day." He persistently advocated that he be granted item veto powers (see the following discussion), and he issued numerous veto threats. Despite these public statements, many conservatives continued to urge Reagan to use the veto more often as a brake on federal spending.

The Veto Threat

For as long as the veto power has existed, so too has the veto threat. Writing in the *Federalist* No. 73, Alexander Hamilton noted that the veto often would have "a silent and unperceived, though forcible, operation" that might give pause to those seeking to challenge the president. President Washington, for example, voiced his displeasure about a tonnage bill that Congress passed just four months into his first term. Because it was too late for Congress to take back or alter the original bill, Congress passed another bill that was more to Washington's liking.

The veto threat can be used as a tool to shape, alter, or deter legislation before it reaches the president's desk. Like the veto itself, however, a threat applied too often loses its potency, and a threat not considered credible is not a threat at all.

Veto threats have been important tools for modern presidents. For example, a legislative coordinator during the Nixon-Ford years estimated that the veto threat resulted in legislative alterations favorable to the president in twenty to thirty cases.[70] President Carter's threat to veto any bill containing tuition tax credits prompted Congress to remove such a program from its 1978 education bill.

Four possible actions can occur in the aftermath of a veto threat: (1) Congress may back down; (2) a compromise bill may be constructed, leading to passage of a modified bill; (3) the president may reconsider; or (4) neither side may back down, and the bill may be passed and vetoed. As Table 5 shows, the public veto threat was not used by Kennedy and Johnson. Although threats were used by Carter, the three Republican presidents (Nixon, Ford, and Reagan), all of whom contended with a Congress controlled partially or entirely by the opposition party, faced the greatest number of confrontations over the threat.

Private Bill Vetoes

About 63 percent of all vetoes involve private bills. A large volume of private bill vetoes is attributable to a rush of war-related pension and other claims. Most of these vetoes were applied by Presidents Cleveland (for Civil War claims), Franklin Roosevelt (for World War I claims), and Truman and Eisenhower (for World War II claims).

Vetoes of private bills are much more likely to be sustained because of the extremely narrow focus of such bills. Given congressional workloads and interests, it is unlikely that the veto of a legislator's pet private bill will spark sufficient interest to cause a serious override effort. Moreover, after passage private bills are subject to a relatively nonpartisan assessment by the appropriate executive departments and agencies. When the recommendation to veto emerges and is carried out, it is perceived in many ways as a nonpolitical judgment, unlike vetoes of public bills.

Pocket Veto

Although the Founders rejected an absolute veto for the president, they nevertheless gave the president a pocket veto, which is in effect an absolute veto. According to Article I, section 7, of the Constitution, "If any bill shall not be returned by the President within ten days (Sundays excepted) after it shall have been presented to him, the same shall be a law, in like manner as if he had signed it, unless the Congress by their adjournment prevent its return, in which case it shall not be a law."

A bill thus automatically becomes law if the president takes no action within ten days, leaving the president unable to block legislation simply by withholding a signature. This provision is modified, however, by the phrase referring to adjournment. This phrase was inserted to prevent

Congress from passing a law objectionable to the president and then quickly adjourning to prevent the president from vetoing the bill. (According to the regular veto procedure a bill must be returned to Congress, but this cannot be done if Congress adjourns to avoid receiving a vetoed bill.) If a bill is pocket vetoed, it dies, and Congress must begin the law-making process again during its next session if it wishes to attempt once more passage of the bill.

Roughly 40 percent of all vetoes have been pocket vetoes, but their use did not become common until after the Civil War. Although the pocket veto has been used frequently, a continuing controversy exists over the question of what constitutes an adjournment by Congress. If the president is able to return a vetoed bill, the pocket veto is not permissible.

The question of the relation between the pocket veto and adjournment has arisen in several court cases. In 1929 the Supreme Court ruled in the *Pocket Veto Case* that the key question concerning when the pocket veto was appropriate was not whether adjournment was final (as in the end of a Congress) or interim (as with a holiday recess), but whether presidents were prevented from returning a vetoed bill to Congress.[71] If they were, the pocket veto was appropriate. In the *Pocket Veto Case* the Court ruled in favor of the pocket veto in question.

In 1938 the Court ruled in *Wright v. United States* that the Congress could designate agents to receive veto messages when it was not in session, just as the executive designated agents to serve as legal representatives to receive messages and the like.[72] As a result of these rulings, use of the regular (also called the return) veto was favored over the absolute pocket veto, as long as Congress designated an agent to receive vetoes. The only time Congress is unable to do this is at the end of its two-year sessions; in the postwar era Congress began to meet year-round.

Two more recent court challenges have questioned a liberal use of the pocket veto. When President Nixon pocket-vetoed a bill during a six-day Christmas recess in 1970, Sen. Edward M. Kennedy (D-Mass.) filed suit, claiming that the pocket veto was unjustified. Kennedy contended that there had been no adjournment and that the bill could have been return-vetoed. Both the federal district court and federal court of appeals ruled the veto unconstitutional, emphasizing that the pocket veto was unjustified as long as duly designated agents were on hand to receive possible veto messages.[73] The Nixon administration declined to appeal the case to the Supreme Court.

During the 1970s both Presidents Ford and Carter avoided pocket vetoes during intra- and intersession adjournments and cooperated with efforts by Congress to formalize procedures for receiving presidential messages during adjournments. This arrangement changed during the Reagan administration, which used the pocket veto twice when the vetoed bill could have been returned. The second incident prompted a court challenge by thirty-three members of Congress. On March 9, 1984, a federal district court judge ruled in favor of the pocket veto of a bill tying aid to El Salvador with that nation's progress on human rights.[74] The judge ruled that the *Pocket Veto Case* had set precedent. A three-judge court of appeals panel then reversed the lower court ruling in a 2-1 decision. The majority ruled that as long as Congress made arrangements to receive veto messages during recesses and adjournments, the return veto was preferred.[75] On appeal, the Supreme Court ruled 6-2 that the case was moot. The case was therefore dismissed without a judgment as to its merits.[76]

The political ambiguity about proper use of the pocket veto thus has played itself out in a series of court disputes. Resolution of the dispute depends on the willingness of the president to seek an accommodative relationship with Congress.

Item Veto

For over one hundred years presidents and others have argued that the presidential veto should be expanded to incorporate the power to veto parts or items of a bill. The call for an item veto has been predicated partly on the bluntness of the existing veto power—presidents may be compelled to veto a bill that includes provisions they favor or to sign a bill that includes provisions they oppose. Congress has long attached "riders" (amendments not related to the bills to which they are attached) to legislation as a means of circumventing a veto. The item veto also has been viewed as a way in which the president can trim excess from spending measures and eliminate special-interest projects. Forty-three state governors currently have item veto powers.

The item veto first appeared in the constitution of the Confederacy in 1861. Although Confederate president Jefferson Davis used the regular veto powers thirty-eight times, he never exercised the item veto. After the Civil War, the item veto was included in Georgia's constitution of 1865 and that of Texas in 1866. It was included in most other state constitutions by about 1915.[77]

In 1873, President Ulysses Grant became the first president to call for the power at the federal level. Three years later the proposal was introduced in Congress, and since then over 150 item veto proposals have been offered in Congress. More recently, President Reagan called for item veto powers for the president in his State of the Union addresses from 1984 to 1988. Other presidents who have called for the power have included Rutherford B. Hayes, Chester A. Arthur, Grover Cleveland, Woodrow Wilson, Franklin Roosevelt, Harry Truman, Dwight Eisenhower, and Gerald Ford.[78] Despite these numerous attempts to gain item veto powers, only one proposal reached the floor of Congress, in 1884.

Opponents of the item veto argue that it would serve principally to enhance the president's already considerable power over the legislative process. Over the last one hundred years the predominant trend in relations between the executive and legislative branches has been a steady rise in presidential influence over virtually every phase of the legislative process. The addition of the item veto would, according to critics, only exacerbate the existing imbalance between the branches.

Accordingly, the claim that presidents would use the power impartially to cut excess spending and special-interest programs overlooks the political and special interests of each president. Nothing could prevent a president from using an item veto to serve political ends by, for example, threatening to item-veto favored programs of presidential opponents, while sparing those of allies. Moreover, an item veto would be effective against only a small proportion of the federal budget, as most of the federal budget is composed of spending resulting from contractual, legal, or other obligations and commitments.[79]

Critics also argue that the existing veto power gives the president an ample, if imperfect, means of dealing with riders and excess spending. The veto threat alone is often incentive enough for Congress to alter legislation. And when that is not effective, presidents have used the veto successfully to force the hand of Congress. This is evident in the frequency of vetoes, their high rates of success, and the fact that Congress stands to suffer as much from legislative bottlenecks as the president. Presidential opponents of the item veto have included Benjamin Harrison, William Howard Taft, and Jimmy Carter.

The experiences of the states provide no ready model for the presidency, critics argue, because state governing systems are centered more heavily around the executive, with legislatures that meet for only part of the year (meaning that governors need greater powers to govern when the legislatures are not in session). Moreover, state governors use their item vetoes for political purposes in ways that critics fear presidents might adopt under similar circumstances.[80]

A practical problem arises from the difficulty in defining and identifying particular items in legislation. So-called pork barrel projects typically are not itemized in legislation but are incorporated into lump sum amounts. The spending for such projects is stipulated in committee reports, not the law itself. This practice is the product of mutual consent between Congress and federal agencies, because it allows agencies some discretion in adapting spending to changing circumstances. In any case, members of Congress seeking to avoid an item veto could find many ways to circumvent the identification of particular items.[81]

Legislative Veto

The legislative veto power, which came into being in the 1930s, allows Congress to maintain some control over administrative actions, while allowing the administrative agencies and the president more discretion to act, subject to later congressional reaction, after Congress has enacted legislation. A legislative veto is action taken by Congress to prevent something from happening. It can be invoked by a vote of both houses of Congress (usually through a concurrent resolution), by a vote of one house (through a simple resolution), or even through the actions of a congressional committee. In 1952, for example, Congress authorized the chair of the House Appropriations Committee to veto proposals made by the director of the budget to amend a budget circular.

A legislative veto, unlike regular legislative action, does not cross the president's desk, although the authority creating each legislative veto must be enacted in prior legislation that does cross the president's desk. In this way, Congress reserves the right to review and disapprove present and future actions of the executive branch.

The legislative veto was first employed during the presidency of Herbert Hoover. In 1930, Hoover asked Congress to enact legislation for reorganization of the executive branch. When Congress failed to do so, he asked for the authority to do it himself, subject to congressional "power of revision." Congress delayed responding until June 1932, when the then Democratic-controlled Congress was reluctant to grant such power to a Republican president. Congress realized, however, that the president was in the best position to oversee such a reorganization, and out of this quandary emerged the legislative veto. Congress reversed the usual legislative procedure by letting the president reorganize, subject to congressional veto, with no authority in the executive to override. Thus, Hoover was allowed to reorganize by executive order, but each order had to be transmitted to Congress and would be undone if disapproved within sixty days by either house.

Since then, the legislative veto has become a standard provision in reorganization legislation and has appeared in many other types of legislation as well. Up to 1983 about two hundred legislative veto provisions had been inserted into legislation. One well-known legislative veto is found in the War Powers Resolution of 1973. According to the provision, Congress may enact a concurrent resolution to force the president to withdraw military forces from hostilities in other nations. A provision of the Budget and Impoundment Control Act of 1974 stipulates that either house can vote to disapprove presidential impoundment of funds and thus compel expenditures. A similar provision is found in the International Security Assistance and Arms Control Act of 1976, which allows Congress to override a decision by the president to sell military hardware to other nations.[82]

Presidents have objected to the idea of the legislative veto by arguing that it represents an improper invasion of executive power. Yet despite this, they have set aside their objections and accepted reorganization authority.

Critics argue that the legislative veto infringes on the executive's constitutional duty to carry out the laws, because of the way Congress uses the veto to direct administrative action. Some also argue that it violates the presentment clause of Article I, section 7, of the Constitution, which says that binding actions emanating from the legislature must be presented to the president for a signature or veto. Finally, the legislative veto is said to reverse the normal relationship between the two branches, since the president or an agency can take an action unless Congress "vetoes" the action.

In arguing for the legislative veto, proponents first point out that Congress legally delegates rule-making authority to executive branch agencies and the president with regularity. Thus Congress may circumscribe or limit that delegated power by making it subject to legislative veto. Second, although the legislative veto is not subject to presidential assent, it is based on prior statutory authority, which must cross the president's desk. Third, in 1976 Supreme Court Justice Byron R. White noted in the case of *Buckley v. Valeo* that the legislative veto "no more invades the President's powers than does a regulation not required to be laid before Congress."[83] Fourth, the legislative veto has been a key political tool for Congress at a time when it has needed such tools to make its oversight more effective.

The arguments for and against the legislative veto came to a head in the 1983 Court case of *Immigration and Naturalization Service v. Chadha*.[84] Speaking for the seven-member majority, Chief Justice Burger said that the legislative veto violated the presentment clause and the principle of bicameralism. (The *Chadha* case involved a one-house veto.) The following month the Court upheld two lower court rulings striking down one- and two-house legislative vetoes.

Despite the sweeping nature of the *Chadha* case the legislative veto is still employed. In fact, from 1983 to 1987 over one hundred legislative veto provisions were implemented through "ingenious and novel methods" developed jointly by Congress and federal agencies. These methods include informal agreements, reliance on arcane bill language, and use of internal congressional rules. Despite President Reagan's stated opposition to the legislative veto, he vetoed none of the bills containing these provisions. One critic of the *Chadha* case has asserted that it has resulted in "a record of non-compliance, subtle evasion, and a system of lawmaking that is now more convoluted, cumbersome, and covert than before." [85] This case is nevertheless an example of a vital political accommodation between the branches that was not impeded even by a sweeping Court ruling.

Appointment Power

Article II, section 2, of the Constitution says that the president shall have the power to nominate,

> with the Advice and Consent of the Senate . . . Ambassadors, other public Ministers and Consuls, Judges of the supreme Court, and all other Officers of the United States, whose Appointments are not herein otherwise provided for, and which shall be established by law; but the Congress may by Law vest the Appointment of such inferior Officers . . . in the President alone, in the Courts . . . or in the Heads of Departments.

The Constitution (Article I, section 6) also forbids members of Congress to serve simultaneously in an executive position, such as a cabinet post, or to serve in any position created by Congress if the position in question was created during the term of a member, or if the salary for the position in question was raised during the member's term.

The Founders clearly paid close attention to many aspects of the appointment power. The appointment process itself involves close interaction between the executive and legislative branches. Its importance is underscored by the roughly sixty thousand appointment cases (most of them military) that arise each year.[86]

Presidential appointments fall into four broad categories: federal court nominees, executive branch officials, ambassadors, and heads of regulatory agencies. The power to nominate belongs, in principle, solely to the president. Alexander Hamilton stated in the *Federalist* No. 66 that the Senate would not choose nominees: "They may defeat one choice of the Executive, and oblige him to make another; but they cannot themselves *choose*—they can only ratify or reject the choice of the President." In fact, many political forces intervene before a name is sent to the Senate.

Senators from the same political party as the president may suggest potential nominees from their home states for judicial, federal marshal, and federal attorney positions. But if dissatisfied with the suggestions of senators, presidents may bargain to find a mutually acceptable nominee. Possible nominees also may be suggested by party leaders, judges, and other executive officials.

Private-interest groups may take a hand as well. The American Bar Association, for example, has formally screened judicial nominees since 1946. Presidents also may consult sympathetic private groups when searching for nominees for agencies and departments related to a group's concerns. Labor unions, for example, take a keen interest in appointments to the position of secretary of labor. The influence of such outside groups is directly related to the extent to which presidents are sympathetic to their concerns. Interest groups play an even more active role after nominees are forwarded to the Senate.

The appointments process is vital to the functioning of an administration. Presidents who pay inadequate attention to the process may wind up with administrative and judicial appointees who are incompetent, unqualified, corrupt, or at odds with the president's philosophy. President Kennedy summarized the problem facing presidents at the beginning of their terms when he said, "For the last four years I spent so much time getting to know people who could help me get elected President that I didn't have time to get to know people who could help me, after I was elected, to be a good president." [87] Richard Nixon faced difficulties filling positions at the beginning of his administration, and both he and Jimmy Carter later reevaluated their appointments, as many positions filled hurriedly at the outset of their administrations were occupied by individuals either inadequately in tune with the goals of the president or simply not well qualified. Ronald Reagan delayed filling many positions during his first year in office to ensure that his nominees conformed with his political philosophy.

Another important factor influencing the course of nominations is "senatorial courtesy," a longstanding informal practice in which presidents and senators defer to the evaluations offered by their fellow senators who represent nominees from (or who are appointed to positions within) their home states. The relative influence of a senator is considerably greater if he or she is in the same political party as the president. Although senatorial courtesy is occasionally violated, senators usually respect the wishes of their colleagues because they want other senators to do the same when individuals are nominated from their own states. Presidents usually respect this courtesy as well to maintain good relations with the Senate, at least when it comes to "advice and consent."

Court Nominations

Presidents make nominations to all federal courts, but Supreme Court nominations attract the most political attention. The Constitution gives the president the power to select nominees, and it gives the Senate the right to confirm or reject them. Historically, the Senate has rejected about one of every five nominees to the Supreme Court. Some critics of this system have suggested erroneously that senatorial rejection of a nominee for political reasons is unconstitutional.[88] The 80 percent confirmation average for Supreme Court nominees, however, indicates that, other things being equal, presidents are entitled to have their nominees confirmed. (The rejection rate was actually higher in the nineteenth century.) And even more to the point, of the nine hundred nominees submitted to the Senate from 1945 to 1974 to fill positions on the federal courts of appeal, federal district courts, and other federal courts, only four were not confirmed.[89]

Two key struggles over rejected Supreme Court nominees in recent years illustrate the interdependence of the two branches when the Senate does not simply accept the president's nomination. The first occurred during President Richard Nixon's term. In May 1969 a vacancy on the Supreme Court was created by the resignation of Justice Abe Fortas. Nixon's nominee to the position was Clement Haynsworth, a competent if undistinguished conservative Southerner who fulfilled Nixon's ideological and regional preferences. During his confirmation hearings, however, Haynsworth demonstrated indifference to the discovery of financial and other improprieties, which the Senate could not overlook especially because Fortas had resigned when charges of similar improprieties surfaced. These and other

Table 6 Federal Judicial Appointments from the President's Political Party, 1888-1984

President	Party	Percentage
Grover Cleveland	Democrat	97.3
Benjamin Harrison	Republican	87.9
William McKinley	Republican	95.7
Theodore Roosevelt	Republican	95.8
William Howard Taft	Republican	82.2
Woodrow Wilson	Democrat	98.6
Warren G. Harding	Republican	97.7
Calvin Coolidge	Republican	94.1
Herbert Hoover	Republican	85.7
Franklin D. Roosevelt	Democrat	96.4
Harry S Truman	Democrat	93.1
Dwight D. Eisenhower	Republican	95.1
John F. Kennedy	Democrat	90.9
Lyndon B. Johnson	Democrat	95.2
Richard Nixon	Republican	93.7
Gerald R. Ford	Republican	81.2
Jimmy Carter	Democrat	94.8
Ronald Reagan	Republican	98.1[a]

Source: Henry J. Abraham, *Justices and Presidents: A Political History of Appointments to the Supreme Court* (New York: Oxford University Press, 1985), 67. Copyright © 1974, 1985 by Henry J. Abraham. Reprinted by permission of the publisher.

a. As of September 1984.

concerns about Haynsworth's civil rights and civil liberties record led the Senate to reject his nomination by a vote of 55-45.[90]

The Senate's rejection of Haynsworth infuriated Nixon, who believed the rejection to be based on Haynsworth's southern conservatism. He followed up the rejection by nominating G. Harrold Carswell, a Florida judge with at best marginal credentials. This appointment was considered "an act of vengeance" by Nixon.[91] As with the Haynsworth nomination, the Senate was disposed initially to ratify Carswell. Investigations revealed, however, that he had at one time firmly supported racial segregation, that he had participated in an effort to keep a Florida golf course segregated, and that he had one of the highest reversal rates of any sitting judge. After several months Carswell too was rejected by the Senate.

After this second stinging rejection Nixon criticized the Senate for robbing him of his right to have his nominations confirmed (although no such right exists). In the spring of 1970 Nixon nominated to the Court a Minnesota judge, Harry A. Blackmun, who was readily confirmed.[92]

A similar scenario occurred in 1987 when President Ronald Reagan moved to fill a Court vacancy left by the June retirement of Lewis Powell, a Nixon appointee. Reagan's nominee was Robert H. Bork, a well-known conservative legal scholar and federal judge. But unlike most Court nominees, Bork had been outspoken over the years about both his judicial philosophy and his opposition to dozens of Supreme Court decisions that expanded civil rights and liberties. His opinions and writings revealed what critics considered extreme conservatism and a rejection of some well-established Court doctrines, such as the right to privacy. Civil rights, women's rights, and civil liberties groups complained bitterly that Bork's views placed him beyond the bounds of even traditional conservatism. Also according to them, his attitudes towards the rights of blacks, women, and others made him unfit to serve on the nation's highest court.[93]

The Bork hearings received unprecedented media attention, and were broadcast on network television. As the hearings progressed, public opposition grew, and private groups on both sides mounted intense campaigns to either oppose or support Bork. After months of hearings and debates the Senate rejected Bork's nomination in October 1987 by the widest margin ever cast against a Supreme Court nominee, 58-42.

Following the Bork rejection Reagan nominated Douglas H. Ginsburg, a California law professor with brief judicial experience. Although Ginsburg was considered to be almost as conservative as Bork, his nomination was not expected to engender as much controversy as that of Bork, given Ginsburg's briefer and less public career. Investigations revealed, however, that Ginsburg had experimented with marijuana, not only as a student, but also while a law professor. This revelation was particularly embarrassing to the White House as the Reagan administration and First Lady Nancy Reagan were engaged in a vigorous antidrug campaign. Thus, the administration pressured Ginsburg to withdraw his name. Had the marijuana question not arisen, Ginsburg's nomination would have encountered difficulty nonetheless because of his conservatism, lack of judicial experience, and hints of conflict-of-interest problems.

Reagan's third nominee was Anthony M. Kennedy, a respected California judge considered to be more moderate than Bork and Ginsburg. The Senate confirmed Kennedy by a unanimous vote, and he took his seat on the Court in February 1988.

Several important observations stem from these admittedly unusual cases. First, initially the Senate is not inclined to resist a presidential nominee, even when senators have personal reservations about a nominee's qualifications or politics. Senate rejection of a judicial nominee invariably engenders resentment and anger in the White House, from which each president exerts significant political resources to see a nomination through to a successful conclusion. *(See Table 6.)*

Second, politics plays a part. All of the rejected nominees described in the preceding account were rejected in part because of their politics. In particular, their stands on civil rights and civil liberties were scrutinized by senators and private interests. Although such scrutiny is by no means limited to conservative judicial nominees (as seen, for example, in Justice Fortas's forced withdrawal as Johnson's nominee to the position of chief justice in 1968), senators take political considerations into account. In the case of Reagan's nominees, liberal senators made it clear that they were not out to oppose all conservative nominees; they cautioned, however, that nominees to the highest court should not be too far to the ideological extreme. Another Reagan appointee to the Court, Antonin Scalia, was ratified by the Senate unanimously in 1986, his well-known conservatism notwithstanding.

Third, timing plays a role. Had Haynsworth been nominated after Carswell instead of before, he might well have been confirmed. Had Bork been nominated for the 1981 Court vacancy (a position that was filled by Sandra Day O'Connor), Reagan might have been able to exert sufficient pressure to obtain Bork's confirmation. Reagan's political strength was greatest in his first year, when the Republicans controlled the Senate. (Party control of the Senate changed after the 1986 elections.)

Fourth, partisanship is also important. The president

is likely to face a more difficult confirmation process when the opposition party controls the Senate, as was the case for the rejections just described.

Fifth, the Senate does not like confrontation over judicial and other appointments. Carswell, for example, was rejected because it was clear that he was less qualified than Haynsworth. The Senate's inclination is to go along with and not challenge presidential appointees.

Presidents select judicial and other nominees hoping that they will act in accordance with the president's ideological leanings. But the record of how Supreme Court justices have voted after joining the Court indicates that it is difficult to predict how an appointee will act after joining the Court. Although presidents have been personally acquainted with about three-fifths of their Supreme Court nominees, one scholar has concluded that one Supreme Court appointee in four has turned out to be quite different from what the appointing president wanted.[94]

President Truman once noted that trying to pack the Supreme Court with loyal appointees "just doesn't work.... Whenever you put a man on the Court, he ceases to be your friend."[95] And President Eisenhower observed in his memoirs that his appointment of Earl Warren as chief justice was the greatest mistake of his presidency. A former Republican governor of California, Warren became (contrary to Eisenhower's expectations) one of the Court's great champions of civil rights, civil liberties, rights of the accused, and a generally more activist Court. This independence demonstrated by Court appointees is explainable by the life terms that they serve and (unlike most other appointees) their location in a separate branch of government.

Other Appointees

The Senate has shown greater deference to presidential appointees to cabinet, ambassadorial, and agency positions than to appointees to judicial positions. From 1945 to 1974 the Senate rejected less than 1 percent of over 3,300 nonjudicial appointees.[96] From 1959 to 1989, the Senate rejected only two cabinet secretary nominees—Lewis L. Strauss in 1959, Eisenhower's nominee for commerce secretary, and John Tower in 1989, George Bush's nominee for defense secretary. These statistics do not, however, take into account prospective nominees whose names were not forwarded to the Senate because of informal opposition or pressure exerted before the actual nomination. *(See Table 7.)*

Questions of competence are sometimes raised, but they rarely have a decisive impact. The nominations of James T. Lynn to serve as secretary of the Department of Housing and Urban Development in 1973 and of Carla A. Hills to the same position two years later (after Lynn's resignation) raised questions about their lack of experience for the job, yet both were confirmed. In 1981 President Reagan nominated California judge and close associate William Clark to serve as an assistant secretary of state for African affairs. During the confirmation hearings Clark exhibited a lack of elementary knowledge of African politics and geography that startled and enraged some senators, yet he was ratified by the Senate.

Both the president and the Senate have been accused of not paying enough attention to the quality of appointments to regulatory agencies. Unlike those in many other appointed positions, the appointed heads of agencies often need substantial knowledge about the object of regulation.

Table 7 Nominations Submitted to and Confirmed by the U.S. Senate, 1967-1984

	Military		Civilian	
Congress	Submitted	Confirmed	Submitted	Confirmed
90th (1967-1968)	109,140	107,623	11,091	10,608
91st (1969-1970)	126,404	126,368	8,060	7,705
92d (1971-1972)	109,970	108,202	7,083	6,707
93d (1973-1974)	127,596	124,581	6,788	6,673
94th (1975-1976)	129,170	125,758	6,132	5,620
95th (1977-1978)	129,476	117,039	8,033	7,691
96th (1979-1980)	147,823	146,560	8,318	8,105
97th (1981-1982)	177,797	177,176	8,467	7,668
98th (1983-1984)	90,312	90,283	7,581	6,979

Source: Roger H. Davidson and Thomas Kephart, "Indicators of Senate Activity and Workload," Congressional Research Service, Report No. 85-133S, June 1985, CRS-72.

Of even greater concern, however, is the tendency to appoint individuals from the industries or sectors being regulated to top agency positions. Such appointments call into question the independence and veracity of subsequent agency actions.[97] *(See Government Agencies and Corporations chapter in Part V.)*

Removal Power

An ongoing debate has accompanied the question of who has the power to remove appointed officials. While the Constitution clearly states that the president and federal judges may be removed by impeachment, it provides little clarity on the matter of removing other appointed officials.

Some scholars and officials have suggested that other executive officers must be impeached to be removed. Most, however, argue that removal rests with either the president as head of the executive branch, or Congress, which creates the offices filled by appointment, allowing it as well to attach conditions and limitations to service in such offices.

The question of removal has been a major concern of several presidents, especially Andrew Johnson. When Johnson tried to suspend and then remove Secretary of War Edwin M. Stanton in violation of the Tenure of Office Act of 1867, he was subjected to a vote of impeachment in the House and a trial in the Senate. (Enacted over Johnson's veto, the act provided for Senate involvement in the removal of executive officials.) After a presidential-congressional clash over the Senate's involvement in removal during the Cleveland administration, the Tenure of Office Act was repealed. The power of the president to remove cabinet officials is now well recognized.

Since repeal of the Tenure of Office Act, the Supreme Court has recognized that Congress may establish grounds for the removal of other appointed officials. Moreover, Congress may remove an official by abolishing the office in which he or she serves. Congress also can establish the terms of office. On occasion Congress has enacted nonbinding resolutions expressing its sense that the president should remove an official. It can apply informal political pressure as well to force the resignation of an appointee. In fact, one study concluded that pressure from Congress resulted in more firings and personnel reassignments than pressure from the president.[98]

At the other extreme, Congress may act to protect an appointee whose job is threatened for inappropriate reasons. In 1968, for example, a procurement specialist, Ernest Fitzgerald, admitted before a Senate committee that the C-5A cargo plane had encountered $2 billion in cost overruns. Because of his admission Fitzgerald was stripped of his civil service protection, demoted, investigated by the air force, and eventually fired. After years of litigation and congressional outcry, Fitzgerald was given back his job, with a promotion, in 1982. Congress has continued to help protect federal officials who reveal agency misdeeds and mistakes from arbitrary suspension, removal, demotion, or reassignment.[99]

The President as Chief Legislator

The Constitution explicitly involves the president in the legislative process, but the president's present-day extensive role in legislative affairs extends far beyond the initial bounds set by the Constitution.

According to Article II, section 3, the president shall give Congress information about the state of the Union, recommend to Congress measures judged "necessary and expedient," and convene "on extraordinary occasions" one or both houses of Congress. The president also makes treaties with the Senate's advice and consent and vetoes bills. Thus, within the ordinary routine of enacting legislation the Constitution allows the president to make proposals to Congress and to veto when legislation emerges. Yet when added together, these powers do not explain how the president has acquired the title of "chief legislator."[100]

Early presidents took great care to avoid trespassing on legislative prerogatives. During his eight years in office, George Washington proposed only three specific measures to Congress and used the veto only twice. Some of Washington's cabinet members, such as Alexander Hamilton, played a more active role by testifying before committees, requesting appropriations, and mobilizing support. Washington's successor, John Adams, faced a more contentious and partisan Congress, and relations deteriorated.

Thomas Jefferson's presidency saw an upturn in relations, aided by close partisan ties between the president and his Democratic-Republican party allies who controlled Congress. Jefferson's own superb political skills helped as well. Members of Jefferson's cabinet considered and actually formulated legislation. In fact, Jefferson's degree of influence over the shape and direction of legislation stood as a high-water mark for presidents of the nineteenth century; not until this century would presidents again wield so much influence over the course of legislation.

The next three presidents—James Madison, James Monroe, and John Quincy Adams—could not match Jefferson's skills, nor were they able to maintain such ascendance over their party. They continued to work with congressional insiders and cabinet members, but the predominant pattern was deference to the legislature in all things legislative.[101] This is evident in a House committee report issued in December 1817 in response to a comment in President Monroe's 1817 message to Congress. In the message, Monroe questioned the constitutional right of Congress to establish and finance internal improvements, and he implicitly threatened to veto any bill along these lines. In response the House report stated that the president's expression of opinion should have no influence whatsoever over congressional actions. Furthermore, should a presidential statement announcing a possible veto be made and deter Congress from enacting a measure it might otherwise have passed, "the Presidential veto would acquire a force unknown to the Constitution, and the legislative body would be shorn of its powers from a want of confidence in its strength."[102] Despite these concerns, Monroe actually vetoed only one bill during his eight years in office.

Legislative reactions to perceived presidential incursions intensified during subsequent administrations. Andrew Jackson was unable to sway congressional leaders and thus appealed directly to the people, using patronage and the veto with considerable effectiveness. (He vetoed twelve bills, more than all of his predecessors combined.) His vetoes, and veto threats, infuriated his opponents in Congress, who accused him of improperly trying to tamper with the legislative process. Critics rejected Jackson's suggestion that congressional leaders should have consulted the president first to avoid a veto and produce better legislation. To these critics the constitutional pronouncement in Article I—"All legislative powers herein granted shall be vested in Congress"—meant plainly that the president was not to intrude until a bill was presented for a presidential signature or veto. This rift over guiding the course of legislation contributed directly to Senate passage in 1834 of a nonbinding motion to censure Jackson.

The ascendance of the Whig Party in the 1830s and 1840s helped to legitimize the "Whiggish" view of the presidency, which emphasized that legislating should be left to the legislature. The country's first Whig president, William Henry Harrison, said in his inaugural address: "I can not conceive that by a fair construction any or either of its [the Constitution's] provisions would be found to constitute the President a part of the legislative power." These sentiments were shared by Whigs and others of the time.

President Abraham Lincoln moved effectively during his first term in office to gain more influence over the flow of legislation. Aided by a wartime crisis and a truncated Congress (the southern states withdrew their representatives at the start of the Civil War), Lincoln proposed legislation and worked for its passage, and he even engaged in some bill drafting. With the ascension of the Radical Republicans after the 1864 elections, Lincoln's influence waned, and Lincoln's successors fared poorly with a postwar Congress that held the political initiative for most of the rest of the century.

Presidents William McKinley and Theodore Roosevelt worked closely with party leaders in Congress. Roosevelt in particular relied on House Speaker Joseph G. Cannon (R-Ill.) to rally support for presidential proposals. Support from the House Speaker was especially crucial during this period because congressional power was at its most hierarchical. From about 1910 on, power in Congress became more and more decentralized, affecting not only the way Congress conducted its business, but also the way Congress interacted with the president.

An important revitalization of presidential influence over legislation occurred during the presidency of Woodrow Wilson. Wilson viewed his role as similar to that of the British prime minister. (He was a close observer and great admirer of the parliamentary system.) To that end he formulated a coordinated series of proposals addressing important national problems, helped draft legislation, used cabinet members to influence Congress, and established his own direct ties to key congressional leaders. Wilson, in fact, became the first president since John Adams personally to deliver his State of the Union address before Congress. The upshot of these efforts was that Wilson obtained passage of a number of pieces of landmark legislation, including the Clayton Antitrust Act, the Federal Reserve Act, and creation of the Federal Trade Commission. The end of Wilson's second term saw a decline in his political fortunes, however, capped by the Senate's ignominious defeat of the Treaty of Versailles.

Wilson's three Republican successors all adopted a more modest attitude toward influencing the legislative process. Like the nineteenth-century Whigs, their conservatism extended to their relations with Congress.

The economic crisis of the 1930s precipitated not only the election of Franklin Roosevelt, but also his unprecedented domination of the legislative agenda. The relationship between the two branches would never be the same again. From the beginning of his first term Roosevelt sought legislative initiative to deal with the depression; in fact, the day after Roosevelt took office, he called a special session of Congress. During the one-hundred-day session, Congress enacted an enormous volume of major New Deal legislation aimed at the country's economic woes. This legislation was then designed and guided through Congress by Roosevelt and his aides. A second great wave of legislative activity (called the second New Deal) occurred from 1934 to 1936, again based on White House initiative.

Roosevelt used all the resources at his command to influence every aspect of the legislative process. He used aides, advisers, and cabinet secretaries to both formulate legislation and shepherd it through Congress. He expanded the role of the Bureau of the Budget to control more firmly the requests of the burgeoning federal bureaucracy. And he employed patronage and used the veto more often than any other president.[103]

In sum, Roosevelt's actions had two important consequences. First, for future presidents his actions set a precedent that placed a high premium on decisive, positive, vigorous legislative leadership. It was a precedent accepted not only by presidents, but also by most members of Congress. Second, Roosevelt presided over the creation of the Executive Office of the President (EOP), which then included, among other offices, the Bureau of the Budget. *(See White House Office chapter in Part V.)* The EOP established the administrative framework that enabled future presidents to exercise legislative leadership. The expectations of such leadership were thus firmly established, as were the mechanisms for that leadership.

Harry Truman worked to establish a comprehensive legislative program for Congress. This effort was hampered, however, by the difficulties in adjusting to peacetime, the strains in foreign alliances, and the many problems associated with building a new White House structure after the unexpected death of Roosevelt. Truman's 1948 messages to Congress assembled for the first time in his presidency the kind of detailed and comprehensive programs that had been associated with his predecessor. His subsequent proposals were even more comprehensive.

When Dwight Eisenhower took office in 1953 he was criticized widely for not proposing a detailed, defined program to Congress. In 1954 "Eisenhower espoused a sweeping concept of the President's initiative in legislation and an elaborate mechanism for its public expression." [104] From this point on, every president would submit a detailed, comprehensive legislative program that would serve as the basis for congressional action in the coming year.

Aside from Franklin Roosevelt, Lyndon Johnson probably had more success in dealing with Congress than any other president. With the assistance of an overwhelmingly Democratic Congress (the famous Eighty-ninth Congress of 1965-1967), he succeeded in enacting an enormous volume of legislation known as his "Great Society" program. These achievements were curtailed first when the Republican party made electoral inroads in the midterm elections of 1966, and later when the country became more deeply enmeshed in the Vietnam War. As Johnson escalated U.S. involvement in the war, more resources had to be drawn from domestic programs. Johnson's critics then grew in both number and intensity over his conduct of the war. An antiwar challenge from within his own party resulted in his decision not to seek reelection in 1968. *(See Presidential Support in Congress, p. 1475, in the Appendix.)*

The political troubles that accompanied the Vietnam War not only interrupted Johnson's Great Society, but also ushered in a period of deadlock between the branches of government. This resulted from, among other things, efforts by Congress to reassert itself in the face of presidential dominance, mostly divided party control of the executive and legislative branches, national economic stagnation, and spreading dissatisfaction with the government's ability to solve national problems. Despite all these difficulties, the president remained at the center of the legislative process.

Extent of the Chief Legislator's Role

The president's involvement in the legislative domain originates not only in custom and precedent, but also in law. According to the Budget and Accounting Act of 1921, for example, the president must present Congress with an annual budget message. The Employment Act of 1946 calls for presidential submission of an annual economic report as well. In addition, hundreds of other presidential messages, reports, communications, and suggestions are sent to Congress to meet legal requirements.[105]

These legal requirements, enacted by Congress over the years, underscore how much Congress relies on the president's annual legislative program. In fact, Congress is critical of presidents when such programs are not forthcoming. In 1953 an important House committee chair reportedly told an Eisenhower administration official, "Don't expect us to start from scratch on what you people want. That's not the way we do things here—*you* draft the bills and *we* work them over." [106] The difference between this attitude and that of Congress in the nineteenth century illustrates how far the president's participation in legislative affairs has evolved.

Liaison

Presidents always have maintained informal relations with congressional leaders. Woodrow Wilson was the first president in this century to lobby personally on Capitol Hill. Franklin Roosevelt sent his top aides directly to the Capitol to push for his proposals, but it was President Truman who first established a White House office to maintain ties between the president and Congress.

The office was enlarged and reorganized under Eisenhower, and it grew to maturity under the guidance of Lawrence O'Brien, special assistant to Presidents Kennedy and Johnson for congressional affairs. O'Brien's office acted as a focal point for the liaison activities of the executive agencies and departments, and he and his staff also spent much time roaming the halls of Congress. The liaison office prepared weekly reports for the president and made projections about the week to come. President Johnson also played an active role in building support in Congress for his programs and proposals.[107]

President Nixon constructed a strong liaison staff, but its judgments and operations were preempted by Nixon's top assistants, including H. R. Haldeman and John Ehrlichman. After two frustrating years, Nixon's liaison head, Bryce Harlow, resigned. Harlow's successors were similarly frustrated by broadside administration attacks against Congress. By 1973 the liaison office had lost its effectiveness, and liaison efforts were left to a few top Nixon aides.

President Carter took office with high expectations, but they were dashed soon by his mishandling of legislative liaison. Frank Moore, Carter's choice to head the liaison office, had been his liaison with the state legislature when Carter was governor of Georgia; but Moore had no Washington experience. He and his staff neglected the early construction of solid relations with an initially receptive Democratic Congress. Moreover, the liaison office was organized by issue categories rather than by regional blocs. These failures combined with the flood of initial legislation forwarded to Congress to produce poor and relatively unproductive relations between the branches. (In contrast, Johnson sent important bills to Congress one at a time.)

President Reagan's initial liaison efforts were successful, despite Republican control of only one house of Congress (the Senate). Early in the Reagan administration, Reagan staff members conducted a study of the first three months of each past administration, beginning with that of Franklin D. Roosevelt. They concluded that their best chance of success lay in working early and hard on a few key proposals. Reagan selected an experienced Washington hand, Max Friedersdorf, to head liaison efforts, and he was also careful to extend personal favors and courtesies to the key congressional leaders of both parties. As a result of these efforts Reagan achieved many early successes, including enactment of his tax cut package.[108]

Central Clearance

Concomitant with the expansion of the president's legislative role, the growth of the federal bureaucracy, and the need for greater fiscal economy, budgetary authority was delegated to the president in 1921 with enactment of the Budget and Accounting Act. This act stated that any agency or department planning to request legislation for the expenditure of funds must first have approval from the newly created Bureau of the Budget (BOB). In the 1930s this "central clearance" process was extended to all executive branch requests for legislation. BOB then determined whether the requests were consistent with the president's legislative priorities. *(See Supporting Organizations chapter in Part V.)*

At the other end of the legislative process BOB also assessed all enrolled bills (those passed by Congress but not yet signed by the president). These were forwarded to the agencies affected, which in turn informed BOB whether the bill should be signed or vetoed by the president. BOB then sent its final recommendation to the president. Communication between the president and the bureau was made easier in 1939 when the office was moved from the Treasury Department to the newly created Executive Office of the President. According to one expert, clearance and enrolled bill processes "lie at the core of the legislative presidency." [109]

From the Franklin Roosevelt period to about 1965 the Bureau of the Budget tried to avoid overt political considerations in its recommendations, concerning itself more directly with budgetary limitations and the objective merits of bills. Primary responsibility for these activities fell to the Legislative Reference Division within BOB. Because of the volume of legislation, BOB recommendations carried considerable weight, as did those of the career civil servants within the bureau who assumed the brunt of the work. Toward the end of his term, however, President Johnson created a high-level, politically appointed position at the bureau. This appointment marked the beginning of a greater general politicization within BOB.

The Johnson White House also began to take a more active role in determining the bureau's political and policy priorities and their relationship to the president's broader agenda. Legislative items of special interest to the president were given higher priority and often were handled by White House aides. This greater White House interest in BOB was accompanied by an expansion of Johnson's domestic policy staff.

When BOB was reconstituted as the Office of Management and Budget (OMB) under Nixon, OMB was given greater managerial responsibilities, and four new politically appointed associate directors assumed key duties. As a consequence, central clearance and assessment of enrolled bills came under the purview of political appointees rather than civil servants. Moreover, OMB was less receptive to the suggestions and recommendations of civil servants and federal agencies, and it increasingly served as an instrument for extending White House policy preferences into these agencies. This process of politicizing OMB accelerated under the Reagan administration.[110]

Winning Support in Congress

Presidents and their staffs rely on personal persuasion to gain congressional approval of presidential initiatives. Although Congress seeks a presidential agenda, it has few inhibitions about changing presidential proposals once consideration begins. Presidents use other informal methods as well to realize their legislative objectives.

Party Leadership

Presidents whose political party controls both houses of Congress begin with an immediate political advantage. Those who have had the greatest success with Congress—such as Thomas Jefferson, Theodore Roosevelt, Woodrow Wilson, Franklin Roosevelt, and Lyndon Johnson—have used party ties to chamber and committee leaders to cement support for important programs. Sometimes, however, presidents have run afoul of their own party leaders. President Kennedy, for example, found that conservative southern Democrats who held influential positions in Congress blocked many of his programs because of ideological differences. President Carter also encountered difficulties with members of his own party in Congress because of his lack of experience and that of his staff.

Even presidents who find the opposition party in control of Congress discover ways of dealing with partisan differences. President Reagan amassed a series of major successes during his first year in office by relying on the Republican majority in the Senate and a working House majority composed of minority Republicans and "Boll Weevil" Democrats (conservative southern Democrats who were sympathetic with many of Reagan's objectives). The centerpiece of Reagan's efforts was a controversial three-year tax cut plan, enacted only a few months after its introduction. Reagan also won passage in 1981 of major shifts in budget priorities, including significant cuts in domestic social programs and a major increase in defense spending.

Patronage

Presidents readily rely on patronage as a means of winning support. Although civil service limits the extent to which federal jobs may be filled by presidential appointment, presidents nevertheless have the authority to fill thousands of federal positions, including judgeships, federal marshal and attorney positions, customs collector posts, and slots on selective service boards. Such appointments can be used to curry favor among members of Congress.

Presidents also can wield substantial personal patronage, such as making campaign trips to the home district of a member of Congress, extending special White House invitations to legislators, and even providing tickets to the president's box at the John F. Kennedy Center for the Performing Arts. Such favors can have an effect on those of either party whose support is sought by the president.

Presidents have great influence as well over the kind of patronage found in distributive (often called pork barrel) policies. Presidents may reward friends and punish enemies by throwing their support to or withholding support from certain distributive policies such as public works projects, construction projects, defense contracts, rivers and harbors work, and agricultural subsidies. President Carter incurred the ire of many in Congress when he attempted to eliminate nineteen water resource projects in 1978; Congress ultimately defeated his efforts. In contrast to Carter, Reagan encouraged water development. Similarly, he overrode the recommendations of his budget director, David Stockman, and continued to back price supports for tobacco growers during the major effort in 1981 to reduce elements of the federal budget. In the case of the water projects, Reagan was lending his support to programs that benefited the western states, which had provided him with vital support during his election. Tobacco supports were of great importance to key southern states, including North Carolina and Virginia.

Another aspect of the president's support for pork barrel projects is illustrated by a study of presidential proposals sent to Congress from 1954 to 1974. It found that presidents propose more distributive policies to Congress during presidential election years than at any other time in the four-year term cycle.[111]

Public Support

One of the president's most important bases of political strength is public support. Abraham Lincoln once noted, "Public sentiment is everything. With public sentiment nothing can fail, without it nothing can succeed."[112] In the early days of his presidency, Lyndon Johnson often quoted poll results to demonstrate the extent of public support for his programs. Later in his presidency, as public support faded, so too did his success with Congress. Likewise, the Watergate revelations eroded Richard Nixon's popular support after his landslide reelection in 1972, thereby sapping his political strength and support for his policy initiatives in Congress.

A remarkable jump in the polls early in Ronald Reagan's first term had an important impact on the passage of his economic program. After the first three months of Reagan's presidency, his public standing according to the polls was about two to one in his favor. Then on March 30, 1981, John Hinckley attempted to assassinate the president. Reagan was hit with a single bullet, but he recovered. According to White House assistant Richard Beal, this incident helped endear the president to the public. "His personal attributes might never have come across without the assassination attempt."[113] Because people admired Reagan's courage, calmness, and humor, his standing in the polls shot up to a three-to-one favorable rating after the assassination attempt. When Reagan's aides then met to decide how best to capitalize on this new reservoir of good feeling, they concluded that enactment of Reagan's economic program should receive priority. Thus, the president's first public speech after the assassination attempt dealt with that subject. *(See Presidential Approval Ratings, Gallup Poll, Truman to Reagan, p. 1465, in the Appendix.)*

A president's standing in the eyes of the public is at its greatest immediately after the presidential election. As a result, presidential resources and opportunities are most plentiful then. Unfortunately, administrations often lack the experience and skills necessary to take full advantage of this so-called honeymoon period. Later in the term, when the requisite skills and experience are on hand, the president invariably stands lower in the polls and thus possesses less of a mandate to act. Presidents thus are best off trying early in the term to enact important programs if they are to realize any benefit from their popularity.[114]

Who Formulates Legislation?

Many scholars have studied the question of who bears the primary responsibility for the formulation and initiation of legislation, and many have argued that the Congress has not received the credit that it deserves. Although Congress waits on the president's annual legislative program, a large number of the ideas and suggestions found in the president's program may in fact come from Congress or elsewhere, such as private-interest groups.

In the first important study of legislative initiative, Lawrence Chamberlain examined ninety major pieces of legislation passed by Congress from 1870 to 1940. According to his results, published in 1946, presidential influence predominated in nineteen cases; congressional influence in thirty-five cases; joint influence in twenty-nine cases; and pressure group influence in seven cases. The study's principal conclusion was that it is "not that the president is less important than generally supposed, but that Congress is more important."[115]

A follow-up study by William Goldsmith applied similar methods to sixty-three major pieces of legislation enacted into law from 1945 to 1964. This study concluded

Table 8 Responsibility for Passage of Major Legislative Proposals

	President		Congress		Joint		Pressure group		Total	
1870-1910	17%	(5)	53%	(16)	20%	(6)	10%	(3)	100%	(30)
1911-1930	12	(4)	48	(16)	27	(9)	12	(4)	99	(33)
1931-1940	37	(10)	11	(3)	52	(14)	0	—	100	(27)
1945-1954	33	(12)	17	(6)	44	(16)	6	(2)	100	(36)
1955-1964	56	(15)	4	(1)	41	(11)	0	—	100	(27)

Source: Robert J. Spitzer, *The Presidency and Public Policy* (University, Ala.: University of Alabama Press, 1983), 92. Reprinted by permission of the publisher.

Note: Variations from 100 percent are due to rounding error. Data taken and readjusted from Lawrence Chamberlain, "The President, Congress, and Legislation," in *The President: Roles and Powers,* ed. David Haight and Larry Johnson (Chicago: Rand McNally, 1965), 301-303, and William Goldsmith, *The Growth of Presidential Power* (New York: Chelsea House, 1974), 3: 1398-1399. Goldsmith claimed to use the same evaluation standards and techniques as Chamberlain. Data from 1870 to 1940 are from the Chamberlain study. Data from 1945 to 1964 are from the Goldsmith study.

that "the President has indeed become a major partner in the legislative process, and . . . very little significant legislation is now passed that either does not emanate from the Executive branch, or is not significantly influenced by executive action at some stage of its legislative history." [116] Another analyst, writing at the height of the Johnson era, concluded: "The President now determines the legislative agenda of Congress almost as thoroughly as the British Cabinet sets the legislative agenda of Parliament." [117]

These conclusions have been challenged by several investigators who have argued that the role of Congress has been undervalued. For example, one study of the period 1940-1967 revealed many areas in which the Congress played a decisive role, including the economy, transportation, agriculture, urban policy, and technology. It concluded that "Congress continues to be an active innovator and very much in the legislative business." [118] Other studies have explored as well what many observers view as Congress's undervalued role in legislative initiation and enactment.[119]

These apparent contradictions can be resolved by recognizing several facts. First, it is often impossible to identify the original source of legislation. And even if it is possible, credit is frequently shared. For example, many of the Great Society initiatives enacted during Lyndon Johnson's presidency actually were adapted from proposals formulated in the 1950s by Democratic members of Congress, who deserve recognition for their initial work. Likewise, President Johnson deserves credit for putting the weight of the presidency behind these proposals and seeing them through to enactment. President Kennedy received credit for enacting the Area Redevelopment Act of 1961, even though several Democratic senators advanced the idea in the late 1950s, when it was successfully blocked by President Eisenhower.

Second, studies such as those just mentioned often are inspired by reactions to the prevailing wisdom shaped by contemporary politics. The Roosevelt and Johnson eras, for example, were periods of relative presidential dominance. But Congress played a more assertive role during the Eisenhower presidency and even more so during the 1970s. Studies with the mid-1960s as their endpoint would almost certainly come to a different conclusion about presidential-congressional relations than studies completed during the mid-1970s, for example.

Third, a reordering of data from different studies often uncovers greater consistencies. For example, when the data from the Chamberlain and Goldsmith studies are reordered, they illustrate that, over time, the president's influence has increased progressively, while that of Congress has declined progressively; joint responsibility is also on the rise. *(See Table 8.)*

Measures of Presidential Success

Factors related to the president's success in dealing with Congress include political party, the kind of policy (for example, domestic or foreign) being addressed by legislation, and term cycle. Personal leadership skills play a role in all of these factors.

Several scores have been used to measure the president's track record in Congress. One such measure is the presidential Boxscore, or success score. From 1954-1975, Congressional Quarterly kept track of proposals that composed the president's annual legislative program (excluding proposals emanating from the executive branch but not specifically endorsed by the president, and those endorsed by the president but not specifically included in the White House program). While the Boxscore provided a ready means for comparing numbers of proposals and their rates of success, it also had its limitations. For example, it did not take into account the relative importance of bills. It included a large number of foreign policy proposals, where the president was more likely to gain congressional approval. It did not indicate which were measures favored by the president but were not included in the formal proposal list because of overwhelming congressional opposition. And it did not take into account measures included solely because the president anticipated that they would be enacted anyway.[120]

Despite these limitations the Boxscore has provided a source of information for those interested in comparing the track records of presidents, variations in their success rates, and the kinds of proposals that presidents have selected for inclusion in their legislative menus. Problems with use of the data arise when the summary percentages are used as the sole indicators of a president's success.

Another measure kept by Congressional Quarterly is presidential support scores. Collected annually since 1953, this measure summarizes all public statements and messages of the president to determine the president's position on pending roll call votes in the House and Senate. These votes may or may not involve presidential proposals. Although support scores indicate how often Congress sup-

Table 9 Presidential Victories on Key Votes, 1957-1978

President	Years	Domestic issues N	% Victories		Foreign and defense issues N	% Victories	
Eisenhower	1957-1960	51	.608	.732	17	.824	.736
Kennedy	1961-1963	47	.702		16	.688	
Johnson	1964-1966	95	.853		17	.647	
Nixon	1969-1972	46	.652		18	.778	
Nixon	1973-1974	20	.500	.565	7	.429	.600
Ford	1974-1976	27	.593		13	.385	
Carter	1977-1978	22	.591		10	1.000	
		President's party only					
Eisenhower	1957-1960	51	.863	.879	17	.882	.853
Kennedy	1961-1962	47	.830		16	.983	
Johnson	1964-1968	95	.926		17	.824	
Nixon	1969-1972	46	.848		18	.833	
Nixon	1973-1974	20	.950	.884	7	1.000	.767
Ford	1974-1976	27	.852		13	.692	
Carter	1977-1978	22	.864		10	.700	
		Opposition party only					
Eisenhower	1957-1960	51	.412	.293	17	.588	.382
Kennedy	1961-1963	47	.128		16	.250	
Johnson	1964-1968	95	.337		17	.412	
Nixon	1969-1972	46	.239		18	.278	
Nixon	1973-1974	20	.300	.217	7	.000	.167
Ford	1974-1976	27	.185		13	.154	
Carter	1977-1978	22	.182		10	.300	

Source: Lee Sigelman, "A Reassessment of the 'Two Presidencies' Thesis," *Journal of Politics* 51, no. 4 (November 1979): 1201. Copyright © 1979 by the Southern Political Association. Reprinted by permission of the author and the University of Texas Press.

ports the president's position, this measure has its limitations. It disregards the reasons for the president's positions on legislation, and it does not indicate which measures are more important to the president. Support scores provide a basis for comparison, however. *(See Presidential Support in Congress, 1953-1988, p. 1475, in Appendix.)*

Presidential support scores are higher than their respective boxscores. Support scores also are usually highest at the start of a presidential term, especially during the honeymoon period.

A third measure utilized by Congressional Quarterly is key votes, pivotal issues of great importance to Congress and the president. To be judged a key vote, a roll call vote must involve a major controversy or constitute an important test of political power or a decision that will have a great impact on the country. Such criteria weed out less important legislative efforts and reveal the priorities and interests of both branches when the political stakes are high.

One important study of key votes found that presidents fared well on key votes from 1957 to 1972, but not as well from 1973 to 1978. Dividing support on key votes by party, the study reported that support from the president's party in Congress remained about the same from 1957 to 1973. After 1973, however, a major drop in support occurred among opposition party members, especially in foreign policy matters.[121] *(See Table 9.)*

Key votes do not focus solely on issues of concern to the president, but, not surprisingly, the president takes a position on most such votes. The usefulness of this measure is limited by the relatively small number of bills that are included in the key votes score each year. In 1957, for example, only five House and five Senate roll call votes (for which individual member votes are recorded) were included, while in 1965, during the height of the Johnson administration, eighteen roll call votes from each chamber were included.

Finally, the number of presidential vetoes and the record for sustaining vetoes sometimes are used as a measure of presidential success. Although veto scores are readily available, by themselves these scores say little about presidential rates of success. The veto is an indisputably important power, but as an aggregate measure it reveals little because of the circumstances under which it is applied and its relatively rare use by most presidents.

The measures of presidential success just described support the proposition that presidents do better when their political party maintains control of Congress. *(See Table 10.)* Thus, virtually all presidents and presidential candidates have devoted political efforts and resources to this end. Like Ronald Reagan, however, some presidents have logged important successes in Congress despite their lack of political party control.

Political scientist George C. Edwards III has concluded that members of the president's party in Congress find that their political future usually is related to that of the president. Thus, when the president's public standing and popularity are high, legislators from the same party face

Table 10 Seats, Votes, and the President's Party in House Elections, 1948-1984

			Seats gained or lost (president's party)[b]		House Democratic vote	
Year	President's party[a]	House seats held (Democratic)	Presidential year	Off year	% Two-party vote	Deviation from the average vote[c] (% points)
1948	Democratic	263	+75		53.2	0.3 R
1950		234		−29	50.0	3.5 R
1952	Republican	211	+22		49.9	3.6 R
1954		232		−18	52.5	1.0 R
1956	Republican	233	−3		51.0	2.5 R
1958		284		−47	56.0	2.5 D
1960	Democratic	263	−21		54.8	1.3 D
1962		258		−5	52.5	1.0 R
1964	Democratic	295	+37		57.3	3.8 D
1966		247		−48	51.3	2.2 R
1968	Republican	243	+5		50.9	2.6 R
1970		254		−12	54.4	0.9 D
1972	Republican	239	+12		52.7	0.8 R
1974		291		−48	58.5	5.0 D
1976	Democratic	292	+1		56.9	3.4 D
1978		276		−16	54.4	0.9 D
1980	Republican	243	+33		51.4	2.1 R
1982		269		−26	56.2	2.7 D
1984	Republican	252	+17		52.9	0.6 R
1948-1984		Mean = 257 seats s = 2.3			Mean = 53.5% s = 2.6	

Source: Democratic seats held are taken from U.S. Bureau of the Census, *Statistical Abstract of the United States* (Washington, D.C.: Government Printing Office, 1979), 507, and the *Statistical Abstract* for 1986, 245. The calculations of seats gained and lost for each party are taken from the same source. The nationwide House vote is supplied by Clerk of the House of Representatives, *Statistics of the Presidential and Congressional Election,* biennial reports, 1948-1984. Cited in Barbara Hinckley, *Stability and Change in Congress* (New York: Harper and Row, 1988), 65.

a. In presidential year elections the president's party is the party of the winning presidential candidate.

b. Because some Congresses will have one or two independents, the number of seats gained or lost for one party will not always equal exactly the number of seats gained or lost for the other.

c. Based on the average vote for 1948-1984 of 53.5 percent Democratic. R and D indicate the party favored by the deviation.

a better chance at reelection and also stand to benefit from presidential favors. Moreover, members of the president's political party feel a sense of personal loyalty to the president, which often transcends ideological or other differences.[122]

Another important factor related to the president's success in dealing with Congress is the kind of policy being addressed by legislation. Studies have demonstrated that presidents have greater success in obtaining passage of foreign policy proposals, for example, than domestic policy proposals, although this trend has varied over time. (For example, Congress challenged presidential foreign policy initiatives more in the 1970s than it had in the past.)

Different kinds of domestic policies also yield various political configurations and thus various political outcomes. Analyst Steven A. Shull has noted that "variations in the content of policies . . . produce variations in the roles and behavior of actors." [123] Several studies have concluded that different policies—such as those dealing with social benefits, civil rights, government management, and agriculture—have different political patterns.[124]

A leading student of policy making, Theodore J. Lowi, has proposed reversing the usual analysis of policy making in Congress and elsewhere. Most examinations of policy making focus on how political relationships affect policies produced by the political system. Lowi proposed instead examining how different kinds of policies affect politics.[125] He then described four kinds of policies—constituent, redistributive, distributive, and regulatory—each of which produces its own unique political pattern.

A study by another analyst applied these four policy types to the presidency, arguing that the kind of policy that presidents proposed to Congress determined the political configuration that ensued, resulting in "four presidencies." The "administrative president" prevails when the president proposes constituent policies related to the running of the government, including those pertaining to government reorganization, election laws, and budgeting. As chief executive the president is perceived as having great authority over such administrative, overhead matters. Thus, the president has the greatest success in dealing with Congress when advancing constituent policy legislation. For the president, this area is less politically rewarding than other policy areas, however, because constituent policies usually attract little attention or interest in the country.

The "public-interest president" results from presidential concern with redistributive policies, which are broad in scope, affecting large groups of people. Examples include social security, welfare, and the progressive income tax. Given the nationwide scope of redistributive policies, Congress looks for presidential leadership in this area. The resulting politics may be contentious, but presidents usually have success in this area. As opposed to constituent policies, the redistributive policies, which are wider in scope and of greater interest to Congress and the country, present presidents with more obstacles. Yet presidents continue to take a strong interest in redistributive policies, which often represent a litmus test of presidential leadership.

The "special-interest president" emerges when the president proposes distributive policies. These policies, which are narrow in scope and purpose, are often labeled patronage or pork barrel policies. Although presidents can exert political influence when proposing these policies to Congress, they must pay careful attention to congressional preferences. Distributive policies—such as construction projects and rivers and harbors legislation—directly affect the economies of the localities where they are targeted, and members of Congress are keenly interested in such projects when they are associated with their districts. Thus, presidents challenging congressional preferences in this area are likely to face a fierce struggle.

Presidents assume a "presidential broker" role when dealing with regulatory policies. These policies affect the formation and enforcement of laws that manipulate economic and social conduct, usually through use of sanctions and penalties. Common examples include regulations on unfair competition, elimination of substandard goods, gun control, and antitrust legislation. Although presidents frequently try to take the lead in this area, they often are frustrated and unsuccessful. By their nature, regulatory policies arouse deep passions in those doing the regulating and those being regulated. Thus, even presidents at the peak of their power (such as Lyndon Johnson after his election in 1964) often find that enactment of such proposals in Congress is extremely difficult. *(See Figure 1.)*

This study of presidential policy making in Congress concluded that presidents have faced comparable political problems in dealing with Congress, according to the kind of policy being proposed. This pattern has held true despite differences in the president's party affiliation, reputed leadership skills, or party support in Congress.[126]

Another factor related to a president's success with Congress is the presidential term cycle. Political scientist Richard E. Neustadt has observed a rhythmic cycle in the presidential term. The first eighteen months usually are devoted to learning the job, establishing routines, and setting patterns with Congress, while the fourth year is a "period of pause," dominated by concern with reelection. By the seventh year national attention is beginning to focus on the president's successor. According to Neustadt, the key years are the third, fifth, and sixth.[127]

A study of presidencies of the 1960s and 1970s concluded that presidential success hinged on two conflicting cycles—one of decreasing influence and one of increasing effectiveness. Presidential resources—and thus influence—are greatest immediately after election or reelection (although the second term holds less potential than the first), when presidents and their staffs possess the least experience and skill. They are therefore in a poor position to exploit their maximal influence. As the term progresses, the administration acquires more experience and skill but loses resources. The capacity for effectiveness then increases, but diminished resources means that success is less likely. Not surprisingly, this paradoxical pattern has been labeled the "No-Win Presidency." According to White House aides, minimizing the no-win problem and maximizing the president's success hinge on a large electoral margin, a high rate of public approval, and presidential party control of Congress.[128]

Forces Promoting Conflict and Cooperation

Structural factors do much to explain the interrelationship between the president and Congress. The impact of these factors is tempered, however, by informal political habits and traditions.

Organization of Congress

The structure and hierarchy of the authority of Congress are related directly to the president's association with the nation's lawmakers. When in the past congressional authority has been concentrated in the hands of a few strong leaders, presidents usually have won congressional support by earning the support of those leaders. Theodore Roosevelt, for example, chalked up important legislative successes because of his close ties to House Speaker Joseph G. Cannon (R-Ill.). Cannon's tenure as Speaker represented an apex of strong congressional leadership.

Since the early 1900s, however, power in Congress has become much more decentralized. Presidents seeking congressional support must now curry favor not only with party and chamber leaders, but also with committee and subcommittee chairs, regional leaders, and spokespersons for particular interests. When President Carter proposed his comprehensive energy program in 1977, no fewer than thirty congressional committees and subcommittees

Figure 1 Arenas of Power Applied to Presidential Policy Making

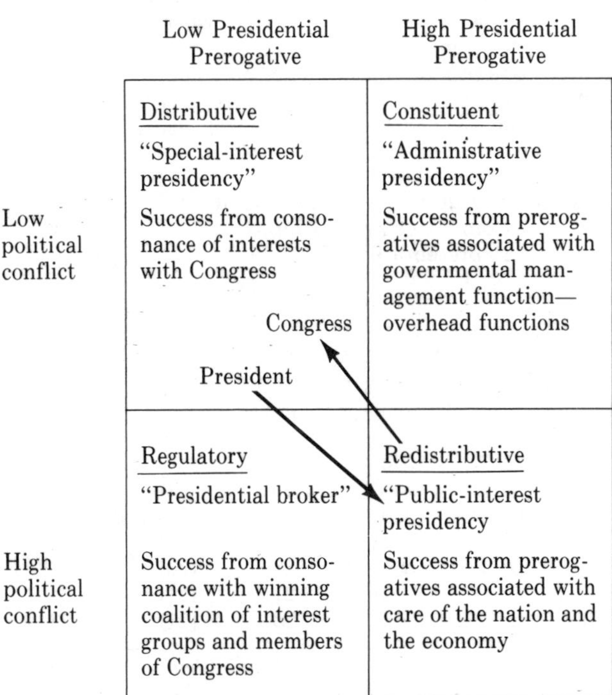

Source: Robert J. Spitzer, *The Presidency and Public Policy* (University, Ala.: University of Alabama Press, 1983), 152. Reprinted by permission of the publisher.

claimed jurisdiction over some portion of the program. In addition, House Speaker Thomas P. (Tip) O'Neill, Jr. (D-Mass.) set up a special ad hoc committee to oversee and coordinate the many facets of the energy legislation.

In short, presidents must be prepared to work within existing channels of congressional authority if they are to be successful. And they must be sensitive to the importance of seniority, the committee and subcommittee system, the role of chamber leaders, and other factors that affect the distribution of power in the legislative branch.

Seniority

Although it is only a custom, seniority has been the principal means of selecting leaders of standing committees and resolving other power-related matters in both houses of Congress. In the seniority system, length of continuous service is rewarded with enhanced power and perquisites within the institution. Length of service in Congress is congressional seniority; length of service on a committee is committee seniority.

Prior to the twentieth century seniority was only one of several criteria used to determine committee leadership positions. But in the latter part of the nineteenth century, as legislation became more complex and the average length of congressional careers increased, reliance on the principle of seniority increased as well (although it came to the House more slowly than to the Senate, where terms were longer and experience was more venerated). In this century the norm of seniority has been violated only occasionally, and then under extraordinary circumstances.[129]

Seniority is the basis for determining influence on congressional committees. The committee chair is typically the most senior member of the majority party, which holds numerical majorities on all committees. The most senior member of the minority party on each committee, known as the ranking minority member, is also accorded some deference for continuous years of committee service. In addition to access to and influence on committees, seniority affects the assignment of office space, access to congressional patronage, and the respect of colleagues.

Table 11 Southern Democratic Membership and Committee Leadership, House of Representatives, 1967-1979

	Southern members (% of all House Democrats)		Southern leaders (% of all chairs)	
Year and Congress	*N* all Democrats	% Southern	*N* all chairs	% Southern
1967 (90th)	(248)	33	(20)	45
1969 (91st)	(243)	33	(21)	38
1971 (92d)	(255)	31	(21)	38
1973 (93d)	(248)	30	(21)	38
1975 (94th)[a]	(291)	28	(20)	50[b]
1977 (95th)	(292)	27	(21)	24
1979 (96th)	(276)	28	(21)	24

Source: Barbara Hinckley, *Stability and Change in Congress* (New York: Harper and Row, 1988), 130.

a. Excludes standing committees newly created for the Ninety-fourth Congress: Budget and Small Business.

b. According to the strict operation of seniority. After the challenges the figure is 35 percent.

Party leaders in both houses are not selected according to seniority, but lengthy service in Congress is generally a necessary perquisite for service as chamber leader. For example, one of the most respected House leaders of the twentieth century was Sam Rayburn. A Democrat from Texas, Rayburn served in the House for twenty-four years before becoming majority leader in 1937. He became Speaker of the House in 1940 and served in that position until his death in 1961. Democrat Tip O'Neill of Massachusetts was elected House majority leader in 1973 after twenty years of service, and he served as Speaker from 1977 until his retirement in 1986.

Because the principle of seniority rewards length of continuous service, it has tended to empower representatives elected from "safe" constituencies—that is, districts or states that reelect their representatives by consistently high percentages. Most often, these have been more conservative, one-party regions. For example, the South was almost entirely Democratic for many years, and southern conservative Democrats controlled many important committee leadership positions from the 1950s to the 1970s. Rural areas in the Midwest and Far West have been Republican strongholds for many years, as have large urban areas for the Democrats.[130] *(See Table 11.)*

Committee System

Congressional committees constitute the heart of Congress. In committees, policy is formulated, reputations are made, and power is wielded. Woodrow Wilson wrote in 1886 that "Congress in session in its Committee rooms is Congress at work." [131]

The importance of committees is seen partly in their workload. Virtually all bills introduced in Congress are referred to one or more committees. During the Ninety-ninth Congress (1985-1986), 7,522 measures were introduced in the House and 4,080 in the Senate. Of these, 664 bills were enacted into law; most of the rest died in committee. In the 100th Congress (1987-1988), the House maintained 22 regular standing committees and 132 subcommittees, while the Senate had 16 standing committees and 85 subcommittees. According to Democratic party caucus rules, in the House no member can chair more than one subcommittee. The Senate also imposes restrictions on chairing multiple committees. As a result, most members of Congress, including very junior members, have the opportunity to wield added power as a chair. Various special, select, and joint committees are engaged in important work as well. *(See Table 12.)*

The average senator sits on ten committees or subcommittees, while the average House member serves on seven. In 1987 Senate committees employed about one thousand staff members, while House committees had a staff of two thousand.

Committees are also recognized for their members' expertise. Deference to committee recommendations reflects the respect accorded committee actions by the full House and Senate.

A committee's work begins by examining its assigned legislation. According to House procedural guidelines, committees "are not infallible, but they have had long familiarity with the subject under discussion, and have made an intimate study of the particular bill before the House and after mature deliberation have made formal recommendations and, other considerations being equal, are entitled to support on the floor." [132]

Table 12 Standing Committees of the 100th Congress, 1987

House committee	Number of subcommittees	Senate committee	Number of subcommittees
Agriculture	8	Agriculture, Nutrition, Forestry	7
Appropriations	13	Appropriations	13
Armed Services	7	Armed Services	6
Banking, Finance, Urban Affairs	8	Banking, Housing, Urban Affairs	4
Budget	0	Budget	0
District of Columbia	3	Commerce, Science, Transportation	8
Education and Labor	8	Energy and Natural Resources	5
Energy and Commerce	6	Environment and Public Works	5
Foreign Affairs	8	Finance	7
Government Operations	7	Foreign Relations	7
House Administration	6	Governmental Affairs	5
Interior and Insular Affairs	6	Judiciary	6
Judiciary	7	Labor and Human Resources	6
Merchant Marine and Fisheries	6	Rules and Administration	0
Post Office and Civil Service	7	Small Business	6
Public Works and Transportation	6	Veterans' Affairs	0
Rules	2		
Science, Space and Technology	7		
Small Business	6		
Standards of Official Conduct	0		
Veterans' Affairs	5		
Ways and Means	6		
Total, 22	132	Total, 16	85

Source: Politics in America: The 100th Congress (Washington, D.C.: Congressional Quarterly Inc., 1987).

After committees receive a bill they may hold hearings to solicit the opinions of government leaders and private interests on the merits of the legislation. This can be done in either the committee or an appropriate subcommittee, or in both. With a positive committee recommendation, the bill is sent to the full chamber for consideration and vote. Expertise, specialization, and experience, then, are the hallmarks of committee work and the foundation for deference to committee and subcommittee actions. Members of Congress who attempt to circumvent the judgment of a committee may find their own pet legislation subject to challenge by others.[133]

All this being said, deference to committees has undergone some change since the 1970s. Committee actions are more likely to be challenged on the floor as members develop expertise on selected issues, as the norm of deference declines, and as greater decentralization takes hold. This move away from traditional committee ascendance is seen partly in challenges to committee leadership.

In the 1970s an influx of new members of Congress prompted a move to grant junior members more influence. In addition, the autonomy of subcommittees was increased, which had the effect of limiting the power of the committee chair.[134] Previously, committee chairs had had the power to name subcommittee chairs, create or abolish subcommittees, call committee meetings, and hire staff. Some committee chairs abused their power, however, by refusing to convene a committee meeting as a means of blocking favored legislation, for example. Most were more circumspect in the use of their powers, and paid careful attention to building a coalition within their committees. Still, the clamor for reform grew. This movement peaked in 1975, when three sitting House Democratic committee chairmen were deposed by the Democratic Caucus—Wright Patman (Texas) from the Banking and Currency Committee, W. R. Poage (Texas) from the Agriculture Committee, and F. Edward Hebert (La.) from the Armed Services Committee. Although seniority was violated in these three cases, it was observed in seventeen others.[135]

After 1975 seniority was observed in every instance until 1985, when the sitting chair of the Armed Services Committee, C. Melvin Price (D-Ill.), was deposed by seventh-ranked Democrat Les Aspin (Wis.). Price was eighty years old at the time, and he had not provided the committee with strong leadership.[136] Although Aspin had begun his career as a maverick liberal on the Armed Services Committee, he had earned the respect of both liberals and conservatives, and he moved quickly to soothe relations among committee members after his election.

Subcommittees

Many committees, such as the House Agriculture and Appropriations committees, have long relied on subcommittees to handle most of the important work. Subcommittees hold the initial hearings and make the first recommendations on bills. Congress relies on the specialization and division of labor represented by subcommittees in dealing with the overwhelming amount of work that it faces annually.

Subcommittees gained a greater role in the 1970s with the adoption of the so-called subcommittee bill of rights. Approved in 1973, this agreement ensured that subcommittees would have clearly defined jurisdictions, could meet with or without the approval of the committee chair, and would have their own budget and staff. Moreover, committee members could choose at least one subcommittee assignment.

Seniority is also the principal basis for determining subcommittee leadership positions, although it is violated more frequently than for committee leadership selection. From 1959 to 1981 about 5 percent of all subcommittee chairs owed their positions to violations of seniority. This percentage remained constant both before and after the changes of the 1970s.[137]

The number of subcommittees has grown, and their workload has increased as well. In the 1950s subcommittees held about 30 percent of all hearings. By the late 1970s this figure had increased to over 90 percent. Their impact was and is felt in committee work, as well as on the chamber floor, where the extension of specialization and decentralization are reflected in the key influence often exerted by subcommittee chairs acting as legislative shepherds. The greater role of subcommittees also has meant that they have generated even more business (hearings, press conferences, etc.) in Congress.[138]

Leaders

Since the post-Civil War period, when the modern two-party system was established in Congress, congressional leadership has been based on partisan divisions. Although members of Congress are elected as representatives of a small geographic region, they also are elected as Republicans or Democrats. The party that holds the numerical majority in each house uses that majority to select chamber leaders.

In the House the chief chamber leader is the Speaker, who also serves as the leader of the majority party. Each party then has its majority and minority floor leaders (depending on which party holds a numerical majority) and majority and minority assistant floor leaders, called whips. *(See Table 13.)*

The Senate has no position comparable to that of the House Speaker. As specified in the Constitution, the U.S. vice president serves as president of the Senate, but this position is ceremonial, and the vice president participates only to cast a tie-breaking vote. The next highest officer is the president pro tempore, also a ceremonial position, which is awarded to the most senior member of the Senate. The most important Senate leaders are the majority and minority floor leaders, followed by the majority and minority whips.

While the committee system is a source of decentralization in Congress, congressional leaders work to provide centralization, coherence, and a measure of party discipline to their chambers. The principal job of the leaders is to rally support for, or opposition to, partisan programs. To do this, they negotiate with committee leaders, resolve jurisdictional disputes between committees, schedule floor action for bills, use rules and procedures to best advantage, and gather support for important votes. Unlike some of their predecessors, modern congressional leaders have limited resources at their disposal. Nevertheless, they can employ persuasion, use bill scheduling authority to reward or punish, influence committee assignments, appoint special committees, direct campaign contributions toward or away from members, and use White House contacts to exert pressure.

Leadership in the modern Congress is problematic compared to leadership patterns of the past. In the Senate of the 1950s, for example, Majority Leader Lyndon Johnson held more personal authority than his successors in the 1970s and 1980s. A few senior, mostly southern leaders prevailed in the Senate during Johnson's tenure; thus, he could advance his goals by dealing with a smaller number of individuals. Decision making itself was more centralized, since fewer committees existed. Staff resources were controlled by a few senior members, the Senate workload was smaller than in later years, its junior members were far less independent-minded than contemporary junior senators, and the institution employed more closed, secretive decision making.[139]

Table 13 Speakers of the House, 1899-1989

Speaker	Dates of service as Speaker	Years of service	Years in House before election as Speaker
David B. Henderson (R-Iowa)	1899-1903	4	16
Joseph G. Cannon (R-Ill.)	1903-1911	8	28
Champ Clark (D-Mo.)	1911-1919	8	16
Frederick H. Gillett (R-Mass.)	1919-1925	6	26
Nicholas Longworth (R-Ohio)	1925-1931	6	20
John N. Garner (D-Texas)	1931-1933	2	28
Henry T. Rainey (D-Ill.)	1933-1934	1	28
Joseph W. Byrns (D-Tenn.)	1935-1936	1	26
William B. Bankhead (D-Ala.)	1936-1940	4	19
Sam Rayburn (D-Texas)	1940-1947, 1949-1953, 1955-1961	17	27
Joseph W. Martin, Jr. (R-Mass.)	1947-1949, 1953-1955	4	22
John W. McCormack (D-Mass.)	1962-1971	9	34
Carl Albert (D-Okla.)	1971-1977	6	24
Thomas P. O'Neill, Jr. (D-Mass.)	1977-1987	10	24
James C. Wright, Jr. (D-Texas)	1987-		32
Average		5.7	24.7

Source: Roger H. Davidson and Walter J. Oleszek, *Congress and Its Members* (Washington, D.C.: CQ Press, 1985), 175.

Note: The House was technically without a Speaker for short periods following the deaths of Rainey and Rayburn. Congress had adjourned, and their successors were not elected until the next Congress convened.

Informal Caucuses

In addition to the fragmenting effects of the committee system, leaders must contend with a vast array of informal caucuses, groups, alliances, cliques, and coalitions that serve to unify like-minded congressional groups. Each party in each chamber has its own party caucus, incorporating a number of particular policy- and issue-related concerns. The House Democratic party caucus also was used to institute many of the reforms of the 1970s. The Boll Weevils, an important party caucus of the 1950s and 1960s composed of conservative southern Democrats, were energized during the 1980s, when they provided President Reagan with key support for his conservative agenda.

Of the other unofficial congressional groups (technically called "legislative service organizations") formed in recent years, some are active and influential, while others are paper organizations that exist mostly to attract favorable public attention. Some state caucuses, composed of representatives from the larger states, have been influential in promoting state and regional concerns.

Various private interests also have encouraged the establishment of congressional caucuses. The American Mushroom Institute, for example, inspired the creation of the Mushroom Caucus in 1977 to protect mushroom producers from foreign competition. And a variety of ethnic groups have promoted ethnic caucuses in Congress. Among the best known and most influential are the black, women's, and Hispanic caucuses. *(See Table 14.)*

Regional and economic interests have prompted the formation of caucuses as well. Representatives of the northeastern states, for example, formed a "Frost Belt" coalition to stem what they believed to be a flow of resources from the Northeast to the Sunbelt states. The Steel Caucus was formed to promote steel-related economic interests.

Assessments of the impact of these groups are divided. Without question, some caucuses have been influential in the passage of important legislation. Some observers view the groups as a positive basis around which like-minded legislators can organize to promote legitimate interests. Critics complain that these caucuses simply add to the list of parochial interests that must be satisfied to transact important business. As House Speaker Tip O'Neill observed, the "House has over-caucused itself." [140]

Consequences

The sum total of these organizational characteristics points to an institution where centrifugal forces predominate, despite the best efforts of chamber leaders. This situation invites presidential leadership in the legislative sphere. As Randall Ripley, an expert on Congress, has observed, "The principal centralizing factor in the legislative equation remains outside Congress in the form of the president and the institutional presidency." [141]

Presidents seeking to establish a positive working relationship with Congress turn first to their party leaders in Congress. This helps strengthen the hand of the president, since it demonstrates respect for the opinions of chamber leaders. Likewise, it helps chamber leaders, as it allows them to represent themselves to the rest of the chamber as a presidential conduit. In addition, presidents must show sensitivity toward important subgovernment leaders, including committee chairs, caucus leaders, and influential private interests. President Reagan, for example, launched a multipronged effort in 1981 to win congressional approval of his controversial economic program. He persuaded several governors to hold meetings with undecided legislators; he contacted Boll Weevil Democrats to line up their support; he sent aides into key local districts to rally public pressure on behalf of the program; and he made a nationwide television appeal to bolster support. The end result was enactment of the program.[142] Presidential success turns on the president's recognition that Congress incorporates numerous decision points. A lack of support at any point can mean the end of a presidential initiative.

Partisan Balance

According to an oft-stated aphorism, the most important single factor accounting for congressional voting patterns is political party affiliation. It is evident, however, that other factors also affect congressional voting, including region, ideology, and peer influence. Students of Congress typically examine roll call votes when studying the impact of political party and other factors, as most important votes are conducted by roll call. Such studies have found that political party voting—those votes in which a majority of one party opposes a majority of the other party—has declined during the twentieth century. Early in the century about two-thirds of all roll call votes were party votes. By the post-World War II period, however, that proportion had fallen to about 50 percent, and then to 40 percent during the 1970s. In contrast, from the 1960s to the 1980s Republicans and Democrats from both houses supported their parties about 70 percent of the time. Admittedly, these apparently strong partisan trends may mask other factors such as region, ideology, or leadership pressure.[143] *(See Table 15.)*

The presence of party voting also is evident in the interest group ratings of congressional voting records undertaken to observe support for liberal, conservative, and labor-related concerns, for example. Such ratings show that Democrats generally receive high scores from labor and liberal groups, whereas Republicans receive high scores from conservative groups.[144]

To the extent that party voting occurs in Congress, it is beneficial to the president when he or she belongs to the majority party. If this is not the case, the president must endeavor to split the majority party coalition and woo support for the minority party. But the president wins no guarantees of loyalty simply by belonging to the party controlling Congress. In 1978, for example, Democratic House Speaker Tip O'Neill and Majority Leader Robert Byrd both deserted President Carter by voting to override his veto of a major public works bill. Although the veto was upheld, many Democrats defended the public works program for the benefits it provided to local constituencies.

The limitations of party ties are illustrated even more clearly by the Johnson presidency. During the Eighty-ninth Congress (1965-1966), Johnson enjoyed a Democratic party advantage in the House of 295 Democrats to 140 Republicans (more than two to one). The legislative accomplishments of that Congress were prolific and well known, including major bills dealing with civil rights, education, and many other social programs. After the 1966 elections the Democrats lost 47 seats in the House, so that the partisan split was then 248 to 187. Although this was still a sizable favorable margin for Johnson and the Democrats, the president found it necessary to draw on liberal Republicans for support. On issues such as rent supplements, open housing, and poverty programs, Johnson lost his working majority, despite having a sixty-one-vote cushion within his own party.[145] And as noted earlier, Presidents Eisenhower and Reagan were able to achieve important successes despite the absence of majority support in one or both houses of Congress.

Table 14 Informal Congressional Groups, 1981

House of Representatives

Democratic
- Conservative Democratic Forum
- Democratic Research Organization
- Democratic Study Group
- New Members' Caucuses for 95th, 96th, and 97th Congresses
- United Democrats of Congress

Republican
- "Gypsy Moths"
- Republican Study Committee
- Republican Clubs for 95th, 96th, and 97th Congresses
- Wednesday Group

Bipartisan
- Ad hoc Congressional Committee for Irish Affairs
- Alcohol Fuels Caucus
- Auto Task Force
- Congressional Ad Hoc Monitoring Group on South Africa
- Congressional Arts Caucus
- Congressional Black Caucus
- Congressional Coal Caucus
- Congressional Port Caucus
- Congressional Shipbuilding Coalition
- Congresswomen's Caucus
- Domestic Energy Supply Coalition
- Export Task Force
- Fair Employment Practices Committee
- Federal Government Service Task Force
- Great Lakes Conference
- Hispanic Caucus
- Industrial Innovation Task Force
- Metropolitan Area Caucus
- Missing in Action Task Force
- Mushroom Caucus
- New England Congressional Caucus
- Northeast-Midwest Economic Advancement Coalition
- Rural Caucus
- Steel Caucus
- Suburban Caucus
- Sun Belt Caucus
- Textile Caucus

Senate

Democratic
- Midwest Conference of Democratic Senators
- Moderate/Conservative Democrats

Republican
- Republican Steering Committee
- Wednesday Club

Bipartisan
- Coal Caucus
- Concerned Senators for the Arts
- Copper Caucus
- Export Caucus
- Freshman Senators
- Northeast-Midwest Coalition
- Rail Caucus
- Steel Caucus
- Western State Coalition

Bicameral, Bipartisan

- Children's Lobby
- Coalition for Peace Through Strength
- Congressional Clearinghouse on the Future
- Environmental and Energy Study Conference
- Friends of Ireland
- High Altitude Coalition
- Jewelry Manufacturing Coalition
- Members of Congress for Peace Through Law
- North American Trade Caucus
- [Pentagon] Reform Caucus
- Pro-Life Caucus
- Solar Coalition
- Tourism Caucus
- Vietnam Era Veterans in Congress

Source: Adapted from Daniel P. Mulhollan, Susan Webb Hammond, and Arthur G. Stevens, Jr., "Informal Groups and Agenda Setting" (Paper delivered at the annual meeting of the Midwest Political Science Association, Cincinnati, Ohio, April 16-18, 1981). Cited in Roger H. Davidson and Walter J. Oleszek, *Congress and Its Members* (Washington, D.C.: CQ Press, 1981), 354.

Presidential Lobbyists

Although the president and the executive branch are now an institutionalized part of the law-making process, representatives of the executive branch engage in congressional lobbying, as do private interests.

Executive lobbying begins, but does not end, with the White House. Its legislative liaison office is relatively small. Under the Reagan administration, for example, it consisted of ten staff members—five who covered the House, four who covered the Senate, and liaison head Ken Duberstein. Extensive liaison work is conducted by the Office of Management and Budget, particularly its Office of Legislative Reference. The latter keeps track of all bills of interest to the executive, whether substantial or minor. In addition, each executive department devotes staff to legislative matters, since these agencies have a direct stake in policy and appropriation actions taken in Congress. The Department of Defense alone has over two hundred staff assigned to liaison work. And by at least one estimate the executive branch has as many as fifteen hundred employees assigned to liaison efforts. Both the White House and the OMB staff

Table 15 Congressional Voting in Support of the President's Position, 1964-1986 (percent)

President and year	House: All Democrats	House: Southern Democrats	House: Republicans	Senate: All Democrats	Senate: Southern Democrats	Senate: Republicans
Johnson						
1964	84	70	42	73	63	52
1965	83	65	46	75	60	55
1966	81	64	45	71	59	53
1967	80	65	51	73	69	63
1968	77	63	59	64	50	57
Nixon						
1969	56	55	65	55	56	74
1970	64	64	79	56	62	74
1971	53	69	79	48	59	76
1972	56	59	74	52	71	77
1973	39	49	67	42	55	70
1974	52	64	71	44	60	65
Ford						
1974	48	52	59	45	55	67
1975	40	48	67	53	67	76
1976	36	52	70	47	61	73
Carter						
1977	69	58	46	77	71	58
1978	67	54	40	74	61	47
1979	70	58	37	75	66	51
1980	71	63	44	71	69	50
Reagan						
1981	46	60	72	52	63	84
1982	43	55	70	46	57	77
1983	30	45	74	45	46	77
1984	37	47	64	45	58	81
1985	31	43	69	36	46	80
1986	26	37	69	39	56	90

Source: Norman J. Ornstein, Thomas E. Mann, and Michael J. Malbin, *Vital Statistics on Congress, 1987-1988* (Washington, D.C.: Congressional Quarterly Inc., 1988), 206-207.

Note: Percentages indicate number of congressional votes supporting the president divided by the total number on which the president had taken a position. The percentages are normalized to eliminate the effects of absences, as follows: support = (support)/(support + opposition).

coordinate departmental liaison activities.[146]

Much executive lobbying consists of routine information gathering. This task is important because it dovetails with the two-pronged nature of lobbying. Lobbyists, whether executive or otherwise, use information to press their case for or against legislation. But members of Congress also rely on lobbyists for information when they are still formulating their own views. Although lobbying by definition involves presenting a one-sided argument rather than a balanced view, lobbyists are experts whose opinions often are valued by sympathetic legislators. Executive lobbyists possess not only expertise, but also the added legitimacy of being part of the government.

Liaison officials must be sensitive to the preferences and leanings of key legislators. The Carter administration, for example, resisted the creation of tax credits designed to aid private and parochial schools. Yet when it encountered an influential legislator, such as a committee chair, who strongly favored such a program, the liaison staff labored to find some compromise or alternate program that might satisfy the chair.

The Carter administration also employed a procedure known as the troublesome bills process. Early in the legislative session OMB compiled a list of bills that were likely to encounter difficulty in Congress. The list then was reviewed regularly by OMB, the domestic policy staff, and liaison personnel to determine what positive steps might be taken to advance these bills. The maintenance of such a list also minimized the likelihood of unwelcome surprises.

Much of the executive lobbying effort is devoted to projecting the preferences of legislators on administration-favored bills. Both Carter and Reagan liaison staffs categorized legislators into those supporting the administration on given bills, those opposed, and those undecided. Executive lobbyists then concentrated on the undecided and those whose commitments were less than firm. The chief executive is often brought in at key moments to apply presidential prestige and personal skills to sway wavering legislators. In June 1981, for example, President Reagan contacted undecided legislators to marshal the support necessary to ensure enactment of his budget package. Even so early in Reagan's term, the liaison staff had little difficulty in identifying the key legislators.

Liaison staff do more than just lobby; they also engage

in policy making. When involved in face-to-face bargaining, liaison staff often must make promises and commitments that constitute policy agreements. For example, in a 1961 meeting with congressional leaders President Kennedy's liaison head, Lawrence O'Brien, found himself agreeing to a level and amount of coverage for the proposed new minimum wage without consulting the White House. Because such situations can arise, the liaison staff must be well informed and have the trust of the president.

Frequently, liaison staff are incorporated into other White House policy groups. Reagan's liaison chief, Ken Duberstein, for example, participated in morning senior White House staff meetings, cabinet council meetings, weekly luncheon meetings with the president, and meetings of the Legislative Strategy Group.

Liaison is often most effective when it does not directly involve the liaison staff. If liaison staff can succeed, for instance, in getting key decision makers together, a favorable and expeditious resolution may be more likely. Similarly, if a key member of Congress adopts and is willing to promote aggressively the president's position, the result is more likely to be favorable to the president. Acting as an institutional insider, a committee chair, for example, can deal effectively with his or her fellow chamber members. The Reagan administration found that House minority leader Robert H. Michel (R-Ill.) and minority whip C. Trent Lott (R-Miss.) were effective in gathering congressional support for key administration initiatives.

Personal presidential persuasion is a decisive lobbying force as well. President Carter disliked such personal lobbying, but he applied it well in a few instances, while Reagan's personal efforts often provided a needed nudge. In one instance, a bill dealing with standby petroleum allocations, championed by conservative Republican senator James A. McClure (Idaho) and opposed by the Reagan administration, passed both houses. The administration considered a veto, but it promised McClure that he could present his case for the bill to the president before the veto decision was made. After McClure did so, Reagan vetoed the bill on March 20, 1982. Both the Senate Republican leader and McClure were contacted after the veto by Reagan, who justified his action. On March 24 the Senate sustained the veto. Despite the defeat of a bill important to McClure, hard feelings were minimized by regular communication and presidential involvement.[147]

The President and the People

Abraham Lincoln once observed, "Public sentiment is everything. With public sentiment nothing can fail, without it nothing can succeed." History has confirmed this observation: Pesidents with a high popular standing are more successful in dealing with Congress than presidents with a low public standing.

Political scientist George C. Edwards III has proposed two explanations for the close connection between a president's popular standing and the willingness of Congress to support the president's program. One posits that legislators believe it is their job to reflect public opinion. When the president's public standing is high, members of Congress are inclined to follow public dictates by supporting the president because such support is in accordance with popular preferences. When the president's standing falls, Congress moves to reflect changing popular sentiments.

The second explanation ties congressional responses to legislators' own electoral fortunes. According to this view, members of Congress believe that their constituents will respond to congressional support for, or opposition to, presidential initiatives. They thus see a link between their own electoral fortunes and the president's popular standing. Members of Congress who oppose a popular president may risk losing support in their home districts. Similarly, opposition to an unpopular president may improve their standing back home.[148] The close electoral tie between the president and the Congress is reflected in the congressional seats gained by the president's party in every presidential election year from 1880 to 1984 except four. Conversely, from 1880 to 1986, the president's party lost seats in every midterm election, with one exception.

These two explanations correspond to those offered by an earlier study, which found that popular perceptions of the president overshadowed popular opinions of Congress, leading to a situation in which Congress was evaluated more positively when the president was regarded more positively, even if Congress was controlled by the opposition party. In short, "a large portion of the general public evaluates Congress by first assessing the President."[149] This finding is supported by the fact that citizens are better informed about, and more interested in, the presidency than in the Congress.

Regardless of the explanation for the connection between congressional support for the president and the president's public standing, the connection itself is well accepted. For the years 1953 to 1976, Edwards examined the connection between the president's popular standing (as measured in Gallup polls) and congressional support for presidential programs (as measured in roll call votes). He found a high correlation between the two, but he noted that members of the House were more likely to respond to fluctuations in the president's popularity than senators. This relationship also was found to be closely related to partisanship.[150]

Presidential Coattails

A successful presidential candidate who is sufficiently popular may aid other party members running for lower offices. When voters decide to vote for members of Congress partly on the basis of the popularity of the presidential candidate at the top of the ticket, the presidential candidate is said to possess coattails. Thus the popularity of a president or presidential candidate can have a direct, measurable impact on members of Congress.

The coattail phenomenon is often discussed, but it is also often misunderstood. Many people assume, for example, that the wider the margin of victory for a presidential candidate, the greater the candidate's pulling power. Many also assume that the coattail effect is present uniformly in every presidential election. Neither assumption is necessarily true. In 1972, for example, Richard Nixon was reelected president by one of the largest margins in the century—over 60 percent. Yet the Republican party picked up only twelve seats in the House and actually lost two seats in the Senate. Indeed, the Republicans might have done even worse had Nixon not done as well, but he demonstrated little in the way of coattails, especially when 1972 is compared with other presidential elections. In fact, in elections where the presidential candidate is struggling in a tight race, he may benefit from a reverse coattail effect—that is, the president may be helped by support for party candidates lower on the ballot.

In 1964, by way of contrast, President Johnson too was elected by a margin of over 60 percent. Yet the Democrats gained thirty-seven seats in the House and one in the Senate, enhancing the already sizable Democratic majority in Congress.

A related question is the size of the parties' majorities in Congress before the election. If one party holds a large congressional majority before an election and gains only modestly after the election, a far greater victory may have occurred than if the party holds a slim lead in Congress but makes the same modest numerical gain.

The coattail effect is important insofar as presidential candidates like to bring as many party allies as possible into Congress to ensure greater legislative success there. Members of Congress elected because of the popularity of the president also may feel a sense of gratitude, identity, and even obligation to the chief executive. A member of Congress who shares party affiliation with the president but feels no similar sense of attachment is more likely to behave independently of the president.

Adequate understanding of the coattail effect depends on understanding the motivations of voters as well as the information derived from vote statistics. The first of these is difficult to study, in part because it is extremely difficult to determine whether voters actually base their votes for lower offices on their choice for president. Although one cannot determine voter motivations from election results, this source of information can help explain the nature and impact of coattails.

One study examined the coattail effect on House races coinciding with presidential elections from 1952 to 1980. It concluded that seventy-six coattail victories occurred during the period (an average of 9.5 per election), ranging from a high of seventeen in Johnson's 1964 race to a low of four in Carter's 1976 election. Of the seventy-six victories, seventy-five involved races in which there was no incumbent. Clearly, a presidential candidate's best chance to benefit from the coattail effect occurs for open seats where the incumbent has either retired, resigned, or died. *(See Table 16.)*

Also according to this study, a president who wins more votes in a district than a House candidate of the same party is not necessarily demonstrating coattails. Such a difference in votes may indicate weak presidential coattails, however, because the president is unable to extend his popularity to the congressional candidate. In close elections such as those in 1960, 1968, and 1976, the president often ran behind or on a par with congressional candidates who nevertheless benefited from coattails.[151]

Many observers believe that the coattail effect is on the decline. This decline has been attributed to the decline of party loyalties among voters and the decline of political parties as vital forces in national elections, reflected in the tendency for candidates to rely more on their own resources (or those of nonparty organizations such as political action committees) to finance election campaigns. This does not imply, however, that the coattail effect is related solely to party ties.

One evidence of the decline of the coattail effect is illustrated by the rise in the number of congressional districts with split results—that is, House districts where the president won a majority of the vote, but the district elected a legislator from the opposition party. The number of districts with split ticket results has increased dramatically since 1920, with a high point reached in 1972. (One would expect a 50 percent result if there were no relationship at all between presidential and congressional elections. *(See Table 17.)*

Table 16 Coattail Victories, House Elections

Year	President	Number of coattails	President tied or ran behind
1952	Eisenhower	13	0
1956	Eisenhower	8	0
1960	Kennedy	7	6
1964	Johnson	17	2
1968	Nixon	10	9
1972	Nixon	12	1
1976	Carter	4	3
1980	Reagan	5	1
Total		76	22

Source: George C. Edwards III, *The Public Presidency: The Pursuit of Popular Support* (New York: St. Martin's Press, 1983), 26.

Despite the best efforts of presidential candidates and party organizations, neither may be able to exert much direct influence over the likelihood of coattails. A downturn in the economy during an election year, for example, may spell the end of coattail possibilities, while an economic upturn may have the opposite effect. Nevertheless, even though the coattail effect lessened during the 1970s and 1980s, it continues to have an impact on congressional and other elections.

Midterm Elections

A similar electoral intersection between the president and Congress is observable during elections held in the middle of presidential terms. The election of all 435 members of the House and one-third of the Senate invites presidential attempts to fortify the executive's party strength in Congress. Yet the overwhelming trend has been the reverse. In every midterm election in this century, except that in 1934, the president's party has lost seats in the House. (With only a third of the Senate elected every two years, its results are a less accurate gauge of the mood of the country.).

This midterm dip has been labeled the "surge and decline" phenomenon. It is predicated on the assumption that the president's party usually does better during presidential years than the national partisan balance would otherwise support because of the strength of the winning presidential candidate. Thus, the system corrects itself in years when the president is not running, with a more nearly normal partisan balance taking hold.

The problem with this explanation is that the correlation between the presidential and congressional vote has declined over the last several decades, and congressional incumbency has become a much more important factor in explaining congressional outcomes. Two other factors also given greater weight in explaining midterm swings are the condition of the economy and the president's popularity.[152] To a great extent midterm elections are perceived as referenda on presidential performance during the previous two years, and the number of seats lost by the president's party—the dominant trend—is related to the state of the economy and the president's popular standing. When such indicators turn down, it is more difficult for the president's

Table 17 Ticket Splitting between Presidential and House Candidates, 1920-1984

Year	Districts[a]	Districts with split results[b]	
		Number	Percentage
1920	344	11	3.2
1924	356	42	11.8
1928	359	68	18.9
1932	355	50	14.1
1936	361	51	14.1
1940	362	53	14.6
1944	367	41	11.2
1948	422	90	21.3
1952	435	84	19.3
1956	435	130	29.9
1960	437	114	26.1
1964	435	145	33.3
1968	435	139	32.0
1972	435	192	44.1
1976	435	124	28.5
1980	435	143	32.8
1984	435	196	45.0

Source: Norman J. Ornstein, Thomas E. Mann, and Michael J. Malbin, *Vital Statistics on Congress, 1987-1988* (Washington, D.C.: Congressional Quarterly Inc., 1988), 62.

a. Before 1952 complete data are not available on every congressional district.

b. Congressional districts carried by a presidential candidate of one party and a House candidate of another party.

party to raise money and field strong candidates for office. If the opposition party is not strongly challenged in a congressional race, the likelihood that the president's party will suffer is greater.

An example of this phenomenon was the 1974 midterm elections. The incumbent president, Repubican Richard Nixon, had suffered precipitously in public standing after his 1972 reelection because of the damaging revelations of the Watergate investigation. Thus, the Republicans—who also were coping with an economic downturn—found it extremely difficult to raise money and select strong candidates for office. Moreover, an unusually large number of legislators (mostly Republican) decided to retire in 1974, thereby enhancing the Democratic challengers' chances. Finally, Democratic antipathy toward Nixon and the Republicans was fanned by revelation of Watergate misdeeds, in part because these offenses were directed against Democratic party leaders. As a result, Democrats at all levels were motivated to run for office, give more money, and otherwise work to defeat the party of Watergate. The net result in Congress was a gain of forty-nine Democratic seats in the House and four in the Senate. Some of the Democratic House gains occurred in districts that had been Republican strongholds.

Evaluation of the president is not the only basis for voter decisions during midterm elections. Despite the long-term erosion of partisanship, political party ties continue to play an important role. A study of midterm elections in the 1970s noted that party identification, incumbency, and personal attributes of candidates were strong predictors of voter choices.[153]

Still, the inexorable erosion of support for the president's party at midterm elections emphasizes the large shadow that the president casts over congressional elections. As the only nationally elected leader the president is a natural referent for voter choices. Moreover, some observers argue that the electorate is more likely to vote against policies or candidates than for them. Given that the president's standing is invariably highest at the start of the term, followed by a decline (although this decline may be mitigated by short-term factors), it is likely that at midterm a president, and his or her political party, will be hurt by critics more than helped by supporters.

It has been suggested that midterm elections may provide a source of affirmation for, or rejection of, the president's issue positions, but there is little reason to believe that this is true. First, experts agree that the public knows little about the positions of congressional candidates on the issues, even the controversial ones. Moreover, voters' awareness of issues during midterm elections is even lower than during presidential elections. Second, many congressional races are not competitive. In 1978, for example, no effective competition was offered in 128 of the 435 congressional races. Third, congressional candidates are likely to deemphasize specific issues in their campaigns, focusing instead on broader abstractions such as government efficiency and invocations of political symbols. Fourth, turnout in midterm elections is low. In 1982, for instance, only 38 percent of the national electorate voted. This level of turnout is not a measure of public opinion, and those who do vote are not representative of the population as a whole. Finally, to the extent that issues are raised in congressional campaigns, they are bound to vary from district to district, in part because they spring from local concerns.[154]

High and Low Presidential Standing

Presidents who stand tall in the eyes of the public possess the political high ground in their dealings with Congress. Presidents who lack high standing face a politically problematic situation in which Congress actually might gain politically from jousting with the president. Presidents have long appreciated the political clout accompanying popular approval, especially when it comes to dealing with Congress.

In the aftermath of his overwhelming victory in 1964, President Johnson moved ahead quickly to enact major legislation, particularly the highly controversial Voting Rights Act of 1965. Despite warnings that the bill was too explosive and that he ought to bide his time more carefully, Johnson knew from his years of Senate experience that presidents had to act when their popularity stood high.

Many presidents before and since have seen the wisdom in capitalizing on public standing to promote important programs in Congress. When presidents are reelected, their annual programs are infused with new proposals as part of the postelection mandate. By the end of their terms, however, a far larger proportion are recycled proposals from earlier in the administration. This trend reflects realization that the president no longer possesses the popular mandate necessary to mount successful drives in Congress for major new legislation. The progressive erosion of the president's public standing results in a more assertive Congress and a less influential president. *(See Table 18.)*

Presidential Leadership Skills

Shortly before leaving office, Harry Truman observed that his successor, former general Dwight Eisenhower, would

Table 18 Presidential Proposals Resubmitted to Congress, 1954-1974

President	Year	Presidential legislative proposals	Presidential proposals previously submitted but not enacted	Resubmitted bills as percentage of legislative proposals
Eisenhower	1954	232	12	5.1
	1955	207	31	15.0
	1956	225	79	35.1
	1957	206	74	35.9
	1958	234	59	25.2
	1959	228	63	27.6
	1960	183	78	42.6
Kennedy	1961	355	—	—
	1962	298	36	12.1
	1963	401	64	16.0
Johnson	1964	217	67	30.9
	1965	469	29	6.2
	1966	371	37	10.0
	1967	431	31	7.2
	1968	414	83	20.0
Nixon	1969	171	—	—
	1970	210	40	19.0
	1971	202	62	30.7
	1972	116	5	4.3
	1973	183	—	—
Nixon/Ford	1974	161	10	6.2

Source: "Presidential Boxscores," *Congressional Quarterly Almanac,* 1954-1974 (Washington, D.C.: Congressional Quarterly Inc., 1955-1975). Table compiled by author.

be in for a rude awakening when he assumed the presidency. Truman predicted: "He'll sit here ... and say, 'Do this! Do that!' *And nothing will happen.* Poor Ike—it won't be a bit like the Army. He'll find it very frustrating."[155]

Political scientist Richard Neustadt made a vital point about the modern American presidency when he quoted President Truman, his former boss. In observing that presidential power to command was both overrated and overstated, he was arguing that presidential power was primarily the power to persuade. Reliance on persuasion and bargaining has become a hallmark of the presidency, Neustadt observed, because the responsibilities, demands, and expectations now inherent in the presidential office have outstripped the powers of the office. As a consequence, presidents must rely on informal bargaining skills to accomplish their goals.

Concern for the appropriate level of presidential leadership skills was articulated by two early twentieth-century presidents. Theodore Roosevelt advocated an aggressive stewardship role for the president. He argued that the president was entitled, even obliged, to act as necessary to promote the needs, goals, and interests of the people, unless such action was explicitly unconstitutional. Roosevelt's successor, William Howard Taft, called instead for a restrained or whiggish view of the presidency, proposing instead that presidents could and should exercise only those powers explicitly granted in the Constitution.[156] Both these approaches require some level of presidential leadership skills, but they vary widely as to the scope and limitation of these skills.

While the philosophical debate over the relative merits of the stewardship and whiggish views of presidential leadership persists, no modern president can ignore the fundamentals of effective executive leadership. To win enactment of important (and therefore usually controversial) legislation, the president cannot simply submit legislation and sit back to wait for the finished product. Specialized coalitions often must be built in Congress, even across party lines. Lyndon Johnson, for example, admitted that he could not have gained passage of key civil rights legislation without the support of moderate Republicans, despite the fact that his party held substantial majorities in both houses.

Often considered one of the most adept legislative strategists ever to occupy the White House, Johnson knew more than most about the key leadership role of the president. Johnson summarized his philosophy when he said: "There is only one way for a President to deal with the Congress, and that is continuously, incessantly, and without interruption."

Although many factors other than the president's leadership skills play a vital role in shaping presidential-congressional relations, presidents are nevertheless the personifications of their administrations. They take personal credit for successes and personal blame for failures (although seldom willingly). More to the point, presidents are personal, readily available reservoirs of influence. They are an administration's handiest political balm.

Some presidents such as Lyndon Johnson bring with them intimate knowledge of Congress, while others acquire such knowledge on the job. As president, Johnson paid close attention to even small legislative details, and he always made himself available to members of Congress who wanted to see him.

Presidents also learn that the timing of legislative maneuvers often contributes to a successful outcome. For example, successful passage of Reagan's economic program owed much to the rise in Reagan's popularity following the

George Tames, *New York Times*

A president's influence over Congress varies with each president's personality. Lyndon Johnson, aggressive as Senate majority leader (shown here with Democratic Senator Theodore Francis Green of Rhode Island), was just as comfortable employing embarrassment and bullying to get his way as president.

1981 attempt on his life. Lyndon Johnson similarly found that sending bills to Congress at the right time was important to a favorable outcome.

Consultation plays a vital role as well in executive-legislative relations. Presidents who do not bother to consult with key members of Congress often find that they have made opponents out of potential allies. President Nixon, for example, probably lost the support of Republican senator Margaret Chase Smith for the Carswell nomination to the Supreme Court when his administration informed members of the Senate that she was going to support Carswell; in fact, she had not made up her mind. Smith eventually voted against Carswell.

Frequently, presidents have found their cabinets to be an important source of expertise and political pressure. Johnson devoted much cabinet meeting time to pending legislation, and he also directed his cabinet secretaries to apply their departments to legislative ends. Cabinet secretaries and lower department officials often testify before congressional committees, and the president can shape that testimony to advantage.

One of the president's most important legislative resources is a personal appeal. Whether over the phone or face to face, such an appeal is usually an effective (although by no means unfailing) means of winning support. Some presidents—such as Johnson, Ford, and Reagan—were frequent and effective users of personal appeals. Others—such as Eisenhower and Carter—were less comfortable with the personal approach. Richard Nixon actively avoided substantive personal contact with members of Congress. Phone calls from members to the president were screened carefully, with most not even getting through to the president himself. His view of himself as more of an administrator than a power broker, as well as his apparent aloofness and detachment, did little to endear Nixon to members of Congress.

As with any resource, the impact of direct involvement by the president may decline if employed too frequently. Presidents usually reserve personal pressure for close votes on important bills and for instances when the president's prestige is on the line. A good example of both of these cases is presidential attempts to defeat a veto override vote. In 1986, for example, Reagan tried to win support for his veto of a congressional effort to block an arms sale to Saudi Arabia by personally contacting twelve senators. One senator who changed his vote to support Reagan's veto was John P. East (R-N.C.). He was persuaded that "the president should be allowed to make foreign policy without being managed at every turn by Congress." In this instance Reagan's veto was upheld by the precise minimum of thirty-four votes.

Although there is no consensus on the extent and effectiveness of bargaining, it is indisputably an integral presidential resource. President Kennedy, for example, struck a bargain with Sen. Robert S. Kerr (D-Okla.) over an Arkansas River project. (The Arkansas River runs through Kerr's home state of Oklahoma.) When Kennedy asked Kerr for help in getting an investment tax credit bill out of the Senate Finance Committee, Kerr responded by raising the Arkansas River bill, insisting on a trade. Kennedy replied, "You know, Bob, I never really understood that Arkansas River bill before today." Kerr's project was supported and enacted; in exchange, Kerr backed the Kennedy bill.

Every president engages in some degree of bargaining, but the technique has its limitations. First, bargaining resources are limited. The president cannot afford to use bargaining or favor trading as a principal means of obtaining action. If bargains are made frequently and explicitly, everyone in Congress will likely want to make such deals. Like personal contact, bargains are most effective when used prudently and implicitly. Moreover, members of Congress may not be swayed by the bargaining option, especially if they are motivated by such factors as constituent pressure, ideology, or party ties. Although presidents use bargaining to pursue their policy objectives, most of the pressure for bargains emanates from Congress.

Sometimes, presidential influence extends to applying

coercion. Strictly speaking, the president can do little to twist arms. Some presidents, such as Eisenhower, found strong-arm tactics distasteful. Even after repeated attacks against him and his administration by Sen. Joseph R. McCarthy (R-Wis.), Eisenhower declined to respond aggressively. Johnson, on the other hand, was not reluctant to employ embarrassment, bullying, and threats to promote his ends.

The Nixon administration also employed arm-twisting tactics, although Nixon himself avoided personal involvement. These tactics came into play in 1969 over such controversial issues as the antiballistic missile system and the Haynsworth and Carswell nominations to the Supreme Court. In addition, the Nixon administration threatened rebellious representatives with reelection trouble. A well-known example is the administration's support of James L. Buckley, who was running for the Senate from New York. Because the Republican incumbent, Charles E. Goodell, had become a strong administration critic, the administration threw its support informally behind Buckley, the nominee of the New York Conservative party. The weight of the Nixon administration helped Buckley defeat Goodell and the Democratic nominee, Richard Ottinger. Despite this and other periodic successes for the arm-twisting technique, it frequently does not work, and it often serves to fan and fortify opposition.

Presidents can provide a variety of services to members of Congress. These include presidential visits to home districts, assistance with favored pork barrel and other projects, patronage appointments, constituent service assistance (such as giving out presidential memorabilia and signed photographs, arranging special White House tours, interceding with federal agencies), access to privileged or other inside information, campaign assistance, and personal favors and amenities for members of Congress (from cuff links to choice theater tickets). The use of amenities and social courtesies builds positive personal relations. Early in his term President Lyndon Johnson was careful to apportion credit for important legislation, but as Vietnam-related criticism mounted, he began to refer to programs as his own, which further eroded his relations with Congress. As with other tactical devices, services and amenities are limited in effectiveness.

In addition to these direct means of influence, presidents can marshal outside pressure, including that exerted by constituents. Thus, presidents may appeal directly to geographic or other constituencies to urge that pressure be placed on representatives. President Kennedy's legislative chief, Lawrence O'Brien, frequently contacted state governors to urge them to pressure state representatives. Federal agencies also may be called on to mobilize support for presidential policies. Farmers, unions, business groups, and regional or other interests may be persuaded to side with the administration in attempting to swing congressional support. President Johnson forged a coalition of the major religious denominations and educational groups in support of the Elementary and Secondary Education Act of 1965 even before the bill was introduced. In fact, Johnson deliberately held the bill until both the National Education Association and the National Catholic Welfare Conference agreed on the bill's basics.[157]

The sheer length of this list of leadership tools available to the president is convincing evidence that presidential persuasion is irresistible when applied firmly and consistently. Yet the actual presidential record suggests almost the opposite. Many examples of all of these factors in operation can be cited, but in fact the persuasive tools and abilities of presidents constitute only one category of factors that influence the legislative process. A penetrating analysis of presidential influence in Congress has concluded that the impact of presidential skills has been overstated, partly because of the tendency for such activities to attract headlines. According to this study, "Presidential legislative skills do not seem to affect support for presidential policies, despite what conventional wisdom leads us to expect." [158]

The Public Presidency

Presidents often use their rhetorical skills to bypass Congress and sway public opinion. The potency of aroused public sentiment already has been summarized. It is not surprising, then, that presidents often seek public favor to build support for major legislation or to head off possible opposition.

One of the best-known examples of presidents seeking public support to sway Congress occurred before the era of television. In 1919 Woodrow Wilson stumped the country to rally support for the beleaguered League of Nations treaty then before the Senate. Although he gave forty speeches in twenty-two days, Wilson's efforts fell short. He suffered exhaustion, then a stroke, and the Senate defeated the treaty by a fifteen-vote margin.

To cite a more recent example, Ronald Reagan met increasing opposition from both Congress and the country to his efforts to cut back on education aid programs. (Polls indicated popular disapproval of Reagan's cutbacks by a two-to-one ratio.) In response, the White House launched a communications offensive, emphasizing the themes of excellence in education, merit pay for teachers, and greater classroom discipline, and Reagan made over twenty-five personal appearances to repeat these themes. Later polls indicated that the public supported Reagan's education program by a two-to-one ratio, even though no programmatic changes had occurred. By altering public perceptions, Reagan also helped alleviate pressure from Congress.

President Johnson also found a public appeal desirable, and even necessary, to impel congressional action. When Johnson's tax surcharge bill stalled in the House Ways and Means Committee, he appealed to the people through several public forums, including his 1968 State of the Union address. The impasse was eventually overcome, despite some congressional resentment over the public approach.

Early in his administration President Carter used a series of television addresses to rally public support for his proposed energy legislation. To symbolize his own commitment to energy conservation, Carter wore a cardigan sweater instead of the traditional suit jacket. But despite his appeal to the public, Carter's energy program faced difficult sailing in Congress.

Presidents also try to take advantage of changing public sentiments. Immediately after the 1968 assassination of Martin Luther King, Jr., President Johnson pressed congressional leaders to act on his Fair Housing Act, which had been stalled in committee for over two years. Within seven days of King's death the bill was signed into law. One day after Robert F. Kennedy's assassination in 1968, Congress enacted the Omnibus Crime Control and Safe Streets Act, even though the bill had been tied up in Congress for more than a year. In both instances, dramatic swings in public sentiment resulting from unforeseen events provided the impetus needed to push a White House-favored proposal through.

The presidential public appeal is nothing new, but many analysts have noted that modern communications technology, along with political changes, have had the effect of encouraging presidents to use the public forum to pressure Congress. Presidents can command network television time almost at will, and no modern president would think of launching a major political effort involving Congress without incorporating public communications channels. Indeed, presidents have progressively expanded their prime time exposure. *(See Figure 2.)*

Political scientist Samuel Kernell has argued that modern presidents "go public" more than their predecessors; they attempt to place themselves, and their proposals, directly before the people in order to improve their political fortunes in Washington. These efforts may target particular groups or segments of the population, but since virtually any presidential action is news, national coverage usually results.

The consequence of this trend is that presidents, their allies, and their foes have all become much more concerned with public relations as a political tactic. Both allies and critics agree that, among modern presidents, "No president has enlisted public strategies to better advantage than has Ronald Reagan." Reagan's acting background dovetailed with a growing understanding of the impact of presidential images to produce a presidency that cultivated Reagan's national image as a means of promoting his congressional agenda.

The idea that modern presidents can obtain powerful political capital from public support is taken further by Theodore J. Lowi. He argues that the country has entered an era in which the government is centered around the presidency. Presidential appeals have taken on a plebiscitary nature—that is, presidents seek popular support or even adoration, as did the autocrats of ancient Rome and the more recent French empires. And, according to Lowi, the forceful ascendance of the personal presidency has come at the expense of the separation of powers (especially in a denigration of the role of Congress) and the two-party system. The cult of presidential personality has been accompanied by expansion of the formal and informal powers of the presidency, although these heightened powers cannot match public expectations. Under these conditions the president may operate outside of the traditional presidential-congressional relations to impel Congress to act in accordance with the president's wishes.

Thus, the powers and skills most important to presidents seeking an effective presidency have changed since the 1950s. Communications skills have always been important, but past presidents known for their communications skills—such as Theodore Roosevelt, Woodrow Wilson, and Franklin Roosevelt—did not rely solely or even primarily on speechmaking and public oration to gain political results in Congress. Modern presidents have found public appeals to be an increasingly important supplement to the traditional bargaining with Congress. With the erosion of strong party ties, the traditional institutional and partisan links between the president and Congress have been further weakened.

Presidents as Leaders

Each president has left a mark on the presidency. Historians, journalists, political scientists, and others pay close attention to the strengths and weaknesses of each president, and they often rank presidents according to their relative "greatness." These rankings have been criticized for their unstated assumptions (such as the assumption that activism equals greatness), their reliance on subjective and reputational considerations, and the lack of agreement about what constitutes greatness. Yet the varying leadership styles of recent presidents reveal much about their dealings with Congress.

Roosevelt. Franklin Roosevelt oversaw the expansion of the modern presidency, in particular the legislative realm. Early in his four-term presidency he shepherded through Congress the enormous volume of legislation that composed his New Deal program. And because he served as president during World War II, he benefited from the wartime deference to presidential authority. In both instances, severe national crises afforded Roosevelt singular opportunities to shape and direct legislative affairs, and even to redefine the president's role. His singular leadership skills were important as well.

As Richard Neustadt has noted, "No president in this century has had a sharper sense of personal power.... No modern President has been more nearly master in the White House.... He wanted power for its own sake; he also wanted what it could achieve."

In addition to the personal enjoyment he derived from the use of power, much of Roosevelt's legacy is his impact on the institution of the presidency. He created the Executive Office of the President and brought the Bureau of the Budget into it from the Treasury Department. He increased staff and other executive resources, and he focused these expanded resources on Congress to provide the necessary presidential input and to ensure the enforcement of presidential preferences.

Roosevelt also knew how to use the media and other external forces to bring pressure to bear on Congress. His celebrated fireside chats highlighted his ability to use the still new electronic medium of radio as a means of rallying public support for his political agenda. Later, during the war years, Roosevelt used the radio to instill confidence and fan patriotic fervor.

For all of Roosevelt's skill, however, he made his share of blunders and suffered his share of defeats. During his second term he miscalculated congressional (and national) sentiments when he proposed increasing the number of seats on the Supreme Court so that he could appoint additional justices more receptive to his agenda. Congress balked at Roosevelt's attempt at "Court packing," and the president suffered no little political humiliation. In the 1938 primaries, Roosevelt ran pro-Roosevelt Democrats against the Democratic legislators who had not been adequately receptive to many of his initiatives in Congress. With one exception, every effort failed, and southern Democrats in particular harbored resentment for years.

Truman. Harry Truman sought to extend the legislative work of his predecessor. His "Fair Deal," which emphasized economic security for Americans, was a continuation of Roosevelt's New Deal. Truman set forth a twenty-one point program, which included proposals related to increasing the minimum wage, urban development, national health insurance, social security, and full employment. Unlike his predecessor, however, Truman met vociferous opposition. In the midterm elections of 1946 the Republicans gained control of both houses for the first time since 1928, and Truman's programs were savaged, as was he in the public press. Nonetheless, he challenged the

Figure 2 Presidential Addresses, 1929-1983 (Yearly Averages for First Three Years of First Term)

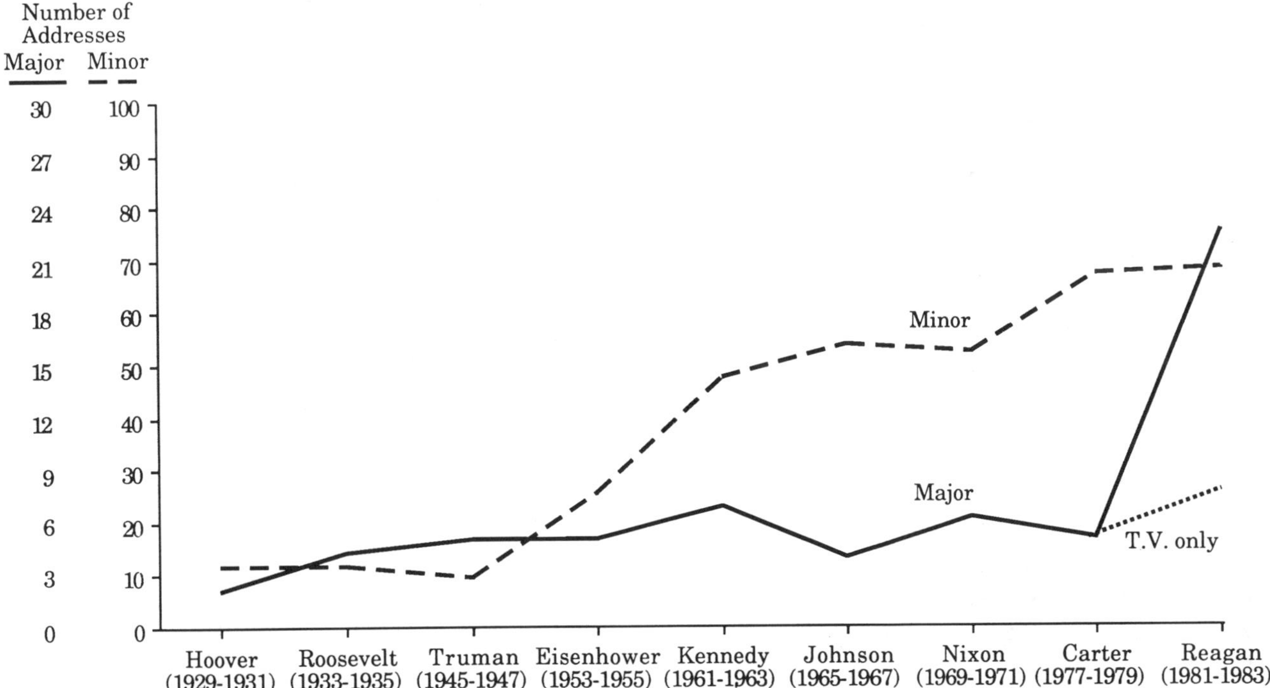

Sources: Data for Hoover, Roosevelt, Truman, Eisenhower, Nixon, and Carter are from William W. Lammers, "Presidential Attention-Focusing Activities," in The President and the American Public, ed. Doris A. Graber (Philadelphia: Institute for the Study of Human Issues, 1982), 152. Data for Kennedy, Johnson, and Reagan are from Public Papers of the President series. See also Samuel Kernell, "The Presidency and the People," in The Presidency and the Political System, ed. Michael Nelson (Washington, D.C.: CQ Press, 1984), 242. Cited in Samuel Kernell, Going Public: New Strategies of Presidential Leadership (Washington, D.C.: CQ Press, 1986), 86.

Note: To eliminate public activities inspired by concerns of reelection rather than governing, only the first three years have been tabulated. For this reason, Gerald Ford's record of public activities during his two and one-half years of office has been ignored.

Republicans head on, and in one of the great upsets in modern presidential elections, he defeated his Republican rival, Thomas E. Dewey in 1948, and carried into office Democratic congressional majorities.

Truman could not match Roosevelt's reputation or adroit leadership skills, but he was not without experience and skill. Truman had served in the Senate for ten years before becoming vice president in 1944, and he both knew and respected the congressional decision-making process. But Roosevelt's death took everyone by surprise, and Truman had little knowledge of White House decision making. He spent his first two years establishing a coherent White House structure to deal with legislative matters. While contributing to the institutionalization process begun by Roosevelt, Truman also took personal interest in and control over legislative matters. The well-known sign he kept on his desk, proclaiming, "The buck stops here," embodied his personal involvement.

Another indication of Truman's attitude was his frequent use of the veto—250 times in eight years. He used his well-known veto of the Taft-Hartley Act in 1947 to enforce his image as defender of the average working man. Truman took special care with his veto messages and worked on them personally. He became enmeshed in the unpopular Korean War during his final two years in office, and suffered a precipitous decline in public standing that was matched only by Nixon's decline during Watergate.

Eisenhower. The election of former general Dwight Eisenhower represented the ascension of a relatively apolitical public figure inexperienced in the ways of civilian governing. Initial assessments of Eisenhower's presidential leadership, such as that of Richard Neustadt, portrayed him as a man who served more out of a sense of duty than a love of power, and as a president who saw his role as that of referee rather than politician in chief.

Yet many presidential observers have argued that Eisenhower's leadership skills have been underrated. Despite facing a Congress controlled by the opposition party for six out of eight years, Eisenhower saw many of his important programs enacted, presided over an era of peace and economic good times, and was elected twice by large margins. Philosophically, he did not share the aggressive activism of his two predecessors. In his first year in office he sent no coordinated legislative program to Congress, but after stern criticism from Congress, he followed through with annual programs for the remainder of his term. His personal role was one of relative detachment compared to his predecessors. He relied more on his staff and organizational hierarchies, and he generally disdained the backslapping, arm-twisting style favored by some politicians.

One revised assessment of Eisenhower's leadership style has argued that it was a "hidden hand"; that is, Ike was in fact "politically astute and informed, engaged in putting his personal stamp on public policy, a president who applied a carefully thought-out conception of leadership to the conduct of his presidency." In addition to the hidden hand, Eisenhower's political strategies included his careful use of language, analysis of the personalities of those with whom he was dealing in assessing options, refusal to engage in personality conflicts, and selective delegation. Eisenhower's leadership style with Congress and the country was relatively low key and detached. He benefited from and relied on his persistent public support. Given the strong opposition congressional leadership of Democratic House Speaker Sam Rayburn and Senate Majority Leader Lyndon Johnson, Eisenhower probably deserves more credit for having leadership skills suited to the circumstances of the time than critics initially conceded.

Kennedy. Although his presidency conveyed a certain mystique, John F. Kennedy entered the White House on a razor-thin margin that left him little in the way of a political base. Congress was in the hands of the Democrats, but southern conservatives held tight reins, and many of Kennedy's most important "New Frontier" initiatives (including Medicare, aid to education, creation of an urban affairs department, establishment of a youth conservation corps, and civil rights) remained bottled up.

Kennedy had served in the Senate for eight years, but he had taken little interest in Senate affairs and in the traditional paths of congressional power. When he became president, his desire to exert leadership was exceeded by political reality and his own inexperience. In the area of civil rights, for example, Kennedy had pledged important advances, but, having lost twenty Democratic seats in the House in the 1960 elections, he failed to win passage of any important civil rights legislation. In response to political pressure, Kennedy did issue a series of executive orders directed at improving civil rights, and he appointed more blacks to judicial and other positions than any of his predecessors. And he achieved some notable legislative successes, including a minimum wage bill, aid to depressed areas, and a housing bill. As leadership specialist Barbara Kellerman has noted, Kennedy might have realized greater successes in areas such as civil rights had he been willing to apply more of the rewards and sanctions available to him. Kennedy lacked "an appreciation of the *politics* of leadership. He failed to exert sufficient influence on those political actors whose support he needed to win."

In terms of staffing, Kennedy shed Eisenhower's formalistic, hierarchical arrangements, preferring instead a flexible arrangement that fed information more directly to him. Kennedy's top aides also had considerable discretion to act on his behalf. Although these mechanisms could have maximized Kennedy's personal ability to have an impact on the legislative process, his fear of outpacing his mandate did much to slow his efforts.

Kennedy's mixed track record in legislative leadership was to some extent overshadowed by a series of dramatic foreign policy developments, including the attempted invasion of Cuba at the Bay of Pigs in 1961, the Cuban missile crisis in 1962, completion of a nuclear test ban treaty in 1963, and the escalating war in Vietnam. Historians and others have speculated about what course the Kennedy administration might have taken had he lived to benefit from the fruits of a strong showing in the 1964 elections. It is difficult to believe, however, that Kennedy could have equaled or surpassed the achievements of his successor.

Johnson. In many respects, Lyndon Johnson was the political opposite of Kennedy. He knew the Congress like few other politicians, having served there since 1937 and risen through the ranks to become majority leader during the Eisenhower administration. As a southerner, he knew how to play to southern Democratic conservatives and Republican leaders in Congress. He also appreciated the subtleties of promoting controversial legislation. In 1964, for example, he succeeded where Kennedy had failed in enacting a major civil rights bill. After the 1964 elections, when the Democrats rolled up large congressional majorities, he stepped up the pace.

Johnson's Great Society followed in the tradition of the legislative agendas of Democratic presidents back to Roosevelt. His successes were considerable during 1965-1966; of eighty-three major Johnson proposals, eighty were enacted. Many of his proposals dated back to the Roosevelt era. Johnson's prodigious record of achievement was the product of both an overwhelming electoral mandate in the 1964 election and his well-known personal leadership skills. To be the object of the "Johnson treatment" was to be stroked, prodded, flattered, bullied, encouraged, and cajoled into supporting the president. Johnson was "the very model of a political president."

Johnson's highly personal, hands-on style was reflected in his staff organization. Johnson actively participated in political and policy matters, reserving most important decisions for himself. Members of his White House staff, of course, were heavily involved in such matters as well. When Johnson's energy was directed at Congress, it produced numerous achievements, but his pattern of close personal involvement served him poorly when his attention turned to Vietnam. As Johnson's public support lessened and the country became more committed to the Vietnam War, Johnson brooked little dissent and less disagreement. He continued to log some legislative successes during the last two years of his administration, but his unwavering commitment to the Vietnam War inexorably sapped resources, political capital, and good will from his legislative agenda. Johnson's considerable leadership skills could not extract him from his own unyielding commitment to fight an increasingly unpopular war.

Nixon. The 1968 elections inaugurated a period of divided government. Although he had served in both houses of Congress and as Eisenhower's vice president for eight years, Richard Nixon failed to carry with him either house of Congress. He was the first president to face this difficulty since Zachary Taylor in 1848.

At the outset of his administration he forwarded over forty legislative proposals to Congress, including election law reform, tax reform, crime-related proposals, welfare reform, and drug control. But despite these early efforts, Nixon encountered problems with Congress almost from the beginning, notably the Haynsworth and Carswell nominations to the Supreme Court. Nixon's initial organizational approach to Congress differed from that of his immediate predecessors. He sought to emulate Eisenhower's strong cabinet model, emphasizing organizational hierarchy and more limited personal involvement by the president in day-to-day decisions. As his term progressed, however, the strong cabinet model was overthrown in favor of an administrative approach, where power was concentrated in the hands of key political aides. During Nixon's first term, he sought to achieve policy successes through legislative remedy. By the second term, however, he had turned increasingly to an administrative strategy that emphasized circumventing congressional channels to the extent possible. This approach suited Nixon's personal leadership style, which emphasized detachment, hierarchy, and managerial values.

Nixon's principal leadership efforts concerned foreign policy. He began to scale down U.S. involvement in Vietnam (although he actually escalated the war, provoking much criticism from Congress and the nation), opened ties to China, and completed the first Strategic Arms Limitation Treaty with the Soviet Union. The Vietnam War was a persistent source of friction between Congress and the White House, with struggles over efforts to end funding for the war and constitutional questions about the extent of Nixon's discretion over the use of U.S. forces. Congress scored several important legislative victories, including passage of the War Powers Resolution.

Nixon's administrative approach conformed to his disdain for congressional critics, and he began to treat his political opponents as enemies. This we-versus-they mentality did much to foster the Watergate scandal, which was marked by efforts to turn the apparatus of government against Nixon's political opponents. Nixon's reelection campaign also diverted resources to political sabotage, dirty tricks, and other illegal activities. As public exposure of Nixon campaign and administration misdeeds surfaced, a siege mentality gripped Nixon and his White House more tightly. Despite the popular mandate accompanying Nixon's landslide 1972 reelection, White House efforts focused increasingly on political damage control. Relations with Congress continued to deteriorate; moreover, Congressional investigations were responsible for Nixon's resignation.

Ford. The presidency of Gerald Ford was the product of historical accident. Had Vice President Spiro T. Agnew not resigned over financial improprieties committed during his tenure as governor of Maryland, Ford never would have become president. Without the benefit of a national campaign, Ford had no opportunity to construct and promote his own political and policy agenda. This simple fact explains much of the difficulty Ford faced with Congress.

Ford's elevation to the presidency was welcomed by a country anxious to put the troubled Nixon presidency behind it. Ford's simple, direct, unassuming style provided a refreshing contrast to the cold and distant Nixon. Congress too welcomed Ford. As House Republican minority leader, he was known as a partisan, but also as a likeable, honest leader. The Ford honeymoon was cut short, however, when he pardoned Richard Nixon. The pardon provoked a sharp drop in Ford's popularity and did little to improve Ford's standing in the Democratic-controlled Congress.

Because the circumstances under which he became president precluded proposal of a full-blown legislative agenda at the beginning of his term, Ford had to rely primarily on a veto strategy in his dealings with a Congress whose Democratic majority had been enhanced significantly in the 1974 midterm elections. The inherent negativity of this approach fanned congressional resentment, and it engendered a public image of Ford as a naysayer. (Ford vetoed sixty-six bills in his two and one-half years in office.) Ford's aides were keenly aware of these problems, but they felt that they had little room to maneuver unless and until Ford won his own mandate in the 1976 elections (although even an election victory might not neutralize the cumulative ill will stemming from sixty-six vetoes).

Ford attempted a major legislative initiative in 1975 when he sent an energy plan to Congress, but Congress, with its greater assertiveness, challenged and revised the Ford proposal. Ford's overall support rate in Congress was among the lowest of any president since approval records were kept. His administrative apparatus was far more open and flexible than that of Nixon's, but it operated less decisively and authoritatively.

It is unclear whether another individual with more adroit leadership skills could have exceeded Ford's performance, given the circumstances. Nevertheless, Ford's presidential leadership style was similar to his style as minority leader—that of a good man with limited vision who held the reins of power loosely.

Carter. Former Georgia governor Jimmy Carter entered the White House as a Washington outsider. Because in his four years as president he failed to shed the outsider status, his legislative record was pockmarked with unfulfilled expectations and outright failures.

Carter's campaign promises filled over one hundred pages, and he meant to carry all of them out. Although Congress was controlled by the president's party, Democrats mistrusted Carter, and Carter did little to assuage the mistrust. He underestimated the importance of building careful relations with key congressional leaders, and he overwhelmed Congress from the start by sending to Capitol Hill numerous important bills all at once. This contrasted with Johnson's practice of sending over one major bill at a time. Carter's experiences testified to Johnson's wisdom.

Carter's top aides, including his legislative liaison chief, Frank Moore, were non-Washingtonians, who were inexperienced in Washington politics and did little to cultivate deep-seated support for the president. The Carter staff was known for not returning phone calls, not informing key legislators of important decisions, and ignoring personal courtesies such as making photo sessions available.

The post-Watergate Congress was not disposed to accept proposals simply because they came from the White House. The composition of Congress also militated against docility and pliability. Of the 289 Democratic House members elected in 1976, 118 had served no more than two terms. The large proportion of junior members was interested in a share of congressional power, and Carter was less disposed than most recent presidents to court members of Congress.

Carter achieved some legislative successes, but most observers saw him as incapable of getting an important program through a Congress controlled by his own party. For example, his 1977 energy package—really an amalgam of different bills—encountered difficulties. Carter tried to rally public support for the program as a means of overcoming congressional hurdles, but he found such support broad and diffuse and insufficient for overcoming conventional congressional obstacles.

With foreign affairs he had more success, most notably the Camp David accords that helped establish bonds between Israel and Egypt. Carter also concluded negotiations for the Panama Canal Treaty, although Senate ratification proved difficult.

Carter's leadership incorporated two divergent tendencies. First, he was a technocrat who immersed himself in the details of complex programs. Second, he was a born-again Christian who espoused high moral standards. What he lacked was a middle-level concern for conventional political relationships.

Reagan. Like Carter, Ronald Reagan ran for president against Washington. Unlike Carter, Reagan's administration labored to gain political insider status, partly by learning from Carter's mistakes. Bringing with him a Republican-controlled Senate (the Democrats retained control of the House) and an electoral mandate based on carrying forty-four states, Reagan labored to lay careful political groundwork from the start.

After conducting a study of the first three months of past presidencies, Reagan's aides concluded that they should push a few selected initiatives and work to restore the informal social courtesies and connections that Carter had neglected. The outsider image successful in the campaign was sublimated after the election in the interest of building better relations with Capitol Hill. Reagan selected Max Friedersdorf, a Washington insider with experience in two previous Republican administrations, as his legislative liaison chief.

Like Carter, Reagan sought to rally public support for high-priority programs, but the Reagan administration paid greater attention to image-building, and Reagan excelled as the "Great Communicator." No president since Eisenhower had demonstrated such enduring personal popularity.

The primary issue thrust for the Reagan administration in 1981 was an economic package, incorporating major increases in defense spending, cuts in social welfare programs, and a major tax cut predicated on supply-side economics. Reagan's political strategies and wide public support resulted in a major policy victory that has been compared to Roosevelt's early successes during the New Deal's first one hundred days. Reagan's political support in Congress stemmed from the Republican Senate majority, the Republican minority in the House, and conservative southern Democrats.

By 1985 Reagan's support level in Congress had dropped to levels comparable to Nixon's low point. In his second term Reagan faced increasingly stiff opposition to several initiatives, including his expensive Strategic Defense Initiative proposal, his advocacy of continued aid to the Nicaraguan contras, continued efforts to cut social programs, and efforts to restrict abortion. In 1986 the Republicans lost control of the Senate. The following year Reagan lost a bitter fight to have Supreme Court nominees Robert H. Bork and Douglas H. Ginsburg confirmed by the Senate. Also in 1972 Congress launched an investigation of the Iran-contra affair, which involved administration efforts to trade U.S. arms for hostages being held in the Middle East and to use profits from the arms sales to fund the Nicaraguan contras. In 1988 grand jury indictments were handed down against the top White House aides participating in the affair.

Despite these pitfalls, Reagan continued to maintain a high level of personal popularity. The enduring appeal of Reagan's personal qualities provided a constant to an otherwise roller-coaster presidency, and earned him the nickname "the Teflon president" ("nothing bad ever stuck to him").

Presidential Purposes and Circumstances

Presidents with ambitious political agendas need the cooperation of Congress more than those with less ambition. But the determinants of presidential ambition are partly beyond presidential control. Dire events such as wars and economic crises impel more active leadership than times of relative placidity. Similarly, if Congress and the people have high expectations for executive leadership, a politically adroit leader will accept the cue.

Political scientist James David Barber proposed a scheme that categorizes presidents according to their level and enjoyment of activity, based on assessments of presidential character. According to this scheme, active-positive presidents exhibit much activity in office and enjoy their high level of activity. These presidents also demonstrate a sense of rational mastery and are ambitious about what they can and will accomplish. This category includes such activist presidents as Franklin Roosevelt, Harry Truman, John Kennedy, Gerald Ford, and Jimmy Carter.

Active-negative presidents also work to accomplish much in office, but they receive a relatively low emotional reward for their efforts. These presidents often encounter crises of their own making because of their inflexibility in dealing with changing circumstances. Although they are ambitious, these presidents find politics more a struggle than a joy. They include Woodrow Wilson, Herbert Hoover, Lyndon Johnson, and Richard Nixon.

Passive-positive presidents are less ambitious and have a more compliant personality that lacks the assertiveness and drive of the actives. These presidents include William Howard Taft, Warren Harding, and Ronald Reagan.

Finally, the passive-negative president combines relatively little ambition with a negative orientation toward the use of power. These presidents would be expected to be the least ambitious about programs, issues, and goals, and include Calvin Coolidge and Dwight Eisenhower.

Although this scheme has been criticized for oversimplifying complex personality traits, the two dimensions summarize the interaction between presidential ambition and action. In the case of Gerald Ford, it illustrates that an active-positive president is not necessarily a successful president. The historical circumstances of the Ford presidency helped shape events. Similarly, Calvin Coolidge was president in a time of peace and relative national prosperity. The Coolidge presidency coincided with the prevailing political philosophy, which favored minimal government involvement in people's lives. When the more ambitious and flexible Franklin Roosevelt became president, the congressional plate was filled with presidential initiatives.

Presidential ambitions thus intersect with the nature of the times, circumstances, and public expectations. From the president's point of view, successful leadership is marked by congressional approval of important presidential initiatives. But from the point of view of Congress, successful presidential leadership incorporates presidential actions marked by close consultation with congressional leaders, flexibility, and respect for congressional procedures and norms.

These general patterns often are shaped by specific events such as crises, which are endemic to presidential and congressional cycles. Nonetheless, every president enters office accompanied by an aura of good feeling. Even in a close, bitterly contested election, supporters and opponents alike in Congress and elsewhere traditionally express hopes for cooperation, respect, and good will. This closing of ranks is seen in the boost in popularity presidents receive immediately after taking office. Honeymoon periods rarely last beyond a few months, however, and presidents need to act quickly after taking office if they are to reap the benefit of initial congressional and popular good will.

Toward the end of presidential terms a reverse phenomenon takes hold. Presidents seeking reelection usually find that Congress is less willing and less rapid in its response to presidential requests as election day nears.

This slowdown occurs partly because members of Congress are more preoccupied with their own reelection campaigns (as is the president), and partly because presidents are furthest in time from their last electoral mandate. Moreover, Congress is less inclined to respond to presidential initiatives until the winner of the upcoming presidential contest is determined. Even in presidential races where the incumbent seems well ahead, guarantees are rarely issued before elections.

When presidents near the completion of their final term (as in the cases of Eisenhower in 1959-1960 and Reagan in 1987-1988) or announce their intention not to seek reelection (as did Truman in 1952 and Johnson in 1968), Congress is least likely to respond to presidential initiatives. During the "lame duck" period at the close of a term, members of Congress are already looking ahead to the next administration and their own reelections. Moreover, presidential administrations often have run their courses by the lame duck period. Presidents who attempt new initiatives at this late point have great difficulty arousing the interest, much less the resources, necessary to ensure enactment.

Some presidential observers have suggested that the president's lame duck status has been exacerbated by the Twenty-second Amendment, enacted in 1951, which limits the president to two terms. Even though the two-term limit had been observed voluntarily before Franklin Roosevelt, the possibility of a third term, some argue, helped keep each presidency a more vigorous institution in its final days. In the modern era, however, presidents are obliged to announce their election intentions well in advance, thereby perpetuating the lame duck problem, regardless of whether a two-term limit exists or not.

Notes

1. For more on the electoral college, see Judith V. Best, *The Case against Direct Election of the President* (Ithaca, N.Y.: Cornell University Press, 1975); Lawrence D. Longley and Alan G. Braun, *The Politics of Electoral College Reform* (New Haven, Conn.: Yale University Press, 1975); Neil R. Peirce, *The People's President: The Electoral College in American History and the Direct Vote Alternative* (New York: Simon and Schuster, 1968).
2. Many have proposed that the electoral cycle be changed so that there is greater connection between congressional and presidential races. See, for example, Donald L. Robinson, ed., *Reforming American Government* (Boulder, Colo.: Westview Press, 1985); Donald L. Robinson, *"To the Best of My Ability"* (New York: Norton, 1987); James L. Sundquist, *Constitutional Reform and Effective Government* (Washington, D.C.: Brookings, 1986).
3. Committee on Responsible Parties, American Political Science Association, *Toward a More Responsible Two-Party System* (New York: Rinehart, 1950), 75. See also President's Commission for a National Agenda for the Eighties, *The Electoral and Democratic Process in the Eighties,* Paul G. Rogers, chairperson (Englewood Cliffs, N.J.: Prentice-Hall, 1981), 35-36.
4. See Max Farrand, *The Records of the Federal Convention of 1787,* 4 vols. (New Haven, Conn.: Yale University Press, 1966), 1:214-215.
5. Sundquist, *Constitutional Reform,* 115.
6. See Robinson, *"To the Best of My Ability,"* 270-271; and Committee on the Constitutional System, *A Bicentennial Analysis of the American Political Structure* (January 1987), 10-11.
7. Quoted in George B. Galloway, *History of the House of Representatives* (New York: Crowell, 1961), 236-237.
8. See Robert J. Spitzer, *The Presidential Veto* (Albany, N.Y.: SUNY Press, 1988), chap. 2.
9. *United States v. Nixon,* 418 U.S. 683 (1974).
10. For example, see Raoul Berger, *Executive Privilege: A Constitutional Myth* (New York: Bantam Books, 1984); Robert G. Dixon, Jr., "Congress, Shared Administration, and Executive Privilege," in *Congress against the President,* ed. Harvey C. Mansfield, Sr. (New York: Praeger, 1975), 125-140; Gary J. Schmitt, "Executive Privilege: Presidential Power to Withhold Information from Congress," in *The Presidency in the Constitutional Order,* ed. Joseph M. Bessette and Jeffrey Tulis (Baton Rouge: Louisiana State University Press, 1981), 154-194.
11. Quoted in Thomas E. Cronin, "Rethinking the Vice-Presidency," in *Rethinking the Presidency,* ed. Thomas E. Cronin (Boston: Little, Brown, 1982), 328.
12. James W. Davis, *The American Presidency: A New Perspective* (New York: Harper and Row, 1987), 396-397; Joel K. Goldstein, *The Modern American Vice Presidency: The Transformation of a Political Institution* (Princeton, N.J.: Princeton University Press, 1981), 4-6.
13. See Michael Dorman, *The Second Man* (New York: Dell, 1970); Paul C. Light, *Vice-Presidential Power: Advice and Influence in the White House* (Baltimore: Johns Hopkins University Press, 1984); Irving G. Williams, *The American Vice-Presidency: A New Look* (Garden City, N.Y.: Doubleday, 1954).
14. Quoted in Louis Fisher, *President and Congress* (New York: Free Press, 1972), 60.
15. An excellent discussion of delegation of power is found in ibid., chap. 3. See also Richard M. Pious, *The American Presidency* (New York: Basic Books, 1979), 213-217.
16. This account is taken from Louis Fisher, *Presidential Spending Power* (Princeton, N.J.: Princeton University Press, 1975), chaps. 1 and 2. For more on budgeting, see Dennis Ippolito, *Congressional Spending* (Ithaca, N.Y.: Cornell University Press, 1981); Lance T. LeLoup, *Budgetary Politics* (Brunswick, Ohio: King's Court Communications, 1986); Howard E. Shuman, *Politics and the Budget* (Englewood Cliffs, N.J.: Prentice-Hall, 1988); Aaron Wildavsky, *The Politics of the Budgetary Process* (Boston: Little, Brown, 1979).
17. *Wayman v. Southart,* 10 Wheat. 1 (1825).
18. *Field v. Clark,* 143 U.S. 649 (1891).
19. *S. W. Hampton, Jr. & Co. v. United States,* 276 U.S. 394 (1928).
20. *United States v. Curtiss-Wright Export Corp.,* 299 U.S. 304 (1936).
21. *Schechter Poultry Corp. v. United States,* 295 U.S. 495 (1935).
22. Quoted in Gerald Gunther, *Constitutional Law* (Mineola, N.Y.: Foundation Press, 1975), 424.
23. See, for example, Theodore J. Lowi, *The End of Liberalism* (New York: Norton, 1979).
24. Louis Fisher, *The Politics of Shared Power: Congress and the Executive,* 2d ed. (Washington, D.C.: CQ Press, 1987), 4.
25. See Aaron Wildavsky, "The Two Presidencies," in *Perspectives on the Presidency,* ed. Aaron Wildavsky (Boston: Little, Brown, 1975), 448-461. Wildavsky noted: "In the realm of foreign policy there has not been a single major issue on which Presidents, when they were serious and determined, have failed" (p. 449). Although Vietnam and subsequent events altered the truth of this statement, an ever-expanding role for the president in foreign policy continues to prevail. For more on the "two presidencies" thesis, see Donald A. Peppers, "The Two Presidencies: Eight Years Later," in ibid., 462-471; Lance T. LeLoup and Steven A. Shull, "Congress versus the Executive: The 'Two Presidencies' Reconsidered," *Social Science Quarterly* 59 (March 1979): 704-719; Lee Sigelman, "A Reassessment of the 'Two Presidencies' Thesis," *Journal of Politics* 41 (November 1979): 1195-1205; Harvey G. Zeidenstein, "The 'Two Presidencies' Thesis Is

Alive and Well and Has Been Living in the U.S. Senate Since 1973," *Presidential Studies Quarterly* 11 (Fall 1981): 511-525; Jeffrey E. Cohen, "A Historical Reassessment of Wildavsky's 'Two Presidencies' Thesis," *Social Science Quarterly* 63 (September 1982): 549-555.

26. Quoted in Gunther, *Constitutional Law,* 422.
27. See Louis Koenig, *The Chief Executive* (New York: Harcourt Brace Jovanovich, 1975), 5-6; Thomas E. Cronin, *The State of the Presidency* (Boston: Little, Brown, 1980), chap. 3; George Reedy, *The Twilight of the Presidency* (New York: New American Library, 1970), chap. 1.
28. Farrand, *The Records of the Federal Convention,* 2:318. As early as 1552 the verb "declare" was synonymous with the verb "commence," as in *to begin* or *initiate.*
29. Quoted in Gunther, *Constitutional Law,* 436; also see Gunther's discussion of war powers. Alexander Hamilton summarized the president's responsibility to Congress in war making in the *Federalist* No. 69. A useful historical accounting of the evolution of war powers is found in Demetrios Caraley, ed., *The President's War Powers: From the Federalists to Reagan* (New York: Academy of Political Science, 1984).
30. See Gunther, *Constitutional Law,* 437-439.
31. For more on this, see Louis Fisher, *Constitutional Conflicts between Congress and the President* (Princeton, N.J.: Princeton University Press, 1985), chap. 9.
32. Quoted in Gunther, *Constitutional Law,* 439.
33. For more on this debate, see Stephen Carter, "The Constitutionality of the War Powers Resolution," *Virginia Law Review* 70 (1984); Kenneth M. Holland, "The War Powers Resolution: An Infringement on the President's Constitutional and Prerogative Powers," in *The Presidency and National Security Policy,* ed. R. Gordon Hoxie (New York: Center for the Study of the Presidency, 1984); Robert Scigliano, "The War Powers Resolution and the War Powers," in *The Presidency in the Constitutional Order,* 115-153; William Spong, Jr., "The War Powers Resolution Revisited: Historical Accomplishment or Surrender?" *William and Mary Law Review* 16 (1975).
34. The Joint Chiefs of Staff, it was later revealed, had unanimously opposed sending the Marines to Lebanon. See Cecil V. Crabb, Jr., and Pat M. Holt, *Invitation to Struggle: Congress, the President, and Foreign Policy* (Washington, D.C.: CQ Press, 1984), 149. In all, 264 Marines were killed and 134 were wounded.
35. Fisher, *Constitutional Conflicts,* 317.
36. See Michael Rubner, "The Reagan Administration, the 1973 War Powers Resolution, and the Invasion of Grenada," *Political Science Quarterly* 100 (Winter 1985-1986): 627-647.
37. See John H. Cushman, Jr., "Iraqui Missile Hits U.S. Navy Frigate in Persian Gulf," *New York Times,* May 18, 1987, A12.
38. *Lowry et al. v. Reagan* (87-2196).
39. John Spanier and Eric M. Uslander, *American Foreign Policy Making and the Democratic Dilemmas* (New York: Holt, Rinehart and Winston, 1985), 73-74.
40. See, for example, Theodore J. Lowi, *Incomplete Conquest: Governing America* (New York: Holt, Rinehart and Winston, 1981), 313-315; Theodore J. Lowi, *The Personal President* (Ithaca, N.Y.: Cornell University Press, 1985), chap. 1. This trend has broken down in a few instances—such as during the Vietnam War and the Iranian hostage crisis—when the involvement stretches on without the prospect of a "winning" outcome.
41. James W. Davis, *The American Presidency: A New Perspective* (New York: Harper and Row, 1987), 196.
42. Larry Berman, *The New American Presidency* (Boston: Little, Brown, 1987), 36-37.
43. See James A. Robinson, *Congress and Foreign Policy-Making* (Homewood, Ill.: Dorsey Press, 1967), 67-69.
44. Koenig, *The Chief Executive,* 215; *Guide to Congress* (Washington, D.C.: Congressional Quarterly Inc., 1971), 202.
45. The Supreme Court case of *United States v. Curtiss Wright* stated: "The President alone has the power to speak or listen as the chief representative of the nation."
46. Crabb and Holt, *Invitation to Struggle,* 14.
47. Fisher, *Constitutional Conflicts,* 269.
48. *Goldwater v. Carter,* 444 U.S. 996 (1979).
49. Bernard Roshco, 'The Polls: Polling on Panama—Si, Don't Know; Hell No!" *Public Opinion Quarterly* 42 (1978): 551-562.
50. These and other basic facts are drawn from Crabb and Holt, *Invitation to Struggle,* chap. 3.
51. William L. Furlong, "Negotiations and Ratifications of the Panama Canal Treaties," in *Congress, the Presidency and American Foreign Policy,* ed. John Spanier and Joseph Nogee (New York: Pergamon Press, 1981), 78.
52. Crabb and Holt, *Invitation to Struggle,* 91.
53. This account is drawn from Stephen J. Flanagan, "The Domestic Politics of SALT II: Implications for the Foreign Policy Process," in *Congress, the Presidency,* chap. 3. See also Spanier and Uslander, *American Foreign Policy Making,* 204-217.
54. This was stated in *United States v. Pink,* 315 U.S. 203 (1942). Although executive agreement power is not stipulated in the Constitution, it generally is recognized as coming from four sources: the presidential responsibility to represent the country in foreign affairs, the presidential authority to receive ambassadors, the president's role as commander in chief of the military, and the president's obligation to "take care that the laws be faithfully executed." See Fisher, *Constitutional Conflicts,* 272-283.
55. See Benjamin I. Page and Mark P. Petracca, *The American Presidency* (New York: McGraw-Hill, 1983), 269-270. The greater presidential reliance on executive agreements is discussed in Loch Johnson and James M. McCormick, "Foreign Policy by Executive Fiat," *Foreign Policy* 28 (Fall 1977).
56. Robert E. DiClerico, *The American President* (Englewood Cliffs, N.J.: Prentice-Hall, 1983), 51.
57. Spanier and Uslander, *American Foreign Policy Making,* 12, 47, 88.
58. This account is taken from Spitzer, *The Presidential Veto,* chap. 3.
59. See Dan Caldwell, "The Jackson-Vanik Amendment," in *Congress, the Presidency,* chap. 1.
60. Jeane Kirkpatrick, "Human Rights and American Foreign Policy: A Symposium," *Commentary* 72 (November 1981): 42-45.
61. For example, Alan Tonelson, "Human Rights: The Bias We Need," *Foreign Policy* 49 (Winter 1982-1983): 52-74.
62. Randall B. Ripley and Grace A. Franklin, *Congress, the Bureaucracy, and Public Policy* (Homewood, Ill.: Dorsey Press, 1987), 190-191.
63. Quoted in Frank Kessler, *The Dilemmas of Presidential Leadership* (Englewood Cliffs, N.J.: Prentice-Hall, 1982), 110.
64. See Crabb and Holt, *Invitation to Struggle,* chap. 6.
65. DiClerico, *The American President,* 51-54.
66. See Jong Lee, "Presidential Vetoes from Washington to Nixon," *Journal of Politics* 37 (May 1975): 522-545; Gary Copeland, "When Congress and the President Collide: Why Presidents Veto Legislation," *Journal of Politics* 45 (August 1983): 696-710; David Rohde and Dennis M. Simon, "Presidential Vetoes and Congressional Response: A Study of Institutional Conflict," *American Journal of Political Science* 29 (August 1985): 397-427.
67. See Spitzer, *The Presidential Veto,* chaps. 2 and 3.
68. Quoted in Herman Finer, *The Presidency* (Chicago: University of Chicago Press, 1960), 75.
69. See Paul Light, *The President's Agenda* (Baltimore: Johns Hopkins University Press, 1982), 111.
70. Stephen J. Wayne, *The Legislative Presidency* (New York: Harper and Row, 1978), 159.
71. *The Pocket Veto Case,* 279 U.S. 644 (1929).
72. *Wright v. United States,* 302 U.S. 583 (1938).
73. See *Kennedy v. Sampson,* 364 F. Supp. 1075 (D.D.C. 1973); and *Kennedy v. Sampson,* 511 F. 2d 430 (D.C.C. 1974).

74. *Barnes v. Carmen,* 582 F. Supp. 163 (1984).
75. *Barnes v. Kline,* 759 F. 2d 21 (1985).
76. *Burke v. Barnes,* 93 L. Ed. 2d 732 (1987).
77. For more on the item veto controversy, see Spitzer, *The Presidential Veto,* chap. 5.
78. For more on arguments for the item veto, see Judith A. Best, "The Item Veto: Would the Founders Approve?" *Presidential Studies Quarterly* 14 (Spring 1984): 183-188; Russell M. Ross and Fred Schwengel, "An Item Veto for the President?" *Presidential Studies Quarterly* 12 (Winter 1982): 66-79.
79. House Committee on the Budget, "The Line-Item Veto: An Appraisal," 98th Cong., 2d sess., February 1984 (Washington, D.C.: Government Printing Office, 1984).
80. See Louis Fisher and Neal Devins, "How Successfully Can the States' Item Veto be Transferred to the President?" *Georgetown Law Journal* 75 (October 1986): 159-197.
81. The item veto proposals are criticized in Thomas E. Cronin and Jeffrey J. Weill, "An Item Veto for the President?" *Congress and the Presidency* 12 (Autumn 1985): 127-151; Fisher, *Constitutional Conflicts,* 159-162; Robert J. Spitzer, "The Item Veto Reconsidered," *Presidential Studies Quarterly* 15 (Summer 1985): 611-617.
82. For more on the legislative veto, see Fisher, *Constitutional Conflicts,* 162-183; Murray Dry, "The Congressional Veto and the Constitutional Separation of Powers," in *The Presidency in the Constitutional Order,* 195-233; Congressional Research Service, "Studies on the Legislative Veto," prepared for the Subcommittee on Rules of the House of the Committee on Rules, U.S. House of Representatives (Washington, D.C.: Government Printing Office, 1980).
83. *Buckley v. Valeo,* 424 U.S. 1 (1976).
84. *Immigration and Naturalization Service v. Chadha,* 462 U.S. 919 (1983).
85. Louis Fisher, "Judicial Misjudgments about the Lawmaking Process: The Legislative Veto Case," *Public Administration Review* 45 (November 1985): 711.
86. Erwin C. Hargrove and Michael Nelson, *Presidents, Politics and Policy* (Baltimore: Johns Hopkins University Press, 1984), 210.
87. Quoted in George C. Edwards III and Stephen J. Wayne, *Presidential Leadership* (New York: St. Martin's Press, 1985), 370.
88. Fisher, *Constitutional Conflicts,* 40.
89. George C. Edwards III, *Presidential Influence in Congress* (San Francisco: Freeman, 1980), 26.
90. Henry J. Abraham, *Justices and Presidents* (New York: Oxford University Press, 1985), 15.
91. Ibid., 16.
92. Ibid., chap. 2.
93. Everett C. Ladd, "The Political Battle for the Federal Courts," *Ladd Report,* no. 7 (New York: Norton, 1988), 10-21.
94. See Robert Scigliano, *The Supreme Court and the Presidency* (New York: Free Press, 1971), 96-99, 146-158.
95. Quoted in Kessler, *The Dilemmas of Presidential Leadership,* 215.
96. Edwards, *Presidential Influence in Congress,* 26.
97. This and other aspects of the appointment process are discussed in Fisher, *Constitutional Conflicts,* chap. 2.
98. Harold Seidman, *Politics, Position, and Power* (New York: Oxford University Press, 1980), 54.
99. Fisher, *The Politics of Shared Power,* 131-134. See also Fisher, *Constitutional Conflicts,* chap. 3.
100. The title of "chief legislator" was popularized by Clinton Rossiter's book *The American Presidency* (New York: New American Library, 1960). Rossiter asserted, "The President alone is in a political, constitutional, and practical position to provide such leadership, and he is therefore expected, within the limits of constitutional and political propriety, to guide Congress in much of its lawmaking activity" (p. 26).
101. Stephen J. Wayne, *The Legislative Presidency* (New York: Harper and Row, 1978), 8-10.
102. *Annals of Congress* (December 15, 1817), 452.
103. Wayne, *The Legislative Presidency,* 12-18.
104. Richard E. Neustadt, "Presidency and Legislation: Planning the President's Program," in *The Presidency,* 559.
105. Fisher, *The Politics of Shared Powers,* 27.
106. Quoted in Neustadt, "Presidency and Legislation," 594.
107. Davis, *The American Presidency,* 159.
108. Harold M. Barger, *The Impossible Presidency* (Glenview, Ill.: Scott, Foresman, 1984), 128-129. For more on legislative liaison, see Abraham Holtzman, *Legislative Liaison* (Chicago: Rand McNally, 1970).
109. Wayne, *The Legislative Presidency,* 72.
110. Ibid., chap. 3; Stephen J. Wayne and James F. C. Hyde, Jr., "Presidential Decision-Making on Enrolled Bills," *Presidential Studies Quarterly* 8 (Summer 1978): 284-296.
111. See Robert J. Spitzer, *The Presidency and Public Policy* (University, Ala.: University of Alabama Press, 1983), 98-100.
112. Quoted in Davis, *The American Presidency,* 163.
113. Sidney Blumenthal, "Marketing the President," *New York Times Magazine,* September 13, 1981, 112.
114. For more on the importance of popularity or "public prestige," see Richard E. Neustedt, *Presidential Power* (New York: Wiley, 1980), chap. 5; and Edwards, *Presidential Influence in Congress,* chap. 4.
115. See Lawrence Chamberlain, *The President, Congress, and Legislation* (New York: Columbia University Press, 1946); and Lawrence Chamberlain, "The President, Congress, and Legislation," in *The President: Roles and Powers,* ed. David Haight and Larry Johnson (Chicago: Rand McNally, 1965), 304.
116. William Goldsmith, *The Growth of Presidential Power* (New York: Chelsea House, 1974), 3: 1400.
117. Samuel Huntington, "Congressional Responses to the Twentieth Century," in *The Congress and America's Future,* ed. David Truman (Englewood Cliffs, N.J.: Prentice-Hall, 1965), 23. Huntington goes on to propose that law making be left to the president and that Congress devote its energies to constituent work and bureaucratic oversight.
118. Ronald C. Moe and Steven C. Teel, "Congress as Policy-Maker: A Necessary Reappraisal," *Political Science Quarterly* 85 (September 1970): 468. See also Hugh Gallagher, "Presidents, Congress, and the Legislative Functions," in *The Presidency Reappraised,* ed. Rexford Tugwell and Thomas E. Cronin (New York: Praeger, 1974), 232-233.
119. See, for example, John R. Johannes, "The President Proposes and Congress Disposes—But Not Always: Legislative Initiative on Capitol Hill," *The Review of Politics* 36 (July 1974): 356-370.
120. The presidential Boxscore is discussed critically in Wayne, *The Legislative Presidency,* 168-171; Thomas E. Cronin, *The State of the Presidency* (Boston: Little, Brown, 1980), 169-173; Spitzer, *The Presidency and Public Policy,* 93-94.
121. Sigelman, "A Reassessment of the Two Presidencies Thesis."
122. Edwards, *Presidential Influence in Congress,* 66.
123. Steven A. Shull, *Domestic Policy Formation* (Westport, Conn.: Greenwood Press, 1983), 10.
124. See Aage R. Clausen, *How Congressmen Decide* (New York: St. Martin's Press, 1973); and John W. Kingdon, *Congressmen's Voting Decisions* (New York: Harper and Row, 1973).
125. Lowi proposed this scheme in "American Business, Public Policy, Case Studies, and Political Theory," *World Politics* 16 (July 1964): 677-715. See also Theodore J. Lowi, "Four Systems of Policy, Politics, and Choice," *Public Administration Review* 32 (July-August 1972): 298-310.
126. Spitzer, *The Presidency and Public Policy,* chap. 7. Shull also applies three of Lowi's four categories to presidential-congressional relations in *Domestic Policy Formation.*
127. Neustadt, *Presidential Power,* 149.
128. Light, *The President's Agenda,* 32, 202-206.
129. The evolution of the seniority system is chronicled in Nelson W. Polsby, Miriam Gallaher, and Barry Rundquist, "The Growth of the Seniority System in the U.S. House of Representatives," *American Poliical Science Review* 63 (September 1969): 787-807.
130. For more on seniority, see Barbara Hinckley, *The Seniority*

System in Congress (Bloomington: Indiana University Press, 1971); and *How Congress Works* (Washington, D.C.: Congressional Quarterly Inc., 1983), 109-112.
131. Woodrow Wilson, *Congressional Government* (Boston: Houghton Mifflin, 1886), 69.
132. Clarence Cannon, *Cannon's Procedure in the House of Representatives* (Washington, D.C.: Government Printing Office, 1963), 221.
133. For more on the rules and procedures followed by committees and Congress as a whole, see Lewis A. Froman, *The Congressional Process* (Boston: Little, Brown, 1967); and Walter J. Oleszek, *Congressional Procedures and the Policy Process* (Washington, D.C.: CQ Press, 1984).
134. See Norman J. Ornstein and David W. Rohde, "Political Parties and Congressional Reform," in *Parties and Elections in an Anti-Party Age,* ed. Jeff Fishel (Bloomington: Indiana University Press, 1978), 280-294.
135. Barbara Hinckley, *Stability and Change in Congress* (New York: Harper and Row, 1988), 123, 138-140.
136. Ibid., 132.
137. Randall Ripley, *Congress: Process and Policy* (New York: Norton, 1983), 66.
138. Hinckley, *Stability and Change in Congress,* 158-163. For more on the committee and subcommittee system, see Richard F. Fenno, *Congressmen in Committees* (Boston: Little, Brown, 1973); Steven S. Smith and Christopher J. Deering, *Committees in Congress* (Washington, D.C.: CQ Press, 1984); *How Congress Works,* 79-108.
139. Roger H. Davidson and Walter J. Oleszek, *Congress and Its Members* (Washington, D.C.: CQ Press, 1981), chap. 6.
140. Quoted in ibid., 352; see also 46, 190, 352-355.
141. Ripley, *Congress: process and Policy,* 160.
142. Davidson and Oleszek, *Congress and Its Members,* 298-300.
143. Hinckley, *Stability and Change in Congress,* 204.
144. Alan R. Gitelson, M. Margaret Conway, and Frank B. Feigert, *American Political Parties* (Boston: Houghton Mifflin, 1984), 270-275.
145. Fred I. Greenstein and Frank B. Feigert, *The American Party System and the American People* (Englewood Cliffs, N.J.: Prentice-Hall, 1985), 133-135.
146. John H. Kessel, *Presidential Parties* (Homewood, Ill.: Dorsey Press, 1984), 138.
147. Ibid., 137-144. See also Wayne, *The Legislative Presidency,* chap. 5; and Holtzman, *Legislative Liaison.*
148. Edwards, *Presidential Influence in Congress,* 88-90.
149. Roger H. Davidson, David M. Kovenock, and Michael K. O'Leary, *Congress in Crisis* (Belmont, Calif.: Wadsworth, 1966), 64.
150. Edwards, *Presidential Influence in Congress,* 90-100.
151. George C. Edwards III, *The Public Presidency* (New York: St. Martin's Press, 1983), 1-4, 83-88. See also Gary C. Jacobson, *The Politics of Congressional Elections* (Boston: Little, Brown, 1983), 131-137; and Barbara Hinckley, *Congressional Elections* (Washington, D.C.: CQ Press, 1981), chap. 7.
152. For more on the relationship between elections and the economy, see Edward R. Tufte, *Political Control of the Economy* (Princeton, N.J.: Princeton University Press, 1978).
153. Hinckley, *Congressional Elections,* 114-131.
154. Edwards, *The Public Presidency,* 25-30.
155. Neustadt, *Presidential Power,* 9.
156. See Theodore Roosevelt, *The Autobiography of Theodore Roosevelt* (New York: Scribner's, 1958), 197-200; and William Howard Taft, *The President and His Powers* (New York: Columbia University Press, 1916), 138-145.
157. See Edwards, *Presidential Influence in Congress,* chaps. 5 and 6. See also Light, *The President's Agenda,* esp. intro. and chap. 1.
158. Edwards, *Presidential Influence in Congress,* 202.
159. Samuel Kernell, *Going Public: New Strategies of Presidential Leadership* (Washington, D.C.: CQ Press, 1986), 4.
160. Theodore J. Lowi, *The Personal President* (Ithaca, N.Y.: Cornell University Press, 1985).
161. These measures are summarized in Steven A. Shull, *Presidential Policy Making* (Brunswick, Ohio: King's Court Communications, 1979), 326-330.
162. The following assessments of individual presidents are drawn partly from Berman, *The New American Presidency,* chaps. 6-8; and Wayne, *The Legislative Presidency,* 32-59.
163. Neustadt, *Presidential Power,* 118-119.
164. Fred I. Greenstein, *The Hidden-Hand Presidency* (New York: Basic Books, 1982), 57.
165. Barbara Kellerman, *The Political Presidency* (New York: Oxford Univerity Press, 1984), 87.
166. Ibid., 155.
167. See Richard P. Nathan, *The Administrative Presidency* (New York: Wiley, 1983).
168. See James David Barber, *The Presidential Character* (Englewood Cliffs, N.J.: Prentice-Hall, 1985). See also Erwin C. Hargrove, *Presidential Leadership* (New York: Macmillan, 1966) for an alternative personality-based scheme.

Selected Bibliography

Binkley, Wilfred E. *President and Congress.* New York: Vintage, 1962.

Crabb, Jr., Cecil V., and Pat M. Holt, eds. *Invitation to Struggle: Congress, the President and Foreign Policy.* Washington, D.C.: CQ Press, 1988.

Edwards III, George C. *Presidential Influence in Congress.* San Francisco: Freeman, 1980.

Fisher, Louis. *Constitutional Conflicts Between Congress and the President.* Princeton, N.J.: Princeton University Press, 1985.

——. *The Politics of Shared Powers.* Washington, D.C.: CQ Press, 1987.

——. *President and Congress.* New York: Free Press, 1972.

Holtzman, Abraham. *Legislative Liaison.* Chicago: Rand McNally, 1970.

Light, Paul C. *The President's Agenda.* Baltimore, Md.: Johns Hopkins University Press, 1981.

Nathan, Richard P. *The Administrative Presidency.* New York: Wiley, 1983.

Polsby, Nelson. *Congress and the Presidency.* Englewood Cliffs, N.J.: Prentice-Hall, 1986.

Spanier, John, and Joseph Nogee, eds. *Congress, the Presidency and American Foreign Policy.* New York: Pergamon Press, 1981.

Spitzer, Robert J. *The Presidency and Public Policy.* University, Ala.: University of Alabama Press, 1983.

Spitzer, Robert J. *The Presidential Veto.* Albany, N.Y.: SUNY Press, 1988.

Sundquist, James L. *The Decline and Resurgence of Congress.* Washington, D.C.: Brookings Institution, 1985.

Wayne, Stephen J. *The Legislative Presidency.* New York: Harper and Row, 1978.

The President and the Supreme Court

The judiciary . . . will always be the least dangerous to the political rights of the Constitution.

—Alexander Hamilton
Federalist No. 78

We have, therefore, reached the point as a Nation where we must take action to save the Constitution from the Court and the Court from itself.

—Franklin D. Roosevelt
March 9, 1937

"In framing a government which is to be administered by men over men," James Madison urged in 1788, "the great difficulty lies in this: you must first enable the government to control the governed; and in the next place oblige it to control itself." The people, he continued, would be the principal control over the newly created American national government. A prudent man, Madison also advised that certain "auxiliary precautions" be taken.[1]

The auxiliary precautions of which Madison spoke involved the structure of and distribution of power within government. His prescription: "Ambition must be made to counteract ambition," power must be made to counteract power. Specifically, he proposed that the "interior structure" of government be arranged so that "its several constituent parts may, by their mutual relations, be the means of keeping each other in their proper places." [2]

Madison's prescription, a system of checks and balances, has been described by Edward S. Corwin as "an invitation to struggle" among the institutions of government.[3] The invitation was accepted. Since the administration of George Washington, the president and Congress have struggled with each other to control foreign and domestic policy. The judicial branch gave notice that it would enter the struggle during Thomas Jefferson's administration. The federal bureaucracy began emerging as a semi-independent branch in the late nineteenth century; by the second third of the twentieth century, it, too, had achieved the status of participant. And federalism ensured that the state governments also have struggled with the national government over the respective powers of each level.

A majority of these struggles have been resolved with minimal or no judicial participation. Members of the executive and legislative branches of government have preferred to settle their disputes through political bargaining and compromise, not litigation. Still, the involvement of the judiciary on occasion has been decisive.

Law delegates legal authority to the institutions of American government; the president acquires authority from the U.S. Constitution and from Congress. When this authority is questioned, the dispute may be submitted to the judiciary. The judiciary resolves these disputes by applying the facts of the dispute to the controlling provisions of law.

The meaning of a law is often unclear. Judges, therefore, must interpret law to resolve the dispute; that is, they must say what the law means. The immediate outcome is a more refined, judge-made definition of legal authority. This definition, in turn, may affect how political power is distributed among the various and competing institutions of government.

Legal authority and *power* are related through different concepts. *Power* means an ability to influence events.[4] The president, for example, may influence Congress to accept a legislative compromise by threatening to veto a bill in its current form. We could say in that case that the president has power over Congress because the president has the capacity to influence the legislative process.

Power is seldom absolute. The amount of power a president, or any other political officer, possesses at any time depends upon the existence and significance of a variety of factors. One such factor is legal authority.

Legal authority is power delegated by law. For example, the constitution delegates veto authority to the president. This authority, in turn, is a source of power for the president, because the president may use that authority to influence the legislative process.

Three important clarifications of legal authority, and its influence on presidential power, should be noted. First, legal authority may come with limitations—it frequently does. Second, legal authority is an important source, but not the only or even the most important source, of political power. Third, grants of legal authority may be overlapping; more than one branch may have the same or similar legal authority. There is ample room for interbranch meddling in the Constitution.

Legal authority is associated with what is called *legitimate power.* If citizens of a country obey a government command because they fear punishment, then the com-

By James Brian Watts

mand is enforced by *coercive power.* Most Americans, for example, file an annual income tax statement with the Internal Revenue Service; many do so because they fear being punished if they do not. Others may file the tax statement because they believe that government has the right to make that command. They would file even if punishment were not possible or likely. Government is exercising legitimate power in this instance because the people obeying believe government has the right to command. Some measure of both is present in all societies.

In the United States, legitimate power is associated strongly with legal authority; the expression "We are a nation of laws, and not of men" says much about American values. The president does not have to surround the Capitol building with troops to enforce a veto; members of Congress accept that the president has a right to veto legislation because the Constitution gives the president that authority.

The relationship between law and political power in the United States, then, flows something like this: law creates legal authority; legal authority confers (or denies) legitimacy; and legitimacy is connected with power. Now, if this flow becomes more specific by inserting the president and judges, we can see how the judiciary influences presidential power. Judges interpret laws that touch on the presidency; these interpretations contribute to the people's perception of the president's legal authority (to the extent that the people accept the legitimacy of this judicial role). Rulings that promote the president's legal authority also tend to promote the legitimacy, thus the power, of presidential actions.

The American Judicial System

The judicial branch *arbitrates* (that is, resolves, or settles) ongoing disputes about powers, obligations, and prohibitions created or governed by law. One party (for example, an individual, business firm, or governmental unit) alleges that another party has violated a law (for example, the U.S. Constitution, a statute enacted by Congress, a regulation promulgated by a bureaucrat, or a treaty made by the president). The two normally will attempt to resolve their differences through a process of bargaining and compromise. If this fails, one of the two may ask a court to resolve the dispute.

The court will resolve the dispute by making several decisions. Four of these are especially important to this discussion. First, the court will *find facts;* that is, it will resolve differences of opinion about what actually happened. Second, the court will decide which laws pertain to this dispute, and it will *interpret* those laws by determining how they govern the outcome of this particular case.

Third, having heard the facts, and having identified and interpreted the relevant provisions of law, the court next decides who wins and who loses. This is done by applying the facts of the case to the law. Fourth, the court will decide on an appropriate remedy for the benefit of the winning party. In a criminal case, for example, the winning party may be the prosecutor representing the government, in which case the court may order the defendant punished by fine or imprisonment. It may also be the defendant, in which case the court will order the charges dismissed and the defendant released from government custody.

This is not the place to discuss the judicial system and process in detail. Many published works already do this.[5] The remaining discussion will be easier to follow, however, if readers understand four characteristics of the judicial system: federalism, hierarchy, adversity, and the reactive nature of the judiciary.

Federalism

Federalism is one of the organizing principles of American politics. It means that a nation's political power is shared by two levels of government. In the United States, the two levels are the national government (usually referred to as the "federal" government) and fifty state governments. The governments of both levels have the power to make laws and to resolve disputes arising from these laws in courts of their own creation. (The federal government sets up its court system; state governments set up theirs.) Each government also determines how its judges are to be selected, decides what types of cases each court may hear (which is called the court's subject matter *jurisdiction*), delegates legal authority to judges, and generally regulates (within limits set by the U.S. Constitution) the trial and appeals, or *appellate*, process.

Federal courts have more influence over presidential power than do all the state courts combined. This is so for two reasons. First, federal courts have *original jurisdiction* in disputes involving federal law. Although state courts may and often do hear cases involving federal law, most cases affecting presidential power, directly or indirectly, are tried in federal court. Even if such a case is filed in state court, Congress has defined procedures for removing it to a federal court.[6] A second reason for the dominance of federal courts in actions affecting presidential power lies in the power of the U.S. Supreme Court as the ultimate interpreter of the Constitution and of laws of the United States. Most of the discussion that follows will be about federal court decisions.

Hierarchy

Hierarchy denotes rank according to specified criteria. It is a characteristic of most large and complex organizations—governments, businesses, and the American judiciary.

One criterion used to rank the various courts of a judicial system is appellate authority; that is, the power to review and modify the decisions of a lower court. The internal structure of every judicial system in the United States—the federal system and the systems of the fifty states, may be described by stating which court has appellate authority over another.

The lowest level in the hierarchy of federal and state judicial systems is the trial courts. They do the bulk of the work of the judicial system. They resolve questions of fact, interpret law, declare the winning party, fashion a remedy for the benefit of the winning party, and command compliance with their orders. Trial courts are given an assortment of names. They include the district, magistrate, and bankruptcy court in the federal system, and the superior court, circuit court, justice of the peace court, municipal court, and traffic court in various state systems. Unless appealed to a higher court, the decisions reached by these courts are final and binding.

Appellate courts are the highest level in the judiciary

because they review and may reverse decisions made by trial courts. Generally, the authority of an appellate court is limited to correcting mistakes made by the trial judge in interpreting a law. The authority of appellate courts to question factual findings of a trial court is severely restricted.

The federal and many state judicial systems have two levels of appellate courts, creating another layer in the hierarchy. An intermediate level handles most appeals from trial courts. The most important courts at this level in the federal system are the courts of appeals for twelve geographically defined areas, or *circuits*. Decisions of intermediate appellate courts may be appealed to the ultimate court of appeals for that system. The U.S. Supreme Court is the ultimate court of appeals for the federal system.

Federal courts primarily adjudicate disputes involving federal law. State courts also adjudicate issues of federal law, especially when a provision of the U.S. Constitution is applicable. For example, driving-under-the-influence-of-alcohol charges normally are matters tried by state courts according to state law. Federal courts typically will not be involved in such disputes. If, however, the defendant charges and presents evidence that the police violated the U.S. Constitution by an illegal search of his or her automobile, thus violating the warrantless-search provision of the Fourth Amendment to the Constitution, then whether the evidence gained through the search may be heard at trial is a matter that is governed by state and federal law. Ultimately, the U.S. Supreme Court may be asked to resolve the limited federal question, but only after the matter has worked its way through the entire hierarchy of state courts. In this limited sense, the U.S. Supreme Court ranks above the highest state appellate court in the judicial hierarchy. If no "federal question" is presented, then the state decision stands.

Adversity

According to Judge Jerome Frank, "litigation is strife. A lawsuit is a kind of fight or combat." [7] But, he continued, it is combat contained within the courts. The judicial process is a civilized alternative to the sword for resolving disputes.

Frank's analogy is apt. Litigation is a fight, and it is a fight between at least two persons whose stakes (property, money, power, freedom, or even life) in the outcome presumably are high. The process is not friendly; it is adversarial.[8]

An adversarial environment can promote or inhibit rational decision making. It can promote rational decision making because the personal and conflicting interests of the opposing parties make it probable that each side will marshal the evidence and legal arguments that offer the strongest support for its side of the case. The court will have the benefit of this work when it attempts to resolve the dispute.

The same incentives also may lead to poorly conceived decisions. Courts depend on the opposing parties to introduce germane evidence. Each side, as has been pointed out already, has a strong incentive to introduce self-serving rather than harmful evidence. In fact, each side has an incentive to obscure the existence of harmful evidence; if the stakes are important enough, self-interest may justify even the risk of perjury. The objective of litigation to the litigants is to win, not promote justice or the public good.

The Reactive Nature of the Judicial Process

Presidents, members of Congress, and judges all feel strongly about certain issues of public policy. All have ample power to influence these issues. Yet a vital difference exists between the power of a president or member of Congress, on the one hand, and a judge, on the other, to effect a change in policy.

Presidents and members of Congress may initiate a policy change without being asked; judges must be asked. The judicial branch makes public policy by answering questions put to it by people outside the judiciary. The reactive nature of the judicial process acts as a restraint on judicial power. This characteristic, therefore, will be discussed in more length under the heading "Restraints on Judicial Power."

Judicial Power

The U.S. Constitution delegates the judicial power of the federal government. Article III, section 1, states, "The judicial Power of the United States, shall be vested in one supreme Court, and in such inferior Courts as the Congress may from time to time ordain and establish." Section 2 continues, "The judicial Power shall extend to all Cases, in Law and Equity, arising under the Constitution, the Laws of the United States, and Treaties made, or which shall be made, under their authority. . . ."

The Constitution says the federal courts shall have judicial power, and it enumerates the types of cases in which this power may be exercised. But it does not say what judicial power is. We may say generally that *judicial power* is the ability to resolve disputes according to law, and to command persons to comply with the outcome. As it has evolved in the United States, this is a great power. Judicial power extends to the common criminal, and it extends to the nation's highest political officers. Even the president and Congress obey judicial commands.

An ability to command presupposes a reason to obey. There are two reasons why people obey judicial commands. First, judicial orders are backed, in most cases, by the coercive power of the United States. If armed marshals are not sufficiently persuasive, then the United States Army should be. But the entire law enforcement and military apparatus of the federal government is commanded by the president. Why should the president enforce orders with which he or she disagrees, especially orders directed by the president personally?

Some other source of power must be available to the courts. This source is *popular legitimacy*. The people of the United States, including the principal political officers, believe for the most part that judges have the legal authority, thus the right, to interpret and command obedience to the law. The president is expected not only to enforce those commands but also to obey commands directed at the office and at subordinates of the president.

Political Insulation of the Judiciary

The American Declaration of Independence was written primarily by lawyers. It is not surprising, therefore, that the text resembles a grand jury indictment, with charges against royal authority enumerated. Among the charges: "He [the king] has made Judges dependent on his Will alone, for the Tenure of their Offices, and the Amount and payment of their Salaries."

Eleven summers later, in 1787, the Founders remembered this royal abuse when drafting the U.S. Constitution. Judges of the national government would not be dependent on the will of the chief executive, or, for that matter, the will of Congress. Judicial power would be lodged in a separate, independent branch.

Members of the federal judiciary (which includes Supreme Court justices) are not elected; they are nominated and, with Senate consent, appointed to their jobs by the president.[9] This permits (but does not require) selection of federal judges on merit. Perhaps of greater importance, it permits federal judges to enter office without being encumbered by promises to an electoral constituency.

The appointments clause insulates federal judges at the time of their appointment. Two other clauses of the Constitution protect them against outside pressure once they take office. Article III, section 2, specifies that federal judges "shall hold their Offices during good Behavior." This protection effectively guarantees federal judges a job for life. They leave office in one of only three ways: death, voluntary resignation or retirement, or legislative impeachment. Impeachment might have been used to remove politically offensive judges; indeed, President Jefferson attempted to use it for this purpose, but his attempt failed. Congress so far has restricted itself to impeachment only on ethical grounds.

Finally, Article III, section 1, prohibits the reduction of judicial salaries during the term of office—which is for life. Neither may Congress coerce nor punish sitting judges by threatened or actual salary reductions.

The constitutional provisions that make the judiciary a separate and independent political branch do not in themselves give the judicial branch power. They do, however, provide judges an environment that is usually not permeated by the expectations and will of other political actors. It is possible to pressure judges; it is not easy.

The Power to Interpret Law

Chief Justice John Marshall wrote, "It is emphatically the province and duty of the judicial department to say what the law is. Those who apply the rule to particular cases, must of necessity expound and interpret that rule." [10] He might have gone further. He might have added: "And those who interpret the rule have the power to make the rule." But he did not. In fact, he disclaimed that power.[11]

Others have been less shy. Bishop Benjamin Hoadly, an Englishman of the eighteenth century, said this about the relationship between interpretation and judicial power: "Nay, whoever hath an absolute authority to interpret any written or spoken laws, it is He who is truly the Law Giver to all intents and purposes, and not the Person who first wrote and spoke them." [12]

American judges have tended to agree. Felix Frankfurter said "judges *are* the Constitution." [13] Charles Evans Hughes expressed the same sentiment: "We are under a Constitution, but the Constitution is what the judges say it is." [14]

Judges interpret law, and by interpreting law they give it final meaning. Consider the power this gives judges.

The U.S. Constitution is the paramount source of American law. Among other things, the Constitution creates the national government, defines the relationship between national and state power, organizes the various branches of the national government, delegates power to the branches it creates, places limits on the exercise of those powers, and defines certain rules for the selection of officers of and the conduct of business in each branch. The Constitution, in other words, says much about American political power.

The institutions of American government, state and federal, also make law. Like the Constitution, these laws affect the distribution of political power. Unlike the Constitution, which is concerned more with political process, these laws also define the ends of politics. Legislators make law by enacting statutes and resolutions, governors and presidents by signing executive orders (and international compacts in the case of the president), bureaucrats by promulgating regulations, and courts by modifying common law (a body of law created by judges to resolve specific disputes).

Laws affecting or exemplifying presidential power may come from all of these sources. Many such laws eventually become the basis for a conflict between two or more persons. Should that occur, should one of these persons ask the judiciary to arbitrate the conflict, and should the judiciary agree to hear the case, then a judge eventually may say, "This is what that law means, and I command you to obey it." The U.S. Supreme Court, for instance, said as much when it ruled that President Harry S Truman's seizure of the nation's steel industry during the Korean War was unconstitutional.

Judicial Review

Judicial review is the power of the judicial branch to determine the constitutionality of government actions (for example, laws, treaties, orders, and police searches), and to require the compliance of affected government officers with its determinations. This power may be used against any branch or officer of either the federal or a state government.

A good example of judicial review is the Supreme Court decision of *Hauenstein v. Lynham.*[15] A Virginia statute provided that real estate owned by aliens who died intestate (without a valid will) would become the property of the state. This law conflicted with a treaty in effect between the United States and Switzerland, which gave heirs of the dead person the right to sell the property and keep the proceeds. The state law was declared in conflict with the treaty, thus unconstitutional.

The U.S. Constitution ranks first in the hierarchy of American law; it is the supreme law of the land. All political acts must conform to the Constitution, whatever the level or branch of government involved.

This much was generally accepted in 1803, the year *Marbury v. Madison* was decided.[16] Not settled was who would measure the constitutional propriety of political actions. Each branch of each level could be the ultimate judge of its own actions. Or, the people themselves could judge the constitutionality of political actions through the electoral process. Or, the judicial branch could settle constitutional conflicts through the usual process of litigation.

The U.S. Supreme Court asserted its claim as final

The Difficulties and Dangers of Interpreting Constitutional Assignments of Presidential Power: The Views of Justice Robert H. Jackson

Like so many other justices, Robert H. Jackson brought a wealth of public experience with him to the U.S. Supreme Court. After serving as legal counsel to the Internal Revenue Bureau and as special counsel to the Securities and Exchange Commission, Jackson was appointed assistant attorney general and, later, solicitor general by President Franklin D. Roosevelt. In 1940, Roosevelt appointed Jackson attorney general, where he served until the president appointed him to the Supreme Court in 1941. In a controversial move, Jackson took a leave of absence from the Court in 1945 to act as chief American prosecutor in the Nuremberg trials of the principal Nazi political and military leaders. He returned to active Court service in 1946, where he remained until his death in 1954.[1]

Jackson is respected for his thoughtful analyses of judicial and political power. The following passages from his concurring opinion in the *Steel Seizure Case* are interesting for three reasons.[2] First, they demonstrate the influence prior experience in the "real world" of politics may have on a judge. Second, they contain a frank admission of this influence. Third, they present the views of at least one justice on the difficulty of applying a difficult set of facts to ambiguous constitutional grants of executive power.

> That comprehensive and undefined presidential powers hold both practical advantages and grave dangers for the country will impress anyone who has served as legal adviser to a President in time of transition and public anxiety. While an interval of detached reflection may temper teachings of that experience, they probably are a more realistic influence on my views than the conventional materials of judicial decision which seem unduly to accentuate doctrine and legal fiction. But as we approach the question of presidential power, we half overcome mental hazards by recognizing them. The opinions of judges, no less than executives and publicists, often suffer the infirmity of confusing the issue of a power's validity with the cause it is invoked to promote, of confounding the permanent executive office with its temporary occupant. The tendency is strong to emphasize transient results upon policies . . . and lose sight of enduring consequences upon the balanced power structure of our Republic.
>
> A judge, like an executive adviser, may be surprised at the poverty of really useful and unambiguous authority applicable to concrete problems of executive power as they actually present themselves. Just what our forefathers did envision, or would have envisioned had they foreseen modern conditions, must be divined from materials almost as enigmatic as the dreams Joseph was called on to interpret for Pharaoh. A century and a half of partisan debate and scholarly speculation yields no net result but only supplies more or less apt quotations from respected sources on each side of any question. They largely cancel each other.

1. *Guide to the Supreme Court* (Washington D.C.: Congressional Quarterly Inc., 1979), 854.
2. *Youngstown Sheet & Tube Co. v. Sawyer,* 343 U.S. 579, 634-635 (1952) (Jackson, J. concurring).

constitutional arbiter in *Marbury*. Writing through Chief Justice Marshall, the Court held that legislative power is subordinate and must be exercised in strict conformity to the Constitution. When a legislative act and a constitutional provision conflict, the judiciary must resolve the conflict in favor of the Constitution. "This," Marshall concluded, "is the very essence of judicial duty." [17] The Court proceeded to declare unconstitutional a section of the Judiciary Act of 1789.

Marshall's logic and decision were not immediately and universally accepted. Nonetheless, for several reasons—the political skill of Marshall, tradition, and the usefulness of the doctrine to Congress—judicial review came to be accepted by the people and political officers of the United States. Judicial review became legitimate.

Legitimation of judicial review "resulted in a quantum leap in the power of American judges." [18] It gave the judicial branch the ultimate power to interpret the Constitution and to command the other branches to obey. Outside the judicial branch, the only formal way of reversing a court interpretation of the Constitution would be by constitutional amendment.

Judicial review is frequently, and accurately, depicted as a negative power, the power to restrain. But this view is also misleading because it is too narrow. Judicial review can be a positive power. It can be used to lend constitutional legitimacy to the actions of political officers, such as occurred when the Supreme Court declared constitutional President Lincoln's naval blockade of Southern ports. Both the positive and the negative aspects of judicial review will be discussed extensively in the next chapter.

Popular Legitimacy

The logic of Marshall's justification for judicial review is not strong. But the continued vitality of the power is not explained by logic. Its vitality, rather, is explained by the legitimacy the American people give the power.

Judicial review is not mentioned in the Constitution. At best, authority for judicial review can be inferred from several constitutional provisions and the general constitutional design. Most Americans, however, would say that the judiciary has both the authority and power to carry out judicial review. They might disagree with specific decisions, but they do not question the right of judges to make those decisions. If for no better reason than tradition, judicial review is considered legitimate.

Popular legitimacy lends power to judicial decisions by making the political costs of defiance or outright disobedience too great for most officials to bear; the people believe that judicial decisions ought to be obeyed. Presidents have defied court orders, but instances of defiance are rare. More commonly, judges have had the power to make presidents enforce the will of the judiciary, even if the formal order is not directed at the president or a subordinate of the president. This is well illustrated by the events surrounding the desegregation of the Little Rock, Arkansas, school system. President Dwight D. Eisenhower enforced the court desegration order with military force, even though he personally believed the order was decided incorrectly. *(See "Dwight D. Eisenhower and the Little Rock Integration Crisis," p. 1170, in this chapter.)*

Popular legitimacy also promotes judicial power by protecting it from undue encroachments by other branches, including the presidency. The best example is the anomaly of the "court packing" episode of 1937. The people of the United States generally supported the New Deal policies of President Franklin D. Roosevelt and as generally opposed the tendency of the Supreme Court to declare many of those policies unconstitutional. Roosevelt's solution to the Court's opposition was to "pack" the Court with justices appointed to fill newly created seats. Despite the popularity of the president and his policies, most Americans opposed this move. Congress refused to enact the requested legislation. *(See "Franklin D. Roosevelt and the 'Court Packing' Episode," p. 1168, in this chapter.)*

Restraints on Judicial Power

Judicial power is not unbounded. It is, in fact, restrained in several important respects. Some of these restraints are internal; that is, they come from within the judiciary. Other restraints come from outside the judicial branch. These are external restraints imposed on judicial power by other political institutions, primarily Congress and the president, but also by constitutional amendment.

The final and perhaps the most comprehensive restraint on judicial power originates with the people of the United States. Judges cannot afford to be either too far ahead or too far behind the prevailing values and expectations of the people.

These categories are distinct, and the following sections address them separately; but readers should keep in mind that the relationships among these various sources of restraint are complex. Congress and the president are separated here; yet the two often act in concert, even if the roles are not public. Moreover, the popular will influences the behavior of Congress and the president as well as the behavior of judges.

Madison may not have consciously directed his prescription at the courts; but it applies nevertheless. Judicial power is controlled partially by the people and partially by the system of institutional checks and balances created by the Constitution.

Internal Restraints

Internal restraints on judicial power are those that originate with individual judges or with the structure or process of judicial decision making. Two already have been discussed: hierarchy and the reactive nature of the judicial process.

Hierarchy restrains judicial power by subjecting lower court decisions to the review of higher courts through the appellate process. The appellate process is typically slow—years may elapse between a trial court's decision and public announcement of the Supreme Court's review of that decision. During the intervening months, the justices may have reviewed other cases involving the same or similar legal issues. Moreover, the justices may have used this time to gauge public reactions to the various decisions made in these cases by trial and appellate courts. Will the public support the Supreme Court's decision? Will Congress or the president? Or, will the Court be alone in attempting to implement an unpopular rule of law? This experience and these perceptions may moderate the Court's decision.

The reactive nature of the judicial process restrains the judiciary by giving judges only a limited ability to initiate public policy. No matter how strongly a judge may feel about a particular issue, he or she cannot influence it until a stranger formally asks them. The request may never come, at least not in the judge's lifetime.

Self Restraint

Justice Oliver Wendell Holmes, Jr., once remarked, "If my fellow citizens want to go to Hell I will help them. It's my job." [19]

Curator's Office, U.S. Supreme Court

Associate Justices Oliver Wendell Holmes, Jr., (1902-1932) and Louis D. Brandeis (1926-1938).

Holmes believed in *judicial restraint.* He believed, that is, that judges ought to defer to decisions made by the president and members of Congress. In Holmes's own case, this required that he vote, most of the time in dissent, to uphold legislative schemes to regulate the economy. He had little confidence in these schemes—he made clear that he thought many were foolish. But he did not allow his personal feelings to guide his voting in these cases. The Constitution gave Congress the power to make the decisions, and make them Congress should.

How much deference a judge feels obliged to accord the two other branches of government will vary by individual judge, and it may vary by the issue being considered. Holmes, for example, qualified his generally deferential attitude toward legislative power by voting against schemes that tended to inhibit freedom of speech. Justice James C. McReynolds, in contrast, tended to vote against economic regulation but in support of measures designed to inhibit speech.

Group Decision Making

Appellate courts may be compared to a committee where each member has one vote. With some exceptions, the side garnering a majority of the votes wins the decision.

Some majority votes are better than others. A bare majority, obtained by a 5-4 vote, or 4-3 vote (if only seven justices are present), is sufficient to win the decision. As a rule, however, the nearer the voting ratio approaches nine-zero, the more desirable the outcome to the majority.

The first reason for this is that a bare majority vote virtually invites continuing challenges by people favoring the minority position, especially when one of the majority justices has indicated some doubt in an earlier or in the current opinion. The hope is that the decision will be reversed or at least limited in a subsequent decision.

The second reason some majority votes are better than others has to do with the legitimacy of the judicial branch. The power of the judiciary derives partly from the perception of the people that judicial decisions are made impartially and objectively. Justices concerned about maintaining judicial power therefore should be conscious that legitimacy is easier to maintain if the judiciary appears to be united rather than divided on an issue. As Walter Murphy, a scholar of the courts, has argued, "It is far more difficult to invoke the sacred mysteries of the cult of the robe for 5-4 rulings than for those which are unanimous or nearly so." [20]

The third reason is especially important in cases involving political power. Political officers outside the judicial branch may have the capacity to ignore, obstruct, or, in some cases, even defy judicial orders. But it is more difficult to defy an order when a court effectively says, by publishing a unanimous opinion, "We—conservatives, liberals, and moderates alike—have considered this issue carefully, and we agree." The full legitimacy of the court is invoked. The unanimous decision of the Supreme Court in *United States v. Nixon*[21] and the Court's practice of reaching unanimous decisions in the civil rights cases of the 1950s illustrate this point.[22]

The events leading to the vote of the Supreme Court in *Dayton v. Dulles* illustrate the rationale and process of judicial bargaining compromise.[23] In response to real and imagined threats to national security from the late 1940s to the mid-1950s, the passport office of the State Department began denying passports to U.S. citizens suspected of being a member of or otherwise supporting a "subversive" organization. Known Communist party members were included in the ban; so was almost anyone else who, in the opinion of the civil servant in charge of the passport office, held suspect views. The decision often was based solely upon a secret informant's report.

Those denied passports were entitled to an administrative appeal. In many cases, however, an appeal had no value since the government refused to divulge the source of the damaging information—the "faceless informer." [24] The applicant could swear to and produce witnesses attesting to his or her loyalty, but he or she could not directly refute the charges since the identity of the informant was not revealed.

Two grounds existed for challenging this procedure. The narrow ground was that the State Department's practice of not divulging the identity of informants had not been authorized by Congress. Should the Supreme Court invalidate the practice on that basis only, then Congress presumably would be free to reinstate the practice merely by changing the law. The second ground was that the right to travel was fundamental and could not be abridged without the applicant first having the opportunity to confront and cross-examine the informant under oath. This ground was constitutional and could not have been reversed by simple congressional action; a constitutional amendment would have been required.

Chief Justice Earl Warren assigned the task of writing the majority opinion to Justice William O. Douglas; Douglas opted for the broad, constitutional ground for invalidating the practice. Once Douglas circulated his draft opinion to the other justices, however, an original 6-3 majority began to crumble. Charles E. Whittaker defected to the dissent outright, and Frankfurter responded by saying he would concur with the Douglas decision, but not for the reasons given—Frankfurter insisted that the narrow, statutory ground be used. Douglas was left with only four of the Court's nine justices joining his draft opinion.

Had this been the final outcome, then Dayton would have won, but the opinion would have been of limited force. First, it would have indicated publicly that the justices were badly divided on the issue—and they were. Second, the constitutional ruling would not have been controlling of the case anyway since a majority of the Court would not have supported this ground.

Douglas eventually revised his draft opinion to gain the Frankfurter vote. As Douglas himself explained, "we [Warren, Hugo Black, William J. Brennan, Jr., and Douglas] have decided to defer to the majority of the Court and accordingly not to reach the constitutional issue." [25]

Precedent

The first question a judge is likely to ask himself or herself upon being asked to resolve a disputed legal issue is, "How have judges before me decided the same or a similar issue?" The judge finds the answer in *legal precedent*—judges' interpretations of law made in previous rulings.

Legal precedent evolves slowly, almost ponderously; there are few significant revolutions in judicial reasoning.[26] Judges usually follow the principle of *stare decisis* (Latin for "let the decision stand"), which means that they accept as authoritative the principles of law established in earlier judicial decisions.

Judges follow this naturally conservative decision-making practice for several reasons. First, the ruling prece-

U.S. Supreme Court

Sandra Day O'Connor became the first woman justice of the Supreme Court September 21, 1981, winning Senate confirmation by a 99-0 vote.

dents often conform to the values of most Americans for at least several years and to the values of judges for perhaps longer.

Second, the controlling interpretations of law presented in earlier decisions may be well reasoned in their original form. Although some interpretations grow stale quickly, the authors of others seem to have foreseen vastly changed social values and conditions. The opinions of John Marshall, for example, written between 1801 and 1835, provide examples of each.

A third justification for adhering to the rule of precedent is quite practical. Law regulates behavior and relationships in the United States. The parties to these relationships make important decisions with the expectation that their relationships will not be upset dramatically by frequent changes in law. Stable precedent leads to stable relationships.

The fourth and final justification recognizes the relationship between popular legitimacy and judicial power. If the people consider the role of the courts as legitimate because judges apparently make their decisions objectively, then the more stable the precedent, the greater the appearance of objectivity. Conversely, frequent reversals of precedent create the risk that the public will perceive judges as being no different from legislators.

External Restraints

Judges restrain themselves. But however important self-restraint may have been in the past, and is expected to be in the future, it is not a certain device for preventing abuse of judicial power. Abuse of judicial power is restrained further by three categories of externally imposed restraints. These are the constitutional amendment, other branches of government, and the people of the United States.

Constitutional Amendment

The ultimate political restraint on judicial power is the constitutional amendment. It is the only way currently available for a Supreme Court interpretation of the Constitution formally to be overruled (excepting, of course, when the Supreme Court reverses itself). It may also be used to reduce or even strip the courts of power.

Despite a promising beginning, the constitutional amendment has been a disappointment for those who might have used it to check judicial power. In 1793, the U.S. Supreme Court accepted for trial a civil suit brought against Georgia by two South Carolina citizens. Georgia refused to defend itself, saying the Court lacked jurisdiction over a state in such circumstances. The Court ruled that jurisdiction was proper and decided against Georgia.[27] The Eleventh Amendment to the U.S. Constitution, which stripped the federal courts of jurisdiction to hear cases in which one state is sued by citizens of another state, was ratified two years later.

The constitutional amendment has never again been used to limit judicial power so directly. Indirectly, however, five amendments have been adopted with the express purpose of overruling a Supreme Court decision.[28] The constitutional amendment holds great promise as a device for limiting judicial power. So far, however, practice has not met promise. The amendment process is too difficult to pursue except in the most unusual circumstances.

Restraints Imposed by Congress

Congress has sufficient authority and power to limit judicial power in several ways. It can create and abolish courts at will except for the U.S. Supreme Court, which the Constitution itself created. Moreover, Congress decides on procedures that must be used by both trial and appellate courts. These rules of procedure govern such activities as what types of evidence the court may hear, who may present this evidence, and what types of information opposing parties may receive before the trial begins. Finally, members of Congress may have a role in shaping public opinion toward the judiciary and toward decisions made by the judiciary. Considering that members of Congress come from every geographic region of the nation, this is not an insignificant power.

Congress has only limited authority to overrule judicial interpretations of law. It may initiate constitutional amendments—the only way outside the judicial system that interpretations of the Constitution can be formally overruled—but has done so rarely. Even when it does propose a constitutional amendment, three-quarters of the states must ratify the proposal for it to be adopted.

Congress also may overrule judicial interpretations of statutory and administrative law by the normal legislative process. Although Congress does this with greater frequency than it proposes constitutional amendments, it does not do so often. For example, the federal courts have rendered many interpretations of the equal employment section of the Civil Rights Act of 1964.[29] Despite this fact, and despite the controversial nature of its subject matter, Congress has overruled the courts in only one instance.[30]

A restraint Congress once used with great effect was based on its constitutional authority to decide what cases the Supreme Court may hear on appeal—that is, to define the court's *jurisdiction*.[31] Although the exact boundaries of this authority are disputed, at least one scholar of the Court, Robert McCloskey, has described it as "a license for Congress to decide whether the Supreme Court will be a significant or a peripheral factor in American government."[32]

Following the South's surrender at Appomattox and President Abraham Lincoln's assassination at Ford's Theatre, control of the national government was centralized in a Congress dominated by Radical Republicans. President Andrew Johnson became politically isolated by a hostile Congress and escaped being removed from office through the impeachment process by one vote in the Senate. These were determined men, and they were determined to impose their will on the formerly rebellious states. They would not tolerate obstruction—not by the president, not by the Supreme Court.

In 1867 William H. McCardle, a newspaper editor, was imprisoned by military forces for publishing articles considered defamatory. He challenged the lawfulness of his imprisonment and sought release by filing a petition for his release in the local federal district court. The writ was issued, but, following a hearing, McCardle was returned to military custody pending an appeal.

The U.S. Supreme Court issued two rulings in the case. First, in 1868, it boldly denied the government's claim that civilian courts lacked jurisdiction to hear the case. Congress responded by amending the Judiciary Act (over President Johnson's veto) to abolish the Supreme Court's jurisdiction to hear appeals from the circuit courts. The Court chose not to challenge Congress this time and, in its second ruling, announced in 1869, held that it now lacked jurisdiction, even though the case had already been accepted when Congress passed the law.[33]

Presidential Restraints

Alexander Hamilton recognized two hundred years ago that judges ultimately depend upon the support of the executive branch, In *Federalist* No. 78 he wrote:

> Whoever attentively considers the different departments of power must perceive that, in a government in which they are separated from each other, the judiciary, from the nature of its functions, will always be the least dangerous to the political rights of the Constitution, because it will be least in a capacity to annoy or injure them. The executive not only dispenses the honors but holds the sword of the community. The legislature not only commands the purse but prescribes the rules by which the duties and rights of every citizen are to be regulated. The judiciary, on the contrary, has no influence on either the sword or the purse; no direction either of the strength or of the wealth of the society, and can take no active resolution whatever. It may truly be said to have neither FORCE nor WILL but merely judgment; and must ultimately depend upon the aid of the executive arm even for the efficacy of its judgments.[34]

A president does not have to defy a court order to restrain judicial power, although such a strategy was employed by President Lincoln. A degree of restraint may be achieved when a president obeys or enforces an order, but not too enthusiastically. Moreover, a president may give the appearance of compliance, but, at the same time, attack the decision in public statements. The legitimacy of the president is protected—no violation of the law is apparent—while that of the judiciary is attacked.

A final means for presidential restraint of the judiciary comes from the authority of the president to appoint federal judges. Article II, section 2, of the Constitution delegates authority to the president to appoint all justices of the Supreme Court and such lower court judges as Congress may choose by legislation. Congress, in fact, has chosen to delegate the most important lower court appointments to the president.

New appointments to federal courts influence the development of precedent. As new appointees replace older judges, the precedents of the past are questioned and, frequently enough, highly qualified or discarded. The values of a new society, a new president, and new judges become part of the law. President Franklin Roosevelt was able eventually to overcome, and thus restrain, a hostile Supreme Court through new appointments; to a lesser extent, Richard Nixon and Ronald Reagan had similar success.

As important as this restraint may be, it is still limited. The president can make appointments only when judges leave a court or Congress creates new positions. The opportunities, therefore, to make new appointments may be few. Jimmy Carter, for example, made no appointments to the Supreme Court, although he made many to newly created appellate and trial court positions.

In addition, presidents have no way of controlling judges once the Senate confirms their nominations. Judges may and do vote independently. President Theodore Roosevelt was disappointed with Holmes, as Eisenhower was with Brennan and Warren. Justices Lewis F. Powell, Jr., and Harry A. Blackmun did not meet the complete political expectations of Nixon, and Sandra Day O'Connor voted several times against positions Reagan advocated.

Restraints Imposed by the Public

Justice Frankfurter argued that Supreme Court decisions largely reflect "that impalpable but controlling thing, the general drift of public opinion."[35]

Public opinion influences judicial decisions first by the fact that judges are members of society. Few judges avoid reading the daily newspapers, as did Holmes, because they think it a potential and undue bias; few refuse to vote, as did Black, because they consider voting a potential conflict of interest. Judges interact with American society in a variety of ways. As Holmes might have put it, judges read life. Part of this reading includes the positions and general drift of public opinion.

Next, public opinion influences how the president, members of Congress, and other political officials may respond to judicial decisions. A court strongly supported by the people may be more certain of executive and legislative support than one that is not. A court whose decisions are firmly at odds with public opinion may count on little support. As the federal judiciary's experience with civil rights cases in the 1950s and early 1960s suggests, judicial decisions strongly opposed by one segment of the public, and only half-heartedly supported by the president, Congress, state and local officials, or other segments of the public, will probably be resisted, and resisted with at least some success.[36]

Ultimately, the great danger to judicial power lies in the possibility that it will lose its public legitimacy. Public legitimacy ensures the independence of the American judiciary and sustains its power. Judges understand this.

Judicial Values and Decisions Affecting the President

Judges resolve most disputes affecting presidential authority by consulting three principal sources: (1) the disputed provisions of the Constitution or an act of Congress, (2) records indicating the intention of those who wrote the disputed text (for example, the *Federalist Papers* and committee reports of the House of Representatives and Senate), and (3) earlier judicial interpretations of the disputed provisions.

Some cases are resolved without difficulty. The text of the disputed law is fairly clear, and it is more so when read in conjunction with records indicating the intention of the law's makers *(Framers' intent)*. Moreover, the law may have already been the subject of one or more court cases, resulting in a body of existing judicial interpretations *(legal precedent)*. The task of the judge in such a situation is not difficult.

Other cases are not resolved so easily. The meaning of the disputed text may be unclear on its face. The judge may then seek guidance by consulting the intention of the framers of the law. Unfortunately, framers' intent, even if it can be found, may not be clear either; conflicting intentions may be discovered within the same records. Finally, the dispute may be somewhat or completely novel to the courts; that is, it may be *a case of first impression.*

The second situation provides judges with the greatest necessity for making law, and the greatest opportunity. It also provides them with a more hospitable environment to interject their own values into the process of interpretation.

That judges have applied their own values (preferences, that is, about what powers the U.S. president ought and ought not have, and what role the judicial branch ought to assume in conflicts involving presidential power) should not be taken to mean that judges have unfettered discretion to shape law. Nor does it mean that they necessarily consider the Constitution and acts of Congress as mere obstacles to be overcome by clever legal craftsmanship. Either assumption would oversimplify and distort the influence of personal values.

Judges start with the assumption that they must resolve the controversy, which in turn may require them to render a definitive interpretation of law; judges cannot say, "Well, I don't know what the law means either, so I just won't make a decision." Without clear guidance from the makers of the law, or from other judges, about what the law means, they have a limited ability to supply a meaning. How much discretion they have in any particular case depends partially upon how much guidance is supplied by the text of the law, the intention of the makers of the law, and the opinions of judges who have already heard and decided the issue.

Values may lead to unity on a court, and they may lead to conflict. Although, for example, the Supreme Court of the middle 1950s consisted of liberals, moderates, and conservatives, leading to split votes in many cases, the justices were mostly unified when the issue before them was government sponsored or enforced racial segregation. The value of "equal protection of the laws" was more powerful in all but a few cases than possibly competing values of state power and judicial restraint.

Five pairs of competing values seem to have had a recurring influence on judicial interpretations of laws affecting presidential power. These values are:

- judicial activism versus judicial restraint
- energy versus restraint in the executive branch
- individual liberty versus societal good
- national versus state power
- expediency versus long-term effect

Tension exists within each of the five pairs, tension that must be resolved by each judge or panel of judges interpreting the law.

Judicial Activism versus Judicial Restraint

Judicial restraint describes an attitude that judges ought to minimize their interference with decisions made by the president or Congress. Judges holding this attitude believe, to varying degrees, that they ought to defer to decisions made by the two other branches. They restrain themselves and thus limit the use of their own power.

Judicial activism, in contrast, is not so much a value held by judges as it is a label describing the tendency of some judges to interfere more often with presidential or congressional decisions than their more restrained colleagues. "Activist" judges do not necessarily view judicial intervention as virtuous (restrained judges do view restraint as a virtue), and they do not necessarily view restraint as a vice. Activist judges, however, do feel that restraint for the sake of restraint may be a vice in particular cases. Their urge to defer to the president or Congress may be offset in those cases by the existence of another, more important value.

American judges, for instance, historically have restrained themselves when the issue before them was presidential conduct of war. They may have disagreed with the presidential policies, and may even have had doubts about the lawfulness of certain policies, but those disagreements and doubts generally were subordinated to their belief that the judicial branch should not interfere. Although restraint has been the dominant value during war, it is not a value that has been held absolutely. On occasion judges have felt they must be more activist, such as when presidential policies have resulted in the infringement of individual rights guaranteed by the Constitution. This happened when the Court declared unconstitutional the military trial of civilians in areas loyal to the Union during the Civil War.[37]

Many reasons may be given to justify judicial restraint. The following is a partial list of these reasons:

- A commitment to democracy would seem to require that judges observe, whenever possible, the choices that democratically elected officials make.
- The Constitution confers primary responsibility for making political decisions on Congress and the president. Judges should not interfere with the constitutional intent.
- Judges are not as competent to make political decisions as executive and legislative officers.
- Judges must preserve the power of the judicial branch. Interfering with decisions made by Congress and the president creates the risk of retaliation and loss of power.
- The judicial process is designed to resolve disputes according to law. This narrow purpose is supported by a variety of rules that tend to narrow the scope of inquiry, the range of evidence considered, and the people involved. Such a restricted decision-making environment is not well suited to consider broader policy issues.
- Judges are not obliged to decide cases based on the rights—the *legal entitlements*—of the contesting parties. Broader questions of social policy are not necessarily relevant, nor are they necessarily considered.

Energy versus Restraint in the Executive

Alexander Hamilton celebrated a presidency with great strength and initiative. He wanted a president with "energy." [38] James Madison was more concerned about the danger created by power being concentrated immoderately in any one branch.[39] Madison saw presidential power would be a means of checking congressional abuse, and congressional power would be a means of checking presidential abuse.

The two compromised and then worked together toward ratification of the U.S. Constitution. The tension between the two views has persisted, however, and is present today. Judges have struggled with but have never resolved this tension. In part, this is because of the vagueness of the Constitution on the issue of executive power, and in part it is because of the urgency of events accompanying many cases to the courts. Judges have an understandable reluctance to be miserly with presidential power, especially in times of crisis; but neither do they want to be overly generous. Energy is an implicit value in some of their decisions, restraint in others.

The conflict between these two competing values has affected judicial review of all categories of presidential power. Generally, judges have been most indulgent of an energetic use of presidential diplomatic and war power. This has been especially true when claimed presidential power is supported by congressional action.[40]

Restraint also is found in cases dealing with presidential domestic power. And in some cases, the two values have collided, resulting in multiple opinions written by different judges.

Two recent decisions of the Supreme Court illustrate this tension. In the first, *Immigration and Naturalization Service v. Chadha,* the Court in 1983 invalidated the legislative veto of executive actions, thus promoting the ability of the president to act with energy and limiting the ability of Congress to restrain that energy.[41] Two justices dissented, Byron White and William Rehnquist.

Five years later, in 1988, the Supreme Court upheld the Independent Counsel Act in *Morrison v. Olson.*[42] (This act created the office of independent counsel, gave it authority to investigate and prosecute criminal acts committed by the president and close associates of the president, and insulated the office to a great extent from presidential interference.) William Rehnquist, now promoted to chief justice, wrote the majority opinion. Rehnquist was joined by White, and six other justices, five of whom had voted against him in *Chadha.* A legislatively devised means of restraining the presidency had been legitimized.

The two cases were similar in that the debate within the Supreme Court in both cases focused on the permissible limits of congressional restraints on presidential power.

The judiciary appears content with following the formula adopted in the compromise of 1787: an independent and energetic presidency, but one that is also capable of being restrained.

National versus State Power

Federalism was incorporated into but was never defined by the U.S. Constitution. The current boundaries between national and state power, such as they exist, are the product of a prolonged political struggle between the two levels, a struggle occasionally settled by military power. The tension between national and state legal authority has been firmly resolved in favor of the national government.

The attitude of the federal judiciary has not been consistent. John Marshall led the Supreme Court in promoting national power—some of his most highly regarded opinions legitimized power claimed by the national government. Marshall's successors, however, have not consistently followed his bias. Under Chief Justice Roger Taney, Marshall's sweeping generalizations about federal supremacy were qualified, although they were not then, nor have they ever been, reversed. And although over a century more of Supreme Court decisions was required to settle the issue decisively, assertions of state over national power are no longer a serious impediment to judicial review of presidential authority in domestic affairs.

The Court has especially upheld the president's supremacy over the states when the issues touched on military and foreign relations. The decision in *United States v. Belmont* provides an example (and an example of how one judge's position on the continuum of national versus state power varied with the issue.)

Justice George Sutherland, appointed to the U.S. Supreme Court by President Warren G. Harding in 1922, is perhaps best remembered as the intellectual leader of the "Four Horsemen," four conservative justices known for their opposition to New Deal legislation. As such, he was a firm opponent of President Franklin D. Roosevelt. But Sutherland also was a firm, even enthusiastic supporter of presidential power in foreign relations. In this respect, he was one of Roosevelt's strongest allies on the Court. His majority opinion in *United States v. Belmont* reveals his views on the state role in foreign relations.

> Governmental power over internal affairs is distributed between the national government and the several states. Governmental power over external affairs is not distributed, but is vested exclusively in the national government....
>
> Plainly, the external powers of the United States are to be exercised without regard to state laws or policies.... In respect of all international negotiations and compacts, and in respect of our foreign relations generally, state lines disappear. As to such purposes the State of New York does not exist.... State constitutions, state laws, and state policies are irrelevant to the inquiry and decision.[43]

If Sutherland, the economic and political conservative, was bothered by the fact that *Belmont* arose from the president's diplomatic recognition of the Soviet Union, it does not show in either his opinion or his vote.

The test for reconciling conflicts between national and state governments was defined as early as 1819 in *McCulloch v. Maryland.*[44] The decision in that case made clear that Congress exercises power granted to it by the Constitution, or one that can be fairly inferred from an explicit grant, and if the exercise of that power is not prohibited by another section of the Constitution, then the power is legitimate. State actions that conflict with a lawful exercise of national power are invalid; they are said to be "preempted" by federal law.

Individual Liberty versus Societal Good

Most Americans agree in principle that government ought to restrict individual liberty for the sake of a larger societal interest. Agreement breaks down, however, when the following questions are asked: "Which activities?" "How extensively?" "For what reasons?" "When?" "By whose authority?"

Legislators, chief executives, and judges must ask and attempt to answer these questions routinely. Some are not difficult. Little debate is required to classify murder, rape, and arson as crimes; little controversy aroused when violators are apprehended, tried, and punished. (Although the severity of the punishment may arouse controversy.) The collective interests of society outweigh whatever interest the individual has in committing these acts.

All issues are not resolved so easily. President Franklin D. Roosevelt, for example, authorized (Congress later ratified the authorization) the virtual imprisonment of over 100,000 American citizens of Japanese ancestry during World War II. Men, women, and children were forcibly removed from their homes and placed in camps surrounded by barbed wire and armed troops. The president did not justify his order with any evidence of disloyalty among the detainees, nor did he subject Americans of German or Italian descent to the same treatment. Only Japanese-Americans were presumed to constitute a risk to national security, and they were presumed to be a risk because they were Japanese-Americans.

The Supreme Court upheld the order in *Korematsu v. United States.*[45] Although, wrote Justice Hugo Black, government restrictions on racial groups are inherently "suspect," the Court was obliged to acknowledge the fact that the United States was at war with Japan, and that the war situation was uncertain at the time the order was signed and implemented. "Pressing public necessity" justified the action constitutionally. (This decision also well exemplifies the tendency of judges to show restraint when reviewing war policies of the president.)

Three justices, Owen J. Roberts, Frank Murphy, and Robert H. Jackson, did not agree, and wrote stinging dissents. National security was valued by all three, but so was individual liberty.

A final irony in this case is that Black, the author of the Court's opinion, and William O. Douglas, Black's colleague on the Supreme Court, are today best known for their prolonged, aggressive, and otherwise consistent use of judicial power to attack racial discrimination and defend individual liberties. The other justices who joined Black's opinion also demonstrated personal commitments to civil rights and civil liberties during their judicial tenure. The controversy presented to them, and to their dissenting companions, was not easily resolved. To most of them, the choice between social good and individual liberty must have been agonizing.

Most cases reaching the judicial branch do not involve a conflict between social good and individual liberty that is as sharply configured as the one resolved by the Court in *Korematsu.* Nevertheless, the conflict persists.

Generally, the Supreme Court has become more skeptical toward claims asserted by the executive of social good, and more protective of individual liberty. This skepticism is illustrated by the treatment the Court gave the government's attempt to suppress publication of the Pentagon Papers in 1971. (The Pentagon Papers were a collection of classified documents that revealed an assortment of embarrassing information about U.S. management of the Vietnam War.)

The government claimed national security justified suppression. The *New York Times* and *Washington Post,* defendants in the case, responded with their First Amendment guarantee of freedom of expression.

The Supreme Court sided this time with the value of individual liberty. As happened in *Korematsu,* however, the decision was not reached easily. Three justices dissented, arguing that the government's claim of national security outweighed the defendants' First Amendment right to publish. And the six justices who did vote against the government and in favor of the First Amendment claim, did so for separately stated reasons.[46]

Individual liberty prevailed, but social good (national security in this case) was not rejected by a majority of the justices as a possible reason for upholding similar government attempts in the future.

Expediency versus Long-term Effect

Tension also arises whenever the president claims legal authority in an environment of urgency. War, rebellion,

Library of Congress

During World War II, President Roosevelt authorized the virtual imprisonment of 100,000 Japanese-Americans who were interned at camps surrounded by barbed wire and armed troops.

and economic depression are not commonplace in American life, but they have occurred. During such emergencies the public insistently demands that government act, act decisively, and act successfully. And it is the president who most keenly feels these demands.

Do emergencies create presidential power? The answer may be yes, and it may be no. It depends on how the question is asked.

If the question is, "Do presidents possess greater power in an emergency than they would in ordinary times?" then the answer is undoubtedly yes. The people tend to unify in support of the president, as do members of Congress and the bureaucracy—the "rally 'round the flag" phenomenon. But political power is not the same thing as legal authority. Legal authority, and the legitimacy that accompanies it, is only one source of political legitimacy and political power. The president may have sufficient political power to respond to an emergency; he or she may not have sufficient legal authority. In some cases, actions deemed necessary by the president may be expressly prohibited by law.

Now, let us consider this question asked in a slightly different and more specific way. "Do presidents possess greater *legal* power during an emergency than they would in ordinary times?" Chief Justice Charles Evans Hughes provides an answer in *Home Building & Loan Assn. v. Blaisdell.*

> Emergency does not create [legal] power. Emergency does not increase granted power or remove or diminish the restrictions imposed upon power granted or reserved. The Constitution was adopted in a period of grave emergency. Its grants of power to the federal government and its limitations of the power of the States were determined in the light of emergency, and they are not altered by emergency. What power was thus granted and what limitations were thus imposed are questions which have always been, and always will be, the subject of close examination under our constitutional system.
>
> While emergency does not create power, emergency may furnish the occasion for the exercise of power.... The constitutional question presented in the light of an emergency is whether the power possessed embraces the particular exercise of it in response to particular conditions.[47]

How should the judicial branch respond? The correct answer is found in Hughes's analysis: either the law contemplates and provides for the emergency, or the president acts without lawful authority. Executive prerogative is a political, not a constitutional device. *(See "Presidential Privileges and Immunities," p. 1176, in this chapter.)*

How will the judicial branch respond? Will judges, as practical persons, find a way to legitimize the power judicially, even if this requires a strained interpretation of law? Will they insist on a rigid adherence to law, regardless of the seriousness of the emergency? Or will they avoid either legitimizing or denying the power to the president by refusing to consider the issue. Each of these responses has its own set of advantages and disadvantages, and each has been made.

Justice Robert H. Jackson has offered what is perhaps the most articulate defense of avoiding the issue. His analysis, it should be noted, follows closely the theory of executive prerogative of John Locke.

> Much is said about the danger to liberty from the Army program for deporting and detaining these citizens of Japanese extraction. But a judicial construction of the due process clause that will sustain this order is a far more subtle blow to liberty than the promulgation of the order itself. A military order, however unconstitutional, is not apt to last longer than the military emergency. Even during that period a succeeding commander may revoke it all. But once a judicial opinion rationalizes such an order to show that it conforms to the Constitution, or rather rationalizes the Constitution to show that the Constitution sanctions such an order, the Court for all time has validated the principle of racial discrimination in criminal procedure and of transplanting American citizens. The principle then lies about like a loaded weapon ready for the hand of any authority that can bring forward a plausible claim of an urgent need. Every repetition imbeds that principle more deeply in our law and thinking and expands it to new purposes. All who observe the work of courts are familiar with what Judge Cardozo described as the tendency of a principle to expand itself to the limit of its logic. A military commander may overstep the bounds of constitutionality, and it is an incident. But if we review and approve, that passing incident becomes the doctrine of the Constitution. There it has a generative power of its own, and all that it creates will be in its own image. Nothing better illustrates this danger than the Court's opinion in this case.[48]

Promoting Presidential Power

The American judicial branch has been a good friend of presidential power. Judges most often have sided with the president when presidential claims of legal authority have been challenged in court. The president's assertion of authority, they have ruled in many and diverse cases, conforms to the Constitution or a valid act of Congress. The judicial branch thus promotes presidential power by legitimizing presidential claims of legal authority to exercise specific uses of power.

The judicial branch also has promoted presidential power by defending presidential authority from invasion by other political officers. State governments have been the principal targets of this protective attitude, although Congress occasionally has discovered that its actions, too, can be invalidated by a circumspect judicial branch.

Legitimizing Presidential Claims of Constitutional Power

Article II, section 2, of the U.S. Constitution grants the president the power, "by and with the Advice and Consent of the Senate, to make treaties, provided two thirds of the Senators present concur." The power to make treaties, the Constitution makes clear, is a shared power. Does this mean that all international agreements signed by the president must be submitted to the Senate for approval?

President Franklin Roosevelt thought not. Following a practice initiated before he took office, Roosevelt made an "executive agreement" with the Soviet Union in 1933. The agreement was not approved by the Senate: in fact, Roosevelt did not even submit it to the Senate for approval. This was one of the grounds asserted in court (though not by the Senate) for ruling the agreement invalid.

Appeals eventually brought the question to the U.S. Supreme Court. The Court ruled in favor of the executive agreement and the president. Senate approval was not required.[49] *(See "International Compacts," p. 1183, in this*

The President versus the Supreme Court:. . .

On August 9, 1974, Richard Nixon became the first president of the United States to resign from office.

His resignation followed events that spanned two years, events first revealed to the public when the press reported that employees of the Nixon reelection campaign committee had burglarized the Democratic National Headquarters located in the now famous Watergate complex of Washington, D.C.

Many institutions of the nation's capital eventually became involved in the drama following the burglary: the president, the Senate, the House of Representatives, the U.S. District Court for the District of Columbia, the Department of Justice, the Federal Bureau of Investigation, and the news media all had critical roles. The case of *United States v. Nixon,* however, concerned primarily four actors: the president, an independent "special prosecutor" selected to investigate and prosecute possible criminal misconduct, the district court, and the Supreme Court of the United States. What emerged from this particular part of the larger drama was a Supreme Court ruling that tended to promote presidential power while contributing directly to Nixon's resignation.

Following an extensive investigation, the special prosecutor presented evidence of criminal misconduct to a federal grand jury. On March 1, 1974, the grand jury returned an indictment charging seven former members of Nixon's cabinet, White House staff, or reelection campaign committee with various crimes. Nixon himself was not indicted, but he was named as an "unindicted coconspirator" by the grand jury in a sealed (secret) part of the record.

On April 18, 1974, the district court issued a subpoena that ordered the president to produce tape recordings of and documents pertaining to conversations he had had with his advisers. The conversations were relevant to the upcoming trial of the seven defendants. Nixon responded with a motion to *quash* (suppress) the subpoena, arguing that certain procedural requirements had not been met and that communications between a president and presidential advisers are protected against disclosure by an *executive privilege.* The district court overruled the president's motion.

Nixon appealed to the U.S. Court of Appeals for the District of Columbia. In response to a petition filed by the special prosecutor, however, an expedited appeal was heard directly by the U.S. Supreme Court. The Supreme Court announced its decision on July 24, 1974.

Writing for a unanimous court, Chief Justice Warren Burger—Nixon's first appointee to the Court—rejected the procedural objections made by the president.[1] His opinion then turned to three arguments made by Nixon about executive privilege.

First, Nixon argued that communications between the president and his advisers are absolutely protected against disclosure by a constitutionally based executive privilege. Candor between the president and his close advisers, by this argument, is necessary for the president to perform his or her constitutionally delegated functions.

The Court agreed, but only partially. Communications between the president and his or her close advisers are presumptively privileged against disclosure. But, the Court continued, the privilege is conditional, not absolute. Whether it applies or not depends on a balancing of the public's interest in having access to the communications against the president's interest in keeping them

---

chapter.)

It is important to note what the Supreme Court did and did not accomplish. It neither created nor authorized a presidential power called the "executive agreement." The power had long been claimed and exercised by American presidents. The president's legal authority, if any existed, came from the Constitution.

The Supreme Court did resolve the issue of whether or not the power was authorized by the Constitution. And by saying that it was authorized, the Court gave the president an ability to say to Congress and the American people, "Making an executive agreement is within my constitutional authority. The United States Supreme Court has said it is."

The Supreme Court had judicially legitimized the executive agreement, and by legitimizing the executive agreement, the Court had associated its own legitimacy as the ultimate interpreter of law with a specific presidential action. To the extent that the people and political officers of the United States accepted Supreme Court rulings as authoritative, they would also accept the claimed power as legitimate.

Judicial scholar Walter F. Murphy explained the relationship as follows:

> The charisma of the Court's prestige has combined with its traditional and legal authority to create a subsidiary but nonetheless important source of judicial power. In a pluralistic society many important public policies adversely affect the aims and interests of a number of powerful individuals and groups. This antagonism not only creates opposition to the wisdom of policies involved but also stirs up controversy as to the very authority of government to pursue such policies. To meet this situation there must be some way of legitimizing political decisions, and the American political system provides for many means. . . . Acting through the ritual of the lawsuit, the Supreme Court plays a significant part in this process by declaring *constitutional* contested policies. Sharing the legitimizing role means the Court has a more positive function to perform than might appear from the superficially negative character of judicial review.[50]

A special predicament for judges occurs when Congress has apparently acquiesced in the exercise of a power by the president, and the exercise of that power not only has become established by long practice, but also has proven to be beneficial.

As president, William Howard Taft followed a practice established by his predecessors when he unilaterally ordered the removal of specified federal lands from private

. . . United States v. Nixon

confidential. The merits of each claim of executive privilege must be evaluated individually.

Nixon's second argument anticipated this ruling. If, he asserted, the privilege is conditional, and not absolute, then it is up to the president alone to determine whether the privilege should apply. Judicial interference with this power of the president would violate the separation of powers doctrine implicit in the Constitution.

The Court disagreed. Certainly, Burger reasoned, the president is obliged to interpret the Constitution. Moreover, interpretations of the Constitution made by the president are entitled to "great respect." But these interpretations are "initial," not final. Final interpretations of the Constitution must be made by the judicial branch.

> Absent a claim of need to protect military, diplomatic, or sensitive national security secrets, we find it difficult to accept the argument that even the very important interest in confidentiality of Presidential communications is significantly diminished by production of such material for *in camera* [closed] inspection with all the protection that a district court will be obliged to provide.[2]

Executive privilege might apply, but that decision would be made by a judge, not the president.

Third, the president contended that the interests of the presidency in this case outweighed the interests of the public in having the communications disclosed.

Again, the Court rejected the president's argument. While agreeing that courts could not proceed against the president as if he were an "ordinary individual," and that the president's need for confidentiality was due great deference, in this case the need of the courts to obtain evidence relevant to a criminal prosecution out-weighed a "generalized" need. Burger wrote, "The very integrity of the judicial system and public confidence in the system depend on full disclosure of all the facts. . . . To ensure that justice is done, it is imperative to the function of the courts that compulsory process be available for the production of evidence needed either by the prosecution or by the defense." [3] The Supreme Court affirmed in full the decision of the district court and ordered the president to surrender the tapes and documents.

For a time, there was some concern over whether the president would comply with the order. He did, and the tapes revealed that Nixon had, in fact, acted to obstruct the criminal investigation following the Watergate burglary. With this revelation, even stalwart congressional supporters of Nixon realized that the president would be impeached by the House and convicted by the Senate if he did not resign.

United States v. Nixon is an example of a president winning a war but losing the main battle. Personally, the decision was a lost battle and, effectively, a lost war to Richard Nixon. He resigned from office in disgrace. To the presidency—a constitutional office, not a person—however, the decision was an important victory. Executive privilege had previously been a political doctrine but not one that the U.S. Supreme Court had legitimized. A question almost as old as the presidency itself had now been settled.

1. The vote was eight to zero against the president. Justice (now chief justice) William Rehnquist, a former assistant attorney general under President Nixon, did not participate in the decision.
2. *United States v. Nixon,* 418 U.S. at 706.
3. Ibid., at 709.

oil and gas exploration, even though the explorations had been approved by Congress. The Court upheld the order in a unanimous opinion by Justice Joseph R. Lamar. Lamar's discussion of *political usage* shows a preference not to upset an arrangement made by tacit approval of Congress.

> It may be argued that while these facts and rulings prove a usage they do not establish its validity. But government is a practical affair intended for practical men. Both officers, law-makers and citizens naturally adjust themselves to any long-continued action of the Executive Department—on the presumption that unauthorized acts would not have been allowed to be so often repeated as to crystallize into a regular practice. That presumption is not reasoning in a circle but the basis of a wise and quieting rule that in determining the meaning of a statute or the existence of a power, weight shall be given to the usage itself—even when the validity of the practice is the subject of investigation.[51]

Lamar continued by saying that past executive practice alone did not mean that the president could "create a power" by a unilateral "course of action." Past practice, however, if "known and acquiesced in by Congress," would at least create a presumption in the minds of judges that Congress had consented.[52]

Legitimizing Congressional Delegations of Power

The example of Roosevelt's executive agreement with the Soviet Union demonstrates how legal power may flow directly from the U.S. Constitution to the president. It also illustrates how the judiciary may ratify, and thus legitimize, an arguable claim to power.

The Constitution also delegates legal power to Congress. Congress, in turn, may delegate a portion of that power to the president. The political function of the judiciary is roughly the same, although the process is complicated by an additional analytical step. The courts must determine (1) whether Congress initially possessed the power it was attempting to delegate, (2) whether the delegation was lawful, and (3) whether the president's exercise of the power conformed to the terms of the delegation.

United States v. Curtiss-Wright Export Corporation provides an example.[53] On May 28, 1934, Congress passed a joint resolution authorizing the president to prohibit the sale of American arms and munitions to Bolivia and Paraguay, the two participants in the Chaco War. President Roosevelt signed a proclamation banning the sales on the same day.

Curtiss-Wright was charged with violating the resolution and the presidential order. The trial court dismissed the charge, however, ruling that Congress had attempted an unlawful delegation of its own authority. This decision was appealed by the United States to the U.S. Supreme Court.

Curtiss-Wright did not challenge the power of Congress to regulate the foreign sale of arms. Article I, section 8, of the Constitution clearly confers that power on Congress. Thus, we can assume that the first part of the three-part test was met—Congress did possess the power it attempted to delegate.

The second part of the test was a point of dispute and was the basis for the trial court's dismissal of the prosecution. Curtiss-Wright objected to the form of the joint resolution since it allowed the president too much discretion in deciding when and how the ban was to be enforced. Justice Sutherland, summarized the defendant's argument, stating that Congress "abdicated its essential functions and delegated them to the Executive." [54]

The Supreme Court rejected this argument, thus reversing the decision of the trial court. Essentially, the Court reasoned that the Constitution differentiates between powers exercised by Congress and the president in foreign and domestic affairs: more latitude is given both branches in foreign affairs. Specifically, Congress may grant the president greater discretion in foreign affairs than it could if the issue were purely domestic.[55]

Finally, Curtiss-Wright insisted that the president had not followed the procedures that Congress had imposed on the president. The Court also rejected this argument.

Again, the Supreme Court did not create either the legal authority or the political power for the president's order. It did, however, say that the authority and power were constitutional, thus legitimate.

The ruling bestowed another important benefit on the president. By holding the order legitimate, the Supreme Court also made the courts available for the prosecution of cases arising out of alleged violations of the order. Had the Court ruled otherwise, the president would have had no way to prosecute violators.

Defending the President against Encroachments by Other Branches

Vietnam and Watergate focused attention on presidential abuse, and the notion of an "imperial presidency" came into vogue. But political imperialism is not initiated exclusively in the White House. It may originate in other branches, and it may be directed at the presidency. This has happened on many occasions.

One such occasion was when Congress attempted to limit the president's constitutionally vested authority to grant pardons during the administration of President Andrew Johnson.

Article II, section 2, of the U.S. Constitution vests in the president the power "to grant Reprieves and Pardons for Offenses against the United States." The pardon power does not extend to impeachments, but otherwise it neither states nor implies limitation. Congress is not mentioned.

Alexander Hamilton justified exclusive delegation of the pardon power in the president by arguing that the timely granting of a pardon by the president could help end a rebellion.[56] It was, in fact, for this purpose, and the purpose of restoring tranquillity to the Union, after the Civil War had ended, that both Abraham Lincoln and Andrew Johnson granted a series of conditional pardons and amnesties to persons aiding the Southern cause. Finally, on Christmas Day, 1868, President Johnson granted a full and unconditional pardon to supporters of the South.

Congress, in the meantime, was overtly hostile to President Johnson and his forgiving policies. Congress wanted to restore domestic tranquillity to the Union, and it wanted to punish the South. Accordingly, the legislative branch enacted a series of laws that indirectly or directly invaded the president's pardon power. A number of these restrictions were challenged in court by former Confederate soldiers or political officers.

Ex parte Garland arose when a person whom President Johnson had pardoned was denied admission to practice law in federal court.[57] The denial was based on an act of Congress that required anyone seeking to practice law in federal court to swear an oath of allegiance to the United States. Part of the required oath affirmed that the applicant had never voluntarily borne arms against the Union or given assistance to those who had.

The U.S. Supreme Court held the law unconstitutional, thus validating the pardon: "This power of the President is not subject to legislative control. Congress can neither limit the effect of his pardon, nor exclude from its exercise any class of offenders. The benign prerogative of mercy reposed in him cannot be fettered by any legislative restrictions." [58]

Congress had tried to limit the president's authority to pardon. The Supreme Court ruled that Congress lacked that authority. By defending the presidency in this manner, the Court did not make the president's authority any greater; it did, however, make that authority more secure.

Limiting Presidential Power

Although the judicial branch has been a good friend of presidential power, it has not permitted this friendship to interfere with its function of resolving disputes according to the law. Presidents occasionally overstep or even abuse their legal authority, and judges occasionally remind presidents of this fact—and of the independent status of the judicial branch.

The judicial branch is a friend of the presidency; it is not a subordinate.

Invalidating Presidential Actions

The U.S. Constitution delegates legal authority to the president; it also limits that authority. Presidents may abuse their authority either by exceeding the boundaries of the delegation or by violating the limitation.

The first principle is illustrated by a Supreme Court decision involving Amos Kendall, postmaster general in the cabinet of President Andrew Jackson. Following the orders of Jackson, Kendall refused to pay a postal contractor for services rendered. Congress then enacted legislation directing the postmaster general to pay the sum owed. Kendall paid some, but not all, of the amount specified by Congress.

The government contractor then sought and obtained a judicial order (writ of mandamus) directing Kendall to pay the disputed amount. Kendall appealed to the Supreme Court, arguing, among other things, that the constitutionally stated obligation of the president to enforce the law implies a corresponding power to forbid their execution. The Court was not persuaded.

Although, reasoned Justice Smith Thompson, the Constitution indeed imposes upon the president an obligation to enforce the law, this obligation does not mean that the president may direct that a law be disobeyed. Kendall's interpretation (Smith pointed out that the president himself did not make the claim) of presidential authority was excessive. The order of the lower court was affirmed.[59]

Kendall v. United States illustrates an instance in which the judicial branch drew a line indicating the limits of presidential authority and then said the president (through his subordinate) had crossed that line. A second decision of the Supreme Court, *Reid v. Covert,* illustrates how a line may be drawn by the existence of a constitutionally protected right.

Exercising his constitutionally granted diplomatic authority, President Franklin D. Roosevelt concluded an executive agreement with Great Britain in 1942 that gave American military courts jurisdiction over civilian dependents of American military personnel for crimes committed within Great Britain. Congress gave effect to this agreement by authorizing military trial of civilians in circumstances covered by the agreement.

The wife of an American air force sergeant was tried and convicted by a military court for murdering her husband in Great Britain. She argued that her conviction was unconstitutional since she was denied, among other things, her constitutionally protected rights to a trial by jury and a grand jury indictment, neither of which is available in military trials.

The Supreme Court agreed. The mere existence of an international agreement, reasoned Justice Hugo Black for the majority, could not itself free the government of limitations imposed by the Constitution. A constitutional limitation on presidential (and congressional) power had been violated.[60]

The Supreme Court ruled in each case that the president had abused his power. In the first case the president had abused his power by exceeding his constitutional authority; in the second by violating an express limitation placed on his authority by the Constitution. In both instances the judiciary denied the legitimacy of the president's action—the president was acting outside of the law.

Invalidating Congressional Delegations

Presidential authority may be conferred by the Constitution directly, by Congress, or, in certain instances, by the two sources together. *Reid v. Covert* involved the latter form of delegation, and it illustrates how the judicial branch may limit presidential power by invalidating congressional delegations of authority to the president.

President Roosevelt made the executive agreement with Great Britain based upon his constitutional authority in the field of foreign relations. Something else was needed, however, to make the agreement fully effective.

Although the president is designated commander in chief of the armed forces of the United States by Article II, section 2, of the Constitution, the grant of authority implicit in this designation is not complete. As is so often the case, presidents share their authority with that given by the Constitution to Congress.

The Private Citizen and Presidential Power: Mr. Wiener versus President Eisenhower

American citizens have limited although important influence on the way political power is allocated. They exert this influence by voting in elections and by supporting organizations that regularly seek to influence the political process, such as local political party organizations. More remotely, private citizens may influence specific controversies by serving on a jury.

These activities usually do not generate conflicts over presidential power. Nevertheless, American citizens have played a critical role in defining the legal authority of the president through the judicial process; it has been individual citizens, in most cases, who have triggered judicial review of claimed political authority by challenging that claim in court, as either plaintiff or defendant.

Myron Wiener, for example, was appointed by President Harry S Truman to the temporary War Claims Commission in 1950. Wiener's appointment, according to the legislation creating the commission, was to coincide with the relatively short life of the commission. The law said nothing about presidential authority to fire commission members. Despite this, President Dwight D. Eisenhower fired Wiener in 1953, informing him that he wanted the commission composed entirely of persons of his own choosing—and, presumably, not of the former president's.

Wiener claimed that the president was without legal authority to fire him and sued to recover the wages he would have earned had he remained a commission member. The president claimed his authority came from the Constitution.

The Supreme Court ruled unanimously in Wiener's favor.[1] The president, the Court held, must have authority from either the Constitution or Congress to fire commission members. He had neither.

Wiener went to court looking for justice—he wanted to be compensated for the money he lost. He got what he wanted. In the process of pursuing his personal claim, however, Wiener also accomplished something of far greater political consequence. He gave the Supreme Court cause to narrow the president's removal power. Wiener may not have cared, but he served as a vehicle for limiting the power of the American president.

1. *Wiener v. United States,* 357 U.S. 349 (1958).

Congress is given authority by Article I, section 8, of the Constitution to make laws it considers "necessary and proper" to regulate the armed forces and to "carry into execution" the president's authority as commander in chief. Thus, it is Congress, and not the president, that defines military crimes and regulates the jurisdiction of military tribunals. And it was Congress that gave effect to Roosevelt's agreement with Great Britain by authorizing the military trial of civilian dependents of U.S. military personnel stationed in foreign nations. The attempted delegation of this authority, the Court ruled, was unconstitutional.

Supporting Congress in Disputes with the President

Congress may limit as well as create presidential authority. This occurs in one of two ways. First, Congress may place restraints directly on the authority it delegates to the president. Second, Congress may place restraints on the authority of the president when the Constitution specifies that Congress and the president are to share that authority.

The Supreme Court ruled in *Kendall v. United States* that Congress may create entitlements and direct that they be paid. As long as the legislatively stated conditions for receiving the entitlement are met, and the president is not given discretion to pay or not pay by the legislation, then the president (or, more often, subordinates of the president) has no choice but to comply.

A modern and frequently litigated variation of the *Kendall* case occurs when Congress confers a benefit on a defined group of people and specifies conditions that must be met before individual members of that group may receive the benefit. For example, Congress has made mentally and physically disabled persons eligible for Social Security benefits under certain conditions.

As part of its effort to reduce the cost of the Social Security program, the Department of Health and Human Services (HHS) under President Ronald Reagan implemented a policy of reviewing the eligibility of existing disability beneficiaries. HHS removed from the benefit rolls those individuals it found no longer met the statutory and administrative eligibility criteria.

Implementation of this policy provoked multiple law suits by former beneficiaries. Many of these found a receptive audience in the judicial branch, leading to rulings that nullified the negative administrative eligibility determinations.[61] By holding HHS to the inferred intent of Congress, these judges had simultaneously denied the president an important power—extensive discretion in exercising authority that had been given by Congress—and had frustrated an important presidential policy.

Congress also may restrain presidential power by defining procedures that must be followed before an executive policy may be made or implemented. The Administrative Procedures Act (APA), which specifies multiple and detailed procedures that administrative agencies must follow before performing actions specified by the act, is the most important example.

In *Morton v. Ruiz,* the Supreme Court ruled that the Bureau of Indian Affairs of the Department of Interior had violated the APA. The agency, according to the Court, had violated the law by not following procedures specified by the APA for making a rule, which, in turn, was applied to deny an applicant benefits conferred by Congress.[62] The agency might well have interpreted the intention of Congress correctly, but it failed to follow the procedures mandated by Congress for making that interpretation.

If Congress delegates authority to the president (to make rules concerning eligibility for benefits, for example), and if Congress accompanies the delegation with procedures that must be followed in the exercise of that authority, then the president is obligated to follow those procedures. This is an important method used by Congress to check the arbitrary abuse of power it delegates to the president. By holding the president to these procedural rules, the judicial branch supports congressional restraints on presidential power.

Congress may even restrain the exercise of authority granted directly to the president by the Constitution. Article II, section 1, of the Constitution vests the "executive Power" of the national government in the president. In addition, Article II, section 2, gives the president broad authority to appoint officers of the executive branch. Other than the impeachment process, nothing is said in the Constitution about the removal of executive officers. The president is neither granted nor denied authority to fire officers of the executive branch.

In *Myers v. United States,* the Supreme Court ruled that Congress could not constitutionally limit the ability of the president to fire postmasters.[63] President Franklin D. Roosevelt interpreted this ruling to mean that he could fire a member of the Federal Trade Commission (FTC) at will, although even the law creating the FTC limited such firings to specified causes. Accordingly, the president fired William E. Humphrey solely for the reason that he and Humphrey disagreed about FTC policy.

The estate of Humphrey (Humphrey died after his discharge) sued the United States to recover the wages Humphrey would have been paid had he continued in office. The estate won.

In *Humphrey's Executor v. United States,* the Supreme Court ruled that Congress could restrict the ability of the president to fire officers of the executive branch when those officers exercised nonexecutive powers delegated to them by Congress.[64] Since commissioners of the FTC were given extensive rule-making and adjudicatory powers by Congress, neither of which was considered executive in nature, the Court concluded that Roosevelt's firing of Humphrey was unlawful.

The Court did not overrule *Myers.* Instead, it distinguished the facts in *Myers* by pointing out that postmasters did not exercise nonexecutive powers.

Humphrey is important because the Court upheld the authority of Congress to restrict a significant executive power of the president: power to fire certain officers of the executive branch. More broadly, it is important because the Court upheld the authority of Congress to place legislative restrictions on powers given directly to the president by the Constitution.

Avoiding the Issue

Americans warmly embrace the notion that the courthouse door is always open. And it is open, but not always. Sometimes the door is firmly closed; at other times it is open, but only narrowly. This applies particularly when a constitutional question of presidential power is at issue.

Goldwater v. Carter is instructive.[65] In 1949, a Communist-led revolution succeeded in expelling Chiang Kai-shek and his government from mainland China. Chiang moved to the island of Taiwan (Formosa), where, protected by American military power, he continued to claim *de jure* (lawful) status as the sole government of China. The Communist government in Beijing (Peking) contested this claim and, in fact, ruled all of mainland China.

The United States initially recognized Chiang's government and backed that recognition with a mutual defense treaty. This policy began to change during the administration of President Nixon as the United States and the People's Republic of China moved toward normal, even friendly, diplomatic relations. On December 15, 1978, President Jimmy Carter formally recognized the Beijing government, thereby severing diplomatic ties between the United States and Taiwan in the process. Carter also abrogated unilaterally (that is, abolished without consulting Congress) the mutual defense treaty between the United States and Taiwan.

Sen. Barry Goldwater challenged the abrogation in court. (The senator, it should be noted, was acting in his own behalf, not on behalf of the Senate.) He argued that since the treaty was ratified by the Senate, it could not be abrogated without prior Senate approval. Both the district court and court of appeals ruled against the senator, whereupon he appealed to the U.S. Supreme Court.

The Supreme Court vacated, or annulled, the judgment of the court of appeals and remanded the case (that is, sent it back) to the district court with instructions that the action be dismissed. In other words, the Court decided not to decide the issue. The courthouse door was closed.

Six justices voted to dismiss the case summarily. Lewis F. Powell, Jr., thought that the issue should be addressed first within the "normal political process" and that a "constitutional impasse" should be reached between the president and at least one house of Congress before the case could be adjudicated. As matters stood, the dispute had not become concrete enough for resolution by the judicial branch; that is, the issue was not "ripe" for adjudication. He voted to dismiss.[66]

William H. Rehnquist agreed with Powell's conclusion, but for different reasons. Rehnquist characterized the question of treaty abrogations as "political," thus not appropriate for judicial resolution. The Constitution, Rehnquist reasoned, confers the treaty-making power on the president and Senate. But the Constitution says nothing about treaty abrogations—no standards are available for judges asked to arbitrate disputes between the president and Congress over their respective authority to terminate treaties. In such circumstances, the issue should be resolved by Congress and the president, not the courts. Rehnquist also voted to dismiss, and three other members of the Court joined him in his statement.[67]

The final member of the Court to vote in favor of dismissal was Thurgood Marshall. He neither filed a statement explaining his reasons nor joined the statements written by Powell or Rehnquist. Byron R. White and Harry A. Blackmun were not prepared either to dismiss the case or affirm the decision of the court of appeals; they voted to set the case for argument. Only William J. Brennan, Jr., voted to affirm the decision of the court of appeals.

What effect does *Goldwater v. Carter* have on presidential power? The decision neither affirms nor denies the legal authority Carter claimed. In effect, the Supreme Court returned the question of constitutional legitimacy to the president, Congress, and the American people. It is as if the case never was tried.

The president may continue to exercise the power and justify its legitimacy with his or her best arguments. The president, however, cannot claim that the Supreme Court has approved the power as being within his or her legal authority; the president cannot invoke the unique power of judges to legitimize claimed political power.

The Supreme Court dismissed *Goldwater v. Carter* because a majority of the justices believed it violated the political question and ripeness doctrines. This decision was within the Court's discretionary power. Other doctrines accord the Court similar discretion, although that discretion is sometimes limited by Congress.

A federal court will not advise the president or Congress on abstract questions of law. An actual *case* and *controversy* must exist. This doctrine was created when five Supreme Court justices declined to certify pension petitions from veterans. The justices reasoned that the legal authority of the judiciary is derived from the Constitution and that the Constitution confers jurisdiction on the courts only if an actual case or controversy exists.[68] The practical import of this rule is that federal judges will not issue advisory opinions.

Not only must a controversy exist at the time a lawsuit is filed, it also must exist throughout the litigation. A court will not attempt to resolve an issue that no longer exists, and it will be dismissed as being *moot*.

Finally, a plaintiff must have *standing* to initiate a lawsuit. This means that a plaintiff must show some direct legal injury that can be attributed to the defendant as a prerequisite to bringing suit. The injury alleged must be specific; it is not sufficient for the plaintiff to show that he or she shared some general injury with the rest of the public. For instance, the Supreme Court held in 1974 that being a taxpayer by itself does not confer standing on a person challenging the constitutionality of secret appropriations for the Central Intelligence Agency.[69]

The reader should be forewarned that the legal rationales for these doctrines are complex and confusing. In some cases, so many exceptions and contradictions exist, that stating a uniform rule is impossible. We should be cautious, therefore, when generalizing about what these doctrines require. It is more profitable to consider them as ways for judges to avoid issues they do not want to decide.

The President and the Judiciary: Cooperation and Conflict

James Madison counseled the American people to accept certain "auxiliary precautions" in the design of the American national government.[70] Power, he advised, should be divided and delegated to separate and independent institutions: legislative, executive, and judicial. Each one of these institutions, moreover, should have the means both of checking abuses committed by the other branches and of defending itself from external encroachments. Intramural conflict within the structure of the American national government would tend to promote liberty.

The two-hundred-year history of U.S. politics gives substantial support to Madison's arguments. Each branch periodically has used its own power to check abuses originating in other branches; each branch periodically has defended itself. Each branch remains independent, yet powerful.

A careful reading of the other sections of this chapter reveals an important lesson about presidential-judicial relations: the federal judiciary has, on balance, been a useful invention to the presidency. The judiciary has legitimized significant claims of presidential diplomatic, war, and economic power. Moreover, various attempts by Congress and the states to limit presidential power have been rebuffed by circumspect judges. Presidents may have cause to complain about judicial decisions on occasion, but they also have reasons to be grateful. The judicial branch has been good to the president.

The generosity of the judiciary, however, has not been unbounded. The Supreme Court said no to George Washington, Abraham Lincoln, Harry S Truman, and Franklin D. Roosevelt. It placed Andrew Jackson and Dwight D. Eisenhower in politically embarrassing positions and lectured Thomas Jefferson about the obligations of the presidency. Richard Nixon became the first president to resign from office; his resignation may be attributed partially to decisions made by various courts.

Such conflicts should not necessarily alarm us. In fact, continuous harmony should be more alarming to us than periodic conflict—if we agree with Madison. Periodic conflict is evidence of a healthy measure of independence among the branches; continuous harmony suggests the successful subjugation of one branch by another.

Still, conflict and confrontation may lead to subjugation, with the judiciary being the losing branch. This nearly occurred in two instances. In the first instance, Thomas Jefferson attempted to remove political opponents from the federal judiciary through the device of legislative impeachment. His attempt failed, and the impeachment device, as Jefferson himself predicted at the time, has never again been used against the judicial branch in an attempt to achieve partisan advantage.

Franklin D. Roosevelt employed a less direct strategy than Jefferson, but it would have had a similar effect. Roosevelt proposed to enlarge the membership of the Supreme Court with new appointees—his appointees—to a size sufficient to offset the votes of justices who consistently opposed his policies. He proposed to "pack the Court." Roosevelt's plan also died in Congress.

Abraham Lincoln employed a different and more successful strategy: he disobeyed an order signed by the chief justice of the United States, Roger Taney. Having no means of enforcing his order in the face of presidentially commanded military force, Taney was forced into a humiliating retreat. The Civil War, Lincoln made clear, would be fought to a successful conclusion with the support of the judiciary if possible, and without it if necessary. American judges were forever reminded of the realities of politics and the relative weakness of their own position.

The final case considered in this section cannot be classified as a confrontation between the judiciary and the presidency. It nevertheless contains a useful lesson. In 1957, Arkansas governor Orval Faubus attempted to obstruct a federal court order with the Arkansas national guard. President Dwight Eisenhower found the job distasteful but backed the judiciary with superior military force. The U.S. Constitution, he believed, required no less.

Thomas Jefferson and the Impeachment Controversy

Thomas Jefferson and John Marshall were Virginians by birth and cousins by blood. Each was to become a "great" in U.S. political history: Jefferson as president and Marshall as chief justice of the United States. They also were to become bitter political enemies.

The personal enmity that existed between these two greats was surely one reason for the most famous, and most dangerous, of the periodic conflicts between the president and the judiciary. There were, however, other less personally motivated factors that should be considered.[71]

First, the Democratic-Republican Jefferson entered the presidency in 1801 following twelve years of Federalist rule, eight years under George Washington, and four under John Adams. The federal judiciary consisted almost entirely of political opponents of the newly inaugurated president.

Second, these Federalist judges had used their offices to support policies anathema to Jefferson. They had routinely applied English judicial precedent when deciding American common law disputes, and they were perceived as being biased in favor of property owners and creditors. Most offensive to Jefferson, they had vigorously enforced the hated Sedition Act, a measure making it a crime to criticize maliciously the president, Congress, or national government.

Third, Jefferson thought that Adams and the then-Federalist-dominated Congress had been patently unfair to him. With only a few days remaining in the Adams administration, Congress had created a number of new judgeships, and the Senate had quickly confirmed the president's hurried appointments to these positions. Denied the presidency and the Congress in the election of 1800, the Federalists thereby secured a power base in the judicial branch.

Jefferson attacked and won an important skirmish. In December 1801 he urged Congress to abolish the federal circuit court system. Congress obliged the president the following March and by so doing effectively eliminated many judgeships filled by Adams. Federalists still controlled the Supreme Court, but their hold on the inferior court was reduced significantly.

A question remained: Would this legislation survive constitutional scrutiny by a hostile Supreme Court? It did, in the 1803 decision of *Stuart v. Laird*.[72] Jefferson's enthusiasm for this result, however, was undoubtedly dampened by an event occurring only a week before.

On February 24, 1803, Chief Justice Marshall announced the opinion of a unanimous Court in *Marbury v. Madison*.[73] William Marbury, the Court held, may have had lawful claim to a judicial commission withheld by Jefferson's secretary of state, James Madison, but that was an issue the Court could not decide. The law conferring jurisdiction on the Court to hear the case was unconstitutional. The Federalist appointee of President John Adams would not sit as a judge.

The decision was both a victory and a loss to Jefferson. Marbury did not get his commission, and that must have been pleasing to the president. But Marshall had in the process lectured the president and his secretary of state about their constitutional responsibilities, and that must have been galling. Finally, Marshall and his Federalist allies on the Court had asserted the power to declare acts of Congress unconstitutional, and that must have been disturbing.

In fact, Jefferson was incensed.

Jefferson might have responded by defying the Court, had defiance been possible. But it was not possible; there was nothing for the president to defy since the Court had imposed no obligation on him. By denying itself a relatively insignificant power (original trial jurisdiction in cases of the type pressed by Marbury) the Court had asserted a more important one—judicial review—and had embarrassed the president in the process. The president's victory a week later in *Stuart* must have seemed insignificant by comparison; and it was.

Only one vacancy occurred on the Supreme Court during Jefferson's first term, when Alfred Moore retired in 1804. And though his place was taken by the able William Johnson, the president was far from achieving the majority he needed to neutralize Marshall and his allies. More direct measures were needed. The impeachment clauses of the Constitution seemed to have promise.

Article III, section 1, of the Constitution provides that judges of the Supreme Court, and inferior courts of the judicial branch, "shall hold their Offices during good Behavior." Under ordinary circumstances, this would have assured Marshall and his Federalist colleagues a life tenure on the Supreme Court. But the circumstances were not ordinary, not to Jefferson and his congressional allies. They wished ardently to rid the judiciary of the Federalists and thought they had found the means in the impeachment clauses.

"The President, Vice President and all civil Officers of the United States," says Article II, section 4, "shall be removed from Office on Impeachment for, and Conviction of, Treason, Bribery, or other high Crimes and Misdemeanors." The power to impeach (roughly equivalent to a criminal indictment) is vested solely within the House of Representatives, according to Article I, section 2; power to try and convict or acquit, impeached officers is conferred on the Senate by Article I, section 3. If both the House and the Senate could have been persuaded to remove the Federalist judges through impeachment, then the way would have been open for Jefferson to have replaced them with his own appointees.

A three-step strategy was developed, with the threat to the judiciary escalating with the progression to each new step. First, the Jeffersonians would attempt the removal of John Pickering, a federal district judge from Maine. Second, if the removal of Pickering was successful, then Congress would move against Samuel Chase, a Supreme Court justice and Federalist ally of Marshall. Third, if Chase were removed, then all Federalists would be removed. The judicial branch would be purged of its Federalist taint, and the purged judges would be replaced by appointees sharing Jefferson's own political values.

The removal of Pickering succeeded. Plagued by insanity and alcoholism, Pickering was incapable of performing his judicial function. Those voting to indict and convict Pickering may have been motivated by partisan more than judicial considerations, but they were justified. Pickering could not do the job.

Chase was not disabled either by insanity or by alcoholism. He could do his job, and he could do it well. And that was the principal—if not the articulated—complaint against him.

Neither Chase nor Jefferson and his allies had clean hands. Chase was prone to making overtly partisan statements from the bench, a number of these being direct and immoderate attacks on the political principles held so dear by the president. Moreover, Chase's conduct as a circuit trial judge led to at least a reasonable basis for believing that partisan bias, not the law, guided his rulings. Chase's behavior would not be tolerated today; constitutional scholar Raoul Berger has argued that it should not have been tolerated then.[74]

Jefferson and his allies were no less partisan. True, Chase committed injudicious conduct from the bench, and this conduct arguably justified removal by impeachment. But the "high crimes and misdemeanors" alleged against Chase in the articles of impeachment failed to enumerate his real "crime"; Chase was a Federalist and, more important, a Federalist in a position to check the president. Chase was a Federalist justice of the Supreme Court.

The House of Representatives voted in favor of impeachment and duly submitted articles of impeachment to the Senate for trial. The outcome seemed certain: Chase would lose.

Marshall was so concerned about the likely outcome, and undoubtedly about what would follow, that he offered a proposal that must be considered somewhat bizarre. Constitutional rulings of the Supreme Court, he suggested, might be appealable to Congress as a whole. This proposal cannot be squared with Marshall's own logic of judicial review announced in *Marbury*.[75]

Marshall may have been desperate at this point, but Jefferson's congressional allies were quite confident. Neither attitude, it turned out, was warranted. A majority of the senators voted to convict Chase, thus remove him from office. Fortunately for Chase, however, the Constitution required (and still requires) that a two-thirds vote of the Senate must be obtained for a conviction. With the defection of six Democratic-Republican senators, the vote fell short of the necessary two-thirds on all counts.

Chase was acquitted, and the immediate threat to Marshall and the Federalist judges passed.

Various explanations have been offered for the failure of the Senate to convict.[76] Edmund Randolph's prosecution of Chase in the Senate was poorly organized and conducted. In contrast, the Chase defense was conducted with great ability. Chase was also a hero of the American revolution, something that engendered, perhaps, some public and congressional sympathy in his behalf. James Madison, more sympathetic than Jefferson to one branch checking the power of another, may have intervened on behalf of Chase. Some of the Democratic-Republican senators who voted to acquit were loyal to Jefferson's vice president, Aaron Burr, who had been dumped from Jefferson's reelection ticket only six days before the Senate vote was taken. Finally, some may have genuinely believed that an emasculated judiciary would, in the end, be more injurious to the nation than a judiciary that was hostile to the current administration.

The consequences of the acquittal are more certain. Plans for using the impeachment process to remove Marshall and his other Federalist colleagues on the Supreme Court were discarded. The independence of the Court was secured for the time being.

Of greater long-term significance, Marshall could now turn his energies toward incorporating his political values into U.S. constitutional doctrine. His views toward protecting property have now been largely discarded. His conviction that national power should be supreme and elastic, however, had become embedded firmly in U.S. constitutional law by the time his tenure as chief justice ended with his death in 1835.

An important political precedent also was established. Had Jefferson succeeded and Chase, Marshall, and the other serving Federalist jurists been removed, then the constitutional grounds for removal by impeachment—"high crimes and misdemeanors"—would have included political disagreement. But Jefferson did not succeed, and his failure established the inverse as precedent: political disagreement alone is not a sufficient basis for removing federal judges through the impeachment process. As Jefferson himself commented at the conclusion of the controversy, "Impeachment is a farce which will not be tried again." [77]

Abraham Lincoln and the Habeas Corpus Controversy

Abraham Lincoln was elected president on November 6, 1860. South Carolina responded by dissolving its ties to the United States on December 20, 1860. By the time Lincoln was inaugurated on March 4, 1861, Mississippi, Florida, Alabama, Georgia, Louisiana, and Texas had followed South Carolina's lead. The Confederate States of America was proclaimed on February 7.

Lincoln inherited a split nation and a presidential decision. If he acquiesced in secession, then the Union would remain split; if he resisted by force, then civil war would surely ensue, perhaps with other southern states assisting in the secessionist cause. Lincoln chose Union and accepted the costs of war.

This policy was made known unmistakably by the Union defense of Ft. Sumter, South Carolina, on April 12-14, 1861. As a result, four more states left the Union: Virginia, Arkansas, Tennessee, and North Carolina. The final battle lines now were drawn, with the eleven states of the Confederacy pitted against the government of the United States.

Claimed geographic boundaries, however, do not convey the true dimensions of the problem Lincoln faced. Although four slave states—Delaware, Maryland, Kentucky, and Missouri—had rejected secession, each one nevertheless contained a substantial number of Confederate sympathizers. Maryland posed a special problem since it, along with Virginia, surrounded Washington, D.C. Southern sympathizers and other opponents of the war effort could be found also in the nonslave states of the North. The president faced a determined and dangerous foe to the South and a population of uncertain loyalty within those states remaining loyal to the Union.

Intent on preserving the Union, Lincoln used the full measure of his constitutional authority as president, and more. He created an army, spent money, and blockaded Southern harbors, all without prior congressional approval. Also unilaterally, he ordered the military arrest and trial of suspected Southern sympathizers, and suspended the writ of *habeas corpus*.

Each one of these orders raised a substantial constitutional issue. It was Lincoln's suspension of *habeas corpus*, however, that led to a direct confrontation between the executive and judicial branches.

Habeas corpus is a judicial order. It commands a government officer to deliver a designated prisoner before the issuing judge. The judge will then determine whether the prisoner is being held lawfully and, if not, will order his or her release. Its purpose is to prevent arbitrary arrest and imprisonment, not to determine innocence or guilt.

The U.S. Constitution speaks of *habeas corpus* in Article I, section 9: "The Privilege of the Writ of Habeas Corpus shall not be suspended, unless when in Cases of Rebellion or Invasion the public Safety may require it." The grounds for suspension stated clearly and apparently met; Lincoln would seem to have acted entirely within the boundaries of his constitutional authority. That was his interpretation of the Constitution, but it was not one that would be shared by the judiciary.

On April 19, 1861, a regiment of Union soldiers marched through Baltimore while in transit from Massachusetts to Washington. A riot ensued, causing the mayor of Baltimore, with the apparent consent of the Maryland governor, to order the destruction of the railroad bridges leading to Baltimore from the North. Lincoln ordered suspension of the writ eight days later.[78]

On May 25, 1861, John Merryman was arrested by military forces, and imprisoned at Ft. McHenry, Maryland. He was charged with treason, stemming from his alleged participation in the destruction of the Baltimore bridges.

At the request of Merryman's counsel, Chief Justice Roger Taney signed a writ of *habeas corpus*, ordering the commanding general of Ft. McHenry, Gen. George Cadwalader, to appear in court with the prisoner. Neither the general nor the prisoner appeared. An aide to the general, however, did appear, and informed Taney that the general had been authorized by the president to suspend the writ. The court, therefore, had no jurisdiction in the matter.

Taney responded by ordering a marshal to produce the general. The marshal could not; the sentries of Ft. McHenry would not let him. He duly reported his failure to the chief justice on the following day.

Realizing the futility of the court's position—the chief justice could not overcome military resistance to his orders without presidential support, and presidential support would not be forthcoming—Taney excused the marshal. The confrontation between Lincoln and Taney had been won by Lincoln.

Taney could not force the president and his generals to comply with his order, but he could explain it. And he did, in his generally authoritative opinion found in *Ex parte Merryman*.[79] The Constitution, reasoned Taney, locates the suspension clause in Article I, the legislative article of the Constitution. Moreover, it is only one of several clauses found in section 9 of this article, all of which expressly limit the power of Congress. Read in this context, the chief justice continued, the clause is clearly intended to limit the occasions on which Congress may suspend the writ; in no sense does it grant affirmative powers to the president. The president's attempt to suspend the writ of *habeas corpus*, he concluded, was unconstitutional.

Taney preserved the law; Lincoln preserved the Union.

Franklin D. Roosevelt and the "Court Packing" Episode

On March 4, 1933, Franklin D. Roosevelt placed his left hand on the Bible, raised his right hand, and faced Charles Evans Hughes, chief justice of the United States. Roosevelt repeated after Hughes: "I do solemnly swear that I will faithfully execute the Office of the President of the United States, and will to the best of my ability, preserve, protect and defend the Constitution of the United States."

Roosevelt entered office facing the greatest national crisis since Abraham Lincoln took the same oath in 1861. Unemployment exceeded 20 percent; the agricultural market was uncertain; banks teetered on collapse. The United States was in the midst of the Great Depression.

Confidence was the theme of the president's first inaugural address: "The only thing we have to fear," he counseled the millions of Americans leaning expectantly toward their radio sets, "is fear itself." He meant to give them confidence, confidence in their economy, and confidence in their government.

The president moved quickly. A "banking holiday" was declared, giving federal auditors time to prune dying banks from the nation's credit system. Measures were soon introduced in Congress, and rapidly enacted, that were designed to attack the evils of unemployment, labor unrest, low wages, and agricultural instability. Extensive regulatory power was given newly created agencies: the National Recovery Administration, the National Labor Relations Board, the Securities and Exchange Commission, and the Agricultural Adjustment Administration. Existing agencies—the Federal Reserve Board and Federal Trade Commission are notable examples—were equipped with new and far-reaching powers. Roosevelt cannot be credited with the many ideas that eventually became a part of his "New Deal," but he does deserve credit for the energy that led to their adoption.[80]

All in government, however, did not share Roosevelt's enthusiasm for a government-administered prescription to the Depression. Supreme Court Justices Willis Van Devanter, James C. McReynolds, George Sutherland, and Pierce Butler were hostile in principle to government economic regulation. Together, they constituted a bloc of four of the five votes needed to invalidate New Deal measures.

A fifth vote was needed for the "four horsemen" of the Supreme Court to prevail. It sometimes came from the chief justice, Charles Evans Hughes; more often it came from Owen J. Roberts; usually, the two would vote together. Even the "liberals" on the Court—Louis D. Brandeis, Harlan Fiske Stone, and Benjamin N. Cardozo—occasionally would vote against the president.

Roosevelt became exasperated, frustrated, and impatient with the Court. Although the Court did not rule against him in every instance, it did rule against him in sufficient quantities and with sufficient regularity for the president to direct his legal and political advisers to find a remedy.

In 1935, a confrontation between the president and the Supreme Court was averted when the Court sustained the government's position in the *Gold Clause Cases.*[81] The victory for the president was narrow, in the vote and in the legal doctrine asserted to justify the majority decision, but it was a victory nonetheless. Roosevelt shelved his intention to follow Lincoln's precedent and defy the Court. A prepared radio address announcing this plan to the American people was also canceled.[82]

A constitutional crisis was avoided, but a political crisis was only delayed. Soon after its decision in the *Gold Clause Cases,* the Supreme Court invalidated the Railroad Retirement Act and the National Industrial Recovery Act.[83] It also declared unconstitutional the president's firing of William E. Humphrey, former chair of the Federal Trade Commission and a vocal critic of New Deal policies.[84] Roosevelt by now was so angry that in January 1936, one cabinet member thought he was "hoping that the Supreme Court [would] make a clean sweep of all New Deal legislation" [85] The people of the United States would then be aroused in adequate numbers and with sufficient intensity that the president would enjoy their support in the anticipated confrontation.

But first the president had to be reelected. He was. Winning 61 percent of the popular vote, and 523 of the 531 electoral votes (he lost only Maine and Vermont), Roosevelt was reelected in 1936 by a margin that exceeded his 1932 landslide victory. At the same time, the Democratic party increased its majorities in both the House and Senate.[86]

Interpreting the 1936 election as a clear and overwhelming expression of support for himself and for his New Deal policies, and enjoying a strong majority in both houses of Congress, the president was now ready to move against the Supreme Court. Victory, he thought, was certain. He thought wrong.

The remedy settled on by Roosevelt has been labeled the "court packing plan," and that is what it was. It was simple in concept. Judicial efficiency, the president argued, was being inhibited by the presence on the Supreme Court of so many elderly justices. Six of these gentlemen were over seventy years old! They needed help, Roosevelt continued, and that is what he proposed to give them. The president, he concluded, should be given authority by Congress to appoint a new justice for each existing member of the Supreme Court reaching the age of seventy. A bill to that effect was introduced in Congress in February 1937.

Roosevelt's proposal was a thinly disguised and poorly conceived method of evading the Supreme Court's power of judicial review. It was a "gimmick," as historian Richard Hofstadter called it,[87] and not a forthright effort to deal with a serious problem. It was soon revealed as such.

The Supreme Court was not suffering from any maladies associated with the age of its membership. In fact, under the leadership of its chief justice, Charles Evans Hughes, efficiency was one of the true virtues of the Court. Hughes made this known to Congress in a passionless but devastating letter. The "nine old men" on the Supreme Court, as Roosevelt was apt to call them, did not need help. Congress agreed, and the bill never passed.

One popular explanation for the failure of Roosevelt's plan in Congress is expressed in the rhyme "a switch in

Russell in The Los Angeles Times
Brown Brothers

time saves nine." Intimidated, so this argument goes, by at least the possibility of court packing and the consequences this would have on an independent judiciary, Hughes and Roberts voted against their own precedents to support the president in a case in which the constitutional validity of the National Labor Relations Board had been challenged.[88]

Whether or not Hughes and Roberts actually changed their votes in response to presidential pressure is debatable and most likely will continue to be debated without resolution.[89] What is clear is that the Roosevelt plan was already in trouble by the time the alleged switch took place. The people of the United States might have supported Roosevelt and his policies, and they might have shared the president's frustrations with the Court. But they also were capable of separating these emotions from a conviction that the independence and integrity of the Supreme Court should be maintained. These views were expressed to an already skeptical Congress.

Jefferson attempted a frontal assault on the Supreme Court, and he failed. Roosevelt tried to outflank the Court. He also failed.

Dwight D. Eisenhower and the Little Rock Integration Crisis

Racial segregation of public schools was declared unconstitutional by the U.S. Supreme Court in the 1954 decision *Brown v. Board of Education.*[90] Resistance—"massive resistance" it came to be called—became the loudest, if not the only, response of southern political leaders.[91]

In 1957, following prolonged litigation, the U.S. Court of Appeals for the Eighth Circuit affirmed an order of the local federal district court, which, in turn, had approved the integration plan submitted by the school board of Little Rock, Arkansas.[92] Compliance with *Brown* in Little Rock would begin with the enrollment of black children in the previously all-white Central High School. The school board had adopted a policy of moderation and compliance. The mayor and police chief of Little Rock were prepared to support that policy.[93]

Gov. Orval E. Faubus was not so prepared. Massive resistance was his strategy, not compliance, and certainly not moderation. If local officials of Little Rock would not resist, then Faubus would do it for them.

Faubus announced that Central High School would not be integrated, judicial order or not, and enforced his decision by deploying troops of the Arkansas national guard around the school. The governor, backed by state military power, had interposed himself between the federal courts and the local school board.

This action presented an immediate crisis to the federal judiciary. Judges command no armies, no forces capable of overcoming armed resistance to its orders. Under the Constitution, only the president has command of the armed forces and of the various law enforcement agencies of the federal government. The judicial branch, as Alexander Hamilton pointed out in 1788, depends on the good will of the president for the enforcement of its orders.[94]

But would President Eisenhower lend his good will to the judiciary? Would he, if necessary, deploy federal troops for that purpose?

The answer was uncertain. Eisenhower himself had given mixed signals to the public. On May 19, 1954, when asked for his reaction to *Brown,* the president had responded: "The Supreme Court has spoken and I am sworn to uphold the constitutional processes in this country; and I will obey." [95] And he said in a September 5, 1957, telegram to Faubus, "The only assurance I can give you is that the Federal Constitution will be upheld by me by every legal means at my command." [96] These statements suggest a president quite ready to take seriously his roles as chief law enforcement officer and, if necessary, commander in chief of the armed forces.

But these were not his only statements on the subject. On July 17, 1957, Eisenhower expressed his opinion that use of federal troops to enforce judicial decisions would not be "a wise thing to do" and expressed his confidence that the law-abiding nature of the American people would not make such action necessary.[97] He refrained from either criticizing or supporting the integration decisions of the judiciary.[98]

Eisenhower also had to be pragmatic. The president, a Republican, needed the cooperation of Congress, and both houses of Congress contained Democratic majorities from 1954 until the end of his administration in January 1961. Many of these Democrats came from the South, as did the powerful chairs of many important House and Senate committees. These were people that Eisenhower would not have wanted to alienate.

Thus, as the 1957 school term was scheduled to begin, the federal judiciary was committed to the racial integration of Central High School, the governor of Arkansas was committed to defiance, and the local school board felt bound to comply with the judicial order but was not sure whether the governor would allow them. The president was committed to supporting the federal judiciary but had announced his reluctance to use federal troops.

Library of Congress

In 1957, facing massive resistance in the South, President Eisenhower ordered federal troops to enforce desegregation at Central High School in Little Rock, Arkansas.

On September 2, the day before the school term was to begin, Faubus ordered the Arkansas national guard to take positions around Central High. A mob formed.[99]

The school board, which neither invited nor wanted the governor's intervention, petitioned the federal district court for a postponement of the integration order. Attorneys for the board cited the presence of the national guard as their justification. The petition was denied.

On September 4, nine black children attempted to enter the school. Their entry, however, was blocked by the national guard. The governor had formally obstructed a judicial order.

The U.S. Justice Department now intervened. It petitioned the district court for an order enjoining the governor and the national guard from further obstruction. The petition was granted and the order entered on September 20, 1957.[100] Faubus now could obstruct the order only at the risk of imprisonment or fine for contempt of court. He withdrew the troops. Central High School became racially integrated on September 23.

By this time, however, the mob outside the school had grown large and violent. President Eisenhower issued a proclamation ordering the mob to disperse and, by executive order, ordered the 101st Airborne Division to maintain the peace and enforce the court's order.[101] The black children were placed under the protection of these troops, and, later, they were protected by Arkansas national guard units placed under federal command by presidential order.

The conflict was rejoined briefly the following year. Citing the turmoil resulting from the racial integration the previous term, the school board of Little Rock petitioned the federal district court for an order delaying integration. The district court granted the order, but the court of appeals reversed. In an unusual opinion *(see box, this page)*, the Supreme Court affirmed the decision of the court of appeals, placed the blame for the turmoil squarely on the governor, and ordered integration to proceed as planned.[102] Faubus offered no obstruction. The battle was renewed, but this time it remained in the courtroom.

President Eisenhower's position on civil rights was complex. On the one hand, the president was skeptical about the ability of federal power to compel an end to segregation. The problem, as he saw it, was in the mind, and minds could not be changed by coercive power. He preferred a moderated, go-slow approach to changing the system—slower, he once admitted, than the courts were requiring at the time.[103]

On the other hand, Eisenhower was committed to the principle that all government officials, governors and presidents included, were bound to observe the Constitution, and that this meant interpretations of the Constitution made by the judiciary. He may have deplored having to use federal troops in Little Rock, but he deplored more the contempt given the federal judiciary (thus, in Eisenhower's mind, the Constitution) by Governor Faubus. "Mob rule," he explained to the nation on September 23, 1957, "cannot be allowed to override the decisions of our courts." [104]

Eisenhower was not aggressive in leading either Congress or the American people toward ending racial segregation, and he has been severely criticized for this lack of aggressiveness.[105] But he did back the judiciary at a critical time; he did, in the end, lend the judiciary his good will.

In somewhat similar circumstances a century earlier, President Andrew Jackson set a precedent of neglect in the *Cherokee Indian Cases*;[106] he had allowed the judiciary to fend for itself in its conflict with Georgia. Eisenhower

The Court's Message of Unity and Determination

The courtroom was called to order as the justices of the U.S. Supreme Court entered and took their seats. The chief justice of the United States, Earl Warren, began to read the opinion of the Court in *Cooper v. Aaron:*

> Opinion of the Court by the Chief Justice, Mr. Justice Black, Mr. Justice Frankfurter, Mr. Justice Douglas, Mr. Justice Burton, Mr. Justice Clark, Mr. Justice Harlan, Mr. Justice Brennan, and Mr. Justice Whitaker.[1]

The "Chief" paused as he intoned each name, looked to the designated justice, and received an acknowledging nod. He continued: "As this case reaches us it raises questions of the highest importance to the maintenance of our federal system of government." [2]

This was high drama for a staid and tradition-bound Supreme Court. The drama did not involve the actual decision of the Court; its order had been announced two weeks before. The drama, rather, involved the manner in which the opinion explaining and justifying that order was delivered.

The tradition was established during the tenure of Chief Justice John Marshall that opinions of the Court would be signed by a single justice, the author of the opinion, or that the opinion would simply be designated *per curiam,* meaning "by the court." Never before had an opinion of the Supreme Court been signed individually by each member, never before had the justice announcing an opinion solicited, and received, visible confirmation—the nod—of the justices joining the opinion. Nor has either procedure been used since.

A message was being sent—to the Arkansas governor, who had announced his intention to defy the Court; to the president, whose military support might be needed to enforce the Court's order; to the political leadership of other southern states and localities, who would likely find themselves embroiled in similar litigation in the near future; and to lower federal court judges, whose cooperation was needed to make judicially mandated racial integration proceed. And, the message was being sent to the American people, whose support the Court also needed.

The message had two themes: we are united, and we are determined. Conservative or liberal, the justices of the Supreme Court would stand together on this issue. Obstruction would not be tolerated.

Whether the message was understood, or even heard, by each of the intended audiences is not known. Governor Faubus protested the ruling but stepped aside and permitted it to be enforced without additional obstruction. Federal troops were no longer required to enforce racial integration of Central High School.

1. *Cooper v. Aaron,* 358 U.S. 1, 4 (1958).
2. Ibid., 4.

might have followed this precedent. He did not. He set his own precedent and set an important ground rule early on in the ensuing struggle between the judiciary and various state governments: if needed, federal military power would be used to back the judiciary.

Constitutional Powers of the President

"The executive Power shall be vested in a President of the United States of America." [107] The president, as this constitutional provision is commonly interpreted, is the chief executive officer of the United States. This is one source of presidential authority over the domestic operations of the U.S. government.

Other sources also are found in the Constitution. The president, say various sections of Article II, shall appoint the principal officers of the executive and judicial branches, execute the laws faithfully, and grant pardons and reprieves. The president is also designated commander in chief of the armed forces of the United States, a designation having domestic implications.

Domestic Power of the President

Much of the president's domestic authority is shared with Congress. The Constitution delegates to Congress extensive authority to regulate a variety of domestic activities. Congress, in turn, has chosen to delegate much of this authority to the executive branch. The Constitution also gives Congress authority to spend money to promote the defense and general welfare of the nation and prohibits the executive branch from spending money not previously appropriated by Congress. It is Congress that creates, empowers, and funds agencies of the executive branch, and it is Congress that determines what these agencies shall and shall not do, and for what purposes the funds they receive may be spent.

Congress also determines which officers of the executive branch may be appointed by the president, which appointments must receive Senate approval, and which employees are protected by the civil service. Few issues of presidentially initiated domestic policy are not affected by congressional action.

Conflict takes place continually between the president and Congress over the content and implementation of domestic policy, as well as the respective authority of each in the process. This conflict may be attributed to a variety of factors. First, the Constitution itself invites conflict by delegating overlapping authority to the two branches. Second, the delegations themselves are ambiguous, a ripe condition for honest disagreement. Third, each branch has sought periodically to aggrandize its own power at the expense of the other.

The Framers of the Constitution created a system of shared power with the foreknowledge and expectation that conflicts between the participants would occur. They did not, however, provide a precise set of instructions about how these conflicts ought to be settled.

Many conflicts or potential conflicts still have not been settled definitively. Others have been settled tacitly by practice or expressly by agreement. Finally, a number of conflicts have been settled by judicial decree.

Judicial attitudes toward the domestic authority of the president have been mixed. It can be said that the judiciary has been especially protective of presidential authority in some instances—the presidential pardon is the best example. In other instances, the reverse has been true.

If conclusions must be made, therefore, about the effect of the judicial branch on the domestic authority of the president, those conclusions must be narrowly drawn. Presidential domestic power has, in many cases, been promoted by judicial interpretation of the Constitution and other laws of the United States. And it has been limited in many other instances.

Enforcement of Laws

The president "shall take Care that the Laws be faithfully executed." [108] This, said former president and chief justice William Howard Taft, is an "especial duty" of the president, one that involves the "widest power" of the office.[109]

Taking care that the laws be executed faithfully involves making decisions about what the law means, which laws deserve the greatest enforcement effort, which transgressors of the law should be investigated and prosecuted, and how vigorously all of this should take place. The laws considered may originate from the Constitution, Congress, or a court. They also may include treaties, executive orders, and administrative regulations.

The "take care clause," finally, imposes an obligation on the president. This obligation is to observe the mandates of the law personally and to ensure compliance by his or her subordinates. The Constitution is not a warrant for the law breaker.

As chief law enforcement officer of the United States, the president is entrusted with the "sword of the community," Alexander Hamilton's poetic way of describing the coercive power of the national government.[110] Thus, the president commands most law enforcement agencies of the executive branch: the Federal Bureau of Investigation, the U.S. Marshals Service, the Coast Guard, and the Federal Aviation Administration are examples. As commander in chief, the president also commands the armed forces of the United States and, when necessary, may employ these to enforce the law.

Also entrusted to the president, in most cases, is the decision to go to court. As chief executive and chief law enforcement officer of the United States, the president ultimately supervises civil actions taken by the Departments of Labor and Treasury, to name only two. Presidents also superintend criminal and civil prosecutions initiated—or, in the case of civil actions, defended—by the Department of Justice. Each local U.S. attorney works at the command of the president, as do the various attorneys assigned to the Anti-Trust, Criminal, Civil Rights, and Civil divisions of the Justice Department.

The amount of power the president possesses as chief law enforcement officer of the United States is primarily a function of two factors, both of which are measured by discretionary authority. The first is how much discretion is vested in the president to decide which laws are to be enforced and which alleged lawbreakers are to be prosecuted. Is the president required, for example, to enforce valid judicial orders, however grudgingly, or is the president permitted to let the courts enforce their own decisions?

The second factor involves coercive force. May the president employ the U.S. marshals to enforce the peace without prior congressional authorization? May, in extreme circumstances, the armed forces be used?

Chief Justice John Marshall provided a basis for answering these questions when he explained the difference between the *discretionary* and *ministerial* (nondiscretionary) authority of the president in *Marbury v. Madison* and the implications of this difference on judicial review of executive actions.

> By the constitution of the United States, the President is invested with certain important political powers, in the exercise of which he is to use his own discretion, and is accountable only to his country in his political character and to his own conscience. To aid him in the performance of these duties, he is authorized to appoint certain officers, who act by his authority and in conformity with his orders.
>
> In such cases, their acts are his acts; and whatever opinion may be entertained of the manner in which executive discretion may be used, still there exists, and can exist, no power to control that discretion. The subjects are political. They respect the nation, not individual rights, and being intrusted to the executive, the decision of the executive is conclusive.... The acts of such an officer, as an officer, can never be examinable by the courts.
>
> But when the legislature proceeds to impose on that officer other duties; when he is directed peremptorily to perform certain acts; when the rights of individuals are dependent on the performance of those acts; he is so far the officer of the law; is amenable to the laws for his conduct; and cannot at his discretion sport away the vested rights of others.
>
> The conclusion of this reasoning is, that where the heads of departments are the political or confidential agents of the executive, merely to execute the will of the President, or rather to act in cases in which the executive possesses a constitutional or legal discretion, nothing can be more perfectly clear than that their acts are only politically [nonjudicially] examinable. But where a specific duty is assigned by law, and individual rights depend upon the performance of that duty, it seems equally clear that the individual who considers himself injured, has a right to resort to the laws of his country for a remedy.[111]

If, to apply Marshall's reasoning, the president is accused of violating the take care clause of the Constitution, and a discretionary act is involved, then a remedy for the transgression must be found within the political process—the ballot, congressional persuasion, or, in extreme cases, removal by impeachment. No judicial remedy is available. If, however, the president's action involved a ministerial obligation, then a remedy may be found by appealing to the judicial branch, as well as the political process.

The implications of this difference on presidential power are clear: the greater the number of law enforcement decisions that are classified as discretionary, the greater the power of the president. The judicial branch has provided some, though not complete, guidance in determining which presidential decisions are discretionary and which are ministerial.

No provision of the Constitution—certainly not the take care clause—authorizes the president to violate or authorize a subordinate to violate a law. In *Kendall v. United States* Justice Smith Thompson commented, "To contend that the obligation imposed on the President to see the laws faithfully executed implies a power to forbid their execution, is a novel construction of the Constitution, and entirely inadmissible."[112] Thus, held the Supreme Court, if Congress directed that a sum of money be paid to an individual, then it was not within the discretion of the president to refuse.

Later decisions of the Court have lent clarity to this issue. If the Constitution confers authority on Congress to regulate a particular matter, and Congress has spoken on the subject, then neither the president nor a subordinate may disregard the legislative decision.[113] Neither is a president empowered to disregard individual rights otherwise ensured by the Constitution.[114] And, should it reach that point, not even presidents may disobey a valid order directed at them by a court of the United States.[115]

None of this should offend American sensibilities; it merely confirms the precept that "no person is above the law." But the issue—and it is more complex than could be conveyed in this limited space—is not so easily resolved. Granted, presidents must obey the law, and they are under an obligation to take care that their subordinates do the same. Does it follow, however, that presidents have no discretion about which laws to enforce or how enthusiastically the resources of the executive branch must be applied to such enforcement?

We might suppose, for example, that the U.S. Attorney for the Southern District of New York (Manhattan) should investigate and prosecute vigorously any violation of federal law. And, we might also suppose that this would be the expectation of the attorney general and of the president. But this is not necessarily the case.

Law enforcement agencies lack the money and personnel to investigate and prosecute all alleged violations of law with equal enthusiasm. (It might be added that the judicial branch could not handle such an increase in its workload either.) The violations must be ranked according to priority, and the resources allocated accordingly. Thus, for the U.S. Attorney in Manhattan, a decision was presumably made, and executed, to focus the government's prosecutorial resources on alleged securities fraud, local government corruption, and the persistent problem of organized crime. We may find it possible to disagree with the priorities chosen, but we cannot disagree with the necessity for establishing and following some system of priorities.

This type of decision falls within the category that Marshall described as "discretionary." Whether or not the president chooses to prosecute is a matter entrusted by the Constitution in the president.[116]

A bizarre event led to an expansive interpretation of the president's authority to use coercive force. Reacting to an adverse ruling by a California federal court in 1888, an embittered Sarah Terry and her husband, David Terry, began threatening and actually assaulting the participating judges. One of these was Stephen J. Field, a justice of the U.S. Supreme Court participating in local trials as a circuit trial judge.

These threats alarmed William H. H. Miller, attorney general to President Benjamin Harrison. Miller ordered his subordinate, U.S. Marshal J. C. Franks, to protect Field while the justice was attending to judicial business in California. Franks assigned David Neagle, a deputy marshal, as Field's bodyguard.

Field and Neagle were dining, when Mr. Terry approached the pair and began assaulting the justice. Neagle identified himself as a marshal and ordered Terry to stop. When it appeared to Neagle that Terry was drawing a weapon, Neagle shot and killed him. Neagle was arrested and charged with murder by California authorities.

The Independent Counsel Case . . .

Article II of the U.S. Constitution delegates the executive power of the United States to the president and imposes on the president the duty to enforce the law. As these provisions have come to be interpreted, the president is the chief law enforcement officer of the United States.

But what happens if the president, or a close associate of the president, is object of a criminal investigation? Can we expect the president or subordinates of the president to be completely objective in investigating and prosecuting wrongdoing in such a situation? Can we expect the American people to give credibility to investigations conducted under these circumstances, even when the investigations are vigorously and objectively pursued?

These questions came to be asked after the 1972 burglary of the Democratic National Headquarters (located in the Watergate complex in Washington, D.C.) by employees of the Nixon White House and the Committee to Re-elect the President. After evidence of a mismanaged and manipulated investigation of the incident had been uncovered, a bipartisan group of U.S. senators passed a resolution calling on the president to appoint a special prosecutor to conduct all future investigations. The president agreed, and Archibald Cox was appointed to the position.

Cox pursued his job aggressively, too aggressively for the beleaguered president. Cox refused to back down from his demand that the president relinquish tape recordings of conversations that had taken place in the Oval Office (the "Watergate tapes"); the president, through his assistant Alexander Haig, ordered that Cox be fired. Haig relayed these instructions to the attorney general, Elliot Richardson, and then to the deputy attorney general, William Ruckelshaus. Both refused to fire Cox, and both resigned. Haig than called the solicitor general, the third-ranking officer of the Justice Department, Robert Bork. Bork fired Cox on Saturday night, October 20, 1973. The event became known as the "Saturday night massacre."

The firing of Cox did not end the president's troubles. Following a public and congressional outcry, Leon Jaworski was appointed as special prosecutor to replace Cox. Jaworski pursued the disputed tapes in the courts and eventually won. Soon after the U.S. Supreme Court decision in *United States v. Nixon*, the president turned over the tapes and resigned. [1]

Congress formalized the office of special prosecutor and made that office independent of the president by enacting the Independent Counsel Act of 1978. [2] The act created the office of Independent Counsel and equipped it with full authority to investigate and prosecute criminal activity allegedly committed by high-ranking members of the executive branch, including the president.

The person filling the office is not a permanent employee of the government. Rather, a separate independent

Neagle sought his release by arguing that he was acting in an official capacity as a law enforcement officer of the United States. The problem with this argument, countered California, was that Congress had not expressly authorized U.S. marshals to protect Supreme Court justices. Without such authorization, Neagle was not cloaked with federal immunity from state prosecution.

This did not deter the Supreme Court from ordering Neagle's release. "There is a peace of the United States," wrote Justice Samuel F. Miller, and it is violated when someone assaults a federal judge attending his or her official duties.[117] A federal marshal may use such force as is necessary to prevent such an assault, with or without prior congressional authorization. "We cannot doubt the power of the President to take measures for the protection of a judge of one of the courts of the United States, who, while in the discharge of the duties of his office, is threatened with a personal attack." [118]

The importance of this case—*In re Neagle*—lies in the ruling of the Court that the take care clause confers authority on the president that does not depend on congressional action. The Constitution itself confers that authority.

The take care clause has been cited by the judiciary to justify unilateral actions taken by the executive branch to enforce treaties (a law of the land equal in status to congressionally enacted statutes)[119] and to protect prisoners in the custody of U.S. marshals.[120] Moreover, the president may unilaterally order the use of force to remove an obstruction to interstate commerce or the transportation of U.S. mail.[121] Congress, to be sure, may regulate when and how such force is used.[122] But in the absence of congressional action the president has the constitutional discretion to deploy force as necessary to ensure that the laws of the United States are observed.

An impressive amount of force is available to the president for law enforcement purposes. Agents of the Federal Bureau of Investigation, Secret Service, Drug Enforcement Administration, and Customs Service, plus the combined forces of the Coast Guard, U.S. Marshals Service, and Border Patrol, constitute a major part, but still only a part, of the federal law enforcement apparatus.

Even the power possessed by these agencies is insufficient at times to enforce the law. Should this occur, then the president may call upon a force that no opposition in the United States can resist: the armed forces of the United States.

Little controversy is aroused when a president deploys troops, including national guard units, at the request of a governor. Much controversy, however, may be expected when a president unilaterally deploys military forces into an area, especially if the governor having jurisdiction opposes the action. Presidents Dwight D. Eisenhower and John F. Kennedy, for example, encountered considerable criticism when they used military force to overcome local resistance to court-ordered school desegregation. But the two presidents were on sound constitutional ground.

In 1894, Pullman workers in Chicago blocked the railroad tracks during a particularly bitter strike. President Grover Cleveland responded by deploying army troops to clear the railroad right-of-way. The president's action was

... The Separation of Powers Tested

counsel is appointed to investigate and possibly prosecute each instance or core of related instances of criminal behavior allegedly committed by one or more persons. The independent counsel is appointed through a somewhat complex process.

First, the chief justice of the United States is empowered to appoint a special panel of three judges or justices drawn from the U.S. courts of appeals or Supreme Court, one of whom must sit on the U.S. Court of Appeals for the District of Columbia. Each appointment is for a two-year term.

Second, upon finding that "reasonable grounds" exist to believe that a person covered by the act has engaged in criminal behavior, the U.S. attorney general is instructed to apply to the special court for the appointment of an independent counsel; the decision of the attorney general to initiate or not initiate appointment of an independent counsel is absolute. Once appointed, the counsel cannot be removed from office except by legislative impeachment or for causes enumerated in the statute.

Investigation and prosecution of possible criminal activity by the president, vice president, attorney general, or others close to the president would no longer be entrusted to the president or presidential subordinates.

A constitutional challenge to this law was mounted by three high-ranking officers of the Department of Justice being investigated by an independent counsel, allegedly for unlawfully obstructing an investigation of the Environmental Protection Agency by the Judiciary Committee of the U.S. House of Representatives. Among other things, the three argued that by vesting in the special three-judge panel the power to appoint the independent counsel, Congress had interfered with the president's constitutional authority to appoint officers of the executive branch, as is provided for in the appointments clause of Article II, section 2, of the Constitution. In addition, they urged that the existence of a judicially appointed and fully empowered independent counsel violated the principle of separation of powers by unduly interfering with the president's executive functions, including the president's duty to "take Care that the Laws be faithfully executed."

A federal district court judge, rejected these arguments but the U.S. Court of Appeals for the District of Columbia reversed that decision. [3] With one justice dissenting, the U.S. Supreme Court reversed the decision of the court of appeals in *Morrison v. Olson.* [4]

1. *United States v. Nixon*, 418 U.S. 683 (1974).
2. PL 95-521.
3. *In re Sealed Case*, 665 F. Supp. 56 (D.D.C. 1987) reversed by 838 F. 2d. 476 (D.C. Cir 1988).
4. *Morrison v. Olson*, 487 U.S. ——, 101 L. Ed. 2d. 569 (1988) reversing *In re Sealed Case*, 838 F. 2d. 476 (D.C. Cir. 1988)

expressly opposed by the Illinois governor. When Cleveland's authority was challenged before the Supreme Court, Justice David Brewer not only upheld the president, but upheld him with these sweeping words:

> The entire strength of the nation may be used to enforce in any part of the land the full and free exercise of all national powers and the security of all rights entrusted by the Constitution to its care. The strong arm of the national government may be put forth to brush away all obstructions to the freedom of interstate commerce or the transportation of the mails. If the emergency arises, the army of the nation, and all its militia, are at the service of the nation to compel obedience to its laws.[123]

Clemency

The president "shall have Power to grant Reprieves and Pardons for Offenses against the United States, except in Cases of Impeachment." [124]

A *reprieve* reduces the severity of a legal penalty that has already been assessed and remains to be inflicted. To a person sentenced to death by a military court, for instance, the president may grant a reprieve that substitutes life imprisonment for the more severe penalty.[125] A *pardon* removes all penalties still existing, including the loss of any rights associated with the conviction. In effect, a pardon restores the person to his or her legal status before conviction; it "blots out" the offense as far as the law is concerned.[126]

Judicial review of various clemency issues generally has resulted in rulings that have enhanced presidential power. The courts have interpreted the president's power expansively, legitimizing claimed presidential authority in the process. They have also protected presidential clemency authority from incursions by Congress.

It is settled that the president may grant a pardon anytime after a criminal act has been committed: before trial, during trial, or after trial and conviction.[127] This rule, established in 1867, was revived briefly as a legal issue when someone sought judicial nullification of the absolute and sweeping pardon granted former president Richard Nixon by his successor, Gerald Ford. The case was dismissed by a federal district court.[128]

It is also well settled that a president may attach conditions to reprieves and pardons. President Eisenhower, for example, commuted to life imprisonment a death sentence imposed by a military court martial. The president specified, however, that the convicted individual could never be released from prison. The Supreme Court upheld the validity of the condition.[129] Similarly, when President Nixon commuted the prison sentence of former Teamsters Union president Jimmy Hoffa, he made it conditional upon Hoffa not reentering union affairs. Hoffa attempted to have this condition removed in federal court, but failed.[130] Had Hoffa violated the condition, the president could have revoked the reprieve.[131]

Reprieves and pardons typically are granted on an individual basis. The president occasionally, however, may find it expedient to grant either form of clemency to defined groups of people by signing an "amnesty." [132] Presidents Abraham Lincoln and Andrew Johnson granted conditional amnesties to Confederate soldiers; Presidents Gerald Ford and Jimmy Carter signed progressively more generous amnesties in favor of Vietnam-era draft evaders. Such amnesties, the Supreme Court held over a century ago, are a proper exercise of the president's clemency authority.[133]

The principal period of conflict between the president and Congress over the president's clemency authority came during the period immediately following the Civil War. Congress, controlled by Radical Republicans, was intent on reconstructing the sections of the South formerly in rebellion. President Andrew Johnson, a Southerner himself, sought reconciliation. Johnson used his clemency power—one of the few powers not requiring some sort of legislative assent—to implement his policy.

What Congress could not do directly—block Johnson's amnesties—it sought to accomplish indirectly. Congress required, for example, that attorneys practicing law in federal court take an oath that they had never participated in an insurrection against the United States. No exemption was provided for persons who had been pardoned.

Augustus Garland, himself a former member of the Confederate legislature, challenged the law, arguing that it unconstitutionally limited the president's clemency authority. The Supreme Court agreed.

"This power of the President," Justice Stephen Field wrote, "is not subject to legislative control." [134] With the disability removed, Garland entered the practice of law, became a U.S. senator from Arkansas, and served as attorney general of the United States under President Grover Cleveland.[135]

However great the clemency authority of the president may be, it is not absolute. First, the Constitution excludes impeachment processes from the clemency authority of the president.[136] Second, the president's authority applies to offenses against the United States; it does not apply to violations of state law. Third, although the president's authority extends to criminal contempt convictions in federal court,[137] the courts have not yet ruled on whether the president's authority may be used to commute sentences or pardon offenses stemming from contempt of Congress or from civil contempt of court. Finally, while Congress may not limit the president's authority to grant reprieves or pardons, it may itself enact amnesty statutes.[138]

Presidential Privileges and Immunities

The "president" is a political office created by Article II of the U.S. Constitution. The person who happens to occupy that office by constitutionally prescribed processes is also the president.

Separating the office from the person is not a difficult task conceptually. The laws of the United States pertaining to the president are neutral; they make no provision for a specific person. Thus, we can speak of the legal authority of the president without reference to any individual. We also can speak of individual presidents.

We cannot, however, speak of the legal authority of a President Ronald Reagan and a President Jimmy Carter as if they were two different things—accounting, of course, for changes in the law. Both have had to operate under the same fundamental set of rules. Decisions of the judiciary in response to Carter's actions are binding on Reagan. Unless reversed or modified, these decisions will also be binding on Reagan's successors.

This fact creates a problem for the judiciary. An interpretation of law made by a judge in response to the actions of one president, even a bad president, is binding on future presidents as well. The office and the political system, not merely the person involved in the immediate controversy, are affected. The judicial branch cannot "proceed against the president as against an ordinary person." [139] The president is not above the law but must be treated with a somewhat different set of procedural rules.

Judges are protective of the president, and for good reason. Questions of war and peace must be dealt with by the president almost daily. So must the overall direction and management of the executive branch and, in important respects, of the legislative branch as well. Unwarranted distractions, including multiple and vexatious lawsuits, are to be discouraged.

The Constitution is another reason for this generally protective attitude. As a separate branch of the United States government, presidents must be able to fulfill their constitutional responsibilities. They must also be able to defend themselves from encroachments attempted by other branches of government, an argument made by James Madison in 1788.[140]

Now, all of this seems reasonable enough on its face. But there are countervailing considerations. Other than removal by impeachment, should presidents be subject to the same standards of accountability for their official actions as other public servants are? Should Congress or litigants in courts have access to the most confidential communications between a president and his or her principal subordinates? Should persons unlawfully and intentionally harmed have a remedy against the president? Against advisers to the president?

The judicial branch has considered and attempted to balance these often competing considerations. The result has been a series of decisions that have gone far to protect the president but that also respect the needs of the other branches.

The Supreme Court has made a distinction between those decisions entrusted to the president's discretion by the Constitution or Congress, and those that have already been made by the Constitution or Congress but that require from the president only implementation or restraint. The Court has ruled that the first type of decision is political and cannot be questioned by a court. If the president has the authority, and if the exercise of that authority violates no other provision of the Constitution, then decisions about how to exercise that authority are outside the scope of judicial competence. *(The distinction between discretionary and ministerial—nondiscretionary—authority is discussed more fully in* *"Enforcement of Laws," p. 1172, in this chapter.)*

Immunity from Personal Liability. The Court has immunized presidents from personal liability as a result of damages caused by their official actions. The Court also has given a limited form of protection to advisers of the president. (The Constitution grants immunity to members of Congress from civil and criminal prosecution in specified circumstances.[141] No such explicit protection is given the president.)

In 1970, A. Ernest Fitzgerald was dismissed by the Air Force, allegedly for revealing contract-cost overruns to Congress. Fitzgerald, a civilian civil service employee, challenged his dismissal in a suit naming President Richard Nixon and other top executive branch officials as defendants. Was the president subject to civil liability for any actions he might have taken with respect to Fitzgerald?

In 1982 the Supreme Court, in a five-to-four decision, ruled that the president could not.[142] Writing for the majority, Justice Lewis Powell stated that the president enjoyed "an absolute immunity" from damages stemming from his "official acts." The nature of the presidential office, Powell reasoned, requires that many decisions be made that are likely to arouse intense feelings and that might lead to numerous lawsuits. The president should be free to make these decisions without the accompanying worry of personal financial loss.

If the president cannot be held liable in civil damage suits, then what about personal aides to the president? In *Harlow v. Fitzgerald,*[143] decided on the same day and involving the same core of facts as *Nixon v. Fitzgerald,* the Court ruled that they could, but only in limited circumstances. Again, Powell wrote for the Court.

Powell refused to accept the argument assserted by Nixon's two former aides, Bryce N. Harlow and Alexander P. Butterfield, that presidential aides necessarily enjoyed a blanket immunity from civil damages derived from their special relationship to the president.[144] A blanket immunity, he concluded, would apply only in those cases in which the aide showed that his or her "responsibility of office embraced a function so sensitive as to require a total shield from liability."[145] Neither Harlow nor Butterfield could maintain such a claim in this instance.

The Court, however, did not totally strip presidential aides of their defensive armor. Presidential aides, Powell recognized, fulfilled important and sensitive functions for the president. It was in the interest of the public that they not be discouraged from doing this by the prospect of lawsuits. Therefore, while they could not be shielded completely from civil liability arising from their official actions, they could and did enjoy a qualified immunity. The test, in each case, was whether their conduct violated "clearly established statutory or constitutional rights of which a reasonable person would have known."[146]

The Supreme Court also has held that cabinet members enjoy a qualified personal immunity from civil liability for actions committed in their official capacity.[147] Federal prosecutors have been more successful in the courts; they have an absolute immunity from personal civil liability.[148] Finally, employees of the federal government, such as law enforcement personnel, are personally liable for damages caused when they violate the law.[149]

Protected Communications. The Supreme Court has granted limited protection to communications between presidents and their advisers.

In 1972, employees of the Committee to Re-elect the President burglarized the offices of the Democratic National Committee. Members of President Nixon's staff authorized and ordered the burglary. The burglars were caught; and in the ensuing investigation by various federal law enforcement agencies, a federal grand jury, a special prosecutor, and committees from both houses of Congress, probable cause was found to suppose that criminal laws had been violated.

During the course of the Senate investigation, Alexander Butterfield, an aide to Nixon, revealed the existence of a large number of tape recordings of conversations by the president. Because these tapes contained evidence that was possibly material to the grand jury's criminal investigation, a subpoena was issued for them to be turned over to the United States District Court for the District of Columbia. The president petitioned the court to quash (suppress) the subpoena, but his motion was overruled. The president appealed.

Through an expedited process, Nixon's appeal was quickly heard and decided by the Supreme Court. The Court first considered and then rejected three procedural arguments made by the president. First, it held that the rules governing appeals to the Supreme Court had been observed. Second, it ruled that the judicial branch was competent to resolve the controversy. Third, it determined that the *Federal Rules of Criminal Procedure* had been followed.

Having disposed of these arguments, the Court turned to the principal constitutional issue in the dispute: the existence and extent of *executive privilege.*

Privileges against being compelled to provide evidence are commonly applied in judicial proceedings. The Fifth Amendment of the U.S. Constitution protects individuals against being compelled to give evidence against themselves in criminal actions. Judicially and legislatively created rules generally afford a privilege against compelled testimony (at the option of the litigant) by a litigant's spouse, physician, attorney, and religious confessor. In each of these cases, the Court found that a public interest in suppressing the evidence outweighed the public interest in hearing it.

Nixon claimed that the Constitution afforded similar protection to the president. Confidentiality of presidential communications, he maintained, was justified by the need to promote candid discussion between the president and his or her subordinates and by the need to protect the independence of the executive branch. Furthermore, he argued, the president has the final say about which communications are privileged.

The Court accepted part of Nixon's argument and rejected the remainder. For Nixon, unfortunately, the part accepted by the Court did not prove adequate to protect him from the subpoena. By a unanimous vote, the Supreme Court upheld the order of the district court and itself ordered Nixon to produce the evidence.

The Constitution, according to the opinion written by Chief Justice Warren E. Burger, does protect the confidentiality of presidential communications; the president's claim that an executive privilege exists was correct. But the privilege is limited, not absolute. It can be maintained only to the extent that it is not outweighed in each case by a more important countervailing public interest.

Burger also stated that it is for the judiciary, as the ultimate interpreter of the Constitution, not the president, to resolve all questions about whether and in what circumstances the privilege should apply. This the Court did.

> In this case we must weigh the importance of the general privilege of confidentiality of Presidential communications in performance of the President's responsibilities against the inroads of such a privilege on the fair administration of criminal justice. The interest in preserving confidentiality is weighty indeed and entitled to great respect.[150]

But the interest of the judiciary in obtaining the evidence was found to be weightier. Burger explained:

> . . . allowance of the privilege to withhold evidence that is demonstrably relevant in a criminal trial would cut deeply into the guarantee of due process of law and gravely impair the basic function of the courts. A Presi-

dent's acknowledged need for confidentiality in the communications of his office is general in nature, whereas the constitutional need for production of relevant evidence in a criminal proceeding is specific and central to the fair adjudication of a particular criminal case in the administration of justice....

We conclude that when the ground for asserting privilege as to subpoenaed materials sought for use in a criminal trial is based only on the generalized interest in confidentiality, it cannot prevail over the fundamental demands of due process of law in the fair administration of criminal justice. The generalized assertion of privilege must yield to the demonstrated, specific need for evidence in a pending criminal trial.[151]

Nixon complied, and resigned.

Two other parts of Burger's opinion merit consideration. First, Burger suggested that conversations affecting national security would be treated more deferentially by the judiciary. Since national security was not involved in the case, however, the Court was not obliged to make a definitive ruling on that issue.

Second, Burger's opinion went to great lengths to instruct lower courts in the proper procedures for treating evidence produced by the president. The Court's desire not to burden the office of the president unnecessarily is evident:

Statements that meet the test of admissibility and relevance must be isolated; all other materials must be excised. At this stage the District Court is not limited to representations of the Special Prosecutor as to the evidence sought by the subpoena; the material will be available to the District Court. It is elementary that *in camera* [secret] inspection of evidence is always a procedure calling for scrupulous protection against any release or publication of material not found by the court, at that stage, probably admissible in evidence and relevant to the issues of the trial for which it is sought. That being true of an ordinary situation, it is obvious that the District Court has a very heavy responsibility to see to it that Presidential conversations, which are either not relevant or not admissible, are accorded that high degree of respect due the President of the United States.[152]

United States v. Nixon was a personal defeat for Nixon, but it may be considered a victory for the office of the president. Presidents had asserted the principle of executive privilege for some time before the Nixon case. By upholding at least the principle of executive privilege, and by emphasizing the responsibility of the judiciary to be especially protective of the president's needs, the Supreme Court legitimized a practice tending to promote presidential power and it limited the authority of judges to intrude upon that practice.

Congress was not involved in the Nixon case. The ruling of the Court, therefore, technically would not necessarily control the outcome of a dispute between the president and Congress over the obligation of the president to comply with a legislative subpoena. The Nixon decision, however, would be important precedent and would support such a congressional claim, at least to the extent that the interests of Congress in making the claim were found to outweigh the president's claim of privilege.

Executive privilege was considered by the Court again in 1977. Again the person asserting the claim was Richard Nixon, now a former president and private citizen.

Following Nixon's departure from office, Congress enacted legislation transferring legal custody and control of presidential papers from the president to the General Services Administration (GSA). The GSA was instructed to return private documents to the president and to preserve the remaining documents. Provisions were made for the protection of sensitive communications.

Nixon argued, among other grounds, that executive privilege was available to former as well as to current presidents. He then asserted that Congress had violated this privilege by transferring custody of the documents from himself to a government agency.

The Court agreed with the president's first contention. Former as well as current presidents may invoke a claim of executive privilege. Ultimately, however, Nixon lost this case as well.

In *Nixon v. Administrator of General Services Administration,* the Court held that it was within the constitutional authority of Congress to regulate the disposition of presidential documents.[153] The documents remained in the custody of the GSA.

Resource Manager of the National Government

The government of the United States is wealthy. In addition to being the largest landowner in the United States, the national government owns title to mineral leases, buildings, ships, aircraft, railroads, and an assortment of office, computer, communications, and scientific equipment.

A measure of assets of the national government also must recognize that the *accounts receivable* of the United States measures in the trillions of dollars: most Americans—individuals and businesses—as well as many foreign individuals, businesses, and governments owe money to the United States in the form of loans or tax obligations.

The Constitution vests in Congress the authority to manage these resources by Article I, section 8. Congress, a legislative assembly not a management enterprise, has delegated much of this authority to the president and officers subordinate to the president.

When the president's authority as chief resource manager of the United States is challenged, the basis of the challenge is usually framed around the issue of *permissible discretion.* If the Constitution or Congress has expressly given the president authority to make a decision, then actions the president takes following upon that delegation is discretionary, thereby outside the scope of judicial review. If, however, the president's authority is ministerial—the president must implement the will of Congress obediently—then the president's actions are subject to judicial review and, if inconsistent with the will of Congress, may be overturned. *(Discretionary and ministerial authority are discussed further under "Enforcement of Laws," p. 1172, in this chapter.)*

Ambiguity about the will of Congress may lead to a greater tolerance by the judiciary when supposedly ministerial authority of the president is challenged. This is especially true if Congress has been aware of the challenged action and has acquiesced. Acquiescence is not the only, or even the most important, actor considered by the judiciary. Congress alone may not amend the Constitution—but the courts occasionally have given it great weight in the past, and may be expected to do so in the future.[154]

One of the least ambiguous provisions of the Constitution has precluded the expenditure of funds by the president without Congress first giving approval. Article I, section 9, states: "No money shall be drawn from the

Treasury, but in consequence of appropriations made by law." No money, not a smudged penny, may otherwise be spent.

Presidents have sometimes violated this provision. Abraham Lincoln spent unappropriated funds to prepare for the Civil War at a time when Congress could not be easily convened; Gerald Ford may have violated this provision when, in the face of prohibitory legislation, he authorized the use of military forces to assist in the rescue and evacuation of Americans from Southeast Asia. These, however, are not the types of political precedents that presidents can reasonably expect to justify in ordinary times.

One of the most controversial issues encountered by the judicial branch has had to do with presidential spending discretion. May the president ignore what amounts to a congressional command to spend a specific amount of money, for a specified purpose, and during a specified time period? In other words, may the president *impound* funds that Congress has appropriated and authorized to be spent?

The judiciary has not resolved the issue fully, partially because successive presidents and congresses have adhered to an accommodation of sorts and partially because the federal courts, particularly the Supreme Court, have evaded the constitutional issue when possible.

Congress does not necessarily condemn impoundment. The response of Congress will predictably depend on the amount of funds impounded, the reason for the impoundment, and in some instances the length of time of the impoundment. No one could fault the president, for example, for refusing to spend money to solve a problem that no longer exists. Thomas Jefferson, for example, refused to spend $50,000 appropriated by Congress to build gunboats when a threat to the United States on the Mississippi River had already abated.[155] Prudent management practices as well as apparent discretionary authority from Congress may justify an occasional presidential impoundment.

If the United States has obligated itself contractually to pay a certain sum to a specified person, and if Congress has appropriated the funds for that purpose and authorized the expenditure, then the president may not unilaterally order or authorize the withholding of payment.[156] The president's authority is ministerial.

A more controversial issue is whether the president may impound funds, against the clear wishes of Congress, when the funds have been appropriated but not obligated to any particular person. (President John F. Kennedy did this when he refused to spend funds appropriated to build the B-70 bombers for the air force, much to the irritation of Congress.) Although the issue has been raised on several occasions, the judiciary has never resolved it. When a decision has been necessary, the courts have preferred to interpret the statute in favor of Congress and then say that resolution of the constitutional issue is not required.[157]

Appointment Power

The president, Article II, section 2, of the U.S. Constitution says, "shall nominate, and by and with the Advice and Consent of the Senate, shall appoint Ambassadors, other public Ministers and Consuls, Judges of the supreme Court, and all other officers of the United States, whose appointments are not otherwise provided for, and which shall be established by Law."

According to the Supreme Court, two categories of federal officers are created by this clause.

> The Constitution for purposes of appointment very clearly divides all its officers into two classes. The primary class required a nomination by the President and confirmation by the Senate. But foreseeing that when offices became numerous, and sudden removals necessary, this mode might be inconvenient, it was provided that, in regard to officers inferior to those specially mentioned, Congress might by law vest their appointment in the President alone, in the courts of law, or in the heads of departments. That all persons who can be said to hold an office under the government about to be established under the Constitution were intended to be included in one or the other of these modes of appointment there can be but little doubt.[158]

Persons appointed by a method not described by the appointments clause may still act as agents of the federal government—they have authority to bind the government in legal relationships—but they cannot be considered commissioned officers nor can they exercise the power of commissioned officers.[159] Such officers include anyone exercising "significant " executive authority.[160]

The respective roles of Congress and the president, and occasionally of the judiciary, in the appointments process is thus demarcated. One category of appointments requires presidential nomination and appointment, and Senate confirmation. Justices of the U.S. Supreme Court and ambassadors fall under this category. A second category of appointments may arise when Congress creates the office through the legislative process. Congress may vest appointment authority for these "inferior officers" in the president, heads of departments, or the judiciary. Congress may also specify that nominations to these posts receive Senate confirmation. Commissioned military officers and federal judges other than Supreme Court justices are examples of officers included in this category. Finally, a vast array of employees who are not commissioned officers of the United States may be appointed in a manner specified by Congress. Most civil servants fall under this category.

Americans have come to expect that Congress will invest in the president the bulk of appointments to so-called inferior offices, subject to Senate confirmation. That expectation is supported by custom and congressional choice; it is not required by the Constitution. Congress, for example, once delegated authority in the courts to appoint election supervisors, a practice that was upheld by the Supreme Court.[161]

The judiciary has been skeptical toward congressional schemes tending to evade the president's appointment authority. A 1976 decision of the Supreme Court, *Buckley v. Valeo,* illustrates this attitude.[162]

Buckley arose when U.S. senator James Buckley of New York launched a multifaceted attack on the Federal Elections Campaign Act (FECA). Some of the arrows launched by Buckley hit target. Among these was his argument that the Federal Elections Commission (FEC), an independent commission established by Congress to regulate federal elections, was unlawfully constituted.

The FECA vested authority to appoint members of the FEC in three officers: the president, the Speaker of the House of Representatives, and the president pro tempore of the Senate. A majority of the appointments went to the Speaker and the president pro tempore.

Buckley had no quarrel with the presence of presidential appointments on the FEC. He objected strenuously, however, to the presence of commission members appointed by the two legislative officers. The FEC, he argued, was granted rule-making, prosecutorial, and quasi-judicial authority by Congress. These were executive, not legislative, functions. This being the case, the only way the FEC could be established lawfully was for Congress to provide for the appointment of FEC commissioners in a manner consistent with the appointments clause of the Constitution. Because the appointments clause did not provide for appointments of such "inferior officers" by legislative officers, the FEC, as constituted, was unconstitutional.

The Supreme Court agreed and declared unconstitutional that section of the FECA providing for the appointment of FEC members. An attempted congressional "end run" around the appointments clause had been blocked. Significant to the power of the president, a general device having the potential for expanded congressional encroachments into a traditional prerogative of the president had been eliminated. This was especially important to the president in the case of independent regulatory agencies, where formal presidential authority generally is limited to appointing agency officers.

Other judicial decisions also have enhanced the president's position with Congress. Although the Senate is not obligated to confirm (or even consider) presidential nominees, it may not revoke its confirmation after confirmation already has been given.[163] Moreover, while Congress may expand the duties of an officer after that officer has received his or her commission, the additional duties must be "germane" to the existing office.[164] Finally, Congress may not specify an appointee in legislation creating an office.

Although the judiciary has generally supported the president in litigation concerning the appointments clause, this support has not been without qualification. A U.S. district court has ruled that a president may not avoid the Senate confirmation process by not submitting the name of an appointee, even if that person is serving in an acting capacity.[165] Moreover, the Supreme Court has restricted the ability of the president to change his or her mind once a resignation has been accepted. If an officer covered by the appointments clause has resigned, and the president has accepted the resignation, then the president cannot reappoint that officer to the formerly held position without Senate confirmation.[166] Finally, in 1988 the court effectively limited the president's appointment power by ruling that special, independent counsel may be appointed by the judicial branch to investigate and prosecute possible criminal activity by the president or close associates of the president.[167] *(See box, The Independent Counsel Case — The Separation of Powers Tested, pp. 1174-1175.)*

Removal Power

The Constitution defines the president's appointment authority with some specificity. It says nothing, however, about removal, except that civil officers of the United States may be removed from office by Congress through the impeachment process.

Must the president seek and obtain the advice and consent of the Senate before firing officers whose original appointment required favorable Senate action? May Congress restrict the authority of the president to terminate officers by specifying a term of office, or by enumerating the causes for which an officer of the executive branch may be fired? What may the president do if neither a term of office nor a list of permissible causes for termination is specified by Congress?

These questions have been largely resolved by a trilogy of Supreme Court decisions. The outcome indicates a sensitivity of the justices to two competing values: the need for the president to exercise a measure of control over officers of the executive branch and the need for Congress to immunize officers performing certain types of "nonexecutive" functions from presidential removal for political reasons.

The Supreme Court first sided squarely with the president in the 1926 decision *Myers v. United States.*[168] In 1920, President Woodrow Wilson dismissed the postmaster of Portland, Oregon, whom he had appointed in 1917. The postmaster sued for the value of his lost wages.

Congress, the former postmaster argued, created the office of postmaster, conferred authority on the president to appoint postmasters, and had authority to impose restrictions on the removal of persons holding that office. In accordance with this authority, Congress had specified a four-year term for postmasters and had provided additionally that Senate consent must be obtained before a president could remove a postmaster before expiration of the statutorily defined term.

The Supreme Court rejected this line of reasoning in *Myers v. United States.* Writing for a majority of the justices, Chief Justice and former president William Howard Taft ruled that the president's removal authority was extensive and came directly from the Constitution. Restrictions placed on this authority by Congress were invalid. The postmaster lost.

Myers might have been interpreted as a signal from the Supreme Court that the president's authority to fire executive officials could not be curbed by Congress; Taft's opinion certainly said as much. And President Franklin D. Roosevelt and his legal advisers could hardly be faulted for making that interpretation.

Upon occupying the White House in 1933, Roosevelt discovered that a number of regulatory commissions were governed by appointees of Republican presidents. One such appointee was William E. Humphrey, a member of the Federal Trade Commission (FTC) since his 1925 appointment by President Calvin Coolidge. Roosevelt requested Humphrey's resignation. When Humphrey refused, the president fired him summarily.

The only justification offered by Roosevelt was a disagreement between the president and Humphrey over policy.[169] This reason, however, had not been listed by Congress as constituting sufficient cause for removal of FTC commissioners.

Humphrey's estate sued—Humphrey had died in the meantime—on the ground that the president had lacked sufficient authority to fire the former commissioner. Relying on the Supreme Court's decision in *Myers,* the government responded by arguing that the president did have sufficient authority; it came from the Constitution. Since the president's authority came directly from the U.S. Constitution, it could not be limited by Congress.

The Supreme Court sided with Humphrey's estate and, implicitly, with Congress. In *Humphrey's Executor v. United States,*[170] the Court distinguished between a postal official, whose responsibilities were purely executive, and a commissioner of the FTC, whose responsibilities were quasi-legislative and quasi-judicial. While the president's authority to fire officers with only executive responsibility could not be curbed by Congress, his or her authority to fire officers with quasi-legislative or quasi-judicial authority could be limited legislatively. Function and legal authority seemed to control the Court's analysis, not location of the officer within the structure of government.

The trilogy was completed in 1958 with *Wiener v.*

United States, a dispute over President Dwight D. Eisenhower's firing of a member of the War Claims Commission.[171] *Humphrey* and *Wiener* seem similar on the surface: both involved the termination of an executive official with quasi-judicial authority. But they differed in one crucial fact: in the former case, Congress had legislatively specified the grounds for removing a commissioner; Congress had not specified any grounds for removal of Wiener. If Congress was silent, did the removal power vest exclusively in the president?

Without dissent, the Court said that it did not. Inaction by Congress does not mean that the president can lawfully discharge an official exercising quasi-judicial authority. The termination must still be justified with a sufficiently important cause. As Eisenhower had not attempted to justify his action, the removal was held unlawful.

Diplomatic Powers of the President

The issue before the U.S. House of Representatives was presidential power. Might President John Adams, in accordance with the Jay Treaty, lawfully order the extradition of a fugitive to Great Britain? Should not extradition petitions be submitted to and resolved by the judicial branch?

No, answered John Marshall, then a representative from Virginia. "The president is the sole organ of the nation in its external relations, and its sole representative with foreign nations. Of consequence, the demand of a foreign nation can only be made on him." [172]

Marshall's view was to prevail. Yet it was not a view that could draw sustenance from any single clause of the Constitution. To the contrary.

Article II, section 2, of the Constitution vests treaty-making authority in the president, providing two-thirds of the senators present at the vote concur. The same article and section also gives the president authority to "appoint Ambassadors, other public Ministers and Consuls ... and all other officers of the United States, whose Appointments are not herein otherwise provided for, and which shall be established by Law." Finally, Article II, section 3, says that the president "shall receive Ambassadors and other public Ministers."

These provisions, it is true, describe a president empowered to have some role in diplomatic relations, but that role cannot be gleaned by a mere reference to these words. Certainly, the preeminent role of the modern president in the making of U.S. foreign policy cannot be attributed solely to these fragments of power floating within the text of the Constitution.

Additional fragments of presidential power seem to be provided by other clauses. The "executive Power," says Article II, section 1, "shall be vested in a President of the United States of America." Section 2 makes the president commander in chief of the armed forces. Finally, section 3 obligates the president to "take Care that the Laws be faithfully executed."

Collectively, and with imagination, these fragments may be assembled into a partial composite of the president as chief diplomat. *(See Chief Diplomat chapter in Part III.)* But it is still only a partial composite, for it is still composed of fragments. Gaps remain.

The composite that is assembled, however, quickly becomes blurred once Congress is considered. In addition to the above-mentioned checks imposed on presidential appointment and treaty making by the Senate, Article I, section 8, of the Constitution enumerates a variety of powers that are given directly to Congress. Thus, to name a few, Congress is delegated legislative authority to raise and appropriate funds, to regulate commerce between the United States and other nations, to declare war, and to make rules governing the operation of the government and armed forces. Also important, Congress is given authority to enact all laws "necessary and proper" for the execution of these powers, as well as all other powers created by the Constitution (for example, the treaty-making power).

Thus, the Constitution does not provide a precise blueprint for the direction of U.S. foreign policy. It presents, rather, a mere sketch of a plan, a sketch that seems to attempt to balance the somewhat competing notions of institutional centralization of power with checks on the exercise of that power. But it does not specify how this balance is to be achieved.

Details of something resembling a blueprint, however, have been penciled in over time. Some of the lines have been drawn through practice; Congress and the president have come to agree by at least tacit convention that certain aspects of U.S. foreign policy shall be conferred primarily on the executive branch. Congress has generally accepted a role consisting of alternatively supporting and checking the executive.

Other lines in the blueprint have been drawn at the insistence of the judicial branch. These lines also contribute to a clearer understanding of the relationship between presidential and congressional power in foreign relations.

In general, the judiciary has promoted presidential diplomatic power by interpreting disputed provisions of the Constitution or congressionally enacted law with the following results:

- the ability of state and local governments to interfere with national or presidential diplomatic prerogatives has been severely restricted;
- the scope of the president's treaty-making authority has been interpreted broadly;
- the ability of the president to conclude executive agreements with foreign nations, without Senate or congressional participation in the process, has been legitimized;
- the ability of state and federal courts to interfere with national or presidential prerogatives has been curtailed.

Still, judicial deference to the president has not been without limitation. Thus, while the general inclination of the judicial branch has been to support the diplomatic authority of the president, it has, at the same time, imposed important restrictions on that authority. These restrictions are of two general types:

- the judicial branch has limited the ability of the president to bargain away constitutionally protected individual rights by way of international compacts;
- the judicial branch has legitimized important Senate and congressional checks on presidential diplomatic authority.

The blueprint is not complete; nor do the prospects of a completed design seem likely. Fragments of power still seem to float on paper, not connected either to president or Congress. Other fragments seem to be connected to the president and Congress, with no clear understanding of which institution shall have the final say. Many of the lines that were drawn at some point in time have been subsequently erased or moved. The design that does exist is replete with erasure smudges.

Special Deference to the President

On May 28, 1934, Congress passed a joint resolution authorizing the president to regulate the sale of U.S. weapons and munitions to Bolivia and Paraguay, the two countries then engaged in the Chaco War. The resolution expressly authorized the president to impose a complete ban on such sales, should he make a finding that such action was warranted. Violators were subjected to criminal prosecution.

President Franklin D. Roosevelt signed a proclamation prohibiting such sales on the same day.

Curtiss-Wright Export Corporation attempted to evade the ban, but was caught. It was indicted by a federal grand jury.

The defense offered by Curtiss-Wright was constitutional. The president's proclamation, it argued, was legislative in character. Because the Constitution confers the legislative authority of the United States on Congress, the proclamation was unlawful. It did not matter, continued the defendant, that Congress had expressly delegated this authority to the president. The delegation itself violated the Constitution. Curtiss-Wright could not be prosecuted for allegedly violating an unconstitutional law.

The Supreme Court disagreed. Congress, the Court ruled in *United States v. Curtiss-Wright Export Corporation,* had acted entirely within the Constitution when it delegated the disputed authority to the president.[173] The president's proclamation was constitutional.

The Court might have ended the matter there; nothing in the case required it to say more. But it went farther.

Sovereign status, wrote Justice George Sutherland, implies the existence of certain inherent powers to conduct international relations. The government of the United States, he continued, became sovereign with the adoption and ratification of the Constitution. Therefore, he concluded, once the United States became sovereign, it axiomatically assumed all those powers attributed to a sovereign nation, except where otherwise limited by the Constitution.

Were the issue purely domestic, Sutherland opined, then the outcome might be different. The Constitution differentiates between the domestic and international power of the national government, with the domestic power being carefully limited. But the issue was not domestic, it was international. The utmost deference of the judicial branch was required.

A central portion of this inherent diplomatic power of the United States is vested in the president, independent of any authority delegated to that office by Congress:

> It is important to bear in mind that we are here dealing not alone with an authority vested in the President by an exertion of legislative power, but with such an authority plus the very delicate plenary and exclusive power of the President as the sole organ of the federal government in the field of international relations—a power which does not require as a basis for its exercise an act of Congress, but which, of course, like every other governmental power, must be exercised in subordination to the applicable provisions of the Constitution.[174]

The president, it seems, had ample power to effect the ban, with or without congressional assent.

Rightly so, continued Sutherland.

> [The president], not Congress, has the better opportunity of knowing the conditions which prevail in foreign countries, and especially is this true in time of war. He has his confidential sources of information. He has his agents in the form of diplomatic, consular and other officials. Secrecy in respect of information gathered by them may be highly necessary, and the premature disclosure of it productive of harmful results.[175]

Sutherland's theory of "inherent" national and presidential diplomatic power is of at least debatable validity.[176] Not debatable, however, is the continued validity of the theme underlying his opinion: deference and support. Judges, we can say generally, are loath to interfere with and are disposed to support presidential decisions about the conduct of U.S. foreign policy.

This attitude of judicial deference is strong, and it is reasonably pervasive. In many cases it will lead judges simply to dismiss the case without making a ruling.

But deference is not certain. In *Baker v. Carr* Justice William J. Brennan, Jr., cautioned that it "rests on reason, not habit." [177]

> . . . it is error to suppose that every case or controversy which touches foreign relations lies beyond judicial cognizance. Our cases in this field seem invariably to show a discriminating analysis of the particular question posed, in terms of the history of its management by the political branches, of its susceptibility to judicial handling in light of its nature and posture in the specific case, and of the possible consequences of judicial action.[178]

Thus, the president may expect general support from the judicial branch when a question of foreign policy is involved. This support may be expressed explicitly, as happens when a presidential decision is considered and upheld. It may also be given implicitly, as when the case is simply dismissed without a ruling. Either way, presidential power is promoted.

The president, however, may not expect such support on all occasions or for just any issue. The judiciary has asserted its power against the president in the past; presidential power has been restricted in the process. The judiciary may be expected to assert itself in the future.

Recognition of Foreign Governments

The president, says Article II, section 2, of the Constitution, "shall appoint Ambassadors, other public Ministers and Consuls," subject to confirmation by the Senate. Section 3 of the second article states that the president "shall receive Ambassadors and other public Ministers." No mention is made of the Senate.

Appointing ambassadors involves more than personnel selection; receiving ambassadors involves more than ceremonial pomp. Combined, the two provisions are generally conceded to confer plenary or complete power on the president to extend, on behalf of the United States, diplomatic recognition to foreign governments.

Recognition has been and remains primarily a political question to be resolved between the president and Congress. Political controversy has surrounded—and surely will continue to surround—presidential decisions to recognize certain governments. U.S. recognition of the Soviet Union, the People's Republic of China, and the Vatican all aroused controversy.

The Supreme Court has assumed that the president has the constitutional authority to extend such recognition. The issue "so strongly defies judicial treatment that without executive recognition a foreign state has been called 'a republic of whose existence we know nothing.' " [179] Should a disagreement arise between Congress and the president over the propriety of a presidential decision to recognize (or not recognize) a foreign government, then Congress will have to rely on its own resources to settle the matter. It should not expect the courtroom door to be open.

Recognition of foreign governments often entails more than the recognition implied by an exchange of ambassadors. The Supreme Court decided that the president's authority to recognize the Soviet Union in 1933 was a sufficient constitutional basis also for making executive agreements with the same government. *(See the following section, "International Compacts.")* Justice William O. Douglas explained in *United States v. Pink:*

> [The authority to recognize foreign governments] is not limited to a determination of the government to be recognized. It includes the power to determine the policy which is to govern the question of recognition. Objections to the underlying policy as well as objections to recognition are to be addressed to the political department [the president] and not to the courts. . . . Recognition is not always absolute: it is sometimes conditional. Power to remove such obstacles to full recognition as settlement of claims of our nationals certainly is a modest implied power of the President who is the "sole organ of the federal government in the field of international relations." Effectiveness in handling the delicate problems of foreign relations requires no less. Unless such a power exists, the power of recognition might be thwarted or seriously diluted. No such obstacle can be placed in the way of rehabilitation of relations between this country and another nation, unless the historic conception of the powers and responsibilities of the President in the conduct of foreign relations is to be drastically revised.[180]

International Compacts

An international compact governs specified aspects of a relationship between the governments of two or more nations. It sets forth mutually binding rights and responsibilities. The subject matter may be routine, such as a cultural exchange agreement between the United States and the Soviet Union. It may also be of great international importance, such as the North Atlantic Defense Treaty of 1949 (which established NATO, the North Atlantic Treaty Organization).

International compacts between the United States and foreign governments may be made by treaty or by executive agreement. According to Article II, section 2, of the U.S. Constitution, a treaty is made by the president, "provided two thirds of the Senators present concur."

An executive agreement is made between the president, or a designated subordinate of the president, and the government of a foreign nation. Unlike a treaty, an executive agreement is not mentioned in the Constitution and is not subject to Senate concurrence. It arose from political usage and gained constitutional legitimacy by Supreme Court review.

Various generalizations have been made to distinguish the two. One is that treaties, because of their constitutional standing, enjoy a higher legal status than do executive agreements. Another generalization is more political than legal and deals with the substance of the compact. Executive agreements, it is said, ought to be used only for lesser issues. The great issues of international diplomacy should be settled by treaties.

Yet, as so often happens, these generalizations may hold true only in limited respects. It is true that one federal appellate court invalidated an executive agreement for reasons that would clearly not have applied to a treaty. *(See discussion of the* Guy Capps *case later in this section.)* And it is also true that executive agreements ordinarily deal with the routine and that treaties are concerned with the more significant issues of foreign policy.

But treaties have also been used to settle routine issues, and executive agreements the most significant. Presidents have even resorted to executive agreements to implement the substance of a proposed treaty after it was rejected by the Senate. Whatever differences exist between the two, they have not, with the one exception mentioned, been defined by the judiciary. *(For further discussion of treaties and executive agreements, see "The Treaty Power," p. 505, and "Executive Agreements," p. 510, in Chief Diplomat chapter of Part III.)*

Judicial review of the president's authority to conclude international agreements has centered on three principal issues: conflict between national and state authority, conflict between presidential and congressional authority, and

The Act of State Doctrine

Were you given the choice, would you permit U.S. courts to adjudicate claims against foreign governments when the gist of the complaint is that these governments violated international law by committing certain actions within their own political jurisdiction? Would you have permitted, for instance, U.S. business firms to file lawsuits in U.S. courts against the government of Cuba for appropriating, without compensation, the firm's assets in Cuba?

You might be tempted to respond, "Of course I would. These companies deserve a fair hearing and they certainly could not get one in a Cuban court."

Such a response might seem appropriate. But before you commit yourself, you should consider the implications. Were U.S. courts to hear claims against a foreign government for acts committed completely within its own geographic boundaries, then U.S. courts would necessarily be placed in the position of questioning at least the legal validity of those actions. Would you want that to happen? More to the point, perhaps, would the president want that to happen? Would the president approve of the judicial branch involving itself in what could become a sensitive area of U.S. foreign policy?

This set of facts was presented to the U.S. Supreme Court in *Banco Nacional de Cuba v. Sabbatino.*[1] In a display of creative law making, and deference to the president, the Court ruled that U.S. courts could not hear the case against the Cuban government. The Court was concerned, as the opinion makes clear, that the judicial branch not interfere with the diplomatic prerogatives of the president. Thus, the "act of state doctrine" was created.

1. *Banco Nacional de Cuba v. Sabbatino,* 376 U.S. 398 (1964). See also *First National City Bank v. Banco Nacional de Cuba,* 406 U.S. 759 (1972).

conflict between the scope of international agreements and the Constitution.

Scope of International Agreements. The scope of the nation's authority to make international agreements is extensive, but it is not unlimited. In 1890 Justice Stephen J. Field had this to say about treaties:

> The treaty power, as expressed in the Constitution, is in terms unlimited except by those restraints which are found in that instrument against the action of the government or of its departments, and those arising from the nature of the government itself and of that of the States.[181]

Few cases have arisen in which the judiciary defined matters that may not be regulated by international agreement. The decisions that do exist make it clear that the president is not authorized to extradite a person to a foreign nation for criminal trial in the absence of either a treaty or congressional authorization[182] and that an international agreement cannot be used to change the character of either a state or the national government or to cede state territory to a foreign nation without the state's consent.[183] Finally, we know that constitutionally guaranteed individual rights, such as the right of nonmilitary personnel to be tried by a jury, may not be bargained away by international agreement.[184]

Treaties are not a heavily litigated issue. And when they are litigated, the judicial branch more often than not will uphold them or simply decline to make a ruling at all. Field's generalization seems to have remained true for the ensuing one hundred years.

Judicial review of conflicts between presidential and Senate or congressional authority has resulted in decisions that have both promoted and limited presidential diplomatic power.

Congress and International Agreements. Although treaties, according to the Constitution, are made with the "Advice and Consent" of the Senate, the Supreme Court has indicated that the Senate has no constitutional right to insist upon participation in the negotiations. Initiating and conducting negotiations lies within the constitutional prerogative of the president.[185] Political prudence, it should be noted, may dictate the inclusion of Senate and even House members in the negotiations; a president would be unwise not to consult with senior Senate and perhaps House members before and during the negotiating process.

The Senate is not obliged constitutionally to concur with or even to consider a proposed treaty. Should either occur, the proposed treaty never would go into effect. Moreover, the Senate may condition its concurrence upon modifications to the text of the treaty, in which case the president must return to the bargaining table with the other signatories. For Senate-imposed conditions to be effective, however, they must be imposed when the Senate approves the treaty; subsequently imposed conditions have no legal effect.[186]

One chain of decisions may tend either to promote or limit presidential diplomatic power. The direction depends on the situation.

A substantial overlap may occur between those matters regulated by treaty and those regulated by congressionally enacted statute. For example, Article I, section 8, of the Constitution vests in Congress authority to regulate immigration. This would also seem to be an appropriate issue for regulation by treaty. What, then, happens when a statute and treaty regulate an issue at the same time but with conflicting results?

The Supreme Court supplied the answer in its 1888 decision of *Whitney v. Robertson:*

> By the Constitution a treaty is placed on the same footing, and made of like obligation, with an act of legislation. Both are declared by that instrument to be the supreme law of the land, and no supreme efficacy is given to either over the other. When the two relate to the same subject, the courts will always endeavor to construe them so as to give effect to both . . . ; but if the two are inconsistent, the one last in debate will control the other. . . .[187]

"The last expression of the sovereign will," the Court said in a later opinion, "must control." [188]

So, Congress effectively may nullify treaties and executive agreements by legislation, and the president, with Senate concurrence, effectively may nullify congressionally enacted legislation by treaty. As a device for checking the power of the other branch, this legal rule is probably of more importance to Congress; Congress has no legal authority to force a president to amend a treaty. It may accomplish the same result, though, by legislation (assuming, if the president opposes this action, that both houses can muster a two-thirds vote to overcome a presidential veto).

The legal ability of the president to bind the United States through an executive agreement had to be challenged eventually, and it was. In 1933, President Franklin Roosevelt concluded such an agreement with the Soviet Union. In accordance with the agreement, the president extended diplomatic recognition to the Moscow government; in return, the Soviet Union transferred to the U.S. government certain financial claims it held against U.S. business firms. The Supreme Court was asked whether a valid agreement could be made without Senate approval.

In 1937 the Supreme Court, speaking through Justice George Sutherland, ruled in favor of the president. In *United States v. Belmont,* Sutherland set forth an expansive theory of presidential authority to make agreements with foreign governments.

> . . . in respect of what was done here, the Executive had authority to speak as the sole organ of that government. The assignment and the agreement in connection therewith did not, as in the case of treaties, as that term is used in the treaty making clause of the Constitution . . . , require the advice and consent of the Senate.[189]

In *Belmont,* the president could claim authority to make an agreement with the Soviet Union in accordance with his constitutionally delegated authority to recognize foreign governments (that is, to appoint and receive ambassadors). Other than constitutional delegations of authority to the president, the Supreme Court has recognized that sufficient authority exists when the president is granted the right to make executive agreements by treaty or congressional delegation.[190]

Like a treaty, an executive agreement is the supreme law of the land, enforceable in all federal and state courts.[191] It can be assumed also that an executive agreement, as is true for a treaty, can be superseded by congressional legislation. Can, however, an executive agreement supersede existing legislation? Can the president overrule Congress by executive agreement?

The Supreme Court has not ruled on this issue. A federal appellate court has, however, and its ruling placed an important limitation on the president's authority to conclude executive agreements. In *United States v. Guy W. Capps, Inc.*, the U.S. Court of Appeals for the Fourth Circuit held unconstitutional an executive agreement that conflicted with an *existing* statute.[192] With concurrence of the Senate, presidents may use a treaty to supersede existing law. But they may not do so by executive agreement.

By recognizing a difference between *executory* and *self-executing* treaties and executive agreements,[193] the Supreme Court has given the entire Congress a limited but important method for exercising political influence over international agreements made by the president, and certainly for insisting upon being consulted during the negotiations.

An *executory* treaty or executive agreement requires legislative action by Congress—beyond Senate concurrence—before the document goes into force. Since the expenditure of funds requires congressional assent,[194] for example, a treaty guaranteeing U.S. financial assistance to another government cannot be fully effective until those funds have been appropriated. Congress may be under an obligation to make the appropriation, but the obligation stems from a desire to support and not embarrass the president. It does not stem from the Constitution.

Self-executing treaties and agreements are effective as soon as they are made. No subsequent congressional action is required for implementation.

A great unresolved issue is whether presidents may abrogate an otherwise valid treaty by their own authority or whether Senate concurrence is required (since Senate concurrence is required to make the treaty in the first place). One respected U.S. jurist, Benjamin Cardozo, thought that the president could; however, Cardozo expressed that opinion while sitting on the New York Court of Appeals and not, as later happened, while sitting as a justice of the U.S. Supreme Court.[195]

Not that the Supreme Court has not been asked to decide the issue. In 1978 President Jimmy Carter announced U.S. diplomatic recognition of the Peoples' Republic of China (mainland China) as the legitimate and only government of China; he severed U.S. diplomatic relations with Nationalist China (Taiwan or Formosa). Had this been the extent of Carter's action, the matter would have been politically controversial, but it would not necessarily have stimulated litigation.

Switching diplomatic relations, however, was not all that Carter accomplished. Without obtaining, or asking for, approval of the Senate, Carter also notified Nationalist China that he would unilaterally abrogate the mutual defense treaty then in effect between the two nations. Sen. Barry Goldwater of Arizona and others challenged this action on the ground that Senate concurrence was required. The president, they argued, had exceeded his constitutional authority.

The Supreme Court summarily dismissed *Goldwater v. Carter*.[196] Various reasons were given by individual justices, but the result of the decision was that the issue would not be resolved by the judicial branch. Treaty abrogation was, and would remain, an issue that must be resolved between the president and the Senate.

Technically, neither the president nor his challengers won. Politically, however, the decision strengthened the power of the president. Although not legitimizing the president's action, the Court did not invalidate it either. Moreover, since Congress is powerless to overrule the president's decision directly (although many devices are available to Congress for indirect retaliation), the president would seem to have come out ahead.

State Governments and International Agreements. Conflicts between national and state sovereignty over national treaty authority have been resolved by the Supreme Court squarely on the side of the national government. Treaties have been held to have preempted contrary provisions of state law in matters such as land title, business operations, and protection of migratory birds.[197] State sovereignty is generally not a barrier to national treaty-making power.

It was once proposed that the Tenth Amendment to the Constitution barred national power in the form of treaties from intruding into traditionally state matters. The Supreme Court decided otherwise in 1920. As Justice Oliver Wendell Holmes explained in *Missouri v. Holland:*

> To answer this question it is not enough to refer to the Tenth Amendment, reserving the powers not delegated to the United States, because by Article 2, Section 2, the power to make treaties is delegated expressly, and by Article 6 treaties made under the authority of the United States, along with the Constitution and laws of the United States made in pursuance thereof, are declared the supreme law of the land. If the treaty is valid there can be no dispute about the validity of the statute under Article I, as a necessary and proper means to execute the powers of the Government.[198]

Now, this passage is replete with references to the Constitution and, in some cases, to settled interpretations of the Constitution. The following summation of Holmes's reasoning explains these references:

1. Article 6 of the U.S. Constitution declares that the Constitution, and treaties and acts of Congress made pursuant to (that is, in accordance with) authority delegated by the Constitution, are the "supreme Law of the Land."
2. The treaty attacked by Missouri in *Missouri v. Holland* was made properly, pursuant to authority delegated to the president by Article II, section 2, of the Constitution.
3. The act of Congress enforcing the treaty was a necessary and proper exercise of congressional authority, as is provided for in Article I, section 8, of the Constitution.
4. Therefore, the treaty and the act are valid.

And what happened to Missouri's Tenth Amendment claim? Consider the text of the amendment: "The powers not delegated to the United States by the Constitution, nor prohibited by it to the States, are reserved to the States respectively, or to the people." The Tenth Amendment, in other words, merely affirms that states may exercise those powers not prohibited by the Constitution or delegated by the Constitution to the national government. It is not an affirmative grant of power to the states. Therefore, once the Court had decided that the treaty and act of Congress were valid, it did not need to inquire further about alleged violation of state prerogatives. In this case, the Tenth Amendment was constitutionally irrelevant.

If not treaties, then what about executive agreements? Here too the Supreme Court sided with the national government, this time with the president expressly. In the 1937 decision of *United States v. Belmont*, the Court ruled that executive agreements also supersede state law.[199]

State Government

We do not think of state governments as active participants in the making of U.S. foreign policy. Nor did the

Framers of the Constitution.

The unhappy experience of the national government under the Articles of Confederation, where states could and often did conduct their own foreign policies, led to a consensus at the Constitutional Convention of 1787 that the future conduct of U.S. diplomacy would be assigned solely to the national government. One Framer, Rufus King of Massachusetts, dismissed states as "deaf" and "dumb" in these matters.[200]

States do not share constitutional authority with the three great institutions of U.S. foreign policy making: the president, the Senate, and the Congress. Where the Constitution mentions states at all, it is in prohibitory language. "No State," says section 10 of Article I, "shall enter into any Treaty, Alliance, or Confederation." Nor, this section continues, may states, "without the Consent of Congress, lay any Imports or Duties on Imports or Exports, except what may be absolutely necessary for executing its inspection laws." Finally, in the next paragraph, states are prohibited, unless given permission by Congress, to "lay any Duty of Tonnage, keep Ships of War in time of Peace, enter into any Agreement or Compact . . . with a foreign Power, or engage in War, unless actually invaded, or in such imminent Danger as will not admit of delay."

The attitude of the judiciary toward state interference with the making of foreign policy by the national government has been unsympathetic. Writing to uphold an executive agreement made between the United States and the Soviet Union, Justice Sutherland of the Supreme Court in 1937 dismissed legal claims asserted by New York in a manner bordering on contemptuous:

> Plainly, the external powers of the United States are to be exercised without regard to state law or policies. . . . In respect of all international negotiations and compacts and in respect of our foreign relations generally, state lines disappear. As to such purposes the State of New York does not exist. Within the field of its powers, whatever the United States rightfully undertakes, it necessarily has warrant to consummate. And when judicial authority is invoked in aid of such consummation, state constitutions, state laws, and state policies are irrelevant to the inquiry and decision.[201]

Sutherland, a conservative justice, did not always agree with his liberal colleague William O. Douglas. But they did agree on this issue. Five years later when the same executive agreement again was challenged, Douglas wrote:

> There are limitations on the sovereignty of the States. No State can rewrite our foreign policy to conform to its own domestic policies. Power over external affairs is not shared by the States; it is vested in the national government exclusively. It need not be exercised as to conform to state laws or state policies whether they be expressed in constitutions, statutes, or judicial decrees. And the policies of States become wholly irrelevant to judicial inquiry when the United States, acting within its constitutional sphere, seeks enforcement of its foreign policy in the courts.[202]

Note the similarities in the two opinions.

Finally, we should consider the blunt analysis of this issue by a contemporary justice of the Supreme Court, Harry A. Blackmun, writing in 1979: "California may not tell this Nation or Japan how to run their foreign policies."[203]

The judiciary has protected treaties and executive agreements from state interference with special vigor. *(See "International Compacts," p. 1183, in this chapter.)* But this circumspect attitude of the courts has extended beyond state interference with U.S. diplomacy in such a direct fashion. States may embarrass the president in quite indirect and even quite unintended ways. By design, or by fortuitous circumstance, the judiciary has occasionally intervened to protect the president from these intrusions. Two specific ways that this has been done are state taxation of foreign commerce and state policies that tend to offend the governments and citizens of other nations.

The "power to tax," Chief Justice John Marshall argued in *McCulloch v. Maryland* in 1819, "involves the power to destroy."[204] To this observation Justice Oliver Wendell Holmes responded over a century later, "Not as long as this court sits."[205]

Marshall made a point worthy of consideration. Taxation is a time-honored method of destroying or discouraging certain types of commercial transactions. So-called sin taxes on alcohol and tobacco products are well-known examples. If states were permitted to tax foreign goods without impediment, thereby giving their own manufacturers a domestic economic advantage, then they probably would. Foreign governments might retaliate.

The Framers of the Constitution anticipated and provided for this contingency. Congress was given full authority to regulate commerce between the United States and foreign nations; the president was given authority to make treaties; and states were expressly prohibited, without prior congressional assent, from taxing imports or exports, unless such taxes were "absolutely necessary" for the enforcement of the state's inspection laws.[206]

The case of an otherwise innocuous state tax illustrates this attitude. California assessed a personal property tax on, among other things, containers used for the international shipment of goods that were temporarily situated in the state. The tax was nondiscriminatory; it applied to all covered goods, whether they were from California, from another U.S. state, or from a foreign country. The tax was also pro-rated, based on the percentage of a tax year that the goods were actually sited in the state.

In 1979, in *Japan Line, Ltd. v. County of Los Angeles,* the Supreme Court of the United States invalidated the tax, as it was applied to containers. The opinion of the Court, written by Justice Blackmun, stressed the dangers of multiple and retaliatory international taxation and of the need for the nation to speak with one voice in foreign relations. Were the California tax permitted to stand, multiple and retaliatory taxes might result, and the policy favoring a unified voice in foreign relations would be violated.[207]

States also interfere with U.S. foreign policy by enforcing policies that offend foreign governments and their people. These policies may be aimed directly at the government in question, or they may be aimed only at people within the political boundaries of the state. Either way, the effect might be to poison the relationship between the United States and a foreign government and people.

A former Oregon inheritance statute exemplifies the first type of offense. Offended themselves over property and inheritance laws found in Communist countries, the Oregon legislature enacted a law that entitled foreign citizens to inherit from Oregon citizens only if Oregon citizens could also inherit from citizens of the foreign country.

This seems like a fair arrangement on its face; the statute merely implemented a policy of reciprocity. The implications, however, were not lost on the Supreme Court. Oregon was patently attempting to punish a foreign nation, and its people, for that nation's political system. In 1968 the Court struck down the statute in *Zschernig v. Miller.*[208]

Offense may also be taken in response to government policies that discriminate against racial and ethnic groups whose immediate or distant ancestry can be traced to another country. Since all people in the United States, other than native American Indians, can trace their origin to one or more foreign country, the possibilities for offense have been numerous.

States were not alone in implementing discriminatory policies. Plenty of room existed for participation in such schemes by the federal government as well, and it did participate. Moreover, the judicial branch cannot be said to have always been free of involvement either. In fact, racially discriminatory policies emanating both from the federal and the various state governments were once given the imprimatur of legitimacy by the judiciary.[209]

At first incrementally,[210] and then with a broader sweep,[211] state (and federal) policies discriminating against racial groups were held in violation of the Constitution. The process of destroying state-sponsored racial discrimination took time, and eventually the judiciary required the active assistance of Congress and the president to do the job properly. But the job was eventually done. Racial prejudice still exists, certainly, but it is no longer embedded in government policy, federal or state.

War Powers

"We have a fighting Constitution,"[212] said Charles Evans Hughes, former chief justice and secretary of state of the United States. It vests power in the national government to wage war, and "to wage war successfully."[213]

Consider the provisions of the U.S. Constitution that touch on the nation's capacity to wage war. Article I, section 8, gives Congress authority to declare war, to raise money through taxation and borrowing, to spend money for the "common Defense and general Welfare," and to regulate interstate and foreign commerce. The same section also provides Congress authority to "grant Letters of Marque and Reprisal" and to raise, support, and regulate the armed forces, including, when called into national service, the militia (national guard) of the states. Finally, Congress may "make all Laws which shall be necessary and proper for carrying into Execution the foregoing Powers, and all other Powers vested by this Constitution in the Government of the United States, or in any Department [branch] or Officer thereof."

Presidents derive their authority to wage war from the Constitution directly and from delegations made to them by Congress. Article II, section 1, of the Constitution vests in the president the "executive Power" of the United States and makes the president "Commander in Chief" of the armed forces. This authority extends to the state militia (national guard) when it is called into national service. Moreover, the president has unilateral authority to grant pardons and reprieves—a bargaining device to end civil insurrection—and, subject to Senate approval, to make treaties and appoint the principal civil and military officers of the national government.

Congress normally is generous to a president during war. Money is raised in sufficient amounts to recruit and support U.S. combat forces. Extensive authority is granted the president to mobilize the home front as well. Essential sectors of the steel, ship-building, aircraft, and automobile industries may come under presidential control, as may retail, transportation, communications, labor, and housing. Even liquor and prostitution may feel the heavy hand of the federal government.

Empowered by a "fighting Constitution" and an agreeable Congress, supported by a demanding populace, presidential power is at its peak during war.

Judges are not disposed to enfeeble a wartime president. Aside from the possibility of being embarrassed by a president who refuses to obey their decrees—with the support of Congress and the people—judges also recognize that extraordinary measures must be taken if war is to be prosecuted successfully. Judges, too, are inclined to support the president. The following passage, written by Chief Justice Harlan Fiske Stone in 1943, exemplifies this attitude:

> The war power of the national government is "the power to wage war successfully." It extends to every matter and activity so related to war as substantially to affect its conduct and progress. The power is not restricted to the winning of victories in the field and the repulse of enemy forces. It embraces every phase of the national defense . . . which attend the rise, prosecution and progress of war.
>
> Since the Constitution commits to the Executive and to Congress the exercise of the war power in all the vicissitudes and conditions of warfare, it has necessarily given them wide scope for the exercise of judgment and discretion in determining the nature and extent of the threatened injury or danger and in the selection of the means for resisting it. Where, as they did here, the conditions call for the exercise of judgment and discretion and for the choice of means by those branches of the government on which the Constitution has placed the responsibility of war making, it is not for any court to sit in review of the wisdom of their actions or substitute its judgment for theirs.[214]

Still, as Hughes also pointed out, the American political system is subject to the Constitution and laws of the United States. War is not a warrant for lawlessness.[215] And though the power and authority of the president is great during war, it is not without limit. Limits are imposed by the Constitution, and limits are imposed by Congress. Limits are occasionally imposed by the judiciary.

Waging War

A preliminary draft of the Constitution gave Congress authority to "make war." Members of the Constitutional Convention raised objections. Would this language bar the president from defending the United States from armed aggression when Congress was not in session? James Madison provided substitute language. Congress would be delegated authority to "declare war." The president, in the meantime, presumably would be authorized to defend the United States.

One ambiguity was resolved, and another one created. The ambiguity has persisted to this day. What legal authority, if any, does the president possess to commit U.S. armed forces to combat in the absence of prior congressional authorization, and in situations in which the United States is not directly attacked? Were, for example, presidential deployment of combat forces to Mexico by James Polk, to Korea by Harry S Truman, and to Grenada by Ronald Reagan illegal?

The judicial branch has never produced a complete answer to this question. But two generalizations may be made: the judicial branch will avoid the issue if possible and will tender its support to the president if necessary.

Where the threat of aggression is clear and immediate, the position of the judicial branch has been to support a unilateral presidential response. The Constitution does not condition national survival upon the assembly and response of Congress.

Determined to maintain the Union in the face of overt southern rebellion, President Abraham Lincoln unilaterally ordered, among other things, a naval blockade of Southern harbors. Ships seeking to "run the blockade" were seized. These ships, along with their cargoes, were then sold at public auction.

The foreign owners of a seized ship brought suit in federal court, seeking recovery of the damages they suffered. Only Congress, they argued, was entrusted by the Constitution with power to declare war. The president had acted unlawfully; neither the Constitution nor Congress had authorized imposition of a naval blockade on the Southern harbors.

True, responded Justice Robert C. Grier in 1863 in *The Prize Cases,* Congress alone has power to declare war.[216] But war may exist in fact, without any declaration being made by any side. When war exists, and threatens the security of the United States, then the president has ample authority as commander in chief to respond: "The President was bound to meet [the insurrection] in the shape it presented itself, without waiting for Congress to baptise it with a name; and no name given to it by him or them could change the fact." President Lincoln could proceed with the Court's blessing.

U.S. military interventions in foreign nations are often justified by the need to protect resident American civilians. President Reagan, for instance, justified the deployment of U.S. combat forces to Grenada in this manner. Reagan's decision was supported by an impressive array of political precedent.

Legal precedent, however, is meager. The Supreme Court, for one, has not ruled on the issue. A lower federal court has, with its opinion written by Supreme Court Justice Samuel Nelson, sitting at the time as a circuit justice.

In 1854, President Franklin Pierce ordered the naval bombardment of Greytown, Nicaragua, in retaliation for a mob assault on a local U.S. diplomat. Compensation for the resulting property damages was demanded in *Durand v. Hollins.*[217] The demand was denied.

Among the powers—indeed the obligations—of the president, wrote Justice Nelson, is the power to protect U.S. citizens at home and abroad. President Pierce, he concluded, acted entirely within his constitutional authority by ordering the bombardment.

Presidential prosecution of a war declared by Congress is entirely lawful and would make an unlikely candidate for judicial review. Of lesser certainty, however, is whether the president may prosecute a war with congressional approval given but with the approval not amounting to a formal declaration. This issue was raised by the state of Massachusetts during the Vietnam War.

The general response of the federal judiciary during the Vietnam era was to dismiss war challenges as essentially political, not justiciable questions (that is, as questions not subject to or capable of court resolution).[218] *Massachusetts v. Laird* was a notable exception.[219] The U.S. Court of Appeals for the First Circuit found that portions of the nation's war power were conferred by the Constitution on Congress and that other portions were conferred on the president directly. Should these two branches concur on a policy of war, even in the absence of a formal declaration, then the policy was constitutional.

The court found at least tacit congressional approval of the Vietnam War. Congress had undoubtedly known about the war, and it had knowingly expanded U.S. military forces and appropriated funds to support the expansion. These and other acts convinced the appellate judges that Congress had given the president its consent. That was sufficient.

Once war is declared, the president's power as commander in chief to deploy combat forces is extensive; in many situations the power is conclusive.[220] The president, incidental to this power, may occupy and rule conquered territory with military force.[221] The actual duration of the occupation is a matter left to the discretion of the president,[222] but congressional assent must be attained before conquered territory may actually be annexed to the United States.[223] Although the Supreme Court has not made a definitive ruling on the issue, it has at least suggested that war may be terminated either by Congress or the president.[224]

Sustaining the War Effort

War requires sacrifice. Most directly, war requires the sacrifice of lives lost in combat. But it also requires other, less extreme sacrifices of the population supporting the general prosecution of war. Business firms are told what to produce and what not to produce. Families are told they must do with less or, in some cases, without scarce products.

In 1952, with the Korean War fully under way, President Harry Truman asked that sacrifices be made mutually by the steel industry and its employees. He asked that the steel industry increase employee wages to correspond somewhat with increased industry profits. To the employees, he asked that a threatened strike be postponed. The war effort, Truman appealed, should not be crippled by a strike. As the industry and employees could not reach an agreement, a strike was scheduled.

The president possessed ample authority to postpone a strike. In 1947, Congress enacted, over Truman's veto, the Labor Management Relations Act, more commonly known today as the Taft-Hartley Act. The 1947 law authorized the president to seek a temporary injunction to stop strikes threatening "the national health or safety." [225] A sixty-day "cooling off period" could have been obtained by invoking this authority.

For political reasons, Truman was reluctant to invoke the Taft-Hartley Act, and did not. Instead, referring to the constitutional authority of the president as chief executive, commander in chief of the armed forces, and chief law enforcement officer, the president ordered the seizure of the steel industry by executive proclamation. His order was challenged by a collection of steel producers and quickly worked its way on appeal to the Supreme Court.

In 1952 the Supreme Court ruled against Truman in the *Steel Seizure Case.*[226] Owing to a number of concurring and dissenting opinions, and the necessity of a majority (five in this case) of the Court agreeing on a rule of law for it to become binding precedent, the opinion for the Court written by Justice Hugo Black must be read narrowly. And a narrow reading of Black's opinion—the part of his opinion that was supported by a majority—focuses on the conflict between presidential and congressional authority.

Congress, Black reasoned, is delegated authority by

the Constitution to regulate interstate commerce, in war and in peace. It exercised this authority generally by enacting labor legislation, and, in particular, by enacting the Taft-Hartley Act. A bit of legislative history then became critical.

During the House debate on the proposed Taft-Hartley bill, an amendment was introduced that would have allowed the president to seize industries during national emergencies. The amendment was rejected by a floor vote.

Congress, then, had constitutional authority to permit a seizure of the type ordered by Truman, and, in fact, it had considered granting the president that authority. But it did not. It rejected the proposal expressly. A conflict thus existed between presidential and congressional authority.

The conflict was resolved in favor of Congress. "The Constitution," Black concluded, "did not subject this lawmaking power of Congress to presidential or military supervision or control." [227]

We cannot say what the Court would have done in the *Steel Seizure Case* had Congress not considered the seizure amendment in 1947; a majority of the justices declined to rule on whether the constitutional authority claimed by Truman would then have been sufficient. With greater certainty—the precedents support such a conclusion—we can say that had Congress adopted the amendment, then the president's order would have been sustained.

The president, in fact, is customarily delegated extensive authority by Congress during war. The Supreme Court has upheld delegations to the president to seize or regulate telegraph lines[228], ships,[229] and housing rentals.[230]

Recognizing that the necessity for regulation may extend to the period following the end of hostilities, the Supreme Court has refused to consider the wisdom of postwar executive regulation of business, when such regulation had been congressionally authorized.[231] Even statutes enacted after hostilities have ended, but designed to ease the readjustment to peace, have been upheld.[232] The requirements of war, and of adjusting to peace, are matters the Court has left to Congress and the president.

Library of Congress

President Truman's seizure of steel mills during the Korean War sparked a firestorm of public protest. The Supreme Court eventually ruled the action illegal.

War Power and Civil Rights

Sacrifices necessitated by war sometimes involve more than lives or property. Civil rights also may be sacrificed, sometimes mildly, and sometimes quite severely. Necessity inevitably will be offered as a justification.

An extensive discussion of how the judicial branch has treated possible wartime deprivations of civil rights by the president would require far more space than is available here. The cases that are described, however, support the argument that the judicial branch will defer to and support a wartime president when possible. This generalization holds true even with particularly liberal justices, as happened in the World War II curfew and exclusion cases discussed in this section.

Still, there is a line beyond which judges will not support the president and will assert the independent power of the judicial branch to invalidate presidential actions. This line is drawn with care and caution. Judges wish neither to inhibit the successful prosecution of a war nor to engage in losing battles with a president who has popular and congressional support.

Using the metaphor "life" to represent the American Republic and "limb" to represent certain rights guaranteed to the citizens of the Republic, President Lincoln argued that a "life is never wisely given to save a limb." [233] Lincoln saved the life but severed many limbs in the process.

His agents were local military commanders. Acting under direct presidential orders, or with express or tacit presidential approval, Lincoln's officers partially or completely supplanted civil with military rule in certain areas of the North and in all areas of the South in rebellion. Rights guaranteed by the Constitution, such as the right to a trial by jury, were suspended in the process.

When a civilian resident of Indiana was arrested by military authorities and then tried and sentenced to be hanged by a military tribunal, the issue of the constitutionality of military rule reached the Supreme Court.

In 1866 the Court, in *Ex parte Milligan,* rejected at the outset any theory that constitutional rights could be suspended merely because an emergency existed. "No doctrine," urged Justice David Davis, "involving more pernicious consequences, was ever invented by the wit of man than that any of the [Constitution's] provisions can be suspended during any of the great exigencies of government." [234] This, David explained, did not mean that military rule could not be used on occasion, but the occasions for its use were severely restricted.

> It will be borne in mind that this is not a question of the power to proclaim martial law, when war exists in a community and the courts and civil authorities are overthrown. Nor is it a question of what rule a military

commander ... can impose on states in rebellion to cripple their resources and quell the insurrection.... If armies were collected in Indiana, they were to be employed in another locality, where the laws were obstructed and the national authority disputed. On her soil there was no hostile foot; if once invaded, that invasion was at an end, and with it all pretext for martial law. Martial law cannot arise from a threatened invasion. The necessity must be actual and present; the invasion real, such as effectually closes the courts and deposes the civilian administration.

It is difficult to see how the safety of the country required martial law in Indiana....

...there are occasions when martial rule can be properly applied. If, in foreign invasion or civil war, the courts are actually closed, and it is impossible to administer criminal justice according to law, then, on the theatre of active military operations, where war really prevails, there is a necessity to furnish a substitute for the civil authority, thus overthrown, to preserve the safety of the army and society; and as no power is left but the military, it is allowed to govern by martial rule until the laws can have their free course. As necessity creates the rule, so it limits its duration; for, if this government is continued after the courts are reinstated, it is a gross usurpation of power. Martial rule can never exist where the courts are open, and in the proper and unobstructed exercise of their jurisdiction.[235]

Thus, the president could lawfully impose military rule in the South, where courts loyal to the United States were closed. But in the North, where judges of the state and federal courts remained loyal to the Republic, Lincoln's officers acted without legal authority.

Almost a century later, the Supreme Court revisited the *Milligan* rule. On December 7, 1941, forces of Imperial Japan attacked a number of U.S. military installations, including those in the Hawaiian Islands. To local military and civilian authorities, the situation was uncertain but dangerous—invasion was a possibility, as indeed had occurred in U.S. outposts in the Philippine Islands, Guam, and Wake Island. The governor of Hawaii proclaimed martial law, in accordance, he stated, with authority given him by Congress. President Franklin D. Roosevelt concurred.

In 1944, a civilian, Lloyd Duncan, was tried and convicted of assaulting two U.S. Navy sentries in violation of military orders. Although Duncan was a civilian, civil courts in Hawaii were open at the time, and the Japanese invasion threat had long since receded, Duncan was tried by a military, not a civilian, tribunal. Duncan challenged his conviction on the ground that the military tribunal lacked jurisdiction over civilians.

The Supreme Court overturned Duncan's conviction in *Duncan v. Kahanamoku.*[236] The opinion by Justice Hugo Black cited *Milligan* with approval, but the decision of the Court, in the end, did not rest on *Milligan*. Instead, Black wrote a narrow opinion, basing the Court's decision on an interpretation of the congressional act purportedly empowering the governor to declare martial law. The result was the same as *Milligan,* but in *Duncan,* the Court avoided the constitutional issue.

A clear exception to the rule that war itself does not justify the suspension of constitutional rights is found with the writ of *habeas corpus,* a judicial order commanding that a person in custody be brought before the court to determine the lawfulness of his or her detention. Article I, section 9, of the Constitution says: "The Privilege of the Writ of Habeas Corpus shall not be suspended, unless when in Cases of Rebellion or Invasion the public Safety may require it." But who has the authority to suspend the writ? Congress? The president? Either? The Constitution does not say.

President Lincoln claimed this power for himself and suspended the writ. Not much time elapsed before his military officers began arresting, and holding without trial, Northern civilians suspected of harboring Southern sympathies.

The Supreme Court did not review the president's action. The chief justice of the United States at the time, however, did, and he ruled against the president. Roger B. Taney, sitting as a circuit trial judge, found conclusive the fact that the Framers had located the suspension clause into Article I of the Constitution, the legislative article. Only Congress, he concluded, was empowered to suspend the writ.

Accordingly, Taney ordered the release of a prisoner held by the military at Ft. McHenry, Maryland.[237] But Lincoln and his general ignored Taney's order.

The judiciary has not been as beneficent toward enemy nations and nationals within the United States, or toward U.S. citizens whose descent can be traced to an enemy nation. As commander in chief, the president unilaterally may subject the residents of conquered territory to military occupation and rule.[238] Foreign civilian and military personnel may be tried and executed for war crimes by military or international tribunals not affording defendants customary due process or other constitutional rights.[239] And, enemy saboteurs who infiltrate the United States during war may be subjected to the jurisdiction of military tribunals, and military hanging if convicted. This rule applies even if the United States is not then being invaded or even mildly threatened with invasion. It also applies to any U.S. citizen who happens to accompany the infiltrators.[240]

Enemy aliens residing within the United States may be subjected to various restrictions by order of the president, including confinement and deportation.[241] Property owned by enemy aliens or nations may be seized summarily.[242]

U.S. citizens may be subjected to similar deprivations during war. Not because they are disloyal but merely because they are identified racially with the enemy nation.

This issue came to the Supreme Court after U.S. citizens of Japanese descent were prosecuted for violating increasingly restrictive measures implemented in response to Japan's December 7, 1941, attack on Pearl Harbor. The first measure was a curfew order imposed on Japanese-Americans living in or in proximity to the Pacific Coast. The second, the "exclusion order," required the evacuation of Japanese-Americans from these areas to "relocation camps" in the interior of the United States. A showing of disloyalty was not required in either case; everyone of Japanese ancestry was subject to the orders.

The curfew order was issued initially by authority of the president as commander in chief and was shortly thereafter ratified by congressional legislation. It was attacked, first, as an unconstitutional delegation of power by Congress and, second, as a violation of the Fifth Amendment to the U.S. Constitution.

Writing for a unanimous Court (although with two concurring opinions), Chief Justice Harlan Fiske Stone upheld the curfew order in *Hirabayashi v. United States.*[243] The Court's decision, he stressed, neither affirmed nor denied the unilateral authority of either the president or Congress to implement a curfew under these circumstances. The decision, rather, rested on the constitutional authority of the president as commander in chief being used in concert with the legislative authority of Congress. An aggregation of legislative and executive authority supported the action.

The question remaining was whether the president and Congress were justified in imposing the curfew. Emphasizing the gravity and uncertainty of the war at the time the curfew was imposed, Stone reasoned that the danger justified the burden.

> That reasonably prudent men charged with the responsibility of our national defense had ample ground for concluding that they must face the danger of invasion, take measures against it, and in making the choice of measure consider our internal situation, cannot be doubted.[244]

The fact that the burden fell on Japanese-Americans, he wrote, was reasonable in view of the circumstances.

The exclusion case was factually similar to the curfew case, except in degree. While the curfew case dealt with an order restricting the movement of Japanese-Americans within designated zones, the exclusion case considered the validity of an order removing Japanese-Americans from these zones altogether and their forced relocation to guarded camps inside the United States. Again, the action was justified by assertions of presidential and congressional power exercised jointly.

The outcome was the same. In *Korematsu v. United States,* the Supreme Court ruled in 1944 that the president and Congress possessed sufficient constitutional authority to order such exclusions, provided that the order was justified by "pressing public necessity." [245] This burden, concluded Justice Hugo Black, had been met by the government.

Unanimity was broken in *Korematsu.* In fact, three vigorous dissents were recorded. Justice Owen J. Roberts indicated that had the government temporarily excluded the Japanese-Americans from specified zones and left the matter at that, then he might have been persuaded to go along. But the government did not leave the matter at simple exclusion; it forced the subjects of the order into what Roberts referred to as "concentration camps." [246]

Justice Frank Murphy attributed the order to one factor: racism. "Justification for the exclusion is sought . . . mainly upon questionable racial and sociological grounds not ordinarily within the realm of expert military judgment." [247] No evidence had been introduced to demonstrate a tendency toward disloyalty among the Japanese-Americans; the basis, rather, for the government's decisions was a collection of racial generalizations for which no support could be given. The action fell "into the ugly abyss of racism." [248]

While anger seems evident in Murphy's dissent, anguish characterizes the dissent of Justice Robert H. Jackson. He, too, thought racism was behind the exclusion order but expressly refused to consider whether the order could have been justified by military necessity. Evidence of necessity was simply not presented, other than the local military commander's "own unsworn, self-serving statement, untested by any cross-examination, that what he did was reasonable." [249]

Jackson's greatest source of anguish, however, appears to have been the participation of the Supreme Court in legitimizing the action. Better, he counseled, to dismiss the case without ruling on its merits than give the exclusion order a gloss of constitutionality: "a judicial construction of the due process clause that will sustain this order is a far more subtle blow to liberty than the promulgation of the order itself." [250]

On the same day that *Korematsu* was decided, the Supreme Court also ruled in another case, *Ex parte Endo,* that Japanese-Americans conceded to be loyal by the government could not be detained against their will.[251] Thus, although the Court had legitimized the exclusion power, it also had limited that power, and signaled its willingness to consider individual petitions for release.

Hirabayashi and *Korematsu* are not decisions that current supporters of the Supreme Court point to with pride. But these cases—perhaps more than any other case or group of cases—well illustrate the great reluctance of the judicial branch to interfere with the prosecution of war by the president and Congress. Even extreme and normally insupportable measures may be tolerated and supported.

The President as Chief Legislator

The U.S. Constitution is explicit: "All legislative powers herein granted shall be vested in a Congress of the United States, which shall consist of a Senate and House of Representatives." [252] Yet we persist in referring to the president as "chief legislator."

Part of the explanation is found in the text of the Constitution. Section 7 of the first article requires that Congress submit to the president all bills, orders, resolutions, or votes requiring the joint assent of both houses. This "presentment clause" then gives the president authority either to approve the act as written, in which case it repassed by both houses with at least a two-thirds vote. In most cases, this veto authority makes the president final arbiter of what becomes law.

The Constitution also commands the president to "give to the Congress information of the state of the Union, and to recommend to their consideration such measures as he shall judge necessary and expedient." [253] This may seem like a fairly innocuous provision, but it does give presidents an important public forum for presenting their own legislative preferences to Congress and, perhaps more important, to the people of the United States. Moreover, by expressly requiring the president to recommend legislation, the Constitution anticipates the institutional jealousies that may exist between Congress and the president and avoids the issue of whether it is proper for an "outsider" to propose legislation.[254]

Article II, section 2, also permits the president to convene special sessions of Congress on "extraordinary occasions," and, should the president deem it proper, to adjourn Congress. This authority is not often used, but it may be important to the president if, for example, a declaration of war is sought or if the two houses of Congress cannot agree on an adjournment date.

These provisions of the Constitution give the president a considerable role in the legislative process. By themselves, however, they do not depict how the actual role of the president in this important process has evolved. This role is much greater than might be deduced from a casual or even a careful reading of the Constitution. The Constitution, for example, gives the president authority to veto legislation originating in Congress; it does not even imply how powerful a political weapon this could become in the hands of an aggressive president. Credit for the development of the president's veto authority as a political asset belongs principally to Presidents Andrew Jackson, John Tyler, and Franklin D. Roosevelt, and not to the Framers of the Constitution.

Nor does the Constitution indicate that the legislative process would evolve into a system whereby Congress frequently would be placed in the position of responding to measures proposed by the president. Yet, that is what has happened. Finally, the Constitution is silent about how the bargaining process between the president and Congress should proceed. The president, it has turned out, possesses numerous powers that may be brought to bear on reluctant members of the House or Senate.

The evolution of the president's powerful role in the legislative process has been defined largely without participation by the judiciary. Certain incidents of the president's power, however, have been adjudicated. Generally, the result has been to promote presidential power.

Presidential Power to Propose Legislation

The Constitution contemplates and authorizes an energetic legislative leader in the White House, and it contemplates and authorizes a submissive Congress. But it does not require either. The relationship between Congress and the president in initiating legislation is one that the Constitution has left to the two branches to define. Politics, not the Constitution, determines how active the president shall be as legislative leader of the United States. *(See Legislative Leader chapter in Part III.)*

Whether motivated by indifference, personal conviction, or fear of a powerful and jealous Congress, most presidents have refrained from attempting an active legislative role. Many of the "forgottens" belong to this list of presidents.

Other presidents have been more active. Secretary of the Treasury Alexander Hamilton actively and openly pursued a legislative program on behalf of his president, George Washington. Thomas Jefferson followed this precedent, although not as openly. And Woodrow Wilson exerted strong leadership with Congress following his inauguration in 1913.

From virtually March 4, 1933, the day on which Franklin Roosevelt was inaugurated, to the present day, major pieces of legislation have been drafted in the White House or in various agencies subordinate to the president.[255] Executive leadership of the legislative process is indeed a characteristic of the modern American presidency.

The judicial branch has not interfered with this arrangement. Nor has it been asked. This fact alone, however, should not be interpreted to mean that the judiciary has not influenced the product of the arrangement. It has. In doing this it has also influenced the power of the president.

If the judiciary interprets presidentially sponsored legislation in a manner that is approved by the president, then the president's power as chief legislator is promoted. But if the judiciary interprets presidentially sponsored legislation in a manner that is disapproved by the president, then the power of the president as chief legislator is narrowed. Two periods of judicial review of presidentially initiated legislation illustrate this point: Supreme Court review of Franklin Roosevelt's New Deal legislation of the 1930s and Supreme Court review of President Lyndon B. Johnson's civil rights legislation of the 1960s.

New Deal Legislation. Events determined Roosevelt's legislative agenda: the nation and much of the world was in the midst of a depression. Rejecting the passive response of his predecessor, Herbert Hoover, Roosevelt moved quickly to assert the power of the national government in an attempt to restore economic stability to the United States. The president needed help in doing this; he asked for it from Congress.

Congress did not quibble. When the president told the legislative body that farmers needed assistance, Congress enacted the Agricultural Adjustment Act. When he told them that jobs had to be created, Congress created and appropriated funds for the Civil Conservation Corps, Works Project Administration, and Public Works Administration. And when the president told Congress that industrial peace was a precondition to economic recovery, Congress enacted the National Labor Relations Act (Wagner Act). In each case, Congress responded to proposals submitted by the White House.

The president thought that these pieces of legislation were needed, and most of Congress and the American people agreed. But a portion of the Supreme Court was not persuaded. Four justices showed a general and persistent hostility toward government regulation of business. Two more justices could be persuaded by the first four to vote with them on certain issues. Only three justices could be counted on to provide the president general, if not uniform, support. Three votes were insufficient to carry a decision.

The Supreme Court did not invalidate the president's legislative agenda as a whole, but it did strike down important parts. In 1935, the Court ruled in *Railroad Retirement Board v. Alton* that Congress was not empowered by the Constitution to mandate and regulate railroad employee retirement plans.[256] *Alton* was followed, in quick succession, by decisions of the Supreme Court declaring unconstitutional the National Industrial Recovery Act,[257] the Agricultural Adjustment Act of 1933,[258] and the Bituminous Coal Conservation Act of 1935.[259]

No one of these decisions can be said to have crippled the New Deal. But there was still cause for anxiety. Other measures, more critical to the president's recovery strategy, were working their way up the judicial appellate structure. Would the Supreme Court treat these in the same dismissive manner?

The president thought that the Court might. His solution, a proposal to "pack" the Supreme Court with new and presumably friendly appointees, provoked a political confrontation involving the president, Congress, and the Court. Congress refused the president's "court packing plan," but the controversy may have alarmed the two justices positioned in the middle, Charles Evans Hughes and Owen J. Roberts, to become more supportive of the president. In 1937, Hughes and Roberts joined with three other justices in declaring the National Labor Relations Act a valid exercise of congressional authority.[260] The obstructionist justices began retiring in 1937, and Roosevelt replaced them with more agreeable appointees. Thereafter, the president's legislative agenda became safe from judicial interference. The power of the judicial branch, in fact, was then used to promote by legitimizing rather than inhibit by invalidating this form of presidential power.

Civil Rights Legislation. The civil rights era of the 1950s and 1960s furnishes additional examples of how judicial authority may be applied to promote presidential law-making authority. Congress, at the urging of President Lyndon Johnson, enacted the Civil Rights Act of 1964 and the Voting Rights Act of 1965. The first piece of legislation targeted various forms of discrimination in, among other things, housing, employment, and public accommodations.

The Voting Rights Act made racial discrimination in voting unlawful and provided a comprehensive scheme for federal supervision of voting in places where discrimination had been a problem in the past. If Johnson's promise of a "Great Society" was to be realized, then judicial support of these laws was essential.

Judicial support was forthcoming. A series of Supreme Court rulings validated the several sections of the Civil Rights Act of 1964[261] and construed them liberally.[262] The Voting Rights Act received equal support from the Court.[263] And again, it interpreted the statute broadly to ensure maximum coverage.[264] The Court had added its own legitimacy to that of Congress and the president when it made these decisions; it also made the considerable resources of the judicial branch available for their enforcement.

The Veto Power

Presidential power in the legislative process is also influenced by the president's authority to disapprove, or "veto," legislation. Article I, section 7, of the Constitution, known as the "presentment clause," says that Congress must "present" to the president all actions requiring and obtaining the joint consent of the House and Senate except on the issue of adjournment. If the president approves the action, then it becomes law. If the president vetoes the action, then it fails to become law unless the veto is overridden by a vote of two-thirds of both houses of Congress.

A veto may be accomplished in one of two ways. First, the president may return the vetoed action to the originating house of Congress, stating in writing the reasons for disapproval. Second, a veto occurs if the president does not sign the action within ten days (Sundays excluded) of the time Congress presents it and if Congress adjourns during that period. The latter method is called a "pocket veto."

The veto must be ranked as one of the most significant presidential powers. With it, the president may prevent enactment of any legislation, and for any reason, provided the veto is not subsequently overridden. Since the power of Congress is defined primarily as the power to make law, and since Congress has rarely demonstrated an ability to override a presidential veto—even the weaker presidents have their way in most cases—the ability of the president to influence the legislative process is partially a function of the extent and scope of this veto authority.

Judicial interpretations of the presentment clause have had a mixed effect on presidential veto power. On the negative side, the Supreme Court ruled in 1798 that the presentment clause does not apply to constitutional amendments proposed by Congress.[265] The president may suggest consideration of an amendment by Congress and work for or against a proposed amendment; however, the president has no formal constitutional authority to block an amendment proposal through a veto.

Of great practical significance is a 1983 Supreme Court decision, *Immigration and Naturalization Service v. Chadha.* In *Chadha,* the authority of Congress to "veto" an executive action through a method not triggering the presentment clause was questioned. The Court held that these methods were improper constitutionally because, for one reason, a "legislative veto" was a legislative act requiring observance of the presentment clause.[266] *(See "Legislative Veto," p. 1195, in this chapter.)*

The presenting provision of the presentment clause also has aroused some controversy. The courts have responded by fashioning an interpretation that accommodates the reality of presidential responsibility.

Recognizing that the modern president must and will travel outside of Washington for extended periods, and that the president must be given sufficient time to consider the merits of a proposed bill, the U.S. court of claims ruled that presidents may insist that a bill be presented to them personally, wherever they may be at the time. The ten-day period allocated to the president for veto consideration begins tolling once this personal service is accomplished and not on the date the bill is passed.[267] Congress, it should be noted, usually will cooperate with the president by making sure that presentation is not accomplished until the president returns to the White House.

Arousing considerably more conflict between Congress and the president has been the pocket veto issue. To review the constitutional provision, a bill presented to and not signed by the president within ten days of presentation (Sundays excepted) will not become law if Congress is adjourned on the tenth day. The president cannot be denied the opportunity to veto a bill simply because Congress has gone home.

The constitutional issue has revolved around definition of the term *adjournment.* Part of a definition has been supplied by the courts. Gaps, however, remain in the definition, leading to a continuing struggle between the legislative and executive branches.

In the *Pocket Veto Case* (1929), the Supreme Court ruled that if Congress had adjourned after its first session (each term of Congress lasts two years, and is divided into two sessions), thus preventing return of the bill by the president, and if the president has not signed the bill, then a pocket veto would be effected after ten days had elapsed from the date of presentation.[268] This decision would seem to have settled the meaning of *adjournment,* but it did not.

When the *Pocket Veto Case* was decided, intersessional breaks typically lasted three to four months. Were the pocket veto clause held not applicable to such breaks, the Court pointed out, then the bill would be kept "in a state of suspended animation," and that would be inconsistent with the Constitution.[269] Moreover, Congress had not authorized any person to receive the president's veto message on its behalf during its adjournment.

Two developments made the applicability of the *Pocket Veto Case* to future bills at least questionable. First, the duration of each session of Congress was soon extended to the point where the session break only lasted for a few weeks. Congress had matured into a full-time legislative assembly. Second, each house of Congress had authorized one of its employees to receive veto messages from the president. The policy of preventing bills from being held in "suspended animation" had been obviated; and presidents could no longer assert that they could not return a vetoed bill for failure of a specified person to receive service.

These changes were acknowledged and found significant by the Supreme Court nine years later. In *Wright v. United States,* the Court ruled that a three-day adjournment by the originating house (the Senate), did not prevent return of a vetoed bill to that house by the president.[270] The duration of the adjournment was short, and the secretary of the Senate had been authorized to receive service during the adjournment. These facts, Chief Justice Charles Evans Hughes explained, distinguished the instant case from the *Pocket Veto Case.*

So, Congress could adjourn for a few days without

The Hard Hat, Delegation, and Law-making Authority

The hard hat is a familiar sight on construction projects. This has not always been the case. Although hard hats were seen on construction sites in the 1960s and early 1970s, they were not worn universally; employees were not required to wear them. Now they do wear hard hats, or they violate the law.

Hard hats make sense to the individual employee—they afford some protection against head injuries caused by falling or flying objects. Moreover, requiring hard hats is a sensible and relatively inexpensive way for employers and insurance companies to reduce the cost of employee injuries. But these factors, however important, do not by themselves explain the universality of the practice. Law does. Examining the evolution of the hard-hat rule gives us insight into the process of delegated rule-making authority.

The Constitution gives Congress the authority to do what is necessary and proper to regulate interstate commerce[1]—a clause that has been construed liberally by the judiciary.[2] Drawing on this authority, Congress enacted the Occupational Safety and Health Act of 1970.[3] One objective of this legislation is "to assure so far as possible every working man and woman in the Nation safe and healthful working conditions."[4]

At this point, Congress might have simply required the wearing of hard hats by statute and designated an agency to investigate and prosecute violations. But Congress did not. It lacked the time and arguably the expertise to develop a comprehensive set of work-place safety rules that would have been necessary to achieve the stated objective. (Current regulations exceed fifteen hundred pages of double-column, fine print.) So, Congress chose to delegate to the Department of Labor the authority to make detailed regulations, or "rules," pertaining to occupational safety and health.[5]

The Administrative Procedures Act defines an *administrative rule* and *rule making* as follows:

> "Rule" means the whole or a part of an agency statement of general or particular applicability and future effect designed to implement, interpret, or prescribe law or policy or describing the organization, procedure, or practice requirements of an agency and includes the approval or prescription for the future of rates wages, corporate or financial structures or reorganization thereof, prices, facilities, appliances, services or allowances therefore or of valuations, costs, or accounting, or practices bearing upon any of the foregoing;
>
> "Rule making" means agency process for formulating, amending, or repealing a rule.[6]

In accordance with this rule-making or quasi-legislative authority delegated by Congress, the secretary of Labor promulgated a series of regulations about the wearing of safety helmets on construction sites. The current rule reads as follows: "Employees working in areas where there is a possible danger of head injury from impact, or from falling or flying objects, or from electrical shock and burns, shall be protected by protective helmets."[7]

Violation of this regulation may result in civil or criminal penalties, including fine or imprisonment.[8]

1. U.S. Constitution, Article I, section 8.
2. See *McCulloch v. Maryland,* 17 U.S. (4 Wheat.) 316 (1819); and *Wickard v. Filburn,* 317 U.S. 111 (1942).
3. PL 91-596 (1970).
4. *United States Code*, vol. 29; section 651(b).
5. *United States Code*, vol. 29; section 655.
6. *United States Code*, vol. 5; section 551(4), (5).
7. *Code of Federal Regulations*; vol. 29; section 1926.100(a) (1987).
8. *United States Code*, vol. 29; section 666.

worrying about a pocket veto. But could it adjourn with the same sense of security for a longer period? A week? Ten days? A month? The Supreme Court did not answer these questions in *Wright* or since then.

The U.S. Court of Appeals for the District of Columbia has addressed this issue and resolved it in favor of Congress. In 1974 the court ruled in *Kennedy v. Sampson* that the pocket veto is not effective during *intra*sessional adjournments of any duration, as long as the originating house previously had authorized an agent to receive the president's veto message.[271] This rule was extended in the 1985 case of *Barnes v. Kline* to apply also to *inter*sessional adjournments.[272] The effect of the latter decision was nullified when the Supreme Court annulled it in 1987.

Delegated Quasi-Legislative Power

The Constitution vests the legislative authority of the United States in Congress. Congress, in turn, has found it convenient to delegate portions of this authority to agencies of the executive branch or to the president directly.

Some of these agencies—such as the Departments of Treasury, State, Defense, and Commerce—are directly subordinate to the president. Others, the so-called independent agencies, are not. The president may influence policy making carried out by these agencies through the presidential authority to appoint their principal officers and through political persuasion, but the president cannot actually direct their activities without prior congressional authorization. The Federal Reserve Board, the Securities and Exchange Commission, and the Federal Trade Commission are examples of independent agencies. *(See Government Agencies and Corporations chapter in Part V.)*

The delegation works in the following manner. Congress enacts a law. This law defines the general objectives of the legislation and designates a specific agency to make detailed rules and regulations to attain those objectives. The outcome, published first in the *Federal Register,* and ultimately codified in the *Code of Federal Regulations,* is a body of law of greater length, and of vastly more detail than is found in the *United States Code.* These rules and regulations are law and are enforced as such by the judiciary.

An example of how this process works is furnished by the hard-hat rule promulgated by the Occupational Safety and Health Administration (OSHA) of the Department of Labor. *(See box, The Hard Hat, Delegation, and Lawmaking Authority, p. 1194.)* Numerous other examples could be supplied: extensive regulation of airline safety by the Federal Aviation Administration of the Department of Transportation, detailed tax rules made by the Internal Revenue Service of the Department of Treasury, and a comprehensive set of standards for meat and dairy products established by the Department of Agriculture.

Each time Congress makes a delegation of this type, it both increases and decreases its own power. Congress increases its power because delegation results in more extensive regulation of an activity than could otherwise be the case—Congress is a busy institution and is limited in how much attention it can give to any particular subject during any single session. As long as the agency follows the will of Congress faithfully, then it acts as an agent of the legislative branch.

But agencies are accorded much discretion in their rule-making activities, and the exercise of this discretion may result in rules that do not conform to the current expectations of Congress. When this occurs, Congress may try to modify or rescind the rule through bargaining, a process that can be politically costly to the legislative branch. If the president backs the agency decision, these costs can be high.

The transfer of power to the executive branch is not complete; Congress still retains influence over the outcome. It may investigate agency practices in public sessions. If it finds that agency rule making does not conform to congressional expectations, Congress may "punish" or threaten to punish the agency by reducing its budget, abolishing positions within the agency, or taking back or restricting some of the authority it had previously granted. If its displeasure is aroused sufficiently, Congress may even abolish the agency. These are powerful bargaining weapons for Congress in its negotiations with rule-making agencies.

More directly, Congress may overrule agency decisions through the legislative process. If an agency promulgates a rule that Congress considers offensive, and if political bargaining does not result in a modification of the rule by the agency, then Congress may amend the rule itself by amending the legislation that gave rule-making authority to the agency in the first place. Although effective, this method is rarely employed; Congress usually considers the political costs too great, particularly if a presidential veto is involved.

To the extent, then, that presidents can use delegated rule-making authority to suit their own purposes, which may or may not coincide with the purposes of Congress, then this authority must be considered a plus for presidential power.

If, as the Constitution states, "all legislative power" of the United States is vested in Congress,[273] then how may OSHA and a large number of other administrative agencies exercise this rule-making authority? How may they constitutionally make law? This question was asked of and had to be resolved by the judiciary.

The judicial branch has not always been consistent in its answer. Language in one Supreme Court opinion, for instance, seemed to indicate a general skepticism about the constitutionality of legislative delegations: "That the legislative power of Congress cannot be delegated is, of course, clear." [274] In practice, however, the judiciary has been indulgent, even enthusiastic, about these delegations. With two notable exceptions, the Supreme Court has upheld every attempt by Congress to delegate legislative authority to the executive branch.[275] By upholding, and thus legitimizing, these delegations, the Court has promoted presidential power.

The Supreme Court has never really articulated a persistently followed justification for delegations of legislative authority. It has never really answered the question: How can this be constitutional? Kenneth Culp Davis, a scholar of administrative law, has argued that all attempts to create constitutional doctrine justifying the practice have failed.[276] If for no other reason, judges permit this delegation of authority because the realities of decision making in the U.S. political system require it.

Delegated legislative authority was once thought to be constitutional because Congress controlled how it would be used by executive agencies through the device of defining general legislative standards. The role of the executive branch was merely to carry out the clear intention of Congress. Indeed, two major pieces of President Franklin Roosevelt's New Deal program were invalidated because they were found to have failed this test.[277]

This doctrine quickly fell into disuse, although it has never been explicitly repudiated. Congress either could not or would not become more precise and frequently enough provided vague standards, or no standards at all. The judiciary decided not to interfere.

In 1942, for example, Congress enacted the Renegotiation Act in an effort to recover the costs incurred by government as a result of excessive profit making by contractors during World War II. The members of Congress who sponsored and considered this legislation presumably understood what constituted an excess profit, but they could not define it in numerical terms. So, they supplied the following definition: "The term 'excessive profits' means any amount of a contract or subcontract price which is found as a result of renegotiation to represent excessive profits." Stripped of verbiage, this definition may be rewritten: "The term 'excessive profits' means . . . excessive profits." Congress then delegated authority to contracting agencies to develop their own definitions of *excess profit.* The Supreme Court upheld this delegation in *Lichter v. United States.*[278]

Other examples are as illuminating. The Economic Stabilization Act of 1970 authorized the president to order price, rent, and wage controls necessary to stabilize the economy. Additional authority was granted the president to make any exceptions to the order that were needed to avoid "gross inequities." [279] President Richard Nixon invoked this authority in 1971 and soon found his order challenged in federal district court. The court upheld the congressional delegation of authority and the president's order.[280] Similar results have been achieved when standards such as "just and reasonable" and "unfair methods of competition" were challenged.[281]

The Legislative Veto

The legislative veto was developed by Congress so that it could delegate portions of its own authority to officers of the executive branch and then exercise some measure of control over how that authority would be used. It is a simple process mechanically.

Congress, as was discussed in the previous section, occasionally finds it expedient to delegate a portion of its own authority to designated officers of the executive branch. It does this through the normal legislative process; that is, a bill or joint resolution is passed and, with the president's approval, becomes law.

The Gulf of Tonkin Resolution of 1964, for example, authorized the president to "take all necessary steps, including the use of armed force, to assist any member or protocol state of the Southeast Asia Collective Defense Treaty" requesting U.S. assistance.[282] Whether this resolution constituted an actual delegation of congressional authority to declare war is debatable. Not debatable, however, is the intention of Congress that the president should be authorized to engage U.S. military forces in combat. Congress was attempting to delegate its constitutional authority to the president. The president used this authority in Vietnam, Laos, and Cambodia.

Congress protected itself. The president's authority, Congress provided in the resolution, could be terminated at any time by a "concurrent resolution of the Congress." [283] Congress arguably had delegated its war-making power to the president, but it also had reserved the right to withdraw that authority at any time and for any reason. Congress had inserted a legislative veto clause into the resolution.

Legislative vetoes could be accomplished by a concurrent resolution passed by both houses of Congress, as was the case with the Gulf of Tonkin Resolution. But a simple resolution passed by either one of the two houses of Congress would often suffice, as would occasionally a mere majority vote of a committee or subcommittee of either house of Congress. None of these three methods, it should be noted, require presentment to the president for possible presidential veto.

The legislative veto was an innovative political device, one that Congress had found useful.[284] With it, Congress could delegate much of its workload, assign many of its political responsibilities to the executive branch, and not lose control over the outcome. Something about the legislative veto, however, disturbed many people. This "something" was well captured by political scientist Louis Fisher when he described the device as a "reversal" of the normal legislative-executive roles in U.S. politics. The executive branch would make the laws and effectively present the product to Congress. Congress, then, would be asked to approve (implicitly by doing nothing) or veto the product.[285] The executive branch assumed the function of Congress, and Congress assumed the function of the president.

However useful the legislative veto may have been to Congress, and arguably to the U.S. political process in general, it was not to survive constitutional scrutiny by the Supreme Court. With only two justices dissenting, the Court in 1983 declared the legislative veto unconstitutional in *Immigration and Naturalization Service v. Chadha*. The legislative veto, the Court ruled, violated both the presentment and bicameral clauses of the Constitution.[286]

Writing for the majority, Chief Justice Warren E. Burger explained:

> The Constitution sought to divide the delegated powers of the new Federal Government into three defined categories, Legislative, Executive, and Judicial, to assure, as nearly as possible, that each branch of government would confine itself to its assigned responsibility. The hydraulic pressure inherent within each of the separate Branches to exceed the outer limits of its power, even to accomplish desirable objectives, must be resisted.[287]

Once Congress had delegated its authority to the executive branch, Burger concluded, it could reverse decisions made in accordance with that authority only if two conditions were met: the legislative veto was passed by both houses of Congress (the specific legislative veto under review involved a simple resolution passed by the House), and the legislative veto was first submitted to the president for possible presidential veto. Separation of powers was the theme of the majority, and this principle had been violated by Congress.

Justice Byron R. White responded in a vigorous dissent, which was joined by Justice (now Chief Justice) William H. Rehnquist. White's first sentence reads: "Today the Court not only invalidates [the legislative veto provision of] the Immigration and Nationality Act, but also sounds the death knell for nearly 200 other statutory provisions in which Congress has reserved a 'legislative veto.' " [288] He continued: "I regret the destructive scope of the Court's holding. It reflects a profoundly different conception of the Constitution than that held by the Courts which sanctioned the modern administrative state." [289] How, White concluded, can the Court approve the delegation by Congress of extensive quasi-legislative authority to the executive branch, yet strike down the only meaningful way at the disposal of Congress to control the exercise of that authority?

Chadha is a clear and explicit attempt by the Supreme Court to protect presidential power from congressional encroachments.

Should Congress attempt to overrule legislative decisions made by executive officers in a manner that conforms to the presentment clause—that is, through the normal legislative process—and should the president veto this attempt, then Congress can succeed only when each house can muster a two-thirds vote to overrule the veto. That is a difficult burden to overcome. Once the authority is delegated, control of how that authority is used is lost.

With the legislative veto, Congress could delegate authority to the president with the understanding that some control could still be exercised over how that authority was used; Congress could veto an executive action with which it disagreed. With the legislative veto held unconstitutional by the Supreme Court, Congress can still influence how the delegated authority is used, but doing so is more difficult. For example, Congress can overrule the executive action by amending the existing law, but it would have to submit the bill to the president.

Because Congress now has greater difficulty influencing the way delegated authority is used by the president (or independent agencies), it may become more reluctant to agree to additional delegations in the future. Will Congress, for example, agree to extend future presidents the same limited authority to reorganize the executive branch that it has since the administration of President Herbert Hoover? Possibly not, according to some scholars of administrative law.[290] Without the check afforded by the legislative veto, Congress also might respond by defining more precise standards that must be followed when discretionary authority is to be exercised. As presidential discretion is restricted by such standards, so is presidential power.

Finally, Congress may delegate authority to the president but condition the exercise of that authority on prior legislative approval. This is currently done in the case of weapons sales to foreign nations. The president is authorized to negotiate these sales but must obtain congressional approval before the transfer actually occurs.

Chadha, then, is an important instance of the judiciary's defending the president against attempted incursions by Congress. For the short term, presidential power has been promoted. It is still too early to assess the long-term implications.

Notes

1. James Madison, "No. 51," in *The Federalist Papers* (New York: Mentor Books, 1961), 322.
2. Ibid., 322, 320.
3. Edward S. Corwin, *The President: Office and Powers, 1787-1984,* 5th rev. ed., ed. Randall W. Bland, Theodore T. Hindson, and Jack W. Peltason (New York: New York University Press, 1984), 201. Corwin was specifically speaking of the provisions of the Constitution concerning foreign affairs. His description, however, captures the entire constitutional design, not just those parts pertaining to the conduct of foreign affairs.
4. For helpful discussions of *power* and related concepts, see Robert A. Dahl, *Modern Political Analysis,* 4th ed. (Englewood Cliffs, N.J.: Prentice-Hall, 1984), 19-47, and David Easton, *A Systems Analysis of Political Life* (Chicago: University of Chicago Press, 1965), 207-211.
5. See, for example, Henry J. Abraham, *The Judicial Process: An Introductory Analysis of the Courts of the United States, England, and France* (New York: Oxford University Press, 1986); Walter F. Murphy and C. Herman Pritchett, *Courts, Judges, & Politics: An Introduction to the Judicial Process,* 4th ed. (New York: Random House, 1986). For a more technical treatment of the subject, see Charles Alan Wright, *Law of Federal Courts,* 4th ed. (St. Paul, Minnesota: West Publishing Co., 1983).
6. 28 U.S.C., section 1441 *et seq.*
7. Jerome Frank, *Courts on Trial: Myth and Reality in American Justice* (New York: Atheneum, 1963), 5.
8. Most state courts and all federal courts, in fact, will not hear a lawsuit unless a real legal dispute exists between at least two parties. This "case" and "controversy" requirement in federal courts stems from an interpretation of Article III, section 2, of the U.S. Constitution by members of the Supreme Court sitting as circuit justices (*Hayburn's Case,* 2 U.S. [2 Dall.] 8 [1792]). Federal courts will not rule on hypothetical questions, including questions of the constitutionality of legislative actions referred to them (even indirectly) by Congress (*Muskrat v. United States,* 219 U.S. 346 [1911]).
9. U.S. Constitution, Article II, section 2.
10. *Marbury v. Madison,* 5 U.S. (1 Cranch) 137, 177 (1803).
11. Marshall said that courts "are mere instruments of the law, and can will nothing" (*Osborn v. Bank of the United States,* 22 U.S. [9 Wheat.] 251, [1824]).
12. Quoted in Jerome Frank, *Courts on Trial: Myth and Reality in American Justice* (New York: Atheneum, 1963), 294.
13. Emphasis original. Felix Frankfurter, Preface to *Mr. Justice Brandeis,* ed. Felix Frankfurter (New Haven: Yale University Press, 1932), unnumbered. Frankfurter made this statement seven years before being appointed to the Supreme Court.
14. Charles Evans Hughes, Speech to the Elmira Chamber of Commerce, May 3, 1907, reprinted in *Addresses* (1908), 139.
15. *Hauenstein v. Lynham,* 100 U.S. 483 (1880).
16. *Marbury,* at 368.
17. Ibid., 389.
18. Walter F. Murphy and C. Herman Pritchett, "Courts and Social Policy," in *Courts, Judges, and Politics: An Introduction to the Judicial Process,* 4th ed., ed. Walter F. Murphy and C. Herman Pritchett (New York: Random House, 1986), 39.
19. Holmes to Laski, March 4, 1920, *Holmes-Laski Letters,* I, ed. Mark DeWolfe Howe (New York: Atheneum, 1963), 249.
20. Walter Murphy, *Elements of Judicial Strategy* (Chicago: University of Chicago Press, 1964), 172.
21. *United States v. Nixon,* 418 U.S. 683 (1974). This case is discussed extensively in the following chapter.
22. See, for example, *Cooper v. Aaron,* 358 U.S. 1 (1958), where the Court not only voted unanimously but punctuated their unity by each justice individually signing the opinion of the Court. This had not been done before, and has not been done since.
23. *Dayton v. Dulles,* 357 U.S. 144 (1958). Except where otherwise noted, the facts contained in this discussion are taken from Bernard Schwartz, *The Unpublished Opinions of the Warren Court* (New York: Oxford University Press, 1985), 45-75.
24. This phrase was used by William O. Douglas in *Peters v. Hobby,* 349 U.S. 331, 350 (1955) (Douglas, J., concurring).
25. William O. Douglas, "Memorandum to the Conference," June 13, 1958, quoted in Schwartz, *Unpublished Opinions of the Warren Court,* 73.
26. See Edward H. Levi, *An Introduction to Legal Reasoning* (Chicago: University of Chicago Press, 1948).
27. *Chisholm v. Georgia,* 2 U.S. (2 Dall.) 16 (1793).
28. These include the Thirteenth, Fourteenth, and Fifteenth Amendments, which were directed at various slavery decisions, most notably *Dred Scott;* the Sixteenth, authorizing a federal income tax, and overruling *Pollock v. Farmers Loan & Trust Co.,* 157 U.S. 429 (1895); and the Twenty-sixth, guaranteeing eighteen-year-olds the right to vote in state elections, and overruling *Oregon v. Mitchell,* 400 U.S. 112 (1970).
29. 42 U.S.C., sections 701 *et seq.*
30. *General Electric Co. v. Gilbert,* 429 U.S. 125 (1978) held that pregnancy benefits were not covered by the sex discrimination provisions of the act. Congress responded by explicitly including these benefits.
31. U.S. Constitution, Article III, section 2.
32. Robert McCloskey, *The American Supreme Court* (Chicago: University of Chicago Press, 1960), 7.
33. *Ex parte McCardle,* 73 U.S. (6 Wall.) 318 (1868) and 74 U.S. (7 Wall.) 264 (1869).
34. Alexander Hamilton, "No. 78," in *The Federalist Papers,* 465.
35. Quoted in Murphy, *Elements of Judiciary Strategy,* 20.
36. See Alexander M. Bickel, *The Least Dangerous Branch: The Supreme Court at the Bar of Politics,* 2d ed. (New Haven: Yale University Press, 1986).
37. *Ex parte Milligan,* 71 U.S. (4 Wall.) 2 (1866).
38. Alexander Hamilton, "Federalist 70," in *The Federalist Papers* (New York: Mentor Books, 1961), 423-431.
39. James Madison, "Federalist 51," in *The Federalist Papers,* 320-325.
40. See Justice Robert H. Jackson's discussion of this point in *Youngstown Sheet and Tube Co. v. Sawyer,* 343 U.S. 579, 635-638 (1952).
41. *Immigration and Naturalization Service v. Chadha,* 462 U.S. 919 (1983).
42. *Morrison v. Olson,* 487 U.S. ___, 101 L. Ed. 2d. 569 (1988).
43. *United States v. Belmont,* 301 U.S. 324, 330-332 (1937).
44. *McCulloch v. Maryland,* 17 U.S. (4 Wheat.) 316 (1819). The Court ruled that Congress was empowered by the Constitution to incorporate a national bank. It held further that a state could not tax the bank.
45. *Korematsu v. United States,* 323 U.S. 214 (1944).
46. *New York Times Co. v. United States,* 403 U.S. 713 (1971).
47. *Home Building & Loan Assn. v. Blaisdell,* 290 U.S. 398, 425-426 (1934).
48. *Korematsu v. United States,* 245-246.
49. *United States v. Belmont,* 301 U.S. 324 (1937).
50. Walter F. Murphy, *Elements of Judicial Strategy* (Chicago: University of Chicago Press, 1964), 17.
51. *United States v. Midwest Oil Company,* 236 U.S. 459, 462-473 (1915).

52. Ibid., 236 U.S. at 474 and 274.
53. *United States v. Curtiss-Wright Export Corporation,* 299 U.S. 304 (1936).
54. Ibid., 315.
55. Much of Justice Sutherland's opinion for the Supreme Court talked about certain "inherent" powers of the national government and president in foreign affairs. The text of this discussion is very quotable and, in fact, is often quoted. Its actual value as precedent is limited, however. President Roosevelt's proclamation was based on powers delegated to him by Congress; it did not mention or depend on either inherent power or power delegated to the president by the Constitution.

    The reader should also note that the domestic-foreign distinction made by Sutherland became less significant as the courts soon adopted the practice of being tolerant of delegations of power in domestic affairs.
56. Alexander Hamilton, "Federalist 74," in *The Federalist Papers,* 447-449.
57. *Ex parte Garland,* 71 U.S. (4 Wall.) 333 (1867).
58. Ibid., 380.
59. *Kendall v. United States,* 37 U.S. (12 Pet.) 524 (1838).
60. *Reid v. Covert,* 354 U.S. 1 (1957).
61. See, for example, *Patti v. Schweiker,* 669 F.2d 582 (9th Cir. 1982).
62. *Morton v. Ruiz,* 415 U.S. 199 (1974).
63. *Myers v. United States,* 272 U.S. 52 (1926).
64. *Humphrey's Executor v. United States,* 295 U.S. 602 (1935).
65. *Goldwater v. Carter,* 444 U.S. 996 (1979).
66. Ibid., at 997-1002 (Powell, J., concurring).
67. Ibid., at 1002-1006 (Rehnquist, J., concurring). Chief Justice Warren Burger and Justices Potter Stewart and John Paul Stevens joined the Rehnquist statement.
68. *Hayburn's Case,* 2 U.S. (2 Dall.) 409 (1792). The refusals were in the form of letters to President Washington. These letters were appended to the decision in *Hayburn's Case* in a footnote inserted by the court reporter. The issue was not officially decided at that time since Congress repealed the legislation the justices found constitutionally offensive. Since that time, however, the views of these justices were made a part of constitutional doctrine. See *Muskrat v. United States,* 219 U.S. 346 (1911).
69. *United States v. Richardson,* 418 U.S. 166 (1974).
70. James Madison, *Federalist* No. 51 (1788), in *The Federalist Papers,* 322.
71. For general accounts of the conflict, see Charles Warren, *The Supreme Court in United States History,* vol. 1 (Boston: Little, Brown, 1826); Albert J. Beveridge, *The Life of John Marshall: Conflict and Construction, 1800-1815,* vol. 3 (Boston: Houghton Mifflin, 1919); and George L. Haskins and Herbert A. Johnson, *History of the Supreme Court of the United States: Foundations of Power: John Marshall, 1801-1815,* vol. 2 (New York: Macmillan, 1981).
72. *Stuart v. Laird,* 5 U.S. (1 Cranch) 298 (1803). (Marshall did not participate in the decision.)
73. *Marbury v. Madison,* 5 U.S. (1 Cranch) 137 (1803).
74. Raoul Berger, *Impeachment: The Constitutional Problems* (Cambridge: Harvard, 1971), 224-251.
75. Beveridge, *John Marshall,* vol. 3, 176-178; Haskins and Johnson, *History of the Supreme Court: John Marshall,* vol. 2, 231-232.
76. See, Haskins and Johnson, *History of the Supreme Court: John Marshall,* vol. 2, 244-245.
77. Beveridge, *Life of John Marshall,* vol. 3, 222.
78. Carl Swisher, *History of the Supreme Court of the United States: The Taney Period, 1836-1864* (New York: Macmillan, 1974), 841-876. This text will be used throughout this section for general historical description of events.
79. *Ex parte Merryman,* 17 Fed. Cas. 144 (C.C.D. Md. 1861).
80. See generally, Arthur M. Schlesinger, Jr., *The Coming of the New Deal* (Boston: Houghton Mifflin, 1959).
81. *Norman v. Baltimore and Ohio Railroad Co.,* 294 U.S. 240 (1935); *Perry v. United States,* 294 U.S. 330 (1935).
82. For accounts of this controversy, see Merlo J. Pusey, *Charles Evans Hughes,* vol. 2 (New York: Macmillan, 1951), 735-737; Arthur M. Schlesinger, Jr., *The Politics of Upheaval* (Boston: Houghton Mifflin, 1960), 255-260.
83. Invalidation of the Railroad Retirement Act is found in *Railroad Retirement Board v. Alton Railroad Co.,* 295 U.S. 495 (1935); and of the National Industrial Recovery Act, in *Schechter Poultry Corp. v. United States,* 295 U.S. 495 (1935).
84. *Humphrey's Executor v. United States,* 295 U.S. 602 (1935).
85. Harold L. Ickes, *The Secret Diaries of Harold L. Ickes: The First Thousand Days, 1933-1936* (New York: Simon and Schuster, 1953), 529-530.
86. *Guide to U.S. Elections* (Washington, D.C.: Congressional Quarterly Inc., 1975), 250-251, 289-290, 928.
87. Richard Hofstadter, *The Age of Reform* (New York: Vintage, 1955), 311.
88. *National Labor Relations Board v. Jones and Laughlin Steel Corp.,* 301 U.S. 1 (1937).
89. Compare, Merlo J. Pusey, *Charles Evans Hughes,* vol. 2 (New York: Macmillan, 1951), with Alpheus T. Mason, *The Supreme Court from Taft to Warren* (Baton Rouge: Louisiana State University, 1958).
90. *Brown v. Board of Education,* 347 U.S. 483 (1954).
91. On political and popular responses to *Brown* and its progeny during the 1950s, see Alexander M. Bickel, *The Least Dangerous Branch: The Supreme Court at the Bar of Politics,* 2d ed. (New Haven: Yale University Press, 1986).
92. *Aaron v. Cooper,* 243 F.2d. 361 (8th Cir. 1957) affirming 143 F.Supp. 855 (E.D. Ark.).
93. See generally, *Cooper v. Aaron,* 353 U.S. 1 (1957).
94. Alexander Hamilton, *Federalist* No. 78 (1788), in *The Federalist Papers,* 464-472.
95. *Public Papers of the Presidents of the United States: Dwight D. Eisenhower, 1954* (Washington, D.C.: U.S. Government Printing Office, 1960), 491.
96. *Public Papers of the Presidents of the United States: Dwight D. Eisenhower, 1957* (Washington, D.C.: U.S. Government Printing Office, 1958), 659.
97. *Public Papers of the Presidents: Eisenhower, 1957,* 546.
98. See his explanation of August 27, 1958, in *Public Papers of the Presidents of the United States: Dwight D. Eisenhower, 1958* (Washington, D.C.: U.S. Government Printing Office, 1959), 647-648.
99. The events summarized in this section are found in *Cooper v. Aaron,* 358 U.S. 1 (1958).
100. *Aaron v. Cooper,* 156 F.Supp. 220 (E.D. Ark 1957) *aff'd* 254 F.2d 797 (8th Cir.).
101. Presidential Proclamation 3204, September 23, 1957, *Federal Register,* vol. 22, no. 186, 7628 (September 25, 1957); and Executive Order 10730, September 24, 1957, *Federal Register,* vol. 22, no. 186, 7628 (September 25, 1957).
102. *Cooper v. Aaron,* 358 U.S. 1 (1958).
103. See, for example, Eisenhower's statement of August 27, 1958, *Public Papers of the Presidents: Eisenhower, 1958,* 647-648; and his letter of July 22, 1957, to Everett E. Hazlett, in *Ike's Letters to a Friend, 1941-1958,* ed. Robert Griffith (Lawrence: University of Kansas Press, 1984), 186-187. See generally, Emmet John Hughes, *The Ordeal of Power: A Political Memoir of the Eisenhower Years* (New York: Atheneum, 1963), 200-201, 241-245.
104. *Public Papers of the Presidents: Eisenhower, 1957,* 693.
105. See, for example, the criticism of Chief Justice Earl Warren, whom Eisenhower appointed to the Supreme Court and who presided over the Court during this period. Earl Warren, *The Memoirs of Earl Warren* (New York: Doubleday, 1977).
106. *Cherokee Nation v. Georgia,* 30 U.S. (5 Pet.) 178 (1831); *Worcester v. Georgia,* 31 U.S. (6 Pet.) 214 (1832).
107. U.S. Constitution, Article II, section 1.
108. U.S. Constitution, Article II, section 3.
109. William Howard Taft, *The Presidency* (New York: Scribner's, 1916), 63.
110. Alexander Hamilton, *Federalist* No. 78 (1788), in *The Feder-*

alist Papers, 465.
111. *Marbury v. Madison*, 5 U.S. (12 Pet.) 524, 613 (1838).
112. *Kendall v. United States*, 12 Pet. 524 (1838).
113. *Youngstown Sheet and Tube Co. v. Sawyer*, 343 U.S. 579 (1952).
114. *Ex parte Milligan*, 71 U.S. (4 Wall.) 2 (1866).
115. *United States v. Nixon*, 418 U.S. 683 (1974).
116. *United States v. Alessio*, 528 F.2d 1079 (9th Cir. 1976).
117. *Cunningham v. Neagle (In re Neagle)*, 135 U.S. 1, 69 (1890).
118. Ibid., 67.
119. *Fong Yue Ting v. United States*, 149 U.S. 698 (1893)
120. *Logan v. United States*, 144 U.S. 263 (1892).
121. *In re Debs*, 158 U.S. 564, 582 (1895).
122. *Stafford v. Wallace*, 258 U.S. 495 (1922).
123. *In re Debs*, 582.
124. U.S. Constitution, Article II, section 2.
125. See, for example, *Schick v. Reed*, 419 U.S. 256 (1974).
126. *Knote v. United States*, 95 U.S. 149, 153 (1877).
127. *Ex parte Garland*, 71 U.S. (4 Wall.) 333, 380 (1867).
128. *Murphy v. Ford*, 390 F.Supp. 1372 (W.D. Mich. 1975).
129. *Schick v. Reed*, 419 U.S. 256 (1974).
130. *Hoffa v. Saxbe*, 378 F.Supp. 1221 (D.D.C. 1974).
131. *Lupo v. Zerbst*, 92 F.2d 362 (5th Cir. 1937), *cert. denied* 303 U.S. 646 (1938).
132. "Amnesties" are simply pardons or reprieves granted to a defined class of people. See Justice Stephen Field's discussion of this issue in *Knote v. United States*, 152-153.
133. *United States v. Klein*, 80 U.S. (13 Wall.) 128 (1872).
134. *Ex parte Garland*, 333, 380. See also *United States v. Klein*, 128.
135. William Howard Taft, *Our Chief Magistrate and His Powers* (New York: Columbia University, 1916), 119-120.
136. U.S. Constitution, Article II, section 2.
137. *Ex parte Grossman*, 267, U.S. 87 (1925).
138. *Brown v. Walker*, 161 U.S. 591 (1896).
139. *United States v. Burr*, 25 F.Cas. 187, 192 (1807) (Marshall, C. J., sitting as trial judge). Quoted with approval in *United States v. Nixon*, 708 and 785.
140. James Madison, *Federalist* No. 51 (1788), in *The Federalist Papers*, 465-466.
141. U.S. Constitution, Article I, section 6.
142. *Nixon v. Fitzgerald*, 457 U.S. 731, 748-758 (1982).
143. *Harlow v. Fitzgerald*, 457 U.S. 800 (1982).
144. Harlow and Butterfield cited *Gravel v. United States*, 408 U.S. 606 (1972), which held that aides to members of Congress do enjoy derivative immunity.
145. *Harlow v. Fitzgerald*, 813.
146. Ibid., 818.
147. *Butz v. Economou*, 483 U.S. 478 (1978); *Mitchell v. Forsyth*, 472 U.S. 511 (1985).
148. *Briscoe v. La Hue*, 460 U.S. 325 (1983).
149. *Bivens v. Six Unknown Agents*, 403 U.S. 388 (1971).
150. *United States v. Nixon*, 711-712.
151. Ibid., 712-713.
152. Ibid., 714-715.
153. *Nixon v. Administrator of General Services*, 433 U.S. 425 (1977).
154. See *United States v. Midwest Oil Co.*, 236 U.S. 459 (1915).
155. Jefferson later released the funds after studying competing gunboat designs. Louis Fisher, *Presidential Spending Power* (Princeton, N.J.: Princeton University Press, 1975).
156. *Kendall v. United States*, 37 U.S. (12 Pet.) 524 (1838).
157. See, for example, *Train v. New York*, 420 U.S. 35 (1975).
158. *United States v. Germaine*, 99 U.S. 508, 509 (1879).
159. Ibid., 508
160. *Buckley v. Valeo*, 424 U.S. 1 (1976).
161. *Ex parte Siebold*, 100 U.S. 371 (1879).
162. *Buckley v. Valeo*. See also *Springer v. Philippine Islands*, 277 U.S. 198 (1928), where the Supreme Court held unconstitutional an attempt by the Philippine legislature to make certain executive appointments. The Philippine Islands were under the administration of the United States at the time.
163. *United States v. Smith*, 286 U.S. 6 (1932).
164. *Shoemaker v. United States*, 147 U.S. 283 (1893).
165. *Williams v. Phillips*, 360 F.Supp. 1363 (D.D.C. 1973).
166. *Mimmack v. United States*, 97 U.S. 426 (1878).
167. *Morrison v. Olson*, 487 U.S. ____, 101 L.Ed. 2d. 569 (1988).
168. *Myers v. United States*, 272 U.S. 52 (1926).
169. This is perhaps an understatement. Trade regulation was to become a fundamental part of Roosevelt's New Deal. Humphrey's views on trade regulation were public: he considered such practices "socialistic." During Humphrey's tenure at the FTC, the commission emphasized self-regulation by business instead of direct government regulation. Arthur M. Schlesinger, Jr., *The Crisis of the Old Order: 1919-1933* (Boston: Houghton Mifflin, 1957), 64-65.
170. *Humphrey's Executor v. United States*, 295 U.S. 602 (1935).
171. *Wiener v. United States*, 357 U.S. 349 (1958). The facts of *Wiener* are discussed on pages 1163, 1180-1181 of this volume.
172. John Marshall, Speech to the U.S. House of Representatives, 6th Congress, March 7, 1800, *Annals of the Congress of the United States* (Washington, D.C.: Gales and Seaton, 1851), 613. John Marshall became chief justice of the United States in 1801 and served in that capacity until 1835.
173. *United States v. Curtiss-Wright Export Corporation*, 299 U.S. 304 (1936).
174. Ibid., 319-320.
175. Ibid., 320. Judicial deference toward the president as chief diplomat has been discussed in a number of judicial opinions. Some of the most influential are: *Baker v. Carr*, 369 U.S. 186 (1962); *Chicago and Southern Air Lines, Inc. v. Waterman Steamship Corp.*, 333 U.S. 103 (1948); and *Oetjen v. Central Leather Co.*, 246 U.S. 297 (1918).
176. See generally the discussion of this issue in Louis Henkin, *Foreign Affairs and the Constitution* (Mineola, N.Y.: Foundation Press, 1972), 19-28.
177. *Baker v. Carr.* Brennan was speaking specifically of duration of war. This statement, however, may be applied consistently to his view of judicial review of foreign policy making, as that view was expressed in the same opinion.
178. Ibid., 211-212.
179. Ibid. See also *Guaranty Trust Co. v. United States*, 304 U.S. 126 (1938).
180. *United States v. Pink*, 315 U.S. 203, 229-230 (1942).
181. *Geofroy v. Riggs*, 133 U.S. 258, 267 (1890).
182. *Valentine v. United States, ex rel Neidecker*, 299 U.S. 5 (1936).
183. *Geofroy v. Riggs*, 266-267.
184. *Reid v. Covert*, 354 U.S. 1 (1957).
185. *United States v. Curtiss-Wright Export Corp.*
186. *Fourteen Diamond Rings v. United States*, 183 U.S. 176 (1901).
187. *Whitney v. Robertson*, 124 U.S. 190, 194 (1888).
188. *The Chinese Exclusion Case*, 130 U.S. 581, 600 (1889).
189. *United States v. Belmont*, 310 U.S. 324, 330 (1937).
190. These decisions are found respectively in *Wilson v. Girard*, 354 U.S. 524 (1957) and *Chicago & S. Air Lines v. Waterman S.S. Corp.*, 333 U.S. 103 (1948).
191. *United States v. Belmont*; *United States v. Pink;* and *Dames & Moore v. Regan*, 453 U.S. 654 (1982) ("Iranian Assets Case").
192. *United States v. Guy W. Capps, Inc.*, 204 F.2d 655 (4th Cir. 1954) *aff'd on other grounds* 348 U.S. 296 (1955).
193. *Cook v. United States*, 288 U.S. 102 (1933).
194. U.S. Constitution, Article I, section 9.
195. *Techt v. Hughes*, 229 N.Y. 222, 128 N.E. 185 (1920).
196. *Goldwater v. Carter*, 444 U.S. 996 (1979).
197. These rulings were respectively made in *Martin v. Hunter's Lessee*, 14 U.S. (1 Wheat.) 304 (1816); *Asakura v. Seattle*, 265 U.S. 332 (1924); and *Missouri v. Holland*, 252 U.S. 416 (1920).
198. *Missouri v. Holland*, 432.
199. *United States v. Belmont.*
200. Jonathan Ellliot, *Debates on the Adoption of the Federal Constitution*, vol. 5 (Philadelphia: Lippincott, 1866), 212.

201. *United States v. Belmont,* 331-332.
202. *United States v. Pink,* 233-234. Douglas, it should be noted, went on to cite with approval and quote a portion of Sutherland's opinion in *Belmont.*
203. *Japan Line, Ltd. v. County of Los Angeles,* 441 U.S. 434 (1979).
204. *McCulloch v. Maryland,* 17 U.S. (4 Wheat.) 316 (1819).
205. *Panhandle Oil Co. v. Mississippi,* 297 U.S. 218 (1928).
206. U.S. Constitution, Article I, sections 8 and 10, and Article II, section 2.
207. *Japan Line, Ltd. v. County of Los Angeles.*
208. *Zschernig v. Miller,* 389 U.S. 429 (1968).
209. See, for example, *Plessy v. Ferguson,* 163 U.S. 537 (1896); and *Chinese Exclusion Case,* 130 U.S. 581 (1888).
210. See, for example, *Shelley v. Kraemer,* 334 U.S. 1 (1948); and *Sweatt v. Painter,* 339 U.S. 629 (1850).
211. *Brown v. Board of Education,* 347 U.S. 483 (1954).
212. Charles Evans Hughes, *The Supreme Court of the United States: Its Foundations, Methods and Achievements* (New York: Columbia University Press, 1928).
213. *Home Building and Loan Assn. v. Blaisdell,* 290 U.S. 398, 426 (1934).
214. *Hirabayashi v. United States,* 320 U.S. 81, 93 (1943). Quoted in Charles Evans Hughes, "War Powers under the Constitution," *American Bar Association Rep.,* vol. 42, 232, 238.
215. See *Blaisdell,* 425-426.
216. *The Prize Cases,* 67 U.S. (2 Black) 635 (1863).
217. *Durand v. Hollins,* Fed. Cases 4186 (C.C. N.Y. 1860).
218. See, for example, *Mora v. McNamara,* 389 U.S. 934 (1967); and *DaCosta v. Laird,* 405 U.S. 979 (1972).
219. *Massachusetts v. Laird,* 451 F.2d 26 (1st Cir. 1971).
220. *Fleming v. Page,* 50 U.S. (9 How.) 603 (1850).
221. *Santiago v. Nogueras,* 214 U.S. 260 (1909).
222. *Neely v. Henkel,* 180 U.S. 109 (1901).
223. *Fleming v. Page.*
224. *Ludeck v. Watkins,* 335 U.S. 160 (1948).
225. 29 U.S.C., sections 141-197.
226. *Youngstown Sheet and Tube Co. v. Sawyer,* 343 U.S. 579 (1952) ("*Steel Seizure Case*").
227. Ibid., 588.
228. *United States v. Russell,* U.S. (13 Wall.) 623 (1871).
229. *Brooks-Scanlon Corp. v. United States,* 265 U.S. 106 (1924).
230. *Woods v. Cloyd W. Miller Co.,* 333 U.S. 138 (1948).
231. Ibid.
232. *Hamilton v. Kentucky Distillers Co.,* 251 U.S. 146 (1919).
233. Abraham Lincoln, letter to Albert G. Hodge, April 4, 1864, *Collected Works,* vol. 7 (Basler, ed. 1953-1955), 281-282. Quoted in Christopher H. Pyle and Richard M. Pious, *The President, Congress, and the Constitution* (New York: Free Press, 1984), 65.
234. *Ex parte Milligan,* 71 U.S. (4 Wall.) 2 (1866).
235. Ibid.
236. *Duncan V. Kahanamoku,* 327 U.S. 304 (1946).
237. *Ex parte Merryman,* F. Cases 9487 (C.C. Md. 1861).
238. *Santiago v. Nogueras,* 214 U.S. 260 (1909); and *Madsen v. Kinsella,* 343 U.S. 341 (1952).
239. *In re Yamashita,* 327 U.S. 1 (1946); and *Johnson v. Eisentrager,* 339 U.S. 763 (1950).
240. *Ex parte Quirin,* 317 U.S. 1 (1942).
241. *Ludecke v. Watkins,* 335 U.S. 160 (1948).
242. *Silesian American Corp. v. Clark,* 332 U.S. 469 (1947).
243. *Hirabayashi v. United States,* 320 U.S. 81 (1943).
244. Ibid., 94.
245. *Korematsu v. United States,* 323 U.S. 214, 216 (1944).
246. Ibid., 225-233.
247. Ibid., 236-237.
248. Ibid., 233.
249. Ibid., 245.
250. Ibid., 245-246.
251. *Ex parte Endo,* 323 U.S. 283 (1944).
252. U.S. Constitution, Article I, section 1.
253. U.S. Constitution, Article II, section 2.
254. The president may recommend legislation to Congress. Specific pieces of legislation, however, must be introduced by a member of Congress, either a representative or a senator. Presidents usually overcome this requirement by having a member of their own party introduce legislation in each house.
255. On the evolution of the legislative role of the president, see Edward S. Corwin, *The President: Office and Powers, 1787-1984,* 5th rev. ed. by Randall W. Bland, Theodore T. Hindson, and Jack W. Peltason (New York: New York University Press, 1984). For an account of Franklin D. Roosevelt's relations with Congress during the early years of his administration, see Arthur M. Schlesinger, Jr., *The Coming of the New Deal* (Boston: Houghton Mifflin, 1959).
256. *Railroad Retirement Board v. Alton,* 295 U.S. 330 (1935).
257. *Schechter Poultry Corp. v. United States,* 295 U.S. 495 (1936).
258. *United States v. Butler,* 297 U.S. 1 (1936).
259. *Carter v. Carter Coal Co.,* 298 U.S. 238 (1936).
260. *National Labor Relations Board v. Jones & Laughlin Steel Corp.,* 301 U.S. 1 (1937).
261. See, for example, *Heart of Atlanta Motel v. United States,* 379 U.S. 241 (1964).
262. See, for example, *Katzenbach v. McClung,* 379 U.S. 294 (1964); and *Daniel v. Paul,* 295 U.S. 298 (1969).
263. *South Carolina v. Katzenbach,* 383 U.S. 301 (1966); and *Katzenbach v. Morgan,* 383 U.S. 641 (1966).
264. See, for example, *Allen v. State Board of Elections,* 393 U.S. 544 (1969).
265. *Hollingsworth v. Virginia,* 3 Dall. 378 (1798). See also *Rhode Island v. Palmer,* 253 U.S. 350 (1920), reaffirming *Hollingsworth,* and *Immigration and Naturalization Service v. Chadha,* 462 U.S. 919, 955 (1983), n. 21, where Chief Justice Warren E. Burger cited *Hollingsworth* in his majority opinion as authority for the proposition that only constitutional amendments are exempt from the requirements of the presentment clause.
266. *Immigration and Naturalization Service v. Chadha*
267. *Eber Brothers Wine and Liquor Corp. v. United States,* 337 F. 2d 624 (Ct. Cl. 1964), *cert. denied,* 380 U.S. 950 (1965).
268. *Pocket Veto Case,* 279 U.S. 655 (1929). Adjournment, however, does not prevent the president from signing the bill, thus allowing it to become law. *La Abra Silver Mining Co. v. United States,* 175 U.S. 473 (1899).
269. *Pocket Veto Case,* 468.
270. *Wright v. United States,* 302 U.S. 583 (1938).
271. *Kennedy v. Sampson,* 511 F. 2d 430 (D.C. Cir. 1974).
272. *Barnes v. Kline,* 759 F. 2d 21 (D.D. Cir. 1985), vacated as moot, 475 U.S. 1044 (1987).
273. U.S. Constitution, Article I, section 1.
274. *United States v. Shreveport Grain & Elevator Co.,* 287 U.S. 77, 85 (1932).
275. The two exceptions are *Panama Refining Co. v. Ryan,* 293 U.S. 388 (1935) and *Schechter Poultry Corp. v. United States.* See generally Kenneth Culp Davis, *Administrative Law Text,* 3d. ed. (St. Paul, Minn.: West, 1972).
276. Davis, *Administrative Law Text,* 26-36.
277. *Panama Refining Co. v. Ryan* and *Schechter Poultry Corp. v. United States.*
278. *Lichter v. United States,* 334 U.S. 742 (1948).
279. PL 91-379, 84 Stat. 799
280. *Amalgamated Meat Cutters v. Connally,* 337 F.Supp. 737 (D.D.C. 1971).
281. The decision upholding the standard of "just and reasonable" is *Tagg Brothers & Moorhead v. United States,* 280 U.S. 420 (1920); of "unfair methods of competition," *Federal Trade Commission v. Gratz,* 253 U.S. 421 (1920).
282. PL 88-408 (1964).
283. PL 88-408 (1964).
284. See Justice Byron White's dissenting opinion for a list of some of the delegations containing legislative vetoes.
285. Louis Fisher, *The President and Congress: Power and Policy* (New York: Free Press, 1972), 82.
286. *Immigration and Naturalization Service v. Chadha.*

287. Ibid., 951.
288. Ibid., 967.
289. Ibid., 1002.
290. Richard J. Pierce, Jr., Sidney A. Shapiro, and Paul R. Verkuil, *Administrative Law and Process* (Mineola, N.Y.: Foundation Press, 1985), 91-93.

Selected Bibliography

Bessette, Joseph M., and Jeffrey Tulis, eds. *The Presidency in the Constitutional Order*. Baton Rouge: Louisiana University Press, 1981.

Corwin, Edward S. *The President: Office and Powers, 1787-1984*. 5th rev. ed. Ed. Randall W. Bland, Theodore T. Hindson, and Jack W. Peltason. New York: New York University Press, 1984.

Cox, Archibald. *The Role of the Supreme Court in American Government*. New York: Oxford University Press, 1976.

Fisher, Louis. *Presidential Spending Power*. Princeton, N.J.: Princeton University Press, 1975.

Henkin, Louis. *Foreign Affairs and the Constitution*. Mineola, N.Y.: Foundation Press, 1972.

Jackson, Robert H. *The Supreme Court in the American System of Government*. New York: Harper and Row, 1955.

McCloskey, Robert G. *The American Supreme Court*. Chicago: University of Chicago Press, 1960.

Murphy, Walter F., and C. Herma Pritchett, eds. *Courts, Judges, and Politics: An Introduction to the Judicial Process*. 4th ed. New York: Random House, 1986.

Pyle, Christopher H., and Richard M. Pious. *The President, Congress, and the Constitution: Power and Legitimacy in American Politics*. New York: Free Press, 1984.

Rossiter, Clinton. *The Supreme Court and the Commander in Chief*. Ithaca, N.Y.: Cornell University Press, 1951.

Schlesinger, Arthur M., Jr. *The Imperial Presidency*. Boston: Houghton Mifflin, 1973.

Schubert, Glendon M. *The Presidency in the Courts*. Minneapolis: University of Minnesota Press, 1957.

Scigliano, Robert. *The Supreme Court and the Presidency*. New York: Free Press, 1971.

Warren, Charles. *The Supreme Court in United States History*. 2 vols. Boston: Little, Brown, 1926.

The President and the Bureaucracy

The Treasury is so large and far-flung and ingrained in its practices that I find it almost impossible to get the action and results I want. . . . But the Treasury is not to be compared with the State Department. You should go through the experience of trying to get any changes in the thinking, policy, and action of the career diplomats. . . . But the Treasury and the State Department put together are nothing compared with the Na-a-vy. . . . To change anything in the Na-a-vy is like punching a feather bed. You punch it with your right and you punch it with your left until you are finally exhausted, and then you find the damn bed just as it was before you started punching.

—Franklin D. Roosevelt

He'll sit here and he'll say, "Do this! Do that!" And nothing will happen. Poor Ike—it won't be a bit like the Army. He'll find it very frustrating.

—Harry S Truman

Before I became president, I realized and was warned that dealing with the federal bureaucracy would be one of the worst problems I would have to face. It has been worse than I had anticipated.

—Jimmy Carter

The term "bureaucracy" does not appear in the U.S. Constitution, yet the bureaucracy is one of the most powerful elements of modern American government. In fact, it is often called the "fourth branch" of government because of its prominence in contemporary politics. Presidents quickly discover that they can accomplish little without help from the bureaucracy; thus, their relationship with it is one of the most important aspects of any administration.

In the minds of many people the term "bureaucracy" conjures up images of red tape, impersonality, and rigidity, and it applies wherever those images are found—from government to universities to large corporations. In this chapter the term is used without any negative connotation; "bureaucracy" simply refers to U.S. government organizations, staffed by unelected public officials, that carry out public policy. Except where noted, the term does not encompass the military.

By Mark E. Byrnes

The bureaucracy is composed of numerous agencies. In this chapter "agency" may refer to one of the cabinet departments, a part of a department, or an entity independent of the departments. "Bureau" is used interchangeably with agency. "Department" refers solely to one of the fourteen cabinet departments. Finally, although it is often intended as a slur, the label "bureaucrat" simply applies here to someone who works in the bureaucracy.

Evolution of the Federal Bureaucracy

The Founders probably would be quite startled by today's federal bureaucracy. Of course, it did not take its present shape suddenly; the bureaucracy has been evolving for well over two hundred years.

Constitutional Foundations

Although the Constitution barely mentions the executive branch and says nothing at all about a bureaucracy, that document is nevertheless crucial to the bureaucracy. The evolution of the bureaucracy has been shaped by what the Founders thought about the executive branch and by what the Constitution says—and does not say—about it. Subsequent constitutional interpretations have played a role as well.

The Founders issued relatively explicit guidelines for the presidency, the Congress, and, to a lesser extent, the judicial system, but they made few references to how the government's decisions were to be executed and thus to the organization and functions of the executive branch. Suggestions made by some delegates to the Constitutional Convention that the details of the executive branch be fleshed out went unheeded. The clauses that eventually were inserted into the Constitution, although brief, at least set the boundaries for the development of the modern bureaucracy.

The position of the executive branch in the Constitution's overall scheme of government is ambiguous. Article II, section 1, states that "the executive Power shall be vested in a President of the United States of America," but it does not spell out exactly what that power includes. The next section provides only some help by specifying two powers. First, the president "may require the Opinion, in writing, of the principal Officer in each of the executive Departments, upon any Subject relating to Duties of their respective Offices." And second, the president "shall nominate, and by and with the Advice and Consent of the Senate, shall appoint Ambassadors, other public Ministers and Consuls, Judges of the Supreme Court, and all other Officers of the United States, whose Appointments are not herein otherwise provided for, and which shall be established by Law." The second power comes with a condition, however: "The Congress may by Law vest the Appointment of such inferior Officers, as they think proper, in the President alone, in the Courts of Law, or in the Heads of Departments." These few provisions are all that the Constitution says specifically about the executive branch.

Organization of Executive Power

The Founders' relative lack of attention to executive power does not mean that they thought it was unimportant. To the contrary, the short yet turbulent history of the American colonies clearly indicated the critical role of administration. The colonists suffered "a long train of abuses" at the hands of British administrators and thus developed an intense distrust of, as well as a healthy respect for, strong executive power.

America's own attempts at administration also taught some lessons. The Continental Congress, intent on avoiding the dangers of executive power, tackled the immense executive task of running the Revolutionary War without outside administrative help. Instead, committees composed of members of Congress were formed to decide even the most minor executive issues. Congress quickly discovered that this system was unwieldy and ineffective, but administration by committees of amateurs serving part time continued throughout the war and under the government established by the Articles of Confederation.

When they met to construct a new form of government, the Founders were determined to correct the executive situation. Aware of the problems created by administrative committees, they agreed that executive functions should be grouped in a limited number of executive departments, each with a single head. While the Constitution does not mandate this specific structure, references to "the principal Officer in each of the executive Departments" and "Heads of Departments" support this interpretation. The major disagreement at the Constitutional Convention concerned how heads of departments would be selected and to whom they would be responsible. The delegates decided that the president, with the advice and consent of the Senate, would choose department heads, but they left the question of responsibility unanswered.

The Constitution gives Congress considerable freedom in deciding how to structure the executive branch. One of the most vital questions facing the First Congress (1789-1791) was removal of officials appointed by the president with Senate approval: Did the president alone have the power to dismiss such officials? Congress debated this issue at length before narrowly deciding that presidents can remove appointees from office on their own authority. That decision made the executive branch technically subordinate to the president, but Congress still holds tremendous influence.

In addition to its power to reject presidential nominations, Congress controls the organization of the executive branch. Congress has the right to establish departments and agencies, to arrange them as it sees fit, and to decide how many employees they have and how those employees are selected. Other congressional powers such as appropriating money and conducting investigations are means of indirect control.

The Constitution grants the president "executive power" to "take Care that the Laws be faithfully executed," but it is ambiguous as to what that power and responsibility entail. Congress settled one issue by its decision that the president has the authority to remove appointed officials from office, but much of the relationship between the president and the executive branch hinges on the attitudes and strategies of individual presidents. In this context the words "executive power," applied to the president by Article II, have been called a "term of uncertain content," the meaning of which can be supplied only by the particular president.[1]

Results of the Constitutional Framework

The Founders' handling of the executive branch demonstrates their fear of centralized government power and their use of checks and balances to ensure that no one part of the U.S. government can subjugate the other parts or the public. Neither the president nor Congress can dominate the executive branch; each checks the other. The president is granted executive power and the right to appoint officials, but that presidential power is countered by the requirement for Senate approval of appointees and by congressional control of the organization of the executive branch. This arrangement vividly illustrates the separation of powers doctrine inherent to the U.S. Constitution.

The constitutional foundations of the executive branch have had some significant ramifications for the development of the bureaucracy and the U.S. government in general. While these foundations have helped prevent excessive concentrations of power, they also have increased the fragmentation of government, making the formulation of coherent public policy difficult. The Constitution's ambiguity and lack of restrictions on the executive branch have allowed the federal bureaucracy to grow to proportions unimagined by the Founders. Finally, the system of dual control of the executive branch by the president and Congress has resulted in a system of limited control.[2] Executive departments and agencies quickly learned to play one branch against the other and to develop an independent power base, thus setting the stage for the historical process that has made the federal bureaucracy one of the most powerful forces in American society.

Growth of the Bureaucracy

The process has been going on for many years, but the growth of the U.S. bureaucracy is still impressive. Although various people and events throughout American history have fueled bureaucratic growth, some periods are particularly noteworthy, including the early period, the Jacksonian era, the Civil War and its aftermath, the Progressive era, and the Roosevelt administration and beyond.

Historical Development

The modern federal bureaucracy has humble beginnings. George Washington's administration began with only three executive departments—State, Treasury, and War—and very few federal workers. The first State Department, for example, had only nine employees.[3] Creation of the U.S. Post Office in 1792 caused a small surge in federal employment, but the entire government work force still numbered only about three thousand in 1801.[4] Although the early bureaucracy was small and informal, competition for jobs was intense. Washington looked for "men of character," whom he knew personally if possible, and could trust to exercise good judgment and to perform competently.

This personalized system of recruitment continued largely unaltered until the presidency of Andrew Jackson (1829-1837), when some important changes took place, as the country was quickly outgrowing its highly informal system of administration. Jackson appointed his friend Amos Kendall to head the Post Office, where lack of structure and established procedures were especially harmful. Kendall made changes—such as setting up clear lines of authority, specifying job descriptions, and establishing strict accounting practices—that replaced informality with routinization. Thus, the bureaucracy began to take on the more formal character that it has today.

Jackson also instituted the "spoils system," in which election winners reward their supporters with federal government jobs. Although Jackson was not the first president to give public jobs to friends and allies, his openness and unapologetic attitude were new. His behavior was not entirely cynical, however, because he based this practice on his support of the idea of "rotation in office."[5] Jackson believed that a regular change of public officials made the government more democratic by giving more people the chance to participate and thereby preventing the rise of a bureaucratic elite unrepresentative of the general public. Jackson was convinced that any reasonably intelligent person could perform the duties of public office.

In the 1860s the Civil War sparked tremendous growth in the size of the bureaucracy but also revealed some of the system's weaknesses. While some corruption and inefficiency undoubtedly afflicted the bureaucracy prior to the war, those problems were highlighted by wartime pressures. Proposals for reform of the bureaucracy soon surfaced and then intensified as scandals over government employment practices appeared in the postwar period. Rapid industrial growth and expansion of government activities placed additional strains on the bureaucracy. Thus, new executive agencies and departments, such as the Departments of Agriculture and Labor, were formed to help meet the increasing demands for government service.

The reform movement got its biggest push in a roundabout and tragic way. Soon after becoming president in 1881 James A. Garfield expressed his displeasure at the spoils system, which forced him to spend a great deal of time selecting appointees to government jobs. One man who failed to get such a job, Charles J. Guiteau, vented his frustration by assassinating Garfield just a few months after Garfield's inauguration. *(See Removal chapter in Part II.)* Public outrage at the killing focused attention on the problems of the spoils system and spurred Congress into action. The Pendleton Act, passed in 1883, reformed the civil service by mandating that federal jobs be granted to the most qualified applicants, rather than those with the best political connections. It also provided those employees with job security, thus ending the mass rotation in office that had occurred with every new president.

The first few decades of the twentieth century also brought sizable increases in the bureaucracy. The Progressive era resulted in the creation of many new agencies, including the Forest Service and the Food and Drug Administration, to fulfill the new tasks assigned to government during the Progressive movement. Similarly, America's entry into World War I resulted in more government activity and therefore more bureaucracy. The greatest influence on the size and role of American bureaucracy, however, was yet to come.

Franklin D. Roosevelt won election to the White House in 1932 on a platform that promised vigorous government action—a "New Deal"—to combat the depression that had plagued the country for three years. Roosevelt kept his promise by persuading Congress to enact a variety of programs. During his first term (1933-1937) Congress passed laws designed by Roosevelt to provide relief to those hardest hit by the depression, to help the wounded economy recover, and to reform the economy to prevent future depressions. These laws not only established more than sixty new bureaucratic agencies, but they also signified a fundamental shift in the role of government in American society.[6] The federal government was now expected to take an active role in fighting the nation's problems, which would require adding to the bureaucracy.

America's tremendous commitment to World War II also led to a burgeoning bureaucracy, most noticeably in the military but also domestically. Another important consequence of the war was the dramatic increase in the amount of money raised and spent by the federal government. From 1940 to 1945 total federal tax collections skyrocketed from approximately $5 billion to almost $44 billion, again enlarging the influence of bureaucracy.[7] Even after Germany and Japan fell, U.S. taxes did not; resources were directed to continued military readiness and domestic social programs. By the early 1950s the number of federal civilian employees had leveled off at about 2.6 million, and that figure has not changed much since then.[8] The importance of bureaucracy has continued to grow, however.

Evansville Courier; Franklin D. Roosevelt Library

Explaining Bureaucratic Growth

What has caused this remarkable growth in the size and scope of the federal bureaucracy? The most obvious answer is that a larger bureaucracy is needed to carry out the new demands placed on government, but more specific reasons can be given.

Scholars often cite four explanations for bureaucratic growth.[9] One explanation maintains that government must have more employees with specialized knowledge to keep up with rapid technological changes taking place throughout society. According to the second explanation, increasing government regulation of the economy and the attendant need for more federal agencies are the primary forces behind expansion of the bureaucracy. The third explanation concerns how the government responds to crises. When a crisis such as a war, an economic depression, or a natural disaster occurs—frequently requiring additional employees and government agencies—the federal government usually takes new measures to end the crisis or limit its effects. Once the crisis has passed, however, the additional bureaucracy is rarely dismantled entirely. The fourth explanation for bureaucratic growth is the political pressure exerted by various segments of society, who demand services from the government and then support the agencies established to fulfill their demands.

Bureaucratic Policy Making

For many years the study of public administration in America was dominated by the notion, espoused by Woodrow Wilson and other political scientists, that politics—the process of deciding what public policy should be—and administration—the process of carrying out those policy decisions—were clearly separable. Within this scenario, the bureaucracy existed solely to implement the policies made by elected officials. While such a description may have been fairly accurate a hundred years ago, the modern American bureaucracy definitely helps form public policy as well as execute it. One reason for this change is the large role played by the federal government in contemporary American life and the tremendous government workload this role generates. The president and Congress cannot possibly make all policy decisions alone.

The organization of the federal government promotes bureaucratic policy making as well. Because of their profound fears of concentrated power the Framers of the U.S. Constitution deliberately created a highly fragmented system of government. Not only do the three branches of the federal government check each other, but the state governments also check the federal government. The political party system that has developed in the United States does little to counter this constitutionally induced fragmentation. U.S. political parties—loose coalitions unable to impose much discipline on their members—generally are more concerned with winning elections than with generating specific policy proposals. The fragmentation of the American political system thus means that there is no centralized control of public policy and that numerous political players—including the federal bureaucracy—can shape the making of policy.[10]

Bureaucratic Tasks

The kinds of tasks assigned to the federal bureaucracy also strengthen its influence on policy making. Most government programs tackle extremely complex problems, and large organizations are needed to run them. For example, preservation of the environment entails handling many complicated problems, so the Environmental Protection Agency must be large enough to do so. Moreover, program size alone can present formidable challenges, as it does to the Social Security Administration, which in fiscal year 1984 issued 35 million checks each month.[11] Public programs also demand expert knowledge, and the federal bureaucracy employs a wide array of specialists to supply this knowledge.

Despite the popular belief that the bureaucracy moves at a snail's pace, it can respond quickly when the need for a new policy arises. For example, in 1982 after the rash of Tylenol™ poisonings, the Food and Drug Administration rapidly established rules requiring tamper-proof medication containers.[12] The bureaucracy is designed to meet such requirements of public policy making and can exert great influence in doing so.

The federal bureaucracy may participate in all stages of setting and implementing public policy, but its main job continues to be implementing policy. The bureaucracy is able to exercise considerable discretion over the implementation of most policies because the laws passed by Congress are usually quite vague. In general, such laws express the goals of Congress and leave it up to the bureaucracy to find the best means of achieving them. The less specific the law, the greater is the bureaucratic influence on the policy.

Lack of time is the major reason that most of the laws passed by Congress are vague. Congress considers hundreds of bills each year and simply does not have time, even with the help of staff, to write laws specific enough to fit every potential situation. Congress also lacks the expert knowledge required to construct highly technical programs. Even if Congress could produce more specific enactments, the bureaucratic discretion accompanying vague legislation probably leads to better policy. The bureaucracy can respond to societal changes affecting policy, and make the appropriate programmatic alterations, more quickly and more easily than Congress.

Self-Interest at Work

According to political scientist Morris P. Fiorina, the growth of bureaucratic policy-making power is based on self-interest. He has contended that the present system is the result of members of Congress, bureaucrats, and voters all pursuing their own self-interests. Because reelection is the foremost goal of members of Congress, their behavior is geared toward achieving that aim. Typical bureaucrats want to see the size and power of their agency increase, which in turn enhances their own status and power. Finally, voters want to get as many benefits as possible from government for the least possible cost.[13]

Congress is engaged in three basic kinds of activities: (1) developing and considering legislation and law making; (2) securing government benefits for members' home districts (so-called "pork barrel" projects); and (3) helping constituents who have problems with the federal government or who request some other kind of assistance (casework). Fiorina has argued that because so many members of Congress are interested primarily in getting reelected, they tend to devote more time and energy to pork barrel and casework activities (from which they reap greater political benefits) at the expense of law making.

Law making is relatively less appealing to the reelection-minded member for two reasons. First, legislation is often controversial, and any stand on divisive issues can upset voters and thus cost the member support in the election. Second, even if the legislation is popular, it is hard to take personal credit for it when hundreds of other people also were involved in its passage.

In contrast, pork barrel and casework efforts present neither difficulty. These tasks are rarely controversial, and the people who benefit not only know who provided the help, but they also usually express their gratitude at the polls. Such gratitude may even withstand a severe political crisis. For example, Democratic representative Gerry E. Studds of Massachusetts was reelected in 1984 despite his highly publicized sexual misconduct the year before. And Democrats Bill Boner and Harold E. Ford of Tennessee were overwhelmingly returned to the House in 1986 in the face of widespread and persistent questioning of their personal incomes.

The ambiguity characteristic of laws passed by Congress serves the interests of individual members of Congress as well. Lawmakers can claim credit for having passed a law to solve a problem, but they also can blame the bureaucracy if constituents are unhappy with the way the law is executed. Ironically, such an arrangement gives legislators more opportunities to do casework for constituents as complaints arise about the law's implementation.

The bureaucracy is a willing partner in this arrangement because it satisfies bureaucrats' drive for more power. Vague laws enable the bureaucracy to decide the specifics of the programs and therefore to exercise tremendous power over policy making. Moreover, the bureaucracy expands as Congress, in its zeal to build political credit, continues to enact imprecise laws that must be carried out by bureaucracy. The outcome, observed Fiorina, is that "more and more bureaucrats promulgate more and more regulations and dispense more and more money." [14]

Most voters are pleased with the system because they benefit from it, and even those concerned about government spending seldom hold individual members of Congress responsible for the overall pattern of federal government expenditures. In general, wrote Fiorina, the system may serve the immediate self-interests of legislators, bureaucrats, and voters, but "the long-term welfare of the United States is no more than an incidental by-product." [15]

Not all scholars have subscribed to Fiorina's view, however. Political scientist Arthur Maass, for example, has asserted that Congress is a responsible and responsive political institution, which overall works for the common good of the American people. Moreover, he has argued that Congress provides a valuable forum for the discussion of different points of view, including those of interest groups, and the generation of new political proposals.[16]

The Modern Federal Bureaucracy

The federal bureaucracy's growth and its policy-making functions have made it one of the most important political forces in this country. Yet it is also one of the least understood political institutions.

Dimensions of the Federal Bureaucracy

Many Americans believe that the federal bureaucracy is growing at an alarming, almost uncontrollable, rate. Part of this perception is based on the pervasive influence of the bureaucracy on American lives. The federal bureaucracy generates rules and regulations that govern the lives of Americans literally from the womb to the tomb, as well as what goes on in the interim. The air they breathe, the food they eat, the cars they drive, the television programs they watch, and virtually all other aspects of American life are affected by bureaucracy. It is thus no wonder that the federal bureaucracy seems to be constantly expanding.

In truth, however, the number of federal government employees is not swelling. About 2.78 million civilians work for the federal government, but that number has not changed significantly in the last thirty-five years. Overall, the number of federal employees has actually declined since the end of World War II, when the government employed 25 percent more people than it did in 1988.[17] The reduction in the work force has not been constant, however, since the size of the bureaucracy varies somewhat over time. It increases during periods of national crisis and then stabilizes or even decreases somewhat as normal conditions return. *(See Tables 1 and 2.)*

Although the U.S. federal bureaucracy is smaller than it used to be, it is still quite large when compared with those of most other countries. The U.S. bureaucracy, on a per capita basis, is twice the size of the British bureaucracy and four times larger than the West German bureaucracy.[18] Only the Soviet Union has a bureaucracy bigger than its U.S. counterpart.

Most federal bureaucrats do not work in Washington, D.C. Only about 350,000, or 12 percent, of the 2.78 million civilian employees are located there.[19] This percentage, as well as the tremendous number of state and local govern-

Table 1 Size of the Federal Executive Bureaucracy for Selected Years

Executive department	Year established	Paid civilian employees		
		1980	1984	1986
Agriculture	1889	126,139	118,809	111,927
Commerce[a]	1913	48,563	35,217	35,408
Defense[b]	1947	960,116	1,043,784	1,087,893
Education	1980	7,364	5,343	4,680
Energy	1977	21,557	16,976	16,674
Health and Human Services[c]	1980	155,662	144,240	136,318
Housing and Urban Development	1965	16,964	12,393	11,545
Interior	1849	77,357	78,661	76,232
Justice	1870	56,327	61,398	65,285
Labor	1913	23,400	18,320	17,841
State	1789	23,497	24,706	25,482
Transportation	1966	72,361	62,781	61,348
Treasury	1789	124,663	130,654	140,669
Total	—	1,713,970	1,753,282	1,791,302

Source: From Gary King and Lyn Ragsdale, *The Elusive Executive: Discovering Statistical Patterns in the Presidency* (Washington, D.C.: CQ Press, 1988), 228.

a. Originally the Department of Commerce and Labor, established in 1903 and split in 1913.

b. Originally the Department of War, established in 1789.

c. Originally the Department of Health, Education and Welfare, established in 1953.

Table 2 Size of Independent Federal Agencies for Selected Years

Agency	Paid civilian employees		
	1980	1984	1986
ACTION	1,837	507	490
American Battle Monuments Commission	386	390	396
Board of Governors, Federal Reserve System	1,498	1,607	1,510
Civil Aeronautics Board	734	357	a
Commission on Civil Rights	304	257	204
Environmental Protection Agency	14,715	13,048	14,081
Equal Employment Opportunity Commission	3,515	3,168	3,156
Export-Import Bank	385	364	340
Farm Credit Administration	271	296	340
Federal Communications Commission	2,244	2,027	1,835
Federal Deposit Insurance Corporation	3,520	4,607	8,408
Federal Emergency Management Agency	3,427	2,691	2,537
Federal Home Loan Bank Board	1,470	1,497	786
Federal Labor Relations Authority	349	323	278
Federal Mediation and Conciliation Service	503	350	331
Federal Trade Commission	1,846	1,318	1,129
General Services Administration	37,654	29,681	24,842
International Trade Commission	424	458	520
Interstate Commerce Commission	1,998	1,071	809
National Aeronautics and Space Administration	23,714	22,085	21,911
National Endowment for the Arts	362	554	276
National Labor Relations Board	2,936	2,720	2,437
National Science Foundation	1,394	1,236	1,170
National Transportation Safety Board	384	348	344
Nuclear Regulatory Commission	3,283	3,678	3,587
Office of Personnel Management	8,280	6,553	6,120
Panama Canal Commission	8,700	8,078	8,292
Railroad Retirement Board	1,795	1,578	1,619
Securities and Exchange Commission	2,056	1,959	1,905
Selective Service System	97	338	290
Small Business Administration	5,804	5,093	5,092
Smithsonian Institution	4,403	4,690	4,797
Tennessee Valley Authority	51,714	33,589	30,680
U.S. Postal Service	660,014	682,653	791,685
Veterans Administration	228,285	239,923	243,833
All other	20,062	18,170	24,447
Total	1,100,363	1,097,262	1,210,477

Source: Gary King and Lyn Ragsdale, *The Elusive Executive: Discovering Statistical Patterns in the Presidency* (Washington, D.C.: CQ Press, 1988), 229.

a. Board was disbanded December 31, 1984.

ment employees nationwide, illustrates how decentralized government is in the United States. Employment at the state and local levels of government has grown dramatically in recent decades: as of 1988, 3.8 million people worked for state governments, and local governments (counties and cities) employed a staggering 9.3 million people.[20]

The power of the federal bureaucracy cannot be judged by the number of its employees alone. While it is true that the number of federal employees has not risen since World War II, the size of the federal budget has increased sharply. In 1950, for example, the federal budget was $46.2 billion—a huge figure that seems minuscule compared with the government's 1986 budget of almost $1 trillion.[21]

The federal government accommodates these vastly larger budgets without hiring more employees to help administer them through a system of proxy, or indirect, administration. Many programs are funded by the federal government and carried out by private organizations or state and local governments. For example, the federal government pays for the food stamp program, but state governments administer it. The practice of proxy administration thus masks the number of people who actually rely on the federal bureaucracy for their livelihood. According to one estimate, for every person who works directly for the federal government, as many as four people may work for it indirectly.[22]

Public Attitudes Toward the Bureaucracy

Bureaucracy has a bad reputation. Deserved or not, criticism is heaped on the bureaucracy by Americans from all walks of life. Much of the public harbors an image of small-minded bureaucrats entrenched in minor offices making life miserable for everyone else by issuing petty regulations and creating miles of red tape. While the U.S.

bureaucracy certainly is not perfect, many of the accusations against it seem unjustified.

The media relishes stories of bureaucratic foul-ups and wastefulness. Some of the incidents revealed in the press are disturbing; others are ruefully amusing. No taxpayer enjoys reading that the Defense Department purchased some $659 ashtrays and $7,000 coffee makers,[23] and few citizens can be comfortable with the knowledge that the Department of Energy included among millions of declassified documents directions on how to build a hydrogen bomb.[24] On the lighter side, it is hard not to smile upon learning that the Department of Health and Human Services sent fifteen chimpanzees to a laboratory to start a chimp breeding program—and that all those chimps were males.[25]

Over the last forty years academics have joined in the chorus of abuse. They tend to castigate the bureaucracy on more general grounds than the media, pointing to organizational problems, policy failures, and excessive political power. One of the first and foremost students of the bureaucracy, German sociologist Max Weber, has warned that bureaucracy is "a power instrument of the first order" which can be a threat to democracy.[26]

Politicians have frequently engaged in bureaucracy bashing as well. In recent years, for example, Sen. William Proxmire (D-Wis.) used his "Golden Fleece" awards to highlight examples of bureaucratic waste, and both Gerald R. Ford and Jimmy Carter included attacks on the bureaucracy in their campaigns for the presidency. But no one has surpassed Ronald Reagan in condemning the federal bureaucracy. His calls to curb the size and spending of the civilian bureaucracy were central to his hallmark pledge to get government "off the backs of the people."

Considering the frequency of assaults on the bureaucracy from these sources, it is hardly surprising that the general public views the bureaucracy negatively. One observer has called the public fear and dislike of bureaucracy "a raging pandemic."[27] Citizens see the bureaucracy as inefficient, unresponsive, and out of control. One survey conducted in the early 1970s by Robert L. Kahn et al. showed that the majority of Americans think government agencies do not treat most people fairly or handle their problems efficiently.[28] In sum, most people believe that the bureaucracy is not doing its job.

Dislike of the bureaucracy is not universal, however, and some observers have come to its defense. They argue that the U.S. bureaucracy, especially when compared with those of other countries, actually performs pretty well.[29] Mistakes occur, of course, but no organization is totally error-free. Moreover, charges of bureaucratic inefficiency often are based on isolated and unrepresentative cases. There is also the question of whether efficiency should be the primary goal of government agencies. For example, the U.S. Postal Service could operate more efficiently if it eliminated home delivery to outlying areas, but then the service it provides obviously would not be the same.

The defenders of the bureaucracy also contend it has become a scapegoat for many of the problems of modern society. It is a convenient target of criticism because it is big, powerful, hard to change, and relatively anonymous. When people become frustrated with government or feel powerless over their lives, they channel their discontent toward the bureaucracy and thus help perpetuate the myth that the bureaucracy is the source of problems, not solutions.

The survey conducted by Kahn et al. lends support to this theory. While respondents were unhappy with the bureaucracy generally, the overwhelming majority had had satisfactory personal encounters with bureaucratic agencies. These results indicate that people cling to bureaucratic stereotypes despite personal experiences to the contrary. Kahn et al. attribute this to a larger pattern of political attitudes in which Americans are patriotic and happy with their own contacts with government but are generally distrustful of politicians and government agencies.[30]

Structure of the Federal Bureaucracy

The federal bureaucracy is extremely complicated. Understanding its place in American life and its relation to the president requires some grasp of its complex structure.

Characteristics of All Bureaucracies

All bureaucracies share certain characteristics.[31] Although many people call any large organization a bureaucracy, the term refers only to entities exhibiting the characteristics described below.

Hierarchy. Each member of a bureaucracy is part of a chain of command, accepting authority from above and exercising authority downward. This hierarchy of authority is vital in performing the large-scale, complex functions usually assigned to bureaucracies. Because each bureaucrat can complete only a small part of the agency's tasks, centralized control is vital in coordinating the work of employees. In general, instruction flows down the hierarchy, while information flows both up and down the chain of command.

Specialization. Bureaucracies have clear divisions of labor. Like a worker on a factory assembly line, each bureaucrat specializes in a limited set of duties and ordinarily becomes an expert in that narrow area. Specific responsibilities usually are developed carefully; in fact, each of the nearly 2.8 million employees of the federal bureaucracy has a written job description.[32] This kind of job specialization allows bureaucracies to shoulder greater loads of more complicated work and do it better and more quickly.

Record Keeping. Bureaucracies are designed to function consistently regardless of changes in personnel, and organized files of records (particularly memoranda and details of decisions made and actions taken) help make this possible. Employees consult agency records to review what has been done in the past, and supervisors use agency records to monitor the work of subordinates. *(See box, Bureaucratic Lingo, p. 1210.)*

Rules. Rules serve some of the same purposes as records. They tell each employee what to do and what not to do in certain situations, thereby facilitating bureaucratic consistency and coordination. Because most employees are highly specialized and supervisors are not always available to advise them, they often do not know how best to handle

Bureaucratic Lingo

Bureaucrats often seem to have a language of their own. The major characteristic of bureaucratic lingo is its lack of clarity and directness. Many bureaucrats apparently adopt "Smith's Principle" when communicating: "If it can be understood, it's not finished yet." [1] For example, in the wake of the explosion of the space shuttle *Challenger,* which killed seven astronauts, the National Aeronautics and Space Administration (NASA) called the explosion an "anomaly." [2] A National Park Service official engaged in some bureaucratic lingo when he termed the service's plan to kill burros in the Grand Canyon, which were eating the vegetation and thus causing erosion, a "direct reduction." [3] The Central Intelligence Agency (CIA) referred to an extermination of a different kind—assassination—as "termination with extreme prejudice" and termed the less violent activity of illegal break-ins as "uncontested physical searches." [4]

Why do bureaucrats engage in such tortuous use of the language? The principal reason is probably to protect themselves and their agencies by burying unpleasant facts under mounds of barely comprehensible verbiage or disguising them with euphemisms. "Acheson's Rule of the Bureaucracy" states that "a memorandum is written not to inform the reader, but to protect the writer." [5] In NASA's case the euphemisms may have eased slightly the emotional situation for everyone concerned, but it also was probably aimed at protecting whatever remnants of the agency's good public image remained after the accident. Similarly, both the CIA and the Park Service official gained some small degree of protection from negative public reaction through their use of euphemistic terminology.

Because lingo requires special skills, the following guidelines for learning to speak and write in "bureaucratese" were devised:

1. Use nouns as if they were verbs.
   Don't say, *"We gave the department this task";* say instead, *"We tasked the department."*
2. Use adjectives as if they were verbs.
   Don't say, *"We put the report in final form";* say instead, *"We finalized the report."*
3. Use several words where one word would do.
   Don't say, *"at this point";* say instead, *"at this point in time."*
4. Never use ordinary words where unusual ones can be found.
   Don't say you *"made a choice";* say you *"selected an option."*
5. No matter what subject you are discussing, employ the language of sports and war.
   Never say *"progress";* say *"breakthrough."* Never speak of a *"compromise";* instead, consider *"adopting a fallback position."*
6. Avoid active verbs.
   Never say, *"Study the problem";* say instead, *"It is felt that the problem should be subjected to further study."* [6]

1. Paul Dickson, *The Official Rules* (New York: Delacorte Press, 1978), 170.
2. "Doublespeak at NASA," *Space World,* February 1987, 7.
3. William Safire, *On Language* (New York: Times Books, 1980).
4. Ibid.
5. Dickson, *The Official Rules,* 1.
6. James Q. Wilson, *American Government: Institutions and Policies,* 2d ed. (Lexington, Mass.: D. C. Heath, 1983), 362.

situations outside their area of specialization. Unfortunately, some rules may be unclear or burdensome to follow and therefore may seem more like annoying red tape than helpful guides.

Impersonal Operation. Bureaucrats strive to handle each business matter objectively, on its merits, rather than emotionally. Such an approach makes the bureaucracy more efficient by keeping employees from becoming mired in the unhappy consequences that sometimes result from bureaucratic decisions, and it ensures a more uniform application of the rules. Thus, impersonality increases fairness. A negative effect is the impression of indifference or coldness that impersonality often leaves with members of the public who come into contact with the bureaucracy, especially those who believe the uniqueness of their situation has been ignored.

Personnel Practices. Bureaucratic personnel systems generally revolve around two factors: merit—ability to do the job well—and seniority—length of employment. Merit is usually the main requirement for employment by the bureaucracy, with qualifications often measured by competitive examinations. Both merit and seniority play a role in promotions.

Size of Operation. Bureaucracies are large. According to scholar Anthony Downs, an organization is large when its highest-ranking leaders know less than half its staff members personally.[33] Bureaucracies must be large enough to handle the extensive chores they are given, but their immense size leads to many of the coordination and control problems and thus structural remedies described in this section. For example, the Defense Department has the gigantic job of providing for U.S. security. Thus, as a huge agency—with over one million paid civilian employees—it enjoys benefits and suffers problems because of its size.

Types of Functions. Bureaucracies generally perform functions that are not carried out elsewhere in society. The economic free market of private organizations acting primarily in their own interests simply does not provide everything society needs. According to Downs, in democratic societies with free markets governments must tackle large societal problems such as pollution; furnish services such as national defense that benefit the entire society;

undertake any major redistribution of income, including welfare programs; regulate the economy; protect consumers; provide law and order; and maintain the government itself.[34]

Organization of the Federal Bureaucracy

The day-to-day activities of the U.S. federal bureaucracy, which consists of many different parts, receives little public attention. Thus, much of the population does not understand how the bureaucracy is organized.

Types of Agencies

Bureaucratic agencies can be sorted into five categories: departments, independent agencies, government corporations, agencies attached to Congress and the president, and other agencies.

Departments. The fourteen executive departments compose the first layer of bureaucracy under the president. The heads of these departments (also known as secretaries) are members of the president's cabinet. Department secretaries and their immediate subordinates are appointed by the president with Senate approval. The departments conduct some of the bureaucracy's most important business and employ over 60 percent of all federal workers.[35] The fourteen executive departments are: Agriculture, Commerce, Defense, Education, Energy, Health and Human Services, Housing and Urban Development, Interior, Justice, Labor, State, Transportation, Treasury, and Veterans Affairs.

Congress determines the number and jurisdiction of cabinet-level departments, but the president can request changes. The Departments of State, Treasury, and War were established in 1789 to meet immediate national needs, while other departments were created as the nation developed and the needs arose. Some departments—such as Justice and Interior—serve the general needs of the entire country. Others—such as Commerce, Labor, Agriculture, and Veterans Affairs—serve particular segments of society.

Each of the fourteen executive departments is broken down into smaller units—offices, administrations, services, and bureaus—which administer the department's programs. The specific functions of these units vary from department to department.[36] Some of these department subunits are the Food Safety and Inspection Service and the Agricultural Marketing Service within the Department of Agriculture, the National Highway Traffic Safety Administration and the Federal Railroad Administration within the Department of Transportation, and the Bureau of African Affairs and the Bureau of International Narcotics Matters within the Department of State. *(See Executive Departments chapter in Part V.)*

Independent Agencies. The approximately sixty independent agencies within the federal bureaucracy, which are roughly equivalent to the department subunits in size and influence, are either independent executive agencies or independent regulatory agencies.[37] Both types exist outside of and independent from the executive departments. Agencies are made independent for several reasons. First, such agencies are less tied to the traditional ways of doing things and thus can be more innovative than the executive departments. Second, with their independent status, these agencies are theoretically less susceptible to outside political pressures. Third, some agencies, such as the National Aeronautics and Space Administration (NASA), are independent simply because their missions do not fall naturally within any of the departments.[38] *(See Government Agencies and Corporations chapter in Part V.)*

Independent executive agencies, usually headed by one person who serves at the president's pleasure, perform a single function and report directly to the president. Presidents wield significant influence over independent executive agencies. Such agencies include NASA, the Central Intelligence Agency, the General Services Administration, and the Environmental Protection Agency.

Independent regulatory agencies regulate parts of the private economic sector to protect the public interest. These agencies are usually headed by a bipartisan group—often called a commission or a board—rather than an individual. Commission members, who serve terms of fixed length, are appointed by the president and approved by the Senate, but they report directly to neither. Independent regulatory agencies—including the Federal Communications Commission, the Federal Trade Commission, and the Securities and Exchange Commission—are designed to operate independently from all three branches of government.

Government Corporations. When confronted with tasks similar to those carried out by private business, the federal government can form a government corporation to take advantage of the rights enjoyed by private corporations. Government corporations have greater freedom of operation than most other government agencies. They can buy and sell property, borrow money, bring legal suits in their own names (and be sued), earn a profit, and even sell stock. Congress finds this structure tempting because it allows transfer of responsibility to a supposedly nonpartisan body and because the costs of such corporations do not appear in the federal budget.

Like private corporations, government corporations are run by boards of directors, whose members come from both political parties and usually serve long, fixed terms. Some of the best-known government corporations are the U.S. Postal Service, the Tennessee Valley Authority, the Federal Deposit Insurance Corporation, and Amtrak. *(See Government Agencies and Corporations chapter in Part V.)*

Presidential and Congressional Agencies. The staffs of both the president and Congress have grown so drastically in recent decades that each now has its own supporting bureaucracy. Not surprisingly, these two bureaucracies frequently clash with other parts of the federal bureaucracy. The White House Office within the Executive Office of the President (EOP) is composed of the president's special assistants, legislative liaisons, and press secretaries. The other supporting organizations within the EOP assist the president primarily with policy issues. One of the most notable agencies is the Office of Management and Budget, which constructs the federal budget and assesses the fiscal side of legislation. Other EOP agencies include the National Security Council and the Council of Economic Advisers. *(See chapter, Executive Office of the President: Supporting Organizations, in Part V.)*

Congress employs about eighteen thousand people,

Abbreviations for Bureaucratic Agencies and Cabinet Departments

ACDA Arms Control and Disarmament Agency
ACIR Advisory Commission on Intergovernmental Relations
BIA Bureau of Indian Affairs
CEA Council of Economic Advisers
CIA Central Intelligence Agency
CPSC Consumer Product Safety Commission
DEA Drug Enforcement Agency
DOD Department of Defense
DOE Department of Energy
DOT Department of Transportation
EEOC Equal Employment Opportunity Commission
EOP Executive Office of the President
EPA Environmental Protection Agency
FAA Federal Aviation Administration
FBI Federal Bureau of Investigation
FCC Federal Communications Commission
FEMA Federal Emergency Management Agency
FDA Food and Drug Administration
FDIC Federal Deposit Insurance Corporation
FEC Federal Election Commission
FRB Federal Reserve Board
FTC Federal Trade Commission
GAO General Accounting Office
GSA General Services Administration
HHS Department of Health and Human Services
HUD Department of Housing and Urban Development
ICC Interstate Commerce Commission
INS Immigration and Naturalization Service
IRS Internal Revenue Service
NASA National Aeronautics and Space Administration
NIH National Institutes of Health
NLRB National Labor Relations Board
NRC Nuclear Regulatory Commission
NSC National Security Council
NSF National Science Foundation
NTSB National Transportation Safety Board
OMB Office of Management and Budget
OPM Office of Personnel Management
OSHA Occupational Safety and Health Administration
SEC Securities and Exchange Commission
SBA Small Business Administration
TVA Tennessee Valley Authority
USDA U.S. Department of Agriculture
USPS U.S. Postal Service
WHO White House Office

who serve on the members' personal staffs, on committee staffs, and in research agencies such as the Library of Congress and the Congressional Budget Office.[39] The General Accounting Office acts as congressional watchdog over federal programs. Other congressional agencies, such as the Government Printing Office, fulfill responsibilities not directly related to policy making.

Other Agencies. In 1985 over 900 advisory committees and 120 minor boards were operating within the federal government.[40] Advisory committees, which can be either temporary or permanent, give expert advice on a wide range of subjects.

Presidents are fond of such committees because their creation demonstrates to the public that the administration cares about the problems being examined and because they provide an opportunity to pay political debts with committee appointments. Examples of the many advisory committees include the President's Science Advisory Committee, the Advisory Committee on Vocational Education, and the Advisory Council to the National Institute of Mental Health.

The same is true of many of the other minor boards and commissions sponsored by the federal government, which usually have no permanent staff and can only make recommendations. Examples of these organizations, which generally are established for a single purpose, include the Grace Commission, which in 1984 made recommendations on how to cut the size of the federal government, and the Rogers Commission, which studied and reported on the explosion of the space shuttle *Challenger* in 1986. *(See Presidential Commissions chapter in Part V.)*

Functions of the Bureaucracy

Bureaucratic functions fall into four categories: regulatory, clientele, regional, and housekeeping.

Regulatory. Congress establishes regulatory agencies to oversee and regulate parts of the private economic sector. Regulatory agencies do not provide services as such; they formulate and enforce rules and regulations. Many independent agencies are regulatory. Prominent examples of regulatory agencies are the Environmental Protection Agency, Federal Trade Commission, National Labor Relations Board, and Interstate Commerce Commission. *(See Government Agencies and Corporations chapter in Part V.)*

Clientele. Clientele agencies address the problems and concerns of a specific segment of society. While such agencies generally are quite responsive to their target groups, these groups do not always approve of what the agencies do. On the contrary, clientele groups can be some of the agencies' harshest critics. Clientele agencies include the Departments of Agriculture, Labor, Veterans Affairs, and Commerce, as well as the Bureau of Indian Affairs and some other independent agencies.

Regional. Some agencies concentrate on specific parts of the country. For example, the Department of Housing and Urban Development devotes most of its attention to the problems of the inner cities, while the Tennessee Valley Authority encourages economic development of the Tennessee Valley region. Other regional agencies include the Mississippi River Commission and the Appalachian Regional Commission.

Housekeeping. Housekeeping agencies serve other government agencies. For example, the General Services Administration supervises most government buildings and oversees contracts for equipment. Another housekeeping agency, the Civil Service Commission, helps run the federal personnel system.

Federal Personnel System

Employees of the federal civilian bureaucracy are hired either through a merit-based system or by presidential appointment. The debate over merit systems versus patronage (political appointments) is an old one. Advocates of merit systems emphasize the goals of recruiting competent employees and maintaining a fairly stable public work force. Supporters of patronage believe that government works better when elected political leaders appoint bureaucrats who can be counted on for their loyalty and enthusiasm. While both kinds of systems are used, in practice some elements of each appear in the other.

Merit System

Merit-based employment began in 1883 with the passage of the Pendleton Act. This act served as the basis for the merit system, until it was modified by the Civil Service Reform Act of 1978. As of 1988, over 90 percent of all federal bureaucrats were working under one of four merit systems: the civil service, the senior executive service, separate merit systems, and the excepted service.[41]

Civil Service. The career civil service system, managed by the Office of Personnel Management (OPM), is the largest merit system, covering three-fifths of federal bureaucracy employees.[42] OPM ensures that employees are hired on the basis of qualifications, promoted on the basis of good performance, and provided with job security.[43] The civil service system revolves around the General Schedule (GS), which classifies positions and sets the pay scale for clerical, administrative, and professional personnel.

The General Schedule lists eighteen grades, from GS-1 to GS-18. Job type and an employee's qualifications determine at what grade the schedule is entered. Clerical employees are placed in the first four grades, while college graduates usually enter at GS-5 and those with advanced degrees at GS-9 or higher.[44] Steps within each grade are decided by seniority, job performance, and type of skill.

Senior Executive Service. In an effort to make the upper stratum of federal employees more productive and more responsive to the president's policy goals, the Civil Service Reform Act of 1978 moved over seven thousand civil service employees from the top three GS grades into the senior executive service (SES). Incentives for SES officials include higher pay and eligibility for financial bonuses, but there are disadvantages as well. For example, SES employees have less job security than other federal employees; they can be transferred or fired with relative ease. Early results indicate that the SES has successfully increased the president's influence over the bureaucracy, but it also has demoralized the program's members and prompted many of them to leave public service.[45]

Separate Merit Systems. Some federal agencies have their own merit personnel systems, independent of OPM control. About 30 percent of federal bureaucrats work under these systems.[46] Although the specific procedures of the separate systems vary from agency to agency, they are created for some of the same reasons: to make recruitment of professionals easier, to give the agency more freedom in hiring and firing than allowed under the civil service system, and to enable closer screening and supervision of applicants and employees.[47]

Separate systems also encourage the notion that employment in these agencies is a career rather than simply a job. Agencies that operate their own personnel systems include the U.S. Postal Service (which has the largest system by far), Department of State (for foreign service officers), Federal Bureau of Investigation, Tennessee Valley Authority, Department of Veterans Affairs, and U.S. Public Health Service.

Excepted Service. Two categories of federal jobs, Schedule A and Schedule B, are excepted from competitive hiring and other merit-based procedures, but very few of the jobs go to political appointees. Both Schedules A and B apply to nonpolicy-making positions that cannot be filled practically using normal civil service system methods. The difference between the two schedules is that applicants for Schedule B jobs must take a noncompetitive exam, while those for Schedule A jobs do not. Many Schedule A employees are lawyers, while Treasury Department bank examiners, among others, fall under Schedule B.

"Name Requests." Despite the formal stress that the merit systems place on hiring on the basis of competitive exams, many jobs are filled by a process known as "name request." Using this process an agency asks the personnel system to recommend the person they want to hire for a particular job. An agency may even write a job description that only the person it wants to employ can fit. About 80 percent of senior-level career openings are filled in this manner.[48]

Occasionally, name requests are initiated by a member of Congress. They are used more often, however, to employ people already known to the agency. This "buddy system" can produce capable employees, especially since many high-caliber job candidates are unwilling to go through the regular slow channels of merit systems, but it does pose some dangers. If abused, it could simply become a way for bureaucrats to give their friends, well qualified or not, government jobs. Moreover, the flow of new ideas into the agency might be slowed if most of the vacancies are filled by people with similar attitudes.

Characteristics of Civil Servants. Employees of the merit systems reflect the diversity of the American population in terms of education, sex, race, social background, income, region of origin, and occupation.[49] People with all sorts of different personal attributes work for the bureaucracy. As scholar Charles T. Goodsell has observed, bureaucrats are "ordinary people." [50]

That ordinariness begins to disappear, however, higher up in the civil service ranks. Officials in the top few grades of the General Schedule tend to fit a common description: a white, middle-aged, male college graduate, with a middle-class background.[51] Political partisanship is another difference between bureaucrats and the general public. Civil servants of all ranks generally favor the Democratic over

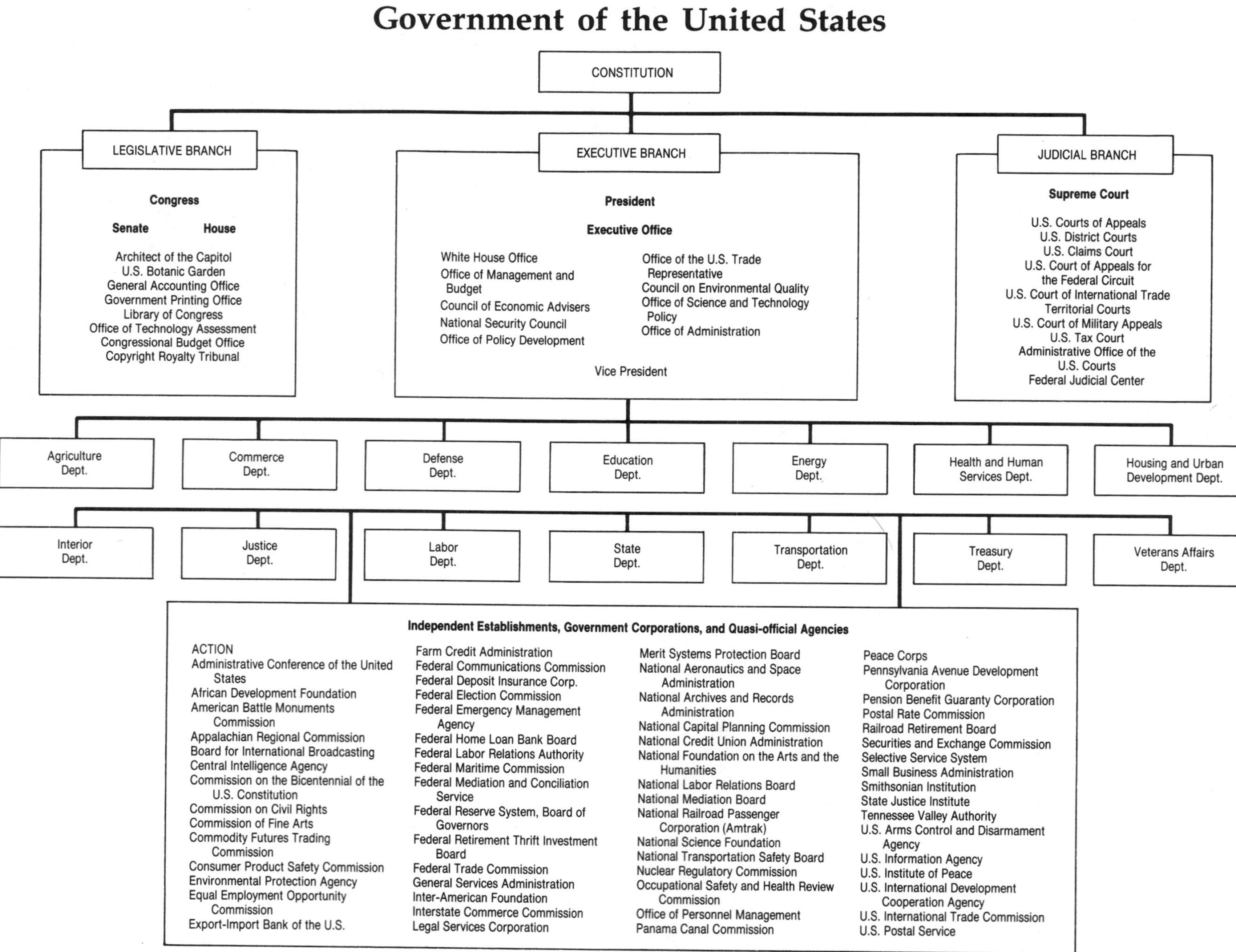
Government of the United States
CONSTITUTION
LEGISLATIVE BRANCH
Congress
Senate
House
Architect of the Capitol
U.S. Botanic Garden
General Accounting Office
Government Printing Office
Library of Congress
Office of Technology Assessment
Congressional Budget Office
Copyright Royalty Tribunal
EXECUTIVE BRANCH
President
Executive Office
White House Office
Office of Management and Budget
Council of Economic Advisers
National Security Council
Office of Policy Development
Office of the U.S. Trade Representative
Council on Environmental Quality
Office of Science and Technology Policy
Office of Administration
Vice President
JUDICIAL BRANCH
Supreme Court
U.S. Courts of Appeals
U.S. District Courts
U.S. Claims Court
U.S. Court of Appeals for the Federal Circuit
U.S. Court of International Trade
Territorial Courts
U.S. Court of Military Appeals
U.S. Tax Court
Administrative Office of the U.S. Courts
Federal Judicial Center
Agriculture Dept.
Commerce Dept.
Defense Dept.
Education Dept.
Energy Dept.
Health and Human Services Dept.
Housing and Urban Development Dept.
Interior Dept.
Justice Dept.
Labor Dept.
State Dept.
Transportation Dept.
Treasury Dept.
Veterans Affairs Dept.
Independent Establishments, Government Corporations, and Quasi-official Agencies
ACTION
Administrative Conference of the United States
African Development Foundation
American Battle Monuments Commission
Appalachian Regional Commission
Board for International Broadcasting
Central Intelligence Agency
Commission on the Bicentennial of the U.S. Constitution
Commission on Civil Rights
Commission of Fine Arts
Commodity Futures Trading Commission
Consumer Product Safety Commission
Environmental Protection Agency
Equal Employment Opportunity Commission
Export-Import Bank of the U.S.
Farm Credit Administration
Federal Communications Commission
Federal Deposit Insurance Corp.
Federal Election Commission
Federal Emergency Management Agency
Federal Home Loan Bank Board
Federal Labor Relations Authority
Federal Maritime Commission
Federal Mediation and Conciliation Service
Federal Reserve System, Board of Governors
Federal Retirement Thrift Investment Board
Federal Trade Commission
General Services Administration
Inter-American Foundation
Interstate Commerce Commission
Legal Services Corporation
Merit Systems Protection Board
National Aeronautics and Space Administration
National Archives and Records Administration
National Capital Planning Commission
National Credit Union Administration
National Foundation on the Arts and the Humanities
National Labor Relations Board
National Mediation Board
National Railroad Passenger Corporation (Amtrak)
National Science Foundation
National Transportation Safety Board
Nuclear Regulatory Commission
Occupational Safety and Health Review Commission
Office of Personnel Management
Panama Canal Commission
Peace Corps
Pennsylvania Avenue Development Corporation
Pension Benefit Guaranty Corporation
Postal Rate Commission
Railroad Retirement Board
Securities and Exchange Commission
Selective Service System
Small Business Administration
Smithsonian Institution
State Justice Institute
Tennessee Valley Authority
U.S. Arms Control and Disarmament Agency
U.S. Information Agency
U.S. Institute of Peace
U.S. International Development Cooperation Agency
U.S. International Trade Commission
U.S. Postal Service

the Republican party, which is not surprising given the Republican preference for small government. Whatever the demographic characteristics of bureaucrats, however, there is little evidence to suggest that those characteristics exert much influence on how public employees do their jobs.[52] jobs.[52]

Presidential Appointments

The president appoints only a small fraction of the government's employees, but those appointees hold some of the most important jobs in the bureaucracy.

Number and Types of Appointments. Relatively few bureaucrats get their jobs through presidential appointment. The president has the authority to appoint only about twenty-seven hundred of the nearly three million civilian federal workers.[53] Most of these are high-level policy-making positions, so while the number of appointments is fairly small, they provide the president with significant leverage over the bureaucracy.

Presidential appointments fall into three major categories: those authorized by statute, Schedule C jobs, and noncareer senior executives. By law the president has the power to appoint numerous officials, including the secretary of each cabinet department and the secretary's immediate subordinates; federal judges, marshals, and attorneys; ambassadors; and members of certain boards and commissions. In addition, the president appoints the White House staff, fills about ten positions in each major independent agency, and names the heads of some minor agencies. Schedule C lists about sixteen hundred jobs at GS-15 and below in the bureaucracy that the president can use for patronage purposes. About eight hundred noncareer senior executives act as advocates for presidential programs at the upper levels of the bureaucracy.

Selection Process. Although twenty-seven hundred positions seem very insignificant when compared to the total number of federal jobs, this number appears much higher when a president faces the task of having to fill each of these positions. Presidents have long found personnel selection an onerous task. Jimmy Carter articulated his frustration shortly after entering office:

> I have learned in my first two and a half weeks why Abraham Lincoln and some of the older Presidents almost went home when they first got to the White House. The handling of personnel appointments, trying to get the right person in the right position at the right time is a very, very difficult question.[54]

Several factors help account for the trouble that presidents often have in deciding on appointees for government posts.[55] Lack of time is a big constraint. Presidents-elect have less than three months between the election and the inauguration to not only search for and recruit people to join the new administration, but also do all the other things necessary to prepare to take office. To make matters worse, presidents-elect and their staffs are often exhausted during this transition period from the just-concluded election campaigns.

The selection process also is hindered by a president's usual compulsion to consider demographic characteristics such as race, sex, geography, religion, and whatever other traits the president believes must be represented among appointees. This constraint persists throughout the president's term in office. Whenever a vacancy occurs, the best-qualified person may be passed over if he or she does not possess the needed demographic characteristics.

Finally, politics influences presidential appointments. The president-elect finds that many of the political IOUs passed out during the campaign are called in during the personnel selection process. Many supporters want either to obtain jobs themselves or to recommend others for positions. Interest groups, members of Congress, and other party loyalists also want a say in the composition of the new administration. The situation becomes even more complicated when the White House and the newly appointed department secretaries do not agree on appointments. The secretaries frequently want control over appointments in their departments, but this hampers presidential efforts to place people in the bureaucracy who will remain loyal to the White House. *(See "Styles and Methods of Appointment," p. 987, in Executive Departments chapter of Part V.)*

Active presidential involvement in the selection process is crucial to its success.[56] Presidents may be tempted to leave this chore mainly to others, but that can lead to long-term trouble. President Richard Nixon, for example, ran into personnel difficulties partly because he was not attentive enough to appointments at the beginning of his administration. In contrast, President Ronald Reagan and his staff devoted much energy to controlling the selection process, with special emphasis placed on recruiting officials who agreed with Reagan's political philosophy. As a result, Reagan was able to exercise greater control over the bureaucracy than any other modern president.[57]

"Government of Strangers." Political scientist Hugh Heclo has asserted that the system for presidential appointments to the executive branch creates a "government of strangers." [58] Appointees are strangers in several respects. The president usually does not know them personally before they are selected, and, aside from cabinet members and a few other top administrators, the president does not get to know them well even after their appointment. Political appointees also generally do not know the other appointees who are asked to serve the president.

Many presidential appointees are strangers to working in the federal government. Because even those with government experience rarely understand all aspects of their new jobs, virtually all newly appointed political executives spend much of their time learning how to do their jobs. This learning process generally takes from twelve to eighteen months, which is a long time considering that the average upper-level presidential appointee keeps the job only about two years.[59] Such a rapid turnover prevents the appointed parts of the bureaucracy from ever being totally settled and ensures that it remains, at least partially, a government of strangers.

Characteristics of Presidential Appointees. The great majority of presidential appointees have economically and socially elite backgrounds.[60] They usually are white, male, middle-aged, affluent urbanites, who are graduates of prestigious schools and members of high-status occupations. About 85 percent of those appointed to the cabinet or subcabinet (deputy secretaries and assistant secretaries in the cabinet departments) have had some prior experience working for the federal government.[61]
Thus, although many presidential appointees have no government experience, those placed in the most senior positions usually do. The executive branch is run mainly by

Table 3 Prior Government Experience of Major Cabinet and Diplomatic Appointees, 1789-1980 (percent)

Period	No experience	Relatively little experience	Considerable experience	Total officials
1789-1800	4.3	4.3	91.4	23
1801-1828	4.2	6.4	89.4	47
1829-1840	—	7.7	92.3	26
1841-1860	—	9.9	90.1	71
1861-1876	12.7	29.1	58.2	55
1877-1896	8.6	31.4	60.0	70
1897-1912	12.1	27.6	60.3	58
1913-1920	25.0	25.0	50.0	24
1921-1932	26.5	18.4	55.1	49
1933-1940	20.0	30.0	50.0	20
1941-1945	6.7	27.6	66.7	15
1946-1952	7.0	9.3	83.7	43
1953-1960	36.6	24.4	39.0	41
1961-1968	9.2	13.8	77.0	65
1969-1976	18.8	18.8	62.4	64
1977-1980	23.1	11.5	65.4	26

Source: Gary King and Lyn Ragsdale, *The Elusive Executive: Discovering Statistical Patterns in the Presidency* (Washington, D.C.: CQ Press, 1988), 244.

Note: "Considerable experience" is defined as having held any prominent federal or state post for four years or more. "Little experience" is defined as having held any other post or a major federal or state post for less than four years.

people knowledgeable about the government. *(See Table 3.)*

Presidential appointees are drawn from many different sources. Some are former politicians or government officials, while others hail from business, universities, "think tanks," law firms, or labor unions. More recent presidents have tended to look for expertise or administrative experience rather than political prominence in their appointees. For the most part, once appointees finish their stint in government, they go back to private life and do not return to government service.[62] This contradicts the commonly held belief that the government is largely controlled by men and women who rotate in and out of public office.

Cabinet

The cabinet consists of the heads of the fourteen major executive departments. In theory, the cabinet meets regularly, debates major issues, and acts as the president's primary advisory group. The cabinet room's location just a few feet away from the Oval Office and its impressive view of the White House Rose Garden seemingly affirm the cabinet's importance in forming the nation's policy. In reality, however, it rarely works that way. The cabinet does serve important political functions, but policy making is not usually one of them. *(See Cabinet chapter in Part V.)*

Cabinet's Place in Government

The Constitution does not mention the cabinet, and no law requires its existence. The cabinet is solely a product of tradition and custom; presidents use it however they see fit. As departmental secretaries, cabinet members serve at the pleasure of the president and can be removed at any time. The president is also free to ignore recommendations made by the cabinet.

Presidential attempts to use the cabinet as a meaningful decision- and policy-making body have almost always failed. Yet virtually every presidential candidate and president-elect pledges to give the cabinet real policy-making power in the new administration, and the public generally approves of that idea. Presidential scholar Robert J. Sickels has suggested some explanations for why presidents continue to express their desire for a policy-making cabinet. First, such sentiments may help presidents recruit cabinet members. Second, promises to decentralize the policy-making process appeal to the long-standing American distrust of concentrated authority. Finally, management plans that make the department secretaries responsible for what happens in their departments sound sensible.[63]

Actual Role of the Cabinet

The cabinet does not play a policy-making role for a variety of reasons. One reason is its lack of legal standing. Because the president does not have to follow or even seek the cabinet's advice, the cabinet can at most only make recommendations. Cabinet members, however, often prefer to save their suggestions for private conversations with the president, partly becuase they are competing with the other cabinet members for the president's time and support and for funds, and partly because they would rather not air private or sensitive topics in a crowded cabinet meeting. Another reason that the cabinet has no policy-making role is that presidents frequently have good reason to wonder where the ultimate loyalties of their cabinet members lay. *(See "Role of Cabinet Members," p. 1217, in this chapter.)*

Although the cabinet is not an effective policy-making body, it still fills some useful roles. Its principal role is to give the president informal advice on matters brought before it. With the diversity of groups that members represent, the cabinet is able to provide a broad spectrum of viewpoints, possibly including some that had not yet occurred to the president. One disadvantage of this approach is that cabinet discussions of issues that do not affect all the departments—and few issues do—can be a waste of time. As Richard Nixon, a veteran of many cabinet meetings, has remarked, the day is "long since passed when it was useful to take an hour and a half to have the Secretary of Defense and the Secretary of State discuss the Secretary of Transportation's new highway proposal."[64]

The cabinet also plays an important symbolic role. The image of the president sitting down at the meeting table with the cabinet in attendance to ponder the important issues of the day is somehow a comforting one. It symbolizes the president's commitment to listening to and consulting with representatives of the major social, economic, and political groups in American society.[65] Elevation of a government agency to the cabinet signifies the nation's commitment to that agency's goals. For example, the two new cabinet departments created during the Carter administration, Energy and Education, demonstrated that Democratic president's commitment to these subjects. Conversely, Reagan's attempt to abolish these new departments indicated his commitment to reducing the size of government. Yet to show his high regard for the nation's veterans, Reagan supported the elevation of the Veterans Administration to a cabinet-level department.

Most recent presidents—including Harry S Truman,

John F. Kennedy, Lyndon B. Johnson, Richard Nixon, and Gerald R. Ford—used the cabinet as an informal discussion group.[66] Jimmy Carter entered office intending to make more extensive use of the cabinet, but he soon became discouraged and scaled back his efforts. Among modern presidents, Dwight D. Eisenhower gave the cabinet its biggest role. He provided it with staff, saw that it held regular meetings, and encouraged it to express independent opinions. Yet even under Eisenhower the cabinet functioned mainly as an advisory body and took no part in making final policy decisions.

Role of Cabinet Members

All cabinet members face an ongoing dilemma: maintaining loyalty to the needs of their respective departments while remaining loyal to the president's policies and programs. Some time after assuming office, department secretaries frequently adopt the positions of the departments they lead—that is, they "marry the natives." Such a development is not too surprising since the secretaries spend much more time with their subordinates in the department and with interest group leaders than they do with the president. Self-interest also prompts secretaries to protect and expand the departments they head. When such a transformation occurs, the secretary often acts more like a representative of the department to the president than the presidential envoy he or she was appointed to be. Presidential goals thus become secondary. This tendency for department secretaries to "go native" is a constant source of frustration for presidents.

Aside from the problem of divided loyalties, the cabinet is characterized by the unequal influence of its members. Presidential scholar Thomas E. Cronin has described two cabinet factions: the inner cabinet, composed of the secretaries of the Departments of State, Defense, Treasury, and Justice, and the outer cabinet, composed of the heads of the remaining departments.[67] Because the inner cabinet departments deal with the most pressing national priorities, and their heads meet regularly with the president, these departments enjoy high status. The president also usually knows these department secretaries better and relies on them more heavily.

Outer cabinet departments have narrower jurisdictions and are subject to stronger congressional and clientele pressure. The secretaries of these departments are more likely to "go native" because each of their departments primarily serves a particular segment of society with strong opinions on how the department should be run. Thus, outer cabinet members generally have less influence with the president not only because of the more limited activities of their departments, but also because the secretaries themselves often put their loyalty to their own departments ahead of their loyalty to the president.

Bureaucratic Power

The federal bureaucracy wields considerable power and can be, depending on the situation, one of the president's primary allies or chief rivals in government and politics. Not all parts of the bureaucracy enjoy the same clout, however. For example, the Selective Service System does not have nearly as much influence as the Department of Defense. Understanding the sources and limits of bureaucratic power is crucial to understanding why the bureaucracy in general is powerful and why certain federal agencies are more powerful than others. Bureaucratic power is one of the key variables in the relationship between the bureaucracy and the president.

Sources of Bureaucratic Power

Bureaucratic power springs from two basic kinds of sources: internal and external. Because no two agencies are exactly alike, no two will draw the same amount of power from the same sources. An agency's specific characteristics largely determine the extent of its power, but it can take certain actions to expand its power.

Internal Sources

Internal sources of power are those inside the bureaucratic agency itself. They include an agency's expertise, control of information, size and complexity, inertia, leadership, cohesion, and popular appeal.

Expertise. Many of today's political issues are so technically complex that only experts on the subject can fully understand them. For example, the intricacies of defense issues such as the Strategic Defense Initiative and of environmental concerns such as the depletion of the ozone layer are beyond the comprehension of most people. Thus, citizens and in turn their political leaders look to bureaucracy for such expertise.

Bureaucratic agencies are large enough to employ specialists in the technical areas within their purview. For example, the Department of Agriculture employs agronomists, soil scientists, economists, and other experts in areas under the department's supervision. Similarly, the State Department houses experts on countries and issues vital to U.S. foreign policy. Unlike members of Congress, who are confronted with dozens of issues at the same time, bureaucratic experts can devote their complete attention to a single project. As of 1981 the federal government employed an impressive number of professionals as its experts: 150,000 engineers and architects, 10,000 doctors, 14,000 scientists, and 31,000 lawyers.[68] Because Americans generally hold professionals in high regard, professionals heighten an agency's prestige.

Bureaucratic experts are usually able to generate effective public policy, or at least policy more effective than that devised by the nonexperts. Political leaders therefore seek expert advice from the bureaucracy when making policy decisions. Experienced politicians realize that they can be saved from embarrassing policy and political errors by consulting with the agency experts.

The respect accorded bureaucrats by politicians enhances the credibility, prestige, and power of their agencies. Despite the frequent antibureaucratic rhetoric spouted by members of Congress and other politicians, they like and fund bureaucratic agencies that produce good results. A kind of cycle is formed: bureaucratic experts study the issues and reach sound conclusions; politicians seek bureaucratic advice and recognize its expertise; agencies play their increased credibility into more power, which they use to maintain and develop their expertise; and the role of the bureaucratic experts in government decision making expands. For example, experts in the Environmental Protection Agency (EPA) advise Congress on the technical aspects of legislation regarding pollution control and other complex environmental issues. Each time Congress accepts EPA's advice, the agency's credibility and influence are enhanced, which in turn generally leads to increased political support for it. EPA takes advantage of that support to expand its expertise—and thus its role in environmental policy making.

Control of Information. Information is the raw material of politics, central to the decision-making process. Thus control of information can greatly influence policy. Largely because of their technical expertise, bureaucratic agencies are asked regularly to advise political leaders on policy issues. The information and recommendations passed along by the agencies shape what comes out of the political decision-making process by shaping much of what goes into it.

From the agency's standpoint the ideal situation is one in which the agency has a monopoly on the information about a particular subject, making that agency an indispensable participant in policy making concerning its area of interest. That situation rarely occurs, however, since information on most issues is widely available from other bureaucratic agencies, universities, interest groups, and congressional staff, among others. Generally, the less available the outside information, the greater is the influence of the agency. For example, the Central Intelligence Agency often enjoys considerable influence because it frequently holds information unavailable from other sources.

The large number of professionals working in the bureaucracy makes the information it provides both more credible and easier to control. The credibility of such information stems from its stamp of professional approval, especially from highly trusted professionals such as physicians and scientists (lawyers and economists, among others, are somewhat less revered). Its control is facilitated by its extremely technical nature or its cryptic jargon, making it unintelligible to the lay public. Bureaucratic professionals can then control the flow of information simply by deciding how much (or how little) of their work to explain to the public.

Natural scientists have enjoyed remarkable bureaucratic success because the sensational scientific achievements of the last few decades—from discovering a vaccine for polio to sending a man to the moon—seem all the more impressive to a public that does not understand how they were accomplished. Political scientist Francis E. Rourke has argued that agencies prosper most when they produce benefits that the public understands and appreciates through methods that it cannot fathom.[69] NASA and the National Science Foundation fit this description.

When the information supplied by a bureaucratic agency does fail to sway political leaders, who frequently have preexisting notions about a policy issue, bureaucrats can appear to be influential by supplying the decision makers with information and advice that matches his or her preconceptions. In fact, politicians ordinarily choose advisers with attitudes similar to their own. This dangerous practice can encourage narrow-mindedness, and presidents are well advised to seek information from as many different sources as possible. President Franklin D. Roosevelt, for example, went to great lengths to get many separate opinions. Whatever advice experts provide, the public usually accepts presidential policy decisions more readily when the policy is perceived to be based on the information and recommendation of experts.

Size and Complexity. The size and complexity of the federal bureaucracy increase its power and autonomy by making it difficult for the president, the Congress, and the courts to exert control over it. Nearly three million civilian bureaucratic employees work in hundreds of separate departments, agencies, offices, corporations, and commissions, and they spend billions of taxpayer dollars and produce hundreds of pages of rules and regulations each year. The federal bureaucracy pervades American society.

In addition to the sheer enormity of the bureaucracy, it is also very complicated. Its functions are highly complex, and its overall organization and overlapping jurisdictions can be perplexing, making it hard to determine which agency is responsible for particular matters. For example, the State Department, the Defense Department, and the National Security Council all participate in foreign policy decisions, as do other agencies, depending on the specific issue. When Jimmy Carter set out to create a separate Department of Education, he discovered that the responsibility for education was distributed throughout the bureaucracy; the Defense Department, for example, handled the education of military dependents stationed overseas.

Another characteristic complicating the bureaucracy is interdependence—the goals and actions of one agency affect other agencies. For example, attempts to reduce America's reliance on imported oil led to the encouragement of practices, such as increased burning of wood and coal, contrary to the environmental goals of fighting air and water pollution.

The dispersion of the bureaucracy also hampers outside control. While the political actors interested in managing the bureaucracy are concentrated in the Washington, D.C., area, bureaucratic agencies are scattered all over the country. Bureaucrats must go where their services are needed, and their presence around the country gives them some protection from outside intervention.

Inertia. Bureaucratic inertia is an internal source of power for the same reason that large size and complexity are power sources—inertia makes outside management of the bureaucracy extremely difficult. It is hard to spur bureaucracies to take new action and equally challenging to stop bureaucratic routines once they have begun. Rourke has expressed this phenomenon in what he calls the "celebrated law" of bureaucratic inertia: "Bureaucracies at rest tend to stay at rest, and bureaucracies in motion tend to stay in motion." [70] Inertia results from several bureaucratic characteristics, including reliance on traditional policies and methods, employees' desire for security, and the potential clash between new policies and the interests of individual bureaucrats and their agencies.

Bureaucratic inertia frustrates presidents, who have a limited time in office and generally want to act quickly and dramatically. Presidents seldom have the patience to wait for the changes they want through the exasperatingly slow and incremental bureaucratic process. The deliberate movement of the bureaucracy can sometimes benefit the president, however, by providing time to reconsider possibly rash decisions. For example, while the military bureaucracy slowly prepared to execute President Nixon's 1969 orders for an air strike against North Korea in retaliation for their destruction of an American plane, Nixon changed his mind.

Momentum—the tendency for bureaucratic agencies to continue established programs—also restricts presidential control. Agencies want to maintain their programs, even if they no longer are productive, to protect their employees and budget. In fact, much bureaucratic activity is mandated by law and cannot be easily changed by the president. For example, over 75 percent of President Reagan's proposed 1987 budget was composed of "uncontrollable" expenditures, including entitlement programs and contractual obligations, which the government was required to fund. The president has relatively little room for maneuvering with so much of the bureaucracy's time and resources already committed.

In contrast to the annoying effects that it has on presidents, bureaucratic inertia does not bother permanent civil servants; they can afford to be patient in the pursuit of their goals. Bureaucrats also benefit from the small but steady growth characteristic of bureaucratic momentum, which eventually will increase their agency's size significantly. Momentum can lead to bad public policy, however. Some scholars have argued that America's deep involvement in the Vietnam War resulted largely from the incremental steps taken by the bureaucratic agencies assigned to oversee America's efforts in Southeast Asia.

Leadership. Another determinate of a bureaucratic agency's power is the quality of its leadership. More than any other individual, an agency's leader affects that agency's power. Whether an appointee or a career civil servant, the leader must exercise a variety of political skills if the agency is to thrive. No one exemplifies the importance of an agency leader better than J. Edgar Hoover, who molded the Federal Bureau of Investigation (FBI) into a potent political force during his nearly fifty-year reign as FBI director.

Agency leaders have two sets of responsibilities: internal and external. Internal duties include building up internal sources of bureaucratic power such as expertise, control of information, and cohesion. Leaders must supervise as well the daily operations of the agency, including overseeing the management of programs and settling disputes. One of the most vital functions of a leader is to create and maintain enthusiasm and commitment to common goals among agency employees. One reason Anne Gorsuch Burford failed dismally as head of the Environmental Protection Agency early in the Reagan administration was her disastrous effect on employees' morale. EPA careerists became dispirited largely because they perceived Burford as hostile to the agency's mission—a perception based on her pro-business record on environmental issues and her voluntary acceptance of cuts in EPA's budget and personnel while she was head of the agency.

The primary external goal of agency leaders is to generate political support for their agencies, especially from the president and Congress. A leader's own reputation plays a crucial role in this effort. A leader who is widely respected and trusted finds the job of gaining support much easier than an unpopular chief. For example, David Stockman's reputation for expertise and candor as the head of the Office of Management and Budget helped that agency take a prominent place in the federal budgeting process.

Relations between agency leaders and the president become tricky when the president's policy desires clash with the best interests of the agency. Much to the dismay of the president, agency heads generally place their interests and those of their agencies first. Since the president can be a powerful ally (or foe), effective agency leaders try to emphasize how their agency is helping to fulfill presidential goals and work to minimize the frequency and severity of clashes with the president.

In dealing with Congress agency leaders must be sensitive to the electoral needs of its members. This entails avoiding actions that could embarrass legislators in their districts and providing quick assistance when they intercede in the bureaucracy on behalf of a constituent with a problem. Agency leaders gain influence over members of Congress by mobilizing political support for the agency in members' districts. This task calls for effective communication and public relations skills. Hoover's legendary success at the FBI was partly attributable to his genius at publicity and his ability to generate public support for his agency. Thus, few elected officials were willing to criticize him.

Much of a leader's external success also depends on the image he or she projects. While the nature of the particular agency has much to do with the leader's image—the director of the Peace Corps, for example, starts out with an inherently better public image than the commissioner of the Internal Revenue Service—the individual's personality and leadership skills make a difference.

Finally, agency leaders must carefully balance their internal and external functions. Sometimes the things done in one sphere can be detrimental in the other.

Cohesion. Cohesion is the commitment felt by bureaucrats to their agency and its goals. Employees who strongly believe in the mission of their agency will generally work harder at their jobs. This sense of cohesion with the agency not only means that employees will accept longer working hours when necessary, but also that they will apply greater dedication and imagination to their jobs. Harder working employees improve an agency's effectiveness, which in turn enhances the agency's political position and power.

Agencies promote this cohesion by carefully recruiting employees who have values or interests similar to those of the agency. Job applicants themselves assist this process; they tend to seek employment in agencies with values that appeal to them. For example, an ecology-minded applicant might well be attracted to the Environmental Protection Agency, while a job seeker interested in consumer rights might gravitate toward the Federal Trade Commission. Agencies also strive to increase their cohesion by conducting orientation programs for new employees as well as by informal socialization into the ways of the organization.

Cohesion comes more easily to some agencies than to others. Agencies that perform clearly identifiable, emotionally attractive functions such as EPA, FBI, the Marine Corps, and the Peace Corps have a natural advantage in cultivating cohesion. Other agencies are not so fortunate. As one scholar has wryly commented, possible slogans such as "the General Accounting Office is looking for a few good accountants" or "the few, the proud, the letter carriers" are less than inspirational.[71]

Popular Appeal. Finally, an agency's popular appeal is an internal source of power that affects its political clout as well as its recruitment of prospective employees. Such appeal helps agencies garner public support—which translates into political clout—and it allows them to develop cohesion.

The functions of some agencies make them inherently more appealing than others. NASA is an excellent example of an agency that traditionally has profited from popular appeal. The glamorous and exciting business of space exploration captures the attention and imagination of the public in a way that few other bureaucratic activities can. For years NASA received hefty budgets partly because of its popular support. The president and Congress, ever sensitive to the preferences of voters, provided those budgets more willingly because of the agency's popularity. NASA's case also illustrates, however, that appeal can be fleeting. The comparative lack of public interest in the space shuttle, NASA's major program during most of the 1970s and 1980s, coupled with the explosion of the *Challenger* in 1986 tarnished the space agency's appeal and weakened its political power.

External Sources

External sources of bureaucratic power are outside the agency itself but within the political arena in which the agency operates. Several of these sources of power also can act as limits to power, however. External sources of power include the president, other bureaucratic agencies, Congress, interest groups, public opinion, and legal protection.

The President. Although the president and the bureaucracy clash frequently, the president may on occasion actively support bureaucratic agencies and their goals. Presidential support is one of the most valuable sources of bureaucratic power. Agencies and individuals blessed with presidential favor enjoy a distinct advantage over those without such status. The Central Intelligence Agency (CIA), having been on both sides of that fence, can attest to the importance of presidential support. In 1961 the CIA lost a great deal of standing and political power when, because of its part in the Bay of Pigs fiasco, it lost the support of President John F. Kennedy.

Presidential support of an agency comes in two forms: diffuse and specific. A president provides diffuse support by approving and backing the general functions and goals of an agency. For example, through his vigorous promotion of the "War on Poverty" Lyndon Johnson gave strong diffuse support to the agencies that helped the needy. And Ronald Reagan's ardent commitment to building up America's national defense lent crucial diffuse support to the Department of Defense.

Presidential advocacy of an agency's particular proposal or program is specific support. While this kind of support is less common than diffuse support, it tends to be quite potent. In a study of eight agencies analyst Stephen A. Shull found that when presidents specifically endorsed an agency's proposal, those proposals received legislative approval and were enacted successfully 76 percent of the time.[72]

Presidential advocacy of an agency's particular proposal or program is specific support. While this kind of support is less common than diffuse support, it tends to be quite potent. In a study of eight agencies analyst Stephen A. Shull found that when presidents specifically endorsed an agency's proposal, those proposals received legislative approval and were enacted 76 percent of the time.[72]

Agencies such as the State Department that work closely with the president and the White House staff have the best chance of gaining presidential support, either diffuse or specific, simply because of regular contact. By giving special emphasis to programs that forward the president's policy objectives or by administering programs in ways favored by the president, other agencies can try, however, to win presidential support. For example, several agencies tried to gain favor with President Carter by stressing managerial efficiency, one of Carter's goals. Agencies seeking presidential support also try to avoid public conflict with the president.

Other Bureaucratic Agencies. Agencies with common interests and goals often find it mutually advantageous to join forces in pursuing their shared objectives—the larger and more influential the coalition, the greater the chance for political success. For example, several agencies, among them the Department of the Interior, the Department of Agriculture, and the Department of Defense, joined NASA in pushing for approval and support of the space shuttle program because they all wanted the regular and inexpensive means of putting satellites into orbit that the program promised.

Some agencies make stronger allies than others. For agencies located within a larger department, it is always useful to have the backing of agencies higher up the departmental chain of command. This is especially true in departments where authority is centralized in the upper echelons of management. One agency that can be a powerful ally for any other is the Office of Management and Budget (OMB), which has considerable influence. OMB constructs the president's annual budget request and holds hearings to determine budget levels for federal agencies. Because Congress rarely appropriates funds in excess of OMB's recommendations, OMB plays a large part in deciding how much money an agency gets every year. Also, all agency requests for additional authority that require congressional approval must be cleared first by OMB.

Other agencies can be quite helpful as well. Agencies with strong ties to either the president, such as the Treasury and Justice departments, or to Congress, such as the Department of Veterans Affairs and the Army Corps of Engineers, make especially good allies. Agencies that provide services to other bureaucratic agencies also can be useful friends. The Office of Personnel Management, for example, oversees the federal merit employment system and thus can affect an agency's recruitment and retention of employees. The General Services Administration, which supervises government buildings and grounds, also provides services essential to the comfort and efficiency of agencies.

Despite the possible benefits of interagency alliances, agencies tend to enter them cautiously, since each organization generally views others as potential rivals. Ironically, agencies that share the most interests are also the ones most likely to fight over jurisdictions and money. Thus, alliances are usually of brief duration. For example, the army, navy, and air force all profit from higher defense spending and work together to help support such spending, but among themselves they maintain an intense and long-standing rivalry.

Congress. Congress is an important external source of bureaucratic power because it controls two of an agency's most vital resources: authority and money. By passing the laws that create, reorganize, or destroy agencies, and stipulate what their functions and authority will be, Congress has the power to shape the bureaucracy at the most basic level. Congressional command over the budget also exerts tremendous influence. While all agencies must have some congressional support, those without much backing from other external sources are particularly dependent on it.

Agencies want not only overall support from Congress as a whole, but also the assistance of individual members of Congress. A member of Congress is one of the best friends an agency can have because legislators more readily accept advice from colleagues than from outsiders. Agencies are especially fortunate when some members of Congress also belong to their organization. For example, the armed services usually have a few lawmakers in their reserve units. These reservists are therefore especially sensitive to the needs of their respective services. Agencies that exert a great deal of influence in particular legislative districts often succeed in gaining the support of the congressional representatives of those districts. The Department of Agriculture, for example, can rely on help from rural legislators.

The congressional committee structure makes some members more important to agencies than others. Because much of the work of Congress is handled by committees and subcommittees that have jurisdiction over certain policy areas, bureaucrats most need the support of members who serve on the committees that oversee their agency. For the most part, committee members enthusiastically support the agencies under their jurisdiction. Exceptions to this rule are the appropriations committees, which are concerned primarily with controlling spending and are therefore more skeptical of agency requests.

Agencies ordinarily receive support from congressional committees fairly easily because, among other reasons, members are assigned to committees on the basis of their backgrounds and the nature of their constituencies. For example, a member of Congress who worked as a banker before entering politics might be appointed to the banking committee, while a member representing a district with areas of great natural beauty or particular natural resources might serve on a committee dealing with the environment. In either case the member probably will be predisposed toward favoring the proposals of agencies working in those areas of interest to the member.

Agencies ensure good relations with Congress by responding quickly to requests made by legislators for information or for help on any problems that legislators' constituents may have with the agency. Agencies also emphasize programs known to interest particular legislators. They may even try to anticipate the political needs and policy preferences of members of Congress and then act accordingly. In general, agencies try to do whatever they can to maintain and increase their congressional support.

Interest Groups. An agency also may receive political support from private interest groups concerned with issues falling within the agency's mandate. For example, the Environmental Protection Agency may receive support from the National Wildlife Federation, the Sierra Club, and manufacturers of pollution-control equipment.

Because bureaucratic agencies and interest groups each command power and resources valuable to the other, their relationship revolves around mutually beneficial trade-offs. On the one hand, an agency's biggest strength is its control over government programs that affect the goals of interest groups. On the other hand, interest groups direct political resources that agencies need to build and keep power. Thus, a general pattern of cooperation is formed: the agency, by listening to the interest group's opinions and providing it with access to the agency's decision makers, allows the interest group to participate in the government's decision-making process, and in return the interest group gives the agency political support. Specific deals usually are not made; instead, the process is one of long-term, implicit bargaining. The connection between the Nuclear Regulatory Commission (NRC) and nuclear plant operators exemplifies this kind of relationship between agencies and interest groups. The NRC and the plant operators maintain a stable, mutually beneficial relationship. The NRC consults the operators on regulation of the nuclear plants, particularly on an issue of vital concern to plant operators: when plants must be shut down. In return for this access to the agency's decision-making process, operators provide the NRC with valuable political support.

Interest groups provide agencies with numerous political services. They include acting as political cheerleaders, heralding the agency's accomplishments and defending it against attackers; providing the agency with both technical data and news of the political situation; and pressuring other political actors, including the president and Congress, to support the agency.

Some interest groups pack more political punch than others. Groups whose members are more dispersed geographically, and thus hail from more congressional districts, enjoy more clout than those whose members are concentrated in a single area. Groups with highly cohesive memberships dedicated to the group's goals and willing to work to achieve them also are at an advantage. Prestige counts as well. Groups whose members are generally respected, such as doctors or scientists, fare better than others. Finally, groups that are organized efficiently and understand how the political system works also tend to succeed more easily.

The National Education Association (NEA), which represents teachers nationwide, is an example of a powerful interest group. Well organized, from the national entity to the many state and local affiliates, with a great deal of political savvy and with a committed membership, the NEA was in the forefront of the successful political battles to establish a separate Department of Education in 1979 and to block President Reagan's attempt to abolish that department a few years later.

Public Opinion. Public opinion constitutes the greatest external bureaucratic power because it underlies virtually all sources of political power in a democratic society. Politicians and the government respond when the American general public evinces an opinion strongly enough. A bureaucratic agency that enjoys strong public support can take primary control of its actions, at least as long as the support lasts. Unfortunately for the agencies, however, the public rarely becomes enthused about bureaucratic issues.

The vast majority of Americans are too busy leading their own lives and worrying about their own problems to be concerned about the bureaucracy. Even when news of a bureaucratic activity reaches citizens, many people do not understand it. For example, one survey of the public found that only 30 percent claimed to understand the functions of the Securities and Exchange Commission.[73] (It did not say, however, how many actually did.) Other agencies were more familiar, but the point is clear.

Even the lesser-known agencies occasionally receive temporary bursts of publicity and public attention. The Nuclear Regulatory Commission, for example, was fairly obscure to the general public until the 1979 nuclear accident at Three Mile Island in Pennsylvania focused attention on the agency. Similarly, as the problem of illegal drugs has climbed higher on the national agenda, the Drug Enforcement Administration has achieved greater public recognition. These episodes of public attention can be quite brief, however, and most recognized agencies sink back into relative obscurity after the crisis that precipitated the publicity has passed.

When the public has no definite opinion about a specific agency, its attitude toward the agency's overall mandate becomes especially important. For example, during the peak of the environmental movement the budget of the Environmental Protection Agency grew dramatically. Likewise, during the late 1970s and early 1980s growing public approval of defense spending led to significantly larger military budgets. Because the public tends to support certain bureaucratic functions over others, agencies performing the favored functions are more likely to generate public support. Opinion polls indicate that the public backs spending on education, health, crime control, treatment for drug addiction, environmental protection, and social security much more strongly than spending on foreign aid, space exploration, and welfare.[74]

Agencies may try to mobilize public opinion on their own behalf by tying the agency and its programs to the kinds of government activities that the public usually supports; capturing the public interest through a pattern of dramatic action, as the FBI has succeeded in doing; or by using the media to spread their message. Whatever an agency's efforts, however, often the only members of the public paying close attention to it are those directly affected by its actions. Even agencies that manage to win public support should not rely on it too heavily as it is apt to change; the recent decline in support for space exploration and NASA illustrates this phenomenon.

Legal Protection. An agency's legal position, the final source of bureaucratic power, usually protects it from many kinds of political attacks. Laws passed by Congress establishing an agency's functions, authority, and place within the government cannot be changed without additional congressional action. The president and other political elites may try to control the bureaucracy through a variety of methods, but they must act within these legal constraints.

Some agencies have more secure legal positions than others. For example, the president can exert greater influence over agencies within the Executive Office of the President than over most independent agencies. To prevent sudden and potentially disruptive shifts in policy, independent agencies that regulate parts of the economy—such as the Federal Reserve Board and the Securities and Exchange Commission—are granted substantial legal protection.

The bureaucracy's various merit employment systems provide a great deal of legal protection. *(See "Federal Personnel System," p. 1213, in this chapter.)* In addition to its other functions, the merit system is designed to give bureaucrats job security. Employees under one of the federal merit systems—over 90 percent of all civilian employees—are protected from being fired for solely partisan political reasons. The days of the spoils system are over, and

UPI/Bettmann Newsphotos

FBI director J. Edgar Hoover sometimes abused his authority. Through illegal wiretaps Hoover gathered embarrassing information on members of Congress and other political leaders, including civil rights leader Martin Luther King, Jr.

the result is a more professional, independent bureaucracy.

Under J. Edgar Hoover, the FBI made effective use of legal protection as a source of bureaucratic power. Although the FBI is part of the Justice Department, Hoover ensured that the statutes governing his agency allowed it considerable autonomy within the department. He also ensured that the laws setting out the FBI's functions gave it tasks that would make the agency look good, such as recovering stolen cars and catching bank robbers, but not messier jobs such as drug enforcement. These and other laws governing the FBI, including the one that enabled the agency to establish its own personnel system, have given the agency tremendous legal protection and therefore have made it more powerful.

Limits to Bureaucratic Power

Just as bureaucratic agencies draw power from many diverse internal and external sources, they also must act within the limits imposed by numerous internal and external political forces. Several sources of bureaucratic power can act as limits to that power as well.

Internal Limits

In a sense the most basic internal constraint facing agencies springs from their internal dynamics, which shapes bureaucratic goals and behavior. Agencies are unlikely to take steps that clash with firmly held agency goals, even if those steps could increase the agency's power. For example, the Environmental Protection Agency probably would gain the political support of wealthy, powerful developers and industrialists if the agency issued regulations making it much easier for their businesses to reap profits at the expense of the environment. Most likely this would not happen, however, since such regulations would contradict the EPA's mission of protecting the environment.

The power of the bureaucracy is limited as well by the personal ethics of bureaucrats. When an agency's goals are objectionable to some of its own employees, they may try to defeat it, or at least they will not support it. Although bureaucrats develop their personal code of ethics in much the same way that nonbureaucrats do, bureaucrats are exposed to additional standards specifically applicable to government employees. The American Society for Public Administration has formally adopted a list of such standards, including admonitions for bureaucrats to be honest, respectful, responsive, and fair.[75]

As limits to bureaucratic power, ethics have advantages and disadvantages. On the positive side, once bureaucrats have accepted ethics, they are in effect constantly; no outsider must be there to apply them. Moreover, bureaucrats may be less likely to evade ethical restraints, since the punishment for doing so comes from their own conscience.

One drawback to relying on ethics is that in many situations the ethical choice is unclear. For example, in weighing an effort to help stop the spread of acquired immune deficiency syndrome (AIDS), which is the more ethical decision: allowing the government or private organizations to provide intravenous drug users with clean needles, or prohibiting such action on the grounds that it might increase drug addiction? Another difficulty is that many ethical concepts themselves are ambiguous; determination of the "fair" thing to do is not always easy. Finally, every individual's code of ethics will differ according to his or her background and training.

For years the American federal bureaucracy has deliberately tried to hire employees who represent a cross section of the country's population. Such a practice ensures not only equal opportunity for government employment, but also nondiscriminatory bureaucratic procedures and policy decisions. The idea is that representatives of any affected groups working in the bureaucracy would recognize discrimination and see that it is eliminated.

External Limits

Restraints on agency power also originate from sources outside the agency itself, including the president, other bureaucratic agencies, Congress, the courts, interest groups, public opinion, and the media.

The President. As the nominal head of the bureaucracy the president needs control over the bureaucracy not only to fulfill the constitutional obligations, but also to exercise "executive power" and to see that the laws are faithfully executed, to help pursue presidential policy objectives. Conflict between the president and the bureaucracy is almost guaranteed because the bureaucracy tends to place its own goals above those of the president. *(See "President's View of the Bureaucracy," p. 1225, in this chapter.)*

Other Bureaucratic Agencies. Bureaucratic agencies work in close proximity to one another, and because their organizational interests differ, they come into conflict and thus limit each other's power. The causes and effects of these conflicts depend upon the agencies involved.

Just as the Office of Management and Budget, the Office of Personnel Management, and other agencies with authority over the bureaucracy can be valuable allies, they also can be formidable enemies. Without the support or at least the neutrality of such offices, the power of other bureaucratic agencies is severely limited. It is, however, a two-way street. If an agency's primary function is to deal with other parts of the bureaucracy, it needs the support of other agencies because it has no clientele outside the bureaucracy. The General Services Administration (GSA), for example, would be in a perilous situation if it antagonized the agencies it serves, since interest groups do not have much incentive to work on the GSA's behalf.

Agencies clash because they are pursuing goals that are either fundamentally opposite or basically the same.[76] The cause of conflict in the first case is obvious; to the extent that one of the agencies succeeds, the other fails. For example, the Department of Agriculture, concerned mainly with the interests of farmers, has differed with the State Department over the issue of grain embargoes. The State Department considers such embargoes useful tools of foreign policy, while the Department of Agriculture sees them as threats to farmers' prosperity.

Agencies working toward the same goals often clash because they feel threatened by one another. Like some animals, bureaucratic agencies stake out their own territory and become defensive when rivals try to invade. For bureaus, their territory is their jurisdiction over certain policy areas; thus, other agencies working in the same areas frequently are perceived as invaders. This fear is not merely paranoia; one law of bureaucratic behavior is that agencies try to expand their jurisdictions, which leads to greater political power.[77] A classic territorial battle is that between the State Department and the president's National Security Council staff over foreign policy making. This kind of competition can limit the power of agencies in two ways: first, by the potential loss of territory to a rival agency; and second, by the necessity to invest precious time and resources in the struggle against other agencies.

Congress. Congress has the power to exert more influence over the bureaucracy than any other external group or institution.[78] Although Congress by no means dominates the bureaucracy, it can guide the bureaucracy in a variety of ways using its legal authority. In practice, however, Congress seldom chooses to use its powers to control the bureaucracy.

The two congressional powers over the bureaucracy—legislation and budgeting—can be potent means of control. By passing legislation, Congress can change or restrict the authority of agencies, or it can take the even more drastic and rarer step of abolishing agencies altogether. Legislation is used frequently and effectively to shape administrative policy. If an agency upsets Congress, it might find its funding cut, or at least its funding threatened. Under such circumstances bureaucrats usually are much more agreeable to the wishes of Congress.

Another method of congressional control is the legislative veto. Until 1983, when the Supreme Court declared some of its uses unconstitutional, the legislative veto allowed one or both houses of Congress to "veto" bureaucratic decisions. Congress passed laws giving agencies the power to take certain actions—enabling the Department of Defense to close military bases, for example—but with the provision that Congress could overturn any decisions it found objectionable.

Congress also influences the bureaucracy through its oversight authority, which entails gathering information on bureaucratic activity. Congress collects this information by holding committee or subcommittee public hearings, conducting staff investigations, and commissioning audits by the General Accounting Office. Oversight can be the first step in the legislative or budgeting process, or it can be an end in itself.[79] Public hearings are an especially effective vehicle for members of Congress to make their views known. The 1987 hearings into the Iran-contra affair, in which Congress delved into the actions of the National Security Council and other agencies, were a vivid example of congressional oversight.

Bureaucratic power is limited as well by congressional influence over who receives top federal jobs. According to the Constitution the president must obtain "the advice and consent" of the Senate in making upper-level appointments to the executive branch, and senators are not shy about giving such advice. Even House members feel free to comment on the president's choices despite their lack of formal authority. Although the Senate consents to the vast majority of presidential nominations, an occasional one is rejected, thereby ensuring continued congressional influence over the leadership of the bureaucracy.

Finally, Congress influences the bureaucracy through its informal contacts with bureaucrats and their agencies, usually in response to a constituent's request for help in dealing with a federal agency. One estimate has placed the total number of such constituent requests at 200,000 annually.[80] Legislators also talk informally to bureaucrats about policy matters. The cumulative effects of these contacts on agencies can be substantial; repeated contacts from Congress may indicate to agencies that some changes are needed.

The Courts. Citizens unhappy with bureaucratic decisions can challenge them in court. If the court has jurisdiction over the matter and sees fit to do so, it can overrule a federal agency action. The judicial system has become immersed in a wide array of administrative issues affecting groups of people, including the drawing of school district boundaries, the running of prison systems, and the oversight of agency employment practices. In addition, the courts hear complaints from individuals dissatisfied with agency decisions as they affect those individuals personally (people denied benefits from government programs, for example).

Judicial involvement in administrative matters has increased as the amount and scope of bureaucratic activity have grown. Since the end of World War II, the federal bureaucracy has expanded in numerous areas, including regulatory activity and the administration of federal government benefit programs. More bureaucratic activity in those areas inevitably has meant more people unhappy with agency decisions, which in turn has resulted in more litigation and thus more opportunities for the courts to intervene in the bureaucracy.

The courts generally review administrative action according to two basic standards: procedural and statutory.[81] The procedural standard is applied when determining whether agencies followed the proper procedures in reaching the decision in question. Agencies must have complied with their own organizational procedures, any procedures mandated by Congress, and the general procedures of due process of law. Thus, agencies are not allowed to ignore the rules even if those rules become inconvenient. Agencies also are required to obey the laws, or statutes, that are on the books. This includes staying within the bounds of legislative intent; taking action beyond what Congress intended is prohibited. The courts are mainly interested in whether these two standards were met, not in the effectiveness or fairness of the agency's policy.

Going to court is an effective strategy for some people dissatisfied with bureaucratic decisions, including environmentalists, who have succeeded in delaying hundreds of construction projects they opposed by filing lawsuits. This is often not a feasible alternative, however. Litigation is slow, risky, and extremely expensive. Even if a citizen wins the case, there is no guarantee that the agency will provide the desired response; it just may start its decision-making process over again.

Interest Groups. Interest groups may be dangerous enemies of agencies for many of the same reasons that make them valuable friends. The political resources that groups mobilize to help agencies they like also can be used against agencies they do not like. Unfortunately for federal agencies, it is nearly impossible to take any action without upsetting some interest groups.

Ironically, often the groups most infuriated by agency decisions are those that normally support the bureau. This is especially likely when the same segment of society is represented by two or more interest groups. Because these groups frequently disagree on issues, the agency has a dilemma; whatever it decides, some proportion of its supporters will be unhappy. For example, American farmers are represented by the National Farmers' Union (NFU) and the American Farm Bureau Federation (AFBF), which traditionally have differed on the issue of government subsidies for agriculture. Thus, the secretary of agriculture is in a no-win situation. By advocating high subsidies, the secretary pleases the NFU but not the AFBF, whereas by promoting lower subsidies, the reverse is true.[82]

Some agencies and interest groups are natural enemies because their goals are incompatible. For example, groups representing developers of natural resources often are frustrated by the Environmental Protection Agency, and businesses frequently bristle at safety regulations imposed by the Occupational Safety and Health Administration. Agencies in this kind of situation must strive not to alienate their friends, since they already have permanent opponents.

Similar inherent enmity is widespread between different interest groups. The National Rifle Association and Handgun Control, Inc., for example, are archenemies. When an agency must act on an issue contested by rival groups, it is guaranteed to draw the ire of one group. The Federal Aviation Administration (FAA), for example, prohibited smoking on short domestic plane flights, leaving antismoking groups overjoyed and representatives of smokers wrathful.

Public Opinion. Public opinion is another political force that can be both a source of and a limit to bureaucratic power. Although the general public seldom pays close attention to the bureaucracy, Americans nevertheless tend to have great expectations about its performance. The bureaucracy is expected to execute its functions effectively and creatively, to be loyal and responsive to citizens, and to be honest and fair.[83] When a bureaucrat or an agency fails to live up to these general expectations or takes an unpopular policy action, negative public reaction can result in political punishment for the offender.

The sporadic episodes of intense public attention that agencies often receive when current events (together with media coverage) highlight their existence and functions—as when plane crashes spotlight the FAA—can be a threat to agencies as well as an opportunity to generate public support.[84] In many cases the agency is making the news because of some dramatic failure or oversight on its part, which often results in calls for changes in the agency—usually an unwelcome prospect for the bureau in question. For example, the Food and Drug Administration captured national attention in the 1960s when use of the drug thalidomide by pregnant women resulted in many babies born with birth defects. Similarly, interest in the Nuclear Regulatory Commission mushroomed in 1979 in the wake of the accident at the Three Mile Island nuclear plant. At other times the cause of attention is less sensational. For example, each time the U.S. Postal Service announces increased postage rates, it is accused of gross inefficiency and its privatization is suggested.

When the public becomes incensed enough about the bureaucracy to want change, it can pressure its elected officials, especially the president and members of Congress, to exert some control over the bureaucracy and make the changes, or it can vote for candidates who promise to take the desired actions. In his campaign for president, Ronald Reagan pledged to scale back the size and power of the bureaucracy, and at least in some areas he fulfilled that promise after entering office.

The public also influences the bureaucracy through informal contacts—personal conversations, phone calls, and letters. Agencies, ever concerned about public support, will likely give serious attention to matters raised frequently through these means. In addition, agencies stay abreast of public opinion by monitoring newspaper editorials and opinion polls. Citizens can make their views known more formally during public hearings that agencies occasionally conduct on controversial issues. Finally, a few agencies regularly consult members of the public throughout the process of policy design and implementation.

The Media. Another limit to bureaucratic power, the news media, is related to public opinion—and helps shape it.[85] Television, radio, newspapers, and magazines play a crucial role in informing the public about the bureaucracy. The media are a blessing for agencies looking for a conduit to provide information or to sell an image to the public, but they also can create problems by reporting agency failures or exposing bureaucratic secrets. The *National Journal* and the *Washington Monthly* devote much attention to the activities of the federal bureaucracy.

Traditionally, American reporters have enjoyed ferreting out juicy government scandals, since the lionization of the two *Washington Post* reporters, Bob Woodward and Carl Bernstein, who were largely responsible for uncovering the Watergate scandal. This tradition has produced investigative reporters hungry for a scoop and skeptical of the official government line.

Reporters' constant need for news can leave them vulnerable to manipulation by the agencies, however. Agencies often feed reporters information designed primarily to make the agency look good. Other inducements used by agencies to capture reporters include special access to sources and advance notice of stories. Although relatively few reporters are captured by agencies, those who are become little more than tools for spreading the agency point of view.

Many parts of the bureaucracy are covered closely by specialized trade journals, which concentrate on a particular agency or group of agencies working in the same field. For example, *Broadcasting Magazine* intensely covers the Federal Communications Commission. While these kinds of publications effectively reach citizens vitally interested in a particular area of policy, the general public usually responds only when the mass media, such as the weekly news magazines or the nightly network newscasts, report on an issue.

President's View of the Bureaucracy

Traditionally, presidents have viewed the federal bureaucracy as one of their biggest political headaches. Rather than a system of compliant agencies faithfully executing the president's will, the bureaucracy is more often—especially from the perspective of the Oval Office—the source of many difficult problems. Presidents may feel a variety of emotions toward the bureaucracy—frustration, anger, disappointment, disdain, boredom, distrust, or despair—but rarely complete satisfaction.

Franklin D. Roosevelt is an excellent example of a president who, unlike most presidents, enjoyed his involvement with the bureaucracy. This is illustrated in a tongue-in-cheek memo written by FDR in response to a minor bureaucratic jurisdictional dispute:

> I agree with the Secretary of the Interior. Please have it carried out so that fur-bearing animals remain in the Department of the Interior.
>
> You might find out if any Alaska bears are still supervised by (a) War Department (b) Department of Agriculture (c) Department of Commerce. They have all had jurisdiction over Alaska bears in the past and many embarrassing situations have been created by the mating of a bear belonging to one Department with a bear belonging to another Department.
>
> F.D.R.
>
> P.S. I don't think the Navy is involved but it may be. Check the Coast Guard. You never can tell![86]

In contrast to FDR, Richard Nixon profoundly distrusted the bureaucracy and had an almost paranoid fear that many bureaucrats were out to get him:

> When a bureaucrat deliberately thumbs his nose, we're going to get him. . . . The little boys over in State particularly, that are against us, will do it: Defense, HEW—those three areas particularly. . . . Now, goddamnit, those are the bad guys—the guys down in the woodwork.[87]

Jimmy Carter expressed his anger toward several bureaucrats who displeased him by telling them, "You are the cause of the problem."[88]

Ronald Reagan's diatribes against the bureaucracy were seemingly endless. Much of his first successful campaign for the White House revolved around his promises to tame the wild bureaucracy and to get the federal government off the backs of the people. As president, such comments continued. Early in his administration Reagan appointees in the Department of Agriculture made the surprising announcement that ketchup was an acceptable substitute for a vegetable in school lunches. In responding to the ensuing criticism, Reagan explained that "somebody got overambitious in the bureaucracy."[89] Reagan made an even more remarkable statement during his 1988 summit conference with Soviet leader Mikhail Gorbachev in Moscow. Reagan exempted Gorbachev and the communist system from any blame for Soviet violations of human rights by saying, incredibly, "I'm blaming [the Soviet] bureaucracy."[90] For Reagan, bureaucracy was apparently responsible not only for creating problems at home, but also for putting the evil into the "evil empire."

Conflicting Goals

Bureaucratic goals frequently conflict with presidential goals. Bureaucrats and presidents play vastly different roles in the political system. Most bureaucratic agencies serve a relatively small segment of the population; the president is responsible to the entire nation. The bureaucracy's main job, at least in theory, is to implement the directions of the president and Congress. While bureaucrats keep their jobs for years, the president, who has only a relatively short time in office, is expected to formulate policy on a large scale and tackle the problems and crises of the day. The president thus wants quick, dramatic government action, the kind hated by bureaucrats. Overall, the starkly different roles and interests of the bureaucracy and the president inevitably lead to conflict.

When the goals of the president and the bureaucracy clash, the bureaucracy often resists the president's plan. This resistance usually is not declared explicitly and often takes the form of passive opposition, but it is real nonetheless. Even presidents who believe that their election to office was a clear mandate from the people cannot escape bureaucratic resistance to change. Arthur M. Schlesinger, Jr., an aide to President Kennedy, wrote: "Getting the bureaucracy to accept new ideas is like carrying a double mattress up a very narrow and winding stairway. It is a terrible job, and you exhaust yourself when you try it. But once you get the mattress up it is awfully hard for anyone else to get it down."[91]

Resistance from the bureaucracy makes the jobs of the president and the White House staff that much harder. Presidents expend a great deal of time and effort developing policy even before it reaches bureaucratic hands: problems must be identified and evaluated, possible solutions weighed, decisions made, political support built, and members of Congress convinced. Then the bureaucracy must be faced. As another Kennedy assistant has said, "Everybody believes in democracy until he gets to the White House and then you begin to believe in dictatorship, because it's so hard to get things done. Every time you turn around, people resist you and even resist their own job."[92]

When President Reagan encountered bureaucratic resistance to the deep budget cuts he proposed early in his term, he responded by saying, perhaps with some justification, that the resisters were "more worried about losing their position than . . about the people they represent."[93] Resistance is not always based on selfish motives, however. During the Nixon administration, the FBI, the CIA, and the Internal Revenue Service all opposed the president's attempts to use their power illegally against his political enemies. Other cases of resistance have been more mundane. In 1977, for example, Jimmy Carter instructed seventy-five federal agencies to draft regulations discouraging federally insured construction projects in low-lying areas where flooding was possible. Two years later only fifteen of those agencies had acted on Carter's order.[94]

Presidential Incentives and the Bureaucracy

The overriding goal of most first-term presidents is reelection, while second-term presidents want to leave their mark on history.[95] Neither objective is easily achieved through close supervision and leadership of the bureaucracy—an activity that fails to inspire the masses. Instead, presidents concentrate on proposing and passing bold new programs, which, regardless of their effectiveness, attract the public's attention and admiration. Presidents have little incentive to worry about how well programs are implemented—the bureaucracy's job—because the public generally does not hold the president accountable for the actual functioning of programs, nor does it give the president credit when those programs run well.

Presidents also tend to concentrate on the broad issues of foreign affairs because in this area they enjoy greater freedom of action from the constraints posed by Congress and the bureaucracy. Moreover, crises that demand immediate presidential attention arise more frequently in foreign affairs than in the domestic realm, and this kind of dramatic action best suits presidential incentives.

Supervision of the bureaucracy is therefore usually low on the president's list of priorities, well below taking valiant action, developing new policies, conducting foreign affairs, and performing the symbolic (but politically valuable) duties of head of state. Even though it is the president's constitutional duty to see that the laws are faithfully executed, lack of presidential attention to administrative detail commonly means that orders are not obeyed and programs do not operate as intended, leading to big problems. David Gergen, an aide to President Reagan, has remarked: "It's unfortunately true that the management of the bureaucracy becomes one of the lowest priorities of almost every administration that comes to this city. Every administration pays a heavy price before it's over." [96]

Presidents do want to control the bureaucracy on certain occasions, however.[97] When they have a particular interest in a program, they want to ensure that the bureaucracy handles it properly. For example, because Richard Nixon was vitally concerned with the issue of busing students for purposes of racial desegregation, he prescribed specific guidelines for the Departments of Justice and Health, Education and Welfare to follow, and he carefully monitored their performance. Presidents also watch the bureaucracy when they want to control government expenditures. Numerous presidents have embarked on budget-cutting plans that started with the bureaucracy.

Partisan politics plays a role as well in how much attention the president gives the bureaucracy. The thousands of presidential appointees to jobs in federal agencies stand a better chance of success when they enter an environment receptive to the president's views. Moreover, appointees welcomed by their prospective agencies ordinarily receive Senate approval more easily. Presidents with some influence over the bureaucracy can act to improve that bureaucratic reception.

Difficulty of Presidential Control

Harry S Truman described with characteristic bluntness his efforts to control the bureaucracy: "I thought I was the president, but when it comes to these bureaucracies I can't make 'em do a damn thing." [98] His successor in the White House did not learn that harsh lesson so well. Six years into Dwight Eisenhower's term, one of his aides said, "The President still feels that when he's decided something, that ought to be the end of it ... and when it bounces back undone or done wrong, he tends to react with shocked surprise." [99] By now the lesson should be clear: all presidents must battle the bureaucratic dragon.

According to a much-quoted maxim, first proposed by an assistant to Franklin Roosevelt, to get anything done, a president must ask for it three times. Bureaucrats feel that only one request from the president means that the matter can be safely ignored. Upon the second request, the president can be told that the matter is being investigated. The third time the president asks, the deed should be done, but presidents rarely ask for anything three times.[100] John Kennedy discovered this maxim's validity when he tried to have a sign that gave directions to the CIA's Langley, Virginia, headquarters taken down. After issuing two directives through proper channels that yielded no results, Kennedy finally telephoned the person in charge of signs in the area and ordered the offending marker removed. "I now understand," he declared, "that for a president to get something done in this country, he's got to say it three times." [101]

Unfortunately, not all cases of bureaucratic resistance are so harmless as the sign that annoyed Kennedy. Soon after entering office Kennedy twice ordered the State Department to remove some obsolete American missiles that were installed in Turkey. The State Department encountered some opposition to the idea from the Turks, and so it simply failed to execute the order, hoping that Kennedy would not press the issue—and he did not. Kennedy was furious and dismayed when he learned, during the October 1962 Cuban missile crisis, that the missiles had not been dismantled. If the United States had bombed the Soviet missiles in Cuba, the American missiles in Turkey would have provided the Soviet Union with a legitimate target for a retaliatory strike—a potential step up the escalatory ladder toward all-out nuclear war.[102] Here, bureaucratic resistance made an already perilous situation even more dangerous.

Another case of potentially deadly bureaucratic obstruction occurred under Richard Nixon. In 1970 Nixon ordered the CIA to destroy its supply of biological weapons. The directive moved down the CIA chain of command to reach the appropriate midlevel official, who disobeyed it. Five years later the illegal toxins were discovered during a routine inventory.

Like Kennedy's hard-fought victory over the sign to the CIA, Nixon also relished a minor win over the bureaucracy. He struggled for over a year to have two old government buildings near the White House demolished. After the structures were eventually destroyed, Nixon summoned his aides and told them with pride and relief, "We have finally gotten something done." [103] But apparently that was small comfort for Nixon. According to his close aide H. R. Haldeman, by his third year in office Nixon "realized that he was virtually powerless to deal with the bureaucracy in every department of government. It was no contest." [104]

Is the situation really as bad for the president as these anecdotes and quotes suggest? Probably not. Even though management of the bureaucracy is no easy task, presidents can improve their performance. One lesson is apparent: the need for followup on presidential orders and programs. Had Kennedy or his personal staff checked on compliance with his instructions to remove the missiles from Turkey and had Nixon followed up on his directive to destroy the CIA weapons, their orders may have been fulfilled satisfactorily.

Presidential Power Over the Bureaucracy

Although presidents find it difficult to exert some control over the bureaucracy, they are far from powerless in their relationship with this sector of the federal government.

Sources of Presidential Power

The Constitution and subsequent statutes grant presidents many powers over federal agencies. While these powers are legally available to all presidents, they cannot be used successfully in every situation; political and personal considerations constrain presidential actions.

Leadership Skills

Presidents need leadership skills because even the most potent power loses effectiveness if used improperly. Political scientists Erwin C. Hargrove and Michael Nelson have identified four skills central to presidential leadership: strategic sense, communication skills, tactical skills, and management of authority.[105] Each of these skills can help the president battle the bureaucracy. The historical circumstances and the president's own talents and preferences influence which type of skill is relied upon most.

A good strategy sense enables the president to understand what kind of general political action the American people want at any particular time, and communication skills help the president capture and hold the public's attention. Franklin Roosevelt's famous "fireside chats" on the radio, in which he allayed the public's fear of the depression and instilled hope for the future, exemplify effective presidential communication. Tactical skills such as timing and persuasion are used in making and carrying out political choices designed to help fulfill goals. Persuasion is one of the most important presidential tactics. In fact, prominent scholar Richard E. Neustadt has argued that "presidential power is the power to persuade."[106] Neustadt supported his assertion with a quote from Harry Truman: "I sit here all day trying to persuade people to do the things they ought to have sense enough to do without my persuading them.... That's all the powers of the president amount to."[107]

Yet another presidential leadership skill—and the one most directly relevant to leadership of the bureaucracy—is the management of authority, which includes supervising the president's staff and organizing the overall government.[108] Presidents need respect, loyalty, honesty, and candor from their personal staffs. Without these attributes, the staff will be of little help to the president. Presidents also need the assistance of the rest of the government—especially the bureaucracy—and such help will most likely be forthcoming if the government is organized efficiently and managed wisely. John F. Kennedy engendered tremendous personal loyalty from his staff, and he worked hard, and fairly successfully, to obtain the best effort from both his staff and the bureaucracy. As one staffer fondly recalled, "You always had the feeling that the most competent ideas would win out."[109]

Effective management of authority helps the president lead the bureaucracy in two important kinds of activities: policy formation and policy implementation. Presidents rely on their staffs and on bureaucrats in the executive departments to construct specific policy proposals that mesh with presidential intentions. Thus, the better managed these workers are, the greater is the likelihood that presidents will receive satisfactory results from them. For example, Richard Nixon instituted a system in which domestic policy proposals were funneled through his aide John R. Ehrlichman, allowing Nixon to maintain his preferred distance from the policy-making process.

Implementation—the carrying out of presidential policies—is by no means automatic. There are so many obstacles to smooth implementation that policies made by the president can be delayed, distorted, or even ignored by those people who are supposed to implement them. While effective management of authority cannot eliminate all problems, it can increase the chances of successful implementation. After numerous implementation problems began appearing in his Great Society program, Lyndon Johnson learned the importance of attention to implementation.

Appointment and Removal Powers

While the approximately twenty-seven hundred presidential appointees to federal agencies are but a small fraction of the total three million federal workers, it is an important fraction because it includes most of the higher-level officials—cabinet members, subcabinet members, and agency heads—who make policy. Presidents can exercise power over the bureaucracy by appointing bureaucrats who share their own political philosophy and who thus are more likely to support and work toward fulfilling the president's political goals.

The removal power complements the appointment power. Although not specifically granted by the Constitution, removal power has been bestowed upon the president by tradition and a string of Supreme Court decisions. Presidents can remove from office appointed officials who fail to perform their duties satisfactorily or who clash with the president on policy matters. In practice, however, presidents rarely fire officials outright; it is usually possible to ease them out of office more gently. Presidents often ask for the resignations of office holders they want ousted or have them informed indirectly that they are no longer welcome. If these alternate methods do not work, presidents can always revert to direct dismissal.

In an effort to avoid some of the personnel problems suffered by Reagan's predecessors, the Reagan administration devoted more time and attention to the appointment process than the administrations of any other recent presidents. Reagan and his close aides painstakingly sought appointees, even for the lower levels of the bureaucracy, who were compatible ideologically with the president. By waiting to fill many top posts, Reagan had fewer bureaucrats around to oppose his proposed budget cuts. Reagan also reshaped the bureaucracy by using provisions of the Civil Service Reform Act of 1978 to reassign or terminate hundreds of influential senior executive service members.

"Think of it! Presidents come and go, but we go on forever!"

Firing Bureaucrats

We have no discipline in this bureaucracy. We never fire anybody. We never reprimand anybody. We never demote anybody. We always promote the sons-of-bitches that kick us in the ass.

President Richard Nixon

President Nixon clearly was not happy about the tremendous job security enjoyed by most bureaucrats. In fact, virtually all presidents have become frustrated with the extreme difficulty encountered when firing bureaucrats. It is enough to make presidents yearn for the good old days of the spoils system, when presidents had much greater control over who held government jobs at all levels.

Ironically, it was widespread dissatisfaction with the spoils system that led to the present situation which so vexes modern presidents. In 1883 Congress responded to concerns that the spoils system bred government inefficiency and corruption by passing the Civil Service Act. This law and a series of others like it placed most government jobs under merit employment systems, which establish and enforce standards for the hiring and firing of employees. People are hired on the basis of their qualifications and fired only when they misbehave in office or fail to perform their duties—not for strictly political reasons.

The merit plans succeeded in crushing the spoils system. In the process of protecting employees from politically motivated dismissal, however, these merit systems have made it hard to fire workers for any reason, including misbehavior and incompetence. To fire a protected bureaucrat is now a time-consuming and convoluted undertaking, requiring much effort and reams of paperwork.

Firing civil servants remains difficult despite the attempt to streamline the process through the Civil Service Reform Act of 1978. The law outlines the following procedure for firing or demoting civil servants: the employee must be given written notice of the proposed action thirty days ahead of time and a reasonable amount of time to prepare a response to the charges. The agency must provide a written decision explaining the reasons for the action. The employee can appeal the agency's decision to the Merit Systems Protection Board (created by the 1978 law specifically for this purpose), which reviews it. Decisions on cases involving alleged discrimination are also reviewed by the Equal Employment Opportunity Commission. As a final step, the employee may take the case to the U.S. Court of Appeals for the Federal District.[1]

The result of this process, according to Carter aide Jody Powell, is that "it is damn near impossible to fire someone from this government for failure to do their job."[2] Statistics back up Powell's assessment: of the nearly 3 million bureaucratic employees, only between 12,000 and 30,000 are fired each year.[3]

Because it is so difficult to fire bureaucrats, presidents (and bosses throughout the bureaucracy) often resort to other ways of handling unwanted subordinates. One of the most common methods is transferring the person in question to another position within the bureaucracy. As Jimmy Carter remarked, it is "easier to promote and transfer incompetent employees than to get rid of them."[4] Richard Nixon described the tactic more bluntly and colorfully:

> There are many unpleasant places where Civil Service people can be sent. . . . We got to get in these departments. . . . Well, maybe he is in the regional office. Fine. Demote him, or send him to the Guam regional office. There's a way. Get him the hell out. . . . Let people know that when they don't produce in this administration, somebody's ass is kicked out.[5]

Other methods of banishing bureaucrats include encouraging early retirement and the more radical move of reorganizing the agency to eliminate the target's job.

One notable exception to the rule that few bureaucrats are fired occurred in 1981, when Ronald Reagan dismissed 11,400 federal air traffic controllers. As members of the Professional Air Traffic Controllers Organization, the controllers were on strike despite a statute prohibiting strikes by federal employees.[6] Not only was Reagan's action upheld by the U.S. Court of Appeals, but a poll indicated that the general public approved of it by a two-to-one margin.[7]

1. Ellen M. Bussey, *Federal Civil Service Law and Procedures: A Basic Guide* (Washington, D.C.: Bureau of National Affairs, Inc., 1984), 7-8, 69-71.
2. George C. Edwards III and Stephen J. Wayne, *Presidential Leadership: Politics and Policy Making* (New York: St. Martin's Press, 1985), 371.
3. David V. Edwards, *The American Political Experience: An Introduction to Government,* 4th ed. (Englewood Cliffs, N.J.: Prentice-Hall, 1988), 280.
4. Edwards and Wayne, *Presidential Leadership,* 372.
5. "Transcript of an April 19, 1971, Meeting Attended by Nixon, Ehrlichman, and Shultz," *New York Times,* July 20, 1974, 14.
6. Richard A. Watson and Norman C. Thomas, *The Politics of the Presidency,* 2d ed. (Washington, D.C.: CQ Press, 1988), 295.
7. Landon Butler, "Reagan Botched the Strike," *Newsweek,* August 31, 1981, 9.

Use of the appointment and removal power to exercise some control over the bureaucracy has its limitations, however. First, a relatively small number of employees are under the president's direct supervision; the vast majority of federal workers enjoy the protection of merit employment systems and thus are insulated from presidential intervention. Presidential appointees frequently have policy-making power, but they still find guiding the bureaucracy difficult because only a few appointees reside in any particular agency. At least in terms of numbers, career civil servants overwhelmingly dominate the bureaucracy. *(See box, Firing Bureaucrats, p. 1229.)*

Second, even if presidential appointees are dedicated to the president's goals, they may not know enough about working in the federal government or in their particular agency to be much help in achieving them. Moreover, they may find themselves unable to buck the deeply ingrained bureaucratic system. With the rapid turnover of presidential appointees, many appointees are ready to leave government service by the time they have learned the ropes.

Third, the president cannot even rely on the undivided loyalty of appointees who are knowledgeable about the bureaucracy because they have personal goals of their own. In addition, appointees wishing to execute a presidential directive almost always need the cooperation of career civil servants, who have their own objectives, which commonly have little similarity to those of the president.

Finally, Congress has much to say about who gets appointed to the bureaucracy. High-ranking appointed officials such as cabinet members must be confirmed by the Senate. Congress also decides which lower-level positions can be filled through presidential appointment and, if it desires, can establish qualifications that must be met by presidential appointees to specific offices. Congress cannot appoint executive officials itself, however, or force the president to fill vacant positions.

Presidential Staff

As Dwight Eisenhower remarked:

> The government of the United States has become too big, too complex, and too pervasive in its influence on all our lives for one individual to pretend to direct the details of its important and critical programming. Competent assistants are mandatory.[110]

The presidential staff plays a big role in virtually all of the president's activities, including management of the bureaucracy.

In 1937 the Committee on Administrative Management, chaired by Louis Brownlow, studied the modern presidency and then issued a report that declared: "The president needs help." [111] The Brownlow Committee recognized that more staff assistance was needed to meet the president's increasing duties and responsibilities. President Franklin Roosevelt and Congress agreed with the committee's recommendations, which spurred a dramatic growth in the size and influence of the president's staff. Since the late 1930s the White House staff has expanded from a few dozen to several hundred employees. The Executive Office of the President (EOP), created in 1939, has likewise evolved into an assortment of powerful offices. *(See chapter, Executive Office of the President: White House Office, in Part V.)*

The White House Office is staffed by the special assistants to the president, including the press secretary, appointments secretary, legal counsel, and various policy and political advisers. Presidents enjoy considerable freedom in staffing and using the White House Office, and they often put their closest and most trusted advisers there. White House staffers have had diverse backgrounds, including the law, the military, journalism, academics, business, and, of course, politics.

The Executive Office of the President is designed to help presidents meet their awesome managerial and policy responsibilities. Although the precise number of EOP employees is difficult to determine because federal workers often are assigned there temporarily, EOP boasts about sixteen hundred full-time workers. The EOP staff has somewhat greater independence than the White House staff, but it remains primarily a servant of the president, playing a crucial role in the president's efforts to control the bureaucracy. Agencies within EOP include the Office of Management and Budget, the National Security Council, the Council of Economic Advisers, and the Office of Policy Development. *(See chapter, Executive Office of the President: Supporting Organizations, in Part V.)*

The president tends to rely heavily on assistants from the White House and executive offices, many of whom the president knows and trusts, unlike appointees to the other executive departments. Often these officials, particularly those working in the White House, are longtime friends or employees of the president; many probably worked on the president's electoral campaign. For example, Jimmy Carter brought fellow Georgians Hamilton Jordan, Bert Lance, and Jody Powell to Washington, and Ronald Reagan appointed old friends such as Michael K. Deaver and Edwin Meese III to important posts.

Presidents use their staffs in efforts to control the bureaucracy by giving the staff authority over bureaucratic programs. The underlying logic is that because the staff is primarily loyal to the president and is thus much less susceptible to influence from outside constituent and interest groups than bureaucrats in the departments, programs overseen by the staff will be run more in accordance with presidential desires. In general, the more suspicious the president is of the bureaucracy, the more likely it is that this strategy will be used. Presidents favorably inclined toward the bureaucracy usually emphasize the appointment of loyalists to the departments. Both presidents Eisenhower and Nixon tried to centralize power over the bureaucracy in the hands of their staffs, while Reagan utilized the tactic in conjunction with carefully chosen appointments to the departments.

Another way presidents use their staffs effectively to control the bureaucracy is by requiring that OMB or other entities that serve the president clear agency decisions. Presidents since Truman have employed this method to examine agency legislative requests, but recent presidents have expanded the practice to include other kinds of agency decisions. Under the Reagan administration central clearance was directed especially at controlling the rules and regulations issued by bureaucratic agencies. In fact, Reagan used this tactic so heavily that it generated opposition from some interest groups and congressional leaders, who attacked it as violating numerous federal statutes and perhaps even the constitutional separation of powers.

By giving control of bureaucratic programs to the White House Office and EOP staffs, the president is able to exert more influence over the bureaucracy, but problems can arise. For example, presidential staffs can bog down quickly when trying to control the bureaucracy. Decisions are inevitably drawn upward, and presidential assistants, distrustful of the department heads, begin handling issues more properly settled in the departments, while department heads, mindful of White House scrutiny, decide questions that could be handled at lower levels. Thus presidential aides soon find themselves immersed in the details of bureaucratic programs rather than concentrating on the broader policy issues facing the president.

Attempts to harness the bureaucracy with the presidential staff typically result in hefty increases in the staff's size. As the staff becomes more involved in the minutiae of bureaucratic decision making, more staff members are needed to deal with specialized matters. And as the staff grows, it takes on many bureaucratic characteristics such as hierarchy, interoffice rivalries, communication problems, overspecialization, and inadequate coordination.[112] Ironically, presidential efforts to control the bureaucracy by using staff actually can transform the presidential staff itself into a bureaucracy.

Presidential distrust and efforts to bypass the executive departments weaken and demoralize the people who work there. Cabinet members and other high-level appointees feel usurped by assistants to the president. Many of their functions are taken over by the president's assistants, who also tend to monopolize the president's time and attention. Civil servants working in the bureaucracy become frustrated when their recommendations are viewed automatically as suspect by the president's staff and when the staff interferes in the normal operation of their departments.

Finally, the president's assistants can become dangerously powerful. Because presidential assistants act in the name of the president, they usually get what they want. In addition, their often overly zealous attempts to protect the president may even seal the president off from the rest of the world.

The tremendous power of presidential staffs raises two problems, one theoretical and one practical. In terms of democratic theory this power is troubling; the men and women who serve on the president's staff are not elected, and their nominations are not directly accountable to the public because Congress has no role in them. And in practical terms the actions taken by the staff, especially those initiated without outside consultation, can be disastrous. Ronald Reagan's powerful National Security Council staff undertook the ill-advised and possibly illegal action that became known as the Iran-contra affair. This action had serious consequences for both American foreign policy and Reagan's political standing.

Reorganization

Presidential reorganization, and therefore control, of the bureaucracy can take several forms: creating new bureaucratic agencies or abolishing existing ones, merging agencies, or moving agencies within departments or to other departments. Presidents and scholars of organizational theory have long placed great faith in the benefits of reorganization. As prominent observers of the federal government's structure Harold Seidman and Robert Gilmour have remarked, "Reorganization has become almost a religion in Washington." [113]

Traditionally reorganization has been hailed by presidents and others as a means of making government more efficient and economical. In fact, reorganization does not appear to be such a means.[114] Despite the rhetoric about efficiency, reorganization is primarily a method for pursuing policy and political objectives. Franklin Roosevelt, a keen political analyst, understood the point: "We have to get over the notion that the purpose of reorganization is economy.... The reason for reorganization is good management." [115] Indeed, presidents can increase their control over the bureaucracy in a number of ways through successful reorganization.

An agency's position within the government greatly influences its power, prestige, and political support. Thus, changes, or threatened changes, in the position of an agency can alter radically its situation and act as leverage for presidents attempting to guide the bureaucracy. For example, President Nixon granted the National Cancer Institute independent and favorable status both to help the agency and to signify his own commitment to fighting the disease. Conversely, Ronald Reagan demonstrated his belief in a limited role for the federal government in education by proposing to abolish the Department of Education. In addition to directly influencing the bureaucracy, presidents can reap other political benefits from reorganization as well. This device gives them the appearance of taking action, provides a method for rewarding political friends and punishing enemies, and assists efforts to centralize executive power in their hands and in the hands of their staff. *(See box, Presidential Reorganization Authority, p. 990.)*

In a series of reorganization acts passed since 1939 Congress has given the president the power to reorganize the executive branch, subject to congressional approval. Presidents have declared frequently that reorganization is needed. Jimmy Carter's statement is typical: "We must give top priority to a drastic and thorough reorganization of the federal bureaucracy." [116] Yet even though Congress usually approves presidential reorganization requests, presidents do not make them very frequently.[117] As with most presidential powers, reorganization has its drawbacks.

Despite the high percentage of congressional approvals, Congress sometimes opposes presidential reorganization plans, particularly when interest groups express strong objections. For example, Richard Nixon's ambitious proposals—including one to merge seven cabinet departments into four "superdepartments"—ran into fatal difficulties in Congress.

Congress also frequently places restrictions on the reorganization power it grants the president. Authorizations, for example, can impose time limits, exempt certain agencies, or prohibit the president from creating or destroying departments.

With its arsenal of potent political weapons the bureaucracy itself can be a formidable opponent to reorganization plans. *(See "Bureaucratic Power," p. 1217, in this chapter.)* Agencies threatened by reorganization proposals fight them with all their considerable might, and many presidents who attempt reorganization do not develop comprehensive political strategies to help them achieve their goals.

Reorganization does offer presidents enhanced control over the bureaucracy but not without significant costs. Presidents attempting to reorganize the bureaucracy ordinarily must invest substantial time, effort, and political resources, all of which are precious commodities. Most presidents are understandably reluctant to expend large amounts of those resources in the mundane realm of bureaucratic reorganization.

Budgetary Powers

As a means of controlling the bureaucracy, the president can influence how much money agencies receive, particularly during the budget process. Although Congress actually appropriates the money that government spends, the president wields power at both the beginning and end of the budget process.

With the help of the Office of Management and Budget, an EOP agency, the president prepares a budget for each year's government spending and presents it to Congress for review. OMB evaluates each federal agency's request for funds and recommends to the president what amount should be placed in the budget. *(See "Office of Management and Budget," p. 950, in Executive Office of the President: Supporting Organizations chapter of Part V.)*

The president makes the final decisions on the proposed budget, based on the advice from the Office of Management and Budget and from other sources such as the Council of Economic Advisers. The amount fixed in the budget by the president and OMB is tremendously important to the agencies. Although Congress is not obligated to accept the president's recommendations, in practice the amounts appropriated by Congress generally follow those recommendations closely.[118]

A president who is unhappy with congressional budget decisions may impound—that is, refuse to spend—funds appropriated by Congress. Presidents have long used this method to control government spending. In the modern era controlling spending also has meant controlling the federal bureaucracy. Controversy over impoundment arose in the early 1970s because President Richard Nixon used the practice prodigiously, prompting Congress to pass legislation stipulating that it can overturn impoundments. Although presidential impoundment of funds is still possible, deferral—delaying expenditures for up to one year, which is harder for Congress to prevent—is an option as well. The most spectacular use of these powers came in 1981, when President Reagan successfully deferred $7 billion and impounded another $14 billion appropriated by Congress.[119]

Yet another means of controlling agency funding is legislative clearance. All agency requests for legislation, even those not requiring additional funding, must be cleared with OMB before going to Congress. Legislative clearance gives the president an opportunity to study the proposals. The president also has certain discretionary powers informally granted by congressional appropriations committees, which allow the presidential transfer of funds from one program to another.[120] Moreover, the president can spend large amounts of money on a confidential basis, including expenditures for intelligence activities.

There are limits, however, to the effectiveness of the president's budgetary powers in controlling the bureaucracy. First, the federal budget is immense, complicated, and—unless the head of OMB is exceptionally sharp (as was Reagan's first OMB chief, David Stockman)—not easy to manipulate. Because the budget process is so complex, it is constructed incrementally; that is, an agency's funding for any one year is based largely on the amount received the previous year. Thus, any changes in an agency's budget will likely be small, since any radical variation from one year to the next rarely occurs. Such stability provides the bureaucracy with a measure of protection from presidential interference.

Second, the budget is highly inflexible. A large proportion of it—perhaps as much as 80 percent—is uncontrollable. Items such as interest on the national debt, payments for contracts already made, and funding for Social Security and other entitlement programs must be included in the budget, thereby reducing the president's ability to direct funds to personal priorities.

Finally, Congress can foil the best-laid presidential plans. Congress takes the budget process very seriously and exercises considerable influence over it. The president's budgetary powers are less effective in cases where Congress disagrees with the president's objective.

Control of Information

The old saying that knowledge is power seems especially applicable to the relationship between the president and the bureaucracy.[121] Expert knowledge is one of the primary sources of bureaucratic power, particularly when the information is not easily available elsewhere. Presidents who become totally dependent on agencies for information are at a disadvantage, whereas those who use their powers wisely not only avoid that problem, but also control information so that they are better able to influence the bureaucracy.

Presidents alone cannot gather and assess all the information they need, however, particularly given the expanded role of the federal government in the twentieth century and the increasing technological complexity of its tasks. Recent presidents have gotten much of the assistance they need from the Executive Office of the President, which is an important alternative and a thoroughly loyal source of information that the president can use to make choices and to counter the bureaucracy.

In recent years the size and information capabilities of EOP have grown, as well as its authority and responsibility. Assistants to the president and EOP staffers frequently act in the president's name, which enhances the president's ability to acquire and disseminate information through subordinates.

Presidents have other sources of information as well. Sources outside the government include newspapers, magazines, television, interest groups, the private sector, and academia. Sources within the government include the federal agencies. When agency jurisdictions overlap, the ensuing duplication of information sources provides a way to collect and verify information. Presidents also may cultivate informal channels of communication to back up formal ones or bypass uncooperative layers of the bureaucracy and extract information from lower-level bureaucrats. This was a favorite tactic of President Kennedy.

Franklin Roosevelt was a master at controlling information. Even though he had comparatively few personal staff assistants, he managed to keep a constant flow of ideas, opinions, and information coming into the Oval Office. He encouraged his staff to brainstorm for new ideas, fostered competition among his staffers, and sought information from a wide array of sources both within and outside the government. All of these strategies helped Roosevelt command the bureaucracy. He depended on no single source for information, and thus no one knew exactly what information he had or what his thinking was. He controlled the information he needed to make knowledgeable political and policy choices.

The acquisition of accurate information can be difficult. Aside from the possibility of factual errors, presidents face other problems. For example, because subordinates tend to filter the information they pass along to superiors, that information can be quite distorted by the time it gets to the top. Subordinates do not necessarily lie, but they often emphasize information that makes them look good and de-emphasize or omit information that is unflattering to them or is unlikely to appeal to their superiors. Information that travels through several layers of hierarchy is therefore often of questionable quality.[122]

Whatever the president's efforts at generating alternate sources of information, inevitably some information—facts on agency performance, for example—must come from bureaucratic agencies themselves. This raises the possibility that agencies will provide information biased in their favor. Moreover, bureaucratic agencies usually operate on the assumption that the president is informed about agency activities only when something out of the ordinary occurs. This tendency further restricts the president's ability to squeeze accurate information from the bureaucracy.

Agenda Setting

The public expects the president to put forth ideas, actions, and proposals—an agenda—designed to solve problems and make the country a better place to live. The president's agenda is then subject to national political consideration and debate. If the president proceeds carefully and effectively, the national agenda can be a powerful political tool used to influence the bureaucracy.

Presidents can use agenda setting to control the bureaucracy by determining what issues agencies must handle. Whether or not agencies support an item placed on the agenda by the president, they must devote time and attention to it. When an agency likes a proposal, it will work for its adoption, and vice versa. In either case, the president, not the bureaucracy, has decided what the issue will be. When President Reagan proposed massive budget cuts for most federal agencies in 1981, he quickly captured the attention of the agencies to be affected.

Because presidents want to give the best possible presentation of their views, their statements on potential agenda issues usually are carefully staged. Using speeches and television appearances the president can reach millions of citizens simultaneously. Presidential addresses to the nation and press conferences are televised regularly, and the network news programs feature stories on the president almost nightly. (In fact, the White House encourages network coverage by staging media events and photo opportunities specifically designed to attract the media's attention.) Television is a more effective tool for some presidents than others. Kennedy, and especially Reagan, were natural performers and communicators; Nixon and Carter were less comfortable in front of the camera.

In addition to having competent communication skills, presidents also must be skilled at limiting the number of items on their agenda.[123] With the gigantic federal deficit there is not enough money to meet all the public's demands or all the president's desires. By limiting their agenda, presidents can concentrate on a few goals and keep public attention focused on them. Carter's agenda suffered when he overloaded it with proposals. Presidents must try as well to establish and move items quickly, particularly early in their terms when they can take advantage of the traditional "honeymoon" period with Congress and the public.

Finally, presidents should attempt to keep a national perspective as well as a long-range view when formulating an agenda, and they should take care not to get too bogged down in details. Jimmy Carter devoted entirely too much time to trivia. According to one of his aides, early in his term Carter diligently checked the arithmetic in budget tables and even personally reviewed the scheduling of the White House tennis court![124]

Planning

Defined by scholars Richard A. Watson and Norman C. Thomas as "anticipating problems and developing solutions to them," planning has long been a hallmark of the private sector, but that is much less the case in government.[125] Recent presidents have used different types of planning to make the bureaucracy and its processes more amenable to presidential direction. These attempts at planning the bureaucracy have yielded only mixed results, however.

One of the first large-scale efforts at government planning was the program planning budgeting system (PPBS), instituted throughout the federal government in 1965 by President Johnson. PPBS sought to improve planning before budget decisions are made, make programs rather than agencies the focus of the budget process, relate budget decisions to long-range national goals, and analyze programs on a cost-benefit basis.[126] The overall aim was to promote rational budgetary decision making. PPBS had worked fairly well in the Department of Defense during the Kennedy administration, and hopes were high for its effectiveness on a broader scale. Those hopes were soon dashed, however, as agencies rebelled against the extensive paperwork required by the system and Congress saw it as a threat to its role in the budgetary process.

A technique similar to PPBS, management-by-objective (MBO), was introduced by Richard Nixon to try to increase presidential direction of the bureaucracy. Under this plan agencies compiled lists of their objectives, ranked in order of priority. Once approved by OMB, these lists were sent to the president for his consent. The objectives then became the standard for evaluating agency performance. MBO offered certain benefits: it quickly uncovered conflicting objectives, facilitated White House oversight of actions accepted by the agencies and the president, and highlighted areas of dispute between the agencies and OMB or the president. But it failed to help agencies formulate their objectives or state them unambiguously, and these facets of the plan were of greatest concern to the president.[127]

Jimmy Carter's principal contribution to planning was zero-base budgeting (ZBB). In theory, agencies justified each year not only their proposed funding increases but also their entire budget—that is, they assumed a zero base. They then estimated their output at various levels of funding (for example, at 80, 90, 100, and 110 percent of current funding), and the estimates were analyzed to determine the influence of the different levels of funding on long-term agency production and objectives.[128] The analysis was then used to make rational budget decisions. In practice, however, ZBB did not operate much differently from the traditional incremental budgeting process.

In addition to the specific defects of particular planning efforts, government planning in general faces significant obstacles. It attempts to apply rationality to the uncertain and occasionally irrational world of politics. The formulation of clear, widely acceptable objectives is rarely easy in a democratic political system. Planners cannot mandate objectives; specific goals are formed, if at all, through the bargaining and compromise inherent in politics—a process that does not guarantee rational decisions. Thus, although presidents can achieve some control over the bureaucracy through planning, that planning inevitably becomes dominated by politics, thereby losing much of its worth.[129]

Executive Orders

Executive orders are presidential proclamations that carry the force of law. The president's power to issue executive orders is essentially a legislative power, since the orders may require agencies or individuals to perform acts not necessarily mandated by Congress. Executive orders may be used to enforce the Constitution or treaties with foreign countries, implement legislative statutes, or direct bureaucratic agencies.[130] Thus, the executive order is a powerful presidential weapon which can be used against the bureaucracy.

Although the Constitution does not grant the power of executive orders explicitly, it does require the president to "take care that the laws be faithfully executed." Occasionally presidents must act quickly and decisively to fulfill this directive, and the executive order is one way of doing so. In addition, modern presidents have maintained that Article II of the Constitution grants them inherent power to take whatever actions they judge to be in the nation's best interests as long as those actions are not prohibited by the Constitution or law.[131] Presidents therefore view executive orders as perfectly acceptable exercises of presidential power, and the Supreme Court generally has upheld this interpretation.

Presidents have used executive orders in such areas as the economy, civil rights, and national security, as well as the bureaucracy. During World War II, Franklin Roosevelt created two powerful agencies—the Office of Price Administration and the Office of Economic Stabilization—through executive orders. Richard Nixon tried, and sometimes succeeded, in using the power to abolish bureaucratic programs and agencies established by Congress. He also took advantage of executive orders to strengthen particular agencies, notably the CIA and the FBI. Executive orders were used as well by Ronald Reagan to curb the bureaucracy's role in promulgating regulations for the private sector.

One problem with executive orders arises from the ambiguous nature of the president's authority to issue them. While the practice itself is clearly accepted, the limits of their use are somewhat vague. This leaves some orders open to questions of their validity. For example, Nixon's 1971 use of executive orders to institute a freeze on wages and prices, even though explicitly allowed by Congress, was challenged in federal court. That particular case was upheld, but as Harry Truman discovered, there is no guarantee of such success in court. His seizure, through executive order, of the steel industry during the Korean War was struck down by the Supreme Court.[132]

Commander in Chief Powers

The Constitution names the president commander in chief of the nation's armed forces. The position also gives the president a great deal of influence over the civilian bureaucracy, where presidential decisions on military questions can affect the funding, status, and support of several bureaucratic agencies. One obvious example is the Department of Defense, which prospered as a result of military decisions made by the Reagan administration. In fact, the traditional though informal role the president plays as commander in chief on domestic issues theoretically makes all agencies subordinate to the president.[133]

Despite the authority that accompanies the role of commander in chief, the president rarely can issue instructions and have them obeyed immediately. As former secretary of state Henry A. Kissinger commented, "The outsider believes a presidential order is consistently followed out. Nonsense."[134] One official in the Nixon administration asserted that frustration over the difficulty in having commands carried out explains certain presidential behavior: "That's why they all love to play Commander in Chief; at least the military *pretends* to obey."[135]

In some instances, however, presidential orders are carried out expeditiously, but unfortunately for presidents, these occasions do not occur too frequently. Political scientist Richard E. Neustadt studied three cases in which presidents issued commands and had them obeyed readily: Truman's dismissal of Gen. Douglas MacArthur, Truman's seizure of the American steel industry during the Korean War, and Eisenhower's use of federal troops to force the desegregation of Little Rock, Arkansas, schools. After examining the circumstances that promoted such obedience, Neustadt concluded that presidential orders are obeyed swiftly only when five conditions are met. First, subordinates must know that the order comes directly from the president, not merely from a presidential staffer. Presidents can ensure that their personal involvement is known by controlling how the announcement of the decision is made. Second, the president's order must be clear and unambiguous; it should state precisely what action the president wants taken. Third, the order must be widely publicized so that any official who disobeys the order draws the attention of the media and the White House. Fourth, whoever receives the order must be able to act on it. There is little reason to expect success if the order cannot possibly be fulfilled. Fifth, recipients of presidential orders must believe that the president has the legitimate authority to issue that particular order; subordinates are more likely to disobey an order that appears to be illegitimate.

Neustadt acknowledged that all five conditions rarely are met simultaneously. He argued that because conditions seldom make it likely that presidential orders will be obeyed rapidly, the primary power of the president is the power to persuade.[136] *(See "Leadership Skills," p. 1225, in this chapter.)*

As Neustadt's analysis clearly emphasized, the president's powers as commander in chief are limited. But even if relatively few presidential directives are obeyed immediately and without question, the power to give those orders is still an important one. Presidential followup or cajoling may be needed to get the desired results, but the president's role as commander in chief is a benefit in dealing with the bureaucracy.

Crisis Leadership

During times of crisis the public expects the president to take charge of the situation, and it ordinarily approves of whatever action the president takes. National crises may include wars, riots, other acts of violence, economic upheavals, and natural disasters such as floods, droughts, blizzards, hurricanes, and earthquakes. The sense of urgency engendered by crises usually means that during crises presidents find that accomplishments come easier, including control of the bureaucracy.

During a war, the most severe kind of crisis, presidents have the greatest freedom of action. They can freeze prices, create new agencies, allocate jobs, and even censor the press.[137] In the past presidential actions have even restricted fundamental civil liberties—for example, Abraham Lincoln suspended habeas corpus during the Civil War and Franklin Roosevelt interned Japanese-American citizens during World War II. In the midst of a crisis presidents find that they can do almost anything in the name of national security.

During the Great Depression of the 1930s FDR got virtually everything he wanted from Congress during his first one hundred days in office, and he used that influence to create much of the modern federal bureaucracy. Many cases of presidential crisis leadership are less dramatic, however, especially when the crises are less severe. For example, Lyndon Johnson directed the effort to rebuild Alaska in the wake of a devastating earthquake in 1964, and Jimmy Carter declared fuel emergencies during the fierce winters of 1976-1979.[138]

Because presidents find the public support of their actions that appears in crises (sometimes called the "rally round the flag" effect) so appealing, they may try to make a genuine problem look like an immediate crisis in an effort to create public support and increase congressional backing. For example, Lyndon Johnson declared "an unconditional war on poverty" in 1964, and Carter described the energy shortage as the "moral equivalent of war" thirteen years later.[139] Johnson made more progress in his War on Poverty than Carter made in the energy crisis for two reasons. First, unlike Carter, Johnson worked long and hard to build congressional support for his programs. Second, LBJ was able to capitalize on emotions dredged up by the assassination of John Kennedy.

Jimmy Carter's experience demonstrates one potential danger of crisis leadership: failure to handle crises effectively can lead to loss of political standing. Carter's mismanagement of the energy crisis seriously wounded his image, but a subsequent crisis that he did not manufacture caused even greater damage. In November 1979 a mob of fanatical Iranians overran the U.S. Embassy in Tehran and captured about fifty Americans. Initially, public support was behind the president, but it steadily decreased as Carter's year-long attempts to free the hostages failed dismally. By most accounts Carter's ineffectual management of the Iranian crisis was a major contributing factor to his defeat in the 1980 election.[140]

Crisis leadership is thus a double-edged sword for presidents. On the one hand, it allows considerable freedom of action, which can be a welcome change from the normal constraints on presidential behavior. The public support for the president characteristic of crises, particularly in their early stages, offers the president additional power. On the other hand, that supply of support is not inexhaustible, and presidents who bungle crises can suffer damaging political setbacks.

Limits to Presidential Power

Although presidents can use a variety of powers in their efforts to control the bureaucracy, each power has its particular disadvantages that limit its usefulness. Unfortunately for presidents, however, those are not the only limits they must confront. Other factors as well hamper presidential attempts to harness the bureaucracy: time constraints, lack of information, "iron triangles," "issue networks," and bureaucratic preferences.

Time Constraints

Time works against presidential endeavors to oversee the bureaucracy in several ways. First, the president and the bureaucracy have wholly different perspectives on time. Longevity is one of the bureaucracy's strongest weapons; many problems facing it diminish after enough time passes. If the president is hostile to a particular agency, for example, the best defense for that agency is often just to wait for the arrival of a new president. Similarly, if conditions do not favor action by an agency, those conditions probably will change eventually.

Presidents do not have the luxury of being able to wait indefinitely. Their relatively short terms in office, as well as their desire to be reelected and then to make a mark on history, demand quick, dramatic action. Thus, with the bureaucracy's seemingly infinite capacity to delay filling presidential requests, the passage of time generally works to the advantage of the bureaucracy and to the disadvantage of the president.

Second, presidents are faced with tremendous daily demands on their time. Even if presidents had more time to devote to controlling the bureaucracy, it is so vast and performs so many functions that becoming fully familiar with it, much less controlling it, would be an impossible task.

Third, the president's staff faces the same kinds of time limitations. They too have many different tasks, and, like the president, they constantly are confronted with unanticipated problems. In the fall of 1978, for example, President Carter and his assistants were dealing with the beginnings of the Iranian revolution, the aftermath of the Camp David meetings, negotiations with the Soviets over the SALT II agreement, secret talks with the Chinese, and trouble with Nicaragua.[141] That is undoubtedly plenty to do, without even considering domestic issues and the bureaucracy.

Finally, even if presidents have abundant time, they are not likely to delve into areas they find uninteresting or unimportant such as the many activities of the bureaucracy. In fact, a lack of presidential concern with the daily operations of many of the bureaucratic agencies is entirely understandable. Lyndon Johnson's response to a reporter's question about something the president considered a "minor administrative matter" clearly makes the point. Johnson roared at the reporter: "Why do you . . . ask me, the leader of the Western World, a chickenshit question like that?"[142]

Lack of Information and Experience

Even with a White House staff numbering in the hundreds the president cannot match the bureaucracy's information on all the activities of the federal bureaucracy and its nearly three million employees. The expertise and specialization of the bureaucracy, perhaps largely because of its size, give it the advantage at information-gathering.

Time constraints also limit the information available to the president and the White House staff. In most cases they have access to the raw information they need, but they do not have time to process and evaluate it. David Stockman, Reagan's first head of OMB, commented on his role in constructing the federal budget:

> I just wish that there were more hours in the day or that we didn't have to do this so fast. I have these stacks of briefing books and I've got to make decisions about specific options. . . . I don't have time, trying to put this whole package together in three weeks, so you just start making snap judgments.[143]

If the president's staff does not even have enough time to consider the budget carefully, it certainly does not have time to generate and assess information about the routine functions of many bureaucratic agencies.

Lack of information can be a particular problem in presidential efforts to oversee the bureaucracy's implementation of programs and directives. Limited time and staff frequently force the president to rely on data provided by the implementing agencies themselves, which naturally raises questions about the information's accuracy. This happens in several policy areas, including health care, desegregation of public schools, and protection of the environment.[144]

Most presidents also suffer from lack of information about the bureaucracy in a broader sense. Few chief executives enter the White House with experience in managing the federal bureaucracy, and some have little background in managing any kind of large organization. Any expectations that they can effectively control the mammoth U.S. bureaucracy immediately after their inauguration are therefore unreasonable.

Five of the last eight American presidents—Truman, Kennedy, Johnson, Nixon, and Ford—spent the bulk of their political careers before assuming the presidency in Congress. Presidential candidates frequently claim that service in Congress is excellent preparation for the White House, but as for handling the bureaucracy, that seems untrue. Congressional contact with the bureaucracy is more cooperative than hierarchical; legislators ask for favors and the agencies are more than happy to respond.[145] This arrangement hardly prepares a president for the much less congenial reception the bureaucracy gives the occupant of the Oval Office.

Moreover, the skills learned in Congress are not especially helpful when managing the bureaucracy as president. Congress revolves around tactics and deal making and, for the most part, leaves an issue behind once legislation is passed. According to Seidman and Gilmour, however, "Unlike a legislator, a president should view the passage of a law as a beginning, not an end." [146] The president is, after all, the chief executive. Training in Congress rarely produces persons interested in or skilled at implementing programs.

George Bush's varied career—including, among other positions, four years in Congress and two years as head of the CIA—would seem to have prepared him well to deal with the bureaucracy. Recent presidents who did not serve in Congress, Jimmy Carter and Ronald Reagan, underwent their political preliminaries as state governors. They perhaps had a slight advantage over former members of Congress who occupied the Oval Office because they assumed the presidency with experience in managing their state bureaucracies. As both Carter and Reagan quickly discovered, however, the huge and complex federal bureaucracy is in an entirely different league than the relatively small state bureaucracies. Franklin Roosevelt was perhaps the president best prepared to tackle the bureaucracy.[147] He not only had experience with the bureaucracy of a large state as governor of New York, but he also had been exposed to the federal bureaucracy when serving as assistant secretary of the navy.

"Iron Triangles"

As the name implies, an "iron triangle" is a strong alliance among three groups of political participants—federal agencies, interest groups, and congressional committees or subcommittees—with stakes in a particular issue. Each member of the alliance, or each point of the triangle, has a mutually beneficial relationship with the other two members, and all members work together to pursue common goals. Iron triangles are sometimes called "subgovernments" because they exert so much influence on government decisions in their policy areas. Hundreds of such alliances have sprung up in Washington.

Iron triangles tend to work behind the scenes. Representatives of the groups involved—agency careerists, interest group lobbyists, and members of Congress and their staffers—discuss policy issues and then agree on preferred outcomes. Likely topics of discussion are proposed legislation, budgetary matters, reorganization plans, personnel concerns, and potential regulations.[148] The interests of the allies do not always coincide completely, but the close personal relationships that frequently form between participants help smooth the differences. Bureaucrats, lobbyists, and, to a lesser extent, members of Congress often hold the same jobs for two decades or more, and thus they have plenty of opportunity to become friends with their allies.

Each side helps the others and receives help in return.[149] From Congress, bureaucrats want generous funding as well as legislation granting them maximum authority and discretion. In return, members of Congress want preferential treatment for their constituencies, technical assistance for their staffs, and often help in drafting legislation. Legislators also turn to interest groups for information and assistance in formulating proposals, as well as financial and political help in their campaigns and sometimes paid speaking engagements. Interest groups, in turn want members of Congress to ensure their access to bureaucratic agencies and to pass and fund programs that benefit the groups. Interest groups rely on Congress as well for help in having group members appointed to and confirmed for key government jobs.

The third side of the triangle connects the interest groups and bureaucratic agencies. Interest groups want to have a strong say in agency decisions, including the writing of regulations, ideally through a formal advisory system that would give the interest group either formal or informal veto power over such decisions. The agencies in turn want the political support of interest groups, including positive congressional testimony and lobbying for additional funds for the agency.

Examples of iron triangles are plentiful. The Department of the Interior; interest groups representing farmers, ranchers, and forestry and mining companies; and various congressional committees (including the Senate Environment Committee and the House Interior Committee, among others) work together to form land- and water-use policies, which are particularly important in the western states. On the issue of highways, the Department of Transportation; interest groups representing the auto, tire, and oil industries; and members of the congressional transportation committees share the driver's seat. One of the more infamous iron triangles is the so-called "military-industrial complex" that dominates the defense system. Its members include the Department of Defense, weapons contractors and related firms, and assorted congressional committees, particularly the armed services committees.

By bringing together the most interested parties on issues and having them work toward common goals, iron triangles greatly influence policy formulation. One effect is continuity in policy, arising from the expertise, longevity, and political clout of iron triangles. Such an effect may benefit the public when presidents are concerned with other matters, but it can also work against the public when citizens are anxious for a change. Moreover, the cozy relationships within iron triangles can result in lax government regulation of the private sector, can stifle free competition by giving some groups preferential treatment, and can penalize the poor or unorganized.[150]

The power of iron triangles limits presidential control of the bureaucracy because agencies within iron triangles always can turn to their congressional and interest group allies for help against the president. An assistant to Jimmy Carter assessed presidential control of the bureaucracy this way: "There isn't any government down there to manage. There is a series of subgovernments pursuing single interests of one kind or another." [151]

Congress is an especially valuable friend of federal agencies, and presidents find that those with strong ties to Congress are the hardest to influence. One career bureaucrat put it bluntly: "I don't care *who* sits in the Oval Office. I depend on Congress for my livelihood." [152] The Army Corps of Engineers, which spreads pork barrel projects across the country, is renowned for its favored status with Congress and for its attendant invulnerability to presidential intervention.

The president can still exercise some influence over agencies, of course, particularly when their iron triangles are weakened—for example, they may clash with other subsystems, receive negative publicity, or suffer from internal dissension. The weapons procurement iron triangle was weakened in 1988 when some of its members were shown to have participated in bribery and fraud. Some observers believed this scandal provided an opportunity for the president to clamp down on wasteful defense spending. And the interests of iron triangles and presidents occasionally do coincide. Thus, their relationships are not always adversarial ones.

"Issue Networks"

Other forces that can impede presidential control of the bureaucracy are what scholar Hugh Heclo has called "issue networks." [153] Like iron triangles, issue networks are coalitions of individuals and groups who want to influence particular areas of executive policy. Issue networks, however, differ from iron triangles in several important respects. Issue networks are larger and more complex than iron triangles, as well as more open and fluid. Participants in such networks have varied backgrounds and may include journalists, academics, foundation officers, lobbyists, White House and congressional staff members, and bureaucrats.[154]

Because issue networks are less structured than iron triangles, people move in and out of them freely, and the networks themselves change as public issues change. Moreover the goals of issue networks are likely to be different than those of iron triangles. Members of iron triangles are interested mainly in pursuing personal benefits—career security for bureaucrats, reelection for members of Congress, and economic gain for most interest groups—whereas those active in issue networks want to influence public policy, perhaps by encouraging rationality and innovation in decision making, promoting greater government efficiency, or pushing specific proposals. Activists in issue networks are generally professionals who enjoy exercising influence over public policy for the prestige, power, and personal satisfaction that such influence offers.

The making of agriculture policy is a good example of an issue network. The Department of Agriculture, farmers' organizations, and the congressional agriculture committees are joined by representatives of other backgrounds and professions in shaping agriculture policy. Nutrition experts, health care professionals, activists concerned with world hunger, and foreign policy analysts (American agricultural products are exported throughout the world) voice their opinions, as do members of "think tanks" and local community groups. Environmentalists concerned with the effects of pesticide use on farms, bankers holding farm mortgages, and energy experts looking at farmers' dependence on imported oil products also take part in the issue network, further illustrating its complexity and openness.

Issue networks sometimes clash with iron triangles. This is not surprising given their conflicting goals: self-interest for iron triangles versus good policy for issue networks (at least their idea of good policy). For example, analysts within the defense issue network but outside the weapons procurement iron triangle criticize the system of purchasing weapons as woefully wasteful. Similarly, environmentalists upset over acid rain battle the iron triangles that protect the "smokestack" industries contributing to the problem.[155]

Issue networks form and operate differently than iron triangles. Networks come into being when concerned citizens realize that they share similar points of view about a particular issue and often disintegrate when that issue is settled. Thus networks appear, disappear, and fluctuate over time, while iron triangles are much more stable. Members of networks want to convince the president and Congress that the network's position is the right one. They also want to have some network members appointed to government posts and to advise the president and Congress regularly of their views.[156] Unlike iron triangles, issue networks seek publicity and use the media to produce and shape public attention. Many members of issue networks are former high government officials, eager for the chance to regain influence over policy making.

Issue networks frustrate presidential control over the bureaucracy in several ways. In general, even though issue networks do not act with the unanimity of iron triangles, they do increase the fragmentation and unpredictability of public policy formulation and therefore the difficulty of presidential control over it.[157] Issue networks draw more people, most of them independent of the president and holding diverse opinions, into the policy-making process. The networks further reduce presidential power by supplying Congress and the bureaucracy with information and political backing that they can use to pursue their own objectives and to thwart presidential intervention.

The conflict that frequently erupts within issue networks can be an advantage to the president, however. Because issue networks are open and contain many diverse participants, disagreements within networks are common. For example, members of the agricultural issue network split sharply on the question of whether embargoes on exports of U.S. agricultural products should be used as tools of foreign policy. Conflicts such as this tend to produce different policy proposals from members of the same issue network. When a variety of proposals are put before the public, the president has an opportunity to weigh the alternatives and assess public opinion before acting. The information generated in such debates is quite useful to the president in making policy decisions. The conflict also may establish the president as the final arbiter of the dispute. Finally, issue networks may lead to better public policy, and enhanced political stature for the president, by increasing the number of experts involved and improving the quality of the debate on policy.

Bureaucratic Preferences

Probably the most important restraint on presidential control of the bureaucracy stems from bureaucratic preferences. Presidents usually find it difficult to get the bureaucracy to do what it does not want to do. One reason for this difficulty is that the bureaucracy does not speak with a single voice. Although it is frequently thought to be a single entity, the federal bureaucracy is composed of hundreds of agencies and millions of employees with various interests and policy preferences. Bureaucratic preferences fall into three basic categories, however: those of agencies, those of civil servants, and those of political appointees.

Federal agencies generally want to survive and, if possible, expand. Thus, any presidential proposals that go counter to those goals are almost certain to draw opposition from the bureaus affected. Not surprisingly then, President Reagan's effort to abolish the Departments of Education and Energy drew vigorous resistance from them.

Agencies may oppose the president as well on matters that do not threaten them directly. For example, an agency occasionally resists the president on behalf of other agencies that are allies. Or an agency may simply disagree with the president's decision and prefer other alternatives when it believes a presidential decision is ill-advised or unworkable. Disagreement also may spring from ideological differences. Many agencies are dominated by employees with liberal predispositions on policy issues.[158] Welfare administrators, for example, opposed the Nixon administration's plan to require able-bodied welfare recipients to work in exchange for their payments, and the proposal eventually was discarded.[159]

The goals of civil servants working within bureaucratic agencies also hamper presidential control of the bureaucracy. Permanent civil servants are committed to their careers and their agencies and its programs.[160] Thus, their preferences, which emphasize their goals of stability and regularity, inevitably clash with those of the president, who usually wants rapid, bold action from the bureaucracy to help fulfill the presidential goals of reelection and historical significance. The security and longevity of civil servants make them formidable opponents of presidential actions they dislike. *(See "Conflicting Goals," p. 1226, in this chapter.)*

Even though they are selected by the president, political appointees too have goals that often conflict with those of the president. Because most appointees serve in government only a short time, they want to establish their reputations quickly. This can entail taking actions that do not toe the presidential line. Conflicting goals also result when political appointees adopt the positions and attitudes of their agencies and become more representatives of their agencies to the president than the other way around. *(See "Role of Cabinet Members," p. 1217, in this chapter.)*

Outcomes of a Complex Relationship

The relationship between the president and the bureaucracy is clearly a complex one, and several important questions about this relationship have not yet been addressed. First, who wins, and why, when the president and the bureaucracy clash? Second, what effects does bureaucratic power have on democratic government? And third, can the president in fact control the bureaucracy?

Explaining Outcomes

Who wins, and why, when the president and the bureaucracy clash? Unfortunately, no precise formula exists to answer this question. Each case differs, and the reasons for outcomes vary according to the specifics of the case. Much of the answer lies, however, in the powers and restraints applicable to the president and the bureaucracy in a particular case (for example, in Ronald Reagan's triumph over the striking air traffic controllers in 1981 or in his failure to keep James G. Watt as his secretary of the interior), which when compared give some indication of the likely outcome of the conflict. Additional factors, including the kind of policy and presidential goal in question come into play as well and must be considered in explaining outcomes.

Types of Policies

The extent and success of presidential efforts to control bureaucratic agencies depend partly upon the type of policy involved. Policies can be separated into two categories: domestic and foreign. Domestic policies can be further divided into distributive, regulatory, and redistributive policies.

Distributive Policies. Conducted nationwide, distributive policies (also called pork barrel policies) work toward general goals and provide benefits directly to the populace.[161] Distributive policies are manifested, for example, in the national park system, the interstate highway system, grants to state and local governments, and federal insurance of bank deposits. The bureaucratic agencies running distributive programs usually are fairly small, but they often participate in powerful iron triangles or issue networks because many distributive programs profit relatively narrow but influential segments of the population, for example, the interstate highway system benefits road contractors and oil companies, among others.

Agencies that implement distributive policies are among the most powerful agencies within the bureaucracy, and thus they are not amenable to presidential control. Their strength stems from the backing of interest groups benefiting from such policies, as well as the enthusiastic support of Congress, which likes distributive policies because of their widespread applicability, political attractiveness, and low political risk. Some distributive agencies are the Army Corps of Engineers, the Department of Education, and the National Park Service.

The functions of agencies handling distributive policies also help shield them from presidential intervention. Because legislation creating the programs is generally vague, the implementing agencies have plenty of latitude in their operations and thus can implement programs as they see fit.[162] Designed to take action and combat problems, distributive agencies also possess ample quantities of expertise, leadership, and cohesion—as well as popular support. In addition, because of their public and congressional support these agencies usually enjoy comfortable budgets.

Presidents, who after all, are politicians too, rarely want to attack popular programs that provide benefits to people all across the country.

Regulatory Policies. Regulatory policies cite government-specified rules of behavior for individuals and institutions, and penalties for violation of those rules.[163] The federal government regulates many aspects of society—including business and industry, public health and safety, natural resources—and enforces federal criminal laws.[164] Because the scope of government regulation is very broad, many bureaucratic agencies participate in its formulation and enforcement. Regulatory agencies include the Interstate Commerce Commission, the Food and Drug Administration, and the Environmental Protection Agency.

Support for regulatory policies is mixed. Activist groups often strongly support the government's regulatory efforts; for example, the Sierra Club and other ecology-minded groups encourage vigorous and stringent regulation of the environment by the EPA. As far as it is aware of governmental regulation, the public is inclined to support it as well. Opposition often comes from the regulated, however, who may assail regulations as unwarranted government intervention. Congress tends to support the principle of government regulation, but in practice it is concerned about the possibility of upsetting constituents and political allies.[165] Overall, the support received by regulatory agencies is significantly less than that for distributive agencies, which is understandable considering that distributive agencies provide benefits, not rules and regulations.

Regulatory agencies also seldom enjoy the other advantages of distributive agencies. For example, most regulatory agencies do not have the large research staffs and expertise that constitute a source of agency power. Strong leadership may be a problem as well because many regulatory agencies are governed not by a single individual but by a board of directors—an arrangement that ordinarily requires greater compromise. Agency cohesion also may be difficult to generate because the functions of regulatory agencies, including the formulation and application of sometimes tedious rules, are relatively less appealing. The Environmental Protection Agency and the Federal Trade Commission are noteworthy exceptions; their employees are frequently zealous and dedicated. Most regulatory agencies are thus not very powerful, leaving them more open to presidential control than other types of agencies. Ironically, the more effective agencies contribute to their own weakness by skillfully making and enforcing rules that engender more active opposition from the regulated.[166]

Presidents exert some influence over regulatory agencies in their appointments of agency heads and manipulation of agencies' proposed budgets, and they can try to persuade agencies to interpret regulations in ways acceptable to the administration. Presidents also control regulatory agencies and policy through the judicial and legislative branches by having the Justice Department file friend-of-the-court briefs in regulatory test cases and by attempting to change regulations through the passage of new legislation. Finally, presidents can choose which regulations the administration will emphasize. By initially appointing EPA administrators who were hostile to the agency's mission, President Reagan clearly signalled that his administration intended to de-emphasize regulation of the environment.[167]

While presidents are able to exercise significant control over regulatory agencies, they often choose not to do so. The political price can be high for intervention in the regulatory arena, as Reagan discovered in his relations with EPA. His moves upset Congress and the public so much that he was forced to back away from his position and to appoint an environmentalist to lead the agency.[168]

Redistributive Policies. Redistributive policies use the taxes taken from one group of people to provide benefits to another group of people.[169] These policies, which are among the most controversial in the country, include Medicaid, housing programs, and a variety of welfare programs. Over half of the federal budget is devoted to redistributive programs.[170]

Public support for redistributive programs varies, largely according to how many and what kind of people benefit from particular programs. Some redistributive programs lean toward being distributive—that is, they spread benefits more widely through society for purposes that are widely approved. The Social Security program, for example, which makes payments to a large segment of the population, is a redistributive program with distributive characteristics. As a general rule the greater the distributive element of a redistributive program, the greater the political support it receives.[171] Not only do such programs have more political backing because they serve more people, but they also are not as likely to be dubbed "welfare," a concept that still rankles many Americans.

The most important task—and thus power—of redistributive agencies is the distribution of funds. Redistributive agencies make and influence funding decisions at several levels. At the highest levels they advise the president and Congress on legislation dealing with redistributive policies and related matters. Agencies frequently even initiate policies themselves. At the agency level daily decisions that affect how money is spent are made in conjunction with oversight of program operations and determination of which individuals are eligible to receive program benefits. Despite the influence of these agencies over spending practices, however, Congress has the final say and usually structures redistributive programs carefully, thereby limiting agency discretion.[172] Examples of redistributive agencies are the Social Security Administration, the Farmers Home Administration, and the Federal Housing Administration.

Because redistributive programs are so large, expertise is an important source of power for the agencies running them. Leadership and cohesion sometimes become power sources for redistributive agencies, but not easily since many of these programs are actually administered at the state and local levels. This also means that there are relatively few redistributive bureaucrats: even though redistributive agencies spend over half the federal budget, only 7 percent of federal employees work in these agencies.[173] Overall, redistributive agencies enjoy more political clout than regulatory agencies but less than distributive ones.

Ideology influences the relationship between presidents and agencies implementing redistributive policies. Conservative presidents are less supportive of redistributive policies and the agencies executing them than liberal presidents. This is especially true of welfare programs that serve only a narrow, and politically inactive, segment of society. But it is unlikely that any president will attack redistributive programs that benefit large numbers of relatively affluent and politically active citizens—as the inviolability of the Social Security system illustrates.

Presidential control of redistributive agencies is affected by two other major issues as well. First, presidents must face the problem of increasingly scarce resources, and redistributive programs are expensive. Second, presidents quickly notice how difficult enforcement of the rules of redistributive programs can be, particularly because the points of service delivery are scattered all over the country.[174] Even though the agencies implementing redistributive policies are not among the more powerful in the federal bureaucracy, presidents can find it difficult to control them. Not only do some of the programs have strong public support, but virtually all of them receive considerable attention from Congress.

Foreign Policy. Presidents devote more time to foreign policy than to domestic issues because they tend to be more interested in it, and because they often believe they can exert greater control over foreign policy than over domestic policy. Presidents view foreign policy achievements as an effective way to increase their popularity, improve their chances for reelection, and make their place in history.[175] As commander in chief of the armed forces, presidents have significant authority over foreign policy questions, particularly issues requiring rapid action. Their power to make treaties with foreign nations and their role as head of state enhance their role in foreign affairs as well. Despite these advantages, however, presidents continue to encounter problems with the bureaucratic agencies that deal most with foreign policy, the Departments of State and Defense.

The State Department, with its deep-seated attitudes and routines, has frustrated presidents for many years. Its foreign service officers, who represent the United States worldwide, are attuned primarily to the goals and procedures of the State Department, not the president. Presidents who try to use the State Department to provide bold new ideas or to carry out risky plans frequently are disappointed.[176]

One challenging aspect of any president's job is controlling the military and dealing with the rivalry that exists among its branches. Moreover, sometimes presidents must contain the Defense Department's enthusiasm for using force in foreign policy and supervise the enormously complicated business of weapons procurement.[177] The Reagan administration's failure to do the latter helps explain the weapons scandal, in which fraud and bribery were uncovered in Pentagon procurement practices, that erupted in 1988.

Problems with the foreign policy bureaucracy have led recent presidents to rely increasingly on their White House national security staff and to make their national security adviser a key player in international relations. Henry A. Kissinger fulfilled this role during Nixon's first term. While such tactics have certain advantages for presidents—including more information, greater discretion and rapid responses to foreign policy issues—they also have some dangers, as shown by the Iran-contra scandal. Heavy reliance on the White House national security staff increases the tension between the White House and the executive agencies, decreases continuity between administrations, and encourages a narrow view of foreign relations.[178]

Presidents who try to control the foreign policy bureaucracy often have two problems.[179] First, agencies sometimes resist fulfilling presidential orders. Because presidents tend to believe that they can shape foreign policy and deal with foreign leaders better on their own than through the bureaucracy, they sometimes make foreign policy decisions without consulting the bureaucracy or against its advice. And when the bureaucracy disagrees with presidential orders, it often resists those orders in the hope that the president will either forget about the matter or have a change of heart. The second problem is that presidential directives sometimes are misunderstood by agencies and thus are not implemented in the way the president intended.

These problems are similar to those that plague presidents in domestic politics. The major difference is that presidents can use their relatively greater authority in foreign policy to counter the problems presented by federal agencies in that area.

Presidential Goals

Although virtually all presidential goals require at least the cooperation if not the assistance of the bureaucracy, some goals are more easily achieved than others. Thus, the nature of those goals is an important variable in the relationship between the president and the bureaucracy.

Presidential scholars Erwin C. Hargrove and Michael Nelson have proposed a cycle theory that categorizes presidents according to their goals.[180] What the public wants at any particular point in time also affects the cycle because skillful presidents adjust their goals to fit the public mood. The three types of presidents identified by Hargrove and Nelson—presidents of achievement, of consolidation, and of preparation—appear in a cycle: a president of consolidation follows a president of achievement, a president of preparation follows a president of consolidation, and a president of achievement follows a president of preparation. Each type of president responds to different cues from the public and generates different goals. Presidents of achievement enter office with a mandate for change from the public and they proceed to propose and get enacted broad and dramatic legislative programs that alter the role of the federal government in American life. Woodrow Wilson, Franklin Roosevelt, Lyndon Johnson, and Ronald Reagan were presidents of achievement.

Presidents of consolidation concentrate on refining, legitimizing, and rationalizing—or consolidating—the changes brought about by their predecessors. They generally pursue no major new programs. Calvin Coolidge, Dwight Eisenhower, and Richard Nixon exemplified this type of president.

Finally, presidents of preparation identify public problems, formulate possible solutions, and lay the political groundwork for the following president of achievement. Theodore Roosevelt, John Kennedy, and Jimmy Carter were presidents of preparation.

Each of the three types of presidents relates differently to the bureaucracy because their goals differ. Presidents of achievement enter office with overwhelming public support for change. That support is short-lived, however; thus, these presidents must act quickly in formulating and passing programs to take advantage of the existing support. One important consequence is that programs often are hastily devised, with little thought given to how they will be implemented—and the implementation state is where the bureaucracy is particularly powerful. Presidents of achievement usually succeed in fulfilling their goals—which can result in big changes for the bureaucracy (as did, for example, FDR's "New Deal" expansion and Reagan's cutbacks on some types of federal spending)—but they often have trouble getting the bureaucracy to implement their programs.

Presidents of consolidation try to solve the implementation problems left by presidents of achievement. They work with the bureaucracy to see that programs run as smoothly and effectually as possible. For example, rather than trying to repeal the Great Society programs passed by Lyndon Johnson, the Nixon administration attempted to make those policies run more efficiently. Good relations with the bureaucracy are therefore especially important for presidents of consolidation, and they are probably maintained more easily because the relationship is basically a cooperative one.

One of the most crucial tasks of presidents of preparation is generating new ideas, a process that usually is carried out by the White House staff, not the bureaucracy. This is not surprising, since the bureaucracy is renowned for its love of routine and its aversion to proposals that conceivably might harm its standing. The bureaucracy still plays a useful role in the process, however, by acting as a devil's advocate and stressing realism and practicality. Because clashes between the president and the bureaucracy can erupt when the president favors an idea unpopular with bureaucrats, presidents of preparation sometimes have stormy relations with the bureaucracy. For example, Jimmy Carter encountered opposition from the Department of Labor when he tried to develop a welfare reform proposal, and he faced resistance from several departments over his proposed urban policies.

Other Influences

Other influences also affect the outcome of clashes between the president and the bureaucracy, including the type of bureaucracy engaged in the conflict. Some agencies outside those in the Executive Office of the President are inherently more receptive to presidential control than others. Sometimes called presidential agencies, these entities ordinarily do not distribute tangible benefits to large areas of the country, nor do they exert direct influence within congressional districts. Presidential agencies include the Justice Department, Central Intelligence Agency, Treasury Department, and the Arms Control and Disarmament Agency.[181]

Other agencies, whose actions affect congressional constituents or districts directly, are more oriented toward Congress. Because such agencies can be valuable politically, Congress tends to take a strong interest in them, while presidential control over them is more tenuous. Congressional agencies include the Departments of Agriculture, Interior, and Veterans Affairs, and the Army Corps of Engineers.

Some agencies do not fit neatly into either category. The president has greater influence over these agencies than over congressional agencies, but not as much as over presidential agencies.[182]

Another consideration in explaining the outcome of presidential-bureaucratic clashes is whether the agency is doing something the president does not like or whether the agency is not doing something the president wants it to do. The president is much more likely to succeed in halting agency action than in instigating agency action.[183] As is true throughout most of the American political system, it is much easier to stop actions than to start them. The president can use, or threaten to use, several powers—including appointment and removal, budgetary measures, and reorganization—to halt the objectionable agency actions. Scholar Dennis D. Riley put the odds of a president being able to stop agency actions at about fifty-fifty.[184]

Unfortunately for the president the odds of being able to get agencies to do something new are much worse. Bureaucratic inertia naturally works against the president, and in some instances the agencies do not have the authority to do what the president desires (here the president's chances are especially slim, since Congress must first be convinced to grant the agency the authority to perform the action in mind). Even when agencies already have the necessary authority, the president must grapple with the reasons why the agency chose not to exercise that authority.[185]

Another factor to be considered in explaining outcomes of the clashes between the president and the bureaucracy is the question of where and how bureaucratic programs are implemented. As difficult as presidents find it to control the federal bureaucracy, that task seems simple compared to the presidential effort required to control the state and local organizations that carry out numerous federal programs.[186]

A final factor is the president's current political standing. The better it is, the easier will be control of the bureaucracy as well as most other political chores.[187]

Bureaucratic Accountability

The tremendous power of the federal bureaucracy raises some important questions about America's democratic government. First, because the bureaucrats who exercise that power are not elected by the public, does the bureaucracy really respond to the public's desires—that is, is the bureaucracy accountable for its actions, and if it is, how so? Second, how much bureaucratic accountability is necessary? And third, should the president be responsible for holding the bureaucracy accountable?

Is the Bureaucracy Accountable?

Some scholars, pointing to the difficulty in holding the bureaucracy accountable, believe that little bureaucratic accountability is exercised in the modern political system. One problem is interpreting the public will. Such a task is tricky enough on major political issues or even election results, but divining the public's desires on the less visible matters ordinarily handled by the bureaucracy is an even more daunting prospect.

The huge size and complexity of the bureaucracy make it hard enough to keep track of what it is doing, much less assess its actions and compare them to the public will. It is also unclear exactly who will do the accounting, as the bureaucracy is technically subordinate to the president, Congress, and the courts, none of whom usually has much incentive to watch the bureaucracy closely.

Despite these obstacles, some observers claim that the federal bureaucracy is reasonably accountable to the public.[188] Scholars Peter Woll and Rochelle Jones even go so far as to assert that "the bureaucracy is at least as accountable and controlled as the three original branches [of the federal government]." [189] This line of argument admits that there is no clear single authority that governs the bureaucracy. Rather, the multiplicity of forces that influences the bureaucracy ensures an adequate degree of accountability. Thus, the will of the public, at least as it manifests itself in interest groups and elected officials, who let the bureaucracy know their feelings, influences bureaucratic behavior.

How Much Accountability Is Necessary?

Almost everyone agrees that some accountability and control over the bureaucracy is needed to see that laws are implemented more or less in accordance with legislative intent and that the bureaucracy is responsive to the needs of the public. But how much accountability is in the public's best interests? Some observers believe that the greater that control, the better, while many others note the benefits of having a bureaucracy with a certain degree of autonomy.

One benefit usually reaped from a bureaucracy with some discretion is better policy. Because bureaucratic agencies have specific functions and use employees with specialized skills to carry them out, bureaucratic discretion is a good thing, the argument goes, as the bureaucrats themselves are best suited to make administrative decisions. Rigid control of the bureaucracy by outsiders may well reduce bureaucratic efficiency, not only because the interference causes inconvenience, but also because outsiders frequently do not know enough about the bureaucracy's functions to exercise control intelligently.[190] As German sociologist and bureaucracy expert Max Weber has observed, bureaucratic expertise and specialization often mean that "the 'political master' finds himself in the position of the 'dilettante' " when trying to control the bureaucracy.[191]

The notion that the bureaucracy must be placed under strict control assumes, probably unfairly, that bureaucrats will somehow misbehave if left to their own devices. But in fact many observers argue that most bureaucrats strive to serve the public interest—perhaps more diligently than some elected officials.[192]

A relatively autonomous bureaucracy can provide other benefits as well by acting as an additional check on the other three branches of government and by making many decisions on its own, without having to consult with those providing oversight. The latter benefit allows the bureaucracy to implement the laws more efficiently and also gives the overseers—whether the president, Congress, or the courts—more time to attend to their own business.

Thus, how much control of the bureaucracy is needed? The answer seems to be some but not too much. As scholar Kenneth J. Meier has written, "Controls should be strong enough to guarantee the responsiveness of bureaucratic policymaking to the policy directives of the people, yet not so strong as to stifle bureaucratic initiative." [193] Although that answer may be frustratingly vague, it also may be the only answer available.

Should the President Do the Accounting?

Many observers of the bureaucracy believe that presidents must take the lead in its control.[194] After all, the president is elected by the entire nation and thus presumably reflects the will of the public. Moreover, the Constitution charges the president with seeing that the laws are executed faithfully, which certainly requires some oversight of the bureaucracy. Most proponents of presidential control of the bureaucracy agree that such control is no easy task, but they disagree over whether the president already possesses the necessary tools for the job. Some scholars contend that the president does have all the powers needed to control the bureaucracy and that it is skillful use of existing powers, rather than the addition of new ones, that is required.[195] Others argue that the president should be granted additional resources and authority to be used in battles against the bureaucracy.[196]

Some doubts about the president's potential role as overseer of the bureaucracy have been raised as well. One reservation is that while presidents are elected on a national basis, those elections are at best only rather vague mandates. Few specific issues are discussed in presidential campaigns; thus, presidential direction of the bureaucracy based on the president's electoral mandate may be stretching things somewhat. Members of Congress also are elected officials; should not they have some say over bureaucratic actions as well? The courts and interest groups too can claim the right to offer input.

The extent of the president's role in supervising the bureaucracy is yet another question that cannot be settled completely. It is widely agreed that the president must take some responsibility for the bureaucracy, but exactly how much is unclear. As a result, it is largely up to presidents themselves to decide how much attention they wish to give to the bureaucracy.

Can Presidents Control the Bureaucracy?

Is presidential control of the bureaucracy possible? According to traditional wisdom, the federal bureaucracy is so intransigent that presidents are incapable of exercising much control over it.[197] The history of several recent presidencies and more contemporary scholarship, however, paint a slightly different picture. Thus, the best answer to the question seems to be that while presidents cannot control everything the bureaucracy does, they can indeed exert significant influence over it.

Although presidents can influence the bureaucracy, it is by no means an easy job. Influencing the bureaucracy is a skill, and presidents who develop and use that skill effectively will enjoy more success with the bureaucracy than those who do not. Presidential scholars Hargrove and Nelson have called this skill "institutional leadership," and they have defined it as the ability of presidents to get the bureaucracy to adopt and work toward presidential goals.[198] Presidents employing this kind of institutional leadership must call on many of the powers of their office.

The experiences of several modern presidents demonstrate that the nation's chief executive can in fact influence the bureaucracy. John Kennedy took primary control of foreign policy making by relying on White House assistants instead of the executive departments, and Lyndon Johnson used his budgetary powers to sway the military bureaucracy. Richard Nixon took advantage of reorganization and other management techniques to achieve some control over the welfare system.[199] Jimmy Carter appointed like-minded people to help pursue his objective of deregulating numerous private sector industries.[200]

No modern president was more successful at controlling the bureaucracy than Ronald Reagan, and his presidency did the most to contradict the notion that presidents are helpless in the face of the massive federal bureaucracy.[201] Reagan was especially careful to appoint bureaucrats who shared his political ideology; in fact, political compatibility was the principal criterion for landing a political job in the Reagan administration.[202] Reagan also used his staff and budget powers effectively. As a result, the federal bureaucracy began working for kinds of policies—items on Reagan's conservative agenda—that were radically different from those put forth by previous presidents, thereby proving that presidents can exert some control over the bureaucracy. Reagan accomplished this feat using constitutional and statutory powers that have been available to presidents for decades.[203]

Some scholars have pointed to several trends that seem to be weakening the bureaucracy's ability to resist the president and enhancing presidential control of the bureaucracy.[204] One of these trends is the decline in the public's belief that experts can solve the nation's most difficult problems, including drug abuse, inner city decay, and international affairs. Because expertise is one of the primary sources of bureaucratic power, the bureaucracy loses strength when its expertise is tarnished. Another trend, arising from the growing number of government programs, is the expanding overlap of agency jurisdictions. The resulting struggles for power among agencies divert their attention from other issues and create stalemates that frequently must be resolved by the White House, giving the president more power. Finally, more and more interest groups are taking part in the policy process and consequently competing. Agencies thus can no longer count on having stable relations with interest groups.

Notes

1. Richard P. Nathan, *The Administrative Presidency* (New York: Wiley, 1983), 2.
2. Michael Nelson, "The Irony of American Bureaucracy," in *Bureaucratic Power in National Policy Making*, 4th ed., ed. Francis E. Rourke (Boston: Little, Brown, 1986), 169.
3. James Q. Wilson, *American Government: Institutions and Policies*, 2d ed. (Lexington, Mass.: D. C. Heath, 1983), 350.
4. Benjamin I. Page and Mark P. Petracca, *The American Presidency* (New York: McGraw-Hill, 1983), 198.
5. Peter K. Eisinger, Dennis L. Dresang, Robert Booth Fowler, et al., *American Politics: The People and the Policy* (Boston: Little, Brown, 1978), 234.
6. Page and Petracca, *The American Presidency*, 201.
7. Wilson, *American Government*, 253.
8. Page and Petracca, *The American Presidency*, 202.
9. George J. Gordon, *Public Administration in America*, 3d ed. (New York: St. Martin's Press, 1986), 17-20.
10. Kenneth J. Meier, *Politics and the Bureaucracy: Policymaking in the Fourth Branch of Government*, 2d ed. (Monterey, Calif.: Brooks/Cole, 1987), 49.
11. Ibid., 50, 89.
12. Ibid., 51.
13. Morris P. Fiorina, "Congress and Bureaucracy: A Profitable Partnership," in Rourke, *Bureaucratic Power*.
14. Ibid., 230.
15. Ibid.
16. Arthur Maass, *Congress and the Common Good* (New York: Basic Books, 1983).
17. Meier, *Politics*, 29.
18. Ibid.
19. Ibid., 30.
20. Ibid., 31.
21. Ibid.
22. Wilson, *American Government*, 353.
23. Meier, *Politics*, 3.
24. Charles T. Goodsell, *The Case for Bureaucracy* (Chatham, N.J.: Chatham House, 1983), 3.
25. Ibid.
26. Ibid., 7-8.
27. Herbert Kaufman, "Fear of Bureaucracy: A Raging Pandemic," *Public Administration Review* (January/February 1981): 1.
28. Robert L. Kahn, Barbara A. Gutek, et al., "Americans Love Their Bureaucrats," in Rourke, *Bureaucratic Power*.
29. Kaufman, "Fear of Bureaucracy"; Goodsell, *The Case for Bureaucracy;* Meier, *Politics*, 4-7.
30. Kahn, "Americans," 290-292.
31. See Anthony Downs, *Inside Bureaucracy* (Boston: Little, Brown, 1967); David Nachmias and David H. Rosenbloom, *Bureaucratic Government USA* (New York: St. Martin's Press, 1980); Eisinger et al., *American Politics*.
32. Nachmias and Rosenbloom, *Bureaucratic Government*, 12.
33. Downs, *Inside Bureaucracy*, 24-25.
34. Ibid., 33-35.
35. Meier, *Politics*, 19.
36. Gordon, *Public Administration*, 9.
37. Meier, *Politics*, 24.
38. Ibid., 25.
39. Ibid., 29.
40. Ibid., 27.
41. Gordon, *Public Administration*, 319.
42. Meier, *Politics*, 33.
43. Ibid.
44. Ibid., 34.
45. Gordon, *Public Administration*, 335.
46. Meier, *Politics*, 36.
47. Ibid.
48. Hugh Heclo, *A Government of Strangers* (Washington, D.C.: Brookings, 1977), 125.
49. Meier, *Politics*, 34-35.
50. Goodsell, *The Case for Bureaucracy*, 82.
51. Wilson, *American Government*, 359.
52. Ibid.
53. Gordon, *Public Administration*, 101.
54. Heclo, *A Government of Strangers*, 94.
55. George C. Edwards III and Stephen J. Wayne, *Presidential Leadership* (New York: St. Martin's Press, 1985), 369-371.
56. Richard A. Watson and Norman C. Thomas, *The Politics of the Presidency*, 2d ed. (Washington, D.C.: CQ Press, 1988), 282.
57. Ibid., 283.
58. Heclo, *A Government of Strangers*.
59. Watson and Thomas, *The Politics of the Presidency*, 283.
60. Heclo, *A Government of Strangers*, 100.
61. Wilson, *American Government*, 320.
62. Heclo, *A Government of Strangers*, 102-103.
63. Robert J. Sickels, *The Presidency: An Introduction* (Englewood Cliffs, N.J.: Prentice-Hall, 1980), 153.
64. Thomas E. Cronin, *The State of the Presidency*, 2d ed. (Boston: Little, Brown, 1980), 266.
65. Watson and Thomas, *The Politics of the Presidency*, 288.
66. Cronin, *The State of the Presidency*, 270.
67. Ibid., 275-278.
68. Meier, *Politics*, 65.
69. Francis E. Rourke, *Bureaucracy, Politics, and Public Policy*, 3d ed. (Boston: Little, Brown, 1984), 94.
70. Ibid., 32.
71. Meier, *Politics*, 70.
72. Ibid., 63.
73. Ibid., 55.
74. Ibid., 56-57.
75. Meier, *Politics*, 172-173.
76. Rourke, *Bureaucracy*, 77.
77. Downs, *Inside Bureaucracy*, 263-264.
78. Dennis D. Riley, *Controlling the Federal Bureaucracy* (Philadelphia: Temple University Press, 1987), 96; and Richard M. Pious, *Essentials of American Politics and Government* (New York: McGraw-Hill, 1987), 459.
79. Meier, *Politics*, 147.
80. Ibid., 149.
81. Ibid., 150-151; and Pious, *Essentials*, 468-469.
82. Wilson, *American Government*, 367.
83. Meier, *Politics*, 112.
84. Rourke, *Bureaucracy*, 51.
85. Ibid., 196-199.

86. Harold Seidman and Robert Gilmour, *Politics, Position, and Power: From the Positive to the Regulatory State*, 4th ed. (New York: Oxford University Press, 1986), 89.
87. Robert Sherrill, *Why They Call It Politics: A Guide to America's Government*, 4th ed. (San Diego: Harcourt Brace Jovanovich, 1984), 260.
88. Cronin, *The State of the Presidency*, 241.
89. David L. Barnett, "A War Reagan's Winning: Taming the Bureaucracy," *U.S. News & World Report*, April 5, 1982, 27.
90. George J. Church, "Good Chemistry," *Time*, June 13, 1988, 14, 21.
91. Sherrill, *Why They Call It Politics*, 251.
92. Cronin, *The State of the Presidency*, 223.
93. Page and Petracca, *The American Presidency*, 217.
94. Ibid.
95. Erwin C. Hargrove, *The Missing Link: The Study of the Implementation of Social Policy* (Washington, D.C.: Urban Institute, 1975), 111.
96. Edwards and Wayne, *Presidential Leadership*, 352-353.
97. Sickels, *The Presidency*, 194-198.
98. David V. Edwards, *The American Political Experience: An Introduction to Government*, 4th ed. (Englewood Cliffs, N.J.: Prentice-Hall, 1988), 289.
99. Richard E. Neustadt, *Presidential Power: The Politics of Leadership from FDR to Carter* (New York: Wiley, 1980), 9.
100. Graham T. Allison, *Essence of Decision: Explaining the Cuban Missile Crisis* (Boston: Little, Brown, 1971).
101. Peter Goldman, "The Bureaucratic Man," *Newsweek*, January 26, 1981, 41.
102. Allison, *Essence of Decision*, 101-102.
103. Edwards and Wayne, *Presidential Leadership*, 380-381.
104. Ibid., 351.
105. Erwin C. Hargrove and Michael Nelson, *Presidents, Politics, and Policy* (New York: Knopf, 1984), 87-90.
106. Neustadt, *Presidential Power*, 25.
107. Ibid., 9.
108. Hargrove and Nelson, *Presidents*, 89.
109. Ibid., 104.
110. Gordon, *Public Administration*, 104.
111. Sickels, *The Presidency*, 173.
112. Cronin, *The State of the Presidency*, 244.
113. Seidman and Gilmour, *Politics*, 3.
114. Rourke, *Public Policy*, 169.
115. Seidman and Gilmour, *Politics*, 13.
116. Riley, *Controlling the Federal Bureaucracy*, 42.
117. Ibid.; and Page and Petracca, *The American Presidency*, 223.
118. Gordon, *Public Administration*, 107.
119. Meier, *Politics*, 161.
120. Watson and Thomas, *The Politics of the Presidency*, 301.
121. See Gordon, *Public Administration*, 111-115.
122. Downs, *Inside Bureaucracy*, 116-118.
123. Edwards and Wayne, *Presidential Leadership*, 252-258.
124. Ibid., 256.
125. Watson and Thomas, *The Politics of the Presidency*, 308.
126. Ibid.; and Gordon, *Public Administration*, 405.
127. Watson and Thomas, *The Politics of the Presidency*, 309; and Gordon, *Public Administration*, 468-469.
128. Gordon, *Public Administration*, 408.
129. Watson and Thomas, *The Politics of the Presidency*, 308.
130. Steffen W. Schmidt, Mack C. Shelley II, and Barbara A. Bardes, *American Government and Politics Today*, 2d ed. (St. Paul, Minn.: West Publishing, 1987), 392.
131. Watson and Thomas, *The Politics of the Presidency*, 296.
132. Ibid., 297.
133. Meier, *Politics*, 164.
134. Page and Petracca, *The American Presidency*, 342.
135. Goldman, "The Bureaucratic Man," 42.
136. Neustadt, *Presidential Power*, 16-21.
137. Sherrill, *Why They Call It Politics*, 32.
138. Gordon, *Public Administration*, 100.
139. Sherrill, *Why They Call It Politics*, 33.
140. Ibid., 34.
141. Edwards and Wayne, *Presidential Leadership*, 200.
142. Riley, *Controlling the Federal Bureaucracy*, 18.
143. Edwards and Wayne, *Presidential Leadership*, 200.
144. Ibid., 363.
145. Meier, *Politics*, 155.
146. Seidman and Gilmour, *Politics*, 70.
147. Sickels, *The Presidency*, 198.
148. Pious, *Essentials*, 469.
149. See Edwards, *The American Political Experience*, 294.
150. Pious, *Essentials*, 470.
151. Goldman, "The Bureaucratic Man," 42.
152. Ibid.
153. Hugh Heclo, "Issue Networks and the Executive Establishment," in *The New American Political System*, ed. Anthony King (Washington, D.C.: American Enterprise Institute, 1978), 87-124.
154. Pious, *Essentials*, 471.
155. Ibid.
156. Ibid., 472.
157. Gordon, *Public Administration*, 81; and Watson and Thomas, *The Politics of the Presidency*, 288.
158. Meier, *Politics*, 164.
159. Edwards and Wayne, *Presidential Leadership*, 366-367.
160. Hargrove, *The Missing Link*, 114.
161. Hargrove and Nelson, *Presidents*, 238-239.
162. Meier, *Politics*, 96-98.
163. Hargrove and Nelson, *Presidents*, 239.
164. Meier, *Politics*, 78.
165. Hargrove and Nelson, *Presidents*, 239.
166. Meier, *Politics*, 87.
167. Hargrove and Nelson, *Presidents*, 240-241.
168. Ibid.
169. Meier, *Politics*, 87.
170. Ibid., 89.
171. Hargrove and Nelson, *Presidents*, 241.
172. Meier, *Politics*, 92-93.
173. Ibid., 89.
174. Hargrove and Nelson, *Presidents*, 242.
175. Edwards and Wayne, *Presidential Leadership*, 308.
176. Hargrove and Nelson, *Presidents*, 243-244.
177. Ibid., 244-245.
178. Edwards and Wayne, *Presidential Leadership*, 308.
179. Hargrove and Nelson, *Presidents*, 248.
180. Ibid., chapter 3.
181. Wilson, *American Government*, 365.
182. Ibid.
183. Riley, *Controlling the Federal Bureaucracy*, 53-54.
184. Ibid.
185. Ibid.
186. Hargrove and Nelson, *Presidents*, 234.
187. Riley, *Controlling the Federal Bureaucracy*, 55.
188. Peter Woll, *American Bureaucracy*, 2d ed. (New York: W. W. Norton, 1977), 246; and Gordon, *Public Administration*, 83.
189. Peter Woll and Rochelle Jones, "The Bureaucracy as a Check on the President," *The Bureaucrat* 3 (April 1974): 19.
190. Riley, *Controlling the Federal Bureaucracy*, 169-170.
191. Max Weber, "Essay on Bureaucracy," in Rourke, *Bureaucratic Power*, 70.
192. Gordon, *Public Administration*, 87-88.
193. Meier, *Politics*, 199.
194. Ibid., 155, 204; and Cronin, *The State of the Presidency*, 225.
195. Meier, *Politics*, 205.
196. Cronin, *The State of the Presidency*, 225-226.
197. Francis E. Rourke, "Grappling with the Bureaucracy," in *Politics and the Oval Office: Towards Presidential Governance*, ed. Arnold J. Meltsner (San Francisco: Institute for Contemporary Studies, 1981), 135.
198. Hargrove and Nelson, *Presidents*, 238.
199. Rourke, "Grappling," 138.
200. Meier, *Politics*, 205.
201. Elizabeth Sanders, "The Presidency and the Bureaucratic State," in *The Presidency and the Political System*, ed. Michael Nelson (Washington, D.C.: CQ Press, 1988), 379.
202. Watson and Thomas, *The Politics of the Presidency*, 310.

203. Sanders, "The Presidency," 379.
204. Rourke, "Grappling," 139-140.

Selected Bibliography

Downs, Anthony. *Inside Bureaucracy.* Boston: Little, Brown, 1967.

Edwards, George C. III, and Stephen J. Wayne. *Presidential Leadership: Politics and Policy Making.* New York: St. Martin's Press, 1985.

Gordon, George J. *Public Administration in America.* 3d ed. New York: St. Martin's Press, 1986.

Hargrove, Erwin C., and Michael Nelson. *Presidents, Politics, and Policy.* New York: Knopf, 1984.

Heclo, Hugh. *A Government of Strangers: Executive Politics in Washington.* Washington, D.C.: Brookings, 1977.

Meier, Kenneth J. *Politics and the Bureaucracy: Policymaking in the Fourth Branch of Government.* 2d ed. Monterey, Calif.: Brooks/Cole, 1987.

Nachmias, David, and David H. Rosenbloom. *Bureaucratic Government USA.* New York: St. Martin's Press, 1980.

Neustadt, Richard E. *Presidential Power: The Politics of Leadership from FDR to Carter.* New York: Wiley, 1980.

Page, Benjamin I., and Mark P. Petracca. *The American Presidency.* New York: McGraw-Hill, 1983.

Pious, Richard M. *Essentials of American Politics and Government.* New York: McGraw-Hill, 1987.

Riley, Dennis D. *Controlling the Federal Bureaucracy.* Philadelphia: Temple University Press, 1987.

Rourke, Francis E. *Bureaucracy, Politics, and Public Policy.* 3d ed. Boston: Little, Brown, 1984.

——, ed. *Bureaucratic Power in National Policy Making.* 4th ed. Boston: Little, Brown, 1986.

Seidman, Harold, and Robert Gilmour. *Politics, Position, and Power: From the Positive to the Regulatory State.* 4th ed. New York: Oxford University Press, 1986.

Watson, Richard A., and Norman C. Thomas. *The Politics of the Presidency.* 2d ed. Washington, D.C.: CQ Press, 1988.

National Park Service

Gutzon Borglum honored Washington, Jefferson, Theodore Roosevelt, and Lincoln by sculpting their faces into Mount Rushmore.

Part VII

The Presidents and the Vice Presidents

Biographies of the Presidents

The Constitution requires only that a president be at least thirty-five years of age, a natural-born citizen or a citizen at the time of the adoption of the Constitution, and a resident within the United States for fourteen years. Although these constitutional requirements disqualify few Americans, the forty persons who have become president have come from a relatively narrow slice of American society.

All presidents have shared several important characteristics. First, all have been men. Through the 1988 election, no woman had been nominated for president by a major political party.

Second, each of the forty presidents descended from northern European ancestors. Moreover, of the forty, only five trace their roots to continental Europe. The ancestors of Martin Van Buren, Theodore Roosevelt, and Franklin D. Roosevelt were Dutch; Herbert C. Hoover's were Swiss; and Dwight D. Eisenhower's were German. The forebears of the thirty-five other presidents came to America primarily from the British Isles.

Third, no president has reached the presidency without significant experience as a public servant. Most presidents have served in at least one elective office at the national or state level. Twenty-four presidents have been members of Congress; fifteen have been governors of a state; and fourteen have been vice presidents. Presidents have also served as cabinet members, diplomats, state legislators, mayors, judges, sheriffs, and prosecutors on their way to higher office. Because George Washington was the first president, he did not have the opportunity to run for Congress, but he served the nation as a general and a delegate to the Continental Congress. Three presidents, Zachary Taylor, Ulysses S. Grant, and Eisenhower, were career generals without civilian political experience. Two others, William Howard Taft and Hoover, never had been elected to a national political office or a governorship but had served the nation as cabinet officers. Taft was Theodore Roosevelt's secretary of war; Hoover was secretary of commerce under Warren G. Harding and Calvin Coolidge.

Beyond these three characteristics common to each of the first forty presidents, two characteristics have been shared by all but one of them: marriage and Protestantism. James Buchanan was the only president who never married. Five others entered the presidency without a wife: Grover Cleveland did not marry until after he became president, and Thomas Jefferson, Van Buren, Andrew Jackson, and Chester A. Arthur took office as widowers. Not until the election of Ronald Reagan in 1980, however, did the American people elect a president who had been divorced.

Until John F. Kennedy became the first Catholic president in 1961, all chief executives had come from Protestant backgrounds with the Episcopalian, Presbyterian, and Unitarian denominations predominating. Although all presidents have professed their belief in God, they have varied widely in their religious convictions and practices. Jefferson's political opponents accused him of being an atheist—a charge he denied. Although Abraham Lincoln frequently quoted the Bible in his speeches, he belonged to no specific denomination and felt compelled early in his political career to make a statement declaring his belief in God. A few presidents have been outwardly religious men. James Garfield was a lay preacher for the Disciples of Christ before beginning his congressional career. Jimmy Carter described himself as a born-again Christian during the 1976 presidential campaign.

If one considers all these characteristics together, a distinct profile of the American president emerges. Presidents typically have been American-born, married men who were at least forty-two years old (Theodore Roosevelt being the youngest to hold office), descended from northern European, Protestant ancestors, and have had some type of public service career at the state or national level.

From this well-defined societal group, however, presidents have come into office from a variety of personal backgrounds.

Some presidents descended from the American aristocracy, including Jefferson, James Madison, John Quincy Adams, John Tyler, William Henry Harrison and his grandson Benjamin Harrison, the Roosevelts, Taft, Kennedy, and George Bush. These presidents had the advantage of wealth and family connections when building their political careers. Other presidents, including Jackson, Lincoln, Andrew Johnson, and Garfield, were self-made men from poor, sometimes destitute circumstances. Several presidents, such as Hoover, Richard Nixon, and Reagan, did not grow up in poverty but received little financial support from their parents as they started their careers.

The educational background of presidents ranges from that of Woodrow Wilson, who earned a Ph.D. from Johns Hopkins University, to Andrew Johnson, who never at-

---

By Daniel C. Diller

tended a school of any type. Other presidents, such as Washington and Lincoln, received only rudimentary formal education. Thirty-one presidents attended college, including every twentieth-century president except Harry S Truman.

Presidents also have worked in all types of professions before starting their careers in public service. The most common profession for presidents has been law; twenty-four were admitted to the bar. Only two, however, of the last nine presidents, Gerald Ford and Nixon, have practiced law. Over half the presidents had some experience in agriculture, either as a plantation owner, dirt farmer, rancher, field worker, or son of a farming family. Seven presidents were teachers. Several others were professional soldiers, merchants, surveyors, or journalists.

Given these differences in wealth, education, and profession, presidents have made progress toward the presidency at different times in their lives. Jackson and Nixon, for example, began their political careers with election to the U.S. House of Representatives at the ages of twenty-nine and thirty-three, respectively. In contrast, Wilson and Reagan were not elected to their first political offices—governor of New Jersey and governor of California, respectively—until they were in their mid-fifties. No one could have foreseen in 1922 that Truman, then the owner of a failing haberdashery who had never gone to college or run for public office, would be president in twenty-three years. In contrast, twenty-three years before John Quincy Adams became president, he had graduated Phi Beta Kappa from Harvard, served as minister to Holland and Prussia, been elected to the Massachusetts state senate, and narrowly lost election to the U.S. House of Representatives.

Thus, despite their similarities, every president has come to office at a different pace, under different circumstances, and with a different set of experiences that affect their leadership.

Just as the pre-presidential experiences of the chief executives have varied, so have their post-presidential experiences. While many chief executives have retired from public life after leaving the presidency, a few have continued their political careers, and several have run again for president. Cleveland was the only president to be reelected president after leaving office. Van Buren, Millard Fillmore, and Theodore Roosevelt ran unsuccessfully for reelection after leaving office. Former president Ulysses S. Grant came close to receiving the Republican nomination in 1880, but the Republican national convention chose dark-horse candidate Garfield instead.

Two former presidents were elected to Congress after retiring from the presidency. John Quincy Adams was elected to the U.S. House of Representatives in 1830 and served there until 1848; he died in the Capitol after suffering a stroke. Andrew Johnson was elected to the Senate in 1875 and served briefly before his death that year. Tyler was elected to the Confederate Congress in 1861 but died before taking his seat. Taft fulfilled his highest personal ambition when Harding appointed him chief justice of the United States in 1921. Taft served on the Court until he retired in 1930.

Most former presidents have served as unofficial advisers to their party or to the incumbent president. Several, including Taft and Hoover, have served on advisory commissions or administrative boards appointed by the incumbent president. And since Coolidge, every president who has survived his term has published an autobiography or memoirs about his time in office.

George Washington

Charles Wilson Peale; Architect of the Capitol Collection

G° Washington

Born: February 22, 1732; Westmoreland County, Virginia
Party: Federalist
Term: April 30, 1789-March 4, 1797
Vice President: John Adams
Died: December 14, 1799; Mount Vernon, Virginia
Buried: Mount Vernon

George Washington was born into a moderately wealthy family, who owned several plantations in northern Virginia. His father, Augustine, had ten children, six with Mary Ball, of which George was the eldest, and four by a previous marriage. When the eleven-year-old George's father died, he was left in the custody of his eldest half brother, Lawrence, whom he loved and admired.

George's early education was adequate, though far from exceptional. He was tutored and attended school on an irregular basis from ages seven to fifteen, but had no formal education beyond grammar school. George's exposure to the well-mannered intellectual atmosphere created by Lawrence compensated for the youngster's limited book learning. He also received an education in the outdoor occupations of Virginia. In his early teens he was already a skilled woodsman, tobacco planter, and surveyor. When George was sixteen, he joined the first of several survey expeditions that he would make to the Virginia frontier.

In 1751 George took the only overseas trip of his life to Barbados with Lawrence, who was suffering from tuberculosis and thus hoping that the Caribbean climate would relieve his condition. There George contracted a mild case of smallpox, which left him scarred. Lawrence died in July 1752, after he and George returned to the colonies.

The following November, Washington began his frontier military career as a major in the Virginia militia. His first assignment was to inform the French commander at Fort Le Boeuf in Pennsylvania that unless the French evacuated the Ohio Valley they risked war. The French refused to budge, ensuring hostilities with the British.

After returning from the mission Washington was promoted to lieutenant colonel with the help of influential friends. In early 1754 he marched west with 160 recruits to reinforce British troops at the fork of the Ohio and Monongahela rivers. During this journey his men fired what many historians regard as the first shots of the French and Indian War. The nervous recruits ambushed a detachment of thirty French soldiers, killing ten, including their commander, Coulon de Jumonville. The attack gained Washington a measure of infamy because Jumonville was on a diplomatic mission to the British. Six weeks later Washington's force was besieged and defeated at Fort Necessity. Before allowing his men to return to Virginia, the French forced Washington to sign a statement written in French, which he did not understand. In it he admitted to being an assassin. Washington's reputation was damaged by the episode, especially among British military officers. Upon returning to Virginia, Washington resigned his commission.

In December 1754 Lawrence's last living child died, and Washington inherited the right to rent Lawrence's estate at Mount Vernon from his late half brother's remarried widow, Ann Lee. In 1761, when Mrs. Lee died, he inherited Mount Vernon outright.

Washington returned to military service in the spring of 1755 when he was appointed aide-de-camp to Maj. Gen. Edward Braddock. After several years of service in the French and Indian War, in which he achieved the rank of colonel, Washington resigned in 1758 to run for the Virginia House of Burgesses. He served there for nine years. He was not known as a dynamic or creative legislator, but he gained the admiration of his colleagues and firsthand knowledge of representative government.

Revolutionary War

As tensions mounted between the British and the colonies, Washington became increasingly involved in the patriot cause. In 1769 he helped lead a movement to establish restrictions on the importation of British goods throughout the colonies. And in 1774 he attended the First Continental Convention in Philadelphia as a delegate from Virginia. Afterward, he returned to Virginia and began training militia forces using his own money. On June 16, 1775, Washington accepted a commission from the Second Continental Convention as the commanding general of the Continental army. Patriot leaders hoped the choice of a military leader from a southern state would unite the colonies behind the rebellion that already had begun in New England.

As a general, Washington's inspirational and administrative abilities were more exceptional than his military knowledge. He made several tactical blunders during the war, including the ill-considered deployment of part of his army in an exposed position on Long Island in 1776, which resulted in the loss of five thousand troops and the British occupation of New York City. Yet despite his lack of experience in commanding large forces, Washington did show flashes of strategic brilliance. The celebrated triumphs of his army at Boston, Trenton, Princeton, and Yorktown demonstrated his superior generalship. Nevertheless, Washington's skill at maintaining morale, inspiring loyalty, and holding his army together, as exemplified during the harsh winter of 1777-1778 at Valley Forge, Pennsylvania, was more crucial to the success of the revolution than his tactical abilities.

After the decisive defeat of the British at Yorktown in 1781, discontent within the Continental army became the primary threat to the young nation. Many soldiers believed that Congress had not compensated them adequately or recognized their service to the nation. In May 1782 Washington angrily rejected an idea proposed by one of his officers that he allow himself to be crowned king. In March 1783 a more serious threat to Republican government emerged. Many officers were considering using the army to depose Congress and set up their own government. Washington addressed an assembly of his officers on March 15 in Newburgh, New York, where he persuaded them to give up their plan and support Congress.

With the war officially ended by the Treaty of Paris, signed on September 3, 1783, Washington retired to Mount Vernon. He managed his plantation until 1787, when he agreed to accept an appointment as one of Virginia's delegates to the Constitutional Convention in Philadelphia. His presence lent legitimacy to the convention, and its delegates unanimously elected him presiding officer. After a long summer of debate during which Washington said little, the convention agreed on a new constitution. Washington and his fellow delegates signed the document on September 17, 1787.

Presidency

Washington was the inevitable choice of his nation to be the first president under the new Constitution. He alone had the nonpartisan reputation needed to transcend sectional and ideological conflicts, so that the United States would have time to establish effective government institutions and gain the trust of the people. In early 1789 presidential electors unanimously elected Washington president. After a triumphant overland journey from Mount Vernon to New York City, during which he was met by cheering crowds at every stop, Washington took the oath of office in New York on April 30, 1789.

During Washington's first term Congress passed the Bill of Rights, and the states that had not yet ratified the Constitution did so. In an attempt to inspire confidence in the federal government and to establish a spirit of national unity Washington toured the northern states in late 1789 and the southern states in the spring of 1791. Mindful of the problems caused by the weakness of the federal government under the Articles of Confederation, Washington was careful throughout his presidency to assert the primacy of the federal government over the states.

Washington was usually deferential toward Congress;

he believed that the president should veto a bill only if it were unconstitutional. He often made decisions after listening to his two most important and eloquent advisers, Secretary of State Thomas Jefferson and Secretary of the Treasury Alexander Hamilton, debate an issue. Secretary of War Henry Knox, Attorney General Edmund Randolph, and Postmaster General Samuel Osgood completed the cabinet. Although Washington endeavored to avoid any partisanship, he usually agreed with Hamilton on important issues. In particular, he backed Hamilton's plans to have the federal government assume the wartime debts of the states and to establish a national bank. After much debate Congress passed both measures, and Washington signed the debt assumption bill in 1790 and the bank bill in 1791.

Washington's primary goal in foreign policy was maintaining the neutrality of the United States in the war between France and Great Britain. Washington believed that the young nation had to avoid alliance entanglements if it were to survive and remain united during its early years. Secretary of State Thomas Jefferson urged that the United States aid France, which had helped the colonies defeat the British in the revolutionary war, but Washington rejected Jefferson's counsel. The president issued a neutrality proclamation on April 22, 1793, which declared that the United States would be "friendly and impartial" toward the belligerents. Jefferson's disputes with Washington's policies led him to resign at the end of 1793. The following year Congress passed the Neutrality Act of 1794, which endorsed Washington's policy of neutrality. In 1795 Washington signed the Jay Treaty with Great Britain. The agreement, which had been negotiated in London by Chief Justice John Jay, increased commerce between the two nations and settled several disputes. The treaty was highly unpopular, however, with pro-French Democratic-Republicans who attacked Washington for concluding what they perceived as a pro-British agreement.

In 1794 Washington faced a domestic crisis when a rebellion broke out in western Pennsylvania over the federal tax on whiskey. Washington believed that he had to put down the rebellion quickly to avoid the impression that the federal government was weak. Thus, he ordered the governors of Pennsylvania, Maryland, New Jersey, and Virginia to supply the federal government with fifteen thousand militia and rode to Pennsylvania to oversee their preparations personally. The show of force was sufficient to quell the Whiskey Rebellion, and Washington never had to lead the militia into battle.

During his presidency Washington strove to avoid partisan politics; he believed that political factions could destroy the unity of the young nation. Thus, in his famous Farewell Address published on September 17, 1796, he cautioned against excessive partisanship as well as foreign influence and permanent alliances. But despite his efforts to prevent the development of parties, before his presidency had ended two factions had already emerged in American politics: the Federalists, with whom Washington most closely identified, led by Alexander Hamilton and Vice President John Adams, and the Democratic-Republicans, led by Thomas Jefferson and House member James Madison.

Retirement

In 1796 Washington refused to consider running for a third term. He had been wounded during his second term by criticism from the Democratic-Republican press over the Jay Treaty and other issues and was anxious to return to the quiet life of a gentleman farmer at Mount Vernon. He spent the last years of his life managing his estate and entertaining friends. In 1799, when war seemed imminent with France, President John Adams asked Washington to accept an appointment as lieutenant general and commander in chief of the army. Washington accepted on the condition that he would not have to take active command of the forces except in an emergency. War with France was averted, and Washington's retirement was not disturbed. On December 12, 1799, after riding about his estate on a cold day, he suddenly fell ill, probably with pneumonia. His condition deteriorated rapidly, and he died on December 14 at Mount Vernon.

Washington married Martha Dandridge Custis on January 6, 1759. Martha was a wealthy widow, who added fifteen thousand acres to Washington's estate. The couple had no children, but they raised Martha's two surviving children from her previous marriage. Martha's daughter, Patsy, died in 1773 as a teenager, and when her son John died in 1781, George and Martha assumed custody of his two children.

Thomas Jefferson, looking back on Washington's life in 1814, wrote:

> His mind was great and powerful without being of the very first order; his penetration strong, though not so acute as that of a Newton, Bacon, or Locke; and as far as he saw, no judgement was ever sounder. It was slow in operation, being little aided by invention or imagination, but sure in conclusion....
>
> Perhaps the strongest feature in his character was prudence, never acting until every circumstance, every consideration, was maturely weighed.... His integrity was most pure, his justice the most inflexible I have ever known.

John Adams

William Winstanley; Adams National Historic Site

John Adams

Born: October 30, 1735; Braintree (now Quincy), Massachusetts
Party: Federalist
Term: March 4, 1797-March 3, 1801
Vice President: Thomas Jefferson
Died: July 4, 1826; Quincy, Massachusetts
Buried: Quincy

John Adams was born into a well-established family of farmers whose descendants had immigrated to Massachusetts from England a century before his birth. He was the oldest of three sons born to John and Susanna Adams. Young John received a grammer school education designed to prepare him for college. He enrolled in Harvard University in 1751 intending to become a Congregational minister. However, before he graduated in 1755 he had decided against a career in the ministry in favor of either law or medicine. After briefly teaching school in Worcester, Adams began studying law. By 1758 he had been admitted to the Massachusetts bar and was practicing law in Braintree.

Adams soon became recognized throughout Massachusetts as an outspoken advocate of colonial causes. He authored Braintree's protest against the British Stamp Act of 1765, which was used as a model for similar protests by many other Massachusetts towns. Adams also published a series of anonymous letters in the *Boston Gazette* in which he theorized that the rights of English citizens were derived solely from God, not from the British monarchy or parliament. In 1770 Adams demonstrated his commitment to due process of the law when he defended the British soldiers on trial for the murder of colonial citizens at the Boston Massacre. His reputation withstood the unpopularity of his action, and the following year he was elected by an overwhelming margin to the Massachusetts state legislature.

In 1774 Adams became a delegate to the First Continental Congress. He was an early and influential advocate of separation from Britain and was appointed to the committee assigned to draft a declaration of independence. Adams retired from Congress in November 1777, intending to return to Massachusetts and his law practice. Within a month, however, Congress appointed him to the American commission in France. He set sail to join Benjamin Franklin and Arthur Lee in Paris on February 13, 1778, but a treaty of alliance had already been concluded by the time he arrived. Adams spent a year in Europe before returning to America in the summer of 1779. Upon his arrival he was elected as a delegate to the Massachusetts constitutional convention. He almost singlehandedly wrote the first draft of the new state constitution, which the convention adopted with only minor changes. He returned to Europe in 1780 where he would spend the next eight years in various diplomatic posts, including minister to Holland and minister to Great Britain. He signed the armistice ending war with the British in 1783 and negotiated several loans and commercial treaties with the European powers.

Adams was serving as envoy to Great Britain when the Constitutional Convention was held, but his *Defense of the Constitutions of Government of the United States,* written while he was in Europe and published in 1787, contained insights into constitutional theory that were cited by delegates to the convention. When Adams received a copy of the Constitution in Great Britain, he immediately gave it his support. By this time he had grown tired of the unwillingness of the British government to improve relations with the United States. He resigned his post and returned to the United States.

When he arrived in Boston on June 17, 1789, he had already been elected to Congress under the new Constitution. He never served in this capacity, because he would also be elected vice president by virtue of his second place finish to George Washington in the balloting for president. Adams was dismayed at winning the vice presidency with only thirty-four votes. The disparity between his total and the unanimous sixty-nine received by Washington was caused by the machinations of Alexander Hamilton, who persuaded many delegates to scatter their second vote to dilute Adam's influence.

Adams dutifully fulfilled his constitutional function of presiding over the Senate. Since the original Senate had only twenty-two members, the vice president was often in a position to break tie votes as prescribed by the Constitution. During Adams's two terms he had twenty-nine opportunities to decide issues with his tie-breaking vote, more than any subsequent vice president. However, he was seldom consulted by Washington on important issues and complained that the vice presidency was an insignificant and mechanical job—a lament of many of the men who would follow Adams in office. Nevertheless, Adams's relationship with Washington remained cordial.

After eight years as vice president, Adams was Washington's heir apparent. Fellow Federalist Alexander Hamilton, however, attempted to arrange the election of a candidate more agreeable to him than Adams. He persuaded a number of Federalist delegates to vote for intended vice-presidential candidate Thomas Pinckney, but not for presidential candidate John Adams. Hamilton hoped that Adams would lose the presidency to Pinckney, who Hamilton believed would be more receptive to his own influence. But the maneuver backfired when many of Adams's supporters withheld their second votes from Pinckney to ensure Adams's victory, thereby allowing Democratic-Republican candidate Thomas Jefferson to finish second and win the vice presidency.

The most important and contentious issue of Adams's presidency was an impending war with France. French vessels had been preying on American shipping since 1795, and, just before Adams's inauguration, Paris issued a decree legitimizing the seizure of virtually any American ship. Adams faced intense political pressure from pro-British Hamiltonians who believed that the United States should join Britain in fighting to prevent French domination of Europe and to preserve American dignity. Jefferson's Democratic-Republicans opposed a war with France, but they did not have the votes in Congress to stop a declaration of war if Adams had wanted one. Adams chose to strengthen the nation's military, particularly the navy, while continuing negotiations with the French. He dispatched John Marshall, Charles C. Pinckney, and Elbridge Gerry to Paris in the summer of 1797 to seek an agreement that would avoid war and end French attacks on American shipping. But the diplomatic mission failed when the American representatives were greeted with demands for a bribe for French foreign minister Tallyrand, a loan to France, and an official apology for Adams's criticisms.

In April 1798 Adams's release of documents relating to the incident (which came to be known as the XYZ affair) aroused American opinion against France and rallied public support behind Adams. By this time an undeclared naval war between the two nations had already begun, and Congress granted Adams's request for further defense measures, including the establishment of the Navy Department. But he resisted calls for a full-scale declared war against France, even though he could have bolstered his own political fortunes by yielding to the militant sentiment of the American public.

While Adams was enthusiastic about building a strong navy, he grudgingly agreed to the enlargement of the army. He asked George Washington to come out of retirement to command it. Washington accepted on the conditions that he would not have to take the field until there was fighting and that Alexander Hamilton would be his second in command in charge of building and training the army. Adams feared giving the powerful and ambitious Hamilton control of the army, but he believed if war did occur Washington's presence was indispensable to the unity of the country, so he assented to Washington's conditions.

In early 1799 France began sending conciliatory signals, which prompted Adams to send another peace commission before the year was over. Hamilton had tried to rally Federalist support for war with France and had proposed a joint British-American venture against Spanish holdings in North America. But increased taxes to support war preparations had diminished public enthusiasm for military adventurism. Adams stood by his policy of avoiding a declared war unless it was forced upon him by the French. The following May when the immediate danger of a land war with France had passed, Adams ordered a drastic reduction in the army. In November word reached the United States that the American delegation had successfully concluded a treaty of peace and commerce with France.

By this time the Democratic-Republicans had taken control of the state legislatures of several key states, thus setting the stage for Adams's defeat in the 1800 presidential election. One of the reasons for the growing disaffection with the Federalist party was its support of the Alien and Sedition Acts. In 1798 the Federalist majority in Congress attempted to put an end to the vituperative attacks on Federalist members of Congress and cabinet members in the Democratic-Republican press. The Sedition Act provided for imprisonment and fines for individuals who wrote, published, or uttered anything false or malicious about federal government officials. The Sedition Act together with the Alien Act of the same year, which gave the president broad authority to deport aliens suspected of subversive activity, constituted the greatest legislated suppression of freedom of expression in the history of the United States. Adams signed these bills into law but was not active in enforcing them. Despite the disunity of the Federalist party and the unpopularity of the Alien and Sedition Acts, the 1800 election was close. Adams received sixty-five electoral votes, eight fewer than Jefferson and Aaron Burr.

Before leaving office Adams pushed for judicial reforms and appointed more than 200 new judges, attorneys, clerks, and marshals. Some of these "midnight appointments" were removed by Jefferson, but many retained their offices. Adams also appointed John Marshall chief justice of the United States, a selection Adams was especially proud of in his later years.

When Adams's term ended, he returned to his farm in Massachusetts without attending Jefferson's inauguration. Adams spent much of his retirement writing his autobiogrpahy and corresponding with former colleagues about politics, philosophy, and religion. He wrote a letter of reconciliation to Thomas Jefferson at the insistence of their mutual friend Dr. Benjamin Rush in December 1811. Jefferson replied immediately, and they established a lasting correspondence. Adams died on July 4, 1826, the fiftieth anniversary of the Declaration of Independence. His last words reportedly were "Thomas Jefferson still lives." Adams had no way of knowing that Jefferson had died only a few hours before.

Adams married Abigail Smith in 1764. Her correspondence with her husband, family, and friends provides a valuable historical record of her husband's activities and the period in which they lived. They had five children: Abigail, John Quincy, Susanna, Charles, and Thomas. Susanna died while she was an infant. John Quincy became a prominent diplomat, congressman, and the sixth president of the United States. Adams's parents were Susanna Boyleston Adams and John Adams, a respected farmer and shoemaker who was active in local politics. The famous New England radical patriot Sam Adams was John's distant cousin.

Thomas Jefferson

Gilbert Stuart; Library of Congress

Th: Jefferson

Born: April 13, 1743; Goochland (now Albemarle) County, Virginia
Party: Democratic-Republican
Term: March 4, 1801-March 4, 1809
Vice Presidents: Aaron Burr; George Clinton
Died: July 4, 1826; Charlottesville, Virginia
Buried: Charlottesville

Thomas Jefferson was the eldest son and third of the ten children of Peter and Jane Jefferson. Peter Jefferson was a wealthy plantation owner, and Jane was a member of the prominent Randolph family, which was descended from British royalty.

As a boy, Thomas received instruction in Latin, Greek, French, mathematics, and philosophy from local scholars. When Peter Jefferson died in 1757, Thomas inherited Shadwell, the thousand-acre Virginia estate on which he was born. In 1760, at the age of seventeen, Thomas entered the College of William and Mary in Williamsburg, Virginia. There he studied vigorously for two years under the tutelage of Dr. William Small, a professor of mathematics, history, and philosophy. He left the college in the spring of 1762, however, without taking a degree.

Jefferson then studied law in Williamsburg for five years under the well-respected lawyer George Wythe. During Jefferson's stay in Williamsburg, Wythe and Small introduced him to many members of Virginia's government, including Francis Fauquier, the royal governor of the colony. In 1767 Jefferson was admitted to the Virginia bar and began a successful legal practice. Two years later he took a seat in Virginia's House of Burgesses. During his six years in that body, Jefferson distinguished himself as a powerful literary stylist. His colleagues often called upon him to draft proclamations and legislative documents.

Jefferson brought his reputation as a gifted writer to the Continental Congress in 1775. The following year, at the age of thirty-three, he was appointed by Congress to the committee charged with writing the Declaration of Independence. His fellow committee members—John Adams, Benjamin Franklin, Robert Livingston, and Roger Sherman—chose him to draft the document. Although the committee made minor changes in Jefferson's original draft and the entire Congress asked that several passages be deleted or modified, the Declaration of Independence was largely Jefferson's work.

Jefferson returned to Virginia in 1776 to a seat in the state legislature. In 1779 he became governor of his home state. His first experience as a chief executive was not impressive. In 1781 he was forced to abandon the Virginia capital of Richmond when British troops advanced upon the city. Some Virginians accused him of cowardice, but after a long debate the Virginia legislature passed a resolution stating that Jefferson's retreat was justified. He declined renomination for governor in 1781.

Diplomat and Secretary of State

In 1784 Congress sent Jefferson to Paris as its minister to France. During his five years at this post, Jefferson witnessed the many events of the French Revolution. He applauded the revolution's stated democratic goals and had many friends among its leaders. Jefferson, like John Adams, missed the drafting of the Constitution because of his diplomatic service in Europe.

In 1789 Jefferson returned to the United States to become the country's first secretary of state. In this capacity Jefferson was more than just the nation's leading diplomat. Like the other members of George Washington's cabinet, Jefferson served as an adviser to Washington on matters outside the area of policy traditionally associated with his position. Washington often preferred to have his cabinet debate issues while he listened dispassionately to their reasoning. In these debates Jefferson was usually pitted against Treasury Secretary Alexander Hamilton. Hamilton, who was closer ideologically to Washington than Jefferson, was undoubtedly the most influential member of the cabinet. On July 31, 1794, he announced that he would resign at the end of the year because of his disagreements with administration policies. In particular, Jefferson objected to Hamilton's creation of a national bank and Washington's strict neutrality between Britain and France despite the 1778 treaty of alliance with France, which Jefferson believed should have been honored.

By 1796 the Democratic-Republican party, which opposed the Federalists, had begun to emerge with Jefferson as its leader. That year he lost the presidential election to John Adams by three electoral votes, and, according to the original election rules of the Constitution, his second-place finish earned him the vice presidency. In this office he actively opposed the policies of Adams and the Federalists.

Presidency

After the election of 1800 the Twelfth Amendment introduced new election rules, which called for the president and vice president to run as a team, thereby eliminating the possibility of a candidate intended for the vice presidency receiving more votes than the presidential candidate. In the 1800 election, however, Jefferson was paired on the Democratic-Republican ticket with Aaron Burr. When the ambitious Burr received as many electoral votes as Jefferson, he refused to concede to his running mate. The tie gave the House of Representatives, where the Federalists and Alexander Hamilton were still in the majority, the responsibility of electing the president. To Hamilton's credit, he worked for the election of Jefferson, his political archenemy, whom he thought less dangerous and more reasonable than Burr. The tie-breaking process took thirty-six ballots, but Jefferson was elected eventually.

Despite the acrimony between the Democratic-Republicans and the Federalists (outgoing president John Adams did not even attend Jefferson's inauguration), Jefferson entered office preaching reconciliation. He transformed the atmosphere surrounding the presidency from the stiff, regal style of Washington and Adams to his own democratic informality. Jefferson immediately freed all persons who had been jailed under the Alien and Sedition Acts enacted during the Adams administration. The Alien Act gave the president the authority to jail or deport aliens in peacetime, and the Sedition Act gave federal authorities broad power to prosecute persons who criticized the government. He also worked with Congress, which had come under the control of his party after the 1800 election, to cut the government budget and federal taxes.

In foreign policy Jefferson acted decisively to meet the threat to American shipping in the Mediterranean from pirates operating from the Barbary Coast of North Africa. American and European nations had been paying tribute to the governments of Morocco, Algiers, Tunis, and Tripoli to protect their ships from harassment. Jefferson, however, refused demands for increased tribute payments and sent a squadron of warships to the Mediterranean to protect U.S. shipping. After U.S. forces defeated Tripoli in a naval war, a treaty was concluded in 1805 that ended tribute payments to that state. The United States continued tribute payments to other North African states, however, until 1816.

Jefferson's most important act during his first term as president was the Louisiana Purchase. In 1803 the French owned the port of New Orleans as well as a vast area that stretched from New Orleans to present-day Montana, known as the Louisiana Territory. Jefferson, fearing that the French could block U.S. navigation of the Mississippi and threaten American settlements in the West, sent ambassadors to France in the hope of purchasing the port of New Orleans. The French instead offered to sell the entire Louisiana Territory. The American representatives, James Monroe and Robert Livingston, saw the opportunity to create an American empire and improve the security of the western frontier. Thus, they struck a deal with French emperor Napoleon to buy all of the Louisiana Territory for $15 million.

Jefferson recognized that to support the agreement he would have to ignore his own principles of strict constructionism, since the Constitution did not specifically authorize the president to acquire territory and Congress had not appropriated money for the purchase. He believed that the purchase would greatly benefit the nation and that the offer from Napoleon might be withdrawn if he hesitated. Therefore, Jefferson approved the deal and urged Congress to ratify it and appropriate funds for the purchase. In the fall of 1803 Congress bowed to his wishes and appropriated the $15 million. With the addition of the 828,000 square miles of the Louisiana Territory, the area of the United States nearly doubled.

In 1804, Jefferson, who was at the height of his popularity, easily won reelection. He lost only two states and defeated Charles C. Pinckney in the electoral college by a vote of 162-14.

Jefferson's second term was troubled by war between Britain and France. In 1806 both powers were blockading each other's ports and seizing American sailors and cargo. Jefferson was determined, however, to not become involved in the war. Thus, he persuaded Congress to pass the Embargo Act of 1807, which prohibited the shipping of U.S. products to other nations. Jefferson hoped that by cutting off all foreign trade he would prevent provocations on the seas that could lead to war.

The Embargo Act was a total failure. It severely hurt American businesses and farmers by denying them export markets. As the U.S. economy stagnated, Federalists and some Democratic-Republicans argued that the federal government's authority to regulate foreign commerce did not give it the power to stop foreign commerce altogether. Many merchants defied the embargo, causing Jefferson to order harsh enforcement measures that led to abuses of civil rights. On March 1, 1809, three days before the end of his term, Jefferson signed the Non-Intercourse Act, which ended the embargo against nations other than Britain and France and made provisions to lift the embargo against those two nations if they stopped violating U.S. neutrality. Despite the unpopularity of the Embargo Act, Jefferson's chosen heir and secretary of state, James Madison, won the 1808 presidential election.

Retirement

When his second term expired Jefferson retired to Monticello, his home outside of Charlottesville, Virginia, which he had designed himself. He devoted his time to managing his estate, entertaining visitors, corresponding with former colleagues, and reveling in his many intellectual pursuits. Jefferson, who suffered from financial troubles caused by his generous entertaining and the defaults by several friends on loans he had cosigned, sold his 6,500-volume library to Congress in 1815. Congress's original collection of books had been burned by the British during the War of 1812. Jefferson's books formed the nucleus of the collection that would become the modern Library of Congress.

In 1819 the University of Virginia was chartered under Jefferson's supervision. He planned the curriculum, chose the faculty, drew up the plans for its buildings, and served as its rector until his death. Jefferson died at Monticello on July 4, 1826, the same day as John Adams and the fiftieth anniversary of the Declaration of Independence. Jefferson is buried at Monticello beneath a gravestone that he willed should read: "Here was buried Thomas Jefferson, Author of the Declaration of American Independence, of the Statute of Virginia for Religious Freedom, and the father of the University of Virginia."

Jefferson married Martha Wayles Skelton, a wealthy twenty-three-year-old widow, on January 1, 1772. The couple had six children, but only two, Martha and Maria, reached maturity. Martha Jefferson's father, John Wayles, died in 1773, leaving a forty-thousand-acre estate to the Jeffersons that doubled their landholdings. Wayles was heavily in debt, however, and Jefferson struggled for many years to pay off the balance. On September 6, 1782, Martha Jefferson died at the age of thirty-three. Little is known about Martha, and there is no authentic portrait of her in existence. Jefferson never remarried.

James Madison

David Edwin; National Portrait Gallery

James Madison

Born: March 16, 1751; Port Conway, Virginia
Party: Democratic-Republican
Term: March 4, 1809-March 4, 1817
Vice Presidents: George Clinton; Elbridge Gerry
Died: June 28, 1836; Orange County, Virginia
Buried: Orange County

James Madison, oldest of the ten children of James and Eleanor Madison, was raised at Montpelier, the family plantation in Virginia. Young James Madison was an excellent scholar. He graduated from the College of New Jersey (now Princeton University) in 1771 and spent an extra six months studying theology under John Witherspoon, president of the college. In 1792 James returned to Virginia to continue his study of law and religion. Like John Adams, he considered entering the ministry after college, but the lure of a political career and the urgency of the patriot cause led him away from the ministry and into public service.

In 1775 he assumed his first government office, a slot on the committee of public safety of his native Orange County. By the spring of 1776 he had earned sufficient notoriety and respect to be elected as a delegate to Virginia's constitutional convention. There he served on the committee that drafted a declaration of rights and was primarily responsible for the constitutional article on religious freedom. As a member of the state constitutional convention, Madison automatically became a state legislator in the new Virginia government. There he met Thomas Jefferson, who became his close friend and political mentor. In 1777 Madison was defeated in his attempt to be elected to the state legislature, but the same year he was elected to the governor's council, an advisory body in which he served governors Patrick Henry and Thomas Jefferson.

Father of the Constitution

In 1780 Madison's political focus was broadened when he was chosen to serve in the Continental Congress, where he worked to bring greater organization to the federal government under the new Articles of Confederation. During this period, however, Madison began to believe that the articles had to be strengthened if the government was going to survive. Congress had no means of implementing its decisions and was completely dependent on the goodwill of the states. For example, in June 1783 Madison had witnessed a band of revolutionary war veterans surround the Philadelphia statehouse where Congress was meeting and demand that the legislators vote them back pay. When Congress asked Pennsylvania for militia to disperse the band, the state government refused. Such humiliations convinced Madison that the federal government had to be restructured.

At the end of 1783 Madison returned to Virginia where he was reelected to the state legislature. He served there until 1786. During this period Madison studied the history of government and began to form ideas about how to strengthen the national government. In September 1786 he attended the Annapolis Convention, a national meeting called to consider trade. Only five states were represented at the convention, but the delegates in Annapolis issued a call for a second national convention to be held in Philadelphia the following year.

Madison led a group of nationalists who wanted to establish a broad mandate for the Philadelphia convention. They urged all thirteen states to send delegates, obtained a congressional endorsement of the convention, and enhanced the prestige of the convention by convincing George Washington to attend. At the Constitutional Convention in Philadelphia in 1787, Madison's extensive study and contemplation of political theory paid off for his nation. More than any other individual, he was responsible for the content of the Constitution produced by the convention. The "Virginia Plan," which served as the basis of the Constitution, was submitted to the convention by Edmund Randolph, but it was largely Madison's work.

Following the convention Madison wrote a series of essays, known as the *Federalist Papers,* with Alexander Hamilton and John Jay. These essays explained and defended the new Constitution, which had to be ratified by the states before it could become law. He also led the successful fight for ratification at Virginia's own ratifying convention in 1788. That year Madison was prevented from being elected to the new U.S. Senate by powerful state legislator and former Virginia governor Patrick Henry, who had opposed the Constitution, Madison won election to the U.S. House of Representatives, however. There he proposed nine amendments to the Constitution, which became the basis for the Bill of Rights.

Madison legislated according to a strict interpretation of the Constitution; he opposed the government's exercise of powers not specifically granted in the document. He fought unsuccessfully against Treasury Secretary Alexander Hamilton's plans to establish a national bank and have the federal government assume the war debts of the states. He also wrote a series of articles, under the name "Helvidius," that argued against the expansion of presidential power and attacked Washington's proclamation of neutrality toward warring Britain and France in 1793 as unconstitutional.

From his position in Congress, Madison assumed a leading role, second only to Thomas Jefferson, in the formation of the Democratic-Republican party. In 1797, after four terms, he retired from Congress.

In 1801, newly elected president Thomas Jefferson appointed Madison secretary of state. He served in this post for all eight years of Jefferson's presidency, and he supported all the president's major diplomatic initiatives, including the Louisiana Purchase.

With Jefferson's support, Madison was nominated for president by the Democratic-Republicans in 1808. Although he lost five northern states, Madison received 122 electoral votes to Federalist Charles C. Pinckney's 47.

Presidency

Madison's presidency focused on issues related to the war under way in Europe between Britain and France. British warships were boarding American commercial ships, seizing cargo, and impressing any sailor they suspected of being British. Members of Congress known as the War Hawks, a group that included Henry Clay and John Calhoun, urged Madison to declare war on the British. The War Hawks, most of whom were from the South and the West, also wanted to launch military adventures into Canada and to halt Indian attacks in the West, which they believed were encouraged by the British. By 1812 Madison saw no alternative to war, and on June 1 he asked Congress for a declaration of war. The declaration passed on June 18, 19-13 in the Senate and 79-49 in the House. That fall, Madison ran for reelection against DeWitt Clinton of New York, the nominee of an anti-Madison faction of the Democratic-Republican party. The Federalists, who did not nominate a candidate, threw their support to Clinton. Madison defeated Clinton 128-89 in the electoral college.

The United States was not prepared for war. Its navy was small compared to the British fleet, and throughout the war the army had great difficulty fulfilling its recruitment goals. Moreover, the nation was not united behind the war effort. The war was opposed by many citizens in the Northeast, who favored the British in their fight with France. In addition, the merchants of that region preferred the occasional seizure of their neutral vessels by the British to a war that could end trade completely. Indeed, some New England Federalists openly discussed secession during the war.

The United States prevailed in several sea battles, and frontier generals William Henry Harrison and Andrew Jackson won decisive victories over Britain's Indian allies, but overall the war went badly for the United States. The worst humiliation occurred in August 1814 when the British occupied Washington, D.C., and burned government buildings, including the Executive Mansion and Capitol. On December 24, 1814, Britain and the United States signed the Treaty of Ghent, which ended the war without resolving the issues for which it had been fought. The British gave no guarantees that it would allow U.S. ships safe passage in the future.

In spite of the many defeats suffered by the United States, the end of the war brought a resurgence of nationalism. The Treaty of Ghent and Andrew Jackson's overwhelming victory over the British at the Battle of New Orleans on January 8, 1815, two weeks after the peace treaty had been signed, convinced many Americans that the war had been won. Federalist opposition to the war crippled that party, leaving Madison's Democratic-Republicans in a commanding position.

Madison's last two years in office were successful ones. Congress backed the president's proposal to appropriate funds to strengthen the armed forces. Madison also supported the establishment of the Second Bank of the United States and increased tariffs to protect U.S. industries.

Retirement

After leaving office Madison returned to Montpelier, his estate in Virginia. He remained a close friend of Thomas Jefferson, who lived thirty miles away. When Jefferson died in 1826 Madison assumed his job as rector of the University of Virginia. In 1829 he cochaired a Virginia convention aimed at revising the state constitution. During his retirement Madison also edited the secret daily record he had kept at the Constitutional Convention, which has been invaluable to historians when reconstructing its events. His wife sold Madison's *Notes on the Federal Convention* to Congress in 1837. The year before Madison had died peacefully at Montpelier at the age of eighty-five.

On September 15, 1794, at the age of forty-three, Madison married widow Dorthea Payne Todd, who was called Dolley. The couple had no children, but they raised Dolley's one surviving child from her previous marriage. Dolley was an outgoing woman who loved entertaining. As first lady her social charms compensated for her husband's reserved nature. After her husband's death Dolley participated in many Washington social functions until her death in 1849.

James Monroe

After painting by C. B. King; Library of Congress

Born: April 28, 1758; Westmoreland County, Virginia
Party: Democratic-Republican
Term: March 4, 1817-March 4, 1825
Vice President: Daniel D. Tompkins
Died: July 4, 1831; New York City
Buried: Richmond, Virginia

James Monroe was the eldest of the five children of Elizabeth and Spence Monroe, a well-established Virginia planter of modest means. James entered the College of William and Mary in Williamsburg, Virginia, when he was sixteen but left two years later to join the Continental army. As a lieutenant he fought in numerous battles, including Trenton, Brandywine, Germantown, and Monmouth. At Trenton he was wounded in the shoulder and promoted to captain for his bravery by Gen. George Washington. In 1778 he was promoted again, to lieutenant colonel, but he was not able to recruit enough Virginia volunteers to form a new regiment that he could command.

Monroe left the army in 1780 to study law under Thomas Jefferson, then governor of Virginia. Monroe quickly developed a close personal and professional relationship with his mentor that lead to a career in politics and public service. In 1782 he was elected to the Virginia legislature and, a year later, he was chosen along with Jefferson to represent Virginia at the Continental Congress in New York City. While in Congress Monroe became an expert on frontier issues after making two fact-finding journeys into the Ohio Valley. When Monroe's third term expired in 1786, he moved to Fredericksburg, Virginia, where he established a law practice. That year Monroe was again elected to the Virginia legislature.

Although Monroe attended the national convention in Annapolis, Maryland, which created momentum for the writing of the Constitution, he was not a delegate to the Constitutional Convention of 1787. His belief that the Constitution gave the president and Senate too much power led him to oppose the document vigorously at Virginia's ratifying convention in 1788. Nevertheless, after ratification by Virginia, he ran for the U.S. House of Representatives but lost to James Madison.

Monroe soon adopted a national political perspective, and when Virginian William Grayson, an anti-Federalist, died in 1790, Monroe was appointed to his Senate seat. In the Senate Monroe worked against Treasury Secretary Alexander Hamilton's fiscal policies. Monroe helped Jefferson and Madison establish the foundations of the Democratic-Republican party that would challenge the Federalists after George Washington's retirement.

In 1794 Washington appointed Monroe ambassador to France. In Paris, however, his outspoken support of the French conflicted with Washington's careful policy of neutrality in the Franco-British war. After the president recalled him in 1796, Monroe published *A View of the Conduct of the Executive* in which he attacked the administration's policies toward France. In 1799 Monroe was elected governor of Virginia and served effectively for three years.

Thomas Jefferson was elected president in 1800, ushering in a period of Democratic-Republican dominance over national affairs. In January 1803, after Monroe's third term as governor of Virginia had expired, Jefferson asked him to travel to France to negotiate the purchase of New Orleans. When Napolean offered to sell not just New Orleans but the entire Louisiana Territory, Monroe and Ambassador Robert Livingston seized the opportunity to double the size of the United States. Acting without authority, they closed the deal for $15 million. The purchase added 828,000 square miles to the United States. Monroe continued to function as a special ambassador in Europe for four more years. He tried unsuccessfully to purchase the Floridas from the Spanish and to conclude a treaty with the British ending that country's capture of American vessels.

Monroe returned to Virginia in 1807 and practiced law until he was again elected governor in 1811. When newly elected president James Madison offered Monroe the post of secretary of state, however, he resigned the governorship to return to national service. Monroe helped write Madison's request for a declaration of war against the British in 1811. The United States was ill-prepared, however, for the War of 1812. The first two years of fighting brought several humiliating defeats, including the capture and burning of Washington, D.C., by the British in August 1814. In September of that year Madison appointed Monroe secretary of war in addition to his duties as secretary of state. Monroe then worked tirelessly to reorganize the nation's defenses and to end the confusion that had prevailed in the War Department. In March 1815, three months after the war ended, an exhausted Monroe resigned as secretary of war and went to his home in Virginia for a rest. He returned to Washington six months later and resumed his duties as secretary of state.

With Madison's backing, Monroe was nominated as the Democratic-Republican presidential candidate in 1816. He easily defeated the Federalist candidate, Sen. Rufus

King of New York, 183-34 in the electoral college. Less than three months after taking office, Monroe followed George Washington's example and toured the Middle Atlantic and New England states. Reacting to the enthusiastic reception of the president in the North, a Boston newspaper declared the time to be a political "era of good feelings." These good feelings extended to the 1820 presidential election. Monroe ran unopposed and received all but one electoral vote that was cast for John Quincy Adams by an elector who wished to preserve George Washington's distinction as the only president ever to be elected unanimously.

Monroe's presidency, however, was not without its problems. When Missouri sought admission to the United States as a slave state, sectional tensions over the slavery issue erupted. Monroe was a slaveholder who believed that the institution should eventually be abolished. He also believed, however, that new states entering the Union had the constitutional right to determine for themselves if they would permit slavery. In 1820, after a lengthy debate, Congress passed the Missouri Compromise. The plan allowed Missouri to enter the Union as a slave state simultaneously with the admission of Maine as a free state. The compromise also prohibited slavery north of latitude 36°30' in the territory acquired in the Louisiana Purchase. Monroe doubted the constitutionality of the plan, but he approved it because he considered it the best way to avoid sectional conflict and possibly the secession of southern states.

In foreign policy Monroe's administration had several notable successes. The Rush-Bagot Agreement signed with Great Britain in 1817 limited the number of warships each country could deploy on the Great Lakes and led to the demilitarization of the Canadian frontier. In 1819 Secretary of State John Quincy Adams concluded a treaty in which Spain transferred control of the Floridas to the United States and agreed to a border dividing the United States and Spanish territory in western North America.

Monroe's administration is best known, however, for the foreign policy doctrine that bears his name and continues to influence U.S. policy toward Latin America. In October 1823 Great Britain suggested that the United States join it in resisting European intervention in Latin America, where several revolutions had succeeded in overthrowing Spanish colonial rule. Although former presidents Jefferson and Madison advised Monroe to accept the British proposal, Monroe was swayed by the arguments of Secretary of State Adams, who advocated an independent U.S. declaration against European intrusions into the Western Hemisphere. In his annual message to Congress in 1823 Monroe announced that the United States intended to stay out of European conflicts and would not interfere in the existing Latin American colonies of the European powers. Monroe warned the Europeans, however, that any attempt to establish new colonies in the Western Hemisphere or interfere in the affairs of independent American nations would be regarded by the United States as an "unfriendly" act. At the time the Monroe Doctrine was issued it had little force because the United States did not possess the military strength to defend Latin America. As the nation developed, however, the Monroe Doctrine became a cornerstone of U.S. foreign policy.

While serving in the Continental Congress in New York in 1785 Monroe met his wife-to-be, Elizabeth Kortright; they married in 1786. The Monroes raised two daughters and had one son who died at the age of two. Monroe experienced financial difficulties after he retired from the presidency and was forced to sell Ash Lawn, one of his two Virginia homes in 1825. After his wife died in 1830, he sold his other Virginia estate, Oak Hill, and moved to New York City to live with his daughter and her husband. On July 4, 1831, Monroe became the third president, along with John Adams and Thomas Jefferson, to die on Independence Day.

John Quincy Adams

Gilbert Stuart and Thomas Sully; Harvard University Art Museums

John Quincy Adams.

Born: July 11, 1767; Braintree (now Quincy), Massachusetts
Party: Democratic-Republican
Term: March 4, 1825-March 4, 1829
Vice President: John C. Calhoun
Died: February 23, 1828; Washington, D.C
Buried: Quincy

John Quincy Adams was the oldest son and second of the children of John and Abigail Adams. He was the only son of a president ever to become president. As a boy in Massachusetts, John Quincy lived through the early stages of the revolutionary war and was an eyewitness to the battle of Bunker Hill. He lived in Europe from 1778 to 1785 while his father served as a diplomat. He was educated at schools in France and the Netherlands and learned to speak several languages. In 1781, when he was just fourteen, he left his family for two years to serve as secretary and translator for Francis Dana, the first U.S. ambassador to Russia.

When Adams returned to America in 1785 he enrolled in Harvard University and graduated two years later. After passing the bar in 1790, he established a law practice in Boston. His distinguished diplomatic career began in 1794 when George Washington appointed him ambassador to the Netherlands. In 1796 he was about to move to Portugal to become ambassador when his father was elected president. President Adams reassigned his son to the post of minister to Prussia, which he held throughout his father's term.

When Thomas Jefferson defeated John Adams in his try for reelection in 1800, John Quincy returned to the United States where he embarked on a legislative career as a Federalist. In 1802 he was elected to the Massachusetts senate, which sent him to the U.S. Senate the following year. Adams, however, angered his fellow Federalists by insisting on considering each issue independently, rather than voting with the party. When he supported President Jefferson's Embargo Act in 1807, the Massachusetts legislature elected his successor six months before his term expired. Adams thus resigned in protest and returned to Massachusetts to practice law and teach at Harvard University.

Despite Adams's Federalist background, Democratic-Republican President James Madison appointed him minister to Russia in 1809. While in St. Petersburg, Adams witnessed Napoleon's disastrous invasion of Russia and declined an appointment to the U.S. Supreme Court. In 1814 Adams was sent to Ghent to head the U.S. delegation to the negotiations seeking an end to the War of 1812. The treaty negotiated by Adams and his delegation and signed on December 24, 1814, extricated the United States from the embarrassing war without having to make significant concessions. Adams was then sent to London where he served as minister to Great Britain until 1817.

President James Monroe called Adams home from London in 1817 to become secretary of state. Adams distinguished himself in this post by conducting successful negotiations with Spain on the cession of the Floridas. The Adams-Onis Treaty with Spain, concluded on February 22, 1819, provided for the transfer of East and West Florida to the United States and the establishment of a border between Spanish and U.S. territory running from the Gulf of Mexico to the Rocky Mountains and along the forty-second parallel to the Pacific Ocean. Historians regard the treaty as a brilliant act of diplomacy, and Adams himself called its conclusion "the most important event of my life." Adams also was the mind behind the Monroe Doctrine, which warned that the United States would oppose any European interference in the internal affairs of an American nation or further European colonization of territory in the Western Hemisphere.

The 1824 presidential election was one of the most confused in U.S. history. The remnants of the Federalist party had faded away during Monroe's presidency, leaving the Democratic-Republican party the only significant party in existence. The Democratic-Republican congressional caucus nominated W. H. Crawford of Georgia as the party's candidate, but several state caucuses refused to be guided by the judgment of this group. Consequently, John Quincy Adams, Andrew Jackson, and Henry Clay were nominated as regional candidates. The four-candidate race split the electoral vote, and no one received the majority required to be elected. Jackson led Adams 99 to 84 votes, with Crawford and Clay receiving 41 and 37 votes, respectively. This stalemate threw the election into the House of Representatives. There Henry Clay, a powerful member of the House, gave his support to Adams, who emerged victorious despite having received less than one-third of the popular vote. Jackson's supporters were furious that their candidate had been denied the presidency. When Adams selected Clay to be his secretary of state, the new president's opponents charged that he had made a "corrupt bargain."

Despite the absence of an electoral mandate and the disadvantage of a Congress poised to oppose him, Adams attempted to implement a program of public improvements. To stimulate the economy he advocated construction of a federally funded system of roads and canals and the implementation of high protective tariffs. He also called for federal funding of a national university, a national observatory, and scientific expeditions. The president's proposals failed, however, to attract significant support. Adams gained respect from certain groups for his antislavery and Indian rights stands, but he was out of step politically with the majority of the American public, especially in the South and West. By his own admission he was not a popular president. When he ran for reelection in 1828 against Andrew Jackson, he did well in his native New England but lost the South and West, and therefore the election, by a landslide.

In 1830 the Twelfth District of Massachusetts elected the former president to the U.S. House of Representatives. Adams welcomed the chance to get back into national politics, free of the burdens and constraints of the presidency. He wrote, "No election or appointment conferred upon me ever gave me so much pleasure." Although not a radical abolitionist, Adams won respect for his conscientious opposition to slavery. He also was a leading congressional critic of the annexation of Texas and the Mexican War. Adams's life of public service ended in February 1848 when he became ill at his desk in the House chamber, fell into a coma, and died two days later in the Capitol.

While serving as a diplomat in Europe in 1797 Adams married Louisa Catherine Johnson, the daughter of Joshua Johnson, a merchant who was also the American consul-general in London. They had four children. Their youngest son, Charles Francis Adams, had a distinguished diplomatic career, serving as minister to Great Britain during the American Civil War.

Andrew Jackson

Library of Congress

Born: March 15, 1767; Waxhaw, South Carolina
Party: Democratic
Term: March 4, 1829-March 4, 1837
Vice Presidents: John C. Calhoun; Martin Van Buren
Died: June 8, 1845; Nashville, Tennessee
Buried: Nashville

Andrew Jackson was the youngest of the three sons of Andrew and Elizabeth Jackson, who had emigrated from Ireland. The couple were poor farmers in the Waxhaw region of South Carolina near the North Carolina border. The boy's father died a few days before Andrew was born from internal injuries sustained while lifting a heavy log. Andrew was raised by his mother, with the help of his uncle and older brother.

By the time he was five Andrew had learned to read at a country school, but he received only a rudimentary education. When he was just thirteen Andrew and his older brother Robert joined the militia. Their oldest brother Hugh had already been killed in the revolutionary war, and Andrew and Robert were wounded and captured by the British in 1781. While a prisoner, Andrew was scarred on the hand by a British officer who struck him with a sabre for refusing to clean the officer's boots. Because the boys contracted smallpox while in a British prison in South Carolina, they were allowed to return to their mother. Andrew's experiences during the war caused him to develop a hatred toward the British that he would feel for the rest of his life.

Andrew's brother Robert died two days after being released by the British, and his mother died later that year. Andrew was then left in the care of his mother's relatives. When he was sixteen he received an inheritance worth several hundred pounds from his paternal grandfather in Ireland. By this time, however, Andrew had adopted a wild lifestyle, and he gambled much of the money away.

In 1784 Jackson moved to Salisbury, North Carolina, where he began studying law in the office of Spruce Macay. He was admitted to the bar and began practicing law in 1787. In 1788 he moved to the new settlement of Nashville, where he became the prosecuting attorney of the Western District of North Carolina, which would become the state of Tennessee.

In 1796 Jackson became a member of the convention that drafted Tennessee's constitution, and that same year he was elected without opposition as Tennessee's first representative to the U.S. House of Representatives. Because Tennessee had become a state shortly before regular congressional elections were to be held, Jackson's term lasted only from December 1796 until March 1797. During his brief tenure in the House he was one of a handful of members to vote against a farewell tribute to George Washington. Jackson was critical of Washington's support for the Jay Treaty, which he believed allowed the British to continue preying on American shipping. Although Jackson declined to run for reelection and returned to Tennessee when his brief term ended, within months he was elected to fill a vacant Senate seat. He served in the Senate from November 1797 to April 1798, when he again resigned. He then returned to Tennessee because of financial difficulties and his dislike of being separated from his family. In November of that year he was appointed to a seat on the Tennessee Superior Court. He served there until 1804, when he resigned to manage his estate.

Although Jackson had become a prominent citizen, he still possessed the temper of his youth. During his years in Tennessee he was involved in several duels and fights. Some of these incidents came to nothing, including a duel in 1803 with Tennessee governor John Sevier in which no shots were fired. In 1806, however, Jackson fought a duel with Charles Dickenson, who had questioned the propriety of Jackson's marriage. Dickenson fired first, wounding Jackson in the chest. The athletic Jackson shrugged off his wound, straightened himself, and mortally wounded Dickenson with his volley. Because Dickenson's bullet was lodged near Jackson's heart, it could not be removed, and caused Jackson periodic pain for the rest of his life. In 1813 Jackson got into a fight with Thomas Hart and Jesse Benton in Nashville. He emerged from the brawl with two bullet wounds, one that almost forced the amputation of his arm.

Military Career

Since 1802 Jackson had held the rank of major general of the Tennessee militia. When the United States declared war on Great Britain in 1812, Jackson offered the services of his militia against the British. The government was slow to accept his offer but eventually sent Jackson to fight the Creek Indians, who were allied with the British. Jackson, whose troops had earlier nicknamed him "Old Hickory" in tribute to his toughness, engineered a five-month campaign that culminated in the decisive defeat of the Creeks at the Battle of Horseshoe Bend, Alabama, on March 27, 1814. Soon after, he was commissioned as a brigadier and then major general in the U.S. Army.

Following a brief campaign in which Jackson's forces captured Pensacola, Florida, from the British, the general was ordered west to defend New Orleans. After a large British force landed near the city, Jackson launched a surprise attack on December 23, 1814, which slowed the British advance. He then ordered his forces to retire to earthen fortifications blocking the route to New Orleans. When the British attacked on January 8, 1815, Jackson's motley army of U.S. regulars, Tennessee backwoodsmen, free blacks, friendly Indians, and pirate Jean Lafitte's crew laid down a deadly fire that left the canefield where the battle was fought littered with British dead. In about a half hour over two thousand British troops were killed or wounded. Only about forty of Jackson's men were killed, wounded, or missing. The decisive victory at New Orleans raised the morale of the nation, which had suffered many embarrassing military defeats during the war, and made Jackson a folk hero.

After the war Jackson remained military commander of the Southern District of the United States. In late 1817, acting on vague orders to defend the frontier near Spanish Florida from Indian attacks, Jackson launched an invasion of Florida that led to the capture of several Spanish posts. When Spain protested, the general was in danger of being reprimanded for exceeding his orders and infringing upon the right of Congress to declare war. Secretary of State John Quincy Adams, however, defended Jackson's actions, which he recognized increased pressure on the Spanish to cede the territory to the United States. President James Monroe stated his qualified support of Jackson's campaign, and in 1819 Adams concluded a treaty in which Spain renounced its claims to the Floridas.

Presidency

Although Jackson denied any interest in seeking the presidency, his supporters in Tennessee maneuvered to make him a candidate. In 1823 Jackson was elected to the U.S. Senate by the Tennessee legislature, sending him back to Washington as an obvious contender for the presidency.

The 1824 election was a confusing affair in which all the candidates were Democratic-Republicans and no one received a majority of electoral votes. One hundred and thirty-three electoral votes were needed for election, but Jackson, the leading vote-getter, received only 99 votes. John Quincy Adams finished second with 84, and William Crawford and Henry Clay received 41 and 37 votes, respectively. The election was thus thrown into the House of Representatives. Jackson lost the election when the House elected Adams after Clay threw his support to the second-place finisher.

The 1828 presidential election, in which Jackson defeated incumbent Adams, was a watershed in American politics. Jackson was not only the first man from the West to be elected president, but also he was the first to have been elected with the overwhelming support of the masses of common farmers and citizens who recently had been enfranchised in most states. Tens of thousands of voters descended on Washington for Jackson's inauguration. After his swearing-in Jackson opened the White House to his supporters, whose rowdy behavior confirmed the perceptions of many members of the conservative eastern political establishment that the country had succumbed to mob rule. The jubilant throngs at the White House broke furniture and china, muddied carpets, and forced Jackson to evacuate the premises for his own safety.

Jackson, like many presidents of his era, faced sectional tensions. In 1832 Congress had passed a high tariff despite the opposition of many southern states. Southerners objected to high tariffs because they protected the manufacturing interests in the North, while trade reprisals from Europe denied the South markets for its agricultural products. In response to the tariff law, the South Carolina legislature declared that the federal tariff was null in that state. Jackson met the challenge to the Constitution by denouncing nullification and requesting authority from Congress to send troops to South Carolina if needed to enforce the tariff. Congress granted this authority, which helped convince South Carolina to accept a compromise tariff bill backed by Jackson. The episode led to the estrangement of Jackson from his vice president, John C. Calhoun, who had supported South Carolina's nullification of the tariff.

Although Jackson was a strong defender of the primacy of the federal government, he did not support all its activities. In 1832 Jackson vetoed the bill that would have rechartered the Second Bank of the United States on the grounds that the bank was unconstitutional and a monopoly that benefited the rich. Jackson's political opponents hoped to turn the issue against him in the 1832 election, but the popular president easily defeated Whig Henry Clay. Unfortunately, the lack of a central bank weakened controls over state and local banks and contributed to the inflation and overspeculation that were partially responsible for the severe depression that began in 1837 after Jackson left office.

On January 30, 1835, Jackson became the first president to be the target of an assassination attempt. As Jackson was emerging from the Capitol, Richard Lawrence fired two pistols at him at point-blank range. Miraculously, both misfired. Jackson went at his assailant with his walking stick as onlookers seized Lawrence. The deluded young man, who claimed Jackson was preventing him from assuming the British throne, later was committed to an insane asylum.

When Jackson's second term expired, he retired to the Hermitage, his estate near Nashville. Although he never again sought public office and suffered from several ailments that left him weak, he retained his avid interest in politics. His support was important to the presidential victories of Martin Van Buren in 1836 and James K. Polk in 1844. Jackson died in 1845 at the Hermitage.

When Jackson met Rachel Donelson Robards in Nashville in 1788, she was separated from but still married to Lewis Robards. But when Jackson married her in 1791, they believed she had been granted a divorce. In late 1793, however, they learned that Rachel's divorce had not become legal until a few months before. Thus, to avoid any legal difficulties Andrew and Rachel repeated their wedding ceremony in January 1794.

Although the couple had no children, in 1810 they adopted Rachel's nephew, whom they renamed Andrew Jackson, Jr. During the 1828 presidential campaign, Jackson's political opponents dredged up old accusations that

Jackson's marriage was improper. Rachel was upset by the scrutiny of her past and longed for a quiet life in Tennessee with her husband. The charges may have affected Rachel's health, for it grew progressively worse, and she eventually died of a heart attack on December 22, 1828, after Jackson had been elected president but before his inauguration.

Martin Van Buren

Library of Congress

M Van Buren

Born: December 5, 1782; Kinderhook, New York
Party: Democratic
Term: March 4, 1837-March 4, 1841
Vice President: Richard M. Johnson
Died: July 24, 1862; Kinderhook
Buried: Kinderhook

Martin Van Buren was the third child of Abraham and Maria Van Buren. Martin's father was a farmer and tavern keeper who had fought in the Revolution. His mother, who had been widowed before marrying Abraham, had two sons and a daughter by her previous marriage.

Van Buren, the first president not of British descent, was raised in the Dutch community of Kinderhook, New York. Despite having received only a rudimentary education as a child, he began studying law when he was only fourteen under Francis Silvester. He moved to New York in 1801 and continued his law studies. After being admitted to the bar in 1803 he returned to Kinderhook and opened a law practice.

In 1808 Van Buren moved to Hudson, New York, where he was appointed surrogate of Columbia County. He began his rapid rise to power in New York politics in 1812 when he was elected to the state senate. He was appointed state attorney general in 1815 and retained his Senate seat while serving in that post. By 1820 Van Buren had become one of the most powerful politicians in New York. Before pursuing a national political career, Van Buren organized the "Albany Regency," a political machine that controlled New York politics through patronage, party newspapers, and a tightly controlled Democratic caucus in the state legislature.

In 1821 the New York State legislature elected Van Buren to the U.S. Senate as a member of the Democratic-Republican party. He was reelected in 1827. While serving in the Senate, Van Buren was one of the most vocal critics of President John Quincy Adams.

Van Buren's rise to the presidency was aided by his association with Andrew Jackson. Although Van Buren and Jackson had little in common but political skill, they became close allies. By 1827 Van Buren had become Jackson's most powerful supporter from the northeastern states. In 1828 Van Buren resigned from the Senate to help Jackson's presidential campaign in New York by running for governor. Jackson was elected president and Van Buren won the governorship, but Van Buren resigned after only three months to become Jackson's secretary of state.

As secretary of state, Van Buren was the most influential member of Jackson's cabinet. He not only became a successful diplomat respected by foreign governments for his discretion and negotiating ability, but he also continued to be Jackson's principal political adviser. In 1831 Van Buren further endeared himself to Jackson, when he concurred with Jackson's defense of Peggy Eaton, Secretary of War John Eaton's wife who had been rejected by Washington society for her alleged past promiscuity. Soon after the Eaton affair Van Buren resigned from his office to allow Jackson to reconstruct his cabinet free of supporters of Van Buren's political rival, Vice President John C. Calhoun. Jackson then appointed Van Buren ambassador to Great Britain, but when the Senate confirmation vote resulted in a tie, Calhoun voted against confirming Van Buren, who had already arrived in London. In 1832 Van Buren replaced Calhoun as Jackson's vice-presidential running mate. The Jackson-Van Buren team was elected easily, and Van Buren continued to exercise influence over Jackson's policies.

In 1836, with President Jackson's backing, Van Buren received the Democratic presidential nomination. The Whig party, believing that no single candidate had a good chance to beat Van Buren, nominated several regional candidates, hoping to divide the electoral vote and force the election into the House of Representatives. Van Buren, however, won a majority of the popular and the electoral vote. He needed 148 electoral votes to win the election outright, and he received 170 votes with William Henry Harrison, his closest Whig opponent, receiving 73 votes.

Van Buren pledged at his inauguration to continue the policies of Jackson, and he reappointed Jackson's cabinet. The former president's economic policies, however, contributed to the depression that dominated Van Buren's presidency and did not subside until he had been defeated for reelection. In 1832 Jackson had vetoed the bill to recharter the National Bank. Without the central control provided by the National Bank, many state and local banks engaged in wild speculation that led to financial disaster.

In 1837 overspeculation and a natural downturn in the business cycle caused many banks and businesses to fail. While unemployment soared, Van Buren followed the conventional economic wisdom of the period by cutting government expenditures. But these restrictive fiscal policies only deepened the depression. Like his mentor, Van Buren also opposed a national bank, but he believed the federal government should handle its own funds rather than placing them in state banks as Jackson had done. He therefore proposed an independent federal treasury system. After several years of political maneuvering and debate Congress passed the Independent Treasury Act in July 1840. It established subtreasuries in seven U.S. cities.

On the issue of slavery Van Buren promoted the moderate course of allowing slavery to continue where it existed but blocking its extension. His opposition to the annexation of Texas, which would have added another slave state to the Union, avoided conflict with Mexico but cost him support in the South and West and damaged his relationship with Andrew Jackson.

Van Buren also had to deal with conflict on the U.S. border with Canada. He refused to support a movement by some U.S. citizens to aid a Canadian attempt to overthrow British rule in Canada. He defused the crisis by issuing a neutrality proclamation and sending Gen. Winfield Scott to Buffalo to enforce the peace. In 1839 a dispute developed over the uncertain legal boundary between Maine and Canada. Maine's governor, John Fairfield, called up a force of Maine militia and was preparing to fight with the Canadians over the issue when Van Buren intervened by negotiating an agreement with the British ambassador to the United States and sending Gen. Scott to Maine to block any military adventure by Fairfield.

In 1840 Van Buren was renominated unanimously by the Democratic party, but Whig William Henry Harrison was a formidable opponent. Not only was Harrison a national hero for his Indian fighting exploits before and during the War of 1812, but also he was portrayed as the candidate of the common man who was truer to Jacksonian principles than Van Buren. Although Van Buren won 47 percent of the popular vote, Harrison trounced him in the electoral college 234-60. Van Buren even failed to win his home state of New York.

Despite his defeat in 1840 Van Buren did not retire from presidential politics. He attempted to run again for his party's nomination in 1844 but was defeated by dark horse candidate James K. Polk, who outflanked Van Buren by openly advocating the annexation of Texas. In 1848 Van Buren ran for president as the candidate of the new antislavery Free Soil party. His long-shot candidacy split the Democratic vote in New York, helping Whig Zachary Taylor win the state and defeat Democrat Lewis Cass by 163-127 electoral votes. In 1850 Van Buren returned to the Democratic party, and he supported Franklin Pierce's presidential candidacy in 1852.

Van Buren was the first former president to tour Europe. From 1853 to 1855 he visited Britain, France, Italy, Belgium, Holland, and Switzerland. During his retirement he wrote *Inquiry into the Origin and Course of Political Parties in the United States.* The manuscript was unfinished when he died in 1862 after suffering severe asthma attacks, but it was edited by his sons and published in 1867.

Van Buren married his childhood sweetheart and distant cousin Hannah Hoes on February 21, 1807. They had four sons and a fifth child who died soon after birth. Hannah died in 1819 before her husband attained national prominence. Van Buren never remarried, and the role of White House hostess was performed by Angelica Singleton Van Buren, the wife of his oldest son and White House secretary, Abraham.

William Henry Harrison

Library of Congress

W H Harrison

Born: February 9, 1773; Berkeley, Virginia
Party: Whig
Term: March 4, 1841-April 4, 1841
Vice President: John Tyler
Died: April 4, 1841; Washington, D.C.
Buried: North Bend, Ohio

William Henry Harrison was the youngest of the seven children of Benjamin and Elizabeth Harrison. William's father, a prosperous Virginia planter who served as a member of the Continental Congress and governor of Virginia, also signed the Declaration of Independence. When William was fourteen his parents sent him to Hampden-Sydney College in his home state. Before graduating, however, he left for Philadelphia to study medicine under Dr. Benjamin Rush, a prominent physician and signer of the Declaration of Independence.

When his father died in 1791, Harrison quit medicine to join the army. He was commissioned as a lieutenant and assigned as an aide to Gen. Anthony Wayne at Fort Washington near Cincinnati. In 1794 Harrison fought in the Battle of Fallen Timbers where General Wayne's forces defeated eight hundred Indians. Harrison was promoted to captain in March 1795 and was given command of Fort Washington late that year.

In 1798 President John Adams appointed Harrison secretary of the Northwest Territory. The following year Harrison traveled to Washington, D.C., as the delegate of the Northwest Territory to Congress. There he worked successfully for legislation that separated the Indiana Territory from the Northwest Territory. In 1800 Adams appointed Harrison governor of the Indiana Territory, a post that he held until 1812. In November 1811 Harrison led the Indiana territorial militia in a battle fought near Tippecanoe Creek against a confederation of Indians under the Shawnee chief Tecumseh. The battle was inconclusive, but it made Harrison a nationally famous Indian fighter. During the War of 1812 Harrison was appointed brigadier general in command of the U.S. Army in the Northwest. Two years after the Battle of Tippecanoe Harrison again met Tecumseh, who had formed an alliance with the British. At the battle of Thames River in Ontario, Harrison's troops decisively defeated the Indians. Tecumseh was killed, and the federation of Indians was broken. The importance of the Thames River battle was overshadowed, however, by Harrison's earlier fight against the Indians, which had earned him the catchy nickname "Tippecanoe."

After the war Harrison was elected first to the U.S. House of Representatives, then to the Ohio senate, and finally to the U.S. Senate. In 1828 Andrew Jackson appointed him ambassador to Colombia, but Harrison served there only eight months before returning to North Bend, Ohio, to manage his farm. In 1834 he accepted an appointment as clerk of his county's court of common pleas to help pay his heavy debts. While serving in this relatively insignificant post, he began campaigning actively for the 1836 presidential nomination of the Whig party.

After witnessing the ease with which popular Democrat Andrew Jackson won two presidential elections, leaders of the Whig party decided that they too needed a candidate who was a war hero from the West. The Whigs thus ran several regional candidates, including Harrison, against Jackson's chosen successor, Martin Van Buren. Van Buren won the election, but Harrison demonstrated his appeal by winning seven states.

Harrison's strong showing in the 1836 presidential election made him the logical Whig candidate in 1840. Even with Andrew Jackson's endorsement, Van Buren's hold on the presidency was vulnerable because of an economic depression that had started in 1837. The Whig's campaign of 1840 was a study in political manipulation of the electorate. Party leaders promoted "Tippecanoe" as a champion of the common man and war hero who was raised in a log cabin and preferred to drink hard cider. Meanwhile, they portrayed Van Buren as the rich person's candidate who lived like a king in the White House. The Whigs buried political issues under a mountain of slogans, songs, picnics, stump speeches, and parades. And the strategy worked, with Harrison receiving 230 electoral votes to Van Buren's 60.

Harrison's inaugural address, delivered on March 4, 1841, while hardly the most memorable in presidential history, was probably the most fateful. A driving rainstorm soaked Harrison as he rode to the Capitol on a white horse and it continued throughout his address, which was the longest inaugural speech ever delivered. It contained over eight thousand words and lasted an hour and forty-five minutes. Ironically, in his speech, he advocated a constitutional amendment limiting presidents to one term in office and pledged to serve only one himself. Harrison caught a severe cold from his long exposure to the elements. On March 27 his condition deteriorated, and he was confined to his bed with what doctors diagnosed as pneumonia. He died on April 4, exactly one month after his inauguration.

Harrison married Anna Symmes on November 25, 1795, while he was an army lieutenant stationed in Ohio. They had six daughters and four sons. One of their sons, John Scott, was the father of Benjamin Harrison, who became the twenty-third president.

John Tyler

G. P. A. Healy; Library of Congress

John Tyler

Born: March 29, 1790; Charles City County, Virginia
Party: Whig
Term: April 6, 1841-March 4, 1845
Vice President: None
Died: January 18, 1862; Richmond, Virginia
Buried: Richmond

John Tyler had much in common with his 1840 presidential running mate, William Henry Harrison. Both men were born in Charles City County, Virginia, and both were sons of prominent Virginia planters who had served as governor of that state.

John was the sixth of the eight children born to John and Mary Tyler. His mother died when he was just seven years old. Throughout his early life John set high goals for himself and attempted to follow his father's example of an active life of public service. He attended William and Mary College in Williamsburg, Virginia, graduating in 1807 when he was just seventeen. He then studied law under his father and was admitted to the bar two years later.

In 1811 Tyler was elected to the Virginia House of Delegates as a Jeffersonian Democratic-Republican. He was reelected five times and remained in office until 1815. During the War of 1812 he served briefly as captain of a Virginia militia company, but he saw no action. In November 1816 he was elected to the U.S. House of Representatives, but he retired from Congress in 1821, citing poor health. During his early political career Tyler was noted for his support of slavery and states' rights.

In 1823 Tyler was again elected to the Virginia House of Delegates, where he served until he was elected governor in 1825. After he resigned the governorship in 1827 he won a seat in the U.S. Senate which he held until 1836.

As a senator, Tyler promoted the compromise tariffs that eased the nullification crises in South Carolina in 1832. Although he doubted that the states could legally nullify federal laws, he vigorously opposed Jackson's threats to use force against South Carolina. In 1836 Tyler resigned his Senate seat after refusing to follow the instructions of the Virginia legislature that he vote for the deletion of a 1833 censure of Andrew Jackson from the Senate *Journal.* The Senate had censured Jackson for his removal of public funds from the Second Bank of the United States without proper congressional approval.

Tyler's unhappiness with Jackson and the Democratic party led him to join the Whig party, despite the antislavery and nationalistic positions of many of its leaders. As one of several regional Whig vice-presidential candidates in 1836, Tyler received forty-seven electoral votes. Democrats Martin Van Buren and Richard Johnson won the presidency and vice presidency, respectively.

Considering their similar beginnings, it is ironic that Tyler was chosen as Harrison's running mate to balance the ticket. Harrison was promoted by the Whigs as "Old Tippecanoe," a tough Indian fighter who, like Andrew Jackson, was a champion of the common people. Tyler added southern gentility and a pro-slavery background that the Whigs hoped would appeal to the South. The Whig campaign of 1840 avoided policy issues and promoted its candidates through parties, parades, songs, and catchy slogans such as "Tippecanoe and Tyler too." The Whig ticket easily defeated President Martin Van Buren, whose popularity had been damaged by an economic depression that had lasted throughout his term.

Tyler appeared destined to have a small role in the Harrison administration. Daniel Webster, Henry Clay, and other Whig leaders had planned to exercise considerable influence over the aging Harrison, and there would be little place for Tyler, whose views were outside the Whig mainstream. Tyler, however, was thrust into the presidency when Harrison died only one month after taking office. The Constitution did not specify whether a vice president was to become president upon the death of an incumbent or merely assume the powers and duties of the office. Since Tyler was neither a Democrat nor a true Whig, leaders of both parties sought to limit his power. Many members of Congress and other national leaders contended that Tyler should be recognized only as acting president. But Tyler ignored his critics and assumed not only the duties of the presidency but also its title and all of its power.

Unlike the aging William Henry Harrison, who would likely have been dominated by Whig party leaders, Tyler adopted policies that were entirely his own. His strict constructionist principles led him to oppose the major goals of the Whig leadership, including the National Bank, high tariffs, and federally funded internal improvements. As a result, he was excommunicated from the Whig party while still president.

Although Tyler had little influence in Congress, he wished to make Texas, which had declared its independence from Mexico in 1836, a part of the United States. He thus oversaw the negotiation of a treaty of annexation with Texas in early 1844. On April 22 of that year he submitted the treaty to the Senate for approval. The Senate, however, rejected the treaty on June 8.

Tyler wished to run for reelection in 1844, but neither of the major political parties wanted to nominate him. He therefore organized a new Democratic-Republican party dedicated to states' rights and the annexation of Texas. He gave up his candidacy, however, when the Democrats nominated James K. Polk, who had the support of Andrew Jackson and also advocated annexing Texas.

On December 4, Tyler, now a lame-duck president, sent his last State of the Union message to Congress. In it he proposed that the Texas annexation treaty be approved by a simple majority of both houses. The proposal was controversial not only because annexation of Texas would have implications for the slavery issue, but also because such a method of granting congressional consent would ignore the constitutional provision requiring a two-thirds vote by the Senate for approval of treaties. The House passed the joint resolution by a vote of 120-98 on January 25, 1845, and the Senate followed suit by a vote of 27-25 on February 27, 1845. Tyler's strategy had worked, and an important legislative precedent was set. Tyler signed the bill into law on March 1, three days before leaving office.

When his term expired, Tyler retired to Sherwood Forest, his Virginia estate. As a private citizen, he remained an outspoken advocate of southern interests. He believed that states had a constitutional right to secede, but he worked to preserve the Union. In early 1861 he presided over the Washington Peace Conference, an eleventh-hour attempt to resolve sectional differences and avoid civil war. When Virginia seceded, however, he pledged his loyalty to the South. In November 1861 Tyler was elected to the new Confederate Congress in Richmond, Virginia. He died there in a hotel room on January 18, 1862, before he could take his seat.

Tyler married Letitia Christian in 1813 on his twenty-third birthday. They had eight children. Mrs. Tyler died in the White House in 1842 after an extended illness. Several months after his first wife's death, Tyler became infatuated with Julia Gardiner, a young socialite from New York. After a year of courtship they were married in New York on June 26, 1844. Tyler had seven children by his second wife giving him a total of fifteen, the most of any president. Tyler's second marriage caused a minor scandal in the capital because his bride was only twenty-four years old. Their wedding came in the wake of a tragic accident on the

Potomac river in which Julia's father, David Gardiner, and several members of Tyler's cabinet were killed. In fact, many members of Washington society, including Julia and the president, were also on board at the time of the accident, when a cannon that was being demonstrated on board the navy frigate *Princeton* exploded.

James K. Polk

Library of Congress

Born: November 2, 1795; Mecklenburg County, North Carolina
Party: Democratic
Term: March 4, 1845-March 4, 1849
Vice President: George M. Dallas
Died: June 15, 1849; Nashville, Tennessee
Buried: Nashville

James Knox Polk was the eldest of the ten children born to Samuel and Jane Polk. Samuel Polk was a prosperous North Carolina farmer who was interested in politics. When James was ten his family moved to Duck River, Tennessee, a settlement without a school on the edge of the frontier. There his parents taught him mathematics and reading. As a boy, Polk was frail and often ill. When he was seventeen he survived an operation to remove gallstones without the benefit of anesthesia. His health improved dramatically after the surgery.

In 1818 Polk graduated from the University of North Carolina with honors. He then moved to Nashville, Tennessee, where he studied law for two years in the office of Felix Grundy before being admitted to the bar.

Polk began his political career in the Tennessee legislature in 1823 at the age of twenty-seven. Two years later he was elected to the U.S. House of Representatives from Andrew Jackson's former district. Polk rose quickly to positions of power in the House, becoming chairman of the Ways and Means Committee, majority leader, and finally Speaker in 1835. During his years in the House he earned the nickname "Young Hickory" because of his unswerving support for Andrew Jackson. In 1839 he left the House when the Democratic party in Tennessee drafted him as its candidate for governor. He won that election and served a two-year term. He ran for reelection in 1841 and 1843 but was defeated both times by the Whig candidate.

At the 1844 Democratic national convention in Baltimore Polk's political career was resurrected dramatically from those gubernatorial defeats. Martin Van Buren was favored to receive the Democratic presidential nomination, but neither he nor his chief rival, Lewis Cass, could muster the two-thirds vote required to secure the nomination. With the balloting hopelessly deadlocked, the convention turned unanimously to Polk as a compromise candidate on the ninth ballot. He thus became the first dark-horse presidential candidate of a major party.

Polk campaigned on an expansionist platform that advocated annexation of Texas and a settlement with Britain that would fix the northern boundary of Oregon at 54°40'. He also received the invaluable endorsement of Andrew Jackson. Polk defeated his better-known Whig opponent, Henry Clay, 170-105 in the electoral college. The election, however, was closer than the electoral vote indicates. Polk received only forty thousand votes more than Clay, and he won New York's thirty-six electoral votes—which would have given Clay a 141-134 victory—by just five thousand votes.

The most important issue confronting the new president was westward expansion. Polk and most of the nation wished to resolve the Oregon boundary question with Great Britain, acquire California and other lands in the Southwest from Mexico, and annex Texas. An agreement signed in 1818 provided for joint U.S.-British ownership of the Oregon Territory, which extended from California to above the fifty-fourth parallel. Although Polk had campaigned on the slogan "54° 40' or fight," the battle cry of those who wanted all of the Oregon Territory, he offered to divide Oregon with the British at the forty-ninth parallel. When the British refused, Congress, at his request, terminated the joint ownership agreement on April 23, 1846. Realizing that lack of a settlement could mean war, the British accepted Polk's original offer.

Three days before Polk's inauguration, President Tyler had signed a joint resolution annexing Texas, as Polk had advocated during his campaign. The southern border of Texas, however, remained in dispute, and tensions with Mexico over Texas and and other territories in the Southwest threatened to lead to war. In 1846 Polk sent U.S. troops under Gen. Zachary Taylor into the territory between the Nueces River and the Rio Grande. The action was provocative, since the area was claimed by both Mexico and Texas but occupied by Mexicans. Polk had already decided to ask Congress for a declaration of war when news reached Washington that Mexican forces had attacked the American contingent. The president then claimed that Mexico was the aggressor and asked Congress to declare war, which it did, despite opposition from some northern lawmakers. American forces under Gen. Zachary Taylor and Gen. Winfield Scott won major victories over the Mexican army and eventually occupied Mexico City. In 1848 Mexico agreed to the treaty of Guadalupe Hidalgo, which ceded California and New Mexico to the United States in return for $15 million and recognized the Rio Grande as the boundary of Texas.

In domestic policy Polk also achieved his major goals. With his backing, Congress narrowly passed the Walker Tariff Act in 1846, which greatly reduced tariffs. Although the bill was opposed in the North, it stimulated free trade and the U.S. economy. Polk also persuaded Congress to pass an independent treasury bill in 1846, which reestablished a system of subtreasuries first set up under Van Buren to handle government funds. Before Polk reestablished the subtreasuries, these funds had been deposited in state banks.

At the beginning of his term, Polk reputedly had told a friend that his four main goals as president were resolution of the territorial dispute over Oregon, acquisition of California and New Mexico, a lowered tariff, and reestablishment of a subtreasury system. He successfully achieved all four goals, and historians generally believe that he provided the strongest presidential leadership between the terms of Presidents Jackson and Abraham Lincoln.

Upon entering office, Polk had declared that he would not run for a second term. He kept his promise in 1848 by not seeking the Democratic presidential nomination. After attending Zachary Taylor's inauguration, the former president left Washington and toured the South on his way to his recently purchased home in Nashville. Polk, who worked long hours and almost never took a day off during his presidency, was not to enjoy a long retirement. The stress of the presidency and his work schedule may have weakened his health. He died in Nashville at the age of fifty-three, only three and a half months after leaving office.

Polk married Sarah Childress on January 1, 1824. She served not only as White House hostess but also as the president's personal secretary. The Polks had no children. After her husband's death Sarah retired in Nashville, Tennessee, where she lived as a widow until her death in 1891.

Zachary Taylor

Library of Congress

Z. Taylor.

Born: November 24, 1784; Orange County, Virginia
Party: Whig
Term: March 4, 1849-July 9, 1850
Vice President: Millard Fillmore
Died: July 9, 1850; Washington, D.C.
Buried: Louisville, Kentucky

Zachary Taylor was born into a prominent family of Virginia planters related to both James Madison and Robert E. Lee. His father, Richard Taylor, had served as an officer in the revolutionary war. When Zachary's mother, Sarah, was pregnant with him, the Taylors left Virginia to establish a farm near Louisville, Kentucky. Zachary, the third of nine children, was born at a friend's home along the way. Because the Kentucky frontier lacked schools, Zachary was given a rudimentary education by occasional tutors and his well-educated parents.

In 1808 at the age of twenty-three Taylor was commissioned as a lieutenant in the army. He participated in William Henry Harrison's Indian campaigns in the Indiana Territory and fought in the Ohio Valley during the War of 1812. After the war he resigned from the army after the war over a dispute about his rank but returned a year later when he was recommissioned as a major. He then served in a series of garrison posts on the frontier. In 1832 Taylor was promoted to colonel during the Black Hawk War and was among the officers who accepted Chief Black Hawk's surrender. He was reassigned in 1837 to Florida where the army was fighting the Seminole Indians. On Christmas Day of that year his troops defeated the Seminoles in a major battle that earned him a promotion to brigadier general, and on May 15, 1838, he assumed command of all forces in Florida. In 1841 Taylor was given command of the southern division of the army and reassigned to Baton Rouge, Louisiana, where he bought a large plantation.

When the United States annexed Texas in 1845, President James K. Polk ordered Taylor to defend it against a Mexican invasion. In January 1846 Polk instructed the general to take the provocative step of deploying his forces on territory claimed by Mexico between the Nueces River and the Rio Grande. When Mexico declared war and launched an attack against Taylor's army, the general invaded Mexico and won a series of quick victories at Palo Alto, Resaca de la Palma, and Monterrey.

Taylor's victories earned him a promotion to major general and popularity among the American public. President Polk, however, recognized that Taylor's heroics made him an attractive Whig presidential candidate and maneuvered to prevent further boosts to the general's reputation. The president ordered Taylor to command a small force of five thousand troops in northern Mexico, while Gen. Winfield Scott was given most of the troops who had served under Taylor and the more glamorous duty of leading an expedition to capture Mexico City. Taylor, however, turned this assignment to his advantage when his soldiers routed twenty thousand Mexicans at Buena Vista in February 1847. The victory made Taylor a hero in the United States, and, as Polk had feared, the Whig party sought to capitalize on "Old Rough and Ready's" popularity by offering him its nomination for president.

Taylor declared that he disliked partisan politics and preferred to run without party affiliation. Eventually, however, he accepted the Whig party's nomination but announced that he thought of himself as a national candidate rather than a Whig candidate. Taylor's reputation as a war hero was enough to earn him a close 163-127 electoral vote victory over Democratic candidate Lewis Cass. Martin Van Buren's third-party candidacy contributed to Taylor's victory by splitting New York's Democratic vote, thereby allowing Taylor to capture the state's thirty-six electoral votes that would have given Cass a majority.

Taylor's primary weakness as a chief executive was his lack of political experience. At Taylor's inauguration James Polk found the general to be "exceedingly ignorant of public affairs." Despite this handicap Taylor refused to be just a Whig figurehead. Among his proposals were greater government aid for agriculture and the development of a transcontinental railroad.

The major issue confronting Taylor was whether slavery would be allowed to exist in the West where territories soon would be applying for statehood. Southerners feared that new states entering the Union, particularly California, would outlaw slavery and upset the equilibrium between slave and free states in Congress. Congressional leaders, led by Henry Clay of Kentucky, attempted to legislate a compromise that would satisfy both the North and the South. Taylor, however, supported the right of states to decide for themselves whether they would permit slavery. He also hoped that the bestowal of statehood on California would bring order to that territory, where local government had been unable to cope with the thousands of settlers who came after the discovery of gold there. He thus encouraged New Mexico and California to apply for statehood and declared that he would oppose the compromise plan being developed by Congress.

Although Taylor was a slave-owning southerner, he believed the Union must be preserved at all costs. He warned southern leaders that if their states rebelled against federal authority because of California statehood or any other issue, he would use the army to enforce the law and preserve the Union. Taylor never had to veto a congressional compromise plan or confront the secession of southern states, however. After sitting through ceremonies at the Washington Monument on a hot July Fourth he fell ill and died in the White House five days later at the age of sixty-five. His vice president, Millard Fillmore, succeeded to the presidency and threw executive support behind the Compromise of 1850, which held the Union together temporarily by making concessions to the South in return for California's entrance into the Union as a free state.

In 1810, while a young army officer, Taylor married Margaret Mackall Smith. They had six children, two of whom died as infants. Their only son, Richard, served as a general in the Confederate army. One of their daughters, Sarah Knox, married Jefferson Davis, who would become president of the Confederacy. She died of malaria only three months after the wedding.

Millard Fillmore

Mathew Brady; Library of Congress

Millard Fillmore

Born: January 7, 1800; Cayuga County, New York
Party: Whig
Term: July 10, 1850-March 4, 1853
Vice President: None
Died: March 8, 1874; Buffalo, New York
Buried: Buffalo

Millard Fillmore was the second oldest of the nine children of Nathaniel and Phoebe Fillmore, a poor New York farm couple. When Millard was fourteen he was apprenticed to a clothmaker, but he bought his freedom from apprenticeship for thirty dollars and took a job teaching school. While teaching, he studied law with a local county judge and was admitted to the bar in 1823.

Fillmore began his political career as a member of New York's Anti-Masonic party, which opposed secret societies in the United States. In 1828 he was elected to the New York State assembly with the support of Anti-Masonic party boss Thurlow Weed. While in the legislature, Fillmore drafted a bill that abolished imprisonment for debtors; it eventually became law. After being reelected twice he left the legislature to establish a lucrative law practice in Buffalo with his future postmaster general, Nathan K. Hall. From 1833 to 1835 and 1837 to 1843 Fillmore served in the U.S. House of Representatives. In 1834 he followed Weed into the Whig party and soon became a prominent member of its northern wing. While in the House, Fillmore was an ally of Sen. Henry Clay (Whig-Ky.). In 1843 Fillmore returned to New York to practice law and enter state politics. He was defeated narrowly for the governorship in 1844 by Democrat Silas Wright but won election as New York's comptroller three years later.

In 1848 the Whigs nominated Mexican War hero Zachary Taylor as their presidential candidate. The party's search for a vice-presidential candidate to balance the ticket with the slave-owning Taylor led to Fillmore, who had impressed many party leaders with his good looks and political skills. The Taylor-Fillmore ticket then narrowly defeated Democrats Lewis Cass and William Butler.

As vice president, Fillmore was excluded from policy making in the Taylor administration, but he dutifully presided over the Senate as that body struggled with the slavery issue. Fillmore was a staunch opponent of slavery, but he believed a moderate course was necessary to preserve the Union. He therefore supported the Compromise of 1850 devised by Sen. Henry Clay. The plan sought to relieve sectional tensions by making concessions to both the North and the South. President Taylor, however, opposed the compromise and was prepared to veto it and use force to put down any rebellions in the South that might result. Fillmore foresaw a close vote in the Senate and informed the president that if a tie vote should occur his conscience obligated him to vote for the compromise despite Taylor's opposition. Before the Senate could vote on the plan, Taylor died suddenly on July 9, 1850.

Because Fillmore believed Taylor's cabinet was against the compromise, he accepted the resignations of all seven men and appointed a new cabinet that supported it. With Taylor dead, the threat of a presidential veto of Clay's plan was removed and work on the compromise moved forward. In September 1850 Fillmore signed a series of bills that made up the Compromise of 1850. Under the compromise, California was admitted to the Union as a free state, the territories of Utah and New Mexico were established without mention of slavery, and Texas was paid $10 million for surrendering its claim to New Mexico. Other provisions made federal officials responsible for capturing and returning runaway slaves and outlawed the slave trade in the District of Columbia while affirming the right to own slaves there. Many southerners objected to the compromise because it set a precedent: it allowed the federal government to pass legislation on slavery rather than leaving the issue to the states. Abolitionists, however, thought the compromise favored the South. They especially detested the Fugitive Slave Law, which Fillmore felt obligated to enforce despite his recognition that in doing so he was committing political suicide. The president believed the compromise would work only if the federal government upheld all of its provisions with equal force.

No one was entirely satisfied with the Compromise of 1850, which did nothing to resolve the slavery issue. It resulted, however, in a few years of relative calm. During this period Fillmore oversaw the modernization of the White House, worked to secure federal funds for railroad construction, and opposed the efforts of private U.S. citizens to overthrow Spanish rule in Cuba. Before Fillmore left office in 1853 he sent Commodore Matthew Perry on a cruise across the Pacific to open up Japan to American trade.

Fillmore attempted to secure the Whig presidential

nomination in 1852, but the convention chose Gen. Winfield Scott, a Mexican War hero, on the fifty-third ballot. Scott then lost to the Democrat Franklin Pierce in a landslide. Fillmore's wife, Abigail, became ill after attending Pierce's inauguration on a cold March day. She died three weeks later, on March 30, 1853.

In 1853 Fillmore lost not only his wife but also his party. After the election of 1852 the Whig party disintegrated. Their most visible leaders, Daniel Webster and Henry Clay, had died in 1852, and Fillmore's enforcement of the Fugitive Slave Act had disaffected many northern Whigs who helped form the new Republican party in 1854. Fillmore declined to join the Republicans and instead accepted the 1856 presidential nomination of the ultraconservative American or "Know-Nothing" party. The Know-Nothings were named for their practice of responding "I know nothing" to questions about their rituals. The party was based on an opposition to immigrants and Catholics. The Know-Nothings believed these groups threatened the United States by plotting against the government and promoting radical ideologies. In the election Fillmore received over 800,000 popular votes but just eight electoral votes. He thus finished a distant third behind Democrat James Buchanan and Republican John Fremont.

After this embarrassment Fillmore retired from politics. In 1858 he married Caroline McIntosh, a wealthy forty-four-year-old widow, and settled in Buffalo. He died of a stroke on March 8, 1874. Fillmore had one son and one daughter by his first wife, Abigail Powers.

Franklin Pierce

Library of Congress

Franklin Pierce

Born: November 23, 1804; Hillsboro, New Hampshire
Party: Democratic
Term: March 4, 1853-March 4, 1857
Vice President: William R. King
Died: October 8, 1869; Concord, New Hampshire
Buried: Concord

Franklin Pierce was the sixth of the eight children born to Anna and Benjamin Pierce. His father, who would become governor of New Hampshire, married Anna after the death of his first wife. Pierce's parents sent him to private schools as a child, and at the age of fifteen he enrolled at Bowdoin College in Brunswick, Maine. Pierce did well at Bowdoin, graduating third in his class in 1824. After college he studied law and was admitted to the bar in 1827. In 1829 he was elected to the New Hampshire legislature while his father was governor.

When he was elected to the U.S. House of Representatives in 1833, Pierce left the New Hampshire legislature, where he had become Speaker of the House. Although Pierce's loyal support of the Jackson administration earned him a second term, he served only a few months because the New Hampshire legislature elected him to the U.S. Senate in 1836. In 1842, however, he retired from the

Senate at the urging of his wife and returned to New Hampshire to practice law. In 1844 President James K. Polk appointed Pierce U.S. district attorney for New Hampshire.

As district attorney and chairman of the Democratic party in New Hampshire, Pierce remained a powerful political figure, but he refused a series of important political appointments, partly because his wife did not want to move back to Washington, D.C. When the president appointed Sen. Levi Woodbury (D-N.H.) to the Supreme Court in 1845, Pierce declined to replace Woodbury in the Senate. The same year he turned down the New Hampshire Democratic gubernatorial nomination. In 1846 Polk offered him the U.S. attorney generalship, but Pierce again refused so he could remain in New Hampshire with his family. After the United States declared war on Mexico, however, Pierce accepted a commission as a colonel and began recruiting a New England regiment. Before he sailed for Mexico in May 1847, he was promoted to brigadier general. Pierce saw little action during his five and one-half months in Mexico because of an intestinal ailment and an injury sustained when his horse fell. Nevertheless, in January 1848 he returned to a hero's welcome in Concord where he resumed his law practice. That same year he again refused the Democratic nomination for governor.

Pierce's rise to the presidency was sudden and unexpected. The 1852 Democratic nominating convention produced a stalemate between James Buchanan, Lewis Cass, William Marcy, and Stephen A. Douglas. Because none of these candidates was able to garner a majority of the votes, the convention began searching for a fifth candidate. On the forty-ninth ballot the Democrats nominated Franklin Pierce, who several months before had announced he would not turn down such a nomination. As a northerner with southern sympathies and a spotless record, Pierce was an acceptable compromise candidate, although he had not served in an elective office since 1842. His Whig opponent was Gen. Winfield Scott, a hero of the Mexican War. Scott's campaign, however, was crippled by the defection of many northern Whigs to the Free Soil Party. Pierce remained in New Hampshire during the months before the election, letting his fellow Democrats, who had united behind his candidacy, campaign for him. The uncontroversial Democratic platform of strict observance of the Compromise of 1850 gained Pierce a 254-42 victory in the electoral college.

Pierce took office advocating tranquillity and prosperity at home and the extension of U.S. territories and commercial interests abroad. Most of his domestic policies favored the South. In his inaugural address he had declared his belief that slavery was constitutional and that "states where it exists are entitled to efficient remedies" to enforce it. The Compromise of 1850 enacted under Millard Fillmore had calmed temporarily tensions over the slavery issue, but that calm did not last through Pierce's presidency. In 1854 Pierce signed the Kansas-Nebraska Act into law. It repealed the 1820 Missouri Compromise that had outlawed slavery north of 36° 30', thereby enabling Kansas to declare itself a slave state if its citizens favored that course. Pierce, who believed that each state should decide for itself whether to permit slavery, strongly supported the act, which had been sponsored by Illinois senator Stephen A. Douglas. The act, however, turned Kansas into a warzone. Proslavery southerners and abolitionist northerners raced into Kansas hoping to seize control of the territory's government for their side. Many atrocities were committed by both groups, causing the territory to be dubbed "Bleeding Kansas."

In international affairs Pierce supported Millard Fillmore's initiative of sending Commodore Matthew Perry to Japan to open that country's ports to western trade. Perry negotiated a treaty that gave U.S. ships access to two ports and guaranteed humane treatment of U.S. sailors shipwrecked off Japan's coasts.

After leaving the presidency in 1857 Pierce never again sought public office. He and his wife, Jane Means Appleton Pierce, traveled in Europe from 1857 to 1859 and then retired to their Concord, New Hampshire, home. They had three sons, two of whom died in infancy. Their third son, eleven-year-old Benjamin, was killed when a train on which he and his parents were passengers wrecked near Andover, Massachusetts, a few weeks before Pierce's inauguration. The tragedy deeply affected Pierce's wife, who remained in a state of mourning during the first two years of Pierce's presidency. Pierce was a close college friend of American author Nathaniel Hawthorne, who wrote Pierce's campaign biography. Pierce was at Hawthorne's bedside when the writer died in 1864.

James Buchanan

Mathew Brady; National Archives

Born: April 23, 1791; Stony Batter, Pennsylvania
Party: Democratic
Term: March 4, 1857-March 4, 1861
Vice President: John C. Breckinridge
Died: June 1, 1868; Lancaster, Pennsylvania
Buried: Lancaster

James Buchanan was the second oldest child and oldest son of the eleven children born to James and Elizabeth Buchanan. Young James grew up working in the family's thriving frontier trading post in Mercersburg, Pennsylvania.

James received an elementary education at common schools and attended a secondary school in Mercersburg before entering Dickinson College in Carlisle, Pennsylvania, in 1807. A year later he was expelled for disorderly conduct, but he was reinstated with the help of the president of the board of trustees of the college. James graduated with honors in 1809 and returned to Lancaster to study law. In 1812 he was admitted to the bar, and the following year he was appointed assistant prosecutor for Lebanon County, Pennsylvania.

In August 1814, after the British burned Washington, D.C., Buchanan joined a company of men from Lancaster that marched to Baltimore to fight the British. The British withdrew from Baltimore soon after the company arrived. The unit was disbanded, and Buchanan returned to Pennsylvania where he was elected to the state assembly. He served two terms before leaving politics to establish a successful law practice.

Buchanan began his national political career in 1820 with his election to the U.S. House of Representatives as a Federalist. He served in the House for ten years. He was a staunch opponent of John Quincy Adams and in 1828 gave his allegiance to Andrew Jackson and the Democratic party. Jackson appointed Buchanan minister to Russia in 1831. While in St. Petersburg, Buchanan negotiated a treaty of commerce favorable to the United States. He returned home in 1833 and was elected to the U.S. Senate by the Pennsylvania legislature the following year. He quickly became a leading conservative Democrat and chairman of the Foreign Relations Committee. Buchanan chose to stay in the Senate despite President Martin Van Buren's offer of the attorney generalship and President John Tyler's offer of a seat on the Supreme Court. When President James K. Polk, for whom Buchanan had campaigned, offered Buchanan the post of secretary of state, however, he accepted. As secretary of state, Buchanan took a leading role in the negotiations with Britain that produced a compromise on fixing the boundary of the Oregon Territory.

After losing the 1848 Democratic presidential nomination to Lewis Cass, Buchanan retired to Lancaster. In 1853, however, he accepted an appointment from President Franklin Pierce as minister to Great Britain. While in Britain, Buchanan collaborated with the U.S. ambassadors to Spain and France in writing the Ostend Manifesto of 1854. This diplomatic report advocated the acquisition of Cuba from Spain by force if Spain refused to sell it. Its intent was to prevent the possibility of a slave uprising on the island that might spread by example to the United States. The document, which was not acted upon, was denounced in the North but increased Buchanan's popularity in the South.

After returning from Britain in 1856, Buchanan was nominated for president by the Democrats. His absence from the country during the bloody fighting in Kansas precipitated by the Kansas-Nebraska Act made him more acceptable than either President Pierce or Senator Stephen Douglas, both of whom had supported the act. Buchanan faced John Fremont of the newly formed Republican party and former president Millard Fillmore of the right-wing American (Know-Nothing) party. Buchanan received only 47 percent of the popular vote but won every southern state in defeating Fremont 174-114 in the electoral college.

Buchanan's presidency was dominated by the tensions between North and South over the slavery issue. Although Buchanan considered slavery to be unjust, he believed people in the southern states had the constitutional right to own slaves. He was a committed Unionist who tried to steer a middle course between the forces for and against slavery, but most of his policies appeared to northerners to favor the South. He enforced the Fugitive Slave Act, tried to quell northern antislavery agitation, and supported the Supreme Court's Dred Scott decision. The latter denied the citizenship of slaves, recognized the right of slaveowners to take their slaves wherever they chose, declared the Missouri Compromise restricting slavery to below 36°30' to be unconstitutional, and implied that neither Congress nor the territorial governments created by Congress had the authority to exclude slavery from the territories. Buchanan not only supported the 7-2 decision, but also lobbied Associate Justice Robert Grier to support it.

The Dred Scott case did not resolve the slavery question as Buchanan had hoped. In 1858 Buchanan split his party when he sent a proslavery constitution written by the minority southern faction in Kansas to Congress and recommended that Kansas be admitted as a slave state. Many Democratic leaders, including Stephen Douglas, denounced the constitution and distanced themselves from Buchanan. The Senate approved the plan to admit Kansas under the proslavery constitution, but the House rejected it. Kansas remained a territory until 1861 and continued to inspire conflict between North and South.

The 1860 election produced the secession crisis that Buchanan had hoped to prevent. When Abraham Lincoln of the antislavery Republican party was elected, southerners began to debate secession. Buchanan supported compromise solutions proposed by members of Congress and other leaders. He backed a proposal to reestablish the Missouri Compromise line and a constitutional amendment that would guarantee the right to own slaves in states that wanted it, but none of the plans was acceptable.

After Lincoln's election secessionists seized most federal forts in the South without much resistance. Buchanan considered secession to be unconstitutional, but he believed that the right to rebel against unjust rule was a basic right of all people and was even embodied in the Declaration of Independence. He also believed that the federal government could wage war against a state or group of states. Therefore, he refrained from responding with force to the acts of rebellion. He did request, however, the power to call out the militia and increase the size of the armed forces, but Congress refused. By the time Buchanan's term ended, seven states had seceded, and the nation was headed toward civil war.

After Lincoln's inauguration Buchanan retired to Wheatland, his home in Lancaster, Pennsylvania. He corresponded with friends and political associates but was not active in public affairs. During his retirement the northern press criticized him for failing to prevent the Civil War and accused him of allowing federal forts to remain vulnerable and participating in plots to arm the South before the war. In an attempt to justify his actions and the policies of his administration, he published his memoirs, *Mr. Buchanan's Administration on the Eve of the Rebellion*, in 1866. Buchanan believed that he vindicated himself through his book, which placed primary blame for the war on northern radicals. Buchanan died at Wheatland in 1868.

Buchanan was the only president never to marry. His close relationship with William R. King, who became vice president under Franklin Pierce, has led some historians to speculate that Buchanan was homosexual. His niece, Harriet Lane, served as White House hostess during his administration. In 1819, while practicing law, he became engaged to Ann Coleman, who was from a wealthy Lancaster family. But after a quarrel with Buchanan she broke the engagement and left for Philadelphia to visit her sister. She died mysteriously a few days later on December 9, 1819, amid rumors that she committed suicide. Her family did not allow Buchanan to attend her funeral.

Abraham Lincoln

Mathew Brady; Library of Congress

Abraham Lincoln

Born: February 12, 1809; near Hodgenville, Kentucky
Party: Republican
Term: March 4, 1861-April 15, 1865
Vice Presidents: Hannibal Hamlin; Andrew Johnson
Died: April 15, 1865; Washington, D.C.
Buried: Springfield, Illinois

Abraham Lincoln was born in a one-room log cabin on a backwoods farm in Kentucky. He was the second of the three children of Nancy and Thomas Lincoln, a poor farmer who also did carpentry work. Abe's younger brother died in infancy, and his mother died when he was nine. In 1819, Thomas Lincoln married Sarah Bush Johnston, who was a loving stepmother to Abe. She brought her three children by her previous marriage into the family.

During Abe's childhood the Lincolns lived on farms in Kentucky and Indiana. Abe attended country schools sporadically, learning to read, write, and do elementary math. He possessed a quick, inquisitive intellect, however, and spent much free time reading the family Bible and whatever books he could borrow. Abe worked at numerous odd jobs while in his teens, including farmhand, grocery store clerk, and ferry boat rower. In 1828 and 1831 he took trips down the Mississippi River to New Orleans as a flatboat deck hand. While in New Orleans during the second trip he reputedly developed his hatred of slavery after witnessing the maltreatment of slaves.

Abe had moved with his family to a farm near Decatur, Illinois, in 1830, but after returning from New Orleans in 1831, he settled in New Salem, Illinois. There he worked in a store and became known for his prowess as a story teller and wrestler. In 1832, Lincoln volunteered to fight Sauk Indians led by Chief Black Hawk. After serving several months in the army, he was discharged without participating in any combat. He returned to New Salem from his military service and made an unprepared attempt to win a seat as a Whig in the Illinois state legislature, but he was defeated.

Later in 1832 Lincoln bought half interest in a general store. When the store failed the following year, Lincoln was left with debts that he would not be able to pay off completely for seventeen years. After his failed business venture, Lincoln was appointed postmaster of New Salem and also worked as a surveyor.

Early Political Career

In 1834 Lincoln ran again for the state legislature and this time won a seat. He began studying law by reading borrowed law books. Shortly after being reelected to a second term in 1836, Lincoln was licensed to practice law. In 1837 he moved to Springfield, Illinois, and began practicing law when the legislature was not in session. He was reelected to the legislature in 1838 and 1840, serving for a time as Whig floor leader.

In 1846 Lincoln was elected to the U.S. House of Representatives. Despite the popularity of the Mexican War in his district, he joined fellow Whigs in denouncing the war as unjust. Lincoln also opposed the extension of slavery into the territories but did not advocate abolishing slavery where it already existed. Lincoln had promised Illinois Whig party leaders that he would serve only one term, so when his term expired he returned to Springfield. He spent the next several years reading and developing his successful law practice.

In 1854 Lincoln ran for the Senate but backed out of the race when his candidacy threatened to split the antislavery vote. Two years later, Lincoln joined the new Republican party, which had formed in 1854. He campaigned for its 1856 presidential candidate, John C. Fremont, who lost to Democrat James Buchanan.

The Illinois Republican party nominated Lincoln for senator in 1858. He faced incumbent Democrat Stephen A. Douglas, author of the Kansas-Nebraska Act of 1854, which was favored by many proslavery Democrats. The act gave the people in the territories of Kansas and Nebraska the option to permit slavery.

Lincoln challenged Douglas to a series of seven debates focusing on slavery that were attended by huge crowds. In the debates Lincoln questioned the morality of slavery and firmly argued against its expansion into territories where it did not exist already. The state legislature elected Douglas over Lincoln 54-46, but the debates made Lincoln famous throughout the country and a credible candidate for the Republican presidential nomination in 1860. During the next two years he made several highly publicized speaking tours, including one to the East in early 1860. His name was placed in nomination at the Republican national convention in Chicago in 1860, but he trailed New York senator William Seward on the first and second ballots. On the third ballot, however, Lincoln secured the nomination.

The Democratic party, meanwhile, split into two factions. Stephen Douglas was nominated by northern Democrats, and Vice President John C. Breckinridge of Kentucky was nominated by southern Democrats. The remnants of the Whig and Know-Nothing parties further complicated the election by joining to nominate John Bell as the candidate of their new Constitutional Union party. Lincoln won the four-candidate race with less than 40 percent of the popular vote. He captured eighteen northern states with 180 out of the total 303 electoral votes. Breckinridge and Bell followed with 72 and 39, respectively. Douglas, who finished second to Lincoln in the popular vote, won only Missouri's 12 electoral votes.

Presidency

Lincoln's election precipitated the secession crisis that the nation had feared for several decades. In December 1860, South Carolina left the Union, followed by six more states early in 1861. The rebelling states formed a confederacy and elected Jefferson Davis as their president.

Lincoln tried to ease southern fears that he intended to abolish slavery. He declared in his first inaugural address that he had no intention or authority to "interfere with the institution of slavery where it already exists." But he warned the southern states that he did not recognize their secession and would enforce federal law and defend the Union. He declared, "In your hands, my dissatisfied fellow-countrymen, and not in mine, is the momentous issue of civil war." War came when rebels attacked and captured Fort Sumter in Charleston harbor in April 1861. The attack on the federal fort signaled the South's unwillingness to return to the Union. On April 15, Lincoln called for seventy-five thousand voluteers to put down the rebellion. Soon after, four more southern states seceded, raising the number of states in the Confederacy to eleven.

During the next three months Lincoln refused to call Congress into session, while he took extraordinary actions to prepare for war, many of which violated the Constitution. He blockaded the South, doubled the size of the armed forces, suspended the writ of *habeas corpus* in some areas, and spent Treasury funds, all without congressional approval. Finally, on July 4, he convened Congress, which ratified most of his war measures.

Lincoln and the North hoped that the rebellion could be put down quickly, but the war turned into a protracted and bloody conflict. The Union won victories in the West under Gen. Ulysses S. Grant; but in the East, Union generals were repeatedly outmaneuvered by Robert E. Lee and other Confederate generals. On January 1, 1863, Lincoln issued the Emancipation Proclamation, which declared that the slaves in the rebellious states were free. *(See "Emancipation Proclamation," p. 1370, in the Appendix.)* So that the proclamation would have greater credibility, he had waited to make this move until after the Union won a victory, which came at the battle of Antietam in September 1862. In July 1863 the Union victory at the Battle of Gettysburg in Pennsylvania put the Confederacy on the defensive. Lincoln traveled to Gettysburg on November 19 where he delivered his famous Gettysburg Address during a ceremony to dedicate the battlefield's cemetery. *(See "Gettysburg Address," p. 1371, in the Appendix.)*

In 1864 Lincoln took an important step toward winning the war when he ordered Grant east to take command of all Union armies. That year Lincoln ran for reelection against Democratic candidate George B. McClellan, one of his former generals. Lincoln had relieved McClellan of his command of the Union army in 1862 because the general was overcautious and ineffective. During the spring of 1864 Lincoln's reelection had been in doubt as Grant's army fought a series of indecisive and costly battles in Virginia at the Wilderness, Spotsylvania, and Cold Harbor. But by September, Union general William T. Sherman had captured Atlanta, and Grant had besieged Petersburg, Virginia. Voters sensed that the Union was close to victory and reelected the president. Lincoln won all but three states and defeated McClellan 212-21 in the electoral college.

During the final year of the war, Grant fought a battle of attrition against Lee's forces in Virginia, while Sherman's army drove though Georgia and North and South Carolina destroying southern crops and industries. Finally, on April 9, 1865, Lee surrendered to Grant at Appomattox Court House in Virginia, ending the four-year war.

In his second inaugural address, delivered on March 4, 1865, Lincoln had proposed a magnanimous peace, saying "with malice toward none, with charity for all, with firmness in the right as God gives us to see the right, let us strive on to finish the work we are in, to bind up the nation's wounds." *(See "Lincoln's Second Inaugural Address," p. 1371, in the Appendix.)*

Lincoln, however, did not have the opportunity to implement his generous reconstruction plans. On April 14, 1865, while watching a production of the play *Our American Cousin* at Ford's Theater in Washington, D.C., he was shot in the back of the head at close range by actor John Wilkes Booth. After shooting Lincoln, Booth jumped from the presidential box to the stage, fled the theater, and rode south. On April 26 federal troops surrounded and killed him at a farm in Virginia. Booth, who had sympathized with the Confederacy, was part of a conspiracy to kill several government officials, including Vice President Andrew Johnson. With the exception of Secretary of State William Seward, who received a nonfatal stab wound at his home, the other targets of assassination escaped harm.

Lincoln was treated by a doctor at the theater, then carried across the street to a house where he died the next morning, April 15, without regaining consciousness. Vice President Johnson took the oath of office later that day. Lincoln's body lay in state in the Capitol and White House before being carried back to Illinois on a train viewed by millions of mourners.

Lincoln married Mary Todd on November 4, 1842. Of their four sons, only Robert, their eldest, reached adulthood. He served as secretary of war under Presidents James A. Garfield and Chester A. Arthur and minister to Great Britain under Benjamin Harrison. Their second son, Edward, died at the age of three; their third son, William, died of typhoid fever in the White House in 1862 at the age of eleven. Their youngest son, Thomas (Tad), survived his father but died at the age of eighteen in 1871.

Lincoln originally had been engaged to marry Mary Todd on January 1, 1841, but their wedding did not take place for reasons that are unclear. Afterwards, Lincoln suffered an emotional and physical breakdown and lived in Kentucky for a period while he recovered. In 1842 Lincoln resumed his relationship with Mary, and they married that year. Their marriage was a stormy one that was complicated by the deaths of their children and Mary's lavish spending, superstitions, and bouts with depression.

Andrew Johnson

Library of Congress

Andrew Johnson

Born: December 29, 1808; Raleigh, North Carolina
Party: Democratic
Term: April 15, 1865-March 4, 1869
Vice President: None
Died: July 31, 1875; Carter's Station, Tennessee
Buried: Greeneville, Tennessee

Andrew Johnson was the younger of the two sons born to Jacob and Mary Johnson. Andrew's father, who died when he was three, was a laborer, and his mother was a seamstress. Neither parent could read or write, and Johnson received no formal education.

When Andrew was thirteen he was apprenticed to a tailor in Raleigh, North Carolina, his birthplace. Andrew's fellow workers taught him to read, although he did not learn to write until several years later. In 1824, after two years as an apprentice, Andrew ran away from his master, James Selby, and worked as a journeyman tailor in Laurens, South Carolina. Although Selby was still offering a reward for his return, Johnson came back to Raleigh in 1826 and convinced his mother and stepfather to move west with him. They settled in Greeneville, Tennessee, where Johnson opened a tailor shop.

In 1828 the people of Greeneville elected the young tailor alderman. After two years on the city council, Johnson was chosen mayor at the age of twenty-one. In 1835 he made the step up to state politics when he was elected as a Democrat to the Tennessee legislature. He espoused the ideals of Andrew Jackson, became an advocate of the common farmer and small business owner, and earned a reputation as a powerful orator. In 1837 he was defeated for a second term in the Tennessee legislature, but he won reelection in 1839. Two years later he was elected to the state senate, and in 1843 his congressional district sent him to the U.S. House of Representatives.

In Washington, Johnson supported the Mexican War and the Compromise of 1850. He served four terms in the House, but an 1853 Whig redistricting plan made his reelection impossible. Consequently, Johnson ran for governor of Tennessee and won two terms before the Tennessee legislature sent him to the U.S. Senate in 1857.

In 1860 Johnson was proposed as a presidential candidate, but he withdrew his name from nomination and supported John Breckinridge. When Abraham Lincoln was elected, Johnson surprised many of his fellow southerners by declaring his loyalty to the Union. He campaigned against the secession of Tennessee, and when his state did secede in June 1861, he was the only southern senator to remain in the Senate. In 1862, after Union forces had captured most of Tennessee, Lincoln appointed Johnson military governor of his state. With Johnson's urging, Tennessee became the only seceding state to outlaw slavery before the 1863 Emancipation Proclamation.

Johnson's loyalty to the Union was rewarded with a vice-presidential nomination in 1864. Lincoln's first-term vice president, Hannibal Hamlin, wanted to be renominated, but Lincoln refused to back his candidacy. Delegates to the National Union convention in Baltimore (the Republican nominating convention expanded to include Democrats loyal to the Union) hoped that having a southern Democrat on the ticket would attract support from northern Democrats and voters in border areas.

Lincoln and Johnson defeated Democrats George McClellan and George Pendleton by 212-21 electoral votes. Some Johnson supporters, however, changed their minds about him when he showed up drunk for the inauguration on March 4, 1865. Lincoln shrugged off the incident and expressed confidence in his vice president.

Johnson served as vice president only six weeks before President Lincoln died on April 15 from a gunshot wound inflicted by assassin John Wilkes Booth. The new president thus faced the immense problem of reconstructing a broken South, which had surrendered six days before. Johnson tried to implement the lenient Reconstruction program envisioned by Lincoln, but he was blocked by radical Republicans in Congress who were intent upon punishing the region and limiting the influence of white southerners in national politics. Johnson successfully vetoed several harsh Reconstruction bills early in his presidency, but in the 1866 congressional elections the radical Republicans gained overwhelming control of Congress and were in a position to override the president's vetoes.

On March 2, 1867, Congress passed the first Reconstruction Act over Johnson's veto. It established martial law in the South, granted universal suffrage to blacks, and limited the voting rights of southern whites. The same day Congress overrode Johnson's veto of the Tenure of Office Act, which prohibited the president from removing without Senate approval any appointee who had been confirmed by the Senate. Johnson's defiance of this act forced a showdown between the president and Congress. On August 12, 1867, while Congress was in recess, Johnson replaced Secretary of War Edwin Stanton with Gen. Ulysses S. Grant without the Senate's approval. On January 13, 1868, the Senate declared the president's action illegal and reinstated Stanton. Gen. Grant complied with the Senate's order, but Johnson again dismissed Stanton and ordered Maj. Gen. Lorenzo Thomas to take Stanton's place. Three days later, on February 24, 1868, the House voted 126-47 to impeach the president. Radical Republicans had been searching for an excuse to impeach Johnson since early 1867.

The president's fate was then in the hands of the Senate, which could remove him from office with a two-thirds vote. On March 13 Johnson's trial began in the Senate chambers with Chief Justice Salmon P. Chase presiding. The Senate voted 35-19 for the impeachment articles, one vote short of the necessary two-thirds needed for conviction. Although Johnson's radical Republican opponents controlled the Senate, seven believed that the charges against Johnson did not warrant his removal and voted against conviction despite the consequences for their political careers. The decisive vote belonged to freshman Sen. Edmund G. Ross (R-Kan.), whose "not guilty" acquitted Johnson.

Although Johnson's presidency was dominated by Reconstruction and his battles with Congress, he and his secretary of state, William H. Seward, achieved a notable foreign policy success in 1867 when they negotiated the purchase of Alaska from Russia for only $7.2 million.

When Johnson's term expired in 1869 he returned to Tennessee, where he ran for the U.S. Senate. He lost that year and was defeated for a seat in the House in 1872. Finally, in 1874 the Tennessee legislature elected him to the Senate. He returned to Washington, where he resumed his fight for more lenient Reconstruction policies. Johnson only served five months of his Senate term before he died of a stroke in 1875 while visiting his daughter at Carter's Station, Tennessee.

Johnson married sixteen-year-old Eliza McCardle on May 17, 1827, in Greeneville, Tennessee, where he had opened a tailor shop. She had received some primary education and was able to teach Johnson, who could already read, to write and do elementary mathematics. The couple had three sons and two daughters. Eliza died in Tennessee less than six months after her husband.

Ulysses S. Grant

Library of Congress

Born: April 27, 1822; Point Pleasant, Ohio
Party: Republican
Term: March 4, 1869-March 4, 1877
Vice Presidents: Schuyler Colfax; Henry Wilson
Died: July 23, 1885; Mount McGregor, New York
Buried: New York City

Ulysses S. Grant was the eldest of the six children born to Jesse and Hanna Grant. Jesse Grant was a tanner, but his son disliked the business and preferred doing chores on the family farm. Grant attended a series of schools as a child, and received an appointment to the United States Military Academy at West Point, New York, in 1839 through the efforts of his father. Although Grant had no interest in a military career, he accepted the appointment.

Grant's name at birth was Hiram Ulysses, but when he enrolled at West Point he reversed the order of these two names. The school, however, officially recorded his name as Ulysses S. Grant. Rather than correct the mistake, Grant adopted West Point's version of his name without expanding his new middle initial. In 1843 Grant graduated twenty-first in his class of thirty-nine at West Point. He did well in mathematics and hoped one day to be a math teacher. He also was recognized for his outstanding handling of horses, a skill he had developed as a boy on his father's farm. His class rank, however, was not high enough to earn him an appointment to the cavalry.

Grant's first assignment was as a second lieuenant in an infantry regiment stationed near St. Louis. In 1844 his unit was transferred to Louisiana, and from there to Texas in 1845. He was among the troops under Gen. Zachary Taylor ordered by President James Polk to occupy the disputed area north of the Rio Grande. When Mexican forces attacked Taylor's forces, Polk persuaded Congress to declare war. Although Grant had deep reservations about the Mexican War's morality, he fought in most of its major battles including Palo Alto, Resaca de la Palma, Monterrey, Vera Cruz, Cerro Gordo, and Chapultepec. He was recognized for his bravery and promoted to first lieutenant after the capture of Mexico City in September 1847.

In July 1848, Grant returned to the United States and was stationed at several posts around the country. In 1852 he reluctantly left his wife and children behind in St. Louis when he was transferred to California. Grant hated being separated from his family and drank heavily to ease his loneliness. Finally, in 1854 after a drinking episode, his commanding officer forced him to resign his commission.

The next few years were humbling ones for Grant. He returned to his family in Missouri where he failed as a farmer and as a real estate broker. In 1860 his younger brother offered him a job as a clerk in their father's hardware and leather store in Galena, Illinois. With no better options, Grant accepted the salary of $800 per year and moved his family to Galena.

Civil War

In April 1861 Grant had worked in the store only eleven months when President Abraham Lincoln called for volunteers to put down the insurrection in the South. Because of his military experience, Grant was appointed colonel of an Illinois regiment in June. He impressed his superiors and in August was promoted to brigadier general. Grant obtained permission from Gen. Henry Halleck in January 1862 to launch a military campaign into the South. On February 6, Grant's troops defeated Confederate forces at Fort Henry, Tennessee. Ten days later he won the first major Union victory of the war, when his forces captured Fort Donelson on the Cumberland River in Tennessee. The battle netted Grant fifteen thousand Confederate prisoners, a promotion to major general, and a national reputation. Grant's demand that the Confederates surrender unconditionally earned him the nickname "Unconditional Surrender" Grant.

Grant moved his troops deeper into Tennessee where on August 6 and 7, 1862, they repelled a furious Confederate surprise attack at Shiloh Church near Pittsburg Landing. Heavy Union casualties at Shiloh prompted some of Lincoln's advisers to urge the president to relieve Grant of his command. Lincoln dismissed their advice, saying, "I can't spare this man. He fights." In July 1862, Grant had gained command of all Union forces in the West when Halleck was promoted to general in chief and transferred to Washington, D.C. During the next twelve months, Grant slowly maneuvered to capture the imposing Confederate fortifications at Vicksburg, Mississippi. On July 4, 1863, the Confederate commander at Vicksburg and twenty thousand troops surrendered to Grant. The victory gave the Union control of the Mississippi River and split the South in two.

In March 1864 President Lincoln promoted Grant to lieutenant general and appointed him general in chief of the army. Grant used his army's numerical superiority to fight a battle of attrition in Virginia against the main body of the Confederate army under Gen. Robert E. Lee. After a year of heavy fighting in which tens of thousands of troops on both sides were killed or wounded, Lee surrendered to Grant at Appomattox Court House in Virginia on April 9, 1865.

After the war Grant toured the South and issued a report advocating a lenient Reconstruction policy. In 1866 he was promoted to the newly established rank of general of the armies of the United States. The following year Grant, who throughout his military career had tried to remain aloof from politics, became involved in a political controversy. President Andrew Johnson had fired Secretary of War Edwin M. Stanton in violation of the Tenure of Office Act, which required the approval of Congress for dismissal of a cabinet member. In August Johnson appointed Grant to take Stanton's place, but the general resigned when Congress reinstated Stanton. Johnson felt betrayed by Grant, whom he hoped would stay in office to force a court battle over the Tenure of Office Act. The split with the Democratic president moved Grant closer to the Republicans. In 1868 they nominated him as their candidate for president. Grant, whose Civil War record had made him the most idolized person in America, received 52.7 percent of the popular vote and defeated Democrat Horatio Seymour 214-80 in the electoral college.

Presidency

When Grant took office, Reconstruction of the South was the primary issue confronting his administration. Grant supported the Reconstruction laws enacted during Andrew Johnson's administration and the ratification of the Fifteenth Amendment giving blacks the right to vote. The amendment was ratified on March 30, 1870. Although Grant opposed blanketing the South with troops to guarantee the rights of blacks and to oversee other aspects of Reconstruction, he did respond to violations of the law with force. As Grant's term progressed, however, many northerners came to believe that federal attempts to keep southern whites from controlling state governments could not go on forever and were causing southern whites to use intimidation and terror to achieve their ends. Grant, therefore, was less willing and able to rally support for an activist Reconstruction policy.

Grant also pursued a conservative financial course. In March 1869, he signed the Public Credit Act, which pledged the government to redeem its debts in gold rather than paper money issued during the Civil War. Grant also advocated a gradual reduction of the pubic debt left over from the war.

In foreign affairs, Grant and Hamilton Fish, his capable secretary of state, successfully negotiated the Treaty of Washington with Great Britain. The treaty, signed in May 1871, provided for the settlement of U.S. claims against Great Britain for destruction caused during the Civil War by the *Alabama* and other ships built in Britain for the Confederacy. Grant was unsuccessful, however, in his attempts to annex Santo Domingo. His personal secretary, Orville Babcock, negotiated a treaty of annexation, but it was rejected by the Senate.

Grant retained his popularity during his first term and in 1872 won an overwhelming victory over Horace Greeley, editor of the *New York Tribune*. Greeley had been nominated by the Democratic party and the Liberal Republican party, a faction of former Republicans pledged to fight corruption and implement a conciliatory policy toward the South. Grant defeated Greeley, 286 electoral votes to 66. Greeley died less than a month after the election.

Like his former commander, Zachary Taylor, Grant had no political experience before becoming president. Although Grant himself was honest, many of his appointees and associates were not; and Grant's administration, particularly his second term, is remembered for its scandals. Before Grant's second inauguration, the Crédit Mobilier scandal was revealed. Grant's outgoing vice president, Schuyler Colfax, and incoming vice president, Henry Wilson, both were implicated in the bribery scheme, which involved skimming profits made from the construction of the transcontinental railroad. In 1875 a Treasury Department investigation revealed that several prominent Republicans, including Orville Babcock, were involved in the Whiskey Ring, a group that had used bribery to avoid taxes on liquor. In 1876 Grant's secretary of war, William Belknap, resigned just before being impeached by the House of Representatives for accepting bribes. In his last annual message to Congress in 1876, Grant acknowledged that he had made mistakes during his presidency but assured its members that "failures have been errors of judgement, not of intent."

Retirement

Upon leaving office Grant embarked with his wife on a round-the-world tour. He traveled in Europe, Africa, and Asia for two and a half years. He received a hero's welcome in foreign capitals and was entertained like royalty by many heads of state. The trip repaired Grant's popularity in the United States, and he was the preconvention favorite for the 1880 Republican presidential nomination. On the first ballot at the Republican convention in Chicago, Grant received 304 of the 378 votes necessary for nomination. Despite the support of Sen. Roscoe Conkling and his New York political machine, the anti-Grant factions had enough strength to prevent the former president's nomination on subsequent ballots. The convention remained deadlocked until the thirty-fifth ballot, when compromise candidate James A. Garfield was nominated.

After the convention, Grant retired from politics and moved to New York City. In May 1884 a brokerage firm in which he was a silent partner failed, and he was forced to sell much of his property to pay his debts. In August of that year he was diagnosed as having cancer. He began writing his memoirs in an attempt to give his family financial security before his death. Although suffering extreme pain, Grant lived longer than his doctors had predicted and finished his memoirs on July 19, 1885, four days before his death. The two-volume *Personal Memoirs of U.S. Grant* sold 300,000 copies and earned Grant's widow nearly a half million dollars in royalties.

Grant married Julia Boggs Dent on August 22, 1848, in St. Louis after he returned from the Mexican War. She was the sister of his West Point roommate. They had three sons and one daughter. Their eldest son rose to the rank of major general in the U.S. Army and served as minister to Austria-Hungary during Benjamin Harrison's administration.

Rutherford B. Hayes

National Portrait Gallery

R B Hayes

Born: October 4, 1822; Delaware, Ohio
Party: Republican
Term: March 4, 1877-March 4, 1881
Vice President: William A. Wheeler
Died: January 17, 1893; Fremont, Ohio
Buried: Fremont

Rutherford Birchard Hayes was the youngest of the five children of Rutherford Hayes, a merchant who died two months before his son's birth. His father's estate was substantial, and his mother, Sophia, was able to send her children to private schools. Hayes enrolled at Kenyon College in Gambier, Ohio, when he was sixteen and graduated four years later, in 1842, as the valedictorian of his class. He studied law for a year at a law firm in Columbus, Ohio, before enrolling in Harvard Law School. In 1845 he graduated and was admitted to the Ohio bar.

In 1846 Hayes practiced law in Lower Sandusky (now Fremont), Ohio, but moved in 1850 to Cincinnati, where he established a thriving law office whose clients included several fugitive slaves. Hayes joined the Republican party when it was formed in the mid-1850s. In 1858 the city council of Cincinnati appointed Hayes to an unexpired term as city solicitor, his first public office. He won reelection to the post in 1859 but was defeated in 1861.

When the Civil War began Hayes was commissioned as a major and given command of a regiment of the Twenty-third Ohio Volunteers, which he had helped organize. He was promoted to lieutenant colonel in October 1861 and colonel in September 1862 after he led a charge at the Battle of South Mountain, Maryland, despite being shot in the arm. In August 1864 he was nominated for the U.S. House of Representatives. When Ohio Republican leaders suggested that he take a furlough to campaign, Hayes replied, "An officer fit for duty, who at this crisis would abandon his post to electioneer for a seat in Congress, ought to be scalped." Hayes's devotion to duty and his bravery in battle, where on several occasions he joined with his troops in hand-to-hand combat against the enemy, impressed voters more than any campaign speech he could have made. After being elected, however, he still refused to leave the army until the war was over. In October 1864, after the battle of Cedar Creek, Virginia, where he was wounded for the fourth time, he was promoted to brigadier general. On June 8, 1865, two months after Robert E. Lee had surrendered at Appomattox, Hayes finally resigned from the army to take his seat in Congress.

Hayes served two terms in the House before being elected governor of Ohio in 1867 in a close race. He was reelected two years later but declined to run for a third term. In 1872 he was defeated in his try for a House seat and turned down an offer from President Ulysses S. Grant of the post of assistant Treasury secretary. He retired to Fremont in 1873 and a year later inherited a large estate from his uncle, Sardis Birchard. Although Hayes did not seek the 1875 Republican nomination for a third term as governor of Ohio, he accepted his party's draft and was elected.

In March 1876 Hayes was put forward as a favorite son presidential candidate by the Ohio delegation at the Republican convention. James G. Blaine of Maine, the preconvention favorite, received the most votes on the first ballot but fell short of the number required for nomination. Blaine's opponents recognized they had to coalesce behind a single candidate and chose Hayes primarily because he was uncontroversial and free of scandal. Despite trailing four other candidates on the first ballot, Hayes was nominated on the seventh.

Hayes's chances for election were weakened by the scandals of the Grant administration, poor economic conditions, and the infrequency of his own campaign appearances. When the votes had been counted, Tilden had beaten Hayes by about 260,000 votes in the popular election and 203-166 in the electoral college. Republican leaders, however, were determined to retain the presidency and challenged the results in Florida, Louisiana, and South Carolina on the grounds that blacks had been intimidated from going to the polls. If the electoral votes of these three states were given to Hayes he would triumph 185-184. Southern Republican election officials from the three disputed states disqualified votes from Democratic precincts and declared Hayes the winner. Democratic leaders from these states accused the Republicans of corruption and sent rival sets of electoral votes to Congress, which was left to deal with the mess. With no way to determine who really deserved the electoral votes, members of Congress struck a deal. Democratic members agreed to the formation of an election commission that favored the Republicans in return for secret assurances that federal troops would be withdrawn from the South. The commission voted 8-7 for Hayes, who was officially declared president on March 4, 1877, just two days before his inauguration.

When Hayes became president he honored the agreement made with the Democrats to withdraw federal troops from the South. This move ended the Reconstruction era and enabled white Democrats to reestablish their political control over the southern states.

Hayes was a well-intentioned president, but the stigma of the deal that had made him president, his quarrels with conservatives in his party, and Democratic control of the House from 1877 to 1879 and the Senate from 1879 to 1881 limited his ability to push legislation through Congress. When Congress tried to stimulate the economy by coining overvalued silver coins, Hayes, an advocate of sound money, vetoed the inflationary measure. Congress, however, passed the bill over Hayes's veto. The president's calls for civil service reform also had little effect, as Congress refused to act on his proposals. In 1877, however, Hayes demonstrated his ability to take decisive action when he dispatched federal troops to stop riots that had broken out in several cities as a result of a nationwide railroad strike.

When his term expired, Hayes retired to Fremont, Ohio, where he managed several farms he had bought. He also promoted humanitarian causes, including prison reform and education opportunities for southern black youth. While returning to Fremont from a business trip, Hayes had a heart attack aboard a train on January 14, 1893. He died three days later.

Hayes married Lucy Ware Webb December 30, 1852, in Cincinnati, Ohio. They had seven sons and one daughter; three of their sons died in infancy. Lucy Hayes was deeply religious and lived according to strict moral principles. Her refusal to allow alcoholic beverages to be served at White House functions made her a symbol of the Women's Christian Temperance Union and earned her the nickname "Lemonade Lucy." She was the first college-educated first lady, having graduated from Wesleyan Female College in Cincinnati.

James A. Garfield

Library of Congress

James A. Garfield.

Born: November 19, 1831; Orange, Ohio
Party: Republican
Term: March 4, 1881-September 19, 1881
Vice President: Chester A. Arthur
Died: September 19, 1881; Elberon, New Jersey
Buried: Cleveland, Ohio

James Abram Garfield was born in a log cabin on an Ohio farm. When he was one year old, his father, Abram, died, leaving his mother, Eliza, to raise James and his three older siblings. After she sold fifty acres of the farm to pay family debts, the Garfields survived by farming just thirty acres. James worked on the farm during the summer months and attended elementary schools in the winter. When he was seventeen he spent a year driving horse and mule teams that pulled barges on the Ohio and Erie Canal.

In 1849 Garfield entered Geauga Seminary in Chester, Ohio, a local denominational secondary school. He paid for his tuition by working as a carpenter. Two years later he enrolled in the Western Reserve Eclectic Institute (later Hiram College). After a semester the school hired him as an English teacher. He taught and studied there until September 1854, when he had saved enough money to enroll at Williams College in Williamstown, Massachusetts. He graduated with honors in 1856 and returned to Hiram, Ohio, where he became president of Western Reserve Eclectic Institute with its five-member faculty. While presiding over the school, Garfield studied law and became known as an eloquent public speaker and preacher. He was elected to the Ohio senate as a Republican in 1859 and was admitted to the bar in 1860.

When the Civil War began in 1861 Garfield received a commission as a lieutenant colonel and command of a regiment of Ohio volunteers. After being promoted to colonel, he led a brigade to a dramatic victory over a superior number of Confederate troops at the battle of Middle Creek, Kentucky, on January 10, 1862. Garfield's success brought him a promotion to brigadier general. He participated in the Battle of Shiloh on April 7, 1862, before falling ill and returning to Ohio in July.

In September 1862, Garfield was elected to the U.S. House of Representatives, but he declined to retire from military service. After the Battle of Chickamauga in September 1863, he was promoted to major general for his bravery, although he had endorsed the battle plan of Gen. William S. Rosecrans that led to the Union defeat.

Garfield resigned his commission in December to take his seat in the House. There his oratory and leadership on important committees made him a prominent Republican member of Congress. Garfield dramatically demonstrated his rhetorical skills on April 15, 1865, the day after President Lincoln was assassinated. When a New York mob threatened to avenge Lincoln's death by destroying the headquarters of the *New York World*, a newspaper that had been a severe critic of Lincoln, Garfield quieted the crowd with a short speech given from the balcony of the New York Stock Exchange. It concluded: "Fellow citizens, God reigns and the government of Washington still lives."

Garfield served in the House until 1880. During this time he supported the harsh Reconstruction policies of the radical wing of his party. In 1877 he served on the election commission formed to decide the disputed outcome of the Hayes-Tilden presidential election of 1876. In fact he helped craft the backroom political deal that made Hayes president. While the Democrats controlled the House during the Hayes presidency, Garfield held the post of Republican minority leader.

At the 1880 Republican national convention the party was sharply divided over whom to nominate for president. President Hayes had declined to run for reelection and could not have won the nomination had he tried. The radical Stalwart faction of the Republican party, headed by New York senator Roscoe Conkling, a powerful political boss, supported former president Ulysses S. Grant, while the less radical Half-Breed faction backed Sen. James G. Blaine (R-Maine). Garfield, who had been elected to the Senate earlier in the year but had not yet taken his seat, had promoted the compromise candidacy of John Sherman of Ohio. The convention, however, nominated Garfield himself on the thirty-sixth ballot. In a gesture to the Stalwarts the convention nominated Chester A. Arthur, a Conkling associate, for vice president.

Garfield faced Democrat Winfield Scott Hancock of Pennsylvania, a hero of the battle of Gettysburg, in the general election. During the campaign the Democrats tried to capitalize on Garfield's role in the Crédit Mobilier bribery scandal that occurred during the Grant administration. Garfield had received a $329 dividend check in 1868 from the Crédit Mobilier holding company but had not actually bought stock in it. The scandal had ruined several other politicians, including Grant's first vice president, Schuyler Colfax, but Garfield's relatively minor role had not crippled his career. Despite the corruption charges and his unpopularity in the South, where he lost every state, Garfield won in the electoral college, 214-155. In the popular vote, however, Garfield received just ten thousand more votes than Hancock.

As president, Garfield's broad-based appointments and support for anticorruption measures angered Stalwarts. On March 23 he appointed Conkling's political rival, William Robertson, to the coveted post of collector of the port of New York. Although Garfield had appointed many Conkling supporters to patronage positions, the powerful senator was determined to block Robertson's confirmation. When Robertson was about to be confirmed, Conkling resigned his seat in protest. The move backfired, however, when the New York State legislature refused to reelect Conkling to the Senate as he had expected.

On July 2, 1881, as Garfield was in the Baltimore and Potomac railroad station in Washington, D.C., on his way to deliver the commencement address at his alma mater, Williams College, he was shot by Charles J. Guiteau. Guiteau shot the president once in the back and fired another bullet that grazed his arm. Garfield was taken to the White House, where he remained for two months while doctors unsuccessfully probed for the bullet that was lodged near his spine. On September 6 the president asked to be moved to Elberon, New Jersey, in the hope that the sea air would help him recover. He died in Elberon on September 19. Ironically, Garfield probably would have survived if his doctors had left the bullet undisturbed rather than searching for it with unsterile instruments, which spread infection.

Guiteau had been captured at the time of the assault and was put on trial in Washington, D.C., two months after the president's death. At the time of the attack the assassin had shouted, "I am a Stalwart; now Arthur is president!" Guiteau, however, was not associated with Roscoe Conkling and the Stalwarts. The assassin believed his distribution of pro-Republican party literature during the 1880 presidential campaign entitled him to a diplomatic appointment. Repeated rejections by the White House angered him, and he claimed to have received a divine vision instructing him to kill the president. The assassin's lawyers argued that their client was insane and should be acquitted, but the jury found him guilty and sentenced him to death. Guiteau was hanged in Washington, D.C., on June 30, 1882.

Garfield married Lucretia Rudolph of Hiram, Ohio, on November 11, 1858. They had five sons and two daughters; two of the children died in infancy. One of their sons, James Rudolph Garfield, served as secretary of the interior under President Theodore Roosevelt.

Chester A. Arthur

Library of Congress

Born: October 5, 1830; Fairfield, Vermont
Party: Republican
Term: September 20, 1881-March 4, 1885
Vice President: None
Died: November 18, 1886; New York City
Buried: Albany, New York

Chester Alan Arthur was one of the nine children of Malvina and William Arthur, a Baptist minister who had emigrated from Northern Ireland. Arthur claimed to have been born in Fairfield, Vermont, but some political enemies claimed that he actually had been born in Canada, where his father had lived at one time. This charge, if true, would have disqualified him for the presidency, but it was never substantiated.

In 1845 at the age of fifteen Arthur enrolled as a sophomore at Union College in Schenectady, New York, where he studied Greek and Latin. He graduated three years later and was one of six in his class to be elected to Phi Beta Kappa, a national honor society. He settled in North Pownal, Vermont, where he taught school at the North Pownal Academy, becoming principal in 1849. While teaching, Arthur studied law, and in 1853 he joined the New York City law firm of Parker and Culver as a clerk. The following year he passed the bar and became a member of the firm. As a laywer, he often defended fugitive slaves and free blacks who suffered discrimination.

Arthur attended the first New York Republican national convention in 1856 and became an active supporter of Republican candidates. In 1860 New York Republican governor Edward D. Morgan rewarded Arthur's political work by appointing him state engineer in chief with the military rank of brigadier general. During the Civil War Arthur served as assistant quartermaster general, inspector general, and finally quartermaster general of the troops of New York. He excelled in these administrative posts, spending state funds efficiently and keeping scrupulous books. He resigned his commission at the beginning of 1863 and returned to his law practice when Democrat Horatio Seymour became governor. He continued his rise in the New York Republican party, however, and by the time Ulysses S. Grant was elected president in 1868, he was Sen. Roscoe Conkling's principal lieutenant in the state's Republican machine.

In 1871, with Conkling's support, President Grant appointed Arthur to one of the most lucrative and coveted offices in government—collector of the port of New York. In this post Arthur oversaw the activities of almost one thousand officials, was in charge of collecting about two-thirds of the country's tariff revenue, and earned an average income of $40,000 per year. But despite Arthur's administrative abilities and basic honesty, President Hayes fired him from the customhouse in 1878 as part of his fight against the spoils system.

The Republican national convention of 1880 pitted New York boss senator Roscoe Conkling and his radical party faction known as the Stalwarts against James G. Blaine and the slightly more moderate Half-Breed faction. Conkling supported former president Ulysses S. Grant for the nomination, but after thirty-six ballots the convention turned to a dark horse candidate, James A. Garfield of Ohio. In an effort to appease the Stalwarts and unify the party, Republican leaders offered the vice presidency to Levi P. Morton, one of Conkling's associates. Conkling, however, was not in a mood to be appeased, and he convinced Morton to reject the offer. When the same offer was made to Arthur, who had never held elective office, he gratefully accepted the nomination despite the objections of Conkling. Garfield and Arthur defeated the Democratic ticket of Winfield Scott Hancock and William H. English by less than ten thousand votes but won in the electoral college, 214-155.

Garfield served only 199 days of his presidential term, however. On July 2, 1881, he was shot by an assassin in Washington, D.C. The gunman, Charles J. Guiteau, declared after the attack, "I am a Stalwart; now Arthur is President!" Garfield initially survived his wounds but died on September 19, after months of failed attempts by his doctors to remove the bullet.

Although Arthur had no connection to Guiteau, he was sensitive to charges that he and the Stalwarts may have been involved in Garfield's death. Therefore, once Arthur had assumed the presidency, he severed his ties to Conkling and the New York political machine. The new president demonstrated his independence by backing the investigations of post office scandals in which several Stalwarts were implicated.

Arthur was not, however, ready to embrace civil service reform, which had been the cause of James Garfield. He advocated instead a continuation of the partisan system of dispensing patronage. Nevertheless, on January 16, 1883, Arthur signed the Pendleton Civil Service Reform Act. The act set up a commission to develop and administer examinations for many federal positions previously filled through patronage.

In economic policy Arthur sought to reduce the government's continuing budget surplus that took money out of the economy. He proposed reducing tariffs, building up the navy, and reducing the federal debt with the surplus. Arthur succeeded in making moderate improvements to the navy and reducing the national debt, but Congress rejected his proposals to cut tariffs.

Upon leaving office Arthur returned to New York City to practice law. He soon accepted the presidency of the New York Arcade Railway Company, which was trying to construct a subway in New York City. In February 1886 Arthur retired after a medical examination revealed that he had Bright's disease, a life-threatening kidney ailment. He died later that year in New York City.

Arthur married Ellen Lewis Herndon on October 25, 1859. They had two sons and one daughter, but their first son died in infancy. Ellen Arthur died on January 12, 1880, five months before her husband was nominated for the vice presidency. Arthur's sister, Mary Arthur McElroy, acted as White House hostess.

Grover Cleveland

Library of Congress

Born: March 18, 1837; Caldwell, New Jersey
Party: Democratic
Terms: March 4, 1885-March 4, 1889; March 4, 1893-March 4, 1897
Vice Presidents: Thomas A. Hendricks; Adlai E. Stevenson
Died: June 24, 1908; Princeton, New Jersey
Buried: Princeton

Grover Cleveland was the fifth of the nine children born to Ann and Richard F. Cleveland, a Presbyterian minister. Grover was originally named Stephen Grover, but he dropped his first name early in his life. In 1853, the year his father died, Grover moved to New York City, where he got a job at a school for the blind. After a year, however, he returned to his family in Holland Patent, New York.

In the spring of 1855 Cleveland traveled west to seek work in Cleveland, Ohio. On the way he stopped to visit relatives in Buffalo, New York, where he decided to stay when his uncle, Lewis F. Allen, offered him a job as a farmhand. A few months later Cleveland went to work as an apprentice clerk in a local law firm. In 1859 he was admitted to the bar and promoted to chief clerk in his firm.

Cleveland had been drafted to fight in the Civil War, but in accordance with the draft laws he had hired a substitute for $300 so he could continue to help support his mother and younger siblings. In 1863 Cleveland accepted an appointment as assistant district attorney of Erie County, New York. Two years later he was defeated in an election for district attorney. With the exception of a two-year term as sheriff of Buffalo from 1871 to 1873, he practiced law for the next sixteen years.

In 1881 he was elected mayor of Buffalo and immediately took action to reform the city administration. His well-deserved reputation as an uncompromising reformer earned him the Democratic nomination for governor of New York in 1882. He easily won the election and assumed office on January 3, 1883. As governor, Cleveland combated corruption and the spoils system with his veto power. He formed an alliance with Theodore Roosevelt, a Republican member of the New York State assembly, to enact legislation reforming New York City's government.

The governor's successes and reform principles made him an attractive presidential candidate in 1884. The Republicans nominated James G. Blaine, a Republican senator from Maine, who had been linked to several scandals. Cleveland's supporters argued that if the Democratic party nominated the reform governor, the reform-minded Republicans, known as Mugwumps might desert their party in sufficient numbers to elect a Democrat to the presidency for the first time since the Civil War. The Democratic delegates at the national convention in Chicago agreed with this strategy, and Cleveland was nominated on the second ballot.

Cleveland's election hopes were damaged, however, when a newspaper report disclosed that he had fathered an illegitimate child, which he continued to support. Cleveland admitted his paternity and instructed his campaign workers to "tell the truth." Cleveland also was attacked for not serving in the Civil War, although Blaine had avoided service as well. Blaine lost many Catholic votes when he failed to repudiate a supporter's accusation less than a week before the election that the Democrats represented "rum, Romanism, and rebellion." In the end Cleveland received just sixty thousand more votes than Blaine and defeated him 219-182 in the electoral college.

During his first term Cleveland attempted to bring to the presidency the same reformist principles that he had followed as governor of New York. For example, he implemented the Pendleton Civil Service Act, signed into law by Chester A. Arthur, which shifted thousands of government jobs from patronage to a merit system of hiring. He also vetoed numerous private pension bills for individual Civil War veterans. Cleveland was unsuccessful, however, in lowering the tariff, which he considered to be unfair to farmers and workers and unnecessary given the large federal budget surplus.

In 1888 Cleveland ran for reelection against Indiana Republican Benjamin Harrison. Despite defeating Harrison by 100,000 votes, Cleveland lost to Harrison in the electoral college 233-168. Had Cleveland won his home state's thirty-six electoral votes as he did in 1884, he would have won the election.

After leaving office Cleveland moved to New York City, where he practiced law. Four years later he was again nominated for president by his party. The 1892 election featured a rematch between Cleveland and President Benjamin Harrison. Cleveland easily defeated Harrison in the electoral college by 277-145 votes but received only 46.3 percent of the popular vote because the third-party candidacy of James Baird Weaver of the People's party drew over a million votes.

Soon after Cleveland took office for the second time the Panic of 1893 sparked a deep economic depression. More than five hundred banks failed, and unemployment rose sharply as businesses went bankrupt. Cleveland believed the depression was caused by inflation and an erosion of business confidence. Thus, with the support of many congressional Republicans, he convinced Congress in 1893 to repeal the mildly inflationary Sherman Silver Purchase Act. He also authorized the purchase of several million ounces of gold from private holders to replenish the government's shrinking gold reserves. Cleveland's policies, however, did not ease the depression.

In 1894 the economic situation worsened when a local strike at the Pullman Palace Car Company near Chicago led to a debilitating railroad strike throughout the Midwest. When violence erupted in Chicago, Cleveland sent federal troops there to break the strike despite the protests of Illinois governor John P. Altgeld. Cleveland's action earned him support from the business community but the enmity of labor organizations. Although the depression had greeted Cleveland as he entered office, he received much of the blame for the nation's economic troubles. After Republicans gained congressional seats in the 1894 midterm elections, Cleveland had difficulty exerting much control over Congress or even his own party. The 1896 Democratic convention nominated William Jennings Bryan for president, and many Democratic candidates distanced themselves from Cleveland.

In foreign affairs Cleveland withdrew in March 1893 a treaty negotiated in the closing months of the Harrison administration that would have annexed Hawaii. He considered the treaty unfair and blocked any further attempt to annex the islands. He also resisted the temptation to yield to public pressure and go to war with Spain over their suppression of a rebellion in Cuba that began in 1895.

Upon leaving office for the second time Cleveland settled in Princeton, New Jersey. He devoted his time to fishing, delivering lectures, and writing books and articles. In 1901 he was appointed to the board of trustees of Princeton University, and in 1904 he became the president of that board while future president Woodrow Wilson served as president of the university. In 1907 Cleveland was elected president of the Association of Presidents of Life Insurance Companies. During his last years Cleveland's heart and kidneys weakened. He died of a heart attack in Princeton, New Jersey, in 1908.

Cleveland married Frances Folsom, the twenty-one-year-old daughter of his former law partner, on June 2, 1886, in a White House ceremony. The couple had three daughters and two sons. Two of the children were born during Cleveland's second term.

Benjamin Harrison

Library of Congress

Benj Harrison

Born: August 20, 1833; North Bend, Ohio
Party: Republican
Term: March 4, 1889-March 4, 1893
Vice President: Levi P. Morton
Died: March 13, 1901; Indianapolis, Indiana
Buried: Indianapolis

Benjamin Harrison was born at his grandfather's home at North Bend, Ohio, the second of the ten children of John and Elizabeth Harrison. Four of the ten children died in infancy. The Harrison family also included John's two surviving daughters from a previous marriage. When Benjamin was seven, his grandfather, William Henry Harrison, became the ninth president of the United States but died after one month in office. Benjamin's great-grandfather, Benjamin Harrison, had been governor of Virginia and a signer of the Declaration of Independence.

After receiving a primary education at a country school and from tutors, Benjamin attended Farmer's College in Cincinnati from 1847 to 1850. He then transferred to Miami University in Oxford, Ohio. He graduated with honors in 1852 and began studying law at a firm in Cincinnati. In 1854 he moved to Indianapolis and established his own practice. A year later he formed a law partnership with William Wallace, a more established Indianapolis lawyer. Within a few years their firm had become one of the most respected in the city.

Soon after moving to Indianapolis Harrison became active in the Republican party. In 1857 he was elected Indianapolis city attorney. The following year he served as secretary of the Indiana Republican central committee, and in 1860 he was elected reporter of the Indiana Supreme Court.

In 1862, during the Civil War, Harrison was commissioned as a colonel and given command of the Seventieth Indiana Volunteers, which he had helped recruit. His regiment guarded railroads in Kentucky and participated in the Atlanta campaign. He gained a reputation as a cold disciplinarian and was unpopular with many of his troops. His unit fought well, however, and he was promoted to brigadier general in 1865.

When the war ended Harrison returned to Indianapolis, where his legal skill, war record, and speeches on behalf of Republican causes made him one of the most famous men in Indiana. In 1876 Harrison received the Republican nomination for governor but lost by five thousand votes to Democrat James D. Williams. Harrison had not sought the nomination and was happy to return to his law practice. He presided over the Indiana Republican convention in 1878 and was chairman of his state's delegation to the Republican national convention in 1880.

In 1881 Harrison was elected to the U.S. Senate, where he chaired the committee on territories. In this capacity he defended the interests of homesteaders and Indians against the railroads. Harrison also was a strong advocate of Civil War veterans and worked to protect and expand their pensions. Harrison ran for reelection in 1886, but the Democrats had gained control of the Indiana legislature two years before and voted him out of office.

At the 1888 Republican national convention in Chicago Harrison was nominated on the eighth ballot to run for president against incumbent Grover Cleveland. The primary issue of the campaign was the tariff, which Harrison promised to raise if elected. Harrison lost the popular vote but won in the electoral college 233-168 with the help of a narrow victory in New York that gave him that state's thirty-six electoral votes.

Harrison enjoyed the luxury of having both houses of Congress controlled by his party. As a result, he was able to implement much of his economic program. In July 1890 he signed the Sherman Antitrust Act and the Sherman Silver Purchase Act. The former outlawed trusts and business combines that restrained trade, while the latter required the Treasury to purchase large quantities of silver with notes that could be redeemed in gold. The silver purchase was inflationary and strained the nation's gold reserves, but Harrison and the Republicans resisted the more damaging proposal of free coinage of silver desired by many indebted farmers from the South and West. Later, in 1890, Harrison signed the McKinley Tariff Act, which was sponsored by House member and future president William McKinley. The act sharply raised tariffs as Harrison had promised, providing protection to some U.S. industries but raising prices for many consumer goods. Harrison constructed several compromises that led to passage of the act.

In foreign policy the Harrison administration enjoyed several successes. Harrison's secretary of state, James G. Blaine, presided over the Inter-American Conference in Washington, D.C., in 1889 and 1890, out of which came the Pan American Union. Blaine also secured an agreement in 1889 with Britain and Germany to preserve the independence of the Samoa Islands under a tripartite protectorate. In 1892 Harrison demanded and received an apology and reparations from Chile for an attack by its citizens on U.S. sailors who were on shore leave in Valparaiso, Chile. He failed, however, in his attempt to annex Hawaii late in his term. An 1803 coup, in which Americans participated, had led to the overthrow of the Hawaiian queen. Thus, the U.S. minister in Hawaii hastily concluded a treaty of ratification with the new provisional government, but Senate Democrats in the Senate blocked the treaty until Harrison's term expired. Incoming president Grover Cleveland withdrew the treaty.

At the end of his term Harrison attended the inauguration of Grover Cleveland, who four years before had accompanied Harrison to the Capitol as the outgoing president. Harrison then returned to Indianapolis, where he resumed his lucrative law practice. In the spring of 1894 he delivered a series of law lectures at Stanford University in Palo Alto, California. Supporters encouraged him to seek the Republican presidential nomination in 1896, but he refused to allow his name to be placed in nomination. From 1897 to 1899 he represented Venezuela in a boundary dispute with Great Britain that was to be decided by an international arbitration tribunal. After he traveled to Paris in 1899 to present his case, the tribunal upheld most of Venezuela's claims. Harrison then toured Europe with his second wife. He died in Indianapolis in 1901 from pneumonia.

On October 20, 1853, Harrison married Caroline Lavinia Scott, whom he had met while attending Miami University. The couple had two children, Russell and Mary. Mrs. Harrison died in the White House on October 25, 1892. Three years after he left office on April 6, 1896, Harrison married thirty-seven-year-old Mary Scott Lord Dimmick, a niece of his first wife. They had one daughter, Elizabeth, who was born when Harrison was sixty-three.

William McKinley

Library of Congress

Born: January 29, 1843; Niles, Ohio
Party: Republican
Term: March 4, 1897-September 14, 1901
Vice Presidents: Garret A. Hobart; Theodore Roosevelt
Died: September 14, 1901; Buffalo, New York
Buried: Canton, Ohio

William McKinley was the seventh of the nine children born to Nancy and William McKinley, an iron founder. The McKinleys moved from Niles, Ohio, to Poland, Ohio, when young William was nine. There he attended Union Seminary, a local private school. He enrolled in Allegheny College in Meadville, Pennsylvania, in 1859 but dropped out the following year because of illness and financial problems. William returned to Poland, where he taught in a country school and worked in the post office.

When the Civil War began in 1861, McKinley enlisted as a private in the Twenty-third Ohio Volunteers—the same unit in which Rutherford B. Hayes began his service as a major. McKinley steadily worked his way up through becoming an officer in September 1862 after the battle of Antietam in Maryland. When the war ended he was a twenty-two-year-old major who had been decorated for bravery.

McKinley chose to leave the army, however, to study law. He worked for two years in the law office of a Youngstown, Ohio, attorney and then polished his legal skills at Albany Law School in New York for a term. He was admitted to the bar in 1867 and opened a law practice in Canton, Ohio. He ran for prosecuting attorney of Stark County as a Republican in 1869 and won despite the county's traditional Democratic voting record. Two years later, however, he was narrowly defeated for reelection.

From 1871 to 1876, McKinley practiced law in Canton and campaigned for Republican candidates. In 1876, when his old commanding officer, Rutherford B. Hayes, was elected president, McKinley won a seat in the U.S. House of Representatives. He served seven consecutive terms in the House until 1891. As a member of Congress, McKinley supported civil service reform, voting rights for blacks, and government coinage of silver. He was best known, however, for his staunch support of high tariffs as a means of protecting U.S. industries. While serving as the chairman of the House Ways and Means Committee he sponsored the McKinley Tariff of 1890, which raised tariff rates to new highs. The tariff brought higher prices for consumers and contributed to voter disaffection for the Republican party. McKinley was voted out of office along with many other Republican members of Congress in 1890.

McKinley returned to Ohio, where he ran for governor successfully. He served two two-year terms, during which he was increasingly promoted as a presidential candidate. In 1892 he served as the chairman of the Republican national convention in Chicago. President Benjamin Harrison was nominated on the first ballot, but McKinley came in second in the balloting.

McKinley's presidential nomination in 1896 did not result from a spontaneous movement on the floor of the Republican convention. With McKinley's approval, Ohio party boss Mark Hanna and other leading Republicans actively promoted McKinley's candidacy in the months leading up to the convention. His nomination was almost ensured when the St. Louis convention convened in June 1896, and the delegates nominated him on the first ballot.

Although McKinley had favored the coinage of silver, he renounced his former position and supported the gold standard in order to win conservative Democrats away from the Democratic nominee, William Jennings Bryan, who was an ardent silver advocate. McKinley waged his campaign from his front porch, speaking to crowds that came to Canton by railroad. In contrast, Bryan traveled more than eighteen thousand miles and delivered hundreds of speeches during his campaign. The Republican nominee received the strong support of business and financial leaders who feared that a Bryan presidency would bring inflation. They helped raise a formidable war chest for McKinley, who won in the electoral college 271-176.

McKinley was severely criticized by Democrats and some Republicans for appointing aging Ohio senator John Sherman as his secretary of state. The appointment was seen as a political payoff to Mark Hanna, who promptly was elected to the vacant Senate seat by the Ohio state legislature.

McKinley's top priority upon entering office was the economy, which had been mired in a depression during much of Cleveland's second term. Congress quickly passed the Dingley Tariff Act of 1897 in response to McKinley's requests. Thereafter, the economy began to grow. Although the tariff bill may not have been the cause of the recovery, McKinley took credit for the improvement of economic conditions.

McKinley's first term, however, was dominated by the Spanish-American War and its results. Americans were disturbed by numerous press accounts of atrocities perpetrated by Spanish colonialists upon Cuban natives. McKinley responded to public pressure for war by sending a war message to Congress on April 11, 1898. Congress declared war two weeks later on April 25. Although the United States was not prepared for the war, victory came easily. Spanish control of Cuba was broken, and the U.S. Asiatic squadron under Commodore George Dewey destroyed the Spanish Pacific fleet in the Battle of Manila Bay. The fighting was over by August. On December 10, 1898, Spain signed a treaty freeing Cuba and ceding the Philippines, Puerto Rico, and Guam to the United States. McKinley agonized over how to deal with the Philippines but decided to take possession of them rather than grant them their independence. He resolved to "uplift and civilize and Christianize" the Filipinos. Insurgents in the Philippines, however, were determined to gain their independence. In 1899 they launched a guerrilla war against the U.S. occupying force, which ended in 1902 with the defeat of the insurgents. The bloody conflict cost more American lives and money than the Spanish-American War.

McKinley took several important steps in other parts of Asia and the Pacific. He oversaw the annexation of Hawaii in 1898 and the partition of the Samoan Islands with Germany in 1899. Secretary of State John Hay negotiated an agreement with European nations in 1900 that established an "Open Door" policy toward China, under which all nations doing business with China would enjoy equal trading rights.

McKinley was renominated without opposition in 1900. His close friend and first-term vice president, Garret Hobart, had died in 1899, however, and the Republican national convention chose Theodore Roosevelt as his running mate. The Democrats again ran William Jennings Bryan, but the nation's economic recovery since McKinley took office gave the Republicans a strong election issue. McKinley improved upon the popular and electoral vote margins of victory he had enjoyed in 1896, defeating Bryan in the electoral college 292-155.

After Roosevelt's nomination, Mark Hanna, who regarded the vice-presidential candidate as an unpredictable reformer, wrote McKinley saying, "Your duty to the country is to live for four years from next March." McKinley would be unable to carry out this duty. Six months after his inauguration, he traveled to Buffalo, New York, to deliver an address at the Pan-American Exposition, a fair celebrating friendship in the Western Hemisphere. The following day the president greeted thousands of people who waited in line to shake his hand at a public reception. Leon Czolgosz, an anarchist disturbed by social injustice, waited in line until it was his turn to shake McKinley's hand. Czolgosz then fired two shots with a concealed .32-caliber revolver that struck McKinley in the chest and stomach.

McKinley was taken first to the emergency medical center at the exposition and then to Milburn House, his Buffalo lodgings. Doctors initially thought the president would recover. Vice President Roosevelt, who had cut his vacation short and rushed to Buffalo upon hearing that the president had been shot, even resumed his holiday when he was informed of the doctors' prognosis. After a week, however, gangrene set in, and McKinley's conditioned deteriorated. He died early in the morning on September 14.

McKinley married Ida Saxton, the daughter of a banker, on January 25, 1871, in Canton, Ohio. The couple had two daughters, but one died as an infant and the other at the age of four. Ida was afflicted with epilepsy and phlebitis for most of her adult life. Despite occasional seizures and her inability to walk without a cane, she presided over most White House social functions.

Theodore Roosevelt

Library of Congress

Theodore Roosevelt

Born: October 27, 1858; New York City
Party: Republican
Term: September 14, 1901-March 4, 1909
Vice President: Charles W. Fairbanks
Died: January 6, 1919; Oyster Bay, New York
Buried: Oyster Bay

Theodore Roosevelt was the second of the four children and the oldest son of Theodore and Martha Roosevelt. His father was a wealthy New York City banker and merchant. Young Theodore was educated by tutors and enjoyed several trips abroad with with family. Throughout his boyhood, he suffered from asthma and other illnesses. When he was thirteen he began a program of vigorous physical exercise that turned him into a healthy, robust young man. Throughout the rest of his life, he would preach the virtues of a strenuous life.

Roosevelt entered Harvard in 1876. An excellent student, he graduated twenty-first in his class in 1880 and was elected to the Phi Beta Kappa honor society. He then enrolled in Columbia Law School but dropped out after a year of study without taking a degree or seeking admission to the bar.

Roosevelt entered politics in 1881 when he was elected to the New York state legislature at the age of twenty-three. He led a group of reform Republicans who fought corruption in the state government. Roosevelt was reelected in 1882 and 1883 but declined to seek reelection after his wife, Alice, and his mother died within hours of each other on February 14, 1884.

From 1884 to 1886, Roosevelt sought refuge from his grief in the Dakota Territory, where he managed a cattle ranch and served for a period as deputy sheriff. He returned to New York City in 1886 and ran unsuccessfully for mayor. After marrying Edith Kermit Carow, he settled into his home, Sagamore Hill, in Oyster Bay, Long Island. There he wrote books on American history and life in the West. His works include *Hunting Trip of a Ranchman*, *Life of Thomas Hart Benton*, *Gouverneur Morris*, *The Winning of the West*, and *Ranch Life and the Hunting Trail*. During his lifetime, Roosevelt wrote more than forty books.

In 1889 Roosevelt returned to public service when President Benjamin Harrison appointed him U.S. civil service commissioner. He was reappointed in 1893 by Democrat Grover Cleveland and served until 1895. As commissioner, Roosevelt fought against the spoils system, which he considered a source of corruption. He revised civil service exams, doubled the number of government positions subject to examination, and increased government employment opportunities for women.

From 1895 to 1897 Roosevelt served as president of the Police Commission of New York City. He moved to Washington, D.C., in 1897 when President William McKinley appointed him assistant secretary of the navy. In this post he fought to increase the size of the U.S. Navy and advocated war with Spain over that country's suppression of an independence movement in Cuba. On February 25, 1898, with Navy Secretary John Long absent from the capital, Roosevelt ordered the Pacific fleet to go to Hong Kong and prepare to destroy the Spanish fleet in the event of a declaration of war. In issuing the order, Roosevelt overstepped the bounds of his authority, but when Commodore George Dewey defeated the Spanish fleet in the Battle of Manila Bay on May 1, 1898, Roosevelt's action was vindicated.

Soon after the United States declared war, Roosevelt resigned from the Navy Department so he could fight in Cuba. He secured the rank of lieutenant colonel and organized a regiment of cavalry that came to be known as the Rough Riders. Although the importance of the Rough Riders to the American victory over the Spanish in Cuba became exaggerated, Roosevelt demonstrated his courage in leading his regiment in a charge up one of the San Juan Hills overlooking Santiago. Despite suffering heavy casualties, the Rough Riders captured the hill.

Roosevelt's exploits in Cuba made him a celebrity in the United States. In November 1898 he received the Republican nomination for governor of New York and was narrowly elected. As governor his political independence and refusal to promote the interests of big business disturbed the power brokers of his party, particularly New York Republican boss Thomas Platt.

In 1900 Platt hoped to get rid of Roosevelt by promoting him as a candidate for vice president. Although Roosevelt declared he did not want the job, he was the popular choice at the Philadelphia Republican national convention, and he accepted the nomination when it was offered to him. Party leaders had mixed feelings about Roosevelt. They recognized that his popularity could win votes for the ticket, but they feared what might happen if McKinley died. Mark Hanna, the Republican national chairman who had overseen McKinley's career, warned his colleagues, "Don't any of you realize that there's only one life between this madman and the White House?"

After the inauguration, Roosevelt presided over a five-day session of the Senate held to confirm presidential appointees. When the session was completed, Congress adjourned until December. Roosevelt, with no other vice-presidential duties to execute, returned to his home on Long Island. On September 6, 1901, Roosevelt was hunting and fishing in Vermont when he learned that President McKinley had been shot. He rushed to Buffalo, where doctors said McKinley would recover from his wounds. Roosevelt wanted to demonstrate to the public that the president was in no danger of death, so he resumed his vacation on September 10. Three days later, however, Roosevelt was informed that McKinley's condition had deteriorated. The vice president arrived in Buffalo on September 14, the day McKinley died. Later in the day he took the oath of office in Buffalo from U.S. District Court Judge John Hazel. At the age of forty-two, Roosevelt became the youngest person ever to serve as president.

Presidency

After McKinley's death, Roosevelt declared, "It shall be my aim to continue absolutely unbroken the policy of President McKinley for the peace, the prosperity, and the honor of our beloved country." Despite retaining McKinley's cabinet, Roosevelt promoted his own policies, which included measures to curb abuses by big business. Soon after taking office he had directed Attorney General Philander Knox to prepare an antitrust suit against Northern Securites Company, a giant railroad trust. The suit was successful in 1904 when the Supreme Court ruled that the company should be dissolved. Although the Roosevelt administration would initiate fewer antitrust suits than the Taft administration, Roosevelt became known as the trust-busting president. In 1902 when a coal strike in Pennsylvania caused shortages and rising coal prices, Roosevelt threatened to take over the mines unless the mine owners submitted to arbitration. The mine owners backed down, and Roosevelt appointed a commission that gave the miners a 10 percent raise.

Roosevelt's most famous act during his first term was his acquisition of land for the Panama Canal. Colombia owned Panama, but in August 1903 the Colombian senate refused to approve a treaty giving the United States the rights to a canal zone six miles wide. Determined to build the canal, Roosevelt later that year supported a revolution in Panama, which, with the help of the U.S. Navy, overthrew Colombian rule. The new Panamanian government agreed to lease the zone to the United States, and construction of the canal began.

In the 1904 presidential election, Roosevelt ran against New York judge Alton B. Parker. Roosevelt lost the South but received over 56 percent of the popular vote, swept the North and West, and easily won in the electoral college, 336-140. He became the first successor president to win the White House in his own right after serving the unfinished term of his predecessor.

During his second term Roosevelt championed many pieces of reform legislation including the Pure Food and Drug Act, the Meat Inspection Act, and the Hepburn Act, which empowered the government to set railroad rates. Roosevelt also continued his conservationist activities begun during his first term. Under Roosevelt the government initiated thirty major federal irrigation projects, added 125 million acres to the national forest reserves, and doubled the number of national parks.

In foreign affairs Roosevelt continued aggressively to promote U.S. interests abroad, often in a manner his critics described as imperialistic. In late 1904 he issued the Roosevelt Corollary to the Monroe Doctrine, which declared that the United States would intervene in Latin American affairs to prevent European nations from intervening there. The following year he put the corollary into practice by taking control of the Santo Domingo customhouses to guarantee that country's European debts. In 1905 he mediated an agreement ending the Russo-Japanese War and was awarded the Nobel Peace Prize for his efforts. In the face of congressional opposition Roosevelt also sent the U.S. fleet on a world cruise that lasted from late 1907 to early 1909. The show of strength was intended to impress other nations, especially Japan, with U.S. resolve to defend its interests and play an active role in world affairs.

Former President

Roosevelt's friend and secretary of war, William Howard Taft, was elected president in 1908 with Roosevelt's backing. Upon leaving office Roosevelt went to Africa to hunt big game with his son Kermit, then toured Europe with his wife before returning to the United States in June 1910. During the next two years Roosevelt became increasingly alienated from Taft, who he felt had abandoned his policies.

In 1912 Roosevelt declared his interest in the Republican nomination for president. He won most of the primaries, but the Republican national convention in Chicago was controlled by supporters of President Taft, who received the nomination. Progressive Republicans organized the Progressive party and persuaded Roosevelt to run. The party was dubbed the "Bull Moose" party, because candidate Roosevelt declared that he felt "as fit as a bull moose."

On October 14, 1912, while campaigning in Milwaukee, Roosevelt was shot in the chest by an assailant. The candidate insisted on delivering a scheduled speech, which lasted almost an hour. He was then rushed from the amazed crowd to a hospital. Wilson and Taft stopped their campaigns while Roosevelt recovered, but the former president was delivering speeches again within two weeks. Roosevelt's heroic campaigning, however, could not overcome the split he had caused among Republicans. Second-place Roosevelt and third-place Taft together received over a million more popular votes than Democrat Woodrow Wilson, but with his opposition divided, Wilson won the election.

The Progressives asked Roosevelt to run for president again in 1916, but Roosevelt declined and supported Republican Charles Evans Hughes, who lost to President Wilson. In 1916 Roosevelt had begun to make plans for raising a volunteer division that he would command if the United States entered World War I. When the United States did enter the war in 1917, he went to the White House to request authority to implement his plans, but Wilson turned him down. During the war, Roosevelt was a leading Republican spokesman and likely would have been his party's candidate for president in 1920 had he lived. He was hospitalized in November 1918 with a severe attack of rheumatism, an ailment from which he suffered during the last years of his life. He returned to Sagamore Hill for Christmas but remained ill. He died in his sleep on January 6, 1919, from an arterial blood clot.

Roosevelt married Alice Hathaway Lee on October 27, 1880, his twenty-second birthday. Alice died on February 14, 1884, of Bright's disease two days after giving birth to the couple's only child, Alice. Roosevelt's mother, Martha Roosevelt, died the same day of typhoid fever. On February 17, 1906, at the White House, Alice married Rep. Nicholas Longworth, who would serve as Speaker of the House from 1925 to 1931.

Roosevelt married Edith Kermit Carow, whom he had known since childhood, on December 2, 1886. They had four sons and one daughter. Their youngest child, Quentin, was killed during World War I while flying a mission over France. Their oldest child, Theodore, Jr., served as assistant secretary of the navy, governor of Puerto Rico, and governor-general of the Philippines during the Harding, Coolidge, and Hoover administrations.

William Howard Taft

Library of Congress

Born: September 15, 1857; Cincinnati, Ohio
Party: Republican
Term: March 4, 1909-March 4, 1913
Vice President: James S. Sherman
Died: March 8, 1931; Washington, D.C.
Buried: Arlington National Cemetery, Virginia

William Howard Taft was the second of the five children of Alphonso and Louisa Taft. William's older brother died in infancy. Alphonso Taft was a prominent Cincinnati lawyer, who served as secretary of war and attorney general under Ulysses S. Grant and later was ambassador to Austria-Hungary and Russia.

After excelling as a scholar and an athlete in high school, William enrolled in Yale in 1874. He graduated four years later, second in his class. He returned to Cincinnati, where he studied law in his father's office and at the Cincinnati Law School. He gained admission to the bar in 1880 and was appointed assistant prosecutor of Hamilton County, Ohio, the following year. In 1882 he served briefly as collector of internal revenue for his Ohio district but resigned rather than fire several employees for political reasons. In 1883 he established a law partnership in Cincinnati with a former partner of his father.

In 1887 Taft was appointed to a vacancy on the state superior court, winning election to his own two-year term on the court the folllowing year. In 1890 President Benjamin Harrison appointed him U.S. solicitor general. Two years later, Harrison appointed him judge of the U.S. Circuit Court, where Taft remained for eight years. During this period the judge also taught at the Cincinnati Law School.

In 1900 President William McKinley appointed Taft president of the U.S. Philippine Commission, which was charged with establishing a civil government on the islands. Taft was reluctant to leave his judgeship, but McKinley persuaded him to go to the Philippines by offering him an eventual appointment to the Supreme Court.

Taft expected to be in the Philippines only a short time, but in 1901, McKinley appointed him governor-general of the islands. In this capacity, Taft reorganized the Filipino court system, acquired land for the Filipinos from the Catholic church, improved roads, harbors, and schools, and encouraged limited self-government. While in the Philippines, Taft twice refused appointment to the Supreme Court, the position he coveted most, because he believed he could not abandon the people of the islands. In 1904, however, he accepted Theodore Roosevelt's appointment as secretary of war under the condition that he would be able to continue supervising U.S. policy toward the Philippines.

As secretary of war, Taft's activities ranged beyond oversight of the army. He visited the Panama Canal site in 1904, negotiated a secret agreement with the Japanese in 1905 pledging noninterference with Japan's affairs in Korea in return for Japan's promise to recognize U.S. influence in the Philippines, served as temporary provisional governor of Cuba in 1906, and oversaw relief efforts after the 1906 San Francisco earthquake. By 1908, Taft's wide government experience, his close friendship with Theodore Roosevelt, and his well-known administrative abilities made him the front-runner for the Republican presidential nomination.

Taft was not anxious to run, but Theodore Roosevelt, Republican party leaders, and his wife persuaded him to seek the presidency. As Roosevelt's chosen successor Taft won the nomination at the 1908 Republican national convention in Chicago on the first ballot. He then defeated Democrat William Jennings Bryan 321-162 in the electoral college.

Upon entering office Taft urged Congress to reduce tariffs. The president, however, angered progressive Republicans, who favored lower tariffs, when he signed the Payne-Aldrich Tariff Act of 1909. The act reduced tariff rates by amounts that most progressives considered insignificant.

Taft showed stronger leadership in his pursuit of antitrust cases. Although Theodore Roosevelt is often remembered as the president who first made wide use of the Sherman Antitrust Act to break up monopolies, Taft's administration brought ninety antitrust suits in four years compared with forty-four during Roosevelt's seven-year presidency. The Standard Oil and American Tobacco companies were among those broken up by the Taft administration. Taft also successfully backed the passage of the Sixteenth Amendment, which authorized a federal income tax.

In foreign affairs Taft instituted a policy that came to be known as "dollar diplomacy." This policy sought to use investments and trade to expand U.S. influence abroad, especially in Latin America. Taft also was willing to use force to maintain order and to protect U.S. business interests in Latin America. He dispatched ships and troops to Honduras in 1911 and Nicaragua in 1910 and again in 1912 to protect American lives and property threatened by revolution. These interventions contributed to Latin American resentment toward the United States.

In 1911 Taft negotiated a trade reciprocity agreement with Canada, which significantly lowered tariffs between the two countries, but the Canadian parliament rejected the agreement later in the year. Taft suffered another foreign policy defeat in 1911 when the Senate attached crippling amendments to his treaty with Britain and France that would have established a process of arbitration to settle international disputes between the signatories. Taft withdrew the treaty rather than sign it.

Theodore Roosevelt had been one of the harshest critics of the arbitration treaty during the ratification fight. Roosevelt also criticized Taft for what the former president considered conservative departures from his progressive policies toward big business and the environment.

In 1912 Taft was nominated by the Republican party for reelection. Roosevelt, who had won most of the Republican primaries that year, protested that he had not received a fair chance to win the nomination at the Republican national convention, which was controlled by Taft supporters. Roosevelt launched a third-party candidacy that doomed Taft's reelection bid. Roosevelt and Taft split the Republican vote, allowing Democrat Woodrow Wilson to capture the presidency. Taft finished in third place with just eight electoral votes.

When Taft's term expired, he accepted a professorship of law at Yale University. While teaching, Taft wrote for law journals and other publications and delivered many lectures around the country. In 1913 he was elected president of the American Bar Association. During World War I President Wilson named him joint chairman of the War Labor Board, which resolved wartime labor disputes.

Although Taft enjoyed his time at Yale, he continued to covet an appointment to the Supreme Court. The election of Taft's friend and fellow Republican Warren G. Harding to the presidency in 1920 opened the door to a Supreme Court appointment. When Chief Justice Edward White died on May 19, 1921, Harding chose Taft to take his place. Taft was a highly capable chief justice who usually rendered moderately conservative opinions. He improved the efficiency of the judicial system and fought successfully for passage of the Judiciary Act of 1925, which increased the Supreme Court's discretion in choosing which cases to accept. As chief justice, Taft administered the presidential oath of office to Calvin Coolidge in 1925 and Herbert Hoover in 1929. Taft resigned as chief justice on February 3, 1930, because of his weak heart. He died a few weeks later from heart failure on March 8.

Taft married Helen Herron June 19, 1886. They had one daughter and two sons. Their oldest son, Robert Alphonso Taft, became one of the most powerful Republicans in the Senate during the late 1940s and early 1950s and was considered as a possible presidential candidate in 1940, 1948, and 1952. Their youngest son, Charles Phelps Taft, served as mayor of Cincinnati from 1955 to 1957.

Woodrow Wilson

Library of Congress

Born: December 28, 1856; Staunton, Virginia
Party: Democrat
Term: March 4, 1913-March 4, 1921
Vice President: Thomas R. Marshall
Died: February 3, 1924; Washington, D.C.
Buried: Washington, D.C.

Woodrow Wilson was the third of the four children born to Janet and Joseph Wilson, a Presbyterian minister. When Wilson was two, his family moved from Staunton, Virginia, to Augusta, Georgia, where his father became pastor of the First Presbyterian Church. As a boy Wilson witnessed the destruction of the Civil War. He claimed later in life that his earliest recollection was hearing a passerby tell his father that "Mr. Lincoln was elected and there was to be war." Although Joseph Wilson was originally from Ohio, he had strong Southern sympathies and served as a chaplain to Confederate troops in the area. The war prevented Woodrow from attending school until he was nine. In 1870, the Wilsons moved to Columbia, South Carolina, where his father taught at a seminary.

Wilson, who was originally named Thomas Woodrow, dropped his first name as a young adult. He enrolled in Davidson College near Charlotte, North Carolina, in 1873. Before the end of the school year, illness forced him to withdraw. After his family moved to Wilmington, North Carolina, he entered Princeton University in 1875. There he earned recognition as a debater, developed a keen interest in government, and decided not to become a minister like his father. After graduation in 1879, he entered law school at the University of Virginia, but in 1880 poor health again forced him to abandon school. He finished his law degree through independent study while living in Wilmington and was admitted to the bar in 1882. He established a law partnership in Atlanta with a law school friend but quit the profession in 1883 to enroll in Johns Hopkins University as a graduate student of history and government.

Educator and Governor

At Johns Hopkins, Wilson distinguished himself as a brilliant student. In 1885 he published his first book, *Congressional Government*, which argued that Congress had become the dominant branch of government and that it should adopt a system of governing patterned after the British Parliament. The book received critical acclaim and served as Wilson's dissertation. In 1885 Bryn Mawr College near Philadelphia hired Wilson as an associate professor of history. He was awarded his doctorate degree in 1886.

Wilson moved to Wesleyan University in Middletown, Connecticut, in 1888. There he taught history and political science and coached the football team. In 1890 he accepted a professorship at Princeton University. In 1902 Princeton's trustees unanimously elected him president of the university.

Wilson regarded his new job as an opportunity to implement his ideas about education. He introduced a system providing for small scholarly discussion groups and close faculty supervision of students. His most cherished reform, however, was his plan to reorganize the residential structure of the college around quadrangle units that he believed would refocus the life of the college away from social and sporting activities toward academics. His "quad plan" was opposed by Princeton's private clubs, which Wilson regarded as bastions of the privileged. Although Wilson's quad plan was eventually rejected, he became known as a crusader for democratic principles in education.

New Jersey's Democratic party leaders proposed to Wilson that he run for governor in 1910. They hoped the notoriety he had gained while president of Princeton and his eloquence could carry him to the New Jersey statehouse. Once elected, party leaders expected to be able to dominate the scholarly Wilson, who had no political experience. Wilson accepted on condition that he would not have to fulfill any promises of patronage. He resigned from Princeton and was elected governor.

Once in office Wilson quickly demonstrated that he was his own man. He pushed a series of reforms through the legislature that attracted national attention including laws establishing direct primaries, worker's compensation, and antitrust measures. His efforts also led to improved regulation of utilities and the reorganization of the public school system. By 1912 Democrats were considering him as a potential presidential candidate.

Wilson entered the 1912 Democratic national convention in Baltimore as an underdog to Speaker of the House Champ Clark. Although Clark led Wilson in the early ballots, he could not muster a majority. On the fourteenth ballot Democratic patriarch William Jennings Bryan abandoned Clark to support Wilson. On the forty-sixth ballot Wilson was finally nominated.

Wilson's election to the presidency was virtually sealed when Teddy Roosevelt split the Republican party by running for president as the candidate of the Progressive party. Of the fifteen million votes cast, Wilson received only 6.3 million, but Republicans divided their votes between Roosevelt and President William Howard Taft. Wilson received 435 electoral votes, while Roosevelt and Taft received 88 and 8 votes, respectively.

Presidency

Once in office, Wilson demonstrated the same independence and innovation he had shown as governor and university president. He delivered his first annual message to Congress in person on April 8, 1913, which no president had done since John Adams. He also established weekly press conferences.

Wilson fulfilled a campaign promise to lower tariffs by signing the Underwood Tariff Act of 1913. The act cut tariff rates to their lowest levels since before the Civil War and provided for the levying of the first income tax since the Sixteenth Amendment had made such taxes legal. At Wilson's urging Congress passed the Federal Reserve Act of 1913, which created a system of regional federal banks to regulate currency and the banking industry. He supported the establishment of the Federal Trade Commission in 1914 to ensure fair business practices. That year he also signed the Clayton Anti-Trust Act, which strengthened the government's powers to break up monopolies. In 1916 Congress passed the Adamson Act at Wilson's request, which established the eight-hour day for railroad workers.

When World War I began in 1914, Wilson announced that the United States would stay out of the conflict. German submarines in the Atlantic Ocean, however, were not observing U.S. neutrality. In May 1915, a German submarine sank the British passenger ship *Lusitania* with more than one hundred Americans aboard. The incident led Wilson to issue several diplomatic protests, until the Germans agreed not to prey on passenger ships and place other restrictions on their submarine warfare.

In 1916 Wilson did not have the luxury of facing a divided Republican party as he had in 1912. The Republicans nominated Supreme Court justice Charles Evans Hughes, and Theodore Roosevelt declined a second third-party candidacy to campaign for the Republican nominee. Wilson campaigned on his domestic accomplishments and his success in keeping the United States out of war. In one of the closest presidential elections in history, Wilson defeated Hughes 277-254 in the electoral college. Had Wilson lost any of the ten states he won with twelve or more electoral votes he would have lost the election.

Wilson, who tried to mediate an end to the war in Europe, called on January 22, 1917, for a "peace without victory" that would end the fighting and the establishment of a league of nations, an international body that would prevent and settle disputes between members. A week after Wilson's speech, however, the Germans, who expected the United States to enter the war soon, announced they would attack without warning any ship passing through a wide zone in the Atlantic. Wilson responded to the submarine offensive by severing diplomatic relations with Germany on February 3. When the Germans continued their submarine warfare in defiance of Wilson's protests, he asked Congress on April 2, 1917, for a declaration of war. Within four days both houses had overwhelmingly passed the declaration.

Congress delegated broad powers to Wilson to marshal the nations resources, build an army, and prosecute the war. He pushed the Selective Service Act through Congress, took control of the railroads, established the War Industries Board to oversee the economy, and instituted many other emergency measures.

With the addition of U.S. troops on the Allied side, the war went badly for Germany. An armistice was signed on November 11, 1918. After U.S. entry into the war, Wilson had outlined a plan for territorial adjustment and maintenance of world peace once the war was over. The basis of this plan was his "Fourteen Points," which included freedom of the seas, removal of trade barriers, an end to secret treaties, and a reduction of armaments. *(See "Wilson's Fourteen Points Speech," p. 1375, in the Appendix.)*

In December 1918, Wilson sailed to France to attend the Versailles peace conference. Europeans hailed the American president as a hero, and he dominated the deliberations of the Allies. Nevertheless, he was forced to make many concessions to European leaders to gain their endorsement of his Fourteen Points and the League of Nations. The treaty produced by the conference imposed a harsh peace on Germany that included heavy war reparations and the loss of its colonies.

Wilson submitted the Treaty of Versailles to the Senate for approval on July 10, 1919, but he could not persuade two-thirds of the Senate to support it. A group of senators led by Republican Henry Cabot Lodge of Massachusetts objected to the provision within the treaty establishing the League of Nations and would not vote for the treaty without attaching reservations that Wilson believed nullified the agreement. On September 4, 1919, Wilson launched a speaking tour of the western states designed to mobilize public support for the treaty. On September 26, after delivering speeches in twenty-nine cities, Wilson became ill in Pueblo, Colorado, and was forced to cancel the rest of his speaking tour. He returned to Washington, D.C., where he suffered a severe stroke on October 2.

The stroke left the president almost entirely incapacitated for several months, and he never completely recovered his strength. While Wilson recuperated, the Senate debated the Treaty of Versailles. Senators split into three major groups: those who supported the treaty, those who sided with Lodge in supporting it only if major reservations were attached, and those who were opposed to the treaty in any form. Wilson refused to compromise with Lodge to gain passage of the treaty and advised his supporters against accepting it with Lodge's reservations. The Senate rejected the treaty on November 19, 1919. Exactly four months later Senate Republican leaders again brought the treaty to a vote in the hope that Democrats would support the Lodge reservations. Democrats in the Senate, however, remained loyal to Wilson and rejected the amended treaty again, while the Republicans blocked the passage of the treaty in its original form. Wilson declared that the American people should decide the issue in the 1920 presidential contest. The public, however, overwhelmingly elected Republican Warren G. Harding over Democrat James M. Cox. Harding refused to back the treaty, and Wilson's fight for U.S. entry into the League of Nations was finished.

When Wilson left office he retired to a home on S Street in Washington, D.C. He formed a law partnership but did not practice. He lived in near seclusion until he died on February 3, 1924, from another stroke.

Wilson married Ellen Louise Axson, the daughter of a Presbyterian minister, on June 24, 1885. They had three daughters. Ellen died on August 6, 1914, in the White House. On December 18, 1915, Wilson married Edith Bolling Galt, a forty-three-year-old widow. After Wilson suffered his stroke in 1919, Edith restricted access to her husband. During Wilson's convalescence he conducted much of his presidential business through Edith. Historians have speculated that she may have made many presidential decisions for her husband.

Warren G. Harding

Library of Congress

Born: November 2, 1865; Corsica, Ohio (now Blooming Grove)
Party: Republican
Term: March 4, 1921-August 2, 1923
Vice President: Calvin Coolidge
Died: August 2, 1923; San Francisco, California
Buried: Marion, Ohio

Warren Gamaliel Harding was the oldest of the eight children of Phoebe and George Harding, who owned a farm in north central Ohio. Warren did farm chores and attended local schools as a boy. He attended tiny Ohio Central College in Iberia, where he edited the school newspaper.

After Harding's graduation in 1882, he taught in a country school for one term, before giving up the profession and moving to Marion, Ohio. There he tried selling insurance and worked briefly for the *Marion Mirror* as a reporter. In 1884 he and two friends bought the *Marion Star*, a bankrupt, four-page newspaper. Harding bought out his friends in 1886 when they lost interest in the enterprise. Gradually, he made the paper a financial success and a political force in Ohio.

In 1892 Harding ran for county auditor but was defeated badly by his Democratic opponent. He remained active in state politics, however, frequently making campaign speeches for Republican candidates. In 1899 he ran for the state senate and was victorious. He won a second term in 1901 and was elected lieutenant governor in 1903. Two years later, however, he refused to be renominated for lieutenant governor in favor of returning to manage his paper in Marion.

In 1909, Harding ran for governor of Ohio but was defeated. He gained national prominence in June 1912 when he delivered the speech nominating William Howard Taft for president at the Republican national convention in Chicago. Two years later, he ran for the U.S. Senate. After winning the Republican party's first direct primary for senator in Ohio, Harding was elected.

As a senator, Harding followed the party line, made many friends, and avoided controversy. He frequently missed role calls and did not introduce any important legislation. He voted for Prohibition and women's suffrage but against the Versailles treaty. Much of his time in the capital was spent drinking, playing poker, and developing political allies.

Harding took his undistinguished record to the 1920 Republican national convention in Chicago. His was one of many names entered into nomination for president, but he was not among the favorites in the early balloting. After four ballots, none of the front-runners could muster a majority of support. Fearing a deadlock that would threaten party unity, Republican leaders retired to a "smoke-filled room" at the Blackstone Hotel. At the urging of Harding's close friend and political mentor, Harry Daugherty, they decided to give the nomination to Harding, who possessed good looks, an amiable personality, and a willingness to be led by the party.

During a "front porch" campaign reminiscent of William McKinley's 1896 campaign, Harding promised a "return to normalcy" after the Wilson years. This promise appealed to American voters, who had lived through a difficult period during World War I and were skeptical of outgoing president Woodrow Wilson's internationalist idealism. In the first presidential election in which women could vote, Harding defeated James M. Cox in a landslide, receiving over sixteen million votes to his opponent's nine million. Harding received 404 electoral votes, while Cox managed to win just eleven states, all in the South, for a total of 127 electoral votes.

In 1919 and 1920 the Senate had rejected Woodrow Wilson's Versailles treaty ending World War I because that body objected to U.S. membership in the League of Nations. Consequently, a separate agreement was needed to make formal the end of the war. In 1921 the Harding administration concluded treaties with Germany, Austria, and Hungary, officially making peace with those nations. In 1921, Harding also called the Washington Disarmament Conference. This meeting, masterminded by Secretary of State Charles Evans Hughes, succeeded in producing a treaty that reduced the navies of the United States, Great Britain, France, Germany, Japan, and Italy.

In domestic policy, Harding cut taxes on high incomes and signed the Fordney-McCumber Act, which raised tariff rates that had been lowered during the Wilson administration. A lasting contribution to U.S. government left by Harding was the Bureau of the Budget (now the Office of Management and Budget), which was created by the Budget Act of 1921.

Harding's administration is best known, however, for the scandals that were revealed after his death. Harding appointed to high government posts many friends and cronies who used their position for personal enrichment. Harding is not known to have participated in the crimes committed by his associates and advisers, but he did little to prevent the corruption within his administration. One of the most famous scandals involved Secretary of the Interior Albert Fall's leasing of government oil reserves at Teapot Dome, Wyoming, and Elk Hills, California, to private interests for a bribe. Fall was later fined and imprisoned for his actions. Secretary of the Navy Edwin Denby, Attorney General Harry Daugherty, and Charles Forbes, head of the Veterans Bureau, also were found to have participated in the scandals.

When the Republicans lost seats in both houses of Congress in the 1922 midterm election, Harding decided to go on a speaking tour in early 1923 to boost his party's and his own popularity. It is also probable that Harding wished to leave Washington to escape the developing rumors about the scandals within his administration.

In Seattle after visiting Alaska, Harding was stricken with pains that were diagnosed as indigestion but which may have been a heart attack. Harding improved but then died suddenly in San Francisco. His doctors suspected a blood clot in the brain may have killed him, but his wife refused to permit an autopsy. The absence of conclusive evidence about his death and the subsequent revelations of scandals led to public speculation that he may have committed suicide or been poisoned, but no evidence of an unnatural death exists. The news of Harding's death brought an outpouring of public grief, and he lay in state at the White House. As details of the scandals of his administration became known in 1923 and 1924, however, Harding's public reputation declined.

Harding married Florence Kling De Wolfe, a divorcee five years his senior, on July 8, 1891, in Marion, Ohio. The couple had no children but raised Florence's child by her first marriage. Harding carried on an affair with Nan Britton, a woman thirty years younger than he, whom he had known since he edited the *Marion Star*. When Harding was a senator, he helped Britton get a job in New York and often visited her. They had one daughter, who was born on October 22, 1919. Britton disclosed the affair three years after Harding's death in her book *The President's Daughter*.

Calvin Coolidge

Library of Congress

Born: July 4, 1872; Plymouth Notch, Vermont
Party: Republican
Term: August 3, 1923-March 4, 1929
Vice President: Charles G. Dawes
Died: January 5, 1933; Northampton, Massachusetts
Buried: Plymouth, Vermont

Calvin Coolidge was the oldest of the two children of Victoria and John Coolidge, who farmed and owned a general store. Calvin was originally named John Calvin after his father, but he dropped his first name when he became an adult. As a boy, Calvin worked on the family farm and attended local public schools. His mother died in 1885 when he was twelve. His younger sister, Abigail, died five years later at the age of fifteen.

As a teenager, Coolidge attended Black River Academy, a local private preparatory school, graduating in 1890. He wanted to attend Amherst College but failed the school's entrance exam that year. He gained admission to Amherst after taking additional courses at St. Johnsbury Academy, another prep school. Coolidge graduated cum laude from Amherst in 1895.

After graduation Coolidge moved to nearby Northampton, Massachusetts, where he got a job as a law clerk. He was admitted to the bar in 1897, started his own law practice, and became involved in Northampton politics as a Republican. He served as a member of the city council, city solicitor, and chairman of the county Republican committee. He suffered his only political defeat in 1905 when he was beaten for a seat on the Northampton school board. In 1906, however, he was elected to the Massachusetts House of Representatives. After two terms, he returned to Northampton in 1909 and was elected mayor the following year.

In 1911 Coolidge won a seat in the state senate. After four one-year terms he was elected lieutenant governor in 1915. He served three one-year terms in this office before being elected governor by a slim margin in 1918.

In September 1919, the Boston police staged a strike that opened the way for a criminal rampage. After two days, Governor Coolidge called out the state militia to keep order in Boston. When Samuel Gompers, head of the American Federation of Labor, accused Coolidge of acting unfairly, Coolidge sent him a wire declaring, "There is no right to strike against the public safety by anybody, anywhere, any time." The statement made Coolidge famous across the country.

Although Coolidge was one of many Republicans whose name was placed in nomination for the presidency at the 1920 Republican national convention in Chicago, he was not a leading candidate for the nomination. The convention was deadlocked between several candidates during the early balloting but eventually turned to Sen. Warren G. Harding of Ohio as a compromise candidate. Harding had been chosen by party leaders who expected their choice for vice president, Wisconsin senator Irvine Lenroot, to be similarly ratified by the convention. When Coolidge's name was put into nomination for vice president after Lenroot's, however, the convention unexpectedly threw its support behind the popular governor. Coolidge received 674 votes to Lenroot's 146 and was chosen on the first ballot.

During the 1920 campaign, Harding and Coolidge promised to raise tariffs to protect U.S. industry and to keep the country out of war and entangling alliances. They won more than 60 percent of the popular vote on their way to a 404-127 victory in the electoral college over Democrats James M. Cox and Franklin D. Roosevelt.

In 1923 Vice President Coolidge was spending the summer in Vermont when a telegraph messenger arrived at his home after midnight on August 3 with the news that President Harding had unexpectedly died in San Francisco. Coolidge's father, who was a notary public, administered the oath of office. The next day Coolidge left for Washington.

Coolidge retained Harding's cabinet, but when the scandals that pervaded the Harding administration were revealed, he asked for the resignations of those involved, including Secretary of the Navy Edwin Denby and Attorney General Harry Daugherty. Coolidge dutifully prosecuted the former Harding administration officials who had committed crimes.

As president, Coolidge quickly became a symbol of simple, practical leadership. Coolidge was fondly called "Silent Cal" by the public because of his quiet, almost sphinxlike demeanor. He was an honest and successful administrator who made the national government more efficient and economical.

Coolidge ran for reelection in 1924 against John W. Davis. Despite the scandals of the Harding administration, Coolidge's personal honesty, his small-town image, and national prosperity carried him to victory. He defeated Davis in the electoral college, 382-136.

During his second term, Coolidge was successful in decreasing the national debt and cutting income taxes. These policies put more money into the hands of consumers and helped stimulate investment. Coolidge's hands-off policies toward business activities, however, deferred needed reforms of the financial industry and encouraged overspeculation that contributed to the stock market crash of 1929 and the subsequent depression.

In foreign relations, Coolidge reestablished diplomatic relations with Mexico severed under Woodrow Wilson and improved relations with other Latin American nations that had been strained since the turn of the century. Although Coolidge opposed U.S. entry into the League of Nations, he backed the multilateral Kellogg-Briand Pact of 1928, which naively outlawed war between nations.

After leaving office, Coolidge retired to Northampton, Massachusetts, where he bought Beeches, a nine-acre estate. During his short retirement Coolidge wrote newspaper columns and served on the board of directors of the New York Life Insurance Company. In January 1933, less than four years after leaving the White House, Coolidge died of a heart attack.

Coolidge married Grace Goodhue on October 4, 1905. Grace had been a teacher at Clarke Institute for the Deaf in Northampton. She died in Northampton in 1957 at the age of 78. The couple had two sons. Their younger son, Calvin, Jr., died in 1924 after developing blood poisoning from a blister formed while playing tennis on the White House court.

Herbert Hoover

Library of Congress

Born: August 10, 1874; West Branch, Iowa
Party: Republican
Term: March 4, 1929-March 4, 1933
Vice President: Charles Curtis
Died: October 20, 1964; New York City
Buried: West Branch

Herbert Clark Hoover was the second of the three children of Jesse and Huldah Hoover. His father, a blacksmith and farm implement merchant, died of typhoid when Herbert was six. When his mother died of pneumonia two years later, he was sent to Oregon to live with an aunt and uncle, who were Quakers like his parents. Herbert attended public schools and worked in his uncle's land settlement office in Salem. He also attended a local business school, where he sharpened his math skills and learned to type.

Hoover took entrance examinations to gain admission to Stanford University, an engineering school being established in California. Despite uneven education, his impressive math skills earned him a spot in Stanford's first freshman class in 1891. Hoover worked his way through college, earning his degree in 1895. After laboring for a few months at a menial mining job in Nevada, Hoover went to San Francisco. There he worked as a typist before an international mining company hired him in 1897 as an engineering assistant. During the next seventeen years, Hoover managed mines in Africa, Asia, Europe, Australia, and the United States. Before the age of forty, he was one of the world's most successful mining engineers and worth several million dollars.

In 1914 when World War I began Hoover was living in London. He served as chairman of a committee of Americans who helped U.S. tourists stranded in Europe to secure passage home. He then became chairman of the Commission for Relief in Belgium, a private charity group. In this capacity he raised funds to aid the people of that war-torn country and made arrangements with the warring nations to distribute the aid.

When the U.S. Congress declared war on Germany in 1917, Hoover returned to the United States, where President Woodrow Wilson appointed him U.S. Food Administrator. In this post Hoover was responsible for stimulating food production and distributing and conserving food supplies. In 1918 Hoover was appointed chairman of the Allied Food Council, which distributed food to millions of Europeans left impoverished by the war. After the war Hoover attended the Versailles Peace Conference as an economic adviser to President Wilson.

Hoover's relief activities made him one of the most famous and admired Americans of his day and a prospective candidate for public office. But his political affiliation was unclear because he had supported Republican Theodore Roosevelt's third party candidacy in 1912 and had worked closely with President Wilson, a Democrat. In 1920, however, Hoover declared that he was a Republican and received some support for the party's presidential nomination, which eventually went to Warren G. Harding.

When Harding was elected president, he appointed Hoover secretary of commerce over the objections of Republican conservatives who regarded Hoover as a liberal. Hoover remained in this post for eight years. He reorganized the department and helped solidify the progress toward an eight-hour workday and a prohibition against child labor. He also became a close economic adviser to both President Harding and Vice President Calvin Coolidge, but he remained free of the scandals that plagued their administration.

Hoover was the popular choice of Republicans for the party's presidential nomination in 1928. Despite the opposition of some conservative party leaders, Hoover was nominated at the Kansas City Republican national convention on the first ballot. He then won the general election over Democrat Al Smith of New York. Hoover received more than twenty-one million popular votes to Smith's fifteen million. Hoover even captured several traditionally Democratic southern states on his way to a 444-87 electoral vote victory.

Hoover had run on a Republican platform that took credit for the prosperity achieved during the 1920s. Ironically, seven months after Hoover's inauguration the October 1929 stock market crash began the economic depression that left about a quarter of the work force unemployed. After the crash Hoover tried to assure the nation that the economy was sound and that business activity would soon recover, but the depression grew worse during his term. Although he had not created the conditions that caused the depression, many Americans blamed him for it.

Hoover tried to fight the growing depression through

limited public works projects, increased government loans to banks and businesses, reductions in the already low income tax, and personal appeals to industry to maintain wages and production levels. But these measures did little to ease the country's economic problems. Hoover's preoccupation with balancing the budget and his belief that federal relief violated the American principle of self reliance prevented him from taking more sweeping actions. Thus, he opposed federal benefit programs to help the poor and unemployed and deficit spending that would have created jobs. He reluctantly signed the Smoot-Hawley Act of 1930, which dramatically raised tariff rates to protect U.S. industries, thereby initiating a trade war that hurt the American and world economies.

Hoover was nominated by the Republicans for a second term but the nation, desperate for relief from the depression, turned against him. His Democratic opponent, Franklin D. Roosevelt, won in a landslide.

Hoover returned to his home in Palo Alto, California, in March 1933. During Franklin Roosevelt's presidency Hoover actively criticized Roosevelt's New Deal programs and the U.S. alliance with the Soviet Union during World War II.

In 1946 President Harry S Truman tapped Hoover's famine relief experience by appointing him chairman of the Famine Emergency Commission, which was charged with preventing starvation in post-World War II Europe. In 1947 Truman appointed Hoover chairman of the Commission on Organization of the Executive Branch of the Government. The "Hoover Commission" recommended hundreds of organizational changes, many of which were adopted, to make the executive branch more efficient. The commission submitted its final report in 1949, but in 1953 President Dwight D. Eisenhower appointed Hoover to chair a second commission on government organization. The second Hoover Commission functioned until 1955.

Hoover retired from government service after 1955 but continued to write on politics and speak at Republican conventions. In 1964 he died in New York City at the age of ninety. He had the second-longest life of any president, with John Adams living 136 days longer.

Hoover married Lou Henry, a fellow student at Stanford and the daughter of a Monterey, California, banker, on February 10, 1899. Their two sons, Herbert, Jr., and Allan, were born while the Hoovers lived in London. Herbert served as under secretary of state from 1954 to 1957.

Franklin D. Roosevelt

Franklin D. Roosevelt Library

Born: January 30, 1882; Hyde Park, New York
Party: Democratic
Term: March 4, 1933-April 12, 1945
Vice Presidents: John N. Garner; Henry A. Wallace; Harry S Truman
Died: April 12, 1945; Warm Springs, Georgia
Buried: Hyde Park

Franklin Delano Roosevelt was the son of James and Sara Roosevelt. He was his mother's only child, but his father, a widower, had a son by his first wife. James Roosevelt was a wealthy lawyer and railroad executive who had inherited a fortune. Sara was also from a wealthy family and had married the fifty-two-year-old James when she was just twenty-six. She and James's first son were both born in 1854.

Franklin lived a sheltered early life. He received his elementary education from private tutors and traveled frequently with his family to Europe. At age fourteen Franklin enrolled in Groton, a private preparatory school in Groton, Massachusetts. After four years there he entered Harvard University in 1900. Although Franklin did not have a distinguished academic record, he graduated in three years and became editor of the campus newspaper.

Roosevelt stayed a fourth year at Harvard as a graduate student of history and economics. He then studied law at Columbia from 1904 until 1907 but left without graduating when he passed the bar. A New York City firm hired him as a law clerk.

Political Career

In 1910 Roosevelt ran for the New York State senate as a Democrat from a traditionally Republican district and surprised Democratic party leaders when he won. He was reelected in 1912 but gave up his seat in 1913, when President Woodrow Wilson appointed him assistant secretary of the navy, a post once held by his distant relative Theodore Roosevelt.

After war broke out in Europe in 1914, Roosevelt argued for greater military preparedness. When the United States entered the war, he twice asked Wilson to transfer him to active service, but the president turned him down saying he was needed where he was. Roosevelt made several trips to Europe to inspect U.S. naval forces. Near the end of the war he developed a plan to hinder German submarine attacks. His "North Sea Mine Barrage," a 240-mile cordon of antisubmarine mines in the Atlantic, reduced allied shipping losses and helped hasten the armistice.

In 1920 Roosevelt resigned from the Navy Department when the Democratic party nominated him for the vice presidency on the ticket with presidential nominee James M. Cox. Democrats hoped that the promising young politician with the famous name could give the ticket a boost, but Cox and Roosevelt were beaten badly by Republicans Warren Harding and Calvin Coolidge.

After the defeat, Roosevelt became a partner in a New York City law firm and accepted a vice presidency in the Fidelity and Deposit Company of Maryland, a surety bond firm.

In 1921 Roosevelt suffered a personal tragedy. While vacationing in New Brunswick he was stricken with poliomyelitis. The attack left him severely crippled and his mother urged him to give up politics and retire to the family estate at Hyde Park. Roosevelt, however, struggled to rehabilitate himself. Over a period of years he built up his arms and chest and eventually was able to walk short distances with the aid of crutches and braces.

On June 26, 1924, Roosevelt returned to national politics when he delivered the presidential nomination speech for New York governor Alfred E. Smith at the Democratic national convention in New York City. Smith did not receive the nomination, but Roosevelt's courageous appearance on crutches at Madison Square Garden increased Roosevelt's popularity and made him a leading figure in the Democratic party. Later that year Roosevelt vacationed in Warm Springs, Georgia, where he hoped to regain the use of his legs by swimming in a natural pool of warm spring water. He made numerous trips to Warm Springs during the rest of his life. In 1927 he founded the Georgia Warm Springs Foundation, an inexpensive treatment center for polio victims.

Al Smith, nominated for president in 1928, urged Roosevelt to run for governor in New York to give the Democratic ticket a boost. Roosevelt at first declined, saying he wanted to concentrate on rehabilitating his legs, but he finally agreed to run when he was nominated by acclamation. Questions of Roosevelt's physical ability to function as governor were dispelled by his vigorous campaigning, often conducted from an automobile. Roosevelt won the election despite Republican presidential candidate Herbert Hoover's victory in New York.

As governor, Roosevelt gave tax relief to New York's farmers and lowered the cost of public utilities to consumers. He was reelected in a landslide in 1930. During his second term he concentrated on easing the suffering caused by the depression.

Roosevelt's success as governor made him a leading candidate for the Democratic presidential nomination in 1932. He entered the convention with a majority of delegates, but he had fewer than the two-thirds necessary to win the nomination. After three ballots he offered to endorse rival John Nance Garner, the Texan Speaker of the House, for vice president, if Garner released his presidential delegates. Garner, recognizing his chances of being nominated for president were slim, accepted the deal and released his ninety delegates to Roosevelt, who was nominated on the fourth ballot. The convention then nominated Garner for vice president.

During the campaign of 1932, Roosevelt exuded confidence and outlined his recovery program, which he called the "New Deal." Although he faced incumbent Republican president Herbert Hoover in the election, Roosevelt was favored to win because many voters blamed Hoover for the severity of the Great Depression. Roosevelt outpolled Hoover by more than seven million votes and won 472-59 in the electoral college.

Before Roosevelt was inaugurated, he became the only president-elect to be the target of an assassination attempt. After Roosevelt had delivered a speech in Florida on February 14, 1933, Giuseppe Zangara, an unemployed bricklayer, fired six shots from a handgun at Roosevelt from twelve yards away. The president-elect, who was sitting in an open car, was uninjured but five other people were shot, including Chicago mayor Anton Cernak, who was killed. Zangara, who had a pathological hatred for rich and powerful figures, was found guilty of murder and electrocuted.

Presidency

Roosevelt took office at the low point of the depression. Most of the nation's banks were closed, industrial production was about half of what it had been in 1928, and as many as 15 million people were unemployed. Roosevelt worked with the new Democratic Congress to enact many New Deal bills during the productive opening period of his presidency, known as the "First Hundred Days." He declared a four-day bank holiday to stop panic withdrawals, abandoned the gold standard, increased government loans to farmers and homeowners, and created federal bank deposit insurance. At Roosevelt's urging, Congress created the Civilian Conservation Corps, which employed tens of thousands of people on conservation projects and passed the Federal Emergency Relief Act, which provided grants to state and local governments for aid to the unemployed. Numerous other measures were passed during the First Hundred Days, which increased public confidence and stimulated the economy.

Business interests feared that the deficit spending required to finance the New Deal would lead to inflation, but injection of federal money into the economy eased the depression. Roosevelt promoted his policies through "fireside chats," radio addresses to the nation from the White House. A second wave of New Deal programs, including Social Security, unemployment insurance, and federal aid to dependent children, was passed in 1934 and 1935.

Roosevelt's New Deal successes made him a popular president. He defeated Kansas governor Alfred M. Landon in the 1936 presidential election in one of the largest landslides in presidential election history. Landon won only Maine and Vermont.

In 1937 Roosevelt suffered one of the biggest defeats of his presidency and squandered political capital won in the 1936 election when he proposed to expand the Supreme Court from nine to as many as fifteen judges. Roosevelt had been frustrated by the conservative court, which had struck down several of his New Deal measures. If the Court were expanded he could appoint judges who would accept his policies. Neither the public nor Congress, however, would go along with Roosevelt's court-packing scheme. Moreover, the episode hardened resistance to the New Deal from Republicans and conservative Democrats.

In 1940 Roosevelt ran for an unprecedented third term against the progressive Republican nominee, Wendell Willkie of Indiana. Roosevelt defeated Willkie 449 to 82 in the electoral college. His popular margin of victory narrowed from four years before, however, in part because some voters objected to Roosevelt's disregard of the unwritten rule that presidents should serve no more than two terms.

In September 1939 Adolph Hitler's Germany had invaded Poland, starting World War II in Europe. Despite strong neutralist sentiments among members of Congress and the general public, Roosevelt recognized that U.S. national security depended on Great Britain's survival. He promised to keep the United States out of the fighting but pressed for the authority to aid Britain and other allied nations in every way short of going to war. In September 1940 Roosevelt violated two neutrality statutes in trading Great Britain fifty outdated destroyers for the right to lease certain British territory in the Western Atlantic for U.S. naval and air bases. In March 1941 Roosevelt persuaded Congress to pass the Lend-Lease Act, which gave the president the power to supply weapons and equipment to "any country whose defense the president deems vital to the defense of the United States." In September of that year, Roosevelt ordered U.S. warships providing protection for supply convoys bound for Britain to attack German vessels on sight. Thus, Roosevelt had engaged the United States in an undeclared naval war months before the nation would enter the war.

On December 7, 1941, the Japanese launched a surprise attack against the U.S. fleet at Pearl Harbor, Hawaii. The next day Roosevelt asked for and received a declaration of war from Congress. Roosevelt shifted his focus and national resources from New Deal reforms to winning the war.

Roosevelt oversaw the development of military strategy and conferred often with British prime minister Winston Churchill. Roosevelt and Churchill met with Soviet leader Joseph Stalin at Tehran in 1943 and Yalta in 1945. At these meetings, the leaders of the three principal allied nations not only discussed wartime strategy, they planned for the postwar order. At Yalta Roosevelt secured a Soviet promise to enter the war against Japan when Germany was defeated in return for territorial concessions in Asia. The allies also set new Polish borders, scheduled a conference in 1945 to establish the United Nations, and agreed to allow occupied countries to construct new governments based on free elections after the war. Many historians have criticized Roosevelt for being too trusting of Stalin, who established Communist puppet states in Eastern Europe after the war.

Although the strain of the wartime presidency had weakened Roosevelt, he ran for a fourth term in 1944. In a fateful move he agreed to the suggestion of his political advisers to drop his third-term vice president Henry A. Wallace, who was considered too liberal. The Democrats nominated Sen. Harry S Truman from Missouri for vice president in Wallace's place. Roosevelt defeated his fourth Republican opponent, New York governor Thomas E. Dewey, 432-99 in the electoral college.

In April 1945, after returning from Yalta, Roosevelt went to Warm Springs, Georgia, for a rest before the conference on the establishment of the United Nations scheduled for later in the month in San Francisco. On April 12, while sitting for a portrait at his cottage, Roosevelt suddenly collapsed from a cerebral hemorrhage and died a few hours later. The same day in Washington, Harry Truman was sworn in as president. The world mourned the dead president as a train carried his body back to the Capitol, where it lay in state at the White House. The train then resumed its journey north to Roosevelt's Hyde Park home, where he was buried.

Roosevelt married Anna Eleanor Roosevelt, a fifth cousin, on March 17, 1905. Eleanor's mother and father died when she was a child, so she was given away at her wedding by her father's brother, President Theodore Roosevelt. The Roosevelts had one daughter and five sons, one of whom died in infancy. Eleanor is regarded as the most active first lady in history up to her time. Besides promoting numerous social causes, she served as her crippled husband's representative at many political and ceremonial functions. After the president's death Eleanor continued to fight for social causes. She died on November 7, 1962.

Harry S Truman

U.S. Navy; Courtesy Harry S. Truman Library

Born: May 8, 1884; Lamar, Missouri
Party: Democratic
Term: April 12, 1945-January 20, 1953
Vice President: Alben W. Barkley
Died: December 26, 1972; Kansas City, Missouri
Buried: Independence, Missouri

Harry S Truman was the oldest of three children born to Martha and John Truman, a mule trader. Harry's parents wanted to give him a middle name in honor of a grandfather but could not decide between his two grandfathers, Anderson Shippe Truman and Solomon Young. Consequently they gave him the middle initial "S," which stood for nothing.

After living in several towns in Missouri, the Trumans settled in Independence, near Kansas City. Harry's poor eyesight prevented him from joining in some outdoor activities as a boy. Instead he learned to play the piano and became a voracious reader. At the age of sixteen he had his first political experience when he worked as a page at the 1900 Democratic national convention in Kansas City, which nominated William Jennings Bryan for president.

After graduating from high school Truman held a succession of jobs, including mail room clerk, bank teller, and bookkeeper. He wanted to go to college, but he and his family could not afford it. In 1906, when Truman was twenty-two, he took over the management of his grandmother's 600-acre farm in Grandview, Missouri. He succeeded at farming and became active in local politics and community organizations.

When the United States entered World War I, Truman received a commission as a first lieutenant. He served with distinction in the Vosges and Meuse-Argonne campaigns as commander of an artillery battery and attained the rank of major before leaving the service in 1919.

Political Career

Upon returing to Missouri, Truman opened a haberdashery in Kansas City with a war buddy. When the store failed in 1922 he ran for judge of the eastern district of Jackson County. He won the election with the support of the powerful Kansas City political boss Tom Pendergast. He failed in his bid for reelection two years later but was elected presiding judge of the court in 1926 and was reelected in 1930. These judgeships were administrative rather than judicial positions. Truman controlled hundreds of patronage jobs and millions of dollars' worth of public works projects.

Truman became well known in the Kansas City area. He retained his close connections to Pendergast and the Kansas City machine but also developed a reputation for honesty. Using his Kansas City political base, Truman launched a campaign for the U.S. Senate and was elected in 1934.

In the Senate Truman supported Franklin D. Roosevelt's New Deal legislation. Despite the conviction of Tom Pendergast for income tax evasion, Truman was reelected by a narrow margin in 1940. During his second term, Truman chaired the Special Committee to Investigate the National Defense Program, which sought to eliminate waste and inefficiency among defense contractors. He also supported Roosevelt's efforts to aid the allies before the entry of the United States into World War II.

In 1944 the Democratic party was set to nominate President Franklin Roosevelt for his fourth term, but the vice-presidential nomination remained in doubt. Vice President Henry Wallace had alienated many Democratic party leaders, who considered his political views too liberal. Robert Hannegan, national chairman of the Democratic party, recommended to Roosevelt that Truman be nominated in place of Wallace, and the president agreed. Truman was nominated for vice president on the second ballot at the Democratic national convention in Chicago. Roosevelt and Truman then defeated Republicans Thomas E. Dewey and John W. Bricker in the general election.

Presidency

Truman served just eighty-two days as vice president. On April 12, 1945, he was summoned to the White House and informed by First Lady Eleanor Roosevelt that the president was dead. Later in the day he took the oath of office at the White House from Chief Justice Harlan F. Stone.

World events forced Truman to become an expert in foreign affairs, an area of policy in which he had little experience before becoming president. Truman's first priority was winning World War II. On May 7 Germany surrendered unconditionally to the allies. In July 1945 Truman traveled to Potsdam, Germany, to discuss the composition of the postwar world with British prime minister Winston Churchill and Soviet premier Joseph Stalin. There the three leaders agreed to divide Germany and its capital, Berlin, into occupation zones.

While at Potsdam, Truman was informed that the United States had successfully tested an atomic bomb. He authorized atomic attacks on Japanese cities to hasten the end of the war. On August 6, 1945, an atomic bomb dropped from a U.S. warplane on Hiroshima killed eighty thousand people. Three days later, another bomb destroyed the city of Nagasaki. Truman's decision to use atomic weapons has been debated by many scholars and military analysts since World War II. Before the bombs were dropped, Japan had sent signals that it might surrender, but Truman believed a quick end of the war was necessary to avoid any need for an invasion of Japan that would cost many U.S. lives. On September 2 the Japanese officially surrendered, ending the war.

Despite U.S.-Soviet cooperation during the war, differences between the two nations developed into a "cold war" by 1946. The United States objected in particular to the Soviet Union's creation of Communist governments in the Eastern European states they had occupied while pushing the Nazi armies back into Germany. Truman vigorously protested Moscow's actions and resolved to contain further Soviet expansionism.

In March 1947 when Britain withdrew its assistance to Greek anti-Communists for economic reasons, Truman proclaimed the Truman Doctrine and asked Congress for $400 million in economic and military aid to prevent Greece and Turkey from falling to Communist insurgents. The Truman Doctrine declared that the United States would aid governments threatened by Communist subversion. Later that year Truman and Secretary of State George Marshall asked Congress to dramatically expand foreign aid by approving the Marshall Plan, a multi-billion-dollar program to rebuild the economies of Western Europe. Congress gave its approval in 1948, and the Marshall Plan became one of the foremost successes of the Truman administration. Later in 1948 when the Soviets closed passage between western Germany and Berlin, which was located within the Soviet occupation zone, Truman used a massive airlift to supply the parts of the city administered by Britain, France, and the United States. The Soviets had hoped to force the United States and its western allies to give up control of their part of Berlin, but Truman's airlift broke the blockade and the Soviets backed down without a military confrontation.

In domestic policy, Truman developed a plan to extend Franklin Roosevelt's New Deal, which the new president called the "Fair Deal." Republicans and conservative Democrats in Congress, however, blocked many of his proposals. He also unsuccessfully backed progressive civil rights legislation. In 1947 Congress overrode Truman's veto of the Taft-Hartley Act, which he claimed unfairly weakened the bargaining power of unions. Five years later he seized and operated steel mills shut down by a strike during the Korean War, a move that the Supreme Court declared unconstitutional. Truman battled postwar inflation with the modest tools at his disposal, but Congress rejected his proposals for more sweeping price-control legislation, and inflation continued to be the most troublesome domestic problem during Truman's years in office.

In 1948 Truman ran for reelection against Thomas E. Dewey. Truman's reelection chances appeared slim when ultra liberal Democrats nominated Henry Wallace for president, and southern Democrats who disliked Truman's strong civil rights platform formed the "Dixiecrat" party and nominated Sen. Strom Thurmond of South Carolina. During the campaign public opinion polls indicated that Dewey would win. Truman, however, used a cross-country, whistle-stop campaign to take his message to the people and won a surprise victory, defeating Dewey 303-189 in the electoral college.

Truman's second term was dominated by the Korean War. On June 24, 1950, troops from Communist North Korea invaded South Korea. Truman sent U.S. troops to Korea under the auspices of the United Nations. UN forces pushed the North Koreans out of South Korea and drove into North Korea in an attempt to unify the country. Communist China entered the war on the side of the North Koreans in late 1950, however, and pushed UN forces back into South Korea. Eventually the war became deadlocked near the thirty-eighth parallel that had divided the two Koreas before the start of the war. Truman was unable to attain a negotiated peace during his presidency.

In 1951 Truman fired Gen. Douglas MacArthur, commander of UN forces in Korea, for insubordination. MacArthur had criticized the Truman administration's conduct of the war, publicly advocated a provocative invasion of China, interfered with Truman's diplomatic gestures, and disobeyed orders. Nevertheless, MacArthur enjoyed a large following in Congress and among the American public, and Truman's popularity sank after he fired the general.

During Truman's years in office the country became consumed with paranoia over Communist subversion. Sen. Joseph R. McCarthy, R-Wis., led a group in Congress who claimed that Communist agents had infiltrated the U.S. government, especially the State Department. McCarthy pointed to the failure of the United States to stop the Communist revolution in China in 1949 as evidence of the Communist sympathies of key U.S. officials. Truman denounced McCarthy but was unable to rally public support against the senator, despite the lack of evidence backing up McCarthy's accusations. After Truman retired, McCarthy became chairman of a Senate investigative subcommittee and accused many citizens of pro-Communist activities before being censured by the Senate in 1954.

From November 1948 until March 1952 the Trumans lived in Blair House across Pennsylvania Avenue from the White House while the executive mansion was being renovated. On November 1, 1950, Harry Truman became the first incumbent president to be the target of an assassination attempt since William McKinley was killed in 1901. Two Puerto Rican nationalists, Griselio Torresola and Oscar Collazo, attacked Blair House with automatic weapons, hoping to fight their way inside to kill the president. Although Truman was not harmed, one Secret Service agent and one of the assassins were killed.

On March 29, 1952, Truman announced that he would not run for reelection in the fall. After leaving office he returned to his home in Independence, Missouri. Truman remained active during his retirement, delivering lectures, commenting on political developments, and overseeing construction of the Truman Library near his home. He published his two-volume memoirs in 1955 and 1956.

Truman married Elizabeth ("Bess") Wallace, whom he had known since his boyhood, on June 28, 1919. The couple had one child, Margaret, who was born in 1924. Margaret attended George Washington University and launched a singing career during her father's presidency.

Dwight D. Eisenhower

Library of Congress

Born: October 14, 1890; Denison, Texas
Party: Republican
Term: January 20, 1953-January 20, 1961
Vice President: Richard M. Nixon
Died: March 28, 1969; Washington, D.C.
Buried: Abilene, Kansas

Dwight David Eisenhower was the third of the seven sons of David and Ida Eisenhower. One of Dwight's younger brothers died in infancy. Dwight was born in Texas, but his family lived there for only a short period. When Dwight was a baby, they returned to Kansas, where they had lived before he was born. Settling in Abilene, David Eisenhower got a job as a mechanic in a creamery. Dwight attended public schools and worked in the creamery after classes. At the age of fourteen, he developed blood poisoning from a severely skinned knee. Dwight's doctor wanted to amputate the leg, warning the Eisenhowers that failure to do so could cost Dwight his life. Despite the risk, the boy refused to let the doctor amputate his leg, and he recovered from the blood poisoning.

Eisenhower lacked the money to attend college, so he worked in the creamery full time upon graduation from high school. After a year, he applied for admission to both the Naval Academy and the Military Academy. He was rejected by Annapolis because he was too old, but he was nominated to West Point. He played football and was an above-average student, graduating sixty-fifth in his class of 164 in 1915.

Military Career

When the United States entered World War I in 1917, Eisenhower served as a troop instructor at several bases in the United States. After the war his assignments included a two-year posting in Panama. In 1925 Eisenhower received an appointment to the Army General Staff School in Leavenworth, Kansas. He graduated in 1926 first in his class of 275, an accomplishment that greatly contributed to his advancement through the ranks. He attended the Army War College in Washington, D.C., in 1928 and then served on the staff of the assistant secretary of war until 1932, when he was appointed as an aide to army chief of staff Gen. Douglas MacArthur. When MacArthur went to the Philippines in 1934 to organize a Filipino army, Eisenhower, by this time a major, accompanied him as a staff officer. While in the Philippines he received his pilot's license.

Eisenhower returned to the United States in early 1940 as a lieutenant colonel. During the next three years he would be promoted above hundreds of senior officers on his way to becoming a full general. When the United States entered World War II in 1941, he was a brigadier general serving as chief of staff of the Third Army in San Antonio, Texas. In February 1942 he was called to Washington, D.C., where he took command of the War Plans Division of the War Department's general staff. In this post he helped draft global strategy and a preliminary plan for the invasion of France from Britain. Eisenhower's skill as a tactician and his reputation as a soldier who could unify military leaders holding diverse points of view led to his appointment in June 1942 as the commanding general of the European Theater of Operations.

In November 1942 Eisenhower directed the successful Allied invasion of North Africa. In 1943 he attained the rank of full general and commanded the Allied invasions of Sicily and Italy. In December 1943 President Roosevelt named Eisenhower supreme commander of all Allied forces in Europe and instructed him to develop a plan for an invasion of France. On June 6, 1944, the forces under Eisenhower's command landed in Normandy in the largest amphibious invasion ever undertaken. The troops gained a beachhead and began driving toward Germany. Eisenhower accepted the surrender of the German army on May 7, 1945.

When the war was over, Eisenhower was one of America's most prominent war heroes. Although he lacked the dramatic presence of Douglas MacArthur, who had commanded U.S. forces in the Pacific during the war, Eisenhower was praised for his ability to rally his troops and his diplomacy with the Allied leaders. After serving as commander of the U.S. occupation zone in Germany, Eisenhower was appointed army chief of staff in November 1945. In 1948 he retired from the military to become president of Columbia University. That year he was approached by both the Democrats and the Republicans as a possible presidential candidate. In 1945 President Harry S Truman had told Eisenhower that he would support Eisenhower if the general wanted to run for president as a Democrat in 1948. Eisenhower, however, declined all offers to run for office and maintained his political neutrality.

In 1950 President Truman asked Eisenhower to return to active service to become supreme commander of the

North Atlantic Treaty Organization (NATO) forces in Europe. During his time in Europe, Eisenhower was again courted by both major political parties. Finally in January 1952 he announced that he would accept the Republican nomination for president if it were offered. He resigned his NATO command in May and was nominated by the Republicans on the first ballot at their national convention in Chicago in July.

Eisenhower's opponent was Gov. Adlai E. Stevenson II of Illinois. Eisenhower avoided detailed discussions of his political positions and relied primarily on his outgoing personality and his popularity as a war hero to win votes. He won a landslide popular-vote victory and defeated Stevenson 442-89 in the electoral college.

Presidency

When Eisenhower became president in 1953 a Korean War settlement was within reach. In December 1952, after the election, he had fulfilled a campaign promise to go to Korea to survey the situation. On July 27, 1953, an armistice was signed ending the war.

Although superpower tensions eased somewhat with the death of Soviet leader Joseph Stalin in March 1953 and the Korean War settlement, the Cold War continued. Eisenhower endorsed Harry Truman's policy of containing Communist expansion but sought to avoid conflict when possible. In 1954 he refused to aid the French garrison surrounded at Dien Bien Phu, Vietnam, by Vietnamese nationalists, who eventually drove the French out of Indochina, and he protested the attack on Egypt by Great Britain, France, and Israel in 1956 over Egypt's nationalization of the Suez Canal. Following the Suez crisis, Eisenhower announced the Eisenhower doctrine, a commitment by the United States to use force to stop international Communist aggression in the Middle East. In accordance with this doctrine, he sent U.S. troops to Lebanon in 1958 when the Lebanese government requested assistance fighting insurgents.

On September 24, 1955, Eisenhower suffered a heart attack that limited his activity for several months. The following June he underwent an operation for an attack of ileitis, an inflamation of the small intestine. Eisenhower's illnesses raised questions about his fitness for a second term. In November 1956, however, the voters reelected him over Democrat Adlai Stevenson by an even larger margin than he had enjoyed in 1952. President Eisenhower was confined to bed a third time in 1957 after suffering a stroke. His periods of disability fueled efforts to develop a procedure for transferring power to the vice president when the president was incapacitated by illness. Such a procedure was established by the Twenty-fifth Amendment, ratified in 1967.

In domestic policy Eisenhower favored anti-inflation policies over measures to stimulate economic growth. He produced budget surpluses in three of the eight years of his presidency, an accomplishment that became all the more noteworthy in the three decades after his retirement, when the federal budget was balanced only once. He also warned of the dangers of the development of a "military-industrial complex" and sought to limit defense spending. He signed bills that compensated farmers for taking land out of production and that initiated the national interstate highway system. Although he was not a leading opponent of racial segregation, he enforced existing civil rights laws. In 1957 he sent federal troops to Little Rock, Arkansas, when local citizens and state officials tried to block integration of public schools.

Eisenhower held several summits with Soviet leaders in attempting to improve U.S.-Soviet relations. He met with Soviet premier Nikolai Bulganin and Allied leaders in 1955 at Geneva and with Soviet premier Nikita Khrushchev in 1959 at Camp David, Maryland. Eisenhower's plans for a 1960 summit, however, were soured when the Soviets shot down an American U-2 reconnaissance plane over the Soviet Union on May 1 of that year. Khrushchev protested the U-2 overflights and refused to attend a summit in Paris with Allied leaders later that month. Eisenhower took full responsibility for the missions and defended them as vital to the security of the United States.

Eisenhower left office at the age of seventy, the oldest person to serve as president up to that time. He retired to his 230-acre farm near Gettysburg, Pennsylvania, where he enjoyed a quiet retirement. He indulged his love for golf, scoring a hole in one in February 1968, and wrote his memoirs, which were published in two volumes in 1965 and 1966. In November 1965 he suffered two heart attacks but recovered. During the spring and summer of 1968 he had a series of heart attacks that confined him to a hospital. He died in March 1969 from a heart attack, two months after his former vice president, Richard Nixon, was elected president.

Eisenhower married Marie ("Mamie") Doud on July 1, 1916. Eisenhower met Mamie, the daughter of a wealthy Denver businessman, shortly after his graduation from West Point. They had two sons, but their first, Doud, died when he was three. Their second son, John Sheldon Eisenhower, was the father of David Eisenhower, who married President Richard Nixon's daughter Julie in 1968. Dwight Eisenhower's youngest brother, Milton, was president of three universities, chaired several government committees, and advised every president from Calvin Coolidge to Richard Nixon.

John F. Kennedy

Library of Congress

Born: May 29, 1917; Brookline, Massachusetts
Party: Democratic
Term: January 20, 1961-November 22, 1963
Vice President: Lyndon B. Johnson
Died: November 22, 1963; Dallas, Texas
Buried: Arlington, Virginia

John Fitzgerald Kennedy was the second of the nine children of Joseph and Rose Kennedy. John's mother was the daughter of a former mayor of Boston. His father was a millionaire who had made his fortune in banking, real estate, and other financial ventures. In 1937 Franklin D. Roosevelt appointed Joseph Kennedy ambassador to Great Britain, a position he resigned in December 1940 when he became pessimistic about Britain's chances for survival during World War II. He returned to the United States, where his advocacy of isolationism caused a falling out with Roosevelt, who did not appoint him to another post.

John graduated in the middle of his class from Choate, a preparatory school in Wallingford, Connecticut. After attending the London School of Economics during the summer of 1935, he enrolled at Princeton University, but an illness forced him to withdraw after two months. In 1936 he entered Harvard University, where he studied economics and political science. Kennedy was an average student, but his grades improved dramatically at the end of his college career and he graduated with honors in 1940. *Why England Slept*, his senior thesis published in book form, was an examination of British appeasement of fascism before World War II.

In 1941 Kennedy tried to enter the army, but he was rejected because of a bad back caused by a football injury. He strengthened his back through exercise and passed the navy's physical later that year. He received a commission as an ensign in October 1941. After attending PT (patrol torpedo) boat training, he was given command of a PT boat in the South Pacific in April 1943. On August 2, 1943, his boat, PT-109, was rammed and sunk by a Japanese destroyer. Eleven of his thirteen crew members survived, and he led them on a four-hour swim to a nearby island. During the swim he towed an injured crew member by a life preserver strap. Kennedy and his crew were rescued after friendly natives took a message carved on a coconut to nearby Allied personnel. After the ordeal Kennedy was sent back to the United States, where he was hospitalized for malaria. In 1944 he underwent a disc operation and was discharged the following year.

Kennedy worked briefly as a reporter for the International News Service, then decided to run for Congress from his Massachusetts district. He was elected in 1946 and served three terms before being elected to the Senate in 1952. In 1954 and 1955, he underwent two more operations for his chronic back condition.

While convalescing, Kennedy wrote *Profiles in Courage*, a book about senators who had demonstrated courage during their careers. The book became a bestseller and earned Kennedy the 1957 Pulitzer Prize for biography.

In 1956 Kennedy tried to secure the Democratic vice-presidential nomination on the ticket with Adlai Stevenson. After leading on the second ballot at the Democratic national convention in Chicago, Kennedy lost the nomination to Sen. Estes Kefauver of Tennessee. Despite this defeat Kennedy's political reputation continued to grow. In 1957 he was assigned to the Senate Foreign Relations Committee, where he gained foreign policy experience. In 1958 he won reelection to the Senate by a record margin in Massachusetts.

By 1960 Kennedy was the leading candidate for the Democratic presidential nomination. His rivals for the nomination were Senate Majority Leader Lyndon Johnson of Texas, Sen. Stuart Symington of Missouri, Sen. Hubert H. Humphrey of Minnesota, and former Democratic presidential candidate Adlai Stevenson. Kennedy prevailed on the first ballot at the Democratic national convention in Los Angeles in July 1960 and convinced Lyndon Johnson, who had finished second, to be his running mate.

Kennedy's opponent was Vice President Richard Nixon. Kennedy and Nixon engaged in a series of four televised debates, the first in presidential election history. Out of almost 69 million votes cast, Kennedy received only 120,000 more than Nixon. Kennedy won in the electoral college 303-219.

Kennedy was the youngest person ever to be elected president, although Theodore Roosevelt was younger than Kennedy when he succeeded to the presidency after the death of William McKinley. Kennedy's youth, idealism, and attractive family would make him one of the most popular presidents of the twentieth century. His administration came to be known as "Camelot" because of its romantic image.

Soon after entering office Kennedy endorsed a CIA plan developed during the Eisenhower presidency to arm, train, and land fourteen hundred Cuban exiles in Cuba in an attempt to overthrow the Communist regime of Fidel Castro. The April 17, 1961, operation, which came to be known as the Bay of Pigs invasion, was a complete failure as twelve hundred of the Cuban exiles were captured. The president accepted full responsibility for the blunder.

Cuba had been the site of Kennedy's greatest foreign policy failure, but it was also the place of his most memorable foreign policy success. In October 1962 Kennedy was informed that aerial reconnaissance photography proved conclusively that the Soviets were building offensive missile bases in Cuba. Kennedy believed Soviet missiles in there would seriously diminish U.S. national security and increase the chances that the Soviets would try to blackmail the United States into concessions in other parts of the world. The president demanded that the bases be dismantled, but he rejected the option of an air strike against the sites in favor of a naval blockade of the island. The confrontation brought the United States and Soviet Union to the brink of nuclear war, but the Soviets ultimately backed down and agreed to remove the missiles.

Tensions decreased following the Cuban missile crisis, but the incident spurred the Soviets to undertake a military buildup that enabled them to achieve nuclear parity with the United States by the late 1960s. In 1963 Kennedy concluded an important arms control treaty with Britain, France, and the Soviet Union that banned nuclear tests in the atmosphere, in outer space, and under water.

Outside of superpower relations, Kennedy increased U.S. involvement in third-world development. In 1961 he established the Peace Corps, an agency that sent skilled volunteers overseas to assist people of underdeveloped countries. He also initiated the Alliance for Progress, an aid program aimed at developing the resources of Latin America.

In domestic policy, Kennedy made substantial progress in furthering the cause of civil rights. He advocated school desegregation, established a program to encourage registration of black voters, issued rules against discrimination in public housing built with federal funds, and appointed an unprecedented number of blacks to public office. Kennedy used federal troops several times to maintain order and enforce the law in the South during the civil rights movement. He sent federal troops and officials to oversee the integration of the University of Mississippi in 1962 and the University of Alabama in 1963. That year he proposed sweeping civil rights legislation, but it did not come to a vote during his lifetime.

Kennedy also tried unsuccessfully to convince Congress to cut taxes. The president's advisers convinced him that a tax cut would stimulate the economy and bring growth without large budget deficits or inflation. After Kennedy's death, President Lyndon Johnson was able to secure passage of the Kennedy tax cut and civil rights legislation.

During the fall of 1963 Kennedy made several trips around the country to build political support for his reelection bid the following year. In late November he scheduled a trip to Texas. While riding through Dallas in an open car on November 22, Kennedy was shot once in the head and once in the neck. He died at a nearby hospital without regaining consciousness. Vice President Lyndon Johnson was sworn in as president that afternoon.

Police quickly apprehended the alleged assassin, Lee Harvey Oswald, a former marine who had once renounced his U.S. citizenship and lived in the Soviet Union. Initial investigations concluded that Oswald had shot Kennedy with a rifle from a sixth-story window of the Texas School Book Depository building. Three days after the shooting, Oswald was murdered in front of millions of television viewers by Jack Ruby, owner of a Dallas nightclub. The Warren Commission, a seven-member panel appointed by President Johnson to investigate the assassination, determined that Oswald acted alone. But Oswald's violent death, his unknown motivation, the difficulty of a single marksman firing several accurate shots so quickly, and other peculiarities surrounding the assassination have fostered speculation that Oswald may have been part of a conspiracy.

Kennedy married Jacqueline Lee Bouvier on September 12, 1953. They had three children, but their youngest son, who had been born several weeks prematurely, died of a respiratory ailment two days after birth on August 9, 1963. Kennedy's children, Caroline and John, Jr., the first young children of a president living in the White House since the Theodore Roosevelt administration, were favorite subjects of the news media. Kennedy's widow, Jacqueline, married Greek shipping millionaire Aristotle Onassis on October 29, 1968.

Lyndon B. Johnson

Lyndon B. Johnson Library

Born: August 27, 1908; Stonewall, Texas
Party: Democratic
Term: November 22, 1963-January 20, 1969
Vice President: Hubert H. Humphrey
Died: January 22, 1973; San Antonio, Texas
Buried: Johnson City, Texas

Lyndon Baines Johnson was the oldest of the five children of Sam and Rebekah Johnson. Lyndon's father and mother were school teachers. His father and both his grandfathers had served in the Texas state legislature. At age five Lyndon moved with his family from Stonewall, Texas, to nearby Johnson City, a small town named for his grandfather. After graduating from high school in 1924, Lyndon traveled to California with a group of friends. He supported himself by working odd jobs, but after a year he hitchhiked his way back to Texas.

Johnson worked on a road gang for a year, then enrolled in Southwest Texas State Teachers College in San Marcos in 1927. He graduated in 1930 and taught high school in Houston for a year before Richard Kleberg, a newly elected member of the U.S. House of Representatives, asked Johnson to come to Washington, D.C., as an aide. Johnson worked for Kleberg from 1931 until 1935. During this period he learned firsthand about the legislative process and became an ardent supporter of President Franklin D. Roosevelt's New Deal policies. Johnson also studied law at Georgetown University during the 1934-1935 school year. He gave up his law studies and his job with Kleberg, however, when Roosevelt appointed him Texas director of the National Youth Administration in 1935. This program sought to help the nation's unemployed youth find employment and go to school.

In 1937 Johnson suddenly was given the opportunity to run for Congress when James P. Buchanan, the House member from Johnson's Texas district, died. Johnson entered the special election held to fill his seat and beat several candidates by campaigning on a pro-Roosevelt platform.

Johnson won reelection to the House in 1938 and 1940 but was narrowly defeated when he ran for a Senate seat in 1941. After the Japanese attacked Pearl Harbor, Johnson was the first House member to volunteer for active duty in the armed forces. He was commissioned as a lieutenant commander in the navy and sent to the South Pacific, where he undertook a fact-finding mission of the Australian combat zone. Johnson's service was short, however, because in July 1942 President Roosevelt ordered all members of Congress to leave the military and return to Washington.

Johnson served in the House until January 1949, when he took the Senate seat he had won the previous November. After just four years his Democratic colleagues elected him minority leader. In January 1955 he was elected majority leader when the Democrats took control of the Senate. Johnson suffered a severe heart attack in July 1955 but recovered fully. During his six years as majority leader, Johnson became known as one of the most skilled legislative leaders in congressional history. His ability to use flattery, coercion, and compromise to get legislation passed was a valuable asset when he became president.

Johnson wanted to run for president in 1960, but he was defeated for the Democratic nomination by Sen. John F. Kennedy of Massachusetts. Kennedy offered the vice presidency to Johnson, however, and the majority leader accepted. Kennedy and Johnson defeated Republicans Richard Nixon and Henry Cabot Lodge in a close election. Many political observers believed Kennedy might not have won without Johnson on the ticket. Johnson's presence was valuable in helping Kennedy win five southern states, including Texas.

Although Johnson was not an insider in the Kennedy administration, he undertook many diplomatic missions, and the president frequently sought his advice, especially on legislative matters. When Kennedy was shot while he rode in a motorcade through Dallas, Johnson was riding in a car behind the president. He followed the president's car to a hospital, where Kennedy was pronounced dead. Johnson then proceeded to the Dallas airport and boarded *Air Force One.* He decided to take the oath of office immediately, rather than wait until he returned to Washington. While the plane sat on the runway, federal Judge Sarah T. Hughes administered the oath of office to Johnson, who became the thirty-sixth president.

In the days following the assassination, Johnson declared his intention to carry out Kennedy's programs and asked Kennedy's cabinet to remain. Johnson, recognizing that public sentiment for the slain president improved his chances of enacting Kennedy's legislative program, vigorously lobbied Congress to pass a civil rights bill and a tax cut. Congress passed both bills in 1964. The tax cut succeeded in stimulating the economy, and the Civil Rights Act of 1964 protected black voting rights, established the Equal Employment Opportunity Commission, and forbade discrimination on account of race or sex by employers, places of public accommodation, and labor unions.

In 1964 Johnson ran for a presidential term of his own against Republican Sen. Barry Goldwater of Arizona. Many Americans were apprehensive that Goldwater's conservative positions were too extreme. Johnson outpolled Goldwater by more than 15 million votes and defeated him 486-52 in the electoral college.

Johnson regarded his landslide victory as a mandate to enact the "Great Society" social programs that he had outlined in his campaign. Johnson's Great Society was a comprehensive plan designed to fight poverty, ignorance, disease, and other social problems. During his second term he guided numerous bills through Congress establishing federal programs that provided expanded aid for medical care, housing, welfare, education, and urban renewal.

Although Johnson had hoped that his administration would be able to concentrate on his Great Society programs, the involvement of the United States in Southeast Asia soon came to dominate his presidency. The government in North Vietnam and guerrillas in South Vietnam were attempting to unify the country under Communist rule by defeating the South Vietnamese regime militarily. Since Vietnam had been split into North and South Vietnam in 1954, the United States had supported the South with weapons, U.S. military advisers, and economic aid. In 1965 Johnson increased the U.S. commitment by sending American combat troops to South Vietnam.

Johnson continued to escalate U.S. involvement in the war in response to Communist provocations and the inability of the South Vietnamese government to defend its country. The growing war diverted attention and dollars away from Johnson's domestic programs. Although many citizens supported the war, by 1966 college campuses had erupted in protest against it. Johnson hoped that each increase in U.S. troop strength and expansion of bombing targets would produce a breakthrough on the battlefield that would lead to a negotiated settlement preserving the independence and security of South Vietnam, but the Communists refused to give up their goal of reunification.

By early 1968 public opinion had swung decisively against the war and Johnson. He recognized that there was a good chance that he might not be renominated for president by his party. Sen. Eugene J. McCarthy of Minnesota and Sen. Robert F. Kennedy of New York, the late president's brother, were running for the Democratic presidential nomination on antiwar platforms and were receiving substantial support. On March 31, 1968, Johnson delivered a television address in which he announced a partial halt to U.S. air attacks on North Vietnam to emphasize the U.S. desire for peace. He then stunned the nation by saying that he would not seek or accept the Democratic nomination for president.

After leaving Washington in 1969, Johnson retired to his ranch near Johnson City, Texas. He wrote a book about his presidential years, *The Vantage Point*, which was published in 1971. On January 22, 1973, Johnson was stricken by a heart attack at his ranch and was pronounced dead on arrival at Brooke Army Medical Center in San Antonio.

Johnson married Claudia Alta Taylor, the daughter of a storekeeper and rancher, on November 17, 1934. During her tenure as first lady, Mrs. Johnson championed efforts to beautify America. Johnson and his wife, who was known as "Lady Bird," had two daughters, Lynda and Luci. Lynda married Charles Robb, who would later serve as governor of and then senator from Virginia.

Richard Nixon

Nixon Project, National Archives

Born: January 9, 1913; Yorba Linda, California
Party: Republican
Term: January 20, 1969-August 9, 1974
Vice Presidents: Spiro T. Agnew; Gerald R. Ford

Richard Milhous Nixon was the second of the five sons of Hannah and Francis Nixon, a lemon farmer. When Richard was nine he moved with his family from Yorba Linda to Whittier, California. There his father managed a combination gas station and general store, and Richard and his brothers attended public schools.

Nixon entered Whittier College in 1930. While at Whittier he played football, participated on the debate team, and was elected president of the student body. He graduated second in his class in 1934 with a degree in history. His academic excellence earned him a tuition scholarship to Duke University law school in Durham, North Carolina. He graduated in 1937 third in his class. He returned to California and joined the law firm of Wingert and Bewley in Whittier, eventually becoming a partner.

When the United States entered World War II in 1941 Nixon quit the law firm and went to Washington, D.C., to help the war effort. He worked briefly as a lawyer in the

Office of Price Administration before applying for a navy commission. He was given the rank of lieutenant (junior grade) and assigned to a navy air transport unit. He served for over a year in the Pacific before being reassigned to the states in 1944. Before leaving active duty in 1946, he had attained the rank of lieutenant commander.

Political Career

In 1945 Nixon was persuaded by a California Republican committee to run for Congress. He faced Democratic House member Jerry Voorhis, who had represented his California district for ten years. In a series of debates Nixon put Voorhis on the defensive by accusing him of being a socialist. Nixon won the election and was reelected in 1948.

In the House Nixon gained a national reputation as an anti-Communist crusader. In August 1948 he was appointed chairman of a subcommittee of the House Committee on Un-American Activities. His subcommittee investigated charges that several government employees were Communists, including Alger Hiss, a former State Department official. In testimony, Hiss denied that he was a Communist. President Truman and other top officials, including some Republicans, denounced the hearings. But Nixon pressed the investigation and found discrepancies that led to Hiss's conviction for perjury.

Nixon won a Senate seat in 1950. Democrats accused him of employing dirty campaign tactics, but his aggressive campaigning and his huge margin of victory impressed many Republican leaders. He became an early supporter of Gen. Dwight D. Eisenhower for the 1952 Republican presidential nomination and was chosen as the party's vice-presidential candidate when Eisenhower was nominated. In September 1952, however, Nixon's candidacy was jeopardized by a *New York Post* story that accused him of using secret funds provided by California business interests for personal expenses. Eisenhower refused to dismiss his running mate but said that Nixon would have to prove that he was "as clean as a hound's tooth." In an emotional televised speech on September 23 viewed by sixty million people, Nixon denied any wrongdoing and said he and his family lived simple lives without the benefit of many luxuries. The address became known as the "Checkers Speech" because, after admitting that he had accepted the gift of a dog his daughter had named "Checkers," he asserted that he would not give it back. The address brought an outpouring of support from the American people and saved Nixon's candidacy.

Dwight Eisenhower's status as a war hero and his pledge to find a settlement to the Korean War brought victory to the Republican ticket. Four years later Nixon was renominated for vice president, despite a "dump Nixon" movement started by several Republican leaders, and was reelected with President Eisenhower. As vice president, Nixon was more visible than many of his predecessors. He chaired several domestic policy committees and made numerous trips overseas, including a 1958 good-will tour of Latin America and a 1959 diplomatic visit to Moscow, where he engaged in a famous spontaneous debate with Soviet premier Nikita Khrushchev on the merits of capitalism and communism.

Nixon ran for president in 1960 and received the Republican nomination. He and his Democratic opponent, Sen. John F. Kennedy of Massachusetts, engaged in the first televised presidential debates in history. Nixon is considered to have lost the important first debate to Kennedy because he appeared tired on camera. Kennedy defeated Nixon by a slim 120,000-vote popular margin but won 303-219 in the electoral college.

After the defeat, Nixon returned to California to practice law. In 1962 he ran for governor but lost to Edmund G. Brown. Following the election he told reporters that they would not "have Richard Nixon to kick around anymore."

In 1963 he moved to New York City, where he joined a law firm. Nixon's political ambitions remained alive, however, and he continued to give speeches on foreign policy. He campaigned for Republican candidates in 1966 and maneuvered for the 1968 Republican presidential nomination. At the Republican national convention in Miami in 1968 he was nominated for president on the first ballot. Nixon promised to end the war in Vietnam and combat rising inflation. In an election that was almost as close as his 1960 loss, Nixon defeated his Democratic opponent, Vice President Hubert H. Humphrey, 301-191 in the electoral college.

Presidency

Nixon's first priority as president was achieving "peace with honor" in Vietnam. He proposed a plan to "Vietnamize" the war by providing the South Vietnamese military with upgraded training and weaponry, while slowly withdrawing U.S. troops from Indochina. Nixon believed that the South Vietnamese armed forces could be built into a force capable of defending their country from North Vietnamese aggression. While this slow withdrawal was taking place, Nixon ordered several controversial military operations, including an invasion of Cambodia in 1970, that increased domestic protests against the war. Nevertheless, the majority of Americans supported Nixon's slow withdrawal. During this period, Nixon's national security adviser, Henry Kissinger, conducted negotiations with the North Vietnamese on ending the war. In January 1973 the Nixon administration finally concluded an agreement that ended direct U.S. participation in the Vietnam War and provided for an exchange of prisoners. Nixon secretly promised South Vietnamese president Nguyen Van Thieu that the United States would not allow his regime to be overthrown by the Communists. These commitments would not be met. The Communists conquered the South in 1975 after Nixon had left office and Congress had placed strict limitations on U.S. military activities in Southeast Asia.

The most notable successes of the Nixon administration came in relations with China and the Soviet Union. In 1972 he became the first American president to travel to Communist China. His summit meeting with Chinese leaders signaled a new beginning for U.S.-Chinese relations, which had been hostile since the Communists came to power in 1949. In 1972 Nixon also became the first incumbent president to travel to Moscow. His summit with Soviet leader Leonid Brezhnev was the result of a relaxation of tensions between the superpowers known as détente. Brezhnev and Nixon signed agreements limiting nuclear weapons and antiballistic-missile systems at the Moscow summit. The Soviet leader returned Nixon's visit in June 1973, when he came to Washington, D.C., for a summit meeting.

Nixon's most significant domestic policy action was his imposition of wage and price controls on August 15, 1971. Nixon took this drastic measure to combat rising inflation that he thought might threaten his reelection chances in 1972. The controls initially slowed inflation, but their removal late in Nixon's presidency, combined with a jump in the price of oil caused by an Arab oil embargo, led to sharp increases in inflation. Prices rose 6.2 percent in 1973 and 11.0 percent in 1974.

The 1971 wage and price controls allowed Nixon to stimulate the economy in 1972 without fear that inflation would skyrocket. With unemployment falling, peace at hand in Vietnam, and the memory of Nixon's dramatic 1972 trips to China and the Soviet Union fresh in the minds of voters, the president was reelected in a landslide. Democratic challenger Sen. George McGovern of South Dakota won only Massachusetts and the District of Columbia.

Despite Nixon's overwhelming election victory, his second term soon became consumed by the Watergate scandal. On June 17, 1972, during the presidential campaign, five men with ties to the Committee for the Reelection of the President were arrested while breaking into the Democratic National Committee headquarters in the Watergate Hotel in Washington, D.C. Investigations of the burglary and the White House's attempt to cover up its connections to the burglars led to disclosure of numerous crimes and improprieties committed by members of the Nixon administration. Several top Nixon officials, including former attorney general John N. Mitchell, chief of staff H. R. Haldeman, and chief domestic adviser John D. Ehrlichman were indicted. Nixon claimed he was innocent of any wrongdoing, but evidence showed that he had participated in the coverup of illegal administration activities. In July 1974 the House Judiciary Committee recommended to the full House that Nixon be impeached for obstruction of justice, abuse of presidential powers, and contempt of Congress.

On August 9, 1974, Richard Nixon became the first president ever to resign from office. Vice President Gerald R. Ford became president. Nixon had chosen Ford to replace his first vice president, Spiro T. Agnew, who had resigned in 1973 because of a scandal unrelated to Watergate. Nixon did not have to face criminal proceedings, however, because on September 8 President Ford granted him a "full, free, and absolute pardon."

After leaving the presidency Nixon wrote extensively about his time in office and world affairs. Although he remained tainted by the Watergate scandal, he was regarded as an elder statesman by many Americans because of his successes in foreign policy. President Ronald Reagan and other officials occasionally asked his advice on dealing with the Soviets and other matters.

Nixon married Thelma Catherine ("Pat") Ryan, a high school typing teacher, on June 21, 1940. Nixon met her while acting in an amateur theater group in Whittier. The couple had two daughters, Patricia and Julie. Patricia married Edward Cox in a White House Rose Garden wedding in 1971. Julie married David Eisenhower, the grandson of President Dwight D. Eisenhower.

Gerald R. Ford

Gerald R. Ford Library

Gerald R. Ford

Born: July 14, 1913; Omaha, Nebraska
Party: Republican
Term: August 9, 1974-January 20, 1977
Vice President: Nelson A. Rockefeller

Gerald Rudolph Ford was the only child of Dorothy and Leslie King, a wool trader. Ford was originally named Leslie Lynch King, Jr., but his parents divorced when he was two. His mother gained custody of the child and moved to her family home in Grand Rapids, Michigan, where she married Gerald R. Ford in 1916. Ford, a paint salesman, adopted young Leslie, who was renamed Gerald Rudolph Ford, Jr. Dorothy and Gerald, Sr., had three sons in addition to Gerald, Jr.

Young Gerald attended public schools in Grand Rapids and became a star football player in high school. He worked in his stepfather's small paint factory and in a restaurant while growing up.

In 1931 Ford enrolled in the University of Michigan. There he studied economics and political science and played center on the football team. Ford played on two national championship teams while at Michigan and was named his team's most valuable player in 1934. He graduated in 1935 with a B average.

Several professional football teams wanted Ford to play for them, but he turned down the offers to become Yale University's boxing coach and an assistant on the football coaching staff. In 1938 he was admitted to Yale's law school. He continued to coach to support himself and finished his law degree in 1941.

Ford practiced law in Grand Rapids for less than a year before joining the navy early in 1942. He was commissioned as an ensign and assigned as a physical education instructor in North Carolina. Ford requested sea duty in 1943 and was transferred to the Pacific, where he became a gunnery officer on the light aircraft carrier *Monterey*. He fought in several major naval battles and achieved the rank of lieutenant commander by the end of the war.

Ford returned to his Grand Rapids law practice in late 1945. He became involved in local politics and decided to run for the U.S. House of Representatives in 1948. With the support of Michigan's powerful Republican senator, Arthur H. Vandenberg, Ford defeated an isolationist Republican incumbent, Bartel Jonkman, in the primary. Ford's district was solidly Republican, so he had little trouble defeating the Democratic candidate in the general election.

Ford won thirteen consecutive terms in the House, always with at least 60 percent of the vote. He turned down an opportunity to run for the Senate in 1952 because he wished to continue in the House where he was building seniority. Ford rose gradually to leadership positions among House Republicans. In 1963 he became chairman of the House Republican Conference, and in 1964 President Lyndon B. Johnson appointed him to the Warren Commission, which investigated the assassination of president John F. Kennedy. The following year, Ford challenged Charles A. Halleck of Indiana for the post of House minority leader. Ford was the choice of most younger Republicans in the House, and he was elected by a vote of 73-67 on January 4, 1965. He remained minority leader for nine years.

In 1973 Vice President Spiro T. Agnew resigned after being accused of income tax evasion and accepting bribes. When the vice presidency is vacant, under terms of the Twenty-fifth Amendment, ratified in 1967, the president nominates a new vice president who then must be confirmed by both houses of Congress. Because the credibility of the administration had been seriously damaged by Agnew and the unfolding Watergate scandal, President Richard Nixon wanted a vice president of unquestioned integrity. He chose Ford, who had developed a reputation for honesty during his years in the House. Nixon announced the appointment of Ford on October 12, 1973, in the East Room of the White House. After two months of scrutiny by Congress, Ford's nomination was approved 92-3 by the Senate and 387-35 by the House. He was sworn in as vice president on December 6.

The Watergate scandal forced President Nixon to resign on August 9, 1974. Later that day Ford became the first president to gain that office without being elected either president or vice president. He nominated former New York governor Nelson A. Rockefeller to be vice president. After a congressional inquiry into Rockefeller's finances, he was confirmed and sworn into office on December 19, 1974.

After taking the oath of office, Ford declared that "our long national nightmare is over." Ford's honest reputation, his friendly relations with Congress, and the public's desire for a return to normalcy led to an initial honeymoon with the American public. Seventy-one percent of respondents to a Gallup poll expressed their approval of the new president, while just 3 percent disapproved.

Ford's honeymoon, however, did not last long. On Sunday morning September 8 he announced to a small group of reporters that he was granting Richard Nixon an unconditional pardon. Ford was sensitive to speculation that he had promised to pardon Nixon in return for his nomination as vice president, so he took the unprecedented action of voluntarily going before a House Judiciary subcommittee to explain the pardon. Ford justified the highly unpopular pardon by saying it was needed to heal the political and social divisions caused by the Watergate scandal. Although no evidence of a secret bargain with Nixon surfaced, the pardon severely damaged Ford's popularity and his chances for election to a term of his own in 1976.

The most pressing domestic problem facing Ford during his term was persistent inflation and a sluggish economy. The president initially attempted to fight inflation by vetoing spending bills and encouraging the Federal Reserve to limit the growth of the money supply. In 1975, however, unemployment had become the more serious problem, and Ford compromised with Congress on a tax cut and a spending plan designed to stimulate the economy. Although inflation and unemployment remained at historically high levels, the nation experienced an economic recovery during late 1975 and 1976.

In foreign affairs Ford attempted to build on President Nixon's expansion of relations with the Soviet Union and China. Congressional restrictions on U.S. military involvement in Southeast Asia prevented Ford from providing military assistance to South Vietnam, which North Vietnam conquered in 1975. When the U.S. merchant ship *Mayaguez* was seized by Cambodia that year, however, he ordered marines to rescue the crew. The operation freed the crew, but forty-one of the rescuers were killed.

In September 1975 Ford was the target of two assassination attempts. On September 5 Lynette Fromme pointed a loaded pistol at the president as he moved through a crowd in Sacramento. A Secret Service agent disarmed her before she could fire. Fromme, a follower of mass murderer Charles Manson, was convicted of attempted assassination and sentenced to life imprisonment. Two weeks later, on September 22, political activist Sara Jane Moore fired a handgun at Ford as he was leaving a hotel in San Francisco. The bullet struck a taxi driver, who received a minor wound. Moore was apprehended by a bystander and two police officers before she could fire a second shot. She, too, was convicted of attempted assassination and sentenced to life in prison.

In early 1976 Ford appeared unlikely to retain the presidency. Even his party's nomination was in doubt, as conservative former California governor Ronald Reagan made a strong bid for the nomination. Ford collected enough delegates in the primaries, however, to narrowly defeat Reagan at the party's convention. In late 1975 Ford had asked Vice President Rockefeller to remove himself from consideration for the vice-presidential nomination in 1976. The president chose Sen. Robert J. Dole of Kansas as his running mate.

Jimmy Carter, the Democratic presidential candidate, was heavily favored to defeat Ford in the general election, but Ford made up ground during the fall campaign. The president, however, was defeated by Carter 297-240 in the electoral college.

After leaving the presidency, Ford retired to Palm Springs, California. In 1979 he published his autobiography, *A Time to Heal.* Ronald Reagan approached Ford about becoming his vice-presidential running mate in 1980, but the former president turned down Reagan's offer.

Ford married Betty Bloomer Warren, a thirty-year-old divorcee and former professional dancer, on October 15, 1948. The Fords had three sons and one daughter. After undergoing medical treatment for her own alcoholism in 1978, Mrs. Ford established the Betty Ford Center for Drug and Alcohol Rehabilitation.

Jimmy Carter

Jimmy Carter Library

Born: October 1, 1924; Plains, Georgia
Party: Democratic
Term: January 20, 1977-January 20, 1981
Vice President: Walter F. Mondale

James Earl Carter, Jr., was the oldest of the four children of James and Lillian Carter. From childhood on, James preferred to be called "Jimmy." His father was a storekeeper, farmer, and insurance broker who believed in segregation. His mother, a registered nurse who provided health care to her poor neighbors, held more progressive views on social and racial issues. Jimmy attended public schools and became a member of the First Baptist Church of Plains, Georgia. This evangelical church profoundly influenced Carter's development, although he did not adopt its conservative political philosophy in his political career.

After high school, Carter briefly attended Georgia Southwestern College in Americus, before being appointed to the U.S. Naval Academy. Carter graduated fifty-ninth in his class of 820 in 1946. His first assignment was as an instructor aboard battleships anchored at Norfolk, Virginia. In 1948 he applied and was accepted for submarine duty. After two and a half years as a crew member on a submarine in the Pacific, he was selected to work in the navy's nuclear submarine program. He became an engineering officer on the *Sea Wolf*, a new atomic submarine under construction. He also took classes in nuclear physics at Union College in Schenectady, New York. After his father died in 1953, however, he decided to retire from the navy.

Carter returned to his home in Plains, where he took over the family peanut farm. He gradually increased his land holdings and started several agriculture-related businesses, including a peanut-shelling plant and a farm-supply business. As Carter's wealth grew he became involved in local politics. He was appointed to the Sumter County School Board in 1955 and served there for seven years. He also served as chairman of the county hospital authority.

In 1962 Carter ran for the Georgia State senate. He lost a primary election but challenged the results because he had personally witnessed a ballot box being stuffed by a supporter of his opponent. His protest was upheld, and he became the Democratic nominee. He was elected and served two terms before declaring his candidacy for governor in 1966. Carter campaigned vigorously but lost in the primary election. In 1970 he surprised political observers by defeating former governor Carl E. Sanders in the Democratic primary, then went on to win the general election.

As governor, Carter openly denounced racial segregation and became a symbol of the "New South." He also reorganized the state government, supported measures to protect the environment, and opened government meetings to the public.

Georgia law prohibited a governor from running for two consecutive terms, so Carter set his sights on the presidency. New federal election laws that provided presidential candidates with campaign funds made it possible for Carter to run for president without the support of wealthy campaign contributors or Democratic party leaders. One month after leaving the Georgia governorship he announced that he was running for the 1976 Democratic presidential nomination.

Carter's candidacy was a longshot. He was an inexperienced, one-term governor from a southern state, who had to defeat several better-known Democrats for the nomination. Carter campaigned tirelessly during 1975 and 1976 and gained national attention by winning the Democratic caucuses in Iowa on January 19, 1976. When he won again in the New Hampshire primary on February 24, he suddenly became the front-runner. Before the June 1976 Democratic national convention in New York he had earned enough delegates in primaries and caucuses to lock up the nomination.

Carter emerged from the convention with a solid lead in public opinion polls over Republican incumbent Gerald R. Ford, whose candidacy suffered from several years of economic troubles and his pardon of former president Richard Nixon. This gap narrowed as the election approached, but Carter won 297-240 in the electoral college.

One of Carter's early presidential goals was to depomp the presidency and make it more responsive to the people. He underscored his intention by walking back to the White

House from the Capitol after his inauguration. Carter conducted frequent press conferences, held meetings in selected towns across the country, carried his own suitbag, and stopped the tradition of having a band play "Hail to the Chief" when he arrived at an occasion. The public liked Carter's open, informal style, but the president could not sustain his initial popularity.

In the late summer of 1977 journalists and government investigators disclosed that Carter's budget director, Bert Lance, had engaged in questionable financial practices during his career as a banker before he joined the Carter administration. For several months Carter defended Lance, a close personal friend, but on September 21, 1977, Lance resigned under the weight of the allegations. Lance was ultimately exonerated when a jury acquitted him of bank fraud charges in 1981, but the Lance affair appeared to contradict Carter's claim that he was holding the officials of his administration to a higher ethical standard than previous presidents had.

The state of the economy did even more damage to Carter's presidency. During the 1976 campaign Carter had criticized President Ford for the high inflation and unemployment the country was suffering. Under Carter, however, the economic situation worsened. Prices had risen 6.5 percent the year Carter took office, but they rose 11.3 percent in 1979 and 13.5 percent in 1980. Unemployment, which stood at about 7.7 percent in 1980 during Carter's reelection campaign, was also higher than most Americans would accept.

In foreign policy, Carter achieved several notable successes. He mediated negotiations between Prime Minister Menachem Begin of Israel and President Anwar Sadat of Egypt. The talks produced the 1979 Camp David Accords, which established peace between those two countries. He also formalized relations with the People's Republic of China on January 1, 1979, and secured Senate approval in 1978 of treaties transferring control of the Panama Canal to Panama on December 31, 1999.

The last two years of Carter's term, however, brought several foreign policy failures. On June 18, 1979, Carter and Soviet leader Leonid Brezhnev signed a treaty in Vienna to limit strategic nuclear weapons, but the Senate was hesitant to approve this agreement known as SALT II. In 1980 Carter withdrew the SALT II treaty after the Soviets invaded Afghanistan in December 1979 to prop up a pro-Communist government there. In response to the Soviet invasion, Carter also imposed a grain embargo and refused to allow the U.S. team to participate in the 1980 Olympic games in Moscow.

On November 4, 1979, Iranian militants stormed the U.S. embassy in Tehran, taking American diplomats and embassy personnel hostage. Carter's efforts to free the hostages, including an abortive helicopter raid in April 1980 in which eight soldiers died, proved ineffective. The hostage crisis dominated the last year of Carter's presidency, and the Iranians did not release the hostages until January 20, 1981, minutes after Carter had left office.

Despite these problems, Carter fought off a challenge for the 1980 Democratic presidential nomination from Sen. Edward M. Kennedy of Massachusetts. Carter's opponent in the general election was conservative former governor Ronald Reagan of California. Reagan defeated Carter 489-49 in the electoral college, with Carter winning only six states and the District of Columbia.

After leaving the presidency, Carter returned to his home in Plains. He lectured and wrote about world affairs and became involved in several voluntary service projects.

Carter married eighteen-year-old Rosalynn Smith, a close friend of his sister Ruth, on July 7, 1946. The Carters had three sons and one daughter. Several of Carter's relatives became national celebrities. His brother, Billy, capitalized on his brother's fame by making numerous public appearances and marketing "Billy Beer." In 1980 he was investigated by Congress for accepting $220,000 from the Libyan government to promote its interests in the United States. Billy was not charged with any crimes, but the affair was an embarrassment to his brother. Carter's mother, who had served in the Peace Corps while in her late sixties and early seventies, made several overseas journeys to represent her son at state funerals and other occasions.

Ronald Reagan

Pete Souza, The White House

Ronald Reagan

Born: February 6, 1911; Tampico, Illinois
Party: Republican
Term: January 20, 1981-January 20, 1989
Vice President: George Bush

Ronald Wilson Reagan was the youngest of the two sons of Nelle and John Reagan, a shoe salesman. When Ronald was nine the family moved from Tampico, Illinois, to nearby Dixon. He attended public schools and worked as a lifeguard at a swimming area in the Rock River. He enrolled in Eureka College near Peoria, Illinois, in 1928. There he played football and was elected president of the student body. He graduated in 1932 with a degree in economics and sociology.

After college Reagan worked as a sportscaster for radio stations in Davenport and Des Moines, Iowa. During a trip to California in 1937 to cover the spring training sessions of the Chicago Cubs baseball team, Reagan was persuaded by an agent for Warner Brothers movie studio to take a screen test. Reagan won the role of a small-town radio announcer in the movie *Love Is on the Air.* The movie began his twenty-eight-year acting career, during which he would make fifty-five movies, including *King's Row, The Hasty Heart*, and *Knute Rockne, All American.*

In 1942 Reagan entered the U.S. Army Air Corps as a second lieutenant and was assigned to make training films. He was discharged in 1945 with the rank of captain. After the war he continued to act in movies but devoted an increasing share of his time to move industry politics. In 1947 he was elected president of the Screen Actors Guild, a labor union representing Hollywood actors. He held that office until 1952 and was reelected to a one-year term in 1959. In October 1947 he appeared as a friendly witness before the House Un-American Activities Committee. He supported the blacklist created by Hollywood producers to deny work to actors and writers suspected of having Communist ties.

Until the late 1940s Reagan had been a staunch Deomcrat, supporting presidents Franklin Roosevelt and Harry Truman. In the late 1940s his political sympathies began to shift to the right as he became more concerned about Communist subversion. He voted for Dwight Eisenhower in 1952 and 1956 and Richard Nixon in 1960. From 1954 to 1962 he served as a spokesman for General Electric. In addition to hosting the television show "GE Theater," he made speeches to factory workers about the virtues of free enterprise and the dangers of too much government regulation. In 1962 Reagan finally abandoned the Democratic party and registered as a Republican.

Political Career

In 1964 Reagan made a televised campaign speech on behalf of Republican presidential candidate Barry Goldwater. The speech established Reagan as an articulate spokesman for the conservative wing of the Republican party and led California Republican leaders to ask him to run for governor. Reagan received the 1966 Republican nomination for governor after winning almost 65 percent of the vote in a five-candidate primary election. He then defeated incumbent Democrat Edmund G. Brown, who had beaten Richard Nixon four years before. Reagan was easily elected to a second term in 1970.

As governor, Reagan succeeded in passing a welfare reform bill that cut the number of Californians on welfare and increased the payments to the remaining welfare recipients. He campaigned for budget cuts and lower taxes, but early in his governorship he signed bills increasing taxes, because he claimed Brown had left the state in financial trouble. Reagan also harshly criticized student protesters on college campuses and cut state funds for higher education during his first term. During his second term, however, the cuts were restored, and by the time he left office state support for higher education was double what it had been when he was first elected.

Reagan received some support for the presidential nomination in 1968, but the party nominated Richard Nixon. Reagan backed President Nixon in 1972, but after declining to run for a third term as governor in 1974 he began campaigning for the presidency. Despite running against incumbent president Gerald R. Ford, Reagan came close to winning the 1976 Republican presidential nomination. Ford received 1,187 delegate votes to Reagan's 1,070 delegate votes at the Republican national convention in Kansas City. When Ford lost the election to Democrat Jimmy Carter, Reagan became the favorite to receive the Republican nomination in 1980.

During the next four years Reagan campaigned for Republican candidates and raised money for his 1980 campaign. He was upset in the Iowa caucuses by George Bush but recovered with a win in the New Hampshire primary. Reagan went on to win all but four of the remaining Republican primaries. He then defeated incumbent Jimmy Carter in the general election, 489 electoral votes to 49.

Presidency

On March 30, 1981, less than three months after he became president, Reagan was shot as he was leaving the Washington Hilton Hotel, where he had spoken to a group of union officials. The assailant, John Hinckley, Jr., fired six shots at Reagan with a .22-caliber pistol. One bullet struck Reagan in the chest and lodged in his left lung. A police officer, a Secret Service agent, and presidential press secretary James Brady were also wounded in the shooting. Reagan was rushed to a nearby hospital, where surgeons removed the bullet. Reagan became the first incumbent president to be wounded by an assailant and survive. Hinckley, who declared he shot the president to impress Jodie Foster, a Hollywood actress, was found not guilty by reason of insanity and placed in St. Elizabeth's Hospital in Washington, D.C.

During 1981 the Reagan administration focused on economic policy. The president pushed a large tax cut through Congress, along with increases in the defense budget and decreases in funding for many domestic programs. Reagan claimed that the tax cut would produce an economic boom that would lower unemployment while ultimately increasing tax revenues that would balance the federal budget. A severe recession that began in late 1981, however, increased unemployment to post-Depression highs.

In early 1983 the economy began to recover. Unlike economic recoveries during the 1970s, however, the expansion was not accompanied by high inflation. In the 1984 presidential election, with the economy prospering, Reagan overwhelmed his Democratic challenger, former vice president Walter F. Mondale, 525-13 in the electoral college. The economic expansion continued through the end of Reagan's term.

Although most Americans were satisfied with the economic recovery, critics charged that it was flawed because low-income groups had fared poorly during the Reagan years, the U.S. trade position had deteriorated, and the federal government had built up huge budget deficits. The last of these problems was particularly troublesome to Reagan, because he had promised in his 1980 campaign to balance the federal budget. Instead, Reagan's military buildup and tax cut had exacerbated the nation's budget deficit problem. In 1981 when Reagan entered office, the budget deficit was $78.9 billion. Two years later it had more than doubled to $207.8 billion, and in 1986 it stood at

$221.2 billion. The national debt had risen from a little over one trillion dollars in 1981 to more than two trillion dollars in 1986. Reagan and the Democratic Congress addressed the debt problem by enacting the Gramm-Rudman-Hollings amendment in 1985. The measure mandated across-the-board spending cuts if the president and Congress could not agree on budget reductions that would reduce the deficit to specified yearly targets.

In foreign affairs, the first five years of Reagan's presidency were characterized by hard-line anti-Communist rhetoric and efforts to block Communist expansion and even overturn pro-Communist governments in the third world. Reagan supported military funding to the anti-Communist Nicaraguan rebels known as the "contras," who were fighting to overthrow the Marxist regime in their country. He also supported aid to anti-Communist guerrillas fighting in Angola and Cambodia, and Afghan rebels fighting Soviet forces that had invaded Afghanistan in 1979. In 1983 Reagan dispatched U.S. troops to Grenada to overthrow the Marxist government and bring stability to the tiny Caribbean island.

With the rise of Mikhail Gorbachev as the leader of the Soviet Union in 1985, however, the president softened his anti-Communist rhetoric and began developing a working relationship with the Soviet leader. During his last three years in office, Reagan held five summits with Gorbachev and signed a treaty banning intermediate nuclear missiles in Europe.

The Reagan administration also took actions to strike back at terrorists in the Middle East, including a 1986 bombing raid on Libya in retaliation for alleged Libyan support for a terrorist bombing of a Berlin nightclub. Reagan's tough antiterrorist posture was undercut late in 1986 when the administration disclosed that the president had approved arms sales to Iran that appeared to be aimed at securing the release of American hostages in Lebanon held by pro-Iranian extremists. Reagan denied that the sale was an arms-for-hostages swap, which would have contradicted his policy of not negotiating with terrorists, but the evidence suggested otherwise.

Investigations revealed that members of the president's National Security Council staff had used the arms sales profits to aid the contras, despite a congressional prohibition then in force against U.S. aid to the contras. Although investigators found no evidence that Reagan had been aware of the diversion of funds to the contras, the scandal led to the resignation of several administration officials. The Tower Commission, appointed by the president to investigate the Iran-contra affair, issued a report in 1987 that was highly critical of the president's detached style of management, which allowed his subordinates to operate without his knowledge.

Despite the Iran-contra affair, Reagan remained one of the most popular presidents of the twentieth century. After Vice President George Bush won the Republican presidential nomination in 1988, Reagan campaigned hard for him. Bush easily defeated Gov. Michael Dukakis of Massachusetts in the November election. When Reagan's term ended, he returned to his home in Bel Air, California, promising to write his memoirs and speak frequently in support of Republican causes and candidates.

Reagan married Jane Wyman, an actress, on January 24, 1940. The couple had one daughter and adopted a son before divorcing in 1948. Reagan then married another actress, Nancy Davis, on March 4, 1952. They had one daughter and one son.

George Bush

The White House

Born: June 12, 1924; Milton, Massachusetts
Party: Republican
Term: January 20, 1989—
Vice President: Dan Quayle

George Herbert Walker Bush was the second of the five children of Prescott and Dorothy Bush. George's father was a wealthy Wall Street banker who represented Connecticut in the U.S. Senate from 1952 to 1963.

George grew up in Greenwich, Connecticut, where he attended a private elementary school before enrolling in the Phillips Academy in Andover, Massachusetts. At this exclusive prep school he excelled in athletics and academics and was elected president of his senior class. He graduated in 1942 and joined the navy, becoming the youngest bomber pilot in that branch of the service.

On September 22, 1944, while flying a mission from the light aircraft carrier *San Jacinto,* Bush was shot down near the Japanese-held island of Chichi Jima. He parachuted safely into the Pacific Ocean and after four hours was rescued by a submarine. Bush received the Distinguished Flying Cross. In December 1944 he was reassigned as a naval flight instructor in Virginia, where he remained until his discharge in September 1945.

After the war Bush enrolled in Yale University and majored in economics. He was also captain of Yale's baseball team, which was beaten in the finals of the College World Series his junior and senior years. He graduated Phi Beta Kappa in 1948.

Bush then moved to Texas, where he gradually made a small fortune in the oil business. He ran for the Senate in 1964 against incumbent Ralph Yarborough, a Democrat. Although he received 200,000 more votes in Texas than Republican presidential nominee Barry Goldwater, Bush lost the election.

In 1966 when reapportionment gave Houston another House seat, Bush ran for it and won. He served on the Ways and Means Committee and became an outspoken supporter of Richard Nixon. Bush was reelected to the House in 1968 when Nixon captured the presidency. Two years later Bush followed Nixon's advice and abandoned his safe House seat to run for the Senate. He was defeated by conservative Democrat Lloyd Bentsen, who would be the Democratic vice-presidential nominee in 1988 on the ticket opposing Bush.

After the 1970 election Nixon appointed Bush ambassador to the United Nations. When Nixon was reelected in 1972, he asked Bush to leave the UN to take over as chair of the Republican National Committee. Bush served in that post during the difficult days of the Watergate scandal. At first he vigorously defended President Nixon. In 1974, however, as the evidence against Nixon mounted, he privately expressed doubts about the president's innocence. Nevertheless, Bush avoided public criticism of the president and concentrated on maintaining Republican party strength despite the president's troubles. On August 7, 1974, Bush wrote a letter asking Nixon to resign, which the president did two days later.

When Vice President Gerald R. Ford succeeded to the presidency upon Nixon's resignation, Bush was a leading candidate to fill the vice-presidential vacancy. Bush wanted the job, but he was bypassed in favor of Gov. Nelson A. Rockefeller of New York. Ford tried to make up the disappointment to Bush by offering him the ambassadorship to Britain or France. Bush chose, however, to take the post of chief of the U.S. Liaison Office in the People's Republic of China.

In 1975 Ford called Bush back to the United States to become director of the Central Intelligence Agency. As CIA chief, Bush's primary goal was restoring the reputation of the agency, which had been damaged by revelations of its illegal and unauthorized activities during the 1970s, including assassination plots against foreign officials and spying on members of the domestic antiwar movement. Bush won bipartisan praise for his efforts to repair the agency's morale and integrity.

After being replaced as CIA director when Democrat Jimmy Carter became president in 1977, Bush returned to Houston to become chairman of the First International Bank. He stayed active in politics by campaigning for Republican candidates before the 1978 midterm election. On January 5, 1979, he formed the "George Bush for President Committee" and declared his intention to seek the presidency. He campaigned full-time during 1979 and established himself as the leading challenger to Republican front-runner Ronald Reagan, when he won the Iowa caucuses on January 21, 1980. During the primary campaign Bush attacked Reagan as an ultraconservative and called his economic proposals "voodoo economics." Reagan, however, prevailed in the primaries and secured enough delegates for the nomination before the Republican national convention in Detroit in July 1980.

At the convention Reagan's team approached former president Ford about running for vice president. When Ford declined, they asked Bush to be the vice-presidential nominee in an attempt to unify the party. Bush accepted, and the Republican ticket defeated President Jimmy Carter and Vice President Walter F. Mondale in a landslide.

Despite Bush's differences with Reagan during the campaign, as vice president he was extremely loyal to the president. When Reagan was wounded by an assailant in 1981, Bush emphasized that Reagan was still president and exerted leadership over the administration in the president's absence.

Bush was frequently called upon to make diplomatic trips overseas. While vice president he visited more than seventy countries. His frequent attendance at state funerals led him to joke that his motto was "I'm George Bush. You die, I fly." Reagan and Bush won a second term in 1984 by easily defeating the Democratic ticket of Walter F. Mondale and Geraldine Ferraro.

Late in Reagan's second term Bush launched his campaign for the presidency. Despite his status as a two-term vice president, he was challenged for the nomination by Senate Minority Leader Robert Dole of Kansas and several other candidates. Dole defeated Bush in the Iowa caucuses, as Bush had defeated Reagan eight years before. In the first primary, in New Hampshire, however, Bush scored a decisive victory and secured the nomination before the end of the primary season.

Bush faced Gov. Michael S. Dukakis of Massachusetts in the general election. President Reagan, who had remained neutral during the primary season, campaigned hard for his vice president. Bush attacked his opponent for liberal policies that Bush said were out of touch with American sentiments, and he promised to continue Ronald Reagan's economic policies and diplomacy with the Soviet Union. Despite the presence of massive budget deficits, Bush also pledged not to raise taxes. Bush overcame speculation about his role in the Reagan administration's Iran-contra affair and criticism of Dan Quayle, his vice-presidential choice, to defeat Dukakis. Bush did not match Reagan's landslide victory of 1984, but he won the election decisively in the electoral college, 426-112.

Bush was praised for his conciliatory gestures toward Congress and Democratic leaders during the transition period. His appointments were also generally well received, except for his defense secretary nominee, former senator John Tower of Texas. After a contentious confirmation battle, the Senate handed Bush the first defeat of his presidency by rejecting Tower's appointment 53-47 on March 9, 1989.

Bush married nineteen-year-old Barbara Pierce, the daughter of a prominent magazine publisher, on January 6, 1945. They had four sons and two daughters. Their daughter Robin died from leukemia in 1953.

Biographies of the Vice Presidents

The vice presidency often has been ridiculed, sometimes by vice presidents themselves, as an insignificant office. Nevertheless, the importance of the vice presidency is obvious given that fourteen vice presidents have become president. Nine succeeded to the presidency after the death or resignation of the incumbent; the five others were elected in their own right.

The biographies of the thirty vice presidents who never became president follow. Although their names are obscure today, they were among the most powerful politicians—and fascinating characters—of their times.

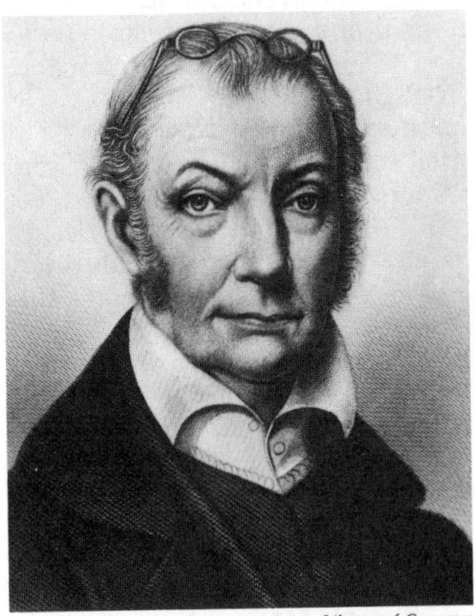

Library of Congress

Aaron Burr

Born: February 6, 1756; Newark, New Jersey
Party: Democratic-Republican
Term: March 4, 1801-March 4, 1805
President: Thomas Jefferson
Died: September 14, 1836; Staten Island, New York
Buried: Princeton, New Jersey

Aaron Burr was born into a family of prominent ministers, headed by his grandfather, the famous theologian and preacher Jonathan Edwards. Burr's father, Rev. Aaron Burr, was the cofounder and second president of Princeton University. His uncle, Timothy Edwards, was a clergyman as well. Shortly after Aaron's birth his parents died, and he and his sister were left in the custody of his uncle.

Burr was only thirteen when he entered Princeton University as a sophomore. He graduated with honors three years later in 1772 and briefly studied theology before abandoning it for a law career. But he had barely begun his legal studies when he received a commission in the army in 1775. Burr joined Gen. George Washington's army at Cambridge, Massachusetts, and served as a captain in Gen. Benedict Arnold's force, which failed to capture Quebec. He then became a member of General Washington's staff until the mutual dislike of the two men resulted in Burr's transfer to the staff of Gen. Israel Putnam. After Burr's promotion to lieutenant colonel he commanded a regiment that fought in the battle of Monmouth (New Jersey) in 1778. The following year he resigned his commission because of illness.

Burr studied law in Albany, New York, until 1782, when he was admitted to the bar. After practicing law in New York City, he was elected to the New York State legislature in 1784. New York governor George Clinton appointed Burr the state's attorney general in 1789, and two years later Burr was elected to the U.S. Senate.

Burr served in the Senate until 1797, then returned to New York. He won a seat in the New York legislature a year later and helped the Democratic-Republican party take control of that body through his organizational work. Burr's reputation for political intrigue and romantic affairs had made him a controversial figure, but his intelligence, charm, and service to the Democratic-Republicans led to his nomination for vice president by that party in 1800.

The electoral procedure in effect through the 1800 election dictated that the candidate who received the second highest number of electoral votes for president became vice president. Each elector voted for two candidates, with no distinction made between a vote for president and a vote for vice president. Although the parties distinguished between their presidential and vice-presidential candidates, nothing prevented a vice-presidential candidate from being elected president if that candidate received more electoral votes than his presidential running mate.

In the election of 1800 this voting procedure resulted in a tie between the Democratic-Republican presidential candidate, Thomas Jefferson, and Burr, his vice-presidential running mate. Both men received seventy-three electoral votes, and Burr refused to concede the election. The

By Daniel C. Diller

responsibility for selecting a president then fell to the House of Representatives, where the Federalists had a majority. After a week and thirty-six ballots, the weary representatives elected Jefferson president. (The confusion of the 1800 election led to the Twelfth Amendment to the Constitution, which was ratified in 1804; it separated the voting for president and vice president.) Predictably, Jefferson did not include Burr in the deliberations of his administration.

Because of Alexander Hamilton's historic reputation as one of the most important Founders of the United States, the romantic mystique that surrounds the antiquated practice of dueling, and the incomprehensibility of a vice president committing murder while in office, Burr will always be remembered as the man who shot and killed Hamilton in a duel on July 11, 1804, at Weehawken, New Jersey. The duel occurred when Burr challenged Hamilton for making derogatory remarks about him during the 1804 New York gubernatorial campaign, which Burr lost to Hamilton's candidate. After Burr mortally wounded Hamilton he fled south to avoid the warrants that had been issued for his arrest in New York and New Jersey. Because federal law did not yet provide for the extradition of criminals from the District of Columbia, Burr returned to the capital. Incredibly, he resumed his duties as presiding officer of the Senate as if nothing had happened.

Even before he left office in 1805 Burr had begun to formulate a treasonous conspiracy. Although the details of Burr's plot are unclear, it is known that he hoped to incite a rebellion in the western regions of the United States, conquer Mexico, and then establish a vast western empire with New Orleans as its capital. While vice president he had proposed to the British ambassador in Washington that he lead a revolt in the western United States in return for £110,000. The offer was rejected, but Burr raised money through other means. He assembled a small force in the summer of 1806 and was preparing to move against Mexico when one of his coconspirators, James Wilkinson, exposed the plot. Burr eventually was arrested and tried for treason in 1807 with Chief Justice John Marshall personally presiding over the case. President Jefferson pushed for a conviction, but, despite evidence that he had planned the conspiracy, Burr was acquitted because he had not yet committed an overt act of treason.

Even after his trial Burr continued to plot ways to gain an empire. In Europe he tried unsuccessfully to convince Napoleon to help him conquer Florida. After living in Europe for four years he returned to the United States in 1812 to be with his only daughter, Theodosia, who was married to Joseph Alston, the governor of South Carolina. She sailed from South Carolina to meet him in New York, but her ship was lost at sea. Burr then settled in New York City and spent the rest of his years practicing law.

Burr had married Theodosia's mother, Theodosia Prevost, in 1782; she died in 1794. In 1833 Burr married Eliza Jumel, a wealthy widow twenty years his junior. She was granted a divorce the day Burr died.

Library of Congress

George Clinton

Born: July 26, 1739; Little Britain, New York
Party: Democratic-Republican
Term: March 4, 1805-April 20, 1812
Presidents: Thomas Jefferson; James Madison
Died: April 20, 1812; Washington, D.C.
Buried: Kingston, New York

Unlike the majority of his contemporaries who reached high office, George Clinton did not have the advantage of being born into a wealthy family. His father was a poor Irish immigrant who could not afford to send George to college. Thus, George went to sea when he was eighteen but returned home after a year. He then fought in the French and Indian War as a lieutenant and gained combat experience during the campaign of 1760 in which the British and their colonial allies captured Montreal.

After the war Clinton studied law in New York City and eventually was admitted to the bar. He then practiced law in his native Ulster County, New York, and in 1765 became district attorney. In 1768 Clinton began his rise in politics when he was elected to the New York assembly. He served in that body until 1775, when he was elected to the Second Continental Congress.

As a prominent public figure with military experience, Clinton was appointed a brigadier general in the New York militia. Gen. George Washington then ordered him to lead his troops in defense of New York in the summer of 1776. Consequently, he was absent from the Continental Congress when the Declaration of Independence was signed, but he had advocated independence before his departure.

Although Clinton's forces were unable to defend Fort Montgomery in the highlands of the Hudson River from advancing British forces under Sir Henry Clinton, the stiff resistance shown by the New York militia enhanced George Clinton's reputation despite his mediocre military skills. In March 1777 Congress granted him the rank of brigadier general in the Continental army to go along with his generalship in the New York militia. He gave up his commissions, however, when he was chosen governor of New York. He assumed the office on July 30, 1777, and served six successive terms until 1795. During the revolutionary war Governor Clinton became known for his harsh treatment of New York's loyalists.

Clinton's power within his home state made him a natural opponent of the new federal Constitution, which, if approved, would limit state sovereignty and slice into his personal power. As the presiding officer at New York's ratifying convention, he did his best to prevent ratification, but the Constitution won approval, 30-27.

Clinton's preeminence in New York gubernatorial elections was not challenged until 1792, when he narrowly defeated John Jay only after he had the votes of three counties invalidated on a technicality. Clinton recognized that his popularity in New York had slipped, and he declined to run for reelection in 1795. Six years later, however, he won another three-year term as governor with the support of his powerful nephew DeWitt Clinton, who manipulated his aging uncle during his last term in office.

Clinton's nomination as the Democratic-Republican candidate for vice president in 1804 stemmed from the new Twelfth Amendment, which linked the fates of a party's presidential and vice-presidential candidates. Vice-presidential nominees were chosen according to their ability to attract votes for their running mates. Although at age sixty-five Clinton's physical and mental capacities were declining, he could still deliver many votes for the Democratic-Republicans in his native New York. As a northerner he also would provide geographic balance to the ticket with Virginian Thomas Jefferson. After Aaron Burr the Democratic-Republicans desired a noncontroversial figure like Clinton for the number two spot. Clinton, who had designs on the presidency, accepted the vice-presidential nomination in the hope that it would be a stepping-stone to the higher office. The Jefferson-Clinton ticket won easily over Federalists Charles Cotesworth Pinckney and Rufus King.

Clinton was regarded unanimously as a poor presiding officer of the Senate. His forgetfulness and inattention to detail caused much parliamentary confusion. He complained that his duties were tiresome, and he spent an increasing proportion of his time at his home in New York rather than at the capital.

Clinton still desired the presidency in 1808, but he was widely regarded as senile. Thus, he had little chance of beating out Jefferson's chosen successor, James Madison, for the Democratic-Republican nomination. Even though Clinton declared his availability for the presidency, the party caucus as expected selected Madison as its nominee, and Clinton bitterly accepted the consolation of yet another vice-presidential nomination. Madison and Clinton were easily elected, but the victory did not soften the vice president's hard feelings. He refused to attend Madison's inauguration and openly opposed the president's policies.

In 1811 Clinton got his chance to strike a blow against Madison and other Democratic-Republican leaders whom he believed had denied him the presidential nomination that he deserved. When the vote on the bill to recharter the Bank of the United States, which Madison favored, was tied in the Senate, Clinton, as vice president, cast the deciding vote against rechartering the bank. On April 20, 1812, at the age of seventy-two, Clinton became the first vice president to die in office.

Clinton married Cornelia Tappan, who was a member of a politically powerful family in New York's Ulster County, on February 7, 1770. They had six children. Cornelia died in 1800, before her husband became vice president.

Library of Congress

Elbridge Gerry

Born: July 17, 1744; Marblehead, Massachusetts
Party: Democratic-Republican
Term: March 4, 1813-November 23, 1814
President: James Madison
Died: November 23, 1914; Washington, D.C.
Buried: Washington, D.C.

Elbridge Gerry was the son of a prosperous Massachusetts merchant. Upon graduating from Harvard in 1752, he entered his father's lucrative importing and shipping business. His resentment of British efforts to tax American commerce drew him into revolutionary circles. Gerry was elected to the General Court of Massachusetts in 1772 and subsequently the Massachusetts Provincial Congress. From his position in this body he managed supply procurement operations for his state's patriot forces in the early days of the American Revolution.

From 1776 to 1781 Gerry served in the Continental Congress. An influential member of its treasury committee, he put his supply procurement experience to use in the service of the Continental Army. He also represented Massachusetts in Congress under the Articles of Confederation from 1783-1785. Gerry signed both the Declaration of Independence and the Articles of Confederation. At the Constitutional Convention he advocated strengthening the federal government. He refused, however, to endorse the document that the convention eventually produced because he thought it gave the federal government too much power over the states. After the Constitution was adopted by Massachusetts, Gerry put his reservations aside and supported the document. He was elected to two terms in the House of Representatives (1789-1793).

In 1797 President Adams sent Gerry, along with John Marshall and Charles C. Pinckney, to France to negotiate a treaty that would head off war between France and the United States. The talks were abandoned by the American side when the French representatives demanded as preconditions to negotiations a bribe for French Foreign Minister Talleyrand, a loan for the French government, and an apology for Adams's recent criticisms. Marshall and Pinckney, who were known to be unsympathetic toward France, left for home. But Gerry stayed in Paris until the following year in the vain hope that his pro-French reputation might create an opening with the French that could lead to a treaty. The bribery incident, which came to be known as the "XYZ affair," after the French representatives who were referred to as "X,Y, and Z" in documents released by Adams, outraged the American public and ushered in several years of undeclared naval warfare with France. Gerry's Federalist opponents accused him of conducting an accommodating diplomacy with an enemy nation, but his reports of France's desire to avoid war contributed to Adams's decision to send another negotiating team to France in 1799.

When Gerry returned to the United States, he ran for the governorship of Massachusetts four consecutive years (1800-1803) without winning. His prospects for election were hampered by his position as a Democratic-Republican in a traditionally Federalist state. Finally, in 1810 and 1811, Gerry was elected to consecutive terms as governor.

Before the Massachusetts elections of 1812, Gerry left his most indelible mark on U.S. political culture. He signed a bill that restructured the senatorial districts of his state so that his party, the Democratic-Republicans, would be likely to win more seats than their actual numbers warranted. Because the map of the new districts was perceived to resemble the outline of a salamander, the redistricting tactic was dubbed a "gerrymander." Gerry had not sponsored the bill, but Federalists were quick to blame him for it. That year he failed to win reelection to his third term as governor.

Despite Gerry's advanced age and his defeat in his home state, his political career was not over. In 1812 the Democratic-Republicans were searching for a northerner to balance their ticket with President James Madison. After DeWitt Clinton of New York and John Langdon of New Hampshire refused the second spot, the party turned to Gerry. He and Madison defeated DeWitt Clinton and Jared Ingersoll, who had formed a coalition of Federalists and maverick Democratic-Republicans.

Gerry fulfilled his constitutional duty of presiding over the Senate despite his weakening health. During his vice presidency he was an outspoken proponent of the War of 1812. He narrowly missed becoming president in 1813 when Madison was stricken by a severe fever. Madison recovered and lived twenty-three years longer, but Gerry died in 1814 while still in office.

Gerry married Ann Thompson, the twenty-year-old daughter of a New York merchant, on January 12, 1786. The couple had ten children. Because of Ann's poor health, she did not move to Washington, D.C., with her husband when he became vice president, but, ironically, she lived thirty-five years after his death.

Library of Congress

Daniel D. Tompkins

Born: June 21, 1774; Fox Meadows (now Scarsdale), New York
Party: Democratic-Republican
Term: March 4, 1817-March 4, 1825
President: James Monroe
Died: June 11, 1825; Tompkinsville, Staten Island, New York
Buried: New York City

Daniel D. Tompkins was born into a family of wealthy farmers in Westchester County, New York. His parents did not give him a middle name, but he added a middle initial to distinguish himself from another boy with the same name. He graduated from Columbia College in 1795 and was admitted to the bar two years later.

Tompkins enjoyed a brilliant early career in New York State politics that was sponsored by New York political boss DeWitt Clinton; Clinton eventually became his political enemy, however. In 1803 Tompkins won a seat in the New York State Assembly. The following year he was elected to the U.S. House of Representatives, but he resigned after he was appointed to the New York Supreme Court. He occupied that post until he was elected governor in 1807. He remained New York's chief executive until his rise to the vice presidency in 1817.

As governor, Tompkins was one of the few political leaders in the Northeast who supported the War of 1812. He borrowed millions of dollars and oversaw the disbursement of funds to pay troops and buy supplies. During his ten years as New York's chief executive, Tompkins also worked for prison reform, better treatment of Indians, and the abolition of slavery in his state. Following his lead, the state legislature passed a bill in 1817 that outlawed slavery as of 1827. In 1814 President James Madison offered Tompkins the post of secretary of state, but he declined the appointment to remain governor of New York.

Tompkins sought the presidential nomination in 1816, but he was forced to settle for the vice presidency because Madison supported James Monroe and Tompkins was not well known outside New York. Like his predecessors George Clinton and Elbridge Gerry, Tompkins provided the Democratic-Republican ticket with geographic balance. Unlike Clinton and Gerry, however, Tompkins had the advantage of being a youthful forty-two years old.

Tompkins's term as vice president was dominated by his fight against charges that he had mismanaged New

York finances while he was governor during the war. Tompkins had indeed failed to keep accurate, detailed records of wartime expenditures and had mixed his personal finances with those of the state. Accounts showed that he owed New York $120,000. In April 1819 the state legislature voted to cancel the vice president's debt by granting him a commission on money he had raised during the war, but Tompkins insisted on a higher commission that would have required the state to pay him a sum in addition to forgiving the debt. His influence in the New York legislature, however, had been damaged by his decision to run for governor against DeWitt Clinton in 1820. Tompkins lost the election and incurred the enmity of Clinton, who snuffed out a movement in the Assembly to give Tompkins the money he claimed. Under Clinton's direction the state filed a suit against the vice president to recover the debt.

Despite the financial scandal hanging over his head, Tompkins was again chosen by the Democratic-Republican party as its candidate for vice president in 1820. Monroe and Tompkins won easily, with only one electoral college vote cast against them. Throughout his second term Tompkins remained preoccupied with his debt problem and devoted little time to the duties of his office. He declined to travel to the capital for the inauguration and was instead given the oath of office in a private ceremony in New York. In 1823, at Tompkins's request, the Senate chose a president pro tempore to preside over its deliberations; Tompkins never again led that body. When his term ended in 1825, he made no attempt to run for another national or state office. Instead, he continued to work to exonerate himself. Weakened by the stress of the scandal and his heavy drinking, he died a year later.

After Tompkins's death, audits finally revealed that New York actually owed him money. His descendants were paid $92,000. In 1827 the law abolishing slavery that had been signed by Tompkins ten years before went into effect. To honor the governor for his efforts to end slavery in the state, a square in New York City was renamed after him.

Tompkins married Hannah Minthorne, a member of a prominent New York family, around 1797. They had eight children.

National Portrait Gallery

John C. Calhoun

Born: March 18, 1782; Abbeville District, South Carolina
Party: Democratic-Republican
Term: March 4, 1825-December 28, 1832
Presidents: John Quincy Adams; Andrew Jackson
Died: March 31, 1850; Washington, D.C.
Buried: Charleston, South Carolina

John Caldwell Calhoun hailed from a family of wealthy and prestigious South Carolina planters. He received his early education at a school in Georgia and entered Yale University in 1802. After graduating in 1804 he studied law in Litchfield, Connecticut, and Abbeville, South Carolina. He was admitted to the South Carolina bar in 1807 and opened a law office in Abbeville. The following year he won a seat in the state legislature, and in 1811 he was elected to the U.S. House of Representatives as a Jeffersonian Democrat.

During the War of 1812 Calhoun gained national fame as a leader of the War Hawks, a group of expansionist members of Congress who helped push the United States toward war with the British. He served three terms in the House and chaired the Foreign Relations Committee. In 1817 President James Monroe appointed Calhoun secretary of war, a post that he held throughout Monroe's presidency.

Calhoun sought the presidency in 1824, but he received less support for the office than either John Quincy Adams or Andrew Jackson. Thus, he gave up his immediate presidential aspirations and maneuvered for the vice presidency. He courted Jackson and Adams and received the support of both men for his vice-presidential candidacy. Adams was elected president by the House of Representatives after neither he nor Jackson received a majority of electoral votes; Calhoun's fence-straddling strategy thus paid off.

Calhoun's quest for the vice presidency was not motivated primarily by his ambition to serve in that office. He saw the post as a stepping-stone to the presidency. Nevertheless, the talented former House member devoted himself to his duties as the presiding officer of the Senate. In this capacity he worked to foil the programs of President Adams, with whom he shared few political goals. The two men vented their antagonism toward one another through letters published in newspapers under pseudonyms.

Calhoun endured a political scandal during his first

term as vice president. It was discovered that, while Calhoun had served as secretary of war under James Monroe, an assistant had awarded a $450,000 military construction contract to the assistant's brother-in-law. Calhoun was accused of receiving a cut of the profits from the deal. After declaring his innocence, the vice president asked the House of Representatives to investigate the matter, and he took a temporary leave of absence while a seven-member committee examined the charges. Six weeks later the committee exonerated Calhoun of any misconduct. The vice president confidently resumed his duties, but the scandal had damaged his reputation.

By 1828 Calhoun's break with John Quincy Adams was complete. The vice president threw his support behind Democratic presidential candidate Andrew Jackson, who in turn backed Calhoun's nomination for a second vice-presidential term. The Jackson-Calhoun ticket easily defeated Adams and Richard Rush of Pennsylvania.

Like John Quincy Adams, Jackson soon became disaffected with his vice president. The split between the two men was first opened in early 1829 not by a political dispute, but by the refusal of Calhoun's wife to accept the wife of Secretary of War John H. Eaton into Washington society. Eaton had met his wife, Peggy O'Neale Timberlake, while he was living in a tavern owned by Peggy and her first husband. Eaton had carried on an affair with Mrs. Timberlake, and, after Mr. Timberlake's death at sea, Eaton followed the advice of his close friend Andrew Jackson and married her. When the wives of prominent politicians in Washington led by Calhoun's wife, Floride, refused to accept Mrs. Eaton as an equal, Jackson blamed his vice president.

The Eaton affair was a small matter compared to Calhoun's increasingly radical opinions on states' rights. During his early career Calhoun had been known as a nationalist. He had not only called for war with the British in 1812, but also supported the National Bank, internal improvements, and a high tariff that many of his fellow southerners opposed. By 1827, however, Calhoun had begun to believe that the southern states needed protection from the high tariffs being imposed by the federal government and the growing antislavery movement in the North. He even wrote anonymously in support of nullification, a concept that allowed a state to nullify within its borders a federal law that it believed was against its interests. Andrew Jackson rejected nullification as an illegal usurpation of national sovereignty by the states. On April 13, 1830, at a Jefferson Day dinner, Jackson resolved to find out whether his vice president's first loyalties were to his country or to his state. The president stared directly at Calhoun as he delivered the toast: "Our Union—it must be preserved." When the vice president replied, "The Union, next to our liberties, most dear," he finally committed himself to South Carolina and the South. As a result, Calhoun no longer had much influence with Jackson, and he lost any chance of eventually attaining the presidency.

In 1832 the Nullification Crisis occurred when South Carolina declared that federal tariffs had no force in the state. But South Carolina leaders agreed to a compromise tariff after Andrew Jackson threatened to send 200,000 troops to that state to enforce the law. Two months before his term was to expire Calhoun resigned the vice presidency in response to Jackson's actions and accepted an appointment to a vacant Senate seat from South Carolina. He remained in that office until 1844, when he resigned to become secretary of state during John Tyler's last year in office. He returned to the Senate in 1845 and served there until his death in 1850. After he left the vice presidency Calhoun did not try to conceal his southern partisanship. He was celebrated in the South for his eloquent advocacy of slavery and states' rights.

Calhoun married Floride Bonneau Calhoun, a wealthy cousin, in January 1811. They had nine children.

Library of Congress

Richard M. Johnson

Born: October 17, 1780; Floyd's Station, Kentucky
Party: Democratic
Term: March 4, 1837-March 4, 1841
President: Martin Van Buren
Died: November 19, 1850; Frankfort, Kentucky
Buried: Frankfort

The son of a wealthy Kentucky landowner, Richard Mentor Johnson studied law at Transylvania University in Lexington, Kentucky, and was admitted to the bar in 1802. After briefly practicing law, Johnson began his political career at the age of twenty-four when he was elected to the Kentucky legislature. Two years later, in 1806, he was elected to the U.S. House of Representatives, where he served until 1819.

Before the War of 1812 Johnson joined with other War Hawks from the South and West in calling for war with Great Britain. When the fighting began, he left the capital without resigning his seat in Congress to become a colonel in command of a regiment of his fellow Kentuckians. In 1813 he skillfully led his troops at the battle of Thames River, where U.S. forces defeated the British and their Indian allies. Johnson, who was seriously wounded in the battle, gained national fame for allegedly killing the Indian chief Tecumseh.

When his wounds healed, Johnson returned to Congress, where he worked to secure military pensions for veterans. In 1816 he authored a bill that granted members of Congress a $1,500 salary instead of a daily allowance for expenses. Although Johnson had justified the salary as a way to encourage Congress to expedite legislative business, the public saw only greed in the law. Johnson responded by supporting the repeal of his own bill. In 1819 he retired from the House and returned to Kentucky, where the state legislature promptly elected him to an unexpired Senate seat. He served in that body until 1829, when he was again elected to the House after losing reelection to the Senate.

In 1824 Johnson backed Henry Clay's presidential bid but switched to Andrew Jackson when Clay threw his support behind John Quincy Adams. Because no candidate had received a majority of electoral votes, the election was decided by the House, which elected Adams. Thereafter, Johnson developed a close political association with Andrew Jackson, who became president in 1829. As a member of Congress, Johnson voted for the president's tariff policies and supported Jackson's stands against the Second Bank of the United States and the use of public funds for internal improvements.

Before the 1836 presidential election Andrew Jackson designated Martin Van Buren as the Democratic party's presidential nominee and pushed for Johnson to be Van Buren's running mate. Jackson probably wanted to reward the Kentuckian for his political loyalty, but the outgoing president also may have believed that Johnson would strengthen Van Buren's candidacy. The Kentuckian gave the ticket geographical balance and a more heroic image. The lore surrounding Johnson's Indian fighting exploits helped to offset the popularity of William Henry Harrison, one of the Whig candidates, who also had a reputation as an Indian fighter and had been Johnson's commanding general at the battle of Thames River.

Despite these contributions to the ticket, the scandals surrounding Johnson's personal life would have prevented his nomination had he not had the support of Jackson, who was still the most powerful and popular political figure in the United States. Johnson was reviled by his fellow politicians for keeping a succession of black mistresses. He had two daughters by his first mistress, Julia Chinn, a mulatto slave he had inherited from his father. Johnson's attempts to introduce his daughters into society as equals offended many powerful southern slaveowners. His vulgar manners and shabby appearance also lost him support.

When it came time to select Van Buren's running mate in 1840, the Democratic party initially ignored Johnson. Even Andrew Jackson had become convinced that Johnson was no longer fit to be vice president. Jackson denounced the colonel's candidacy, saying it would cost "thousands of votes." Thus, rather than renominate Johnson, the Democratic convention chose to allow individual states to nominate vice-presidential candidates. Enough states nominated Johnson, however, to get his name on the ballot. Van Buren and Johnson tried to repeat their success of 1836, but they faced a better-organized Whig party, which had coalesced behind William Henry Harrison. The economic depression that had plagued Van Buren's presidency and a shrewd Whig campaign that relied on catchy slogans and generous quantities of hard cider brought Harrison victory.

After leaving the vice presidency in 1841 Johnson returned to Kentucky, where he again served in the state legislature until 1842. Two years later he sought the Democratic presidential nomination at the Baltimore national convention, but his favorite-son candidacy received little support. In 1850 the ailing sixty-nine-year-old was elected to the Kentucky legislature for the final time; however, he died of a stroke without ever taking up his legislative duties.

Library of Congress

George M. Dallas

Born: July 10, 1792; Philadelphia, Pennsylvania
Party: Democratic
Term: March 4, 1845-March 4, 1849
President: James K. Polk
Died: December 31, 1864; Philadelphia
Buried: Philadelphia

George Mifflin Dallas was born into a wealthy Philadelphia family. His father, Alexander Dallas, had served as secretary of the Treasury under James Madison. George was groomed for college by Philadelphia's best tutors. After graduating from Princeton University in 1810, he went to work in his father's law office. He was admitted to the bar in 1813. That year he traveled to Russia to serve as a private secretary to Albert Gallatin, the U.S. minister in St. Petersburg. When he returned in 1814, he worked for his father in the Treasury Department and later on the legal staff of the Second Bank of the United States. During the 1820s Dallas became increasingly active in politics. He supported the presidential candidacy of John C. Calhoun in 1824. After Andrew Jackson's strong showing in that election, however, Dallas became a Jacksonian Democrat.

Dallas began his own political career in 1828 when he was elected mayor of Philadelphia. In 1829 he accepted an appointment as U.S. district attorney for eastern Pennsylvania. Two years later his state legislature sent him to the U.S. Senate, where he served out an unexpired term. Although Dallas remained personally loyal to President Jackson, he favored the rechartering of the National Bank, which Jackson successfully opposed. When his senatorial term expired in 1833, Dallas returned to Pennsylvania, where he served as state attorney general until 1835. Martin Van Buren appointed him minister to Russia in 1837, but he resigned the post in 1839, claiming there was little work for a U.S. minister to do there. Upon his return to Pennsylvania, he reestablished his law practice while remaining active in state politics.

In 1844 the Democratic national convention, meeting in Baltimore, Maryland, chose Sen. Silas Wright of New York as James K. Polk's running mate. Wright, who was in Washington, D.C., refused to accept the nomination because his close political associate, Martin Van Buren, had been denied the top spot on the ticket. Wright had received the news of his nomination by telegraph and had wired his answer back to the convention. Democratic leaders, however, wanted to make sure the new invention had not made a mistake and sent a messenger to Washington. By the time the confirmation of Wright's refusal reached Baltimore, many of the delegates had gone home.

Those delegates still in Baltimore gathered early the next morning to select another candidate. On the second ballot they nominated Dallas to balance the ticket with Polk, who was from Tennessee. Polk and Dallas defeated Whigs Henry Clay and Theodore Frelinghuysen by 170-105 in the electoral college, with Pennsylvania's twenty-six votes contributing to the margin of victory.

Dallas believed that a vice president should support the administration's policies even when in disagreement with them. In 1846 he demonstrated his devotion to this principle by breaking a tie vote in the Senate on a low-tariff bill supported by Polk, in spite of his state's strong protectionist sentiment. The vice president's action was attacked so bitterly in Pennsylvania that he arranged to move his family to Washington, D.C., because he feared for their safety.

By voting for the low-tariff bill, Dallas had hoped to win support in the South and West for his own presidential candidacy in 1848. At the Democratic national convention that year he received only a handful of votes on the first ballot; Democrats were skeptical of a candidate who probably could not even win his home state. The convention chose instead Sen. Lewis Cass of Michigan, and Dallas retired from politics. In 1856 President Franklin Pierce appointed Dallas minister to Great Britain, a post he retained under James Buchanan. In 1861 he returned to Philadelphia, where he lived until he died suddenly on the last day of 1864.

Dallas married Sophia Nicklin in Philadelphia on May 23, 1816. The couple, who took their family with them on diplomatic missions to Europe, had eight children. Dallas, Texas, is named after George Dallas, who was vice president when Texas was admitted to the Union on December 29, 1845.

Library of Congress

William R. King

Born: April 7, 1786; Sampson County, North Carolina
Party: Democratic
Term: March 24, 1853-April 18, 1853
President: Franklin Pierce
Died: April 18, 1853; Dallas County, Alabama
Buried: Selma, Alabama

William Rufus Devane King was the son of well-to-do North Carolina planters William and Margaret King. Young William graduated from the University of North Carolina in 1803. After studying law in Fayetteville, North Carolina, he was admitted to the bar in 1806.

King entered politics in 1807 at the age of twenty-one when he won a two-year term in the North Carolina House of Commons. In 1810 he was elected to the U.S. House of Representatives, where he sided with the War Hawks, who supported the War of 1812 with Great Britain. He resigned from the House in 1816, however, to undertake a diplomatic mission to Italy and Russia.

When he returned to the United States in 1818, King moved to Alabama and bought a plantation. He was a delegate to the convention that established Alabama's state government, and he was elected to the U.S. Senate in 1820 as one of Alabama's first senators. During his long career in the Senate King was a strong supporter of Andrew Jackson's policies. He served as president pro tempore of the Senate from 1836 to 1841.

In 1844 King left the Senate after twenty-four years when President John Tyler appointed him minister to France. While in Paris he helped secure French acquiescence to the U.S. annexation of Texas. He returned to Alabama in 1846 and was defeated for reelection to the Senate. Two years later, however, King was appointed by the governor of Alabama to fill an unexpired Senate seat. He served as chairman of the Senate Foreign Relations Committee, and, when Millard Fillmore became president following the death of Zachary Taylor in 1850, the Senate selected King to take over Fillmore's duties as presiding officer of the Senate.

During King's time in Washington, D.C., he was surrounded by an air of personal scandal. His lack of a wife and his intimate friendship with James Buchanan, with whom he shared an apartment while the two men served in the Senate, led to speculation that he was a homosexual. King also was ridiculed for his fastidious dressing habits and his insistence on wearing a wig long after they had gone out of style. Andrew Jackson referred to King as "Miss Nancy." Like Richard M. Johnson, however, King overcame the gossip about his private life to obtain the vice presidency.

In 1852 the Democrats chose King to balance the ticket with their dark horse presidential candidate, Franklin Pierce of New Hampshire. The choice of King was also intended to satisfy supporters of James Buchanan, who had sought the presidential nomination. King, however, was already ill with tuberculosis when he received the nomination. His condition deteriorated rapidly before the election, and he was not able to campaign. King's condition did not raise much concern among voters, however, as the Pierce-King team defeated Whigs Winfield Scott and William Alexander Graham by an electoral college vote of 254-42.

After the election King traveled to Cuba in the hope that the Caribbean climate would heal him. There on March 24, 1853, with the special permission of Congress, he became the only executive officer of the United States to take the oath of office on foreign soil. King realized that he was weakening and asked the U.S. government for a ship to take him back to the United States to die. The U.S. Navy steamship *Fulton* transported him to Mobile, Alabama. He reached his plantation, King's Bend, on April 17 and died the next day. King served just twenty-five days of his term, fewer than any other vice president.

Library of Congress

John C. Breckinridge

Born: January 21, 1821; Lexington, Kentucky
Party: Democratic
Term: March 4, 1857-March 4, 1861
President: James Buchanan
Died: May 17, 1875; Lexington
Buried: Lexington

John Cabell Breckinridge was born into a prominent Kentucky family. His grandfather, John Breckinridge, had represented Kentucky in the Senate and had served as attorney general under Thomas Jefferson. His father, Joseph Cabell Breckinridge, was an influential lawyer and politician.

Breckinridge attended Centre College in Danville, Kentucky, graduating in 1839. After studying law at the College of New Jersey (later Princeton University) and Transylvania College in Lexington, Kentucky, he was admitted to the bar in 1841. He opened a law practice in Burlington, Iowa, but returned to Kentucky after two years. By 1845 he had established a successful law partnership in Lexington.

In 1846 he declined to fight in the Mexican War. The following year, however, after delivering a moving speech honoring the state's war dead in front of thousands of people, he was given a commission as a major and sent to Mexico. Although he arrived after most of the fighting was over, he was able to add military experience to his political credentials.

In 1849 Breckinridge was elected to the Kentucky legislature as a Democrat. Two years later he upset the Whig candidate for a seat in the U.S. House of Representatives from Henry Clay's former district. In 1855, after two terms, Breckinridge left Congress to resume his law practice in Kentucky and improve his finances. That year he also turned down President Franklin Pierce's offer of the ambassadorship to Spain.

The 1856 Democratic national convention nominated Pennsylvanian James Buchanan for president and Breckinridge for vice president. Buchanan easily defeated John C. Fremont of the new Republican party, whose election many Americans feared would bring civil war. Breckinridge was a capable presiding officer of the Senate. The handsome and eloquent vice president was so popular in his home state that, sixteen months before his vice-presidential term was to expire, he was elected to a term in the U.S. Senate, which was to begin when he left the vice presidency.

In 1860 southern Democrats nominated Breckinridge for the presidency, while Illinois Senator Stephen A. Douglas was nominated by Democrats in the North. Breckinridge had not encouraged this split in his party, but he accepted the nomination. He declared that he favored preserving the Union and that it could be saved if slavery were not prohibited in the territories. Breckinridge finished second with seventy-two electoral votes from eleven southern states. Abraham Lincoln received less than 40 percent of the popular vote, but with three other candidates splitting the vote—Breckinridge, Douglas, and John Bell of the Constitutional Union party—Lincoln won 180 electoral votes and the presidency.

As a lame-duck vice president, Breckinridge worked with Democratic leaders who searched vainly for a compromise that would prevent civil war. After Lincoln's inauguration Breckinridge returned to Kentucky, whose leaders were debating the future of their state. Breckinridge was in favor of secession, but he accepted the state's declaration of neutrality. When Congress reconvened on July 4, 1861, he took his seat in the Senate. Throughout the summer he defended the right of southern states to secede and opposed Lincoln's efforts to raise an army to put down the insurrection.

In September Union and Confederate armies invaded Kentucky. When the Union army won control of the state, Breckinridge offered his services to the South and was indicted for treason by the federal government. He joined the Confederate army and was commissioned as a brigadier general. After serving at the battle of Shiloh in April 1862, he was promoted to major general. He led troops at the battles of Vicksburg, Murfreesboro, Chickamauga, Chattanooga, and Cold Harbor. In February 1865 Confederate president Jefferson Davis appointed Breckinridge secretary of war.

When the South surrendered in April 1865, Breckinridge feared that he would be captured and prosecuted as a traitor. He and his small party eluded federal troops for two months as they made their way through the South and across the water to Cuba. For three and a half years Breckinridge lived in Europe and Canada while he waited for the treason charge against him to be dropped. On Christmas Day 1868 President Andrew Johnson declared an amnesty for all who had participated in the insurrection. The following March Breckinridge returned to Kentucky, where crowds greeted him as a hero. He settled in Lexington and resumed his law practice. He died at the age of fifty-four after undergoing his second unsuccessful liver operation.

Breckinridge married Mary Burch of Lexington, Kentucky on December 12, 1843. They had five children. Although Mary suffered through several periods of poor health during her lifetime, she lived for thirty-two years after her husband's death.

Library of Congress

Hannibal Hamlin

Born: August 27, 1809; Paris Hill, Maine
Party: Republican
Term: March 4, 1861-March 4, 1865
President: Abraham Lincoln
Died: July 4, 1891; Bangor, Maine
Buried: Bangor

Hannibal Hamlin's ancestors were among the first settlers in Maine. His father, Cyrus, was a Harvard-educated doctor, who also dabbled in farming and small-town politics. Hannibal's parents intended to send him to college and even gave him a prep school education, but family financial troubles forced him to abandon his college plans. He worked as a surveyor, printer, schoolteacher, and farmer before deciding to study law.

In Portland, Maine, Hamlin studied law in the office of Samuel C. Fessenden, the leading antislavery activist in the state. Hamlin was admitted to the bar in 1833 and established a lucrative law practice in Hampden, Maine. In 1836 he was elected as a Democrat to the Maine House of Representatives. During his five years in that body he served three one-year terms as Speaker.

In 1843 Hamlin was elected to the U.S. House of Representatives, where he served two terms. Then in 1847, after a brief stint back in the Maine legislature, that body elected him to the U.S. Senate. While in the Senate, Hamlin became an outspoken opponent of slavery. He supported Democrat Franklin Pierce in the 1852 presidential election, but in 1856 his abolitionist sentiments caused him to defect to the new Republican party. He was elected governor of Maine in 1857 but resigned after serving only a few weeks when he once again was elected to the Senate.

The 1860 Republican national convention nominated Abraham Lincoln of Illinois for president. Republican leaders correctly saw that Lincoln had little chance to win electoral votes in the South, even if a southerner were nominated for the vice presidency. Consequently, giving the ticket geographic balance meant choosing a northeasterner for vice president. Republican leaders were also looking for a candidate who would satisfy William H. Seward, the powerful New York senator who had hoped to be the presidential nominee. The convention settled on Hamlin, who met both requirements and had the proper antislavery credentials. Lincoln and Hamlin faced a divided Democratic party and won the election with less than 40 percent of the popular vote.

Hamlin, who criticized the president's circumspect approach to emancipation, had little influence within the Lincoln administration. Hamlin disliked the vice presidency, not only because of his lack of power, but also because the office did not allow him to dispense any patronage, which for Hamlin had been the foremost reward of political success. Although well qualified to preside over the Senate, Hamlin spent little time in this capacity. Routinely, he presided over a new session of the Senate only until it chose a president pro tempore, after which he returned to Maine.

Despite Hamlin's misgivings about the vice presidency, he wanted a second term. Lincoln, however, believed that Hamlin's view toward the South had become too radical and did not support his candidacy. The 1864 National Union convention, a coalition of Republicans and pro-Union Democrats, nominated Tennessee Democrat Andrew Johnson to run with Lincoln. Republican leaders hoped Johnson would be better able than Hamlin to attract votes in border states and among northern Democrats.

After retiring from the vice presidency Hamlin served for a year as collector of the port of Boston and two years as president of a railroad company. In 1868 Maine again elected him to the Senate. He served two terms during which he was associated with the radical Republicans who advocated harsh Reconstruction policies. Hamlin retired from politics in 1881 but secured an appointment as minister to Spain. During his year and a half in Europe he and his wife traveled widely on the Continent, occasionally showing up in Madrid to perform the minimum duties of his post.

In late 1882 Hamlin returned to Maine, where he enjoyed a quiet retirement. He died of heart failure on July 4, 1891, at the age of eighty-one.

Hamlin married Sarah Emery on December 10, 1833, in Paris Hill, Maine. The couple had four children before she died in 1855. On September 25, 1856, Hamlin married Ellen Vesta Emery, a younger half-sister of his first wife. They had two sons; the younger was born while Hamlin was vice president.

Library of Congress

Schuyler Colfax

Born: March 23, 1823; New York City
Party: Republican
Term: March 4, 1869-March 4, 1873
President: Ulysses S. Grant
Died: January 13, 1885; Mankato, Minnesota
Buried: South Bend, Indiana

Schuyler Colfax was the son of Schuyler and Hannah Colfax. His father died in 1822, and his mother married George Matthews in 1832. Schuyler attended public schools in New York City until he was ten. In 1836 he moved with his family to New Carlisle, Indiana, where he studied law but never passed the bar. His interest in politics stemmed from his writing for newspapers, which he began at age sixteen. In 1841 Schuyler's stepfather, who was county auditor, appointed his stepson deputy auditor, a post Schuyler then occupied for eight years.

Colfax became active in state politics in 1842 when he began a two-year term as enrolling clerk of the Indiana Senate. In 1845 Colfax became part owner of the *South Bend Free Press*. He changed its name to the *St. Joseph Valley Register* and used it to support Whig candidates and issues. Colfax attended several state and national Whig conventions and ran unsuccessfully for the U.S. House of Representatives in 1851. When the Republican party was formed, Colfax became a member and helped build a Republican organization in Indiana. In 1855 he was elected to the U.S. House of Representatives, where he served for the next fourteen years until he became vice president in 1869. During his last five and a half years in the House, he held the office of Speaker.

At the 1868 Republican national convention Colfax actively sought the vice presidency. He hoped the Republican presidential nominee, Ulysses S. Grant, would serve only one four-year term, thereby setting the stage for his own nomination for president in 1872. Colfax emerged from a crowd of favorite-son candidates to receive the vice-presidential nomination on the fifth ballot despite being from Indiana, a state contiguous to Grant's home state of Illinois. Grant, however, was the most celebrated hero of the Civil War, and a geographically balanced ticket was not necessary for victory. He and Colfax easily defeated Democrats Horatio Seymour and Francis P. Blair, Jr., 214-80 in the electoral college. Like most nineteenth-century vice presidents, Colfax did not play a significant role in his running mate's administration.

During Colfax's rise in government he had gained a reputation for political intrigue. He was known as the "Smiler" and "Great Joiner" for his propensity to join any club or organization that would accept him. Abraham Lincoln had called Colfax a "friendly rascal." Events would show, however, that Colfax was not just an opportunistic and manipulative politician; he was also corrupt.

A September 1872 newpaper exposé implicated Colfax in the Crédit Mobilier scandal. In 1867 Congress had appropriated funds for the construction of the Union Pacific Railroad. The director of the railroad, Oakes Ames (R-Mass.), who was also a House member, set up a holding company, Crédit Mobilier of America, in which he deposited millions of dollars of money appropriated for the railroad. He proceeded to bribe other members of Congress not to expose his corruption and to support legislation favorable to the railroad by selling them shares of stock in the holding company at bargain prices. While Speaker of the House, Colfax had received twenty shares of Crédit Mobilier stock and substantial dividends from those shares. His defense of his actions was unconvincing, and he fell back on the argument that his mistakes while in Congress should not affect his tenure as vice president. Some members of Congress considered impeaching him, but, because his term was about to expire, they dropped the matter. Colfax then claimed he had been exonerated, but his political reputation was ruined.

When Colfax left office, he made a good living by touring the country delivering lectures. He died of a stroke in 1885 after changing trains in subzero weather during a lecture tour of Minnesota.

Colfax married Evelyn Clark on October 10, 1844. His wife, who had no children, died in 1863 while he was Speaker of the House. On November 18, 1868, he married Ellen Wade, a niece of Sen. Benjamin F. Wade (R-Ohio), who had been Colfax's primary rival for the 1868 vice-presidential nomination. The couple had one child, Schuyler Colfax III. Colfax's grandfather, William Colfax, had been the commander of George Washington's bodyguard during the Revolutionary War.

Library of Congress

Henry Wilson

Born: February 16, 1812; Farmington, New Hampshire
Party: Republican
Term: March 4, 1873-November 22, 1875
President: Ulysses S. Grant
Died: November 22, 1875; Washington, D.C.
Buried: Natick, Massachusetts

Henry Wilson was born Jeremiah Jones Colbath, the son of Abigail and Winthrop Colbath, a poor New Hampshire sawmill worker. When Jeremiah was ten, he was indentured to a farmer, for whom he labored for over ten years for room and board. During his free hours he educated himself by reading hundreds of borrowed books. On his twenty-first birthday Jeremiah was given his freedom as well as six sheep and a pair of oxen. He broke with the hard life he had led by selling the livestock for eighty-five dollars and legally changing his name to Henry Wilson.

Wilson then walked over one hundred miles to Natick, Massachusetts, where he apprenticed himself to a shoemaker. He learned the trade within a month, bought his freedom from his master, and went into business for himself. By the time he was twenty-seven Wilson owned a shoe factory that employed as many as one hundred people. Although Wilson was accumulating a modest fortune, his political ambitions were stronger than his desire for wealth. He continued to read voraciously and developed his speaking skills at the Natick Debating Society. In 1840 Wilson was elected as a Whig to the Massachusetts legislature, where he served for most of the next twelve years.

Wilson left the Whig party in 1848 because of its indecisiveness on the slavery issue. He helped form the

Free Soil party and edited the *Boston Republican*, a party organ, from 1848 to 1851. He joined the ultraconservative American (Know Nothing) party in 1854 but walked out of its 1855 convention when it too failed to take a strong stand against slavery.

Earlier in 1855 Wilson had been elected to the U.S. Senate by the Massachusetts legislature to fill an unexpired term. He served in the Senate until 1873, when he became vice president. Wilson joined the Republican party after his rejection of the Know Nothings. He made many enemies among southern members of Congress for his harsh attacks in the Senate against slavery. His fear of assassination led him to carry a pistol and make plans for his family to be provided for in the event of his death. In addition to his activism against slavery, Wilson also established himself as an advocate of the rights of factory workers.

During the Civil War Wilson served as chairman of the Senate Committee on Military Affairs. In this capacity he earned praise from military and political leaders for his effective legislative leadership in raising and supporting the huge Union army. After the war he supported the harsh Reconstruction program of the radical Republicans and voted for Andrew Johnson's impeachment in 1868. Wilson's Reconstruction views softened late in his Senate career after he toured the South and West extensively.

Wilson was nominated to be President Ulysses S. Grant's vice-presidential running mate at the 1872 Republican national convention in Philadelphia. Like his vice-presidential predecessor, Schuyler Colfax, Wilson had been involved in the Crédit Mobilier scandal. A few weeks before the 1872 presidential election the *New York Sun* broke the story that several members of Congress, including Wilson, were involved in the bribery scheme. Wilson, however, claimed that he had returned the twenty Crédit Mobilier shares he had purchased before he reaped any profit from them. Although Wilson was not exonerated by the congressional committees investigating the scandal until several months after the election, his troubles did not affect the election's outcome. The highly popular president Grant easily defeated Democrat Horace Greeley 286-66 in the electoral college.

Shortly after the election Wilson suffered a stroke. When he recovered, he claimed to be in good health, but he was a poor presiding officer of the Senate. In 1875, he died from a second stroke with a year and a half left in his term.

Wilson married sixteen-year-old Harriet Malvina Howe on October 28, 1840. She died of cancer on May 28, 1870. They had one son, Henry Hamilton Wilson, who distinguished himself as a Union officer during the Civil War. He died in 1866 while still in the army.

Library of Congress

William A. Wheeler

Born: June 30, 1819; Malone, New York
Party: Republican
Term: March 4, 1877-March 4, 1881
President: Rutherford B. Hayes
Died: June 4, 1887; Malone
Buried: Malone

William Almon Wheeler was the second of the two children of Eliza and Almon Wheeler. Although William's father was a lawyer, he left virtually no estate when he died in 1827. William worked his way through a preparatory academy, and in 1838 he enrolled in the University of Vermont, where he led a Spartan existence. He had so little money that at one point he lived on bread and water for several weeks. After two years these financial problems forced Wheeler to drop out of college before graduating.

He returned to his home in Malone, New York, where he studied law with a local lawyer. He was admitted to the New York bar in 1845 and served as district attorney of Franklin County from 1846 to 1849. In 1850 he was elected to the New York State legislature as a Whig. Upon leaving the assembly in 1851 he took over the management of a Malone bank, and two years later he became a trustee for the mortgage holders of the Northern Railway. Like many northern Whigs, Wheeler switched his loyalty to the Republican party in the mid-1850s. From 1858 to 1860 he served in the New York State Senate, where as president pro tempore he gained experience presiding over a legislature.

In 1861 Wheeler was elected to the U.S. House of Representatives, his first national office. He served only one term but remained active in New York politics. In 1867 he was chosen to preside over the New York constitutional convention because he was on good terms with the New York Republican machine while retaining his independence. He was reelected to the U.S. House in 1869 and served there until he became vice president in 1877.

Wheeler was best known not for his legislative skill or political acumen but for his scrupulous honesty. He demonstrated this quality during the "Salary Grab" of 1873, in which Congress voted itself a 50 percent pay raise and back pay of $5,000. Wheeler voted against the measure, and, when it was passed, he returned the back pay. His most notable accomplishment during his time in the House was his service on a congressional committee that investigated an election dispute in Louisiana in 1874. He developed a compromise known as the "Wheeler adjustment" that resolved the dispute and ended the threat of civil unrest.

When Wheeler's name was put into contention for the vice presidency at the 1876 Republican national convention, he was virtually unknown. Earlier in the year when someone had suggested a Hayes-Wheeler ticket, Hayes commented in a letter to his wife, "Who is Wheeler?" Despite his lack of prominence, Wheeler received the vice-presidential nomination because he was from New York, he had a spotless reputation, and the convention delegates were anxious to go home.

The election of 1876 involved the uncontroversial Wheeler in one of the most intense political controversies in American history. Although the Hayes-Wheeler ticket received a minority of the popular vote and their Democratic opponents appeared to win the electoral college, Republican leaders challenged the election results in several southern states. After months of political maneuvers and backroom deals, a congressionally appointed electoral commission ruled in favor of Hayes and Wheeler.

Wheeler was a conscientious presiding officer of the Senate, but he had little enthusiasm for his office. He frequently referred to Benjamin Franklin's comment that the vice presidency was so insignificant that its occupant should be called "His Superfluous Highness."

Wheeler welcomed the end of his term as vice president. He quietly retired to Malone, where he lived the last six years of his life. He had married Mary King on September 17, 1845. She died in March 1876, three months before he was nominated for the vice presidency. The couple had no children, and, when Wheeler's sister died shortly after his wife, he was left without any immediate family. Although Hayes had never met Wheeler before 1876, they became close friends during their time in office. The widowed vice president spent many evenings at the White House with Hayes and his wife, Lucy.

Library of Congress

Thomas A. Hendricks

Born: September 7, 1819; near Zanesville, Ohio
Party: Democratic
Term: March 4, 1885-November 25, 1885
President: Grover Cleveland
Died: November 25, 1885; Indianapolis, Indiana
Buried: Indianapolis

Thomas Andrews Hendricks was born in Ohio, the son of John and Jane Hendricks. In 1820, when Thomas was a baby, the family moved to Indiana, where Thomas grew up working on the family farm in Shelby County. He attended local schools before enrolling in Hanover College near Madison, Indiana. After his graduation in 1841, Thomas began to study law in Shelbyville, Indiana. In 1843 he traveled to Chambersburg, Pennsylvania, to study law under an uncle who was a judge. He returned to Shelbyville the following year, passed the bar, and established a successful law practice.

Hendricks entered politics in 1848 when he was elected to the Indiana legislature. In 1850 he served as a delegate to the convention called to revise the Indiana constitution. At the convention he supported a proposal to prohibit blacks from entering the state. He was elected to the U.S. House of Representatives in 1851 and again in 1852 when the state constitution mandated that House elections be held in even-numbered years. While in the House, Hendricks aligned himself with the policies of Democratic senator Stephen A. Douglas of Illinois. Hendricks was a strong supporter of Douglas's Kansas-Nebraska Act, which permitted Kansas to decide for itself whether it would be a slave state or free state and precipitated a bloody war in that territory. Hendricks lost reelection to the House in 1854, but President Franklin Pierce appointed him commissioner of the general land office, a post he occupied until 1859.

In 1860 Hendricks ran for governor of Indiana but was defeated by Republican Henry S. Lane. When the Democratic party gained control of the Indiana legislature in 1863, Hendricks was elected to the U.S. Senate. During his single term he was a leading critic of Lincoln's leadership during the war. Hendricks supported appropriations to pay for troops, weapons, and supplies, but he opposed the Emancipation Proclamation, the draft, and many other wartime measures. After the war he backed President Andrew Johnson's magnanimous Reconstruction plan and worked against the Thirteenth Amendment, which abolished slavery, and the Fourteenth Amendment, which gave blacks the rights of U.S. citizens. Hendricks claimed that the black slave was "inferior and no good would come from his freedom."

In 1868 Hendricks again was nominated as his party's candidate for governor of Indiana, but he lost the election. The following year, when his Senate term expired, he retired to Indianapolis, where he resumed his law practice. In 1872, however, he ran for governor for the third time and was finally elected by a narrow 1,148-vote margin.

In 1872 the national prominence attained by Hendricks was demonstrated when he received forty-two of the sixty-two electoral votes for president won by fellow Democrat Horace Greeley, who had died between the election and the electoral college vote. Four years later the Democrats nominated Hendricks as Samuel J. Tilden's vice-presidential running mate. The presence of Hendricks on the ticket helped Tilden carry Indiana and seemingly the election. The Republicans, however, disputed the election results in several southern states, and an election commission that favored the Republicans ruled in favor of the Republican presidential candidate, Rutherford B. Hayes.

Hendricks was nominated again for vice president in 1884 to balance the ticket with New Yorker Grover Cleveland. Like eight years before, his popularity helped the Democrats carry Indiana, but this time they won the election. Cleveland and Hendricks defeated Republicans James

G. Blaine and John A. Logan 219-182 in the electoral college and by just sixty thousand votes in the popular balloting.

As vice president, Hendricks presided over only a one-month session of the Senate called to consider President Cleveland's cabinet nominations. Hendricks died in his home in Indianapolis two weeks before the Senate was scheduled to resume its business in December. The vice president had served less than nine months of his term.

Hendricks married Eliza C. Morgan of North Bend, Ohio, on September 26, 1845. They had one child, Morgan, who died when he was three years old. Eliza died at the age of eighty in 1903.

Library of Congress

Levi P. Morton

Born: May 16, 1824; Shoreham, Vermont
Party: Republican
Term: March 4, 1889-March 4, 1893
President: Benjamin Harrison
Died: May 16, 1920; Rhinebeck, New York
Buried: Rhinebeck

Levi Parsons Morton was the son of Lucretia and Daniel Morton, an Episcopalian minister. His ancestors arrived in New England before 1650. He received a modest education as a boy and never attended college.

Morton began his climb in the business world as a clerk in a Hanover, New Hampshire, store. He later worked in Boston for an import company and by 1855 owned his own wholesale business in New York City. He suffered a financial setback in 1861 because the Civil War debts owed to him by southerners went unpaid. He was able to pay his own creditors, however, and in 1863 established a Wall Street banking firm. Over the next thirteen years he accumulated a large personal fortune and developed his firm, Morton, Bliss & Company, into one of the most powerful financial institutions in the United States.

In 1876 Morton decided to try his hand at politics. He ran unsuccessfully for a seat in the U.S. House of Representatives from Manhattan's wealthy Eleventh District but won the seat two years later. Morton was reelected to Congress in 1880, but he resigned his House seat when President James A. Garfield appointed him minister to France.

The 1880 Republican national convention nominated dark horse James A. Garfield of Ohio as president instead of former president Ulysses S. Grant, who was allied with Morton's political mentor, Republican senator Roscoe Conkling of New York. As a gesture to the Conkling faction, Garfield offered the vice-presidential nomination to Morton, who refused on the instructions of Conkling. Instead, the nomination went to another Conkling ally, Chester A. Arthur, who accepted the nomination against Conkling's wishes.

Had Grant been nominated and elected, Morton would have likely been nominated Treasury secretary, a post that the New York banker coveted. After Garfield won the election, however, he sought to limit the influence of the Conkling faction and chose William Windom of Minnesota to be Treasury secretary. Morton's fund-raising efforts on behalf of Garfield were rewarded by an appointment as minister to France, where for four years Morton lived in splendor and threw lavish parties for European royalty. Morton, who had relinquished his House seat to go to France, returned to the United States in 1885 hopeful of winning a Senate seat, but his election campaigns for the Senate in 1885 and 1887 were unsuccessful.

In 1888 Morton was offered the vice-presidential slot on the Republican ticket with Indianan Benjamin Harrison. Having seen Chester Arthur succeed to the presidency when Garfield was killed by an assassin in 1881, Morton did not refuse the nomination a second time. During the 1888 campaign Morton concentrated on doing what he knew best—raising money. Although Harrison and Morton lost the popular election by ten thousand votes to President Grover Cleveland and Allen G. Thurman, they won in the electoral college 233-168.

Morton fulfilled his duties as presiding officer of the Senate conscientiously. During one Democratic filibuster in late 1890 and early 1891, Morton opposed the position of his own party and refused to cooperate with Republican attempts to end the filibuster. The Democrats stopped the legislation, however, and Morton's standing in the Republican party was damaged. He was willing to accept a second vice-presidential term, but Republican party leaders dropped him for fellow New Yorker Whitelaw Reid.

In 1895 Morton ran successfully for governor of New York with the support of Sen. Thomas C. Platt (R-N.Y.), the most powerful figure in New York politics. Morton, however, displayed the same independence that he had shown as vice president and refused to be part of Platt's machine. In particular, he angered his machine supporters by advocating civil service reform. Morton hoped to be his party's presidential nominee in 1896 (his name was entered as a favorite-son candidate), but William McKinley was the clear choice of the party bosses and the convention. When Morton's term as governor ended in January 1897, he retired from politics to manage his business interests. He formed the Morton Trust Company in 1899 and merged it with the Guaranty Trust Company in 1909.

Morton spent much of his retirement traveling or at Ellerslie, his thousand-acre estate in Rhinebeck, New York. He died there in 1920 on his ninety-sixth birthday.

On October 15, 1856, Morton married Lucy Young Kimball, who died in 1871 before her husband entered politics. They had one daughter, who died in infancy. Morton then married Anna Livingson Street on February 12, 1873, and the couple had five daughters. Anna died at Ellerslie in 1918, two years before her husband.

Library of Congress

Adlai E. Stevenson

Born: October 25, 1835; Christian County, Kentucky
Party: Democratic
Term: March 4, 1893-March 4, 1897
President: Grover Cleveland
Died: June 14, 1914; Chicago, Illinois
Buried: Bloomington, Illinois

Adlai Ewing Stevenson was the second of the seven children of Eliza and John Stevenson, a slave-owning Kentucky planter. As a boy, Adlai worked on the farm and obtained an elementary education at local schools. When Adlai was sixteen, his family moved to Bloomington, Illinois, where he taught school and attended briefly Illinois Wesleyan University. He then enrolled in Centre College in Danville, Kentucky. In 1857, after two years of study, he left Centre without a degree when the death of his father forced him to resume teaching to supplement his family's income. While teaching, Adlai studied law and was admitted to the bar in 1858.

That same year Stevenson opened a law office in Metamora, Illinois. He also became a Democrat and a follower of Illinois senator Stephen A. Douglas. In 1864 Stevenson won his first elective office, state's attorney for the Metamora judicial district. After four years in the post Stevenson moved back to Bloomington and resumed his successful career as a lawyer.

In 1874 Stevenson was elected to the U.S. House of Representatives. He was defeated for reelection in 1876 but won his seat back in 1878. After his term expired in 1881 he returned to private life.

In 1885 President Grover Cleveland appointed Stevenson first assistant postmaster. In this office Stevenson was in charge of firing postmasters appointed by the previous Republican administrations. Cleveland believed that, despite the traditional practice, government employees should not be fired simply because they belonged to the party out of power. But Cleveland's fellow Democrats were not as magnanimous. They demanded that Cleveland replace Republicans with loyal Democrats. Stevenson agreed and wrote a letter to the *New York World*, a Democratic paper, supporting patronage. Under pressure from his party, Cleveland relented and gave Stevenson permission to proceed with the mass removal of Republican postmasters. Although Stevenson was known for his tact and amiability, he made many enemies in the process of firing tens of thousands of people and earned the nickname, the "Headsman." Cleveland appointed Stevenson to the Supreme Court in 1889, but the Republican majority in the Senate refused to confirm the nomination of a man who had just fired tens of thousands of their fellow party members.

Stevenson went to the 1892 Democratic national convention as the chairman of the Illinois delegation. There he received the party's nomination for vice president. By choosing Stevenson, the Democrats improved their chances of winning Illinois, a large, traditionally Republican state. Stevenson's support of bimetallism, the coinage of money based on both gold and silver, also appealed to many citizens in the South and West who believed that having more money in circulation would increase their buying power and the country's economic health. With Stevenson on the ticket, Illinois voted for a Democratic presidential candidate for the first time since 1856. Cleveland and Stevenson defeated Republican incumbent Benjamin Harrison and vice-presidential candidate Whitelaw Reid 277-145 in the electoral college.

As vice president, Stevenson made many friends in the Senate, where he was regarded as a good presiding officer. And, although he was on friendly terms with President Cleveland, Stevenson was not a regular participant in policy making. In July 1893, when Cleveland secretly underwent surgery for mouth cancer, Stevenson was not even informed.

In 1900 Stevenson again received the Democratic nomination for vice president on a ticket with William Jennings Bryan, but they were defeated by incumbent William McKinley and vice-presidential nominee Theodore Roosevelt. In 1908 the Illinois Democratic party honored the aging Stevenson with its nomination for governor. He lost, however, to Republican Charles Deneen in a close election. After this defeat Stevenson retired from politics. His book, *Something of Men I Have Known*, a collection of speeches and political anecdotes, was published in 1909. In 1914 Stevenson died of heart failure following prostate surgery.

On December 20, 1866, Stevenson married Letitia Green, whom he had met while attending Centre College, where her father served as president. They did not marry, however, until they met again nearly a decade later after she had moved to Illinois. Letitia died on Christmas Day in 1913, a few months before her husband. The Stevensons had three girls and a boy. Their son, Lewis, managed his father's vice-presidential campaign in 1892 and served as his father's private secretary while he was in office. Lewis was the father of Adlai Stevenson II, who was the Democratic nominee for president in 1952 and 1956.

Library of Congress

Garret A. Hobart

Born: June 3, 1844; Long Branch, New Jersey
Party: Republican
Term: March 4, 1897-November 21, 1899
President: William McKinley
Died: November 21, 1899; Paterson, New Jersey
Buried: Paterson

Garret Augustus Hobart was the eldest son of Addison and Sophia Hobart, who owned a store and a small farm. When Garret was sixteen, he enrolled in Rutgers College in New Jersey. There he majored in math and English and graduated with honors in 1863. Garret then taught school briefly before moving to Paterson, New Jersey, to work in the law office of Socrates Tuttle, a close friend of his father. Garret was admitted to the bar in 1869.

After serving as Paterson city counsel in 1871, Hobart entered state politics and in 1872 was elected to the state assembly. He became speaker in 1874 at the age of thirty. Two years later he won election to the state senate, where he served two three-year terms. Hobart left the state senate in 1882 but continued to be a leading figure in New Jersey politics. From 1880 to 1891 he was chairman of the state Republican committee. Although Hobart was not a well-known figure outside of New Jersey, he had become a member of the Republican National Committee in 1884 and was acquainted with the leading Republicans around the country, including Ohio boss Mark Hanna.

Although Hobart was enthusiastic about his political career, he considered it a hobby. Most of his energies went into his legal and business career. He served as president of the Passaic, New Jersey, water company and was director of several banks. By the time he entered national politics, he had amassed a fortune.

In 1896 the Republican party was confident of recapturing the White House. Grover Cleveland and the Democrats had received much of the blame for the economic and labor troubles of the previous four years. The Democrats nominated William Jennings Bryan as president and Arthur Sewall as vice president. The Republicans countered with William McKinley of Ohio and a conservative platform that advocated the gold standard. Republican party leaders wanted a gold supporter from the East as the vice-presidential candidate to balance the ticket and reinforce their commitment to hard money. They found their candidate in Hobart, who was an outspoken advocate of the gold standard. In his acceptance speech at the Republican national convention in St. Louis, Hobart uttered one of the most famous quotes of his era: "An honest dollar, worth 100 cents everywhere, cannot be coined out of fifty-three cents of silver, plus a legislative fiat."

Despite Bryan's stirring campaign speeches, the Republicans won the 1896 election 271-176 in the electoral college. Hobart's presence on the ticket helped the Republicans win New Jersey for the first time since Ulysses S. Grant's success there in 1872.

The last vice president of the nineteenth century proved to be one of the most able and influential. Despite never having held national office, Hobart understood national political issues and became one of McKinley's closest friends and advisers. The press often referred to Hobart as the "Assistant President." He also was credited with presiding over the Senate with energy and fairness.

Hobart became ill in the spring of 1899. He left the capital to recuperate in New Jersey, but he died at his home in Paterson in November. Hobart received stirring eulogies in the nation's newspapers, and his funeral was attended by President McKinley and many other top government officials. Paterson erected a bronze statue of Hobart in front of its city hall next to a statue of Alexander Hamilton.

Hobart married Jennie Tuttle on July 21, 1869. While Hobart was vice president, they entertained lavishly at their rented mansion on Lafayette Square near the White House. The couple had two children, Garret, Jr., and his older sister Fannie. Fannie died in 1895 from diptheria while on a tour of Europe with her family. Mrs. Hobart died on January 8, 1941, at the age of ninety-one. She wrote two books about her experiences, *Memories*, published in 1930, and *Second Lady*, published in 1933.

Library of Congress

Charles W. Fairbanks

Born: May 11, 1852; near Unionville Center, Ohio
Party: Republican
Term: March 4, 1905-March 4, 1909
President: Theodore Roosevelt
Died: June 4, 1918; Indianapolis, Indiana
Buried: Indianapolis

Charles Warren Fairbanks was born in a one-room log cabin on a farm in Ohio. His parents, Loriston and Mary Fairbanks, were Methodist abolitionists who helped runaway slaves before the Civil War. As a child, Charles worked on the family farm and attended a district school. Despite his humble background, he enrolled in Ohio Wesleyan University in Delaware, Ohio, at the age of fifteen. He worked his way through college and graduated in 1872.

He was admitted to the bar in 1874 and moved to Indianapolis. He quickly built a reputation as an attorney specializing in railroad litigation. While accumulating a fortune from his law practice, Fairbanks became involved in politics. He supported various Republican candidates, including fellow Indianan Benjamin Harrison. By 1896 he was one of the state's leading Republicans, although he had never held public office. That year his keynote address at the Republican national convention brought him national acclaim. In 1897 he was elected to the U.S. Senate.

In the Senate Fairbanks was one of President William McKinley's most consistent supporters. Republican leaders considered Fairbanks for the vice-presidential nomination in 1900, but he decided to remain in the Senate. For Fairbanks, who had presidential ambitions, the decision was a bad one; Theodore Roosevelt was nominated instead.

Fairbanks had planned to run for the presidency after McKinley served out his second term, but McKinley's assassination in 1901 eliminated any chance of his nomination for the presidency in 1904. Theodore Roosevelt assumed the presidency and became so popular that he was the inevitable choice of his party for a second term.

In 1904 Fairbanks settled for the vice-presidential nomination. Roosevelt would have preferred someone else, but he accepted Fairbanks, who was the choice of the party's conservative wing. While Roosevelt remained aloof in Washington, Fairbanks campaigned vigorously across the country. Roosevelt and Fairbanks easily defeated Democrats Alton B. Parker and Henry G. Davis.

While serving as McKinley's vice president, Theodore Roosevelt had advocated a greater role for the occupant of nation's second highest office. As president, however, Roosevelt made no effort to involve Fairbanks in his administration. He had a low opinion of Fairbanks and was disdainful of Fairbanks's persistent maneuverings to set himself up as the Republican nominee in 1908. Roosevelt's endorsement of Secretary of War William Howard Taft ensured that Fairbanks would not get the nomination.

After finishing his vice-presidential term, Fairbanks never again held public office, but he remained a powerful figure in national and state politics. His fellow Indiana Republicans supported his bid for the presidential nomination in 1916, but his favorite-son candidacy was unsuccessful. He asked that his name not be placed in nomination for the vice presidency that year, but, when it was, he accepted. The election was extremely close and remained in doubt until the day after the voting. Fairbanks, responding to news reports that the Republican ticket had won, even sent a congratulatory telegram to his presidential running mate, Charles Evans Hughes. Woodrow Wilson and Thomas Marshall, however, won in the electoral college 277-254.

After the defeat Fairbanks retired from politics. When World War I began, he was appointed to the Indiana State Council of Defense. He died in 1918 at the age of sixty-six after a speaking tour supporting the war effort.

In 1874 Fairbanks married Cornelia Cole, whom he had met at Ohio Wesleyan University, where they co-edited the college newspaper. The couple had five children. Cornelia died on October 24, 1913. The second largest city in Alaska is named after Fairbanks, who sat on a senatorial commission on Alaskan affairs.

Library of Congress

James S. Sherman

Born: October 24, 1855; Utica, New York
Party: Republican
Term: March 4, 1909-October 30, 1912
President: William Howard Taft
Died: October 30, 1912; Utica
Buried: Utica

James Schoolcraft Sherman was the son of Richard and Mary Sherman. James's father was a newspaper editor and a Democratic politician who held minor offices at the state and national levels. After attending both public and private schools, James enrolled at Hamilton College in Clinton, New York, where he earned a bachelor's degree in 1878 and a law degree in 1879. He then moved back to Utica, where he joined his brother-in-law's law firm.

Despite his family's Democratic affiliation, Sherman chose to enter politics as a Republican. In 1884 he was elected mayor of Utica, an office once held by his brother, who was a Democrat. Two years later Sherman won a seat in the U.S. House of Representatives, where he served from 1887 to 1891 and 1893 to 1909. As a member of Congress, Sherman was known best for his amiability and his parliamentary skills. He became close friends with Republican leaders Thomas B. Reed (R-Maine) and Joseph G. Cannon (R-Ill.), both of whom served as Speaker during Sherman's tenure in the House. Reed and Cannon frequently called on Sherman to preside over House debates.

In 1908 Theodore Roosevelt had pushed Republican party leaders to nominate William Howard Taft as his successor to the presidency, but Roosevelt did not express a strong preference for a vice-presidential candidate. When congressional Republicans led by Cannon backed Sherman's nomination for vice president, Taft and Roosevelt agreed. Sherman, like Taft, was nominated on the first ballot at the Republican national convention in Chicago.

During the 1908 campaign Sherman was accused of misconduct. Edmund Burke, a California lawyer, claimed that he and Sherman had obtained tens of thousands of acres of Indian land in New Mexico at bargain prices through bribery and Sherman's influence as chairman of the House Committee on Indian affairs. The Democrats, however, did not press the scandal issue, and the Republicans denounced the unproven charges as an attempt to slander their candidate. Taft and Sherman easily defeated William Jennings Bryan and John W. Kern 321-162 in the electoral college.

As vice president, Sherman got to do what he did best—preside over a legislative body. He won praise from both parties for his handling of the Senate. Sherman was not a close confidant of Taft, who did not like his vice president's ties to New York Republican machine politicians, but early in their term the running mates shared a regular golf game together and became more friendly.

Even before becoming vice president, Sherman suffered from Bright's disease, a kidney ailment. He became seriously ill in the spring of 1908 but recovered in time to accept the vice-presidential nomination. During his vice presidency he experienced occasional periods of illness that prevented him from presiding over the Senate. Nevertheless, he was renominated in 1912 along with Taft. In the fall he became very ill, and on October 20, 1912, he died of complications caused by his kidney condition. He was the only vice president who died before election day after having been nominated for a second term.

Because the election was just six days away, the Republican party did not have time to choose a replacement for Sherman. His death, however, did not affect the outcome of the election. Democrat Woodrow Wilson swept to victory when Theodore Roosevelt's third party candidacy split the Republican vote.

Sherman married Carrie Babcock on January 26, 1881, while he practiced law in Utica; they had three sons. Sherman's wife died in 1931 in Utica at the age of seventy-four.

Library of Congress

Thomas R. Marshall

Born: March 14, 1854; North Manchester, Indiana
Party: Democratic
Term: March 4, 1913-March 4, 1921
President: Woodrow Wilson
Died: June 1, 1925; Washington, D.C.
Buried: Indianapolis, Indiana

Thomas Riley Marshall was the son of Martha and Daniel Marshall, a country doctor. Thomas was born in Indiana, but as a boy he lived in Illinois, Kansas, and Missouri before his family resettled in Indiana. He was educated at public schools and attended Wabash College in Crawfordsville, Indiana. He graduated in 1873 and was selected for membership in Phi Beta Kappa, a national honor society.

After college Marshall studied law and was admitted to the bar in 1875. He then embarked on a successful legal career in Columbia City, Indiana. Although Marshall became friends with many prominent Democratic politicians, he never ran for office until he was nominated for governor of the state in 1908 at the age of fifty-four. Marshall's candidacy seemed a long shot, since Indiana had not had a Democratic governor since 1892. Nevertheless, he won the election by more than ten thousand votes, overcoming the coattails of Republican presidential nominee William Howard Taft, who carried Indiana by fifteen thousand votes.

As governor, Marshall opposed capital punishment (he issued many pardons), Prohibition, and voting rights for women. Because Indiana barred a governor from seeking two consecutive terms, Marshall planned to return to Columbia City when his four-year term expired. In 1912, however, Indiana Democratic party leader Thomas Taggart backed Marshall for vice president. Marshall received the number two slot on the Democratic ticket with Woodrow Wilson. Wilson and Marshall faced a Republican party divided by Theodore Roosevelt's third party candidacy. The Democrats received less than 42 percent of the popular vote but won 435 electoral votes to Roosevelt's 88 votes and President William Howard Taft's 8 votes.

While serving as vice president, Marshall gained a national reputation for his dry humor. After listening to Sen. Joseph L. Bristow (R-Kan.) deliver a long speech on the needs of the country, he remarked in a voice loud enough for many in the Senate chamber to overhear, "What this country needs is a really good five-cent cigar." This line was reported in newspapers and immediately became his most famous utterance. During his political career he declined to run for Congress on the grounds that he "might be elected."

The vice presidency was among the targets of Marshall's wit. He told a story about two brothers: "One ran away to sea; the other was elected vice president. And nothing was ever heard of either of them again." He also likened his position to "a man in a cataleptic fit; he cannot speak; he cannot move; he suffers no pain; he is perfectly conscious of all that goes on, but has no part in it."

Both President Wilson and Vice President Marshall were renominated for a second term. In the 1916 election, however, they were opposed by a Republican party united behind Charles Evans Hughes and former vice president Charles W. Fairbanks. Wilson and Marshall narrowly defeated Hughes and Fairbanks 277-254 in the electoral college.

Marshall's most significant action as vice president may have been something he did not do. When President Wilson returned to the United States after negotiating the Versailles treaty, he encountered strong Senate opposition to U.S. entry into the League of Nations that was to be created by the treaty. In response, Wilson toured the country trying to build support for ratification. The stress of the tour caused Wilson to suffer a nervous breakdown and a stroke. With Wilson paralyzed, many people advised Marshall to assume the presidency. At that time, however, there was no provision in the Constitution for the removal of an incapacitated president by the vice president. Marshall refused to make any move to replace Wilson because he believed such a move would set a bad precedent and might divide the government and the nation. Marshall merely took over many of Wilson's ceremonial duties to lighten the weakened president's work load.

When Marshall's second term expired in 1921 he retired to Indianapolis. He was the first vice president since Daniel D. Tompkins to serve two full terms. Marshall occupied his time by writing syndicated articles, delivering lectures, and traveling. Just before his death at the age of seventy-one, he finished writing *Recollections*, a book containing many of his humorous stories and witticisms.

Marshall married twenty-three-year-old Lois Kimsey on October 2, 1895. The couple had no children but took care of a foster child for a period while they lived in Washington. It is said that the couple spent only two nights of their twenty-nine-year marriage apart.

Library of Congress

Charles G. Dawes

Born: August 27, 1865; Marietta, Ohio
Party: Republican
Term: March 4, 1925-March 4, 1929
President: Calvin Coolidge
Died: April 23, 1951; Evanston, Illinois
Buried: Chicago, Illinois

Charles Gates Dawes was the son of Mary and Rufus Dawes, a Civil War general who served one term in the House of Representatives. Charles's great-great-grandfather was William Dawes, who rode with Paul Revere to alert the people near Boston that British troops were approaching on April 18, 1775.

Dawes attended Marietta College in Marietta, Ohio, graduating in 1884. He earned his law degree from Cincinnati Law School in 1886 and joined a Lincoln, Nebraska, law firm the following year. His practice grew as he became known for his expertise on banking issues and his opposition to discriminatory railway freight rates.

In 1894 Dawes bought gas and light companies in Evanston, Illinois, and LaCrosse, Wisconsin. He moved to Chicago to oversee his new business ventures. He soon expanded his profitable utility operations and was joined in business by his three brothers.

Since his days in Lincoln, Dawes had been active in the Republican party. He directed William McKinley's early 1896 presidential campaign in Illinois and became the campaign finance director after McKinley won the nomination. After McKinley became president in 1897, he appointed Dawes comptroller of the currency. In 1902 Dawes resigned and ran unsuccessfully for the Senate in Illinois. He returned to Chicago, where he organized the Central Trust Company of Illinois and became its president. The bank's success made him one of the leading financiers in the nation.

When the United States entered World War I, Dawes asked for a commission and was made a major in the Seventeenth Engineers. Soon after, his close friend, Gen. John J. Pershing, commander of the American Expeditionary Force in Europe, appointed him chief purchasing agent for the American army. Dawes oversaw the purchase and transportation of millions of tons of supplies for the troops in Europe. He retired from the army in 1919 with the rank of brigadier general. He became a popular figure after the war when he answered a petty congressional inquiry into his wartime purchasing records by exclaiming, "Hell and Maria, we weren't trying to keep a set of books, we were trying to win the war!"

President Warren G. Harding offered to appoint Dawes secretary of the treasury in 1921, but Dawes chose instead a one-year assignment as director of the new Bureau of the Budget. In 1923 Dawes was appointed chairman of the Allied Reparations Commission, formed to study Germany's budget and make recommendations on restructuring payments of its World War I reparations. He helped to develop the "Dawes Plan," adopted in August 1924, which reduced German reparation payments and provided for a foreign loan to stimulate the German economy. For his efforts Dawes was awarded the Nobel Peace Prize in 1925.

In 1924 the Republican party nominated Gov. Frank Lowden of Illinois as the vice-presidential candidate on the ticket with President Calvin Coolidge. When Lowden turned down the nomination, the convention turned to Dawes, who accepted. Coolidge and Dawes defeated Democrats John W. Davis and Charles W. Bryan 382-136 in the electoral college.

On inauguration day Dawes stole some of the limelight from President Coolidge when he demanded in his inaugural speech that the Senate pass new rules limiting filibusters. As vice president, Dawes became active in Senate politics, where he worked behind the scenes for naval appropriations, banking reforms, and farm relief programs. When President Coolidge announced he would not run for another term, Dawes also declared he would not seek reelection.

After leaving the vice presidency, Dawes was appointed ambassador to Great Britain in 1929 by President Herbert Hoover. He served there until January 1932, when Hoover appointed him director of the Reconstruction Finance Corporation (RFC), a government agency charged with making loans to banks and businesses in financial trouble. He resigned after several months to return to Chicago to reorganize his old bank into the City National Bank and Trust Company. He was criticized for securing an RFC loan for the bank shortly after resigning as the agency's director, but the loan helped return his bank to financial stability and it was properly repaid.

Dawes married Caro Blymer on January 24, 1889. When Dawes died in 1951 at the age of eighty-five, they had been married sixty-two years. Mrs. Dawes died on October 3, 1957. The couple had two children and later adopted two more. Dawes was a talented amateur composer, whose "Melody in A Major" was published in 1911. The piece became a popular song in 1951, when it was set to lyrics and retitled, "It's All in the Game."

Library of Congress

Charles Curtis

Born: January 25, 1860; North Topeka, Kansas
Party: Republican
Term: March 4, 1929-March 4, 1933
President: Herbert Hoover
Died: February 8, 1936; Washington, D.C.
Buried: Topeka, Kansas

Charles Curtis was the older of the two children of Oren and Ellen Curtis. Charles's father was a drifter who had two sons by a previous marriage, which had ended in divorce. When Ellen Curtis died in 1863, Oren left Charles and his sister in the care of their two grandmothers and joined the Union cavalry. He remained in the cavalry after the war and seldom saw his children. His daughter by a third marriage would develop a close relationship with Charles.

After living with his paternal grandmother, Permelia Curtis, from 1863 to 1866, Charles spent three years with his maternal grandmother, Julie Pappan. Mrs. Pappan, who was half Kaw Indian, lived on an Indian reservation in Kansas. During this period Charles became such a skilled horseman that he was able to supplement his income as a teenager by riding race horses at county fairs.

After 1869 Charles again lived with Permelia Curtis in North Topeka, Kansas. He had attended a mission school on the reservation, but he had fallen behind his classmates in North Topeka. Nevertheless, he graduated from a public high school in 1879. He then clerked for a Topeka lawyer and was admitted to the bar in 1881.

Curtis practiced law in Topeka for several years before being elected county attorney in 1885. His vigorous prosecution of Prohibition violators brought him statewide recognition. He returned to his law practice in 1889 but stayed active in local politics.

In 1892 Curtis was elected to the U.S. House of Representatives. His greatest strength as a politician was staying in contact with his constituents. He kept information about persons throughout his district so he would be able to answer their mail with a personal touch and call them by name on campaign trips. This attention to detail helped Curtis win seven consecutive terms.

In 1907 Curtis shifted from the House to the Senate when he was elected by the Kansas legislature to fill several months of an unexpired term. The legislature elected him to a term of his own that year, and he served until 1913, when he was defeated for reelection. In 1914, however, he was elected to the Senate in the first election in which senators were chosen by popular vote according to the new Seventeenth Amendment.

Curtis served in the Senate until 1929. He supported Prohibition, voting rights for women, and bills benefiting farmers and Indians. He rarely introduced bills or made speeches, preferring to influence legislation through personal consultations and back-room meetings with other senators. He became Republican whip in 1915 and Senate majority leader in 1924.

Curtis wanted the Republican presidential nomination in 1928, and his name was placed in nomination at the Republican national convention in Kansas City, Missouri, along with several other candidates. Herbert Hoover, however, was nominated on the first ballot. Party leaders chose Curtis for vice president because he was a political conservative from a farm state who could balance the ticket with Hoover, a liberal Californian. With the nation enjoying prosperity after eight years of Republican presidential leadership, Hoover and Curtis had little trouble defeating Democrats Alfred E. Smith and Joseph T. Robinson.

As vice president, Curtis faithfully supported Republican policies. Although he had served thirty-four years in Congress, he considered the vice presidency to be an office with higher status and asked colleagues who had called him "Charley" for decades to address him as "Mr. Vice President."

Hoover and Curtis were renominated in 1932, but the Great Depression had turned voters against the Republicans. They were defeated by Franklin D. Roosevelt and John Nance Garner 472-59 in the electoral college. After leaving the vice presidency, Curtis practiced law in Washington, D.C. He died of a heart attack in 1936.

On November 27, 1884, Curtis married Anna E. Baird, whom he had met in high school. They had three children. Anna died in 1924, five years before Curtis became vice president. The vice president's half-sister, Dolly Gann, who worked as his secretary during his years in Congress, served as his official hostess.

Library of Congress

John Nance Garner

Born: November 22, 1868; near Detroit, Texas
Party: Democratic
Term: March 4, 1933-January 20, 1941
President: Franklin D. Roosevelt
Died: November 7, 1967; Uvalde, Texas
Buried: Uvalde

John Nance Garner was the oldest of the six children of Sarah and John Garner, a former soldier in the Confederate cavalry. Young John attended a Texas country school until the fourth grade, when he stopped going because of poor health. Thereafter he was tutored by a maiden aunt.

Garner enrolled at Vanderbilt University in Nashville, Tennessee, when he was eighteen, but he returned to Texas in less than a month, considering himself scholastically unprepared for college. Rather than go back to school, he studied law under local attorneys. He was admitted to the bar in 1890 and opened a law practice in the northeast Texas city of Clarksville, about fifteen miles from where he was born.

While Garner was in Clarksville, doctors tentatively diagnosed him as having tuberculosis and advised him to move to a drier climate. He took their advice and in 1892 relocated to Uvalde, in west Texas, a town of about 2,500 people. He joined a local law firm and regained his health. Through shrewd investing, he gradually acquired thousands of acres of land, three banks, and numerous businesses that made him a millionaire.

Garner was elected a judge of Uvalde County in 1893. He served until 1896, when he returned to his law practice. Two years later he was elected to the Texas house of representatives. After two terms there, he won a seat in the U.S. House in 1902. When Woodrow Wilson was elected president in 1913, Garner gained a seat on the powerful Ways and Means Committee and soon developed into one of Wilson's most important congressional allies. Garner served in the House continuously until 1933, becoming minority leader in 1928 and Speaker on December 7, 1931.

In 1932 Garner ran for the Democratic presidential nomination. In the early balloting at the party's national convention in Chicago, he was a distant third place behind front-runner Franklin D. Roosevelt and the 1928 Democratic presidential candidate, Alfred E. Smith. After the third ballot the convention appeared to be headed for a deadlock. More than half the delegates favored Roosevelt, but he could not secure the two-thirds needed for nomination. Rather than see the party divided, Garner agreed to release his ninety delegates from Texas and California. The addition of Garner's delegates gave Roosevelt enough votes for the nomination. Roosevelt then supported Garner for the vice-presidential nomination, which the Texas representative received on the first ballot. The Roosevelt and Garner camps claimed they had not traded Garner's delegates for his nomination, but they convinced few political observers. Roosevelt and Garner were swept into office by a landslide victory over President Herbert Hoover and Vice President Charles Curtis.

Garner had reservations about taking the vice presidency because he had long aspired to the speakership of the House and had attained his goal less than a year before being nominated for vice president. Indeed, during his vice presidency, Garner would remark that his office was "not worth a bucket of warm spit." Garner, however, had wanted the party to be united for the 1932 election and believed that holding the vice presidency increased his chances of eventually becoming president.

Unlike many previous vice presidents, Garner remained active. He attended cabinet meetings and used his congressional contacts and experience to help push Franklin Roosevelt's New Deal legislation through Congress in 1933. Roosevelt and Garner were reelected in 1936, but during their second term a split developed between them. Garner was alarmed by the enhancement of executive power under Roosevelt and opposed the president's plan to increase the number of Supreme Court justices in 1937. The vice president also thought that deficit spending on Roosevelt's New Deal social programs should be cut back. In response, the president excluded Garner from many important White House meetings.

In December 1939 Garner announced he was a candidate for president, but Roosevelt chose to break precedent and seek a third term. Garner denounced the president's action, but Roosevelt was nominated by acclamation in 1940, with Garner receiving only a handful of votes at the Democratic national convention in Chicago. After this disappointment, Garner quit politics and retired to Uvalde. He died in 1967, two weeks before his ninety-ninth birthday. He lived longer than any other vice president or president.

Garner married Mariette Rheiner on November 25, 1895. They had met on a train shortly after he moved to Uvalde. Their one son, Tully, was born in 1896.

Henry A. Wallace

Library of Congress

Born: October 7, 1888; Adair County, Iowa
Party: Democratic
Term: January 20, 1941-January 20, 1945
President: Franklin D. Roosevelt
Died: November 18, 1965; Danbury, Connecticut
Buried: Des Moines, Iowa

Henry Agard Wallace was the son of May and Henry C. Wallace, a magazine editor and secretary of agriculture under Warren G. Harding and Calvin Coolidge. Henry attended public school in central Iowa and graduated in 1910 from Iowa State University in Ames with a degree in animal husbandry.

After college Wallace worked as a writer and editor on his father's magazine, *Wallaces' Farmer*, one of the most influential agricultural journals in the United States. He also conducted plant breeding experiments and farmed a small plot of land. He became associate editor of the magazine in 1916 and editor in 1924.

Despite his father's Republicanism, Wallace left the party during the late 1920s because he believed the high tariffs advocated by the Republicans hurt farmers and he supported farm export bills that President Calvin Coolidge had vetoed. Wallace backed Democrat Alfred E. Smith for president in 1928 and Franklin D. Roosevelt in 1932.

In 1933 Wallace entered public service when President Roosevelt appointed him secretary of agriculture. Wallace traveled to all forty-eight states during his first year in office to survey the plight of the farmers, who had endured low commodity prices since the 1920s. Armed with the Agriculture Adjustment Act of 1933, a measure giving the secretary of agriculture broad powers to address the farm crisis, Wallace began subsidy payments to farmers who took fields out of production, authorized the slaughter of millions of hogs to raise prices, and introduced systematic controls to prevent overproduction. He also supported Secretary of State Cordell Hull's efforts to negotiate with foreign nations tariff reductions that increased world trade and opened up markets for U.S. agricultural products.

In 1940 a rift developed between Roosevelt and Vice President John Nance Garner that caused Democratic leaders to look for a new vice-presidential candidate. During Wallace's two terms as agriculture secretary, he had supported virtually all of the president's programs, including his unpopular attempt to increase the number of Supreme Court justices in 1937. This loyalty and Wallace's popularity in farm states led Roosevelt to support him as Garner's replacement. Many Democrats, however, did not want Wallace. Not only did they consider him to be too liberal, they were suspicious of his unconventional personal philosophy, which was influenced by Eastern religions and mysticism. Nevertheless, when Roosevelt insisted that he would not run for a third term without Wallace as his running mate, the 1940 Democratic national convention in Chicago gave Wallace the nomination on the first ballot. Roosevelt and Wallace easily defeated Republicans Wendell Willkie and Charles L. McNary 449-82 in the electoral college. The vice presidency was the only office to which Wallace was ever elected.

Wallace was an active vice president. He made goodwill tours of Latin America, China, and Soviet Asia. He also became an outspoken advocate of an internationalist post-World War II foreign policy in which the United States would cooperate closely with the Soviet Union and provide economic and technical assistance to underdeveloped nations.

By 1944 Wallace's liberal views had alienated many Democratic leaders, who urged Roosevelt to drop him from the ticket. Roosevelt said he wanted to keep Wallace, but that he would also accept either Supreme Court Justice William O. Douglas or Sen. Harry Truman of Missouri. This weak endorsement ended Wallace's chances for a second term, and Truman was nominated. Roosevelt and Truman then defeated Thomas E. Dewey and William W. Bricker in the general election.

Even after being dropped from the ticket, Wallace campaigned hard for Roosevelt and Truman. Roosevelt rewarded him by naming him secretary of commerce in 1945. After Roosevelt died in April of that month, Wallace became concerned that President Truman would abandon Roosevelt's policy of friendship toward the Soviet Union. In July 1946 he wrote to the president, urging him to recognize Soviet security interests that Wallace believed were legitimate. When Wallace spoke out against Truman's tough policy toward the Soviets in September 1946, Truman fired him.

While the people of the United States were becoming increasingly alarmed by the threat of Communist expansion and subversion, Wallace continued to speak out in favor of cooperation between the superpowers. On December 29, 1947, he announced his intention to run for the presidency as the candidate of the Progressive party. Wallace's candidacy hurt Truman's chances of being elected in 1948, especially since southern Democrats had also formed a separate party and nominated Sen. Strom Thurmond of South Carolina to run for president. The endorsement of Wallace by the American Communist party, however, reinforced perceptions that he was at best a naive dreamer and at worst a Communist. Wallace received barely more than 2 percent of the vote and won no states. Truman overcame the divisions within his party to win the election.

After his defeat, Wallace retired to his farm in South Salem, New York. By 1952 Wallace's attitudes toward the Soviet Union had undergone a transformation. He published *Why I Was Wrong*, a book that explained his newfound distrust of the Soviet Union.

Wallace married Ilo Browne on May 30, 1914. They had two sons and a daughter. Before his death in 1965, Wallace spent much of his retirement conducting agricultural experiments.

Library of Congress

Alben W. Barkley

Born: November 24, 1877; Lowes, Kentucky
Party: Democratic
Term: January 20, 1949-January 20, 1953
President: Harry S Truman
Died: April 30, 1956; Lexington, Virginia
Buried: Paducah, Kentucky

Alben William Barkley was the son of Electra and John Barkley, a poor tobacco farmer and railroad worker. Alben, who was born in a log cabin, worked on his father's farm and attended country schools.

At age fourteen he entered Marvin College in Clinton, Kentucky. He paid his tuition by working as a janitor at the college. After graduating in 1897, he studied law for a year at Emory University in Oxford, Georgia. He then moved to Paducah, Kentucky, and got a job in a law office. He was admitted to the bar in 1901 and attended the University of Virginia Law School during the summer of 1902 to sharpen his legal skills.

Entering Democratic politics, Barkley won his first election in 1905, becoming prosecuting attorney of McCracken County, Kentucky. In 1909 he was elected county judge, an administrative rather than a judicial position that was primarily responsible for building and maintaining public roads. Barkley ran for the U.S. House of

Representatives in 1912 and won a seat he held continuously until he became a senator in 1927.

In Congress Barkley was a staunch supporter of President Woodrow Wilson. He backed Wilson's decision to enter World War I and voted for the Versailles Treaty. Although he supported most liberal causes, he gained a reputation as a political compromiser who would make political deals when it was in the interests of his constituents. He also was renowned for his speaking ability, which combined a bombastic style with homespun humor and wisdom. He delivered the keynote addresses at the 1932, 1936, and 1948 Democratic national conventions.

After Barkley was reelected to the Senate in 1932, Democratic Majority Leader Joseph Robinson of Arkansas appointed him assistant majority leader. In 1937, with the support of the White House, Barkley was elected majority leader when Robinson died. Barkley supported both Roosevelt's New Deal social programs and his aid to Britain and its allies before World War II. He remained majority leader until 1946, when the Republicans gained control of the Senate and he became minority leader.

In 1948 Truman's first choice for vice president was Supreme Court Justice William O. Douglas, but Douglas turned him down. Barkley had long wanted to be president, but Franklin Roosevelt's four-term grip on the Democratic presidential nomination prevented him from running. Now, at the age of seventy, Barkley was unwilling to challenge an incumbent Democratic president for the nomination, but he decided that he wanted to be vice president. He telephoned Truman during the convention to tell him he would accept a nomination as his running mate. Truman agreed to support his candidacy, and the convention nominated him by acclamation. Although opinion polls indicated that the Democrats would lose, Truman and Barkley campaigned tirelessly around the country and defeated Republicans Thomas E. Dewey and Earl Warren.

Although Barkley, at seventy-one, was the oldest vice president ever to take office, he had an active term. He lobbied Congress to support administration programs and made many ceremonial appearances. His grandson called him the "Veep," a title that stuck with the office of vice president even after Barkley had left.

In 1952 Barkley announced his interest in the presidential nomination, but he received little support because of his age. He retired briefly but was elected to the Senate in 1954 by the voters of Kentucky. He died in 1956 from a heart attack suffered during a speaking engagement at Washington and Lee College in Lexington, Virginia.

Barkley married Dorothy Brower on June 23, 1903. They had four children. Dorothy died in 1947 after a long illness. Barkley became the only incumbent vice president ever to marry, when he wed Jane Rucker Hadley, a thirty-eight-year-old St. Louis widow, on November 18, 1949.

Library of Congress

Hubert H. Humphrey

Born: May 27, 1911; Wallace, South Dakota
Party: Democratic
Term: January 20, 1965-January 20, 1969
President: Lyndon B. Johnson
Died: January 13, 1978; Waverly, Minnesota
Buried: Minneapolis, Minnesota

Hubert Horatio Humphrey, Jr., was the second of the four children of Hubert and Christine Humphrey. His father was a druggist and his mother was a Norwegian immigrant who had come to the United States in her teens. Hubert, Jr., was born above the family drugstore in Wallace, South Dakota. When he was four, the Humphreys moved to Doland, South Dakota, where his father ran another drugstore. Hubert attended public schools in Doland and was the valedictorian of his high school class.

Humphrey enrolled in the University of Minnesota in 1929, but he left the following year because of family financial troubles caused by the Great Depression. He helped his father run a drugstore in Huron, South Dakota, where his family had moved. In 1932 Humphrey entered the Denver School of Pharmacy and was licensed as a registered pharmacist in 1933. Humphrey managed the family drugstore when his father, who had been active in local politics as a Democrat, won a seat in the South Dakota state legislature.

In 1937 Humphrey returned to the University of Minnesota. He graduated *magna cum laude* in 1939 with a degree in political science and was elected to the Phi Beta Kappa honor society. He then enrolled in graduate school at Louisiana State University, where he had received a teaching assistantship. After earning his master's degree in 1940, he again returned to the University of Minnesota, hoping to earn a doctorate, but financial problems forced him to withdraw after less than a year.

Color blindness and a double hernia disqualified Humphrey from military service during World War II. Instead, he served as state director for War Production Training and later became assistant director of the state War Manpower Administration. While serving in these administrative posts, he made many political contacts, especially among labor organizations.

In 1943 Humphrey ran for mayor of Minneapolis on the Democratic ticket. He had the support of labor unions and intellectuals at the University of Minnesota, but he lost by a close vote. Two years later, after helping to forge an alliance between the Minnesota Democratic and Farmer Labor parties, he was elected mayor in his second try. He gained a reputation as a hardworking reformer and easily won a second term as mayor in 1947.

In 1948 Humphrey ran for the Senate. His advocacy of a civil rights platform at the 1948 Democratic convention in Philadelphia won him national recognition and helped him defeat his Republican opponent, Sen. Joseph Ball. In the Senate, Humphrey became a leading supporter of legislation promoting civil rights and welfare programs. He was easily reelected in 1954 and 1960.

Humphrey announced his candidacy for his party's presidential nomination in January 1960, but he withdrew after doing poorly against John F. Kennedy in the primaries. In 1961 Humphrey became Senate majority whip and helped guide several of President Kennedy's legislative proposals, including the nuclear test ban treaty and the Civil Rights Act of 1964, to approval.

In 1964 President Lyndon Johnson chose Humphrey as his running mate after securing a promise from the senator that he would remain loyal to the administration even if he disagreed with specific policies. Johnson and Humphrey defeated Republicans Barry M. Goldwater and William E. Miller by more than sixteen million popular votes.

As vice president, Humphrey was not a member of Johnson's inner circle of advisers. Nevertheless, he worked hard to help push Johnson's Great Society social programs through Congress and made several good will tours of foreign nations, including two trips to Vietnam.

After Johnson announced on March 31, 1968, that he would not seek another term, Humphrey entered the race. His nomination was secure when his main rival, Sen. Robert F. Kennedy of New York, was assassinated in Los Angeles on June 5. Humphrey's campaign was burdened by the unpopularity of the Vietnam War and the unfavorable media attention given violent protests at the Democratic national convention in Chicago. He was defeated 301-191 in the electoral college but received only a half million fewer votes than Richard Nixon out of more than sixty-three million cast.

After leaving the vice presidency in 1969 Humphrey taught at Macalester College in St. Paul, Minnesota. In 1970 he returned to the Senate after winning the seat vacated by retiring Democrat Eugene J. McCarthy. Humphrey entered the race for the 1972 Democratic presidential nomination after the campaign of Sen. Edmund S. Muskie, his 1968 vice-presidential running mate, sputtered. The nomination, however, went to Sen. George McGovern of South Dakota. Humphrey considered running for the presidency again in 1976, but he announced in April of that year that he would not be a candidate.

In August 1976 doctors detected an advanced cancer in Humphrey's prostate and bladder. Surgery failed to arrest the cancer. Despite his illness, the voters of Minnesota reelected him to the Senate in 1976. His Senate colleagues honored him by electing him deputy president pro tempore, a post created especially for him. Humphrey's fortitude and high spirits during the year preceding his death won him admiration around the country. He died at his Waverly, Minnesota, home on January 13, 1978.

Humphrey married Muriel Buck on September 3, 1936. They had one daughter and three sons. Their oldest son, Hubert H. Humphrey III, became attorney general of Minnesota. Muriel Humphrey was appointed to her husband's Senate seat after his death and served until January 3, 1979.

Library of Congress

Spiro T. Agnew

Born: November 9, 1918; Baltimore, Maryland
Party: Republican
Term: January 20, 1969-October 10, 1973
President: Richard M. Nixon

Spiro Theodore Agnew was the son of Theofrastos and Margaret Agnew. Spiro's father, whose original name was Anagnostopoulos, immigrated to the United States from Greece in 1897. He settled in Baltimore, Maryland, where he became the owner of a successful restaurant. Spiro's Greek ancestry was not a major factor in his childhood. He was raised in his mother's Episcopalian church, attended public schools, and preferred to be called "Ted."

Agnew enrolled in Johns Hopkins University in Baltimore in 1937 with the intention of studying chemistry, but he dropped out after two years. He then took classes at the Baltimore Law School at night, while holding a succession of jobs during the day, including supermarket manager and insurance claims adjuster.

In 1941 Agnew was drafted into the army and assigned to officer candidate school at Fort Knox, Kentucky. He was commissioned as a lieutenant in 1942. While serving with the Tenth Armored Division during World War II, he saw combat in France and Germany.

Agnew returned to the Baltimore Law School after the war and earned his law degree in 1947. He then opened a law office in Towson, Maryland, a Baltimore suburb. Agnew had been a Democrat, but he switched to the Republican party in the late 1940s and actively supported local Republican candidates. In 1957 he was appointed to the Zoning Board of Appeals of Baltimore County. In 1962 he ran for executive of the county, a post with responsibilities similar to those of a mayor. He won the election, becoming the first Republican in the twentieth century to be elected executive of Baltimore County.

Agnew ran for governor of Maryland in 1966. During the campaign he acquired a reputation as a liberal, in part because his Democratic opponent, George Mahoney, was a segregationist, while Agnew took a strong stand on civil rights. Substantial support from blacks and liberal Democrats helped Agnew defeat Mahoney decisively, despite the Democratic party's three-to-one advantage over the Republicans among Maryland's registered voters.

Agnew fulfilled many of his campaign promises in his first year as governor. With the cooperation of the Maryland legislature he reformed the state's tax code, increased aid to the poor, passed an open housing law, repealed the ban on racial intermarriage, liberalized the abortion law, and enacted strict regulations to reduce water pollution. In 1968, however, Agnew appeared to shift to the right. In particular, his uncompromising response to race riots in Baltimore after the assassination of civil rights leader Martin Luther King, Jr., in April 1968 caused observers to question his liberal image. Agnew called out the National Guard and had thousands of blacks arrested. He then met with black leaders and scolded them for failing to control the rioting, even though many of the leaders had made an earnest effort to stop the riots.

On August 7, 1968, Agnew placed Richard Nixon's name in nomination for president at the Republican national convention in Miami. The following morning, after Nixon had secured the nomination, he surprised many observers by announcing that he had chosen Agnew as his running mate. Agnew was virtually unknown outside of Maryland, but Nixon hoped that his new running mate would appeal to southern voters who might be drawn to the third party candidacy of former Alabama governor George C. Wallace.

During the 1968 campaign, Agnew made several political blunders that betrayed his lack of national political experience. His claim that Democratic presidential candidate Hubert H. Humphrey was "squishy soft on communism" rekindled memories of Nixon's extreme anti-communist rhetoric during the 1940s and 1950s. Agnew also used the derogatory term "Polack" in a statement referring to a person of Polish ancestry and remarked in an interview that "If you've seen one city slum, you've seen them all." Nixon and Agnew overcame these mistakes to defeat Democrats Hubert H. Humphrey and Edmund S. Muskie 301-191 in the electoral college.

As vice president, Agnew had little influence on policy decisions, but he became the administration's hard-line spokesman against liberal members of the news media, Vietnam war protesters, and other Nixon opponents. In 1972 Nixon and Agnew were reelected in a landslide. Early in 1973 Agnew's noninvolvement in the Watergate scandal made him a potential contender for his party's presidential nomination in 1976.

In August 1973, however, the U.S. attorney in Baltimore disclosed that Agnew was under investigation for receiving bribes from contractors during his years as Baltimore County executive and governor of Maryland. Agnew claimed he was innocent, but his lawyers worked out a plea bargain in which the vice president agreed to resign, plead "no contest" to income tax evasion, and pay a $10,000 fine and $150,000 in back taxes. In return, the Justice Department agreed not to prosecute Agnew for taking bribes. Agnew resigned the vice presidency on October 10, 1973. Two days later Nixon nominated Gerald R. Ford to replace him.

Early in 1974 Agnew was disbarred. He decided to write a novel to pay his debts, and in 1976 he published *The Canfield Decision*, a story about a U.S. vice president who becomes involved with Iranian militants. Agnew also opened Pathlite, Inc., a profitable consulting service for firms doing business in the Middle East. In 1980 he published his autobiography, *Go Quietly. . .or Else*, in which he claims he was innocent of the crimes that forced his resignation.

Agnew married Elinor "Judy" Judefind on May 27, 1942. The couple had met while Agnew worked in an insurance office. They had four children.

Library of Congress

Nelson A. Rockefeller

Born: July 8, 1908; Bar Harbor, Maine
Party: Republican
Term: December 19, 1974-January 20, 1977
President: Gerald R. Ford
Died: January 26, 1979; New York City
Buried: North Tarrytown, New York

Nelson Aldrich Rockefeller was the second of the six children of Abby and John D. Rockefeller, Jr. Nelson's paternal grandfather was John D. Rockefeller, the billionaire philanthropist who founded Standard Oil. Nelson's maternal grandfather was Nelson W. Aldrich, a senator from Rhode Island.

After attending private schools in New York City, Nelson enrolled in Dartmouth College in 1926. Although hindered by dyslexia, he graduated with a degree in economics in 1930 and was named to the Phi Beta Kappa honor fraternity. Rockefeller then helped manage the numerous holdings of the Rockefeller family, including real estate properties in New York City. From 1935 to 1940 he served as director of the Standard Oil subsidiary in Venezuela. During this period he developed an intense interest in Latin American affairs.

In 1940 Rockefeller entered public service when President Franklin D. Roosevelt appointed him coordinator of a new agency, the Office for Coordination of Commercial and Cultural Relations between the American Republics. During World War II the agency was renamed the Office of Inter-American Affairs. In 1944 Roosevelt transferred Rockefeller to the State Department, where he became assistant secretary for Latin American affairs. After clashing with other State Department officials in 1945, Rockefeller was asked by incoming secretary James F. Byrnes to resign. In 1950 Rockefeller returned to government when President Harry Truman appointed him to chair the Advisory Board on International Development. When the president did not commit himself to acting on the board's recommendations, Rockefeller resigned in 1951.

Rockefeller supported Dwight Eisenhower's successful bid for the presidency in 1952, and in 1953 Eisenhower appointed him under secretary of the newly created Department of Health, Education, and Welfare. In 1954 Rockefeller became special assistant to the president for foreign affairs, but he resigned in 1955 after conflicts with Secretary of State John Foster Dulles. From 1953 to 1958 Rockefeller also chaired Eisenhower's Advisory Committee on Government Organization, which studied ways to reorganize the government.

Rockefeller was elected governor of New York as a Republican in 1958. In this office he supported civil rights legislation and urban renewal and oversaw the expansion of New York's state university system. He was reelected governor in 1962, 1966, and 1970. In September 1971, after inmates had taken hostages at the state prison in Attica, Rockefeller ordered more than a thousand policemen to storm the cellblock. This controversial action culminated in the deaths of thirty-four prisoners and nine hostages.

Rockefeller wanted to be president and unsuccessfully sought the Republican nomination before all three presidential elections during the 1960s. He was a leading candidate for the nomination in 1964, but he lost it to Sen. Barry M. Goldwater of Arizona. Rockefeller suffered from an image problem. Although he was conservative on many issues, including law enforcement, military spending, and superpower relations, he was seen as an urbane liberal by the conservatives who dominated his party during the 1960s.

Rockefeller resigned from the governorship on December 18, 1973, to establish the National Commission on Critical Choices for Americans, an organization devoted to developing new national policy options.

On August 20, 1974, President Gerald R. Ford, who had succeeded to the presidency from the vice presidency after the resignation of President Richard Nixon, nominated Rockefeller for vice president. The sixty-six-year-old Rockefeller had considered another run for the presidency in 1976, but knowing his chances of being elected were small, he accepted the nomination. Under the Twenty-fifth Amendment, Rockefeller's appointment had to be approved by a majority of both houses of Congress. The confirmation hearings lasted throughout the fall as committees examined the nominee's vast financial holdings for potential conflicts of interest. Finally on December 19, 1974, he was sworn in as the forty-first vice president.

Rockefeller chaired several boards and commissions as vice president, including a commission set up by the president to investigate the CIA. At Ford's request, Rockefeller announced on November 3, 1975, that he would not accept the Republican nomination for vice president. Ford believed he could attract more votes in the Republican primaries without Rockefeller. Nevertheless, the vice president remained loyal to Ford. He delivered the speech nominating Sen. Robert J. Dole of Kansas as the Republican vice-presidential nominee and campaigned for the Ford-Dole ticket.

After leaving the vice presidency in 1977, Rockefeller returned to New York to manage various family business and philanthropic enterprises. He died of a heart attack in his Manhattan townhouse while in the company of Megan Marshack, a twenty-six-year-old assistant.

Rockefeller married Mary Todhunter ("Tod") Clark, a member of a prominent Philadelphia family, on June 23, 1930. They had three sons and two daughters. The couple became estranged during Rockefeller's first term as governor and divorced in 1962. In May 1963 he married Margaretta ("Happy") Murphy, with whom he had two sons.

White House

Walter F. Mondale

Born: January 5, 1928; Ceylon, Minnesota
Party: Democratic
Term: January 20, 1977-January 20, 1981
President: Jimmy Carter

Walter Frederick Mondale was the second of the three sons of Claribel and Theodore Mondale, a Methodist minister who served as pastor of a succession of churches in southern Minnesota. Theodore married Claribel in 1925 after the death of his first wife, with whom he also had three sons. In 1946 Walter, who was nicknamed "Fritz," graduated from Elmore (Minnesota) High School, where he excelled in athletics and music.

Mondale then entered Macalester College in St. Paul. He dropped out in 1949 when his father died, but he resumed his education at the University of Minnesota the following year. After graduating with honors in 1951, he enlisted in the army. He was discharged with the rank of corporal after serving two years at Fort Knox, Kentucky. Mondale then returned to the University of Minnesota, where he earned his law degree in 1956. That year he was admitted to the Minnesota bar and began practicing law.

Since Mondale's college years, he had been active in the Minnesota Democratic party. He became a follower of Hubert H. Humphrey in 1946 when Humphrey was mayor of Minneapolis. In 1948, when Humphrey ran successfully for the Senate, Mondale managed Humphrey's campaign in Minnesota's Second Congressional District. Mondale also worked on the campaign of Orville Freeman, who was elected governor of Minnesota in 1954, and served as Freeman's campaign chairman in his successful bid for reelection in 1958.

That year Freeman appointed Mondale special assistant to Minnesota's attorney general. When the attorney general resigned in 1960, Freeman appointed Mondale to serve out the remaining eight months of the term. Mondale was elected to the post in 1960 and reelected in 1962. As attorney general, he won praise for his enforcement of civil rights, antitrust, and consumer protection laws.

When Humphrey resigned from the Senate in 1964 after being elected vice president, Minnesota governor Karl Rolvaag appointed Mondale to Humphrey's seat. Mondale was elected to a term of his own in 1966 and reelected in 1972. In the Senate Mondale compiled a consistently liberal voting record on domestic issues. He became a leading advocate of civil rights legislation, Lyndon Johnson's Great

Society social programs, and bills benefiting farm workers, Indians, children, and the elderly. In foreign policy he was less consistent. He supported U.S. participation in the Vietnam War until 1968. He then sided with those members of Congress who sought to limit U.S. military involvement in Southeast Asia.

In 1974 Mondale took time off from his Senate duties to campaign across the country for the 1976 Democratic presidential nomination. He abandoned his candidacy after several months when he failed to attract significant support. Jimmy Carter, the eventual Democratic presidential nominee, however, selected Mondale to be his vice-presidential running mate. Carter said he chose Mondale because the Minnesota senator was qualified to assume the presidency, had substantial Washington experience that would complement Carter's "outsider" image, and gave the ticket geographic balance. On October 15, 1976, Mondale engaged Republican vice-presidential candidate Robert J. Dole in the first televised debate between vice-presidential candidates in U.S. election history. Most observers believed Mondale won the debate. Carter and Mondale defeated President Gerald R. Ford and Dole 297-240 in the electoral college.

Mondale was deeply involved in Carter administration policy making. He helped choose cabinet officers and draft policy proposals. He also met with Carter alone at least once a week and had an open invitation to attend any White House meeting. During Carter's first week in office he demonstrated Mondale's importance by sending him as a personal emissary to Western Europe and Japan. In 1980 Carter and Mondale were renominated, but a sagging economy and the Iran hostage crisis weakened their chances for reelection. They were easily defeated by Republicans Ronald Reagan and George Bush.

In 1984 Mondale was the front-runner of a pack of Democrats seeking the party's presidential nomination. Mondale overcame early primary successes by Sen. Gary Hart of Colorado to win the nomination. Mondale made history by choosing Rep. Geraldine Ferraro of New York as his running mate. She was the first woman to be nominated as vice president by a major political party. Mondale and Ferraro, however, faced President Ronald Reagan and Vice President George Bush, who were running for reelection during a period of economic prosperity. The Democrats won only Minnesota and the District of Columbia as they were buried in a forty-nine-state Republican landslide. After the election, Mondale retired from politics and returned to Minnesota.

Mondale married Joan Adams, the daughter of a Presbyterian minister, on December 27, 1955. They had two sons and a daughter.

AP

Dan Quayle

Born: February 4, 1947; Indianapolis
Party: Republican
Term: January 20, 1989-—
President: George Bush

James Danforth Quayle III was the eldest of the four children of James and Corinne Quayle. Since childhood, James was called "Dan." His maternal grandfather was Eugene C. Pulliam, a conservative Indiana newspaper publisher who amassed a fortune close to a billion dollars. In 1955 Dan moved with his family from Indiana to Phoenix, Arizona, where his father helped manage the family's newspaper interests in that state. While Dan was in high school, the Quayles moved back to Indiana, where his father took over as publisher of the *Huntington Herald-Press*, one of the family newspapers.

In 1965 Quayle enrolled in DePauw University, a small liberal arts college in Greencastle, Indiana, which was heavily endowed by his family. Quayle played on the golf team and compiled a mediocre academic record. Upon graduation in 1969 Quayle lost his student deferment and became eligible for the military draft. With the help of family friends, however, Quayle secured a place in the Indiana National Guard, an action that made military service in Vietnam unlikely.

While serving in the National Guard one weekend a month, Quayle attended Indiana University Law School at night and held a series of jobs in Indiana state government. With the help of his family he was hired as a clerk in the attorney general's office and later as an administrative assistant to Indiana governor Edgar Whitcomb. After graduating from law school in 1974, Quayle opened a law practice in Huntington and worked as associate publisher of the *Huntington Herald-Press*.

In 1976 local Republican leaders asked Quayle to run for Congress against eight-term incumbent Democrat Edward Roush. Quayle waged an energetic campaign and won despite his inexperience. He served two terms in the House before challenging Democrat Birch Bayh for his Senate seat in 1980. With the help of conservative groups, Quayle unseated Bayh after a tough campaign in which both sides used negative advertisements.

Quayle performed in the Senate with greater diligence than he had shown during his four years in the House. As a member of the Armed Services Committee, he supported most defense spending programs, including President Ronald Reagan's Strategic Defense Initiative missile defense system, but he also advocated reforms in the Pentagon's procurement process. Although Quayle sided with Senate conservatives on most issues, he occasionally demonstrated independence. In 1982 he worked with liberal senator Edward M. Kennedy on a consensus job training bill that was enacted into law despite the initial opposition of the administration. In 1986 the Democrats were unable to attract a prominent challenger, and Quayle was reelected to his seat with 61 percent of the vote.

In August 1988 Republican presidential nominee George Bush surprised the nation by naming the forty-one-year-old Quayle to be his running mate. Quayle had been mentioned as a possible vice-presidential candidate, but he was considered a long shot behind several better-known Republicans, including Rep. Jack F. Kemp of New York, Sen. Robert J. Dole of Kansas, and Sen. Alan K. Simpson of Wyoming.

Within hours of the announcement, Quayle became the subject of controversy. Journalists focused on Quayle's decision to enter the National Guard rather than risk being drafted. Not only did the action conflict with his hawkish posture in Congress, it appeared that Quayle had used his family's influence to avoid having to fight in Vietnam. Negative reports also pointed to his unimpressive academic record and his apparent use of family influence to gain admittance to the Indiana University Law School. Quayle had committed no crimes, but the media's portrait of a wealthy underachiever who used his family's connections to avoid service in Vietnam and further his career threatened to damage Bush's election chances. Some Republicans advised Bush to withdraw Quayle's nomination, but Bush stuck by his choice.

National polls in the months after the convention showed that Quayle was hurting Bush's popularity. Bush campaign strategists sought to limit Quayle's visibility by seldom having him appear with Bush and assigning him to campaign in smaller cities. Most observers also believed that Democratic vice-presidential nominee Lloyd Bentsen defeated Quayle in their one televised debate. Nevertheless, by late September Bush and Quayle had built a solid lead in public opinion polls that they held through election day. They defeated Massachusetts governor Michael S. Dukakis and Bentsen 426-112 in the electoral college. Quayle took the oath of office on January 20, 1989, becoming the forty-fourth vice president of the United States.

Quayle married Marilyn Tucker on November 18, 1972. The couple met in law school and practiced law together for a brief period before Quayle entered politics. They had two sons and a daughter.

Appendix

U.S. Presidents and Vice Presidents

President and political party	Born	Died	Age at inaugu-ration	Native of	Elected from	Term of service	Vice president
George Washington (F)	1732	1799	57	Va.	Va.	April 30, 1789-March 4, 1793	John Adams
George Washington (F)			61			March 4, 1793-March 4, 1797	John Adams
John Adams (F)	1735	1826	61	Mass.	Mass.	March 4, 1797-March 4, 1801	Thomas Jefferson
Thomas Jefferson (DR)	1743	1826	57	Va.	Va.	March 4, 1801-March 4, 1805	Aaron Burr
Thomas Jefferson (DR)			61			March 4, 1805-March 4, 1809	George Clinton
James Madison (DR)	1751	1836	57	Va.	Va.	March 4, 1809-March 4, 1813	George Clinton
James Madison (DR)			61			March 4, 1813-March 4, 1817	Elbridge Gerry
James Monroe (DR)	1758	1831	58	Va.	Va.	March 4, 1817-March 4, 1821	Daniel D. Tompkins
James Monroe (DR)			62			March 4, 1821-March 4, 1825	Daniel D. Tompkins
John Q. Adams (DR)	1767	1848	57	Mass.	Mass.	March 4, 1825-March 4, 1829	John C. Calhoun
Andrew Jackson (D)	1767	1845	61	S.C.	Tenn.	March 4, 1829-March 4, 1833	John C. Calhoun
Andrew Jackson (D)			65			March 4, 1833-March 4, 1837	Martin Van Buren
Martin Van Buren (D)	1782	1862	54	N.Y.	N.Y.	March 4, 1837-March 4, 1841	Richard M. Johnson
W. H. Harrison (W)	1773	1841	68	Va.	Ohio	March 4, 1841-April 4, 1841	John Tyler
John Tyler (W)	1790	1862	51	Va.	Va.	April 6, 1841-March 4, 1845	
James K. Polk (D)	1795	1849	49	N.C.	Tenn.	March 4, 1845-March 4, 1849	George M. Dallas
Zachary Taylor (W)	1784	1850	64	Va.	La.	March 4, 1849-July 9, 1850	Millard Fillmore
Millard Fillmore (W)	1800	1874	50	N.Y.	N.Y.	July 10, 1850-March 4, 1853	
Franklin Pierce (D)	1804	1869	48	N.H.	N.H.	March 4, 1853-March 4, 1857	William R. King
James Buchanan (D)	1791	1868	65	Pa.	Pa.	March 4, 1857-March 4, 1861	John C. Breckinridge
Abraham Lincoln (R)	1809	1865	52	Ky.	Ill.	March 4, 1861-March 4, 1865	Hannibal Hamlin
Abraham Lincoln (R)			56			March 4, 1865-April 15, 1865	Andrew Johnson
Andrew Johnson (R)	1808	1875	56	N.C.	Tenn.	April 15, 1865-March 4, 1869	
Ulysses S. Grant (R)	1822	1885	46	Ohio	Ill.	March 4, 1869-March 4, 1873	Schuyler Colfax
Ulysses S. Grant (R)			50			March 4, 1873-March 4, 1877	Henry Wilson
Rutherford B. Hayes (R)	1822	1893	54	Ohio	Ohio	March 4, 1877-March 4, 1881	William A. Wheeler
James A. Garfield (R)	1831	1881	49	Ohio	Ohio	March 4, 1881-Sept. 19, 1881	Chester A. Arthur
Chester A. Arthur (R)	1830	1886	50	Vt.	N.Y.	Sept. 20, 1881-March 4, 1885	
Grover Cleveland (D)	1837	1908	47	N.J.	N.Y.	March 4, 1885-March 4, 1889	Thomas A. Hendricks
Benjamin Harrison (R)	1833	1901	55	Ohio	Ind.	March 4, 1889-March 4, 1893	Levi P. Morton
Grover Cleveland (D)	1837	1908	55			March 4, 1893-March 4, 1897	Adlai E. Stevenson
William McKinley (R)	1843	1901	54	Ohio	Ohio	March 4, 1897-March 4, 1901	Garret A. Hobart
William McKinley (R)			58			March 4, 1901-Sept. 14, 1901	Theodore Roosevelt
Theodore Roosevelt (R)	1858	1919	42	N.Y.	N.Y.	Sept. 14, 1901-March 4, 1905	
Theodore Roosevelt (R)			46			March 4, 1905-March 4, 1909	Charles W. Fairbanks
William H. Taft (R)	1857	1930	51	Ohio	Ohio	March 4, 1909-March 4, 1913	James S. Sherman
Woodrow Wilson (D)	1856	1924	56	Va.	N.J.	March 4, 1913-March 4, 1917	Thomas R. Marshall
Woodrow Wilson (D)			60			March 4, 1917-March 4, 1921	Thomas R. Marshall
Warren G. Harding (R)	1865	1923	55	Ohio	Ohio	March 4, 1921-Aug. 2, 1923	Calvin Coolidge
Calvin Coolidge (R)	1872	1933	51	Vt.	Mass.	Aug. 3, 1923-March 4, 1925	
Calvin Coolidge (R)			52			March 4, 1925-March 4, 1929	Charles G. Dawes
Herbert Hoover (R)	1874	1964	54	Iowa	Calif.	March 4, 1929-March 4, 1933	Charles Curtis
Franklin D. Roosevelt (D)	1882	1945	51	N.Y.	N.Y.	March 4, 1933-Jan. 20, 1937	John N. Garner
Franklin D. Roosevelt (D)			55			Jan. 20, 1937-Jan. 20, 1941	John N. Garner
Franklin D. Roosevelt (D)			59			Jan. 20, 1941-Jan. 20, 1945	Henry A. Wallace
Franklin D. Roosevelt (D)			63			Jan. 20, 1945-April 12, 1945	Harry S Truman
Harry S Truman (D)	1884	1972	60	Mo.	Mo.	April 12, 1945-Jan. 20, 1949	
Harry S Truman (D)			64			Jan. 20, 1949-Jan. 20, 1953	Alben W. Barkley
Dwight D. Eisenhower (R)	1890	1969	62	Texas	N.Y.	Jan. 20, 1953-Jan. 20, 1957	Richard Nixon
Dwight D. Eisenhower (R)			66		Pa.	Jan. 20, 1957-Jan. 20, 1961	Richard Nixon
John F. Kennedy (D)	1917	1963	43	Mass.	Mass.	Jan. 20, 1961-Nov. 22, 1963	Lyndon B. Johnson
Lyndon B. Johnson (D)	1908	1973	55	Texas	Texas	Nov. 22, 1963-Jan. 20, 1965	
Lyndon B. Johnson (D)			56			Jan. 20, 1965-Jan. 20, 1969	Hubert H. Humphrey
Richard Nixon (R)	1913		56	Calif.	N.Y.	Jan. 20, 1969-Jan. 20, 1973	Spiro T. Agnew
Richard Nixon (R)			60		Calif.	Jan. 20, 1973-Aug. 9, 1974	Spiro T. Agnew Gerald R. Ford
Gerald R. Ford (R)	1913		61	Neb.	Mich.	Aug. 9, 1974-Jan. 20, 1977	Nelson A. Rockefeller
Jimmy Carter (D)	1924		52	Ga.	Ga.	Jan. 20, 1977-Jan. 20, 1981	Walter F. Mondale
Ronald Reagan (R)	1911		69	Ill.	Calif.	Jan. 20, 1981-Jan. 20, 1985	George Bush
Ronald Reagan (R)			73			Jan. 20, 1985-Jan. 20, 1989	George Bush
George Bush (R)	1924		64	Mass.	Texas	Jan. 20, 1989-	Dan Quayle

Source: Presidential Elections Since 1789, 4th ed. (Washington, D.C.: Congressional Quarterly Inc., 1987), 4.

Note: D—Democrat; DR—Democratic-Republican; F—Federalist; R—Republican; W—Whig.

Documents and Texts

The documentary history of the presidency is long and extensive. It begins before the actual creation of the office at the Constitutional Convention of 1787 with documents from the American Revolution that helped to prepare the way for the presidency. It includes official messages and orders by individual presidents, presidential speeches, Supreme Court decisions, congressional resolutions, and other official and unofficial documents.

In compiling this section of the Appendix, an effort has been made to include the most important presidential documents (a sort of "Top 40" from the history of the office), with an emphasis on the twentieth-century presidency. But no pretense is made to comprehensiveness; for reasons of space, many important documents had to be omitted. In addition, most of the documents in this Appendix have been edited to retain only the most important material. Omissions are indicated by ellipses (. . .).

A more complete and less heavily edited compilation of presidential documents may be found in Michael Nelson, ed., *Historic Documents on the Presidency: 1776-1989,* also published by Congressional Quarterly Inc.

Declaration of Independence

On June 11, 1776, the responsibility to "prepare a declaration" of independence was assigned by the Continental Congress, meeting in Philadelphia, to five members: John Adams, Benjamin Franklin, Thomas Jefferson, Robert Livingston, and Roger Sherman. Impressed by his talents as a writer, the committee asked Jefferson to compose a draft. After modifying Jefferson's draft the committee turned it over to Congress on June 28. On July 2 Congress voted to declare independence; on the evening of July 4, it approved the Declaration of Independence.

The Declaration is best remembered for its ringing preamble, which affirms the "self-evident" truths that "all men are created equal, that they are endowed by their Creator with certain unalienable Rights, that among these are Life, Liberty, and the pursuit of Happiness." But, at the time, the more important part of the Declaration was what followed the preamble: the list of "a long train of abuses and usurpations" against the American colonists by the British government. The charges detailed the abuses that made it "necessary for one people [the Americans] to dissolve the political bands which have connected them with another [the British]." Although many of the more than two dozen specific alleged abuses were acts of Parliament, all were attributed to King George III. The indictment—and the Declaration as a whole—thus contributed to the idea that a strong executive was a threat to the fundamental liberties of the people.

Headnotes by Michael Nelson

In Congress, July 4, 1776,

The Unanimous Declaration of the
Thirteen United States of America,

When in the Course of human events, it becomes necessary for one people to dissolve the political bands which have connected them with another, and to assume among the Powers of the earth, the separate and equal station to which the Laws of Nature and of Nature's God entitle them, a decent respect to the opinions of mankind requires that they should declare the causes which impel them to the separation.

We hold these truths to be self-evident, that all men are created equal, that they are endowed by their Creator with certain unalienable Rights, that among these are Life, Liberty and the pursuit of Happiness. That to secure these rights, Governments are instituted among Men, deriving their just powers from the consent of the governed. That whenever any form of Government becomes destructive of these ends, it is the Right of the People to alter or to abolish it, and to institute new Government, laying its foundation on such principles and organizing its powers in such form, as to them shall seem most likely to effect their Safety and Happiness. Prudence, indeed, will dictate that Government long established should not be changed for light and transient causes; and accordingly all experience hath shown, that mankind are more disposed to suffer, while evils are sufferable, than to right themselves by abolishing the forms to which they are accustomed. But when a long train of abuses and usurpations, pursuing invariably the same Object evinces a design to reduce them under absolute Despotism, it is their right, it is their duty, to throw off such Government, and to provide new Guards for their future security. —Such has been the patient sufferance of these Colonies; and such is now the necessity which constrains them to alter their former Systems of Government. The history of the present King of Great Britain is a history of repeated injuries and usurpations, all having in direct object the establishment of an absolute Tyranny over these States. To prove this, let Facts be submitted to a candid world.

He has refused his Assent to Laws, the most wholesome and necessary for the public good.

He has forbidden his Governors to pass Laws of immediate and pressing importance, unless suspended in their operation till his Assent should be obtained; and when so suspended, he has utterly neglected to attend to them.

He has refused to pass other Laws for the accommodation of large districts of people, unless those people would relinquish the right of Representation in the Legislature, a right inestimable to them and formidable to tyrants only.

He has called together legislative bodies at places unusual, uncomfortable, and distant from the depository of their Public Records, for the sole purpose of fatiguing them into compliance with his measures.

He has dissolved Representative Houses repeatedly, for opposing with manly firmness his invasions on the rights of the people.

He has refused for a long time, after such dissolutions, to cause others to be elected; whereby the Legislative Powers, incapable of Annihilation, have returned to the People at large for their exercise; the State remaining in the mean time exposed to all the dangers of invasion from without, and convulsions within.

He has endeavored to prevent the population of these States; for that purpose obstructing the Laws of Naturalization of Foreigners; refusing to pass others to encourage their migration hither, and raising the conditions of new Appropriations of Lands.

He has obstructed the Administration of Justice, by refusing his Assent to Laws for establishing Judiciary Powers.

He has made Judges dependent on his Will alone, for the tenure of their offices, and the amount and payment of their salaries.

He has erected a multitude of New Offices, and sent hither swarms of Officers to harass our People, and eat out their substance.

He has kept among us, in times of peace, Standing Armies without the Consent of our legislature.

He has affected to render the Military independent of and superior to the Civil Power.

He has combined with others to subject us to a jurisdiction foreign to our constitution, and unacknowledged by our laws; giving his Assent to their acts of pretended legislation:

For quartering large bodies of armed troops among us:

For protecting them, by a mock Trial, from Punishment for any Murders which they should commit on the Inhabitants of these States:

For cutting off our Trade with all parts of the world:

For imposing taxes on us without our Consent:

For depriving us in many cases, of the benefits of Trial by Jury:

For transporting us beyond Seas to be tried for pretended offences:

For abolishing the free System of English Laws in a neighbouring Province, establishing therein an Arbitrary government, and enlarging its Boundaries so as to render it at once an example and fit instrument for introducing the same absolute rule into these Colonies:

For taking away our Charters, abolishing our most valuable Laws, and altering fundamentally the Forms of our Governments:

For suspending our own Legislature, and declaring themselves invested with Power to legislate for us in all cases whatsoever.

He has abdicated Government here, by declaring us out of his Protection and waging War against us.

He has plundered our seas, ravaged our Coasts, burnt our towns, and destroyed the lives of our people.

He is at this time transporting large armies of foreign mercenaries to compleat the works of death, desolation and tyranny, already begun with circumstances of Cruelty & perfidy scarcely parallel in the most barbarous ages, and totally unworthy the Head of a civilized nation.

He has constrained our fellow Citizens taken Captive on the high Seas to bear Arms against their Country, to become the executioners of their friends and Brethren, or to fall themselves by their Hands.

He has excited domestic insurrections amongst us, and has endeavoured to bring on the inhabitants of our frontiers, the merciless Indian Savages, whose known rule of warfare, is an undistinguished destruction of all ages, sexes and conditions.

In every stage of these Oppressions We have Petitioned for Redress in the most humble terms: Our repeated Petitions have been answered only by repeated injury. A Prince, whose character is thus marked by every act which may define a Tyrant, is unfit to be the ruler of a free People.

Nor have We been wanting in attention to our British brethren. We have warned them from time to time of attempts by their legislature to extend an unwarrantable jurisdiction over us. We have reminded them of the circumstances of our emigration and settlement here. We have appealed to their native justice and magnanimity, and we have conjured them by the ties of our common kindred to disavow these usurpations, which would inevitably interrupt our connections and correspondence. They too have been deaf to the voice of justice and of consanguinity. We must, therefore, acquiesce in the necessity, which denounces our Separation, and hold them, as we hold the rest of mankind, Enemies in War, in Peace Friends.

We, therefore, the Representatives of the United States of America, in General Congress, Assembled, appealing to the Supreme Judge of the world for the rectitude of our intentions, do, in the Name, and by Authority of the good People of these Colonies, solemnly publish and declare, That these United Colonies are, and of Right ought to be Free and Independent States; that they are Absolved from all Allegiance to the British Crown, and that all political connection between them and the State of Great Britain, is and ought to be totally dissolved; and that as Free and Independent States, they have full Power to levy War, conclude Peace, contract Alliances, establish Commerce, and to do all other Acts and Things which Independent States may of right do. And for the support of this Declaration, with a firm reliance on the Protection of Divine Providence, we mutually pledge to each other our Lives, our Fortunes and our sacred Honor.

JOHN HANCOCK.

New Hampshire:
Josiah Bartlett,
William Whipple,
Matthew Thornton.

Massachusetts-Bay:
Samuel Adams,
John Adams,
Robert Treat Paine,
Elbridge Gerry.

Rhode Island:
Stephen Hopkins,
William Ellery.

Connecticut:
Roger Sherman,
Samuel Huntington,
William Williams,
Oliver Wolcott.

New York:
William Floyd,
Philip Livingston,
Francis Lewis,
Lewis Morris.

Pennsylvania:
Robert Morris,
Benjamin Harris,
Benjamin Franklin,
John Morton,
George Clymer,
James Smith,
George Taylor,
James Wilson,
George Ross.

Delaware:
Caesar Rodney,
George Read,
Thomas McKean.

Georgia:
Button Gwinnett,
Lyman Hall,
George Walton.

Maryland:	Samuel Chase, William Paca, Thomas Stone, Charles Carroll of Carrollton.
Virginia:	George Wythe, Richard Henry Lee, Thomas Jefferson, Benjamin Harrison, Thomas Nelson Jr., Francis Lightfoot Lee, Carter Braxton.
North Carolina:	William Hooper, Joseph Hewes, John Penn.
South Carolina:	Edward Rutledge, Thomas Heyward Jr., Thomas Lynch Jr., Arthur Middleton.
New Jersey:	Richard Stockton, John Witherspoon, Francis Hopkinson, John Hart, Abraham Clark.

Articles of Confederation

On June 11, 1776, the same day that it created a five-member committee to prepare the Declaration of Independence, the Continental Congress appointed a thirteen-member committee (one from each state) to draft a "plan of confederation." The two decisions were closely connected: a new and independent nation needed a government of some sort. The committee recommended the Articles of Confederation to Congress on July 12; Congress adopted the plan on November 15, 1777; and unanimous ratification by the states finally came on March 1, 1781.

Written at a time when hostility against a strong central government (the British) and executive power (the king and his royal governors in each colony) was at its height, the Articles, not surprisingly, provided for a weak central government with no executive at all. Congress—a unicameral body in which each state was represented equally—was the sole organ of the new national government. It had no power to levy taxes or to enforce any laws that it passed. Even the powers that it did have—such as to raise an army and navy, regulate coinage and borrow money, and adjudicate disputes among the states—were hard to exercise, because any proposed law required a two-thirds majority for passage. (To amend the Articles required unanimity.)

The Articles of Confederation provided a barely adequate framework for fighting and winning the Revolutionary War: the presence of a common enemy fostered a certain amount of unity among the states. But when the British were defeated in 1783, the national government found it increasingly difficult to unite the country to confront the new challenges of peace.

To all to whom these Presents shall come, we the undersigned Delegates of the States affixed to our Names send greeting. Whereas the Delegates of the United States of America in Congress assembled did on the fifteenth day of November in the Year of our Lord One Thousand Seven Hundred and Seventy seven, and in the Second Year of the Independence of America agree to certain articles of Confederation and perpetual Union between the States of Newhampshire, Massachusetts-bay, Rhodeisland and Providence Plantations, Connecticut, New York, New Jersey, Pennsylvania, Delaware, Maryland, Virginia, North-Carolina, South-Carolina and Georgia in the Words following, viz. "Articles of Confederation and perpetual Union between the states of Newhampshire, Massachusetts-bay, Rhodeisland and Providence Plantations, Connecticut, New-York, New-Jersey, Pennsylvania, Delaware, Maryland, Virginia, North-Carolina, South-Carolina and Georgia.

Article I. The Stile of this confederacy shall be "The United States of America."

Article II. Each state retains its sovereignty, freedom and independence, and every Power, Jurisdiction and Right, which is not by this confederation expressly delegated to the United States, in Congress assembled.

Article III. The said states hereby severally enter into a firm league of friendship with each other, for their common defence, the security of their Liberties, and their mutual and general welfare, binding themselves to assist each other, against all force offered to, or attacks made upon them, or any of them, on account of religion, sovereignty, trade, or any other pretence whatever.

Article IV. The better to secure the perpetuate mutual friendship and intercourse among the people of the different states in this union, the free inhabitants of each of these states, paupers, vagabonds and fugitives from Justice excepted, shall be entitled to all privileges and immunities of free citizens in the several states; and the people of each state shall have free ingress and regress to and from any other state, and shall enjoy therein all the privileges of trade and commerce, subject to the same duties, impositions and restrictions as the inhabitants thereof respectively, provided that such restriction shall not extend so far as to prevent the removal of property imported into any state, to any other state of which the Owner is an inhabitant; provided also that no imposition, duties or restriction shall be laid by any state, on the property of the united states, or either of them.

If any Person guilty of, or charged with treason, felony, or other high misdemeanor in any state, shall flee from Justice, and be found in any of the united states, he shall upon demand of the Governor or executive power, of the state from which he fled be delivered up and removed to the state having jurisdiction of his offence.

Full faith and credit shall be given in each of these states to the records, acts and judicial proceedings of the courts and magistrates of every other state.

Article V. For the more convenient management of the general interests of the united states, delegates shall be annually appointed in such manner as the legislature of each state shall direct, to meet in Congress on the first Monday in November, in every year, with a power reserved to each state, to recall its delegates, or any of them, at any time within the year, and to send others in their stead, for the remainder of the Year.

No state shall be represented in Congress by less than two, nor by more than seven Members; and no person shall be capable of being a delegate for more than three years in any term of six years; nor shall any person, being a delegate, be capable of holding any office under the united states, for which he, or another for his benefit receives any salary, fees or emolument of any kind.

Each state shall maintain its own delegates in a meeting of the states, and while they act as members of the committee of the states.

In determining questions in the united states, in Congress assembled, each state shall have one vote.

Freedom of speech and debate in Congress shall not be impeached or questioned in any Court, or place out of Congress, and the members of congress shall be protected in their persons from arrests and imprisonments, during the time of their going to and from, and attendance on congress, except for treason, felony, or breach of the peace.

Article VI. No state without the Consent of the united states in congress assembled, shall send any embassy to, or receive any embassy from, or enter into any conference, agreement, or alliance or treaty with any King, prince or state; nor shall any person holding any office of profit or trust under the united states, or any of them, accept of any present, emolument, office or title of any kind whatever from any king, prince or foreign state; nor shall the united states in congress assembled, or any of them, grant any title of nobility.

No two or more states shall enter into any treaty, confederation or alliance whatever between them, without the consent of the united states in congress assembled, specifying accurately the purposes for which the same is to be entered into, and how long it shall continue.

No state shall lay any imposts or duties, which may interfere with any stipulations in treaties, entered into by the united states in congress assembled, with any king, prince or state, in pursuance of any treaties already proposed by congress, to the courts of France and Spain.

No vessels of war shall be kept up in time of peace by any state, except such number only, as shall be deemed necessary by the united states in congress assembled, for the defence of such state, or its trade; nor shall any body of forces be kept up by any state, in time of peace, except such number only, as in the judgment of the united states, in congress assembled, shall be deemed requisite to garrison the forts necessary for the defence of such state; but every state shall always keep up a well regulated and disciplined militia, sufficiently armed and accoutred, and shall provide and constantly have ready for use, in public stores, a due number of field pieces and tents, and a proper quantity of arms, ammunition and camp equipage.

No state shall engage in any war without the consent of the united states in Congress assembled, unless such state be actually invaded by enemies, or shall have received certain advice of a resolution being formed by some nation of Indians to invade such state; and the danger is so imminent as not to admit of a delay, till the united states in congress assembled can be consulted: nor shall any state grant commissions to any ships or vessels of war, nor letters of marque or reprisal, except it be after a declaration of war by the united states in congress assembled, and then only against the kingdom or state and the subjects thereof, against which war has been so declared, and under such regulations as shall be established by the united states in congress assembled, unless such state be infested by pirates, in which case vessels of war may be fitted out for that occasion, and kept so long as the danger shall continue, or until the united states in congress assembled shall determine otherwise.

Article VII. When land-forces are raised by any state for the common defence, all officers of or under the rank of colonel, shall be appointed by the legislature of each state respectively by whom such forces shall be raised, or in such manner as such state shall direct, and all vacancies shall be filled up by the state which first made the appointment.

Article VIII. All charges of war, and all other expences that shall be incurred for the common defence or general welfare, and allowed by the united states in congress assembled, shall be defrayed out of a common treasury, which shall be supplied by the several states, in proportion to the value of all land within each state, granted to or surveyed for any Person, as such land and the buildings and improvements thereon shall be estimated according to such mode as the united states in congress assembled, shall from time to time direct and appoint. The taxes for paying that proportion shall be laid and levied by the authority and direction of the legislatures of the several states within the time agreed upon by the united states in congress assembled.

Article IX. The united states in congress assembled, shall have the sole and exclusive right and power of determining on peace and war, except in the cases mentioned in the sixth article—of sending and receiving ambassadors—entering into treaties and alliances, provided that no treaty of commerce shall be made whereby the legislative power of the respective states shall be restrained from imposing such imposts and duties on foreigners, as their own people are subjected to, or from prohibiting the exportation or importation of any species of goods or commodities whatsoever—of establishing rules for deciding in all cases, what capture on land or water shall be legal, and in what manner prizes taken by land or naval forces in the service of the united states shall be divided or appropriated—of granting letters of marque and reprisal in times of peace—appointing courts for the trial of piracies and felonies committed on the high seas and establishing courts for receiving and determining finally appeals in all cases of captures, provided that no member of congress shall be appointed a judge of any of the said courts.

The united states in congress assembled shall also be the last resort on appeal in all disputes and differences now subsisting or that hereafter may arise between two or more states concerning boundary, jurisdiction or any other cause whatever; which authority shall always be exercised in the manner following. Whenever the legislative or executive authority or lawful agent of any state in controversy with another shall present a petition to congress, stating the matter in question and praying for a hearing, notice thereof shall be given by order of congress to the legislative or executive authority of the other state in controversy, and a day assigned for the appearance of the parties by their lawful agents, who shall then be directed to appoint by joint consent, commissioners or judges to constitute a court for hearing and determining the matter in question: but if they cannot agree, congress shall name three persons out of each of the united states, and from the list of such persons each party shall alternately strike out one, the petitioners beginning, until the number shall be reduced to thirteen; and from that number not less than seven, nor more than nine names as congress shall direct, shall in the presence of congress be drawn out by lot, and the persons whose names shall be so drawn or any five of them, shall be commissioners or judges, to hear and finally determine the controversy, so always as a major part of the judges who shall hear the cause shall agree in the determination: and if either party shall neglect to attend at the day appointed, without shewing reasons, which congress shall judge sufficient, or being present shall refuse to strike, the congress shall proceed to nominate three persons out of each state, and the secretary of congress shall strike in behalf of such party absent or refusing; and the judgment and sentence of the court to be appointed, in the manner before prescribed, shall be final and conclusive; and if any of the parties shall refuse to submit to the authority of such court, or to appear to defend their claim or cause, the court shall nevertheless proceed to pronounce sentence, or judgment, which shall in like manner be final and decisive, the judgment or sentence and other proceedings being in either case transmitted to congress, and lodged among the acts of congress for the security of the parties concerned: provided that every commissioner, before he sits in judgment, shall take an oath to be administered by one of the judges of the supreme or superior court of the state, where the cause shall be tried, "well and truly to hear and determine the matter in question, according to the best of his judgment, without favour, affection or hope of reward:" provided also that no state shall be deprived of territory for the benefit of the united states.

All controversies concerning the private right of soil claimed under different grants of two or more states, whose jurisdictions as they may respect such lands, and the states which passed such grants are adjusted, the said grants or either of them being at the same time claimed to have originated antecedent to such settlement of jurisdiction, shall on the petition of either party to the congress of the united states, be finally determined as near as may be in the same manner as is before prescribed for deciding disputes respecting territorial jurisdiction between different states.

The united states in congress assembled shall also have the sole and exclusive right and power of regulating the alloy and value of coin struck by their own authority, or by that of the respective states—fixing the standard of weights and measures throughout the united states—regulating the trade and managing all affairs with the Indians, not members of any of the states, provided that the legislative right of any state within its own limits be not infringed or violated—establishing and regulating post-offices from one state to another, throughout all the united states, and exacting such postage on the papers passing thro' the same as may be requisite to defray the expences of the said office—appointing all officers of the land forces, in the service of the united states, excepting regimental officers—appointing all the officers of the naval forces, and commissioning all officers whatever in the service of the united states—making rules for the government and regulation of the said land and naval forces, and directing their operations.

The united states in congress assembled shall have authority to appoint a committee, to sit in the recess of congress, to be denominated "A Committee of the States," and to consist of one delegate from each state; and to appoint such other committees and civil officers as may be necessary for managing the general affairs of the united states under their direction—to appoint one of their number to preside, provided that no person be allowed to serve in the office of president more than one year in any term of three years; to ascertain the necessary sums of Money to be raised for the service of the united states, and to appropriate and apply the same for defraying the public expences—to borrow money, or emit bills on the credit of the united states, transmitting every half year to the respective states an account of the sums of money so borrowed or emitted,—to build and equip a navy—to agree upon the number of land forces, and to make requisitions from each state for its quota, in proportion to the number of white inhabitants in such state; which requisition shall be binding, and thereupon the legislature of each state shall appoint the regimental officers, raise the men and cloath, arm and equip them in a soldier like manner, at the expence of the united states, and the officers and men so cloathed, armed and equipped shall march to the place appointed, and within the time agreed on by the united states in congress assembled: But if the united states in congress assembled shall, on consideration of circumstances judge proper that any state should not raise men, or should raise a smaller number than its quota, and that any other state should raise a greater number of men than the quota thereof, such extra number shall be raised, officered, cloathed, armed and equipped in the same manner as the quota of such state, unless the legislature of such state shall judge that such extra number cannot be safely spared out of the same, in which case they shall raise, officer, cloath, arm and equip as many of such extra number as they judge can be safely spared. And the officers and men so cloathed, armed and equipped, shall march to the place appointed, and within the time agreed on by the united states in congress assembled.

The united states in congress assembled shall never engage in a war, nor grant letters of marque and reprisal in time of peace, nor enter into any treaties or alliances, nor coin money, nor regulate the value thereof, nor ascertain the sums and expences necessary for the defence and welfare of the united states, or any of them, nor emit bills, nor borrow money on the credit of the united states, nor appropriate money, nor agree upon the number of vessels of war, to be built or purchased, or the number of land or sea forces to be raised, nor appoint a commander in chief of the army or navy, unless nine states assent to the same: nor shall a question on any other point, except for adjourning from day to day be determined, unless by the votes of a majority of the united states in congress assembled.

The congress of the united states shall have power to adjourn to any time within the year, and to any place within the united states, so that no period of adjournment be for a longer duration than the space of six Months, and shall publish the Journal of their proceedings monthly, except such parts thereof relating to treaties, alliances or military operations as in their judgment require secresy; and the yeas and nays of the delegates of each state on any question shall be entered on the Journal, when it is desired by any delegate; and the delegates of a state, or any of them, at his or their request shall be furnished with a transcript of the said Journal, except such parts as are above excepted, to lay before the legislatures of the several states.

Article X. The committee of the states, or any nine of them, shall be authorised to execute, in the recess of congress, such of the powers of congress as the united states in congress assembled, by the consent of nine states, shall from time to time think expedient to vest them with; provided that no power be delegated to the said committee, for the exercise of which, by the articles of confederation, the voice of nine states in the congress of the united states assembled is requisite.

Article XI. Canada acceding to this confederation, and joining in the measures of the united states, shall be admitted into, and entitled to all the advantages of this union: but no other colony shall be admitted into the same, unless such admission be agreed to by nine states.

Article XII. All bills of credit emitted, monies borrowed and debts contracted by, or under the authority of congress, before the assembling of the united states, in pursuance of the present confederation, shall be deemed and considered as a charge against the united states, for payment and satisfaction whereof the said united states, and the public faith are hereby solemnly pledged.

Article XIII. Every state shall abide by the determinations of the united states in congress assembled, on all questions which by this confederation are submitted to them. And the Articles of this confederation shall be inviolably observed by every state, and the union shall be perpetual; nor shall any alteration at any time hereafter be made in any of them; unless such alteration be agreed to in a congress of the united states, and be afterwards confirmed by the legislatures of every state.

And Whereas it has pleased the Great Governor of the World to incline the hearts of the legislatures we respectively represent in congress, to approve of, and to authorize us to ratify the said articles of confederation and perpetual union. Know Ye that we the under-signed delegates, by virtue of the power and authority to us given for that purpose, do by these presents, in the name and in behalf of our respective constituents, fully and entirely ratify and confirm each and every of the said articles of confederation and perpetual union, and all and singular the matters and things therein contained: And we do further solemnly plight and engage the faith of our respective constituents, that they shall abide by the determinations of the united states in congress assembled, on all questions, which by the said confederation are submitted to them. And that the articles thereof shall be inviolably observed by the states we respectively represent, and that the union shall be perpetual. In Witness whereof we have hereunto set our hands in Congress. Done at Philadelphia in the state of Pennsylvania the ninth Day of July in the Year of our Lord one Thousand seven Hundred and Seventy-eight, and in the third year of the independence of America.

New Hampshire: Josiah Bartlett, John Wentworth Jr.

Massachusetts: John Hancock, Samuel Adams, Elbridge Gerry, Francis Dana, James Lovell, Samuel Holten.

Rhode Island: William Ellery, Henry Marchant, John Collins.

Connecticut: Roger Sherman, Samuel Huntington, Oliver Wolcott, Titus Hosmer, Andrew Adams.

New York: James Duane, Francis Lewis, William Duer, Gouverneur Morris.

New Jersey: John Witherspoon, Nathaniel Scudder.

Pennsylvania: Robert Morris, Daniel Roberdeau, Jonathan Bayard Smith, William Clingan, Joseph Reed.

Delaware: Thomas McKean, John Dickinson, Nicholas Van Dyke.

Maryland: John Hanson, Daniel Carroll.

Virginia: Richard Henry Lee, John Banister, Thomas Adams, John Harvie, Francis Lightfoot Lee.

North Carolina: John Penn, Cornelius Harnett, John Williams.

South Carolina: Henry Laurens, William Henry Drayton, John Mathews, Richard Hutson, Thomas Heyward Jr.

Georgia: John Walton, Edward Telfair, Edward Langworthy.

The Virginia Plan of Union

James Madison of Virginia not only helped to orchestrate the calling of the Constitutional Convention of 1787, he arrived in Philadelphia several days before it began and drafted a proposed plan of government to lay before the delegates. Madison, who was only thirty-six years old and lacked a strong national reputation, persuaded the governor of his state, Edmund Randolph, to introduce the plan on May 29, the convention's first day of business.

The Virginia Plan proposed a radical departure from the Articles of Confederation—a strong, three-branch national government whose powers would make it superior to the states. The legislature would have two houses, not one, and would be apportioned according to population, not state equality. In addition, the new government would have an executive and a judicial branch. The executive would be chosen by the legislature, but was otherwise undefined in the plan.

The Virginia Plan was endorsed in principle by the delegates to the convention, and it provided a working agenda for their deliberations.

1. Resolved that the Articles of Confederation ought to be so corrected and enlarged as to accomplish the objects proposed by their institution; namely "common defence, security of liberty and general welfare."

2. Resolved therefore that the rights of suffrage in the National Legislature ought to be proportioned to the Quotas of contribution, or to the number of free inhabitants, as the one or the other rule may seem best in different cases.

3. Resolved that the National Legislature ought to consist of two branches.

4. Resolved that the members of the first branch of the National Legislature ought to be elected by the people of the several States every   for the terms of   ; to be of the age of   years at least, to receive liberal stipends by which they may be compensated for the devotion of their time to public service, to be ineligible to any office established by a particular State, or under the authority of the United States, except those peculiarly belonging to the functions of the first branch, during the term of service, and for the space of   after its expiration; to be incapable of reelection for the space of   after the expiration of their term of service, and to be subject to recall.

5. Resolved that the members of the second branch of the National Legislature ought to be elected by those of the first, out of a proper number of persons nominated by the individual Legislatures, to be of the age of   years at least; to hold their offices for a term sufficient to ensure their independency; to receive liberal stipends, by which they may be compensated for the devotion of their time to public service; and to be ineligible to any office established by a particular State, or under the authority of the United States, except those peculiarly belonging to the functions of the second branch, during the term of service, and for the space of   after the expiration thereof.

6. Resolved that each branch ought to possess the right of originating Acts; that the National Legislature ought to be impowered to enjoy the Legislative Rights vested in Congress by the Confederation and moreover to legislate in all cases to which the separate States are incompetent, or in which the harmony of the United States may be interrupted by the exercise of individual Legislation; to negative all laws passed by the several States, contravening in the opinion of the National Legislature the articles of Union; and to call forth the force of the Union against any member of the Union failing in its duty under the articles thereof.

7. Resolved that a National Executive be instituted; to be chosen by the National Legislature for the term of   years; to receive punctually, at stated times, a fixed compensation for the services rendered, in which no increase or diminution shall be made so as to affect the Magistracy, existing at the time of the increase or diminution, and to be ineligible a second time; and that besides a general authority to execute the National laws, it ought to enjoy the Executive rights vested in Congress by the Confederation.

8. Resolved that the Executive and a convenient number of the National Judiciary, ought to compose a Council or revision with authority to examine every act of the National Legislature before it shall operate, and every act of a particular Legislature before a Negative thereon shall be final; and that the dissent of the said Council shall amount to a rejection, unless the Act of the National Legislature be passed again, or that of a particular Legislature be again negatived by   of the members of each branch.

9. Resolved that a National Judiciary be established to consist of one or more supreme tribunals, and of inferior tribunals to be chosen by the National Legislature, to hold their offices during good behavior; and to receive punctually at stated times fixed compensation for their services, in which no increase or diminution shall be made so as to affect the persons actually in office at the time of such increase or diminution. That the jurisdiction of the inferior tribunals shall be to hear and determine in the first instance, and of the supreme tribunal to hear and determine in the dernier resort, all piracies and felonies on the high seas, captures from an enemy; cases in which foreigners or citizens of other States applying to such jurisdictions may be interested, or which respect the collection of the National revenue; impeachments of any National officers, and questions which may involve the national peace and harmony.

10. Resolved that provision ought to be made for the admission of States lawfully arising within the limits of the United States, whether from a voluntary junction of Government and Territory or otherwise, with the consent of a number of voices in the National legislature less than the whole.

11. Resolved that a Republican Government and the territory of each State, except in the instance of a voluntary junction of Government and territory, ought to be guaranteed by the United States to each State.

12. Resolved that provision ought to be made for the continuance of Congress and their authorities and privileges, until a given day after the reform of the articles of Union shall be adopted, and for the completion of all their engagements.

13. Resolved that provision ought to be made for the amendment of the Articles of Union whensoever it shall seem necessary, and that the assent of the National Legislature ought not to be required thereto.

14. Resolved that the Legislative, Executive and Judiciary powers within the several States ought to be bound by oath to support the articles of Union.

15. Resolved that the amendments which shall be offered to the Confederation, by the Convention ought at a proper time, or times, after the approbation of Congress to be submitted to an assembly or assemblies of Representatives, recommended by the several Legislatures to be expressly chosen by the people, to consider and decide thereon.

Constitution of the United States

The United States Constitution was written at a convention that Congress called on February 21, 1787, for the purpose of recommending amendments to the Articles of Confederation. Every state but Rhode Island sent delegates to Philadelphia, where the convention met that summer. The delegates decided to write an entirely new constitution, completing their labors on September 17. Nine states (the number the Constitution itself stipulated as sufficient) ratified by June 21, 1788.

The presidency is the most original feature of the Constitution. Described mainly in Article II, it was created as a strong, unitary office. The president was to be elected by an electoral college to a four-year term and was empowered, among other things, to recommend and veto congressional acts, appoint judges and executive officials, command the army and navy, negotiate treaties, and issue pardons. Congress could impeach and remove a president for committing acts of "Treason, Bribery, or other High Crimes and Misdemeanors." The Constitution also created the vice presidency and charged the vice president to be president of the Senate and standby successor to the president.

Numerous constitutional amendments have dealt with the presidency. For example, the Twenty-second Amendment (1951) imposes a two-term limit on the president and the Twenty-fifth Amendment (1967) provides for both vacancies in the vice presidency and situations of presidential disability.

We the People of the United States, in Order to form a more perfect Union, establish Justice, insure domestic Tranquility, provide for the common defence, promote the general Welfare, and secure the Blessings of Liberty to ourselves and our Posterity, do ordain and establish this Constitution for the United States of America.

Article I

Section 1. All legislative Powers herein granted shall be vested in a Congress of the United States, which shall consist of a Senate and House of Representatives.

Section 2. The House of Representatives shall be composed of Members chosen every second Year by the People of the several States, and the Electors in each State shall have the Qualifications requisite for Electors of the most numerous Branch of the State Legislature.

No Person shall be a Representative who shall not have attained to the age of twenty five Years, and been seven Years a Citizen of the United States, and who shall not, when elected, be an Inhabitant of that State in which he shall be chosen.

[Representatives and direct Taxes shall be apportioned among the several States which may be included within this Union, according to their respective Numbers, which shall be determined by adding to the whole Number of free Persons, including those bound to Service for a Term of Years, and excluding Indians not taxed, three fifths of all other Persons.][1] The actual Enumeration shall be made within three Years after the first Meeting of the Congress of the United States, and within every subsequent Term of ten Years, in such Manner as they shall by Law direct. The Number of Representatives shall not exceed one for every thirty Thousand, but each State shall have at Least one Representative; and until such enumeration shall be made, the State of New Hampshire shall be entitled to chuse three, Massachusetts eight, Rhode-Island and Providence Plantations one, Connecticut five, New-York six, New Jersey four, Pennsylvania eight, Delaware one, Maryland six, Virginia ten, North Carolina five, South Carolina five, and Georgia three.

When vacancies happen in the Representation from any State, the Executive Authority thereof shall issue Writs of Election to fill such Vacancies.

The House of Representatives shall chuse their Speaker and other Officers; and shall have the sole Power of Impeachment.

Section 3. The Senate of the United States shall be composed of two Senators from each State, [chosen by the Legislature thereof,][2] for six Years; and each Senator shall have one Vote.

Immediately after they shall be assembled in Consequence of the first Election, they shall be divided as equally as may be into three Classes. The Seats of the Senators of the first Class shall be vacated at the Expiration of the second Year, of the second Class at the Expiration of the fourth Year, and of the third Class at the Expiration of the sixth Year, so that one third may be chosen every second Year; [and if Vacancies happen by Resignation, or otherwise, during the Recess of the Legislature of any State, the Executive thereof may make temporary Appointments until the next Meeting of the Legislature, which shall then fill such Vacancies.][3]

No Person shall be a Senator who shall not have attained to the Age of thirty Years, and been nine Years a Citizen of the United States, and who shall not, when elected, be an Inhabitant of that State for which he shall be chosen.

The Vice President of the United States shall be President of the Senate, but shall have no Vote, unless they be equally divided.

The Senate shall chuse their other Officers, and also a President pro tempore, in the Absence of the Vice President, or when he shall exercise the Office of President of the United States.

The Senate shall have the sole Power to try all Impeachments. When sitting for that Purpose, they shall be on Oath or Affirmation. When the President of the United States is tried the Chief Justice shall preside: And no Person shall be convicted without the Concurrence of two thirds of the Members present.

Judgment in Cases of Impeachment shall not extend further than to removal from Office, and disqualification to hold and enjoy any Office of honor, Trust or Profit under the United States: but the Party convicted shall nevertheless be liable and subject to Indictment, Trial, Judgment and Punishment, according to Law.

Section 4. The Times, Places and Manner of holding Elections for Senators and Representatives, shall be prescribed in each State by the Legislature thereof; but the Congress may at any time by Law make or alter such Regulations, except as to the Places of chusing Senators.

The Congress shall assemble at least once in every Year, and such Meeting shall [be on the first Monday in December],[4] unless they shall by Law appoint a different Day.

Section 5. Each House shall be the Judge of the Elections, Returns and Qualifications of its own Members, and a Majority of each shall constitute a Quorum to do Business; but a smaller Number may adjourn from day to day, and may be authorized to compel the Attendance of absent Members, in such Manner, and under such Penalties as each House may provide.

Each House may determine the Rules of its Proceedings, punish its Members for disorderly Behaviour, and, with the Concurrence of two thirds, expel a Member.

Each House shall keep a Journal of its Proceedings, and from time to time publish the same, excepting such Parts as may in their Judgment require Secrecy; and the Yeas and Nays of the Members of either House on any question shall, at the Desire of one fifth of those Present, be entered on the Journal.

Neither House, during the Session of Congress, shall, without the Consent of the other, adjourn for more than three days, nor to any other Place than that in which the two Houses shall be sitting.

Section 6. The Senators and Representatives shall receive a Compensation for their Services, to be ascertained by Law, and paid out of the Treasury of the United States. They shall in all Cases, except Treason, Felony and Breach of the Peace, be privileged from Arrest during their Attendance at the Session of their respective Houses, and in going to and returning from the same; and for any Speech or Debate in either House, they shall not be questioned in any other Place.

No Senator or Representative shall, during the Time for which he was elected, be appointed to any civil Office under the Authority of the United States, which shall have been created, or the Emoluments whereof shall have been encreased during such time; and no Person holding any Office under the United States, shall be a Member of either House during his Continuance in Office.

Section 7. All Bills for raising Revenue shall originate in the House of Representatives; but the Senate may propose or concur with amendments as on other Bills.

Every Bill which shall have passed the House of Representatives and the Senate, shall, before it become a Law, be presented to the President of the United States; If he approve he shall sign it, but if not he shall return it, with his Objections to that House in which it shall have originated, who shall enter the Objections at large on their Journal, and proceed to reconsider it. If after such Reconsideration two thirds of that House shall agree to pass the Bill, it shall be sent, together with the Objections, to the other House, by which it shall likewise be reconsidered, and if approved by two thirds of that House, it shall become a Law. But in all such Cases the Votes of both Houses shall be determined by yeas and Nays, and the Names of the Persons voting for and against the Bill shall be entered on the Journal of each House respectively. If any Bill shall not be returned by the President within ten Days (Sundays excepted) after it shall have been presented to him, the Same shall be a Law, in like Manner as if he had signed it, unless the Congress by their Adjournment prevent its Return, in which Case it shall not be a Law.

Every Order, Resolution, or Vote to which the Concurrence of the Senate and House of Representatives may be necessary (except on a question of Adjournment) shall be presented to the President of the United States; and before the Same shall take Effect, shall be approved by him, or being disapproved by him, shall be repassed by two thirds of the Senate and House of Representatives, according to the Rules and Limitations prescribed in the Case of a Bill.

Section 8. The Congress shall have Power To lay and collect Taxes, Duties, Imposts and Excises, to pay the Debts and provide for the common Defence and general Welfare of the United States; but all Duties, Imposts and Excises shall be uniform throughout the United States;

To borrow Money on the credit of the United States;

To regulate Commerce with foreign Nations, and among the several States, and with the Indian Tribes;

To establish an uniform Rule of Naturalization, and uniform Laws on the subject of Bankruptcies throughout the United States;

To coin Money, regulate the Value thereof, and of foreign Coin, and fix the Standard of Weights and Measures;

To provide for the Punishment of counterfeiting the Securities and current Coin of the United States;

To establish Post Offices and post Roads;

To promote the Progress of Science and useful Arts, by securing for limited Times to Authors and Inventors the exclusive Right to their respective Writings and Discoveries;

To constitute Tribunals inferior to the supreme Court;

To define and punish Piracies and Felonies commited on the high Seas, and Offences against the Law of Nations;

To declare War, grant Letters of Marque and Reprisal, and make Rules concerning Captures on Land and Water;

To raise and support Armies, but no Appropriation of Money to that Use shall be for a longer Term than two Years;

To provide and maintain a Navy;

To make Rules for the Government and Regulation of the land and naval Forces;

To provide for calling forth the Militia to execute the Laws of the Union, suppress Insurrections and repel Invasions;

To provide for organizing, arming, and disciplining, the Militia, and for governing such Part of them as may be employed in the Service of the United States, reserving to the States respectively, the Appointment of the Officers, and the Authority of training the Militia according to the discipline prescribed by Congress;

To exercise exclusive Legislation in all Cases whatsoever, over such District (not exceeding ten Miles square) as may, by Cession of Particular States, and the Acceptance of Congress, become the Seat of the Government of the United States, and to exercise like Authority over all Places purchased by the Consent of the Legislature of the State in which the Same shall be, for the Erection of Forts, Magazines, Arsenals, dock-Yards, and other needful Buildings; —And

To make all Laws which shall be necessary and proper for carrying into Execution the foregoing Powers, and all other Powers vested by this Constitution in the Government of the United States, or in any Department or Officer thereof.

Section 9. The Migration or Importation of such Persons as any of the States now existing shall think proper to admit, shall not be prohibited by the Congress prior to the Year one thousand eight hundred and eight, but a Tax or duty may be imposed on such Importation, not exceeding ten dollars for each Person.

The Privilege of the Writ of Habeas Corpus shall not be suspended, unless when in Cases of Rebellion or Invasion the public Safety may require it.

No Bill of Attainder or ex post facto Law shall be passed.

No capitation, or other direct, Tax shall be laid, unless in Proportion to the Census of Enumeration herein before directed to be taken.[5]

No Tax or Duty shall be laid on Articles exported from any State.

No Preference shall be given by any Regulation of Commerce or Revenue to the Ports of one State over those of another; nor shall Vessels bound to, or from, one State, be obliged to enter, clear or pay Duties in another.

No Money shall be drawn from the Treasury, but in Consequence of Appropriations made by Law; and a regular Statement and Account of the Receipts and Expenditures of all public Money shall be published from time to time.

No Title of Nobility shall be granted by the United States: And no Person holding any Office of Profit or Trust under them, shall, without the Consent of the Congress, accept of any present, Emolument, Office, or Title, of any kind whatever, from any King, Prince or foreign State.

Section 10. No State shall enter into any Treaty, Alliance, or Confederation; grant Letters of Marque and Reprisal; coin Money; emit Bills of Credit; make any Thing but gold and silver Coin a Tender in Payment of Debts; pass any Bill of Attainder, ex post facto Law, or Law impairing the Obligation of Contracts, or grant any Title of Nobility.

No State shall, without the Consent of the Congress, lay any Imposts or Duties on Imports or Exports, except what may be absolutely necessary for executing it's inspection Laws: and the net Produce of all Duties and Imposts, laid by any State on Imports or Exports, shall be for the Use of the Treasury of the United States; and all such Laws shall be subject to the Revision and Controul of the Congress.

No State shall, without the Consent of Congress, lay any Duty of Tonnage, keep Troops, or Ships of War in time of Peace, enter into any Agreement or Compact with another State, or with a foreign Power, or engage in War, unless actually invaded, or in such imminent Danger as will not admit of delay.

Article II

Section 1. The executive Power shall be vested in a President of the United States of America. He shall hold his Office during the Term of four Years, and, together with the Vice President, chosen for the same Term, be elected, as follows.

Each State shall appoint, in such Manner as the Legislature thereof may direct, a Number of Electors, equal to the whole Number of Senators and Representatives to which the State may be entitled in the Congress: but no Senator or Representative, or Person holding an Office of Trust or Profit under the United States, shall be appointed an Elector.

[The Electors shall meet in their respective States, and vote by Ballot for two Persons, of whom one at least shall not be an Inhabitant of the same State with themselves. And they shall make a List of all the Persons voted for, and of the Number of Votes for each; which List they shall sign and certify, and transmit sealed to the Seat of the Government of the United States, directed to the President of the Senate. The President of the Senate shall, in the Presence of the Senate and House of Representatives, open all the Certificates, and the Votes shall then be counted. The Person having the greatest Number of Votes shall be the President, if such Number be a Majority of the whole Number of Electors appointed; and if there be more than one who have such Majority, and have an equal Number of Votes, then the House of

Representatives shall immediately chuse by Ballot one of them for President; and if no Person have a Majority, then from the five highest on the list the said House shall in like Manner chuse the President. But in chusing the President, the Votes shall be taken by States, the Representation from each State having one Vote; a quorum for this Purpose shall consist of a Member or Members from two thirds of the States, and a Majority of all the States shall be necessary to a Choice. In every Case, after the Choice of the President, the Person having the greatest Number of Votes of the Electors shall be the Vice President. But if there should remain two or more who have equal Votes, the Senate shall chuse from them by Ballot the Vice President.][6]

The Congress may determine the Time of chusing the Electors, and the Day on which they shall give their Votes; which Day shall be the same throughout the United States.

No Person except a natural born Citizen, or a Citizen of the United States, at the time of the Adoption of this Constitution, shall be eligible to the Office of President; neither shall any Person be eligible to that Office who shall not have attained to the Age of thirty five Years, and been fourteen Years a Resident within the United States.

In Case of the Removal of the President from Office, or of his Death, Resignation, or Inability to discharge the Powers and Duties of the said Office,[7] the Same shall devolve on the Vice President, and the Congress may by Law provide for the Case of Removal, Death, Resignation or Inability, both of the President and Vice President, declaring what Officer shall then act as President, and such Officer shall act accordingly, until the Disability be removed, or a President shall be elected.

The President shall, at stated Times, receive for his Services, a Compensation, which shall neither be encreased nor diminished during the Period for which he shall have been elected, and he shall not receive within that Period any other Emolument from the United States, or any of them.

Before he enter on the Execution of his Office, he shall take the following Oath or Affirmation: —"I do solemnly swear (or affirm) that I will faithfully execute the Office of President of the United States, and will to the best of my Ability, preserve, protect and defend the Constitution of the United States."

Section 2. The President shall be Commander in Chief of the Army and Navy of the United States, and of the Militia of the several States, when called into the actual Service of the United States; he may require the Opinion, in writing, of the principal Officer in each of the executive Departments, upon any Subject relating to the Duties of their respective Offices, and he shall have Power to grant Reprieves and Pardons for Offenses against the United States, except in Cases of Impeachment.

He shall have Power, by and with the Advice and Consent of the Senate, to make Treaties, provided two thirds of the Senators present concur; and he shall nominate, and by and with the Advice and Consent of the Senate, shall appoint Ambassadors, other public Ministers and Consuls, Judges of the supreme Court, and all other Officers of the United States, whose Appointments are not herein otherwise provided for, and which shall be established by Law: but the Congress may by Law vest the Appointment of such inferior Officers, as they think proper, in the President alone, in the Courts of Law, or in the Heads of Departments.

The President shall have Power to fill up all Vacancies that may happen during the Recess of the Senate, by granting Commissions which shall expire at the End of their next Session.

Section 3. He shall from time to time give to the Congress Information of the State of the Union, and recommend to their Consideration such Measures as he shall judge necessary and expedient; he may, on extraordinary Occasions, convene both Houses, or either of them, and in Case of Disagreement between them, with Respect to the Time of Adjournment, he may adjourn them to such Time as he shall think proper; he shall receive Ambassadors and other public Ministers; he shall take Care that the Laws be faithfully executed, and shall Commission all the Officers of the United States.

Section 4. The President, Vice President and all Civil Officers of the United States, shall be removed from office on Impeachment for, and Conviction of, Treason, Bribery, or other high Crimes and Misdemeanors.

Article III

Section 1. The judicial Power of the United States, shall be vested in one supreme Court, and in such inferior Courts as the Congress may from time to time ordain and establish. The Judges, both of the supreme and inferior Courts, shall hold their Offices during good Behaviour, and shall, at stated Times, receive for their Services, a Compensation, which shall not be diminished during their Continuance in Office.

Section 2. The judicial Power shall extend to all Cases, in Law and Equity, arising under this Constitution, the Laws of the United States, and Treaties made, or which shall be made, under their Authority; —to all Cases affecting Ambassadors, other public Ministers and Consuls; —to all Cases of admiralty and maritime Jurisdiction; —to Controversies to which the United States shall be a Party; —to Controversies between two or more States; —between a State and Citizens of another State;[8] —between Citizens of different States; —between Citizens of the same State claiming Lands under Grants of different States, and between a State, or the Citizens thereof, and foreign States, Citizens or Subjects.[8]

In all Cases affecting Ambassadors, other public Ministers and Consuls, and those in which a State shall be Party, the supreme Court shall have original Jurisdiction. In all the other Cases before mentioned, the supreme Court shall have appellate Jurisdiction, both as to Law and Fact, with such Exceptions, and under such Regulations as the Congress shall make.

The Trial of all Crimes, except in cases of Impeachment, shall be by Jury; and such Trial shall be held in the State where the said Crimes shall have been committed; but when not committed within any State, the Trial shall be at such Place or Places as the Congress may by Law have directed.

Section 3. Treason against the United States, shall consist only in levying War against them, or in adhering to their Enemies, giving them Aid and Comfort. No Person shall be convicted of Treason unless on the Testimony of two Witnesses to the same overt Act, or on Confession in open Court.

The Congress shall have Power to declare the Punishment of Treason, but no Attainder of Treason shall work Corruption of Blood, or Forfeiture except during the Life of the Person attainted.

Article IV

Section 1. Full Faith and Credit shall be given in each State to the public Acts, Records, and judicial Proceedings of every other State. And the Congress may by general Laws prescribe the Manner in which such Acts, Records and Proceedings shall be proved, and the Effect thereof.

Section 2. The Citizens of each State shall be entitled to all Privileges and Immunities of Citizens in the several States.

A Person charged in any State with Treason, Felony, or other Crime, who shall flee from Justice, and be found in another State, shall on Demand of the executive Authority of the State from which he fled, be delivered up, to be removed to the State having Jurisdiction of the Crime.

[No Person held to Service or Labour in one State, under the Laws thereof, escaping into another, shall, in Consequence of any Law or Regulation therein, be discharged from such Service or Labour, but shall be delivered up on Claim of the Party to whom such Service or Labour may be due.][9]

Section 3. New States may be admitted by the Congress into this Union; but no new State shall be formed or erected within the

Jurisdiction of any other State; nor any State be formed by the Junction of two or more States, or Parts of States, without the Consent of the Legislatures of the States concerned as well as of the Congress.

The Congress shall have Power to dispose of and make all needful Rules and Regulations respecting the Territory or other Property belonging to the United States; and nothing in this Constitution shall be so construed as to Prejudice any Claims of the United States, or of any particular State.

Section 4. The United States shall guarantee to every State in this Union a Republican Form of Government, and shall protect each of them against Invasion; and on Application of the Legislature, or of the Executive (when the Legislature cannot be convened) against domestic Violence.

Article V

The Congress, whenever two thirds of both Houses shall deem it necessary, shall propose Amendments to this Constitution, or, on the Application of the Legislatures of two thirds of the several States, shall call a Convention for proposing Amendments, which, in either Case, shall be valid to all Intents and Purposes, as Part of this Constitution, when ratified by the Legislatures of three fourths of the several States, or by Conventions in three fourths thereof, as the one or the other Mode of Ratification may be proposed by the Congress; Provided [that no Amendment which may be made prior to the Year One thousand eight hundred and eight shall in any Manner affect the first and fourth Clauses in the Ninth Section of the first Article; and][10] that no State, without its Consent, shall be deprived of its equal Suffrage in the Senate.

Article VI

All Debts contracted and Engagements entered into, before the Adoption of this Constitution, shall be as valid against the United States under this Constitution, as under the Confederation.

This Constitution, and the Laws of the United States which shall be made in Pursuance thereof; and all Treaties made, or which shall be made, under the Authority of the United States, shall be the supreme Law of the Land; and the Judges in every State shall be bound thereby, any Thing in the Constitution or Laws of any State to the Contrary notwithstanding.

The Senators and Representatives before mentioned, and the Members of the several State Legislatures, and all executive and judicial Officers, both of the United States and of the several States, shall be bound by Oath or Affirmation, to support this Constitution; but no religious Test shall ever be required as a Qualification to any Office or public Trust under the United States.

Article VII

The Ratification of the Conventions of nine States, shall be sufficient for the Establishment of this Constitution between the States so ratifying the Same. Done in Convention by the Unanimous Consent of the States present the Seventeenth Day of September in the Year of our Lord one thousand seven hundred and Eighty seven and of the Independence of the United States of America the Twelfth. In witness whereof We have hereunto subscribed our Names, George Washington, President and deputy from Virginia.

New Hampshire: John Langdon, Nicholas Gilman.

Massachusetts: Nathaniel Gorham, Rufus King.

Connecticut: William Samuel Johnson, Roger Sherman.

New York: Alexander Hamilton.

New Jersey: William Livingston, David Brearley, William Paterson, Jonathan Dayton.

Pennsylvania: Benjamin Franklin, Thomas Mifflin, Robert Morris, George Clymer, Thomas FitzSimons, Jared Ingersoll, James Wilson, Gouverneur Morris.

Delaware: George Read, Gunning Bedford Jr., John Dickinson, Richard Bassett, Jacob Broom.

Maryland: James McHenry, Daniel of St. Thomas Jenifer, Daniel Carroll.

Virginia: John Blair, James Madison Jr.

North Carolina: William Blount, Richard Dobbs Spaight, Hugh Williamson.

South Carolina: John Rutledge, Charles Cotesworth Pinckney, Charles Pinckney, Pierce Butler.

Georgia: William Few, Abraham Baldwin.

[The language of the original Constitution, not including the Amendments, was adopted by a convention of the states on Sept. 17, 1787, and was subsequently ratified by the states on the following dates: Delaware, Dec. 7, 1787; Pennsylvania, Dec. 12, 1787; New Jersey, Dec. 18, 1787; Georgia, Jan. 2, 1788; Connecticut, Jan. 9, 1788; Massachusetts, Feb. 6, 1788; Maryland, April 28, 1788; South Carolina, May 23, 1788; New Hampshire, June 21, 1788.

Ratification was completed on June 21, 1788.

The Constitution subsequently was ratified by Virginia, June 25, 1788; New York, July 26, 1788; North Carolina, Nov. 21, 1789; Rhode Island, May 29, 1790; and Vermont, Jan. 10, 1791.]

Amendments

Amendment I

(First ten amendments ratified December 15, 1791.)

Congress shall make no law respecting an establishment of religion, or prohibiting the free exercise thereof; or abridging the freedom of speech, or of the press; or the right of the people peaceably to assemble, and to petition the Government for a redress of grievances.

Amendment II

A well regulated Militia, being necessary to the security of a free State, the right of the people to keep and bear Arms, shall not be infringed.

Amendment III

No Soldier shall, in time of peace be quartered in any house, without the consent of the Owner, nor in time of war, but in a manner to be prescribed by law.

Amendment IV

The right of the people to be secure in their persons, houses, papers, and effects, against unreasonable searches and seizures, shall not be violated, and no Warrants shall issue, but upon probable cause, supported by Oath or affirmation, and particularly describing the place to be searched, and the persons or things to be seized.

Amendment V

No person shall be held to answer for a capital, or otherwise infamous crime, unless on a presentment or indictment of a Grand Jury, except in cases arising in the land or naval forces, or in the Militia, when in actual service in time of War or public danger; nor shall any person be subject for the same offence to be twice put in jeopardy of life or limb; nor shall be compelled in any criminal case to be a witness against himself, nor be deprived of life, liberty, or property, without due process of law; nor shall private property be taken for public use, without just compensation.

Amendment VI

In all criminal prosecutions, the accused shall enjoy the right to a speedy and public trial, by an impartial jury of the State and district wherein the crime shall have been committed, which district shall have been previously ascertained by law, and to be informed of the nature and cause of the accusation; to be confronted with the witnesses against him; to have compulsory process for obtaining witnesses in his favor, and to have the Assistance of Counsel for his defence.

Amendment VII

In Suits at common law, where the value in controversy shall exceed twenty dollars, the right of trial by jury shall be preserved, and no fact tried by a jury, shall be otherwise re-examined in any Court of the United States, than according to the rules of the common law.

Amendment VIII

Excessive bail shall not be required, nor excessive fines imposed, nor cruel and unusual punishments inflicted.

Amendment IX

The enumeration in the Constitution, of certain rights, shall not be construed to deny or disparage others retained by the people.

Amendment X

The powers not delegated to the United States by the Constitution, nor prohibited by it to the States, are reserved to the States respectively, or to the people.

Amendment XI *(Ratified February 7, 1795)*

The Judicial power of the United States shall not be construed to extend to any suit in law or equity, commenced or prosecuted against one of the United States by Citizens of another State, or by Citizens or Subjects of any Foreign State.

Amendment XII *(Ratified June 15, 1804)*

The Electors shall meet in their respective states and vote by ballot for President and Vice-President, one of whom, at least, shall not be an inhabitant of the same state with themselves; they shall name in their ballots the person voted for as President, and in distinct ballots the person voted for as Vice-President, and they shall make distinct lists of all persons voted for as President, and of all persons voted for as Vice-President, and of the number of votes for each, which lists they shall sign and certify, and transmit sealed to the seat of the government of the United States, directed to the President of the Senate; —The President of the Senate shall, in the presence of the Senate and House of Representatives, open all the certificates and the votes shall then be counted; —The person having the greatest number of votes for President, shall be the President, if such number be a majority of the whole number of Electors appointed; and if no person have such majority, then from the persons having the highest numbers not exceeding three on the list of those voted for as President, the House of Representatives shall choose immediately, by ballot, the President. But in choosing the President, the votes shall be taken by states, the representation from each state having one vote; a quorum for this purpose shall consist of a member or members from two-thirds of the states, and a majority of all the states shall be necessary to a choice. [And if the House of Representatives shall not choose a President whenever the right of choice shall devolve upon them, before the fourth day of March next following, then the Vice-President shall act as President, as in the case of the death or other constitutional disability of the President—][11] The person having the greatest number of votes as Vice-President, shall be the Vice-President, if such number be a majority of the whole number of Electors appointed, and if no person have a majority, then from the two highest numbers on the list, the Senate shall choose the Vice-President; a quorum for the purpose shall consist of two-thirds of the whole number of Senators, and a majority of the whole number shall be necessary to a choice. But no person constitutionally ineligible to the office of President shall be eligible to that of Vice-President of the United States.

Amendment XIII *(Ratified December 6, 1865)*

Section 1. Neither slavery nor involuntary servitude, except as a punishment for crime whereof the party shall have been duly convicted, shall exist within the United States, or any place subject to their jurisdiction.

Section 2. Congress shall have power to enforce this article by appropriate legislation.

Amendment XIV *(Ratified July 9, 1868)*

Section 1. All persons born or naturalized in the United States and subject to the jurisdiction thereof, are citizens of the United States and of the State wherein they reside. No State shall make or enforce any law which shall abridge the privileges or immunities of citizens of the United States; nor shall any State deprive any person of life, liberty, or property, without due process of law; nor deny to any person within its jurisdiction the equal protection of the laws.

Section 2. Representatives shall be apportioned among the several States according to their respective numbers, counting the whole number of persons in each State, excluding Indians not taxed. But when the right to vote at any election for the choice of electors for President and Vice President of the United States, Representatives in Congress, the Executive and Judicial officers of a State, or the members of the Legislature thereof, is denied to any of the male inhabitants of such State, being twenty-one years of age,[12] and citizens of the United States, or in any way abridged, except for participation in rebellion, or other crime, the basis of representation therein shall be reduced in the proportion which the number of such male citizens shall bear to the whole number of male citizens twenty-one years of age in such State.

Section 3. No person shall be a Senator or Representative in Congress, or elector of President and Vice President, or hold any office, civil or military, under the United States, or under any State, who, having previously taken an oath, as a member of Congress, or as an officer of the United States, or as a member of any State legislature, or as an executive or judicial officer of any State, to support the Constitution of the United States, shall have engaged in insurrection or rebellion against the same, or given aid or comfort to the enemies thereof. But Congress may by a vote of two-thirds of each House, remove such disability.

Section 4. The validity of the public debt of the United States, authorized by law, including debts incurred for payment of pensions and bounties for services in suppressing insurrection or rebellion, shall not be questioned. But neither the United States nor any State shall assume or pay any debt or obligation incurred in aid of insurrection or rebellion against the United States, or any claim for the loss or emancipation of any slave; but all such debts, obligations and claims shall be held illegal and void.

Section 5. The Congress shall have power to enforce, by appropriate legislation, the provisions of this article.

Amendment XV *(Ratified February 3, 1870)*

Section 1. The right of citizens of the United States to vote shall not be denied or abridged by the United States or by any State on account of race, color, or previous condition of servitude.

Section 2. The Congress shall have power to enforce this article by appropriate legislation.

Amendment XVI *(Ratified February 3, 1913)*

The Congress shall have power to lay and collect taxes on incomes, from whatever source derived, without apportionment among the several States, and without regard to any census or enumeration.

Amendment XVII *(Ratified April 8, 1913)*

The Senate of the United States shall be composed of two Senators from each State, elected by the people thereof, for six years; and each Senator shall have one vote. The electors in each State shall have the qualifications requisite for electors of the most numerous branch of the State legislatures.

When vacancies happen in the representation of any State in the Senate, the executive authority of such State shall issue writs of election to fill such vacancies: *Provided,* That the legislature of any State may empower the executive thereof to make temporary appointments until the people fill the vacancies by election as the legislature may direct.

This amendment shall not be so construed as to affect the election or term of any Senator chosen before it becomes valid as part of the Constitution.

[Amendment XVIII *(Ratified January 16, 1919)*

Section 1. After one year from the ratification of this article the manufacture, sale, or transportation of intoxicating liquors within, the importation thereof into, or the exportation thereof from the United States and all territory subject to the jurisdiction thereof for beverage purposes is hereby prohibited.

Section 2. The Congress and the several States shall have concurrent power to enforce this article by appropriate legislation.

Section 3. This article shall be inoperative unless it shall have been ratified as an amendment to the Constitution by the legislatures of the several States, as provided in the Constitution, within seven years from the date of the submission hereof to the States by the Congress.][13]

Amendment XIX *(Ratified August 18, 1920)*

The right of citizens of the United States to vote shall not be denied or abridged by the United States or by any State on account of sex.

Congress shall have power to enforce this article by appropriate legislation.

Amendment XX *(Ratified January 23, 1933)*

Section 1. The terms of the President and Vice President shall end at noon on the 20th day of January, and the terms of Senators and Representatives at noon on the 3d day of January, of the years in which such terms would have ended if this article had not been ratified; and the terms of their successors shall then begin.

Section 2. The Congress shall assemble at least once in every year, and such meeting shall begin at noon on the 3d day of January, unless they shall by law appoint a different day.

Section 3.[14] If, at the time fixed for the beginning of the term of the President, the President elect shall have died, the Vice President elect shall become President. If a President shall not have been chosen before the time fixed for the beginning of his term, or if the President elect shall have failed to qualify, then the Vice President elect shall act as President until a President shall have qualified; and the Congress may by law provide for the case wherein neither a President elect nor a Vice President elect shall have qualified, declaring who shall then act as President, or the manner in which one who is to act shall be selected, and such person shall act accordingly until a President or Vice President shall have qualified.

Section 4. The Congress may by law provide for the case of the death of any of the persons from whom the House of Representatives may choose a President whenever the right of choice shall have devolved upon them, and for the case of the death of any of the persons from whom the Senate may choose a Vice President whenever the right of choice shall have devolved upon them.

Section 5. Sections 1 and 2 shall take effect on the 15th day of October following the ratification of this article.

Section 6. This article shall be inoperative unless it shall have been ratified as an amendment to the Constitution by the legislatures of three-fourths of the several States within seven years from the date of its submission.

Amendment XXI *(Ratified December 5, 1933)*

Section 1. The eighteenth article of amendment to the Constitution of the United States is hereby repealed.

Section 2. The transportation or importation into any State, Territory or possession of the United States for delivery or use therein of intoxicating liquors, in violation of the laws thereof, is hereby prohibited.

Section 3. This article shall be inoperative unless it shall have been ratified as an amendment to the Constitution by conventions in the several States, as provided in the Constitution, within seven years from the date of the submission hereof to the States by the Congress.

Amendment XXII *(Ratified February 27, 1951)*

Section 1. No person shall be elected to the office of the President more than twice, and no person who has held the office of President, or acted as President, for more than two years of a term to which some other person was elected President shall be elected to the office of the President more than once. But this Article shall not apply to any person holding the office of President when this Article was proposed by the Congress, and shall not prevent any person who may be holding the office of President, or acting as President, during the term within which this Article becomes operative from holding the office of President or acting as President during the remainder of such term.

Section 2. This Article shall be inoperative unless it shall have been ratified as an amendment to the Constitution by the legislatures of three-fourths of the several States within seven years from the date of its submission to the States by the Congress.

Amendment XXIII *(Ratified March 29, 1961)*

Section 1. The District constituting the seat of Government of the United States shall appoint in such manner as the Congress may direct:

A number of electors of President and Vice President equal to the whole number of Senators and Representatives in Congress to which the District would be entitled if it were a State, but in no event more than the least populous State; they shall be in addition to those appointed by the States, but they shall be considered, for the purposes of the election of President and Vice President, to be electors appointed by a State; and they shall meet in the District and perform such duties as provided by the twelfth article of amendment.

Section 2. The Congress shall have power to enforce this article by appropriate legislation.

Amendment XXIV *(Ratified January 23, 1964)*

Section 1. The right of citizens of the United States to vote in any primary or other election for President or Vice President, for electors for President or Vice President, or for Senator or Representative in Congress, shall not be denied or abridged by the United States or any State by reason of failure to pay any poll tax or other tax.

Section 2. The Congress shall have power to enforce this article by appropriate legislation.

Amendment XXV *(Ratified February 10, 1967)*

Section 1. In case of the removal of the President from office or of his death or resignation, the Vice President shall become President.

Section 2. Whenever there is a vacancy in the office of the Vice President, the President shall nominate a Vice President who shall take office upon confirmation by a majority vote of both Houses of Congress.

Section 3. Whenever the President transmits to the President pro tempore of the Senate and the Speaker of the House of Representatives his written declaration that he is unable to discharge the powers and duties of his office, and until he transmits to them a written declaration to the contrary, such powers and duties shall be discharged by the Vice President as Acting President.

Section 4. Whenever the Vice President and a majority of either the principal officers of the executive departments or of such other body as Congress may by law provide, transmit to the President pro tempore of the Senate and the Speaker of the House of Representatives their written declaration that the President is unable to discharge the powers and duties of his office, the Vice President shall immediately assume the powers and duties of the office as Acting President.

Thereafter, when the President transmits to the President pro tempore of the Senate and the Speaker of the House of Representatives his written declaration that no inability exists, he shall resume the powers and duties of his office unless the Vice President and a majority of either the principal officers of the executive department or of such other body as Congress may by law provide, transmit within four days to the President pro tempore of the Senate and the Speaker of the House of Representatives their written declaration that the President is unable to discharge the powers and duties of his office. Thereupon Congress shall decide the issue, assembling within forty-eight hours for that purpose if not in session. If the Congress, within twenty-one days after receipt of the latter written declaration, or, if Congress is not in session, within twenty-one days after Congress is required to assemble, determines by two-thirds vote of both houses that the President is unable to discharge the powers and duties of his office, the Vice President shall continue to discharge the same as Acting President; otherwise, the President shall resume the powers and duties of his office.

Amendment XXVI *(Ratified July 1, 1971)*

Section 1. The right of citizens of the United States, who are eighteen years of age or older, to vote shall not be denied or abridged by the United States or by any State on account of age.

Section 2. The Congress shall have power to enforce this article by appropriate legislation.

Notes

1. The part in brackets was changed by section 2 of the Fourteenth Amendment.
2. The part in brackets was changed by section 1 of the Seventeenth Amendment.
3. The part in brackets was changed by the second paragraph of the Seventeenth Amendment.
4. The part in brackets was changed by section 2 of the Twentieth Amendment.
5. The Sixteenth Amendment gave Congress the power to tax incomes.
6. The material in brackets has been superseded by the Twelfth Amendment.
7. This provision has been affected by the Twenty-fifth Amendment.
8. These clauses were affected by the Eleventh Amendment.
9. This paragraph has been superseded by the Thirteenth Amendment.
10. Obsolete.
11. The part in brackets has been superseded by section 3 of the Twentieth Amendment.
12. See the Twenty-sixth Amendment.
13. This Amendment was repealed by section 1 of the Twenty-first Amendment.
14. See the Twenty-fifth Amendment.

The Federalist, No. 70

During the months that the proposed Constitution was being considered for ratification by the states, a number of newspaper articles were written by Alexander Hamilton, James Madison, and John Jay under the pseudonym "Publius" to explain and defend the Constitution. The papers later were gathered together in a book called The Federalist *(or* The Federalist Papers*).*

Federalist Nos. 69-77, written by Hamilton, deal with the presidency. His most memorable defense of the office may be found in No. 70. In it, he squarely addresses the argument that a one-person executive is a threat to liberty. Instead, Hamilton writes, only a properly designed unitary executive can provide those qualities of "energy" that a republican government needs.

There is an idea, which is not without its advocates, that a vigorous executive is inconsistent with the genius of republican government. The enlightened well-wishers to this species of government must at least hope that the supposition is destitute of foundation; since they can never admit its truth, without at the same time admitting the condemnation of their own principles. Energy in the executive is a leading character in the definition of good government. It is essential to the protection of the community against foreign attacks; it is not less essential to the steady administration of the laws; to the protection of property against those irregular and high-handed combinations which sometimes interrupt the ordinary course of justice; to the security of liberty against the enterprises and assaults of ambition, of faction, and of anarchy. Every man the least conversant in Roman history knows how often that republic was obliged to take refuge in the absolute power of a single man, under the formidable title of dictator, as well against the intrigues of ambitious individuals who aspired to the tyranny, and the seditions of whole classes of the community whose conduct threatened the existence of all government, as against the invasions of external enemies who menaced the conquest and destruction of Rome.

There can be no need, however, to multiply arguments or examples on this head. A feeble executive implies a feeble execution of the government. A feeble execution is but another phrase for a bad execution; and a government ill executed, whatever it may be in theory, must be, in practice, a bad government.

Taking it for granted, therefore, that all men of sense will agree in the necessity of an energetic executive, it will only remain to inquire, what are the ingredients which constitute this energy? How far can they be combined with those other ingredients which constitute safety in the republican sense? And how far does this combination characterize the plan which has been reported by the convention?

The ingredients which constitute energy in the executive are unity; duration; an adequate provision for its support; and competent powers.

The ingredients which constitute safety in the republican sense are a due dependence on the people, and a due responsibility.

Those politicians and statesmen who have been the most celebrated for the soundness of their principles and for the justness of their views have declared in favor of a single executive and a numerous legislature. They have, with great propriety, considered energy as the most necessary qualification of the former, and have regarded this as most applicable to power in a single hand; while they have, with equal propriety, considered the latter as best adapted to deliberation and wisdom, and best calculated to conciliate the confidence of the people and to secure their privileges and interests.

That unity is conducive to energy will not be disputed. Decision, activity, secrecy, and dispatch will generally characterize the proceedings of one man in a much more eminent degree than the proceedings of any greater number; and in proportion as the number is increased, these qualities will be diminished.

This unity may be destroyed in two ways: either by vesting the power in two or more magistrates of equal dignity and authority, or by vesting it ostensibly in one man, subject in whole or in part to the control and cooperation of others, in the capacity of counselors to him. Of the first, the two consuls of Rome may serve as an example; of the last, we shall find examples in the constitutions of several of the States. New York and New Jersey, if I recollect right, are the only States which have intrusted the executive authority wholly to single men. Both these methods of destroying the unity of the executive have their partisans; but the votaries of an executive council are the most numerous. They are both liable, if not equal, to similar objections, and may in most lights be examined in conjunction.

The experience of other nations will afford little instruction on this head. As far, however, as it teaches anything, it teaches us not to be enamored of plurality in the executive. . . .

Whenever two or more persons are engaged in any common enterprise or pursuit, there is always danger of difference of opinion. If it be a public trust or office in which they are clothed with equal dignity and authority, there is peculiar danger of personal emulation and even animosity. From either, and especially from all these causes, the most bitter dissensions are apt to spring. Whenever these happen, they lessen the respectability, waken the authority, and distract the plans and operations of those whom they divide. If they should unfortunately assail the supreme executive magistracy of a country, consisting of a plurality of persons, they might impede or frustrate the most important measures of the government in the most critical emergencies of the state. And what is still worse, they might split the community into the most violent and irreconcilable factions, adhering differently to the different individuals who composed the magistracy. . . .

Upon the principles of a free government, inconveniences from the source just mentioned must necessarily be submitted to in the formation of the legislature; but it is unnecessary, and therefore unwise, to introduce them into the constitution of the executive. It is here too that they may be most pernicious. In the legislature, promptitide of decision is oftener an evil than a benefit. The differences of opinion, and the jarring of parties in that department of the government, though they may sometimes obstruct salutary plans, yet often promote deliberation and circumspection, and serve to check excesses in the majority. When a resolution too is once taken, the opposition must be at an end. That resolution is a law, and resistance to it punishable. But no favorable circumstances palliate or atone for the disadvantages of dissension in the executive department. Here they are pure and unmixed. There is no point at which they cease to operate. They serve to embarrass and weaken the execution of the plan or measure to which they relate, from the first step to the final conclusion of it. They constantly counteract those qualities in the executive which are the most necessary ingredients in its composition—vigor and expedition, and this without any counterbalancing good. In the conduct of war, in which the energy of the executive is the bulwark of the national security, everything would be to be apprehended from its plurality.

It must be confessed that these observations apply with principal weight to the first case supposed—that is, to a plurality of magistrates of equal dignity and authority, a scheme, the advocates for which are not likely to form a numerous sect; but they apply, though not with equal yet with considerable weight to the project of a council, whose concurrence is made constitutionally necessary to the operations of the ostensible executive. An artful cabal in that council would be able to distract and to enervate the whole system of administration. If no such cabal should exist, the mere diversity of views and opinions would alone be sufficient to tincture the exercise of the executive authority with a spirit of habitual feebleness and dilatoriness.

But one of the weightiest objections to a plurality in the executive, and which lies as much against the last as the first plan is that it tends to conceal faults and destroy responsibility. . . . It often becomes impossible, admidst mutual accusations, to determine on whom the blame or the punishment of a pernicious measure, or series of pernicious measures, ought really to fall. . . .

A little consideration will satisfy us that the species of security sought for in the multiplication of the executive is unattainable. Numbers must be so great as to render combination difficult, or they are rather a source of danger than of security. The united credit and influence of several individuals must be more formidable to liberty than the credit and influence of either of them separately. When power, therefore, is placed in the hands of so small a number of men as to admit of their interests and views being easily combined in a common enterprise, by an artful leader, it becomes more liable to abuse, and more dangerous when abused, than if it be lodged in the hands of one man, who, from the very circumstance of his being alone, will be more narrowly watched and more readily suspected, and who cannot unite so great a mass of influence as when he is associated with others. . . .

I will only add that, prior to the appearance of the Constitution, I rarely met with an intelligent man from any of the States who did not admit, as the result of experience, that the UNITY of the executive of this State was one of the best of the distinguishing features of our Constitution.

Washington's Farewell Address

George Washington had hoped to retire from public life at the end of his first term as president—he even asked James Madison to draft a farewell address in 1792—but was prevailed upon to serve another term. In 1796 Washington resolved to retire after his second term expired in 1797. Weaving together Madison's draft, a new draft by Alexander Hamilton, and his own words and ideas, Washington wrote (the address was never spoken to an audience) a long address directly to his "friends and fellow citizens" (not Congress) and released it to the Daily American Advertiser, *a Philadelphia newspaper, where it was published on September 19. Newspapers around the country reprinted what soon became known as the "Farewell Address," setting off a national wave of tributes and expressions of thanks. By disseminating word of his decision to retire three months before the presidential election, Washington also forestalled any effort to reelect him.*

The Farewell Address reviews Washington's career of public service, then looks ahead to the long-term future of the new nation. Washington was especially concerned about threats to national unity. He dwelled at length on two such threats—the rise of political parties and the inclination among Americans to choose sides in disputes between England and France.

Friends, and Fellow-Citizens:

The period for a new election of a Citizen, to administer the Executive Government of the United States, being not far distant, and the time actually arrived, when your thoughts must be employed in designating the person, who is to be clothed with that important trust, it appears to me proper, especially as it may conduce to a more distinct expression of the public voice, that I should now apprise you of the resolution I have formed, to decline being considered among the number of those, out of whom a choice is to be made. . . .

The acceptance of, and continuance hitherto in, the office to which your suffrages have twice called me, have been a uniform sacrifice of inclination to the opinion of duty, and to a deference for what appeared to be your desire.—I constantly hoped, that it would have been much earlier in my power, consistently with motives, which I was not at liberty to disregard, to return to that retirement, from which I had been reluctantly drawn.—The strength of my inclination to do this, previous to the last election, had even led to the preparation of an address to declare it to you; but mature reflection on the then perplexed and critical nature of our affairs with foreign Nations, and the unanimous advice of persons entitled to my confidence, impelled me to abandon the idea.—

I rejoice that the state of your concerns, external as well as internal, no longer renders the pursuit of inclination incompatible with the sentiment of duty, or propriety; and am persuaded, whatever partiality may be retained for my services, that in the present circumstances of our country, you will not disapprove my determination to retire.

The impressions, with which I first undertook the arduous trust, were explained on the proper occasion.—In the discharge of this trust, I will only say, that I have, with good intentions, contributed towards the organization and administration of the government, the best exertions of which a very fallible judgment was capable.—Not unconscious, in the outset, of the inferiority of my qualifications, experience in my own eyes, perhaps still more in the eyes of others, has strengthened the motives to diffidence of myself; and every day the increasing weight of years admonishes me more and more, that the shade of retirement is as necessary to me as it will be welcome.—Satisfied, that, if any circumstances have given peculiar value to my services, they were temporary, I have the consolation to believe, that, while choice and prudence invite me to quit the political scene, patriotism does not forbid it. . . .

Here, perhaps, I ought to stop.—But a solicitude for your welfare, which cannot end but with my life, and the apprehension of danger, natural to that solicitude, urge me on an occasion like the present, to offer to your solemn contemplation, and to recommend to your frequent review, some sentiments; which are the results of much reflection, of no inconsiderable observation, and which appear to me all-important to the permanency of your felicity as a People.—These will be offered to you with the more freedom, as you can only see in them the disinterested warnings of a parting friend, who can possibly have no personal motive to bias his counsels.—Nor can I forget, as an encouragement to it your indulgent reception of my sentiments on a former and not dissimilar occasion.

Interwoven as is the love of liberty with every ligament of your hearts, no recommendation of mine is necessary to fortify or confirm the attachment.—

The Unity of Government which constitutes you one people, is also now dear to you.—It is justly so;—for it is a main Pillar in the Edifice of your real independence; the support of your tranquility at home; your peace abroad; of your safety; of your prosperity; of that very Liberty, which you so highly prize.—But as it is easy to foresee, that from different causes, and from different quarters, much pains will be taken, many artifices employed, to weaken in your minds the conviction of this truth;—as this is the point in your political fortress against which the batteries of internal and external enemies will be most constantly and actively (though often covertly and insidiously) directed, it is of infinite moment, that you should properly estimate the immense value of your national Union to your collective and individual happiness;—that you should cherish a cordial, habitual, and immoveable attachment to it; accustoming yourselves to think and speak of it as of the Palladium of your political safety and prosperity; watching for its preservation with jealous anxiety; discountenancing whatever may suggest even a suspicion that it can in any event be abandoned, and indignantly frowning upon the first dawning of every attempt to alienate any portion of our Country from the rest, or to enfeeble the sacred ties which now link together the various parts. . . .

. . . Let me now . . . warn you in the most solemn manner against the baneful effects of the Spirit of Party, generally.

This Spirit, unfortunately, is inseparable from our nature, having its root in the strongest passions of the human mind.—It exists under different shapes in all Governments, more or less stifled, controuled, or repressed; but, in those of the popular form, it is seen in its greatest rankness, and is truly their worst enemy. . . .

It serves always to distract the Public Councils, and enfeeble the Public administration.—It agitates the community with ill-founded jealousies and false alarms, kindles the animosity of one part against another, foments occasionally riot and insurrection.—

It opens the doors to foreign influence and corruption, which find a facilitated access to the Government itself through the channels of party passions. Thus the policy and the will of one country, are subjected to the policy and will of another.

There is an opinion that parties in free countries are useful checks upon the Administration of the Government, and serve to keep alive the Spirit of Liberty.—This within certain limits is probably true—and in Governments of a Monarchical cast, Patriotism may look with indulgence, if not with favour, upon the spirit of party.—But in those of the popular character, in Governments purely elective, it is a spirit not to be encouraged.—From their natural tendency, it is certain there will always be enough of that spirit for every salutary purpose,—and there being constant danger of excess, the effort ought to be, by force of public opinion, to mitigate and assuage it.—A fire not to be quenched; it demands a uniform vigilance to prevent its bursting into a flame, lest, instead of warning, it should consume. . . .

Observe good faith and justice towards all Nations. Cultivate peace and harmony with all.—Religion and Morality enjoin this conduct; and can it be that good policy does not equally enjoin it?—It will be worthy of a free, enlightened, and, at no distant period, a great nation, to give to mankind the magnanimous and too novel example of a People always guided by an exalted justice and benevolence.—Who can doubt that in the course of time and things, the fruits of such a plan would richly repay any temporary advantages, which might be lost by a steady adherence to it? Can it be, that Providence has not connected the permanent felicity of a Nation with its virtue? The experiment, at least, is recommended by every sentiment which ennobles human nature.—Alas! is it rendered impossible by its vices?

In the execution of such a plan nothing is more essential than that permanent, inveterate antipathies against particular nations and passionate attachments for others should be excluded; and that in place of them just and amicable feelings towards all should be cultivated.—The Nation, which indulges towards another an habitual hatred or an habitual fondness, is in some degree a slave. It is a slave to its animosity or to its affection, either of which is sufficient to lead it astray from its duty and its interest.—Antipathy in one nation against another disposes each more readily to offer insult and injury, to lay hold of slight causes of umbrage, and to be haughty and intractable, when accidental or trifling occasions of dispute occur.—Hence frequent collisions, obstinate, envenomed and bloody contests.—The Nation promoted by ill-will and resentment sometimes impels to War the Government, contrary to the best calculations of policy.—The Government sometimes participates in the national propensity, and adopts through passion what reason would reject;—at other times, it makes the animosity of the Nation subservient to projects of hostility instigated by pride, ambition, and other sinister and pernicious motives.—The peace often, sometimes perhaps the Liberty, of Nations has been the victim. . . .

The great rule of conduct for us, in regard to foreign Nations, is, in extending our commercial relations, to have with them as little *Political* connection as possible.—So far as we have already formed engagements, let them be fulfilled with perfect good faith.—Here let us stop. . . .

In offering to you, my Countrymen, these counsels of an old and affectionate friend, I dare not hope they will make the strong and lasting impression, I could wish,—that they will controul the usual current of the passions, or prevent our Nation from running the course which has hitherto marked the destiny of Nations.—But if I may even flatter myself, that they may be productive of some partial benefit; some occasional good; that they may now and then recur to moderate the fury of party spirit, to warn against the mischiefs of foreign intrigue, to guard against the impostures of pretended patriotism, this hope will be a full recompense for the solicitude for your welfare, by which they have been dictated.—

How far in the discharge of my official duties, I have been guided by the principles which have been delineated, the public Records and other evidences of my conduct must witness to You, and to the World.—To myself, the assurance of my own conscience is, that I have at least believed myself to be guided by them. . . .

. . . With me, a predominant motive has been to endeavour to gain time to our country to settle and mature its yet recent institutions, and to progress without interruption to that degree of strength and consistency, which is necessary to give it, humanly speaking, the command of its own fortunes.

Though, in reviewing the incidents of my Administration, I am unconscious of intentional error—I am nevertheless too sensible of my defects not to think it probable that I may have committed many errors.—Whatever they may be I fervently beseech the Almighty to avert or mitigate the evils to which they may tend.—I shall also carry with me the hope that my country will never cease to view them with indulgence; and that after forty-five years of my life dedicated to its service, with an upright zeal, the faults of incompetent abilities will be consigned to oblivion, as myself must soon be to the mansions of rest.

Relying on its kindness in this as in other things, and actuated by that fervent love towards it, which is so natural to a man, who views in it the native soil of himself and his progenitors for several generations;—I anticipate with pleasing expectation that retreat, in which I promise myself to realize, without alloy, the sweet enjoyment of partaking, in the midst of my fellow-citizens, the benign influence of good Laws under a free Government,—the ever favourite object of my heart, and the happy reward, as I trust, of our mutual cares, labours, and dangers.

Jefferson's First Inaugural Address

Despite George Washington's warnings about the dangers of party strife, his retirement from the presidency in 1797 loosed spirits of angry partisanship in the land. The Federalist party, which won the election of 1796, passed laws (notably the Alien and Sedition Acts of 1798) to stifle public criticism and undermine the opposition Democratic-Republican party; the Democratic-Republicans quickly passed resolutions in Kentucky and Virginia to deny the federal government's right to impose its laws on resisting states.

In an 1800 rematch of the 1796 presidential election, Thomas Jefferson, the Democratic-Republican candidate, ran against the Federalist president John Adams. This time Jefferson won. The very fact of his inaugural address on March 4, 1801, was significant—it was the first inauguration in the new capital city of Washington and it marked the first peaceful transfer of power from one political party to another in the new nation. But the address also was significant because of what Jefferson said. Resisting the temptation to proclaim a partisan triumph, the new president insisted that "every difference of opinion is not a difference of principle. We have called by different names brethren of the same principle. We are all Republicans, we are all Federalists."

Friends and Fellow-Citizens. . . .

During the contest of opinion through which we have passed the animation of discussions and of exertions has sometimes worn an aspect which might impose on strangers unused to think freely and to speak and to write what they think; but this being now decided by the voice of the nation, announced according to the rules of the Constitution, all will, of course, arrange themselves under the will of the law, and unite in common efforts for the common good. All, too, will bear in mind this sacred principle, that though the will of the majority is in all cases to prevail, that will to be rightful must be reasonable; that the minority possess their equal rights, which equal law must protect, and to violate would be oppression. Let us, then, fellow-citizens, unite with one heart and one mind. Let us restore to social intercourse that harmony and affection without which liberty and even life itself are but dreary things. And let us reflect that, having banished from our land that religious intolerance under which mankind so long bled and suffered, we have yet gained little if we countenance a political intolerance as despotic, as wicked, and capable of as bitter and bloody persecutions. During the throes and convulsions of the ancient world, during the agonizing spasms of infuriated man, seeking through blood and slaughter his long-lost liberty, it was not wonderful that the agitation of the billows should reach even this distant and peaceful shore; that this should be more felt and feared by some and less by others, and should divide opinions as to measures of safety. But every difference of opinion is not a difference of principle. We have called by different names brethren of the same principle. We are all Republicans, we are all Federalists. If there be any among us who would wish to dissolve this Union or to change its republican form, let them stand undisturbed as monuments of the safety with which error of opinion may be tolerated where reason is left free to combat it. I know, indeed, that some honest men fear that a republican government can not be strong, that this Government is not strong enough; but would the honest patriot, in the full time of successful experiment, abandon a government which has so far kept us free and firm on the theoretic and visionary fear that this Government, the world's best hope, may by possibility want energy to preserve itself? I trust not. I believe this, on the contrary, the strongest Government on earth. I believe it the only one where every man, at the call of the law, would fly to the standard of the law, and would meet invasions of the public order as his own personal concern. Sometimes it is said that man can not be trusted with the government of himself. Can he, then, be trusted with the government of others? Or have we found angels in the forms of kings to govern him? Let history answer this question.

Let us, then, with courage and confidence pursue our own Federal and Republican principles, our attachment to union and representative government. Kindly separated by nature and a wide ocean from the exterminating havoc of one quarter of the globe; too high-minded to endure the degradations of the others; possessing a chosen country, with room enough for our descendants to the thousandth and thousandth generation; entertaining a due sense of our equal right to the use of our faculties, to the acquisitions of our own industry, to honor and confidence from our fellow-citizens, resulting not from birth, but from our actions and their sense of them; enlightened by a benign religion, professed, indeed, and practiced in various forms, yet all of them inculcating honesty, truth, temperance, gratitude, and the love of man; acknowledging and adoring an overruling Providence, which by all its dispensations proves that it delights in the happiness of man here and his greater happiness hereafter—with all these blessings, what more is necessary to make us a happy and a prosperous people? Still one thing more, fellow-citizens—a wise and frugal Government, which shall restrain men from injuring one another, shall leave them otherwise free to regulate their own pursuits of industry and improvement, and shall not take from the mouth of labor the bread it has earned. This is the sum of good government, and this is necessary to close the circle of our felicities.

About to enter, fellow-citizens, on the exercise of duties which comprehend everything dear and valuable to you, it is proper you should understand what I deem the essential principles of our Government, and consequently those which ought to shape its Administration. I will compress them within the narrowest compass they will bear, stating the general principle, but not all its limitations. Equal and exact justice to all men, of whatever state or persuasion, religious or political; peace, commerce, and honest friendship with all nations, entangling alliances with none; the support of the State governments in all their rights, as the most competent administrations for our domestic concerns and the surest bulwarks against antirepublican tendencies; the preservation of the General Government in its whole constitutional vigor, as the sheet anchor of our peace at home and safety abroad; a jealous care of the right of election by the people—a mild and safe corrective of abuses which are lopped by the sword of revolution where peaceable remedies are unprovided; absolute acquiescence in the decisions of the majority, the vital principle of republics, from which is not appeal but to force, the vital principle and immediate parent of despotism; a well-disciplined militia, our best reliance in peace and for the first moments of war, till regulars may relieve them; the supremacy of the civil over the military authority; economy in the public expense, that labor may be lightly burthened; the honest payment of our debts and sacred preservation of the public faith; encouragement of agriculture, and of commerce as its handmaid; the diffusion of information and arraignment of all abuses at the bar of the public reason; freedom of religion; freedom of the press, and freedom of person under the protection of the habeas corpus, and trial by juries impartially selected. These principles form the bright constellation which has gone before us and guided our steps through an age of revolution and reformation. The wisdom of our sages and blood of our heroes have been devoted to their attainment. They should be the creed of our political faith, the text of civic instruction, the touchstone by which to try the services of those we trust; and should we wander from them in moments of error or of alarm, let us hasten to retrace our steps and to regain the road which alone leads to peace, liberty, and safety.

I repair, then, fellow-citizens, to the post you have assigned me. With experience enough in subordinate offices to have seen the difficulties of this the greatest of all, I have learnt to expect that it will rarely fall to the lot of imperfect man to retire from this station with the reputation and the favor which bring him into it. Without pretensions to that high confidence you reposed in our first and greatest revolutionary character, whose preëminent services had entitled him to the first place in his country's love and destined for him the fairest page in the volume of faithful history, I ask so much confidence only as may give firmness and effect to the legal administration of your affairs. I shall often go wrong through defect of judgment. When right, I shall often be thought wrong by those whose positions will not command a view of the whole ground. I ask your indulgence for my own errors, which will never be intentional, and your support against the errors of others, who may condemn what they would not if seen in all its parts. The approbation implied by your suffrage is a great consolation to me for the past, and my future solicitude will be to retain the good opinion of those who have bestowed it in advance, to conciliate that of others by doing them all the good in my power, and to be instrumental to the happiness and freedom of all.

Relying, then, on the patronage of your good will, I advance with obedience to the work, ready to retire from it whenever you become sensible how much better choice it is in your power to make. And may that Infinite Power which rules the destinies of the universe lead our councils to what is best, and give them a favorable issue for your peace and prosperity.

The Monroe Doctrine

President James Monroe is best known for the doctrine that bears his name. It was proclaimed in response to two foreign policy disputes in which the United States was involved during the early 1820s. The first was a Russian claim of land along the Pacific coast, from the Bering Straits south to some unspecified location. The other arose from rumored European plans to recolonize the newly independent nations of previously Spanish South America.

After frequent consultations with the cabinet and with former presidents Thomas Jefferson and James Madison during the fall of 1823, Monroe and Secretary of State John Quincy Adams resolved to declare the "new world" of the Americas off-limits to new attempts at colonization by the "old world" of Europe.

The Monroe Doctrine had almost no immediate effect: as it turned out, Europe was not planning to recolonize South America anyway; as for the Russians, they continued their efforts in the Pacific northwest. In later years, however, presidents invoked the doctrine on several occasions to assert special U.S. influence in South America.

This document is without doubt the most famous public statement ever delivered by James Monroe. It is quite possibly the most renowned doctrine ever promulgated by an American statesman—anywhere, at any time. Contrary to popular opinion, however, it was not delivered as a separate, isolated statement of American policy; rather, it was contained in Monroe's Seventh Annual Message to Congress (1823). In essence, the Doctrine consists of two basic points: that the two American continents are no longer to be considered subjects for future European colonization, and that any attempt by European powers to extend their influence into the Western Hemisphere would be considered dangerous to the peace and safety of the United States.

Fellow-Citizens of the Senate and House of Representatives....

At the proposal of the Russian Imperial Government, made through the minister of the Emperor residing here, a full power and instructions have been transmitted to the minister of the United States at St. Petersburg to arrange by amicable negotiation the respective rights and interests of the two nations on the northwest coast of this continent. A similar proposal had been made by His Imperial Majesty to the Government of Great Britain, which has likewise been acceded to. The Government of the United States has been desirous by this friendly proceeding of manifesting the great value which they have invariably attached to the friendship of the Emperor and their solicitude to cultivate the best understanding with his Government. In the discussions to which this interest has given rise and in the arrangements by which they may terminate the occasion has been judged proper for asserting, as a principle in which the rights and interests of the United States are involved, that the American continents, by the free and independent condition which they have assumed and maintain, are henceforth not to be considered as subjects for future colonization by any European powers....

It was stated at the commencement of the last session that a great effort was then making in Spain and Portugal to improve the condition of the people of those countries, and that it appeared to be conducted with extraordinary moderation. It need scarcely be remarked that the result has been so far very different from what was then anticipated. Of events in that quarter of the globe, with which we have so much intercourse and from which we derive our origin, we have always been anxious and interested spectators. The citizens of the United States cherish sentiments the most friendly in favor of the liberty and happiness of their fellow-men on that side of the Atlantic. In the wars of the European powers in matters relating to themselves we have never taken any part, nor does it comport with our policy to do so. It is only when our rights are invaded or seriously menaced that we resent injuries or make preparation for our defense. With the movements in this hemisphere we are of necessity more immediately connected, and by causes which must be obvious to all enlightened and impartial observers. The political system of the allied powers is essentially different in this respect from that of America. This difference proceeds from that which exists in their respective Governments; and to the defense of our own, which has been achieved by the loss of so much blood and treasure, and matured by the wisdom of their most enlightened citizens, and under which we have enjoyed unexampled felicity, this whole nation is devoted. We owe it, therefore, to candor and to the amicable relations existing between the United States and those powers to declare that we should consider any attempt on their part to extend their system to any portion of this hemisphere as dangerous to our peace and safety. With the existing colonies or dependencies of any European power we have not interfered and shall not interfere. But with the Governments who have declared their independence and maintained it, and whose independence we have, on great consideration and on just principles, acknowledged, we could not view any interposition for the purpose of oppressing them, or controlling in any other manner their destiny, by any European power in any other light than as the manifestation of an unfriendly disposition toward the United States. In the war between those new Governments and Spain we declared our neutrality at the time of their recognition, and to this we have adhered, and shall continue to adhere, provided no change shall occur which, in the judgment of the competent authorities of this Government, shall make a corresponding change on the part of the United States indispensable to their security.

The late events in Spain and Portugal shew that Europe is still unsettled. Of this important fact no stronger proof can be adduced than that the allied powers should have thought it proper, on any principle satisfactory to themselves, to have interposed by force in the internal concerns of Spain. To what extent such interposition may be carried, on the same principle, is a question in which all independent powers whose governments differ from theirs are interested, even those most remote, and surely none more so than the United States. Our policy in regard to Europe, which was adopted at an early stage of the wars which have so long agitated that quarter of the globe, nevertheless remains the same, which is, not to interfere in the internal concerns of any of its powers; to consider the government *de facto* as the legitimate government for us; to cultivate friendly relations with it, and to preserve those relations by a frank, firm, and manly policy, meeting in all instances the just claims of every power, submitting to injuries from none. But in regard to those continents circumstances are eminently and conspicuously different. It is impossible that the allied powers should extend their political system to any portion of either continent without endangering our peace and happiness; nor can anyone believe that our southern brethren, if left to themselves, would adopt it of their own accord. It is equally impossible, therefore, that we should behold such interposition in any form with indifference. If we look to the comparative strength and resources of Spain and those new Governments, and their distance from each other, it must be obvious that she can never subdue them. It is still the true policy of the United States to leave the parties to themselves, in the hope that other powers will pursue the same course....

Jackson's Bank Bill Veto

Andrew Jackson's veto of a bill passed by Congress to renew the Bank of the United States's charter was politically important at the time and of enduring importance as a bold assertion of presidential power.

Politically, the bank was a bastion of everything Jackson opposed—the East, the commercial elite, and the National Republican party (soon to be known as the Whigs). Indeed, bank president Nicholas Biddle, encouraged by Henry Clay, the National Republican candidate for president in 1832, asked Congress to renew the bank's charter four years before the old charter was scheduled to expire in 1836 because Clay thought (erroneously) that a veto by Jackson would be a good issue in the election.

Jackson's veto message reflected an expansive view of the powers of the presidency. Previously, presidents had felt constrained to veto bills only on constitutional grounds, and an earlier version of the bank bill had been judged constitutional by the Supreme Court. But Jackson, in the first part of his message, attacked the bank renewal as bad public policy, setting a precedent for future presidents casting future vetoes. He went on to assert that the president and Congress have as much right to interpret the Constitution as the Court.

To the Senate:

The bill "to modify and continue" the act entitled "An act to incorporate the subscribers to the Bank of the United States" was presented to me on the 4th July instant. Having considered it with that solemn regard to the principles of the Constitution which the day was calculated to inspire, and come to the conclusion that it ought not to become a law, I herewith return it to the Senate, in which it originated, with my objections. . . .

The present [bank] . . . enjoys an exclusive privilege of banking under the authority of the general government, a monopoly of its favor and support, and, as a necessary consequence, almost a monopoly of the foreign and domestic exchange. The powers, privileges, and favors bestowed upon it in the original charter, by increasing the value of the stock far above its par value, operated as a gratuity of many millions to the stockholders. . . .

The act before me proposes another gratuity to the holders of the same stock. . . .

Every monopoly and all exclusive privileges are granted at the expense of the public, which ought to receive a fair equivalent. The many millions which this act proposes to bestow on the stockholders of the existing bank must come directly or indirectly out of the earnings of the American people. . . .

It is maintained by the advocates of the bank that its constitutionality in all its features ought to be considered as settled by precedent and by the decision of the Supreme Court. To this conclusion I cannot assent. Mere precedent is a dangerous source of authority and should not be regarded as deciding questions of constitutional power except where the acquiescence of the people and the states can be considered as well settled. So far from this being the case on this subject, an argument against the bank might be based on precedent. One Congress in 1791 decided in favor of a bank; another in 1811 decided against it. One Congress in 1815 decided against a bank; another in 1816 decided in its favor. Prior to the present Congress, therefore, the precedents drawn from that source were equal. If we resort to the states, the expressions of legislative, judicial, and executive opinions against the bank have been probably to those in its favor as 4 to 1. . . .

If the opinion of the Supreme Court covered the whole ground of this act, it ought not to control the coordinate authorities of this government. The Congress, the executive, and the court must each for itself be guided by its own opinion of the Constitution. Each public officer who takes an oath to support the Constitution swears that he will support it as he understands it and not as it is understood by others. It is as much the duty of the House of Representatives, of the Senate, and of the President to decide upon the constitutionality of any bill or resolution which may be presented to them for passage or approval as it is of the supreme judges when it may be brought before them for judicial decision. The opinion of the judges has no more authority over Congress than the opinion of Congress has over the judges, and on that point the President is independent of both. The authority of the Supreme Court must not, therefore, be permitted to control the Congress or the executive when acting in their legislative capacities, but to have only such influence as the force of their reasoning may deserve. . . .

The government is the only *"proper"* judge where its agents should reside and keep their offices, because it best knows where their presence will be *"necessary."* It cannot, therefore, be *"necessary"* or *"proper"* to authorize the bank to locate branches where it pleases to perform the public service, without consulting the government and contrary to its will. The principle laid down by the Supreme Court concedes that Congress cannot establish a bank for purposes of private speculation and gain, but only as a means of executing the delegated powers of the general government. By the same principle a branch bank cannot constitutionally be established for other than public purposes. The power which this act gives to establish two branches in any state, without the injunction or request of the government and for other than public purposes, is not *"necessary"* to the due *"execution"* of the powers delegated to the Congress. . . .

The principle is conceded that the states cannot rightfully tax the operations of the general government. They cannot tax the money of the government deposited in the state banks nor the agency of those banks remitting it; but will any man maintain that their mere selection to perform this public service for the general government would exempt the state banks and their ordinary business from state taxation? Had the United States, instead of establishing a bank at Philadelphia, employed a private banker to keep and transmit their funds, would it have deprived Pennsylvania of the right to tax his bank and his usual banking operations? . . .

It can not be *"necessary"* to the character of the bank as a fiscal agent of the government that its private business should be exempted from that taxation to which all the state banks are liable, nor can I conceive it *"proper"* that the substantive and most essential powers reserved by the states shall be thus attacked and annihilated as a means of executing the powers delegated to the general government. It may be safely assumed that none of those sages who had an agency in forming or adopting our Constitution ever imagined that any portion of the taxing power of the states not prohibited to them nor delegated to Congress was to be swept away and annihilated as a means of executing certain powers delegated to Congress.

If our power over means is so absolute that the Supreme Court will not call in question the constitutionality of an act of Congress the subject of which "is not prohibited, and is really calculated to effect any of the objects entrusted to the government," although, as in the case before me, it takes away powers expressly granted to Congress and rights scrupulously reserved to the states, it becomes us to proceed in our legislation with the utmost caution. Though not directly, our own powers and the rights of the states may be indirectly legislated away in the use of means to execute substantive powers.

We may not enact that Congress shall not have the power of exclusive legislation over the District of Columbia, but we may pledge the faith of the United States that as a means of executing other powers it shall not be exercised for twenty years or forever. We may not pass an act prohibiting the states to tax the banking business carried on within their limits, but we may, as a means of executing our powers over other objects, place that business in the hands of our agents and then declare it exempt from state taxation in their hands. Thus may our own powers and the rights of the states, which we cannot directly curtail or invade, be frittered away and extinguished in the use of means employed by us to execute other powers. That a bank of the United States, competent to all the duties which may be required by the government, might be so organized as not to infringe on our own delegated powers or the reserved rights of the states I do not entertain a doubt. . . .

Under such circumstances the bank comes forward and asks a renewal of its charter for a term of fifteen years upon conditions which not only operate as a gratuity to the stockholders of many millions of dollars but will sanction any abuses and legalize any encroachments. . . .

The bank is professedly established as an agent of the executive branch of the government, and its constitutionality is maintained on that ground. Neither upon the propriety of present action nor upon the provisions of this act was the executive consulted. It has had no opportunity to say that it neither needs nor wants an agent clothed with such powers and favored by such exemptions. There is nothing in its legitimate functions which makes it necessary or proper. Whatever interest or influence, whether public or private, has given birth to this act, it cannot be found either in the wishes or necessities of the Executive Department, by which present action is deemed premature, and the powers conferred upon its agent not only unnecessary but dangerous to the government and country.

It is to be regretted that the rich and powerful too often bend the acts of government to their selfish purposes. Distinctions in society will always exist under every just government. Equality of talents, of education, or of wealth cannot be produced by human institutions. In the full enjoyment of the gifts of Heaven and the fruits of superior industry, economy, and virtue, every man is equally entitled to protection by law; but when the laws undertake to add to these natural and just advantages artificial distinctions, to grant titles, gratuities, and exclusive privileges, to make the rich richer and the potent more powerful, the humble members of society—the farmers, mechanics, and laborers—who have neither the time nor the means of securing like favors to themselves, have a right to complain of the injustice of their government. There are no necessary evils in government. Its evils exist only in its abuses. If it would confine itself to equal protection, and, as Heaven does it rains, shower its favors alike on the high and the low, the rich and the poor, it would be an unqualified blessing. In the act before me there seems to be a wide and unnecessary departure from these just principles.

Nor is our government to be maintained or our Union preserved by invasions of the rights and powers of the several states. In thus attempting to make our general government strong, we make it weak. Its true strength consists in leaving individuals and states as much as possible to themselves—in making itself felt, not in its power, but in its beneficence; not in its control, but in its protection; not in binding the states more closely to the center, but leaving each to move unobstructed in its proper orbit.

Experience should teach us wisdom. Most of the difficulties our government now encounters and most of the dangers which impend over our Union have sprung from an abandonment of the legitimate objects of government by our national legislation and the adoption of such principles as are embodied in this act. Many of our rich men have not been content with equal protection and equal benefits but have besought us to make them richer by act of Congress. By attempting to gratify their desires, we have in the results of our legislation arrayed section and section, interest against interest, and man against man, in a fearful commotion which threatens to shake the foundations of our Union.

It is time to pause in our career to review our principles and, if possible, revive that devoted patriotism and spirit of compromise which distinguished the sages of the Revolution and the fathers of our Union. If we cannot at once, in justice to interests vested under improvident legislation, make our government what it ought to be, we can at least take a stand against all new grants of monopolies and exclusive privileges, against any prostitution of our government to the advancement of a few at the expense of the many, and in favor of compromise and gradual reform in our code of laws and system of political economy.

The Emancipation Proclamation

To Abraham Lincoln, the Civil War was a crusade not to end slavery, but to preserve the Union. "If I could save the Union without freeing any *slave, I would do it," he wrote in a letter to the* New York Herald. *In the face of continuing Union frustration on the battlefield, however, Lincoln's hands-off policy on slavery jeopardized the support of abolitionists at home and European governments abroad. During the summer of 1862 Lincoln resolved to move against slavery, but he heeded the advice of his cabinet that he wait until after the Union Army had won a battle. A partial military victory at Antietam in September was occasion enough, and on September 22, 1862, Lincoln issued a preliminary Emancipation Proclamation. The rebellious states were told that unless they laid down their arms by January 1, 1863, their slaves would be legally free.*

On New Year's Day, 1863, Lincoln signed the Emancipation Proclamation at a White House ceremony, saying, "I never, in my life, felt more certain that I was doing right than I do in signing this paper." Few slaves were freed right away, since the only slaves to whom the proclamation applied were in states that the Confederacy controlled. But abolitionists and European public opinion rallied to the North's cause and, in the long run, slavery was ended as the Union Army regained more and more southern territory.

By the President of the United States of America:

A Proclamation.

Whereas on the 22d day of September, A.D. 1862, a proclamation was issued by the President of the United States, containing, among other things, the following, to wit:

"That on the 1st day of January, A.D. 1863, all persons held as slaves within any state or designated part of a State the people whereof shall then be in rebellion against the United States shall be then, thenceforward, and forever free; and the executive government of the United States, including the military and naval authority thereof, will recognize and maintain the freedom of such persons and will do no act or acts to repress such persons, or any of them, in any efforts they may make for their actual freedom.

"That the executive will on the 1st day of January aforesaid, by proclamation, designate the States and parts of States, if any, in which the people thereof, respectively, shall then be in rebellion against the United States; and the fact that any State or the people thereof shall on that day be in good faith represented in the Congress of the United States by members chosen thereto at elections wherein a majority of the qualified voters of such States shall have participated shall, in the absence of strong countervailing testimony, be deemed conclusive evidence that such State and the people thereof are not then in rebellion against the United States."

Now, therefore, I, Abraham Lincoln, President of the United States, by virtue of the power in me vested as Commander-in-Chief of the Army and Navy of the United States in time of actual armed rebellion against the authority and government of the United States, and as a fit and necessary war measure for suppressing said rebellion, do, on this 1st day of January, A.D. 1863, and in accordance with my purpose so to do, publicly proclaim for the full period of one hundred days from the first day above mentioned, order and designate as the State and parts of States wherein the people thereof, respectively, are this day in rebellion against the United States the following, to wit:

Arkansas, Texas, Louisiana (except the parishes of St. Bernard, Plaquemines, Jefferson, St. John, St. Charles, St. James, Ascension, Assumption, Terrebonne, Lafourche, St. Mary, St. Martin, and Orleans, including the city of New Orleans), Mississippi, Alabama, Florida, Georgia, South Carolina, North Carolina, and Virginia (except the forty-eight counties designated as West Virginia, and also the counties of Berkeley, Accomac, Northhampton, Elizabeth City, York, Princess Anne, and Norfolk, including the cities of Norfolk and Portsmouth), and which excepted parts are for the present left precisely as if this proclamation were not issued.

And by virtue of the power and for the purpose aforesaid, I do order and declare that all persons held as slaves within said designated States and parts of States are, and henceforward shall be, free; and that the Executive Government of the United States, including the military and naval authorities thereof, will recognize and maintain the freedom of said persons.

And I hereby enjoin upon the people so declared to be free to abstain from all violence, unless in necessary self-defense; and I recommend to them that, in all cases when allowed, they labor faithfully for reasonable wages.

And I further declare and make known that such persons of suitable condition will be received into the armed service of the United States to garrison forts, positions, stations, and other places, and to man vessels of all sorts in said service.

And upon this act, sincerely believed to be an act of justice, warranted by the Constitution upon military necessity, I invoke the considerate judgment of mankind and the gracious favor of Almighty God.

The Gettysburg Address

On November 18, 1863, Abraham Lincoln rode a train from Washington to Gettysburg, Pennsylvania, to attend the next day's dedication of a cemetery in which six thousand casualties of the Battle of Gettysburg were buried. The battle, fought in early July, had helped to turn the tide of the Civil War in the Union's favor. Lincoln was not the main speaker at the dedication—that honor fell to former senator and renowned orator Edward Everett, who delivered a lengthy and moving address. Instead, Lincoln spoke briefly after Everett was finished.

The brilliance of the Gettysburg Address is that in the space of around 250 words it solemnly and honestly acknowledges the awful pain of "these honored dead" while placing the war in which they had fought into the context of the struggle to attain "government of the people, by the people, for the people" that had begun "four score and seven years ago" in 1776. That struggle, Lincoln urged, must continue into "a new birth of freedom" so that the soldiers would "not have died in vain."

Four score and seven years ago our fathers brought forth on this continent, a new nation, conceived in Liberty, and dedicated to the proposition that all men are created equal.

Now we are engaged in a great civil war, testing whether that nation or any nation so conceived and so dedicated, can long endure. We are met on a great battle-field of that war. We have come to dedicate a portion of that field, as a final resting place for those who here gave their lives that that nation might live. It is altogether fitting and proper that we should do this.

But, in a larger sense, we can not dedicate—we can not consecrate—we can not hallow—this ground. The brave men, living and dead, who struggled here, have consecrated it, far above our poor power to add or detract. The world will little note, nor long remember what we say here, but it can never forget what they did here. It is for us the living, rather, to be dedicated here to the unfinished work which they who fought here have thus far so nobly advanced. It is rather for us to be here dedicated to the great task remaining before us—that from these honored dead we take increased devotion to that cause for which they gave the last full measure of devotion—that we here highly resolve that these dead shall not have died in vain—that this nation, under God, shall have a new birth of freedom—and that government of the people, by the people, for the people, shall not perish from the earth.

Lincoln's Second Inaugural Address March 4, 1865

Abraham Lincoln delivered his second inaugural address, which could not have lasted more than five minutes, on March 4, 1865, almost four years after the beginning of the Civil War. Six hundred thousand people had died in the war, but it clearly was drawing to an end. (Indeed, Confederate general Robert E. Lee surrendered to Union general Ulysses S. Grant at Appomattox courthouse in Virginia only a month later, on April 9.)

In style, Lincoln's second inaugural address is biblical—he quotes from the Old Testament, describes the hand of Providence in the war, and writes in cadences reminiscent of the King James Version. In substance, the address is tolerant and conciliatory toward the almost-defeated South, whose people he refers to as "adversaries," not enemies. His concluding plea for "malice toward none" in the effort to "bind up the nation's wounds" is almost as well remembered as the first and last sentences of the Gettysburg Address.

Fellow-Countrymen:

At this second appearing to take the oath of the presidential office there is less occasion for an extended address than there was at the first. Then a statement somewhat in detail of a course to be pursued seemed fitting and proper. Now, at the expiration of four years, during which public declarations have been constantly called forth on every point and phase of the great contest which still absorbs the attention and engrosses the energies of the nation, little that is new could be presented. The progress of our arms, upon which all else chiefly depends, is as well known to the public as to myself, and it is, I trust, reasonably satisfactory and encouraging to all. With high hope for the future, no prediction in regard to it is ventured.

On the occasion corresponding to this four years ago all thoughts were anxiously directed to an impending civil war. All dreaded it, all sought to avert it. While the inaugural address was being delivered from this place, devoted altogether to *saving* the Union without war, insurgent agents were in the city seeking to *destroy* it without war—seeking to dissolve the Union and divide effects by negotiation. Both parties deprecated war, but one of them would *make* war rather than let the nation survive, and the other would *accept* war rather than let it perish, and the war came.

One eighth of the whole population was colored slaves, not distributed generally over the Union, but localized in the southern part of it. These slaves constituted a peculiar and powerful interest. All knew that this interest was somehow the cause of the war. To strengthen, perpetuate, and extend this interest was the object for which the insurgents would rend the Union even by war, while the Government claimed no right to do more than to restrict the territorial enlargement of it. Neither party expected for the war the magnitude or the duration which it has already attained. Neither anticipated that the *cause* of the conflict might cease with or even before the conflict itself should cease. Each looked for an easier triumph, and a result less fundamental and astounding. Both read the same Bible and pray to the same God, and each invokes His aid against the other. It may seem strange that any men should dare to ask a just God's assistance in wringing their bread from the sweat of other men's faces, but let us judge not, that we be not judged. The prayers of both could not be answered. That of neither has been answered fully. The Almighty has His own purposes. "Woe unto the world because of offenses; for it must needs be that offenses come, but woe to that man by whom the offense cometh." If we shall suppose that American slavery is one of those offenses which, in the providence of God, must needs come, but which, having continued through His appointed time, He now wills to remove, and that he gives to both North and South this terrible war as the woe due to those by whom the offense came, shall we discern therein any departure from those divine attributes which the believers in a living God always ascribe to Him? Fondly do we hope, fervently do we pray, that this mighty scourge of war may speedily pass away. Yet, if God wills that it continue until all the wealth piled by the bondsman's two hundred and fifty years of unrequited toil shall be sunk, and until every drop of blood drawn with the lash shall be paid by another drawn with the sword, as was said three thousand years ago, so still it must be said, "The judgments of the Lord are true and righteous altogether."

With malice toward none, with charity for all, with firmness in the right as God gives us to see the right, let us strive on to finish the work we are in, to bind up the nation's wounds, to care for him who shall have borne the battle and for his widow and his orphan, to do all which may achieve and cherish a just and lasting peace among ourselves and with all nations.

Impeachment of Andrew Johnson

The Constitution stipulates that the president "shall be removed from Office on Impeachment for, and Convic-

tion of, Treason, Bribery, or other High Crimes and Misdemeanors." The House of Representatives is charged to impeach the president by majority vote; the Senate, with the chief justice of the United States presiding, then tries the president and decides whether to convict and remove. A two-thirds majority of senators is required to do so.

Andrew Johnson, who was elected vice president in 1864 and succeeded to the presidency when President Abraham Lincoln was assassinated in 1865, is the only president to undergo the entire impeachment process. Johnson was very unpopular in the Republican-controlled Congress because he wished to pursue a conciliatory policy of Reconstruction toward the southern states that had seceded from the Union and been defeated in the Civil War. The major formal charge against Johnson, however, was that he had violated the Tenure of Office Act of 1867 by firing Secretary of War Edwin M. Stanton without obtaining the Senate's approval. The House impeached him on that charge on March 2 and 3, 1868, and on May 16 and 26 the Senate voted for conviction and removal by a margin of 35 to 19—one vote shy of the required two-thirds majority. Johnson served out the remainder of the term.

Articles of Impeachment

ARTICLES EXHIBITED BY THE HOUSE OF REPRESENTATIVES OF THE UNITED STATES, IN THE NAME OF THEMSELVES AND ALL THE PEOPLE OF THE UNITED STATES, AGAINST ANDREW JOHNSON, PRESIDENT OF THE UNITED STATES, IN MAINTENANCE AND SUPPORT OF THEIR IMPEACHMENT AGAINST HIM FOR HIGH CRIMES AND MISDEMEANORS IN OFFICE.

Article I

That said Andrew Johnson, President of the United States, on the 21st day of February, A.D. 1868, at Washington, in the District of Columbia, unmindful of the high duties of his office, of his oath of office, and of the requirement of the Constitution that he should take care that the laws be faithfully executed, did unlawfully and in violation of the Constitution and laws of the United States issue an order in writing for the removal of Edwin M. Stanton from the office of Secretary for the Department of War, said Edwin M. Stanton having been theretofore duly appointed and commissioned, by and with the advice and consent of the Senate of the United States, as such Secretary; and said Andrew Johnson, President of the United States, on the 12th day of August, A.D. 1867, and during the recess of said Senate, having suspended by his order Edwin M. Stanton from said office, and within twenty days after the first day of the next meeting of said Senate—that is to say, on the 12th day of December, in the year last aforesaid—having reported to said Senate such suspension, with the evidence and reasons for his action in the case and the name of the person designated to perform the duties of such office temporarily until the next meeting of the Senate; and said Senate thereafterwards, on the 13th day of January, A.D. 1868, having duly considered the evidence and reasons reported by said Andrew Johnson for said suspension, and having refused to concur in said suspension, whereby and by force of the provisions of an act entitled "An act regulating the tenure of certain civil offices," passed March 2, 1867, said Edwin M. Stanton did forthwith resume the functions of his office, whereof the said Andrew Johnson had then and there due notice; and said Edwin M. Stanton, by reason of the premises, on said 21st day of February, being lawfully entitled to hold said office of Secretary for the Department of War; which said order for the removal of said Edwin M. Stanton is in substance as follows; that is to say:

EXECUTIVE MANSION,
Washington, D.C., February 21, 1868.

HON. EDWIN M. STANTON,
Washington, D.C.

SIR: By virtue of the power and authority vested in me as President by the Constitution and laws of the United States, you are hereby removed from office as Secretary for the Department of War, and your functions as such will terminate upon the receipt of this communication.

You will transfer to Brevet Major-General Lorenzo Thomas, Adjutant-General of the Army, who has this day been authorized and empowerd to act as secretary of War ad interim, all records, books, papers, and other public property now in your custody and charge.

Respectfully yours,

ANDREW JOHNSON.

Which order was unlawfully issued with intent then and there to violate the act entitled "An act regulating the tenure of certain civil offices," passed March 2, 1867, and with the further intent, contrary to the provisions of said act, in violation thereof, and contrary to the provisions of the Constitution of the United States, and without the advice and consent of the Senate of the United States, the said Senate then and there being in session, to remove said Edwin M. Stanton from the office of Secretary for the Department of War, the said Edwin M. Stanton being then and there Secretary for the Department of War, and being then and there in the due and lawful execution and discharge of the duties of said office; whereby said Andrew Johnson, President of the United States, did then and there commit and was guilty of a high misdemeanor in office. . . .

[Articles II through IX omitted]

Article X

That said Andrew Johnson, President of the United States, unmindful of the high duties of his office and the dignity and proprieties thereof, and of the harmony and courtesies which ought to exist and be maintained between the executive and legislative branches of the Government of the United States, designing and intending to set aside the rightful authority and powers of Congress, did attempt to bring disgrace, ridicule, hatred, contempt, and reproach to the Congress of the United States and the several branches thereof, to impair and destroy the regard and respect of all the good people of the United States for the Congress and legislative power thereof (which all officers of the Government ought inviolably to preserve and maintain) and to excite the odium and resentment of all the good people of the United States against Congress and the laws by it duly and constitutionally enacted; and, in pursuance of his said design and intent, openly and publicly, and before divers assemblages of the citizens of the United States, convened in divers parts thereof to meet and receive said Andrew Johnson as the Chief Magistrate of the United States, did, on the 18th day of August, A.D. 1866, and on divers other days and times, as well before as afterwards, make and deliver with a loud voice certain intemperate, inflammatory, and scandalous harrangues, and did therein utter loud threats and bitter menaces, as well against Congress as the laws of the United States, duly enacted thereby, amid the cries, jeers, and laughter of the multitudes then assembled and in hearing, . . .

SCHUYLER COLFAX,
Speaker of the House of Representatives

EDWARD McPHERSON,
Clerk of the House of Representatives

Pendleton Act

The effort to reform the federal civil service by replacing the "spoils system" (under which government employees were hired and fired by elected officials) with a "merit system" (under which personnel decisions would be made nonpolitically, according to ability) was a prominent feature of American politics after the Civil War. In 1881 President James A. Garfield was assassinated by Charles Guiteau, who was enraged that he had not received a government job as reward for his labors on behalf of Garfield's candidacy in the 1880 election. In the atmosphere of revulsion against spoils that followed the assassination, Congress passed the Pendleton Act of 1883.

The Pendleton Act created the Civil Service Commission and stated several ideals that were to guide its labors. Partisan activity and family and personal connections as reasons for hiring, promoting, and firing government employees were to be replaced by competitive examinations and performance-based promotion and retention policies. In the short term, only 10 percent of the federal civil service was covered by the new rules, but the act empowered the president to extend the coverage to additional categories of employees. Over time, virtually the entire civil service became "merit"-based by virtue of presidential decisions.

An act to regulate and improve the civil service of the United States.

Be it enacted . . . , That the President is authorized to appoint, by and with the advice and consent of the Senate, three persons, not more than two of whom shall be adherents of the same party, as Civil Service Commissioners, and said three commissioners shall constitute the United States Civil Service Commission. Said commissioners shall hold no other official place under the United States.

SEC. 2. That it shall be the duty of said commissioners:

FIRST. To aid the President, as he may request, in preparing suitable rules for carrying this act into effect, and when said rules shall have been promulgated it shall be the duty of all officers of the United States in the departments and offices to which any such rules may relate to aid, in all proper ways, in carrying said rules, and any modifications thereof, into effect.

SECOND. And, among other things, said rules shall provide and declare, as nearly as the first conditions of good administration will warrant, as follows:

First, for open, competitive examinations for testing the fitness of applicants for the public service now classified or to be classified hereunder. Such examinations shall be practical in their character, and so far as may be shall relate to those matters which will fairly test the relative capacity and fitness of the persons examined to discharge the duties of the service into which they seek to be appointed.

Second, that all the offices, places, and employments so arranged or to be arranged in classes shall be filled by selections according to grade from among those graded highest as the results of such competitive examinations.

Third, appointments to the public service aforesaid in the departments at Washington shall be apportioned among the several States and Territories and the District of Columbia upon the basis of population as ascertained at the last preceding census. . . .

Fourth, that there shall be a period of probation before any absolute appointment or employment aforesaid.

Fifth, that no person in the public service is for that reason under any obligations to contribute to any political fund, or to render any political service, and that he will not be removed or otherwise prejudiced for refusing to do so.

Sixth, that no person in said service has any right to use his official authority or influence to coerce the political action of any person or body. . . .

SEC. 6. . . . That from time to time [the secretary of the Treasury,] the Postmaster-General, and each of the heads of departments mentioned in . . . [Section 158] . . . of the Revised Statutes, and each head of an office, shall, on the direction of the President, and for facilitating the execution of this act, respectively revise any then existing classification or arrangement of those in their respective departments and offices, and shall, for the purposes of the examination herein provided for, include in one or more of such classes, so far as practicable, subordinate places, clerks, and officers in the public service pertaining to their respective departments not before classified for examinations. . . .

SEC. 8. That no person habitually using intoxicating beverages to excess shall be appointed to, or retained in, any office, appointment, or employment to which the provisions of this act are applicable.

SEC. 9. That whenever there are already two or more members of a family in the public service in the grades covered by this act, no other member of such family shall be eligible to appointment to any of said grades.

SEC. 10. That no recommendation of any person who shall apply for office or place under the provisions of this act which may be given by any Senator or member of the House of Representatives, except as to the character or residence of the applicant, shall be received or considered by any person concerned in making any examination or appointment under this act. . . .

Theodore Roosevelt's "New Nationalism" Speech

Theodore Roosevelt voluntarily stepped down as president at the end of his term in 1909, two years shy of his fiftieth birthday. His "New Nationalism" speech was delivered almost a year and a half later, at the August 31, 1910, dedication of the John Brown Battlefield at Osawatomie, Kansas. In between those two dates, Roosevelt had witnessed the inauguration of his chosen successor, William Howard Taft, as president, then had become increasingly disillusioned with Taft's conservative leadership.

When it was delivered, the New Nationalism speech (the phrase was writer Herbert Croly's) was widely regarded as the kickoff to another presidential candidacy. In truth, Roosevelt did seek the Republican nomination in 1912 and, when Taft was nominated instead, ran as the Progressive, or "Bull Moose" candidate. (Both he and Taft lost to Woodrow Wilson.)

But Roosevelt's speech is of greatest enduring interest because it embodies the philosophy that he brought to political life in general and to the presidency in particular. He warned of the dangers of rising concentrations of corporate power and, by implication, union power. Bigness in the private sector was not intrinsically bad, Roosevelt argued, but big business and big labor were prone to commit abuses of power that could be checked only by a large and active federal government. Within that government, the president must be "the steward of the public welfare."

I stand for the square deal. But when I say that I am for the square deal, I mean not merely that I stand for fair play under the present rules of the game but that I stand for having those rules changed so as to work for a more substantial equality of opportunity and of reward for equally good service. . . .

Now, this means that our government, national and state, must be freed from the sinister influence or control of special interests. . . . We must drive the special interests out of politics. . . . For every special interest is entitled to justice, but not one is entitled to a vote in Congress, to a voice on the bench, or to representation in any public office. The Constitution guarantees protection to property, and we must make that promise good. But it does not give the right of suffrage to any corporation.

The true friend of property, the true conservative, is he who insists that property shall be the servant and not the master of the commonwealth; who insists that the creature of man's making shall be the servant and not the master of the man who made it. The citizens of the United States must effectively control the mighty commercial forces which they have themselves called into being. There can be no effective control of corporations while their political activity remains. To put an end to it will be neither a short nor an easy task, but it can be done.

We must have complete and effective publicity of corporate affairs so that the people may know beyond peradventure whether the corporations obey the law and whether their management entitles them to the confidence of the public. It is necessary that laws should be passed to prohibit the use of corporate funds directly or indirectly for political purposes; it is still more necessary that such laws should be thoroughly enforced. Corporate expenditures for political purposes, and especially such expenditures by public service corporations, have supplied one of the principal sources of corruption in our political affairs.

It has become entirely clear that we must have government supervision of the capitalization, not only of public service corporations, including, particularly, railways, but of all corporations doing an interstate business. I do not wish to see the nation forced into the ownership of the railways if it can possibly be avoided, and the only alternative is thoroughgoing and effective regulation, which shall be based on a full knowledge of all the facts, including a physical valuation of property. . . .

We have come to recognize that franchises should never be granted, except for a limited time, and never without proper provision for compensation to the public. It is my personal belief that the same kind and degree of control and supervision which should be exercised over public service corporations should be extended also to combinations which control necessaries of life, such as meat, oil, and coal, or which deal in them on an important scale. I have no doubt that the ordinary man who has control of them is much like ourselves. I have no doubt he would like to do well, but I want to have enough supervision to help him realize that desire to do well.

I believe that the officers, and, especially, the directors, of corporations should be held personally responsible when any corporation breaks the law.

Combinations in industry are the result of an imperative economic law which cannot be repealed by political legislation. The effort at prohibiting all combination has substantially failed. The way out lies, not in attempting to prevent such combinations but in completely controlling them in the interest of the public welfare. For that purpose the Federal Bureau of Corporations is an agency of first importance. Its powers, and, therefore, its efficiency, as well as that of the Interstate Commerce Commission, should be largely increased. We have a right to expect from the Bureau of Corporations and from the Interstate Commerce Commission a very high grade of public service. We should be as sure of the proper conduct of the interstate railways and the proper management of interstate business as we are now sure of the conduct and management of the national banks, and we should have as effective supervision in one case as in the other. . . .

There is a widespread belief among our people that, under the methods of making tariffs which have hitherto obtained, the special interests are too influential. Probably this is true of both the big special interests and the little special interests. These methods have put a premium on selfishness, and, naturally, the selfish big interests have gotten more than their smaller, though equally selfish, brothers. The duty of Congress is to provide a method by which the interest of the whole people shall be all that receives consideration. To this end there must be an expert tariff commission, wholly removed from the possibility of political pressure or of improper business influence. Such a commission can find the real difference between cost of production, which is mainly the difference of labor cost here and abroad. As fast as its recommendations are made, I believe in revising one schedule at a time. A general revision of the tariff almost inevitably leads to logrolling and the subordination of the general public interest to local and special interests.

The absence of effective state and, especially, national restraint upon unfair money getting has tended to create a small class of enormously wealthy and economically powerful men whose chief object is to hold and increase their power. The prime need is to change the conditions which enable these men to accumulate power which it is not for the general welfare that they should hold or exercise. . . . This, I know, implies a policy of a far more active governmental interference with social and economic conditions in this country than we have yet had, but I think we have got to face the fact that such an increase in governmental control is now necessary.

No man should receive a dollar unless that dollar has been fairly earned. Every dollar received should represent a dollar's worth of service rendered—not gambling in stocks but service rendered. The really big fortune, the swollen fortune, by the mere fact of its size, acquires qualities which differentiate it in kind as well as in degree from what is possessed by men of relatively small means. Therefore, I believe in a graduated income tax on big fortunes, and in another tax which is far more easily collected and far more effective—a graduated inheritance tax on big fortunes, properly safeguarded against evasion and increasing rapidly in amount with the size of the estate.

The people of the United States suffer from periodical financial panics to a degree substantially unknown among the other nations which approach us in financial strength. There is no reason why we should suffer what they escape. It is of profound importance that our financial system should be promptly investigated and so thoroughly and effectively revised as to make it certain that hereafter our currency will no longer fail at critical times to meet our needs. . . .

Nothing is more true than that excess of every kind is followed by reaction; a fact which should be pondered by reformer and reactionary alike. We are face to face with new conceptions of the relations of property to human welfare, chiefly because certain advocates of the rights of property as against the rights of men have been pushing their claims too far. The man who wrongly holds that every human right is secondary to his profit must now give way to the advocate of human welfare, who rightly maintains that every man holds his property subject to the general right of the community to regulate its use to whatever degree the public welfare may require it.

But I think we may go still further. The right to regulate the use of wealth in the public interest is universally admitted. Let us admit also the right to regulate the terms and conditions of labor, which is the chief element of wealth, directly in the interest of the common good. The fundamental thing to do for every man is to give him a chance to reach a place in which he will make the greatest possible contribution to the public welfare. Understand what I say there. Give him a chance, not push him up if he will not be pushed. Help any man who stumbles; if he lies down, it is a poor job to try to carry him; but if he is a worthy man, try your best to see that he gets a chance to show the worth that is in him.

No man can be a good citizen unless he has a wage more than sufficient to cover the bare cost of living and hours of labor short enough so that after his day's work is done he will have time and energy to bear his share in the management of the community, to help in carrying the general load. We keep countless men from being good citizens by the conditions of life with which we surround them. We need comprehensive workmen's compensation acts, both state and national laws to regulate child labor and work for women, and, especially, we need in our common schools not merely education in book learning but also practical training for daily life and work. We need to enforce better sanitary conditions for our workers and to extend the use of safety appliances for our workers in industry and commerce, both within and between the states. Also, friends, in the interest of the workingman himself we need to set our faces like flint against mob violence just as against corporate greed; against violence and injustice and lawlessness by wage workers just as much as against lawless cunning and greed and selfish arrogance of employers.

If I could ask but one thing of my fellow countrymen, my request would be that, whenever they go in for reform, they remember the two sides, and that they always exact justice from one side as much as from the other. I have small use for the public servant who can always see and denounce the corruption of the capitalist, but who cannot persuade himself to say a word about lawless mob violence. And I have equally small use for the man, be he a judge on the bench, or editor of a great paper, or wealthy and influential private citizen, who can see clearly enough and denounce the lawlessness of mob violence, but whose eyes are closed so that he is blind when the question is one of corruption in business on a gigantic scale. . . .

I do not ask for overcentralization; but I do ask that we work in a spirit of broad and far-reaching nationalism when we work for what concerns our people as a whole. We are all Americans. Our common interests are as broad as the continent. I speak to you here in Kansas exactly as I would speak in New York or Georgia, for the most vital problems are those which affect us all alike. The national government belongs to the whole American people, and where the whole American people are interested, that interest can be guarded effectively only by the national government. The betterment which we seek must be accomplished, I believe, mainly through the national government.

The American people are right in demanding that New Nationalism, without which we cannot hope to deal with new problems. The New Nationalism puts the national need before sectional or personal advantage. It is impatient of the utter confusion that results from local legislatures attempting to treat national issues as local issues. It is still more impatient of the impotence which springs from overdivision of governmental powers, the impotence which makes it possible for local selfishness or for legal cunning, hired by wealthy special interests, to bring national activities to a deadlock. This New Nationalism regards the executive power as the steward of the public welfare. It demands of the judiciary that it shall be interested primarily in human welfare rather than in property, just as it demands that the representative body shall represent all the people rather than any one class or section of people. . . .

One of the fundamental necessities in a representative government such as ours is to make certain that the men to whom the people delegate their power shall serve the people by whom they are elected and not the special interests. I believe that every national officer, elected or appointed, should be forbidden to perform any service or receive any compensation, directly or indirectly, from interstate corporations; and a similar provision could not fail to be useful within the states.

The object of government is the welfare of the people. The material progress and prosperity of a nation are desirable chiefly so far as they lead to the moral and material welfare of all good citizens. Just in proportion as the average man and woman are honest, capable of sound judgment and high ideals, active in public affairs—but, first of all, sound in their homelife, and the father and mother of healthy children whom they bring up well—just so far, and no farther, we may count our civilization a success. We must have—I believe we have already—a genuine and permanent moral awakening, without which no wisdom of legislation or administration really means anything; and, on the other hand, we must try to secure the social and economic legislation without which any improvement due to purely mortal agitation is necessarily evanescent.

Wilson's "Fourteen Points" Speech

Almost from the moment the United States entered World War I in 1917, President Woodrow Wilson wanted to issue a clear statement of U.S. objectives in the war against Germany. He was dissuaded from doing so by the argument that any such statement could foster disagreement among the other Allied governments. In December 1917, however, the new Bolshevik government in Russia released copies of the old tsarist government's secret treaties with the Allies, charging that the documents proved that both sides in the war were fighting only in pursuit of selfish national interests. In response to Russia's action, Wilson resolved to publish a statement of U.S. objectives that was more idealistic.

The "Fourteen Points" speech (each point described a U.S. war aim) was delivered to Congress on January 8, 1918. The speech was successful both as an answer to the Russians and as the initial framework for peace. The armistice agreement that ended the war on November 11, 1918, recognized the fourteen points as the basis for a negotiated settlement. Much of its idealism was lost in the writing of the Treaty of Versailles, but Wilson's proposal to create a League of Nations was accepted. Much to Wilson's disappointment, the U.S. Senate refused to allow the United States to join the league.

. . . We entered this war because violations of right had occurred which touched us to the quick and made the life of our own people impossible unless they were corrected and the world secured once for all against their recurrence. What we demand in this war, therefore, is nothing peculiar to ourselves. It is that the world be made fit and safe to live in; and particularly that it be made safe for every peace-loving nation which, like our own, wishes to live its own life, determine its own institutions, be assured of justice and fair dealing by the other peoples of the world as against force and selfish aggression. All the peoples of the world are in effect partners in this interest, and for our own part we see very clearly that unless justice be done to others it will not be done to us. The program of the world's peace, therefore, is our program; and that program, as we see it, is this:

I. Open covenants of peace, openly arrived at, after which there shall be no private international understandings of any kind but diplomacy shall proceed always frankly and in the public view.

II. Absolute freedom of navigation upon the seas, outside territorial waters, alike in peace and in war, except as the seas may be closed in whole or in part by international action for the enforcement of international covenants.

III. The removal, so far as possible, of all economic barriers and the establishment of an equality of trade conditions among all the nations consenting to the peace and associating themselves for its maintenance.

IV. Adequate guarantees given and taken that national armaments will be reduced to the lowest point consistent with domestic safety.

V. A free, open-minded, and absolutely impartial adjustment of all colonial claims, based upon a strict observance of the principle that in determining all such questions of sovereignty the interests of the populations concerned must have equal weight with the equitable claims of the government whose title is to be determined.

VI. The evacuation of all Russian territory and such a settlement of all questions affecting Russia as will secure the best and freest cooperation of the other nations of the world in obtaining for her an unhampered and unembarrassed opportunity for the independent determination of her own political development and national policy and assure her of a sincere welcome into the society of free nations under institutions of her own choosing; and, more than a welcome, assistance also of every kind that she may need and may herself desire. The treatment accorded Russia by her sister nations in the months to come will be the acid test of their good will, of their comprehension of her needs as distinguished from their own interests, and of their intelligent and unselfish sympathy.

VII. Belgium, the whole world will agree, must be evacuated and restored, without any attempt to limit the sovereignty which she enjoys in common with all other free nations. No other single act will serve as this will serve to restore confidence among the nations in the laws which they have themselves set and determined for the government of their relations with one another. Without this healing act the whole structure and validity of internal law is forever impaired.

VIII. All French territory should be freed and the invaded portions restored, and the wrong done to France by Prussia in 1871 in the matter of Alsace-Lorraine, which has unsettled the peace of the world for nearly fifty years, should be righted, in order that peace may once more be made secure in the interest of all.

IX. A readjustment of the frontiers of Italy should be effected along clearly recognizable lines of nationality.

X. The peoples of Austria-Hungary, whose place among the nations we wish to see safeguarded and assured, should be accorded the freest opportunity of autonomous development.

XI. Rumania, Serbia, and Montenegro should be evacuated; occupied territories restored; Serbia accorded free and secure access to the sea; and the relations of the several Balkan states to one another determined by friendly counsel along historically established lines of allegiance and nationality; and international guarantees of the political and economic independence and territorial integrity of the several Balkan states should be entered into.

XII. The Turkish portions of the present Ottoman Empire should be assured a secure sovereignty, but the other nationalities which are now under Turkish rule should be assured an undoubted security of life and an absolutely unmolested opportunity of autonomous development, and the Dardanelles should be permanently opened as a free passage to the ships and commerce of all nations under international guarantees.

XIII. An independent Polish state should be erected which should include the territories inhabited by indisputably Polish populations, which should be assured a free and secure access to the sea, and whose political and economic independence and territorial integrity should be guaranteed by international covenant.

XIV. A general association of nations must be formed under specific covenants for the purpose of affording mutual guarantees of political independence and territorial integrity to great and small states alike. . . .

We have spoken now, surely, in terms too concrete to admit of any further doubt or question. An evident principle runs through the whole program I have outlined. It is the principle of justice to all peoples and nationalities, and their right to live on equal terms of liberty and safety with one another, whether they be strong or weak. Unless this principle be made its foundation no part of the structure of international justice can stand. The people of the United States could act upon no other principle; and to the vindication of this principle they are ready to devote their lives, their honor, and everything that they possess. The moral climax of this the culminating and final war for human liberty has come, and they are ready to put their own strength, their own highest purpose, their own integrity and devotion to the test.

Teapot Dome Resolution

Warren G. Harding, who was president from 1921 until his death in 1923, presided over one of the most corrupt administrations in history. The most notorious scandal of his tenure involved the naval oil reserves at Teapot Dome, Wyoming, and Elk Hills, California. In 1921 Secretary of the Interior Albert B. Fall persuaded Secretary of the Navy Edwin Denby to transfer these oil fields to the Interior Department, with Harding's approval. Fall then leased them without competitive bidding—Teapot Dome to Harry Sinclair's Mammoth Oil Co. and Elk Hills to Edward L. Doheny's Pan-American Co. In October 1923, after an eighteen-month investigation and two months after Harding's death, a Senate committee exposed the scandal in public hearings.

The Teapot Dome scandal eventually led to the resignation of Denby, the cancellation of the oil leases, the firing of Attorney General Harry M. Daugherty, who had refused to cooperate with the Senate investigation and had ordered federal agents to spy on certain senators, and the imprisonment of Sinclair and Fall. Congress cancelled the leases by a joint resolution adopted February 8, 1924. President Calvin Coolidge, who succeeded Harding, heeded Congress's call to investigate and prosecute vigorously.

A joint resolution directing the President to institute and prosecute suits to cancel certain leases of oil lands and incidental contracts, and for other purposes.

Whereas it appears from evidence taken by the Committee on Public Lands and Surveys of the United States Senate that certain lease of naval reserve No. 3, in the State of Wyoming, bearing date April 7, 1922, made in form by the Government of the United States, through Albert B. Fall, Secretary of the Interior, and Edwin Denby, Secretary of the Navy, as lessor, to the Mammoth Oil Co., as lessee, and that certain contract between the Government of the United States and the Pan American Petroleum & Transport Co., dated April 25, 1922, signed by Edward C. Finney, Acting Secretary of the Interior, and Edwin Denby, Secretary of the Navy, relating among other things to the construction of oil tanks at Pearl Harbor, Territory of Hawaii, and that certain lease of naval reserve No. 1, in the State of California, bearing date December 11, 1922, made in form by the Government of the United States through Albert B. Fall, Secretary of the Interior, and Edwin Denby, Secretary of the Navy, as lessor, to the Pan American Petroleum Co., as lessee, were executed under circumstances indicating fraud and corruption; and

Whereas the said leases and contract were entered into without authority on the part of the officers purporting to act in the execution of the same for the United States and in violation of the laws of Congress; and

Whereas such leases and contract were made in defiance of the settled policy of the Government adhered to through three successive administrations, to maintain in the ground a great reserve supply of oil adequate to the needs of the Navy in any emergency threatening the national security: Therefore be it

Resolved, etc., That the said leases and contract are against the public interest and that the lands embraced therein should be recovered and held for the purpose to which they were dedicated; and

Resolved further, That the President of the United States be, and he hereby is, authorized and directed immediately to cause suit to be instituted and prosecuted for the annulment and cancellation of the said leases and contract and all contracts incidental or supplemental thereto, to enjoin further extraction of oil from the said reserves under said lease or from the territory covered by the same, to secure any further appropriate incidental relief, and to prosecute such other actions or proceedings, civil and criminal, as may be warranted by the facts in relation to the making of the said leases and contract.

And the President is further authorized and directed to appoint, by and with the advice and consent of the Senate, special counsel who shall have charge and control of the prosecution of such litigation, anything in the statutes touching the powers of the Attorney General of the Department of Justice to the contrary notwithstanding.

Franklin D. Roosevelt's First Inaugural Address

Franklin D. Roosevelt was the last president to be inaugurated on March 4; the Twentieth Amendment (1933) advanced the start of the president's term to January 20. During the long winter between Roosevelt's election victory over President Herbert C. Hoover in November 1932 (the most overwhelming defeat of an incumbent president in history) and his inauguration, the depression that had sunk the nation into economic inactivity had worsened. Factories to produce goods and land to grow food and other crops were abundant but had fallen into disuse.

Roosevelt saw his main challenge as restoring the people's confidence and raising their morale. In the best-remembered line from his address, he proclaimed that "the only thing we have to fear is fear itself—nameless, unreasoning, unjustified terror which paralyzes needed efforts to convert retreat into advance." Roosevelt pledged to pursue active and helpful government policies to combat the depression, using and perhaps extending the full powers of the presidency to do so.

Roosevelt's distant relative, former president Theodore Roosevelt, had been the first to describe the presidency as a "bully pulpit" for moral leadership. Franklin Roosevelt made full use of the pulpit in 1933 and afterward. In response to his first inaugural address, half a million people wrote him to express their thanks and support, an unprecedented outpouring of mail.

President Hoover, Mr. Chief Justice, my friends:

This is a day of national consecration, and I am certain that my fellow-Americans expect that on my induction into the Presidency I will address them with a candor and a decision which the present situation of our nation impels.

This is pre-eminently the time to speak the truth, the whole truth, frankly and boldly. Nor need we shrink from honestly facing conditions in our country today. This great nation will endure as it has endured, will revive and will prosper.

So first of all let me assert my firm belief that the only thing we have to fear is fear itself—nameless, unreasoning, unjustified terror which paralyzes needed efforts to convert retreat into advance.

In every dark hour of our national life a leadership of frankness and vigor has met with that understanding and support of the people themselves which is essential to victory. I am convinced that you will again give that support to leadership in these critical days.

In such a spirit on my part and on yours we face our common difficulties. They concern, thank God, only material things. Values have shrunken to fantastic levels; taxes have risen; our ability to pay has fallen, government of all kinds is faced by serious curtailment of income; the means of exchange are frozen in the currents of trade; the withered leaves of industrial enterprise lie on every side; farmers find no markets for their produce; the savings of many years in thousands of families are gone.

More important, a host of unemployed citizens face the grim problem of existence, and an equally great number toil with little return. Only a foolish optimist can deny the dark realities of the moment.

Yet our distress comes from no failure of substance. We are stricken by no plague of locusts. Compared with the perils which our forefathers conquered because they believed and were not afraid, we have still much to be thankful for. Nature still offers her bounty and human efforts have multiplied it. Plenty is at our doorstep, but a generous use of it languishes in the very sight of the supply.

Primarily, this is because the rulers of the exchange of mankind's goods have failed through their own stubbornness and their own incompetence, have admitted their failure and abdicated. Practices of the unscrupulous money changers stand indicted in the court of public opinion, rejected by the hearts and minds of men. True, they have tried, but their efforts have been cast in the pattern of an outworn tradition. Faced by failure of credit, they have proposed only the lending of more money.

Stripped of the lure of profit by which to induce our people to follow their false leadership, they have resorted to exhortations, pleading tearfully for restored confidence. They know only the rules of a generation of self-seekers.

They have no vision, and when there is no vision the people perish.

The money changers have fled from their high seats in the temple of our civilization. We may now restore that temple to the ancient truths.

The measure of the restoration lies in the extent to which we apply social values more noble than mere monetary profit.

Happiness lies not in the mere possession of money; it lies in the joy of achievement, in the thrill of creative effort.

The joy and moral stimulation of work no longer must be forgotten in the mad chase of evanescent profits. These dark days will be worth all they cost us if they teach us that our true destiny is not to be ministered unto but to minister to ourselves and to our fellow-men.

Recognition of the falsity of material wealth as the standard of success goes hand in hand with the abandonment of the false belief that public office and high political position are to be valued only by the standards of pride of place and personal profit; and there must be an end to a conduct in banking and in business which too often has given to a sacred trust the likeness of callous and selfish wrongdoing.

Small wonder that confidence languishes, for it thrives only on honesty, on honor, on the sacredness of obligations, on faithful protection, on unselfish performance. Without them it cannot live.

Restoration calls, however, not for changes in ethics alone. This nation asks for action, and action now.

Our greatest primary task is to put people to work. This is no unsolvable problem if we face it wisely and courageously.

It can be accomplished in part by direct recruiting by the government itself, treating the task as we would treat the emergency of a war, but at the same time, through this employment accomplishing greatly needed projects to stimulate and reorganize the use of our natural resources.

Hand in hand with this, we must frankly recognize the overbalance of population in our industrial centers and, by engaging on a national scale in the redistribution, endeavor to provide a better use of the land for those best fitted for the land.

The task can be helped by definite efforts to raise the values of agricultural products and with this the power to purchase the output of our cities.

It can be helped by preventing realistically the tragedy of the growing loss, through foreclosure, of our small homes and our farms.

It can be helped by insistence that the Federal, State and local governments act forthwith on the demand that their cost be drastically reduced.

It can be helped by the unifying of relief activities which today are often scattered, uneconomical and unequal. It can be helped by national planning for and supervision of all forms of transportation and of communications and other utilities which have a definitely public character.

There are many ways in which it can be helped, but it can never be helped merely by talking about it. We must act, and act quickly.

Finally, in our progress toward a resumption of work we require two safeguards against a return of the evils of the old order; there must be a strict supervision of all banking and credits and investments; there must be an end to speculation with other people's money, and there must be provision for an adequate but sound currency.

These are the lines of attack. I shall presently urge upon a new Congress in special session detailed measures for their fulfillment, and I shall seek the immediate assistance of the several States. . . .

I am prepared under my constitutional duty to recommend the measures that a stricken nation in the midst of a stricken world may require.

These measures, or such other measures as the Congress may build out of its experience and wisdom, I shall seek, within my constitutional authority, to bring to speedy adoption.

But in the event that the Congress shall fail to take one of these two courses, and in the event that the national emergency is still critical, I shall not evade the clear course of duty that will then confront me.

I shall ask the Congress for the one remaining instrument to meet the crisis—broad executive power to wage a war against the emergency as great as the power that would be given me if we were in fact invaded by a foreign foe.

For the trust reposed in me I will return the courage and the devotion that befit the time. I can do no less.

We face the arduous days that lie before us in the warm courage of national unity; with the clear consciousness of seeking old and precious moral values; with the clean satisfaction that comes from the stern performance of duty by old and young alike.

We aim at the assurance of a rounded and permanent national life.

We do not distrust the future of essential democracy. The people of the United States have not failed. In their need they have registered a mandate that they want direct, vigorous action.

They have asked for discipline and direction under leadership. They have made me the present instrument of their wishes. In the spirit of the gift I take it.

In this dedication of a nation we humbly ask the blessing of God. May He protect each and every one of us! May He guide me in the days to come!

United States v. Curtiss-Wright Export Corporation

This landmark Supreme Court case endorsed an expansive view of presidential power in foreign affairs, which was all the more remarkable because the Court had been unusually hostile to the New Deal domestic policies of President Franklin D. Roosevelt. Indeed, the author of the Court's December 21, 1936, opinion, Justice George Sutherland, was one of the New Deal's most ardent judicial foes. Yet in U.S. v. Curtiss-Wright *(299 U.S. 304), Sutherland and all but one of his fellow justices (James C. McReynolds) promulgated a constitutional theory that regarded "the President as the sole organ of the federal government in the field of international relations."*

The case was triggered by the government's effort to limit a war between Bolivia and Paraguay. Congress had empowered the president to prohibit the sale of U.S.-made arms to the two nations. The Curtiss-Wright corporation was charged with conspiring to sell machine guns to Bolivia in violation of the president's order not to do so. It challenged the law under which the president acted by saying that it involved an unconstitutional delegation of power from Congress to the president.

. . . It will contribute to the elucidation of the question if we first consider the differences between the powers of the federal government in respect of foreign or external affairs and those in respect of domestic or internal affairs. That there are differences between them, and that these differences are fundamental, may not be doubted.

The two classes of powers are different, both in respect of their origin and their nature. The broad statement that the federal government can exercise no powers except those specifically enumerated in the Constitution and such implied powers as are necessary and proper to carry into effect the enumerated powers, is categorically true only in respect of our internal affairs. In that field, the primary purpose of the Constitution was to carve from the general mass of legislative powers *then possessed by the states* such portions as it was thought desirable to vest in the federal government, leaving those not included in the enumeration still in the States. That this doctrine applies only to powers which the states had, is self evident. And since the states severally never possessed international powers, such powers could not have been carved from the mass of state powers but obviously were transmitted to the United States from some other source. During the colonial period, those powers were possessed exclusively by and were entirely under control of the Crown. . . .

As a result of the separation from Great Britain by the colonies acting as a unit, the powers of external sovereignty passed from the Crown not to the colonies severally, but to the colonies in their collective and corporate capacity as the United States of America. . . .

The Union existed before the Constitution, which was ordained and established among other things to form "a more perfect Union.". . .

It results that the investment of the federal government with the powers of external sovereignty did not depend upon the affirmative grants of the Constitution. The powers to declare and wage war, to conclude peace, to make treaties, to maintain diplomatic relations with other sovereignties, if they had never been mentioned in the Constitution, would have vested in the federal government as necessary concomitants of nationality. . . .

Not only, as we have shown, is the federal power over external affairs in origin and essential character different from that over internal affairs, but participation in the exercise of the power is significantly limited. In this vast external realm, with its important, complicated, delicate and manifold problems, the President alone has the power to speak or listen as a representative of the nation. He *makes* treaties with the advice and consent of the Senate; but he alone negotiates. Into the field of negotiation the Senate cannot intrude; and Congress itself is powerless to invade it. . . .

It is important to bear in mind that we are here dealing not only with an authority vested in the President by an exertion of legislative power, but with such an authority plus the very delicate, plenary and exclusive power of the President as the sole organ of the federal government in the field of international relations—a power which does not require as a basis for its exercise an act of Congress, but which, of course, like every other government power, must be exercised in subordination to the applicable provisions of the Constitution. It is quite apparent that if, in the maintenance of our international relations, embarrassment—perhaps serious embarrassment—is to be avoided and success for our aims achieved, congressional legislation which is to be made effective through negotiation and inquiry within the international field must often accord to the President a degree of discretion and freedom from statutory restriction which would not be admissible were domestic affairs alone involved. Moreover he, not Congress, has the better opportunity of knowing the conditions which prevail in foreign countries, and especially is this true in time of war. He has his confidential sources of information. He has his agents in the form of diplomatic, consular and other officials. Secrecy in respect of information gathered by them may be highly necessary and the premature disclosure of it productive of harmful results. . . .

In the light of the foregoing observations, it is evident that this court should not be in haste to apply a general rule which will have the effect of condemning legislation like that under review as constituting an unlawful delegation of legislative power. The principles which justify such legislation find overwhelming support in the unbroken legislative practice which has prevailed almost from the inception of the national government to the present day. . . .

Franklin D. Roosevelt's "Four Freedoms" Speech

After World War I the United States sank into a mood of isolationism in foreign policy that was embodied by the slogan, "America first!" Beginning in 1937 President Franklin D. Roosevelt tried to alert the nation to the "solidarity and interdependence about the modern world, . . . which makes it impossible for any nation completely to isolate itself from political and economic upheavals in the rest of the world." But public response was tepid to his call to "quarantine" aggressor nations for the sake of national self-interest.

In 1941 Roosevelt took another tack in his effort to promote U.S. aid to nations that were at war with the Axis powers of Germany, Italy, and Japan. In his January 6, 1941, State of the Union address, Roosevelt appealed to American idealism by citing "four essential human freedoms" to which all people were entitled. The first two—freedom of speech and expression and freedom of reli-

gion—derived from the Bill of Rights to the Constitution. The third—freedom from want—extended the New Deal view of economic sufficiency to the international arena. The fourth was freedom from fear, which ultimately meant widespread disarmament.

The "Four Freedoms" speech roused public support for Roosevelt's lend-lease program of military aid to Great Britain and the Soviet Union and was incorporated into the Atlantic Charter, which stated Allied war aims.

. . . Let us say to the democracies:

We Americans are vitally concerned in your defense of freedom. We are putting forth our energies, our resources and our organizing powers to give you the strength to regain and maintain a free world. We shall send you in ever-increasing numbers, ships, planes, tanks, guns. That is our purpose and our pledge. . . .

Yes, and we must prepare, all of us prepare, to make the sacrifices that the emergency—almost as serious as war itself—demands. Whatever stands in the way of speed and efficiency in defense, in defense preparations at any time, must give way to the national need.

A free nation has the right to expect full cooperation from all groups. A free nation has the right to look to the leaders of business, of labor and of agriculture to take the lead in stimulating effort, not among other groups but within their own groups. . . .

As men do not live by bread alone, they do not fight by armament alone. Those who man our defenses and those behind them who build our defenses must have the stamina and the courage which come from unshakable belief in the manner of life which they are defending. The mighty action that we are calling for cannot be based on a disregard for all the things worth fighting for.

The nation takes great satisfaction and much strength from the things which have been done to make its people conscious of their individual stakes in the preservation of democratic life in America. Those things have toughened the fiber of our people, have renewed their faith and strengthened their devotion to the institutions we make ready to protect.

Certainly this is no time for any of us to stop thinking about the social and economic problems which are the root cause of the social revolution which is today a supreme factor in the world. For there is nothing mysterious about the foundations of a healthy and strong democracy.

The basic things expected by our people of their political and economic systems are simple. They are:

Equality of opportunity for youth and for others.

Jobs for those who can work.

Security for those who need it.

The ending of special privilege for the few.

The preservation of civil liberties for all.

The employment of the fruits of scientific progress in a wider and constantly rising standard of living.

These are the simple, the basic things that must never be lost sight of in the turmoil and unbelievable complexity of our modern world. The inner and abiding strength of our economic and political systems is dependent upon the degree to which they fulfill these expectations. . . .

I have called for personal sacrifice, and I am assured of the willingness of almost all Americans to respond to that call. A part of the sacrifice means the payment of more money in taxes. In my budget message I will recommend that a greater portion of this great defense program be paid for from taxation than we are paying for today. No person should try, or be allowed to get rich out of the program, and the principle of tax payments in accordance with ability to pay should be constantly before our eyes to guide our legislation.

If the Congress maintains these principles the voters, putting patriotism ahead of pocketbooks, will give you their applause.

In the future days which we seek to make secure, we look forward to a world founded upon four essential human freedoms.

The first is freedom of speech and expression—everywhere in the world.

The second is freedom of every person to worship God in his own way—everywhere in the world.

The third is freedom from want, which, translated into world terms, means economic understanding which will secure to every nation a healthy peacetime life for its inhabitants—everywhere in the world.

The fourth is freedom from fear, which, translated into world terms means a world-wide reduction of armaments to such a point and in such a thorough fashion that no nation will be in a position to commit an act of physical aggression against any neighbor—anywhere in the world.

That is no vision of a distant millenium. It is a definite basis for a kind of world attainable in our own time and generation. That kind of world is the very antithesis of the so-called "new order" of tyranny which the dictators seek to create with crash of a bomb.

To that new order we oppose the greater conception—the moral order. A good society is able to face schemes of world domination and foreign revolutions alike without fear.

Since the beginning of our American history we have been engaged in change, in a perpetual, peaceful revolution, a revolution which goes on steadily, quietly, adjusting itself to changing conditions without the concentration camp or the quicklime in the ditch. The world order which we seek is the cooperation of free countries, working together in a friendly, civilized society.

This nation has placed its destiny in the hands, heads and hearts of its millions of free men and women, and its faith in freedom under the guidance of God. Freedom means the supremacy of human rights everywhere. Our support goes to those who struggle to gain those rights and keep them. Our strength is our unity of purpose.

To that high concept there can be no end save victory.

Truman's Point Four Message

On January 20, 1949, President Harry S Truman delivered an inaugural address organized around four main points. He especially emphasized Point Four, in which he called for "a bold new program for making the benefits of our scientific advances and industrial progress available for the improvement and growth of underdeveloped areas." Part of Truman's motive was altruistic; the underdeveloped nations were suffering economically. Part of the motive was political. The United States had been laboring to halt the spread of communism in Europe and wanted to do the same in Africa, Asia, and South America.

The Point Four program was spelled out in detail in a special message that Truman sent to Congress on June 24, 1949. In 1950 Congress passed the Act for International Development and also appropriated money for the technical assistance program of the United Nations.

U.S. foreign aid falls into two main categories: military aid and economic aid. The latter originated with Truman's Point Four program.

To the Congress of the United States:

In order to enable the United States, in cooperation with other countries, to assist the peoples of economically under-developed areas to raise their standards of living, I recommend the enactment of legislation to authorize an expanded program of technical assistance for such areas, and an experimental program for encouraging the outflow of private investment beneficial to their economic development. These measures are the essential first steps in an undertaking which will call upon private enterprise and voluntary organizations in the United States, as well as the Government, to take part in a constantly growing effort to improve economic conditions in the less developed regions of the world.

The grinding poverty and the lack of economic opportunity for many millions of people in the economically under-developed parts of Africa, the Near and Far East, and certain regions of Central and South America, constitute one of the greatest challenges of the world today. In spite of their age-old economic and social handicaps, the peoples in these areas have in recent decades been stirred and awakened. The spread of industrial civilization, the growing understanding of modern concepts of government, and the impact of two world wars have changed their lives and their outlook. They are eager to play a greater part in the community of nations.

All these areas have a common problem. They must create a firm economic base for the democratic aspirations of their citizens. Without such an economic base, they will be unable to meet the expectations which the modern world has aroused in their peoples. If they are frustrated and disappointed, they may turn to false doctrines which hold that the way of progress lies through tyranny. . . .

The major effort in such a program must be local in character; it must be made by the people of the under-developed areas themselves. It is essential, however, to the success of their effort that there be help from abroad. In some cases, the peoples of these areas will be unable to begin their part of this great enterprise without initial aid from other countries.

The aid that is needed falls roughly into two categories. The first is the technical, scientific and managerial knowledge necessary to economic development. This category includes not only medical and educational knowledge, and assistance and advice in such basic fields as sanitation, communications, road building and governmental services, but also, and perhaps most important, assistance in the survey of resources and in planning for long-range economic development.

The second category is production goods—machinery and equipment—and financial assistance in the creation of productive enterprises. The under-developed areas need capital for port and harbor development, roads and communications, irrigation and drainage projects, as well as for public utilities and the whole range of extractive, processing and manufacturing industries. Much of the capital required can be provided by these areas themselves, in spite of their low standards of living. But much must come from abroad.

The two categories of aid are closely related. Technical assistance is necessary to lay the groundwork for productive investment. Investment, in turn, brings with it technical assistance. In general, however, technical surveys of resources and of the possibilities of economic development must precede substantial capital investment. Furthermore, in many of the areas concerned, technical assistance in improving sanitation, communications or education is required to create conditions in which capital investment can be fruitful. . . .

In addition to our participation in this work of the United Nations, much of the technical assistance required can be provided directly by the United States to countries needing it. A careful examination of the existing information concerning the under-developed countries shows particular need for technicians and experts with United States training in plant and animal diseases, malaria and typhus control, water supply and sewer systems, metallurgy and mining, and nearly all phases of industry.

It has already been shown that experts in these fields can bring about tremendous improvements. For example, the health of the people of many foreign communities has been greatly improved by the work of United States sanitary engineers in setting up modern water supply systems. The food supply of many areas has been increased as the result of the advice of United States agricultural experts in the control of animal diseases and the improvement of crops. These are only examples of the wide range of benefits resulting from the careful application of modern techniques to local problems. The benefits which a comprehensive program of expert assistance will make possible can only be revealed by studies and surveys undertaken as a part of the program itself. . . .

Many of these conditions of instability in under-developed areas which deter foreign investment are themselves a consequence of the lack of economic development which only foreign investment can cure. Therefore, to wait until stable conditions are assured before encouraging the outflow of capital to under-developed areas would defer the attainment of our objectives indefinitely. It is necessary to take vigorous action now to break out of this vicious circle.

Since the development of under-developed economic areas is of major importance in our foreign policy, it is appropriate to use the resources of the government to accelerate private efforts toward that end. . . .

The enactment of these two legislative proposals, the first pertaining to technical assistance and the second to the encouragement of foreign investment, will contitute a national endorsement of a program of major importance in our efforts for world peace and economic stability. Nevertheless, these measures are only the first steps. We are here embarking on a venture that extends far into the future. We are at the beginning of a rising curve of activity, private, governmental and international, that will continue for many years to come. It is all the more important, therefore, that we start promptly. . . .

Before the peoples of these areas we hold out the promise of a better future through the democratic way of life. It is vital that we move quickly to bring the meaning of that promise home to them in their daily lives.

Youngstown Sheet and Tube Co. v. Sawyer

On April 8, 1952, President Harry S Truman ordered Secretary of Commerce Charles Sawyer to seize the nation's privately owned steel mills and keep them in operation. Truman acted partly out of the fear that an impending strike of the steel unions would jeopardize U.S. ability to maintain its military effort in the Korean War. His order was challenged quickly and was ruled unconstitutional by the Supreme Court on June 2, 1952, in Youngstown Sheet and Tube Co. v. Sawyer *(343 U.S. 579).*

Although Truman lost the case, his constitutional claim that the president has an inherent, unstated constitutional power to act in national emergencies was accepted, to one degree or another, by a majority of the justices. Justice Hugo L. Black, delivering the opinion of the Court, rejected this claim (as did Justice William O. Douglas). But the three dissenting justices (Chief Justice Fred M. Vinson and Justices Sherman Minton and Stanley F. Reed) and at least two of the justices who voted with Black endorsed it to one degree or another. Justice Robert H. Jackson, for example, voted with Black, but only because Congress had expressly denied the president powers of seizure. But Jackson argued that an inherent executive power did exist.

[Justice Black delivered the opinion of the Court.]

We are asked to decide whether the President was acting within his constitutional power when he issued an order directing the Secretary of Commerce to take possession of and operate most of the Nation's steel mills. The mill owners argue that the President's order amounts to lawmaking, a legislative function which the Constitution has expressly confided to the Congress and not to the President. The Government's position is that the order was made on findings of the President that his action was necessary to avert a national catastrophe which would inevitably result from a stoppage of steel production, and that in meeting this grave emergency the President was acting within the aggregate of his constitutional powers as the Nation's Chief Executive and the Commander in Chief of the Armed Forces of the United States. . . .

Two crucial issues have developed: *First.* Should final determination of the constitutional validity of the President's order be made in this case which has proceeded no further than the preliminary injunction stage? *Second.* If so, is the seizure order within the constitutional power of the President? . . .

The President's power, if any, to issue the order must stem either from an act of Congress or from the Constitution itself. There is no statute that expressly authorizes the President to take possession of property as he did here. Nor is there any act of Congress to which our attention has been directed from which such a power can fairly be implied. Indeed, we do not understand the Government to rely on statutory authorization for this seizure. . . .

Moreover, the use of the seizure technique to solve labor disputes in order to prevent work stoppages was not only unauthorized by any congressional enactment; prior to this controversy, Congress had refused to adopt that method of settling labor disputes. When the Taft-Hartley Act was under consideration in 1947, Congress rejected an amendment which would have authorized such governmental seizures in cases of emergency. . . .

It is clear that if the President had authority to issue the order he did, it must be found in some provisions of the Constitution. And it is not claimed that express constitutional language grants this power to the President. The contention is that presidential power should be implied from the aggregate of his powers under the Constitution. Particular reliance is placed on provisions in Article II which say that "the executive Power shall be vested in a President . . ."; that "he shall take Care that the Laws be faithfully executed"; and that he "shall be Commander in Chief of the Army and Navy of the United States."

The order cannot properly be sustained as an exercise of the President's military power as Commander in Chief of the Armed Forces. The Government attempts to do so by citing a number of cases upholding broad powers in military commanders engaged in day-to-day fighting in a theater of war. Such cases need not concern us here. Even though "theater of war" be an expanding concept, we cannot with faithfulness to our constitutional system hold that the Commander in Chief of the Armed Forces has the ultimate power as such to take possession of private property in order to keep labor disputes from stopping production. This is a job for the Nation's lawmakers, not for its military authorities.

Nor can the seizure order be sustained because of the several constitutional provisions that grant executive power to the President. In the framework of our Constitution, the President's power to see that the laws are faithfully executed refutes the idea that he is to be a lawmaker. The Constitution limits his functions in the lawmaking process to the recommending of laws he thinks wise and the vetoing of laws he thinks bad. And the Constitution is neither silent nor equivocal about who shall make laws which the President is to execute. The first section of the first article says that "All legislative Powers herein granted shall be vested in a Congress of the United States. . . ." After granting many powers to the Congress, Article I goes on to provide that Congress may "make all Laws which shall be necessary and proper for carrying into Execution the foregoing Powers and all other Powers vested by this Constitution in the Government of the United States, or in any Department or Officer thereof." . . .

It is said that other Presidents without congressional authority have taken possession of private business enterprises in order to settle labor disputes. But even if this be true, Congress has not thereby lost its exclusive constitutional authority to make laws necessary and proper to carry out the powers vested by the Constitution "in the Government of the United States, or in any Department or Officer thereof."

The Founders of this Nation entrusted the law-making power to the Congress alone in both good and bad times. It would do no good to recall the historical events, the fears of power and the hopes for freedom that lay behind their choice. Such a review would but confirm our holding that this seizure order cannot stand.

The Judgment of the District Court is affirmed.

[Dissent by Chief Justice Vinson, in which Justice Reed and Justice Minton joined.]

. . . Those who suggest that this is a case involving extraordinary powers should be mindful that these are extraordinary times. A world not yet recovered from the devastation of World War II has been forced to face the threat of another and more terrifying global conflict. . . .

The steel mills were seized for a public use. The power of eminent domain, invoked in this case, is an essential attribute of sovereignty and has long been recognized as a power of the Federal Government. . . .

Admitting that the Government could seize the mills, plaintiffs claim that the implied power of eminent domain can be exercised only under an Act of Congress; under no circumstances, they say, can that power be exercised by the President unless he can point to an express provision in enabling legislation. This was the view adopted by the District Judge when he granted the preliminary injunction. . . .

Under this view, the President is left powerless at the very moment when the need for action may be most pressing and when no one, other than he, is immediately capable of action. Under this view, he is left powerless because a power not expressly given to Congress is nevertheless found to rest exclusively with Congress. . . .

Eisenhower's Farewell Address

President Dwight D. Eisenhower was the first president to deliver a televised farewell address, three days before the end of his second term on January 17, 1961. Eisenhower's departing speech is the best-remembered such address since George Washington's in 1796.

President Eisenhower was not renowned as an orator, yet his speech was both thoughtful and moving. Although he was best known as the general who had served as supreme commander of the Allied forces during World War II, his speech warned the nation to keep a close watch on the "military-industrial complex" (a term he coined). Eisenhower also cautioned against the excesses of technology and warned the nation not to overreact to crises foreign and domestic.

At the time, Eisenhower's farewell address was not so well suited to the mood of the country as President John F. Kennedy's bold and challenging inaugural address, which was delivered three days later. As time went by, however, the wisdom of the farewell address became better appreciated.

My fellow Americans:

Three days from now, after half a century in the service of our country, I shall lay down the responsibilities of office as, in traditional and solemn ceremony, the authority of the Presidency is vested in my successor.

This evening I come to you with a message of leave-taking and farewell, and to share a few final thoughts with you, my countrymen. . . .

Throughout America's adventure in free government, our basic purposes have been to keep the peace; to foster progress in human achievement, and to enhance liberty, dignity and integrity among people and among nations. To strive for less would be unworthy of a free and religious people. Any failure traceable to arrogance, or our lack of comprehension or readiness to sacrifice would inflict upon us grievous hurt both at home and abroad.

Progress toward these noble goals is persistently threatened by the conflict now engulfing the world. It commands our whole attention, absorbs our very beings. We face a hostile ideology—global in scope, atheistic in character, ruthless in purpose, and insidious in method. Unhappily the danger it poses promises to be of indefinite duration. To meet it successfully, there is called for, not so much the emotional and transitory sacrifices of crisis, but rather those which enable us to carry forward steadily, surely, and without complaint the burdens of a prolonged and complex struggle—with liberty the stake. Only thus shall we remain, despite every provocation, on our charted course toward permanent peace and human betterment.

Crises there will continue to be. In meeting them, whether foreign or domestic, great or small, there is a recurring temptation to feel that some spectacular and costly action could become the miraculous solution to all current difficulties. A huge increase in newer elements of our defense; development of unrealistic programs to cure every ill in agriculture; a dramatic expansion in basic and applied research—these and many other possibilities, each possibly promising in itself, may be suggested as the only way to the road we wish to travel.

But each proposal must be weighed in the light of a broader consideration: the need to maintain balance in and among national programs—balance between the private and the public economy, balance between cost and hoped for advantage—balance between the clearly necessary and the comfortably desirable; balance between our essential requirements as a nation and the duties imposed by the nation upon the individual; balance between actions of the moment and the national welfare of the future. Good judgment seeks balance and progress; lack of it eventually finds imbalance and frustration.

The record of many decades stands as proof that our people and their government have, in the main, understood these truths and have responded to them well, in the face of stress and threat. But threats, new in kind or degree, constantly arise. I mention two only. . . .

Until the latest of our world conflicts, the United States had no armaments industry. American makers of plowshares could, with time and as required, make swords as well. But now we can no longer risk emergency improvision of national defense; we have been compelled to create a permanent armaments industry of vast proportions. Added to this, three and a half million men and women are directly engaged in the defense establishment. We annually spend on military security more than the net income of all United States corporations.

This conjunction of an immense military establishment and a large arms industry is new in the American experience. The total influence—economic, political, even spiritual—is felt in every city, every State house, every office of the Federal government. We recognize the imperative need for this development. Yet we must not fail to comprehend its grave implications. Our toil, resources and livelihood are all involved; so is the very structure of our society.

In the councils of government, we must guard against the acquisition of unwarranted influence, whether sought or unsought, by the military-industrial complex. The potential for the disastrous rise of misplaced power exists and will persist.

We must never let the weight of this combination endanger our liberties or democratic processes. We should take nothing for granted. Only an alert and knowledgeable citizenry can compel the proper meshing of the huge industrial and military machinery of defense with our peaceful methods and goals, so that security and liberty may prosper together.

Akin to, and largely responsible for the sweeping changes in our industrial-military posture, has been the technological revolution during recent decades.

In this revolution, research has become central; it also becomes more formalized, complex, and costly. A steadily increasing share is conducted for, by, or by the direction of, the Federal government.

Today, the solitary inventor, tinkering in his shop, has been overshadowed by task forces of scientists in laboratories and testing fields. In the same fashion, the free university, historically the fountainhead of free ideas and scientific discovery, has experienced a revolution in the conduct of research. Partly because of the huge costs involved, a government contract becomes virtually a substitute for intellectual curiosity. For every old blackboard there are now hundreds of new electronic computers.

The prospect of domination of the nation's scholars by Federal employment, project allocations, and the power of money is ever present—and is gravely to be regarded.

Yet, in holding scientific research and discovery in respect, as we should, we must also be alert to the equal and opposite danger that public policy could itself become the captive of a scientific-technological elite.

It is the task of statesmanship to mold, to balance, and to integrate these and other forces, new and old, within the principle of our democratic system—ever aiming toward the supreme goals of our free society.

Another factor in maintaining balance involves the element of time. As we peer into society's future, we—you and I, and our government—must avoid the impulse to live only for today, plundering, for our own ease and convenience, the precious resources of tomorrow. We cannot mortgage the material assets of our grandchildren without risking the loss also of their political and spiritual heritage. We want democracy to survive for all generations to come, not to become the insolvent phantom of tomorrow. . . .

To all the peoples of the world, I once more give expression to America's prayerful and continuing aspiration:

We pray that peoples of all faiths, all races, all nations, may have their great human needs satisfied; that those now denied opportunity shall come to enjoy it to the full; that all who yearn for freedom may experience its spiritual blessings; that those who have freedom will understand, also, its heavy responsibilities; that all who are insensitive to the needs of others will learn charity; that the scourges of poverty, disease and ignorance will be made to disappear from the earth, and that, in the goodness of time, all peoples will come to live together in a peace guaranteed by the binding force of mutual respect and love.

Kennedy's Inaugural Address

John F. Kennedy was elected president in 1960, at the end of Dwight D. Eisenhower's second term. The contrasts between the two presidents were dramatic and visible: the youngest man ever to be elected president was replacing the oldest man to leave the office up to that time; a Democrat was replacing a Republican; and an advocate of change and energy was replacing a defender of caution, prudence, and restraint.

Kennedy's inaugural, delivered January 20, 1961, on a bright but bitterly cold day, accentuated all of these contrasts. He emphasized his youth by noting that "the torch has been passed to a new generation of Americans—born in this century." He reached out to the Soviet Union: "Let us never negotiate out of fear. But let us never fear to negotiate." But he also pledged that "we shall pay any price, bear any burden, meet any hardship, support any friend, oppose any foe to assure the survival and the success of liberty." Finally, in the best-remembered phrase of his presidency, Kennedy summoned the idealism of the American people: "ask not what your country can do for you—ask what you can do for your country."

We observe today not a victory of party but a celebration of freedom—symbolizing an end as well as a beginning—signifying renewal as well as change. For I have sworn before you and Almighty God the same solemn oath our forebears prescribed nearly a century and three quarters ago.

The world is very different now. For man holds in his mortal hands the power to abolish all forms of human poverty and all forms of human life. And yet the same revolutionary beliefs for which our forebears fought are still at issue around the globe—the belief that the rights of man come not from the generosity of the state but from the hand of God.

We dare not forget today that we are the heirs of that first revolution. Let the word go forth from this time and place, to friend and foe alike, that the torch has been passed to a new generation of Americans—born in this century, tempered by war, disciplined by a hard and bitter peace, proud of our ancient heritage—and unwilling to witness or permit the slow undoing of those human rights to which this nation has always been committed, and to which we are committed today at home and around the world.

Let every nation know, whether it wishes us well or ill, that we shall pay any price, bear any burden, meet any hardship, support any friend, oppose any foe to assure the survival and the success of liberty.

This much we pledge—and more.

To those old allies whose cultural and spiritual origins we share, we pledge the loyalty of faithful friends. United, there is little we cannot do in a host of cooperative ventures. Divided, there is little we can do—for we dare not meet a powerful challenge at odds and split asunder.

To those new states whom we welcome to the ranks of the free, we pledge our word that one form of colonial control shall not have passed away merely to be replaced by a far more iron tyranny. We shall not always expect to find them supporting our view. But we shall always hope to find them strongly supporting their own freedom—and to remember that, in the past, those who foolishly sought power by riding the back of the tiger ended up inside.

To those peoples in the huts and villages of half the globe struggling to break the bonds of mass misery, we pledge our best efforts to help them help themselves, for whatever period is required—not because the communists may be doing it, not because we seek their votes, but beause it is right. If a free society cannot help the many who are poor, it cannot save the few who are rich.

To our sister republics south of our border, we offer a special pledge—to convert our good words into good deeds—in a new alliance for progress—to assist free men and free governments in casting off the chains of poverty. But this peaceful revolution of hope cannot become the prey of hostile powers. Let all our neighbors know that we shall join with them to oppose aggression or subversion anywhere in the Americas. And let every other power know that this Hemisphere intends to remain the master of its own house.

To that world assembly of sovereign states, the United Nations, our last best hope in an age where the intruments of war have far outpaced the instruments of peace, we renew our pledge of support—to prevent it from becoming merely a forum for invective—to strengthen its shield of the new and the weak—and to enlarge the area in which its writ may run.

Finally, to those nations who would make themselves our adversary, we offer not a pledge but a request: that both sides begin anew the quest for peace, before the dark powers of destruction unleashed by science engulf all humanity in planned or accidental self-destruction.

We dare not tempt them with weakness. For only when our arms are sufficient beyond doubt can we be certain beyond doubt that they will never be employed.

But neither can two great and powerful groups of nations take comfort from our present course—both sides overburdened by the cost of modern weapons, both rightly alarmed by the steady spread of the deadly atom, yet both racing to alter that uncertain balance of terror that stays the hand of mankind's final war.

So let us begin anew—remembering on both sides that civility is not a sign of weakness, and sincerity is always subject to proof. Let us never negotiate out of fear. But let us never fear to negotiate.

Let both sides explore what problems unite us instead of belaboring those problems which divide us.

Let both sides, for the first time, formulate serious and precise proposals for the inspection and control of arms—and bring the absolute power to destroy other nations under the absolute control of all nations.

Let both sides seek to invoke the wonders of science instead of its terrors. Together let us explore the stars, conquer the deserts, eradicate disease, tap the ocean depths and encourage the arts and commerce.

Let both sides unite to heed in all corners of the earth the command of Isaiah—to "undo the heavy burdens . . . (and) let the oppressed go free."

And if a beach-head of cooperation may push back the jungle of suspicion, let both sides join in creating a new endeavor, not a new balance of power, but a new world of law, where the strong are just and the weak secure and the peace preserved.

All this will not be finished in the first one hundred days. Nor will it be finished in the first one thousand days, nor in the life of this Administration, nor even perhaps in our lifetime on this planet. But let us begin.

In your hands, my fellow citizens, more than mine, will rest the final success or failure of our course. Since this country was founded, each generation of Americans has been summoned to give testimony to its national loyalty. The graves of young Americans who answered the call to service surround the globe.

Now the trumpet summons us again—not as a call to bear arms, though arms we need—not a call to battle, though embattled we are—but a call to bear the burden of a long twilight struggle, year in and year out, "rejoicing in hope, patient in tribulation"—a struggle against the common enemies of man: tyranny, poverty, disease and war itself.

Can we forge against these enemies a grand and global alliance, North and South, East and West, that can assure a more fruitful life for all mankind? Will you join in that historic effort?

In the long history of the world, only a few generations have been granted the role of defending freedom in its hours of maximum danger. I do not shrink from this responsibility—I welcome it. I do not believe that any of us would exchange places with any other people or any other generation. The energy, the faith, the devotion which we bring to this endeavor will light our country and all who serve it—and the glow from that fire can truly light the world.

And so, my fellow Americans: ask not what your country can do for you—ask what you can do for your country.

My fellow citizens of the world: ask not what America will do for you, but what together we can do for the freedom of man.

Finally, whether you are citizens of America or citizens of the world, ask of us here the same high standards of strength and sacrifice which we ask of you. With a good conscience our only sure reward, with history the final judge of our deeds, let us go forth to lead the land we love, asking His blessing and His help, but knowing that here on earth God's work must truly be our own.

The Cuban Missile Crisis

On October 15, 1962, President John F. Kennedy received photographic evidence that the Soviet Union had installed offensive nuclear missiles, aimed at the United States, just ninety miles from U.S. soil in Cuba. Kennedy secretly formed an "executive committee" (ExCom) of high administration officials to prepare a U.S. response. With advice from the committee, Kennedy decided to confront the Soviet Union by imposing a naval blockade around Cuba to prevent Soviet ships from bringing in supplies. Publicly and privately, Kennedy then demanded that the Soviet missiles be withdrawn. Nuclear war between the United States and the Soviet Union seemed more likely than at any other time in history.

Soviet reaction to the U.S. blockade and demand was hard to ascertain. A conciliatory message from Soviet leader Nikita Khrushchev was received on October 26; a harsh one followed on October 27. Kennedy decided to ignore the latter and reply to the former. Kennedy's October 27 letter to Khrushchev laid out the basis of the agreement that ended the crisis: the Soviet missiles would be removed in return for a U.S. pledge not to invade Cuba.

President Kennedy's Letter to Khrushchev

Dear Mr. Chairman:

I have read your letter of October 26th with great care and welcomed the statement of your desire to seek a prompt solution to the problem. The first thing that needs to be done, however, is for work to cease on offensive missile bases in Cuba and for all weapons systems in Cuba capable of offensive use to be rendered inoperable, under effective United Nations arrangements.

Assuming this is done promptly, I have given my representatives in New York instructions that will permit them to work out this weekend—in cooperation with the Acting Secretary General and your representative—an arrangement for a permanent solution to the Cuban problem along the lines suggested in your letter of October 26th. As I read your letter, the key elements of your proposals—which seem generally acceptable as I understand them—are as follows:

1) You would agree to remove these weapons systems from Cuba under appropriate United Nations observation and supervision; and undertake, with suitable safeguards, to halt the further introduction of such weapons systems into Cuba.

2) We, on our part, would agree—upon the establishment of adequate arrangements through the United Nations to ensure the carrying out and continuation of these commitments—(a) to remove promptly the quarantine measures now in effect and (b) to give assurances against an invasion of Cuba. I am confident that other nations of the Western Hemisphere would be prepared to do likewise.

If you will give your representative similar instructions, there is no reason why we should not be able to complete these arrangements and announce them to the world within a couple of days. The effect of such a settlement on easing world tensions would enable us to work toward a more general arrangement regarding "other armaments," as proposed in your second letter which you made public. I would like to say again that the United States is very much interested in reducing tensions and halting the arms race; and if your letter signifies that you are prepared to discuss a detente affecting NATO and the Warsaw Pact, we are quite prepared to consider with our allies any useful proposals.

But the first ingredient, let me emphasize, is the cessation of work on missile sites in Cuba and measures to render such weapons inoperable, under effective international guarantees. The continuation of this threat, or a prolonging of this discussion concerning Cuba by linking these problems to the broader questions of European and world security, would surely lead to an intensification of the Cuban crisis and a grave risk to the peace of the world. For this reason I hope we can quickly agree along the lines outlined in this letter and in your letter of October 26th.

Lyndon B. Johnson's "Great Society" Speech

Vice President Lyndon B. Johnson succeeded to the presidency when President John F. Kennedy was assassinated on November 22, 1963. Although Johnson initially offered "Let us continue" as the watchword of his presidency, he was more concerned to make his own mark on history. Within a few months, Johnson chose the phrase "Great Society" as the theme for his administration. In a May 22, 1964, commencement address at the University of Michigan, he developed the theme in detail.

According to Johnson, the United States already had become "the rich society and the powerful society" and now was challenged to reach "upward." The effort to build a Great Society would have two main goals. The first was "an end to poverty and racial injustice." The other was "to advance the quality of our American civilization."

As president, Johnson was able to create and enact a number of new programs to address the goals of the Great Society, including Medicare, Medicaid, highway beautification, the National Endowment for the Arts, civil rights legislation, and others.

. . . The purpose of protecting the life of our Nation and preserving the liberty of our citizens is to pursue the happiness of our people. Our success in that pursuit is the test of our success as a nation. For a century we labored to settle and to subdue a continent. For half a century, we called upon unbounded invention and untiring industry to create an order of plenty for all of our people. The challenge of the next half century is whether we have the wisdom to use that wealth to enrich and elevate our national life, and to advance the quality of our American civilization.

Your imagination, your initiative and your indignation will determine whether we build a society where progress is the servant of our needs, or a society where old values and new visions are buried under unbridled growth.

For in your time we have the opportunity to move not only toward the rich society and the powerful society, but upward to the Great Society. The Great Society rests on abundance and liberty for all. It demands an end to poverty and racial injustice, to which we are totally committed in our time. But that is just the beginning.

The Great Society is a place where every child can find knowledge to enrich his mind and to enlarge his talents. It is a place where leisure is a welcome chance to build and reflect, not a feared cause of boredom and restlessness. It is a place where the city of man serves not only the needs of the body and the demands of commerce, but the desire for beauty and the hunger for community.

It is a place where man can renew contact with nature. It is a place which honors creation for its own sake and for what it adds to the understanding of the race. It is a place where men are more concerned with the quality of their goals than the quantity of their goods. But most of all, the great society is not a safe harbor, a resting place, a final objective, a finished work. It is a challenge constantly renewed, beckoning us toward a destiny where the meaning of our lives matches the marvelous products of our labor.

So I want to talk to you today about three places where we begin to build the Great Society—in our cities, in our countryside, and in our classrooms. . . .

Aristotle said, "Men come together in cities in order to live, but they remain together in order to live the good life."

It is harder and harder to live the good life in American cities today. The catalogue of ills is long: There is the decay of the centers and the despoiling of the suburbs. There is not enough housing for our people or transportation for our traffic. Open land is vanishing and old landmarks are violated. Worst of all, expansion is eroding the precious and time-honored values of community with neighbors and communion with nature. The loss of these values breeds loneliness and boredom and indifference. Our society will never be great until our cities are great. Today the frontier of imagination and innovation is inside those cities, and not beyond their borders. . . .

A second place where we begin to build the Great Society is in our countryside. We have always prided ourselves on being not only America the strong and America the free, but America the beautiful. Today that beauty is in danger. The water we drink, the food we eat, the very air that we breathe, are threatened with pollution. Our parks are overcrowded. Our seashores overburdened. Green fields and dense forests are disappearing.

A few years ago we were greatly concerned about the Ugly American. Today we must act to prevent an Ugly America.

For once the battle is lost, once our natural splendor is destroyed, it can never be recaptured. And once man can no longer walk with beauty or wonder at nature, his spirit will wither and his sustenance be wasted.

A third place to build the Great Society is in the classrooms of America. There your children's lives will be shaped. Our society will not be great until every young mind is set free to scan the farthest reaches of thought and imagination. We are still far from that goal. . . . In many places, classrooms are overcrowded and curricula are outdated. Most of our qualified teachers are underpaid, and many of our paid teachers are unqualified.

So we must give every child a place to sit and a teacher to learn from. Poverty must not be a bar to learning, and learning must offer an escape from poverty.

But more classrooms and more teachers are not enough. We

must seek an educational system which grows in excellence as it grows in size. This means better training for our teachers. It means preparing youth to enjoy their hours of leisure as well as their hours of labor. It means exploring new techniques of teaching, to find new ways to stimulate the love of learning and the capacity for creation.

These are three of the central issues of the Great Society. While our government has many programs directed at those issues, I do not pretend that we have the full answer to those problems. But I do promise this: We are going to assemble the best thought and the broadest knowledge from all over the world to find those answers for America....

There are those timid souls who say this battle cannot be won, that we are condemned to a soulless wealth. I do not agree. We have the power to shape the civilization that we want. But we need your will, your labor, your hearts, if we are to build that kind of society.

Those who came to this land sought to build more than just a new country. They sought a free world.

So I have come here today to your campus to say that you can make their vision our reality. Let us from this moment begin our work so that in the future men will look back and say: It was then, after a long and weary way, that man turned the exploits of his genius to the full enrichment of his life.

Thank you. Goodbye.

Johnson's Gulf of Tonkin Message

Two themes dominated the five-year presidency of Lyndon B. Johnson: the Great Society and the war in Vietnam. In early 1964 Johnson aides privately prepared a congressional resolution that would give the president a virtual blank check to conduct the Vietnam War as he saw fit. Johnson feared that such a proposal would generate too much controversy. But on August 4, 1964, reports reached Washington (they were proved false much later) that U.S. naval vessels had been attacked by North Vietnamese patrol boats in the Gulf of Tonkin near North Vietnam. The next day, Johnson sent a message to Congress urging passage of "a Resolution expressing the support of Congress for all necessary action to protect our armed forces and to assist nations covered by the SEATO [Southeast Asia Treaty Organization] treaty," including South Vietnam. On August 6 the Gulf of Tonkin Resolution passed unanimously in the House of Representatives and with only two dissenting votes in the Senate. In later years, as the U.S. war effort became much larger and more controversial, Johnson cited the resolution as providing ample justification for his administration's policies. Privately, he compared it to "grandma's nightshirt—it covered everything."

To the Congress of the United States:

Last night I announced to the American people that the North Vietnamese regime had conducted further deliberate attacks against U.S. naval vessels operating in international waters, and that I had therefore directed air action against gun boats and supporting facilities used in these hostile operations. This air action has now been carried out with substantial damage to the boats and facilities. Two U.S. aircraft were lost in the action.

After consultation with the leaders of both parties in the Congress, I further announced a decision to ask the Congress for a Resolution expressing the unity and determination of the United States in supporting freedom and in protecting peace in Southeast Asia.

These latest actions of the North Vietnamese regime have given a new and grave turn to the already serious situation in Southeast Asia. Our commitments in that area are well known to the Congress. They were first made in 1954 by President Eisenhower. They were further defined in the Southeast Asia Collective Defense Treaty approved by the Senate in February 1955.

This Treaty with its accompanying protocol obligates the United States and other members to act in accordance with their Constitutional processes to meet Communist aggression against any of the parties or protocol states.

Our policy in Southeast Asia has been consistent and unchanged since 1954. I summarized it on June 2 in four simple propositions:

1. *America keeps her word.* Here as elsewhere, we must and shall honor our commitments.

2. *The issue is the future of Southeast Asia as a whole.* A threat to any nation in that region is a threat to all, and a threat to us.

3. *Our purpose is peace.* We have no military, political or territorial ambitions in the area.

4. *This is not just a jungle war, but a struggle for freedom on every front of human activity.* Our military and economic assistance to South Vietnam and Laos in particular has the purpose of helping these countries to repel aggression and strengthen their independence.

The threat to the free nations of Southeast Asia has long been clear. The North Vietnamese regime has constantly sought to take over South Vietnam and Laos. This Communist regime has violated the Geneva Accords for Vietnam. It has systematically conducted a campaign of subversion, which includes the direction, training, and supply of personnel and arms for the conduct of guerrilla warfare in South Vietnamese territory. In Laos, the North Vietnamese regime has maintained military forces, used Laotian territory for infiltration into South Vietnam, and most recently carried out combat operations—all in direct violation of the Geneva Agreements of 1962.

In recent months, the actions of the North Vietnamese regime have become steadily more threatening. In May, following new acts of Communist aggression in Laos, the United States undertook reconnaissance flights over Laotian territory, at the request of the Government of Laos. These flights had the essential mission of determining the situation in territory where Communist forces were preventing inspection by the International Control Commission. When the Communists attacked these aircraft, I responded by furnishing escort fighters with instructions to fire when fired upon. Thus, these latest North Vietnamese attacks on our naval vessels are not the first direct attack on armed forces of the United States.

As President of the United States I have concluded that I should now ask the Congress, on its part, to join in affirming the national determination that all such attacks will be met, and that the U.S. will continue in its basic policy of assisting the free nations of the area to defend their freedom.

As I have repeatedly made clear, the United States intends no rashness, and seeks no wider war. We must make it clear to all that the United States is united in its determination to bring about the end of Communist subversion and aggression in the area. We seek the full and effective restoration of the international agreements signed in Geneva in 1954, with respect to South Vietnam, and again in Geneva in 1962, with respect to Laos.

I recommend a Resolution expressing the support of the Congress for all necessary action to protect our armed forces and to assist nations covered by the SEATO Treaty. At the same time, I assure the Congress that we shall continue readily to explore any avenues of political solution that will effectively guarantee the removal of Communist subversion and the preservation of the independence of the nations of the area.

The Resolution could well be based upon similar resolutions enacted by the Congress in the past—to meet the threat to Formosa in 1955, to meet the threat to the Middle East in 1957, and to meet the threat in Cuba in 1962. It could state in the simplest terms the resolve and support of the Congress for action to deal appropriately with attacks against our armed forces and to defend freedom and preserve peace in southeast Asia in accordance with the obligations of the United States under the southeast Asia Treaty. I urge the Congress to enact such a Resolution promptly and thus to give convincing evidence to the aggressive Communist nations, and to the world as a whole, that our policy in Southeast Asia will be carried forward—and that the peace and security of the area will be preserved.

The events of this week would in any event have made the passage of a Congressional Resolution essential. But there is an additional reason for doing so at a time when we are entering on three months of political campaigning. Hostile nations must understand that in such a period the United States will continue to protect its national interests, and that in these matters there is no division among us.

Nixon's China Trip Announcement

On July 15, 1971, President Richard Nixon appeared on national television to read a three-and-one-half minute announcement that he would be traveling to China sometime in early 1972 at the invitation of the Chinese government. The purpose would be "to seek the normalization of relations" between the United States and the People's Republic of China. Nixon made the trip, which was the product of two years of secret negotiations, in February 1972.

Nixon's visit ended more than twenty years of hostility between the two nations, tracing back to the 1949 revolution in China in which Communist forces led by Mao Tse-tung had overthrown the government of Chiang Kai-shek, a close ally of the United States. Ironically, Nixon's entire political career had been based on anticommunism, including strong support for Chiang, who had fled to the island of Formosa, claiming to be leader of the true government of China. Yet, as president, Nixon saw an opportunity for the United States to take advantage of the hostility between China and the Soviet Union. Many analysts believed that only a staunch anticommunist like Nixon could have ended U.S. hostility to the most populous nation in the world without provoking widespread political opposition.

Good evening.

I have requested this television time tonight to announce a major development in our efforts to build a lasting peace in the world.

As I have pointed out on a number of occasions over the past three years, there can be no stable and enduring peace without the participation of the Peoples Republic of China and its 750 million people. That is why I have undertaken initiatives in several areas to open the door for more normal relations between our two countries.

In pursuance of that goal, I sent Dr. Kissinger, my Assistant for National Security Affairs, to Peking during his recent world tour for the purpose of having talks with Premier Chou En-lai. The announcement I shall now read is being issued simultaneously in Peking and in the United States.

Premier Chou En-lai and Dr. Henry Kissinger, President Nixon's Assistant for National Security Affairs, held talks in Peking from July 9 to 11, 1971. Knowing of President Nixon's expressed desire to visit the Peoples Republic of China, Premier Chou En-lai, on behalf of the Government of the Peoples Republic of China, has extended an invitation to President Nixon to visit China at an appropriate date before May 1972. President Nixon has accepted the invitation with pleasure.

The meeting between the leaders of China and the United States is to seek the normalization of relations between the two countries and also to exchange views on questions of concern to the two sides. In anticipation of the inevitable speculation which will follow this announcement, I want to put our policy in the clearest possible context.

Our action in seeking a new relationship with the Peoples Republic of China will not be at the expense of our old friends. It is not directed against any other nation. We seek friendly relations with all nations. Any nation can be our friend without being any other nation's enemy.

I have taken this action because of my profound conviction that all nations will gain from a reduction of tensions and a better relationship between the United States and the Peoples Republic of China.

It is in that spirit that I will undertake what I deeply hope will become a journey for peace, peace not just for our generation, but for future generations on this earth we share together.

Thank you and good night.

Resignation of Vice President Agnew

Vice President Spiro T. Agnew, who was elected with President Richard Nixon in 1968 and reelected in 1972, resigned on October 10, 1973, as part of a plea bargain with federal prosecutors. The Justice Department had uncovered extensive evidence that Agnew received bribes from contractors while serving as county executive of Baltimore County, Maryland, governor of Maryland, and vice president. It was prepared to indict Agnew for conspiracy, extortion, bribery, and tax charges. In return for his resignation, however, Agnew was allowed (also on October 10) to plead nolo contendere (no contest) to one count of income tax evasion. He was fined $10,000 and sentenced to three years of unsupervised probation.

On the day of Agnew's resignation, the Justice Department submitted a forty-page document to a federal grand jury in Baltimore that listed the payoffs Agnew had accepted.

II. The Relationship between Mr. Agnew and Allen Green.

Shortly after Mr. Angew's election in November 1966 as governor of Maryland, he complained to Allen Green, principal of a large engineering firm, about the financial burdens to be imposed upon Mr. Agnew by his role as Governor. Green responded by saying that his company had benefited from state work and had been able to generate some cash funds from which he would be willing to provide Mr. Agnew with some financial assistance. Mr. Agnew indicated that he would be grateful for such assistance.

Beginning shortly thereafter, Green delivered to Mr. Agnew six to nine times a year an envelope containing between $2,000 and $3,000 in cash. Green's purpose was to elicit from the Agnew administration as much state work for his engineering firm as possible. The purpose was clearly understood by Governor Agnew. . . .

Green continued to make cash payments to Vice President Agnew three or four times a year up to and including December 1972. These payments were usually about $2,000 each. The payments were made both in Mr. Agnew's vice presidential office and at his residence in the Sheraton-Park Hotel, Washington, D.C. The payments were not discontinued until after the initiation of the Baltimore County investigation by the United States Attorney for the District of Maryland in January 1973.

III. The Relationship between Mr. Agnew and Lester Matz.

Lester Matz, a principal in another large engineering firm, began making corrupt payments while Mr. Agnew was County Executive of Baltimore County in the early 1970s. In those days, Matz paid 5 percent of his fees from Baltimore County contracts in cash to Mr. Agnew through one of Mr. Agnew's close associates.

After Mr. Agnew became Governor of Maryland, Matz decided to make his payments directly to Governor Agnew. He made no payments until that summer of 1968 when he and his partner calculated that they owed Mr. Agnew approximately $20,000 in consideration for the work which their firm had already received from the Governor's administration. The $20,000 in cash was generated in an illegal manner and was given by Matz to Governor Agnew in a manila envelope in Governor Agnew's office on or about July 16, 1968....

Matz made no further corrupt payments to Mr. Agnew until shortly after Mr. Agnew became Vice President, at which time Matz calculated that he owed Mr. Agnew approximately $10,000 more from jobs and fees which the Matz firm had received from Governor Agnew's administration since July 1968. After generating $10,000 in cash in an illegal manner, Matz met with Mr. Agnew in the Vice President's office and gave him approximately $10,000 cash in an envelope....

In or around April 1971, Matz made a cash payment to Vice President Agnew of $2,500 in return for the awarding by the General Services Administration of a contract to a small engineering firm in which Matz had a financial ownership interest. An intermediary was instrumental in the arrangement for that particular corrupt payment.

Proposed Articles of Impeachment of Richard Nixon

On June 17, 1972, burglars secretly employed by the Committee to Re-elect the President were caught breaking into the offices of the Democratic National Committee in Washington's Watergate Hotel. The chain of command that had authorized the break-in, as well as a host of other illegal and unethical campaign activities, reached high into the Nixon administration. In an effort to avoid embarrassing revelations, President Richard Nixon and some of his closest aides responded to news of the burglary by trying to obstruct official investigations into what had happened.

Through a combination of activities—including diligent investigations by reporters Bob Woodward and Carl Bernstein of the Washington Post, *thorough hearings by a special bipartisan Senate committee chaired by Democratic senator Sam Ervin of North Carolina, testimony by John Dean and other participants in the Watergate affair, and the release of secret White House tape recordings—evidence of Nixon's involvement in the Watergate coverup was brought to light.*

In February 1974 the House of Representatives charged its Judiciary Committee to consider impeaching the president for "High Crimes and Misdemeanors." Between July 27 and 29 the committee voted to recommend three articles of impeachment to the full House. Article I describes Nixon's role in the Watergate coverup, Article II details other abuses of power by the president, and Article III charges Nixon with contempt of Congress for his failure to honor the Judiciary Committee's subpoenas, mostly for certain tape recordings. Two other proposed articles—one dealing with Nixon's secret bombings of Cambodia, the other with his income taxes—were rejected by the committee on July 30.

Article I

In his conduct of the office of President of the United States, Richard M. Nixon, in violation of his constitutional oath faithfully to execute the office of President of the United States and, to the best of his ability, preserve, protect, and defend the Constitution of the United States, and in violation of his constitutional duty to take care that the laws be faithfully executed, has prevented, obstructed, and impeded the administration of justice, in that:

On June 17, 1972, and prior thereto, agents of the Committee for the Re-Election of the President committed unlawful entry of the headquarters of the Democratic National Committee in Washington, District of Columbia, for the purpose of securing political intelligence. Subsequent thereto, Richard M. Nixon, using the powers of his high office, engaged personally and through his close subordinates and agents, in a course of conduct or plan designed to delay, impede, and obstruct the investigation of such unlawful entry; to cover up, conceal and protect those responsible; and to conceal the existence and scope of other unlawful covert activities.

The means used to implement this course of conduct or plan included one or more of the following:

(1) making false or misleading statements to lawfully authorized investigative officers and employees of the United States;

(2) withholding relevant and material evidence or information from lawfully authorized investigative officers and employees of the United States;

(3) approving, condoning, acquiescing in, and counseling witnesses with respect to the giving of false or misleading statements to lawfully authorized investigative officers and employees of the United States and false or misleading testimony in duly instituted judicial and congressional proceedings;

(4) interfering or endeavoring to interfere with the conduct of investigations by the Department of Justice of the United States, the Federal Bureau of Investigation, the Office of Watergate Special Prosecution Force, and Congressional Committees;

(5) approving, condoning, and acquiescing in, the surreptitious payment of substantial sums of money for the purpose of obtaining the silence or influencing the testimony of witnesses, potential witnesses or individuals who participated in such unlawful entry and other illegal activities;

(6) endeavoring to misuse the Central Intelligence Agency, an agency of the United States;

(7) disseminating information received from officers of the Department of Justice of the United States to subjects of investigations conducted by lawfully authorized investigative officers and employees of the United States, for the purpose of aiding and assisting such subjects in their attempts to avoid criminal liability;

(8) making or causing to be made false or misleading public statements for the purpose of deceiving the people of the United States into believing that a thorough and complete investigation had been conducted with respect to allegations of misconduct on the part of personnel of the executive branch of the United States and personnel of the Committee for the Re-Election of the President, and that there was no involvement of such personnel in such misconduct; or

(9) endeavoring to cause prospective defendants, and individuals duly tried and convicted, to expect favored treatment and consideration in return for their silence or false testimony, or rewarding individuals for their silence or false testimony.

In all of this, Richard M. Nixon has acted in a manner contrary to his trust as President and subversive of constitutional government, to the great prejudice of the cause of law and justice and to the manifest injury of the people of the United States.

Wherefore Richard M. Nixon, by such conduct, warrants impeachment and trial, and removal from office.

[—Adopted July 27 by a 27-11 vote]

Article II

Using the powers of the office of President of the United States, Richard M. Nixon, in violation of his constitutional oath faithfully to execute the office of President of the United States and, to the best of his ability, preserve, protect, and defend the Constitution of the United States, and in disregard of his constitutional duty to take care that the laws be faithfully executed, has repeatedly engaged in conduct violating the constitutional rights of citizens, impairing the due and proper administration of justice and the conduct of lawful inquiries, or contravening the laws governing agencies of the executive branch and the purposes of these agencies.

This conduct has included one or more of the following:

(1) He has, acting personally and through his subordinates and agents, endeavored to obtain from the Internal Revenue Service, in violation of the constitutional rights of citizens, confidential information contained in income tax returns for purposes not authorized by law, and to cause, in violation of the constitutional rights of citizens, income tax audits or other income tax investigations to be initiated or conducted in a discriminatory manner.

(2) He misused the Federal Bureau of Investigation, the Secret Service, and other executive personnel, in violation or disregard of the constitutional rights of citizens, by directing or authorizing such agencies or personnel to conduct or continue electronic surveillance or other investigations for purposes unrelated to national security, the enforcement of laws, or any other lawful function of his office; he did direct, authorize, or permit the use of information obtained thereby for purposes unrelated to national security, the enforcement of laws, or any other lawful function of his office; and he did direct the concealment of certain records made by the Federal Bureau of Investigation of electronic surveillance.

(3) He has, acting personally and through his subordinates and agents, in violation or disregard of the constitutional rights of citizens, authorized and permitted to be maintained a secret investigative unit within the office of the President, financed in part with money derived from campaign contributions, which unlawfully utilized the resources of the Central Intelligence Agency, engaged in covert and unlawful activities, and attempted to prejudice the constitutional right of an accused to a fair trial.

(4) He has failed to take care that the laws were faithfully executed by failing to act when he knew or had reason to know that his close subordinates endeavored to impede and frustrate lawful inquiries by duly constituted executive, judicial, and legislative entities concerning the unlawful entry into the headquarters of the Democratic National Committee, and the cover up thereof, and concerning other unlawful activities including those relating to the confirmation of Richard Kleindienst as Attorney General of the United States, the electronic surveillance of private citizens, the break-in into the offices of Dr. Lewis Fielding and the campaign financing practices of the Committee to Re-elect the President.

(5) In disregard of the rule of law, he knowingly misused the executive branch, including the Federal Bureau of Investigation, the Criminal Division, and the Office of Watergate Special Prosecution Force, of the Department of Justice, and the Central Intelligence Agency, in violation of his duty to take care that the laws be faithfully executed.

In all of this, Richard M. Nixon has acted in a manner contrary to his trust as President and subversive of constitutional government, to the great prejudice of the cause of law and justice and to the manifest injury of the people of the United States.

Wherefore Richard M. Nixon, by such conduct, warrants impeachment and trial, and removal from office.

[—Adopted July 29 by a 28-10 vote]

Article III

In his conduct of the office of President of the United States, Richard M. Nixon, contrary to his oath faithfully to execute the office of President of the United States and, to the best of his ability, preserve, protect, and defend the Constitution of the United States, and in violation of his constitutional duty to take care that the laws be faithfully executed, has failed without lawful cause of excuse to produce papers and things as directed by duly authorized subpoenas issued by the Committee on the Judiciary of the House of Representatives on April 11, 1974, May 15, 1974, May 30, 1974, and June 24, 1974, and willfully disobeyed such subpoenas. The subpoenaed papers and things were deemed necessary by the Committee in order to resolve by direct evidence fundamental, factual questions relating to Presidential direction, knowledge, or approval of actions demonstrated by other evidence to be substantial grounds for impeachment of the President. In refusing to produce these papers and things Richard M. Nixon, substituting his judgment as to what materials were necessary for the inquiry, interposed the powers of the Presidency against the lawful subpoenas of the House of Representatives, thereby assuming to himself functions and judgments necessary to the exercise of the sole power of impeachment vested by the Constitution in the House of Representatives.

In all of this, Richard M. Nixon has acted in a manner contrary to his trust as President and subversive of constitutional government, to the great prejudice of the cause of law and justice, and to the manifest injury of the people of the United States.

Wherefore, Richard M. Nixon by such conduct, warrants impeachment and trial, and removal from office.

[—Adopted July 30 by a 21-17 vote]

Nixon's "Smoking-Gun" Tape

In 1973 the special Senate Watergate committee learned that President Richard Nixon had installed a secret, voice-activated taping system in the Oval Office and other presidential offices. Under severe political and legal pressure, Nixon released many of the tape recordings but withheld others. On July 24, 1974, just before the House Judiciary Committee voted to recommend articles of impeachment, a unanimous U.S. Supreme Court ordered Nixon to release more tapes in the case of United States v. Nixon.

Included in the tapes, which Nixon made public August 5, was a ninety-five-minute Oval Office meeting between the president and his chief of staff, H. R. Haldeman. At that meeting, Nixon instructed Haldeman to have the Central Intelligence Agency (CIA) falsely tell the Federal Bureau of Investigation (FBI) that the FBI should tread lightly in its investigation because the June 17, 1972, Watergate break-in was a CIA activity.

The June 23 tape was the "smoking gun" in the Watergate investigation—the first piece of evidence that indisputably demonstrated Nixon's active role in the coverup. Republicans in Congress, including members of the House Judiciary Committee who had voted against recommending impeachment, publicly denounced Nixon, all but guaranteeing that the House of Representatives would vote to impeach the president and that the Senate would vote to convict. On August 9, 1974, Nixon became the first U.S. president to resign the office.

Haldeman. Now, on the investigation, you know the Democratic break-in thing, we're back in the problem area because the FBI is not under control, because Gray [acting FBI director L. Patrick Gray III] doesn't exactly know how to control it and they have—their investigation is now leading into some productive areas—because they've been able to trace the money—not through the money itself—but through the bank sources—the banker. And, and it goes in some directions we don't want it to go. Ah, also there have been some things—like an informant came in off the street to the FBI in Miami who was a photographer or has a friend who is a photographer who developed some films through this guy Barker [Bernard L. Barker, one of the five men caught in the Watergate break-in] and the films had pictures of Democratic National Committee letterhead documents and things. So it's things like that that are filtering in. Mitchell [former attorney general John N. Mitchell] came up with yesterday, and [White House counsel] John Dean analyzed very carefully last night and concludes, concurs now with Mitchell's recommendation that the only way to solve this, and we're set up beautifully to do it, ah, in that and that—the only network that paid any attention to it last night was NBC—they did a massive story on the Cuban thing.

President. That's right.

H. That the way to handle this now is for us to have Walters [deputy CIA director Vernon A. Walters] call Pat Gray and just say, "Stay to hell out of this—this is ah, business here we don't want you to go any further on it." That's not an unusual development, and ah, that would take care of it.

P. What about Pat Gray—you mean Pat Gray doesn't want to?

P. Pat does want to. He doesn't know how to, and he doesn't have, he doesn't have any basis for doing it. Given this, he will then have the basis. He'll call Mark Felt in [W. Mark Felt, FBI deputy associate director in 1972], and the two of them—and Mark Felt wants to cooperate because he's ambitious—

P. Yeah.

H. He'll call him in and say, "We've got the signal from across the river to put the hold on this." And that will fit rather well because the FBI agents who are working the case, at this point, feel that's what it is.

P. This is CIA? They've traced the money? Who'd they trace it to?

H. Well they've traced it to a name, but they haven't gotten to the guy yet.

P. Would it be somebody here?

H. Ken Dahlberg.

P. Who the hell is Ken Dahlberg?

H. He gave $25,000 in Minnesota and, ah, the check went directly to this guy Barker.

P. It isn't from the Committee, though, from [Nixon reelection committee finance chairman Maurice H.] Stans?

H. Yeah. It is. It's directly traceable and there's some more through some Texas people that went to the Mexican bank which can also be traced to the Mexican bank—they'll get their names today.

H. —And (pause)

P. Well, I mean, there's no way—I'm just thinking if they don't cooperate, what do they say? That they were approached by the Cubans. That's what Dahlberg has to say, the Texans too, that they—

H. Well, if they will. But then we're relying on more and more people all the time. That's the problem and they'll stop if we could take this other route.

P. All right.

H. And you seem to think the thing to do is get them to stop?

P. Right, fine.

H. They say the only way to do that is from White House instructions. And it's got to be to Helms [CIA director Richard C. Helms] and to—ah, what's his name...? Walters.

P. Walters.

H. And the proposal would be that [domestic policy adviser John D.] Ehrlichman and I call them in, and say, ah—

P. All right, fine. How do you call him in—I mean you just—well, we protected Helms from one hell of a lot of things.

H. That's what Ehrlichman says.

P. Of course, this Hunt [E. Howard Hunt, Jr., a White House consultant], that will uncover a lot of things. You open that scab there's a hell of a lot of things and we just feel that it would be very detrimental to have this thing go any further. This involves these Cubans, Hunt, and a lot of hanky-panky that we have nothing to do with ourselves. Well what the hell, did Mitchell know about this?

H. I think so. I don't think he knew the details, but I think he knew.

P. He didn't know how it was going to be handled though—with Dahlberg and the Texans and so forth? Well who was the asshole that did? Is it Liddy? [G. Gordon Liddy, former FBI agent] Is that the fellow? He must be a little nuts!

H. He is.

P. I mean he just isn't well screwed on is he? Is that the problem?

H. No, but he was under pressure, apparently, to get more information, and as he got more pressure, he pushed the people harder to move harder—

P. Pressure from Mitchell?

H. Apparently.

P. Oh, Mitchell. Mitchell was at the point (unintelligible).

H. Yes.

P. All right, fine, I understand it all. We won't second-guess Mitchell and the rest. Thank God it wasn't Colson [Charles W. Colson, White House special counsel].

H. The FBI interviewed Colson yesterday. They determined that would be a good thing to do. To have him take an interrogation, which he did, and that—the FBI guys working the case concluded that there were one or two possibilities—one, that this was a White House—they don't think that there is anything at the Election Committee—they think it was either a White House operation and they had some obscure reasons for it—non-political, or it was a—Cuban and the CIA. And after their interrogation of Colson yesterday, they concluded it was not the White House, but are now convinced it is a CIA thing, so the CIA turnoff would—

P. Well, not sure of their analysis, I'm not going to get that involved. I'm (unintelligible).

H. No, sir, we don't want you to.

P. You call them in.

H. Good deal.

P. Play it tough. That's the way they play it and that's the way we are going to play it.

H. O.K.

P. When I saw that news summary, I questioned whether it's a bunch of crap, but I thought, er, well it's good to have them off us awhile, because when they start bugging us, which they have, our little boys will not know how to handle it. I hope they will though.

H. You never know.

P. Good.

[Other matters are discussed. Then the conversation returns to the break-in coverup strategy.]

P. When you get in—when you get in (unintelligible) people, say, "Look the problem is that this will open the whole, the whole Bay of Pigs thing, and the President just feels that ah, without going into the details—don't, don't lie to them to the extent to say there is no involvement, but just say this is a comedy of errors, without getting into it, the President believes that it is going to open the whole Bay of Pigs thing up again. And, ah, because these people are plugging for (unintelligible) and that they should call the FBI in and (unintelligible) don't go any further into this case period! (Inaudible) our cause—

H. Get more done for our cause by the opposition than by us.

P. Well, can you get it done?

H. I think so.

Nixon's Resignation Speech

After protesting many times that he would defend his presidency until the end, President Richard Nixon announced in a televised address August 8, 1974, that he would resign effective noon the next day. Impeachment and conviction were certain—also for Nixon to fight on would cost him the extensive benefits that former presidents receive and increase the likelihood that he would be prosecuted for his role in the Watergate coverup.

In his speech, Nixon admitted only to having made mistaken judgments, claiming that even "they were made in what I believed at the time to be the best interest of the Nation." He also suggested that but for the political hopelessness of his position, and the paralysis that a long impeachment process would cause in the government, the right thing to do would be to continue his fight for vindication.

Good evening.

This is the 37th time I have spoken to you from this office, where so many decisions have been made that shaped the history of this Nation. Each time I have done so to discuss with you some matter that I believe affected the national interest.

In all the decisions I have made in my public life, I have always tried to do what was best for the Nation. Throughout the long and difficult period of Watergate, I have felt it was my duty to persevere, to make every possible effort to complete the term of office to which you elected me.

In the past few days, however, it has become evident to me that I no longer have a strong enough political base in the Congress to justify continuing that effort. As long as there was a base, I felt strongly that it was necessary to see the constitutional process through to its conclusion. . . .

But with the disappearance of that base, I now believe that the constitutional purpose has been served, and there is no longer a need for the process to be prolonged. . . .

I have never been a quitter. To leave office before my term is completed is abhorrent to every instinct in my body. But as President, I must put the interest of America first. America needs a full-time President and a full-time Congress, particularly at this time with problems we face at home and abroad.

To continue to fight through the months ahead for my personal vindication would almost totally absorb the time and attention of both the President and the Congress in a period when our entire focus should be on the great issues of peace abroad and prosperity without inflation at home.

Therefore, I shall resign the Presidency effective at noon tomorrow. Vice President Ford will be sworn in as President at that hour in this office.

As I recall the high hopes for America with which we began this second term, I feel a great sadness that I will not be here in this office working on your behalf to achieve those hopes in the next 2½ years. But in turning over direction of the Government to Vice President Ford, I know, as I told the Nation when I nominated him for that office 10 months ago, that the leadership of America will be in good hands. . . .

By taking this action, I hope that I will have hastened the start of that process of healing which is so desperately needed in America.

I regret deeply any injuries that may have been done in the course of the events that led to this decision. I would say only that if some of my judgments were wrong, and some were wrong, they were made in what I believed at the time to be the best interest of the Nation.

To those who have stood with me during these past difficult months, to my family, my friends, to many others who joined in supporting my cause because the believed it was right, I will be eternally grateful for your support.

And to those who have not felt able to give me your support, let me say I leave with no bitterness toward those who have opposed me, because all of us, in the final analysis, have been concerned with the good of the country, however our judgments might differ.

So, let us all now join together in affirming that common commitment and in helping our new President succeed for the benefit of all Americans.

I shall leave this office with regret at not completing my term, but with gratitude for the privilege of serving as your President for the past 5½ years. These years have been a momentous time in the history of our Nation and the world. They have been a time of achievement in which we can all be proud, achievements that represent the shared efforts of the Administration, the Congress, and the people.

But the challenges ahead are equally great, and they, too, will require the support and the efforts of the Congress and the people working in cooperation with the new Administration.

We have ended America's longest war, but in the work of securing a lasting peace in the world, the goals ahead are even more far-reaching and more difficult. We must complete a structure of peace so that it will be said of this generation, our generation of Americans, by the people of all nations, not only that we ended one war but that we prevented future wars.

We have unlocked the doors that for a quarter of a century stood between the United States and the People's Republic of China.

We must now ensure that the one quarter of the world's people who live in the People's Republic of China will be and remain not our enemies but our friends.

In the Middle East, 100 million people in the Arab countries, many of whom have considered us their enemy for nearly 20 years, now look on us as their friends. We must continue to build on that friendship so that peace can settle at last over the Middle East and so that the cradle of civilization will not become its grave.

Together with the Soviet Union we have made the crucial breakthroughs that have begun the process of limiting nuclear arms. But we must set as our goal not just limiting but reducing and finally destroying these terrible weapons so that they cannot destroy civilization and so that the threat of nuclear war will no longer hang over the world and the people.

We have opened the new relation with the Soviet Union. We must continue to develop and expand that new relationship so that the two strongest nations of the world will live together in cooperation rather than confrontation.

Around the world, in Asia, in Africa, in Latin America, in the Middle East, there are millions of people who live in terrible poverty, even starvation. We must keep as our goal turning away from production for war and expanding production for peace so that people everywhere on this earth can at last look forward in their children's time, if not in our own time, to having the necessities for a decent life.

Here in America, we are fortunate that most of our people have not only the blessings of liberty but also the means to live full and good and, by the world's standards, even abundant lives. We must press on, however, toward a goal of not only more and better jobs but of full opportunity for every American and of what we are striving so hard right now to achieve, prosperity without inflation.

For more than a quarter of a century in public life I have shared in the turbulent history of this era. I have fought for what I believed in. I have tried to the best of my ability to discharge those duties and meet those responsibilities that were entrusted to me.

Sometimes I have succeeded and sometimes I have failed, but always I have taken heart from what Theodore Roosevelt once said about the man in the arena, "whose face is marred by dust and sweat and blood, who strives valiantly, who errs and comes short again and again because there is not effort without error and shortcoming, but who does actually strive to do the deed, who knows the great enthusiasms, the great devotions, who spends himself in a worthy cause, who at the best knows in the end the triumphs of high achievements and who at the worst, if he fails, at least fails while daring greatly."

I pledge to you tonight that as long as I have a breath of life in my body, I shall continue in that spirit. I shall continue to work for the great causes to which I have been dedicated throughout my years as a Congressman, a Senator, a Vice President, and President, the cause of peace not just for America but among all nations, prosperity, justice, and opportunity for all of our people.

There is one cause above all to which I have been devoted and to which I shall always be devoted for as long as I live.

When I first took the oath of office as President 5½ years ago, I made this sacred commitment, to "consecrate my office, my energies, and all the wisdom I can summon to the cause of peace among nations."

I have done my very best in all the days since to be true to that pledge. As a result of these efforts, I am confident that the world is a safer place today, not only for the people of America but for the people of all nations, and that all of our children have a better chance than before of living in peace rather than dying in war.

This, more than anything, is what I hoped to achieve when I sought the Presidency. This, more than anything, is what I hope will be my legacy to you, to our country, as I leave the Presidency.

To have served in this office is to have felt a very personal sense of kinship with each and every American. In leaving it, I do so with this prayer: May God's grace be with you in all the days ahead.

Ford's Remarks on Becoming President

Section 2 of the Twenty-fifth Amendment (1967) charges the president to fill a vacancy in the vice presidency by nominating a new vice president, subject to the approval of both houses of Congress, voting separately. When Vice President Spiro T. Agnew resigned in 1973, President Richard Nixon nominated House minority leader Gerald R. Ford of Michigan to be vice president. Congress confirmed the nomination overwhelmingly.

From the moment of his appointment, Ford was aware that he might be called upon to serve as president if Nixon either resigned or was removed from office. When Nixon's resignation took effect at noon on August 9, 1974, Ford was sworn in by Chief Justice Warren E. Burger. In his brief remarks, Ford proclaimed that "our long national nightmare is over." Aware that he was the first unelected vice president to become president, Ford said: "I am acutely aware that you have not elected me your President by your ballots, and so I ask that you confirm me as your President with your prayers."

Mr. Chief Justice, my dear friends, my fellow Americans:

The oath that I have taken is the same oath that was taken by George Washington and by every President under the Constitution. But I assume the Presidency under extraordinary circumstances, never before experienced by Americans. This is an hour of history that troubles our minds and hurts our hearts.

Therefore, I feel it is my first duty to make an unprecedented compact with my countrymen. Not an inaugural address, not a fireside chat, not a campaign speech—just a little straight talk among friends. And I intend it to be the first of many.

I am acutely aware that you have not elected me as your President by your ballots, and so I ask you to confirm me as your President with your prayers. And I hope that such prayers will be the first of many.

If you have not chosen me by secret ballot, neither have I gained office by any secret promises. I have not campaigned either for the Presidency or the Vice Presidency. I have not subscribed to any partisan platform. I am indebted to no man, and only to one woman—my dear wife—as I begin this very difficult job.

I have not sought this enormous responsibility, but I will not shirk it. Those who nominated and confirmed me as Vice President were my friends and are my friends. They were of both parties, elected by all the people and acting under the Constitution in their name. It is only fitting then that I should pledge to them and to you that I will be the President of all the people.

Thomas Jefferson said the people are the only sure reliance for the preservation of our liberty. And down the years, Abraham Lincoln renewed this American article of faith saying, "Is there any better way or equal hope in the world?"

I intend, on Monday next, to request of the Speaker of the House of Representatives and the President pro tempore of the Senate the privilege of appearing before the Congress to share with my former colleagues and with you, the American people, my views on the priority business of the Nation and to solicit your views and their views. And may I say to the Speaker and the others, if I could meet with you right after these remarks, I would appreciate it.

Even though this is late in an election year, there is no way we can go forward except together and no way anybody can win except by serving the people's urgent needs. We cannot stand still or slip backwards. We must go forward now together.

To the peoples and the governments of all friendly nations, and I hope that could encompass the whole world, I pledge an uninterrupted and sincere search for peace. America will remain strong and united, but its strength will remain dedicated to the safety and sanity of the entire family of man, as well as to our own precious freedom.

I believe that truth is the glue that holds governments together, not only our Government, but civilization itself. That bond, though strained, is unbroken at home and abroad.

In all my public and private acts as your President, I expect to follow my instincts of openness and candor with full confidence that honesty is always the best policy in the end.

My fellow Americans, our long national nightmare is over. Our Constitution works; our great Republic is a Government of laws and not of men. Here the people rule. But there is a higher power, by whatever name we honor him, who ordains not only righteousness but love, not only justice but mercy.

As we bind up the internal wounds of Watergate, more painful and more poisonous than those of foreign wars, let us restore the golden rule to our political process, and let brotherly love purge our hearts of suspicion and of hate.

In the beginning, I asked you to pray for me. Before closing, I ask again your prayers, for Richard Nixon and his family. May our former President, who brought peace to millions, find it for himself. May God bless and comfort his wonderful wife and daughters, whose love and loyalty will forever be a shining legacy to all who bear the lonely burdens of the White House.

I can only guess at those burdens, although I have witnessed at close hand the tragedies that befell three Presidents and the lesser trials of others.

With all the strength and all the good sense I have gained from life, with all the confidence my family, my friends, and my dedicated staff impart to me, and with the good will of countless Americans I have encountered in recent visits to 40 states, I now solemnly reaffirm my promise I made to you last December 6: to uphold the Constitution, to do what is right as God gives me to see the right, and to do the very best I can for America.

God helping me, I will not let you down.

Thank you.

The Nixon Pardon

President Richard Nixon's resignation on August 9, 1974, left him subject to indictment, trial, and possible conviction for obstructing justice in the Watergate investigation. On September 8, President Gerald R. Ford used the pardon power of his office to grant Nixon a "full, free and absolute pardon ... for all offenses against the United States which he ... has committed or may have committed."

In announcing the pardon, Ford noted several reasons for his decision, including the former president's health and mental anguish and the difficulty of securing a fair trial. More than anything else, though, Ford argued that someone must write "The End" to the "American tragedy" of the Watergate affair, lest "ugly passions ... again be aroused."

Ford paid a severe political price for the Nixon pardon. He was roundly criticized and his approval rating dropped 20 percentage points in the polls.

... The Constitution is the supreme law of our land and it governs our actions as citizens. Only the laws of God, which govern our consciences, are superior to it. As we are a nation under God, so I am sworn to uphold our laws with the help of God. And I have sought such guidance and searched my own conscience with special diligence to determine the right thing for me to do with respect to my predecessor in this place, Richard Nixon, and his loyal wife and family.

Theirs is an American tragedy in which we all have played a part. It could go on and on and on, or someone must write "The End" to it.

I have concluded that only I can do that. And if I can, I must.

There are no historic or legal precedents to which I can turn in this matter, none that precisely fit the circumstances of a private citizen who has resigned the presidency of the United States. But it is common knowledge that serious allegations and accusations hang like a sword over our former President's head, threatening his health, as he tries to reshape his life, a great part of which was spent in the service of this country and by the mandate of its people.

After years of bitter controversy and divisive national debate, I have been advised and I am compelled to conclude that many months and perhaps more years will have to pass before Richard Nixon could obtain a fair trial by jury in any jurisdiction of the United States under governing decisions of the Supreme Court.

I deeply believe in equal justice for all Americans, whatever their station or former station. The law, whether human or divine, is no respecter of persons but the law is a respecter of reality. The facts as I see them are that a former President of the United States, instead of enjoying equal treatment with any other citizen accused of violating the law, would be cruelly and excessively penalized either in preserving the presumption of his innocence or in obtaining a speedy determination of his guilt in order to repay a legal debt to society.

During this long period of delay and potential litigation, ugly passions would again be aroused, and our people would again be polarized in their opinions, and the credibility of our free institutions of government would again be challenged at home and abroad. In the end, the courts might well hold that Richard Nixon had been denied due process and the verdict of history would even more be inconclusive with respect to those charges arising out of the period of his presidency of which I am presently aware.

But it is not the ultimate fate of Richard Nixon that most concerns me—though surely it deeply troubles every decent and every compassionate person. My concern is the immediate future of this great country. In this I dare not depend upon my personal sympathy as a longtime friend of the former President nor my professional judgment as a lawyer. And I do not.

As President, my greatest concern must always be the greatest good of all the people of the United States, whose servant I am.

As a man, my first consideration is to be true to my own convictions and my own conscience.

My conscience tells me clearly and certainly that I cannot prolong the bad dreams that continue to reopen a chapter that is closed. My conscience tells me that only I, as President, have the constitutional power to firmly shut and seal this book. My conscience says it is my duty, not merely to proclaim domestic tranquility, but to use every means that I have to ensure it.

I do believe that the buck stops here, that I cannot rely upon public opinion polls to tell me what is right. I do believe that right makes might, and that if I am wrong 10 angels swearing I was right would make no difference. I do believe with all my heart and mind and spirit that I, not as President, but as a humble servant of God, will receive justice without mercy if I fail to show mercy.

Finally, I feel that Richard Nixon and his loved ones have suffered enough, and will continue to suffer no matter what I do, no matter what we as a great and good nation can do together to make his goal of peace come true.

Now, therefore, I, Gerald R. Ford, President of the United States, pursuant to the pardon power conferred upon me by Article II, Section 2, of the Constitution, have granted and by these presents do grant a full, free, and absolute pardon unto Richard Nixon for all offenses against the United States which he, Richard Nixon, has committed or may have committed or taken part in during the period from January 20, 1969, through August 9, 1974.

In witness whereof, I have hereunto set my hand this 8th day of September in the year of our Lord Nineteen Hundred Seventy Four, and of the independence of the United States of America the 199th.

Carter's Remarks on the Signing of the Camp David Accords

On September 17, 1978, American president Jimmy Carter, Israeli prime minister Menachem Begin, and Egyptian president Anwar Sadat concluded thirteen days of negotiations at Camp David by announcing that two agreements had been signed. Taken together, the two documents—called "A Framework for Peace in the Middle East Agreed to at Camp David" and "A Framework for the Conclusion of a Peace Treaty Between Egypt and Israel"—provided an outline for peace in the Middle East. The former attempted (unsuccessfully, it later turned out) to provide a structure to settle the issue of control of the West Bank, which Israel had seized from the Arab nation of Jordan in the June 1967 war. The latter, which proved to be more successful, provided in part for the return of Israeli-occupied territory in the Sinai desert to Egypt in return for a treaty of peace between the two nations. The agreements were announced jointly by Carter, Begin, and Sadat on the evening of September 17. Both foreign leaders praised Carter effusively for keeping the negotiations going and bringing them to a successful conclusion.

When we first arrived at Camp David, the first thing upon which we agreed was to ask the people of the world to pray that our negotiations would be successful. Those prayers have been answered far beyond any expectations. We are privileged to witness tonight a significant achievement in the cause of peace, an achievement none thought possible a year ago, or even a month ago, an achievement that reflects the courage and wisdom of these two leaders.

Through 13 long days at Camp David, we have seen them display determination and vision and flexibility which was needed to make this agreement come to pass. All of us owe them our gratitude and respect. They know that they will always have my personal admiration.

There are still great difficulties that remain and many hard issues to be settled. The questions that have brought warfare and bitterness to the Middle East for the last 30 years will not be settled overnight. But we should all recognize the substantial achievements that have been made.

One of the agreements that President Sadat and Prime Minister Begin are signing tonight is entitled, "A Framework For Peace in the Middle East."

This framework concerns the principles and some specifics in the most substantive way which will govern a comprehensive peace settlement. It deals specifically with the future of the West Bank and Gaza, and the need to resolve the Palestinian problem in all its aspects. The framework document proposes a five-year transitional period in the West Bank and Gaza during which the Israeli military government will be withdrawn and a self-governing authority will be elected with full autonomy.

It also provides for Israeli forces to remain in specified locations during this period to protect Israel's security.

The Palestinians will have the right to participate in the determination of their own future, in negotiations which will resolve the final status of the West Bank and Gaza, and then to produce an Israeli-Jordanian peace treaty.

These negotiations will be based on all the provisions and all the principles of the United Nations Security Council Resolution 242. And it provides that Israel may live in peace within secure and recognized borders.

This great aspiration of Israel has been certified without constraint with the greatest degree of enthusiasm by President Sadat, the leader of one of the greatest nations on earth.

The other document is entitled, "Framework For the Conclusion of a Peace Treaty," between Egypt and Israel.

It provides for the full exercise of Egyptian sovereignty over the Sinai. It calls for the full withdrawal of Israeli forces from the Sinai; and after an interim withdrawal which will be accomplished very quickly, the establishment of normal, peaceful relations between the two countries, including diplomatic relations.

Together with accompanying letters, which we will make public tomorrow, these two Camp David agreements provide the basis for progress and peace throughout the Middle East.

There is one issue on which agreement has not been reached. Egypt states that the agreement to remove Israeli settlements from Egyptian territory is a prerequisite to a peace treaty. Israel states that the issue of Israeli settlements should be resolved during the peace negotiations. That is a substantial difference.

Within the next two weeks, the Knesset [Israel's parliament] will decide on the issue of these settlements.

Tomorrow night, I will go before the Congress to explain these agreements more fully, and to talk about their implications for the United States, and for the world. For the moment, and in closing, I want to speak more personally about my admiration for all those who have taken part in this process, and my hope that the promise of this moment will be fulfilled.

During the last two weeks the members of all three delegations have spent endless hours, day and night, talking, negotiating, grappling with problems that have divided their people for 30 years. Whenever there was a danger that human energy would fail, or patience would be exhausted, or good will would run out—and there were such moments—these two leaders and the able advisers in all delegations found the resources within them to keep the chances for peace alive.

Well, the long days at Camp David are over. But many months of difficult negotiations still lie ahead.

I hope that the foresight and the wisdom that have made this session a success will guide these leaders and the leaders of all nations as they continue the process toward peace.

Thank you very much.

Jimmy Carter's "Crisis of Confidence" Speech

Summer 1979 was a time of oil shortages, raging inflation, and widespread dissatisfaction with the leadership of President Jimmy Carter. In July, Carter cancelled a scheduled televised address on energy and retreated to the presidential compound at Camp David, Maryland, to reflect on the underlying causes of the energy crisis. During the course of the next week, he met there with more than a hundred invited visitors, including political, business, labor, and religious leaders. He also made some unannounced helicopter visits to speak with average families in their homes. On July 15 Carter gave a televised speech from the White House that, while dealing with energy, dwelt on the "crisis of confidence" that he believed was enfeebling the country.

Carter began with an extended mea culpa, quoting criticisms of his leadership from some of the people with whom he had spoken during his Camp David retreat. He then described "a fundamental threat to American democracy," namely, a "crisis of the American spirit" that was marked by loss of faith in the country and confidence in the future. "Restoring that faith and that confidence in America is now the most important task we face," Carter concluded.

Although Carter never spoke the word, his address soon became known as the "malaise speech." In 1980 Republican Ronald Reagan defeated Carter in his bid for reelection after proclaiming repeatedly that the United States was not lacking in confidence, but in leadership.

Good evening.

This is a special night for me. Exactly three years ago on July 15, 1976, I accepted the nomination of my party to run for President of the United States. I promised you a President who is not isolated from the people, who feels your pain and who shares your dreams and who draws his strength and his wisdom from you.

During the past 3 years I have spoken to you on many occasions about national concerns, the energy crisis, reorganizing the Government, our Nation's economy and issues of war and especially peace. But over those years the subjects of the speeches, the talks and the press conferences have become increasingly narrow, focused more and more on what the isolated world of Washington thinks is important. Gradually you have heard more and more about what the Government thinks or what the Government should be doing and less and less about our Nation's hopes, our dreams and our vision of the future.

Ten days ago I had planned to speak to you again about a very important subject—energy. For the fifth time I would have described the urgency of the problem and laid out a series of legislative recommendations to the Congress. But as I was preparing to speak, I began to ask myself the same question that I now know has been troubling many of you. Why have we not been able to get together as a nation to resolve our serious energy problem?

It's clear that the true problems of our Nation are much deeper—deeper than gasoline lines or energy shortages, deeper even than inflation or recession. And I realize more than ever that as President I need your help. So, I decided to reach out and to listen to the voices of America.

I invited to Camp David people from almost every segment of our society—business and labor, teachers and preachers, Governors, mayors and private citizens. And then I left Camp David to listen to other Americans, men and women like you. It has been an extraordinary 10 days, and I want to share with you what I've heard.

First of all, I got a lot of personal advice. Let me quote a few of the typical comments that I wrote down.

This from a southern Governor: "Mr. President, you are not leading this Nation—you're just managing the Government."

"You don't see the people enough any more."

"Some of your Cabinet members don't seem loyal. There is not enough discipline among your disciples."

"Don't talk to us about politics or the mechanics of government, but about an understanding of our common good."

"Mr. President, we're in trouble. Talk to us about blood and sweat and tears."

"If you lead, Mr. President, we will follow."

Many people talked about themselves and about the condition of our Nation. This from a young woman in Pennsylvania: "I feel so far from government. I feel like ordinary people are excluded from political power."

And this from a young Chicano: "Some of us have suffered from recession all our lives."

"Some people have wasted energy, but others haven't had anything to waste."

And this from a religious leader: "No material shortage can touch the important things like God's love for us or our love for one another."

And I like this one particularly from a black woman who happens to be the mayor of a small Mississippi town: "The big shots are not the only ones who are important. Remember, you can't sell anything on Wall Street unless someone digs it up somewhere else first."

This kind of summarized a lot of other statements: "Mr. President, we are confronted with a moral and a spiritual crisis."...

These 10 days confirmed my belief in the decency and the strength and the wisdom of the American people, but it also bore out some of my longstanding concerns about our Nation's underlying problems.

I know, of course, being President, that government actions and legislation can be very important. That is why I've worked hard to put my campaign promises into law—and I have to admit, with just mixed success. But after listening to the American people I have been reminded again that all the legislation in the world can't fix what's wrong with America. So, I want to speak to you first tonight about a subject even more serious than energy or inflation. I want to talk to you right now about a fundamental threat to American democracy.

I do not mean our political and civil liberties. They will

endure. And I do not refer to the outward strength of America, a nation that is at peace tonight everywhere in the world, with unmatched economic power and military might.

The threat is nearly invisible in ordinary ways. It is a crisis of confidence. It is a crisis that strikes at the very heart and soul and spirit of our national will. We can see this crisis in the growing doubt about the meaning of our own lives and in the loss of a unity of purpose for our Nation.

The erosion of our confidence in the future is threatening to destroy the social and the political fabric of America.

The confidence that we have always had as a people is not simply some romantic dream or a proverb in a dusty book that we read just on the Fourth of July. It is the idea we founded our Nation on and has guided our development as a people. Confidence in the future has supported everything else—public institutions and private enterprise, our own families, and the very Constitution of the United States. Confidence has defined our course and has served as a link between generations. We've always believed in something called progress. We've always had a faith that the days of our children would be better than our own.

Our people are losing that faith, not only in government itself, but in the ability as citizens to serve as the ultimate rulers and shapers of our democracy. As a people we know our past and we are proud of it. Our progress has been part of the living history of America, even the world. We always believed that we were part of a great movement of humanity itself called democracy, involved in the search for freedom and that belief has always strengthened us in our purpose. But just as we are losing our confidence in the future, we are also beginning to close the door on our past.

In a Nation that was proud of hard work, strong families, close knit communities, and our faith in God, too many of us now tend to worship self-indulgence and consumption. Human identity is no longer defined by what one does, but by what one owns. But we've discovered that owning things and consuming things does not satisfy our longing for meaning. We've learned that piling up material goods cannot fill the emptiness of lives which have no confidence or purpose.

The symptoms of this crisis of the American spirit are all around us. For the first time in the history of our country the majority of our people believe that the next 5 years will be worse than the past 5 years. Two-thirds of our people do not even vote. The productivity of American workers is actually dropping and the willingness of Americans to save for the future has fallen below that of all other people in the Western world.

As you know, there is a growing disrespect for government and for churches and for schools, the news media, and other institutions. This is not a message of happiness or reassurance, but it is the truth and it is a warning.

These changes did not happen overnight. They've come upon us gradually over the last generation, years that were filled with shocks and tragedy.

We were sure that ours was a nation of the ballot, not the bullet, until the murders of John Kennedy and Robert Kennedy and Martin Luther King Jr. We were taught that our armies were always invincible and our causes were always just, only to suffer the agony of Vietnam. We respected the Presidency as a place of honor until the shock of Watergate.

We remember when the phrase "sound as a dollar," was an expression of absolute dependability, until 10 years of inflation began to shrink our dollars and our savings. We believed that our Nation's resources were limitless until 1973 when we had to face a growing dependence on foreign oil.

These wounds are still very deep. They have never been healed.

Looking for a way out of this crisis, our people have turned to the Federal Government and found it isolated from the mainstream of our Nation's life. Washington, D.C., has become an island. The gap between our citizens and our government has never been so wide. The people are looking for honest answers, not easy answers; clear leadership, not false claims and evasiveness and politics as usual.

What you see too often in Washington and elsewhere around the country is a system of government that seems incapable of action. You see a Congress twisted and pulled in every direction by hundreds of well-financed and powerful special interests.

You see every extreme position defended to the last vote, almost to the last breath by one unyielding group or another. You often see a balanced and a fair approach that demands sacrifice, a little sacrifice from everyone, abandoned like an orphan without support and without friends.

Often you see paralysis and stagnation and drift. You don't like it, and neither do I. What can we do?

First of all, we must face the truth and then we can change our course. We simply must have faith in each other, faith in our ability to govern ourselves and faith in the future of this Nation.

Restoring that faith and that confidence to America is now the most important task we face. It is a true challenge of this generation of Americans.

One of the visitors to Camp David last week put it this way: "We've got to stop crying and start sweating, stop talking and start walking, stop cursing and start praying. The strength we need will not come from the White House, but from every house in America."

We know the strength of America. We are strong. We can regain our unity. We can regain our confidence. We are the heirs of generations who survived threats much more powerful and awesome than those that challenge us now. Our fathers and mothers were strong men and women who shaped a new society during the Great Depression, who fought world wars and who carved out a new charter of peace for the world.

We ourselves are the same Americans who just 10 years ago put a man on the moon. We are the generation that dedicated our society to the pursuit of human rights and equality. And we are the generation that will win the war on the energy problem and in that process rebuild the unity and confidence of America. . . .

Reagan's First Inaugural Address

In the 1980 presidential election, Ronald Reagan defeated President Jimmy Carter by the largest electoral vote majority in history against an incumbent president. His inauguration also was unprecedented in some ways. Reagan was the oldest person ever to be inaugurated as president. He was inaugurated on the West Front of the Capitol, not the traditional East Front. And he coordinated part of his speech with television cameras, which showed pictures of the Washington Monument, the Jefferson and Lincoln Memorials, and Arlington National Cemetery as he spoke of them.

Reagan's inaugural on January 20, 1981, advanced the two main themes of his political career, his 1980 campaign, and, subsequently, of his presidency: the ills of big government and a fervent optimism that national problems could be overcome. "In this present crisis, he said, "government is not the solution to our problem; government is the problem."

To a few of us here today this is a solemn and most momentous occasion. And, yet, in the history of our Nation it is a commonplace occurrence. The orderly transfer of authority as called for in the Constitution routinely takes place, as it has for almost two centuries, and few of us stop to think how unique we really are. In the eyes of many in the world, this every-4-year ceremony we accept as normal is nothing less than a miracle.

Mr. President, I want our fellow citizens to know how much you did to carry on this tradition. By your gracious cooperation in the transition process you have shown a watching world that we are a united people pledged to maintaining a political system which guarantees individual liberty to a greater degree than any other, and I thank you and your people for all your help in maintaining the continuity which is the hallmark of our Republic.

The business of our Nation goes forward. These United States are confronted with an economic affliction of great proportions. We suffer from the longest and one of the worst sustained inflations in our national history. It distorts our economic decisions, penalizes thrift and crushes the struggling young and the fixed-income elderly alike. It threatens to shatter the lives of millions of our people.

Idle industries have cast workers into unemployment, human misery, and personal indignity. Those who do work are denied a fair return for their labor by a tax system which penalizes successful achievement and keeps us from maintaining full productivity.

But great as our tax burden is, it has not kept pace with public spending. For decades we have piled deficit upon deficit, mortgaging our future and our children's future for the temporary convenience of the present. To continue this long trend is to guarantee tremendous social, cultural, political, and economic upheavals.

You and I, as individuals, can, by borrowing, live beyond our means, but for only a limited period of time. Why, then, should we think that collectively, as a nation, we're not bound by that same limitation? We must act today in order to preserve tomorrow. And let there be no misunderstanding—we are going to begin to act, beginning today.

The economic ills we suffer have come upon us over several decades. They will not go away in days, weeks, or months, but they will go away. They will go away because we as Americans have the capacity now, as we've had in the past, to do whatever needs to be done to preserve this last and greatest bastion of freedom.

In this present crisis, government is not the solution to our problem; government is the problem. From time to time we've been tempted to believe that society has become too complex to be managed by self-rule, that government by an elite group is superior to government for, by, and of the people. Well, if no one among us is capable of governing himself, then who among us has the capacity to govern someone else? All of us together—in and out of government—must bear the burden. The solutions we seek must be equitable with no one group singled out to pay a higher price.

We hear much of special interest groups. Well, our concern must be for a special interest group that has been too long neglected. It knows no sectional boundaries or ethnic and racial divisions, and it crosses political party lines. It is made up of men and women who raise our food, patrol our streets, man our mines and factories, teach our children, keep our homes, and heal us when we're sick—professionals, industrialists, shopkeepers, clerks, cabbies, and truck drivers. They are, in short, "We the people," this breed called Americans.

Well, this administration's objective will be a healthy, vigorous, growing economy that provides equal opportunities for all Americans with no barriers born of bigotry or discrimination. Putting America back to work means putting all Americans back to work. Ending inflation means freeing all Americans from the terror of runaway living costs. All must share in the productive work of this "new beginning," and all must share in the bounty of a revived economy. With the idealism and fair play which are the core of our system and our strength, we can have a strong and prosperous America at peace with itself and the world.

So, as we begin, let us take inventory. We are a nation that has a government—not the other way around. And this makes us special among the nations of the Earth. Our government has no power except that granted it by the people. It is time to check and reverse the growth of government which shows signs of having grown beyond the consent of the governed.

It is my intention to curb the size and influence of the Federal establishment and to demand recognition of the distinction between the powers granted to the Federal Government and those reserved to the States or to the people. All of us need to be reminded that the Federal Government did not create the States; the States created the Federal Government.

Now so there will be no misunderstanding, it's not my intention to do away with government. It is rather to make it work—work with us, not over us; to stand by our side, not ride on our back. Government can and must provide opportunity, not smother it; foster productivity, not stifle it.

If we look to the answer as to why for so many years we achieved so much, prospered as no other people on Earth, it was because here in this land we unleashed the energy and individual genius of man to a greater extent than has ever been done before. Freedom and the dignity of the individual have been more available and assured here than in any other place on Earth. The price for this freedom at times has been high. But we have never been unwilling to pay that price.

It is no coincidence that our present troubles parallel and are proportionate to the intervention and intrusion in our lives that result from unnecessary and excessive growth of government. . . .

Well, I believe we, the Americans of today, are ready to act worthy of ourselves, ready to do what must be done to ensure happiness and liberty for ourselves, our children, and our children's children. And as we renew ourselves here in our own land, we will be seen as having greater strength throughout the world. We will again be the exemplar of freedom and a beacon of hope for those who do not now have freedom.

To those neighbors and allies who share our ideal of freedom, we will strengthen our historic ties and assure them of our support and firm commitment. We will match loyalty with loyalty. We will strive for mutually beneficial relations. We will not use our friendship to impose on their sovereignty, for our own sovereignty is not for sale.

As for the enemies of freedom, those who are potential adversaries, they will be reminded that peace is the highest aspiration of the American people. We will negotiate for it, sacrifice for it; we will not surrender for it now or ever.

Our forbearance should never be misunderstood. Our reluctance for conflict should not be misjudged as a failure of will. When action is required to preserve our national security, we will act. We will maintain sufficient strength to prevail if need be, knowing that if we do so we have the best chance of never having to use that strength.

Above all we must realize that no arsenal or no weapon in the arsenals of the world is so formidable as the will and moral courage of free men and women. It is a weapon our adversaries in today's world do not have. It is a weapon that we as Americans do have. Let that be understood by those who practice terrorism and prey upon their neighbors.

I'm told that tens of thousands of prayer meetings are being held on this day, and for that I'm deeply grateful. We are a nation under God, and I believe God intended for us to be free. It would be fitting and good, I think, if each Inaugural Day in future years it should be declared a day of prayer.

This is the first time in our history that this ceremony has been held, as you've been told, on this West Front of the Capitol. Standing here, one faces a magnificent vista, opening up on this city's special beauty and history. At the end of this open mall are those shrines to the giants on whose shoulders we stand.

Directly in front of me, the monument to a monumental man. George Washington, father of our country. A man of humility who came to greatness reluctantly. He led America out of revolutionary victory into infant nationhood. Off to one side, the stately memorial to Thomas Jefferson. The Declaration of Independence flames with his eloquence. And then, beyond the Reflecting Pool, the dignified columns of the Lincoln Memorial. Whoever would understand in his heart the meaning of America will find it in the life of Abraham Lincoln.

Beyond these monuments to heroism is the Potomac River, and on the far shore the sloping hills of Arlington National Cemetery, with its row upon row of simple white markers bearing crosses or Stars of David. They add up to only a tiny fraction of the price that has been paid for our freedom.

Each one of those markers is a monument to the kind of hero I spoke of earlier. Their lives ended in places called Belleau Wood, The Argonne, Omaha Beach, Salerno, and halfway around the world on Guadalcanal, Tarawa, Pork Chop Hill, the Chosin Reservoir, and in a hundred rice paddies and jungles of a place called Vietnam. Under one such marker lies a young man, Martin Treptow, who left his job in a small town barbershop in 1917 to go to France with the famed Rainbow Division. There, on the western front, he was killed trying to carry a message between battalions under heavy artillery fire.

We're told that on his body was found a diary. On the flyleaf under the heading, "My Pledge," he had written these words: "America must win this war. Therefore I will work, I will save, I will sacrifice, I will endure, I will fight cheerfully and do my utmost, as if the issue of the whole struggle depended on me alone."

The crisis we are facing today does not require of us the kind of sacrifice that Martin Treptow and so many thousands of others were called upon to make. It does require, however, our best effort, and our willingness to believe in ourselves and to believe in our capacity to perform great deeds, to believe that together and with God's help we can and will resolve the problems which confront us.

And after all, why shouldn't we believe that? We are Americans.

God bless you, and thank you.

Reagan's Economic Plan Speech

President Ronald Reagan became known to the nation as the "Great Communicator" because of his skill, developed during a long career as a movie and television actor and public speaker, at appealing directly to the public in televised speeches from the Oval Office of the White House. Reagan's first such speech, delivered February 5, 1981, was one of his most successful. In it, he asked the American people to support his economic plan of dramatic reductions in a range of domestic federal programs and of sweeping reductions in federal income taxes. At one point, the president dramatized the nation's economic woes by holding a dollar in one hand and thirty-six cents (which he had borrowed from an aide) in the other: the coins represented the decline in the value of the dollar since 1960.

Reagan's speech had its intended effect: an unusually large outpouring of letters, telegrams, and telephone calls urging Congress to support the president's proposed policies. Within a few months, most of the Reagan economic plan was enacted.

Good evening. I am speaking to you tonight to give you a report on the state of our Nation's economy. I regret to say that we are in the worst economic mess since the Great Depression. . . .

Let me try to put this in personal terms. Here is a dollar such as you earned, spent, or saved in 1960. Here is a quarter, a dime, and a penny—36¢. That's what this 1960 dollar is worth today. And if the present inflation rate should continue three more years, that dollar of 1960 will be worth a quarter. What initiative is there to save? And if we don't save we are short of the investment capital needed for business and industry expansion. Workers in Japan and West Germany save several times the percentage of their income than Americans do.

What's happened to that American dream of owning a home? Only ten years ago a family could buy a home and the monthly payment averaged little more than a quarter—27¢ out of each dollar earned. Today it takes 42¢ out of every dollar of income. So, fewer than 1 out of 11 families can afford to buy their first new home.

Regulations adopted by government with the best of intentions have added $666 to the cost of an automobile. It is estimated that altogether regulations of every kind, on shopkeepers, farmers, and major industries add $100 billion or more to the cost of the goods and services we buy. And then another $20 billion is spent by government handling the paperwork created by those regulations.

I'm sure you are getting the idea that the audit presented to me found government policies of the last few decades responsible for our economic troubles. We forgot or just overlooked the fact that government—any government—has a built-in tendency to grow. Now, we all had a hand in looking to government for benefits as if government had some sources of revenue other than our earnings. Many if not most of the things we thought of or that government offered to us seemed attractive. . . .

By 1960 our national debt stood at $284 billion. Congress in 1971 decided to put a ceiling of $400 billion on our ability to borrow. Today the debt is $934 billion. So-called temporary increases or extensions in the debt ceiling have been allowed 21 times in these 10 years and now I have been forced to ask for another increase in the debt ceiling or the government will be unable to function past the middle of February and I've only been here 16 days. Before we reach the day when we can reduce the debt ceiling we may in spite of our best efforts see a national debt in excess of a trillion dollars. Now this is a figure literally beyond our comprehension.

We know now that inflation results from all that deficit spending. Government has only two ways of getting money other than raising taxes. It can go into the money market and borrow, competing with its own citizens and driving up interest rates, which it has done, or it can print money, and it's done that. Both methods are inflationary. . . .

One way out would be to raise taxes so that government need not borrow or print money. But in all these years of government growth we've reached—indeed surpassed—the limit of our people's tolerance or ability to bear an increase in the tax burden.

Prior to World War II, taxes were such that on the average we only had to work just a little over one month each year to pay our total Federal, state and local tax bill. Today we have to work four months to pay that bill.

Some say shift the tax burden to business and industry but business doesn't pay taxes. Oh, don't get the wrong idea, business is being taxed—so much so that we are being priced out of the world market. But business must pass its costs of operation and that includes taxes, onto the customer in the price of the product. Only people pay taxes—all the taxes. Government just uses business in a kind of sneaky way to help collect the taxes. They are hidden in the price and we aren't aware of how much tax we actually pay. Today, this once great industrial giant of ours has the lowest rate of gain in productivity of virtually all the industrial nations with whom we must compete in the world market here in America against foreign automobiles, steel and a number of other products.

Japanese production of automobiles is almost twice as great per worker as it is in America. Japanese steel workers out-produce their American counterparts by about 25 percent.

Now this isn't because they are better workers. I'll match the American working man or woman against anyone in the world. But we have to give them the tools and equipment that workers in the other industrial nations have.

We invented the assembly line and mass production, but punitive tax policies and excessive and unnecessary regulations plus government borrowing have stifled our ability to update plant and equipment. When capital investment is made it's too often for some unproductive alterations demanded by government to meet various of its regulations.

Excessive taxation of individuals has robbed us of incentive and made overtime unprofitable. . . .

All of you who are working know that even with cost-of-living pay raises you can't keep up with inflation. In our progressive tax system as you increase the number of dollars you earn you find yourself moved up into higher tax brackets, paying a higher tax rate just for trying to hold your own. The result? Your standard of living is going down.

Over the past decades we've talked of curtailing government spending so that we can then lower the tax burden. Sometimes we've even taken a run at doing that. But there were always those who told us taxes couldn't be cut until spending was reduced. Well, you know, we can lecture our children about extravagance until we run out of voice and breath. Or we can cure their extravagance by simply reducing their allowance.

It is time to recognize that we have come to a turning point. We are threatened with an economic calamity of tremendous proportions and the old business as usual treatment can't save us.

Together, we must chart a different course. We must increase productivity. That means making it possible for industry to modernize and make use of the technology which we ourselves invented: that means putting Americans back to work. And that means above all bringing government spending back within government revenues which is the only way, together with increased productivity that we can reduce and, yes, eliminate inflation.

In the past we've tried to fight inflation one year and then when unemployment increased turn the next year to fighting unemployment with more deficit spending as a pump primer. So again, up goes inflation. It hasn't worked. We don't have to choose between inflation and unemployment—they go hand in hand. It's time to try something different and that's what we're going to do.

I've already placed a freeze on hiring replacements for those who retire or leave government service. I have ordered a cut in government travel, the number of consultants to the government, and the buying of office equipment and other items. I have put a freeze on pending regulations and set up a task force under Vice President Bush to review regulations with an eye toward getting rid of as many as possible. I have decontrolled oil. And I am eliminating that ineffective Council on Wage and Price Stability.

But it will take more, much more and we must realize there is no quick fix. At the same time, however, we cannot delay in implementing an economic program aimed at both reducing rates to stimulate productivity and reducing the growth in government spending to reduce unemployment and inflation.

On February 18th, I will present in detail an economic program to Congress embodying the features I have just stated. It will propose budget cuts in virtually every department of government. It is my belief that these actual budget cuts will only be a part of the savings. As our Cabinet Secretaries take charge of their departments, they will search out areas of waste, extravagance, and costly administrative overhead which could yield additional and substantial reductions.

Now at the same time we're doing this, we must go forward with a tax relief package. I shall ask for a 10 percent reduction across the board in personal income tax rates for each of the next three years. Proposals will also be submitted for accelerated depreciation allowances for business to provide necessary capital so as to create jobs.

Now, here again, in saying this, I know that language, as I said earlier, can get in the way of a clear understanding of what our program is intended to do. Budget cuts can sound as if we are going to reduce total government spending to a lower level than was spent the year before. This is not the case. The budgets will increase as our population increases and each year we'll see spending increases to match that growth. Government revenues will increase as the economy grows, but the burden will be lighter for each individual because the economic base will have been expanded by reason of the reduced rates....

Now, in all of this we will of course work closely with the Federal Reserve System toward the objective of a stable monetary policy.

Our spending cuts will not be at the expense of the truly needy. We will, however, seek to eliminate benefits to those who are not really qualified by reason of need....

We can create the incentives which take advantage of the genius of our economic system—a system, as Walter Lippmann observed more than 40 years ago, which for the first time in history gave men "a way of producing wealth in which the good fortune of others multiplied their own."

Our aim is to increase our national wealth so all will have more not just redistribute what we already have which is just a sharing of scarcity. We can begin to reward hard work and risk-taking, by forcing this government to live within its means.

Over the years we've let negative economic forces run out of control. We've stalled the judgment day. We no longer have that luxury. We're out of time.

And to you my fellow citizens, let us join in a new determination to rebuild the foundation of our society; to work together to act responsibly. Let us do so with the most profound respect for that which must be preserved as well as with sensitive understanding and compassion for those who must be protected.

We can leave our children with an unrepayable massive debt and a shattered economy or we can leave them liberty in a land where every individual has the opportunity to be whatever God intended us to be. All it takes is a little common sense and recognition of our ability. Together we can forge a new beginning for America.

Thank you and good night.

Temporary Transfer of Power from Reagan to Bush

Section 3 of the Twenty-fifth Amendment (1967) created a procedure for a disabled president to transfer temporarily the powers and duties of the office to the vice president. President Ronald Reagan was criticized for not invoking the amendment after he was shot in March 1981. On July 13, 1985, preparing for cancer surgery, Reagan transferred power to Vice President George Bush, the first such transfer in history. Following the new constitutional procedure, Reagan sent separate letters to the Speaker of the House of Representatives and the president pro tempore of the Senate to announce both the beginning of the transfer and the end, later the same day. For eight hours, Bush was acting president.

Curiously, although Reagan's transfer of power to Bush clearly fell under the terms of the Twenty-fifth Amendment, his letter to the Speaker and president pro tempore stated that he thought the action was inappropriate to the situation.

Dear Mr. President: (Dear Mr. Speaker:)

I am about to undergo surgery during which time I will be briefly and temporarily incapable of discharging the Constitutional powers and duties of the Office of the President of the United States.

After consultation with my counsel and the Attorney General, I am mindful of the provisions of Section 3 of the 25th Amendment to the Constitution and of the uncertainties of its application to such brief and temporary periods of incapacity. I do not believe that the drafters of this Amendment intended its application to situations such as the instant one.

Nevertheless, consistent with my long-standing arrangement with Vice President George Bush, and not intending to set a precedent binding anyone privileged to hold this Office in the future, I have determined and it is my intention and direction that Vice President George Bush shall discharge those powers and duties in my stead commencing with the administration of anesthesia to me in this instance.

I shall advise you and the Vice President when I determine that I am able to resume the discharge of the Constitutional powers and duties of this Office.

May God bless this Nation and us all.

Dear Mr. President: (Dear Mr. Speaker:)

Following up on my letter to you of this date, please be advised I am able to resume the discharge of the Constitutional powers and duties of the Office of the President of the United States. I have informed the Vice President of my determination and my resumption of those powers.

Bush's Inaugural Address

George Bush was the first incumbent vice president to be elected president since Martin Van Buren was elected in 1836. Although Bush's twenty-five-year career in public life included service in Congress and in three administrations, his success in being nominated and elected president could be traced mainly to his association with President Ronald Reagan. Bush's presidential campaign oscillated between harsh invective against his Democratic opponent, Gov. Michael S. Dukakis of Massachusetts, and calls for a "kinder, gentler nation."

Both during the transition period between election and inauguration and in his inaugural address on January 20, 1989, Bush stressed the latter theme, pledging his administration "to make kinder the face of a nation and gentler the face of the world." While stressing continuity with the Reagan administration, he said repeatedly that a "new breeze is blowing" in the nation and the world.

Bush pledged his administration to work with the Democratic Congress, seeking bipartisan solutions to the budget deficit, drugs, the homeless, and other problems.

. . . We meet on democracy's front porch. A good place to talk as neighbors, and as friends. For this is a day when our nation is made whole, when our differences, for a moment, are suspended.

And my first act as President is a prayer and I ask you to bow your heads:

"Heavenly Father, we bow our heads and thank you for your love. Accept our thanks for the peace that yields this day and the shared faith that makes its continuance likely. Make us strong to do your work, willing to heed and hear your will, and write on our hearts these words: 'Use power to help people.' For we are given power not to advance our own purposes, nor to make a great show in the world, nor a name. There is but one just use of power, and it is to serve people. Help us to remember, Lord. Amen."

I come before you and assume the presidency at a moment rich with promise. We live in a peaceful, prosperous time, but we can make it better.

For a new breeze is blowing, and a world refreshed by freedom seems reborn; for in man's heart, if not in fact, the day of the dictator is over. The totalitarian era is passing, its old ideas blown away like leaves from an ancient lifeless tree. . . .

America today is a proud, free nation, decent and civil—a place we cannot help but love. We know in our hearts, not loudly and proudly, but as a simple fact, that this country has meaning beyond what we see, and that our strength is a force for good.

But have we changed as a nation even in our time? Are we enthralled with material things, less appreciative of the nobility of work and sacrifice?

My friends, we are not the sum of our possessions. They are not the measure of our lives. In our hearts we know what matters. We cannot hope only to leave our children a bigger car, a bigger bank account. We must hope to give them a sense of what it means to be a loyal friend, a loving parent, a citizen who leaves his home, his neighborhood and town better than he found it.

And what do we want the men and women who work with us to say when we are no longer there? That we were more driven to succeed than anyone around us? Or that we stopped to ask if a sick child had gotten better, and stayed a moment there to trade a word of friendship.

No President, no government, can teach us to remember what is best in what we are. But if the man you have chosen to lead this government can help make a difference; if he can celebrate the quieter, deeper successes that are made not of gold and silk, but of better hearts and finer souls; if he can do these things, then he must.

America is never wholly herself unless she is engaged in high moral principle. We as a people have such a purpose today. It is to make kinder the face of the nation and gentler the face of the world.

My friends, we have work to do. There are the homeless, lost and roaming—there are the children who have nothing, no love, no normalcy—there are those who cannot free themselves of enslavement to whatever addiction—drugs, welfare, the demoralization that rules the slums. There is crime to be conquered, the rough crime of the streets. There are young women to be helped who are about to become mothers of children they can't care for and might not love. They need our care, our guidance, and our education; though we bless them for choosing life.

The old solution, the old way, was to think that public money alone could end these problems. But we have learned that that is not so. And in any case, our funds are low. We have a deficit to bring down. We have more will than wallet; but will is what we need.

We will make the hard choices, looking at what we have, perhaps allocating it differently, making our decisions based on honest need and prudent safety.

And then we will do the wisest thing of all: We will turn to the only resource we have that in times of need always grows: the goodness and the courage of the American people.

And I am speaking of a new engagement in the lives of others—a new activism, hands-on and involved, that gets the job done. We must bring in the generations, harnessing the unused talent of the elderly and the unfocused energy of the young. For not only leadership is passed from generation to generation, but so is stewardship. And the generation born after the Second World War has come of age.

I have spoken of a thousand points of light—of all the community organizations that are spread like stars throughout the nation, doing good.

We will work hand in hand, encouraging, sometimes leading, sometimes being led, rewarding. We will work on this in the White House, in the Cabinet agencies. I will go to the people and the programs that are the brighter points of light, and I will ask every member of my government to become involved.

The old ideas are new again because they're not old, they are timeless: duty, sacrifice, commitment, and a patriotism that finds its expression in taking part and pitching in.

We need a new engagement, too, between the Executive and the Congress.

The challenges before us will be thrashed out with the House and Senate. We must bring the federal budget into balance. And we must ensure that America stands before the world united: strong, at peace, and fiscally sound. But, of course, things may be difficult.

We need compromise; we've had dissension. We need harmony; we've had a chorus of discordant voices.

For Congress, too, has changed in our time. There has grown a certain divisiveness. We have seen the hard looks and heard the statements in which not each other's ideas are challenged, but each other's motives. And our great parties have too often been far apart and untrusting of each other.

It's been this way since Vietnam. That war cleaves us still. But, friends, that war began in earnest a quarter of a century ago; and surely the statute of limitations has been reached. This is a fact: The final lesson of Vietnam is that no great nation can long afford to be sundered by a memory.

A new breeze is blowing—and the old bipartisanship must be made new again. . . .

To the world, too, we offer new engagement and a renewed vow: We will stay strong to protect the peace. The "offered hand" is a reluctant fist; once made strong, it can be used with great effect.

There are today Americans who are held against their will in foreign lands, and Americans who are unaccounted for. Assistance can be shown here, and will be long remembered. Good will begets good will. Good faith can be a spiral that endlessly moves on.

"Great nations like great men must keep their word." When America says something, America means it, whether a treaty or an agreement or a vow made on marble steps. We will always try to speak clearly, for candor is a compliment. But subtlety, too, is good and has its place.

While keeping our alliances and friendships around the world strong, ever strong, we will continue the new closeness with the Soviet Union, consistent both with our security and with progress. One might say that our new relationship in part reflects the triumph of hope and strength over experience. But hope is good.

And so is strength. And vigilance. . . .

Our children are watching in schools throughout our great land. And to them I say, thank you for watching democracy's big day. For democracy belongs to us all, and freedom is like a beautiful kite that can go higher and higher with the breeze.

And to all I say: No matter what your circumstances or where you are, you are part of this day, you are part of the life of our great nation.

A President is neither prince nor pope, and I don't seek "a window on men's souls." In fact, I yearn for a greater tolerance, an easy-goingness about each other's attitudes and way of life.

There are few clear areas in which we as a society must rise up united and express our intolerance. And the most obvious now is drugs. And when that first cocaine was smuggled in on a ship, it may as well have been a deadly bacteria, so much has it hurt the body, the soul of our country. There is much to be done and to be said, but take my word for it: This scourge will stop.

And so, there is much to do; and tomorrow the work begins.

And I do not mistrust the future; I do not fear what is ahead. For our problems are large, but our heart is larger. Our challenges are great, but our will is greater. And if our flaws are endless, God's love is truly boundless.

Some see leadership as high drama, and the sound of trumpets calling. And sometimes it is that. But I see history as a book with many pages—and each day we fill a page with acts of hopefulness and meaning.

The new breeze blows, a page turns, the story unfolds—and so today a chapter begins: a small and stately story of unity, diversity, and generosity—shared, and written, together. Thank you. God bless you. And God bless the United States of America.

Backgrounds of U.S. Presidents

President	Age at first political office	First political office	Last political office[a]	Age at becoming president	State of residence[b]	Father's occupation	Higher education[c]	Occupation
1. Washington (1789-1797)	17	County surveyor	Commander in chief	57	Va.	Farmer	None	Farmer, surveyor
2. Adams, J. (1797-1801)	39	Surveyor of highways	Vice president	61	Mass.	Farmer	Harvard	Farmer, lawyer
3. Jefferson (1801-1809)	26	State legislator	Vice president	58	Va.	Farmer	William and Mary	Farmer, lawyer
4. Madison (1809-1817)	25	State legislator	Secretary of state	58	Va.	Farmer	Princeton	Farmer
5. Monroe (1817-1825)	24	State legislator	Secretary of state	59	Va.	Farmer	William and Mary	Lawyer, farmer
6. Adams, J. Q. (1825-1829)	27	Minister to Netherlands	Secretary of state	58	Mass.	Farmer, lawyer	Harvard	Lawyer
7. Jackson (1829-1837)	21	Prosecuting attorney	U.S. Senate	62	Tenn.	Farmer	None	Lawyer
8. Van Buren (1837-1841)	30	Surrogate of county	Vice president	55	N.Y.	Tavern keeper	None	Lawyer
9. Harrison, W. H. (1841)	26	Territorial delegate to Congress	Minister to Colombia	68	Ind.	Farmer	Hampden-Sydney	Military
10. Tyler (1841-1845)	21	State legislator	Vice president	51	Va.	Planter, lawyer	William and Mary	Lawyer
11. Polk (1845-1849)	28	State legislator	Governor	50	Tenn.	Surveyor	U. of North Carolina	Lawyer
12. Taylor (1849-1850)	—	None	a	65	Ky.	Collector of internal revenue	None	Military
13. Fillmore (1850-1853)	28	State legislator	Vice president	50	N.Y.	Farmer	None	Lawyer
14. Pierce (1853-1857)	25	State legislator	U.S. district attorney	48	N.H.	General	Bowdoin	Lawyer
15. Buchanan (1857-1861)	22	Assistant county prosecutor	Minister to Great Britain	65	Pa.	Farmer	Dickinson	Lawyer
16. Lincoln (1861-1865)	25	State legislator	U.S. House of Representatives	52	Ill.	Farmer, carpenter	None	Lawyer
17. Johnson, A. (1865-1869)	20	City alderman	Vice president	57	Tenn.	Janitor-porter	None	Tailor
18. Grant (1869-1877)	—	None	a	47	Ohio	Tanner	West Point	Military
19. Hayes (1877-1881)	36	City solicitor	Governor	55	Ohio	Farmer	Kenyon	Lawyer
20. Garfield (1881)	28	State legislator	U.S. Senate	50	Ohio	Canal worker	Williams	Educator, lawyer
21. Arthur (1881-1885)	31	State engineer	Vice president	51	N.Y.	Minister	Union	Lawyer
22. Cleveland (1885-1889) 24. (1893-1897)	26	Assistant district attorney	Governor	48	N.Y.	Minister	None	Lawyer
23. Harrison, B. (1889-1893)	24	City attorney	U.S. Senate	56	Ind.	Military	Miami of Ohio	Lawyer
25. McKinley (1897-1901)	26	Prosecuting attorney	Governor	54	Ohio	Ironmonger	Allegheny	Lawyer
26. Roosevelt, T. (1901-1909)	24	State legislator	Vice president	43	N.Y.	Businessman	Harvard	Lawyer, author

President	Age at first political office	First political office	Last political office[a]	Age at becoming president	State of residence[b]	Father's occupation	Higher education[c]	Occupation
27. Taft (1909-1913)	24	Assistant prosecuting attorney	Secretary of war	52	Ohio	Lawyer	Yale	Lawyer
28. Wilson (1913-1921)	54	Governor	Governor	56	N.J.	Minister	Princeton	Educator
29. Harding (1921-1923)	35	State legislator	U.S. Senate	56	Ohio	Physician, editor	Ohio Central	Newspaper editor
30. Coolidge (1923-1929)	26	City councilman	Vice president	51	Mass.	Storekeeper	Amherst	Lawyer
31. Hoover (1929-1933)	43	Relief and food administrator	Secretary of commerce	55	Calif.	Blacksmith	Stanford	Mining engineer
32. Roosevelt, F. (1933-1945)	28	State legislator	Governor	49	N.Y.	Businessman, landowner	Harvard	Lawyer
33. Truman (1945-1953)	38	County judge (commissioner)	Vice president	61	Mo.	Farmer, livestock	None	Clerk, store owner
34. Eisenhower (1953-1961)	—	None	a	63	Kan.	Mechanic	West Point	Military
35. Kennedy (1961-1963)	29	U.S. House of Representatives	U.S. Senate	43	Mass.	Businessman	Harvard	Newspaper reporter
36. Johnson, L. (1963-1969)	23	Assistant to member, U.S. House of Representatives	Vice president	55	Texas	Farmer, real estate	Southwest Texas State Teacher's College	Educator
37. Nixon (1969-1974)	29	Office of Price Administration	Vice president	56	Calif.	Streetcar conductor	Whittier	Lawyer
38. Ford (1974-1977)	36	U.S. House of Representatives	Vice president	61	Mich.	Businessman	U. of Michigan	Lawyer
39. Carter (1977-1981)	38	County Board of Education	Governor	52	Ga.	Farmer, businessman	U.S. Naval Academy	Farmer, businessman
40. Reagan (1981-1989)	55	Governor	Governor	69	Calif.	Shoe salesman	Eureka	Entertainer
41. Bush (1989-)	42	U.S. House of Representatives	Vice president	64	Texas	Businessman, U.S. senator	Yale	Businessman

Source: Richard A. Watson and Norman C. Thomas, *The Politics of the Presidency,* 2d ed. (Washington, D.C.: CQ Press, 1988), 515-519.

a. This category refers to the last civilian office held before the presidency. Taylor, Grant, and Eisenhower had served as generals before becoming president.

b. The state is where the president spent his important adult years, not necessarily where he was born.

c. Refers to undergraduate education.

Electoral College Votes, 1789-1988

Under Article II, section 1 of the Constitution, each presidential elector had two votes and was required to cast each vote for a different person. The person receiving the highest number of votes from a majority of electors was elected president; the person receiving the second highest total became vice president. Since there were sixty-nine electors in 1789, Washington's sixty-nine votes constituted a unanimous election. After ratification of the Twelfth Amendment in 1804, electors were required to designate which of their two votes was for president and which was for vice president. The first four tables show *all* electoral votes cast in the elections of 1789, 1792, 1796, and 1800; the tables for 1804 and thereafter show only the electoral votes cast for president. A breakdown of electoral votes for vice president is given elsewhere in the Appendix. *(See "Electoral Votes for Vice President, 1804-1988," p. 1429.)*

1789

States	Electoral Votes[a]	Washington	Adams	Jay	Harrison	Rutledge	Hancock	Clinton	Huntington	Milton	Armstrong	Lincoln	Telfair
Connecticut[b]	(14)	7	5	-	-	-	-	-	2	-	-	-	-
Delaware	(6)	3	-	3	-	-	-	-	-	-	-	-	-
Georgia[b]	(10)	5	-	-	-	-	-	-	-	2	1	1	1
Maryland[c]	(16)	6	-	-	6	-	-	-	-	-	-	-	-
Massachusetts	(20)	10	10	-	-	-	-	-	-	-	-	-	-
New Hampshire	(10)	5	5	-	-	-	-	-	-	-	-	-	-
New Jersey[b]	(12)	6	1	5	-	-	-	-	-	-	-	-	-
New York[d]	(16)	-	-	-	-	-	-	-	-	-	-	-	-
North Carolina[e]	(14)	-	-	-	-	-	-	-	-	-	-	-	-
Pennsylvania[b]	(20)	10	8	-	-	-	2	-	-	-	-	-	-
Rhode Island[e]	(6)	-	-	-	-	-	-	-	-	-	-	-	-
South Carolina[b]	(14)	7	-	-	-	6	1	-	-	-	-	-	-
Virginia[f]	(24)	10	5	1	-	-	1	3	-	-	-	-	-
Totals	(182)	69	34	9	6	6	4	3	2	2	1	1	1

1792

States	Electoral Votes [1]	Washington	Adams	Clinton	Jefferson	Burr
Connecticut	(18)	9	9	-	-	-
Delaware	(6)	3	3	-	-	-
Georgia	(8)	4	-	4	-	-
Kentucky	(8)	4	-	-	4	-
Maryland[g]	(20)	8	8	-	-	-
Massachusetts	(32)	16	16	-	-	-
New Hampshire	(12)	6	6	-	-	-
New Jersey	(14)	7	7	-	-	-
New York	(24)	12	-	12	-	-
North Carolina	(24)	12	-	12	-	-
Pennsylvania[b]	(30)	15	14	1	-	-
Rhode Island	(8)	4	4	-	-	-
South Carolina[b]	(16)	8	7	-	-	1
Vermont[g]	(8)	3	3	-	-	-
Virginia	(42)	21	-	21	-	-
Totals	(270)	132	77	50	4	1

1796

States	Electoral Votes[a]	J. Adams	Jefferson	T. Pinckney	Burr	S. Adams	Ellsworth	Clinton	Jay	Iredell	Henry	Johnston	Washington	C. Pinckney
Connecticut[a]	(18)	9	-	4	-	-	-	-	5	-	-	-	-	-
Delaware	(6)	3	-	3	-	-	-	-	-	-	-	-	-	-
Georgia	(8)	-	4	-	-	-	-	4	-	-	-	-	-	-
Kentucky	(8)	-	4	-	4	-	-	-	-	-	-	-	-	-
Maryland[a]	(20)	7	4	4	3	-	-	-	-	-	2	-	-	-
Massachusetts[a]	(32)	16	-	13	-	-	1	-	-	-	-	2	-	-
New Hampshire	(12)	6	-	-	-	-	6	-	-	-	-	-	-	-
New Jersey	(14)	7	-	7	-	-	-	-	-	-	-	-	-	-
New York	(24)	12	-	12	-	-	-	-	-	-	-	-	-	-
North Carolina[a]	(24)	1	11	1	6	-	-	-	-	3	-	-	1	1
Pennsylvania[a]	(30)	1	14	2	13	-	-	-	-	-	-	-	-	-
Rhode Island	(8)	4	-	-	-	-	4	-	-	-	-	-	-	-
South Carolina	(16)	-	8	8	-	-	-	-	-	-	-	-	-	-
Tennessee	(6)	-	3	-	3	-	-	-	-	-	-	-	-	-
Vermont	(8)	4	-	4	-	-	-	-	-	-	-	-	-	-
Virginia[a]	(42)	1	20	1	1	15	-	3	-	-	-	-	1	-
Totals	(276)	71	68	59	30	15	11	7	5	3	2	2	2	1

1800

States	Electoral Votes[a]	Jefferson[h]	Burr[h]	Adams	Pinckney	Jay
Connecticut	(18)	-	-	9	9	-
Delaware	(6)	-	-	3	3	-
Georgia	(8)	4	4	-	-	-
Kentucky	(8)	4	4	-	-	-
Maryland[b]	(20)	5	5	5	5	-
Massachusetts	(32)	-	-	16	16	-
New Hampshire	(12)	-	-	6	6	-
New Jersey	(14)	-	-	7	7	-
New York	(24)	12	12	-	-	-
North Carolina[b]	(24)	8	8	4	4	-
Pennsylvania[b]	(30)	8	8	7	7	-
Rhode Island[b]	(8)	-	-	4	3	1
South Carolina	(16)	8	8	-	-	-
Tennessee	(6)	3	3	-	-	-
Vermont	(8)	-	-	4	4	-
Virginia	(42)	21	21	-	-	-
Totals	(276)	73	73	65	64	1

1804

States	Electoral Votes	Jefferson	Pinckney
Connecticut	(9)	-	9
Delaware	(3)	-	3
Georgia	(6)	6	-
Kentucky	(8)	8	-
Maryland[b]	(11)	9	2
Massachusetts	(19)	19	-
New Hampshire	(7)	7	-
New Jersey	(8)	8	-
New York	(19)	19	-
North Carolina	(14)	14	-
Ohio	(3)	3	-
Pennsylvania	(20)	20	-
Rhode Island	(4)	4	-
South Carolina	(10)	10	-
Tennessee	(5)	5	-
Vermont	(6)	6	-
Virginia	(24)	24	-
Totals	(176)	162	14

1808

States	Electoral Votes	Madison	Pinckney	Clinton
Connecticut	(9)	-	9	-
Delaware	(3)	-	3	-
Georgia	(6)	6	-	-
Kentucky[i]	(8)	7	-	-
Maryland[b]	(11)	9	2	-
Massachusetts	(19)	-	19	-
New Hampshire	(7)	-	7	-
New Jersey	(8)	8	-	-
New York[b]	(19)	13	-	6
North Carolina[b]	(14)	11	3	-
Ohio	(3)	3	-	-
Pennsylvania	(20)	20	-	-
Rhode Island	(4)	-	4	-
South Carolina	(10)	10	-	-
Tennessee	(5)	5	-	-
Vermont	(6)	6	-	-
Virginia	(24)	24	-	-
Totals	(176)	122	47	6

1812

States	Electoral Votes	Madison	Clinton
Connecticut	(9)	-	9
Delaware	(4)	-	4
Georgia	(8)	8	-
Kentucky	(12)	12	-
Louisiana	(3)	3	-
Maryland[b]	(11)	6	5
Massachusetts	(22)	-	22
New Hampshire	(8)	-	8
New Jersey	(8)	-	8
New York	(29)	-	29
North Carolina	(15)	15	-
Ohio[j]	(8)	7	-
Pennsylvania	(25)	25	-
Rhode Island	(4)	-	4
South Carolina	(11)	11	-
Tennessee	(8)	8	-
Vermont	(8)	8	-
Virginia	(25)	25	-
Totals	(218)	128	89

1816

States	Electoral Votes	Monroe	King
Connecticut	(9)	-	9
Delaware[k]	(4)	-	3
Georgia	(8)	8	-
Indiana	(3)	3	-
Kentucky	(12)	12	-
Louisiana	(3)	3	-
Maryland[k]	(11)	8	-
Massachusetts	(22)	-	22
New Hampshire	(8)	8	-
New Jersey	(8)	8	-
New York	(29)	29	-
North Carolina	(15)	15	-
Ohio	(8)	8	-
Pennsylvania	(25)	25	-
Rhode Island	(4)	4	-
South Carolina	(11)	11	-
Tennessee	(8)	8	-
Vermont	(8)	8	-
Virginia	(25)	25	-
Totals	(221)	183	34

1820

States	Electoral Votes	Monroe	Adams
Alabama	(3)	3	-
Connecticut	(9)	9	-
Delaware	(4)	4	-
Georgia	(8)	8	-
Illinois	(3)	3	-
Indiana	(3)	3	-
Kentucky	(12)	12	-
Louisiana	(3)	3	-
Maine	(9)	9	-
Maryland	(11)	11	-
Massachusetts	(15)	15	-
Mississippi[l]	(3)	2	-
Missouri	(3)	3	-
New Hampshire[b]	(8)	7	1
New Jersey	(8)	8	-
New York	(29)	29	-
North Carolina	(15)	15	-
Ohio	(8)	8	-
Pennsylvania[l]	(25)	24	-
Rhode Island	(4)	4	-
South Carolina	(11)	11	-
Tennessee[l]	(8)	7	-
Vermont	(8)	8	-
Virginia	(25)	25	-
Totals	(235)	231	1

1824

States	Electoral Votes	Jackson	Adams	Crawford	Clay
Alabama	(5)	5	-	-	-
Connecticut	(8)	-	8	-	-
Delaware[b]	(3)	-	1	2	-
Georgia	(9)	-	-	9	-
Illinois[b]	(3)	2	1	-	-
Indiana	(5)	5	-	-	-
Kentucky	(14)	-	-	-	14
Louisiana[b]	(5)	3	2	-	-
Maine	(9)	-	9	-	-
Maryland[b]	(11)	7	3	1	-
Massachusetts	(15)	-	15	-	-
Mississippi	(3)	3	-	-	-
Missouri	(3)	-	-	-	3
New Hampshire	(8)	-	8	-	-
New Jersey	(8)	8	-	-	-
New York[b]	(36)	1	26	5	4
North Carolina	(15)	15	-	-	-
Ohio	(16)	-	-	-	16
Pennsylvania	(28)	28	-	-	-
Rhode Island	(4)	-	4	-	-
South Carolina	(11)	11	-	-	-
Tennessee	(11)	11	-	-	-
Vermont	(7)	-	7	-	-
Virginia	(24)	-	-	24	-
Totals	(261)	99[m]	84	41	37

1828

States	Electoral Votes	Jackson	Adams	States	Electoral Votes	Jackson	Adams
Alabama	(5)	5	-	New Hampshire	(8)	-	8
Connecticut	(8)	-	8	New Jersey	(8)	-	8
Delaware	(3)	-	3	New York[b]	(36)	20	16
Georgia	(9)	9	-	North Carolina	(15)	15	-
Illinois	(3)	3	-	Ohio	(16)	16	-
Indiana	(5)	5	-	Pennsylvania	(28)	28	-
Kentucky	(14)	14	-	Rhode Island	(4)	-	4
Louisiana	(5)	5	-	South Carolina	(11)	11	-
Maine[b]	(9)	1	8	Tennessee	(11)	11	-
Maryland[b]	(11)	5	6	Vermont	(7)	-	7
Massachusetts	(15)	-	15	Virginia	(24)	24	-
Mississippi	(3)	3	-				
Missouri	(3)	3	-	Totals	(261)	178	83

1832

States	Electoral Votes	Jackson	Clay	Floyd	Wirt
Alabama	(7)	7	-	-	-
Connecticut	(8)	-	8	-	-
Delaware	(3)	-	3	-	-
Georgia	(11)	11	-	-	-
Illinois	(5)	5	-	-	-
Indiana	(9)	9	-	-	-
Kentucky	(15)	-	15	-	-
Louisiana	(5)	5	-	-	-
Maine	(10)	10	-	-	-
Maryland[n]	(10)	3	5	-	-
Massachusetts	(14)	-	14	-	-
Mississippi	(4)	4	-	-	-
Missouri	(4)	4	-	-	-
New Hampshire	(7)	7	-	-	-
New Jersey	(8)	8	-	-	-
New York	(42)	42	-	-	-
North Carolina	(15)	15	-	-	-
Ohio	(21)	21	-	-	-
Pennsylvania	(30)	30	-	-	-
Rhode Island	(4)	-	4	-	-
South Carolina	(11)	-	-	11	-
Tennessee	(15)	15	-	-	-
Vermont	(7)	-	-	-	7
Virginia	(23)	23	-	-	-
Totals	(288)	219	49	11	7

1836

States	Electoral Votes	Van Buren	Harrison°	White°	Webster°	Mangum
Alabama	(7)	7	-	-	-	-
Arkansas	(3)	3	-	-	-	-
Connecticut	(8)	8	-	-	-	-
Delaware	(3)	-	3	-	-	-
Georgia	(11)	-	-	11	-	-
Illinois	(5)	5	-	-	-	-
Indiana	(9)	-	9	-	-	-
Kentucky	(15)	-	15	-	-	-
Louisiana	(5)	5	-	-	-	-
Maine	(10)	10	-	-	-	-
Maryland	(10)	-	10	-	-	-
Massachusetts	(14)	-	-	-	14	-
Michigan	(3)	3	-	-	-	-
Mississippi	(4)	4	-	-	-	-
Missouri	(4)	4	-	-	-	-
New Hampshire	(7)	7	-	-	-	-
New Jersey	(8)	-	8	-	-	-
New York	(42)	42	-	-	-	-
North Carolina	(15)	15	-	-	-	-
Ohio	(21)	-	21	-	-	-
Pennsylvania	(30)	30	-	-	-	-
Rhode Island	(4)	4	-	-	-	-
South Carolina	(11)	-	-	-	-	11
Tennessee	(15)	-	-	15	-	-
Vermont	(7)	-	7	-	-	-
Virginia	(23)	23	-	-	-	-
Totals	(294)	170	73	26	14	11

1840

States	Electoral Votes	Harrison	Van Buren
Alabama	(7)	-	7
Arkansas	(3)	-	3
Connecticut	(8)	8	-
Delaware	(3)	3	-
Georgia	(11)	11	-
Illinois	(5)	-	5
Indiana	(9)	9	-
Kentucky	(15)	15	-
Louisiana	(5)	5	-
Maine	(10)	10	-
Maryland	(10)	10	-
Massachusetts	(14)	14	-
Michigan	(3)	3	-
Mississippi	(4)	4	-
Missouri	(4)	-	4
New Hampshire	(7)	-	7
New Jersey	(8)	8	-
New York	(42)	42	-
North Carolina	(15)	15	-
Ohio	(21)	21	-
Pennsylvania	(30)	30	-
Rhode Island	(4)	4	-
South Carolina	(11)	-	11
Tennessee	(15)	15	-
Vermont	(7)	7	-
Virginia	(23)	-	23
Totals	(294)	234	60

1844

States	Electoral Votes	Polk	Clay	States	Electoral Votes	Polk	Clay
Alabama	(9)	9	-	Missouri	(7)	7	-
Arkansas	(3)	3	-	New Hampshire	(6)	6	-
Connecticut	(6)	-	6	New Jersey	(7)	-	7
Delaware	(3)	-	3	New York	(36)	36	-
Georgia	(10)	10	-	North Carolina	(11)	-	11
Illinois	(9)	9	-	Ohio	(23)	-	23
Indiana	(12)	12	-	Pennsylvania	(26)	26	-
Kentucky	(12)	-	12	Rhode Island	(4)	-	4
Louisiana	(6)	6	-	South Carolina	(9)	9	-
Maine	(9)	9	-	Tennessee	(13)	-	13
Maryland	(8)	-	8	Vermont	(6)	-	6
Massachusetts	(12)	-	12	Virginia	(17)	17	-
Michigan	(5)	5	-				
Mississippi	(6)	6	-	Totals	(275)	170	105

1848

States	Electoral Votes	Taylor	Cass	States	Electoral Votes	Taylor	Cass
Alabama	(9)	-	9	Missouri	(7)	-	7
Arkansas	(3)	-	3	New Hampshire	(6)	-	6
Connecticut	(6)	6	-	New Jersey	(7)	7	-
Delaware	(3)	3	-	New York	(36)	36	-
Florida	(3)	3	-	North Carolina	(11)	11	-
Georgia	(10)	10	-	Ohio	(23)	-	23
Illinois	(9)	-	9	Pennsylvania	(26)	26	-
Indiana	(12)	-	12	Rhode Island	(4)	4	-
Iowa	(4)	-	4	South Carolina	(9)	-	9
Kentucky	(12)	12	-	Tennessee	(13)	13	-
Louisiana	(6)	6	-	Texas	(4)	-	4
Maine	(9)	-	9	Vermont	(6)	6	-
Maryland	(8)	8	-	Virginia	(17)	-	17
Massachusetts	(12)	12	-	Wisconsin	(4)	-	4
Michigan	(5)	-	5				
Mississippi	(6)	-	6	Totals	(290)	163	127

1852

States	Electoral Votes	Pierce	Scott	States	Electoral Votes	Pierce	Scott
Alabama	(9)	9	-	Missouri	(9)	9	-
Arkansas	(4)	4	-	New Hampshire	(5)	5	-
California	(4)	4	-	New Jersey	(7)	7	-
Connecticut	(6)	6	-	New York	(35)	35	-
Delaware	(3)	3	-	North Carolina	(10)	10	-
Florida	(3)	3	-	Ohio	(23)	23	-
Georgia	(10)	10	-	Pennsylvania	(27)	27	-
Illinois	(11)	11	-	Rhode Island	(4)	4	-
Indiana	(13)	13	-	South Carolina	(8)	8	-
Iowa	(4)	4	-	Tennessee	(12)	-	12
Kentucky	(12)	-	12	Texas	(4)	4	-
Louisiana	(6)	6	-	Vermont	(5)	-	5
Maine	(8)	8	-	Virginia	(15)	15	-
Maryland	(8)	8	-	Wisconsin	(5)	5	-
Massachusetts	(13)	-	13				
Michigan	(6)	6	-	Totals	(296)	254	42
Mississippi	(7)	7	-				

1856

States	Electoral Votes	Buchanan	Fremont	Fillmore
Alabama	(9)	9	-	-
Arkansas	(4)	4	-	-
California	(4)	4	-	-
Connecticut	(6)	-	6	-
Delaware	(3)	3	-	-
Florida	(3)	3	-	-
Georgia	(10)	10	-	-
Illinois	(11)	11	-	-
Indiana	(13)	13	-	-
Iowa	(4)	-	4	-
Kentucky	(12)	12	-	-
Louisiana	(6)	6	-	-
Maine	(8)	-	8	-
Maryland	(8)	-	-	8
Massachusetts	(13)	-	13	-
Michigan	(6)	-	6	-
Mississippi	(7)	7	-	-
Missouri	(9)	9	-	-
New Hampshire	(5)	-	5	-
New Jersey	(7)	7	-	-
New York	(35)	-	35	-
North Carolina	(10)	10	-	-
Ohio	(23)	-	23	-
Pennsylvania	(27)	27	-	-
Rhode Island	(4)	-	4	-
South Carolina	(8)	8	-	-
Tennessee	(12)	12	-	-
Texas	(4)	4	-	-
Vermont	(5)	-	5	-
Virginia	(15)	15	-	-
Wisconsin	(5)	-	5	-
Totals	(296)	174	114	8

1860

States	Electoral Votes	Lincoln	Breckinridge	Bell	Douglas
Alabama	(9)	-	9	-	-
Arkansas	(4)	-	4	-	-
California	(4)	4	-	-	-
Connecticut	(6)	6	-	-	-
Delaware	(3)	-	3	-	-
Florida	(3)	-	3	-	-
Georgia	(10)	-	10	-	-
Illinois	(11)	11	-	-	-
Indiana	(13)	13	-	-	-
Iowa	(4)	4	-	-	-
Kentucky	(12)	-	-	12	-
Louisiana	(6)	-	6	-	-
Maine	(8)	8	-	-	-
Maryland	(8)	-	8	-	-
Massachusetts	(13)	13	-	-	-
Michigan	(6)	6	-	-	-
Minnesota	(4)	4	-	-	-
Mississippi	(7)	-	7	-	-
Missouri	(9)	-	-	-	9
New Hampshire	(5)	5	-	-	-
New Jersey[b]	(7)	4	-	-	3
New York	(35)	35	-	-	-
North Carolina	(10)	-	10	-	-
Ohio	(23)	23	-	-	-
Oregon	(3)	3	-	-	-
Pennsylvania	(27)	27	-	-	-
Rhode Island	(4)	4	-	-	-
South Carolina	(8)	-	8	-	-
Tennessee	(12)	-	-	12	-
Texas	(4)	-	4	-	-
Vermont	(5)	5	-	-	-
Virginia	(15)	-	-	15	-
Wisconsin	(5)	5	-	-	-
Totals	(303)	180	72	39	12

1864

States[p]	Electoral Votes	Lincoln	McClellan
California	(5)	5	-
Connecticut	(6)	6	-
Delaware	(3)	-	3
Illinois	(16)	16	-
Indiana	(13)	13	-
Iowa	(8)	8	-
Kansas	(3)	3	-
Kentucky	(11)	-	11
Maine	(7)	7	-
Maryland	(7)	7	-
Massachusetts	(12)	12	-
Michigan	(8)	8	-
Minnesota	(4)	4	-
Missouri	(11)	11	-
Nevada[q]	(3)	2	-
New Hampshire	(5)	5	-
New Jersey	(7)	-	7
New York	(33)	33	-
Ohio	(21)	21	-
Oregon	(3)	3	-
Pennsylvania	(26)	26	-
Rhode Island	(4)	4	-
Vermont	(5)	5	-
West Virginia	(5)	5	-
Wisconsin	(8)	8	-
Totals	(234)	212	21

1868

States[r]	Electoral Votes	Grant	Seymour
Alabama	(8)	8	-
Arkansas	(5)	5	-
California	(5)	5	-
Connecticut	(6)	6	-
Delaware	(3)	-	3
Florida	(3)	3	-
Georgia	(9)	-	9
Illinois	(16)	16	-
Indiana	(13)	13	-
Iowa	(8)	8	-
Kansas	(3)	3	-
Kentucky	(11)	-	11
Louisiana	(7)	-	7
Maine	(7)	7	-
Maryland	(7)	-	7
Massachusetts	(12)	12	-
Michigan	(8)	8	-
Minnesota	(4)	4	-
Missouri	(11)	11	-
Nebraska	(3)	3	-
Nevada	(3)	3	-
New Hampshire	(5)	5	-
New Jersey	(7)	-	7
New York	(33)	-	33
North Carolina	(9)	9	-
Ohio	(21)	21	-
Oregon	(3)	-	3
Pennsylvania	(26)	26	-
Rhode Island	(4)	4	-
South Carolina	(6)	6	-
Tennessee	(10)	10	-
Vermont	(5)	5	-
West Virginia	(5)	5	-
Wisconsin	(8)	8	-
Totals	(294)	214	80

1872

States	Electoral Votes	Grant	Hendricks[s]	Brown[s]	Jenkins[s]	Davis[s]
Alabama	(10)	10	-	-	-	-
Arkansas[t]	(6)	-	-	-	-	-
California	(6)	6	-	-	-	-
Connecticut	(6)	6	-	-	-	-
Delaware	(3)	3	-	-	-	-
Florida	(4)	4	-	-	-	-
Georgia[u]	(11)	-	-	6	2	-
Illinois	(21)	21	-	-	-	-
Indiana	(15)	15	-	-	-	-
Iowa	(11)	11	-	-	-	-
Kansas	(5)	5	-	-	-	-
Kentucky	(12)	-	8	4	-	-
Louisiana[t]	(8)	-	-	-	-	-
Maine	(7)	7	-	-	-	-
Maryland	(8)	-	8	-	-	-
Massachusetts	(13)	13	-	-	-	-
Michigan	(11)	11	-	-	-	-
Minnesota	(5)	5	-	-	-	-
Mississippi	(8)	8	-	-	-	-
Missouri	(15)	-	6	8	-	1
Nebraska	(3)	3	-	-	-	-
Nevada	(3)	3	-	-	-	-
New Hampshire	(5)	5	-	-	-	-
New Jersey	(9)	9	-	-	-	-
New York	(35)	35	-	-	-	-
North Carolina	(10)	10	-	-	-	-
Ohio	(22)	22	-	-	-	-
Oregon	(3)	3	-	-	-	-
Pennsylvania	(29)	29	-	-	-	-
Rhode Island	(4)	4	-	-	-	-
South Carolina	(7)	7	-	-	-	-
Tennessee	(12)	-	12	-	-	-
Texas	(8)	-	8	-	-	-
Vermont	(5)	5	-	-	-	-
Virginia	(11)	11	-	-	-	-
West Virginia	(5)	5	-	-	-	-
Wisconsin	(10)	10	-	-	-	-
Totals	(366)	286	42	18	2	1

1876

States	Electoral Votes	Hayes	Tilden	States	Electoral Votes	Hayes	Tilden
Alabama	(10)	-	10	Missouri	(15)	-	15
Arkansas	(6)	-	6	Nebraska	(3)	3	-
California	(6)	6	-	Nevada	(3)	3	-
Colorado	(3)	3	-	New Hampshire	(5)	5	-
Connecticut	(6)	-	6	New Jersey	(9)	-	9
Delaware	(3)	-	3	New York	(35)	-	35
Florida[v]	(4)	4	-	North Carolina	(10)	-	10
Georgia	(11)	-	11	Ohio	(22)	22	-
Illinois	(21)	21	-	Oregon[v]	(3)	3	-
Indiana	(15)	-	15	Pennsylvania	(29)	29	-
Iowa	(11)	11	-	Rhode Island	(4)	4	-
Kansas	(5)	5	-	South Carolina[v]	(7)	7	-
Kentucky	(12)	-	12	Tennessee	(12)	-	12
Louisiana[v]	(8)	8	-	Texas	(8)	-	8
Maine	(7)	7	-	Vermont	(5)	5	-
Maryland	(8)	-	8	Virginia	(11)	-	11
Massachusetts	(13)	13	-	West Virginia	(5)	-	5
Michigan	(11)	11	-	Wisconsin	(10)	10	-
Minnesota	(5)	5	-				
Mississippi	(8)	-	8	Totals	(369)	185	184

1880

States	Electoral Votes	Garfield	Hancock	States	Electoral Votes	Garfield	Hancock
Alabama	(10)	-	10	Missouri	(15)	-	15
Arkansas	(6)	-	6	Nebraska	(3)	3	-
California[b]	(6)	1	5	Nevada	(3)	-	3
Colorado	(3)	3	-	New Hampshire	(5)	5	-
Connecticut	(6)	6	-	New Jersey	(9)	-	9
Delaware	(3)	-	3	New York	(35)	35	-
Florida	(4)	-	4	North Carolina	(10)	-	10
Georgia	(11)	-	11	Ohio	(22)	22	-
Illinois	(21)	21	-	Oregon	(3)	3	-
Indiana	(15)	15	-	Pennsylvania	(29)	29	-
Iowa	(11)	11	-	Rhode Island	(4)	4	-
Kansas	(5)	5	-	South Carolina	(7)	-	7
Kentucky	(12)	-	12	Tennessee	(12)	-	12
Louisiana	(8)	-	8	Texas	(8)	-	8
Maine	(7)	7	-	Vermont	(5)	5	-
Maryland	(8)	-	8	Virginia	(11)	-	11
Massachusetts	(13)	13	-	West Virginia	(5)	-	5
Michigan	(11)	11	-	Wisconsin	(10)	10	-
Minnesota	(5)	5	-				
Mississippi	(8)	-	8	Totals	(369)	214	155

1884

States	Electoral Votes	Cleveland	Blaine	States	Electoral Votes	Cleveland	Blaine
Alabama	(10)	10	-	Missouri	(16)	16	-
Arkansas	(7)	7	-	Nebraska	(5)	-	5
California	(8)	-	8	Nevada	(3)	-	3
Colorado	(3)	-	3	New Hampshire	(4)	-	4
Connecticut	(6)	6	-	New Jersey	(9)	9	-
Delaware	(3)	3	-	New York	(36)	36	-
Florida	(4)	4	-	North Carolina	(11)	11	-
Georgia	(12)	12	-	Ohio	(23)	-	23
Illinois	(22)	-	22	Oregon	(3)	-	3
Indiana	(15)	15	-	Pennsylvania	(30)	-	30
Iowa	(13)	-	13	Rhode Island	(4)	-	4
Kansas	(9)	-	9	South Carolina	(9)	9	-
Kentucky	(13)	13	-	Tennessee	(12)	12	-
Louisiana	(8)	8	-	Texas	(13)	13	-
Maine	(6)	-	6	Vermont	(4)	-	4
Maryland	(8)	8	-	Virginia	(12)	12	-
Massachusetts	(14)	-	14	West Virginia	(6)	6	-
Michigan	(13)	-	13	Wisconsin	(11)	-	11
Minnesota	(7)	-	7				
Mississippi	(9)	9	-	Totals	(401)	219	182

1888

States	Electoral Votes	Harrison	Cleveland	States	Electoral Votes	Harrison	Cleveland
Alabama	(10)	-	10	Missouri	(16)	-	16
Arkansas	(7)	-	7	Nebraska	(5)	5	-
California	(8)	8	-	Nevada	(3)	3	-
Colorado	(3)	3	-	New Hampshire	(4)	4	-
Connecticut	(6)	-	6	New Jersey	(9)	-	9
Delaware	(3)	-	3	New York	(36)	36	-
Florida	(4)	-	4	North Carolina	(11)	-	11
Georgia	(12)	-	12	Ohio	(23)	23	-
Illinois	(22)	22	-	Oregon	(3)	3	-
Indiana	(15)	15	-	Pennsylvania	(30)	30	-
Iowa	(13)	13	-	Rhode Island	(4)	4	-
Kansas	(9)	9	-	South Carolina	(9)	-	9
Kentucky	(13)	-	13	Tennessee	(12)	-	12
Louisiana	(8)	-	8	Texas	(13)	-	13
Maine	(6)	6	-	Vermont	(4)	4	-
Maryland	(8)	-	8	Virginia	(12)	-	12
Massachusetts	(14)	14	-	West Virginia	(6)	-	6
Michigan	(13)	13	-	Wisconsin	(11)	11	-
Minnesota	(7)	7	-				
Mississippi	(9)	-	9	Totals	(401)	233	168

1892

States	Electoral Votes	Cleveland	Harrison	Weaver
Alabama	(11)	11	-	-
Arkansas	(8)	8	-	-
California[b]	(9)	8	1	-
Colorado	(4)	-	-	4
Connecticut	(6)	6	-	-
Delaware	(3)	3	-	-
Florida	(4)	4	-	-
Georgia	(13)	13	-	-
Idaho	(3)	-	-	3
Illinois	(24)	24	-	-
Indiana	(15)	15	-	-
Iowa	(13)	-	13	-
Kansas	(10)	-	-	10
Kentucky	(13)	13	-	-
Louisiana	(8)	8	-	-
Maine	(6)	-	6	-
Maryland	(8)	8	-	-
Massachusetts	(15)	-	15	-
Michigan	(14)	5	9	-
Minnesota	(9)	-	9	-
Mississippi	(9)	9	-	-
Missouri	(17)	17	-	-
Montana	(3)	-	3	-
Nebraska	(8)	-	8	-
Nevada	(3)	-	-	3
New Hampshire	(4)	-	4	-
New Jersey	(10)	10	-	-
New York	(36)	36	-	-
North Carolina	(11)	11	-	-
North Dakota	(3)	1	1	1
Ohio	(23)	1	22	-
Oregon	(4)	-	3	1
Pennsylvania	(32)	-	32	-
Rhode Island	(4)	-	4	-
South Carolina	(9)	9	-	-
South Dakota	(4)	-	4	-
Tennessee	(12)	12	-	-
Texas	(15)	15	-	-
Vermont	(4)	-	4	-
Virginia	(12)	12	-	-
Washington	(4)	-	4	-
West Virginia	(6)	6	-	-
Wisconsin	(12)	12	-	-
Wyoming	(3)	-	3	-
Totals	(444)	277	145	22

1896

States	Electoral Votes	McKinley	Bryan
Alabama	(11)	-	11
Arkansas	(8)	-	8
California[b]	(9)	8	1
Colorado	(4)	-	4
Connecticut	(6)	6	-
Delaware	(3)	3	-
Florida	(4)	-	4
Georgia	(13)	-	13
Idaho	(3)	-	3
Illinois	(24)	24	-
Indiana	(15)	15	-
Iowa	(13)	13	-
Kansas	(10)	-	10
Kentucky[b]	(13)	12	1
Louisiana	(8)	-	8
Maine	(6)	6	-
Maryland	(8)	8	-
Massachusetts	(15)	15	-
Michigan	(14)	14	-
Minnesota	(9)	9	-
Mississippi	(9)	-	9
Missouri	(17)	-	17
Montana	(3)	-	3
Nebraska	(8)	-	8
Nevada	(3)	-	3
New Hampshire	(4)	4	-
New Jersey	(10)	10	-
New York	(36)	36	-
North Carolina	(11)	-	11
North Dakota	(3)	3	-
Ohio	(23)	23	-
Oregon	(4)	4	-
Pennsylvania	(32)	32	-
Rhode Island	(4)	4	-
South Carolina	(9)	-	9
South Dakota	(4)	-	4
Tennessee	(12)	-	12
Texas	(15)	-	15
Utah	(3)	-	3
Vermont	(4)	4	-
Virginia	(12)	-	12
Washington	(4)	-	4
West Virginia	(6)	6	-
Wisconsin	(12)	12	-
Wyoming	(3)	-	3
Totals	(447)	271	176

1900

States	Electoral Votes	McKinley	Bryan	States	Electoral Votes	McKinley	Bryan
Alabama	(11)	-	11	Nebraska	(8)	8	-
Arkansas	(8)	-	8	Nevada	(3)	-	3
California	(9)	9	-	New Hampshire	(4)	4	-
Colorado	(4)	-	4	New Jersey	(10)	10	-
Connecticut	(6)	6	-	New York	(36)	36	-
Delaware	(3)	3	-	North Carolina	(11)	-	11
Florida	(4)	-	4	North Dakota	(3)	3	-
Georgia	(13)	-	13	Ohio	(23)	23	-
Idaho	(3)	-	3	Oregon	(4)	4	-
Illinois	(24)	24	-	Pennsylvania	(32)	32	-
Indiana	(15)	15	-	Rhode Island	(4)	4	-
Iowa	(13)	13	-	South Carolina	(9)	-	9
Kansas	(10)	10	-	South Dakota	(4)	4	-
Kentucky	(13)	-	13	Tennessee	(12)	-	12
Louisiana	(8)	-	8	Texas	(15)	-	15
Maine	(6)	6	-	Utah	(3)	3	-
Maryland	(8)	8	-	Vermont	(4)	4	-
Massachusetts	(15)	15	-	Virginia	(12)	-	12
Michigan	(14)	14	-	Washington	(4)	4	-
Minnesota	(9)	9	-	West Virginia	(6)	6	-
Mississippi	(9)	-	9	Wisconsin	(12)	12	-
Missouri	(17)	-	17	Wyoming	(3)	3	-
Montana	(3)	-	3				
				Totals	(447)	292	155

1904

States	Electoral Votes	Roosevelt	Parker	States	Electoral Votes	Roosevelt	Parker
Alabama	(11)	-	11	Nebraska	(8)	8	-
Arkansas	(9)	-	9	Nevada	(3)	3	-
California	(10)	10	-	New Hampshire	(4)	4	-
Colorado	(5)	5	-	New Jersey	(12)	12	-
Connecticut	(7)	7	-	New York	(39)	39	-
Delaware	(3)	3	-	North Carolina	(12)	-	12
Florida	(5)	-	5	North Dakota	(4)	4	-
Georgia	(13)	-	13	Ohio	(23)	23	-
Idaho	(3)	3	-	Oregon	(4)	4	-
Illinois	(27)	27	-	Pennsylvania	(34)	34	-
Indiana	(15)	15	-	Rhode Island	(4)	4	-
Iowa	(13)	13	-	South Carolina	(9)	-	9
Kansas	(10)	10	-	South Dakota	(4)	4	-
Kentucky	(13)	-	13	Tennessee	(12)	-	12
Louisiana	(9)	-	9	Texas	(18)	-	18
Maine	(6)	6	-	Utah	(3)	3	-
Maryland[b]	(8)	1	7	Vermont	(4)	4	-
Massachusetts	(16)	16	-	Virginia	(12)	-	12
Michigan	(14)	14	-	Washington	(5)	5	-
Minnesota	(11)	11	-	West Virginia	(7)	7	-
Mississippi	(10)	-	10	Wisconsin	(13)	13	-
Missouri	(18)	18	-	Wyoming	(3)	3	-
Montana	(3)	3	-				
				Totals	(476)	336	140

1908

States	Electoral Votes	Taft	Bryan	States	Electoral Votes	Taft	Bryan
Alabama	(11)	-	11	Nebraska	(8)	-	8
Arkansas	(9)	-	9	Nevada	(3)	-	3
California	(10)	10	-	New Hampshire	(4)	4	-
Colorado	(5)	-	5	New Jersey	(12)	12	-
Connecticut	(7)	7	-	New York	(39)	39	-
Delaware	(3)	3	-	North Carolina	(12)	-	12
Florida	(5)	-	5	North Dakota	(4)	4	-
Georgia	(13)	-	13	Ohio	(23)	23	-
Idaho	(3)	3	-	Oklahoma	(7)	-	7
Illinois	(27)	27	-	Oregon	(4)	4	-
Indiana	(15)	15	-	Pennsylvania	(34)	34	-
Iowa	(13)	13	-	Rhode Island	(4)	4	-
Kansas	(10)	10	-	South Carolina	(9)	-	9
Kentucky	(13)	-	13	South Dakota	(4)	4	-
Louisiana	(9)	-	9	Tennessee	(12)	-	12
Maine	(6)	6	-	Texas	(18)	-	18
Maryland[b]	(8)	2	6	Utah	(3)	3	-
Massachusetts	(16)	16	-	Vermont	(4)	4	-
Michigan	(14)	14	-	Virginia	(12)	-	12
Minnesota	(11)	11	-	Washington	(5)	5	-
Mississippi	(10)	-	10	West Virginia	(7)	7	-
Missouri	(18)	18	-	Wisconsin	(13)	13	-
Montana	(3)	3	-	Wyoming	(3)	3	-
				Totals	(483)	321	162

1912

States	Electoral Votes	Wilson	Roosevelt	Taft	States	Electoral Votes	Wilson	Roosevelt	Taft
Alabama	(12)	12	-	-	Nebraska	(8)	8	-	-
Arizona	(3)	3	-	-	Nevada	(3)	3	-	-
Arkansas	(9)	9	-	-	New Hampshire	(4)	4	-	-
California[b]	(13)	2	11	-	New Jersey	(14)	14	-	-
Colorado	(6)	6	-	-	New Mexico	(3)	3	-	-
Connecticut	(7)	7	-	-	New York	(45)	45	-	-
Delaware	(3)	3	-	-	North Carolina	(12)	12	-	-
Florida	(6)	6	-	-	North Dakota	(5)	5	-	-
Georgia	(14)	14	-	-	Ohio	(24)	24	-	-
Idaho	(4)	4	-	-	Oklahoma	(10)	10	-	-
Illinois	(29)	29	-	-	Oregon	(5)	5	-	-
Indiana	(15)	15	-	-	Pennsylvania	(38)	-	38	-
Iowa	(13)	13	-	-	Rhode Island	(5)	5	-	-
Kansas	(10)	10	-	-	South Carolina	(9)	9	-	-
Kentucky	(13)	13	-	-	South Dakota	(5)	-	5	-
Louisiana	(10)	10	-	-	Tennessee	(12)	12	-	-
Maine	(6)	6	-	-	Texas	(20)	20	-	-
Maryland	(8)	8	-	-	Utah	(4)	-	-	4
Massachusetts	(18)	18	-	-	Vermont	(4)	-	-	4
Michigan	(15)	-	15	-	Virginia	(12)	12	-	-
Minnesota	(12)	-	12	-	Washington	(7)	-	7	-
Mississippi	(10)	10	-	-	West Virginia	(8)	8	-	-
Missouri	(18)	18	-	-	Wisconsin	(13)	13	-	-
Montana	(4)	4	-	-	Wyoming	(3)	3	-	-
					Totals	(531)	435	88	8

1916

States	Electoral Votes	Wilson	Hughes	States	Electoral Votes	Wilson	Hughes
Alabama	(12)	12	-	Nebraska	(8)	8	-
Arizona	(3)	3	-	Nevada	(3)	3	-
Arkansas	(9)	9	-	New Hampshire	(4)	4	-
California	(13)	13	-	New Jersey	(14)	-	14
Colorado	(6)	6	-	New Mexico	(3)	3	-
Connecticut	(7)	-	7	New York	(45)	-	45
Delaware	(3)	-	3	North Carolina	(12)	12	-
Florida	(6)	6	-	North Dakota	(5)	5	-
Georgia	(14)	14	-	Ohio	(24)	24	-
Idaho	(4)	4	-	Oklahoma	(10)	10	-
Illinois	(29)	-	29	Oregon	(5)	-	5
Indiana	(15)	-	15	Pennsylvania	(38)	-	38
Iowa	(13)	-	13	Rhode Island	(5)	-	5
Kansas	(10)	10	-	South Carolina	(9)	9	-
Kentucky	(13)	13	-	South Dakota	(5)	-	5
Louisiana	(10)	10	-	Tennessee	(12)	12	-
Maine	(6)	-	6	Texas	(20)	20	-
Maryland	(8)	8	-	Utah	(4)	4	-
Massachusetts	(18)	-	18	Vermont	(4)	-	4
Michigan	(15)	-	15	Virginia	(12)	12	-
Minnesota	(12)	-	12	Washington	(7)	7	-
Mississippi	(10)	10	-	West Virginia[b]	(8)	1	7
Missouri	(18)	18	-	Wisconsin	(13)	-	13
Montana	(4)	4	-	Wyoming	(3)	3	-
				Totals	(531)	277	254

1920

States	Electoral Votes	Harding	Cox	States	Electoral Votes	Harding	Cox
Alabama	(12)	-	12	Nebraska	(8)	8	-
Arizona	(3)	3	-	Nevada	(3)	3	-
Arkansas	(9)	-	9	New Hampshire	(4)	4	-
California	(13)	13	-	New Jersey	(14)	14	-
Colorado	(6)	6	-	New Mexico	(3)	3	-
Connecticut	(7)	7	-	New York	(45)	45	-
Delaware	(3)	3	-	North Carolina	(12)	-	12
Florida	(6)	-	6	North Dakota	(5)	5	-
Georgia	(14)	-	14	Ohio	(24)	24	-
Idaho	(4)	4	-	Oklahoma	(10)	10	-
Illinois	(29)	29	-	Oregon	(5)	5	-
Indiana	(15)	15	-	Pennsylvania	(38)	38	-
Iowa	(13)	13	-	Rhode Island	(5)	5	-
Kansas	(10)	10	-	South Carolina	(9)	-	9
Kentucky	(13)	-	13	South Dakota	(5)	5	-
Louisiana	(10)	-	10	Tennessee	(12)	12	-
Maine	(6)	6	-	Texas	(20)	-	20
Maryland	(8)	8	-	Utah	(4)	4	-
Massachusetts	(18)	18	-	Vermont	(4)	4	-
Michigan	(15)	15	-	Virginia	(12)	-	12
Minnesota	(12)	12	-	Washington	(7)	7	-
Mississippi	(10)	-	10	West Virginia	(8)	8	-
Missouri	(18)	18	-	Wisconsin	(13)	13	-
Montana	(4)	4	-	Wyoming	(3)	3	-
				Totals	(531)	404	127

1924

States	Electoral Votes	Coolidge	Davis	La Follette
Alabama	(12)	-	12	-
Arizona	(3)	3	-	-
Arkansas	(9)	-	9	-
California	(13)	13	-	-
Colorado	(6)	6	-	-
Connecticut	(7)	7	-	-
Delaware	(3)	3	-	-
Florida	(6)	-	6	-
Georgia	(14)	-	14	-
Idaho	(4)	4	-	-
Illinois	(29)	29	-	-
Indiana	(15)	15	-	-
Iowa	(13)	13	-	-
Kansas	(10)	10	-	-
Kentucky	(13)	13	-	-
Louisiana	(10)	-	10	-
Maine	(6)	6	-	-
Maryland	(8)	8	-	-
Massachusetts	(18)	18	-	-
Michigan	(15)	15	-	-
Minnesota	(12)	12	-	-
Mississippi	(10)	-	10	-
Missouri	(18)	18	-	-
Montana	(4)	4	-	-
Nebraska	(8)	8	-	-
Nevada	(3)	3	-	-
New Hampshire	(4)	4	-	-
New Jersey	(14)	14	-	-
New Mexico	(3)	3	-	-
New York	(45)	45	-	-
North Carolina	(12)	-	12	-
North Dakota	(5)	5	-	-
Ohio	(24)	24	-	-
Oklahoma	(10)	-	10	-
Oregon	(5)	5	-	-
Pennsylvania	(38)	38	-	-
Rhode Island	(5)	5	-	-
South Carolina	(9)	-	9	-
South Dakota	(5)	5	-	-
Tennessee	(12)	-	12	-
Texas	(20)	-	20	-
Utah	(4)	4	-	-
Vermont	(4)	4	-	-
Virginia	(12)	-	12	-
Washington	(7)	7	-	-
West Virginia	(8)	8	-	-
Wisconsin	(13)	-	-	13
Wyoming	(3)	3	-	-
Totals	(531)	382	136	13

1928

States	Electoral Votes	Hoover	Smith
Alabama	(12)	-	12
Arizona	(3)	3	-
Arkansas	(9)	-	9
California	(13)	13	-
Colorado	(6)	6	-
Connecticut	(7)	7	-
Delaware	(3)	3	-
Florida	(6)	6	-
Georgia	(14)	-	14
Idaho	(4)	4	-
Illinois	(29)	29	-
Indiana	(15)	15	-
Iowa	(13)	13	-
Kansas	(10)	10	-
Kentucky	(13)	13	-
Louisiana	(10)	-	10
Maine	(6)	6	-
Maryland	(8)	8	-
Massachusetts	(18)	-	18
Michigan	(15)	15	-
Minnesota	(12)	12	-
Mississippi	(10)	-	10
Missouri	(18)	18	-
Montana	(4)	4	-
Nebraska	(8)	8	-
Nevada	(3)	3	-
New Hampshire	(4)	4	-
New Jersey	(14)	14	-
New Mexico	(3)	3	-
New York	(45)	45	-
North Carolina	(12)	12	-
North Dakota	(5)	5	-
Ohio	(24)	24	-
Oklahoma	(10)	10	-
Oregon	(5)	5	-
Pennsylvania	(38)	38	-
Rhode Island	(5)	-	5
South Carolina	(9)	-	9
South Dakota	(5)	5	-
Tennessee	(12)	12	-
Texas	(20)	20	-
Utah	(4)	4	-
Vermont	(4)	4	-
Virginia	(12)	12	-
Washington	(7)	7	-
West Virginia	(8)	8	-
Wisconsin	(13)	13	-
Wyoming	(3)	3	-
Totals	(531)	444	87

1932

States	Electoral Votes	Roosevelt	Hoover	States	Electoral Votes	Roosevelt	Hoover
Alabama	(11)	11	-	Nevada	(3)	3	-
Arizona	(3)	3	-	New Hampshire	(4)	-	4
Arkansas	(9)	9	-	New Jersey	(16)	16	-
California	(22)	22	-	New Mexico	(3)	3	-
Colorado	(6)	6	-	New York	(47)	47	-
Connecticut	(8)	-	8	North Carolina	(13)	13	-
Delaware	(3)	-	3	North Dakota	(4)	4	-
Florida	(7)	7	-	Ohio	(26)	26	-
Georgia	(12)	12	-	Oklahoma	(11)	11	-
Idaho	(4)	4	-	Oregon	(5)	5	-
Illinois	(29)	29	-	Pennsylvania	(36)	-	36
Indiana	(14)	14	-	Rhode Island	(4)	4	-
Iowa	(11)	11	-	South Carolina	(8)	8	-
Kansas	(9)	9	-	South Dakota	(4)	4	-
Kentucky	(11)	11	-	Tennessee	(11)	11	-
Louisiana	(10)	10	-	Texas	(23)	23	-
Maine	(5)	-	5	Utah	(4)	4	-
Maryland	(8)	8	-	Vermont	(3)	-	3
Massachusetts	(17)	17	-	Virginia	(11)	11	-
Michigan	(19)	19	-	Washington	(8)	8	-
Minnesota	(11)	11	-	West Virginia	(8)	8	-
Mississippi	(9)	9	-	Wisconsin	(12)	12	-
Missouri	(15)	15	-	Wyoming	(3)	3	-
Montana	(4)	4	-				
Nebraska	(7)	7	-	Totals	(531)	472	59

1936

States	Electoral Votes	Roosevelt	Landon	States	Electoral Votes	Roosevelt	Landon
Alabama	(11)	11	-	Nevada	(3)	3	-
Arizona	(3)	3	-	New Hampshire	(4)	4	-
Arkansas	(9)	9	-	New Jersey	(16)	16	-
California	(22)	22	-	New Mexico	(3)	3	-
Colorado	(6)	6	-	New York	(47)	47	-
Connecticut	(8)	8	-	North Carolina	(13)	13	-
Delaware	(3)	3	-	North Dakota	(4)	4	-
Florida	(7)	7	-	Ohio	(26)	26	-
Georgia	(12)	12	-	Oklahoma	(11)	11	-
Idaho	(4)	4	-	Oregon	(5)	5	-
Illinois	(29)	29	-	Pennsylvania	(36)	36	-
Indiana	(14)	14	-	Rhode Island	(4)	4	-
Iowa	(11)	11	-	South Carolina	(8)	8	-
Kansas	(9)	9	-	South Dakota	(4)	4	-
Kentucky	(11)	11	-	Tennessee	(11)	11	-
Louisiana	(10)	10	-	Texas	(23)	23	-
Maine	(5)	-	5	Utah	(4)	4	-
Maryland	(8)	8	-	Vermont	(3)	-	3
Massachusetts	(17)	17	-	Virginia	(11)	11	-
Michigan	(19)	19	-	Washington	(8)	8	-
Minnesota	(11)	11	-	West Virginia	(8)	8	-
Mississippi	(9)	9	-	Wisconsin	(12)	12	-
Missouri	(15)	15	-	Wyoming	(3)	3	-
Montana	(4)	4	-				
Nebraska	(7)	7	-	Totals	(531)	523	8

1940

States	Electoral Votes	Roosevelt	Willkie	States	Electoral Votes	Roosevelt	Willkie
Alabama	(11)	11	-	Nevada	(3)	3	-
Arizona	(3)	3	-	New Hampshire	(4)	4	-
Arkansas	(9)	9	-	New Jersey	(16)	16	-
California	(22)	22	-	New Mexico	(3)	3	-
Colorado	(6)	-	6	New York	(47)	47	-
Connecticut	(8)	8	-	North Carolina	(13)	13	-
Delaware	(3)	3	-	North Dakota	(4)	-	4
Florida	(7)	7	-	Ohio	(26)	26	-
Georgia	(12)	12	-	Oklahoma	(11)	11	-
Idaho	(4)	4	-	Oregon	(5)	5	-
Illinois	(29)	29	-	Pennsylvania	(36)	36	-
Indiana	(14)	-	14	Rhode Island	(4)	4	-
Iowa	(11)	-	11	South Carolina	(8)	8	-
Kansas	(9)	-	9	South Dakota	(4)	-	4
Kentucky	(11)	11	-	Tennessee	(11)	11	-
Louisiana	(10)	10	-	Texas	(23)	23	-
Maine	(5)	-	5	Utah	(4)	4	-
Maryland	(8)	8	-	Vermont	(3)	-	3
Massachusetts	(17)	17	-	Virginia	(11)	11	-
Michigan	(19)	-	19	Washington	(8)	8	-
Minnesota	(11)	11	-	West Virginia	(8)	8	-
Mississippi	(9)	9	-	Wisconsin	(12)	12	-
Missouri	(15)	15	-	Wyoming	(3)	3	-
Montana	(4)	4	-				
Nebraska	(7)	-	7	Totals	(531)	449	82

1944

States	Electoral Votes	Roosevelt	Dewey	States	Electoral Votes	Roosevelt	Dewey
Alabama	(11)	11	-	Nevada	(3)	3	-
Arizona	(4)	4	-	New Hampshire	(4)	4	-
Arkansas	(9)	9	-	New Jersey	(16)	16	-
California	(25)	25	-	New Mexico	(4)	4	-
Colorado	(6)	-	6	New York	(47)	47	-
Connecticut	(8)	8	-	North Carolina	(14)	14	-
Delaware	(3)	3	-	North Dakota	(4)	-	4
Florida	(8)	8	-	Ohio	(25)	-	25
Georgia	(12)	12	-	Oklahoma	(10)	10	-
Idaho	(4)	4	-	Oregon	(6)	6	-
Illinois	(28)	28	-	Pennsylvania	(35)	35	-
Indiana	(13)	-	13	Rhode Island	(4)	4	-
Iowa	(10)	-	10	South Carolina	(8)	8	-
Kansas	(8)	-	8	South Dakota	(4)	-	4
Kentucky	(11)	11	-	Tennessee	(12)	12	-
Louisiana	(10)	10	-	Texas	(23)	23	-
Maine	(5)	-	5	Utah	(4)	4	-
Maryland	(8)	8	-	Vermont	(3)	-	3
Massachusetts	(16)	16	-	Virginia	(11)	11	-
Michigan	(19)	19	-	Washington	(8)	8	-
Minnesota	(11)	11	-	West Virginia	(8)	8	-
Mississippi	(9)	9	-	Wisconsin	(12)	-	12
Missouri	(15)	15	-	Wyoming	(3)	-	3
Montana	(4)	4	-				
Nebraska	(6)	-	6	Totals	(531)	432	99

1948

States	Electoral Votes	Truman	Dewey	Thurmond
Alabama	(11)	-	-	11
Arizona	(4)	4	-	-
Arkansas	(9)	9	-	-
California	(25)	25	-	-
Colorado	(6)	6	-	-
Connecticut	(8)	-	8	-
Delaware	(3)	-	3	-
Florida	(8)	8	-	-
Georgia	(12)	12	-	-
Idaho	(4)	4	-	-
Illinois	(28)	28	-	-
Indiana	(13)	-	13	-
Iowa	(10)	10	-	-
Kansas	(8)	-	8	-
Kentucky	(11)	11	-	-
Louisiana	(10)	-	-	10
Maine	(5)	-	5	-
Maryland	(8)	-	8	-
Massachusetts	(16)	16	-	-
Michigan	(19)	-	19	-
Minnesota	(11)	11	-	-
Mississippi	(9)	-	-	9
Missouri	(15)	15	-	-
Montana	(4)	4	-	-
Nebraska	(6)	-	6	-
Nevada	(3)	3	-	-
New Hampshire	(4)	-	4	-
New Jersey	(16)	-	16	-
New Mexico	(4)	4	-	-
New York	(47)	-	47	-
North Carolina	(14)	14	-	-
North Dakota	(4)	-	4	-
Ohio	(25)	25	-	-
Oklahoma	(10)	10	-	-
Oregon	(6)	-	6	-
Pennsylvania	(35)	-	35	-
Rhode Island	(4)	4	-	-
South Carolina	(8)	-	-	8
South Dakota	(4)	-	4	-
Tennessee[b]	(12)	11	-	1
Texas	(23)	23	-	-
Utah	(4)	4	-	-
Vermont	(3)	-	3	-
Virginia	(11)	11	-	-
Washington	(8)	8	-	-
West Virginia	(8)	8	-	-
Wisconsin	(12)	12	-	-
Wyoming	(3)	3	-	-
Totals	(531)	303	189	39

1952

States	Electoral Votes	Eisenhower	Stevenson
Alabama	(11)	-	11
Arizona	(4)	4	-
Arkansas	(8)	-	8
California	(32)	32	-
Colorado	(6)	6	-
Connecticut	(8)	8	-
Delaware	(3)	3	-
Florida	(10)	10	-
Georgia	(12)	-	12
Idaho	(4)	4	-
Illinois	(27)	27	-
Indiana	(13)	13	-
Iowa	(10)	10	-
Kansas	(8)	8	-
Kentucky	(10)	-	10
Louisiana	(10)	-	10
Maine	(5)	5	-
Maryland	(9)	9	-
Massachusetts	(16)	16	-
Michigan	(20)	20	
Minnesota	(11)	11	-
Mississippi	(8)	-	8
Missouri	(13)	13	-
Montana	(4)	4	-
Nebraska	(6)	6	-
Nevada	(3)	3	-
New Hampshire	(4)	4	-
New Jersey	(16)	16	-
New Mexico	(4)	4	-
New York	(45)	45	-
North Carolina	(14)	-	14
North Dakota	(4)	4	-
Ohio	(25)	25	-
Oklahoma	(8)	8	-
Oregon	(6)	6	-
Pennsylvania	(32)	32	-
Rhode Island	(4)	4	-
South Carolina	(8)	-	8
South Dakota	(4)	4	-
Tennessee	(11)	11	-
Texas	(24)	24	-
Utah	(4)	4	-
Vermont	(3)	3	-
Virginia	(12)	12	-
Washington	(9)	9	-
West Virginia	(8)	-	8
Wisconsin	(12)	12	-
Wyoming	(3)	3	-
Totals	(531)	442	89

1956

States	Electoral Votes	Eisenhower	Stevenson	Jones
Alabama[b]	(11)	-	10	1
Arizona	(4)	4	-	-
Arkansas	(8)	-	8	-
California	(32)	32	-	-
Colorado	(6)	6	-	-
Connecticut	(8)	8	-	-
Delaware	(3)	3	-	-
Florida	(10)	10	-	-
Georgia	(12)	-	12	-
Idaho	(4)	4	-	-
Illinois	(27)	27	-	-
Indiana	(13)	13	-	-
Iowa	(10)	10	-	-
Kansas	(8)	8	-	-
Kentucky	(10)	10	-	-
Louisiana	(10)	10	-	-
Maine	(5)	5	-	-
Maryland	(9)	9	-	-
Massachusetts	(16)	16	-	-
Michigan	(20)	20	-	-
Minnesota	(11)	11	-	-
Mississippi	(8)	-	8	-
Missouri	(13)	-	13	-
Montana	(4)	4	-	-
Nebraska	(6)	6	-	-
Nevada	(3)	3	-	-
New Hampshire	(4)	4	-	-
New Jersey	(16)	16	-	-
New Mexico	(4)	4	-	-
New York	(45)	45	-	-
North Carolina	(14)	-	14	-
North Dakota	(4)	4	-	-
Ohio	(25)	25	-	-
Oklahoma	(8)	8	-	-
Oregon	(6)	6	-	-
Pennsylvania	(32)	32	-	-
Rhode Island	(4)	4	-	-
South Carolina	(8)	-	8	-
South Dakota	(4)	4	-	-
Tennessee	(11)	11	-	-
Texas	(24)	24	-	-
Utah	(4)	4	-	-
Vermont	(3)	3	-	-
Virginia	(12)	12	-	-
Washington	(9)	9	-	-
West Virginia	(8)	8	-	-
Wisconsin	(12)	12	-	-
Wyoming	(3)	3	-	-
Totals	(531)	457	73	1

1960

States	Electoral Votes	Kennedy	Nixon	Byrd
Alabama[b]	(11)	5	-	6
Alaska	(3)	-	3	-
Arizona	(4)	-	4	-
Arkansas	(8)	8	-	-
California	(32)	-	32	-
Colorado	(6)	-	6	-
Connecticut	(8)	8	-	-
Delaware	(3)	3	-	-
Florida	(10)	-	10	-
Georgia	(12)	12	-	-
Hawaii	(3)	3	-	-
Idaho	(4)	-	4	-
Illinois	(27)	27	-	-
Indiana	(13)	-	13	-
Iowa	(10)	-	10	-
Kansas	(8)	-	8	-
Kentucky	(10)	-	10	-
Louisiana	(10)	10	-	-
Maine	(5)	-	5	-
Maryland	(9)	9	-	-
Massachusetts	(16)	16	-	-
Michigan	(20)	20	-	-
Minnesota	(11)	11	-	-
Mississippi	(8)	-	-	8
Missouri	(13)	13	-	-
Montana	(4)	-	4	-
Nebraska	(6)	-	6	-
Nevada	(3)	3	-	-
New Hampshire	(4)	-	4	-
New Jersey	(16)	16	-	-
New Mexico	(4)	4	-	-
New York	(45)	45	-	-
North Carolina	(14)	14	-	-
North Dakota	(4)	-	4	-
Ohio	(25)	-	25	-
Oklahoma	(8)	-	7	1
Oregon	(6)	-	6	-
Pennsylvania	(32)	32	-	-
Rhode Island	(4)	4	-	-
South Carolina	(8)	8	-	-
South Dakota	(4)	-	4	-
Tennessee	(11)	-	11	-
Texas	(24)	24	-	-
Utah	(4)	-	4	-
Vermont	(3)	-	3	-
Virginia	(12)	-	12	-
Washington	(9)	-	9	-
West Virginia	(8)	8	-	-
Wisconsin	(12)	-	12	-
Wyoming	(3)	-	3	-
Totals	(537)	303	219	15

1964

States	Electoral Votes	Johnson	Goldwater
Alabama	(10)	-	10
Alaska	(3)	3	-
Arizona	(5)	-	5
Arkansas	(6)	6	-
California	(40)	40	-
Colorado	(6)	6	-
Connecticut	(8)	8	-
Delaware	(3)	3	-
District of Columbia	(3)	3	-
Florida	(14)	14	-
Georgia	(12)	-	12
Hawaii	(4)	4	-
Idaho	(4)	4	-
Illinois	(26)	26	-
Indiana	(13)	13	-
Iowa	(9)	9	-
Kansas	(7)	7	-
Kentucky	(9)	9	-
Louisiana	(10)	-	10
Maine	(4)	4	-
Maryland	(10)	10	-
Massachusetts	(14)	14	-
Michigan	(21)	21	-
Minnesota	(10)	10	-
Mississippi	(7)	-	7
Missouri	(12)	12	-
Montana	(4)	4	-
Nebraska	(5)	5	-
Nevada	(3)	3	-
New Hampshire	(4)	4	-
New Jersey	(17)	17	-
New Mexico	(4)	4	-
New York	(43)	43	-
North Carolina	(13)	13	-
North Dakota	(4)	4	-
Ohio	(26)	26	-
Oklahoma	(8)	8	-
Oregon	(6)	6	-
Pennsylvania	(29)	29	-
Rhode Island	(4)	4	-
South Carolina	(8)	-	8
South Dakota	(4)	4	-
Tennessee	(11)	11	-
Texas	(25)	25	-
Utah	(4)	4	-
Vermont	(3)	3	-
Virginia	(12)	12	-
Washington	(9)	9	-
West Virginia	(7)	7	-
Wisconsin	(12)	12	-
Wyoming	(3)	3	-
Totals	(538)	486	52

1968

States	Electoral Votes	Nixon	Humphrey	Wallace
Alabama	(10)	-	-	10
Alaska	(3)	3	-	-
Arizona	(5)	5	-	-
Arkansas	(6)	-	-	6
California	(40)	40	-	-
Colorado	(6)	6	-	-
Connecticut	(8)	-	8	-
Delaware	(3)	3	-	-
District of Columbia	(3)	-	3	-
Florida	(14)	14	-	-
Georgia	(12)	-	-	12
Hawaii	(4)	-	4	-
Idaho	(4)	4	-	-
Illinois	(26)	26	-	-
Indiana	(13)	13	-	-
Iowa	(9)	9	-	-
Kansas	(7)	7	-	-
Kentucky	(9)	9	-	-
Louisiana	(10)	-	-	10
Maine	(4)	-	4	-
Maryland	(10)	-	10	-
Massachusetts	(14)	-	14	-
Michigan	(21)	-	21	-
Minnesota	(10)	-	10	-
Mississippi	(7)	-	-	7
Missouri	(12)	12	-	-
Montana	(4)	4	-	-
Nebraska	(5)	5	-	-
Nevada	(3)	3	-	-
New Hampshire	(4)	4	-	-
New Jersey	(17)	17	-	-
New Mexico	(4)	4	-	-
New York	(43)	-	43	-
North Carolina[b]	(13)	12	-	1
North Dakota	(4)	4	-	-
Ohio	(26)	26	-	-
Oklahoma	(8)	8	-	-
Oregon	(6)	6	-	-
Pennsylvania	(29)	-	29	-
Rhode Island	(4)	-	4	-
South Carolina	(8)	8	-	-
South Dakota	(4)	4	-	-
Tennessee	(11)	11	-	-
Texas	(25)	-	25	-
Utah	(4)	4	-	-
Vermont	(3)	3	-	-
Virginia	(12)	12	-	-
Washington	(9)	-	9	-
West Virginia	(7)	-	7	-
Wisconsin	(12)	12	-	-
Wyoming	(3)	3	-	-
Totals	(538)	301	191	46

1972

States	Electoral Votes	Nixon	McGovern	Hospers
Alabama	(9)	9	-	-
Alaska	(3)	3	-	-
Arizona	(6)	6	-	-
Arkansas	(6)	6	-	-
California	(45)	45	-	-
Colorado	(7)	7	-	-
Connecticut	(8)	8	-	-
Delaware	(3)	3	-	-
District of Columbia	(3)	-	3	-
Florida	(17)	17	-	-
Georgia	(12)	12	-	-
Hawaii	(4)	4	-	-
Idaho	(4)	4	-	-
Illinois	(26)	26	-	-
Indiana	(1)	13	-	-
Iowa	(8)	8	-	-
Kansas	(7)	7	-	-
Kentucky	(9)	9	-	-
Louisiana	(10)	10	-	-
Maine	(4)	4	-	-
Maryland	(10)	10	-	-
Massachusetts	(14)	-	14	-
Michigan	(21)	21	-	-
Minnesota	(10)	10	-	-
Mississippi	(7)	7	-	-
Missouri	(12)	12	-	-
Montana	(4)	4	-	-
Nebraska	(5)	5	-	-
Nevada	(3)	3	-	-
New Hampshire	(4)	4	-	-
New Jersey	(17)	17	-	-
New Mexico	(4)	4	-	-
New York	(41)	41	-	-
North Carolina	(13)	13	-	-
North Dakota	(3)	3	-	-
Ohio	(25)	25	-	-
Oklahoma	(8)	8	-	-
Oregon	(6)	6	-	-
Pennsylvania	(27)	27	-	-
Rhode Island	(4)	4	-	-
South Carolina	(8)	8	-	-
South Dakota	(4)	4	-	-
Tennessee	(10)	10	-	-
Texas	(26)	26	-	-
Utah	(4)	4	-	-
Vermont	(3)	3	-	-
Virginia[b]	(12)	11	-	1
Washington	(9)	9	-	-
West Virginia	(6)	6	-	-
Wisconsin	(11)	11	-	-
Wyoming	(3)	3	-	-
Totals	(538)	520	17	1

1976

States	Electoral Votes	Carter	Ford	Reagan
Alabama	(9)	9	-	-
Alaska	(3)	-	3	-
Arizona	(6)	-	6	-
Arkansas	(6)	6	-	-
California	(45)	-	45	-
Colorado	(7)	-	7	-
Connecticut	(8)	-	8	-
Delaware	(3)	3	-	-
District of Columbia	(3)	3	-	-
Florida	(17)	17	-	-
Georgia	(12)	12	-	-
Hawaii	(4)	4	-	-
Idaho	(4)	-	4	-
Illinois	(26)	-	26	-
Indiana	(13)	-	13	-
Iowa	(8)	-	8	-
Kansas	(7)	-	7	-
Kentucky	(9)	9	-	-
Louisiana	(10)	10	-	-
Maine	(4)	-	4	-
Maryland	(10)	10	-	-
Massachusetts	(14)	14	-	-
Michigan	(21)	-	21	-
Minnesota	(10)	10	-	-
Mississippi	(7)	7	-	-
Missouri	(12)	12	-	-
Montana	(4)	-	4	-
Nebraska	(5)	-	5	-
Nevada	(3)	-	3	-
New Hampshire	(4)	-	4	-
New Jersey	(17)	-	17	-
New Mexico	(4)	-	4	-
New York	(41)	41	-	-
North Carolina	(13)	13	-	-
North Dakota	(3)	-	3	-
Ohio	(25)	25	-	-
Oklahoma	(8)	-	8	-
Oregon	(6)	-	6	-
Pennsylvania	(27)	27	-	-
Rhode Island	(4)	4	-	-
South Carolina	(8)	8	-	-
South Dakota	(4)	-	4	-
Tennessee	(10)	10	-	-
Texas	(26)	26	-	-
Utah	(4)	-	4	-
Vermont	(3)	-	3	-
Virginia	(12)	-	12	-
Washington[b]	(9)	-	8	1
West Virginia	(6)	6	-	-
Wisconsin	(11)	11	-	-
Wyoming	(3)	-	3	-
Totals	(538)	297	240	1

1980

States	Electoral Votes	Reagan	Carter	States	Electoral Votes	Reagan	Carter
Alabama	(9)	-	9	Montana	(4)	-	4
Alaska	(3)	-	3	Nebraska	(5)	-	5
Arizona	(6)	-	6	Nevada	(3)	-	3
Arkansas	(6)	-	6	New Hampshire	(4)	-	4
California	(45)	-	45	New Jersey	(17)	-	17
Colorado	(7)	-	7	New Mexico	(4)	-	4
Connecticut	(8)	-	8	New York	(41)	-	41
Delaware	(3)	-	3	North Carolina	(13)	-	13
District of Columbia	(3)	3	-	North Dakota	(3)	-	3
Florida	(17)	-	17	Ohio	(25)	-	25
Georgia	(12)	12	-	Oklahoma	(8)	-	8
Hawaii	(4)	4	-	Oregon	(6)	-	6
Idaho	(4)	-	4	Pennsylvania	(27)	-	27
Illinois	(26)	-	26	Rhode Island	(4)	4	-
Indiana	(13)	-	13	South Carolina	(8)	-	8
Iowa	(8)	-	8	South Dakota	(4)	-	4
Kansas	(7)	-	7	Tennessee	(10)	-	10
Kentucky	(9)	-	9	Texas	(26)	-	26
Louisiana	(10)	-	10	Utah	(4)	-	4
Maine	(4)	-	4	Vermont	(3)	-	3
Maryland	(10)	10	-	Virginia	(12)	-	12
Massachusetts	(14)	-	14	Washington	(9)	-	9
Michigan	(21)	-	21	West Virginia	(6)	6	-
Minnesota	(10)	10	-	Wisconsin	(11)	-	11
Mississippi	(7)	-	7	Wyoming	(3)	-	3
Missouri	(12)	-	12	Totals	(538)	49	489

1984

States	Electoral Votes	Reagan	Mondale	States	Electoral Votes	Reagan	Mondale
Alabama	(9)	9	-	Montana	(4)	4	-
Alaska	(3)	3	-	Nebraska	(5)	5	-
Arizona	(7)	7	-	Nevada	(4)	4	-
Arkansas	(6)	6	-	New Hampshire	(4)	4	-
California	(47)	47	-	New Jersey	(16)	16	-
Colorado	(8)	8	-	New Mexico	(5)	5	-
Connecticut	(8)	8	-	New York	(36)	36	-
Delaware	(3)	3	-	North Carolina	(13)	13	-
District of Columbia	(3)	-	3	North Dakota	(3)	3	-
Florida	(21)	21	-	Ohio	(23)	23	-
Georgia	(12)	12	-	Oklahoma	(8)	8	-
Hawaii	(4)	4	-	Oregon	(7)	7	-
Idaho	(4)	4	-	Pennsylvania	(25)	25	-
Illinois	(24)	24	-	Rhode Island	(4)	4	-
Indiana	(12)	12	-	South Carolina	(8)	8	-
Iowa	(8)	8	-	South Dakota	(3)	3	-
Kansas	(7)	7	-	Tennessee	(11)	11	-
Kentucky	(9)	9	-	Texas	(29)	29	-
Louisiana	(10)	10	-	Utah	(5)	5	-
Maine	(4)	4	-	Vermont	(3)	3	-
Maryland	(10)	10	-	Virginia	(12)	12	-
Massachusetts	(13)	13	-	Washington	(10)	10	-
Michigan	(20)	20	-	West Virginia	(6)	6	-
Minnesota	(10)	-	10	Wisconsin	(11)	11	-
Mississippi	(7)	7	-	Wyoming	(3)	3	-
Missouri	(11)	11	-	Totals	(538)	525	13

1988

States	Electoral Votes	Bush	Dukakis	Bentsen
Alabama	(9)	9	-	-
Alaska	(3)	3	-	-
Arizona	(7)	7	-	-
Arkansas	(6)	6	-	-
California	(47)	47	-	-
Colorado	(8)	8	-	-
Connecticut	(8)	8	-	-
Delaware	(3)	3	-	-
District of Columbia	(3)	-	3	-
Florida	(21)	21	-	-
Georgia	(12)	12	-	-
Hawaii	(4)	-	4	-
Idaho	(4)	4	-	-
Illinois	(24)	24	-	-
Indiana	(12)	12	-	-
Iowa	(8)	-	8	-
Kansas	(7)	7	-	-
Kentucky	(9)	9	-	-
Louisiana	(10)	10	-	-
Maine	(4)	4	-	-
Maryland	(10)	10	-	-
Massachusetts	(13)	-	13	-
Michigan	(20)	20	-	-
Minnesota	(10)	-	10	-
Mississippi	(7)	7	-	-
Missouri	(11)	11	-	-
Montana	(4)	4	-	-
Nebraska	(5)	5	-	-
Nevada	(4)	4	-	-
New Hampshire	(4)	4	-	-
New Jersey	(16)	16	-	-
New Mexico	(5)	5	-	-
New York	(36)	-	36	-
North Carolina	(13)	13	-	-
North Dakota	(3)	3	-	-
Ohio	(23)	23	-	-
Oklahoma	(8)	8	-	-
Oregon	(7)	-	7	-
Pennsylvania	(25)	25	-	-
Rhode Island	(4)	-	4	-
South Carolina	(8)	8	-	-
South Dakota	(3)	3	-	-
Tennessee	(11)	11	-	-
Texas	(29)	29	-	-
Utah	(5)	5	-	-
Vermont	(3)	3	-	-
Virginia	(12)	12	-	-
Washington	(10)	-	10	-
West Virginia[b]	(6)	-	5	1
Wisconsin	(11)	-	11	-
Wyoming	(3)	3	-	-
Totals	(538)	426	111	1

Source: Guide to U.S. Elections, 2d ed. (Washington, D.C.: Congressional Quarterly Inc., 1985), 269-313.

a. Before 1804, under Article II, section 1, of the Constitution, each elector cast two votes—each for a different person. The electors did not distinguish between votes for president and vice president. The candidate receiving the second-highest total became vice president. The Twelfth Amendment, ratified in 1804, required electors to vote separately for president and vice president. See "The Twelfth Amendment," p. 159, in the Electoral Process chapter of Part II.

b. The state's electoral votes were split among two or more candidates. The district system of choosing electors accounted for split electoral votes in Maryland in 1804, 1808, 1812, 1824, 1828, and 1832; North Carolina in 1808; Illinois in 1824; and Maine and New York in 1828.

When electors were chosen by state legislatures, they sometimes chose persons loyal to more than one candidate. This caused the division of electoral votes in New York in 1808 and 1824, Delaware in 1824, and Louisiana in 1824.

Later in the nineteenth century and early in the twentieth, splits came about because several states allowed voters to choose individual electors, with electors of different parties sometimes being chosen.

Yet another cause for split electoral votes is the so-called "faithless elector," who breaks ranks and votes for a candidate not supported by his or her party. This happened in 1796 when a Pennsylvania Federalist elector voted for Democratic-Republican Thomas Jefferson instead of Federalist John Adams; in 1820 when a New Hampshire Democratic-Republican elector voted for John Quincy Adams instead of the party nominee, James Monroe; in 1948 when Preston Parks, a Truman elector in Tennessee, voted for the States Rights Dèmocratic (Dixiecrat) nominee, Gov. Strom Thurmond of South Carolina; in 1956 when W. F. Turner, a Stevenson elector in Alabama, voted for a local judge, Walter B. Jones; in 1960 when Henry D. Irwin, a Nixon elector in Oklahoma, voted for Sen. Harry F. Byrd, D-Va.; in 1968 when Dr. Lloyd W. Bailey, a Nixon elector in North Carolina, voted for George C. Wallace, the American Independent party candidate; in 1972 when Roger L. MacBride, a Nixon elector in Virginia, voted for John Hospers, the Libertarian party candidate; in 1976 when Mike Padden, a Ford elector in Washington State, voted for former governor Ronald Reagan of California; and in 1988 when Margaret Leach, a Dukakis elector in West Virginia, voted for Dukakis's running mate, Sen. Lloyd Bentsen of Texas.

c. 1789: Two Maryland electors did not vote.

d. 1789: Not voting. Because of a dispute between its two chambers, the New York legislature failed to choose electors.

e. 1789: Not voting because North Carolina had not yet ratified the Constitution.

f. 1789: Two Virginia electors did not vote and the state's electoral votes were split among five candidates.

g. 1792: Two Maryland electors and one Vermont elector did not vote.

h. 1800: Because of the Jefferson-Burr tie, the election was decided (in Jefferson's favor) by the House of Representatives. See "Jefferson's 1800 Victory," p. 268, in the Electoral Process chapter of Part II.

i. 1808: One Kentucky elector did not vote.

j. 1812: One Ohio elector did not vote.

k. 1816: One Delaware and three Maryland electors did not vote.

l. 1820: One elector each from Mississippi, Pennsylvania, and Tennessee did not vote.

m. 1824: Because no candidate received a majority of the electoral votes, the election was decided (in Adams's favor) by the House of Representatives.

n. 1832: Two Maryland electors did not vote and the state's electoral votes were split between Jackson and Clay.

o. 1836: For an explanation of the Whigs' strategy in running several candidates, see "Van Buren's 1836 Win," p. 274, in the Electoral Process chapter of Part II.

p. 1864: Eleven Southern states—Alabama, Arkansas, Florida, Georgia, Louisiana, Mississippi, North Carolina, South Carolina,

Tennessee, Texas, and Virginia—had seceded from the Union and did not vote.

q. 1864: One Nevada elector did not vote.

r. 1868: Mississippi, Texas, and Virginia were not yet readmitted to the Union and did not participate in the election.

s. 1872: Liberal Republican and Democratic presidential candidate Horace Greeley died November 29, 1872. In the electoral college, eighteen electors who had been pledged to Greeley cast their presidential electoral votes for B. Gratz Brown, Greeley's running mate.

t. 1872: Congress refused to accept the electoral votes of Arkansas and Louisiana because of disruptive conditions during Reconstruction.

u. 1872: Three Georgia electoral votes cast for Greeley were not counted.

v. 1876: The electoral votes of Florida, Louisiana, Oregon, and South Carolina were disputed. See "The Compromise of 1876," p. 286, in the Electoral Process chapter of Part II.

Electoral Votes for Vice President, 1804-1988

The following list gives the electoral votes for vice president from 1804 to 1988. Unless indicated by a note, the state-by-state breakdown of electoral votes for each vice-presidential candidate was the same as for his or her party's presidential candidate.

Prior to 1804, under Article II, section 1, of the Constitution, each elector cast two votes—each vote for a different person. The electors did not distinguish between votes for president and vice president. The candidate receiving the second highest total became vice president. The Twelfth Amendment, ratified in 1804, required electors to vote separately for president and vice president.

In some cases, persons received electoral votes although they had never been formally nominated. The word *candidate* is used in this section to designate persons receiving electoral votes.

Year	Candidate	Electoral votes
1804	George Clinton (Democratic-Republican)	162
	Rufus King (Federalist)	14
1808	George Clinton (Democratic-Republican)[a]	113
	John Langdon (Democratic-Republican)	9
	James Madison (Democratic-Republican)	3
	James Monroe (Democratic-Republican)	3
	Rufus King (Federalist)	47
1812	Elbridge Gerry (Democratic-Republican)[b]	131
	Jared Ingersoll (Federalist)	86
1816	Daniel D. Tompkins (Democratic-Republican)	183
	John E. Howard (Federalist)[c]	22
	James Ross (Federalist)	5
	John Marshall (Federalist)	4
	Robert G. Harper (Federalist)	3
1820	Daniel D. Tompkins (Democratic-Republican)[d]	218
	Richard Rush (Democratic-Republican)	1
	Richard Stockton (Federalist)	8
	Daniel Rodney (Federalist)	4
	Robert G. Harper (Federalist)	1
1824	John C. Calhoun (Democratic-Republican)[e]	182
	Nathan Sanford (Democratic-Republican)	30
	Nathaniel Macon (Democratic-Republican)	24
	Andrew Jackson (Democratic-Republican)	13
	Martin Van Buren (Democratic-Republican)	9
	Henry Clay (Democratic-Republican)	2
1828	John C. Calhoun (Democratic-Republican)[f]	171
	William Smith (Independent Democratic-Republican)	7
	Richard Rush (National Republican)	83
1832	Martin Van Buren (Democratic)[g]	189
	William Wilkins (Democratic)	30
	Henry Lee (Independent Democratic)	11
	John Sergeant (National Republican)	49
	Amos Ellmaker (Anti-Masonic)	7
1836	Richard M. Johnson (Democratic)[h]	147
	William Smith (Independent Democratic)	23
	Francis Granger (Whig)	77
	John Tyler (Whig)	47

Year	Candidate	Electoral votes
1840	John Tyler (Whig)	234
	Richard M. Johnson (Democratic)[i]	48
	L. W. Tazewell (Democratic)	11
	James K. Polk (Democratic)	1
1844	George M. Dallas (Democratic)	170
	Theodore Frelinghuysen (Whig)	105
1848	Millard Fillmore (Whig)	163
	William O. Butler (Democratic)	127
1852	William R. King (Democratic)	254
	William A. Graham (Whig)	42
1856	John C. Breckinridge (Democratic)	174
	William L. Dayton (Republican)	114
	Andrew J. Donelson (American)	8
1860	Hannibal Hamlin (Republican)	180
	Joseph Lane (Southern Democratic)	72
	Edward Everett (Constitutional Union)	39
	Herschel V. Johnson (Democratic)	12
1864	Andrew Johnson (Republican)	212
	George H. Pendleton (Democratic)	21
1868	Schuyler Colfax (Republican)	214
	Francis P. Blair (Democratic)	80
1872	Henry Wilson (Republican)	286
	Benjamin G. Brown (Democratic)[j]	47
	Alfred H. Colquitt (Democratic)	5
	John M. Palmer (Democratic)	3
	Thomas E. Bramlette (Democratic)	3
	William S. Groesbeck (Democratic)	1
	Willis B. Machen (Democratic)	1
	George W. Julian (Liberal Republican)	5
	Nathaniel P. Banks (Liberal Republican)	1
1876	William A. Wheeler (Republican)	185
	Thomas A. Hendricks (Democratic)	184
1880	Chester A. Arthur (Republican)	214
	William H. English (Democratic)	155
1884	Thomas A. Hendricks (Democratic)	219
	John A. Logan (Republican)	182
1888	Levi P. Morton (Republican)	233
	Allen G. Thurman (Democratic)	168
1892	Adlai E. Stevenson (Democratic)	277
	Whitelaw Reid (Republican)	145
	James G. Field (Populist)	22
1896	Garret A. Hobart (Republican)	271
	Arthur Sewall (Democratic)[k]	149
	Thomas E. Watson (Populist)	27
1900	Theodore Roosevelt (Republican)	292
	Adlai E. Stevenson (Democratic)	155
1904	Charles W. Fairbanks (Republican)	336
	Henry G. Davis (Democratic)	140
1908	James S. Sherman (Republican)	321
	John W. Kern (Democratic)	162
1912	Thomas R. Marshall (Democratic)	435

Year	Candidate	Electoral votes
	Hiram W. Johnson (Progressive)	88
	Nicholas M. Butler (Republican)	8
1916	Thomas R. Marshall (Democratic)	277
	Charles W. Fairbanks (Republican)	254
1920	Calvin Coolidge (Republican)	404
	Franklin D. Roosevelt (Democratic)	127
1924	Charles G. Dawes (Republican)	382
	Charles W. Bryan (Democratic)	136
	Burton K. Wheeler (Progressive)	13
1928	Charles Curtis (Republican)	444
	Joseph T. Robinson (Democratic)	87
1932	John N. Garner (Democratic)	472
	Charles Curtis (Republican)	59
1936	John N. Garner (Democratic)	523
	Frank Knox (Republican)	8
1940	Henry A. Wallace (Democratic)	449
	Charles L. McNary (Republican)	82
1944	Harry S Truman (Democratic)	432
	John W. Bricker (Republican)	99
1948	Alben W. Barkley (Democratic)	303
	Earl Warren (Republican)	189
	Fielding L. Wright (States' Rights Democratic)	39
1952	Richard Nixon (Republican)	442
	John J. Sparkman (Democratic)	89
1956	Richard Nixon (Republican)	457
	Estes Kefauver (Democratic)	73
	Herman Talmadge (Democratic)	1
1960	Lyndon B. Johnson (Democratic)	303
	Strom Thurmond (Democratic)[l]	14
	Henry Cabot Lodge (Republican)	219
	Barry Goldwater (Republican)	1
1964	Hubert H. Humphrey (Democratic)	486
	William E. Miller (Republican)	52
1968	Spiro T. Agnew (Republican)	301
	Edmund S. Muskie (Democratic)	191
	Curtis E. LeMay (American Independent)	46
1972	Spiro T. Agnew (Republican)	520
	R. Sargent Shriver (Democratic)	17
	Theodora Nathan (Libertarian)	1
1976	Walter F. Mondale (Democratic)	297
	Robert Dole (Republican)[m]	241
1980	George Bush (Republican)	489
	Walter F. Mondale (Democratic)	49
1984	George Bush (Republican)	525
	Geraldine A. Ferraro (Democratic)	13
1988	Dan Quayle (Republican)	426
	Lloyd Bentsen (Democratic)[n]	111
	Michael S. Dukakis (Democratic)	1

Source: *Guide to U.S. Elections,* 2d ed. (Washington, D.C.: Congressional Quarterly Inc., 1985), 314-315.

a. New York cast 13 presidential electoral votes for Democratic-Republican James Madison and 6 votes for Clinton; for vice president, New York cast 13 votes for Clinton, 3 votes for Madison, and 3 votes for Monroe.

Langdon received Ohio's 3 votes and Vermont's 6 votes.

b. The state-by-state vote for Gerry was the same as for Democratic-Republican presidential candidate Madison, except for Massachusetts and New Hampshire. Massachusetts cast 2 votes for Gerry and 20 votes for Ingersoll; New Hampshire cast 1 vote for Gerry and 7 votes for Ingersoll.

c. Four Federalists received vice-presidential electoral votes: Howard—Massachusetts, 22 votes; Ross—Connecticut, 5 votes; Marshall—Connecticut, 4 votes; Harper—Delaware, 3 votes.

d. The state-by-state vote for Tompkins was the same as for Democratic-Republican presidential candidate Monroe, except for Delaware, Maryland, and Massachusetts. Delaware cast 4 votes for Rodney; Maryland cast 10 votes for Tompkins and 1 for Harper; Massachusetts cast 7 votes for Tompkins and 8 for Stockton.

New Hampshire, which cast 7 presidential electoral votes for Monroe and 1 vote for John Quincy Adams, cast 7 vice-presidential electoral votes for Tompkins and 1 vote for Rush.

e. The state-by-state vice-presidential electoral vote was as follows:

Calhoun—Alabama, 5 votes; Delaware, 1 vote; Illinois, 3 votes; Indiana, 5 votes; Kentucky, 7 votes; Louisiana, 5 votes; Maine, 9 votes; Maryland, 10 votes; Massachusetts, 15 votes; Mississippi, 3 votes; New Hampshire, 7 votes; New Jersey, 8 votes; New York, 29 votes; North Carolina, 15 votes; Pennsylvania, 28 votes; Rhode Island, 3 votes; South Carolina, 11 votes; Tennessee, 11 votes; Vermont, 7 votes.

Sanford—Kentucky, 7 votes; New York, 7 votes; Ohio, 16 votes.

Macon—Virginia, 24 votes.

Jackson—Connecticut, 8 votes; Maryland, 1 vote; Missouri, 3 votes; New Hampshire, 1 vote.

Van Buren—Georgia, 9 votes.

Clay—Delaware, 2 votes.

f. The state-by-state vote for Calhoun was the same as for Democratic-Republican presidential candidate Jackson, except for Georgia, which cast 2 votes for Calhoun and 7 votes for Smith.

g. The state-by-state vote for Van Buren was the same as for Democratic-Republican presidential candidate Jackson, except for Pennsylvania, which cast 30 votes for Wilkins.

South Carolina cast 11 presidential electoral votes for Independent Democratic presidential candidate Floyd and 11 votes for Independent Democratic vice-presidential candidate Lee.

Vermont cast 7 presidential electoral votes for Anti-Masonic candidate Wirt and 7 vice-presidential electoral votes for Wirt's running mate, Ellmaker.

h. The state-by-state vote for Johnson was the same as for Democratic presidential candidate Van Buren, except for Virginia, which cast 23 votes for Smith.

Granger's state-by-state vote was the same as for Whig presidential candidate Harrison, except for Maryland and Massachusetts. Maryland cast 10 presidential electoral votes for Harrison and 10 vice-presidential votes for Tyler; Massachusetts cast 14 presidential electoral votes for Whig candidate Webster and 14 vice-presidential votes over Granger.

Tyler received 11 votes from Georgia, 10 from Maryland, 11 from South Carolina, and 15 from Tennessee.

No vice-presidential candidate received a majority of the electoral vote. As a result, the Senate, for the only time in history, selected the vice president under the provisions of the 12th Amendment. Johnson was elected vice president by a vote of 33 to 16 over Granger.

i. The Democratic party did not nominate a vice-presidential candidate in 1840. Johnson's state-by-state vote was the same as for presidential candidate Van Buren, except for South Carolina and Virginia. South Carolina cast 11 votes for Tazewell. Virginia cast 23 presidential electoral votes for Van Buren, 22 vice-presidential votes for Johnson, and 1 vice-presidential vote for Polk.

j. Liberal Republican and Democratic presidential candidate Horace Greeley died November 29, 1872. As a result, 18 electors pledged to Greeley cast their presidential electoral votes for Brown, Greeley's running mate.

The vice-presidential vote was as follows:

Brown—Georgia, 5 votes; Kentucky, 8 votes; Maryland, 8 votes; Missouri, 6 votes; Tennessee, 12 votes; Texas, 8 votes.

Colquitt—Georgia, 5 votes.

Palmer—Missouri, 3 votes.
Bramlette—Kentucky, 3 votes.
Groesbeck—Missouri, 1 vote.
Machen—Kentucky, 1 vote.
Julian—Missouri, 5 votes.
Banks—Georgia, 1 vote.

k. The state-by-state vote for Sewell was the same as for Democratic-Populist candidate William Jennings Bryan, except for the following states, which cast electoral votes for Watson: Arkansas, 3 votes; Louisiana, 4; Missouri, 4; Montana, 1; Nebraska, 4; North Carolina, 5; South Dakota, 2; Utah, 1; Washington, 2; Wyoming, 1.

l. Democratic electors carried Alabama's 11 electoral votes. Five of the electors were pledged to the national Democratic ticket of Kennedy and Johnson. Six electors ran unpledged and voted for Harry F. Byrd for president and Strom Thurmond for vice president.

Mississippi's 8 electors voted for Byrd and Thurmond.

In Oklahoma, the Republican ticket of Nixon and Lodge carried the state, but 1 of the state's 8 electors voted for Byrd for president and Goldwater for vice president.

m. One Republican elector from the state of Washington cast his presidential electoral vote for Reagan instead of the Republican nominee, Ford. But he voted for Dole, Ford's running mate, for vice president. Dole thus received one more electoral vote than Ford.

n. One Democratic elector from West Virginia cast her vice-presidential electoral vote for Dukakis, the Democratic nominee for president, and her presidential vote for his running mate, Bentsen.

Also-Rans: Electoral Vote Winners Who Did Not Become President or Vice President

This directory provides biographical summaries of candidates who received electoral votes for president or vice president but never served in those offices. Included are a number of prominent third-party candidates who received popular votes but no electoral votes. The material is organized as follows: name, state of residence in the year or years when the individual received electoral votes, party or parties with which the individual was identified when he or she received electoral votes, date of birth, date of death (where applicable), major offices held, and the year or years when the person received electoral votes. For third-party candidates who received no electoral votes, the dates indicate the year or years in which they were candidates. *(See biographies of presidents and vice presidents in Part VII.)*

For the elections of 1789, 1792, 1796, and 1800, presidential electors did not vote separately for president or vice president. It was, therefore, difficult in many cases to determine whether an individual receiving electoral votes in these elections was a candidate for president or vice president. Where no determination could be made from the sources consulted by Congressional Quarterly, the year in which the individual received electoral votes is given with no specification as to whether the individual was a candidate for president or vice president.

ADAMS, Charles Francis - Mass. (Free Soil) August 18, 1807-November 21, 1886; House, 1859-1861; minister to Great Britain, 1861-1868. Candidacy: VP - 1848.

ADAMS, Samuel - Mass. (Federalist) September 27, 1722-October 2, 1803; Continental Congress, 1774-1782; signer of Declaration of Independence; governor, 1794-1797. Candidacy: 1796.

ANDERSON, John B. - Ill. (Republican, Independent) February 15, 1922—; state's attorney, 1956-1960; House, 1961-1980. Candidacy: P - 1980.

ARMSTRONG, James - Pa. (Federalist) August 29, 1748-May 6, 1828; House, 1793-1795. Candidacy: 1789.

BANKS, Nathaniel Prentice - Mass. (Liberal Republican) January 30, 1816-September 1, 1894; House, 1853-1857, 1865-1873, 1875-1879, 1889-1891; governor, 1858-1861. Candidacy: VP - 1872.

BELL, John - Tenn. (Constitutional Union) February 15, 1797-September 10, 1869; House, 1827-1841; Speaker of the House, 1834-1835; secretary of war, 1841; Senate, 1847-1859. Candidacy: P - 1860.

BENSON, Allan Louis - N.Y. (Socialist) November 6, 1871-August 19, 1940; writer, editor; founder of *Reconstruction Magazine,* 1918. Candidacy: P - 1916.

BENTSEN, Lloyd Millard, Jr. - Texas (Democratic) February 11, 1921—; House, 1948-1955; Senate 1971—. Candidacy: VP - 1988.

BIDWELL, John - Calif. (Prohibition) August 5, 1819-April 4, 1900; California pioneer; major in Mexican War; House, 1865-1867. Candidacy: P - 1892.

BIRNEY, James Gillespie - N.Y. (Liberty) February 4, 1792-November 25, 1857; Kentucky Legislature, 1816-1817; Alabama Legislature, 1819-1820. Candidacies: P - 1840, 1844.

BLAINE, James Gillespie - Maine (Republican) January 31, 1830-January 27, 1893; House, 1863-1876; Speaker of the House, 1869-1875; Senate, 1876-1881; secretary of state, 1881, 1889-1892; president, first Pan American Congress, 1889. Candidacy: P - 1884.

BLAIR, Francis Preston, Jr. - Mo. (Democratic) February 19, 1821-July 8, 1875; House, 1857-1859, 1860, 1861-1862, 1863-1864; Senate, 1871-1873. Candidacy: VP - 1868.

BRAMLETTE, Thomas E. - Ky. (Democratic) January 3, 1817-January 12, 1875; governor, 1863-1867. Candidacy: VP - 1872.

BRICKER, John William - Ohio (Republican) September 6, 1893-March 22, 1986; attorney general of Ohio, 1933-1937; governor, 1939-1945; Senate, 1947-1959. Candidacy: VP - 1944.

BROWN, Benjamin Gratz - Mo. (Democratic) May 28, 1826-December 13, 1885; Senate, 1863-1867; governor, 1871-1873. Candidacy: VP - 1872.

BRYAN, Charles Wayland - Neb. (Democratic) February 10, 1867-March 4, 1945; governor, 1923-1925, 1931-1935; Candidacy: VP - 1924.

BRYAN, William Jennings - Neb. (Democratic, Populist) March 19, 1860-July 26, 1925; House, 1891-1895; secretary of state, 1913-1915. Candidacies: P - 1896, 1900, 1908.

BUTLER, Benjamin Franklin - Mass. (Greenback, Anti-Monopoly) November 5, 1818-January 11, 1893; House, 1867-1875, 1877-1879; governor, 1883-1884. Candidacy: P - 1884.

BUTLER, Nicholas Murray - N.Y. (Republican) April 2, 1862-December 7, 1947; president, Columbia University, 1901-1945; president, Carnegie Endowment for International Peace, 1925-1945. Candidacy: VP - 1912. (Substituted as candidate after October 30 death of nominee James S. Sherman.)

BUTLER, William Orlando - Ky. (Democratic) April 19, 1791-August 6, 1880; House, 1939-1943. Candidacy: VP - 1848.

BYRD, Harry Flood - Va. (States' Rights Democratic, Independent Democratic) June 10, 1887-October 20, 1966; governor, 1926-1930; Senate, 1933-1965. Candidacies: P - 1956, 1960.

CASS, Lewis - Mich. (Democratic) October 9, 1782-June 17, 1866; military and civil governor of Michigan Territory, 1813-1831; secretary of war, 1831-1836; minister to France, 1836-1842; Senate, 1845-1848, 1849-1857; secretary of state, 1857-1860. Candidacy: P - 1848.

CLAY, Henry - Ky. (Democratic-Republican, National Republican, Whig) April 12, 1777-June 29, 1852; Senate, 1806-1807, 1810-1811, 1831-1842, 1849-1852; House, 1811-1814, 1815-1821, 1823-1825; Speaker of the House, 1811-1814, 1815-1820, 1823-1825; secretary of state, 1825-1829. Candidacies: P - 1824, 1832, 1844.

CLINTON, De Witt - N.Y. (Independent Democratic-Republican, Federalist) March 2, 1769-February 11, 1828; Senate, 1802-1803; mayor of New York, 1803-1807, 1810, 1811, 1813, 1814; governor, 1817-1823, 1825-1828. Candidacy: P - 1812.

COLQUITT, Alfred Holt - Ga. (Democratic) April 20, 1824-March 26, 1894; House, 1853-1855; governor, 1877-1882; Senate, 1883-1894. Candidacy: VP - 1872.

COX, James Middleton - Ohio (Democratic) March 31, 1870-July 15, 1957; House, 1909-1913; governor, 1913-1915, 1917-1921. Candidacy: P - 1920.

CRAWFORD, William Harris - Ga. (Democratic-Republican) February 24, 1772-September 15, 1834; Senate, 1807-1813; president pro tempore of the Senate, 1812-13; secretary of war, 1815-1816; secretary of the treasury, 1816-1825. Candidacy: P - 1824.

DAVIS, David - Ill. (Democratic) March 9, 1815-June 26, 1886; associate justice of U.S. Supreme Court, 1862-1877; Senate, 1877-1883. Candidacy: P - 1872.

DAVIS, Henry Gassaway - W.Va. (Democratic) November 16, 1823-March 11, 1916; Senate, 1871-1883; chairman of Pan American Railway Committee, 1901-1916. Candidacy: VP - 1904.

DAVIS, John William - W.Va. (Democratic) April 13, 1873-March 24, 1955; House, 1911-1913; solicitor general, 1913-18; ambassador to Great Britain, 1918-1921. Candidacy: P - 1924.

DAYTON, William Lewis - N.J. (Republican) February 17, 1807-December 1, 1864; Senate, 1842-1851; minister to France, 1861-1864. Candidacy: VP - 1856.

DEBS, Eugene Victor - Ind. (Socialist) November 5, 1855-October 20, 1926; Indiana Legislature, 1885; president, American Railway Union, 1893-1897. Candidacies: P - 1900, 1904, 1908, 1912, 1920.

DEWEY, Thomas Edmund - N.Y. (Republican) March 24, 1902-March 16, 1971; district attorney, New York County, 1937-1941; governor, 1943-1955. Candidacies: P - 1944, 1948.

DOLE, Robert Joseph - Kan. (Republican) July 22, 1923—; House, 1961-1969; Senate, 1969—. Candidacy: VP - 1976.

DONELSON, Andrew Jackson - Tenn. (American "Know-Nothing") August 25, 1799-June 26, 1871; minister to Prussia, 1846-1848; minister to Germany, 1848-1849. Candidacy: VP - 1856.

DOUGLAS, Stephen Arnold - Ill. (Democratic) April 23, 1813-June 3, 1861; House, 1843-1847; Senate, 1847-1861. Candidacy: P - 1860.

DUKAKIS, Michael Stanley - Mass. (Democratic) November 3, 1933—; governor, 1975-1979, 1983—. Candidacy: P - 1988.

EAGLETON, Thomas Francis - Mo. (Democratic) September 4, 1929—; attorney general of Missouri, 1961-1965; lieutenant governor, 1965-1968; Senate, 1968-1987. Candidacy: VP - 1972. (Resigned from Democratic ticket July 31; replaced by R. Sargent Shriver, Jr.)

ELLMAKER, Amos - Pa. (Anti-Masonic) February 2, 1787-November 28, 1851; House, 1815; attorney general of Pennsylvania, 1816-1819, 1828-1829. Candidacy: VP - 1832.

ELLSWORTH, Oliver - Conn. (Federalist) April 29, 1745-November 26, 1807; Continental Congress, 1777-1884; Senate, 1789-1796; chief justice of United States, 1796-1800; minister to France, 1799. Candidacy: 1796.

ENGLISH, William Hayden - Ind. (Democratic) August 27, 1822-February 7, 1896; House, 1853-1861. Candidacy: VP - 1880.

EVERETT, Edward - Mass. (Constitutional Union) April 11, 1794-January 15, 1865; House, 1825-1835; governor, 1836-1840; minister to Great Britain, 1841-1845; president of Harvard University, 1846-1849; secretary of state, 1852-1853; Senate, 1853-1854. Candidacy: VP - 1860.

FERRARO, Geraldine Anne - N.Y. (Democratic) August 26, 1935—; assistant district attorney, Queens County, 1974-1978; House, 1979-1985. Candidacy: VP-1984.

FIELD, James Gaven - Va. (Populist) February 24, 1826-October 12, 1901; major in the Confederate Army, 1861-1865; attorney general of Virginia, 1877-1882. Candidacy: VP - 1892.

FISK, Clinton Bowen - N.J. (Prohibition) December 8, 1828-July 9, 1890; Civil War brevet major general; founder of Fisk University, 1866; member, Board of Indian Commissioners, 1874, president, 1881-1890. Candidacy: P - 1888.

FLOYD, John - Va. (Independent Democratic) April 24, 1783-August 17, 1837; House, 1817-1829; governor, 1830-1834. Candidacy: P - 1832.

FRELINGHUYSEN, Theodore - N.J. (Whig) March 28, 1787-April 12, 1862; attorney general of New Jersey, 1817-1829; Senate, 1829-1835; president of Rutgers College, 1850-1862. Candidacy: VP - 1844.

FREMONT, John Charles - Calif. (Republican) January 21, 1813-July 13, 1890; explorer and Army officer in West before 1847; Senate, 1850-1851; governor of Arizona Territory, 1878-1881. Candidacy: P - 1856.

GOLDWATER, Barry Morris - Ariz. (Republican) January 1, 1909—; Senate, 1953-1965, 1969-1987. Candidacies: VP - 1960; P - 1964.

GRAHAM, William Alexander - N.C. (Whig) September 5, 1804-August 11, 1875; Senate, 1840-1843; governor, 1845-1849; secretary of the Navy, 1850-1852; Confederate Senate, 1864. Candidacy: VP - 1852.

GRANGER, Francis - N.Y (Whig) December 1, 1792-August 31, 1868; House, 1835-1837, 1839-1841, 1841-1843; postmaster general, 1841. Candidacy: VP - 1836.

GREELEY, Horace - N.Y. (Liberal Republican, Democratic) February 3, 1811-November 29, 1872; founder and editor, *New York Tribune*, 1841-1872; House, 1848-1849. Candidacy: P - 1872.

GRIFFIN, S. Marvin - Ga. (American Independent) September 4, 1907-June 13, 1982; governor, 1955-1959. Candidacy: VP - 1968. (Substituted as candidate until permanent candidate Curtis LeMay was chosen.)

GROESBECK, William Slocum - Ohio (Democratic) July 24, 1815-July 7, 1897; House, 1857-1859; delegate to International Monetary Conference in Paris, 1878. Candidacy: VP - 1872.

HALE, John Parker - N.H. (Free Soil) March 31, 1806-November 19, 1873; House, 1843-1845; Senate, 1847-1853, 1855-1865; minister to Spain, 1865-1869. Candidacy: P - 1852.

HANCOCK, John - Mass. (Federalist) January 12, 1737-October 8, 1793; Continental Congress, 1775-1780, 1785-1786; president of Continental Congress, 1775-1777; governor, 1780-1785, 1787-1793. Candidacy: 1789.

HANCOCK, Winfield Scott - Pa. (Democratic) February 14, 1824-February 9, 1886; brigadier general, commander of II Army Corps, Civil War. Candidacy: P - 1880.

HARPER, Robert Goodloe - Md. (Federalist) January 1765-January 14, 1825; House, 1795-1801; Senate, 1816. Candidacies: VP - 1816, 1820.

HARRISON, Robert H. - Md. 1745-1790; chief justice, General Court of Maryland, 1781. Candidacy: 1789.

HENRY, John - Md. (Democratic-Republican) November 1750-December 16, 1798; Continental Congress, 1778-1781, 1784-1787; Senate, 1789-1797; governor, 1797-1798. Candidacy - 1796.

HOSPERS, John - Calif. (Libertarian) June 9, 1918—; director of school of philosophy at University of Southern California. Candidacy: P - 1972.

HOWARD, John Eager - Md. (Federalist) June 4, 1752-October 12, 1827; Continental Congress, 1784-1788; governor, 1788-1791; Senate, 1796-1803. Candidacy: VP - 1816.

HUGHES, Charles Evans - N.Y. (Republican) April 11, 1862-August 27, 1948; governor, 1907-1910; associate justice of U.S. Supreme Court, 1910-1916; secretary of state, 1921-1925; chief justice of United States, 1930-1941. Candidacy: P - 1916.

HUNTINGTON, Samuel - Conn., July 3, 1731-January 5, 1796; Continental Congress, 1776-1784; president of Continental Congress, 1779-1781, 1783; governor, 1786-1796. Candidacy: 1789.

INGERSOLL, Jared - Pa. (Federalist) October 24, 1749-October 31, 1822; Continental Congress, 1780-1781; Constitutional Convention, 1787. Candidacy: VP - 1812.

IREDELL, James - N.C. (Federalist) October 5, 1751-October 20, 1799; associate justice of U.S. Supreme Court, 1790-1799. Candidacy: 1796.

JAY, John - N.Y. (Federalist) December 12, 1745-May 17, 1829; Continental Congress, 1774-1777, 1778-1779; president of Continental Congress, 1778-1779; minister to Spain, 1779; chief justice of United States, 1789-1795; governor, 1795-1801. Candidacies: 1789, 1796, 1800.

JENKINS, Charles Jones - Ga. (Democratic) January 6, 1805-June 14, 1883; governor, 1865-1868. Candidacy: P - 1872.

JOHNSON, Herschel Vespasian - Ga. (Democratic) September 18, 1812-August 16, 1880; Senate, 1848-1849; governor, 1853-1857; senator, Confederate Congress, 1862-1865. Candidacy: VP - 1860.

JOHNSON, Hiram Warren - Calif. (Progressive) September 2, 1866-August 6, 1945; governor, 1911-1917; Senate, 1917-1945. Candidacy: VP - 1912.

JOHNSTON, Samuel - N.C. (Federalist) December 15, 1733-August 18, 1816; Continental Congress, 1780-1782; Senate, 1789-1793. Candidacy: 1796.

JONES, Walter Burgwyn - Ala. (Independent Democratic) October 16, 1888-August 1, 1963; Alabama Legislature, 1919-1920; Alabama circuit court judge, 1920-1935; presiding judge, 1935-1963. Candidacy: P - 1956.

JULIAN, George Washington - Ind. (Free Soil, Liberal Republican) May 5, 1817-July 7, 1899; House, 1849-1851, 1861-1871. Candidacies: VP - 1852, 1872.

KEFAUVER, Estes - Tenn. (Democratic) July 26, 1903-August 10, 1963; House, 1939-1949; Senate, 1949-1963. Candidacy: VP - 1956.

KERN, John Worth - Ind. (Democratic) December 20, 1849-August 17, 1917; Senate, 1911-17. Candidacy: VP - 1908.

KING, Rufus - N.Y. (Federalist) March 24, 1755-April 29, 1827; Continental Congress, 1784-1787; Constitutional Convention, 1787; Senate, 1789-1796, 1813-1825; minister to Great Britain, 1796-1803, 1825-1826. Candidacies: VP - 1804, 1808; P - 1816.

KNOX, Franklin - Ill. (Republican) January 1, 1874-April 28, 1944; secretary of the Navy, 1940-1944. Candidacy: VP - 1936.

LA FOLLETTE, Robert Marion - Wis. (Progressive) June 14, 1855-June 18, 1925; House, 1885-1891; governor, 1901-1906; Senate, 1906-1925. Candidacy: P - 1924.

LANDON, Alfred Mossman - Kan. (Republican) September 9, 1887-October 12, 1987; governor, 1933-1937. Candidacy: P-1936.

LANE, Joseph - Ore. (Southern Democratic) December 14, 1801-April 19, 1881; governor of Oregon Territory, 1849-1850, May 16-19, 1853; House (territorial delegate), 1851-1859; Senate, 1859-1861. Candidacy: VP - 1860.

LANGDON, John - N.H. (Democratic-Republican) June 25, 1741-September 18, 1819; Continental Congress, 1775-1776, 1783; governor, 1788-1789; 1805-1809, 1810-1812; Senate, 1789-1801; first president pro tempore of the Senate, 1789. Candidacy: VP - 1808.

LEE, Henry - Mass. (Independent Democratic) February 4, 1782-February 6, 1867; merchant and publicist. Candidacy: VP - 1832.

LeMAY, Curtis Emerson - Ohio (American Independent) November 15, 1906—; Air Force chief of staff, 1961-1965. Candidacy: VP - 1968.

LEMKE, William - N.D. (Union) August 13, 1878-May 30, 1950; House, 1933-1941, 1943-1950. Candidacy: P - 1936.

LINCOLN, Benjamin - Mass. (Federalist) January 24, 1733-May 9, 1810; major general in Continental Army, 1777-1781; secretary of war, 1781-1783. Candidacy: 1789.

LODGE, Henry Cabot, Jr. - Mass. (Republican) July 5, 1902-February 27, 1985; Senate, 1937-1944, 1947-1953; ambassador to United Nations, 1953-1960; ambassador to Republic of Vietnam, 1963-1964, 1965-1967. Candidacy: VP - 1960.

LOGAN, John Alexander - Ill. (Republican) February 9, 1826-December 26, 1886; House, 1859-1862, 1867-1871; Senate, 1871-1877, 1879-1886. Candidacy: VP - 1884.

MACHEN, Willis Benson - Ky. (Democratic) April 10, 1810-September 29, 1893; Confederate Congress, 1861-1865; Senate, 1872-1873. Candidacy: VP - 1872.

MACON, Nathaniel - N.C. (Democratic-Republican) December 17, 1757-June 29, 1837; House, 1791-1815; Speaker of the House, 1801-1807; Senate, 1815-1828. Candidacy: VP - 1824.

MANGUM, Willie Person - N.C. (Independent Democrat) May 10, 1792-September 7, 1861; House, 1823-1826; Senate, 1831-1836, 1840-1853. Candidacy: P - 1836.

MARSHALL, John - Va. (Federalist) September 24, 1755-July 6, 1835; House 1799-1800; secretary of state, 1800-1801; chief justice of United States, 1801-1835. Candidacy: VP - 1816.

McCARTHY, Eugene Joseph - Minn. (Independent) March 29, 1916—; House, 1949-1959; Senate, 1959-1971. Candidacy: P-1976.

McCLELLAN, George Brinton - N.J. (Democratic) December 3, 1826-October 29, 1885; general-in-chief of Army of the Potomac, 1861; governor, 1878-1881. Candidacy: P - 1864.

McGOVERN, George Stanley - S.D. (Democratic) July 19, 1922—; House, 1957-1961; Senate, 1963-1981. Candidacy: P - 1972.

McNARY, Charles Linza - Ore. (Republican) June 12, 1874-February 25, 1944; state Supreme Court judge, 1913-1915; Senate, May 29, 1917-November 5, 1918, December 18, 1918-February 25, 1944. Candidacy: VP - 1940.

MILLER, William Edward - N.Y. (Republican) March 22, 1914-June 24, 1983; House, 1951-1965; chairman of Republican National Committee, 1961-1964. Candidacy: VP - 1964.

MILTON, John - Ga. circa 1740 - circa 1804; secretary of state, Georgia, circa 1778, 1781, 1783. Candidacy: 1789.

MUSKIE, Edmund Sixtus - Maine (Democratic) March 28, 1914—; governor, 1955-1959; Senate, 1959-1980; secretary of state, 1980-1981. Candidacy: VP - 1968.

NATHAN, Theodora Nathalia - Ore. (Libertarian) February 9, 1923—; broadcast journalist; National Judiciary Committee, Libertarian Party, 1972-1975; vice chairperson, Oregon Libertarian Party, 1974-1975. Candidacy: VP - 1972.

PALMER, John McAuley - Ill. (Democratic, National Democratic) September 13, 1817-September 25, 1900; governor, 1869-1873; Senate, 1891-1897. Candidacies: VP - 1872; P - 1896.

PARKER, Alton Brooks - N.Y. (Democratic) May 14, 1852-May 10, 1926; chief justice of N.Y. Court of Appeals, 1898-1904. Candidacy: P - 1904.

PENDLETON, George Hunt - Ohio (Democratic) July 19, 1825-November 24, 1889; House, 1857-1865; Senate, 1879-1885; minister to Germany, 1885-1889. Candidacy: VP - 1864.

PINCKNEY, Charles Cotesworth - S.C. (Federalist) February 25, 1746-August 16, 1825; president, state Senate, 1779; minister to France, 1796. Candidacies: VP - 1800; P - 1804, 1808.

PINCKNEY, Thomas - S.C. (Federalist) October 23, 1750-November 2, 1828; governor, 1787-1789; minister to Great Britain, 1792-1796; envoy to Spain, 1794-1795; House, 1797-1801. Candidacy: 1796.

REID, Whitelaw - N.Y. (Republican) October 27, 1837-December 15, 1912; minister to France, 1889-1892; editor-in-chief, *New York Tribune,* 1872-1905. Candidacy: VP - 1892.

ROBINSON, Joseph Taylor - Ark. (Democratic) August 26, 1872-July 14, 1937; House, 1903-1913; governor, January 16-March 8, 1913; Senate, 1913-1937; Senate minority leader, 1923-1933; Senate majority leader, 1933-1937. Candidacy: VP - 1928.

RODNEY, Daniel - Del. (Federalist) September 10, 1764-September 2, 1846; governor, 1814-1817; House, 1822-1823; Senate, 1826-1827. Candidacy: VP - 1820.

ROSS, James - Pa. (Federalist) July 12, 1762-November 27, 1847; Senate, 1794-1803. Candidacy: VP - 1816.

RUSH, Richard - Pa. (Democratic-Republican, National-Republican) August 29, 1780-July 30, 1859; attorney general, 1814-1817; minister to Great Britain, 1817-1824; secretary of the Treasury, 1825-1828. Candidacies: VP - 1820, 1828.

RUTLEDGE, John - S.C. (Federalist) September 1739-July 23, 1800; Continental Congress, 1774-1776, 1782-1783; governor, 1779-1782; Constitutional Convention, 1787; associate justice of U.S. Supreme Court, 1789-1791. Candidacy: 1789.

SANFORD, Nathan - N.Y. (Democratic-Republican) November 5, 1777-October 17, 1838; Senate, 1815-1821, 1826-1831. Candidacy: VP - 1824.

SCHMITZ, John George - Calif. (American Independent) August 12, 1930—; House, 1970-1973. Candidacy: P - 1972.

SCOTT, Winfield - N.J. (Whig) June 13, 1786-May 29, 1866; general-in-chief of U.S. Army, 1841-1861. Candidacy: P - 1852.

SERGEANT, John - Pa. (National-Republican) December 5, 1779-November 23, 1852; House, 1815-1823, 1827-1829, 1837-1841. Candidacy: VP - 1832.

SEWALL, Arthur - Maine (Democratic) November 25, 1835-September 5, 1900; Democratic National Committee member, 1888-1896. Candidacy: VP - 1896.

SEYMOUR, Horatio - N.Y. (Democratic) May 31, 1810-February 12, 1886; governor, 1853-1855, 1863-1865. Candidacy: P - 1868.

SHRIVER, Robert Sargent, Jr. - Md. (Democratic) November 9, 1915—; director, Peace Corps, 1961-1966; director, Office of Economic Opportunity, 1964-1968; ambassador to France, 1968-1970. Candidacy: VP - 1972. (Replaced Thomas F. Eagleton on Democratic ticket August 8.)

SMITH, Alfred Emanuel - N.Y. (Democratic) December 30, 1873-October 4, 1944; governor, 1919-1921, 1923-1929. Candidacy: P - 1928.

SMITH, William - S.C., Ala. (Independent Democratic-Republican) September 6, 1762-June 26, 1840; Senate, 1816-1823, 1826-1831. Candidacies: VP - 1828, 1836.

SPARKMAN, John Jackson - Ala. (Democratic) December 20, 1899-November 16, 1985; House, 1937-1946; Senate, 1946-1979. Candidacy: VP - 1952.

STEVENSON, Adlai Ewing II - Ill. (Democratic) February 5, 1900-July 14, 1965; assistant to the secretary of Navy, 1941-1944; assistant to the secretary of state, 1945; governor, 1949-1953; ambassador to United Nations, 1961-1965. Candidacies: P - 1952, 1956.

STOCKTON, Richard - N.J. (Federalist) April 17, 1764-March 7, 1828; Senate, 1796-1799; House, 1813-1815. Candidacy: VP - 1820.

TALMADGE, Herman Eugene - Ga. (Independent Democratic) August 9, 1913—; governor, 1947, 1948-1955; Senate, 1957-1981. Candidacy: VP - 1956.

TAYLOR, Glen Hearst - Idaho (Progressive) April 12, 1904-April 28, 1984; Senate, 1945-1951. Candidacy: VP - 1948.

TAZEWELL, Littleton Waller - Va. (Democratic) December 17, 1774-May 6, 1860; House, 1800-1801; Senate, 1824-1832; governor, 1834-1836. Candidacy: VP - 1840.

TELFAIR, Edward - Ga. (Democratic-Republican) 1735-September 17, 1807; Continental Congress, 1778-1782, 1784-1785, 1788-1789; governor, 1786, 1790-1793. Candidacy: 1789.

THOMAS, Norman Mattoon - N.Y. (Socialist) November 20, 1884-December 19, 1968; Presbyterian minister, 1911-1931; author and editor. Candidacies: P - 1928, 1932, 1936, 1940, 1944, 1948.

THURMAN, Allen Granberry - Ohio (Democratic) November 13, 1813-December 12, 1895; House, 1845-1847; Ohio Supreme Court, 1851-1856; Senate, 1869-1881. Candidacy: VP - 1888.

THURMOND, James Strom - S.C. (States' Rights Democrat, Democratic, Republican) December 5, 1902—; governor, 1947-1951; Senate, 1954-1956, 1956—. Candidacies: P - 1948; VP - 1960.

TILDEN, Samuel Jones - N.Y. (Democratic) February 9, 1814-August 4, 1886; governor, 1875-1877. Candidacy: P - 1876.

WALLACE, George Corley - Ala. (American Independent) August 25, 1919—; governor, 1963-1967, 1971-1979, 1983-1987. Candidacy: P - 1968.

WARREN, Earl - Calif. (Republican) March 19, 1891-July 9, 1974; governor, 1943-1953; chief justice of United States, 1953-1969. Candidacy: VP - 1948.

WATSON, Thomas Edward - Ga. (Populist) September 5, 1856-September 26, 1922; House, 1891-1893; Senate, 1921-1922. Candidacies: VP - 1896; P - 1904, 1908.

WEAVER, James Baird - Iowa (Greenback, Populist) June 12, 1833-February 6, 1912; House, 1879-1881, 1885-1889; Candidacies: P - 1880, 1892.

WEBSTER, Daniel - Mass. (Whig) January 18, 1782-October 24, 1852; House, 1813-1817, 1823-1827; Senate, 1827-1841, 1845-1850; secretary of state, 1841-1843, 1850-1852. Candidacy: P - 1836.

WHEELER, Burton Kendall - Mont. (Progressive) February 27, 1882-January 6, 1975; Senate, 1923-1947. Candidacy: VP - 1924.

WHITE, Hugh Lawson - Tenn. (Whig) October 30, 1773-April 10, 1840; Senate,

October 25, 1825-March 3, 1835, October 6, 1835-January 13, 1840. Candidacy: P - 1836.

WILKINS, William - Pa. (Democratic) December 20, 1779-June 23, 1865; Senate, 1831-1834; minister to Russia, 1834-1835; House, 1843-1844; secretary of war, 1844-1845. Candidacy: VP - 1832.

WILLKIE, Wendell Lewis - N.Y. (Republican) February 18, 1892-October 8, 1944; utility executive, 1933-1940. Candidacy: P - 1940.

WIRT, William - Md. (Anti-Masonic) November 8, 1772-February 18, 1834; attorney general, 1817-1829. Candidacy: P - 1832.

WRIGHT, Fielding Lewis - Miss. (States' Rights Democratic) May 16, 1895-May 4, 1956; governor, 1946-1952. Candidacy: VP - 1948.

Source: Guide to U.S. Elections, 2d ed. (Washington, D.C.: Congressional Quarterly Inc., 1985), 442-448.

Summary of Presidential Elections, 1824-1988

Year	No. of states	Candidates		Electoral vote		Popular vote	
1824[a]	24	Dem.-Rep. Andrew Jackson	Dem.-Rep. John Q. Adams	Dem.-Rep. 99 38%	Dem.-Rep. 84 32%	Dem.-Rep. 151,271 41.3%	Dem.-Rep. 113,122 30.9%
1828	24	Dem.-Rep. Andrew Jackson	Nat.-Rep. John Q. Adams	Dem.-Rep. 178 68%	Nat.-Rep. 83 32%	Dem.-Rep. 642,553 56.0%	Nat.-Rep. 500,897 43.6%
1832[b]	24	Dem. Andrew Jackson	Nat.-Rep. Henry Clay	Dem. 219 76%	Nat.-Rep. 49 17%	Dem. 701,780 54.2%	Nat.-Rep. 484,205 37.4%
1836[c]	26	Dem. Martin Van Buren	Whig William H. Harrison	Dem. 170 58%	Whig 73 25%	Dem. 764,176 50.8%	Whig 550,816 36.6%
1840	26	Dem. Martin Van Buren	Whig William H. Harrison	Dem. 60 20%	Whig 234 80%	Dem. 1,275,390 52.9%	Whig 1,128,854 46.8%
1844	26	Dem. James Polk	Whig Henry Clay	Dem. 170 62%	Whig 105 38%	Dem. 1,339,494 49.5%	Whig 1,300,004 48.1%
1848	30	Dem. Lewis Cass	Whig Zachary Taylor	Dem. 127 44%	Whig 163 56%	Dem. 1,361,393 47.3%	Whig 1,223,460 42.5%
1852	31	Dem. Franklin Pierce	Whig Winfield Scott	Dem. 254 86%	Whig 42 14%	Dem. 1,607,510 50.8%	Whig 1,386,942 43.9%

Year	No. of states	Candidates		Electoral Vote		Popular Vote	
		Dem.	Rep.	Dem.	Rep.	Dem.	Rep.
1856[d]	31	James Buchanan	John C. Fremont	174 59%	114 39%	1,836,072 45.3%	1,342,345 33.1%
1860[e]	33	Stephen A. Douglas Herschel V. Johnson	Abraham Lincoln Hannibal Hamlin	12 4%	180 59%	1,380,202 29.5%	1,865,908 39.8%
1864[f]	36	George B. McClellan George H. Pendleton	Abraham Lincoln Andrew Johnson	21 9%	212 91%	1,812,807 45.0%	2,218,388 55.0%
1868[g]	37	Horatio Seymour Francis P. Blair, Jr.	Ulysses S. Grant Schuyler Colfax	80 27%	214 73%	2,708,744 47.3%	3,013,650 52.7%
1872[h]	37	Horace Greeley Benjamin Gratz Brown	Ulysses S. Grant Henry Wilson		286 78%	2,834,761 43.8%	3,598,235 55.6%
1876	38	Samuel J. Tilden Thomas A. Hendricks	Rutherford B. Hayes William A. Wheeler	184 50%	185 50%	4,288,546 51.0%	4,034,311 47.9%
1880	38	Winfield S. Hancock William H. English	James A. Garfield Chester A. Arthur	155 42%	214 58%	4,444,260 48.2%	4,446,158 48.3%
1884	38	Grover Cleveland Thomas A. Hendricks	James G. Blaine John A. Logan	219 55%	182 45%	4,874,621 48.5%	4,848,936 48.2%
1888	38	Grover Cleveland Allen G. Thurman	Benjamin Harrison Levi P. Morton	168 42%	233 58%	5,534,488 48.6%	5,443,892 47.8%
1892[i]	44	Grover Cleveland Adlai E. Stevenson	Benjamin Harrison Whitelaw Reid	277 62%	145 33%	5,551,883 46.1%	5,179,244 43.0%
1896	45	William J. Bryan Arthur Sewall	William McKinley Garret A. Hobart	176 39%	271 61%	6,511,495 46.7%	7,108,480 51.0%

Year	No. of states	Candidates		Electoral Vote		Popular Vote	
		Dem.	Rep.	Dem.	Rep.	Dem.	Rep.
1900	45	William J. Bryan Adlai E. Stevenson	William McKinley Theodore Roosevelt	155 35%	292 65%	6,358,345 45.5%	7,218,039 51.7%
1904	45	Alton B. Parker Henry G. Davis	Theodore Roosevelt Charles W. Fairbanks	140 29%	336 71%	5,028,898 37.6%	7,626,593 56.4%
1908	46	William J. Bryan John W. Kern	William H. Taft James S. Sherman	162 34%	321 66%	6,406,801 43.0%	7,676,258 51.6%
1912[j]	48	Woodrow Wilson Thomas R. Marshall	William H. Taft James S. Sherman	435 82%	8 2%	6,293,152 41.8%	3,486,333 23.2%
1916	48	Woodrow Wilson Thomas R. Marshall	Charles E. Hughes Charles W. Fairbanks	277 52%	254 48%	9,126,300 49.2%	8,546,789 46.1%
1920	48	James M. Cox Franklin D. Roosevelt	Warren G. Harding Calvin Coolidge	127 24%	404 76%	9,140,884 34.2%	16,133,314 60.3%
1924[k]	48	John W. Davis Charles W. Bryant	Calvin Coolidge Charles G. Dawes	136 26%	382 72%	8,386,169 28.8%	15,717,553 54.1%
1928	48	Alfred E. Smith Joseph T. Robinson	Herbert C. Hoover Charles Curtis	87 16%	444 84%	15,000,185 40.8%	21,411,991 58.2%
1932	48	Franklin D. Roosevelt John N. Garner	Herbert C. Hoover Charles Curtis	472 89%	59 11%	22,825,016 57.4%	15,758,397 39.6%
1936	48	Franklin D. Roosevelt John N. Garner	Alfred M. London Frank Knox	523 98%	8 2%	27,747,636 60.8%	16,679,543 36.5%
1940	48	Franklin D. Roosevelt Henry A. Wallace	Wendell L. Willkie Charles L. McNary	449 85%	82 15%	27,263,448 54.7%	22,336,260 44.8%
1944	48	Franklin D. Roosevelt Harry S Truman	Thomas E. Dewey John W. Bricker	432 81%	99 19%	25,611,936 53.4%	22,013,372 45.9%
1948[l]	48	Harry S Truman Alben W. Barkley	Thomas E. Dewey Earl Warren	303 57%	189 36%	24,105,587 49.5%	21,970,017 45.1%
1952	48	Adlai E. Stevenson John J. Sparkman	Dwight D. Eisenhower Richard M. Nixon	89 17%	442 83%	27,314,649 44.4%	33,936,137 55.1%
1956[m]	48	Adlai E. Stevenson Estes Kefauver	Dwight D. Eisenhower Richard M. Nixon	73 14%	457 86%	26,030,172 42.0%	35,585,245 57.4%
1960[n]	50	John F. Kennedy Lyndon B. Johnson	Richard M. Nixon Henry Cabot Lodge	303 56%	219 41%	34,221,344 49.7%	34,106,671 49.5%
1964	50*	Lyndon B. Johnson Hubert H. Humphrey	Barry Goldwater William E. Miller	486 90%	52 10%	43,126,584 61.1%	27,177,838 38.5%
1968[o]	50*	Hubert H. Humphrey Edmund S. Muskie	Richard M. Nixon Spiro T. Agnew	191 36%	301 56%	31,274,503 42.7%	31,785,148 43.4%
1972[p]	50*	George McGovern Sargent Shriver	Richard M. Nixon Spiro T. Agnew	17 3%	520 97%	29,171,791 37.5%	47,170,179 60.7%
1976[q]	50*	Jimmy Carter Walter F. Mondale	Gerald R. Ford Robert Dole	297 55%	240 45%	40,830,763 50.1%	39,147,793 48.0%
1980	50*	Jimmy Carter Walter F. Mondale	Ronald Reagan George Bush	49 9%	489 91%	35,483,883 41.0%	43,904,153 50.7%
1984	50*	Walter F. Mondale Geraldine Ferraro	Ronald Reagan George Bush	13 2%	525 98%	37,577,185 40.6%	54,455,075 58.8%
1988[r]	50*	Michael S. Dukakis Lloyd Bentsen	George Bush Dan Quayle	111 21%	426 79%	41,809,083 45.6%	48,886,097 53.4%

Source: 1824-1984—*Guide to U.S. Elections,* 2d ed. (Washington, D.C.: Congressional Quarterly Inc.), 1985—329-366; 1988—Federal Election Commission.

Note: Dem.-Rep.—Democratic-Republican; Nat.-Rep.—National-Republican; Dem.—Democratic; Rep.—Republican.

a. 1824: All four candidates represented Democratic-Republican factions. William H. Crawford polled 41 electoral votes and Henry Clay polled 37 votes. Because no candidate received a majority, the election was decided (in Adams's favor) by the House of Representatives.
b. 1832: 2 electoral votes were not cast.
c. 1836: Other Whig candidates receiving electoral votes were Hugh L. White, who polled 26 votes, and Daniel Webster, who polled 14 votes.
d. 1856: Millard Fillmore, Whig-American, polled 8 electoral votes.
e. 1860: John C. Breckinridge, Southern Democrat, polled 72 electoral votes. John Bell, Constitutional Union, polled 39 electoral votes.
f. 1864: 81 electoral votes were not cast.
g. 1868: 23 electoral votes were not cast.
h. 1872: Horace Greeley, Democrat, died after the election. In the electoral college, Democratic electoral votes went to Thomas Hendricks, 42 votes; B. Gratz Brown, 18 votes; Charles J. Jenkins, 2 votes; and David Davis, 1 vote. 17 electoral votes were not cast.
i. 1892: James B. Weaver, People's party, polled 22 electoral votes.
j. 1912: Theodore Roosevelt, Progressive party, polled 86 electoral votes.
k. 1924: Robert M. La Follette, Progressive party, polled 13 electoral votes.
l. 1948: J. Strom Thurmond, States' Rights party, polled 39 electoral votes.
m. 1956: Walter B. Jones, Democrat, polled 1 electoral vote.
n. 1960: Harry Flood Byrd, Democrat, polled 15 electoral votes.
o. 1968: George C. Wallace, American Independent party, polled 46 electoral votes.
p. 1972: John Hospers, Libertarian party, polled 1 electoral vote.
q. 1976: Ronald Reagan, Republican, polled 1 electoral vote.
r. 1988: Lloyd Bentsen, the Democratic vice presidential nominee, polled 1 electoral vote for president.
* Fifty states plus District of Columbia.

Political Party Nominees, 1831-1988

The following pages contain a comprehensive list of major and minor party nominees for president and vice president since 1831, when the first nominating convention was held by the Anti-Masonic party. In many cases, minor parties made only token efforts at a presidential campaign. Often, third-party candidates declined to run after being nominated by the convention, or their names appeared on the ballots of only a few states. In some cases the names of minor candidates did not appear on any state ballots and they received only a scattering of write-in votes, if any.

1832 Election

Democratic party
President: Andrew Jackson, Tennessee
Vice president: Martin Van Buren, New York
National Republican party
President: Henry Clay, Kentucky
Vice president: John Sergeant, Pennsylvania
Independent party
President: John Floyd, Virginia
Vice president: Henry Lee, Massachusetts
Anti-Masonic party
President: William Wirt, Maryland
Vice president: Amos Ellmaker, Pennsylvania

1836 Election

Democratic party
President: Martin Van Buren, New York
Vice president: Richard Mentor Johnson, Kentucky
Whig party
President: William Henry Harrison, Hugh Lawson White, Daniel Webster
Vice president: Francis Granger, John Tyler

The Whigs nominated regional candidates in 1836 hoping that each candidate would carry his region and deny Democrat Van Buren an electoral vote majority. Webster was the Whig candidate in Massachusetts; Harrison in the rest of New England, the Middle Atlantic states, and the West; and White in the South.

Granger was the running mate of Harrison and Webster. Tyler was White's running mate.

1840 Election

Whig party
President: William Henry Harrison, Ohio
Vice president: John Tyler, Virginia
Democratic party
President: Martin Van Buren, New York

The Democratic convention adopted a resolution that left the choice of vice-presidential candidates to the states. Democratic electors divided their vice-presidential votes among incumbent Richard M. Johnson (forty-eight votes), Littleton W. Tazewell (eleven votes), and James K. Polk (one vote).

Liberty party
President: James Gillespie Birney, New York
Vice president: Thomas Earle, Pennsylvania

1844 Election

Democratic party
President: James Knox Polk, Tennessee
Vice president: George Mifflin Dallas, Pennsylvania
Whig party
President: Henry Clay, Kentucky
Vice president: Theodore Frelinghuysen, New Jersey
Liberty party
President: James Gillespie Birney, New York
Vice president: Thomas Morris, Ohio
National Democratic party
President: John Tyler, Virginia
Vice president: None

Tyler withdrew in favor of the Democrat, Polk.

1848 Election

Whig party
President: Zachary Taylor, Louisiana
Vice president: Millard Fillmore, New York
Democratic party
President: Lewis Cass, Michigan
Vice president: William Orlando Butler, Kentucky
Free Soil party
President: Martin Van Buren, New York
Vice president: Charles Francis Adams, Massachusetts
Free Soil (Barnburners—Liberty party)
President: John Parker Hale, New Hampshire
Vice president: Leicester King, Ohio

Later John Parker Hale relinquished the nomination.

National Liberty party
President: Gerrit Smith, New York
Vice president: Charles C. Foote, Michigan

1852 Election

Democratic party
President: Franklin Pierce, New Hampshire
Vice president: William Rufus De Vane King, Alabama
Whig party
President: Winfield Scott, New Jersey
Vice president: William Alexander Graham, North Carolina
Free Soil
President: John Parker Hale, New Hampshire
Vice president: George Washington Julian, Indiana

1856 Election

Democratic party
President: James Buchanan, Pennsylvania
Vice president: John Cabell Breckinridge, Kentucky
Republican party
President: John Charles Fremont, California
Vice president: William Lewis Dayton, New Jersey
American (Know-Nothing) party
President: Millard Fillmore, New York
Vice president: Andrew Jackson Donelson, Tennessee
Whig party (the "Silver Grays")
President: Millard Fillmore, New York

Vice president: Andrew Jackson Donelson, Tennessee
North American party
President: Nathaniel Prentice Banks, Massachusetts
Vice president: William Freame Johnson, Pennsylvania
Banks and Johnson declined the nominations and gave their support to the Republicans.

1860 Election

Republican party
President: Abraham Lincoln, Illinois
Vice president: Hannibal Hamlin, Maine
Democratic party
President: Stephen Arnold Douglas, Illinois
Vice president: Herschel Vespasian Johnson, Georgia
Southern Democratic party
President: John Cabell Breckinridge, Kentucky
Vice president: Joseph Lane, Oregon
Constitutional Union party
President: John Bell, Tennessee
Vice president: Edward Everett, Massachusetts

1864 Election

Republican party
President: Abraham Lincoln, Illinois
Vice president: Andrew Johnson, Tennessee
Democratic party
President: George Brinton McClellan, New York
Vice president: George Hunt Pendleton, Ohio
Independent Republican party
President: John Charles Fremont, California
Vice president: John Cochrane, New York
Fremont and Cochrane declined the nominations and gave their support to the Republicans.

1868 Election

Republican party
President: Ulysses Simpson Grant, Illinois
Vice president: Schuyler Colfax, Indiana
Democratic party
President: Horatio Seymour, New York
Vice president: Francis Preston Blair, Jr., Missouri

1872 Election

Republican party
President: Ulysses Simpson Grant, Illinois
Vice president: Henry Wilson, Massachusetts
Liberal Republican party
President: Horace Greeley, New York
Vice president: Benjamin Gratz Brown, Missouri
Independent Liberal Republican party (Opposition party)
President: William Slocum Groesbeck, Ohio
Vice president: Frederick Law Olmsted, New York
Democratic party
President: Horace Greeley, New York
Vice president: Benjamin Gratz Brown, Missouri
Straight-Out Democratic party
President: Charles O'Conor, New York
Vice president: John Quincy Adams, Massachusetts
Prohibition party
President: James Black, Pennsylvania
Vice president: John Russell, Michigan
People's party (Equal Rights party)
President: Victoria Claflin Woodhull, New York
Vice president: Frederick Douglass
Labor Reform party
President: David Davis, Illinois
Vice president: Joel Parker, New Jersey
Liberal Republican Party of Colored Men
President: Horace Greeley, New York
Vice president: Benjamin Gratz Brown, Missouri
National Working Men's party
President: Ulysses Simpson Grant, Illinois
Vice president: Henry Wilson, Massachusetts

1876 Election

Republican party
President: Rutherford Birchard Hayes, Ohio
Vice president: William Almon Wheeler, New York
Democratic party
President: Samuel Jones Tilden, New York
Vice president: Thomas Andrews Hendricks, Indiana
Greenback party
President: Peter Cooper, New York
Vice president: Samuel Fenton Cary, Ohio
Prohibition party
President: Green Clay Smith, Kentucky
Vice president: Gideon Tabor Stewart, Ohio
American National party
President: James B. Walker, Illinois
Vice president: Donald Kirkpatrick, New York

1880 Election

Republican party
President: James Abram Garfield, Ohio
Vice president: Chester Alan Arthur, New York
Democratic party
President: Winfield Scott Hancock, Pennsylvania
Vice president: William Hayden English, Indiana
Greenback Labor party
President: James Baird Weaver, Iowa
Vice president: Benjamin J. Chambers, Texas
Prohibition party
President: Neal Dow, Maine
Vice president: Henry Adams Thompson, Ohio
American party
President: John Wolcott Phelps, Vermont
Vice president: Samuel Clarke Pomeroy, Kansas *

1884 Election

Democratic party
President: Grover Cleveland, New York
Vice president: Thomas Andrews Hendricks, Indiana
Republican party
President James Gillespie Blaine, Maine
Vice president: John Alexander Logan, Illinois
Anti-Monopoly party
President: Benjamin Franklin Butler, Massachusetts
Vice president: Absolom Madden West, Mississippi
Greenback party
President: Benjamin Franklin Butler, Massachusetts
Vice president: Absolom Madden West, Mississippi
Prohibition party
President: John Pierce St. John, Kansas
Vice president: William Daniel, Maryland
American Prohibition party
President: Samuel Clark Pomeroy, Kansas
Vice president: John A. Conant, Connecticut

Equal Rights party
President: Belva Ann Bennett Lockwood, District of Columbia
Vice president: Marietta Lizzie Bell Stow, California

1888 Election

Republican party
President: Benjamin Harrison, Indiana
Vice president: Levi Parsons Morton, New York
Democratic party
President: Grover Cleveland, New York
Vice president: Allen Granberry Thurman, Ohio
Prohibition party
President: Clinton Bowen Fisk, New Jersey
Vice president: John Anderson Brooks, Missouri *
Union Labor party
President: Alson Jenness Streeter, Illinois
Vice president: Charles E. Cunningham, Arkansas *
United Labor party
President: Robert Hall Cowdrey, Illinois
Vice president: William H. T. Wakefield, Kansas *
American party
President: James Langdon Curtis, New York
Vice president: Peter Dinwiddie Wigginton, California *
Equal Rights party
President: Belva Ann Bennett Lockwood, District of Columbia
Vice president: Alfred Henry Love, Pennsylvania *
Industrial Reform party
President: Albert E. Redstone, California *
Vice president: John Colvin, Kansas *

1892 Election

Democratic party
President: Grover Cleveland, New York
Vice president: Adlai Ewing Stevenson, Illinois
Republican party
President: Benjamin Harrison, Indiana
Vice president: Whitelaw Reid, New York
People's Party of America
President: James Baird Weaver, Iowa
Vice president: James Gaven Field, Virginia
Prohibition party
President: John Bidwell, California
Vice president: James Britton Cranfill, Texas
Socialist Labor party
President: Simon Wing, Massachusetts
Vice president: Charles Horatio Matchett, New York *

1896 Election

Republican party
President: William McKinley, Ohio
Vice president: Garret Augustus Hobart, New Jersey
Democratic party
President: William Jennings Bryan, Nebraska
Vice president: Arthur Sewall, Maine
People's party (Populist)
President: William Jennings Bryan, Nebraska
Vice president: Thomas Edward Watson, Georgia
National Democratic party
President: John McAuley Palmer, Illinois
Vice president: Simon Bolivar Buckner, Kentucky
Prohibition party
President: Joshua Levering, Maryland
Vice president: Hale Johnson, Illinois *
Socialist Labor party
President: Charles Horatio Matchett, New York
Vice president: Matthew Maguire, New Jersey
National party
President: Charles Eugene Bentley, Nebraska
Vice president: James Haywood Southgate, North Carolina *
National Silver party (Bi-Metallic League)
President: William Jennings Bryan, Nebraska
Vice president: Arthur Sewall, Maine

1900 Election

Republican party
President: William McKinley, Ohio
Vice president: Theodore Roosevelt, New York
Democratic party
President: William Jennings Bryan, Nebraska
Vice president: Adlai Ewing Stevenson, Illinois
Prohibition party
President: John Granville Wooley, Illinois
Vice president: Henry Brewer Metcalf, Rhode Island
Social-Democratic party
President: Eugene Victor Debs, Indiana
Vice president: Job Harriman, California
People's party (Populist—Anti-Fusionist faction)
President: Wharton Barker, Pennsylvania
Vice president: Ignatius Donnelly, Minnesota
Socialist Labor party
President: Joseph Francis Malloney, Massachusetts
Vice president: Valentine Remmel, Pennsylvania
Union Reform party
President: Seth Hockett Ellis, Ohio
Vice president: Samuel T. Nicholson, Pennsylvania
United Christian party
President: Jonah Fitz Randolph Leonard, Iowa
Vice president: David H. Martin, Pennsylvania
People's party (Populist—Fusionist faction)
President: William Jennings Bryan, Nebraska
Vice president: Adlai Ewing Stevenson, Illinois
Silver Republican party
President: William Jennings Bryan, Nebraska
Vice president: Adlai Ewing Stevenson, Illinois
National party
President: Donelson Caffery, Louisiana
Vice president: Archibald Murray Howe, Massachusetts *

1904 Election

Republican party
President: Theodore Roosevelt, New York
Vice president: Charles Warren Fairbanks, Indiana
Democratic party
President: Alton Brooks Parker, New York
Vice president: Henry Gassaway Davis, West Virginia
Socialist party
President: Eugene Victor Debs, Indiana
Vice president: Benjamin Hanford, New York
Prohibition party
President: Silas Comfort Swallow, Pennsylvania
Vice president: George W. Carroll, Texas
People's party (Populist)
President: Thomas Edward Watson, Georgia
Vice president: Thomas Henry Tibbles, Nebraska

Socialist Labor party
President: Charles Hunter Corregan, New York
Vice president: William Wesley Cox, Illinois
Continental party
President: Austin Holcomb
Vice president: A. King, Missouri

1908 Election

Republican party
President: William Howard Taft, Ohio
Vice president: James Schoolcraft Sherman, New York
Democratic party
President: William Jennings Bryan, Nebraska
Vice president: John Worth Kern, Indiana
Socialist party
President: Eugene Victor Debs
Vice president: Benjamin Hanford
Prohibition party
President: Eugene Wilder Chafin, Illinois
Vice president: Aaron Sherman Watkins, Ohio
Independence party
President: Thomas Louis Hisgen, Massachusetts
Vice president: John Temple Graves, Georgia
People's party (Populist)
President: Thomas Edward Watson, Georgia
Vice president: Samuel Williams, Indiana
Socialist Labor party
President: August Gillhaus, New York
Vice president: Donald L. Munro, Virginia
United Christian party
President: Daniel Braxton Turney, Illinois
Vice president: Lorenzo S. Coffin, Iowa

1912 Election

Democratic party
President: Woodrow Wilson, New Jersey
Vice president: Thomas Riley Marshall, Indiana
Progressive party ("Bull Moose" party)
President: Theodore Roosevelt, New York
Vice president: Hiram Warren Johnson, California
Republican party
President: William Howard Taft, Ohio
Vice president: James Schoolcraft Sherman, New York
Sherman died October 30; he was replaced by Nicholas Murray Butler, New York.
Socialist party
President: Eugene Victor Debs, Indiana
Vice president: Emil Seidel, Wisconsin
Prohibition party
President: Eugene Wilder Chafin, Illinois
Vice president: Aaron Sherman Watkins, Ohio
Socialist Labor party
President: Arthur Elmer Reimer, Massachusetts
Vice president: August Gillhaus, New York [a]

1916 Election

Democratic party
President: Woodrow Wilson, New Jersey
Vice president: Thomas Riley Marshall, Indiana
Republican party
President: Charles Evans Hughes, New York
Vice president: Charles Warren Fairbanks, Indiana
Socialist party
President: Allan Louis Benson, New York
Vice president: George Ross Kirkpatrick, New Jersey
Prohibition party
President: James Franklin Hanly, Indiana
Vice president: Ira Landrith, Tennessee
Socialist Labor party
President: Arthur Elmer Reimer, Massachusetts *
Vice president: Caleb Harrison, Illinois *
Progressive party
President: Theodore Roosevelt, New York
Vice president: John Milliken Parker, Louisiana

1920 Election

Republican party
President: Warren Gamaliel Harding, Ohio
Vice president: Calvin Coolidge, Massachusetts
Democratic party
President: James Middleton Cox, Ohio
Vice president: Franklin Delano Roosevelt, New York
Socialist party
President: Eugene Victor Debs, Indiana
Vice president: Seymour Stedman, Illinois
Farmer Labor party
President: Parley Parker Christensen, Utah
Vice president: Maximilian Sebastian Hayes, Ohio
Prohibition party
President: Aaron Sherman Watkins, Ohio
Vice president: David Leigh Colvin, New York
Socialist Labor party
President: William Wesley Cox, Missouri
Vice president: August Gillhaus, New York
Single Tax party
President: Robert Colvin Macauley, Pennsylvania
Vice president: R. G. Barnum, Ohio
American party
President: James Edward Ferguson, Texas
Vice president: William J. Hough

1924 Election

Republican party
President: Calvin Coolidge, Massachusetts
Vice president: Charles Gates Dawes, Illinois
Democratic party
President: John William Davis, West Virginia
Vice president: Charles Wayland Bryan, Nebraska
Progressive party
President: Robert La Follette, Wisconsin
Vice president: Burton Kendall Wheeler, Montana
Prohibition party
President: Herman Preston Faris, Missouri
Vice president: Marie Caroline Brehm, California
Socialist Labor party
President: Frank T. Johns, Oregon
Vice president: Verne L. Reynolds, New York
Socialist party
President: Robert La Follette, New York
Vice president: Burton Kendall Wheeler, Montana
Workers party (Communist party)
President: William Zebulon Foster, Illinois
Vice president: Benjamin Gitlow, New York
American party
President: Gilbert Owen Nations, District of Columbia
Vice president: Charles Hiram Randall, California [b]
Commonwealth Land party
President: William J. Wallace, New Jersey
Vice president: John Cromwell Lincoln, Ohio

Farmer Labor party
President: Duncan McDonald, Illinois *
Vice president: William Bouck, Washington *
Greenback party
President: John Zahnd, Indiana *
Vice president: Roy M. Harrop, Nebraska *

1928 Election

Republican party
President: Herbert Clark Hoover, California
Vice president: Charles Curtis, Kansas
Democratic party
President: Alfred Emanuel Smith, New York
Vice president: Joseph Taylor Robinson, Arkansas
Socialist party
President: Norman Mattoon Thomas, New York
Vice president: James Hudson Maurer, Pennsylvania
Workers party (Communist party)
President: William Zebulon Foster, Illinois
Vice president: Benjamin Gitlow, New York
Socialist Labor party
President: Verne L. Reynolds, Michigan
Vice president: Jeremiah D. Crowley, New York
Prohibition party
President: William Frederick Varney, New York
Vice president: James Arthur Edgerton, Virginia
Farmer Labor party
President: Frank Elbridge Webb, California
Vice president: Will Vereen, Georgia [c]
Greenback party
President: John Zahnd, Indiana *
Vice president: Wesley Henry Bennington, Ohio *

1932 Election

Democratic party
President: Franklin Delano Roosevelt, New York
Vice president: John Nance Garner, Texas
Republican party
President: Herbert Clark Hoover, California
Vice president: Charles Curtis, Kansas
Socialist party
President: Norman Mattoon Thomas, New York
Vice president: James Hudson Maurer, Pennsylvania
Communist party
President: William Zebulon Foster, Illinois
Vice president: James William Ford, New York
Prohibition party
President: William David Upshaw, Georgia
Vice president: Frank Stewart Regan, Illinois
Liberty party
President: William Hope Harvey, Arkansas
Vice president: Frank B. Hemenway, Washington
Socialist Labor party
President: Verne L. Reynolds, New York
Vice president: John W. Aiken, Massachusetts
Farmer Labor party
President: Jacob Sechler Coxey, Ohio
Vice president: Julius J. Reiter, Minnesota
Jobless party
President: James Renshaw Cox, Pennsylvania
Vice president: V. C. Tisdal, Oklahoma
National party
President: Seymour E. Allen, Massachusetts

1936 Election

Democratic party
President: Franklin Delano Roosevelt, New York
Vice president: John Nance Garner, Texas
Republican party
President: Alfred Mossman Landon, Kansas
Vice president: Frank Knox, Illinois
Union party
President: William Lemke, North Dakota
Vice president: Thomas Charles O'Brien, Massachusetts
Socialist party
President: Norman Mattoon Thomas, New York
Vice president: George A. Nelson, Wisconsin
Communist party
President: Earl Russell Browder, Kansas
Vice president: James William Ford, New York
Prohibition party
President: David Leigh Colvin, New York
Vice president: Alvin York, Tennessee
Socialist Labor party
President: John W. Aikin, Massachusetts
Vice president: Emil F. Teichert, New York
National Greenback party
President: John Zahnd, Indiana *
Vice president: Florence Garvin, Rhode Island *

1940 Election

Democratic party
President: Franklin Delano Roosevelt, New York
Vice president: Henry Agard Wallace, Iowa
Republican party
President: Wendell Lewis Willkie, New York
Vice president: Charles Linza McNary, Oregon
Socialist party
President: Norman Mattoon Thomas, New York
Vice president: Maynard C. Krueger, Illinois
Prohibition party
President: Roger Ward Babson, Massachusetts
Vice president: Edgar V. Moorman, Illinois
Communist party (Workers party)
President: Earl Russell Browder, Kansas
Vice president: James William Ford, New York
Socialist Labor party
President: John W. Aiken, Massachusetts
Vice president: Aaron M. Orange, New York
Greenback party
President: John Zahnd, Indiana *
Vice president: James Elmer Yates, Arizona *

1944 Election

Democratic party
President: Franklin Delano Roosevelt, New York
Vice president: Harry S Truman, Missouri
Republican party
President: Thomas Edmund Dewey, New York
Vice president: John William Bricker, Ohio
Socialist party
President: Norman Mattoon Thomas, New York
Vice president: Darlington Hoopes, Pennsylvania
Prohibition party
President: Claude A. Watson, California
Vice president: Andrew Johnson, Kentucky
Socialist Labor party
President: Edward A. Teichert, Pennsylvania

Vice president: Arla A. Albaugh, Ohio
America First party
President: Gerald Lyman Kenneth Smith, Michigan
Vice president: Henry A. Romer, Ohio

1948 Election

Democratic party
President: Harry S Truman, Missouri
Vice president: Alben William Barkley, Kentucky
Republican party
President: Thomas Edmund Dewey, New York
Vice president: Earl Warren, California
States' Rights Democratic party
President: James Strom Thurmond, South Carolina
Vice president: Fielding Lewis Wright, Mississippi
Progressive party
President: Henry Agard Wallace, Iowa
Vice president: Glen Hearst Taylor, Idaho
Socialist party
President: Norman Mattoon Thomas, New York
Vice president: Tucker Powell Smith, Michigan
Prohibition party
President: Claude A. Watson, California
Vice president: Dale Learn, Pennsylvania
Socialist Labor party
President: Edward A. Teichert, Pennsylvania
Vice president: Stephen Emery, New York
Socialist Workers party
President: Farrell Dobbs, New York
Vice president: Grace Carlson, Minnesota
Christian Nationalist party
President: Gerald Lyman Kenneth Smith, Missouri
Vice president: Henry A. Romer, Ohio
Greenback party
President: John G. Scott, New York
Vice president: Granville B. Leeke, Indiana *
Vegetarian party
President: John Maxwell, Illinois
Vice president: Symon Gould, New York *

1952 Election

Republican party
President: Dwight David Eisenhower, New York
Vice president: Richard Milhous Nixon, California
Democratic party
President: Adlai Ewing Stevenson, Illinois
Vice president: John Jackson Sparkman, Alabama
Progressive party
President: Vincent William Hallinan, California
Vice president: Charlotta A. Bass, New York
Prohibition party
President: Stuart Hamblen, California
Vice president: Enoch Arden Holtwick, Illinois
Socialist Labor party
President: Eric Hass, New York
Vice president: Stephen Emery, New York
Socialist party
President: Darlington Hoopes, Pennsylvania
Vice president: Samuel Herman Friedman, New York
Socialist Workers party
President: Farrell Dobbs, New York
Vice president: Myra Tanner Weiss, New York
America First party
President: Douglas MacArthur, Wisconsin
Vice president: Harry Flood Byrd, Virginia
American Labor party
President: Vincent William Hallinan, California
Vice president: Charlotta A. Bass, New York
American Vegetarian party
President: Daniel J. Murphy, California
Vice president: Symon Gould, New York *
Church of God party
President: Homer Aubrey Tomlinson, New York
Vice president: Willie Isaac Bass, North Carolina *
Constitution party
President: Douglas MacArthur, Wisconsin
Vice president: Harry Flood Byrd, Virginia
Greenback party
President: Frederick C. Proehl, Washington
Vice president: Edward J. Bedell, Indiana
Poor Man's party
President: Henry B. Krajewski, New Jersey
Vice president: Frank Jenkins, New Jersey

1956 Election

Republican party
President: Dwight David Eisenhower, Pennsylvania
Vice president: Richard Milhous Nixon, California
Democratic party
President: Adlai Ewing Stevenson, Illinois
Vice president: Estes Kefauver, Tennessee
States' Rights party
President: Thomas Coleman Andrews, Virginia
Vice president: Thomas Harold Werdel, California
Ticket also favored by Constitution party.
Prohibition party
President: Enoch Arden Holtwick, Illinois
Vice president: Edward M. Cooper, California
Socialist Labor party
President: Eric Hass, New York
Vice president: Georgia Cozzini, Wisconsin
Texas Constitution party
President: William Ezra Jenner, Indiana *
Vice president: Joseph Bracken Lee, Utah *
Socialist Workers party
President: Farrell Dobbs, New York
Vice president: Myra Tanner Weiss, New York
American Third party
President: Henry Krajewski, New Jersey
Vice president: Ann Marie Yezo, New Jersey
Socialist party
President: Darlington Hoopes, Pennsylvania
Vice president: Samuel Herman Friedman, New York
Pioneer party
President: William Langer, North Dakota *
Vice president: Burr McCloskey, Illinois *
American Vegetarian party
President: Herbert M. Shelton, California *
Vice president: Symon Gould, New York *
Greenback party
President: Frederick C. Proehl, Washington
Vice president: Edward Kirby Meador, Massachusetts *
States' Rights Party of Kentucky
President: Harry Flood Byrd, Virginia
Vice president: William Ezra Jenner, Indiana
South Carolinians for Independent Electors
President: Harry Flood Byrd, Virginia
Christian National party
President: Gerald Lyman Kenneth Smith
Vice president: Charles I. Robertson

1960 Election

Democratic party
President: John Fitzgerald Kennedy, Massachusetts
Vice president: Lyndon Baines Johnson, Texas
Republican party
President: Richard Milhous Nixon, California
Vice president: Henry Cabot Lodge, Massachusetts
National States' Rights party
President: Orval Eugene Faubus, Arkansas
Vice president: John Geraerdt Crommelin, Alabama
Socialist Labor party
President: Eric Hass, New York
Vice president: Georgia Cozzini, Wisconsin
Prohibition party
President: Rutherford Losey Decker, Missouri
Vice president: Earle Harold Munn, Michigan
Socialist Workers party
President: Farrell Dobbs, New York
Vice president: Myra Tanner Weiss, New York
Conservative Party of New Jersey
President: Joseph Bracken Lee, Utah
Vice president: Kent H. Courtney, Louisiana
Conservative Party of Virginia
President: C. Benton Coiner, Virginia
Vice president: Edward M. Silverman, Virginia
Constitution party (Texas)
President: Charles Loten Sullivan, Mississippi
Vice president: Merritt B. Curtis, District of Columbia
Constitution party (Washington)
President: Merritt B. Curtis, District of Columbia
Vice president: B. N. Miller
Greenback party
President: Whitney Hart Stocomb, California *
Vice president: Edward Kirby Meador, Massachusetts *
Independent Afro-American party
President: Clennon King, Georgia
Vice president: Reginald Carter
Tax Cut party (America First party; American party)
President: Lar Daly, Illinois
Vice president: Merritt Barton Curtis, District of Columbia
Theocratic party
President: Homer Aubrey Tomlinson, New York
Vice president: Raymond L. Teague, Alaska *
Vegetarian party
President: Symon Gould, New York
Vice president: Christopher Gian-Cursio, Florida

1964 Election

Democratic party
President: Lyndon Baines Johnson, Texas
Vice president: Hubert Horatio Humphrey, Minnesota
Republican party
President: Barry Morris Goldwater, Arizona
Vice president: William Edward Miller, New York
Socialist Labor party
President: Eric Hass, New York
Vice president: Henning A. Blomen, Massachusetts
Prohibition party
President: Earle Harold Munn, Michigan
Vice president: Mark Shaw, Massachusetts
Socialist Workers party
President: Clifton DeBerry, New York
Vice president: Edward Shaw, New York
National States' Rights party
President: John Kasper, Tennessee
Vice president: J. B. Stoner, Georgia
Constitution party
President: Joseph B. Lightburn, West Virginia
Vice president: Theodore C. Billings, Colorado
Independent States' Rights party
President: Thomas Coleman Andrews, Virginia
Vice president: Thomas H. Werdel, California *
Theocratic party
President: Homer Aubrey Tomlinson, New York
Vice president: William R. Rogers, Missouri *
Universal party
President: Kirby James Hensley, California
Vice president: John O. Hopkins, Iowa

1968 Election

Republican party
President: Richard Milhous Nixon, New York
Vice president: Spiro Theodore Agnew, Maryland
Democratic party
President: Hubert Horatio Humphrey, Minnesota
Vice president: Edmund Sixtus Muskie, Maine
American Independent party
President: George Corley Wallace, Alabama
Vice president: Curtis Emerson LeMay, Ohio
LeMay replaced S. Marvin Griffin, who originally had been selected.
Peace and Freedom party
President: Eldridge Cleaver
Vice president: Judith Mage, New York
Socialist Labor party
President: Henning A. Blomen, Massachusetts
Vice president: George Sam Taylor, Pennsylvania
Socialist Workers party
President: Fred Halstead, New York
Vice president: Paul Boutelle, New Jersey
Prohibition party
President: Earle Harold Munn, Sr., Michigan
Vice president: Rolland E. Fisher, Kansas
Communist party
President: Charlene Mitchell, California
Vice president: Michael Zagarell, New York
Constitution party
President: Richard K. Troxell, Texas
Vice president: Merle Thayer, Iowa
Freedom and Peace party
President: Dick Gregory (Richard Claxton Gregory), Ill.
Patriotic party
President: George Corley Wallace, Alabama
Vice president: William Penn Patrick, California
Theocratic party
President: William R. Rogers, Missouri
Universal party
President: Kirby James Hensley, California
Vice president: Roscoe B. MacKenna

1972 Election

Republican party
President: Richard Milhous Nixon, California
Vice president: Spiro Theodore Agnew, Maryland
Democratic party
President: George Stanley McGovern, South Dakota
Vice president: Thomas Francis Eagleton, Missouri
Eagleton resigned and was replaced on August 8, 1972,

by Robert Sargent Shriver, Jr., Maryland, selected by the Democratic National Committee.
American Independent party
  President: John George Schmitz, California
  Vice president: Thomas Jefferson Anderson, Tennessee
Socialist Workers party
  President: Louis Fisher, Illinois
  Vice president: Genevieve Gunderson, Minnesota
Socialist Labor party
  President: Linda Jenness, Georgia
  Vice president: Andrew Pulley, Illinois
Communist party
  President: Gus Hall, New York
  Vice president: Jarvis Tyner
Prohibition party
  President: Earle Harold Munn, Sr., Michigan
  Vice president: Marshall Uncapher
Libertarian party
  President: John Hospers, California
  Vice president: Theodora Nathan, Oregon
People's party
  President: Benjamin McLane Spock
  Vice president: Julius Hobson, District of Columbia
America First party
  President: John V. Mahalchik
  Vice president: Irving Homer
Universal party
  President: Gabriel Green
  Vice president: Daniel Fry

1976 Election

Democratic party
  President: James Earl (Jimmy) Carter, Jr., Georgia
  Vice president: Walter Frederick Mondale, Minnesota
Republican party
  President: Gerald Rudolph Ford, Michigan
  Vice president: Robert Joseph Dole, Kansas
Independent candidate
  President: Eugene Joseph McCarthy, Minnesota
  Vice president: none [d]
Libertarian party
  President: Roger MacBride, Virginia
  Vice president: David P. Bergland, California
American Independent party
  President: Lester Maddox, Georgia
  Vice president: William Dyke, Wisconsin
American party
  President: Thomas J. Anderson, Tennessee
  Vice president: Rufus Shackleford, Florida
Socialist Workers party
  President: Peter Camejo, California
  Vice president: Willie Mae Reid, California
Communist party
  President: Gus Hall, New York
  Vice president: Jarvis Tyner, New York
People's party
  President: Margaret Wright, California
  Vice president: Benjamin Spock, New York
U.S. Labor party
  President: Lyndon H. LaRouche, Jr., New York
  Vice president: R. W. Evans, Michigan
Prohibition party
  President: Benjamin C. Bubar, Maine
  Vice president: Earl F. Dodge, Colorado
Socialist Labor party
  President: Jules Levin, New Jersey
  Vice president: Constance Blomen, Massachusetts
Socialist party
  President: Frank P. Zeidler, Wisconsin
  Vice president: J. Quinn Brisben, Illinois
Restoration party
  President: Ernest L. Miller
  Vice president: Roy N. Eddy
United American party
  President: Frank Taylor
  Vice president: Henry Swan

1980 Election[e]

Republican party
  President: Ronald Wilson Reagan, California
  Vice president: George Herbert Walker Bush, Texas
Democratic party
  President: James Earl (Jimmy) Carter, Jr., Georgia
  Vice president: Walter Frederick Mondale, Minnesota
National Unity Campaign
  President: John B. Anderson, Illinois
  Vice president: Patrick Joseph Lucey, Wisconsin
Libertarian party
  President: Edward E. Clark, California
  Vice president: David Koch, New York
Citizens party
  President: Barry Commoner, New York
  Vice president: LaDonna Harris, New Mexico
Communist party
  President: Gus Hall, New York
  Vice president: Angela Davis, California
American Independent party
  President: John Richard Rarick, Louisiana
  Vice president: Eileen M. Shearer, California
Socialist Workers party
  President: Andrew Pulley, Illinois
  Vice president: Matilde Zimmermann

  President: Clifton DeBerry, California
  Vice president: Matilde Zimmermann

  President: Richard Congress, Ohio
  Vice president: Matilde Zimmermann
Right to Life party
  President: Ellen McCormack, New York
  Vice president: Carroll Driscoll, New Jersey
Peace and Freedom party
  President: Maureen Smith, California
  Vice president: Elizabeth Barron
Workers World party
  President: Deirdre Griswold, New Jersey
  Vice president: Larry Holmes, New York
Statesman party
  President: Benjamin C. Bubar, Maine
  Vice president: Earl F. Dodge, Colorado
Socialist party
  President: David McReynolds, New York
  Vice president: Diane Drufenbrock, Wisconsin
American party
  President: Percy L. Greaves, New York
  Vice president: Frank L. Varnum, California

  President: Frank W. Shelton, Utah
  Vice president: George E. Jackson

Middle Class party
President: Kurt Lynen, New Jersey
Vice president: Harry Kieve, New Jersey
Down With Lawyers party
President: Bill Gahres, New Jersey
Vice president: J. F. Loghlin, New Jersey
Independent party
President: Martin E. Wendelken
Natural Peoples party
President: Harley McLain, North Dakota
Vice president: Jewelie Goeller, North Dakota

1984 Election [f]

Republican party
President: Ronald Wilson Reagan, California
Vice president: George Herbert Walker Bush, Texas
Democratic party
President: Walter Fritz Mondale, Minnesota
Vice president: Geraldine Anne Ferraro, New York
Libertarian party
President: David P. Bergland, California
Vice president: Jim Lewis, Connecticut
Independent party
President: Lyndon H. LaRouche, Jr., Virginia
Vice president: Billy Davis, Mississippi
Citizens party
President: Sonia Johnson, Virginia
Vice president: Richard Walton, Rhode Island
Populist party
President: Bob Richards, Texas
Vice president: Maureen Kennedy Salaman, California
Independent Alliance party
President: Dennis L. Serrette, New Jersey
Vice president: Nancy Ross, New York
Communist party
President: Gus Hall, New York
Vice president: Angela Davis, California
Socialist Workers party
President: Mel Mason, California
Vice president: Andrea Gonzalez, New York
Workers World party
President: Larry Holmes, New York
Vice president: Gloria La Riva, California
President: Gavrielle Holmes, New York
Vice president: Milton Vera
American party
President: Delmar Davis, Tennessee
Vice president: Traves Brownlee, Delaware
Workers League party
President: Ed Winn, New York
Vice presidents: Jean T. Brust, Helen Halyard, Edward Bergonzi
Prohibition party
President: Earl F. Dodge, Colorado
Vice president: Warren C. Martin, Kansas

1988 Election [g]

Democratic party
President: Michael Stanley Dukakis, Massachusetts
Vice president: Lloyd Millard Bentsen, Jr., Texas
Republican party
President: George Herbert Walker Bush, Texas
Vice president: James Danforth Quayle, Indiana
Libertarian party
President: Ronald Ernest Paul, Texas
Vice president: Andre Marrou
New Alliance party
President: Lenora B. Fulani, New York
Vice president: Joyce Dattner
Populist party
President: David E. Duke, Louisiana
Vice president: Floyd C. Parker
Consumer party
President: Eugene Joseph McCarthy, Minnesota
Vice president: Florence Rice
American Independent party
President: James C. Griffin, California
Vice president: Charles J. Morsa
National Economic Recovery party
President: Lyndon H. LaRouche, Jr., Virginia
Vice president: Debra H. Freeman
Right to Life party
President: William A. Marra, New Jersey
Vice president: Joan Andrews
Workers League party
President: Edward Winn, New York
Vice president: Barry Porster
Socialist Workers party
President: James Warren, New Jersey
Vice president: Kathleen Mickells
Peace and Freedom party
President: Herbert Lewin
Vice president: Vikki Murdock
Prohibition party
President: Earl F. Dodge, Colorado
Vice president: George D. Ormsby
Workers World party
President: Larry Holmes, New York
Vice president: Gloria La Riva, California
Socialist party
President: Willa Kenoyer, Minnesota
Vice president: Ron Ehrenreich
American party
President: Delmar Dennis, Tennessee
Vice president: Earl Jepson
Grassroots party
President: Jack E. Herer
Vice president: (no first name listed) Beal
Independent party
President: Louie Youngkeit, Utah
Third World Assembly
President: John G. Martin, District of Columbia
Vice president: Cleveland Sparrow

Source: 1832-1984—*Guide to U.S. Elections,* 2d ed. (Washington, D.C.: Congressional Quarterly Inc., 1985), 239-247; 1988—Elections Research Center.

* Candidates appeared in Joseph Nathan Kane, *Facts About the Presidents*, 4th ed. (New York: H. W. Wilson, 1981), but could not be verified in another source.

a. 1912: Arthur M. Schlesinger's *History of American Presidential Elections* (New York: McGraw-Hill, 1971) lists the Socialist Labor party vice-presidential candidate as Francis. No first name is given.
b. 1924: Richard M. Scammon's *America at the Polls* (Pittsburgh: University of Pittsburgh Press, 1965) lists the American party vice-presidential candidate as Leander L. Pickett.
c. 1928: *America at the Polls* lists the Farmer Labor party vice-presidential candidate as L. R. Tillman.
d. 1976: McCarthy, who ran as an independent with no party designation, had no national running mate, favoring the elimination of the office. But because various state laws required a running mate, he had different ones in different states, amounting to nearly two dozen, all political unknowns.
e. 1980: In several cases vice-presidential nominees were different from those listed for most states, and the Socialist Workers and American party nominees for president varied from state to state. For example, because Pulley, the major standard bearer for the Socialist Workers party was only twenty-nine years old, his name was not allowed on the ballot on some states (the Constitution requires presidential candidates to be at least thirty-five years old). Hence, the party ran other candidates in those states. In a number of states candidates appeared on the ballot with variants of the party designations listed, without any party designation, or with entirely different party names.
f. 1984: Both Larry Holmes and Gavrielle Holmes were standard bearers of the Workers World party. Of the two, Larry Holmes was listed on more state ballots. Milton Vera was Gavrielle Holmes's vice-presidential running mate in Ohio and Rhode Island. The Workers League party had three vice-presidential running mates: Jean T. Brust in Illinois; Helen Halyard in Michigan, New Jersey, and Pennsylvania; and Edward Bergonzi in Minnesota and Ohio.
g. 1988: In several cases, a party's vice-presidential candidate varied from state to state. Candidates' full names and states were not available from some parties.

Party Affiliations in Congress and the Presidency, 1789-1989

		House		Senate		
Year	Congress	Majority party	Principal minority party	Majority party	Principal minority party	President
1789-1791	1st	Ad-38	Op-26	Ad-17	Op-9	F (Washington)
1791-1793	2d	F-37	DR-33	F-16	DR-13	F (Washington)
1793-1795	3d	DR-57	F-48	F-17	DR-13	F (Washington)
1795-1797	4th	F-54	DR-52	F-19	DR-13	F (Washington)
1797-1799	5th	F-58	DR-48	F-20	DR-12	F (John Adams)
1799-1801	6th	F-64	DR-42	F-19	DR-13	F (John Adams)
1801-1803	7th	DR-69	F-36	DR-18	F-13	DR (Jefferson)
1803-1805	8th	DR-102	F-39	DR-25	F-9	DR (Jefferson)
1805-1807	9th	DR-116	F-25	DR-27	F-7	DR (Jefferson)
1807-1809	10th	DR-118	F-24	DR-28	F-6	DR (Jefferson)
1809-1811	11th	DR-94	F-48	DR-28	F-6	DR (Madison)
1811-1813	12th	DR-108	F-36	DR-30	F-6	DR (Madison)
1813-1815	13th	DR-112	F-68	DR-27	F-9	DR (Madison)
1815-1817	14th	DR-117	F-65	DR-25	F-11	DR (Madison)
1817-1819	15th	DR-141	F-42	DR-34	F-10	DR (Monroe)
1819-1821	16th	DR-156	F-27	DR-35	F-7	DR (Monroe)
1821-1823	17th	DR-158	F-25	DR-44	F-4	DR (Monroe)
1823-1825	18th	DR-187	F-26	DR-44	F-4	DR (Monroe)
1825-1827	19th	Ad-105	J-97	Ad-26	J-20	C (John Q. Adams)
1827-1829	20th	J-119	Ad-94	J-28	Ad-20	C (John Q. Adams)
1829-1831	21st	D-139	NR-74	D-26	NR-22	D (Jackson)
1831-1833	22d	D-141	NR-58	D-25	NR-21	D (Jackson)
1833-1835	23d	D-147	AM-53	D-20	NR-20	D (Jackson)
1835-1837	24th	D-145	W-98	D-27	W-25	D (Jackson)
1837-1839	25th	D-108	W-107	D-30	W-18	D (Van Buren)
1839-1841	26th	D-124	W-118	D-28	W-22	D (Van Buren)
1841-1843	27th	W-133	D-102	W-28	D-22	W (W. Harrison) W (Tyler)
1843-1845	28th	D-142	W-79	W-28	D-25	W (Tyler)
1845-1847	29th	D-143	W-77	D-31	W-25	D (Polk)
1847-1849	30th	W-115	D-108	D-36	W-21	D (Polk)
1849-1851	31st	D-112	W-109	D-35	W-25	W (Taylor) W (Fillmore)
1851-1853	32d	D-140	W-88	D-35	W-24	W (Fillmore)
1853-1855	33d	D-159	W-71	D-38	W-22	D (Pierce)
1855-1857	34th	R-108	D-83	D-40	R-15	D (Pierce)
1857-1859	35th	D-118	R-92	D-36	R-20	D (Buchanan)
1859-1861	36th	R-114	D-92	D-36	R-26	D (Buchanan)
1861-1863	37th	R-105	D-43	R-31	D-8	R (Lincoln)
1863-1865	38th	R-102	D-75	R-36	D-9	R (Lincoln)
1865-1867	39th	U-149	D-42	U-42	D-10	R (Lincoln) R (A. Johnson)
1867-1869	40th	R-143	D-49	R-42	D-11	R (A. Johnson)
1869-1871	41st	R-149	D-63	R-56	D-11	R (Grant)
1871-1873	42d	R-134	D-104	R-52	D-17	R (Grant)
1873-1875	43d	R-194	D-92	R-49	D-19	R (Grant)
1875-1877	44th	D-169	R-109	R-45	D-29	R (Grant)
1877-1879	45th	D-153	R-140	R-39	D-36	R (Hayes)
1879-1881	46th	D-149	R-130	D-42	R-33	R (Hayes)
1881-1883	47th	R-147	D-135	R-37	D-37	R (Garfield) R (Arthur)
1883-1885	48th	D-197	R-118	R-38	D-36	R (Arthur)
1885-1887	49th	D-183	R-140	R-43	D-34	D (Cleveland)
1887-1889	50th	D-169	R-152	R-39	D-37	D (Cleveland)
1889-1891	51st	R-166	D-159	R-39	D-37	R (B. Harrison)
1891-1893	52nd	D-235	R-88	R-47	D-39	R (B. Harrison)
1893-1895	53rd	D-218	R-127	D-44	R-38	D (Cleveland)
1895-1897	54th	R-244	D-105	R-43	D-39	D (Cleveland)

Year	Congress	House: Majority party	House: Principal minority party	Senate: Majority party	Senate: Principal minority party	President
1897-1899	55th	R-204	D-113	R-47	D-34	R (McKinley)
1899-1901	56th	R-185	D-163	R-53	D-26	R (McKinley)
1901-1903	57th	R-197	D-151	R-55	D-31	R (McKinley)
						R (T. Roosevelt)
1903-1905	58th	R-208	D-178	R-57	D-33	R (T. Roosevelt)
1905-1907	59th	R-250	D-136	R-57	D-33	R (T. Roosevelt)
1907-1909	60th	R-222	D-164	R-61	D-31	R (T. Roosevelt)
1909-1911	61st	R-219	D-172	R-61	D-32	R (Taft)
1911-1913	62d	D-228	R-161	R-51	D-41	R (Taft)
1913-1915	63d	D-291	R-127	D-51	R-44	D (Wilson)
1915-1917	64th	D-230	R-196	D-56	R-40	D (Wilson)
1917-1919	65th	D-216	R-210	D-53	R-42	D (Wilson)
1919-1921	66th	R-240	D-190	R-49	D-47	D (Wilson)
1921-1923	67th	R-301	D-131	R-59	D-37	R (Harding)
1923-1925	68th	R-225	D-205	R-51	D-43	R (Coolidge)
1925-1927	69th	R-247	D-183	R-56	D-39	R (Coolidge)
1927-1929	70th	R-237	D-195	R-49	D-46	R (Coolidge)
1929-1931	71st	R-267	D-167	R-56	D-39	R (Hoover)
1931-1933	72d	D-220	R-214	R-48	D-47	R (Hoover)
1933-1935	73d	D-310	R-117	D-60	R-35	D (F. Roosevelt)
1935-1937	74th	D-319	R-103	D-69	R-25	D (F. Roosevelt)
1937-1939	75th	D-331	R-89	D-76	R-16	D (F. Roosevelt)
1939-1941	76th	D-261	R-164	D-69	R-23	D (F. Roosevelt)
1941-1943	77th	D-268	R-162	D-66	R-28	D (F. Roosevelt)
1943-1945	78th	D-218	R-208	D-58	R-37	D (F. Roosevelt)
1945-1947	79th	D-242	R-190	D-56	R-38	D (F. Roosevelt)
						D (Truman)
1947-1949	80th	R-245	D-188	R-51	D-45	D (Truman)
1949-1951	81st	D-263	R-171	D-54	R-42	D (Truman)
1951-1953	82d	D-234	R-199	D-49	R-47	D (Truman)
1953-1955	83d	R-221	D-211	R-48	D-47	R (Eisenhower)
1955-1957	84th	D-232	R-203	D-48	R-47	R (Eisenhower)
1957-1959	85th	D-233	R-200	D-49	R-47	R (Eisenhower)
1959-1961	86th	D-283	R-153	D-64	R-34	R (Eisenhower)
1961-1963	87th	D-263	R-174	D-65	R-35	D (Kennedy)
1963-1965	88th	D-258	R-177	D-67	R-33	D (Kennedy)
						D (L. Johnson)
1965-1967	89th	D-295	R-140	D-68	R-32	D (L. Johnson)
1967-1969	90th	D-247	R-187	D-64	R-36	D (L. Johnson)
1969-1971	91st	D-243	R-192	D-57	R-43	R (Nixon)
1971-1973	92d	D-254	R-180	D-54	R-44	R (Nixon)
1973-1975	93d	D-239	R-192	D-56	R-42	R (Nixon)
						R (Ford)
1975-1977	94th	D-291	R-144	D-60	R-37	R (Ford)
1977-1979	95th	D-292	R-143	D-61	R-38	D (Carter)
1979-1981	96th	D-276	R-157	D-58	R-41	D (Carter)
1981-1983	97th	D-243	R-192	R-53	D-46	R (Reagan)
1983-1985	98th	D-269	R-165	R-54	D-46	R (Reagan)
1985-1987	99th	D-252	R-182	R-53	D-47	R (Reagan)
1987-1989	100th	D-258	R-177	D-55	R-45	R (Reagan)
1989-1991	101st	D-260	R-175	D-55	R-45	R (Bush)

Source: American Leaders, 1789-1987 (Washington, D.C.: Congressional Quarterly Inc., 1987).

Note: AD—Administration; AM—Anti-Masonic; C—Coalition; D—Democratic; DR—Democratic-Republican; F—Federalist; J—Jacksonian; NR—National Republican; Op—Opposition; R—Republican; U—Unionist; W—Whig. Figures are for the beginning of the first session of each Congress.

Cabinet Members and Other Officials

George Washington, 1789-1797

Chief Justice	John Jay	1789-95
	Oliver Ellsworth	1796-97
Vice President	John Adams	1789-97
Secretary of State	Thomas Jefferson	1789-93
	Edmund Randolph	1794-95
	Timothy Pickering	1795-97
Secretary of the Treasury	Alexander Hamilton	1789-95
	Oliver Wolcott, Jr.	1795-97
Secretary of War	Henry Knox	1789-95
	Timothy Pickering	1795-96
	James McHenry	1796-97
Attorney General	Edmund Randolph	1789-94
	William Bradford	1794-95
	Charles Lee	1795-97
Postmaster General	Samuel Osgood	1789-91
	Timothy Pickering	1791-95
	Joseph Habersham	1795-97

John Adams, 1797-1801

Chief Justice	Oliver Ellsworth	1797-1800
	John Marshall	1801
Vice President	Thomas Jefferson	1797-1801
Secretary of State	Thomas Pickering	1797-1800
	John Marshall	1800-01
Secretary of the Treasury	Oliver Wolcott, Jr.	1797-1800
	Samuel Dexter	1801
Secretary of War	James McHenry	1797-1800
	Samuel Dexter	1800-01
Attorney General	Charles Lee	1797-1801
Postmaster General	Joseph Habersham	1797-1801
Secretary of the Navy	Benjamin Stoddert	1798-1801

Thomas Jefferson, 1801-1809

Chief Justice	John Marshall	1801-09
Vice President	Aaron Burr	1801-05
	George Clinton	1805-09
Secretary of State	James Madison	1801-09
Secretary of the Treasury	Samuel Dexter	1801
	Albert Gallatin	1801-09
Secretary of War	Henry Dearborn	1801-09
Attorney General	Levi Lincoln	1801-04
	Robert Smith	1805
	John Breckinridge	1805-06
	Caesar A. Rodney	1807-09
Postmaster General	Joseph Habersham	1801
	Gideon Granger	1801-09
Secretary of the Navy	Benjamin Stoddert	1801
	Henry Dearborn	1801
	Robert Smith	1801-09

James Madison, 1809-1817

Chief Justice	John Marshall	1809-17
Vice President	George Clinton	1809-13
	Elbridge Gerry	1813-14
Secretary of State	Robert Smith	1809-11
	James Monroe	1811-17
Secretary of the Treasury	Albert Gallatin	1809-14
	George W. Campbell	1814
	Alexander J. Dallas	1814-16
	William H. Crawford	1816-17
Secretary of War	John Smith	1809
	John Armstrong	1813-14
	James Monroe	1814-15
	William H. Crawford	1815-16
	George Graham	1816-17
Attorney General	Caesar A. Rodney	1809-11
	William Pinkney	1811-14
	Richard Rush	1814-17
Postmaster General	Gideon Granger	1809-14
	Return J. Meigs, Jr.	1814-17
Secretary of the Navy	Robert Smith	1809
	Charles W. Goldsborough	1809, 13
	Paul Hamilton	1809-12
	William Jones	1813-14
	Benjamin Homans	1814
	Benjamin W. Crowninshield	1815-17

James Monroe, 1817-1825

Chief Justice	John Marshall	1817-25
Vice President	Daniel D. Tompkins	1817-25
Secretary of State	John Graham	1817
	Richard Rush	1817
	John Quincy Adams	1817-25
Secretary of the Treasury	William H. Crawford	1817-25
Secretary of War	George Graham	1817
	John C. Calhoun	1817-25
Attorney General	Richard Rush	1817
	William Wirt	1817-25
Postmaster General	Return J. Meigs, Jr.	1817-23
	John McLean	1823-25
Secretary of the Navy	Benjamin W. Crowninshield	1817-18
	John C. Calhoun	1818
	Smith Thompson	1819-23
	John Rodgers	1823
	Samuel L. Southard	1823-25

John Quincy Adams, 1825-1829

Chief Justice	John Marshall	1825-29
Vice President	John C. Calhoun	1825-29
Secretary of State	Daniel Brent	1825
	Henry Clay	1825-29
Secretary of the Treasury	Samuel Southard	1825
	Richard Rush	1825-29
Secretary of War	James Barbour	1825-28
	Samuel Southard	1828
	Peter B. Porter	1828-29
Attorney General	William Wirt	1825-29
Postmaster General	John McLean	1825-29
Secretary of the Navy	Samuel L. Southard	1825-29

Andrew Jackson, 1829-1837

Chief Justice	John Marshall	1829-35
	Roger B. Taney	1836-37
Vice President	John C. Calhoun	1829-32
	Martin Van Buren	1833-37
Secretary of State	James A. Hamilton	1829
	Martin Van Buren	1829-31
	Edward Livingston	1831-33
	Louis McLane	1833-34
	John Forsyth	1834-37
Secretary of the Treasury	Samuel D. Ingham	1829-31
	Asbury Dickins	1831
	Louis McLane	1831-33
	William J. Duane	1833
	Roger B. Taney	1833-34
	McClintock Young	1834
	Levi Woodbury	1834-37
Secretary of War	John H. Eaton	1829-31
	Philip G. Randolph	1831
	Roger B. Taney	1831
	Lewis Cass	1831-36
	Carey A. Harris	1836
	Benjamin F. Butler	1837
Attorney General	John M. Berrien	1829-31
	Roger B. Taney	1831-33
	Benjamin F. Butler	1833-37
Postmaster General	John McLean	1829
	William T. Barry	1829-35
	Amos Kendall	1835-37
Secretary of the Navy	Charles Hay	1829
	John Branch	1829-31
	John Boyle	1831
	Levi Woodbury	1831-34
	Mahlon Dickerson	1834-37

Martin Van Buren, 1837-1842

Chief Justice	Roger B. Taney	1837-41
Vice President	Richard M. Johnson	1837-41
Secretary of State	John Forsyth	1837-41
Secretary of the Treasury	Levi Woodbury	1837-41
Secretary of War	Benjamin F. Butler	1837
	Joel R. Poinsett	1837-41
Attorney General	Benjamin F. Butler	1837-38
	Felix Grundy	1838-40
	Henry D. Gilpin	1840-41
Postmaster General	Amos Kendall	1837-40
	John M. Niles	1840-41
Secretary of the Navy	Mahlon Dickerson	1837-38
	James K. Paulding	1838-41

William H. Harrison, 1841

Chief Justice	Roger B. Taney	1841
Vice President	John Tyler	1841
Secretary of State	J. L. Martin	1841
	Daniel Webster	1841
Secretary of the Treasury	McClintock Young	1841
	Thomas Ewing	1841
Secretary of War	John Bell	1841
Attorney General	John J. Crittenden	1841
Postmaster General	Selah Reeve Hobbie	1841
	Francis Granger	1841
Secretary of the Navy	John Simms	1841
	George E. Badger	1841

John Tyler, 1841-1845

Chief Justice	Roger B. Taney	1841-45
Vice President	*None*	
Secretary of State	Daniel Webster	1841-43
	Hugh S. Legaré	1843
	William S. Derrick	1843
	Abel P. Upshur	1843-44
	John Nelson	1844
	John C. Calhoun	1844-45
Secretary of the Treasury	Thomas Ewing	1841
	McClintock Young	1841
	Walter Forward	1841-43
	McClintock Young	1843
	John C. Spencer	1843-44
	McClintock Young	1844
	George M. Bibb	1844-45
Secretary of War	John Bell	1841
	Albert Lea	1841
	John C. Spencer	1841-43
	James M. Porter	1843-44
	William Wilkins	1844-45
Attorney General	John J. Crittenden	1841
	Hugh S. Legaré	1841-43
	John Nelson	1843-45
Postmaster General	Francis Granger	1841
	Selah Reeve Hobbie	1841
	Charles A. Wickliffe	1841-45
Secretary of the Navy	George E. Badger	1841
	John Simms	1841
	Abel P. Upshur	1841-43
	David Henshaw	1843-44
	Thomas W. Gilmer	1844
	Lewis Warrington	1844
	John Y. Mason	1844-45

James K. Polk, 1845-1849

Chief Justice	Roger B. Taney	1845-49
Vice President	George M. Dallas	1845-49
Secretary of State	John C. Calhoun	1845
	James Buchanan	1845-49
Secretary of the Treasury	George M. Bibb	1845
	Robert J. Walker	1845-49
Secretary of War	William Wilkins	1845-49
	William L. Marcy	1845-49
Attorney General	John Nelson	1845
	John Y. Mason	1845-46
	Nathan Clifford	1846-48
	Isaac Toucey	1848-49
Postmaster General	Charles A. Wickliffe	1845
	Cave Johnson	1845-49
Secretary of the Navy	John Y. Mason	1845
	George Bancroft	1845-46
	John Y. Mason	1846-49

Zachary Taylor, 1849-1850

Chief Justice	Roger B. Taney	1849-50
Vice President	Millard Fillmore	1849-50
Secretary of State	James Buchanan	1849
	John M. Clayton	1849-50
Secretary of the Treasury	Robert J. Walker	1849
	McClintock Young	1849
	W. M. Meredith	1849-50

Secretary of War	William L. Marcy	1849
	Reverdy Johnson	1849
	G. W. Crawford	1849-50
Attorney General	Isaac Toucey	1849
	Reverdy Johnson	1849-50
Postmaster General	Cave Johnson	1849
	Selah Reeve Hobbie	1849
	Jacob Collamer	1849-50
Secretary of the Navy	John Y. Mason	1849
	William B. Preston	1849-50
Secretary of the Interior	Thomas Ewing	1849-50

Millard Fillmore, 1850-1853

Chief Justice	Roger B. Taney	1850-53
Vice President	*None*	
Secretary of State	John Clayton	1850
	Daniel Webster	1850-52
	Charles M. Conrad	1852
Secretary of the Treasury	William M. Meredith	1850
	Thomas Corwin	1850-53
Secretary of War	George W. Crawford	1850
	Samuel J. Anderson	1850
	Winfield Scott	1850
	Charles M. Conrad	1850-53
Attorney General	Reverdy Johnson	1850
	John J. Crittenden	1850-53
Postmaster General	Jacob Collamer	1850
	Nathan K. Hall	1850-52
	Samuel D. Hubbard	1852-53
Secretary of the Navy	William B. Preston	1850
	Lewis Warrington	1850
	William A. Graham	1850-52
	John P. Kennedy	1852-53
Secretary of the Interior	Thomas Ewing	1850
	Daniel Goddard	1850
	T. M. T. McKennan	1850
	A. H. H. Stuart	1850-53

Franklin Pierce, 1853-1857

Chief Justice	Roger B. Taney	1853-57
Vice President	William R. D. King	1853
Secretary of State	William Hunter	1853
	William L. Marcy	1853-57
Secretary of the Treasury	Thomas Corwin	1853
	James Guthrie	1853-57
Secretary of War	Charles M. Conrad	1853
	Jefferson Davis	1853-57
	Samuel Cooper	1857
Attorney General	John J. Crittenden	1853
	Caleb Cushing	1853-57
Postmaster General	Samuel Hubbard	1853
	James Campbell	1853-57
Secretary of the Navy	John P. Kennedy	1853
	James C. Dobbin	1853-57
Secretary of the Interior	Alexander H. H. Stuart	1853
	Robert McClelland	1853-57

James Buchanan, 1857-1861

Chief Justice	Roger B. Taney	1857-61
Vice President	John C. Breckinridge	1857-61
Secretary of State	William L. Marcy	1857
	Lewis Cass	1857-60
	William Hunter	1860
	Jeremiah S. Black	1860-61
Secretary of the Treasury	James Guthrie	1857
	Howell Cobb	1857-60
	Isaac Toucey	1860
	Phillip F. Thomas	1860-61
	John A. Dix	1861
Secretary of War	Samuel Cooper	1857
	John B. Floyd	1857-61
	Joseph Holt	1861
Attorney General	Caleb Cushing	1857
	Jeremiah S. Black	1857-60
	Edwin M. Stanton	1860-61
Postmaster General	James Campbell	1857
	Aaron V. Brown	1857-59
	Horatio King	1859
	Joseph Holt	1859-61
	Horatio King	1861
Secretary of the Navy	John C. Dobbin	1857
	Isaac Toucey	1857-61
Secretary of the Interior	Robert McClelland	1857
	Jacob Thompson	1857-61
	Moses Kelly	1861

Abraham Lincoln, 1861-1865

Chief Justice	Roger B. Taney	1861-64
	Salmon P. Chase	1864-65
Vice President	Hannibal Hamlin	1861-65
	Andrew Johnson	1865
Secretary of State	Jeremiah S. Black	1861
	William H. Seward	1861-65
Secretary of the Treasury	John A. Dix	1861
	Salmon P. Chase	1861-64
	George Harrington	1864
	William P. Fessenden	1864-65
	George Harrington	1865
	Hugh McCulloch	1865
Secretary of War	Joseph Holt	1861
	Simon Cameron	1861-62
	Edwin M. Stanton	1862-65
Attorney General	Edward McMasters Stanton	1861
	Edward Bates	1861-64
	James Speed	1864-65
Postmaster General	Horatio King	1861
	Montgomery Blair	1861-64
	William Dennison	1864-65
Secretary of the Navy	Isaac Toucey	1861
	Gideon Welles	1861-65
Secretary of the Interior	Moses Kelly	1861
	Caleb B. Smith	1861-63
	John P. Usher	1863-65

Andrew Johnson, 1865-1869

Chief Justice	Salmon P. Chase	1865-69
Vice President	*None*	
Secretary of State	William H. Seward	1865-69
Secretary of the Treasury	Hugh McCulloch	1865-69
Secretary of War	Edwin M. Stanton	1865-67
	Ulysses S. Grant	1867-68
	Edwin M. Stanton	1868
	John M. Schofield	1868-69
Attorney General	James Speed	1865-66
	J. Hubley Ashton	1866
	Henry Stanbery	1866-68
	Orville Hickman Browning	1868

Postmaster General	William Dennison	1865-66
	Alexander W. Randall	1866-69
Secretary of the Navy	Gideon Welles	1865-69
Secretary of the Interior	John P. Usher	1865
	James Harlan	1865-66
	Orville H. Browning	1866-69

Ulysses S. Grant, 1869-1877

Chief Justice	Salmon P. Chase	1869-73
	Morrison R. Waite	1874-77
Vice President	Schuyler Colfax	1869-73
	Henry Wilson	1873-75
Secretary of State	William H. Seward	1869
	Elihu B. Washburne	1869
	Hamilton Fish	1869-77
Secretary of the Treasury	Hugh McCulloch	1869
	John F. Hartley	1869
	George S. Boutwell	1869-73
	William A. Richardson	1873-74
	Benjamin H. Bristow	1874-76
	Charles F. Conant	1876
	Lot M. Morrill	1876-77
Secretary of War	John M. Schofield	1869
	John A. Rawlins	1869
	William T. Sherman	1869
	William W. Belknap	1869-76
	Alphonso Taft	1876
	James D. Cameron	1876-77
Attorney General	William M. Evarts	1869
	J. Hubley Ashton	1869
	Ebenezer Rockwood Hoar	1869-70
	Amos T. Akerman	1870-71
	George H. Williams	1872-75
	Edwards Pierrepont	1875-76
	Alphonso Taft	1876-77
Postmaster General	St. John B. L. Skinner	1869
	John A. J. Creswell	1869-74
	James W. Marshall	1874
	Marshall Jewell	1874-76
	James N. Tyner	1876-77
Secretary of the Navy	William Faxon	1869
	Adolph E. Borie	1869
	George M. Robeson	1869-77
Secretary of the Interior	William T. Otto	1869
	Jacob D. Cox	1869-70
	Columbus Delano	1870-75
	Benjamin R. Cowen	1875
	Zachariah Chandler	1875-77

Rutherford B. Hayes, 1877-1881

Chief Justice	Morrison R. Waite	1877-81
Vice President	William A. Wheeler	1877-81
Secretary of State	Hamilton Fish	1877
	William M. Evarts	1877-81
Secretary of the Treasury	Lot M. Morrill	1877
	John Sherman	1877-81
Secretary of War	James D. Cameron	1877
	George W. McCrary	1877-79
	Alexander Ramsey	1879-81
Attorney General	Alphonso Taft	1877
	Charles Devens	1877-81
Postmaster General	James N. Tyrer	1877
	David M. Key	1877-80
	Horace Maynard	1880-81
Secretary of the Navy	George M. Robeson	1877
	Richard W. Thompson	1877-81
	Alexander Ramsey	1880
	Nathan Goff, Jr.	1881
Secretary of the Interior	Zachariah Chandler	1877
	Carl Schurz	1877-81

James A. Garfield, 1881

Chief Justice	Morrison R. Waite	1881
Vice President	Chester A. Arthur	1881
Secretary of State	William M. Evarts	1881
	James G. Blaine	1881
Secretary of the Treasury	Henry F. French	1881
	William Windom	1881
Secretary of War	Alexander Ramsey	1881
	Robert T. Lincoln	1881
Attorney General	Charles Devens	1881
	Wayne MacVeagh	1881
Postmaster General	Horace Maynard	1881
	Thomas L. James	1881
Secretary of the Navy	Nathan Goff	1881
	William H. Hunt	1881
Secretary of the Interior	Carl Schurz	1881
	Samuel J. Kirkwood	1881

Chester A. Arthur, 1881-1885

Chief Justice	Morrison R. Waite	1881-85
Vice President	*None*	
Secretary of State	James G. Blaine	1881
	Frederick T. Frelinghuysen	1881-85
Secretary of the Treasury	William Windom	1881
	Charles J. Folger	1881-84
	Charles E. Coon	1884
	Henry F. French	1884
	Walter Q. Gresham	1884
	Hugh McCullock	1884-85
Attorney General	Wayne MacVeagh	1881
	Samuel F. Phillips	1881
	Benjamin H. Brewster	1882-85
Postmaster General	Thomas L. James	1881
	Timothy O. Howe	1882-83
	Frank Hatton	1883
	Walter Q. Gresham	1883-84
	Frank Hatton	1884-85
Secretary of the Navy	William H. Hunt	1881-82
	William E. Chandler	1882-85
Secretary of the Interior	Samuel J. Kirkwood	1881-82
	Henry M. Teller	1882-85

Grover Cleveland, 1885-1889

Chief Justice	Morrison R. Waite	1885-88
	Melville W. Fuller	1888-89
Vice President	Thomas A. Hendricks	1885
Secretary of State	Frederick T. Frelinghuysen	1885
	Thomas F. Bayard	1885-89
Secretary of the Treasury	Hugh McCulloch	1885
	Daniel Manning	1885-87
	Charles S. Fairchild	1887-89
Secretary of War	Robert T. Lincoln	1881-85
	William C. Endicott	1885-89

Attorney General	Benjamin H. Brewster	1885
	Augustus H. Garland	1885-89
Postmaster General	Frank Hatton	1885
	William F. Vilas	1885-88
	Don M. Dickinson	1888-89
Secretary of the Navy	William E. Chandler	1885
	William C. Whitney	1885-89
Secretary of the Interior	Merritt Joslyn	1885
	Lucius Q. C. Lamar	1885-88
	Henry L. Muldrow	1888
	William F. Vilas	1888-89
Secretary of Agriculture	Norman J. Colman	1889

Benjamin Harrison, 1889-1893

Chief Justice	Melville W. Fuller	1889-93
Vice President	Levi P. Morton	1889-93
Secretary of State	Thomas F. Bayard	1889
	James G. Blaine	1889-92
	William F. Wharton	1892
	John W. Foster	1892-93
	William F. Wharton	1893
Secretary of the Treasury	Charles S. Fairchild	1889
	William Windom	1889-91
	Alvred B. Nettleton	1891
	Charles Foster	1891-93
Secretary of War	William C. Endicott	1889
	Redfield Proctor	1889-91
	Lewis A. Grant	1891
	Stephen B. Elkins	1891-93
Attorney General	Augustus H. Garland	1889
	William H. H. Miller	1889-93
Postmaster General	Donald M. Dickinson	1889
	John Wanamaker	1889-93
Secretary of the Navy	William C. Whitney	1889
	Benjamin F. Tracy	1889-93
Secretary of the Interior	William F. Vilas	1889
	John W. Noble	1889-93
Secretary of Agriculture	Norman J. Colman	1889
	Jeremiah M. Rusk	1889-93

Grover Cleveland, 1893-1897

Chief Justice	Melville W. Fuller	1893-97
Vice President	Adlai E. Stevenson	1893-97
Secretary of State	William F. Wharton	1893
	Walter Q. Gresham	1893-95
	Edwin F. Uhl	1895
	Alvey A. Adee	1895
	Richard Olney	1895-97
Secretary of the Treasury	Charles Foster	1893
	John G. Carlisle	1893-97
Secretary of War	Stephen B. Elkins	1893
	Daniel S. Lamont	1893-97
Attorney General	William H. H. Miller	1893
	Richard Olney	1893-95
	Judson Harmon	1895-97
Postmaster General	John Wanamaker	1893
	Wilson S. Bissel	1893-95
	William L. Wilson	1895-97
Secretary of the Navy	Benjamin F. Tracy	1893
	Hilary A. Herbert	1893-97
Secretary of the Interior	John W. Noble	1893
	Hoke Smith	1893-96
	John M. Reynolds	1896
	David R. Francis	1896-97
Secretary of Agriculture	Jeremiah M. Rusk	1893
	Julius Sterling Morton	1893-97

William McKinley, 1897-1901

Chief Justice	Melville W. Fuller	1897-1901
Vice President	Garret A. Hobart	1897-99
	Theodore Roosevelt	1901
Secretary of State	Richard Olney	1897
	John Sherman	1897-98
	William R. Day	1898
	Alvey A. Adee	1898
	John Hay	1898-1901
Secretary of the Treasury	John G. Carlisle	1897
	Lyman J. Gage	1897-1901
Secretary of War	Daniel S. Lamont	1897
	Russell A. Alger	1897-99
	Elihu Root	1899-1901
Attorney General	Judson Harmon	1897
	Joseph McKenna	1897-98
	John K. Richards	1898
	John W. Griggs	1898-1901
	John K. Richards	1901
	Philander C. Knox	1901
Postmaster General	William L. Wilson	1897
	James A. Gary	1897-98
	Charles E. Smith	1898-1901
Secretary of the Navy	Hilary A. Herbert	1897
	John D. Long	1897-1901
Secretary of the Interior	David R. Francis	1897
	Cornelius N. Bliss	1897-99
	Ethan A. Hitchcock	1899-1901
Secretary of Agriculture	Julius S. Morton	1897
	James Wilson	1897-1901

Theodore Roosevelt, 1901-1909

Chief Justice	Melville W. Fuller	1901-09
Vice President	Charles W. Fairbanks	1905-09
Secretary of State	John Hay	1901-05
	Francis B. Loomis	1905
	Elihu Root	1905-09
	Robert Bacon	1909
Secretary of the Treasury	Lyman J. Gage	1901-02
	Leslie M. Shaw	1902-07
	George B. Cortelyou	1907-09
Secretary of War	Elihu Root	1901-04
	William H. Taft	1904-08
	Luke E. Wright	1908-09
Attorney General	Philander C. Knox	1901-04
	William H. Moody	1904-06
	Charles J. Bonaparte	1906-09
Postmaster General	Charles E. Smith	1901-02
	Henry C. Payne	1902-04
	Robert J. Wynne	1904-05
	George B. Cortelyou	1905-07
	George von L. Meyer	1907-09
Secretary of the Navy	John D. Long	1901-02
	William H. Moody	1902-04
	Paul Morton	1904-05
	Charles J. Bonaparte	1905-06
	Victor H. Metcalf	1906-08
	Truman H. Newberry	1908-09
Secretary of the Interior	Ethan A. Hitchcock	1901-07
	James R. Garfield	1907-09
Secretary of Agriculture	James Wilson	1901-09

Secretary of Commerce and Labor	George B. Cortelyou	1903-04
	Victor H. Metcalf	1904-06
	Oscar S. Straus	1906-09

William H. Taft, 1909-1913

Chief Justice	Melville W. Fuller	1909-10
	Edward D. White	1910-13
Vice President	James Schoolcraft Sherman	1909-12
Secretary of State	Roger Bacon	1909
	Philander C. Knox	1909-13
Secretary of the Treasury	George B. Cortelyou	1909
	Franklin Mac Veagh	1909-13
Secretary of War	Luke E. Wright	1909
	Jacob M. Dickinson	1909-11
	Henry L. Stimson	1911-13
Attorney General	Charles J. Bonaparte	1909
	George W. Wichersham	1909-13
Postmaster General	George von L. Meyer	1909
	Frank H. Hitchcock	1909-13
Secretary of the Navy	Truman H. Newberry	1909
	George von L. Meyer	1909-13
Secretary of the Interior	James Rudolph Garfield	1909
	Richard A. Ballinger	1909-11
	Walter L. Fisher	1911-13
Secretary of Agriculture	James Wilson	1909-13
Secretary of Commerce and Labor	Oscar S. Straus	1909
	Charles Nagel	1909-13

Woodrow Wilson, 1913-1921

Chief Justice	Edward D. White	1913-21
Vice President	Thomas R. Marshall	1913-21
Secretary of State	Philander C. Knox	1913
	William Jennings Bryan	1913-15
	Robert Lansing	1915-20
	Frank L. Polk	1920
	Bainbridge Colby	1920-21
Secretary of the Treasury	Franklin MacVeagh	1913
	William G. McAdoo	1913-18
	Carter Glass	1918-20
	David F. Houston	1920-21
Secretary of War	Henry L. Stimson	1913
	Lindley M. Garrison	1913-16
	Hugh L. Scott	1916
	Newton D. Baker	1916-21
Attorney General	George W. Wickersham	1913
	James C. McReynolds	1913-14
	Thomas W. Gregory	1914-19
	A. Mitchell Palmer	1919-21
Postmaster General	Frank H. Hitchcock	1913
	Albert S. Burleson	1913-21
Secretary of the Navy	George von L. Meyer	1913
	Josephus Daniels	1913-21
Secretary of the Interior	Walter L. Fisher	1913
	Franklin K. Lane	1913-20
	John B. Payne	1920-21
Secretary of Agriculture	James Wilson	1913
	David F. Houston	1913-20
	Edwin T. Meredith	1920-21
Secretary of Commerce	Charles Nagel	1913
	William C. Redfield	1913-19
	Joshua W. Alexander	1919-21
Secretary of Labor	Charles Nagel	1913
	William B. Wilson	1913-21

Warren G. Harding, 1921-1923

Chief Justice	Edward D. White	1921
	William Howard Taft	1921-23
Vice President	Calvin Coolidge	1921-23
Secretary of State	Bainbridge Colby	1921
	Charles Evans Hughes	1921-23
Secretary of the Treasury	David F. Houston	1921
	Andrew W. Mellon	1921-23
Secretary of War	Newton D. Baker	1921
	John W. Weeks	1921-23
Attorney General	Alexander M. Palmer	1921
	Harry M. Daugherty	1921-23
Postmaster General	Albert S. Burleson	1921
	Will H. Hays	1921-22
	Hubert Work	1922-23
	Harry S. New	1923
Secretary of the Navy	Josephus Daniels	1921
	Edwin Denby	1921-23
Secretary of the Interior	John B. Payne	1921
	Albert B. Fall	1921-23
	Hubert Work	1923
Secretary of Agriculture	Edwin T. Meredith	1921
	Henry C. Wallace	1921-23
Secretary of Commerce	Joshua W. Alexander	1921
	Herbert Hoover	1921-23
Secretary of Labor	William B. Wilson	1921
	James J. Davis	1921-23

Calvin Coolidge, 1923-1929

Chief Justice	William Howard Taft	1923-29
Vice President	Charles G. Dawes	1925-29
Secretary of State	Charles Evans Hughes	1923-25
	Frank B. Kellogg	1925-29
Secretary of the Treasury	Andrew W. Mellon	1923-29
Secretary of War	John W. Weeks	1923-25
	Dwight F. Davis	1925-29
Attorney General	Harry M. Daugherty	1923-24
	Harlan F. Stone	1924-25
	James M. Beck	1925
	John G. Sargent	1925-29
Postmaster General	Harry S. New	1923-29
Secretary of the Navy	Edwin Denby	1923-24
	Curtis D. Wilbur	1924-29
Secretary of the Interior	Hubert Work	1923-28
	Roy O. West	1928-29
Secretary of Agriculture	Henry C. Wallace	1923-24
	Howard M. Gore	1924-25
	William M. Jardine	1925-29
Secretary of Commerce	Herbert Hoover	1923-28
	William F. Whiting	1928-29
Secretary of Labor	James J. Davis	1923-29

Herbert C. Hoover, 1929-1933

Chief Justice	William Howard Taft	1929-30
	Charles Evans Hughes	1930-33
Vice President	Charles Curtis	1929-33
Secretary of State	Frank B. Kellogg	1929
	Henry L. Stimson	1929-33
Secretary of the Treasury	Andrew W. Mellon	1929-32
	Ogden L. Mills	1932-33
Secretary of War	Dwight F. Davis	1929
	James W. Good	1929
	Patrick J. Hurley	1929-33

Attorney General	John G. Sargent	1929
	William D. Mitchell	1929-33
Postmaster General	Harry S. New	1929
	Walter F. Brown	1929-33
Secretary of the Navy	Curtis D. Wilbur	1929
	Charles Francis Adams	1929-33
Secretary of the Interior	Roy O. West	1929
	Ray Lyman Wilbur	1929-33
Secretary of Agriculture	William M. Jardine	1929
	Arthur M. Hyde	1929-33
Secretary of Commerce	William F. Whiting	1929
	Robert P. Lamont	1929-32
	Roy D. Chapin	1932-33
Secretary of Labor	James J. Davis	1929-30
	William N. Doak	1930-33

Franklin D. Roosevelt, 1933-1945

Chief Justice	Charles Evans Hughes	1933-41
	Harlan Fiske Stone	1941-45
Vice President	John Nance Garner	1933-41
	Henry A. Wallace	1941-45
	Harry S Truman	1945
Secretary of State	Cordell Hull	1933-44
	Edward R. Stettinius, Jr.	1944-45
Secretary of the Treasury	W. H. Woodin	1933-34
	Henry Morgenthau, Jr.	1934-45
Secretary of War	George H. Dren	1933-36
	Harry H. Woodring	1936-40
	Henry L. Stimson	1940-45
Attorney General	Homer S. Cummings	1933-39
	Frank Murphy	1939-40
	Robert H. Jackson	1940-41
	Francis Biddle	1941-45
Postmaster General	James A. Farley	1933-40
	Frank C. Walker	1940-45
Secretary of the Navy	Claude A. Swanson	1933-39
	Charles Edison	1939-40
	Frank Knox	1940-44
	James Forrestal	1944-45
Secretary of the Interior	Harold L. Ickes	1933-45
Secretary of Agriculture	Henry A. Wallace	1933-40
	Claude R. Wickard	1940-45
Secretary of Commerce	Daniel C. Roper	1933-38
	Harry L. Hopkins	1938-40
	Jesse H. Jones	1940-45
	Henry A. Wallace	1945
Secretary of Labor	Frances Perkins	1933-45

Harry S Truman, 1945-1953

Chief Justice	Harlan Fiske Stone	1945-46
	Frederick M. Vinson	1946-53
Vice President	Alben W. Barkley	1949-53
Secretary of State	Edward R. Stettinius, Jr.	1945
	James F. Byrnes	1945-47
	George C. Marshall	1947-49
	Dean G. Acheson	1949-53
Secretary of the Treasury	Henry Morgenthau, Jr.	1945
	Frederick M. Vinson	1945-46
	John W. Snyder	1946-53
Secretary of War	Henry L. Stimson	1945
	Robert P. Patterson	1945-47
	Kenneth C. Royall	1947
Secretary of Defense	James V. Forrestal	1947-49
	Louis A. Johnson	1949-50
	George C. Marshall	1950-51
	Robert A. Lovett	1951-53
Attorney General	Francis Biddle	1945
	Thomas C. Clark	1945-49
	J. Howard McGrath	1949-52
	James P. McGranery	1952-53
Postmaster General	Frank C. Walker	1945
	Robert E. Hannegan	1945-47
	Jesse M. Donaldson	1947-53
Secretary of the Navy	James V. Forrestal	1945-47
Secretary of the Interior	Harold L. Ickes	1945-46
	Julius A. Krug	1946-49
	Oscar L. Chapman	1949-53
Secretary of Agriculture	Claude R. Wichard	1945
	Clinton P. Anderson	1945-48
	Charles F. Brannan	1948-53
Secretary of Commerce	Henry A. Wallace	1945-46
	W. Averell Harriman	1946-48
	Charles Sawyer	1948-53
Secretary of Labor	Frances Perkins	1945
	Lewis B. Schwellenbach	1945-48
	Maurice J. Tobin	1948-53

Dwight D. Eisenhower, 1953-1961

Chief Justice	Frederick M. Vinson	1953
	Earl Warren	1953-61
Vice President	Richard M. Nixon	1953-61
Secretary of State	John Foster Dulles	1953-59
	Christian A. Herter	1959-61
Secretary of the Treasury	George M. Humphrey	1953-57
	Robert B. Anderson	1957-61
Secretary of Defense	Charles E. Wilson	1953-57
	Neil H. McElroy	1957-59
	Thomas S. Gates, Jr.	1959-61
Attorney General	Herbert Brownell, Jr.	1953-58
	William P. Rogers	1958-61
Postmaster General	Arthur E. Summerfield	1953-61
Secretary of the Interior	Douglas McKay	1953-56
	Fred A. Seaton	1956-61
Secretary of Agriculture	Ezra Taft Benson	1953-61
Secretary of Commerce	Sinclair Weeks	1953-58
	Lewis L. Strauss	1958-59
	Frederick H. Mueller	1959-61
Secretary of Labor	Martin P. Durkin	1953
	James P. Mitchell	1953-61
Secretary of Health, Education, and Welfare	Oveta Culp Hobby	1953-55
	Marion B. Folson	1955-58
	Arthur S. Flemming	1958-61

John F. Kennedy, 1961-1963

Chief Justice	Earl Warren	1961-63
Vice President	Lyndon B. Johnson	1961-63
Secretary of State	Dean Rusk	1961-63
Secretary of the Treasury	C. Douglas Dillon	1961-63
Secretary of Defense	Robert S. McNamara	1961-63
Attorney General	Robert F. Kennedy	1961-63
Postmaster General	J. Edward Day	1961-63
	John A. Gronouski, Jr.	1963
Secretary of the Interior	Stewart L. Udall	1961-63
Secretary of Agriculture	Orville L. Freeman	1961-63
Secretary of Commerce	Luther H. Hodges	1961-63

Secretary of Labor	Arthur J. Goldberg	1961-62
	W. Willard Wirtz	1962-63
Secretary of Health, Education, and Welfare	Abraham A. Ribicoff	1961-62
	Anthony J. Celebrezze	1962-63

Lyndon B. Johnson, 1963-1969

Chief Justice	Earl Warren	1963-69
Vice President	Hubert Humphrey	1965-69
Secretary of State	Dean Rusk	1963-69
Secretary of the Treasury	C. Douglas Dillon	1963-65
	Henry H. Fowler	1965-68
	Joseph W. Barr	1968-69
Secretary of Defense	Robert S. McNamara	1963-68
	Clark Clifford	1968-69
Attorney General	Robert F. Kennedy	1963-65
	Nicholas deB. Katzenbach	1965-67
	Ramsey Clark	1967-69
Postmaster General	John A. Gronouski, Jr.	1963-65
	Lawrence Francis O'Brien	1965-68
	W. Marvin Watson	1968-69
Secretary of the Interior	Stewart Lee Udall	1963-69
Secretary of Agriculture	Orville Lothrop Freeman	1963-69
Secretary of Commerce	Luther H. Hodges	1963-65
	John T. Connor	1965-67
	Alexander B. Trowbridge	1967-68
	C. R. Smith	1968-69
Secretary of Labor	W. Willard Wirtz	1963-69
Secretary of Health, Education, and Welfare	Anthony J. Celebrezze	1963-65
	John William Gardner	1965-68
	Wilbur J. Cohen	1968-69
Secretary of Housing and Urban Development	Robert C. Weaver	1966-68
	Robert C. Wood	1969
Secretary of Transportation	Alan S. Boyd	1967-69

Richard M. Nixon, 1969-1974

Chief Justice	Earl Warren	1969
	Warren Earl Burger	1969-74
Vice President	Spiro Agnew	1969-73
	Gerald R. Ford	1973-74
Secretary of State	William P. Rogers	1969-73
	Henry A. Kissinger	1973-74
Secretary of the Treasury	David M. Kennedy	1969-71
	John B. Connally, Jr.	1971-72
	George P. Shultz	1972-74
	William E. Simon	1974
Secretary of Defense	Melvin R. Laird	1969-73
	Elliot L. Richardson	1973
	James R. Schlesinger	1973-74
Attorney General	John N. Mitchell	1969-72
	Richard G. Kleindienst	1972-73
	Elliot L. Richardson	1973
	Robert H. Bork	1973
	William B. Saxbe	1974
Postmaster General *	Wilton M. Blount	1969-71
Secretary of the Interior	Walter J. Hickel	1969-70
	Rogers C. B. Morton	1971-74
Secretary of Agriculture	Clifford M. Hardin	1969-71
	Earl L. Butz	1971-74
Secretary of Commerce	Maurice H. Stans	1969-72
	Peter G. Peterson	1972-73
	Frederick B. Dent	1973-74
Secretary of Labor	George P. Shultz	1969-70
	James D. Hodgson	1970-73
	Peter J. Brennan	1973-74
Secretary of Health, Education and Welfare	Robert H. Finch	1969-70
	Elliot L. Richardson	1970-73
	Caspar W. Weinberger	1973-74
Secretary of Housing and Urban Development	George Romney	1969-73
	James T. Lynn	1973-74
Secretary of Transportation	John A. Volpe	1969-73
	Claude S. Brinegar	1973-74

* *Abolished as Cabinet position in 1971.*

Gerald R. Ford, 1974-1977

Chief Justice	Warren Earl Burger	1974-77
Vice President	Nelson A. Rockefeller	1974-77
Secretary of State	Henry A. Kissinger	1974-77
Secretary of the Treasury	William E. Simon	1974-77
Secretary of Defense	James R. Schlesinger	1974-75
	Donald H. Rumsfeld	1975-77
Attorney General	William B. Saxbe	1974-75
	Edward H. Levi	1975-77
Secretary of the Interior	Rogers C. B. Morton	1974-75
	Stanley K. Hathaway	1975
	Thomas S. Kleppe	1975-77
Secretary of Agriculture	Earl L. Butz	1974-76
	John A. Knebel	1976-77
Secretary of Commerce	Frederick B. Dent	1974-75
	Rogers C. B. Morton	1975-76
	Elliot L. Richardson	1976-77
Secretary of Labor	Peter J. Brennan	1974-75
	John T. Dunlop	1975-76
	William J. Usery, Jr.	1976-77
Secretary of Health, Education, and Welfare	Caspar W. Weinberger	1974-75
	F. David Mathews	1975-77
Secretary of Housing and Urban Development	James T. Lynn	1974-75
	Carla Anderson Hills	1975-77
Secretary of Transportation	Claude S. Brinegar	1974-75
	William T. Coleman, Jr.	1975-77

Jimmy Carter 1977-1981

Chief Justice	Warren Earl Burger	1977-81
Vice President	Walter F. Mondale	1977-81
Secretary of State	Cyrus R. Vance	1977-80
	Edmund S. Muskie	1980-81
Secretary of the Treasury	W. Michael Blumenthal	1977-79
	George W. Miller	1979-81
Secretary of Defense	Harold Brown	1977-81
Attorney General	Griffin B. Bell	1977-79
	Benjamin R. Civiletti	1979-81
Secretary of the Interior	Cecil D. Andrus	1977-81
Secretary of Agriculture	Robert S. Bergland	1977-81
Secretary of Commerce	Juanita M. Kreps	1977-80
	Philip M. Klutznick	1980-81
Secretary of Labor	F. Ray Marshall	1977-81
Secretary of Health, Education, and Welfare	Joseph A. Califano, Jr.	1977-79
	Patricia Roberts Harris	1979-81
Secretary of Housing and Urban Development	Particia Roberts Harris	1977-79
	Moon Landrieu	1979-81
Secretary of Transportation	Brock Adams	1977-79
	Neil E. Goldschmidt	1979-81
Secretary of Energy	James R. Schlesinger	1977-79
	Charles W. Duncan	1979-81
Secretary of Education	Shirley M. Hufstedler	1979-81

Ronald Reagan, 1981-1989

Chief Justice	Warren Earl Burger	1981-86
	William Rehnquist	1986-89
Vice President	George Bush	1981-89
Secretary of State	Alexander Haig	1981-82
	George P. Shultz	1982-89
Secretary of the Treasury	Donald T. Regan	1981-85
	James A. Baker	1985-88
	Nicholas F. Brady	1988-89
Secretary of Defense	Caspar Weinberger	1981-87
	Frank Carlucci	1987-89
Attorney General	William French Smith	1981-85
	Edwin Meese	1985-88
	Dick Thornburgh	1988-89
Secretary of the Interior	James G. Watt	1981-83
	William P. Clark	1983-85
	Donald Hodel	1985-89
Secretary of Agriculture	John R. Block	1981-86
	Richard E. Lyng	1986-89
Secretary of Commerce	Malcolm Baldrige	1981-87
	C. William Verity	1987-89
Secretary of Labor	Raymond J. Donovan	1981-85
	William E. Brock	1985-87
	Ann McLaughlin	1987-89
Secretary of Health and Human Services	Richard S. Schweiker	1981-83
	Margaret M. Heckler	1983-85
	Dr. Otis R. Bowen	1985-89
Secretary of Housing and Urban Development	Samuel R. Pierce, Jr.	1981-89
Secretary of Transportation	Andrew L. Lewis	1981-83
	Elizabeth H. Dole	1983-87
	James H. Burnley	1987-89
Secretary of Energy	James B. Edwards	1981-83
	Donald P. Hodel	1983-85
	John S. Herrington	1985-89
Secretary of Education	Terrel H. Bell	1981-85
	William J. Bennett	1985-88
	Lauro F. Cavazos	1988-89

George Bush, 1989-

Chief Justice	William Rehnquist	1989-
Vice President	Dan Quayle	1989-
Secretary of State	James A. Baker	1989-
Secretary of the Treasury	Nicholas F. Brady	1989-
Secretary of Defense	Richard B. Cheney	1989-
Attorney General	Dick Thornburgh	1989-
Secretary of the Interior	Manuel Lujan, Jr.	1989-
Secretary of Agriculture	Clayton Yeutter	1989-
Secretary of Commerce	Robert A. Mosbacher	1989-
Secretary of Labor	Elizabeth H. Dole	1989-
Secretary of Health and Human Services	Louis W. Sullivan	1989-
Secretary of Housing and Urban Development	Jack F. Kemp	1989-
Secretary of Transportation	Samuel K. Skinner	1989-
Secretary of Energy	James Watkins	1989-
Secretary of Education	Lauro F. Cavazos	1989-

Presidential Approval Ratings, Gallup Poll, Truman to Reagan (percent)

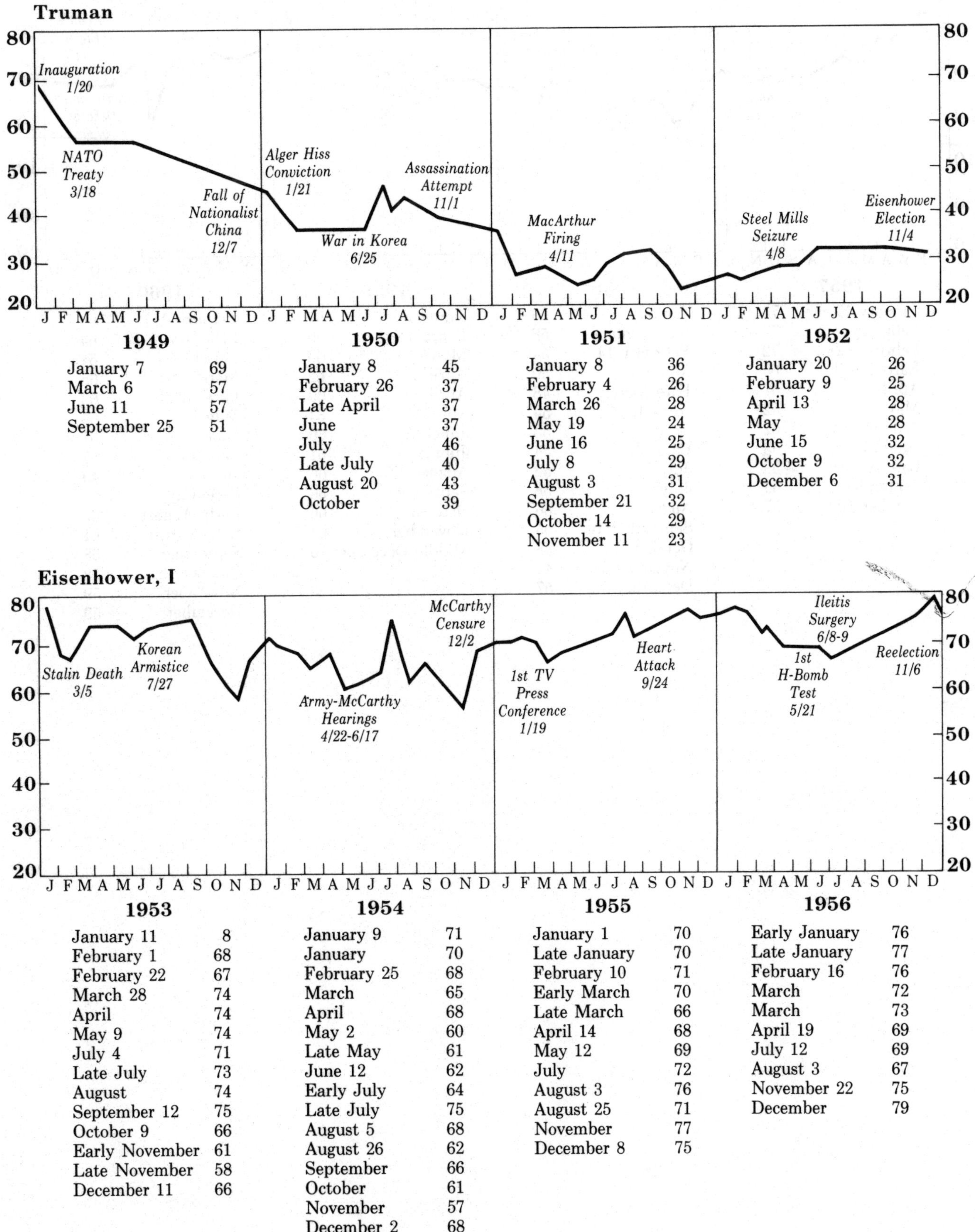

1949

January 7	69
March 6	57
June 11	57
September 25	51

1950

January 8	45
February 26	37
Late April	37
June	37
July	46
Late July	40
August 20	43
October	39

1951

January 8	36
February 4	26
March 26	28
May 19	24
June 16	25
July 8	29
August 3	31
September 21	32
October 14	29
November 11	23

1952

January 20	26
February 9	25
April 13	28
May	28
June 15	32
October 9	32
December 6	31

1953

January 11	8
February 1	68
February 22	67
March 28	74
April	74
May 9	74
July 4	71
Late July	73
August	74
September 12	75
October 9	66
Early November	61
Late November	58
December 11	66

1954

January 9	71
January	70
February 25	68
March	65
April	68
May 2	60
Late May	61
June 12	62
Early July	64
Late July	75
August 5	68
August 26	62
September	66
October	61
November	57
December 2	68

1955

January 1	70
Late January	70
February 10	71
Early March	70
Late March	66
April 14	68
May 12	69
July	72
August 3	76
August 25	71
November	77
December 8	75

1956

Early January	76
Late January	77
February 16	76
March	72
March	73
April 19	69
July 12	69
August 3	67
November 22	75
December	79

Eisenhower, II

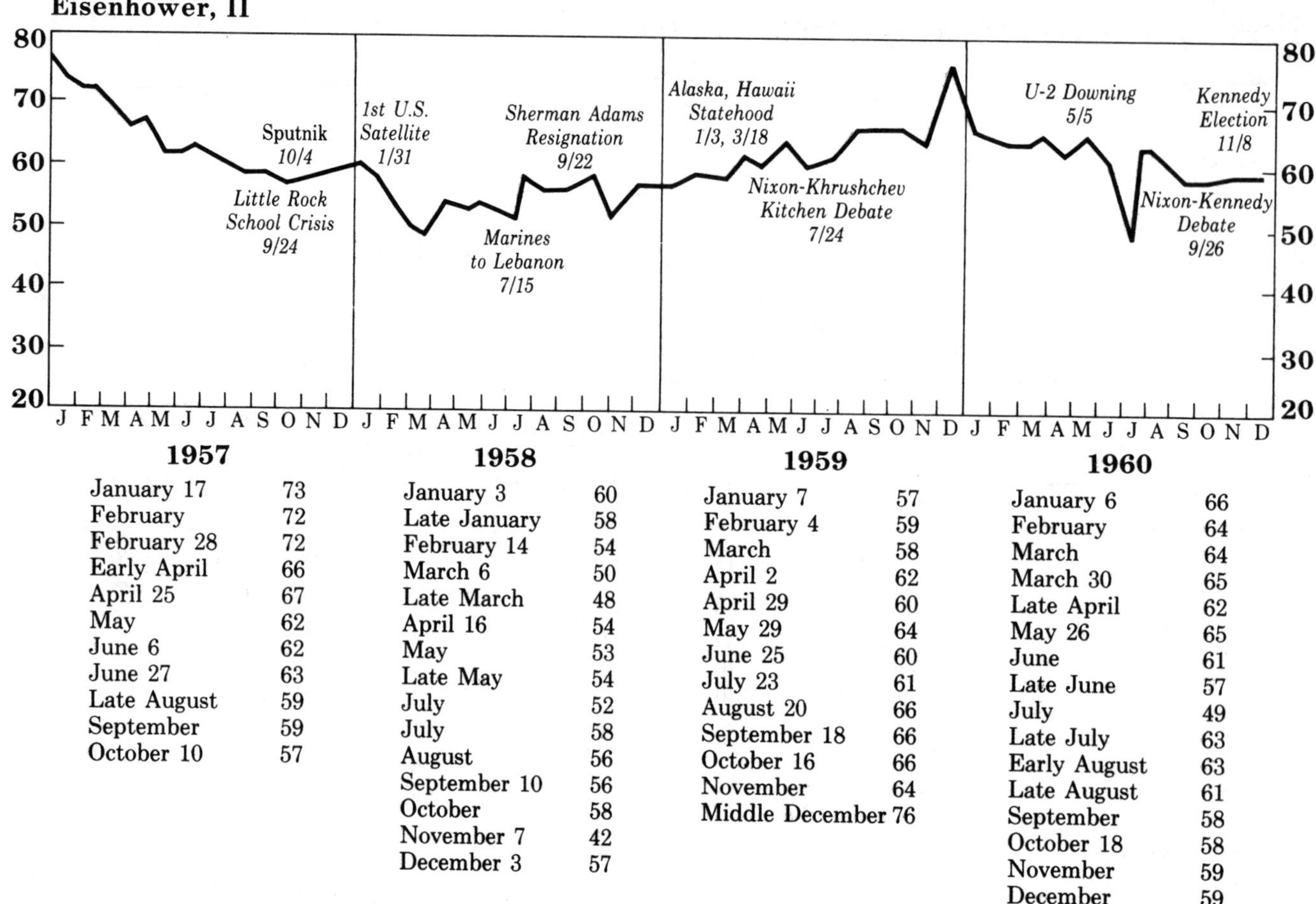

1957

January 17	73
February	72
February 28	72
Early April	66
April 25	67
May	62
June 6	62
June 27	63
Late August	59
September	59
October 10	57

1958

January 3	60
Late January	58
February 14	54
March 6	50
Late March	48
April 16	54
May	53
Late May	54
July	52
July	58
August	56
September 10	56
October	58
November 7	42
December 3	57

1959

January 7	57
February 4	59
March	58
April 2	62
April 29	60
May 29	64
June 25	60
July 23	61
August 20	66
September 18	66
October 16	66
November	64
Middle December	76

1960

January 6	66
February	64
March	64
March 30	65
Late April	62
May 26	65
June	61
Late June	57
July	49
Late July	63
Early August	63
Late August	61
September	58
October 18	58
November	59
December	59

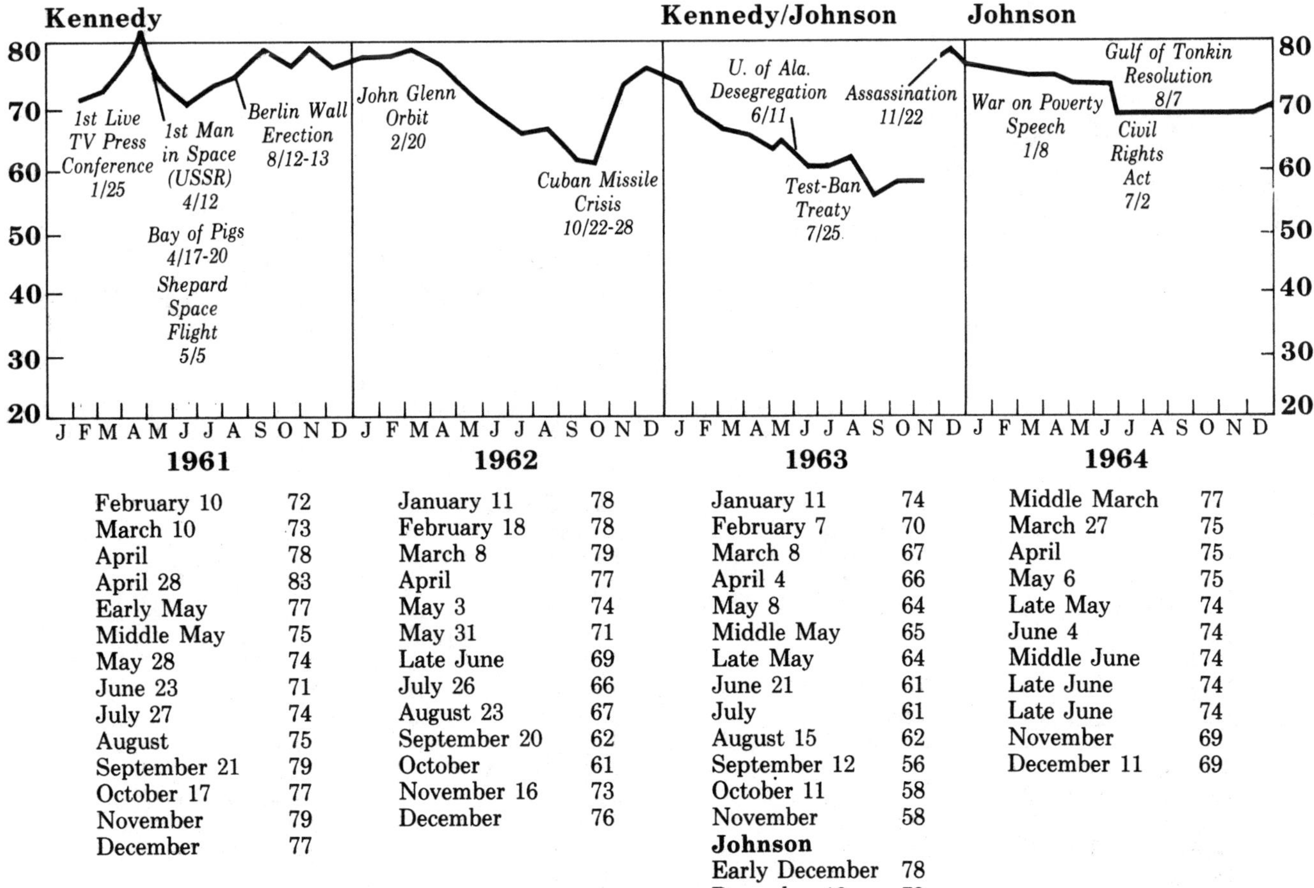

1961	
February 10	72
March 10	73
April	78
April 28	83
Early May	77
Middle May	75
May 28	74
June 23	71
July 27	74
August	75
September 21	79
October 17	77
November	79
December	77

1962	
January 11	78
February 18	78
March 8	79
April	77
May 3	74
May 31	71
Late June	69
July 26	66
August 23	67
September 20	62
October	61
November 16	73
December	76

1963	
January 11	74
February 7	70
March 8	67
April 4	66
May 8	64
Middle May	65
Late May	64
June 21	61
July	61
August 15	62
September 12	56
October 11	58
November	58
Johnson	
Early December	78
December 12	79

1964	
Middle March	77
March 27	75
April	75
May 6	75
Late May	74
June 4	74
Middle June	74
Late June	74
Late June	74
November	69
December 11	69

Johnson

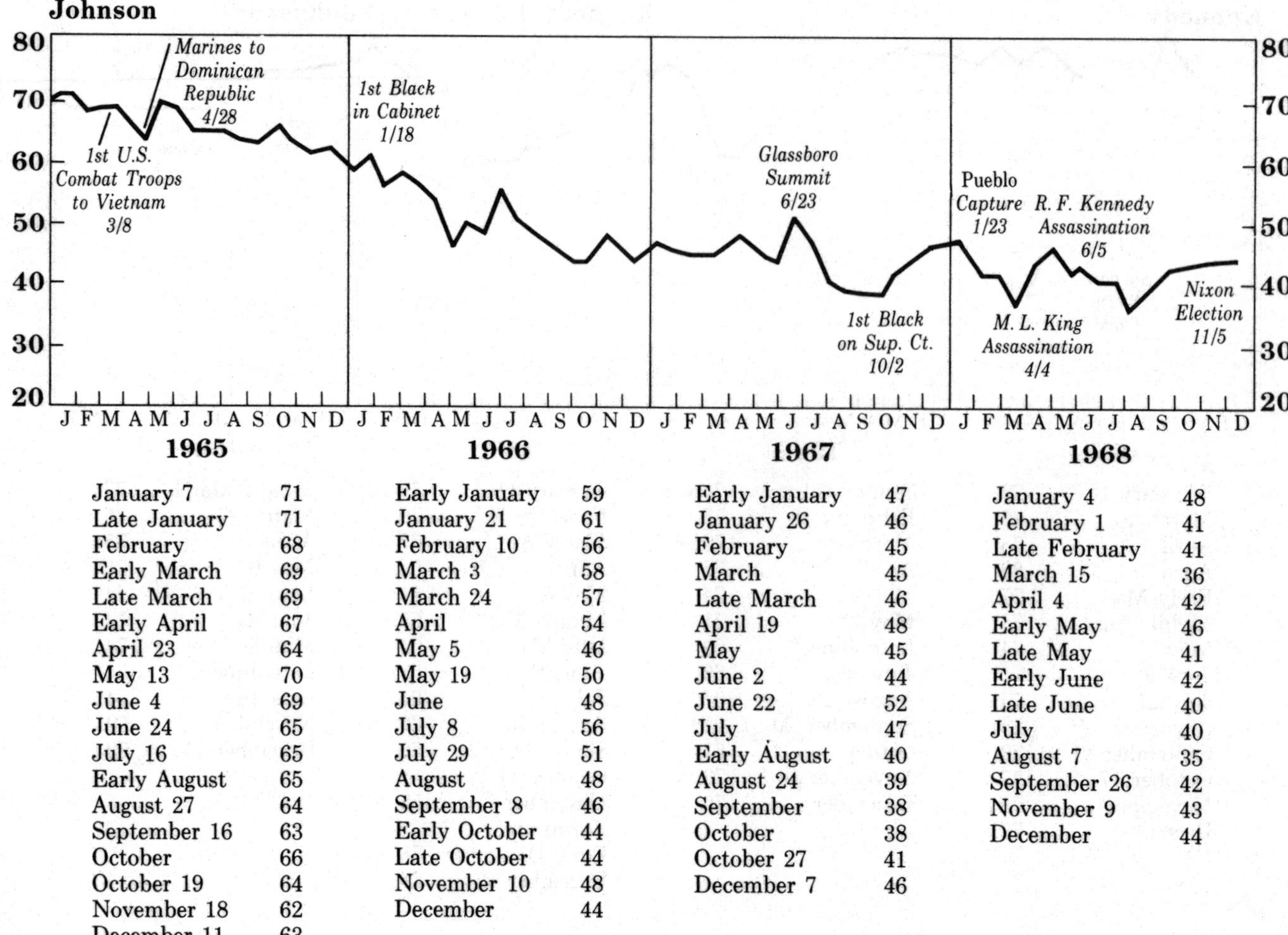

1965		1966		1967		1968	
January 7	71	Early January	59	Early January	47	January 4	48
Late January	71	January 21	61	January 26	46	February 1	41
February	68	February 10	56	February	45	Late February	41
Early March	69	March 3	58	March	45	March 15	36
Late March	69	March 24	57	Late March	46	April 4	42
Early April	67	April	54	April 19	48	Early May	46
April 23	64	May 5	46	May	45	Late May	41
May 13	70	May 19	50	June 2	44	Early June	42
June 4	69	June	48	June 22	52	Late June	40
June 24	65	July 8	56	July	47	July	40
July 16	65	July 29	51	Early August	40	August 7	35
Early August	65	August	48	August 24	39	September 26	42
August 27	64	September 8	46	September	38	November 9	43
September 16	63	Early October	44	October	38	December	44
October	66	Late October	44	October 27	41		
October 19	64	November 10	48	December 7	46		
November 18	62	December	44				
December 11	63						

Nixon, I

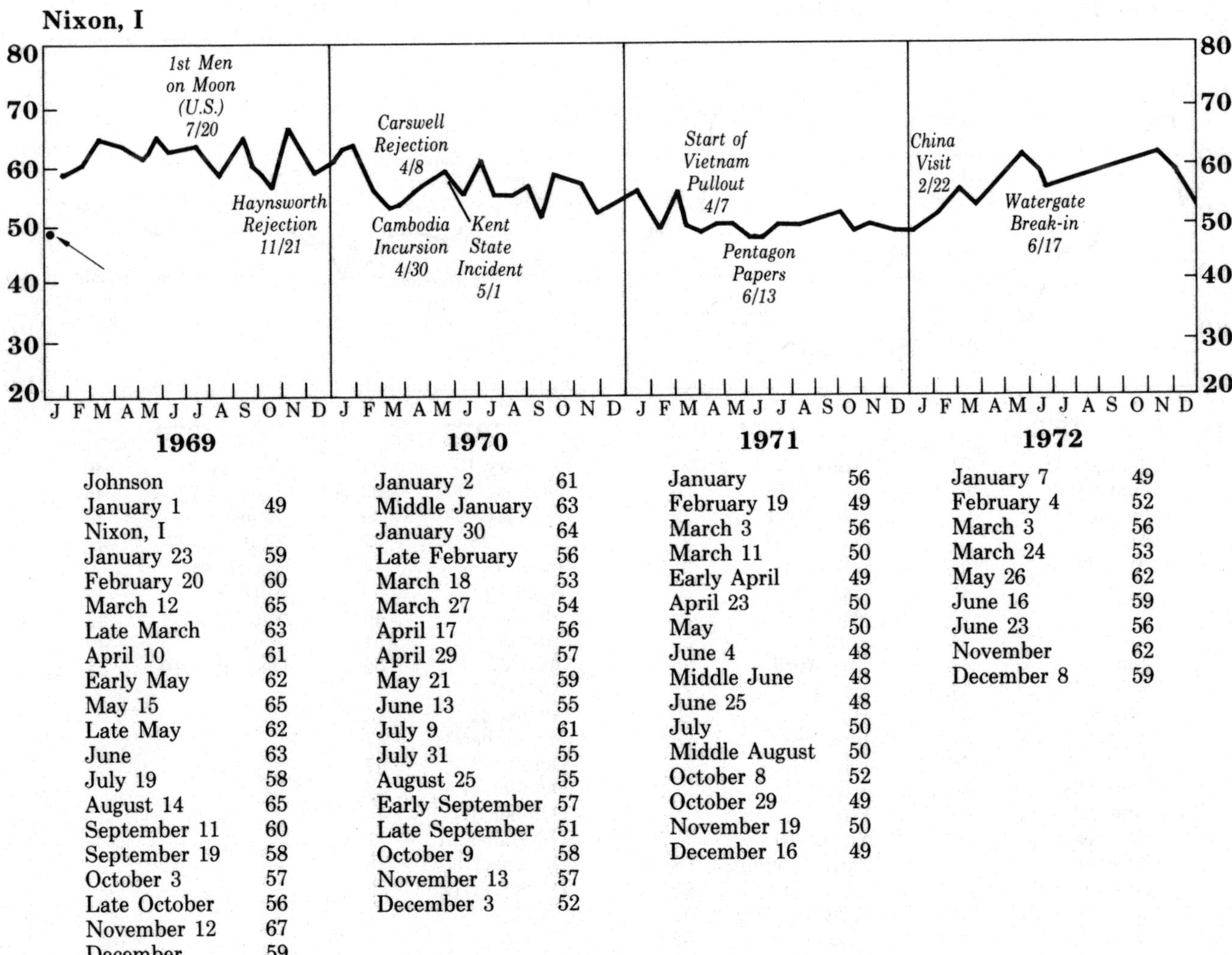

1969

Johnson	
January 1	49
Nixon, I	
January 23	59
February 20	60
March 12	65
Late March	63
April 10	61
Early May	62
May 15	65
Late May	62
June	63
July 19	58
August 14	65
September 11	60
September 19	58
October 3	57
Late October	56
November 12	67
December	59

1970

January 2	61
Middle January	63
January 30	64
Late February	56
March 18	53
March 27	54
April 17	56
April 29	57
May 21	59
June 13	55
July 9	61
July 31	55
August 25	55
Early September	57
Late September	51
October 9	58
November 13	57
December 3	52

1971

January	56
February 19	49
March 3	56
March 11	50
Early April	49
April 23	50
May	50
June 4	48
Middle June	48
June 25	48
July	50
Middle August	50
October 8	52
October 29	49
November 19	50
December 16	49

1972

January 7	49
February 4	52
March 3	56
March 24	53
May 26	62
June 16	59
June 23	56
November	62
December 8	59

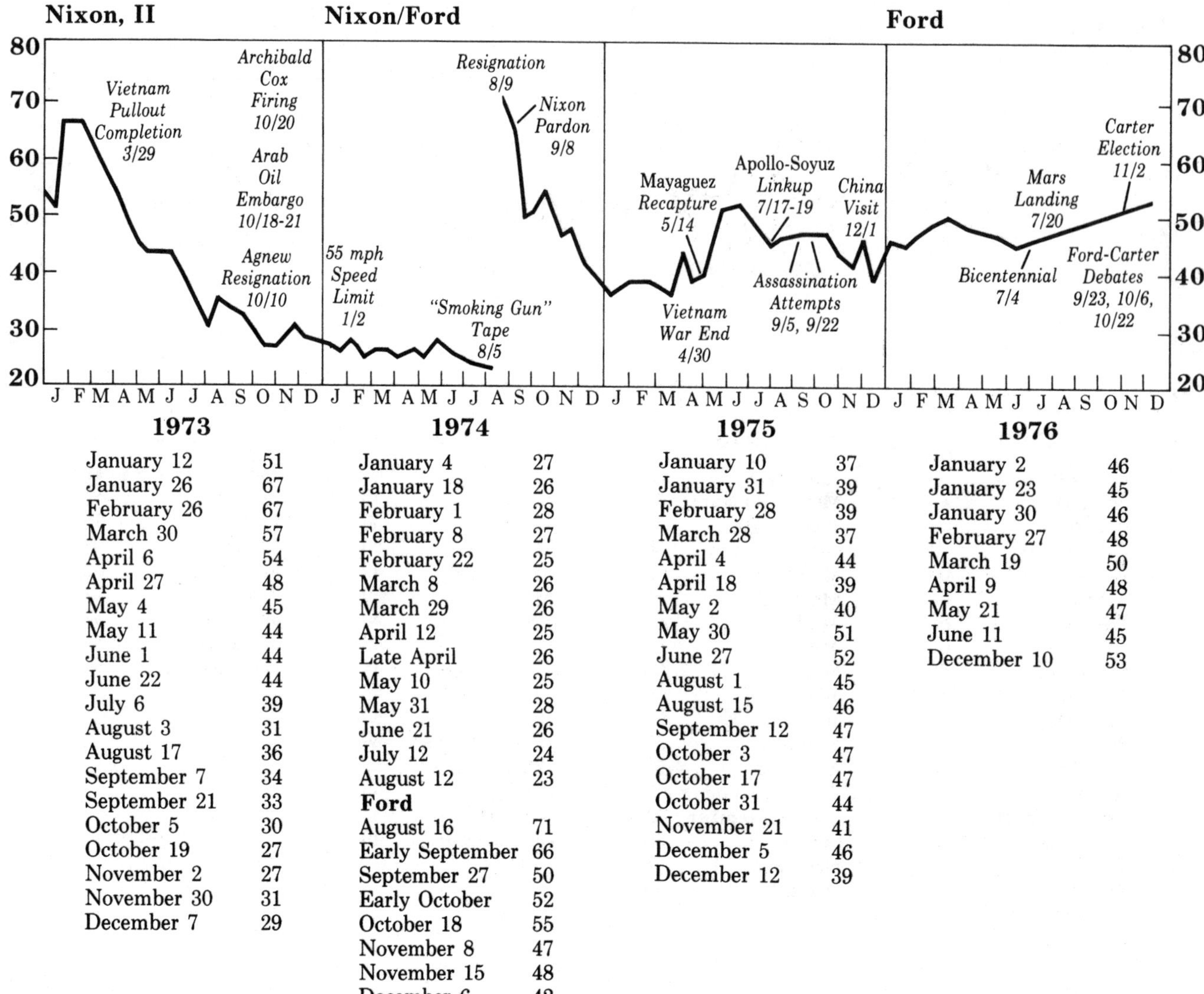

1973	
January 12	51
January 26	67
February 26	67
March 30	57
April 6	54
April 27	48
May 4	45
May 11	44
June 1	44
June 22	44
July 6	39
August 3	31
August 17	36
September 7	34
September 21	33
October 5	30
October 19	27
November 2	27
November 30	31
December 7	29

1974	
January 4	27
January 18	26
February 1	28
February 8	27
February 22	25
March 8	26
March 29	26
April 12	25
Late April	26
May 10	25
May 31	28
June 21	26
July 12	24
August 12	23
Ford	
August 16	71
Early September	66
September 27	50
Early October	52
October 18	55
November 8	47
November 15	48
December 6	42

1975	
January 10	37
January 31	39
February 28	39
March 28	37
April 4	44
April 18	39
May 2	40
May 30	51
June 27	52
August 1	45
August 15	46
September 12	47
October 3	47
October 17	47
October 31	44
November 21	41
December 5	46
December 12	39

1976	
January 2	46
January 23	45
January 30	46
February 27	48
March 19	50
April 9	48
May 21	47
June 11	45
December 10	53

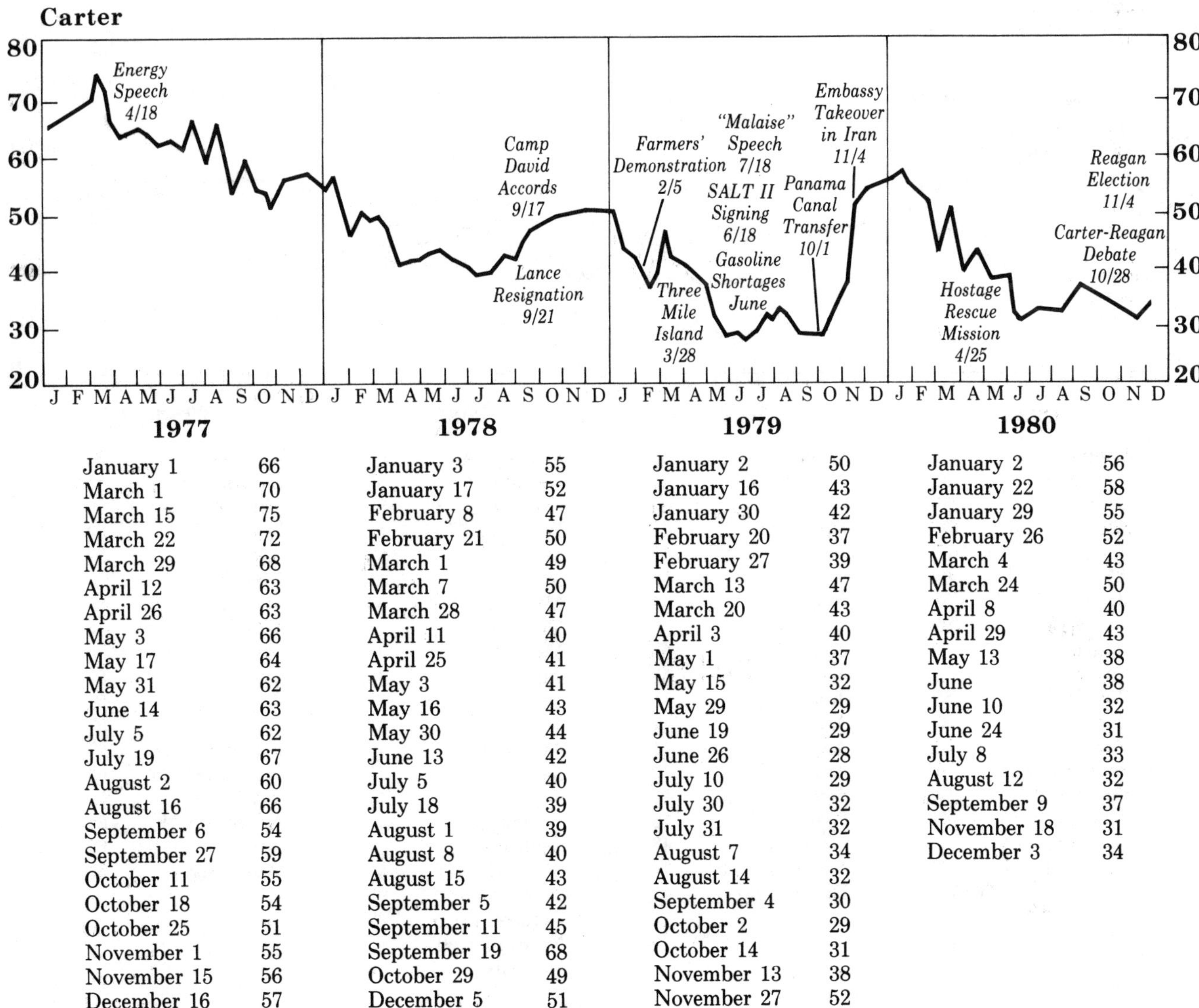

1977

Date	Rating
January 1	66
March 1	70
March 15	75
March 22	72
March 29	68
April 12	63
April 26	63
May 3	66
May 17	64
May 31	62
June 14	63
July 5	62
July 19	67
August 2	60
August 16	66
September 6	54
September 27	59
October 11	55
October 18	54
October 25	51
November 1	55
November 15	56
December 16	57

1978

Date	Rating
January 3	55
January 17	52
February 8	47
February 21	50
March 1	49
March 7	50
March 28	47
April 11	40
April 25	41
May 3	41
May 16	43
May 30	44
June 13	42
July 5	40
July 18	39
August 1	39
August 8	40
August 15	43
September 5	42
September 11	45
September 19	68
October 29	49
December 5	51

1979

Date	Rating
January 2	50
January 16	43
January 30	42
February 20	37
February 27	39
March 13	47
March 20	43
April 3	40
May 1	37
May 15	32
May 29	29
June 19	29
June 26	28
July 10	29
July 30	32
July 31	32
August 7	34
August 14	32
September 4	30
October 2	29
October 14	31
November 13	38
November 27	52
December 4	54

1980

Date	Rating
January 2	56
January 22	58
January 29	55
February 26	52
March 4	43
March 24	50
April 8	40
April 29	43
May 13	38
June	38
June 10	32
June 24	31
July 8	33
August 12	32
September 9	37
November 18	31
December 3	34

Reagan, I

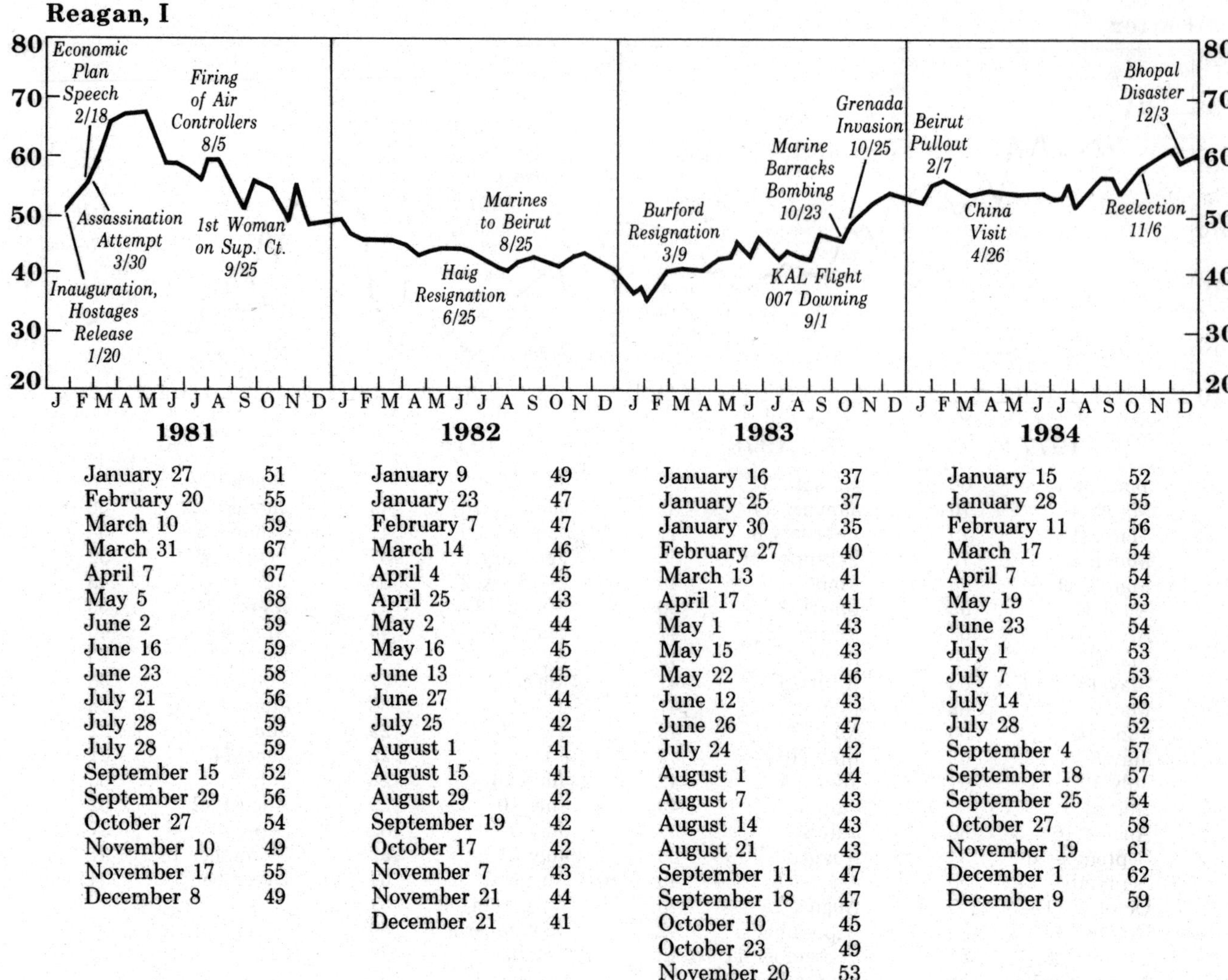

1981		1982		1983		1984	
January 27	51	January 9	49	January 16	37	January 15	52
February 20	55	January 23	47	January 25	37	January 28	55
March 10	59	February 7	47	January 30	35	February 11	56
March 31	67	March 14	46	February 27	40	March 17	54
April 7	67	April 4	45	March 13	41	April 7	54
May 5	68	April 25	43	April 17	41	May 19	53
June 2	59	May 2	44	May 1	43	June 23	54
June 16	59	May 16	45	May 15	43	July 1	53
June 23	58	June 13	45	May 22	46	July 7	53
July 21	56	June 27	44	June 12	43	July 14	56
July 28	59	July 25	42	June 26	47	July 28	52
July 28	59	August 1	41	July 24	42	September 4	57
September 15	52	August 15	41	August 1	44	September 18	57
September 29	56	August 29	42	August 7	43	September 25	54
October 27	54	September 19	42	August 14	43	October 27	58
November 10	49	October 17	42	August 21	43	November 19	61
November 17	55	November 7	43	September 11	47	December 1	62
December 8	49	November 21	44	September 18	47	December 9	59
		December 21	41	October 10	45		
				October 23	49		
				November 20	53		
				December 11	54		

Reagan, II

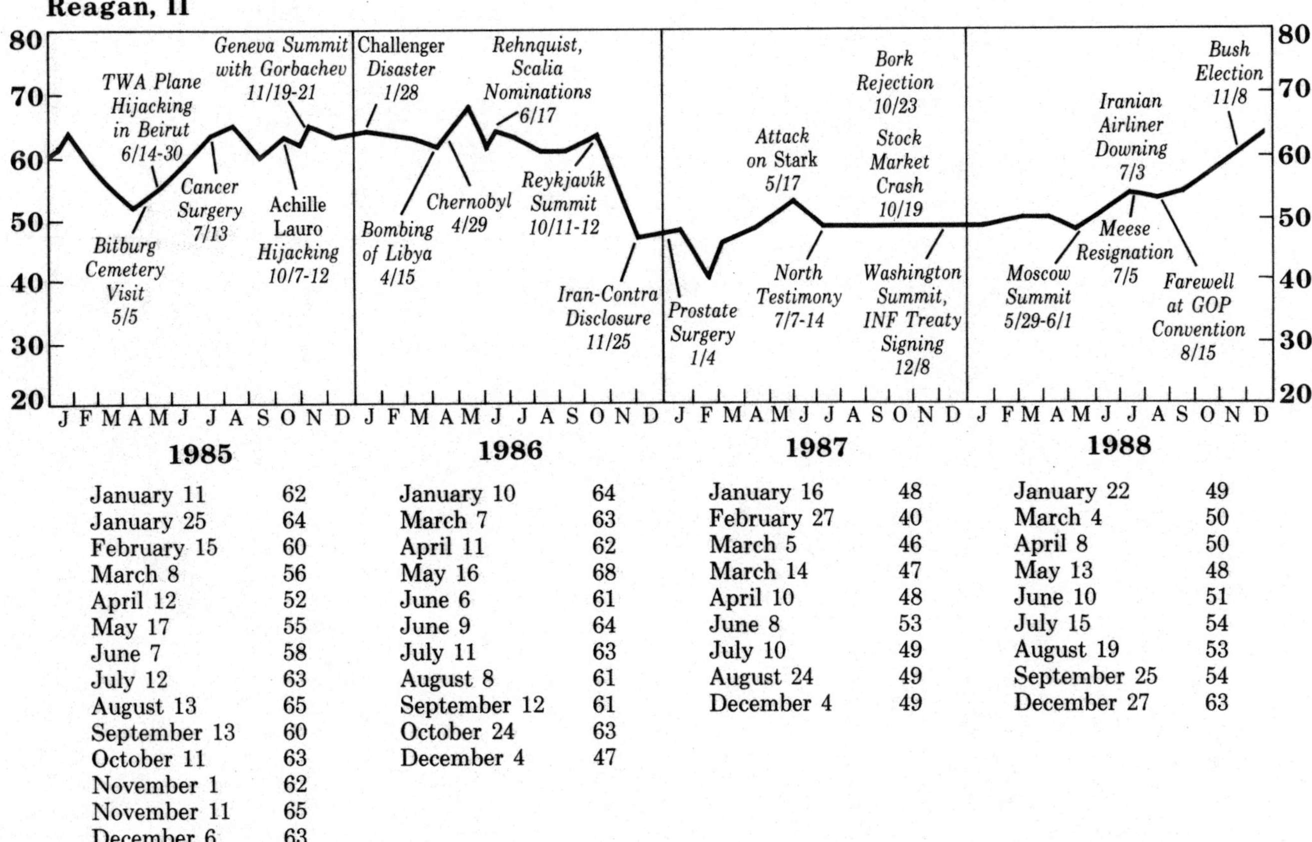

1985

January 11	62
January 25	64
February 15	60
March 8	56
April 12	52
May 17	55
June 7	58
July 12	63
August 13	65
September 13	60
October 11	63
November 1	62
November 11	65
December 6	63

1986

January 10	64
March 7	63
April 11	62
May 16	68
June 6	61
June 9	64
July 11	63
August 8	61
September 12	61
October 24	63
December 4	47

1987

January 16	48
February 27	40
March 5	46
March 14	47
April 10	48
June 8	53
July 10	49
August 24	49
December 4	49

1988

January 22	49
March 4	50
April 8	50
May 13	48
June 10	51
July 15	54
August 19	53
September 25	54
December 27	63

Sources: Gary King and Lyn Ragsdale, *The Elusive Executive: Discovering Statistical Patterns in the Presidency* (Washington, D.C.: CQ Press, 1988) 295-307. Ratings 1977-1984 coded and calculated by the authors from their analysis of the original Gallup survey data. Ratings 1949-1976 adapted by King and Ragsdale from the *Gallup Opinion Index*, Report 182, October-November 1980, 13-59. Ratings 1985-1988 from a Gallup Organization compilation, "Reagan's Job Performance," February 1989.

Presidential Support in Congress, 1953-1988

Studies of congressional voting behavior have been a staple of Congressional Quarterly for more than forty years. For the presidential support study, CQ tries to determine what the president personally, as distinct from other administration officials, does and does not want in the way of legislative action by analyzing the president's messages to Congress, press conference remarks, and other public statements and documents. Members must be aware of the position when the vote is taken.

By the time an issue reaches a vote, it may differ from the original form in which the president expressed opposition or support. In such cases, CQ analyzes the measure to determine whether, on balance, the features favored by the president outweigh those opposed or vice versa. Only then is the vote classified.

In general, analysts who use the CQ study should do so cautiously, taking into account its strengths and weaknesses. It is a useful gauge of long-term trends in presidential-congressional relations, and it has served as a key yardstick for political scientists.

The study's usefulness diminishes, however, as the need for detail rises. It masks controversies that never reach a roll-call vote on the floor. In the Senate, particularly, legislation of considerable substance often passes by voice vote. When a committee kills a bill the president supports, this goes unrecorded in the vote study.

It is also important to consider the matters that do make it to the floor.

The study also gives equal weight to every vote, no matter its actual importance.

Presidential Success on Votes, 1953-1988

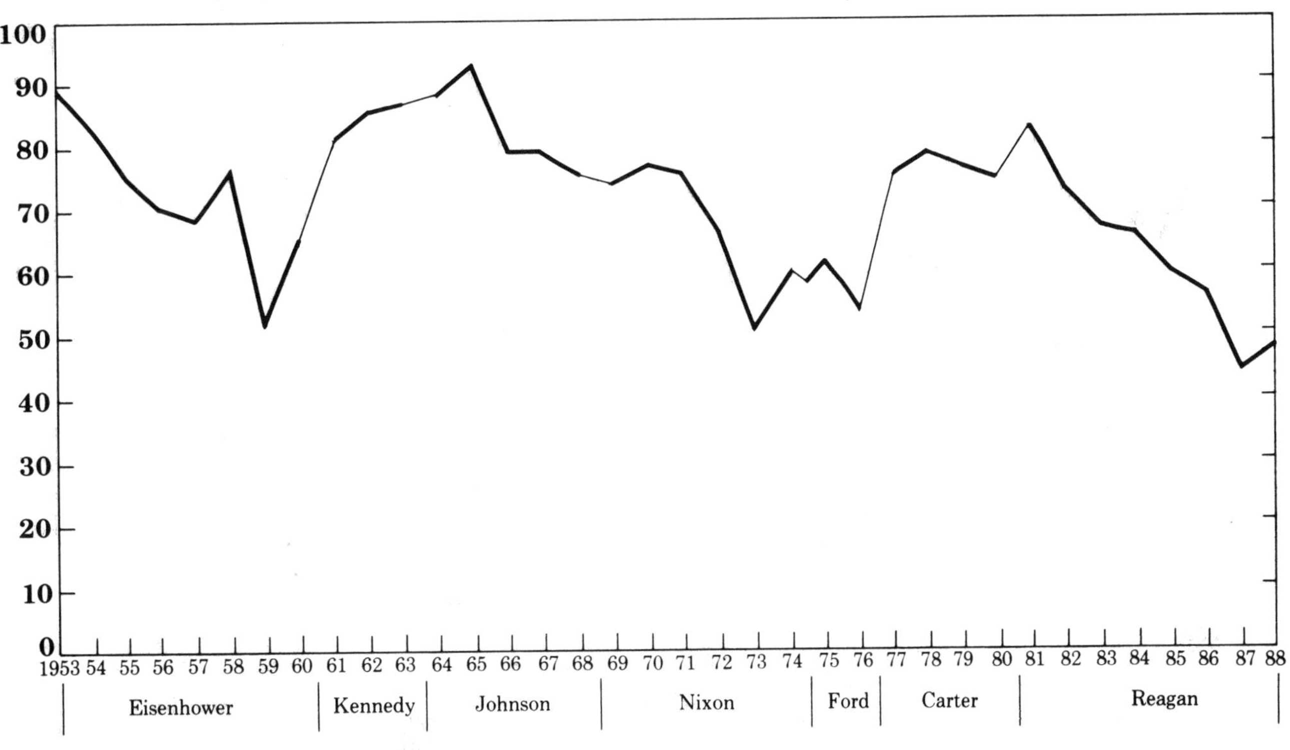

Eisenhower		Kennedy		Johnson		Nixon		Ford		Carter		Reagan	
1953	89.0	1961	81.0	1964	88.0	1969	74.0	1974	58.2	1977	75.4	1981	82.4
1954	82.8	1962	85.4	1965	93.0	1970	77.0	1975	61.0	1978	78.3	1982	72.4
1955	75.0	1963	87.1	1966	79.0	1971	75.0	1976	53.8	1979	76.8	1983	67.1
1956	70.0			1967	79.0	1972	66.0			1980	75.1	1984	65.8
1957	68.0			1968	75.0	1973	50.6					1985	59.9
1958	76.0					1974	59.6					1986	56.1
1959	52.0											1987	43.5
1960	65.0											1988	47.4

Source: Congressional Quarterly Weekly Report, November 19, 1988, 3324-3330.

Note: Percentages based on votes on which presidents took a clear position.

Index